Merriam-Webster's
Deluxe
Dictionary

TENTH COLLEGIATE® EDITION

The Reader's Digest Association, Inc.
Pleasantville, New York / Montreal

Published by The Reader's Digest Association, Inc.
Pleasantville, New York 10570

Also published as *Merriam-Webster's Collegiate Dictionary, Deluxe Edition*
by Merriam-Webster, Incorporated

READER'S DIGEST GENERAL BOOKS

Editor, U.S. General Books	David Palmer
Executive Editor	Gayla Visalli
Managing Editor	Christopher Cavanaugh
Editorial Director, History, Religion, and Reference Books	Edmund H. Harvey, Jr.
Design Director, History, Religion, and Reference Books	Irene Ledwith

Address any comments about *Merriam-Webster's Deluxe Dictionary* to
Reader's Digest, Editor-in-Chief, Illustrated Reference Books, Reader's Digest Road, Pleasantville, NY 10570

To order additional copies of *Merriam-Webster's Deluxe Dictionary,* call 1-800-846-2100.

You can also visit us on the World Wide Web at http://www.readersdigest.com

Library of Congress Cataloging in Publication Data

Merriam-Webster's deluxe dictionary. — 10th collegiate ed.
 p. cm.
Newly illustrated edition of: Merriam-Webster's collegiate dictionary. 10th ed. 1998.
 Includes index.
 ISBN 0-7621-0300-0
 1. English language—Dictionaries. I. Merriam-Webster, Inc. II. Merriam-Webster's collegiate dictionary.
PE1628.M3645 1998
423—dc21 98-18666

Printed in the United States of America

5 6 02 01 00

Contents

Preface ... 6a

Explanatory Notes ... 7a

Guide to Pronunciation ... 23a

Pronunciation Symbols ... 28a

A Dictionary of the English Language ... 1

Abbreviations and Symbols for Chemical Elements ... 2157

Foreign Words and Phrases ... 2169

Biographical Names ... 2176

Geographical Names ... 2225

Signs and Symbols ... 2321

A Handbook of Style ... 2325

Index ... 2339

Preface

Merriam-Webster's Deluxe Dictionary, Tenth Collegiate Edition has been specially created by its editors to serve the needs of a broad audience: every person who reads, writes, speaks, and listens to English words, that is, everyone who uses English to communicate. This work is solidly based on the most popular American college-level dictionary, *Merriam-Webster's Collegiate Dictionary, Tenth Edition.* That book is the latest volume in a distinguished series of dictionaries that goes back to 1898. The book you are holding incorporates almost all—and certainly all the essential features—of the *Collegiate Dictionary* and adds a good deal besides. In this dictionary the reader will find a number of new, enhanced, or expanded features not found all together in any other work, and the combination makes this an unusually valuable tool for the entire family when there is a need to "look it up."

The heart and soul of any dictionary is its main vocabulary, the dictionary proper, and the ever-expanding vocabulary of our language exerts considerable pressure on the contents of that section. Words and senses are born far more rapidly than they die out. The main vocabulary of this dictionary contains over 10,000 words and senses of words that have established themselves in English since the preceding edition of the *Collegiate Dictionary* was created in the 1980s. And the treatment of all the words and senses is as nearly exhaustive as the compass of an abridged work permits. As in all Merriam-Webster dictionaries, the information given is based on a collection of 15,000,000 citations maintained in the offices of Merriam-Webster, Incorporated. These citations show words used in a wide range of printed sources, and the collection is constantly being augmented through the efforts of the editorial staff. Thus, the user of this dictionary may be confident that entries are based on current as well as older material. The citation files now hold 6,000,000 more examples than were available to the editors of *Webster's Third New International Dictionary, Unabridged,* published in 1961, and 2,000,000 more than the editors of the Ninth Edition of the *Collegiate Dictionary* had at their disposal. This time the editors also had available to them a machine-readable corpus of over 20,000,000 words of text drawn from the wide and constantly changing range of publications that supply the paper slips in the citation file.

Those entries known to be trademarks or service marks are so labeled and are treated in accordance with a formula approved by the United States Trademark Association. No entry in this dictionary, however, should be regarded as affecting the validity of any trademark or service mark.

The best special features of the parent work have been brought over intact into this dictionary. These features include pictorial illustrations that supplement and clarify definitions, paragraphs that discuss and exemplify the small differences in meaning that keep synonyms separate from each other, and brief, pointed discussions of some matters of confused or disputed usage. In addition, the dates of first use provided at most main entries have proven popular with users of the *Collegiate Dictionary* and appear as well in the present work. In the case of the illustrations and the usage paragraphs, the numbers of each have been substantially increased for this book, to make it even more informative than its original.

At the same time, many features are entirely new to this edition. To the paragraphs on synonyms and usages we have added hundreds of paragraphs of a completely different type, called word histories. These set forth in easy, straightforward prose the often surprising and entertaining story of how an English word came to be or how its meaning evolved over time. Similarly, each letter section of the main vocabulary is introduced by a short history of the letter itself.

Other new features are meant to make this dictionary more inviting to the eye than dictionaries commonly are, and easier to use at the same time. The type employed here is larger and more readable than what one has to deal with in other dictionaries of similar scope. Most definitions in this dictionary begin on a new line and are thus much easier for the eye to locate. The reliance of the dictionary text upon such techniques of compression as frequent abbreviations and special symbols like the swung dash has been nearly eliminated from the main vocabulary and very greatly reduced in the back matter. Color, carefully determined in each case to be authentic, has been added to all the pictorial illustrations. Another important use of color is in the blocks that appear in the third column of many right-hand pages. These hold the three kinds of explanatory paragraphs—word history, usage, and synonym—in one convenient place. Taken together, all these new features should make *Merriam-Webster's Deluxe Dictionary* a positive pleasure to use as well as a clear, accurate source of information about English words.

The front matter of this book establishes a context for understanding what this dictionary is and how it may be used most effectively. The Explanatory Notes answer the user's questions about the conventions, devices, and techniques by which the editors have been able to present mountains of information in a single volume. All users of the dictionary are urged to read this section through and then consult it for special information as the need arises. The Guide to Pronunciation serves both to show how the pronunciations in the book are arrived at and to explain the mechanics of the respelling system in which they are set down.

The back matter contains six sections from the *Collegiate Dictionary.* They are Abbreviations and Symbols for Chemical Elements; Foreign Words and Phrases that occur frequently in English texts but have not become part of the English vocabulary; thousands of proper names brought together under the separate headings Biographical Names and Geographical Names; a gathering of important Signs and Symbols that cannot readily be alphabetized; and a Handbook of Style in which various stylistic conventions (as of punctuation and capitalization) are summarized and exemplified.

The publishers said of the original 1898 *Collegiate Dictionary* that "for the book as a whole we venture to claim that in its class and for its purpose it has no superior and no equal." The editors of Merriam-Webster, Incorporated who produced this special dictionary have no less confidence in what they have created. They offer it to people everywhere who need information about the vocabulary of English, in the assurance that it will prove a reliable companion.

Explanatory Notes

Entries

MAIN ENTRIES

A boldface letter or a combination of such letters, including punctuation marks and diacritics where needed, that is set flush with the left-hand margin of each column of type is a main entry or entry word. The main entry may consist of letters set solid, of letters joined by a hyphen or a diagonal, or of letters separated by one or more spaces:

> [1]**alone** . . . *adjective*
>
> **au·to–da–fé** . . . *noun*
>
> **and/or** . . . *conjunction*
>
> **automatic pilot** *noun*

The material in lightface type that follows each main entry on the same line and on succeeding indented lines explains and justifies its inclusion in the dictionary.

Variation in the styling of compound words in English is frequent and widespread. It is often completely acceptable to choose freely among open, hyphenated, and closed alternatives (as *lifestyle, life-style,* or *life style*). However, to show all the stylings that are found for English compounds would require space that can be better used for other information. So this dictionary limits itself to a single styling for a compound:

> **peace·mak·er**
>
> **pell–mell**
>
> **boom box**

When a compound is widely used and one styling predominates, that styling is shown. When a compound is uncommon or when the evidence indicates that two or three stylings are approximately equal in frequency, the styling shown is based on the analogy of parallel compounds.

ORDER OF MAIN ENTRIES

The main entries follow one another in alphabetical order letter by letter without regard to intervening spaces or hyphens: *battle royal* follows *battlement* and *earth-shattering* follows *earthshaking.* Those containing an Arabic numeral are alphabetized as if the numeral were spelled out: *3-D* comes between *three-color* and *three-decker.* Those that often begin with the abbreviation *St.* in common usage have the abbreviation spelled out: *Saint Anthony's fire.*

Full words come before parts of words made up of the same letters. Solid compounds come first and are followed by hyphenated compounds and then open compounds. Lowercase entries come before entries that begin with a capital letter:

> **semi** . . . *noun*
>
> **semi-** . . . *prefix*
>
> **take·out** . . . *noun*
>
> **take–out** . . . *adjective*
>
> **take out** . . . *transitive verb*

> **tim·o·thy** . . . *noun*
>
> **Tim·o·thy** . . . *noun*

HOMOGRAPHS

When one main entry has exactly the same written form as another, the two are distinguished by superscript numerals preceding each word:

> [1]**melt** . . . *verb* [1]**pine** . . . *noun*
>
> [2]**melt** *noun* [2]**pine** *intransitive verb*

Sometimes such homographs are related: the two entries *melt* are derived from the same root. Sometimes there is no relationship: the two entries *pine* are unrelated beyond the accident of spelling. The order of homographs is usually historical: the one first used in English is entered first. A homograph derived from an earlier homograph by functional shift, however, follows its parent immediately, with the result that occasionally one homograph appears ahead of another that is older in usage. For example, of the three entries *kennel* the second (a verb) is derived from the first (a noun). Even though the unrelated third entry *kennel* was used in English many years before the second, it follows the two related entries.

GUIDE WORDS

A pair of guide words is printed at the top of each page. The entries that fall alphabetically between the guide words are found on that page.

It is important to remember that alphabetical order rather than position of an entry on the page determines the selection of guide words. The first guide word is the alphabetically first entry on the page. The second guide word is usually the alphabetically last entry on the page:

> **game** **gamut**

The entry need not be a main entry. Another boldface word—a variant, an inflected form, or a defined or undefined run-on—may be selected as a guide word. For this reason the last printed main entry on a page is not always the last entry alphabetically:

> **Gentoo** **geomagnetism**

On the page where these guide words are used, *geomagnetic storm* is the last printed entry, but *geomagnetism,* an undefined run-on at *geomagnetic,* is the last entry alphabetically and so has been chosen as the second guide word.

All guide words must themselves be in alphabetical order from page to page throughout the dictionary; thus, the alphabetically last entry on a page is not used if it follows alphabetically the first guide word on the next page:

> **Giemsa stain** **gillied**

On the page where these guide words are found, *gillying,* an inflected form at the entry [2]*gillie,* is the last entry alphabetically, but it is not used as the second guide word because it follows alphabetically the entry *gillnet,* which is the first guide word on the next page. To use *gillying* would violate the alphabetical order of guide words from page to page, and so the inflected form *gillied* is the second guide word instead.

END-OF-LINE DIVISION

The centered dots within entry words indicate division points at which a hyphen may be put at the end of a line of print or writing. Thus the noun *pos·si·bil·i·ty* may be ended on one line with:

> pos-
> possi-
> possibil-
> possibili-

and continued on the next with:

> sibility
> bility
> ity
> ty

Centered dots are not shown after a single initial letter or before a single terminal letter because printers seldom cut off a single letter:

> **aswirl** . . . *adjective*
>
> **mouthy** . . . *adjective*
>
> **idea** . . . *noun*

Nor are they shown at second and succeeding homographs unless these differ among themselves:

> ¹**re·form** . . . *verb* ¹**min·ute** . . . *noun*
>
> ²**reform** *noun* ²**minute** *transitive verb*
>
> ³**reform** *adjective* ³**mi·nute** . . . *adjective*

There are acceptable alternative end-of-line divisions just as there are acceptable variant spellings and pronunciations. It is, for example, all but impossible to produce a convincing argument that either of the divisions *aus·ter·i·ty, au·ster·i·ty* is better than the other. But space cannot be taken for entries like *aus·ter·i·ty or au·ster·i·ty,* and *au·s·ter·i·ty* would likely be confusing to many. No more than one division is, therefore, shown for an entry in this dictionary.

Many words have two or more common pronunciation variants, and the same end-of-line division is not always appropriate for each of them. The division *pi·an·ist,* for example, best fits the variant \pē-'a-nist\ whereas the division *pi·a·nist* best fits the variant \'pē-ə-nist\. In instances like this, the division falling farther to the left is used, regardless of the order of the pronunciations:

> **pi·a·nist** \pē-'a-nist, 'pē-ə-\

A double hyphen ⸗ at the end of a line in this dictionary (as in the etymology at *dally*) stands for a hyphen that belongs at that point in a hyphenated word and that is retained when the word is written as a unit on one line.

VARIANTS

When a main entry is followed by the word *or* and another spelling, the two spellings are equal variants. Both are standard, and either one may be used according to personal inclination:

> **ocher** *or* **ochre**

If two variants joined by *or* are out of alphabetical order, they remain equal variants. The one printed first is, however, slightly more common than the second:

> **plow** *or* **plough**

When another spelling is joined to the main entry by the word *also,* the spelling after *also* is a secondary variant and occurs less frequently than the first:

> **can·cel·la·tion** *also* **can·cel·ation**

Secondary variants belong to standard usage and may be used according to personal inclination. If there are two secondary variants, the second is joined to the first by *or.* Once the word *also* is used to signal a secondary variant, all following variants are joined by *or:*

> ¹**Shake·spear·ean** *or* **Shake·spear·ian**
> *also* **Shak·sper·ean** *or* **Shak·sper·ian**

Variants whose spelling places them alphabetically more than a column away from the main entry are entered at their own alphabetical places and usually not at the main entry:

> ¹**jibe** . . . *variant of* GIBE
>
> ³**rime, rimester** *variant of* RHYME, RHYME-
> STER

Variants having a usage label appear only at their own alphabetical places:

> **metre** . . . *chiefly British variant of* METER
>
> **agin** . . . *dialect variant of* AGAINST

RUN-ON ENTRIES

A main entry may be followed by one or more derivatives or by a homograph with a different functional label. These are run-on entries. Each is introduced on a new line by a boldface dash and each has a functional label. They are not defined, however, since their meanings are readily derivable from the meaning of the root word:

> **slay** . . . *verb* . . .
> — **slay·er** *noun*
>
> **spir·it·ed** . . . *adjective* . . .
> — **spir·it·ed·ly** *adverb*
> — **spir·it·ed·ness** *noun*
>
> **stac·ca·to** . . . *adjective* . . .
> — **staccato** *adverb*
> — **staccato** *noun*

A main entry may be followed by one or more phrases containing the entry word or an inflected form of it. These are also run-on entries. Each is introduced on a new line by a boldface dash but there is no functional label. They are, however, defined since their meanings are more than the sum of the meanings of their elements:

> ¹**hole** . . . *noun* . . .
> — **in the hole :** . . .
>
> ¹**live** . . . *verb* . . .
> — **live it up :** . . .

Defined phrases of this sort are run on at the entry constituting the first major element in the phrase. The first major element is ordinarily a verb or a noun, but when these are absent another part of speech may serve instead:

> ¹**but** . . . *conjunction* . . .
> — **but what :** . . .

When there are variants, however, the run-on appears at the entry constituting the first major invariable element in the phrase:

> ¹**clock** . . . *noun* . . .
> — **kill the clock** *or* **run out the clock**
> **:** . . .

¹hand . . . *noun* . . .
— **on all hands** *or* **on every hand**
: . . .

A run-on entry is an independent entry with respect to function and status. Labels at the main entry do not apply unless they are repeated.

Attention is called to the definition of *vocabulary entry* in this book. The term *dictionary entry* includes all vocabulary entries as well as all boldface entries in the separate sections of the back matter headed "Abbreviations and Symbols for Chemical Elements," "Foreign Words and Phrases," "Biographical Names," and "Geographical Names."

Pronunciation

Pronunciation is indicated between a pair of reversed virgules \ \ following the entry word. The symbols used are listed in the chart printed on the page facing the first page of the dictionary proper. An abbreviated list appears at the bottom of the third column of each right-hand page of the vocabulary. Explanations of the symbols are given in the Guide to Pronunciation.

SYLLABLES

A hyphen is used in the pronunciation to show syllabic division. These hyphens sometimes coincide with the centered dots in the entry word that indicate end-of-line division; sometimes they do not:

ab·sen·tee \ˌab-sən-'tē\

¹met·ric \'me-trik\

STRESS

A high-set mark \'\ indicates primary (strongest) stress or accent; a low-set mark \ˌ\ indicates secondary (medium) stress or accent:

heart·beat \'härt-ˌbēt\

The stress mark stands at the beginning of the syllable that receives the stress.

Stress marks are an indication of the relative prominence of the syllables in a word. In running speech the primary stress can vary in English words for several contextual and semantic reasons. Because the variation is so great, this book shows the primary stress of a word in its pronunciation as a single word out of context.

VARIANT PRONUNCIATIONS

The presence of variant pronunciations indicates that not all educated speakers pronounce words the same way. A second-place variant is not to be regarded as less acceptable than the pronunciation that is given first. It may, in fact, be used by as many educated speakers as the first variant, but the requirements of the printed page make one precede the other:

apri·cot \'a-prə-ˌkät, 'ā-\

for·eign \'fȯr-ən, 'fär-\

A variant that is appreciably less common than the preceding variant is preceded by the word *also* :

¹al·loy \'a-ˌlȯi *also* ə-'lȯi\

A variant preceded by *sometimes* is even less common, though it does occur in educated speech:

in·vei·gle \in-'vā-gəl *sometimes* -'vē-\

Sometimes a regional label precedes a variant:

¹great \'grāt, *Southern also* 'gre(ə)t\

The label *dial* precedes a variant that is noteworthy or common in a dialect or dialects of American English, but that is not considered to be a standard pronunciation:

ask \'ask, 'åsk; *dialect* 'aks\

The symbol \÷\ is placed before a pronunciation variant that occurs in educated speech but that is considered by some to be unacceptable:

cu·po·la \'kyü-pə-lə, ÷-ˌlō\

This symbol refers only to the immediately following variant and not to subsequent variants separated from it by a comma or a semicolon.

PARENTHESES IN PRONUNCIATIONS

Symbols enclosed by parentheses represent elements that are present in the pronunciation of some speakers but are absent from the pronunciation of other speakers, or elements that are present in some but absent from other utterances of the same speaker:

¹twin·kle \'twiŋ-kəl\ *verb* . . . **twin·kling** \-k(ə-)liŋ\

sat·is·fac·to·ry \ˌsa-təs-'fak-t(ə-)rē\

re·sponse \ri-'spän(t)s\

Thus, the parentheses at *twinkling* mean that there are some who pronounce the \ə\ between \k\ and \l\ and others who do not pronounce it.

PARTIAL AND ABSENT PRONUNCIATIONS

When a main entry has less than a full pronunciation, the missing part is to be supplied from a pronunciation in a preceding entry or within the same pair of reversed virgules:

cham·pi·on·ship \-ˌship\

Ma·dei·ra \mə-'dir-ə, -'der-\

The pronunciation of the first three syllables of *championship* is found at the main entry *champion* :

¹cham·pi·on \'cham-pē-ən\

The hyphens before and after \'der\ in the pronunciation of *Madeira* indicate that both the first and the last parts of the pronunciation are to be taken from the immediately preceding pronunciation.

Partial pronunciations are usually shown when two or more variants have a part in common. When a variation of stress is involved, a partial pronunciation may be terminated at the stress mark which stands at the beginning of a syllable not shown:

di·verse \dī-'vərs, də-', 'dī-ˌ\

an·cho·vy \'an-ˌchō-vē, an-'\

In general, no pronunciation is indicated for open compounds consisting of two or more English words that have own-place entry:

witch doctor *noun*

A pronunciation is shown, however, for any element of an open compound that does not have entry at its own alphabetical place:

Oc·cam's razor \'ä-kəmz-\

sieve of Er·a·tos·the·nes \-,er-ə-'täs-thə-
,nēz\

Only the first entry in a sequence of numbered homographs is given a pronunciation if their pronunciations are the same:

¹re·ward \ri-'word\

²reward

Pronunciations are shown for obsolete words only if they occur in Shakespeare:

clois·tress \'klȯi-strəs\ *noun* . . .
obsolete

The pronunciation of unpronounced derivatives and compounds run on at a main entry is a combination of the pronunciation at the main entry and the pronunciation of the suffix or final element as given at its alphabetical place in the vocabulary:

— **oval·ness** *noun*

— **shot in the dark**

Thus, the pronunciation of *ovalness* is the sum of the pronunciations given at *oval* and *-ness* ; that of *shot in the dark,* the sum of the pronunciation of the four elements that make up the phrase.

Functional Labels

An italic label indicating a part of speech or some other functional classification follows the pronunciation or, if no pronunciation is given, the main entry. The eight traditional parts of speech are indicated as follows:

¹bold . . . *adjective*

hand·some·ly . . . *adverb*

¹but . . . *conjunction*

oops . . . *interjection*

bo·le·ro . . . *noun*

²under . . . *preposition*

some·one . . . *pronoun*

¹shrink . . . *verb*

If a verb is both transitive and intransitive, the labels *transitive verb* and *intransitive verb* introduce the subdivisions:

flat·ten . . . *verb* . . .
transitive verb . . .
intransitive verb . . .

If there is no subdivision, *transitive verb* or *intransitive verb* takes the place of *verb*:

²fleece *transitive verb*

ap·per·tain . . . *intransitive verb*

Labeling a verb as transitive, however, does not preclude occasional intransitive use (as in absolute constructions).

Other italicized labels used to indicate functional classifications that are not traditional parts of speech are:

poly- *combining form*

-logy *noun combining form*

-iferous *adjective combining
form*

super- *prefix*

Gram·my . . . *service mark*

¹-ic *adjective suffix*

²-ward *or* **-wards** *adverb
suffix*

-itis *noun suffix*

-ize *verb suffix*

NC–17 . . . *certification mark*

Ly·cra . . . *trademark*

-nd *symbol*

¹may . . . *verbal auxiliary*

gid·dap . . . *verb imperative*

me·thinks . . . *impersonal
verb*

Two functional labels are sometimes combined:

zilch . . . *adjective or noun*

afloat . . . *adjective or adverb*

Inflected Forms

In comparison with some other languages English does not have many inflected forms. Of those which it has, several are inflected forms of words belonging to small, closed groups (as the personal pronouns or the demonstratives). These forms can readily be found at their own alphabetical places with a full entry (as *whom,* the objective case form of *who*) or with a cross-reference in small capital letters to another entry (as *those,* the plural form of *that*).

Most other inflected forms, however, are covered explicitly or by implication at the main entry for the base form. These are the plurals of nouns, the principal parts of verbs (the past tense, the past participle when it differs from the past tense, and the present participle), and the comparative and superlative forms of adjectives and adverbs. In general, it may be said that when these inflected forms are created in a manner considered regular in English (as by adding *-s* or *-es* to nouns, *-ed* and *-ing* to verbs, and *-er* and *-est* to adjectives and adverbs) and when it seems that there is nothing about the formation likely to give the dictionary user doubts, the inflected form is not shown in order to save space for information more likely to be sought. Inflected forms are also not shown at undefined run-ons or at some entries bearing a limiting label:

gour·mand . . . *noun* . . .
— **gour·man·dize** . . . *intransitive verb*

¹fem·i·nine . . . *adjective* . . .
— **fem·i·nine·ness** . . . *noun*

²lake *noun* . . .
— **laky** . . . *adjective*

²cote . . . *transitive verb* . . . *obsolete* **:** to
pass by

crouse . . . *adjective* . . .
chiefly Scottish **:** BRISK, LIVELY

On the other hand, if the inflected form is created in an irregular way or if the dictionary user is likely to have doubts about it (even though it is formed regularly), the inflected form is shown in boldface, either in full or cut back to a convenient and easily recognizable point. Full details about the kinds of entries at which inflected forms are shown and the kinds at which they are not shown are given in the three following sections.

NOUNS

The plurals of nouns are shown in this dictionary when suffixation brings about a change of final *-y* to *-i-*, when the noun ends in a consonant plus *-o* or in *-ey,* when the noun ends in *-oo,* when the noun has an irregular plural or a zero plural or a foreign

plural, when the noun is a compound that pluralizes any element but the last, when a final consonant is doubled, when the noun has variant plurals, and when it is believed that the dictionary user might have reasonable doubts about the spelling of the plural or when the plural is spelled in a way contrary to expectations:

> [2]**spy** *noun, plural* **spies**
>
> **si·lo** . . . *noun, plural* **silos**
>
> [1]**ro·deo** . . . *noun, plural* **ro·de·os**
>
> [2]**shampoo** *noun, plural* **shampoos**
>
> [1]**mouse** . . . *noun, plural* **mice**
>
> **moose** . . . *noun, plural* **moose**
>
> **cri·te·ri·on** . . . *noun, plural* **-ria**
>
> **son–in–law** . . . *noun, plural* **sons–in–law**
>
> [1]**quiz** . . . *noun, plural* **quiz·zes**
>
> [1]**fish** . . . *noun, plural* **fish** *or* **fish·es**
>
> **cor·gi** . . . *noun, plural* **corgis**
>
> [3]**dry** *noun, plural* **drys**

Cutback inflected forms are used when the noun has three or more syllables:

> **ame·ni·ty** . . . *noun, plural* **-ties**

The plurals of nouns are usually not shown when the base word is unchanged by suffixation, when the noun is a compound whose second element is readily recognizable as a regular free form entered at its own place, or when the noun is unlikely to occur in the plural:

> [1]**night** . . . *noun*
>
> [2]**crunch** *noun*
>
> **fore·foot** . . . *noun*
>
> **mo·nog·a·my** . . . *noun*

Nouns that are plural in form and that regularly occur in plural construction are labeled *noun plural*:

> **munch·ies** . . . *noun plural*

Nouns that are plural in form but that are not always construed as plurals are appropriately labeled:

> **ro·bot·ics** . . . *noun plural but singular in construction*
>
> **two bits** *noun plural but singular or plural in construction*

A noun that is singular in construction takes a singular verb when it is used as a subject; a noun that is plural in construction takes a plural verb when it is used as a subject.

VERBS

The principal parts of verbs are shown in this dictionary when suffixation brings about a doubling of a final consonant or an elision of a final *-e* or a change of final *-y* to *-i-*, when final *-c* changes to *-ck* in suffixation, when the verb ends in *-ey*, when the inflection is irregular, when there are variant inflected forms, and when it is believed that the dictionary user might have reasonable doubts about the spelling of an inflected form or when the inflected form is spelled in a way contrary to expectations:

> [2]**snag** *transitive verb* **snagged; snag·ging**
>
> [1]**move** . . . *verb* **moved; mov·ing**

> [1]**cry** . . . *verb* **cried; cry·ing**
>
> [2]**frolic** *intransitive verb* **frol·icked; frol·ick·ing**
>
> [1]**sur·vey** . . . *verb* **sur·veyed; sur·vey·ing**
>
> [1]**drive** . . . *verb* **drove** . . . ; **driv·en** . . . ; **driv·ing**
>
> [2]**bus** *verb* **bused** *or* **bussed; bus·ing** *or* **bus·sing**
>
> [2]**visa** *transitive verb* **vi·saed** . . . ; **vi·sa·ing**
>
> [2]**chagrin** *transitive verb* **cha·grined** . . . ; **cha·grin·ing**

The principal parts of a regularly inflected verb are shown when it is desirable to indicate the pronunciation of one of the inflected forms:

> **learn** . . . *verb* **learned** \'lərnd, 'lərnt\; **learn·ing**
>
> **rip·en** . . . *verb* **rip·ened; rip·en·ing** \'rī·pə·niŋ, 'rīp·niŋ\

Cutback inflected forms are often used when the verb has three or more syllables, when it is a disyllable that ends in *-l* and has variant spellings, and when it is a compound whose second element is readily recognized as an irregular verb:

> **elim·i·nate** . . . *transitive verb* **-nat·ed; -nat·ing**
>
> [3]**quarrel** *intransitive verb* **-reled** *or* **-relled; -rel·ing** *or* **-rel·ling**
>
> [1]**re·take** . . . *transitive verb* **-took** . . . ; **-tak·en** . . . ; **-tak·ing**

The principal parts of verbs are usually not shown when the base word is unchanged by suffixation or when the verb is a compound whose second element is readily recognizable as a regular free form entered at its own place:

> [1]**jump** . . . *verb*
>
> **pre·judge** . . . *transitive verb*

Another inflected form of English verbs is the third person singular of the present tense, which is regularly formed by the addition of *-s* or *-es* to the base form of the verb. This inflected form is not shown except at a handful of entries (as *have* and *do*) for which it is in some way anomalous.

ADJECTIVES & ADVERBS

The comparative and superlative forms of adjectives and adverbs are shown in this dictionary when suffixation brings about a doubling of a final consonant or an elision of a final *-e* or a change of final *-y* to *-i-*, when the word ends in *-ey*, when the inflection is irregular, and when there are variant inflected forms:

> [1]**red** . . . *adjective* **red·der; red·dest**
>
> [1]**tame** . . . *adjective* **tam·er; tam·est**
>
> [1]**kind·ly** . . . *adjective* **kind·li·er; -est**
>
> [1]**ear·ly** . . . *adverb* **ear·li·er; -est**
>
> **dic·ey** . . . *adjective* **dic·i·er; -est**
>
> [1]**good** . . . *adjective* **bet·ter** . . . ; **best**
>
> [1]**bad** . . . *adjective* **worse** . . . ; **worst**
>
> [1]**far** . . . *adverb* **far·ther** . . . *or* **fur·ther** . . . ; **far·thest** *or* **fur·thest**

The superlative forms of adjectives and adverbs of two or more syllables are usually cut back:

> [3]**fancy** *adjective* **fan·ci·er; -est**

The comparative and superlative forms of regularly inflected adjectives and adverbs are shown when it is desirable to indicate the pronunciation of the inflected forms:

> [1]**young** . . . *adjective* **youn·ger** \'yəŋ-gər\;
> **youn·gest** \'yəŋ-gəst\

The inclusion of inflected forms in *-er* and *-est* at adjective and adverb entries means nothing more about the use of *more* and *most* with these adjectives and adverbs than that their comparative and superlative degrees may be expressed in either way; *lazier* or *more lazy; laziest* or *most lazy.*

At a few adjective entries only the superlative form is shown:

> [3]**mere** . . . *adjective, superlative* **mer·est**

The absence of the comparative form indicates that there is no evidence of its use.

The comparative and superlative forms of adjectives and adverbs are not shown when the base word is unchanged by suffixation or when the word is a compound whose second element is readily recognizable as a regular free form entered at its own place:

> [1]**near** . . . *adverb*

> **un·wary** . . . *adjective*

The comparative and superlative forms of adverbs are not shown when they are identical with the inflected forms of a preceding adjective homograph:

> [1]**hot** . . . *adjective* **hot·ter; hot·test**

> [2]**hot** *adverb*

Capitalization

Most entries in this dictionary begin with a lowercase letter. A few of these have an italicized label *often capitalized*, which indicates that the word is as likely to be capitalized as not, that it is as acceptable with an uppercase initial as it is with one in lowercase. Some entries begin with an uppercase letter, which indicates that the word is usually capitalized. The absence of an initial capital or of an *often capitalized* label indicates that the word is not ordinarily capitalized:

> **lunk·head** . . . *noun*

> **gar·gan·tuan** . . . *adjective, often capitalized*

> **Mo·hawk** . . . *noun*

The capitalization of entries that are open or hyphenated compounds is similarly indicated by the form of the entry or by an italicized label:

> **obstacle course** *noun*

> **neo-Dar·win·ian** . . . *adjective, often N capitalized*

> **off–off–Broadway** *noun, often both Os capitalized*

> **un–Amer·i·can** . . . *adjective*

> **Dutch oven** *noun*

> **Old Glory** *noun*

A word that is capitalized in some senses and lowercase in others shows variations from the form of the main entry by the use of italicized labels at the appropriate senses:

> **re·nais·sance** . . . *noun* . . .
> **1** *capitalized* . . .
> **2** *often capitalized*

> **Shet·land** . . . *noun* . . .
> **2** *often not capitalized*

> **Trin·i·ty** . . . *noun* . . .
> **2** *not capitalized*

Attributive Nouns

The italicized label *often attributive* placed after the functional label *noun* indicates that the noun is often used as an adjective equivalent in attributive position before another noun:

> **gold** . . . *noun, often attributive*

> **busi·ness** . . . *noun, often attributive*

Examples of the attributive use of these nouns are *gold chain* and *business ethics.*

While any noun may occasionally be used attributively, the label *often attributive* is limited to those having broad attributive use. This label is not used when an adjective homograph (as *iron* or *paper*) is entered. And it is not used at open compounds (as *X ray*) that may be used attributively with an inserted hyphen (as in *X-ray therapy*).

Etymology

The matter in square brackets preceding the definition is the etymology. Meanings given in roman type within these brackets are not definitions of the entry, but are meanings of the Middle English, Old English, or non-English words within the brackets.

The etymology traces a vocabulary entry as far back as possible in English (as to Old English), tells from what language and in what form it came into English, and (except in the case of such words outside the general vocabulary of English as *bascule* and *zloty*) traces the pre-English source as far back as possible if the source is an Indo-European language. These etyma are printed in italics.

OLD, MIDDLE, AND MODERN ENGLISH

The etymology usually gives the Middle English and the Old English forms of words in the following style:

> [1]**nap** . . . *intransitive verb* . . . [Middle English *nappen,* from Old English *hnappian* . . .]

> [1]**old** . . . *adjective* [Middle English, from Old English *eald* . . .]

An etymology in which a word is traced back to Middle English but not to Old English indicates that the word is found in Middle English but not in those texts that have survived from the Old English period:

¹slab . . . *noun* [Middle English *slabbe*]

¹stale . . . *adjective* . . . [Middle English, aged (of ale), not fresh; akin to Middle Dutch *stel* stale]

An etymology in which a word is traced back directly to Old English with no intervening mention of Middle English indicates that the word has not survived continuously from Old English times to the present. Rather, it died out after the Old English period and has been revived in modern times:

ge·mot . . . *noun* [Old English *gemōt* . . .]

thegn . . . *noun* [Old English . . .]

An etymology is not usually given for a word created in English by the combination of existing constituents or by functional shift. This indicates that the identity of the constituents is expected to be self-evident to the user.

book·shelf . . . *noun* . . . : an open shelf for holding books

¹fire·proof . . . *adjective* . . . : proof against or resistant to fire

off–put·ting . . . *adjective* . . . : that puts off : REPELLENT, DISCONCERTING

penal code *noun* . . . : a code of laws concerning crimes and offenses and their punishment

³stalk *noun* . . . **1** : the act of stalking

In the case of a family of words obviously related to a common English word but differing from it by containing various easily recognizable suffixes, an etymology is usually given only at the base word, even though some of the derivatives may have been formed in a language other than English:

¹equal . . . *adjective* [Middle English, from Latin *aequalis,* from *aequus* level, equal] . . . **1 a** (1) : of the same measure, quantity, amount, or number as another

equal·i·ty . . . *noun* . . . **1** : the quality or state of being equal

equal·ize . . . *transitive verb* **1** : to make equal

While *equalize* was formed in Modern English, *equality* was actually borrowed into Middle English (via Middle French) from Latin *aequalitas.*

LANGUAGES OTHER THAN ENGLISH

The etymology gives the language from which words borrowed into English have come. It also gives the form or a transliteration of the word in that language if the form differs from that in English:

¹mar·ble . . . *noun* [Middle English, from Old French *marbre,* from Latin *marmor,* from Greek *marmaros*]

pome·gran·ate . . . *noun* [Middle English *poumgrenet,* from Middle French *pomme grenate,* literally, seedy apple]

souk . . . *noun* [Arabic *sūq* market]

In a few cases the expression "ultimately from" replaces the more usual "from." This expression indicates that one or more intermediate steps have been omitted in tracing the derivation of the form preceding the expression from the form following it:

tri·lo·bite . . . *noun* [ultimately from Greek *trilobos* three-lobed, from *tri-* + *lobos* lobe]

Words cited from certain American Indian languages and from some other languages that are infrequently printed have been rendered with the phonetic symbols used by scholars of those languages. These symbols include the following: a raised dot to the right of a vowel letter to mark vowel length; a hook below a vowel letter to mark nasality; an apostrophe over a consonant letter to mark glottal release; a superscript *w* to the right of a consonant letter to mark labialization; the symbol ɔ to render \ȯ\; the symbol *i* to render a high central vowel; the Greek letters β, δ, and γ to render voiced labial, dental, and velar fricatives; the symbol *x* to render \k\; the symbol ʔ to render a glottal stop; and the symbol λ ("crossed lambda") for a voiceless lateral affricate. Examples of these symbols can be found at etymologies for the words *Athabascan, babassu, coho, geoduck, muskellunge, obeah, potlatch,* and *sego lily.*

WORDS OF UNKNOWN ORIGIN

When the source of a word appearing as a main entry is unknown, the expression "origin unknown" is usually used. Only in exceptional circumstances (as with some ethnic names) does the absence of an etymology mean that it has not been possible to furnish an informative etymology. More often, it means that no etymology is believed to be necessary. This is the case, for instance, with most of the entries identified as variants and with many derivatives.

ETYMOLOGIES OF TECHNICAL WORDS

Much of the technical vocabulary of the sciences and other specialized studies consists of words or word elements that are current in two or more languages, with only such slight modifications as are necessary to adapt them to the structure of the individual language in each case. Many words and word elements of this kind have become sufficiently a part of the general vocabulary of English as to require entry in an abridged dictionary. Because of the vast extent of the relevant published material in many languages and in many scientific and other specialized fields, it is impracticable to ascertain the language of origin of every such term. Yet it would not be accurate to formulate a statement about the origin of any such term in a way that could be interpreted as implying that it was coined in English. Accordingly, whenever a term that is entered in this dictionary belongs recognizably to this class of internationally current terms and whenever no positive evidence is at hand to show that it was coined in English, the etymology recognizes its international status and the possibility that it originated elsewhere than in English by use of the label International Scientific Vocabulary:

mega·watt . . . *noun* [International Scientific Vocabulary]

phy·lo·ge·net·ic . . . *adjective* [International Scientific Vocabulary, from New Latin *phylogenesis* . . .]

¹-ol *noun suffix* [International Scientific Vocabulary, from *alcohol*]

COMPRESSION OF INFORMATION

An etymology giving the name of a language (including Middle English or Old English) and not giving the foreign (or Middle English or Old English) form indicates that this form is the same as that of the entry word:

ka·pok . . . *noun* [Malay]

¹po·grom . . . *noun* [Yiddish, from Russian . . .]

¹**dumb** . . . *adjective* [Middle English, from Old English . . .]

An etymology giving the name of a language (including Middle English or Old English) and the form in that language but not giving the foreign (or Middle English or Old English) meaning indicates that this meaning is the same as that expressed in the first definition in the entry:

> ¹**wea·ry** . . . *adjective* . . . [Middle English *wery*, from Old English *wērig* . . .] . . .
> **1 :** exhausted in strength . . .

When a word from a foreign language (or Middle English or Old English) is a key element in the etymologies of several related entries that are found close together, the meaning of the word is usually given at only one of the entries:

> **ve·lo·ce** . . . *adverb or adjective* [Italian, from Latin *veloc-, velox*]
>
> **ve·loc·i·pede** . . . *noun* [French *vélocipède,* from Latin *veloc-, velox* + *ped-, pes* foot — more at FOOT]
>
> **ve·loc·i·ty** . . . *noun* . . . [Middle French *velocité,* from Latin *velocitat-, velocitas,* from *veloc-, velox* quick; probably akin to Latin *vegēre* to enliven — more at WAKE]

When an etymology includes the expression "by alteration" and the altered form is not cited, the form is the term given in small capital letters as the definition:

> **crit·ter** . . . *noun* [by alteration] . . .
> **:** CREATURE

When the origin of a word is traced to the name of a person or place not further identified, additional information may be found in the Biographical Names or Geographical Names section in the back matter:

> **far·ad** . . . *noun* [Michael *Faraday*]
>
> **jodh·pur** . . . *noun* [*Jodhpur,* India]

RELATED WORDS

When a word of Indo-European origin has been traced back to the earliest language in which it is attested, words descended from the same Indo-European base in other languages (especially Old High German, Latin, Greek, and Sanskrit) are usually given:

> **na·vel** . . . *noun* [Middle English, from Old English *nafela;* akin to Old High German *nabalo* navel, Latin *umbilicus,* Greek *omphalos*]
>
> ¹**wind** . . . *noun* . . . [Middle English, from Old English; akin to Old High German *wint* wind, Latin *ventus,* Greek *aēnai* to blow, Sanskrit *vāti* it blows]

Sometimes, however, to avoid space-consuming repetition, the expression "more at" directs the user to another entry where the cognates are given:

> **ho·ly** . . . *adjective* . . . [Middle English, from Old English *hālig;* akin to Old English *hāl* whole — more at WHOLE]

Besides the use of "akin to" to denote relatedness, some etymologies make special use of "akin to" as part of a longer formula "of — origin; akin to —." This formula indicates that a word was borrowed from some language belonging to a group of languages whose name is inserted in the blank before the word *origin,* that it is impossible to say that the word in question is a borrowing of a particular attested word in a particular language of the source group, and that the form cited in the blank after the expression *akin to* is related to the word in question as attested within the source group:

> **ba·nana** . . . *noun* . . . [Spanish or Portuguese; Spanish, from Portuguese, of African origin; akin to Wolof *banäna* banana]
>
> ²**brier** *noun* [French *bruyère* heath, from Middle French *bruiere,* from (assumed) Vulgar Latin *brucaria,* from Late Latin *brucus* heather, of Celtic origin; akin to Old Irish *froech* heather; akin to Greek *ereikē* heather]

This last example shows the two contrasting uses of "akin to." The word cited immediately after "of Celtic origin; akin to" is an attested Celtic word descended from the same etymon as the unattested Celtic source of the Latin word. The word cited after the second "akin to" is evidence that the Celtic etymon has deeper relations within Indo-European.

Word History Paragraphs

Word history paragraphs are provided for a number of words with especially interesting origins. Such paragraphs explain word origins in greater detail than is possible in etymologies. A brown-shaded diamond after the last definition of a word signals that a word history paragraph discussing that word can be found in the right-hand column on that page or on the facing page to the right:

> **den·im** . . . *noun* [French (*serge*) *de Nîmes* serge of Nîmes, France] (1965)
> **1 a :** a firm durable twilled usually cotton fabric woven with colored warp and white filling threads **b :** a similar fabric woven in colored stripes
> **2** *plural* **:** overalls or trousers usually of blue denim ◇

The paragraph itself is set on a light-brown background:

> ◇ WORD HISTORY
> **denim** It is not unusual for fabrics to be named after the places where they were originally made. Nîmes is a city in France known traditionally for its textiles. A heavy serge produced there became known as *serge de Nîmes,* meaning literally, "serge from Nîmes." The "s" in *Nîmes* is not pronounced in French, so when the name of the fabric came into English in the late 17th century, it was often written *serge de Nim* and later *serge denim.* In time the latter was shortened to *denim.*

When a word is included in the word history paragraph of a different entry, the main entry for that word is followed by a run-on "***word history*** see _____" which refers to the entry where the word history paragraph appears.

Dates

At most main entries a date will be found enclosed in parentheses before the boldface colon or number that introduces the first sense:

> **som·bre·ro** . . . *noun* . . . [Spanish, from *sombra* shade] (1599)

: a high-crowned hat of felt or straw with a very wide brim worn especially in the Southwest and Mexico

This is the date of the earliest recorded use in English, as far as it could be determined, of the sense which the date precedes. Several caveats are appropriate at this point. First, a few classes of main entries that are not complete words (as prefixes, suffixes, and combining forms) or are not generic words (as trademarks and names of figures from mythology) are not given dates. Second, the date given applies only to the first sense of the word entered in this dictionary and not necessarily to the word's very earliest meaning in English. Many words, especially those with long histories, have obsolete, archaic, or uncommon senses that are not entered in this dictionary, and such senses have been excluded from consideration in determining the date:

> **¹slur** . . . *noun* [obsolete English dialect *slur* thin mud, from Middle English *sloor;* akin to Middle High German *slier* mud] (1609)
> **1 a** : an insulting or disparaging remark or innuendo : ASPERSION

The 1609 date is for a sense of *slur* synonymous with *aspersion*. *Slur* also has an obsolete sense, "thin mud," that was recorded as early as the fifteenth century; but since this sense is not entered, it is ignored for purposes of dating. Third, the printed date should not be taken to mark the very first time that the word—or even the sense—was used in English. Many words were certainly in spoken use for decades or even longer before they passed into the written language. The date is for the earliest written or printed use that the editors have been able to discover. This fact means further that any date is subject to change as evidence of still earlier use may emerge, and many dates given now can confidently be expected to yield to others in future printings and editions.

A date will appear in one of three different styles:

> **put·tee** . . . *noun* [Hindi *paṭṭī* strip of cloth, from Sanskrit *paṭṭikā*] (1886)
> **1** : a cloth strip wrapped around the leg from ankle to knee

> **¹moon·light** . . . *noun* (14th century) : the light of the moon

> **¹thrall** . . . *noun* [Middle English *thral,* from Old English *thrǽl,* from Old Norse *thrǽll*] (before 12th century)
> **1 a** : a servant slave : BONDMAN; *also* : SERF

The style that names a year (as 1886) is the one used for the period from the sixteenth century to the present. The style that names only a century (as 14th century) is the one used for the period from the twelfth century through the fifteenth century, a span that roughly approximates the period of Middle English. The style (before 12th century) is used for the period before the twelfth century back to the earliest records of English, a span that approximates the period of Old English. Words first attested after 1500 can usually be dated to a single year because the precise dates of publication of modern printed texts are known. If a word must be dated from a modern text of uncertain chronology, it will be assigned the latest possible date of the text's publication prefixed by the word *circa*. For words from the Old and Middle English periods the examples of use on which the dates depend very often occur in manuscripts which are themselves of uncertain date and which may record a text whose date of composition is highly conjectural. To date words from these periods by year would frequently give a quite misleading impression of the state of our knowledge, and so the broader formulas involving centuries are used instead.

Each date reflects a particular instance of the use of a word, most often within a continuous text. In cases where the earliest appearance of a word dated by year is not from continuous text but from a source (as a dictionary or glossary) that defines or explains the word instead of simply using it, the year is preceded by *circa*:

> **magnesium sulfate** *noun* (circa 1890)
> : a sulfate of magnesium . . .

In such instances, *circa* indicates that while the source providing the date attests that the word was in use in the relevant sense at that time, it does not offer an example of the normal use of the word and thus gives no better than an approximate date for such use. For the example above no use has so far been found that is earlier than its appearance (spelled *magnesium sulphate*) as an entry in Webster's International Dictionary, published in 1890, so the date is given with the qualifying abbreviation.

Usage

USAGE LABELS

Three types of status labels are used in this dictionary—temporal, regional, and stylistic—to signal that a word or a sense of a word is not part of the standard vocabulary of English.

The temporal label *obsolete* means that there is no evidence of use since 1755:

> **¹per·du** . . . *noun* . . .
> *obsolete*

> **gov·ern·ment** . . . *noun* . . .
> **2** *obsolete*

The label *obsolete* is a comment on the word being defined. When a thing, as distinguished from the word used to designate it, is obsolete, appropriate orientation is usually given in the definition:

> **¹cat·a·pult** . . . *noun* . . .
> **1** : an ancient military device for hurling missiles

> **far·thin·gale** . . . *noun* . . .
> : a support (as of hoops) worn especially in the 16th century beneath a skirt to expand it at the hipline

The temporal label *archaic* means that a word or sense once in common use is found today only sporadically or in special contexts:

> **¹goody** . . . *noun* . . .
> *archaic*

> **lon·gi·tude** . . . *noun* . . .
> **2** *archaic*

A word or sense limited in use to a specific region of the U.S. has a regional label. Some regional labels correspond loosely to areas defined in Hans Kurath's *Word Geography of the Eastern United States.* The adverb *chiefly* precedes a label when the word has some currency outside the specified region, and a double label is used to indicate considerable currency in each of two specific regions:

> **pung** . . . *noun* . . .
> *New England*

> **ban·quette** . . . *noun* . . .
> **1** . . . **b** *Southern*

> **³pas·tor** . . . *noun* . . .
> *chiefly Southwest*

> **do·gie** . . . *noun* . . .
> *chiefly West*

> **gal·lery** . . . *noun* . . .
> **2** . . . **b** *Southern & Midland*

¹pot·latch . . . *noun* . . .
2 *Northwest*

smear·case . . . *noun* . . .
chiefly Midland

crul·ler . . . *noun* . . .
2 *Northern & Midland*

Words current in all regions of the U.S. have no label.

A word or sense limited in use to one of the other countries of the English-speaking world has an appropriate regional label:

cutty sark . . . *noun* . . .
chiefly Scottish

lar·ri·kin . . . *noun* . . .
chiefly Australian

in·da·ba . . . *noun* . . .
chiefly South African

spal·peen . . . *noun* . . .
chiefly Irish

¹bon·net . . . *noun* . . .
2 a *British*

book off *intransitive verb* . . .
Canadian

¹din·kum . . . *adjective* . . .
Australian & New Zealand

gar·ron . . . *noun* . . .
Scottish & Irish

The label *dialect* indicates that the pattern of use of a word or sense is too complex for summary labeling: it usually includes several regional varieties of American English or of American and British English:

least·ways . . . *adverb* . . .
dialect

The label *dialect British* indicates currency in several dialects of the Commonwealth; *dialect English* indicates currency in one or more provincial dialects of England:

bo·gle . . . *noun* . . .
dialect British

¹hob . . . *noun* . . .
1 *dialect English*

The stylistic label *slang* is used with words or senses that are especially appropriate in contexts of extreme informality, that usually have a currency not limited to a particular region or area of interest, and that are composed typically of shortened or altered forms or extravagant or facetious figures of speech:

⁴barb *noun* . . .
slang **:** BARBITURATE

²skin·ny *noun* . . .
slang **:** inside information **:** DOPE

main squeeze *noun* . . .
slang **:** one's principal romantic partner

There is no satisfactory objective test for slang, especially with reference to a word out of context. No word, in fact, is invariably slang, and many standard words can be given slang applications.

The stylistic label *nonstandard* is used for a few words or senses that are disapproved by many but that have some currency in reputable contexts:

learn . . . *verb* . . .
2 a *nonstandard*

ir·re·gard·less . . . *adverb* . . .
nonstandard

The stylistic label *substandard* is used for those words or senses that conform to a widespread pattern of usage that differs in choice of word or form from that of the prestige group of the community:

is . . . *present 3d singular of* BE, *dialect present 1st & 2d singular of* BE, *substandard present plural of* BE

A subject label or guide phrase is sometimes used to indicate the specific application of a word or sense:

knock·about . . . *adjective* . . .
3 *of a sailing vessel*

²break *noun* . . .
5 . . . **d** *mining*

²up *adjective* . . .
5 *of a quark*

In general, however, subject orientation is given in the definition:

Di·do . . . *noun* . . .
: a legendary queen of Carthage in Virgil's *Aeneid* who kills herself when Aeneas leaves her

je·té . . . *noun* . . .
: a springing jump in ballet made from one foot to the other in any direction

ILLUSTRATIONS OF USAGE

Definitions are sometimes followed by verbal illustrations that show a typical use of the word in context. These illustrations are enclosed in angle brackets:

¹key . . . *noun* . . .
3 a . . . <the *key* to a riddle>

nary . . . *adjective*
. . . <*nary* a person wanted to go>

²plummet *intransitive verb* . . .
2 . . . <prices *plummeted*>

¹true . . . *adjective* . . .
8 . . . <in the *truest* sense>

turn off *transitive verb* . . .
4 . . . <*turn* the water *off*>

Illustrative quotations are also used to show words in typical contexts:

con·flict·ed . . . *adjective*
. . . <this unhappy and *conflicted* modern woman —John Updike>

Omissions in quotations are indicated by suspension points:

alien·ation . . . *noun*
. . . <*alienation* . . . from the values of one's society and family —S.L. Halleck>

USAGE NOTES

Definitions are sometimes followed by usage notes that give supplementary information about such matters as idiom, syntax, semantic relationship, and status. A usage note is introduced by a lightface dash:

²cry *noun* . . .
11 : . . . — usually used in the phrase *a far cry*

²drum . . . *transitive verb* . . .
2 : . . . — usually used with *out*

¹so . . . *adverb* . . .
1 a : . . . — often used as a substitute for a
preceding clause

¹sfor·zan·do . . . *adjective or adverb* . . .
: . . . — used as a direction in music

grin·go . . . *noun* . . .
: . . . — often used disparagingly

pissed . . . *adjective* . . .
1 . . . **:** . . . — sometimes considered vul-
gar

hajji . . . *noun* . . .
: . . . — often used as a title

Two or more usage notes are separated by a semicolon:

²thine *pronoun* . . .
: that which belongs to thee — used with-
out a following noun as a pronoun equiva-
lent in meaning to the adjective *thy*; used
especially in ecclesiastical or literary lan-
guage and still surviving in the speech of
Friends especially among themselves

Sometimes a usage note calls attention to one or more terms
with the same denotation as the main entry:

water moccasin *noun* . . .
1 : a venomous semiaquatic pit viper
(*Agkistrodon piscivorus*) chiefly of the south-
eastern U.S. that is closely related to the cop-
perhead — called also *cottonmouth, cotton-
mouth moccasin*

The called-also terms are shown in italic type. If such a term falls
alphabetically more than a column away from the main entry, it is
entered at its own place with the sole definition being a synony-
mous cross-reference to the entry where it appears in the usage
note:

cot·ton·mouth . . . *noun* . . .
: WATER MOCCASIN

cottonmouth moccasin *noun* . . .
: WATER MOCCASIN

Sometimes a usage note is used in place of a definition. Some
function words (as conjunctions and prepositions) have little or
no semantic content; most interjections express feelings but are
otherwise untranslatable into meaning; and some other words (as
oaths and honorific titles) are more amenable to comment than to
definition:

¹of . . . *preposition* . . .
1 — used as a function word to indicate a
point of reckoning

¹oyez . . . *verb imperative* . . .
— used by a court or public crier to gain
attention before a proclamation

¹or . . . *conjunction* . . .
1 — used as a function word to indicate an
alternative

gol·ly . . . *interjection* . . .
— used as a mild oath or to express surprise

sir . . . *noun* . . .
2 a — used as a usually respectful form of
address

USAGE PARAGRAPHS

Brief usage paragraphs are provided for a number of entries
that are considered to present problems of confused or disputed
usage. A usage paragraph typically summarizes the historical

background of the item and its associated body of opinion, com-
pares these with available evidence of current usage, and often
adds a few words of suitable advice for the dictionary user.

A small green-shaded square after the last definition of a word
signals that a usage paragraph discussing that word can be found
in the right-hand column on that page or on the facing page to the
right:

ag·gra·vate . . . *transitive verb* . . .
1 *obsolete* **a :** to make heavy **:** BURDEN **b**
: INCREASE
2 : to make worse, more serious, or more se-
vere **:** intensify unpleasantly <problems have
been *aggravated* by neglect>
3 a : to rouse to displeasure or anger by
usually persistent and often petty goading **b**
: to produce inflammation in □

The paragraph itself is set on a green background. Where
appropriate, discussion in the paragraph is keyed by sense num-
ber to the definition of the meaning in question. Most paragraphs
incorporate appropriate verbal illustrations and illustrative quota-
tions to clarify and exemplify the points being made:

□ USAGE
Aggravate Although *aggravate* has
been used in sense 3a since the 17th
century, it has been the object of disap-
proval only since about 1870. It is used in
expository prose <when his silly conceit
. . . about his not-very-good early work
has begun to *aggravate* us —William Sty-
ron> but seems to be more common in
speech and casual writing <a good profes-
sion for him, because bus drivers get *ag-
gravated* —Jackie Gleason (interview,
1986)> <& now this letter comes to *aggra-
vate* me a thousand times worse —Mark
Twain (letter, 1864)>. Sense 2 is far more
common than sense 3a in published prose.
Such is not the case, however, with *aggra-
vation* and *aggravating*. *Aggravation* is
used in sense 3 somewhat more than in its
earlier senses; *aggravating* has practically
no use other than to express annoyance.

When a second word is also discussed in a paragraph, the main
entry for that word is followed by a run-on "***usage*** see_____"
which refers to the entry where the paragraph may be found:

²af·fect . . . *verb*
. . . ***usage*** see EFFECT

When a word that has its own usage paragraph is also dis-
cussed in a usage paragraph at another entry, the word's usage
paragraph is followed by a cross-reference to the other entry.

Definitions

DIVISION OF SENSES

A boldface colon is used in this dictionary to introduce a defi-
nition:

¹coo·per . . . *noun* . . .
: one that makes or repairs wooden casks or
tubs

It is also used to separate two or more definitions of a single
sense:

un·cage . . . *transitive verb* . . .
: to release from or as if from a cage **:** free
from restraint

Boldface Arabic numerals separate the senses of a word that has more than one sense:

> ²**savage** *noun* . . .
> **1 :** a person belonging to a primitive society
> **2 :** a brutal person
> **3 :** a rude or unmannerly person

Boldface lowercase letters separate the subsenses of a word:

> ¹**grand** . . . *adjective* . . .
> **5 a :** LAVISH, SUMPTUOUS . . . **b :** marked by a regal form and dignity **c :** fine or imposing in appearance or impression **d :** LOFTY, SUBLIME

Lightface numerals in parentheses indicate a further division of subsenses:

> **take out** . . . *transitive verb* . . .
> **1 a** (1) **:** DEDUCT, SEPARATE (2) **:** EXCLUDE, OMIT (3) **:** WITHDRAW, WITHHOLD

A lightface colon following a definition and immediately preceding two or more subsenses indicates that the subsenses are subsumed by the preceding definition:

> ²**crunch** *noun* . . .
> **3 :** a tight or critical situation: as **a :** a critical point in the buildup of pressure between opposing elements . . . **b :** a severe economic squeeze . . . **c :** SHORTAGE

> **se·quoia** . . . *noun* . . .
> **:** either of two huge coniferous California trees of the bald cypress family that may reach a height of over 300 feet (90 meters): **a :** BIG TREE **b :** REDWOOD 3a

The word *as* may or may not follow the lightface colon. Its presence (as at ²*crunch*) indicates that the following subsenses are typical or significant examples. Its absence (as at *sequoia*) indicates that the subsenses which follow are exhaustive.

The system of separating the various senses of a word by numerals and letters is a lexical convenience. It reflects something of their semantic relationship, but it does not evaluate senses or set up a hierarchy of importance among them.

Sometimes a particular semantic relationship between senses is suggested by the use of one of four italic sense dividers: *especially, specifically, also,* or *broadly.*

The sense divider *especially* is used to introduce the most common meaning subsumed in the more general preceding definition:

> ²**slick** *adjective* . . .
> **3 a :** characterized by subtlety or nimble wit **:** CLEVER; *especially* **:** WILY

The sense divider *specifically* is used to introduce a common but highly restricted meaning subsumed in the more general preceding definition:

> **pon·tiff** . . . *noun* . . .
> **2 :** BISHOP; *specifically* **:** POPE

The sense divider *also* is used to introduce a meaning that is closely related to but may be considered less important than the preceding sense:

> **chi·na** . . . *noun* . . .
> **1 :** PORCELAIN; *also* **:** vitreous porcelain wares (as dishes, vases, or ornaments) for domestic use

The sense divider *broadly* is used to introduce an extended or wider meaning of the preceding definition:

> **flot·sam** . . . *noun* . . .
> **1 :** floating wreckage of a ship or its cargo; *broadly* **:** floating debris

ORDER OF SENSES

The order of senses within an entry is historical: the sense known to have been first used in English is entered first. This is not to be taken to mean, however, that each sense of a multisense word developed from the immediately preceding sense. It is altogether possible that sense 1 of a word has given rise to sense 2 and sense 2 to sense 3, but frequently sense 2 and sense 3 may have arisen independently of one another from sense 1.

When a numbered sense is further subdivided into lettered subsenses, the inclusion of particular subsenses within a sense is based upon their semantic relationship to one another, but their order is likewise historical: subsense 1a is earlier than 1b, 1b is earlier than 1c, and so forth. Divisions of subsenses indicated by lightface numerals in parentheses are also in historical order with respect to one another. Subsenses may be out of historical order, however, with respect to the broader numbered senses:

> ¹**job** . . . *noun* . . . (circa 1627)
> **1 a :** a piece of work; *especially* **:** a small miscellaneous piece of work undertaken on order at a stated rate **b :** the object or material on which work is being done **c :** something produced by or as if by work <do a better *job* next time> **d :** an example of a usually specified type **:** ITEM <this *job* is round-necked and sleeveless —Lois Long>
> **2 a :** something done for private advantage <suspected the whole incident was a put-up *job*> **b :** a criminal enterprise; *specifically* **:** ROBBERY **c :** a damaging or destructive bit of work <did a *job* on him>
> **3 a** (1) **:** something that has to be done **:** TASK (2) **:** an undertaking requiring unusual exertion <it was a real *job* to talk over that noise> **b :** a specific duty, role, or function **c :** a regular remunerative position **d** *chiefly British* **:** state of affairs — used with *bad* or *good* <it was a good *job* you didn't hit the old man —E. L. Thomas>

At *job* the date indicates that the earliest unit of meaning, sense 1a, was born in the seventeenth century, and it is readily apparent how the following subsenses are linked to it and to each other by the idea of work. Even subsense 1d is so linked, because while it does not apply exclusively to manufactured items, it often does so, as the illustrative quotation suggests. Yet 1d did not exist before the 1920s, while 2a and 3a(1) both belong to the seventeenth century, although they are later than 1a. Even the very last subsense, 3d, is earlier than 1d, as it is found in the works of Dickens.

Historical order also determines whether transitive or intransitive senses are given first at verbs which have both kinds. If the earliest sense is transitive, all the transitive senses precede all the intransitive senses.

OMISSION OF A SENSE

Occasionally the dictionary user, having turned to an entry, may not find a particular sense that was expected or hoped for. This usually means no more than that the editors judged the sense insufficiently common or otherwise important to include in a dictionary of this scope. Such a sense will frequently be found at the appropriate entry in a dictionary (as Webster's Third New International Dictionary) that has room for less common words and meanings. One special case is worth noting, however.

At times it would be possible to include the definition of a meaning at more than one entry (as at a simple verb and a verb-adverb collocation or at a verb and an adjective derived from a participle of that verb). To save space for other information such double coverage is avoided, and the meaning is generally defined only at the base form. For the derivative term the meaning is then considered to be essentially self-explanatory and is not defined. For example *cast off* has a sense "to get rid of" in

such typical contexts as "cast off all restraint," and so has the simple verb *cast* in contexts like "cast all restraint to the winds." This meaning is defined as sense 1e(2) of *cast* and is omitted from the entry *cast off*, where the dictionary user will find a number of senses that cannot be considered self-explanatory in relation to the entries for *cast* and *off*. Likewise, the entry for the adjective *picked* gives only one sense—"CHOICE, PRIME"—which is not the meaning of *picked* in such a context as "the picked fruit lay stacked in boxes awaiting shipment." A definition suitable for this use is not given at *picked* because one is given at the first homograph *pick*, the verb from which the adjective *picked* is derived, as sense 3a—"to gather by plucking."

INFORMATION AT INDIVIDUAL SENSES

Information coming between the entry word and the first definition of a multisense word applies to all senses and subsenses. Information applicable only to some senses or subsenses is given between the appropriate boldface numeral or letter and the symbolic colon. A variety of kinds of information is offered in this way:

²**palm** *noun* . . .
 3 [Latin *palmus,* from *palma*]

²**rally** *noun* . . .
 4 *also* **ral·lye**

¹**disk** *or* **disc** . . . *noun* . . .
 4 . . . **b** *usually disc*

cru·ci·fix·ion . . . *noun* . . .
 1 a *capitalized*

¹**tile** . . . *noun* . . .
 1 *plural* **tiles** *or* **tile a** . . .

del·i·ca·tes·sen . . . *noun plural* . . .
 1 . . .
 2 *singular, plural* **delicatessens**

fix·ing . . . *noun* . . .
 2 *plural*

²**die** . . . *noun, plural* **dice** . . . *or* **dies**
. . .
 1 *plural* **dice** . . .
 2 *plural* **dies** . . .
 3 *plural* **dies**

¹**folk** . . . *noun, plural* **folk** *or* **folks** . . .
 4 *folks plural*

At *palm* the subetymology indicates that the third sense, while ultimately derived from the same source (Latin *palma*) as the other senses of the word, has a different immediate etymon (Latin *palmus*), from which it receives its meaning. At *rally* one is told that in the fourth sense the word has a variant spelling not used for other senses and that this variant is a secondary or less common one. At *disk* the italic label of sense 4b indicates that, while the spelling *disk* is overall somewhat the more common (since it precedes *disc* out of alphabetical order at the beginning of the entry), *disc* is the usual spelling for this particular sense. At *crucifixion* the label *capitalized* points out the one meaning of the word in which it is capitalized. At the first homograph *tile* no plural is shown at the beginning of the entry because the usual plural, *tiles,* is regular. The subsenses of sense 1, however, have a zero plural as well as the usual one, and so both plurals appear in boldface at sense 1. At *delicatessen* the situation is different: the entry as a whole is labeled a plural noun, but sense 2 is used as a singular. In this sense *delicatessen* can take the plural ending *-s* when needed, a fact that is indicated by the appearance of the plural in boldface at the sense. At *fixing* the italic abbreviation simply means that when used in this sense the word is always written in its plural form, *fixings*. At the second homograph *die* the actual distribution of the variant plurals can be given sense by sense in italic type because both variants are shown in boldface earlier in the entry. At the first homograph *folk* a singular noun is

shown with variant plurals of nearly equal frequency, when all senses are taken into account. The fourth sense, however, is unique in being always plural in form and construction. The form of the plural for this sense is *folks,* as shown, and the placement of the form before the label instead of after it (as at the senses of *die*) means that this sense is always plural.

When an italicized label or guide phrase follows a boldface numeral, the label or phrase applies only to that specific numbered sense and its subsenses. It does not apply to any other boldface numbered senses:

¹**boot** . . . *noun* . . .
 1 *archaic* . . .
 2 *chiefly dialect* . . .
 3 *obsolete* . . .

¹**fa·vor** . . . *noun* . . .
 2 *archaic* **a** . . . **b** (1) . . . (2) . . .
 3

At *boot* the *archaic* label applies only to sense 1, the *chiefly dialect* label only to sense 2, and the *obsolete* label only to sense 3. At *favor* the *archaic* label applies to all the subsenses of sense 2 but not to sense 3.

When an italicized label or guide phrase follows a boldface letter, the label or phrase applies only to that specific lettered sense and its subsenses. It does not apply to any other boldface lettered senses:

²**stour** *noun* . . .
 1 a *archaic* . . . **b** *dialect British*

The *archaic* label applies to sense 1a but not to sense 1b. The *dialect British* label applies to sense 1b but not to sense 1a.

When an italicized label or guide phrase follows a parenthesized numeral, the label or phrase applies only to that specific numbered sense:

in·car·na·tion . . . *noun* . . .
 1a (1) . . . (2) *capitalized*

The label *capitalized* applies to sense 1a(2) and to no other subsenses of the word.

Names of Plants & Animals

The entries that define the common or vernacular names (as *peach* and *lion*) of plants and animals or sometimes a related term (as *streptomycin*), if a common name is rare or does not exist, employ in part the formal, codified, New Latin vocabulary of biological systematics. This vocabulary has been developed and used by biologists in accordance with international codes of botanical and zoological nomenclature for the purpose of identifying and indicating the relationships of plants and animals. This system of names classifies organisms into a hierarchy of groups—taxa—with each kind of organism having one—and only one—correct name and belonging to one—and only one—taxon at each level of classification in the hierarchy.

This contrasts with the system of common or vernacular names which is determined by popular usage and in which one organism may have several names (as *mountain lion, cougar,* and *painter*), different organisms may have the same name (as *dolphin*), and there may be variation in meaning or overlapping of the categories denoted by the names (as *whale, dolphin,* and *porpoise*).

The fundamental taxon is the genus. It includes a group of closely related kinds of plants (as *Prunus,* which includes the wild and cultivated cherries, apricots, peaches, and almonds) or animals (as *Canis,* which includes domestic dogs, coyotes, jackals, and wolves). The genus name is a capitalized singular noun.

The unique name of each kind of organism or species—the binomial or species name—consists of a singular capitalized genus name combined with an uncapitalized specific epithet. The name for a variety or subspecies—the trinomial, variety name, or subspecies name—adds a similar varietal or subspecific epithet. The cultivated cabbage (*Brassica oleracea capitata*), the cauliflower (*Brassica oleracea botrytis*), and brussels sprouts (*Brassica oleracea gemmifera*) belong to the same species (*Brassica oleracea*) of cole.

Names of taxa higher than the genus (as family, order, and class) are capitalized plural nouns that are often used with singular verbs and that are not abbreviated in normal use. No two genera of animals in good standing are permitted to have the same name, nor are any two genera of plants in good standing. Since the botanical and zoological codes are independent, however, a plant genus and an animal genus may have the same name. Thus, a number of cabbage butterflies (as *Pieris rapae*) are placed in a genus of animals with the same name as the plant genus to which the Japanese andromeda (*Pieris japonica*) belongs. Although no two higher taxa of plants are permitted to have the same name, the rules of zoological nomenclature do not apply to taxa above the family so that rarely some widely separated groups may receive the same taxonomic name (as the ordinal name Decapoda in the entry *decapod*) from different specialists.

The taxonomic names of biological nomenclature used in this dictionary are enclosed in parentheses and usually come immediately after the primary orienting noun. Genus names as well as binomials and trinomials are italicized, but names of taxa above the genus are not italicized:

> **¹bee·tle** . . . *noun* . . .
> **1 :** any of an order (Coleoptera) of insects having four wings of which the outer pair are modified into stiff elytra that protect the inner pair when at rest

> **rob·in** . . . *noun* . . .
> **1 a :** a small chiefly European thrush (*Erithacus rubecula*) resembling a warbler and having a brownish olive back and orangish face and breast **b :** any of various Old World songbirds that are related to or resemble the European robin
> **2 :** a large North American thrush (*Turdus migratorius*) with olivaceous to slate gray upperparts, blackish head and tail, black and whitish streaked throat, and dull reddish breast and underparts

> **strep·to·my·cin** . . . *noun* . . .
> **:** an antibiotic organic base $C_{21}H_{39}N_7O_{12}$ produced by a soil actinomycete (*Streptomyces griseus*), active against many bacteria, and used especially in the treatment of infections (as tuberculosis) by gram-negative bacteria

Sometimes two or more different New Latin names can be found used in current literature for the same organism or group. This happens when older monographs and field guides are kept in print after name changes occur, when there are legitimate differences of opinion about the validity of names, and when the rules of priority do not apply or are not applied. To help the reader in recognizing an organism or group, some entries in this dictionary give two taxonomic names connected by the word *synonym*:

> **li·on** . . . *noun* . . .
> **1 a** . . . **:** a large heavily-built social cat (*Panthera leo* synonym *Leo leo*) of open or rocky areas chiefly of sub-Saharan Africa . . .

Taxonomic names are used in this dictionary to provide precise technical identifications through which defined terms may be pursued in technical writings. Because of their specialized nature taxonomic names do not have separate entry. However, many common names are derived directly from the names of taxa and especially genera with little or no modification. It is particularly important to distinguish between a common name and the genus name from which it is derived without a change in spelling, as these names appear in print. The common name (as clostridium or drosophila) is not usually capitalized or italicized but does have a plural (as clostridia or drosophilas) which often has an ending different from that of the singular. In contrast the genus name (as *Clostridium* or *Drosophila*) is capitalized and italicized but never takes a plural. A common name in plural form (as coleoptera) may sometimes be spelled like the name of a taxon, but it is not usually capitalized.

The entries defining the names of plants and animals are usually oriented to higher taxa by other vernaculars (as by *alga* at *seaweed* or *thrush* at *robin*) or by technical adjectives (as by *composite* at *daisy*, *leguminous* at *pea*, or *oscine* at *warbler*) so that the name of a higher taxon may often be found by consulting an entry defining a more inclusive common name or a term related to it. Among the higher plants, except for the composites and legumes and a few tropical groups, such orientation is by a vernacular family name linked at the corresponding taxonomic entry to its technical equivalent:

> **²rose** . . . *noun* . . .
> **1 a :** any of a genus (*Rosa* of the family Rosaceae, the rose family) of usually prickly shrubs with pinnate leaves and showy flowers . . .

> **ap·ple** . . . *noun, often attributive* . . .
> **1 :** the fleshy usually rounded and red, yellow, or green edible pome fruit of a tree (genus *Malus*) of the rose family; *also* **:** an apple tree

A genus name may be abbreviated to its initial letter when it is used more than once in senses not separated by a boldface number:

> **nas·tur·tium** . . . *noun* . . .
> **:** any of a genus (*Tropaeolum* of the family Tropaeolaceae, the nasturtium family) of herbs of Central and South America with showy spurred flowers and pungent seeds; *especially* **:** either of two widely cultivated ornamentals (*T. majus* and *T. minus*)

Cross-Reference

Four different kinds of cross-references are used in this dictionary: directional, synonymous, cognate, and inflectional. In each instance the cross-reference is readily recognized by the lightface small capitals in which it is printed.

A cross-reference following a lightface dash and beginning with *see* or *compare* is a directional cross-reference. It directs the dictionary user to look elsewhere for further information. A *compare* cross-reference is regularly appended to a definition; a *see* cross-reference may stand alone:

> **wel·ter·weight** . . . *noun*
> . . . — compare LIGHTWEIGHT, MIDDLEWEIGHT

> **¹ri·al** . . . *noun*
> . . . — see MONEY table

A cross-reference immediately following a boldface colon is a synonymous cross-reference. It may stand alone as the only definitional matter for an entry or for a sense or subsense of an entry; it may follow an analytical definition; it may be one of two synonymous cross-references separated by a comma:

> **gar·ban·zo** . . . *noun* . . .
> **:** CHICKPEA

> **¹ne·glect** . . . *transitive verb* . . .
> **1 :** to give little attention or respect to
> **:** DISREGARD

²**main** *adjective* . . .
 1 : CHIEF, PRINCIPAL

A synonymous cross-reference indicates that a definition at the entry cross-referred to can be substituted as a definition for the entry or the sense or subsense in which the cross-reference appears.

A cross-reference following an italic *variant of* is a cognate cross-reference:

kaf·tan *variant of* CAFTAN

Sometimes a cognate cross-reference has a limiting label preceding *variant of* as a specific indication that the variant is not standard English:

haul·ier . . . *British variant of* HAULER

²**hist** . . . *dialect variant of* HOIST

sher·ris . . . *archaic variant of* SHERRY

A cross-reference following an italic label that identifies an entry as an inflected form of a noun, of an adjective or adverb, or of a verb is an inflectional cross-reference. Inflectional cross-references appear only when the inflected form falls at least a column away from the entry cross-referred to:

calves *plural of* CALF

³**wound** . . . *past and past participle of* WIND

When guidance seems needed as to which one of several homographs or which sense of a multisense word is being referred to, a superscript numeral may precede the cross-reference or a sense number may follow it or both:

¹**toss** . . . *transitive verb* . . .
 3 . . . **c :** MATCH 5a

When a word is included in a synonym paragraph, the main entry for that word is followed by a run-on "**synonym** see _____" which refers to the entry where the synonym paragraph appears:

²**respond** *verb* . . . **synonym** see ANSWER

When a word is a main entry at which there is a synonym paragraph and is also included in another paragraph elsewhere, the paragraph at the main entry is followed by a run-on "See in addition _____" which refers to the entry where the other paragraph may be found:

¹**nat·u·ral** . . . *adjective* . . .
 15 : of an off-white or beige color ☆

> ☆ SYNONYMS
> **Natural, ingenuous, naive, unsophisticated, artless** mean free from pretension or calculation . . . See in addition REGULAR.

¹**reg·u·lar** . . . *adjective* . . .
 5 : of, relating to, or constituting the permanent standing military force of a state <*regular* army> <*regular* soldiers> ☆

> ☆ SYNONYMS
> **Regular, normal, typical, natural** mean being of the sort or kind that is expected as usual, ordinary, or average . . .

Synonyms

Brief paragraphs discriminating words of closely associated meaning from one another have been placed at a number of entries. A small blue-shaded star after the last definition of a word signals that a synonym paragraph discussing that word can be found in the right-hand column on that page or on the facing page to the right:

²**answer** . . . *intransitive verb* . . .
 6 : to offer a solution for; *especially* **:** SOLVE ☆

The paragraph itself is set on a blue background and begins with a list of the words to be discussed in it, followed by a concise statement of the element of meaning that the words have in common. The discriminations are amplified with verbal illustrations:

> ☆ SYNONYMS
> **Answer, respond, reply, rejoin, retort** mean to say, write, or do something in return. ANSWER implies the satisfying of a question, demand, call, or need <*answered* all the questions>. RESPOND may suggest an immediate or quick reaction <*responded* eagerly to a call for volunteers>. REPLY implies making a return commensurate with the original question or demand <an invitation that requires you to *reply*>. REJOIN often implies sharpness or quickness in answering <"who asked you?" she *rejoined*>. RETORT suggests responding to an explicit charge or criticism by way of retaliation <he *retorted* to the attack with biting sarcasm>.

Combining Forms, Prefixes & Suffixes

An entry that begins or ends with a hyphen is a word element that forms part of an English compound:

mega- *or* **meg-** *combining form* . . .
 1 . . . **b** . . . <*mega*hit>

-logy *noun combining form* . . .
 1 . . . <phrase*ology*>

-lyze *verb combining form* . . . <electro*lyze*>

-like *adjective combining form* . . . <bell-*like*> <lady*like*>

pre- *prefix* . . .
 1 a (1) . . . <*pre*historic>

¹**-ory** . . . *noun suffix* . . .
 1 . . . <observat*ory*>

¹**-ic** *adjective suffix* . . .
 2 a . . . <alderman*ic*>

²**-ly** *adverb suffix* . . .
 1 a . . . <slow*ly*>

-ize *verb suffix* . . .
 2 a . . . <crystall*ize*>

Combining forms, prefixes, and suffixes are entered in this dictionary for three reasons: to make easier the writing of etymologies of words in which these word elements occur over and over again; to make understandable the meaning of many undefined run-ons which for reasons of space would be omitted if they had

to be given etymologies and definitions; and to make recogniz-
able the meaningful elements of new words that are not well
enough established in the language to warrant dictionary entry.

Lists of Undefined Words

Lists of undefined words occur after the entries of these prefixes
and combining forms:

anti-	**multi-**	**re-**
co-	**non-**	**self-**

counter-	**out-**	**sub-**
hyper-	**over-**	**super-**
inter-	**post-**	**ultra-**
mis-	**pre-**	**un-**

These words are not defined because they are self-explanatory;
their meanings are simply the sum of a meaning of the prefix or
combining form and a meaning of the root word. Centered dots
are shown to save the dictionary user the trouble of consulting
another entry. The lists are not exhaustive of all the words that
might be, or actually have been, formed with these prefixes and
combining forms. The dictionary has room for only the most
common or important examples.

Guide to Pronunciation

Pronunciation is not an intrinsic component of the dictionary. For some languages, such as Spanish, Swahili, and Serbo-Croatian, the correspondence between orthography and pronunciation is so close that a dictionary need only spell a word correctly to indicate its pronunciation. Modern English, however, displays no such consistency in sound and spelling, and so a dictionary of English must devote considerable attention to the pronunciation of the language. The English lexicon contains numerous eye rhymes such as *love, move,* and *rove,* words which do not sound alike despite their similar spellings. On the other hand, it also contains rhyming words such as *breeze, cheese, ease, frieze,* and *sleaze* whose rhymes are all spelled differently.

This grand mismatch between words that look alike and words that sound alike does at least serve to record something of the history of the English-speaking peoples and their language. Spelling often indicates whether a word comes down from the native Anglo-Saxon word stock or was adopted in successive ages from the speech of a missionary monk chanting Latin, a seafaring Viking dickering in Old Norse, a Norman nobleman giving orders in French, or a young immigrant to turn-of-the-century America. For example, the sound \sh\ is spelled as *sh* in native English *shore,* as *ch* in the French loan *champagne,* as *sk* in one pronunciation of the Norwegian loan *ski,* as *si* in the Renaissance Latin loan *emulsion,* and as *sch* in the recent Yiddish loan *schlepp.* English vowels present different complexities of sound and spelling, due in large part to the fact that William Caxton introduced printing to England in A.D. 1476, many decades before the sound change known as the Great Vowel Shift had run its course. With the rise of printing came an increasingly fixed set of spelling conventions, but the conventionalized spellings soon lost their connection to pronunciation as the vowel shift continued. The stressed vowels of *sane* and *sanity* are therefore identical in spelling though now quite different in quality. For the trained observer the vagaries of English orthography contain a wealth of linguistic history; for most others, however, this disparity between sound and spelling is just a continual nuisance at school or work.

Readers often turn to the dictionary wanting to learn the exact pronunciation of a word, only to discover that the word may have several pronunciations, as is the case for *deity, economic, envelope,* and *greasy,* among many others. The inclusion of variant pronunciations disappoints those who want their dictionary to list one "correct" pronunciation. In truth, though, there can be no objective standard for correct pronunciation other than the usage of thoughtful and, in particular, educated speakers of English. Among such speakers one hears much variation in pronunciation. Dictionaries of English before the modern era usually ignored pronunciation variants, instead indicating a single pronunciation by marking the entry word with diacritics to indicate stress and letter values. These systems were cumbersome, however, and reflected the dialectal biases of the editors more than the facts about how a word was actually spoken. Lexicographers came eventually to recognize the need for separate respellings which could record the entire range of accepted variants along with appropriate notes about dialectal distribution or usage.

This dictionary records many types of variation in pronunciation. Distinctions between British and American speech are frequently noted, as are differences among the three major dialect areas of the U.S.—Northern, Southern, and Midland. Words that have distinctive pronunciations in Canada, such as *decal* and *khaki,* have those pronunciations duly noted. Pronunciations peculiar to certain spheres of activity are also represented, as for example the variants of *athwart* and *tackle* heard in nautical use. Finally, a wide range of unpredictable variations are included, such as the pronunciation of *economic* with either \e\ or \ē\. Unpredictable variations frequently cut across the boundaries of geographical dialects, sometimes running along the lines of social class, ethnicity, or gender instead. In fine, this dictionary attempts to include—either explicitly or by implication—all pronunciation variants of a word that are used by educated speakers of the English language.

The pronunciations in this dictionary are informed chiefly by the Merriam-Webster pronunciation file. This file contains citations that are transcriptions of words used by native speakers of English in the course of utterances heard in speeches, interviews, and conversations. In this extensive collection of 3 × 5 slips of paper, one finds the pronunciations of a host of people: politicians, professors, curators, artists, musicians, doctors, engineers, preachers, activists, journalists, and many others. The Merriam-Webster pronunciation editors have been collecting these citations from live speech and from radio, television, and shortwave broadcasts since the 1930s. It is primarily on the basis of this large and growing file that questions of usage and acceptability in pronunciation are answered. All of the pronunciations recorded in this book can be documented as falling within the range of generally acceptable variation, unless they are accompanied by a restricting usage note or symbol or a regional label.

No system of indicating pronunciation is self-explanatory. The following discussion sets out the signification and use of the pronunciation symbols in this book, with special attention to those areas where experience has shown that dictionary users may have questions. More detailed information can be found in the Guide to Pronunciation in Webster's Third New International Dictionary. The order of symbols discussed below is the same as the order on the page of Pronunciation Symbols, with the exception that the symbols which are not letter characters are here listed first. Those characters which have corresponding symbols in the International Phonetic Alphabet (IPA) are shown with their IPA equivalents.

\ \ All pronunciation information is printed between reversed virgules. Pronunciation symbols are printed in roman type and all other information, such as labels and notes, is printed in italics.

\ˈ ˌ\ A high-set stress mark precedes a syllable with primary (strongest) stress; a low-set mark precedes a syllable with secondary (medium) stress; a third level of weak stress requires no mark at all: \ˈpen-mən-ˌship\.

Since the nineteenth century the International Phonetics Association has recommended that stress marks precede the stressed syllable, and linguists worldwide have adopted this practice on the basic principle that before a syllable can be uttered the speaker must know what degree of stress to give it. In accordance with the practice of French phoneticians, no stress marks are shown in the transcription of words borrowed from French whose pronunciations have not been anglicized, as at *ancien régime* and *émeute*.

\ - \ Hyphens are used to separate syllables in pronunciation transcriptions. In actual speech, of course, there is no pause between the syllables of a word. The placement of hyphens is based on phonetic principles, such as vowel length, nasalization, variation due to the position of a consonant in a syllable, and other nuances of the spoken word. The syllable breaks shown in this book reflect the careful pronunciation of a single word out of context. Syllabication tends to change in rapid or running speech: a consonant at the end of a syllable may shift into a following syllable, and unstressed vowels may be elided. The numerous variations in pronunciation that a word may have in running speech are of interest to phoneticians but are well outside the scope of a dictionary of general English.

The centered dots in boldface entry words indicate potential end-of-line division points and not syllabication. These division points are determined by considerations of both morphology and pronunciation, among others. A detailed discussion of end-of-line division is contained in the article on Division in Boldface Entry Words in Webster's Third New International Dictionary. In this book a consistent approach has been pursued, both toward word division based on traditional formulas and toward syllabication based on phonetic principles. As a result, the hyphens indicating syllable breaks and the centered dots indicating end-of-line division often do not fall in the same places.

\ () \ Parentheses are used in pronunciations to indicate that whatever is symbolized between them is present in some utterances but not in others; thus *factory* \'fak-t(ə-)rē\ is pronounced both \'fak-tə-rē\ and \'fak-trē\, *industry* \'in-(,)dəs-trē\ is pronounced both \'in-dəs-trē\ and \'in-,dəs-trē\. In some phonetic environments, as in *fence* \'fen(t)s\ and *boil* \'bȯi(ə)l\, it may be difficult to determine whether the sound shown in parentheses is or is not present in a given utterance; even the usage of a single speaker may vary considerably.

\ , ; \ Variant pronunciations are separated by commas; groups of variants are separated by semicolons. The order of variants does not mean that the first is in any way preferable to or more acceptable than the others. All of the variants in this book, except those restricted by a regional or usage label, are widely used in acceptable educated speech. If evidence reveals that a particular variant is used more frequently than another, the former will be given first. This should not, however, prejudice anyone against the second or subsequent variants. In many cases the numerical distribution of variants is equal but one of them, of course, must be printed first.

\ ÷ \ The obelus, or division sign, is placed before a pronunciation variant that occurs in educated speech but that is considered by some to be questionable or unacceptable. This symbol is used sparingly and primarily for variants that have been objected to over a period of time in print by commentators on usage, in schools by teachers, or in correspondence that has come to the Merriam-Webster editorial department. In most cases the objection is based on orthographic or etymological arguments. For instance, the second variant of *cupola* \'kyü-pə-lə, ÷-,lō\, though used frequently in speech, is objected to because *a* is very rarely pronounced \ō\ in English. The pronunciations \'fe-byə-,wer-ē\ and \'fe-bə-,wer-ē\ (indicated simultaneously by the use of parentheses) are similarly marked at the entry for *February*

\÷'fe-b(y)ə-,wer-ē, 'fe-brə-\, even though they are the most frequently heard pronunciations, because some people insist that both *r*'s should be pronounced. The obelus applies only to that portion of the transcription which it immediately precedes and not to any other variants following.

\ ə \ in unstressed syllables as in b**a**nana, c**o**llide, **a**but (IPA [ə]). This neutral vowel, called *schwa*, may be represented orthographically by any of the letters *a, e, i, o, u, y*, and by many combinations of letters. In running speech unstressed vowels are regularly pronounced as \ə\ in American and British speech. Unstressed \ə\ often intrudes between a stressed vowel and a following \l\ or \r\ though it is not represented in the spelling, as in *eel* \'ē(ə)l\ and *sour* \'saů(-ə)r\.

\ 'ə, ,ə \ in stressed syllables as in h**u**mdr**u**m, **a**but (IPA [ʌ]).

\ ᵊ \ immediately preceding \l\, \n\, \m\, \ŋ\, as in bat**tle**, cot**ton**, and one pronunciation of o**pen** \'ō-pᵊm\ and of **and** \ᵊŋ\ as in one pronunciation of the phrase *lock and key* \,läk-ᵊŋ-'kē\. The symbol \ᵊ\ preceding these consonants does not itself represent a sound. It signifies instead that the following consonant is syllabic; that is, the consonant itself forms the nucleus of a syllable that does not contain a vowel.

In the pronunciation of some French or French-derived words \ᵊ\ is placed immediately after \l\, \m\, \r\ to indicate one nonsyllabic pronunciation of these consonants, as in the French words ta**ble** "table," pris**me** "prism," and ti**tre** "title," each of which in isolation and in some contexts is a one-syllable word.

\ ər \ as in f**ur**ther, m**er**ger, b**ir**d (IPA [ɝ, ɚ]). (See the section on \r\.) The anglicized pronunciation of the vowel \œ\ is represented in this book as \ə(r)\. (See the section on \œ\.)

\ 'ər-, 'ə-r \ as in two different pronunciations of *hurry*. Most U.S. speakers pronounce \'hər-ē\ with the \ər\ representing the same sounds as in *bird* \'bərd\. Usually in metropolitan New York and southern England and frequently in New England and the southeastern U.S. the vowel is much the same as the vowel of *hum* followed by a syllable-initial variety of \r\. This pronunciation of *hurry* is represented as \'hə-rē\ in this book. Both types of pronunciation are shown for words composed of a single meaningful unit (or *morpheme*) as in *current, hurry,* and *worry*. In words such as *furry, stirring,* and *purring* in which a vowel or vowel-initial suffix is added to a word ending in *r* or *rr* (as *fur, stir,* and *purr*), the second type of pronunciation outlined above is heard only occasionally and is not shown in this dictionary.

\ a \ as in m**a**t, m**a**p, m**a**d, g**a**g, sn**a**p, p**a**tch (IPA [æ]). Some variation in this vowel is occasioned by the consonant that follows it; thus, for some speakers *map, mad,* and *gag* have noticeably different vowel sounds. There is a very small number of words otherwise identical in pronunciation that these speakers may distinguish solely by variation of this vowel, as in the two words *can* (put into cans; be able) in the sentence "Let's can what we can." However, this distinction is sufficiently infrequent that the traditional practice of using a single symbol is followed in this book.

\ ā \ as in d**ay**, f**a**de, d**a**te, **a**orta, dr**a**pe, c**a**pe (IPA [e, eɪ, ei]). In most English speech this is actually a diphthong. In lowland South Carolina, in coastal Georgia and Florida, and occasionally elsewhere \ā\ is pronounced as a monophthong. As a diphthong \ā\ has a first element \e\ or monophthongal \ā\ and a second element \i\.

\ä\ as in bother, cot, and, with most American speakers, father, cart (IPA [α]). The symbol \ä\ represents the vowel of *cot, cod,* and the stressed vowel of *collar* in the speech of those who pronounce this vowel differently from the vowel in *caught, cawed,* and *caller,* represented by \ȯ\. In U.S. speech \ä\ is pronounced with little or no rounding of the lips, and it is fairly long in duration, especially before voiced consonants. In southern England \ä\ is usually accompanied by some lip rounding and is relatively short in duration. The vowel \ȯ\ generally has appreciable lip rounding. Some U.S. speakers (a perhaps growing minority) do not distinguish between *cot—caught, cod—cawed,* and *collar—caller,* usually because they lack or have less lip rounding in the words transcribed with \ȯ\. Though the symbols \ä\ and \ȯ\ are used throughout this book to distinguish the members of the above pairs and similar words, the speakers who rhyme these pairs will automatically reproduce a sound that is consistent with their own speech.

In words such as *card* and *cart* most U.S. speakers have a sequence of sounds that we transcribe as \är\. Most speakers who do not pronounce \r\ before another consonant or a pause, however, do not rhyme *card* with either *cod* or *cawed* and do not rhyme *cart* with either *cot* or *caught.* The pronunciation of *card* and *cart* by such speakers, although not shown in this dictionary, would be transcribed as \'kȧd\ and \'kȧt\. Speakers of r-dropping dialects will automatically substitute \ȧ\ for the transcribed \är\. (See the sections on \ȧ\ and \r\.)

\ȧ\ as in father as pronounced by those who do not rhyme it with *bother* (IPA [a, ɐ]). The pronunciation of this vowel varies regionally. In eastern New England and southern England it is generally pronounced farther forward in the mouth than \ä\ but not as far forward as \a\. In New York City and the southeastern U.S. it may have much the same quality as \ä\ but somewhat greater duration.

In areas in which \r\ is not pronounced before another consonant or a pause, \ȧ\ occurs for the sequence transcribed in this book as \är\. (See the sections on \ä\ and \r\.) In these areas \ȧ\ also occurs with varying frequency in a small group of words in which *a* in the spelling is followed by a consonant letter other than *r* and is not preceded by *w* or *wh,* as in *father, calm, palm,* and *tomato* but not in *watch, what,* or *swap* (though \ȧ\ does sometimes occur in *waft*). Especially in southern England and, less consistently, in eastern New England \ȧ\ occurs in certain words in which \a\ is the usual American vowel and in most of which the vowel is followed by \f\, \th\, \s\, or by \n\ and another consonant, as in the words *after, bath, mask,* and *slant.*

The symbol \ȧ\ is also used in the transcription of some foreign-derived words and names. This vowel, as in French *patte* "paw" and *chat* "cat," is intermediate between \a\ and \ä\ and is similar in quality to the \ȧ\ heard in eastern New England.

\au̇\ as in now, loud, out (IPA [aʊ, au]). The initial element of this diphthong may vary from \a\ to \ȧ\ or \ä\, the first being more common in Southern and south Midland speech than elsewhere. In coastal areas of the southern U.S. and in parts of Canada this diphthong is often realized as \ou̇\ when immediately preceding a voiceless consonant, as in the noun *house* and in *out.*

\b\ as in baby, rib (IPA [b]).

\ch\ as in chin, nature \'nā-chər\ (IPA [tʃ]). Actually, this sound is \t\ + \sh\. The distinction between the phrases *why choose* and *white shoes* is maintained by a difference in the syllabication of the \t\ and the \sh\ in each case and the consequent use of different varieties (or *allophones*) of \t\.

\d\ as in did, adder (IPA [d]). (See the section on \t\ below for a discussion of the flap allophone of \d\.)

\e\ as in bet, bed, peck (IPA [ɛ]). In Southern and Midland dialects this vowel before nasal consonants often has a raised articulation that approximates \i\, so that *pen* has nearly the pronunciation \'pin\.

\'ē, ͵ē\ in stressed syllables as in beat, nosebleed, evenly, easy (IPA [i]).

\ē\ in unstressed syllables, as in easy, mealy (IPA [i, ɪ, ɪ]). Though the fact is not shown in this book, some dialects such as southern British and southern U.S. often, if not usually, pronounce \i\ instead of unstressed \ē\.

\f\ as in fifty, cuff (IPA [f]).

\g\ as in go, big, gift (IPA [g]).

\h\ as in hat, ahead (IPA [h]).

\hw\ as in whale as pronounced by those who do not have the same pronunciation for both *whale* and *wail.* Most U.S. speakers distinguish these two words as \'hwā(ə)l\ and \'wā(ə)l\ respectively, though frequently in the U.S. and usually in southern England \'wā(ə)l\ is used for both. Some linguists consider \hw\ to be a single sound, a voiceless \w\ (IPA [ʍ]).

\i\ as in tip, banish, active (IPA [ɪ]).

\ī\ as in site, side, buy, tripe (IPA [aɪ, ai, αɪ, αi]). Actually, this sound is a diphthong, usually composed of \ä\ + \i\ or \ȧ\ + \i\. In Southern speech, especially before a pause or voiced consonant, as in *shy* and *five,* the second element \i\ may not be pronounced (IPA [aː]). Chiefly in eastern Virginia, coastal South Carolina, and parts of Canada the diphthong is approximately \'ə\ + \i\ before voiceless consonants, as in *nice* and *write* (IPA [ʌɪ]).

\j\ as in job, gem, edge, join, judge. Actually, this sound is \d\ + \zh\ (IPA [dʒ]). Assuming the anglicization of *Jeanne d'Arc* as \zhän-'därk\, the distinction between the sentences *They betray John Dark* and *They betrayed Jeanne d'Arc* is maintained by a difference in the syllabication of the \d\ and the \zh\ in each case and the consequent use of different varieties (or *allophones*) of \d\.

\k\ as in kin, cook, ache (IPA [k]).

\k̲\ as in German ich "I," Buch "book," and one pronunciation of English loch. Actually, there are two distinct sounds in German; the \k̲\ in *ich* (IPA [ç]) is pronounced toward the front of the mouth and the \k̲\ in *Buch* is pronounced toward the back (IPA [x]). In English, however, no two words otherwise identical are distinguished by these two varieties of \k̲\, and therefore only a single symbol is necessary.

\l\ as in lily, pool (IPA [l, ɫ]). In words such as *battle* and *fiddle* the \l\ is a syllabic consonant (IPA [l̩]). (See the section on \ᵊ\ above.)

\m\ as in murmur, dim, nymph (IPA [m]). In pronunciation variants of some words, such as *open* and *happen,* \m\ is a syllabic consonant (IPA [m̩]). (See the section on \ᵊ\ above.)

\n\ as in **n**o, ow**n** (IPA [n]). In words such as *cotton* and *sudden,* the \n\ is a syllabic consonant (IPA [n̩]). (See the section on \ᵊ\ above.)

\ⁿ\ indicates that a preceding vowel or diphthong is pronounced with the nasal passages open, as in French *un bon vin blanc* \œⁿ-bōⁿ-vaⁿ-bläⁿ\ "a good white wine."

\ŋ\ as in si**ng** \'siŋ\, si**ng**er \'siŋ-ər\, fi**ng**er \'fiŋ-gər\, i**nk** \'iŋk\ (IPA [ŋ]). In some rare contexts \ŋ\ may be a syllabic consonant (IPA [ŋ̩]). (See the section on \ᵊ\ above.)

\ō\ as in b**o**ne, kn**ow**, b**eau** (IPA [o, oʊ, ou]). Especially in positions of emphasis, such as when it is word final or when as primary stress, \ō\ tends to become diphthongal, moving from \ō\ toward a second element \u̇\. In southern England and in some U.S. speech, particularly in the Philadelphia area and in the Pennsylvania-Ohio-West Virginia border area, the first element is often approximately \ə\. In coastal South Carolina, Georgia, and Florida stressed \ō\ is often monophthongal when final, but when a consonant follows it is often a diphthong moving from \ō\ to \ə\. In this book the symbol \ō\ represents all of the above variants. As an unstressed vowel before another vowel, \ō\ is often pronounced as a schwa with slight lip rounding that is separated from the following vowel by the glide \w\, as in *following* \'fä-lə-wiŋ\. This reduced variant is not usually shown at individual entries.

\ȯ\ as in s**aw**, **a**ll, gn**aw**, c**au**ght (IPA [ɔ]). (See the section on \ä\.)

\œ\ as in French b**oeu**f "beef," German H**ö**lle "hell" (IPA [œ]). This vowel, which occurs only in foreign-derived terms and names, can be approximated by attempting to pronounce the vowel \e\ with the lips moderately rounded as for the vowel \u̇\. This vowel is often anglicized as the \ər\ of *bird* by those who do not "drop their r's" or as the corresponding vowel of *bird* used by those who do (see the section on \r\). Where this anglicization is shown, it is represented as \ə(r)\.

\ō�softer(œ̄)\ as in French f**eu** "fire," German H**ö**hle "hole" (IPA [ø]). This vowel, which occurs primarily in foreign-derived terms and names, can be approximated by attempting to pronounce a monophthongal vowel \ā\ with the lips fully rounded as for the vowel \ü\. This vowel also occurs in Scots and thus is used in the pronunciation of *guidwillie*, mainly restricted to Scotland.

\ȯi\ as in c**oi**n, destr**oy** (IPA [ɔɪ, ɔi]). In some Southern speech, especially before a consonant in the same word, the second element may disappear or be replaced by \ə\. Some utterances of *drawing* and *sawing* have a sequence of vowel sounds identical to that in *coin,* but because *drawing* and *sawing* are analyzed by many as two-syllable words they are transcribed with a parenthesized hyphen: \'drȯ(-)iŋ\, \'sȯ(-)iŋ\.

\p\ as in **p**e**pp**er, li**p** (IPA [p]).

\r\ as in **r**ed, **r**a**r**ity, ca**r**, bea**r**d. What is transcribed here as \r\ in reality represents several distinct sounds. Before a stressed vowel \r\ denotes a continuant produced with the tongue tip slightly behind the teethridge (IPA [ɹ]). This sound is usually voiceless when it follows a voiceless stop, as in *pray, tree,* and *cram.* After a vowel in the same syllable \r\ is most often a semi-vowel characterized by retroflexion of the tongue tip. The sequences \ar\, \är\, \er\, \ir\, \ȯr\, \u̇r\, and \ər\ may then be considered diphthongs. In some speech the retroflexion of the \r\ occurs throughout the articulation of the vowel, but in other cases the first vowel glides into a retroflex articulation. In the latter cases a brief transition vowel is sometimes heard; this variable and nondistinctive glide is not transcribed in this book, but is considered implicit in the symbol \r\.

In Received Pronunciation \r\ is sometimes pronounced as a flap (IPA [ɾ]) in the same contexts in which \t\ and \d\ occur as flaps in American English. (See the section on \t\ below.) Occasionally the flap may be heard after consonants, as in *bright* and *grow.* In other dialects of British English, particularly Scottish, \r\ may be pronounced as an alveolar trill (IPA [r]) or as a uvular trill (IPA [R]). In some dialects, especially those of the southeastern U.S., eastern New England, New York City, and southern England, \r\ is not pronounced after a vowel in the same syllable. This is often, if somewhat misleadingly, referred to as r-dropping. In these dialects *r* is pronounced as a nonsyllabic \ə\ when it occurs in these positions or there may be no sound corresponding to the *r* ; thus *beard, corn,* and *assured* may be pronounced as \'biəd\, \'kȯən\, and \ə-'shu̇əd\ or, usually with some lengthening of the vowel sound, as \'bid\, \'kȯn\, and \ə-'shu̇d\. In *car, card,* and *cart* those who do not pronounce \r\ generally have a vowel which we would transcribe as \ä\, usually pronounced with some lengthening and without a following \ə\. (See the sections on \ä\ and \à\.) The stressed vowel of *bird* and *hurt* in r-dropping speech is similar to the vowel used by r-keepers in the same words but without the simultaneous raising of the center and/or tip of the tongue. In the U.S. most speakers of r-dropping dialects will pronounce \r\ before consonants in some words or in some contexts. Because it is determined by the phonetic context, r-dropping is not explicitly represented in this dictionary; speakers of r-dropping dialects will automatically substitute the sounds appropriate to their own speech.

\s\ as in **s**ource, le**ss** (IPA [s]).

\sh\ as in **sh**y, mi**ss**ion, ma**ch**ine, spe**ci**al (IPA [ʃ]). Actually, this is a single sound, not two. When the two sounds \s\ and \h\ occur in sequence, they are separated by a hyphen in this book, as in *grasshopper* \'gras-ˌhä-pər\.

\t\ as in **t**ie, a**tt**ack, la**t**e, la**t**er, la**tt**er (IPA [t]). In some contexts, as when a stressed or unstressed vowel precedes and an unstressed vowel or \ᵊl\ follows, the sound represented by *t* or *tt* is pronounced in most American speech as a voiced flap produced by the tongue tip tapping the teethridge (IPA [ɾ]). In similar contexts the sound represented by *d* or *dd* has the same pronunciation. Thus, the pairs *ladder* and *latter, leader* and *liter, parody* and *parity* are often homophones. At the end of a syllable \t\ often has an incomplete articulation with no release, or it is accompanied or replaced by a glottal closure. When \t\ occurs before the syllabic consonant \ᵊn\ as in *button* \'bə-tᵊn\, the glottal allophone is often heard. This may reflect a syllabication of \t\ with the preceding stressed syllable (i.e. \'bət-ᵊn\).

\th\ as in **th**in, e**th**er (IPA [θ]). Actually, this is a single sound, not two. When the two sounds \t\ and \h\ occur in sequence they are separated by a hyphen in this book, as in *knighthood* \'nīt-ˌhu̇d\.

\th\ as in **th**en, ei**th**er, **th**is (IPA [ð]). Actually, this is a single sound, not two. The difference between \th\ and \th\ is that the former is pronounced without and the latter with vibration of the vocal cords.

\ü\ as in r**u**le, y**ou**th, uni**o**n \'yün-yən\, f**ew** \'fyü\ (IPA [u]). As an unstressed vowel before another vowel,

\ü\ is often pronounced as a schwa with slight lip rounding that is separated from the following vowel by the glide \w\, as *valuing* \'val-yə-wiŋ\. This reduced variant is not usually shown at individual entries. Younger speakers of American English often use a more centralized and less rounded pronunciation of \ü\ in certain words (as *news* and *musician*), both in stressed and especially in unstressed syllables.

\ u̇ \ as in p**u**ll, w**oo**d, b**oo**k, curable \'kyu̇r-ə-bəl\, fury \'fyu̇r-ē\ (IPA [ʊ]).

\ ʉ \ as in German f**ü**llen "to fill," h**ü**bsch "handsome" (IPA [ʏ]). This vowel, which occurs only in foreign-derived terms and names, can be approximated by attempting to pronounce the vowel \i\ with the lips moderately rounded as for the vowel \u̇\.

\ ʉ \ as in French r**u**e "street," German f**ü**hlen "to feel" (IPA [y]). This vowel, which occurs only in foreign-derived terms and names, can be approximated by attempting to pronounce the vowel \ē\ with the lips fully rounded as for the vowel \ü\.

\ v \ as in **v**i**v**id, in**v**ite (IPA [v]).

\ w \ as in **w**e, a**w**ay (IPA [w]).

\ y \ as in **y**ard, **y**oung, cue \'kyü\, curable \'kyu̇r-ə-bəl\, few \'fyü\, fury \'fyu̇r-ē\, union \'yün-yən\ (IPA [j]). The sequences \lyü\, \syü\, and \zyü\ in the same syllable, as in *lewd, suit,* and *presume,* are common in southern British speech but are rare in American speech and only \lü\, \sü\, and \zü\ are shown in this dictionary. A sequence of \h\ and \y\ as in *hue* and *huge* is pronounced by some speakers as a \k̲\ articulated toward the front of the mouth (IPA [ç]).

In English \y\ does not occur at the end of a syllable after a vowel. In a few words of French origin whose pronunciation has not been anglicized, a postvocalic \y\ is transcribed, as in *mille-feuille* \mēl-fœy\ and in *rouille* \'rü-ē, rüy\. The sound represented is the consonantal \y\ of *yard.*

\ ʸ \ indicates that during the articulation of the preceding consonant the tongue has substantially the position it has for the articulation of the \y\ of *yard,* as in French *digne* \dē-nʸ\ "worthy." Thus \ʸ\ does not itself represent a sound but rather modifies the preceding symbol.

\ z \ as in **z**one, rai**s**e (IPA [z]).

\ zh \ as in vi**si**on, a**z**ure \'a-zhər\ (IPA [ʒ]). Actually, this is a single sound, not two. When the two sounds \z\ and \h\ occur in sequence, they are separated by a hyphen in this book, as in *hogshead* \'hȯgz-ˌhed, 'hägz-\.

Pronunciation Symbols

For more information see the Guide to Pronunciation.

ə . . . b**a**n**a**na, c**o**llide, **a**but

ˈə, ˌə̰ . . . h**u**mdr**u**m, abut

. . . immediately preceding \l\, \n\, \m\, \ŋ\, as in batt**le**, mitt**en**, eat**en**, and sometimes op**en** \ˈō-p°m\, lock **and** key \-°n-\; immediately following \l\, \m\, \r\, as often in French tabl**e**, prism**e**, titr**e**

ər . . . furth**er**, merg**er**, bi**r**d

ˈər-} ˈə-r} . . . as in two different pronunciations of h**urr**y \ˈhər-ē, ˈhə-rē\

a . . . m**a**t, m**a**p, m**a**d, g**a**g, sn**a**p, p**a**tch

ā . . . d**a**y, f**a**de, d**a**te, **a**orta, dr**a**pe, c**a**pe

ä . . . b**o**ther, c**o**t, and, with most American speakers, f**a**ther, c**a**rt

à . . . f**a**ther as pronounced by speakers who do not rhyme it with *bother*; French p**a**tte

aù . . . n**ow**, l**ou**d, **ou**t

b . . . **b**a**b**y, ri**b**

ch . . . **ch**in, nature \ˈnā-**ch**ər\

d . . . **d**i**d**, a**dd**er

e . . . b**e**t, b**e**d, p**e**ck

ˈē, ˌē . . . b**ea**t, nosebl**ee**d, **e**venly, **ea**sy

ē . . . eas**y**, meal**y**

f . . . **f**i**f**ty, cu**ff**

g . . . **g**o, bi**g**, **g**ift

h . . . **h**at, a**h**ead

hw . . . **wh**ale as pronounced by those who do not have the same pronunciation for both *whale* and *wail*

i . . . t**i**p, ban**i**sh, act**i**ve

ī . . . s**i**te, s**i**de, b**uy**, tr**i**pe

j . . . **j**ob, **g**em, e**dge**, **j**oin, **j**u**dge**

k . . . **k**in, **c**ook, a**ch**e

k̲ . . . German i**ch**, Bu**ch**; one pronunciation of lo**ch**

l . . . **l**i**l**y, poo**l**

m . . . **m**ur**m**ur, di**m**, ny**m**ph

n . . . **n**o, ow**n**

ⁿ . . . indicates that a preceding vowel or diphthong is pronounced with the nasal passages open, as in French *un bon vin blanc* \œ̄ⁿ-bōⁿ-vaⁿ-bläⁿ\

ŋ . . . si**ng** \ˈsiŋ\, si**ng**er \ˈsiŋ-ər\, fi**ng**er \ˈfiŋ-gər\, i**n**k \ˈiŋk\

ō . . . b**o**ne, kn**ow**, b**eau**

ȯ . . . s**aw**, **a**ll, gn**aw**, c**augh**t

œ . . . French b**oeu**f, German H**ö**lle

ōœ . . . French f**eu**, German H**öh**le

ȯi . . . c**oi**n, destr**oy**

p . . . **p**e**pp**er, li**p**

r . . . **r**ed, ca**r**, **r**a**r**ity

s . . . **s**ource, le**ss**

sh . . . as in **sh**y, mi**ss**ion, ma**ch**ine, spe**ci**al (actually, this is a single sound, not two); with a hyphen between, two sounds as in *grasshopper* \ˈgras-ˌhä-pər\

t . . . **t**ie, a**tt**ack, la**t**e, la**t**er, la**tt**er

th . . . as in **th**in, e**th**er (actually, this is a single sound, not two); with a hyphen between, two sounds as in *knighthood* \ˈnīt-ˌhu̇d\

t̲h̲ . . . **th**en, ei**th**er, **th**is (actually, this is a single sound, not two)

ü . . . r**u**le, y**ou**th, union \ˈyün-yən\, few \ˈfyü\

u̇ . . . p**u**ll, w**oo**d, b**oo**k, curable \ˈkyu̇r-ə-bəl\, fury \ˈfyu̇r-ē\

ᵫ . . . German f**ü**llen, h**ü**bsch

ūᵫ . . . French r**u**e, German f**üh**len

v . . . **v**i**v**id, gi**v**e

w . . . **w**e, a**w**ay

y . . . **y**ard, **y**oung, cue \ˈkyü\, mute \ˈmyüt\, union \ˈyün-yən\

ʸ . . . indicates that during the articulation of the sound represented by the preceding character the front of the tongue has substantially the position it has for the articulation of the first sound of *yard*, as in French *digne* \dēnʸ\

z . . . **z**one, rai**s**e

zh . . . as in vi**si**on, azure \ˈa-zhər\ (actually, this is a single sound, not two); with a hyphen between, two sounds as in *hogshead* \ˈhȯgz-ˌhed, ˈhägz-\

\ . . . slant line used in pairs to mark the beginning and end of a transcription: \ˈpen\

ˈ . . . mark preceding a syllable with primary (strongest) stress: \ˈpen-mən-ˌship\

ˌ . . . mark preceding a syllable with secondary (medium) stress: \ˈpen-mən-ˌship\

- . . . mark of syllable division

() . . . indicate that what is symbolized between is present in some utterances but not in others: *factory* \ˈfak-t(ə-)rē\

÷ . . . indicates that many regard as unacceptable the pronunciation variant immediately following: *cupola* \ˈkyü-pə-lə, ÷-ˌlō\

A *A is the first letter of the English Alphabet and of most alphabets that are closely related. It comes from Latin A, which was itself descended, via Etruscan, from Greek A (alpha). The Greek letter, in turn, was borrowed from the first letter of the Phoenician alphabet, ' aleph. That letter represented a consonant sound called the glottal stop, pronounced something like a cough. Since the Greeks did not use the glottal stop, they assigned the letter to their own equivalent of the vowel sound (pronounced "ah") following the glottal stop in Phoenician ' aleph. In modern English, A represents various sounds, including the short a in* bad *and the long a in* fate. *The two small forms of* a *developed through gradual transformation of the capital form. First, the horizontal bar of A dropped out; next, it was replaced by a line slanting upward from the bottom of the left leg to the center of the right leg; then, the triangle thus formed was rounded to the left to form a loop; and, eventually, the right upward stroke was curved leftward or shortened and straightened to a vertical position.*

¹a \'ā\ *noun, plural* **a's** *or* **as** \'āz\ *often capitalized, often attributive* (before 12th century)
1 a : the 1st letter of the English alphabet **b :** a graphic representation of this letter **c :** a speech counterpart of orthographic *a*
2 : the 6th tone of a C-major scale
3 : a graphic device for reproducing the letter *a*
4 : one designated *a* especially as the 1st in order or class
5 a : a grade rating a student's work as superior in quality **b :** one graded or rated with an A
6 : something shaped like the letter A

²a \ə, (')ā, *Canadian* 'ā\ *indefinite article* [Middle English, from Old English *ān* one — more at ONE] (before 12th century)
1 — used as a function word before singular nouns when the referent is unspecified ⟨*a* man overboard⟩ and before number collectives and some numbers ⟨*a* dozen⟩
2 : the same ⟨birds of *a* feather⟩ ⟨swords all of *a* length⟩
3 a — used as a function word before a singular noun followed by a restrictive modifier ⟨*a* man who was here yesterday⟩ **b :** ANY ⟨*a* man who is sick can't work⟩ **c** — used as a function word before a mass noun to denote a particular type or instance ⟨*a* bronze made in ancient times⟩ ⟨glucose is *a* simple sugar⟩ **d** — used as a function word before a proper noun representing an example or type ⟨the attractions of *a* Boston or *a* Cleveland⟩
4 — used as a function word with nouns to form adverbial phrases of quantity, amount, or degree ⟨felt *a* little tired⟩ □

³a \ə *also* (')ā\ *preposition* [Middle English, from Old English *a-, an, on*] (before 12th century)
1 *chiefly dialect* **:** ON, IN, AT
2 : in, to, or for each ⟨twice *a* week⟩ ⟨five dollars *a* dozen⟩
usage see ²A

⁴a \ə, (ˌ)ā\ *verb* [Middle English, contraction of *have*] (14th century)
archaic **:** HAVE ⟨I might *a* had husbands afore now —John Bunyan⟩

⁵a \ə\ *preposition* [Middle English, by contraction] (15th century)
: OF — often attached to the preceding word ⟨kind*a*⟩ ⟨lott*a*⟩

¹a- \ə\ *prefix* [Middle English, from Old English]
1 : on **:** in **:** at ⟨*a*bed⟩
2 : in (such) a state or condition ⟨*a*fire⟩
3 : in (such) a manner ⟨*a*loud⟩
4 : in the act or process of ⟨gone *a*-hunting⟩ ⟨*a*tingle⟩

²a- \(')ā *also* (')a *or* (')ä\ *or* **an-** \(')an\ *prefix* [Latin & Greek; Latin, from Greek — more at UN-]
: not **:** without ⟨*a*sexual⟩ — *a*- before consonants other than *h* and sometimes even before *h*, *an*- before vowels and usually before *h* ⟨*a*chromatic⟩ ⟨*a*historical⟩ ⟨*an*astigmatic⟩ ⟨*an*hydrous⟩

-a- *combining form* [International Scientific Vocabulary]
: replacing carbon especially in a ring ⟨*a*za-⟩

-a \ə\ *noun suffix* [New Latin, from *-a* (as in *magnesia*)]
: OXIDE ⟨silica⟩

aah \'ä, *often prolonged and/or followed by* ə\ *intransitive verb* (1953)
: to exclaim in amazement, joy, or surprise ⟨one finds oneself oohing and *aah*ing over the exciting new TV commercials —Walter Goodman⟩
— **aah** *noun*

aard·vark \'ärd-ˌvärk\ *noun* [obsolete Afrikaans, from Afrikaans *aard* earth + *vark* pig] (1827)
: a large burrowing nocturnal ungulate mammal (*Orycteropus afer*) of sub-Saharan Africa that has a long snout, extensile tongue, powerful claws, large ears, and heavy tail and feeds especially on termites and ants

aardvark

aard·wolf \-ˌwu̇lf\ *noun* [Afrikaans, from *aard* + *wolf*] (1833)
: a maned striped nocturnal mammal (*Proteles cristatus*) of southern and eastern Africa that resembles the related hyenas and feeds chiefly on insects and especially termites

aardwolf

Aar·on \'ar-ən, 'er-\ *noun* [Late Latin, from Greek *Aarōn*, from Hebrew *Ahărōn*]
: a brother of Moses and high priest of the Hebrews

Aar·on·ic \a-'rä-nik, e-\ *adjective* (circa 1828)
1 : of or stemming from Aaron
2 : of or relating to the lower order of the Mormon priesthood

ab \'ab\ *noun* (1983)
: an abdominal muscle — usually used in plural

Ab \'äb, 'äv, 'ȯv\ *noun* [Hebrew *Ābh*] (circa 1771)
: the 11th month of the civil year or the 5th month of the ecclesiastical year in the Jewish calendar — see MONTH table

ab- \(ˌ)ab, əb\ *prefix* [Middle English, from Old French & Latin; Old French, from Latin *ab-, abs-, a-*, from *ab, a* — more at OF]
: from **:** away **:** off ⟨*ab*axial⟩

aba \ə-'bä, ä-'ba\ *noun* [Arabic *'abā*] (1811)
1 : a loose sleeveless outer garment worn as traditional dress by men in the Middle East
2 : a fabric woven from the hair of camels or goats

ab·a·ca \ˌa-bə-'kä, 'a-bə-ˌ\ *noun* [Spanish *abacá*, from Tagalog *abaká*] (circa 1818)
1 : a strong fiber obtained from the leafstalk of a banana (*Musa textilis*) native to the Philippines — called also *Manila hemp*
2 : the plant that yields abaca

aback \ə-'bak\ *adverb* (before 12th century)
1 *archaic* **:** BACKWARD, BACK
2 : in a position to catch the wind upon the forward surface of a square sail
3 : by surprise **:** UNAWARES ⟨was taken *aback* by her sharp retort⟩

abac·te·ri·al \ˌā-(ˌ)bak-'tir-ē-əl\ *adjective* (circa 1935)
: not caused by or characterized by the presence of bacteria ⟨*abacterial* prostatitis⟩

aba·cus \'a-bə-kəs, ə-'ba-\ *noun, plural* **aba·ci** \'a-bə-ˌsī, -ˌkē; ə-'ba-ˌkī\ *or* **aba·cus·es** [Latin, from Greek *abak-, abax*, literally, slab] (14th century)
1 : an instrument for performing calculations by sliding counters along rods in grooves
2 : a slab that forms the uppermost member or division of the capital of a column

abacus 1

¹abaft \ə-'baft\ *preposition* [¹*a-* + *baft* (aft)] (1594)
: to the rear of; *specifically* **:** toward the stern from

²abaft *adverb* (1628)
: toward or at the stern **:** AFT

ab·a·lo·ne \ˌa-bə-'lō-nē, 'a-bə-ˌ\ *noun* [American Spanish *abulón*, from Rumsen (American

□ **USAGE**
a In speech and writing *a* is used before a consonant sound ⟨*a* door⟩ ⟨*a* human⟩. Before a vowel sound *an* is usual ⟨*an* icicle⟩ ⟨*an* honor⟩ but especially in speech *a* is used occasionally, more often in some dialects than in others ⟨*a* apple⟩ ⟨*a* hour⟩ ⟨*a* obligation⟩. Before a consonant sound represented by a vowel letter *a* is usual ⟨*a* one⟩ ⟨*a* union⟩ but *an* also occurs though less frequently now than formerly ⟨*an* unique⟩ ⟨such *an* one⟩. Before unstressed or weakly stressed syllables with initial *h* both *a* and *an* are used in writing ⟨*a* historic⟩ ⟨*an* historic⟩ but in speech *an* is more frequent whether \h\ is pronounced or not. In the King James Version of the Old Testament and occasionally in writing and speech *an* is used before *h* in a stressed syllable ⟨*an* huntress⟩ ⟨*an* hundred⟩ ⟨children are *an* heritage of the Lord —Psalms 127:3 (Authorized Version)⟩.

Indian language of Monterey Bay, Calif.) *au‧lon*] (1850)
: any of a genus (*Haliotis*) of edible rock‧clinging gastropod mollusks that have a flattened shell slightly spiral in form, lined with mother-of-pearl, and with a row of apertures along its outer edge

¹**aban‧don** \ə-'ban-dən\ *transitive verb* [Middle English *abandounen*, from Middle French *abandoner*, from *abandon*, noun, surrender, from *a bandon* in one's power] (14th century)
1 a : to give up to the control or influence of another person or agent **b :** to give up with the intent of never again claiming a right or interest in
2 : to withdraw from often in the face of danger or encroachment ⟨*abandon* ship⟩
3 : to withdraw protection, support, or help from
4 : to give (oneself) over unrestrainedly
5 a : to cease from maintaining, practicing, or using ⟨*abandoned* their native language⟩ **b :** to cease intending or attempting to perform ⟨*abandoned* the escape⟩ ☆
— **aban‧don‧er** *noun*
— **aban‧don‧ment** \-dən-mənt\ *noun*

²**abandon** *noun* (1822)
: a thorough yielding to natural impulses; *especially* **:** ENTHUSIASM, EXUBERANCE ⟨with reckless *abandon*⟩

aban‧doned \ə-'ban-dənd\ *adjective* (14th century)
1 : wholly free from restraint
2 : given up : FORSAKEN

à bas \ä-'bä\ [French] (circa 1897)
: down with ⟨*à bas* the profiteers⟩

abase \ə-'bās\ *transitive verb* **abased; abas‧ing** [Middle English *abassen*, from Middle French *abaisser*, from *a-* (from Latin *ad-*) + (assumed) Vulgar Latin *bassiare* to lower] (15th century)
1 *archaic* **:** to lower physically
2 : to lower in rank, office, prestige, or esteem
— **abase‧ment** \-'bā-smənt\ *noun*

abash \ə-'bash\ *transitive verb* [Middle English *abaishen*, from (assumed) Middle French *abaiss-*, *abair* to astonish, alteration of Middle French *esbair*, from *ex-* + *baer* to yawn — more at ABEYANCE] (14th century)
: to destroy the self-possession or self-confidence of **:** DISCONCERT
synonym see EMBARRASS
— **abash‧ment** \-mənt\ *noun*

abate \ə-'bāt\ *verb* **abat‧ed; abat‧ing** [Middle English, from Old French *abattre* to beat down — more at REBATE] (13th century)
transitive verb
1 a : to put an end to ⟨*abate* a nuisance⟩ **b :** NULLIFY ⟨*abate* a writ⟩
2 a : to reduce in degree or intensity **:** MODERATE **b :** to reduce in value or amount **:** make less especially by way of relief ⟨*abate* a tax⟩
3 : DEDUCT, OMIT ⟨*abate* part of the price⟩
4 a : to beat down or cut away so as to leave a figure in relief **b** *obsolete* **:** BLUNT
5 : DEPRIVE
intransitive verb
1 : to decrease in force or intensity
2 a : to become defeated or become null or void **b :** to decrease in amount or value ☆
— **abat‧er** *noun*

abate‧ment \ə-'bāt-mənt\ *noun* (14th century)
1 : the act or process of abating **:** the state of being abated
2 : an amount abated; *especially* **:** a deduction from the full amount of a tax

ab‧a‧tis \'a-bə-,tē, 'a-bə-təs\ *noun, plural* **ab‧a‧tis** \'a-bə-,tēz\ *or* **ab‧a‧tis‧es** \'a-bə-tə-səz\ [French, from *abattre*] (1766)
: a defensive obstacle formed by felled trees with sharpened branches facing the enemy

ab‧at‧toir \'a-bə-,twär, -,twȯr, -,tȯr\ *noun* [French, from *abattre*] (1820)
: SLAUGHTERHOUSE

ab‧ax‧i‧al \(,)a-'bak-sē-əl\ *adjective* (1857)

: situated out of or directed away from the axis ⟨the *abaxial* or lower surface of a leaf⟩

ab‧ba‧cy \'a-bə-sē\ *noun, plural* **-cies** [Middle English *abbatie*, from Late Latin *abbatia*] (15th century)
: the office, dignity, jurisdiction, or tenure of an abbot

Ab‧bas‧id \ə-'ba-səd, 'a-bə-səd\ *noun* (1788)
: a member of a dynasty of caliphs (750–1258) ruling the Islamic empire especially from their capital Baghdad and claiming descent from Abbas the uncle of Muhammad

ab‧ba‧tial \ə-'bā-shəl, a-\ *adjective* (circa 1642)
: of or relating to an abbot, abbess, or abbey

ab‧bé \a-'bā, 'a-,bā\ *noun* [French, from Late Latin *abbat-, abbas*] (1530)
: a member of the French secular clergy in major or minor orders — used as a title

ab‧bess \'a-bəs\ *noun* [Middle English *abbesse*, from Old French, from Late Latin *abbatissa*, feminine of *abbat-, abbas*] (13th century)
: a woman who is the superior of a convent of nuns

Abbe‧vil‧li‧an \,ab-'vi-lē-ən, ,a-bə-\ *adjective* [*Abbeville*, France] (circa 1934)
: of or relating to an early Lower Paleolithic culture of Europe characterized by bifacial stone hand axes

ab‧bey \'a-bē\ *noun, plural* **abbeys** [Middle English, from Old French *abaïe*, from Late Latin *abbatia* abbey, from *abbat-, abbas*] (13th century)
1 a : a monastery ruled by an abbot **b :** a convent ruled by an abbess
2 : an abbey church

ab‧bot \'a-bət\ *noun* [Middle English *abbod*, from Old English, from Late Latin *abbat-, abbas*, from Late Greek *abbas*, from Aramaic *abbā* father] (before 12th century)
: the superior of a monastery for men

ab‧bre‧vi‧ate \ə-'brē-vē-,āt\ *transitive verb* **-at‧ed; -at‧ing** [Middle English, from Late Latin *abbreviatus*, past participle of *abbreviare* — more at ABRIDGE] (15th century)
: to make briefer; *especially* **:** to reduce to a shorter form intended to stand for the whole
synonym see SHORTEN
— **ab‧bre‧vi‧a‧tor** \-,ā-tər\ *noun*

ab‧bre‧vi‧a‧tion \ə-,brē-vē-'ā-shən\ *noun* (15th century)
1 : the act or result of abbreviating **:** ABRIDGMENT
2 : a shortened form of a written word or phrase used in place of the whole ⟨*amt* is an *abbreviation* for *amount*⟩

ABC \,ā-(,)bē-'sē\ *noun, plural* **ABC's** *or* **ABCs** \-'sēz\ (13th century)
1 : ALPHABET — usually used in plural
2 a : the rudiments of reading, writing, and spelling — usually used in plural **b :** the rudiments of a subject

ABD \,ā-(,)bē-'dē\ *noun, plural* **ABDs** *also* **ABD's** [all but *d*issertation] (1965)
: a doctoral candidate who has completed required courses and examinations but not a dissertation

Ab‧di‧as \ab-'dī-əs\ *noun* [Late Latin, from Greek]
: OBADIAH

ab‧di‧cate \'ab-di-,kāt\ *verb* **-cat‧ed; -cat‧ing** [Latin *abdicatus*, past participle of *abdicare*, from *ab-* + *dicare* to proclaim — more at DICTION] (1541)
transitive verb
1 : to cast off **:** DISCARD
2 : to relinquish (as sovereign power) formally
intransitive verb
: to renounce a throne, high office, dignity, or function ☆
— **ab‧di‧ca‧ble** \-kə-bəl\ *adjective*
— **ab‧di‧ca‧tion** \,ab-di-'kā-shən\ *noun*
— **ab‧di‧ca‧tor** \'ab-di-,kā-tər\ *noun*

ab‧do‧men \'ab-də-mən, -,dō-; əb-'dō-mən, ab-\ *noun* [Middle French & Latin; Middle French, from Latin] (1615)
1 : the part of the body between the thorax and the pelvis; *also* **:** the cavity of this part of the trunk containing the chief viscera
2 : the posterior section of the body behind the thorax in an arthropod — see INSECT illustration
— **ab‧dom‧i‧nal** \ab-'dä-mə-n°l, əb-, -'däm-n°l\ *adjective*
— **ab‧dom‧i‧nal‧ly** \-ē\ *adverb*

ab‧du‧cens nerve \ab-'dü-,senz-, -'dyü-\ *noun* [New Latin *abducent-, abducens*, from Latin, present participle of *abducere*] (1947)
: either of the 6th pair of cranial nerves that are motor nerves supplying the rectus on the outer and lateral side of each eye — called also *abducens*

ab‧du‧cent nerve \ab-'dü-s°nt-, -'dyü-\ *noun* (1875)
: ABDUCENS NERVE

ab‧duct \ab-'dəkt, əb-; *2 also* 'ab-,\ *transitive verb* [Latin *abductus*, past participle of *abducere*, literally, to lead away, from *ab-* + *ducere* to lead — more at TOW] (1834)
1 : to carry off (as a person) by force
2 : to draw or spread away (as a limb or the fingers) from a position near or parallel to the median axis of the body or from the axis of a limb
— **ab‧duc‧tor** \-'dək-tər\ *noun*

ab‧duc‧tion \ab-'dək-shən, əb-\ *noun* (1666)
1 : the action of abducting **:** the condition of being abducted
2 : the unlawful carrying away of a woman for marriage or intercourse

abeam \ə-'bēm\ *adverb or adjective* (circa 1836)
: off to the side of a ship or plane especially at a right angle to the middle of the ship or plane's length

¹**abe‧ce‧dar‧i‧an** \,ā-bē-(,)sē-'der-ē-ən\ *noun* [Middle English *abecedary*, from Medieval Latin *abecedarium* alphabet, from Late Latin,

neuter of *abecedarius* of the alphabet, from the letters *a + b + c + d*] (1603)
: one learning the rudiments of something (as the alphabet)
²**abecedarian** *adjective* (1665)
1 a : of or relating to the alphabet **b :** alphabetically arranged
2 : RUDIMENTARY
abed \ə-'bed\ *adverb or adjective* (13th century)
: in bed
Abel \'ā-bəl\ *noun* [Late Latin, from Greek, from Hebrew *Hebhel*]
: a son of Adam and Eve killed by his brother Cain
abe·lia \ə-'bēl-yə\ *noun* [New Latin, from Clarke *Abel* (died 1826) English botanist] (circa 1899)
: any of a genus (*Abelia*) of shrubs of Asian or Mexican origin having opposite leaves and white, red, or pink flowers
abe·li·an \ə-'bē-lē-ən\ *adjective, often capitalized* [Niels *Abel* (died 1829) Norwegian mathematician] (circa 1909)
: COMMUTATIVE 2 ⟨*abelian* group⟩ ⟨*abelian* ring⟩
Abe·na·ki \ˌa-bə-'nä-kē\ *noun, plural* **Abenaki** *or* **Abenakis** (1721)
1 : a member of a group of American Indian peoples of northern New England and adjoining parts of Quebec
2 : either of the two Algonquian languages spoken by the Abenaki peoples
Ab·er·deen An·gus \ˈa-bər-ˌdēn-'aŋ-gəs\ *noun* [*Aberdeen & Angus*, counties in Scotland] (1862)
: ANGUS
¹**ab·er·rant** \a-'ber-ənt, ə-; 'a-bə-rənt, -ˌber-ənt\ *adjective* [Latin *aberrant-, aberrans*, present participle of *aberrare* to go astray, from *ab-* + *errare* to wander, err] (circa 1780)
1 : straying from the right or normal way
2 : deviating from the usual or natural type **:** ATYPICAL
— **ab·er·rance** \-ən(t)s\ *noun*
— **ab·er·ran·cy** \-ən(t)-sē\ *noun*
— **ab·er·rant·ly** *adverb*
²**aberrant** *noun* (1938)
1 : an aberrant group, individual, or structure
2 : a person whose behavior departs substantially from the standard
ab·er·rat·ed \'a-bə-ˌrā-təd\ *adjective* [Latin *aberratus*, past participle of *aberrare*] (1893)
: ABERRANT
ab·er·ra·tion \ˌa-bə-'rā-shən\ *noun* [Latin *aberration-, aberratio*] (1594)
1 : the fact or an instance of being aberrant especially from a moral standard or normal state
2 : failure of a mirror, refracting surface, or lens to produce exact point-to-point correspondence between an object and its image
3 : unsoundness or disorder of the mind
4 : a small periodic change of apparent position in celestial bodies due to the combined effect of the motion of light and the motion of the observer
5 : an aberrant individual
— **ab·er·ra·tion·al** \-shnəl, -shə-nᵊl\ *adjective*
abet \ə-'bet\ *transitive verb* **abet·ted; abet·ting** [Middle English *abetten*, from Middle French *abeter*, from Old French, from *a-* (from Latin *ad-*) + *beter* to bait, of Germanic origin; akin to Old English *bǣtan* to bait] (14th century)
1 : to actively second and encourage (as an activity or plan) **:** FORWARD
2 : to assist or support in the achievement of a purpose ⟨*abetted* the thief in his getaway⟩
synonym see INCITE
— **abet·ment** \-mənt\ *noun*
— **abet·tor** *or* **abet·ter** \ə-'be-tər\ *noun*
abey·ance \ə-'bā-ən(t)s\ *noun* [Middle French *abeance* expectation, from *abaer* to desire, from *a-* + *baer* to yawn, from Medieval Latin *batare*] (1660)

1 : temporary inactivity **:** SUSPENSION
2 : a lapse in succession during which there is no person in whom a title is vested
abey·ant \-ənt\ *adjective* [back-formation from *abeyance*] (circa 1859)
: being in abeyance
ab·hor \əb-'hȯr, ab-\ *transitive verb* **ab·horred; ab·hor·ring** [Middle English *abhorren*, from Latin *abhorrēre*, from *ab-* + *horrēre* to shudder — more at HORROR] (15th century)
: to regard with extreme repugnance **:** LOATHE
synonym see HATE
— **ab·hor·rer** \-'hȯr-ər\ *noun*
ab·hor·rence \əb-'hȯr-ən(t)s, -'här-\ *noun* (1660)
1 a : the act or state of abhorring **b :** the feeling of one who abhors
2 : one that is abhorred
ab·hor·rent \-ənt\ *adjective* [Latin *abhorrent-, abhorrens*, present participle of *abhorrēre*] (1599)
1 a *archaic* **:** strongly opposed **b :** feeling or showing abhorrence
2 : not agreeable **:** CONTRARY ⟨a notion *abhorrent* to their philosophy⟩
3 : being so repugnant as to stir up positive antagonism ⟨acts *abhorrent* to every right-minded person⟩
— **ab·hor·rent·ly** *adverb*
Abib \ä-'vēv\ *noun* [Hebrew *Ābhībh*, literally, ear of grain] (1535)
: the 1st month of the ancient Hebrew calendar corresponding to Nisan — see MONTH table
abid·ance \ə-'bī-dᵊn(t)s\ *noun* (1647)
1 : an act or state of abiding **:** CONTINUANCE
2 : COMPLIANCE ⟨*abidance* by the rules⟩
abide \ə-'bīd\ *verb* **abode** \-'bōd\ *or* **abid·ed; abid·ing** [Middle English, from Old English *ābīdan*, from *ā-*, perfective prefix + *bīdan* to bide; akin to Old High German *ir-*, perfective prefix] (before 12th century)
transitive verb
1 : to wait for **:** AWAIT
2 a : to endure without yielding **:** WITHSTAND **b :** to bear patiently **:** TOLERATE ⟨cannot *abide* such bigots⟩
3 : to accept without objection ⟨will *abide* your decision⟩
intransitive verb
1 : to remain stable or fixed in a state
2 : to continue in a place **:** SOJOURN
synonym see BEAR, CONTINUE
— **abid·er** *noun*
— **abide by 1 :** to conform to **2 :** to acquiesce in
abid·ing \ə-'bī-diŋ\ *adjective* (14th century)
: ENDURING, CONTINUING ⟨an *abiding* interest in nature⟩
— **abid·ing·ly** *adverb*
ab·i·gail \'a-bə-ˌgāl\ *noun* [*Abigail*, servant in *The Scornful Lady*, a play by Francis Beaumont & John Fletcher] (1671)
: a lady's personal maid
abil·i·ty \ə-'bi-lə-tē\ *noun, plural* **-ties** [Middle English *abilite*, from Middle French *habilité*, from Latin *habilitat-, habilitas*, from *habilis* apt, skillful — more at ABLE] (14th century)
1 a : the quality or state of being able ⟨*ability* of the soil to hold water⟩; *especially* **:** physical, mental, or legal power to perform **b :** competence in doing **:** SKILL
2 : natural aptitude or acquired proficiency ⟨children whose *abilities* warrant higher education⟩
-ability *also* **-ibility** *noun suffix* [Middle English *-abilite, -ibilite*, from Middle French *-abilité, -ibilité*, from Latin *-abilitas, -ibilitas*, from *-abilis, -ibilis* + *-tas* -ty]
: capacity, fitness, or tendency to act or be acted on in a (specified) way ⟨agglutin*ability*⟩
ab in·i·tio \ˌab-ə-'ni-shē-ˌō\ *adverb* [Latin] (1599)
: from the beginning

abio·gen·e·sis \ˌā-ˌbī-ō-'je-nə-səs\ *noun* [New Latin, from ²*a-* + *bio-* + Latin *genesis*] (1870)
: the supposed spontaneous origination of living organisms directly from lifeless matter
— **abi·og·e·nist** \ˌā-(ˌ)bī-'ä-jə-nist\ *noun*
abio·gen·ic \ˌā-ˌbī-ō-'je-nik\ *adjective* (1891)
: not produced by the action of living organisms
— **abio·gen·i·cal·ly** \-ni-k(ə-)lē\ *adverb*
abi·o·log·i·cal \ˌā-ˌbī-ə-'lä-ji-kəl\ *adjective* (1868)
: not biological; *especially* **:** not involving or produced by organisms ⟨*abiological* synthesis of amino acids⟩
abi·ot·ic \ˌā-(ˌ)bī-'ä-tik\ *adjective* (circa 1893)
: not biotic **:** ABIOLOGICAL ⟨the *abiotic* environment⟩
— **abi·ot·i·cal·ly** \-ti-k(ə-)lē\ *adverb*
ab·ject \'ab-ˌjekt\ *adjective* [Middle English, from Latin *abjectus*, from past participle of *abicere* to cast off, from *ab-* + *jacere* to throw — more at JET] (15th century)
1 : sunk to or existing in a low state or condition ⟨to lowest pitch of *abject* fortune thou art fallen —John Milton⟩
2 a : cast down in spirit **:** SERVILE, SPIRITLESS ⟨a man made *abject* by suffering⟩ **b :** showing utter hopelessness or resignation ⟨*abject* surrender⟩
3 : expressing or offered in a humble and often ingratiating spirit ⟨*abject* flattery⟩ ⟨an *abject* apology⟩
synonym see MEAN
— **ab·ject·ly** \'ab-ˌjekt(t)-lē, ab-\ *adverb*
— **ab·ject·ness** \-ˌjekt(t)-nəs, -'jek(t)-\ *noun*
ab·jec·tion \ab-'jek-shən\ *noun* (14th century)
1 : a low or downcast state **:** DEGRADATION
2 : the act of making abject **:** HUMBLING, REJECTION ⟨I protest . . . this vile *abjection* of youth to age —G. B. Shaw⟩
ab·ju·ra·tion \ˌab-jə-'rā-shən\ *noun* (15th century)
1 : the act or process of abjuring
2 : an oath of abjuring
ab·jure \ab-'jùr\ *transitive verb* **ab·jured; ab·jur·ing** [Middle English, from Middle French or Latin; Middle French *abjurer*, from Latin *abjurare*, from *ab-* + *jurare* to swear — more at JURY] (15th century)
1 a : to renounce upon oath **b :** to reject solemnly
2 : to abstain from **:** AVOID ⟨*abjure* extravagance⟩ ☆
— **ab·jur·er** *noun*
ab·late \a-'blāt\ *verb* **ab·lat·ed; ab·lat·ing** [Latin *ablatus* (past participle of *auferre* to remove), from *ab-* + *latus*, past participle of

☆ **SYNONYMS**

Abjure, renounce, forswear, recant, retract mean to withdraw one's word or professed belief. ABJURE implies a firm and final rejecting or abandoning often made under oath ⟨*abjured* the errors of his former faith⟩. RENOUNCE often equals ABJURE but may carry the meaning of disclaim or disown ⟨*renounced* abstract art and turned to portrait painting⟩. FORSWEAR may add to ABJURE an implication of perjury or betrayal ⟨I cannot *forswear* my principles⟩. RECANT stresses the withdrawing or denying of something professed or taught ⟨if they *recant* they will be spared⟩. RETRACT applies to the withdrawing of a promise, an offer, or an accusation ⟨the newspaper had to *retract* its allegations against the mayor⟩.

ferre — more at UKASE, BEAR, TOLERATE] (1542)
transitive verb
: to remove especially by cutting, abrading, or evaporating
intransitive verb
: to become ablated; *especially* : VAPORIZE 1
ab·la·tion \a-'blā-shən\ *noun* (15th century)
: the process of ablating: as **a** : surgical removal **b** : loss of a part (as ice from a glacier or the outside of a nose cone) by melting or vaporization
¹ab·la·tive \'a-blə-tiv\ *adjective* (15th century)
: of, relating to, or constituting a grammatical case expressing typically the relations of separation and source and also frequently such relations as cause or instrument
— **ablative** *noun*
²ab·la·tive \a-'blā-tiv\ *adjective* (circa 1569)
1 : of or relating to ablation
2 : tending to ablate (*ablative* material on a nose cone)
— **ab·la·tive·ly** *adverb*
ablative absolute \'a-blə-tiv-\ *noun* (circa 1828)
: a construction in Latin in which a noun or pronoun and its adjunct both in the ablative case form together an adverbial phrase expressing generally the time, cause, or an attendant circumstance of an action
ab·laut \'ä-blaut, 'a-; 'äp-,laut\ *noun* [German, from *ab* away from + *Laut* sound] (1849)
: a systematic variation of vowels in the same root or affix or in related roots or affixes especially in the Indo-European languages that is usually paralleled by differences in use or meaning (as in *sing, sang, sung, song*)
ablaze \ə-'blāz\ *adjective or adverb* (1801)
1 : being on fire
2 : radiant with light or emotion (his face all *ablaze* with excitement —Bram Stoker)
able \'ā-bəl\ *adjective* **abler** \-b(ə-)lər\; **ablest** \-b(ə-)ləst\ [Middle English, from Middle French, from Latin *habilis* apt, from *habēre* to have — more at HABIT] (14th century)
1 a : having sufficient power, skill, or resources to accomplish an object **b** : susceptible to action or treatment
2 : marked by intelligence, knowledge, skill, or competence
— **ably** \'ā-b(ə-)lē\ *adverb*
-able *also* **-ible** *adjective suffix* [Middle English, from Old French, from Latin *-abilis, -ibilis,* from *-a-, -i-,* verb stem vowels + *-bilis* capable or worthy of]
1 : capable of, fit for, or worthy of (being so acted upon or toward) — chiefly in adjectives derived from verbs (break*able*) (collect*ible*)
2 : tending, given, or liable to (agree*able*) (perish*able*)
— **-ably** *also* **-ibly** *adverb suffix*
able–bod·ied \,ā-bəl-'bä-dēd\ *adjective* (circa 1622)
: having a sound strong body
able–bodied seaman *noun* (circa 1909)
: ABLE SEAMAN
able seaman *noun* (1702)
: an experienced deck-department seaman qualified to perform routine duties at sea
abloom \ə-'blüm\ *adjective* (1855)
: abounding with blooms : BLOOMING (parks *abloom* with roses)
ab·lut·ed \ə-'blü-təd, a-\ *adjective* [back-formation from *ablution*] (1650)
: washed clean
ab·lu·tion \ə-'blü-shən, a-\ *noun* [Middle English, from Middle French or Latin; Middle French, from Latin *ablution-, ablutio,* from *abluere* to wash away, from *ab-* + *luere* to wash; akin to Latin *lavere* to wash — more at LYE] (1533)
1 a : the washing of one's body or part of it (as in a religious rite) **b** *plural* : the act or action of bathing

2 *plural, British* : a building housing bathing and toilet facilities on a military base
— **ab·lu·tion·ary** \-shə-,ner-ē\ *adjective*
ABM \,ā-(,)bē-'em\ *noun, plural* **ABM's** *or* **ABMs** \-'emz\ (1963)
: ANTIBALLISTIC MISSILE
Ab·na·ki \ab-'nä-kē\ *variant of* ABENAKI
ab·ne·gate \'ab-ni-,gāt\ *transitive verb* **-gated; -gat·ing** [back-formation from *abnegation*] (1623)
1 : DENY, RENOUNCE (*abnegated* their God)
2 : SURRENDER, RELINQUISH (*abnegated* her powers)
— **ab·ne·ga·tor** \-,gā-tər\ *noun*
ab·ne·ga·tion \,ab-ni-'gā-shən\ *noun* [Late Latin *abnegation-, abnegatio,* from Latin *abnegare* to refute, from *ab-* + *negare* to deny — more at NEGATE] (14th century)
: DENIAL; *especially* : SELF-DENIAL
¹ab·nor·mal \(,)ab-'nȯr-məl, əb-\ *adjective* [alteration of French *anormal,* from Medieval Latin *anormalis,* from Latin *a-* + Late Latin *normalis* normal] (circa 1836)
: deviating from the normal or average : UNUSUAL, EXCEPTIONAL (*abnormal* behavior)
— **ab·nor·mal·ly** \-mə-lē\ *adverb*
²abnormal *noun* (1912)
: an abnormal person
ab·nor·mal·i·ty \,ab-nər-'ma-lə-tē, -(,)nȯr-\ *noun, plural* **-ties** (1854)
1 : the quality or state of being abnormal
2 : something abnormal
abnormal psychology *noun* (circa 1903)
: a branch of psychology concerned with mental and emotional disorders (as neuroses, psychoses, and mental deficiency) and with certain incompletely understood normal phenomena (as dreams and hypnosis)
abo \'a-(,)bō\ *noun, plural* **ab·os** (1908)
Australian : ABORIGINE — often used disparagingly
¹aboard \ə-'bȯrd, -'bȯrd\ *adverb or adjective* (14th century)
1 : ALONGSIDE
2 a : on, onto, or within a vehicle (as a car or ship) **b** : in or into a group, association, or organization (her second promotion since coming *aboard*)
3 *baseball* : on base
²aboard *preposition* (15th century)
: ON, ONTO, WITHIN (go *aboard* ship) (*aboard* a plane)
ABO blood group \,ā-(,)bē-'ō-\ *noun* (1949)
: any of the four blood groups A, B, AB, and O comprising the ABO system
abode \ə-'bōd\ *noun* [Middle English *abod,* from *abiden* to abide] (13th century)
1 *obsolete* : WAIT, DELAY
2 : a temporary stay : SOJOURN
3 : the place where one abides : HOME
aboil \ə-'bȯi(ə)l\ *adjective or adverb* (1810)
1 : being at the boiling point : BOILING
2 : intensely excited or stirred up (the meeting was *aboil* with controversy)
abol·ish \ə-'bä-lish\ *transitive verb* [Middle English *abolisshen,* from Middle French *aboliss-,* stem of *abolir,* from Latin *abolēre;* probably akin to *adolescere* to grow up — more at ADULT] (15th century)
1 : to end the observance or effect of : ANNUL
2 : DESTROY
— **abol·ish·able** \-li-shə-bəl\ *adjective*
— **abol·ish·er** *noun*
— **abol·ish·ment** \-mənt\ *noun*
ab·o·li·tion \,a-bə-'li-sh°n\ *noun* [Middle French, from Latin *abolition-, abolitio,* from *abolēre*] (1529)
1 : the act of abolishing : the state of being abolished
2 : the abolishing of slavery
— **ab·o·li·tion·ary** \-'li-sh°n-,er-ē\ *adjective*
ab·o·li·tion·ism \-'li-sh°n-,i-zəm\ *noun* (1808)
: principles or measures fostering abolition especially of slavery

— **ab·o·li·tion·ist** \-ist\ *noun or adjective*
ab·oma·sum \,a-bō-'mā-səm\ *noun, plural* **-sa** \-sə\ [New Latin, from Latin *ab-* + *omasum* ox's tripe] (circa 1706)
: the fourth compartment of the ruminant stomach that follows the omasum and has a true digestive function — compare RUMEN, RETICULUM
— **ab·oma·sal** \-səl\ *adjective*
A–bomb \'ā-,bäm\ *noun* (1945)
: ATOMIC BOMB 1
abom·i·na·ble \ə-'bäm-nə-bəl, -'bä-mə-\ *adjective* (14th century)
1 : worthy of or causing disgust or hatred : DETESTABLE (the *abominable* treatment of the poor)
2 : quite disagreeable or unpleasant (*abominable* weather)
— **abom·i·na·bly** \-blē\ *adverb*
abominable snow·man \-'snō-mən, -,man\ *noun, often A&S capitalized* (1921)
: a mysterious creature with human or apelike characteristics reported to exist in the high Himalayas — called also *yeti*
abom·i·nate \ə-'bä-mə-,nāt\ *transitive verb* **-nat·ed; -nat·ing** [Latin *abominatus,* past participle of *abominari,* literally, to deprecate as an ill omen, from *ab-* + *omin-, omen* omen] (1644)
: to hate or loathe intensely : ABHOR
synonym see HATE
— **abom·i·na·tor** \-,nā-tər\ *noun*
abom·i·na·tion \ə-,bä-mə-'nā-shən\ *noun* (14th century)
1 : something abominable
2 : extreme disgust and hatred : LOATHING
ab·oral \(,)a-'bȯr-əl, -'bȯr-\ *adjective* (1857)
: situated opposite to or away from the mouth (a sea urchin's *aboral* surface)
— **ab·oral·ly** \-ə-lē\ *adverb*
¹ab·orig·i·nal \,a-bə-'rij-nəl, -'ri-jə-n°l\ *adjective* (1667)
1 : being the first or earliest known of its kind present in a region (*aboriginal* forests) (*aboriginal* rocks)
2 a : of or relating to aborigines **b** *often capitalized* : of or relating to the indigenous peoples of Australia
synonym see NATIVE
— **ab·orig·i·nal·ly** *adverb*
²aboriginal *noun* (1767)
1 : ABORIGINE 1
2 *often capitalized* : ABORIGINE 2
ab·orig·i·ne \,a-bə-'rij-(,)nē, -'ri-jə-\ *noun* [Latin *aborigines,* plural, from *ab origine* from the beginning] (1533)
1 : an aboriginal inhabitant especially as contrasted with an invading or colonizing people
2 *often capitalized* : a member of any of the indigenous peoples of Australia
¹aborn·ing \ə-'bȯr-niŋ\ *adverb* [¹a- + English dialect *borning* (birth)] (1916)
: while being born or produced (a resolution that died *aborning*)
²aborning *adjective* (1943)
: being born or produced (the *aborning* fiasco)
¹abort \ə-'bȯrt\ *verb* [Latin *abortus,* past participle of *aboriri* to miscarry, from *ab-* + *oriri* to rise, to be born — more at ORIENT] (1580)
intransitive verb
1 : to bring forth premature or stillborn offspring
2 : to become checked in development so as to degenerate or remain rudimentary
transitive verb
1 a : to induce the abortion of or give birth to prematurely **b** : to terminate the pregnancy of before term
2 a : to terminate prematurely : CANCEL (*abort* a project) (*abort* a spaceflight) **b** : to stop in the early stages (*abort* a disease)
— **abort·er** *noun*
²abort *noun* (1944)
: the premature termination of a flight (as of

an aircraft or spacecraft), a mission, or an action or procedure relating to a flight ⟨a launch *abort*⟩

abor·ti·fa·cient \ə-ˌbȯr-tə-'fā-shənt\ *noun* (1873)
: an agent (as a drug) that induces abortion
— **abortifacient** *adjective*

abor·tion \ə-'bȯr-shən\ *noun* (1547)
1 : the termination of a pregnancy after, accompanied by, resulting in, or closely followed by the death of the embryo or fetus: as **a** : spontaneous expulsion of a human fetus during the first 12 weeks of gestation — compare MISCARRIAGE **b** : induced expulsion of a human fetus **c** : expulsion of a fetus by a domestic animal often due to infection at any time before completion of pregnancy — compare CONTAGIOUS ABORTION
2 : MONSTROSITY
3 : arrest of development (as of a part or process) resulting in imperfection; *also* : a result of such arrest

abor·tion·ist \-sh(ə-)nist\ *noun* (1871)
: one who induces abortions

abor·tive \ə-'bȯr-tiv\ *adjective* (14th century)
1 *obsolete* : prematurely born
2 : FRUITLESS, UNSUCCESSFUL
3 : imperfectly formed or developed
4 : tending to cut short □
— **abor·tive·ly** *adverb*
— **abor·tive·ness** *noun*

ABO system \ˌā-(ˌ)bē-'ō-\ *noun* (1944)
: the basic system of antigens of human blood behaving in heredity as an allelic unit to produce any of the ABO blood groups

abound \ə-'bau̇nd\ *intransitive verb* [Middle English, from Middle French *abonder*, from Latin *abundare*, from *ab-* + *unda* wave — more at WATER] (14th century)
1 : to be present in large numbers or in great quantity : be prevalent
2 : to be copiously supplied ⟨life *abounded* in mysteries —Norman Mailer⟩ ⟨institutions *abound* with evidence of his success —*Johns Hopkins Magazine*⟩

¹about \ə-'bau̇t\ *adverb* [Middle English, from Old English *abūtan*, from *¹a-* + *būtan* outside — more at BUT] (before 12th century)
1 a : reasonably close to ⟨*about* a year ago⟩ **b** : ALMOST ⟨*about* starved⟩ **c** : on the verge of — usually used with *be* and a following infinitive ⟨is *about* to join the army⟩; used with a negative to express intention or determination ⟨not *about* to quit⟩
2 : on all sides : AROUND
3 a : in rotation **b** : around the outside
4 : HERE AND THERE
5 : in the vicinity : NEAR
6 : in succession : ALTERNATELY ⟨turn *about* is fair play⟩
7 : in the opposite direction ⟨face *about*⟩ ⟨the other way *about*⟩

²about *preposition* (before 12th century)
1 : in a circle around : on every side of : AROUND
2 a : in the immediate neighborhood of : NEAR **b** : on or near the person of **c** : in the makeup of ⟨a mature wisdom *about* him⟩ **d** : at the command of ⟨has his wits *about* him⟩
3 : engaged in ⟨act as if they know what they're *about* —T. S. Matthews⟩
4 a : with regard to : CONCERNING **b** : concerned with **c** : fundamentally concerned with or directed toward ⟨poker is *about* money —David Mamet⟩
5 : over or in different parts of

³about *adjective* (1815)
1 : moving from place to place; *specifically* : being out of bed
2 : AROUND 2

about–face \ə-'bau̇t-'fās\ *noun* [from the imperative phrase *about face*] (1861)
1 : a 180° turn to the right from the position of attention

2 : a reversal of direction
3 : a reversal of attitude, behavior, or point of view
— **about–face** *intransitive verb*

about–turn \-'tərn\ *noun* (1893)
British : ABOUT-FACE

¹above \ə-'bəv\ *adverb* [Middle English, from Old English *abufan*, from *a-* + *bufan* above, from *be-* + *ufan* above; akin to Old English *ofer* over] (before 12th century)
1 a : in the sky : OVERHEAD **b** : in or to heaven
2 a : in or to a higher place **b** : higher on the same page or on a preceding page **c** : UPSTAIRS **d** : above zero ⟨10 degrees *above*⟩
3 : in or to a higher rank or number ⟨30 and *above*⟩
4 *archaic* : in addition : BESIDES
5 : UPSTAGE

²above *preposition* (before 12th century)
1 : in or to a higher place than : OVER
2 a : superior to (as in rank, quality, or degree) **b** : out of reach of **c** : in preference to **d** : too proud or honorable to stoop to
3 : exceeding in number, quantity, or size : more than
4 : as distinct from and in addition to ⟨heard the whistle *above* the roar of the crowd⟩

³above *noun, plural* **above** (13th century)
1 a : something that is above **b** : a person whose name is written above
2 a : a higher authority **b** : HEAVEN □

⁴above *adjective* (1604)
: written or discussed higher on the same page or on a preceding page
usage see ³ABOVE

above all *adverb* (14th century)
: before every other consideration : ESPECIALLY

¹above·board \ə-'bəv-ˌbȯrd, -ˌbȯrd\ *adverb* [from the difficulty of cheating at cards when the hands are above the table] (1594)
: in a straightforward manner : OPENLY

²aboveboard *adjective* (1648)
: free from all traces of deceit or duplicity

above·ground \ə-'bəv-ˌgrau̇nd\ *adjective* (1878)
1 : located or occurring on or above the surface of the ground
2 : existing, produced, or published by or within the establishment ⟨*aboveground* movies⟩

ab ovo \ab-'ō-(ˌ)vō\ *adverb* [Latin, literally, from the egg] (circa 1586)
: from the beginning

ab·ra·ca·dab·ra \ˌa-brə-kə-'da-brə\ *noun* [Late Latin] (1565)
1 : a magical charm or incantation
2 : unintelligible language

abrade \ə-'brād\ *verb* **abrad·ed; abrad·ing** [Latin *abradere* to scrape off, from *ab-* + *radere* to scrape — more at RODENT] (1677) *transitive verb*
1 a : to rub or wear away especially by friction : ERODE **b** : to irritate or roughen by rubbing
2 : to wear down in spirit : IRRITATE, WEARY *intransitive verb*
: to undergo abrasion
— **abrad·able** \-'brā-də-bəl\ *adjective*
— **abrad·er** *noun*

Abra·ham \'ā-brə-ˌham\ *noun* [Late Latin, from Greek *Abraam*, from Hebrew *'Abhrāhām*]
: an Old Testament patriarch regarded by Jews as the founder of the Hebrew people through his son Isaac and by Muslims as the founder of the Arab peoples through his son Ishmael

abra·sion \ə-'brā-zhən\ *noun* [Medieval Latin *abrasion-, abrasio*, from Latin *abradere*] (circa 1656)
1 a : a wearing, grinding, or rubbing away by friction **b** : IRRITATION
2 : an abraded area of the skin or mucous membrane

¹abra·sive \ə-'brā-siv, -ziv\ *noun* (1853)
: a substance (as emery or pumice) used for abrading, smoothing, or polishing

²abrasive *adjective* (1875)
1 : tending to abrade
2 : causing irritation ⟨*abrasive* manners⟩
— **abra·sive·ly** *adverb*
— **abra·sive·ness** *noun*

ab·re·ac·tion \ˌa-brē-'ak-shən\ *noun* [part translation of German *Abreagierung* catharsis, from *ab* off, away (from Old High German *aba*) + *Reagierung* reaction, from Latin *re-agere* to react — more at OF, REACT] (1912)
: the expression and emotional discharge of unconscious material (as a repressed idea or emotion) by verbalization especially in the presence of a therapist
— **ab·re·act** \-'akt\ *verb*

abreast \ə-'brest\ *adverb or adjective* (15th century)
1 : beside one another with bodies in line ⟨columns of men five *abreast*⟩
2 : up to a particular standard or level especially of knowledge of recent developments ⟨keeps *abreast* of the latest trends⟩

abridge \ə-'brij\ *transitive verb* **abridged; abridg·ing** [Middle English *abregen*, from Middle French *abregier*, from Late Latin *abbreviare*, from Latin *ad-* + *brevis* short — more at BRIEF] (14th century)
1 a *archaic* : DEPRIVE **b** : to reduce in scope : DIMINISH ⟨attempts to *abridge* the right of free speech⟩
2 : to shorten in duration or extent ⟨modern transportation that *abridges* distance⟩
3 : to shorten by omission of words without sacrifice of sense : CONDENSE
synonym see SHORTEN
— **abridg·er** *noun*

abridg·ment *or* **abridge·ment** \ə-'brij-mənt\ *noun* (15th century)
1 : the action of abridging : the state of being abridged
2 : a shortened form of a work retaining the general sense and unity of the original

abroach \ə-'brōch\ *adverb or adjective* (14th century)
1 : in a condition for letting out a liquid (as wine) ⟨a cask set *abroach*⟩
2 : in action or agitation : ASTIR ⟨mischiefs that I set *abroach* —Shakespeare⟩

abroad \ə-'brȯd\ *adverb or adjective* (13th century)
1 : over a wide area : WIDELY

□ **USAGE**

abortive Sense 2 has been objected to occasionally since the 1880s. These objections depend upon an etymological argument that the suffix *-ive* implies continuation, repetition, or tendency, rather than completion; therefore, something unsuccessful must be *aborted*, rather than *abortive*. This argument ignores the whole history of the word in English; from Shakespeare's time and earlier *abortive* has meant, literally and figuratively, "aborted." One may safely ignore this objection, as other writers have ⟨our first design, my friend, has prov'd *abortive* —Joseph Addison⟩ ⟨the *abortive* coup against him in October —Elizabeth Drew⟩.

above Although still objected to by some, the use of *above* as a noun in sense 1a ⟨none of the *above*⟩ ⟨the *above* is Theseus's opinion —William Blake⟩ and as an adjective ⟨without the *above* reserve —O. W. Holmes (died 1935)⟩ ⟨I was brought up on the *above* words —Viscount Montgomery⟩ has been long established as standard.

\ə\ **abut** \ᵊ\ **kitten** \ər\ **further** \a\ **ash** \ā\ **ace**
\ä\ **mop, mar** \au̇\ **out** \ch\ **chin** \e\ **bet** \ē\ **easy**
\g\ **go** \i\ **hit** \ī\ **ice** \j\ **job** \ŋ\ **sing** \ō\ **go**
\ȯ\ **law** \ȯi\ **boy** \th\ **thin** \t̲h̲\ **the** \ü\ **loot** \u̇\ **foot**
\y\ **yet** \zh\ **vision** *see also* Guide to Pronunciation

2 : away from one's home
3 : beyond the boundaries of one's country
4 : in wide circulation : ABOUT
5 : wide of the mark : ASTRAY

ab·ro·gate \'a-brə-ˌgāt\ *transitive verb* **-gat·ed; -gat·ing** [Latin *abrogatus,* past participle of *abrogare,* from *ab-* + *rogare* to ask, propose a law — more at RIGHT] (1526) **1 :** to abolish by authoritative action : ANNUL **2 :** to treat as nonexistent ⟨*abrogating* their responsibilities⟩
synonym see NULLIFY
— **ab·ro·ga·tion** \ˌa-brə-'gā-shən\ *noun*

abrupt \ə-'brəpt\ *adjective* [Latin *abruptus,* from past participle of *abrumpere* to break off, from *ab-* + *rumpere* to break — more at REAVE] (1591) **1 a :** characterized by or involving action or change without preparation or warning : UNEXPECTED ⟨came to an *abrupt* stop⟩ ⟨an *abrupt* turn to the left⟩ ⟨an *abrupt* decision to retire⟩ **b :** unceremoniously curt ⟨an *abrupt* manner⟩ **c :** lacking smoothness or continuity ⟨an *abrupt* transition⟩ **2 :** giving the impression of being cut or broken off; *especially* **:** involving a sudden steep rise or drop ⟨*abrupt* hills⟩ ⟨a high *abrupt* bank bounded the stream⟩
synonym see PRECIPITATE, STEEP
— **abrupt·ly** \ə-'brəp(t)-lē\ *adverb*
— **abrupt·ness** \ə-'brəp(t)-nəs\ *noun*

abrup·tion \ə-'brəp-shən\ *noun* (1606)
: a sudden breaking off or away

ABS \ˌā-(ˌ)bē-'es\ *noun* [acrylonitrile-butadiene-styrene] (1966)
: a tough rigid plastic used especially for automobile parts and building materials

ab·scess \'ab-ˌses\ *noun, plural* **ab·scess·es** \'ab-ˌse-səz, -ˌsēz; -sə-səz\ [Latin *abscessus,* literally, act of going away, from *abscedere* to go away, from *abs-, ab-* + *cedere* to go] (1615)
: a localized collection of pus surrounded by inflamed tissue
— **ab·scessed** \-ˌsest\ *adjective*

ab·scise \ab-'sīz\ *verb* **ab·scised; ab·scis·ing** [Latin *abscisus,* past participle of *abscidere,* from *abs-* + *caedere* to cut] (1612) *transitive verb*
: to cut off by abscission
intransitive verb
: to separate by abscission

ab·scis·ic acid \ab-ˌsi-zik-, -ˌsik-\ *noun* [*abscision* (variant of *abscission*) + *-ic*] (1968)
: a plant hormone $C_{15}H_{20}O_4$ that is a sesquiterpene widespread in nature and that typically promotes leaf abscission and dormancy and has an inhibitory effect on cell elongation

ab·sci·sin \'ab-sə-sən, ab-'si-s°n\ *noun* [*abscision* + *-in*] (1961)
: ABSCISIC ACID

ab·scis·sa \ab-'si-sə\ *noun, plural* **abscis·sas** *also* **ab·scis·sae** \-'si-(ˌ)sē\ [New Latin, from Latin, feminine of *abscissus,* past participle of *abscindere* to cut off, from *ab-* + *scindere* to cut — more at SHED] (1694)
: the horizontal coordinate of a point in a plane Cartesian coordinate system obtained by measuring parallel to the x-axis — compare ORDINATE

AP abscissa of point *P*

ab·scis·sion \ab-'si-zhən\ *noun* [Latin *abscission-, abscissio,* from *abscindere*] (15th century) **1 :** the act or process of cutting off : REMOVAL **2 :** the natural separation of flowers, fruit, or leaves from plants at a special separation layer

ab·scond \ab-'skänd, əb-\ *intransitive verb* [Latin *abscondere* to hide away, from *abs-* + *condere* to store up, conceal — more at CONDIMENT] (circa 1578)
: to depart secretly and hide oneself
— **ab·scond·er** *noun*

ab·seil \'ab-ˌsāl, -ˌsīl\ *intransitive verb* [German *abseilen,* from *ab* down, off + *Seil* rope] (1941)
chiefly British **:** RAPPEL

ab·sence \'ab-sən(t)s\ *noun* (14th century) **1 :** the state of being absent **2 :** the period of time that one is absent **3 :** WANT, LACK ⟨an *absence* of detail⟩ **4 :** inattention to present surroundings or occurrences ⟨*absence* of mind⟩

¹ab·sent \'ab-sənt\ *adjective* [Middle English, from Middle French, from Latin *absent-, absens,* present participle of *abesse* to be absent, from *ab-* + *esse* to be — more at IS] (14th century) **1 :** not present or attending : MISSING **2 :** not existing : LACKING ⟨danger in a situation where power is *absent* —M. H. Trytten⟩ **3 :** INATTENTIVE, PREOCCUPIED
— **ab·sent·ly** *adverb*

²ab·sent \ab-'sent, 'ab-ˌ\ *transitive verb* (15th century)
: to keep (oneself) away

³ab·sent \'ab-sənt\ *preposition* (1945)
: in the absence of : WITHOUT

ab·sen·tee \ˌab-sən-'tē\ *noun* (1605)
: one that is absent: as **a :** a proprietor that lives away from his or her estate or business **b :** one missing from work or school
— **absentee** *adjective*

absentee ballot *noun* (1932)
: a ballot submitted (as by mail) in advance of an election by a voter who is unable to be present at the polls

ab·sen·tee·ism \ˌab-sən-'tē-ˌi-zəm\ *noun* (1829) **1 :** prolonged absence of an owner from his or her property **2 :** chronic absence (as from work or school); *also* **:** the rate of such absence

ab·sent·mind·ed \ˌab-sənt-'mīn-dəd\ *adjective* (1854) **1 :** lost in thought and unaware of one's surroundings or actions : PREOCCUPIED; *also* **:** given to absence of mind **2 :** indicative of or resulting from preoccupation or absence of mind
— **ab·sent·mind·ed·ly** *adverb*
— **ab·sent·mind·ed·ness** *noun*

absent without leave *adjective* (circa 1919)
: absent without authority from one's place of duty in the armed forces

ab·sinthe *also* **ab·sinth** \'ab-(ˌ)sin(t)th\ *noun* [French *absinthe,* from Latin *absinthium,* from Greek *apsinthion*] (1612) **1 :** WORMWOOD 1; *especially* **:** a common European wormwood (*Artemisia absinthium*) **2 :** a green liqueur flavored with wormwood or a substitute, anise, and other aromatics

ab·so·lute \'ab-sə-ˌlüt, ˌab-sə-'\ *adjective* [Middle English *absolut,* from Latin *absolutus,* from past participle of *absolvere* to set free, absolve] (14th century) **1 a :** free from imperfection : PERFECT **b :** free or relatively free from mixture : PURE ⟨*absolute* alcohol⟩ **c :** OUTRIGHT, UNMITIGATED ⟨an *absolute* lie⟩ **2 :** being, governed by, or characteristic of a ruler or authority completely free from constitutional or other restraint **3 a :** standing apart from a normal or usual syntactical relation with other words or sentence elements ⟨the absolute construction *this being the case* in the sentence "this being the case, let us go"⟩ **b** *of an adjective or possessive pronoun* **:** standing alone without a modified substantive ⟨*blind* in "help the blind" and *ours* in "your work and ours" are *absolute*⟩ **c** *of a verb* **:** having no object in the particular construction under consideration though normally transitive ⟨*kill* in "if looks could kill" is an *absolute* verb⟩ **4 :** having no restriction, exception, or qualification ⟨an *absolute* requirement⟩ ⟨*absolute* freedom⟩

5 : POSITIVE, UNQUESTIONABLE ⟨*absolute* proof⟩ **6 a :** independent of arbitrary standards of measurement **b :** relating to or derived in the simplest manner from the fundamental units of length, mass, and time ⟨*absolute* electric units⟩ **c :** relating to, measured on, or being a temperature scale based on absolute zero ⟨*absolute* temperature⟩; *specifically* **:** KELVIN ⟨10° *absolute*⟩ **7 :** FUNDAMENTAL, ULTIMATE ⟨*absolute* knowledge⟩ **8 :** perfectly embodying the nature of a thing ⟨*absolute* justice⟩ **9 :** being self-sufficient and free of external references or relationships ⟨an *absolute* term in logic⟩ ⟨*absolute* music⟩ **10 :** being the true distance from an aircraft to the earth's surface ⟨*absolute* altitude⟩
— **absolute** *noun*
— **ab·so·lute·ness** *noun*

absolute ceiling *noun* (circa 1920)
: the maximum height above sea level at which a particular airplane can maintain horizontal flight under standard air conditions — called also *ceiling*

absolute convergence *noun* (circa 1909)
: convergence of a mathematical series when the absolute values of the terms are taken

absolute humidity *noun* (1867)
: the amount of water vapor present in a unit volume of air — compare RELATIVE HUMIDITY

ab·so·lute·ly \'ab-sə-ˌlüt-lē, ˌab-sə-'\ *adverb* (14th century) **1 :** in an absolute manner or condition — often used as an intensive ⟨*absolutely* brilliant⟩ **2 :** with respect to absolute values ⟨an *absolutely* convergent series⟩

absolute magnitude *noun* (1902)
: the intrinsic luminosity of a celestial body (as a star) if viewed from a distance of 10 parsecs — compare APPARENT MAGNITUDE

absolute pitch *noun* (1864) **1 :** the position of a tone in a standard scale independently determined by its rate of vibration **2 :** the ability to recognize or sing a given isolated note

absolute space *noun* (circa 1889)
: SPACE 4b

absolute value *noun* (1907) **1 :** a nonnegative number equal in numerical value to a given real number **2 :** the positive square root of the sum of the squares of the real and imaginary parts of a complex number

absolute zero *noun* (1848)
: a theoretical temperature characterized by complete absence of heat and equivalent to exactly $-273.15°C$ or $-459.67°F$

ab·so·lu·tion \ˌab-sə-'lü-shən\ *noun* (13th century)
: the act of absolving; *specifically* **:** a remission of sins pronounced by a priest (as in the sacrament of reconciliation)

ab·so·lut·ism \'ab-sə-ˌlü-ˌti-zəm\ *noun* (1830) **1 a :** a political theory that absolute power should be vested in one or more rulers **b :** government by an absolute ruler or authority : DESPOTISM **2 :** advocacy of a rule by absolute standards or principles **3 :** an absolute standard or principle
— **ab·so·lut·ist** \-ˌlü-tist\ *noun or adjective*
— **ab·so·lu·tis·tic** \ˌab-sə-(ˌ)lü-'tis-tik\ *adjective*

ab·so·lu·tive \ˌab-sə-'lü-tiv\ *adjective* (1952)
: of, being, or relating to an inflectional morpheme that typically marks the subject of an intransitive verb or the direct object of a transitive verb in an ergative language

ab·so·lut·ize \'ab-sə-ˌlü-ˌtīz\ *transitive verb* **-ized; -iz·ing** (1919)
: to make absolute : convert into an absolute

ab·solve \əb-'zälv, -'sälv, -'zölv, -'sölv *also* without l\ *transitive verb* **ab·solved; ab-**

solv·ing [Middle English, from Latin *absolvere*, from *ab-* + *solvere* to loosen — more at SOLVE] (15th century)
1 : to set free from an obligation or the consequences of guilt
2 : to remit (a sin) by absolution
synonym see EXCULPATE
— **ab·solv·er** *noun*

ab·sorb \əb-'sȯrb, -'zȯrb\ *transitive verb* [Middle French *absorber*, from Latin *absorbēre*, from *ab-* + *sorbēre* to suck up; akin to Lithuanian *surbti* to sip, Greek *rophein* to gulp down] (15th century)
1 : to take in and make part of an existent whole 〈the capacity of China to *absorb* invaders〉
2 a : to suck up or take up 〈a sponge *absorbs* water〉 〈charcoal *absorbs* gas〉 〈plant roots *absorb* water〉 **b :** to take in **:** ACQUIRE, LEARN 〈convictions *absorbed* in youth —M. R. Cohen〉 **c :** USE UP, CONSUME 〈the fever *absorbed* her strength〉
3 : to engage or engross wholly 〈*absorbed* in thought〉
4 a (1) **:** to receive without recoil or echo 〈provided with a sound-*absorbing* surface〉 (2) **:** ENDURE, SUSTAIN 〈*absorbing* hardships〉 (3) **:** ASSUME, BEAR 〈the expenses were *absorbed* by the company〉 **b :** to transform (radiant energy) into a different form usually with a resulting rise in temperature 〈the earth *absorbs* the sun's rays〉
— **ab·sorb·abil·i·ty** \əb-ˌsȯr-bə-'bi-lə-tē, -ˌzȯr-\ *noun*
— **ab·sorb·able** \əb-'sȯr-bə-bəl, -'zȯr-\ *adjective*
— **ab·sorb·er** *noun*

ab·sor·bance \əb-'sȯr-bən(t)s, -'zȯr-\ *noun* (1947)
: the ability of a layer of a substance to absorb radiation expressed mathematically as the negative common logarithm of transmittance

ab·sor·ben·cy \əb-'sȯr-bən(t)-sē, -'zȯr-\ *noun, plural* **-cies** (1859)
1 : the quality or state of being absorbent
2 *or* **ab·sor·ban·cy :** ABSORBANCE

ab·sor·bent *also* **ab·sor·bant** \-bənt\ *adjective* [Latin *absorbent-, absorbens,* present participle of *absorbēre*] (1718)
: able to absorb 〈as *absorbent* as a sponge〉
— **absorbent** *also* **absorbant** *noun*

ab·sorb·ing *adjective* (1876)
: fully taking one's attention **:** ENGROSSING 〈an *absorbing* novel〉
— **ab·sorb·ing·ly** \-biŋ-lē\ *adverb*

ab·sorp·tance \əb-'sȯrp-tən(t)s, -'zȯrp-\ *noun* [*absorp*tion + -*ance*] (circa 1931)
: the ratio of the radiant energy absorbed by a body to that incident upon it

ab·sorp·tion \əb-'sȯrp-shən, -'zȯrp-\ *noun* [French & Latin; French, from Latin *absorption-, absorptio,* from *absorbēre*] (1741)
1 a : the process of absorbing or of being absorbed — compare ADSORPTION **b :** interception of radiant energy or sound waves
2 : entire occupation of the mind 〈*absorption* in his work〉
— **ab·sorp·tive** \-tiv\ *adjective*

absorption band *noun* (1867)
: a dark band in an absorption spectrum

absorption line *noun* (circa 1889)
: a dark line in an absorption spectrum

absorption spectrum *noun* (1879)
: an electromagnetic spectrum in which a decrease in intensity of radiation at specific wavelengths or ranges of wavelengths characteristic of an absorbing substance is manifested especially as a pattern of dark lines or bands

ab·sorp·tiv·i·ty \əb-ˌsȯrp-'ti-və-tē, -ˌzȯrp-\ *noun, plural* **-ties** (circa 1859)
: the property of a body that determines the fraction of incident radiation absorbed by the body

ab·stain \əb-'stān, ab-\ *intransitive verb* [Middle English *absteinen,* from Middle French *abstenir,* from Latin *abstinēre,* from *abs-, ab-* + *tenēre* to hold — more at THIN] (14th century)
: to refrain deliberately and often with an effort of self-denial from an action or practice
— **ab·stain·er** *noun*

ab·ste·mi·ous \ab-'stē-mē-əs\ *adjective* [Latin *abstemius,* from *abs-* + *-temius;* akin to Latin *temetum* intoxicating drink] (1609)
: marked by restraint especially in the consumption of food or alcohol; *also* **:** reflecting such restraint 〈an *abstemious* diet〉
— **ab·ste·mi·ous·ly** *adverb*
— **ab·ste·mious·ness** *noun*

ab·sten·tion \əb-'sten(t)-shən, ab-\ *noun* [Late Latin *abstention-, abstentio,* from Latin *abstinēre*] (1521)
: the act or practice of abstaining
— **ab·sten·tious** \-shəs\ *adjective*

ab·sti·nence \'ab-stə-nən(t)s\ *noun* [Middle English, from Middle French, from Latin *abstinentia,* from *abstinent-, abstinens,* present participle of *abstinēre*] (14th century)
1 : voluntary forbearance especially from indulgence of an appetite or craving or from eating some foods **:** ABSTENTION
2 : habitual abstaining from intoxicating beverages
— **ab·sti·nent** \-nənt\ *adjective*
— **ab·sti·nent·ly** *adverb*

¹ab·stract \ab-'strakt, 'ab-\ *adjective* [Medieval Latin *abstractus,* from Latin, past participle of *abstrahere* to drag away, from *abs-, ab-* + *trahere* to pull, draw] (14th century)
1 a : disassociated from any specific instance 〈*abstract* entity〉 **b :** difficult to understand **:** ABSTRUSE 〈*abstract* problems〉 **c :** insufficiently factual **:** FORMAL 〈possessed only an *abstract* right〉
2 : expressing a quality apart from an object 〈the word *poem* is concrete, *poetry* is *abstract*〉
3 a : dealing with a subject in its abstract aspects **:** THEORETICAL 〈*abstract* science〉 **b :** IMPERSONAL, DETACHED 〈the *abstract* compassion of a surgeon —*Time*〉
4 : having only intrinsic form with little or no attempt at pictorial representation or narrative content 〈*abstract* painting〉
— **ab·stract·ly** \ab-'strak(t)-lē, 'ab-ˌ\ *adverb*
— **ab·stract·ness** \ab-'strak(t)-nəs, 'ab-ˌ\ *noun*

²ab·stract \'ab-ˌstrakt, *in sense 2 also* ab-'\ *noun* [Middle English, from Latin *abstractus*] (15th century)
1 : a summary of points (as of a writing) usually presented in skeletal form; *also* **:** something that summarizes or concentrates the essentials of a larger thing or several things
2 : an abstract thing or state
3 : ABSTRACTION 4a

³ab·stract \ab-'strakt, 'ab-ˌ, *in sense 3 usually* 'ab-ˌ\ (1542)
transitive verb
1 : REMOVE, SEPARATE
2 : to consider apart from application to or association with a particular instance
3 : to make an abstract of **:** SUMMARIZE
4 : to draw away the attention of
5 : STEAL, PURLOIN
intransitive verb
: to make an abstraction
— **ab·stract·able** \-'strak-tə-bəl, -ˌstrak-\ *adjective*
— **ab·strac·tor** *or* **ab·stract·er** \-tər\ *noun*

ab·stract·ed \ab-'strak-təd, 'ab-ˌ\ *adjective* (1643)
1 : PREOCCUPIED, ABSENTMINDED 〈the *abstract*ed look of a professor〉
2 : ABSTRACT 4 〈*abstracted* geometric shapes〉
— **ab·stract·ed·ly** *adverb*
— **ab·stract·ed·ness** *noun*

abstract expressionism *noun* (1951)

: an artistic movement of the mid-20th century comprising diverse styles and techniques and emphasizing especially an artist's liberty to convey attitudes and emotions through nontraditional and usually nonrepresentational means
— **abstract expressionist** *noun or adjective*

ab·strac·tion \ab-'strak-shən, əb-\ *noun* (1549)
1 a : the act or process of abstracting **:** the state of being abstracted **b :** an abstract idea or term
2 : absence of mind or preoccupation
3 : abstract quality or character
4 a : an abstract composition or creation in art **b :** ABSTRACTIONISM
— **ab·strac·tion·al** \-shnəl, -shə-nᵊl\ *adjective*
— **ab·strac·tive** \ab-'strak-tiv, 'ab-ˌ\ *adjective*

ab·strac·tion·ism \ab-'strak-shə-ˌni-zəm, əb-\ *noun* (1926)
: the principles or practice of creating abstract art
— **ab·strac·tion·ist** \-sh(ə-)nist\ *adjective or noun*

abstract of title (1858)
: a summary statement of the successive conveyances and other facts on which a title to a piece of land rests

ab·struse \əb-'strüs, ab-\ *adjective* [Latin *abstrusus,* from past participle of *abstrudere* to conceal, from *abs-, ab-* + *trudere* to push — more at THREAT] (1599)
: difficult to comprehend **:** RECONDITE 〈the *abstruse* calculations of mathematicians〉
— **ab·struse·ly** *adverb*
— **ab·struse·ness** *noun*

ab·stru·si·ty \-'strü-sə-tē\ *noun, plural* **-ties** (1646)
1 : the quality or state of being abstruse **:** ABSTRUSENESS
2 : something that is abstruse

¹ab·surd \əb-'sərd, -'zərd\ *adjective* [Middle French *absurde,* from Latin *absurdus,* from *ab-* + *surdus* deaf, stupid] (1557)
1 : ridiculously unreasonable, unsound, or incongruous
2 : having no rational or orderly relationship to human life **:** MEANINGLESS; *also* **:** lacking order or value
3 : dealing with the absurd or with absurdism
— **ab·surd·ly** *adverb*
— **ab·surd·ness** *noun*

²absurd *noun* (1946)
: the state or condition in which human beings exist in an irrational and meaningless universe and in which human life has no ultimate meaning — usually used with *the*

ab·surd·ism \əb-'sər-ˌdi-zəm, -'zər-\ *noun* (1946)
: a philosophy based on the belief that the universe is irrational and meaningless and that the search for order brings the individual into conflict with the universe — compare EXISTENTIALISM
— **ab·surd·ist** \-dist\ *noun or adjective*

ab·sur·di·ty \əb-'sər-də-tē, -'zər-\ *noun, plural* **-ties** (1528)
1 : the quality or state of being absurd **:** ABSURDNESS
2 : something that is absurd

abub·ble \ə-'bə-bəl\ *adjective* (circa 1869)
1 : being in the process of bubbling
2 : being in a state of agitated activity or motion **:** ASTIR

abuild·ing \ə-'bil-diŋ\ *adjective* (1535)
: being in the process of building or of being built

\ə\ **abut**　\ᵊ\ **kitten**　\ər\ **further**　\a\ **ash**　\ā\ **ace**
\ä\ **mop, mar**　\au̇\ **out**　\ch\ **chin**　\e\ **bet**　\ē\ **easy**
\g\ **go**　\i\ **hit**　\ī\ **ice**　\j\ **job**　\ŋ\ **sing**　\ō\ **go**
\ȯ\ **law**　\ȯi\ **boy**　\th\ **thin**　\t̲h̲\ **the**　\ü\ **loot**　\u̇\ **foot**
\y\ **yet**　\zh\ **vision**　　*see also* Guide to Pronunciation

abu·lia \ä-'bü-lē-ə, -'byü-, ə-\ *noun* [New Latin, from ²*a-* + Greek *boulē* will] (circa 1864) **:** abnormal lack of ability to act or to make decisions
— **abu·lic** \-lik\ *adjective*

abun·dance \ə-'bən-dən(t)s\ *noun* (14th century)
1 : an ample quantity **:** PROFUSION
2 : AFFLUENCE, WEALTH
3 : relative degree of plentifulness ⟨low *abundances* of uranium and thorium —H. C. Urey⟩

abun·dant \-dənt\ *adjective* [Middle English, from Middle French, from Latin *abundant-, abundans*, present participle of *abundare* to abound] (14th century)
1 a : marked by great plenty (as of resources) ⟨a fair and *abundant* land⟩ **b :** amply supplied **:** ABOUNDING ⟨an area *abundant* with bird life⟩
2 : occurring in abundance **:** AMPLE ⟨*abundant* rainfall⟩
synonym see PLENTIFUL
— **abun·dant·ly** *adverb*

¹abuse \ə-'byüs\ *noun* [Middle English, from Middle French *abus*, from Latin *abusus*, from *abuti* to consume, from *ab-* + *uti* to use] (15th century)
1 : a corrupt practice or custom
2 : improper or excessive use or treatment **:** MISUSE ⟨drug *abuse*⟩
3 *obsolete* **:** a deceitful act **:** DECEPTION
4 : language that condemns or vilifies usually unjustly, intemperately, and angrily
5 : physical maltreatment ☆

²abuse \ə-'byüz\ *transitive verb* **abused; abus·ing** (15th century)
1 : to put to a wrong or improper use ⟨*abuse* a privilege⟩
2 *obsolete* **:** DECEIVE
3 : to use so as to injure or damage **:** MALTREAT
4 : to attack in words **:** REVILE
— **abus·able** \-'byü-zə-bəl\ *adjective*
— **abus·er** *noun*

abu·sive \ə-'byü-siv, -ziv\ *adjective* (1583)
1 : characterized by wrong or improper use or action; *especially* **:** CORRUPT ⟨*abusive* financial practices⟩
2 a : using harsh insulting language **:** characterized by or serving for abuse **b :** physically injurious ⟨*abusive* behavior⟩
— **abu·sive·ly** *adverb*
— **abu·sive·ness** *noun*

abut \ə-'bət\ *verb* **abut·ted; abut·ting** [Middle English *abutten*, partly from Old French *aboter* to border on, from *a-* (from Latin *ad-*) + *bout* blow, end, from *boter* to strike; partly from Old French *abuter* to come to an end, from *a-* + *but* end, aim — more at ¹BUTT, ⁴BUTT] (15th century)
intransitive verb
1 : to touch along a border or with a projecting part ⟨land *abuts* on the road⟩
2 a : to terminate at a point of contact **b :** to lean for support
transitive verb
1 : to border on
2 : to cause to abut

abu·ti·lon \ə-'byü-t'l-ˌän, -t'l-ən\ *noun* [New Latin, genus name, from Arabic *awbūtīlūn* abutilon] (circa 1578)
: any of a genus (*Abutilon*) of plants of the mallow family often having lobed leaves and solitary bell-shaped flowers

abut·ment \ə-'bət-mənt\ *noun* (1644)
1 : the place at which abutting occurs
2 : the part of a structure (as an arch or a bridge) that directly receives thrust or pressure

abut·tals \ə-'bə-t'lz\ *noun plural* (1630)
: the boundaries of lands with respect to adjacent lands

abut·ter \ə-'bə-tər\ *noun* (1673)
: one that abuts; *specifically* **:** the owner of a contiguous property

abut·ting *adjective* (1599)
: that abuts or serves as an abutment **:** ADJOINING, BORDERING

abuzz \ə-'bəz\ *adjective* (1859)
: filled or resounding with or as if with a buzzing sound ⟨a lake *abuzz* with outboards⟩ ⟨a town *abuzz* with excitement⟩

aby *or* **abye** \ə-'bī\ *transitive verb* [Middle English *abien*, from Old English *ābycgan*, from *ā-* + *bycgan* to buy — more at ABIDE, BUY] (before 12th century)
archaic **:** to suffer a penalty for

abysm \ə-'bi-zəm\ *noun* [Middle English *abime*, from Middle French *abisme*, modification of Late Latin *abyssus*] (14th century)
: ABYSS ⟨the dark backward and *abysm* of time —Shakespeare⟩

abys·mal \ə-'biz-məl, a-\ *adjective* (circa 1656)
1 a : having immense or fathomless extension downward, backward, or inward ⟨an *abysmal* cliff⟩ **b :** immeasurably great **:** PROFOUND ⟨*abysmal* ignorance⟩ **c :** immeasurably low or wretched ⟨*abysmal* living conditions of the poor⟩
2 : ABYSSAL
— **abys·mal·ly** \-mə-lē\ *adverb*

abyss \ə-'bis, a- *also* 'a-(ˌ)bis\ *noun* [Middle English *abissus*, from Late Latin *abyssus*, from Greek *abyssos*, from *abyssos*, adjective, bottomless, from *a-* + *byssos* depth; perhaps akin to Greek *bathys* deep] (14th century)
1 : the bottomless gulf, pit, or chaos of the old cosmogonies
2 a : an immeasurably deep gulf or great space **b :** intellectual or moral depths

abys·sal \ə-'bi-səl\ *adjective* (1691)
1 : UNFATHOMABLE a
2 : of or relating to the bottom waters of the ocean depths

abyssal plain *noun* (1954)
: any of the great flat areas of ocean floor

Ab·ys·sin·i·an cat \ˌa-bə-'si-nē-ən-, -'sin-yən-\ *noun* [*Abyssinia*, kingdom in Africa] (1876)
: any of a breed of small slender cats of African origin with short brownish hair ticked with bands of darker color

Abyssinian cat

ac- — see AD-

-ac *noun suffix* [New Latin *-acus*, from Greek *-akos*, variant of *-ikos* *-ic* after stems ending in *-i*-]
: one affected with ⟨hemophili*ac*⟩

aca·cia \ə-'kā-shə\ *noun* [New Latin, genus name, from Latin, acacia tree, from Greek *akakia*] (14th century)
1 : GUM ARABIC
2 : any of a large genus (*Acacia*) of leguminous shrubs and trees of warm regions with leaves pinnate or reduced to phyllodes and white or yellow flower clusters

ac·a·deme \'a-kə-ˌdēm, ˌa-kə-'-\ *noun* [Latin *Academus* (in the phrase *inter silvas Academi* among the groves of Academus), from Greek *Akadēmos* — more at ACADEMY] (1588)
1 a : a place of instruction **:** SCHOOL **b :** the academic life, community, or world ⟨in the halls of *academe*⟩
2 : ACADEMIC; *especially* **:** PEDANT

ac·a·de·mia \ˌa-kə-'dē-mē-ə\ *noun* [New Latin, from Latin, academy] (1946)
: ACADEME 1b

¹ac·a·dem·ic \ˌa-kə-'de-mik\ *noun* (1587)
1 : a member of an institution of learning
2 : one who is academic in background, outlook, or methods
3 *plural* **:** academic subjects

²academic *also* **ac·a·dem·i·cal** \-mi-kəl\ *adjective* (1588)
1 a : of, relating to, or associated with an academy or school especially of higher learning **b :** of or relating to performance in academic courses ⟨*academic* excellence⟩ **c :** very learned but inexperienced in practical matters

⟨*academic* thinkers⟩ **d :** based on formal study especially at an institution of higher learning
2 : of or relating to literary or artistic rather than technical or professional studies
3 a : THEORETICAL, SPECULATIVE ⟨an *academic* question⟩ **b :** having no practical or useful significance
4 : conforming to the traditions or rules of a school (as of literature or art) or an official academy **:** CONVENTIONAL
— **ac·a·dem·i·cal·ly** \-mi-k(ə-)lē\ *adverb*

academic freedom *noun* (1901)
: freedom to teach or to learn without interference (as by government officials)

ac·a·de·mi·cian \ˌa-kə-də-'mi-shən, ə-ˌka-də-\ *noun* (1748)
1 a : a member of an academy for promoting science, art, or literature **b :** a follower of an artistic or philosophical tradition or a promoter of its ideas
2 : ACADEMIC

ac·a·dem·i·cism \ˌa-kə-'de-mə-ˌsi-zəm\ *also* **acad·e·mism** \ə-'ka-də-ˌmi-zəm\ *noun* (1610)
1 : the doctrines of Plato's Academy; *specifically* **:** the skeptical doctrines of the later Academy holding that nothing can be known — compare PYRRHONISM
2 : a formal academic quality (as in art or music)
3 : purely speculative thoughts and attitudes

academic year *noun* (circa 1934)
: the annual period of sessions of an educational institution usually beginning in September and ending in June

acad·e·my \ə-'ka-də-mē\ *noun*, *plural* **-mies** [Latin *academia*, from Greek *Akadēmeia*, from *Akadēmeia*, gymnasium where Plato taught, from *Akadēmos* Attic mythological hero] (1549)
1 a : a school usually above the elementary level; *especially* **:** a private high school **b :** a high school or college in which special subjects or skills are taught **c :** higher education — used with *the* ⟨the functions of the *academy* in modern society⟩
2 *capitalized* **a :** the school for advanced education founded by Plato **b :** the philosophical doctrines associated with Plato's Academy
3 : a society of learned persons organized to advance art, science, or literature
4 : a body of established opinion widely accepted as authoritative in a particular field ◇

Aca·di·an \ə-'kā-dē-ən, a-\ *noun* (1705)
1 : a native or inhabitant of Acadia
2 : a descendant of the French-speaking inhabitants of Acadia expelled after the French loss of the colony in 1755; *especially* **:** CAJUN
— **Acadian** *adjective*

acan·tho·ceph·a·lan \ə-ˌkan(t)-thə-'se-fə-lən\ *noun* [ultimately from Greek *akantha* thorn, spine + *kephalē* head — more at CEPHALIC] (circa 1909)
: SPINY-HEADED WORM

— **acanthocephalan** *adjective*

acan·thus \ə-'kan(t)-thəs\ *noun, plural* **acanthus** [New Latin, genus name, from Greek *akanthos,* an acanthus, from *akantha* thorn] (1616)
1 : any of a genus (*Acanthus* of the family Acanthaceae, the acanthus family) of prickly herbs of the Mediterranean region
2 : an ornamentation (as in a Corinthian capital) representing or suggesting the leaves of the acanthus

acanthus 2

a cap·pel·la *also* **a ca·pel·la** \ˌä-kə-'pe-lə\ *adverb or adjective* [Italian *a cappella* in chapel style] (circa 1864)
: without instrumental accompaniment

ac·a·ri·a·sis \ˌa-kə-'rī-ə-səs\ *noun* (1828)
: infestation with or disease caused by mites

acar·i·cide \ə-'kar-ə-ˌsīd\ *noun* [*acar*us + *-i-* + *-cide*] (circa 1879)
: a pesticide that kills mites and ticks
— **acar·i·cid·al** \ə-ˌkar-ə-'sī-dᵊl\ *adjective*

ac·a·rid \'a-kə-rəd\ *noun* (1881)
: any of an order (Acarina) of arachnids including the mites and ticks; *especially* **:** a typical mite (family Acaridae)
— **acarid** *adjective*

ac·a·rus \'a-kə-rəs\ *noun, plural* **-ri** \-ˌrī\ [New Latin, genus name, from Greek *akari,* a mite] (1658)
: MITE; *especially* **:** one of a formerly extensive genus (*Acarus*)

acat·a·lec·tic \(ˌ)ā-ˌka-tə-'lek-tik\ *adjective* [Late Latin *acatalecticus,* from *acatalectus,* from Greek *akatalēktos,* from *a-* + *katalēgein* to leave off — more at CATALECTIC] (1589)
: not catalectic ⟨*acatalectic* verse⟩
— **acatalectic** *noun*

acau·les·cent \ˌā-kò-'le-sᵊnt\ *adjective* [*a-* + Latin *caulis* stem — more at HOLE] (1854)
: having no stem or appearing to have none

ac·cede \ak-'sēd, ik-\ *intransitive verb* **ac·ced·ed; ac·ced·ing** [Middle English, from Latin *accedere* to go to, be added, from *ad-* + *cedere* to go] (15th century)
1 a : to become a party (as to an agreement) **b :** to express approval or give consent **:** give in to a request or demand
2 *archaic* **:** APPROACH
3 : to enter upon an office or position
synonym see ASSENT

¹**ac·ce·le·ran·do** \(ˌ)ä-ˌche-lə-'rän-(ˌ)dō; ik-ˌse-, (ˌ)ak-\ *adverb or adjective* [Italian, literally, accelerating, from Latin *accelerandum,* gerund of *accelerare*] (circa 1842)
: gradually faster — used as a direction in music

²**accelerando** *noun, plural* **-dos** (1889)
: a gradual increase in tempo

ac·cel·er·ant \ik-'se-lə-rənt, ak-\ *noun* (1916)
: a substance used to accelerate a process (as the spreading of a fire)

ac·cel·er·ate \-lə-ˌrāt\ *verb* **-at·ed; -at·ing** [Latin *acceleratus,* past participle of *accelerare,* from *ad-* + *celer* swift — more at HOLD] (circa 1530)
transitive verb
1 : to bring about at an earlier time
2 : to cause to move faster; *also* **:** to cause to undergo acceleration
3 a : to hasten the progress or development of **b :** INCREASE ⟨*accelerate* food production⟩
4 a : to enable (a student) to complete a course in less than usual time **b :** to speed up (as a course of study)
intransitive verb
1 a : to move faster **:** gain speed **b :** GROW, INCREASE ⟨inflation was *accelerating*⟩
2 : to follow an accelerated educational program

ac·cel·er·at·ing·ly \-ˌrā-tiŋ-lē\ *adverb*

ac·cel·er·a·tion \ik-ˌse-lə-'rā-shən, (ˌ)ak-\ *noun* (1531)
1 : the act or process of accelerating **:** the state of being accelerated
2 : the rate of change of velocity with respect to time; *broadly* **:** change of velocity

acceleration of gravity (circa 1889)
: the acceleration of a body in free fall under the influence of earth's gravity expressed as the rate of increase of velocity per unit of time and assigned the standard value of 980.665 centimeters per second per second

acceleration principle *noun* (circa 1941)
: a theory in economics: an increase or decrease in income induces a corresponding but magnified change in investment

ac·cel·er·a·tive \ik-'se-lə-ˌrā-tiv, ak-\ *adjective* (1751)
: of, relating to, or tending to cause acceleration **:** ACCELERATING

ac·cel·er·a·tor \ik-'se-lə-ˌrā-tər, ak-\ *noun* (1611)
: one that accelerates: as **a :** a muscle or nerve that speeds the performance of an action **b :** a device (as a pedal) for controlling the speed of a motor vehicle engine **c :** a substance that speeds a chemical reaction **d :** an apparatus for imparting high velocities to charged particles (as electrons)

ac·cel·er·om·e·ter \ik-ˌse-lə-'rä-mə-tər, ak-\ *noun* [International Scientific Vocabulary *acceler*ation + *-o-* + *-meter*] (circa 1890)
: an instrument for measuring acceleration or for detecting and measuring vibrations

¹**ac·cent** \'ak-ˌsent, ak-\ *transitive verb* [Middle French *accenter,* from *accent* intonation, from Latin *accentus,* from *ad-* + *cantus* song — more at CHANT] (1530)
1 a : to pronounce with accent **:** STRESS **b :** to mark with a written or printed accent
2 : to give prominence to **:** make more prominent

²**ac·cent** \'ak-ˌsent, *chiefly British* -sənt\ *noun* (1538)
1 : a distinctive manner of expression: as **a :** an individual's distinctive or characteristic inflection, tone, or choice of words — usually used in plural **b :** a way of speaking typical of a particular group of people and especially of the natives or residents of a region
2 : an articulative effort giving prominence to one syllable over adjacent syllables; *also* **:** the prominence thus given a syllable
3 : rhythmically significant stress on the syllables of a verse usually at regular intervals
4 *archaic* **:** UTTERANCE
5 a : a mark (as ´, `, ^) used in writing or printing to indicate a specific sound value, stress, or pitch, to distinguish words otherwise identically spelled, or to indicate that an ordinarily mute vowel should be pronounced **b :** an accented letter
6 a : greater stress given to one musical tone than to its neighbors **b :** ACCENT MARK 2
7 a : emphasis laid on a part of an artistic design or composition **b :** an emphasized detail or area; *especially* **:** a small detail in sharp contrast with its surroundings **c :** a substance or object used for emphasis
8 : a mark placed to the right of a letter or number and usually slightly above it: as **a :** a double prime **b :** PRIME
9 : special concern or attention **:** EMPHASIS ⟨an *accent* on youth⟩
— **ac·cent·less** \-ləs\ *adjective*

accent mark *noun* (circa 1889)
1 : ACCENT 5a, 8
2 a : a symbol used to indicate musical stress **b :** a mark placed after a letter designating a note of music to indicate in which octave the note occurs

ac·cen·tu·al \ak-'sen(t)-sh(ə-)wəl, ik-\ *adjective* [Latin *accentus*] (1610)
: of, relating to, or characterized by accent;

specifically **:** based on accent rather than on quantity or syllabic recurrence ⟨*accentual* poetry⟩
— **ac·cen·tu·al·ly** *adverb*

ac·cen·tu·ate \ik-'sen(t)-shə-ˌwāt, ak-\ *transitive verb* **-at·ed; -at·ing** [Medieval Latin *accentuatus,* past participle of *accentuare,* from Latin *accentus*] (circa 1731)
: ACCENT, EMPHASIZE; *also* **:** INTENSIFY ⟨*accentuates* the feeling of despair⟩
— **ac·cen·tu·a·tion** \ik-ˌsen(t)-shə-'wā-shən, (ˌ)ak-\ *noun*

ac·cept \ik-'sept, ak- *also* ek-\ *verb* [Middle English, from Middle French *accepter,* from Latin *acceptare,* frequentative of *accipere* to receive, from *ad-* + *capere* to take — more at HEAVE] (14th century)
transitive verb
1 a : to receive willingly ⟨*accept* a gift⟩ **b :** to be able or designed to take or hold (something applied or added) ⟨a surface that will not *accept* ink⟩
2 : to give admittance or approval to ⟨*accept* her as one of the group⟩
3 a : to endure without protest or reaction ⟨*accept* poor living conditions⟩ **b :** to regard as proper, normal, or inevitable ⟨the idea is widely *accepted*⟩ **c :** to recognize as true **:** BELIEVE ⟨refused to *accept* the explanation⟩
4 a : to make a favorable response to ⟨*accept* an offer⟩ **b :** to agree to undertake (a responsibility) ⟨*accept* a job⟩
5 : to assume an obligation to pay; *also* **:** to take in payment ⟨we don't *accept* personal checks⟩
6 : to receive (a legislative report) officially
intransitive verb
: to receive favorably something offered — usually used with *of*
— **ac·cept·ing·ly** \-'sep-tiŋ-lē\ *adverb*
— **ac·cept·ing·ness** \-tiŋ-nəs\ *noun*

ac·cept·able \ik-'sep-tə-bəl, ak- *also* ek-\ *adjective* (14th century)
1 : capable or worthy of being accepted ⟨no compromise would be *acceptable*⟩
2 a : WELCOME, PLEASING ⟨compliments are always *acceptable*⟩ **b :** barely satisfactory or adequate ⟨performances varied from excellent to *acceptable*⟩
— **ac·cept·abil·i·ty** \ik-ˌsep-tə-'bi-lə-tē, (ˌ)ak-, ek-\ *noun*
— **ac·cept·able·ness** \ik-'sep-tə-bəl-nəs, ak-\ *noun*
— **ac·cept·ably** \-blē\ *adverb*

ac·cep·tance \ik-'sep-tən(t)s, ak-\ *noun* (1574)
1 : an agreeing either expressly or by conduct to the act or offer of another so that a contract is concluded and the parties become legally bound

2 : the quality or state of being accepted or acceptable
3 : the act of accepting **:** the fact of being accepted **:** APPROVAL
4 a : the act of accepting a time draft or bill of exchange for payment when due according to the specified terms **b :** an accepted draft or bill of exchange
5 : ACCEPTATION 2

ac·cep·tant \-tənt\ *adjective* (1851)
: willing to accept **:** RECEPTIVE

ac·cep·ta·tion \,ak-,sep-'tā-shən\ *noun* (15th century)
1 : ACCEPTANCE; *especially* **:** favorable reception or approval
2 : a generally accepted meaning of a word or understanding of a concept

ac·cept·ed *adjective* (15th century)
: generally approved or used
— **ac·cept·ed·ly** *adverb*

ac·cept·er \ik-'sep-tər, ak-\ *noun* (1585)
1 : one that accepts
2 : ACCEPTOR

ac·cep·tive \ak-'sep-tiv\ *adjective* (1596)
1 : ACCEPTABLE
2 : RECEPTIVE

ac·cep·tor \ik-'sep-tər, ak-\ *noun* (14th century)
1 : ACCEPTER 1
2 : one that accepts an order or a bill of exchange
3 : an atom, molecule, or subatomic particle capable of receiving another entity (as an electron) especially to form a compound — compare DONOR 3a

¹ac·cess \'ak-,ses *also* ik-'ses\ *noun* [Middle English, from Middle French & Latin; Middle French *acces* arrival, from Latin *accessus* approach, from *accedere* to approach — more at ACCEDE] (14th century)
1 a : ONSET 2 **b :** a fit of intense feeling **:** OUTBURST
2 a : permission, liberty, or ability to enter, approach, communicate with, or pass to and from **b :** freedom or ability to obtain or make use of **c :** a way or means of access **d :** the act or an instance of accessing
3 : an increase by addition ⟨a sudden *access* of wealth⟩

²access *transitive verb* (1962)
: to get at **:** gain access to ⟨*accessed* the computer by phone⟩

ac·ces·si·ble \ik-'se-sə-bəl, ak-, ek-\ *adjective* (15th century)
1 : providing access
2 a : capable of being reached ⟨*accessible* by rail⟩; *also* **:** being within reach ⟨fashions at *accessible* prices⟩ **b :** easy to speak or deal with ⟨*accessible* people⟩
3 : capable of being influenced **:** OPEN
4 : capable of being used or seen **:** AVAILABLE
5 : capable of being understood or appreciated ⟨the author's most *accessible* stories⟩ ⟨an *accessible* film⟩
— **ac·ces·si·bil·i·ty** \-,se-sə-'bi-lə-tē\ *noun*
— **ac·ces·si·ble·ness** \-'se-sə-bəl-nəs\ *noun*
— **ac·ces·si·bly** \-blē\ *adverb*

¹ac·ces·sion \ik-'se-shən, ak-\ *noun* (1588)
1 a : increase by something added **b :** acquisition of additional property (as by growth or increase of existing property)
2 : something added **:** ACQUISITION
3 : the act of assenting or agreeing
4 a : the act of becoming joined **:** ADHERENCE **b :** the act by which one nation becomes party to an agreement already in force between other powers
5 a : an act of coming near or to **:** APPROACH, ADMITTANCE **b :** the act of coming to high office or a position of honor or power
6 : a sudden fit or outburst **:** ACCESS
— **ac·ces·sion·al** \-'sesh-nəl, -'se-shə-nᵊl\ *adjective*

²accession *transitive verb* (1892)
: to record in order of acquisition

ac·ces·so·ri·al \,ak-sə-'sōr-ē-əl, -'sòr-\ *adjective* (1726)
1 : of or relating to an accessory ⟨*accessorial* liability⟩
2 : of, relating to, or constituting an accession **:** SUPPLEMENTARY ⟨*accessorial* services⟩

ac·ces·so·rise *British variant of* ACCESSORIZE

ac·ces·so·rize \ik-'se-sə-,rīz, ak-\ *verb* **-rized; -riz·ing** (1939)
transitive verb
: to furnish with accessories
intransitive verb
: to wear clothing accessories

¹ac·ces·so·ry *also* **ac·ces·sa·ry** \ik-'se-sə-rē, ak-, ek-, -'ses-rē, *also* ə-'se-\ *noun, plural* **-ries** (15th century)
1 a : a person not actually or constructively present but contributing as an assistant or instigator to the commission of an offense — called also *accessory before the fact* **b :** a person who knowing that a crime has been committed aids or shelters the offender with intent to defeat justice — called also *accessory after the fact*
2 a : a thing of secondary or subordinate importance **:** ADJUNCT **b :** an object or device not essential in itself but adding to the beauty, convenience, or effectiveness of something else ⟨auto *accessories*⟩ ⟨clothing *accessories*⟩

²accessory *adjective* (1607)
1 : assisting as a subordinate; *especially* **:** contributing to a crime but not as the chief agent
2 : aiding or contributing in a secondary way **:** SUPPLEMENTARY
3 : present in a minor amount and not essential as a constituent ⟨an *accessory* mineral in a rock⟩

accessory fruit *noun* (circa 1900)
: a fruit (as the apple) of which a conspicuous part consists of tissue other than that of the ripened ovary

accessory nerve *noun* (circa 1842)
: either of a pair of motor nerves that are the 11th cranial nerves of higher vertebrates, arise from the medulla and the upper part of the spinal cord, and supply chiefly the pharynx and muscles of the upper chest, back, and shoulders

access time *noun* (1950)
: the time lag between the time stored information (as in a computer) is requested and the time it is delivered

ac·ciac·ca·tu·ra \(,)ä-,chä-kə-'tùr-ə\ *noun* [Italian, literally, crushing] (circa 1819)
: a discordant note sounded with a principal note or chord and immediately released

ac·ci·dence \'ak-sə-dən(t)s, -,den(t)s\ *noun* [Middle English, from Middle French, from Latin *accidentia* inflections of words, nonessential qualities, plural of *accident-, accidens*, noun] (15th century)
: a part of grammar that deals with inflections

ac·ci·dent \'ak-sə-dənt, -,dent; 'aks-dənt\ *noun* [Middle English, from Middle French, from Latin *accident-, accidens* nonessential quality, chance, from present participle of *accidere* to happen, from *ad-* + *cadere* to fall — more at CHANCE] (14th century)
1 a : an unforeseen and unplanned event or circumstance **b :** lack of intention or necessity **:** CHANCE ⟨met by *accident* rather than by design⟩
2 a : an unfortunate event resulting especially from carelessness or ignorance **b :** an unexpected and medically important bodily event especially when injurious ⟨a cerebrovascular *accident*⟩ **c :** an unexpected happening causing loss or injury which is not due to any fault or misconduct on the part of the person injured but for which legal relief may be sought
3 : a nonessential property or quality of an entity or circumstance ⟨*accident* of nationality⟩

¹ac·ci·den·tal \,ak-sə-'den-tᵊl\ *adjective* (14th century)

1 : arising from extrinsic causes **:** INCIDENTAL, NONESSENTIAL
2 a : occurring unexpectedly or by chance **b :** happening without intent or through carelessness and often with unfortunate results ☆
— **ac·ci·den·tal·ly** \-'dent-lē, -'den-tᵊl-ē\ *also* **ac·ci·dent·ly** \-'dent-lē\ *adverb*
— **ac·ci·den·tal·ness** \-'den-tᵊl-nəs\ *noun*

²accidental *noun* (1651)
1 : a nonessential property
2 a : a note foreign to a key indicated by a signature **b :** a prefixed sign indicating an accidental

accident insurance *noun* (1866)
: insurance against loss through accidental bodily injury to the insured

accident–prone *adjective* (1926)
1 : having a greater than average number of accidents
2 : having personality traits that predispose to accidents

ac·cid·ie \'ak-sə-dē\ *noun* (13th century)
: ACEDIA

ac·cip·i·ter \ak-'si-pə-tər, ik-\ *noun* [New Latin, genus name, from Latin, hawk] (circa 1828)
: any of a genus (*Accipiter*) of medium-sized forest-inhabiting hawks that have short broad wings and a long tail and a characteristic flight pattern of several quick flaps and a glide
— **ac·cip·i·trine** \-'si-pə-,trīn\ *adjective or noun*

¹ac·claim \ə-'klām\ *verb* [Latin *acclamare*, literally, to shout at, from *ad-* + *clamare* to shout — more at CLAIM] (1633)
transitive verb
1 : APPLAUD, PRAISE
2 : to declare by acclamation
intransitive verb
: to shout praise or applause
— **ac·claim·er** *noun*

²acclaim *noun* (1667)
1 : the act of acclaiming
2 : PRAISE, APPLAUSE

ac·cla·ma·tion \,a-klə-'mā-shən\ *noun* [Latin *acclamation-, acclamatio*, from *acclamare*] (1585)
1 : a loud eager expression of approval, praise, or assent
2 : an overwhelming affirmative vote by cheers, shouts, or applause rather than by ballot

ac·cli·mate \'a-klə-,māt; ə-'klī-mət, -,māt\ *verb* **-mat·ed; -mat·ing** [French *acclimater*, from *a-* (from Latin *ad-*) + *climat* climate] (1792)
: ACCLIMATIZE

ac·cli·ma·tion \,a-klə-'mā-shən, -,klī-\ *noun* (1826)
: ACCLIMATIZATION; *especially* **:** physiological adjustment by an organism to environmental change

ac·cli·ma·tise *British variant of* ACCLIMATIZE

ac·cli·ma·ti·za·tion \ə-,klī-mə-tə-'zā-shən\ *noun* (1830)
: the process or result of acclimatizing

ac·cli·ma·tize \ə-'klī-mə-,tīz\ *verb* **-tized; -tiz·ing** (1836)
transitive verb

☆ **SYNONYMS**
Accidental, fortuitous, casual, contingent mean not amenable to planning or prediction. ACCIDENTAL stresses chance ⟨any resemblance to actual persons is entirely *accidental*⟩. FORTUITOUS so strongly suggests chance that it often connotes entire absence of cause ⟨a series of *fortuitous* events⟩. CASUAL stresses lack of real or apparent premeditation or intent ⟨a *casual* encounter with a stranger⟩. CONTINGENT suggests possibility of happening but stresses uncertainty and dependence on other future events for existence or occurrence ⟨the *contingent* effects of the proposed law⟩.

: to adapt to a new temperature, altitude, climate, environment, or situation
intransitive verb
: to become acclimatized
— **ac·cli·ma·tiz·er** *noun*
ac·cliv·i·ty \ə-'kli-və-tē, a-\ *noun, plural* **-ties** [Latin *acclivitas,* from *acclivis* ascending, from *ad-* + *clivus* slope — more at DECLIVITY] (1614)
: an ascending slope (as of a hill)
ac·co·lade \'a-kə-ˌlād, -ˌläd\ *noun* [French, from *accoler* to embrace, from (assumed) Vulgar Latin *accollare,* from Latin *ad-* + *collum* neck — more at COLLAR] (1623)
1 a : a ceremonial embrace **b :** a ceremony or salute conferring knighthood
2 a : a mark of acknowledgment : AWARD **b :** an expression of praise
3 : a brace or a line used in music to join two or more staffs carrying simultaneous parts
ac·com·mo·date \ə-'kä-mə-ˌdāt\ *verb* **-dat·ed; -dat·ing** [Latin *accommodatus,* past participle of *accommodare,* from *ad-* + *commodare* to make fit, from *commodus* suitable — more at COMMODE] (1550)
transitive verb
1 : to make fit, suitable, or congruous
2 : to bring into agreement or concord : RECONCILE
3 : to provide with something desired, needed, or suited (as a helpful service, a loan, or lodgings)
4 a : to make room for **b :** to hold without crowding or inconvenience
5 : to give consideration to : allow for ⟨*accommodate* the special interests of various groups⟩
intransitive verb
: to adapt oneself; *also* : to undergo visual accommodation
synonym see ADAPT, CONTAIN
— **ac·com·mo·da·tive** \-ˌdā-tiv\ *adjective*
— **ac·com·mo·da·tive·ness** *noun*
ac·com·mo·dat·ing *adjective* (1775)
: HELPFUL, OBLIGING
— **ac·com·mo·dat·ing·ly** \-ˌdā-tiŋ-lē\ *adverb*
ac·com·mo·da·tion \ə-ˌkä-mə-'dā-shən\ *noun* (1603)
1 : something supplied for convenience or to satisfy a need: as **a :** lodging, food, and services or traveling space and related services — usually used in plural ⟨tourist *accommodations* on the boat⟩ ⟨overnight *accommodations*⟩ **b :** a public conveyance (as a train) that stops at all or nearly all points **c :** LOAN
2 : the act of accommodating : the state of being accommodated: as **a :** the providing of what is needed or desired for convenience **b :** ADAPTATION, ADJUSTMENT **c :** a reconciliation of differences : SETTLEMENT **d :** the automatic adjustment of the eye for seeing at different distances effected chiefly by changes in the convexity of the crystalline lens; *also* : the range over which such adjustment is possible
— **ac·com·mo·da·tion·al** \-shnəl, -shə-nᵊl\ *adjective*
¹ac·com·mo·da·tion·ist \-'dā-sh(ə-)nist\ *noun* (1964)
: a black who adapts to the ideals or attitudes of whites ⟨making Uncle Toms, compromisers, and *accommodationists* . . . thoroughly ashamed —Ossie Davis⟩
²accommodationist *adjective* (1964)
: favoring or practicing accommodation or compromise
accommodation ladder *noun* (1769)
: a light ladder or stairway hung over the side of a ship for ascending from or descending to small boats
ac·com·mo·da·tor \ə-'kä-mə-ˌdā-tər\ *noun* (circa 1630)
: one that accommodates; *especially* : a part-time or special-occasion domestic worker
ac·com·pa·ni·ment \ə-'kəm-pə-nē-mənt, -'kəmp-nē-\ *noun* (circa 1744)

1 : an instrumental or vocal part designed to support or complement a melody
2 a : an addition (as an ornament) intended to give completeness or symmetry : COMPLEMENT **b :** an accompanying situation or occurrence : CONCOMITANT
ac·com·pa·nist \ə-'kəmp-nist, -'kəm-pə-\ *noun* (circa 1828)
: one (as a pianist) who plays an accompaniment
ac·com·pa·ny \ə-'kəmp-nē, -'kämp-; -'kəm-pə-, -'käm-\ *verb* **-nied; -ny·ing** [Middle English *accompanien,* from Middle French *acompaignier,* from *a-* (from Latin *ad-*) + *compaing* companion — more at COMPANION] (15th century)
transitive verb
1 : to go with as an associate or companion
2 : to perform an accompaniment to or for
3 a : to cause to be in association ⟨*accompanied* their advice with a warning⟩ **b :** to be in association with ⟨the pictures that *accompany* the text⟩
intransitive verb
: to perform an accompaniment
ac·com·plice \ə-'käm-pləs, -'kəm-\ *noun* [alteration (from incorrect division of *a complice*) of *complice*] (1589)
: one associated with another especially in wrongdoing
ac·com·plish \ə-'käm-plish, -'kəm-\ *transitive verb* [Middle English *accomplisshen,* from Middle French *acompliss-,* stem of *acomplir,* from (assumed) Vulgar Latin *accomplēre,* from Latin *ad-* + *complēre* to fill up — more at COMPLETE] (14th century)
1 : to bring about (a result) by effort ⟨have much to *accomplish* today⟩ ⟨regretted that he had never *accomplished* a marriage for her —Francis Hackett⟩
2 : to bring to completion : FULFILL ⟨we can *accomplish* the job in an hour⟩
3 : to succeed in reaching (a stage in a progression) ⟨would starve before *accomplishing* half the distance —W. H. Hudson (died 1922)⟩
4 *archaic* **a :** to equip thoroughly **b :** PERFECT
synonym see PERFORM
— **ac·com·plish·able** \-pli-shə-bəl\ *adjective*
— **ac·com·plish·er** *noun*
ac·com·plished *adjective* (15th century)
1 a : proficient as the result of practice or training ⟨an *accomplished* dancer⟩ **b :** having many social accomplishments
2 : established beyond doubt or dispute ⟨an *accomplished* fact⟩
ac·com·plish·ment \ə-'käm-plish-mənt, -'kəm-\ *noun* (15th century)
1 : the act of accomplishing : COMPLETION
2 : something that has been accomplished : ACHIEVEMENT
3 a : a quality or ability equipping one for society **b :** a special skill or ability acquired by training or practice
¹ac·cord \ə-'kȯrd\ *verb* [Middle English, from Old French *acorder,* from (assumed) Vulgar Latin *accordare,* from Latin *ad-* + *cord-, cor* heart — more at HEART] (12th century)
transitive verb
1 : to bring into agreement : RECONCILE
2 : to grant or give especially as appropriate, due, or earned
intransitive verb
1 *archaic* **:** to arrive at an agreement
2 *obsolete* **:** to give consent
3 : to be consistent or in harmony : AGREE
synonym see GRANT
²accord *noun* [Middle English, from Old French *acort,* from *acorder*] (14th century)
1 a : AGREEMENT, CONFORMITY ⟨acted in *accord* with the company's policy⟩ **b :** a formal reaching of agreement : COMPACT, TREATY
2 : balanced interrelationship : HARMONY
3 *obsolete* **:** ASSENT
4 : voluntary or spontaneous impulse to act ⟨gave generously of their own *accord*⟩

ac·cor·dance \ə-'kȯr-dᵊn(t)s\ *noun* (14th century)
1 : AGREEMENT, CONFORMITY ⟨in *accordance* with a rule⟩
2 : the act of granting
ac·cor·dant \-dᵊnt\ *adjective* (14th century)
1 : CONSONANT, AGREEING
2 : HARMONIOUS, CORRESPONDENT
— **ac·cor·dant·ly** *adverb*
according as *conjunction* (1500)
1 : in accord with the way in which
2 a : depending on how **b :** depending on whether : IF
ac·cord·ing·ly \ə-'kȯr-diŋ-lē\ *adverb* (14th century)
1 : in accordance : CORRESPONDINGLY
2 : CONSEQUENTLY, SO
according to *preposition* (14th century)
1 : in conformity with
2 : as stated or attested by
3 : depending on
¹ac·cor·di·on \ə-'kȯr-dē-ən\ *noun* [German *Akkordion,* from *Akkord* chord, from French *accord,* from Old French *acort*] (1831)
: a portable keyboard wind instrument in which the wind is forced past free reeds by means of a hand-operated bellows
— **ac·cor·di·on·ist** \-dē-ə-nist\ *noun*
²accordion *adjective* (1885)
: folding or creased or hinged to fold like an accordion ⟨an *accordion* pleat⟩ ⟨an *accordion* door⟩

accordion

ac·cost \ə-'kȯst, -'käst\ *transitive verb* [Middle French *accoster,* ultimately from Latin *ad-* + *costa* rib, side — more at COAST] (1612)
: to approach and speak to often in a challenging or aggressive way
ac·couche·ment \ˌa-ˌküsh-'mäⁿ, ə-'küsh-ˌ\ *noun* [French] (1803)
: the time or act of giving birth
ac·cou·cheur \ˌa-ˌkü-'shər\ *noun* [French] (1759)
: one that assists at a birth; *especially* : OBSTETRICIAN
¹ac·count \ə-'kaúnt\ *noun* (14th century)
1 *archaic* **:** RECKONING, COMPUTATION
2 a : a record of debit and credit entries to cover transactions involving a particular item or a particular person or concern **b :** a statement of transactions during a fiscal period and the resulting balance
3 a : a statement explaining one's conduct **b :** a statement or exposition of reasons, causes, or motives ⟨no satisfactory *account* of these phenomena⟩ **c :** a reason for an action : BASIS ⟨on that *account* I must refuse⟩
4 a : a formal business arrangement providing for regular dealings or services (as banking, advertising, or store credit) and involving the establishment and maintenance of an account; *also* : CLIENT, CUSTOMER **b :** money deposited in a bank account and subject to withdrawal by the depositor
5 a : VALUE, IMPORTANCE ⟨it's of no *account* to me⟩ **b :** ESTEEM ⟨stood high in their *account*⟩
6 : ADVANTAGE ⟨turned her wit to good *account*⟩
7 a : careful thought : CONSIDERATION ⟨have to take many things into *account*⟩ **b :** a usually mental record : TRACK ⟨keep *account* of all you do⟩

8 : a description of facts, conditions, or events **:** REPORT, NARRATIVE ⟨the newspaper *account* of the fire⟩ ⟨by all *accounts* they're well-off⟩; *also* **:** PERFORMANCE ⟨a straightforward *account* of the sonata⟩
— on account : with the price charged to one's account
— on account of : for the sake of **:** by reason of
— on no account : under no circumstances
— on one's own account 1 : on one's own behalf **2 :** at one's own risk **3 :** by oneself **:** on one's own
²**account** *verb* [Middle English, from Middle French *acompter*, from *a-* (from Latin *ad-*) + *compter* to count] (14th century)
transitive verb
1 : to think of as **:** CONSIDER ⟨*accounts* himself lucky⟩
2 : to probe into **:** ANALYZE
intransitive verb
1 : to furnish a justifying analysis or explanation — used with *for* ⟨couldn't *account* for the loss⟩
2 a : to be the sole or primary factor — used with *for* ⟨the pitcher *accounted* for all three putouts⟩ **b :** to bring about the capture, death, or destruction of something ⟨*accounted* for two rabbits⟩
ac·count·abil·i·ty \ə-ˌkauṅ-tə-ˈbi-lə-tē\ *noun* (1794)
: the quality or state of being accountable; *especially* **:** an obligation or willingness to accept responsibility or to account for one's actions ⟨public officials lacking *accountability*⟩
ac·count·able \ə-ˈkauṅ-tə-bəl\ *adjective* (14th century)
1 : subject to giving an account **:** ANSWERABLE
2 : capable of being accounted for **:** EXPLAINABLE
synonym see RESPONSIBLE
— ac·count·able·ness \-ˈkauṅ-tə-bəl-nəs\ *noun*
— ac·count·ably \-blē\ *adverb*
ac·coun·tan·cy \ə-ˈkauṅ-t°n(t)-sē\ *noun* (1854)
: the profession or practice of accounting
¹**ac·coun·tant** \ə-ˈkauṅ-t°nt\ *noun* (15th century)
1 : one that gives an account or is accountable
2 : one who is skilled in the practice of accounting or who is in charge of public or private accounts
— ac·coun·tant·ship \-t°n(t)-ˌship\ *noun*
²**accountant** *adjective* (15th century)
obsolete **:** ACCOUNTABLE, ANSWERABLE ⟨I stand *accountant* for as great a sin —Shakespeare⟩
account executive *noun* (1931)
: a business executive (as in an advertising agency) responsible for dealing with a client's account
ac·count·ing \ə-ˈkauṅ-tiŋ\ *noun* (circa 1716)
1 : the system of recording and summarizing business and financial transactions and analyzing, verifying, and reporting the results; *also* **:** the principles and procedures of accounting
2 a : work done in accounting or by accountants **b :** an instance of applied accounting or of the settling or presenting of accounts
account payable *noun, plural* **accounts payable** (circa 1936)
: the balance due to a creditor on a current account
account receivable *noun, plural* **accounts receivable** (1936)
: a balance due from a debtor on a current account
ac·cou·tre *or* **ac·cou·ter** \ə-ˈkü-tər\ *transitive verb* **-cou·tred** *or* **-cou·tered; -cou·tring** *or* **-cou·ter·ing** \-ˈkü-tə-riŋ, -ˈkü-triŋ\ [French *accoutrer*, from Middle French *acoustrer*, from *a-* + *costure* seam, from (assumed)

Vulgar Latin *consutura* — more at COUTURE] (1596)
: to provide with equipment or furnishings **:** OUTFIT
synonym see FURNISH
ac·cou·tre·ment *or* **ac·cou·ter·ment** \ə-ˈkü-trə-mənt, -ˈkü-tər-mənt\ *noun* (1549)
1 a : EQUIPMENT, TRAPPINGS; *specifically* **:** a soldier's outfit usually not including clothes and weapons — usually used in plural **b :** an accessory item of clothing or equipment — usually used in plural
2 *archaic* **:** the act of accoutring
3 : an identifying and often superficial characteristic or device — usually used in plural ⟨*accoutrements* of power that define our diplomacy —Elizabeth Drew⟩
ac·cred·it \ə-ˈkre-dət\ *transitive verb* [Latin *accreditus*, past participle of *accredere* to give credence to, from *ad-* + *credere* to believe — more at CREED] (1535)
1 : to give official authorization to or approval of: **a :** to provide with credentials; *especially* **:** to send (an envoy) with letters of authorization **b :** to recognize or vouch for as conforming with a standard **c :** to recognize (an educational institution) as maintaining standards that qualify the graduates for admission to higher or more specialized institutions or for professional practice
2 : to consider or recognize as outstanding
3 : ATTRIBUTE, CREDIT
synonym see APPROVE
— ac·cred·i·table \-də-tə-bəl\ *adjective*
— ac·cred·i·ta·tion \ə-ˌkre-də-ˈtā-shən, -ˈdā-\ *noun*
ac·crete \ə-ˈkrēt\ *verb* **ac·cret·ed; ac·cret·ing** [back-formation from *accretion*] (1784)
intransitive verb
: to grow or become attached by accretion
transitive verb
: to cause to adhere or become attached; *also* **:** ACCUMULATE
ac·cre·tion \ə-ˈkrē-shən\ *noun* [Latin *accretion-, accretio*, from *accrescere* — more at ACCRUE] (1615)
1 : the process of growth or enlargement by a gradual buildup: as **a :** increase by external addition or accumulation (as by adhesion of external parts or particles) **b :** the increase of land by the action of natural forces
2 : a product of accretion; *especially* **:** an extraneous addition ⟨*accretions* of grime⟩
— ac·cre·tion·ary \-shə-ˌner-ē\ *adjective*
— ac·cre·tive \ə-ˈkrē-tiv\ *adjective*
¹**ac·cru·al** \ə-ˈkrü-əl\ *noun* (1880)
1 : the action or process of accruing
2 : something that accrues or has accrued
²**accrual** *adjective* (1917)
: being a method of accounting that recognizes income when earned and expenses when incurred regardless of when cash is received or disbursed
ac·crue \ə-ˈkrü\ *verb* **ac·crued; ac·cru·ing** [Middle English *acreuen*, probably from Middle French *acreue* increase, from *acreistre* to increase, from Latin *accrescere*, from *ad-* + *crescere* to grow — more at CRESCENT] (15th century)
intransitive verb
1 : to come into existence as a legally enforceable claim
2 a : to come about as a natural growth, increase, or advantage ⟨the wisdom that *accrues* with age⟩ **b :** to come as a direct result of some state or action ⟨rewards due to the feminine will *accrue* to me —Germaine Greer⟩
3 : to accumulate or be added periodically ⟨interest *accrues* on a daily basis⟩
transitive verb
: to accumulate or have due after a period of time ⟨*accrue* vacation time⟩
— ac·cru·able \-ˈkrü-ə-bəl\ *adjective*
— ac·crue·ment \-ˈkrü-mənt\ *noun*

ac·cul·tur·ate \ə-ˈkəl-chə-ˌrāt, a-\ *transitive verb* **-at·ed; -at·ing** [back-formation from *acculturation*] (1930)
: to change through acculturation
ac·cul·tur·a·tion \ə-ˌkəl-chə-ˈrā-shən, a-\ *noun* (1880)
1 : cultural modification of an individual, group, or people by adapting to or borrowing traits from another culture; *also* **:** a merging of cultures as a result of prolonged contact
2 : the process by which a human being acquires the culture of a particular society from infancy
— ac·cul·tur·a·tion·al \-shnəl, -shə-n°l\ *adjective*
— ac·cul·tur·a·tive \ə-ˈkəl-chə-ˌrā-tiv, a-\ *adjective*
ac·cu·mu·late \ə-ˈkyü-m(y)ə-ˌlāt\ *verb* **-lat·ed; -lat·ing** [Latin *accumulatus*, past participle of *accumulare*, from *ad-* + *cumulare* to heap up — more at CUMULATE] (15th century)
transitive verb
: to gather or pile up especially little by little **:** AMASS ⟨*accumulate* a fortune⟩
intransitive verb
: to increase gradually in quantity or number
ac·cu·mu·la·tion \ə-ˌkyü-m(y)ə-ˈlā-shən\ *noun* (15th century)
1 : something that has accumulated or has been accumulated
2 : the action or process of accumulating **:** the state of being or having accumulated
3 : increase or growth by addition especially when continuous or repeated ⟨*accumulation* of interest⟩
ac·cu·mu·la·tive \ə-ˈkyü-m(y)ə-ˌlā-tiv, -lə-\ *adjective* (circa 1651)
1 : CUMULATIVE ⟨an age of rapid and *accumulative* change⟩
2 : tending or given to accumulation
— ac·cu·mu·la·tive·ly *adverb*
— ac·cu·mu·la·tive·ness *noun*
ac·cu·mu·la·tor \ə-ˈkyü-m(y)ə-ˌlā-tər\ *noun* (1748)
: one that accumulates: as **a :** a device (as in a hydraulic system) in which a fluid is collected and especially in which it is kept under pressure as a means of storing energy **b** *British* **:** STORAGE BATTERY **c :** a part (as in a computer) where numbers are totaled or stored
ac·cu·ra·cy \ˈa-kyə-rə-sē, ˈa-k(ə-)rə-\ *noun, plural* **-cies** (1662)
1 : freedom from mistake or error **:** CORRECTNESS
2 a : conformity to truth or to a standard or model **:** EXACTNESS **b :** degree of conformity of a measure to a standard or a true value — compare PRECISION 2a
ac·cu·rate \ˈa-kyə-rət, ˈa-k(ə-)rət\ *adjective* [Latin *accuratus*, from past participle of *accurare* to take care of, from *ad-* + *cura* care] (1596)
1 : free from error especially as the result of care ⟨an *accurate* diagnosis⟩
2 : conforming exactly to truth or to a standard **:** EXACT ⟨providing *accurate* color⟩
3 : able to give an accurate result ⟨an *accurate* gauge⟩
synonym see CORRECT
— ac·cu·rate·ly \ˈa-kyə-rət-lē, ˈa-k(ə-)rət-, ˈa-k(y)ərt-\ *adverb*
— ac·cu·rate·ness \-kyə-rət-nəs, -k(ə-)rət-nəs\ *noun*
ac·cursed \ə-ˈkərst, -ˈkər-səd\ *or* **ac·curst** \ə-ˈkərst\ *adjective* [Middle English *acursed*, from past participle of *acursen* to consign to destruction with a curse, from *a-* (from Old English *ā*, perfective prefix) + *cursen* to curse — more at ABIDE] (13th century)
1 : being under or as if under a curse
2 : DAMNABLE
— ac·curs·ed·ly \-ˈkər-səd-lē\ *adverb*
— ac·curs·ed·ness \-ˈkər-səd-nəs\ *noun*
ac·cus·al \ə-ˈkyü-zəl\ *noun* (1594)
: ACCUSATION

ac·cu·sa·tion \ˌa-kyə-'zā-shən, -ˌ(ˌ)kyü-\ *noun* (14th century)
1 : the act of accusing : the state or fact of being accused
2 : a charge of wrongdoing

¹ac·cu·sa·tive \ə-'kyü-zə-tiv\ *adjective* [Middle English, from Middle French or Latin; Middle French *accusatif*, from Latin *accusativus*, from *accusatus*, past participle of *accusare*] (15th century)
1 : of, relating to, or being the grammatical case that marks the direct object of a verb or the object of any of several prepositions
2 : ACCUSATORY

²accusative *noun* (circa 1620)
: the accusative case of a language : a form in the accusative case

ac·cu·sa·to·ry \ə-'kyü-zə-ˌtōr-ē, -ˌtȯr-\ *adjective* (14th century)
: containing or expressing accusation : ACCUSING

ac·cuse \ə-'kyüz\ *verb* **ac·cused; ac·cus·ing** [Middle English, from Old French *acuser*, from Latin *accusare* to call to account, from *ad-* + *causa* lawsuit] (14th century)
transitive verb
1 : to charge with a fault or offense : BLAME
2 : to charge with an offense judicially or by a public process
intransitive verb
: to bring an accusation
— **ac·cus·er** \ə-'kyü-zər\ *noun*
— **ac·cus·ing·ly** \-'kyü-ziŋ-lē\ *adverb*

ac·cused *noun, plural* **accused** (1593)
: one charged with an offense; *especially* : the defendant in a criminal case

ac·cus·tom \ə-'kəs-təm\ *transitive verb* [Middle English, from Middle French *acostumer*, from *a-* (from Latin *ad-*) + *costume* custom] (15th century)
: to make familiar with something through use or experience
— **ac·cus·tom·ation** \-ˌkəs-tə-'mā-shən\ *noun*

ac·cus·tomed \ə-'kəs-təmd\ *adjective* (15th century)
1 : often used or practiced : CUSTOMARY ⟨her *accustomed* cheerfulness⟩
2 : adapted to existing conditions ⟨eyes *accustomed* to the dark⟩
3 : being in the habit or custom ⟨*accustomed* to making decisions⟩
synonym see USUAL
— **ac·cus·tomed·ness** \-təm(d)-nəs\ *noun*

AC/DC \ˌā-(ˌ)sē-'dē-(ˌ)sē\ *adjective* [from the likening of a bisexual person to an electrical appliance which can operate on either alternating or direct current] (circa 1960)
: BISEXUAL 1b

¹ace \'ās\ *noun* [Middle English *as*, from Middle French, from Latin, unit, a copper coin] (14th century)
1 a : a die face marked with one spot **b** : a playing card marked in its center with one pip **c** : a domino end marked with one spot
2 : a very small amount or degree : PARTICLE
3 : a point scored especially on a service (as in tennis or handball) that an opponent fails to touch
4 : a golf score of one stroke on a hole; *also* : a hole made in one stroke
5 : a combat pilot who has brought down at least five enemy airplanes
6 : one that excels at something
— **ace in the hole 1** : an ace dealt face down to a player (as in stud poker) and not exposed until the showdown **2** : an effective and decisive argument or resource held in reserve
— **within an ace of** : on the point of : very near to ⟨came *within an ace of* winning⟩

²ace *transitive verb* **aced; ac·ing** (1923)
1 : to score an ace against (an opponent)
2 : to make (a hole in golf) in one stroke
3 : to gain a decisive advantage over : DEFEAT
— usually used with *out*

4 : to earn a high grade on (as on an examination); *especially* : to get an A on

³ace *adjective* (1926)
: of first or high rank or quality

-aceae *noun plural suffix* [New Latin, from Latin, feminine plural of *-aceus* -aceous]
: plants of the nature of ⟨Ros*aceae*⟩ — in names of families of plants

ace·dia \ə-'sē-dē-ə\ *noun* [Late Latin, from Greek *akēdeia*, from *a-* + *kēdos* care, grief — more at HATE] (1607)
: APATHY, BOREDOM

ACE inhibitor \ˌā-(ˌ)sē-'ē-; 'ās-\ *noun* [*a*ngiotensin *c*onverting *e*nzyme] (1985)
: any of a group of antihypertensive drugs (as captopril) that relax arteries and promote renal excretion of salt and water by inhibiting the activity of angiotensin converting enzyme

Acel·da·ma \ə-'sel-də-mə\ *noun* [Greek *Akeldama*, from Aramaic *ḥăqēl děmā*, literally, field of blood]
: the potter's field bought with the money Judas had been paid for betraying Christ

acel·lu·lar \(ˌ)ā-'sel-yə-lər\ *adjective* (1940)
1 : containing no cells ⟨*acellular* vaccines⟩
2 : not divided into cells : consisting of a single complex cell — used especially of protozoa and ciliates

acen·tric \(ˌ)ā-'sen-trik\ *adjective* (1937)
: lacking a centromere ⟨*acentric* chromosomes⟩

-aceous *adjective suffix* [Latin *-aceus*]
1 a : characterized by : full of ⟨setac*eous*⟩ **b** : consisting of ⟨diatom*aceous*⟩ : having the nature or form of ⟨tuff*aceous*⟩
2 a : of or relating to a group of animals typified by (such) a form ⟨cetac*eous*⟩ or characterized by (such) a feature ⟨crustac*eous*⟩ **b** : of or relating to a plant family ⟨solan*aceous*⟩

aceph·a·lous \(ˌ)ā-'sef-ə-ləs, ə-'se-\ *adjective* [Greek *akephalos*, from *a-* + *kephalē* head — more at CEPHALIC] (circa 1731)
1 : lacking a head or having the head reduced
2 : lacking a governing head or chief

ace·quia \ə-'sā-kē-ə, ä-\ *noun* [Spanish, from Arabic *as-sāqiyah* the irrigation stream] (1844)
Southwest : an irrigation ditch or canal

acerb \ə-'sərb, a-\ *adjective* [French or Latin; French *acerbe*, from Latin *acerbus*; akin to Latin *acer* sharp — more at EDGE] (1622)
: ACERBIC

ac·er·bate \'a-sər-ˌbāt\ *transitive verb* **-bat·ed; -bat·ing** (circa 1731)
: IRRITATE, EXASPERATE

acer·bic \ə-'sər-bik, a-\ *adjective* (1865)
: acid in temper, mood, or tone
— **acer·bi·cal·ly** \-bi-k(ə-)lē\ *adverb*

acer·bi·ty \ə-'bə-tē\ *noun, plural* **-ties** (1572)
: the quality of being acerbic

ac·er·o·la \ˌa-sə-'rō-lə\ *noun* [American Spanish, from Spanish, fruit of a shrub (*Crataegus azarolus*), from Arabic *az-zu'rūr*] (1945)
: any of various West Indian shrubs (genus *Malpighia*) with mildly acid cherrylike fruits very rich in vitamin C

acet- *or* **aceto-** *combining form* [French & Latin; French *acét-*, from Latin *acet-*, from *acetum* vinegar; akin to *acēre* to be sour, *acer* sharp — more at EDGE]
: acetic acid : acetyl ⟨*acetyl*⟩

ac·e·tab·u·lum \-'ta-byə-ləm\ *noun, plural* **-lums** *or* **-la** \-lə\ [Latin, literally, vinegar cup, from *acetum* vinegar] (1661)
1 : a ventral sucker of a trematode
2 : the cup-shaped socket in the hipbone
— **ac·e·tab·u·lar** \-lər\ *adjective*

ac·e·tal \'a-sə-ˌtal\ *noun* [German *Azetal*, from *azet-* acet- + *A*lkohol alcohol] (1853)
: any of various compounds characterized by the grouping $C(OR)_2$ and obtained especially by heating aldehydes or ketones with alcohols

ac·et·al·de·hyde \ˌa-sə-'tal-də-ˌhīd\ *noun* [International Scientific Vocabulary] (1877)
: a colorless volatile water-soluble liquid aldehyde C_2H_4O used chiefly in organic synthesis

acet·amide \ə-'se-tə-ˌmīd, ˌa-sə-'ta-ˌmīd\ *noun* [International Scientific Vocabulary] (1873)
: a white crystalline amide C_2H_5NO of acetic acid used especially as a solvent and in organic synthesis

acet·amin·o·phen \ə-ˌsē-tə-'mi-nə-fən, ˌa-sə-tə-\ *noun* [*acet-* + *amino* + *phen*ol] (1958)
: a crystalline compound $C_8H_9NO_2$ that is a hydroxy derivative of acetanilide and is used in chemical synthesis and in medicine to relieve pain and fever

ac·et·an·i·lide *or* **ac·et·an·i·lid** \ˌa-sə-'ta-nə-ˌlīd, -ləd\ *noun* [International Scientific Vocabulary] (circa 1864)
: a white crystalline compound C_8H_9NO that is derived from aniline and acetic acid and is used especially to relieve pain or fever

ac·e·tate \'a-sə-ˌtāt\ *noun* (1827)
1 : a salt or ester of acetic acid
2 : CELLULOSE ACETATE; *also* : something (as a textile fiber) made from cellulose acetate
3 : a phonograph recording disk made of an acetate or coated with cellulose acetate

ac·et·azol·amide \ˌa-sə-tə-'zō-lə-ˌmīd, -'zä-, -məd\ *noun* [*acet-* + *azole* + *amide*] (1954)
: a diuretic drug $C_4H_6N_4O_3S_2$ used especially in the treatment of edema associated with congestive heart failure and of glaucoma

ace·tic acid \ə-'sē-tik-\ *noun* [probably from French *acétique*, from Latin *acetum* vinegar] (1808)
: a colorless pungent liquid acid $C_2H_4O_2$ that is the chief acid of vinegar and that is used especially in synthesis (as of plastics)

acetic anhydride *noun* (1876)
: a colorless liquid $C_4H_6O_3$ with a pungent odor used in organic synthesis (as of cellulose acetate and aspirin)

ace·ti·fy \ə-'sē-tə-ˌfī, -'se-\ *transitive verb* **-fied; -fy·ing** (circa 1828)
: to turn into acetic acid or vinegar
— **ace·ti·fi·ca·tion** \-ˌsē-tə-fə-'kā-shən, -ˌse-\ *noun*

ace·to·ace·tic acid \ˌa-sə-(ˌ)tō-ə-ˌsē-tik-, ə-ˌsē-tō-\ *noun* [part translation of German *Azetessigsäure*, from *azet-* acet- + *Essigsäure* acetic acid] (circa 1900)
: an unstable acid $C_4H_6O_3$ that is a ketone body found in abnormal quantities in the blood and urine in some conditions (as diabetes)

ac·e·tone \'a-sə-ˌtōn\ *noun* [German *Azeton*, from Latin *acetum*] (1839)
: a volatile fragrant flammable liquid ketone C_3H_6O used chiefly as a solvent and in organic synthesis and found in abnormal quantities in diabetic urine
— **ac·e·ton·ic** \ˌa-sə-'tä-nik\ *adjective*

ace·to·ni·trile \ə-ˌsē-tō-'nī-trəl, ˌa-sə-tō-, -ˌtrīl\ *noun* (circa 1869)
: the colorless liquid nitrile CH_3CN of acetic acid used chiefly in organic synthesis and as a solvent

ace·to·phe·net·i·din \ˌa-sə-(ˌ)tō-fə-'ne-tə-dən, ə-ˌsē-tō-\ *noun* [International Scientific Vocabulary] (1910)
: PHENACETIN

ace·tous \ə-'sē-təs, 'a-sə-təs\ *adjective* (1778)
: relating to or producing vinegar ⟨*acetous* fermentation⟩; *also* : SOUR, VINEGARY

ace·tyl \ə-'sē-t³l, 'a-sə-; ˌa-sə-ˌtēl\ *noun* (circa 1864)
: the radical CH_3CO- of acetic acid — often used in combination

acet·y·late \ə-'se-t³l-ˌāt\ *transitive verb* **-lat·ed; -lat·ing** (circa 1900)
: to introduce the acetyl radical into (a compound)
— **acet·y·la·tion** \-ˌse-t³l-'ā-shən\ *noun*

— **acet·y·la·tive** \-'set-ºl-,ā-tiv\ *adjective*

ace·tyl·cho·line \ə,se-tºl-'kō-,lēn, -sē-; 'a-sə-,tēl-\ *noun* [International Scientific Vocabulary] (1906)
: a neurotransmitter $C_7H_{17}NO_3$ released at autonomic synapses and neuromuscular junctions and formed enzymatically in the tissues from choline

ace·tyl·cho·lin·es·ter·ase \-,kō-lə-'nes-tə-,rās, -,rāz\ *noun* (1947)
: an enzyme that occurs especially in some nerve endings and in the blood and promotes the hydrolysis of acetylcholine

acetyl CoA \-,kō-'ā\ *noun* (circa 1959)
: ACETYL COENZYME A

acetyl coenzyme A *noun* (1952)
: a compound $C_{25}H_{38}N_7O_{17}P_3S$ formed as an intermediate in metabolism and active as a coenzyme in biological acetylations

acet·y·lene \ə-'se-tºl-ən, -tºl-,ēn\ *noun* (1864)
: a colorless gaseous hydrocarbon HC≡CH used chiefly in organic synthesis and as a fuel (as in welding and soldering)
— **acet·y·le·nic** \ə-,se-tºl-'ē-nik, -'e-nik\ *adjective*

ace·tyl·sa·lic·y·late \ə-,sē-tºl-sə-'li-sə-,lāt\ *noun* (circa 1960)
: a salt or ester of acetylsalicylic acid

ace·tyl·sal·i·cyl·ic acid \ə-'sē-tºl-,sa-lə-,si-lik-\ *noun* [International Scientific Vocabulary] (1897)
: ASPIRIN 1

ac·ey–deuc·ey *also* **ac·ey–deu·cy** \,ā-sē-'dü-sē, -'dyü-\ *noun* (1925)
: a variation of backgammon in which a throw of a 1-2 wins extra turns

¹Achae·an \ə-'kē-ən\ *or* **Achai·an** \-'kī-ən, -'kā-ən\ *adjective* (1567)
: of, relating to, or characteristic of Achaea; *broadly* : of or relating to Greece

²Achaean *or* **Achaian** *noun* (1607)
: a native or inhabitant of Achaea; *broadly* : GREEK

Ach·ae·me·ni·an \,a-kə-'mē-nē-ən\ *adjective* (1717)
: of or relating to the Achaemenids

Achae·me·nid \ə-'kē-mə-nəd\ *noun, plural* **-menids** *also* **-men·i·dae** \,a-kə-'me-nə-,dē\ [Greek *Achaimenides,* from *Achaimenes,* 7th century B.C. Persian king, founder of the dynasty + *-ides* (patronymic suffix)] (1889)
: a member of the ruling house of ancient Persia generally considered historically important from the assumption of power by Cyrus the Great (559 B.C.) to the overthrow of Darius III (330 B.C.)

acha·la·sia \,ā-kə-'lā-zh(ē-)ə\ *noun* [New Latin, from *a-* + Greek *chalasis* slackening + New Latin *-ia*] (1914)
: failure of a ring of muscle (as the anal sphincter or one of the esophagus) to relax

Acha·tes \ə-'kā-tēz\ *noun* [Latin]
: a faithful companion of Aeneas in Virgil's *Aeneid*

¹ache \'āk\ *intransitive verb* **ached; aching** [Middle English *aken,* from Old English *acan*] (before 12th century)
1 a : to suffer a usually dull persistent pain **b** : to become distressed or disturbed (as with anxiety or regret) **c** : to feel compassion
2 : to experience a painful eagerness or yearning

²ache *noun* (before 12th century)
1 : a usually dull persistent pain
2 : a condition marked by aching

achene \ə-'kēn\ *noun* [New Latin *achaenium,* from *a-* + Greek *chainein* to yawn — more at YAWN] (1855)
: a small dry indehiscent one-seeded fruit (as of a sunflower) developing from a simple ovary and usually having a thin pericarp attached to the seed at only one point

Ach·er·on \'a-kə-,rän, -rən\ *noun* [Greek *Acherōn*]
: a river in Hades

Acheu·le·an *or* **Acheu·li·an** \ə-'shü-lē-ən\ *adjective* [French *acheuléen,* from Saint *Acheul,* near Amiens, France] (circa 1909)
: of or relating to a Lower Paleolithic culture typified by bifacial tools with round cutting edges

à che·val \,ä-shə-'väl\ *adverb* [French, literally, on horseback] (1832)
1 : with a leg on each side : ASTRIDE
2 : in such a way as to be played or chanced simultaneously on two numbers or events (as in roulette)

achieve \ə-'chēv\ *verb* **achieved; achieving** [Middle English *acheven,* from Middle French *achever* to finish, from *a-* (from Latin *ad-*) + *chief* end, head — more at CHIEF] (14th century)
transitive verb
1 : to carry out successfully : ACCOMPLISH ⟨*achieve* a gradual increase in production⟩
2 : to get or attain as the result of exertion : REACH ⟨*achieved* a high degree of skill⟩ ⟨*achieved* greatness⟩
intransitive verb
: to attain a desired end or aim : become successful
synonym see PERFORM
— **achiev·able** \-'chē-və-bəl\ *adjective*
— **achiev·er** *noun*

achieved *adjective* (1918)
: brought to or marked by a high degree of development or refinement : FINISHED ⟨fully *achieved* poems⟩

achieve·ment \ə-'chēv-mənt\ *noun* (15th century)
1 : the act of achieving : ACCOMPLISHMENT
2 a : a result gained by effort **b** : a great or heroic deed
3 : the quality and quantity of a student's work
synonym see FEAT

Achil·les \ə-'ki-lēz\ *noun* [Latin, from Greek *Achilleus*]
: the greatest warrior among the Greeks at Troy and slayer of Hector

Achilles' heel *noun* [from the story that Achilles was vulnerable only in the heel] (1864)
: a vulnerable point

Achilles tendon *noun* (circa 1879)
: the strong tendon joining the muscles in the calf of the leg to the bone of the heel

ach·ing \'ā-kin\ *adjective* (13th century)
1 : that aches ⟨an *aching* back⟩
2 : causing or reflecting distress, deep emotion, or longing ⟨*aching* country ballads⟩
— **ach·ing·ly** *adverb*

achlor·hyd·ria \,ā-,klor-'hi-drē-ə, -,klòr-\ *noun* [New Latin, from *a-* + International Scientific Vocabulary *chlor-* + *hydr-* + New Latin *-ia*] (1898)
: absence of hydrochloric acid from the gastric juice
— **achlor·hy·dric** \-'hi-drik, -'hī-\ *adjective*

achon·drite \(,)ā-'kän-,drīt\ *noun* (circa 1904)
: a stony meteorite without rounded grains
— **achon·drit·ic** \,ā-,kän-'dri-tik\ *adjective*

achon·dro·pla·sia \,ā-,kän-drə-'plā-zh(ē-)ə\ *noun* [New Latin, from *a-* + *chondr-* + *-plasia*] (circa 1893)
: a genetic disorder disturbing normal growth of cartilage, resulting in a form of dwarfism characterized by a usually normal torso and shortened limbs, and usually inherited as an autosomal dominant
— **achon·dro·plas·tic** \-'plas-tik\ *adjective*

ach·ro·mat \'a-krə-,mat\ *noun* (1900)
: ACHROMATIC LENS

ach·ro·mat·ic \,a-krə-'ma-tik, (,)ā-\ *adjective* (1766)
1 : refracting light without dispersing it into its constituent colors : giving images practically free from extraneous colors ⟨an *achromatic* telescope⟩

2 : not readily colored by the usual staining agents
3 : possessing no hue : being or involving black, gray, or white : NEUTRAL ⟨*achromatic* visual sensations⟩
4 : being without accidentals or modulation : DIATONIC
— **ach·ro·mat·i·cal·ly** \-ti-k(ə-)lē\ *adverb*
— **achro·ma·tism** \(,)ā-'krō-mə-,ti-zəm, a-\ *noun*
— **achro·ma·tize** \(,)ā-'krō-mə-,tīz, a-\ *transitive verb*

achromatic lens *noun* (circa 1864)
: a lens made by combining lenses of different glasses having different focal powers so that the light emerging from the lens forms an image practically free from unwanted colors

achy \'ā-kē\ *adjective* **ach·i·er; ach·i·est** (1875)
: afflicted with aches
— **ach·i·ness** *noun*

acic·u·lar \ə-'si-kyə-lər\ *adjective* [Late Latin *acicula* (diminutive of Latin *acus* needle) + English *-ar* — more at ACUTE] (1794)
: shaped like a needle ⟨*acicular* leaves⟩ ⟨*acicular* crystals⟩

¹ac·id \'a-səd\ *adjective* [French or Latin; French *acide,* from Latin *acidus,* from *acēre* to be sour — more at ACET-] (1626)
1 a : sour, sharp, or biting to the taste **b** : sharp, biting, or sour in manner, disposition, or nature ⟨an *acid* individual⟩ **c** : sharply clear, discerning, or pointed ⟨an *acid* wit⟩ **d** : piercingly intense and often jarring ⟨*acid* yellow⟩
2 a : of, relating to, or being an acid; *also* : having the reactions or characteristics of an acid ⟨*acid* soil⟩ ⟨an *acid* solution⟩ **b** *of salts and esters* : derived by partial exchange of replaceable hydrogen ⟨*acid* sodium carbonate $NaHCO_3$⟩ **c** : containing or involving the use of an acid (as in manufacture) **d** : marked by or resulting from an abnormally high concentration of acid ⟨*acid* indigestion⟩
3 : relating to or made by a process (as in making steel) in which the furnace is lined with acidic material and an acidic slag is used
4 : rich in silica ⟨*acid* rocks⟩
— **ac·id·ly** *adverb*
— **ac·id·ness** *noun*

²acid *noun* (1696)
1 : a sour substance; *specifically* : any of various typically water-soluble and sour compounds that in solution are capable of reacting with a base to form a salt, redden litmus, and have a pH less than 7, that are hydrogen-containing molecules or ions able to give up a proton to a base, or that are substances able to accept an unshared pair of electrons from a base
2 : something incisive, biting, or sarcastic ⟨a social satire dripping with *acid*⟩
3 : LSD
— **ac·idy** \'a-sə-dē\ *adjective*

ac·id–fast \'a-səd-,fast\ *adjective* (1903)
: not easily decolorized by acids

ac·id·head \-,hed\ *noun* (1966)
: an individual who uses LSD

acid·ic \ə-'si-dik, a-\ *adjective* (1880)
1 : acid-forming
2 : ACID

acid·i·fi·er \ə-'si-də-,fī(-ə)r, a-\ *noun* (circa 1828)
: one that acidifies; *especially* : a substance used to increase soil acidity

acid·i·fy \-,fī\ *transitive verb* **-fied; -fy·ing** (1797)
1 : to make acid
2 : to convert into an acid
— **acid·i·fi·ca·tion** \-,si-də-fə-'kā-shən\ *noun*

acid·i·met·ric \ə-,si-də-'me-trik\ *adjective* (1900)
: of or relating to the precise determination of the amount of acid present in a solution
— **ac·i·dim·e·ter** \,a-sə-'di-mə-tər\ *noun*
— **ac·i·dim·e·try** \-'di-mə-trē\ *noun*

acid·i·ty \ə-'si-də-tē, a-\ *noun, plural* **-ties** (1620)
1 : the quality, state, or degree of being acid
2 : the state of being excessively acid
acid·o·phil \ə-'si-də-,fil, a-\ *also* **acid·o·phile** \-,fil\ *noun* (circa 1900)
: a substance, tissue, or organism that stains readily with acid stains
— **acidophil** *also* **acidophile** *adjective*
ac·i·do·phil·ic \,a-sə-dō-'fi-lik\ *adjective* (circa 1900)
1 : staining readily with acid stains **:** ACIDOPHIL
2 : preferring or thriving in a relatively acid environment
ac·i·doph·i·lus milk \,a-sə-'dä-f(ə-)ləs-\ *noun* [New Latin *Lactobacillus acidophilus,* literally, acidophilic lactobacillus] (1921)
: milk fermented by any of several bacteria and used therapeutically to change the intestinal flora
ac·i·do·sis \,a-sə-'dō-səs\ *noun* [New Latin] (1900)
: an abnormal condition characterized by reduced alkalinity of the blood and of the body tissues
— **ac·i·dot·ic** \-'dä-tik\ *adjective*
acid phosphatase *noun* (1949)
: a phosphatase (as the phosphomonoesterase from the prostate gland) optimally active in acid medium
acid precipitation *noun* (1979)
: precipitation (as rain or snow) having increased acidity caused by environmental factors (as atmospheric pollutants)
acid rain *noun* (1858)
: acid precipitation in the form of rain
acid rock *noun* (1966)
: rock music with lyrics and sound relating to or suggestive of drug-induced experiences
acid test *noun* (1912)
: a severe or crucial test
acid·u·late \ə-'si-jə-,lāt\ *transitive verb* **-lat·ed; -lat·ing** [Latin *acidulus*] (1732)
: to make acid or slightly acid
— **acid·u·la·tion** \-,si-jə-'lā-shən\ *noun*
acid·u·lent \ə-'si-jə-lənt\ *adjective* [French *acidulant,* from present participle of *aciduler* to acidulate, from Latin *acidulus*] (1834)
: ACIDULOUS
acid·u·lous \ə-'si-jə-ləs\ *adjective* [Latin *acidulus,* from *acidus*] (1769)
: somewhat acid or harsh in taste or manner
ac·i·nar \'a-sə-nər, -,när\ *adjective* (1936)
: of, relating to, or comprising an acinus (pancreatic *acinar* cells)
ac·i·nus \'a-sə-nəs\ *noun, plural* **-ni** \-,nī\ [New Latin, from Latin, berry, berry seed] (circa 1751)
: any of the small sacs terminating the ducts of some exocrine glands and lined with secretory cells
— **ac·i·nous** \-nəs\ *adjective*
ack-ack \'ak-,ak\ *noun* [British signalmen's former telephone pronunciation of *AA,* abbreviation of *antiaircraft*] (1926)
: an antiaircraft gun; *also* **:** antiaircraft fire
ackee *variant of* AKEE
ac·knowl·edge \ik-'nä-lij, ak-\ *transitive verb* **-edged; -edg·ing** [*ac-* (as in *accord*) + *knowledge*] (15th century)
1 : to recognize the rights, authority, or status of
2 : to disclose knowledge of or agreement with
3 a : to express gratitude or obligation for **b :** to take notice of **c :** to make known the receipt of
4 : to recognize as genuine or valid (*acknowledge* a debt) ☆
ac·knowl·edged \-lijd\ *adjective* (1598)
: generally recognized, accepted, or admitted
— **ac·knowl·edged·ly** \-lijd-lē, -li-jəd-\ *adverb*
ac·knowl·edg·ment *or* **ac·knowl·edge·ment** \ik-'nä-lij-mənt, ak-\ *noun* (1594)

1 a : the act of acknowledging **b :** recognition or favorable notice of an act or achievement
2 : a thing done or given in recognition of something received
3 : a declaration or avowal of one's act or of a fact to give it legal validity
ac·me \'ak-mē\ *noun* [Greek *akmē* point, highest point — more at EDGE] (1620)
: the highest point or stage; *also* **:** one that represents perfection of the thing expressed
synonym SEE SUMMIT
ac·ne \'ak-nē\ *noun* [Greek *aknē* eruption of the face, manuscript variant of *akmē,* literally, point] (circa 1828)
: a disorder of the skin caused by inflammation of the skin glands and hair follicles; *specifically* **:** a form found chiefly in adolescents and marked by pimples especially on the face
— **ac·ned** \-nēd\ *adjective*
acock \ə-'käk\ *adjective or adverb* (1846)
: being in a cocked position
acoe·lo·mate \(,)ā-'sē-lə-,māt\ *noun* (circa 1889)
: an invertebrate lacking a coelom; *especially* **:** one belonging to the group comprising the flatworms and nemerteans and characterized by bilateral symmetry and a digestive cavity that is the only internal cavity
— **acoelomate** *adjective*
acold \ə-'kōld\ *adjective* (14th century)
archaic **:** COLD, CHILLED (the owl, for all his feathers, was *acold* —John Keats)
ac·o·lyte \'a-kə-,līt\ *noun* [Middle English, from Middle French & Medieval Latin; Middle French, from Medieval Latin *acoluthus,* from Middle Greek *akolouthos,* from Greek, adjective, following, from *a-, ha-* together (akin to Greek *homos* same) + *keleuthos* path] (14th century)
1 : one who assists the clergyman in a liturgical service by performing minor duties
2 : one who attends or assists **:** FOLLOWER
ac·o·nite \'a-kə-,nīt\ *noun* [Middle French or Latin; from Latin *aconitum,* from Greek *akoniton*] (1578)
1 : MONKSHOOD
2 : the dried tuberous root of a common monkshood (*Aconitum napellus*) formerly used as a sedative and anodyne
acorn \'ā-,kȯrn, -kərn\ *noun* [Middle English *akern,* from Old English *æcern;* akin to Old English *æcer* field, Middle High German *ackeran* acorns collectively, Old Irish *áirne* sloe, Lithuanian *uoga* berry] (before 12th century)
: the nut of the oak usually seated in or surrounded by a hard woody cupule of indurated bracts

acorn

acorn squash *noun* (1937)
: an acorn-shaped dark green winter squash with a ridged surface and sweet yellow to orange flesh
acorn worm *noun* (circa 1889)
: any of a class (Enteropneusta) of burrowing wormlike marine animals having an acorn-shaped proboscis and classified with the hemichordates

acorn squash

acous·tic \ə-'kü-stik\ *or* **acous·ti·cal** \-sti-kəl\ *adjective* [Greek *akoustikos* of hearing, from *akouein* to hear — more at HEAR] (1605)
1 : of or relating to the sense or organs of hearing, to sound, or to the science of sounds (*acoustic* apparatus of the ear) (*acoustic* energy): as **a :** deadening or absorbing sound (*acoustic* tile) **b :** operated by or utilizing sound waves

2 : of, relating to, or being a musical instrument whose sound is not electronically modified
— **acous·ti·cal·ly** \-k(ə-)lē\ *adverb*
ac·ous·ti·cian \,a-,kü-'sti-shən, ə-,kü-\ *noun* (1859)
: a specialist in acoustics
acous·tics \ə-'kü-stiks\ *noun plural* (1683)
1 *singular in construction* **:** a science that deals with the production, control, transmission, reception, and effects of sound
2 *also* **acoustic :** the qualities that determine the ability of an enclosure (as an auditorium) to reflect sound waves in such a way as to produce distinct hearing
ac·quaint \ə-'kwānt\ *transitive verb* [Middle English, from Old French *acointier,* from *acointe* familiar, from Latin *accognitus,* past participle of *accognoscere* to recognize, from *ad- + cognoscere* to know — more at COGNITION] (14th century)
1 : to cause to know personally (was *acquainted* with the mayor)
2 : to make familiar **:** cause to know firsthand
synonym SEE INFORM
ac·quain·tance \ə-'kwān-t°n(t)s\ *noun* (14th century)
1 a : the state of being acquainted **b :** personal knowledge **:** FAMILIARITY
2 a : the persons with whom one is acquainted (should auld *acquaintance* be forgot —Robert Burns) **b :** a person whom one knows but who is not a particularly close friend
— **ac·quain·tance·ship** \-,ship\ *noun*
ac·qui·esce \,a-kwē-'es\ *intransitive verb* **-esced; -esc·ing** [French *acquiescer,* from Latin *acquiescere,* from *ad- + quiescere* to be quiet — more at QUIESCENT] (circa 1620)
: to accept, comply, or submit tacitly or passively — often used with *in* and sometimes with *to*
synonym SEE ASSENT
ac·qui·es·cence \-'e-s°n(t)s\ *noun* (1612)
1 : the act of acquiescing **:** the state of being acquiescent
2 : an instance of acquiescing
ac·qui·es·cent \-'e-s°nt\ *adjective* [Latin *acquiescent-, acquiescens,* present participle of *acquiescere*] (1753)
: inclined to acquiesce
— **ac·qui·es·cent·ly** *adverb*
ac·quir·able \ə-'kwī-rə-bəl\ *adjective* (1646)
: capable of being acquired
ac·quire \ə-'kwīr\ *transitive verb* **ac·quired; ac·quir·ing** [Middle English *aqueren,* from Middle French *aquerre,* from Latin *acquirere,* from *ad- + quaerere* to seek, obtain] (15th century)

1 : to get as one's own: **a :** to come into possession or control of often by unspecified means **b :** to come to have as a new or added characteristic, trait, or ability (as by sustained effort or natural selection) ⟨*acquire* fluency in French⟩ ⟨bacteria that *acquire* tolerance to antibiotics⟩
2 : to locate and hold (a desired object) in a detector ⟨*acquire* a target by radar⟩

acquired immune deficiency syndrome *noun* (1982)
: AIDS

acquired immunodeficiency syndrome *noun* (1982)
: AIDS

acquired taste *noun* (1858)
: one that is not easily or immediately liked or appreciated

ac·quire·ment \ə-ˈkwīr-mənt\ *noun* (1630)
1 : a skill of mind or body usually resulting from continued endeavor
2 : the act of acquiring

ac·qui·si·tion \ˌa-kwə-ˈzi-shən\ *noun* [Middle English *acquisicioun*, from Middle French or Latin; Middle French *acquisition*, from Latin *acquisition-*, *acquisitio*, from *acquirere*] (14th century)
1 : the act of acquiring
2 : something acquired or gained
— **ac·qui·si·tion·al** \-shnəl, -shə-nᵊl\ *adjective*
— **ac·quis·i·tor** \ə-ˈkwi-zə-tər\ *noun*

ac·quis·i·tive \ə-ˈkwi-zə-tiv\ *adjective* (1846)
: strongly desirous of acquiring and possessing
synonym see COVETOUS
— **ac·quis·i·tive·ly** *adverb*
— **ac·quis·i·tive·ness** *noun*

ac·quit \ə-ˈkwit\ *transitive verb* **ac·quit·ted; ac·quit·ting** [Middle English *aquiten*, from Old French *aquiter*, from *a-* (from Latin *ad-*) + *quite* free of — more at QUIT] (13th century)
1 a *archaic* **:** to pay off (as a claim or debt) **b** *obsolete* **:** REPAY, REQUITE
2 : to discharge completely (as from an obligation or accusation) ⟨the court *acquitted* the prisoner⟩
3 : to conduct (oneself) usually satisfactorily especially under stress ⟨the recruits *acquitted* themselves like veterans⟩
synonym see BEHAVE, EXCULPATE
— **ac·quit·ter** *noun*

ac·quit·tal \ə-ˈkwi-tᵊl\ *noun* (15th century)
: a setting free from the charge of an offense by verdict, sentence, or other legal process

ac·quit·tance \ə-ˈkwi-tᵊn(t)s\ *noun* (14th century)
: a document evidencing a discharge from an obligation; *especially* **:** a receipt in full

acr- *or* **acro-** *combining form* [Middle French or Greek; Middle French *acro-*, from Greek *akr-*, *akro-*, from *akros* topmost, extreme; akin to Greek *akmē* point — more at EDGE]
1 : beginning **:** end **:** tip ⟨*acronym*⟩
2 a : top **:** peak **:** summit ⟨*acropetal*⟩ **b :** height ⟨*acrophobia*⟩

acre \ˈā-kər\ *noun* [Middle English, from Old English *æcer*; akin to Old High German *ackar* field, Latin *ager*, Greek *agros*, and perhaps to Latin *agere* to drive — more at AGENT] (before 12th century)
1 a *archaic* **:** a field especially of arable land or pastureland **b** *plural* **:** LANDS, ESTATE
2 : any of various units of area; *specifically* **:** a unit in the U.S. and England equal to 43,560 square feet (4047 square meters) — see WEIGHT table
3 : a broad expanse or great quantity ⟨*acres* of free publicity⟩

acre·age \ˈā-k(ə-)rij\ *noun* (1859)
: area in acres **:** ACRES

acre–foot \ˈā-kər-ˈfu̇t\ *noun* (1900)
: the volume (as of irrigation water) that would cover one acre to a depth of one foot

acre–inch \ˈā-kər-ˈinch\ *noun* (circa 1909)
: one twelfth of an acre-foot

ac·rid \ˈa-krəd\ *adjective* [modification of Latin *acr-*, *acer* sharp — more at EDGE] (1712)
1 : sharp and harsh or unpleasantly pungent in taste or odor **:** IRRITATING
2 : deeply or violently bitter **:** ACRIMONIOUS ⟨an *acrid* denunciation⟩
synonym see CAUSTIC
— **acrid·i·ty** \a-ˈkri-də-tē, ə-\ *noun*
— **ac·rid·ly** \ˈa-krəd-lē\ *adverb*
— **ac·rid·ness** *noun*

ac·ri·dine \ˈa-krə-ˌdēn\ *noun* (circa 1877)
: a colorless crystalline compound $C_{13}H_9N$ occurring in coal tar and important as the parent compound of dyes and pharmaceuticals

acridine orange *noun* (circa 1909)
: a basic orange dye structurally related to acridine and used especially to stain nucleic acids

ac·ri·fla·vine \ˌa-krə-ˈflā-ˌvēn, -vən\ *noun* [*acridine* + *flavine*] (1917)
: a yellow dye $C_{14}H_{14}N_3Cl$ used as an antiseptic especially for wounds

Ac·ri·lan \ˈa-krə-ˌlan, -lən\ *trademark*
— used for an acrylic fiber

ac·ri·mo·ni·ous \ˌa-krə-ˈmō-nē-əs\ *adjective* (1775)
: caustic, biting, or rancorous especially in feeling, language, or manner ⟨an *acrimonious* dispute⟩
— **ac·ri·mo·ni·ous·ly** *adverb*
— **ac·ri·mo·ni·ous·ness** *noun*

ac·ri·mo·ny \ˈa-krə-ˌmō-nē\ *noun, plural* **-nies** [Middle French or Latin; Middle French *acrimonie*, from Latin *acrimonia*, from *acr-*, *acer*] (1542)
: harsh or biting sharpness especially of words, manner, or disposition

ac·ri·tarch \ˈa-kri-ˌtärk\ *noun* [Greek *akritos* uncertain (from *a-* + *kritos*, verbal of *krinein* to decide) + *archē* beginning — more at CERTAIN, ARCH-] (1963)
: any of a group of fossil one-celled marine planktonic organisms of uncertain and possibly various taxonomic affinities held to represent the earliest known eukaryotes

ac·ro·bat \ˈa-krə-ˌbat\ *noun* [French & Greek; French *acrobate*, from Greek *akrobatēs*, from *akros* + *bainein* to go — more at COME] (1825)
1 : one that performs gymnastic feats requiring skillful control of the body
2 a : one skillful at exercises of intellectual or artistic dexterity **b :** one adept at swiftly changing or adapting a position or viewpoint ⟨a political *acrobat*⟩
— **ac·ro·bat·ic** \ˌa-krə-ˈba-tik\ *adjective*
— **ac·ro·bat·i·cal·ly** \-ti-k(ə-)lē\ *adverb*

ac·ro·bat·ics \ˌa-krə-ˈba-tiks\ *noun plural but singular or plural in construction* (1882)
1 : the art, performance, or activity of an acrobat
2 : a spectacular, showy, or startling performance or demonstration involving great agility or complexity

ac·ro·cen·tric \ˌa-krō-ˈsen-trik\ *adjective* (1945)
: having the centromere situated so that one chromosomal arm is much shorter than the other
— **acrocentric** *noun*

ac·ro·lect \ˈa-krə-ˌlekt\ *noun* [*acr-* + *-lect* (as in *dialect*)] (1964)
: the language variety of a speech community closest to the standard or prestige form of a language

acro·le·in \ə-ˈkrō-lē-ən\ *noun* [International Scientific Vocabulary *acr-* (from Latin *acr-*, *acer*) + Latin *olēre* to smell — more at ODOR] (circa 1857)
: a colorless irritant pungent liquid aldehyde C_3H_4O used chiefly in organic synthesis

ac·ro·meg·a·ly \ˌa-krō-ˈme-gə-lē\ *noun* [International Scientific Vocabulary] (1889)
: chronic hyperpituitarism marked by progressive enlargement of hands, feet, and face

— **ac·ro·me·gal·ic** \-mə-ˈga-lik\ *adjective or noun*

ac·ro·nym \ˈa-krə-ˌnim\ *noun* [*acr-* + *-onym*] (1943)
: a word (as *radar* or *snafu*) formed from the initial letter or letters of each of the successive parts or major parts of a compound term
— **ac·ro·nym·ic** \ˌa-krə-ˈni-mik\ *adjective*
— **ac·ro·nym·i·cal·ly** \-mi-k(ə-)lē\ *adverb*

acrop·e·tal \ə-ˈkrä-pə-tᵊl, a-\ *adjective* [*acr-* + *-petal* (as in *centripetal*)] (1875)
: proceeding from the base toward the apex or from below upward ⟨*acropetal* development of floral buds⟩
— **acrop·e·tal·ly** \-tᵊl-ē\ *adverb*

ac·ro·pho·bia \ˌa-krə-ˈfō-bē-ə\ *noun* [New Latin] (circa 1892)
: abnormal dread of being at a great height
— **ac·ro·phobe** \ˈa-krə-ˌfōb\ *noun*

acrop·o·lis \ə-ˈkrä-pə-ləs\ *noun* [Greek *akropolis*, from *akr-* *acr-* + *polis* city — more at POLICE] (1662)
: the upper fortified part of an ancient Greek city (as Athens); *also* **:** a usually fortified height of a city or district elsewhere (as in Central America)

ac·ro·some \ˈa-krə-ˌsōm\ *noun* [International Scientific Vocabulary] (1899)
: an anterior prolongation of a spermatozoon that releases egg-penetrating enzymes
— **ac·ro·so·mal** \ˌa-krə-ˈsō-məl\ *adjective*

¹across \ə-ˈkrȯs, *chiefly dialect* -ˈkrȯst\ *adverb* [Middle English *acros*, from Anglo-French *an crois*, from *an* in (from Latin *in*) + *crois* cross, from Latin *crux*] (14th century)
1 : in a position reaching from one side to the other **:** CROSSWISE
2 : to or on the opposite side
3 : so as to be understandable, acceptable, or successful ⟨get an argument *across*⟩

²across *preposition* (1591)
1 a : from one side to the opposite side of **:** OVER, THROUGH ⟨swam *across* the river⟩ **b :** on the opposite side of ⟨lives *across* the street from us⟩
2 : so as to intersect or pass through at an angle ⟨sawed *across* the grain of the wood⟩
3 : so as to find or meet ⟨came *across* your football in the hall closet⟩
4 a : THROUGHOUT ⟨obvious interest *across* the nation —Robert Goralski⟩ **b :** so as to include or take into consideration all classes or categories ⟨*across* differences, they insist, there can be no rational dialogue —Huston Smith⟩

³across *adjective* (1646)
: being in a crossed position

across–the–board *adjective* (1945)
1 : placed to win if a competitor wins, places, or shows ⟨an *across-the-board* racing bet⟩
2 : embracing or affecting all classes or categories **:** BLANKET ⟨an *across-the-board* price increase⟩

acros·tic \ə-ˈkrȯs-tik, -ˈkräs-\ *noun* [Middle French & Greek; Middle French *acrostiche*, from Greek *akrostichis*, from *akr-* *acr-* + *stichos* line; akin to *steichein* to go — more at STAIR] (1530)
1 : a composition usually in verse in which sets of letters (as the initial or final letters of the lines) taken in order form a word or phrase or a regular sequence of letters of the alphabet
2 : ACRONYM
— **acrostic** *also* **acros·ti·cal** \-ti-kəl\ *adjective*
— **acros·ti·cal·ly** \-ti-k(ə-)lē\ *adverb*

ac·ryl·am·ide \ˌa-krᵊl-ˈa-ˌmīd, ə-ˈkri-lə-\ *noun* [*acrylic* + *amide*] (1946)
: an amide C_3H_5NO that is derived from acrylic acid, that polymerizes readily, and that is used in the manufacture of synthetic textile fibers

ac·ry·late \ˈa-krə-ˌlāt\ *noun* (1873)
1 : a salt or ester of acrylic acid
2 : ACRYLIC RESIN

¹acryl·ic \ə-'kri-lik\ *adjective* [International Scientific Vocabulary *acrolein* + *-yl* + ¹*-ic*] (1855)
1 : of or relating to acrylic acid or its derivatives ⟨*acrylic* polymers⟩
2 : made or consisting of an acrylic ⟨an *acrylic* window⟩

²acrylic *noun* (1942)
1 a : ACRYLIC RESIN **b :** a paint in which the vehicle is an acrylic resin **c :** a painting done in an acrylic resin
2 : ACRYLIC FIBER

acrylic acid *noun* (circa 1855)
: an unsaturated liquid acid $C_3H_4O_2$ that polymerizes readily to form useful products (as constituents for varnishes and lacquers)

acrylic fiber *noun* (1951)
: a quick-drying synthetic textile fiber made by polymerization of acrylonitrile usually with other monomers

acrylic resin *noun* (1936)
: a glassy thermoplastic made by polymerizing acrylic or methacrylic acid or a derivative of either and used for cast and molded parts or as coatings and adhesives

ac·ry·lo·ni·trile \ˌa-krə-lō-'nī-trəl, -ˌtrēl\ *noun* (1893)
: a colorless volatile flammable liquid nitrile C_3H_3N used chiefly in organic synthesis and for polymerization

¹act \'akt\ *noun* [Middle English, partly from Latin *actus* doing, act, from *agere* to drive, do; partly from Latin *actum* thing done, record, from neuter of *actus*, past participle of *agere* — more at AGENT] (14th century)
1 a : the doing of a thing **:** DEED **b :** something done voluntarily
2 : a state of real existence rather than possibility
3 : the formal product of a legislative body **:** STATUTE; *also* **:** a decision or determination of a sovereign, a legislative council, or a court of justice
4 : the process of doing **:** ACTION ⟨caught in the *act*⟩
5 *often capitalized* **:** a formal record of something done or transacted
6 : one of the principal divisions of a theatrical work (as a play or opera)
7 a : one of successive parts or performances (as in a variety show or circus) **b :** the performer or performers in such an act **c :** a performance or presentation identified with a particular individual or group **d :** the sum of a person's actions or effects that serve to create an impression or set an example ⟨a hard *act* to follow⟩
8 : a display of affected behavior **:** PRETENSE

²act (1594)
transitive verb
1 a : to represent or perform by action especially on the stage **b :** FEIGN, SIMULATE **c :** IMPERSONATE
2 *obsolete* **:** ACTUATE, ANIMATE
3 : to play the part of as if in a play ⟨*act* the man of the world⟩
4 : to behave in a manner suitable to ⟨*act* your age⟩
intransitive verb
1 a : to perform on the stage **b :** to behave as if performing on the stage **:** PRETEND
2 : to take action **:** MOVE ⟨think before *acting*⟩ ⟨*acted* favorably on the recommendation⟩
3 : to conduct oneself **:** BEHAVE ⟨*act* like a fool⟩
4 : to perform a specified function **:** SERVE ⟨trees *acting* as a windbreak⟩
5 : to produce an effect **:** WORK ⟨wait for a medicine to *act*⟩
6 *of a play* **:** to be capable of being performed ⟨the play *acts* well⟩
7 : to give a decision or award ⟨adjourned without *acting* on the bill⟩
— **act·abil·i·ty** \ˌak-tə-'bi-lə-tē\ *noun*
— **act·able** \'ak-tə-bəl\ *adjective*

Ac·tae·on \ak-'tē-ən\ *noun* [Latin, from Greek *Aktaiōn*]
: a hunter turned into a stag and killed by his own hounds for having seen Artemis bathing

ACTH \ˌā-(ˌ)sē-(ˌ)tē-'āch\ *noun* [adrenocorticotropic *hormone*] (1944)
: a protein hormone of the anterior lobe of the pituitary gland that stimulates the adrenal cortex — called also *adrenocorticotropic hormone*

ac·tin \'ak-tən\ *noun* [International Scientific Vocabulary, from Latin *actus*] (1942)
: a cellular protein found especially in microfilaments (as those comprising myofibrils) and active in muscular contraction, cellular movement, and maintenance of cell shape

actin- *or* **actini-** *or* **actino-** *combining form* [New Latin, ray, from Greek *aktin-*, *aktino-*, from *aktin-*, *aktis*; perhaps akin to Old English *ūhte* morning twilight, Latin *noct-*, *nox* night — more at NIGHT]
1 : having a radiate form ⟨*actino*lite⟩
2 : actinic radiation (as X rays) ⟨*actino*meter⟩

¹act·ing \'ak-tiŋ\ *noun* (1664)
: the art or practice of representing a character on a stage or before cameras

²acting *adjective* (1797)
1 : holding a temporary rank or position **:** performing services temporarily ⟨*acting* president⟩
2 a : suitable for stage performance ⟨an *acting* play⟩ **b :** prepared with directions for actors ⟨an *acting* text of a play⟩

ac·tin·i·an \ak-'ti-nē-ən\ *noun* [New Latin *actinia*, from Greek *aktin-*, *aktis*] (1888)
: SEA ANEMONE

ac·tin·ic \ak-'ti-nik\ *adjective* (1844)
: of, relating to, resulting from, or exhibiting actinism
— **ac·tin·i·cal·ly** \-ni-k(ə-)lē\ *adverb*

ac·ti·nide \'ak-tə-ˌnīd\ *noun* [International Scientific Vocabulary] (1945)
: any of the members of the series of elements that begins with actinium or thorium and ends with lawrencium — see PERIODIC TABLE table

ac·tin·ism \'ak-tə-ˌni-zəm\ *noun* (1844)
: the property of radiant energy especially in the visible and ultraviolet spectral regions by which chemical changes are produced

ac·tin·i·um \ak-'ti-nē-əm\ *noun* [New Latin] (1900)
: a radioactive trivalent metallic element that resembles lanthanum in chemical properties and that is found especially in pitchblende — see ELEMENT table

ac·tin·o·lite \ak-'ti-nᵊl-ˌīt\ *noun* (circa 1828)
: a bright or grayish green amphibole occurring in fibrous, radiate, or columnar forms

ac·ti·nom·e·ter \ˌak-tə-'nä-mə-tər\ *noun* (1833)
: any of various instruments for measuring the intensity of incident radiation; *especially* **:** one in which the intensity of radiation is measured by the speed of a photochemical reaction
— **ac·ti·no·me·tric** \-nō-'me-trik\ *adjective*
— **ac·ti·nom·e·try** \-'nä-mə-trē\ *noun*

ac·ti·no·mor·phic \ˌak-(ˌ)ti-nō-'mór-fik, -tə-nō-; ak-ˌti-nō-\ *adjective* [International Scientific Vocabulary] (1900)
: being radially symmetrical and capable of division by any longitudinal plane into essentially symmetrical halves ⟨an *actinomorphic* tulip flower⟩
— **ac·ti·no·mor·phy** \'ak-tə-nō-ˌmór-fē, ak-'ti-nō-\ *noun*

ac·ti·no·my·ces \ˌak-(ˌ)ti-nō-'mī-ˌsēz, -tə-nō-; ak-ˌti-nō-\ *noun, plural* **actinomyces** [New Latin, genus name, from *actin-* + Greek *mykēt-*, *mykēs* fungus; akin to Greek *myxa* mucus — more at MUCUS] (1882)
: any of a genus (*Actinomyces*) of filamentous or rod-shaped bacteria that includes usually commensal and sometimes pathogenic forms inhabiting mucosal surfaces especially of the oral cavity of warm-blooded vertebrates

ac·ti·no·my·cete \-'mī-ˌsēt, -mī-'sēt\ *noun* [ultimately from Greek *aktin-*, *aktis* + *mykēt-*, *mykēs*] (1911)
: any of an order (Actinomycetales) of filamentous or rod-shaped bacteria (as the actinomyces and streptomyces)
— **ac·ti·no·my·ce·tous** \-mī-'sē-təs\ *adjective*

ac·ti·no·my·cin \-'mī-sᵊn\ *noun* (1940)
: any of various red or yellow-red mostly toxic polypeptide antibiotics isolated from soil bacteria (especially *Streptomyces antibioticus*); *specifically* **:** one used to inhibit DNA or RNA synthesis

ac·ti·no·my·co·sis \-mī-'kō-səs\ *noun* [New Latin] (1882)
: infection with or disease caused by actinomycetes; *especially* **:** a chronic disease of cattle, swine, and humans characterized by hard granulomatous masses usually in the mouth and jaw
— **ac·ti·no·my·cot·ic** \-'kä-tik\ *adjective*

ac·ti·non \'ak-tə-ˌnän\ *noun* [New Latin, from *actinium*] (1926)
: a gaseous radioactive isotope of radon that has a half-life of about 4 seconds

ac·tion \'ak-shən\ *noun* (14th century)
1 : the initiating of a proceeding in a court of justice by which one demands or enforces one's right; *also* **:** the proceeding itself
2 : the bringing about of an alteration by force or through a natural agency
3 : the manner or method of performing: **a** **:** the deportment of an actor or speaker or his expression by means of attitude, voice, and gesture **b :** the style of movement of the feet and legs (as of a horse) **c :** a function of the body or one of its parts
4 : an act of will
5 a : a thing done **:** DEED **b :** the accomplishment of a thing usually over a period of time, in stages, or with the possibility of repetition **c** *plural* **:** BEHAVIOR, CONDUCT ⟨unscrupulous *actions*⟩ **d :** INITIATIVE, ENTERPRISE ⟨a man of *action*⟩
6 a (1) **:** an engagement between troops or ships (2) **:** combat in war ⟨gallantry in *action*⟩ **b** (1) **:** an event or series of events forming a literary composition (2) **:** the unfolding of the events of a drama or work of fiction (3) **:** PLOT **:** the movement of incidents in a plot **c :** the combination of circumstances that constitute the subject matter of a painting or sculpture
7 a : an operating mechanism **b :** the manner in which a mechanism or instrument operates
8 a : the price movement and trading volume of a commodity, security, or market **b :** the process of betting including the offering and acceptance of a bet and determination of a winner **c :** an opportunity for financial gain ⟨a piece of the *action*⟩
9 : the most vigorous, productive, or exciting activity in a particular field, area, or group ⟨they itch to go where the *action* is —D. J. Henahan⟩

ac·tion·able \'ak-sh(ə-)nə-bəl\ *adjective* (1591)
: subject to or affording ground for an action or suit at law
— **ac·tion·ably** \-blē\ *adverb*

ac·tion·less \'ak-shən-ləs\ *adjective* (circa 1817)
: marked by inaction **:** IMMOBILE

action painting *noun* (1952)
: abstract expressionism marked especially by the use of spontaneous techniques (as dribbling, splattering, or smearing)
— **action painter** *noun*

action potential *noun* (1926)
: a momentary change in electrical potential

\ə\ abut \ᵊ\ kitten \ər\ further \a\ ash \ā\ ace
\ä\ mop, mar \aů\ out \ch\ chin \e\ bet \ē\ easy
\g\ go \i\ hit \ī\ ice \j\ job \ŋ\ sing \ō\ go
\ò\ law \òi\ boy \th\ thin \t̲h̲\ the \ü\ loot \ů\ foot
\y\ yet \zh\ vision *see also* Guide to Pronunciation

(as between the inside of a nerve cell and the extracellular medium) that occurs when a cell or tissue has been activated by a stimulus

ac·ti·vate \'ak-tə-ˌvāt\ *verb* **-vat·ed; -vat·ing** (1626)
transitive verb
: to make active or more active: as **a** (1) **:** to make (as molecules) reactive or more reactive (2) **:** to convert (as a provitamin) into a biologically active derivative **b :** to make (a substance) radioactive **c :** to treat (as carbon or alumina) so as to improve adsorptive properties **d** (1) **:** to set up or formally institute (as a military unit) with the necessary personnel and equipment (2) **:** to put (an individual or unit) on active duty
intransitive verb
: to become active
— **ac·ti·va·tion** \ˌak-tə-'vā-shən\ *noun*
— **ac·ti·va·tor** \'ak-tə-ˌvā-tər\ *noun*
activated carbon *noun* (1921)
: a highly adsorbent powdered or granular carbon made usually by carbonization and chemical activation and used chiefly for purifying by adsorption — called also *activated charcoal*
activation analysis *noun* (1949)
: NEUTRON ACTIVATION ANALYSIS
activation energy *noun* (1940)
: the minimum amount of energy required to convert a normal stable molecule into a reactive molecule
ac·tive \'ak-tiv\ *adjective* [Middle English, from Middle French or Latin; Middle French *actif,* from Latin *activus,* from *actus,* past participle of *agere* to drive, do — more at AGENT] (14th century)
1 : characterized by action rather than by contemplation or speculation
2 : producing or involving action or movement
3 a *of a verb form or voice* **:** asserting that the person or thing represented by the grammatical subject performs the action represented by the verb ⟨*hits* in "he hits the ball" is *active*⟩ **b :** expressing action as distinct from mere existence or state
4 : quick in physical movement **:** LIVELY
5 : marked by vigorous activity **:** BUSY ⟨the stock market was *active*⟩
6 : requiring vigorous action or exertion ⟨*active* sports⟩
7 : having practical operation or results **:** EFFECTIVE ⟨an *active* law⟩
8 a : disposed to action **:** ENERGETIC ⟨took an *active* interest⟩ **b :** engaged in an action or activity ⟨an *active* club member⟩ **c** *of a volcano* **:** currently erupting or likely to erupt — compare DORMANT 2a, EXTINCT 1b **d :** characterized by emission of large amounts of electromagnetic energy ⟨an *active* galactic nucleus⟩
9 : engaged in full-time service especially in the armed forces ⟨*active* duty⟩
10 : marked by present operation, transaction, movement, or use ⟨*active* account⟩
11 a : capable of acting or reacting **:** reacting readily ⟨*active* nitrogen⟩ **b :** tending to progress or to cause degeneration ⟨*active* tuberculosis⟩ **c** *of an electronic circuit element* **:** capable of controlling voltages or currents **d** (1) **:** requiring the expenditure of energy ⟨*active* calcium ion uptake⟩ (2) **:** functioning by the emission of radiant energy ⟨radar is an *active* sensor⟩
12 : still eligible to win the pot in poker
13 : moving down the line **:** visiting in the set — used of couples in contredanses or square dances
— **active** *noun*
— **ac·tive·ly** *adverb*
— **ac·tive·ness** *noun*
active immunity *noun* (circa 1903)
: usually long-lasting immunity that is acquired through production of antibodies within the organism in response to the presence of antigens — compare PASSIVE IMMUNITY
active transport *noun* (1963)
: movement of a chemical substance by the expenditure of energy through a gradient (as across a cell membrane) in concentration or electrical potential and opposite to the direction of normal diffusion
ac·tiv·ism \'ak-ti-ˌvi-zəm\ *noun* (1915)
: a doctrine or practice that emphasizes direct vigorous action especially in support of or opposition to one side of a controversial issue
— **ac·tiv·ist** \-vist\ *noun or adjective*
— **ac·tiv·is·tic** \ˌak-ti-'vis-tik\ *adjective*
ac·tiv·i·ty \ak-'ti-və-tē\ *noun, plural* **-ties** (1530)
1 : the quality or state of being active
2 : vigorous or energetic action **:** LIVELINESS
3 : natural or normal function: as **a :** a process (as digestion) that an organism carries on or participates in by virtue of being alive **b :** a similar process actually or potentially involving mental function; *specifically* **:** an educational procedure designed to stimulate learning by firsthand experience
4 : an active force
5 a : a pursuit in which a person is active **b :** a form of organized, supervised, often extracurricular recreation
6 : an organizational unit for performing a specific function; *also* **:** its function or duties
act of God (circa 1859)
: an extraordinary interruption by a natural cause (as a flood or earthquake) of the usual course of events that experience, prescience, or care cannot reasonably foresee or prevent
ac·to·my·o·sin \ˌak-tə-'mī-ə-sən\ *noun* [International Scientific Vocabulary *actin + -o- + myosin*] (1942)
: a viscous contractile complex of actin and myosin concerned together with ATP in muscular contraction
ac·tor \'ak-tər *also* -ˌtȯr\ *noun* (15th century)
1 : one that acts **:** DOER
2 a : one who represents a character in a dramatic production **b :** a theatrical performer **c :** one that behaves as if acting a part
3 : one that takes part in any affair
— **ac·tor·ish** \-tə-rish\ *adjective*
act out *transitive verb* (1611)
1 a : to represent in action ⟨children *act out* what they read⟩ **b :** to translate into action ⟨unwilling to *act out* their beliefs⟩
2 : to express (as an impulse or a fantasy) directly in overt behavior without modification to comply with social norms
ac·tress \'ak-trəs\ *noun* (1676)
: a woman who is an actor
— **ac·tressy** \-trə-sē\ *adjective*
usage see -ESS
Acts \'akts\ *noun plural but singular in construction*
: a book in the New Testament narrating the beginnings of the Christian Church — called also *Acts of the Apostles;* see BIBLE table
ac·tu·al \'ak-ch(ə-w)əl, -sh(ə-w)əl\ *adjective* [Middle English *actuel,* from Middle French, from Late Latin *actualis,* from Latin *actus* act] (14th century)
1 *obsolete* **:** ACTIVE
2 a : existing in act and not merely potentially **b :** existing in fact or reality ⟨*actual* and imagined conditions⟩ **c :** not false or apparent ⟨*actual* costs⟩
3 : existing or occurring at the time **:** CURRENT ⟨caught in the *actual* commission of a crime⟩
actual cash value *noun* (circa 1946)
: money equal to the cost of replacing lost, stolen, or damaged property after depreciation
ac·tu·al·i·ty \ˌak-chə-'wa-lə-tē, ˌak-shə-\ *noun, plural* **-ties** (1652)
1 : the quality or state of being actual
2 : something that is actual **:** FACT, REALITY ⟨possible risks which have been seized upon as *actualities* —T. S. Eliot⟩
ac·tu·al·ize \'ak-ch(ə-w)ə-ˌlīz, -sh(ə-w)ə-ˌlīz\ *verb* **-ized; -iz·ing** (1701)
transitive verb
: to make actual **:** REALIZE
intransitive verb
: to become actual
— **ac·tu·al·iza·tion** \ˌak-ch(ə-w)ə-lə-'zā-shən, -sh(ə-w)ə-lə-\ *noun*
ac·tu·al·ly \'ak-ch(ə-w)ə-lē, -sh(ə-w)ə-lē; 'aksh-lē, 'aks-\ *adverb* (15th century)
1 : in act or in fact **:** REALLY ⟨nominally but not *actually* independent —Karl Loewenstein⟩ ⟨don't know how old they *actually* are⟩ ⟨*actually,* they just arrived⟩
2 : in point of fact — in truth — used to suggest something unexpected ⟨I have *actually* been invited⟩ ⟨he could *actually* read the Greek⟩
ac·tu·ar·i·al \ˌak-chə-'wer-ē-əl, -shə-\ *adjective* (1869)
1 : of or relating to actuaries
2 : relating to statistical calculation especially of life expectancy
— **ac·tu·ar·i·al·ly** \-ē-ə-lē\ *adverb*
ac·tu·ary \'ak-chə-ˌwer-ē, -shə-\ *noun, plural* **-ar·ies** [Latin *actuarius* shorthand writer, alteration of *actarius,* from *actum* record — more at ACTIVE] (1553)
1 *obsolete* **:** CLERK, REGISTRAR
2 : one who calculates insurance and annuity premiums, reserves, and dividends
ac·tu·ate \'ak-chə-ˌwāt, -shə-\ *transitive verb* **-at·ed; -at·ing** [Medieval Latin *actuatus,* past participle of *actuare* to execute, from Latin *actus* act] (1645)
1 : to put into mechanical action or motion
2 : to move to action
synonym see MOVE
— **ac·tu·a·tion** \ˌak-chə-'wā-shən, -shə-\ *noun*
ac·tu·a·tor \'ak-chə-ˌwā-tər, -shə-\ *noun* (circa 1864)
: one that actuates; *specifically* **:** a mechanical device for moving or controlling something
act up *intransitive verb* (1903)
1 : to act in a way different from that which is normal or expected: as **a :** to behave in an unruly, recalcitrant, or capricious manner **b :** SHOW OFF **c :** to function improperly ⟨this typewriter is *acting up* again⟩
2 : to become active or acute after being quiescent ⟨her rheumatism started to *act up*⟩
acu·ity \ə-'kyü-ə-tē, a-\ *noun, plural* **-ities** [Middle French *acuité,* from Late Latin *acuitat-, acuitas,* from Latin *acuere*] (1543)
: keenness of perception **:** SHARPNESS
acu·le·ate \ə-'kyü-lē-ət\ *adjective* [Latin *aculeatus* having stings, from *aculeus* sting, from *acus*] (1875)
: relating to or being hymenopterans (as bees, ants, and many wasps) of a division (Aculeata) typically having the ovipositor modified into a sting
acu·men \ə-'kyü-mən, 'a-kyə-mən\ *noun* [Latin *acumin-, acumen,* literally, point, from *acuere*] (circa 1580)
: keenness and depth of perception, discernment, or discrimination especially in practical matters **:** SHREWDNESS
synonym see DISCERNMENT
acu·mi·nate \ə-'kyü-mə-nət\ *adjective* (1646)
: tapering to a slender point
acu·pres·sure \'a-kyə-ˌpre-shər, 'a-kə-\ *noun* (1958)
: SHIATSU
acu·punc·ture \-ˌpəŋ(k)-chər\ *noun* [Latin *acus* + English *puncture*] (1684)
: an originally Chinese practice of puncturing the body (as with needles) at specific points to cure disease or relieve pain (as in surgery)
— **acu·punc·tur·ist** \-ˌpəŋ(k)-chə-rist\ *noun*
acute \ə-'kyüt\ *adjective* **acut·er; acut·est** [Latin *acutus,* past participle of *acuere* to sharpen, from *acus* needle; akin to Latin *acer* sharp — more at EDGE] (14th century)

1 a (1) **:** characterized by sharpness or severity ⟨*acute* pain⟩ (2) **:** having a sudden onset, sharp rise, and short course ⟨*acute* disease⟩ **b :** lasting a short time ⟨*acute* experiments⟩
2 : ending in a sharp point: as **a :** being or forming an angle measuring less than 90 degrees ⟨*acute* angle⟩ **b :** composed of acute angles ⟨*acute* triangle⟩
3 a *of an accent mark* **:** having the form ´ **b :** marked with an acute accent **c :** of the variety indicated by an acute accent
4 a : marked by keen discernment or intellectual perception especially of subtle distinctions **:** PENETRATING ⟨an *acute* thinker⟩ **b :** responsive to slight impressions or stimuli ⟨*acute* hearing⟩
5 : felt, perceived, or experienced intensely ⟨*acute* distress⟩
6 : seriously demanding urgent attention ☆
— **acute·ly** *adverb*
— **acute·ness** *noun*
acy·clic \(ˌ)ā-ˈsī-klik, -ˈsi-\ *adjective* (1878)
: not cyclic: as **a :** not disposed in whorls or cycles **b :** having an open-chain structure **:** ALIPHATIC ⟨an *acyclic* compound⟩
acy·clo·vir \(ˌ)ā-ˈsī-klō-ˌvir\ *noun* [²a- + cycl- + virus] (1979)
: a cyclic nucleoside $C_8H_{11}N_5O_3$ used especially to treat the symptoms of the genital form of herpes simplex
ac·yl \ˈa-səl\ *noun, often attributive* [International Scientific Vocabulary, from *acid*] (1899)
: a radical RCO− derived usually from an organic acid by removal of the hydroxyl from all acid groups — often used in combination
ac·yl·ate \ˈa-sə-ˌlāt\ *transitive verb* **-at·ed; -at·ing** (1907)
: to introduce an acyl group into
— **ac·yl·a·tion** \ˌa-sə-ˈlā-shən\ *noun*
¹ad \ˈad\ *noun, often attributive* (1841)
1 : ADVERTISEMENT 2
2 : ADVERTISING
²ad *noun* (1947)
: ADVANTAGE 4
ad- *or* **ac-** *or* **af-** *or* **ag-** *or* **al-** *or* **ap-** *or* **as-** *or* **at-** *prefix* [Middle English, from Middle French, Old French & Latin; Middle French, from Old French, from Latin, from *ad* — more at AT]
1 : to **:** toward — usually *ac-* before *c, k,* or *q* ⟨*acculturation*⟩ and *af-* before *f* ⟨*affluent*⟩ and *ag-* before *g* ⟨*aggradation*⟩ and *al-* before *l* ⟨*alliteration*⟩ and *ap-* before *p* ⟨*apportion*⟩ and *as-* before *s* ⟨*assuasive*⟩ and *at-* before *t* ⟨*attune*⟩ and *ad-* before other sounds but sometimes *ad-* even before one of the listed consonants ⟨*adsorb*⟩
2 : near **:** adjacent to — in this sense always in the form *ad-* ⟨*adrenal*⟩
¹-ad \ˌad, əd\ *adverb suffix* [Latin *ad*]
: in the direction of **:** toward ⟨cephal*ad*⟩
²-ad *noun suffix* [probably from New Latin *-ad-, -as,* from Greek, suffix denoting descent from or connection with]
: member of a botanical group ⟨bromeli*ad*⟩
Ada \ˈā-də\ *trademark*
— used for a structured computer programming language
ad·age \ˈa-dij\ *noun* [Middle French, from Latin *adagium,* from *ad-* + *-agium* (akin to *aio* I say); akin to Greek *ē* he said] (1548)
: a saying often in metaphorical form that embodies a common observation □
¹ada·gio \ə-ˈdä-j(ē-ˌ)ō, ä-, -zh(ē-ˌ)ō\ *adverb or adjective* [Italian, from *ad* to + *agio* ease] (1724)
: at a slow tempo — used chiefly as a direction in music
²adagio *noun, plural* **-gios** (1754)
1 : a musical composition or movement in adagio tempo
2 : a ballet duet by a man and woman or a mixed trio displaying difficult feats of balance, lifting, or spinning
¹Ad·am \ˈa-dəm\ *noun* [Middle English, from Late Latin, from Greek, from Hebrew *Ādhām*]

1 : the first man and father by Eve of Cain and Abel
2 : the unregenerate nature of man — used especially in the phrase *the old Adam*
— **Adam·ic** \ə-ˈda-mik\ *or* **Adam·i·cal** \-mi-kəl\ *adjective*
²Adam *adjective* [Robert *Adam* & James *Adam*] (1872)
: of, relating to, or being an 18th century decorative style (as of furniture) characterized by straight lines, surface decoration, and conventional designs (as festooned garlands and medallions)
ad·a·mance \ˈa-də-mən(t)s\ *noun* (1954)
: ADAMANCY
ad·a·man·cy \-mən(t)-sē\ *noun* [²adamant + -cy] (1937)
: OBSTINACY
adam–and–eve \ˌa-də-mən-ˈ(d)ēv\ *noun* (1807)
: PUTTYROOT
¹ad·a·mant \ˈa-də-mənt, -ˌmant\ *noun* [Middle English, from Middle French, from Latin *adamant-, adamas* hardest metal, diamond, from Greek] (14th century)
1 : a stone (as a diamond) formerly believed to be of impenetrable hardness
2 : an unbreakable or extremely hard substance
²adamant *adjective* (1923)
: unshakable or immovable especially in opposition **:** UNYIELDING
synonym see INFLEXIBLE
— **ad·a·mant·ly** *adverb*
ad·a·man·tine \ˌa-də-ˈman-ˌtēn, -ˌtīn, -ˈman-tᵊn\ *adjective* [Middle English, from Latin *adamantinus,* from Greek *adamantinos,* from *adamant-, adamas*] (13th century)
1 : made of or having the quality of adamant
2 : rigidly firm **:** UNYIELDING
3 : resembling the diamond in hardness or luster
Adam's apple *noun* (circa 1775)
: the projection in the front of the neck formed by the largest cartilage of the larynx
Adam's needle *noun* (circa 1760)
: an often cultivated yucca (*Yucca filamentosa*) of coastal pine barrens of the eastern U.S. with a basal rosette of sharp-tipped leaves having loose threads along the margins
adapt \ə-ˈdapt, a-\ *verb* [French or Latin; French *adapter,* from Latin *adaptare,* from *ad-* + *aptare* to fit, from *aptus* apt, fit] (15th century)
transitive verb
: to make fit (as for a specific or new use or situation) often by modification
intransitive verb
: to become adapted ☆
— **adapt·ed·ness** *noun*
adapt·able \ə-ˈdap-tə-bəl, a-\ *adjective* (1800)
: capable of being adapted **:** SUITABLE
synonym see PLASTIC
— **adapt·abil·i·ty** \-ˌdap-tə-ˈbi-lə-tē\ *noun*
ad·ap·ta·tion \ˌa-ˌdap-ˈtā-shən, -dəp-\ *noun* (1610)
1 : the act or process of adapting **:** the state of being adapted
2 : adjustment to environmental conditions: as **a :** adjustment of a sense organ to the intensity or quality of stimulation **b :** modification of an organism or its parts that makes it more fit for existence under the conditions of its environment
3 : something that is adapted; *specifically* **:** a composition rewritten into a new form
— **ad·ap·ta·tion·al** \-shnəl, -shə-nᵊl\ *adjective*
— **ad·ap·ta·tion·al·ly** *adverb*
adapt·er *also* **adap·tor** \ə-ˈdap-tər, a-\ *noun* (1801)
1 : one that adapts
2 a : a device for connecting two parts (as of different diameters) of an apparatus **b :** an attachment for adapting apparatus for uses not originally intended

adap·tion \ə-ˈdap-shən, a-\ *noun* (1704)
: ADAPTATION
adap·tive \ə-ˈdap-tiv, a-\ *adjective* (1824)
: showing or having a capacity for or tendency toward adaptation
— **adap·tive·ly** *adverb*
— **adap·tive·ness** *noun*
— **ad·ap·tiv·i·ty** \ˌa-ˌdap-ˈti-və-tē\ *noun*
adaptive radiation *noun* (1902)
: evolutionary diversification of a generalized ancestral form with production of a number of adaptively specialized forms
Adar \ä-ˈdär, ˈä-\ *noun* [Middle English, from Hebrew *Ădhār*] (14th century)
: the 6th month of the civil year or the 12th month of the ecclesiastical year in the Jewish calendar — see MONTH table
Adar She·ni \ä-ˌdär-shä-ˈnē\ *noun* [Hebrew *Ădhār Shēnī* second Adar] (circa 1901)
: VEADAR
ad·ax·i·al \(ˌ)a-ˈdak-sē-əl\ *adjective* (circa 1900)

☆ **SYNONYMS**
Acute, critical, crucial mean of uncertain outcome. ACUTE stresses intensification of conditions leading to a culmination or breaking point ⟨an *acute* housing shortage⟩. CRITICAL adds to ACUTE implications of imminent change, of attendant suspense, and of decisiveness in the outcome ⟨the war has entered a *critical* phase⟩. CRUCIAL suggests a dividing of the ways and often a test or trial involving the determination of a future course or direction ⟨a *crucial* vote⟩. See in addition SHARP.

Adapt, adjust, accommodate, conform, reconcile mean to bring one thing into correspondence with another. ADAPT implies a modification according to changing circumstances ⟨*adapted* themselves to the warmer climate⟩. ADJUST suggests bringing into a close and exact correspondence or harmony such as exists between parts of a mechanism ⟨*adjusted* the budget to allow for inflation⟩. ACCOMMODATE may suggest yielding or compromising to effect a correspondence ⟨*accommodated* his political beliefs in order to win⟩. CONFORM applies to bringing into accordance with a pattern, example, or principle ⟨refused to *conform* to society's idea of morality⟩. RECONCILE implies the demonstration of the underlying compatibility of things that seem to be incompatible ⟨tried to *reconcile* what they said with what I knew⟩.

□ **USAGE**
adage Quite a few commentators call *old adage* redundant because they say *adage* means "an old saying," a phrase Noah Webster did use in his definition of 1828. But *old* has been absent from Merriam-Webster definitions for more than 50 years—adages simply are not always old ⟨the popular *adage* is that 12 years is the ideal median age —Michael Jackson⟩. Even so, *old* has gone with *adage* from the beginning ⟨that old *adage* 'Much courtesy, much subtlety' —Thomas Nashe (1594)⟩. It is sometimes used actually to impute age ⟨racegoers remembered the old *adage,* "Second in the Trial, first in the Derby" —Audax Minor⟩ and is sometimes merely casual ⟨the old *adage* "misery loves company" —Natalie Babbitt⟩. It may be used where it seems apt.

\ə\ **abut** \ᵊ\ **kitten** \ər\ **further** \a\ **ash** \ā\ **ace**
\ä\ **mop, mar** \aů\ **out** \ch\ **chin** \e\ **bet** \ē\ **easy**
\g\ **go** \i\ **hit** \ī\ **ice** \j\ **job** \ŋ\ **sing** \ō\ **go**
\ȯ\ **law** \ȯi\ **boy** \th\ **thin** \t̶h\ **the** \ü\ **loot** \ů\ **foot**
\y\ **yet** \zh\ **vision** *see also* Guide to Pronunciation

: situated on the same side as or facing the axis (as of an organ) ⟨the *adaxial* or upper surface of a leaf⟩

add \'ad\ *verb* [Middle English, from Latin *addere,* from *ad-* + *-dere* to put — more at DO] (14th century)
transitive verb
1 : to join or unite so as to bring about an increase or improvement ⟨*adds* 60 acres to his land⟩ ⟨wine *adds* a creative touch to cooking⟩
2 : to say further **:** APPEND
3 : to combine (numbers) into an equivalent simple quantity or number
4 : to include as a member of a group ⟨don't forget to *add* me in⟩
intransitive verb
1 a : to perform addition **b :** to come together or unite by addition
2 a : to serve as an addition ⟨the movie will *add* to his fame⟩ **b :** to make an addition ⟨*add*-ed to her savings⟩
— **add·able** *or* **add·ible** \'a-də-bəl\ *adjective*

ad·dax \'a-ˌdaks\ *noun, plural* **ad·dax·es** [Latin] (1693)
: a large light-colored Saharan antelope (*Addax nasomaculatus*) that has long spiralling horns

ad·dend \'a-ˌdend, ə-'dend\ *noun* [short for *addendum*] (1674)
: a number to be added to another

ad·den·dum \ə-'den-dəm\ *noun, plural* **-den·da** \-'den-də\ [Latin, neuter of *addendus,* gerundive of *addere*] (1684)
1 : a thing added **:** ADDITION
2 : a supplement to a book — often used in plural but singular in construction

¹ad·der \'a-dər\ *noun* [Middle English, alteration (by false division of *a naddre*) of *naddre,* from Old English *nædre;* akin to Old High German *nātara* adder, Latin *natrix* water snake] (14th century)
1 : the common venomous viper (*Vipera berus*) of Europe; *broadly* **:** a terrestrial viper (family Viperidae)
2 : any of several North American snakes (as the hognose snakes) that are harmless but are popularly believed to be venomous

²add·er \'a-dər\ *noun* (1580)
: one that adds; *especially* **:** a device (as in a computer) that performs addition

adder 1

ad·der's-tongue \'a-dərz-ˌtəŋ\ *noun* (1578)
1 : any of a genus (*Ophioglossum,* family Ophioglossaceae) of small ferns having a spore-bearing stalk resembling a serpent's tongue
2 : DOGTOOTH VIOLET

¹ad·dict \ə-'dikt\ *transitive verb* [Latin *addictus,* past participle of *addicere* to favor, from *ad-* + *dicere* to say — more at DICTION] (1534)
1 : to devote or surrender (oneself) to something habitually or obsessively ⟨*addicted* to gambling⟩
2 : to cause addiction to a substance in

²ad·dict \'a-(ˌ)dikt\ *noun* (1909)
1 : one who is addicted to a substance
2 : DEVOTEE ⟨a detective novel *addict*⟩

ad·dic·tion \ə-'dik-shən, a-\ *noun* (1599)
1 : the quality or state of being addicted ⟨*addiction* to reading⟩
2 : compulsive need for and use of a habit-forming substance (as heroin, nicotine, or alcohol) characterized by tolerance and by well-defined physiological symptoms upon withdrawal; *broadly* **:** persistent compulsive use of a substance known by the user to be harmful

ad·dic·tive \-'dik-tiv\ *adjective* (1939)
: causing or characterized by addiction

Ad·di·son's disease \'a-də-sənz-\ *noun* [Thomas *Addison* (died 1860) English physician] (circa 1856)
: a destructive disease marked by deficient adrenocortical secretion and characterized by extreme weakness, loss of weight, low blood pressure, gastrointestinal disturbances, and brownish pigmentation of the skin and mucous membranes

ad·di·tion \ə-'di-shən, a-\ *noun* [Middle English, from Middle French, from Latin *addition-, additio,* from *addere*] (14th century)
1 : a part added (as to a building or residential section)
2 : the result of adding **:** INCREASE
3 : the act or process of adding; *especially* **:** the operation of combining numbers so as to obtain an equivalent simple quantity
4 : direct chemical combination of substances into a single product
— **in addition :** ²BESIDES, ALSO
— **in addition to :** combined or associated with **:** ¹BESIDES 2

ad·di·tion·al \-'dish-nəl, -'di-shə-n°l\ *adjective* (1646)
: existing by way of addition **:** ADDED

ad·di·tion·al·ly \-'dish-nə-lē, -'di-shən-lē, -'di-shə-n°l-ē\ *adverb* (circa 1665)
: in or by way of addition **:** FURTHERMORE

¹ad·di·tive \'a-də-tiv\ *adjective* (1699)
1 : of, relating to, or characterized by addition
2 : produced by addition
3 : characterized by, being, or producing effects (as drug responses or gene products) that when the causative factors act together are the sum of their individual effects
— **ad·di·tive·ly** *adverb*
— **ad·di·tiv·i·ty** \ˌa-də-'ti-və-tē\ *noun*

²additive *noun* (1945)
: a substance added to another in relatively small amounts to effect a desired change in properties ⟨food *additives*⟩

additive identity *noun* (1960)
: an identity element (as 0 in the group of whole numbers under the operation of addition) that in a given mathematical system leaves unchanged any element to which it is added

additive inverse *noun* (1958)
: a number that when added to a given number gives zero ⟨the *additive inverse* of 4 is −4⟩ — compare OPPOSITE 3

¹ad·dle \'a-d°l\ *adjective* [Middle English *adel* filth, from Old English *adela;* akin to Middle Low German *adele* liquid manure] (1592)
1 *of an egg* **:** ROTTEN
2 : CONFUSED

²addle *verb* **ad·dled; ad·dling** \'ad-liŋ, 'a-d°l-iŋ\ (circa 1712)
transitive verb
: to throw into confusion **:** CONFOUND
intransitive verb
1 : to become rotten **:** SPOIL
2 : to become confused

ad·dle-pat·ed \ˌa-d°l-ˌpā-təd\ *adjective* (1630)
1 : being mixed up **:** CONFUSED
2 : ECCENTRIC

¹add-on *noun* (1946)
: something added on: as **a :** a sum or amount added on **b :** something (as an accessory or added feature) that enhances the thing it is added to

²add-on \'a-ˌdän, -ˌdòn\ *adjective* (1955)
1 : being or able to be added on
2 : able to be added to ⟨*add-on* certificates of deposit⟩

¹ad·dress \ə-'dres, a- *also* 'a-ˌdres\ *verb* [Middle English *adressen,* from Middle French *adresser,* from *a-* (from Latin *ad-*) + *dresser* to arrange — more at DRESS] (14th century)
transitive verb
1 *archaic* **a :** DIRECT, AIM **b :** to direct to go **:** SEND
2 a : to direct the efforts or attention of (oneself) ⟨will *address* himself to the problem⟩ **b**

: to deal with **:** TREAT ⟨intrigued by the chance to *address* important issues —I. L. Horowitz⟩
3 *archaic* **:** to make ready; *especially* **:** DRESS
4 a : to communicate directly ⟨*addresses* his thanks to his host⟩ **b :** to speak or write directly to; *especially* **:** to deliver a formal speech to
5 a : to mark directions for delivery on ⟨*address* a letter⟩ **b :** to consign to the care of another (as an agent or factor)
6 : to greet by a prescribed form
7 : to adjust the club preparatory to hitting (a golf ball)
8 : to identify (as a peripheral or memory location) by an address or a name for information transfer
intransitive verb
obsolete **:** to direct one's speech or attentions
— **ad·dress·er** *noun*

²ad·dress \ə-'dres, *for 5 & 7 & 4 also* 'a-ˌdres\ *noun* (1539)
1 : dutiful and courteous attention especially in courtship — usually used in plural
2 a : readiness and capability for dealing (as with a person or problem) skillfully and smoothly **:** ADROITNESS **b** *obsolete* **:** a making ready; *also* **:** a state of preparedness
3 a : manner of bearing oneself ⟨a man of rude *address*⟩ **b :** manner of speaking or singing **:** DELIVERY
4 : a formal communication; *especially* **:** a prepared speech delivered to a special audience or on a special occasion
5 a : a place where a person or organization may be communicated with **b :** directions for delivery on the outside of an object (as a letter or package) **c :** the designation of place of delivery placed between the heading and salutation on a business letter
6 : a preparatory position of the player and club in golf
7 : a location (as in the memory of a computer) where particular information is stored; *also* **:** the digits that identify such a location
synonym see TACT

ad·dress·able \ə-'dre-sə-bəl\ *adjective* (1953)
1 : able to be addressed **:** directly accessible ⟨*addressable* registers in a computer⟩
2 : of or relating to a subscription television system that uses decoders addressable by the system operator
— **ad·dress·abil·i·ty** \ə-ˌdre-sə-'bi-lə-tē\ *noun*

ad·dress·ee \ˌa-ˌdre-'sē, ə-ˌdre-'sē\ *noun* (1810)
: one to whom something is addressed

ad·duce \ə-'düs *also* -'dyüs\ *transitive verb* **ad·duced; ad·duc·ing** [Latin *adducere,* literally, to lead to, from *ad-* + *ducere* to lead — more at TOW] (15th century)
: to offer as example, reason, or proof in discussion or analysis
— **ad·duc·er** *noun*

¹ad·duct \ə-'dəkt, a-\ *transitive verb* [Latin *adductus,* past participle of *adducere*] (circa 1839)
: to draw (as a limb) toward or past the median axis of the body; *also* **:** to bring together (similar parts) ⟨*adduct* the fingers⟩
— **ad·duc·tive** \-'dək-tiv\ *adjective*

²ad·duct \'a-ˌdəkt\ *noun* [German *Addukt,* from Latin *adductus*] (1941)
: a chemical addition product

ad·duc·tion \ə-'dək-shən, a-\ *noun* (14th century)
1 : the action of adducting **:** the state of being adducted
2 : the act or action of adducing

ad·duc·tor \-'dək-tər\ *noun* [New Latin, from Latin, one that draws to, from *adductus*] (1615)
1 : a muscle that draws a part toward the median line of the body or toward the axis of an extremity
2 : a muscle that closes the valves of a bivalve mollusk

add up (1850)
intransitive verb
1 a : to come to the expected total ⟨the bill doesn't *add up*⟩ **b :** to form an intelligible pattern **:** make sense ⟨her story just doesn't *add up*⟩
2 a : AMOUNT 1b — used with *to* ⟨the play *adds up* to a lot of laughs⟩ **b :** to amount to a lot ⟨just a little each time, but it all *adds up*⟩
transitive verb
: to form an opinion of ⟨*added* him *up* at a glance⟩

-ade *noun suffix* [Middle English, from Middle French, from Old Provençal *-ada,* from Late Latin *-ata,* from Latin, feminine of *-atus* -ate]
1 : act **:** action ⟨block*ade*⟩
2 : product; *especially* **:** sweet drink ⟨lime*ade*⟩

Adé·lie penguin \ə-'dā-lē-\ *noun* [*Adélie* Coast, Antarctica] (1907)
: a small antarctic penguin (*Pygoscelis adeliae*) — called also *Adélie*

Adélie penguin

-adelphous *adjective combining form* [probably from New Latin *-adelphus,* from Greek *adelphos* brother, from *ha-, a-* together (akin to *homos* same) + *delphys* womb — more at SAME, DOLPHIN]
: having (such or so many) stamen fascicles ⟨mon*adelphous*⟩

aden- *or* **adeno-** *combining form* [New Latin, from Greek, from *aden-, adēn;* akin to Latin *inguen* groin]
: gland ⟨*adenine*⟩ **:** adenoid ⟨*adeno*virus⟩

ad·e·nine \'a-dⁿ-ẹ̄n\ *noun* [International Scientific Vocabulary, from its presence in glandular tissue] (1885)
: a purine base $C_5H_5N_5$ that codes hereditary information in the genetic code in DNA and RNA — compare CYTOSINE, GUANINE, THYMINE, URACIL

ad·e·ni·tis \ˌa-dⁿ-'ī-təs\ *noun* [New Latin] (circa 1848)
: inflammation of a gland; *especially* **:** LYMPHADENITIS

ad·e·no·car·ci·no·ma \ˌa-dⁿ-(ˌ)ō-ˌkär-sⁿ-'ō-mə\ *noun* [New Latin] (circa 1889)
: a malignant tumor originating in glandular epithelium
— **ad·e·no·car·ci·no·ma·tous** \-mə-təs\ *adjective*

ad·e·no·hy·poph·y·sis \-hī-'pä-fə-səs\ *noun, plural* **-y·ses** \-fə-ˌsēz\ [New Latin] (1935)
: the anterior glandular lobe of the pituitary gland
— **ad·e·no·hy·poph·y·se·al** \-(ˌ)hī-ˌpä-fə-'sē-əl\ *or* **ad·e·no·hy·po·phys·i·al** \-ˌhī-pə-'fi-zē-əl\ *adjective*

¹ad·e·noid \'a-dⁿ-ˌóid, 'a-dⁿ-ˌnóid\ *noun* [Greek *adenoeidēs* glandular, from *adēn*] (circa 1890)
: an enlarged mass of lymphoid tissue at the back of the pharynx characteristically obstructing breathing — usually used in plural

²adenoid *adjective* (circa 1947)
1 : of or relating to the adenoids
2 : relating to, affected with, or associated with abnormally enlarged adenoids ⟨a severe *adenoid* condition⟩ ⟨*adenoid* facies⟩

ad·e·noi·dal \ˌa-dⁿ-'ói-dⁿl\ *adjective* (1919)
: exhibiting the characteristics (as snoring, mouth breathing, and voice nasality) of one affected with abnormally enlarged adenoids **:** ADENOID ⟨an *adenoidal* tenor⟩ — not usually used technically

ad·e·no·ma \ˌa-dⁿ-'ō-mə\ *noun, plural* **-mas** *also* **-ma·ta** \-mə-tə\ [New Latin *adenomat-, adenoma*] (1870)
: a benign tumor of a glandular structure or of glandular origin
— **ad·e·no·ma·tous** \-mə-təs\ *adjective*

aden·o·sine \ə-'de-nə-ˌsēn, -sən\ *noun* [International Scientific Vocabulary, blend of *adenine* and *ribose*] (circa 1909)
: a nucleoside $C_{10}H_{13}N_5O_4$ that is a constituent of RNA yielding adenine and ribose on hydrolysis

adenosine diphosphate *noun* (1938)
: ADP

adenosine mo·no·phos·phate \-ˌmä-nə-'fäs-ˌfāt, -ˌmō-\ *noun* (1950)
: AMP

adenosine 3',5'–monophosphate \-ˌthrē-ˌfīv-\ *noun* (1970)
: CYCLIC AMP

adenosine tri·phos·pha·tase \-trī-'fäs-fə-ˌtās, -ˌtāz\ *noun* (1943)
: ATPASE

adenosine tri·phos·phate \-trī-'fäs-ˌfāt\ *noun* (1938)
: ATP

ad·e·no·vi·rus \ˌa-dⁿn-ō-'vī-rəs\ *noun* (1956)
: any of a group of DNA-containing viruses originally identified in human adenoid tissue, causing respiratory diseases (as catarrh), and including some capable of inducing malignant tumors in experimental animals
— **ad·e·no·vi·ral** \-rəl\ *adjective*

ad·e·nyl·ate cy·clase \ə-ˌde-nⁿl-ət-'sī-ˌklās, -ˌāt-, -ˌklāz; ˌa-dⁿn-i-lət-, -ə-ˌlāt-\ *noun* (1968)
: an enzyme that catalyzes the formation of cyclic AMP from ATP

ad·e·nyl cyclase \'a-dⁿn-ˌil-\ *noun* [*adenine* + *-yl*] (1968)
: ADENYLATE CYCLASE

ad·e·nyl·ic acid \'a-dⁿn-i-lik-\ *noun* (1894)
: AMP

¹ad·ept \'a-ˌdept, ə-'dept, a-'\ *noun* [New Latin *adeptus* alchemist who has attained the knowledge of how to change base metals into gold, from Latin, past participle of *adipisci* to attain, from *ad-* + *apisci* to reach — more at APT] (1709)
: a highly skilled or well-trained individual **:** EXPERT ⟨an *adept* at chess⟩

²adept \ə-'dept *also* 'a-ˌdept\ *adjective* (circa 1691)
: thoroughly proficient **:** EXPERT
synonym see PROFICIENT
— **adept·ly** \ə-'dep-(t)lē, a-\ *adverb*
— **adept·ness** \-'dep(t)-nəs\ *noun*

ad·e·qua·cy \'a-di-kwə-sē\ *noun, plural* **-cies** (1808)
: the quality or state of being adequate

ad·e·quate \-kwət\ *adjective* [Latin *adaequatus,* past participle of *adaequare* to make equal, from *ad-* + *aequare* to equal — more at EQUABLE] (circa 1617)
1 : sufficient for a specific requirement ⟨*adequate* taxation of goods⟩; *also* **:** barely sufficient or satisfactory ⟨her first performance was merely *adequate*⟩
2 : lawfully and reasonably sufficient
synonym see SUFFICIENT
— **ad·e·quate·ly** *adverb*
— **ad·e·quate·ness** *noun*

ad eun·dem \ˌa-dē-'ən-dəm\ *or* **ad eundem gra·dum** \-'grā-dəm\ *adverb or adjective* [New Latin *ad eundem gradum*] (1711)
: to, in, or of the same rank — used especially of the honorary granting of academic standing or a degree by a university to one whose actual work was done elsewhere

¹à deux \(ˌ)ä-'də(r), (ˌ)à-dœ̄\ *adjective* [French] (1886)
: involving two people especially in private ⟨a cozy evening *à deux*⟩

²à deux *adverb* (1927)
: privately or intimately with only two present ⟨dined *à deux*⟩

ad·here \ad-'hir, əd-\ *verb* **ad·hered; ad·her·ing** [Middle French or Latin; Middle French *adhérer,* from Latin *adhaerēre,* from *ad-* + *haerēre* to stick] (1536)
intransitive verb
1 : to give support or maintain loyalty
2 *obsolete* **:** ACCORD 3

3 : to hold fast or stick by or as if by gluing, suction, grasping, or fusing
4 : to bind oneself to observance
transitive verb
: to cause to stick fast
synonym see STICK

ad·her·ence \-'hir-ən(t)s\ *noun* (1531)
1 : the act, action, or quality of adhering
2 : steady or faithful attachment **:** FIDELITY

¹ad·her·ent \ad-'hir-ənt, əd-\ *adjective* [Middle English, from Middle French or Latin; Middle French *adhérent,* from Latin *adhaerent-, adhaerens,* present participle of *adhaerēre*] (15th century)
1 : able or tending to adhere
2 : connected or associated with especially by contract
3 : ADNATE
— **ad·her·ent·ly** *adverb*

²adherent *noun* (15th century)
: one that adheres: as **a :** a follower of a leader, party, or profession **b :** a believer in or advocate especially of a particular idea or church
synonym see FOLLOWER

ad·he·sion \ad-'hē-zhən, əd-\ *noun* [French or Latin; French *adhésion,* from Latin *adhaesion-, adhaesio,* from *adhaerēre*] (1624)
1 : steady or firm attachment **:** ADHERENCE
2 : the action or state of adhering
3 : the abnormal union of separate tissue surfaces by new fibrous tissue resulting from an inflammatory process; *also* **:** the newly formed uniting tissue
4 : agreement to join ⟨*adhesion* of all nations to a copyright convention⟩
5 : the molecular attraction exerted between the surfaces of bodies in contact
— **ad·he·sion·al** \-'hēzh-nəl, -'hē-zhə-nⁿl\ *adjective*

¹ad·he·sive \-'hē-siv, -ziv\ *adjective* (1670)
1 : tending to remain in association or memory
2 : tending to adhere or cause adherence
3 : prepared for adhering
— **ad·he·sive·ly** *adverb*
— **ad·he·sive·ness** *noun*

²adhesive *noun* (1912)
1 : an adhesive substance (as glue or cement)
2 : a postage stamp with a gummed back

adhesive binding *noun* (1955)
: PERFECT BINDING
— **ad·he·sive–bound** \-ˌbaúnd\ *adjective*

adhesive tape *noun* (1928)
: tape coated on one side with an adhesive mixture; *especially* **:** one used for covering wounds

¹ad hoc \'ad-'häk, -'hōk; 'äd-'hōk\ *adverb* [Latin, for this] (1659)
: for the particular end or case at hand without consideration of wider application

²ad hoc *adjective* (1879)
1 a : concerned with a particular end or purpose ⟨an *ad hoc* investigating committee⟩ **b :** formed or used for specific or immediate problems or needs ⟨*ad hoc* solutions⟩
2 : fashioned from whatever is immediately available **:** IMPROVISED ⟨large *ad hoc* parades and demonstrations —Nat Hentoff⟩

¹ad ho·mi·nem \(')ad-'hä-mə-ˌnem, -nəm\ *adjective* [New Latin, literally, to the person] (1598)
1 : appealing to feelings or prejudices rather than intellect
2 : marked by an attack on an opponent's character rather than by an answer to the contentions made

²ad hominem *adverb* (1962)
: in an ad hominem manner ⟨was arguing *ad hominem*⟩

\ə\ abut \ⁿ\ kitten \ər\ further \a\ ash \ā\ ace
\ä\ mop, mar \aú\ out \ch\ chin \e\ bet \ē\ easy
\g\ go \i\ hit \ī\ ice \j\ job \ŋ\ sing \ō\ go
\ó\ law \ói\ boy \th\ thin \t̲h\ the \ü\ loot \ú\ foot
\y\ yet \zh\ vision *see also* Guide to Pronunciation

adi·a·bat·ic \,a-dē-ə-'ba-tik, ,ā-,dī-ə-\ *adjective* [Greek *adiabatos* impassable, from *a-* + *diabatos* passable, from *diabainein* to go across, from *dia-* + *bainein* to go — more at COME] (1870)
: occurring without loss or gain of heat ⟨*adiabatic* expansion of a body of air⟩
— **adi·a·bat·i·cal·ly** \-ti-k(ə-)lē\ *adverb*

adieu \ə-'dü, a-, -'dyü\ *noun, plural* **adieus** *or* **adieux** \-'düz, -'dyüz\ [Middle English, from Middle French, from *a* (from Latin *ad*) + *Dieu* God, from Latin *Deus* — more at DEITY] (14th century)
: FAREWELL — often used interjectionally

ad in·fi·ni·tum \,ad-,in-fə-'nī-təm *also* ,äd-\ *adverb or adjective* [Latin] (1610)
: without end or limit

¹ad in·ter·im \'ad-'in-tə-rəm, -,rim *also* ,äd-\ *adverb* [Latin] (1787)
: for the intervening time : TEMPORARILY

²ad interim *adjective* (1818)
: made or serving ad interim

adi·os \,ä-dē-'ōs, ,a-\ *interjection* [Spanish *adiós*, from *a* (from Latin *ad*) + *Dios* God, from Latin *Deus*] (1837)
— used to express farewell

adip- *or* **adipo-** *combining form* [Latin *adip-, adeps,* probably from Greek *aleipha* fat, oil, from *aleiphein* to rub with oil — more at ALIPHATIC]
: fat ⟨*adipo*cyte⟩

adip·ic acid \ə-'di-pik-\ *noun* [International Scientific Vocabulary] (1877)
: a white crystalline dicarboxylic acid $C_6H_{10}O_4$ formed by oxidation of various fats and also made synthetically for use especially in the manufacture of nylon

ad·i·po·cyte \'a-di-pō-,sīt\ *noun* (1959)
: FAT CELL

ad·i·pose \'a-də-,pōs\ *adjective* [New Latin *adiposus*, from Latin *adip-, adeps*] (1743)
: of or relating to animal fat; *broadly* : FAT
— **ad·i·pos·i·ty** \,a-də-'pä-sə-tē\ *noun*

adipose tissue *noun* (1854)
: connective tissue in which fat is stored and which has the cells distended by droplets of fat

ad·it \'a-dət\ *noun* [Latin *aditus* approach, from *adire* to go to, from *ad-* + *ire* to go — more at ISSUE] (1602)
: a nearly horizontal passage from the surface in a mine

ad·ja·cen·cy \ə-'jā-s°n(t)-sē\ *noun, plural* **-cies** (1646)
1 : something that is adjacent
2 : the quality or state of being adjacent : CONTIGUITY

ad·ja·cent \ə-'jā-s°nt\ *adjective* [Middle English, from Middle French or Latin; Middle French, from Latin *adjacent-, adjacens,* present participle of *adjacēre* to lie near, from *ad-* + *jacēre* to lie; akin to Latin *jacere* to throw — more at JET] (15th century)
1 a : not distant : NEARBY ⟨the city and *adjacent* suburbs⟩ **b :** having a common endpoint or border ⟨*adjacent* lots⟩ ⟨*adjacent* sides of a triangle⟩ **c :** immediately preceding or following
2 *of two angles* **:** having the vertex and one side in common ☆
— **ad·ja·cent·ly** *adverb*

ad·jec·ti·val \,a-jik-'tī-vəl\ *adjective* (1797)
1 : ADJECTIVE
2 : characterized by the use of adjectives
— **ad·jec·ti·val·ly** \-və-lē\ *adverb*

¹ad·jec·tive \'a-jik-tiv *also* -'a-jə-tiv\ *adjective* [Middle English, from Middle French or Late Latin; Middle French *adjectif,* from Late Latin *adjectivus,* from Latin *adjectus,* past participle of *adicere* to throw to, from *ad-* + *jacere* to throw — more at JET] (14th century)
1 : of, relating to, or functioning as an adjective ⟨an *adjective* clause⟩
2 : not standing by itself : DEPENDENT
3 : requiring or employing a mordant ⟨*adjective* dyes⟩

4 : PROCEDURAL ⟨*adjective* law⟩
— **ad·jec·tive·ly** *adverb*

²adjective *noun* (14th century)
: a word belonging to one of the major form classes in any of numerous languages and typically serving as a modifier of a noun to denote a quality of the thing named, to indicate its quantity or extent, or to specify a thing as distinct from something else

ad·join \ə-'jȯin, a-\ *verb* [Middle English, from Middle French *adjoindre,* from Latin *adjungere,* from *ad-* + *jungere* to join — more at YOKE] (14th century)
transitive verb
1 : to add or attach by joining
2 : to lie next to or in contact with
intransitive verb
: to be close to or in contact with one another

ad·join·ing *adjective* (15th century)
: touching or bounding at a point or line
synonym see ADJACENT

ad·joint \'a-,jȯint\ *noun* [French, from past participle of *adjoindre* to adjoin] (1907)
: the transpose of a matrix in which each element is replaced by its cofactor

ad·journ \ə-'jərn\ *verb* [Middle English *ajournen,* from Middle French *ajourner,* from *a-* (from Latin *ad-*) + *jour* day — more at JOURNEY] (15th century)
transitive verb
: to suspend indefinitely or until a later stated time
intransitive verb
1 : to suspend a session indefinitely or to another time or place
2 : to move to another place

ad·journ·ment \-mənt\ *noun* (1607)
1 : the act of adjourning
2 : the state or interval of being adjourned

ad·judge \ə-'jəj\ *transitive verb* **ad·judged; ad·judg·ing** [Middle English *ajugen,* from Middle French *ajugier,* from Latin *adjudicare,* from *ad-* + *judicare* to judge — more at JUDGE] (14th century)
1 a : to decide or rule upon as a judge : ADJUDICATE **b :** to pronounce judicially : RULE
2 *archaic* **:** SENTENCE, CONDEMN
3 : to hold or pronounce to be : DEEM ⟨*adjudge* the book a success⟩
4 : to award or grant judicially in a case of controversy

ad·ju·di·cate \ə-'jü-di-,kāt\ *verb* **-cat·ed; -cat·ing** (1775)
transitive verb
: to settle judicially
intransitive verb
: to act as judge
— **ad·ju·di·ca·tive** \-,kā-tiv, -kə-\ *adjective*
— **ad·ju·di·ca·tor** \-,kā-tər\ *noun*

ad·ju·di·ca·tion \ə-,jü-di-'kā-shən\ *noun* [French or Late Latin; French, from Late Latin *adjudicatio,* from Latin *adjudicare*] (1691)
1 : the act or process of adjudicating
2 a : a judicial decision or sentence **b :** a decree in bankruptcy
— **ad·ju·di·ca·to·ry** \-'jü-di-kə-,tōr-ē, -,tȯr-\ *adjective*

¹ad·junct \'a-,jəŋ(k)t\ *noun* [Latin *adjunctum,* from neuter of *adjunctus,* past participle of *adjungere*] (1588)
1 : something joined or added to another thing but not essentially a part of it
2 a : a word or word group that qualifies or completes the meaning of another word or other words and is not itself a main structural element in its sentence **b :** an adverb or adverbial (as *heartily* in "Most children eat heartily" or *at noon* in "We will leave at noon") attached to the verb of a clause especially to express a relation of time, place, frequency, degree, or manner — compare DISJUNCT 2
3 : an associate or assistant of another
— **ad·junc·tive** \a-'jəŋ(k)-tiv, ə-\ *adjective*

²adjunct *adjective* (1595)
1 : added or joined as an accompanying object or circumstance

2 : attached in a subordinate or temporary capacity to a staff ⟨an *adjunct* psychiatrist⟩
— **ad·junct·ly** \'a-,jəŋ(k)-tlē, -,jəŋ-klē\ *adverb*

ad·junc·tion \a-'jəŋ(k)-shən\ *noun* (1618)
: the act or process of adjoining

ad·ju·ra·tion \,a-jə-'rā-shən\ *noun* (1611)
1 : a solemn oath
2 : an earnest urging or advising
— **ad·jur·a·to·ry** \ə-'jur-ə-,tōr-ē, -,tȯr-\ *adjective*

ad·jure \ə-'jur\ *transitive verb* **ad·jured; ad·jur·ing** [Middle English, from Middle French & Latin; Middle French *ajurer,* from Latin *adjurare,* from *ad-* + *jurare* to swear — more at JURY] (14th century)
1 : to command solemnly under or as if under oath or penalty of a curse
2 : to urge or advise earnestly
synonym see BEG

ad·just \ə-'jəst\ *verb* [Middle English *ajusten,* from Middle French *ajuster* to gauge, adjust, from *a-* (from Latin *ad-*) + *juste* right, exact — more at JUST] (14th century)
transitive verb
1 a : to bring to a more satisfactory state: (1) : SETTLE, RESOLVE (2) : RECTIFY **b :** to make correspondent or conformable : ADAPT **c :** to bring the parts of to a true or more effective relative position ⟨*adjust* a carburetor⟩
2 : to reduce to a system : REGULATE
3 : to determine the amount to be paid under an insurance policy in settlement of (a loss)
intransitive verb
1 : to adapt or conform oneself (as to new conditions)
2 : to achieve mental and behavioral balance between one's own needs and the demands of others
synonym see ADAPT
— **ad·just·abil·i·ty** \-,jəs-tə-'bi-lə-tē\ *noun*
— **ad·just·able** \-'jəs-tə-bəl\ *adjective*
— **ad·jus·tive** \-'jəs-tiv\ *adjective*

adjustable rate mortgage *noun* (1981)
: a mortgage having an interest rate which is usually initially lower than that of a mortgage with a fixed rate but is adjusted periodically according to the cost of funds to the lender

ad·just·ed *adjective* (circa 1674)
1 : accommodated to suit a particular set of circumstances or requirements
2 : having achieved an often specified and usually harmonious relationship with the environment or with other individuals ⟨a well-*adjusted* schoolchild⟩

ad·just·er *also* **ad·jus·tor** \ə-'jəs-tər\ *noun* (1673)
: one that adjusts; *especially* : an insurance agent who investigates personal or property damage and makes estimates for effecting settlements

ad·just·ment \ə-'jəs(t)-mənt\ *noun* (1644)
1 : the act or process of adjusting
2 : a settlement of a claim or debt in a case in which the amount involved is uncertain or full payment is not made
3 : the state of being adjusted
4 : a means (as a mechanism) by which things are adjusted one to another

☆ **SYNONYMS**
Adjacent, adjoining, contiguous, juxtaposed mean being in close proximity. ADJACENT may or may not imply contact but always implies absence of anything of the same kind in between ⟨a house with an *adjacent* garage⟩. ADJOINING definitely implies meeting and touching at some point or line ⟨had *adjoining* rooms at the hotel⟩. CONTIGUOUS implies having contact on all or most of one side ⟨offices in all 48 *contiguous* states⟩. JUXTAPOSED means placed side by side especially so as to permit comparison and contrast ⟨a skyscraper *juxtaposed* to a church⟩.

5 : a correction or modification to reflect actual conditions
— **ad·just·men·tal** \ə-,jəs(t)-'men-tᵊl, ,a-,jəs(t)-\ adjective
ad·ju·tan·cy \'a-jə-tən(t)-sē\ noun (1775)
: the office or rank of an adjutant
ad·ju·tant \'a-jə-tənt\ noun [Latin adjutant-, adjutans, present participle of adjutare to help — more at AID] (1539)
1 : a staff officer in the army, air force, or marine corps who assists the commanding officer and is responsible especially for correspondence
2 : one who helps **:** ASSISTANT
adjutant general noun, plural **adjutants general** (1645)
1 : the chief administrative officer of an army who is responsible especially for the administration and preservation of personnel records
2 : the chief administrative officer of a major military unit (as a division or corps)
¹**ad·ju·vant** \'a-jə-vənt\ adjective [French or Latin; French, from Latin adjuvant-, adjuvans, present participle of adjuvare to aid — more at AID] (1574)
1 : serving to aid or contribute **:** AUXILIARY
2 : assisting in the prevention, amelioration, or cure of disease ⟨adjuvant chemotherapy following surgery⟩
²**adjuvant** noun (1609)
: one that helps or facilitates: as **a :** an ingredient (as in a prescription or a solution) that modifies the action of the principal ingredient **b :** something (as a drug or method) that enhances the effectiveness of medical treatment **c :** a substance enhancing the immune response to an antigen
Ad·le·ri·an \äd-'lir-ē-ən, ad-\ adjective [Alfred Adler] (1924)
: of, relating to, or being a theory and technique of psychotherapy emphasizing the importance of feelings of inferiority, a will to power, and overcompensation in neurotic processes
¹**ad–lib** \'ad-'lib\ verb **ad–libbed; ad–lib·bing** [ad lib] (1919)
transitive verb
: to deliver spontaneously
intransitive verb
: to improvise especially lines or a speech
— **ad–lib** noun
²**ad–lib** adjective (1935)
: spoken, composed, or performed without preparation
ad lib adverb [New Latin ad libitum] (circa 1811)
1 : in accordance with one's wishes
2 : without restraint or limit
¹**ad li·bi·tum** \(,)ad-'li-bə-təm\ adverb [New Latin, in accordance with desire] (1610)
: AD LIB ⟨rats fed ad libitum⟩
²**ad libitum** adjective (circa 1801)
: omissible according to a performer's wishes — used as a direction in music; compare OBBLIGATO
ad·man \'ad-,man\ noun (1909)
: a person who writes, solicits, or places advertisements
ad·mass \'ad-,mas\ noun, often attributive [advertising + mass] (1955)
chiefly British **:** mass-media advertising; also **:** the society influenced by it
ad·mea·sure \ad-'me-zhər, -'mā-\ transitive verb **-sured; -sur·ing** [Middle English amesuren, from Middle French amesurer, from a- (from Latin ad-) + mesurer to measure] (1641)
: to determine the proper share of **:** APPORTION
ad·mea·sure·ment \-'me-zhər-mənt, -'mā-\ noun (1523)
1 : determination and apportionment of shares
2 : determination or comparison of dimensions
3 : DIMENSIONS, SIZE
Ad·me·tus \ad-'mē-təs\ noun [Latin, from Greek Admētos]

: a king of Pherae who is saved by Apollo from his fated death when his wife Alcestis offers to die in his place
ad·min·is·ter \əd-'mi-nə-stər\ verb **-is·tered; -is·ter·ing** \-st(ə-)riŋ\ [Middle English administren, from Middle French administrer, from Latin administrare, from ad- + ministrare to serve, from minister servant — more at MINISTER] (14th century)
transitive verb
1 : to manage or supervise the execution, use, or conduct of ⟨administer a trust fund⟩
2 a : to mete out **:** DISPENSE ⟨administer punishment⟩ **b :** to give ritually ⟨administer the last rites⟩ **c :** to give remedially ⟨administer a dose of medicine⟩
intransitive verb
1 : to perform the office of administrator
2 : to furnish a benefit **:** MINISTER ⟨administer to an ailing friend⟩
3 : to manage affairs
— **ad·min·is·tra·ble** \-strə-bəl\ adjective
— **ad·min·is·trant** \-strənt\ noun
ad·min·is·trate \-,strāt\ verb **-trat·ed; -trat·ing** [Latin administratus, past participle of administrare] (circa 1617)
: ADMINISTER
ad·min·is·tra·tion \əd-,mi-nə-'strā-shən, (,)ad-\ noun (14th century)
1 : performance of executive duties **:** MANAGEMENT
2 : the act or process of administering
3 : the execution of public affairs as distinguished from policy-making
4 a : a body of persons who administer **b** often capitalized **:** a group constituting the political executive in a presidential government **c :** a governmental agency or board
5 : the term of office of an administrative officer or body
ad·min·is·tra·tive \əd-'mi-nə-,strā-tiv, -strə-\ adjective (circa 1731)
: of or relating to administration or an administration **:** EXECUTIVE
— **ad·min·is·tra·tive·ly** adverb
administrative county noun (1949)
: a British local administrative unit often not coincident with an older county
administrative law noun (1896)
: law dealing with the establishment, duties, and powers of and available remedies against authorized agencies in the executive branch of the government
ad·min·is·tra·tor \əd-'mi-nə-,strā-tər, -,strā-,tór\ noun (15th century)
1 : a person legally vested with the right of administration of an estate
2 a : one that administers especially business, school, or governmental affairs **b :** a priest appointed to administer a diocese or parish temporarily
ad·min·is·tra·trix \-,mi-nə-'strā-triks\ noun, plural **-tra·tri·ces** \-'strā-trə-,sēz\ [New Latin] (circa 1623)
: a woman administrator especially of an estate
ad·mi·ra·ble \'ad-m(ə-)rə-bəl\ adjective (15th century)
1 : deserving the highest esteem **:** EXCELLENT
2 obsolete **:** exciting wonder **:** SURPRISING
— **ad·mi·ra·bil·i·ty** \,ad-m(ə-)rə-'bi-lə-tē\ noun
— **ad·mi·ra·ble·ness** \'ad-m(ə-)rə-bəl-nəs\ noun
— **ad·mi·ra·bly** \-blē\ adverb
ad·mi·ral \'ad-m(ə-)rəl\ noun [Middle English, from Middle French amiral admiral & Medieval Latin admiralis emir, admirallus admiral, from Arabic amīr-al- commander of the (as in amīr-al-baḥr commander of the sea)] (15th century)
1 archaic **:** the commander in chief of a navy
2 a : FLAG OFFICER **b :** a commissioned officer in the navy or coast guard who ranks above a vice admiral and whose insignia is four stars — compare GENERAL

3 archaic **:** FLAGSHIP
4 : any of several brightly colored butterflies (family Nymphalidae) ◇
admiral of the fleet (1660)
: the highest-ranking officer of the British navy
ad·mi·ral·ty \'ad-m(ə-)rəl-tē\ noun (15th century)
1 capitalized **:** the executive department or officers formerly having general authority over British naval affairs
2 : the court having jurisdiction over questions of maritime law; also **:** the system of law administered by admiralty courts
ad·mi·ra·tion \,ad-mə-'rā-shən\ noun (15th century)
1 archaic **:** WONDER
2 : an object of esteem
3 : delighted or astonished approbation
ad·mire \əd-'mīr\ verb **ad·mired; ad·mir·ing** [Middle French admirer, from Latin admirari, from ad- + mirari to wonder, from mirus astonishing] (1579)
transitive verb
1 archaic **:** to marvel at
2 : to regard with admiration
intransitive verb
dialect **:** to like very much ⟨I would admire to know why not —A. H. Lewis⟩
synonym see REGARD
— **ad·mir·er** noun
— **ad·mir·ing·ly** \-'mī-riŋ-lē\ adverb
ad·mis·si·ble \əd-'mi-sə-bəl, ad-\ adjective [French, from Medieval Latin admissibilis, from Latin admissus, past participle of admittere] (circa 1611)
1 : capable of being allowed or conceded **:** PERMISSIBLE ⟨evidence legally admissible in court⟩
2 : capable or worthy of being admitted ⟨admissible to the university⟩
— **ad·mis·si·bil·i·ty** \-,mi-sə-'bi-lə-tē\ noun
ad·mis·sion \əd-'mi-shən, ad-\ noun (15th century)
1 a : the act or process of admitting **b :** the state or privilege of being admitted **c :** a fee paid at or for admission
2 a : the granting of an argument or position not fully proved **b :** acknowledgment that a fact or statement is true
synonym see ADMITTANCE

◇ WORD HISTORY
admiral　It is a curiosity of history that admiral, a word meaning "naval commander," ultimately has its source in Arabic, the language of a desert people who acquired their seafaring skills largely from the Mediterranean peoples they dominated after the great Islamic expansion of the 7th century. As a name for a Muslim chieftain, the Arabic word amīr "commander" appears as early as the 9th century in Medieval Latin documents, in forms such as amiratus, admirandus, and admirallus. These display a variety of suffixes and an extraneous d through confusion with the Latin verb admirari "to admire." The ending -allus is probably from the Arabic definite article al, which actually belongs to the following word in phrases such as amīr al-alī "supreme commander." The specific application of admirallus to a commander of a fleet originated in 12th century Sicily, when it was ruled by the Normans. This usage was acquired by the Genoese and then spread to the rest of western Europe, including France and England.

\ə\ abut \ᵊ\ kitten \ər\ further \a\ ash \ā\ ace
\ä\ mop, mar \aů\ out \ch\ chin \e\ bet \ē\ easy
\g\ go \i\ hit \ī\ ice \j\ job \ŋ\ sing \ō\ go
\ó\ law \ói\ boy \th\ thin \t͟h\ the \ü\ loot \ů\ foot
\y\ yet \zh\ vision　　see also Guide to Pronunciation

— **ad·mis·sive** \-'mi-siv\ *adjective*

ad·mit \əd-'mit, ad-\ *verb* **ad·mit·ted; ad·mit·ting** [Middle English *admitten,* from Latin *admittere,* from *ad-* + *mittere* to send] (15th century)
transitive verb
1 a : to allow scope for **:** PERMIT ⟨admits no possibility of misunderstanding⟩ **b :** to concede as true or valid ⟨admitted making a mistake⟩
2 : to allow entry (as to a place, fellowship, or privilege) ⟨an open window had *admitted* rain⟩ ⟨admitted to the club⟩
intransitive verb
1 : to give entrance or access
2 a : ALLOW, PERMIT ⟨admits of two interpretations⟩ **b :** to make acknowledgment — used with *to*
synonym see ACKNOWLEDGE

ad·mit·tance \əd-'mi-t⁰n(t)s, ad-\ *noun* (1536)
1 : permission to enter (as a place or office) **:** ENTRANCE
2 : the reciprocal of the impedance of a circuit ☆

ad·mit·ted·ly \əd-'mi-təd-lē, ad-\ *adverb* (1804)
1 : as has been or must be admitted ⟨an *admittedly* inadequate treatment⟩
2 : it must be admitted ⟨admittedly, we took a chance⟩

ad·mix \ad-'miks\ *transitive verb* [back-formation from obsolete *admixt* mingled (with), from Middle English, from Latin *admixtus*] (1533)
: to mix in

ad·mix·ture \ad-'miks-chər\ *noun* [Latin *admixtus,* past participle of *admiscēre* to mix with, from *ad-* + *miscēre* to mix — more at MIX] (1605)
1 a : the action of mixing **b :** the fact of being mixed
2 a : something added by mixing **b :** a product of mixing **:** MIXTURE

ad·mon·ish \ad-'mä-nish\ *transitive verb* [Middle English *admonesten,* from Middle French *admonester,* from (assumed) Vulgar Latin *admonestare,* alteration of Latin *admonēre* to warn, from *ad-* + *monēre* to warn — more at MIND] (14th century)
1 a : to indicate duties or obligations to **b :** to express warning or disapproval to especially in a gentle, earnest, or solicitous manner
2 : to give friendly earnest advice or encouragement to
synonym see REPROVE
— **ad·mon·ish·er** *noun*
— **ad·mon·ish·ing·ly** \-ni-shiŋ-lē\ *adverb*
— **ad·mon·ish·ment** \-mənt\ *noun*

ad·mo·ni·tion \ˌad-mə-'ni-shən\ *noun* [Middle English *amonicioun,* from Middle French *amonition,* from Latin *admonition-, admonitio,* from *admonēre*] (14th century)
1 : gentle or friendly reproof
2 : counsel or warning against fault or oversight

ad·mon·i·to·ry \əd-'mä-nə-ˌtōr-ē, -ˌtȯr-\ *adjective* (1594)
: expressing admonition **:** WARNING
— **ad·mon·i·to·ri·ly** \-ˌmä-nə-'tȯr-ə-lē, -'tȯr-\ *adverb*

ad·nate \'ad-ˌnāt\ *adjective* [Latin *adnatus, adgnatus,* past participle of *adgnasci* to be born in addition, grow later — more at AGNATE] (1661)
: grown to a usually unlike part especially along a margin ⟨a calyx *adnate* to the ovary⟩
— **ad·na·tion** \ad-'nā-shən\ *noun*

ad nau·se·am \ad-'nȯ-zē-əm *also* -ˌam\ *adverb* [Latin] (1647)
: to a sickening or excessive degree

ad·nexa \ad-'nek-sə\ *noun plural* [New Latin, from Latin *annexa,* neuter plural of *annexus,* past participle of *annectere* to bind to — more at ANNEX] (1899)

: conjoined, subordinate, or associated anatomic parts
— **ad·nex·al** \-səl\ *adjective*

ado \ə-'dü\ *noun* [Middle English, from *at do,* from *at* + *don,* do to do] (14th century)
1 : fussy bustling excitement **:** TO-DO
2 : time-wasting bother over trivial details ⟨wrote the paper without further *ado*⟩
3 : TROUBLE, DIFFICULTY

ado·be \ə-'dō-bē\ *noun* [Spanish, from Arabic *aṭ-ṭūb* the brick, from Coptic *tōbe* brick] (1748)
1 : a brick or building material of sun-dried earth and straw
2 : a structure made of adobe bricks
3 : a heavy clay used in making adobe bricks; *broadly* **:** alluvial or playa clay in desert or arid regions
— **ado·be·like** \-ˌlīk\ *adjective*

adobe 2

ado·bo \ə-'dō-bō, ä-'thō-bō\ *noun, plural* **-bos** [Spanish] (circa 1951)
: a Philippine dish of fish or meat marinated in a sauce usually containing vinegar and garlic, browned in fat, and simmered in the marinade

ad·o·les·cence \ˌa-d⁰l-'e-s⁰n(t)s\ *noun* (15th century)
1 : the state or process of growing up
2 : the period of life from puberty to maturity terminating legally at the age of majority
3 : a stage of development (as of a language or culture) prior to maturity

¹ad·o·les·cent \-s⁰nt\ *noun* [French, from Latin *adolescent-, adolescens,* present participle of *adolescere* to grow up — more at ADULT] (15th century)
: one that is in the state of adolescence

²adolescent *adjective* (1785)
1 : of, relating to, or being in adolescence
2 : emotionally or intellectually immature
— **ad·o·les·cent·ly** *adverb*

Ado·nai \ˌä-də-'nȯi, -'nī\ *noun* [Hebrew *ădhōnāy*] (14th century)
— used as a name of the God of the Hebrews

Ado·nis \ə-'dä-nəs, -'dō-\ *noun* [Latin, from Greek *Adōnis*]
1 : a youth loved by Aphrodite who is killed at hunting by a wild boar and restored to Aphrodite from Hades for a part of each year
2 : a very handsome young man

adopt \ə-'däpt\ *transitive verb* [Middle English, from Middle French or Latin; Middle French *adopter,* from Latin *adoptare,* from *ad-* + *optare* to choose] (1500)
1 : to take by choice into a relationship; *especially* **:** to take voluntarily (a child of other parents) as one's own child
2 : to take up and practice or use ⟨adopted a moderate tone⟩
3 : to accept formally and put into effect ⟨adopt a constitutional amendment⟩
4 : to choose (a textbook) for required study in a course ☆
— **adopt·abil·i·ty** \-ˌdäp-tə-'bi-lə-tē\ *noun*
— **adopt·able** \-'däp-tə-bəl\ *adjective*
— **adopt·er** *noun*

adopt·ee \ə-ˌdäp-'tē\ *noun* (1892)
: one that is adopted

adop·tion \ə-'däp-shən\ *noun* (14th century)
: the act of adopting **:** the state of being adopted

adop·tion·ism *or* **adop·tian·ism** \-shə-ˌni-zəm\ *noun, often capitalized* (1874)
: the doctrine that Jesus of Nazareth became the Son of God by adoption
— **adop·tion·ist** \-sh(ə-)nist\ *noun, often capitalized*

adop·tive \ə-'däp-tiv\ *adjective* (15th century)
1 : made or acquired by adoption ⟨the *adoptive* father⟩
2 : tending to adopt

3 : of or relating to adoption
— **adop·tive·ly** *adverb*

ador·able \ə-'dȯr-ə-bəl, -'dȯr-\ *adjective* (1611)
1 : worthy of being adored
2 : extremely charming ⟨an *adorable* child⟩
— **ador·abil·i·ty** \-ˌdȯr-ə-'bi-lə-tē, -ˌdȯr-\ *noun*
— **ador·able·ness** \-'dȯr-ə-bəl-nəs, -'dȯr-\ *noun*
— **ador·ably** \-blē\ *adverb*

ad·o·ra·tion \ˌa-də-'rā-shən\ *noun* (1528)
: the act of adoring **:** the state of being adored

adore \ə-'dȯr, -'dȯr\ *transitive verb* **ador·ing** [Middle English *adouren,* from Middle French *adorer,* from Latin *adorare,* from *ad-* + *orare* to speak, pray — more at ORATION] (14th century)
1 : to worship or honor as a deity or as divine
2 : to regard with loving admiration and devotion ⟨adored his daughter⟩
3 : to be extremely fond of ⟨adores pecan pie⟩
synonym see REVERE
— **ador·er** *noun*
— **ador·ing·ly** *adverb*

adorn \ə-'dȯrn\ *transitive verb* [Middle English, from Middle French *adorner,* from Latin *adornare,* from *ad-* + *ornare* to furnish — more at ORNATE] (14th century)
1 : to enhance the appearance of especially with beautiful objects
2 : to enliven or decorate as if with ornaments ⟨people of fashion who *adorned* the Court⟩ ☆

☆ SYNONYMS

Admittance, admission mean permitted entrance. ADMITTANCE is usually applied to mere physical entrance to a locality or a building ⟨members must show their cards upon *admittance* to the club⟩. ADMISSION applies to entrance or formal acceptance (as into a club) that carries with it rights, privileges, standing, or membership ⟨two recommendations are required for *admission* to the club⟩.

Adopt, embrace, espouse mean to take an opinion, policy, or practice as one's own. ADOPT implies accepting something created by another or foreign to one's nature ⟨forced to *adopt* new policies⟩. EMBRACE implies a ready or happy acceptance ⟨embraced the customs of their new homeland⟩. ESPOUSE adds an implication of close attachment to a cause and a sharing of its fortunes ⟨espoused the cause of women's rights⟩.

Adorn, decorate, ornament, embellish, beautify, deck, garnish mean to enhance the appearance of something by adding something unessential. ADORN implies an enhancing by something beautiful in itself ⟨a diamond necklace *adorned* her neck⟩. DECORATE suggests relieving plainness or monotony by adding beauty of color or design ⟨decorate a birthday cake⟩. ORNAMENT and EMBELLISH imply the adding of something extraneous, ORNAMENT stressing the heightening or setting off of the original ⟨a white house *ornamented* with green shutters⟩, EMBELLISH often stressing the adding of superfluous or adventitious ornament ⟨embellish a page with floral borders⟩. BEAUTIFY adds to EMBELLISH a suggestion of counterbalancing plainness or ugliness ⟨will *beautify* the grounds with flower beds⟩. DECK implies the addition of something that contributes to gaiety, splendor, or showiness ⟨a house all *decked* out for Christmas⟩. GARNISH suggests decorating with a small final touch and is used especially in referring to the serving of food ⟨an entrée *garnished* with parsley⟩.

adorn·ment \-mənt\ *noun* (14th century)
1 : the action of adorning **:** the state of being adorned
2 : something that adorns
ADP \ˌā-(ˌ)dē-ˈpē\ *noun* [adenosine *d*iphosphate] (1944)
: an ester of adenosine that is reversibly converted to ATP for the storing of energy by the addition of a high-energy phosphate group — called also *adenosine diphosphate*
ad rem \(ˌ)ad-ˈrem\ *adverb or adjective* [Latin, to the thing] (1599)
: to the point or purpose **:** RELEVANTLY
adren- *or* **adreno-** *combining form* [*adrenal*]
1 : adrenal glands ⟨*adreno*cortical⟩
2 : adrenaline ⟨*adren*ergic⟩
¹ad·re·nal \ə-ˈdrē-n°l\ *adjective* [*ad-* + *renal*] (1875)
: of, relating to, or derived from the adrenal glands or their secretions ⟨*adrenal* steroids⟩
²adrenal *noun* (1882)
: ADRENAL GLAND
ad·re·nal·ec·to·my \ə-ˌdrē-n°l-ˈek-tə-mē\ *noun* (circa 1910)
: surgical removal of one or both adrenal glands
— **ad·re·nal·ec·to·mized** \-ˌmīzd\ *adjective*
adrenal gland *noun* (1875)
: either of a pair of complex endocrine organs near the anterior medial border of the kidney consisting of a mesodermal cortex that produces glucocorticoid, mineralocorticoid, and androgenic hormones and an ectodermal medulla that produces epinephrine and norepinephrine — called also *adrenal, suprarenal gland*
Adren·a·lin \ə-ˈdre-n°l-ən\ *trademark*
— used for a preparation of levorotatory epinephrine
adren·a·line \ə-ˈdre-n°l-ən\ *noun* (1901)
: EPINEPHRINE — often used in nontechnical contexts ⟨the fans were jubilant, raucous, their *adrenaline* running high —W. P. Kinsella⟩
ad·ren·er·gic \ˌa-drə-ˈnər-jik\ *adjective* [*adren-* + *ergic*] (1934)
1 : liberating or activated by adrenaline or a substance like adrenaline ⟨an *adrenergic* nerve⟩
2 : resembling adrenaline especially in physiological action ⟨*adrenergic* drugs⟩
— **ad·ren·er·gi·cal·ly** \-ji-k(ə-)lē\ *adverb*
ad·re·no·chrome \ə-ˈdrē-nō-ˌkrōm\ *noun* (circa 1913)
: a red-colored mixture of quinones derived from epinephrine by oxidation
ad·re·no·cor·ti·cal \ə-ˌdrē-nō-ˈkȯr-ti-kəl\ *adjective* (1936)
: of, relating to, or derived from the cortex of the adrenal glands
ad·re·no·cor·ti·co·ste·roid \-ˌkȯr-ti-kō-ˈstir-ˌȯid *also* -ˈster-\ *noun* (1960)
: a steroid obtained from, resembling, or having physiological effects like those of the adrenal cortex
ad·re·no·cor·ti·co·tro·pic \ə-ˌdrē-nō-ˌkȯr-ti-kō-ˈtrō-pik\ *also* **ad·re·no·cor·ti·co·tro·phic** \-ˈtrō-fik\ *adjective* (1936)
: acting on or stimulating the adrenal cortex ⟨*adrenocorticotropic* activity⟩
adrenocorticotropic hormone *noun* (1937)
: ACTH
ad·re·no·cor·ti·co·tro·pin \-ˈtrō-pən\ *also* **ad·re·no·cor·ti·co·tro·phin** \-ˈtrō-fən\ *noun* (1952)
: ACTH
Adria·my·cin \ˌā-drē-ə-ˈmī-s°n, ˌa-drē-\ *trademark*
— used for a preparation of the hydrochloride of doxorubicin
adrift \ə-ˈdrift\ *adverb or adjective* (1624)
1 : without motive power and without anchor or mooring
2 : without ties, guidance, or security
3 : free from restraint or support

adroit \ə-ˈdrȯit\ *adjective* [French, from Old French, from *a-* (from Latin *ad-*) + *droit* right, droit] (1652)
: having or showing skill, cleverness, or resourcefulness in handling situations ⟨an *adroit* leader⟩
synonym see CLEVER, DEXTEROUS
— **adroit·ly** *adverb*
— **adroit·ness** *noun*
ad·sci·ti·tious \ˌad-sə-ˈti-shəs\ *adjective* [Latin *adscitus*, from past participle of *adsciscere* to admit, adopt, from *ad-* + *sciscere* to get to know, from *scire* to know — more at SCIENCE] (1620)
: derived or acquired from something extrinsic **:** ADVENTITIOUS
ad·sorb \ad-ˈsȯrb, -ˈzȯrb\ *verb* [*ad-* + ab*sorb*] (1882)
transitive verb
: to take up and hold by adsorption
intransitive verb
: to become adsorbed
— **ad·sorb·able** \-ˈsȯr-bə-bəl, -ˈzȯr-\ *adjective*
— **ad·sorb·er** \-ˈsȯr-bər, -ˈzȯr-\ *noun*
ad·sor·bate \ad-ˈsȯr-bət, -ˈzȯr-, -ˌbāt\ *noun* (1928)
: an adsorbed substance
ad·sor·bent \-bənt\ *noun* (1917)
: a usually solid substance that adsorbs another substance
— **adsorbent** *adjective*
ad·sorp·tion \ad-ˈsȯrp-shən, -ˈzȯrp-\ *noun* [*ad-* + ab*sorption*] (1882)
: the adhesion in an extremely thin layer of molecules (as of gases, solutes, or liquids) to the surfaces of solid bodies or liquids with which they are in contact — compare ABSORPTION
— **ad·sorp·tive** \-ˈsȯrp-tiv, -ˈzȯrp-\ *adjective*
ad·u·lar·ia \ˌa-jə-ˈlar-ē-ə, ˌa-dyə-, -ˈler-\ *noun* [Italian, from French *adulaire*, from *Adula*, Swiss mountain group] (1798)
: a transparent or translucent orthoclase
ad·u·late \ˈa-jə-ˌlāt, ˈa-dyə-; ˈa-d°l-ˌāt\ *transitive verb* **-lat·ed; -lat·ing** [back-formation from *adulation*, from Middle English, from Middle French, from Latin *adulation-, adulatio*, from *adulari* to fawn on (of dogs), flatter] (1777)
: to flatter or admire excessively or slavishly
— **ad·u·la·tion** \ˌa-jə-ˈlā-shən, ˌa-dyə-; ˌa-d°l-ˈā-\ *noun*
— **ad·u·la·tor** \ˈa-jə-ˌlā-tər, ˈa-dyə-; ˈa-d°l-ˌā-\ *noun*
— **ad·u·la·to·ry** \-lə-ˌtȯr-ē, -ˌtȯr-\ *adjective*
¹adult \ə-ˈdəlt, ˈa-ˌdəlt\ *adjective* [Latin *adultus*, past participle of *adolescere* to grow up, from *ad-* + *-olescere* (from *alescere* to grow) — more at OLD] (1531)
1 : fully developed and mature **:** GROWN-UP
2 : of, relating to, intended for, or befitting adults ⟨an *adult* approach to a problem⟩
3 : dealing in or with explicitly sexual material ⟨*adult* bookstores⟩ ⟨*adult* movies⟩
— **adult·hood** \ə-ˈdəlt-ˌhu̇d\ *noun*
— **adult·ly** \ə-ˈdəlt-lē, ˈa-ˌdəlt-\ *adverb*
— **adult·ness** \ə-ˈdəlt-nəs, ˈa-ˌdəlt-\ *noun*
²adult *noun* (1658)
: one that is adult; *especially* **:** a human being after an age (as 21) specified by law
— **adult·like** \ə-ˈdəlt-ˌlīk\ *adjective*
adult education *noun* (1851)
: CONTINUING EDUCATION
adul·ter·ant \ə-ˈdəl-t(ə-)rənt\ *noun* (circa 1755)
: an adulterating substance or agent
— **adulterant** *adjective*
¹adul·ter·ate \ə-ˈdəl-tə-ˌrāt\ *transitive verb* **-at·ed; -at·ing** [Latin *adulteratus*, past participle of *adulterare*, from *ad-* + *alter* other — more at ELSE] (1531)
: to corrupt, debase, or make impure by the addition of a foreign or inferior substance or

element; *especially* **:** to prepare for sale by replacing more valuable with less valuable or inert ingredients
— **adul·ter·a·tor** \-ˌrā-tər\ *noun*
²adul·ter·ate \ə-ˈdəl-t(ə-)rət\ *adjective* (1590)
1 : tainted with adultery **:** ADULTEROUS
2 : being adulterated **:** SPURIOUS
adul·ter·a·tion \ə-ˌdəl-tə-ˈrā-shən\ *noun* (1506)
1 : the process of adulterating **:** the condition of being adulterated
2 : an adulterated product
adul·ter·er \ə-ˈdəl-tər-ər\ *noun* (1513)
: a person who commits adultery; *especially* **:** a man who commits adultery
adul·ter·ess \ə-ˈdəl-t(ə-)rəs\ *noun* (1611)
: a woman who commits adultery
adul·ter·ine \ə-ˈdəl-tə-ˌrīn, -ˌrēn\ *adjective* (1542)
1 a : marked by adulteration **:** SPURIOUS **b :** ILLEGAL
2 : born of adultery
adul·ter·ous \ə-ˈdəl-t(ə-)rəs\ *adjective* (1606)
: relating to, characterized by, or given to adultery
— **adul·ter·ous·ly** *adverb*
adul·tery \ə-ˈdəl-t(ə-)rē\ *noun, plural* **-ter·ies** [Middle English, alteration of *avoutrie*, from Middle French, from Latin *adulterium*, from *adulter* adulterer, back-formation from *adulterare*] (15th century)
: voluntary sexual intercourse between a married man and someone other than his wife or between a married woman and someone other than her husband; *also* **:** an act of adultery
ad·um·brate \ˈa-dəm-ˌbrāt, a-ˈdəm-\ *transitive verb* **-brat·ed; -brat·ing** [Latin *adumbratus*, past participle of *adumbrare*, from *ad-* + *umbra* shadow — more at UMBRAGE] (1581)
1 : to foreshadow vaguely **:** INTIMATE
2 a : to give a sketchy representation or outline of **b :** to suggest or disclose partially
3 : OVERSHADOW, OBSCURE
— **ad·um·bra·tion** \ˌa-(ˌ)dəm-ˈbrā-shən\ *noun*
— **ad·um·bra·tive** \a-ˈdəm-brə-tiv\ *adjective*
— **ad·um·bra·tive·ly** *adverb*
adust \ə-ˈdəst\ *adjective* [Middle English, from Latin *adustus*, past participle of *adurere* to set fire to, from *ad-* + *urere* to burn — more at EMBER] (15th century)
1 : SCORCHED, BURNED
2 *archaic* **:** of a sunburned appearance
3 *archaic* **:** of a gloomy appearance or disposition
ad va·lo·rem \ˌad-və-ˈlōr-əm, -ˈlȯr-\ *adjective* [Latin, according to the value] (1698)
: imposed at a rate percent of value ⟨*ad valorem* tax on goods⟩
¹ad·vance \əd-ˈvan(t)s\ *verb* **ad·vanced; ad·vanc·ing** [Middle English *advauncen*, from Old French *avancier*, from (assumed) Vulgar Latin *abantiare*, from Late Latin *abante* in front, from Latin *ab-* + *ante* before — more at ANTE-] (15th century)
transitive verb
1 : to accelerate the growth or progress of
2 : to bring or move forward
3 : to raise to a higher rank
4 *archaic* **:** to lift up **:** RAISE
5 a : to bring forward in time; *especially* **:** to make earlier ⟨*advance* the date of the meeting⟩
b : to place later in time
6 : to bring forward for notice, consideration, or acceptance **:** PROPOSE
7 : to supply or furnish in expectation of repayment
8 : to raise in rate **:** INCREASE ⟨*advance* the rent⟩

\ə\ **abut** \°\ **kitten** \ər\ **further** \a\ **ash** \ā\ **ace** \ä\ **mop, mar** \au̇\ **out** \ch\ **chin** \e\ **bet** \ē\ **easy** \g\ **go** \i\ **hit** \ī\ **ice** \j\ **job** \ŋ\ **sing** \ō\ **go** \ȯ\ **law** \ȯi\ **boy** \th\ **thin** \t̲h̲\ **the** \ü\ **loot** \u̇\ **foot** \y\ **yet** \zh\ **vision** *see also* Guide to Pronunciation

intransitive verb
1 : to move forward : PROCEED
2 : to make progress : INCREASE ⟨*advance* in age⟩
3 : to rise in rank, position, or importance
4 : to rise in rate or price ☆
— **ad·vanc·er** *noun*

²**advance** *noun* (1668)
1 : a moving forward
2 a : progress in development ⟨mistaking material *advance* for spiritual enrichment —H. J. Laski⟩ **b** : a progressive step : IMPROVEMENT ⟨an *advance* in medical technique⟩
3 : a rise in price, value, or amount
4 : a first step or approach made ⟨her attitude discouraged all *advances*⟩
5 : a provision of something (as money or goods) before a return is received; *also* : the money or goods supplied
— **in advance** : before a deadline or an anticipated event
— **in advance of** : AHEAD OF

³**advance** *adjective* (1701)
1 : made, sent, or furnished ahead of time ⟨*advance* sales⟩
2 : going or situated before ⟨an *advance* party of soldiers⟩

ad·vanced *adjective* (1534)
1 : far on in time or course ⟨a man *advanced* in years⟩
2 a : being beyond others in progress or ideas ⟨tastes a bit too *advanced* for the times⟩ **b** : being beyond the elementary or introductory ⟨*advanced* chemistry⟩ **c** : greatly developed beyond an initial stage ⟨the most *advanced* scientific methods⟩ ⟨*advanced* weapons systems⟩

advanced degree *noun* (1928)
: a university degree (as a master's or doctor's degree) higher than a bachelor's

Advanced level *noun* (1947)
: A LEVEL

advance man *noun* (1906)
: an employee who makes arrangements and handles publicity in advance of an appearance or engagement by the employer (as a political candidate or a circus)

ad·vance·ment \əd-'van(t)-smənt\ *noun* (1599)
1 : the action of advancing : the state of being advanced: **a** : promotion or elevation to a higher rank or position **b** : progression to a higher stage of development
2 : an improved feature : IMPROVEMENT

¹**ad·van·tage** \əd-'van-tij\ *noun* [Middle English *avantage*, from Middle French, from *avant* before, from Late Latin *abante*] (1523)
1 : superiority of position or condition ⟨higher ground gave the enemy the *advantage*⟩
2 : a factor or circumstance of benefit to its possessor ⟨lacked the *advantages* of an education⟩
3 a : BENEFIT, GAIN; *especially* : benefit resulting from some course of action ⟨a mistake which turned out to our *advantage*⟩ **b** *obsolete* : INTEREST 2a
4 : the first point won in tennis after deuce
— **to advantage** : so as to produce a favorable impression or effect

²**advantage** *transitive verb* **-taged; -taging** (1549)
: to give an advantage to : BENEFIT

ad·van·ta·geous \ˌad-ˌvan-'tā-jəs, -vən-\ *adjective* (1598)
: giving an advantage : FAVORABLE
— **ad·van·ta·geous·ly** *adverb*
— **ad·van·ta·geous·ness** *noun*

ad·vec·tion \ad-'vek-shən\ *noun* [Latin *advection-, advectio* act of bringing, from *advehere* to carry to, from *ad-* + *vehere* to carry — more at WAY] (1910)
: the usually horizontal movement of a mass of fluid (as air or an ocean current); *also* : transport (as of pollutants or plankton) by such movement
— **ad·vect** \-'vekt\ *transitive verb*

— **ad·vec·tive** \-'vek-tiv\ *adjective*
Ad·vent \'ad-ˌvent, *chiefly British* -vənt\ *noun* [Middle English, from Medieval Latin *adventus*, from Latin, arrival, from *advenire*] (12th century)
1 : the period beginning four Sundays before Christmas and observed by some Christians as a season of prayer and fasting
2 a : the coming of Christ at the Incarnation **b** : SECOND COMING
3 *not capitalized* : a coming into being or use ⟨the *advent* of spring⟩ ⟨the *advent* of pasteurization⟩ ⟨the *advent* of personal computers⟩

Ad·vent·ism \'ad-ˌven-ˌti-zəm\ *noun* (1874)
1 : the doctrine that the second coming of Christ and the end of the world are near at hand
2 : the principles and practices of Seventh-Day Adventists
— **Ad·vent·ist** \əd-'ven-tist, ad-', 'ad-ˌ\ *adjective or noun*

ad·ven·ti·tia \ˌad-vən-'ti-shə, -(ˌ)ven-\ *noun* [New Latin, alteration of Latin *adventicia*, neuter plural of *adventicius* coming from outside, from *adventus*, past participle] (1876)
: an external chiefly connective tissue covering of an organ; *especially* : the external coat of a blood vessel
— **ad·ven·ti·tial** \-shəl\ *adjective*

ad·ven·ti·tious \ˌad-(ˌ)ven-'ti-shəs, -vən-\ *adjective* [Latin *adventicius*] (1603)
1 : coming from another source and not inherent or innate
2 : arising or occurring sporadically or in other than the usual location ⟨*adventitious* roots⟩
— **ad·ven·ti·tious·ly** *adverb*

ad·ven·tive \ad-'ven-tiv\ *adjective* (circa 1859)
1 : introduced but not fully naturalized
2 : ADVENTITIOUS 2
— **adventive** *noun*

Advent Sunday *noun* (15th century)
: the first Sunday in Advent

¹**ad·ven·ture** \əd-'ven-chər\ *noun* [Middle English *aventure*, from Old French, from (assumed) Vulgar Latin *adventura*, from Latin *adventus*, past participle of *advenire* to arrive, from *ad-* + *venire* to come — more at COME] (14th century)
1 a : an undertaking usually involving danger and unknown risks **b** : the encountering of risks ⟨the spirit of *adventure*⟩
2 : an exciting or remarkable experience ⟨an *adventure* in exotic dining⟩
3 : an enterprise involving financial risk

²**adventure** *verb* **ad·ven·tured; ad·ven·tur·ing** \-'ven-ch(ə-)riŋ\ (14th century)
transitive verb
1 : to expose to danger or loss : VENTURE
2 : to venture upon : TRY
intransitive verb
1 : to proceed despite risk
2 : to take the risk

ad·ven·tur·er \əd-'ven-ch(ə-)rər\ *noun* (1539)
1 : one that adventures: as **a** : SOLDIER OF FORTUNE **b** : one that engages in risky commercial enterprises for profit
2 : one who seeks unmerited wealth or position especially by playing on the credulity or prejudice of others

ad·ven·ture·some \əd-'ven-chər-səm\ *adjective* (circa 1731)
: inclined to take risks : VENTURESOME
— **ad·ven·ture·some·ness** *noun*

ad·ven·tur·ess \əd-'ven-ch(ə-)rəs\ *noun* (1754)
: a female adventurer; *especially* : one who seeks position or livelihood by questionable means

ad·ven·tur·ism \əd-'ven-chə-ˌri-zəm\ *noun* (1932)
: improvisation or experimentation (as in politics or military or foreign affairs) in the absence or in defiance of accepted plans or principles
— **ad·ven·tur·ist** \-'ven-ch(ə-)rist\ *noun*

— **ad·ven·tur·is·tic** \-ˌven-chə-'ris-tik\ *adjective*

ad·ven·tur·ous \əd-'ven-ch(ə-)rəs\ *adjective* (14th century)
1 a : disposed to seek adventure or to cope with the new and unknown ⟨an *adventurous* explorer⟩ **b** : INNOVATIVE ⟨an *adventurous* artistic style⟩
2 : characterized by unknown dangers and risks ⟨an *adventurous* journey⟩ ☆
— **ad·ven·tur·ous·ly** *adverb*
— **ad·ven·tur·ous·ness** *noun*

¹**ad·verb** \'ad-ˌvərb\ *noun* [Middle English *adverbe*, from Middle French, from Latin *adverbium*, from *ad-* + *verbum* word — more at WORD] (14th century)
: a word belonging to one of the major form classes in any of numerous languages, typically serving as a modifier of a verb, an adjective, another adverb, a preposition, a phrase, a clause, or a sentence, expressing some relation of manner or quality, place, time, degree, number, cause, opposition, affirmation, or denial, and in English also serving to connect and to express comment on clause content — compare ADJUNCT, CONJUNCT, DISJUNCT

²**adverb** *adjective* (1879)
: ADVERBIAL

ad·ver·bi·al \ad-'vər-bē-əl\ *adjective* (1611)
: of, relating to, or having the function of an adverb
— **adverbial** *noun*
— **ad·ver·bi·al·ly** \-ə-lē\ *adverb*

ad verbum \(ˌ)ad-'vər-bəm\ *adverb* [Latin] (circa 1580)
: to a word : VERBATIM

ad·ver·sar·i·al \ˌad-və-'ser-ē-əl\ *adjective* (1926)
: of, relating to, or characteristic of an adversary or adversary procedures : ADVERSARY

¹**ad·ver·sary** \'ad-və(r)-ˌser-ē\ *noun, plural* **-sar·ies** (14th century)
: one that contends with, opposes, or resists : ENEMY
— **ad·ver·sari·ness** *noun*

☆ SYNONYMS
Advance, promote, forward, further mean to help (someone or something) to move ahead. ADVANCE stresses effective assisting in hastening a process or bringing about a desired end ⟨*advance* the cause of peace⟩. PROMOTE suggests an encouraging or fostering and may denote an increase in status or rank ⟨a campaign to *promote* better health⟩. FORWARD implies an impetus forcing something ahead ⟨a wage increase would *forward* productivity⟩. FURTHER suggests a removing of obstacles in the way of a desired advance ⟨used the marriage to *further* his career⟩.

Adventurous, venturesome, daring, daredevil, rash, reckless, foolhardy mean exposing oneself to danger more than required by good sense. ADVENTUROUS implies a willingness to accept risks but not necessarily imprudence ⟨*adventurous* pioneers⟩. VENTURESOME implies a jaunty eagerness for perilous undertakings ⟨*venturesome* stunt pilots⟩. DARING heightens the implication of fearlessness in courting danger ⟨*daring* mountain climbers⟩. DAREDEVIL stresses ostentation in daring ⟨*daredevil* motorcyclists⟩. RASH suggests imprudence and lack of forethought ⟨a *rash* decision⟩. RECKLESS implies heedlessness of probable consequences ⟨a *reckless* driver⟩. FOOLHARDY suggests a recklessness that is inconsistent with good sense ⟨only a *foolhardy* sailor would venture into this storm⟩.

²**adversary** *adjective* (14th century)
1 : of, relating to, or involving an adversary
2 : having or involving antagonistic parties or opposing interests ⟨divorce can be an *adversary* proceeding⟩

ad·ver·sa·tive \əd-'vər-sə-tiv, ad-\ *adjective* (15th century)
: expressing antithesis, opposition, or adverse circumstance ⟨the *adversative* conjunction *but*⟩
— **adversative** *noun*
— **ad·ver·sa·tive·ly** *adverb*

ad·verse \ad-'vərs, 'ad-,\ *adjective* [Middle English, from Middle French *advers*, from Latin *adversus*, past participle of *advertere*] (14th century)
1 : acting against or in a contrary direction **:** HOSTILE ⟨hindered by *adverse* winds⟩
2 a : opposed to one's interests ⟨an *adverse* verdict⟩ ⟨heard testimony *adverse* to their position⟩; *especially* **:** UNFAVORABLE ⟨*adverse* criticism⟩ **b :** causing harm **:** HARMFUL ⟨*adverse* drug effects⟩
3 *archaic* **:** opposite in position □
— **ad·verse·ly** *adverb*
— **ad·verse·ness** *noun*

ad·ver·si·ty \ad-'vər-sə-tē\ *noun, plural* **-ties** (13th century)
1 : a state or condition contrary to one of well-being
2 : an instance of adversity
synonym see MISFORTUNE

¹**ad·vert** \ad-'vərt\ *intransitive verb* [Middle English *adverten*, from Middle French & Latin; Middle French *advertir*, from Latin *advertere*, from *ad-* + *vertere* to turn — more at WORTH] (15th century)
1 : to turn the mind or attention — used with *to* ⟨*adverted* to the speaker⟩
2 : to call attention in the course of speaking or writing **:** make reference — used with *to* ⟨*adverted* to foreign-language sources⟩

²**ad·vert** \'ad-,vərt\ *noun* (1860)
chiefly British **:** ADVERTISEMENT

ad·ver·tence \ad-'vər-t°n(t)s\ *noun* (14th century)
1 : the action or process of adverting **:** ATTENTION
2 : ADVERTENCY 1

ad·ver·ten·cy \-t°n(t)-sē\ *noun, plural* **-cies** (1646)
1 : the quality or state of being advertent **:** HEEDFULNESS
2 : ADVERTENCE 1

ad·ver·tent \-t°nt\ *adjective* [Latin *advertent-, advertens*, present participle of *advertere*] (1671)
: giving attention **:** HEEDFUL
— **ad·ver·tent·ly** *adverb*

ad·ver·tise \'ad-vər-,tīz\ *verb* **-tised; -tis·ing** [Middle English, from Middle French *advertiss-*, stem of *advertir*] (15th century)
transitive verb
1 : to make something known to **:** NOTIFY
2 a : to make publicly and generally known ⟨*advertising* their readiness to make concessions⟩ **b :** to announce publicly especially by a printed notice or a broadcast **c :** to call public attention to especially by emphasizing desirable qualities so as to arouse a desire to buy or patronize **:** PROMOTE
intransitive verb
: to issue or sponsor advertising ⟨*advertise* for a secretary⟩
— **ad·ver·tis·er** *noun*

ad·ver·tise·ment \,ad-vər-'tīz-mənt; əd-'vər-təz-mənt, -tə-smənt\ *noun* (15th century)
1 : the act or process of advertising
2 : a public notice; *especially* **:** one published in the press or broadcast over the air

ad·ver·tis·ing *noun* (1762)
1 : the action of calling something to the attention of the public especially by paid announcements
2 : ADVERTISEMENTS ⟨the magazine contains much *advertising*⟩

3 : the business of preparing advertisements for publication or broadcast

ad·ver·tize, ad·ver·tize·ment *British variant of* ADVERTISE, ADVERTISEMENT

ad·ver·to·ri·al \,ad-vər-'tōr-ē-əl, -'tòr-\ *noun* [blend of *advertisement* and *editorial*] (1946)
: an advertisement that imitates editorial format

ad·vice \əd-'vīs\ *noun* [Middle English, from Middle French *avis*, probably from the phrase *ce m'est a vis* that appears to me, part translation of Latin *mihi visum est* it seemed so to me, I decided] (14th century)
1 : recommendation regarding a decision or course of conduct **:** COUNSEL ⟨he shall have power, by and with the *advice* and consent of the Senate, to make treaties —*U.S. Constitution*⟩
2 : information or notice given — usually used in plural
3 : an official notice concerning a business transaction

ad·vis·able \əd-'vī-zə-bəl\ *adjective* (1582)
: fit to be advised or done **:** PRUDENT
synonym see EXPEDIENT
— **ad·vis·abil·i·ty** \-,vī-zə-'bi-lə-tē\ *noun*
— **ad·vis·able·ness** \-'vī-zə-bəl-nəs\ *noun*
— **ad·vis·ably** \-blē\ *adverb*

ad·vise \əd-'vīz\ *verb* **ad·vised; ad·vis·ing** [Middle English, from Middle French *aviser*, from *avis*] (14th century)
transitive verb
1 a : to give advice to **:** COUNSEL ⟨*advise* her to try a drier climate⟩ **b :** CAUTION, WARN ⟨*advise* them of the consequences⟩ **c :** RECOMMEND ⟨*advise* prudence⟩
2 : to give information or notice to **:** INFORM ⟨*advise* them of their rights⟩
intransitive verb
1 : to give advice ⟨*advise* on legal matters⟩
2 : to take counsel **:** CONSULT ⟨*advise* with your parents⟩
— **ad·vis·er** *also* **ad·vi·sor** \-'vī-zər\ *noun*

ad·vised \əd-'vīzd\ *adjective* (14th century)
: thought out **:** CONSIDERED — often used in combination ⟨ill-*advised* plans⟩
— **ad·vis·ed·ly** \-'vī-zəd-lē\ *adverb*

ad·vis·ee \əd-,vī-'zē\ *noun* (1824)
: one that is advised

ad·vise·ment \əd-'vīz-mənt\ *noun* (14th century)
1 : careful consideration **:** DELIBERATION
2 : the act or process of advising (as a college student)

¹**ad·vi·so·ry** \əd-'vīz-rē, -'vī-zə-\ *adjective* (1778)
1 : having or exercising power to advise
2 : containing or giving advice

²**advisory** *noun, plural* **-ries** (1936)
: a report giving information (as on the weather) and often recommending action to be taken

ad·vo·ca·cy \'ad-və-kə-sē\ *noun* (15th century)
: the act or process of advocating or supporting a cause or proposal

advocacy journalism *noun* (1970)
: journalism that advocates a cause or expresses a viewpoint
— **advocacy journalist** *noun*

¹**ad·vo·cate** \'ad-və-kət, -,kāt\ *noun* [Middle English *advocat*, from Middle French, from Latin *advocatus*, from past participle of *advocare* to summon, from *ad-* + *vocare* to call, from *voc-, vox* voice — more at VOICE] (14th century)
1 : one that pleads the cause of another; *specifically* **:** one that pleads the cause of another before a tribunal or judicial court
2 : one that defends or maintains a cause or proposal

²**ad·vo·cate** \-,kāt\ *transitive verb* **-cat·ed; -cat·ing** (1599)
: to plead in favor of
synonym see SUPPORT
— **ad·vo·ca·tion** \,ad-və-'kā-shən\ *noun*

— **ad·vo·ca·tive** \'ad-və-,kā-tiv\ *adjective*
— **ad·vo·ca·tor** \-,kā-tər\ *noun*

ad·vow·son \əd-'vaú-z°n\ *noun* [Middle English, from Old French *avoueson*, from Medieval Latin *advocation-, advocatio*, from Latin, act of calling, from *advocare*] (14th century)
: the right in English law of presenting a nominee to an ecclesiastical benefice

ady·nam·ic \,ā-(,)dī-'na-mik, ,a-də-'na-\ *adjective* [Greek *adynamia* lack of strength, from *a-* + *dynamis* power, from *dynasthai* to be able] (1829)
: characterized by or causing a loss of strength or function ⟨*adynamic* ileus⟩

ad·y·tum \'a-də-təm\ *noun, plural* **-ta** \-tə\ [Latin, from Greek *adyton*, neuter of *adytos* not to be entered, from *a-* + *dyein* to enter] (1611)
: the innermost sanctuary in an ancient temple open only to priests **:** SANCTUM

adze *also* **adz** \'adz\ *noun* [Middle English *adse*, from Old English *adesa*] (before 12th century)
: a cutting tool that has a thin arched blade set at right angles to the handle and is used chiefly for shaping wood

ad·zu·ki bean \ad-'zü-kē-\ *noun* [Japanese *azuki*] (1795)
: an annual bushy leguminous plant (*Vignis angularis* synonym *Phaseolus angularis*) widely grown in Japan and China for its seeds which are used as food and to produce a flour; *also* **:** its seed — called also *adzuki*

adze

ae \'ā\ *adjective* [Middle English (northern dialect) *a*, alteration of *an*] (1737)
chiefly Scottish **:** ONE

Ae·a·cus \'ē-ə-kəs\ *noun* [Latin, from Greek *Aiakos*]
: a son of Zeus who is given the Myrmidons as followers and becomes on his death a judge of the underworld

ae·cio·spore \'ē-shə-,spōr, 'ē-sə-, -,spòr\ *noun* (1905)
: one of the spores arranged within an aecium in a series like a chain

ae·ci·um \'ē-shē-əm, 'ē-sē-\ *noun, plural* **-cia** \-shē-ə, -sē-\ [New Latin, from Greek *aikia* outrage, assault, from *aikēs, aeikēs* unseemly, from *a-* + *-eikēs*, from *eikenai* to seem] (1905)

□ USAGE

adverse Here are a few observations to help with the use of *adverse* and *averse*. *Adverse* is often used attributively ⟨under *adverse* circumstances⟩ ⟨an *adverse* reaction⟩ while *averse* is rarely so used. It is more often a thing than a person that is adverse ⟨the whole Parliamentary tradition . . . is *adverse* to it —Sir Winston Churchill⟩. When used with *to* and of people, *adverse* and *averse* are pretty much synonymous, but *adverse* generally refers to opinion or intention ⟨was *adverse* to his union with this young lady —George Meredith⟩ and *averse* to feeling or inclination ⟨I am not *averse* to pillorying the innocent —John Barth⟩. But this is a subtle distinction and is not observed universally, even by respected writers ⟨liked to settle herself and was *adverse* to complications —Carson McCullers⟩ ⟨Her Majesty . . . was by no means *averse* to reforms —Edith Sitwell⟩.

\ə\ abut \°\ kitten \ər\ further \a\ ash \ā\ ace
\ä\ mop, mar \aú\ out \ch\ chin \e\ bet \ē\ easy
\g\ go \i\ hit \ī\ ice \j\ job \ŋ\ sing \ō\ go
\ò\ law \òi\ boy \th\ thin \th\ the \ü\ loot \ú\ foot
\y\ yet \zh\ vision *see also* Guide to Pronunciation

: the fruiting body of a rust fungus in which the first binucleate spores are usually produced
— **ae·cial** \-sh(ē-)əl\ *adjective*

ae·des \ā-ē-(ˌ)dēz\ *noun, plural* **aedes** [New Latin, genus name, from Greek *aēdēs* unpleasant, from *a-* + *ēdos* pleasure; akin to Greek *hēdys* sweet — more at SWEET] (circa 1909)
: any of a genus (*Aedes*) of mosquitoes including the vector of yellow fever, dengue, and other diseases
— **ae·dine** \-ē-ˌdīn\ *adjective*

ae·dile \ē-ˌdīl, ē-dⁿl\ *noun* [Latin *aedilis*, from *aedes* temple — more at EDIFY] (1540)
: an official in ancient Rome in charge of public works and games, police, and the grain supply

Ae·ge·an \i-ˈjē-ən\ *adjective* [Latin *Aegaeus*, from Greek *Aigaios*] (1550)
1 : of or relating to the arm of the Mediterranean Sea east of Greece
2 : of or relating to the chiefly Bronze Age civilization of the islands of the Aegean Sea and the countries adjacent to it

ae·gis \ˈē-jəs *also* ˈā-\ *noun* [Latin, from Greek *aigis*, literally, goatskin, from *aig-, aix* goat; akin to Armenian *ayc* goat] (1611)
1 : a shield or breastplate emblematic of majesty that was associated with Zeus and Athena
2 a : PROTECTION ⟨under the *aegis* of the constitution⟩ **b** : controlling or conditioning influence ⟨many American mothers, under the *aegis* of benevolent permissiveness . . . actually neglect their children —*Time*⟩
3 a : AUSPICES, SPONSORSHIP ⟨under the *aegis* of the museum⟩ **b** : control or guidance especially by an individual, group, or system ⟨acted under the court's *aegis*⟩ ◆

Ae·gis·thus \i-ˈjis-thəs\ *noun* [Latin, from Greek *Aigisthos*]
: a lover of Clytemnestra slain with her by her son Orestes

-aemia *chiefly British variant of* -EMIA

Ae·ne·as \i-ˈnē-əs\ *noun* [Latin, from Greek *Aineias*]
: a son of Anchises and Aphrodite, defender of Troy, and hero of Virgil's *Aeneid*

Ae·ne·o·lith·ic \ā-ˌē-nē-ō-ˈli-thik\ *adjective* [Latin *aeneus* of copper or bronze, from *aes* copper, bronze — more at ORE] (1901)
: of or relating to a transitional period between the Neolithic and Bronze ages in which some copper was used

¹Ae·o·li·an \ē-ˈō-lē-ən, ē-ˈōl-yən\ *adjective* (1605)
1 *often capitalized* : of or relating to Aeolus
2 : giving forth or marked by a moaning or sighing sound or musical tone produced by or as if by the wind

²aeolian *variant of* EOLIAN

¹Ae·o·li·an \ē-ˈō-lē-ən, ā-, -ˈōl-yən\ *adjective* (1589)
: of or relating to Aeolis or its inhabitants

²Aeolian *noun* (circa 1889)
1 : a member of a group of Greek peoples of Thessaly and Boeotia that colonized Lesbos and the adjacent coast of Asia Minor
2 : AEOLIC

aeolian harp *noun* (1791)
: a box-shaped musical instrument having stretched strings usually tuned in unison on which the wind produces varying harmonics over the same fundamental tone

¹Ae·ol·ic \ē-ˈä-lik\ *adjective* (1674)
: AEOLIAN

²Aeolic *noun* (1902)
: a group of ancient Greek dialects used by the Aeolians

Ae·o·lus \ˈē-ə-ləs\ *noun* [Latin, from Greek *Aiolos*]
: the Greek god of the winds

ae·on *or* **eon** \ˈē-ən, ˈē-ˌän\ *noun* [Latin, from Greek *aiōn* — more at AYE] (1647)
1 : an immeasurably or indefinitely long period of time : AGE
2 a *usually* **eon** : a very large division of geo-

logic time usually longer than an era **b** : a unit of geologic time equal to one billion years

ae·o·ni·an \ē-ˈō-nē-ən\ *or* **ae·on·ic** \-ˈä-nik\ *adjective* (1765)
: lasting for an immeasurably or indefinitely long period of time

ae·py·or·nis \ˌē-pē-ˈȯr-nəs\ *noun* [New Latin, genus name, from Greek *aipys* high + *ornis* bird — more at ERNE] (1851)
: any of a group (genus *Aepyornis* or order Aepyornithiformes) of gigantic ratite birds known only from remains found in Madagascar — called also *elephant bird*

aer- *or* **aero-** *combining form* [Middle English *aero-*, from Middle French, from Latin, from Greek *aer-, aero-*, from *aēr*]
1 a : air : atmosphere ⟨*aer*ate⟩ ⟨*aero*biology⟩ **b** : air and ⟨*aero*space⟩
2 : gas ⟨*aero*sol⟩
3 : aviation ⟨*aero*drome⟩

aer·ate \ˈa(-ə)r-ˌāt, ˈe(-ə)r-\ *transitive verb* **aer·at·ed; aer·at·ing** (1794)
1 : to supply (the blood) with oxygen by respiration
2 : to supply or impregnate (as the soil or a liquid) with air
3 a *British* : CARBONATE 2 **b** : to make light or sparkling
— **aer·a·tion** \ˌa(-ə)r-ˈā-shən, ˌe(-ə)r-\ *noun*

aer·a·tor \ˈa(-ə)r-ˌā-tər, ˈe(-ə)r-\ *noun* (1861)
: one that aerates; *especially* : an apparatus for aerating something (as sewage)

aer·en·chy·ma \ˌa-ˈreŋ-kə-mə, ˌer-\ *noun* [New Latin] (circa 1893)
: the spongy modified cork tissue of many aquatic plants that facilitates gaseous exchange and maintains buoyancy

¹ae·ri·al \ˈar-ē-əl, ˈer-; ā-ˈir-ē-əl\ *adjective* [Latin *aerius*, from Greek *aerios*, from *aēr*] (1604)
1 a : of, relating to, or occurring in the air or atmosphere **b** : existing or growing in the air rather than in the ground or in water **c** : high in the air ⟨*aerial* spires⟩ **d** : operating or operated overhead on elevated cables or rails ⟨an *aerial* tram⟩
2 : suggestive of air: as **a** : lacking substance **b** : FANCIFUL, ETHEREAL ⟨visions of *aerial* joy —P. B. Shelley⟩
3 a : of or relating to aircraft ⟨*aerial* navigation⟩ **b** : designed for use in, taken from, or operating from or against aircraft **c** : effected by means of aircraft ⟨*aerial* transportation⟩
4 : of, relating to, or gained by the forward pass in football
— **ae·ri·al·ly** \-ə-lē\ *adverb*

²aer·i·al \ˈar-ē-əl, ˈer-\ *noun* (1902)
1 : ANTENNA 2
2 : FORWARD PASS

ae·ri·al·ist \ˈar-ē-ə-list, ˈer-, ā-ˈir-\ *noun* (1905)
: one that performs feats in the air or above the ground especially on the trapeze

aerial ladder *noun* (1904)
: a mechanically operated extensible ladder usually mounted on a fire truck

aerial perspective *noun* (1720)
: the expression of space in painting by gradation of color and distinctness

ae·rie \ˈar-ē, ˈer-, ˈir-, ˈā-(ə-)rē\ *noun* [Medieval Latin *aerea*, from Old French *aire*, probably from (assumed) Vulgar Latin *agrum* origin, nest, lair, from Latin *ager* field — more at ACRE] (1581)
1 : the nest of a bird on a cliff or a mountaintop
2 *obsolete* : a brood of birds of prey
3 : an elevated often secluded dwelling, structure, or position

aero \ˈa(-ə)r-(ˌ)ō, ˈe(-ə)r-\ *adjective* [*aero-*] (1874)
: of or relating to aircraft or aeronautics ⟨an *aero* engine⟩

aer·o·bat·ics \ˌar-ə-ˈba-tiks, ˌer-\ *noun plural but singular or plural in construction* [*aer-* + acro*batics*] (circa 1911)

: spectacular flying feats and maneuvers (as rolls and dives)
— **aer·o·bat·ic** \-tik\ *adjective*

aer·obe \ˈa(-ə)r-ˌōb, ˈe(-ə)r-\ *noun* [French *aérobie*, from *aéro-* aer- + *-bie* (from Greek *-bion*, from *bios* life) — more at QUICK] (1886)
: an organism (as a bacterium) that lives only in the presence of oxygen

aer·o·bic \ˌa(-ə)r-ˈō-bik, ˌe(-ə)r-\ *adjective* (1884)
1 : living, active, or occurring only in the presence of oxygen ⟨*aerobic* respiration⟩
2 : of, relating to, or induced by aerobes ⟨*aerobic* fermentation⟩
3 : involving, utilizing, or used in aerobics ⟨an *aerobic* workout⟩ ⟨*aerobic* fitness⟩
— **aer·o·bi·cal·ly** \-bi-k(ə-)lē\ *adverb*

aer·o·bics \-biks\ *noun plural* (1967)
1 *singular or plural in construction* : a system of physical conditioning involving exercises (as running, walking, swimming, or calisthenics) strenuously performed so as to cause marked temporary increase in respiration and heart rate
2 : aerobic exercises

aero·bi·ol·o·gy \ˌar-ō-bī-ˈä-lə-jē\ *noun* [*aer-* + *biology*] (circa 1937)
: the science dealing with the occurrence, transportation, and effects of airborne materials (as viruses, pollen, or pollutants)
— **aero·bi·o·log·i·cal** \-ˌbī-ə-ˈlä-ji-kəl\ *adjective*

aero·bi·o·sis \ˌar-ō-bī-ˈō-səs, ˌer-, -bē-\ *noun, plural* **-o·ses** \-ˌsēz\ [New Latin] (circa 1900)
: life in the presence of air or oxygen

aero·brake \ˈar-ō-ˌbrāk, ˈer-\ *transitive verb* (1965)
: to decelerate (as a spacecraft) by passage through a planetary atmosphere

aero·drome \ˈar-ə-ˌdrōm, ˈer-\ *noun* (1908) *chiefly British* : AIRFIELD

aero·dy·nam·i·cist \ˌar-ō-dī-ˈna-mə-sist, ˌer-\ *noun* (1926)
: one who specializes in aerodynamics

aero·dy·nam·ics \-ˈna-miks\ *noun plural but singular or plural in construction* (circa 1837)
: a branch of dynamics that deals with the motion of air and other gaseous fluids and with the forces acting on bodies in motion relative to such fluids
— **aero·dy·nam·ic** \-mik\ *also* **aero·dy·nam·i·cal** \-mi-kəl\ *adjective*
— **aero·dy·nam·i·cal·ly** \-mi-k(ə-)lē\ *adverb*

aero·dyne \ˈar-ə-ˌdīn, ˈer-\ *noun* [*aerodynamic*] (circa 1906)
: a heavier-than-air aircraft (as an airplane, helicopter, or glider) — compare AEROSTAT

aero·elas·tic·i·ty \ˌar-ō-ˌē-ˌlas-ˈti-sə-tē, ˌer-, -i-ˌlas-\ *noun* (1935)

◇ WORD HISTORY
aegis When we speak of something as being "under the aegis of" another, we mean that it is under the authority, sponsorship, or control of another. The basic idea is that whatever is in the subordinate position is being protected. In ancient Greece the word *aigis* meant literally "goatskin," but literal usage was uncommon. More frequently, *aigis* referred to a protective mantle, presumably of goat hide, or perhaps a shield, brandished by the god Zeus. Sometimes he entrusted the aegis to other deities, especially his daughter Athena. In its center the aegis bore an image of the Gorgon Medusa's head, and its border was decorated with golden fringe according to Homer. The aegis became a familiar classical reference in English literature, and by the 18th century the word *aegis* was being used figuratively for other kinds of seemingly impregnable protection.

: distortion (as from bending or flexing) in a structure (as an airplane wing or a building) caused by aerodynamic forces
— **aero·elas·tic** \-'las-tik\ *adjective*

aer·o·em·bo·lism \,ar-ō-'em-bə-,li-zəm, ,er-\ *noun* (circa 1939)
: a condition equivalent to bends caused by a rapid ascent to high altitudes and resulting exposure to rapidly lowered air pressure

aero·foil \'ar-ə-,fȯil, 'er-\ *noun* (1907) *chiefly British* **:** AIRFOIL

aero·gram *or* **aero·gramme** \'ar-ə-,gram, 'er-\ *noun* (1899)
: AIR LETTER 2

aer·og·ra·pher's mate \,a-'rä-grə-fərz-, ,e-\ *noun* (circa 1952)
: a navy petty officer specializing in meteorology

aer·o·lite \'ar-ə-,līt, 'er-\ *noun* (circa 1815)
: a stony meteorite

aero·mag·net·ic \,ar-ō-mag-'ne-tik, ,er-\ *adjective* (1948)
: of, relating to, or derived from a study of the earth's magnetic field especially from the air ⟨an *aeromagnetic* survey⟩

aero·me·chan·ics \-mə-'ka-niks\ *noun plural but singular or plural in construction* (circa 1909)
: mechanics that deals with the equilibrium and motion of gases and of solid bodies immersed in them

aero·med·i·cine \-'me-də-sən\ *noun* (1942)
: a branch of medicine that deals with the diseases and disorders arising from flying and the associated physiological and psychological problems
— **aero·med·i·cal** \-'me-di-kəl\ *adjective*

aer·om·e·ter \a(-ə)r-'ä-mə-tər, ,e(-ə)r-\ *noun* [probably from French *aéromètre*, from *aér-* + *-mètre* -meter] (1794)
: an instrument for ascertaining the weight or density of air or other gases

aero·naut \'ar-ə-,nȯt, 'er-, -,nät\ *noun* [French *aéronaute*, from *aér-* aer- + Greek *nautēs* sailor — more at NAUTICAL] (1784)
: one that operates or travels in an airship or balloon

aero·nau·tics \,ar-ə-'nȯ-tiks, ,er-, -'nä-\ *noun plural but singular in construction* (circa 1824)
1 : a science dealing with the operation of aircraft
2 : the art or science of flight
— **aero·nau·ti·cal** \-ti-kəl\ *also* **aero·nau·tic** \-tik\ *adjective*
— **aero·nau·ti·cal·ly** \-ti-k(ə-)lē\ *adverb*

aer·on·o·my \a(-ə)r-'ä-nə-mē, ,e(-ə)r-\ *noun* (1957)
: a science that deals with the physics and chemistry of the upper atmosphere of planets
— **aer·on·o·mer** \-mər\ *noun*
— **aer·o·nom·ic** \,ar-ə-'nä-mik, ,er-\ *or* **aer·o·nom·i·cal** \-mi-kəl\ *adjective*
— **aer·on·o·mist** \,a(-ə)r-'ä-nə-mist, ,e(-ə)r-\ *noun*

aero·plane \'ar-ə-,plān, 'er-\ *noun* [French *aéroplane*, from *aéro-* aer- + *-plane*, probably from feminine of *plan* flat, level, from Latin *planus* — more at FLOOR] (1873) *chiefly British* **:** AIRPLANE

aero·sol \'ar-ə-,säl, 'er-, -,sȯl\ *noun* (1923)
1 : a suspension of fine solid or liquid particles in gas ⟨smoke, fog, and mist are *aerosols*⟩
2 : a substance (as an insecticide or cosmetic) dispensed from a pressurized container especially as an aerosol; *also* **:** the container for this

aero·sol·ize \-'sä-,līz, -,sȯ-, -sə-\ *transitive verb* **-ized; -iz·ing** (1944)
: to disperse as an aerosol
— **aero·sol·iza·tion** \,ar-ə-,sä-lə-'zā-shən, -,sȯ-, -sə-\ *noun*

¹aero·space \'ar-ō-,spās, 'er-\ *noun* (circa 1958)
1 : space comprising the earth's atmosphere and the space beyond

2 : a physical science that deals with aerospace
3 : the aerospace industry

²aerospace *adjective* (1958)
: of or relating to aerospace, to vehicles used in aerospace or the manufacture of such vehicles, or to travel in aerospace ⟨*aerospace* research⟩ ⟨*aerospace* profits⟩ ⟨*aerospace* medicine⟩

aerospace plane *noun* (1960)
: an airplane designed to be able to reach low earth orbit

aero·stat \-,stat\ *noun* [French *aérostat*, from *aér-* + *-stat*] (1784)
: a lighter-than-air aircraft (as a balloon or blimp) — compare AERODYNE

aero·stat·ics \,ar-ō-'sta-tiks, ,er-\ *noun plural but singular or plural in construction* [modification of New Latin *aerostatica*, from *aer-* + *statica* statics] (1784)
: a branch of statics that deals with the equilibrium of gaseous fluids and of solid bodies immersed in them

aero·ther·mo·dy·nam·ics \-,thər-mə-(,)dī-'na-miks\ *noun plural but singular or plural in construction* (1949)
: the thermodynamics of gases and especially of air
— **aero·ther·mo·dy·nam·ic** \-mik\ *adjective*

¹aery \'ar-ē, 'er-ē, 'ā-ə-rē\ *adjective* **aer·i·er; -est** [Latin *aerius* — more at AERIAL] (14th century)
: having an aerial quality **:** ETHEREAL ⟨*aery* visions⟩
— **aer·i·ly** \'ar-ə-lē, 'er-\ *adverb*

²aery *like* AERIE\ *variant of* AERIE

Aes·cu·la·pi·an \,es-k(y)ə-'lā-pē-ən\ *adjective* [*Aesculapius*, Greco-Roman god of medicine, from Latin, from Greek *Asklēpios*] (1605)
: of or relating to Aesculapius or the healing art ◇

Ae·sir \'ā-,zir, -,sir\ *noun plural* [Old Norse *Æsir*, plural of *āss* god]
: the principal race of Norse gods

Ae·so·pi·an \ē-'sō-pē-ən, -'sä-\ *also* **Ae·sop·ic** \-'sä-pik\ *adjective* (1728)
1 : of, relating to, or characteristic of Aesop or his fables
2 : conveying an innocent meaning to an outsider but a hidden meaning to a member of a conspiracy or underground movement ⟨*Aesopian* language⟩

aes·thete \'es-,thēt, *British usually* 'ēs-\ *noun* [back-formation from *aesthetic*] (1881)
: one having or affecting sensitivity to the beautiful especially in art

¹aes·thet·ic \es-'the-tik, is-, *British usually* ēs-\ *or* **aes·thet·i·cal** \-ti-kəl\ *adjective* [German *ästhetisch*, from New Latin *aestheticus*, from Greek *aisthētikos* of sense perception, from *aisthanesthai* to perceive — more at AUDIBLE] (1798)
1 a : of, relating to, or dealing with aesthetics or the beautiful ⟨*aesthetic* theories⟩ **b :** ARTISTIC ⟨a work of *aesthetic* value⟩ **c :** pleasing in appearance **:** ATTRACTIVE ⟨easy-to-use keyboards, clear graphics, and other ergonomic and *aesthetic* features —Mark Mehler⟩
2 : appreciative of, responsive to, or zealous about the beautiful; *also* **:** responsive to or appreciative of what is pleasurable to the senses
— **aes·thet·i·cal·ly** \-ti-k(ə-)lē\ *adverb*

²aesthetic *noun* (1822)
1 *plural but singular or plural in construction* **:** a branch of philosophy dealing with the nature of beauty, art, and taste and with the creation and appreciation of beauty
2 : a particular theory or conception of beauty or art **:** a particular taste for or approach to what is pleasing to the senses and especially sight ⟨modernist *aesthetics*⟩ ⟨staging new ballets which reflected the *aesthetic* of the new nation —Mary Clarke & Clement Crisp⟩

3 *plural* **:** a pleasing appearance or effect **:** BEAUTY ⟨appreciated the *aesthetics* of the gemstones⟩

aesthetic distance *noun* (1938)
: the frame of reference that an artist creates by the use of technical devices in and around the work of art to differentiate it psychologically from reality

aes·the·ti·cian \,es-thə-'ti-shən\ *noun* (1829)
: a specialist in aesthetics

aes·thet·i·cism \es-'the-tə-,si-zəm, is-\ *noun* (1855)
1 : a doctrine that the principles of beauty are basic to other and especially moral principles
2 : devotion to or emphasis on beauty or the cultivation of the arts

aes·thet·i·cize \-,sīz\ *transitive verb* **-cized; -ciz·ing** (1864)
: to make aesthetic

aes·ti·val \'es-tə-vəl\ *variant of* ESTIVAL

aes·ti·vate, aes·ti·va·tion *variant of* ESTIVATE, ESTIVATION

aether *variant of* ETHER 2a

ae·ti·ol·o·gy *chiefly British variant of* ETIOLOGY

af- — see AD-

¹afar \ə-'fär\ *adverb* [Middle English *afer*, from *on fer* at a distance and *of fer* from a distance] (14th century)
: from, to, or at a great distance ⟨roamed *afar*⟩
: far away

²afar *noun* (14th century)
: a great distance ⟨saw him from *afar*⟩

afeard *or* **afeared** \ə-'fird\ *adjective* [Middle English *afered*, from Old English *āfǣred*, past participle of *āfǣran* to frighten, from *ā-*, perfective prefix + *fǣran* to frighten — more at ABIDE, FEAR] (before 12th century) *dialect* **:** AFRAID

afe·brile \(,)ā-'fe-,brīl *also* -'fē-\ *adjective* (1875)
: not marked by fever

af·fa·ble \'a-fə-bəl\ *adjective* [Middle French, from Latin *affabilis*, from *affari* to speak to, from *ad-* + *fari* to speak — more at BAN] (15th century)
1 : being pleasant and at ease in talking to others
2 : characterized by ease and friendliness
synonym see GRACIOUS
— **af·fa·bil·i·ty** \,a-fə-'bi-lə-tē\ *noun*
— **af·fa·bly** \-blē\ *adverb*

af·fair \ə-'far, -'fer\ *noun* [Middle English & Middle French; Middle English *affaire*, from Middle French, from *a faire* to do] (14th century)
1 a *plural* **:** commercial, professional, public, or personal business **b :** MATTER, CONCERN
2 : a procedure, action, or occasion only

◇ WORD HISTORY
Aesculapian Aesculapius or Asclepius was the god of healing in Greco-Roman religious belief. The son of Apollo and the nymph Coronis, he was raised by the Centaur Chiron, who taught him the arts of medicine. According to one myth, Aesculapius was struck dead by one of Zeus's thunderbolts for bringing Hippolytus back to life. Snakes were the god's sacred emblems, and he was believed to be incarnate in them. It was in the figure of a snake that he was introduced into Rome during a time of pestilence. His branched staff with a snake coiled around it became the traditional symbol for medicine and is today the official insignia of the American Medical Association.

\ə\ abut \ᵊ\ kitten \ər\ further \a\ ash \ā\ ace
\ä\ mop, mar \au̇\ out \ch\ chin \e\ bet \ē\ easy
\g\ go \i\ hit \ī\ ice \j\ job \ŋ\ sing \ō\ go
\ȯ\ law \ȯi\ boy \th\ thin \t͟h\ the \ü\ loot \u̇\ foot
\y\ yet \zh\ vision *see also* Guide to Pronunciation

vaguely specified; *also* : an object or collection of objects only vaguely specified ⟨their house was a 2-story *affair*⟩
3 *also* **af·faire a** : a romantic or passionate attachment typically of limited duration : LIAISON 2b **b** : a matter occasioning public anxiety, controversy, or scandal : CASE

¹af·fect \'a-,fekt\ *noun* [Middle English, from Latin *affectus,* from *afficere*] (14th century)
1 *obsolete* : FEELING, AFFECTION
2 : the conscious subjective aspect of an emotion considered apart from bodily changes
usage see EFFECT

²af·fect \ə-'fekt, a-\ *verb* [Middle English, from Middle French & Latin; Middle French *affecter,* from Latin *affectare,* frequentative of *afficere* to influence, from *ad-* + *facere* to do — more at DO] (15th century)
transitive verb
1 *archaic* : to aim at
2 a *archaic* : to have affection for **b** : to be given to : FANCY ⟨*affect* flashy clothes⟩
3 : to make a display of liking or using : CULTIVATE ⟨*affect* a worldly manner⟩
4 : to put on a pretense of : FEIGN ⟨*affect* indifference, though deeply hurt⟩
5 : to tend toward ⟨drops of water *affect* roundness⟩
6 : FREQUENT
intransitive verb
obsolete : INCLINE 2
synonym see ASSUME
usage see EFFECT

³affect *transitive verb* [Middle English, from *affectus,* past participle of *afficere*] (15th century)
: to produce an effect upon: as **a** : to produce a material influence upon or alteration in ⟨paralysis *affected* his limbs⟩ **b** : to act upon (as a person or a person's mind or feelings) so as to effect a response : INFLUENCE ☆
usage see EFFECT
— **af·fect·abil·i·ty** \-,fek-tə-'bi-lə-tē\ *noun*
— **af·fect·able** \-'fek-tə-bəl\ *adjective*

af·fec·ta·tion \,a-,fek-'tā-shən\ *noun* (1548)
1 a : the act of taking on or displaying an attitude or mode of behavior not natural to oneself or not genuinely felt **b** : speech or conduct not natural to oneself : ARTIFICIALITY
2 *obsolete* : a striving after
synonym see POSE

af·fect·ed \ə-'fek-təd, a-\ *adjective* (1587)
1 : INCLINED, DISPOSED ⟨was well *affected* toward her⟩
2 a : given to affectation **b** : assumed artificially or falsely : PRETENDED ⟨an *affected* interest in art⟩
— **af·fect·ed·ly** *adverb*
— **af·fect·ed·ness** *noun*

af·fect·ing \ə-'fek-tiŋ, a-\ *adjective* (1720)
: evoking a strong emotional response
synonym see MOVING
— **af·fect·ing·ly** \-tiŋ-lē\ *adverb*

af·fec·tion \ə-'fek-shən\ *noun* [Middle English, from Old French *affection,* from Latin *affection-, affectio,* from *afficere*] (13th century)
1 : a moderate feeling or emotion
2 : tender attachment : FONDNESS ⟨she had a deep *affection* for her parents⟩
3 a (1) : a bodily condition (2) : DISEASE, MALADY **b** : ATTRIBUTE ⟨shape and weight are *affections* of bodies⟩
4 *obsolete* : PARTIALITY, PREJUDICE
5 : the feeling aspect (as in pleasure) of consciousness
6 a : PROPENSITY, DISPOSITION **b** *archaic* : AFFECTATION 1
7 : the action of affecting : the state of being affected
synonym see FEELING
— **af·fec·tion·less** \-ləs\ *adjective*

af·fec·tion·al \ə-'fek-shnəl, -shə-n³l\ *adjective* (1859)
: of or relating to the affections
— **af·fec·tion·al·ly** *adverb*

af·fec·tion·ate \ə-'fek-sh(ə-)nət\ *adjective* (15th century)
1 *obsolete* : INCLINED, DISPOSED
2 : having affection or warm regard : LOVING
3 : proceeding from affection : TENDER ⟨*affectionate* care⟩
— **af·fec·tion·ate·ly** *adverb*

af·fec·tioned \-shənd\ *adjective* (1555)
archaic : having a tendency, disposition, or inclination : DISPOSED

af·fec·tive \a-'fek-tiv\ *adjective* (1623)
1 : relating to, arising from, or influencing feelings or emotions : EMOTIONAL ⟨*affective* disorders⟩
2 : expressing emotion ⟨*affective* language⟩
— **af·fec·tive·ly** *adverb*
— **af·fec·tiv·i·ty** \,a-,fek-'ti-və-tē\ *noun*

af·fect·less \'a-,fekt-ləs, a-'fekt-\ *adjective* (1967)
: showing or expressing no emotion; *also* : UNFEELING ⟨a ruthless *affectless* society⟩
— **af·fect·less·ness** *noun*

af·fen·pin·scher \'a-fən-,pin-chər\ *noun* [German, from *Affe* ape + *Pinscher,* a breed of hunting dog] (1903)
: any of a breed of toy dogs with a wiry black, red, tan, or gray coat, erect ears, large round eyes, and bushy eyebrows, chin tuft, and mustache

¹af·fer·ent \'a-fə-rənt, -,fer-ənt\ *adjective* [Latin *afferent-, afferens,* present participle of *afferre* to bring to, from *ad-* + *ferre* to bear — more at BEAR] (circa 1847)
: bearing or conducting inward; *specifically* : conveying impulses toward a nerve center (as the brain or spinal cord) — compare EFFERENT
— **af·fer·ent·ly** *adverb*

²afferent *noun* (1949)
: an afferent anatomical part (as a nerve)

¹af·fi·ance \ə-'fī-ən(t)s\ *noun* [Middle English, from Middle French, from *affier* to pledge, trust, from Medieval Latin *affidare* to pledge, from Latin *ad-* + (assumed) Vulgar Latin *fidare* to trust — more at FIANCÉ] (14th century)
archaic : TRUST, CONFIDENCE

²affiance *transitive verb* **-anced; -anc·ing** (1555)
: to solemnly promise (oneself or another) in marriage : BETROTH

af·fi·ant \ə-'fī-ənt\ *noun* [Middle French, from present participle of *affier*] (1807)
: one that swears to an affidavit; *broadly* : DEPONENT

af·fi·cio·na·do *variant of* AFICIONADO

af·fi·da·vit \,a-fə-'dā-vət\ *noun* [Medieval Latin, he has made an oath, from *affidare*] (1593)
: a sworn statement in writing made especially under oath or on affirmation before an authorized magistrate or officer

¹af·fil·i·ate \ə-'fi-lē-,āt\ *verb* **-at·ed; -at·ing** [Medieval Latin *affiliatus,* past participle of *affiliare* to adopt as a son, from Latin *ad-* + *filius* son — more at FEMININE] (1761)
transitive verb
1 a : to bring or receive into close connection as a member or branch **b** : to associate as a member ⟨*affiliates* herself with the local club⟩
2 : to trace the origin of
intransitive verb
: to connect or associate oneself : COMBINE
— **af·fil·i·a·tion** \-,fī-lē-'ā-shən\ *noun*

²af·fil·i·ate \ə-'fi-lē-ət, -,āt\ *noun* (1879)
: an affiliated person or organization

af·fil·i·at·ed \-lē-,ā-təd\ *adjective* (1795)
: closely associated with another typically in a dependent or subordinate position ⟨the university and its *affiliated* medical school⟩

¹af·fine \a-'fīn, ə-\ *noun* [Middle French *affin,* from Latin *affinis,* from *affinis* related] (circa 1509)
: a relative by marriage : IN-LAW

²affine *adjective* [Latin *affinis,* adjective] (1918)
: of, relating to, or being a transformation (as a translation, a rotation, or a uniform stretching) that carries straight lines into straight lines and parallel lines into parallel lines but may alter distance between points and angles between lines ⟨*affine* geometry⟩
— **af·fine·ly** *adverb*

af·fined \a-'fīnd, ə-\ *adjective* (1597)
1 : joined in a close relationship : CONNECTED
2 : bound by obligation

af·fin·i·ty \ə-'fi-nə-tē\ *noun, plural* **-ties** [Middle English *affinite,* from Middle French or Latin; Middle French *afinité,* from Latin *affinitas,* from *affinis* bordering on, related by marriage, from *ad-* + *finis* end, border] (14th century)
1 : relationship by marriage
2 a : sympathy marked by community of interest : KINSHIP **b** (1) : an attraction to or liking for something ⟨people with an *affinity* to darkness —Mark Twain⟩ ⟨pork and fennel have a natural *affinity* for each other —Abby Mandel⟩ (2) : an attractive force between substances or particles that causes them to enter into and remain in chemical combination **c** : a person especially of the opposite sex having a particular attraction for one
3 a : likeness based on relationship or causal connection ⟨found an *affinity* between the teller of a tale and the craftsman —Mary McCarthy⟩ ⟨this investigation, with *affinities* to a case history, a psychoanalysis, a detective story and a novel — Oliver Sacks⟩ **b** : a relation between biological groups involving resemblance in structural plan and indicating a common origin
synonym see ATTRACTION

affinity chromatography *noun* (1970)
: chromatography in which a macromolecule (as a protein) is isolated and purified by passing it in solution through a column treated with a substance having a ligand for which the macromolecule has an affinity that causes it to be retained on the column

affinity group *noun* (1970)
: a group of people having a common interest or goal or acting together for a specific purpose (as for a chartered tour)

af·firm \ə-'fərm\ *verb* [Middle English *affermen,* from Middle French *afermer,* from Latin *affirmare,* from *ad-* + *firmare* to make firm, from *firmus* firm — more at FIRM] (14th century)
transitive verb
1 a : VALIDATE, CONFIRM **b** : to state positively
2 : to assert (as a judgment or decree) as valid or confirmed
3 : to express dedication to

intransitive verb
1 : to testify or declare by affirmation as distinguished from swearing an oath
2 : to uphold a judgment or decree of a lower court
synonym see ASSERT
— **af·firm·able** \ə-ˈfər-mə-bəl\ *adjective*
— **af·fir·mance** \ə-ˈfər-mən(t)s\ *noun*
af·fir·ma·tion \ˌa-fər-ˈmā-shən\ *noun* (15th century)
1 a : the act of affirming **b :** something affirmed **:** a positive assertion
2 : a solemn declaration made under the penalties of perjury by a person who conscientiously declines taking an oath
¹**af·fir·ma·tive** \ə-ˈfər-mə-tiv\ *adjective* (15th century)
1 : asserting a predicate of a subject
2 : asserting that the fact is so
3 : POSITIVE ⟨*affirmative* approach⟩
4 : favoring or supporting a proposition or motion
— **af·fir·ma·tive·ly** *adverb*
²**affirmative** *noun* (15th century)
1 : an expression (as the word *yes*) of affirmation or assent
2 : an affirmative proposition
3 : the side that upholds the proposition stated in a debate
affirmative action *noun* (1965)
: an active effort to improve the employment or educational opportunities of members of minority groups and women
¹**af·fix** \ə-ˈfiks, a-\ *transitive verb* [Latin *affixus,* past participle of *affigere* to fasten to, from *ad-* + *figere* to fasten — more at FIX] (1533)
1 : to attach physically ⟨*affix* a stamp to a letter⟩
2 : to attach in any way **:** ADD, APPEND ⟨*affix* a signature to a document⟩
3 : IMPRESS ⟨*affixed* my seal⟩
synonym see FASTEN
— **af·fix·able** \-ˈfik-sə-bəl\ *adjective*
— **af·fix·a·tion** \ˌa-ˌfik-ˈsā-shən\ *noun*
— **af·fix·ment** \ə-ˈfik-smənt, a-\ *noun*
²**af·fix** \ˈa-ˌfiks\ *noun* (1612)
1 : one or more sounds or letters occurring as a bound form attached to the beginning or end of a word, base, or phrase or inserted within a word or base and serving to produce a derivative word or an inflectional form
2 : APPENDAGE
— **af·fix·al** \-ˌfik-səl\ *or* **af·fix·i·al** \a-ˈfik-sē-əl\ *adjective*
af·fla·tus \ə-ˈflā-təs, a-\ *noun* [Latin, act of blowing or breathing on, from *afflare* to blow on, from *ad-* + *flare* to blow — more at BLOW] (1660)
: a divine imparting of knowledge or power **:** INSPIRATION
af·flict \ə-ˈflikt\ *transitive verb* [Middle English, from Latin *afflictus,* past participle of *affligere* to cast down, from *ad-* + *fligere* to strike — more at PROFLIGATE] (14th century)
1 *obsolete* **a :** HUMBLE **b :** OVERTHROW
2 a : to distress so severely as to cause persistent suffering or anguish **b :** TROUBLE, INJURE
☆
af·flic·tion \ə-ˈflik-shən\ *noun* (14th century)
1 : the state of being afflicted
2 : the cause of persistent pain or distress
3 : great suffering
af·flic·tive \ə-ˈflik-tiv\ *adjective* (circa 1611)
: causing affliction **:** DISTRESSING, TROUBLESOME
— **af·flic·tive·ly** *adverb*
af·flu·ence \ˈa-(ˌ)flü-ən(t)s *also* a-ˈflü- *or* ə-\ *noun* (14th century)
1 a : an abundant flow or supply **:** PROFUSION
b : abundance of property **:** WEALTH
2 : a flowing to or toward a point **:** INFLUX
af·flu·en·cy \-ən(t)-sē\ *noun, plural* **-cies** (1664)
: AFFLUENCE

¹**af·flu·ent** \-ənt\ *adjective* [Middle English, from Middle French, from Latin *affluent-, affluens,* present participle of *affluere* to flow to, flow abundantly, from *ad-* + *fluere* to flow — more at FLUID] (15th century)
1 : flowing in abundance ⟨*affluent* streams⟩ ⟨*affluent* creativity⟩
2 : having a generously sufficient and typically increasing supply of material possessions ⟨our *affluent* society⟩
synonym see RICH
— **af·flu·ent·ly** *adverb*
²**affluent** *noun* (1828)
1 : a tributary stream
2 : an affluent person
af·ford \ə-ˈfȯrd, -ˈfȯrd\ *transitive verb* [Middle English *aforthen,* from Old English *geforthian* to carry out, from *ge-,* perfective prefix + *forthian* to carry out, from *forth* — more at CO-, FORTH] (14th century)
1 a : to manage to bear without serious detriment ⟨you can't *afford* to neglect your health⟩
b : to be able to bear the cost of ⟨can't *afford* to be out of work long⟩ ⟨able to *afford* a new car⟩
2 : to make available, give forth, or provide naturally or inevitably ⟨the sun *affords* warmth to the earth⟩ ⟨the roof *afforded* a fine view⟩
synonym see GIVE
— **af·ford·abil·i·ty** \-ˌfȯr-də-ˈbi-lə-tē, -ˌfȯr-\ *noun*
— **af·ford·able** \-ˈfȯr-də-bəl, -ˈfȯr-\ *adjective*
— **af·ford·ably** \ə-ˈfȯr-də-blē, -ˈfȯr-\ *adverb*
af·for·es·ta·tion \(ˌ)a-ˌfȯr-ə-ˈstā-shən, ə-, -ˌfär-\ *noun* [Medieval Latin *afforestation-, afforestatio,* from *afforestare* to put under forest laws, from Latin *ad-* + Medieval Latin *foresta, forestis* forest] (1615)
: the act or process of establishing a forest especially on land not previously forested
— **af·for·est** \a-ˈfȯr-əst, -ˈfär-\ *transitive verb*
¹**af·fray** \ə-ˈfrā\ *noun* [Middle English, from Middle French, from *affreer* to startle] (14th century)
: FRAY, BRAWL
²**affray** *transitive verb* [Middle English *affraien,* from Middle French *affreer*] (14th century)
archaic **:** STARTLE, FRIGHTEN
af·fri·cate \ˈa-fri-kət\ *noun* [probably from German *Affrikata,* from Latin *africata,* feminine of *africatus,* past participle of *africare* to rub against, from *ad-* + *fricare* to rub — more at FRICTION] (1880)
: a stop and its immediately following release into a fricative that are considered to constitute a single phoneme (as the \t\ and \sh\ of \ch\ in *choose*)
— **af·fric·a·tive** \a-ˈfri-kə-tiv, ə-\ *noun or adjective*
¹**af·fright** \ə-ˈfrīt\ *transitive verb* [Middle English *afyrht, afright* frightened, from Old English *āfyrht,* past participle of *āfyrhtan* to frighten, from *ā-,* perfective prefix + *fyrhtan* to fear; akin to Old English *fyrhto* fright — more at ABIDE, FRIGHT] (before 12th century)
: FRIGHTEN, ALARM
²**affright** *noun* (1596)
: sudden and great fear **:** TERROR
¹**af·front** \ə-ˈfrənt\ *transitive verb* [Middle English *afronten,* from Middle French *afronter* to defy, from (assumed) Vulgar Latin *affrontare,* from Latin *ad-* + *front-, frons* forehead] (14th century)
1 a : to insult especially to the face by behavior or language **b :** to cause offense to ⟨a system of law about both family and marriage that *affronted* lay society —J. H. Mundy⟩
2 a : to face in defiance **:** CONFRONT ⟨*affront* death⟩ **b** *obsolete* **:** to encounter face-to-face
3 : to appear directly before
synonym see OFFEND

²**affront** *noun* (1533)
1 *obsolete* **:** a hostile encounter
2 : a deliberate offense **:** INSULT ⟨an *affront* to his dignity⟩
af·fu·sion \ə-ˈfyü-zhən\ *noun* [Late Latin *affusion-, affusio,* from Latin *affundere* to pour on, from *ad-* + *fundere* to pour — more at FOUND] (1615)
: an act of pouring a liquid on (as in baptism)
Af·ghan \ˈaf-ˌgan *also* -gən\ *noun* [Persian *afghān* Pashtun] (1767)
1 a (1) **:** PASHTUN (2) **:** PASHTO **b :** a native or inhabitant of Afghanistan
2 *not capitalized* **:** a blanket or shawl of colored wool knitted or crocheted in strips or squares
3 *not capitalized* **:** a Turkoman carpet of large size and long pile woven in geometric designs
4 : AFGHAN HOUND
— **Afghan** *adjective*
Afghan hound *noun* (1925)
: any of a breed of tall slim swift hunting dogs of Near Eastern origin with a coat of silky thick hair and a long silky topknot

Afghan hound

af·gha·ni \af-ˈga-nē, -ˈgä-\ *noun* [Persian *afghānī,* literally, of the Pashtuns] (1927)
— see MONEY table
afi·cio·na·da \ə-ˌfi-sh(ē-)ə-ˈnä-də, -fē-, -sē-ə-, -ˌdä\ *noun* [Spanish, feminine of *aficionado*] (1952)
: a female aficionado
afi·cio·na·do \-ˈnä-(ˌ)dō\ *noun, plural* **-dos** [Spanish, from past participle of *aficionar* to inspire affection, from *afición* affection, from Latin *affection-, affectio* — more at AFFECTION] (1845)
: a person who likes, knows about, and appreciates a usually fervently pursued interest or activity **:** DEVOTEE ⟨*aficionados* of the bullfight⟩ ⟨movie *aficionados*⟩
afield \ə-ˈfē(ə)ld\ *adverb or adjective* (before 12th century)
1 : to, in, or on the field ⟨was weak at bat but strong *afield*⟩
2 : away from home **:** ABROAD
3 : out of the way **:** ASTRAY ⟨irrelevant remarks that carried us far *afield*⟩
afire \ə-ˈfīr\ *adjective or adverb* (13th century)
: being on fire **:** BLAZING
aflame \ə-ˈflām\ *adjective or adverb* (1555)
: AFIRE

☆ **SYNONYMS**
Afflict, try, torment, torture, rack
mean to inflict on a person something that is hard to bear. AFFLICT is a general term and applies to the causing of pain or suffering or of acute annoyance, embarrassment, or any distress ⟨ills that *afflict* the elderly⟩. TRY suggests imposing something that strains the powers of endurance or of self-control ⟨children often *try* their parents' patience⟩. TORMENT suggests persecution or the repeated inflicting of suffering or annoyance ⟨a horse *tormented* by flies⟩. TORTURE adds the implication of causing unbearable pain or suffering ⟨*tortured* by a sense of guilt⟩. RACK stresses straining or wrenching ⟨a body *racked* by pain⟩.

\ə\ abut \ᵊ\ kitten \ər\ **further** \a\ ash \ā\ ace
\ä\ mop, mar \aù\ **out** \ch\ **chin** \e\ bet \ē\ **easy**
\g\ go \i\ hit \ī\ ice \j\ job \ŋ\ sing \ō\ go
\ò\ law \òi\ boy \th\ thin \t̲h̲\ the \ü\ loot \ù\ foot
\y\ yet \zh\ vision *see also* Guide to Pronunciation

af·la·tox·in \,a-flə-'täk-sən\ *noun* [New Latin *Aspergillus flavus,* species of mold + English *toxin*] (1962)
: any of several carcinogenic mycotoxins that are produced especially in stored agricultural crops (as peanuts) by molds (as *Aspergillus flavus*)

afloat \ə-'flōt\ *adjective or adverb* [Middle English *aflot,* from Old English *on flot,* from *on* + *flot,* from *flot* deep water, sea; akin to Old English *flēotan* to float — more at FLEET] (before 12th century)
1 a : borne on or as if on the water **b :** being at sea
2 : free of difficulties : SELF-SUFFICIENT ⟨the inheritance kept them *afloat* for years⟩
3 a : circulating about ⟨nasty stories were *afloat*⟩ **b :** ADRIFT

aflut·ter \ə-'flə-tər\ *adjective* (1830)
1 : being in a flutter : FLUTTERING
2 : nervously excited
3 : filled with or marked by the presence of fluttering things ⟨roofs *aflutter* with flags⟩

afoot \ə-'fut\ *adverb or adjective* (13th century)
1 : on foot
2 : in the process of development : UNDER WAY ⟨something out of the ordinary was *afoot* —Hamilton Basso⟩

afore \ə-'fōr, -'fȯr\ *adverb or conjunction or preposition* [Middle English, from Old English *onforan,* from *on* + *foran* before — more at BEFORE] (before 12th century)
chiefly dialect **:** BEFORE

afore·men·tioned \-'men(t)-shənd\ *adjective* (1587)
: mentioned previously

afore·said \-,sed\ *adjective* (14th century)
: said or named before or above

afore·thought \-,thȯt\ *adjective* (1581)
: previously in mind : PREMEDITATED, DELIBERATE ⟨with malice *aforethought*⟩

a for·ti·o·ri \,ä-,fȯr-shē-'ōr-,ī, ,ä-,fȯr-shē-'ōr-ē, -,fȯr-tē-, -'ȯr-\ *adverb* [New Latin, literally, from the stronger (argument)] (1588)
: with greater reason or more convincing force — used in drawing a conclusion that is inferred to be even more certain than another ⟨the man of prejudice is, *a fortiori,* a man of limited mental vision⟩

afoul of \ə-'faủ-ləv\ *preposition* (1824)
1 : in or into conflict with
2 : in or into collision or entanglement with

Afr- *or* **Afro-** *combining form* [Latin *Afr-, Afer*]
: African ⟨*Afro*-American⟩ : African and ⟨*Afro*-Asiatic⟩

afraid \ə-'frād, *Southern also* ə-'fred\ *adjective* [Middle English *affraied,* from past participle of *affraien* to frighten — more at AFFRAY] (14th century)
1 : filled with fear or apprehension ⟨*afraid* of machines⟩ ⟨*afraid* for his job⟩
2 : filled with concern or regret over an unwanted situation ⟨I'm *afraid* I won't be able to go⟩
3 : having a dislike for something ⟨*afraid* of hard work⟩
synonym see FEARFUL

A-frame \'ā-,frām\ *noun* (circa 1909)
1 : a support structure shaped like the letter A
2 : a building typically having triangular front and rear walls and a roof reaching to the ground

afreet *or* **afrit** \'a-,frēt, ə-'frēt\ *noun* [Arabic *'ifrīt*] (1786)
: a powerful evil jinni, demon, or monstrous giant in Arabic mythology

afresh \ə-'fresh\ *adverb* (15th century)
: from a fresh beginning : ANEW, AGAIN

¹Af·ri·can \'a-fri-kən *also* 'ä-\ *noun* (before 12th century)
1 : a native or inhabitant of Africa
2 : a person and especially a black person of African ancestry

²African *adjective* (1564)
: of, relating to, or characteristic of the continent of Africa or its people
— Af·ri·can·ness \-kə(n)-nəs\ *noun*

Af·ri·ca·na \,a-fri-'ka-nə, -'kä-, -'kā- *also* ,ä-\ *noun plural* (1908)
: materials (as books, documents, or artifacts) relating to African history and culture

Af·ri·can–Amer·i·can \,a-fri-kə-nə-'mer-ə-kən *also* ,ä-\ *noun* (1984)
: AFRO-AMERICAN
— African–American *adjective*

African buffalo *noun* (1902)
: CAPE BUFFALO

African daisy *noun* (circa 1889)
: any of a genus (*Arctotis*) of widely cultivated composite herbs

Af·ri·can·der *or* **Af·ri·kan·der** \,a-fri-'kan-dər\ *noun* [Afrikaans *Afrikaner, Afrikaander,* literally, Afrikaner] (1852)
: any of a breed of tall red large-horned humped southern African cattle used chiefly for meat or draft

African elephant *noun* (1607)
: ELEPHANT 1a

Af·ri·can·ise *British variant of* AFRICANIZE

Af·ri·can·ism \'a-fri-kə-,ni-zəm *also* 'ä-\ *noun* (1641)
1 : a characteristic feature (as a custom or belief) of African culture
2 : a characteristic feature of an African language occurring in a non-African language
3 : allegiance to the traditions, interests, or ideals of Africa

Af·ri·can·ist \-nist\ *noun* (1895)
: a specialist in African languages or cultures

Af·ri·can·ize \-,nīz\ *transitive verb* **-ized; -iz·ing** (1853)
1 : to cause to acquire a distinctively African trait
2 : to bring under the influence, control, or cultural or civil supremacy of Africans and especially black Africans
— Af·ri·can·iza·tion \,a-fri-kə-nə-'zā-shən *also* ,ä-\ *noun*

Africanized bee *noun* (1974)
: a honeybee that originated in Brazil as an accidental hybrid between an aggressive African subspecies (*Apis mellifera scutellata*) and previously established European honeybees and has spread to Mexico and the southernmost U.S. by breeding with local bees producing populations retaining most of the African bee's traits — called also *Africanized honeybee, killer bee*

African mahogany *noun* (1842)
: MAHOGANY 1b

African violet *noun* (1902)
: any of several tropical African gesneriads (especially *Saintpaulia ionantha*) widely grown as houseplants for their velvety fleshy leaves and showy purple, pink, or white flowers

¹Af·ri·kaans \,a-fri-'kän(t)s, ,ä-, -'känz, 'a-fri-,, 'ä-\ *noun* [Afrikaans, from *afrikaans,* adjective, African, from obsolete Afrikaans *afrikanisch,* from Latin *africanus*] (1908)
: a language developed from 17th century Dutch that is one of the official languages of the Republic of South Africa

²Afrikaans *adjective* (1923)
: of or relating to Afrikaners or Afrikaans

Af·ri·ka·ner \,a-fri-'kä-nər\ *noun, often attributive* [Afrikaans, literally, African, from Latin *africanus*] (1824)
: a South African of European descent whose native language is Afrikaans
— Af·ri·ka·ner·dom \-dəm\ *noun*

¹Af·ro \'a-(,)frō\ *adjective* [probably from *Afro-American*] (1938)
: characterized by or being a hairstyle of tight curls in a full evenly rounded shape

²Afro *noun, plural* **Afros** (1968)
: an Afro hairstyle

Af·ro-Amer·i·can \,a-frō-ə-'mer-ə-kən\ *noun* (1853)
: an American of African and especially of black African descent
— Afro–American *adjective*

Af·ro-Asi·at·ic \,a-frō-,ā-zhē-'a-tik, -zē- *also* -shē-\ *adjective* (1953)
: of, relating to, or being a family of languages widely distributed over southwestern Asia and Africa comprising the Semitic, Egyptian, Berber, Cushitic, and Chadic subfamilies

Afro

Af·ro·cen·tric \,a-frō-'sen-trik\ *adjective* (1966)
: centered on or derived from Africa or the Africans
— Af·ro·cen·trism \-,tri-zəm\ *noun*

¹aft \'aft\ *adverb* [Middle English *afte* back, from Old English *æftan* from behind, behind; akin to Old English *æfter*] (1628)
: near, toward, or in the stern of a ship or the tail of an aircraft ⟨called all hands *aft*⟩

²aft *adjective* (1816)
: REARWARD, AFTER 2 ⟨the *aft* decks⟩

³aft *Scottish variant of* OFT

¹af·ter \'af-tər\ *adverb* [Middle English, from Old English *æfter;* akin to Old High German *aftar* after, and probably to Old English *of* of] (before 12th century)
: following in time or place : AFTERWARD, BEHIND, LATER ⟨we arrived shortly *after*⟩ ⟨returned 20 years *after*⟩

²after *preposition* (before 12th century)
1 a : behind in place **b** (1) **:** subsequent to in time or order (2) **:** subsequent to and in view of ⟨*after* all our advice⟩
2 — used as a function word to indicate the object of a stated or implied action ⟨go *after* gold⟩ ⟨was asking *after* you⟩
3 : so as to resemble: as **a :** in accordance with **b :** with the name of or a name derived from that of **c :** in the characteristic manner of **d :** in imitation of

³after *conjunction* (before 12th century)
: subsequently to the time when

⁴after *adjective* (before 12th century)
1 : later in time ⟨in *after* years⟩
2 : located toward the rear and especially toward the stern of a ship or tail of an aircraft

⁵af·ter \'äf-tər\ *verbal auxiliary* (1800)
chiefly Irish — used with a present participle to indicate action completed and especially just completed ⟨the poor old man is *after* dying on me —J. M. Synge⟩

⁶after *noun* (circa 1902)
: AFTERNOON

after all *adverb* (1846)
1 : in spite of considerations or expectations to the contrary : NEVERTHELESS ⟨decided to take the train *after all*⟩ ⟨didn't rain *after all*⟩
2 — used as a sentence modifier to emphasize something to be taken into consideration ⟨literature which is *after all* only a special department of reading —W. W. Watt⟩

af·ter·birth \'af-tər-,bərth\ *noun* (1587)
: the placenta and fetal membranes that are expelled after delivery

af·ter·burn·er \-,bər-nər\ *noun* (1947)
1 : a device incorporated into the tail pipe of a turbojet engine for injecting fuel into the hot exhaust gases and burning it to provide extra thrust
2 : a device for burning or catalytically destroying unburned or partially burned carbon compounds in exhaust (as from an automobile)

af·ter·care \-,ker, -,kar\ *noun* (1894)
: the care, treatment, help, or supervision given to persons discharged from an institution (as a hospital)

af·ter·clap \-,klap\ *noun* (14th century)

: an unexpected damaging or unsettling event following a supposedly closed affair

af·ter·deck \-,dek\ *noun* (1897)
: the part of a deck abaft amidships

af·ter·ef·fect \'af-tə-rə-,fekt\ *noun* (1817)
: an effect that follows its cause after an interval

af·ter·glow \'af-tər-,glō\ *noun* (1871)
1 : a reflection of past splendor, success, or emotion
2 : a glow remaining where a light has disappeared

af·ter–hours \,af-tər-'aủ(-ə)rz\ *adjective* (1929)
: engaged in or operating after a legal or conventional closing time ⟨*after-hours* drinking⟩ ⟨an *after-hours* club⟩

af·ter·im·age \'af-tər-,i-mij\ *noun* (1874)
: a usually visual sensation occurring after stimulation by its external cause has ceased

af·ter·life \'af-tər-,līf\ *noun* (circa 1593)
1 : an existence after death
2 : a later period in one's life

af·ter·mar·ket \-,mär-kət\ *noun* (1940)
1 : the market for parts and accessories used in the repair or enhancement of a product (as an automobile)
2 : a secondary market available after sales in the original market are finished ⟨a movie in the videocassette *aftermarket*⟩

af·ter·math \-,math\ *noun* [⁴*after* + *math* (mowing, crop)] (1523)
1 : a second-growth crop — called also *rowen*
2 : CONSEQUENCE, RESULT ⟨stricken with guilt as an *aftermath* of the accident⟩
3 : the period immediately following a usually ruinous event ⟨in the *aftermath* of the war⟩

af·ter·most \-,mōst\ *adjective* (1773)
: farthest aft

af·ter·noon \,af-tər-'nün\ *noun* (13th century)
1 : the part of day between noon and sunset
2 : a relatively late period (as of time or life) ⟨in the *afternoon* of the 19th century⟩
— afternoon *adjective*

af·ter·noons \-'nünz\ *adverb* (1896)
: in the afternoon repeatedly **:** on any afternoon

af·ter·piece \'af-tər-,pēs\ *noun* (1779)
: a short usually comic entertainment performed after a play

af·ters \'af-tərz\ *noun plural* (circa 1909)
British **:** DESSERT

af·ter·shave \'af-tər-,shāv\ *noun* (1946)
: a usually scented lotion for use on the face after shaving

af·ter·shock \-,shäk\ *noun* (1894)
1 : a minor shock following the main shock of an earthquake
2 : an aftereffect of a distressing or traumatic event

af·ter·taste \-,tāst\ *noun* (circa 1798)
: persistence of a sensation (as of flavor or an emotion) after the stimulating agent or experience has gone

af·ter–tax \-'taks\ *adjective* (1954)
: remaining after payment of taxes and especially of income tax ⟨an *after-tax* profit⟩

af·ter·thought \-,thȯt\ *noun* (circa 1661)
1 : an idea occurring later
2 : a part, feature, or device not thought of originally

af·ter·time \-,tīm\ *noun* (1597)
: FUTURE

af·ter·ward \'af-tə(r)-wərd\ *or* **af·ter·wards** \-wərdz\ *adverb* (13th century)
: at a later or succeeding time **:** SUBSEQUENTLY, THEREAFTER

af·ter·word \-,wərd\ *noun* (1890)
: EPILOGUE 1

af·ter·world \-,wərld\ *noun* (1596)
: a future world **:** a world after death

ag \'ag\ *adjective* (circa 1918)
: of or relating to agriculture ⟨*ag* schools⟩

ag- — see AD-

Aga·da \ə-'gä-də, -'gȯ-\ *variant of* HAGGADAH

again \ə-'gen, -'gin, -'gān\ *adverb* [Middle English, opposite, again, from Old English *ongēan* opposite, back, from *on* + *gēn, gēan* still, again; akin to Old English *gēan-* against, Old High German *gegin* against, toward] (13th century)
1 : in return **:** BACK ⟨swore he would pay him *again* when he was able —Shakespeare⟩
2 : another time **:** once more **:** ANEW ⟨I shall not look upon his like *again* —Shakespeare⟩
3 : on the other hand ⟨he might go, and *again* he might not⟩
4 : in addition **:** BESIDES ⟨*again*, there is another matter to consider⟩

again and again *adverb* (1604)
: OFTEN, REPEATEDLY

¹against \ə-'gen(t)st, -'gin(t)st, -'gān(t)st\ *preposition* [Middle English, alteration of *againes*, from *again*] (13th century)
1 a : in opposition or hostility to **b :** contrary to ⟨*against* the law⟩ **c :** in competition with **d :** as a basis for disapproval of ⟨had nothing *against* him⟩
2 a : directly opposite **:** FACING **b** *obsolete* **:** exposed to
3 : compared or contrasted with
4 a : in preparation or provision for **b :** as a defense or protection from
5 a : in the direction of and into contact with **b :** in contact with
6 : in a direction opposite to the motion or course of **:** counter to
7 a : as a counterbalance to **b :** in exchange for **c :** as a charge on
8 : before the background of

²against *conjunction* (14th century)
archaic **:** in preparation for the time when ⟨throw on another log of wood *against* father comes home —Charles Dickens⟩

Ag·a·mem·non \,a-gə-'mem-,nän, -nən\ *noun* [Latin, from Greek *Agamemnōn*]
: a king of Mycenae and leader of the Greeks in the Trojan War

aga·mete \(,)ā-'ga-,mēt *also* -gə-'mēt\ *noun* [International Scientific Vocabulary, from Greek *agametos* unmarried, from *a-* + *gamein* to marry, from *gamos* marriage] (circa 1920)
: an asexual reproductive cell (as a spore)

agam·ic \(,)ā-'ga-mik\ *adjective* [Greek *agamos* unmarried, from *a-* + *gamos*] (1850)
: ASEXUAL, PARTHENOGENETIC

agam·ma·glob·u·lin·emia \,ā-,ga-mə-,gläb-yə-lə-'nē-mē-ə\ *noun* [New Latin, from *a-* + International Scientific Vocabulary *gamma globulin* + New Latin *-emia*] (circa 1952)
: a condition in which the body forms few or no gamma globulins or antibodies

— agam·ma·glob·u·lin·emic \-'nē-mik\ *adjective*

aga·mo·sper·my \(,)ā-'ga-mə-,spər-mē, 'a-gə-mō-,spər-\ *noun* [Greek *agamos* + English *-spermy*] (1944)
: APOGAMY; *specifically* **:** apogamy in which sexual union is not completed and the embryo is produced from the innermost layer of the integument of the female gametophyte

ag·a·pan·thus \,a-gə-'pan(t)-thəs\ *noun, plural* **-thus** *also* **-thuses** [New Latin, genus name, from Greek *agapē* + *anthos* flower — more at ANTHOLOGY] (circa 1789)
: any of several African plants (genus *Agapanthus*) of the lily family cultivated for their umbels of showy blue or purple flowers

¹aga·pe \ä-'gä-(,)pā, 'ä-gə-,pā\ *noun* [Late Latin, from Greek *agapē*, literally, love] (1607)
1 : LOVE FEAST
2 : LOVE 4a

²agape \ə-'gāp *also* -'gap\ *adjective or adverb* (1667)
1 : wide open **:** GAPING
2 : being in a state of wonder

agar \'ä-gər\ *noun* [Malay *agar-agar*] (1889)
1 : a gelatinous colloidal extractive of a red alga (as of the genera *Gelidium, Gracilaria,* and *Eucheuma*) used especially in culture media or as a gelling and stabilizing agent in foods

2 : a culture medium containing agar

agar–agar \,ä-gər-'ä-gər\ *noun* [Malay] (1820)
: AGAR

aga·ric \'a-gər-ik, ə-'gar-ik\ *noun* [Latin *agaricum*, a fungus, from Greek *agarikon*] (15th century)
1 : the dried fruiting body of a fungus (*Fomes officinalis* synonym *Polyporus officinalis*) formerly used in medicine
2 : any of a family (Agaricaceae) of fungi with the sporophore usually resembling an umbrella and with numerous gills on the underside of the cap

aga·rose \'a-gə-,rōs, 'ä-, -,rōz\ *noun* (1964)
: a polysaccharide obtained from agar and used especially as a supporting medium in gel electrophoresis

ag·ate \'a-gət\ *noun, often attributive* [Middle French, from Latin *achates,* from Greek *achatēs*] (1570)
1 : a fine-grained variegated chalcedony having its colors arranged in stripes, blended in clouds, or showing mosslike forms
2 : something made of or fitted with agate: as **a :** a drawplate used by gold-wire drawers **b :** a playing marble of agate
3 : a size of type approximately 5½ point

agate line *noun* (circa 1935)
: a space one column wide and 1/14 inch deep used as a unit of measurement in classified advertising

agate ware *noun* (1857)
1 : pottery veined and mottled to resemble agate
2 : an enameled iron or steel ware for household utensils

aga·ve \ə-'gä-vē\ *noun* [New Latin *Agave*, genus name, from Latin, a daughter of Cadmus, from Greek *Agauē*] (circa 1797)
: any of a genus (*Agave*) of the family Agavaceae (the agave family) of plants having spiny-margined leaves and flowers in tall spreading panicles and including some cultivated for their fiber or sap or for ornament

agave

agaze \ə-'gāz\ *adjective* (circa 1902)
: engaged in the act of gazing

¹age \'āj\ *noun* [Middle English, from Old French *aage,* from (assumed) Vulgar Latin *aetaticum,* from Latin *aetat-, aetas,* from *aevum* lifetime — more at AYE] (13th century)
1 a : the time of life at which some particular qualification, power, or capacity arises or rests ⟨the voting *age* is 18⟩; *specifically* **:** MAJORITY **b :** one of the stages of life **c :** the length of an existence extending from the beginning to any given time ⟨a boy 10 years of *age*⟩ **d :** LIFETIME **e :** an advanced stage of life
2 : a period of time dominated by a central figure or prominent feature ⟨the *age* of Pericles⟩: as **a :** a period in history or human progress ⟨the *age* of reptiles⟩ ⟨the *age* of exploration⟩ **b :** a cultural period marked by the prominence of a particular item ⟨entering the atomic *age*⟩ **c :** a division of geologic time that is usually shorter than an epoch
3 a : the period contemporary with a person's lifetime or with his or her active life **b :** a long time — usually used in plural ⟨haven't seen him in *ages*⟩ **c :** GENERATION
4 : an individual's development measured in terms of the years requisite for like development of an average individual
synonym see PERIOD

²age *verb* **aged; ag·ing** *or* **age·ing** (14th century)
intransitive verb
1 : to become old **:** show the effects or the characteristics of increasing age
2 : to acquire a desirable quality (as mellowness or ripeness) by standing undisturbed for some time ⟨letting cheese *age*⟩
transitive verb
1 : to cause to become old
2 : to bring to a state fit for use or to maturity
— **ag·er** \'ā-jər\ *noun*

-age *noun suffix* [Middle English, from Old French, from Latin *-aticum*]
1 : aggregate **:** collection ⟨track*age*⟩
2 a : action **:** process ⟨haul*age*⟩ **b :** cumulative result of ⟨break*age*⟩ **c :** rate of ⟨dos*age*⟩
3 : house or place of ⟨orphan*age*⟩
4 : state **:** rank ⟨peon*age*⟩
5 : charge ⟨post*age*⟩

aged \'ā-jəd, 'ājd; 'ājd *for 1b*\ *adjective* (15th century)
1 : grown old: as **a :** of an advanced age **b :** having attained a specified age ⟨a man *aged* 40 years⟩
2 : typical of old age
— **ag·ed·ness** \'ā-jəd-nəs\ *noun*

age–group \'āj-,grüp\ *noun* (1904)
: a segment of a population that is of approximately the same age or is within a specified range of ages

age·ism *also* **ag·ism** \'ā-(,)ji-zəm\ *noun* (1969)
: prejudice or discrimination against a particular age-group and especially the elderly
— **age·ist** *also* **ag·ist** \-jist\ *adjective*

age·less \'āj-ləs\ *adjective* (1651)
1 : not growing old or showing the effects of age
2 : TIMELESS, ETERNAL ⟨*ageless* truths⟩
— **age·less·ly** *adverb*
— **age·less·ness** *noun*

age·long \'āj-,lȯŋ\ *adjective* (1810)
: lasting for an age **:** EVERLASTING

age–mate \-,māt\ *noun* (1583)
: one who is of about the same age as another

agen·cy \'ā-jən(t)-sē\ *noun, plural* **-cies** (1658)
1 : the capacity, condition, or state of acting or of exerting power **:** OPERATION
2 : a person or thing through which power is exerted or an end is achieved **:** INSTRUMENTALITY ⟨communicated through the *agency* of the ambassador⟩
3 a : the office or function of an agent **b :** the relationship between a principal and his agent
4 : an establishment engaged in doing business for another ⟨an advertising *agency*⟩
5 : an administrative division (as of a government) ⟨the *agency* for consumer protection⟩

agency shop *noun* (circa 1946)
: a shop in which the union serves as the agent for and receives dues and assessments from all employees in the bargaining unit regardless of union membership

agen·da \ə-'jen-də\ *noun* [Latin, neuter plural of *agendum*, gerundive of *agere*] (1871)
1 : a list or outline of things to be considered or done ⟨*agendas* of faculty meetings⟩
2 : an underlying often ideological plan or program ⟨a political *agenda*⟩
— **agen·da·less** \-də-ləs\ *adjective*

agen·dum \-dəm\ *noun, plural* **-da** \-də\ *or* **-dums** [Latin] (circa 1847)
1 : AGENDA
2 : an item on an agenda

agen·e·sis \(,)ā-'je-nə-səs\ *noun* [New Latin] (circa 1879)
: lack or failure of development (as of a body part)

agent \'ā-jənt\ *noun* [Middle English, from Medieval Latin *agent-*, *agens*, from Latin, present participle of *agere* to drive, lead, act, do; akin to Old Norse *aka* to travel in a vehicle, Greek *agein* to drive, lead] (15th century)

1 : one that acts or exerts power
2 a : something that produces or is capable of producing an effect **:** an active or efficient cause **b :** a chemically, physically, or biologically active principle
3 : a means or instrument by which a guiding intelligence achieves a result
4 : one who is authorized to act for or in the place of another: as **a :** a representative, emissary, or official of a government ⟨crown *agent*⟩ ⟨federal *agent*⟩ **b :** one engaged in undercover activities (as espionage) **:** SPY ⟨secret *agent*⟩ **c :** a business representative (as of an athlete or entertainer) ⟨a theatrical *agent*⟩

agent–general *noun, plural* **agents–general** (1833)
: a chief agent; *specifically* **:** the representative in England of a British dominion

agent·ing \'ā-jən-tiŋ\ *noun* (1681)
: the business or activities of an agent

Agent Orange *noun* [so called from the identifying color stripe on its container] (1970)
: an herbicide widely used as a defoliant in the Vietnam War that is composed of 2,4-D and 2,4,5-T and contains dioxin as a contaminant

agent pro·vo·ca·teur \'ä-,zhäⁿ-prō-,vä-kə-'tər, 'ä-jənt-\ *noun, plural* **agents provo·cateurs** \'ä-,zhäⁿ-prō-,vä-kə-'tər, 'ä-jən(t)s-prō-\ [French, literally, provoking agent] (1877)
: one employed to associate with suspected persons and by pretending sympathy with their aims to incite them to some incriminating action

agent·ry \'ā-jən-trē\ *noun, plural* **-ries** (1925)
: the office, duties, or activities of an agent

age of consent (1504)
: the age at which one is legally competent to give consent especially to marriage or to sexual intercourse

age of reason (circa 1794)
1 : a period characterized by a prevailing belief in the use of reason; *especially* **:** the 18th century in England and France
2 : the time of life when one begins to be able to distinguish right from wrong

age–old \'ā-'jōld\ *adjective* (1904)
: having existed for ages **:** ANCIENT

ag·er·a·tum \,a-jə-'rā-təm\ *noun, plural* **-tum** *also* **-tums** [New Latin, genus name, from Greek *agēratos* ageless, from *a-* + *gēras* old age — more at GERONT-] (1866)
: any of a genus (*Ageratum*) of tropical American composite herbs often cultivated for their small showy heads of blue or white flowers; *also* **:** a related blue-flowered plant (*Eupatorium coelestinum*)

Ag·ga·dah \ə-'gä-də, -'gȯ-\ *variant of* HAGGADAH

Ag·ge·us \a-'gē-əs\ *noun* [Late Latin *Aggaeus*, from Greek *Aggaios*, from Hebrew *Ḥaggai*]
: HAGGAI

¹ag·gie \'a-gē\ *noun, often capitalized* [*agricultural* + *-ie*] (1902)
: an agricultural school or college; *also* **:** a student at such an institution

²aggie *noun* [*agate* + *-ie*] (1915)
: a playing marble; *specifically* **:** AGATE 2b

ag·gior·na·men·to \ə-,jȯr-nə-'men-(,)tō\ *noun, plural* **-tos** [Italian, from *aggiornare* to bring up to date, from *a* to (from Latin *ad-*) + *giorno* day, from Late Latin *diurnum* day — more at JOURNEY] (1963)
: a bringing up to date **:** MODERNIZATION ⟨dedicated to the *aggiornamento* of the church⟩

¹ag·glom·er·ate \ə-'glä-mə-,rāt\ *transitive verb* **-at·ed; -at·ing** [Latin *agglomeratus*, past participle of *agglomerare* to heap up, join, from *ad-* + *glomer-*, *glomus* ball — more at CLAM] (1684)
: to gather into a ball, mass, or cluster

²ag·glom·er·ate \-rət\ *adjective* (1684)
: gathered into a ball, mass, or cluster; *specifically* **:** clustered or growing together but not coherent ⟨an *agglomerate* flower head⟩

³ag·glom·er·ate \-rət\ *noun* (1830)
1 : a rock composed of volcanic fragments of various sizes and degrees of angularity
2 : a jumbled mass or collection **:** AGGLOMERATION

ag·glom·er·a·tion \ə-,glä-mə-'rā-shən\ *noun* (1774)
1 : the action or process of collecting in a mass
2 : a heap or cluster of usually disparate elements ⟨urban *agglomerations* knit together by the new railways —*Times Literary Supplement*⟩
— **ag·glom·er·a·tive** \-'glä-mə-,rā-tiv\ *adjective*

ag·glu·ti·na·bil·i·ty \ə-,glü-tᵊn-ə-'bi-lə-tē\ *noun* (1901)
: capacity (as of red blood cells) to be agglutinated
— **ag·glu·ti·na·ble** \ə-'glü-tᵊn-ə-bəl\ *adjective*

¹ag·glu·ti·nate \ə-'glü-tᵊn-,āt\ *verb* **-nat·ed; -nat·ing** [Latin *agglutinatus*, past participle of *agglutinare* to glue to, from *ad-* + *glutinare* to glue, from *glutin-*, *gluten* glue — more at CLAY] (1586)
transitive verb
1 : to cause to adhere **:** FASTEN
2 : to combine into a compound **:** attach to a base as an affix
3 : to cause to undergo agglutination
intransitive verb
1 : to unite or combine into a group or mass
2 : to form words by agglutination

²ag·glu·ti·nate \-tᵊn-ət, -tᵊn,āt\ *noun* (1952)
: a clump of agglutinated material (as blood cells or mineral particles in soil)

ag·glu·ti·na·tion \ə-,glü-tᵊn-'ā-shən\ *noun* (1541)
1 : the action or process of agglutinating
2 : a mass or group formed by the union of separate elements
3 : the formation of derivational or inflectional words by putting together constituents of which each expresses a single definite meaning
4 : a reaction in which particles (as red blood cells or bacteria) suspended in a liquid collect into clumps and which occurs especially as a serologic response to a specific antibody

ag·glu·ti·na·tive \ə-'glü-tᵊn-,ā-tiv, -ə-tiv\ *adjective* (1634)
1 : ADHESIVE
2 : characterized by linguistic agglutination

ag·glu·ti·nin \ə-'glü-tᵊn-ən\ *noun* [International Scientific Vocabulary *agglutin*ation + *-in*] (1902)
: a substance (as an antibody) producing agglutination

ag·glu·ti·no·gen \ə-'glü-tᵊn-ə-jən\ *noun* [*agglutin*in + *-o-* + *-gen*] (1904)
: an antigen whose presence results in the formation of an agglutinin
— **ag·glu·ti·no·gen·ic** \-,glü-tᵊn-ə-'je-nik\ *adjective*

ag·gra·da·tion \,a-grə-'dā-shən\ *noun* [*ad-* + *gradation*] (1898)
: a modification of the earth's surface in the direction of uniformity of grade by deposition

ag·gran·dise *British variant of* AGGRANDIZE

ag·gran·dize \ə-'gran-,dīz *also* 'a-grən-\ *transitive verb* **-dized; -diz·ing** [French *agrandiss-*, stem of *agrandir*, from *a-* (from Latin *ad-*) + *grandir* to increase, from Latin *grandire*, from *grandis* great] (1634)
1 : to make great or greater **:** INCREASE, ENLARGE
2 : to make appear great or greater **:** praise highly
3 : to enhance the power, wealth, position, or reputation of ⟨exploited the situation to *aggrandize* himself⟩
— **ag·gran·dize·ment** \ə-'gran-dəz-mənt, -,dīz-; ,a-grən-'dīz-\ *noun*
— **ag·gran·diz·er** \ə-'gran-,dī-zər *also* 'a-grən-\ *noun*

ag·gra·vate \'a-grə-ˌvāt\ *transitive verb* **-vat·ed; -vat·ing** [Latin *aggravatus,* past participle of *aggravare* to make heavier, from *ad-* + *gravare* to burden, from *gravis* heavy — more at GRIEVE] (1530)
1 *obsolete* **a :** to make heavy **:** BURDEN **b :** INCREASE
2 : to make worse, more serious, or more severe **:** intensify unpleasantly ⟨problems have been *aggravated* by neglect⟩
3 a : to rouse to displeasure or anger by usually persistent and often petty goading **b :** to produce inflammation in □

aggravated assault *noun* (1925)
: an assault that is more serious than a common assault: as **a :** an assault combined with an intent to commit a crime **b :** any of various assaults so defined by statute

aggravating *adjective* (1775)
: arousing displeasure, impatience, or anger
usage see AGGRAVATE

ag·gra·va·tion \ˌa-grə-'vā-shən\ *noun* (circa 1555)
1 : an act or circumstance that intensifies or makes worse
2 : the act, action, or result of aggravating; *especially* **:** an increasing in seriousness or severity
3 : IRRITATION, PROVOCATION
usage see AGGRAVATE

¹**ag·gre·gate** \'a-gri-gət\ *adjective* [Middle English *aggregat,* from Latin *aggregatus,* past participle of *aggregare* to add to, from *ad-* + *greg-, grex* flock] (15th century)
: formed by the collection of units or particles into a body, mass, or amount **:** COLLECTIVE: as **a** (1) **:** clustered in a dense mass or head ⟨an *aggregate* flower⟩ (2) **:** formed from several separate ovaries of a single flower ⟨*aggregate* fruit⟩ **b :** composed of mineral crystals of one or more kinds or of mineral rock fragments **c :** taking all units as a whole ⟨*aggregate* sales⟩
— **ag·gre·gate·ly** *adverb*
— **ag·gre·gate·ness** *noun*

²**ag·gre·gate** \-ˌgāt\ *transitive verb* **-gat·ed; -gat·ing** (15th century)
1 : to collect or gather into a mass or whole
2 : to amount in the aggregate to **:** TOTAL

³**ag·gre·gate** \-gət\ *noun* (15th century)
1 : a mass or body of units or parts somewhat loosely associated with one another
2 : the whole sum or amount **:** SUM TOTAL
3 a : an aggregate rock **b :** any of several hard inert materials (as sand, gravel, or slag) used for mixing with a cementing material to form concrete, mortar, or plaster **c :** a clustered mass of individual soil particles varied in shape, ranging in size from a microscopic granule to a small crumb, and considered the basic structural unit of soil
4 : SET 21
5 : MONETARY AGGREGATE
— **in the aggregate :** considered as a whole **:** COLLECTIVELY ⟨dividends for the year amounted *in the aggregate* to 25 million dollars⟩

ag·gre·ga·tion \ˌa-gri-'gā-shən\ *noun* (1547)
1 : a group, body, or mass composed of many distinct parts or individuals
2 a : the collecting of units or parts into a mass or whole **b :** the condition of being so collected
— **ag·gre·ga·tion·al** \-shnəl, -shə-nʰl\ *adjective*

ag·gre·ga·tive \'a-gri-ˌgā-tiv\ *adjective* (1644)
1 : of or relating to an aggregate
2 : tending to aggregate
— **ag·gre·ga·tive·ly** *adverb*

ag·gress \ə-'gres\ *intransitive verb* (circa 1714)
: to commit aggression **:** act aggressively

ag·gres·sion \ə-'gre-shən\ *noun* [Latin *aggression-, aggressio* attack, from *aggredi* to attack, from *ad-* + *gradi* to step, go — more at GRADE] (1611)

1 : a forceful action or procedure (as an unprovoked attack) especially when intended to dominate or master
2 : the practice of making attacks or encroachments; *especially* **:** unprovoked violation by one country of the territorial integrity of another
3 : hostile, injurious, or destructive behavior or outlook especially when caused by frustration

ag·gres·sive \ə-'gre-siv\ *adjective* (1824)
1 a : tending toward or exhibiting aggression ⟨*aggressive* behavior⟩ **b :** marked by combative readiness ⟨an *aggressive* fighter⟩
2 a : marked by obtrusive energy **b :** marked by driving forceful energy or initiative **:** ENTERPRISING ⟨an *aggressive* salesman⟩
3 : strong or emphatic in effect or intent ⟨*aggressive* colors⟩ ⟨*aggressive* flavors⟩
4 : more severe, intensive, or comprehensive than usual especially in dosage or extent ⟨*aggressive* chemotherapy⟩ ☆
— **ag·gres·sive·ly** *adverb*
— **ag·gres·sive·ness** *noun*
— **ag·gres·siv·i·ty** \ˌa-gre-'si-və-tē\ *noun*

ag·gres·sor \ə-'gre-sər\ *noun* (1646)
: one that commits or practices aggression

ag·grieve \ə-'grēv\ *transitive verb* **ag·grieved; ag·griev·ing** [Middle English *agreven,* from Middle French *agrever,* from Latin *aggravare* to make heavier] (14th century)
1 : to give pain or trouble to **:** DISTRESS
2 : to inflict injury on
synonym see WRONG

ag·grieved \ə-'grēvd\ *adjective* (14th century)
1 : troubled or distressed in spirit
2 a : suffering from an infringement or denial of legal rights ⟨*aggrieved* minority groups⟩ **b :** showing or expressing grief, injury, or offense ⟨an *aggrieved* plea⟩
— **ag·griev·ed·ly** \-'grē-vəd-lē\ *adverb*

ag·grieve·ment \ə-'grēv-mənt\ *noun* (1847)
: the quality or state of being aggrieved

ag·gro \'a-(ˌ)grō\ *noun, plural* **aggros** [probably *aggr*avation + ¹*-o*] (1969)
1 *British* **:** deliberately aggressive, provoking, or violent behavior
2 *British* **:** EXASPERATION, IRRITATION

aghast \ə-'gast\ *adjective* [Middle English *agast,* from past participle of *agasten* to frighten, from *a-* (perfective prefix) + *gasten* to frighten — more at ABIDE, GAST] (13th century)
: struck with terror, amazement, or horror **:** SHOCKED

ag·ile \'a-jəl, -ˌjīl\ *adjective* [Middle French, from Latin *agilis,* from *agere* to drive, act — more at AGENT] (1581)
1 : marked by ready ability to move with quick easy grace
2 : having a quick resourceful and adaptable character ⟨an *agile* mind⟩
— **ag·ile·ly** \-jə(l)-lē, -ˌjī(l)-lē\ *adverb*

agil·i·ty \ə-'ji-lə-tē\ *noun, plural* **-ties** (15th century)
: the quality or state of being agile **:** NIMBLENESS, DEXTERITY ⟨played with increasing *agility*⟩

agin \ə-'gin\ *dialect variant of* AGAINST

aging *present participle of* AGE

ag·ism *variant of* AGEISM

ag·i·tate \'a-jə-ˌtāt\ *verb* **-tat·ed; -tat·ing** [Latin *agitatus,* past participle of *agitare,* frequentative of *agere* to drive — more at AGENT] (15th century)
transitive verb
1 a *obsolete* **:** to give motion to **b :** to move with an irregular, rapid, or violent action ⟨the storm *agitated* the sea⟩
2 : to excite and often trouble the mind or feelings of **:** DISTURB
3 a : to discuss excitedly and earnestly **b :** to stir up public discussion of

intransitive verb
: to attempt to arouse public feeling ⟨*agitated* for better schools⟩
synonym see SHAKE, DISCOMPOSE
— **ag·i·tat·ed·ly** *adverb*
— **ag·i·ta·tion** \ˌa-jə-'tā-shən\ *noun*
— **ag·i·ta·tion·al** \-shnəl, -shə-nʰl\ *adjective*

ag·i·ta·tive \'a-jə-ˌtā-tiv\ *adjective* (1687)
: causing or tending to cause agitation

ag·i·ta·to \ˌa-jə-'tä-(ˌ)tō\ *adverb or adjective* [Italian, literally, agitated, from Latin *agitatus*] (circa 1801)
: in a restless and agitated manner — used as a direction in music

ag·i·ta·tor \'a-jə-ˌtā-tər\ *noun* (circa 1734)
: one that agitates: as **a :** one who stirs up public feeling on controversial issues ⟨political *agitators*⟩ **b :** a device or an apparatus for stirring or shaking

ag·it·prop \'a-jət-ˌpräp\ *noun* [Russian, from *agit*atsiya agitation + *prop*aganda] (1935)
: PROPAGANDA; *especially* **:** political propaganda promulgated chiefly in literature, drama, music, or art
— **agitprop** *adjective*

Aglaia \ə-'glī-ə, -'glä-ə\ *noun* [Latin, from Greek]
: one of the three Graces

aglare \ə-'glar, -'gler\ *adjective* (1872)
: GLARING ⟨his eyes *aglare* with fury⟩

agleam \ə-'glēm\ *adjective* (1870)
: gleaming especially with reflected light

☆ SYNONYMS
Aggressive, militant, assertive, self-assertive mean obtrusively energetic especially in pursuing particular goals. AGGRESSIVE implies a disposition to dominate often in disregard of others' rights or in determined and energetic pursuit of one's ends ⟨was taught to be *aggressive* in his business dealings⟩. MILITANT also implies a fighting disposition but suggests not self-seeking but devotion to a cause, movement, or principle ⟨*militant* protesters held a rally against racism⟩. ASSERTIVE suggests bold self-confidence in expression of opinion ⟨the more *assertive* speakers dominated the forum⟩. SELF-ASSERTIVE connotes forwardness or brash self-confidence ⟨a *self-assertive* young executive climbing the corporate ladder⟩.

□ USAGE
aggravate Although *aggravate* has been used in sense 3a since the 17th century, it has been the object of disapproval only since about 1870. It is used in expository prose ⟨when his silly conceit . . . about his not-very-good early work has begun to *aggravate* us —William Styron⟩ but seems to be more common in speech and casual writing ⟨a good profession for him, because bus drivers get *aggravated* —Jackie Gleason (interview, 1986)⟩ ⟨& now this letter comes to *aggravate* me a thousand times worse —Mark Twain (letter, 1864)⟩. Sense 2 is far more common than sense 3a in published prose. Such is not the case, however, with *aggravation* and *aggravating. Aggravation* is used in sense 3 somewhat more than in its earlier senses; *aggravating* has practically no use other than to express annoyance.

\ə\ abut \ʰ\ kitten \ər\ further \a\ ash \ā\ ace
\ä\ mop, mar \aù\ out \ch\ chin \e\ bet \ē\ easy
\g\ go \i\ hit \ī\ ice \j\ job \ŋ\ sing \ō\ go
\ò\ law \òi\ boy \th\ thin \th\ the \ü\ loot \ù\ foot
\y\ yet \zh\ vision *see also* Guide to Pronunciation

ag·let \'a-glət\ *noun* [Middle English, from Middle French *aguillette, aiguillette,* diminutive of *aguille, aiguille* needle, from Late Latin *acicula, acucula* ornamental pin, diminutive of Latin *acus* needle, pin — more at ACUTE] (15th century)
1 : the plain or ornamental tag covering the ends of a lace or point
2 : any of various ornamental studs, cords, or pins worn on clothing

agley \ə-'glā, -'glē, -'glī\ *adverb* [Scots, from [1]*a-* + *gley* to squint] (1785)
chiefly Scottish **:** AWRY, WRONG ⟨the best-laid schemes o' mice an' men gang aft *agley* —Robert Burns⟩

aglit·ter \ə-'gli-tər\ *adjective* (1865)
: glittering especially with reflected light

aglow \ə-'glō\ *adjective* (1817)
: glowing especially with warmth or excitement

agly·cone \a-'glī-,kōn\ *also* **agly·con** \-,kän\ *noun* [International Scientific Vocabulary *a-* (from Greek *ha-, a-* together) + *glyc-* + *-one, -on*] (1925)
: an organic compound (as a phenol or alcohol) combined with the sugar portion of a glycoside

[1]ag·nate \'ag-,nāt\ *noun* [Latin *agnatus,* from past participle of *agnasci* to be born in addition to, from *ad-* + *nasci* to be born — more at NATION] (1534)
1 : a relative whose kinship is traceable exclusively through males
2 : a paternal kinsman

[2]agnate *adjective* (1782)
1 : ALLIED, AKIN
2 : related through male descent or on the father's side
— **ag·nat·ic** \ag-'na-tik\ *adjective*

Ag·ne·an \'äg-nē-ən\ *noun* [*Agni,* ancient kingdom in Turkestan] (1939)
: TOCHARIAN A

ag·nize \ag-'nīz\ *transitive verb* **ag·nized; ag·niz·ing** [Latin *agnoscere* to acknowledge (from *ad-* + *noscere* to know) + English *-ize* (as in *recognize*) — more at KNOW] (1535)
archaic **:** RECOGNIZE, ACKNOWLEDGE

ag·no·men \ag-'nō-mən\ *noun, plural* **-nom·i·na** \-'nä-mə-nə\ *or* **-no·mens** [Latin, irregular from *ad-* + *nomen* name — more at NAME] (1665)
: an additional cognomen given to a person by the ancient Romans (as in honor of some achievement)

ag·no·sia \ag-'nō-zhə, -shə\ *noun* [New Latin, from Greek *agnōsia* ignorance, from *a-* + *gnōsis* knowledge, from *gignōskein*] (circa 1900)
: loss or diminution of the ability to recognize familiar objects or stimuli usually as a result of brain damage

[1]ag·nos·tic \ag-'näs-tik, əg-\ *noun* [Greek *agnōstos* unknown, unknowable, from *a-* + *gnōstos* known, from *gignōskein* to know — more at KNOW] (1869)
: a person who holds the view that any ultimate reality (as God) is unknown and probably unknowable; *broadly* **:** one who is not committed to believing in either the existence or the nonexistence of God or a god ◇
— **ag·nos·ti·cism** \-tə-,si-zəm\ *noun*

[2]agnostic *adjective* (1873)
1 : of, relating to, or being an agnostic or the beliefs of agnostics
2 : NONCOMMITTAL, UNDOGMATIC

Ag·nus Dei \,äg-,nùs-'dā(-,ē), -,nüs-; ,än-yùs-; ,ag-nəs-\ *noun* [Middle English, from Late Latin, lamb of God; from its opening words] (14th century)
1 : a liturgical prayer addressed to Christ as Savior
2 : an image of a lamb often with a halo and a banner and cross that is used as a symbol of Christ

ago \ə-'gō\ *adjective or adverb* [Middle English *agon, ago,* from past participle of *agon*

to pass away, from Old English *āgān,* from *ā-* (perfective prefix) + *gān* to go — more at ABIDE, GO] (14th century)
: earlier than the present time ⟨10 years *ago*⟩

agog \ə-'gäg\ *adjective* [Middle French *en gogues* in mirth] (1559)
: full of intense interest or excitement **:** EAGER ⟨kids all *agog* over new toys⟩

Agnus Dei

[1]a–go–go \ä-'gō-(,)gō, ə-\ *noun* [*Whisky à Gogo,* café and discotheque in Paris, France, from French *à gogo* galore, from Middle French] (1965)
: a nightclub for dancing to pop music **:** DISCO

[2]a–go–go *adjective* (1965)
1 : GO-GO 1
2 : being in a whirl of motion
3 : being up-to-date — often used postpositively

-agogue *noun combining form* [French & New Latin; French, from Late Latin *-agogus* promoting the expulsion of, from Greek *-agōgos,* from *agein* to lead; New Latin *-agogon,* from Greek, neuter of *-agōgos* — more at AGENT]
: substance that promotes the secretion or expulsion of ⟨emmen*agogue*⟩

agon \'ä-,gän, ä-'gōn\ *noun* [Greek *agōn*] (1600)
: CONTEST, CONFLICT; *especially* **:** the dramatic conflict between the chief characters in a literary work

ag·o·nal \'a-gə-n°l\ *adjective* (1901)
: of, relating to, or associated with agony and especially the death agony

agone \ə-'gòn *also* -'gän\ *adjective or adverb* (14th century)
archaic **:** AGO

ag·o·nise, agonised, agonising *British variant of* AGONIZE, AGONIZED, AGONIZING

ag·o·nist \'a-gə-nist\ *noun* [Late Latin *agonista* competitor, from Greek *agōnistēs,* from *agōnizesthai* to contend, from *agōn*] (circa 1623)
1 : one that is engaged in a struggle
2 [from *antagonist*] **a :** a muscle that is controlled by the action of an antagonist with which it is paired **b :** a chemical substance capable of combining with a receptor on a cell and initiating a reaction or activity — compare ANTAGONIST 2b

ag·o·nis·tic \,a-gə-'nis-tik\ *adjective* (1648)
1 : of or relating to the athletic contests of ancient Greece
2 : ARGUMENTATIVE
3 : striving for effect **:** STRAINED
4 : of, relating to, or being aggressive or defensive social interaction (as fighting, fleeing, or submitting) between individuals usually of the same species
— **ag·o·nis·ti·cal·ly** \-ti-k(ə-)lē\ *adverb*

ag·o·nize \'a-gə-,nīz\ *verb* **-nized; -niz·ing** (1583)
transitive verb
: to cause to suffer agony **:** TORTURE
intransitive verb
1 : to suffer agony, torture, or anguish ⟨*agonizes* over every decision⟩
2 : STRUGGLE

agonized *adjective* (1583)
: characterized by, suffering, or expressing agony

agonizing *adjective* (1593)
: causing agony **:** PAINFUL
— **ag·o·niz·ing·ly** *adverb*

ag·o·ny \'a-gə-nē\ *noun, plural* **-nies** [Middle English *agonie,* from Late Latin *agonia,* from Greek *agōnia* struggle, anguish, from *agōn* gathering, contest for a prize, from *agein* to lead, celebrate — more at AGENT] (14th century)

1 a : intense pain of mind or body **:** ANGUISH, TORTURE **b :** the struggle that precedes death
2 : a violent struggle or contest
3 : a strong sudden display (as of joy or delight) **:** OUTBURST ◇
synonym see DISTRESS

agony column *noun* (1863)
: a newspaper column of personal advertisements relating especially to missing relatives or friends

[1]ag·o·ra \'a-gə-rə\ *noun, plural* **-ras** *or* **-rae** \-,rē, -,rī\ [Greek, from *ageirein* to gather] (1589)
: a gathering place; *especially* **:** the marketplace in ancient Greece

[2]ago·ra \,ä-gə-'rä\ *noun, plural* **ago·rot** \-'rōt\ [New Hebrew *ăgōrāh,* from Hebrew, a small coin] (1963)
— see *shekel* at MONEY table

ag·o·ra·pho·bia \,a-g(ə-)rə-'fō-bē-ə\ *noun* [New Latin, from Greek *agora* + New Latin *-phobia*] (1873)
: abnormal fear of being helpless in an embarrassing or unescapable situation that is characterized especially by the avoidance of open or public places
— **ag·o·ra·phobe** \'a-g(ə-)rə-,fōb\ *noun*
— **ag·o·ra·pho·bic** \-'fō-bik\ *adjective or noun*

agou·ti \ə-'gü-tē\ *noun* [French, from Spanish *agutí,* from Tupi] (1625)
1 : any of a genus (*Dasyprocta*) of tropical American rodents about the size of a rabbit
2 : a grizzled color of fur resulting from the barring of each hair in several alternate dark and light bands

agouti 1

agrafe *or* **agraffe** \ə-'graf\ *noun* [French *agrafe*] (1643)
: a hook-and-loop fastening; *especially* **:** an ornamental clasp used on armor or costumes

◇ WORD HISTORY

agnostic The word *agnostic* owes its origin to a particular occasion on the evening of April 21, 1869, when it was coined by the English biologist Thomas Henry Huxley at an organizational meeting of the Metaphysical Society. The precise etymological route by which Huxley arrived at his coinage has been a matter of debate. Two decades after the fact, the coiner himself recalled that the word seemed "suggestively antithetic to the 'gnostic' of church history" and so he chose it on that basis. In any event, *agnostic* is undoubtedly rooted in *agnōstos,* a Greek word meaning "unknown" or "unknowable." The ending *-ic* was probably suggested by the previously established English word *gnostic.*

agony In ancient Greece the word *agōn* denoted any large public assembly. As the Greeks placed a high value on athletic skills, assemblies on festival days featured athletic contests, the prototype of our modern Olympic Games. The word *agōn* by association with public games came to denote any competitive event. The struggle to win, as well as the pain accompanying the struggle, was called *agōnia,* which began also to be applied to any intense pain, physical or mental. The irony is that English *agony,* a word synonymous with intense pain of mind or body, ultimately comes from a word for a festive game.

agran·u·lo·cyte \(ˌ)ā-'gran-yə-lō-ˌsīt\ *noun* (circa 1923)
: a white blood cell without cytoplasmic granules

agran·u·lo·cy·to·sis \ˌā-ˌgran-yə-lō-ˌsī-'tō-səs\ *noun, plural* **-to·ses** \-'tō-ˌsēz\ [New Latin] (1927)
: an acute febrile condition marked by severe decrease in blood granulocytes and often associated with the use of certain drugs

ag·ra·pha \'a-grə-fə\ *noun plural* [Greek, neuter plural of *agraphos* unwritten, from *a-* + *graphein* to write — more at CARVE] (1890)
: sayings of Jesus not in the canonical gospels but found in other New Testament or early Christian writings

agraph·ia \(ˌ)ā-'gra-fē-ə\ *noun* [New Latin, from ²*a-* + Greek *graphein* to write] (1871)
: the pathologic loss of the ability to write

¹agrar·i·an \ə-'grer-ē-ən, -'grar-\ *adjective* [Latin *agrarius*, from *agr-, ager* field — more at ACRE] (1618)
1 : of or relating to fields or lands or their tenure
2 a : of, relating to, or characteristic of farmers or their way of life **b :** organized or designed to promote agricultural interests ⟨an *agrarian* political party⟩ ⟨*agrarian* reforms⟩

²agrarian *noun* (1818)
: a member of an agrarian party or movement

agrar·i·an·ism \-ē-ə-ˌni-zəm\ *noun* (1830)
: a social or political movement designed to bring about land reforms or to improve the economic status of the farmer

agree \ə-'grē\ *verb* **agreed; agree·ing** [Middle English, from Middle French *agreer*, from *a gre* at will, from *a* (from Latin *ad*) + *gre* will, pleasure, from Latin *gratum,* neuter of *gratus* pleasing, agreeable — more at GRACE] (15th century)
transitive verb
1 : ADMIT, CONCEDE ⟨*agrees* that he is right⟩
2 *chiefly British* **:** to settle on by common consent **:** ARRANGE ⟨I *agreed* rental terms with him —Eric Bennett⟩
intransitive verb
1 : to accept or concede something (as the views or wishes of another) ⟨*agree* to a plan⟩
2 a : to achieve or be in harmony (as of opinion, feeling, or purpose) ⟨we *agree* in our taste in music⟩ **b :** to get along together **c :** to come to terms
3 a : to be similar **:** CORRESPOND ⟨both copies *agree*⟩ **b :** to be consistent ⟨the story *agrees* with the facts⟩
4 : to be fitting, pleasing, or healthful **:** SUIT ⟨this climate *agrees* with him⟩
5 : to have an inflectional form denoting identity or other regular correspondence in a grammatical category (as gender, number, case, or person) ☆

agree·able \ə-'grē-ə-bəl\ *adjective* (14th century)
1 : pleasing to the mind or senses especially as according well with one's tastes or needs ⟨an *agreeable* companion⟩ ⟨an *agreeable* change⟩
2 : ready or willing to agree or consent
3 : being in harmony **:** CONSONANT
— **agree·abil·i·ty** \-ˌgrē-ə-'bi-lə-tē\ *noun*
— **agree·able·ness** \-'grē-ə-bəl-nəs\ *noun*
— **agree·ably** \-blē\ *adverb*

agree·ment \ə-'grē-mənt\ *noun* (15th century)
1 a : the act or fact of agreeing **b :** harmony of opinion, action, or character **:** CONCORD
2 a : an arrangement as to a course of action **b :** COMPACT, TREATY
3 a : a contract duly executed and legally binding **b :** the language or instrument embodying such a contract

ag·ri·busi·ness \'a-grə-ˌbiz-nəs, -nəz\ *noun* [*agriculture* + *business*] (circa 1955)
: an industry engaged in the producing operations of a farm, the manufacture and distribu-

tion of farm equipment and supplies, and the processing, storage, and distribution of farm commodities

ag·ri·busi·ness·man \ˌa-grə-'biz-nəs-ˌman, -mən, -nəz-\ *noun* (1961)
: a person who works in or manages an agribusiness

ag·ri·cul·tur·al \ˌa-gri-'kəl-ch(ə-)rəl\ *adjective* (1776)
: of, relating to, used in, or concerned with agriculture
— **ag·ri·cul·tur·al·ly** *adverb*

ag·ri·cul·ture \'a-gri-ˌkəl-chər\ *noun* [Middle English, from Middle French, from Latin *agricultura,* from *ager* field + *cultura* cultivation — more at ACRE, CULTURE] (15th century)
: the science, art, or practice of cultivating the soil, producing crops, and raising livestock and in varying degrees the preparation and marketing of the resulting products **:** FARMING
— **ag·ri·cul·tur·ist** \ˌa-gri-'kəl-ch(ə-)rist\ *or* **ag·ri·cul·tur·al·ist** \-ch(ə-)rə-list\ *noun*

ag·ri·mo·ny \'a-grə-ˌmō-nē\ *noun, plural* **-nies** [Middle English, from Middle French & Latin; Middle French *aigremoine,* from Latin *agrimonia,* manuscript variant of *argemonia,* from Greek *argemōnē*] (14th century)
: any of a genus (*Agrimonia* and especially *A. eupatoria*) of herbs of the rose family having compound leaves, slender spikes of small yellow flowers, and fruits like burs

agro- *combining form* [French, from Greek, from *agros* field — more at ACRE]
1 : of or belonging to fields or soil **:** agricultural ⟨*agro*chemical⟩
2 : agricultural and ⟨*agro*-industrial⟩

ag·ro·chem·i·cal \ˌa-grō-'ke-mi-kəl\ *also* **ag·ri·chem·i·cal** \ˌa-gri-\ *noun* (1956)
: an agricultural chemical (as an herbicide or an insecticide)

ag·ro·for·est·ry \ˌa-grō-'fȯr-ə-strē, -'fär-\ *noun* (1977)
: land management for the simultaneous production of food, crops, and trees; *also* **:** the science of agroforestry
— **ag·ro·for·est·er** \-stər\ *noun*

ag·ro·in·dus·tri·al \ˌa-grō-in-'dəs-trē-əl\ *adjective* (1940)
: of or relating to production (as of power for industry and water for irrigation) for both industrial and agricultural purposes

agron·o·my \ə-'grä-nə-mē\ *noun* [probably from French *agronomie,* from *agro-* + *-nomie* -nomy] (1814)
: a branch of agriculture dealing with field-crop production and soil management
— **ag·ro·nom·ic** \ˌa-grə-'nä-mik\ *adjective*
— **ag·ro·nom·i·cal·ly** \-mi-k(ə-)lē\ *adverb*
— **agron·o·mist** \ə-'grä-nə-mist\ *noun*

aground \ə-'grau̇nd\ *adverb or adjective* (14th century)
1 : on the ground ⟨planes aloft and *aground*⟩
2 : on or onto the shore or the bottom of a body of water ⟨a ship run *aground*⟩

ague \'ā-(ˌ)gyü\ *noun* [Middle English, from Middle French *aguë,* from Medieval Latin (*febris*) *acuta,* literally, sharp fever, from Latin, feminine of *acutus* sharp — more at ACUTE] (14th century)
1 : a fever (as malaria) marked by paroxysms of chills, fever, and sweating that recur at regular intervals
2 : a fit of shivering **:** CHILL
— **agu·ish** \'ā-ˌgyü-ish\ *adjective*

ah \'ä\ *interjection* [Middle English] (13th century)
— used to express delight, relief, regret, or contempt

aha \ä-'hä\ *interjection* [Middle English] (14th century)
— used to express surprise, triumph, or derision

ahead \ə-'hed\ *adverb or adjective* (1596)
1 a : in a forward direction or position **:** FORWARD **b :** in front
2 : in, into, or for the future ⟨plan *ahead*⟩

3 : in or toward a more advantageous position ⟨helped others to get *ahead*⟩
4 : at or to an earlier time **:** in advance ⟨make payments *ahead*⟩

ahead of *preposition* (1748)
1 : in front or advance of
2 : in excess of

ahem \ə-'hem\ *a throat-clearing sound; often read as* ə-'hem\ *interjection* [imitative] (1763)
— used especially to attract attention

ahim·sa \ə-'him-ˌsä\ *noun* [Sanskrit *ahiṁsā* noninjury] (1875)
: the Hindu and Buddhist doctrine of refraining from harming any living being

ahis·tor·i·cal \ˌā-his-'tȯr-i-kəl, -'tär-\ *or* **ahis·tor·ic** \-ik\ *adjective* (1945)
: not concerned with or related to history, historical development, or tradition ⟨the *ahistorical* attitudes of the radicals⟩

ahold \ə-'hōld\ *noun* [probably from the phrase *a hold*] (1872)
: HOLD ⟨if you could get *ahold* of a representative —Norman Mailer⟩

A horizon \'ā-\ *noun* (1936)
: the uppermost dark-colored layer of a soil consisting largely of partly disintegrated organic debris

ahoy \ə-'hȯi\ *interjection* [*a-* (as in *aha*) + *hoy*] (1751)
— used in hailing ⟨ship *ahoy*⟩

Ah·ri·man \'är-i-mən, -ˌmän\ *noun* [Persian, modification of Avestan *aṅro mainyuš* hostile spirit]
: Ahura Mazda's antagonist who is a spirit of darkness and evil in Zoroastrianism

Ahu·ra Maz·da \ə-ˌhu̇r-ə-'maz-də, ä-ˌhu̇r-\ *noun* [Avestan *Ahuramazda,* literally, wise god]
: the Supreme Being represented as a deity of goodness and light in Zoroastrianism

Ai·as \'ī-əs\ *noun* [Greek]
: AJAX

ai·blins \'ā-blənz\ *adverb* [*able* + *-lings, -lins* -lings] (circa 1605)
chiefly Scottish **:** PERHAPS

¹aid \'ād\ *verb* [Middle English *eyden,* from Middle French *aider,* from Latin *adjutare,* frequentative of *adjuvare,* from *ad-* + *juvare* to help] (15th century)
transitive verb
: to provide with what is useful or necessary in achieving an end
intransitive verb
: to give assistance
— **aid·er** *noun*

²aid *noun* (15th century)
1 : a subsidy granted to the king by the English parliament until the 18th century for an extraordinary purpose
2 a : the act of helping **b :** help given **:** ASSISTANCE; *specifically* **:** tangible means of assistance (as money or supplies)

\ə\ abut \ᵊ\ kitten \ər\ **further** \a\ ash \ā\ ace
\ä\ mop, mar \au̇\ out \ch\ chin \e\ bet \ē\ easy
\g\ go \i\ hit \ī\ ice \j\ job \ŋ\ sing \ō\ go
\ȯ\ law \ȯi\ boy \th\ thin \t͟h\ the \ü\ loot \u̇\ foot
\y\ yet \zh\ vision *see also* Guide to Pronunciation

3 a : an assisting person or group — compare AIDE **b :** something by which assistance is given **:** an assisting device ⟨an *aid* to understanding⟩ ⟨a visual *aid*⟩; *especially* **:** HEARING AID
4 : a tribute paid by a vassal to his lord

aide \\'ād\ *noun* [short for *aide-de-camp*] (1777)
: a person who acts as an assistant; *specifically* **:** a military officer acting as assistant to a superior

aide-de-camp \\,ād-di-'kamp, -'käⁿ\ *noun,* *plural* **aides-de-camp** \\,ād(z)-di-\ [French *aide de camp,* literally, camp assistant] (1670)
: a military aid; *also* **:** a civilian aide usually to an executive

aide-mé·moire \\,ād-mām-'wär\ *noun, plural* **aide-mémoire** [French, from *aider* to aid + *mémoire* memory] (1846)
1 : an aid to the memory; *especially* **:** a mnemonic device
2 : a written summary or outline of important items of a proposed agreement or diplomatic communication

aid·man \\'ād-,man\ *noun* (1944)
: an army medical corpsman attached to a field unit

AIDS \\'ādz\ *noun* [acquired *immunodeficiency syndrome*] (1982)
: a disease of the human immune system that is caused by infection with HIV, that is characterized cytologically especially by severe reduction in the numbers of helper T cells, that in modern industrialized nations occurs especially in homosexual and bisexual men and in intravenous users of illicit drugs, that is commonly transmitted in blood and bodily secretions (as semen), and that renders the subject highly vulnerable to life-threatening conditions (as Pneumocystis carinii pneumonia) and to some that become life-threatening (as Kaposi's sarcoma)

AIDS-related complex *noun* (1984)
: a group of symptoms (as fever, weight loss, and lymphadenopathy) that is associated with the presence of antibodies to HIV and is followed by the development of AIDS in a certain proportion of cases

AIDS virus *noun* (1985)
: HIV

ai·grette \\ā-'gret, 'ā-,\ *noun* [French, plume, egret, from Middle French — more at EGRET] (1630)
1 : a spray of feathers (as of the egret) for the head
2 : a spray of gems worn on a hat or in the hair

ai·guille \\ā-'gwē(ə)l, -'gwē\ *noun* [French, literally, needle — more at AGLET] (1816)
: a sharp-pointed pinnacle of rock

ai·guil·lette \\,ā-gwi-'let\ *noun* [French — more at AGLET] (1816)
: AGLET; *specifically* **:** a shoulder cord worn by designated military aides — compare FOURRAGÈRE

ai·ki·do \\,ī-ki-'dō, ī-'kē-(,)dō\ *noun* [Japanese *aikidō,* from *ai-* match, coordinate + *ki* breath, spirit + *dō* art, way] (1956)
: a Japanese art of self-defense employing locks and holds and utilizing the principle of nonresistance to cause an opponent's own momentum to work against him

¹ail \\'ā(ə)l\ *verb* [Middle English *eilen,* from Old English *eglan;* akin to Gothic *agljan* to harm] (before 12th century)
transitive verb
: to give physical or emotional pain, discomfort, or trouble to
intransitive verb
: to have something the matter; *especially* **:** to suffer ill health

²ail *noun* (13th century)
: AILMENT

ai·lan·thus \\ā-'lan(t)-thəs\ *noun* [New Latin, from Amboinese *ai lanito,* literally, tree (of) heaven] (1807)

: any of a small Asian genus (*Ailanthus* of the family Simaroubaceae, the ailanthus family) of chiefly tropical trees and shrubs with bitter bark, pinnate leaves, and terminal panicles of ill-scented greenish flowers

ai·le·ron \\'ā-lə-,rän\ *noun* [French, from diminutive of *aile* wing — more at AISLE] (1909)
: a movable airfoil at the trailing edge of an airplane wing that is used for imparting a rolling motion especially in banking for turns — see AIRPLANE illustration

ail·ment \\'ā(ə)l-mənt\ *noun* (circa 1706)
1 : a bodily disorder or chronic disease
2 : UNREST, UNEASINESS

ai·lu·ro·phile \\ī-'lur-ə-,fīl, ā-\ *noun* [Greek *ailouros* cat] (1927)
: a cat fancier **:** a lover of cats

ai·lu·ro·phobe \\-,fōb\ *noun* (1905)
: a person who hates or fears cats

¹aim \\'ām\ *verb* [Middle English, from Middle French *aesmer* & *esmer;* Middle French *aesmer,* from Old French, from *a-* (from Latin *ad-*) + *esmer* to estimate, from Latin *aestimare*] (14th century)
intransitive verb
1 : to direct a course; *specifically* **:** to point a weapon at an object
2 : ASPIRE, INTEND ⟨*aims* to reform the government⟩
transitive verb
1 *obsolete* **:** GUESS, CONJECTURE
2 a : POINT **b :** to direct to or toward a specified object or goal ⟨a program *aimed* at reducing pollution⟩

²aim *noun* (14th century)
1 *obsolete* **:** MARK, TARGET
2 a : the pointing of a weapon at a mark **b :** the ability to hit a target **c :** a weapon's accuracy or effectiveness
3 *obsolete* **a :** CONJECTURE, GUESS **b :** the directing of effort toward a goal
4 : a clearly directed intent or purpose
synonym see INTENTION
— **aim·less** \\-ləs\ *adjective*
— **aim·less·ly** *adverb*
— **aim·less·ness** *noun*

ain \\'än\ *adjective* [probably from Old Norse *eiginn*] (1721)
Scottish **:** OWN

ain't \\'änt\ [contraction of *are not*] (1778)
1 : am not **:** are not **:** is not
2 : have not **:** has not
3 : do not **:** does not **:** did not — used in some varieties of Black English □

Ai·nu \\'ī-(,)nü\ *noun, plural* **Ainu** *or* **Ainus** [Ainu *aynu* person] (1819)
1 : a member of an indigenous people of the Japanese archipelago, the Kuril Islands, and part of Sakhalin Island
2 : the language of the Ainu people

ai·o·li \\(,)ī-'ō-lē, (,)ā-\ *noun* [Provençal, from *ai* garlic + *oli* oil] (circa 1900)
: a sauce made of crushed garlic, egg yolks, olive oil, and lemon juice and sometimes potato **:** garlic mayonnaise

¹air \\'ar, 'er\ *noun, often attributive* [Middle English, from Middle French, from Latin *aer,* from Greek *aēr*] (14th century)
1 a *archaic* **:** BREATH **b :** the mixture of invisible odorless tasteless gases (as nitrogen and oxygen) that surrounds the earth **c :** a light breeze
2 a : empty space **b :** NOTHINGNESS ⟨vanished into thin *air*⟩ **c :** a sudden severance of relations ⟨she gave me the *air*⟩
3 [probably translation of Italian *aria*] **a :** TUNE, MELODY **b** *Elizabethan & Jacobean music* **:** an accompanied song or melody in usually strophic form **c :** the chief voice part or melody in choral music
4 a : outward appearance of a thing ⟨an *air* of luxury⟩ **b :** a surrounding or pervading influence **:** ATMOSPHERE ⟨an *air* of mystery⟩ **c :** the look, appearance, or bearing of a person especially as expressive of some personal quality

or emotion **:** DEMEANOR ⟨an *air* of dignity⟩ **d :** an artificial or affected manner ⟨put on *airs*⟩
5 : public utterance ⟨he gave *air* to his opinion⟩
6 : COMPRESSED AIR
7 a (1) **:** AIRCRAFT ⟨go by *air*⟩ (2) **:** AVIATION ⟨*air* safety⟩ ⟨*air* rights⟩ (3) **:** AIR FORCE ⟨*air* headquarters⟩ **b :** the medium of transmission of radio waves; *also* **:** RADIO, TELEVISION ⟨went on the *air*⟩
8 : a football offense utilizing primarily the forward pass ⟨trailing by 20 points, the team took to the *air*⟩
9 : an air-conditioning system
synonym see POSE
— **air·less** \\-ləs\ *adjective*
— **air·less·ness** *noun*
— **in the air :** in wide circulation **:** ABOUT
— **up in the air :** not yet settled

²air (1530)
transitive verb
1 : to expose to the air for drying, purifying, or refreshing **:** VENTILATE — often used with *out*
2 : to expose to public view or bring to public notice
3 : to transmit by radio or television ⟨*air* a program⟩
intransitive verb
1 : to become exposed to the open air
2 : to become broadcast ⟨the program *airs* daily⟩
synonym see EXPRESS

air bag *noun* (1969)
: an automobile safety device consisting of a bag designed to inflate automatically in front of an occupant in case of collision

air ball *noun* (1981)
: a missed shot in basketball that fails to touch the rim and backboard

air base *noun* (1915)
: a military base intended chiefly for the operation of aircraft

air bladder *noun* (1731)
: a sac containing gas and especially air; *especially* **:** a hydrostatic organ present in most fishes that serves as an accessory respiratory organ

air·boat \\'ar-,bōt, 'er-\ *noun* (1946)
: a shallow-draft boat driven by an airplane propeller and steered by an airplane rudder

air·borne \\-,bōrn, -,bȯrn\ *adjective* (1641)
1 : done or being in the air **:** being off the ground: as **a :** carried through the air (as by an

aircraft) **b :** supported especially by aerodynamic forces or propelled through the air by force

2 : trained for deployment by air and especially by parachute

air brake *noun* (1871)

1 : a brake operated by a piston driven by compressed air

2 : a surface that may be projected into the airstream for increasing drag and lowering the speed of an airplane

¹air·brush \-,brəsh\ *noun* (circa 1889)

: an atomizer for applying by compressed air a fine spray (as of paint or liquid color)

²airbrush *transitive verb*

: to paint, treat, or alter with an airbrush

air·burst \-,bərst\ *noun* (1917)

: the burst of a shell or bomb in the air

air·bus \-,bəs\ *noun* (1945)

: a short-range or medium-range subsonic jet passenger airplane

air chief marshal *noun* (1919)

: a commissioned officer in the British air force who ranks with a general in the army

air commodore *noun* (1919)

: a commissioned officer in the British air force who ranks with a brigadier in the army

air–con·di·tion \,ar-kən-'di-shən, ,er-\ *transitive verb* [back-formation from *air conditioning*] (1933)

: to equip (as a building) with an apparatus for washing air and controlling its humidity and temperature; *also* **:** to subject (air) to these processes

 — **air con·di·tion·er** \-'di-sh(ə-)nər\ *noun*

 — **air–con·di·tion·ing** \-'di-sh(ə-)niŋ\ *noun*

air·craft \'ar-,kraft, 'er-\ *noun, plural* **aircraft** *often attributive* (1850)

: a vehicle (as an airplane or balloon) for traveling through the air

aircraft carrier *noun* (1919)

: a warship with a flight deck on which airplanes can be launched and landed

air·crew \'ar-,krü, 'er-\ *noun* (1921)

: the crew manning an airplane

air–cush·ion vehicle *noun* (circa 1962)

: HOVERCRAFT

air dam *noun* (1965)

: a device attached to the underside of the front of an automobile to improve stability, aerodynamic performance, and engine cooling by redirecting the flow of air

air·date \-,dāt\ *noun* (1971)

: the scheduled date of a broadcast

air·drome \'ar-,drōm, 'er-\ *noun* [alteration of *aerodrome*] (1917)

: AIRPORT

air·drop \-,dräp\ *noun* (circa 1945)

: delivery of cargo or personnel by parachute from an airplane in flight

 — **air–drop** *transitive verb*

 — **air–drop·pa·ble** \-,drä-pə-bəl\ *adjective*

air–dry \-'drī\ *adjective* (1856)

: dry to such a degree that no further moisture is given up on exposure to air

Aire·dale terrier \,ar-,dāl-, ,er-\ *noun* [*Airedale,* valley of the Aire river, England] (1880)

: any of a breed of large terriers with a hard, wiry, black-and-tan coat — called also *Airedale*

air·er \'ar-ər, 'er-\ *noun* (circa 1847)

British **:** a frame on which clothes are aired or dried

air·fare \'ar-,far, 'er-,fer\ *noun* (1918)

: fare for travel by airplane

air·field \-,fēld\ *noun* (1927)

: an area of land from which aircraft operate: as **a :** AIRPORT **b :** AIR BASE

air·flow \-,flō\ *noun* (circa 1911)

: a flow of air; *specifically* **:** the motion of air (as around parts of an airplane in flight) relative to the surface of a body immersed in it

air·foil \-,fȯil\ *noun* (circa 1922)

: a body (as an airplane wing or propeller

blade) designed to provide a desired reaction force when in motion relative to the surrounding air

air force *noun* (1917)

1 : the military organization of a nation for air warfare

2 : a unit of the U.S. Air Force higher than a division and lower than a command

air·frame \-,frām\ *noun* (1931)

: the structure of an aircraft, rocket vehicle, or missile without the power plant

air·freight \-'frāt\ *noun* (1929)

: freight transport by air in volume; *also* **:** the charge for this service

 — **airfreight** *transitive verb*

air·glow \-,glō\ *noun* (circa 1950)

: light that is observed especially during the night, that originates in the high atmosphere of a planet (as the earth), and that is associated with photochemical reactions of gases caused by solar radiation

air gun *noun* (circa 1753)

1 : a gun from which a projectile is propelled by compressed air

2 : any of various hand tools that work by compressed air; *especially* **:** AIRBRUSH

¹air·head \-,hed\ *noun* [¹*air* + *-head* (as in *beachhead*)] (circa 1944)

: an area in hostile territory secured usually by airborne troops for further use in bringing in troops and materiel by air

²airhead *noun* (1972)

: a mindless or stupid person

 — **air·head·ed** \-,he-dəd\ *adjective*

air·hole \-,hōl\ *noun* (1766)

: a hole to admit or discharge air

air·ing \'ar-iŋ, 'er-\ *noun* (circa 1606)

1 : exposure to air or heat for drying or freshening

2 : exposure to or exercise in the open air especially to promote health or fitness

3 : exposure to public view or notice

4 : a radio or television broadcast

air lane *noun* (circa 1910)

: a path customarily followed by airplanes

air letter *noun* (1920)

1 : an airmail letter

2 : a sheet of airmail stationery that can be folded and sealed with the message inside and the address outside

air·lift \'ar-,lift, 'er-\ *noun* (1945)

: a system of transporting cargo or passengers by aircraft usually to or from an otherwise inaccessible area

 — **airlift** *transitive verb*

air·line \'ar-,līn\ *noun* (1910)

: an air transportation system including its equipment, routes, operating personnel, and management

air line *noun* (1813)

: a straight line through the air between two points

air·lin·er \-,lī-nər\ *noun* (1908)

: an airplane operated by an airline

air lock *noun* (1857)

1 : an intermediate chamber with two airtight doors or openings to permit passage between two dissimilar spaces (as two places of unequal atmospheric pressure)

2 : a stoppage of flow caused by air being in a part where liquid ought to circulate

air·mail \'ar-,mā(ə)l, 'er-\ *noun* (1913)

: the system of transporting mail by aircraft; *also* **:** the mail thus transported

 — **airmail** *transitive verb*

air·man \-mən\ *noun* (1873)

1 : a civilian or military pilot, aviator, or aviation technician

2 : an enlisted man in the air force: as **a :** an enlisted man of one of the three ranks below sergeant **b :** an enlisted man ranking above an airman basic and below an airman first class

airman basic *noun* (circa 1961)

: an enlisted man of the lowest rank in the air force

airman first class *noun* (1952)

: an enlisted man in the air force ranking above an airman and below a sergeant

air·man·ship \'ar-mən-,ship, 'er-\ *noun* (1908)

: skill in piloting or navigating airplanes

air marshal *noun* (1919)

: a commissioned officer in the British air force who ranks with a lieutenant general in the army

air mass *noun* (1893)

: a body of air extending hundreds or thousands of miles horizontally and sometimes as high as the stratosphere and maintaining as it travels nearly uniform conditions of temperature and humidity at any given level

air mattress *noun* (1926)

: MATTRESS 1b

Air Medal *noun* (1942)

: a U.S. military decoration awarded for meritorious achievement while participating in an aerial flight

air mile *noun* (1919)

: a mile in air travel

air–mind·ed \'ar-'mīn-dəd, 'er-\ *adjective* (1924)

: interested in aviation or in air travel

 — **air–mind·ed·ness** *noun*

air·mo·bile \-,mō-bəl, -,bēl, -,bīl\ *adjective* (1965)

: of, relating to, or being a military unit whose members are transported to combat areas usually by helicopter

air·park \-,pärk\ *noun* (1929)

: a small airport usually near an industrial area

air piracy *noun* (1948)

: the hijacking of a flying airplane **:** SKYJACKING

air·plane \'ar-,plān, 'er-\ *noun* [alteration of *aeroplane*] (1907)

: a powered heavier-than-air aircraft that has fixed wings from which it derives most of its lift

airplane: *1* weather radar, *2* cockpit, *3* jet engine, *4* engine pod, *5* pylon, *6* wing, *7* vertical stabilizer, *8* rudder, *9, 10* tabs, *11* elevator, *12* horizontal stabilizer, *13* inboard flap, *14* inboard spoiler, *15, 16* tabs, *17* aileron, *18* outboard flap, *19* outboard spoiler, *20* sound suppressor, *21* thrust reverser, *22* cabin air intake, *23* fuselage, *24* nose landing gear

air plant *noun* (1841)

1 : EPIPHYTE

2 : BRYOPHYLLUM

air·play \-,plā\ *noun* (1966)

: the playing of a musical recording on the air by a radio station

air pocket *noun* (1912)

: a condition of the atmosphere (as a local down current) that causes an airplane to drop suddenly

air police *noun* (1944)

: the military police of an air force

air·port \'ar-,pȯrt, 'er-, -,pȯrt\ *noun* (1919)

: a place from which aircraft operate that usually has paved runways and maintenance facilities and often serves as a terminal

air·post \-'pōst\ *noun* (circa 1927)
: AIRMAIL

air·pow·er \-,paü(-ə)r\ *noun* (1908)
: the military strength of a nation's air force

air pump *noun* (1660)
: a pump for exhausting air from a closed space or for compressing air or forcing it through other apparatus

air raid *noun* (1914)
: an attack by armed airplanes on a surface target — usually hyphened when used attributively ⟨*air-raid* shelter⟩

air rifle *noun* (1886)
: a rifle whose projectile (as a BB or pellet) is propelled by compressed air or carbon dioxide

air right *noun* (1922)
: a property right to the space above a surface area or object

air sac *noun* (circa 1828)
1 : one of the air-filled spaces in the body of a bird connected with the air passages of the lungs
2 : ALVEOLUS 1b
3 : a thin-walled dilation of a trachea occurring in many insects

air·screw \'ar-,skrü, 'er-\ *noun* (1894)
chiefly British : an airplane propeller

air·ship \-,ship\ *noun* (1819)
: a lighter-than-air aircraft having propulsion and steering systems

air show *noun* (1950)
: an exhibition of aircraft and aviation skills

air·sick \-,sik\ *adjective* (1785)
: affected with motion sickness associated with flying
— **air·sick·ness** *noun*

air·space \-,spās\ *noun* (1911)
: the space lying above the earth or above a certain area of land or water; *especially* : the space lying above a nation and coming under its jurisdiction

air·speed \-,spēd\ *noun* (circa 1909)
: the speed (as of an airplane) with relation to the air — compare GROUND SPEED

air·stream \-,strēm\ *noun* (1869)
: a current of air; *specifically* : AIRFLOW

air·strip \-,strip\ *noun* (1942)
: a runway without normal air base or airport facilities

¹airt \'ärt, 'ert\ *noun* [Middle English *art*, from Scottish Gaelic *àirt*] (15th century)
chiefly Scottish : compass point : DIRECTION

²airt *transitive verb* (circa 1782)
chiefly Scottish : DIRECT, GUIDE

air taxi *noun* (1920)
: a small commercial airplane used for short flights between localities not served by scheduled airlines

air·tight \'ar-,tīt, 'er-\ *adjective* (1760)
1 : impermeable to air or nearly so
2 a : having no noticeable weakness, flaw, or loophole ⟨an *airtight* argument⟩ **b** : permitting no opportunity for an opponent to score ⟨an *airtight* defense⟩
— **air·tight·ness** *noun*

air·time \-,tīm\ *noun* (1942)
1 : the time at which a radio or television broadcast is scheduled to begin
2 : the time or any part thereof that a radio or television station is on the air

air–to–air \,ar-tə-'(w)ar, ,er-tə-'(w)er\ *adjective* (1941)
: launched from one airplane in flight at another ⟨*air-to-air* missiles⟩; *also* : involving aircraft in flight ⟨*air-to-air* combat⟩

air vice–marshal *noun* (1919)
: a commissioned officer in the British air force who ranks with a major general in the army

air·wave \'ar-,wāv, 'er-\ *adjective* (1944)
: of, created for, or heard on the airwaves

air·waves \-,wāvz\ *noun plural* (1928)
: the medium of radio and television transmission — not used technically

air·way \-,wā\ *noun* (1849)
1 : a passage for a current of air (as in a mine or to the lungs)
2 : a designated route along which airplanes fly from airport to airport; *especially* : such a route equipped with navigational aids
3 : AIRLINE
4 : a channel of a designated radio frequency for broadcasting or other radio communication

air·wor·thy \-,wər-thē\ *adjective* (1829)
: fit for operation in the air ⟨an *airworthy* airplane⟩
— **air·wor·thi·ness** *noun*

airy \'ar-ē, 'er-\ *adjective* **air·i·er; -est** (14th century)
1 a : of or relating to air : ATMOSPHERIC **b** : high in the air : LOFTY ⟨*airy* perches⟩ **c** : performed in air : AERIAL ⟨*airy* leaps⟩
2 : UNREAL, ILLUSORY ⟨*airy* romances⟩
3 a : being light and graceful in movement or manner : SPRIGHTLY, VIVACIOUS ⟨an *airy* laugh⟩ **b** : ETHEREAL ⟨*airy* fantasy⟩
4 a : open to the free circulation of air ⟨an *airy* front porch⟩ **b** : having openings or spaces ⟨*airy* lacework⟩
5 : AFFECTED, PROUD ⟨*airy* condescension⟩
— **air·i·ly** \'ar-ə-lē, 'er-\ *adverb*
— **air·i·ness** \-ē-nəs\ *noun*

airy–fairy \-'far-ē, -'fer-ē\ *adjective* (1869)
1 *chiefly British* : DELICATE, FAIRYLIKE
2 *chiefly British* : lacking substance or purpose ⟨in . . . an *airy-fairy*, unserious, insufficiently careful fashion —*Times Literary Supplement*⟩

aisle \'ī(ə)l\ *noun* [Middle English *ile*, alteration of *ele*, from Middle French, wing, from Latin *ala*; akin to Old English *eaxl* shoulder, Latin *axis* axletree — more at AXIS] (15th century)
1 : the side of a church nave separated by piers from the nave proper
2 a : a passage (as in a theater or railroad passenger car) separating sections of seats **b** : a passage (as in a store or warehouse) for inside traffic

aisle·way \-,wā\ *noun* (1926)
: AISLE 2b

ait \'āt\ *noun* [Middle English *eyt*, alteration of Old English *īggoth*, from *īg* island — more at ISLAND] (before 12th century)
British : a little island

aitch \'āch\ *noun* [French *hache*, from (assumed) Vulgar Latin *hacca*] (circa 1580)
: the letter h

aitch·bone \'āch-,bōn\ *noun* [Middle English *hachbon*, alteration (resulting from incorrect division of *a nachebon*) of (assumed) Middle English *nachebon*, from Middle English *nache* buttock (from Middle French, from Late Latin *natica*, from Latin *natis*) + *bon* bone] (15th century)
1 : the hipbone especially of cattle
2 : the cut of beef containing the aitchbone

ajar \ə-'jär\ *adjective or adverb* [earlier *on char*, from *on* + *char* turn — more at CHARE] (15th century)
: slightly open ⟨a door *ajar*⟩

Ajax \'ā-,jaks\ *noun* [Latin, from Greek *Aias*]
1 : a Greek hero in the Trojan War who kills himself because the armor of Achilles is awarded to Odysseus
2 : a fleet-footed Greek hero in the Trojan War

aju·ga \'a-jə-gə\ *noun, plural* **-ga** *or* **-gas** [New Latin, from ²*a-* + Latin *jugum* yoke — more at YOKE] (circa 1899)
: ¹BUGLE

Akan \'ä-,kän\ *noun, plural* **Akan** *or* **Akans** (1694)
1 : a member of any of the Akan-speaking peoples (as the Ashanti)
2 : a Kwa language of southern Ghana and the southeast Ivory Coast

akee \'a-,kē, a-'kē\ *noun* [origin unknown] (1794)
: the fleshy fruit of an African tree (*Blighia sapida*) of the soapberry family grown in the

Caribbean area, Florida, and Hawaii that is edible when ripe but has a toxic pink raphe attaching the aril to the seed and toxic arils when immature or overripe; *also* : the tree

AK-47 \'ā-,kā-,fŏr-tē-'se-vᵊn, -,fŏr-\ *noun* [Russian *avtomat Kalashnikova 1947* Kalashnikov automatic rifle of 1947] (1968)
: a Soviet-designed 7.62 mm (.30 cal.) gas-operated magazine-fed rifle for automatic or semiautomatic fire

akim·bo \ə-'kim-(,)bō\ *adjective or adverb* [Middle English *in kenebowe*] (15th century)
1 : having the hand on the hip and the elbow turned outward
2 : set in a bent position ⟨a tailor sitting with legs *akimbo*⟩

akin \ə-'kin\ *adjective* (1586)
1 : related by blood : descended from a common ancestor or prototype
2 : essentially similar, related, or compatible

Aki·ta \ə-'kē-tə, ä-\ *noun* [from *Akita*, Japan] (1928)
: any of a breed of large muscular dogs of Japanese origin

Ak·ka·di·an \ə-'kā-dē-ən\ *noun* (circa 1855)
1 : an extinct Semitic language of ancient Mesopotamia
2 : a Semitic inhabitant of central Mesopotamia before 2000 B.C.
— **Akkadian** *adjective*

ak·va·vit \'ä-kwə-,vēt, 'äk-vä-\ *variant of* AQUAVIT

al- — see AD-

¹-al *adjective suffix* [Middle English, from Old French & Latin; Old French, from Latin *-alis*]
: of, relating to, or characterized by ⟨directional⟩ ⟨fictional⟩

²-al *noun suffix* [Middle English *-aille*, from Old French, from Latin *-alia*, neuter plural of *-alis*]
: action : process ⟨rehearsal⟩

³-al *noun suffix* [French, from *alcool* alcohol, from Medieval Latin *alcohol*]
: aldehyde ⟨furfural⟩

ala \'ā-lə\ *noun, plural* **alae** \-,lē\ [Latin — more at AISLE] (1738)
: a wing or a winglike anatomic process or part
— **alar** \'ā-lər\ *adjective*
— **ala·ry** \-lə-rē\ *adjective*

à la *also* **a la** \,ä-(,)lä, ,ä-lə, ,a-lə\ *preposition* [French *à la*] (1589)
: in the manner of

al·a·bas·ter \'a-lə-,bas-tər\ *noun* [Middle English *alabastre*, from Middle French, from Latin *alabaster* vase of alabaster, from Greek *alabastros*] (14th century)
1 : a compact fine-textured usually white and translucent gypsum often carved into vases and ornaments
2 : a hard compact calcite or aragonite that is translucent and sometimes banded
— **alabaster** *or* **al·a·bas·trine** \,a-lə-'bas-trən\ *adjective*

à la carte *also* **a la carte** \,ä-lə-'kärt, ,a-lə-\ *adverb or adjective* [French, by the bill of fare] (1826)
: according to a menu that prices each item separately

alack \ə-'lak\ *interjection* [Middle English] (15th century)
— used to express sorrow or regret

alac·ri·ty \ə-'la-krə-tē\ *noun* [Latin *alacritas*, from *alacr-, alacer* lively, eager] (15th century)
: promptness in response : cheerful readiness ⟨accepted the invitation of the president with *alacrity*⟩
— **alac·ri·tous** \-krə-təs\ *adjective*

Alad·din \ə-'la-dᵊn\ *noun*
: a youth in the *Arabian Nights' Entertainments* who comes into possession of a magic lamp

à la grecque \,ä-lə-'grek, ,a-lə-\ *adjective, often G capitalized* [French, in the Greek manner] (circa 1925)

: served in a sauce made of olive oil, lemon juice, and several seasonings (as fennel, coriander, sage, and thyme)

à la king \ˌä-lə-'kiŋ, ˌa-lə-\ *adjective* (1919)
: served in a cream sauce with mushrooms and pimiento or green peppers ⟨chicken *à la king*⟩

al·a·me·da \ˌa-lə-'mē-də, -'mā-\ *noun* [Spanish, from *álamo* poplar] (1797)
: a public promenade bordered with trees

à la mode *also* **a la mode** \ˌä-lə-'mōd, ˌa-lə-\ *adjective* [French, according to the fashion] (1650)
1 : FASHIONABLE, STYLISH
2 : topped with ice cream

al·a·nine \'a-lə-ˌnēn\ *noun* [German *Alanin,* irregular from *Aldehyd* aldehyde] (circa 1879)
: a simple nonessential crystalline amino acid $C_3H_7NO_2$

al·a·nyl \'a-lə-ˌnil\ *noun* [International Scientific Vocabulary *alan*ine + *-yl*] (circa 1928)
: an acyl radical of alanine

¹alarm \ə-'lärm\ *also* **ala·rum** \ə-'lär-əm, -'lar-, *British also* -'ler-\ *noun* [Middle English *alarme, alarom,* from Middle French *alarme,* from Old Italian *all'arme,* literally, to the arms] (14th century)
1 *usually* alarum, *archaic* **:** a call to arms ⟨the angry trumpet sounds *alarum* —Shakespeare⟩
2 : a signal (as a loud noise or flashing light) that warns or alerts; *also* **:** a device that signals ⟨set the *alarm* to wake me at seven⟩
3 : sudden sharp apprehension and fear resulting from the perception of imminent danger
4 : a warning notice
synonym see FEAR

²alarm *also* **alarum** *transitive verb* (1605)
1 : DISTURB, EXCITE
2 : to give warning to
3 : to strike with fear
— alarm·ing·ly \-'lär-miŋ-lē\ *adverb*

alarm clock *noun* (1697)
: a clock that can be set to sound an alarm at a desired time

alarm·ism \ə-'lär-ˌmi-zəm\ *noun* (1867)
: the often unwarranted exciting of fears or warning of danger
— alarm·ist \-mist\ *noun or adjective*

alarm reaction *noun* (1936)
: the initial reaction of an organism (as increased hormonal activity) to stress

alarums and excursions *noun plural* (1592)
1 : martial sounds and the movement of soldiers across the stage — used as a stage direction in Elizabethan drama
2 : clamor, excitement, and feverish or disordered activity

alas \ə-'las\ *interjection* [Middle English, from Old French, from *a* ah + *las* weary, from Latin *lassus* — more at LASSITUDE] (13th century)
— used to express unhappiness, pity, or concern

Alas·kan malamute \ə-'las-kən-\ *noun* (1938)
: any of a breed of powerful heavy-coated deep-chested dogs of Alaskan origin that have erect ears, heavily cushioned feet, and a plumy tail

Alas·ka time \ə-'las-kə-\ *noun* (1945)
: the time of the 9th time zone west of Greenwich that includes most of Alaska

¹alate \'ā-ˌlāt\ *adjective* [Latin *alatus,* from *ala*] (1668)
: having wings or a winglike part

²alate *noun* (1941)
: a winged insect (as an aphid) of a kind having winged and wingless forms

alb \'alb\ *noun* [Middle English *albe,* from Old English, from Medieval Latin *alba,* from Latin, feminine of *albus* white; akin to Greek *alphos* white leprous spot] (before 12th century)
: a full-length white linen ecclesiastical vestment with long sleeves that is gathered at the waist with a cincture

al·ba·core \'al-bə-ˌkōr, -ˌkȯr\ *noun, plural* **-core** *or* **-cores** [Portuguese *albacor,* from Arabic *al-bakūrah* the albacore] (1579)
: a large pelagic tuna (*Thunnus alalunga*) with long pectoral fins that is a source of canned tuna; *broadly* **:** any of various tunas (as a bonito)

albacore

Al·ba·nian \al-'bā-nē-ən, -nyən *also* ȯl-\ *noun* (1579)
1 : a native or inhabitant of Albania
2 : the Indo-European language of the Albanian people — see INDO-EUROPEAN LANGUAGES table
— Albanian *adjective*

al·ba·tross \'al-bə-ˌtrȯs, -ˌträs\ *noun, plural* **-tross** *or* **-tross·es** [probably alteration of obsolete *alcatrace* frigate bird, from Spanish or Portuguese *alcatraz* pelican, from Arabic *al-ghaṭṭās,* a kind of sea eagle] (1672)
1 : any of a family (Diomedeidae) of large web-footed seabirds that have long slender wings, are excellent gliders, and include the largest seabirds
2 a : something that causes persistent deep concern or anxiety **b :** something that greatly hinders accomplishment **:** ENCUMBRANCE

albatross 1

al·be·do \al-'bē-(ˌ)dō\ *noun, plural* **-dos** [Late Latin, whiteness, from Latin *albus*] (circa 1859)
: reflective power; *specifically* **:** the fraction of incident radiation (as light) that is reflected by a surface or body (as the moon or a cloud)

al·be·it \ȯl-'bē-ət, al-\ *conjunction* [Middle English, literally, all though it be] (14th century)
: conceding the fact that **:** even though

Al·bi·gen·ses \ˌal-bə-'jen-ˌsēz\ *noun plural* [Medieval Latin, plural of *Albigensis,* literally, inhabitant of Albi, from *Albiga* (Albi), France] (1625)
: members of a Catharistic sect of southern France flourishing primarily in the 12th and 13th centuries
— Al·bi·gen·sian \-'jen(t)-shən, -'jen(t)-sē-ən\ *adjective or noun*
— Al·bi·gen·sian·ism \-shə-ˌni-zəm, -sē-ə-ˌ\ *noun*

al·bi·nism \'al-bə-ˌni-zəm, al-'bī-\ *noun* (1836)
: the condition of an albino
— al·bi·nis·tic \ˌal-bə-'nis-tik\ *adjective*

al·bi·no \al-'bī-(ˌ)nō\ *noun, plural* **-nos** [Portuguese, from Spanish, from *albo* white, from Latin *albus*] (1777)
: an organism exhibiting deficient pigmentation; *especially* **:** a human being or nonhuman mammal that is congenitally deficient in pigment and usually has a milky or translucent skin, white or colorless hair, and eyes with pink or blue iris and deep-red pupil

al·bi·not·ic \ˌal-bə-'nä-tik\ *adjective* [*albino* + *-tic* (as in *melanotic*)] (1872)
1 : of, relating to, or affected with albinism
2 : tending toward albinism

Al·bi·on \'al-bē-ən\ *noun* [Latin] (before 12th century)
1 : Great Britain
2 : England

al·bite \'al-ˌbīt\ *noun* [Swedish *albit,* from Latin *albus*] (circa 1843)
: a triclinic usually white feldspar consisting of a sodium aluminum silicate

— al·bit·ic \al-'bit-ik\ *adjective*

al·bum \'al-bəm\ *noun* [Latin, a white tablet, from neuter of *albus*] (1612)
1 a : a book with blank pages used for making a collection (as of autographs, stamps, or photographs) **b :** a paperboard container for a phonograph record **c :** one or more recordings (as on tape or disc) produced as a single unit ⟨a 2-record *album*⟩
2 : a collection usually in book form of literary selections, musical compositions, or pictures **:** ANTHOLOGY

al·bu·men \al-'byü-mən; 'al-ˌbyü-, -byə-\ *noun* [Latin, from *albus*] (1599)
1 : the white of an egg — see EGG illustration
2 : ALBUMIN

al·bu·min \al-'byü-mən; 'al-ˌbyü-, -byə-\ *noun* [International Scientific Vocabulary *album*en + *-in*] (1869)
: any of numerous simple heat-coagulable water-soluble proteins that occur in blood plasma or serum, muscle, the whites of eggs, milk, and other animal substances and in many plant tissues and fluids

al·bu·min·ous \al-'byü-mə-nəs\ *adjective* (1791)
: relating to, containing, or having the properties of albumen or albumin

al·bu·min·uria \ˌ(ˌ)al-ˌbyü-mə-'nùr-ē-ə, -'nyùr-\ *noun* [New Latin] (circa 1842)
: the presence of albumin in the urine often symptomatic of kidney disease
— al·bu·min·uric \-'nùr-ik, -'nyùr-\ *adjective*

al·ca·ic \al-'kā-ik\ *adjective, often capitalized* [Late Latin *Alcaicus* of Alcaeus, from Greek *Alkaïkos,* from *Alkaios* Alcaeus, (flourished about 600 B.C.) Greek poet] (circa 1637)
: relating to or written in a verse or strophe marked by complicated variation of a dominant iambic pattern
— alcaic *noun, often capitalized*

al·cai·de *or* **al·cay·de** \al-'kī-dē\ *noun* [Spanish *alcaide,* from Arabic *al-qā'id* the captain] (1502)
: a commander of a castle or fortress (as among Spaniards, Portuguese, or Moors)

al·cal·de \al-'käl-dē\ *noun* [Spanish, from Arabic *al-qāḍī* the judge] (1565)
: the chief administrative and judicial officer of a Spanish town

al·ca·zar \al-'kä-zər, -'ka-\ *noun* [Spanish *alcázar,* from Arabic *al-qaṣr* the castle] (circa 1615)
: a Spanish fortress or palace

Al·ces·tis \al-'ses-təs\ *noun* [Latin, from Greek *Alkēstis*]
: the wife of Admetus who dies for her husband and is restored to him by Hercules

al·che·mist \'al-kə-mist\ *noun* (15th century)
: a person who studies or practices alchemy
— al·che·mis·tic \ˌal-kə-'mis-tik\ *also* **al·che·mis·ti·cal** \-ti-kəl\ *adjective*

al·che·mize \'al-kə-ˌmīz\ *transitive verb* **-mized; -miz·ing** (1597)
: to change by alchemy **:** TRANSMUTE

al·che·my \'al-kə-mē\ *noun* [Middle English *alkamie, alquemie,* from Middle French or Medieval Latin; Middle French *alquemie,* from Medieval Latin *alchymia,* from Arabic *al-kīmiyā',* from *al* the + *kīmiyā'* alchemy, from Late Greek *chēmeia*] (14th century)
1 : a medieval chemical science and speculative philosophy aiming to achieve the transmutation of the base metals into gold, the discovery of a universal cure for disease, and the discovery of a means of indefinitely prolonging life
2 : a power or process of transforming something common into something special

3 : an inexplicable or mysterious transmuting
— **al·chem·i·cal** \-mi-kəl\ *also* **al·chem·ic** \al-'ke-mik\ *adjective*
— **al·chem·i·cal·ly** \-mi-k(ə-)lē\ *adverb*

Alc·me·ne \alk-'mē-nē\ *noun* [Greek *Alkmēnē*]
: the mother of Hercules by Zeus in the form of her husband Amphitryon

al·co·hol \'al-kə-ˌhȯl\ *noun* [New Latin, from Medieval Latin, powdered antimony, from Old Spanish, from Arabic *al-kuhul* the powdered antimony, from *koḥl* kohl] (1672)
1 a : ethanol especially when considered as the intoxicating agent in fermented and distilled liquors **b** : drink (as whiskey or beer) containing ethanol **c** : a mixture of ethanol and water that is usually 95 percent ethanol
2 : any of various compounds that are analogous to ethanol in constitution and that are hydroxyl derivatives of hydrocarbons

¹**al·co·hol·ic** \ˌal-kə-'hȯ-lik, -'hä-\ *adjective* (1790)
1 a : of, relating to, or caused by alcohol **b** : containing alcohol
2 : affected with alcoholism
— **al·co·hol·i·cal·ly** \-li-k(ə-)lē\ *adverb*

²**alcoholic** *noun* (circa 1890)
: a person affected with alcoholism

al·co·hol·ism \'al-kə-ˌhȯ-ˌli-zəm, -kə-hə-\ *noun* (1860)
1 : continued excessive or compulsive use of alcoholic drinks
2 : poisoning by alcohol; *especially* : a complex chronic psychological and nutritional disorder associated with excessive and usually compulsive drinking

Al·co·ran \ˌal-kə-'ran\ *noun* [Middle English, from Middle French or Medieval Latin; Middle French & Medieval Latin, from Arabic *al-qurʾān*, literally, the reading] (14th century)
archaic : KORAN

al·cove \'al-ˌkōv\ *noun* [French *alcôve*, from Spanish *alcoba*, from Arabic *al-qubbah* the arch] (1676)
1 a : a small recessed section of a room : NOOK **b** : an arched opening (as in a wall) : NICHE
2 : SUMMERHOUSE 2
— **al·coved** \-ˌkōvd\ *adjective*

al·cy·o·nar·i·an \ˌal-sē-ə-'nar-ē-ən\ *noun* [ultimately from Greek *alkyoneion*, a zoophyte, from neuter of *alkyoneios* of a kingfisher, from *alkyon* kingfisher; from its resemblance to a kingfisher's nest] (1878)
: any of a subclass (Alcyonaria) of colonial anthozoans (as the sea pen) having polyps with eight branched tentacles and eight septa

Al·cy·o·ne \al-'sī-ə-(ˌ)nē\ *noun* [Latin, from Greek *Alkyonē*]
: the brightest star in the Pleiades

Al·deb·a·ran \al-'de-bə-rən\ *noun* [Arabic *al-dabarān*, literally, the follower]
: a red star of the first magnitude that is seen in the eye of Taurus and is the brightest star in the Hyades

al·de·hyde \'al-də-ˌhīd\ *noun* [German *Aldehyd*, from New Latin *al. dehyd.*, abbreviation of *alcohol dehydrogenatum* dehydrogenated alcohol] (circa 1846)
: ACETALDEHYDE; *broadly* : any of various highly reactive compounds typified by acetaldehyde and characterized by the group CHO
— **al·de·hy·dic** \ˌal-də-'hī-dik\ *adjective*

al den·te \äl-'den-(ˌ)tā, al-\ *adjective* [Italian; literally, to the tooth] (1935)
: cooked just enough to retain a somewhat firm texture

al·der \'ȯl-dər\ *noun* [Middle English, from Old English *alor*; akin to Old High German *elira* alder, Latin *alnus*] (before 12th century)
: any of a genus (*Alnus*) of toothed-leaved trees or shrubs of the birch family that have catkins which become woody, that grow in moist ground, and that have wood used in turnery

al·der·man \'ȯl-dər-mən\ *noun* [Middle English, from Old English *ealdorman*, from *ealdor* parent (from *eald* old) + *man* — more at OLD] (before 12th century)
1 : a person governing a kingdom, district, or shire as viceroy for an Anglo-Saxon king
2 a : a magistrate formerly ranking next below the mayor in an English or Irish city or borough **b** : a high-ranking member of a borough or county council in Ireland or formerly in England chosen by elected members
3 : a member of a city legislative body
— **al·der·man·ic** \ˌȯl-dər-'ma-nik\ *adjective*

al·der·wom·an \'ȯl-dər-ˌwu̇-mən\ *noun* [*alder-* (as in *alderman*) + *woman*] (1768)
: a female member of a city legislative body

al·dol \'al-ˌdȯl, -ˌdōl\ *noun* [International Scientific Vocabulary *ald*ehyde + ¹-*ol*] (1874)
: a colorless beta-hydroxy aldehyde $C_4H_8O_2$ used especially in organic synthesis; *broadly* : any of various similar aldehydes
— **al·dol·iza·tion** \ˌal-ˌdȯ-lə-'zā-shən, -ˌdō-\ *noun*

al·dol·ase \'al-də-ˌlās, -ˌlāz\ *noun* [*aldol* + *-ase*] (1940)
: a crystalline enzyme that occurs widely in living systems and catalyzes reversibly the cleavage of a phosphorylated fructose into triose sugars

al·dose \'al-ˌdōs, -ˌdōz\ *noun* [International Scientific Vocabulary *ald*ehyde + *-ose*] (1894)
: a sugar containing one aldehyde group per molecule

al·do·ste·rone \al-'däs-tə-ˌrōn; ˌal-dō-'ster-ˌōn, -'stir-; 'al-dō-stə-ˌrōn\ *noun* [*ald*ehyde + *-o-* + *-sterone*] (1954)
: a steroid hormone $C_{21}H_{28}O_5$ of the adrenal cortex that functions in the regulation of the salt and water balance of the body

al·do·ste·ron·ism \al-'däs-tə-rə-ˌni-zəm; ˌal-dō-'ster-(ˌ)ō-, -'stir-; ˌal-dō-stə-'rō-\ *noun* (1955)
: a condition that is characterized by excessive secretion of aldosterone and typically by loss of body potassium, muscular weakness, and elevated blood pressure

al·drin \'ȯl-drən, 'al-\ *noun* [Kurt *Alder* (died 1958) German chemist + English ¹-*in*] (1949)
: an exceedingly poisonous cyclodiene insecticide $C_{12}H_8Cl_6$

ale \'ā(ə)l\ *noun* [Middle English, from Old English *ealu;* akin to Old Norse *ǫl* ale, Lithuanian *alus*] (before 12th century)
1 : an alcoholic beverage brewed especially by rapid fermentation from an infusion of malt with the addition of hops
2 : an English country festival at which ale is the principal beverage

ale·a·tor·ic \ˌā-lē-ə-'tȯr-ik, -'tär-\ *adjective* [Latin *aleatorius*] (1961)
: characterized by chance or indeterminate elements ⟨*aleatoric* music⟩

ale·a·to·ry \'ā-lē-ə-ˌtȯr-ē, -ˌtȯr-\ *adjective* [Latin *aleatorius* of a gambler, from *aleator* gambler, from *alea* a dice game] (1693)
1 : depending on an uncertain event or contingency as to both profit and loss ⟨an *aleatory* contract⟩
2 : relating to luck and especially to bad luck
3 : ALEATORIC

alee \ə-'lē\ *adverb* (14th century)
: on or toward the lee — compare AWEATHER

ale·house \'ā(ə)l-ˌhau̇s\ *noun* (before 12th century)
: a place where ale is sold to be drunk on the premises

Al·e·man·nic \ˌa-lə-'ma-nik\ *noun* [Late Latin *alemanni*, of Germanic origin; akin to Gothic *alamans* totality of people] (circa 1797)
: the group of dialects of German spoken in Alsace, Switzerland, and southwestern Germany

alem·bic \ə-'lem-bik\ *noun* [Middle English, from Middle French & Medieval Latin; Middle French *alambic* & Medieval Latin *alem-*

bicum, from Arabic *al-anbīq*, from *al* the + *anbīq* still, from Late Greek *ambik-, ambix* alembic, from Greek, cap of a still] (14th century)
1 : an apparatus used in distillation
2 : something that refines or transmutes as if by distillation ⟨philosophy . . . filtered through the *alembic* of Plato's mind —B. T. Shropshire⟩

alembic 1

alen·çon \ə-'len-ˌsän, -'len(t)-sən\ *noun, often capitalized* [*Alençon*, France] (1865)
: a delicate needlepoint lace

aleph \'ä-ˌlef, -ləf\ *noun* [Hebrew *āleph*, probably from *eleph* ox] (14th century)
: the 1st letter of the Hebrew alphabet — see ALPHABET table

aleph–null \-'nəl\ *noun* (circa 1909)
: the number of elements in the set of all integers which is the smallest transfinite cardinal number

¹**alert** \ə-'lərt\ *adjective* [Italian *all'erta*, literally, on the ascent] (1618)
1 a : watchful and prompt to meet danger or emergency **b** : quick to perceive and act
2 : ACTIVE, BRISK
synonym see WATCHFUL, INTELLIGENT
— **alert·ly** *adverb*
— **alert·ness** *noun*

²**alert** *noun* (1796)
1 : the state of readiness of those warned by an alert
2 : an alarm or other signal of danger
3 : the period during which an alert is in effect
— **on the alert** : on the lookout especially for danger or opportunity

³**alert** *transitive verb* (circa 1868)
1 : to call to a state of readiness : WARN
2 : to make aware of ⟨*alerted* the public to the dangers of pesticides⟩

-ales *noun plural suffix* [New Latin, from Latin, plural of *-alis* -al]
: plants consisting of or related to — in the names of orders of plants ⟨Conifer*ales*⟩

al·eu·rone \'al-yə-ˌrōn\ *noun* [German *Aleuron*, from Greek, flour; akin to Armenian *alam* I grind] (1869)
: protein matter in the form of minute granules or grains occurring in seeds in endosperm or in a special peripheral layer

Aleut \ˌa-lē-'üt, 'a-lē-ˌ; ə-'lüt\ *noun* [Russian] (1780)
1 : a member of a people of the Aleutian and Shumagin islands and the western part of Alaska Peninsula
2 : the language of the Aleuts

A level *noun* (1951)
1 : the second of three standardized British examinations in a secondary school subject used as a qualification for university entrance; *also* : successful completion of an A-level examination in a particular subject — called also *Advanced level;* compare O LEVEL, S LEVEL
2 a : the level of education required to pass an A-level examination **b** : a course leading to an A-level examination

al·e·vin \'a-lə-vən\ *noun* [French, from Old French, from *alever* to lift up, rear (offspring), from Latin *allevare*, from *ad-* + *levare* to raise — more at LEVER] (1868)
: a young fish; *especially* : a newly hatched salmon when still attached to the yolk sac

¹**ale·wife** \'ā(ə)l-ˌwīf\ *noun* (15th century)
: a woman who keeps an alehouse

²**alewife** *noun* [perhaps alteration of obsolete *allowes*, a kind of shad, from French *alose* shad, from Old French, from Late Latin *alausa*] (1633)
: a clupeid food fish (*Alosa pseudoharengus*) very abundant along the Atlantic coast; *also* : any of several related fishes (as the menhaden)

al·ex·an·der \,a-lig-'zan-dər, ,e-\ *noun, often capitalized* (1928)
: an iced cocktail made from crème de cacao, sweet cream, and gin or brandy

Al·ex·an·dri·an \,a-lig-'zan-drē-ən, ,e-\ *adjective* (circa 1860)
1 : of or relating to Alexander the Great
2 : HELLENISTIC

al·ex·an·drine \-'zan-,drēn, -drən, -,drīn\ *noun, often capitalized* [Middle French *alexandrin*, adjective, from *Alexandre* Alexander the Great; from its use in a poem on Alexander] (1667)
: a line of verse of 12 syllables consisting regularly of 6 iambs with a caesura after the 3d iamb
— alexandrine *adjective*

al·ex·an·drite \-'zan-,drīt\ *noun* [German *Alexandrit*, from *Alexander I* Russian emperor] (circa 1880)
: a grass-green chrysoberyl that shows a red color by transmitted or artificial light

alex·ia \ə-'lek-sē-ə\ *noun* [New Latin, from *a-* + Greek *lexis* speech, from *legein* to speak — more at LEGEND] (1878)
: aphasia marked by loss of ability to read

Al·fa \'al-fə\ (1952)
— a communications code word for the letter *a*

al·fal·fa \al-'fal-fə\ *noun* [Spanish, modification of Arabic dialect *al-faṣfaṣah* the alfalfa] (1845)
: a deep-rooted European leguminous plant (*Medicago sativa*) widely grown for hay and forage

alfalfa weevil *noun* (1912)
: a small dark brown European weevil (*Hypera postica*) that is now a widespread pest of alfalfa in North America

al·fil·a·ria \,(,)al-,fi-lə-'rē-ə\ *noun* [American Spanish *alfilerillo*, from Spanish, diminutive of *alfiler* pin, modification of Arabic *al-khilāl* the thorn] (1868)
: a European weed (*Erodium cicutarium*) of the geranium family grown for forage in the western U.S.

al·for·ja \al-'fȯr-(,)hä\ *noun* [Spanish, from Arabic *al-khurj*] (1611)
West **:** SADDLEBAG

al·fres·co \al-'fres-(,)kō\ *adjective or adverb* [Italian] (1753)
: taking place or located in the open air **:** OUTDOOR, OUTDOORS ⟨an *alfresco* lunch⟩ ⟨an *alfresco* restaurant⟩

word history *see* FRESCO

al·ga \'al-gə\ *noun, plural* **al·gae** \'al-(,)jē\ *also* **algas** [Latin, seaweed] (1551)
: a plant or plantlike organism of any of several phyla, divisions, or classes of chiefly aquatic usually chlorophyll-containing nonvascular organisms of polyphyletic origin that usually include the green, yellow-green, brown, and red algae in the eukaryotes and the blue-green algae in the prokaryotes
— al·gal \-gəl\ *adjective*

al·ga·ro·ba *also* **al·gar·ro·ba** \,al-gə-'rō-bə\ *noun* [Spanish *algarroba*, from Arabic *al-kharrūbah* the carob] (1577)
1 : CAROB 1
2 [Mexican Spanish, from Spanish] **:** MESQUITE; *also* **:** its pods

al·ge·bra \'al-jə-brə\ *noun* [Medieval Latin, from Arabic *al-jabr*, literally, the reduction] (1551)
1 : a generalization of arithmetic in which letters representing numbers are combined according to the rules of arithmetic
2 : any of various systems or branches of mathematics or logic concerned with the properties and relationships of abstract entities (as complex numbers, matrices, sets, vectors, groups, rings, or fields) manipulated in symbolic form under operations often analogous to those of arithmetic — compare BOOLEAN ALGEBRA
— al·ge·bra·ist \-,brä-ist\ *noun*

al·ge·bra·ic \,al-jə-'brā-ik\ *adjective* (1662)
1 : relating to, involving, or according to the laws of algebra
2 : involving only a finite number of repetitions of addition, subtraction, multiplication, division, extraction of roots, and raising to powers ⟨*algebraic* equation⟩ — compare TRANSCENDENTAL
— al·ge·bra·i·cal·ly \-'brā-ə-k(ə-)lē\ *adverb*

algebraic number *noun* (1904)
: a root of an algebraic equation with rational coefficients

-algia *noun combining form* [Greek, from *algos* pain]
: pain ⟨neur*algia*⟩

al·gi·cide *or* **al·gae·cide** \'al-jə-,sīd\ *noun* (1904)
: an agent used to kill algae
— al·gi·cid·al \,al-jə-'sī-dᵊl\ *adjective*

al·gid \'al-jəd\ *adjective* [Latin *algidus*, from *algēre* to feel cold] (circa 1623)
: COLD

al·gin \'al-jən\ *noun* (1883)
: any of various colloidal substances (as an alginate or alginic acid) derived from marine brown algae and used especially as emulsifiers or thickeners

al·gi·nate \'al-jə-,nāt\ *noun* (circa 1909)
: a salt or ester of alginic acid

al·gin·ic acid \(,)al-'ji-nik-\ *noun* [International Scientific Vocabulary *algin* + ¹-*ic*] (1885)
: an insoluble colloidal acid $(C_6H_8O_6)_n$ that in the form of its salts is a constituent of the cell walls of brown algae

Al·gol \'al-,gäl, -,gȯl\ *noun* [Arabic *al-ghūl*, literally, the ghoul]
: a binary star in the constellation Perseus whose larger member orbits and eclipses the smaller brighter star causing periodic variation in brightness

AL·GOL *or* **Al·gol** \'al-,gäl, -,gȯl\ *noun* [*algo*rithmic *l*anguage] (1959)
: an algebraic computer programming language used especially in mathematical and scientific applications

al·go·lag·nia \,al-gō-'lag-nē-ə\ *noun* [New Latin, from Greek *algos* pain + Greek *lagneia* lust, from *lagnos* lustful — more at SLACK] (circa 1900)
: a perversion (as sadism or masochism) characterized by pleasure and especially sexual gratification in inflicting or suffering pain
— al·go·lag·ni·ac \-'lag-nē-,ak\ *noun*

al·gol·o·gy \al-'gä-lə-jē\ *noun* (1849)
: the study or science of algae — called also *phycology*
— al·go·log·i·cal \,al-gə-'lä-ji-kəl\ *adjective*
— al·gol·o·gist \al-'gä-lə-jist\ *noun*

Al·gon·qui·an \al-'gän-kwē-ən, -'gäŋ-\ *or* **Al·gon·quin** \-kwən\ *or* **Al·gon·ki·an** \-'gäŋ-kē-ən\ *also* **Al·gon·kin** \-'gäŋ-kən\ *noun* [Canadian French *Algonquin*] (1625)
1 *usually* Algonquin **a :** an American Indian people of the Ottawa river valley **b :** the dialect of Ojibwa spoken by these people
2 *usually* Algonquian **a :** a family of American Indian languages spoken by peoples from Labrador to Carolina and westward into the Great Plains **b :** a member of the peoples speaking Algonquian languages

al·go·rithm \'al-gə-,ri-thəm\ *noun* [alteration of Middle English *algorisme*, from Old French & Medieval Latin; Old French, from Medieval Latin *algorismus*, from Arabic *al-khuwārizmi*, from *al-Khuwārizmi* (flourished A.D. 825) Arab mathematician] (circa 1894)
: a procedure for solving a mathematical problem (as of finding the greatest common divisor) in a finite number of steps that frequently involves repetition of an operation; *broadly* **:** a step-by-step procedure for solving a problem or accomplishing some end especially by a computer

— al·go·rith·mic \,al-gə-'rith-mik\ *adjective*
— al·go·rith·mi·cal·ly \-mi-k(ə-)lē\ *adverb*

Al·ham·bra \al-'ham-brə\ *noun* [Spanish, from Arabic *al-ḥamrā* the red house] (1612)
: the palace of the Moorish kings at Granada, Spain

¹alias \'ā-lē-əs, 'āl-yəs\ *adverb* [Latin, otherwise, from *alius* other — more at ELSE] (15th century)
: otherwise called **:** otherwise known as

²alias *noun* (1605)
: an assumed or additional name

Ali Ba·ba \,a-lē-'bä-bə, ,ä-lē-\ *noun*
: a woodcutter in the *Arabian Nights' Entertainments* who enters the cave of the Forty Thieves by using the password *Sesame*

¹al·i·bi \'a-lə-,bī\ *noun* [Latin, elsewhere, from *alius*] (1743)
1 : the plea of having been at the time of the commission of an act elsewhere than at the place of commission; *also* **:** the fact or state of having been elsewhere at the time
2 : an excuse usually intended to avert blame or punishment (as for failure or negligence) ◆
synonym *see* APOLOGY

²alibi *verb* **-bied; -bi·ing** (1909)
transitive verb
: to exonerate by an alibi **:** furnish an excuse for
intransitive verb
: to offer an excuse

Al·ice–in–Won·der·land \'a-lə-sən-'wən-dər-,land\ *adjective* [from *Alice's Adventures in Wonderland* (1865) by Lewis Carroll] (1925)
: suitable to a world of fantasy or illusion **:** UNREAL

ali·cy·clic \,a-lə-'sī-klik, -'si-klik\ *adjective* [International Scientific Vocabulary *aliphatic* + *cyclic*] (1891)
: of, relating to, or being an organic compound that contains a ring but is not aromatic — compare ALIPHATIC

al·i·dade \'a-lə-,dād\ *noun* [Middle English *alidatha*, from Medieval Latin *alhidada*, from Arabic *al-'iḍādah* the revolving radius of a circle] (15th century)
: a rule equipped with simple or telescopic sights and used for determination of direction: as **a :** a part of an astrolabe **b :** a part of a surveying instrument consisting of the telescope and its attachments

¹alien \'ā-lē-ən, 'āl-yən\ *adjective* [Middle English, from Middle French, from Latin *alienus*, from *alius*] (14th century)

\ə\ **abut** \ᵊ\ **kitten** \ər\ **further** \a\ **ash** \ā\ **ace**
\ä\ **mop, mar** \au̇\ **out** \ch\ **chin** \e\ **bet** \ē\ **easy**
\g\ **go** \i\ **hit** \ī\ **ice** \j\ **job** \ŋ\ **sing** \ō\ **go**
\ȯ\ **law** \ȯi\ **boy** \th\ **thin** \t̲h̲\ **the** \ü\ **loot** \u̇\ **foot**
\y\ **yet** \zh\ **vision** *see also* **Guide to Pronunciation**

1 a : belonging or relating to another person, place, or thing **:** STRANGE **b :** relating, belonging, or owing allegiance to another country or government **:** FOREIGN
2 : differing in nature or character typically to the point of incompatibility
synonym see EXTRINSIC
— **alien·ly** adverb
— **alien·ness** \-lē-ən-nəs, -yən-nəs\ noun
²**alien** noun (14th century)
1 : a person of another family, race, or nation
2 : a foreign-born resident who has not been naturalized and is still a subject or citizen of a foreign country; broadly **:** a foreign-born citizen
3 : EXTRATERRESTRIAL
³**alien** transitive verb (14th century)
1 : ALIENATE, ESTRANGE
2 : to make over (as property)
alien·able \'āl-yə-nə-bəl, 'ā-lē-ə-nə-\ adjective (1611)
: transferable to another's ownership
— **alien·abil·i·ty** \āl-yə-nə-'bi-lə-tē, ,ā-lē-ə-nə-\ noun
alien·age \'āl-yə-nij, 'ā-lē-ə-nij\ noun (1809)
: the status of an alien
alien·ate \'ā-lē-ə-,nāt, 'āl-yə-\ transitive verb **-at·ed; -at·ing** (circa 1509)
1 : to make unfriendly, hostile, or indifferent where attachment formerly existed
2 : to convey or transfer (as property or a right) usually by a specific act rather than the due course of law
3 : to cause to be withdrawn or diverted
synonym see ESTRANGE
— **alien·ator** \-,nā-tər\ noun
alien·ation \,ā-lē-ə-'nā-shən, ,āl-yə-\ noun (14th century)
1 : a withdrawing or separation of a person or a person's affections from an object or position of former attachment **:** ESTRANGEMENT ⟨alienation . . . from the values of one's society and family —S. L. Halleck⟩
2 : a conveyance of property to another
alien·ee \-'nē\ noun (1531)
: one to whom property is transferred
alien·ism \'ā-lē-ə-,ni-zəm, 'āl-yə-\ noun (1808)
: ALIENAGE
alien·ist \-nist\ noun [French aliéniste, from aliéné insane, from Latin alienatus, past participle of alienare to estrange, from alienus] (1864)
: PSYCHIATRIST
alien·or \,ā-lē-ə-'nȯr, ,āl-yə-\ noun (circa 1552)
: one who transfers property to another
¹**alight** \ə-'līt\ intransitive verb **alight·ed** also **alit** \ə-'lit\; **alight·ing** [Middle English, from Old English ālīhtan, from ā- (perfective prefix) + līhtan to alight — more at ABIDE, LIGHT] (before 12th century)
1 : to come down from something (as a vehicle): as **a :** DISMOUNT **b :** DEPLANE
2 : to descend from or as if from the air and come to rest **:** LAND, SETTLE
3 archaic **:** to come by chance
— **alight·ment** noun
²**alight** adjective (15th century)
1 chiefly British **:** being on fire
2 : lighted up
align also **aline** \ə-'līn\ verb [French aligner, from Old French, from a- (from Latin ad-) + ligne line, from Latin linea] (circa 1693)
transitive verb
1 : to bring into line or alignment
2 : to array on the side of or against a party or cause
intransitive verb
1 : to get or fall into line
2 : to be in or come into precise adjustment or correct relative position
— **align·er** noun
align·ment also **aline·ment** \ə-'līn-mənt\ noun (1790)
1 : the act of aligning or state of being

aligned; especially **:** the proper positioning or state of adjustment of parts (as of a mechanical or electronic device) in relation to each other
2 a : a forming in line **b :** the line thus formed
3 : the ground plan (as of a railroad or highway) in distinction from the profile
4 : an arrangement of groups or forces in relation to one another ⟨new alignments within the political party⟩
¹**alike** \ə-'līk\ adverb (14th century)
: in the same manner, form, or degree **:** EQUALLY ⟨was denounced by teachers and students alike⟩
²**alike** adjective [Middle English ilik, ilich (from Old English gelīc) & alik, alteration of Old English onlīc, from on + līc body — more at LIKE] (15th century)
: exhibiting close resemblance without being identical ⟨alike in their beliefs⟩
— **alike·ness** noun
¹**al·i·ment** \'a-lə-mənt\ noun [Middle English, from Latin alimentum, from alere to nourish — more at OLD] (15th century)
: FOOD, NUTRIMENT; also **:** SUSTENANCE ⟨there was nothing there of conversational aliment —Kingsley Amis⟩
²**al·i·ment** \-,ment\ transitive verb (15th century)
: to give aliment to **:** NOURISH, SUSTAIN
al·i·men·ta·ry \,a-lə-'men-t(ə-)rē\ adjective (1615)
1 : of or relating to nourishment or nutrition
2 : furnishing sustenance or maintenance
alimentary canal noun (1764)
: the tubular passage that extends from mouth to anus and functions in digestion and absorption of food and elimination of residual waste
al·i·men·ta·tion \,a-lə-mən-'tā-shən, -,men-\ noun (circa 1656)
: the act or process of affording nutriment or nourishment ⟨intravenous alimentation⟩
al·i·mo·ny \'a-lə-,mō-nē\ noun, plural **-nies** [Latin alimonia sustenance, from alere] (1656)
1 : an allowance made to one spouse by the other for support pending or after legal separation or divorce
2 : the means of living **:** MAINTENANCE
A-line \'ā-,līn\ adjective (1964)
: having a flared bottom and a close-fitting top — used of a garment ⟨an A-line skirt⟩
al·i·phat·ic \,a-lə-'fa-tik\ adjective [International Scientific Vocabulary, from Greek aleiphat-, aleiphar oil, from aleiphein to smear; perhaps akin to Greek lipos fat — more at LEAVE] (1889)
: of, relating to, or being an organic compound having an open-chain structure (as an alkane) — compare ALICYCLIC, AROMATIC 2
al·i·quot \'a-lə-,kwät, -kwət\ adjective [Medieval Latin aliquotus, from Latin aliquot some, several, from alius other + quot how many — more at ELSE, QUOTE] (1570)
1 : contained an exact number of times in something else — used of a divisor or part ⟨5 is an aliquot part of 15⟩ ⟨an aliquot portion of a solution⟩
2 : FRACTIONAL ⟨an aliquot part of invested capital⟩
— **aliquot** noun
A-list \'ā-,list\ noun (1980)
: a list or group of individuals of the highest level of society, excellence, or eminence
alit·er·a·cy \,ā-'li-tər-ə,sē, ə-'\ noun (1984)
: the quality or state of being able to read but uninterested in doing so
— **alit·er·ate** \-'li-tər-ət\ adjective or noun
alive \ə-'līv\ adjective [Middle English, from Old English on life, from on + līf life] (before 12th century)
1 : having life **:** not dead or inanimate
2 : still in existence, force, or operation **:** ACTIVE ⟨kept hope alive⟩
3 : knowing or realizing the existence of **:** SENSITIVE ⟨alive to the danger⟩
4 : marked by alertness, energy, or briskness

5 : marked by much life, animation, or activity **:** SWARMING ⟨streets alive with traffic⟩
6 — used as an intensive following the noun ⟨the proudest boy alive⟩
synonym see AWARE
— **alive·ness** noun
ali·yah or **ali·ya** \ä-'lē-(,)yä, ,ä-lē-'yä\ noun [New Hebrew 'alīyāh, from Hebrew, ascent] (circa 1934)
: the immigration of Jews to Israel
aliz·a·rin \ə-'li-zə-rən\ noun [probably from French alizarine] (circa 1835)
1 : an orange or red crystalline compound $C_{14}H_8O_4$ formerly prepared from madder and now made synthetically and used especially to dye Turkey reds and in making red pigments
2 : any of various acid, mordant, and solvent dyes derived like alizarin proper from anthraquinone
al·ka·hest \'al-kə-,hest\ noun [New Latin alchahest] (1641)
: the universal solvent believed by alchemists to exist
— **al·ka·hes·tic** \,al-kə-'hes-tik\ adjective
al·ka·li \'al-kə-,lī\ noun, plural **-lies** or **-lis** [Middle English, from Medieval Latin, from Arabic al-qili the ashes of the plant saltwort] (14th century)
1 : a soluble salt obtained from the ashes of plants and consisting largely of potassium or sodium carbonate; broadly **:** a substance (as a hydroxide or carbonate of an alkali metal) having marked basic properties — compare BASE 7a
2 : ALKALI METAL
3 : a soluble salt or a mixture of soluble salts present in some soils of arid regions in quantity detrimental to agriculture
alkali metal noun (circa 1885)
: any of the univalent mostly basic metals of group I of the periodic table comprising lithium, sodium, potassium, rubidium, cesium, and francium — see PERIODIC TABLE table
al·ka·lim·e·ter \,al-kə-'li-mə-tər\ noun [French alcalimètre, from alcali alkali + -mètre -meter] (circa 1828)
: an apparatus for measuring the strength or the amount of alkali in a mixture or solution
— **al·ka·lim·e·try** \-'lim-ə-trē\ noun
al·ka·line \'al-kə-lən, -,līn\ adjective (1677)
: of, relating to, containing, or having the properties of an alkali or alkali metal **:** BASIC; especially, of a solution **:** having a pH of more than 7
— **al·ka·lin·i·ty** \,al-kə-'li-nə-tē\ noun
alkaline battery noun (1941)
: a long-lived dry cell that has an alkaline electrolyte which decreases corrosion of the cell — called also alkaline cell
alkaline earth metal noun (circa 1903)
: any of the bivalent strongly basic metals of group II of the periodic table comprising beryllium, magnesium, calcium, strontium, barium, and radium — called also alkaline earth; see PERIODIC TABLE table
alkaline phosphatase noun (1949)
: any of the phosphatases that are optimally active in alkaline medium and occur in especially high concentrations in bone, the liver, the kidneys, and the placenta
al·ka·lin·ize \'al-kə-lə-,nīz\ transitive verb **-ized; -iz·ing** (1800)
: to make alkaline
— **al·ka·lin·iza·tion** \,al-kə-,li-nə-'zā-shən, -lə-nə-\ noun
al·ka·loid \'al-kə-,lȯid\ noun (circa 1831)
: any of numerous usually colorless, complex, and bitter organic bases (as morphine or codeine) containing nitrogen and usually oxygen that occur especially in seed plants
— **al·ka·loi·dal** \,al-kə-'lȯi-dᵊl\ adjective
al·ka·lo·sis \,al-kə-'lō-səs\ noun (1911)
: an abnormal condition of increased alkalinity of the blood and tissues
— **al·ka·lot·ic** \-'lä-tik\ adjective
al·kane \'al-,kān\ noun [alkyl + -ane] (1899)

: any of numerous saturated hydrocarbons; *specifically* : any of a series of open-chain hydrocarbons C_nH_{2n+2} (as methane and butane) — called also *paraffin*

al·ka·net \'al-kə-ˌnet\ *noun* [Middle English, from Old Spanish *alcaneta,* diminutive of *alcana* henna shrub, from Medieval Latin *alchanna,* from Arabic *al-ḥinnā'* the henna] (14th century)
1 a : a European plant (*Alkanna tinctoria*) of the borage family; *also* : its root **b** : a red dyestuff prepared from the root
2 : a plant (*Anchusa officinalis*) of the borage family with delicate usually blue flowers

al·kene \'al-ˌkēn\ *noun* [International Scientific Vocabulary *alkyl* + *-ene*] (1899)
: any of numerous unsaturated hydrocarbons having one double bond; *specifically* : any of a series of open-chain hydrocarbons C_nH_{2n} (as ethylene)

alk·ox·ide \al-'käk-ˌsīd, -səd\ *noun* [*alkyl* + *oxide*] (circa 1889)
: a basic salt derived from an alcohol by the replacement of the hydroxyl hydrogen with a metal

alk·oxy \'al-ˌkäk-sē\ *adjective* [International Scientific Vocabulary *alkyl* + *oxygen*] (circa 1925)
: of, relating to, or containing a univalent radical composed of an alkyl group united with oxygen — often used in combination

al·kyd \'al-kəd\ *noun* [blend of *alkyl* and *acid*] (1929)
1 : any of numerous synthetic resins that are used especially for protective coatings and in paint
2 : a paint in which the vehicle is an alkyd resin

¹al·kyl \'al-kəl\ *adjective* (1882)
: having a monovalent organic group and especially one C_nH_{2n+1} (as methyl) derived from an alkane (as methane)

²alkyl *noun* [probably from German, from *Alkohol* alcohol] (1952)
: a compound of one or more alkyl groups with a metal ⟨mercury *alkyls*⟩

alkylating agent *noun* (1900)
: a substance that causes replacement of hydrogen by an alkyl group especially in a biologically important molecule; *specifically* : one with mutagenic activity that inhibits cell division and growth and is used to treat some cancers

al·kyl·ation \ˌal-kə-'lā-shən\ *noun* (1900)
: the act or process of introducing one or more alkyl groups into a compound (as to increase octane number in a motor fuel)
— **al·kyl·ate** \'al-kə-ˌlāt\ *transitive verb*

al·kyne \'al-ˌkīn\ *noun* [*alkyl* + *-yne,* alteration of *-ine*] (circa 1909)
: any of a series of open-chain hydrocarbons C_nH_{2n-2} (as acetylene) having one triple bond

¹all \'ȯl\ *adjective* [Middle English *all, al,* from Old English *eall;* akin to Old High German *all* all] (before 12th century)
1 a : the whole amount or quantity of ⟨needed *all* the courage they had⟩ ⟨sat up *all* night⟩ **b** : as much as possible ⟨spoke in *all* seriousness⟩
2 : every member or individual component of ⟨*all* men will go⟩ ⟨*all* five children were present⟩
3 : the whole number or sum of ⟨*all* the angles of a triangle are equal to two right angles⟩
4 : EVERY ⟨*all* manner of hardship⟩
5 : any whatever ⟨beyond *all* doubt⟩
6 : nothing but : ONLY : **a** : completely taken up with, given to, or absorbed by ⟨became *all* attention⟩ **b** : having or seeming to have (some physical feature) in conspicuous excess or prominence ⟨*all* legs⟩ **c** : paying full attention with ⟨*all* ears⟩
7 *dialect* : used up : entirely consumed — used especially of food and drink

8 : being more than one person or thing ⟨who *all* is coming⟩
synonym see WHOLE
— **all the** : as much of . . . as : as much of a . . . as ⟨*all the* home I ever had⟩

²all *adverb* (before 12th century)
1 a : WHOLLY, QUITE ⟨sat *all* alone⟩ — often used as an intensive ⟨*all* out of proportion⟩ ⟨*all* over the yard⟩ **b** : selected as the best (as at a sport) within an area or organization — used in combination ⟨*all*-league halfback⟩
2 *obsolete* : ONLY, EXCLUSIVELY
3 *archaic* : JUST
4 : so much ⟨*all* the better for it⟩
5 : for each side : APIECE ⟨the score is two *all*⟩

³all *pronoun* (before 12th century)
1 : the whole number, quantity, or amount : TOTALITY ⟨*all* that I have⟩ ⟨*all* of us⟩ ⟨*all* of the books⟩
2 : EVERYBODY, EVERYTHING ⟨gave equal attention to *all*⟩ ⟨that is *all*⟩
— **all in all** : on the whole : GENERALLY ⟨*all in all,* things might have been worse⟩
— **and all** : and everything else especially of a kind suggested by a previous context ⟨cards to fill out with . . . numbers *and all* —Sally Quinn⟩

⁴all *noun* (1593)
: the whole of one's possessions, resources, or energy ⟨gave his *all* for the cause⟩

all- *or* **allo-** *combining form* [Greek, from *allos* other — more at ELSE]
1 : other : different : atypical ⟨*allo*gamous⟩ ⟨*allo*tropy⟩
2 *allo-* : isomeric form or variety of (a specified chemical compound) ⟨*allo*purinol⟩
3 *allo-* : being one of a group whose members together constitute a structural unit especially of a language ⟨*allo*phone⟩

¹al·la breve \ˌa-lə-'brev, ˌä-lə-'bre-(ˌ)vā\ *noun* [Italian, literally, according to the breve] (circa 1740)
: the sign marking a piece or passage to be played alla breve; *also* : a passage so marked

²alla breve *adverb or adjective* (circa 1823)
: in duple or quadruple time with the beat represented by the half note **alla breve**

Al·lah \'ä-lə, 'a-lə, 'ä-ˌlä, ä-'lä\ *noun* [Arabic *al-lāh*] (1584)
: GOD 1a — used in Islam

all along *adverb* (1670)
: all the time ⟨knew the truth *all along*⟩

¹all–Amer·i·can \ˌȯ-lə-'mer-ə-kən\ *adjective* (1888)
1 a *also* **all–Amer·i·ca** : selected (as by a poll of journalists) as one of the best in the U.S. in a particular category at a particular time ⟨an *all-American* quarterback⟩ **b** : having only all-American participants ⟨an *all-American* basketball team⟩
2 : composed wholly of American elements
3 : representative or typical of the U.S. or its ideals ⟨an *all-American* boy⟩ ⟨her *all-American* optimism⟩
4 : of or relating to the American nations as a group

²all–American *noun* (1920)
: one (as an athlete) that is voted all-American

al·lan·to·in \ə-'lan-tə-wən\ *noun* [probably from German, from New Latin *allantois* + German *-in*] (circa 1845)
: a crystalline oxidation product $C_4H_6N_4O_3$ of uric acid used to promote healing of local wounds and infections

al·lan·to·is \ə-'lan-tə-wəs\ *noun, plural* **al·lan·to·i·des** \ˌa-lən-'tō-ə-ˌdēz, ˌa-ˌlan-\ [New Latin, ultimately from Greek *allant-, allas* sausage] (1646)
: a vascular fetal membrane of reptiles, birds, and mammals that is formed as a pouch from the hindgut and that in placental mammals is intimately associated with the chorion in formation of the placenta

— **al·lan·to·ic** \ˌa-lən-'tō-ik, ˌa-ˌlan-\ *adjective*

al·lar·gan·do \ˌä-lär-'gän-(ˌ)dō\ *adjective or adverb* [Italian, widening, verbal of *allargare* to widen, from *al-* (from Latin *ad-*) + *largare* to widen] (circa 1893)
: becoming gradually slower and more stately — used as a direction in music

all–around \ˌȯ-lə-'raund\ *adjective* (1867)
1 : considered in or encompassing all aspects : COMPREHENSIVE ⟨the best *all-around* performance so far⟩
2 : competent in many fields ⟨an *all-around* performer⟩
3 : having general utility or merit

al·lay \ə-'lā, ə-\ *verb* [Middle English *alayen,* from Old English *ālecgan,* from *ā-* (perfective prefix) + *lecgan* to lay — more at ABIDE, LAY] (14th century)
transitive verb
1 : to subdue or reduce in intensity or severity : ALLEVIATE ⟨expect a breeze to *allay* the heat⟩
2 : to make quiet : CALM
intransitive verb
obsolete : to diminish in strength : SUBSIDE
synonym see RELIEVE

all but *adverb* (1593)
: very nearly : ALMOST ⟨would be *all but* impossible⟩

all clear *noun* (1902)
: a signal that a danger has passed

all–day \'ȯl-'dā\ *adjective* (circa 1870)
: lasting for, occupying, or appearing throughout an entire day ⟨an *all-day* trip⟩

al·lée \ä-'lā, a-\ *noun* [French, from Middle French *alee* — more at ALLEY] (1759)
: a walkway lined with trees or tall shrubs

al·le·ga·tion \ˌa-li-'gā-shən\ *noun* (15th century)
1 : the act of alleging
2 : a positive assertion; *specifically* : a statement by a party to a legal action of what the party undertakes to prove
3 : an assertion unsupported and by implication regarded as unsupportable ⟨vague *allegations* of misconduct⟩

al·lege \ə-'lej\ *transitive verb* **al·leged; al·leg·ing** [Middle English *alleggen,* from Middle French *alleguer,* from Latin *allegare* to dispatch, cite, from *ad-* + *legare* to depute — more at LEGATE] (14th century)
1 *archaic* : to adduce or bring forward as a source or authority
2 : to assert without proof or before proving ⟨the newspaper *alleges* the mayor's guilt⟩
3 : to bring forward as a reason or excuse

al·leged \ə-'lejd, -'le-jəd\ *adjective* (1509)
1 : asserted to be true or to exist ⟨an *alleged* miracle⟩
2 : questionably true or of a specified kind : SUPPOSED, SO-CALLED ⟨bought an *alleged* antique vase⟩
3 : accused but not proven or convicted ⟨an *alleged* gangster⟩
— **al·leg·ed·ly** \-'le-jəd-lē\ *adverb*

Al·le·ghe·ny spurge \'a-lə-ˌgā-nē- *also* -ˌge-nē-\ *noun* [*Allegheny* Mountains, U.S.A.] (circa 1936)
: a low herb or subshrub (*Pachysandra procumbens*) of the box family widely grown as a ground cover

al·le·giance \ə-'lē-jən(t)s\ *noun* [Middle English *allegeaunce,* modification of Middle French *ligeance,* from Old French, from *lige* liege] (14th century)
1 a : the obligation of a feudal vassal to his liege lord **b** (1) : the fidelity owed by a subject or citizen to a sovereign or government (2) : the obligation of an alien to the government under which the alien resides

2 : devotion or loyalty to a person, group, or cause
synonym see FIDELITY
— **al·le·giant** \-jənt\ *adjective*

al·le·gor·i·cal \ˌa-lə-ˈgȯr-i-kəl, -ˈgär-\ *adjective* (1528)
1 : of, relating to, or having the characteristics of allegory
2 : having hidden spiritual meaning that transcends the literal sense of a sacred text
— **al·le·gor·i·cal·ly** \-k(ə-)lē\ *adverb*
— **al·le·gor·i·cal·ness** \-kəl-nəs\ *noun*

al·le·go·rise *British variant of* ALLEGORIZE

al·le·go·rist \ˈa-lə-ˌgȯr-əst, -ˌgȯr-\ *noun* (1684)
: a creator of allegory

al·le·go·ri·za·tion \ˌa-lə-ˌgȯr-ə-ˈzā-shən, -ˌgȯr-, -gər-\ *noun* (1847)
: allegorical representation or interpretation

al·le·go·rize \ˈa-lə-ˌgȯr-ˌīz, -ˌgȯr-, -gər-\ *verb* **-rized; -riz·ing** (1581)
intransitive verb
1 : to give allegorical explanations
2 : to compose or use allegory
transitive verb
1 : to treat or explain as an allegory
2 : to make into allegory
— **al·le·go·riz·er** *noun*

al·le·go·ry \ˈa-lə-ˌgȯr-ē, -ˌgȯr-\ *noun, plural* **-ries** [Middle English *allegorie,* from Latin *allegoria,* from Greek *allēgoria,* from *allēgorein* to speak figuratively, from *allos* other + *-ēgorein* to speak publicly, from *agora* assembly — more at ELSE, AGORA] (14th century)
1 : the expression by means of symbolic fictional figures and actions of truths or generalizations about human existence; *also* **:** an instance (as in a story or painting) of such expression
2 : a symbolic representation **:** EMBLEM 2

¹**al·le·gret·to** \ˌa-lə-ˈgre-(ˌ)tō, ˌä-lə-\ *adverb or adjective* [Italian, diminutive of *allegro*] (circa 1740)
: faster than andante but not so fast as allegro — used as a direction in music

²**allegretto** *noun, plural* **-tos** (circa 1846)
: a musical composition or movement in allegretto tempo

¹**al·le·gro** \ə-ˈle-(ˌ)grō, -ˈlä-\ *noun, plural* **-gros** (1683)
: a musical composition or movement in allegro tempo

²**allegro** *adverb or adjective* [Italian, merry, from (assumed) Vulgar Latin *alecrus* lively, alteration of Latin *alacr-, alacer*] (circa 1721)
: at a brisk lively tempo — used as a direction in music

al·lele \ə-ˈlē(ə)l\ *noun* [German *Allel,* short for *Allelomorph*] (1928)
1 : any of the alternative forms of a gene that may occur at a given locus
2 : either of a pair of alternative Mendelian characters (as smooth and wrinkled seed in the pea)
— **al·le·lic** \-ˈlē-lik, -ˈle-\ *adjective*
— **al·lel·ism** \-ˈlē(ə)-ˌli-zəm, -ˈle-\ *noun*

allelo- *combining form* [Greek *allēlon* of each other, from *allos . . . allos* one . . . the other, from *allos* other — more at ELSE]
1 : alternative ⟨*allelo*morph⟩
2 : reciprocal ⟨*allelo*pathy⟩

al·le·lo·morph \ə-ˈlē-lə-ˌmȯrf, -ˈle-lə-\ *noun* (1902)
: ALLELE
— **al·le·lo·mor·phic** \ə-ˌlē-lə-ˈmȯr-fik, -ˌle-lə-\ *adjective*
— **al·le·lo·mor·phism** \ə-ˈlē-lə-ˌmȯr-ˌfi-zəm, -ˈle-lə-\ *noun*

al·le·lop·a·thy \ə-ˈlē-lə-ˌpa-thē, -ˈle-lə-; *also* ˌa-lə-ˈlä-pə-thē\ *noun* [International Scientific Vocabulary] (1948)
: the suppression of growth of one plant species by another due to the release of toxic substances

— **al·le·lo·path·ic** \ə-ˌlē-lə-ˈpa-thik, -ˌlə-lə-\ *adjective*

al·le·lu·ia \ˌa-lə-ˈlü-yə\ *interjection* [Middle English, from Late Latin, from Greek *allēlouia,* from Hebrew *halălūyāh* praise ye Jehovah] (14th century)
: HALLELUJAH

al·le·mande \ˈa-lə-ˌman(d), -mən, -, ˌmänd, *1a & 2 also* ˌa-lə-ˈ\ *noun, often capitalized* [French, from feminine of *allemand* German] (1685)
1 : a musical composition or movement (as in a baroque suite) in moderate tempo and duple or quadruple time
2 a : a 17th and 18th century court dance developed in France from a German folk dance
b : a dance step with arms interlaced

all–em·brac·ing \ˌȯl-im-ˈbrā-siŋ\ *adjective* (circa 1649)
: COMPLETE, SWEEPING

Al·len wrench \ˈa-lən-\ *noun* [Allen Manufacturing Co., Hartford, Conn.] (1943)
: an L-shaped hexagonal metal bar either end of which fits the socket of a screw or bolt

al·ler·gen \ˈa-lər-jən\ *noun* [International Scientific Vocabulary *allergy* + *-gen*] (1910)
: a substance that induces allergy
— **al·ler·gen·ic** \ˌa-lər-ˈje-nik\ *adjective*
— **al·ler·ge·nic·i·ty** \ˌa-lər-jə-ˈni-sə-tē\ *noun*

al·ler·gic \ə-ˈlər-jik\ *adjective* (1911)
1 : of, relating to, inducing, or affected by allergy
2 : having an aversion ⟨*allergic* to work⟩

al·ler·gist \ˈa-lər-jist\ *noun* (1928)
: a specialist in allergy

al·ler·gy \ˈa-lər-jē\ *noun, plural* **-gies** [German *Allergie,* from *all-* + Greek *ergon* work — more at WORK] (1910)
1 : altered bodily reactivity (as hypersensitivity) to an antigen in response to a first exposure ⟨a bee venom *allergy* so severe that a second sting may be fatal⟩
2 : exaggerated or pathological reaction (as by sneezing, respiratory embarrassment, itching, or skin rashes) to substances, situations, or physical states that are without comparable effect on the average individual
3 : medical practice concerned with allergies
4 : a feeling of antipathy or repugnance

al·le·thrin \ˈa-lə-thrən\ *noun* [*allyl* + *pyrethrin*] (1950)
: a light yellow viscous oily synthetic insecticide $C_{19}H_{26}O_3$ used especially in household aerosols

al·le·vi·ate \ə-ˈlē-vē-ˌāt\ *transitive verb* **-at·ed; -at·ing** [Late Latin *alleviatus,* past participle of *alleviare,* from Latin *ad-* + *levis* light — more at LIGHT] (15th century)
: RELIEVE, LESSEN: as **a :** to make (as suffering) more bearable ⟨her sympathy *alleviated* his distress⟩ **b :** to partially remove or correct
synonym see RELIEVE
— **al·le·vi·a·tion** \ə-ˌlē-vē-ˈā-shən\ *noun*
— **al·le·vi·a·tor** \-ˈlē-vē-ˌā-tər\ *noun*

¹**al·ley** \ˈa-lē\ *noun, plural* **alleys** [Middle English, from Middle French *alee,* from Old French, from *aler* to go] (14th century)
1 : a garden or park walk bordered by trees or bushes
2 a (1) **:** a grassed enclosure for bowling or skittles (2) **:** a hardwood lane for bowling; *also* **:** a room or building housing a group of such lanes **b :** the space on each side of a tennis doubles court between the sideline and the service sideline **c :** an area in a baseball outfield between two outfielders when they are in normal positions
3 : a narrow street; *especially* **:** a thoroughfare through the middle of a block giving access to the rear of lots or buildings
— **up one's alley** *also* **down one's alley :** suited to one's own tastes or abilities

²**alley** *noun, plural* **alleys** [by shortening and alteration from *alabaster*] (1720)

: a playing marble; *especially* **:** one of superior quality

al·ley–oop \ˌa-lē-ˈyüp\ *noun* [alteration of *allez-oop,* cry of a circus acrobat about to leap, probably from French *allez,* 2d person plural imperative of *aller* to go + English *-oop,* perhaps alteration of *up*] (1967)
: a basketball play in which a leaping player catches a pass above the basket and immediately dunks the ball; *also* **:** the usually looping pass thrown on such a play

al·ley·way \ˈa-lē-ˌwā\ *noun* (1788)
1 : a narrow passageway
2 : ALLEY 3

All Fools' Day *noun* (1712)
: APRIL FOOLS' DAY

all fours *noun plural* (1563)
1 a : all four legs of a quadruped **b :** the two legs and two arms of a person when used to support the body
2 *singular in construction* **:** any of various card games in which points are scored for the high trump, low trump, jack of trumps, and game

all get–out \ˈȯl-ˌget-ˌaut, -ˈgit-\ *noun* (1884)
: the utmost conceivable degree — used in comparisons to suggest something superlative ⟨is handsome as *all get-out* and has a deft way with the ladies —John McCarten⟩

all hail *interjection* (14th century)
— used to express greeting, welcome, or acclamation

All·hal·lows \ȯl-ˈha-(ˌ)lōz, -ˌləz\ *noun, plural* **Allhallows** [short for *All Hallows' Day*] (1503)
: ALL SAINTS' DAY

al·li·a·ceous \ˌa-lē-ˈā-shəs\ *adjective* [Latin *allium* garlic] (1792)
: resembling garlic or onion especially in smell or taste

al·li·ance \ə-ˈlī-ən(t)s\ *noun* (13th century)
1 a : the state of being allied **:** the action of allying **b :** a bond or connection between families, states, parties, or individuals ⟨a closer *alliance* between government and industry⟩
2 : an association to further the common interests of the members; *specifically* **:** a confederation of nations by treaty
3 : union by relationship in qualities **:** AFFINITY
4 : a treaty of alliance

al·lied \ə-ˈlīd, ˈa-ˌlīd\ *adjective* (14th century)
1 : having or being in close association **:** CONNECTED ⟨a strong personal pride *allied* with the utmost probity⟩ ⟨two families *allied* by marriage⟩
2 : joined in alliance by compact or treaty; *specifically, capitalized* **:** of or relating to the nations united against Germany and its allies in World War I or those united against the Axis powers in World War II
3 a : related especially by common properties or qualities ⟨heraldry and *allied* subjects⟩ **b :** related genetically

allies *plural of* ALLY

al·li·ga·tor \ˈa-lə-ˌgā-tər\ *noun* [Spanish *el lagarto* the lizard, from *el* the (from Latin *ille* that) + *lagarto* lizard, from (assumed) Vulgar Latin *lacertus,* from Latin *lacertus, lacerta* — more at LIZARD] (1579)
1 a : either of two crocodilians (genus *Alligator*) having broad heads not tapering to the snout and a special pocket in the upper jaw for reception of the enlarged lower fourth tooth **b :** CROCODILIAN

alligator 1a

2 : leather made from alligator hide

alligator clip *noun* (circa 1941)

: a spring-loaded clip that has jaws resembling an alligator's and is used for making temporary electrical connections

alligator clip

al·li·ga·tor pear *noun* [by folk etymology from Spanish *aguacate* — more at AVOCADO] (1763)
: AVOCADO

alligator snapper *noun* (1884)
: a snapping turtle (*Macrochelys temminckii*) of the rivers of the Gulf states that may reach nearly 150 pounds (68 kilograms) in weight and 5 feet (1.5 meters) in length

all-im·por·tant \ˌȯ-lim-'pȯr-tᵊnt, -tᵊnt\ *adjective* (1839)
: of very great or greatest importance 〈an *all-important* question〉

all-in \ˈȯ-'lin\ *adjective* (1890)
1 *chiefly British* **:** ALL-INCLUSIVE
2 *chiefly British* **:** being almost without restrictions 〈*all-in* wrestling〉

all in *adjective* (1903)
: TIRED, EXHAUSTED 〈after a day of wood-splitting he was *all in*〉

all-in·clu·sive \ˌȯ-lin-'klü-siv, -ziv\ *adjective* (circa 1855)
: including everything 〈a broader and more nearly *all-inclusive* view〉
— **all-in·clu·sive·ness** *noun*

al·lit·er·ate \ə-'li-tə-ˌrāt\ *verb* **-at·ed; -at·ing** [back-formation from *alliteration*] (1816)
intransitive verb
1 : to form an alliteration
2 : to write or speak alliteratively
transitive verb
: to arrange or place so as to make alliteration 〈*alliterate* syllables in a sentence〉

al·lit·er·a·tion \ə-ˌli-tə-'rā-shən\ *noun* [*ad-* + Latin *littera* letter] (circa 1656)
: the repetition of usually initial consonant sounds in two or more neighboring words or syllables (as *w*ild and *w*oolly, *thr*eatening *thr*ongs) — called also *head rhyme, initial rhyme*

al·lit·er·a·tive \ə-'li-tər-ə-tiv, -tə-ˌrā-tiv\ *adjective* (1764)
: of, relating to, or marked by alliteration
— **al·lit·er·a·tive·ly** *adverb*

al·li·um \ˈa-lē-əm\ *noun* [New Latin, genus name, from Latin, garlic] (1807)
: any of a large genus (*Allium*) of bulbous herbs of the lily family including the onion, garlic, chive, leek, and shallot

all-night \ˈȯl-'nīt\ *adjective* (1888)
1 : lasting throughout the night 〈an *all-night* poker game〉
2 : open throughout the night 〈an *all-night* diner〉

all-night·er \ˈȯl-'nī-tər\ *noun* (1967)
: something that lasts all night; *specifically* **:** an all-night study session

allo- — see ALL-

al·lo·an·ti·body \ˌa-lō-'an-ti-ˌbä-dē\ *noun* (1964)
: an antibody produced following introduction of an alloantigen into the system of an individual of a species lacking that particular antigen — called also *isoantibody*

al·lo·an·ti·gen \ˌa-lō-'an-ti-jən\ *noun* (1964)
: an antigen present only in some individuals (as of a particular blood group) of a species and capable of inducing the production of an isoantibody by individuals which lack it — called also *isoantigen*

al·lo·ca·ble \ˈa-lə-kə-bəl\ *adjective* (1916)
: capable of being allocated

al·lo·cate \ˈa-lə-ˌkāt\ *transitive verb* **-cat·ed; -cat·ing** [Medieval Latin *allocatus,* past participle of *allocare,* from Latin *ad-* + *locare* to place, from *locus* place — more at STALL] (circa 1641)
1 : to apportion for a specific purpose or to particular persons or things **:** DISTRIBUTE 〈*allo-*

cate tasks among human and automated components〉
2 : to set apart or earmark **:** DESIGNATE 〈*allocate* a section of the building for special research purposes〉
— **al·lo·cat·able** \-ˌkā-tə-bəl\ *adjective*
— **al·lo·ca·tion** \ˌa-lə-'kā-shən\ *noun*
— **al·lo·ca·tor** \ˈa-lə-ˌkā-tər\ *noun*

al·lo·cu·tion \ˌa-lə-'kyü-shən\ *noun* [Latin *allocution-, allocutio,* from *alloqui* to speak to, from *ad-* + *loqui* to speak] (1615)
: a formal speech; *especially* **:** an authoritative or hortatory address

all of *adverb* (1829)
: FULLY 〈she's *all of* 20 years old〉

al·log·a·mous \ə-'lä-gə-məs\ *adjective* (circa 1890)
: reproducing by cross-fertilization
— **al·log·a·my** \-mē\ *noun*

al·lo·ge·ne·ic \ˌa-lə-jə-'nē-ik\ *also* **al·lo·gen·ic** \-'je-nik\ *adjective* [*all-* + *-geneic* (as in *syngeneic*)] (1961)
: involving, derived from, or being individuals of the same species that are sufficiently unlike genetically to interact antigenically

al·lo·graft \ˈa-lə-ˌgraft\ *noun* (1961)
: a homograft between allogeneic individuals
— **allograft** *transitive verb*

al·lo·graph \ˈa-lə-ˌgraf\ *noun* (1951)
1 : a letter of an alphabet in a particular shape (as A or a)
2 : a letter or combination of letters that is one of several ways of representing one phoneme (as *pp* in *hopping* representing the phoneme \p\)
— **al·lo·graph·ic** \ˌa-lə-'gra-fik\ *adjective*

al·lom·e·try \ə-'lä-mə-trē\ *noun* (1936)
: relative growth of a part in relation to an entire organism or to a standard; *also* **:** the measure and study of such growth
— **al·lo·me·tric** \ˌa-lə-'me-trik\ *adjective*

allomorph *noun* [*allo-* + *morph*eme] (1945)
: one of a set of forms that a morpheme may take in different contexts 〈the *-s* of *cats,* the *-en* of *oxen,* and the zero suffix of *sheep* are *allomorphs* of the English plural morpheme〉
— **al·lo·mor·phic** \ˌa-lə-'mȯr-fik\ *adjective*
— **al·lo·mor·phism** \ˈa-lə-ˌmȯr-ˌfi-zəm\ *noun*

al·longe \a-'lōⁿzh\ *noun* [French, literally, lengthening] (circa 1859)
: RIDER 2a

al·lo·pat·ric \ˌa-lə-'pa-trik\ *adjective* [*all-* + Greek *patra* fatherland, from *patēr* father — more at FATHER] (1942)
: occurring in different geographical areas or in isolation 〈*allopatric* speciation〉 — compare SYMPATRIC
— **al·lo·pat·ri·cal·ly** \-tri-k(ə-)lē\ *adverb*
— **al·lop·a·try** \ə-'lä-pə-trē\ *noun*

al·lo·phane \ˈa-lə-ˌfān\ *noun* [Greek *allophanēs* appearing otherwise, from *all-* + *phainesthai* to appear, middle voice of *phainein* to show — more at FANCY] (circa 1821)
: an amorphous translucent mineral of various colors often occurring in incrustations or stalactite forms and consisting of a hydrous aluminum silicate

al·lo·phone \ˈa-lə-ˌfōn\ *noun* [*allo-* + *phone*] (1938)
: one of two or more variants of the same phoneme 〈the aspirated \p\ of *pin* and the unaspirated \p\ of *spin* are *allophones* of the phoneme \p\〉
— **al·lo·phon·ic** \ˌa-lə-'fä-nik\ *adjective*

al·lo·poly·ploid \ˌa-lō-'pä-li-ˌplȯid\ *noun* (1928)
: a polyploid individual or strain having a chromosome set composed of two or more chromosome sets derived more or less completely from different species
— **allopolyploid** *adjective*
— **al·lo·poly·ploi·dy** \-ˌplȯi-dē\ *noun*

al·lo·pu·ri·nol \ˌa-lō-'pyúr-ə-ˌnȯl, -ˌnōl\ *noun* [*all-* + *purine* + ¹*-ol*] (1964)

: a drug C₅H₄N₄O used to promote excretion of uric acid

all-or-none \ˌȯ-lər-'nən\ *adjective* (1900)
: marked either by entire or complete operation or effect or by none at all 〈*all-or-none* response of a nerve cell〉

all-or-noth·ing \-'nə-thiŋ\ *adjective* (1765)
1 : ALL-OR-NONE
2 a : accepting no less than everything 〈he's an *all-or-nothing* perfectionist〉 **b :** risking everything 〈an *all-or-nothing* combat strategy〉

al·lo·sau·rus \ˌa-lə-'sȯr-əs\ *noun* [New Latin, from Greek *all-* + *sauros* lizard] (1899)
: any of a genus (*Allosaurus*) of huge carnivorous North American theropod dinosaurs of the Upper Jurassic period

al·lo·ste·ric \ˌa-lō-'ster-ik, -'stir-\ *adjective* [*all-* + *steric*] (1962)
: of, relating to, or being a change in the shape and activity of a protein (as an enzyme) that results from combination with another substance at a point other than the chemically active site
— **al·lo·ste·ri·cal·ly** \-i-k(ə-)lē\ *adverb*
— **al·lo·ste·ry** \ˈa-lō-ˌster-ē, -ˌstir-\ *noun*

al·lot \ə-'lät\ *transitive verb* **al·lot·ted; al·lot·ting** [Middle English *alotten,* from Middle French *aloter,* from *a-* (from Latin *ad-*) + *lot,* of Germanic origin; akin to Old English *hlot* lot] (15th century)
1 : to assign as a share or portion 〈*allot* 10 minutes for the speech〉
2 : to distribute by or as if by lot 〈*allot* seats to the press〉
— **al·lot·ter** *noun*

al·lo·te·tra·ploid \ˌa-lō-'te-trə-ˌplȯid\ *noun* (1930)
: AMPHIDIPLOID
— **al·lo·te·tra·ploi·dy** \-ˌplȯi-dē\ *noun*

al·lot·ment \ə-'lät-mənt\ *noun* (1574)
1 : the act of allotting **:** APPORTIONMENT
2 : something that is allotted; *especially, chiefly British* **:** a plot of land let to an individual for cultivation

al·lo·trope \ˈa-lə-ˌtrōp\ *noun* [International Scientific Vocabulary, back-formation from *allotropy*] (1889)
: a form showing allotropy

al·lot·ro·py \ə-'lä-trə-pē\ *noun, plural* **-pies** (1850)
: the existence of a substance and especially an element in two or more different forms (as of crystals) usually in the same phase
— **al·lo·trop·ic** \ˌa-lə-'trä-pik\ *adjective*

all' ot·ta·va \ˌa-lə-'tä-və, ˌä-lō-\ *adverb or adjective* [Italian, at the octave] (circa 1823)
: OTTAVA

al·lot·tee \ə-ˌlä-'tē\ *noun* (1846)
: one to whom an allotment is made

al·lo·type \ˈa-lə-ˌtīp\ *noun* (1960)
: an alloantigen that is part of a plasma protein (as an antibody)
— **al·lo·typ·ic** \ˌa-lə-'ti-pik\ *adjective*
— **al·lo·typ·i·cal·ly** \-pi-k(ə-)lē\ *adverb*
— **al·lo·typy** \ˈa-lə-ˌtī-pē\ *noun*

all-out \ˈȯ-'laút\ *adjective* (1908)
1 : made with maximum effort **:** THOROUGHGOING 〈an *all-out* effort to win the contest〉
2 : FULL-BLOWN 2

all out *adverb* (1895)
: with full determination or enthusiasm **:** with maximum effort — used chiefly in the phrase *go all out*

¹all-over \ˈȯ-ˌlō-vər\ *adjective* (1859)
: covering the whole extent or surface 〈a sweater with an *allover* pattern〉

²allover *noun* (1838)
1 : an embroidered, printed, or lace fabric with a design covering most of the surface

\ə\ abut \ᵊ\ kitten \ər\ further \a\ ash \ā\ ace
\ä\ mop, mar \aú\ out \ch\ chin \e\ bet \ē\ easy
\g\ go \i\ hit \ī\ ice \j\ job \ŋ\ sing \ō\ go
\ȯ\ law \ȯi\ boy \th\ thin \th\ the \ü\ loot \ú\ foot
\y\ yet \zh\ vision *see also* Guide to Pronunciation

2 : a pattern or design in which a single unit is repeated so as to cover an entire surface

all over *adverb* (1577)
1 : over the whole extent ⟨decorated *all over* with a flower pattern⟩
2 : EVERYWHERE ⟨looked *all over* for the book⟩
3 : in every respect **:** THOROUGHLY ⟨she is her mother *all over*⟩

al·low \ə-'laủ\ *verb* [Middle English, from Middle French *alouer* to place, (from Medieval Latin *allocare*) & *allouer* to approve, from Latin *allaudare* to extol, from *ad-* + *laudare* to praise — more at ALLOCATE] (14th century)
transitive verb
1 a : to assign as a share or suitable amount (as of time or money) ⟨*allow* an hour for lunch⟩ **b :** to reckon as a deduction or an addition ⟨*allow* a gallon for leakage⟩
2 a *chiefly Southern & Midland* **:** to be of the opinion **:** THINK **b** *dialect* **:** SAY, STATE **c :** to express an opinion — usually used with *as how* or *that*
3 *chiefly Southern & Midland* **:** INTEND, PLAN
4 : ADMIT, CONCEDE ⟨must *allow* that money causes problems in marriage⟩
5 a : PERMIT ⟨doesn't *allow* people to smoke in his home⟩ **b :** to forbear or neglect to restrain or prevent ⟨*allow* the dog to roam⟩
intransitive verb
1 : to make a possibility **:** ADMIT — used with *of* ⟨evidence that *allows* of only one conclusion⟩
2 : to give consideration to circumstances or contingencies — used with *for* ⟨*allow* for expansion⟩

al·low·able \ə-'laủ-ə-bəl\ *adjective* (15th century)
: PERMISSIBLE
— **al·low·ably** \-blē\ *adverb*

¹al·low·ance \ə-'laủ-ən(t)s\ *noun* (14th century)
1 a : a share or portion allotted or granted **b :** a sum granted as a reimbursement or bounty or for expenses ⟨salary includes cost-of-living *allowance*⟩; *especially* **:** a sum regularly provided for personal or household expenses ⟨each child has an *allowance*⟩ **c :** a fixed or available amount ⟨provide an *allowance* of time for recreation⟩ **d :** a reduction from a list price or stated price ⟨a trade-in *allowance*⟩
2 : an imposed handicap (as in a horse race)
3 : an allowed dimensional difference between mating parts of a machine
4 : the act of allowing **:** PERMISSION
5 : a taking into account of mitigating circumstances or contingencies

²allowance *transitive verb* **-anced; -anc·ing** (circa 1828)
1 *archaic* **:** to put on a fixed allowance (as of food and drink)
2 *archaic* **:** to supply in a fixed or regular quantity

al·low·ed·ly \ə-'laủ-əd-lē\ *adverb* (1602)
: by allowance **:** ADMITTEDLY

al·lox·an \ə-'läk-sən\ *noun* [German, from *Al*lantoin + *Ox*alsäure oxalic acid + *-an*] (1853)
: a crystalline compound $C_4H_2N_2O_4$ causing diabetes mellitus when injected into experimental animals

¹al·loy \'a-ˌlói *also* ə-'lói\ *noun* [French *aloi*, from Old French *alei*, from *aleir* to combine, from Latin *alligare* to bind — more at ALLY] (1604)
1 : the degree of mixture with base metals **:** FINENESS
2 : a substance composed of two or more metals or of a metal and a nonmetal intimately united usually by being fused together and dissolving in each other when molten; *also* **:** the state of union of the components
3 a : an admixture that lessens value **b :** an impairing alien element
4 : a compound, mixture, or union of different things ⟨an ethnic *alloy* of many peoples⟩

5 *archaic* **:** a metal mixed with a more valuable metal to give durability or some other desired quality

²al·loy \ə-'lói *also* 'a-ˌlói\ (1661)
transitive verb
1 a : TEMPER, MODERATE **b :** to impair or debase by admixture
2 : to reduce the purity of by mixing with a less valuable metal
3 : to mix so as to form an alloy
intransitive verb
: to lend itself to being alloyed ⟨iron *alloys* well⟩

all–pow·er·ful \'ól-'paủ-(ə)r-fəl\ *adjective* (1667)
: having complete or sole power

all–pur·pose \-'pər-pəs\ *adjective* (1928)
: suited for many purposes or uses

¹all right *adjective* (1701)
1 : SATISFACTORY, AGREEABLE ⟨whatever you decide is *all right* with me⟩
2 : SAFE, WELL ⟨he was ill but he's *all right* now⟩
3 : GOOD, PLEASING — often used as a generalized term of approval ⟨an *all right* guy⟩
usage see ALRIGHT

²all right *adverb* (1837)
1 : very well ⟨*all right*, let's go⟩
2 : beyond doubt **:** CERTAINLY ⟨she has pneumonia *all right*⟩
3 : well enough **:** SATISFACTORILY ⟨does *all right* in school⟩
usage see ALRIGHT

all–round \'ól-'raủnd\ *variant of* ALL-AROUND

all–round·er \'ól-'raủn-dər\ *noun* (1875)
British **:** one that is all-around

All Saints' Day *noun* (circa 1798)
: November 1 observed in Western liturgical churches as a Christian feast in honor of all the saints

All Souls' Day *noun* (14th century)
: November 2 observed in some Christian churches as a day of prayer for the souls of the faithful departed

all·spice \'ól-ˌspīs\ *noun* (1621)
1 : the berry of a West Indian tree (*Pimenta dioica*) of the myrtle family; *also* **:** the allspice tree
2 : a mildly pungent and aromatic spice prepared from allspice berries

¹all–star \'ól-'stär\ *adjective* (1889)
: composed wholly or chiefly of stars or of outstanding performers or participants ⟨an *all-star* cast⟩

²all–star \'ól-ˌstär\ *noun* (circa 1934)
: a member of an all-star team

all that *adverb* (1945)
: to an indicated or suggested extent or degree **:** SO ⟨didn't take his threats *all that* seriously⟩

all–time \'ól-ˌtīm\ *adjective* (1914)
1 : FULL-TIME 1
2 : being for or of all time up to and including the present; *especially* **:** exceeding all others of all time ⟨an *all-time* best-seller⟩

all told *adverb* (1850)
: with everything taken into account **:** in all

al·lude \ə-'lüd\ *intransitive verb* **al·lud·ed; al·lud·ing** [Latin *alludere*, literally, to play with, from *ad-* + *ludere* to play — more at LUDICROUS] (1533)
: to make indirect reference ⟨*alluded* vaguely to personal problems⟩; *broadly* **:** REFER

¹al·lure \ə-'lủr\ *transitive verb* **al·lured; al·lur·ing** [Middle English *aluren*, from Middle French *alurer*, from Old French *a-* (from Latin *ad-*) + *loire* lure — more at LURE] (15th century)
: to entice by charm or attraction
synonym see ATTRACT
— **al·lure·ment** \-'lủr-mənt\ *noun*
— **al·lur·ing·ly** *adverb*

²allure *noun* (1548)
: power of attraction or fascination **:** CHARM

al·lu·sion \ə-'lü-zhən\ *noun* [Late Latin *allusion-, allusio*, from Latin *alludere*] (1548)

1 : an implied or indirect reference especially in literature; *also* **:** the use of such references
2 : the act of alluding or hinting at
— **al·lu·sive** \-'lü-siv, -ziv\ *adjective*
— **al·lu·sive·ly** *adverb*
— **al·lu·sive·ness** *noun*

¹al·lu·vi·al \ə-'lü-vē-əl\ *adjective* (1802)
: relating to, composed of, or found in alluvium ⟨*alluvial* soil⟩ ⟨*alluvial* diamonds⟩

²alluvial *noun* (1866)
: an alluvial deposit

alluvial fan *noun* (1873)
: the alluvial deposit of a stream where it issues from a gorge upon a plain or of a tributary stream at its junction with the main stream

alluvial fan

al·lu·vi·on \ə-'lü-vē-ən\ *noun* [Latin *alluvion-, alluvio*, from *alluere* to flow past, deposit (of water), from *ad-* + *lavere* to wash — more at LYE] (1536)
1 : the wash or flow of water against a shore
2 : FLOOD, INUNDATION
3 : ALLUVIUM
4 : an accession to land by the gradual addition of matter (as by deposit of alluvium) that then belongs to the owner of the land to which it is added; *also* **:** the land so added

al·lu·vi·um \-vē-əm\ *noun, plural* **-vi·ums** *or* **-via** \-vē-ə\ [Medieval Latin, alteration of Latin *alluvio*] (circa 1656)
: clay, silt, sand, gravel, or similar detrital material deposited by running water

¹al·ly \ə-'lī, 'a-ˌlī\ *verb* **al·lied; al·ly·ing** [Middle English *allien*, from Old French *alier*, from Latin *alligare* to bind to, from *ad-* + *ligare* to bind — more at LIGATURE] (14th century)
transitive verb
1 : to unite or form a connection between **:** ASSOCIATE ⟨*allied* himself with a wealthy family by marriage⟩
2 : to connect or form a relation between (as by likeness or compatibility) **:** RELATE
intransitive verb
: to form or enter into an alliance

²al·ly \'a-ˌlī, ə-'lī\ *noun, plural* **allies** (1598)
1 : a sovereign or state associated with another by treaty or league
2 : a plant or animal linked to another by genetic or taxonomic proximity
3 : one that is associated with another as a helper **:** AUXILIARY

-ally *adverb suffix* ['-*al* + -*ly*]
: ²-LY ⟨terrific*ally*⟩ — in adverbs formed from adjectives in -*ic* with no alternative form in -*ical*

al·lyl \'a-ləl\ *adjective* [International Scientific Vocabulary, from Latin *allium* garlic] (1854)
: being or containing the unsaturated univalent group C_3H_5-

al·lyl·ic \ə-'li-lik, a-\ *adjective* (1857)
: involving or characteristic of an allyl group

al·ma·gest \'al-mə-ˌjest\ *noun* [Middle English *almageste*, from Middle French & Medieval Latin, from Arabic *al-majusti*, the Arabic version of Ptolemy's astronomy treatise, from *al* the + Greek *megistē* (*syntaxis*), literally, greatest (composition)] (14th century)
: any of several early medieval treatises on a branch of knowledge

al·ma ma·ter \ˌal-mə-'mä-tər\ *noun* [Latin, fostering mother] (1696)
1 : a school, college, or university which one has attended or from which one has graduated
2 : the song or hymn of a school, college, or university

al·ma·nac \'ól-mə-ˌnak, 'al-\ *noun* [Middle

English *almenak,* from Medieval Latin *almanach,* probably from Arabic *al-manākh* the almanac] (14th century)
1 : a publication containing astronomical and meteorological data for a given year and often including a miscellany of other information
2 : a usually annual publication containing statistical, tabular, and general information

al·man·dine \'al-mən-,dēn, -,dīn\ *noun* [Middle English *alemaundine,* from Middle French *alemandine,* alteration of *alabandine,* from Medieval Latin *alabandina,* from *Alabanda,* ancient city in Asia Minor] (15th century)
: ALMANDITE

al·man·dite \'al-mən-,dīt\ *noun* [alteration of *almandine*] (circa 1868)
: a deep red garnet consisting of an iron aluminum silicate

¹al·mighty \ol-'mī-tē\ *adjective* [Middle English, from Old English *ealmihtig,* from *eall* all + *mihtig* mighty] (before 12th century)
1 *often capitalized* **:** having absolute power over all ⟨*Almighty* God⟩
2 : relatively unlimited in power
3 : great in magnitude or seriousness
— **al·mighti·ness** *noun*

²almighty *adverb* (1833)
: to a great degree **:** EXTREMELY ⟨although he did not precisely starve, he was *almighty* hungry —W. A. Swanberg⟩

Almighty *noun* (before 12th century)
: GOD 1 — used with *the*

al·mond \'ä-mənd, 'a-, 'äl-, 'al-\ *noun* [Middle English *almande,* from Middle French, from Late Latin *amandula,* alteration of Latin *amygdala,* from Greek *amygdalē*] (14th century)
1 a : the drupaceous fruit of a small tree (*Prunus dulcis* synonym *P. amygdalus*) of the rose family with flowers and young fruit resembling those of the peach; *especially* **:** its ellipsoidal edible kernel used as a nut **b** **:** any of several similar fruits
2 : a tree that produces almonds

almond 1a

al·mond–eyed \-,īd\ *adjective* (1870)
: having narrow slant almond-shaped eyes

al·mo·ner \'al-mə-nər, 'ä-mə-\ *noun* [Middle English *almoiner,* from Middle French *almosnier,* from *almosne* alms, from Late Latin *eleemosyna*] (15th century)
1 : one who distributes alms
2 *British* **:** a social-service worker in a hospital

¹al·most \'ol-,mōst, ol-'\ *adverb* [Middle English, from Old English *ealmǣst,* from *eall* + *mǣst* most] (before 12th century)
: very nearly but not exactly or entirely

²almost *adjective* (1709)
: very near but not quite ⟨an *almost* failure⟩

alms \'ä(l)mz, *New England also* 'ämz\ *noun, plural* **alms** [Middle English *almesse, almes,* from Old English *ælmesse, ælmes,* from Late Latin *eleemosyna* alms, from Greek *eleēmosynē* pity, alms, from *eleēmōn* merciful, from *eleos* pity] (before 12th century)
1 *archaic* **:** CHARITY
2 : something (as money or food) given freely to relieve the poor
— **alms·giv·er** \-,gi-vər\ *noun*
— **alms·giv·ing** \-,gi-viŋ\ *noun*

alms·house \-,haús\ *noun* (14th century)
1 *British* **:** a privately financed home for the poor
2 : POORHOUSE

alms·man \-mən\ *noun* (before 12th century)
: a recipient of alms

al·ni·co \'al-ni-,kō\ *noun* [*al*uminum + *ni*ckel + *co*balt] (1935)
: a powerful permanent-magnet alloy containing iron, nickel, aluminum, and one or more of the elements cobalt, copper, and titanium

al·oe \'a-(,)lō\ *noun* [Middle English, from Late Latin, from Latin, dried juice of aloe leaves, from Greek *aloē*] (before 12th century)
1 *plural* **:** the fragrant wood of an East Indian tree (*Aquilaria agallocha*) of the mezereon family
2 a : any of a large genus (*Aloe*) of succulent chiefly southern African plants of the lily family with basal leaves and spicate flowers **b** **:** the dried juice of the leaves of various aloes used especially formerly as a purgative — usually used in plural but singular in construction

aloe vera \-'ver-ə, -'vir-\ *noun* [New Latin, species name, from *Aloe* + Latin *vera,* feminine of *verus* true — more at VERY] (circa 1936)
: an aloe (*Aloe barbadensis* synonym *A. vera*) whose leaves furnish an emollient extract used especially in cosmetics and skin creams; *also* **:** such a preparation

¹aloft \ə-'loft\ *adverb* [Middle English, from Old Norse *ā lopt,* from *ā* on, in + *lopt* air — more at ON, LOFT] (13th century)
1 : at or to a great height
2 : in the air; *especially* **:** in flight (as in an airplane) ⟨meals served *aloft*⟩
3 : at, on, or to the masthead or the higher rigging

²aloft *preposition* (14th century)
: on top of **:** ABOVE ⟨bright signs *aloft* hotels⟩

alog·i·cal \(,)ä-'lä-ji-kəl\ *adjective* (1694)
: being outside the bounds of that to which logic can apply
— **alog·i·cal·ly** \-k(ə-)lē\ *adverb*

alo·ha \ə-'lō-,(h)ä, ä-, -(h)ə\ *interjection* [Hawaiian, from *aloha* love] (1820)
— used as a greeting or farewell

aloha shirt *noun* (1940)
: HAWAIIAN SHIRT

¹alone \ə-'lōn\ *adjective* [Middle English, from *al* all + *one* one] (13th century)
1 : separated from others **:** ISOLATED
2 : exclusive of anyone or anything else **:** ONLY
3 a : considered without reference to any other ⟨the children *alone* would eat that much⟩ **b** **:** INCOMPARABLE, UNIQUE ⟨*alone* among their contemporaries in this respect⟩ ☆
— **alone·ness** \-'lōn-nəs\ *noun*

²alone *adverb* (13th century)
1 : SOLELY, EXCLUSIVELY
2 : without aid or support

¹along \ə-'loŋ\ *preposition* [Middle English, from Old English *andlang,* from *and-* against + *lang* long — more at ANTE-] (before 12th century)
1 : in a line parallel with the length or direction of
2 : in the course of
3 : in accordance with **:** IN

²along *adverb* (14th century)
1 : FORWARD, ON ⟨move *along*⟩
2 : from one to another ⟨word was passed *along*⟩
3 a : in company **:** as a companion ⟨brought his wife *along*⟩ — often used with *with* ⟨walked to school *along* with her friends⟩ **b** **:** in association — used with *with* ⟨work *along* with colleagues⟩
4 : sometime within a specified or implied extent of time — usually used with *about* ⟨*along* about July 17⟩ **b** **:** at or to an advanced point ⟨plans are far *along*⟩
5 : in addition **:** ALSO — often used with *with* ⟨a bill came *along* with the package⟩
6 : at hand **:** as a necessary or useful item ⟨brought an extra one *along*⟩ ⟨had his gun *along*⟩
7 : on hand **:** THERE ⟨tell him I'll be *along* to see him⟩

along of *preposition* [Middle English *ilong on,* from Old English *gelang on,* from *ge-,* associative prefix + *lang* — more at CO-] (before 12th century)
dialect **:** BECAUSE OF

along·shore \ə-'loŋ-'shōr, -'shór\ *adverb or adjective* (1779)
: along the shore or coast ⟨walked *alongshore*⟩ ⟨*alongshore* currents⟩

¹along·side \-'sīd\ *adverb* (1707)
1 : along the side **:** in parallel position
2 : at the side **:** close by ⟨a guard with a prisoner *alongside*⟩

²alongside *preposition* (1793)
1 a : along the side of **b** **:** BESIDE 1
2 a : in company with ⟨men she has been working *alongside* —Richard Halloran⟩ **b** **:** in addition to ⟨a special category *alongside* the awards it annually presents —*Horizon*⟩

alongside of *preposition* (1781)
: ALONGSIDE

¹aloof \ə-'lüf\ *adverb* [obsolete *aloof* to windward, from ¹*a-* + *louf, luf* luff] (circa 1540)
: at a distance

²aloof *adjective* (1608)
: removed or distant either physically or emotionally ⟨the *aloof* composer neither worried nor cared about public opinion —Mary Jane Matz⟩ ⟨he stood *aloof* from worldly success —John Buchan⟩
synonym *see* INDIFFERENT
— **aloof·ly** *adverb*
— **aloof·ness** *noun*

al·o·pe·cia \,a-lə-'pē-sh(ē-)ə\ *noun* [Middle English *allopicia,* from Latin *alopecia,* from Greek *alōpekia,* from *alōpek-, alōpēx* fox; akin to Armenian *aluēs* fox, Sanskrit *lopāśa*] (14th century)
: loss of hair, wool, or feathers **:** BALDNESS
— **al·o·pe·cic** \-'pē-sik\ *adjective*

aloud \ə-'laùd\ *adverb* [Middle English, from ¹*a-* + *loud*] (13th century)
1 *archaic* **:** in a loud manner **:** LOUDLY
2 : with the speaking voice

alow \ə-'lō\ *adverb* [Middle English, from ¹*a-* + *low*] (13th century)
: BELOW ⟨*alow* in the ship's hold⟩

alp \'alp\ *noun* [back-formation from *Alps,* mountain system of Europe] (15th century)
1 : a high rugged mountain
2 : something suggesting an alp in height, size, or ruggedness

al·paca \al-'pa-kə\ *noun* [Spanish, from Aymara *allpaqa*] (1811)
1 : a domesticated mammal (*Lama pacos*) especially of Peru that is probably descended from the guanaco
2 a : wool of the alpaca **b** (1) **:** a thin cloth

\ə\ **abut** \ᵊ\ **kitten** \ər\ **further** \a\ **ash** \ā\ **ace**
\ä\ **mop, mar** \aú\ **out** \ch\ **chin** \e\ **bet** \ē\ **easy**
\g\ **go** \i\ **hit** \ī\ **ice** \j\ **job** \ŋ\ **sing** \ō\ **go**
\o\ **law** \ói\ **boy** \th\ **thin** \t͟h\ **the** \ü\ **loot** \ú\ **foot**
\y\ **yet** \zh\ **vision** *see also* Guide to Pronunciation

made of or containing this wool (2) **:** a rayon or cotton imitation of this cloth

al·pen·glow \'al-pən-ˌglō\ *noun* [part translation of German *Alpenglühen,* from *Alpen* Alps + *Glühen* glow] (1871)
: a reddish glow seen near sunset or sunrise on the summits of mountains

alpaca 1

al·pen·horn \'al-pən-ˌhȯrn\ *or* **alp·horn** \'alp-ˌhȯrn\ *noun* [German, from *Alpen* + *Horn* horn] (1864)
: a straight wooden horn 5 to 14 feet (about 1.5 to 4.3 meters) in length used chiefly by Swiss herdsmen

al·pen·stock \'al-pən-ˌstäk\ *noun* [German, from *Alpen* + *Stock* staff] (1829)
: a long iron-pointed staff used in mountain climbing

¹al·pha \'al-fə\ *noun* [Middle English, from Latin, from Greek, of Semitic origin; akin to Hebrew *āleph* aleph] (13th century)
1 : the 1st letter of the Greek alphabet — see ALPHABET table
2 : something that is first **:** BEGINNING
3 : ALPHA WAVE
4 : ALPHA PARTICLE

²alpha *adjective* (1863)
1 : closest in the structure of an organic molecule to a particular group or atom — symbol α ⟨α-substitution⟩
2 : socially dominant especially in a group of animals
3 : ALPHABETIC

al·pha–ad·ren·er·gic \'al-fə-ˌa-drə-'nər-jik\ *adjective* (1966)
: of, relating to, or being an alpha-receptor ⟨*alpha-adrenergic* blocking action⟩

alpha and omega *noun* [from the fact that alpha and omega are respectively the first and last letters of the Greek alphabet] (1526)
1 : the beginning and ending
2 : the principal element

al·pha·bet \'al-fə-ˌbet, -bət\ *noun* [Middle English *alphabete,* from Late Latin *alphabetum,* from Greek *alphabētos,* from *alpha* + *bēta* beta] (1513)
1 a : a set of letters or other characters with which one or more languages are written especially if arranged in a customary order **b :** a system of signs or signals that serve as equivalents for letters
2 : RUDIMENTS, ELEMENTS

al·pha·bet·ic \ˌal-fə-'be-tik\ *or* **al·pha·bet·i·cal** \-ti-kəl\ *adjective* (1567)
1 : arranged in the order of the letters of the alphabet
2 : of, relating to, or employing an alphabet
— **al·pha·bet·i·cal·ly** \-ti-k(ə-)lē\ *adverb*

al·pha·bet·iza·tion \ˌal-fə-ˌbe-tə-'zā-shən\ *noun* (1889)
1 : the act or process of alphabetizing
2 : an alphabetically arranged series, list, or file

al·pha·bet·ize \'al-fə-bə-ˌtīz\ *transitive verb* **-ized; -iz·ing** (1796)
1 : to arrange alphabetically
2 : to furnish with an alphabet
— **al·pha·bet·iz·er** *noun*

alphabet soup *noun* (1934)
: a hodgepodge especially of initials (as of the names of organizations)

al·pha·fe·to·pro·tein \ˌal-fə-ˌfē-tō-'prō-ˌtēn, -'prō-tē-ən\ *noun* (1968)
: a fetal blood protein present abnormally in adults with some cancers (as of the liver) and normally in the amniotic fluid of pregnant women with high or low levels tending to be associated with certain birth defects (as spina bifida or Down's syndrome)

alpha globulin *noun* [International Scientific Vocabulary] (1923)
: any of several globulins of plasma or serum that have at alkaline pH the greatest electrophoretic mobility next to albumin — compare BETA GLOBULIN, GAMMA GLOBULIN

al·pha–he·lix \ˌal-fə-'hē-liks\ *noun* (1955)
: the coiled structural arrangement of many proteins consisting of a single chain of amino acids stabilized by hydrogen bonds
— **al·pha–he·li·cal** \-'he-li-kəl, -'hē-li-\ *adjective*

alpha iron *noun* (1902)
: the form of iron stable below 910°C

al·pha·mer·ic \ˌal-fə-'mer-ik\ *adjective* [*alphabetic* + nu*meric*] (circa 1952)
: ALPHANUMERIC

al·pha·nu·mer·ic \-nu̇-'mer-ik, -nyu̇-\ *also* **al·pha·nu·mer·i·cal** \-i-kəl\ *adjective* [*alphabetic* + *numeric, numerical*] (1950)
1 : consisting of both letters and numbers and often other symbols (as punctuation marks and mathematical symbols) ⟨an *alphanumeric* code⟩; *also* **:** being a character in an alphanumeric system
2 : capable of using or displaying alphanumeric characters
— **al·pha·nu·mer·i·cal·ly** \-i-k(ə-)lē\ *adverb*
— **al·pha·nu·mer·ics** \-iks\ *noun plural*

alpha particle *noun* (1903)
: a positively charged nuclear particle identical with the nucleus of a helium atom that consists of two protons and two neutrons and is ejected at high speed in certain radioactive transformations — called also *alpha, alpha ray*

alpha privative *noun* (1590)
: the prefix *a-* or *an-* expressing negation in Greek and in English

al·pha–re·cep·tor \'al-fə-ri-ˌsep-tər\ *noun* (1961)
: any of a group of receptors postulated to exist on nerve cell membranes of the sympathetic nervous system to explain the specificity of certain adrenergic agents in affecting only some sympathetic activities (as vasoconstriction, relaxation of intestinal muscle, and contraction of most smooth muscle)

alpha wave *noun* (1936)
: an electrical rhythm of the brain with a frequency of 8 to 13 cycles per second that is often associated with a state of wakeful relaxation — called also *alpha, alpha rhythm*

Al·phe·us \al-'fē-əs\ *noun* [Latin, from Greek *Alpheios*]
: a Greek river-god who pursues the nymph Arethusa and is finally united with her

al·pine \'al-ˌpīn\ *noun* (circa 1828)
1 : a plant native to alpine or boreal regions that is often grown for ornament
2 *capitalized* **:** a person possessing Alpine physical characteristics

Alpine *adjective* (15th century)
1 *often not capitalized* **:** of, relating to, or resembling the Alps or any mountains
2 *often not capitalized* **:** of, relating to, or growing in the biogeographic zone including the elevated slopes above timberline
3 : of or relating to a physical type characterized by a broad head, stockiness, medium height, and brown hair or eyes often regarded as constituting a branch of the Caucasian race
4 : of or relating to competitive ski events consisting of slalom and downhill racing — compare NORDIC

al·pin·ism \'al-pə-ˌni-zəm\ *noun, often capitalized* (1884)
: mountain climbing in the Alps or other high mountains
— **al·pin·ist** \-nist\ *noun*

al·ready \ȯl-'re-dē, 'ȯl-\ *adverb* [Middle English *al redy,* from *al redy,* adjective, wholly ready, from *al* all + *redy* ready] (14th century)
1 : prior to a specified or implied past,

present, or future time **:** by this time **:** PREVIOUSLY ⟨he had *already* left when I called⟩
2 — used as an intensive ⟨all right *already*⟩ ⟨enough *already*⟩

al·right \(ˌ)ȯl-'rīt, 'ȯl-\ *adverb or adjective* (1887)
: ALL RIGHT □

Al·sa·tian \al-'sā-shən\ *noun* [Medieval Latin *Alsatia* Alsace] (1917)
: GERMAN SHEPHERD

al·sike clover \'al-ˌsak-, -ˌsīk-\ *noun* [*Alsike,* Sweden] (1852)
: a European perennial clover (*Trifolium hybridum*) much used as a forage plant

al·so \'ȯl(t)-(ˌ)sō, 'ȯl-\ *adverb* [Middle English, from Old English *eallswā,* from *eall* all + *swā* so — more at SO] (before 12th century)
1 : LIKEWISE 1
2 : in addition **:** BESIDES, TOO

al·so-ran \-ˌran\ *noun* (1896)
1 : a horse or dog that finishes out of the money in a race
2 : a contestant that does not win
3 : one that is of little importance especially competitively ⟨was just an *also-ran* in the scramble for . . . privileges —C. A. Buss⟩

Al·ta·ic \al-'tā-ik\ *adjective* (circa 1828)
1 : of or relating to the Altai Mountains
2 : of, relating to, or constituting the Turkic, Tungusic, and Mongolian language families collectively

Al·tair \al-'tīr, -'tar, -'ter, 'al-\ *noun* [Arabic *al-ṭā'ir,* literally, the flier]
: the brightest star in the constellation Aquila

al·tar \'ȯl-tər\ *noun, often attributive* [Middle English *alter,* from Old English *altar,* from Latin *altare;* probably akin to Latin *adolēre* to burn up] (before 12th century)
1 : a usually raised structure or place on which sacrifices are offered or incense is burned in worship
2 : a table on which the eucharistic elements are consecrated or which serves as a center of worship or ritual

altar boy *noun* (1772)
: a boy who assists the celebrant in a liturgical service

altar call *noun* (1946)
: an appeal by an evangelist to worshipers to come forward to signify their decision to commit their lives to Christ

altar of repose *often A&R capitalized* (circa 1872)
: REPOSITORY 2

al·tar·piece \'ȯl-tər-ˌpēs\ *noun* (1644)
: a work of art that decorates the space above and behind an altar

altar rail *noun* (1860)
: a railing in front of an altar separating the chancel from the body of the church

altar stone *noun* (14th century)
: a stone slab with a compartment containing the relics of martyrs that forms an essential part of a Roman Catholic altar

alt·az·i·muth \(ˌ)al-'taz-məth, -'ta-zə-\ *noun, often attributive* [International Scientific Vocabulary *alt*itude + *azimuth*] (1860)
: a telescope mounted so that it can swing horizontally and vertically; *also* **:** any of several other similarly mounted instruments

□ **USAGE**

alright The one-word spelling *alright* appeared some 75 years after *all right* itself had reappeared from a 400-year-long absence. Since the early 20th century some critics have insisted *alright* is wrong, but it has its defenders and its users. It is less frequent than *all right* but remains in common use especially in journalistic and business publications. It is quite common in fictional dialogue, and is used occasionally in other writing ⟨the first two years of medical school were *alright* —Gertrude Stein⟩.

ALPHABET TABLE

Showing the letters of five non-Roman alphabets and the transliterations used in the etymologies

HEBREW[1,4]			ARABIC[3,4]					GREEK[7]			RUSSIAN[8]			SANSKRIT[11]			
א	aleph	' [2]	ا	ل			alif	[5]	A α	alpha	a	А а	a	अ	a	ञ	ñ
ב	beth	b, bh	ب	ب	ﺒ	ﺑ	bā	b	B β	beta	b	Б б	b	आ	ā	ट	ṭ
ג	gimel	g, gh	ت	ت	ﺘ	ﺗ	tā	t	Γ γ	gamma	g, n	В в	v	इ	i	ठ	ṭh
ד	daleth	d, dh	ث	ث	ﺜ	ﺛ	thā	th				Г г	g	ई	ī	ड	ḍ
ה	he	h	ج	ج	ﺠ	ﺟ	jīm	j	Δ δ	delta	d	Д д	d	उ	u	ढ	ḍh
			ح	ح	ﺤ	ﺣ	ḥā	ḥ	E ε	epsilon	e	Е е	e	ऊ	ū	ण	ṇ
ו	waw	w	خ	خ	ﺨ	ﺧ	khā	kh	Z ζ	zeta	z	Ж ж	zh	ऋ	ṛ	त	t
ז	zayin	z	د	د			dāl	d	H η	eta	ē	З з	z	ॠ	ṝ	थ	th
ח	heth	ḥ	ذ	ذ			dhāl	dh	Θ θ	theta	th	И и Й й	i, ĭ	ऌ	ḷ	द	d
ט	teth	ṭ	ر	ﺮ			rā	r	I ι	iota	i	К к	k	ॡ	ḹ	ध	dh
			ز	ﺰ			zāy	z	K κ	kappa	k	Л л	l			न	n
י	yod	y	س	ﺲ	ﺴ	ﺳ	sīn	s	Λ λ	lambda	l	М м	m	ए	e	प	p
כ ך	kaph	k, kh	ش	ﺶ	ﺸ	ﺷ	shīn	sh	M μ	mu	m	Н н	n	ऐ	ai	फ	ph
ל	lamed	l	ص	ﺺ	ﺼ	ﺻ	ṣād	ṣ	N ν	nu	n	О о	o	ओ	o	ब	b
מ ם	mem	m	ض	ﺾ	ﻀ	ﺿ	ḍād	ḍ	Ξ ξ	xi	x	П п	p	औ	au	भ	bh
נ ן	nun	n	ط	ط	ﻄ	ﻃ	ṭā	ṭ	O o	omicron	o	Р р	r	ं	ṁ	म	m
ס	samekh	s	ظ	ظ	ﻈ	ﻇ	ẓā	ẓ	Π π	pi	p	С с	s	ः	ḥ	य	y
ע	ayin	'	ع	ع	ﻌ	ﻋ	'ayn	'	P ρ	rho	r, rh	Т т	t	क	k	र	r
פ ף	pe	p, ph	غ	غ	ﻐ	ﻏ	ghayn	gh	Σ σ ς	sigma	s	У у	u	ख	kh	ल	l
צ ץ	sadhe	ṣ	ف	ف	ﻔ	ﻓ	fā	f	T τ	tau	t	Ф ф	f	ग	g	व	v
ק	qoph	q	ق	ق	ﻘ	ﻗ	qāf	q	Υ υ	upsilon	y, u	Х х	kh	घ	gh	श	ś
ר	resh	r	ك	ك	ﻜ	ﻛ	kāf	k	Φ φ	phi	ph	Ц ц	ts	ङ	ṅ	ष	ṣ
ש	sin	ś	ل	ل	ﻠ	ﻟ	lām	l	X χ	chi	ch	Ч ч	ch	च	c	स	s
ש	shin	sh	م	م	ﻤ	ﻣ	mīm	m	Ψ ψ	psi	ps	Ш ш	sh	छ	ch	ह	h
ת	taw	t, th	ن	ن	ﻨ	ﻧ	nūn	n	Ω ω	omega	ō	Щ щ	shch	ज	j		
			ه	ه	ﻬ	ﻫ	hā	h[6]				Ъ ъ[9]	''	झ	jh		
			و	ﻮ			wāw	w				Ы ы	y				
			ي	ي	ﻴ	ﻳ	yā	y				Ь ь[10]	'				
												Э э	e				
												Ю ю	yu				
												Я я	ya				

1 See ALEPH, BETH, etc., in the vocabulary. Where two forms of a letter are given, the one at the right is the form used at the end of a word. 2 Not represented in transliteration when initial. 3 The left column shows the form of each Arabic letter that is used when it stands alone, the second column its form when it is joined to the preceding letter, the third column its form when it is joined to both the preceding and the following letter, and the right column its form when it is joined to the following letter only. In the names of the Arabic letters, *ā*, *ī*, and *ū* respectively are pronounced like *a* in *father*, *i* in *machine*, *u* in *rude*. 4 Hebrew and Arabic are written from right to left. The Hebrew and Arabic letters are all primarily consonants; a few of them are also used secondarily to represent certain vowels, but full indication of vowels, when provided at all, is by means of a system of dots or strokes adjacent to the consonantal characters. 5 Alif represents no sound in itself, but is used principally as an indicator of the presence of a glottal stop (transliterated ' medially and finally; not represented in transliteration when initial) and as the sign of a long *a*. 6 When ة has two dots above it (ة), it is called *tā marbūta* and, if it immediately precedes a vowel, is transliterated *t* instead of *h*. 7 See ALPHA, BETA, GAMMA, etc., in the vocabulary. The letter gamma is transliterated *n* only before velars; the letter upsilon is transliterated *u* only as the final element in diphthongs. 8 See CYRILLIC in the vocabulary. 9 This sign indicates that the immediately preceding consonant is not palatalized even though immediately followed by a palatal vowel. 10 This sign indicates that the immediately preceding consonant is palatalized even though not immediately followed by a palatal vowel. 11 The alphabet shown here is the Devanagari. When vowels are combined with preceding consonants they are indicated by various strokes or hooks instead of by the signs here given, or, in the case of short *a*, not written at all. Thus the character क represents *ka*; the character का, *kā*; the character कि, *ki*; the character की, *kī*; the character कु, *ku*; the character कू, *kū*; the character कृ, *kṛ*; the character कॄ, *kṝ*; the character के, *ke*; the character कै, *kai*; the character को, *ko*; the character कौ, *kau*; and the character क्, *k* without any following vowel. There are also many compound characters representing combinations of two or more consonants.

al·ter \'òl-tər\ *verb* **al·tered; al·ter·ing** \-t(ə-)riŋ\ [Middle English, from Middle French *alterer*, from Medieval Latin *alterare*, from Latin *alter* other (of two); akin to Latin *alius* other — more at ELSE] (14th century)
transitive verb
1 : to make different without changing into something else
2 : CASTRATE, SPAY
intransitive verb
: to become different
synonym see CHANGE
— **al·ter·abil·i·ty** \,òl-t(ə-)rə-'bi-lə-tē\ *noun*
— **al·ter·able** \'òl-t(ə-)rə-bəl\ *adjective*
— **al·ter·ably** \-blē\ *adverb*
— **al·ter·er** \-tər-ər\ *noun*

al·ter·ation \,òl-tə-'rā-shən\ *noun* (14th century)
1 : the act or process of altering **:** the state of being altered
2 : the result of altering **:** MODIFICATION

al·ter·cate \'òl-tər-,kāt\ *intransitive verb* **-cat·ed; -cat·ing** [Latin *altercatus*, past participle of *altercari*, from *alter*] (1530)
: to dispute angrily or noisily **:** WRANGLE

al·ter·ca·tion \,òl-tər-'kā-shən\ *noun* (14th century)
: a noisy heated angry dispute; *also* **:** noisy controversy

al·ter ego \,òl-tər-'ē-(,)gō *also* -'e-(,)gō\ *noun* [Latin, literally, second I] (1537)
: a second self: as **a :** a trusted friend **b :** the opposite side of a personality **c :** COUNTERPART 3

¹al·ter·nate \US & Canadian 'òl-tər-nət *also* 'al-; *chiefly British* òl-'tər-\ *adjective* [Latin *alternatus*, past participle of *alternare*, from *alternus* alternate, from *alter*] (1513)
1 : occurring or succeeding by turns ⟨a day of *alternate* sunshine and rain⟩
2 a : arranged first on one side and then on the other at different levels or points along an axial line ⟨*alternate* leaves⟩ — compare OPPOSITE **b :** arranged one above or alongside the other
3 : every other **:** every second ⟨he works on *alternate* days⟩
4 : constituting an alternative ⟨took the *alternate* route home⟩
5 : ALTERNATIVE 3
— **al·ter·nate·ly** *adverb*

²al·ter·nate \'òl-tər-,nāt *also* 'al-\ *verb* **-nat·ed; -nat·ing** (1599)
transitive verb
1 : to perform by turns or in succession
2 : to cause to alternate
intransitive verb
: to change from one to another repeatedly ⟨rain *alternated* with sun⟩

³al·ter·nate \same as ¹\ *noun* (1717)
1 : ALTERNATIVE
2 : one that substitutes for or alternates with another

alternate angle *noun* (1660)
: one of a pair of angles with different vertices and on opposite sides of a transversal at its intersection with two other lines: **a :** one of a pair of angles inside the two intersected lines — called also *alternate interior angle* **b :** one of a pair of angles outside the two intersected lines — called also *alternate exterior angle*

alternate interior angles *a*, *a'*, *b*, *b'*; alternate exterior angles *c*, *c'*, *d*, *d'*

alternating current *noun* (1839)
: an electric current that reverses its direction at regularly recurring intervals — abbreviation *AC*

alternating group *noun* (1904)
: a permutation group whose elements comprise those permutations of *n* objects which

can be formed from the original order by making consecutively an even number of interchanges of pairs of objects

alternating series *noun* (circa 1909)
: a mathematical series in which consecutive terms are alternatively positive and negative

al·ter·na·tion \,òl-tər-'nā-shən *also* ,al-\ *noun* (15th century)
1 a : the act or process of alternating or causing to alternate **b :** alternating occurrence **:** SUCCESSION
2 : INCLUSIVE DISJUNCTION
3 : the occurrence of different allomorphs or allophones

alternation of generations (1858)
: the occurrence of two or more forms differently produced in the life cycle of a plant or animal usually involving the regular alternation of a sexual with an asexual generation

¹al·ter·na·tive \òl-'tər-nə-tiv, al-\ *adjective* (1540)
1 : ALTERNATE 1
2 : offering or expressing a choice ⟨several *alternative* plans⟩
3 : existing or functioning outside the established cultural, social, or economic system ⟨*alternative* newspaper⟩ ⟨*alternative* lifestyles⟩; *also* **:** different from the usual or conventional ⟨*alternative* fuels⟩
— **al·ter·na·tive·ly** *adverb*
— **al·ter·na·tive·ness** *noun*

²alternative *noun* (1624)
1 a : a proposition or situation offering a choice between two or more things only one of which may be chosen **b :** an opportunity for deciding between two or more courses or propositions
2 a : one of two or more things, courses, or propositions to be chosen **b :** something which can be chosen instead ⟨the only *alternative* to intervention⟩ ☐
synonym see CHOICE

alternative school *noun* (1972)
: an elementary or secondary school with a nontraditional curriculum

al·ter·na·tor \'òl-tər-,nā-tər *also* 'al-\ *noun* (1892)
: an electric generator for producing alternating current

alt·horn \'alt-,hòrn\ *noun* [German, from *alt* alto + *Horn* horn] (1859)
: an alto saxhorn

al·though *also* **al·tho** \òl-'thō\ *conjunction* [Middle English *although*, from *al* all + *though*] (14th century)
: in spite of the fact that **:** even though

al·tim·e·ter \al-'ti-mə-tər, 'al-tə-,mē-tər\ *noun* [Latin *altus* + English *-meter*] (circa 1828)
: an instrument for measuring altitude; *especially* **:** an aneroid barometer designed to register changes in atmospheric pressure accompanying changes in altitude
— **al·tim·e·try** \al-'ti-mə-trē\ *noun*

al·ti·pla·no \,al-ti-'plä-(,)nō\ *noun, plural* **-nos** [American Spanish, from Latin *altus* + *planum* plain] (1919)
: a high plateau or plain **:** TABLELAND

al·ti·tude \'al-tə-,tüd *also* -,tyüd\ *noun* [Middle English, from Latin *altitudo* height, depth, from *altus* high, deep — more at OLD] (14th century)
1 a : the angular elevation of a celestial object above the horizon **b :** the vertical elevation of an object above a surface (as sea level or land) of a planet or natural satellite **c** (1) **:** a perpendicular line segment from a vertex of a geometric figure (as a triangle or a pyramid) to the opposite side or the opposite side extended or from a side or face to a parallel side or face or the side or face extended (2) **:** the length of an altitude
2 : a high level (as of quality or feeling) ⟨the *altitudes* of his anger⟩

3 a : vertical distance or extent **b :** position at a height **c :** an elevated region **:** EMINENCE — usually used in plural
synonym see HEIGHT
— **al·ti·tu·di·nal** \,al-tə-'tüd-ᵊn-əl, -'tyü-\ *adjective*
— **al·ti·tu·di·nous** \-ᵊn-əs\ *adjective*

altitude sickness *noun* (1920)
: the effects (as nosebleed or nausea) of oxygen deficiency in the blood and tissues developed in rarefied air at high altitudes

¹al·to \'al-(,)tō\ *noun, plural* **altos** [Italian, literally, high, from Latin *altus*] (circa 1724)
1 a : COUNTERTENOR **b :** CONTRALTO
2 : the second highest voice part in a 4-part chorus
3 : a member of a family of instruments having a range lower than that of the treble or soprano; *especially* **:** an alto saxophone

²alto *adjective* (circa 1724)
: relating to or having the range or part of an alto

al·to·cu·mu·lus \,al-tō-'kyü-myə-ləs\ *noun, plural* **-li** \-,lī, -,lē\ [New Latin, from Latin *altus* + New Latin *-o-* + *cumulus*] (1894)
: a fleecy cloud formation consisting of large whitish globular cloudlets with shaded portions — see CLOUD illustration

¹al·to·geth·er \,òl-tə-'ge-thər\ *adverb* [Middle English *altogedere*, from *al* all + *togedere* together] (13th century)
1 : WHOLLY, COMPLETELY ⟨an *altogether* different problem⟩ ⟨stopped crying *altogether*⟩
2 : in all **:** ALL TOLD ⟨spent a hundred dollars *altogether*⟩
3 : on the whole **:** in the main ⟨*altogether* their efforts were successful⟩

²altogether *noun* (1894)
: NUDE — used with *the* ⟨posed in the *altogether*⟩

al·to–re·lie·vo *or* **al·to–ri·lie·vo** \,al-(,)tō-ri-'lē-(,)vō, ,äl-(,)tō-rēl-'yä-(,)vō\ *noun, plural* **alto–relievos** *or* **al·to–ri·lie·vi** \,äl-(,)tō-rēl-'yä-(,)vē\ [Italian *altorilievo*] (1664)
1 : HIGH RELIEF
2 : a sculpture in high relief

al·to·stra·tus \,al-tō-'strā-təs, -'stra-\ *noun, plural* **-ti** \-,tī\ [New Latin, from Latin *altus* + New Latin *-o-* + *stratus*] (1894)
: a cloud formation similar to cirrostratus but darker and at a lower level — see CLOUD illustration

al·tri·cial \al-'tri-shəl\ *adjective* [Latin *altric-, altrix*, feminine of *altor* one who nourishes, from *alere* to nourish — more at OLD] (1872)
: being hatched or born or having young that are hatched or born in a very immature and helpless condition so as to require care for some time ⟨*altricial* birds⟩ — compare PRECOCIAL

al·tru·ism \'al-trü-,i-zəm\ *noun* [French *altruisme*, from *autrui* other people, from Old French, oblique case form of *autre* other, from Latin *alter*] (1853)
1 : unselfish regard for or devotion to the welfare of others
2 : behavior by an animal that is not beneficial to or may be harmful to itself but that benefits others of its species

— **al·tru·ist** \-trü-ist\ *noun*
— **al·tru·is·tic** \ˌal-trü-'is-tik\ *adjective*
— **al·tru·is·ti·cal·ly** \-ti-k(ə-)lē\ *adverb*

al·u·la \'al-yə-lə\ *noun, plural* **-lae** \-ˌlē, -ˌlī\ [New Latin, from Latin, diminutive of *ala* wing — more at AISLE] (1772)
: the process of a bird's wing corresponding to the thumb and bearing a few short quills — called also *bastard wing*

¹al·um \'a-ləm\ *noun* [Middle English, from Middle French *alum, alun,* from Latin *alumen*] (14th century)
1 : a potassium aluminum sulfate KAl$(SO_4)_2 \cdot 12H_2O$ or an ammonium aluminum sulfate $NH_4Al(SO_4)_2 \cdot 12H_2O$ used especially as an emetic and as an astringent and styptic
2 : any of various double salts isomorphous with potassium aluminum sulfate
3 : ALUMINUM SULFATE

²alum \ə-'ləm\ *noun* [by shortening] (1930)
: ALUMNUS, ALUMNA

alu·mi·na \ə-'lü-mə-nə\ *noun* [New Latin, from Latin *alumin-, alumen* alum] (1801)
: aluminum oxide Al_2O_3 occuring native as corundum and in hydrated forms (as in bauxite)

alu·mi·nate \-nət\ *noun* (1841)
: a compound of alumina with a metallic oxide

al·u·min·i·um \ˌal-yə-'mi-nē-əm\ *noun* [New Latin, from *alumina*] (1812)
chiefly British : ALUMINUM

alu·mi·nize \ə-'lü-mə-ˌnīz\ *transitive verb* **-nized; -niz·ing** (1934)
: to treat or coat with aluminum

alu·mi·no·sil·i·cate \ə-ˌlü-mə-nō-'si-lə-ˌkāt, -'si-li-kət\ *noun* [Latin *alumin-, alumen* + *-o-* + International Scientific Vocabulary *silicate*] (1907)
: a combined silicate and aluminate

alu·mi·nous \ə-'lü-mə-nəs\ *adjective* (15th century)
: of, relating to, or containing alum or aluminum

alu·mi·num \ə-'lü-mə-nəm\ *noun, often attributive* [New Latin, from *alumina*] (1812)
: a bluish silver-white malleable ductile light trivalent metallic element that has good electrical and thermal conductivity, high reflectivity, and resistance to oxidation and is the most abundant metal in the earth's crust where it always occurs in combination — see ELEMENT table

aluminum sulfate *noun* (1873)
: a white salt $Al_2(SO_4)_3$ usually made by treating bauxite with sulfuric acid and used in making paper, in water purification, and in tanning

alum·na \ə-'ləm-nə\ *noun, plural* **-nae** \-(ˌ)nē *also* -ˌnī\ [Latin, feminine of *alumnus*] (1879)
1 : a girl or woman who has attended or has graduated from a particular school, college, or university
2 : a girl or woman who is a former member, employee, contributor, or inmate

alum·nus \ə-'ləm-nəs\ *noun, plural* **-ni** \-ˌnī\ [Latin, foster son, pupil, from *alere* to nourish — more at OLD] (1645)
1 : one who has attended or has graduated from a particular school, college, or university
2 : one who is a former member, employee, contributor, or inmate

al·um·root \'a-ləm-ˌrüt, -ˌrút\ *noun* (1813)
: any of a genus (*Heuchera*) of North American herbs of the saxifrage family having basal rounded or lobed toothed leaves; *especially* : one (*H. americana*) of eastern North America

al·u·nite \'al-yə-ˌnīt, 'a-lə-\ *noun* [French, from *alun* alum] (1868)
: a mineral that consists of a hydrous potassium aluminum sulfate and occurs in massive form or in rhombohedral crystals

al·ve·o·lar \al-'vē-(ə-)lər\ *adjective* (1799)
1 : of, relating to, resembling, or having alveoli; *especially* : relating to or consti-

tuting the part of the jaws where the teeth arise, the air-containing cells of the lungs, or glands with secretory cells about a central space
2 : articulated with the tip of the tongue touching or near the teethridge
— **al·ve·o·lar·ly** *adverb*

al·ve·o·late \-lət\ *adjective* (circa 1823)
: pitted like a honeycomb ⟨*alveolate* pollen⟩

al·ve·o·lus \al-'vē-ə-ləs\ *noun, plural* **-li** \-ˌlī, -(ˌ)lē\ [New Latin, from Latin, diminutive of *alveus* cavity, hollow, from *alvus* belly, beehive; akin to Lithuanian *aulys* beehive, Greek *aulos* tube, flute] (circa 1706)
1 : a small cavity or pit: as **a** : a socket for a tooth **b** : an air-containing cell of the lungs **c** : an acinus of a compound gland **d** : a cell or compartment of a honeycomb
2 : TEETHRIDGE

al·way \'ól-(ˌ)wā\ *adverb* [Middle English *alwey, alneway,* from Old English *ealne weg,* literally, all the way, from *ealne* (accusative of *eall* all) + *weg* (accusative) way — more at WAY] (14th century)
archaic : ALWAYS

al·ways \'ól-wēz, -wəz, -(ˌ)wāz *also* 'ó-\ *adverb* [Middle English *alwayes,* from *alwey*] (14th century)
1 : at all times : INVARIABLY
2 : FOREVER, PERPETUALLY
3 : at any rate : in any event ⟨as a last resort one can *always* work⟩

Al·yce clover \'a-ləs-\ *noun* [probably by folk etymology from New Latin *Alysicarpus,* genus name, from Greek *halysis* chain + *karpos* fruit] (1941)
: a low spreading annual Old World legume (*Alysicarpus vaginalis*) used in the southern U.S. as a cover crop and for hay and forage

alys·sum \ə-'li-səm\ *noun* [New Latin, from Greek *alysson,* plant believed to cure rabies, from neuter of *alyssos* curing rabies, from *a-* + *lyssa* rabies] (1548)
1 : any of a genus (*Alyssum*) of Old World herbs of the mustard family with small usually yellow racemose flowers
2 : SWEET ALYSSUM

Alz·hei·mer's disease \'älts-ˌhī-mərz-, 'alts-\ *noun* [Alois *Alzheimer* (died 1915) German physician] (1912)
: a degenerative disease of the central nervous system characterized especially by premature senile mental deterioration — called also *Alzheimer's* ◇

am [Middle English, from Old English *eom;* akin to Old Norse *em* am, Latin *sum,* Greek *eimi*] *present 1st singular of* BE

AM \'ā-ˌem\ *noun, often attributive* [amplitude modulation] (1940)
: a broadcasting system using amplitude modulation; *also* : a radio receiver of such a system

ama \'ä-(ˌ)mä\ *noun, plural* **amas** *or* **ama** [Japanese] (1946)
: a Japanese diver especially for pearls

amah \'ä-(ˌ)mä\ *noun* [Portuguese *ama* wet nurse, from Medieval Latin *amma*] (1839)
: an Oriental female servant; *especially* : a Chinese nurse

amain \ə-'mān\ *adverb* (1540)
1 : with all one's might ⟨attacking a huge rack of beef with a cleaver, she flailed away *amain* —Jay Jacobs⟩
2 *archaic* **a** : at full speed **b** : in great haste
3 *archaic* : to a high degree : EXCEEDINGLY ⟨they whom I favour thrive in wealth *amain* —John Milton⟩

Am·a·le·kite \'a-mə-lə-ˌkīt, ə-'ma-lə-ˌkīt\ *noun* [Hebrew *'Ămālēqī,* plural from *'Ămālēq* Amalek, grandson of Esau] (1560)
: a member of an ancient nomadic people living south of Canaan

amal·gam \ə-'mal-gəm\ *noun* [Middle English *amalgame,* from Middle French, from Medieval Latin *amalgama*] (15th century)
1 : an alloy of mercury with another metal that

is solid or liquid at room temperature according to the proportion of mercury present and is used especially in making tooth cements
2 : a mixture of different elements : COMBINATION

amal·gam·ate \-gə-ˌmāt\ *transitive verb* **-at·ed; -at·ing** (1617)
: to unite in or as if in an amalgam; *especially* : to merge into a single body
synonym see MIX
— **amal·gam·ator** \-ˌmā-tər\ *noun*

amal·gam·ation \ə-ˌmal-gə-'mā-shən\ *noun* (1612)
1 a : the action or process of amalgamating : UNITING **b** : the state of being amalgamated
2 : the result of amalgamating : AMALGAM
3 : CONSOLIDATION, MERGER ⟨*amalgamation* of two corporations⟩

aman·dine \ˌä-män-'dēn\ *adjective* [French] (1945)
: prepared or served with almonds

am·a·ni·ta \ˌa-mə-'nī-tə, -'nē-\ *noun* [New Latin, genus name, from Greek *amanitai,* plural, a kind of fungus] (1899)
: any of a genus (*Amanita*) of white-spored fungi that typically have a volva and an annulus about the stipe and that includes some deadly poisonous forms

am·a·ni·tin \-'nī-t°n, -'nē-\ *noun* [*amanita* + *-in*] (circa 1847)
: a highly toxic peptide that is produced by the death cap and that selectively inhibits mammalian RNA polymerase

amanita

aman·ta·dine \ə-'man-tə-ˌdēn\ *noun* [International Scientific Vocabulary *amantad-* (alteration of *adamantane,* $C_{10}H_{16}$) + *amine*] (1964)
: a drug used especially as the hydrochloride $C_{10}H_{17}N \cdot HCl$ to prevent infection (as by an influenza virus) by interfering with virus penetration into host cells

aman·u·en·sis \ə-ˌman-yə-'wen(t)-səs\ *noun, plural* **-en·ses** \-(ˌ)sēz\ [Latin, from (*servus*) *a manu* slave with secretarial duties] (1619)
: one employed to write from dictation or to copy manuscript

am·a·ranth \'a-mə-ˌran(t)th\ *noun* [Latin *amarantus,* a flower, from Greek *amaranton,* from neuter of *amarantos* unfading, from *a-* + *marainein* to waste away] (1548)

◇ **WORD HISTORY**

Alzheimer's disease Alzheimer's disease is named after the German neurologist Alois Alzheimer (1864–1915). The majority of his medical contributions centered on the structure of nerve tissue. In 1906 he undertook the autopsy of a 55-year-old patient who had died with severe dementia. In examining the brain he noted the abnormal presence of neuritic plaques, structures that had previously been found only in the brains of quite elderly patients. He also noted a neurofibrillary tangle (an abnormal fibrous structure within the neurons) that had not been previously described and whose presence signaled the discovery of a new disease entity. In 1907 Alzheimer published his classic description of premature senile dementia. The disease was later named *Alzheimersche Krankheit* (German for "Alzheimer's disease") by the psychiatrist Emil Kraepelin.

1 : any of a large genus (*Amaranthus* of the family Amaranthaceae, the amaranth family) of coarse herbs including forms cultivated as food crops and various pigweeds
2 : a flower that never fades
3 : a red azo dye
am·a·ran·thine \ˌa-mə-'ran(t)-thən, -'ran-ˌthīn\ *adjective* (1667)
1 a : of or relating to an amaranth **b** : UNDYING
2 : of the color amaranth
am·a·ret·to \ˌa-mə-'re-(ˌ)tō, ˌä-\ *noun* [Italian, diminutive of *amaro* bitter, from Latin *amarus*] (1945)
1 am·a·ret·ti \-(ˌ)tē\ *plural* : macaroons made with bitter almonds
2 *often capitalized* : an almond-flavored liqueur
am·a·ryl·lis \ˌa-mə-'ri-ləs\ *noun* [New Latin, genus name, probably from Latin, name of a shepherdess in Virgil's *Eclogues*] (circa 1794)
: an autumn-flowering South African bulbous herb (*Amaryllis belladonna* of the family Amaryllidaceae, the amaryllis family) widely grown for its deep red to whitish umbellate flowers; *also* : a plant of any of several related genera (as *Hippeastrum* or *Sprekelia*)
amass \ə-'mas\ *verb* [Middle French *amasser*, from Old French, from *a*- (from Latin *ad*-) + *masser* to gather into a mass, from *masse* mass] (15th century)
transitive verb
1 : to collect for oneself : ACCUMULATE ⟨amass a great fortune⟩
2 : to collect into a mass : GATHER ⟨must select rather than simply *amass* details⟩
intransitive verb
: to come together : ASSEMBLE
— **amass·er** *noun*
— **amass·ment** \-mənt\ *noun*
am·a·teur \'a-mə-(ˌ)tər, -ˌtür, -ˌtyür, -ˌchür, -chər\ *noun, often attributive* [French, from Latin *amator* lover, from *amare* to love] (1784)
1 : DEVOTEE, ADMIRER
2 : one who engages in a pursuit, study, science, or sport as a pastime rather than as a profession
3 : one lacking in experience and competence in an art or science ☆
— **am·a·teur·ish** \ˌa-mə-'tər-ish, -'t(y)ùr-, -'chùr-, -'chər-\ *adjective*
— **am·a·teur·ish·ly** *adverb*
— **am·a·teur·ish·ness** *noun*
— **am·a·teur·ism** \'a-mə-ˌtər-ˌi-zəm, -ˌt(y)ùr-, -ˌchùr-, -ˌtə-ˌri-, -ˌchə-ˌri-\ *noun*
Ama·ti \ä-'mä-tē, ə-\ *noun, plural* **Amatis** (1833)
: a violin made by a member of the Amati family of Cremona
am·a·tive \'a-mə-tiv\ *adjective* [Medieval Latin *amativus*, from Latin *amatus*, past participle of *amare*] (1636)
: AMOROUS 1, 3
— **am·a·tive·ly** *adverb*
— **am·a·tive·ness** *noun*
am·a·to·ry \'a-mə-ˌtōr-ē, -ˌtòr-\ *adjective* (1599)
: of, relating to, or expressing sexual love
am·au·ro·sis \ˌa-mò-'rō-səs\ *noun, plural* **-ro·ses** \-ˌsēz\ [New Latin, from Greek *amaurōsis*, literally, dimming, from *amauroun* to dim, from *amauros* dim] (circa 1657)
: partial or complete loss of sight occurring especially without an externally perceptible change in the eye
— **am·au·rot·ic** \-'rä-tik\ *adjective*
amaurotic idiocy *noun* (1896)
: any of several recessive genetic conditions characterized by the accumulation of lipid-containing cells in the viscera and nervous system, mental retardation, and impaired vision or blindness; *especially* : TAY-SACHS DISEASE
¹amaze \ə-'māz\ *verb* **amazed; amaz·ing** [Middle English *amasen*, from Old English

āmasian, from *ā*- (perfective prefix) + (assumed) *masian* to confuse — more at ABIDE] (before 12th century)
transitive verb
1 *obsolete* : BEWILDER, PERPLEX
2 : to fill with wonder : ASTOUND
intransitive verb
: to show or cause astonishment
synonym see SURPRISE
— **amaz·ed·ly** \-'mā-zəd-lē\ *adverb*
²amaze *noun* (15th century)
: AMAZEMENT
amaze·ment \ə-'māz-mənt\ *noun* (1595)
1 *obsolete* : CONSTERNATION, BEWILDERMENT
2 : the quality or state of being amazed
3 : something that amazes
amaz·ing·ly \ə-'mā-ziŋ-lē\ *adverb* (1673)
1 : to an amazing degree ⟨amazingly low prices⟩
2 : what is amazing ⟨amazingly, the runnerup was only two seconds behind —Jim Doherty⟩
am·a·zon \'a-mə-ˌzän, -zən\ *noun* [Middle English, from Latin, from Greek *Amazōn*] (14th century)
1 *capitalized* : a member of a race of female warriors of Greek mythology
2 : a tall strong often masculine woman
Am·a·zo·nian \ˌa-mə-'zō-nē-ən, -nyən\ *adjective* (1594)
1 : relating to, resembling, or befitting an Amazon or an amazon
2 : of or relating to the Amazon River or its valley
am·a·zon·ite \'a-mə-zə-ˌnīt\ *noun* [*Amazon* River] (circa 1879)
: an apple-green or bluish-green microcline
am·a·zon·stone \-zən-ˌstōn\ *noun* (1836)
: AMAZONITE
am·bage \'am-bij\ *noun, plural* **am·ba·ges** \am-'bā-(ˌ)jēz, 'am-bi-jəz\ [back-formation from Middle English *ambages*, from Middle French or Latin; Middle French, from Latin, from *ambi*- + *agere* to drive — more at AGENT] (14th century)
1 *archaic* : AMBIGUITY, CIRCUMLOCUTION — usually used in plural
2 *plural, archaic* : indirect ways or proceedings
am·bas·sa·dor \am-'ba-sə-dər, əm-, im-, -ˌdòr, -'bas-dər\ *noun* [Middle English *ambassadour*, from Middle French *ambassadeur*, ultimately of Germanic origin; akin to Old High German *ambaht* service] (14th century)
1 : an official envoy; *especially* : a diplomatic agent of the highest rank accredited to a foreign government or sovereign as the resident representative of his own government or sovereign or appointed for a special and often temporary diplomatic assignment
2 a : an authorized representative or messenger **b** : an unofficial representative ⟨traveling abroad as *ambassadors* of goodwill⟩
— **am·bas·sa·do·ri·al** \-ˌba-sə-'dòr-ē-əl, -ˌdòr-\ *adjective*
— **am·bas·sa·dor·ship** \-'ba-sə-dər-ˌship\ *noun*
ambassador–at–large *noun, plural* **ambassadors–at–large** (1908)
: a minister of the highest rank not accredited to a particular foreign government or sovereign
am·bas·sa·dress \am-'ba-sə-drəs, əm-, im-\ *noun* (1594)
1 : a woman who is an ambassador
2 : the wife of an ambassador
am·beer \'am-ˌbir\ *noun* [probably alteration of *amber*; from its color] (1848)
chiefly Southern & southern Midland : TOBACCO JUICE
¹am·ber \'am-bər\ *noun* [Middle English *ambre*, from Middle French, from Medieval Latin *ambra*, from Arabic *'anbar* ambergris] (14th century)
1 : a hard yellowish to brownish translucent fossil resin that takes a fine polish and is used chiefly in making ornamental objects (as beads)

2 : a variable color averaging a dark orange yellow
²amber *adjective* (15th century)
1 : consisting of amber
2 : resembling amber; *especially* : having the color amber
am·ber·gris \'am-bər-ˌgris, -ˌgrē(s)\ *noun* [Middle English *ambregris*, from Middle French *ambre gris*, from *ambre* + *gris* gray — more at GRIZZLE] (15th century)
: a waxy substance found floating in or on the shores of tropical waters, believed to originate in the intestines of the sperm whale, and used in perfumery as a fixative
am·ber·i·na \ˌam-bə-'rē-nə\ *noun* [from *Amberina*, a trademark] (1885)
: a late 19th century American clear glassware of a graduated color that shades from ruby to amber
am·ber·jack \-ˌjak\ *noun* [from its color] (circa 1893)
: any of several carangid fishes (genus *Seriola*); *especially* : a large vigorous sport fish (*S. dumerili*) of the western Atlantic
ambi- *prefix* [Latin *ambi*-, *amb*- both, around; akin to Latin *ambo* both, Greek *amphō* both, *amphi* around — more at BY]
: both ⟨*ambivalence*⟩
am·bi·dex·ter·i·ty \ˌam-bi-(ˌ)dek-'ster-ə-tē\ *noun* (1593)
: the quality or state of being ambidextrous
am·bi·dex·trous \ˌam-bi-'dek-strəs\ *adjective* [Late Latin *ambidexter*, from Latin *ambi*- + *dexter* right-hand — more at DEXTER] (1646)
1 : using both hands with equal ease
2 : unusually skillful : VERSATILE
3 : characterized by duplicity : DOUBLE-DEALING
— **am·bi·dex·trous·ly** *adverb*
am·bi·ence *or* **am·bi·ance** \'am-bē-ən(t)s, 'äm-bē-än(t)s; ä"-byä"s\ *noun* [French *ambiance*, from *ambiant* ambient] (1889)
: a feeling or mood associated with a particular place, person, or thing : ATMOSPHERE
¹am·bi·ent \'am-bē-ənt\ *adjective* [Latin *ambient-, ambiens*, present participle of *ambire* to go around, from *ambi*- + *ire* to go — more at ISSUE] (1596)
: existing or present on all sides : ENCOMPASSING
²ambient *noun* (1624)
: an encompassing atmosphere : ENVIRONMENT
am·bi·gu·i·ty \ˌam-bə-'gyü-ə-tē\ *noun, plural* **-ties** (15th century)
1 a : the quality or state of being ambiguous especially in meaning **b** : an ambiguous word or expression
2 : UNCERTAINTY
am·big·u·ous \am-'bi-gyə-wəs\ *adjective* [Latin *ambiguus*, from *ambigere* to be undecided, from *ambi*- + *agere* to drive — more at AGENT] (1528)

1 a : doubtful or uncertain especially from obscurity or indistinctness ⟨eyes of an *ambiguous* color⟩ **b :** INEXPLICABLE
2 : capable of being understood in two or more possible senses or ways
synonym see OBSCURE
— **am·big·u·ous·ly** *adverb*
— **am·big·u·ous·ness** *noun*
am·bi·sex·u·al \,am-bi-'sek-sh(ə-)wəl, -'sek-shəl\ *adjective* (1939)
: BISEXUAL
— **ambisexual** *noun*
— **am·bi·sex·u·al·i·ty** \-,sek-shə-'wa-lə-tē\ *noun*
am·bit \'am-bət\ *noun* [Middle English, from Latin *ambitus,* from *ambire*] (1597)
1 : CIRCUIT, COMPASS
2 : the bounds or limits of a place or district
3 : a sphere of action, expression, or influence
: SCOPE
¹am·bi·tion \am-'bi-shən\ *noun* [Middle English, from Middle French or Latin; Middle French, from Latin *ambition-, ambitio,* literally, act of soliciting for votes, from *ambire*] (14th century)
1 a : an ardent desire for rank, fame, or power **b :** desire to achieve a particular end
2 : the object of ambition
3 : a desire for activity or exertion ⟨felt sick and had no *ambition*⟩ ☆ ◇
— **am·bi·tion·less** \-ləs\ *adjective*
²ambition *transitive verb* (1664)
: to have as one's ambition **:** DESIRE
am·bi·tious \am-'bi-shəs\ *adjective* (14th century)
1 a : having or controlled by ambition **b :** having a desire to achieve a particular goal
: ASPIRING
2 : resulting from, characterized by, or showing ambition
— **am·bi·tious·ly** *adverb*
— **am·bi·tious·ness** *noun*
am·biv·a·lence \am-'bi-və-lən(t)s\ *noun* [International Scientific Vocabulary] (1918)
1 : simultaneous and contradictory attitudes or feelings (as attraction and repulsion) toward an object, person, or action
2 a : continual fluctuation (as between one thing and its opposite) **b :** uncertainty as to which approach to follow
— **am·biv·a·lent** \-lənt\ *adjective*
— **am·biv·a·lent·ly** *adverb*
am·bi·ver·sion \,am-bi-'vər-zhən, -shən\ *noun* [ambi- + -version (as in *introversion*)] (1927)
: the personality configuration of an ambivert
am·bi·vert \'am-bi-,vərt\ *noun* [ambi- + -vert (as in *introvert*)] (1927)
: a person having characteristics of both extrovert and introvert
¹am·ble \'am-bəl\ *intransitive verb* **am·bled; am·bling** \-b(ə-)liŋ\ [Middle English, from Middle French *ambler,* from Latin *ambulare* to walk, from *ambi- + -ulare* (verb base akin to Middle Welsh *el* he may go, Greek *ēlythe* he went) — more at ELASTIC] (14th century)
: to go at or as if at an amble **:** SAUNTER
— **am·bler** \-b(ə-)lər\ *noun*
²amble *noun* (14th century)
1 a : an easy gait of a horse in which the legs on the same side of the body move together **b :** ⁷RACK b
2 : an easy gait
3 : a leisurely walk
am·blyg·o·nite \am-'bli-gə-,nīt\ *noun* [German *Amblygonit,* from Greek *amblygōnios* obtuse-angled, from *amblys* blunt, dull + *gōnia* angle — more at MOLLIFY, -GON] (circa 1828)
: a mineral that consists of basic lithium aluminum phosphate commonly containing sodium and fluorine and occurs in white cleavable masses
am·bly·opia \,am-blē-'ō-pē-ə\ *noun* [New Latin, from Greek *amblyōpia,* from *amblys + -ōpia* -opia] (circa 1706)

: dimness of sight especially in one eye without apparent change in the eye structures — called also *lazy eye*
— **am·bly·opic** \-'ō-pik, -'ä-pik\ *adjective*
Am·boi·nese \,am-,bȯi-'nēz, -'nēs, am-'bȯi-,\ *or* **Am·bo·nese** \,am-bə-'nēz, -'nēs\ *noun, plural* **Amboinese** *or* **Ambonese** (circa 1864)
1 : a native or inhabitant of Ambon
2 : the group of closely related Austronesian languages spoken on Ambon
— **Amboinese** *or* **Ambonese** *adjective*
am·boy·na *or* **am·boi·na** \am-'bȯi-nə\ *noun* [*Amboina,* Moluccas, Indonesia] (circa 1859)
: a mottled curly-grained wood of a leguminous tree (*Pterocarpus indicus*) of southeastern Asia
am·bro·sia \am-'brō-zh(ē-)ə\ *noun* [Latin, from Greek, literally, immortality, from *ambrotos* immortal, from *a- + -mbrotos* (akin to *brotos* mortal) — more at MURDER] (15th century)
1 a : the food of the Greek and Roman gods **b :** the ointment or perfume of the gods
2 : something extremely pleasing to taste or smell
3 : a dessert made of oranges and shredded coconut ◇
— **am·bro·sial** \-zh(ē-)əl\ *adjective*
— **am·bro·sial·ly** \-zh(ē-)ə-lē\ *adverb*
ambrosia beetle *noun* (circa 1900)
: any of various small wood-boring beetles (family Scolytidae) that cultivate a fungus on which they feed and raise their larvae
am·bro·type \'am-brə-,tīp\ *noun* [Greek *am-brotos* + English *type*] (1858)
: a positive picture made of a photographic negative on glass backed by a dark surface
am·bry \'am-brē; 'äm-rē, 'ȯm-\ *noun, plural* **ambries** [Middle English *almery,* from Middle French *almarie, armarie,* from Latin *armarium,* from *arma* weapons — more at ARM] (14th century)
1 *dialect chiefly British :* PANTRY
2 : a recess in a church wall (as for holding sacramental vessels)
ambs·ace \'äm-,zās\ *noun* [Middle English *ambes ace,* from Old French, from *ambes* both + *as* aces] (13th century)
archaic : the lowest throw at dice; *also*
: something worthless or unlucky
am·bu·la·cral \,am-byə-'la-krəl, -'lā-\ *adjective* (1836)
: of, relating to, or being any of the radial areas of echinoderms along which run the principal nerves, blood vessels, and elements of the water-vascular system ⟨*ambulacral* grooves⟩
am·bu·la·crum \-krəm\ *noun, plural* **-cra** \-krə\ [New Latin, from Latin, alley, from *ambulare* to walk — more at AMBLE] (1837)
: an ambulacral area or part
am·bu·lance \'am-byə-lən(t)s, -bə- *also* -,lan(t)s\ *noun* [French, from (*hôpital*) *ambulant,* literally, ambulant field hospital, from *ambulant itinerant,* from Latin *ambulant-, ambulans,* present participle of *ambulare*] (1809)
: a vehicle equipped for transporting the injured or sick
ambulance chaser *noun* (1897)
: a lawyer or lawyer's agent who incites accident victims to sue for damages
— **ambulance chasing** *noun*
am·bu·lant \'am-byə-lənt\ *adjective* (1619)
: moving about **:** AMBULATORY
am·bu·late \-,lāt\ *intransitive verb* **-lat·ed; -lat·ing** [Latin *ambulatus,* past participle of *ambulare*] (circa 1623)
: to move from place to place **:** WALK
— **am·bu·la·tion** \,am-byə-'lā-shən\ *noun*
¹am·bu·la·to·ry \'am-byə-lə-,tōr-ē, -,tȯr-\ *adjective* (1622)
1 : of, relating to, or adapted to walking; *also* **:** occurring during a walk
2 : moving from place to place **:** ITINERANT

3 : capable of being altered ⟨a will is *ambulatory* until the testator's death⟩
4 a : able to walk about and not bedridden **b :** performed on or involving an ambulatory patient or an outpatient ⟨*ambulatory* medical care⟩ ⟨an *ambulatory* electrocardiogram⟩
— **am·bu·la·to·ri·ly** \,am-byə-lə-'tȯr-ə-lē, -'tȯr-\ *adverb*
²ambulatory *noun, plural* **-ries** (circa 1616)
: a sheltered place (as in a cloister or church) for walking
am·bus·cade \'am-bə-,skād, ,am-bə-'\ *noun* [Middle French *embuscade,* modification of Old Italian *imboscata,* from *imboscare* to place in ambush, from *in* (from Latin) + *bosco* forest, of Germanic origin; akin to Old High German *busc* forest — more at IN, BUSH] (circa 1588)
: AMBUSH
— **ambuscade** *verb*
— **am·bus·cad·er** *noun*

\ə\ abut \ˌ,ə̇\ kitten \ər\ further \a\ ash \ā\ ace
\ä\ mop, mar \au̇\ out \ch\ chin \e\ bet \ē\ easy
\g\ go \i\ hit \ī\ ice \j\ job \ŋ\ sing \ō\ go
\ȯ\ law \ȯi\ boy \th\ thin \th\ the \ü\ loot \u̇\ foot
\y\ yet \zh\ vision *see also* Guide to Pronunciation

¹am·bush \'am-ˌbu̇sh\ *verb* [Middle English *embushen*, from Middle French *embuschier*, from *en* in (from Latin *in*) + *busche* stick of firewood] (14th century)
transitive verb
1 : to station in ambush
2 : to attack from an ambush **:** WAYLAY
intransitive verb
: to lie in wait **:** LURK
— **am·bush·er** *noun*
— **am·bush·ment** \-mənt\ *noun*
²ambush *noun* (15th century)
1 : a trap in which concealed persons lie in wait to attack by surprise
2 : the persons stationed in ambush; *also* **:** their concealed position
3 : an attack especially from an ambush
ame·ba, ame·boid *variant of* AMOEBA, AMOEBOID
am·e·bi·a·sis \ˌa-mi-'bī-ə-səs\ *noun, plural* **-a·ses** \-ˌsēz\ (1905)
: infection with or disease caused by amoebas (especially *Entamoeba histolytica*)
ame·bic dysentery \ə-'mē-bik-\ *noun* (1891)
: acute human intestinal amebiasis caused by an amoeba (*Entamoeba histolytica*) and marked by dysentery, gripes, and erosion of the intestinal wall
ame·bo·cyte *variant of* AMOEBOCYTE
ameer *variant of* EMIR
ame·lio·rate \ə-'mēl-yə-ˌrāt, -'mē-lē-ə-\ *verb* **-rat·ed; -rat·ing** [alteration of *meliorate*] (1767)
transitive verb
: to make better or more tolerable
intransitive verb
: to grow better
synonym see IMPROVE
— **ame·lio·ra·tion** \-ˌmēl-yə-'rā-shən, -ˌmē-lē-ə-\ *noun*
— **ame·lio·ra·tive** \-'mēl-yə-ˌrā-tiv, -'mē-lē-ə-\ *adjective*
— **ame·lio·ra·tor** \-ˌrā-tər\ *noun*
— **ame·lio·ra·to·ry** \-rə-ˌtōr-ē, -ˌtòr-\ *adjective*
am·e·lo·blast \'a-mə-lō-ˌblast\ *noun* [obsolete *amel* enamel (Middle English, ultimately from Old French *esmail*) + *-o-* + *-blast* — more at ENAMEL] (1882)
: one of a group of columnar cells that produce and deposit enamel on the surface of a developing vertebrate tooth
amen \(')ä-'men, (')ā-; 'ä- *when sung*\ *interjection* [Middle English, from Old English, from Late Latin, from Greek *amēn*, from Hebrew *āmēn*] (before 12th century)
— used to express solemn ratification (as of an expression of faith) or hearty approval (as of an assertion)
ame·na·ble \ə-'mē-nə-bəl, -'me-\ *adjective* [probably from (assumed) Anglo-French, from Middle French *amener* to lead up, from Old French, from *a-* (from Latin *ad-*) + *mener* to lead, from Late Latin *minare* to drive, from Latin *minari* to threaten — more at MOUNT] (1596)
1 : liable to be brought to account **:** ANSWERABLE ⟨citizens *amenable* to the law⟩
2 a : capable of submission (as to judgment or test) **:** SUITED ⟨the data is *amenable* to analysis⟩ **b :** readily brought to yield, submit, or cooperate **c :** WILLING 1 ⟨was *amenable* to spending more time at home⟩
synonym see RESPONSIBLE, OBEDIENT
— **ame·na·bil·i·ty** \-ˌmē-nə-'bil-ət-ē, -ˌme-\ *noun*
— **ame·na·bly** \-'mē-nə-blē, -'me-\ *adverb*
amen corner \ˌā-ˌmen-\ *noun* (1860)
: a conspicuous corner in a church occupied by fervent worshipers
amend \ə-'mend\ *verb* [Middle English, from Old French *amender*, modification of Latin *emendare*, from *e, ex* out + *menda* fault; akin

to Latin *mendax* lying, *mendicus* beggar, and perhaps to Sanskrit *mindā* physical defect] (13th century)
transitive verb
1 : to put right; *especially* **:** to make emendations in (as a text)
2 a : to change or modify for the better **:** IMPROVE ⟨*amend* the situation⟩ **b :** to alter especially in phraseology; *especially* **:** to alter formally by modification, deletion, or addition ⟨*amend* the constitution⟩
intransitive verb
: to reform oneself
synonym see CORRECT
— **amend·able** \-'men-də-bəl\ *adjective*
— **amend·er** *noun*
amen·da·to·ry \ə-'men-də-ˌtōr-ē, -ˌtòr-\ *adjective* [*amend* + *-atory* (as in *emendatory*)] (circa 1828)
: CORRECTIVE
amend·ment \ə-'men(d)-mənt\ *noun* (13th century)
1 : the act of amending **:** CORRECTION
2 : a material (as compost or sand) that aids plant growth indirectly by improving the condition of the soil
3 a : the process of amending by parliamentary or constitutional procedure **b :** an alteration proposed or effected by this process ⟨the 18th *amendment*⟩
amends \ə-'men(d)z\ *noun plural but singular or plural in construction* [Middle English *amendes*, from Middle French, plural of *amende* reparation, from *amender*] (14th century)
: compensation for a loss or injury **:** RECOMPENSE ⟨make *amends*⟩
ame·ni·ty \ə-'me-nə-tē, -'mē-\ *noun, plural* **-ties** [Middle English *amenite*, from Latin *amoenitat-, amoenitas*, from *amoenus* pleasant] (14th century)
1 a : the quality of being pleasant or agreeable **b** (1) **:** the attractiveness and value of real estate or of a residential structure (2) **:** a feature conducive to such attractiveness and value
2 : something (as a conventional social gesture) that conduces to smoothness or pleasantness of social relationships
3 : something that conduces to comfort, convenience, or enjoyment
amen·or·rhea \ˌā-ˌme-nə-'rē-ə, ˌä-\ *noun* [New Latin, from *a-* + Greek *mēn* month + New Latin *-o-* + *-rrhea* — more at MOON] (1804)
: abnormal absence or suppression of menses
— **amen·or·rhe·ic** \-'rē-ik\ *adjective*
ament \'a-mənt, 'ā-\ *noun* [New Latin *amentum*, from Latin, thong, strap] (1791)
: CATKIN
— **amen·tif·er·ous** \-mən-'ti-f(ə-)rəs\ *adjective*
amen·tia \(ˌ)ā-'men(t)-sh(ē-)ə, (ˌ)ä-\ *noun* [New Latin, from Latin, madness, from *ament-, amens* mad, from *a-* (from *ab-*) + *ment-, mens* mind — more at MIND] (14th century)
: MENTAL RETARDATION; *specifically* **:** a condition of lack of development of intellectual capacity
Am·er·asian \ˌa-mə-'rā-zhən, -shən\ *noun* [*American* + *Asian*] (1953)
: a person of mixed American and Asian descent; *especially* **:** one fathered by an American and especially an American serviceman in Asia
amerce \ə-'mərs\ *transitive verb* **amerced; amerc·ing** [Middle English *amercien*, from Anglo-French *amercier*, from Old French *a merci* at (one's) mercy] (15th century)
: to punish by a fine whose amount is fixed by the court; *broadly* **:** PUNISH
— **amerce·ment** \-'mər-smənt\ *noun*
— **amer·cia·ble** \-'mər-sē-ə-bəl, -'mər-shə-bəl\ *adjective*
¹Amer·i·can \ə-'mer-ə-kən, -'mər-, -'mar-, -i-kən\ *noun* (1578)

1 : an American Indian of North America or South America
2 : a native or inhabitant of North America or South America
3 : a citizen of the U.S.
4 : AMERICAN ENGLISH
²American *adjective* (1598)
1 : of or relating to America
2 : of or relating to the U.S. or its possessions or original territory
— **Amer·i·can·ness** \-kə(n)-nəs\ *noun*
Amer·i·ca·na \ə-ˌmer-ə-'kä-nə, -ˌmər-, -ˌmar-, -'ka-nə\ *noun plural* (1841)
1 : materials concerning or characteristic of America, its civilization, or its culture; *broadly* **:** things typical of America
2 : American culture
American chameleon *noun* (1881)
: a lizard (*Anolis carolinensis*) of the southeastern U.S. that can vary its skin color from green to brown and is often kept as a pet
American cheese *noun* (1804)
: a process cheese made from American cheddar
American dog tick *noun* (1927)
: a common North American ixodid tick (*Dermacentor variabilis*) especially of dogs and humans that is an important vector of Rocky Mountain spotted fever and tularemia — called also *dog tick*
American dream *noun, often D capitalized* (1931)
: an American social ideal that stresses egalitarianism and especially material prosperity
American eel *noun* (circa 1949)
: a yellow to greenish-brown eel (*Anguilla rostrata*) that is lighter below, has 103 to 111 vertebrae, is found in fresh and coastal waters along the Atlantic coasts of North America, and is held to spawn in or near the Sargasso Sea
American elm *noun* (1813)
: a large elm (*Ulmus americana*) with gradually spreading branches and pendulous branchlets that is common in eastern North America
American English *noun* (1806)
: the English language as spoken in the U.S. — used especially with the implication that it is clearly distinguishable from British English yet not so divergent as to be a separate language
Amer·i·ca·nese \ə-ˌmer-ə-kə-'nēz, -ˌmər-, -ˌmar-, -i-kə-, -'nēs\ *noun* (1882)
: AMERICAN ENGLISH
American foxhound *noun* (circa 1891)
: any of an American breed of foxhounds smaller than the English foxhound but with longer ears and a short glossy coat usually of black, tan, and white
American Indian *noun* (1732)
: a member of any of the aboriginal peoples of the western hemisphere except usually the Eskimos; *especially* **:** an American Indian of North America and especially the U.S.
Amer·i·can·isa·tion, Amer·i·can·ise *British variant of* AMERICANIZATION, AMERICANIZE
Amer·i·can·ism \ə-'mer-ə-kə-ˌni-zəm, -'mər-, -'mar-\ *noun* (1781)
1 : a characteristic feature of American English especially as contrasted with British English
2 : attachment or allegiance to the traditions, interests, or ideals of the U.S.
3 a : a custom or trait peculiar to America **b :** the political principles and practices essential to American culture
Amer·i·can·ist \-kə-nist\ *noun* (1881)
1 : a specialist in American culture or history
2 : a specialist in the languages or cultures of the aboriginal inhabitants of America
Amer·i·can·iza·tion \ə-ˌmer-ə-kə-nə-'zā-shən, -ˌmər-, -ˌmar-\ *noun* (1858)
1 : the act or process of Americanizing

2 : instruction of foreigners (as immigrants) in English and in U.S. history, government, and culture

Amer·i·can·ize \ə-'mer-ə-kə-ˌnīz, -'mər-, -'mar-\ *verb* **-ized; -iz·ing** (1797)
transitive verb
1 : to cause to acquire or conform to American characteristics
2 : to bring (as an area) under the political, cultural, or commercial influence of the U.S.
intransitive verb
: to acquire or conform to American traits **:** assimilate to American life or culture

American pit bull terrier *noun* (1950)
: any of a breed of dogs developed to combine the traits of terriers and bulldogs that have extremely powerful jaws and great strength and tenacity — called also *pit bull terrier*

American plan *noun* (1856)
: a hotel plan whereby the daily rates cover the costs of the room and three meals — compare EUROPEAN PLAN

American saddlebred *noun* (1948)
: any of a breed of 3-gaited or 5-gaited saddle horses developed chiefly in Kentucky from Thoroughbreds and smooth-gaited stock — called also *American saddle horse*

American saddlebred

American short·hair *noun* (1974)
: any of a breed of cats with a usually solid-colored or tabby coat; *broadly :* SHORTHAIR

American Sign Language *noun* (1960)
: a sign language for the deaf in which meaning is conveyed by a system of articulated hand gestures and their placement relative to the upper body

American Staffordshire terrier *noun* (1971)
: a strong stocky terrier of a breed originally developed for dogfighting

American Standard Version *noun* (1901)
: an American version of the Bible that is based on the Revised Version and was published in 1901 — called also *American Revised Version*

American trotter *noun* (1894)
: STANDARDBRED

American water spaniel *noun* (1947)
: any of a breed of medium-sized spaniels of American origin that have a thick curly chocolate or liver-colored coat

am·er·i·ci·um \ˌa-mə-'ri-shē-əm, -sē-\ *noun* [New Latin, from *America* + New Latin *-ium*] (1946)
: a radioactive metallic element produced by bombardment of plutonium with high-energy neutrons — see ELEMENT table

Am·er·in·di·an \ˌa-mə-'rin-dē-ən\ *noun* [*American* + *Indian*] (circa 1898)
: AMERICAN INDIAN
— **Am·er·ind** \'a-mə-ˌrind\ *noun or adjective*
— **Amerindian** *adjective*

Ame·slan \'a-məs-ˌlan, 'am-ˌslan\ *noun* (1972)
: AMERICAN SIGN LANGUAGE

Ames test \'āmz-\ *noun* [Bruce N. Ames (born 1928) American biochemist] (1977)
: a test for identifying potential carcinogens by studying their mutagenic effect on bacteria

am·e·thyst \'a-mə-thəst, -ˌ(ˌ)thist\ *noun* [Middle English *amatiste,* from Old French & Latin; Old French, from Latin *amethystus,* from Greek *amethystos,* literally, remedy against drunkenness, from *a-* + *methyein* to be drunk, from *methy* wine — more at MEAD] (13th century)

1 a : a clear purple or bluish violet variety of crystallized quartz that is much used as a jeweler's stone **b :** a deep purple variety of corundum
2 : a moderate purple ◇
— **am·e·thys·tine** \ˌa-mə-'this-tən\ *adjective*

am·e·tro·pia \ˌa-mə-'trō-pē-ə\ *noun* [New Latin, from Greek *ametros* without measure (from *a-* + *metron* measure) + New Latin *-opia* — more at MEASURE] (1875)
: an abnormal refractive condition (as myopia, hyperopia, or astigmatism) of the eye in which images fail to focus upon the retina
— **am·e·tro·pic** \-'trō-pik, -'trä-\ *adjective*

Am·har·ic \am-'har-ik; am-'här-, äm-\ *noun* (1813)
: a Semitic language that is the official language of Ethiopia
— **Amharic** *adjective*

ami·a·ble \'ā-mē-ə-bəl\ *adjective* [Middle English, from Middle French, from Late Latin *amicabilis* friendly, from Latin *amicus* friend; akin to Latin *amare* to love] (14th century)
1 *archaic :* PLEASING, ADMIRABLE
2 a : generally agreeable ⟨an *amiable* comedy⟩
b : being friendly, sociable, and congenial ☆
— **ami·a·bil·i·ty** \ˌā-mē-ə-'bi-lə-tē\ *noun*
— **ami·a·ble·ness** \'ā-mē-ə-bəl-nəs\ *noun*
— **ami·a·bly** \-blē\ *adverb*

am·i·ca·ble \'a-mi-kə-bəl\ *adjective* [Middle English, from Late Latin *amicabilis*] (15th century)
: characterized by friendly goodwill **:** PEACEABLE ☆
— **am·i·ca·bil·i·ty** \ˌa-mi-kə-'bi-lə-tē\ *noun*
— **am·i·ca·ble·ness** \'a-mi-kə-bəl-nəs\ *noun*
— **am·i·ca·bly** \-blē\ *adverb*

am·ice \'a-məs\ *noun* [Middle English *amis,* probably from Middle French, plural of *amit,* from Medieval Latin *amictus,* from Latin, cloak, from *amicire* to wrap around, from *am-, amb-* around + *jacere* to throw — more at AMBI-, JET] (13th century)
: a liturgical vestment made of an oblong piece of cloth usually of white linen and worn about the neck and shoulders and partly under the alb

ami·cus \ə-'mē-kəs, -'mī-\ *noun, plural* **ami·ci** \-'mē-ˌkē, -'mī-ˌsī\ (1951)
: AMICUS CURIAE

amicus cu·ri·ae \-'kyùr-ē-ˌī, -'kùr-, -i-ˌē\ *noun, plural* **amici curiae** [New Latin, literally, friend of the court] (1612)
: one (as a professional person or organization) that is not a party to a particular litigation but that is permitted by the court to advise it in respect to some matter of law that directly affects the case in question

amid \ə-'mid\ *or* **amidst** \-'midst, -'mitst\ *preposition* [*amid* from Middle English *amidde,* from Old English *onmiddan,* from *on* + *middan,* dative of *midde* mid; *amidst* from Middle English *amiddes,* from *amidde* + *-es* -s] (before 12th century)
1 : in or into the middle of **:** surrounded by **:** AMONG
2 a : DURING **b :** with the accompaniment of ⟨resigned *amid* rumors of misconduct⟩

am·i·dase \'a-mə-ˌdās, -ˌdāz\ *noun* [International Scientific Vocabulary] (1921)
: an enzyme that hydrolyzes acid amides usually with the liberation of ammonia

am·ide \'a-ˌmīd, -məd\ *noun* [International Scientific Vocabulary, from New Latin *ammonia*] (circa 1847)
1 : an inorganic compound derived from ammonia by replacement of an atom of hydrogen with another element (as a metal)
2 : an organic compound derived from ammonia or an amine by replacement of ammoniacal hydrogen with an acyl group — compare AMINE, IMIDE

ami·do \ə-'mīd-(ˌ)dō, 'a-mə-ˌdō\ *adjective* [International Scientific Vocabulary *amide* + *-o-*] (1877)
: relating to or containing an organic amide group — often used in combination

am·i·dol \'a-mə-ˌdòl, -ˌdōl\ *noun* [German, from *Amidol,* a trademark] (1892)
: a colorless crystalline salt $C_6H_8N_2O \cdot 2HCl$ used chiefly as a photographic developer

amid·ships \ə-'mid-ˌships\ *adverb* (1692)
1 : in or toward the part of a ship midway between bow and stern
2 : in or toward the middle

ami·go \ə-'mē-(ˌ)gō, ä-\ *noun, plural* **-gos** [Spanish, from Latin *amicus* — more at AMIABLE] (1837)
: FRIEND

amine \ə-'mēn, 'a-ˌmēn\ *noun* [International Scientific Vocabulary, from New Latin *ammonia*] (1863)
: any of a class of organic compounds derived from ammonia by replacement of hydrogen with one or more alkyl groups — compare AMIDE 2

ami·no \ə-'mē-(ˌ)nō\ *adjective* [International Scientific Vocabulary *amine* + *-o-*] (1904)
: relating to, being, or containing an amine group — often used in combination

\ə\ abut \ᵊ\ kitten \ər\ further \a\ ash \ā\ ace
\ä\ mop, mar \aù\ out \ch\ chin \e\ bet \ē\ easy
\g\ go \i\ hit \ī\ ice \j\ job \ŋ\ sing \ō\ go
\ò\ law \òi\ boy \th\ thin \th̲\ the \ü\ loot \ù\ foot
\y\ yet \zh\ vision *see also* Guide to Pronunciation

amino acid *noun* (1898)
: an amphoteric organic acid containing the amino group NH_2; *especially* : any of the alpha-amino acids that are the chief components of proteins and are synthesized by living cells or are obtained as essential components of the diet

ami·no·ac·id·uria \ə-ˌmē-nō-ˌa-sə-'dùr-ē-ə,-'dyùr\ *noun* [New Latin] (circa 1923)
: a condition in which one or more amino acids are excreted in excessive amounts

ami·no·ben·zo·ic acid \ə-ˌmē-nō-ben-'zō-ik-\ *noun* [International Scientific Vocabulary] (1904)
: any of three crystalline derivatives $C_7H_7NO_2$ of benzoic acid; *especially* : PARA-AMINO-BENZOIC ACID

ami·no·pep·ti·dase \ə-ˌmē-nō-'pep-tə-ˌdās, -ˌdāz\ *noun* (1943)
: an enzyme that hydrolyzes peptides by acting on the peptide bond next to a terminal amino acid containing a free amino group

am·i·noph·yl·line \ˌa-mə-'nä-fə-lən\ *noun* [*amino* + *theophylline*] (1934)
: a theophylline derivative $C_{16}H_{24}N_{10}O_4$ used especially to stimulate the heart in congestive heart failure and to dilate the air passages in respiratory disorders

am·i·nop·ter·in \ˌa-mə-'näp-tə-rən\ *noun* [*amino* + *pter*oylglutamic acid + *-in*] (1948)
: a derivative of glutamic acid $C_{19}H_{20}N_8O_5$ used especially as a rodenticide

ami·no·py·rine \ə-ˌmē-nō-'pīr-ˌēn\ *noun* [International Scientific Vocabulary, from *amino* + anti*pyrine*] (circa 1936)
: a crystalline compound $C_{13}H_{17}N_3O$ formerly used to relieve pain and fever but now largely abandoned for this purpose because of the occurrence of fatal agranulocytosis as a side effect in some users

ami·no·sal·i·cyl·ic acid \ə-ˌmē-nō-ˌsa-lə-'si-lik-\ *noun* (1925)
: any of four isomeric derivatives $C_7H_7NO_3$ of salicylic acid that have a single amino group; *especially* : PARA-AMINOSALICYLIC ACID

ami·no·trans·fer·ase \-'tran(t)s-fə-ˌrās, -ˌrāz\ *noun* (circa 1965)
: TRANSAMINASE

amir *variant of* EMIR

Amish \'ä-mish, 'a-, 'ā-\ *adjective* [probably from German *amisch*, from Jacob *Amman* or *Amen* (flourished 1693) Swiss Mennonite bishop] (1844)
: of or relating to a strict sect of Mennonite followers of Amman that settled in America chiefly in the 18th century
— **Amish** *noun*

¹amiss \ə-'mis\ *adverb* (13th century)
1 a : in a mistaken way : WRONGLY ⟨if you think he is guilty, you judge *amiss*⟩ **b** : ASTRAY ⟨something had gone *amiss*⟩
2 : in a faulty way : IMPERFECTLY

²amiss *adjective* (14th century)
1 : not being in accordance with right order
2 : FAULTY, IMPERFECT
3 : out of place in given circumstances — usually used with a negative ⟨a few remarks may not be *amiss* here⟩

ami·to·sis \ˌā-mī-'tō-səs\ *noun* [New Latin, from ²*a-* + *mitosis*] (1894)
: cell division by simple cleavage of the nucleus and division of the cytoplasm without spindle formation or appearance of chromosomes
— **ami·tot·ic** \-'tä-tik\ *adjective*
— **ami·tot·i·cal·ly** \-ti-k(ə-)lē\ *adverb*

am·i·trip·ty·line \ˌa-mə-'trip-tə-ˌlēn\ *noun* [*amino* + *tryp*tophan + *-yl* + ²*-ine*] (1961)
: a tricyclic antidepressant drug $C_{20}H_{23}N$

am·i·trole \'a-mə-ˌtrōl\ *noun* [*amino* + *triazole*] (circa 1960)
: a systemic herbicide $C_2H_4N_4$ used in areas other than food croplands

am·i·ty \'a-mə-tē\ *noun, plural* **-ties** [Middle English *amite,* from Middle French *amité,* from Medieval Latin *amicitas,* from Latin *amicus* friend — more at AMIABLE] (15th century)
: FRIENDSHIP; *especially* : friendly relations between nations

am·me·ter \'a-ˌmē-tər\ *noun* [*ampere* + *-meter*] (1882)
: an instrument for measuring electric current in amperes

am·mine \'a-ˌmēn, a-'mēn\ *noun* [International Scientific Vocabulary *ammonia* + ²*-ine*] (1897)
1 : a molecule of ammonia as it exists in a coordination complex ⟨hex-*ammine*-cobalt chloride $Co(NH_3)_6Cl_3$⟩
2 : a compound that contains an ammine

am·mo \'a-(ˌ)mō\ *noun* [by shortening & alteration] (1911)
: AMMUNITION

am·mo·nia \ə-'mō-nyə\ *noun* [New Latin, from Latin *sal ammoniacus* sal ammoniac, literally, salt of Ammon, from Greek *ammōniakos* of Ammon, from *Ammōn* Ammon, Amen, an Egyptian god near one of whose temples it was prepared] (circa 1799)
1 : a pungent colorless gaseous alkaline compound of nitrogen and hydrogen NH_3 that is very soluble in water and can easily be condensed to a liquid by cold and pressure
2 : AMMONIA WATER

am·mo·ni·ac \ə-'mō-nē-ˌak\ *noun* [Middle English & Latin; Middle English, from Latin *ammoniacum,* from Greek *ammōniakon,* from neuter of *ammōniakos* of Ammon] (15th century)
: the aromatic gum resin of a Persian herb (*Dorema ammoniacum*) of the carrot family used as an expectorant and stimulant and in plasters

am·mo·ni·a·cal \ˌa-mə-'nī-ə-kəl\ *also* **am·mo·ni·ac** \ə-'mō-nē-ˌak\ *adjective* (1798)
: of, relating to, containing, or having the properties of ammonia

am·mo·ni·ate \ə-'mō-nē-ˌāt\ *transitive verb* **-at·ed; -at·ing** (circa 1928)
1 : to combine or impregnate with ammonia or an ammonium compound
2 : to subject to ammonification
— **am·mo·ni·a·tion** \-ˌmō-nē-'ā-shən\ *noun*

ammonia water *noun* (circa 1928)
: a water solution of ammonia

am·mo·ni·fi·ca·tion \ə-ˌmä-nə-fə-'kā-shən, -ˌmō-nə\ *noun* (1886)
1 : the act or process of ammoniating
2 : decomposition with production of ammonia or ammonium compounds especially by the action of bacteria on nitrogenous organic matter
— **am·mo·ni·fy** \-ˌfī\ *verb*

am·mo·nite \'a-mə-ˌnīt\ *noun* [New Latin *ammonites,* from Latin *cornu Ammonis,* literally, horn of Ammon] (1758)
: any of a subclass (Ammonoidea) of extinct cephalopods with flat spiral shells that were especially abundant in the Mesozoic age
— **am·mo·nit·ic** \ˌa-mə-'ni-tik\ *adjective*

ammonite

Am·mon·ite \'a-mə-ˌnīt\ *noun* [Late Latin *Ammonites,* from Hebrew '*Ammōn* Ammon (son of Lot), descendant of Ammon] (1537)
: a member of a Semitic people who in Old Testament times lived east of the Jordan between the Jabbok and the Arnon
— **Ammonite** *adjective*

am·mo·ni·um \ə-'mō-nē-əm\ *noun* [New Latin, from *ammonia*] (1808)
: an ion NH_4^+ derived from ammonia by combination with a hydrogen ion and known in compounds (as salts) that resemble in properties the compounds of the alkali metals

ammonium carbonate *noun* (circa 1881)
: a carbonate of ammonium; *specifically* : the commercial mixture of the bicarbonate and carbamate used especially in smelling salts

ammonium chloride *noun* (1869)
: a white crystalline volatile salt NH_4Cl that is used in dry cells and as an expectorant — called also *sal ammoniac*

ammonium cyanate *noun* (circa 1881)
: an inorganic white crystalline salt NH_4CNO that can be converted into organic urea

ammonium hydroxide *noun* (1904)
: a weakly basic compound NH_4OH that is formed when ammonia dissolves in water and that exists only in solution

ammonium nitrate *noun* (circa 1881)
: a colorless crystalline salt NH_4NO_3 used in explosives and fertilizers and in veterinary medicine

ammonium phosphate *noun* (circa 1881)
: a phosphate of ammonium; *especially* : DIAMMONIUM PHOSPHATE

ammonium sulfate *noun* (circa 1881)
: a colorless crystalline salt $(NH_4)_2SO_4$ used chiefly as a fertilizer

am·mo·noid \'a-mə-ˌnòid\ *noun* (1884)
: AMMONITE

am·mu·ni·tion \ˌam-yə-'ni-shən\ *noun* [obsolete French *amunition,* from Middle French, alteration of *munition*] (circa 1626)
1 a : the projectiles with their fuses, propelling charges, or primers fired from guns **b** : CARTRIDGES **c** : explosive military items (as grenades or bombs)
2 : material for use in attacking or defending a position ⟨*ammunition* for the defense lawyers⟩

am·ne·sia \am-'nē-zhə\ *noun* [New Latin, from Greek *amnēsia* forgetfulness, alteration of *amnēstia*] (1786)
1 : loss of memory due usually to brain injury, shock, fatigue, repression, or illness
2 : a gap in one's memory
3 : the selective overlooking or ignoring of those events or acts that are not favorable or useful to one's purpose or position
— **am·ne·si·ac** \-zhē-ˌak, -zē-\ *or* **am·ne·sic** \-zik, -sik\ *adjective or noun*

am·nes·ty \'am-nə-stē\ *noun, plural* **-ties** [Greek *amnēstia* forgetfulness, from *amnēstos* forgotten, from *a-* + *mnasthai* to remember — more at MIND] (1580)
: the act of an authority (as a government) by which pardon is granted to a large group of individuals
— **amnesty** *transitive verb*

am·nio·cen·te·sis \ˌam-nē-ō-(ˌ)sen-'tē-səs\ *noun, plural* **-te·ses** \-ˌsēz\ [New Latin, from *amnion* + *centesis* puncture, from Greek *kentesis,* from *kentein* to prick — more at CENTER] (1957)
: the surgical insertion of a hollow needle through the abdominal wall and into the uterus to obtain amniotic fluid especially for the determination of fetal sex or chromosomal abnormality

am·ni·on \'am-nē-ˌän, -ən\ *noun, plural* **amnions** *or* **am·nia** \-nē-ə\ [New Latin, from Greek, caul, from *amnos* lamb — more at YEAN] (1667)
1 : a thin membrane forming a closed sac about the embryos of reptiles, birds, and mammals and containing a serous fluid in which the embryo is immersed
2 : a membrane analogous to the amnion and occurring in various invertebrates
— **am·ni·ot·ic** \ˌam-nē-'ä-tik\ *adjective*

am·ni·ote \'am-nē-ˌōt\ *noun* [New Latin *Amniota,* from *amnion*] (circa 1909)
: any of a group (Amniota) of vertebrates that undergo embryonic development within an amnion and include the birds, reptiles, and mammals
— **amniote** *adjective*

amniotic fluid *noun* (1855)
: the serous fluid in which the embryo is suspended within the amnion

amniotic sac *noun* (circa 1881)

: AMNION

amo·bar·bi·tal \,a-mō-'bär-bə-,tȯl\ *noun* [*amyl* + *-o-* + *barbital*] (1949)
: a barbiturate $C_{11}H_{18}N_2O_3$ used as a hypnotic and sedative; *also* : its sodium salt

amoe·ba \ə-'mē-bə\ *noun, plural* **-bas** or **-bae** \-(,)bē\ [New Latin, genus name, from Greek *amoibē* change, from *ameibein* to change — more at MIGRATE] (1855)
: any of a large genus (*Amoeba*) of naked rhizopod protozoans with lobed and never anastomosing pseudopodia, without permanent organelles or supporting structures, and of wide distribution in fresh and salt water and moist terrestrial environments; *broadly* : a naked rhizopod or other amoeboid protozoan

amoeba:
1 pseudopodium,
2 nucleus, *3* contractile vacuole, *4* food vacuole

— **amoe·bic** \-bik\ *adjective*

am·oe·bi·a·sis *variant of* AMEBIASIS

amoe·bo·cyte \ə-'mē-bə-,sīt\ *noun* (1892)
: a cell (as a phagocyte) having amoeboid form or movements

amoe·boid \ə-'mē-,bȯid\ *adjective* (1856)
: resembling an amoeba specifically in moving or changing in shape by means of protoplasmic flow

¹**amok** \ə-'mək, -'mäk\ *noun* [Malay *amok*] (1665)
: a murderous frenzy that occurs chiefly among Malays ◆

²**amok** *adverb* (1672)
1 : in a murderously frenzied state
2 a : in a violently raging manner ⟨a virus that had run *amok*⟩ **b :** in an undisciplined, uncontrolled, or faulty manner ⟨films . . . about computers run *amok* —*People*⟩

³**amok** *adjective* (1944)
: possessed with or motivated by a murderous or violently uncontrollable frenzy

amo·le \ə-'mō-lē\ *noun* [American Spanish, from Nahuatl *amōlli* soap] (1831)
: a plant part (as a root) possessing detergent properties and serving as a substitute for soap; *also* : a plant (as a yucca or agave) so used

among \ə-'məŋ\ *preposition* [*among* from Middle English, from Old English *on gemonge*, from *on* + *gemonge*, dative of *gemong* crowd, from *ge-* (associative prefix) + *-mong* (akin to Old English *mengan* to mix); *amongst* from Middle English *amonges*, from *among* + *-es* -s — more at CO-, MINGLE] (before 12th century)
1 : in or through the midst of : surrounded by
2 : in company or association with ⟨living *among* artists⟩
3 : by or through the aggregate of ⟨discontent *among* the poor⟩
4 : in the number or class of ⟨wittiest *among* poets⟩ ⟨*among* other things she was president of her college class⟩
5 : in shares to each of ⟨divided *among* the heirs⟩
6 a : through the reciprocal acts of ⟨quarrel *among* themselves⟩ **b :** through the joint action of ⟨made a fortune *among* themselves⟩
usage see BETWEEN

amon·til·la·do \ə-,män-tə-'lä-(,)dō, -ti(l)-'yä-(,)thō\ *noun, plural* **-dos** [Spanish, literally, done in the manner of *Montilla*, town in Andalusia] (1825)
: a medium dry sherry

amor·al \(,)ā-'mȯr-əl, (,)a-, -'mär-\ *adjective* (1882)
1 a : being neither moral nor immoral; *specifically* : lying outside the sphere to which moral judgments apply ⟨science as such is completely *amoral* —W. S. Thompson⟩ **b :** lacking moral sensibility ⟨infants are *amoral*⟩

2 : being outside or beyond the moral order or a particular code of morals ⟨*amoral* customs⟩
— **amor·al·ism** \-'li-zəm\ *noun*
— **amo·ral·i·ty** \,ā-mə-'ra-lə-tē, ,a-, -(,)mȯ-\ *noun*
— **amor·al·ly** \ā-'mȯr-ə-lē, (,)a-, -'mär-\ *adverb*

amo·ret·to \,a-mə-'re-(,)tō, ,ä-\ *noun, plural* **-ti** \-(,)tē\ *or* **-tos** [Italian, diminutive of *amore* love, cupid, from Latin *amor*] (1622)
: CUPID, CHERUB 2

am·or·ist \'a-mə-rist\ *noun* (1581)
1 : a devotee of love and especially sexual love : GALLANT
2 : one that writes about romantic love
— **am·or·is·tic** \,a-mə-'ris-tik\ *adjective*

Am·o·rite \'a-mə-,rīt\ *noun* [Hebrew *Ĕmōrī*] (1535)
: a member of one of various Semitic peoples living in Mesopotamia, Syria, and Palestine during the 3d and 2d millennia B.C.
— **Amorite** *adjective*

am·o·rous \'a-mə-rəs, 'am-rəs\ *adjective* [Middle English, from Middle French, from Medieval Latin *amorosus*, from Latin *amor* love, from *amare* to love] (14th century)
1 : strongly moved by love and especially sexual love ⟨*amorous* women⟩
2 : being in love : ENAMORED — usually used with *of* ⟨*amorous* of the girl⟩
3 a : indicative of love ⟨received *amorous* glances from her partner⟩ **b :** of or relating to love ⟨an *amorous* novel⟩
— **am·o·rous·ly** *adverb*
— **am·o·rous·ness** *noun*

amor·phous \ə-'mȯr-fəs\ *adjective* [Greek *amorphos*, from *a-* + *morphē* form] (circa 1731)
1 a : having no definite form : SHAPELESS ⟨an *amorphous* cloud mass⟩ **b :** being without definite character or nature : UNCLASSIFIABLE ⟨an *amorphous* segment of society⟩ **c :** lacking organization or unity ⟨an *amorphous* style⟩
2 : having no real or apparent crystalline form : UNCRYSTALLIZED ⟨an *amorphous* mineral⟩
— **amor·phous·ly** *adverb*
— **amor·phous·ness** *noun*

amort \ə-'mȯrt\ *adjective* [short for *all-a-mort*, by folk etymology from Middle French *a la mort* to the death] (1590)
archaic : being at the point of death

am·or·ti·za·tion \,a-mər-tə-'zā-shən *also* ə-,mȯr-\ *noun* (circa 1859)
1 : the act or process of amortizing
2 : the result of amortizing

am·or·tize \'a-mər-,tīz *also* ə-'mȯr-\ *transitive verb* **-tized; -tiz·ing** [Middle English *amortisen* to deaden, alienate in mortmain, modification of Middle French *amortiss-*, stem of *amortir*, from (assumed) Vulgar Latin *admortire* to deaden, from Latin *ad-* + *mort-, mors* death — more at MURDER] (1882)
1 : to provide for the gradual extinguishment of (as a mortgage) usually by contribution to a sinking fund at the time of each periodic interest payment
2 : to amortize an expenditure for ⟨*amortize* intangibles⟩ ⟨*amortize* the new factory⟩
— **am·or·tiz·able** \-,tī-zə-bəl\ *adjective*

Amos \'ā-məs\ *noun* [Hebrew *Āmōs*]
1 : a Hebrew prophet of the 8th century B.C.
2 : a prophetic book of canonical Jewish and Christian Scripture — see BIBLE table

am·o·site \'a-mə-,sīt, -,zīt\ *noun* [*Amosa* (from *As*bestos *M*ines of *S*outh Africa) + ¹*-ite*] (circa 1918)
: an iron-rich amphibole that is a variety of asbestos

¹**amount** \ə-'maunt\ *intransitive verb* [Middle English, from Middle French *amonter*, from *amont* upward, from *a-* (from Latin *ad-*) + *mont* mountain — more at MOUNT] (14th century)
1 a : to be equivalent ⟨acts that *amount* to treason⟩ **b :** to reach in kind or quality ⟨wants

her son to *amount* to something⟩ ⟨doesn't *amount* to much⟩
2 : to reach a total : add up ⟨the bill *amounts* to $10⟩

²**amount** *noun* (1710)
1 a : the total number or quantity : AGGREGATE **b :** the quantity at hand or under consideration ⟨has an enormous *amount* of energy⟩
2 : the whole effect, significance, or import
3 : a principal sum and the interest on it □

amour \ə-'mur, ä-, a-\ *noun* [Middle English, love, affection, from Middle French, from Old Provençal *amor*, from Latin, from *amare* to love] (14th century)
: a usually illicit love affair; *also* : LOVER

amour pro·pre \,a-,mur-'prȯpr°, ,ä-, -'pròpr°\ *noun* [French *amour-propre*, literally, love of oneself] (1775)
: SELF-ESTEEM

amox·i·cil·lin \ə-,mäk-sē-'si-lən\ *noun* [*amino* + *ox-* + *penicillin*] (1973)
: a semisynthetic penicillin $C_{16}H_{19}N_3O_5S$ derived from ampicillin

amox·y·cil·lin *British variant of* AMOXICILLIN

Amoy \ä-'mȯi, a-, ə-\ *noun* (1904)
: the dialect of Chinese spoken in and near Amoy in southeastern China

amp \'amp\ *noun* [by shortening] (1886)
1 : AMPERE
2 : AMPLIFIER; *also* : a unit consisting of an electronic amplifier and a loudspeaker

AMP \,ā-,em-'pē\ *noun* [*a*denosine *m*ono*p*hosphate] (1951)
: a mononucleotide of adenine $C_{10}H_{12}N_5O_3H_2PO_4$ that was originally isolated from mammalian muscle and is reversibly convert-

□ **USAGE**

amount *Number* is regularly used with count nouns ⟨a large *number* of mistakes⟩ ⟨any *number* of times⟩ while *amount* is mainly used with mass nouns ⟨annual *amount* of rainfall⟩ ⟨a substantial *amount* of money⟩. The use of *amount* with count nouns has been frequently criticized; it usually occurs when the number of things is thought of as a mass or collection ⟨glad to furnish any *amount* of black pebbles —*New Yorker*⟩ ⟨a substantial *amount* of film offers —Lily Tomlin⟩ or when money is involved ⟨a substantial *amount* of loans —E. R. Black⟩.

◇ **WORD HISTORY**

amok From the earliest Portuguese contacts with Southeast Asia in the sixteenth century, travelers have reported on a psychiatric disorder peculiar to the region that afflicts only men and is known in Malay as *amok*. In its typical modern manifestation, a man affected by amok first goes through a period of brooding and then explodes into homicidal frenzy, seizing a parang (a short sword) and cutting down everyone in his path, whether relative, friend, or stranger. If the man is not first killed by efforts to stop him, he eventually collapses in exhaustion, with no recollection of the episode. The phrase *run amuck* (translating the Malay verb *mengamok*) was being used in English to describe any undisciplined behavior by the late 17th century, and it occurs in the poetry of Alexander Pope ("Satire's my weapon, but I'm too discreet/To run a muck, and tilt at all I meet"). Most English speakers are probably no longer aware of the literal violence that the Malay word describes.

\ə\ abut \ə\ kitten \ər\ further \a\ ash \ā\ ace
\ä\ mop, mar \au̇\ out \ch\ chin \e\ bet \ē\ easy
\g\ go \i\ hit \ī\ ice \j\ job \ŋ\ sing \ō\ go
\ȯ\ law \ȯi\ boy \th\ thin \t͟h\ the \ü\ loot \u̇\ foot
\y\ yet \zh\ vision *see also* Guide to Pronunciation

ible to ADP and ATP in metabolic reactions — called also *adenosine monophosphate, adenylic acid;* compare CYCLIC AMP

am·per·age \'am-p(ə-)rij, -ˌpir-ij\ *noun* (1893) : the strength of a current of electricity expressed in amperes

am·pere \'am-ˌpir *also* -ˌper\ *noun* [André-Marie *Ampère*] (1881) **1 :** the practical meter-kilogram-second unit of electric current that is equivalent to a flow of one coulomb per second or to the steady current produced by one volt applied across a resistance of one ohm **2 :** the base unit of electric current in the International System of Units that is equal to a constant current which when maintained in two straight parallel conductors of infinite length and negligible circular sections one meter apart in a vacuum produces between the conductors a force equal to 2×10^{-7} newton per meter of length ◈

ampere–hour *noun* (1885) : a unit quantity of electricity equal to the quantity carried past any point of a circuit in one hour by a steady current of one ampere

ampere–turn *noun* (1884) : the meter-kilogram-second unit of magnetomotive force equal to the magnetomotive force around a path that links with one turn of wire carrying an electric current of one ampere

am·per·o·met·ric \ˌam-pir-ə-'me-trik\ *adjective* [*ampere* + *-o-* + *-metric*] (1940) : relating to or being a chemical titration in which the measurement of the electric current flowing under an applied potential difference between two electrodes in a solution is used for detecting the end point

am·per·sand \'am-pər-ˌsand\ *noun* [alteration of *and* (&) *per se and,* literally, (the character) & by itself (is the word) *and*] (1835) : a character typically & standing for the word *and* ◈

am·phet·amine \am-'fe-tə-ˌmēn, -mən\ *noun* [International Scientific Vocabulary *a*lpha + *m*ethyl + *ph*en- + *et*hyl + *amine*] (1938) : a racemic compound $C_9H_{13}N$ or one of its derivatives (as dextroamphetamine or methamphetamine) frequently abused as a stimulant of the central nervous system but used clinically especially as the sulfate or hydrochloride salt to treat hyperactive children and the symptoms of narcolepsy and as a short-term appetite suppressant in dieting

amphi- *or* **amph-** *prefix* [Latin *amphi-* around, on both sides, from Greek *amphi-, amph-,* from *amphi* — more at AMBI-] : on both sides : of both kinds : both ⟨*amphi*brach⟩ ⟨*amphi*diploid⟩

am·phib·ia \am-'fi-bē-ə\ *noun plural* (1607) : AMPHIBIANS

am·phib·i·an \-bē-ən\ *noun* [ultimately from Greek *amphibion* amphibious being, from neuter of *amphibios*] (1835) **1 :** an amphibious organism; *especially* : any of a class (Amphibia) of cold-blooded vertebrates (as frogs, toads, or salamanders) intermediate in many characters between fishes and reptiles and having gilled aquatic larvae and air-breathing adults **2 :** an airplane designed to take off from and land on either land or water — **amphibian** *adjective*

am·phib·i·ous \am-'fi-bē-əs\ *adjective* [Greek *amphibios,* literally, living a double life, from *amphi-* + *bios* mode of life — more at QUICK] (1643) **1 :** combining two characteristics **2 a :** relating to or adapted for both land and water ⟨*amphibious* vehicles⟩ **b :** executed by coordinated action of land, sea, and air forces organized for invasion; *also* : trained or organized for such action ⟨*amphibious* forces⟩ **3 :** able to live both on land and in water ⟨*amphibious* plants⟩ — **am·phib·i·ous·ly** *adverb* — **am·phib·i·ous·ness** *noun*

am·phi·bole \'am(p)-fə-ˌbōl\ *noun* [French, from Late Latin *amphibolus,* from Greek *amphibolos* ambiguous, from *amphiballein* to throw round, doubt, from *amphi-* + *ballein* to throw — more at DEVIL] (circa 1823) **1 :** HORNBLENDE **2 :** any of a group of complex silicate minerals with like crystal structures that contain calcium, sodium, magnesium, aluminum, and iron ions or a combination of them

am·phib·o·lite \am-'fi-bə-ˌlīt\ *noun* (1833) : a usually metamorphic rock consisting essentially of amphibole

am·phi·bol·o·gy \ˌam(p)-fə-'bä-lə-jē\ *noun, plural* **-gies** [Middle English *amphibologie,* from Late Latin *amphibologia,* alteration of Latin *amphibolia,* from Greek, from *amphibolos*] (14th century) : a sentence or phrase (as "nothing is good enough for you") susceptible of more than one interpretation

am·phib·o·ly \am-'fi-bə-lē\ *noun, plural* **-lies** [Late Latin *amphibolia*] (circa 1588) : AMPHIBOLOGY

am·phi·brach \'am(p)-fə-ˌbrak\ *noun* [Latin *amphibrachys,* from Greek, literally, short at both ends, from *amphi-* + *brachys* short — more at BRIEF] (1589) : a metrical foot consisting of a long syllable between two short syllables in quantitative verse or of a stressed syllable between two unstressed syllables in accentual verse ⟨*romantic* is an accentual *amphibrach*⟩ — **am·phi·brach·ic** \ˌam(p)-fə-'bra-kik\ *adjective*

am·phic·ty·o·ny \am-'fik-tē-ə-nē\ *noun, plural* **-nies** [Greek *amphiktyonia*] (1835) : an association of neighboring states in ancient Greece to defend a common religious center; *broadly* : an association of neighboring states for their common interest — **am·phic·ty·on·ic** \(ˌ)am-ˌfik-tē-'ä-nik\ *adjective*

am·phi·dip·loid \ˌam(p)-fi-'di-ˌplȯid\ *noun* (1930) : an interspecific hybrid having a complete diploid chromosome set from each parent form — called also *allotetraploid* — **amphidiploid** *adjective* — **am·phi·dip·loi·dy** \-ˌplȯi-dē\ *noun*

am·phim·a·cer \am-'fi-mə-sər\ *noun* [Latin *amphimacrus,* from Greek *amphimakros,* literally, long at both ends, from *amphi-* + *makros* long — more at MEAGER] (1589) : a metrical foot consisting of a short syllable between two long syllables in quantitative verse or of an unstressed syllable between two stressed syllables in accentual verse ⟨*twenty-two* is an accentual *amphimacer*⟩

am·phim·ix·is \ˌam(p)-fi-'mik-səs\ *noun, plural* **-mix·es** \-ˌsēz\ [New Latin, from *amphi-* + Greek *mixis* mingling, from *mignynai* to mix — more at MIX] (1893) : the union of gametes in sexual reproduction

Am·phi·on \am-'fī-ən\ *noun* [Latin, from Greek *Amphiōn*] : a musician of Greek mythology who builds the walls of Thebes by charming the stones into place with his lyre

am·phi·ox·us \ˌam(p)-fē-'äk-səs\ *noun, plural* **-oxi** \-ˌsī\ *or* **-ox·us·es** [New Latin, from *amphi-* + Greek *oxys* sharp] (1847) : any of a genus (Branchiostoma) of lancelets; *broadly* : LANCELET

am·phi·path·ic \ˌam(p)-fə-'pa-thik\ *adjective* [*amphi-* + *-pathic* (as in *empathic*)] (1945) : AMPHIPHILIC

am·phi·phil·ic \-'fi-lik\ *adjective* (1950) : of, relating to, or being a compound (as a surfactant) consisting of molecules having a polar water-soluble group attached to a water-insoluble hydrocarbon chain; *also* : being a molecule of such a compound — **am·phi·phile** \'am(p)-fə-ˌfīl\ *noun*

am·phi·ploid \'am(p)-fi-ˌplȯid\ *adjective* (1945)

of an interspecific hybrid **:** having at least one complete diploid set of chromosomes derived from each parent species — **amphiploid** *noun* — **am·phi·ploi·dy** \-ˌplȯi-dē\ *noun*

am·phi·pod \-ˌpäd\ *noun* [ultimately from Greek *amphi-* + *pod-, pous* foot — more at FOOT] (1835) : any of a large order (Amphipoda) of small crustaceans (as the beach flea) with a laterally compressed body — **amphipod** *adjective*

am·phi·pro·style \ˌam(p)-fi-'prō-ˌstīl\ *adjective* [Latin *amphiprostylos,* from Greek, from *amphi-* + *prostylos* having pillars in front, from *pro-* + *stylos* pillar — more at STEER] (1850) : having columns at each end only ⟨an *amphiprostyle* building⟩ — **amphiprostyle** *noun*

am·phis·bae·na \ˌam(p)-fəs-'bē-nə\ *noun* [Latin, from Greek *amphisbaina,* from *amphis* on both sides (from *amphi* around) + *bainein* to walk, go — more at BY, COME] (14th century) : a serpent in classical mythology having a head at each end and capable of moving in either direction — **am·phis·bae·nic** \-nik\ *adjective*

am·phi·the·ater \'am(p)-fə-ˌthē-ə-tər *also* 'am-pə-ˌthē-\ *noun* [Latin *amphitheatrum,* from Greek *amphitheatron,* from *amphi-* + *theatron* theater] (14th century) **1 :** an oval or circular building with rising tiers of seats ranged about an open space and used in ancient Rome especially for contests and spectacles **2 a :** a very large auditorium **b :** a room with a gallery from which doctors and students may observe surgical operations **c :** a rising gallery in a modern theater **d :** a flat or gently sloping area surrounded by abrupt slopes **3 :** a place of public games or contests — **am·phi·the·at·ric** \ˌam(p)-fə-thē-'a-trik *also* ˌam-pə-thē-\ *or* **am·phi·the·at·ri·cal** \-tri-kəl\ *adjective* — **am·phi·the·at·ri·cal·ly** \-tri-k(ə-)lē\ *adverb*

ampere The *ampere* was named in honor of the French physicist André-Marie Ampère (1775–1836). Ampère is credited with founding, naming, and developing the science of electrodynamics. He was the formulator of two laws in electromagnetism relating magnetic fields to electric currents. The first person to develop techniques for measuring electricity, he invented an instrument that was a forerunner of the galvanometer. In 1881 an international congress on electricity adopted *ampere* as a term for the standard unit of electric current.

ampersand For pupils studying Latin in the grammar schools of late medieval and Tudor England, the traditional practice was to spell words by syllables. When a single letter formed a whole word (like *I*) or a complete syllable (like the first *i-* in *iris*), it was followed by the words *per se,* which in Latin means "by itself." Thus in the schoolroom *I* became *I per se, I.* Because the character &, a symbol for *and,* was placed after *z* in primers and treated like any other letter of the alphabet, it too was spelled out orally as "and per se, and." Frequent use of the phrase and diminishing recognition of its literal meaning shrank it to *ampersand* by the 19th century. The character & is a development of ⅋, a ligature of *et,* the Latin word for "and."

Am·phit·ry·on \am-'fi-trē-ən\ *noun* [Greek *Amphitryōn*]
: the husband of Alcmene

am·pho·ra \'am(p)-fə-rə\ *noun, plural* **-rae** \-ˌrē, -ˌrī\ *or* **-ras** [Latin, modification of Greek *amphoreus, amphiphoreus,* from *amphi- + phoreus* bearer, from *pherein* to bear — more at BEAR] (14th century)
1 : an ancient Greek jar or vase with a large oval body, narrow cylindrical neck, and two handles that rise almost to the level of the mouth
2 : a 2-handled vessel shaped like an amphora

amphora 1

am·pho·ter·ic \ˌam(p)-fə-'ter-ik\ *adjective* [International Scientific Vocabulary, from Greek *amphoteros* each of two, from *amphō* both — more at AMBI-] (circa 1849)
: partly one and partly the other; *specifically* : capable of reacting chemically either as an acid or as a base

am·pho·ter·i·cin B \ˌam(p)-fə-'ter-ə-sən-'bē\ *noun* [*amphoteric* + [1]-*in*] (1955)
: an antifungal antibiotic obtained from a soil actinomycete (*Streptomyces nodosus*) and used especially to treat systemic fungal infections

am·pi·cil·lin \ˌam-pə-'si-lən\ *noun* [*amino + penicillin*] (1961)
: a penicillin $C_{16}H_{19}N_3O_4S$ that is effective against gram-negative and gram-positive bacteria and is used to treat various infections of the urinary, respiratory, and intestinal tracts

am·ple \'am-pəl\ *adjective* **am·pler** \-p(ə-)lər\; **am·plest** \-p(ə-)ləst\ [Middle French, from Latin *amplus*] (15th century)
1 : generous or more than adequate in size, scope, or capacity ⟨there was room for an *ample* garden⟩
2 : generously sufficient to satisfy a requirement or need ⟨they had *ample* money for the trip⟩
3 : BUXOM, PORTLY ⟨an *ample* figure⟩
synonym see SPACIOUS, PLENTIFUL
— **am·ple·ness** \-pəl-nəs\ *noun*
— **am·ply** \-plē\ *adverb*

am·plex·us \am-'plek-səs\ *noun* [New Latin, from Latin, embrace, from *amplecti* to embrace, from *am-, amb-* around + *plectere* to braid — more at AMBI-, PLY] (circa 1927)
: the mating embrace of a frog or toad during which eggs are shed into the water and there fertilized

am·pli·dyne \'am-plə-ˌdīn\ *noun* [*amplifier* + Greek *dynamis* power — more at DYNAMIC] (1940)
: a direct-current generator that precisely controls a large power output whenever a small power input is varied in the field winding of the generator

am·pli·fi·ca·tion \ˌam-plə-fə-'kā-shən\ *noun* (1546)
1 a : an act, example, or product of amplifying **b :** a usually massive replication especially of a gene or DNA sequence (as in a polymerase chain reaction)
2 a : the particulars by which a statement is expanded **b :** an expanded statement

am·pli·fi·er \'am-plə-ˌfī-(ə-)r\ *noun* (1542)
: one that amplifies; *specifically* : an electronic device (as in a stereo system) for amplifying voltage, current, or power

am·pli·fy \-ˌfī\ *verb* **-fied; -fy·ing** [Middle English *amplifien,* from Middle French *amplifier,* from Latin *amplificare,* from *amplus*] (15th century)
transitive verb
1 : to expand (as a statement) by the use of detail or illustration or by closer analysis
2 a : to make larger or greater (as in amount, importance, or intensity) **:** INCREASE **b :** to increase the strength or amount of; *especially* **:** to make louder **c :** to cause (a gene or DNA sequence) to undergo amplification
intransitive verb
: to expand one's remarks or ideas
synonym see EXPAND

am·pli·tude \-ˌtüd, -ˌtyüd\ *noun* (1542)
1 : the quality or state of being ample **:** FULLNESS
2 : the extent or range of a quality, property, process, or phenomenon: as **a :** the extent of a vibratory movement (as of a pendulum) measured from the mean position to an extreme **b :** the maximum departure of the value of an alternating current or wave from the average value
3 : ARGUMENT 6b

amplitude modulation *noun* (1921)
: modulation of the amplitude of a radio carrier wave in accordance with the strength of the audio or other signal; *also* : a broadcasting system using such modulation — compare FREQUENCY MODULATION

am·poule *or* **am·pule** *also* **am·pul** \'am-ˌpyü(ə)l, -ˌpül\ *noun* [Middle English *ampulle* flask, from Old English & Old French; Old English *ampulle* & Old French *ampoule,* from Latin *ampulla*] (1886)
1 : a hermetically sealed small bulbous glass vessel that is used to hold a solution for hypodermic injection
2 : a vial resembling an ampoule

am·pul·la \am-'pu̇-lə, 'am-ˌpyü-lə\ *noun, plural* **-lae** \-(ˌ)lē, -ˌlī\ [Middle English, from Old English, from Latin, diminutive of *amphora*] (before 12th century)
1 : a glass or earthenware flask with a globular body and two handles used especially by the ancient Romans to hold ointment, perfume, or wine
2 : a saccular anatomic swelling or pouch
— **am·pul·la·ry** \am-'pu̇-lər-ē, 'am-pyə-ˌler-ē\ *adjective*

am·pu·tate \'am-pyə-ˌtāt\ *transitive verb* **-tat·ed; -tat·ing** [Latin *amputatus,* past participle of *amputare,* from *am-, amb-* around + *putare* to cut, prune — more at AMBI-] (1638)
: to remove by or as if by cutting; *especially* : to cut (as a limb) from the body
— **am·pu·ta·tion** \ˌam-pyə-'tā-shən\ *noun*

am·pu·tee \ˌam-pyə-'tē\ *noun* (1910)
: one that has had a limb amputated

am·trac *or* **am·track** \'am-ˌtrak\ *noun* [*amphibious + tractor*] (1944)
: a flat-bottomed military vehicle that moves on tracks on land or water

amuck \ə-'mək\ *variant of* AMOK

am·u·let \'am-yə-lət\ *noun* [Latin *amuletum*] (1584)
: a charm (as an ornament) often inscribed with a magic incantation or symbol to protect the wearer against evil (as disease or witchcraft) or to aid him

amuse \ə-'myüz\ *verb* **amused; amus·ing** [Middle French *amuser,* from Old French, from *a-* (from Latin *ad-*) + *muser* to muse] (15th century)
transitive verb
1 a *archaic* : to divert the attention of so as to deceive **b** *obsolete* : to occupy the attention of **:** ABSORB **c** *obsolete* : DISTRACT, BEWILDER
2 a : to entertain or occupy in a light, playful, or pleasant manner ⟨*amuse* the child with a story⟩ **b :** to appeal to the sense of humor of ⟨the joke doesn't *amuse* me⟩
intransitive verb
obsolete : MUSE ☆
— **amus·ed·ly** \-'myü-zəd-lē\ *adverb*
— **amus·er** *noun*
— **amus·ive** \ə-'myü-zəv, -səv\ *adjective*

amuse·ment \ə-'myüz-mənt\ *noun* (1603)
1 : a means of amusing or entertaining ⟨what are her favorite *amusements*⟩
2 : the condition of being amused ⟨his *amusement* knew no bounds⟩
3 : pleasurable diversion **:** ENTERTAINMENT ⟨plays the piano for *amusement*⟩

amusement park *noun* (1909)
: a commercially operated park having various devices for entertainment (as a merry-go-round and roller coaster) and usually booths for the sale of food and drink

amus·ing \ə-'myü-zin\ *adjective* (1712)
: giving amusement **:** DIVERTING
— **amus·ing·ly** \-zin-lē\ *adverb*
— **amus·ing·ness** *noun*

amyg·da·la \ə-'mig-də-lə\ *noun, plural* **-lae** \-ˌlē, -ˌlī\ [New Latin, from Latin, almond, from Greek *amygdalē*] (circa 1860)
: the one of the four basal ganglia in each cerebral hemisphere that is part of the limbic system and consists of an almond-shaped mass of gray matter in the anterior extremity of the temporal lobe — called also *amygdaloid nucleus*

amyg·da·lin \-lən\ *noun* [Latin *amygdala*] (1651)
: a white crystalline cyanogenetic glucoside $C_{20}H_{27}NO_{11}$ found especially in the seeds of the apricot, peach, and bitter almond

amyg·da·loid \-ˌlȯid\ *adjective* [Greek *amygdaloeidēs,* from *amygdalē*] (1836)
1 : almond-shaped
2 : of, relating to, or affecting an amygdala

amyg·da·loi·dal \ə-ˌmig-də-'lȯi-dᵊl\ *adjective* (1813)
: of, being, or containing small cavities in igneous rock that are filled with deposits of different minerals (as chalcedony or calcite)
— **amyg·da·loid** \ə-'mig-də-ˌlȯid\ *noun*

am·yl \'a-məl\ *noun* [Latin *amylum* + English *-yl*] (1850)
: a univalent hydrocarbon radical C_5H_{11}— that occurs in various isomeric forms and is derived from pentane

amyl- *or* **amylo-** *combining form* [Latin *amylum,* from Greek *amylon,* from neuter of *amylos* unmilled (of grain), from *a- + mylē* mill — more at MEAL]
: starch ⟨*amylo*plast⟩

amyl acetate *noun* (circa 1881)
: BANANA OIL

amyl alcohol *noun* (1863)
: any of eight isomeric alcohols $C_5H_{12}O$ used especially as solvents and in making esters; *also* : a commercially produced mixture of amyl alcohols used especially as a solvent

am·y·lase \'a-mə-ˌlās, -ˌlāz\ *noun* (1893)
: any of a group of enzymes (as amylopsin) that catalyze the hydrolysis of starch and glycogen or their intermediate hydrolysis products

amyl nitrite *noun* (circa 1881)
: a pale yellow pungent flammable liquid ester $C_5H_{11}NO_2$ of commercial amyl alcohol and nitrous acid — compare POPPER 2

am·y·loid \-ˌlȯid\ *noun* (1872)
: a waxy translucent substance consisting of protein in combination with polysaccharides

☆ **SYNONYMS**
Amuse, divert, entertain mean to pass or cause to pass the time pleasantly. AMUSE suggests that one's attention is engaged lightly or frivolously ⟨*amuse* yourselves while I prepare dinner⟩. DIVERT implies the distracting of the attention from worry or routine occupation especially by something funny ⟨a light comedy to *divert* the tired businessman⟩. ENTERTAIN suggests supplying amusement or diversion by specially prepared or contrived methods ⟨a magician *entertaining* children at a party⟩.

that is deposited in some animal organs and tissues under abnormal conditions (as Alzheimer's disease)
— **amyloid** *adjective*

am·y·loid·o·sis \,a-mə-,lói-'dō-səs\ *noun* [New Latin] (circa 1900)
: a disorder characterized by the deposition of amyloid in bodily organs and tissues

am·y·lo·lyt·ic \,a-mə-lō-'li-tik\ *adjective* [New Latin *amylolysis*, from *amyl-* + *-lysis*] (1876)
: characterized by or capable of the enzymatic splitting of starch into soluble products ⟨*amylolytic* enzymes⟩ ⟨*amylolytic* activity⟩

am·y·lo·pec·tin \,a-mə-lō-'pek-tən\ *noun* (1905)
: a component of starch that has a high molecular weight and branched structure and does not tend to gel in aqueous solutions

am·y·lo·plast \'a-mə-(,)lō-,plast\ *noun* (1886)
: a colorless plastid that forms and stores starch

am·y·lop·sin \,a-mə-'läp-sən\ *noun* [*amyl-* + *-psin* (as in *trypsin*)] (circa 1881)
the amylase of the pancreatic juice

am·y·lose \'a-mə-,lōs, -,lōz\ *noun* (1877)
a component of starch characterized by its straight chains of glucose units

amyo·to·nia \,ā-,mī-ə-'tō-nē-ə\ *noun* [New Latin] (circa 1919)
: deficiency of muscle tone

amyo·tro·phic lateral sclerosis \,ā-,mī-ə-'trō-fik-, -'trä-\ *noun* [*²a-* + *my-* + *-trophic*] (circa 1889)
: a rare progressive degenerative fatal disease affecting the spinal cord, usually beginning in middle age, and characterized especially by increasing and spreading muscular weakness — called also *Lou Gehrig's disease*

Am·y·tal \'a-mə-,tól\ *trademark*
— used for amobarbital

¹an \ən, (')an\ *indefinite article* [Middle English, from Old English *ān* one — more at ONE] (before 12th century)
: ²A
usage see ²A

²an \ən, an\ *preposition* (before 12th century)
: ³A 2
usage see ²A

³an *or* **an'** *conjunction* (12th century)
1 *see* AND\ : AND
2 \'an\ *archaic* : IF

an- — see ²A-

¹-an *or* **-ian** *also* **-ean** *noun suffix* [-*an* & *-ian* from Middle English *-an*, *-ian*, from Old French & Latin; Old French *-ien*, from Latin *-ianus*, from *-i-* + *-anus*, from *-anus*, adjective suffix; *-ean* from such words as *Mediterranean*, *European*]
1 : one that is of or relating to ⟨American⟩ ⟨Bostonian⟩
2 : one skilled in or specializing in ⟨phonetician⟩

²-an *or* **-ian** *also* **-ean** *adjective suffix*
1 : of or belonging to ⟨American⟩ ⟨Floridian⟩
2 : characteristic of : resembling ⟨Mozartean⟩

³-an *noun suffix* [International Scientific Vocabulary *-an*, *-ane*, alteration of *-ene*, *-ine*, & *-one*]
1 : unsaturated organic compound ⟨furan⟩
2 : anhydride of a carbohydrate ⟨dextran⟩

¹ana \'a-nə\ *adverb* [Middle English, from Medieval Latin, from Greek, at the rate of, literally, up] (14th century)
: of each an equal quantity — used in prescriptions

²ana \'a-nə, 'ä-, 'ā-\ *noun, plural* **ana** *or* **anas** [-*ana*] (circa 1751)
1 : a collection of the memorable sayings of a person
2 : a collection of anecdotes or interesting information about a person or a place

ana- *or* **an-** *prefix* [Latin, from Greek, up, back, again, from *ana* up — more at ON]
1 : up : upward ⟨anabolism⟩
2 : back : backward ⟨anatropous⟩

-ana *or* **-iana** *noun plural suffix* [New Latin, from Latin, neuter plural of *-anus* -an & *-ianus* -ian]
: collected items of information especially anecdotal or bibliographical concerning ⟨Americana⟩

ana·bap·tism \,a-nə-'bap-,ti-zəm\ *noun* [New Latin *anabaptismus*, from Late Greek *anabaptismos* rebaptism, from *anabaptizein* to rebaptize, from Greek *ana-* again + *baptizein* to baptize] (1577)
1 *capitalized* **a** : the doctrine or practices of the Anabaptists **b** : the Anabaptist movement
2 : the baptism of one previously baptized

Ana·bap·tist \-'bap-tist\ *noun* (1532)
: a Protestant sectarian of a radical movement arising in the 16th century and advocating the baptism and church membership of adult believers only, nonresistance, and the separation of church and state
— **Anabaptist** *adjective*

anab·a·sis \ə-'na-bə-səs\ *noun, plural* **-a·ses** \-,sēz\ [Greek, inland march, from *anabainein* to go up or inland, from *ana-* + *bainein* to go — more at COME] (circa 1706)
1 : a going or marching up : ADVANCE; *especially* : a military advance
2 [from the retreat of Greek mercenaries in Asia Minor described in the *Anabasis* of Xenophon] : a difficult and dangerous military retreat

an·a·bat·ic \,a-nə-'ba-tik\ *adjective* [Greek *anabatos*, verbal of *anabainein*] (1853)
: moving upward : RISING ⟨an *anabatic* wind⟩

anabolic steroid *noun* (1961)
: any of a group of usually synthetic hormones that increase constructive metabolism and are sometimes abused by athletes in training to increase temporarily the size of their muscles

anab·o·lism \ə-'na-bə-,li-zəm\ *noun* [International Scientific Vocabulary *ana-* + metabolism] (1886)
: the constructive part of metabolism concerned especially with macromolecular synthesis — compare CATABOLISM
— **an·a·bol·ic** \,a-nə-'bä-lik\ *adjective*

anach·ro·nism \ə-'na-krə-,ni-zəm\ *noun* [probably from Middle Greek *anachronismos*, from *anachronizesthai* to be an anachronism, from Late Greek *anachronizein* to be late, from Greek *ana-* + *chronos* time] (circa 1646)
1 : an error in chronology; *especially* : a chronological misplacing of persons, events, objects, or customs in regard to each other
2 : a person or a thing that is chronologically out of place; *especially* : one from a former age that is incongruous in the present
— **anach·ro·nis·tic** \ə-,na-krə-'nis-tik\ *also* **ana·chron·ic** \a-nə-'krä-nik\ *adjective*
— **anach·ro·nis·ti·cal·ly** \ə-,na-krə-'nis-ti-k(ə-)lē\ *adverb*
— **anach·ro·nous** \ə-'na-krə-nəs\ *adjective*
— **anach·ro·nous·ly** *adverb*

an·a·clit·ic \,a-nə-'kli-tik\ *adjective* [Greek *anaklitos*, verbal of *anaklinein* to lean upon, from *ana-* + *klinein* to lean — more at LEAN] (1922)
: of, relating to, or characterized by the direction of love toward an object (as the mother) that satisfies nonsexual needs (as hunger)

an·a·co·lu·thon \,a-nə-kə-'lü-,thän\ *noun, plural* **-tha** \-thə\ *also* **-thons** [Late Latin, from Late Greek *anakolouthon* inconsistency in logic, from Greek, neuter of *anakolouthos* inconsistent, from *an-* + *akolouthos* following, from *ha-*, *a-* together + *keleuthos* path] (circa 1706)
: syntactical inconsistency or incoherence within a sentence; *especially* : a shift in an unfinished sentence from one syntactic construction to another (as in "you really ought—well, do it your own way")
— **an·a·co·lu·thic** \-thik\ *adjective*
— **an·a·co·lu·thi·cal·ly** \-thi-k(ə-)lē\ *adverb*

an·a·con·da \,a-nə-'kän-də\ *noun* [probably modification of Sinhalese *henakandayā*, a slender green snake] (1768)
: a large semiaquatic constricting snake (*Eunectes murinus*) of the boa family of tropical South America that may reach a length of 30 feet (9.1 meters); *broadly* : any of the large constricting snakes

anac·re·on·tic \ə-,na-krē-'än-tik\ *noun* (1656)
: a poem in the manner of Anacreon; *especially* : a drinking song or light lyric
◇

Anacreontic *adjective* [Latin *anacreonticus*, from *Anacreont-*, *Anacreon* Anacreon, from Greek *Anakreont-*, *Anakreōn*] (1611)
1 : of, relating to, or resembling the poetry of Anacreon
2 : convivial or amatory in tone or theme

anaconda

an·a·cru·sis \,a-nə-'krü-səs\ *noun, plural* **-cru·ses** \-,sēz\ [New Latin, from Greek *anakrousis* beginning of a song, from *ana-* *krouein* to begin a song, from *ana-* + *krouein* to strike, beat; akin to Lithuanian *kraušyti* to strike] (1830)
1 : one or more syllables at the beginning of a line of poetry that are regarded as preliminary to and not a part of the metrical pattern
2 : UPBEAT; *specifically* : one or more notes or tones preceding the first downbeat of a musical phrase

an·a·dama bread \,a-nə-'da-mə-\ *noun* [origin unknown] (1954)
: a leavened bread made with flour, cornmeal, and molasses

an·a·dem \'a-nə-,dem\ *noun* [Latin *anadema*, from Greek *anadēma*, from *anadein* to wreathe, from *ana-* + *dein* to bind — more at DIADEM] (1604)
archaic : a wreath for the head : GARLAND

ana·di·plo·sis \,a-nə-də-'plō-səs, ,a-nə-(,)dī-'plō-\ *noun, plural* **-plo·ses** \-,sēz\ [Late Latin, from Greek *anadiplōsis*, literally, repetition, from *anadiploun* to double, from *ana-* + *diploun* to double — more at DIPLOMA] (circa 1550)
: repetition of a prominent and usually the last word in one phrase or clause at the beginning of the next (as in "rely on his honor—honor such as his?")

anad·ro·mous \ə-'na-drə-məs\ *adjective* [Greek *anadromos* running upward, from

anadramein to run upward, from *ana-* + *dramein* to run — more at DROMEDARY] (circa 1753)

: ascending rivers from the sea for breeding ⟨shad are *anadromous*⟩ — compare CATADROMOUS

anae·mia, anae·mic *chiefly British variant of* ANEMIA, ANEMIC

an·aer·obe \'a-nə-ˌrōb; (ˌ)an-'a(-)r-ˌōb, -'e(-ə)r-\ *noun* [International Scientific Vocabulary] (1884)
: an anaerobic organism

an·aer·o·bic \ˌa-nə-'rō-bik; ˌan-ˌa(-ə)-, -ˌe(-ə)-\ *adjective* (circa 1881)
1 a : living, active, occurring, or existing in the absence of free oxygen ⟨*anaerobic* respiration⟩ **b :** of, relating to, or being activity in which the body incurs an oxygen debt ⟨*anaerobic* exercise⟩
2 : relating to or induced by anaerobes
— **an·aer·o·bi·cal·ly** \-bi-k(ə-)lē\ *adverb*

an·aero·bi·o·sis \ˌa-nə-rō-(ˌ)bī-'ō-səs, -bē-; ˌan-ˌa(-ə)-, -ˌe(-ə)-\ *noun, plural* **-o·ses** \-'ō-ˌsēz\ [New Latin] (circa 1889)
: life in the absence of air or free oxygen

an·aes·the·sia, an·aes·thet·ic *chiefly British variant of* ANESTHESIA, ANESTHETIC

ana·gen·e·sis \ˌa-nə-'je-nə-səs\ *noun* [New Latin] (1889)
: evolutionary change producing a single lineage in which one taxon replaces another without branching — compare CLADOGENESIS

ana·glyph \'a-nə-ˌglif\ *noun* [Late Latin *anaglyphus* embossed, from Greek *anaglyphos,* from *anaglyphein* to emboss, from *ana-* + *glyphein* to carve — more at CLEAVE] (1651)
1 : a sculptured, chased, or embossed ornament worked in low relief
2 : a stereoscopic motion or still picture in which the right component of a composite image usually red in color is superposed on the left component in a contrasting color to produce a three-dimensional effect when viewed through correspondingly colored filters in the form of spectacles
— **ana·glyph·ic** \ˌa-nə-'gli-fik\ *adjective*

an·ag·no·ri·sis \ˌa-ˌnag-'nòr-ə-səs\ *noun, plural* **-ri·ses** \-ˌsēz\ [Greek *anagnōrisis,* from *anagnōrizein* to recognize, from *ana-* + *gnōrizein* to make known; akin to Greek *gnōrimos* well-known, *gignōskein* to come to know — more at KNOW] (circa 1800)
: the point in the plot especially of a tragedy at which the protagonist recognizes his or her or some other character's true identity or discovers the true nature of his or her own situation

an·a·go·ge *or* **an·a·go·gy** \'a-nə-ˌgō-jē\ *noun, plural* **-ges** *or* **-gies** [Late Latin *anagoge,* from Late Greek *anagōgē,* from Greek, reference, from *anagein* to refer, from *ana-* + *agein* to lead — more at AGENT] (15th century)
: interpretation of a word, passage, or text (as of Scripture or poetry) that finds beyond the literal, allegorical, and moral senses a fourth and ultimate spiritual or mystical sense
— **an·a·gog·ic** \ˌa-nə-'gä-jik\ *or* **an·a·gog·i·cal** \-ji-kəl\ *adjective*
— **an·a·gog·i·cal·ly** \-ji-k(ə-)lē\ *adverb*

¹an·a·gram \'a-nə-ˌgram\ *noun* [probably from Middle French *anagramme,* from New Latin *anagrammat-, anagramma,* modification of Greek *anagrammatismos,* from *anagrammatizein* to transpose letters, from *ana-* + *grammat-, gramma* letter — more at GRAM] (1589)
1 : a word or phrase made by transposing the letters of another word or phrase
2 *plural but singular in construction* **:** a game in which words are formed by rearranging the letters of other words or by arranging letters taken (as from a stock of cards or blocks) at random
— **an·a·gram·mat·ic** \ˌa-nə-grə-'ma·tik\ *also* **an·a·gram·mat·i·cal** \-ti-kəl\ *adjective*

— **an·a·gram·mat·i·cal·ly** \-ti-k(ə-)lē\ *adverb*

²anagram *transitive verb* **-grammed; -gram·ming** (1630)
1 : ANAGRAMMATIZE
2 : to rearrange (the letters of a text) in order to discover a hidden message

an·a·gram·ma·tize \ˌa-nə-'gra-mə-ˌtīz\ *transitive verb* **-tized; -tiz·ing** (1588)
: to transpose (as letters in a word) so as to form an anagram
— **an·a·gram·ma·ti·za·tion** \-ˌgra-mə-tə-'zā-shən\ *noun*

anal \'ā-nᵊl\ *adjective* (1769)
1 : of, relating to, or situated near the anus ⟨*anal* fin⟩
2 a : of, relating to, characterized by, or being the stage of psychosexual development in psychoanalytic theory during which the child is concerned especially with its feces **b :** of, relating to, characterized by, or being personality traits (as parsimony, meticulousness, and ill humor) considered typical of fixation at the anal stage of development ⟨*anal* disposition⟩ ⟨*anal* neatness⟩
— **anal·ly** \-nᵊl-ē\ *adverb*

anal·cime \ə-'nal-ˌsēm\ *noun* [French, from Greek *analkimos* weak, from *an-* + *alkimos* strong, from *alkē* strength] (1803)
: a white or slightly colored mineral that consists of hydrated silicate of sodium and aluminum and occurs in various igneous rocks in massive form or in crystals

anal·cite \ə-'nal-ˌsīt\ *noun* (1868)
: ANALCIME

an·a·lects \'a-nᵊl-ˌek(t)s\ *also* **an·a·lec·ta** \ˌa-nᵊl-'ek-tə\ *noun plural* [New Latin *analecta,* from Greek *analekta,* neuter plural of *analektos,* verbal of *analegein* to collect, from *ana-* + *legein* to gather — more at LEGEND] (1652)
: selected miscellaneous written passages

an·a·lem·ma \ˌa-nə-'le-mə\ *noun* [Latin, sundial on a pedestal, from Greek *analēmma,* lofty structure, sundial, from *analambanein* to take up, restore, from *ana-* + *lambanein* to take — more at LATCH] (1832)
: a plot or graph of the position of the sun in the sky at a certain time of day (as noon) at one locale measured at regular intervals throughout the year that has the shape of a figure 8; *also* **:** a scale (as on a globe or sundial) based on such a plot that shows the sun's position for each day of the year or that allows local mean time to be determined
— **an·a·lem·mat·ic** \ˌa-nə-le-'ma-tik, -lə-\ *adjective*

an·a·lep·tic \ˌa-nə-'lep-tik\ *noun* [Greek *analēptikos,* from *analambanein*] (1671)
: a drug that stimulates the central nervous system
— **analeptic** *adjective*

an·al·ge·sia \ˌa-nᵊl-'jē-zh(ē-)ə, -zē-ə\ *noun* [New Latin, from Greek *analgēsia,* from *an-* + *algēsis* sense of pain, from *algein* to suffer pain, from *algos* pain] (circa 1706)
: insensibility to pain without loss of consciousness
— **an·al·ge·sic** \-'jē-zik, -sik\ *adjective or noun*
— **an·al·get·ic** \-'je-tik\ *adjective or noun*

anal·i·ty \ā-'na-lə-tē\ *noun, plural* **-ties** (1939)
: the psychological state or quality of being anal

an·a·log \'a-nᵊl-ˌòg, -ˌäg\ *adjective* (1948)
1 : of, relating to, or being an analogue
2 a : of, relating to, or being a mechanism in which data is represented by continuously variable physical quantities **b :** of or relating to an analog computer **c :** being a timepiece having hour and minute hands

analog computer *noun* (1948)
: a computer that operates with numbers represented by directly measurable quantities (as voltages or rotations) — compare DIGITAL COMPUTER, HYBRID COMPUTER

an·a·log·i·cal \ˌa-nᵊl-'ä-ji-kəl\ *also* **an·a·log·ic** \-jik\ *adjective* (1609)
1 : of, relating to, or based on analogy
2 : expressing or implying analogy
— **an·a·log·i·cal·ly** \-ji-k(ə-)lē\ *adverb*

anal·o·gist \ə-'na-lə-jist\ *noun* (circa 1828)
: one who searches for or reasons from analogies

anal·o·gize \-ˌjīz\ *verb* **-gized; -giz·ing** (1655)
intransitive verb
: to use or exhibit analogy
transitive verb
: to compare by analogy

anal·o·gous \ə-'na-lə-gəs\ *adjective* [Latin *analogus,* from Greek *analogos,* literally, proportionate, from *ana-* + *logos* reason, ratio, from *legein* to gather, speak — more at LEGEND] (1646)
1 : showing an analogy or a likeness that permits one to draw an analogy
2 : being or related to as an analogue
synonym see SIMILAR
— **anal·o·gous·ly** *adverb*
— **anal·o·gous·ness** *noun*

¹an·a·logue *or* **an·a·log** \'a-nᵊl-ˌòg, -ˌäg\ *noun* [French *analogue,* from *analogue* analogous, from Greek *analogos*] (1826)
1 : something that is analogous or similar to something else
2 : an organ similar in function to an organ of another animal or plant but different in structure and origin
3 *usually analog* **:** a chemical compound that is structurally similar to another but differs slightly in composition (as in the replacement of one atom by an atom of a different element or in the presence of a particular functional group)
4 : a food product made by combining a less expensive food (as soybeans or whitefish) with additives to give the appearance and taste of a more expensive food (as beef or crab)

²an·a·logue *chiefly British variant of* ANALOG

anal·o·gy \ə-'na-lə-jē\ *noun, plural* **-gies** (15th century)
1 : inference that if two or more things agree with one another in some respects they will probably agree in others
2 a : resemblance in some particulars between things otherwise unlike **:** SIMILARITY **b :** comparison based on such resemblance
3 : correspondence between the members of pairs or sets of linguistic forms that serves as a basis for the creation of another form
4 : correspondence in function between anatomical parts of different structure and origin
— compare HOMOLOGY
synonym see LIKENESS

an·al·pha·bet \(ˌ)an-'al-fə-ˌbet, -bət\ *noun* [Greek *analphabētos* not knowing the alphabet, from *an-* + *alphabētos* alphabet] (circa 1889)
: one who cannot read **:** ILLITERATE
— **an·al·pha·bet·ic** \ˌan-ˌal-fə-'be-tik\ *adjective or noun*
— **an·al·pha·bet·ism** \(ˌ)an-'al-fə-bə-ˌti-zəm\ *noun*

anal·y·sand \ə-'na-lə-ˌsand\ *noun* [*analyse* + *-and* (as in *multiplicand*)] (1917)
: one who is undergoing psychoanalysis

an·a·lyse *chiefly British variant of* ANALYZE

anal·y·sis \ə-'na-lə-səs\ *noun, plural* **-y·ses** \-ˌsēz\ [New Latin, from Greek, from *analyein* to break up, from *ana-* + *lyein* to loosen — more at LOSE] (1581)

1 : separation of a whole into its component parts
2 a : the identification or separation of ingredients of a substance **b :** a statement of the constituents of a mixture
3 a : proof of a mathematical proposition by assuming the result and deducing a valid statement by a series of reversible steps **b** (1) **:** a branch of mathematics concerned mainly with functions and limits (2) **:** CALCULUS 1b
4 a : an examination of a complex, its elements, and their relations **b :** a statement of such an analysis
5 a : a method in philosophy of resolving complex expressions into simpler or more basic ones **b :** clarification of an expression by an elucidation of its use in discourse
6 : the use of function words instead of inflectional forms as a characteristic device of a language
7 : PSYCHOANALYSIS
analysis of variance (circa 1939)
: analysis of variation in an experimental outcome and especially of a statistical variance in order to determine the contributions of given factors or variables to the variance
analysis si·tus \-'sī-təs, -'sē-, -,tüs\ *noun* [New Latin, literally, analysis of situation] (circa 1909)
: TOPOLOGY 2a(1)
an·a·lyst \'a-nᵊl-əst\ *noun* [French *analyste*, from *analyse* analysis] (1656)
1 : a person who analyzes or who is skilled in analysis
2 : PSYCHOANALYST
an·a·lyt·ic \,a-nᵊl-'i-tik\ *or* **an·a·lyt·i·cal** \-ti-kəl\ *adjective* [Late Latin *analyticus*, from Greek *analytikos*, from *analyein*] (1601)
1 : of or relating to analysis or analytics; *especially* **:** separating something into component parts or constituent elements
2 : being a proposition (as "no bachelor is married") whose truth is evident from the meaning of the words it contains — compare SYNTHETIC
3 : skilled in or using analysis especially in thinking or reasoning ⟨a keenly *analytic* person⟩
4 : characterized by analysis rather than inflection ⟨*analytic* languages⟩
5 : PSYCHOANALYTIC
6 : treated or treatable by or using the methods of algebra and calculus
7 a *of a function of a real variable* **:** capable of being expanded in a Taylor's series in powers of $x - h$ in some neighborhood of the point h **b** *of a function of a complex variable* **:** differentiable at every point in some neighborhood of a given point or points
— **an·a·lyt·i·cal·ly** \-ti-k(ə-)lē\ *adverb*
— **an·a·ly·tic·i·ty** \,a-nᵊl-ə-'ti-sə-tē\ *noun*
analytic geometry *noun* (circa 1886)
: the study of geometric properties by means of algebraic operations upon symbols defined in terms of a coordinate system — called also *coordinate geometry*
analytic philosophy *noun* (1936)
: a philosophical movement that seeks the solution of philosophical problems in the analysis of propositions or sentences — called also *philosophical analysis; compare* ORDINARY=LANGUAGE PHILOSOPHY
an·a·lyt·ics \,a-nᵊl-'i-tiks\ *noun plural but singular or plural in construction* (circa 1590)
: the method of logical analysis
an·a·ly·za·tion \,a-nᵊl-ə-'zā-shən\ *noun* (1742)
: ANALYSIS
an·a·lyze \'a-nᵊl-,īz\ *transitive verb* **-lyzed; -lyz·ing** [probably irregular from *analysis*] (1587)
1 : to study or determine the nature and relationship of the parts of by analysis ⟨*analyze* a traffic pattern⟩
2 : to subject to scientific or grammatical analysis

3 : PSYCHOANALYZE ☆
— **an·a·lyz·abil·i·ty** \,a-nᵊl-,ī-zə-'bi-lə-tē\ *noun*
— **an·a·lyz·able** \'a-nᵊl-,ī-zə-bəl\ *adjective*
— **an·a·lyz·er** \-,ī-zər\ *noun*
an·am·ne·sis \,a-,nam-'nē-səs\ *noun, plural* **-ne·ses** \-,sēz\ [New Latin, from Greek *anamnēsis*, from *anamimnēskesthai* to remember, from *ana-* + *mimnēskesthai* to remember — more at MIND] (circa 1593)
1 : a recalling to mind **:** REMINISCENCE
2 : a preliminary case history of a medical or psychiatric patient
an·am·nes·tic \-'nes-tik\ *adjective* [Greek *anamnēstikos* easily recalled, from *anamimnēskesthai*] (circa 1753)
1 : of or relating to an anamnesis
2 : of or relating to a secondary response to an immunogenic substance after serum antibodies can no longer be detected in the blood
ana·mor·phic \,a-nə-'mȯr-fik\ *adjective* [New Latin *anamorphosis* distorted optical image] (circa 1925)
: producing, relating to, or marked by intentional distortion (as by unequal magnification along perpendicular axes) of an image ⟨an *anamorphic* lens⟩
An·a·ni·as \,a-nə-'nī-əs\ *noun* [Greek, probably from Hebrew *Ḥānanyāh*]
1 : an early Christian struck dead for lying
2 : LIAR
an·a·pest \'a-nə-,pest\ *noun* [Latin *anapaestus*, from Greek *anapaistos*, literally, struck back (a dactyl reversed), from *ana-* + *-paistos*, verbal of *paiein* to strike] (circa 1678)
: a metrical foot consisting of two short syllables followed by one long syllable or of two unstressed syllables followed by one stressed syllable (as *unabridged*)
— **an·a·pes·tic** \,a-nə-'pes-tik\ *adjective or noun*
ana·phase \'a-nə-,fāz\ *noun* [International Scientific Vocabulary] (1887)
: the stage of mitosis and meiosis in which the chromosomes move toward the poles of the spindle
— **ana·pha·sic** \,a-nə-'fā-zik\ *adjective*
ana·phor \'a-nə-,fȯr\ *noun, plural* **anaphors** *also* **anaph·o·ra** \ə-'na-f(ə-)rə\ [back=formation from *anaphoric*] (1975)
: a word or phrase with an anaphoric function
anaph·o·ra \ə-'na-f(ə-)rə\ *noun* [Late Latin, from Late Greek, from Greek, act of carrying back, reference, from *anapherein* to carry back, refer, from *ana-* + *pherein* to carry — more at BEAR] (circa 1589)
1 : repetition of a word or expression at the beginning of successive phrases, clauses, sentences, or verses especially for rhetorical or poetic effect ⟨Lincoln's "we cannot dedicate—we cannot consecrate—we cannot hallow—this ground" is an example of *anaphora*⟩ — compare EPISTROPHE
2 : use of a grammatical substitute (as a pronoun or a pro-verb) to refer to the denotation of a preceding word or group of words; *also* **:** the relation between a grammatical substitute and its antecedent
an·a·phor·ic \,a-nə-'fȯr-ik, -'fär-\ *adjective* (1904)
: of or relating to anaphora ⟨an *anaphoric* usage⟩; *especially* **:** being a word or phrase that takes its reference from another word or phrase and especially from a preceding word or phrase — compare CATAPHORIC
— **ana·phor·i·cal·ly** \-i-k(ə-)lē\ *adverb*
an·aph·ro·di·si·ac \a-,na-frə-'dē-zē-,ak, -zhē-, -'di-zē-\ *adjective* (1823)
: inhibiting or discouraging sexual desire
— **anaphrodisiac** *noun*
ana·phy·lac·tic \,a-nə-fə-'lak-tik\ *adjective* (1907)
: of, relating to, affected by, or causing anaphylaxis or anaphylactic shock
— **ana·phy·lac·ti·cal·ly** \-ti-k(ə-)lē\ *adverb*

— **ana·phy·lac·toid** \-'lak-,tȯid\ *adjective*
anaphylactic shock *noun* (1910)
: an often severe and sometimes fatal systemic reaction in a susceptible individual upon exposure to a specific antigen (as wasp venom or penicillin) after previous sensitization that is characterized especially by respiratory symptoms, fainting, itching, and urticaria
ana·phy·lax·is \-'lak-səs\ *noun, plural* **-lax·es** \-,sēz\ [New Latin, from *ana-* + pro*phylaxis*] (1907)
1 : hypersensitivity (as to foreign proteins or drugs) resulting from sensitization following prior contact with the causative agent
2 : ANAPHYLACTIC SHOCK
ana·pla·sia \,a-nə-'plā-zh(ē-)ə\ *noun* [New Latin] (circa 1909)
: reversion of cells to a more primitive or undifferentiated form
— **ana·plas·tic** \-'plas-tik\ *adjective*
ana·plas·mo·sis \,a-nə-,plaz-'mō-səs\ *noun, plural* **-mo·ses** \-,sēz\ [New Latin, from *Anaplasma*, genus name, from *ana-* + *plasma* (protoplasm)] (1920)
: a tick-borne disease of cattle and sheep caused by a bacterium (*Anaplasma marginale*) and characterized especially by anemia without blood-tinged urine and by jaundice
an·arch \'a-,närk\ *noun* [back-formation from *anarchy*] (1667)
: a leader or advocate of revolt or anarchy
an·ar·chic \a-'när-kik, ə-\ *also* **an·ar·chi·cal** \-ki-kəl\ *adjective* (1649)
1 a : of, relating to, or advocating anarchy **b :** likely to bring about anarchy ⟨*anarchic* violence⟩
2 : lacking order, regularity, or definiteness ⟨*anarchic* art forms⟩
— **an·ar·chi·cal·ly** \-k(ə-)lē\ *adverb*
an·ar·chism \'a-nər-,ki-zəm, -,när-\ *noun* (1642)
1 : a political theory holding all forms of governmental authority to be unnecessary and undesirable and advocating a society based on voluntary cooperation and free association of individuals and groups
2 : the advocacy or practice of anarchistic principles
an·ar·chist \'a-nər-kist, -,när-\ *noun* (1678)
1 : one who rebels against any authority, established order, or ruling power
2 : one who believes in, advocates, or promotes anarchism or anarchy; *especially* **:** one who uses violent means to overthrow the established order
— **anarchist** *or* **an·ar·chis·tic** \,a-nər-'kis-tik, -(,)när-\ *adjective*
an·ar·cho–syn·di·cal·ism \a-,när-kō-'sin-di-kə-,li-zəm, ,a-nər-kō-\ *noun* (circa 1928)
: SYNDICALISM
— **an·ar·cho–syn·di·cal·ist** \-kə-list\ *noun or adjective*
an·ar·chy \'a-nər-kē, -,när-\ *noun* [Medieval Latin *anarchia*, from Greek, from *anarchos* having no ruler, from *an-* + *archos* ruler — more at ARCH-] (1539)

☆ **SYNONYMS**
Analyze, dissect, break down mean to divide a complex whole into its parts or elements. ANALYZE suggests separating or distinguishing the component parts of something (as a substance, a process, a situation) so as to discover its true nature or inner relationships (*analyzed* the problem of the trade deficit). DISSECT suggests a searching analysis by laying bare parts or pieces for individual scrutiny (commentators *dissected* every word of the President's statement). BREAK DOWN implies a reducing to simpler parts or divisions (*break down* the budget).

1 a : absence of government **b :** a state of lawlessness or political disorder due to the absence of governmental authority **c :** a utopian society of individuals who enjoy complete freedom without government
2 a : absence or denial of any authority or established order **b :** absence of order **:** DISORDER ⟨not manicured plots but a wild *anarchy* of nature —Israel Shenker⟩
3 : ANARCHISM

ana·sar·ca \ˌa-nə-ˈsär-kə\ *noun* [New Latin, from *ana-* + Greek *sark-, sarx* flesh — more at SARCASM] (14th century)
: generalized edema with accumulation of serum in the connective tissue
— **ana·sar·cous** \-kəs\ *adjective*

An·a·sa·zi \ˌä-nə-ˈsä-zē\ *noun, plural* **Anasazi** [Navajo *anaasází*, literally, enemy ancestors] (1938)
: a prehistoric American Indian inhabitant of the canyons of northern Arizona and New Mexico and southwestern Colorado

an·as·tig·mat \a-ˈnas-tig-ˌmat, ˌa-nə-ˈstig-\ *noun* [German, back-formation from *anastigmatisch* anastigmatic] (1890)
: an anastigmatic lens

an·a·stig·mat·ic \ˌa-nə-(ˌ)stig-ˈma-tik, ˌa-ˌnas-tig-\ *adjective* [International Scientific Vocabulary] (1890)
: not astigmatic — used especially of lenses that are able to form approximately point images of object points

anas·to·mose \ə-ˈnas-tə-ˌmōz, -ˌmōs\ *verb* **-mosed; -mos·ing** [probably back-formation from *anastomosis*] (1697)
transitive verb
: to connect or join by anastomosis
intransitive verb
: to communicate by anastomosis

anas·to·mo·sis \ə-ˌnas-tə-ˈmō-səs\ *noun, plural* **-mo·ses** \-ˌsēz\ [Late Latin, from Greek *anastomōsis*, from *anastomoun* to provide with an outlet, from *ana-* + *stoma* mouth, opening — more at STOMACH] (1541)
1 : the union of parts or branches (as of streams, blood vessels, or leaf veins) so as to intercommunicate **:** INOSCULATION
2 : a product of anastomosis **:** NETWORK
— **anas·to·mot·ic** \-ˈmä-tik\ *adjective*

anas·tro·phe \ə-ˈnas-trə-(ˌ)fē\ *noun* [Medieval Latin, from Greek *anastrophē*, literally, turning back, from *anastrephein* to turn back, from *ana-* + *strephein* to turn] (circa 1550)
: inversion of the usual syntactical order of words for rhetorical effect — compare HYSTERON PROTERON

an·a·tase \ˈa-nə-ˌtās, -ˌtāz\ *noun* [French, from Greek *anatasis* extension, from *anateinein* to extend, from *ana-* + *teinein* to stretch — more at THIN] (circa 1828)
: a tetragonal form of titanium dioxide used especially as a white pigment

anath·e·ma \ə-ˈna-thə-mə\ *noun* [Late Latin *anathemat-, anathema*, from Greek, thing devoted to evil, curse, from *anatithenai* to set up, dedicate, from *ana-* + *tithenai* to place, set — more at DO] (1526)
1 a : one that is cursed by ecclesiastical authority **b :** someone or something intensely disliked or loathed — usually used as a predicate nominative ⟨this notion was *anathema* to most of his countrymen —S. J. Gould⟩
2 a : a ban or curse solemnly pronounced by ecclesiastical authority and accompanied by excommunication **b :** the denunciation of something as accursed **c :** a vigorous denunciation **:** CURSE ◇

anath·e·ma·tize \-ˌtīz\ *transitive verb* **-tized; -tiz·ing** (1566)
: to pronounce an anathema upon
synonym *see* EXECRATE

An·a·to·lian \ˌa-nə-ˈtō-lē-ən, -ˈtōl-yən\ *noun* (1590)
1 : a native or inhabitant of Anatolia and specifically of the western plateau lands of Turkey in Asia

2 : a branch of the Indo-European language family that includes a group of extinct languages of ancient Anatolia — see INDO-EUROPEAN LANGUAGES table
— **Anatolian** *adjective*

anat·o·mise *British variant of* ANATOMIZE

anat·o·mist \ə-ˈna-tə-mist\ *noun* (1543)
1 : a student of anatomy; *especially* **:** one skilled in dissection
2 : one who analyzes minutely and critically ⟨an *anatomist* of urban society⟩

anat·o·mize \-ˌmīz\ *transitive verb* **-mized; -miz·ing** (15th century)
1 : to cut in pieces in order to display or examine the structure and use of the parts **:** DISSECT
2 : ANALYZE

anat·o·my \ə-ˈna-tə-mē\ *noun, plural* **-mies** [Late Latin *anatomia* dissection, from Greek *anatomē*, from *anatemnein* to dissect, from *ana-* + *temnein* to cut] (14th century)
1 : a branch of morphology that deals with the structure of organisms
2 : a treatise on anatomic science or art
3 : the art of separating the parts of an organism in order to ascertain their position, relations, structure, and function **:** DISSECTION
4 *obsolete* **:** a body dissected or to be dissected
5 : structural makeup especially of an organism or any of its parts
6 : a separating or dividing into parts for detailed examination **:** ANALYSIS
7 a (1) **:** SKELETON (2) **:** MUMMY **b :** the human body
— **an·a·tom·ic** \ˌa-nə-ˈtä-mik\ *or* **an·a·tom·i·cal** \-mi-kəl\ *adjective*
— **an·a·tom·i·cal·ly** \-mi-k(ə-)lē\ *adverb*

anat·ro·pous \ə-ˈna-trə-pəs\ *adjective* (circa 1846)
: having or being an ovule inverted so that the micropyle is bent down to the funiculus to which the body of the ovule is united

-ance *noun suffix* [Middle English, from Old French, from Latin *-antia*, from *-ant-, -ans* -ant + *-ia* -y]
1 : action or process ⟨further*ance*⟩ **:** instance of an action or process ⟨perform*ance*⟩
2 : quality or state **:** instance of a quality or state ⟨protuber*ance*⟩
3 : amount or degree ⟨conduct*ance*⟩

an·ces·tor \ˈan-ˌses-tər *also* -səs-\ *noun* [Middle English *ancestre*, from Old French, from Latin *antecessor* predecessor, from *antecedere* to go before, from *ante-* + *cedere* to go — more at CEDE] (13th century)
1 a : one from whom a person is descended and who is usually more remote in the line of descent than a grandparent **b :** FOREFATHER 2
2 : FORERUNNER, PROTOTYPE
3 : a progenitor of a more recent or existing species or group

ancestor worship *noun* (1854)
: the custom of venerating deceased ancestors who are considered still a part of the family and whose spirits are believed to have the power to intervene in the affairs of the living

an·ces·tral \an-ˈses-trəl\ *adjective* (15th century)
: of, relating to, or inherited from an ancestor ⟨*ancestral* estates⟩
— **an·ces·tral·ly** \-trə-lē\ *adverb*

an·ces·tress \ˈan-ˌses-trəs\ *noun* (1580)
: a female ancestor

an·ces·try \ˈan-ˌses-trē\ *noun* (14th century)
1 : line of descent **:** LINEAGE; *especially* **:** honorable, noble, or aristocratic descent
2 : persons initiating or comprising a line of descent **:** ANCESTORS

An·chi·ses \an-ˈkī-(ˌ)sēz, aŋ-\ *noun* [Latin, from Greek *Anchisēs*]
: the father of Aeneas rescued by his son from the burning city of Troy

¹an·chor \ˈaŋ-kər\ *noun, often attributive* [Middle English *ancre*, from Old English *ancor*, from Latin *anchora*, from Greek *ankyra*;

akin to Old English *anga* hook — more at ANGLE] (before 12th century)
1 : a device usually of metal attached to a ship or boat by a cable and cast overboard to hold it in a particular place by means of a fluke that digs into the bottom
2 : a reliable or principal support **:** MAINSTAY
3 : something that serves to hold an object firmly
4 : an object shaped like a ship's anchor
5 : an anchorman or anchorwoman
6 : the member of a team (as a relay team) that competes last
7 : a large business (as a department store) that attracts customers and other businesses to a shopping center or mall
— **an·chor·less** \-ləs\ *adjective*
— **at anchor :** being anchored

anchor 1: *A* yachtsman's: *1* ring, *2* stock, *3* shank, *4* bill, *5* fluke, *6* arm, *7* throat, *8* crown; *B* grapnel; *C* mushroom

²anchor *verb* **an·chored; an·chor·ing** \-k(ə-)riŋ\ (13th century)
transitive verb
1 : to hold in place in the water by an anchor
2 : to secure firmly **:** FIX
3 : to act or serve as an anchor for ⟨it is she who is *anchoring* the rebuilding campaign —G. D. Boone⟩ ⟨*anchoring* the evening news⟩
intransitive verb
1 : to cast anchor
2 : to become fixed

an·chor·age \ˈaŋ-k(ə-)rij\ *noun* (15th century)

◇ WORD HISTORY
anathema The word *anathema* is of Greek origin, a derivative of the verb *anatithenai*, which means "to set up, dedicate." In the Septuagint, an influential Greek translation of the Hebrew scriptures, *anathema* was used to mean "something offered to God," and could refer either to a revered object or an object representing destruction brought about in the name of the Lord. Since the objects symbolic of consecrated destruction were often the spoils of war stripped from the bodies of despised enemies, *anathema* came to signify something odious or accursed. In the New Testament, Paul uses the term in the sense of a curse and the forced exclusion of a person from the Christian community. In Medieval Latin *anathema* was used interchangeably with *excommunicatio* and was pronounced chiefly against unrepentant heretics. In English the word *anathema* has been and continues to be used in its ecclesiastical sense. By the 18th century, however, its use in a broadened sense for "the denunciation of anything as accursed" is attested. That secular use continues to be common, as does the transferred sense, "someone or something intensely disliked."

\ə\ abut \ᵊ\ kitten \ər\ **further** \a\ ash \ā\ ace
\ä\ mop, mar \aù\ out \ch\ chin \e\ bet \ē\ easy
\g\ go \i\ hit \ī\ ice \j\ job \ŋ\ sing \ō\ go
\ò\ law \òi\ boy \th\ thin \t̲h̲\ the \ü\ loot \ù\ foot
\y\ yet \zh\ vision *see also* Guide to Pronunciation

1 a : a place where vessels anchor : a place suitable for anchoring **b** : the act of anchoring : the condition of being anchored
2 : a means of securing : a source of reassurance ⟨this *anchorage* of Christian hope —T. O. Wedel⟩
3 : something that provides a secure hold
an·cho·ress \'aŋ-k(ə-)rəs\ *or* **an·cress** \-krəs\ *noun* [Middle English *ankeresse*, from *anker* hermit, from Old English *ancor*, from Old Irish *anchara*, from Late Latin *anachoreta*] (14th century)
: a woman who is an anchorite
an·cho·rite \'aŋ-kə-ˌrīt\ *also* **an·cho·ret** \-ˌret\ *noun* [Middle English, from Medieval Latin *anchorita*, alteration of Late Latin *anachoreta*, from Late Greek *anachōrētēs*, from Greek *anachōrein* to withdraw, from *ana-* + *chōrein* to make room, from *chōros* place] (15th century)
: one who lives in seclusion usually for religious reasons
— **an·cho·rit·ic** \ˌaŋ-kə-'ri-tik\ *adjective*
— **an·cho·rit·i·cal·ly** \-ti-k(ə-)lē\ *adverb*
an·chor·man \'aŋ-kər-ˌman\ *noun* (1911)
1 : one who is last: as **a** : the member of a team who competes last ⟨the *anchorman* on a relay team⟩ **b** : one who has the lowest scholastic standing in a graduating class
2 : a broadcaster (as on a news program) who introduces reports by other broadcasters and usually reads the news
3 : MODERATOR 2c
an·chor·peo·ple \-ˌpē-pəl\ *noun plural* (1974)
: ANCHORPERSONS
an·chor·per·son \-ˌpər-s°n\ *noun* (1973)
: an anchorman or anchorwoman
an·chor·wom·an \-ˌwu̇-mən\ *noun* (1973)
: a woman who anchors a broadcast
an·cho·ve·ta *also* **an·cho·vet·ta** \ˌan-chō-'ve-tə\ *noun* [Spanish *anchoveta*, diminutive of *anchova*] (1940)
: a small anchovy (*Cetengraulis mysticetus*) of the Pacific coast of North America
an·cho·vy \'an-ˌchō-vē, an-'\ *noun, plural* **-vies** *or* **-vy** [Spanish *anchova*] (1596)
: any of a family (Engraulidae) of small fishes resembling herrings; *especially* : a common Mediterranean fish (*Engraulis encrasicholus*) used especially in appetizers, as a garnish, and for making sauces and relishes
an·cien ré·gime \ä°s-ya°-rä-'zhēm\ *noun* [French, literally, old regime] (1794)
1 : the political and social system of France before the Revolution of 1789
2 : a system or mode no longer prevailing
1an·cient \'ān(t)-shənt, 'āŋ(k)-shənt\ *adjective* [Middle English *ancien*, from Middle French, from (assumed) Vulgar Latin *anteanus*, from Latin *ante* before — more at ANTE-] (14th century)
1 : having had an existence of many years
2 : of or relating to a remote period, to a time early in history, or to those living in such a period or time; *especially* : of or relating to the historical period beginning with the earliest known civilizations and extending to the fall of the western Roman Empire in A.D. 476
3 : having the qualities of age or long existence: **a** : VENERABLE **b** : OLD-FASHIONED, ANTIQUE
synonym see OLD
— **an·cient·ness** *noun*
2ancient *noun* (1502)
1 : an aged living being ⟨a penniless *ancient*⟩
2 : one who lived in ancient times: **a** *plural* : the civilized people of antiquity; *especially* : those of the classical nations **b** : one of the classical authors ⟨Plutarch and other *ancients*⟩
3 : an ancient coin
3ancient *noun* [alteration of *ensign*] (1554)
1 *archaic* : ENSIGN, STANDARD, FLAG
2 *obsolete* : the bearer of an ensign
ancient history *noun* (1595)
1 : the history of ancient times

2 : knowledge or information that is widespread and has lost its initial freshness or importance : common knowledge
an·cient·ly *adverb* (1502)
: in ancient times : long ago
an·cient·ry \-shən-trē\ *noun* (1580)
: ANTIQUITY, ANCIENTNESS
an·cil·la \an-'si-lə\ *noun, plural* **-lae** \-(ˌ)lē\ [Latin, female servant] (1902)
: an aid to achieving or mastering something difficult
an·cil·lary \'an(t)-sə-ˌler-ē, *especially British* an-'si-lə-rē\ *adjective* (1667)
1 : SUBORDINATE, SUBSIDIARY ⟨the main factory and its *ancillary* plants⟩
2 : AUXILIARY, SUPPLEMENTARY ⟨the need for *ancillary* evidence⟩
— **ancillary** *noun*
an·con \'aŋ-ˌkän\ *noun, plural* **an·co·nes** \aŋ-'kō-nēz\ [Latin, from Greek *ankōn* elbow; akin to Old English *anga* hook — more at ANGLE] (circa 1706)
: a bracket, elbow, or console used as an architectural support
-ancy *noun suffix* [Latin *-antia* — more at -ANCE]
: quality or state ⟨piqu*ancy*⟩
an·cy·lo·sto·mi·a·sis \ˌaŋ-ki-ˌlō-stə-'mī-ə-səs, ˌan(t)-sə-\ *noun, plural* **-a·ses** \-ˌsēz\ [New Latin, from *Ancylostoma*, genus of hookworms, from Greek *ankylos* hooked (akin to Old English *anga* hook) + *stoma* mouth — more at ANGLE, STOMACH] (1887)
: infestation with or disease caused by hookworms; *especially* : a lethargic anemic state in humans due to blood loss from hookworms feeding in the small intestine
and \ən(d), (ˈ)an(d), *usually* °n(d) *after* t, d, s *or* z, *often* °m *after* p *or* b, *sometimes* °ŋ *after* k *or* g\ *conjunction* [Middle English, from Old English; akin to Old High German *unti* and] (before 12th century)
1 — used as a function word to indicate connection or addition especially of items within the same class or type; used to join sentence elements of the same grammatical rank or function
2 a — used as a function word to express logical modification, consequence, antithesis, or supplementary explanation **b** — used as a function word to join one finite verb (as *go, come, try*) to another so that together they are logically equivalent to an infinitive of purpose ⟨come *and* see me⟩
3 *obsolete* : IF
4 — used in logic to form a conjunction
— **and so forth** \ən-'sō-ˌförth, -ˌförth\ **1** : and others or more of the same or similar kind **2** : further in the same or similar manner **3** : and the rest **4** : and other things
— **and so on** \ən-'sō-ˌön, -ˌän\ : and so forth
AND \'and\ *noun* (1949)
: a logical operator that requires both of two inputs to be present or two conditions to be met for an output to be made or a statement to be executed
An·da·lu·sian \ˌan-də-'lü-zhən\ *noun* [*Andalusia*, Spain] (1966)
: any of a breed of horses of Spanish origin that have a high-stepping gait
an·da·lu·site \ˌan-də-'lü-ˌsīt\ *noun* [French *andalousite*, from *Andalousie* Andalusia, region in Spain] (circa 1828)
: a mineral consisting of a silicate of aluminum usually in thick orthorhombic prisms of various colors
1an·dan·te \än-'dän-(ˌ)tā, -'dän-tē; an-'dan-tē\ *adverb or adjective* [Italian, literally, going, present participle of *andare* to go] (1724)
: moderately slow — usually used as a direction in music
2andante *noun* (1784)
: a musical composition or movement in andante tempo

1an·dan·ti·no \ˌän-ˌdän-'tē-(ˌ)nō\ *adverb or adjective* [Italian, diminutive of *andante*] (1819)
: slightly faster than andante — used as a direction in music
2andantino *noun, plural* **-nos** (1845)
: a musical composition or movement in andantino tempo
an·des·ite \'an-di-ˌzīt\ *noun* [German *Andesit*, from *Andes*] (1850)
: an extrusive usually dark grayish rock consisting essentially of oligoclase or feldspar
— **an·des·it·ic** \ˌan-di-'zi-tik\ *adjective*
and how *adverb* (1865)
— used to emphasize the preceding idea ⟨having a great time—*and how!*⟩
and·iron \'an-ˌdī(-ə)rn\ *noun* [Middle English *aundiren*, modification of Middle French *andier*] (14th century)
: either of a pair of metal supports for firewood used on a hearth and made of a horizontal bar mounted on short legs with usually a vertical shaft surmounting the front end
and/or \'an-ˌdȯr\ *conjunction* (1853)
— used as a function word to indicate that two words or expressions are to be taken together or individually ⟨language comprehension *and/or* production —David Crystal⟩
an·dou·ille \än-'dü-ē, ˌän-dü-ē\ *noun* [French, from Old French *andoille*, from (assumed) Vulgar Latin *inductilia*, neuter plural of *inductilis* made by insertion, from Latin *inductus*, past participle of *inducere* to insert, bring in — more at INDUCE] (1605)
: a highly spiced smoked pork sausage
an·douill·ette \ˌän-dü-'yet\ *noun* [French, diminutive of *andouille*] (1611)
: a fresh pork sausage made with tripe or chitterlings
andr- *or* **andro-** *combining form* [Latin, from Greek, from *andr-, anēr*; akin to Oscan *nerman*, Sanskrit *nar-*, Old Irish *nert* strength]
1 : male human being ⟨*andro*centric⟩
2 : male ⟨*andro*ecium⟩
an·dra·dite \an-'drä-ˌdīt, 'an-drə-ˌdīt\ *noun* [José B. de *Andrada* e Silva (died 1838) Brazilian geologist] (1868)
: a garnet of any of various colors ranging from yellow and green to brown and black
an·dro·cen·tric \ˌan-drə-'sen-trik\ *adjective* (1903)
: dominated by or emphasizing masculine interests or a masculine point of view
An·dro·cles \'an-drə-ˌklēz\ *noun* [Latin, from Greek *Androklēs*]
: a fabled Roman slave spared in the arena by a lion from whose foot he had years before extracted a thorn
an·droe·ci·um \an-'drē-shē-əm, -sē-əm\ *noun, plural* **-cia** \-shē-ə, -sē-ə\ [New Latin, from *andr-* + Greek *oikion*, diminutive of *oikos* house — more at VICINITY] (circa 1839)
: the aggregate of stamens in the flower of a seed plant
an·dro·gen \'an-drə-jən\ *noun* [International Scientific Vocabulary] (1936)
: a male sex hormone (as testosterone)
— **an·dro·gen·ic** \ˌan-drə-'je-nik\ *adjective*
an·dro·gen·e·sis \ˌan-drō-'je-nə-səs\ *noun* [New Latin] (circa 1900)
: development of an embryo containing only paternal chromosomes due to failure of the egg to participate in fertilization
— **an·dro·ge·net·ic** \-jə-'ne-tik\ *adjective*
an·dro·gyne \'an-drə-ˌjīn\ *noun* [Middle French, from Latin *androgynus*] (1552)
: one that is androgynous
an·drog·y·nous \an-'drä-jə-nəs\ *adjective* [Latin *androgynus* hermaphrodite, from Greek *androgynos*, from *andr-* + *gynē* woman — more at QUEEN] (1651)
1 : having the characteristics or nature of both male and female
2 a : neither specifically feminine nor masculine ⟨the *androgynous* pronoun *them*⟩ **b** : suitable to or for either sex ⟨*androgynous* clothing⟩

3 : having traditional male and female roles obscured or reversed ⟨an *androgynous* marriage⟩

— **an·drog·y·ny** \-nē\ *noun*

an·droid \'an-ˌdrȯid\ *noun* [Late Greek *androeidēs* manlike, from Greek *andr-* + *-oeidēs* -oid] (circa 1751)

: a mobile robot usually with a human form

An·drom·a·che \an-'drä-mə-(ˌ)kē\ *noun* [Latin, from Greek *Andromachē*]

: the wife of Hector

an·drom·e·da \an-'drä-mə-də\ *noun* [New Latin *Andromeda*, genus name, from Latin] (circa 1760)

: any of several evergreen shrubs (genera *Pieris* and *Andromeda*) of the heath family; *especially* : JAPANESE ANDROMEDA

An·drom·e·da \an-'drä-mə-də\ *noun* [Latin, from Greek *Andromedē*]

1 : an Ethiopian princess of Greek mythology rescued from a monster by her future husband Perseus

2 [Latin (genitive *Andromedae*)] : a northern constellation directly south of Cassiopeia between Pegasus and Perseus

an·dros·ter·one \an-'dräs-tə-ˌrōn\ *noun* [International Scientific Vocabulary] (1934)

: an androgenic hormone that is a hydroxy ketone $C_{19}H_{30}O_2$ found in human male and female urine

ane \'ān\ *adjective or noun or pronoun* (before 12th century)

chiefly Scottish : ONE

-ane *noun suffix* [International Scientific Vocabulary *-an*, *-ane*, alteration of *-ene*, *-ine*, & *-one*]

1 : ³-AN 1 ⟨fur*ane*⟩

2 : saturated hydrocarbon ⟨alk*ane*⟩ ⟨meth*ane*⟩

an·ec·dot·age \'a-nik-ˌdō-tij\ *noun* (1823)

1 : the telling of anecdotes; *also* : ANECDOTES

2 : garrulous old age

an·ec·dot·al \ˌa-nik-'dō-t³l\ *adjective* (1836)

1 a : of, relating to, or consisting of anecdotes ⟨an *anecdotal* biography⟩ **b** : ANECDOTIC 2 ⟨my *anecdotal* uncle⟩

2 : based on or consisting of reports or observations of usually unscientific observers ⟨*anecdotal* evidence⟩

3 : of, relating to, or being the depiction of a scene suggesting a story ⟨*anecdotal* painting⟩ ⟨*anecdotal* detail⟩

— **an·ec·dot·al·ly** \-t³l-ē\ *adverb*

an·ec·dot·al·ist \ˌa-nik-'dō-t³l-ist\ *or* **an·ec·dot·ist** \'a-nik-ˌdō-tist\ *noun* (1837)

: one who is given to or is skilled in telling anecdotes

— **an·ec·dot·al·ism** \-t³l-ˌi-zəm\ *noun*

an·ec·dote \'a-nik-ˌdōt\ *noun, plural* **anec·dotes** *also* **an·ec·dota** \ˌa-nik-'dō-tə\ [French, from Greek *anekdota* unpublished items, from neuter plural of *anekdotos* unpublished, from *a-* + *ekdidonai* to publish, from *ex* out + *didonai* to give — more at EX-, DATE] (circa 1721)

: a usually short narrative of an interesting, amusing, or biographical incident ◇

an·ec·dot·ic \ˌa-nik-'dä-tik\ *or* **an·ec·dot·i·cal** \-'dä-ti-kəl\ *adjective* (circa 1744)

1 : ANECDOTAL 1a

2 : given to or skilled in telling anecdotes

— **an·ec·dot·i·cal·ly** \-'dä-ti-k(ə-)lē\ *adverb*

an·echo·ic \ˌa-ni-'kō-ik\ *adjective* (1946)

: free from echoes and reverberations ⟨an *anechoic* chamber⟩

an·elas·tic \ˌa-n³l-'as-tik\ *adjective* (1947)

: relating to the property of a substance in which there is no definite relation between stress and strain

— **an·elas·tic·i·ty** \-n³l-ˌas-'ti-sə-tē, -'tis-tē\ *noun*

anem- *or* **anemo-** *combining form* [Greek, from *anemos* — more at ANIMATE]

: wind ⟨*anem*ometer⟩

ane·mia \ə-'nē-mē-ə\ *noun* [New Latin, from Greek *anaimia* bloodlessness, from *a-* + *-aimia* -emia] (1824)

1 a : a condition in which the blood is deficient in red blood cells, in hemoglobin, or in total volume **b** : ISCHEMIA

2 : lack of vitality

ane·mic \ə-'nē-mik\ *adjective* (1858)

1 : relating to or affected with anemia

2 a : lacking force, vitality, or spirit ⟨an *anemic* rendition of the song⟩ ⟨*anemic* efforts at enforcement⟩ **b** : lacking interest or savor : INSIPID ⟨*anemic* wines⟩ **c** : lacking in substance or quantity ⟨*anemic* returns on an investment⟩ ⟨*anemic* attendance⟩

— **ane·mi·cal·ly** \-mi-k(ə-)lē\ *adverb*

anemo·graph \ə-'ne-mə-ˌgraf\ *noun* (1865)

: a recording anemometer

an·e·mom·e·ter \ˌa-nə-'mä-mə-tər\ *noun* (circa 1751)

: an instrument for measuring and indicating the force or speed of the wind

an·e·mom·e·try \ˌa-nə-'mä-mə-trē\ *noun* (1847)

: the process of ascertaining the force, speed, and direction of wind or an airflow

anem·o·ne \ə-'ne-mə-nē\ *noun* [Latin, from Greek *anemōnē*] (1548)

1 : any of a large genus (*Anemone*) of the buttercup family having lobed or divided leaves and showy flowers without petals but with conspicuous often colored sepals — called also *windflower*

2 : SEA ANEMONE

an·e·moph·i·lous \ˌa-nə-'mä-fə-ləs\ *adjective* (1874)

: pollinated by wind

an·en·ceph·a·ly \ˌan-(ˌ)en-'se-fə-lē\ *noun, plural* **-lies** [²*a-* + *encephal-* + ²*-y*] (circa 1889)

: congenital absence of all or a major part of the brain

— **an·en·ce·phal·ic** \-ˌen(t)-sə-'fa-lik\ *adjective*

anent \ə-'nent\ *preposition* [Middle English *onevent*, *anent*, from Old English *on efen* alongside, from *on* + *efen* even] (13th century)

: ABOUT, CONCERNING

an·er·oid \'a-nə-ˌrȯid\ *adjective* [French *anéroïde*, from Greek *a-* + Late Greek *nēron* water, from Greek, neuter of *nearos*, *nēros* fresh; akin to Greek *neos* new — more at NEW] (circa 1848)

: using no liquid; *specifically* : operating by the effect of outside air pressure on a diaphragm forming one wall of an evacuated container ⟨*aneroid* barometer⟩

an·es·the·sia \ˌa-nəs-'thē-zhə\ *noun* [New Latin, from Greek *anaisthēsia* insensibility, from *a-* + *aisthēsis* perception, from *aisthanesthai* to perceive — more at AUDIBLE] (circa 1721)

: loss of sensation with or without loss of consciousness

an·es·the·si·ol·o·gist \-ˌthē-zē-'ä-lə-jist\ *noun* (1942)

: ANESTHETIST; *specifically* : a physician specializing in anesthesiology

an·es·the·si·ol·o·gy \-jē\ *noun* (circa 1914)

: a branch of medical science dealing with anesthesia and anesthetics

¹an·es·thet·ic \ˌa-nəs-'the-tik\ *adjective* (1846)

1 : of, relating to, or capable of producing anesthesia

2 : lacking awareness or sensitivity ⟨unmoved and quite *anesthetic* to his presence —S. J. Perelman⟩

— **an·es·thet·i·cal·ly** \-ti-k(ə-)lē\ *adverb*

²anesthetic *noun* (1848)

1 : a substance that produces anesthesia

2 : something that brings relief : PALLIATIVE

anes·the·tist \ə-'nes-thə-tist, *British* -'nēs-\ *noun* (1882)

: one who administers anesthetics

anes·the·tize \-thə-ˌtīz\ *transitive verb* **-tized; -tiz·ing** (1848)

: to subject to anesthesia

an·es·trous \(ˌ)an-'es-trəs\ *adjective* (circa 1909)

1 : not exhibiting estrus

2 : of or relating to anestrus

an·es·trus \-trəs\ *noun* [New Latin] (1927)

: the period of sexual quiescence between two periods of sexual activity in cyclically breeding mammals

an·eu·ploid \'an-yü-ˌplȯid\ *adjective* (1926)

: having or being a chromosome number that is not an exact multiple of the usually haploid number — compare EUPLOID

— **aneuploid** *noun*

— **an·eu·ploi·dy** \-ˌplȯi-dē\ *noun*

an·eu·rysm *also* **an·eu·rism** \'an-yə-ˌri-zəm\ *noun* [Greek *aneurysma*, from *aneurynein* to dilate, from *ana-* + *eurynein* to stretch, from *eurys* wide — more at EURY-] (15th century)

: an abnormal blood-filled dilatation of a blood vessel and especially an artery resulting from disease of the vessel wall

— **an·eu·rys·mal** \ˌan-yə-'riz-məl\ *adjective*

anew \ə-'nü, -'nyü\ *adverb* [Middle English *of newe*, from Old English *of nīwe*, from *of* + *nīwe* new] (before 12th century)

1 : for an additional time : AFRESH

2 : in a new or different form

an·frac·tu·os·i·ty \(ˌ)an-ˌfrak-chə-'wä-sə-tē, -shə-\ *noun, plural* **-ties** (1596)

1 : the quality or state of being anfractuous

2 : a winding channel or course; *especially* : an intricate path or process (as of the mind)

an·frac·tu·ous \an-'frak-chə-wəs, -shə-\ *adjective* [French *anfractueux*, from Late Latin *anfractuosus*, from Latin *anfractus* coil, bend, from *an-* (from *ambi-* around) + *-fractus*, from *frangere* to break — more at AMBI-, BREAK] (1621)

: full of windings and intricate turnings : TORTUOUS

an·gel \'ān-jəl\ *noun* [Middle English, from Old English *engel* & Old French *angele*; both from Late Latin *angelus*, from Greek *angelos*, literally, messenger] (before 12th century)

1 a : a spiritual being superior to man in power and intelligence; *especially* : one in the lowest rank in the celestial hierarchy **b** *plural* : an order of angels — see CELESTIAL HIERARCHY

◇ WORD HISTORY

anecdote Procopius, a 6th century historian and official at the court of the eastern Roman emperor Justinian, published two important historical works in his lifetime. A third work, however, did not begin to circulate until after his death. Entitled *Anekdota*, "unpublished things," it contained bitter attacks on the emperor Justinian and his wife, Theodora, as well as on many other noted officials in Constantinople. Some of these attacks are in the form of juicy bits of scandalous gossip. Procopius's work is often referred to as *Historia Arcana* or *Secret History*. It was the original title that became a byword, however. Procopius's title first appeared in English in its Medieval Latin form, *anecdota*, and then as *anecdotes*, borrowed from French. When first used in the latter half of the 17th century, these plurals meant "unpublished secret history." By the 18th century, the word was being used in the singular, *anecdote*, and in the sense familiar to us today.

\ə\ abut \ᵊ\ kitten \ər\ further \a\ ash \ā\ ace
\ä\ mop, mar \au̇\ out \ch\ chin \e\ bet \ē\ easy
\g\ go \i\ hit \ī\ ice \j\ job \ŋ\ sing \ō\ go
\ȯ\ law \ȯi\ boy \th\ thin \th\ the \ü\ loot \u̇\ foot
\y\ yet \zh\ vision *see also* Guide to Pronunciation

2 : an attendant spirit or guardian
3 : a white-robed winged figure of human form in fine art
4 : MESSENGER, HARBINGER ⟨*angel* of death⟩
5 : a person like an angel (as in looks or behavior)
6 *Christian Science* **:** inspiration from God
7 : one (as a backer of a theatrical venture) who aids or supports with money or influence
8 : ANGELFISH
— **an·gel·ic** \an-'je-lik\ *or* **an·gel·i·cal** \-li-kəl\ *adjective*
— **an·gel·i·cal·ly** \-li-k(ə-)lē\ *adverb*
angel dust *noun* (1973)
: PHENCYCLIDINE
An·ge·le·no \,an-jə-'lē-(,)nō\ *noun, plural* **-nos** [American Spanish *angeleño*, from Los *Angeles*, Calif.] (1888)
: a native or resident of Los Angeles, Calif.
an·gel·fish \'ān-jəl-,fish\ *noun* (1668)
1 : any of several compressed bright-colored bony fishes (family Pomacanthidae) of warm seas
2 : SCALARE
angel food cake *noun* (1920)
: a usually white sponge cake made of flour, sugar, and whites of eggs
angel–hair pasta \'an-jəl-,her-, -,har-\ *noun* (1981)
: pasta smaller in diameter than vermicelli
an·gel·i·ca \an-'je-li-kə\ *noun* [New Latin, genus name, from Medieval Latin, from Late Latin, feminine of *angelicus* angelic, from Late Greek *angelikos*, from Greek, of a messenger, from *angelos*] (1527)
1 a : any of a genus (*Angelica*) of herbs of the carrot family; *especially* **:** a Eurasian biennial or perennial (*A. archangelica*) whose roots and fruit yield a flavoring oil **b :** a confection prepared from angelica
2 *capitalized* **:** a sweet fortified wine produced in California
angelica tree *noun* (1785)
: HERCULES'-CLUB 1
an·gel·ol·o·gy \,ān-jə-'lä-lə-jē\ *noun, often capitalized* (circa 1828)
: the theological doctrine of angels or its study
— **an·gel·ol·o·gist** \-jist\ *noun*
An·ge·lus \'an-jə-ləs\ *noun* [Medieval Latin, from Late Latin, angel; from the first word of the opening versicle] (1658)
1 : a devotion of the Western church that commemorates the Incarnation and is said in the morning, at noon, and in the evening
2 : a bell announcing the time for the Angelus
¹anger *verb* **an·gered; an·ger·ing** \-g(ə-)riŋ\ (13th century)
transitive verb
: to make angry
intransitive verb
: to become angry
²an·ger \'aŋ-gər\ *noun* [Middle English, affliction, anger, from Old Norse *angr* grief; akin to Old English *enge* narrow, Latin *angere* to strangle, Greek *anchein*] (14th century)
1 : a strong feeling of displeasure and usually of antagonism
2 : RAGE 2 ☆
— **an·ger·less** \-ləs\ *adjective*
An·ge·vin \'an-jə-vən\ *adjective* [French, from Old French, from Medieval Latin *andegavinus*, from *Andegavia* Anjou] (1769)
: of, relating to, or characteristic of Anjou or the Plantagenets
— **Angevin** *noun*
angi- *or* **angio-** *combining form* [New Latin, from Greek *angei-, angeio-,* from *angeion* vessel, blood vessel, diminutive of *angos* vessel]
1 : blood or lymph vessel **:** blood vessels and ⟨*angioma*⟩ ⟨*angio*cardiography⟩
2 : pericarp ⟨*angiosperm*⟩
an·gi·na \an-'jī-nə, 'an-jə-\ *noun* [Latin, throat inflammation, from Greek *anchonē* strangling, from *anchein* to strangle] (1578)
: a disease marked by spasmodic attacks of in-

tense suffocative pain: as **a :** a severe inflammatory or ulcerated condition of the mouth or throat **b :** ANGINA PECTORIS
— **an·gi·nal** \an-'jī-n°l, 'an-jə-\ *adjective*
angina pec·to·ris \-'pek-t(ə-)rəs\ *noun* [New Latin, literally, angina of the chest] (1744)
: a disease marked by brief paroxysmal attacks of chest pain precipitated by deficient oxygenation of the heart muscles
an·gio·car·di·og·ra·phy \'an-jē-ō-,kär-dē-'ä-grə-fē\ *noun* (1938)
: the roentgenographic visualization of the heart and its blood vessels after injection of a radiopaque substance
— **an·gio·car·dio·graph·ic** \-dē-ə-'graf-ik\ *adjective*
an·gio·gen·e·sis \,an-jē-ō-'je-nə-səs\ *noun* [New Latin] (1899)
: the formation and differentiation of blood vessels
— **an·gio·gen·ic** \-'je-nik\ *adjective*
an·gio·gram \'an-jē-ə-,gram\ *noun* (1933)
: a roentgenogram made by angiography
an·gi·og·ra·phy \,an-jē-'ä-grə-fē\ *noun* (1933)
: the roentgenographic visualization of the blood vessels after injection of a radiopaque substance
— **an·gio·graph·ic** \,an-jē-ə-'gra-fik\ *adjective*
an·gi·o·ma \,an-jē-'ō-mə\ *noun* [New Latin] (1871)
: a tumor composed chiefly of blood vessels or lymph vessels
— **an·gi·o·ma·tous** \-mə-təs\ *adjective*
an·gio·plas·ty \'an-jē-ə-,plas-tē\ *noun, plural* **-ties** (circa 1919)
: surgical repair of a blood vessel; *especially* **:** BALLOON ANGIOPLASTY
an·gio·sperm \'an-jē-ə-,spərm\ *noun* [ultimately from New Latin *angi-* + Greek *sperma* seed — more at SPERM] (circa 1828)
: any of a class (Angiospermae) or division (Magnoliophyta) of vascular plants (as magnolias, grasses, oaks, roses, and daisies) that have the ovules and seeds enclosed in an ovary, form the embryo and endosperm by double fertilization, and typically have each flower surrounded by a perianth composed of two sets of floral envelopes comprising the calyx and corolla — called also *flowering plant*
— **an·gio·sper·mous** \,an-jē-ə-'spər-məs\ *adjective*
an·gio·ten·sin \,an-jē-ō-'ten(t)-sən\ *noun* [*angi-* + hyper*tension* + *-in*] (circa 1961)
: either of two forms of a kinin of which one has marked vasoconstrictive action; *also* **:** a synthetic amide derivative of the physiologically active form used to treat some forms of hypotension
angiotensin converting enzyme *noun* (1970)
: a proteolytic enzyme that converts the physiologically inactive form of angiotensin to the active vasoconstrictive form
¹an·gle \'aŋ-gəl\ *noun* [Middle English, from Middle French, from Latin *angulus*] (14th century)
1 : a corner whether constituting a projecting part or a partially enclosed space ⟨they sheltered in an *angle* of the building⟩
2 a : the figure formed by two lines extending from the same point; *also* **:** DIHEDRAL ANGLE **b** **:** a measure of an angle or of the amount of turning necessary to bring one line or plane into coincidence with or parallel to another
3 a : the precise viewpoint from which something is observed or considered; *also* **:** the aspect seen from such an angle **b** (1) **:** a special approach, point of attack, or technique for accomplishing an objective (2) **:** an often improper or illicit method of obtaining advantage ⟨he always had an *angle* to beat the other fellow⟩
4 : a sharply divergent course ⟨the road went off at an *angle*⟩

5 : a position to the side of an opponent in football from which a player may block his opponent more effectively or without penalty — usually used in the phrases *get an angle* or *have an angle*
— **an·gled** \-gəld\ *adjective*
²angle *verb* **an·gled; an·gling** \-g(ə-)liŋ\ (1741)
intransitive verb
: to turn or proceed at an angle
transitive verb
1 : to turn, move, or direct at an angle
2 : to present (as a news story) from a particular or prejudiced point of view
³angle *intransitive verb* **an·gled; an·gling** \-g(ə-)liŋ\ [Middle English *angelen*, from *angel* fishhook, from Old English, from *anga* hook; akin to Old High German *ango* hook, Latin *uncus*, Greek *onkos* barbed hook, *ankos* glen] (15th century)
1 : to fish with a hook
2 : to use artful means to attain an objective ⟨*angled* for an invitation⟩
An·gle \'aŋ-gəl\ *noun* [Latin *Angli*, plural, of Germanic origin; akin to Old English *Engle* Angles] (before 12th century)
: a member of a Germanic people that invaded England along with the Saxons and Jutes in the 5th century A.D. and merged with them to form the Anglo-Saxon peoples
angle bracket *noun* (circa 1956)
: BRACKET 3b
angle iron *noun* (circa 1853)
1 : an iron cleat for joining parts of a structure at an angle
2 : a piece of structural steel rolled with an L-shaped section
angle of attack *noun* (1908)
: the acute angle between the direction of the relative wind and the chord of an airfoil
angle of depression (1790)
: the angle formed by the line of sight and the horizontal plane for an object below the horizontal
angle of elevation (circa 1737)
: the angle formed by the line of sight and the horizontal plane for an object above the horizontal
angle of incidence (1628)
: the angle that a line (as a ray of light) falling on a surface or interface makes with the normal drawn at the point of incidence — see CRITICAL ANGLE illustration
angle of reflection (1638)
: the angle between a reflected ray and the normal drawn at the point of incidence to a reflecting surface
angle of refraction (circa 1737)
: the angle between a refracted ray and the normal drawn at the point of incidence to the interface at which refraction occurs

☆ **SYNONYMS**
Anger, ire, rage, fury, indignation, wrath mean an intense emotional state induced by displeasure. ANGER, the most general term, names the reaction but in itself conveys nothing about intensity or justification or manifestation of the emotional state (tried to hide his *anger*). IRE, more frequent in literary contexts, may suggest greater intensity *than anger*, often with an evident display of feeling (cheeks flushed dark with *ire*). RAGE suggests loss of self-control from violence of emotion (screaming with *rage*). FURY is overmastering destructive rage that can verge on madness (in her *fury* she accused everyone around her of betrayal). INDIGNATION stresses righteous anger at what one considers unfair, mean, or shameful (a refusal to listen that caused general *indignation*). WRATH is likely to suggest a desire or intent to revenge or punish (rose in his *wrath* and struck his tormentor to the floor).

an·gler \'aŋ-glər\ noun (15th century)
1 : one that angles
2 : ANGLERFISH

ang·ler·fish \-ˌfish\ noun (circa 1889)
: any of several pediculate fishes (as the goosefishes); *especially* **:** MONKFISH

angle shot noun (circa 1922)
: a picture taken with the camera pointed at an angle from the horizontal

an·gle·site \'aŋ-gəl-ˌsīt, -glə-\ noun [French *anglésite,* from *Anglesey* Island, Wales] (circa 1841)
: a mineral consisting of lead sulfate formed by the oxidation of galena

an·gle·worm \'aŋ-gəl-ˌwərm\ noun (1832)
: EARTHWORM

An·gli·an \'aŋ-glē-ən\ noun (1726)
1 : a member of the Angles
2 : the Old English dialects of Mercia and Northumbria
— Anglian *adjective*

An·gli·can \'aŋ-gli-kən\ *adjective* [Medieval Latin *anglicanus,* from *anglicus* English, from Latin *Angli* Angles] (1635)
1 : of or relating to the established episcopal Church of England and churches of similar faith and order in communion with it
2 : of or relating to England or the English nation
— Anglican *noun*
— An·gli·can·ism \-kə-ˌni-zəm\ *noun*

an·gli·ce \'aŋ-glə-(ˌ)sē\ *adverb, often capitalized* [Medieval Latin, adverb of *anglicus*] (1602)
: in English; *especially* **:** in readily understood English ⟨the city of Napoli, *anglice* Naples⟩

an·gli·cise *often capitalized, variant of* ANGLICIZE

an·gli·cism \'aŋ-glə-ˌsi-zəm\ *noun, often capitalized* [Medieval Latin *anglicus* English] (1642)
1 : a characteristic feature of English occurring in another language
2 : adherence or attachment to English customs or ideas

An·gli·cist \'aŋ-glə-sist\ noun (1930)
: a specialist in English linguistics

an·gli·cize \'aŋ-glə-ˌsīz\ *transitive verb* **-cized; -ciz·ing** *often capitalized* (1710)
1 : to make English in quality or characteristics
2 : to adapt (a foreign word or phrase) to English usage; *especially* **:** to borrow into English without alteration of form or spelling and with or without change in pronunciation
— an·gli·ci·za·tion \ˌaŋ-glə-sə-'zā-shən\ *noun, often capitalized*

an·gling \'aŋ-gliŋ\ noun (15th century)
: the action of one who angles; *especially* **:** the action or sport of fishing with hook and line

An·glist \'aŋ-glist\ noun (1888)
: ANGLICIST

An·glo \'aŋ-(ˌ)glō\ noun, plural **Anglos** [in sense 2, from American Spanish, short for Spanish *angloamericano* Anglo-American] (1800)
1 : ANGLO-AMERICAN
2 : a white inhabitant of the U.S. of non-Hispanic descent
— Anglo *adjective*

An·glo- *combining form* [New Latin, from Late Latin *Angli*]
1 \'aŋ-(ˌ)glō, -glə\ **:** English ⟨*Anglo*-Norman⟩
2 \-(ˌ)glō\ **:** English and ⟨*Anglo*-Japanese⟩

An·glo–Amer·i·can \ˌaŋ-glō-ə-'mer-ə-kən\ noun (circa 1782)
: a North American whose native language is English; *especially* **:** an inhabitant of the U.S. of English origin or descent
— Anglo–American *adjective*

An·glo–Cath·o·lic \-'kath-lik, -'ka-thə-\ *adjective* (1838)
: of or relating to a High Church movement in Anglicanism emphasizing its continuity with historic Catholicism and fostering Catholic dogmatic and liturgical traditions

— Anglo–Catholic *noun*
— An·glo–Ca·thol·i·cism \-kə-'thä-lə-ˌsi-zəm\ *noun*

An·glo–French \-'french\ noun (circa 1884)
: the French language used in medieval England

An·glo·ma·nia \-'mā-nē-ə, -nyə\ noun (1787)
: an absorbing or pervasive interest in England or things English

An·glo–Nor·man \-'nȯr-mən\ noun (1735)
1 : any of the Normans living in England after the Norman conquest of 1066
2 : the form of Anglo-French used by Anglo-Normans
— Anglo–Norman *adjective*

An·glo·phile \'aŋ-glə-ˌfīl\ *also* **An·glo·phil** \-ˌfil\ noun [French, from *anglo-* + *-phile*] (1883)
: one who greatly admires or favors England and things English
— Anglophile *or* **An·glo·phil·ic** \ˌaŋ-glə-'fi-lik\ *adjective*

An·glo·phil·ia \ˌaŋ-glə-'fi-lē-ə\ noun (1896)
: unusual admiration or partiality for England, English ways, or things English
— An·glo·phil·i·ac \-lē-ˌak\ *adjective*

An·glo·phobe \'aŋ-glə-ˌfōb\ noun [probably from French, from *anglo-* + *-phobe*] (1866)
: one who is averse to or dislikes England and things English
— An·glo·pho·bia \ˌaŋ-glə-'fō-bē-ə\ noun
— An·glo·pho·bic \-'fō-bik\ *adjective*

an·glo·phone \'aŋ-glə-ˌfōn\ *adjective, often capitalized* (1965)
: consisting of or belonging to an English-speaking population especially in a country where two or more languages are spoken
— Anglophone *noun*

An·glo–Sax·on \ˌaŋ-glō-'sak-sən\ noun [New Latin *Anglo-Saxones,* plural, alteration of Medieval Latin *Angli Saxones,* from Latin *Angli* Angles + Late Latin *Saxones* Saxons] (before 12th century)
1 : a member of the Germanic peoples conquering England in the 5th century A.D. and forming the ruling class until the Norman conquest — compare ANGLE, JUTE, SAXON
2 a : ENGLISHMAN; *specifically* **:** a person descended from the Anglo-Saxons **b :** a white gentile of an English-speaking nation
3 *capitalized* **a :** ANGORA CAT **b :** ANGORA GOAT
c : ANGORA RABBIT

Angora cat noun [*Angora* (Ankara), Turkey] (1819)
: a long-haired domestic cat; *specifically* **:** any of a breed that differs from the Persian in having a narrower head and slighter body

Angora goat noun (1833)
: any of a breed or variety of the domestic goat raised for its long silky hair which is the true mohair

Angora rabbit noun (1849)
: any of a breed of long-haired usually white rabbits with red eyes that is raised for fine wool

Angora goat

an·gry \'aŋ-grē\ *adjective* **an·gri·er; -est** (14th century)
1 : feeling or showing anger **:** WRATHFUL
2 a : indicative of or proceeding from anger ⟨*angry* words⟩ **b :** seeming to show anger or to threaten in an angry manner ⟨an *angry* sky⟩
3 : painfully inflamed ⟨an *angry* rash⟩

— an·gri·ly \-grə-lē\ *adverb*
— an·gri·ness \-grē-nəs\ *noun*

angry young man noun (1941)
1 : an outspoken critic of or protester against an economic condition or social injustice
2 : one of a group of mid-20th century British authors whose works express the bitterness of the lower classes toward the established socio-political system and toward the mediocrity and hypocrisy of the middle and upper classes

Angora rabbit

angst \'äŋ(k)st, 'aŋ(k)st\ noun [Danish & German; Danish, from German] (circa 1942)
: a feeling of anxiety, apprehension, or insecurity

ang·strom \'aŋ-strəm *also* 'ȯŋ-\ noun [Anders J. *Ångström*] (1892)
: a unit of length equal to one ten-billionth of a meter

¹an·guish \'aŋ-gwish\ noun [Middle English *angwisshe,* from Old French *angoisse,* from Latin *angustiae,* plural, straits, distress, from *angustus* narrow; akin to Old English *enge* narrow — more at ANGER] (13th century)
: extreme pain, distress, or anxiety
synonym SEE SORROW

²anguish (14th century)
intransitive verb
: to suffer anguish
transitive verb
: to cause to suffer anguish

an·guished *adjective* (14th century)
1 : suffering anguish **:** TORMENTED ⟨the *anguished* martyrs⟩
2 : expressing anguish **:** AGONIZED ⟨*anguished* cries⟩

an·gu·lar \'aŋ-gyə-lər\ *adjective* [Middle French or Latin; Middle French *angulaire,* from Latin *angularis,* from *angulus* angle] (15th century)
1 a : forming an angle **:** sharp-cornered **b :** having one or more angles
2 : measured by an angle ⟨*angular* distance⟩
3 a : stiff in character or manner **:** lacking smoothness or grace **b :** lean and having prominent bone structure
— an·gu·lar·ly *adverb*

angular acceleration noun (1883)
: the rate of change per unit time of angular velocity

an·gu·lar·i·ty \ˌaŋ-gyə-'lar-ə-tē\ noun, plural **-ties** (1642)
1 : the quality of being angular
2 *plural* **:** angular outlines or characteristics

angular momentum noun (1870)
: a vector quantity that is a measure of the rotational momentum of a rotating body or system, that is equal in classical physics to the product of the angular velocity of the body or system and its moment of inertia with respect to the rotation axis, and that is directed along the rotation axis

angular velocity noun (1819)
: the rate of rotation around an axis usually expressed in radians or revolutions per second or per minute

an·gu·la·tion \ˌaŋ-gyə-'lā-shən\ noun (1869)
1 : the action of making angular
2 : an angular position, formation, or shape

An·gus \'aŋ-gəs\ noun [*Angus,* county in Scotland] (1842)
: any of a breed of usually black hornless beef cattle originating in Scotland

an·he·do·nia \ˌan-(ˌ)hē-'dō-nē-ə, -nyə\ noun [New Latin, from ²a- + Greek hēdonē pleasure — more at HEDONISM] (1897)
: a psychological condition characterized by inability to experience pleasure in normally pleasurable acts
— **an·he·don·ic** \-'dä-nik\ adjective

an·hin·ga \an-'hiŋ-gə\ noun [Portuguese, from Tupi] (1769)
: any of a genus (Anhinga) of fish-eating birds related to the cormorants but distinguished by a longer neck and sharply pointed rather than hooked bill; especially : one (A. anhinga) occurring from the southern U.S. to Argentina

an·hy·dride \(ˌ)an-'hī-ˌdrīd\ noun (1863)
: a compound derived from another (as an acid) by removal of the elements of water

an·hy·drite \-ˌdrīt\ noun [German Anhydrit, from Greek anydros] (circa 1823)
: a mineral consisting of an anhydrous calcium sulfate that is usually massive and white or slightly colored

an·hy·drous \-drəs\ adjective [Greek anydros, from a- + hydōr water — more at WATER] (1819)
: free from water and especially water of crystallization

ani \ä-'nē\ noun [Spanish aní, or Portuguese ani, from Tupi ani] (circa 1823)
: any of a genus (Crotophaga) of black cuckoos of the warmer parts of America

anile \'a-ˌnīl, 'ā-\ adjective [Latin anilis, from anus old woman] (1652)
: of or resembling a doddering old woman; especially : SENILE
— **anil·i·ty** \a-'ni-lə-tē, ā-, ə-\ noun

an·i·line \'a-nªl-ən\ noun [German Anilin, from Anil indigo, from French, from Portuguese, from Arabic an-nīl the indigo plant, from Sanskrit nīla indigo, from feminine of nīla dark blue] (1850)
: an oily liquid poisonous amine $C_6H_5NH_2$ obtained especially by the reduction of nitrobenzene and used chiefly in organic synthesis (as of dyes)

aniline dye noun (1864)
: a dye made by the use of aniline or one chemically related to such a dye; broadly : a synthetic organic dye

ani·lin·gus \ˌā-ni-'liŋ-gəs\ or **ani·linc·tus** \-'liŋ(k)-təs\ noun [New Latin, from anus + -i- + -lingus, -linctus (as in cunnilingus, cunnilinctus)] (1949)
: erotic stimulation achieved by contact between mouth and anus

an·i·ma \'a-nə-mə\ noun [New Latin, from Latin, soul] (1923)
: an individual's true inner self that in the analytic psychology of C. G. Jung reflects archetypal ideals of conduct; also : an inner feminine part of the male personality — compare ANIMUS, PERSONA

an·i·mad·ver·sion \ˌa-nə-ˌmad-'vər-zhən, -məd-, -'vər-shən\ noun [Latin animadversion-, animadversio, from animadvertere] (1599)
1 : a critical and usually censorious remark — often used with on
2 : adverse criticism

an·i·mad·vert \-'vərt\ verb [Latin animadvertere to pay attention to, censure, from animum advertere, literally, to turn the mind to] (15th century)
transitive verb
archaic : NOTICE, OBSERVE
intransitive verb
: to make an animadversion

¹**an·i·mal** \'a-nə-məl\ noun [Latin, from animale, neuter of animalis animate, from anima soul — more at ANIMATE] (14th century)
1 : any of a kingdom (Animalia) of living things including many-celled organisms and often many of the single-celled ones (as protozoans) that typically differ from plants in having cells without cellulose walls, in lacking chlorophyll and the capacity for photosynthe-

sis, in requiring more complex food materials (as proteins), in being organized to a greater degree of complexity, and in having the capacity for spontaneous movement and rapid motor responses to stimulation
2 a : one of the lower animals as distinguished from human beings b : MAMMAL; broadly : VERTEBRATE
3 : a human being considered chiefly as physical or nonrational; also : this nature
4 : an individual with a particular interest or aptitude ⟨a political animal⟩
5 : MATTER, THING ⟨the theater . . . is an entirely different animal —Arthur Miller⟩; also : CREATURE 1c ◇
— **an·i·mal-like** \-mə(l)-ˌlīk\ adjective

²**animal** adjective (1615)
1 : of, relating to, resembling, or derived from animals
2 a : of or relating to the physical or sentient as contrasted with the intellectual or rational b : SENSUAL, FLESHLY
3 : of or relating to the animal pole of an egg or to the part from which ectoderm normally develops
synonym see CARNAL
— **an·i·mal·ly** \-mə-lē\ adverb

animal control noun (1957)
: an office or department responsible for enforcing ordinances relating to the control, impoundment, and disposition of animals

animal cracker noun (1898)
: a small cookie in the shape of an animal

an·i·mal·cule \ˌa-nə-'mal-(ˌ)kyü(ə)l\ also **an·i·mal·cu·lum** \-'mal-kyə-ləm\ noun, plural -cules also -cu·la \-kyə-lə\ [New Latin animalculum, diminutive of Latin animal] (1662)
: a minute usually microscopic organism

animal heat noun (1779)
: heat produced in the body of a living animal by functional chemical and physical activities

animal husbandry noun (1919)
: a branch of agriculture concerned with the production and care of domestic animals

an·i·mal·ier \ˌa-nə-mə-'lir\ noun [French, from animal animal, from Latin] (1912)
: a sculptor or painter of animal subjects

an·i·mal·ism \'a-nə-mə-ˌli-zəm\ noun (1831)
: ANIMALITY
— **an·i·mal·is·tic** \ˌa-nə-mə-'lis-tik\ adjective

an·i·mal·i·ty \ˌa-nə-mə-'ma-lə-tē\ noun (1615)
1 : qualities associated with animals: a : VITALITY b : a natural unrestrained unreasoned response to physical drives or stimuli
2 : the animal nature of human beings

an·i·mal·ize \'a-nə-mə-ˌlīz\ transitive verb -ized; -iz·ing (1741)
1 : to represent in animal form
2 : to cause to be or act like an animal
— **an·i·mal·iza·tion** \ˌa-nə-mə-lə-'zā-shən\ noun

animal kingdom noun (1776)
: a basic group of natural objects that includes all living and extinct animals — compare MINERAL KINGDOM, PLANT KINGDOM

animal magnetism noun (1784)
1 : a mysterious force claimed by Mesmer to enable him to hypnotize patients
2 : a magnetic charm or appeal; especially : SEX APPEAL

animal model noun (1976)
: an animal sufficiently like humans in its anatomy, physiology, or response to a pathogen to be used in medical research in order to obtain results that can be extrapolated to human medicine

animal pole noun (1887)
: the point on the surface of an egg that is diametrically opposite to the vegetal pole and usually marks the most active part of the protoplasm or the part containing least yolk

animal rights noun plural but singular in construction (1879)
: fair and humane treatment of animals — often used attributively

animal spirits noun plural (1543)
1 sometimes **animal spirit** obsolete : the nervous energy that is the source of physical sensation and movement
2 : vivacity arising from physical health and energy

animal starch noun (circa 1860)
: GLYCOGEN

¹**an·i·mate** \'a-nə-mət\ adjective [Middle English, from Latin animatus, past participle of animare to give life to, from anima breath, soul; akin to Old English ōthian to breathe, Latin animus spirit, Greek anemos wind, Sanskrit aniti he breathes] (15th century)
1 : possessing or characterized by life : ALIVE
2 : full of life : ANIMATED
3 : of or relating to animal life as opposed to plant life
4 : referring to a living thing ⟨an animate noun⟩
— **an·i·mate·ly** adverb
— **an·i·mate·ness** noun

²**an·i·mate** \-ˌmāt\ transitive verb -mat·ed; -mat·ing (15th century)
1 : to give spirit and support to : ENCOURAGE
2 a : to give life to b : to give vigor and zest to
3 : to move to action
4 a : to make or design in such a way as to create apparently spontaneous lifelike movement b : to produce in the form of an animated cartoon
synonym see QUICKEN

an·i·mat·ed \-ˌmā-təd\ adjective (1534)
1 a : endowed with life or the qualities of life : ALIVE ⟨viruses that can behave as animated bodies or inert crystals⟩ b : full of movement and activity c : full of vigor and spirit : LIVELY ⟨an animated discussion⟩
2 : having the appearance of something alive
3 : made in the form of an animated cartoon
synonym see LIVELY
— **an·i·mat·ed·ly** adverb

animated cartoon noun (1915)
1 : a motion picture made from a series of drawings simulating motion by means of slight progressive changes in the drawings
2 : ANIMATION 2a

an·i·ma·tion \ˌa-nə-'mā-shən\ noun (1597)
1 : the act of animating : the state of being animate or animated
2 a : a motion picture made by photographing successive positions of inanimate objects (as puppets or mechanical parts) b : ANIMATED CARTOON 1
3 : the preparation of animated cartoons

an·i·ma·to \ˌä-nə-'(ˌ)tō, ˌa-\ adverb or adjective [Italian, from Latin animatus] (circa 1724)
: with animation — used as a direction in music

an·i·ma·tor \'a-nə-ˌmā-tər\ noun (1611)
1 : one that animates ⟨the prime animator of the movement⟩
2 : an artist who creates drawings for an animated cartoon

an·i·mism \'a-nə-ˌmi-zəm\ noun [German Animismus, from Latin anima soul] (1832)
1 : a doctrine that the vital principle of organic development is immaterial spirit

◇ WORD HISTORY
animal Latin anima means "breath," the vital principle that distinguishes living things from dead ones, and the adjective derivative animalis means "having breath." Though plants may be said to breathe insofar as they take in certain gases from the atmosphere and release others, this is not a process seen by the naked eye. Thus the Latin noun animal, derived from animalis, is used to designate those living beings that breathe perceptibly, and so is our word, borrowed from Latin.

2 : attribution of conscious life to objects in and phenomena of nature or to inanimate objects
3 : belief in the existence of spirits separable from bodies
— **an·i·mist** \-mist\ *noun*
— **an·i·mis·tic** \ˌa-nə-'mis-tik\ *adjective*

an·i·mos·i·ty \ˌa-nə-'mä-sə-tē\ *noun, plural* **-ties** [Middle English *animosite,* from Middle French or Late Latin; Middle French *animosité,* from Late Latin *animositat-, animositas,* from Latin *animosus* spirited, from *animus*] (1605)
: ill will or resentment tending toward active hostility **:** an antagonistic attitude
synonym see ENMITY

an·i·mus \'a-nə-məs\ *noun* [Latin, spirit, mind, courage, anger] (1816)
1 : basic attitude or governing spirit **:** DISPOSITION, INTENTION
2 : a usually prejudiced and often spiteful or malevolent ill will
3 : an inner masculine part of the female personality in the analytic psychology of C. G. Jung — compare ANIMA
synonym see ENMITY

an·ion \'a-ˌnī-ən\ *noun* [Greek, neuter of *aniōn,* present participle of *anienai* to go up, from *ana-* + *ienai* to go — more at ISSUE] (1834)
: the ion in an electrolyzed solution that migrates to the anode; *broadly* **:** a negatively charged ion

an·ion·ic \ˌa-(ˌ)nī-'ä-nik\ *adjective* (circa 1920)
1 : of or relating to anions
2 : characterized by an active and especially surface-active anion

anis- *or* **aniso-** *combining form* [New Latin, from Greek, from *anisos,* from *a-* + *isos* equal]
: unequal ⟨*aniso*tropic⟩

an·ise \'a-nəs\ *noun* [Middle English *anis,* from Middle French, from Latin *anisum,* from Greek *annēson, anison*] (14th century)
: an herb (*Pimpinella anisum*) of the carrot family having carminative and aromatic seeds; *also* **:** ANISEED

ani·seed \'a-nə(s)-ˌsēd\ *noun* [Middle English *anis seed,* from *anis* + *seed*] (14th century)
: the seed of anise often used as a flavoring in liqueurs and in cooking

an·is·ei·ko·nia \ˌa-nə-ˌsī-'kō-nē-ə\ *noun* [New Latin, from *anis-* + Greek *eikōn* image — more at ICON] (1934)
: a defect of binocular vision in which the two retinal images of an object differ in size
— **an·is·ei·kon·ic** \-'kä-nik\ *adjective*

an·is·ette \ˌa-nə-'set, -'zet\ *noun* [French, from *anis*] (1837)
: a usually colorless sweet liqueur flavored with aniseed

an·isog·a·mous \ˌa-(ˌ)nī-'sä-gə-məs\ *adjective* (1891)
: characterized by fusion of heterogamous gametes or of individuals that usually differ chiefly in size ⟨*anisogamous* reproduction⟩
— **an·isog·a·my** \-(ˌ)nī-'sä-gə-mē\ *noun*

an·iso·me·tro·pia \ˌa-ˌnī-sə-mə-'trō-pē-ə\ *noun* [New Latin, from Greek *anisometros* of unequal measure (from *anis-* + *metron* measure) + New Latin *-opia* — more at MEASURE] (circa 1880)
: unequal refractive power in the two eyes
— **an·iso·me·tro·pic** \-'trä-pik, -'trō-\ *adjective*

an·iso·trop·ic \ˌa-ˌnī-sə-'trä-pik\ *adjective* (1879)
: exhibiting properties with different values when measured in different directions ⟨an *anisotropic* crystal⟩
— **an·iso·trop·i·cal·ly** \-pi-k(ə-)lē\ *adverb*
— **an·isot·ro·py** \-(ˌ)nī-'sä-trə-pē\ *also* **an·isot·ro·pism** \-ˌpi-zəm\ *noun*

an·ker·ite \'aŋ-kə-ˌrīt\ *noun* [German *Ankerit,* from M. J. *Anker* (died 1843) Austrian mineralogist] (circa 1843)

: a dolomitic iron-containing mineral

ankh \'äŋk\ *noun* [Egyptian *'nḫ* live] (1888)
: a cross having a loop for its upper vertical arm and serving especially in ancient Egypt as an emblem of life

ankh

an·kle \'aŋ-kəl\ *noun* [Middle English *ankel,* from Old English *anclēow;* akin to Old High German *anchlāo* ankle] (before 12th century)
1 : the joint between the foot and the leg; *also* **:** the region of this joint
2 : the joint between the cannon bone and pastern (as in the horse)

an·kle·bone \'aŋ-kəl-ˌbōn, ˌaŋ-kəl-'\ *noun* (14th century)
: ²TALUS 1

an·klet \'aŋ-klət\ *noun* (1819)
1 : something (as an ornament) worn around the ankle
2 : a short sock reaching slightly above the ankle

an·ky·lo·saur \'aŋ-kə-lō-ˌsȯr\ *noun* [New Latin *Ankylosauria,* from *Ankylosaurus*] (1949)
: any of a suborder (Ankylosauria) of herbivorous Cretaceous dinosaurs having a long low-lying thickset body covered dorsally with bony plates

an·ky·lo·sau·rus \ˌaŋ-kə-lō-'sȯr-əs\ *noun* [New Latin, genus name, from Greek *ankylos* + *sauros* lizard] (1908)
: any of a North American genus (*Ankylosaurus*) of large ankylosaurs having a bony club at the end of the tail

an·ky·lose \'aŋ-ki-ˌlōs, -ˌlōz\ *verb* **-losed; -los·ing** [back-formation from *ankylosis*] (1787)
transitive verb
: to unite or stiffen by ankylosis
intransitive verb
: to undergo ankylosis

an·ky·lo·sis \ˌaŋ-ki-'lō-səs\ *noun, plural* **-lo·ses** \-ˌsēz\ [New Latin, from Greek *ankylōsis,* from *ankyloun* to make crooked, from *ankylos* crooked — more at ANGLE] (1713)
1 : stiffness or fixation of a joint by disease or surgery
2 : union of separate bones or hard parts to form a single bone or part
— **an·ky·lot·ic** \-'lät-ik\ *adjective*

an·ky·lo·sto·mi·a·sis \ˌaŋ-ki-lō-stə-'mī-ə-səs\ *variant of* ANCYLOSTOMIASIS

an·la·ge \'än-ˌlä-gə\ *noun, plural* **-gen** \-gən\ *also* **-ges** \-gəz\ [German, literally, act of laying on] (1892)
: the foundation of a subsequent development; *especially* **:** PRIMORDIUM

an·na \'ä-nə\ *noun* [Hindi *ānā*] (1708)
1 : a former monetary unit of Burma, India, and Pakistan equal to ¹⁄₁₆ rupee
2 : a coin representing one anna

an·nal·ist \'a-nᵊl-ist\ *noun* (circa 1611)
: a writer of annals **:** CHRONICLER
— **an·nal·is·tic** \ˌa-nᵊl-'is-tik\ *adjective*

an·nals \'a-nᵊlz\ *noun plural* [Latin *annales,* from plural of *annalis* yearly — more at ANNUAL] (1542)
1 : a record of events arranged in yearly sequence
2 : historical records **:** CHRONICLES
3 : records of the activities of an organization

An·nam·ese \ˌa-nə-'mēz, -'mēs\ *noun, plural* **Annamese** [*Annam,* region of Vietnam] (1826)
1 *or* **An·nam·ite** \'a-nə-ˌmīt\ **:** a native or inhabitant of Annam
2 : VIETNAMESE 2
— **Annamese** *adjective*
— **Annamite** *adjective*

an·nat·to \ə-'nä-(ˌ)tō\ *noun* [Carib *annoto* tree producing annatto] (1629)
: a yellowish red dyestuff made from the pulp

around the seeds of a tropical tree (*Bixa orellana,* family Bixaceae); *also* **:** the tree that yields annatto

an·neal \ə-'nē(ə)l\ *verb* [Middle English *anelen* to set on fire, from Old English *onǣlan,* from *on* + *ǣlan* to set on fire, burn, from *āl* fire; akin to Old English *ǣled* fire, Old Norse *eldr*] (1664)
transitive verb
1 a : to heat and then cool (as steel or glass) usually for softening and making less brittle; *also* **:** to cool slowly usually in a furnace **b :** to heat and then cool (nucleic acid) in order to separate strands and induce combination at lower temperature especially with complementary strands of a different species
2 : STRENGTHEN, TOUGHEN
intransitive verb
: to be capable of combining with complementary nucleic acid by a process of heating and cooling

an·ne·lid \'a-nᵊl-əd, 'a-nə-ˌlid\ *noun* [ultimately from Latin *anellus* little ring — more at ANNULET] (1834)
: any of a phylum (Annelida) of usually elongated segmented coelomate invertebrates (as earthworms, various marine worms, and leeches)
— **annelid** *adjective*
— **an·nel·i·dan** \ə-'ne-lə-dᵊn, a-\ *adjective or noun*

¹an·nex \ə-'neks, 'a-ˌneks\ *transitive verb* [Middle English, from Middle French *annexer,* from Old French, from *annexe* joined, from Latin *annexus,* past participle of *annectere* to bind to, from *ad-* + *nectere* to bind] (14th century)
1 : to attach as a quality, consequence, or condition
2 *archaic* **:** to join together materially **:** UNITE
3 : to add to something earlier, larger, or more important
4 : to incorporate (a country or other territory) within the domain of a state
5 : to obtain or take for oneself
— **an·nex·ation** \ˌa-ˌnek-'sā-shən\ *noun*
— **an·nex·ation·al** \-shnəl, -shə-nᵊl\ *adjective*
— **an·nex·ation·ist** \-sh(ə-)nist\ *noun*

²an·nex \'a-ˌneks, -niks\ *noun* (1501)
: something annexed as an expansion or supplement: as **a :** an added stipulation or statement **:** APPENDIX **b :** a subsidiary or supplementary structure **:** WING

an·nexe \'a-ˌneks, -niks\ *chiefly British variant of* ²ANNEX

An·nie Oak·ley \ˌa-nē-'ō-klē\ *noun, plural* **Annie Oakleys** [*Annie Oakley* (died 1926) American markswoman; from the resemblance of a punched pass to a playing card with bullet holes through the spots] (circa 1910)
: a free ticket

an·ni·hi·late \ə-'nī-ə-ˌlāt\ *verb* **-lat·ed; -lat·ing** [Late Latin *annihilatus,* past participle of *annihilare* to reduce to nothing, from Latin *ad-* + *nihil* nothing — more at NIL] (1525)
transitive verb
1 a : to cause to be of no effect **:** NULLIFY **b :** to destroy the substance or force of
2 : to regard as of no consequence
3 : to cause to cease to exist; *especially* **:** KILL
4 a : to destroy a considerable part of ⟨bombs *annihilated* the city⟩ **b :** to vanquish completely **:** ROUT ⟨*annihilated* the visitors 56–0⟩
intransitive verb
of a particle and its antiparticle **:** to vanish or cease to exist by coming together and changing into other forms of energy (as radiation or particles)
— **an·ni·hi·la·tion** \-ˌnī-ə-'lā-shən\ *noun*

— **an·ni·hi·la·tor** \-,lā-tər\ *noun*
— **an·ni·hi·la·to·ry** \-'nī-ə-lə-,tōr-ē, -,tȯr-\ *adjective*
an·ni·ver·sa·ry \,a-nə-'vərs-rē, -'vər-sə-\ *noun, plural* **-ries** [Middle English *anniversarie,* from Medieval Latin *anniversarium,* from Latin, neuter of *anniversarius* returning annually, from *annus* year + *versus,* past participle of *vertere* to turn — more at ANNUAL, WORTH] (13th century)
1 : the annual recurrence of a date marking a notable event
2 : the celebration of an anniversary
an·no Do·mi·ni \,a-(,)nō-'dä-mə-nē, -'dō-, -,nī\ *adverb, often A capitalized* [Medieval Latin, in the year of the Lord] (1530)
— used to indicate that a time division falls within the Christian era
an·no he·gi·rae \-hi-'jī-(,)rē, -'he-jə-,rē\ *adverb, often A&H capitalized* [New Latin, in the year of the Hegira] (circa 1889)
— used to indicate that a time division falls within the Islamic era
an·no·tate \'a-nə-,tāt\ *verb* **-tat·ed; -tat·ing** [Latin *annotatus,* past participle of *annotare,* from *ad-* + *notare* to mark — more at NOTE] (1733)
intransitive verb
: to make or furnish critical or explanatory notes or comment
transitive verb
: to make or furnish annotations for (as a literary work or subject)
— **an·no·ta·tive** \-,tā-tiv\ *adjective*
— **an·no·ta·tor** \-,tā-tər\ *noun*
an·no·ta·tion \,a-nə-'tā-shən\ *noun* (15th century)
1 : a note added by way of comment or explanation
2 : the act of annotating
an·nounce \ə-'naún(t)s\ *verb* **-nounced; -nounc·ing** [Middle English, from Middle French *annoncer,* from Latin *annuntiare,* from *ad-* + *nuntiare* to report, from *nuntius* messenger] (15th century)
transitive verb
1 : to make known publicly **:** PROCLAIM ⟨*announced* the appointment⟩
2 a : to give notice of the arrival, presence, or readiness of ⟨*announce* dinner⟩ **b :** to indicate beforehand **:** FORETELL
3 : to serve as an announcer of
intransitive verb
1 : to serve as an announcer
2 a : to declare one's candidacy **b :** to declare oneself politically — used with *for* or *against*
synonym see DECLARE
an·nounce·ment \ə-'naún(t)-smənt\ *noun* (1798)
1 : the act of announcing or of being announced
2 : a public notification or declaration
3 : a piece of formal stationery designed for a social or business announcement
an·nounc·er \ə-'naún(t)-sər\ *noun* (circa 1611)
: one that announces: as **a :** a person who introduces television or radio programs, makes commercial announcements, or gives station identification **b :** a person who describes and comments on the action in a broadcast sports event
an·noy \ə-'nȯi\ *verb* [Middle English *anoien,* from Middle French *enuier,* from Late Latin *inodiare* to make loathsome, from Latin *in* + *odium* hatred — more at ODIUM] (13th century)
transitive verb
1 : to disturb or irritate especially by repeated acts
2 : to harass especially by quick brief attacks
intransitive verb
: to cause annoyance ☆
— **an·noy·er** *noun*
an·noy·ance \ə-'nȯi-ən(t)s\ *noun* (14th century)

1 : the act of annoying or of being annoyed
2 : the state or feeling of being annoyed **:** VEXATION
3 : a source of vexation or irritation **:** NUISANCE
an·noy·ing *adjective* (14th century)
: causing vexation **:** IRRITATING
— **an·noy·ing·ly** \-in-lē\ *adverb*
¹**an·nu·al** \'an-yə(-wə)l\ *adjective* [Middle English, from Middle French & Late Latin; Middle French *annuel,* from Late Latin *annualis,* blend of Latin *annuus* yearly (from *annus* year) and Latin *annalis* yearly (from *annus* year); probably akin to Gothic *athnam* (dative plural) years, Sanskrit *atati* he walks, goes] (14th century)
1 : covering the period of a year ⟨*annual* rainfall⟩
2 : occurring or happening every year or once a year **:** YEARLY ⟨an *annual* reunion⟩
3 : completing the life cycle in one growing season
— **an·nu·al·ly** *adverb*
²**annual** *noun* (14th century)
1 : an event that occurs yearly
2 : a publication appearing yearly
3 : something that lasts one year or season; *specifically* **:** an annual plant
an·nu·al·ize \'an-yə(-wə)-,līz\ *transitive verb* **-ized; -iz·ing** (1918)
: to calculate or adjust to reflect a rate based on a full year ⟨quarterly returns yielding at an *annualized* rate of 7 percent⟩
annual ring *noun* (circa 1879)
: the layer of wood produced by a single year's growth of a woody plant
an·nu·itant \ə-'nü-ət-ənt, -'nyü-\ *noun* (1720)
: a beneficiary of an annuity
an·nu·ity \ə-'nü-ə-tē, -'nyü-\ *noun, plural* **-ities** [Middle English *annuite,* from Middle French *annuité,* from Medieval Latin *annuitat-, annuitas,* from Latin *annuus* yearly] (15th century)
1 : a sum of money payable yearly or at other regular intervals
2 : the right to receive an annuity
3 : a contract or agreement providing for the payment of an annuity
an·nul \ə-'nəl\ *transitive verb* **an·nulled; an·nul·ling** [Middle English *annullen,* from Middle French *annuller,* from Late Latin *annullare,* from Latin *ad-* + *nullus* not any — more at NULL] (15th century)
1 : to reduce to nothing **:** OBLITERATE
2 : to make ineffective or inoperative **:** NEUTRALIZE ⟨*annul* the drug's effect⟩
3 : to declare or make legally invalid or void ⟨wants the marriage *annulled*⟩
synonym see NULLIFY
an·nu·lar \'an-yə-lər\ *adjective* [Middle French or Medieval Latin; Middle French *annulaire,* from Medieval Latin *anularis,* from Latin *anulus*] (1571)
: of, relating to, or forming a ring ⟨an *annular* skin lesion⟩
annular eclipse *noun* (1771)
: an eclipse in which a thin outer ring of the sun's disk is not covered by the apparently smaller dark disk of the moon
an·nu·late \'an-yə-lət, -,lāt\ *adjective* (circa 1823)
: furnished with or composed of rings **:** RINGED
an·nu·la·tion \,an-yə-'lā-shən\ *noun* (1829)
: a ringlike anatomical structure
an·nu·let \'an-yə-lət\ *noun* [modification of Middle French *annelet,* diminutive of *anel,* from Latin *anellus,* diminutive of *anulus*] (1598)
1 : a little ring
2 : a small architectural molding or ridge forming a ring
an·nul·ment \ə-'nəl-mənt\ *noun* (15th century)
1 : the act of annulling **:** the state of being annulled

2 : a judicial pronouncement declaring a marriage invalid
an·nu·lus \'an-yə-ləs\ *noun, plural* **-li** \-,lī, -(,)lē\ *also* **-lus·es** [Medieval Latin, from Latin *anulus* finger ring, from *anus* ring — more at ANUS] (1563)
1 : RING
2 : a part, structure, or marking resembling a ring: as **a :** a line of cells around a fern sporangium that ruptures the sporangium by contracting **b :** a growth ring (as on the scale of a fish) that is used in estimating age
an·nun·ci·ate \ə-'nən(t)-sē-,āt\ *transitive verb* **-at·ed; -at·ing** (circa 1536)
: ANNOUNCE
an·nun·ci·a·tion \ə-,nən(t)-sē-'ā-shən\ *noun* [Middle English *annunciacioun,* from Middle French *anunciation,* from Late Latin *annuntiation-, annuntiatio,* from Latin *annuntiare* — more at ANNOUNCE] (14th century)
1 *capitalized* **:** March 25 observed as a church festival in commemoration of the announcement of the Incarnation to the Virgin Mary
2 : the act of announcing or of being announced **:** ANNOUNCEMENT
an·nun·ci·a·tor \ə-'nən(t)-sē-,ā-tər\ *noun* (circa 1753)
: one that annunciates; *specifically* **:** a usually electrically controlled signal board or indicator
— **an·nun·ci·a·to·ry** \-sē-ə-,tōr-ē, -,tȯr-\ *adjective*
an·nus mi·ra·bi·lis \,a-nəs-mə-'rä-bə-ləs, ,ä-\ *noun, plural* **an·ni mi·ra·bi·les** \'a-,nī-mə-'rä-bə-,lēz, 'ä-(,)nē-mə-'rä-bə-,lās\ [New Latin, literally, wonderful year] (1660)
: a remarkable or notable year
an·ode \'a-,nōd\ *noun* [Greek *anodos* way up, from *ana-* + *hodos* way] (1834)
1 : the electrode of an electrochemical cell at which oxidation occurs: as **a :** the positive terminal of an electrolytic cell **b :** the negative terminal of a galvanic cell
2 : the electron-collecting electrode of an electron tube — compare CATHODE
— **an·od·ic** \a-'nä-dik\ *also* **an·od·al** \-'nō-dᵊl\ *adjective*
— **an·od·i·cal·ly** \-di-k(ə-)lē\ *also* **an·od·al·ly** \-dᵊl-ē\ *adverb*
an·od·ize \'a-nə-,dīz\ *transitive verb* **-ized; -iz·ing** (1931)
: to subject (a metal) to electrolytic action as the anode of a cell in order to coat with a protective or decorative film
— **an·od·iza·tion** \,a-,nō-də-'zā-shən, ,a-nə-\ *noun*
¹**an·o·dyne** \'a-nə-,dīn\ *adjective* [Latin *anodynos,* from Greek *anōdynos,* from *a-* + *odynē* pain; probably akin to Old English *etan* to eat] (1543)
1 : serving to assuage pain
2 : not likely to offend or arouse tensions **:** INNOCUOUS
²**anodyne** *noun* (circa 1550)
1 : something that soothes, calms, or comforts ⟨the *anodyne* of bridge, a comfortable book, or sport —Harrison Smith⟩

☆ **SYNONYMS**
Annoy, vex, irk, bother mean to upset a person's composure. ANNOY implies a wearing on the nerves by persistent petty unpleasantness ⟨their constant complaining *annoys* us⟩. VEX implies greater provocation and stronger disturbance and usually connotes anger but sometimes perplexity or anxiety ⟨*vexed* by her teenager's failure to pick up his room⟩. IRK stresses difficulty in enduring and the resulting weariness or impatience of spirit ⟨careless waste *irks* the boss⟩. BOTHER suggests interference with comfort or peace of mind ⟨don't *bother* me while I'm reading⟩. See in addition WORRY.

2 : a drug that allays pain

anoint \ə-'nóint\ *transitive verb* [Middle English, from Middle French *enoint,* past participle of *enoindre,* from Latin *inunguere,* from *in-* + *unguere* to smear — more at OINTMENT] (14th century)

1 : to smear or rub with oil or an oily substance

2 a : to apply oil to as a sacred rite especially for consecration **b :** to choose by or as if by divine election; *also* **:** to designate as if by a ritual anointment

— **anoint·er** *noun*

— **anoint·ment** \-mənt\ *noun*

anointing of the sick (circa 1884)

: EXTREME UNCTION

ano·le \ə-'nō-lē\ *noun* [probably from French *anolis,* from Arawak of the Lesser Antilles] (circa 1753)

: any of a genus (*Anolis* of the family Iguanidae) of arboreal American lizards (as the American chameleon) that have a brightly colored dewlap and the ability to change color

anom·a·lous \ə-'nä-mə-ləs\ *adjective* [Late Latin *anomalus,* from Greek *anōmalos,* literally, uneven, from *a-* + *homalos* even, from *homos* same — more at SAME] (1655)

1 : inconsistent with or deviating from what is usual, normal, or expected **:** IRREGULAR, UNUSUAL

2 a : of uncertain nature or classification **b :** marked by incongruity or contradiction **:** PARADOXICAL

synonym see IRREGULAR

— **anom·a·lous·ly** *adverb*

— **anom·a·lous·ness** *noun*

anom·a·ly \ə-'nä-mə-lē\ *noun, plural* **-lies** (1603)

1 : the angular distance of a planet from its perihelion as seen from the sun

2 : deviation from the common rule **:** IRREGULARITY

3 : something different, abnormal, peculiar, or not easily classified

an·o·mie *also* **an·o·my** \'a-nə-mē\ *noun* [French *anomie,* from Middle French, from Greek *anomia* lawlessness, from *anomos* lawless, from *a-* + *nomos* law, from *nemein* to distribute — more at NIMBLE] (1933)

: social instability resulting from a breakdown of standards and values; *also* **:** personal unrest, alienation, and uncertainty that comes from a lack of purpose or ideals

— **ano·mic** \ə-'nä-mik, -'nō-\ *adjective*

anon \ə-'nän\ *adverb* [Middle English, from Old English *on ān,* from *on* in + *ān* one — more at ON, ONE] (before 12th century)

1 *archaic* **:** at once **:** IMMEDIATELY

2 : SOON, PRESENTLY

3 : after a while **:** LATER

an·o·nym \'a-nə-,nim\ *noun* (1812)

1 : one who is anonymous

2 : PSEUDONYM

an·o·nym·i·ty \,a-nə-'ni-mə-tē\ *noun, plural* **-ties** (1820)

1 : the quality or state of being anonymous

2 : one that is anonymous

anon·y·mous \ə-'nä-nə-məs\ *adjective* [Late Latin *anonymus,* from Greek *anōnymos,* from *a-* + *onyma* name — more at NAME] (1631)

1 : not named or identified ⟨an *anonymous* author⟩ ⟨they wish to remain *anonymous*⟩

2 : of unknown authorship or origin ⟨an *anonymous* tip⟩

3 : lacking individuality, distinction, or recognizability ⟨the *anonymous* faces in the crowd⟩ ⟨the gray *anonymous* streets —William Styron⟩

— **anon·y·mous·ly** *adverb*

— **anon·y·mous·ness** *noun*

anoph·e·les \ə-'nä-fə-,lēz\ *noun* [New Latin, genus name, from Greek *anōphelēs* useless, from *a-* + *ophelos* advantage, help; akin to Greek *ophellein* to increase, Armenian *aweli* more] (1899)

: any of a genus (*Anopheles*) of mosquitoes that includes all mosquitoes which transmit malaria to humans

— **anoph·e·line** \-,līn\ *adjective or noun*

an·o·rak \'a-nə-,rak\ *noun* [Danish, from Inuit (Greenland) *annoraaq*] (1922)

: a usually pullover hooded jacket long enough to cover the hips

¹**an·o·rec·tic** \,a-nə-'rek-tik\ *also* **an·o·ret·ic** \-'re-tik\ *adjective* [Greek *anorektos,* from *a-* + *oregein* to reach after — more at RIGHT] (circa 1894)

1 a : lacking appetite **b :** ANOREXIC 2

2 : causing loss of appetite

²**anorectic** *also* **anoretic** *noun* (circa 1957)

1 : an anorectic agent

2 : ANOREXIC

an·orex·ia \,a-nə-'rek-sē-ə, -'rek-shə\ *noun* [New Latin, from Greek, from *a-* + *orexis* appetite, from *oregein*] (1598)

1 : loss of appetite especially when prolonged

2 : ANOREXIA NERVOSA

anorexia ner·vo·sa \-(,)nər-'vō-sə, -zə\ *noun* [New Latin, nervous anorexia] (1873)

: a serious disorder in eating behavior primarily of young women in their teens and early twenties that is characterized especially by a pathological fear of weight gain leading to faulty eating patterns, malnutrition, and usually excessive weight loss

¹**an·orex·ic** \,a-nə-'rek-sik\ *adjective* (circa 1907)

1 : ANORECTIC

2 : affected with or as if with anorexia nervosa

²**anorexic** *noun* (1912)

: a person affected with anorexia nervosa

an·orex·i·gen·ic \,a-nə-,rek-sə-'ge-nik\ *adjective* (1948)

: ANORECTIC 2

an·or·thite \ə-'nòr-,thīt\ *noun* [French, from *a-* + Greek *orthos* straight] (1833)

: a white, grayish, or reddish feldspar occurring in many igneous rocks

— **an·or·thit·ic** \,a-nòr-'thi-tik\ *adjective*

an·or·tho·site \ə-'nòr-thə-,sīt\ *noun* [French *anorthose,* a feldspar, from *a-* + Greek *orthos* — more at ORTH-] (1863)

: a granular plutonic igneous rock composed almost exclusively of a soda-lime feldspar (as labradorite)

— **an·or·tho·si·tic** \ə-,nòr-thə-'si-tik\ *adjective*

an·os·mia \a-'näz-mē-ə\ *noun* [New Latin, from *a-* + Greek *osmē* smell — more at ODOR] (circa 1811)

: loss or impairment of the sense of smell

— **an·os·mic** \-mik\ *adjective*

¹**an·oth·er** \ə-'nə-<u>th</u>ər *also* a- *or* ā-\ *adjective* (12th century)

1 : different or distinct from the one first considered ⟨the same scene viewed from *another* angle⟩

2 : some other ⟨do it *another* time⟩

3 : being one more in addition to one or more of the same kind ⟨have *another* piece of pie⟩

²**another** *pronoun* (13th century)

1 : an additional one of the same kind **:** one more

2 : one that is different from the first or present one

3 : one of a group of unspecified or indefinite things ⟨in one way or *another*⟩

anoth·er–guess \ə-'nə-<u>th</u>ər-,ges\ *adjective* [alteration of *anothergates,* from ¹*another* + *gate*] (1644)

archaic **:** of another sort

an·ovu·la·to·ry \(,)an-'äv-yə-lə-,tōr-ē, -'ōv-, -,tòr-\ *adjective* (1934)

1 : not involving or accompanied by ovulation ⟨*anovulatory* bleeding⟩

2 : suppressing ovulation

an·ox·emia \,a-,näk-'sē-mē-ə\ *noun* [New Latin] (circa 1881)

: a condition of subnormal oxygenation of the arterial blood

— **an·ox·emic** \-mik\ *adjective*

an·ox·ia \a-'näk-sē-ə\ *noun* [New Latin] (1931)

: hypoxia especially of such severity as to result in permanent damage

an·ox·ic \(,)a-'näk-sik\ *adjective* (1920)

1 : of, relating to, or affected with anoxia

2 : greatly deficient in oxygen **:** OXYGENLESS ⟨*anoxic* water⟩

an·ser·ine \'an(t)-sə-,rīn\ *adjective* [Latin *anserinus,* from *anser* goose — more at GOOSE] (circa 1828)

: of, relating to, or resembling a goose

¹**an·swer** \'an(t)-sər\ *noun* [Middle English, from Old English *andswaru* (akin to Old Norse *andsvar* answer); akin to Old English *and-* against, *swerian* to swear — more at ANTE-] (before 12th century)

1 a : something spoken or written in reply to a question **b :** a correct response

2 : a reply to a legal charge or suit **:** PLEA; *also* **:** DEFENSE

3 : something done in response or reaction ⟨his only *answer* was to walk out⟩

4 : a solution of a problem

5 : one that imitates, matches, or corresponds to another ⟨television's *answer* to the news magazines⟩

²**answer** *verb* **an·swered; an·swer·ing** \'an(t)s-riŋ, 'an(t)-sə-\ (before 12th century)

intransitive verb

1 : to speak or write in reply

2 a : to be or make oneself responsible or accountable **b :** to make amends **:** ATONE

3 : to be in conformity or correspondence ⟨*answered* to the description⟩

4 : to act in response to an action performed elsewhere or by another

5 : to be adequate **:** SERVE

transitive verb

1 a : to speak or write in reply to **b :** to say or write by way of reply

2 : to reply in rebuttal, justification, or explanation

3 a : to correspond to ⟨*answers* the description⟩ **b :** to be adequate or usable for **:** FULFILL

4 *obsolete* **:** to atone for

5 : to act in response to ⟨*answered* the call to arms⟩

6 : to offer a solution for; *especially* **:** SOLVE ☆

— **an·swer·er** \'an(t)-sər-ər\ *noun*

an·swer·able \'an(t)s-rə-bəl, 'an(t)-sə-\ *adjective* (1536)

1 *archaic* **:** SUITABLE, ADEQUATE

2 : liable to be called to account **:** RESPONSIBLE

3 *archaic* **:** CORRESPONDING, SIMILAR

4 : capable of being refuted

synonym see RESPONSIBLE

answering machine *noun* (1961)

: a machine that receives telephone calls by playing a recorded message and usually by recording messages from callers

☆ **SYNONYMS**

Answer, respond, reply, rejoin, retort mean to say, write, or do something in return. ANSWER implies the satisfying of a question, demand, call, or need ⟨*answered* all the questions⟩. RESPOND may suggest an immediate or quick reaction ⟨*responded* eagerly to a call for volunteers⟩. REPLY implies making a return commensurate with the original question or demand ⟨an invitation that requires you to *reply*⟩. REJOIN often implies sharpness or quickness in answering ⟨"who asked you?" she *rejoined*⟩. RETORT suggests responding to an explicit charge or criticism by way of retaliation ⟨he *retorted* to the attack with biting sarcasm⟩.

\ə\ **abut** \ᵊ\ **kitten** \ər\ **further** \a\ **ash** \ā\ **ace**
\ä\ **mop, mar** \aù\ **out** \ch\ **chin** \e\ **bet** \ē\ **easy**
\g\ **go** \i\ **hit** \ī\ **ice** \j\ **job** \ŋ\ **sing** \ō\ **go**
\ò\ **law** \òi\ **boy** \th\ **thin** \<u>th</u>\ **the** \ü\ **loot** \ù\ **foot**
\y\ **yet** \zh\ **vision** *see also* Guide to Pronunciation

answering service *noun* (1941)
: a commercial service that answers telephone calls for its clients

ant \'ant\ *noun* [Middle English *ante, emete,* from Old English *æmette;* akin to Old High German *āmeiza* ant] (before 12th century)
: any of a family (Formicidae) of colonial hymenopterous insects with a complex social organization and various castes performing special duties
— **ants in one's pants :** impatience for action or activity **:** RESTLESSNESS

ant- — see ANTI-

¹-ant *noun suffix* [Middle English, from Old French, from -*ant*, present participle suffix, from Latin -*ant-, -ans,* present participle suffix of first conjugation, from -*a-* (stem vowel of first conjugation) + -*nt-, -ns,* present participle suffix; akin to Old English -*nde,* present participle suffix, Greek -*nt-, -n,* participle suffix]
1 a : one that performs (a specified action) **:** personal or impersonal agent ⟨claim*ant*⟩ ⟨cool*ant*⟩ **b :** thing that promotes (a specified action or process) ⟨expector*ant*⟩
2 : one connected with ⟨annuit*ant*⟩
3 : thing acted upon (in a specified manner) ⟨inhal*ant*⟩

²-ant *adjective suffix*
1 : performing (a specified action) or being (in a specified condition) ⟨somnambul*ant*⟩
2 : promoting (a specified action or process) ⟨expector*ant*⟩

an·ta \'an-tə\ *noun, plural* **antas** *or* **an·tae** \-ˌtē, -ˌtī\ [Latin; akin to Old Norse *ǫnd* anteroom] (1598)
: a pier produced by thickening a wall at its termination

A anta

ant·ac·id \(ˌ)ant-'a-səd, 'an-ˌta-\ *noun* (1732)
: an agent that counteracts or neutralizes acidity
— **antacid** *adjective*

An·tae·an \an-'tē-ən\ *adjective* [*Antaeus,* a giant overcome by Hercules] (1921)
1 : MAMMOTH
2 : having superhuman strength

an·tag·o·nism \an-'ta-gə-ˌni-zəm\ *noun* (circa 1828)
1 a : opposition of a conflicting force, tendency, or principle ⟨the *antagonism* of democracy to dictatorship⟩ **b :** actively expressed opposition or hostility ⟨*antagonism* between factions⟩
2 : opposition in physiological action; *especially* **:** interaction of two or more substances such that the action of any one of them on living cells or tissues is lessened
synonym see ENMITY

an·tag·o·nist \-nist\ *noun* (1594)
1 : one that contends with or opposes another **:** ADVERSARY, OPPONENT
2 : an agent of physiological antagonism: as **a :** a muscle that contracts with and limits the action of an agonist with which it is paired — called also *antagonistic muscle* **b :** a chemical that acts within the body to reduce the physiological activity of another chemical substance (as an opiate); *especially* **:** one that opposes the action on the nervous system of a drug or a substance occurring naturally in the body by combining with and blocking its nervous receptor — compare AGONIST 2b

an·tag·o·nis·tic \(ˌ)an-ˌta-gə-'nis-tik\ *adjective* (1632)
: marked by or resulting from antagonism
— **an·tag·o·nis·ti·cal·ly** \-ti-k(ə-)lē\ *adverb*

an·tag·o·nize \an-'ta-gə-ˌnīz\ *transitive verb* **-nized; -niz·ing** [Greek *antagōnizesthai,* from *anti-* + *agōnizesthai* to struggle, from *agōn* contest — more at AGONY] (circa 1742)
1 : to act in opposition to **:** COUNTERACT
2 : to incur or provoke the hostility of

ant·arc·tic \(ˌ)ant-'ärk-tik, -'är-tik\ *adjective,* *often capitalized* [Middle English *antartik,* from Latin *antarcticus,* from Greek *antarktikos,* from *anti-* + *arktikos* arctic] (14th century)
: of or relating to the south pole or to the region near it

antarctic circle *noun, often A&C capitalized* (1556)
: the parallel of latitude that is approximately 66½ degrees south of the equator and that circumscribes the southern frigid zone

An·tar·es \an-'tar-(ˌ)ēz, -'ter-\ *noun* [Greek *Antarēs*]
: a giant red star of very low density that is the brightest star in Scorpio

ant·bear \'ant-ˌbar, -ˌber\ *noun* (circa 1889)
: AARDVARK

ant cow *noun* (1875)
: an aphid from which ants obtain honeydew

¹an·te \'an-tē\ *noun* [*ante-*] (1838)
1 : a poker stake usually put up before the deal to build the pot ⟨the dealer called for a dollar *ante*⟩
2 : COST, PRICE ⟨these improvements would raise the *ante*⟩

²ante *verb* **an·ted; an·te·ing** (1845)
transitive verb
: to put up (an ante); *also* **:** PAY, PRODUCE — often used with *up*
intransitive verb
: PAY UP — often used with *up*

ante- *prefix* [Middle English, from Latin, from *ante* before, in front of; akin to Old English *and-* against, Greek *anti* before, against — more at END]
1 a : prior **:** earlier ⟨*ante*date⟩ **b :** anterior **:** forward ⟨*ante*room⟩
2 a : prior to **:** earlier than ⟨*ante*diluvian⟩ **b :** in front of ⟨*ante*choir⟩

ant·eat·er \'ant-ˌē-tər\ *noun* (1764)
: any of several mammals that feed largely or entirely on ants or termites: as **a :** any of a family (Myrmecophagidae) of New World edentates with a long narrow snout, a long tongue, and large salivary glands that includes the giant anteater and tamandua **b :** PANGOLIN **c :** ECHIDNA **d :** AARDVARK

an·te·bel·lum \ˌan-ti-'be-ləm\ *adjective* [Latin *ante bellum* before the war] (circa 1847)
: existing before a war; *especially* **:** existing before the Civil War

an·te·cede \ˌan-tə-'sēd\ *transitive verb* **-ced·ed; -ced·ing** [Latin *antecedere*] (1624)
: PRECEDE

an·te·ced·ence \-'sē-d°n(t)s\ *noun* (1651)
: PRIORITY, PRECEDENCE

¹an·te·ced·ent \ˌan-tə-'sē-d°nt\ *noun* [Middle English, from Medieval Latin & Latin; Medieval Latin *antecedent-, antecedens,* from Latin, what precedes, from neuter of *antecedent-, antecedens,* present participle of *antecedere* to go before, from *ante-* + *cedere* to go] (14th century)
1 : a substantive word, phrase, or clause whose denotation is referred to by a pronoun (as *John* in "Mary saw John and called to him"); *broadly* **:** a word or phrase replaced by a substitute
2 : the conditional element in a proposition (as *if A* in "if A, then B")
3 : the first term of a mathematical ratio
4 a : a preceding event, condition, or cause **b** *plural* **:** the significant events, conditions, and traits of one's earlier life
5 a : PREDECESSOR; *especially* **:** a model or stimulus for later developments **b** *plural* **:** ANCESTORS, PARENTS

²antecedent *adjective* (14th century)
: PRIOR
synonym see PRECEDING
— **an·te·ced·ent·ly** *adverb*

an·te·ces·sor \ˌan-ti-'se-sər\ *noun* [Middle English *antecessour,* from Latin *antecessor* — more at ANCESTOR] (14th century)
: one that goes before **:** PREDECESSOR

an·te·cham·ber \'an-ti-ˌchām-bər\ *noun* [French *antichambre,* from Middle French, from Italian *anti-* (from Latin *ante-*) + Middle French *chambre* room] (circa 1656)
: ANTEROOM

an·te·chap·el \-ˌcha-pəl\ *noun* (1703)
: a vestibule or anteroom to a chapel or church

an·te·choir \'an-ti-ˌkwī-(ə)r\ *noun* (circa 1889)
: a space enclosed or reserved for the clergy and choristers at the entrance to a choir

¹an·te·date \'an-ti-ˌdāt\ *noun* (15th century)
: a date assigned to an event or document earlier than the actual date of the event or document

²an·te·date \'an-ti-ˌdāt, ˌan-ti-'\ *transitive verb* (1572)
1 a : to date as of a time prior to that of execution **b :** to assign to a date prior to that of actual occurrence
2 *archaic* **:** ANTICIPATE
3 : to precede in time

an·te·di·lu·vi·an \ˌan-ti-də-'lü-vē-ən, -(ˌ)dī-\ *adjective* [*ante-* + Latin *diluvium* flood — more at DELUGE] (1646)
1 : of or relating to the period before the flood described in the Bible
2 : made, evolved, or developed a long time ago ⟨an *antediluvian* automobile⟩
— **antediluvian** *noun*

an·te·fix \'an-ti-ˌfiks\ *noun, plural* **-fix·ae** \-ˌfik-ˌsē\ *or* **-fix·es** \-ˌfik-səz\ [Latin *antefixum,* from neuter of *antefixus,* past participle of *antefigere* to fasten before, from *ante-* + *figere* to fasten — more at FIX] (1832)
: an ornament at the eaves of a classical building concealing the ends of the joint tiles of the roof

an·te·lope \'an-t°l-ˌōp\ *noun, plural* **-lope** *or* **-lopes** [Middle English, fabulous heraldic beast, probably from Middle French *antelop* savage animal with sawlike horns, from Medieval Latin *anthalopus,* from Late Greek *antholop-, antholops*] (15th century)
1 a : any of various ruminant mammals (family Bovidae) chiefly of Africa and southwest Asia that differ from the true oxen especially in lighter racier build and horns directed upward and backward **b :** PRONGHORN
2 : leather from antelope hide

an·te me·ri·di·em \ˌan-ti-mə-'ri-dē-əm, -dē-ˌem\ *adjective* [Latin] (1563)
: being before noon — abbreviation *a.m.*

an·te·mor·tem \-'mòr-təm\ *adjective* [Latin *ante mortem*] (1883)
: preceding death

an·te·na·tal \-'nā-t°l\ *adjective* (1817)
: PRENATAL ⟨*antenatal* diagnosis of birth defects⟩
— **an·te·na·tal·ly** \-ē\ *adverb*

an·ten·na \an-'te-nə\ *noun, plural* **-nae** \-(ˌ)nē\ *or* **-nas** [Medieval Latin, from Latin, sail yard] (1646)
1 *plural* **-nae :** one of a pair of slender movable segmented sensory organs on the head of insects, myriapods, and crustaceans — see INSECT illustration
2 : a usually metallic device (as a rod or wire) for radiating or receiving radio waves
3 *antennae plural* **:** a special sensitivity or receptiveness ⟨his political *antennae* proved to be shrewder than ever —Erich Segal⟩ ◆
— **an·ten·nal** \-'te-n°l\ *adjective*

an·ten·nule \an-'ten-(ˌ)yü(ə)l\ *noun* (1845)
: a small antenna or similar appendage
— **an·ten·nu·lar** \-'ten-yə-lər\ *adjective*

an·te·nup·tial \ˌan-ti-'nəp-shəl, -chəl; ÷-shə-wəl, ÷-chə-\ *adjective* (1818)
: PRENUPTIAL

an·te·pen·di·um \ˌan-ti-'pen-dē-əm\ *noun, plural* **-di·ums** *or* **-dia** \-dē-ə\ [Medieval Latin, from Latin *ante-* + *pendēre* to hang — more at PENDANT] (circa 1696)
: a hanging for the front of an altar, pulpit, or lectern

an·te·pe·nult \ˌan-ti-'pē-ˌnəlt, -pi-'\ *also* **an·te·pen·ul·ti·ma** \-pi-'nəl-tə-mə\ *noun* [Late

Latin *antepaenultima*, feminine of *antepaenultimus* preceding the next to last, from Latin *ante-* + *paenultimus* penultimate] (1581)
: the third syllable of a word counting from the end (as *cu* in *accumulate*)
— **an·te·pen·ul·ti·mate** \-pi-'nəl-tə-mət\ *adjective or noun*

an·te·post \'an-ti-ˌpōst\ *adjective* (1902)
British : relating to or being wagers on a horse race made especially before the day of the race

an·te·ri·or \an-'tir-ē-ər\ *adjective* [Latin, comparative of *ante* before — more at ANTE-] (1541)
1 a : situated before or toward the front **b** : situated near or toward the head or part most nearly corresponding to a head
2 : coming before in time or development
synonym see PRECEDING
— **an·te·ri·or·ly** *adverb*

an·te·room \'an-ti-ˌrüm, -ˌrum\ *noun* (1762)
: an outer room that leads to another room and that is often used as a waiting room

anth- — see ANTI-

an·thel·min·tic \ˌant-hel-'min-tik, ˌan-ˌthel-\ *adjective* [*anti-* + Greek *helminth-, helmis* worm] (1684)
: expelling or destroying parasitic worms especially of the intestine
— **anthelmintic** *noun*

an·them \'an(t)-thəm\ *noun* [Middle English *antem*, from Old English *antefn*, from Late Latin *antiphona*, from Late Greek *antiphōna*, plural of *antiphōnon*, from Greek, neuter of *antiphōnos* responsive, from *anti-* + *phōnē* sound — more at BAN] (before 12th century)
1 a : a psalm or hymn sung antiphonally or responsively **b** : a sacred vocal composition with words usually from the Scriptures
2 : a song or hymn of praise or gladness

an·the·mi·on \an-'thē-mē-ən\ *noun, plural* **-mia** \-mē-ə\ [Greek, from diminutive of *anthemon* flower, from *anthos* — more at ANTHOLOGY] (1865)
: a flat ornament of floral form (as in relief sculpture or in painting)

an·ther \'an(t)-thər\ *noun* [New Latin *anthera*, from Latin, medicine made from flowers, from Greek *anthēra*, from feminine of *anthēros* flowery, from *anthos*] (circa 1706)
: the part of a stamen that produces and contains pollen and is usually borne on a stalk — see FLOWER illustration
— **an·ther·al** \-thə-rəl\ *adjective*

an·ther·id·i·um \ˌan(t)-thə-'ri-dē-əm\ *noun, plural* **-id·ia** \-dē-ə\ [New Latin, from *anthera*] (1854)
: the male reproductive organ of some cryptogamous plants
— **an·ther·id·i·al** \-dē-əl\ *adjective*

an·the·sis \an-'thē-səs\ *noun* [New Latin, from Greek *anthēsis* bloom, from *anthein* to flower, from *anthos*] (circa 1823)
: the action or period of opening of a flower

ant·hill \'ant-ˌhil\ *noun* (14th century)
: a mound of debris thrown up by ants or termites in digging their nest

an·tho·cy·a·nin \ˌan(t)-thə-'sī-ə-nən\ *also* **an·tho·cy·an** \-'sī-ən, -ˌan\ *noun* [Greek *anthos* + *kyanos* dark blue] (1839)
: any of various soluble glycoside pigments producing blue to red coloring in flowers and plants

an·thol·o·gist \an-'thä-lə-jist\ *noun* (1805)
: a compiler of an anthology

an·thol·o·gize \-ˌjīz\ *transitive verb* **-gized; -giz·ing** (1892)
: to compile, publish, or include in an anthology
— **an·thol·o·giz·er** \-ˌjī-zər\ *noun*

an·thol·o·gy \an-'thä-lə-jē\ *noun, plural* **-gies** [New Latin *anthologia* collection of epigrams, from Middle Greek, from Greek, flower gathering, from *anthos* flower + *logia* collecting, from *legein* to gather; akin to Sanskrit *andha* herb — more at LEGEND] (1640)

1 : a collection of selected literary pieces or passages or works of art or music
2 : ASSORTMENT ⟨an *anthology* of threadbare clichés of . . . bistro cuisine —Jay Jacobs⟩
— **an·tho·log·i·cal** \ˌan(t)-thə-'lä-ji-kəl\ *adjective*

an·thoph·i·lous \an-'thä-fə-ləs\ *adjective* [International Scientific Vocabulary, from Greek *anthos* + English *-philous*] (1883)
: feeding upon or living among flowers ⟨*anthophilous* insects⟩

an·tho·phyl·lite \ˌan(t)-thə-'fi-ˌlīt, (ˌ)an-'thä-fə-\ *noun* [German *Anthophyllit*, from New Latin *anthophyllum*, from Greek *anthos* + *phyllon* leaf — more at BLADE] (circa 1828)
: an orthorhombic mineral of the amphibole group that is essentially a silicate of magnesium and iron and is usually lamellar or fibrous and when fibrous is one of the less common forms of asbestos

an·tho·zo·an \ˌan(t)-thə-'zō-ən\ *noun* [ultimately from Greek *anthos* + *zōion* animal; akin to Greek *zōē* life — more at QUICK] (circa 1889)
: any of a class (Anthozoa) of marine coelenterates (as the corals and sea anemones) having polyps with radial partitions
— **anthozoan** *adjective*

an·thra·cene \'an(t)-thrə-ˌsēn\ *noun* (1863)
: a crystalline aromatic hydrocarbon $C_{14}H_{10}$ obtained from coal-tar distillation

an·thra·cite \'an(t)-thrə-ˌsīt\ *noun* [Greek *anthrakitis*, from *anthrak-, anthrax* coal] (1812)
: a hard natural coal of high luster differing from bituminous coal in containing little volatile matter and in burning very cleanly — called also *hard coal*
— **an·thra·cit·ic** \ˌan(t)-thrə-'si-tik\ *adjective*

an·thrac·nose \an-'thrak-ˌnōs\ *noun* [French, from Greek *anthrak-, anthrax* + *nosos* disease] (1886)
: any of numerous destructive plant diseases caused by imperfect fungi and characterized especially by necrotic lesions

an·thra·ni·late \an-'thra-nᵊl-ˌāt, ˌan-thrə-'ni-ˌlāt\ *noun* (1921)
: a salt or ester of anthranilic acid

an·thra·nil·ic acid \ˌan(t)-thrə-'ni-lik-\ *noun* [International Scientific Vocabulary *anthracene* + *aniline*] (1881)
: a crystalline acid $NH_2C_6H_4COOH$ used as an intermediate in the manufacture of dyes (as indigo), pharmaceuticals, and perfumes

an·thra·qui·none \ˌan(t)-thrə-kwi-'nōn, -'kwi-ˌnōn\ *noun* [probably from French, from *anthracene* + *quinone*] (1869)
: a yellow crystalline ketone $C_{14}H_8O_2$ often derived from anthracene and used especially in the manufacture of dyes

an·thrax \'an-ˌthraks\ *noun* [Middle English *antrax* carbuncle, from Latin *anthrax*, from Greek, coal, carbuncle] (1876)
: an infectious disease of warm-blooded animals (as cattle and sheep) caused by a spore-forming bacterium (*Bacillus anthracis*), transmissible to humans especially by the handling of infected products (as wool), and characterized by external ulcerating nodules or by lesions in the lungs

anthrop- *or* **anthropo-** *combining form* [Latin *anthropo-*, from Greek *anthrōp-, anthrōpo-*, from *anthrōpos*]
: human being ⟨*anthrop*ogenic⟩

an·throp·ic \an-'thrä-pik\ *or* **an·throp·i·cal** \-pi-kəl\ *adjective* [Greek *anthrōpikos*, from *anthrōpos*] (circa 1806)
: of or relating to human beings or the period of their existence on earth

anthropic principle *noun* (1974)
: either of two principles in cosmology: **a** : conditions that are observed in the universe must allow the observer to exist — called also *weak anthropic principle* **b** : the universe must have properties that make inevitable the existence of intelligent life — called also *strong anthropic principle*

an·thro·po·cen·tric \ˌan(t)-thrə-pə-'sen-trik\ *adjective* (1863)
1 : considering human beings as the most significant entity of the universe
2 : interpreting or regarding the world in terms of human values and experiences
— **an·thro·po·cen·tri·cal·ly** \-tri-k(ə-)lē\ *adverb*
— **an·thro·po·cen·tric·i·ty** \-pō-(ˌ)sen-'tri-sə-tē\ *noun*
— **an·thro·po·cen·trism** \-'sen-ˌtri-zəm\ *noun*

an·thro·po·gen·ic \-pə-'je-nik\ *adjective* (1923)
: of, relating to, or resulting from the influence of human beings on nature ⟨*anthropogenic* pollutants⟩

an·thro·poid \'an(t)-thrə-ˌpóid\ *noun* [Greek *anthrōpoeidēs* resembling a human, from *anthrōpos*] (1832)
1 : APE 1b
2 : a person resembling an ape ⟨the howling *anthropoids* of the Hookworm Belt —H. L. Mencken⟩
— **anthropoid** *adjective*

anthropoid ape *noun* (circa 1837)
: APE 1b

an·thro·pol·o·gy \ˌan(t)-thrə-'pä-lə-jē\ *noun* [New Latin *anthropologia*, from *anthrop-* + *-logia* -logy] (1593)
1 : the science of human beings; *especially* : the study of human beings in relation to distribution, origin, classification, and relationship of races, physical character, environmental and social relations, and culture
2 : theology dealing with the origin, nature, and destiny of human beings
— **an·thro·po·log·i·cal** \-pə-'lä-ji-kəl\ *adjective*
— **an·thro·po·log·i·cal·ly** \-ji-k(ə-)lē\ *adverb*
— **an·thro·pol·o·gist** \ˌan(t)-thrə-'pä-lə-jist\ *noun*

an·thro·pom·e·try \ˌan(t)-thrə-'pä-mə-trē\ *noun* [French *anthropométrie*, from *anthrop-* + *-métrie* -metry] (circa 1839)
: the study of human body measurements especially on a comparative basis
— **an·thro·po·met·ric** \-pə-'me-trik\ *adjective*

an·thro·po·morph \'an(t)-thrə-pə-ˌmórf\ *noun* (1894)
: a stylized human figure (as in prehistoric art)

an·thro·po·mor·phic \ˌan(t)-thrə-pə-'mór-fik\ *adjective* [Late Latin *anthropomorphus* of

\ə\ abut \ᵊ\ kitten \ər\ further \a\ ash \ā\ ace
\ä\ mop, mar \aú\ out \ch\ chin \e\ bet \ē\ easy
\g\ go \i\ hit \ī\ ice \j\ job \ŋ\ sing \ō\ go
\ò\ law \òi\ boy \th\ thin \t̷h\ the \ü\ loot \ú\ foot
\y\ yet \zh\ vision *see also* Guide to Pronunciation

human form, from Greek *anthrōpomorphos*, from *anthrōp-* + *-morphos* -morphous] (1827)
1 : described or thought of as having a human form or human attributes ⟨*anthropomorphic* deities⟩
2 : ascribing human characteristics to nonhuman things ⟨*anthropomorphic* supernaturalism⟩
— **an·thro·po·mor·phi·cal·ly** \-fi-k(ə-)lē\ *adverb*
an·thro·po·mor·phism \-ˌfi-zəm\ *noun* (1753)
: an interpretation of what is not human or personal in terms of human or personal characteristics : HUMANIZATION
— **an·thro·po·mor·phist** \-fist\ *noun*
an·thro·po·mor·phize \-ˌfīz\ *verb* **-phized; -phiz·ing** (1845)
transitive verb
: to attribute human form or personality to
intransitive verb
: to attribute human form or personality to things not human
— **an·thro·po·mor·phi·za·tion** \-ˌmȯr-fə-'zā-shən\ *noun*
an·thro·po·pa·thism \ˌan(t)-thrə-'pä-pə-ˌthi-zəm, -pō-'pa-ˌthi-\ *noun* [Late Greek *anthrōpopatheia* humanity, from Greek *anthrōpopathēs* having human feelings, from *anthrōp-* + *pathos* experience — more at PATHOS] (1847)
: the ascription of human feelings to something not human
an·thro·poph·a·gous \ˌan(t)-thrə-'pä-fə-gəs\ *adjective* (circa 1828)
: feeding on human flesh
— **an·thro·poph·a·gy** \-fə-jē\ *noun*
an·thro·poph·a·gus \-fə-gəs\ *noun, plural* **-a·gi** \-fə-ˌgī, -ˌjī, -ˌgē\ [Latin, from Greek *anthrōpophagos*, from *anthrōp-* + *-phagos* -phagous] (1552)
: MAN-EATER, CANNIBAL
an·thro·pos·o·phy \ˌan(t)-thrə-'pä-sə-fē\ *noun* (1916)
: a 20th century religious system growing out of theosophy and centering on human development
an·thur·ium \an-'thùr-ē-əm, -'thyùr-\ *noun* [New Latin, from Greek *anthos* flower + *oura* tail — more at ANTHOLOGY, ASS] (circa 1839)
: any of a genus (*Anthurium*) of tropical American plants of the arum family with large often highly colored leaves, a cylindrical spadix, and a colored spathe
¹an·ti \'an-ˌtī, 'an-tē\ *noun, plural* **antis** [*anti-*] (1788)
: one that is opposed
²anti *adjective* (1857)
: OPPOSED
³anti *preposition* (1953)
: opposed to : AGAINST
anti- *or* **ant-** *or* **anth-** *prefix* [*anti-* from Middle English, from Middle French & Latin; Middle French, from Latin, against, from Greek, from *anti*; *ant-* from Middle English, from Latin, against, from Greek, from *anti*; *anth-* from Latin, against, from Greek, from *anti* — more at ANTE-]
1 a : of the same kind but situated opposite, exerting energy in the opposite direction, or pursuing an opposite policy ⟨*anticlinal*⟩ **b** : one that is opposite in kind to ⟨*anticlimax*⟩
2 a : opposing or hostile to in opinion, sympathy, or practice ⟨*anti*-Semite⟩ **b** : opposing in effect or activity ⟨*antacid*⟩
3 : serving to prevent, cure, or alleviate ⟨*anti*-anxiety⟩
4 : combating or defending against ⟨*antiaircraft*⟩ ⟨*antimissile*⟩

an·ti·ac·a·dem·ic
an·ti–ac·ne
an·ti·ad·min·is·tra·tion
an·ti·ag·gres·sion
an·ti·ag·ing
an·ti–AIDS
an·ti·al·co·hol
an·ti·al·co·hol·ism
an·ti·alien
an·ti·al·ler·gen·ic
an·ti·ane·mia
an·ti·apart·heid
an·ti·aph·ro·di·si·ac
an·ti·aris·to·crat·ic
an·ti·ar·thrit·ic
an·ti·ar·thri·tis
an·ti·as·sim·i·la·tion
an·ti·asth·ma
an·ti·au·thor·i·tar·i·an
an·ti·au·thor·i·tar·i·an·ism
an·ti·au·thor·i·ty
an·ti·back·lash
an·ti·bi·as
an·ti·bill·board
an·ti·boss
an·ti·bour·geois
an·ti·boy·cott
an·ti–Brit·ish
an·ti·bug
an·ti·bu·reau·crat·ic
an·ti·bur·glar
an·ti·bur·glary
an·ti·cak·ing
an·ti·cap·i·tal·ism
an·ti·cap·i·tal·ist
an·ti·car·cin·o·gen
an·ti·car·ci·no·gen·ic
an·ti·car·ies
an·ti–Cath·o·lic
an·ti–Ca·thol·i·cism
an·ti·cel·lu·lite
an·ti·cen·sor·ship
an·ti·cho·les·ter·ol
an·ti–Chris·tian
an·ti–Chris·tian·i·ty
an·ti·church
an·ti·cig·a·rette
an·ti·city
an·ti·clas·si·cal
an·ti·cling
an·ti·clot·ting
an·ti·cold
an·ti·col·li·sion
an·ti·co·lo·nial
an·ti·co·lo·nial·ism
an·ti·co·lo·nial·ist
an·ti·com·mer·cial
an·ti·com·mer·cial·ism
an·ti·com·mu·nism
an·ti·com·mu·nist
an·ti·con·glom·er·ate
an·ti·con·ser·va·tion
an·ti·con·ser·va·tion·ist
an·ti·con·sum·er
an·ti·con·ven·tion·al
an·ti·cor·po·rate
an·ti·cor·ro·sion
an·ti·cor·ro·sive
an·ti·cor·rup·tion
an·ti·coun·ter·feit·ing
an·ti·crack
an·ti·cre·ative
an·ti·crime
an·ti·cru·el·ty
an·ti·cult
an·ti·cul·tur·al
an·ti·dan·druff
an·ti–Dar·win·i·an
an·ti–Dar·win·ism
an·ti·def·a·ma·tion
an·ti·de·pres·sion
an·ti·de·seg·re·ga·tion
an·ti·de·sert·i·fi·ca·tion
an·ti·des·ic·cant
an·ti·de·vel·op·ment
an·ti·di·a·bet·ic
an·ti·di·ar·rhe·al
an·ti·di·lu·tion
an·ti·dis·crim·i·na·tion
an·ti·dog·mat·ic
an·ti·draft
an·ti·eco·nom·ic
an·ti·ed·u·ca·tion·al
an·ti·egal·i·tar·i·an
an·ti·elite
an·ti·elit·ism
an·ti·elit·ist
an·ti·emet·ic
an·ti–En·glish
an·ti·en·tro·pic
an·ti·ep·i·lep·sy
an·ti·ep·i·lep·tic
an·ti·erot·ic
an·ti·es·tab·lish·ment
an·ti·es·tro·gen
an·ti·evo·lu·tion
an·ti·evo·lu·tion·ary
an·ti·evo·lu·tion·ism
an·ti·evo·lu·tion·ist
an·ti·fam·i·ly
an·ti·fas·cism
an·ti·fas·cist
an·ti·fash·ion
an·ti·fash·ion·able
an·ti·fa·tigue
an·ti·fe·male
an·ti·fem·i·nine
an·ti·fem·i·nism
an·ti·fem·i·nist
an·ti·fil·i·bus·ter
an·ti·flu
an·ti·foam
an·ti·foam·ing
an·ti·fog·ging
an·ti·fore·clo·sure
an·ti·for·eign
an·ti·for·eign·er
an·ti·for·mal·ist
an·ti·fraud
an·ti–French
an·ti·fric·tion
an·ti·fur
an·ti·gam·bling
an·ti·gay
an·ti–Ger·man
an·ti·glare
an·ti·gov·ern·ment
an·ti·growth
an·ti·guer·ril·la
an·ti·gun
an·ti·her·pes
an·ti·hi·er·ar·chi·cal
an·ti·hi·jack
an·ti·his·tor·i·cal
an·ti·ho·mo·sex·u·al
an·ti·hu·man·ism
an·ti·hu·man·is·tic
an·ti·hu·man·i·tar·i·an
an·ti·hunt·er
an·ti·hunt·ing
an·ti·hys·ter·ic
an·ti–ic·ing
an·ti–ideo·log·i·cal
an·ti·im·pe·ri·al·ism
an·ti·im·pe·ri·al·ist
an·ti·in·cum·bent
an·ti·in·fec·tive
an·ti·in·fla·tion
an·ti·in·fla·tion·ary
an·ti·in·sti·tu·tion·al
an·ti·in·te·gra·tion
an·ti·in·tru·sion
an·ti–Ital·ian
an·ti·jam
an·ti·jam·ming
an·ti–Jap·a·nese
an·ti–Jew·ish
an·ti·kick·back
an·ti·knock
an·ti·la·bor
an·ti·leak
an·ti·lep·ro·sy
an·ti·lib·er·al
an·ti·lib·er·al·ism
an·ti·lib·er·tar·i·an
an·ti·lit·er·ate
an·ti·lit·ter
an·ti·lit·ter·ing
an·ti·log·i·cal
an·ti·lynch·ing
an·ti·ma·cho
an·ti·ma·lar·ia
an·ti·male
an·ti·man
an·ti·man·age·ment
an·ti·mar·i·jua·na
an·ti·mar·ket
an·ti·ma·te·ri·al·ism
an·ti·ma·te·ri·al·ist
an·ti·mech·a·nist
an·ti·merg·er
an·ti·met·a·bol·ic
an·ti·meta·phys·i·cal
an·ti·mil·i·ta·rism
an·ti·mil·i·ta·rist
an·ti·mil·i·tary
an·ti·mis·ce·ge·na·tion
an·ti·mis·sile
an·ti·mod·ern
an·ti·mod·ern·ist
an·ti·mo·nar·chi·cal
an·ti·mon·ar·chist
an·ti·mo·nop·o·list
an·ti·mo·nop·o·ly
an·ti·mos·qui·to
an·ti·mu·si·cal
an·ti·nar·ra·tive
an·ti·na·tion·al
an·ti·na·tion·al·ist
an·ti·nat·u·ral
an·ti·na·ture
an·ti·nau·sea
an·ti–Na·zi
an·ti–Ne·gro
an·ti·nep·o·tism
an·ti·noise
an·ti·obe·si·ty
an·ti·ob·scen·i·ty
an·ti·or·ga·ni·za·tion
an·ti·pa·pal
an·ti·par·ty
an·ti·pes·ti·cide
an·ti·pi·ra·cy
an·ti·plague
an·ti·plaque
an·ti·plea·sure
an·ti·poach·ing
an·ti·po·lice
an·ti·po·lit·i·cal
an·ti·pol·i·tics
an·ti·pop·u·lar
an·ti·porn
an·ti·por·no·graph·ic
an·ti·por·nog·ra·phy
an·ti·pot
an·ti·pov·er·ty
an·ti·pred·a·tor
an·ti·press
an·ti·prof·i·teer·ing
an·ti·pro·gres·sive
an·ti·pros·ti·tu·tion
an·ti·pru·rit·ic
an·ti·ra·bies
an·ti·rac·ism
an·ti·rac·ist
an·ti·rack·e·teer·ing
an·ti·ra·dar
an·ti·rad·i·cal
an·ti·rad·i·cal·ism
an·ti·rape
an·ti·ra·tio·nal
an·ti·ra·tio·nal·ism
an·ti·ra·tio·nal·ist
an·ti·ra·tio·nal·i·ty
an·ti·re·al·ism
an·ti·re·al·ist
an·ti·re·ces·sion
an·ti·re·ces·sion·ary
an·ti·red
an·ti·re·duc·tion·ism
an·ti·re·duc·tion·ist
an·ti·re·flec·tion
an·ti·re·flec·tive
an·ti·re·form
an·ti·reg·u·la·to·ry
an·ti·re·li·gion
an·ti·re·li·gious
an·ti·rev·o·lu·tion·ary
an·ti·ri·ot
an·ti·rit·u·al·ism
an·ti·rock
an·ti·roll
an·ti·ro·man·tic
an·ti·ro·man·ti·cism
an·ti·roy·al·ist
an·ti–Rus·sian
an·ti·rust
an·ti·sat·el·lite
an·ti·schizo·phre·nia
an·ti·schiz·o·phren·ic
an·ti·sci·ence
an·ti·sci·en·tif·ic
an·ti·se·cre·cy
an·ti·seg·re·ga·tion
an·ti·sei·zure
an·ti·sen·ti·men·tal
an·ti·sep·a·rat·ist
an·ti·sex
an·ti·sex·ist
an·ti·sex·u·al
an·ti·sex·u·al·i·ty
an·ti·shark
an·ti·ship
an·ti·shock
an·ti·shop·lift·ing
an·ti·skid
an·ti·slav·ery
an·ti·sleep
an·ti·slip
an·ti·smog
an·ti·smoke
an·ti·smok·er
an·ti·smok·ing
an·ti·smug·gling
an·ti·smut
an·ti·snob
an·ti·so·cial·ist
an·ti–So·viet
an·ti–So·vi·et·ism
an·ti·spec·u·la·tion
an·ti·spec·u·la·tive
an·ti·spend·ing
an·ti–Sta·lin·ist
an·ti·stick
an·ti·sto·ry
an·ti·stress
an·ti·strike
an·ti·stu·dent
an·ti·sub·ma·rine
an·ti·sub·si·dy
an·ti·sub·ver·sion
an·ti·sub·ver·sive
an·ti·sui·cide
an·ti·syph·i·lit·ic
an·ti·take·over
an·ti·tank
an·ti·tar·nish
an·ti·tax
an·ti·tech·no·log·i·cal
an·ti·tech·nol·o·gy
an·ti·ter·ror·ism
an·ti·ter·ror·ist
an·ti·theft
an·ti·the·o·ret·i·cal
an·ti·to·bac·co
an·ti·to·tal·i·tar·i·an
an·ti·tra·di·tion·al
an·ti·tu·ber·cu·lar
an·ti·tu·ber·cu·lo·sis
an·ti·tu·ber·cu·lous
an·ti·tu·mor

an·ti·tu·mor·al
an·ti·ty·phoid
an·ti·ul·cer
an·ti·un·em·ploy-
 ment
an·ti·union
an·ti·uni·ver·si·ty
an·ti·ur·ban
an·ti·vi·o·lence
an·ti·vi·ral
an·ti·vi·rus

an·ti·vivi·sec·tion
an·ti·vivi·sec·tion·ist
an·ti·war
an·ti·wear
an·ti·wel·fare
an·ti–West
an·ti–West·ern
an·ti·whal·ing
an·ti·wom·an
an·ti·wrin·kle
an·ti–Zi·on·ist

an·ti·abor·tion \,an-tē-ə-'bȯr-shən, ,an-,tī-\ *adjective* (1971)
: opposed to abortion ⟨*antiabortion* lobbyists⟩
— **an·ti·abor·tion·ist** \-sh(ə-)nist\ *noun*

an·ti·air \,an-tē-'ar, -'er, -,tī-\ *adjective* (1925)
: ANTIAIRCRAFT

¹an·ti·air·craft \-'ar-,kraft, -'er-\ *adjective* (1914)
: designed for or concerned with defense against air attack

²antiaircraft *noun* (1926)
: antiaircraft guns or their fire

an·ti–Amer·i·can \-ə-'mer-ə-kən, -'mər-, -'mar-, -i-kən\ *adjective* (1773)
: opposed or hostile to the people or the government policies of the U.S.
— **an·ti–Amer·i·can·ism** \-kə-,ni-zəm\ *noun*

an·ti·anx·i·ety \-(,)aŋ-'zī-ə-tē\ *adjective* (1962)
: tending to prevent or relieve anxiety ⟨*antianxiety* drugs⟩

an·ti·ar·rhyth·mic \,an-tē-(,)ā-'rith-mik, ,an-,tī-\ *adjective* (1954)
: tending to prevent or relieve cardiac arrhythmia ⟨an *antiarrhythmic* agent⟩

an·ti·art \-'ärt\ *noun* (1937)
: art based on premises antithetical to traditional or popular art forms; *specifically* **:** DADA

an·ti·aux·in \-'ȯk-sən\ *noun* (1949)
: a plant substance that opposes or suppresses the natural effect of an auxin

an·ti·bac·te·ri·al \,an-ti-bak-'tir-ē-əl, ,an-,tī-\ *adjective* (circa 1897)
: directed or effective against bacteria
— **antibacterial** *noun*

an·ti·bal·lis·tic missile \,an-ti-bə-'lis-tik-, ,an-,tī-\ *noun* (circa 1959)
: a missile for intercepting and destroying ballistic missiles

an·ti·bi·o·sis \-bī-'ō-səs, -bē-\ *noun* [New Latin] (1899)
: antagonistic association between organisms to the detriment of one of them or between one organism and a metabolic product of another

¹an·ti·bi·ot·ic \,an-ti-bī-'ä-tik, -,tī-; ,an-ti-bē-\ *adjective* (1894)
1 : tending to prevent, inhibit, or destroy life
2 : of or relating to antibiotics or to antibiosis
— **an·ti·bi·ot·i·cal·ly** \-ti-k(ə-)lē\ *adverb*

²antibiotic *noun* (1943)
: a substance produced by or a semisynthetic substance derived from a microorganism and able in dilute solution to inhibit or kill another microorganism

an·ti·black \-'blak\ *adjective* (1952)
: opposed or hostile to black people
— **an·ti·black·ism** \-'bla-,ki-zəm\ *noun*

an·ti·body \'an-ti-,bä-dē\ *noun* (1900)
: any of a large number of proteins of high molecular weight that are produced normally by specialized B cells after stimulation by an antigen and act specifically against the antigen in an immune response, that are produced abnormally by some cancer cells, and that typically consist of four subunits including two heavy chains and two light chains — called also *immunoglobulin*

an·ti·busi·ness \,an-ti-'biz-nəs, ,an-tī-, -nəz\ *adjective* (1938)
: antagonistic toward business and especially big business

an·ti·bus·ing \-'bə-siŋ\ *adjective* (circa 1969)
: opposed to the busing of schoolchildren ⟨*antibusing* parents⟩ ⟨*antibusing* campaign⟩

¹an·tic \'an-tik\ *noun* [Italian *antico* ancient thing or person, from *antico* ancient, from Latin *antiquus* — more at ANTIQUE] (1529)
1 : an attention-drawing often wildly playful or funny act or action **:** CAPER ⟨childish *antics*⟩
2 *archaic* **:** a performer of a grotesque or ludicrous part **:** BUFFOON ◇

²antic *adjective* (1548)
1 *archaic* **:** GROTESQUE, BIZARRE
2 a : characterized by clownish extravagance or absurdity **b :** whimsically gay **:** FROLICSOME
— **an·ti·cal·ly** \-ti-k(ə-)lē\ *adverb*

an·ti·can·cer \,an-,tī-'kan(t)-sər, ,an-ti-\ *adjective* (1926)
: used against or tending to arrest cancer ⟨*anticancer* drugs⟩ ⟨*anticancer* activity⟩ ⟨*anticancer* effects⟩

an·ti·cho·lin·er·gic \-,kō-lə-'nər-jik\ *adjective* (1942)
: opposing or blocking the physiologic action of acetylcholine
— **anticholinergic** *noun*

an·ti·cho·lin·es·ter·ase \-'nes-tə-,rās, -,rāz\ *noun* (1942)
: a substance (as neostigmine) that inhibits a cholinesterase by combination with it

An·ti·christ \'an-ti-,krīst, -,tī-\ *noun* [Middle English *anticrist,* from Old English & Late Latin; Old English *antecrist,* from Late Latin *Antichristus,* from Greek *Antichristos,* from *anti-* + *Christos* Christ] (before 12th century)
1 : one who denies or opposes Christ; *specifically* **:** a great antagonist expected to fill the world with wickedness but to be conquered forever by Christ at his second coming
2 : a false Christ

an·tic·i·pant \an-'ti-sə-pənt\ *adjective* (1626)
: EXPECTANT, ANTICIPATING — usually used with *of*
— **anticipant** *noun*

an·tic·i·pate \an-'ti-sə-,pāt\ *verb* **-pat·ed;**
-pat·ing [Latin *anticipatus,* past participle of *anticipare,* from *ante-* + *-cipare* (from *capere* to take) — more at HEAVE] (1532)
transitive verb
1 : to give advance thought, discussion, or treatment to
2 : to meet (an obligation) before a due date
3 : to foresee and deal with in advance **:** FORESTALL
4 : to use or expend in advance of actual possession
5 : to act before (another) often so as to check or counter
6 : to look forward to as certain **:** EXPECT
intransitive verb
: to speak or write in knowledge or expectation of later matter
synonym SEE FORESEE, PREVENT
— **an·tic·i·pat·able** \-,pā-tə-bəl\ *adjective*
— **an·tic·i·pa·tor** \-,pā-tər\ *noun*

an·tic·i·pa·tion \(,)an-,ti-sə-'pā-shən\ *noun* (14th century)
1 a : a prior action that takes into account or forestalls a later action **b :** the act of looking forward; *especially* **:** pleasurable expectation
2 : the use of money before it is available
3 a : visualization of a future event or state **b :** an object or form that anticipates a later type
4 : the early sounding of one or more tones of a succeeding chord to form a temporary dissonance — compare SUSPENSION
synonym SEE PROSPECT

an·tic·i·pa·to·ry \an-'ti-sə-pə-,tōr-ē, -,tȯr-\ *adjective* (1669)
: characterized by anticipation **:** ANTICIPATING

an·ti·cler·i·cal \,an-ti-'kler-i-kəl, ,an-,tī-\ *adjective* (1845)
: opposed to clericalism or to the interference or influence of the clergy in secular affairs
— **anticlerical** *noun*
— **an·ti·cler·i·cal·ism** \-kə-,li-zəm\ *noun*

an·ti·cli·mac·tic \-klī-'mak-tik, -klə-\ *also*
an·ti·cli·mac·ti·cal \-ti-kəl\ *adjective* (1898)
: of, relating to, or marked by anticlimax
— **an·ti·cli·mac·ti·cal·ly** \-ti-k(ə-)lē\ *adverb*

an·ti·cli·max \-'klī-,maks\ *noun* (1710)
1 : the usually sudden transition in discourse from a significant idea to a trivial or ludicrous idea; *also* **:** an instance of this transition
2 : an event (as at the end of a series) that is strikingly less important than what has preceded it

an·ti·cli·nal \,an-ti-'klī-n°l\ *adjective* [*anti-* + Greek *klinein* to lean — more at LEAN] (1882)
: occurring at right angles to the surface or circumference of a plant organ ⟨an *anticlinal* pattern of cell walls⟩

an·ti·cline \'an-ti-,klīn\ *noun* (circa 1861)
: an arch of stratified rock in which the layers bend downward in opposite directions from the crest — compare SYNCLINE

cross section of strata showing anticline

an·ti·clock·wise \,an-ti-'kläk-,wīz, ,an-,tī-\ *adjective or adverb* (1898)
chiefly British **:** COUNTERCLOCKWISE

an·ti·co·ag·u·lant \-kō-'a-gyə-lənt\ *noun* (circa 1905)
: a substance that hinders the clotting of blood
— **anticoagulant** *adjective*

an·ti·co·don \-'kō-,dän\ *noun* (1965)
: a triplet of nucleotide bases in transfer RNA that identifies the amino acid carried and binds to a complementary codon in messenger RNA during protein synthesis at a ribosome

an·ti·com·pet·i·tive \-kəm-'pe-tə-tiv\ *adjective* (1952)
: tending to reduce or discourage competition

an·ti·con·vul·sant \-kən-'vəl-sənt\ *also* **an·ti·con·vul·sive** \-siv\ *adjective* (1734)
: used or tending to control or to prevent convulsions (as in epilepsy)
— **anticonvulsant** *also* **anticonvulsive** *noun*

an·ti·cy·clone \,an-ti-'sī-,klōn\ *noun* (1877)
1 : a system of winds that rotates about a center of high atmospheric pressure clockwise in the northern hemisphere and counterclockwise in the southern, that usually advances at 20 to 30 miles (about 30 to 50 kilometers) per hour, and that usually has a diameter of 1500 to 2500 miles (2400 to 4000 kilometers)
2 : HIGH 2
— **an·ti·cy·clon·ic** \-sī-'klä-nik\ *adjective*

an·ti·dem·o·crat·ic \,an-ti-,de-mə-'kra-tik, ,an-,tī-\ *adjective* (1837)
: opposed or hostile to the theories or policies of democracy

¹an·ti·de·pres·sant \-di-'pre-s°nt\ *adjective* (1961)

◇ WORD HISTORY

antic The fantastic mural paintings found in the ruins of ancient Roman buildings were, by reason of their age, *antichi*—"ancient things"—to the Italians of the Renaissance. In Renaissance England, on the other hand, any similarly fantastic painting—of whatever vintage—that showed strange combinations of human, animal, and floral forms came to be called *antike* or *anticke,* from the Italian word for "ancient," *antico.* And any odd gesture or strange behavior reminiscent of such artwork became an *antic.*

\ə\ abut \ᵊ\ kitten \ər\ further \a\ ash \ā\ ace
\ä\ mop, mar \au̇\ out \ch\ chin \e\ bet \ē\ easy
\g\ go \i\ hit \ī\ ice \j\ job \ŋ\ sing \ō\ go
\ȯ\ law \ȯi\ boy \th\ thin \t͟h\ the \ü\ loot \u̇\ foot
\y\ yet \zh\ vision *see also* Guide to Pronunciation

: used or tending to relieve or prevent psychic depression

²**antidepressant** *noun* (1962)
: an antidepressant drug — compare TRICYCLIC ANTIDEPRESSANT

an·ti·de·riv·a·tive \-di-'ri-və-tiv\ *noun* (circa 1942)
: INDEFINITE INTEGRAL

an·ti·di·uret·ic hormone \ˌan-ti-ˌdī-yủ-'re-tik-\ *noun* (1942)
: VASOPRESSIN

an·ti·dot·al \ˌan-ti-'dō-t°l\ *adjective* (1646)
: of, relating to, or acting as an antidote
— **an·ti·dot·al·ly** \-t°l-ē\ *adverb*

an·ti·dote \'an-ti-ˌdōt\ *noun* [Middle English antidot, from Latin antidotum, from Greek antidotos, from feminine of antidotos given as an antidote, from antididonai to give as an antidote, from anti- + didonai to give — more at DATE] (15th century)
1 : a remedy to counteract the effects of poison
2 : something that relieves, prevents, or counteracts ⟨an antidote to the mechanization of our society⟩
— **antidote** *transitive verb*

an·ti·drom·ic \ˌan-ti-'drä-mik\ *adjective* [anti- + Greek dromos racecourse, running — more at DROMEDARY] (circa 1927)
: proceeding or conducting in a direction opposite to the usual one — used especially of a nerve impulse or fiber
— **an·ti·drom·i·cal·ly** \-mi-k(ə-)lē\ *adverb*

an·ti·drug \'an-ˌtī-ˌdrəg, ˌan-tī-'-\ *adjective* (1970)
: acting against or opposing illicit drugs or their use ⟨antidrug activist⟩ ⟨antidrug program⟩

an·ti·dump·ing \ˌan-ti-'dəm-piŋ, ˌan-ˌtī-\ *adjective* (1915)
: designed to discourage the importation and sale of foreign goods at prices well below domestic prices ⟨antidumping tariffs⟩

an·ti·elec·tron \ˌan-tē-ə-'lek-ˌträn, ˌan-ˌtī-\ *noun* (1931)
: POSITRON

an·ti·fed·er·al·ist \ˌan-ti-'fe-d(ə-)rə-list, ˌan-ˌtī-\ *noun, often A&F capitalized* (1787)
: a member of the group that opposed the adoption of the U.S. Constitution

an·ti·fer·ro·mag·net·ic \-ˌfer-ō-mag-'ne-tik\ *adjective* (1936)
: FERRIMAGNETIC
— **an·ti·fer·ro·mag·net** \-'mag-nət\ *noun*
— **an·ti·fer·ro·mag·net·i·cal·ly** \-mag-'ne-ti-k(ə-)lē\ *adverb*
— **an·ti·fer·ro·mag·net·ism** \-'mag-nə-ˌti-zəm\ *noun*

an·ti·fer·til·i·ty \-fər-'ti-lə-tē\ *adjective* (1953)
: capable of or tending to reduce or destroy fertility : CONTRACEPTIVE ⟨antifertility agents⟩

an·ti·flu·o·ri·da·tion·ist \-ˌflủr-ə-'dā-sh(ə-)nist, -ˌflōr-, -ˌflȯr-\ *noun* (1961)
: a person opposed to the fluoridation of public water supplies

an·ti·foul·ing \-'faủ-liŋ\ *adjective* (1895)
: intended to prevent fouling of underwater structures (as the bottoms of ships) ⟨antifouling paint⟩

an·ti·freeze \'an-ti-ˌfrēz\ *noun* (1924)
: a substance added to a liquid (as the water in an automobile engine) to lower its freezing point

an·ti·fun·gal \ˌan-ti-'fəŋ-gəl, ˌan-ˌtī-\ *adjective* (1945)
: destroying fungi; *also* : inhibiting the growth of fungi
— **antifungal** *noun*

an·ti·gen \'an-ti-jən, -ˌjen\ *noun* [German, from French antigène, from anticorps antibody + -gène -gen] (1908)
: a usually protein or carbohydrate substance (as a toxin or enzyme) capable of stimulating an immune response
— **an·ti·gen·ic** \ˌan-ti-'je-nik\ *adjective*

— **an·ti·gen·i·cal·ly** \-ni-k(ə-)lē\ *adverb*
— **an·ti·ge·nic·i·ty** \-jə-'ni-sə-tē\ *noun*

antigenic determinant *noun* (1950)
: EPITOPE

an·ti·glob·u·lin \ˌan-ti-'glä-byə-lən, ˌan-ˌtī-\ *noun* (circa 1909)
: an antibody that combines with and precipitates globulin

Antig·o·ne \an-'ti-gə-(ˌ)nē\ *noun* [Greek Antigonē]
: a daughter of Oedipus and Jocasta who buries her brother Polynices' body against the order of her uncle Creon

¹**an·ti·grav·i·ty** \ˌan-ti-'gra-və-tē, ˌan-ˌtī-\ *adjective* (1944)
: reducing, canceling, or protecting against the effect of gravity

²**antigravity** *noun* (1949)
: a hypothetical effect resulting from cancellation or reduction of a gravitational field

an·ti·he·mo·phil·ic factor \-ˌhē-mə-'fi-lik-\ *noun* (1947)
: FACTOR VIII

an·ti·he·ro \'an-ti-ˌhē-(ˌ)rō, ˌan-ˌtī-, -ˌhir-(ˌ)ō\ *noun* (1714)
: a protagonist or notable figure who is conspicuously lacking in heroic qualities
— **an·ti·he·ro·ic** \ˌan-ti-hi-'rō-ik, ˌan-ˌtī-\ *adjective*

an·ti·her·o·ine \ˌan-ti-'her-ə-wən, ˌan-ˌtī-\ *noun* (1907)
: a female antihero

an·ti·his·ta·mine \-'his-tə-ˌmēn, -mən\ *noun* (1946)
: any of various compounds that counteract histamine in the body and that are used for treating allergic reactions (as hay fever) and cold symptoms
— **antihistamine** *adjective*
— **an·ti·his·ta·min·ic** \-ˌhis-tə-'mi-nik\ *adjective or noun*

an·ti·hu·man \-'hyü-mən, -'yü-\ *adjective* (1854)
1 : acting or being against humanity
2 : reacting strongly with human antigens

an·ti·hy·per·ten·sive \-ˌhī-pər-'ten(t)-siv\ *noun* (circa 1957)
: a substance that is effective against high blood pressure
— **antihypertensive** *adjective*

an·ti·id·io·type \ˌan-tē-'i-dē-ə-ˌtīp, ˌan-ti-\ *noun* (1975)
: an antibody that treats another antibody as an antigen and suppresses its immunoreactivity
— **an·ti·id·io·typ·ic** \-ˌi-dē-ə-'ti-pik\ *adjective*

an·ti·in·flam·ma·to·ry \-in-'fla-mə-ˌtōr-ē, -tȯr-\ *adjective* (circa 1957)
: counteracting inflammation
— **anti–inflammatory** *noun*

an·ti·in·tel·lec·tu·al \-ˌin-t°l-'ek-ch(ə-w)əl, -'ek-shwəl\ *adjective* (1936)
: opposing or hostile to intellectuals or to an intellectual view or approach
— **anti–intellectual** *noun*
— **an·ti·in·tel·lec·tu·al·ism** \-'ek-chə-(wə-)li-zəm, -'ek-shwə-\ *noun*

an·ti·leu·ke·mic \-lü-'kē-mik\ *adjective* (1951)
: counteracting the effects of leukemia

an·ti·life \-'līf\ *adjective* (1929)
: antagonistic or antithetical to life or to normal human values

an·ti·lock \'an-ˌtī-ˌläk, 'an-ti-\ *adjective* (1974)
: being a braking system for a motor vehicle designed to keep the wheels from locking by electronically controlled pulsed application of the brake for each wheel

an·ti·log \'an-ti-ˌlȯg, 'an-ˌtī-, -ˌläg\ *noun* (1910)
: ANTILOGARITHM

an·ti·log·a·rithm \ˌan-ti-'lȯ-gə-ˌri-thəm, ˌan-ˌtī-, -'lä-\ *noun* (1675)
: the number corresponding to a given logarithm

an·ti·ma·cas·sar \ˌan-ti-mə-'ka-sər\ *noun*

[anti- + Macassar (oil) (a hairdressing)] (1852)
: a cover to protect the back or arms of furniture

an·ti·mag·net·ic \ˌan-ti-mag-'ne-tik, ˌan-ˌtī-\ *adjective* (1946)
of a watch : having a balance unit composed of alloys that will not remain magnetized

an·ti·ma·lar·i·al \-mə-'ler-ē-əl\ *adjective* (circa 1893)
: serving to prevent, check, or cure malaria
— **antimalarial** *noun*

an·ti·mat·ter \'an-ti-ˌma-tər, 'an-ˌtī-\ *noun* (1950)
: matter composed of antiparticles

an·ti·me·tab·o·lite \ˌan-ti-mə-'ta-bə-ˌlīt, ˌan-ˌtī-\ *noun* (1945)
: a substance that replaces or inhibits an organism's utilization of a metabolite

an·ti·mi·cro·bi·al \ˌan-ti-mī-'krō-bē-əl\ *adjective* (circa 1910)
: destroying or inhibiting the growth of microorganisms
— **antimicrobial** *noun*

an·ti·mis·sile missile \ˌan-ti-'mi-səl-, ˌan-ˌtī-; *chiefly British* ˌan-ti-'mi-ˌsīl-\ *noun* (circa 1956)
: ANTIBALLISTIC MISSILE

an·ti·mi·tot·ic \ˌan-ti-mī-'tä-tik, ˌan-ˌtī-\ *adjective* (1970)
: inhibiting or disrupting mitosis ⟨antimitotic agents⟩ ⟨antimitotic activity⟩
— **antimitotic** *noun*

an·ti·mo·ni·al \ˌan-tə-'mō-nē-əl\ *adjective* (1605)
: of, relating to, or containing antimony
— **antimonial** *noun*

an·ti·mo·nide \'an-ti-mə-ˌnīd\ *noun* (1863)
: a binary compound of antimony with a more positive element

an·ti·mo·ny \'an-tə-ˌmō-nē\ *noun* [Middle English antimonie, from Medieval Latin antimonium] (15th century)
1 : STIBNITE
2 : a trivalent and pentavalent metalloid element that is commonly metallic silvery white, crystalline, and brittle and that is used especially as a constituent of alloys and semiconductors — see ELEMENT table

an·ti·my·cin A \ˌan-ti-'mī-s°n-'ä\ *noun* [anti- + -mycin] (1949)
: a crystalline antibiotic $C_{28}H_{40}N_2O_9$ used especially as a fungicide, insecticide, and miticide — called also *antimycin*

an·ti·neo·plas·tic \ˌan-ti-ˌnē-ə-'plas-tik, ˌan-ˌtī-\ *adjective* (1954)
: inhibiting or preventing the growth and spread of neoplasms or malignant cells

an·ti·neu·tri·no \-nü-'trē-(ˌ)nō, -nyü-\ *noun* (1934)
: the antiparticle of the neutrino

an·ti·neu·tron \-'nü-ˌträn, -'nyü-\ *noun* (1942)
: the antiparticle of the neutron

ant·ing \'an-tiŋ\ *noun* (1936)
: bird behavior in which ants are rubbed on the feathers to obtain chemicals (as formic acid) from the ants

an·ti·node \'an-ti-ˌnōd, 'an-ˌtī-\ *noun* [International Scientific Vocabulary] (1882)
: a region of maximum amplitude situated between adjacent nodes in a vibrating body
— **an·ti·nod·al** \ˌan-ti-'nō-d°l, ˌan-ˌtī-\ *adjective*

an·ti·no·mi·an \ˌan-ti-'nō-mē-ən\ *noun* [Medieval Latin antinomus, from Latin anti- + Greek nomos law] (1645)
1 : one who holds that under the gospel dispensation of grace the moral law is of no use or obligation because faith alone is necessary to salvation
2 : one who rejects a socially established morality
— **antinomian** *adjective*
— **an·ti·no·mi·an·ism** \-mē-ə-ˌni-zəm\ *noun*

an·tin·o·my \an-'ti-nə-mē\ *noun, plural* **-mies** [German *Antinomie*, from Latin *antinomia* conflict of laws, from Greek, from *anti-* + *nomos* law — more at NIMBLE] (1592)
1 : a contradiction between two apparently equally valid principles or between inferences correctly drawn from such principles
2 : a fundamental and apparently unresolvable conflict or contradiction ⟨*antinomies* of beauty and evil, freedom and slavery —Stephen Holden⟩
— **an·ti·nom·ic** \,an-ti-'nä-mik\ *adjective*

an·ti·nov·el \'an-ti-,nä-vəl, 'an-,tī-\ *noun* (1958)
: a work of fiction that lacks most or all of the traditional features of the novel
— **an·ti·nov·el·ist** \-,näv-list, -,nä-və-\ *noun*

an·ti·nu·cle·ar \,an-ti-'nü-klē-ər, ,an-,tī-, -'nyü-, ÷-kyə-lər\ *adjective* (1958)
1 : tending to react with cell nuclei or their components (as DNA) ⟨*antinuclear* antibodies⟩
2 : opposing the use or production of nuclear power plants

an·ti·nu·cle·on \-'n(y)ü-klē-,än\ *noun* (1946)
: the antiparticle of a nucleon

an·ti·nuke \-'nük, -'nyük\ *adjective* (1975)
: ANTINUCLEAR 2

an·ti·ox·i·dant \,an-tē-'äk-sə-dənt, ,an-,tī-\ *noun* (1926)
: a substance that inhibits oxidation or reactions promoted by oxygen or peroxides
— **antioxidant** *adjective*

an·ti·ozon·ant \-'ō-(,)zō-nənt\ *noun* (1954)
: a substance that opposes ozonization or protects against it

an·ti·par·al·lel \,an-ti-'par-ə-,lel, ,an-,tī-, -ləl\ *adjective* (circa 1660)
: parallel but oppositely directed or oriented ⟨*antiparallel* electron spins⟩ ⟨two *antiparallel* chains of nucleotides comprise DNA⟩

an·ti·par·a·sit·ic \,an-ti-,par-ə-'si-tik, ,an-,tī-\ *adjective* (circa 1860)
: acting against parasites

an·ti·par·ti·cle \'an-ti-,pär-ti-kəl, 'an-,tī-\ *noun* (1934)
: a subatomic particle identical to another subatomic particle in mass but opposite to it in electric and magnetic properties (as sign of charge) that when brought together with its counterpart produces mutual annihilation; *especially* : a subatomic particle not found in ordinary matter

an·ti·pas·to \,an-ti-'pas-(,)tō, ,än-ti-, -'päs-\ *noun, plural* **-ti** \-(,)tē\ [Italian, from *anti-* (from Latin *ante-*) + *pasto* food, from Latin *pastus*, from *pascere* to feed — more at FOOD] (1590)
: any of various typically Italian hors d'oeuvres; *also* : a plate of these served especially as the first course of a meal

an·ti·pa·thet·ic \,an-ti-pə-'the-tik, (,)an-,ti-pə-\ *adjective* (1640)
1 : having a natural aversion; *also* : not sympathetic : HOSTILE
2 : arousing antipathy ⟨mountains . . . are *antipathetic* to me —Havelock Ellis⟩
— **an·ti·pa·thet·i·cal·ly** \-ti-k(ə-)lē\ *adverb*

an·tip·a·thy \an-'ti-pə-thē\ *noun, plural* **-thies** [Latin *antipathia*, from Greek *antipatheia*, from *antipathēs* of opposite feeling, from *anti-* + *pathos* experience — more at PATHOS] (1601)
1 *obsolete* : opposition in feeling
2 : settled aversion or dislike : DISTASTE
3 : an object of aversion
synonym see ENMITY

an·ti·per·son·nel \,an-ti-,pər-s°n-'el, ,an-,tī-\ *adjective* (1939)
: designed for use against military personnel ⟨an *antipersonnel* mine⟩

an·ti·per·spi·rant \-'pər-sp(ə-)rənt\ *noun* (1943)
: a preparation used to check perspiration

an·ti·phlo·gis·tic \-flə-'jis-tik\ *adjective* (1769)
: ANTI-INFLAMMATORY

an·ti·phon \'an-tə-fən, -,fän\ *noun* [Middle English *antiphone*, from Middle French, from Late Latin *antiphona* — more at ANTHEM] (15th century)
1 : a psalm, anthem, or verse sung responsively
2 : a verse usually from Scripture said or sung before and after a canticle, psalm, or psalm verse as part of the liturgy

¹an·tiph·o·nal \an-'ti-fə-n°l\ *noun* (1537)
: ANTIPHONARY

²antiphonal *adjective* (1719)
: of, relating to, or suggesting an antiphon or antiphony
— **an·tiph·o·nal·ly** \-n°l-ē\ *adverb*

an·tiph·o·nary \an-'ti-fə-,ner-ē\ *noun, plural* **-nar·ies** (15th century)
1 : a book containing a collection of antiphons
2 : a book containing the choral parts of the Divine Office

an·tiph·o·ny \an-'ti-fə-nē\ *noun, plural* **-nies** (1592)
: responsive alternation between two groups especially of singers

an·tiph·ra·sis \an-'ti-frə-səs\ *noun, plural* **-ra·ses** \-,sēz\ [Late Latin, from Greek, from *anti-* + *phrasis* diction — more at PHRASE] (1533)
: the usually ironic or humorous use of words in senses opposite to the generally accepted meanings (as in "this giant of 3 feet 4 inches")

¹an·tip·o·dal \an-'ti-pə-d°l\ *adjective* (1646)
1 : of or relating to the antipodes; *specifically* : situated at the opposite side of the earth or moon ⟨an *antipodal* meridian⟩ ⟨an *antipodal* continent⟩
2 : diametrically opposite ⟨an *antipodal* point on a sphere⟩
3 : entirely opposed ⟨a system *antipodal* to democracy⟩

²antipodal *noun* (1919)
: any of three cells in the female gametophyte of most angiosperms that are grouped at the end of the embryo sac farthest from the micropyle — called also *antipodal cell*

an·ti·pode \'an-tə-,pōd\ *noun, plural* **an·tip·o·des** \an-'ti-pə-,dēz\ [Middle English *antipodes*, plural, persons dwelling at opposite points on the globe, from Latin, from Greek, from plural of *antipod-, antipous* with feet opposite, from *anti-* + *pod-, pous* foot — more at FOOT] (1549)
1 : the parts of the earth diametrically opposite — usually used in plural; often used of Australia and New Zealand
2 : the exact opposite or contrary
— **an·tip·o·de·an** \(,)an-,ti-pə-'dē-ən\ *adjective or noun*

an·ti·po·et·ic \,an-ti-pō-'e-tik, ,an-,tī-\ *adjective* (1847)
: of, relating to, or characterized by opposition to traditional poetic technique or style

an·ti·pol·lu·tion \-pə-'lü-shən\ *adjective* (1924)
: designed to prevent, reduce, or eliminate pollution ⟨*antipollution* laws⟩
— **antipollution** *noun*

an·ti·pope \'an-ti-,pōp\ *noun* [Middle English *antepope*, from Middle French *antipape*, from Medieval Latin *antipapa*, from *anti-* + *papa* pope] (15th century)
: one elected or claiming to be pope in opposition to the pope canonically chosen

an·ti·pro·ton \,an-ti-'prō-,tän, ,an-,tī-\ *noun* (1940)
: the antiparticle of the proton

an·ti·psy·chot·ic \,an-ti-sī-'kä-tik\ *noun* (1966)
: NEUROLEPTIC
— **antipsychotic** *adjective*

an·ti·py·ret·ic \-pī-'re-tik\ *noun* (circa 1681)
: an agent that reduces fever
— **antipyretic** *adjective*

an·ti·py·rine \-'pīr-,ēn\ *noun* [from *Antipyrine*, a trademark] (1884)
: an analgesic and antipyretic $C_{11}H_{12}N_2O$ formerly widely used but now largely replaced in oral use by less toxic substances (as aspirin)

¹an·ti·quar·i·an \,an-tə-'kwer-ē-ən\ *noun* (1610)
: one who collects or studies antiquities

²antiquarian *adjective* (1771)
1 : of or relating to antiquarians or antiquities
2 : dealing in old or rare books
— **an·ti·quar·i·an·ism** \-ē-ə-,ni-zəm\ *noun*

an·ti·quark \'an-ti-,kwärk, 'an-,tī-\ *noun* (1964)
: the antiparticle of the quark

an·ti·quary \'an-tə-,kwer-ē\ *noun, plural* **-quar·ies** (1586)
: ANTIQUARIAN

an·ti·quate \'an-tə-,kwāt\ *transitive verb* **-quat·ed; -quat·ing** [Late Latin *antiquatus*, past participle of *antiquare*, from Latin *antiquus*] (1596)
: to make old or obsolete
— **an·ti·qua·tion** \,an-tə-'kwā-shən\ *noun*

an·ti·quat·ed *adjective* (1623)
1 : OBSOLETE ⟨an *antiquated* calendar⟩
2 : outmoded or discredited by reason of age : being out of style or fashion ⟨*antiquated* methods of farming⟩
3 : advanced in age
synonym see OLD

¹an·tique \(,)an-'tēk\ *noun* (1530)
1 : a relic or object of ancient times
2 a : a work of art, piece of furniture, or decorative object made at an earlier period and according to various customs laws at least 100 years ago **b** : a manufactured product (as an automobile) from an earlier period

²an·tique \(,)an-'tēk, *in verse often* 'an-tik\ *adjective* [Middle French, from Latin *antiquus*, from *ante* before — more at ANTE-] (1534)
1 : existing since or belonging to earlier times : ANCIENT ⟨*antique* trade routes to the Orient⟩
2 a : being in the style or fashion of former times ⟨*antique* manners and graces⟩ **b** : made in or representative of the work of an earlier period ⟨*antique* mirrors⟩; *also* : being an antique
3 : selling or exhibiting antiques ⟨an *antique* show⟩
synonym see OLD

³an·tique \(,)an-'tēk\ *verb* **-tiqued; -tiqu·ing** (1923)
transitive verb
: to finish or refinish in antique style : give an appearance of age to
intransitive verb
: to shop around for antiques
— **an·tiqu·er** \an-'tē-kər\ *noun*

an·tiq·ui·ty \an-'ti-kwə-tē\ *noun, plural* **-ties** (13th century)
1 : ancient times; *especially* : those before the Middle Ages
2 : the quality of being ancient
3 *plural* **a** : relics or monuments (as coins, statues, or buildings) of ancient times **b** : matters relating to the life or culture of ancient times
4 : the people of ancient times

an·ti·ra·chit·ic \,an-ti-rə-'ki-tik, ,an-,tī-\ *adjective* (circa 1860)
: used or tending to prevent the development of rickets ⟨an *antirachitic* vitamin⟩

an·ti·re·jec·tion \,an-ti-ri-'jek-shən, ,an-,tī-\ *adjective* (1968)
: used or tending to prevent organ transplant rejection ⟨*antirejection* drugs⟩ ⟨*antirejection* treatment⟩

an·ti·rheu·mat·ic \-rú-'ma-tik\ *adjective* (1817)

\ə\ abut \°\ kitten \ər\ further \a\ ash \ā\ ace
\ä\ mop, mar \aú\ out \ch\ chin \e\ bet \ē\ easy
\g\ go \i\ hit \ī\ ice \j\ job \ŋ\ sing \ō\ go
\o\ law \oí\ boy \th\ thin \th\ the \ü\ loot \ú\ foot
\y\ yet \zh\ vision *see also* Guide to Pronunciation

: alleviating or preventing rheumatism ⟨*antirheumatic* therapy⟩ ⟨*antirheumatic* drugs⟩
— **antirheumatic** *noun*

an·ti–roll bar \'an-ˌtī-ˌrōl-\ *noun* (1951)
: SWAY BAR

an·tir·rhi·num \ˌan-tə-'rī-nəm\ *noun* [New Latin, genus name, from Latin, snapdragon, from Greek *antirrhinon,* from *anti-* like (from *anti* against, equivalent to) + *rhin-, rhis* nose — more at ANTI-] (1548)
: SNAPDRAGON

antis *plural of* ANTI

an·ti·scor·bu·tic \ˌan-ti-skȯr-'byü-tik, ˌan-ˌtī-\ *adjective* (1725)
: counteracting scurvy ⟨the *antiscorbutic* vitamin is vitamin C⟩
— **antiscorbutic** *noun*

an·ti–Sem·i·tism \ˌan-ti-'se-mə-ˌti-zəm, ˌan-ˌtī-\ *noun* (1882)
: hostility toward or discrimination against Jews as a religious, ethnic, or racial group
— **an·ti–Se·mit·ic** \-sə-'mi-tik\ *adjective*
— **an·ti–Sem·ite** \-'se-ˌmīt\ *noun*

an·ti·sense \'an-ˌtī-ˌsen(t)s, 'an-ti-\ *adjective* [*anti-* + non*sense*] (1984)
: having a complementary sequence to a segment of genetic material (as mRNA) and serving to inhibit gene function ⟨*antisense* nucleotides⟩ ⟨*antisense* RNA⟩ — compare MISSENSE, NONSENSE

an·ti·sep·sis \ˌan-tə-'sep-səs\ *noun* (1875)
: the inhibiting of the growth and multiplication of microorganisms by antiseptic means

¹an·ti·sep·tic \ˌan-tə-'sep-tik\ *adjective* [*anti-* + Greek *sēptikos* putrefying, septic] (1751)
1 a : opposing sepsis, putrefaction, or decay; *especially* : preventing or arresting the growth of microorganisms (as on living tissue) **b** : acting or protecting like an antiseptic
2 : relating to or characterized by the use of antiseptics
3 a : scrupulously clean : ASEPTIC **b** : extremely neat or orderly; *especially* : neat to the point of being bare or uninteresting **c** : free from what is held to be contaminating
4 : coldly impersonal ⟨an *antiseptic* greeting⟩
— **an·ti·sep·ti·cal·ly** \-ti-k(ə-)lē\ *adverb*

²antiseptic *noun* (1751)
: a substance that checks the growth or action of microorganisms especially in or on living tissue; *also* : GERMICIDE

an·ti·se·rum \'an-ti-ˌsir-əm, 'an-ˌtī-, -ˌser-\ *noun* [International Scientific Vocabulary] (1901)
: a serum containing antibodies

an·ti·so·cial \ˌan-ti-'sō-shəl, ˌan-ˌtī-\ *adjective* (1797)
1 : averse to the society of others : UNSOCIABLE
2 : hostile or harmful to organized society; *especially* : being or marked by behavior deviating sharply from the social norm
— **an·ti·so·cial·ly** \-shə-lē\ *adverb*

an·ti·so·lar \-'sō-lər\ *noun* (circa 1890)
: being or having a direction away from the sun ⟨the *antisolar* point⟩

an·ti·spas·mod·ic \-spaz-'mä-dik\ *adjective* (1763)
: capable of preventing or relieving spasms or convulsions
— **antispasmodic** *noun*

an·ti·stat \-'stat\ *or* **an·ti·stat·ic** \-'sta-tik\ *adjective* (1952)
: reducing, removing, or preventing the buildup of static electricity

an·tis·tro·phe \an-'tis-trə-(ˌ)fē\ *noun* [Late Latin, from Greek *antistrophē,* from *anti-* + *strophē* strophe] (circa 1550)
1 a : the repetition of words in reversed order **b** : the repetition of a word or phrase at the end of successive clauses
2 a : a returning movement in Greek choral dance exactly answering to a previous strophe **b** : the part of a choral song delivered during the antistrophe
— **an·ti·stroph·ic** \ˌan-tə-'strä-fik\ *adjective*

— an·ti·stroph·i·cal·ly \-fi-k(ə-)lē\ *adverb*

an·ti·sym·met·ric \-sə-'me-trik\ *adjective* (1923)
: relating to or being a relation (as "is a subset of") that implies equality of any two quantities for which it holds in both directions ⟨the relation *R* is *antisymmetric* if *aRb* and *bRa* implies $a = b$⟩

an·tith·e·sis \an-'ti-thə-səs\ *noun, plural* **-e·ses** \-ˌsēz\ [Late Latin, from Greek, literally, opposition, from *antitithenai* to oppose, from *anti-* + *tithenai* to set — more at DO] (1529)
1 a (1) : the rhetorical contrast of ideas by means of parallel arrangements of words, clauses, or sentences (as in "action, not words" or "they promised freedom and provided slavery") (2) : OPPOSITION, CONTRAST ⟨the *antithesis* of prose and verse⟩ **b** (1) : the second of two opposing constituents of an antithesis (2) : the direct opposite
2 : the second stage of a dialectic process

an·ti·thet·i·cal \ˌan-tə-'the-ti-kəl\ *also* **an·ti·thet·ic** \-'the-tik\ *adjective* (1583)
1 : constituting or marked by antithesis
2 : being in direct and unequivocal opposition
synonym see OPPOSITE
— an·ti·thet·i·cal·ly \-ti-k(ə-)lē\ *adverb*

an·ti·throm·bin \ˌan-ti-'thräm-bən, ˌan-ˌtī-\ *noun* (circa 1911)
: any of a group of substances that inhibit blood clotting by inactivating thrombin

an·ti·thy·roid \ˌan-ti-'thī-ˌrȯid\ *adjective* (1908)
: able to counteract excessive thyroid activity ⟨*antithyroid* drugs⟩

an·ti·tox·ic \-'täk-sik\ *adjective* (circa 1890)
1 : counteracting toxins
2 : being or containing antitoxins ⟨*antitoxic* serum⟩

an·ti·tox·in \ˌan-ti-'täk-sən\ *noun* [International Scientific Vocabulary] (circa 1890)
: an antibody that is capable of neutralizing the specific toxin (as a specific causative agent of disease) that stimulated its production in the body and is produced in animals for medical purposes by injection of a toxin or toxoid with the resulting serum being used to counteract the toxin in other individuals; *also* : an antiserum containing antitoxins

an·ti·trades \'an-ti-ˌtrādz, 'an-ˌtī-\ *noun plural* (1875)
: the westerly winds above the trade winds

an·ti·trust \ˌan-ti-'trəst, ˌan-ˌtī-\ *adjective* (1890)
: of, relating to, or being legislation against or opposition to trusts or combinations; *specifically* : consisting of laws to protect trade and commerce from unlawful restraints and monopolies or unfair business practices

an·ti·trust·er \-'trəs-tər\ *noun* (1947)
: one who advocates or enforces antitrust provisions of the law

an·ti·tus·sive \-'tə-siv\ *noun* (circa 1909)
: a cough suppressant
— antitussive *adjective*

an·ti–uto·pia \ˌan-ti-yü-'tō-pē-ə, ˌan-ˌtī-\ *noun* (1966)
1 : DYSTOPIA 1
2 : a work describing an anti-utopia
— an·ti–uto·pi·an \-pē-ən\ *adjective or noun*

an·ti·ven·in \ˌan-ti-'ve-nən, ˌan-ˌtī-\ *noun* [International Scientific Vocabulary] (1895)
: an antitoxin to a venom; *also* : an antiserum containing such antitoxin

an·ti·vi·ta·min \'an-ti-ˌvī-tə-mən, *British usually* -ˌvi-\ *noun* (1927)
: a substance that makes a vitamin metabolically ineffective

an·ti·white \ˌan-ti-'hwīt, ˌan-ˌtī-, -'wīt\ *adjective* (1906)
: opposed or hostile to people belonging to a light-skinned race

ant·ler \'ant-lər\ *noun* [Middle English *auntteler,* from Middle French *antoillier,* from (as-

sumed) Vulgar Latin *anteoculare,* from neuter of *anteocularis,* from Latin *ante-* + *oculus* eye — more at EYE] (14th century)
: one of the paired deciduous solid bone processes that arise from the frontal bone on the head of an animal of the deer family; *also* : a branch of an antler
— ant·lered \-lərd\ *adjective*

ant lion *noun* (1815)
: any of various neuropterous insects (as of the genus *Myrmeleon*) having a long-jawed larva that digs a conical pit in which it lies in wait to catch insects (as ants) on which it feeds

ant lion: *1* larva, *2* adult

An·to·ni·an \an-'tō-nē-ən\ *noun* [Latin *Antonius* Anthony] (circa 1907)
: a member of one of several monastic communities (as the Armenian Antonians) that follow a rule devised by Saint Anthony

an·to·no·ma·sia \ˌan-tə-nō-'mā-zh(ē-)ə, (ˌ)an-ˌtä-nə-\ *noun* [Latin, use of an epithet for a proper name, from Greek, from *antonomazein* to call by a new name, from *anti-* + *onomazein* to name, from *onoma* name — more at NAME] (circa 1550)
: the use of a proper name to designate a member of a class (as a *Solomon* for a *wise ruler*); *also* : the use of an epithet or title in place of a proper name (as *the Bard* for *Shakespeare*)

an·to·nym \'an-tə-ˌnim\ *noun* (1870)
: a word of opposite meaning ⟨the usual *antonym* of *good* is *bad*⟩
— an·to·nym·ic \ˌan-tə-'ni-mik\ *adjective*
— an·ton·y·mous \an-'tä-nə-məs\ *adjective*
— an·ton·y·my \-mē\ *noun*

an·tre \'an-tər\ *noun* [French, from Latin *antrum*] (1604)
: CAVE 1

an·trum \'an-trəm\ *noun, plural* **an·tra** \-trə\ [Late Latin, from Latin, cave, from Greek *antron;* akin to Armenian *ayr* cave] (circa 1751)
: the cavity of a hollow organ or a sinus
— an·tral \-trəl\ *adjective*

ant·sy \'ant-sē\ *adjective* (1838)
1 : impatient of restraint; *especially* : FIDGETY
2 : NERVOUS, APPREHENSIVE

Anu·bis \ə-'nü-bəs, -'nyü-\ *noun* [Latin, from Greek *Anoubis,* from Egyptian *inpw*]
: a jackal-headed god in Egyptian mythology who leads the dead to judgment

an·uran \ə-'nyür-ən, a-, -'nùr-\ *adjective or noun* [ultimately from Greek *a-* + *oura* tail — more at ASS] (1900)
: any of an order (Anura) of amphibians comprising the frogs, toads, and tree toads all of which lack a tail in the adult stage and have long strong hind limbs suited to leaping and swimming
— anuran *adjective*

an·uria \ə-'nyür-ē-ə, a-, -'nùr-\ *noun* [New Latin] (1838)
: absence or defective excretion of urine
— an·uric \-'nyür-ik, -'nùr-\ *adjective*

anus \'ā-nəs\ *noun* [Latin, ring, anus; perhaps akin to Old Irish *ánne* ring] (15th century)
: the posterior opening of the alimentary canal

an·vil \'an-vəl\ *noun* [Middle English *anfilt,* from Old English; akin to Old High German *anafalz* anvil; akin to Latin *pellere* to beat — more at FELT] (before 12th century)
1 : a heavy usually steel-faced iron block on which metal is shaped (as by hand hammering)
2 : INCUS

anx·i·ety \aŋ-'zī-ə-tē\ *noun, plural* **-eties** [Latin *anxietas,* from *anxius*] (circa 1525)

1 a : painful or apprehensive uneasiness of mind usually over an impending or anticipated ill **b :** fearful concern or interest **c :** a cause of anxiety
2 : an abnormal and overwhelming sense of apprehension and fear often marked by physiological signs (as sweating, tension, and increased pulse), by doubt concerning the reality and nature of the threat, and by self-doubt about one's capacity to cope with it
synonym see CARE

an·xi·o·lyt·ic \ˌaŋ-zē-ō-'li-tik, ˌaŋ(k)-sē-\ *noun* [anxiety + -o- + -lytic] (1965)
: a drug that relieves anxiety
— anxiolytic *adjective*

anx·ious \'aŋ(k)-shəs\ *adjective* [Latin *anxius*; akin to Latin *angere* to strangle, distress — more at ANGER] (circa 1616)
1 : characterized by extreme uneasiness of mind or brooding fear about some contingency **:** WORRIED
2 : characterized by, resulting from, or causing anxiety **:** WORRYING
3 : ardently or earnestly wishing □
synonym see EAGER
— anx·ious·ly *adverb*
— anx·ious·ness *noun*

¹any \'e-nē\ *adjective* [Middle English, from Old English *ǣnig*; akin to Old High German *einag* any, Old English *ān* one — more at ONE] (before 12th century)
1 : one or some indiscriminately of whatever kind: **a :** one or another taken at random ⟨ask *any* man you meet⟩ **b :** EVERY — used to indicate one selected without restriction ⟨*any* child would know that⟩
2 : one, some, or all indiscriminately of whatever quantity: **a :** one or more — used to indicate an undetermined number or amount ⟨have you *any* money⟩ **b :** ALL — used to indicate a maximum or whole ⟨needs *any* help he can get⟩ **c :** a or some without reference to quantity or extent ⟨grateful for *any* favor at all⟩
3 a : unmeasured or unlimited in amount, number, or extent ⟨*any* quantity you desire⟩ **b :** appreciably large or extended ⟨could not endure it *any* length of time⟩

²any *pronoun, singular or plural in construction* (before 12th century)
1 : any person or persons **:** ANYONE
2 a : any thing or things **b :** any part, quantity, or number

³any *adverb* (14th century)
: to any extent or degree **:** AT ALL ⟨was never *any* good⟩

any·body \-ˌbä-dē, -bə-\ *pronoun* (14th century)
: any person **:** ANYONE □

any·how \-ˌhau̇\ *adverb* (1690)
1 a : in any manner whatever **b :** in a haphazard manner
2 a : at any rate **b :** in any event

any·more \ˌe-nē-'mȯr, -'mȯr\ *adverb* (14th century)
1 : any longer ⟨I was not moving *anymore* with my feet —Anaïs Nin⟩
2 : at the present time **:** NOW ⟨hardly a day passes without rain *anymore*⟩ □

any·one \'e-nē-(ˌ)wən\ *pronoun* (1536)
: any person at all
usage see ANYBODY

any·place \-ˌplās\ *adverb* (1916)
: in any place **:** ANYWHERE

¹any·thing \-ˌthiŋ\ *pronoun* (before 12th century)
: any thing whatever **:** any such thing

²anything *adverb* (before 12th century)
: AT ALL

any·time \'e-nē-ˌtīm\ *adverb* (1926)
: at any time whatever

any·way \-ˌwā\ *adverb* (13th century)
1 : ANYWISE
2 : in any case **:** ANYHOW

any·ways \-ˌwāz\ *adverb* (13th century)

1 a *archaic* **:** ANYWISE **b** *dialect* **:** to any degree at all
2 *chiefly dialect* **:** ANYHOW, ANYWAY

¹any·where \-ˌ(h)wer, -ˌ(h)war, -ˌ(h)wər\ *adverb* (14th century)
1 : at, in, or to any place or point
2 : to any extent **:** AT ALL
3 — used as a function word to indicate limits of variation ⟨*anywhere* from 40 to 60 students⟩

²anywhere *noun* (1924)
: any place

any·wheres \-ˌ(h)werz, -ˌ(h)warz, -ˌ(h)wərz\ *adverb* (1775)
chiefly dialect **:** ANYWHERE

any·wise \'e-nē-ˌwīz\ *adverb* (13th century)
: in any way whatever **:** AT ALL

An·zac \'an-ˌzak\ *noun* [Australian and New Zealand Army Corps] (1915)
: a soldier from Australia or New Zealand

A–OK \ˌā-(ˌ)ō-'kā\ *adverb or adjective* (1959)
: very definitely OK

A1 \'ā-'wən\ *adjective* (1837)
1 : having the highest possible classification — used of a ship
2 : of the finest quality **:** FIRST-RATE

ao·rist \'ā-ə-rəst, 'e-ə-\ *noun* [Late Latin & Greek; Late Latin *aoristos*, from Greek, from *aoristos* undefined, from *a* + *horistos* definable, from *horizein* to define — more at HORIZON] (1581)
: an inflectional form of a verb typically denoting simple occurrence of an action without reference to its completeness, duration, or repetition
— aorist *or* **ao·ris·tic** \ˌā-ə-'ris-tik, ˌe-ə-\ *adjective*
— ao·ris·ti·cal·ly \-ti-k(ə-)lē\ *adverb*

aor·ta \ā-'ȯr-tə\ *noun, plural* **-tas** *or* **-tae** \-tē\ [New Latin, from Greek *aortē*, from *aeirein* to lift] (1543)
: the great arterial trunk that carries blood from the heart to be distributed by branch arteries through the body — see HEART illustration
— aor·tic \-'ȯr-tik\ *adjective*

aortic arch *noun* (1903)
: one of the arterial branches in vertebrate embryos that exist in a series of pairs with one on each side of the embryo, connect the ventral arterial system lying anterior to the heart to the dorsal arterial system above the alimentary tract, and persist in adult fishes but are reduced or much modified in the adult of higher forms

aor·tog·ra·phy \ˌā-ȯr-'tä-grə-fē\ *noun* (circa 1935)
: arteriography of the aorta
— aor·to·graph·ic \(ˌ)ā-ˌȯr-tə-'gra-fik\ *adjective*

aou·dad \'au̇-ˌdad, 'ä- u̇-\ *noun* [French, from Berber *audad*] (1861)
: a wild bovine (*Ammotragus lervia*) of North Africa that is closely related to goats and sheep and has been introduced into the southwestern U.S.

à ou·trance \ˌä-ü-'trä^ns\ *adverb* [French] (1883)
: to the limit **:** UNSPARINGLY

¹ap- — see AD-

²ap- — see APO-

apace \ə-'pās\ *adverb* [Middle English, probably from Middle French *à pas* on step] (14th century)
1 : at a quick pace **:** SWIFTLY
2 : ABREAST — used with *of* or *with*

Apache \ə-'pa-chē, *in sense 3* ə-'pash\ *noun, plural* **Apache** *or* **Apach·es** \-'pa-chēz; -'pash, -'pa-shəz\ [American Spanish, perhaps from Zuni *ʔaˑpacu* Navajo, Apachean] (1745)
1 : a member of a group of American Indian peoples of the southwestern U.S.
2 : any of the Athabascan languages of the Apache people
3 *not capitalized* [French, from *Apache*

Apache Indian] **a :** a member of a gang of criminals especially in Paris **b :** RUFFIAN
— Apach·e·an \ə-'pa-chē-ən\ *adjective or noun*

ap·a·nage *variant of* APPANAGE

ap·a·re·jo \ˌa-pə-'rā-(ˌ)(h)ō\ *noun, plural* **-jos** [American Spanish] (1844)
: a packsaddle of stuffed leather or canvas

¹apart \ə-'pärt\ *adverb* [Middle English, from Middle French *a part*, literally, to the side] (14th century)
1 a : at a little distance ⟨tried to keep *apart*

anxious The opinion that *anxious* must not be used to mean "eager" was formed in the U.S. at the beginning of the 20th century. British commentators have largely ignored the problem—after all, sense 3 of *anxious* had been established in British English for 160 years before American commentators decided it must be wrong ⟨his manner was perhaps the more seductive, because he ne'er seem'd *anxious* to seduce —Lord Byron (1824)⟩. Of course, it was just as firmly established in American English too ⟨at any hour of the day or night, I have been *anxious* to improve the nick of time —Henry David Thoreau (1854)⟩. But the topic is still dear to the hearts of American commentators, few of whom notice that the use is standard.

anybody The indefinite pronouns *anybody* and *anyone* share with other indefinite pronouns the characteristic of taking a singular verb and, more often than not, a plural pronoun in reference. The use of the plural pronoun—*they, their, them*—has traditionally been disapproved by those who insist that agreement in number is more important than avoidance of gender-specific third-person singular pronouns. But use of the plural pronouns has long been established ⟨as *anybody* in their senses would have done —Jane Austen (1814)⟩ ⟨if *anybody* thinks that kings, nobles, or priests are good conservators of the public happiness send them here —Thomas Jefferson (letter from Paris, 1786)⟩ and increasing resistance to generic *he* seems to be easing their acceptance. Usage is still mixed ⟨I had never examined all the papers left by *anybody* after his death —Donald Winch⟩ ⟨isn't interested in serving lunch or having *anyone* get their own —Andy Rooney⟩.

anymore Although both *anymore* and *any more* are found in written use, in the 20th century *anymore* is the more common styling. *Anymore* is regularly used in negative ⟨no one can be natural *anymore* —May Sarton⟩, interrogative ⟨do you read much *anymore*?⟩, and conditional ⟨if you do that *anymore*, I'll leave⟩ contexts and in certain positive constructions ⟨the Washingtonian is too sophisticated to believe *anymore* in solutions —Russell Baker⟩. In many regions of the U.S. the use of *anymore* in sense 2 is quite common in positive constructions, especially in speech ⟨everybody's cool *anymore* —Bill White⟩ ⟨every time we leave the house *anymore*, I play a game called "Stump the Housebreaker" —Erma Bombeck⟩. The positive use appears to have been of Midland origin, but it is now reported to be widespread in all speech areas of the U.S. except New England.

from the family squabbles〉 **b :** away from one another in space or time 〈towns 20 miles *apart*〉
2 a : as a separate unit **:** INDEPENDENTLY 〈viewed *apart*, his arguments were unsound〉 **b :** so as to separate one from another 〈found it hard to tell the twins *apart*〉
3 : excluded from consideration **:** ASIDE 〈a few blemishes *apart*, the novel is excellent〉
4 : in or into two or more parts **:** to pieces 〈coming *apart* at the seams〉
²apart *adjective* (1786)
1 : SEPARATE, ISOLATED
2 : holding different opinions **:** DIVIDED
— **apart·ness** *noun*
apart from *preposition* (1833)
: other than **:** BESIDES
apart·heid \ə-'pär-ˌtāt, -ˌtīt\ *noun* [Afrikaans, from Dutch, from *apart* apart + *-heid* -hood] (1947)
1 : racial segregation; *specifically* **:** a policy of segregation and political and economic discrimination against non-European groups in the Republic of South Africa
2 : SEPARATION, SEGREGATION 〈I favor *apartheid* of smokers —L. E. Bellin〉 〈sexual *apartheid*〉
apart·ment \ə-'pärt-mənt\ *noun* [French *appartement*, from Italian *appartamento*] (1641)
1 : a room or set of rooms fitted especially with housekeeping facilities and usually leased as a dwelling
2 : a building containing several individual apartments
— **apart·men·tal** \ə-ˌpärt-'men-t°l\ *adjective*
apartment hotel *noun* (1909)
: a hotel containing apartments as well as accommodations for transients
apartment house *noun* (1874)
: a building containing separate residential apartments — called also *apartment building*
ap·a·thet·ic \ˌa-pə-'the-tik\ *adjective* (1744)
1 : having or showing little or no feeling or emotion **:** SPIRITLESS
2 : having little or no interest or concern **:** INDIFFERENT
synonym see IMPASSIVE
— **ap·a·thet·i·cal·ly** \-ti-k(ə-)lē\ *adverb*
ap·a·thy \'a-pə-thē\ *noun* [Greek *apatheia*, from *apathēs* without feeling, from *a-* + *pathos* emotion — more at PATHOS] (1603)
1 : lack of feeling or emotion **:** IMPASSIVENESS
2 : lack of interest or concern **:** INDIFFERENCE
ap·a·tite \'a-pə-ˌtīt\ *noun* [German *Apatit*, from Greek *apatē* deceit] (1803)
: any of a group of calcium phosphate minerals occurring variously as hexagonal crystals, as granular masses, or in fine-grained masses as the chief constituent of phosphate rock and of bones and teeth; *especially* **:** calcium phosphate fluoride
apato·sau·rus \ə-ˌpa-tə-'sȯr-əs\ *noun* [New Latin, from Greek *apatē* + *sauros* lizard] (circa 1899)
: BRONTOSAURUS
¹ape \'āp\ *noun* [Middle English, from Old English *apa;* akin to Old High German *affo* ape] (before 12th century)
1 a : MONKEY; *especially* **:** one of the larger tailless or short-tailed Old World forms **b :** any of two families (Pongidae and Hylobatidae) of large tailless semierect primates (as the chimpanzee, gorilla, orangutan, or gibbon) — called also *anthropoid, anthropoid ape*
2 a : MIMIC **b :** a large uncouth person
— **ape·like** \'āp-ˌlīk\ *adjective*
²ape *transitive verb* **aped; ap·ing** (1632)
: to copy closely but often clumsily and ineptly
synonym see COPY
— **ap·er** *noun*
³ape *adjective* (circa 1955)
: being beyond restraint **:** CRAZY, WILD — usually used in the phrase *go ape*

apeak \ə-'pēk\ *adjective or adverb* [alteration of earlier *apike*, probably from French *à pic* vertically] (1596)
: being in a vertical position 〈with oars *apeak*〉
ape–man \'āp-ˌman, -'man\ *noun* (1879)
: a primate (as an australopithecine) intermediate in character between Homo sapiens and the higher apes
aper·çu \ˌa-per-sǖ, ˌa-pər-'sü\ *noun, plural* **aper·çus** \-sǖ(z), -'süz\ [French, from *aperçu*, past participle of *apercevoir* to perceive, from Old French *aperceivre*, from *a-* (from Latin *ad-*) + *perceivre* to perceive — more at PERCEIVE] (1828)
1 : a brief survey or sketch **:** OUTLINE
2 : an immediate impression; *especially* **:** INSIGHT 2
ape·ri·ent \ə-'pir-ē-ənt\ *adjective* [Latin *aperient-, aperiens,* present participle of *aperire*] (1626)
: gently moving the bowels **:** LAXATIVE
— **aperient** *noun*
ape·ri·od·ic \ˌā-ˌpir-ē-'ä-dik\ *adjective* (1879)
1 : of irregular occurrence 〈*aperiodic* floods〉
2 : not having periodic vibrations **:** not oscillatory
— **ape·ri·od·i·cal·ly** \-di-k(ə-)lē\ *adverb*
— **ape·ri·o·dic·i·ty** \-ē-ə-'di-sə-tē\ *noun*
aper·i·tif \ə-ˌper-ə-'tēf, ä-; ä-ˌpər-(ə-)'tēf\ *noun* [French *apéritif* aperient, aperitif, from Middle French *apéritif,* adjective, aperient, from Medieval Latin *aperitivus,* irregular from Latin *aperire*] (1894)
: an alcoholic drink taken before a meal as an appetizer
ap·er·ture \'ap-ə(r)-ˌchu̇r, -chər, -ˌtyu̇r, -ˌtu̇r\ *noun* [Middle English, from Latin *apertura,* from *apertus,* past participle of *aperire* to open] (15th century)
1 : an opening or open space **:** HOLE
2 a : the opening in a photographic lens that admits the light **b :** the diameter of the stop in an optical system that determines the diameter of the bundle of rays traversing the instrument **c :** the diameter of the objective lens or mirror of a telescope
apet·al·ous \(ˌ)ā-'pe-t°l-əs\ *adjective* (circa 1706)
: having no petals
apex \'ā-ˌpeks\ *noun, plural* **apex·es** *or* **api·ces** \'ā-pə-ˌsēz, 'a-\ [Latin] (1601)
1 a : the uppermost point **:** VERTEX 〈the *apex* of a mountain〉 **b :** the narrowed or pointed end **:** TIP 〈the *apex* of the tongue〉
2 : the highest or culminating point 〈the *apex* of his career〉
synonym see SUMMIT
Ap·gar score \'ap-ˌgär-\ *noun* [Virginia *Apgar* (died 1974) American anesthesiologist] (1962)
: an index used to evaluate the condition of a newborn infant based on a rating of 0, 1, or 2 for each of the five characteristics of color, heart rate, response to stimulation of the sole of the foot, muscle tone, and respiration with 10 being a perfect score
aphaer·e·sis \ə-'fer-ə-səs\ *noun, plural* **-e·ses** \-ˌsēz\ [Late Latin, from Greek *aphairesis,* literally, taking off, from *aphairein* to take away, from *apo-* + *hairein* to take] (circa 1550)
: the loss of one or more sounds or letters at the beginning of a word (as in *round* for *around* and *coon* for *raccoon*)
— **aph·ae·ret·ic** \ˌa-fə-'re-tik\ *adjective*
aph·a·nite \'a-fə-ˌnīt\ *noun* [French, from Greek *aphanēs* invisible, from *a-* + *phainesthai* to appear — more at PHENOMENON] (circa 1828)
: a dark rock of such close texture that its separate grains are invisible to the naked eye
— **aph·a·nit·ic** \ˌa-fə-'ni-tik\ *adjective*
apha·sia \ə-'fā-zh(ē-)ə\ *noun* [New Latin, from Greek, from *a-* + *-phasia*] (1867)

: loss or impairment of the power to use or comprehend words usually resulting from brain damage
— **apha·sic** \-zik\ *noun or adjective*
aph·e·lion \a-'fēl-yən\ *noun, plural* **-elia** \-yə\ [New Latin, from *apo-* + Greek *hēlios* sun — more at SOLAR] (1656)
: the point in the path of a celestial body (as a planet) that is farthest from the sun — compare PERIHELION
aph·e·sis \'a-fə-səs\ *noun, plural* **-e·ses** \-ˌsēz\ [New Latin, from Greek, release, from *aphienai* to let go, from *apo-* + *hienai* to send — more at JET] (1880)
: aphaeresis consisting of the loss of a short unaccented vowel (as in *lone* for *alone*)
— **aphet·ic** \ə-'fe-tik\ *adjective*
— **aphet·i·cal·ly** \-ti-k(ə-)lē\ *adverb*
aphid \'ā-fəd *also* 'a-fəd\ *noun* (1884)
: any of numerous very small sluggish homopterous insects (superfamily Aphidoidea) that suck the juices of plants
aphid lion *noun* (1949)
: any of several insect larvae (as a lacewing or ladybug larva) that feed on aphids — called also *aphis lion*
aphis \'ā-fəs *also* 'a-fəs\ *noun, plural* **aphi·des** \'ā-fə-ˌdēz, 'a-fə-\ [New Latin *Aphid-, Aphis,* genus name] (1771)
: any of a genus (*Aphis*) of aphids; *broadly* **:** APHID
apho·nia \(ˌ)ā-'fō-nē-ə\ *noun* [New Latin, from Greek *aphōnia,* from *aphōnos* voiceless, from *a-* + *phōnē* sound — more at BAN] (1778)
: loss of voice and of all but whispered speech
— **apho·nic** \-'fä-nik, -'fō-\ *adjective*
aph·o·rism \'a-fə-ˌri-zəm\ *noun* [Middle French *aphorisme,* from Late Latin *aphorismus,* from Greek *aphorismos* definition, from *aphorizein* to define, from *apo-* + *horizein* to bound — more at HORIZON] (1528)
1 : a concise statement of a principle
2 : a terse formulation of a truth or sentiment **:** ADAGE
— **aph·o·rist** \-rist\ *noun*
— **aph·o·ris·tic** \ˌa-fə-'ris-tik\ *adjective*
— **aph·o·ris·ti·cal·ly** \-ti-k(ə-)lē\ *adverb*
aph·o·rize \'a-fə-ˌrīz\ *intransitive verb* **-rized; -riz·ing** (1669)
: to write or speak in or as if in aphorisms
apho·tic \(ˌ)ā-'fō-tik\ *adjective* (circa 1900)
: being the deep zone of an ocean or lake receiving too little light to permit photosynthesis
aph·ro·di·si·ac \ˌa-frə-'dē-zē-ˌak, -'di-zē-\ *noun* [Greek *aphrodisiakos* sexual, gem with aphrodisiac properties, from *aphrodisia* heterosexual pleasures, from neuter plural of *aphrodisios* of Aphrodite, from *Aphroditē*] (1719)
1 : an agent (as a food or drug) that arouses or is held to arouse sexual desire
2 : something that excites
— **aphrodisiac** *also* **aph·ro·di·si·a·cal** \ˌa-frə-di-'sī-ə-kəl, -'zī-\ *adjective*
Aph·ro·di·te \ˌa-frə-'dī-tē\ *noun* [Greek *Aphroditē*]
: the Greek goddess of love and beauty — compare VENUS
api·ar·i·an \ˌā-pē-'er-ē-ən\ *adjective* (1801)
: of or relating to beekeeping or bees
api·a·rist \'ā-pē-ə-rist, -pē-ˌer-ist\ *noun* (1816)
: BEEKEEPER
api·ary \'ā-pē-ˌer-ē\ *noun, plural* **-ar·ies** [Latin *apiarium,* from *apis* bee] (1654)
: a place where bees are kept; *especially* **:** a collection of hives or colonies of bees kept for their honey
api·cal \'ā-pi-kəl *also* 'a-pi-\ *adjective* [probably from New Latin *apicalis,* from Latin *apic-, apex*] (1828)
1 : of, relating to, or situated at an apex
2 : of, relating to, or formed with the tip of the tongue 〈*n, l,* and *r* are *apical* consonants〉
— **api·cal·ly** \-k(ə-)lē\ *adverb*
apical dominance *noun* (1947)

: inhibition of the growth of lateral buds by the terminal bud of a shoot

apical meristem *noun* (circa 1934)
: a meristem at the apex of a root or shoot that is responsible for increase in length

apic·u·late \ə-'pi-kyə-lət, ā-\ *adjective* [New Latin *apiculus,* diminutive of Latin *apic-, apex*] (1830)
: ending abruptly in a small distinct point ⟨an *apiculate* leaf⟩

api·cul·ture \'ā-pə-ˌkəl-chər\ *noun* [probably from French, from Latin *apis* bee + French *culture*] (1864)
: the keeping of bees especially on a large scale
— **api·cul·tur·al** \ˌā-pə-'kəl-ch(ə-)rəl\ *adjective*
— **api·cul·tur·ist** \-ch(ə-)rist\ *noun*

apiece \ə-'pēs\ *adverb* (15th century)
: for each one **:** INDIVIDUALLY

Apis \'ā-pəs\ *noun* [Latin, from Greek, from Egyptian *ḥp*]
: a sacred bull worshiped by the ancient Egyptians

ap·ish \'ā-pish\ *adjective* (1532)
: resembling an ape: as **a :** extremely silly or affected **b :** given to slavish imitation
— **ap·ish·ly** *adverb*
— **ap·ish·ness** *noun*

APL \ˌā-(ˌ)pē-'el\ *noun* [*a* programming language] (1966)
: a computer programming language designed especially for the concise representation of algorithms

ap·la·nat·ic \ˌa-plə-'na-tik\ *adjective* [*a-* + Greek *planasthai* to wander — more at PLANET] (1794)
: free from or corrected for spherical aberration ⟨an *aplanatic* lens⟩

aplas·tic anemia \(ˌ)ā-'plas-tik-\ *noun* (1928)
: anemia that is characterized by defective function of the blood-forming organs (as the bone marrow) and is caused by toxic agents (as chemicals or X rays) or is idiopathic in origin

¹aplen·ty \ə-'plen-tē\ *adjective* (1830)
: being in plenty or abundance — used postpositively ⟨money *aplenty* for all his needs⟩

²aplenty *adverb* (1846)
1 : in abundance **:** PLENTIFULLY
2 : very much **:** EXTREMELY ⟨scared *aplenty*⟩

ap·lite \'a-ˌplīt\ *noun* [probably from German *Aplit,* from Greek *haploos* simple — more at HAPL-] (1879)
: a fine-grained light-colored granite consisting almost entirely of quartz and feldspar
— **ap·lit·ic** \a-'pli-tik\ *adjective*

aplomb \ə-'pläm, -'pləm\ *noun* [French, literally, perpendicularity, from Middle French, from *a plomb,* literally, according to the plummet] (1828)
: complete and confident composure or self-assurance **:** POISE
synonym see CONFIDENCE

ap·nea \'ap-nē-ə\ *noun* [New Latin, from *a-* + *-pnea*] (circa 1719)
1 : transient cessation of respiration
2 : ASPHYXIA
— **ap·ne·ic** \-nē-ik\ *adjective*

ap·noea *chiefly British variant of* APNEA

apo- *or* **ap-** *prefix* [Middle English, from Middle French & Latin; Middle French, from Latin, from Greek, from *apo* — more at OF]
1 : away from **:** off ⟨*aphelion*⟩
2 : detached **:** separate ⟨*apogamy*⟩
3 : formed from **:** related to ⟨*apomorphine*⟩

apoc·a·lypse \ə-'pä-kə-ˌlips\ *noun* [Middle English, revelation, Revelation, from Late Latin *apocalypsis,* from Greek *apokalypsis,* from *apokalyptein* to uncover, from *apo-* + *kalyptein* to cover — more at HELL] (13th century)
1 a : one of the Jewish and Christian writings of 200 B.C. to A.D. 150 marked by pseudonymity, symbolic imagery, and the expectation of

an imminent cosmic cataclysm in which God destroys the ruling powers of evil and raises the righteous to life in a messianic kingdom **b** capitalized **:** REVELATION 3
2 a : something viewed as a prophetic revelation **b :** ARMAGEDDON

apoc·a·lyp·tic \ə-ˌpä-kə-'lip-tik\ *also* **apoc·a·lyp·ti·cal** \-ti-kəl\ *adjective* (1663)
1 : of, relating to, or resembling an apocalypse
2 : forecasting the ultimate destiny of the world **:** PROPHETIC
3 : foreboding imminent disaster or final doom **:** TERRIBLE
4 : wildly unrestrained **:** GRANDIOSE
5 : ultimately decisive **:** CLIMACTIC
— **apoc·a·lyp·ti·cal·ly** \-ti-k(ə-)lē\ *adverb*

apoc·a·lyp·ti·cism \-tə-ˌsi-zəm\ *or* **apoc·a·lyp·tism** \ə-'pä-kə-ˌlip-ˌti-zəm\ *noun* (1884)
: apocalyptic expectation; *especially* **:** a doctrine concerning an imminent end of the world and an ensuing general resurrection and final judgment

apoc·a·lyp·tist \ə-'pä-kə-ˌlip-tist\ *noun* (1835)
: the writer of an apocalypse

apo·chro·mat·ic \ˌa-pə-krō-'ma-tik\ *adjective* [International Scientific Vocabulary] (1887)
: free from chromatic and spherical aberration ⟨an *apochromatic* lens⟩

apoc·o·pe \ə-'pä-kə-(ˌ)pē\ *noun* [Late Latin, from Greek *apokopē,* literally, cutting off, from *apokoptein* to cut off, from *apo-* + *koptein* to cut — more at CAPON] (circa 1550)
: the loss of one or more sounds or letters at the end of a word (as in *sing* from Old English *singan*)

apo·crine \'a-pə-krən, -ˌkrīn, -ˌkrēn\ *adjective* [International Scientific Vocabulary *apo-* + Greek *krinein* to separate — more at CERTAIN] (1926)
: producing a fluid secretion by pinching off one end of the secretory cell while leaving the rest intact ⟨an *apocrine* gland⟩; *also* **:** produced by an apocrine gland

apoc·ry·pha \ə-'pä-krə-fə\ *noun plural but singular or plural in construction* [Medieval Latin, from Late Latin, neuter plural of *apocryphus* secret, not canonical, from Greek *apokryphos* obscure, from *apokryptein* to hide away, from *apo-* + *kryptein* to hide — more at CRYPT] (14th century)
1 : writings or statements of dubious authenticity
2 capitalized **a :** books included in the Septuagint and Vulgate but excluded from the Jewish and Protestant canons of the Old Testament — see BIBLE table **b :** early Christian writings not included in the New Testament ◇

apoc·ry·phal \-fəl\ *adjective* (1590)
1 : of doubtful authenticity **:** SPURIOUS
2 *often* capitalized **:** of or resembling the Apocrypha
synonym see FICTITIOUS
— **apoc·ry·phal·ly** \-fə-lē\ *adverb*
— **apoc·ry·phal·ness** *noun*

apo·dic·tic \ˌa-pə-'dik-tik\ *also* **apo·deic·tic** \-'dīk-tik\ *adjective* [Latin *apodicticus,* from Greek *apodeiktikos,* from *apodeiknynai* to demonstrate, from *apo-* + *deiknynai* to show — more at DICTION] (circa 1645)
: expressing or of the nature of necessary truth or absolute certainty
— **apo·dic·ti·cal·ly** \-ti-k(ə-)lē\ *adverb*

apod·o·sis \ə-'pä-də-səs\ *noun,* plural **-o·ses** \-ˌsēz\ [New Latin, from Greek, from *apodidonai* to give back, deliver, from *apo-* + *didonai* to give — more at DATE] (circa 1638)
: the main clause of a conditional sentence — compare PROTASIS

apo·en·zyme \ˌa-pō-'en-ˌzīm\ *noun* [International Scientific Vocabulary] (1936)
: a protein that forms an active enzyme system

by combination with a coenzyme and determines the specificity of this system for a substrate

apog·a·my \ə-'pä-gə-mē\ *noun* [International Scientific Vocabulary] (circa 1878)
: development of a sporophyte from a gametophyte without fertilization
— **apog·a·mous** \ə-'pä-gə-məs\ *adjective*

apo·gee \'a-pə-(ˌ)jē\ *noun* [French *apogée,* from New Latin *apogaeum,* from Greek *apogaion,* from neuter of *apogeios, apogaios* far from the earth, from *apo-* + *gē, gaia* earth] (1594)

apogee 1

1 : the point in the orbit of an object (as a satellite) orbiting the earth that is at the greatest distance from the center of the earth; *also* **:** the point farthest from a planet or a satellite (as the moon) reached by an object orbiting it — compare PERIGEE
2 : the farthest or highest point **:** CULMINATION ⟨Aegean civilization reached its *apogee* in Crete⟩
— **apo·ge·an** \ˌa-pə-'jē-ən\ *adjective*

apo·li·po·pro·tein \ˌa-pō-ˌlī-pō-'prō-ˌtēn, -ˌli-, -ˌtē-ən\ *noun* (1970)
: a protein that combines with a lipid to form a lipoprotein

apo·lit·i·cal \ˌā-pə-'li-ti-kəl\ *adjective* (1935)
1 : having no interest or involvement in political affairs; *also* **:** having an aversion to politics or political affairs
2 : having no political significance
— **apo·lit·i·cal·ly** \-k(ə-)lē\ *adverb*

Ap·ol·lin·i·an \ˌa-pə-'li-nē-ən\ *adjective* (1924)
: APOLLONIAN

Apol·lo \ə-'pä-(ˌ)lō\ *noun* [Latin *Apollin-, Apollo,* from Greek *Apollōn*]
: the Greek and Roman god of sunlight, prophecy, music, and poetry

Ap·ol·lo·ni·an \ˌa-pə-'lō-nē-ən\ *adjective* (1663)
1 : of, relating to, or resembling the god Apollo

\ə\ abut \ᵊ\ kitten \ər\ further \a\ ash \ā\ ace \ä\ mop, mar \aů\ out \ch\ chin \e\ bet \ē\ easy \g\ go \i\ hit \ī\ ice \j\ job \ŋ\ sing \ō\ go \ó\ law \ói\ boy \th\ thin \th\ the \ü\ loot \ů\ foot \y\ yet \zh\ vision *see also* Guide to Pronunciation

2 : harmonious, measured, ordered, or balanced in character — compare DIONYSIAN

Apol·lyon \ə-ˈpäl-yən, -ˈpä-lē-ən\ noun [Greek Apollyōn] : the angel of the bottomless pit in the Book of Revelation

¹apol·o·get·ic \ə-ˌpä-lə-ˈje-tik\ noun (15th century) : APOLOGETICS 1

²apologetic adjective [Greek apologētikos, from apologeisthai to defend, from apo- + logos speech] (1649)
1 a : offered in defense or vindication ⟨the apologetic writings of the early Christians⟩ **b** : offered by way of excuse or apology ⟨an apologetic smile⟩
2 : regretfully acknowledging fault or failure : CONTRITE ⟨was apologetic about his mistake⟩
— **apol·o·get·i·cal·ly** \-ti-k(ə-)lē\ adverb

apol·o·get·ics \-tiks\ noun plural but singular or plural in construction (circa 1733)
1 : systematic argumentative discourse in defense (as of a doctrine)
2 : a branch of theology devoted to the defense of the divine origin and authority of Christianity

apo·lo·gia \ˌa-pə-ˈlō-j(ē-)ə\ noun [Late Latin] (1784) : a defense especially of one's opinions, position, or actions ⟨the finest apologia or explanation of what drives a man to devote his life to pure mathematics —British Book News⟩
synonym see APOLOGY

apol·o·gise British variant of APOLOGIZE

apol·o·gist \ə-ˈpä-lə-jist\ noun (1640) : one who speaks or writes in defense of someone or something

apol·o·gize \-ˌjīz\ intransitive verb **-gized; -giz·ing** (1597) : to make an apology
— **apol·o·giz·er** noun

ap·o·logue \ˈa-pə-ˌlóg, -ˌläg\ noun [French, from Latin apologus, from Greek apologos, from apo- + logos speech, narrative] (circa 1555) : an allegorical narrative usually intended to convey a moral

apol·o·gy \ə-ˈpä-lə-jē\ noun, plural **-gies** [Middle French or Late Latin; Middle French apologie, from Late Latin apologia, from Greek, from apo- + logos speech — more at LEGEND] (1533)
1 a : a formal justification : DEFENSE **b** : EXCUSE 2a
2 : an admission of error or discourtesy accompanied by an expression of regret
3 : a poor substitute : MAKESHIFT ☆

apo·lune \ˈa-pə-ˌlün\ noun [apo- + Latin luna moon — more at LUNAR] (circa 1968) : the point in the path of a body orbiting the moon that is farthest from the center of the moon — compare PERILUNE

apo·mict \ˈa-pə-ˌmikt\ noun [probably back-formation from International Scientific Vocabulary apomictic, from apo- + Greek mignynai to mix — more at MIX] (circa 1938) : one produced or reproducing by apomixis
— **apo·mic·tic** \ˌa-pə-ˈmik-tik\ adjective
— **apo·mic·ti·cal·ly** \-ti-k(ə-)lē\ adverb

apo·mix·is \ˌa-pə-ˈmik-səs\ noun, plural **-mix·es** \-ˌsēz\ [New Latin, from apo- + Greek mixis act of mixing, from mignynai] (1913) : reproduction (as apogamy or parthenogenesis) involving specialized generative tissues but not dependent on fertilization

apo·mor·phine \ˌa-pə-ˈmór-ˌfēn\ noun [International Scientific Vocabulary] (1888) : a crystalline morphine derivative $C_{17}H_{17}NO_2$ that is a dopamine agonist and is administered as the hydrochloride for its powerful emetic action

apo·neu·ro·sis \ˌa-pə-nù-ˈrō-səs, -nyù-\ noun [New Latin, from Greek aponeurōsis, from

aponeurousthai to pass into a tendon, from apo- + neuron sinew — more at NERVE] (1676) : a broad flat sheet of dense fibrous collagenous connective tissue that covers, invests, and forms the terminations and attachments of various muscles
— **apo·neu·rot·ic** \-ˈrä-tik\ adjective

ap·o·phthegm \ˈa-pə-ˌthem\ variant of APOTHEGM

apo·phyl·lite \ˌa-pə-ˈfi-ˌlīt, ə-ˈpä-fə-ˌlīt\ noun [French, from apo- + Greek phyllon leaf — more at BLADE] (1810) : a mineral composed of a hydrous potassium calcium silicate that is related to the zeolites and is usually found in transparent square prisms or white or grayish masses

apoph·y·sis \ə-ˈpä-fə-səs\ noun, plural **-y·ses** \-ˌsēz\ [New Latin, from Greek, from apo- + phyein to bring forth — more at BE] (1646) : an expanded or projecting part especially of an organism
— **apoph·y·se·al** \-ˌpä-fə-ˈsē-əl\ adjective

ap·o·plec·tic \ˌa-pə-ˈplek-tik\ adjective [French or Late Latin; French apoplectique, from Late Latin apoplecticus, from Greek apoplēktikos, from apoplēssein] (1611)
1 : of, relating to, or causing stroke
2 : affected with, inclined to, or showing symptoms of stroke
3 : of a kind to cause or apparently cause stroke ⟨an apoplectic rage⟩; also : greatly excited or angered
— **ap·o·plec·ti·cal·ly** \-ti-k(ə-)lē\ adverb

ap·o·plexy \ˈa-pə-ˌplek-sē\ noun [Middle English apoplexie, from Middle French & Late Latin; Middle French, from Late Latin apoplexia, from Greek apoplēxia, from apoplēssein to cripple by a stroke, from apo- + plēssein to strike — more at PLAINT] (15th century) : STROKE 5

aport \ə-ˈpórt, -ˈpòrt\ adverb (1627) : on or toward the left side of a ship ⟨put the helm hard aport⟩

apo·se·mat·ic \ˌa-pə-si-ˈma-tik\ adjective (1890) : being conspicuous and serving to warn ⟨aposematic coloration⟩
— **apo·se·mat·i·cal·ly** \-ti-k(ə-)lē\ adverb

ap·o·si·o·pe·sis \ˌa-pə-ˌsī-ə-ˈpē-səs\ noun, plural **-pe·ses** \-ˌsēz\ [Late Latin, from Greek aposiōpēsis, from aposiōpan to be fully silent, from apo- + siōpan to be silent, from siōpē silence] (1578) : the leaving of a thought incomplete usually by a sudden breaking off (as in "his behavior was—but I blush to mention that")
— **ap·o·si·o·pet·ic** \-ˈpe-tik\ adjective

apos·po·ry \ˈa-pə-ˌspór-ē, -ˌspòr-; ə-ˈpäs-pə-rē\ noun (1884) : production of gametophytes directly from diploid cells of the sporophytes without spore formation (as in certain ferns and mosses)
— **apos·po·rous** \ˈa-pə-ˌspór-əs, -ˌspòr-; ə-ˈpäs-pə-rəs\ adjective

apos·ta·sy \ə-ˈpäs-tə-sē\ noun, plural **-sies** [Middle English apostasie, from Late Latin apostasia, from Greek, literally, revolt, from aphistasthai to revolt, from apo- + histasthai to stand — more at STAND] (14th century)
1 : renunciation of a religious faith
2 : abandonment of a previous loyalty : DEFECTION

apos·tate \ə-ˈpäs-ˌtāt, -tət\ noun (14th century) : one who commits apostasy
— **apostate** adjective

apos·ta·tise British variant of APOSTATIZE

apos·ta·tize \ə-ˈpäs-tə-ˌtīz\ intransitive verb **-tized; -tiz·ing** (1611) : to commit apostasy

a pos·te·ri·o·ri \ˌä-pō-ˌstir-ē-ˈór-ē, -ˌster-; ˌä-(ˌ)pä-ˌstir-ē-ˈór-ˌī, -(ˌ)pō-, -ˈor-ē; -ˈór-\ adjective [Latin, literally, from the latter] (1588)

1 : INDUCTIVE
2 : relating to or derived by reasoning from observed facts — compare A PRIORI
— **a posteriori** adverb

apos·tle \ə-ˈpä-səl\ noun [Middle English, from Old French & Old English; Old French apostle & Old English apostol, both from Late Latin apostolus, from Greek apostolos, from apostellein to send away, from apo- + stellein to send] (before 12th century)
1 : one sent on a mission: as **a** : one of an authoritative New Testament group sent out to preach the gospel and made up especially of Christ's 12 original disciples and Paul **b** : the first prominent Christian missionary to a region or group
2 a : a person who initiates a great moral reform or who first advocates an important belief or system **b** : an ardent supporter : ADHERENT ⟨an apostle of liberty⟩
3 : the highest ecclesiastical official in some church organizations
4 : one of a Mormon administrative council of 12 men
— **apos·tle·ship** \-ˌship\ noun

Apostles' Creed noun (circa 1658) : a Christian statement of belief ascribed to the Twelve Apostles and used especially in public worship

apos·to·late \ə-ˈpäs-tə-ˌlāt, -lət\ noun [Late Latin apostolatus, from apostolus] (14th century)
1 : the office or mission of an apostle
2 : an association of persons dedicated to the propagation of a religion or a doctrine

ap·os·tol·ic \ˌa-pə-ˈstä-lik\ adjective (13th century)
1 a : of or relating to an apostle **b** : of, relating to, or conforming to the teachings of the New Testament apostles
2 a : of or relating to a succession of spiritual authority from the apostles held (as by Roman Catholics, Anglicans, and Eastern Orthodox) to be perpetuated by successive ordinations of bishops and to be necessary for valid sacraments and orders **b** : PAPAL
— **apos·to·lic·i·ty** \ə-ˌpäs-tə-ˈli-sə-tē\ noun

apostolic delegate noun (circa 1907) : an ecclesiastical representative of the Holy See to the Catholic hierarchy of another country

Apostolic Father noun (1828) : a church father of the first or second century A.D.

¹apos·tro·phe \ə-ˈpäs-trə-(ˌ)fē\ noun [Latin, from Greek apostrophē, literally, active of turning away, from apostrephein to turn away, from apo- + strephein to turn] (1533)

: the addressing of a usually absent person or a usually personified thing rhetorically ⟨Carlyle's "O Liberty, what things are done in thy name!" is an example of *apostrophe*⟩
— **ap·os·troph·ic** \ˌa-pə-'strä-fik\ *adjective*
²**apostrophe** *noun* [Middle French & Late Latin; Middle French, from Late Latin *apostrophus*, from Greek *apostrophos*, from *apostrophos* turned away, from *apostrephein*] (1727)
: a mark ' used to indicate the omission of letters or figures, the possessive case, or the plural of letters or figures
— **apostrophic** *adjective*
apos·tro·phise *British variant of* APOSTROPHIZE
apos·tro·phize \ə-'päs-trə-ˌfīz\ *verb* **-phized; -phiz·ing** (1718)
transitive verb
: to address by or in apostrophe
intransitive verb
: to make use of apostrophe
apothecaries' measure *noun* (circa 1900)
: a system of liquid units of measure used chiefly by pharmacists
apothecaries' weight *noun* (1765)
: a system of weights used chiefly by pharmacists — see WEIGHT table
apoth·e·cary \ə-'pä-thə-ˌker-ē\ *noun, plural* **-car·ies** [Middle English *apothecarie*, from Medieval Latin *apothecarius*, from Late Latin, shopkeeper, from Latin *apotheca* storehouse, from Greek *apothēkē*, from *apotithenai* to put away, from *apo- + tithenai* to put — more at DO] (14th century)
1 : one who prepares and sells drugs or compounds for medicinal purposes
2 : PHARMACY
apo·the·ci·um \ˌa-pə-'thē-shē-əm, -sē-\ *noun, plural* **-cia** \-shē-ə, -sē-\ [New Latin, from Latin *apotheca*] (1830)
: a spore-bearing structure in many lichens and fungi consisting of a discoid or cupped body bearing asci on the exposed flat or concave surface
— **apo·the·cial** \-sh(ē-)əl, -sē-əl\ *adjective*
ap·o·thegm \'a-pə-ˌthem\ *noun* [Greek *apophthegmat-, apophthegma*, from *apophthengesthai* to speak out, from *apo- + phthengesthai* to utter] (circa 1587)
: a short, pithy, and instructive saying or formulation : APHORISM
— **ap·o·theg·mat·ic** \ˌa-pə-theg-'ma-tik\ *adjective*
ap·o·them \'a-pə-ˌthem\ *noun* [International Scientific Vocabulary *apo- + -them* (from Greek *thema* something laid down, theme)] (circa 1856)
: the perpendicular from the center of a regular polygon to one of the sides
apo·the·o·sis \ə-ˌpä-thē-'ō-səs, ˌa-pə-'thē-ə-səs\ *noun, plural* **-o·ses** \-ˌsēz\ [Late Latin, from Greek *apotheōsis*, from *apotheoun* to deify, from *apo- + theos* god] (circa 1580)
1 : elevation to divine status : DEIFICATION
2 : the perfect example : QUINTESSENCE ⟨this is the literary *apotheosis* of the shaggy dog story —Thomas Sutcliffe⟩
— **apo·the·o·size** \ə-'pä-thē-ə-ˌsīz, ə-ˌpä-thē-ə-\ *transitive verb*
apo·tro·pa·ic \ˌa-pə-trō-'pā-ik\ *adjective* [Greek *apotropaios*, from *apotrepein* to avert, from *apo- + trepein* to turn] (1883)
: designed to avert evil ⟨an *apotropaic* ritual⟩
— **apo·tro·pa·i·cal·ly** \-'pā-ə-k(ə-)lē\ *adverb*
Ap·pa·la·chian \ˌa-pə-'lā-ch(ē-)ən, -'la-, -sh(ē-)ən\ *noun* (1888)
: a white native or resident of the Appalachian mountain area
Appalachian dulcimer *noun* (1962)
: DULCIMER 2
ap·pall *also* **ap·pal** \ə-'pol\ *verb* **ap·palled; ap·pall·ing** [Middle English, from Middle French *apalir*, from Old French, from *a-* (from Latin *ad-*) *+ palir* to grow pale, from Latin

pallescere, inchoative of *pallēre* to be pale — more at FALLOW] (14th century)
intransitive verb
obsolete : WEAKEN, FAIL
transitive verb
: to overcome with consternation, shock, or dismay
synonym see DISMAY
ap·pall·ing *adjective* (1817)
: inspiring horror, dismay, or disgust ⟨living under *appalling* conditions⟩
— **ap·pall·ing·ly** *adverb*
Ap·pa·loo·sa \ˌa-pə-'lü-sə\ *noun* [origin unknown] (1947)
: any of a breed of rugged saddle horses developed in western North America and usually having a white or solid-colored coat with small spots

Appaloosa

ap·pa·nage \'a-pə-nij\ *noun*
[French *apanage,* from Old French, from *apaner* to provide for a younger offspring, from Medieval Latin *appanare,* from Latin *ad- + panis* bread — more at FOOD] (1602)
1 a : a grant (as of land or revenue) made by a sovereign or a legislative body to a dependent member of the royal family or a principal vassal **b** : a property or privilege appropriated to or by a person as something due
2 : a rightful endowment or adjunct
ap·pa·rat \'a-pə-ˌrat, ˌä-pə-'rät\ *noun* [Russian] (1941)
: APPARATUS 2
ap·pa·rat·chik \ˌä-pə-'rä(t)-chik\ *noun, plural* **-chiks** *also* **-chi·ki** \-chi-kē\ [Russian, from *apparat*] (1941)
1 : a member of a Communist apparat
2 : an official blindly devoted to superiors or to the organization
ap·pa·ra·tus \ˌa-pə-'ra-təs, -'rā-\ *noun, plural* **-tus·es** *or* **-tus** [Latin, from *apparare* to prepare, from *ad- + parare* to prepare — more at PARE] (circa 1628)
1 a : a set of materials or equipment designed for a particular use **b** : a group of anatomical or cytological parts functioning together ⟨mitotic *apparatus*⟩ **c** : an instrument or appliance designed for a specific operation
2 : the functional processes by means of which a systematized activity is carried out: as **a** : the machinery of government **b** : the organization of a political party or an underground movement
¹**ap·par·el** \ə-'par-əl\ *transitive verb* **-eled** *or* **-elled; -el·ing** *or* **-el·ling** [Middle English *appareillen,* from Middle French *apareillier* to prepare, from (assumed) Vulgar Latin *appariculare,* from Latin *apparare*] (14th century)
1 : to put clothes on : DRESS
2 : ADORN, EMBELLISH
²**apparel** *noun* (14th century)
1 : the equipment (as sails and rigging) of a ship
2 : personal attire : CLOTHING
3 : something that clothes or adorns ⟨the bright *apparel* of spring⟩
ap·par·ent \ə-'par-ənt, -'per-\ *adjective* [Middle English, from Middle French *aparent,* from Latin *apparent-, apparens,* present participle of *apparēre* to appear] (14th century)
1 : open to view : VISIBLE
2 : clear or manifest to the understanding
3 : appearing as actual to the eye or mind
4 : having an indefeasible right to succeed to a title or estate
5 : manifest to the senses or mind as real or true on the basis of evidence that may or may not be factually valid ⟨the air of spontaneity is perhaps more *apparent* than real —J. R. Sutherland⟩ ☆

— **ap·par·ent·ness** \-'par-ənt-nəs, -'per-\ *noun*
ap·par·ent·ly \-lē\ *adverb* (1566)
: it seems apparent ⟨the window had *apparently* been forced open⟩ ⟨*apparently,* we're supposed to wait here⟩
apparent magnitude *noun* (1875)
: the luminosity of a celestial body (as a star) as observed from the earth — compare ABSOLUTE MAGNITUDE
apparent time *noun* (1694)
: the time of day indicated by the hour angle of the sun or by a sundial
ap·pa·ri·tion \ˌa-pə-'ri-shən\ *noun* [Middle English *apparicioun,* from Late Latin *apparition-, apparitio* appearance, from Latin *apparēre*] (15th century)
1 a : an unusual or unexpected sight : PHENOMENON **b** : a ghostly figure
2 : the act of becoming visible : APPEARANCE
— **ap·pa·ri·tion·al** \-'rish-nəl, -'ri-shə-nᵊl\ *adjective*
ap·pa·ri·tor \ə-'par-ə-tər\ *noun* [Latin, from *apparēre*] (15th century)
: an official formerly sent to carry out the orders of a magistrate, judge, or court
¹**ap·peal** \ə-'pē(ə)l\ *noun* (13th century)
1 : a legal proceeding by which a case is brought before a higher court for review of the decision of a lower court
2 : a criminal accusation
3 a : an application (as to a recognized authority) for corroboration, vindication, or decision **b** : an earnest plea : ENTREATY
4 : the power of arousing a sympathetic response : ATTRACTION ⟨movies had a great *appeal* for him⟩
²**appeal** *verb* [Middle English *appelen* to accuse, appeal, from Middle French *apeler,* from Latin *appellare,* from *appellere* to drive to, from *ad- + pellere* to drive — more at FELT] (14th century)
transitive verb
1 : to charge with a crime : ACCUSE
2 : to take proceedings to have (a lower court's decision) reviewed in a higher court
intransitive verb
1 : to take a lower court's decision to a higher court for review
2 : to call upon another for corroboration, vindication, or decision
3 : to make an earnest request
4 : to arouse a sympathetic response
— **ap·peal·abil·i·ty** \-ˌpē-lə-'bi-lə-tē\ *noun*
— **ap·peal·able** \-'pē-lə-bəl\ *adjective*
— **ap·peal·er** *noun*

\ə\ abut \ᵊ\ kitten \ər\ further \a\ ash \ā\ ace
\ä\ mop, mar \au̇\ out \ch\ chin \e\ bet \ē\ easy
\g\ go \i\ hit \ī\ ice \j\ job \ŋ\ sing \ō\ go
\ȯ\ law \ȯi\ boy \th\ thin \t̲h̲\ the \ü\ loot \u̇\ foot
\y\ yet \zh\ vision *see also* Guide to Pronunciation

ap·peal·ing \ə-'pē-liŋ\ *adjective* (1813)
1 : marked by earnest entreaty **:** IMPLORING
2 : having appeal **:** PLEASING
— **ap·peal·ing·ly** \-liŋ-lē\ *adverb*

ap·pear \ə-'pir\ *intransitive verb* [Middle English *apperen*, from Old French *aparoir*, from Latin *apparēre*, from *ad-* + *parēre* to show oneself] (13th century)
1 a : to be or come in sight ⟨the sun *appears* on the horizon⟩ **b :** to show up ⟨*appears* promptly at eight each day⟩
2 : to come formally before an authoritative body ⟨must *appear* in court today⟩
3 : to have an outward aspect **:** SEEM ⟨*appears* happy enough⟩
4 : to become evident or manifest ⟨there *appears* to be evidence to the contrary⟩
5 : to come into public view ⟨first *appeared* on a television variety show⟩ ⟨the book *appeared* in print a few years ago⟩
6 : to come into existence ⟨hominids *appeared* late in the evolutionary chain⟩

ap·pear·ance \ə-'pir-ən(t)s\ *noun* (14th century)
1 a : external show **:** SEMBLANCE ⟨although hostile, he preserved an *appearance* of neutrality⟩ **b :** outward aspect **:** LOOK ⟨had a fierce *appearance*⟩ **c** *plural* **:** outward indication ⟨trying to keep up *appearances*⟩
2 a : a sense impression or aspect of a thing ⟨the blue of distant hills is only an *appearance*⟩ **b :** the world of sensible phenomena
3 a : the act, action, or process of appearing **b :** the presentation of oneself in court as a party to an action often through the representation of an attorney
4 : something that appears **:** PHENOMENON **b :** an instance of appearing **:** OCCURRENCE

ap·pease \ə-'pēz\ *transitive verb* **appeased; ap·peas·ing** [Middle English *appesen*, from Middle French *apaisier*, from *a-* (from Latin *ad-*) + *pais* peace — more at PEACE] (14th century)
1 : to bring to a state of peace or quiet **:** CALM
2 : to cause to subside **:** ALLAY ⟨*appeased* my hunger⟩
3 : PACIFY, CONCILIATE; *especially* **:** to buy off (an aggressor) by concessions usually at the sacrifice of principles
synonym see PACIFY
— **ap·peas·able** \-'pē-zə-bəl\ *adjective*
— **ap·pease·ment** \-'pēz-mənt\ *noun*
— **ap·peas·er** *noun*

¹**ap·pel·lant** \ə-'pe-lənt\ *adjective* (14th century)
: of or relating to an appeal **:** APPELLATE
²**appellant** *noun* (15th century)
: one that appeals; *specifically* **:** one that appeals from a judicial decision or decree

ap·pel·late \ə-'pe-lət\ *adjective* [Latin *appellatus*, past participle of *appellare*] (1768)
: of, relating to, or recognizing appeals; *specifically* **:** having the power to review the judgment of another tribunal ⟨an *appellate* court⟩

ap·pel·la·tion \ˌa-pə-'lā-shən\ *noun* (15th century)
1 : an identifying name or title **:** DESIGNATION
2 *archaic* **:** the act of calling by a name
3 : a geographical name (as of a region, village or vineyard) under which a winegrower is authorized to identify and market wine

ap·pel·la·tive \ə-'pe-lə-tiv\ *adjective* (15th century)
1 : of or relating to a common noun
2 : of, relating to, or inclined to the giving of names
— **ap·pel·la·tive** *noun*
— **ap·pel·la·tive·ly** *adverb*

ap·pel·lee \ˌa-pə-'lē\ *noun* (1531)
: one against whom an appeal is taken

ap·pend \ə-'pend\ *transitive verb* [Middle English, from Middle French *appendre*, from Late Latin *appendere*, from Latin, to weigh, from *ad-* + *pendere* to weigh — more at PENDANT] (14th century)
1 : ATTACH, AFFIX

2 : to add as a supplement or appendix (as in a book)

ap·pend·age \ə-'pen-dij\ *noun* (1649)
1 : an adjunct to something larger or more important **:** APPURTENANCE
2 : a subordinate or derivative body part; *especially* **:** a limb or analogous part (as a seta)
3 : a dependent or subordinate person

ap·pen·dant \ə-'pen-dənt\ *adjective* (15th century)
1 : belonging as a right by prescription — used of annexed land in English law
2 : associated as an attendant circumstance
3 : attached as an appendage ⟨a seal *appendant* to a document⟩
— **appendant** *noun*

ap·pen·dec·to·my \ˌa-pən-'dek-tə-mē, ˌa-ˌpen-\ *noun, plural* **-mies** [Latin *appendic-, appendix* + English *-ectomy*] (circa 1895)
: surgical removal of the vermiform appendix

ap·pen·di·cec·to·my \ə-ˌpen-də-'sek-tə-mē\ *noun, plural* **-mies** (1894)
British **:** APPENDECTOMY

ap·pen·di·ci·tis \ə-ˌpen-də-'sī-təs\ *noun* [New Latin] (1886)
: inflammation of the vermiform appendix

ap·pen·dic·u·lar \ˌa-pən-'di-kyə-lər\ *adjective* (1651)
: of or relating to an appendage and especially a limb ⟨the *appendicular* skeleton⟩

ap·pen·dix \ə-'pen-diks\ *noun, plural* **-dix·es** or **-di·ces** \-də-ˌsēz\ [Latin *appendic-, appendix*, from *appendere*] (1542)
1 a : APPENDAGE **b :** supplementary material usually attached at the end of a piece of writing
2 : a bodily outgrowth or process; *specifically* **:** VERMIFORM APPENDIX

ap·per·ceive \ˌa-pər-'sēv\ *transitive verb* **-ceived; -ceiv·ing** [French *apercevoir*] (1876)
: to have apperception of

ap·per·cep·tion \-'sep-shən\ *noun* [French *aperception*, from *apercevoir*, from Middle French *aperceivre*, from *a-* (from Latin *ad-*) + *perceivre* to perceive] (1753)
1 : introspective self-consciousness
2 : mental perception; *especially* **:** the process of understanding something perceived in terms of previous experience
— **ap·per·cep·tive** \-'sep-tiv\ *adjective*

ap·per·tain \ˌa-pər-'tān\ *intransitive verb* [Middle English *apperteinen*, from Middle French *apartenir*, from Late Latin *appertinēre*, from Latin *ad-* + *pertinēre* to belong — more at PERTAIN] (14th century)
: to belong or be connected as a rightful part or attribute **:** PERTAIN

ap·pe·tence \'a-pə-tən(t)s\ *noun* (1610)
: APPETENCY

ap·pe·ten·cy \-tən(t)-sē\ *noun, plural* **-cies** [Latin *appetentia*, from *appetent-, appetens*, present participle of *appetere*] (1631)
: a fixed and strong desire **:** APPETITE
— **ap·pe·tent** \-tənt\ *adjective*

ap·pe·tis·er, ap·pe·tis·ing *British variant of* APPETIZER, APPETIZING

ap·pe·tite \'a-pə-ˌtīt\ *noun* [Middle English *apetit*, from Middle French, from Latin *appetitus*, from *appetere* to strive after, from *ad-* + *petere* to go to — more at FEATHER] (14th century)
1 : any of the instinctive desires necessary to keep up organic life; *especially* **:** the desire to eat
2 a : an inherent craving ⟨an insatiable *appetite* for work⟩ **b :** TASTE, PREFERENCE ⟨the cultural *appetites* of the time —J. D. Hart⟩
— **ap·pe·ti·tive** \-ˌtī-tiv\ *adjective*

ap·pe·tiz·er \'a-pə-ˌtī-zər\ *noun* (1859)
: a food or drink that stimulates the appetite and is usually served before a meal

ap·pe·tiz·ing \-ˌtī-ziŋ\ *adjective* (1653)
: appealing to the appetite especially in appearance or aroma; *also* **:** appealing to one's taste ⟨an *appetizing* display of merchandise⟩

synonym see PALATABLE
— **ap·pe·tiz·ing·ly** \-ziŋ-lē\ *adverb*

ap·plaud \ə-'plȯd\ *verb* [Middle English, from Middle French or Latin; Middle French *applaudir*, from Latin *applaudere*, from *ad-* + *plaudere* to applaud] (15th century)
intransitive verb
: to express approval especially by clapping the hands
transitive verb
1 : to express approval of **:** PRAISE ⟨*applaud* her efforts to lose weight⟩
2 : to show approval of especially by clapping the hands
— **ap·plaud·able** \-'plȯ-də-bəl\ *adjective*
— **ap·plaud·ably** \-blē\ *adverb*
— **ap·plaud·er** *noun*

ap·plause \ə-'plȯz\ *noun* [Medieval Latin *applausus*, from Latin, beating of wings, from *applaudere*] (15th century)
1 : marked commendation **:** ACCLAIM ⟨the kind of *applause* every really creative writer wants —Robert Tallant⟩
2 : approval publicly expressed (as by clapping the hands)

ap·ple \'a-pəl\ *noun, often attributive* [Middle English *appel*, from Old English *æppel*; akin to Old High German *apful* apple, Old Irish *ubull*, Old Church Slavonic *ablŭko*] (before 12th century)
1 : the fleshy usually rounded and red, yellow, or green edible pome fruit of a tree (genus *Malus*) of the rose family; *also* **:** an apple tree
2 : a fruit or other vegetable production suggestive of an apple — compare OAK APPLE
— **apple of one's eye :** one that is highly cherished ⟨his daughter is the *apple of his eye*⟩

apple butter *noun* (circa 1774)
: a thick brown spread made by cooking apples with sugar and spices usually in cider

ap·ple·cart \-ˌkärt\ *noun* (1788)
: a plan, system, situation, or undertaking that may be disrupted or terminated ⟨upset the *applecart*⟩

ap·ple–cheeked \'a-pəl-ˌchēkt\ *adjective* (1864)
: having cheeks the color of red apples

ap·ple·jack \-ˌjak\ *noun* (1816)
: brandy distilled from hard cider; *also* **:** an alcoholic beverage traditionally made by freezing hard cider and siphoning off the concentrated liquor

ap·ple–knock·er \-ˌnä-kər\ *noun* (1919)
: RUSTIC

apple maggot *noun* (1867)
: a dipteran fly (*Rhagoletis pomonella*) whose larva burrows in and feeds especially on apples

ap·ple–pie \'a-pəl-'pī\ *adjective* (1780)
1 : EXCELLENT, PERFECT ⟨*apple-pie* order⟩
2 : of, relating to, or characterized by traditionally American values (as honesty or simplicity) ⟨is the epitome of *apple-pie* wholesomeness⟩

ap·ple–pol·ish \'a-pəl-ˌpä-lish\ *verb* [from the traditional practice of schoolchildren bringing a shiny apple as a gift to their teacher] (1935)
intransitive verb
: to attempt to ingratiate oneself **:** TOADY
transitive verb
: to curry favor with (as by flattery)
— **ap·ple–pol·ish·er** *noun*

ap·ple·sauce \-ˌsȯs\ *noun* (1739)
1 : a relish or dessert made of apples stewed to a pulp and sweetened
2 *slang* **:** BUNKUM, NONSENSE

apple scab *noun* (circa 1899)
: a disease of apple trees caused by a fungus (*Venturia inaequalis*) producing dark blotches or lesions on the leaves, fruit, and sometimes the young twigs

ap·pli·ance \ə-'plī-ən(t)s\ *noun* (1561)
1 : an act of applying
2 a : a piece of equipment for adapting a tool or machine to a special purpose **:** ATTACHMENT

b : an instrument or device designed for a particular use; *specifically* : a household or office device (as a stove, fan, or refrigerator) operated by gas or electric current **c** *British* : FIRE ENGINE

3 *obsolete* : COMPLIANCE

synonym see IMPLEMENT

ap·pli·ca·ble \'a-pli-kə-bəl *also* ə-'pli-kə-\ *adjective* (1660)

: capable of or suitable for being applied : APPROPRIATE ⟨statutes *applicable* to the case⟩

synonym see RELEVANT

— **ap·pli·ca·bil·i·ty** \ˌa-pli-kə-'bi-lə-tē *also* ə-ˌpli-kə-\ *noun*

ap·pli·cant \'a-pli-kənt\ *noun* (circa 1782)

: one who applies ⟨a job *applicant*⟩

ap·pli·ca·tion \ˌa-plə-'kā-shən\ *noun* [Middle English *applicacioun*, from Latin *application-, applicatio* inclination, from *applicare*] (15th century)

1 : an act of applying: **a** (1) : an act of putting to use ⟨*application* of new techniques⟩ (2) : a use to which something is put ⟨new *applications* for old remedies⟩ (3) : a program (as a word processor or a spreadsheet) that performs one of the important tasks for which a computer is used **b** : an act of administering or superposing ⟨*application* of paint to a house⟩ **c** : assiduous attention ⟨succeeds by *application* to her studies⟩

2 a : REQUEST, PETITION ⟨an *application* for financial aid⟩ **b** : a form used in making a request

3 : the practical inference to be derived from a discourse (as a moral tale)

4 : a medicated or protective layer or material ⟨an oily *application* for dry skin⟩

5 : capacity for practical use ⟨words of varied *application*⟩

ap·pli·ca·tive \'a-plə-ˌkā-tiv, ə-'pli-kə-\ *adjective* (1638)

1 : APPLICABLE, PRACTICAL

2 : put to use : APPLIED

— **ap·pli·ca·tive·ly** *adverb*

ap·pli·ca·tor \'a-plə-ˌkā-tər\ *noun* (1659)

: one that applies; *specifically* : a device for applying a substance (as medicine or polish)

ap·pli·ca·to·ry \'a-pli-kə-ˌtōr-ē, -ˌtör-, ə-'pli-kə-\ *adjective* (1649)

: capable of being applied

ap·plied \ə-'plīd\ *adjective* (1656)

1 : put to practical use ⟨*applied* art⟩; *especially* : applying general principles to solve definite problems ⟨*applied* sciences⟩

2 : working in an applied science ⟨an *applied* physicist⟩

¹ap·pli·qué \ˌa-plə-'kā\ *noun* [French, past participle of *appliquer* to put on, from Latin *applicare*] (1801)

: a cutout decoration fastened to a larger piece of material

²appliqué *transitive verb* **-quéd; -qué·ing** (1881)

: to apply (as a decoration or ornament) to a larger surface : OVERLAY

ap·ply \ə-'plī\ *verb* **ap·plied; ap·ply·ing** [Middle English *applien*, from Middle French *aplier*, from Latin *applicare*, from *ad-* + *plicare* to fold — more at PLY] (14th century)

transitive verb

1 a : to put to use especially for some practical purpose ⟨*applies* pressure to get what he wants⟩ **b** : to bring into action ⟨*apply* the brakes⟩ **c** : to lay or spread on ⟨*apply* varnish⟩ **d** : to put into operation or effect ⟨*apply* a law⟩ **2** : to employ diligently or with close attention ⟨should *apply* yourself to your work⟩

intransitive verb

1 : to have relevance or a valid connection ⟨this rule *applies* to freshmen only⟩

2 : to make an appeal or request especially in the form of a written application ⟨*apply* for a job⟩

— **ap·pli·er** \-'plī(-ə)r\ *noun*

ap·pog·gia·tu·ra \ə-ˌpä-jə-'tür-ə\ *noun* [Italian, literally, support] (1753)

: an embellishing note or tone preceding an essential melodic note or tone and usually written as a note of smaller size

ap·point \ə-'point\ *verb* [Middle English, from Middle French *apointier* to arrange, from *a-* (from Latin *ad-*) + *point* point] (14th century)

transitive verb

1 a : to fix or set officially ⟨*appoint* a trial date⟩ **b** : to name officially ⟨will *appoint* her director of the program⟩ **c** *archaic* : ARRANGE **d** : to determine the disposition of (an estate) to someone by virtue of a power of appointment

2 : to provide with complete and usually appropriate or elegant furnishings or equipment

intransitive verb

: to exercise a power of appointment

synonym see FURNISH

ap·poin·tee \ə-ˌpoin-'tē, ˌa-\ *noun* (1768)

1 : one who is appointed

2 : one to whom an estate is appointed

ap·point·ive \ə-'poin-tiv\ *adjective* (1881)

: of, relating to, or filled by appointment ⟨an *appointive* office⟩

ap·point·ment \ə-'point-mənt\ *noun* (15th century)

1 a : an act of appointing : DESIGNATION **b** : the designation by virtue of a vested power of a person to enjoy an estate

2 : an arrangement for a meeting : ENGAGEMENT

3 : EQUIPMENT, FURNISHINGS — usually used in plural

4 : a nonelective office or position ⟨holds an academic *appointment*⟩

ap·por·tion \ə-'pōr-shən, -'pör-\ *transitive verb* **-tioned; -tion·ing** \-sh(ə-)niŋ\ [Middle French *apportionner*, from *a-* (from Latin *ad-*) + *portionner* to portion] (1574)

: to divide and share out according to a plan; *especially* : to make a proportionate division or distribution of

— **ap·por·tion·able** \-shə-nə-bəl\ *adjective*

ap·por·tion·ment \-shən-mənt\ *noun* (1579)

: an act or result of apportioning; *especially* : the apportioning of representatives or taxes among the states according to U.S. law

ap·pose \a-'pōz\ *transitive verb* **ap·posed; ap·pos·ing** [Middle French *aposer*, from Old French, from *a-* + *poser* to put — more at POSE] (1596)

1 *archaic* : to put before : apply (one thing) to another

2 : to place in juxtaposition or proximity

ap·po·site \'a-pə-zət\ *adjective* [Latin *appositus*, from past participle of *apponere* to place near, from *ad-* + *ponere* to put — more at POSITION] (1621)

: highly pertinent or appropriate : APT

synonym see RELEVANT

— **ap·po·site·ly** *adverb*

— **ap·po·site·ness** *noun*

ap·po·si·tion \ˌa-pə-'zi-shən\ *noun* (15th century)

1 a : a grammatical construction in which two usually adjacent nouns having the same referent stand in the same syntactical relation to the rest of a sentence (as *the poet* and *Burns* in "a biography of the poet Burns") **b** : the relation of one of such a pair of nouns or noun equivalents to the other

2 a : an act or instance of apposing; *specifically* : the deposition of successive layers upon those already present (as in cell walls) **b** : the state of being apposed

— **ap·po·si·tion·al** \-'zish-nəl, -'zi-shə-nᵊl\ *adjective*

ap·pos·i·tive \ə-'pä-zə-tiv, a-\ *adjective* (1693)

: of, relating to, or standing in grammatical apposition

— **appositive** *noun*

— **ap·pos·i·tive·ly** *adverb*

ap·prais·al \ə-'prā-zəl\ *noun* (1817)

: an act or instance of appraising; *especially* : a valuation of property by the estimate of an authorized person

ap·praise \ə-'prāz\ *transitive verb* **ap·praised; ap·prais·ing** [Middle English *appreisen*, from Middle French *aprisier* to apprize] (15th century)

1 : to set a value on : estimate the amount of

2 : to evaluate the worth, significance, or status of; *especially* : to give an expert judgment of the value or merit of

synonym see ESTIMATE

— **ap·prais·ee** \ə-ˌprā-'zē\ *noun*

— **ap·praise·ment** \-'prāz-mənt\ *noun*

— **ap·prais·er** *noun*

— **ap·prais·ing·ly** \-'prā-ziŋ-lē\ *adverb*

— **ap·prais·ive** \-'prā-ziv\ *adjective*

ap·pre·cia·ble \ə-'prē-shə-bəl, -'pri-sh(ē-)ə-bəl\ *adjective* (1818)

: capable of being perceived or measured

synonym see PERCEPTIBLE

— **ap·pre·cia·bly** \-blē\ *adverb*

ap·pre·ci·ate \ə-'prē-shē-ˌāt, -'pri- *also* -'prē-sē-\ *verb* **-at·ed; -at·ing** [Late Latin *appretiatus*, past participle of *appretiare*, from Latin *ad-* + *pretium* price — more at PRICE] (1655)

transitive verb

1 a : to grasp the nature, worth, quality, or significance of ⟨*appreciate* the difference between right and wrong⟩ **b** : to value or admire highly ⟨*appreciates* our work⟩ **c** : to judge with heightened perception or understanding : be fully aware of ⟨must see it to *appreciate* it⟩ **d** : to recognize with gratitude ⟨certainly *appreciates* your kindness⟩

2 : to increase the value of

intransitive verb

: to increase in number or value ☆

— **ap·pre·ci·a·tor** \-ˌā-tər\ *noun*

— **ap·pre·cia·to·ry** \-'prē-shə-ˌtōr-ē, -'pri-shə-, -ˌtör-\ *adjective*

ap·pre·ci·a·tion \ə-ˌprē-shē-'ā-shən, -ˌpri- *also* -ˌprē-sē-\ *noun* (1604)

1 a : JUDGMENT, EVALUATION; *especially* : a favorable critical estimate **b** : sensitive awareness; *especially* : recognition of aesthetic values **c** : an expression of admiration, approval, or gratitude

2 : increase in value

ap·pre·cia·tive \ə-'prē-shə-tiv, -'pri- *also* -'prē-shē-ˌā-\ *adjective* (circa 1698)

: having or showing appreciation

— **ap·pre·cia·tive·ly** *adverb*

— **ap·pre·cia·tive·ness** *noun*

ap·pre·hend \ˌa-pri-'hend\ *verb* [Middle English, from Latin *apprehendere*, literally, to seize, from *ad-* + *prehendere* to seize — more at GET] (15th century)

transitive verb

1 : ARREST, SEIZE ⟨*apprehend* a thief⟩

☆ SYNONYMS

Appreciate, value, prize, treasure, cherish mean to hold in high estimation. APPRECIATE often connotes sufficient understanding to enjoy or admire a thing's excellence ⟨*appreciates* fine wine⟩. VALUE implies rating a thing highly for its intrinsic worth ⟨*values* our friendship⟩. PRIZE implies taking a deep pride in something one possesses ⟨Americans *prize* their freedom⟩. TREASURE emphasizes jealously safeguarding something considered precious ⟨a *treasured* memento⟩. CHERISH implies a special love and care for something ⟨*cherishes* her children above all⟩. See in addition UNDERSTAND.

2 a : to become aware of **:** PERCEIVE **b :** to anticipate especially with anxiety, dread, or fear **3 :** to grasp with the understanding **:** recognize the meaning of
intransitive verb
: UNDERSTAND, GRASP

ap·pre·hen·si·ble \ˌa-pri-'hen(t)-sə-bəl\ *adjective* (circa 1631)
: capable of being apprehended
— **ap·pre·hen·si·bly** \-blē\ *adverb*

ap·pre·hen·sion \ˌa-pri-'hen(t)-shən\ *noun* [Middle English, from Late Latin *apprehension-, apprehensio,* from Latin *apprehendere*] (14th century)
1 a : the act or power of perceiving or comprehending ⟨a person of dull *apprehension*⟩ **b :** the result of apprehending mentally **:** CONCEPTION ⟨according to popular *apprehension*⟩
2 : seizure by legal process **:** ARREST
3 : suspicion or fear especially of future evil **:** FOREBODING

ap·pre·hen·sive \-'hen(t)-siv\ *adjective* (14th century)
1 : capable of apprehending or quick to do so **:** DISCERNING
2 : having apprehension **:** COGNIZANT
3 : viewing the future with anxiety or alarm
synonym see FEARFUL
— **ap·pre·hen·sive·ly** *adverb*
— **ap·pre·hen·sive·ness** *noun*

¹ap·pren·tice \ə-'pren-təs\ *noun* [Middle English *aprentis,* from Middle French, from Old French, from *aprendre* to learn, from Latin *apprendere, apprehendere*] (14th century)
1 a : one bound by indenture to serve another for a prescribed period with a view to learning an art or trade **b :** one who is learning by practical experience under skilled workers a trade, art, or calling
2 : an inexperienced person **:** NOVICE ⟨an *apprentice* in cooking⟩
— **ap·pren·tice·ship** \-tə(sh)-ˌship, -təsˌship\ *noun*

²apprentice *verb* -ticed; -tic·ing (1596)
transitive verb
: to set at work as an apprentice; *especially* **:** to bind to an apprenticeship by contract or indenture
intransitive verb
: to serve as an apprentice

ap·pressed \a-'prest\ *adjective* [Latin *appressus,* past participle of *apprimere* to press to, from *ad-* + *premere* to press — more at PRESS] (1791)
: pressed close to or lying flat against something ⟨leaves *appressed* against the stem⟩

ap·pres·so·ri·um \ˌa-pre-'sōr-ē-əm, -'sȯr-\ *noun, plural* -ria \-ē-ə\ [New Latin, from Latin *apprimere*] (1897)
: the flattened thickened tip of a hyphal branch by which some parasitic fungi are attached to their host

ap·prise \ə-'prīz\ *transitive verb* **ap·prised; ap·pris·ing** [French *appris,* past participle of *apprendre* to learn, teach, from Old French *aprendre*] (1694)
: to give notice to **:** TELL
synonym see INFORM

ap·prize \ə-'prīz\ *transitive verb* **ap·prized; ap·priz·ing** [Middle English *apprisen,* from Middle French *apriser,* from Old French *aprisier,* from *a-* (from Latin *ad-*) + *prisier* to appraise — more at PRIZE] (14th century)
: VALUE, APPRECIATE

¹ap·proach \ə-'prōch\ *verb* [Middle English *approchen,* from Old French *aprochier,* from Late Latin *appropiare,* from Latin *ad-* + *prope* near; akin to Latin *pro* before — more at FOR] (13th century)
transitive verb
1 a : to draw closer to **:** NEAR **b :** to come very near to **:** be almost the same as ⟨its mathematics *approaches* mysticism —Theodore Sturgeon⟩ ⟨as the quantity *x approaches* zero⟩
2 a : to make advances to especially in order to create a desired result ⟨was *approached* by

several Broadway producers⟩ **b :** to take preliminary steps toward accomplishment or full knowledge or experience of ⟨*approach* the subject with an open mind⟩
intransitive verb
1 : to draw nearer
2 : to make an approach in golf

²approach *noun* (15th century)
1 a : an act or instance of approaching ⟨the *approach* of summer⟩ **b :** APPROXIMATION ⟨in this book he makes his closest *approach* to greatness⟩
2 a : the taking of preliminary steps toward a particular purpose ⟨experimenting with new lines of *approach*⟩ **b :** a particular manner of taking such steps ⟨a highly individual *approach* to language⟩
3 : a means of access **:** AVENUE
4 a : a golf shot from the fairway toward the green **b :** the steps taken by a bowler before he delivers the ball; *also* **:** the part of the alley behind the foul line from which the bowler delivers the ball
5 : the descent of an aircraft toward a landing place

ap·proach·able \ə-'prō-chə-bəl\ *adjective* (1571)
: capable of being approached **:** ACCESSIBLE; *specifically* **:** easy to meet or deal with
— **ap·proach·abil·i·ty** \-ˌprō-chə-'bi-lə-tē\ *noun*

ap·pro·bate \'a-prə-ˌbāt\ *transitive verb* **-bat·ed; -bat·ing** [Middle English, from Latin *approbatus,* past participle of *approbare* — more at APPROVE] (15th century)
: APPROVE, SANCTION
— **ap·pro·ba·to·ry** \'a-prə-bə-ˌtōr-ē, ə-'prō-bə-, -ˌtȯr-\ *adjective*

ap·pro·ba·tion \ˌa-prə-'bā-shən\ *noun* (14th century)
1 *obsolete* **:** PROOF
2 a : an act of approving formally or officially **b :** COMMENDATION, PRAISE

¹ap·pro·pri·ate \ə-'prō-prē-ˌāt\ *transitive verb* **-at·ed; -at·ing** [Middle English, from Late Latin *appropriatus,* past participle of *appropriare,* from Latin *ad-* + *proprius* own] (15th century)
1 : to take exclusive possession of **:** ANNEX ⟨no one should *appropriate* a common benefit⟩
2 : to set apart for or assign to a particular purpose or use ⟨*appropriate* money for the research program⟩
3 : to take or make use of without authority or right
— **ap·pro·pri·a·ble** \-prē-ə-bəl\ *adjective*
— **ap·pro·pri·a·tor** \-prē-ˌā-tər\ *noun*

²ap·pro·pri·ate \ə-'prō-prē-ət\ *adjective* (15th century)
: especially suitable or compatible **:** FITTING
synonym see FIT
— **ap·pro·pri·ate·ly** *adverb*
— **ap·pro·pri·ate·ness** *noun*

ap·pro·pri·a·tion \ə-ˌprō-prē-'ā-shən\ *noun* (14th century)
1 : an act or instance of appropriating
2 : something that has been appropriated; *specifically* **:** money set aside by formal action for a specific use
— **ap·pro·pri·a·tive** \-'prō-prē-ˌā-tiv\ *adjective*

ap·prov·able \ə-'prü-və-bəl\ *adjective* (15th century)
: capable or worthy of being approved
— **ap·prov·ably** \-blē\ *adverb*

ap·prov·al \ə-'prü-vəl\ *noun* (1616)
: an act or instance of approving **:** APPROBATION
— **on approval :** subject to a prospective buyer's acceptance or refusal ⟨stamps sent to collectors *on approval*⟩

ap·prove \ə-'prüv\ *verb* **ap·proved; ap·prov·ing** [Middle English, from Middle French *aprover,* from Latin *approbare,* from *ad-* + *probare* to prove — more at PROVE] (14th century)

transitive verb
1 *obsolete* **:** PROVE, ATTEST
2 : to have or express a favorable opinion of ⟨couldn't *approve* such conduct⟩
3 a : to accept as satisfactory ⟨hopes she will *approve* the date of the meeting⟩ **b :** to give formal or official sanction to **:** RATIFY ⟨Congress *approved* the proposed budget⟩
intransitive verb
: to take a favorable view ⟨doesn't *approve* of fighting⟩ ☆
— **ap·prov·ing·ly** \-'prü-viŋ-lē\ *adverb*

approved school *noun* (1932)
British **:** a school for juvenile delinquents

¹ap·prox·i·mate \ə-'präk-sə-mət\ *adjective* [Late Latin *approximatus,* past participle of *approximare* to come near, from Latin *ad-* + *proximare* to come near — more at PROXIMATE] (15th century)
1 : located close together ⟨*approximate* leaves⟩
2 : nearly correct or exact ⟨an *approximate* solution⟩
— **ap·prox·i·mate·ly** *adverb*

²ap·prox·i·mate \-ˌmāt\ *verb* **-mat·ed; -mat·ing** (15th century)
transitive verb
1 a : to bring near or close **b :** to bring (cut edges of tissue) together
2 : to come near or to be close to in position, value, or characteristics ⟨a child tries to *approximate* his parents' speech⟩
intransitive verb
: to come close — usually used with *to*

ap·prox·i·ma·tion \ə-ˌpräk-sə-'mā-shən\ *noun* (15th century)
1 : the act or process of drawing together
2 : the quality or state of being close or near ⟨an *approximation* to the truth⟩ ⟨an *approximation* of justice⟩
3 : something that is approximate; *especially* **:** a mathematical quantity that is close in value to but not the same as a desired quantity
— **ap·prox·i·ma·tive** \-'präk-sə-ˌmā-tiv\ *adjective*

ap·pur·te·nance \ə-'pərt-nən(t)s, -'pər-t°n-ən(t)s\ *noun* (14th century)
1 : an incidental right (as a right-of-way) attached to a principal property right and passing in possession with it
2 : a subordinate part or adjunct ⟨the *appurtenance* of welcome is fashion and ceremony —Shakespeare⟩
3 *plural* **:** accessory objects **:** APPARATUS

ap·pur·te·nant \ə-'pərt-nənt, -'pər-t°n-ənt\ *adjective* [Middle English *apertenant,* from Middle French, from Old French, present participle of *apartenir* to belong — more at APPERTAIN] (14th century)
1 : constituting a legal accompaniment
2 : AUXILIARY, ACCESSORY
— **appurtenant** *noun*

aprax·ia \(ˌ)ā-'prak-sē-ə\ *noun* [New Latin, from Greek, inaction, from *a-* + *praxis* action, from *prassein* to do — more at PRACTICAL] (circa 1881)
: loss or impairment of the ability to execute complex coordinated movements without impairment of the muscles or senses

☆ **SYNONYMS**
Approve, endorse, sanction, accredit, certify mean to have or express a favorable opinion of. APPROVE often implies no more than this but may suggest considerable esteem or admiration ⟨the parents *approve* of the marriage⟩. ENDORSE suggests an explicit statement of support ⟨publicly *endorsed* her for Senator⟩. SANCTION implies both approval and authorization ⟨the President *sanctioned* covert operations⟩. ACCREDIT and CERTIFY usually imply official endorsement attesting to conformity to set standards ⟨the board voted to *accredit* the college⟩ ⟨must be *certified* to teach⟩.

— **aprac·tic** \-'prak-tik\ *or* **aprax·ic** \-'prak-sik\ *adjective*

après \(ₐ)ä-'prā, ä-ₚrä; 'a-ₓ\ *preposition* [French *après-*, from *après* after] (1967)
: AFTER ⟨*après* tennis⟩ — usually used in combination ⟨*après*-theater party⟩

après-ski \ₐä-ₚrä-'skē, ₚa-\ *noun, often attributive* [French *après* after + *ski* ski, skiing] (1951)
: social activity (as at a ski lodge) after a day's skiing

apri·cot \'a-prə-ₚkät, 'ā-\ *noun, often attributive* [alteration of earlier *abrecock*, ultimately from Arabic *al-birqūq* the apricot, ultimately from Latin (*persicum*) *praecox*, literally, early ripening (peach) — more at PRECOCIOUS] (1551)
1 a : the oval orange-colored fruit of a temperate-zone tree (*Prunus armeniaca*) resembling the related peach and plum in flavor **b** : a tree that bears apricots
2 : a variable color averaging a moderate orange ◇

April \'ā-prəl\ *noun* [Middle English, from Old French & Latin; Old French *avrill*, from Latin *Aprilis*] (before 12th century)
: the 4th month of the Gregorian calendar

April fool *noun* (1687)
: the butt of a joke or trick played on April Fools' Day; *also* : such a joke or trick

April Fools' Day *noun* (1854)
: April 1 characteristically marked by the playing of practical jokes

a pri·o·ri \ₐä-prē-'ȯr-ē, ₐa-; ₐä-(ₓ)prī-'ȯr-ī, -ₚprē-'ȯr-ē; -'ȯr-\ *adjective* [Latin, literally, from the former] (1652)
1 a : DEDUCTIVE **b** : relating to or derived by reasoning from self-evident propositions — compare A POSTERIORI **c** : presupposed by experience
2 a : being without examination or analysis : PRESUMPTIVE **b** : formed or conceived beforehand
— **a priori** *adverb*
— **apri·or·i·ty** \-'ȯr-ə-tē\ *noun*

apron \'ā-prən, -pərn\ *noun, often attributive* [Middle English, alteration (resulting from false division of *a napron*) of *napron*, from Middle French *naperon*, diminutive of *nape* cloth, modification of Latin *mappa* napkin] (15th century)
1 : a garment usually of cloth, plastic, or leather usually tied around the waist and used to protect clothing or adorn a costume
2 : something that suggests or resembles an apron in shape, position, or use: as **a** : the lower member under the sill of the interior casing of a window **b** : an upward or downward vertical extension of a bathroom fixture (as a sink or tub) **c** : an endless belt for carrying material **d** : an extensive fan-shaped deposit of detritus **e** : the part of the stage in front of the proscenium arch **f** : the area along the waterfront edge of a pier or wharf **g** : a shield (as of concrete or gravel) to protect against erosion (as of a waterway) by water **h** : the extensive paved part of an airport immediately adjacent to the terminal area or hangars ◇
— **aproned** \-prənd, -pərnd\ *adjective*

apron string *noun* (1542)
: the string of an apron — usually used in plural as a symbol of dominance or complete control ⟨though 40 years old he was still tied to his mother's *apron strings*⟩

¹ap·ro·pos \ₐa-prə-'pō, 'a-prə-ₓ\ *adverb* [French *à propos*, literally, to the purpose] (1668)
1 : at an opportune time : SEASONABLY
2 : BY THE WAY

²apropos *adjective* (1686)
: being both relevant and opportune
synonym see RELEVANT

³apropos *preposition* (1910)
: APROPOS OF

apropos of *preposition* (1746)

: with regard to : CONCERNING

apro·tic \(ₓ)ā-'prō-tik\ *adjective* [²*a*- + *proton* + ¹-*ic*] (1931)
of a solvent : incapable of acting as a proton donor

apse \'aps\ *noun* [Medieval Latin & Latin; Medieval Latin *apsis*, from Latin] (1822)
1 : APSIS 1
2 : a projecting part of a building (as a church) that usually semicircular in plan and vaulted

ap·si·dal \'ap-sə-dʰl\ *adjective* (1846)
: of or relating to an apse or apsis

ap·sis \'ap-səs\ *noun, plural* **ap·si·des** \-sə-ₚdēz\ [New Latin *apsid-, apsis*, from Latin, arch, orbit, from Greek *hapsid-, hapsis*, from *haptein* to fasten] (1658)
1 : the point in an astronomical orbit at which the distance of the body from the center of attraction is either greatest or least
2 : APSE 2

apt \'apt\ *adjective* [Middle English, from Latin *aptus*, literally, fastened, from past participle of *apere* to fasten; akin to Latin *apisci* to grasp, obtain, *apud* near, Hittite *ḫap-* to attach] (14th century)
1 : unusually fitted or qualified : READY ⟨proved an *apt* tool in the hands of the conspirators⟩
2 a : having a tendency : LIKELY ⟨plants *apt* to suffer from drought⟩ **b** : ordinarily disposed : INCLINED ⟨*apt* to accept what is plausible as true⟩
3 : suited to a purpose; *especially* : being to the point ⟨an *apt* quotation⟩
4 : keenly intelligent and responsive
synonym see FIT, QUICK
usage see LIABLE
— **apt·ly** \'ap(t)-lē\ *adverb*
— **apt·ness** \'ap(t)-nəs\ *noun*

ap·ter·ous \'ap-tə-rəs\ *adjective* [Greek *apteros*, from *a*- + *pteron* wing — more at FEATHER] (1775)
: lacking wings ⟨*apterous* insects⟩

ap·ter·yx \'ap-tə-riks\ *noun* [New Latin, from *a*- + Greek *pteryx* wing; akin to Greek *pteron*] (1813)
: KIWI

ap·ti·tude \'ap-tə-ₚtüd, -ₚtyüd\ *noun* [Middle English, from Medieval Latin *aptitudo*, from Late Latin, fitness, from Latin *aptus*] (15th century)
1 a : INCLINATION, TENDENCY **b** : a natural ability : TALENT
2 : capacity for learning : APTNESS
3 : general suitability
synonym see GIFT
— **ap·ti·tu·di·nal** \ₐap-tə-'tü-dʰn-əl, -'tyü-\ *adjective*
— **ap·ti·tu·di·nal·ly** *adverb*

aptitude test *noun* (1923)
: a standardized test designed to predict an individual's ability to learn certain skills

ap·y·rase \'a-pə-ₚrās, -ₚrāz\ *noun* [adenosine + *py*rophosphate + -*ase*] (1945)
: any of several enzymes that hydrolyze ATP with the liberation of phosphate and energy

aqua \'ä-kwə *also* 'a-\ *noun* [Latin — more at ISLAND] (14th century)
1 *plural* **aquae** \'ä-ₓkwī *also* 'a-(ₓ)kwē\ : WATER; *especially* : WATER 5a(2)
2 *plural* **aquas** : a light greenish blue color

aqua·cade \'ä-kwə-ₚkād, 'a-\ *noun* [*Aquacade*, a water spectacle originally at Cleveland, Ohio] (1937)
: a water spectacle that consists usually of exhibitions of swimming and diving with musical accompaniment

aqua·cul·ture *also* **aqui·cul·ture** \'ä-kwə-ₚkəl-chər, 'a-\ *noun* [Latin *aqua* + English -*culture* (as in *agriculture*)] (1867)
: the cultivation of the natural produce of water (as fish or shellfish)
— **aqua·cul·tur·al** \ₐä-kwə-'kəl-ch(ə-)rəl, ₚa-\ *adjective*
— **aqua·cul·tur·ist** \-ch(ə-)rist\ *noun*

aqua for·tis \'ä-kwə-'fȯr-təs, 'a-\ *noun* [New Latin *aqua fortis,* literally, strong water] (15th century)
: NITRIC ACID

Aqua–Lung \'ä-kwə-ₚləŋ, 'a-\ *trademark*
— used for an underwater breathing apparatus

aqua·ma·rine \ₐä-kwə-mə-'rēn, ₚa-\ *noun* [New Latin *aqua marina*, from Latin, sea water] (1677)
1 : a transparent beryl that is blue, blue-green, or green in color
2 : a pale blue to light greenish blue

aqua·naut \'ä-kwə-ₚnȯt, 'a-, -ₚnät\ *noun* [Latin *aqua* + English -*naut* (as in *aeronaut*)] (1881)
: a scuba diver who lives and operates both inside and outside an underwater shelter for an extended period

¹aqua·plane \'ä-kwə-ₚplān, 'a-\ *noun* (1914)
: a board towed behind a speeding motorboat and ridden by a person standing on it
— **aqua·plan·er** *noun*

²aquaplane *intransitive verb* (circa 1923)
1 : to ride on an aquaplane
2 *British* : HYDROPLANE

aqua re·gia \-'rē-j(ē-)ə\ *noun* [New Latin, literally, royal water] (1610)
: a mixture of nitric and hydrochloric acids that dissolves gold or platinum

aqua·relle \ₐa-kwə-'rel, ₚä-\ *noun* [French,

◇ WORD HISTORY
apricot The apricot is native to China and was probably not introduced to the Mediterranean region before the first century B.C. We assume that the fruit which the Roman poet Martial called *persica praecocia*, literally, "early-ripening peaches," was the apricot. A Greek form of the second word in this phrase, *praikokion*, migrated to the eastern end of the Mediterranean, and when the Arabs entered this area in the early Middle Ages, they turned *praikokion* into *barqūq* or *birqūq*. In areas that they occupied, such as Sicily and the Iberian Peninsula, the Arabs revived apricot cultivation. Arabic *al-barqūq* "the apricot" entered Spanish as *albaricoque*, Portuguese as *albricoque*, and Catalan as *albercoc* or *abercoc*. The earliest English form of the word, *aprecock*, appears to be borrowed from French *abricot* (itself also from Iberian Romance). The change of *b* to *p* (notable also in German *Aprikose*) was perhaps by association with Latin *apricus* "sunny, warmed by sunshine."

apron In late Medieval French a diminutive form of *nape*, meaning "tablecloth," was *naperon*, which was usually used for a small cloth placed over a more elegant tablecloth to protect it from stains. This word appears in English of the 14th century as *napron;* like its French source, *napron* denoted a protective cloth, but one that was placed over clothing rather than on a table. Because in connected speech it is often difficult to tell where word boundaries fall, *a napron* was incorrectly understood as *an apron*. The new form *apron* had effectively replaced *napron* by the 17th century, completely obscuring the etymological relation of *apron* to *napkin*, the name for yet another kind of protective cloth. Curiously, the modern French word for "apron," *tablier,* has undergone a similar sense shift; originally a derivative of *table* "table," in Old French it meant "tablecloth."

\ə\ **abut** \ᵊ\ **kitten** \ər\ **further** \a\ **ash** \ā\ **ace** \ä\ **mop, mar** \au̇\ **out** \ch\ **chin** \e\ **bet** \ē\ **easy** \g\ **go** \i\ **hit** \ī\ **ice** \j\ **job** \ŋ\ **sing** \ō\ **go** \ȯ\ **law** \ȯi\ **boy** \th\ **thin** \t͟h\ **the** \ü\ **loot** \u̇\ **foot** \y\ **yet** \zh\ **vision** *see also* Guide to Pronunciation

from obsolete Italian *acquarella* (now *acque-rello*), from *acqua* water, from Latin *aqua*] (1869)
: a drawing usually in transparent watercolor
— **aqua·rell·ist** \-'re-list\ *noun*

Aquar·i·an \ə-'kwar-ē-ən, -'kwer-\ *noun* (1911)
: AQUARIUS 2b
— **Aquarian** *adjective*

aquar·ist \ə-'kwar-ist, -'kwer-\ *noun* (circa 1893)
: a person who keeps or maintains an aquarium

aquar·i·um \ə-'kwar-ē-əm, -'kwer-\ *noun, plural* **-i·ums** *or* **-ia** \-ē-ə\ [probably alteration of *aquatic vivarium*] (circa 1847)
1 : a container (as a glass tank) or an artificial pond in which living aquatic animals or plants are kept
2 : an establishment where aquatic collections of living organisms are kept and exhibited

Aquar·i·us \-ē-əs\ *noun* [Latin (genitive *Aquarii*), literally, water carrier]
1 : a constellation south of Pegasus pictured as a man pouring water
2 a : the 11th sign of the zodiac in astrology — see ZODIAC table **b** : one born under the sign of Aquarius

¹**aquat·ic** \ə-'kwä-tik, -'kwa-\ *adjective* (1642)
1 : growing or living in or frequenting water ⟨*aquatic* mosquito larvae⟩
2 : taking place in or on water ⟨*aquatic* sports⟩
— **aquat·i·cal·ly** \-ti-k(ə-)lē\ *adverb*

²**aquatic** *noun* (circa 1600)
1 : an aquatic animal or plant
2 *plural but singular or plural in construction* : water sports

aqua·tint \'a-kwə-,tint, 'ä-\ *noun* [Italian *acqua tinta* dyed water] (1782)
: a method of etching a printing plate so that tones similar to watercolor washes can be reproduced; *also* : a print made from a plate so etched
— **aquatint** *transitive verb*
— **aqua·tint·er** *noun*
— **aqua·tint·ist** \-,tin-tist\ *noun*

aqua·vit \'ä-kwə-,vēt\ *noun* [Swedish, Danish, & Norwegian *akvavit*, from Medieval Latin *aqua vitae*] (1890)
: a clear Scandinavian liquor flavored with caraway seeds
word history see WHISKEY

aqua vi·tae \,a-kwə-'vī-tē, ,ä-\ *noun* [Middle English, from Medieval Latin, literally, water of life] (15th century)
: a strong alcoholic liquor (as brandy)
word history see WHISKEY

aq·ue·duct \'a-kwə-,dəkt\ *noun* [Latin *aquaeductus*, from *aquae* (genitive of *aqua*) + *ductus* act of leading — more at DUCT] (1538)
1 a : a conduit for water; *especially* : one for carrying a large quantity of flowing water **b** : a structure for conveying a canal over a river or hollow
2 : a canal or passage in a part or organ

aque·ous \'ā-kwē-əs, 'a-\ *adjective* [Medieval Latin *aqueus*, from Latin *aqua*] (1646)
1 a : of, relating to, or resembling water **b** : made from, with, or by water
2 : of or relating to the aqueous humor

aqueous humor *noun* (1643)
: a transparent fluid occupying the space between the crystalline lens and the cornea of the eye

aqui·fer \'a-kwə-fər, 'ä-\ *noun* [New Latin, from Latin *aqua* + *-fer*] (1901)
: a water-bearing stratum of permeable rock, sand, or gravel
— **aquif·er·ous** \a-'kwi-fə-rəs, ä-\ *adjective*

Aq·ui·la \'a-kwə-lə *also* ə-'kwi-lə\ *noun* [Latin (genitive *Aquilae*), literally, eagle]
: a constellation in the northern hemisphere represented by the figure of an eagle

aq·ui·le·gia \,a-kwə-'lē-j(ē-)ə\ *noun* [New Latin] (1871)
: COLUMBINE

aq·ui·line \'a-kwə-,līn, -lən\ *adjective* [Latin *aquilinus*, from *aquila* eagle] (1646)
1 : curving like an eagle's beak ⟨an *aquiline* nose⟩
2 : of, relating to, or resembling an eagle
— **aq·ui·lin·i·ty** \,a-kwə-'li-nə-tē\ *noun*

aquiv·er \ə-'kwi-vər\ *adjective* (1883)
: marked by trembling or quivering ⟨all *aquiver* with excitement⟩

ar \'är\ *noun* [Middle English] (14th century)
: the letter *r*

-ar *adjective suffix* [Middle English, from Latin *-aris*, alteration of *-alis* -al]
: of or relating to ⟨molecul*ar*⟩ : being ⟨spectacul*ar*⟩ : resembling ⟨oracul*ar*⟩

Ar·ab \'ar-əb, 'er-; *dialect also* 'ā-,rab\ *noun* [Middle English, from Latin *Arabus, Arabs*, from Greek *Arab-, Araps*] (14th century)
1 a : a member of the Semitic people of the Arabian peninsula **b** : a member of an Arabic-speaking people
2 : ARABIAN HORSE
— **Arab** *adjective*

¹**ar·a·besque** \,ar-ə-'besk\ *adjective* [French, from Italian *arabesco* Arabian in fashion, from *arabo* Arab, from Latin *Arabus*] (circa 1656)
: of, relating to, or being in the style of arabesque or an arabesque

²**arabesque** *noun* (1786)
1 : an ornament or style that employs flower, foliage, or fruit and sometimes animal and figural outlines to produce an intricate pattern of interlaced lines
2 : a posture in ballet in which the body is bent forward from the hip on one leg with one arm extended forward and the other arm and leg backward

arabesque 1

3 : an elaborate or intricate pattern ⟨richly pierced by an *arabesque* of wormholes —John Chase⟩ ⟨as lawyers . . . perform their procedural *arabesques* —Daniel Okrent⟩

¹**Ara·bi·an** \ə-'rā-bē-ən\ *noun* (14th century)
1 : a native or inhabitant of Arabia
2 : ARABIAN HORSE

²**Arabian** *adjective* (14th century)
: ARABIC 1

Arabian horse *noun* (1737)
: any of a breed of swift compact horses developed in Arabia and usually having gray or chestnut silky hair

¹**Ar·a·bic** \'ar-ə-bik\ *noun* (14th century)
: a Semitic language originally of the Arabs of the Hejaz and Nejd that is now the prevailing speech of a wide region of southwestern Asia and northern Africa

²**Arabic** *adjective* (1526)
1 : of, relating to, or characteristic of Arabia or the Arabs
2 : of, relating to, or constituting Arabic
3 : expressed in or utilizing Arabic numerals

arab·i·ca \ə-'ra-bə-kə\ *noun, often attributive* [New Latin, specific epithet of *Coffea arabica*, from Latin, feminine of *Arabicus* Arabian] (1922)
1 : an evergreen shrub or tree (*Coffea arabica*) yielding seeds that produce a high-quality coffee and form a large portion of the coffee of commerce
2 : the seeds of arabica

Arabic alphabet *noun* (1841)
: an alphabet of 28 letters derived from the Aramaic alphabet which is used for writing Arabic and also with adaptations for other languages of the Islamic world

arab·i·cize \ə-'ra-bə-,sīz\ *transitive verb* **-cized; -ciz·ing** *often capitalized* (1872)
1 : to adapt (a language or elements of a language) to the phonetic or structural pattern of Arabic
2 : ARABIZE 1

— **arab·i·ci·za·tion** \ə-,ra-bə-sə-'zā-shən\ *noun*

Arabic numeral *noun* (circa 1847)
: any of the number symbols 0, 1, 2, 3, 4, 5, 6, 7, 8, 9 — see NUMBER table

arab·i·nose \ə-'ra-bə-,nōs, -,nōz\ *noun* [International Scientific Vocabulary *arabin* (the solid principle in gum arabic, from *gum arabic* + ¹-*in*) + -*ose*] (circa 1884)
: a white crystalline aldose sugar $C_5H_{10}O_5$ occurring especially in vegetable gums

ara·bi·no·side \,ar-ə-'bi-nə-,sīd, ə-'ra-bə-nō-,sīd\ *noun* (1927)
: a glycoside that yields arabinose on hydrolysis

Ar·ab·ise *British variant of* ARABIZE

Ar·ab·ism \'ar-ə-,bi-zəm\ *noun* (1614)
1 : a characteristic feature of Arabic occurring in another language
2 : devotion to Arab interests, culture, aspirations, or ideals

Ar·ab·ist \'ar-ə-bist\ *noun* (1753)
1 : a specialist in the Arabic language or in Arabic culture
2 : a person who favors Arab interests and positions in international affairs

Ar·ab·ize \'ar-ə-,bīz\ *transitive verb* **-ized; -iz·ing** (1883)
1 a : to cause to acquire Arabic customs, manners, speech, or outlook **b** : to modify (a population) by intermarriage with Arabs
2 : ARABICIZE 1
— **Ar·ab·i·za·tion** \,ar-ə-bə-'zā-shən\ *noun*

¹**ar·a·ble** \'ar-ə-bəl\ *adjective* [Middle French or Latin; Middle French, from Latin *arabilis*, from *arare* to plow; akin to Old English *erian* to plow, Greek *aroun*] (15th century)
1 : fit for or used for the growing of crops
2 *British* : engaged in, produced by, or being the cultivation of arable land
— **ar·a·bil·i·ty** \,ar-ə-'bi-lə-tē\ *noun*

²**arable** *noun* (1576)
chiefly British : land fit or used for the growing of crops; *also* : a plot of such land

ar·a·chi·don·ic acid \,ar-ə-kə-'dä-nik-\ *noun* [New Latin *Arachid-, Arachis* + English -*onic* (as in *gluconic acid*)] (1913)
: a liquid unsaturated fatty acid $C_{20}H_{32}O_2$ that occurs in most animal fats, is a precursor of prostaglandins, and is considered essential in animal nutrition

ar·a·chis oil \'ar-ə-kəs-\ *noun* [New Latin *Arachis*, genus that includes the peanut, from Greek *arakis*, diminutive of *arakos*, a legume] (circa 1889)
: PEANUT OIL

arach·nid \ə-'rak-nəd, -,nid\ *noun* [New Latin *Arachnida*, from Greek *arachnē* spider] (1869)
: any of a class (Arachnida) of arthropods comprising chiefly terrestrial invertebrates, including the spiders, scorpions, mites, and ticks, and having a segmented body divided into two regions of which the anterior bears four pairs of legs but no antennae
— **arachnid** *adjective*

¹**arach·noid** \ə-'rak-,nòid\ *adjective* (1789)
1 : of or relating to a thin membrane of the brain and spinal cord that lies between the dura mater and the pia mater
2 : covered with or composed of soft loose hairs or fibers

²**arachnoid** *noun* [New Latin *arachnoides*, from Greek *arachnoeidēs*, like a cobweb, from *arachnē* spider, spider's web] (circa 1847)
: an arachnoid membrane

³**arachnoid** *adjective* [New Latin *Arachn*ida + English -*oid*] (1852)
: resembling or related to the arachnids

ar·a·go·nite \ə-'ra-gə-,nīt, 'ar-ə-gə-\ *noun* [German *Aragonit*, from *Aragon*, Spain] (1803)
: a mineral similar to calcite in consisting of calcium carbonate but differing from calcite in its orthorhombic crystallization, greater density, and less distinct cleavage

— **ara·go·nit·ic** \ə-,ra-gə-'ni-tik, ,ar-ə-gə-\ *adjective*

ar·ak *variant of* ARRACK

Ar·a·mae·an \,ar-ə-'mē-ən\ *noun* [Latin *Aramaeus,* from Greek *Aramaios,* from Hebrew *'Ărām* Aram, ancient name for Syria] (1839)
1 : ARAMAIC
2 : a member of a Semitic people of the second millennium B.C. in Syria and Upper Mesopotamia
— **Aramaean** *adjective*

Ar·a·ma·ic \,ar-ə-'mā-ik\ *noun* (1882)
: a Semitic language known since the ninth century B.C. as the speech of the Aramaeans and later used extensively in southwest Asia as a commercial and governmental language and adopted as their customary speech by various non-Aramaean peoples including the Jews after the Babylonian exile

Aramaic alphabet *noun* (1925)
1 : an extinct North Semitic alphabet dating from the ninth century B.C. which was for several centuries the commercial alphabet of southwest Asia and the parent of other alphabets (as Syriac and Arabic)
2 : the square Hebrew alphabet as distinguished from the early Hebrew alphabet

ar·a·mid \'ar-ə-məd, -,mid\ *noun* [aromatic poly*amide*] (1972)
: any of a group of lightweight but very strong heat-resistant synthetic aromatic polyamide materials that are fashioned into fibers, filaments, or sheets and used especially in textiles and plastics

Arap·a·ho *or* **Arap·a·hoe** \ə-'ra-pə-,hō\ *noun, plural* **-ho** *or* **-hos** *or* **-hoe** *or* **-hoes** (1812)
1 : a member of an American Indian people of the plains region ranging from Saskatchewan and Manitoba to New Mexico and Texas
2 : the Algonquian language of the Arapaho people

Arau·ca·ni·an \ə-,raü-'kä-nē-ən, ,ar-ȯ-'kä-\ *also* **Arau·can** \ə-'raü-kən\ *noun* [Spanish *araucano,* from *Arauco,* former province in Chile] (1809)
1 : a member of a group of Indian peoples of south central Chile and adjacent regions of Argentina
2 : the language of the Araucanian people that constitutes an independent language family
— **Araucanian** *adjective*

ar·au·car·ia \,ar-ȯ-'kar-ē-ə\ *noun* [New Latin, from *Arauco*] (1809)
: any of a genus (*Araucaria* of the family Araucariaceae, the araucaria family) of South American or Australian coniferous trees that resemble pines and are often grown as ornamentals
— **ar·au·car·i·an** \-ē-ən\ *adjective*

Ar·a·wak \'ar-ə-,wäk, -,wak\ *noun, plural* **Arawak** *or* **Arawaks** (1769)
1 : a member of an Indian people of the Arawakan group now living chiefly along the coast of Guyana
2 : the language of the Arawak people

Ar·a·wak·an \,ar-ə-'wä-\ *noun, plural* **Arawakan** *or* **Arawakans** (1901)
1 : a member of a group of Indian peoples of South America and the West Indies
2 : the language family of the Arawakan peoples

arb \'ärb\ *noun* (1979)
: ARBITRAGEUR

ar·ba·lest *or* **ar·ba·list** \'är-bə-list\ *noun* [Middle English *arblast,* from Old English, from Old French *arbaleste,* from Late Latin *arcuballista,* from Latin *arcus* bow + *ballista* — more at ARROW] (before 12th century)
: a crossbow especially of medieval times

ar·bi·ter \'är-bə-tər\ *noun* [Middle English *arbitre,* from Middle French, from Latin *arbitr-, arbiter*] (14th century)
1 : a person with power to decide a dispute **:** JUDGE

2 : a person or agency having the power of deciding

arbiter el·e·gan·ti·a·rum \-,e-lə-,gan-shē-'är-əm, -'er-\ *noun* [Latin, literally, arbiter of refinements] (1818)
: a person who prescribes, rules on, or is a recognized authority on matters of social behavior and taste

ar·bi·tra·ble \'är-bə-trə-bəl, är-'bi-\ *adjective* (1531)
: subject to decision by arbitration

¹ar·bi·trage \'är-bə-,träzh\ *noun* [French, from Middle French, arbitration, from Old French, from *arbitrer* to render judgment, from Latin *arbitrari,* from *arbitr-, arbiter*] (1875)
1 : the nearly simultaneous purchase and sale of securities or foreign exchange in different markets in order to profit from price discrepancies
2 : the purchase of the stock of a takeover target especially with a view to selling it profitably to the raider

²arbitrage *intransitive verb* **-traged; -traging** (1900)
: to engage in arbitrage

ar·bi·tra·geur \,är-bə-(,)trä-'zhər\ *or* **ar·bi·trag·er** \'är-bə-,trä-zhər\ *noun* [French *arbitrageur,* from *arbitrage*] (1870)
: one that practices arbitrage

ar·bi·tral \'är-bə-trəl\ *adjective* (1609)
: of or relating to arbiters or arbitration

ar·bit·ra·ment \är-'bi-trə-mənt\ *noun* [Middle English, from Middle French *arbitrement,* from *arbitrer*] (15th century)
1 *archaic* **:** the right or power of deciding
2 : the settling of a dispute by an arbiter
3 : the judgment given by an arbitrator

ar·bi·trary \'är-bə-,trer-ē\ *adjective* (15th century)
1 : depending on individual discretion (as of a judge) and not fixed by law ⟨the manner of punishment is *arbitrary*⟩
2 a : not restrained or limited in the exercise of power **:** ruling by absolute authority ⟨an *arbitrary* government⟩ **b :** marked by or resulting from the unrestrained and often tyrannical exercise of power ⟨protection from *arbitrary* arrest and detention⟩
3 a : based on or determined by individual preference or convenience rather than by necessity or the intrinsic nature of something ⟨an *arbitrary* standard⟩ ⟨take any *arbitrary* positive number⟩ ⟨*arbitrary* division of historical studies into watertight compartments —A. J. Toynbee⟩ **b :** existing or coming about seemingly at random or by chance or as a capricious and unreasonable act of will ⟨when a task is not seen in a meaningful context it is experienced as being *arbitrary* —Nehemiah Jordan⟩
— **ar·bi·trari·ly** \,är-bə-'trer-ə-lē\ *adverb*
— **ar·bi·trar·i·ness** \'är-bə-,trer-ē-nəs\ *noun*

ar·bi·trate \'är-bə-,trāt\ *verb* **-trat·ed; -trating** (1592)
transitive verb
1 *archaic* **:** DECIDE, DETERMINE
2 : to act as arbiter upon
3 : to submit or refer for decision to an arbiter ⟨agreed to *arbitrate* their differences⟩
intransitive verb
: to act as arbitrator
— **ar·bi·tra·tive** \-,trā-tiv\ *adjective*

ar·bi·tra·tion \,är-bə-'trā-shən\ *noun* (15th century)
: the action of arbitrating; *especially* **:** the hearing and determination of a case in controversy by an arbiter
— **ar·bi·tra·tion·al** \-sh(ə-)nəl\ *adjective*

ar·bi·tra·tor \'är-bə-,trā-tər\ *noun* (15th century)
: one that arbitrates **:** ARBITER

¹ar·bor \'är-bər\ *noun* [Middle English *erber* plot of grass, arbor, from Middle French *her-*

bier plot of grass, from *herbe* herb, grass] (14th century)
: a shelter of vines or branches or of latticework covered with climbing shrubs or vines

²arbor *noun* [Latin, tree, shaft] (1659)
1 : a spindle or axle of a wheel
2 : a main shaft or beam
3 : a shaft on which a revolving cutting tool is mounted
4 : a spindle on a cutting machine that holds the work to be cut

arbor- *or* **arbori-** *combining form* [Latin *arbor*]
: tree ⟨*arbori*culture⟩

Arbor Day *noun* [Latin *arbor* tree] (1872)
: a day designated for planting trees

ar·bo·re·al \är-'bōr-ē-əl, -'bȯr-\ *adjective* [Latin *arboreus* of a tree, from *arbor*] (circa 1667)
1 : of, relating to, or resembling a tree
2 : inhabiting or frequenting trees ⟨*arboreal* monkeys⟩
— **ar·bo·re·al·ly** \-ə-lē\ *adverb*

ar·bo·re·ous \-ē-əs\ *adjective* (1646)
: ARBOREAL ⟨an *arboreous* palm⟩

ar·bo·res·cent \,är-bə-'re-sᵊnt\ *adjective* (1675)
: resembling a tree in properties, growth, structure, or appearance
— **ar·bo·res·cence** \-sᵊn(t)s\ *noun*

ar·bo·re·tum \,är-bə-'rē-təm\ *noun, plural* **-retums** *or* **-re·ta** \-'rē-tə\ [New Latin, from Latin, plantation of trees, from *arbor*] (1838)
: a place where trees, shrubs, and herbaceous plants are cultivated for scientific and educational purposes

ar·bor·i·cul·ture \'är-bər-ə-,kəl-chər, är-'bȯr-ə-\ *noun* [*arbori-* + *-culture* (as in *agriculture*)] (1828)
: the cultivation of trees and shrubs especially for ornamental purposes
— **ar·bor·i·cul·tur·al** \,är-bər-ə-'kəl-chər-əl, är-,bȯr-ə-\ *adjective*

ar·bor·ist \'är-bə-rist\ *noun* (1578)
: a specialist in the care and maintenance of trees

ar·bor·i·za·tion \,är-bə-rə-'zā-shən\ *noun* (1794)
: formation of or into an arborescent figure or arrangement; *also* **:** such a figure or arrangement (as a dendritic process of a nerve cell)

ar·bor·ize \'är-bə-,rīz\ *intransitive verb* **-ized; -iz·ing** (1847)
: to branch freely and repeatedly

ar·bor·vi·tae \,är-bər-'vī-tē\ *noun* [New Latin *arbor vitae,* literally, tree of life] (1646)
: any of various evergreen trees and shrubs (especially genus *Thuja*) of the cypress family that usually have closely overlapping or compressed scale leaves and are often grown for ornament and in hedges

ar·bour *chiefly British variant of* ARBOR

ar·bo·vi·rus \'är-bə-,vī-rəs\ *noun* [*arthropodborne virus*] (1957)
: any of various RNA viruses (as the causative agents of encephalitis, yellow fever, and dengue) transmitted by arthropods

ar·bu·tus \är-'byü-təs\ *noun* [New Latin, from Latin, strawberry tree] (1548)
1 : any of a genus (*Arbutus*) of shrubs and trees of the heath family with white or pink flowers and red or orange berries
2 : a creeping plant (*Epigaea repens*) of the heath family that occurs in eastern North America and bears fragrant pink or white flowers in early spring

¹arc \'ärk\ *noun* [Middle English *ark,* from Middle French *arc* bow, from Latin *arcus* bow, arch, arc — more at ARROW] (14th century)

1 : the apparent path described above and below the horizon by a celestial body (as the sun)
2 : something arched or curved
3 : a sustained luminous discharge of electricity across a gap in a circuit or between electrodes; *also* **:** ARC LAMP
4 : a continuous portion (as of a circle or ellipse) of a curved line
5 : degree measurement on the circumference of a circle — used especially in the phrase *of arc* ⟨11 minutes 3 seconds *of arc*⟩
²arc *intransitive verb* **arced** \'ärkt\; **arc·ing** \'är-kiŋ\ (1893)
1 : to form an electric arc
2 : to follow an arc-shaped course ⟨the missile *arced* across the sky⟩
³arc *adjective* [*arc sine* arc or angle (corresponding to the) sine (of so many degrees)] (circa 1949)
: INVERSE 2 — used with the trigonometric functions and hyperbolic functions
ar·cade \är-'kād\ *noun* [French, from Italian *arcata*, from *arco* arch, from Latin *arcus*] (1725)
1 : a long arched building or gallery
2 : an arched covered passageway or avenue (as between shops)
3 : a series of arches with their columns or piers
4 : an amusement center having coin-operated games
ar·cad·ed \-'kā-dəd\ *adjective* (1805)
: having, formed in, or decorated with arches or arcades ⟨*arcaded* streets⟩ ⟨an *arcaded* bowl⟩
ar·ca·dia \är-'kā-dē-ə\ *noun, often capitalized* [*Arcadia*, region of ancient Greece frequently chosen as background for pastoral poetry] (circa 1890)
: a region or scene of simple pleasure and quiet
ar·ca·di·an \är-'kā-dē-ən\ *adjective, often capitalized* (1589)
1 : idyllically pastoral; *especially* **:** idyllically innocent, simple, or untroubled
2 a : of or relating to Arcadia or the Arcadians
b : of or relating to Arcadian
Ar·ca·di·an \är-'kā-dē-ən\ *noun* (1590)
1 *often not capitalized* **:** a person who lives a simple quiet life
2 : a native or inhabitant of Arcadia
3 : the dialect of ancient Greek used in Arcadia
ar·cad·ing \är-'kā-diŋ\ *noun* (1849)
: a series of arches or arcades used in the construction or decoration especially of a building
Ar·ca·dy \'är-kə-dē\ *noun* (14th century)
: ARCADIA
ar·cane \är-'kān\ *adjective* [Latin *arcanus*] (1547)
: known or knowable only to the initiate **:** SECRET ⟨the *arcane* rites of a mystery cult⟩; *broadly* **:** MYSTERIOUS, OBSCURE ⟨the technical consultant's *arcane* explanations⟩
ar·ca·num \är-'kā-nəm\ *noun, plural* **-na** \-nə\ [Latin, from neuter of *arcanus* secret, from *arca* chest — more at ARK] (15th century)
1 : mysterious knowledge, language, or information accessible only by the initiate — usually used in plural
2 : ELIXIR 1
arc·co·sine \(,)är(k)-'kō-,sīn\ *noun* (circa 1884)
: the inverse function to the cosine ⟨if *y* is the cosine of *θ*, then *θ* is the *arccosine* of *y*⟩
¹arch \'ärch\ *noun* [Middle English *arche*, from Middle French, from (assumed) Vulgar Latin *arca*, from Latin *arcus* — more at ARROW] (14th century)
1 : a typically curved structural member spanning an opening and serving as a support (as for the wall or other weight above the opening)
2 a : something resembling an arch in form or function; *especially* **:** either of two vaulted portions of the bony structure of the foot that

impart elasticity to it **b :** a curvature having the form of an arch
3 : ARCHWAY

arch 1: *1* round: *imp* impost, *sp* springer, *v* voussoir, *k* keystone, *ext* extrados, *int* intrados; *2* horseshoe; *3* lancet; *4* ogee; *5* trefoil; *6* basket-handle; *7* Tudor

²arch (15th century)
transitive verb
1 : to cover or provide with an arch
2 : to form into an arch
intransitive verb
1 : to form an arch
2 : to take an arch-shaped course
³arch *adjective* [¹*arch*] (1547)
1 : PRINCIPAL, CHIEF ⟨your *arch* opponent⟩
2 a : MISCHIEVOUS, SAUCY **b :** marked by a deliberate and often forced irony, brashness, or impudence
— **arch·ly** *adverb*
— **arch·ness** *noun*
¹arch- *prefix* [Middle English *arche-*, *arch-*, from Old English & Old French; Old English *arce-*, from Late Latin *arch-* & Latin *archi-*; Old French *arch-*, from Late Latin *arch-* & Latin *archi-*, from Greek *arch-*, *archi-*, from *archein* to begin, rule; akin to Greek *archē* beginning, rule, *archos* ruler]
1 : chief **:** principal ⟨*arch*fiend⟩
2 : extreme **:** most fully embodying the qualities of the kind ⟨*arch*conservative⟩
²arch- — see ARCHI-
¹-arch *noun combining form* [Middle English *-arche*, from Old French & Late Latin & Latin; Old French *-arche*, from Late Latin *-archa*, from Latin *-arches*, *-archus*, from Greek *-archēs*, *-archos*, from *archein*]
: ruler **:** leader ⟨matri*arch*⟩
²-arch *adjective combining form* [probably from German, from Greek *archē* beginning]
: having (such) a point or (so many) points of origin ⟨end*arch*⟩
archae- *or* **archaeo-** *also* **archeo-** *combining form* [Greek *archaio-*, from *archaios* ancient, from *archē* beginning]
: ancient **:** primitive ⟨*archaeo*pteryx⟩ ⟨*Archeo*zoic⟩
ar·chae·bac·te·ri·um \,är-kē-,bak-'tir-ē-əm\ *noun* [New Latin] (1977)
: any of a class (Archaeobacteria) or a separate kingdom (Archaebacteria) of primitive bacteria including methane-producing forms, some red halophilic forms, and others of harsh hot acidic environments
ar·chaeo·as·tron·o·my \,är-kē-(,)ō-ə-'strä-nə-mē\ *noun* (1971)
: the study of the astronomy of ancient cultures
ar·chae·ol·o·gy *or* **ar·che·ol·o·gy** \,är-kē-'ä-lə-jē\ *noun* [French *archéologie*, from Late Latin *archaeologia* antiquarian lore, from Greek *archaiologia*, from *archaio-* + *-logia* -logy] (1837)
1 : the scientific study of material remains (as fossil relics, artifacts, and monuments) of past human life and activities
2 : remains of the culture of a people **:** ANTIQUITIES
— **ar·chae·o·log·i·cal** \,är-kē-ə-'lä-ji-kəl\ *adjective*
— **ar·chae·o·log·i·cal·ly** \-k(ə-)lē\ *adverb*
— **ar·chae·ol·o·gist** \,är-kē-'ä-lə-jist\ *noun*
ar·chae·op·ter·yx \,är-kē-'äp-tə-riks\ *noun*

[New Latin, from *archae-* + Greek *pteryx* wing; akin to Greek *pteron* wing — more at FEATHER] (1859)
: a primitive crow-sized bird (genus *Archaeopteryx*) of the Upper Jurassic period of Europe having reptilian characteristics (as teeth and a long bony tail)
ar·cha·ic \är-'kā-ik\ *adjective* [French or Greek; French *archaïque*, from Greek *archaïkos*, from *archaios*] (1832)
1 : having the characteristics of the language of the past and surviving chiefly in specialized uses
2 : of, relating to, or characteristic of an earlier or more primitive time **:** ANTIQUATED ⟨*archaic* legal traditions⟩
3 *capitalized* **:** of or belonging to the early or formative phases of a culture or a period of artistic development; *especially* **:** of or belonging to the period leading up to the classical period of Greek culture
4 : surviving from an earlier period; *specifically* **:** typical of a previously dominant evolutionary stage
5 *capitalized* **:** of or relating to the period from about 8000 B.C. to 1000 B.C. and the North American cultures of that time
synonym see OLD
— **ar·cha·i·cal·ly** \-i-k(ə-)lē\ *adverb*
archaic smile *noun* (1889)
: an expression that resembles a smile and is characteristic of early Greek sculpture
ar·cha·ism \'är-kē-,i-zəm, -(,)ā-,i-\ *noun* [New Latin *archaïsmus*, from Greek *archaïsmos*, from *archaios*] (1643)
1 : the use of archaic diction or style
2 : an instance of archaic usage
3 : something archaic; *especially* **:** something (as a practice or custom) that is outmoded or old-fashioned
— **ar·cha·ist** \-ist\ *noun*
— **ar·cha·is·tic** \,är-kē-'is-tik, -(,)kā-\ *adjective*
— **ar·cha·ize** \'är-kē-,īz, -(,)kā-\ *verb*
arch·an·gel \'är-,kān-jəl\ *noun* [Middle English, from Old French or Late Latin; Old French *archangele*, from Late Latin *archangelus*, from Greek *archangelos*, from *archi-* + *angelos* angel] (12th century)
1 : a chief angel
2 *plural* **:** an order of angels — see CELESTIAL HIERARCHY
— **arch·an·gel·ic** \,är-(,)kan-'je-lik\ *adjective*
arch·bish·op \(,)ärch-'bi-shəp\ *noun* [Middle English, from Old English *arcebiscop*, from Late Latin *archiepiscopus*, from Late Greek *archiepiskopos*, from *archi-* + *episkopos* bishop — more at BISHOP] (before 12th century)
: a bishop at the head of an ecclesiastical province or one of equivalent honorary rank
arch·bish·op·ric \-shə-(,)prik\ *noun* (before 12th century)
1 : the see or province over which an archbishop exercises authority
2 : the jurisdiction or office of an archbishop
arch·con·ser·va·tive \(,)ärch-kən-'sər-və-tiv\ *noun* (1934)
: an extreme conservative
— **archconservative** *adjective*
arch·dea·con \(,)ärch-'dē-kən\ *noun* [Middle English *archedeken*, from Old English *arcediacon*, from Late Latin *archidiaconus*, from Late Greek *archidiakonos*, from Greek *archi-* + *diakonos* deacon] (before 12th century)
: a clergyman having the duty of assisting a diocesan bishop in ceremonial functions or administrative work
arch·dea·con·ry \-kən-rē\ *noun, plural* **-ries** (1779)
: the district or residence of an archdeacon
arch·di·o·cese \(,)ärch-'dī-ə-səs, -,sēz, -,sēs\ *noun, plural* **-ces·es** \-'dī-ə-,sēz, -,sē-zəz, -sə-səz, -sə-,sēz\ (1844)
: the diocese of an archbishop

— **arch·di·oc·e·san** \ˌärch-dī-'ä-sə-sən\ *adjective*

arch·du·cal \(ˌ)ärch-'dü-kəl, -'dyü-\ *adjective* [French *archiducal,* from *archiduc*] (1665)
: of or relating to an archduke or archduchy

arch·duch·ess \-'də-chəs\ *noun* [French *archiduchesse,* feminine of *archiduc* archduke, from Middle French *archeduc*] (1618)
1 : the wife or widow of an archduke
2 : a woman having in her own right a rank equal to that of an archduke

arch·duchy \-'də-chē\ *noun* [French *archiduché,* from Middle French *archeduché,* from *arche-* arch- + *duché* duchy] (1680)
: the territory of an archduke or archduchess

arch·duke \-'dük, -'dyük\ *noun* [Middle French *archeduc,* from *arche-* arch- + *duc* duke] (circa 1530)
1 : a sovereign prince
2 : a prince of the imperial family of Austria
— **arch·duke·dom** \-dəm\ *noun*

Ar·che·an *or* **Ar·chae·an** \är-'kē-ən\ *adjective* [Greek *archaios*] (1872)
1 : of, relating to, or being the earliest eon of geological history or the corresponding system of rocks — see GEOLOGIC TIME table
2 : PRECAMBRIAN
— **Archean** *noun*

ar·che·go·ni·al \ˌär-ki-'gō-nē-əl\ *adjective* (1865)
: of or relating to an archegonium; *also*
: ARCHEGONIATE

¹ar·che·go·ni·ate \-nē-ət\ *adjective* (circa 1888)
: bearing archegonia

²archegoniate *noun* (circa 1903)
: a plant (as a moss, fern, horsetail, or club moss) that bears archegonia

ar·che·go·ni·um \-nē-əm\ *noun, plural* **-nia** \-nē-ə\ [New Latin, from Greek *archegonos* originator, from *archein* to begin + *gonos* procreation; akin to Greek *gignesthai* to be born — more at ARCH-, KIN] (1854)
: the flask-shaped female sex organ of bryophytes, lower vascular plants (as ferns), and some gymnosperms

arch·en·e·my \(ˌ)ärch-'e-nə-mē\ *noun, plural* **-mies** (1550)
: a principal enemy

arch·en·ter·on \är-'ken-tə-ˌrän, -rən\ *noun* [New Latin] (1877)
: the cavity of a gastrula forming a primitive gut

Ar·cheo·zo·ic *also* **Ar·chaeo·zo·ic** \ˌär-kē-ə-'zō-ik\ *adjective* (1872)
: ARCHEAN 1
— **Archeozoic** *noun*

ar·cher \'är-chər\ *noun* [Middle English, from Old French, from Late Latin *arcarius,* alteration of *arcuarius,* from *arcuarius* of a bow, from Latin *arcus* bow — more at ARROW] (14th century)
1 : a person who uses a bow and arrow
2 *capitalized* **:** SAGITTARIUS

ar·cher·fish \'är-chər-ˌfish\ *noun* (circa 1889)
: a small East Indian fish (*Toxotes jaculator*) that catches insects by stunning them with water ejected from its mouth; *also* **:** any of various related fish of similar habits

ar·chery \'är-chə-rē\ *noun* (15th century)
1 : the art, practice, or skill of shooting with bow and arrow
2 : an archer's weapons
3 : a body of archers

ar·che·spo·ri·um \ˌär-ki-'spōr-ē-əm, -'spȯr-\ *noun, plural* **-spo·ria** \-ē-ə\ [New Latin, from *arche-* (as in *archegonium*) + *-sporium* (from *spora* spore)] (circa 1889)
: the cell or group of cells from which spore mother cells develop
— **ar·che·spo·ri·al** \ˌär-ki-'spōr-ē-əl, -'spȯr-\ *adjective*

ar·che·type \'är-ki-ˌtīp\ *noun* [Latin *archetypum,* from Greek *archetypon,* from neuter of *archetypos* archetypal, from *archein* + *typos* type] (1545)

1 : the original pattern or model of which all things of the same type are representations or copies **:** PROTOTYPE; *also* **:** a perfect example
2 : IDEA 1a
3 : an inherited idea or mode of thought in the psychology of C. G. Jung that is derived from the experience of the race and is present in the unconscious of the individual
— **ar·che·typ·al** \ˌär-ki-'tī-pəl\ *also* **ar·che·typ·i·cal** \-'ti-pi-kəl\ *adjective*
— **ar·che·typ·al·ly** \-pə-lē\ *adverb*

arch·fiend \(ˌ)ärch-'fēnd\ *noun* (1667)
: a chief fiend; *especially* **:** SATAN

archi- *or* **arch-** *prefix* [French or Latin; French, from Latin, from Greek — more at ARCH-]
: primitive **:** original **:** primary ⟨*archenteron*⟩

ar·chi·di·ac·o·nal \ˌär-ki-dī-'a-kə-nᵊl\ *adjective* [Late Latin *archidiaconus* archdeacon] (15th century)
: of or relating to an archdeacon

ar·chi·epis·co·pal \ˌär-kē-ə-'pis-kə-pəl\ *adjective* [Medieval Latin *archiepiscopalis,* from Late Latin *archiepiscopus* archbishop — more at ARCHBISHOP] (1611)
: of or relating to an archbishop
— **ar·chi·epis·co·pal·ly** \-p(ə-)lē\ *adverb*

ar·chi·epis·co·pate \-pət, -ˌpāt\ *noun* (1792)
: ARCHBISHOPRIC

ar·chil \'är-chəl\ *noun* [Middle English *orchell*] (15th century)
1 : a violet dye obtained from lichens (genera *Roccella* and *Lecanora*)
2 : a lichen that yields archil

ar·chi·man·drite \ˌär-kə-'man-ˌdrīt\ *noun* [Late Latin *archimandrites,* from Late Greek *archimandritēs,* from Greek *archi-* + Late Greek *mandra* monastery, from Greek, fold, pen] (1591)
: a dignitary in an Eastern church ranking below a bishop; *specifically* **:** the superior of a large monastery or group of monasteries

Ar·chi·me·des' **screw** \ˌär-kə-'mē-dēz-\ *noun* [*Archimedes*] (circa 1859)
: a device made of a tube bent spirally around an axis or of a broad-threaded screw encased by a cylinder and used to raise water

Archimedes' screw

ar·chi·pe·lag·ic \ˌär-kə-pə-'la-jik, ˌär-kə-pə-\ *adjective* (1841)
: of, relating to, or located in an archipelago

ar·chi·pel·a·go \ˌär-kə-'pe-lə-ˌgō, ˌär-chə-\ *noun, plural* **-goes** *or* **-gos** [Italian *Arcipelago* Aegean Sea, from Italian *Arcipelago,* literally, chief sea, from *arci-* (from Latin *archi-*) + Greek *pelagos* sea — more at PLAGAL] (1502)
1 : an expanse of water with many scattered islands
2 : a group of islands

ar·chi·tect \'är-kə-ˌtekt\ *noun* [Middle French *architecte,* from Latin *architectus,* from Greek *architektōn* master builder, from *archi-* + *tektōn* builder, carpenter — more at TECHNICAL] (1563)
1 : a person who designs buildings and advises in their construction
2 : a person who designs and guides a plan or undertaking ⟨the *architect* of American foreign policy⟩

ar·chi·tec·ton·ic \ˌär-kə-ˌtek-'tä-nik\ *adjective* [Latin *architectonicus,* from Greek *architektonikos,* from *architektōn*] (1645)
1 : of, relating to, or according with the principles of architecture **:** ARCHITECTURAL
2 : having an organized and unified structure that suggests an architectural design
— **ar·chi·tec·ton·i·cal·ly** \-ni-k(ə-)lē\ *adverb*

ar·chi·tec·ton·ics \-'tä-niks\ *noun plural but*

singular or plural in construction, *also* **ar·chi·tec·ton·ic** \-nik\ (1660)
1 : the science of architecture
2 a : the unifying structural design of something **b :** the system of structure

ar·chi·tec·tur·al \ˌär-kə-'tek-chə-rəl, -'tek-shrəl\ *adjective* (circa 1794)
1 : of or relating to architecture **:** conforming to the rules of architecture
2 : having or conceived of as having a single unified overall design, form, or structure
— **ar·chi·tec·tur·al·ly** *adverb*

ar·chi·tec·ture \'är-kə-ˌtek-chər\ *noun* (1555)
1 : the art or science of building; *specifically* **:** the art or practice of designing and building structures and especially habitable ones
2 a : formation or construction as or as if as the result of conscious act ⟨the *architecture* of the garden⟩ **b :** a unifying or coherent form or structure ⟨the novel lacks *architecture*⟩
3 : architectural product or work
4 : a method or style of building
5 : the manner in which the components of a computer or computer system are organized and integrated

ar·chi·trave \'är-kə-ˌtrāv\ *noun* [Middle French, from Old Italian, from *archi-* + *trave* beam, from Latin *trab-, trabs* — more at THORP] (1563)
1 : the lowest division of an entablature resting in classical architecture immediately on the capital of the column — see ENTABLATURE illustration
2 : the molding around a rectangular opening (as a door)

ar·chi·val \är-'kī-vəl\ *adjective* (circa 1828)
: of, relating to, contained in, or constituting archives

¹ar·chive \'är-ˌkīv\ *noun* [French & Latin; French, from Latin *archivum,* from Greek *archeion* government house (in plural, official documents), from *archē* rule, government — more at ARCH-] (1603)
: a place in which public records or historical documents are preserved; *also* **:** the material preserved — often used in plural

²archive *transitive verb* **ar·chived; ar·chiv·ing** (1926)
: to file or collect (as records or documents) in or as if in an archive

ar·chi·vist \'är-kə-vist, -ˌkī-\ *noun* (1753)
: a person in charge of archives

ar·chi·volt \'är-kə-ˌvōlt\ *noun* [Italian *archivolto,* from Medieval Latin *archivoltum*] (circa 1731)
: an ornamental molding around an arch corresponding to an architrave

ar·chon \'är-ˌkän, -kən\ *noun* [Latin, from Greek *archōn,* from present participle of *archein*] (1579)
1 : a chief magistrate in ancient Athens
2 : a presiding officer

ar·cho·saur \'är-kə-ˌsȯr\ *noun* [New Latin *Archosauria,* from Greek *archōn* + *sauros* lizard] (1933)
: any of a subclass (Archosauria) of reptiles comprising the dinosaurs, pterosaurs, and crocodilians
— **ar·cho·sau·ri·an** \ˌär-kə-'sȯr-ē-ən\ *adjective*

arch·priest \(ˌ)ärch-'prēst\ *noun* (14th century)
: a priest of preeminent rank

arch·way \'ärch-ˌwā\ *noun* (1802)
: a way or passage under an arch; *also* **:** an arch over a passage

-archy *noun combining form, plural* **-archies** [Middle English *-archie,* from Middle French, from Latin *-archia,* from Greek, from *archein* to rule — more at ARCH-]

: rule : government ⟨squire*archy*⟩

arc lamp *noun* (1882)
: an electric lamp that produces light by an arc made when a current passes between two incandescent electrodes surrounded by gas — called also *arc light*

ar·co \'är-(ˌ)kō\ *adverb or adjective* [Italian, from *arco* bow, from Latin *arcus* — more at ARROW] (1806)
: with the bow — usually used as a direction in music for players of stringed instruments; compare PIZZICATO

arc·sine \(ˌ)ärk-'sīn\ *noun* (circa 1909)
: the inverse function to the sine ⟨if *y* is the sine of θ, then θ is the *arcsine* of *y*⟩

arc·tan·gent \(ˌ)ärk-'tan-jənt\ *noun* (circa 1909)
: the inverse function to the tangent ⟨if *y* is the tangent of θ, then θ is the *arctangent* of *y*⟩

¹arc·tic \'ärk-tik, 'är-tik\ *adjective* [Middle English *artik*, from Latin *arcticus*, from Greek *arktikos*, from *arktos* bear, Ursa Major, north; akin to Latin *ursus* bear, Sanskrit *ṛkṣa*] (14th century)
1 *often capitalized* : of or relating to the north pole or the region near it
2 a : a bitter cold : FRIGID **b** : cold in temper or mood ⟨an *arctic* smile⟩
— **arc·ti·cal·ly** \-ti-k(ə-)lē\ *adverb*

²arc·tic \'är-tik, 'ärk-tik\ *noun* (1867)
: a rubber overshoe reaching to the ankle or above

arctic char *noun* (circa 1902)
: a Holarctic char (*Salvelinus alpinus*) of arctic waters occurring in freshwater or anadromous populations

arctic circle *noun, often A&C capitalized* (1834)
: the parallel of latitude that is approximately 66½ degrees north of the equator and that circumscribes the northern frigid zone

arctic fox *noun* (1772)
: a small migratory Holarctic fox (*Alopex lagopus*) especially of coastal arctic and alpine tundra

arctic tern *noun* (1844)
: a Holarctic tern (*Sterna paradisaea*) that breeds in arctic regions and migrates to southern Africa and South America

Arc·tu·rus \ärk-'tùr-əs, -'tyùr-\ *noun* [Latin, from Greek *Arktouros*, literally, bear watcher] : a giant fixed star of the first magnitude in Boötes

ar·cu·ate \'är-kyə-wət, -ˌwāt\ *adjective* [Latin *arcuatus*, past participle of *arcuare* to bend like a bow, from *arcus* bow] (1626)
: curved like a bow ⟨an *arcuate* cloud⟩
— **ar·cu·ate·ly** *adverb*

-ard *also* **-art** *noun suffix* [Middle English, from Old French, of Germanic origin; akin to Old High German *-hart* (in personal names such as *Gērhart* Gerard), Old English *heard* hard]
: one that is characterized by performing some action, possessing some quality, or being associated with some thing especially conspicuously or excessively ⟨bragg*art*⟩ ⟨dull*ard*⟩ ⟨poll*ard*⟩

ar·den·cy \'är-d°n(t)-sē\ *noun* (1549)
: the quality or state of being ardent

ar·dent \'är-d°nt\ *adjective* [Middle English, from Middle French, from Latin *ardent-, ardens*, present participle of *ardēre* to burn, from *ardor*] (14th century)
1 : characterized by warmth of feeling typically expressed in eager zealous support or activity
2 : FIERY, HOT ⟨an *ardent* sun⟩
3 : SHINING, GLOWING ⟨*ardent* eyes⟩
synonym see IMPASSIONED
— **ar·dent·ly** *adverb*

ardent spirits *noun plural* (1833)
: strong distilled liquors

ar·dor \'är-dər\ *noun* [Middle English *ardour*, from Middle French & Latin; Middle French, from Latin *ardor* burning, heat, ardor, from *aridus* dry — more at ARID] (14th century)

1 a : an often restless or transitory warmth of feeling ⟨the sudden *ardors* of youth⟩ **b** : extreme vigor or energy : INTENSITY **c** : ZEAL **d** : LOYALTY
2 : sexual excitement
synonym see PASSION

ar·dour *chiefly British variant of* ARDOR

ar·du·ous \'är-jə-wəs, -dyù-wəs\ *adjective* [Latin *arduus* high, steep, difficult; akin to Old Irish *ard* high] (1538)
1 a : hard to accomplish or achieve : DIFFICULT ⟨years of *arduous* training⟩ **b** : marked by great labor or effort : STRENUOUS ⟨a life of *arduous* toil —A. C. Cole⟩
2 : hard to climb : STEEP
synonym see HARD
— **ar·du·ous·ly** *adverb*
— **ar·du·ous·ness** *noun*

¹are [Middle English, from Old English *earun*; akin to Old Norse *eru, erum* are, Old English *is* is] *present 2d singular or present plural of* BE

²are \'är, 'er, 'är\ *noun* [French, from Latin *area*] (circa 1819)
— see METRIC SYSTEM table

ar·ea \'är-ē-ə, -'er-; 'ā-rē-ə\ *noun* [Latin, open space, threshing floor; perhaps akin to Latin *arēre* to be dry — more at ARID] (1538)
1 : a level piece of ground
2 : the surface included within a set of lines; *specifically* : the number of unit squares equal in measure to the surface — see METRIC SYSTEM table, WEIGHT table
3 : the scope of a concept, operation, or activity : FIELD ⟨the whole *area* of foreign policy⟩
4 : AREAWAY ⟨went down the steps into the *area* of a house —James Joyce⟩
5 : a particular extent of space or surface or one serving a special function: as **a** : a part of the surface of the body **b** : a geographic region
6 : a part of the cerebral cortex having a particular function
— **ar·e·al** \-ē-əl\ *adjective*
— **ar·e·al·ly** \-ə-lē\ *adverb*

area code *noun* (1961)
: a 3-digit number that identifies each telephone service area in a country (as the U.S. or Canada)

ar·ea·way \'är-ē-ə-ˌwā, 'er-; 'ā-rē-\ *noun* (1899)
: a sunken space affording access, air, and light to a basement

are·ca \ə-'rē-kə, 'ar-i-kə\ *noun* [New Latin, from Portuguese, from Malayalam *aṭakka*] (1510)
: any of several tropical Asian palms (*Areca* or related genera); *especially* : BETEL PALM

arec·o·line \ə-'re-kə-ˌlēn\ *noun* [International Scientific Vocabulary *areca* + ¹-*ol* + ²-*ine*] (1899)
: a toxic parasympathomimetic alkaloid $C_8H_{13}NO_2$ that is used as a veterinary anthelmintic and occurs naturally in betel nuts

are·na \ə-'rē-nə\ *noun* [Latin *harena, arena* sand, sandy place] (1600)
1 : an area in a Roman amphitheater for gladiatorial combats
2 a : an enclosed area used for public entertainment **b** : a building containing an arena
3 a : a sphere of interest, activity, or competition ⟨the political *arena*⟩ **b** : a place or situation for controversy ⟨in the public *arena*⟩

ar·e·na·ceous \ˌar-ə-'nā-shəs\ *adjective* [Latin *arenaceus*, from *arena*] (1646)
1 : resembling, made of, or containing sand or sandy particles
2 : growing in sandy places

arena theater *noun* (1943)
: THEATER-IN-THE-ROUND

ar·e·nic·o·lous \ˌar-ə-'ni-kə-ləs\ *adjective* [Latin *arena* + English -*i*- + -*colous*] (circa 1859)
: living, burrowing, or growing in sand

aren't \'ärnt, 'är-ənt\ (1810)
1 : are not
2 : am not — used in questions

ar·eo·cen·tric \ˌar-ē-ō-'sen-trik\ *adjective* [Greek *Areios* of Ares, from *Arēs*] (1877)
: having or relating to the planet Mars as a center

are·o·la \ə-'rē-ə-lə\ *noun, plural* **-lae** \-ˌlē\ *or* **-las** [New Latin, from Latin, small open space, diminutive of *area*] (1664)
: a small area between things or about something; *especially* : a colored ring (as about the nipple, a vesicle, or a pustule)
— **are·o·lar** \-lər\ *adjective*
— **are·o·late** \-lət\ *adjective*

ar·e·ole \'ar-ē-ˌōl\ *noun* (circa 1934)
: a small pit or cavity

Ar·e·op·a·gite \ˌar-ē-'ä-pə-ˌgīt, -ˌjīt\ *noun* (14th century)
: a member of the Areopagus
— **Ar·e·op·a·git·ic** \-ˌä-pə-'ji-tik\ *adjective*

Ar·e·op·a·gus \ˌar-ē-'ä-pə-gəs\ *noun* [Latin, from Greek *Areios pagos*, from *Areios pagos* (literally, hill of Ares), a hill in Athens where the tribunal met] (1586)
: the supreme tribunal of Athens

Ar·es \'ar-(ˌ)ēz, 'er-\ *noun* [Greek *Arēs*]
: the Greek god of war — compare MARS

arête \ə-'rāt\ *noun* [French, literally, fish bone, from Late Latin *arista*, from Latin, beard of grain] (1838)
: a sharp-crested ridge in rugged mountains

Ar·e·thu·sa \ˌar-ə-'thü-zə, -'thyü-\ *noun* [Latin, from Greek *Arethousa*]
: a wood nymph who is changed into a spring while fleeing the advances of the river-god Alpheus

ar·ga·li \'är-gə-lē\ *noun* [Mongolian] (circa 1774)
: a large wild sheep (*Ovis ammon*) of Asia that is noted for its large horns

Ar·gand diagram \ˌär-'gän-, -'gan-\ *noun* [Jean Robert *Argand* (died 1825) Swiss mathematician] (1908)
: a system of rectangular coordinates in which the complex number $x + iy$ is represented by the point whose coordinates are x and y

ar·gent \'är-jənt\ *noun* [Middle English, from Middle French & Latin; Middle French, from Latin *argentum;* akin to Greek *argyros* silver, *argos* white, Sanskrit *rajata* whitish, silvery] (15th century)
1 *archaic* : the metal silver; *also* : WHITENESS
2 : the heraldic color silver or white
— **argent** *adjective*

ar·gen·tif·er·ous \ˌär-jən-'ti-f(ə-)rəs\ *adjective* (1801)
: containing silver

¹ar·gen·tine \'är-jən-ˌtīn, -ˌtēn\ *adjective* (15th century)
: SILVER, SILVERY

²argentine *noun* (1577)
: SILVER; *also* : any of various similar materials

ar·gen·tite \'är-jən-ˌtīt\ *noun* (circa 1837)
: native silver sulfide having a metallic luster and dark lead-gray color and constituting a valuable ore of silver

ar·gil \'är-jəl\ *noun* [Middle English, from Latin *argilla*, from Greek *argillos;* akin to Greek *argos* white] (14th century)
: CLAY; *especially* : POTTER'S CLAY

ar·gil·la·ceous \ˌär-jə-'lā-shəs\ *adjective* (circa 1731)
: of, relating to, or containing clay or clay minerals : CLAYEY

ar·gil·lite \'är-jə-ˌlīt\ *noun* (1795)
: a compact argillaceous rock cemented by silica and having no slaty cleavage

ar·gi·nase \'är-jə-ˌnās, -ˌnāz\ *noun* [International Scientific Vocabulary] (1904)
: a crystalline enzyme that converts naturally occurring arginine into ornithine and urea

ar·gi·nine \'är-jə-ˌnēn\ *noun* [German *Arginin*] (1886)
: a crystalline basic amino acid $C_6H_{14}N_4O_2$ derived from guanidine

Ar·give \'är-ˌjīv, -ˌgīv\ *adjective* [Latin *Argivus,* from Greek *Argeios,* literally, of Argos, from *Argos* city-state of ancient Greece] (1598)
: of or relating to the Greeks or Greece and especially the Achaean city of Argos or the surrounding territory of Argolis
— Argive *noun*

ar·gle–bar·gle \ˌär-gəl-'bär-gəl\ *noun* [reduplication of Scots & English *argle,* alteration of *argue*] (1872)
chiefly British **:** ARGY-BARGY

Ar·go \'är-(ˌ)gō\ *noun* [Latin (genitive *Argus*), from Greek *Argō*]
: a large constellation in the southern hemisphere lying principally between Canis Major and the Southern Cross

ar·gol \'är-ˌgȯl\ *noun* [Middle English *argoile,* from Anglo-French *argoil*] (14th century)
: crude tartar deposited in wine casks during aging

ar·gon \'är-ˌgän\ *noun* [Greek, neuter of *argos* idle, lazy, from *a-* + *ergon* work; from its relative inertness — more at WORK] (1894)
: a colorless odorless inert gaseous element found in the air and in volcanic gases and used especially in welding, lasers, and electric bulbs — see ELEMENT table

ar·go·naut \'är-gə-ˌnȯt, -ˌnät\ *noun* [Latin *Argonautes,* from Greek *Argonautēs,* from *Argō,* ship in which the Argonauts sailed + *nautēs* sailor — more at NAUTICAL] (14th century)
1 a *capitalized* **:** any of a band of heroes sailing with Jason in quest of the Golden Fleece **b** **:** an adventurer engaged in a quest
2 : PAPER NAUTILUS

ar·go·sy \'är-gə-sē\ *noun, plural* **-sies** [modification of Italian *ragusea* Ragusan vessel, from *Ragusa,* Dalmatia (now Dubrovnik, Croatia)] (1587)
1 : a large ship; *especially* **:** a large merchant ship ⟨three of your argosies are . . . come to harbor —Shakespeare⟩
2 : a fleet of ships
3 : a rich supply ⟨an *argosy* of railway folklore —F. P. Donovan⟩

ar·got \'är-gət, -(ˌ)gō\ *noun* [French] (1860)
: an often more or less secret vocabulary and idiom peculiar to a particular group ⟨shoved into a taxi by a porter whose *argot* I couldn't understand —Allen Tate⟩

ar·gu·able \'är-gyü-ə-bəl\ *adjective* (circa 1611)
1 : open to argument, dispute, or question
2 : that can be plausibly or convincingly argued

ar·gu·ably \'är-gyü-(ə-)blē\ *adverb* (1890)
: it can be argued ⟨the word is *arguably* useful⟩ ⟨*arguably* the busiest airport in the world⟩

ar·gue \'är-(ˌ)gyü\ *verb* **ar·gued; ar·gu·ing** [Middle English, from Middle French *arguer* to accuse, reason & Latin *arguere* to demonstrate, prove; Middle French *arguer,* from Latin *argutare* to prate, frequentative of *arguere;* akin to Hittite *arkuwai-* to plead, respond] (14th century)
intransitive verb
1 : to give reasons for or against something
: REASON
2 : to contend or disagree in words **:** DISPUTE
transitive verb
1 : to give evidence of **:** INDICATE
2 : to consider the pros and cons of **:** DISCUSS
3 : to prove or try to prove by giving reasons
: MAINTAIN
4 : to persuade by giving reasons **:** INDUCE
synonym see DISCUSS
— ar·gu·er \-gyə-wər\ *noun*

ar·gu·fy \'är-gyə-ˌfī\ *verb* **-fied; -fy·ing** (1771)
transitive verb
: DISPUTE, DEBATE
intransitive verb
: WRANGLE
— ar·gu·fi·er \-ˌfī(-ə)r\ *noun*

ar·gu·ment \'är-gyə-mənt\ *noun* [Middle English, from Middle French, from Latin *argumentum,* from *arguere*] (14th century)
1 *obsolete* **:** an outward sign **:** INDICATION
2 a : a reason given in proof or rebuttal **b** **:** discourse intended to persuade
3 a : the act or process of arguing **:** ARGUMENTATION **b** **:** a coherent series of statements leading from a premise to a conclusion **c** **:** QUARREL, DISAGREEMENT
4 : an abstract or summary especially of a literary work ⟨a later editor added an *argument* to the poem⟩
5 : the subject matter especially of a literary work
6 a : one of the independent variables upon whose value that of a function depends **b** **:** a substantive (as the direct object of a transitive verb) that is required by a predicate in grammar **c** **:** the angle assigned to a complex number when it is plotted in a complex plane using polar coordinates — called also *amplitude;* compare ABSOLUTE VALUE 2

ar·gu·men·ta·tion \ˌär-gyə-mən-'tā-shən, -ˌmen-\ *noun* (15th century)
1 : the act or process of forming reasons and of drawing conclusions and applying them to a case in discussion
2 : DEBATE, DISCUSSION

ar·gu·men·ta·tive \ˌär-gyə-'men-tə-tiv\ *also* **ar·gu·men·tive** \-'men-tiv\ *adjective* (15th century)
1 : characterized by argument **:** CONTROVERSIAL
2 : given to argument **:** DISPUTATIOUS
— ar·gu·men·ta·tive·ly *adverb*

ar·gu·men·tum \ˌär-gyə-'men-təm\ *noun, plural* **-men·ta** \-'men-tə\ [Latin] (1690)
: ARGUMENT 3b

Ar·gus \'är-gəs\ *noun* [Latin, from Greek *Argos*]
1 : a hundred-eyed monster of Greek mythology
2 : a watchful guardian

Ar·gus–eyed \'är-gəs-ˌīd\ *adjective* (1603)
: vigilantly observant

ar·gy–bar·gy \ˌär-jē-'bär-jē, ˌär-gē-'bär-gē\ *noun* [reduplication of Scots & English dialect *argy,* alteration of *argue*] (1887)
chiefly British **:** a lively discussion **:** ARGUMENT, DISPUTE

ar·gyle *also* **ar·gyll** \'är-ˌgī(ə)l, är-'\ *noun, often capitalized* [*Argyle, Argyll,* branch of the Scottish clan of Campbell, from whose tartan the design was adapted] (1899)
: a geometric knitting pattern of varicolored diamonds in solid and outline shapes on a single background color; *also* **:** a sock knit in this pattern

ar·hat \'är-(ˌ)hət\ *noun* [Sanskrit, from present participle of *arhati* he deserves; akin to Greek *alphein* to gain] (1870)
: a Buddhist who has reached the stage of enlightenment
— ar·hat·ship \-ˌship\ *noun*

argyle

aria \'är-ē-ə\ *noun* [Italian, literally, atmospheric air, modification of Latin *aer*] (circa 1724)
1 : AIR, MELODY, TUNE; *specifically* **:** an accompanied elaborate melody sung (as in an opera) by a single voice
2 : a striking solo performance (as in a movie)

Ar·i·ad·ne \ˌar-ē-'ad-nē\ *noun* [Latin, from Greek *Ariadnē*]
: a daughter of Minos who helps Theseus escape the labyrinth

¹Ar·i·an \'ar-ē-ən, 'er-\ *adjective* (14th century)
: of or relating to Arius or his doctrines especially that the Son is not of the same substance as the Father but was created as an agent for creating the world
— Ar·i·an·ism \-ə-ˌni-zəm\ *noun*

²Arian *noun* (14th century)
: a supporter of Arian doctrines

³Ar·i·an \'er-ē-ən, 'ar-\ *noun* (1917)
: ARIES 2b

-ar·i·an *noun suffix* [Latin *-arius* -ary]
1 : believer ⟨necessit*arian*⟩ **:** advocate ⟨latitudin*arian*⟩
2 : producer ⟨disciplin*arian*⟩

ar·i·bo·fla·vin·osis \ˌā-ˌrī-bə-ˌflā-və-'nō-səs\ *noun* [New Latin] (1939)
: a deficiency disease due to inadequate intake of riboflavin and characterized by sores on the mouth

ar·id \'ar-əd\ *adjective* [French or Latin; French *aride,* from Latin *aridus,* from *arēre* to be dry; akin to Sanskrit *āsa* ash, Old English *asce*] (1652)
1 : excessively dry; *specifically* **:** having insufficient rainfall to support agriculture
2 : lacking in interest and life **:** JEJUNE
— arid·i·ty \ə-'ri-də-tē, a-\ *noun*
— ar·id·ness \'ar-əd-nəs\ *noun*

Ar·i·el \'ar-ē-əl, 'er-\ *noun*
: a prankish spirit in Shakespeare's *The Tempest*

Ar·i·es \'er-ˌēz, 'ar-, -ē-ˌēz\ *noun* [Latin (genitive *Arietis*), literally, ram; perhaps akin to Greek *eriphos* kid, Old Irish *heirp* she-goat]
1 : a constellation between Pisces and Taurus pictured as a ram
2 a : the first sign of the zodiac in astrology — see ZODIAC table **b** **:** one born under the sign of Aries

ari·et·ta \ˌär-ē-'e-tə, ˌar-\ *noun* [Italian, diminutive of *aria*] (circa 1724)
: a short aria

aright \ə-'rīt\ *adverb* [Middle English, from Old English *ariht,* from ¹*a-* + *riht* right] (before 12th century)
: RIGHT, CORRECTLY ⟨if I remember *aright*⟩

Arik·a·ra \ə-'ri-kə-rə\ *noun, plural* **Arikara** (1811)
1 : a member of an American Indian people of the Missouri River Valley in North Dakota
2 : the language of the Arikara

ar·il \'ar-əl\ *noun* [probably from New Latin *arillus,* from Medieval Latin, raisin, grape seed] (1794)
: an exterior covering or appendage of some seeds (as of the yew) that develops after fertilization as an outgrowth from the ovule stalk
— ar·il·late \'ar-ə-ˌlāt\ *adjective*

ari·o·so \ˌär-ē-'ō-(ˌ)sō, -(ˌ)zō\ *noun, plural* **-sos** *also* **-si** \-(ˌ)sē, -(ˌ)zē\ [Italian, from *aria*] (circa 1724)
: a musical passage or composition having a mixture of free recitative and metrical song

arise \ə-'rīz\ *intransitive verb* **arose** \-'rōz\; **aris·en** \-'ri-z°n\; **aris·ing** \-'rī-ziŋ\ [Middle English, from Old English *ārīsan,* from *ā-,* perfective prefix + *rīsan* to rise — more at ABIDE] (before 12th century)
1 : to get up **:** RISE
2 a : to originate from a source **b** **:** to come into being or to attention
3 : ASCEND
synonym see SPRING

aris·ta \ə-'ris-tə\ *noun, plural* **-tae** \-(ˌ)tē, -ˌtī\ *or* **-tas** [New Latin, from Latin, beard of grain] (1691)
: a bristlelike structure or appendage
— aris·tate \-ˌtāt\ *adjective*

aris·to \ə-'ris-(ˌ)tō\ *noun, plural* **-tos** [by shortening] (1864)
: ARISTOCRAT

ar·is·toc·ra·cy \ˌar-ə-'stä-krə-sē\ *noun, plural* **-cies** [Middle French & Late Latin; Middle French *aristocratie,* from Late Latin *aristocratia,* from Greek *aristokratia,* from *aristos* best + *-kratia* -cracy] (1561)
1 : government by the best individuals or by a small privileged class

2 a : a government in which power is vested in a minority consisting of those believed to be best qualified **b :** a state with such a government
3 : a governing body or upper class usually made up of an hereditary nobility
4 : the aggregate of those believed to be superior

aris·to·crat \ə-'ris-tə-ˌkrat, a-; 'ar-ə-stə-\ *noun* (1789)
1 : a member of an aristocracy; *especially* **:** NOBLE
2 a : one who has the bearing and viewpoint typical of the aristocracy **b :** one who favors aristocracy
3 : one believed to be superior of its kind ⟨the *aristocrat* of Southern resorts —*Southern Living*⟩

aris·to·crat·ic \ə-ˌris-tə-'kra-tik, (ˌ)a-ˌris-tə-, ˌar-ə-stə-\ *adjective* [Middle French *aristocratique,* from Medieval Latin *aristocraticus,* from Greek *aristokratikos,* from *aristokratia*] (1602)
1 : belonging to, having the qualities of, or favoring aristocracy
2 a : socially exclusive ⟨an *aristocratic* neighborhood⟩ **b :** SNOBBISH
— **aris·to·crat·i·cal·ly** \-ti-k(ə-)lē\ *adverb*
Ar·is·to·te·lian *also* **Ar·is·to·te·lean** \ˌar-ə-stə-'tēl-yən\ *adjective* [Latin *Aristoteles* Aristotle, from Greek *Aristotelēs*] (1607)
: of or relating to the Greek philosopher Aristotle or his philosophy
— **Aristotelian** *noun*
— **Ar·is·to·te·lian·ism** \-yə-ˌni-zəm\ *noun*
arith·me·tic \ə-'rith-mə-ˌtik\ *noun* [Middle English *arsmetrik,* from Old French *arismetique,* from Latin *arithmetica,* from Greek *arithmētikē,* from feminine of *arithmētikos* arithmetical, from *arithmein* to count, from *arithmos* number; akin to Old English *rīm* number, and perhaps to Greek *arariskein* to fit] (15th century)
1 a : a branch of mathematics that deals usually with the nonnegative real numbers including sometimes the transfinite cardinals and with the application of the operations of addition, subtraction, multiplication, and division to them **b :** a treatise on arithmetic
2 : COMPUTATION, CALCULATION
— **ar·ith·met·ic** \ˌar-ith-'me-tik\ *or* **ar·ith·met·i·cal** \-ti-kəl\ *adjective*
— **ar·ith·met·i·cal·ly** \-ti-k(ə-)lē\ *adverb*
— **arith·me·ti·cian** \ə-ˌrith-mə-'ti-shən\ *noun*
arithmetic mean *noun* (1767)
: a value that is computed by dividing the sum of a set of terms by the number of terms
arithmetic progression *noun* (1594)
: a progression (as 3, 5, 7, 9) in which the difference between any term and its predecessor is constant
-arium *noun suffix, plural* **-ariums** *or* **-aria** [Latin, from neuter of *-arius* -ary]
: thing or place relating to or connected with ⟨planet*arium*⟩
ark \'ärk\ *noun* [Middle English, from Old English *arc,* from Latin *arca* chest; akin to Latin *arcēre* to hold off, defend, Greek *arkein,* Hittite *hark-* to have, hold] (before 12th century)
1 a : a boat or ship held to resemble that in which Noah and his family were preserved from the Flood **b :** something that affords protection and safety
2 a : the sacred chest representing to the Hebrews the presence of God among them **b :** a repository traditionally in or against the wall of a synagogue for the scrolls of the Torah
ar·kose \'är-ˌkōs, -ˌkōz\ *noun* [French] (1839)
: a sandstone characterized by feldspar fragments that is derived from granite or gneiss which has disintegrated rapidly
— **ar·ko·sic** \(ˌ)är-'kō-sik, -zik\ *adjective*
¹arm \'ärm\ *noun* [Middle English, from Old English *earm;* akin to Latin *armus* shoulder, Sanskrit *īrma* arm] (before 12th century)

1 : a human upper limb; *especially* **:** the part between the shoulder and the wrist
2 : something like or corresponding to an arm: as **a :** the forelimb of a vertebrate **b :** a limb of an invertebrate animal **c :** a branch or lateral shoot of a plant **d :** a slender part of a structure, machine, or an instrument projecting from a main part, axis, or fulcrum **e :** the end of a ship's yard; *also* **:** the part of an anchor from the crown to the fluke — see ANCHOR illustration **f :** any of the usually two parts of a chromosome lateral to the centromere
3 : an inlet of water (as from the sea)
4 : a narrow extension of a larger area, mass, or group
5 : POWER, MIGHT ⟨the long *arm* of the law⟩
6 : a support (as on a chair) for the elbow and forearm
7 : SLEEVE
8 : the ability to throw or pitch a baseball well; *also* **:** a player having such ability
9 : a functional division of a group, organization, institution, or activity ⟨the logistical *arm* of the air force⟩
— **arm·less** \'ärm-ləs\ *adjective*
— **arm·like** \-ˌlīk\ *adjective*
— **arm in arm :** with arms linked together ⟨walked down the street *arm in arm*⟩
²arm *verb* [Middle English *armen,* from Old French *armer,* from Latin *armare,* from *arma* weapons, tools; akin to Latin *ars* skill, Greek *harmos* joint, *arariskein* to fit] (12th century)
transitive verb
1 : to furnish or equip with weapons
2 : to furnish with something that strengthens or protects
3 : to fortify morally
4 : to equip or ready for action or operation ⟨*arm* a bomb⟩
intransitive verb
: to prepare oneself for struggle or resistance
³arm *noun, often attributive* [Middle English *armes* (plural) weapons, from Old French, from Latin *arma*] (13th century)
1 a : a means (as a weapon) of offense or defense; *especially* **:** FIREARM **b :** a combat branch (as of an army) **c :** an organized branch of national defense (as the navy)
2 *plural* **a :** the hereditary heraldic devices of a family **b :** heraldic devices adopted by a government
3 *plural* **a :** active hostilities **:** WARFARE **b :** military service
— **up in arms :** aroused and ready to undertake hostilities
ar·ma·da \är-'mä-də, -'mā- *also* -'ma-\ *noun* [Spanish, from Medieval Latin *armata* army, fleet, from Latin, feminine of *armatus,* past participle of *armare* to arm, from *arma*] (1533)
1 : a fleet of warships
2 : a large force or group usually of moving things ⟨an *armada* of fishing boats⟩
ar·ma·dil·lo \ˌär-mə-'di-(ˌ)lō\ *noun, plural* **-los** [Spanish, from diminutive of *armado* armed one, from Latin *armatus*] (1577)
: any of a family (Dasypodidae) of burrowing edentate mammals found from the southern U.S. to Argentina and having the body and head encased in an armor of small bony plates

armadillo

Ar·ma·ged·don \ˌär-mə-'ge-dᵊn\ *noun* [Greek *Armageddōn, Harmagedōn,* scene of the battle foretold in Revelation 16:14–16] (1534)
1 a : the site or time of a final and conclusive battle between the forces of good and evil **b :** the battle taking place at Armageddon
2 : a usually vast decisive conflict or confrontation

Ar·ma·gnac \'är-mən-ˌyak\ *noun* [French, from *Armagnac,* region in southwest France] (1850)
: a brandy produced in the Gers department of France
ar·ma·ment \'är-mə-mənt *also* 'ärm-mənt\ *noun* [French *armement,* from Latin *armamenta* (plural) utensils, military or naval equipment, from *armare*] (1699)
1 : a military or naval force
2 a : the aggregate of a nation's military strength **b :** WEAPONS, ARMS
3 : the process of preparing for war
ar·ma·men·tar·i·um \ˌär-mə-ˌmen-'ter-ē-əm, -mən-\ *noun, plural* **-tar·ia** \-ē-ə\ [Latin, armory, from *armamenta*] (circa 1860)
1 : the equipment and methods used especially in medicine
2 : matter available or utilized for an undertaking or field of activity ⟨a whole *armamentarium* of devices to create an illusion of real life —Kenneth Rexroth⟩
arm and a leg *noun* (1967)
: an exorbitant price
ar·ma·ture \'är-mə-ˌchur, -chər, -ˌtyur, -ˌtur\ *noun* [Latin *armatura* armor, equipment, from *armatus*] (15th century)
1 : an organ or structure (as teeth or thorns) for offense or defense
2 a : a piece of soft iron or steel that connects the poles of a magnet or of adjacent magnets **b :** a usually rotating part of an electric machine (as a generator or motor) which consists essentially of coils of wire around a metal core and in which electric current is induced or in which the input current interacts with a magnetic field to produce torque **c :** the movable part of an electromagnetic device (as a loudspeaker) **d :** a framework used by a sculptor to support a figure being modeled in a plastic material **e :** FRAMEWORK 1b ⟨the *armature* of the book derives from fourteenth century England —Stanley Kauffmann⟩
arm·band \'ärm-ˌband\ *noun* (1797)
: a band usually worn around the upper part of a sleeve for identification or in mourning
¹arm·chair \'ärm-ˌcher, -ˌchar\ *noun* (1633)
: a chair with armrests
²armchair *adjective* (1886)
1 : remote from direct dealing with problems **:** theoretical rather than practical ⟨*armchair* strategists⟩
2 : sharing vicariously in another's experiences ⟨an *armchair* traveler⟩
¹armed \'ärmd\ *adjective* (13th century)
1 a : furnished with weapons **b :** furnished with something that provides security, strength, or efficacy
2 : marked by the maintenance of armed forces in readiness
²armed *adjective* (1606)
: having an arm or arms especially of a specified kind or number — usually used in combination ⟨long-*armed*⟩ ⟨two-*armed*⟩
armed forces *noun plural* (1943)
: the combined military, naval, and air forces of a nation — called also *armed services*
Ar·me·nian \är-'mē-nē-ən, -nyən\ *noun* (1537)
1 : a member of a people dwelling chiefly in Armenia and neighboring areas (as Turkey or Azerbaijan)
2 : the Indo-European language of the Armenians — see INDO-EUROPEAN LANGUAGES table
3 : a member of the Armenian church established by Saint Gregory the Illuminator that adheres to the decisions of the first three ecumenical councils
— **Armenian** *adjective*
arm·ful \'ärm-ˌful\ *noun, plural* **arm·fuls** \-ˌfulz\ *or* **arms·ful** \'ärmz-ˌful\ (1579)
: as much as the arm or arms can hold
arm·hole \'ärm-ˌhōl\ *noun* (circa 1775)
: an opening for the arm in a garment
ar·mi·ger \'är-mi-jər\ *noun* [Medieval Latin,

from Latin, armor-bearer, from *armiger* bearing arms, from *arma* arms + *gerere* to carry] (1762)
1 : SQUIRE
2 : one entitled to bear heraldic arms
— **ar·mig·er·al** \är-'mi-jə-rəl\ *adjective*
ar·mig·er·ous \är-'mi-jər-əs\ *adjective* (circa 1731)
: bearing heraldic arms
ar·mil·la·ry sphere \'är-mə-,ler-ē-, är-'mi-lə-rē-\ *noun* [French *sphère armillaire,* from Medieval Latin *armilla,* from Latin, bracelet, iron ring, from *armus* shoulder — more at ARM] (1664)
: an old astronomical instrument composed of rings showing the positions of important circles of the celestial sphere
Ar·min·i·an \är-'mi-nē-ən\ *adjective* (1618)
: of or relating to Arminius or his doctrines opposing the absolute predestination of strict Calvinism and maintaining the possibility of salvation for all
— **Arminian** *noun*
— **Ar·min·i·an·ism** \-nē-ə-,ni-zəm\ *noun*
ar·mi·stice \'är-mə-stəs\ *noun* [French or New Latin; French, from New Latin *armistitium,* from Latin *arma* + *-stitium* (as in *solstitium* solstice)] (circa 1707)
: temporary suspension of hostilities by agreement between the opponents **:** TRUCE
Armistice Day *noun* [from the armistice terminating World War I on November 11, 1918] (1919)
: VETERANS DAY — used before the official adoption of *Veterans Day* in 1954
arm·let \'ärm-lət\ *noun* (1535)
1 : a band (as of cloth or metal) worn around the upper arm
2 : a small arm (as of the sea)
arm·load \'ärm-,lōd\ *noun* (1906)
: ARMFUL
arm·lock \-,läk\ *noun* (1905)
: HAMMERLOCK
ar·moire \ärm-'wär, *Southern also* 'är-mər\ *noun* [Middle French, from Old French *armaire,* from Latin *armarium,* from *arma*] (1571)
: a usually tall cupboard or wardrobe
ar·mor \'är-mər\ *noun* [Middle English *armure,* from Old French, from Latin *armatura* — more at ARMATURE] (13th century)
1 : defensive covering for the body; *especially* **:** covering (as of metal) used in combat
2 : a quality or circumstance that affords protection (the *armor* of prosperity)
3 : a protective outer layer (as of a ship, a plant or animal, or a cable)
4 : armored forces and vehicles (as tanks)
— **armor** *transitive verb*
— **ar·mored** \-mərd\ *adjective*
— **ar·mor·less** \-mər-ləs\ *adjective*
armored scale *noun* (circa 1903)
: any of a family (Diaspididae) of scale insects having a firm covering of wax best developed in the female
ar·mor·er \'är-mər-ər\ *noun* (14th century)
1 : one that makes armor or arms
2 : one that repairs, assembles, and tests firearms
ar·mo·ri·al \är-'mōr-ē-əl, -'mȯr-\ *adjective* [*armory* (heraldry)] (1610)
: of, relating to, or bearing heraldic arms
— **ar·mo·ri·al·ly** \-ē-ə-lē\ *adverb*

armor 1:
1 helmet, 2 gorget, 3 shoulder piece, 4 pallette, 5 breastplate, 6 brassard, 7 elbow piece, 8 skirt of tasses, 9 tuille, 10 gauntlet, 11 cuisse, 12 knee piece, 13 jambeau, 14 solleret

Ar·mor·i·can \är-'mȯr-i-kən, -'mär-\ *or* **Ar·mor·ic** \-ik\ *noun* (circa 1645)
: a native or inhabitant of Armorica; *especially* **:** BRETON
— **Armorican** *or* **Armoric** *adjective*
ar·mory \'ärm-rē, 'är-mə-\ *noun, plural* **ar·mor·ies** (14th century)
1 a : a supply of arms for defense or attack **b :** a collection of available resources
2 : a place where arms and military equipment are stored; *especially* **:** one used for training reserve military personnel
3 : a place where arms are manufactured
ar·mour, ar·moury *chiefly British variant of* ARMOR, ARMORY
arm·pit \'ärm-,pit\ *noun* (14th century)
1 : the hollow beneath the junction of the arm and shoulder
2 : the least desirable place **:** PIT (77th Street Station . . . was the *armpit* of detective duty —Joseph Wambaugh)
arm·rest \-,rest\ *noun* (circa 1889)
: a support for the arm
arm's length *noun* (circa 1909)
1 : a distance discouraging personal contact or familiarity (kept people at *arm's length*)
2 : the condition or fact that the parties to a transaction are independent and on an equal footing
— **arm's–length** *adjective*
arm–twist·ing \-,twis-tiŋ\ *noun* (1948)
: the use of direct personal pressure in order to achieve a desired end (for all the *arm-twisting,* the . . . vote on the measure was unexpectedly tight —*Newsweek*)
— **arm–twist** \-,twist\ *verb*
arm wrestling *noun* (1973)
: a form of wrestling in which two opponents sit face to face gripping usually their right hands, set corresponding elbows firmly on a surface (as a tabletop), and attempt to force each other's arm down — called also *Indian wrestling*
ar·my \'är-mē\ *noun, plural* **armies** [Middle English *armee,* from Middle French, from Medieval Latin *armata* — more at ARMADA] (14th century)
1 a : a large organized body of armed personnel trained for war especially on land **b :** a unit capable of independent action and consisting usually of a headquarters, two or more corps, and auxiliary troops **c** *often capitalized* **:** the complete military organization of a nation for land warfare
2 : a great multitude (an *army* of bicycles —Norm Fruchter)
3 : a body of persons organized to advance a cause
army ant *noun* (1874)
: any of a subfamily (Dorylinae) of aggressive nomadic tropical ants that prey on insects and spiders
ar·my·worm \'är-mē-,wərm\ *noun* (1816)
: any of numerous moths whose larvae travel in multitudes from field to field destroying grass, grain, and other crops; *especially* **:** the common armyworm (*Pseudaletia unipuncta*) of the northern U.S.
ar·ni·ca \'är-ni-kə\ *noun* [New Latin] (circa 1753)
: any of a genus (*Arnica*) of composite herbs including some with bright yellow ray flowers
ar·oid \'ar-,ȯid, 'er-\ *adjective* [New Latin *Arum*] (circa 1890)
: of or relating to the arum family
— **aroid** *noun*
aroint \ə-'rȯint\ *verb imperative* [origin unknown] (1605)
archaic **:** BEGONE (*aroint* thee, witch —Shakespeare)
aro·ma \ə-'rō-mə\ *noun* [Middle English *aromat* spice, from Old French, from Latin *aromat-, aroma,* from Greek *arōmat-, arōma*] (1814)
1 a : a distinctive pervasive and usually pleasant or savory smell; *broadly* **:** ODOR **b :** the

odor of a wine imparted by the grapes from which it is made
2 : a distinctive quality or atmosphere **:** FLAVOR (the *aroma* of enjoyment —Stella D. Gibbons)
synonym see SMELL
aro·ma·ther·a·py \ə-,rō-mə-'ther-ə-pē\ *noun* [French *aromathérapie,* from Latin *aroma* + French *thérapie* therapy] (1969)
: massage of the body and especially of the face with a preparation of fragrant essential oils extracted from herbs, flowers, and fruits
— **aro·ma·ther·a·pist** \-pist\ *noun*
¹ar·o·mat·ic \,ar-ə-'ma-tik\ *adjective* (14th century)
1 : of, relating to, or having aroma: **a :** FRAGRANT **b :** having a strong smell **c :** having a distinctive quality
2 *of an organic compound* **:** characterized by increased chemical stability resulting from the delocalization of electrons in a ring system (as benzene) containing usually multiple conjugated double bonds — compare ALICYCLIC, ALIPHATIC
synonym see ODOROUS
— **ar·o·mat·i·cal·ly** \-ti-k(ə-)lē\ *adverb*
— **aro·ma·tic·i·ty** \,ar-ə-mə-'ti-sə-tē, ə-,rō-mə-\ *noun*
²aromatic *noun* (15th century)
1 : an aromatic plant or plant part; *especially* **:** an aromatic herb or spice
2 : an aromatic organic compound
aro·ma·tize \ə-'rō-mə-,tīz\ *transitive verb* **-tized; -tiz·ing** (15th century)
1 : to make aromatic **:** FLAVOR
2 : to convert into one or more aromatic compounds
— **aro·ma·ti·za·tion** \-,rō-mə-tə-'zā-shən\ *noun*
arose *past of* ARISE
¹around \ə-'raund\ *adverb* [Middle English, from ¹*a-* + ²*round*] (14th century)
1 a : in a circle or in circumference (the wheel goes *around*) (a tree five feet *around*) **b :** in, along, or through a circuit (the road goes *around* by the lake)
2 a : on all or various sides **:** in every or any direction (papers lying *around*) (nothing for miles *around*) **b :** in close from all sides so as to surround (people crowded *around*) **c :** in or near one's present place or situation (wait *around* awhile)
3 a : here and there **:** from one place to another (travels *around* on business) **b :** to a particular place (come *around* for dinner)
4 a : in rotation or succession (another winter comes *around*) **b :** from beginning to end **:** THROUGH (mild the year *around*) **c :** in order (the other way *around*)
5 : in or to an opposite direction or position (turn *around*)
6 : with some approach to exactness **:** APPROXIMATELY (cost *around* $5)
²around *preposition* (14th century)
1 a : on all sides of **b :** so as to encircle or enclose (seated *around* the table) **c :** so as to avoid or get past **:** on or to another side of (find a way *around* their objections) (went *around* the lake) (*around* the corner) **d :** NEAR (lives *around* Chicago) (*around* the turn of the century)
2 : in all directions outward from (look *around* you)
3 : here and there in or throughout (barnstorming *around* the country)
4 : so as to have a center or basis in (a society organized *around* kinship ties)
³around *adjective* (1849)
1 : ABOUT 1 (has been up and *around* for two days)

2 : being in existence, evidence, or circulation 〈the most intelligent of the artists *around* today —R. M. Coates〉
— **been around :** gone through many varied experiences **:** become worldly-wise
around–the–clock *adjective* (1943)
: being in effect, continuing, or lasting 24 hours a day **:** CONSTANT
arouse \ə-ˈraůz\ *verb* **aroused; arous·ing** [*a-* (as in *arise*) + *rouse*] (1593)
transitive verb
1 : to awaken from sleep
2 : to rouse or stimulate to action or to physiological readiness for activity **:** EXCITE 〈the book *aroused* debate〉
intransitive verb
: to awake from sleep **:** STIR
— **arous·al** \ə-ˈraů-zəl\ *noun*
ar·peg·gi·ate \är-ˈpe-jē-ˌāt\ *transitive verb* **-at·ed; -at·ing** (1953)
: to play (as a chord or passage) in arpeggio
ar·peg·gio \är-ˈpe-jē-ˌō, -ˈpe-jō\ *noun, plural* **-gios** [Italian, from *arpeggiare* to play on the harp, from *arpa* harp, of Germanic origin; akin to Old High German *harpha* harp] (circa 1724)
1 : production of the tones of a chord in succession and not simultaneously
2 : a chord played in arpeggio
ar·pent \är-ˈpäⁿ\ *noun, plural* **ar·pents** \-ˈpäⁿ(z)\ [Middle French] (1580)
1 : any of various old French units of land area; *especially* **:** one used in French sections of Canada and the U.S. equal to about 0.85 acre (0.34 hectare)
2 : a unit of length equal to one side of a square arpent
ar·que·bus \ˈär-kwi-(ˌ)bəs, -kə-bəs\ *variant of* HARQUEBUS
ar·rack \ˈar-ək, ə-ˈrak\ *noun* [Arabic *ʽaraq* sweet juice, liquor] (1521)
: an Asian alcoholic beverage like rum that is distilled from a fermented mash of malted rice with toddy or molasses
ar·raign \ə-ˈrān\ *transitive verb* [Middle English *arreinen*, from Middle French *araisner*, from Old French, from *a-* (from Latin *ad-*) + *raisnier* to speak, from (assumed) Vulgar Latin *rationare*, from Latin *ration-*, *ratio* reason — more at REASON] (14th century)
1 : to call (a defendant) before a court to answer to an indictment **:** CHARGE
2 : to accuse of wrong, inadequacy, or imperfection
— **ar·raign·ment** \-mənt\ *noun*
ar·range \ə-ˈrānj\ *verb* **-ranged; -rang·ing** [Middle English *arangen*, from Middle French *arangier*, from Old French, from *a-* + *rengier* to set in a row, from *reng* row — more at RANK] (1789)
transitive verb
1 : to make preparations for **:** PLAN 〈*arranged* a reception for the visitor〉
2 : to put into a proper order or into a correct or suitable sequence, relationship, or adjustment 〈*arrange* flowers in a vase〉 〈*arrange* cards alphabetically〉
3 a : to adapt (a musical composition) by scoring for voices or instruments other than those for which originally written **b :** ORCHESTRATE
4 : to bring about an agreement or understanding concerning **:** SETTLE 〈*arrange* an exchange of war prisoners〉
intransitive verb
1 : to bring about an agreement or understanding 〈*arranged* to have a table at the restaurant〉
2 : to make preparations **:** PLAN 〈*arranged* for a vacation with his family〉
synonym see ORDER
— **ar·rang·er** \ə-ˈrān-jər\ *noun*
ar·range·ment \ə-ˈrānj-mənt\ *noun* (1690)
1 a : the state of being arranged **:** ORDER 〈everything in neat *arrangement*〉 **b :** the act of arranging 〈the *arrangement* of the details was quickly accomplished〉

2 : something arranged: as **a :** a preliminary measure **:** PREPARATION 〈travel *arrangements*〉 **b :** an adaptation of a musical composition by rescoring **c :** an informal agreement or settlement especially on personal, social, or political matters 〈*arrangements* under the new regime〉
3 : something made by arranging parts or things together 〈a floral *arrangement*〉
ar·rant \ˈar-ənt\ *adjective* [alteration of *errant*] (1553)
: being notoriously without moderation **:** EXTREME 〈we are *arrant* knaves, all; believe none of us —Shakespeare〉
— **ar·rant·ly** *adverb*
ar·ras \ˈar-əs\ *noun, plural* **arras** [Middle English, from *Arras*, France] (15th century)
1 : a tapestry of Flemish origin used especially for wall hangings and curtains
2 : a wall hanging or screen of tapestry
¹**ar·ray** \ə-ˈrā\ *transitive verb* [Middle English, from Old French *arayer*, from (assumed) Vulgar Latin *arredare*, from Latin *ad-* + a base of Germanic origin; akin to Gothic *garaiths* arranged — more at READY] (14th century)
1 : to dress or decorate especially in splendid or impressive attire **:** ADORN
2 a : to set or place in order **:** DRAW UP, MARSHAL **b :** to set or set forth in order (as a jury) for the trial of a cause
— **ar·ray·er** *noun*
²**array** *noun* (14th century)
1 a : a regular and imposing grouping or arrangement **:** ORDER 〈lined up . . . in soldierly *array* —Donald Barthelme〉 **b :** an orderly listing of jurors impaneled
2 a : CLOTHING, ATTIRE **b :** rich or beautiful apparel **:** FINERY
3 : a body of soldiers **:** MILITIA 〈the baron and his feudal *array*〉
4 : an imposing group **:** large number 〈faced a whole *array* of problems〉
5 a (1) **:** a number of mathematical elements arranged in rows and columns (2) **:** a data structure in which similar elements of data are arranged in a table **b :** a series of statistical data arranged in classes in order of magnitude
6 : a group of elements forming a complete unit 〈an antenna *array*〉
ar·rear \ə-ˈrir\ *noun* [Middle English *arrere* behind, backward, from Middle French, from (assumed) Vulgar Latin *ad retro* backward, from Latin *ad* to + *retro* backward, behind — more at AT, RETRO-] (1620)
1 : the state of being behind in the discharge of obligations — usually used in plural 〈in *arrears* with the rent〉
2 a : an unfinished duty — usually used in plural 〈*arrears* of work that have piled up〉 **b :** an unpaid and overdue debt — usually used in plural 〈paying off the *arrears* of the past several months〉
ar·rear·age \-ij\ *noun* (14th century)
1 : the condition of being in arrears
2 : something that is in arrears; *especially* **:** something unpaid and overdue
¹**ar·rest** \ə-ˈrest\ *transitive verb* [Middle English *aresten*, from Middle French *arester* to rest, arrest, from (assumed) Vulgar Latin *arrestare*, from Latin *ad-* + *restare* to remain — more at REST] (14th century)
1 a : to bring to a stop 〈sickness *arrested* his activities〉 **b :** CHECK, SLOW **c :** to make inactive 〈an *arrested* tumor〉
2 : SEIZE, CAPTURE; *specifically* **:** to take or keep in custody by authority of law
3 : to catch suddenly and engagingly
— **ar·rest·er** *or* **ar·res·tor** \-ˈres-tər\ *noun*
— **ar·rest·ment** \-ˈres(t)-mənt\ *noun*
²**arrest** *noun* (14th century)
1 a : the act of stopping **b :** the condition of being stopped or inactive
2 : the taking or detaining in custody by authority of law
— **under arrest :** in legal custody
ar·res·tant \ə-ˈres-tənt\ *noun* (1962)

: a substance that stimulates an insect to stop locomotion
ar·rest·ee \ə-ˌres-ˈtē\ *noun* (1944)
: one that is under arrest
ar·rest·ing \ə-ˈres-tiŋ\ *adjective* (1792)
: catching the attention **:** STRIKING, IMPRESSIVE
— **ar·rest·ing·ly** \-tiŋ-lē\ *adverb*
ar·rhyth·mia \ā-ˈrith-mē-ə\ *noun* [New Latin, from Greek, lack of rhythm, from *arrhythmos* unrhythmical, from *a-* + *rhythmos* rhythm] (circa 1860)
: an alteration in rhythm of the heartbeat either in time or force
ar·rhyth·mic \-mik\ *adjective* [Greek *arrhythmos*] (1853)
: lacking rhythm or regularity 〈*arrhythmic* locomotor activity〉
ar·ri·ère–ban \ˌar-ē-ˌer-ˈbän, -ˈban\ *noun* [French] (1523)
: a proclamation of a king (as of France) calling his vassals to arms; *also* **:** the body of vassals summoned
ar·ri·ère–pen·sée \-pä̃-ˈsā\ *noun* [French, from *arrière* in back + *pensée* thought] (1824)
: mental reservation
ar·ris \ˈar-əs\ *noun, plural* **arris** *or* **ar·ris·es** [probably modification of Middle French *areste*, literally, fishbone, from Late Latin *arista* — more at ARÊTE] (1677)
: the sharp edge or salient angle formed by the meeting of two surfaces especially in moldings
ar·riv·al \ə-ˈrī-vəl\ *noun* (14th century)
1 : the act of arriving
2 : the attainment of an end or state
3 : one that has recently reached a destination
ar·rive \ə-ˈrīv\ *intransitive verb* **ar·rived; ar·riv·ing** [Middle English *ariven*, from Old French *ariver*, from (assumed) Vulgar Latin *arripare* to come to shore, from Latin *ad-* + *ripa* shore — more at RIVE] (13th century)
1 a : to reach a destination **b :** to make an appearance 〈the guests have *arrived*〉
2 a *archaic* **:** HAPPEN **b :** to be near in time **:** COME 〈the moment has *arrived*〉
3 : to achieve success
— **ar·riv·er** *noun*
— **arrive at :** to reach by effort or thought 〈*arrived* at a decision〉
ar·ri·vé \ˌar-i-ˈvā\ *noun* [French, from past participle of *arriver* to arrive, from Old French *ariver*] (1925)
: one who has risen rapidly to success, power, or fame
ar·ri·viste \-ˈvēst\ *noun* [French, from *arriver*] (1901)
: one that is a new and uncertain arrival (as in social position or artistic endeavor)
ar·ro·ba \ə-ˈrō-bə\ *noun* [Spanish & Portuguese, from Arabic *ar-rub*ʽ, literally, the quarter] (1555)
1 : an old Spanish unit of weight equal to about 25 pounds
2 : an old Portuguese unit of weight equal to about 32 pounds
ar·ro·gance \ˈar-ə-gən(t)s\ *noun* (14th century)
: a feeling or an impression of superiority manifested in an overbearing manner or presumptuous claims
ar·ro·gant \-gənt\ *adjective* [Middle English, from Latin *arrogant-*, *arrogans*, present participle of *arrogare*] (14th century)
1 : exaggerating or disposed to exaggerate one's own worth or importance in an overbearing manner 〈an *arrogant* official〉
2 : proceeding from or characterized by arrogance 〈*arrogant* manners〉
synonym see PROUD
— **ar·ro·gant·ly** *adverb*
ar·ro·gate \-ˌgāt\ *transitive verb* **-gat·ed; -gat·ing** [Latin *arrogatus*, past participle of *arrogare*, from *ad-* + *rogare* to ask — more at RIGHT] (1537)
1 a : to claim or seize without justification **b :** to make undue claims to having **:** ASSUME

2 : to claim on behalf of another : ASCRIBE
— **ar·ro·ga·tion** \ˌar-ə-'gā-shən\ noun
ar·ron·disse·ment \ə-'rän-də-smənt, ˌar-ˌōⁿ-(ˌ)dē-'smäⁿ\ noun [French] (1807)
1 : an administrative district of some large French cities
2 : the largest division of a French department
¹ar·row \'ar-(ˌ)ō\ noun [Middle English arwe, from Old English; akin to Gothic arhwazna arrow, Latin arcus bow, arch, arc] (before 12th century)
1 : a missile weapon shot from a bow and usually having a slender shaft, a pointed head, and feathers at the butt
2 : something shaped like an arrow; especially : a mark (as on a map or signboard) to indicate direction

arrow 1

²arrow intransitive verb (1827)
: to move fast and straight like an arrow in flight : DART
ar·row·head \'ar-ō-ˌhed, 'ar-ə-\ noun (14th century)
1 a : a wedge-shaped piercing tip usually fixed to an arrow
2 : something resembling an arrowhead

arrowhead 1

3 : any of a genus (Sagittaria) of marsh or aquatic plants of the water-plantain family with leaves shaped like arrowheads
ar·row·root \-ˌrüt, -ˌrut\ noun (1696)
1 a : any of a genus (Maranta of the family Marantaceae, the arrowroot family) of tropical American plants with tuberous roots; especially : one (M. arundinacea) whose roots yield an easily digested edible starch **b** : any of several plants (as coontie) that yield starch
2 : starch yielded by an arrowroot
ar·row·wood \-ˌwud\ noun (1709)
: any of several common viburnums (especially Viburnum dentatum) of the eastern U.S.
ar·row·worm \-ˌwərm\ noun (circa 1889)
: any of a phylum (Chaetognatha) of small planktonic wormlike marine organisms having curved bristles on either side of the head for seizing prey
ar·row·y \'ar-ə-wē\ adjective (1637)
1 : resembling or suggesting an arrow; especially : swiftly moving
2 : consisting of arrows
ar·roy·o \ə-'roi-(ˌ)ō, -ə\ noun, plural **-royos** [Spanish] (1843)
1 : a watercourse (as a creek) in an arid region
2 : a water-carved gully or channel
ar·roz con po·llo \ä-'rōth-(ˌ)kòn-'pōl-(ˌ)yō, -'pō-(ˌ)yō\ noun [Spanish, literally, rice with chicken] (1938)
: chicken cooked with rice and usually flavored with saffron
arse variant of ASS
ar·se·nal \'ärs-nəl, 'är-s°n-əl\ noun [Italian arsenale, ultimately from Arabic dār ṣinā'ah house of manufacture] (1555)
1 a : an establishment for the manufacture or storage of arms and military equipment **b** : a collection of weapons
2 : STORE, REPERTORY ⟨the team's arsenal of veteran players⟩
ar·se·nate \'ärs-nət, 'är-s°n-ət, -s°n-ˌāt\ noun (1800)
: a salt or ester of an arsenic acid

¹ar·se·nic \'ärs-nik, -s°n-ik\ noun [Middle English, yellow orpiment, from Middle French & Latin; Middle French, from Latin arsenicum, from Greek arsenikon, arrhenikon, from Syriac zarnīg, of Iranian origin; akin to Avestan zaranya gold, Sanskrit hari yellowish — more at YELLOW] (14th century)
1 : a trivalent and pentavalent solid poisonous element that is commonly metallic steel-gray, crystalline, and brittle — see ELEMENT table
2 : a poisonous trioxide As_2O_3 or As_4O_6 of arsenic used especially as an insecticide or weed killer — called also arsenic trioxide
²ar·sen·ic \är-'se-nik\ adjective (1801)
: of, relating to, or containing arsenic especially with a valence of five
ar·sen·i·cal \är-'se-ni-kəl\ adjective (1605)
: of, relating to, containing, or caused by arsenic ⟨arsenical poisoning⟩
— **arsenical** noun
ar·se·nide \'är-s°n-ˌīd\ noun (circa 1859)
: a binary compound of arsenic with a more positive element
ar·se·ni·ous \är-'sē-nē-əs\ adjective (1818)
: of, relating to, or containing arsenic especially when trivalent
ar·se·nite \'är-s°n-ˌīt\ noun (1800)
: a salt or ester of an arsenious acid
ar·se·no·py·rite \ˌär-s°n-ō-'pī-ˌrīt\ noun (1881)
: a mineral consisting of a combined sulfide and arsenide of iron occurring in prismatic orthorhombic crystals or in masses or grains
ar·sine \är-'sēn, 'är-ˌ\ noun [International Scientific Vocabulary, from arsenic] (1876)
: a colorless flammable extremely poisonous gas AsH_3 with an odor like garlic; also : a derivative of arsine
ar·sis \'är-səs\ noun, plural **ar·ses** \-ˌsēz\ [Late Latin & Greek; Late Latin, raising of the voice, accented part of foot, from Greek, upbeat, less important part of foot, literally, act of lifting, from aeirein, airein to lift] (14th century)
1 a : the lighter or shorter part of a poetic foot especially in quantitative verse **b** : the accented or longer part of a poetic foot especially in accentual verse
2 : the unaccented part of a musical measure — compare THESIS
ar·son \'är-s°n\ noun [Anglo-French arsoun, alteration of Old French arsin act of burning, from ars, past participle of ardre to burn, from Latin ardēre — more at ARDOR] (circa 1680)
: the willful or malicious burning of property (as a building) especially with criminal or fraudulent intent
— **ar·son·ist** \-ist\ noun
— **ar·son·ous** \-əs\ adjective
ars·phen·a·mine \ärs-'fe-nə-ˌmēn, -mən\ noun [International Scientific Vocabulary arsenic + phenamine] (1917)
: a light-yellow toxic hygroscopic powder $C_{12}Cl_2H_{14}As_2N_2O_2 \cdot 2H_2O$ formerly used in the treatment especially of syphilis and yaws
¹art \'ärt, ərt\ [Middle English, from Old English eart; akin to Old Norse est, ert (thou) art, Old English is is] archaic present 2d singular of BE
²art \'ärt\ noun [Middle English, from Old French, from Latin art-, ars — more at ARM] (13th century)
1 : skill acquired by experience, study, or observation ⟨the art of making friends⟩
2 a : a branch of learning: (1) : one of the humanities (2) plural : LIBERAL ARTS **b** archaic : LEARNING, SCHOLARSHIP
3 : an occupation requiring knowledge or skill ⟨the art of organ building⟩
4 a : the conscious use of skill and creative imagination especially in the production of aesthetic objects; also : works so produced **b** (1) : FINE ARTS (2) : one of the fine arts (3) : a graphic art
5 a archaic : a skillful plan **b** : the quality or state of being artful

6 : decorative or illustrative elements in printed matter ☆
-art — see -ARD
art de·co \ˌärt-'de-ˌkō; ˌär(t)-dā-'kō, 'är(t)-'dā-(ˌ)kō\ noun, often A&D capitalized [French Art Déco, from Exposition Internationale des Arts Décoratifs et Industriels Modernes, an exposition of modern decorative and industrial arts held in Paris, France, in 1925] (1966)
: a popular design style of the 1920s and 1930s characterized especially by bold outlines, geometric and zigzag forms, and the use of new materials (as plastic)
ar·te·fact chiefly British variant of ARTIFACT
ar·tel \är-'tel; -'telʸ\ noun [Russian artel'] (1884)
: a workers' or craftsmen's cooperative in Russia and later the U.S.S.R
Ar·te·mis \'är-tə-məs\ noun [Greek]
: a Greek moon goddess often portrayed as a virgin huntress — compare DIANA
ar·te·mi·sia \ˌär-tə-'mi-zh(ē-)ə, -zē-ə\ noun [New Latin, from Latin, artemisia, from Greek, wormwood] (14th century)
: any of a genus (Artemisia) of aromatic composite herbs and shrubs (as sagebrush) — compare WORMWOOD 1
arteri- or **arterio-** combining form [Greek artēri-, artērio-, from artēria artery]
1 : artery ⟨arteriogram⟩
2 : arterial and ⟨arteriovenous⟩
¹ar·te·ri·al \är-'tir-ē-əl\ adjective (15th century)
1 a : of or relating to an artery **b** : relating to or being the bright red blood present in most arteries that has been oxygenated in lungs or gills
2 : of, relating to, or constituting through traffic
— **ar·te·ri·al·ly** \-ē-ə-lē\ adverb
²arterial noun (1932)
: a through street or highway
ar·te·rio·gram \är-'tir-ē-ə-ˌgram\ noun [International Scientific Vocabulary] (1929)
: a roentgenogram of an artery made by arteriography
ar·te·ri·og·ra·phy \är-ˌtir-ē-'ä-grə-fē\ noun, plural **-phies** [International Scientific Vocabulary] (1929)
: the roentgenographic visualization of an artery after injection of a radiopaque substance
— **ar·te·rio·graph·ic** \-ē-ə-'gra-fik\ adjective
ar·te·ri·ole \är-'tir-ē-ˌōl\ noun [French or New Latin; French artériole, probably from New Latin arteriola, diminutive of Latin arteria] (circa 1847)
: any of the small terminal twigs of an artery that ends in capillaries
— **ar·te·ri·o·lar** \-ˌtir-ē-'ō-ˌlär, -lər\ adjective

\ə\ abut \ᵊ\ kitten \ər\ further \a\ ash \ā\ ace
\ä\ mop, mar \aú\ out \ch\ chin \e\ bet \ē\ easy
\g\ go \i\ hit \ī\ ice \j\ job \ŋ\ sing \ō\ go
\ò\ law \òi\ boy \th\ thin \th\ the \ü\ loot \u\ foot
\y\ yet \zh\ vision see also Guide to Pronunciation

ar·te·rio·scle·ro·sis \är-ˌtir-ē-ō-sklə-'rō-səs\ *noun* [New Latin] (1881)
: a chronic disease characterized by abnormal thickening and hardening of the arterial walls with resulting loss of elasticity
— **ar·te·rio·scle·rot·ic** \-'rä-tik\ *adjective or noun*

ar·te·rio·ve·nous \-'vē-nəs\ *adjective* [International Scientific Vocabulary] (circa 1880)
: of, relating to, or connecting the arteries and veins ⟨an *arteriovenous* fistula⟩

ar·ter·i·tis \ˌär-tə-'rī-təs\ *noun* [New Latin] (1836)
: arterial inflammation

ar·tery \'är-tə-rē, 'är-trē\ *noun, plural* **-ter·ies** [Middle English *arterie,* from Latin *arteria,* from Greek *artēria;* akin to Greek *aortē* aorta] (14th century)
1 : any of the tubular branching muscular- and elastic-walled vessels that carry blood from the heart through the body
2 : a channel (as a river or highway) of transportation or communication; *especially* : the main channel in a branching system

ar·te·sian well \är-'tē-zhən\ *noun* [French *artésien,* literally, of Artois, from Old French, from *Arteis* Artois, France] (1842)
1 : a well in which water is under pressure; *especially* : one in which the water flows to the surface naturally
2 : a deep well

art film *noun* (1926)
: a motion picture produced as an artistic effort

art form *noun* (1868)
1 : a recognized form (as a symphony) or medium (as sculpture) of artistic expression
2 : an unconventional form or medium in which impulses regarded as artistic may be expressed ⟨describe pinball as a great American *art form* —Tom Buckley⟩

art·ful \'ärt-fəl\ *adjective* (1615)
1 : performed with or showing art or skill ⟨an *artful* performance on the violin⟩
2 a : using or characterized by art and skill : DEXTEROUS ⟨an *artful* prose stylist⟩ **b** : adroit in attaining an end often by insinuating or indirect means : WILY ⟨an *artful* cross-examiner⟩
3 : ARTIFICIAL ⟨trim walks and *artful* bowers —William Wordsworth⟩
synonym see SLY
— **art·ful·ly** \-fə-lē\ *adverb*
— **art·ful·ness** *noun*

art glass *noun* (1926)
: articles of glass designed primarily for decorative purposes; *especially* : novelty glassware

art historical *adjective* (1933)
: of or relating to the history of art
— **art historically** *adverb*

art house *noun* (1951)
: ART THEATER

arthr- *or* **arthro-** *combining form* [Latin, from Greek, from *arthron;* akin to Greek *arariskein* to fit — more at ARM]
: joint ⟨*arthr*opathy⟩

ar·thral·gia \är-'thral-j(ē-)ə\ *noun* [New Latin] (circa 1848)
: neuralgic pain in one or more joints
— **ar·thral·gic** \-jik\ *adjective*

ar·thrit·ic \är-'thri-tik\ *adjective* (14th century)
1 : of, relating to, or affected with arthritis
2 : being or showing effects associated with aging ⟨*arthritic* anxiety⟩
— **arthritic** *noun*
— **ar·thrit·i·cal·ly** \-ti-k(ə-)lē\ *adverb*

ar·thri·tis \är-'thrī-təs\ *noun, plural* **-thrit·i·des** \-'thri-tə-ˌdēz\ [Latin, from Greek, from *arthron*] (1543)
: inflammation of joints due to infectious, metabolic, or constitutional causes; *also* : a specific arthritic condition

ar·throd·e·sis \är-'thrä-də-səs\ *noun, plural* **-e·ses** \-ˌsēz\ [New Latin, from *arthr-* + Greek *desis* binding, from *dein* to bind] (circa 1901)
: the surgical immobilization of a joint so that the bones grow solidly together

ar·throp·a·thy \är-'thrä-pə-thē\ *noun, plural* **-thies** (circa 1860)
: a disease of a joint

ar·thro·pod \'är-thrə-ˌpäd\ *noun* [New Latin *Arthropoda,* from *arthr-* + Greek *pod-, pous* foot — more at FOOT] (1877)
: any of a phylum (Arthropoda) of invertebrate animals (as insects, arachnids, and crustaceans) that have a segmented body and jointed appendages, a usually chitinous exoskeleton molted at intervals, and a dorsal anterior brain connected to a ventral chain of ganglia
— **arthropod** *adjective*
— **ar·throp·o·dan** \är-'thrä-pə-dən\ *adjective*

ar·thros·co·py \är-'thräs-kə-pē\ *noun* (circa 1935)
: visual examination of the interior of a joint (as the knee) with a special surgical instrument; *also* : joint surgery using an arthroscope
— **ar·thro·scope** \'är-thrə-ˌskōp\ *noun*
— **ar·thro·scop·ic** \ˌär-thrə-'skä-pik\ *adjective*

ar·thro·sis \är-'thrō-səs\ *noun, plural* **-thro·ses** \-ˌsēz\ [New Latin, from Greek *arthrōsis* jointing, articulation, from *arthroun* to articulate, from *arthron*] (1634)
1 : an articulation between bones
2 : a degenerative disease of a joint

ar·thro·spore \'är-thrə-ˌspōr, -ˌspor\ *noun* (1895)
: OIDIUM 1b

Ar·thur \'är-thər\ *noun*
: a legendary king of the Britons whose story is based on traditions of a 6th century military leader

Ar·thu·ri·an \är-'thur-ē-ən, -'thyur-\ *adjective* (1612)
: of or relating to King Arthur and his court

ar·ti·choke \'är-tə-ˌchōk\ *noun* [Italian dialect *articiocco,* ultimately from Arabic *al-khurshūf* the artichoke] (1530)
1 : a tall composite herb (*Cynara scolymus*) like a thistle with coarse pinnately incised leaves; *also* : its edible immature flower head which is cooked as a vegetable
2 : JERUSALEM ARTICHOKE

¹ar·ti·cle \'är-ti-kəl\ *noun* [Middle English, from Old French, from Latin *articulus* joint, division, diminutive of *artus* joint, limb; akin to Greek *arariskein* to fit — more at ARM] (13th century)
1 a : a distinct often numbered section of a writing **b** : a separate clause **c** : a stipulation in a document (as a contract or a creed) **d** : a nonfictional prose composition usually forming an independent part of a publication (as a magazine)
2 : an item of business : MATTER
3 : any of a small set of words or affixes (as *a, an,* and *the*) used with nouns to limit or give definiteness to the application
4 : a member of a class of things; *especially* : an item of goods ⟨*articles* of value⟩
5 : a thing of a particular and distinctive kind ⟨the genuine *article*⟩

²article *transitive verb* **ar·ti·cled; ar·ti·cling** \-k(ə-)liŋ\ (1820)
: to bind by articles (as of apprenticeship)

article of faith (15th century)
: a basic belief

ar·tic·u·la·ble \är-'ti-kyə-lə-bəl\ *adjective* (1833)
: capable of being articulated

ar·tic·u·la·cy \är-'ti-kyə-lə-sē\ *noun* (1918)
chiefly British : the quality or state of being articulate

ar·tic·u·lar \är-'ti-kyə-lər\ *adjective* [Middle English *articuler,* from Latin *articularis,* from *articulus*] (15th century)
: of or relating to a joint ⟨*articular* cartilage⟩

¹ar·tic·u·late \är-'ti-kyə-lət\ *adjective* [Latin *articulatus* jointed, past participle of *articulare,* from *articulus*] (1586)
1 a : divided into syllables or words meaningfully arranged : INTELLIGIBLE **b** : able to speak **c** : expressing oneself readily, clearly, or effectively; *also* : expressed in this manner
2 a : consisting of segments united by joints : JOINTED ⟨*articulate* animals⟩ **b** : distinctly marked off
— **ar·tic·u·late·ly** *adverb*
— **ar·tic·u·late·ness** *noun*

²ar·tic·u·late \-ˌlāt\ *verb* **-lat·ed; -lat·ing** (1594)
transitive verb
1 a : to utter distinctly ⟨*articulating* each note in the musical phrase⟩ **b** : to give clear and effective utterance to : put into words ⟨*articulate* one's grievances⟩ **c** : to give definition to (as a shape or object) ⟨shades of gray were chosen to *articulate* different spaces —Carol Vogel⟩
2 a : to unite by means of a joint : JOINT **b** : to form or fit into a systematic whole ⟨*articulating* a program for all school grades⟩
intransitive verb
1 : to utter articulate sounds
2 : to become united or connected by or as if by a joint
— **ar·tic·u·la·tive** \-lə-tiv, -ˌlā-\ *adjective*
— **ar·tic·u·la·tor** \-ˌlā-tər\ *noun*

ar·tic·u·lat·ed \-ˌlā-təd\ *adjective* (1899)
of a vehicle : having a hinge or pivot connection especially to allow negotiation of sharp turns ⟨*articulated* lorry⟩ ⟨*articulated* bus⟩

ar·tic·u·la·tion \(ˌ)är-ˌti-kyə-'lā-shən\ *noun* (15th century)
1 a : a joint or juncture between bones or cartilages in the skeleton of a vertebrate **b** : a movable joint between rigid parts of an animal
2 a : the action or manner of jointing or interrelating **b** : the state of being jointed or interrelated
3 a : the act of giving utterance or expression **b** : the act or manner of articulating sounds **c** : an articulated utterance or sound; *specifically* : CONSONANT
4 : OCCLUSION 1b

ar·tic·u·la·to·ry \är-'ti-kyə-lə-ˌtōr-ē, -ˌtor-\ *adjective* (1818)
: of or relating to articulation

ar·ti·fact \'är-ti-ˌfakt\ *noun* [Latin *arte* by skill (ablative of *art-, ars* skill) + *factum,* neuter of *factus,* past participle of *facere* to do — more at ARM, DO] (1821)
1 a : something created by humans usually for a practical purpose; *especially* : an object remaining from a particular period ⟨caves containing prehistoric *artifacts*⟩ **b** : something characteristic of or resulting from a human institution or activity ⟨self-consciousness . . . turns out to be an *artifact* of our education system —*Times Literary Supplement*⟩
2 : a product of artificial character (as in a scientific test) due usually to extraneous (as human) agency
— **ar·ti·fac·tu·al** \ˌär-ti-'fak-chə(-wə)l, -'fak-shwəl\ *adjective*

ar·ti·fice \'är-tə-fəs\ *noun* [Middle French, from Latin *artificium,* from *artific-, artifex* artificer, from *art-, ars* + *facere*] (circa 1604)
1 a : clever or artful skill : INGENUITY ⟨believing that characters had to be created from within rather than with *artifice* —Garson Kanin⟩ **b** : an ingenious device or expedient
2 a : an artful stratagem : TRICK **b** : false or insincere behavior ⟨social *artifice*⟩
synonym see TRICK, ART

ar·ti·fi·cer \är-'ti-fə-sər, 'är-tə-fə-sər\ *noun* (14th century)
1 : a skilled or artistic worker or craftsman
2 : one that makes or contrives : DEVISER ⟨had been the *artificer* of his own fortunes —*Times Literary Supplement*⟩

ar·ti·fi·cial \ˌär-tə-'fi-shᵊl\ *adjective* (14th century)

1 : humanly contrived often on a natural model **:** MAN-MADE ⟨an *artificial* limb⟩ ⟨*artificial* diamonds⟩
2 a : having existence in legal, economic, or political theory **b :** caused or produced by a human and especially social or political agency ⟨an *artificial* price advantage⟩ ⟨*artificial* barriers of discrimination —R. C. Weaver⟩
3 *obsolete* **:** ARTFUL, CUNNING
4 a : lacking in natural or spontaneous quality ⟨an *artificial* smile⟩ ⟨an *artificial* excitement⟩ **b :** IMITATION, SHAM ⟨*artificial* flavor⟩
5 : based on differential morphological characters not necessarily indicative of natural relationships ⟨an *artificial* key for plant identification⟩
— **ar·ti·fi·ci·al·i·ty** \ˌär-tə-ˌfi-shē-'a-lə-tē\ *noun*
— **ar·ti·fi·cial·ly** \-'fi-shᵊl-ē\ *adverb*
— **ar·ti·fi·cial·ness** \-'fi-shəl-nəs\ *noun*
artificial horizon *noun* (1920)
: a gyroscopic flight instrument designed to indicate aircraft attitude with respect to the true horizon

artificial insemination *noun* (1897)
: introduction of semen into the uterus or oviduct by other than natural means
artificial intelligence *noun* (1956)

artificial horizon (showing plane banking left): *a* miniature airplane, *b* horizon line

1 : the capability of a machine to imitate intelligent human behavior
2 : a branch of computer science dealing with the simulation of intelligent behavior in computers
artificial respiration *noun* (1852)
: the rhythmic forcing of air into and out of the lungs of a person whose breathing has stopped
ar·til·ler·ist \är-'ti-lə-rist\ *noun* (1781)
: GUNNER, ARTILLERYMAN
ar·til·lery \är-'ti-lər-ē, -'til-rē\ *noun, plural* **-ler·ies** [Middle English *artillerie*, from Middle French, from *artillier* to equip, arm, alteration of Old French *atillier*, from (assumed) Vulgar Latin *apticulare*, from Latin *aptare* to don, prepare, fit — more at ADAPT] (15th century)
1 : weapons (as bows, slings, and catapults) for discharging missiles
2 a : large bore crew-served mounted firearms (as guns, howitzers, and rockets) **:** ORDNANCE **b :** a branch of an army armed with artillery
3 : means of impressing, arguing, or persuading
ar·til·lery·man \-mən\ *noun* (1635)
: a soldier in the artillery
ar·tio·dac·tyl \ˌär-tē-ō-'dak-tᵊl\ *noun* [New Latin *Artiodactyla*, from Greek *artios* fitting, even-numbered + *daktylos* finger, toe; akin to Greek *arariskein* to fit — more at ARM] (circa 1879)
: any of an order (Artiodactyla) of ungulates (as the camel or pig) with an even number of functional toes on each foot
— **artiodactyl** *adjective*
ar·ti·san \'är-tə-zən, -sən, *chiefly British* ˌär-tə-'zan\ *noun* [Middle French, ultimately from Old Italian *artigiano*, from *arte* art, from Latin *art-, ars*] (1538)
: CRAFTSMAN
— **ar·ti·san·al** \-zə-nᵊl, -sə-, -'za-\ *adjective*
— **ar·ti·san·ship** \-ˌship\ *noun*
art·ist \'är-tist\ *noun* (circa 1507)
1 a *obsolete* **:** one skilled or versed in learned arts **b** *archaic* **:** PHYSICIAN **c** *archaic* **:** ARTISAN
2 a : one who professes and practices an imaginative art **b :** a person skilled in one of the fine arts
3 : a skilled performer; *especially* **:** ARTISTE

4 : one who is adept at something ⟨con *artist*⟩ ⟨strikeout *artist*⟩
ar·tiste \är-'tēst\ *noun* [French] (1823)
: a skilled adept public performer; *specifically* **:** a musical or theatrical entertainer
ar·tis·tic \är-'tis-tik\ *adjective* (circa 1753)
1 : of, relating to, or characteristic of art or artists ⟨*artistic* subjects⟩ ⟨an *artistic* success⟩
2 : showing imaginative skill in arrangement or execution ⟨*artistic* photography⟩
— **ar·tis·ti·cal·ly** \-ti-k(ə-)lē\ *adverb*
art·ist·ry \'är-tə-strē\ *noun* (1868)
1 : artistic quality of effect or workmanship ⟨the *artistry* of his novel⟩
2 : artistic ability ⟨the *artistry* of the violinist⟩ ⟨a lawyer's *artistry* in persuading juries⟩
art·less \'ärt-ləs\ *adjective* (1589)
1 : lacking art, knowledge, or skill **:** UNCULTURED
2 a : made without skill **:** CRUDE **b :** free from artificiality **:** NATURAL ⟨*artless* grace⟩
3 : free from guile or craft **:** sincerely simple
synonym see NATURAL
— **art·less·ly** *adverb*
— **art·less·ness** *noun*
art mo·derne \ˌär(t)-mō-'dern\ *noun, often A&M capitalized* [French — more at ART DECO] (1931)
: ART DECO
art nou·veau \ˌär(t)-nü-'vō\ *noun, often A&N capitalized* [French, literally, new art] (1908)
: a design style of late 19th century origin characterized especially by sinuous lines and foliate forms
Arts and Crafts *noun* (1888)
: a movement in European and American design during the late 19th and early 20th centuries promoting handcraftsmanship over industrial mass production
art song *noun* (1890)
: a usually through-composed lyric song with melody and accompaniment
art·sy \'ärt-sē\ *adjective* (1902)
: ARTY
artsy–craftsy \ˌärt-sē-'kraf(t)-sē\ *also* **arty–crafty** \är-tē-'kraf-tē\ *adjective* [from the phrase *arts and crafts*] (1902)
: ARTY
art theater *noun* (1923)
: a theater that specializes in the presentation of art films
art·work \'ärt-ˌwərk\ *noun* (1877)
1 a : an artistic production ⟨an 8-foot metal *artwork*⟩ **b :** artistic work ⟨*artwork* being sold on the sidewalk⟩
2 a : ART 6 **b :** material (as a drawing or photograph) prepared for reproduction in printed matter
arty \'är-tē\ *adjective* **art·i·er; -est** (1901)
: showily or pretentiously artistic ⟨*arty* lighting and photography⟩
— **art·i·ly** \'är-tᵊl-ē\ *adverb*
— **art·i·ness** \'är-tē-nəs\ *noun*
aru·gu·la \ə-'rü-gə-lə, -gyə-\ *noun* [probably from Italian dialect; akin to Italian dialect (Lombardy) *arigola* arugula, Italian *ruca* — more at ROCKET] (1967)
: a yellowish-flowered European herb (*Eruca vesicaria*) of the mustard family cultivated for its foliage which is used especially in salads — called also *garden rocket, rocket, rugola*
ar·um \'ar-əm, 'er-\ *noun* [New Latin, from Latin *arum*, from Greek *aron*] (14th century)
: any of a genus (*Arum* of the family Araceae, the arum family) of Old World plants having usually arrow-shaped leaves and a showy spathe partially enclosing a spadix; *broadly* **:** a plant of the arum family
¹-ary \US *usually* ˌer-ē *when an unstressed syllable precedes,* ə-rē *or* rē *when a stressed syllable precedes; British usually* ə-rē *or* rē *in all cases*\ *noun suffix* [Middle English *-arie*, from Old French & Latin; Old French *-aire, -arie*, from Latin *-arius, -aria, -arium*, from *-arius*, adjective suffix]

1 : thing belonging to or connected with; *especially* **:** place of ⟨ov*ary*⟩
2 : person belonging to, connected with, or engaged in ⟨function*ary*⟩
²-ary *adjective suffix* [Middle English *-arie*, from Middle French & Latin; Middle French *-aire*, from Latin *-arius*]
: of, relating to, or connected with ⟨budget*ary*⟩
¹Ary·an \'ar-ē-ən, 'er-; 'är-yən\ *adjective* [Sanskrit *ārya* noble, belonging to the people speaking an Indo-European dialect who migrated into northern India] (1839)
1 : INDO-EUROPEAN
2 a : of or relating to a hypothetical ethnic type illustrated by or descended from early speakers of Indo-European languages **b :** NORDIC **c** — used in Nazism to designate a supposed master race of non-Jewish Caucasians having especially Nordic features
3 : of or relating to Indo-Iranian or its speakers
²Aryan *noun* (1851)
1 : INDO-EUROPEAN
2 a : NORDIC **b :** GENTILE
ar·yl \'ar-əl\ *adjective* [International Scientific Vocabulary *ar*omatic + *-yl*] (1906)
: having or being a univalent organic group (as phenyl) derived from an aromatic hydrocarbon by the removal of one hydrogen atom — often used in combination
ar·y·te·noid \ˌar-ə-'tē-ˌnȯid, ə-'ri-tᵊn-ˌȯid\ *adjective* [New Latin *arytaenoides*, from Greek *arytainoeidēs*, literally, ladle-shaped, from *arytaina* ladle] (circa 1751)
1 : relating to or being either of two small laryngeal cartilages to which the vocal cords are attached
2 : relating to or being either of a pair of small muscles or an unpaired muscle of the larynx
— **arytenoid** *noun*
¹as \əz, (ˌ)az\ *adverb* [Middle English, from Old English *eallswā* likewise, just as — more at ALSO] (before 12th century)
1 : to the same degree or amount ⟨*as* deaf as a post⟩ ⟨twice *as* long⟩
2 : for instance ⟨various trees, *as* oak or pine⟩
3 : when considered in a specified form or relation — usually used before a preposition or a participle ⟨my opinion *as* distinguished from his⟩
²as *conjunction* (12th century)
1 : AS IF ⟨looks *as* he had seen a ghost —S. T. Coleridge⟩
2 : in or to the same degree in which ⟨deaf *as* a post⟩ — usually used as a correlative after an adjective or adverb modified by adverbial *as* or *so* ⟨*as* cool *as* a cucumber⟩
3 : in the way or manner that ⟨do *as* I do⟩
4 : in accordance with what or the way in which ⟨quite good *as* boys go⟩
5 : WHILE, WHEN ⟨spilled the milk *as* she got up⟩
6 : regardless of the degree to which **:** THOUGH ⟨improbable *as* it seems, it's true⟩
7 : for the reason that **:** BECAUSE, SINCE ⟨stayed home *as* she had no car⟩
8 : that the result is ⟨so clearly guilty *as* to leave no doubt⟩
usage see LIKE
— **as is :** in the presently existing condition without modification ⟨bought the clock at an auction *as* is⟩
— **as it were :** as if it were so **:** in a manner of speaking
³as *pronoun* (12th century)
1 : THAT, WHO, WHICH — used after *same* or *such* ⟨in the same building *as* my brother⟩ ⟨tears such *as* angels weep —John Milton⟩ and chiefly dialect after a substantive not modified

\ə\ **abut** \ᵊ\ **kitten** \ər\ **further** \a\ **ash** \ā\ **ace**
\ä\ **mop, mar** \au̇\ **out** \ch\ **chin** \e\ **bet** \ē\ **easy**
\g\ **go** \i\ **hit** \ī\ **ice** \j\ **job** \ŋ\ **sing** \ō\ **go**
\ȯ\ **law** \ȯi\ **boy** \th\ **thin** \t͟h\ **the** \ü\ **loot** \u̇\ **foot**
\y\ **yet** \zh\ **vision** *see also* Guide to Pronunciation

by *same* or *such* ⟨that kind of fruit *as* maids call medlars —Shakespeare⟩ **2 :** a fact that ⟨is a foreigner, *as* is evident from his accent⟩

⁴as *preposition* (13th century) **1 a :** LIKE 2 ⟨all rose *as* one man⟩ **b :** LIKE 1a ⟨his face was *as* a mask —Max Beerbohm⟩ **2 :** in the capacity, character, condition, or role of ⟨works *as* an editor⟩

⁵as \'as\ *noun, plural* **as·ses** \'a-,sēz, 'a-səz\ [Latin] (1540) **1 a :** a bronze coin of the ancient Roman republic **b :** a unit of value equivalent to an *as* coin **2 :** LIBRA 2a

as- — see AD-

asa·fet·i·da *or* **asa·foe·ti·da** \,a-sə-'fe-tə-də, -'fē-; *Southern also* -'fi-tə-də\ *noun* [Middle English *asafetida*, from Medieval Latin *asafoetida*, from Persian *azā* mastic + Latin *foetida*, feminine of *foetidus* fetid] (14th century) **:** the fetid gum resin of various oriental plants (genus *Ferula*) of the carrot family formerly used in medicine as an antispasmodic and in folk medicine as a general prophylactic against disease

asa·na \'ä-sə-nə\ *noun* [Sanskrit *āsana* manner of sitting, from *āste* he sits; akin to Greek *hēsthai* to sit, Hittite *es*-] (circa 1934) **:** any of various yogic postures

Asan·te \ə-'san-tē, -'sän-\ *noun, plural* **Asante** (1721) **:** ASHANTI

as·bes·tos \as-'bes-təs, az-\ *noun* [Middle English *albestron* mineral supposed to be inextinguishable when set on fire, probably from Middle French, from Medieval Latin *asbeston*, alteration of Latin *asbestos*, from Greek, unslaked lime, from *asbestos* inextinguishable, from *a*- + *sbennynai* to quench] (1607) **:** any of several minerals (as chrysotile) that readily separate into long flexible fibers, that have been implicated as causes of certain cancers, and that have been used especially formerly as fireproof insulating materials

as·bes·to·sis \,as-,bes-'tō-səs, ,az-\ *noun, plural* **-to·ses** \-,sēz\ (1927) **:** a pneumoconiosis due to asbestos particles

asc- *or* **asco-** *combining form* [New Latin, from *ascus*] **:** ascus ⟨*asco*carp⟩

as·ca·ri·a·sis \,as-kə-'rī-ə-səs\ *noun, plural* **-a·ses** \-,sēz\ [New Latin] (circa 1888) **:** infestation with or disease caused by ascarids

as·ca·rid \'as-kə-rəd\ *noun* [ultimately from Late Latin *ascarid-, ascaris* intestinal worm, from Greek *askarid-, askaris*, probably by back-formation from *askarizein* to jump, throb, alteration of *skarizein*, from *skairein* to gambol] (circa 1890) **:** any of a family (Ascaridae) of nematode worms that includes the common roundworm (*Ascaris lumbricoides*) parasitic in the human intestine

as·ca·ris \'as-kə-rəs\ *noun, plural* **as·car·i·des** \a-'skar-ə-,dēz\ (14th century) **:** ASCARID

as·cend \ə-'send\ *verb* [Middle English, from Latin *ascendere*, from *ad*- + *scandere* to climb — more at SCAN] (14th century) *intransitive verb* **1 a :** to move upward **b :** to slope upward **2 a :** to rise from a lower level or degree **b :** to go back in time or in order of genealogical succession *transitive verb* **1 :** to go or move up ⟨*ascend* a staircase⟩ **2 :** to succeed to **:** OCCUPY ⟨*ascend* the throne⟩ — **as·cend·able** *or* **as·cend·ible** \-'sen-də-bəl\ *adjective*

as·cen·dance *also* **as·cen·dence** \ə-'sen-dən(t)s\ *noun* (1742) **:** ASCENDANCY

as·cen·dan·cy *also* **as·cen·den·cy** \ə-'sen-dən(t)-sē\ *noun* (1712)

: governing or controlling influence **:** DOMINATION

¹as·cen·dant *also* **as·cen·dent** \ə-'sen-dənt\ *noun* [Middle English *ascendent*, from Medieval Latin *ascendent-, ascendens*, from Latin, present participle of *ascendere*] (14th century) **1 :** the point of the ecliptic or degree of the zodiac that rises above the eastern horizon at any moment **2 :** a state or position of dominant power or importance **3 :** a lineal or collateral relative in the ascending line

²ascendant *also* **ascendent** *adjective* (1591) **1 a :** moving upward **:** RISING **b :** directed upward ⟨an *ascendant* stem⟩ **2 a :** SUPERIOR **b :** DOMINANT — **as·cen·dant·ly** *adverb*

as·cend·er \ə-'sen-dər, 'a-\ *noun* (circa 1867) **:** the part of a lowercase letter (as b) that rises above the main body of the letter; *also* **:** a letter that has such a part

as·cend·ing \ə-'sen-diŋ\ *adjective* (1599) **1 a :** mounting or sloping upward **b :** rising or increasing to higher levels, values, or degrees ⟨*ascending* powers of *x*⟩ **2 :** rising upward usually from a more or less prostrate base or point of attachment

as·cen·sion \ə-'sen(t)-shən\ *noun* [Middle English, from Latin *ascension-, ascensio*, from *ascendere*] (14th century) **:** the act or process of ascending

as·cen·sion·al \ə-'sench-nəl, ə-'sen(t)-shə-nᵊl\ *adjective* (1594) **:** of or relating to ascension or ascent

Ascension Day *noun* (14th century) **:** the Thursday 40 days after Easter observed in commemoration of Christ's ascension into Heaven

as·cen·sive \ə-'sen(t)-siv\ *adjective* (1646) **:** rising or tending to rise

as·cent \ə-'sent, a-\ *noun* [irregular from *ascend*] (circa 1596) **1 a :** the act of rising or mounting upward **:** CLIMB **b :** an upward slope or rising grade **:** ACCLIVITY **c :** the degree of elevation **:** INCLINATION, GRADIENT **2 :** an advance in social status or reputation **:** PROGRESS **3 :** a going back in time or upward in order of genealogical succession

as·cer·tain \,a-sər-'tān\ *transitive verb* [Middle English *acertainen*, from Middle French *acertainer*, from *a*- (from Latin *ad*-) + *certain*] (15th century) **1** *archaic* **:** to make certain, exact, or precise **2 :** to find out or learn with certainty **synonym** *see* DISCOVER — **as·cer·tain·able** \-'tā-nə-bəl\ *adjective* — **as·cer·tain·ment** \-'tān-mənt\ *noun*

as·ce·sis \a-'sē-səs\ *noun, plural* **-ce·ses** \-'sē-(,)sēz\ [Late Latin or Greek; Late Latin, from Greek *askēsis*, literally, exercise, from *askein*] (1873) **:** SELF-DISCIPLINE, ASCETICISM

as·cet·ic \ə-'se-tik, a-\ *also* **as·cet·i·cal** \-ti-kəl\ *adjective* [Greek *askētikos*, literally, laborious, from *askētēs* one that exercises, hermit, from *askein* to work, exercise] (1646) **1 :** practicing strict self-denial as a measure of personal and especially spiritual discipline **2 :** austere in appearance, manner, or attitude **synonym** *see* SEVERE — **ascetic** *noun* — **as·cet·i·cal·ly** \-ti-k(ə-)lē\ *adverb* — **as·cet·i·cism** \-'se-tə-,si-zəm\ *noun*

as·cid·i·an \ə-'si-dē-ən\ *noun* [New Latin *Ascidia*, group comprising tunicates, from *Ascidium*, genus name, from Greek *askidion*, diminutive of *askos* wineskin, bladder] (1856) **:** any of a class (Ascidiacea) of solitary or colonial sessile tunicates that have an oral and an atrial siphon — called also *sea squirt*

ASCII \'as-(,)kē\ *noun* [*A*merican *S*tandard *C*ode for *I*nformation *I*nterchange] (1963) **:** a code for representing alphanumeric information

as·ci·tes \ə-'sī-tēz\ *noun, plural* **ascites** [Middle English *aschytes*, from Late Latin *ascites*, from Greek *askitēs*, from *askos*] (14th century) **:** accumulation of serous fluid in the spaces between tissues and organs in the cavity of the abdomen — **as·cit·ic** \-'si-tik\ *adjective*

as·cle·pi·ad \ə-'sklē-pē-əd, a-, -,ad\ *noun* [ultimately from Greek *asklēpiad-, asklēpias* swallowwort, from *Asklēpios*, Greek god of medicine] (1859) **:** MILKWEED

as·co·carp \'as-kə-,kärp\ *noun* (circa 1887) **:** the mature fruiting body of an ascomycetous fungus; *broadly* **:** such a body with its enclosed asci, spores, and paraphyses — **as·co·car·pic** \,as-kə-'kär-pik\ *adjective*

as·co·go·ni·um \,as-kə-'gō-nē-əm\ *noun, plural* **-nia** \-nē-ə\ [New Latin] (1875) **:** the female sex organ in ascomycetous fungi

as·co·my·cete \,as-kō-'mī-,sēt, -,mī-'sēt\ *noun* [ultimately from Greek *askos* + *mykēt-, mykēs* fungus; akin to Greek *myxa* mucus — more at MUCUS] (1875) **:** any of a class (Ascomycetes) or subdivision (Ascomycotina) of higher fungi (as yeasts or molds) with septate hyphae and spores formed in asci — **as·co·my·ce·tous** \-,mī-'sē-təs\ *adjective*

ascor·bate \ə-'skòr-,bāt, -bət\ *noun* (1941) **:** a salt of ascorbic acid

ascor·bic acid \ə-'skòr-bik-\ *noun* [International Scientific Vocabulary *a*- + New Latin *scorbutus* scurvy — more at SCORBUTIC] (1933) **:** VITAMIN C

as·co·spore \'as-kə-,spōr, -,spòr\ *noun* (1875) **:** any of the spores contained in an ascus — **as·co·spor·ic** \,as-kə-'spōr-ik, -'spòr-\ *adjective*

as·cot \'as-kət, -,kät\ *noun* [*Ascot* Heath, racetrack near Ascot, England] (1898) **:** a broad neck scarf that is looped under the chin

as·cribe \ə-'skrīb\ *transitive verb* **as·cribed;** **as·crib·ing** [Middle English, from Latin *ascribere*, from *ad*- + *scribere* to write — more at SCRIBE] (15th century) **:** to refer to a supposed cause, source, or author ☆ — **as·crib·able** \-'skrī-bə-bəl\ *adjective*

ascribed *adjective* (1972) **:** acquired or assigned arbitrarily (as at birth) ⟨*ascribed* social status⟩

as·crip·tion \ə-'skrip-shən\ *noun* [Late Latin *ascription-, ascriptio*, from Latin, written addition, from *ascribere*] (1600) **1 :** the act of ascribing **:** ATTRIBUTION

☆ **SYNONYMS**
Ascribe, attribute, assign, impute, credit mean to lay something to the account of a person or thing. ASCRIBE suggests an inferring or conjecturing of cause, quality, authorship ⟨forged paintings formerly *ascribed* to masters⟩. ATTRIBUTE suggests less tentativeness than ASCRIBE, less definiteness than ASSIGN ⟨*attributed* to Rembrandt but possibly done by an associate⟩. ASSIGN implies ascribing with certainty or after deliberation ⟨*assigned* the bones to the Cretaceous Period⟩. IMPUTE suggests ascribing something that brings discredit by way of accusation or blame ⟨tried to *impute* sinister motives to my actions⟩. CREDIT implies ascribing a thing or especially an action to a person or other thing as its agent, source, or explanation ⟨*credited* his teammates for his success⟩.

2 : arbitrary placement (as at birth) in a particular social status

as·crip·tive \ə-'skrip-tiv\ *adjective* (1650)
: relating to, marked by, or involving ascription

as·cus \'as-kəs\ *noun, plural* **as·ci** \'as-ˌkī, -ˌkē, 'a-ˌsī\ [New Latin, from Greek *askos* wineskin, bladder] (1830)
: the membranous oval or tubular spore case of an ascomycete

as·dic \'az-(ˌ)dik\ *noun* [from *asdics* underwater echo ranging, probably from *Anti-Submarine Division* (British Admiralty department 1916–18) + *-ics*] (1939)
chiefly British : SONAR

word history see SONAR

-ase *noun suffix* [French, from *diastase*]
: enzyme ⟨prote*ase*⟩

asep·sis \(ˌ)ā-'sep-səs, ə-\ *noun* [New Latin] (1892)
1 : the condition of being aseptic
2 : the methods of making or keeping aseptic

asep·tic \(ˌ)ā-'sep-tik, ə-\ *adjective* [International Scientific Vocabulary] (circa 1859)
1 a : preventing infection ⟨*aseptic* techniques⟩ **b :** free or freed from pathogenic microorganisms ⟨an *aseptic* operating room⟩
2 : lacking vitality, emotion, or warmth ⟨the bureaucrat's world is prim and proper and *aseptic* —R. M. Weaver⟩
— **asep·ti·cal·ly** \-ti-k(ə-)lē\ *adverb*

asex·u·al \(ˌ)ā-'sek-sh(ə-)wəl, -'sek-shəl\ *adjective* (1830)
1 : lacking sex or functional sex organs ⟨*asexual* plants⟩
2 a : involving or reproducing by reproductive processes (as cell division, spore formation, fission, or budding) that do not involve the union of individuals or germ cells ⟨*asexual* reproduction⟩ **b :** produced by asexual reproduction ⟨*asexual* spores⟩
3 : devoid of sexuality ⟨an *asexual* relationship⟩
— **asex·u·al·i·ty** \ˌā-ˌsek-shə-'wa-lə-tē\ *noun*
— **asex·u·al·ly** \(ˌ)ā-'sek-sh(ə-)wə-lē, -ˌsek-sh(ə-)lē\ *adverb*

¹as far as *conjunction* (14th century)
: to the extent or degree that ⟨is safe, *as far as* we know⟩ — often used in expressions like "as far as (something) goes" and "as far as (something) is concerned" to mean "with regard to (something)" ⟨we felt pretty safe *as far as* the fire was concerned —Mark Twain⟩ or in expressions like "as far as (someone) is concerned" to mean "in (someone's) opinion" ⟨*as far as* I'm concerned, it's a mistake⟩

²as far as *preposition* (1523)
: with regard to : CONCERNING ⟨neatly groomed and, *as far as* clothes, casual looking —*N.Y. Times*⟩ ⟨*as far as* being mentioned in the Ten Commandments, I think it is —Billy Graham⟩ — chiefly in oral use

as for *preposition* (1533)
: with regard to : CONCERNING ⟨*as for* the others, they'll arrive later⟩

As·gard \'as-ˌgärd, 'az-\ *noun* [Old Norse *āsgarthr*]
: the home of the Norse gods

¹ash \'ash\ *noun* [Middle English *asshe*, from Old English *æsc*; akin to Old High German *ask* ash, Latin *ornus* mountain ash] (before 12th century)
1 : any of a genus (*Fraxinus*) of trees of the olive family with pinnate leaves, thin furrowed bark, and gray branchlets
2 : the tough elastic wood of an ash
3 [Old English *æsc*, name of the corresponding runic letter] **:** the ligature æ used in Old English and some phonetic alphabets to represent a low front vowel \a\

²ash *noun, often attributive* [Middle English *asshe*, from Old English *asce* — more at ARID] (before 12th century)
1 : something that symbolizes grief, repentance, or humiliation

2 a : the solid residue left when combustible material is thoroughly burned or is oxidized by chemical means **b :** fine particles of mineral matter from a volcanic vent
3 *plural* **:** the remains of the dead human body after cremation or disintegration
4 *plural* **:** deathly pallor ⟨the lip of *ashes* and the cheek of flame —Lord Byron⟩
5 *plural* **:** RUINS
— **ash·less** \-ləs\ *adjective*

³ash *transitive verb* (1894)
: to convert into ash

ashamed \ə-'shāmd\ *adjective* [Middle English, from Old English *āscamod*, past participle of *āscamian* to shame, from *ā-* (perfective prefix) + *scamian* to shame — more at ABIDE, SHAME] (before 12th century)
1 a : feeling shame, guilt, or disgrace **b :** feeling inferior or unworthy
2 : restrained by anticipation of shame ⟨was *ashamed* to beg⟩
— **asham·ed·ly** \-'shā-məd-lē\ *adverb*

Ashan·ti \ə-'shan-tē, -'shän-\ *noun, plural* **Ashanti** *or* **Ashantis** [Twi *àsànté*] (1721)
1 : a member of a people of southern Ghana
2 : the dialect of Akan spoken by the Ashanti people

ash–blond *or* **ash–blonde** \'ash-'bländ\ *adjective* (1903)
: pale or grayish blond ⟨*ash-blond* hair⟩

Ash·can \'ash-ˌkan\ *adjective* (1939)
: of or relating to a group of 20th century American painters who depicted city life realistically ⟨*Ashcan* school⟩

ash can *noun* (1899)
1 : a metal receptacle for refuse
2 *slang* **:** DEPTH CHARGE

¹ash·en \'a-shən\ *adjective* (before 12th century)
: of, relating to, or made from ash wood

²ashen *adjective* (14th century)
: resembling ashes (as in color); *especially* : deathly pale ⟨a face *ashen* and haggard⟩

Ash·er \'a-shər\ *noun* [Hebrew *Āshēr*]
: a son of Jacob and the traditional eponymous ancestor of one of the tribes of Israel

ash·fall \'ash-ˌfȯl\ *noun* (1923)
: a deposit of volcanic ash

Ash·ke·nazi \ˌäsh-kə-'nä-zē, ˌash-kə-'na-\ *noun, plural* **-naz·im** \-'nä-zəm, -'na-\ [Late Hebrew *Ashkĕnāzī*, from *Ashkĕnāz*, medieval rabbinical name for Germany] (1839)
: a member of one of the two great divisions of Jews comprising the eastern European Yiddish-speaking Jews — compare SEPHARDI
— **Ash·ke·naz·ic** \-'nä-zik, -'na-\ *adjective*

ash·lar \'ash-lər\ *noun* [Middle English *asheler*, from Middle French *aisselier* traverse beam, from Old French, from *ais* board, from Latin *axis*, alteration of *assis*] (14th century)
1 : hewn or squared stone; *also* : masonry of such stone
2 : a thin squared and dressed stone for facing a wall of rubble or brick

ashore \ə-'shȯr, -'shȯr\ *adverb* (1582)
: on or to the shore

as how *conjunction* (1771)
: THAT ⟨allowed *as how* she was glad to be here⟩

ash·ram \'äsh-rəm, -ˌräm; 'ash-ˌram\ *noun* [Sanskrit *āśrama*, from *śrama* religious exercise] (1917)
1 : a secluded dwelling of a Hindu sage; *also* : the group of disciples instructed there
2 : a religious retreat

Ash·to·reth \'ash-tə-ˌreth\ *noun* [Hebrew *'Ashtōreth*]
: ASTARTE

ash·tray \'ash-ˌtrā\ *noun* (1887)
: a receptacle for tobacco ashes and for cigar and cigarette butts

Ashur \'ä-ˌshu̇r\ *noun* [Akkadian *Ashūr*]
: the chief deity of the Assyrians

Ash Wednesday *noun* (14th century)
: the first day of Lent — see EASTER table

ashy \'a-shē\ *adjective* **ash·i·er; -est** (14th century)
1 : of or relating to ashes
2 : ASHEN

Asi·a·go \ˌä-zhē-'ä-(ˌ)gō, ˌä-sē-, -shē-\ *noun* [*Asiago,* town in Italy] (1938)
: a pungent hard yellow cheese of Italian origin suitable for grating

¹Asian \'ā-zhən *also* -shən\ *adjective* (1550)
: of, relating to, or characteristic of the continent of Asia or its people □

²Asian *noun* (circa 1890)
: a native or inhabitant of Asia

Asian–Amer·i·can \-ə-'mər-ə-kən\ *noun* (1974)
: an American of Asian descent
— **Asian–American** *adjective*

Asian elephant *noun* (1981)
: ELEPHANT 1b

Asian influenza *noun* (1957)
: influenza caused by a mutant strain of the influenza virus isolated during the 1957 epidemic in Asia — called also *Asian flu*

Asi·at·ic \ˌā-zhē-'a-tik, -zē-\ *adjective* (1602)
: ASIAN — sometimes taken to be offensive
— **Asiatic** *noun*
usage see ASIAN

Asiatic cholera *noun* (1831)
: cholera of Asian origin that is caused by virulent strains of the cholera vibrio (*Vibrio cholerae*)

Asiatic elephant *noun* (1930)
: ELEPHANT 1b

¹aside \ə-'sīd\ *adverb* (14th century)
1 : to or toward the side ⟨stepped *aside*⟩
2 : away from others or into privacy ⟨pulled him *aside*⟩
3 : out of the way especially for future use : AWAY ⟨putting *aside* savings⟩
4 : away from one's thought or consideration ⟨jesting *aside*⟩

²aside *preposition* (1592)
obsolete : BEYOND, PAST

³aside *noun* (circa 1751)
1 : an utterance meant to be inaudible to someone; *especially* : an actor's speech heard by the audience but supposedly not by other characters
2 : a straying from the theme : DIGRESSION

aside from *preposition* (1818)
1 : in addition to : BESIDES
2 : EXCEPT FOR

as if *conjunction* (13th century)
1 : as it would be if ⟨it was *as if* he had lost his last friend⟩
2 : as one would do if ⟨he ran *as if* ghosts were chasing him⟩
3 : THAT ⟨it seemed *as if* the day would never end⟩

as·i·nine \'a-sᵊn-ˌīn\ *adjective* [Latin *asininus*, from *asinus* ass] (15th century)
1 : marked by inexcusable failure to exercise

□ USAGE
Asian As we move toward the end of the 20th century, *Asian* is the preferred word especially in ethnic reference, because *Asiatic* is held to be at least mildly offensive. *Asiatic* appears to have been the more common term up until the 1940s, when it began to be considered offensive, especially as associated with the policies of colonialism. While *Asian* prevails today, *Asiatic* still has some use as a geographical designator ⟨the *Asiatic* side of the Bosporus⟩. Such use appears to be more frequent in British English than in American.

\ə\ abut \ᵊ\ kitten \ər\ further \a\ ash \ā\ ace
\ä\ mop, mar \au̇\ out \ch\ chin \e\ bet \ē\ easy
\g\ go \i\ hit \ī\ ice \j\ job \ŋ\ sing \ō\ go
\ȯ\ law \ȯi\ boy \th\ thin \th\ the \ü\ loot \u̇\ foot
\y\ yet \zh\ vision *see also* Guide to Pronunciation

intelligence or sound judgment ⟨an *asinine* excuse⟩
2 : of, relating to, or resembling an ass
synonym see SIMPLE
— **as·i·nine·ly** *adverb*
— **as·i·nin·i·ty** \ˌa-sə-'ni-nə-tē\ *noun*
ask \'ask, 'åsk; *dialect* 'aks\ *verb* **asked**
\'as(k)t, 'åsk(t)t, 'åsk; *dialect* 'akst\ **ask·ing**
[Middle English, from Old English *āscian;*
akin to Old High German *eiscōn* to ask,
Lithuanian *eiškoti* to seek, Sanskrit *icchati* he
seeks] (before 12th century)
transitive verb
1 a : to call on for an answer **b :** to put a question about **c :** SPEAK, UTTER ⟨*ask* a question⟩
2 a : to make a request of ⟨she *asked* her
teacher for help⟩ **b :** to make a request for ⟨she
asked help from her teacher⟩
3 : to call for **:** REQUIRE
4 : to set as a price ⟨*asked* $3000 for the car⟩
5 : INVITE
intransitive verb
1 : to seek information
2 : to make a request ⟨*asked* for food⟩
3 : LOOK — often used in the phrase *ask for
trouble* ☆ ☆ □
— **ask·er** *noun*
askance \ə-'skan(t)s\ *also* **askant** \-'skant\
adverb [origin unknown] (circa 1530)
1 : with a side-glance **:** OBLIQUELY
2 : with disapproval or distrust **:** SCORNFULLY
as·ke·sis \ə-'skē-səs\ *variant of* ASCESIS
askew \ə-'skyü\ *adverb or adjective* [probably
from ¹*a-* + *skew*] (1573)
: out of line **:** AWRY ⟨the picture hung *askew*⟩
— **askew·ness** *noun*
asking price *noun* (1755)
: the price at which something is offered for
sale
¹**aslant** \ə-'slant\ *adverb or adjective* (14th
century)
: in a slanting direction **:** OBLIQUELY
²**aslant** *preposition* (1602)
: over or across in a slanting direction
¹**asleep** \ə-'slēp\ *adjective* [Middle English
aslepe, from Old English *on slǣpe*] (13th century)
1 : being in a state of sleep
2 : DEAD
3 : lacking sensation **:** NUMB
4 a : INACTIVE, DORMANT **b :** not alert **:** INDIFFERENT
²**asleep** *adverb* (13th century)
1 : into a state of sleep
2 : into the sleep of death
3 : into a state of inactivity, sluggishness, or
indifference
as long as *conjunction* (15th century)
1 : provided that ⟨can do as they like *as long
as* they have a B average⟩
2 : INASMUCH AS, SINCE ⟨*as long as* you're going, I'll go too⟩
aslope \ə-'slōp\ *adjective or adverb* (14th century)
: being in a sloping or slanting position or direction
aso·cial \(ˌ)ā-'sō-shəl\ *adjective* (1883)
: not social: as **a :** rejecting or lacking the capacity for social interaction **b :** ANTISOCIAL
as of *preposition* (1900)
: ON, AT, FROM — used to indicate a time or
date at which something begins or ends ⟨takes
effect *as of* July 1⟩
¹**asp** \'asp\ *noun* [Middle English, from Old
English *æspe*] (before 12th century)
: ASPEN
²**asp** *noun* [Middle English *aspis,* from Latin,
from Greek] (14th century)
: a small venomous snake of Egypt usually
held to be a cobra (*Naja haje*)
as·par·a·gine \ə-'spar-ə-ˌjēn\ *noun* [French,
from Latin *asparagus*] (1813)
: a nonessential amino acid $C_4H_8N_2O_3$ that is
an amide of aspartic acid

as·par·a·gus \ə-'spar-ə-gəs\ *noun, plural*
-gus [New Latin, genus name, from Latin, asparagus plant, from Greek *asparagos;* perhaps
akin to Greek *spargan* to swell] (1548)
: any of a genus (*Asparagus*) of Old World perennial plants of the lily family having much-branched
stems, minute scalelike leaves, and narrow usually
filiform branchlets that function as leaves; *especially* **:** one (*A. officinalis*)
widely cultivated for its
edible young shoots

asparagus

as·par·tame \'as-pər-ˌtām, ə-'spär-ˌtām\ *noun*
[*aspartic* acid + *phenylalanine* + *methyl* + *ester*] (1972)
: a crystalline compound $C_{14}H_{18}N_2O_5$ that is a
diamide synthesized from phenylalanine and
aspartic acid and that is used as a low-calorie
sweetener
as·par·tate \ə-'spär-ˌtāt\ *noun* (1863)
: a salt or ester of aspartic acid
as·par·tic acid \ə-'spär-tik-\ *noun* [International Scientific Vocabulary, irregular from
Latin *asparagus*] (1863)
: a crystalline amino acid $C_4H_7NO_4$ found especially in plants
as·pect \'as-ˌpekt\ *noun* [Middle English,
from Latin *aspectus,* from *aspicere* to look at,
from *ad-* + *specere* to look — more at SPY]
(14th century)
1 a : the position of planets or stars with respect to one another held by astrologers to influence human affairs; *also* **:** the apparent position (as conjunction) of a body in the solar
system with respect to the sun **b :** a position
facing a particular direction **:** EXPOSURE ⟨the
house has a southern *aspect*⟩ **c :** the manner of
presentation of a plane to a fluid through
which it is moving or to a current
2 a (1) **:** appearance to the eye or mind (2) **:** a
particular appearance of countenance **:** MIEN **b**
: a particular status or phase in which something appears or may be regarded ⟨studied every *aspect* of the question⟩
3 *archaic* **:** an act of looking **:** GAZE
4 a : the nature of the action of a verb as to its
beginning, duration, completion, or repetition
and without reference to its position in time **b**
: a set of inflected verb forms that indicate aspect
— **as·pec·tu·al** \a-'spek-chə(-wə)l\ *adjective*
aspect ratio *noun* (1907)
: a ratio of one dimension to another: as **a**
: the ratio of span to mean chord of an airfoil
b : the ratio of the width of a television or
motion-picture image to its height
as·pen \'as-pən\ *noun* [Middle English, of an
aspen, from *asp* aspen, from Old English
æspe; akin to Old High German *aspa* aspen,
Russian *osina*] (1596)
: any of several poplars (especially *Populus
tremula* of Europe and *P. tremuloides* and *P.
grandidentata* of North America) with leaves
that flutter in the lightest wind because of their
flattened petioles
as per \'az-ˌpər\ *preposition* (1859)
: in accordance with **:** ACCORDING TO
— **as per usual :** as usual
as·per·ges \ə-'spər-(ˌ)jēz\ *noun* [Latin, thou
wilt sprinkle, from *aspergere*] (circa 1587)
: a ceremony of sprinkling altar and people
with holy water
as·per·gil·lo·sis \ˌas-pər-(ˌ)ji-'lō-səs\ *noun,
plural* **-lo·ses** \-ˌsēz\ (1898)
: infection with or disease caused (as in poultry) by molds (genus *Aspergillus*)
as·per·gil·lum \ˌas-pər-'ji-ləm\ *noun, plural*
-la \-lə\ *or* **-lums** [New Latin, from Latin *aspergere*] (1649)

: a brush or small perforated container with a
handle that is used for
sprinkling holy water in
a liturgical service
as·per·gil·lus \-'ji-ləs\
noun, plural **-gil·li** \-'ji-ˌlī\ [New Latin, genus
name, from *aspergillum*]
(circa 1847)
: any of a genus (*Aspergillus*) of ascomycetous fungi with branched radiate sporophores
including many common molds

aspergillum

as·per·i·ty \a-'sper-ə-tē, ə-\ *noun, plural* **-ties**
[Middle English *asprete,* from Old French
aspreté, from *aspre* rough, from Latin *asper,*
from (assumed) Old Latin *absperos,* from *ab-*
ab- + *-speros;* akin to Sanskrit *apasphura* repelling, Latin *spernere* to spurn — more at
SPURN] (13th century)
1 : RIGOR, SEVERITY
2 a : roughness of surface **:** UNEVENNESS; *also*

: a tiny projection from a surface **b** : roughness of sound
3 : roughness of manner or of temper : HARSHNESS

as·perse \ə-'spərs, a-\ *transitive verb* **aspersed; as·pers·ing** [Latin *aspersus,* past participle of *aspergere,* from *ad- + spargere* to scatter — more at SPARK] (15th century)
1 : SPRINKLE; *especially* : to sprinkle with holy water
2 : to attack with evil reports or false or injurious charges
synonym see MALIGN

as·per·sion \ə-'spər-zhən, -shən\ *noun* (circa 1587)
1 : a sprinkling with water especially in religious ceremonies
2 a : the act of calumniating **b** : a calumnious expression ⟨cast *aspersions* on her integrity⟩

¹as·phalt \'as-,fȯlt *also* 'ash-, *especially British* -,falt\ *also* **as·phal·tum** \as-'fȯl-təm, *especially British* -'fal-\ *noun* [Middle English *aspalt,* from Late Latin *aspaltus,* from Greek *asphaltos*] (14th century)
1 : a dark bituminous substance that is found in natural beds and is also obtained as a residue in petroleum refining and that consists chiefly of hydrocarbons
2 : an asphaltic composition used for pavements and as a waterproof cement
— **as·phal·tic** \as-'fȯl-tik, *especially British* -'fal-\ *adjective*

²asphalt *transitive verb* (circa 1859)
: to cover with asphalt : PAVE 1

as·phalt·ite \'as-,fȯl-,tīt, *especially British* -,fal-\ *noun* (circa 1899)
: a native asphalt occurring in vein deposits below the surface of the ground

asphalt jungle *noun* (1920)
: a big city or a specified part of a big city

as·pher·ic \(,)ā-'sfir-ik, -'sfer-\ *or* **as·pher·i·cal** \-i-kəl\ *adjective* (circa 1922)
: departing slightly from the spherical form especially in order to correct for spherical aberration ⟨an *aspheric* lens⟩

as·pho·del \'as-fə-,del\ *noun* [Latin *asphodelus,* from Greek *asphodelos*] (1597)
: any of various Old World usually perennial herbs (especially genera *Asphodelus* and *Asphodeline*) of the lily family with flowers in usually long erect racemes

as·phyx·ia \as-'fik-sē-ə, əs-\ *noun* [New Latin, from Greek, stopping of the pulse, from *a-* + *sphyzein* to throb] (1778)
: a lack of oxygen or excess of carbon dioxide in the body that is usually caused by interruption of breathing and that causes unconsciousness

as·phyx·i·ate \-sē-,āt\ *verb* **-at·ed; -at·ing** (1836)
transitive verb
: to cause asphyxia in; *also* : to kill or make unconscious by inadequate oxygen, presence of noxious agents, or other obstruction to normal breathing
intransitive verb
: to become asphyxiated
— **as·phyx·i·a·tion** \-,fik-sē-'ā-shən\ *noun*

¹as·pic \'as-pik\ *noun* [Middle French, alteration of *aspe,* from Latin *aspis*] (1530)
obsolete : ²ASP

²aspic *noun* [French, literally, asp] (1789)
: a clear savory jelly (as of fish or meat stock) used as a garnish or to make a meat, fish, or vegetable mold

as·pi·dis·tra \,as-pə-'dis-trə\ *noun* [New Latin, irregular from Greek *aspid-, aspis* shield] (1822)
: an Asian plant (*Aspidistra elatior*) of the lily family that has large basal leaves and is often grown as a foliage plant

¹as·pi·rant \'as-p(ə-)rənt, ə-'spī-rənt\ *noun* (1738)
: one who aspires ⟨presidential *aspirants*⟩

²aspirant *adjective* (1814)

: seeking to attain a desired position or status

¹as·pi·rate \'as-p(ə-)rət\ *noun* (1617)
1 : an independent sound \h\ or a character (as the letter *h*) representing it
2 : a consonant having aspiration as its final component ⟨in English the \p\ of *pit* is an *aspirate*⟩
3 : material removed by aspiration

²as·pi·rate \'as-pə-,rāt\ *transitive verb* **-rat·ed; -rat·ing** [Latin *aspiratus,* past participle of *aspirare*] (circa 1700)
1 : to pronounce (a vowel or a consonant) with aspiration (sense 1a)
2 a : to draw by suction **b** : to remove (as blood) by aspiration **c** : to take into the lungs by aspiration

as·pi·ra·tion \,as-pə-'rā-shən\ *noun* (14th century)
1 a : audible breath that accompanies or comprises a speech sound **b** : the pronunciation or addition of an aspiration; *also* : the symbol of an aspiration
2 : a drawing of something in, out, up, or through by or as if by suction: as **a** : the act of breathing and especially of breathing in **b** : the withdrawal of fluid or tissue from the body **c** : the taking of foreign matter into the lungs with the respiratory current
3 a : a strong desire to achieve something high or great **b** : an object of such desire
synonym see AMBITION
— **as·pi·ra·tion·al** \-'rā-sh(ə-)nəl\ *adjective*

as·pi·ra·tor \'as-pə-,rā-tər\ *noun* (1804)
: an apparatus for producing suction or moving or collecting materials by suction; *especially* : a hollow tubular instrument connected with a partial vacuum and used to remove fluid or tissue or foreign bodies from the body

as·pire \ə-'spīr\ *intransitive verb* **as·pired; as·pir·ing** [Middle English, from Middle French or Latin; Middle French *aspirer,* from Latin *aspirare,* literally, to breathe upon, from *ad- + spirare* to breathe] (14th century)
1 : to seek to attain or accomplish a particular goal ⟨*aspired* to a career in medicine⟩
2 : ASCEND, SOAR
— **as·pir·er** *noun*

as·pi·rin \'as-p(ə-)rən\ *noun, plural* **aspirin** *or* **aspirins** [International Scientific Vocabulary, from *acetyl + spir*aeic acid (former name of salicylic acid), from New Latin *Spiraea,* genus of shrubs — more at SPIREA] (1899)
1 : a white crystalline derivative $C_9H_8O_4$ of salicylic acid used for relief of pain and fever
2 : a tablet of aspirin

as regards *also* **as respects** *preposition* (1840)
: in regard to : with respect to

¹ass \'as\ *noun* [Middle English, from Old English *assa,* probably from Old Irish *asan,* from Latin *asinus*] (before 12th century)
1 : any of several hardy gregarious African or Asian perissodactyl mammals (genus *Equus*) smaller than the horse and having long ears; *especially* : an African mammal (*E. asinus*) that is the ancestor of the donkey
2 : a stupid, obstinate, or perverse person — often compounded with a preceding adjective ⟨don't be a smart-*ass*⟩; often considered vulgar

²ass \'as\ *or* **arse** \'as, 'ärs\ *noun* [Middle English *ars, ers,* from Old English *ærs, ears;* akin to Old High German & Old Norse *ars* buttocks, Greek *orrhos* buttocks, *oura* tail] (before 12th century)
1 a : BUTTOCKS — often used in emphatic reference to a specific person ⟨get your *ass* over here⟩ ⟨saved my *ass*⟩; often considered vulgar **b** : ANUS — often considered vulgar
2 : SEXUAL INTERCOURSE — usually considered vulgar

³ass *adverb* [²*ass*] (1955)
— used as a postpositive intensive especially with words of derogatory implication ⟨fancy-*ass*⟩; often considered vulgar

as·sai \ä-'sī\ *adverb* [Italian, from (assumed) Vulgar Latin *ad satis* enough — more at ASSET] (circa 1724)
: VERY — used with tempo direction in music ⟨allegro *assai*⟩

as·sail \ə-'sā(ə)l\ *transitive verb* [Middle English, from Old French *asaillir,* from (assumed) Vulgar Latin *assalire,* alteration of Latin *assilire* to leap upon, from *ad- + salire* to leap — more at SALLY] (13th century)
: to attack violently with blows or words
synonym see ATTACK
— **as·sail·able** \-'sā-lə-bəl\ *adjective*
— **as·sail·ant** \-'sā-lənt\ *noun*

As·sam·ese \,a-sə-'mēz, -'mēs\ *noun, plural* **Assamese** (1826)
1 : a native or inhabitant of Assam, India
2 : the Indo-Aryan language of Assam
— **Assamese** *adjective*

as·sas·sin \ə-'sa-s°n\ *noun* [Medieval Latin *assassinus,* from Arabic *hashshāshīn,* plural of *hashshāsh* one who smokes or chews hashish, from *hashīsh* hashish] (circa 1520)
1 *capitalized* : one of a secret order of Muslims that at the time of the Crusades terrorized Christians and other enemies by secret murder committed under the influence of hashish
2 : a person who commits murder; *especially* : one who murders a politically important person either for hire or from fanatical motives

as·sas·si·nate \ə-'sa-s°n-,āt\ *transitive verb* **-nat·ed; -nat·ing** (1607)
1 : to injure or destroy unexpectedly and treacherously
2 : to murder by sudden or secret attack usually for impersonal reasons
synonym see KILL
— **as·sas·si·na·tion** \-,sa-s°n-'ā-shən\ *noun*
— **as·sas·si·na·tor** \-'sa-s°n-,ā-tər\ *noun*

assassin bug *noun* (1895)
: any of a family (Reduviidae) of bugs that are usually predatory on insects though some (as a conenose) suck the blood of mammals — called also *reduviid*

¹as·sault \ə-'sȯlt\ *noun* [Middle English *assaut,* from Old French, from (assumed) Vulgar Latin *assaltus,* from *assalire*] (14th century)
1 a : a violent physical or verbal attack **b** : a military attack usually involving direct combat with enemy forces **c** : a concerted effort (as to reach a goal or defeat an adversary)
2 a : a threat or attempt to inflict offensive physical contact or bodily harm on a person (as by lifting a fist in a threatening manner) that puts the person in immediate danger of or in apprehension of such harm or contact — compare BATTERY 1b **b** : RAPE

²assault (15th century)
transitive verb
1 : to make an assault on
2 : RAPE
intransitive verb
: to make an assault
synonym see ATTACK
— **as·sault·er** *noun*
— **as·saul·tive** \-'sȯl-tiv\ *adjective*
— **as·saul·tive·ly** *adverb*
— **as·saul·tive·ness** *noun*

assault boat *noun* (1941)
: a small portable boat used in an amphibious military attack or in land warfare for crossing rivers or lakes

assault rifle *noun* (1975)
: any of various automatic or semiautomatic rifles designed for military use with large capacity magazines

¹as·say \'a-,sā, a-'sā\ *noun* [Middle English, from Old French *essai, assai* test, effort — more at ESSAY] (14th century)

\ə\ **abut** \°\ **kitten** \ər\ **further** \a\ **ash** \ā\ **ace**
\ä\ **mop, mar** \au̇\ **out** \ch\ **chin** \e\ **bet** \ē\ **easy**
\g\ **go** \i\ **hit** \ī\ **ice** \j\ **job** \ŋ\ **sing** \ō\ **go**
\ȯ\ **law** \ȯi\ **boy** \th\ **thin** \th̷\ **the** \ü\ **loot** \u̇\ **foot**
\y\ **yet** \zh\ **vision** *see also* Guide to Pronunciation

1 *archaic* **:** TRIAL, ATTEMPT
2 : examination and determination as to characteristics (as weight, measure, or quality)
3 : analysis (as of an ore or drug) to determine the presence, absence, or quantity of one or more components
4 : a substance to be assayed; *also* **:** the tabulated result of assaying
²**as·say** \a-ˈsā, ˈa-ˌsā\ (14th century)
transitive verb
1 : TRY, ATTEMPT
2 a : to analyze (as an ore) for one or more specific components **b :** to judge the worth of **:** ESTIMATE
intransitive verb
: to prove up in an assay
— **as·say·er** *noun*
assed \ˈast\ *adverb* (1932)
: ³ASS — used in combination ⟨smart-*assed*⟩; often considered vulgar
as·se·gai *or* **as·sa·gai** \ˈa-si-ˌgī\ *noun* [ultimately from Arabic *az-zaghāya* the assegai, from *al-* the + *zaghāya* assegai] (1600)
: a slender hardwood spear or light javelin usually tipped with iron and used in southern Africa
as·sem·blage \ə-ˈsem-blij, *for 3 also* ˌa-ˌsäm-ˈbläzh\ *noun* (1690)
1 : a collection of persons or things **:** GATHERING
2 : the act of assembling **:** the state of being assembled
3 a : an artistic composition made from scraps, junk, and odds and ends (as of paper, cloth, wood, stone, or metal) **b :** the art of making assemblages
as·sem·blag·ist \-bli-jist, -ˈblä-zhist\ *noun* (1965)
: an artist who specializes in assemblages
as·sem·ble \ə-ˈsem-bəl\ *verb* **as·sem·bled; as·sem·bling** \-b(ə-)liŋ\ [Middle English, from Old French *assembler*, from (assumed) Vulgar Latin *assimulare*, from Latin *ad-* + *simul* together — more at SAME] (13th century)
transitive verb
1 : to bring together (as in a particular place or for a particular purpose)
2 : to fit together the parts of
intransitive verb
: to meet together **:** CONVENE
synonym see GATHER
as·sem·bler \-b(ə-)lər\ *noun* (1635)
1 : one that assembles
2 a : a computer program that automatically converts instructions written in assembly language into machine language **b :** ASSEMBLY LANGUAGE
as·sem·bly \ə-ˈsem-blē\ *noun, plural* **-blies** [Middle English *assemblee*, from Middle French, from Old French, from *assembler*] (14th century)
1 : a company of persons gathered for deliberation and legislation, worship, or entertainment
2 *capitalized* **:** a legislative body; *specifically* **:** the lower house of a legislature
3 : ASSEMBLAGE 1, 2
4 : a signal for troops to assemble or fall in
5 a : the fitting together of manufactured parts into a complete machine, structure, or unit of a machine **b :** a collection of parts so assembled
6 : the translation of assembly language to machine language by an assembler
assembly language *noun* (circa 1964)
: a programming language that consists of instructions that are mnemonic codes for corresponding machine language instructions
assembly line *noun* (1914)
1 : an arrangement of machines, equipment, and workers in which work passes from operation to operation in direct line until the product is assembled
2 : a process for turning out a finished product in a mechanically efficient manner ⟨academic *assembly lines*⟩

as·sem·bly·man \ə-ˈsem-blē-mən\ *noun* (1647)
: a member of an assembly
Assembly of God (1952)
: a congregation belonging to a Pentecostal body founded in the U.S. in 1914
as·sem·bly·wom·an \-ˌwu̇-mən\ *noun* (1969)
: a woman who is a member of an assembly
¹**as·sent** \ə-ˈsent, a-\ *intransitive verb* [Middle English, from Old French *assenter*, from Latin *assentari*, from *assentire*, from *ad-* + *sentire* to feel — more at SENSE] (14th century)
: to agree to something especially after thoughtful consideration **:** CONCUR ☆
— **as·sen·tor** *or* **as·sent·er** \-ˈsen-tər\ *noun*
²**assent** *noun* (14th century)
: an act of assenting **:** ACQUIESCENCE, AGREEMENT
as·sen·ta·tion \ˌa-sᵊn-ˈtā-shən, ˌa-ˌsen-\ *noun* (15th century)
: ready assent especially when insincere or obsequious
as·sert \ə-ˈsərt, a-\ *transitive verb* [Latin *assertus*, past participle of *asserere*, from *ad-* + *serere* to join — more at SERIES] (circa 1604)
1 : to state or declare positively and often forcefully or aggressively
2 a : to demonstrate the existence of ⟨*assert* his manhood —James Joyce⟩ **b :** POSIT, POSTULATE ☆
— **assert oneself :** to compel recognition especially of one's rights
as·sert·ed·ly \ə-ˈsər-təd-lē, a-\ *adverb* (1937)
: by positive and usually unsubstantiated assertion **:** ALLEGEDLY
as·ser·tion \ə-ˈsər-shən, a-\ *noun* (15th century)
: the act of asserting; *also* **:** DECLARATION, AFFIRMATION
as·ser·tive \ə-ˈsər-tiv, a-\ *adjective* (circa 1619)
1 : disposed to or characterized by bold or confident assertion
2 : having a strong or distinctive flavor or aroma ⟨*assertive* wines⟩
synonym see AGGRESSIVE
— **as·ser·tive·ly** *adverb*
— **as·ser·tive·ness** *noun*
assertiveness training *noun* (1975)
: a method of training individuals to act in a bold self-confident manner
asses *plural of* AS *or of* ASS
as·sess \ə-ˈses, a-\ *transitive verb* [Middle English, probably from Medieval Latin *assessus*, past participle of *assidēre*, from Latin, to sit beside, assist in the office of a judge — more at ASSIZE] (15th century)
1 : to determine the rate or amount of (as a tax)
2 a : to impose (as a tax) according to an established rate **b :** to subject to a tax, charge, or levy
3 : to make an official valuation of (property) for the purposes of taxation
4 : to determine the importance, size, or value of
5 : to charge (a player or team) with a foul or penalty
synonym see ESTIMATE
— **as·sess·able** \-ˈse-sə-bəl\ *adjective*
as·sess·ment \ə-ˈses-mənt, a-\ *noun* (1534)
1 : the action or an instance of assessing **:** APPRAISAL
2 : the amount assessed
as·ses·sor \ə-ˈse-sər\ *noun* (14th century)
1 : an official who assists a judge or magistrate
2 : one that assesses; *especially* **:** an official who assesses property for taxation
as·set \ˈa-ˌset *also* -sət\ *noun* [back-formation from *assets*, singular, sufficient property to pay debts and legacies, from Anglo-French *asetz*, from Old French *assez* enough, from (assumed) Vulgar Latin *ad satis*, from Latin

ad to + *satis* enough — more at AT, SAD] (1531)
1 *plural* **a :** the property of a deceased person subject by law to the payment of his or her debts and legacies **b :** the entire property of a person, association, corporation, or estate applicable or subject to the payment of debts
2 : ADVANTAGE, RESOURCE ⟨his wit is his chief *asset*⟩
3 a : an item of value owned **b** *plural* **:** the items on a balance sheet showing the book value of property owned
as·sev·er·ate \ə-ˈse-və-ˌrāt\ *transitive verb* **-at·ed; -at·ing** [Latin *asseveratus*, past participle of *asseverare*, from *ad-* + *severus* severe] (1791)
: to affirm or aver positively or earnestly
— **as·sev·er·a·tion** \-ˌse-və-ˈrā-shən\ *noun*
— **as·sev·er·a·tive** \-ˈse-və-ˌrā-tiv\ *adjective*
ass·hole \ˈas-ˌ(h)ōl\ *noun* (14th century)
1 : ANUS — usually considered vulgar
2 a : a stupid, incompetent, or detestable person — usually considered vulgar **b :** a despicable place — usually used in the phrase *asshole of the universe;* usually considered vulgar
as·si·du·ity \ˌa-sə-ˈdü-ə-tē, -ˈdyü-\ *noun, plural* **-ities** (1596)
1 : the quality or state of being assiduous **:** DILIGENCE
2 : persistent personal attention — usually used in plural
as·sid·u·ous \ə-ˈsij-wəs, -ˈsi-jə-\ *adjective* [Latin *assiduus*, from *assidēre*] (1660)
: marked by careful unremitting attention or persistent application ⟨an *assiduous* book collector⟩ ⟨tended her garden with *assiduous* attention⟩
synonym see BUSY
— **as·sid·u·ous·ly** *adverb*
— **as·sid·u·ous·ness** *noun*

☆ SYNONYMS

Assent, consent, accede, acquiesce, agree, subscribe mean to concur with what has been proposed. ASSENT implies an act involving the understanding or judgment and applies to propositions or opinions ⟨voters *assented* to the proposal⟩. CONSENT involves the will or feelings and indicates compliance with what is requested or desired ⟨*consented* to their daughter's going⟩. ACCEDE implies a yielding, often under pressure, of assent or consent ⟨officials *acceded* to the prisoners' demands⟩. ACQUIESCE implies tacit acceptance or forbearance of opposition ⟨*acquiesced* to his boss's wishes⟩. AGREE sometimes implies previous difference of opinion or attempts at persuasion ⟨finally *agreed* to come along⟩. SUBSCRIBE implies not only consent or assent but hearty approval and active support ⟨*subscribes* wholeheartedly to the idea⟩.

Assert, declare, affirm, protest, avow mean to state positively usually in anticipation of denial or objection. ASSERT implies stating confidently without need for proof or regard for evidence ⟨*asserted* that modern music is just noise⟩. DECLARE stresses open or public statement ⟨*declared* her support for the candidate⟩. AFFIRM implies conviction based on evidence, experience, or faith ⟨*affirmed* the existence of an afterlife⟩. PROTEST emphasizes affirming in the face of denial or doubt ⟨*protested* that he really had been misquoted⟩. AVOW stresses frank declaration and acknowledgment of personal responsibility for what is declared ⟨*avowed* that all investors would be repaid in full⟩. See in addition MAINTAIN.

¹as·sign \ə-'sīn\ *transitive verb* [Middle English, from Old French *assigner,* from Latin *assignare,* from *ad-* + *signare* to mark, from *signum* mark, sign] (13th century)
1 : to transfer (property) to another especially in trust or for the benefit of creditors
2 a : to appoint to a post or duty ⟨*assigned* them to light duty⟩ ⟨*assigned* me two clerks⟩ **b :** to appoint as a duty or task ⟨*assigns* 20 pages for homework⟩
3 : to fix or specify in correspondence or relationship ⟨*assign* counsel to the defendant⟩ ⟨*assign* a value to the variable⟩
4 a : to ascribe as a motive, reason, or cause especially after deliberation **b :** to consider to belong to (a specified period of time)
synonym see ASCRIBE
— **as·sign·abil·i·ty** \-ˌsī-nə-'bi-lə-tē\ *noun*
— **as·sign·able** \-'sī-nə-bəl\ *adjective*
— **as·sign·er** \ə-'sī-nər\ *or* **as·sign·or** \ˌa-sə-'nȯr, ˌa-ˌsī-, ə-ˌsī-\ *noun*

²assign *noun* (15th century)
: ASSIGNEE 3 ⟨heirs and *assigns*⟩

as·si·gnat \ˌa-(ˌ)sēn-'yä, 'a-sig-ˌnat\ *noun* [French, from Latin *assignatus,* past participle of *assignare*] (1790)
: a bill issued as currency by the French Revolutionary government (1789–96) on the security of expropriated lands

as·sig·na·tion \ˌa-sig-'nā-shən\ *noun* (15th century)
1 : the act of assigning or the assignment made
2 : an appointment of time and place for a meeting; *especially* **:** TRYST ⟨returned from an *assignation* with his mistress —W. B. Yeats⟩

assigned risk *noun* (1946)
: a poor risk (as an accident-prone motorist) that insurance companies would normally reject but are forced to insure by state law

as·sign·ee \ˌa-sə-'nē, ˌa-ˌsī-, ə-ˌsī-\ *noun* (14th century)
1 : a person to whom an assignment is made
2 : a person appointed to act for another
3 : a person to whom a right or property is legally transferred

as·sign·ment \ə-'sīn-mənt\ *noun* (14th century)
1 : the act of assigning
2 a : a position, post, or office to which one is assigned **b :** a specified task or amount of work assigned or undertaken as if assigned by authority
3 : the transfer of property; *especially* **:** the transfer of property to be held in trust or to be used for the benefit of creditors
synonym see TASK

as·sim·i·la·ble \ə-'si-mə-lə-bəl\ *adjective* (1667)
: capable of being assimilated
— **as·sim·i·la·bil·i·ty** \-ˌsi-mə-lə-'bi-lə-tē\ *noun*

¹as·sim·i·late \ə-'si-mə-ˌlāt\ *verb* **-lat·ed; -lat·ing** [Middle English, from Medieval Latin *assimilatus,* past participle of *assimilare,* from Latin *assimulare* to make similar, from *ad-* + *simulare* to make similar, simulate] (15th century)
transitive verb
1 a : to take in and appropriate as nourishment **:** absorb into the system **b :** to take into the mind and thoroughly comprehend
2 a : to make similar **b :** to alter by assimilation **c :** to absorb into the culture or mores of a population or group
3 : COMPARE, LIKEN
intransitive verb
: to become assimilated ☐
— **as·sim·i·la·tor** \-ˌlā-tər\ *noun*

²as·sim·i·late \-lət, -ˌlāt\ *noun* (1935)
: something that is assimilated

as·sim·i·la·tion \ə-ˌsi-mə-'lā-shən\ *noun* (15th century)
1 a : an act, process, or instance of assimilating **b :** the state of being assimilated
2 : the incorporation or conversion of nutri-

ents into protoplasm that in animals follows digestion and absorption and in higher plants involves both photosynthesis and root absorption
3 : change of a sound in speech so that it becomes identical with or similar to a neighboring sound ⟨the usual *assimilation* of \z\ to \sh\ in the phrase *his shoe*⟩
4 : the process of receiving new facts or of responding to new situations in conformity with what is already available to consciousness

as·sim·i·la·tion·ist \-sh(ə-)nist\ *noun* (1899)
: a person who advocates a policy of assimilating differing racial or cultural groups
— **as·sim·i·la·tion·ism** \-shə-ˌni-zəm\ *noun*
— **as·sim·i·la·tion·ist** *adjective*

as·sim·i·la·tive \ə-'si-mə-ˌlā-tiv, -lə-tiv\ *adjective* (14th century)
: of, relating to, or causing assimilation

as·sim·i·la·to·ry \ə-'si-mə-lə-ˌtȯr-ē, -ˌtȯr-\ *adjective* (circa 1847)
: ASSIMILATIVE

As·sin·i·boin *or* **As·sin·i·boine** \ə-'si-nə-ˌbȯin\ *noun, plural* **-boin** *or* **-boins** *or* **boine** *or* **-boines** [Ojibwa dialect *assiniʼpwaʼn,* literally, stone Sioux] (1804)
: a member of an American Indian people originally of the area between the upper Missouri and middle Saskatchewan rivers

¹as·sist \ə-'sist\ *verb* [Middle French or Latin; Middle French *assister* to help, stand by, from Latin *assistere,* from *ad-* + *sistere* to cause to stand; akin to Latin *stare* to stand — more at STAND] (15th century)
transitive verb
: to give usually supplementary support or aid to
intransitive verb
1 : to give support or aid ⟨*assisted* at the stove⟩ ⟨another surgeon *assisted* on the operation⟩
2 : to be present as a spectator ⟨the ideal figures *assisting* at Italian holy scenes —Mary McCarthy⟩

²assist *noun* (1597)
1 : an act of assistance **:** AID
2 : the action (as a throw or pass) of a player who enables a teammate to make a putout or score a goal; *also* **:** official credit given for such an action
3 : a mechanical device that provides assistance

as·sis·tance \ə-'sis-tən(t)s\ *noun* (14th century)
: the act of assisting or the help supplied **:** AID ⟨financial and technical *assistance*⟩

as·sis·tant \-tənt\ *noun* (15th century)
: a person who assists **:** HELPER; *also* **:** a person holding an assistantship
— **assistant** *adjective*

assistant professor *noun* (1851)
: a member of a college or university faculty who ranks above an instructor and below an associate professor
— **assistant professorship** *noun*

as·sis·tant·ship \ə-'sis-tən(t)-ˌship\ *noun* (1948)
: a paid appointment awarded annually to a qualified graduate student that requires part-time teaching, research, or residence hall duties

as·size \ə-'sīz\ *noun* [Middle English *assise,* from Old French, session, settlement, from *asseoir* to seat, from (assumed) Vulgar Latin *assedēre,* from Latin *assidēre* to sit beside, assist in the office of a judge, from *ad-* + *sedēre* to sit — more at SIT] (14th century)
1 a : a judicial inquest **b :** an action to be decided by such an inquest, the writ for instituting it, or the verdict or finding rendered by the jury
2 a : the former periodical sessions of the superior courts in English counties for trial of civil and criminal cases — usually used in

plural **b :** the time or place of holding such a court, the court itself, or a session of it — usually used in plural

¹as·so·ci·ate \ə-'sō-shē-ˌāt, -sē-\ *verb* **-at·ed; -at·ing** [Middle English *associat* associated, from Latin *associatus,* past participle of *associare* to unite, from *ad-* + *sociare* to join, from *socius* companion — more at SOCIAL] (14th century)
transitive verb
1 : to join as a partner, friend, or companion
2 *obsolete* **:** to keep company with **:** ATTEND
3 : to join or connect together **:** COMBINE
4 : to bring together or into relationship in any of various intangible ways (as in memory or imagination)
intransitive verb
1 : to come or be together as partners, friends, or companions
2 : to combine or join with other parts **:** UNITE
synonym see JOIN

²as·so·ci·ate \ə-'sō-shē-ət, -sē-, -ˌāt, -shət\ *adjective* (14th century)
1 : closely connected (as in function or office) with another
2 : closely related especially in the mind
3 : having secondary or subordinate status ⟨*associate* membership in a society⟩

³as·so·ci·ate *same as* ²\ *noun* (1533)
1 : one associated with another: as **a :** PARTNER, COLLEAGUE **b :** COMPANION, COMRADE
2 a : an entry-level member (as of a learned society, professional organization, or profession) **b :** EMPLOYEE, WORKER
3 *often capitalized* **:** a degree conferred especially by a junior college ⟨*associate* in arts⟩
— **as·so·ci·ate·ship** \-ˌship\ *noun*

associate professor *noun* (1822)
: a member of a college or university faculty who ranks above an assistant professor and below a professor
— **associate professorship** *noun*

as·so·ci·a·tion \ə-ˌsō-sē-'ā-shən, -shē-\ *noun* (1535)
1 a : the act of associating **b :** the state of being associated **:** COMBINATION, RELATIONSHIP
2 : an organization of persons having a common interest **:** SOCIETY
3 : something linked in memory or imagination with a thing or person
4 : the process of forming mental connections or bonds between sensations, ideas, or memories
5 : the aggregation of chemical species to form (as with hydrogen bonds) loosely bound complexes
6 : a major unit in ecological community organization characterized by essential uniformity and usually by two or more dominant species
— **as·so·ci·a·tion·al** \-sh(ə-)nᵊl\ *adjective*

association area *noun* (circa 1909)
: an area of the cerebral cortex that functions in linking and coordinating the sensory and motor areas

association football *noun* (1873)
: SOCCER

as·so·ci·a·tion·ism \ə-ˌsō-sē-'ā-shə-ˌni-zəm, -ˌsō-shē-\ *noun* (1875)
: a reductionist school of psychology that

☐ USAGE
assimilate When *assimilate* is followed by a preposition, transitive senses 2a and 2c commonly take *to* and *into* and less frequently *with;* 2b regularly takes *to;* sense 3 most often takes *to* and sometimes *with.* The most frequent prepositions used with the intransitive sense are *to* and *into.*

\ə\ abut \ᵊ\ kitten \ər\ further \a\ ash \ā\ ace
\ä\ mop, mar \aù\ out \ch\ chin \e\ bet \ē\ easy
\g\ go \i\ hit \ī\ ice \j\ job \ŋ\ sing \ō\ go
\ȯ\ law \ȯi\ boy \th\ thin \th\ the \ü\ loot \ù\ foot
\y\ yet \zh\ vision *see also* Guide to Pronunciation

holds that the content of consciousness can be explained by the association and reassociation of irreducible sensory and perceptual elements
— **as·so·ci·a·tion·ist** \-'ā-sh(ə-)nist\ *noun*
— **as·so·ci·a·tion·is·tic** \-,ā-shə-'nis-tik\ *adjective*

as·so·cia·tive \ə-'sō-shē-,ā-tiv, -sē-, -shə-tiv\ *adjective* (1812)
1 : of or relating to association especially of ideas or images
2 : dependent on or acquired by association or learning
3 : of, having, or being the property of producing the same result no matter which pair of elements next to each other in a mathematical expression is used to perform a given operation first if the elements in the expression are listed in a fixed order ⟨addition is *associative* since (a + b) + c = a + (b + c)⟩
— **as·so·cia·tive·ly** *adverb*
— **as·so·cia·tiv·i·ty** \-,sō-shē-ə-'ti-və-tē, -sē-, -shə-'ti-\ *noun*

associative learning *noun* (1957)
: a learning process in which discrete ideas and percepts become linked to one another

associative neuron *noun* (1935)
: a neuron that conveys impulses from one neuron to another

as·soil \ə-'sòi(ə)l\ *transitive verb* [Middle English, from Old French *assoldre,* from Latin *absolvere* to absolve] (13th century)
1 *archaic* **:** ABSOLVE, PARDON
2 *archaic* **:** ACQUIT, CLEAR
3 *archaic* **:** EXPIATE
— **as·soil·ment** \-mənt\ *noun, archaic*

as·so·nance \'a-sə-nən(t)s\ *noun* [French, from Latin *assonare* to answer with the same sound, from *ad-* + *sonare* to sound, from *so·nus* sound — more at SOUND] (1727)
1 : resemblance of sound in words or syllables
2 a : relatively close juxtaposition of similar sounds especially of vowels **b :** repetition of vowels without repetition of consonants (as in *stony* and *holy*) used as an alternative to rhyme in verse
— **as·so·nant** \-nənt\ *adjective or noun*
— **as·so·nant·al** \,a-sə-'nan-t°l\ *adjective*

as soon as *conjunction* (14th century)
: immediately or at or shortly after the time that

as·sort \ə-'sòrt\ *verb* [Middle French *assortir,* from *a-* (from Latin *ad-*) + *sorte* sort] (15th century)
transitive verb
1 : to distribute into groups of a like kind **:** CLASSIFY
2 : to supply with an assortment (as of goods)
intransitive verb
1 : to agree in kind **:** HARMONIZE
2 : to keep company **:** ASSOCIATE
— **as·sort·er** *noun*

as·sor·ta·tive \ə-'sòr-tə-tiv\ *adjective* (1897)
: being nonrandom mating based on like or unlike characteristics
— **as·sor·ta·tive·ly** \-lē\ *adverb*

as·sort·ed \-'sòr-təd\ *adjective* (circa 1797)
1 : suited especially by nature or character ⟨an ill-*assorted* pair⟩
2 : consisting of various kinds ⟨*assorted* chocolates⟩

as·sort·ment \-'sòrt-mənt\ *noun* (1611)
1 a : the act of assorting **b :** the state of being assorted
2 : a collection of assorted things or persons

as·suage \ə-'swāj *also* -'swāzh *or* -'swäzh\ *transitive verb* **as·suaged; as·suag·ing** [Middle English *aswagen,* from Old French *assouagier,* from (assumed) Vulgar Latin *assuaviare,* from Latin *ad-* + *suavis* sweet — more at SWEET] (14th century)
1 : to lessen the intensity of (something that pains or distresses) **:** EASE
2 : PACIFY, QUIET
3 : to put an end to by satisfying **:** APPEASE, QUENCH
synonym see RELIEVE
— **as·suage·ment** \-mənt\ *noun*

as·sua·sive \ə-'swā-siv, -ziv\ *adjective* (1708)
: SOOTHING, CALMING

as·sume \ə-'süm\ *transitive verb* **as·sumed; as·sum·ing** [Middle English, from Latin *assumere,* from *ad-* + *sumere* to take — more at CONSUME] (15th century)
1 a : to take up or in **:** RECEIVE **b :** to take into partnership, employment, or use
2 a : to take to or upon oneself **:** UNDERTAKE **b :** PUT ON, DON
3 : to take control of
4 : to pretend to have or be **:** FEIGN ⟨*assumed* an air of confidence in spite of her dismay⟩
5 : to take as granted or true **:** SUPPOSE
6 : to take over (the debts of another) as one's own ☆
— **as·sum·abil·i·ty** \-,sü-mə-'bi-lə-tē\ *noun*
— **as·sum·able** \-'sü-mə-bəl\ *adjective*
— **as·sum·ably** \-blē\ *adverb*

as·sum·ing *adjective* (1695)
: PRETENTIOUS, PRESUMPTUOUS

as·sump·sit \ə-'səm(p)-sət\ *noun* [New Latin, he undertook, from Latin *assumere* to undertake] (1590)
1 : an express or implied promise or contract not under seal on which an action may be brought
2 a : a former common-law action brought to recover damages alleged from the breach of an assumpsit **b :** an action to recover damages for breach of a contract

as·sump·tion \ə-'səm(p)-shən\ *noun* [Middle English, from Late Latin *assumption-, assumptio* taking up, from Latin *assumere*] (13th century)
1 a : the taking up of a person into heaven **b** *capitalized* **:** August 15 observed in commemoration of the Assumption of the Virgin Mary
2 : a taking to or upon oneself ⟨the *assumption* of a new position⟩
3 : the act of laying claim to or taking possession of something ⟨the *assumption* of power⟩
4 : ARROGANCE, PRETENSION
5 a : an assuming that something is true **b :** a fact or statement (as a proposition, axiom, postulate, or notion) taken for granted
6 : the taking over of another's debts

as·sump·tive \ə-'səm(p)-tiv\ *adjective* (1611)
: of, relating to, or based on assumption

as·sur·ance \ə-'shùr-ən(t)s\ *noun* (14th century)
1 : the act or action of assuring: as **a :** PLEDGE, GUARANTEE **b :** the act of conveying real property; *also* **:** the instrument by which it is conveyed **c** *chiefly British* **:** INSURANCE
2 : the state of being assured: as **a :** SECURITY **b :** a being certain in the mind ⟨the puritan's *assurance* of salvation⟩ **c :** confidence of mind or manner **:** easy freedom from self-doubt or uncertainty; *also* **:** excessive self-confidence **:** BRASHNESS, PRESUMPTION
3 : something that inspires or tends to inspire confidence ⟨gave repeated *assurances* of goodwill⟩
synonym see CONFIDENCE

as·sure \ə-'shùr\ *transitive verb* **as·sured; as·sur·ing** [Middle English, from Middle French *assurer,* from Medieval Latin *assecurare,* from Latin *ad-* + *securus* secure] (14th century)
1 : to make safe (as from risks or against overthrow) **:** INSURE
2 : to give confidence to ⟨and hereby we know that we are of the truth, and shall *assure* our hearts —1 John 3:19 (Authorized Version)⟩
3 : to make sure or certain **:** CONVINCE ⟨glancing back to *assure* himself no one was following⟩
4 : to inform positively ⟨I *assure* you that we will do better next time⟩
5 : to make certain the coming or attainment of **:** GUARANTEE ⟨worked hard to *assure* accuracy⟩
synonym see ENSURE

¹as·sured \ə-'shùrd\ *adjective* (15th century)
1 : characterized by certainty or security **:** GUARANTEED ⟨an *assured* market⟩
2 a : SELF-ASSURED **b :** SELF-SATISFIED
3 : satisfied as to the certainty or truth of a matter ⟨rest *assured* we got what we came for⟩
— **as·sured·ness** \-'shùr-əd-nəs, -'shùrd-\ *noun*

²assured *noun, plural* **assured** *or* **assureds** (1755)
: INSURED

as·sured·ly \ə-'shùr-əd-lē\ *adverb* (14th century)
1 : without a doubt **:** CERTAINLY
2 : in an assured manner **:** CONFIDENTLY

as·sur·er \ə-'shùr-ər\ *or* **as·sur·or** \ə-'shùr-ər, ə-,shùr-'òr\ *noun* (1607)
: one that assures **:** INSURER

as·sur·gent \ə-'sər-jənt\ *adjective* [Latin *assurgent-, assurgens,* present participle of *assurgere* to rise, from *ad-* + *surgere* to rise — more at SURGE] (1578)
: moving upward **:** RISING; *especially* **:** ASCENDANT 1b

As·syr·i·an \ə-'sir-ē-ən\ *noun* (15th century)
1 : a native or inhabitant of ancient Assyria
2 : the dialect of Akkadian spoken by the Assyrians
— **Assyrian** *adjective*

As·syr·i·ol·o·gy \ə-,sir-ē-'ä-lə-jē\ *noun* (1828)
: the science or study of the history, language, and antiquities of ancient Assyria and Babylonia
— **As·syr·i·o·log·i·cal** \-,sir-ē-ə-'lä-ji-kəl\ *adjective*
— **As·syr·i·ol·o·gist** \-'ä-lə-jist\ *noun*

-ast *noun suffix* [Middle English, from Latin *-astes,* from Greek *-astēs,* from verbs in *-azein*]
: one connected with ⟨ecdysi*ast*⟩

astar·board \ə-'stär-bərd\ *adverb* (circa 1630)
: toward or on the starboard side of a ship ⟨put the helm hard *astarboard*⟩

As·tar·te \ə-'stär-tē\ *noun* [Latin, from Greek *Astartē*]
: the Phoenician goddess of fertility and of sexual love

as·ta·tine \'as-tə-,tēn\ *noun* [Greek *astatos* unsteady, from *a-* + *statos* standing, from *histanai* to cause to stand — more at STAND] (1947)
: a radioactive halogen element discovered by bombarding bismuth with alpha particles and also formed by radioactive decay — see ELEMENT table

as·ter \'as-tər\ *noun* (1664)
1 [New Latin, from Latin, *aster,* from Greek *aster-, astēr* star, aster — more at STAR] **a :** any of various chiefly fall-blooming leafy-stemmed composite herbs (*Aster* and closely

☆ **SYNONYMS**
Assume, affect, pretend, simulate, feign, counterfeit, sham mean to put on a false or deceptive appearance. ASSUME often implies a justifiable motive rather than an intent to deceive (*assumed* an air of cheerfulness around the patients). AFFECT implies making a false show of possessing, using, or feeling (*affected* an interest in art). PRETEND implies an overt and sustained false appearance (*pretended* that nothing had happened). SIMULATE suggests a close imitation of the appearance of something (cosmetics that *simulate* a suntan). FEIGN implies more artful invention than PRETEND, less specific mimicry than SIMULATE (*feigned* sickness). COUNTERFEIT implies achieving the highest degree of verisimilitude of any of these words (an actor *counterfeiting* drunkenness). SHAM implies an obvious falseness that fools only the gullible (*shammed* a most unconvincing limp).

related genera) with often showy heads containing disk flowers or both disk and ray flowers **b :** CHINA ASTER
2 [New Latin, from Greek *aster-, astēr*] **:** a system of microtubules arranged radially about a centriole at either end of the mitotic or meiotic spindle

-aster *noun suffix* [Middle English, from Latin, suffix denoting partial resemblance]
: one that is inferior or not genuine ⟨criticaster⟩

as·te·ria \a-'stir-ē-ə\ *noun* [Latin, a precious stone, from Greek, feminine of *asterios* starry, from *aster-, astēr*] (1903)
: a gemstone cut to show asterism

as·te·ri·at·ed \-ē-,ā-təd\ *adjective* [Greek *asterios*] (1816)
: exhibiting asterism ⟨*asteriated* sapphire⟩

¹as·ter·isk \'as-tə-,risk, *especially in plural also* ÷-,rik\ *noun* [Middle English, *astarisc,* from Late Latin *asteriscus,* from Greek *asteriskos,* literally, little star, diminutive of *aster-, astēr*] (14th century)
: the character * used in printing or writing as a reference mark, as an indication of the omission of letters or words, to denote a hypothetical or unattested linguistic form, or for various arbitrary meanings
— **as·ter·isk·less** \-ləs\ *adjective*
²asterisk *transitive verb* (circa 1733)
: to mark with an asterisk **:** STAR

as·ter·ism \'as-tə-,ri-zəm\ *noun* [Greek *asterismos,* from *asterizein* to arrange in constellations, from *aster-, astēr*] (1598)
1 a : CONSTELLATION **b :** a small group of stars
2 : a star-shaped figure exhibited by some crystals by reflected light (as in a star sapphire) or by transmitted light (as in some mica)

astern \ə-'stərn\ *adverb or adjective* (1627)
1 : behind a ship
2 : at or toward the stern of a ship
3 : STERNFOREMOST, BACKWARD

¹as·ter·oid \'as-tə-,ròid\ *noun* [Greek *asteroeidēs* starlike, from *aster-, astēr*] (1802)
1 : any of the small celestial bodies found especially between the orbits of Mars and Jupiter
2 : STARFISH
— **as·ter·oi·dal** \,as-tə-'ròi-d°l\ *adjective*
²asteroid *adjective* (1854)
1 : resembling a star ⟨*asteroid* bodies in sporotrichosis⟩
2 : of or resembling a starfish

asteroid belt *noun* (1952)
: the region of interplanetary space between the orbits of Mars and Jupiter in which most asteroids are found

aster yellows *noun plural* (1922)
: a widespread disease that affects more than 40 families of plants, is characterized especially by yellowing and dwarfing, and is caused by a mycoplasma transmitted by leafhoppers

as·the·nia \as-'thē-nē-ə\ *noun* [New Latin, from Greek *astheneia,* from *asthenēs* weak, from *a- + sthenos* strength] (1802)
: lack or loss of strength **:** DEBILITY

as·then·ic \as-'the-nik\ *adjective* (1789)
1 : of, relating to, or exhibiting asthenia **:** WEAK
2 : ECTOMORPHIC 2

as·theno·sphere \as-'the-nə-,sfir\ *noun* [Greek *asthenēs* weak + English *-o-* + *sphere*] (1914)
: a hypothetical zone of a celestial body (as the earth) which lies beneath the lithosphere and within which the material is believed to yield readily to persistent stresses
— **as·theno·spher·ic** \-,the-nə-'sfir-ik, -'sfer-\ *adjective*

asth·ma \'az-mə, *British* 'as-\ *noun* [Middle English *asma,* from Medieval Latin, modification of Greek *asthma*] (14th century)
: a condition often of allergic origin that is marked by continuous or paroxysmal labored breathing accompanied by wheezing, by a

sense of constriction in the chest, and often by attacks of coughing or gasping
— **asth·mat·ic** \az-'ma-tik, *British* as-\ *adjective or noun*
— **asth·mat·i·cal·ly** \-ti-k(ə-)lē\ *adverb*

as though *conjunction* (13th century)
: AS IF

as·tig·mat·ic \,as-tig-'ma-tik\ *adjective* [*a-* + Greek *stigmat-, stigma* stigma] (1849)
1 : affected with, relating to, or correcting astigmatism
2 : showing incapacity for observation or discrimination ⟨an *astigmatic* fanaticism, a disregard for the facts —*N.Y. Herald Tribune*⟩
— **astigmatic** *noun*

astig·ma·tism \ə-'stig-mə-,ti-zəm\ *noun* (1849)
1 : a defect of an optical system (as a lens) causing rays from a point to fail to meet in a focal point resulting in a blurred and imperfect image
2 : a defect of vision due to astigmatism of the refractive system of the eye and especially to corneal irregularity
3 : distorted understanding suggestive of the blurred vision of an astigmatic person

astil·be \ə-'stil-(,)bē\ *noun* [New Latin, from ²*a-* + Greek *stilbē,* feminine of *stilbos* sparkling]
: any of a genus (*Astilbe*) of chiefly Asian perennials of the saxifrage family having simple or usually compound leaves and widely cultivated for their panicles of white or red flowers

astir \ə-'stər\ *adjective* (1823)
1 : exhibiting activity
2 : being out of bed **:** UP

As·ti Spu·man·te \'äs-tē-spü-'män-(,)tē, 'as-tē-, -spü-'man-\ *noun* [Italian, from *Asti,* Italy + Italian *spumante* effervescent, literally, foaming] (1908)
: a sweet sparkling white wine made in and around the village of Asti in Piedmont

as to *preposition* (14th century)
1 : AS FOR, ABOUT ⟨at a loss *as to* how to explain the error⟩
2 : ACCORDING TO, BY ⟨graded *as to* size and color⟩

as·ton·ied \ə-'stä-nēd\ *adjective* [Middle English, from past participle of *astonien*] (14th century)
1 *archaic* **:** deprived briefly of the power to act **:** DAZED
2 *archaic* **:** filled with consternation or dismay

as·ton·ish \ə-'stä-nish\ *transitive verb* [probably from earlier *astony* (from Middle English *astonen, astonien,* from Old French *estoner,* from — assumed — Vulgar Latin *extonare,* from Latin *ex-* + *tonare* to thunder) + *-ish* (as in *abolish*) — more at THUNDER] (1535)
1 *obsolete* **:** to strike with sudden fear
2 : to strike with sudden and usually great wonder or surprise
synonym see SURPRISE

as·ton·ish·ing \-ni-shiŋ\ *adjective* (1543)
: causing astonishment **:** SURPRISING
— **as·ton·ish·ing·ly** \-shiŋ-lē\ *adverb*

as·ton·ish·ment \ə-'stä-nish-mənt\ *noun* (circa 1586)
1 a : the state of being astonished **b :** CONSTERNATION **c :** AMAZEMENT
2 : a cause of amazement or wonder

¹as·tound \ə-'staùnd\ *adjective* [Middle English *astoned,* from past participle of *astonen*] (14th century)
archaic **:** overwhelmed with astonishment or amazement **:** ASTOUNDED
²astound *transitive verb* (1634)
: to fill with bewilderment or wonder
synonym see SURPRISE

as·tound·ing \ə-'staùn-diŋ\ *adjective* (1586)
: causing astonishment or amazement
— **as·tound·ing·ly** \-diŋ-lē\ *adverb*

astr- *or* **astro-** *combining form* [Middle English *astro-,* from Old French, from Latin *astr-, astro-,* from Greek, from *astron* — more at STAR]

: star **:** heavens **:** outer space **:** astronomical ⟨*astrophysics*⟩

¹astrad·dle \ə-'stra-d°l\ *adverb* (1703)
: on or above and extending onto both sides **:** ASTRIDE
²astraddle *preposition* (1935)
: with one leg on each side of **:** ASTRIDE

as·tra·gal \'as-tri-gəl\ *noun* [Latin *astragalus,* from Greek *astragalos* anklebone, molding; akin to Greek *astakos* lobster, *osteon* bone — more at OSSEOUS] (1563)
1 : a narrow half-round molding
2 : a projecting strip on the edge of a folding door

as·tra·khan \'as-trə-kən, -,kan\ *noun, often capitalized* [*Astrakhan,* Russia] (1766)
1 : karakul of Russian origin
2 : a cloth with a usually wool, curled, and looped pile resembling karakul

as·tral \'as-trəl\ *adjective* [Late Latin *astralis,* from Latin *astrum* star, from Greek *astron*] (1605)
1 : of, relating to, or coming from the stars ⟨*astral* influences⟩ ⟨unusual *astral* occurrences⟩
2 : of or relating to a mitotic or meiotic aster
3 : of or consisting of a supersensible substance held in theosophy to be next above the tangible world in refinement
4 a : VISIONARY **b :** elevated in station or position **:** EXALTED
— **as·tral·ly** \-trə-lē\ *adverb*

astray \ə-'strā\ *adverb or adjective* [Middle English, from Middle French *estraié* wandering, from *estraier* to stray — more at STRAY] (14th century)
1 : off the right path or route **:** STRAYING
2 : in error **:** away from what is proper or desirable

¹astride \ə-'strīd\ *adverb* (1664)
1 : with one leg on each side **:** astride a horse ⟨she rode *astride,* not sidesaddle⟩
2 : with the legs stretched wide apart ⟨standing *astride*⟩
²astride *preposition* (1713)
1 : on or above and with one leg on each side of
2 : placed or lying on both sides of
3 : extending over or across **:** SPANNING, BRIDGING

as·trin·gen·cy \ə-'strin-jən(t)-sē\ *noun* (1601)
: the quality or state of being astringent

¹as·trin·gent \-jənt\ *adjective* [probably from Middle French, from Latin *astringent-, astringens,* present participle of *astringere* to bind fast, from *ad-* + *stringere* to bind tight — more at STRAIN] (1541)
1 : able to draw together the soft organic tissues **:** STYPTIC, PUCKERY ⟨*astringent* lotions⟩ ⟨an *astringent* fruit⟩
2 : suggestive of an astringent effect upon tissue **:** rigidly severe **:** AUSTERE ⟨dry *astringent* comments⟩; *also* **:** PUNGENT, CAUSTIC
— **as·trin·gent·ly** *adverb*
²astringent *noun* (1626)
: an astringent agent or substance

as·tro·bi·ol·o·gy \,as-trō-(,)bī-'ä-lə-jē\ *noun* (1955)
: EXOBIOLOGY
— **as·tro·bi·ol·o·gist** \-(,)bī-'ä-lə-jist\ *noun*

as·tro·cyte \'as-trə-,sīt\ *noun* [International Scientific Vocabulary] (1898)
: a star-shaped cell (as of the neuroglia)
— **as·tro·cyt·ic** \,as-trə-'si-tik\ *adjective*

as·tro·cy·to·ma \,as-trə-sī-'tō-mə\ *noun, plural* **-mas** *or* **-ma·ta** \-mə-tə\ [New Latin] (circa 1923)
: a nerve-tissue tumor composed of astrocytes
as·tro·dome \'as-trə-,dōm\ *noun* [International Scientific Vocabulary] (1941)
: a transparent dome in the upper surface of an airplane from within which the navigator makes celestial observations
as·tro·labe \'as-trə-,lāb *also* -,lab\ *noun* [Middle English, from Middle French & Medieval Latin; Middle French, from Medieval Latin *astrolabium*, from Late Greek *astrolabion*, from Greek *astrolabos*, from *astr-* + *lambanein* to take — more at LATCH] (14th century)
: a compact instrument used to observe and calculate the position of celestial bodies before the invention of the sextant

astrolabe

as·trol·o·ger \ə-'strä-lə-jər\ *noun* (14th century)
: one who practices astrology
as·trol·o·gy \ə-'strä-lə-jē\ *noun* [Middle English *astrologie*, from Middle French, from Latin *astrologia*, from Greek, from *astr-* + *-logia* -logy] (14th century)
1 *archaic* : ASTRONOMY
2 : the divination of the supposed influences of the stars and planets on human affairs and terrestrial events by their positions and aspects
— **as·tro·log·i·cal** \,as-trə-'lä-ji-kəl\ *adjective*
— **as·tro·log·i·cal·ly** \-k(ə-)lē\ *adverb*
as·trom·e·try \ə-'strä-mə-trē\ *noun* (circa 1859)
: a branch of astronomy that deals with measurements (as of positions and movements) of celestial bodies
— **as·tro·me·tric** \,as-trə-'me-trik\ *adjective*
as·tro·naut \'as-trə-,nòt, -,nät\ *noun* [*astr-* + *-naut* (as in *aeronaut*)] (1929)
: a person who travels beyond the earth's atmosphere; *also* : a trainee for spaceflight
as·tro·nau·tics \,as-trə-'nò-tiks, -'nä-\ *noun plural but singular or plural in construction* (1928)
: the science of the construction and operation of vehicles for travel in space beyond the earth's atmosphere
— **as·tro·nau·tic** \-tik\ *or* **as·tro·nau·ti·cal** \-ti-kəl\ *adjective*
— **as·tro·nau·ti·cal·ly** \-ti-k(ə-)lē\ *adverb*
as·tron·o·mer \ə-'strä-nə-mər\ *noun* (14th century)
: one who is skilled in astronomy or who makes observations of celestial phenomena
as·tro·nom·i·cal \,as-trə-'nä-mi-kəl\ *also* **as·tro·nom·ic** \-mik\ *adjective* (1556)
1 : of or relating to astronomy
2 : enormously or inconceivably large or great 〈*astronomical* numbers〉
— **as·tro·nom·i·cal·ly** \-mi-k(ə-)lē\ *adverb*
astronomical unit *noun* (1903)
: a unit of length used in astronomy equal to the mean distance of the earth from the sun or about 93 million miles (150 million kilometers)
as·tron·o·my \ə-'strä-nə-mē\ *noun, plural* **-mies** [Middle English *astronomie*, from Old French, from Latin *astronomia*, from Greek, from *astr-* + *-nomia* -nomy] (13th century)
: the study of objects and matter outside the earth's atmosphere and of their physical and chemical properties
as·tro·pho·tog·ra·phy \,as-(,)trō-fə-'tä-grə-fē\ *noun* [International Scientific Vocabulary] (circa 1858)

: photography as used in astronomical investigations
— **as·tro·pho·to·graph** \-'fō-tə-,graf\ *noun*
— **as·tro·pho·tog·ra·pher** \-fə-'tä-grə-fər\ *noun*
as·tro·phys·ics \,as-trə-'fi-ziks\ *noun plural but singular or plural in construction* [International Scientific Vocabulary] (1890)
: a branch of astronomy dealing especially with the behavior, physical properties, and dynamic processes of celestial objects and phenomena
— **as·tro·phys·i·cal** \-zi-kəl\ *adjective*
— **as·tro·phys·i·cal·ly** \-zi-k(ə-)lē\ *adverb*
— **as·tro·phys·i·cist** \-'fi-zə-sist, -'fiz-sist\ *noun*
as·tute \ə-'stüt, a-, -'styüt\ *adjective* [Latin *astutus*, from *astus* craft] (circa 1611)
: having or showing shrewdness and perspicacity 〈an *astute* observer〉 〈*astute* remarks〉; *also* : CRAFTY, WILY
synonym see SHREWD
— **as·tute·ly** *adverb*
— **as·tute·ness** *noun*
As·ty·a·nax \ə-'stī-ə-,naks\ *noun* [Greek]
: a son of Hector and Andromache hurled by the Greeks from the walls of Troy
asun·der \ə-'sən-dər\ *adverb or adjective* (14th century)
1 : into parts 〈torn *asunder*〉
2 : apart from each other in position 〈wide *asunder*〉
aswarm \ə-'swòrm\ *adjective* (circa 1869)
: filled to overflowing : SWARMING 〈streets *aswarm* with people〉
¹as well as *conjunction* (15th century)
: and in addition : AND 〈brave *as well as* loyal〉
²as well as *preposition* (1589)
: in addition to : BESIDES 〈the coach, *as well as* the team, is ready〉
aswirl \ə-'swər(-ə)l\ *adjective* (1877)
: being in a swirl : SWIRLING
aswoon \ə-'swün\ *adjective* (14th century)
: being in a swoon : DAZED
asy·lum \ə-'sī-ləm\ *noun* [Middle English, from Latin, from Greek *asylon*, neuter of *asylos* inviolable, from *a-* + *sylon* right of seizure] (15th century)
1 : an inviolable place of refuge and protection giving shelter to criminals and debtors : SANCTUARY
2 : a place of retreat and security : SHELTER
3 a : the protection or inviolability afforded by an asylum : REFUGE **b** : protection from arrest and extradition given especially to political refugees by a nation or by an embassy or other agency enjoying diplomatic immunity
4 : an institution for the care of the destitute or sick and especially the insane
asym·met·ri·cal \,ā-sə-'me-tri-kəl\ *or* **asym·met·ric** \-trik\ *adjective* [Greek *asymmetria* lack of proportion, from *asymmetros* ill-proportioned, from *a-* + *symmetros* symmetrical] (1690)
1 : not symmetrical
2 *usually* asymmetric, *of a carbon atom* : bonded to four different atoms or groups
— **asym·met·ri·cal·ly** \-tri-k(ə-)lē\ *adverb*
— **asym·me·try** \(,)ā-'si-mə-trē\ *noun*
asymp·tom·at·ic \,ā-,sim(p)-tə-'ma-tik\ *adjective* (1927)
: presenting no symptoms of disease
— **asymp·tom·at·i·cal·ly** \-ti-k(ə-)lē\ *adverb*
as·ymp·tote \'a-səm(p)-,tōt\ *noun* [probably from (assumed) New Latin *asymptotus*, from Greek *asymptōtos* not meeting, from *a-* + *sympiptein* to meet — more at SYMPTOM] (1656)
: a straight line associated with a curve such that as a point moves along an infinite branch of the curve the distance from the point to the line approaches zero and the slope of the curve at the point approaches the slope of the line

— **as·ymp·tot·ic** \,a-səm(p)-'tä-tik\ *adjective*
— **as·ymp·tot·i·cal·ly** \-ti-k(ə-)lē\ *adverb*
asyn·ap·sis \,ā-sə-'nap-səs\ *noun, plural* **-ap·ses** \-,sēz\ [New Latin ²*a-* + *synapsis*] (1930)
: failure of pairing of homologous chromosomes in meiosis

asymptotes to the hyperbola

asyn·chro·nous \(,)ā-'siŋ-krə-nəs, -'sin-\ *adjective* (1748)
1 : not synchronous
2 : of, used in, or being digital communication (as between computers) in which there is no timing requirement for transmission and in which the start of each character is individually signaled by the transmitting device
— **asyn·chro·nous·ly** *adverb*
asyn·chro·ny \-krə-nē\ *or* **asyn·chro·nism** \-krə-,ni-zəm\ *noun* (1875)
: the quality or state of being asynchronous
: absence or lack of concurrence in time
as·yn·det·ic \,a-sⁿ-'de-tik\ *adjective* (circa 1864)
: marked by asyndeton
— **as·yn·det·i·cal·ly** \-ti-k(ə-)lē\ *adverb*
asyn·de·ton \ə-'sin-də-,tän, (,)ā-'sin-\ *noun, plural* **-tons** *or* **-ta** \-də-tə\ [Late Latin, from Greek, from neuter of *asyndetos* unconnected, from *a-* + *syndetos* bound together, from *syndein* to bind together, from *syn-* + *dein* to bind — more at DIADEM] (1555)
: omission of the conjunctions that ordinarily join coordinate words or clauses (as in "I came, I saw, I conquered")
¹at \ət, 'at\ *preposition* [Middle English, from Old English *æt*; akin to Old High German *az* at, Latin *ad*] (before 12th century)
1 — used as a function word to indicate presence or occurrence in, on, or near 〈staying *at* a hotel〉 〈*at* a party〉 〈sick *at* heart〉
2 — used as a function word to indicate the goal of an indicated or implied action or motion 〈aim *at* the target〉 〈creditors are *at* him again〉
3 — used as a function word to indicate that with which one is occupied or employed 〈*at* work〉 〈*at* the controls〉 〈good *at* chess〉
4 — used as a function word to indicate situation in an active or passive state or condition 〈*at* liberty〉 〈*at* rest〉
5 — used as a function word to indicate the means, cause, or manner 〈sold *at* auction〉 〈laughed *at* my joke〉 〈act *at* your own discretion〉
6 a — used as a function word to indicate the rate, degree, or position in a scale or series 〈the temperature *at* 90〉 〈*at* first〉 **b** — used as a function word to indicate age or position in time 〈will retire *at* 65〉
²at \'ät\ *noun, plural* **at** [Lao] (1955)
— see **kip** at MONEY table
at- — see AD-
At·a·brine \'a-tə-brən, -,brēn\ *trademark*
— used for quinacrine
atac·tic \(,)ā-'tak-tik\ *adjective* [International Scientific Vocabulary ²*a-* + *-tactic*] (1957)
: of, relating to, or being a polymer exhibiting no stereochemical regularity of structure 〈*atactic* polypropylene〉 — compare ISOTACTIC
At·a·lan·ta \,a-tᵊl-'an-tə\ *noun* [Latin, from Greek *Atalantē*]
: a fleet-footed huntress in Greek mythology who challenges her suitors to a race and is defeated by Hippomenes when she stops to pick up three golden apples he has dropped
at all *adverb* (14th century)
: in any way or respect : to the least extent or degree : under any circumstances 〈doesn't smoke *at all*〉
at·a·man \,a-tə-'man\ *noun* [Russian] (1835)
: HETMAN

at·a·mas·co lily \ˌa-tə-'mas-(ˌ)kō-\ *noun* [Virginia Algonquian *atamusco*] (1743)
: any of a genus (*Zephyranthes*) of American bulbous herbs of the amaryllis family with pink, white, or yellowish flowers; *especially* **:** one (*Z. atamasco*) of the southeastern U.S. with white flowers usually tinged with purple

at·a·rac·tic \ˌa-tə-'rak-tik\ *or* **at·a·rax·ic** \-'rak-sik\ *noun* [ataractic from Greek *ataraktos* calm, from *a-* + *tarassein* to disturb; *ataraxic* from Greek *ataraxia* calmness, from *a-* + *tarassein*] (1955)
: TRANQUILIZER 2
— **ataractic** *or* **ataraxic** *adjective*

at·a·vism \'a-tə-ˌvi-zəm\ *noun* [French *atavisme*, from Latin *atavus* ancestor, from *at-* (probably akin to *atta* daddy) + *avus* grandfather — more at UNCLE] (1833)
1 a : recurrence in an organism of a trait or character typical of an ancestral form and usually due to genetic recombination **b :** recurrence of or reversion to a past style, manner, outlook, or approach ⟨architectural *atavism*⟩ **2 :** one that manifests atavism **:** THROWBACK
— **at·a·vis·tic** \ˌa-tə-'vis-tik\ *adjective*
— **at·a·vis·ti·cal·ly** \-ti-k(ə-)lē\ *adverb*

atax·ia \ə-'tak-sē-ə, (ˌ)ā-\ *noun* [Greek, from *a-* + *tassein* to put in order] (1670)
: an inability to coordinate voluntary muscular movements that is symptomatic of some nervous disorders
— **atax·ic** \-sik\ *adjective*

at bat *noun* (1884)
: an official time at bat charged to a baseball batter except when he walks, sacrifices, is hit by a pitched ball, or is interfered with by the catcher ⟨three hits in five *at bats*⟩

ate *past of* EAT

Ate \'ä-tē, 'ā-(ˌ)tē; 'ä-ˌtā\ *noun* [Greek *Atē*]
: a Greek goddess personifying foolhardy and ruinous impulse

¹-ate *noun suffix* [Middle English *-at*, from Old French, from Latin *-atus, -atum*, masculine & neuter of *-atus*, past participle ending]
1 : one acted upon (in a specified way) ⟨distill*ate*⟩
2 [New Latin *-atum*, from Latin] **:** chemical compound or complex anion derived from a (specified) compound or element ⟨phenol*ate*⟩; *especially* **:** salt or ester of an acid with a name ending in *-ic* and not beginning with *hydro-* ⟨bor*ate*⟩

²-ate *noun suffix* [Middle English *-at*, from Old French, from Latin *-atus*, from *-a-*, stem vowel of 1st conjugation + *-tus*, suffix of verbal nouns]
1 : office **:** function **:** rank **:** group of persons holding a (specified) office or rank or having a (specified) function ⟨vicar*ate*⟩
2 : state **:** dominion **:** jurisdiction ⟨emir*ate*⟩ ⟨khan*ate*⟩

³-ate *adjective suffix* [Middle English *-at*, from Latin *-atus*, from past participle ending of 1st conjugation verbs, from *-a-*, stem vowel of 1st conjugation + *-tus*, past participle suffix — more at -ED]
: marked by having ⟨crani*ate*⟩

⁴-ate *verb suffix* [Middle English *-aten*, from Latin *-atus*, past participle ending]
: act on (in a specified way) ⟨insul*ate*⟩ **:** cause to be modified or affected by ⟨camphor*ate*⟩ **:** cause to become ⟨activ*ate*⟩ **:** furnish with ⟨capacit*ate*⟩

-ated *adjective suffix*
: ³-ATE ⟨pile*ated*⟩

at·el·ec·ta·sis \ˌa-tᵊl-'ek-tə-səs\ *noun, plural* **-ta·ses** \-ˌsēz\ [New Latin, from Greek *atelēs* incomplete, defective (from *a-* ²a- + *telos* end) + *ektasis* extension, from *ekteinein* to stretch out, from *ex-* + *teinein* to stretch — more at TELOS, THIN] (1859)
: collapse of the expanded lung; *also* **:** defective expansion of the pulmonary alveoli at birth

ate·lier \ˌa-tᵊl-'yā\ *noun* [French, from Middle French *astelier* woodpile, from *astele* splinter, from Late Latin *astella*, diminutive of Latin *astula*] (1699)
1 : an artist's or designer's studio or workroom
2 : WORKSHOP

ate·moya \ˌä-tə-'mòi-ə, ˌa-\ *noun* [*ates* sweetsop (from Tagalog) + cheri*moya*] (1914)
: a white-pulped tropical fruit of a tree that is a hybrid of the sweetsop and the cherimoya

a tem·po \ä-'tem-(ˌ)pō\ *adverb or adjective* [Italian] (circa 1740)
: in time — used as a direction in music to return to the original tempo

atem·po·ral \(ˌ)ā-'tem-p(ə-)rəl\ *adjective* (1870)
: independent of or unaffected by time **:** TIMELESS

Ate·ri·an \ə-'tir-ē-ən\ *adjective* [French *atérien*, from Bir el-*Ater* (Constantine), Algeria] (1928)
: of or relating to a Paleolithic culture of northern Africa characterized by Mousterian features, tanged arrow points, and leaf-shaped spearheads

Ath·a·bas·can \ˌa-thə-'bas-kən\ *or* **Ath·a·pas·kan** \-'pas-\ *also* **Ath·a·bas·kan** \-'bas-\ *or* **Ath·a·pas·can** \-'pas-\ *noun* [*Athabasca*, a Cree band, from Cree dialect *aδapaska'w*, name for the area east of Lake Athabasca, literally, (where) there are reeds one after another] (1846)
1 : a family of American Indian languages spoken primarily in western Canada, Alaska, and the U.S. Southwest
2 : a member of a people speaking an Athabascan language

Ath·a·na·sian \ˌa-thə-'nā-zhən, -shən\ *adjective* (1586)
: of or relating to Athanasius or his advocacy of the homoousian doctrine against Arianism

Athanasian Creed *noun* (1586)
: a Christian creed originating in Europe about A.D. 400 and relating especially to the Trinity and Incarnation

athe·ism \'ā-thē-ˌi-zəm\ *noun* [Middle French *athéisme*, from *athée* atheist, from Greek *atheos* godless, from *a-* + *theos* god] (1546)
1 *archaic* **:** UNGODLINESS, WICKEDNESS
2 a : a disbelief in the existence of deity **b :** the doctrine that there is no deity

athe·ist \'ā-thē-ist\ *noun* (1571)
: one who denies the existence of God
— **athe·is·tic** \ˌā-thē-'is-tik\ *or* **athe·is·ti·cal** \ˌā-thē-'is-ti-kəl\ *adjective*
— **athe·is·ti·cal·ly** \-ti-k(ə-)lē\ *adverb*

athe·ling \'a-thə-liŋ, -thə-\ *noun* [Middle English, from Old English *ætheling*, from *æthelu* nobility, akin to Old High German *adal* nobility] (before 12th century)
: an Anglo-Saxon prince or nobleman; *especially* **:** the heir apparent or a prince of the royal family

Athe·na \ə-'thē-nə\ *or* **Athe·ne** \-nē\ *noun* [Latin *Athena*, from Greek *Athēnē*]
: the Greek goddess of wisdom — compare MINERVA

ath·e·nae·um *or* **ath·e·ne·um** \ˌa-thə-'nē-əm\ *noun* [Latin *Athenaeum*, a school in ancient Rome for the study of arts, from Greek *Athēnaion*, a temple of Athena, from *Athēnē*] (1799)
1 : a building or room in which books, periodicals, and newspapers are kept for use
2 : a literary or scientific association

athe·o·ret·i·cal \ˌā-ˌthē-ə-'re-ti-kəl, -ˌthi-(ə-)r'e-\ *adjective* (1969)
: not based on or concerned with theory

athero- *combining form* [Greek *athēra*]
: atheroma ⟨*athero*genic⟩

ath·ero·gen·e·sis \ˌa-thə-rō-'je-nə-səs\ *noun* (1953)
: the process of developing atheroma

ath·ero·gen·ic \-'je-nik\ *adjective* (1954)
: relating to or producing degenerative changes in arterial walls ⟨*atherogenic* diet⟩

ath·er·o·ma \ˌa-thə-'rō-mə\ *noun* [New Latin *atheromat-, atheroma*, from Latin, a tumor containing matter resembling gruel, from Greek *athērōma*, from *athēra* gruel] (1875)
1 : fatty degeneration of the inner coat of the arteries
2 : an abnormal fatty deposit in an artery
— **ath·er·o·ma·tous** \-'rō-mə-təs\ *adjective*

ath·ero·scle·ro·sis \ˌa-thə-rō-sklə-'rō-səs\ *noun* [New Latin] (1910)
: an arteriosclerosis characterized by atheromatous deposits in and fibrosis of the inner layer of the arteries
— **ath·ero·scle·rot·ic** \-sklə-'rä-tik\ *adjective*

athirst \ə-'thərst\ *adjective* [Middle English, from Old English *ofthyrst*, past participle of *ofthyrstan* to suffer from thirst, from *of* off, from + *thyrstan* to thirst — more at OF] (before 12th century)
1 *archaic* **:** THIRSTY
2 : having a strong eager desire ⟨I that for ever feel *athirst* for glory —John Keats⟩
synonym see EAGER

ath·lete \'ath-ˌlēt, ÷'a-thə-ˌlēt\ *noun* [Middle English, from Latin *athleta*, from Greek *athlētēs*, from *athlein* to contend for a prize, from *athlon* prize, contest] (15th century)
: a person who is trained or skilled in exercises, sports, or games requiring physical strength, agility, or stamina

athlete's foot *noun* (1928)
: ringworm of the feet

ath·let·ic \ath-'le-tik, ÷ˌa-thə-'le-\ *adjective* (1636)
1 : of or relating to athletes or athletics
2 : characteristic of an athlete; *especially* **:** VIGOROUS, ACTIVE
3 : MESOMORPHIC
4 : used by athletes
— **ath·let·i·cal·ly** \-ti-k(ə-)lē\ *adverb*
— **ath·let·i·cism** \-'le-tə-ˌsi-zəm\ *noun*

ath·let·ics \ath-'le-tiks, ÷ˌa-thə-'le-\ *noun plural but singular or plural in construction* (1727)
1 : exercises, sports, or games engaged in by athletes
2 : the practice or principles of athletic activities

athletic supporter *noun* (1927)
: a supporter for the genitals worn by men participating in sports or strenuous activities

at-home \ət-'hōm\ *adjective* (1951)
1 : intended or suitable for one's home ⟨an *at-home* dress⟩
2 : being or occurring at one's home ⟨*at-home* entertainment⟩

at home *noun* (1745)
: a reception given at one's home

-athon *noun combining form* [marathon]
: event or activity lasting a long time ⟨talk*athon*⟩

ath·ro·cyte \'a-thrə-ˌsīt\ *noun* [Greek *athroos* together, collected + International Scientific Vocabulary *-cyte*] (1938)
: a cell that has the ability to store up substances of an excretory nature

¹athwart \ə-'thwȯrt, *nautical often* -'thȯrt\ *preposition* (15th century)
1 : ACROSS
2 : in opposition to ⟨a procedure directly *athwart* the New England prejudices —R. G. Cole⟩

²athwart *adverb* (circa 1500)
1 : across especially in an oblique direction
2 : in opposition to the right or expected course ⟨and quite *athwart* goes all decorum —Shakespeare⟩

athwart·ship \-ˌship\ *adjective* (1879)

: being across the ship from side to side ⟨*athwartship* and longitudinal framing⟩

athwart·ships \-ˌships\ *adverb* (1718)
: across the ship from side to side

atilt \ə-ˈtilt\ *adverb or adjective* (1562)
1 : in a tilted position
2 : with lance in hand ⟨run *atilt* at death —Shakespeare⟩

atin·gle \ə-ˈtiŋ-gəl\ *adjective* (1855)
: tingling especially with excitement

-ation *noun suffix* [Middle English *-acioun,* from Old French *-ation,* from Latin *-ation-, -atio,* from *-a-,* stem vowel of 1st conjugation + *-tion-, -tio,* noun suffix]
: action or process ⟨flirt*ation*⟩ : something connected with an action or process ⟨discolor*ation*⟩

-ative *adjective suffix* [Middle English, from Middle French *-atif,* from Latin *-ativus,* from *-atus* -ate + *-ivus* -ive]
: of, relating to, or connected with ⟨authorita*tive*⟩ : tending to ⟨talk*ative*⟩

At·ka mackerel \ˈat-kə-, ˈät-\ *noun* [Atka Island, Alaska] (1893)
: a greenling (*Pleurogrammus monopterygius*) of Alaska and adjacent regions valued as a food fish

¹At·lan·te·an \ˌat-ˌlan-ˈtē-ən, ət-ˈlan-tē-\ *adjective* (1667)
: of, relating to, or resembling Atlas : STRONG

²Atlantean *adjective* (circa 1828)
: of or relating to Atlantis

At·lan·tic \ət-ˈlan-tik, at-\ *adjective* (1601)
1 a : of, relating to, or found in, on, or near the Atlantic Ocean **b** : of, relating to, or found on or near the east coast of the U.S.
2 : of or relating to the nations that border the Atlantic Ocean ⟨the *Atlantic* community⟩

Atlantic croaker *noun* (circa 1949)
: a small fish (*Micropogonias undulatus*) of the Gulf coast and the Atlantic coast — called also *hardhead*

At·lan·ti·cism \-ˈlan-tə-ˌsi-zəm\ *noun* (1950)
: a policy of military cooperation between European powers and the U.S.
— **At·lan·ti·cist** \-sist\ *noun*

Atlantic salmon *noun* (1902)
: SALMON 1a

Atlantic time *noun* (circa 1909)
: the time of the fourth time zone west of Greenwich that includes the Canadian Maritime Provinces, Puerto Rico, and the Virgin Islands

At·lan·tis \ət-ˈlan-təs, at-\ *noun* [Latin, from Greek, from *Atlas*]
: a fabled island in the Atlantic that according to legend sank beneath the sea

at·las \ˈat-ləs\ *noun* [Latin *Atlant-, Atlas,* from Greek]
1 *capitalized* : a Titan who for his part in the Titans' revolt against the gods is forced by Zeus to support the heavens on his shoulders
2 *capitalized* : one who bears a heavy burden
3 a : a bound collection of maps often including illustrations, informative tables, or textual matter **b** : a bound collection of tables, charts, or plates
4 : the first vertebra of the neck
5 *plural usually* **at·lan·tes** \ət-ˈlan-(ˌ)tēz, at-\ : a male figure used like a caryatid as a supporting column or pilaster — called also *telamon* ◇

atlas 5

at·latl \ˈät-ˌlä-t²l\ *noun* [Nahuatl *ahtlatl*] (1871)
: a device for throwing a spear or dart that consists of a rod or board with a projection (as a hook or thong) at the rear end to hold the weapon in place until released

At·li \ˈät-lē\ *noun* [Old Norse]
: a king of the Huns figuring in Germanic legend and corresponding to the historical Attila

at·man \ˈät-mən, -ˌmän\ *noun, often capitalized* [Sanskrit *ātman,* literally, breath, soul; akin to Old English *ǣthm* breath] (1785)
1 *Hinduism* : the innermost essence of each individual
2 *Hinduism* : the supreme universal self : BRAHMA 2

at·mom·e·ter \at-ˈmä-mə-tər\ *noun* [Greek *atmos* + English *-meter*] (1815)
: an instrument for measuring the evaporating capacity of the air

at·mo·sphere \ˈat-mə-ˌsfir\ *noun* [New Latin *atmosphaera,* from Greek *atmos* vapor + Latin *sphaera* sphere] (1677)
1 a : the gaseous envelope of a celestial body (as a planet) **b** : the whole mass of air surrounding the earth
2 : the air of a locality
3 : a surrounding influence or environment ⟨an *atmosphere* of hostility⟩
4 : a unit of pressure equal to the pressure of the air at sea level or approximately 14.7 pounds per square inch (101,325 pascals)
5 a : the overall aesthetic effect of a work of art **b** : a dominant aesthetic or emotional effect or appeal
— **at·mo·sphered** \-ˌsfird\ *adjective*

at·mo·spher·ic \ˌat-mə-ˈsfir-ik, -ˈsfer-\ *adjective* (1783)
1 a : of, relating to, or occurring in the atmosphere **b** : resembling the atmosphere : AIRY
2 : having, marked by, or contributing aesthetic or emotional atmosphere
— **at·mo·spher·i·cal·ly** \-i-k(ə-)lē\ *adverb*

at·mo·spher·ics \-iks\ *noun plural* (1915)
1 : audible disturbances produced in radio receiving apparatus by atmospheric electrical phenomena (as lightning); *also* : the electrical phenomena causing these disturbances
2 : actions (as official statements) intended to create or suggest a particular atmosphere or mood in politics and especially international relations; *also* : the mood so created or suggested
3 : realistic detail added (as to a literary work) to create a mood

atoll \ˈa-ˌtȯl, -ˌtäl, -ˌtōl, ˈā-\ *noun* [Divehi (Indo-Aryan language of the Maldive Islands) *atolu*] (1625)
: a coral island consisting of a reef surrounding a lagoon

atoll

at·om \ˈa-təm\ *noun* [Middle English, from Latin *atomus,* from Greek *atomos,* from *atomos* indivisible, from *a-* + *temnein* to cut] (15th century)
1 : one of the minute indivisible particles of which according to ancient materialism the universe is composed
2 : a tiny particle : BIT
3 : the smallest particle of an element that can exist either alone or in combination
4 : the atom considered as a source of vast potential energy ◇

atom·ic \ə-ˈtä-mik\ *adjective* (1678)
1 a : of, relating to, or concerned with atoms ⟨*atomic* physics⟩ **b** : NUCLEAR 2 ⟨*atomic* energy⟩
2 a : marked by acceptance of the theory of atomism **b** : ATOMISTIC 2
3 : MINUTE
4 *of a chemical element* : existing in the state of separate atoms
— **atom·i·cal·ly** \-mi-k(ə-)lē\ *adverb*

atomic bomb *noun* (1914)

1 : a bomb whose violent explosive power is due to the sudden release of energy resulting from the splitting of nuclei of a heavy chemical element (as plutonium or uranium) by neutrons in a very rapid chain reaction — called also *atom bomb*
2 : a nuclear weapon (as a hydrogen bomb)

atomic clock *noun* (1938)
: a precision clock that depends for its operation on an electrical oscillator regulated by the natural vibration frequencies of an atomic system (as a beam of cesium atoms)

atomic mass *noun* (1898)
: the mass of an atom usually expressed in atomic mass units; *also* : ATOMIC WEIGHT

atomic mass unit *noun* (circa 1942)
: a unit of mass for expressing masses of atoms, molecules, or nuclear particles equal to $\frac{1}{12}$ the mass of a single atom of the most abundant carbon isotope ^{12}C — called also *dalton*

atomic number *noun* (1821)
: an experimentally determined number characteristic of a chemical element that represents the number of protons in the nucleus which in a neutral atom equals the number of electrons outside the nucleus and that determines the place of the element in the periodic table — see ELEMENT table

atomic reactor *or* **atomic pile** *noun* (1945)
: REACTOR 3b

atomic theory *noun* (circa 1847)
1 : a theory of the nature of matter: all material substances are composed of minute particles or atoms of a comparatively small number of kinds and all the atoms of the same kind are uniform in size, weight, and other properties

◇ WORD HISTORY

atlas In Greek myth, the Titan Atlas, following the defeat of the Titans in a war with Zeus and the other gods, was punished by being forced to support the heavens on his shoulders. A representation of Atlas as a man bearing on his back the globe of the earth became a conventional title-page illustration in bound volumes of maps during the 16th century. In 1585, the Flemish mathematician and mapmaker Gerhardus Mercator initiated a series of map collections with a flowery Latin title that can be translated as *Atlas, or Cosmographical Reflections on the Edifice of the World and the Representation of its Form.* The word *atlas* eventually became the generic term for a book of maps in most languages of Europe, including English.

atom For ancient Greek thinkers, ideas about the nature of matter and motion, what we think of as physics, were inseparable from philosophical reflections about existence and plurality. On grounds that a modern physicist would consider philosophical rather than experimental, Leucippus and his better-known student Democritus decided that matter was not infinitely divisible, but rather consisted of particles of being separated by empty space. These particles of being that made up all things were called *atoma sōmata* "indivisible bodies." The later Greek word *atomos,* borrowed into Latin as *atomus* and into French as *atome,* was used in Epicurean philosophy. Long after ancient Greece and Rome the concept was taken up again by early experimental science in the 17th century. With the development of modern atomic chemistry in the 19th and 20th centuries, the atoms of Democritus proved real enough, though they were not indivisible after all, and the splitting of their nuclei was discovered to be the source of enormous energy.

2 : any of several theories of the structure of the atom; *especially* **:** one based on experimentation and theoretical considerations holding that the atom is composed essentially of a small positively charged comparatively heavy nucleus surrounded by a comparatively large arrangement of electrons

atomic weight *noun* (1820)
: the mass of one atom of an element; *specifically* **:** the average mass of an atom of an element as it occurs in nature that is expressed in atomic mass units — see ELEMENT table

at·om·ise, at·om·is·er *British variant of* ATOMIZE, ATOMIZER

at·om·ism \'a-tə-,mi-zəm\ *noun* (1678)
1 : a doctrine that the physical or physical and mental universe is composed of simple indivisible minute particles
2 : INDIVIDUALISM 1
— **at·om·ist** \-mist\ *noun*

at·om·is·tic \,a-tə-'mis-tik\ *adjective* (1809)
1 : of or relating to atoms or atomism
2 : composed of many simple elements; *also* **:** characterized by or resulting from division into unconnected or antagonistic fragments ⟨an *atomistic* society⟩
— **at·om·is·ti·cal·ly** \-ti-k(ə-)lē\ *adverb*

at·om·ize \'a-tə-,mīz\ *transitive verb* **-ized; -iz·ing** (1845)
1 : to treat as made up of many discrete units
2 : to reduce to minute particles or to a fine spray
3 : DIVIDE, FRAGMENT
4 : to subject to attack by nuclear weapons
— **at·om·iza·tion** \,a-tə-mə-'zā-shən\ *noun*

at·om·iz·er \'a-tə-,mī-zər\ *noun* (1865)
: an instrument for atomizing usually a perfume, disinfectant, or medicament

atom smasher *noun* (1937)
: ACCELERATOR d

at·o·my \'a-tə-mē\ *noun, plural* **-mies** [irregular from Latin *atomi,* plural of *atomus* atom] (1591)
: a tiny particle **:** ATOM, MITE

aton·al \(,)ā-'tō-n°l, (,)a-\ *adjective* [²a- + tonal] (1922)
: marked by avoidance of traditional musical tonality; *especially* **:** organized without reference to key or tonal center and using the tones of the chromatic scale impartially
— **aton·al·ism** \-n°l-,i-zəm\ *noun*
— **aton·al·ist** \-ist\ *noun*
— **ato·nal·i·ty** \,ā-tō-'na-lə-tē, ,a-\ *noun*
— **aton·al·ly** \(,)ā-'tō-n°l-ē, (,)a-\ *adverb*

atone \ə-'tōn\ *verb* **atoned; aton·ing** [Middle English, to become reconciled, from *at on* in harmony, from *at + on* one] (1593)
transitive verb
1 *obsolete* **:** RECONCILE
2 : to supply satisfaction for **:** EXPIATE
intransitive verb
: to make amends

atone·ment \ə-'tōn-mənt\ *noun* (1513)
1 *obsolete* **:** RECONCILIATION
2 : the reconciliation of God and man through the sacrificial death of Jesus Christ
3 : reparation for an offense or injury **:** SATISFACTION
4 *Christian Science* **:** the exemplifying of man's oneness with God

aton·ic \(,)ā-'tä-nik, (,)a-\ *adjective* (1792)
1 : characterized by atony
2 : uttered without accent or stress

at·o·ny \'a-t°n-ē\ *noun* [Late Latin *atonia,* from Greek, from *atonos* without tone, from *a- + tonos* tone] (1693)
: lack of physiological tone especially of a contractile organ

¹atop \ə-'täp\ *preposition* (1655)
: on top of

²atop *adverb or adjective* (1658)
: on, to, or at the top

at·o·py \'a-tə-pē\ *noun* [Greek *atopia* uncommonness, from *atopos* out of the way, uncommon, from *a- + topos* place] (1923)
: a probably hereditary allergy characterized

by symptoms (as asthma, hay fever, or hives) produced upon exposure to the exciting antigen without inoculation
— **atop·ic** \(,)ā-'tä-pik, -'tō-\ *adjective*

-ator *noun suffix* [Middle English *-atour,* from Old French & Latin; Old French, from Latin *-ator,* from *-a-,* stem vowel of 1st conjugation + *-tor,* agent suffix]
: one that does ⟨totaliz*ator*⟩

ATP \,ā-,tē-'pē\ *noun* [adenosine *tri*phosphate] (1939)
: a phosphorylated nucleoside $C_{10}H_{16}N_5O_{13}P_3$ of adenine that supplies energy for many biochemical cellular processes by undergoing enzymatic hydrolysis especially to ADP — called also *adenosine triphosphate*

ATPase \,ā-,tē-'pē-,ās, -,āz\ *noun* (1946)
: an enzyme that hydrolyzes ATP; *especially* **:** one that hydrolyzes ATP to ADP and inorganic phosphate

at·ra·bil·ious \,a-trə-'bil-yəs\ *adjective* [Latin *atra bilis* black bile] (1651)
1 : given to or marked by melancholy **:** GLOOMY
2 : ILL-NATURED, PEEVISH
— **at·ra·bil·ious·ness** *noun*

at·ra·zine \'a-trə-,zēn\ *noun* [perhaps from *amino + triazine*] (1962)
: a photosynthesis-inhibiting persistent herbicide $C_8H_{14}ClN_5$ used especially to kill annual weeds and quack grass

atrem·ble \ə-'trem-bəl\ *adjective* (1862)
: shaking involuntarily **:** TREMBLING ⟨he was white as death and all *atremble* —Robert Coover⟩

atre·sia \ə-'trē-zhə\ *noun* [New Latin, from ²a- + Greek *trēsis* perforation, from *tetrainein* to pierce — more at THROW] (circa 1807)
1 : absence or closure of a natural passage of the body
2 : absence or disappearance of an anatomical part (as an ovarian follicle) by degeneration

Atreus \'ā-,trüs, -trē-əs\ *noun* [Greek]
: a king of Mycenae and father of Agamemnon and Menelaus

atrial natriuretic factor *noun* (1984)
: a peptide hormone secreted by the cardiac atria that stimulates natriuresis and diuresis and helps regulate blood pressure

atrio·ven·tric·u·lar \,ā-trē-ō-ven-'tri-kyə-lər, -vən-\ *adjective* [New Latin *atrium* + English *ventricular*] (circa 1860)
: of, relating to, or located between an atrium and ventricle of the heart

atrioventricular node *noun* (circa 1934)
: a small mass of tissue in the right atrioventricular region of higher vertebrates through which impulses from the sinoatrial node are passed to the ventricles

atrip \ə-'trip\ *adjective* (1796)
of an anchor **:** AWEIGH

atri·um \'ā-trē-əm\ *noun, plural* **atria** \-trē-ə\ *also* **atri·ums** [Latin] (1577)
1 : the central room of a Roman house
2 *plural usually* **atriums** **:** a rectangularly shaped open patio around which a house is built; *also* **:** a many-storied court in a building (as a hotel) usually with a skylight
3 [New Latin, from Latin] **:** an anatomical cavity or passage; *especially* **:** the chamber or either of the chambers of the heart that receives blood from the veins and forces it into the ventricle or ventricles — see HEART illustration
— **atri·al** \-trē-əl\ *adjective*

atro·cious \ə-'trō-shəs\ *adjective* [Latin *atroc-, atrox* gloomy, atrocious, from *atr-, ater* black + *-oc-, -ox* (akin to Greek *ōps* eye) — more at EYE] (1669)
1 : extremely wicked, brutal, or cruel **:** BARBARIC
2 : APPALLING, HORRIFYING ⟨the *atrocious* weapons of modern war⟩
3 a : utterly revolting **:** ABOMINABLE ⟨*atrocious* working conditions⟩ **b :** of very poor quality ⟨*atrocious* handwriting⟩

— **atro·cious·ly** *adverb*
— **atro·cious·ness** *noun*

atroc·i·ty \ə-'trä-sə-tē\ *noun, plural* **-ties** (1534)
1 : the quality or state of being atrocious
2 : an atrocious act, object, or situation ⟨the . . . sufferings and *atrocities* of trench warfare —Aldous Huxley⟩

at·ro·phy \'a-trə-fē\ *noun, plural* **-phies** [Late Latin *atrophia,* from Greek, from *atrophos* ill fed, from *a- + trephein* to nourish] (1601)
1 : decrease in size or wasting away of a body part or tissue; *also* **:** arrested development or loss of a part or organ incidental to the normal development or life of an animal or plant
2 : a wasting away or progressive decline **:** DEGENERATION ⟨the *atrophy* of freedom⟩ ⟨was not a solitude of *atrophy,* of negation, but of perpetual flowering —Willa Cather⟩
— **atro·phic** \(,)ā-'trō-fik\ *adjective*
— **atrophy** \'a-trə-fē, -,fī\ *verb*

at·ro·pine \'a-trə-,pēn\ *noun* [German *Atropin,* from New Latin *Atropa,* genus name of belladonna, from Greek *Atropos,* one of the three Fates] (1836)
: a racemic mixture of hyoscyamine obtained from any of various solanaceous plants (as belladonna) and used especially in the form of its sulfate for its anticholinergic effects (as pupil dilation or inhibition of smooth muscle spasms)

att *variant of* ²AT

at·ta·boy \'a-də-,boi\ *interjection* [probably alteration of *that's the boy*] (1909)
— used to express encouragement, approval, or admiration

at·tach \ə-'tach\ *verb* [Middle English, from Middle French *attacher,* from Old French *estachier,* from *estache* stake, of Germanic origin; akin to Old English *staca* stake] (14th century)
transitive verb
1 : to take by legal authority especially under a writ ⟨*attached* the property⟩
2 a : to bring (oneself) into an association **b :** to assign temporarily
3 : to bind by personal ties (as of affection or sympathy) ⟨was strongly *attached* to his family⟩
4 : to make fast (as by tying or gluing) ⟨*attach* a label to a package⟩
5 : to associate especially as a property **:** ATTRIBUTE ⟨*attached* great importance to public opinion polls⟩
intransitive verb
: to become attached **:** ADHERE
synonym see FASTEN
— **at·tach·able** \-'ta-chə-bəl\ *adjective*

at·ta·ché \,a-tə-'shā, ,a-,ta-, ə-,ta-\ *noun* [French, past participle of *attacher*] (1829)
1 : a technical expert on the diplomatic staff of his country at a foreign capital ⟨a military *attaché*⟩
2 : ATTACHÉ CASE

at·ta·ché case \,a-,ta-'shā-, ,a-tə-; ə-'ta-(,)shā-\ *noun* (1904)
1 : a small thin suitcase used especially for carrying business papers
2 : BRIEFCASE

at·tached \ə-'tacht\ *adjective* (1854)
: permanently fixed when adult ⟨*attached* barnacles⟩

at·tach·ment \ə-'tach-mənt\ *noun* (14th century)
1 : a seizure by legal process; *also* **:** the writ or precept commanding such seizure
2 a : the state of being personally attached **:** FIDELITY ⟨*attachment* to a cause⟩ **b :** affectionate regard ⟨a deep *attachment* to nature⟩

\ə\ abut \°\ kitten \ər\ further \a\ ash \ā\ ace
\ä\ mop, mar \au̇\ out \ch\ chin \e\ bet \ē\ easy
\g\ go \i\ hit \ī\ ice \j\ job \ŋ\ sing \ō\ go
\o̯\ law \oi\ boy \th\ thin \th\ the \ü\ loot \u̇\ foot
\y\ yet \zh\ vision *see also* Guide to Pronunciation

3 : a device attached to a machine or implement
4 : the physical connection by which one thing is attached to another
5 : the process of physically attaching

¹at·tack \ə-'tak\ *verb* [Middle French *attaquer,* from (assumed) Old Italian *estaccare* to attach, from *stacca* stake, of Germanic origin; akin to Old English *staca*] (1600)
transitive verb
1 : to set upon or work against forcefully
2 : to assail with unfriendly or bitter words
3 : to begin to affect or to act on injuriously
4 : to set to work on
5 : to threaten (a piece in chess) with immediate capture
intransitive verb
: to make an attack ☆
— **at·tack·er** *noun*
²attack *noun* (1661)
1 : the act of attacking with physical force or unfriendly words **:** ASSAULT
2 : a belligerent or antagonistic action
3 a : a fit of sickness; *especially* **:** an active episode of a chronic or recurrent disease **b :** a period of being strongly affected by something (as a desire or mood)
4 a : an offensive or scoring action ⟨won the game with an eight-hit *attack*⟩ **b :** offensive players or the positions taken up by them
5 : the setting to work on some undertaking ⟨made a new *attack* on the problem⟩
6 : the beginning of destructive action (as by a chemical agent)
7 : the act or manner of beginning a musical tone or phrase
at·tack·man \-,man\ *noun* (1940)
: a player (as in lacrosse) assigned to an offensive zone or position
at·tain \ə-'tān\ *verb* [Middle English *atteynen,* from Old French *ataindre,* from (assumed) Vulgar Latin *attangere,* alteration of Latin *attingere,* from *ad-* + *tangere* to touch — more at TANGENT] (14th century)
transitive verb
1 : to reach as an end **:** GAIN, ACHIEVE ⟨*attain* a goal⟩
2 : to come into possession of **:** OBTAIN ⟨he *attained* preferment over his fellows⟩
3 : to come to as the end of a progression or course of movement ⟨they *attained* the top of the hill⟩ ⟨*attain* a ripe old age⟩
intransitive verb
: to come or arrive by motion, growth, or effort — usually used with *to*
— **at·tain·a·bil·i·ty** \-,tā-nə-'bi-lə-tē\ *noun*
— **at·tain·able** \-'tā-nə-bəl\ *adjective*
at·tain·der \ə-'tān-dər\ *noun* [Middle English *attaynder,* from Middle French *ataindre* to accuse, attain] (15th century)
1 : extinction of the civil rights and capacities of a person upon sentence of death or outlawry usually after a conviction of treason
2 obsolete : DISHONOR
at·tain·ment \ə-'tān-mənt\ *noun* (1549)
1 : the act of attaining **:** the condition of being attained
2 : something attained **:** ACCOMPLISHMENT ⟨scientific *attainments*⟩
¹at·taint \ə-'tānt\ *transitive verb* [Middle English *attaynten,* from Middle French *ataint,* past participle of *ataindre*] (14th century)
1 : to affect by attainder
2 a : INFECT, CORRUPT **b** *archaic* **:** TAINT, SULLY
3 *archaic* **:** ACCUSE
²attaint *noun* (1592)
obsolete **:** a stain upon honor or purity **:** DISGRACE
at·tar \'a-tər, 'a-,tär\ *noun* [Persian *'aṭir* perfumed, from Arabic, from *'iṭr* perfume] (1798)
: a fragrant essential oil (as from rose petals); *also* **:** FRAGRANCE
¹at·tempt \ə-'tem(p)t\ *transitive verb* [Middle English, from Middle French & Latin; Middle French *attempter,* from Latin *attemptare,* from

ad- + *temptare* to touch, try — more at TEMPT] (14th century)
1 : to make an effort to do, accomplish, solve, or effect ⟨*attempted* to swim the swollen river⟩
2 *archaic* **:** TEMPT
3 *archaic* **:** to try to subdue or take by force **:** ATTACK ☆
— **at·tempt·able** \-'tem(p)-tə-bəl\ *adjective*
²attempt *noun* (1534)
1 a : the act or an instance of attempting; *especially* **:** an unsuccessful effort **b :** something resulting from or representing an attempt ⟨surrounded by . . . a few *attempts* at rose bushes —Marian Engel⟩
2 : ATTACK, ASSAULT ⟨an *attempt* on the life of the president⟩
at·tend \ə-'tend\ *verb* [Middle English, from Old French *atendre,* from Latin *attendere,* literally, to stretch to, from *ad-* + *tendere* to stretch — more at THIN] (14th century)
transitive verb
1 : to pay attention to
2 : to look after **:** take charge of ⟨campsites . . . *attended* by park rangers —Jackson Rivers⟩
3 a : to go or stay with as a companion, nurse, or servant **b :** to visit professionally as a physician
4 *archaic* **a :** to wait for **b :** to be in store for
5 : to be present with **:** ACCOMPANY
6 : to be present at **:** go to ⟨*attend* law school⟩
intransitive verb
1 : to apply oneself ⟨*attend* to your work⟩
2 : to apply the mind or pay attention **:** HEED
3 a : to be ready for service ⟨ministers who *attend* upon the king⟩ **b :** to be present
4 *obsolete* **:** WAIT, STAY
5 : to direct one's attention **:** SEE ⟨I'll *attend* to that⟩
— **at·tend·er** *noun*
at·ten·dance \ə-'ten-dən(t)s\ *noun* (14th century)
1 : the act or fact of attending ⟨a physician in *attendance*⟩
2 a : the persons or number of persons attending ⟨daily *attendance* at the fair⟩ **b :** the number of times a person attends
attendance officer *noun* (1884)
: one employed by a public-school system to investigate the continued absences of pupils
¹at·ten·dant \ə-'ten-dənt\ *noun* (15th century)
1 : one who attends another to perform a service; *especially* **:** an employee who waits on customers
2 : something that accompanies **:** CONCOMITANT
3 : ATTENDEE
²attendant *adjective* (15th century)
1 : accompanying, waiting upon, or following in order to perform service ⟨Cherub and Seraph . . . *attendant* on their Lord —John Milton⟩
2 : accompanying or following as a consequence or result ⟨problems *attendant* upon pollution⟩
at·tend·ee \ə-,ten-'dē, ,a-\ *noun* (1937)
: a person who is present on a given occasion or at a given place ⟨*attendees* at a convention⟩
at·tend·ing \ə-'ten-din\ *adjective* (circa 1923)
: serving as a physician on the staff of a teaching hospital ⟨*attending* surgeon⟩
at·ten·tion \ə-'ten(t)-shən; *sense 4 often* (ə-),ten(ch)-'hət\ *noun* [Middle English *attencioun,* from Latin *attention-, attentio,* from *attendere*] (14th century)
1 a : the act or state of attending especially through applying the mind to an object of sense or thought **b :** a condition of readiness for such attention involving especially a selective narrowing or focusing of consciousness and receptivity
2 : OBSERVATION, NOTICE; *especially* **:** consideration with a view to action ⟨a problem requiring prompt *attention*⟩
3 a : an act of civility or courtesy especially in

courtship **b :** sympathetic consideration of the needs and wants of others **:** ATTENTIVENESS
4 : a position assumed by a soldier with heels together, body erect, arms at the sides, and eyes to the front — often used as a command
— **at·ten·tion·al** \-'ten(t)-sh(ə-)nəl\ *adjective*
attention deficit disorder *noun* (1980)
: a syndrome of learning and behavioral problems that is not caused by any serious underlying physical or mental disorder and is characterized especially by difficulty in sustaining attention, by impulsive behavior (as in speaking out of turn), and usually by excessive activity
attention line *noun* (1925)
: a line usually placed above the salutation in a business letter directing the letter to one specified
attention span *noun* (1934)
: the length of time during which an individual is able to concentrate or remain interested
at·ten·tive \ə-'ten-tiv\ *adjective* (14th century)
1 : MINDFUL, OBSERVANT ⟨*attentive* to what he is doing⟩
2 : heedful of the comfort of others **:** SOLICITOUS
3 : offering attentions in or as if in the role of a suitor
— **at·ten·tive·ly** *adverb*
— **at·ten·tive·ness** *noun*
¹at·ten·u·ate \ə-'ten-yə-,wāt\ *verb* **-at·ed; -at·ing** [Latin *attenuatus,* past participle of *attenuare* to make thin, from *ad-* + *tenuis* thin — more at THIN] (15th century)
transitive verb
1 : to make thin or slender
2 : to make thin in consistency **:** RAREFY
3 : to lessen the amount, force, magnitude, or value of **:** WEAKEN
4 : to reduce the severity, virulence, or vitality of
intransitive verb
: to become thin, fine, or less
— **at·ten·u·a·tion** \-,ten-yə-'wā-shən\ *noun*
²at·ten·u·ate \ə-'ten-yə-wət\ *adjective* (15th century)

1 : attenuated especially in thickness, density, or force
2 : tapering gradually usually to a long slender point ⟨*attenuate* leaves⟩
at·ten·u·a·tor \-yə-ˌwā-tər\ *noun* (1924)
: a device for attenuating; *especially* **:** one for reducing the amplitude of an electrical signal without appreciable distortion
at·test \ə-'test\ *verb* [Middle French *attester,* from Latin *attestari,* from *ad-* + *testis* witness — more at TESTAMENT] (1596)
transitive verb
1 a : to affirm to be true or genuine; *specifically* **:** to authenticate by signing as a witness
b : to authenticate officially
2 : to establish or verify the usage of
3 : to be proof of **:** MANIFEST ⟨her record *attests* her integrity⟩
4 : to put on oath
intransitive verb
: to bear witness **:** TESTIFY ⟨*attest* to a belief⟩
synonym see CERTIFY
— **at·tes·ta·tion** \ˌa-ˌtes-'tā-shən, ˌa-tə-'stā-\ *noun*
— **at·test·er** \ə-'tes-tər\ *noun*
at·tic \'a-tik\ *noun* [French *attique,* from *attique* of Attica, from Latin *Atticus*] (circa 1696)
1 : a low story or wall above the main order of a facade in the classical styles
2 : a room behind an attic
3 : a room or a space immediately below the roof of a building **:** GARRET
4 : something resembling an attic (as in being used for storage) ◈
¹At·tic \'a-tik\ *adjective* [Latin *Atticus* of Attica, from Greek *Attikos,* from *Attikē* Attica, Greece] (1599)
1 : of, relating to, or having the characteristics of Athens or its ancient civilization
2 : marked by simplicity, purity, and refinement ⟨an *Attic* prose style⟩
²Attic *noun* (circa 1771)
: a dialect of ancient Greek originally used in Attica and later the literary language of the Greek-speaking world
at·ti·cism \'a-tə-ˌsi-zəm\ *noun, often capitalized* (1593)
1 : a witty or well-turned phrase
2 : a characteristic feature of Attic Greek occurring in another language or dialect
¹at·tire \ə-'tīr\ *transitive verb* **at·tired; at·tir·ing** [Middle English, from Old French *atirier,* from *a-* (from Latin *ad-*) + *tire* order, rank, of Germanic origin; akin to Old English *tīr* glory, ornament] (14th century)
: to put garments on **:** DRESS, ARRAY; *especially* **:** to clothe in fancy or rich garments
²attire *noun* (14th century)
1 : DRESS, CLOTHES; *especially* **:** splendid or decorative clothing
2 : the antlers or antlers and scalp of a stag or buck
at·ti·tude \'a-tə-ˌtüd, -ˌtyüd\ *noun* [French, from Italian *attitudine,* literally, aptitude, from Late Latin *aptitudin-, aptitudo* fitness — more at APTITUDE] (1668)
1 : the arrangement of the parts of a body or figure **:** POSTURE
2 : a position assumed for a specific purpose ⟨a threatening *attitude*⟩
3 : a ballet position similar to the arabesque in which the raised leg is bent at the knee
4 a : a mental position with regard to a fact or state **b :** a feeling or emotion toward a fact or state
5 : the position of an aircraft or spacecraft determined by the relationship between its axes and a reference datum (as the horizon or a particular star)
6 : an organismic state of readiness to respond in a characteristic way to a stimulus (as an object, concept, or situation)
7 a : a negative or hostile state of mind **b :** a cocky or arrogant manner
at·ti·tu·di·nal \ˌa-tə-'tü-dᵊn-əl, -'tyü-\ *adjec-*

tive [*attitude* + *-inal* (as in *aptitudinal,* from Latin *aptitudin-, aptitudo*)] (1831)
: relating to, based on, or expressive of personal attitudes or feelings ⟨*attitudinal* judgment⟩
— **at·ti·tu·di·nal·ly** \-ə-lē\ *adverb*
at·ti·tu·di·nise *British variant of* ATTITUDINIZE
at·ti·tu·di·nize \ˌa-tə-'tü-dᵊn-ˌīz, -'tyü-\ *intransitive verb* **-nized; -niz·ing** (1784)
: to assume an affected mental attitude **:** POSE
at·to- \'a-(ˌ)tō\ *combining form* [International Scientific Vocabulary, from Danish or Norwegian *atten* eighteen, from Old Norse *āttjān;* akin to Old English *eahtatīene* eighteen]
: one quintillionth (10^{-18}) part of ⟨*atto*gram⟩
at·torn \ə-'tərn\ *intransitive verb* [Middle English *attournen,* from Middle French *atorner,* from Old French, from *a-* (from Latin *ad-*) + *torner* to turn] (15th century)
: to agree to be tenant to a new owner or landlord of the same property
— **at·torn·ment** \-mənt\ *noun*
at·tor·ney \ə-'tər-nē\ *noun, plural* **-neys** [Middle English *attourney,* from Middle French *atorné,* past participle of *atorner*] (14th century)
: one who is legally appointed to transact business on another's behalf; *specifically* **:** a legal agent qualified to act for suitors and defendants in legal proceedings
— **at·tor·ney·ship** \-ˌship\ *noun*
attorney–at–law *noun, plural* **attorneys–at–law** (1768)
: a practitioner in a court of law who is legally qualified to prosecute and defend actions in such court on the retainer of clients
attorney general *noun, plural* **attorneys general** *or* **attorney generals** (1585)
: the chief law officer of a nation or state who represents the government in litigation and serves as its principal legal adviser
at·tract \ə-'trakt\ *verb* [Middle English, from Latin *attractus,* past participle of *attrahere,* from *ad-* + *trahere* to pull, draw] (15th century)
transitive verb
: to cause to approach or adhere: as **a :** to pull to or draw toward oneself or itself ⟨a magnet *attracts* iron⟩ **b :** to draw by appeal to natural or excited interest, emotion, or aesthetic sense **:** ENTICE ⟨*attract* attention⟩
intransitive verb
: to exercise attraction ☆
— **at·trac·tor** \-'trak-tər\ *noun*
at·trac·tance \-tən(t)s\ *noun* (1948)
: ATTRACTANCY
at·trac·tan·cy \ə-'trak-tən(t)-sē\ *noun* (1948)
: the quality or capacity (as of a pheromone) of attracting
at·trac·tant \ə-'trak-tənt\ *noun* (1920)
: a substance (as of a pheromone) that attracts insects or other animals
at·trac·tion \ə-'trak-shən\ *noun* (14th century)
1 a : the act, process, or power of attracting **b :** personal charm
2 : the action or power of drawing forth a response **:** an attractive quality
3 : a force acting mutually between particles of matter, tending to draw them together, and resisting their separation
4 : something that attracts or is intended to attract people by appealing to their desires and tastes ⟨coming *attractions*⟩ ☆
at·trac·tive \ə-'trak-tiv\ *adjective* (14th century)
1 : having or relating to the power to attract ⟨*attractive* forces between molecules⟩ ⟨an *attractive* offer⟩
2 : arousing interest or pleasure **:** CHARMING ⟨an *attractive* smile⟩
— **at·trac·tive·ly** *adverb*
— **at·trac·tive·ness** *noun*
¹at·tri·bute \'a-trə-ˌbyüt\ *noun* [Middle English, from Latin *attributus,* past participle of

attribuere to attribute, from *ad-* + *tribuere* to bestow — more at TRIBUTE] (14th century)
1 : an inherent characteristic; *also* **:** an accidental quality
2 : an object closely associated with or belonging to a specific person, thing, or office ⟨a scepter is the *attribute* of power⟩; *especially* **:** such an object used for identification in painting or sculpture
3 : a word ascribing a quality; *especially* **:** ADJECTIVE
synonym see QUALITY
²at·trib·ute \ə-'tri-ˌbyüt, -byət\ *transitive verb* **-ut·ed; -ut·ing** (1530)

☆ SYNONYMS

Attract, allure, charm, captivate, fascinate, enchant mean to draw another by exerting a powerful influence. ATTRACT applies to any degree or kind of ability to exert influence over another ⟨students *attracted* by the school's locale⟩. ALLURE implies an enticing by what is fair, pleasing, or seductive ⟨an *alluring* smile⟩. CHARM implies the power of casting a spell over the person or thing affected and so compelling a response ⟨*charmed* by their hospitality⟩, but it may, like CAPTIVATE, suggest no more than evoking delight or admiration ⟨her performances *captivated* audiences⟩. FASCINATE suggests a magical influence and tends to stress the ineffectiveness of attempts to resist ⟨a story that continues to *fascinate* children⟩. ENCHANT is perhaps the strongest of these terms in stressing the appeal of the agent and the degree of delight evoked in the subject ⟨hopelessly *enchanted* by her beauty⟩.

Attraction, affinity, sympathy mean the relationship existing between things or persons that are naturally or involuntarily drawn together. ATTRACTION implies the possession by one thing of a quality that pulls another to it ⟨felt an *attraction* to danger⟩. AFFINITY implies a susceptibility or predisposition on the part of the one drawn ⟨an *affinity* for mathematics⟩. SYMPATHY implies a reciprocal or natural relation between two things that are both susceptible to the same influence ⟨two minds in *sympathy*⟩.

◇ WORD HISTORY

attic The ancient Greek city-state of Athens included the whole of the Attic peninsula, the region called Attica. Typical of the Attic or Athenian style of architecture is the use of pilasters, rectangular columns projecting from, but attached to, the wall. These take the place of the freestanding and usually rounded pillars common in other architectural styles. Occasionally the large columns and entablature that form the facade of a building are surmounted by a similar but smaller decorative structure, whose columns are usually pilasters, rather than pillars. Because this small upper order is in the Attic style, the French named it *attique*. The English borrowed the word as *attic,* and extended its meaning, originally in the phrases *attic story* and *attic floor,* to designate the top story of any building just under the roof. So a word that was once associated with an elegant architectural style now names what is usually no more than a lowly storage area.

\ə\ **abut** \ᵊ\ **kitten** \ər\ **further** \a\ **ash** \ā\ **ace**
\ä\ **mop, mar** \aú\ **out** \ch\ **chin** \e\ **bet** \ē\ **easy**
\g\ **go** \i\ **hit** \ī\ **ice** \j\ **job** \ŋ\ **sing** \ō\ **go**
\ó\ **law** \ói\ **boy** \th\ **thin** \t̲h̲\ **the** \ü\ **loot** \ú\ **foot**
\y\ **yet** \zh\ **vision** *see also* Guide to Pronunciation

1 : to explain by indicating a cause ⟨*attributed* his success to his coach⟩ **2 a :** to regard as a characteristic of a person or thing **b :** to reckon as made or originated in an indicated fashion ⟨*attributed* the invention to a Russian⟩ **c :** CLASSIFY, DESIGNATE
synonym see ASCRIBE
— **at·trib·ut·able** \-byü-tə-bəl, -byə-\ *adjective*

at·tri·bu·tion \ˌa-trə-'byü-shən\ *noun* (1651) **1 :** the act of attributing; *especially* **:** the ascribing of a work (as of literature or art) to a particular author or artist **2 :** an ascribed quality, character, or right
— **at·tri·bu·tion·al** \-sh(ə-)nᵊl\ *adjective*

at·trib·u·tive \ə-'tri-byə-tiv\ *adjective* (1606) **1 :** relating to or of the nature of an attribute **:** ATTRIBUTING **2 :** joined directly to a modified noun without a linking verb (as *city* in *city streets*)
— **attributive** *noun*
— **at·trit·u·tive·ly** *adverb*

at·trit·ed \ə-'trī-təd\ *adjective* (1760) **:** worn by attrition

at·tri·tion \ə-'tri-shən, a-\ *noun* [Latin *attrition-*, *attritio*, from *atterere* to rub against, from *ad-* + *terere* to rub — more at THROW] (14th century) **1** [Middle English *attricioun*, from Medieval Latin *attrition-*, *attritio*, from Latin] **:** sorrow for one's sins that arises from a motive other than that of the love of God **2 :** the act of rubbing together **:** FRICTION; *also* **:** the act of wearing or grinding down by friction **3 :** the act of weakening or exhausting by constant harassment, abuse, or attack **4 :** a reduction in numbers usually as a result of resignation, retirement, or death
— **at·tri·tion·al** \-'tri-sh(ə-)nᵊl\ *adjective*

at·tune \ə-'tün, -'tyün\ *transitive verb* (1596) **1 :** to bring into harmony **:** TUNE **2 :** to make aware or responsive ⟨*attune* businesses to changing trends⟩
— **at·tune·ment** \-mənt\ *noun*

atwit·ter \ə-'twi-tər\ *adjective* (1833) **:** nervously concerned **:** EXCITED ⟨gossips *atwitter* with speculation —*Time*⟩

atyp·i·cal \(ˌ)ā-'ti-pi-kəl\ *adjective* (1885) **:** not typical **:** IRREGULAR, UNUSUAL
— **atyp·i·cal·i·ty** \ˌā-ˌti-pə-'ka-lə-tē\ *noun*
— **atyp·i·cal·ly** \(ˌ)ā-'ti-pi-k(ə-)lē\ *adverb*

au·bade \ō-'bäd\ *noun* [French, from Middle French, from Old Provençal *aubada*, from *alba*, *auba* dawn, from (assumed) Vulgar Latin *alba*, from Latin, feminine of *albus* white — more at ALB] (circa 1678) **1 :** a song or poem greeting the dawn **2 a :** a morning love song **b :** a song or poem of lovers parting at dawn **3 :** morning music — compare NOCTURNE

au·berge \ō-'berzh\ *noun* [French, from Middle French, of Germanic origin; akin to Old High German *heriberga* military quarters — more at HARBOR] (1599) **:** INN 1a

au·ber·gine \'ō-bər-ˌzhēn\ *noun* [French, from Catalan *albergínia*, from Arabic *al-bādhinjān* the eggplant] (1794) **1** *chiefly British* **:** EGGPLANT 1 **2 :** EGGPLANT 2

¹au·burn \'ò-bərn\ *adjective* [Middle English *auborne* blond, from Middle French, from Medieval Latin *alburnus* whitish, from Latin *alburnum* sapwood] (15th century) **1 :** of the color auburn **2 :** of a reddish brown color

²auburn *noun* (1613) **:** a moderate brown

Au·bus·son \ˌō-bə-'sōⁿ\ *noun* [*Aubusson*, town in France] (1851) **:** a figured scenic tapestry used for wall hangings and upholstery; *also* **:** a rug woven to resemble Aubusson tapestry

au cou·rant \ˌō-ku̇-'räⁿ\ *adjective* [French, literally, in the current] (1762)

1 a : fully informed **:** UP-TO-DATE **b :** FASHIONABLE, STYLISH **2 :** fully familiar **:** CONVERSANT

¹auc·tion \'ȯk-shən\ *noun* [Latin *auction-*, *auctio*, from *augēre* to increase — more at EKE] (1595) **1 :** a sale of property to the highest bidder **2 :** the act or process of bidding in some card games

²auction *transitive verb* **auc·tioned; auc·tion·ing** \-sh(ə-)niŋ\ (circa 1798) **:** to sell at auction ⟨*auctioned* off his library⟩

auction bridge *noun* (1908) **:** a bridge game differing from contract bridge in that tricks made in excess of the contract are scored toward game

auc·tion·eer \ˌȯk-shə-'nir\ *noun* (circa 1708) **:** an agent who sells goods at auction

auc·to·ri·al \ȯk-'tȯr-ē-əl, -'tȯr-\ *adjective* [Latin *auctor* author — more at AUTHOR] (1821) **:** of or relating to an author

au·da·cious \ȯ-'dā-shəs\ *adjective* [Middle French *audacieux*, from *audace* boldness, from Latin *audacia*, from *audac-*, *audax* bold, from *audēre* to dare, from *avidus* eager — more at AVID] (1550) **1 a :** intrepidly daring **:** ADVENTUROUS ⟨an *audacious* mountain climber⟩ **b :** recklessly bold **:** RASH **2 :** contemptuous of law, religion, or decorum **:** INSOLENT **3 :** marked by originality and verve
— **au·da·cious·ly** *adverb*
— **au·da·cious·ness** *noun*

au·dac·i·ty \ȯ-'da-sə-tē\ *noun*, *plural* **-ties** [Middle English *audacite*, from Latin *audac-*, *audax*] (15th century) **1 :** the quality or state of being audacious: as **a :** intrepid boldness **b :** bold or arrogant disregard of normal restraints **2 :** an audacious act — usually used in plural
synonym see TEMERITY

au·di·al \'ȯ-dē-əl\ *adjective* [*audio* + *¹-al*] (1966) **:** of, relating to, or affecting the sense of hearing **:** AURAL

¹au·di·ble \'ȯ-də-bəl\ *adjective* [Late Latin *audibilis*, from Latin *audire* to hear; akin to Greek *aisthanesthai* to perceive, Sanskrit *āvis* evidently] (1529) **:** heard or capable of being heard
— **au·di·bil·i·ty** \ˌȯ-də-'bi-lə-tē\ *noun*
— **au·di·bly** \'ȯ-də-blē\ *adverb*

²audible *noun* (1962) **:** a substitute offensive or defensive play called at the line of scrimmage in football

au·di·ence \'ȯ-dē-ən(t)s, 'ä-\ *noun* [Middle English, from Middle French, from Latin *audientia*, from *audient-*, *audiens*, present participle of *audire*] (14th century) **1 :** the act or state of hearing **2 a :** a formal hearing or interview ⟨an *audience* with the pope⟩ **b :** an opportunity of being heard ⟨I would succeed if I were once given an *audience*⟩ **3 a :** a group of listeners or spectators **b :** a reading, viewing, or listening public **4 :** a group of ardent admirers or devotees **:** FOLLOWING

au·dile \'ȯ-ˌdīl\ *adjective* [*auditory* + *-ile* (as in *tactile*)] (1897) **:** AUDITORY

aud·ing \'ȯ-diŋ\ *noun* [Latin *audire* + English *¹-ing*] (circa 1949) **:** the process of hearing, recognizing, and interpreting spoken language

¹au·dio \'ȯ-dē-ˌō\ *adjective* [*audio-*] (1916) **1 :** of or relating to acoustic, mechanical, or electrical frequencies corresponding to normally audible sound waves which are of frequencies approximately from 15 to 20,000 hertz **2 a :** of or relating to sound or its reproduction and especially high-fidelity reproduction **b :** relating to or used in the transmission or re-

ception of sound — compare VIDEO **c :** of, relating to, or utilizing recorded sound

²audio *noun* (1934) **1 :** an audio signal; *broadly* **:** SOUND **2 :** the section of television or motion-picture equipment that deals with sound **3 :** the transmission, reception, or reproduction of sound

audio- *combining form* [Latin *audire* to hear] **1 :** hearing ⟨*audio*meter⟩ **2 :** sound ⟨*audio*phile⟩ **3 :** auditory and ⟨*audio*visual⟩

au·dio–an·i·ma·tron·ic \ˌȯ-dē-ō-ˌa-nə-mə-'trä-nik\ *adjective* [from *Audio-Animatronics*, a trademark] (1964) **:** being or consisting of a lifelike electromechanical figure of a person or animal that has synchronized movement and sound

au·dio·cas·sette \ˌȯ-dē-(ˌ)ō-kə-'set, -ka-\ *noun* (1971) **:** an audiotape recording mounted in a cassette

au·dio·gen·ic \ˌȯ-dē-ō-'je-nik\ *adjective* (1941) **:** produced by frequencies corresponding to sound waves — used especially of epileptoid responses

au·dio·gram \'ȯ-dē-ō-ˌgram\ *noun* (1927) **:** a graphic representation of the relation of vibration frequency and the minimum sound intensity for hearing

au·dio–lin·gual \ˌȯ-dē-ō-'liŋ-gwəl *also* -gyə-wəl\ *adjective* (1960) **:** involving a drill routine of listening and speaking in language learning

au·di·ol·o·gy \ˌȯ-dē-'ä-lə-jē\ *noun* (1946) **:** a branch of science dealing with hearing; *specifically* **:** therapy of individuals having impaired hearing
— **au·di·o·log·i·cal** \-ē-ə-'lä-ji-kəl\ *also* **au·di·o·log·ic** \-ē-ə-'lä-jik\ *adjective*
— **au·di·ol·o·gist** \-ē-'ä-lə-jist\ *noun*

au·di·om·e·ter \ˌȯ-dē-'ä-mə-tər\ *noun* (1879) **:** an instrument used in measuring the acuity of hearing
— **au·dio·met·ric** \-dē-ō-'me-trik\ *adjective*
— **au·di·om·e·try** \-dē-'ä-mə-trē\ *noun*

au·dio·phile \'ȯ-dē-ō-ˌfīl\ *noun* (1951) **:** a person who is enthusiastic about high-fidelity sound reproduction

au·dio·tape \'ȯ-dē-ō-ˌtāp\ *noun* (1958) **:** a tape recording of sound

au·dio·vi·su·al \ˌȯ-dē-(ˌ)ō-'vi-zhə-wəl, -zhəl\ *adjective* (1937) **1 :** designed to aid in learning or teaching by making use of both hearing and sight **2 :** of or relating to both hearing and sight

au·dio·vi·su·als \-zhə-wəlz, -zhəlz\ *noun plural* (1955) **:** audiovisual teaching materials (as filmstrips accompanied by recordings)

¹au·dit \'ȯ-dət\ *noun* [Middle English, from Latin *auditus* act of hearing, from *audire*] (15th century) **1 a :** a formal examination of an organization's or individual's accounts or financial situation **b :** the final report of an audit **2 :** a methodical examination and review
— **au·dit·able** \-di-tə-bəl\ *adjective*

²audit *transitive verb* (15th century) **1 :** to perform an audit of or for ⟨*audit* the books⟩ ⟨*audit* the company⟩ **2 :** to attend (a course) without working for or expecting to receive formal credit

¹au·di·tion \ȯ-'di-shən\ *noun* [Middle French or Latin; Middle French, from Latin *audition-*, *auditio*, from *audire*] (1599) **1 :** the power or sense of hearing **2 :** the act of hearing; *especially* **:** a critical hearing ⟨an *audition* of new recordings⟩ **3 :** a trial performance to appraise an entertainer's merits

²audition *verb* **au·di·tioned; au·di·tion·ing** \-'di-sh(ə-)niŋ\ (1934) *transitive verb* **:** to test especially in an audition

intransitive verb
: to give a trial performance

au·di·tor \'ȯ-də-tər\ *noun* (14th century)
1 : a person authorized to examine and verify accounts
2 : one that hears or listens; *especially* : one that is a member of an audience
3 : a person who audits a course of study
4 : a person who hears (as a court case) in the capacity of judge

au·di·to·ri·um \,ȯ-də-'tōr-ē-əm, -'tȯr-\ *noun*, *plural* **-riums** *or* **-ria** \-ē-ə\ [Latin, literally, lecture room] (circa 1751)
1 : the part of a public building where an audience sits
2 : a room, hall, or building used for public gatherings

¹au·di·to·ry \'ȯ-də-ˌtōr-ē, -ˌtȯr-\ *noun* [Middle English *auditorie,* from Latin *auditorium*] (14th century)
1 *archaic* : AUDIENCE
2 *archaic* : AUDITORIUM

²au·di·to·ry *adjective* [Late Latin *auditorius*] (1578)
: of, relating to, or experienced through hearing
— **au·di·to·ri·ly** *adverb*

auditory nerve *noun* (1724)
: either of the 8th pair of cranial nerves connecting the inner ear with the brain and transmitting impulses concerned with hearing and balance — see EAR illustration

auditory tube *noun* (1907)
: EUSTACHIAN TUBE

audit trail *noun* (1954)
: a record of a sequence of events (as actions performed by a computer) from which a history may be reconstructed

Auf·klä·rung \'aὐf-ˌkler-əŋ, -ˌὐŋ\ *noun* [German] (1842)
: ENLIGHTENMENT 2

auf Wie·der·seh·en \aὐf-'vē-dər-ˌzā(-ə)n\ *interjection* [German, literally, till seeing again] (1885)
— used to express farewell

Au·ge·an \ȯ-'jē-ən\ *adjective* [Latin *Augeas,* king of Elis, from Greek *Augeias;* from the legend that his stable, left neglected for 30 years, was finally cleaned by Hercules] (1599)
: extremely formidable or difficult and occasionally distasteful ⟨an *Augean* task⟩

Augean stable *noun* (1635)
: a condition or place marked by great accumulation of filth or corruption

au·ger \'ȯ-gər\ *noun* [Middle English, alteration (resulting from false division of *a nauger*) of *nauger,* from Old English *nafogār;* akin to Old High German *nabugēr* auger, Old English *nafu* nave, *gār* spear — more at NAVE, GORE] (before 12th century)
: any of various tools or devices having a helical shaft or member that are used for boring holes (as in wood, earth, or ice) or moving loose material (as snow) ◊

Au·ger effect \(ˌ)ō-'zhā-\ *noun* [Pierre V. *Auger* (born 1899) French physicist] (1931)
: a process in which an atom that has been ionized through the emission of an electron with energy in the X-ray range undergoes a transition in which a second electron is emitted rather than an X-ray photon — called also *Auger process*

auger:
1, 2 screw,
3 tapering
pod

Auger electron *noun* (1939)
: an electron emitted from an atom in the Auger effect

Auger electron spectroscopy *noun* (1970)
: an instrumental method for determining the chemical composition of a material's surface by bombardment with an electron beam to produce Auger electrons whose energy spectra are characteristic of their parent atoms — called also *Auger spectroscopy*

¹aught \'ȯt, 'ät\ *pronoun* [Middle English, from Old English *āwiht,* from *ā* ever + *wiht* creature, thing — more at AYE, WIGHT] (before 12th century)
1 : ANYTHING
2 : ALL, EVERYTHING ⟨for *aught* I care⟩ ⟨for *aught* we know⟩

²aught *adverb* (13th century)
archaic : AT ALL

³aught *noun* [alteration (resulting from false division of *a naught*) of *naught*] (1872)
1 : ZERO, CIPHER
2 *archaic* : NONENTITY, NOTHING

au·gite \'ȯ-ˌjīt\ *noun* [Latin *augites,* a precious stone, from Greek *augitēs*] (1804)
1 : an aluminous usually black or dark green pyroxene that is found in igneous rocks
2 : PYROXENE
— **au·git·ic** \ȯ-'ji-tik\ *adjective*

¹aug·ment \ȯg-'ment\ *verb* [Middle English, from Middle French *augmenter,* from Late Latin *augmentare,* from Latin *augmentum* increase, from *augēre* to increase — more at EKE] (14th century)
transitive verb
1 : to make greater, more numerous, larger, or more intense ⟨the impact of the report was *augmented* by its timing⟩
2 : to add an augment to
3 : SUPPLEMENT ⟨*augmented* her scholarship by working nights⟩
intransitive verb
: to become augmented
synonym see INCREASE
— **aug·ment·er** *or* **aug·men·tor** \-'men-tər\ *noun*

²aug·ment \'ȯg-ˌment\ *noun* (circa 1771)
: a vowel prefixed or a lengthening of the initial vowel to mark past time especially in Greek and Sanskrit verbs

aug·men·ta·tion \ˌȯg-mən-'tā-shən, -ˌmen-\ *noun* (14th century)
1 a : the act or process of augmenting **b** : the state of being augmented
2 : something that augments : ADDITION

¹aug·men·ta·tive \ȯg-'men-tə-tiv\ *adjective* (15th century)
1 : able to augment
2 : indicating large size and sometimes awkwardness or unattractiveness — used of words and affixes; compare DIMINUTIVE

²augmentative *noun* (1804)
: an augmentative word or affix

aug·ment·ed \ȯg-'men-təd\ *adjective* (1825)
of a musical interval : made one half step greater than major or perfect ⟨an *augmented* fifth⟩

augmented matrix *noun* (circa 1949)
: a matrix whose elements are the coefficients of a set of simultaneous linear equations with the constant terms of the equations entered in an added column

au gra·tin \ō-'grä-tᵊn, ȯ-, -'gra-\ *adjective* [French, literally, with the burnt scrapings from the pan] (1806)
: covered with bread crumbs or grated cheese and browned (as under a broiler)

¹au·gur \'ȯ-gər\ *noun* [Latin; akin to Latin *augēre*] (14th century)
1 : an official diviner of ancient Rome
2 : one held to foretell events by omens

²augur (1601)
transitive verb
1 : to foretell especially from omens
2 : to give promise of : PRESAGE ⟨higher pay *augurs* a better future⟩
intransitive verb
: to predict the future especially from omens

au·gu·ry \'ȯ-gyə-rē, -gə-\ *noun*, *plural* **-ries** (14th century)
1 : divination from auspices or omens; *also* : an instance of this
2 : OMEN, PORTENT

au·gust \ȯ-'gəst, 'ȯ-(ˌ)gəst\ *adjective* [Latin *augustus;* akin to Latin *augur*] (1664)
: marked by majestic dignity or grandeur

— **au·gust·ly** *adverb*
— **au·gust·ness** \ȯ-'gəs(t)-nəs, 'ȯ-(ˌ)gəs(t)-\ *noun*

Au·gust \'ȯ-gəst\ *noun* [Middle English, from Old English, from Latin *Augustus,* from *Augustus* Caesar] (before 12th century)
: the 8th month of the Gregorian calendar

Au·gus·tan \ȯ-'gəs-tən, ə-\ *adjective* (1704)
1 : of, relating to, or characteristic of Augustus Caesar or his age
2 : of, relating to, or characteristic of the neoclassical period in England
— **Augustan** *noun*

¹Au·gus·tin·i·an \ˌȯ-gə-'sti-nē-ən\ *noun* (1602)
1 : a member of an Augustinian order; *specifically* : a friar of the Hermits of Saint Augustine founded in 1256 and devoted to educational, missionary, and parish work
2 : a follower of Saint Augustine

²Augustinian *adjective* (1674)
1 : of or relating to Saint Augustine or his doctrines
2 : of or relating to any of several orders under a rule ascribed to Saint Augustine
— **Au·gus·tin·i·an·ism** \-nē-ə-ˌni-zəm\ *noun*

au jus \ō-'zhü(s), -'jüs; ō-zhæ\ *adjective* [French, literally, with juice] (circa 1919)
of meat : served in the juice obtained from roasting

auk \'ȯk\ *noun* [Norwegian or Icelandic *alk, alka,* from Old Norse *ālka*] (1674)
: any of several black-and-white short-necked diving seabirds (family Alcidae) that breed in colder parts of the northern hemisphere

auk·let \'ȯ-klət\ *noun* (1886)
: any of several small auks of the North Pacific coasts

auld \'ȯl(d), 'äl(d)\ *adjective* (14th century)
chiefly Scottish : OLD

auk

auld lang syne \ˌȯl(d)-ˌ(l)aŋ-'zīn, ˌȯl(d)-\ *noun* [Scots, literally, old long ago] (1692)
: the good old times

au na·tu·rel \ˌō-ˌna-tə-'rel, -ˌna-chə-\ *adjective* [French] (1817)
1 : cooked or served plainly
2 a : being in natural style or condition **b** : NUDE

aunt \'ant, 'änt\ *noun* [Middle English, from Old French *ante,* from Latin *amita;* akin to Old High German *amma* mother, nurse, Greek *amma* nurse] (14th century)

◇ **WORD HISTORY**
auger *Auger,* like *apron,* arose because it is hard to be sure of word boundaries in connected speech. *Auger* began its life in Old English as *nafogār,* a compound of *nafu* "nave of a wheel" and *gār* "spear," a "nave-spear" being the tool used to bore a hole through the hub of a wheel into which the axle could be inserted. By Middle English, *nafogār* had shrunk to *nauger,* obscuring the original sense of the compound. Already in Middle English, the combination of indefinite article and noun was spelled as both *an auger* and *a nauger,* an indication that younger generations of speakers who heard the word in connected speech were unsure whether it began with a consonant or a vowel. The form *auger* emerged as dominant in the 17th century.

1 : the sister of one's father or mother
2 : the wife of one's uncle
— **aunt·hood** \-ˌhu̇d\ *noun*
— **aunt·like** \-ˌlīk\ *adjective*
— **aunt·ly** *adjective*

Aunt Sal·ly \-'sa-lē\ *noun, plural* **Aunt Sal·lies** [*Aunt Sally,* name given to an effigy of a woman smoking a pipe set up as an amusement attraction at English fairs for patrons to throw missiles at] (1898)
British **:** an object of criticism or contention; *especially* **:** one that is set up to invite criticism or be easily refuted

au pair \'ō-ˌpar, -ˌper\ *noun, plural* **au pairs** \-ˌparz, -ˌperz\ [French, on even terms] (1960)
: a usually young foreign person who does domestic work for a family in return for room and board and the opportunity to learn the family's language

au poivre \ō-'pwäv(r⁹)\ *adjective* [French, with pepper] (1971)
: prepared or served with a generous amount of usually coarsely ground black pepper ⟨steak *au poivre*⟩

au·ra \'ȯr-ə\ *noun* [Middle English, from Latin, puff of air, breeze, from Greek; probably akin to Greek *aēr* air] (1732)
1 a : a subtle sensory stimulus (as an aroma) **b :** a distinctive atmosphere surrounding a given source ⟨the place had an *aura* of mystery⟩
2 : a luminous radiation **:** NIMBUS
3 : a subjective sensation (as of lights) experienced before an attack of some disorders (as epilepsy or a migraine)
4 : an energy field that is held to emanate from a living being

au·ral \'ȯr-əl\ *adjective* [Latin *auris* ear — more at EAR] (1847)
: of or relating to the ear or to the sense of hearing
— **au·ral·ly** \-ə-lē\ *adverb*

aurar *plural of* EYRIR

au·re·ate \'ȯr-ē-ət\ *adjective* [Middle English *aureat,* from Medieval Latin *aureatus* decorated with gold, from Latin *aureus*] (15th century)
1 : of a golden color or brilliance
2 : marked by grandiloquent and rhetorical style

au·re·ole \'ȯr-ē-ˌōl\ *or* **au·re·o·la** \ȯ-'rē-ə-lə, ə-\ *noun* [Middle English *aureole* heavenly crown worn by saints, from Medieval Latin *aureola,* from Latin, feminine of *aureolus* golden, diminutive of *aureus*] (13th century)
1 a : a radiant light around the head or body of a representation of a sacred personage **b :** something resembling an aureole ⟨an *aureole* of hair⟩
2 : RADIANCE, AURA ⟨an *aureole* of youth and health⟩
3 : the luminous area surrounding the sun or other bright light when seen through thin cloud or mist **:** CORONA
4 : a ring-shaped zone around an igneous intrusion
— **aureole** *transitive verb*

Au·reo·my·cin \ˌȯr-ē-ō-'mī-s⁹n\ *trademark*
— used for a preparation of the hydrochloride of chlortetracycline

au·re·us \'ȯr-ē-əs\ *noun, plural* **-rei** \-ē-ˌī\ [Latin, literally, golden, from *aurum* gold; akin to Old Prussian *ausis* gold] (1609)
: a gold coin of ancient Rome varying in weight from ⅟₃₀ to ⅟₇₀ libra

au re·voir \ˌō-rə-'vwär, ˌȯr-, *French* ȯr(-ə)-vwàr\ *noun* [French, literally, till seeing again] (1694)
: GOOD-BYE — often used interjectionally

au·ric \'ȯr-ik\ *adjective* [Latin *aurum*] (circa 1828)
: of, relating to, or derived from gold

au·ri·cle \'ȯr-i-kəl\ *noun* [Latin *auricula,* from diminutive of *auris* ear — more at EAR] (15th century)
1 a : an atrium of a heart **b :** PINNA 2b **c :** an anterior ear-shaped pouch in each atrium of the human heart
2 : an angular or ear-shaped lobe, process, or appendage

au·ric·u·la \ȯ-'ri-kyə-lə\ *noun* [New Latin, from Latin, external ear] (1655)
: a yellow-flowered Alpine primrose (*Primula auricula*)

au·ric·u·lar \ȯ-'ri-kyə-lər\ *adjective* (15th century)
1 : told privately ⟨an *auricular* confession⟩
2 : understood or recognized by the sense of hearing
3 : of, relating to, or using the ear or the sense of hearing
4 : of or relating to an auricle

au·ric·u·late \ȯ-'ri-kyə-lət\ *adjective* (1713)
: having auricles

au·rif·er·ous \ȯ-'ri-f(ə-)rəs\ *adjective* [Latin *aurifer,* from *aurum* + *-fer* -ferous] (1727)
: containing gold

Au·ri·ga \ȯ-'rī-gə\ *noun* [Latin, literally, charioteer]
: a constellation between Perseus and Gemini

Au·rig·na·cian \ˌȯr-ēn-'yä-shən\ *adjective* [French *aurignacien,* from *Aurignac,* France] (1909)
: of or relating to an Upper Paleolithic culture marked by finely made artifacts of stone and bone, paintings, and engravings

au·rochs \'au̇r-ˌäks, 'ȯr-\ *noun, plural* **aurochs** [German, from Old High German *ūrohso,* from *ūro* aurochs + *ohso* ox; akin to Old English *ūr* aurochs — more at OX] (1766)
1 : an extinct large long-horned wild ox (*Bos primigenius*) of Europe that is the ancestor of domestic cattle
2 : WISENT

au·ro·ra \ə-'rōr-ə, ȯ-, -'rȯr-\ *noun, plural* **auroras** *or* **au·ro·rae** \-(ˌ)ē\ [Latin — more at EAST] (14th century)
1 : DAWN
2 *capitalized* **:** the Roman goddess of dawn — compare EOS
3 : a luminous phenomenon that consists of streamers or arches of light appearing in the upper atmosphere of a planet's magnetic polar regions and is caused by the emission of light from atoms excited by electrons accelerated along the planet's magnetic field lines
— **au·ro·ral** \-əl\ *adjective*
— **au·ro·re·an** \-ē-ən\ *adjective*

aurora aus·tra·lis \-ȯ-'strä-ləs, -ä-'strä-\ *noun* [New Latin, literally, southern dawn] (1741)
: an aurora that occurs in earth's southern hemisphere — called also *southern lights*

aurora bo·re·al·is \-ˌbȯr-ē-'a-ləs, -ˌbȯr-\ *noun* [New Latin, literally, northern dawn] (1717)
: an aurora that occurs in earth's northern hemisphere — called also *northern lights*

aus·cul·tate \'ȯ-skəl-ˌtāt\ *transitive verb* **-tat·ed; -tat·ing** [back-formation from *auscultation*] (circa 1860)
: to examine by auscultation
— **aus·cul·ta·to·ry** \ȯ-'skəl-tə-ˌtōr-ē, -ˌtȯr-\ *adjective*

aus·cul·ta·tion \ˌȯ-skəl-'tā-shən\ *noun* [Latin *auscultation-, auscultatio* act of listening, from *auscultare* to listen; akin to Latin *auris* ear — more at EAR] (circa 1828)
: the act of listening to sounds arising within organs (as the lungs) as an aid to diagnosis and treatment

aus·land·er \'au̇s-ˌlen-dər, -ˌlan-\ *noun* [German *Ausländer*] (1936)
: OUTSIDER, FOREIGNER

aus·pice \'ȯs-pəs\ *noun, plural* **aus·pic·es** \-pə-səz, -ˌsēz\ [Latin *auspicium,* from *auspic-, auspex* diviner by birds, from *avis* bird + *specere* to look, look at — more at AVIARY, SPY] (1533)
1 : observation by an augur especially of the flight and feeding of birds to discover omens
2 *plural* **:** kindly patronage and guidance
3 : a prophetic sign; *especially* **:** a favorable sign

aus·pi·cious \ȯ-'spi-shəs\ *adjective* (1593)
1 : affording a favorable auspice **:** PROPITIOUS ⟨made an *auspicious* beginning⟩
2 : attended by good auspices **:** PROSPEROUS ⟨an *auspicious* year⟩
synonym see FAVORABLE
— **aus·pi·cious·ly** *adverb*
— **aus·pi·cious·ness** *noun*

Aus·sie \'ȯ-sē, 'ä-sē, *British & Australian usually* 'ȯ-zē\ *noun* [*Australian* + *-ie*] (1917)
: a native or inhabitant of Australia

aus·ten·ite \'ȯs-tə-ˌnīt, 'äs-\ *noun* [French, from Sir W. C. Roberts-*Austen* (died 1902) English metallurgist] (1902)
: a solid solution in iron of carbon and sometimes other solutes that occurs as a constituent of steel under certain conditions
— **aus·ten·it·ic** \ˌȯs-tə-'ni-tik, ˌäs-\ *adjective*

aus·tere \ȯ-'stir *also* -'ster\ *adjective* [Middle English, from Middle French, from Latin *austerus,* from Greek *austēros* harsh, severe; akin to Greek *hauos* dry — more at SERE] (14th century)
1 a : stern and cold in appearance or manner **b :** SOMBER, GRAVE ⟨an *austere* critic⟩
2 : morally strict **:** ASCETIC
3 : markedly simple or unadorned ⟨an *austere* office⟩ ⟨an *austere* style of writing⟩
4 : giving little or no scope for pleasure ⟨*austere* diets⟩
5 *of a wine* **:** having the flavor of acid or tannin predominant over fruit flavors usually indicating a capacity for aging
synonym see SEVERE
— **aus·tere·ly** *adverb*
— **aus·tere·ness** *noun*

aus·ter·i·ty \ȯ-'ster-ə-tē *also* -'stir-\ *noun, plural* **-ties** (14th century)
1 : the quality or state of being austere
2 a : an austere act, manner, or attitude **b :** an ascetic practice
3 : enforced or extreme economy

¹Austr- *or* **Austro-** *combining form* [Latin, from *Austr-, Auster* south wind]
: south ⟨*Austro*asiatic⟩

²Austr- *or* **Austro-** *combining form* [probably from New Latin, from *Austria*]
: Austrian and ⟨*Austro*-Hungarian⟩

¹aus·tral \'ȯs-trəl, 'äs-\ *adjective* [Middle English, from Latin *australis,* from *Austr-, Auster*] (14th century)
1 : of or relating to the Southern hemisphere
2 *capitalized* **:** AUSTRALIAN

²aus·tral \au̇-'sträl\ *noun, plural* **aus·tral·es** \-'strä-ˌläs\ *also* **australs** \-'strä-ləs\ [Spanish] (1985)
: the basic monetary unit of Argentina 1985–91

Aus·tra·lia Day \ȯ-'sträl-yə-, ä-, ə-\ *noun* (1911)
: a national holiday in Australia commemorating the landing of the British at Sydney Cove in 1788 and observed on the Monday of or next following Jan. 26

¹Aus·tra·lian \ȯ-'sträl-yən, ä-, ə-\ *adjective* (1814)
1 : of, relating to, or characteristic of the continent or commonwealth of Australia, its inhabitants, or the languages spoken there
2 : of, relating to, or being a biogeographic region that comprises Australia, the islands north of it from Celebes eastward, Tasmania, New Zealand, and Polynesia

²Australian *noun* (1814)
1 : a native or inhabitant of the Australian commonwealth
2 : a group of about 200 languages spoken by the aboriginal inhabitants of Australia

Australian ballot *noun* (1888)
: an official ballot printed at public expense on which the names of all the candidates and proposals appear and which is distributed only at the polling place and marked in secret

Australian cattle dog *noun* (1926)
: any of a breed of medium-sized dogs that were developed in Australia to herd cattle and that have upright ears and a red or blue mottled coat

Aus·tra·lian·ism \ȯ-'strāl-yə-ˌni-zəm, ˌä-, ə-\ *noun* (1883)
: a characteristic feature of Australian English

Australian cattle dog

Australian pine *noun* (1919)
: any of several casuarinas (especially *Casuarina equisetifolia*) now widely grown as ornamentals in warm regions

Australian Rules football *noun* (1904)
: a game resembling rugby that is played between two teams of 18 players on a field 180–190 yards long that has four goalposts at each end

Australian shepherd *noun* (1964)
: any of a breed of bobtailed medium-sized dogs developed in America and often used in herding

Australian terrier *noun* (1903)
: any of a breed of small rather short-legged wirehaired terriers of Australian origin usually having a tan and blue or sandy coat

Aus·tra·loid \'ȯs-trə-ˌlȯid, 'äs-\ *adjective* [*Australia* + English *-oid*] (1901)
in some classifications : of or relating to a racial group including the Australian aborigines and other peoples of southern Asia and Pacific islands

Australian terrier

— **Australoid** *noun*

aus·tra·lo·pith·e·cine \ȯ-ˌstrā-lō-'pi-thə-ˌsīn, ä-; ˌȯs-trə-, äs-\ *noun* [ultimately from Latin *australis* + Greek *pithēkos* ape] (1943)
: any of a genus (*Australopithecus*) of extinct southern and eastern African hominids that include gracile and robust forms with near-human dentition and a relatively small brain
— **australopithecine** *adjective*

Austrian pine *noun* (1858)
: a tall European pine (*Pinus nigra*) widely cultivated for ornament and having needles in clusters of two

Aus·tro·asi·at·ic \'ȯs-(ˌ)trō-ˌā-zhē-'a-tik, -zē-'a-, 'äs- *also* -ˌā-shē-\ *adjective* (1922)
: of, relating to, or constituting a family of languages of south and southeast Asia that includes Mon-Khmer and Munda as subfamilies

Aus·tro·ne·sian \ˌȯs-trə-'nē-zhən, äs-, -shən\ *adjective* [*Austronesia*, islands of the southern Pacific] (1925)
: of, relating to, or constituting a family of languages spoken in the area extending from Madagascar eastward through the Malay Peninsula and Archipelago to Hawaii and Easter Island and including practically all the native languages of the Pacific islands with the exception of the Australian and Papuan languages

aut- *or* **auto-** *combining form* [Greek, from *autos* same, -self, self]
1 : self : same one ⟨*auti*sm⟩ ⟨*auto*biography⟩
2 : automatic : self-acting ⟨*auto*pilot⟩

au·ta·coid \'ȯ-tə-ˌkȯid\ *noun* [*aut-* + Greek *akos* remedy; probably akin to Old Irish *ícc* cure] (1914)
: a physiologically active substance (as serotonin, bradykinin, or angiotensin) produced by and acting within the body

au·tar·chic \ȯ-'tär-kik\ *adjective* (1883)
: AUTARKIC
— **au·tar·chi·cal** \-ki-kəl\ *adjective*

¹**au·tar·chy** \'ȯ-ˌtär-kē\ *noun* [by alteration] (1617)
: AUTARKY

²**autarchy** *noun, plural* **-chies** [Greek *autarchia,* from *aut-* + *-archia* -archy] (1665)
: absolute sovereignty : AUTOCRACY

au·tar·kic \ȯ-'tär-kik\ *adjective* (1936)
: of, relating to, or marked by autarky
— **au·tar·ki·cal** \-ki-kəl\ *adjective*

au·tar·ky \'ȯ-ˌtär-kē\ *noun* [German *Autarkie,* from Greek *autarkeia,* from *autarkēs* self-sufficient, from *aut-* + *arkein* to defend, suffice — more at ARK] (1657)
1 : SELF-SUFFICIENCY, INDEPENDENCE; *specifically* : national economic self-sufficiency and independence
2 : a policy of establishing a self-sufficient and independent national economy

aut·ecol·o·gy \ȯ-ti-'kä-lə-jē, ˌȯt-ē-\ *noun* [International Scientific Vocabulary] (1910)
: ecology dealing with individual organisms or individual species of organisms
— **aut·eco·log·i·cal** \ˌȯt-ˌē-kə-'lä-ji-kəl, -ˌe-kə-\ *adjective*

au·teur \ō-'tər\ *noun* [French, originator, author, from Old French *autor,* from Latin *auctor* — more at AUTHOR] (1967)
: a film director whose practice accords with the auteur theory
— **au·teur·ist** \-ist\ *adjective or noun*

au·teur theory \ō-'tər\ *noun* (1962)
: a view of filmmaking in which the director is considered the primary creative force in a motion picture

au·then·tic \ə-'then-tik, ȯ-\ *adjective* [Middle English *autentik,* from Middle French *autentique,* from Late Latin *authenticus,* from Greek *authentikos,* from *authentēs* perpetrator, master, from *aut-* + *-hentēs* (akin to Greek *anyein* to accomplish, Sanskrit *sanoti* he gains)] (14th century)
1 *obsolete* : AUTHORITATIVE
2 a : worthy of acceptance or belief as conforming to or based on fact ⟨paints an *authentic* picture of our society⟩ **b** : conforming to an original so as to reproduce essential features ⟨an *authentic* reproduction of a colonial farmhouse⟩ **c** : made or done the same way as an original ⟨*authentic* Mexican fare⟩
3 : not false or imitation : REAL, ACTUAL ⟨based on *authentic* documents⟩ ⟨an *authentic* cockney accent⟩
4 a *of a church mode* : ranging upward from the keynote — compare PLAGAL 1 **b** *of a cadence* : progressing from the dominant chord to the tonic — compare PLAGAL 2
5 : true to one's own personality, spirit, or character ☆
— **au·then·ti·cal·ly** \-ti-k(ə-)lē\ *adverb*
— **au·then·tic·i·ty** \ˌȯ-ˌthen-'ti-sə-tē, -thən-\ *noun*

au·then·ti·cate \ə-'then-ti-ˌkāt, ȯ-\ *transitive verb* **-cat·ed; -cat·ing** (1653)
: to prove or serve to prove the authenticity of
synonym see CONFIRM
— **au·then·ti·ca·tion** \-ˌthen-ti-'kā-shən\ *noun*
— **au·then·ti·ca·tor** \-'then-ti-ˌkā-tər\ *noun*

¹**au·thor** \'ȯ-thər\ *noun* [Middle English *auctour,* from Old North French, from Latin *auctor* promoter, originator, author, from *augēre* to increase — more at EKE] (14th century)
1 a : one that originates or creates : SOURCE ⟨software *authors*⟩ ⟨the *author* of this crime⟩ **b** *capitalized* : GOD 1
2 : the writer of a literary work (as a book)
— **au·tho·ri·al** \ȯ-'thȯr-ē-əl, -'thȯr-\ *adjective*

²**author** *transitive verb* (1596)
: to be the author of

au·thor·ess \'ȯ-th(ə-)rəs\ *noun* (15th century)
: a woman author

au·tho·rise *British variant of* AUTHORIZE

au·thor·i·tar·i·an \ȯ-ˌthär-ə-'ter-ē-ən, ə-, -ˌthȯr-\ *adjective* (1879)
1 : of, relating to, or favoring blind submission to authority ⟨had *authoritarian* parents⟩
2 : of, relating to, or favoring a concentration of power in a leader or an elite not constitutionally responsible to the people
— **authoritarian** *noun*
— **au·thor·i·tar·i·an·ism** \-ē-ə-ˌni-zəm\ *noun*

au·thor·i·ta·tive \ə-'thär-ə-ˌtā-tiv, ȯ-, -'thȯr-\ *adjective* (1605)
1 a : having or proceeding from authority : OFFICIAL ⟨*authoritative* church doctrine⟩ **b** : showing evident authority : DEFINITIVE ⟨a most *authoritative* literary critique⟩
2 : DICTATORIAL 2
— **au·thor·i·ta·tive·ly** *adverb*
— **au·thor·i·ta·tive·ness** *noun*

au·thor·i·ty \ə-'thär-ə-tē, ȯ-, -'thȯr-\ *noun, plural* **-ties** [Middle English *auctorite,* from Old French *auctorité,* from Latin *auctoritat-, auctoritas* opinion, decision, power, from *auctor*] (13th century)
1 a (1) : a citation (as from a book or file) used in defense or support (2) : the source from which the citation is drawn **b** (1) : a conclusive statement or set of statements (as an official decision of a court) (2) : a decision taken as a precedent (3) : TESTIMONY **c** : an individual cited or appealed to as an expert
2 a : power to influence or command thought, opinion, or behavior **b** : freedom granted by one in authority : RIGHT
3 a : persons in command; *specifically* : GOVERNMENT **b** : a governmental agency or corporation to administer a revenue-producing public enterprise ⟨the transit *authority*⟩
4 a : GROUNDS, WARRANT ⟨had excellent *authority* for believing the claim⟩ **b** : convincing force ⟨lent *authority* to the performance⟩
synonym see INFLUENCE, POWER

au·tho·ri·za·tion \ˌȯ-th(ə-)rə-'zā-shən\ *noun* (15th century)
1 : the act of authorizing
2 : an instrument that authorizes : SANCTION

au·tho·rize \'ȯ-thə-ˌrīz\ *transitive verb* **-rized; -riz·ing** (14th century)
1 : to establish by or as if by authority : SANCTION ⟨a custom *authorized* by time⟩
2 : to invest especially with legal authority : EMPOWER ⟨*authorized* to act for her husband⟩
3 *archaic* : JUSTIFY 1a
— **au·tho·riz·er** *noun*

Authorized Version *noun* (1824)
: a revision of the English Bishops' Bible carried out under James I, published in 1611, and widely used by Protestants — called also *King James Version*

au·thor·ship \'ȯ-thər-ˌship\ *noun* (1710)
1 : the profession of writing

☆ **SYNONYMS**
Authentic, genuine, bona fide mean being actually and exactly what is claimed. AUTHENTIC implies being fully trustworthy as according with fact ⟨an *authentic* account of the perilous journey⟩; it can also stress painstaking or faithful imitation of an original ⟨an *authentic* reproduction⟩ ⟨*authentic* Vietnamese cuisine⟩. GENUINE implies actual character not counterfeited, imitated, or adulterated ⟨*genuine* piety⟩ ⟨*genuine* maple syrup⟩; it also connotes definite origin from a source ⟨a *genuine* Mark Twain autograph⟩. BONA FIDE implies good faith and sincerity of intention ⟨a *bona fide* offer for the stock⟩.

\ə\ abut \ᵊ\ kitten \ər\ further \a\ ash \ā\ ace
\ä\ mop, mar \au̇\ out \ch\ chin \e\ bet \ē\ easy
\g\ go \i\ hit \ī\ ice \j\ job \ŋ\ sing \ō\ go
\ȯ\ law \ȯi\ boy \th\ thin \th\ the \ü\ loot \u̇\ foot
\y\ yet \zh\ vision *see also* Guide to Pronunciation

2 : the source (as the author) of a piece of writing, music, or art
3 : the state or act of writing, creating, or causing

au·tism \'ò-ˌti-zəm\ *noun* (1912)
1 : absorption in self-centered subjective mental activity (as daydreams, fantasies, delusions, and hallucinations) usually accompanied by marked withdrawal from reality
2 : a mental disorder originating in infancy that is characterized by self-absorption, inability to interact socially, repetitive behavior, and language dysfunction (as echolalia)
— **au·tis·tic** \ò-'tis-tik\ *adjective or noun*
— **au·tis·ti·cal·ly** \-ti-k(ə-)lē\ *adverb*

au·to \'ò-(ˌ)tō, 'ä-\ *noun, plural* **autos** (1899)
: AUTOMOBILE

auto- — see AUT-

au·to·an·ti·body \ˌò-ō-(ˌ)tō-'an-ti-ˌbä-dē\ *noun* (circa 1910)
: an antibody active against a tissue constituent of the individual producing it

au·to·bahn \'ò-tō-ˌbän, 'aù-\ *noun* [German, from *Auto* + *Bahn* road] (1937)
: a German, Swiss, or Austrian expressway

au·to·bi·og·ra·phy \ˌò-tə-bī-'ä-grə-fē, -bē-\ *noun* (1771)
: the biography of a person narrated by himself
— **au·to·bi·og·ra·pher** \-fər\ *noun*
— **au·to·bio·graph·i·cal** \-ˌbī-ə-'gra-fi-kəl\ *also* **au·to·bio·graph·ic** \-fik\ *adjective*
— **au·to·bio·graph·i·cal·ly** \-fi-k(ə-)lē\ *adverb*

au·to·bus \'ò-tō-ˌbəs\ *noun* [*auto* + *bus*] (1899)
: OMNIBUS 1

au·to·ca·tal·y·sis \ˌò-tō-kə-'ta-lə-səs\ *noun, plural* **-y·ses** \-ˌsēz\ [New Latin] (1891)
: catalysis of a reaction by one of its products
— **au·to·cat·a·lyt·ic** \-ˌka-tə-'li-tik\ *adjective*
— **au·to·cat·a·lyt·i·cal·ly** \-ti-k(ə-)lē\ *adverb*

au·to·ceph·a·lous \ˌò-tō-'se-f(ə-)ləs\ *adjective* [Late Greek *autokephalos*, from Greek *aut-* + *kephalē* head — more at CEPHALIC] (1863)
: being independent of external and especially patriarchal authority — used especially of Eastern national churches
— **au·to·ceph·a·ly** \-fə-lē\ *noun*

au·toch·thon \ò-'täk-thən\ *noun, plural* **-thons** *or* **-tho·nes** \-thə-ˌnēz\ [Greek *autochthōn*, from *aut-* + *chthōn* earth — more at HUMBLE] (1590)
: one (as a person, plant, or animal) that is autochthonous

au·toch·tho·nous \ò-'täk-thə-nəs\ *adjective* (1805)
1 : INDIGENOUS, NATIVE ⟨an *autochthonous* people⟩
2 : formed or originating in the place where found ⟨*autochthonous* rock⟩ ⟨an *autochthonous* infection⟩
— **au·toch·tho·nous·ly** *adverb*

¹**au·to·clave** \'ò-tō-ˌklāv\ *noun* [French, from *aut-* + Latin *clavis* key — more at CLAVICLE] (1876)
: an apparatus in which special conditions (as high or low pressure or temperature) can be established for a variety of applications; *especially* **:** an apparatus (as for sterilizing) using superheated steam under high pressure

²**autoclave** *transitive verb* **-claved; -claving** (1911)
: to treat in an autoclave

au·to·cor·re·la·tion \ˌò-tō-ˌkòr-ə-'lā-shən, -ˌkär-\ *noun* (1950)
: the correlation between paired values of a function of a mathematical or statistical variable taken at usually constant intervals that indicates the degree of periodicity of the function

au·toc·ra·cy \ò-'tä-krə-sē\ *noun, plural* **-cies** (1655)

1 : the authority or rule of an autocrat
2 : government in which one person possesses unlimited power
3 : a community or state governed by autocracy

au·to·crat \'ò-tə-ˌkrat\ *noun* [French *autocrate*, from Greek *autokratēs* ruling by oneself, absolute, from *aut-* + *-kratēs* ruling — more at -CRAT] (1803)
1 : a person (as a monarch) ruling with unlimited authority
2 : one who has undisputed influence or power

au·to·crat·ic \ˌò-tə-'kra-tik\ *also* **au·to·crat·i·cal** \-ti-kəl\ *adjective* (1823)
1 : of, relating to, or being an autocracy **:** ABSOLUTE ⟨an *autocratic* government⟩
2 : characteristic of or resembling an autocrat **:** DESPOTIC ⟨an *autocratic* ruler⟩
— **au·to·crat·i·cal·ly** \-ti-k(ə-)lē\ *adverb*

au·to·cross \'ò-tō-ˌkròs, 'ä-tō-\ *noun* [*auto* + moto*cross*] (1963)
: an automobile gymkhana

au·to·da·fé \ˌaù-tō-də-'fā, ˌò-tō-\ *noun, plural* **au·tos·da·fé** \-tōz-də-\ [Portuguese *auto da fé*, literally, act of the faith] (1723)
: the ceremony accompanying the pronouncement of judgment by the Inquisition and followed by the execution of sentence by the secular authorities; *broadly* **:** the burning of a heretic

au·to·di·dact \ˌò-tō-'dī-ˌdakt, -ˌdī-', -də-\ *noun* [Greek *autodidaktos* self-taught, from *aut-* + *didaktos* taught, from *didaskein* to teach] (1748)
: a self-taught person
— **au·to·di·dac·tic** \-dī-'dak-tik, -də-\ *adjective*

au·toe·cious \ò-'tē-shəs\ *adjective* [*aut-* + Greek *oikia* house — more at VICINITY] (circa 1882)
: passing through all life stages on the same host ⟨*autoecious* rusts⟩
— **au·toe·cious·ly** *adverb*
— **au·to·e·cism** \-'tē-ˌsi-zəm\ *noun*

au·to·er·o·tism \ˌò-tō-'er-ə-ˌti-zəm\ *or* **au·to·erot·i·cism** \-i-'rä-tə-ˌsi-zəm\ *noun* (1898)
1 : sexual feeling arising without known external stimulation
2 : sexual gratification obtained solely through stimulation by oneself of one's own body
— **au·to·erot·ic** \-i-'rä-tik\ *adjective*

au·tog·a·my \ò-'tä-gə-mē\ *noun* [International Scientific Vocabulary] (1877)
: SELF-FERTILIZATION: as **a :** pollination of a flower by its own pollen **b :** conjugation of two sister cells or sister nuclei of protozoans or fungi
— **au·tog·a·mous** \-məs\ *adjective*

au·tog·e·nous \ò-'tä-jə-nəs\ *also* **au·to·gen·ic** \ˌò-tə-'je-nik\ *adjective* [Greek *autogenēs*, from *aut-* + *-genēs* born, produced — more at -GEN] (1846)
1 : produced independently of external influence or aid **:** ENDOGENOUS
2 : originating or derived from sources within the same individual ⟨an *autogenous* graft⟩ ⟨*autogenous* vaccine⟩
3 : not requiring a meal of blood to produce eggs ⟨*autogenous* mosquitoes⟩
— **au·tog·e·nous·ly** *adverb*
— **au·tog·e·ny** \ò-'tä-jə-nē\ *noun*

au·to·gi·ro *or* **au·to·gy·ro** \ˌò-tō-'jīr-(ˌ)ō\ *noun, plural* **-ros** [from *Autogiro*, a trademark] (1923)
: a rotary-wing aircraft that employs a propeller for forward motion and a freely rotating rotor for lift

au·to·graft \'ò-tō-ˌgraft\ *noun* (circa 1913)

: a tissue or organ that is transplanted from one part to another of the same body
— **autograft** *transitive verb*

¹**au·to·graph** \'ò-tə-ˌgraf\ *noun* [Late Latin *autographum*, from Latin, neuter of *autographus* written with one's own hand, from Greek *autographos*, from *aut-* + *-graphos* written — more at -GRAPH] (circa 1644)
: something written or made with one's own hand: **a :** an original manuscript or work of art
b : a person's handwritten signature
— **au·tog·ra·phy** \ò-'tä-grə-fē\ *noun*

²**autograph** *transitive verb* (1818)
1 : to write with one's own hand
2 : to write one's signature in or on

³**autograph** *adjective* (1832)
: being in the writer's own handwriting **:** not copied or duplicated ⟨an *autograph* letter⟩

au·to·graph·ic \ˌò-tə-'gra-fik\ *adjective* (1810)
1 : of, relating to, or constituting an autograph
2 a *of an instrument* **:** SELF-RECORDING **b** *of a record* **:** recorded by a self-recording instrument
— **au·to·graph·i·cal·ly** \-fi-k(ə-)lē\ *adverb*

Au·to·harp \'ò-tō-ˌhärp\ *trademark*
— used for a zither with button-controlled dampers for selected strings

au·to·hyp·no·sis \ˌò-tō-hip-'nō-səs\ *noun* [New Latin] (1903)
: self-induced and usually automatic hypnosis
— **au·to·hyp·not·ic** \-'nä-tik\ *adjective*

au·to·im·mune \-im-'yün\ *adjective* (1952)
: of, relating to, or caused by autoantibodies or lymphocytes that attack molecules, cells, or tissues of the organism producing them ⟨*autoimmune* diseases⟩
— **au·to·im·mu·ni·ty** \-'yü-nə-tē\ *noun*
— **au·to·im·mu·ni·za·tion** \-ˌim-yə-nə-'zā-shən *also* -im-ˌyü-\ *noun*

au·to·in·fec·tion \-in-'fek-shən\ *noun* [International Scientific Vocabulary] (1903)
: reinfection with larvae produced by parasitic worms already in the body

au·to·in·tox·i·ca·tion \-in-ˌtäk-sə-'kā-shən\ *noun* [International Scientific Vocabulary] (1887)
: a state of being poisoned by toxic substances produced within the body

au·to·load·ing \ˌò-tō-'lō-diŋ\ *adjective* (1923)
: SEMIAUTOMATIC b

au·tol·o·gous \ò-'tä-lə-gəs\ *adjective* [*aut-* + *-ologous* (as in *homologous*)] (circa 1921)
: derived from the same individual ⟨*autologous* blood transfusion⟩

au·tol·y·sate \ò-'tä-lə-ˌsāt, -ˌzāt\ *also* **au·tol·y·zate** \-ˌzāt\ *noun* (1910)
: a product of autolysis

au·to·lyse *British variant of* AUTOLYZE

au·tol·y·sis \-lə-səs\ *noun* [New Latin] (1902)
: breakdown of all or part of a cell or tissue by self-produced enzymes
— **au·to·lyt·ic** \ˌò-tᵊl-'i-tik\ *adjective*

au·to·lyze \'ò-tō-ˌlīz\ *verb* **-lyzed; -lyzing** [back-formation from *autolysis*] (1903)
intransitive verb
: to undergo autolysis
transitive verb
: to subject to autolysis

au·to·mak·er \'ò-tō-ˌmā-kər, 'ä-tō-\ *noun* (circa 1905)
: a manufacturer of automobiles

au·to·man \'ò-tō-ˌman, 'ä-tō-\ *noun* (1952)
: AUTOMAKER

Au·to·mat \'ò-tə-ˌmat\ *service mark*
— used for a cafeteria in which food is obtained especially from vending machines

au·to·mate \'ò-tə-ˌmāt\ *verb* **-mat·ed; -mat·ing** [back-formation from *automation*] (1952)
transitive verb
1 : to operate by automation
2 : to convert to largely automatic operation **:** AUTOMATIZE

autogiro

intransitive verb
: to undergo automation
— **au·to·mat·able** \-ˌmā-tə-bəl\ *adjective*
automated teller machine *noun* (1981)
: a computerized electronic machine that performs basic banking functions (as handling check deposits or issuing cash withdrawals) — called also *automatic teller, automatic teller machine*

¹**au·to·mat·ic** \ˌȯ-tə-'ma-tik\ *adjective* [Greek *automatos* self-acting, from *aut-* + *-matos* (akin to Latin *ment-, mens* mind) — more at MIND] (1748)
1 a : largely or wholly involuntary; *especially* **:** REFLEX 5 ⟨*automatic* blinking of the eyelids⟩ **b :** acting or done spontaneously or unconsciously **c :** done or produced as if by machine **:** MECHANICAL ⟨the answers were *automatic*⟩
2 : having a self-acting or self-regulating mechanism
3 *of a firearm* **:** using either gas pressure or force of recoil and mechanical spring action for repeatedly ejecting the empty cartridge shell, introducing a new cartridge, and firing it
synonym see SPONTANEOUS
— **au·to·mat·i·cal·ly** \-ti-k(ə-)lē\ *adverb*
— **au·to·ma·tic·i·ty** \-mə-'ti-sə-tē, -ma-\ *noun*

²**automatic** *noun* (1902)
1 : a machine or apparatus that operates automatically: as **a :** an automatic firearm **b :** an automatic gear-shifting mechanism
2 : a semiautomatic firearm
3 : AUDIBLE
automatic pilot *noun* (1916)
1 : AUTOPILOT 1
2 : a state or condition in which activity or behavior is regulated automatically in a predetermined or instinctive manner ⟨would go on *automatic pilot* and repeat all his standard denunciations —G. J. Church⟩
automatic writing *noun* (1883)
: writing produced without conscious intention as if of telepathic or spiritualistic origin
au·to·ma·tion \ˌȯ-tə-'mā-shən\ *noun* [¹*automatic*] (circa 1948)
1 : the technique of making an apparatus, a process, or a system operate automatically
2 : the state of being operated automatically
3 : automatically controlled operation of an apparatus, process, or system by mechanical or electronic devices that take the place of human organs of observation, effort, and decision
au·tom·a·tism \ȯ-'tä-mə-ˌti-zəm\ *noun* [French *automatisme,* from *automate* automaton, from Latin *automaton*] (1838)
1 a : the quality or state of being automatic **b :** an automatic action
2 : the power or fact of moving or functioning without conscious control either independently of external stimuli (as in the beating of the heart) or under the influence of external stimuli (as in pupil dilation)
3 : a theory that views the body as a machine and consciousness as a noncontrolling adjunct of the body
4 : suspension of the conscious mind to release subconscious images ⟨*automatism* —the surrealist trend toward spontaneity and intuition —*Elle*⟩
— **au·tom·a·tist** \-'tä-mə-tist\ *noun or adjective*
au·tom·a·tize \ȯ-'tä-mə-ˌtīz\ *transitive verb* **-tized; -tiz·ing** [¹*automatic*] (1952)
: to make automatic
— **au·tom·a·ti·za·tion** \ȯ-ˌtä-mə-tə-'zā-shən, -ˌtī-'zā-\ *noun*
au·tom·a·ton \ȯ-'tä-mə-tən, -mə-ˌtän\ *noun, plural* **-atons** *or* **-a·ta** \-mə-tə, -mə-ˌtä\ [Latin, from Greek, neuter of *automatos*] (1645)
1 : a mechanism that is relatively self-operating; *especially* **:** ROBOT
2 : a machine or control mechanism designed to follow automatically a predetermined sequence of operations or respond to encoded instructions
3 : an individual who acts in a mechanical fashion

¹**au·to·mo·bile** \'ȯ-tə-mō-ˌbēl, ˌȯ-tə-mō-'bē(ə)l, ˌȯ-tə-'mō-ˌbēl\ *adjective* [French, from *aut-* + *mobile*] (1883)
: AUTOMOTIVE

²**automobile** *noun* (circa 1889)
: a usually four-wheeled automotive vehicle designed for passenger transportation
— **au·to·mo·bile** *intransitive verb*
— **au·to·mo·bil·ist** \-'bē-list, -ˌbē-\ *noun*
au·to·mo·bil·i·ty \ˌȯ-tō-mə-'bi-lə-tē, -mō-\ *noun* (1903)
: the use of automobiles as the major means of transportation
au·to·mor·phism \ˌȯ-tə-'mȯr-ˌfi-zəm\ *noun* [*aut-* + *isomorphism*] (1903)
: an isomorphism of a set (as a group) with itself
au·to·mo·tive \ˌȯ-tə-'mō-tiv\ *adjective* (1898)
1 : of, relating to, or concerned with self-propelled vehicles or machines
2 : SELF-PROPELLED
au·to·nom·ic \ˌȯ-tə-'nä-mik\ *adjective* (1898)
1 : acting or occurring involuntarily ⟨*autonomic* reflexes⟩
2 : relating to, affecting, or controlled by the autonomic nervous system or its effects or activity ⟨*autonomic* drugs⟩
— **au·to·nom·i·cal·ly** \-mi-k(ə-)lē\ *adverb*
autonomic nervous system *noun* (1898)
: a part of the vertebrate nervous system that innervates smooth and cardiac muscle and glandular tissues and governs involuntary actions (as secretion and peristalsis) and that consists of the sympathetic nervous system and the parasympathetic nervous system
au·ton·o·mist \ȯ-'tä-nə-mist\ *noun* (1865)
: one who advocates autonomy
au·ton·o·mous \ȯ-'tä-nə-məs\ *adjective* [Greek *autonomos* independent, from *aut-* + *nomos* law — more at NIMBLE] (1800)
1 : of, relating to, or marked by autonomy
2 a : having the right or power of self-government **b :** undertaken or carried on without outside control **:** SELF-CONTAINED ⟨an *autonomous* school system⟩
3 a : existing or capable of existing independently ⟨an *autonomous* zooid⟩ **b :** responding, reacting, or developing independently of the whole ⟨an *autonomous* growth⟩
4 : controlled by the autonomic nervous system
synonym see FREE
— **au·ton·o·mous·ly** *adverb*
au·ton·o·my \-mē\ *noun, plural* **-mies** (circa 1623)
1 : the quality or state of being self-governing; *especially* **:** the right of self-government
2 : self-directing freedom and especially moral independence
3 : a self-governing state
au·to·pi·lot \'ȯ-tō-ˌpī-lət\ *noun* (1935)
1 : a device for automatically steering ships, aircraft, and spacecraft
2 : AUTOMATIC PILOT 2
au·to·poly·ploid \ˌȯ-tō-'pä-li-ˌplȯid\ *noun* (1930)
: an individual or strain whose chromosome complement consists of more than two complete copies of the genome of a single ancestral species
— **autopolyploid** *adjective*
— **au·to·poly·ploi·dy** \-ˌplȯi-dē\ *noun*
au·top·sy \'ȯ-ˌtäp-sē, 'ȯ-təp-\ *noun, plural* **-sies** [Greek *autopsia* act of seeing with one's own eyes, from *aut-* + *opsis* sight, appearance — more at OPTIC] (1678)
1 : an examination of a body after death to determine the cause of death or the character and extent of changes produced by disease
2 : a critical examination, evaluation, or assessment of someone or something past
— **autopsy** *transitive verb*

au·to·ra·dio·gram \ˌȯ-tō-'rā-dē-ə-ˌgram\ *noun* (1949)
: AUTORADIOGRAPH
au·to·ra·dio·graph \ˌȯ-tō-'rā-dē-ə-ˌgraf\ *noun* [International Scientific Vocabulary] (1903)
: an image produced on a photographic film or plate by the radiations from a radioactive substance in an object which is in close contact with the emulsion
— **au·to·ra·dio·graph·ic** \-ˌrā-dē-ə-'gra-fik\ *adjective*
— **au·to·ra·di·og·ra·phy** \-ˌrā-dē-'ä-grə-fē\ *noun*
au·to·ro·ta·tion \-rō-'tā-shən\ *noun* (1918)
: the turning of the rotor of an autogiro or a helicopter with the resulting lift caused solely by the aerodynamic forces induced by motion of the rotor along its flight path
— **au·to·ro·tate** \-'rō-ˌtāt\ *intransitive verb*
au·to·route \'ȯ-tō-ˌrüt, -ˌraůt\ *noun* [French, from *automobile* + *route*] (1951)
: an expressway especially in France
autos–da–fé *plural of* AUTO-DA-FÉ
au·to·sex·ing \'ȯ-tō-ˌsek-siŋ\ *adjective* (1936)
: exhibiting different characters in the two sexes at birth or hatching
au·to·some \'ȯ-tə-ˌsōm\ *noun* (circa 1906)
: a chromosome other than a sex chromosome
— **au·to·so·mal** \ˌȯ-tə-'sō-məl\ *adjective*
— **au·to·so·mal·ly** \-mə-lē\ *adverb*
au·to·stra·da \ˌaů-tō-'strä-də, ˌȯ-tō-\ *noun, plural* **-stradas** *or* **-stra·de** \-'strä-(ˌ)dā\ [Italian, from *auto*mobile + *strada* street, from Late Latin *strata* paved road — more at STREET] (1927)
: an expressway especially in Italy
au·to·sug·ges·tion \ˌȯ-tō-sə(g)-'jes-chən, -'jesh-\ *noun* [International Scientific Vocabulary] (1890)
: an influencing of one's own attitudes, behavior, or physical condition by mental processes other than conscious thought **:** SELF-HYPNOSIS
— **au·to·sug·gest** \-sə(g)-'jest\ *transitive verb*
au·to·te·lic \ˌȯ-tō-'te-lik, -'tē-\ *adjective* [Greek *autotelēs,* from *aut-* + *telos* end — more at TELOS] (circa 1901)
: having a purpose in and not apart from itself
au·to·tet·ra·ploid \ˌȯ-tō-'te-trə-ˌplȯid\ *noun* (1930)
: an individual or strain whose chromosome complement consists of four copies of a single genome due to doubling of an ancestral chromosome complement
— **autotetraploid** *adjective*
— **au·to·tet·ra·ploi·dy** \-ˌplȯi-dē\ *noun*
au·tot·o·my \ȯ-'tä-tə-mē\ *noun* [International Scientific Vocabulary] (1897)
: reflex separation of a part (as an appendage) from the body **:** division of the body into two or more pieces
— **au·tot·o·mous** \-məs\ *adjective*
— **au·tot·o·mize** \-ˌmīz\ *verb*
au·to·trans·form·er \ˌȯ-tō-tran(t)s-'fȯr-mər\ *noun* (1895)
: a transformer in which the primary and secondary coils have part or all of their turns in common
au·to·trans·fu·sion \ˌȯ-tō-tran(t)s-'fyü-zhən\ *noun* (circa 1923)
: return of autologous blood to the patient's own circulatory system
au·to·troph \'ȯ-tə-ˌtrōf, -ˌträf\ *noun* [German, from *autotroph,* adjective] (1938)
: an autotrophic organism

\ə\ abut \ᵊ\ kitten \ər\ further \a\ ash \ā\ ace
\ä\ mop, mar \aů\ out \ch\ chin \e\ bet \ē\ easy
\g\ go \i\ hit \ī\ ice \j\ job \ŋ\ sing \ō\ go
\ȯ\ law \ȯi\ boy \th\ thin \t͟h\ the \ü\ loot \ů\ foot
\y\ yet \zh\ vision *see also* Guide to Pronunciation

au·to·tro·phic \ˌȯ-tə-'trō-fik\ *adjective* [probably from German *autotroph*, from Greek *autotrophos* supplying one's own food, from *aut-* + *trephein* to nourish] (circa 1900)
1 : needing only carbon dioxide or carbonates as a source of carbon and a simple inorganic nitrogen compound for metabolic synthesis
2 : not requiring a specified exogenous factor for normal metabolism
— **au·to·tro·phi·cal·ly** \-fi-k(ə-)lē\ *adverb*
— **au·tot·ro·phy** \ȯ-'tä-trə-fē\ *noun*
au·to·wor·ker \'ȯ-tō-ˌwər-kər, 'ä-\ *noun* (1941)
: a person employed in the automobile manufacturing industry
au·tox·i·da·tion \ȯ-ˌtäk-sə-'dā-shən\ *noun* (1883)
: oxidation by direct combination with oxygen (as in air) at ordinary temperatures
au·tumn \'ȯ-təm\ *noun* [Middle English *autumpne*, from Latin *autumnus*] (14th century)
1 : the season between summer and winter comprising in the northern hemisphere usually the months of September, October, and November or as reckoned astronomically extending from the September equinox to the December solstice — called also *fall*
2 : a period of maturity or incipient decline ⟨in the *autumn* of life⟩
— **au·tum·nal** \ȯ-'təm-nəl\ *adjective*
— **au·tum·nal·ly** \-nə-lē\ *adverb*
autumn crocus *noun* (1885)
: an autumn-blooming colchicum (*Colchicum autumnale*)
au·tun·ite \ō-'tə-ˌnīt, 'ȯ-t°n-\ *noun* [*Autun*, town in France] (circa 1852)
: a radioactive lemon-yellow mineral occurring in tabular crystals with basal cleavage and in scales like mica
aux·e·sis \ȯg-'zē-səs, ȯk-'sē-\ *noun* [New Latin, from Greek *auxēsis* increase, growth, from *auxein* to increase — more at EKE] (circa 1848)
: GROWTH; *specifically* **:** increase of cell size without cell division
— **aux·et·ic** \-'ze-tik, -'se-\ *adjective or noun*
¹**aux·il·ia·ry** \ȯg-'zil-yə-rē, -'zil-rē, -'zi-lə-\ *adjective* [Latin *auxiliaris*, from *auxilium* help; akin to Latin *augēre* to increase — more at EKE] (15th century)
1 a : offering or providing help **b :** functioning in a subsidiary capacity ⟨an *auxiliary* branch of the state university⟩
2 *of a verb* **:** accompanying another verb and typically expressing person, number, mood, or tense
3 a : SUPPLEMENTARY **b :** constituting a reserve ⟨an *auxiliary* power plant⟩
4 : equipped with sails and a supplementary inboard engine
²**auxiliary** *noun, plural* **-ries** (1601)
1 a : an auxiliary person, group, or device; *specifically* **:** a member of a foreign force serving a nation at war **b :** a Roman Catholic titular bishop assisting a diocesan bishop and not having the right of succession — called also *auxiliary bishop*
2 : an auxiliary boat or ship
3 : an auxiliary verb
aux·in \'ȯk-sən\ *noun* [International Scientific Vocabulary, from Greek *auxein*] (1934)
1 : any of various usually acidic organic substances that promote cell elongation in plant shoots and usually regulate other growth processes (as root initiation): as **a :** INDOLEACETIC ACID **b :** any of various synthetic substances (as 2,4-D) resembling indoleacetic acid in activity and used especially in research and agriculture
2 : PLANT HORMONE
— **aux·in·ic** \ȯk-'si-nik\ *adjective*
auxo·troph \'ȯk-sə-ˌtrōf, -ˌträf\ *noun* (1950)
: an auxotrophic strain or individual

auxo·tro·phic \ˌȯk-sə-'trō-fik\ *adjective* [Greek *auxein* to increase + *-o-* + English *-trophic*] (1944)
: requiring a specific growth substance beyond the minimum required for normal metabolism and reproduction by the parental or wild-type strain ⟨*auxotrophic* mutants of bacteria⟩
— **aux·ot·ro·phy** \ȯk-'sä-trə-fē\ *noun*
¹**avail** \ə-'vā(ə)l\ *verb* [Middle English, probably from *a-* (as in *abaten* to abate) + *vailen* to avail, from Old French *valoir* to be of worth, from Latin *valēre* — more at WIELD] (14th century)
intransitive verb
: to be of use or advantage **:** SERVE ⟨our best efforts did not *avail*⟩
transitive verb
1 : to be of use or advantage to **:** PROFIT
2 : to result in **:** bring about ⟨his efforts *availed* him nothing⟩
— **avail oneself of** *also* **avail of :** to make use of **:** take advantage of
²**avail** *noun* (15th century)
1 : advantage toward attainment of a goal or purpose **:** USE ⟨effort was of little *avail*⟩
2 *plural* **:** profits or proceeds especially from a business or from the sale of property
avail·abil·i·ty \ə-ˌvā-lə-'bi-lə-tē\ *noun, plural* **-ties** (1803)
1 : the quality or state of being available
2 : an available person or thing
avail·able \ə-'vā-lə-bəl\ *adjective* (15th century)
1 *archaic* **:** having a beneficial effect
2 : VALID — used of a legal plea or charge
3 : present or ready for immediate use
4 : ACCESSIBLE, OBTAINABLE ⟨articles *available* in any drugstore⟩
5 : qualified or willing to do something or to assume a responsibility ⟨*available* candidates⟩
6 : present in such chemical or physical form as to be usable (as by a plant) ⟨*available* nitrogen⟩ ⟨*available* water⟩
— **avail·able·ness** *noun*
— **avail·ably** \-blē\ *adverb*
¹**av·a·lanche** \'a-və-ˌlanch\ *noun* [French, from French dialect *lavantse*, *avalantse*] (1771)
1 : a large mass of snow, ice, earth, rock, or other material in swift motion down a mountainside or over a precipice
2 : a sudden great or overwhelming rush or accumulation of something ⟨office workers tied down with an *avalanche* of paperwork⟩
3 : a cumulative process in which photons or accelerated charge carriers produce additional photons or charge carriers through collisions (as with gas molecules)
²**avalanche** *verb* **-lanched; -lanch·ing** (1872)
intransitive verb
: to descend in an avalanche
transitive verb
: OVERWHELM, FLOOD
Av·a·lon \'a-və-ˌlän\ *noun*
: a paradise to which Arthur is carried after his death
avant \ä-ˌvän(t), 'a-, -ˌvȯn(t), -ˌvōⁿ\ *adjective* [French *avant-* fore-, front, from *avant* before, from Latin *abante*] (1965)
: culturally or stylistically advanced **:** AVANT-GARDE ⟨*avant* jazz⟩
¹**avant–garde** \ˌä-ˌvän(t)-'gärd, ˌa-, ˌä-; ə-'vänt-ˌ; ˌa-ˌvōⁿ-', ˌa-ˌvȯn(t)-'\ *noun* [French, vanguard] (1910)
: an intelligentsia that develops new or experimental concepts especially in the arts
— **avant–gard·ism** \-'gär-ˌdi-zəm\ *noun*
— **avant–gard·ist** \-'gär-dist\ *noun*
²**avant–garde** *adjective* (1925)
: of or relating to an avant-garde ⟨*avant-garde* writers⟩
av·a·rice \'a-və-rəs, 'av-rəs\ *noun* [Middle English, from Old French, from Latin *avaritia*, from *avarus* avaricious, from *avēre* to crave — more at AVID] (14th century)

: excessive or insatiable desire for wealth or gain **:** GREEDINESS, CUPIDITY
av·a·ri·cious \ˌa-və-'ri-shəs\ *adjective* (15th century)
: greedy of gain **:** excessively acquisitive especially in seeking to hoard riches
synonym see COVETOUS
— **av·a·ri·cious·ly** *adverb*
— **av·a·ri·cious·ness** *noun*
avas·cu·lar \(ˌ)ā-'vas-kyə-lər\ *adjective* (circa 1900)
: having few or no blood vessels ⟨*avascular* tissue⟩
— **avas·cu·lar·i·ty** \ˌā-ˌvas-kyə-'lar-ə-tē\ *noun*
avast \ə-'vast\ *verb imperative* [perhaps from Dutch *houd vast* hold fast] (1681)
— a nautical command to stop or cease
av·a·tar \'a-və-ˌtär\ *noun* [Sanskrit *avatāra* descent, from *avatarati* he descends, from *ava-* away + *tarati* he crosses over — more at UKASE, THROUGH] (1784)
1 : the incarnation of a Hindu deity (as Vishnu)
2 a : an incarnation in human form **b :** an embodiment (as of a concept or philosophy) often in a person
3 : a variant phase or version of a continuing basic entity
avaunt \ə-'vȯnt, -'vänt\ *adverb* [Middle English, from Middle French *avant*, from Latin *abante* forward, before, from *ab* from + *ante* before — more at OF, ANTE-] (15th century)
: AWAY, HENCE
ave \'ā-(ˌ)vā\ *noun* [Middle English, from Latin, hail] (13th century)
1 : an expression of greeting or of leave-taking **:** HAIL, FAREWELL
2 *often capitalized* **:** AVE MARIA
avel·lan \ə-'ve-lən\ *or* **avel·lane** \ə-'ve-ˌlān, 'a-və-ˌlän\ *adjective* [Latin *abellana, avellana* filbert, from feminine of *Abellanus* of Abella, from *Abella*, ancient town in Italy] (1611)
of a heraldic cross **:** having the four arms shaped like conventionalized filberts — see CROSS illustration
Ave Ma·ria \ˌä-(ˌ)vā-mə-'rē-ə\ *noun* [Middle English, from Medieval Latin, hail, Mary] (13th century)
: HAIL MARY
avenge \ə-'venj\ *transitive verb* **avenged; aveng·ing** [Middle English *avengen*, probably from *a-* (as in *abaten* to abate) + *vengen* to avenge, from Old French *vengier* — more at VENGEANCE] (14th century)
1 : to take vengeance for or on behalf of
2 : to exact satisfaction for (a wrong) by punishing the wrongdoer
— **aveng·er** *noun*
av·ens \'a-vənz\ *noun, plural* **avens** [Middle English *avence*, from Old French] (13th century)
: any of a genus (*Geum*) of perennial herbs of the rose family with white, purple, or yellow flowers
av·en·tail \'a-vən-ˌtāl\ *noun* [Middle English, modification of Old French *ventaille*] (14th century)
: VENTAIL
aven·tu·rine \ə-'ven-chə-ˌrēn, -rən\ *noun* [French, from *aventure* chance — more at ADVENTURE] (1811)
1 : glass containing opaque sparkling particles of foreign material usually copper or chromic oxide
2 : a translucent quartz spangled throughout with scales of mica or other mineral
av·e·nue \'a-və-ˌnü, -ˌnyü\ *noun* [Middle French, from feminine of *avenu*, past participle of *avenir* to come to, from Latin *advenire* — more at ADVENTURE] (1600)
1 : a way of access **:** ROUTE
2 : a channel for pursuing a desired object ⟨*avenues* of communication⟩
3 a *chiefly British* **:** the principal walk or driveway to a house situated off a main road **b**

: a broad passageway bordered by trees
4 : an often broad street or road

aver \ə-'vər\ *transitive verb* **averred; aver-ring** [Middle English *averren*, from Middle French *averer*, from Medieval Latin *adverare* to confirm as authentic, from Latin *ad-* + *verus* true — more at VERY] (15th century)
1 a : to verify or prove to be true in pleading a cause **b** : to allege or assert in pleading
2 : to declare positively

¹**av·er·age** \'a-v(ə-)rij\ *noun* [from earlier *average* proportionally distributed charge for damage at sea, modification of Middle French *avarie* damage to ship or cargo, from Old Italian *avaria*, from Arabic *'awārīyah* damaged merchandise] (1735)
1 a : a single value (as a mean, mode, or median) that summarizes or represents the general significance of a set of unequal values **b** : MEAN 1b
2 a : an estimation of or approximation to an arithmetic mean **b** : a level (as of intelligence) typical of a group, class, or series ⟨above the *average*⟩
3 : a ratio expressing the average performance especially of an athletic team or an athlete computed according to the number of opportunities for successful performance ☆
— on average *or* **on the average** : taking the typical example of the group under consideration ⟨prices have increased *on average* by five percent⟩

²**average** *adjective* (1770)
1 : equaling an arithmetic mean
2 a : being about midway between extremes ⟨a man of *average* height⟩ **b** : not out of the ordinary : COMMON ⟨the *average* person⟩
— av·er·age·ly *adverb*
— av·er·age·ness *noun*

³**average** *verb* **av·er·aged; av·er·ag·ing** (1769)
intransitive verb
1 a : to be or come to an average ⟨the gain *averaged* out to 20 percent⟩ **b** : to have a medial value of ⟨a color *averaging* a pale purple⟩
2 : to buy on a falling market or sell on a rising market additional shares or commodities so as to obtain a more favorable average price — usually used with *down* or *up*
transitive verb
1 : to do, get, or have on the average or as an average sum or quantity ⟨*averages* 12 hours of work a day⟩
2 : to find the arithmetic mean of (a series of unequal quantities)
3 a : to bring toward the average **b** : to divide among a number proportionally

aver·ment \ə-'vər-mənt\ *noun* (15th century)
1 : the act of averring
2 : something that is averred : AFFIRMATION

averse \ə-'vərs\ *adjective* [Latin *aversus*, past participle of *avertere*] (1597)
: having an active feeling of repugnance or distaste ⟨*averse* to strenuous exercise⟩
synonym see DISINCLINED
usage see ADVERSE
— averse·ly *adverb*
— averse·ness *noun*

aver·sion \ə-'vər-zhən, -shən\ *noun* (1596)
1 *obsolete* : the act of turning away
2 a : a feeling of repugnance toward something with a desire to avoid or turn from it ⟨regards drunkenness with *aversion*⟩ **b** : a settled dislike : ANTIPATHY ⟨expressed an *aversion* to parties⟩ **c** : a tendency to extinguish a behavior or to avoid a thing or situation and especially a usually pleasurable one because it is or has been associated with a noxious stimulus
3 : one that is the object of aversion

aversion therapy *noun* (1946)
: therapy intended to change habits or antisocial behavior by inducing dislike for them through association with a noxious stimulus

aver·sive \ə-'vər-siv, -ziv\ *adjective* (1923)
: tending to avoid or causing avoidance of a noxious or punishing stimulus ⟨behavior modification by *aversive* stimulation⟩
— aver·sive·ly *adverb*
— aver·sive·ness *noun*

avert \ə-'vərt\ *transitive verb* [Middle English, from Middle French *avertir*, from Latin *avertere*, from *ab-* + *vertere* to turn — more at WORTH] (15th century)
1 : to turn away or aside (as the eyes) in avoidance
2 : to see coming and ward off : AVOID

Aves·ta \ə-'ves-tə\ *noun* [Middle Persian *Avastāk*, literally, original text] (1856)
: the book of the sacred writings of Zoroastrianism

Aves·tan \-tən\ *noun* (1856)
: an ancient Iranian language in which the sacred books of Zoroastrianism were written — see INDO-EUROPEAN LANGUAGES table
— Avestan *adjective*

av·gas \'av-,gas\ *noun* [aviation gasoline] (1943)
: gasoline for airplanes

av·go·lem·o·no \äv-gō-'le-mə-(,)nō\ *noun* [New Greek *augolemono*, from *augo* egg + *lemoni* lemon] (1961)
: a soup or sauce made of chicken stock, rice, egg yolks, and lemon sauce

avi·an \'ā-vē-ən\ *adjective* [Latin *avis*] (1870)
: of, relating to, or derived from birds

avi·ary \'ā-vē-,er-ē\ *noun, plural* **-ar·ies** [Latin *aviarium*, from *avis* bird; akin to Greek *aetos* eagle] (1577)
: a place for keeping birds confined

avi·ate \'ā-vē-,āt, 'a-\ *intransitive verb* **-at·ed; -at·ing** [back-formation from *aviation*] (1887)
: to navigate the air (as in an airplane)

avi·a·tion \,ā-vē-'ā-shən, ,a-\ *noun, often attributive* [French, from Latin *avis*] (1866)
1 : the operation of heavier-than-air aircraft
2 : military airplanes
3 : airplane manufacture, development, and design

avi·a·tor \'ā-vē-,ā-tər, 'a-\ *noun* (1887)
: the operator or pilot of an aircraft and especially an airplane

aviator glasses *noun plural* (1968)
: eyeglasses having a lightweight metal frame and relatively large usually tinted lenses

avi·a·trix \,ā-vē-'ā-triks, 'a-\ *noun, plural* **-trix·es** \-trik-səz\ *or* **-tri·ces** \-trə-,sēz\ (1910)
: a woman aviator

avi·cul·ture \'ā-və-,kəl-chər, 'a-\ *noun* [Latin *avis* + English *culture*] (circa 1879)
: the raising and care of birds and especially of wild birds in captivity
— avi·cul·tur·ist \,ā-və-'kəl-ch(ə-)rist, ,a-\ *noun*

av·id \'a-vəd\ *adjective* [French or Latin; French *avide*, from Latin *avidus*, from *avēre* to desire, crave; akin to Welsh *ewyllys* desire, Old Irish *con-oí* he protects] (1769)
1 : desirous to the point of greed : urgently eager : GREEDY ⟨*avid* for publicity⟩
2 : characterized by enthusiasm and vigorous pursuit ⟨*avid* readers⟩
synonym see EAGER
— av·id·ly *adverb*
— av·id·ness *noun*

av·i·din \'a-və-dən\ *noun* [from its avidity for biotin] (1941)
: a protein found in egg white that inactivates biotin by combining with it

avid·ity \ə-'vi-də-tē, a-\ *noun, plural* **-ities** (15th century)
1 : the quality or state of being avid: **a** : keen eagerness **b** : consuming greed
2 : AFFINITY 2b(2)

avi·fau·na \,ā-və-'fo-nə, ,a-, -'fä-nə\ *noun* [New Latin, from Latin *avis* + New Latin *fauna*] (1874)
: the birds or the kinds of birds of a region, period, or environment
— avi·fau·nal \-'fo-nᵊl, -'fä-\ *adjective*

avi·on·ics \,ā-vē-'ä-niks, ,a-\ *noun plural* [aviation electronics] (1949)
: electronics designed for use in aerospace vehicles
— avi·on·ic \-nik\ *adjective*

avir·u·lent \(,)ā-'vir-(y)ə-lənt\ *adjective* [International Scientific Vocabulary] (circa 1900)
: not virulent — compare NONPATHOGENIC

avi·ta·min·osis \,ā-,vī-tə-mə-'nō-səs\ *noun, plural* **-o·ses** \-,sēz\ [New Latin] (1919)
: disease (as pellagra) resulting from a deficiency of one or more vitamins
— avi·ta·min·ot·ic \-mə-'nä-tik\ *adjective*

A–V node \,ā-'vē-, 'ā-\ *noun* (1949)
: ATRIOVENTRICULAR NODE

avo \'a-(,)vü\ *noun, plural* **avos** [Portuguese, from *avo* fractional part, from *-avo* ordinal suffix (as in *oitavo* eighth, from Latin *octavus*) — more at OCTAVE] (circa 1909)
— see *pataca* at MONEY table

avo·ca·do \,ä-və-'kä-(,)dō, ,a-\ *noun, plural* **-dos** *also* **-does** [modification of Spanish *aguacate*, from Nahuatl *āhuacatl* avocado, testicle] (1697)
1 : a pulpy green to purple nutty-flavored edible fruit of any of various tropical American trees (genus *Persea* especially *P. americana*) of the laurel family; *also* : a tree bearing avocados
2 : a light yellowish green ◇

☆ **SYNONYMS**
Average, mean, median, norm mean something that represents a middle point. AVERAGE is exactly or approximately the quotient obtained by dividing the sum total of a set of figures by the number of figures (scored an *average* of 85 on tests). MEAN may be the simple average or it may represent value midway between two extremes ⟨a high of 70° and a low of 50° give a *mean* of 60°⟩. MEDIAN applies to the value that represents the point at which there are as many instances above as there are below ⟨*average* of a group of persons earning 3, 4, 5, 8, and 10 dollars a day is 6 dollars, whereas the *median* is 5 dollars⟩. NORM means the computed or estimated average of performance of a significantly large group, class, or grade ⟨scores about the *norm* for 5th grade arithmetic⟩.

◇ **WORD HISTORY**
avocado We owe the avocado, along with chocolate and the tomato, to pre-Columbian Middle America, and the words for these tasty items to Nahuatl, the language of several important Indian peoples, including the Aztecs, who lived in the area that is now Mexico City. The Nahuatl word for the avocado was *āhuacatl*, which also means "testicle"—one sense presumably being a metaphor for the other, though we do not know which came first. This word was borrowed into Spanish as *aguacate*, though by a peculiar twist of folk etymology some American Spanish speakers modified it to *abocado*, identical with *abocado* or *abogado* "advocate, lawyer." This modification eventually lost out to *aguacate* in almost all varieties of overseas Spanish, but not before it was borrowed into French (as *avocat*) and English (as *avocato* or *avocado*) in the late 17th century. Nahuatl *āhaucatl* also occurred in the compound *āhuacamōlli*, literally, "avocado sauce," borrowed into Spanish as *guacamole*, which American English borrowed several centuries later.

\ə\ abut \ᵊ\ kitten \ər\ further \a\ ash \ā\ ace \ä\ mop, mar \aů\ out \ch\ chin \e\ bet \ē\ easy \g\ go \i\ hit \ī\ ice \j\ job \ŋ\ sing \ō\ go \ȯ\ law \ȯi\ boy \th\ thin \t̲h̲\ the \ü\ loot \ů\ foot \y\ yet \zh\ vision *see also* Guide to Pronunciation

avocado pear *noun* (1830)
chiefly British **:** AVOCADO 1

av·o·ca·tion \,a-və-'kā-shən\ *noun* [Latin *avocation-, avocatio,* from *avocare* to call away, from *ab-* + *vocare* to call, from *voc-, vox* voice — more at VOICE] (circa 1617)
1 *archaic* **:** DIVERSION, DISTRACTION
2 : customary employment **:** VOCATION
3 : a subordinate occupation pursued in addition to one's vocation especially for enjoyment **:** HOBBY

av·o·ca·tion·al \,a-və-'kā-sh(ə-)nəl\ *adjective* (1921)
1 : of or relating to an avocation ⟨an *avocational* interest in sports⟩
2 : being such by avocation ⟨an *avocational* musician⟩
— **av·o·ca·tion·al·ly** \-sh(ə-)nə-lē\ *adverb*

av·o·cet \'a-və-,set\ *noun* [French & Italian; French *avocette,* from Italian *avocetta*] (1766)
: any of a genus (*Recurvirostra*) of rather large long-legged shorebirds with webbed feet and slender upward-curving bill

avocet

Avo·ga·dro's num·ber \,a-və-'gä-(,)drōz-, ,a-və-, -'ga-\ *noun* [Count Amedeo *Avogadro*] (1924)
: the number 6.023×10^{23} indicating the number of atoms or molecules in a mole of any substance — called also *Avogadro number*

avoid \ə-'void\ *transitive verb* [Middle English, from Middle French *esvuidier,* from *es-* (from Latin *ex-*) + *vuidier* to empty — more at VOID] (14th century)
1 : to make legally void **:** ANNUL ⟨*avoid* a plea⟩
2 *obsolete* **:** VOID, EXPEL
3 a : to keep away from **:** SHUN **b :** to prevent the occurrence or effectiveness of **c :** to refrain from
4 *archaic* **:** to depart or withdraw from **:** LEAVE
synonym *see* ESCAPE
— **avoid·able** \-'voi-də-bəl\ *adjective*
— **avoid·ably** \-blē\ *adverb*
— **avoid·er** *noun*

avoid·ance \ə-'void-ᵊn(t)s\ *noun* (14th century)
1 *obsolete* **a :** an action of emptying, vacating, or clearing away **b :** OUTLET
2 : ANNULMENT
3 : an act or practice of avoiding or withdrawing from something

¹av·oir·du·pois \,a-vər-də-'poiz, 'a-vər-də-\ *noun* [Middle English *avoir de pois* goods sold by weight, from Old French, literally, goods of weight] (15th century)
1 : AVOIRDUPOIS WEIGHT
2 : WEIGHT, HEAVINESS; *especially* **:** personal weight

²avoirdupois *adjective* (1755)
: expressed in avoirdupois weight ⟨one ounce *avoirdupois*⟩

avoirdupois weight *noun* (1619)
: the series of units of weight based on the pound of 16 ounces and the ounce of 16 drams — see WEIGHT table

avouch \ə-'vauch\ *transitive verb* [Middle English, to cite as authority, from Middle French *avochier* to summon, from Latin *advocare* — more at ADVOCATE] (15th century)
1 : to declare as a matter of fact or as a thing that can be proved **:** AFFIRM
2 : to vouch for **:** CORROBORATE
3 a : to acknowledge (as an act) as one's own **b :** CONFESS, AVOW

avouch·ment \-mənt\ *noun* (1574)
: an act of avouching **:** AVOWAL

avow \ə-'vau\ *transitive verb* [Middle English, from Middle French *avouer,* from Latin *advocare*] (14th century)

1 : to declare assuredly
2 : to declare openly, bluntly, and without shame ⟨ever ready to *avow* his reactionary outlook⟩
synonym *see* ACKNOWLEDGE, ASSERT
— **avow·er** \-'vau(-ə)r\ *noun*

avow·al \ə-'vau(-ə)l\ *noun* (circa 1732)
: an open declaration or acknowledgment

avow·ed·ly \ə-'vau-əd-lē\ *adverb* (1656)
1 : with open acknowledgment **:** FRANKLY ⟨an *avowedly* hostile review⟩
2 : by unsupported assertion or profession alone **:** ALLEGEDLY ⟨politicians remain skeptical of . . . *avowedly* democratic intentions —Jerry Kirshenbaum⟩

avulse \ə-'vəls\ *transitive verb* **avulsed; avuls·ing** [Latin *avulsus,* past participle of *avellere* to tear off, from *ab-* + *vellere* to pluck — more at VULNERABLE] (circa 1765)
: to separate by avulsion

avul·sion \ə-'vəl-shən\ *noun* (1622)
: a forcible separation or detachment: as **a :** a tearing away of a body part accidentally or surgically **b :** a sudden cutting off of land by flood, currents, or change in course of a body of water; *especially* **:** one separating land from one person's property and joining it to another's

avun·cu·lar \ə-'vən-kyə-lər\ *adjective* [Latin *avunculus* maternal uncle — more at UNCLE] (1831)
1 : of or relating to an uncle
2 : suggestive of an uncle especially in kindliness or geniality ⟨*avuncular* indulgence⟩
— **avun·cu·lar·i·ty** \ə-,vən-kyə-'la-rə-tē\ *noun*
— **avun·cu·lar·ly** \ə-'vən-kyə-lər-lē\ *adverb*

aw \'ò\ *interjection* (1852)
— used to express mild disappointment, gentle entreaty, or real or mock sympathy or sentiment

await \ə-'wāt\ *verb* [Middle English, from Old North French *awaitier,* from *a-* (from Latin *ad-*) + *waitier* to watch — more at WAIT] (13th century)
transitive verb
1 *obsolete* **:** to lie in wait for
2 a : to wait for **b :** to remain in abeyance until ⟨a treaty *awaiting* ratification⟩
3 : to be in store for ⟨wonders what *awaits* him next⟩
intransitive verb
1 *obsolete* **:** ATTEND
2 : to stay or be in waiting **:** WAIT
3 : to be in store

¹awake \ə-'wāk\ *verb* **awoke** \-'wōk\ *also* **awaked** \-'wākt\; **awo·ken** \-'wō-kən\ *or* **awaked** *also* **awoke; awak·ing** [Middle English *awaken* (from Old English *awacan, onwacan,* from ¹*a-, on* + *wacan* to awake) & *awakien,* from Old English *awacian,* from ¹*a-* + *wacian* to be awake — more at WAKE] (before 12th century)
intransitive verb
1 : to cease sleeping
2 : to become aroused or active again
3 : to become conscious or aware of something ⟨*awoke* to the possibilities⟩
transitive verb
1 : to arouse from sleep or a sleeplike state ⟨*awoken* by the storm⟩
2 : to make active **:** stir up ⟨*awoke* old memories⟩ □

²awake *adjective* (13th century)
: fully conscious, alert, and aware **:** not asleep
synonym *see* AWARE

awak·en \ə-'wā-kən\ *verb* **awak·ened; awak·en·ing** \-'wāk-niŋ, -'wā-kə-\ [Middle English, from Old English *awæcnian,* from *a-* + *wæcnian* to waken] (before 12th century)
: AWAKE
— **awak·en·er** \-'wāk-nər, -'wā-kə-\ *noun*

¹award \ə-'wòrd\ *transitive verb* [Middle English, to decide, from Old North French *eswarder,* from *es-* (from Latin *ex-*) + *warder* to guard, of Germanic origin; akin to Old High German *wartēn* to watch — more at WARD] (14th century)
1 : to give by judicial decree or after careful consideration
2 : to confer or bestow as being deserved or merited or needed ⟨*award* scholarships to disadvantaged students⟩
synonym *see* GRANT
— **award·able** \-'wòr-də-bəl\ *adjective*
— **award·ee** \-,wòr-'dē\ *noun*
— **award·er** \-'wòr-dər\ *noun*

²award *noun* (14th century)
1 a : a judgment or final decision; *especially* **:** the decision of arbitrators in a case submitted to them **b :** the document containing the decision of arbitrators
2 : something that is conferred or bestowed especially on the basis of merit or need

aware \ə-'war, -'wer\ *adjective* [Middle English *iwar,* from Old English *gewær,* from *ge-* (associative prefix) + *wær* wary — more at CO-, WARY] (before 12th century)
1 *archaic* **:** WATCHFUL, WARY
2 : having or showing realization, perception, or knowledge ☆
— **aware·ness** *noun*

awash \ə-'wòsh, -'wäsh\ *adjective* (1833)

1 a : alternately covered and exposed by waves or tide **b :** washing about **:** AFLOAT **c :** covered with water **:** FLOODED
2 : filled, covered, or completely overrun as if by a flood ⟨a movie *awash* in sentimentality⟩

¹away \ə-'wā\ *adverb* (before 12th century)
1 : on the way **:** ALONG ⟨get *away* early⟩
2 : from this or that place **:** HENCE, THENCE ⟨go *away*⟩
3 a : in a secure place or manner ⟨locked *away*⟩ **b :** in another direction ⟨look *away*⟩
4 : out of existence **:** to an end ⟨echoes dying *away*⟩
5 : from one's possession ⟨gave *away* a fortune⟩
6 : steadily onward **:** UNINTERRUPTEDLY ⟨clocks ticking *away*⟩
7 : by a long distance or interval **:** FAR ⟨*away* back in 1910⟩

²away *adjective* (14th century)
1 : absent from a place **:** GONE ⟨*away* for the weekend⟩
2 : distant in space or time ⟨a lake 10 miles *away*⟩ ⟨the season is two months *away*⟩
3 : played on an opponent's grounds ⟨home and *away* games⟩
4 *baseball* **:** OUT ⟨two *away* in the ninth⟩
— away·ness *noun*

¹awe \'ò\ *noun* [Middle English, from Old Norse *agi;* akin to Old English *ege* awe, Greek *achos* pain] (13th century)
1 : an emotion variously combining dread, veneration, and wonder that is inspired by authority or by the sacred or sublime ⟨stood in *awe* of the king⟩ ⟨regard nature's wonders with *awe*⟩
2 *archaic* **a :** DREAD, TERROR **b :** the power to inspire dread

²awe *transitive verb* **awed; aw·ing** (13th century)
: to inspire with awe

aweary \ə-'wir-ē\ *adjective* (1537)
archaic **:** being weary

aweath·er \ə-'we-thər\ *adverb* (1599)
: on or toward the weather or windward side
— compare ALEE

awed \'òd\ *adjective* (1592)
: showing awe ⟨*awed* respect⟩

aweigh \ə-'wā\ *adjective* (1670)
: raised just clear of the bottom — used of an anchor

awe·less *or* **aw·less** \'ò-ləs\ *adjective* (14th century)
1 : feeling no awe
2 *obsolete* **:** inspiring no awe

awe·some \'ò-səm\ *adjective* (1598)
1 : expressive of awe ⟨*awesome* tribute⟩
2 a : inspiring awe ⟨an *awesome* task⟩ **b :** TERRIFIC 2, 3; *especially* **:** EXTRAORDINARY
— awe·some·ly *adverb*
— awe·some·ness *noun*

awe·struck \-,strək\ *also* **awe·strick·en** \-,stri-kən\ *adjective* (1634)
: filled with awe

¹aw·ful \'ò-fəl\ *adjective* (13th century)
1 : inspiring awe
2 : filled with awe: as **a** *obsolete* **:** AFRAID, TERRIFIED **b :** deeply respectful or reverential
3 : extremely disagreeable or objectionable
4 : exceedingly great — used as an intensive ⟨an *awful* lot of money⟩ □
— aw·ful·ly \'ò-fə-lē, *especially as adverb of adjective senses 3 & 4* -flē\ *adverb*
— aw·ful·ness \-fəl-nəs\ *noun*

²awful *adverb* (1818)
: VERY, EXTREMELY ⟨*awful* tired⟩

awhile \ə-'hwī(ə)l, ə-'wī(ə)l\ *adverb* (before 12th century)
: for a while □

awhirl \ə-'hwər(-ə)l, -'wər(-ə)l\ *adjective* (1883)
: being in a whirl

awk·ward \'ò-kwərd\ *adjective* [Middle English *awkeward* in the wrong direction, from *awke* turned the wrong way, from Old Norse

ǫfugr; akin to Old High German *abuh* turned the wrong way] (1530)
1 *obsolete* **:** PERVERSE
2 *archaic* **:** UNFAVORABLE, ADVERSE
3 a : lacking dexterity or skill (as in the use of hands) ⟨*awkward* with a needle and thread⟩ **b :** showing the result of a lack of expertness ⟨*awkward* pictures⟩
4 a : lacking ease or grace (as of movement or expression) **b :** lacking the right proportions, size, or harmony of parts **:** UNGAINLY
5 a : lacking social grace and assurance **b :** causing embarrassment ⟨an *awkward* moment⟩
6 : not easy to handle or deal with **:** requiring great skill, ingenuity, or care ⟨an *awkward* load⟩ ⟨an *awkward* diplomatic situation⟩ ☆
— awk·ward·ly *adverb*
— awk·ward·ness *noun*

awl \'òl\ *noun* [Middle English *al*, from Old Norse *alr;* akin to Old High German *āla* awl, Sanskrit *ārā*] (before 12th century)
: a pointed tool for marking surfaces or piercing small holes (as in leather or wood)

awn \'òn\ *noun* [Middle English, from Old English *agen*, from Old Norse *ǫgn;* akin to Old High German *agana* awn, Old English *ecg* edge — more at EDGE] (12th century)

awls

: one of the slender bristles that terminate the glumes of the spikelet in some cereal and other grasses
— awned \'ònd\ *adjective*
— awn·less \'òn-ləs\ *adjective*

aw·ning \'ò-niŋ, 'ä-niŋ\ *noun* [origin unknown] (1624)
: a rooflike cover extending over or in front of a place (as over the deck or in front of a door or window) as a shelter
— aw·ninged \-niŋd\ *adjective*

awoke *past and past participle of* AWAKE
awoken *past participle of* AWAKE

¹AWOL \'ā-,wòl, ,ā-,də-bəl-yü-,ō-'el\ *adjective or adverb, sometimes not capitalized* [absent without leave] (1919)
: ABSENT WITHOUT LEAVE; *broadly* **:** absent often without notice or permission ⟨the place looked as if its caretaker had been *AWOL* for some time —Daniel Ford⟩

²AWOL *noun, sometimes not capitalized* (1919)
: a person who is AWOL

awry \ə-'rī\ *adverb or adjective* (14th century)
1 : in a turned or twisted position or direction **:** ASKEW
2 : off the correct or expected course **:** AMISS

aw–shucks \'ò-,shəks\ *adjective* (1951)
: being or marked by an unsophisticated, self-conscious, or self-effacing manner

¹ax *or* **axe** \'aks\ *noun* [Middle English, from Old English *æcs;* akin to Old High German *ackus* ax, Latin *ascia*, Greek *axinē*] (before 12th century)
1 : a cutting tool that consists of a heavy edged head fixed to a handle with the edge parallel to the handle and that is used especially for felling trees and chopping and splitting wood
2 : a hammer with a sharp edge for dressing or spalling stone
3 : abrupt removal (as from employment or from a budget) — sometimes used in the phrase *get the ax*
4 : a musical instrument (as a guitar or a saxophone)
— ax to grind : an ulterior often selfish purpose to further

²ax *or* **axe** *transitive verb* **axed; ax·ing** (1679)
1 a : to shape, dress, or trim with an ax **b :** to chop, split, or sever with an ax

2 : to remove abruptly (as from employment or from a budget)

ax·el \'ak-səl, 'äk-\ *noun, often capitalized* [*Axel* Paulsen (died 1938) Norwegian figure skater] (1930)
: a jump in figure skating from the outer forward edge of one skate with 1½ turns taken in the air and a return to the outer backward edge of the other skate

axe·nic \(,)ā-'zē-nik, -'zē-\ *adjective* [²a- + Greek *xenos* strange] (1942)
: free from other living organisms
— axe·ni·cal·ly \-ni-k(ə-)lē\ *adverb*

ax·i·al \'ak-sē-əl\ *adjective* (circa 1847)
1 : of, relating to, or having the characteristics of an axis
2 a : situated around, in the direction of, on, or along an axis **b :** extending in a direction essentially perpendicular to the plane of a cyclic structure (as of cyclohexane) ⟨*axial* hydrogens⟩ — compare EQUATORIAL
— ax·i·al·i·ty \,ak-sē-'a-lə-tē\ *noun*
— ax·i·al·ly \'ak-sē-ə-lē\ *adverb*

axial skeleton *noun* (1872)
: the skeleton of the trunk and head

ax·il \'ak-səl, -,sil\ *noun* [New Latin *axilla*, from Latin] (1794)

☆ **SYNONYMS**
Awkward, clumsy, maladroit, inept, gauche mean not marked by ease (as of performance, movement, or social conduct). AWKWARD is widely applicable and may suggest unhandiness, inconvenience, lack of muscular control, embarrassment, or lack of tact ⟨periods of *awkward* silence⟩. CLUMSY implies stiffness and heaviness and so may connote inflexibility, unwieldiness, or lack of ordinary skill ⟨a *clumsy* mechanic⟩. MALADROIT suggests a tendency to create awkward situations ⟨a *maladroit* politician⟩. INEPT often implies complete failure or inadequacy ⟨a hopelessly *inept* defense attorney⟩. GAUCHE implies the effects of shyness, inexperience, or ill breeding ⟨felt *gauche* and unsophisticated at formal parties⟩.

□ **USAGE**
awful Many grammarians take issue with the senses of *awful* and *awfully* that do not convey the etymological connection with *awe*. However, senses 3 and 4 of the adjective were used in speech and casual writing by the late 18th century ⟨it is an *awful* while since you have heard from me —John Keats (letter)⟩ ⟨there was an *awful* crowd —Sir Walter Scott (letter)⟩ ⟨this is an *awful* thing to say to oil painters —William Blake⟩. Adverbial use of *awful* as an intensifier began to appear in print in the early 19th century, as did the senses of *awfully* corresponding to senses 3 and 4 of the adjective. Both adverbs remain in widespread use ⟨a sad state of affairs and *awful* tough on art —H. L. Mencken⟩ ⟨the *awfully* rich young American —Henry James⟩ ⟨decided to play it so *awfully* safe —A. M. Schlesinger (born 1917)⟩.

awhile Although considered a solecism by many commentators, *awhile*, like several other adverbs of time and place, is often used as the object of a preposition ⟨for *awhile* there is a silence —Lord Dunsany⟩.

\ə\ **abut** \ə\ **kitten** \ər\ **further** \a\ **ash** \ā\ **ace**
\ä\ **mop, mar** \au̇\ **out** \ch\ **chin** \e\ **bet** \ē\ **easy**
\g\ **go** \i\ **hit** \ī\ **ice** \j\ **job** \ŋ\ **sing** \ō\ **go**
\ȯ\ **law** \ȯi\ **boy** \th\ **thin** \th\ **the** \ü\ **loot** \u̇\ **foot**
\y\ **yet** \zh\ **vision** *see also* Guide to Pronunciation

: the angle between a branch or leaf and the axis from which it arises

ax·il·la \ag-'zi-lə, ak-'si-\ *noun, plural* **-lae** \-(,)lē, -,lī\ *or* **-las** [Latin, diminutive of *ala* wing, upper arm, armpit, axil — more at AISLE] (1616)
: the cavity beneath the junction of a forelimb and the body; *especially* : ARMPIT

ax·il·lar \ag-'zi-lər, ak-'si-, 'ag-zə-, 'ak-sə-, -,lär\ *noun* (1541)
: an axillary part (as a feather)

¹ax·il·lary \'ak-sə-,ler-ē\ *adjective* (1615)
1 : of, relating to, or located near the axilla
2 : situated in or growing from an axil ⟨*axillary* buds⟩

²axillary *noun, plural* **-lar·ies** (circa 1889)
: one of the feathers arising from the axilla and closing the space between the flight feathers and body of a flying bird

ax·i·ol·o·gy \,ak-sē-'ä-lə-jē\ *noun* [Greek *axios* + International Scientific Vocabulary *-logy*] (1908)
: the study of the nature, types, and criteria of values and of value judgments especially in ethics
— **ax·i·o·log·i·cal** \,ak-sē-ə-,lä-ji-kəl\ *adjective*
— **ax·i·o·log·i·cal·ly** \-ji-k(ə-)lē\ *adverb*

ax·i·om \'ak-sē-əm\ *noun* [Latin *axioma*, from Greek *axiōma*, literally, something worthy, from *axioun* to think worthy, from *axios* worth, worthy; akin to Greek *agein* to weigh, drive — more at AGENT] (15th century)
1 : a maxim widely accepted on its intrinsic merit
2 : a statement accepted as true as the basis for argument or inference : POSTULATE 1
3 : an established rule or principle or a self-evident truth

ax·i·om·at·ic \,ak-sē-ə-'ma-tik\ *adjective* [Middle Greek *axiōmatikos*, from Greek, honorable, from *axiōmat-, axiōma*] (1797)
1 : taken for granted : SELF-EVIDENT
2 : based on or involving an axiom or system of axioms ⟨*axiomatic* set theory⟩
— **ax·i·om·at·i·cal·ly** \-ti-k(ə-)lē\ *adverb*

ax·i·omat·isa·tion *chiefly British variant of* AXIOMATIZATION

ax·i·omat·iza·tion \,ak-sē-ə-,ma-tə-'zā-shən, -sē-,ä-mə-tə-\ *noun* (1931)
: the act or process of reducing to a system of axioms
— **ax·i·om·a·tize** \-sē-'ä-mə-,tīz\ *transitive verb*

axiom of choice (1942)
: an axiom in set theory that is equivalent to Zorn's lemma: for every collection of nonempty sets there is a function which chooses an element from each set

ax·ion \'ak-sē-(,)än\ *noun* [*axi*al + ²*-on*] (1978)
: a hypothetical subatomic particle of low mass and energy that is postulated to exist because of certain properties of the strong force

ax·is \'ak-səs\ *noun, plural* **ax·es** \-,sēz\ [Latin, axis, axle; akin to Old English *eax* axis, axle, Greek *axōn*, Lithuanian *ašis*, Sanskrit *akṣa*] (14th century)
1 a : a straight line about which a body or a geometric figure rotates or may be supposed to rotate **b** : a straight line with respect to which a body or figure is symmetrical — called also *axis of symmetry* **c** : a straight line that bisects at right angles a system of parallel chords of a curve and divides the curve into two symmetrical parts **d** : one of the reference lines of a coordinate system
2 a : the second vertebra of the neck on which the head and first vertebra turn as on a pivot **b** : any of various central, fundamental, or axial parts
3 : a plant stem
4 : one of several imaginary lines assumed in describing the positions of the planes by which a crystal is bounded and the positions of atoms in the structure of the crystal

5 : a main line of direction, motion, growth, or extension
6 a : an implied line in painting or sculpture through a composition to which elements in the composition are referred **b** : a line actually drawn and used as the basis of measurements in an architectural or other working drawing
7 : any of three fixed lines of reference in an aircraft that run in the longitudinal, lateral, and vertical directions, are mutually perpendicular, and usually pass through the aircraft's center of gravity
8 : PARTNERSHIP, ALLIANCE

Axis *adjective* (1938)
: of or relating to the three powers Germany, Italy, and Japan engaged against the Allied nations in World War II

axi·sym·met·ric \,ak-si-sə-'me-trik\ *also* **axi·sym·met·ri·cal** \-tri-kəl\ *adjective* [*axis* + *symmetric*] (1893)
: symmetric in respect to an axis
— **axi·sym·me·try** \-'si-mə-trē\ *noun*

ax·le \'ak-səl\ *noun* [Middle English *axel-* (as in *axeltre*)] (14th century)
1 a : a pin or shaft on or with which a wheel or pair of wheels revolves **b** (1) : a fixed bar or beam with bearings at its ends on which wheels (as of a cart) revolve (2) : the spindle of such a beam
2 *archaic* : AXIS

axle·tree \-,(,)trē\ *noun* [Middle English *axeltre*, from Old Norse *ǫxultrē*, from *ǫxull* axle + *trē* tree] (14th century)
: AXLE 1b(1)

ax·man \'ak-smən\ *noun* (1671)
: one who wields an ax

Ax·min·ster \'ak-,smin(t)-stər\ *noun* [*Axminster*, town in England] (1818)
: a machine-woven carpet with pile tufts inserted mechanically in a variety of textures and patterns

ax·o·lotl \'ak-sə-,lä-t³l\ *noun* [Nahuatl *āxōlōtl*] (circa 1768)
: any of several salamanders (genus *Ambystoma* especially *A. mexicanum* and *A. tigrinum*) of mountain lakes of Mexico and the western U.S. that ordinarily live and breed without metamorphosing

ax·on \'ak-,sän\ *also* **ax·one** \-,sōn\ *noun* [New Latin *axon*, from Greek *axōn*] (circa 1899)
: a usually long and single nerve-cell process that usually conducts impulses away from the cell body
— **ax·o·nal** \'ak-sə-n³l; ak-'sä-, -'sō-\ *adjective*

ax·o·neme \'ak-sə-,nēm\ *noun* [Greek *axōn* axis + *nēma* thread, from *nēn* to spin — more at NEEDLE] (1901)
: the fibrillar bundle of a flagellum or cilium that usually consists of nine pairs of microtubules arranged in a ring around a single central pair
— **ax·o·ne·mal** \,ak-sə-'nē-məl\ *adjective*

ax·o·no·met·ric \,ak-sə-nō-'me-trik\ *adjective* [Greek *axōn* axis + English *-metric*] (1908)
: being or prepared by the projection of objects on the drawing surface so that they appear inclined with three sides showing and with horizontal and vertical distances drawn to scale but diagonal and curved lines distorted ⟨an *axonometric* drawing⟩

axo·plasm \'ak-sə-,pla-zəm\ *noun* [*axon* + *-plasm*] (1900)
: the protoplasm of an axon
— **axo·plas·mic** \,ak-sə-'plaz-mik\ *adjective*

ay \'ī\ *interjection* [Middle French *aymi* ay me] (14th century)
— usually used with following *me* to express sorrow or regret

ayah \'ī-ə; 'ä-yə, -(,)yä\ *noun* [Hindi *āyā*, from Portuguese *aia*, from Latin *avia* grandmother] (1779)
: a nurse or maid native to India

aya·hua·sca \,ī-yə-'hwäs-kə, -'wäs-\ *noun* [American Spanish] (1949)
: an hallucinogenic beverage prepared from the bark of a South American vine (*Banisteriopsis caapi* of the family Malpighiaceae)

aya·tol·lah \,ī-ə-'tō-lə, -'tä-, -'tə-, 'ī-ə-,\ *noun* [Persian, literally, sign of God, from Arabic *āya* sign, miracle + *allāh* God] (1953)
: a religious leader among Shiite Muslims — used as a title of respect especially for one who is not an imam

¹aye *also* **ay** \'ā\ *adverb* [Middle English, from Old Norse *ei*; akin to Old English *ā* always, Latin *aevum* age, lifetime, Greek *aiōn* age] (13th century)
: ALWAYS, CONTINUALLY, EVER ⟨love that will *aye* endure —W. S. Gilbert⟩

²aye *also* **ay** \'ī\ *adverb* [perhaps from Middle English *ye, yie* — more at YEA] (1576)
: YES ⟨*aye, aye*, sir⟩

³aye *also* **ay** \'ī\ *noun, plural* **ayes** (1589)
: an affirmative vote or voter ⟨the *ayes* have it⟩

aye–aye \'ī-,ī\ *noun* [French, from Malagasy *aiay*] (circa 1781)
: a small primitive nocturnal forest-dwelling primate (*Daubentonia madagascariensis*) of northern Madagascar that has a round head, large eyes and ears, and long thin fingers

ayin \'ī-ən\ *noun* [Hebrew *'ayin*, literally, eye] (1823)
: the 16th letter of the Hebrew alphabet — see ALPHABET table

Ay·ma·ra \,ī-mə-'rä\ *noun, plural* **Aymara** *or* **Aymaras** [Spanish *aymará*] (1860)
1 : a member of an Indian people of Bolivia and Peru
2 : the language of the Aymara people

Ayr·shire \'ar-,shir, 'er-, -shər; 'ash-,ir\ *noun* [*Ayrshire*, Scotland] (1856)
: any of a breed of hardy dairy cattle originated in Ayr and usually marked with blotches of red or brown with white

az- *or* **azo-** *combining form* [International Scientific Vocabulary, from French *azote* nitrogen, from *a-* ²*a-* + *-zote*, probably from Greek *zōtikos* maintaining life, from *zōē* life — more at QUICK]
: containing nitrogen especially as the bivalent group N=N ⟨*azine*⟩

aza- *or* **az-** *combining form* [International Scientific Vocabulary *az-* + *-a-*]
: containing nitrogen in place of carbon and usually the bivalent group NH for the group CH_2 or a single trivalent nitrogen atom for the group CH ⟨*aza*thioprine⟩

aza·lea \ə-'zāl-yə\ *noun* [New Latin, genus name, from Greek, feminine of *azaleos* dry, from *azein* to parch, dry; akin to Hittite *ḫat-* to dry up and probably to Latin *ador* emmer] (1767)
: any of a subgenus (*Azalea*) of rhododendrons with funnel-shaped corollas and usually deciduous leaves including many species and hybrid forms cultivated as ornamentals

aza·thi·o·prine \,a-zə-'thī-ə-,prēn\ *noun* [*aza-* + *thi-* + *purine*] (1962)
: a purine antimetabolite $C_9H_7N_7O_2S$ used especially as an immunosuppressant

Aza·zel \ə-'zā-zəl, 'a-zə-,zel\ *noun* [Hebrew *'ăzāzēl*]
: an evil spirit of the wilderness to which a scapegoat was sent by the ancient Hebrews in a ritual of atonement

azeo·trope \'ā-zē-ə-,trōp\ *noun* [²*a-* + *zeo-* (from Greek *zein* to boil) + *-trope* something changed, from Greek *tropos* turn — more at YEAST, TROPE] (1938)
: a liquid mixture that is characterized by a constant minimum or maximum boiling point which is lower or higher than that of any of the components

azide \'ā-,zīd, 'a-\ *noun* (circa 1904)
: a compound containing the group N_3 combined with an element or radical

az·i·do \'a-zə-(,)dō\ *adjective* [International Scientific Vocabulary *azide* + *-o-*] (circa 1926)

: relating to or containing the univalent group N₃ — often used in combination

az·i·do·thy·mi·dine \ə-ˌzī-dō-'thī-mə-ˌdēn\ *noun* (1974)

: an antiviral drug $C_{10}H_{13}N_5O_4$ that inhibits replication of some retroviruses (as HIV) and is used to treat AIDS — called also *AZT, zidovudine*

az·i·muth \'az-məth, 'a-zə-\ *noun* [Middle English, from (assumed) Medieval Latin, from Arabic *as-sumūt* the azimuth, plural of *as-samt* the way] (14th century)

1 : an arc of the horizon measured between a fixed point (as true north) and the vertical circle passing through the center of an object usually in astronomy and navigation clockwise from the north point through 360 degrees **2 :** horizontal direction expressed as the angular distance between the direction of a fixed point (as the observer's heading) and the direction of the object

— **az·i·muth·al** \ˌa-zə-'mə-thəl\ *adjective*

— **az·i·muth·al·ly** \-'mə-thə-lē\ *adverb*

azimuthal equidistant projection *noun* (1942)

: a map projection of the surface of the earth so centered at any given point that a straight line radiating from the center to any other point represents the shortest distance and can be measured to scale

azine \'ā-ˌzēn, 'a-\ *noun* (1887)

: a compound of the general formula RCH=NH=CHR or R₂C=NN=CR₂ formed by the action of hydrazine on aldehydes or ketones

azo \'ā-(ˌ)zō, 'a-\ *adjective* [*az-*] (circa 1879)

: relating to or containing the bivalent group N=N united at both ends to carbon

azo dye *noun* (1884)

: any of numerous dyes containing azo groups

azo·ic \(ˌ)ā-'zō-ik\ *adjective* [²a- + Greek *zōē* life — more at QUICK] (circa 1847)

: having no life; *especially* **:** of or relating to the part of geologic time that antedates life — compare ARCHEOZOIC

azole \'ā-ˌzōl, 'a-\ *noun* (circa 1899)

: any of numerous compounds characterized by a 5-membered ring containing at least one nitrogen atom

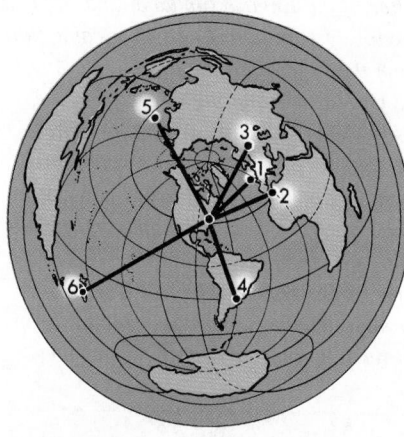

azimuthal equidistant projection, centered on Washington, D.C.: *1* London, *2* Algiers, *3* Moscow, *4* Rio de Janeiro, *5* Tokyo, *6* Auckland

azon·al \(ˌ)ā-'zō-n°l\ *adjective* (1938)

: of, relating to, or being a soil or a major group of soils lacking well-developed horizons often because of immaturity — compare INTRAZONAL, ZONAL

azo·o·sper·mia \(ˌ)ā-ˌzō-ə-'spər-mē-ə\ *noun* [New Latin, from Greek *azoos* lifeless (from *a-* ²a- + *zōē* life) + *sperma* semen, seed — more at SPERM] (circa 1881)

: absence of spermatozoa from the seminal fluid

azo·te·mia \ˌā-zō-'tē-mē-ə\ *noun* [International Scientific Vocabulary *azote* nitrogen + New Latin *-emia* — more at AZ-] (circa 1900)

: an excess of nitrogenous bodies in the blood as a result of kidney insufficiency — compare UREMIA

— **azo·te·mic** \-mik\ *adjective*

az·oth \'a-ˌzóth\ *noun* [Arabic *az-zā'ūq* the mercury] (15th century)

1 : mercury regarded by alchemists as the first principle of metals

2 : the universal remedy of Paracelsus

azo·to·bac·ter \ā-'zō-tə-ˌbak-tər\ *noun* [New Latin, genus name, from International Scientific Vocabulary *azote* + New Latin *bacterium*] (1910)

: any of a genus (*Azotobacter*) of large rod-shaped or spherical bacteria occurring in soil and sewage and fixing atmospheric nitrogen

azo·tu·ria \ˌā-zō-'tùr-ē-ə, -'tyùr-\ *noun* [International Scientific Vocabulary *azote* + New Latin *-uria*] (circa 1838)

: an abnormal condition of horses characterized by an excess of urea or other nitrogenous substances in the urine and muscle damage especially to the hindquarters

AZT \ˌā-(ˌ)zē-'tē\ *noun* (1985)

: AZIDOTHYMIDINE

Az·tec \'az-ˌtek\ *noun* [Spanish *azteca*, from Nahuatl *aztēcah*, plural of *aztēcatl*] (1787)

1 a : a member of a Nahuatl-speaking people that founded the Mexican empire conquered by Cortes in 1519 **b :** a member of any people under Aztec influence

2 : NAHUATL

— **Az·tec·an** \'az-ˌte-kən, ˌaz-'te-\ *adjective*

azure \'a-zhər\ *noun* [Middle English *asur*, from Old French *azur*, probably from Old Spanish, modification of Arabic *lāzaward*, from Persian *lāzhuward*] (14th century)

1 *archaic* **:** LAPIS LAZULI

2 a : the blue color of the clear sky **b :** the heraldic color blue

3 : the unclouded sky

— **azure** *adjective*

azur·ite \'a-zhə-ˌrīt\ *noun* [French, from *azur* azure] (circa 1868)

1 : a mineral that consists of blue basic carbonate of copper and is a copper ore

2 : a semiprecious stone derived from azurite

¹azy·gos \ā-'zī-gəs\ *noun* [New Latin, from Greek, unyoked, from *a-* + *zygon* yoke — more at YOKE] (1646)

: an azygos anatomical part

²azy·gos *also* **azy·gous** \(ˌ)ā-'zī-gəs\ *adjective* (1681)

: not being one of a pair **:** SINGLE ⟨an *azygos* vein⟩

B

B *is the second letter of the English alphabet and of most alphabets that are closely related to English. It came into these alphabets from the Latin, into the Latin (by way of Etruscan) from the Greek, and into the Greek from the Phoenician, where it was called* beth. B *usually represents the voiced bilabial stop, the consonant sound pronounced at the beginning of the English word* banana; *in a few English words it is silent, as in de*b*t and tom*b. *In related languages English* b *corresponds to German* b (B*ruder "brother"), Latin* f (f*rater "brother,"* f*ero "I bear"), Greek* ph (p*hero "I bear"), and Sanskrit* bh (b*harati "he bears"). The small* b *developed from the capital form through the shrinking and eventual disappearance of the upper lobe, together with a reduction in the overall size of the letter.*

b \'bē\ *noun, plural* **b's** *or* **bs** \'bēz\ *often capitalized, often attributive* (before 12th century)
1 a : the 2d letter of the English alphabet **b :** a graphic representation of this letter **c :** a speech counterpart of orthographic *b*
2 : the 7th tone of a C-major scale
3 : a graphic device for reproducing the letter *b*
4 : one designated *b* especially as the 2d in order or class
5 a : a grade rating a student's work as good but short of excellent **b :** one graded or rated with a B
6 : something shaped like the letter B
baa \'ba, 'bä\ *intransitive verb* **baaed; baa-ing** [imitative] (circa 1586)
: to make the bleat of a sheep
— **baa** *noun*
baal \'bā-(ə)l\ *noun, plural* **baals** *or* **baa-lim** \'bā-(ə)ləm, 'bä-ə-,lim\ *often capitalized* [Hebrew *ba'al* lord] (14th century)
: any of numerous Canaanite and Phoenician local deities
— **baal-ism** \'bā-(ə-)li-zəm\ *noun, often capitalized*
baas \'bäs\ *noun* [Afrikaans, from Dutch] (1785)
South African **:** BOSS, MASTER — used especially by nonwhites when speaking to or about Europeans in positions of authority
ba-ba \'bä-(,)bä, -bə\ *noun* [French, from Polish, literally, old woman] (1827)
: a rich cake soaked in a rum and sugar syrup
ba-bas-su \,bä-bə-'sü\ *noun* [Portuguese *babaçú*, from (assumed) Tupi *iwaβasu*, from Tupi *iwa* fruit + *βasu* large] (1917)
: a tall pinnate-leaved palm (*Orbignya barbosiana*) of Brazil with hard-shelled nuts yielding a valuable oil
bab-bitt \'ba-bət\ *noun* [Isaac *Babbitt* (died 1862) American inventor] (1900)
: an alloy used for lining bearings; *especially* **:** one containing tin, copper, and antimony — called also *babbitt metal*
— **bab-bitt-ed** \-bə-təd\ *adjective*
Bab-bitt \'ba-bət\ *noun* [George F. *Babbitt*, character in the novel *Babbitt* (1922) by Sinclair Lewis] (1923)
: a business or professional man who conforms unthinkingly to prevailing middle-class standards ◇
— **Bab-bitt-ry** \-bə-trē\ *noun*
— **Bab-itty** \-tē\ *adjective*
bab-ble \'ba-bəl\ *verb* **bab-bled; bab-bling** \-b(ə-)liŋ\ [Middle English *babelen*, probably of imitative origin] (13th century)
intransitive verb
1 a : to talk enthusiastically or excessively **b :** to utter meaninglessly or unintelligible sounds
2 : to make sounds as though babbling
transitive verb
1 : to utter in an incoherently or meaninglessly repetitive manner

2 : to reveal by talk that is too free
— **babble** *noun*
— **bab-ble-ment** \-bəl-mənt\ *noun*
— **bab-bler** \-b(ə-)lər\ *noun*
babe \'bāb\ *noun* [Middle English, probably of imitative origin] (14th century)
1 a : INFANT, BABY **b** *slang* **:** GIRL, WOMAN
2 : a naive inexperienced person — used especially in the phrase *babe in the woods*
Ba-bel \'bā-bəl, 'ba-\ *noun* [Hebrew *Bābhel*, from Akkadian *bāb-ilu* gate of god]
1 : a city in Shinar where the building of a tower is held in Genesis to have been halted by the confusion of tongues
2 *often not capitalized* **a :** a confusion of sounds or voices **b :** a scene of noise or confusion
ba-be-sia \bə-'bē-zh(ē-)ə\ *noun* [New Latin, from Victor *Babeş* (died 1926) Romanian bacteriologist] (1911)
: any of a genus (*Babesia*) of sporozoans parasitic in mammalian red blood cells (as in Texas fever) and transmitted by the bite of a tick — called also *piroplasm*
bab-e-si-o-sis \,ba-bə-'zī-ə-səs\ *noun* [New Latin] (1911)
: an infection with or disease caused by babesias
Ba-bin-ski reflex \bə-'bin-skē-\ *noun* [J.F.F. *Babinski* (died 1932) French neurologist] (1900)
: a reflex movement in which when the sole is tickled the big toe turns upward instead of downward and which is normal in infancy but indicates damage to the central nervous system (as in the pyramidal tracts) later in life — called also *Babinski sign, Ba-bin-ski's reflex* \-skēz-\
bab-i-ru-sa \,ba-bə-'rü-sə, ,bä-\ *noun* [Malay, from *babi* pig + *rusa* deer] (1673)
: a large wild swine (*Babyrousa babyrussa*) of Indonesia
ba-boon \ba-'bün, *chiefly British* bə-\ *noun* [Middle English *babewin*, from Middle French *babouin*, from *baboue* grimace] (15th century)
: any of a genus (*Papio*) of large gregarious primates of Africa and southwestern Asia having a long square naked muzzle; *also* **:** any of several closely related primates
ba-bu *also* **ba-boo** \'bä-(,)bü\ *noun, often attributive* [Hindi *bābū*, literally, father] (1776)
1 : a Hindu gentleman — a form of address corresponding to *Mr.*
2 a : an Indian clerk who writes English **b :** an Indian having some education in English — often used disparagingly
ba-bul \bə-'bül\ *noun* [Persian *babūl*] (1780)
: an acacia tree (*Acacia nilotica* synonym *A. arabica*) widespread in India and northern Africa that yields gum arabic and tannins as well as fodder and timber

ba-bush-ka \bə-'büsh-kə, -'büsh-\ *noun* [Russian, grandmother, diminutive of *baba* old woman] (1938)
1 a : a usually triangularly folded kerchief for the head **b :** a head covering resembling a babushka
2 : an elderly Russian woman

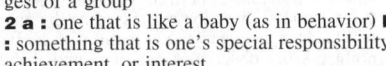

¹ba-by \'bā-bē\ *noun, plural* **babies** [Middle English, from *babe*] (14th century)
1 a (1) **:** an extremely young child; *especially* **:** INFANT (2) **:** an extremely young animal **b :** the youngest of a group

babushka 1a

2 a : one that is like a baby (as in behavior) **b :** something that is one's special responsibility, achievement, or interest
3 *slang* **a :** GIRL, WOMAN — often used in address **b :** BOY, MAN — often used in address
4 : PERSON, THING ⟨is one tough *baby*⟩
— **ba-by-hood** \-bē-,hüd\ *noun*
— **ba-by-ish** \-ish\ *adjective*
²baby *adjective* (1591)
1 : of, relating to, or being a baby
2 : much smaller than the usual ⟨*baby* carrots⟩ ⟨a *baby* flattop⟩ ⟨take two *baby* steps⟩
³baby *transitive verb* **ba-bied; ba-by-ing** (1742)
1 : to tend to indulge with often excessive or inappropriate care and solicitude ⟨*babying* their only child⟩
2 : to operate or treat with care ⟨*baby* a new motor⟩ ⟨*babying* a sore knee⟩
synonym see INDULGE
baby blue *noun* (1889)
: a pale blue
baby blue-eyes \-'blü-,īz\ *noun plural but singular or plural in construction* (1887)
: a delicate blue-flowered California herb (*Nemophila menziesii*) of the waterleaf family
baby boom *noun* (1941)
: a marked rise in birthrate (as in the U.S. immediately following the end of World War II)
— **baby boomer** *noun*
baby bust *noun* (1971)
: a marked decline in birthrate
— **baby buster** *noun*
baby carriage *noun* (1866)
: a small four-wheeled carriage often with a folding top for pushing a baby around in — called also *baby buggy*
baby grand *noun* (circa 1903)
: a small grand piano
Bab-y-lon \'ba-bə-,län, -lən\ *noun* [*Babylon*, ancient city of Babylonia] (14th century)
: a city devoted to materialism and sensual pleasure

◇ **WORD HISTORY**
Babbitt *Babbitt* and *Babbittry* are words that sum up all the values, attitudes, and mores associated with the American middle class during the 1920's. Both derive from the protagonist of *Babbitt*, a satirical novel by Sinclair Lewis published in 1922. George F. Babbitt epitomizes the unimaginative and self-important businessmen that Lewis found typical of the provincial cities and towns of Middle America. A real estate agent by profession and a conformist by nature, Babbitt is a compulsive booster and joiner in his native Zenith, "The Zip City." Despite his evident prosperity and status in the community, he remains vaguely dissatisfied with his life. Although he makes tentative attempts at rebellion through brief encounters with artists, bohemians, and socialists and by having an extramarital affair, Babbitt finds his need for social acceptance greater than his desire for escape and he ends as he began.

¹**Bab·y·lo·nian** \‚ba-bə-'lō-nyən, -nē-ən\ *noun* (1564)
1 : a native or inhabitant of ancient Babylonia or Babylon
2 : the form of the Akkadian language used in ancient Babylonia
²**Babylonian** *adjective* (1596)
1 : of, relating to, or characteristic of Babylonia or Babylon, the Babylonians, or Babylonian
2 : marked by luxury, extravagance, or the pursuit of sensual pleasure ⟨the *Babylonian* halls of the big hotel —G. K. Chesterton⟩ ⟨the *Babylonian* delights of the city⟩
baby's breath *noun* (circa 1890)
: GYPSOPHILA; *especially* **:** a perennial herb (*Gypsophila paniculata*) or an annual herb (*G. elegans*) commonly used in floral arrangements
ba·by–sit \'bā-bē-‚sit\ *verb* **-sat** \-‚sat\; **-sit·ting** [back-formation from *baby-sitter*] (1947)
intransitive verb
: to care for children usually during a short absence of the parents; *broadly* **:** to give care ⟨*baby-sit* for a neighbor's pets⟩
transitive verb
: to baby-sit for; *broadly* **:** MIND, TEND ⟨*baby-sit* house plants⟩ ⟨police *baby-sitting* a witness⟩
— **ba·by–sit·ter** *noun*
baby talk *noun* (1836)
1 a : the syntactically imperfect speech or phonetically modified forms used by small children learning to talk **b :** the consciously imperfect or altered speech used by adults in speaking to small children
2 : oversimplified speech or writing
baby tooth *noun* (1939)
: MILK TOOTH
bac·ca·lau·re·ate \‚ba-kə-'lȯr-ē-ət, -'lär-\ *noun* [Medieval Latin *baccalaureatus,* from *baccalaureus* bachelor, alteration of *baccalarius*] (circa 1649)
1 : the degree of bachelor conferred by universities and colleges
2 a : a sermon to a graduating class **b :** the service at which this sermon is delivered
bac·ca·rat \‚bä-kə-'rä, ‚ba-\ *noun* [French *baccara*] (1865)
: a card game resembling chemin de fer in which three hands are dealt and players may bet either or both hands against the dealer's; *also* **:** a two-handed version in which players may bet on or against the dealer
Bac·chae \'ba-‚kē, -‚kī\ *noun plural* [Latin, from Greek *Bakchai,* from *Bakchos* Bacchus] (circa 1909)
1 : the female attendants or priestesses of Bacchus
2 : the women participating in the Bacchanalia
¹**bac·cha·nal** \'ba-kə-nᵊl, 'bä-; ‚ba-kə-'nal, ‚bä-kə-'näl\ *noun* [Latin, shrine of Bacchus, probably back-formation from *Bacchanalia*] (1550)
1 : ORGY 2, 3
2 a : a devotee of Bacchus; *especially* **:** one who celebrates the Bacchanalia **b :** REVELER
²**bac·cha·nal** \'ba-kə-nᵊl\ *adjective* (1550)
: of, relating to, or suggestive of the Bacchanalia **:** BACCHANALIAN
bac·cha·na·lia \‚ba-kə-'nāl-yə, 'bä-\ *noun, plural* **bacchanalia** [Latin, from *Bacchus*] (1591)
1 *plural, capitalized* **:** a Roman festival of Bacchus celebrated with dancing, song, and revelry
2 : ORGY 2, 3
— **bac·cha·na·lian** \-'nāl-yən\ *adjective or noun*
bac·chant \bə-'kant, -'känt; 'ba-kənt, 'bä-\ *noun, plural* **bacchants** *or* **bacchantes** \bə-'kants, -'känts, -'kan-tēz, -'kän-tēz\ [Latin *bacchant-, bacchans,* from present participle of *bacchari* to take part in the orgies of Bacchus] (1699)
: BACCHANAL
— **bacchant** *adjective*

bac·chante \bə-'kant, -'känt; -'kan-tē, -'kän-\ *noun* [French, from Latin *bacchant-, bacchans*] (1579)
: a priestess or female follower of Bacchus **:** MAENAD
bac·chic \'ba-kik, 'bä-\ *adjective, often capitalized* (1669)
: of, relating to, or suggestive of Bacchus or the Bacchanalia **:** BACCHANALIAN
Bac·chus \'ba-kəs, 'bä-\ *noun* [Latin, from Greek *Bakchos*]
: the Greek god of wine — called also *Dionysus*
¹**bach** \'bach\ *noun* (1855)
: BACHELOR 3a
²**bach** *intransitive verb* (1870)
: to live as a bachelor — often used with *it*
³**bach** *noun* [²*bach*] (1925)
New Zealand **:** a small house or weekend cottage
¹**bach·e·lor** \'bach-lər, 'ba-chə-\ *noun* [Middle English *bacheler,* from Old French] (14th century)
1 : a young knight who follows the banner of another
2 : a person who has received what is usually the lowest degree conferred by a four-year college, university, or professional school ⟨*bachelor* of arts⟩
3 a : an unmarried man **b :** a male animal (as a fur seal) without a mate during breeding time
— **bach·e·lor·dom** \-dəm\ *noun*
— **bach·e·lor·hood** \-‚hüd\ *noun*
²**bachelor** *adjective* (1857)
1 : suitable for or occupied by a single person ⟨a *bachelor* apartment⟩
2 : UNMARRIED ⟨*bachelor* women⟩ ⟨*bachelor* parents⟩
bach·e·lor·ette \‚bach-lə-'ret, ‚ba-chə-\ *noun* (1938)
: a bachelor woman
bachelor's button *noun* (1847)
: a European composite (*Centaurea cyanus*) having flower heads with blue, pink, or white rays that is often cultivated in North America — called also *cornflower*
ba·cil·la·ry \'ba-sə-‚ler-ē, bə-'si-lə-rē\ *or* **ba·cil·lar** \bə-'si-lər, 'ba-sə-lər\ *adjective* [Medieval Latin & New Latin *bacillus*] (1865)
1 : shaped like a rod; *also* **:** consisting of small rods
2 : of, relating to, or caused by bacilli
ba·cil·lus \bə-'si-ləs\ *noun, plural* **-li** \-‚lī *also* -lē\ [New Latin, from Medieval Latin, small staff, rod, diminutive of Latin *baculus* staff, alteration of *baculum*] (circa 1879)
1 : any of a genus (*Bacillus*) of aerobic rod-shaped gram-positive bacteria producing endospores that do not thicken the rod and including many saprophytes and some parasites (as *B. anthracis* of anthrax); *broadly* **:** a straight rod-shaped bacterium
2 : BACTERIUM; *especially* **:** a disease-producing bacterium
bac·i·tra·cin \‚ba-sə-'trā-sᵊn\ *noun* [New Latin *Bacillus subtilis* (species of bacillus producing the toxin) + Margaret *Tracy* (born about 1936) American child in whose tissues it was found] (1945)
: a toxic polypeptide antibiotic isolated from a bacillus (*Bacillus subtilis*) and usually used topically especially against gram-positive bacteria
¹**back** \'bak\ *noun* [Middle English, from Old English *bæc;* akin to Old High German *bah* back] (before 12th century)
1 a (1) **:** the rear part of the human body especially from the neck to the end of the spine (2) **:** the body considered as the wearer of clothes (3) **:** capacity for labor, effort, or endurance (4) **:** the back considered as the seat of one's awareness of duty or failings ⟨get off my *back*⟩ **b :** the part of a lower animal (as a quadruped) corresponding to the human back **c :** SPINAL COLUMN **d :** BACKBONE 4

2 a : the side or surface opposite the front or face **:** the rear part; *also* **:** the farther or reverse side **b :** something at or on the back for support ⟨*back* of a chair⟩ **c :** a place away from the front ⟨sat in *back*⟩
3 : a position in some games (as football or soccer) behind the front line of players; *also* **:** a player in this position
— **backed** \'bakt\ *adjective*
— **back·less** \'bak-ləs\ *adjective*
— **back of one's hand** *or* **back of the hand :** a show of contempt
— **back of one's mind :** the remote part of one's mind where thoughts and memories are stored to be drawn on
— **behind one's back :** without one's knowledge **:** in secret
— **in back of :** BEHIND
²**back** *adverb* (14th century)
1 a : to, toward, or at the rear **b :** in or into the past **:** backward in time; *also* **:** AGO **c :** to or at an angle off the vertical **d** (1) **:** under restraint (2) **:** in a delayed or retarded condition
2 a : to, toward, or in a place from which a person or thing came **b :** to or toward a former state **c :** in return or reply
³**back** *adjective* (15th century)
1 a : being at or in the back ⟨*back* door⟩ **b :** distant from a central or main area ⟨*back* roads⟩ **c :** articulated at or toward the back of the oral passage ⟨*back* vowels⟩
2 : having returned or been returned
3 : being in arrears **:** OVERDUE
4 : moving or operating backward **:** REVERSE
5 : not current ⟨*back* numbers of a magazine⟩
6 : constituting the final 9 holes of an 18-hole golf course
⁴**back** (1548)
transitive verb
1 a : to support by material or moral assistance — usually used with *up* **b :** SUBSTANTIATE **c :** to assume financial responsibility for **d :** to provide musical accompaniment for — often used with *up*
2 a : to cause to go back or in reverse **b :** to articulate (a sound) with the tongue farther back
3 a : to furnish with a back **b :** to be at the back of
intransitive verb
1 : to move backward — often used with *up*
2 *of the wind* **:** to shift counterclockwise — compare VEER
3 : to have the back in the direction of something
synonym SEE SUPPORT, RECEDE
— **back·er** \'ba-kər\ *noun*
— **back and fill 1 :** to manage the sails of a ship so as to keep it clear of obstructions as it floats down with the current of a river or channel **2 :** to take opposite positions alternately **:** SHILLY-SHALLY
— **back into :** to get into inadvertently ⟨*backed into* the antiques business⟩
back·ache \'bak-‚āk\ *noun* (1601)
: a pain in the lower back
back–and–forth *noun* (1941)
: DISCUSSION 1, GIVE-AND-TAKE; *also* **:** EXCHANGE 1
back and forth *adverb* (1613)
: backward and forward; *also* **:** between two places or persons
back away *intransitive verb* (1919)
: to move away (as from a stand on an issue)
back bacon *noun* (1947)
chiefly British **:** CANADIAN BACON
back·beat \'bak-‚bēt\ *noun* (1928)
: a steady pronounced rhythm stressing the second and fourth beats of a four-beat measure
back·bench *noun* (1874)

\ə\ abut \ᵊ\ kitten \ər\ further \a\ ash \ā\ ace
\ä\ mop, mar \aȯ\ out \ch\ chin \e\ bet \ē\ easy
\g\ go \i\ hit \ī\ ice \j\ job \ŋ\ sing \ō\ go
\ȯ\ law \ȯi\ boy \th\ thin \t͟h\ the \ü\ loot \u̇\ foot
\y\ yet \zh\ vision *see also* Guide to Pronunciation

: a bench in a British legislature (as the House of Commons) occupied by rank-and-file members — compare FRONT BENCH
— **back·bench·er** \-'ben-chər\ *noun*
back·bite \-ˌbīt\ *verb* **-bit; -bit·ten; -bit·ing** (12th century)
transitive verb
: to say mean or spiteful things about
intransitive verb
: to backbite a person
— **back·bit·er** *noun*
backbiting \'bak-ˌbī-tiŋ\ *noun* (12th century)
: malicious comment about one not present
back·block \-ˌbläk\ *noun* (1870)
Australian & New Zealand : BOONDOCKS 2 — usually used in plural
back·board \-ˌbōrd, -ˌbȯrd\ *noun* (1761)
: a board placed at or serving as the back of something; *especially* : a rounded or rectangular board behind the basket on a basketball court which serves to keep missed shots from going out-of-bounds and from which the ball can be made to rebound into the basket
back·bone \-'bōn, -ˌbōn\ *noun* (14th century)
1 : SPINAL COLUMN, SPINE
2 : something that resembles a backbone: as **a** : a chief mountain ridge, range, or system **b** : the foundation or most substantial or sturdiest part of something **c** : the longest chain of atoms or groups of atoms in a usually long molecule (as a polymer or protein)
3 : firm and resolute character
4 : SPINE 1c
back·break·ing \-ˌbrā-kiŋ\ *adjective* (1870)
: extremely tiring or demanding : OPPRESSIVE ⟨*backbreaking* labor⟩ ⟨*backbreaking* rents⟩
— **back·break·er** \-kər\ *noun*
back burner *noun* (1963)
: the condition of being out of active consideration or development — usually used in the phrase *on the back burner*
back channel *noun* (1975)
: a secret, unofficial, or irregular means of communication
— **back–channel** *adjective*
back·chat \'bak-ˌchat\ *noun* (1901)
1 : BACK TALK
2 : gossip or bantering conversation
back–check \-ˌchek\ *intransitive verb* (1937)
: to skate back toward one's own goal while closely defending against the offensive rushes of an opposing player in ice hockey
— **back–check·er** \-ˌche-kər\ *noun*
back·cloth \-ˌklȯth\ *noun* (1886)
chiefly British : BACKDROP
back·coun·try \-ˌkən-trē\ *noun, often attributive* (1746)
: a remote undeveloped rural area
back·court \-ˌkōrt, -ˈkȯrt\ *noun* (1890)
1 : the area near or nearest the back boundary lines or back wall of the playing area in a net or court game
2 : a basketball team's defensive half of the court; *also* : the part of the offensive half of the court farthest from the goal
3 : the basketball players who play the backcourt
back·court·man \-mən\ *noun* (1954)
: a guard on a basketball team
¹**back·cross** \'bak-ˌkrȯs\ *transitive verb* (1904)
: to cross (a first-generation hybrid) with one of the parental types
²**backcross** *noun* (1918)
: a mating that involves backcrossing; *also* : an individual produced by backcrossing
back·date \'bak-ˌdāt\ *transitive verb* (1944)
: to put a date earlier than the actual one on ⟨*backdate* a memo⟩; *also* : to make retroactive ⟨*backdate* pension rights⟩
back dive *noun* (circa 1934)
: a dive from a position facing the diving board
back·door \'bak-ˌdōr, -ˈdȯr\ *adjective* (1805)
: INDIRECT, DEVIOUS
back down *intransitive verb* (1849)

: to withdraw from a commitment or position
back–drop \'bak-ˌdräp\ *noun* (1913)
1 : a painted cloth hung across the rear of a stage
2 : BACKGROUND
— **backdrop** *transitive verb*
back·field \-ˌfēld\ *noun* (1920)
: the football players whose positions are behind the line of scrimmage; *also* : the positions themselves
back·fill \-ˌfil\ (1908)
transitive verb
: to refill (as an excavation) usually with excavated material
intransitive verb
: to backfill an excavation
— **backfill** *noun*
¹**back·fire** \-ˌfīr\ *noun* (1839)
1 : a fire started to check an advancing fire by clearing an area
2 : a loud noise caused by the improperly timed explosion of fuel mixture in the cylinder of an internal combustion engine
²**backfire** *intransitive verb* (1886)
1 : to make or undergo a backfire
2 : to have the reverse of the desired or expected effect
back·fit \'bak-ˌfit\ *transitive verb* (1967)
: RETROFIT
— **backfit** *noun*
back·flow \-ˌflō\ *noun* (1884)
: a flowing back or returning toward a source
back–formation *noun* (1889)
1 : a word formed by subtraction of a real or supposed affix from an already existing longer word (as *burgle* from *burglar*)
2 : the formation of back-formations
back·gam·mon \'bak-ˌga-mən, bak-'\ *noun* [perhaps from ³*back* + Middle English *gamen, game* game] (circa 1645)
: a board game played with dice and counters in which players try to be the first to gather their pieces into one corner and then systematically remove them from the board
¹**back·ground** \'bak-ˌgrau̇nd\ *noun, often attributive* (1672)
1 a : the scenery or ground behind something **b** : the part of a painting representing what lies behind objects in the foreground
2 : an inconspicuous position
3 a : the conditions that form the setting within which something is experienced **b** (1) : the circumstances or events antecedent to a phenomenon or development (2) : information essential to understanding of a problem or situation **c** : the total of a person's experience, knowledge, and education
4 a : intrusive sound or radiation that interferes with received or recorded electronic signals **b** : a more or less steady level of noise above which the effect (as radioactivity) being measured by an apparatus (as a Geiger counter) is detected; *especially* : a somewhat steady level of radiation in the natural environment (as from cosmic rays) ☆
²**background** *transitive verb* (1768)
: to provide with background
back·ground·er \'bak-ˌgrau̇n-dər\ *noun* (1960)
: an off-the-record briefing for reporters
background music *noun* (1928)
: music to accompany the dialogue or action of a motion picture or radio or television drama
background radiation *noun* (1969)
: the microwave radiation pervading the universe that has the spectral energy distribution of a blackbody having a temperature of 2.7 K and that is the principle evidence supporting the big bang theory — called also *cosmic background radiation*
¹**back·hand** \'bak-ˌhand\ *noun* (1657)
1 a : a stroke (as in tennis) made with the back of the hand turned in the direction of movement; *also* : the side on which such

strokes are made **b** : a catch (as in baseball) made to the side of the body opposite the hand being used
2 : handwriting whose strokes slant downward from left to right
²**backhand** *adjective* (1695)
: made with a backhand ⟨a *backhand* tennis stroke⟩
³**backhand** *or* **backhand·ed** \-'han-dəd\ *adverb* (1889)
: with a backhand
⁴**backhand** *transitive verb* (circa 1935)
: to do, hit, or catch backhand
back·hand·ed \'bak-'han-dəd\ *adjective* (1800)
1 : INDIRECT, DEVIOUS; *especially* : SARCASTIC ⟨a *backhanded* compliment⟩
2 : using or made with a backhand
— **back·hand·ed·ly** *adverb*
back·hand·er \-dər\ *noun* (1960)
British : BRIBE
back·hoe \-ˌhō\ *noun* (1928)
: an excavating machine having a bucket that is attached to a rigid bar hinged to a boom and that is drawn toward the machine in operation
back·house \-ˌhau̇s\ *noun* (circa 1847)
: PRIVY 1a
back·ing \'ba-kiŋ\ *noun* (1793)
1 : something forming a back
2 a : SUPPORT, AID **b** : endorsement especially of a warrant by a magistrate
back judge *noun* (circa 1966)
: a football official whose duties include keeping the game's official time and identifying eligible pass receivers
back·land \'bak-ˌland\ *noun* (1681)
: BACKCOUNTRY, HINTERLAND — usually used in plural
back·lash \'bak-ˌlash\ *noun* (1815)
1 a : a sudden violent backward movement or reaction **b** : the play between adjacent movable parts (as in a series of gears); *also* : the jar caused by this when the parts are put into action
2 : a snarl in that part of a fishing line wound on the reel
3 : a strong adverse reaction (as to a recent political or social development)
— **back·lash·er** *noun*
back·light \-ˌlīt\ *noun* (circa 1846)
: illumination from behind; *also* : the source of such illumination
— **backlight** *transitive verb*
back·list \'bak-ˌlist\ *noun* (1964)

backhand 1a

: a list of books kept in print as distinguished from books newly published

¹**back·log** \-ˌlȯg, -ˌläg\ *noun* (1684)
1 : a large log at the back of a hearth fire
2 : an accumulation of tasks unperformed or materials not processed

²**backlog** *verb* (1963)
: ACCUMULATE

back matter *noun* (1947)
: matter following the main text of a book

back mutation *noun* (1939)
: mutation of a previously mutated gene to its former condition

back of *preposition* (1694)
: BEHIND

back of beyond (1816)
: a remote place

back off *intransitive verb* (1938)
: BACK DOWN

back–office \ˈbak-ˈä-fəs, -ˈȯ-fəs\ *adjective* (1953)
: of or relating to the inner workings of a business or institution : INTERNAL ⟨*back-office* operations⟩

back out *intransitive verb* (1807)
: to withdraw especially from a commitment or contest

¹**back·pack** \ˈbak-ˌpak\ *noun* (1914)
1 a : a load carried on the back **b** : a camping pack (as of canvas or nylon) supported by a usually aluminum frame and carried on the back
2 : a piece of equipment designed for use while being carried on the back

²**backpack** (1927)
transitive verb
: to carry (food or equipment) on the back especially in hiking
intransitive verb
: to hike with a backpack
— **back·pack·er** *noun*

back·ped·al \ˈbak-ˌpe-d°l\ *intransitive verb* (1901)
: to retreat or move backward

back·rest \-ˌrest\ *noun* (1859)
: a rest for the back

back·room \ˈbak-ˈrüm, -ˈrùm\ *adjective* (1940)
: made or operating in an inconspicuous way : BEHIND-THE-SCENES ⟨*backroom* deals⟩ ⟨a *backroom* politician⟩

back room *noun* (1592)
1 : a room situated in the rear
2 : the meeting place of a directing group that exercises its authority in an inconspicuous and indirect way

back·saw \ˈbak-ˌsȯ\ *noun* (circa 1877)
: a saw with a metal rib along its back

back·scat·ter \-ˌska-tər\ *or* **back·scat·ter·ing** \-tə-riŋ\ *noun* (1940)
: the scattering of radiation or particles in a direction opposite to that of the incident radiation due to reflection from particles of the medium traversed; *also* : the radiation or particles so reversed in direction
— **backscatter** *transitive verb*

back–scratch·ing \ˈbak-ˌskra-chiŋ\ *noun* (1924)
: the reciprocal exchange of favors, services, assistance, or praise

back·seat \-ˈsēt\ *noun* (1829)
1 : a seat in the back (as of an automobile)
2 : an inferior position ⟨won't take a *backseat* to anyone⟩

back·set \ˈbak-ˌset\ *noun* (1721)
: SETBACK

back·side \-ˈsīd\ *noun* (circa 1500)
: BUTTOCKS — often used in plural

back·slap \-ˌslap\ (1926)
transitive verb
: to display excessive or effusive goodwill for
intransitive verb
: to express excessive cordiality or goodwill
— **backslap** *noun*
— **back·slap·per** *noun*

back·slide \-ˌslīd\ *intransitive verb* **-slid** \-ˌslid\; **-slid** *or* **-slid·den** \-ˌsli-d°n\; **-slid·ing** \-ˌslī-diŋ\ (1581)
1 : to lapse morally or in the practice of religion
2 : to revert to a worse condition : RETROGRESS
— **back·slid·er** \-ˌslī-dər\ *noun*

back·space \-ˌspās\ *intransitive verb* (1911)
: to move back one space in a text with each depression of a key
— **backspace** *noun*

back·spin \-ˌspin\ *noun* (circa 1909)
: a backward rotary motion of a ball

back·splash \ˈbak-ˌsplash\ *noun* (1947)
: a vertical surface (as of tiles) designed to protect the wall behind a stove or countertop

back·stab·bing \-ˌsta-biŋ\ *noun* (1946)
: betrayal (as by a verbal attack against one not present) especially by a false friend
— **back·stab** \-ˌstab\ *verb*
— **back·stab·ber** \-ˌsta-bər\ *noun*

¹**back·stage** \ˈbak-ˈstāj\ *adjective* (1916)
1 : of, relating to, or occurring in the area behind the proscenium and especially in the dressing rooms
2 : of or relating to the private lives of theater people
3 : of or relating to the inner working or operation (as of an organization)

²**back·stage** \ˈbak-ˈstāj\ *adverb* (1923)
1 : in or to a backstage area
2 : in private : SECRETLY

back·stairs \-ˌstarz, -ˌsterz\ *adjective* (1663)
1 : SECRET, FURTIVE ⟨*backstairs* political deals⟩
2 : SORDID, SCANDALOUS ⟨*backstairs* gossip⟩

back·stay \-ˌstā\ *noun* (1626)
1 : a stay extending from the mastheads to the side of a ship and slanting aft
2 : a strengthening or supporting device at the back (as of a carriage or a shoe)

back·stitch \-ˌstich\ *noun* (1611)
: a stitch sewn one stitch length backward on the front side and two stitch lengths forward on the reverse side to form a solid line of stitching on both sides
— **backstitch** *verb*

¹**back·stop** \-ˌstäp\ *noun* (1851)
1 : something at the back serving as a stop: as **a** : a screen or fence for keeping a ball from leaving the field of play **b** : a stop (as a pawl) that prevents a backward movement (as of a wheel)
2 : a player (as the catcher) positioned behind the batter

²**backstop** *transitive verb* (1941)
1 : SUPPORT, BOLSTER
2 : to serve as a backstop to

back·street \ˈbak-ˌstrēt\ *noun* (15th century)
: a street away from the main thoroughfares

back·stretch \ˈbak-ˌstrech\ *noun* (1839)
: the side opposite the homestretch on a racecourse

back·stroke \-ˌstrōk\ *noun* (1879)
: a swimming stroke executed on the back and usually consisting of alternating circular arm pulls and a flutter kick

back·swept \-ˌswept\ *adjective* (circa 1918)
: swept or slanting backward

back swimmer *noun* (1862)
: an aquatic bug (family Notonectidae) that swims on its back

back·swing \ˈbak-ˌswiŋ\ *noun* (1899)
: the movement of a club, racket, bat, or arm backward to a position from which the forward or downward swing is made

back·sword \-ˌsōrd, -ˌsȯrd\ *noun* (1609)
: a single-edged sword

back talk *noun* (1858)
: impudent, insolent, or argumentative replies

back–to–back *adjective or adverb* (15th century)
1 : facing in opposite directions and often touching
2 : coming one after the other : CONSECUTIVE

back·track \ˈbak-ˌtrak\ *intransitive verb* (1904)

1 a : to retrace one's course **b** : to go back to an earlier point in a sequence
2 : to reverse a position

back·up \-ˌəp\ *noun, often attributive* (1951)
1 a : one that serves as a substitute or support ⟨a *backup* plan⟩ **b** : musical accompaniment
2 : an accumulation caused by a stoppage in the flow ⟨traffic *backup*⟩
3 : the act or an instance of backing up a computer's hard disk

back up (1837)
intransitive verb
: to accumulate in a congested state ⟨traffic *backed up* for miles⟩
transitive verb
1 : to move into a position behind (a teammate) in order to assist on a play
2 : HOLD BACK 1
3 : to make copies of the computer files on a hard disk) to protect against loss of data

¹**back·ward** \ˈbak-wərd\ *or* **back·wards** \-wərdz\ *adverb* (14th century)
1 a : toward the back **b** : with the back foremost
2 a : in a reverse or contrary direction or way **b** : toward the past **c** : toward a worse state
— **bend over backward** *or* **lean over backward** : to make extreme efforts (as at concession)

²**backward** *adjective* (14th century)
1 a : directed or turned backward **b** : done or executed backward
2 : DIFFIDENT, SHY
3 : retarded in development
— **back·ward·ly** *adverb*
— **back·ward·ness** *noun*

³**backward** *noun* (1610)
: the part behind or past

back·wash \ˈbak-ˌwȯsh, -ˌwäsh\ *noun* (1876)
1 : a backward flow or movement (as of water or air) produced especially by a propelling force; *also* : the fluid that is moving backward
2 : CONSEQUENCE, AFTERMATH

back·wa·ter \-ˌwȯ-tər, -ˌwä-\ *noun* (1629)
1 a : water backed up in its course by an obstruction, an opposing current, or the tide **b** : a body of water (as an inlet or tributary) that is out of the main current of a larger body
2 : an isolated or backward place or condition

back·woods \-ˈwùdz\ *noun plural but singular or plural in construction, often attributive* (1709)
1 : wooded or partly cleared areas far from cities
2 : a remote or culturally backward area
— **back·woodsy** \-ˈwùd-zē\ *adjective*

back·woods·man \ˌbak-ˈwùdz-mən, ˈbak-ˌ\ *noun* (1774)
: one who lives in the backwoods

back·wrap \-ˌrap\ *noun* (1951)
: a wraparound garment (as a skirt) that fastens in the back

back·yard \-ˈyärd\ *noun* (1659)
1 : an area at the rear of a house
2 : an area that is one's special domain

ba·con \ˈbā-kən\ *noun* [Middle English, from Middle French, of Germanic origin; akin to Old High German *bahho* side of bacon, *bah* back] (14th century)
: a side of a pig cured and smoked

Ba·co·ni·an \bā-ˈkō-nē-ən\ *adjective* (1812)
1 : of, relating to, or characteristic of Francis Bacon or his doctrines
2 : of or relating to those who believe that Francis Bacon wrote the works usually attributed to Shakespeare
— **Baconian** *noun*

bac·ter·emia \ˌbak-tə-ˈrē-mē-ə\ *noun* [New Latin, alteration of *bacteriemia*, from *bacteri-* + *-emia*] (circa 1890)

\ə\ abut	\°\ kitten	\ər\ further	\a\ ash	\ā\ ace	
\ä\ mop, mar	\aù\ out	\ch\ chin	\e\ bet	\ē\ easy	
\g\ go	\i\ hit	\ī\ ice	\j\ job	\ŋ\ sing	\ō\ go
\ȯ\ law	\ȯi\ boy	\th\ thin	\t̠h\ the	\ü\ loot	\ù\ foot
\y\ yet	\zh\ vision	*see also* Guide to Pronunciation			

: the usually transient presence of bacteria in the blood
— **bac·ter·emic** \-mik\ *adjective*
bacteri- or **bacterio-** *combining form* [New Latin *bacterium*]
: bacteria ⟨*bacteriolysis*⟩
bac·te·ria \bak-'tir-ē-ə\ *noun, plural* **-ri·as** [plural of *bacterium*] (1884)
: a group (as a genus, species, or strain) of bacteria — used chiefly in nontechnical writing and in news broadcasts □
bac·te·ri·al \bak-'tir-ē-əl\ *adjective* (1871)
: of, relating to, or caused by bacteria ⟨*bacterial* infection⟩
— **bac·te·ri·al·ly** \-ə-lē\ *adverb*
bac·te·ri·cid·al \bak-,tir-ə-'sī-dᵊl\ *adjective* (1878)
: destroying bacteria
— **bac·te·ri·cid·al·ly** \-dᵊl-ē\ *adverb*
— **bac·te·ri·cide** \-'tir-ə-,sīd\ *noun*
bac·ter·in \'bak-tə-rən\ *noun* (circa 1912)
: a suspension of killed or attenuated bacteria for use as a vaccine
bac·te·rio·chlo·ro·phyll \bak-,tir-ē-ō-'klȯr-ə-,fil, -'klȯr-, -fəl\ *noun* (1938)
: a pyrrole derivative in photosynthetic bacteria related to the chlorophyll of higher plants
bac·te·rio·cin \bak-'tir-ē-ə-sən\ *noun* [International Scientific Vocabulary *bacteri-* + *-cin* (as in *colicin*)] (1954)
: an antibiotic (as colicin) produced by bacteria
bac·te·ri·ol·o·gy \(,)bak-,tir-ē-'ä-lə-jē\ *noun* [International Scientific Vocabulary] (1884)
1 : a science that deals with bacteria and their relations to medicine, industry, and agriculture
2 : bacterial life and phenomena
— **bac·te·ri·o·log·ic** \bak-,tir-ē-ə-'lä-jik\ or **bac·te·ri·o·log·i·cal** \-'lä-ji-kəl\ *adjective*
— **bac·te·ri·o·log·i·cal·ly** \-ji-k(ə-)lē\ *adverb*
— **bac·te·ri·ol·o·gist** \(,)bak-,tir-ē-'ä-lə-jist\ *noun*
bac·te·ri·ol·y·sis \(,)bak-,tir-ē-'ä-lə-səs\ *noun* [New Latin] (1900)
: destruction or lysis of bacterial cells
— **bac·te·ri·o·lyt·ic** \bak-,tir-ē-ə-'li-tik\ *adjective*
bac·te·rio·phage \bak-'tir-ē-ə-,fāj also -,fäzh\ *noun* [International Scientific Vocabulary] (1920)
: a virus that infects bacteria
— **bac·te·ri·oph·a·gy** \(,)bak-,tir-ē-'ä-fə-jē\ *noun*
bac·te·rio·rho·dop·sin \bak-,tir-ē-ə-rō-'däp-sin\ *noun* (1974)
: a purple-pigmented protein found in the outer membrane of a bacterium (*Halobacterium halobium*) that converts light energy into chemical energy in the synthesis of ATP
bac·te·rio·sta·sis \bak-,tir-ē-ō-'stā-səs\ *noun* [New Latin] (1920)
: inhibition of the growth of bacteria without destruction
bac·te·rio·stat \-'tir-ē-ō-,stat\ *noun* (1920)
: an agent that causes bacteriostasis
— **bac·te·rio·stat·ic** \-,tir-ē-ō-'sta-tik\ *adjective*
bac·te·ri·um \bak-'tir-ē-əm\ *noun, plural* **-ria** \-ē-ə\ [New Latin, from Greek *baktērion* staff] (circa 1849)
: any of a group (as Kingdom Procaryotae or Kingdom Monera) of prokaryotic unicellular round, spiral, or rod-shaped single-celled microorganisms that are often aggregated into colonies or motile by means of flagella, that live in soil, water, organic matter, or the bodies of plants and animals, and that are autotrophic, saprophytic, or parasitic in nutrition and important because of their biochemical effects and pathogenicity
bac·te·ri·uria \bak-,tir-ē-'yu̇r-ē-ə\ *noun* [New Latin] (1900)
: the presence of bacteria in the urine

bac·te·rize \'bak-tə-,rīz\ *transitive verb* **-rized; -riz·ing** (1914)
: to subject to bacterial action
— **bac·te·ri·za·tion** \,bak-tə-rə-'zā-shən\ *noun*
bac·te·roid \'bak-tə-,rȯid\ *noun* (1878)
: an irregularly shaped bacterium (as a rhizobium) found especially in root nodules of legumes
Bac·tri·an camel \'bak-trē-ən-\ *noun* (1609)
: CAMEL 1b
¹**bad** \'bad\ *adjective* **worse** \'wərs\; **worst** \'wərst\ [Middle English] (14th century)
1 a : failing to reach an acceptable standard : POOR **b** : UNFAVORABLE ⟨make a *bad* impression⟩ **c** : not fresh : SPOILED ⟨*bad* fish⟩ **d** : not sound : DILAPIDATED ⟨the house was in *bad* condition⟩
2 a : morally objectionable **b** : MISCHIEVOUS, DISOBEDIENT
3 : inadequate or unsuited to a purpose ⟨a *bad* plan⟩ ⟨*bad* lighting⟩
4 : DISAGREEABLE, UNPLEASANT ⟨*bad* news⟩
5 a : INJURIOUS, HARMFUL **b** : SERIOUS, SEVERE ⟨in *bad* trouble⟩ ⟨a *bad* cough⟩
6 : INCORRECT, FAULTY ⟨*bad* grammar⟩
7 a : suffering pain or distress ⟨felt generally *bad*⟩ **b** : UNHEALTHY, DISEASED ⟨*bad* teeth⟩
8 : SORROWFUL, SORRY
9 : INVALID, VOID ⟨a *bad* check⟩
10 bad·der; bad·dest *slang* **a** : GOOD, GREAT **b** : TOUGH, MEAN
— **bad·ness** *noun*
²**bad** *noun* (15th century)
1 : something that is bad
2 : an evil or unhappy state
³**bad** *adverb* (1681)
: BADLY □
¹**bad·ass** \-,as\ *adjective* (1956)
: ready to cause or get into trouble : MEAN — often considered vulgar
²**badass** *noun* (1984)
: a person who is badass — often considered vulgar
bad blood *noun* (1825)
: ill feeling : BITTERNESS
bad·die or **bad·dy** \'ba-dē\ *noun, plural* **baddies** (1937)
: one that is bad; *especially* : an opponent of the hero (as in fiction or motion pictures)
bade *past and past participle of* BID
badge \'baj\ *noun* [Middle English *bage, bagge*] (14th century)
1 : a device or token especially of membership in a society or group
2 : a characteristic mark
3 : an emblem awarded for a particular accomplishment
— **badge** *transitive verb*
¹**bad·ger** \'ba-jər\ *noun* [probably from *badge*; from the white mark on its forehead] (1523)
1 a : any of various burrowing mammals (especially *Taxidea taxus* and *Meles meles*) that are related to the weasels and are widely distributed in the northern hemisphere **b** : the pelt or fur of a badger
2 *capitalized* : a native or resident of Wisconsin — used as a nickname
²**badger** *transitive verb* [from the sport of baiting badgers] (1794)
: to harass or annoy persistently
synonym *see* BAIT
ba·di·nage \,ba-dᵊn-'äzh\ *noun* [French] (circa 1658)
: playful repartee : BANTER
bad·land \'bad-,land\ *noun* (1851)
: a region marked by intricate erosional sculpturing, scanty vegetation, and fantastically formed hills — usually used in plural
bad·ly \'bad-lē\ *adverb* (14th century)
1 : in a bad manner ⟨played *badly*⟩
2 : to a great or intense degree ⟨want something *badly*⟩
usage *see* BAD

bad·min·ton \'bad-,min-t³n\ *noun* [*Badminton*, residence of the Duke of Beaufort, England] (1874)
: a court game played with light long-handled rackets and a shuttlecock volleyed over a net
bad—mouth \'bad-,mau̇th, -,mau̇th\ *transitive verb* (1942)
: to criticize severely
bad news *noun plural but singular in construction* (1930)
: one that is troublesome, unwelcome, or dangerous ⟨stay away from him, he's *bad news*⟩
Bae·de·ker \'bā-di-kər, 'be-\ *noun* [Karl *Baedeker* (died 1859) German publisher of guidebooks] (1924)
: GUIDEBOOK
¹**baf·fle** \'ba-fəl\ *transitive verb* **baf·fled; baf·fling** \-f(ə-)liŋ\ [probably alteration of Middle English (Scots) *bawchillen* to denounce, discredit publicly] (circa 1590)
1 : to defeat or check (as a person) by confusing or puzzling : DISCONCERT
2 : to check or break the force or flow of by or as if by a baffle
synonym *see* FRUSTRATE
— **baf·fle·ment** \-fəl-mənt\ *noun*
— **baf·fler** \-f(ə-)lər\ *noun*
— **baf·fling·ly** \'ba-fliŋ-lē\ *adverb*
²**baffle** *noun* (circa 1900)
: a device (as a plate, wall, or screen) to deflect, check, or regulate flow (as of a fluid, light, or sound)
— **baf·fled** \'ba-fəld\ *adjective*

□ USAGE
bacteria *Bacteria* is regularly a plural in scientific and pedagogical use; in speech and in journalism it is also used as a singular ⟨caused by a *bacteria* borne by certain tiny ticks —*Wall Street Journal*⟩ ⟨more resistant to chlorine and elevated water temperatures than other *bacterias* —Allan Bruckheim, M.D., *Chicago Tribune*⟩. This journalistic use is found in British as well as American sources.

bad *Bad* is a 17th century adverb that is not nearly as old as its relatives *bad,* adjective, and *badly,* adverb. It is interchangeable with *badly* in many constructions, and while these constructions are grammatically correct, they are more common in speech than in edited prose ⟨I didn't do too *bad* —Denny McLain⟩ ⟨I wanted to get a mandolin real *bad* —Bill Holt⟩ ⟨the luxurious . . . irresponsibility that is the nicest thing about being *bad* sick —James Jones⟩. After *feel* both *bad* and *badly* are in common use. There are several strands to this mixed usage. Present-day teaching says that *feel* is a linking verb and must be followed by the adjective *bad,* but 19th century teaching said that *bad* referred to morals or behavior and that *badly* should be used for health. Further, some adverbs, like *differently* or *strongly,* are regularly used after *feel;* other adverbs, like *angrily* or *sadly,* are not. And the choice between *feel bad* and *feel badly* is related to the choice between *feel well* and *feel good.* Many people choose *well* for health and *good* for mental state, and many choose *bad* for health and *badly* for mental state ⟨we feel very *badly* about your only having one turkey —James Thurber⟩. But many others do not make that distinction ⟨I feel *bad* about not having written you —E. B. White⟩. So the controversy over *feel bad* and *feel badly* is not as simple as it is often made out to be. The writer will have to make a choice situation by situation, and, whatever that choice is, some people will agree and some will not.

¹**bag** \'bag *also* 'bäg\ *noun* [Middle English *bagge*, from Old Norse *baggi*] (13th century) **1 :** a usually flexible container that may be closed for holding, storing, or carrying something: as **a :** PURSE; *especially* **:** HANDBAG **b :** a bag for game **c :** SUITCASE **2 :** something resembling a bag: as **a :** a pouched or pendulous bodily part or organ; *especially* **:** UDDER **b :** a puffed-out sag or bulge in cloth **c :** a square white stuffed canvas bag to mark a base in baseball **3 :** the amount contained in a bag **4 a :** a quantity of game taken; *also* **:** the maximum legal quantity of game **b :** an assortment or collection especially of nonmaterial things ⟨a *bag* of tricks⟩ **5 :** an unattractive woman **6 :** something one likes or does regularly or well; *also* **:** one's characteristic way of doing things — **in the bag :** SURE, CERTAIN ⟨her nomination was *in the bag*⟩

²**bag** *verb* **bagged; bag·ging** (15th century) *intransitive verb* **1 :** to swell out **:** BULGE **2 :** to hang loosely *transitive verb* **1 :** to cause to swell **2 :** to put into a bag **3 a :** to take (animals) as game **b :** to get possession of especially by strategy or stealth **c :** CAPTURE, SEIZE **d :** to shoot down **:** DESTROY **synonym** see CATCH — **bag·ger** *noun*

ba·gasse \bə-'gas\ *noun* [French] (circa 1826) **:** plant residue (as of sugarcane or grapes) left after a product (as juice) has been extracted

bag·a·telle \,ba-gə-'tel\ *noun* [French, from Italian *bagattella*] (1633) **1 :** TRIFLE 1 **2 :** any of various games involving the rolling of balls into scoring areas **3 :** a short literary or musical piece in light style

ba·gel \'bā-gəl\ *noun* [Yiddish *beygl*, from (assumed) Middle High German *böugel* ring, from Middle High German *bouc* ring, from Old High German; akin to Old English *bēag* ring, *būgan* to bend — more at BOW] (1932) **:** a hard glazed doughnut-shaped roll

bag·ful \'bag-,fül\ *noun* (15th century) **1 :** as much or as many as a bag will hold **2 :** a large number or amount ⟨had a *bagful* of tricks⟩

¹**bag·gage** \'ba-gij\ *noun* [Middle English *bagage*, from Middle French, from *bague* bundle] (15th century) **1 :** suitcases, trunks, and personal belongings of travelers **:** LUGGAGE **2 :** transportable equipment especially of a military force **3 :** things (as objects, circumstances, or beliefs) that get in the way **:** IMPEDIMENTA

²**baggage** *noun* [probably modification of Middle French *bagasse*, from Old Provençal *bagassa*] (1594) **1 :** a contemptible woman; *especially* **:** PROSTITUTE **2 :** a young woman

bag·ging \'ba-giŋ\ *noun* (1732) **:** material (as cloth) for bags

bag·gy \'ba-gē\ *adjective* **bag·gi·er; -est** (1831) **:** loose, puffed out, or hanging like a bag ⟨*baggy* trousers⟩ — **bag·gi·ly** \'ba-gə-lē\ *adverb* — **bag·gi·ness** \'ba-gē-nəs\ *noun*

bag·house \'bag-,haús\ *noun* (1914) **:** a device or facility in which particulates are removed from a stream of exhaust gases (as from a blast furnace) as the stream passes through a large cloth bag; *also* **:** the bag used to filter the gas stream

bag lady *noun* (1979)

: a homeless woman who roams the streets of a large city carrying her possessions in shopping bags

bag·man \'bag-mən\ *noun* (1765) **1** *chiefly British* **:** TRAVELING SALESMAN **2 :** a person who on behalf of another collects or distributes illicitly gained money

ba·gnio \'ban-(,)yō\ *noun, plural* **bagnios** [Italian *bagno*, literally, public baths (from the Turks' use of Roman baths at Constantinople as prisons), from Latin *balneum*, from Greek *balaneion*] (1599) **1** *obsolete* **:** PRISON **2 :** BORDELLO

bag of waters (circa 1881) **:** the double-walled fluid-filled sac that encloses and protects the fetus in the womb and that breaks releasing its fluid during the birth process

bag·pipe \'bag-,pīp\ *noun* (14th century) **:** a wind instrument consisting of a reed melody pipe and from one to five drones with air supplied continuously either by a bag with valve-stopped mouth tube or by bellows — often used in plural — **bag·pip·er** \-,pī-pər\ *noun*

bagpipe

ba·guette \ba-'get\ *noun* [French, literally, rod] (1926) **1 :** a gem having the shape of a narrow rectangle; *also* **:** the shape itself **2 :** a long thin loaf of French bread

bag·wig \'bag-,wig\ *noun* (1717) **:** an 18th century wig with the back hair enclosed in a small silk bag

bag·worm \-,wərm\ *noun* (1862) **:** any of a family (Psychidae) of moths with wingless females and plant-feeding larvae that live in a silk case covered with plant debris; *especially* **:** one (*Thyridopteryx ephemeraeformis*) often destructive to deciduous and evergreen trees of the eastern U.S.

bah \'bä, 'ba\ *interjection* (1600) — used to express disdain or contempt

Ba·ha·i \bä-'hä-,ē, -'hī\ *noun, plural* **Baha·is** [Persian *bahā'ī*, literally, of glory, from *bahā* glory] (1889) **:** an adherent of a religious movement originating in Iran in the 19th century and emphasizing the spiritual unity of mankind — **Baha'i** *adjective* — **Ba·ha·ism** \-'hä-,i-zəm, -'hī-,i-\ *noun* — **Ba·ha·ist** \-'hä-(,)ist\ *noun*

Ba·ha·sa In·do·ne·sia \bə-,hä-sə-,in-də-'nē-zhə, -shə\ *noun* [Indonesian *bahasa indonésia*, literally, Indonesian language] (1952) **:** INDONESIAN 2b

Ba·hia grass \bə-'hē-ə-\ *noun* [*Bahia*, state in Brazil] (circa 1927) **:** a perennial tropical American grass (*Paspalum notatum*) used in the southern U.S. as a lawn grass

baht \'bät\ *noun, plural* **baht** *also* **bahts** [Thai *bàad*] (1828) — see MONEY table

¹**bail** \'bā(ə)l\ *noun* [Middle English *baille*, from Middle French, bucket, from Medieval Latin *bajula* water vessel, from feminine of Latin *bajulus*] (14th century) **:** a container used to remove water from a boat

²**bail** *transitive verb* (1613) **1 :** to clear (water) from a boat by dipping and

throwing over the side — usually used with *out* **2 :** to clear water from by dipping and throwing — usually used with *out* — **bail·er** *noun*

³**bail** *noun* [Middle English, custody, bail, from Middle French, custody, from *baillier* to have in charge, deliver, from Medieval Latin *bajulare* to control, from Latin, to carry a load, from *bajulus* porter] (15th century) **1 :** the temporary release of a prisoner in exchange for security given for the due appearance of the prisoner **2 :** security given for the release of a prisoner on bail **3 :** one who provides bail

⁴**bail** *transitive verb* (1548) **1 :** to release under bail **2 :** to procure the release of by giving bail — often used with *out* **3 :** to help from a predicament — used with *out* ⟨*bailing* out impoverished countries⟩ — **bail·able** *adjective*

⁵**bail** *noun* [Middle English *beil, baile*, probably of Scandinavian origin; akin to Swedish *bygel* bow, hoop; akin to Old English *būgan* to bend — more at BOW] (15th century) **1 a :** a supporting half hoop **b :** a hinged bar for holding paper against the platen of a typewriter **2 :** a usually arched handle (as of a kettle or pail)

⁶**bail** *transitive verb* [Anglo-French *baillier*, from French] (1768) **:** to deliver (personal property) in trust to another for a special purpose and for a limited period

⁷**bail** *noun* [perhaps from ⁵*bail*] (1844) *chiefly British* **:** a device for confining or separating animals

bail·ee \bā-'lē\ *noun* (1528) **:** the person to whom personal property is bailed

bai·ley \'bā-lē\ *noun, plural* **baileys** [Middle English *bailli*, palisade, bailey, from Old French *baille, balie*] (13th century) **1 :** the outer wall of a castle or any of several walls surrounding the keep **2 :** a courtyard within the external wall or between two outer walls of a castle

bai·lie \'bā-lē\ *noun* [Middle English] (14th century) **1** *chiefly dialect* **:** BAILIFF **2 :** a Scottish municipal magistrate corresponding to an English alderman

bai·liff \'bā-ləf\ *noun* [Middle English *baillif, bailie*, from Old French *baillif*, from *bail* custody, jurisdiction — more at BAIL] (14th century) **1 a :** an official employed by a British sheriff to serve writs and make arrests and executions **b :** a minor officer of some U.S. courts usually serving as a messenger or usher **2** *chiefly British* **:** one who manages an estate or farm — **bai·liff·ship** \-,ship\ *noun*

bai·li·wick \'bā-li-,wik\ *noun* [Middle English *baillifwik*, from *baillif* + *wik* dwelling place, village, from Old English *wīc*, from Latin *vicus* village — more at VICINITY] (15th century) **1 :** the office or jurisdiction of a bailiff **2 :** a special domain

bail·ment \'bā(ə)l-mənt\ *noun* (1554) **:** the act of bailing a person or personal property

bail·or \bā-'lór, 'bā-lər\ *or* **bail·er** \'bā-lər\ *noun* (1602)

: a person who delivers personal property to another in trust

bail·out \'bā-ˌlaùt\ *noun* (1951)
: a rescue (as of a corporation) from financial distress

bail out *intransitive verb* (1930)
1 : to parachute from an aircraft
2 : to abandon a harmful or difficult situation; *also* : LEAVE, DEPART

bails·man \'bā(ə)lz-mən\ *noun* (1862)
: one who gives bail for another

bairn \'barn, 'bern\ *noun* [Middle English *bern, barn,* from Old English *bearn* & Old Norse *barn;* akin to Old High German *barn* child] (before 12th century)
chiefly Scottish : CHILD

¹bait \'bāt\ *verb* [Middle English, from Old Norse *beita;* akin to Old English *bǣtan* to bait, *bītan* to bite] (13th century)
transitive verb
1 a : to persecute or exasperate with unjust, malicious, or persistent attacks **b** : TEASE
2 a : to harass (as a chained animal) with dogs usually for sport **b** : to attack by biting and tearing
3 a : to furnish with bait **b** : ENTICE, LURE
4 : to give food and drink to (an animal) especially on the road
intransitive verb
archaic : to stop for food and rest when traveling ☆
— bait·er *noun*

²bait *noun* [Middle English, from Old Norse *beit* pasturage & *beita* food; akin to Old English *bītan* to bite] (14th century)
1 a : something used in luring especially to a hook or trap **b** : a poisonous material placed where it will be eaten by usually wild animals considered undesirable or deleterious
2 : LURE, TEMPTATION

bait and switch *noun* (1967)
: a sales tactic in which a customer is attracted by the advertisement of a low-priced item but is then encouraged to buy a higher-priced one

bai·za \'bī-(ˌ)zä\ *noun, plural* **baiza** *or* **bai·zas** [Arabic, from Hindi *paisā*] (1970)
— see *rial* at MONEY table

baize \'bāz\ *noun* [Middle French *baies,* plural of *baie* baize, from feminine of *bai* bay-colored] (1578)
: a coarse woolen or cotton fabric napped to imitate felt

¹bake \'bāk\ *verb* **baked; bak·ing** [Middle English, from Old English *bacan;* akin to Old High German *bahhan* to bake, Greek *phōgein* to roast] (before 12th century)
transitive verb
1 : to cook (as food) by dry heat especially in an oven
2 : to dry or harden by subjecting to heat
intransitive verb
1 : to prepare food by baking it
2 : to become baked
3 : to become extremely hot
— bak·er *noun*

²bake *noun* (1565)
1 : the act or process of baking
2 : a social gathering at which a baked food is served
3 : baked food ⟨a *bake* sale⟩

Ba·ke·lite \'bā-kə-ˌlīt, -ˌklīt\ *trademark*
— used for any of various synthetic resins and plastics

baker's dozen *noun* (1596)
: THIRTEEN

baker's yeast *noun* (1854)
: a yeast (as *Saccharomyces cerevisiae*) used or suitable for use as leaven

bak·ery \'bā-k(ə-)rē\ *noun, plural* **-er·ies** (circa 1820)
: a place for baking or selling baked goods

bake·shop \'bāk-ˌshäp\ *noun* (1789)
: BAKERY

baking powder *noun* (1850)
: a powder used as a leavening agent in making baked goods (as quick breads) that con-

sists of a carbonate, an acid substance, and starch or flour

baking soda *noun* (1881)
: SODIUM BICARBONATE

bak·la·va \ˌbä-klə-'vä\ *noun* [Turkish] (1653)
: a dessert made of thin pastry, nuts, and honey

bak·sheesh \'bak-ˌshēsh, bak-'\ *noun* [Persian *bakhshīsh,* from *bakhshīdan* to give; akin to Greek *phagein* to eat, Sanskrit *bhajati* he allots] (1775)
: payment (as a tip or bribe) to expedite service

BAL \ˌbē-(ˌ)ā-'el\ *noun* [British Anti-*L*ewisite] (1942)
: DIMERCAPROL

Ba·laam \'bā-ləm\ *noun* [Greek, from Hebrew *Bil'ām*]
: an Old Testament prophet who is reproached by the ass he is riding and rebuked by God's angel while on the way to meet with an enemy of Israel

bal·a·cla·va \ˌba-lə-'klä-və, -'kla-\ *noun* [*Balaclava,* Crimea, where a battle of the Crimean War was fought] (1881)
: a knit cap for the head and neck — called also *balaclava helmet*

bal·a·lai·ka \ˌba-lə-'lī-kə\ *noun* [Russian] (1788)
: a usually 3-stringed instrument of Russian origin with a triangular body played by plucking or strumming

¹bal·ance \'ba-lən(t)s\ *noun* [Middle English, from Old French, from (assumed) Vulgar Latin *bilancia,* from Late Latin *bilanc-, bilanx* having two scalepans, from Latin *bi- + lanc-, lanx* plate] (13th century)
1 : an instrument for weighing: as **a** : a beam that is supported freely in the center and has two pans of equal weight suspended from its ends **b** : a device that uses the elasticity of a spiral spring for measuring weight or force **c** *capitalized* : LIBRA
2 : a means of judging or deciding
3 : a counterbalancing weight, force, or influence
4 : an oscillating wheel operating with a hairspring to regulate the movement of a timepiece
5 a : stability produced by even distribution of weight on each side of the vertical axis **b** : equipoise between contrasting, opposing, or interacting elements **c** : equality between the totals of the two sides of an account
6 a : an aesthetically pleasing integration of elements **b** : the juxtaposition in writing of syntactically parallel constructions containing similar or contrasting ideas
7 a : physical equilibrium **b** : the ability to retain one's balance
8 a : weight or force of one side in excess of another **b** : something left over : REMAINDER **c** : an amount in excess especially on the credit side of an account
9 : mental and emotional steadiness
— bal·anced \-lən(t)st\ *adjective*
— in the balance *or* **in balance** : with the fate or outcome about to be determined
— on balance : with all things considered

²balance *verb* **bal·anced; bal·anc·ing** (1588)
transitive verb
1 a (1) : to compute the difference between the debits and credits of (an account) (2) : to pay the amount due on : SETTLE **b** (1) : to arrange so that one set of elements exactly equals another ⟨*balance* a mathematical equa-

balalaika

tion⟩ (2) : to complete (a chemical equation) so that the same number of atoms and electric charges of each kind appears on each side
2 a : COUNTERBALANCE, OFFSET **b** : to equal or equalize in weight, number, or proportion
3 : to weigh in or as if in a balance
4 a : to bring to a state or position of equipoise **b** : to poise in or as if in balance **c** : to bring into harmony or proportion
intransitive verb
1 : to become balanced or established in balance
2 : to be an equal counterpoise
3 : WAVER 1 ⟨*balances* and temporizes on matters that demand action⟩

balance beam *noun* (circa 1949)
1 : a narrow wooden beam supported in a horizontal position approximately four feet above the floor and used for balancing feats in gymnastics
2 : an event in gymnastics competition in which the balance beam is used

balance of payments (1844)
: a summary of the international transactions of a country or region over a period of time including commodity and service transactions, capital transactions, and gold movements

balance of power (1701)
: an equilibrium of power sufficient to discourage or prevent one nation or party from imposing its will on or interfering with the interests of another

balance of trade (1668)
: the difference in value over a period of time between a country's imports and exports

bal·anc·er \'ba-lən(t)-sər\ *noun* (15th century)
: one that balances; *specifically* : HALTERE

balance sheet *noun* (circa 1771)
: a statement of financial condition at a given date

balance wheel *noun* (1669)
1 : a wheel that regulates or stabilizes the motion of a mechanism
2 : a balancing or stabilizing force

balancing act *noun* (1954)
: an attempt to cope with several often conflicting factors or situations at the same time

Ba·lante \bə-'länt\ *noun, plural* **Balante** *or* **Balantes** [French, from Balante *Bulanda*] (circa 1895)
1 : a member of a people of Senegal and Guinea-Bissau
2 : the language of the Balante people

bal·as \'ba-ləs\ *noun* [Middle English, from Middle French *balais,* from Arabic *balakhsh,* from *Balakhshān,* ancient region of Afghanistan] (15th century)
: a ruby spinel of a pale rose-red or orange

ba·la·ta \bə-'lä-tə\ *noun* [Spanish, from Carib] (1860)
: a substance like gutta-percha that is the dried juice of tropical American trees (especially *Manilkara bidentata*) of the sapodilla family and is used especially in belting and golf balls; *also* : a tree yielding it

☆ **SYNONYMS**
Bait, badger, heckle, hector, chivy, hound mean to harass by efforts to break down. BAIT implies wanton cruelty or delight in persecuting a helpless victim ⟨*baited* the chained dog⟩. BADGER implies pestering so as to drive a person to confusion or frenzy ⟨*badgered* her father for a car⟩. HECKLE implies persistent annoying or belligerent interruptions of a speaker ⟨drunks *heckled* the stand-up comic⟩. HECTOR carries an implication of bullying and domineering ⟨football players *hectored* by their coach⟩. CHIVY suggests persecution by teasing or nagging ⟨*chivied* the new student mercilessly⟩. HOUND implies unrelenting pursuit and harassing ⟨*hounded* by creditors⟩.

bal·boa \bal-'bō-ə\ *noun* [Spanish, from Vasco Núñez de *Balboa*] (circa 1909)
— see MONEY table

bal·brig·gan \bal-'bri-gən\ *noun* [*Balbriggan*, town in Ireland] (1885)
: a knitted cotton fabric used especially for underwear or hosiery

bal·co·ny \'bal-kə-nē\ *noun, plural* **-nies** [Italian *balcone*, from Old Italian, large window, of Germanic origin; akin to Old High German *balko* beam — more at BALK] (1618)
1 : a platform that projects from the wall of a building and is enclosed by a parapet or railing
2 : an interior projecting gallery in a public building (as a theater)
— **bal·co·nied** \-nēd\ *adjective*

¹bald \'bȯld\ *adjective* [Middle English *balled*; probably akin to Danish *bældet* bald, Latin *fulica* coot, Greek *phalios* having a white spot] (14th century)
1 a : lacking a natural or usual covering (as of hair, vegetation, or nap) **b** : having little or no tread ⟨*bald* tires⟩
2 : UNADORNED
3 : UNDISGUISED, PALPABLE
4 : marked with white
synonym see BARE
— **bald·ish** \'bȯl-dish\ *adjective*
— **bald·ly** \'bȯl(d)-lē\ *adverb*
— **bald·ness** \'bȯl(d)-nəs\ *noun*

²bald (1602)
transitive verb
: to make bald
intransitive verb
: to become bald

bal·da·chin \'bȯl-də-kən, 'bal-\ *or* **bal·da·chi·no** \,bal-də-'kē-(,)nō, ,bäl-\ *noun, plural* **baldachins** *or* **baldachinos** [Italian *baldacchino*, from *Baldacco* Baghdad, Iraq] (1537)
1 : a cloth canopy fixed or carried over an important person or a sacred object
2 : a rich embroidered fabric of silk and gold
3 : an ornamental structure resembling a canopy used especially over an altar

bald cypress *noun* (1709)
1 : either of two large swamp trees (*Taxodium distichum* and *T. ascendens* of the family Taxodiaceae, the bald cypress family) of the southern U.S. that are related to the sequoias
2 : the hard red wood of bald cypress that is much used for shingles

bald eagle *noun* (1688)
: an eagle (*Haliaeetus leucocephalus*) of North America that is brown when young with white only on the undersides of the wings but in full adult plumage has white head and neck feathers and a white tail

bald eagle

Bal·der \'bȯl-dər\ *noun* [Old Norse *Baldr*]
: the son of Odin and Frigga and Norse god of light and peace slain through the trickery of Loki by a mistletoe sprig

bal·der·dash \'bȯl-dər-,dash\ *noun* [origin unknown] (1674)
: NONSENSE

bald–faced \'bȯl(d)-'fāst\ *adjective* (1943)
: BAREFACED

bald·head \'bȯld-,hed\ *noun* (1535)
: a bald-headed person

balding *adjective* (1938)
: getting bald ⟨bespectacled and *balding*⟩

bald·pate \'bȯl(d)-,pāt\ *noun* (1592)
1 : BALDHEAD
2 : a North American wigeon (*Anas americana*) with a large white patch on each wing and in the male a white crown

bal·dric \'bȯl-drik\ *noun* [Middle English *baudry*, *baudrik*, from Middle French *baudré*, from Old French *baldrei*] (14th century)
: an often ornamented belt worn over one shoulder to support a sword or bugle

¹bale \'bā(ə)l\ *noun* [Middle English, from Old English *bealu*; akin to Old High German *balo* evil, Old Church Slavonic *bolĭ* sick person] (before 12th century)
1 : great evil
2 : WOE, SORROW

²bale *noun* [Middle English, from Middle French, of Germanic origin; akin to Old High German *balla* ball] (14th century)
: a large bundle of goods; *specifically* : a large closely pressed package of merchandise bound and usually wrapped ⟨a *bale* of paper⟩ ⟨a *bale* of hay⟩

³bale *transitive verb* **baled; bal·ing** (1760)
: to make up into a bale
— **bal·er** *noun*

ba·leen \bə-'lēn, 'ba-,lēn\ *noun* [Middle English *baleine* whale, baleen, from Latin *balaena* whale; akin to Greek *phallaina* whale] (14th century)
: a horny substance found in two rows of plates from 2 to 12 feet long attached along the upper jaws of baleen whales

baleen whale *noun* (1874)
: any of a suborder (Mysticeti) of usually large whales lacking teeth but having baleen which is used to filter chiefly small marine crustaceans (as krill) out of large quantities of seawater

bale·fire \'bā(ə)l-,fīr\ *noun* [Middle English, from Old English *bǣlfȳr* funeral fire, from *bǣl* pyre + *fȳr* fire] (before 12th century)
: an outdoor fire often used as a signal fire

bale·ful \-fəl\ *adjective* (before 12th century)
1 : deadly or pernicious in influence
2 : foreboding evil : OMINOUS
synonym see SINISTER
— **bale·ful·ly** \-fə-lē\ *adverb*
— **bale·ful·ness** \-fəl-nəs\ *noun*

Ba·li·nese \,bä-li-'nēz, ,ba-, -'nēs\ *noun* [Dutch *Balinees*, from *Bali* island of Indonesia] (1967)
: any of a breed of slender long-haired cats that originated as a spontaneous mutation of the Siamese

¹balk \'bȯk\ *noun* [Middle English *balke*, from Old English *balca*; akin to Old High German *balko* beam, Latin *fulcire* to prop, Greek *phalanx* log, phalanx] (before 12th century)
1 : a ridge of land left unplowed as a dividing line or through carelessness
2 : BEAM, RAFTER
3 : HINDRANCE, CHECK
4 a : the space behind the balkline on a billiard table **b** : any of the outside divisions made by the balklines
5 : failure of a player to complete a motion; *especially* : an illegal motion of the pitcher in baseball while in position

²balk (15th century)
transitive verb
1 *archaic* : to pass over or by
2 : to check or stop by or as if by an obstacle : BLOCK
intransitive verb
1 : to stop short and refuse to proceed
2 : to refuse abruptly — used with *at*
3 : to commit a balk in sports
synonym see FRUSTRATE
— **balk·er** *noun*

bal·kan·ize \'bȯl-kə-,nīz\ *transitive verb* **-ized; -iz·ing** *often capitalized* [*Balkan* Peninsula] (1919)
: to break up (as a region or group) into smaller and often hostile units
— **bal·kan·i·za·tion** \,bȯl-kə-nə-'zā-shən\ *noun, often capitalized*

balk·line \'bȯk-,klīn\ *noun* (1839)
1 : a line across a billiard table near one end behind which the cue balls are placed in making opening shots
2 a : one of four lines parallel to the cushions of a billiard table dividing it into nine compartments **b** : a billiards game that sets restrictions in scoring caroms according to these lines

balky \'bȯ-kē\ *adjective* **balk·i·er; -est** (1847)
: refusing or likely to refuse to proceed, act, or function as directed or expected ⟨a *balky* mule⟩
synonym see CONTRARY
— **balk·i·ness** *noun*

¹ball \'bȯl\ *noun, often attributive* [Middle English *bal*, from Old Norse *bǫllr*; akin to Old English *bealluc* testis, Old High German *balla* ball, Old English *blāwan* to blow] (13th century)
1 : a round or roundish body or mass: as **a** : a spherical or ovoid body used in a game or sport **b** : EARTH, GLOBE **c** : a spherical or conical projectile; *also* : projectiles used in firearms **d** : a roundish protuberant anatomic structure; *especially* : the rounded eminence at the base of the thumb or big toe
2 a : TESTIS — often considered vulgar **b** *plural* (1) : NONSENSE — often used interjectionally; often considered vulgar (2) : NERVE 3 — often considered vulgar
3 : a game in which a ball is thrown, kicked, or struck; *also* : the quality of play in such a game
4 a : a pitch not swung at by the batter that fails to pass through the strike zone **b** : a hit or thrown ball in various games ⟨foul *ball*⟩
— **on the ball 1** : COMPETENT, KNOWLEDGEABLE, ALERT ⟨the other introductory essay . . . is much more *on the ball* —*Times Literary Supplement*⟩ ⟨keep *on the ball*⟩ **2** : of ability or competence ⟨if the teacher has something *on the ball*, the pupils won't squirm much —*New Yorker*⟩

²ball (1658)
transitive verb
1 : to form or gather into a ball ⟨*balled* the paper into a wad⟩
2 : to have sexual intercourse with — usually considered vulgar
intransitive verb
1 : to form or gather into a ball
2 : to engage in sexual intercourse — usually considered vulgar

³ball *noun* [French *bal*, from Old French, from *baller* to dance, from Late Latin *ballare*, from Greek *ballizein*] (circa 1639)
1 : a large formal gathering for social dancing
2 : a very pleasant experience : a good time ⟨had a *ball* on their vacation⟩

bal·lad \'ba-ləd\ *noun* [Middle English *balade* ballade, song, from Middle French, from Old Provençal *balada* dance, song sung while dancing, from *balar* to dance, from Late Latin *ballare*] (14th century)
1 a : a narrative composition in rhythmic verse suitable for singing **b** : an art song accompanying a traditional ballad
2 : a simple song : AIR
3 : a popular song; *especially* : a slow romantic or sentimental song
— **bal·lad·ic** \bə-'la-dik, ba-\ *adjective*

bal·lade \bə-'läd, ba-\ *noun* [Middle English *balade*, from Middle French, ballad, ballade] (14th century)

\ə\ abut	\ᵊ\ kitten	\ər\ further	\a\ ash	\ā\ ace	
\ä\ mop, mar	\au̇\ out	\ch\ chin	\e\ bet	\ē\ easy	
\g\ go	\i\ hit	\ī\ ice	\j\ job	\ŋ\ sing	\ō\ go
\ȯ\ law	\ȯi\ boy	\th\ thin	\t͟h\ the	\ü\ loot	\u̇\ foot
\y\ yet	\zh\ vision	see also Guide to Pronunciation			

1 : a fixed verse form consisting usually of three stanzas with recurrent rhymes, an envoi, and an identical refrain for each part
2 : a musical composition usually for piano suggesting the epic ballad
bal·lad·eer \ˌba-lə-'dir\ *noun* (1830)
: a singer of ballads
bal·lad·ist \'ba-lə-dist\ *noun* (1858)
: one who writes or sings ballads
bal·lad·ry \'ba-lə-drē\ *noun* (1596)
1 : the composing or performing of ballads
2 : BALLADS
ballad stanza *noun* (circa 1934)
: a stanza consisting of four lines with the first and third lines unrhymed iambic tetrameters and the second and fourth lines rhymed iambic trimeters
ball–and–socket joint *noun* (1809)
1 : a joint in which a ball moves within a socket so as to allow rotary motion in every direction within certain limits
2 : an articulation (as the hip joint) in which the rounded head of one bone fits into a cuplike cavity of the other and admits movement in any direction

ball-and-socket joint 1

¹**bal·last** \'ba-ləst\ *noun* [probably from Low German, of Scandinavian origin; akin to Danish & Swedish *barlast* ballast; perhaps akin to Old English *bær* bare & to Old English *hlæst* load, *hladan* to load — more at LADE] (1530)
1 : a heavy substance used to improve the stability and control the draft of a ship or the ascent of a balloon
2 : something that gives stability (as in character or conduct)
3 : gravel or broken stone laid in a railroad bed or used in making concrete
4 : a device used to provide the starting voltage or to stabilize the current in a circuit (as of a fluorescent lamp)
— in ballast *of a ship* : having only ballast for a load
²**ballast** *transitive verb* (1538)
1 : to steady or equip with or as if with ballast
2 : to fill in (as a railroad bed) with ballast
ball bearing *noun* (1883)
: a bearing in which the journal turns upon loose hardened steel balls that roll easily in a race; *also* : one of the balls in such a bearing
ball boy *noun* (1903)
: a male tennis court attendant who retrieves balls for the players
ball·car·ri·er \'bȯl-ˌkar-ē-ər\ *noun* (1935)
: the football player carrying the ball on an offensive play
ball cock *noun* (1790)
: an automatic valve whose opening and closing are controlled by a spherical float at the end of a lever
ball control *noun* (1928)
: an offensive strategy (as in football) in which a team tries to maintain possession of the ball for extended periods of time
bal·le·ri·na \ˌba-lə-'rē-nə\ *noun* [Italian, from *ballare* to dance, from Late Latin] (1815)
: a woman who is a ballet dancer : DANSEUSE
bal·let \'ba-ˌlā, ba-'\ *noun* [French, from Italian *balletto*, diminutive of *ballo* dance, from *ballare*] (1634)
1 a : a theatrical art form using dancing, music, and scenery to convey a story, theme, or atmosphere **b :** dancing in which conventional poses and steps are combined with light flowing figures (as leaps and turns)
2 : music for a ballet
3 : a group that performs ballets
— bal·let·ic \ba-'le-tik\ *adjective*
bal·let·o·mane \ba-'le-tə-ˌmān\ *noun* [*ballet* + *-o-* + *-mane* (from *mania*)] (1930)
: a devotee of ballet

— bal·let·o·ma·nia \-ˌle-tə-'mā-nē-ə, -nyə\ *noun*
ball–flow·er \'bȯl-ˌflaů(-ə)r\ *noun* (1845)
: an architectural ornament consisting of a ball in the flower-shaped hollow of a circular mold
ball game *noun* (1848)
1 : a game played with a ball
2 a : a set of circumstances : SITUATION ⟨a whole new *ball game*⟩ **b :** CONTEST 1
ball girl *noun* (1926)
: a female tennis court attendant who retrieves balls for the players
ball handler *noun* (1948)
: a player who controls the ball in any of various games; *especially* : a player who is skilled at handling the ball (as in basketball)
— ball·han·dling *noun*
bal·lis·ta \bə-'lis-tə\ *noun, plural* **-tae** \-ˌtē\ [Latin, from (assumed) Greek *ballistēs*, from *ballein* to throw — more at DEVIL] (14th century)
: an ancient military engine often in the form of a crossbow for hurling large missiles
bal·lis·tic \bə-'lis-tik\ *adjective* [Latin *ballista*] (circa 1775)
1 : of or relating to ballistics or to a body in motion according to the laws of ballistics
2 : suddenly and extremely upset or angry : WILD — usually used with *go*
— bal·lis·ti·cal·ly \-ti-k(ə-)lē\ *adverb*
ballistic missile *noun* (1954)
: a missile guided in the ascent of a high-arch trajectory and freely falling in the descent
bal·lis·tics \bə-'lis-tiks\ *noun plural but singular or plural in construction* (circa 1753)
1 a : the science of the motion of projectiles in flight **b :** the flight characteristics of a projectile
2 a : the study of the processes within a firearm as it is fired **b :** the firing characteristics of a firearm or cartridge
ball joint *noun* (circa 1884)
: BALL-AND-SOCKET JOINT 1
ball lightning *noun* (1857)
: a rare form of lightning consisting of luminous balls that may move along solid objects or float in the air
ball mill *noun* (1903)
: a pulverizing machine consisting of a rotating drum which contains pebbles or metal balls as the grinding implements
ball of fire (circa 1900)
: a person of unusual energy, vitality, or drive
ball of wax (circa 1953)
: AFFAIR, CONCERN ⟨the whole *ball of wax*⟩
bal·lon \ba-'lō^n\ *noun* [French, literally, balloon] (1830)
: lightness of movement that exaggerates the duration of a ballet dancer's jump
bal·lo·net \ˌba-lə-'nā\ *noun* [French *ballonnet*, diminutive of *ballon*] (1902)
: a compartment of variable volume within the interior of a balloon or airship used to control ascent and descent
¹**bal·loon** \bə-'lün\ *noun* [French *ballon* large football, balloon, from Italian dialect *ballone* large football, augmentative of *balla* ball, of Germanic origin] (1783)
1 : a nonporous bag of tough light material filled with heated air or a gas lighter than air so as to rise and float in the atmosphere
2 : an inflatable bag (as of rubber) usually used as a toy or for decoration
3 : the outline enclosing words spoken or thought by a figure especially in a cartoon
²**balloon** *adjective* (circa 1786)
1 : relating to, resembling, or suggesting a balloon ⟨a *balloon* sleeve⟩
2 : being or having a final installment that is much larger than preceding ones in a term or installment note
³**balloon** (1841)
intransitive verb
1 : to swell or puff out : EXPAND ⟨*ballooned* to 200 pounds⟩
2 : to ascend or travel in a balloon

3 : to increase rapidly
transitive verb
: INFLATE, INCREASE
balloon angioplasty *noun* (1980)
: dilatation of an atherosclerotically obstructed artery by the passage of a balloon catheter through the vessel to the area of disease where inflation of the catheter compresses the plaque against the vessel wall
balloon catheter *noun* (1961)
: a catheter with an inflatable tip that is used especially to measure blood pressure in a blood vessel or to expand a partly closed or obstructed bodily passage or tube (as a coronary artery)
bal·loon·ing \bə-'lü-niŋ\ *noun* (1784)
: the act or sport of riding in a balloon
bal·loon·ist \-nist\ *noun* (1784)
: a person who rides in a balloon
balloon tire *noun* (1923)
: a low-pressure pneumatic tire with a flexible carcass and large cross section designed to provide cushioning
balloon vine *noun* (1836)
: a tropical American vine (*Cardiospermum halicacabum*) of the soapberry family bearing large ornamental pods
¹**bal·lot** \'ba-lət\ *noun* [Italian *ballotta*, from Italian dialect, diminutive of *balla* ball] (1549)
1 a : a small ball used in secret voting **b :** a sheet of paper used to cast a secret vote
2 a : the action or system of secret voting **b :** the right to vote **c :** VOTE 1a
3 : the number of votes cast
4 : the drawing of lots ◇
²**ballot** *intransitive verb* (1580)
: to vote or decide by ballot
— bal·lot·er *noun*
ballot box *noun* (circa 1680)
1 : a box for receiving ballots
2 : BALLOT 2a
¹**ball·park** \'bȯl-ˌpärk\ *noun* (1899)
1 : a park in which ball games (as baseball) are played
2 : a range (as of prices or views) within which comparison or compromise is possible
— in the ballpark : approximately correct
²**ballpark** *adjective* [from the expression *in the ballpark*] (1967)
: approximately correct ⟨a *ballpark* figure⟩
ball·play·er \'bȯl-ˌplā-ər\ *noun* (1619)
: a person who plays ball; *especially* : a baseball player
ball·point \-ˌpȯint\ *noun* (1953)
: a pen having as the writing point a small rotating metal ball that inks itself by contact with an inner magazine
ball·room \'bȯl-ˌrüm, -ˌrům\ *noun* (1736)
: a large room used for dances

balls–up \'bȯl-ˌzəp\ *noun* (1939)
British : FOUL-UP
ball·sy \'bȯl-zē\ *adjective* **ball·si·er; -est**
[¹*ball*] (1959)
: aggressively tough : GUTSY — sometimes considered vulgar
ball up (1885)
transitive verb
: to make a mess of : CONFUSE, MUDDLE
intransitive verb
: to become badly muddled or confused
ball valve *noun* (1839)
: a valve in which a ball regulates the aperture by its rise and fall due to fluid pressure, a spring, or its own weight
bally \'ba-lē\ *adjective or adverb* [euphemism for *bloody,* adjective, adverb] (1885)
British — used as an intensive
bal·ly·hoo \'ba-lē-ˌhü\ *noun, plural* **-hoos** [origin unknown] (1901)
1 : a noisy attention-getting demonstration or talk
2 : flamboyant, exaggerated, or sensational advertising or propaganda
— **ballyhoo** *transitive verb*
bal·ly·rag \-ˌrag\ *variant of* BULLYRAG
balm \'bä(l)m, *New England also* 'bäm\ *noun* [Middle English *basme, baume,* from Old French, from Latin *balsamum* balsam] (13th century)
1 : a balsamic resin; *especially* : one from small tropical evergreen trees (genus *Commiphora* of the family Burseraceae)
2 : an aromatic preparation (as a healing ointment)
3 : any of several aromatic plants of the mint family; *especially* : LEMON BALM
4 : a spicy aromatic odor
5 : a soothing restorative agency
bal·ma·caan \ˌbal-mə-'kan, -'kän\ *noun* [*Balmacaan,* estate near Inverness, Scotland] (1919)
: a loose single-breasted overcoat usually having raglan sleeves and a short turnover collar
balm of Gil·e·ad \-'gi-lē-əd\ [*Gilead,* region of ancient Palestine known for its balm] (1703)
1 : a small evergreen African and Asian tree (*Commiphora meccanensis* of the family Burseraceae) with aromatic leaves; *also* : a fragrant oleoresin from this tree
2 : an agency that soothes, relieves, or heals
3 : either of two poplars: **a** : a hybrid northern tree (*Populus gileadensis*) with broadly cordate leaves that are pubescent especially on the underside **b** : BALSAM POPLAR
bal·mor·al \bal-'mȯr-əl, -'mär-\ *noun* [*Balmoral* Castle, Scotland] (1859)
1 : a laced boot or shoe
2 *often capitalized* : a round flat cap with a top projecting all around
balmy \'bä-mē, 'bäl-mē, *New England also* 'bä-mē\ *adjective* **balm·i·er; -est** (15th century)
1 a : having the qualities of balm : SOOTHING **b** : MILD
2 : CRAZY, FOOLISH
— **balm·i·ly** \-mə-lē\ *adverb*
— **balm·i·ness** \-mē-nəs\ *noun*
bal·ne·ol·o·gy \ˌbal-nē-'ä-lə-jē\ *noun* [International Scientific Vocabulary, from Latin *balneum* bath — more at BAGNIO] (circa 1879)
: the science of the therapeutic use of baths
¹**ba·lo·ney** \bə-'lō-nē\ *variant of* BOLOGNA
²**baloney** *noun* [*bologna*] (1923)
: pretentious nonsense : BUNKUM — often used as a generalized expression of disagreement
bal·sa \'bȯl-sə\ *noun* [Spanish] (circa 1600)
1 : a small raft or boat; *specifically* : one made of tightly bundled reeds and used on Lake Titicaca
2 : a tropical American tree (*Ochroma pyramidale* synonym *O. lagopus*) of the silk-cotton family with extremely light strong wood used especially for floats; *also* : its wood

bal·sam \'bȯl-səm\ *noun* [Latin *balsamum,* from Greek *balsamon,* probably of Semitic origin; akin to Hebrew *bāshām* balsam] (before 12th century)
1 a : an aromatic and usually oily and resinous substance flowing from various plants; *especially* : any of several resinous substances containing benzoic or cinnamic acid and used especially in medicine **b** : a preparation containing resinous substances and having a balsamic odor
2 a : a balsam-yielding tree; *especially* : BALSAM FIR **b** : IMPATIENS; *especially* : a common garden ornamental (*Impatiens balsamina*)
3 : BALM 5
— **bal·sam·ic** \bȯl-'sa-mik\ *adjective*
balsam fir *noun* (1805)
: a resinous American fir (*Abies balsamea*) that is widely used for pulpwood and as a Christmas tree and is the source of Canada balsam
balsamic vinegar *noun* [translation of Italian *aceto balsamico,* literally, curative vinegar] (1982)
: an aged Italian vinegar made from the must of white grapes
balsam poplar *noun* (1819)
: a North American poplar (*Populus balsamifera*) that is often cultivated as a shade tree and has buds thickly coated with an aromatic resin — called also *balm of Gilead, tacamahac*
Bal·ti \'bəl-tē, 'bȯl-\ *noun* (1901)
: a Tibeto-Burman language of northern Kashmir
Bal·tic \'bȯl-tik\ *adjective* [Medieval Latin (*mare*) *balticum* Baltic Sea] (circa 1590)
1 : of or relating to the Baltic Sea or to the states of Lithuania, Latvia, and Estonia
2 : of or relating to a branch of the Indo-European language family containing Latvian, Lithuanian, and Old Prussian — see INDO-EUROPEAN LANGUAGES table
Bal·ti·more oriole \'bȯl-tə-ˌmȯr-, -ˌmȯr-, -mər-\ *noun* [George Calvert, Lord *Baltimore*] (1808)
: a northern oriole (*Icterus galbula galbula*) of the eastern and central U.S. and southern Canada in which the male has a solid black head and the female usually has an olive brown back and orange yellow underside
Bal·to–Slav·ic \ˌbȯl-(ˌ)tō-'slä-vik, -'sla-\ *noun* (1896)
: a subgroup of Indo-European languages consisting of the Baltic and the Slavic branches — see INDO-EUROPEAN LANGUAGES table
Ba·lu·chi \bə-'lü-chē\ *noun, plural* **Baluchis** *also* **Baluchi** [Persian *Balūchī* of the Baluchis, from *Balūch, Baloch* Baluchi] (1616)
1 : a member of an Indo-Iranian people of Baluchistan
2 : the Iranian language of the Baluchi people
bal·us·ter \'ba-lə-stər\ *noun* [French *balustre,* from Italian *balaustro,* from *balaustra* wild pomegranate flower, from Latin *balaustium,* from Greek *balaustion;* from its shape] (1602)
1 : an object or vertical member (as the leg of a table, a round in a chair back, or the stem of a glass) having a vaselike or turned outline
2 : an upright often vase-shaped support for a rail
bal·us·trade \'ba-lə-ˌsträd\ *noun* [French, from Italian *balaustrata,* from *balaustro*] (1644)
1 : a row of balusters topped by a rail
2 : a low parapet or barrier
— **bal·us·trad·ed** \-ˌsträ-dəd\ *adjective*
bam *noun* [imitative] (1930)
: a dull resounding noise (as of a hard blow or impact) — often used interjectionally
Bam·ba·ra \bäm-'bär-ə\ *noun, plural* **Bambara** *or* **Bambaras** (1883)
1 : a member of an African people of the upper Niger
2 : a Mande language of the Bambara people

bam·bi·no \bam-'bē-(ˌ)nō, bäm-\ *noun, plural* **-nos** *or* **-ni** \-(ˌ)nē\ [Italian, diminutive of *bambo* child] (1722)
1 *plural usually* **bambini** : a representation of the infant Christ
2 : CHILD, BABY
bam·boo \(ˌ)bam-'bü, 'bam-ˌ\ *noun, plural* **bamboos** *often attributive* [Malay *bambu*] (1586)
: any of various chiefly tropical woody or arborescent grasses (as of the genera *Bambusa, Arundinaria,* and *Dendrocalamus*) including some with hollow stems used for building, furniture, or utensils and young shoots used for food

bamboo

bamboo curtain *noun, often B&C capitalized* (1949)
: a political, military, and ideological barrier isolating an area of the Orient
bam·boo·zle \bam-'bü-zəl\ *transitive verb* **-boo·zled; -boo·zling** \-'büz-liŋ, -'bü-zə-\ [origin unknown] (1703)
: to deceive by underhanded methods : DUPE, HOODWINK
— **bam·boo·zle·ment** \-'bü-zəl-mənt\ *noun*
¹**ban** \'ban\ *verb* **banned; ban·ning** [Middle English *bannen* to summon, curse, from Old English *bannan* to summon; akin to Old High German *bannan* to command, Latin *fari* to speak, Greek *phanai* to say, *phōnē* sound, voice] (12th century)
transitive verb
1 *archaic* : CURSE
2 : to prohibit especially by legal means ⟨*ban* discrimination⟩; *also* : to prohibit the use, performance, or distribution of ⟨*ban* a book⟩ ⟨*ban* a pesticide⟩
intransitive verb
: to utter curses or maledictions
²**ban** *noun* [Middle English, partly from *bannen* & partly from Old French *ban,* of Germanic origin; akin to Old High German *bannan* to command] (14th century)
1 : the summoning in feudal times of the king's vassals for military service
2 : ANATHEMA, EXCOMMUNICATION
3 : MALEDICTION, CURSE
4 : legal or formal prohibition
5 : censure or condemnation especially through social pressure
³**ban** \'bän\ *noun, plural* **ba·ni** \'bä-(ˌ)nē\ [Romanian] (1880)
— see *leu* at MONEY table
Ba·nach space \'bä-ˌnäk-, -nək-\ *noun* [Stefan *Banach* (died 1945) Polish mathematician] (1949)
: a normed vector space for which the field of multipliers comprises the real or complex numbers and in which every Cauchy sequence converges to a point in the space
ba·nal \bə-'nal, ba-, -'nàl; 'bā-nal; 'bā-nᵊl\ *adjective* [French, from Middle French, of compulsory feudal service, possessed in common, commonplace, from *ban*] (1840)
: lacking originality, freshness, or novelty : TRITE
synonym see INSIPID

— **ba·nal·i·ty** \bə-'na-lə-tē *also* bā- *or* ba-\ *noun*
— **ba·nal·ize** \bə-'na-,līz, ba-, -'nà-; bā-'na-; 'bā-nᵊl-,īz\ *transitive verb*
— **ba·nal·ly** \bə-'nal-lē, ba-, -'nàl-; bā-'nal-; 'bā-nᵊl-(l)ē\ *adverb*
ba·nana \bə-'na-nə, *especially British* -'nä-\ *noun, often attributive* [Spanish or Portuguese; Spanish, from Portuguese, of African origin; akin to Wolof *banäna* banana] (1597)
1 : an elongated usually tapering tropical fruit with soft pulpy flesh enclosed in a soft usually yellow rind **2 :** any of several widely cultivated perennial herbs (genus *Musa* of the family Musaceae, the banana family) bearing bananas in compact pendent bunches

banana 2

banana oil *noun* (1926)
: a colorless liquid acetate $C_7H_{14}O_2$ of amyl alcohol that has a pleasant fruity odor and is used as a solvent and in the manufacture of artificial fruit essences
banana republic *noun* (1935)
: a small dependent country usually of the tropics; *especially* **:** one run despotically
ba·nan·as \bə-'na-nəz, *especially British* -'nä-\ *adjective* (1968)
: CRAZY ⟨go *bananas*⟩ ⟨drives me *bananas*⟩
word history see NUTS
banana seat *noun* (1965)
: an elongated bicycle saddle
bananas Fos·ter \-'fòs-tər, -'fäs-\ *noun* [Richard *Foster*, friend of New Orleans restaurateur Owen E. Brennan, at whose restaurant the dish was first made] (1976)
: a dessert of bananas flamed (as with rum) and served with ice cream
banana split *noun* (1920)
: ice cream served on a banana sliced in half lengthwise and usually garnished with flavored syrups, fruits, nuts, and whipped cream
ba·nau·sic \bə-'nò-sik, -zik\ *adjective* [Greek *banausikos* of an artisan, nonintellectual, vulgar, from *banausos* artisan] (1845)
: relating to or concerned with earning a living — used pejoratively ⟨contempt for the *banausic* occupations —T. S. Eliot⟩; *also* **:** UTILITARIAN, PRACTICAL ⟨such mundane and *banausic* considerations as comfort and durability —G. B. Boyer⟩
¹band \'band\ *noun* [in senses 1 & 2, from Middle English *band, bond* something that constricts, from Old Norse *band;* akin to Old English *bindan* to bind; in other senses, from Middle English *bande* strip, from Middle French, from (assumed) Vulgar Latin *binda,* of Germanic origin; akin to Old High German *binta* fillet; akin to Old English *bindan* to bind, *bend* fetter] (12th century)
1 : something that confines or constricts while allowing a degree of movement
2 : something that binds or restrains legally, morally, or spiritually
3 : a strip serving to join or hold things together: as **a :** BELT 2 **b :** a cord or strip across the back of a book to which the sections are sewn
4 : a thin flat encircling strip especially for binding: as **a :** a close-fitting strip that confines material at the waist, neck, or cuff of clothing **b :** a strip of cloth used to protect a newborn baby's navel — called also *belly-band* **c :** a ring of elastic
5 a : a strip (as of living tissue or rock) or a stripe (as on an animal) differentiable (as by color, texture, or structure) from the adjacent

material or area **b :** a more or less well-defined range of wavelengths, frequencies, or energies **c :** RANGE 7a
6 : a narrow strip serving chiefly as decoration: as **a :** a narrow strip of material applied as trimming to an article of dress **b** *plural* **:** a pair of strips hanging at the front of the neck as part of a clerical, legal, or academic dress **c :** a ring without raised portions
7 : TRACK 1e(2)
²band (15th century)
transitive verb
1 : to affix a band to or tie up with a band
2 : to finish or decorate with a band
3 : to gather together **:** UNITE ⟨*banded* themselves together for protection⟩
intransitive verb
: to unite for a common purpose — often used with *together* ⟨have *banded* together in hopes of attacking the blight that is common to them all —J. B. Conant⟩
— **band·er** *noun*
³band *noun* [Middle French *bande* troop, from Old Provençal *banda,* of Germanic origin; akin to Gothic *bandwo* sign, standard — more at BANNER] (15th century)
: a group of persons, animals, or things; *especially* **:** a group of musicians organized for ensemble playing and using chiefly woodwinds, brass, and percussion instruments — compare ORCHESTRA
¹ban·dage \'ban-dij\ *noun* [Middle French, from *bande*] (1599)
1 : a strip of fabric used especially to dress and bind up wounds
2 : a flexible strip or band used to cover, strengthen, or compress something
²bandage *transitive verb* **ban·daged; ban·dag·ing** (1774)
: to bind, dress, or cover with a bandage
Band–Aid \'ban-,dād\ *trademark*
— used for a small adhesive strip with a gauze pad for covering minor wounds
ban·dan·na *or* **ban·dana** \ban-'da-nə\ *noun* [Hindi *bã̄dhnū* tie-dyeing, cloth so dyed, from *bã̄dhnā* to tie, from Sanskrit *badhnāti* he ties; akin to Old English *bindan*] (1741)
: a large often colorfully patterned handkerchief
¹band·box \'ban(d)-,bäks\ *noun* (1631)
1 : a usually cylindrical box of paperboard or thin wood for holding light articles of attire
2 : a structure (as a baseball park) having relatively small interior dimensions
²bandbox *adjective* (1844)
: exquisitely neat, clean, or ordered as if just taken from a bandbox ⟨a *bandbox* perfection of appearance⟩
— **bandbox** *adverb*
ban·deau \ban-'dō\ *noun, plural* **ban·deaux** \-'dōz\ [French, diminutive of *bande*] (1706)
1 : a fillet or band especially for the hair
2 : BRASSIERE; *also* **:** a band-shaped covering for the breasts
band·ed \'ban-dəd\ *adjective* (1787)
: having or marked with bands
ban·de·ril·la \,ban-də-'rē(l)-yə\ *noun* [Spanish, diminutive of *bandera* banner] (1797)
: a decorated barbed dart that the banderillero thrusts into the neck or shoulders of the bull in a bullfight
ban·de·ril·le·ro \,ban-də-(,)rē(l)-'yer-(,)ō\ *noun, plural* **-ros** [Spanish, from *banderilla*] (1797)
: one who thrusts in the banderillas in a bullfight
ban·de·role *or* **ban·de·rol** \'ban-də-,rōl\ *noun* [French *banderole,* from Italian *banderuola,* diminutive of *bandiera* banner, of Germanic origin; akin to Gothic *bandwo* sign] (1562)
1 : a long narrow forked flag or streamer
2 : a long scroll bearing an inscription or a device
ban·di·coot \'ban-di-,küt\ *noun* [Telugu *pandikokku*] (1813)

1 : any of several very large rats (genera *Bandicota* and *Nesokia*) of southern Asia destructive to crops
2 : any of a family (Peramelidae) of small insectivorous and herbivorous marsupial mammals of Australia, Tasmania, and New Guinea
ban·dit \'ban-dət\ *noun* [Italian *bandito,* from past participle of *bandire* to banish, of Germanic origin; akin to Old High German *bannan* to command — more at BAN] (1591)
1 *plural also* **ban·dit·ti** \ban-'di-tē\ **:** an outlaw who lives by plunder; *especially* **:** a member of a band of marauders
2 : ROBBER
3 : an enemy plane
— **ban·dit·ry** \'ban-də-trē\ *noun*
band·lead·er \'band-,lē-dər\ *noun* (1894)
: the conductor of a band (as a dance band)
band·mas·ter \'ban(d)-,mas-tər\ *noun* (1858)
: BANDLEADER; *especially* **:** a conductor of a military or concert band
ban·dog \'ban-,dòg\ *noun* [Middle English *bandogge,* from *band + dogge* dog] (14th century)
: a dog kept tied to serve as a watchdog or because of its ferocity
ban·do·lier *or* **ban·do·leer** \,ban-də-'lir\ *noun* [Middle French *bandouliere,* ultimately from Old Spanish *bando* band, of Germanic origin; akin to Gothic *bandwo*] (circa 1577)
: a belt worn over the shoulder and across the breast often for the suspending or supporting of some article (as cartridges) or as a part of an official or ceremonial dress
ban·dore \'ban-,dōr, -,dòr\ *or* **ban·do·ra** \ban-'dōr-ə, -'dòr-\ *noun* [Spanish *bandurria* or Portuguese *bandurra,* from Late Latin *pandura* 3-stringed lute, from Greek *pandoura*] (1566)
: a bass stringed instrument resembling a guitar
band–pass filter \'ban(d)-,pas-\ *noun* (1926)
: a filter that transmits only frequencies within a selected band
band saw *noun* (circa 1864)
: a saw in the form of an endless steel belt running over pulleys; *also* **:** a power sawing machine using this device
band shell *noun* (1926)
: a bandstand having at the rear a sounding board shaped like a huge concave seashell
bands·man \'ban(d)z-mən\ *noun* (circa 1842)
: a member of a musical band
band·stand \'ban(d)-,stand\ *noun* (1859)
1 : a usually roofed platform on which a band or orchestra performs outdoors
2 : a platform in a ballroom or nightclub on which musicians perform
band·wag·on \'band-,wa-gən\ *noun* (1855)
1 : a usually ornate and high wagon for a band of musicians especially in a circus parade
2 : a popular party, faction, or cause that attracts growing support — often used in such phrases as *climb on the bandwagon*
3 : a current or fashionable trend
band·width \'band-,width\ *noun* (circa 1937)
1 : a range within a band of wavelengths, frequencies, or energies; *especially* **:** a range of radio frequencies which is occupied by a modulated carrier wave, which is assigned to a service, or over which a device can operate
2 : the data transfer rate of an electronic communications system
¹ban·dy \'ban-dē\ *verb* **ban·died; ban·dy·ing** [probably from Middle French *bander* to be tight, to bandy, from *bande* strip — more at BAND] (1577)
transitive verb
1 : to bat (as a tennis ball) to and fro
2 a : to toss from side to side or pass about from one to another often in a careless or inappropriate manner **b :** EXCHANGE; *especially* **:** to exchange (words) argumentatively **c :** to discuss lightly or banteringly **d :** to use in a glib or offhand manner — often used with

about ⟨*bandy* these statistics about with considerable bravado —Richard Pollak⟩
3 *archaic* **:** to band together
intransitive verb
1 *obsolete* **:** CONTEND
2 *archaic* **:** UNITE

²**bandy** *noun* [perhaps from Middle French *bandé*, past participle of *bander*] (1693)
: a game similar to hockey and believed to be its prototype

³**bandy** *adjective* [probably from *bandy* (hockey stick)] (1687)
1 *of legs* **:** BOWED
2 : BOWLEGGED
— **ban·dy–legged** \'ban-dē-₁legd; ₁ban-dē-'le-gəd, -'lā-\ *adjective*

¹**bane** \'bān\ *noun* [Middle English, from Old English *bana*; akin to Old High German *bano* death] (before 12th century)
1 a *obsolete* **:** KILLER, SLAYER **b :** POISON **c :** DEATH, DESTRUCTION ⟨stop the way of those that seek my *bane* —Philip Sidney⟩ **d :** WOE
2 : a source of harm or ruin **:** CURSE ⟨national frontiers have been more of a *bane* than a boon for mankind —D. C. Thomson⟩

²**bane** *transitive verb* **baned; ban·ing** (1578)
obsolete **:** to kill especially with poison

³**bane** *noun* [Middle English (northern dialect) *ban*, from Old English *bān*] (before 12th century)
chiefly Scottish **:** BONE

bane·ber·ry \'bān-₁ber-ē\ *noun* (1755)
: any of several perennial herbs (genus *Actaea*) of the buttercup family having acrid poisonous berries; *also* **:** one of the berries

bane·ful \'bān-fəl\ *adjective* (1579)
1 : productive of destruction or woe **:** seriously harmful ⟨a *baneful* influence⟩
2 *archaic* **:** POISONOUS
synonym see PERNICIOUS
— **bane·ful·ly** \-fə-lē\ *adverb*

¹**bang** \'baŋ\ *verb* [probably of Scandinavian origin; akin to Icelandic *banga* to hammer] (circa 1550)
transitive verb
1 : to strike sharply **:** BUMP
2 : to knock, beat, or thrust vigorously often with a sharp noise
3 : to have sexual intercourse with — often considered vulgar
intransitive verb
1 : to strike with a sharp noise or thump
2 : to produce a sharp often metallic explosive or percussive noise or series of such noises

²**bang** *noun* (circa 1550)
1 : a resounding blow
2 : a sudden loud noise — often used interjectionally
3 a : a sudden striking effect **b :** a quick burst of energy ⟨start off with a *bang*⟩ **c :** THRILL ⟨I get a *bang* out of all this —W. H. Whyte⟩
— **bang for the buck** *also* **bang for one's buck :** value received from outlay or effort ⟨investment is yielding less *bang for the buck* —Fortune⟩

³**bang** *adverb* (1828)
: RIGHT, DIRECTLY ⟨ran *bang* up against more trouble⟩

⁴**bang** *noun* [probably short for *bangtail* (short tail)] (1878)
: a fringe of banged hair — usually used in plural

⁵**bang** *transitive verb* (1878)
: to cut (as front hair) short and squarely across

ban·ga·lore torpedo \'baŋ-gə-₁lōr-, -₁lȯr-\ *noun* [*Bangalore*, India] (1913)
: a metal tube that contains explosives and a firing mechanism and is used to cut barbed wire and detonate buried mines

bang away *intransitive verb* (circa 1889)
1 : to work with determined effort ⟨students *banging away* at their homework⟩

2 : to attack persistently ⟨police are going to keep *banging away* at you —Erle Stanley Gardner⟩

bang·er \'baŋ-ər\ *noun* (circa 1919)
1 *British* **:** SAUSAGE
2 *British* **:** FIRECRACKER
3 *British* **:** JALOPY

bang·kok \'baŋ-₁käk, baŋ-'\ *noun* [earlier *bangkok*, a fine straw, from *Bangkok*, Thailand] (1916)
: a hat woven of fine palm fiber in the Philippines

ban·gle \'baŋ-gəl\ *noun* [Hindi *baṅglī*] (1787)
1 : a stiff usually ornamental bracelet or anklet slipped or clasped on
2 : an ornamental disk that hangs loosely (as on a bracelet)

bang on *adjective* (1936)
chiefly British **:** exactly correct or appropriate

Bang's disease \'baŋz-\ *noun* [Bernhard L. F. *Bang* (died 1932) Danish veterinarian] (circa 1929)
: BRUCELLOSIS; *specifically* **:** contagious abortion of cattle caused by a brucella (*Brucella abortus*)

bang·tail \'baŋ-₁tāl\ *noun* [*bangtail* (short tail)] (1921)
: RACEHORSE

bang–up \'baŋ-₁əp\ *adjective* [³*bang*] (1810)
: FIRST-RATE, EXCELLENT ⟨a *bang-up* job⟩

bang up *transitive verb* [¹*bang*] (1920)
: to cause extensive damage to

bani *plural of* ³BAN

ban·ish \'ba-nish\ *transitive verb* [Middle English, from Middle French *baniss-*, stem of *banir*, of Germanic origin; akin to Old High German *bannan* to command — more at BAN] (14th century)
1 : to require by authority to leave a country
2 : to drive out or remove from a home or place of usual resort or continuance
3 : to clear away **:** DISPEL ⟨his discovery *banishes* anxiety —Stringfellow Barr⟩ ☆
— **ban·ish·er** *noun*
— **ban·ish·ment** \-nish-mənt\ *noun*

ban·is·ter \'ba-nəs-tər\ *noun* [alteration of *baluster*] (1667)
1 : BALUSTER 2
2 a : a handrail with its supporting posts **b :** HANDRAIL
— **ban·is·tered** \-tərd\ *adjective*

ban·jax \'ban-₁jaks\ *transitive verb* [origin unknown] (1939)
chiefly Irish **:** DAMAGE, RUIN; *also* **:** SMASH

ban·jo \'ban-(₁)jō\ *noun, plural* **banjos** *also* **banjoes** [probably of African origin; akin to Kimbundu *mbanza*, a similar instrument] (1739)
: a musical instrument with a drumlike body, a fretted neck, and usually four or five strings which may be plucked or strummed
— **ban·jo·ist** \-₁jō-ist\ *noun*

banjo clock *noun* (1903)
: a pendulum clock whose shape suggests a banjo

¹**bank** \'baŋk\ *noun* [Middle English, probably of Scandinavian origin; akin to Old Norse *bakki* bank; akin to Old English *benc* bench — more at BENCH] (13th century)
1 : a mound, pile, or ridge raised above the surrounding level: as **a :** a piled-up mass of cloud or fog **b :** an undersea elevation rising especially from the continental shelf
2 : the rising ground bordering a lake, river, or sea or forming the edge of a cut or hollow
3 a : a steep slope (as of a hill) **b :** the lateral inward tilt of a surface along a curve or of a vehicle (as an airplane) when taking a curve
4 : a protective or cushioning rim or piece ◆

²**bank** (1590)

banjo

transitive verb
1 a : to raise a bank about **b :** to cover (as a fire) with fresh fuel and adjust the draft of air so as to keep in an inactive state **c :** to build (a curve) with the roadbed or track inclined laterally upward from the inside edge
2 : to heap or pile in a bank
3 : to drive (a ball in billiards) into a cushion
4 : to form or group in a tier
intransitive verb
1 : to rise in or form a bank — often used with *up* ⟨clouds would *bank* up about midday, and showers fall —William Beebe⟩
2 a : to incline an airplane laterally **b** (1) **:** to incline laterally (2) **:** to follow a curve or incline ⟨skiers *banking* around the turn⟩

³**bank** *noun* [Middle English, from Middle French or Old Italian; Middle French *banque*, from Old Italian *banca*, literally, bench, of Germanic origin; akin to Old English *benc*] (15th century)
1 a : an establishment for the custody, loan, exchange, or issue of money, for the extension of credit, and for facilitating the transmission of funds **b** *obsolete* **:** the table, counter, or place of business of a money changer
2 : a person conducting a gambling house or game; *specifically* **:** DEALER
3 : a supply of something held in reserve: as **a :** the fund of supplies (as money, chips, or pieces) held by the banker or dealer for use in a game **b :** a fund of pieces belonging to a game (as dominoes) from which the players draw
4 : a place where something is held available ⟨memory *bank*⟩; *especially* **:** a depot for the collection and storage of a biological product of human origin for medical use ⟨blood *bank*⟩

⁴**bank** (circa 1751)

☆ **SYNONYMS**
Banish, exile, deport, transport mean to remove by authority from a state or country. BANISH implies compulsory removal from a country not necessarily one's own ⟨*banished* for seditious activities⟩. EXILE may imply compulsory removal or an enforced or voluntary absence from one's own country ⟨a writer who *exiled* himself for political reasons⟩. DEPORT implies sending out of the country an alien who has illegally entered or whose presence is judged inimical to the public welfare ⟨illegal aliens will be *deported*⟩. TRANSPORT implies sending a convicted criminal to an overseas penal colony ⟨a convict who was *transported* to Australia⟩.

◇ **WORD HISTORY**
bank Long before the days of automatic teller machines, money transactions took place between individuals over a table or counter. The medieval Italian word for such a counter was *banco*. As the transactions of financial institutions became more complex than simple exchanges of money across a counter, especially in Italian cities such as Florence and Venice, the word *banco* was extended to the institution itself. Italian banking practices spread to the rest of Europe, and with them went the word *banco*, usually via the feminine variant *banca*—hence late medieval French *banque* and late Middle English *banke*. In Italian, *banca*, possibly influenced by the feminine gender of the French noun, has now largely supplanted *banco* in the sense "bank."

intransitive verb
1 : to manage a bank
2 : to deposit money or have an account in a bank
transitive verb
: to deposit in a bank
— **bank on :** to depend or rely on
⁵**bank** *noun* [Middle English *banc* bench, from Old French, of Germanic origin; akin to Old English *benc*] (1614)
1 : a group or series of objects arranged together in a row or a tier: as **a :** a set of elevators **b :** a row or tier of telephones
2 : one of the horizontal and usually secondary or lower divisions of a headline
bank·able \ˈbaŋ-kə-bəl\ *adjective* (1818)
1 : acceptable to or at a bank
2 : sure to bring in a profit ⟨Hollywood's most *bankable* star —Sidney Sheldon⟩
— **bank·abil·i·ty** \ˌbaŋ-kə-ˈbi-lə-tē\ *noun*
bank·book \ˈbaŋk-ˌbu̇k\ *noun* (1714)
: the depositor's book in which a bank records deposits and withdrawals — called also *passbook*
bank·card \-ˌkärd\ *noun* (1970)
: a credit card issued by a bank
bank discount *noun* (1841)
: the interest discounted in advance on a note and computed on the face value of the note
¹**bank·er** \ˈbaŋ-kər\ *noun* (1534)
1 : one that engages in the business of banking
2 : the player who keeps the bank in various games
— **bank·er·ly** \-lē\ *adjective*
²**banker** *noun* (1666)
: a man or boat employed in the cod fishery on the Newfoundland banks
³**banker** *noun* (1677)
: a sculptor's or mason's workbench
banker's acceptance *noun* (circa 1924)
: a short-term credit instrument issued by an importer's bank that guarantees payment of an exporter's invoice
bank holiday *noun* (1871)
1 *British* **:** LEGAL HOLIDAY
2 : a period when banks in general are closed often by government fiat
bank·ing *noun* (1735)
: the business of a bank or a banker
bank money *noun* (1904)
: a medium of exchange consisting chiefly of checks and drafts
bank·note \ˈbaŋk-ˌnōt\ *noun* (1695)
: a promissory note issued by a bank payable to bearer on demand without interest and acceptable as money
¹**bank·roll** \ˈbaŋk-ˌkrōl\ *noun* (1887)
: supply of money **:** FUNDS
²**bankroll** *transitive verb* (1928)
: to supply the capital for or pay the cost of ⟨a business or project⟩
— **bank·roll·er** *noun*
¹**bank·rupt** \ˈbaŋ-(ˌ)krəpt\ *noun* [modification of Middle French & Old Italian; Middle French *banqueroute* bankruptcy, from Old Italian *bancarotta*, from *banca* bank + *rotta* broken, from Latin *rupta*, feminine of *ruptus*, past participle of *rumpere* to break — more at BANK, REAVE] (1533)
1 a : a person who has done any of the acts that by law entitle his creditors to have his estate administered for their benefit **b :** a person judicially declared subject to having his estate administered under the bankrupt laws for the benefit of his creditors **c :** a person who becomes insolvent
2 : one who is destitute of a particular thing ⟨a moral *bankrupt*⟩
²**bankrupt** *adjective* (1570)
1 a : reduced to a state of financial ruin **:** IMPOVERISHED; *specifically* **:** legally declared a bankrupt ⟨the company went *bankrupt*⟩ **b :** of or relating to bankrupts or bankruptcy ⟨*bankrupt* laws⟩

2 a : BROKEN, RUINED ⟨a *bankrupt* professional career⟩ **b :** exhausted of valuable qualities **:** STERILE ⟨a *bankrupt* old culture⟩ **c :** DESTITUTE — used with *of* or *in* ⟨*bankrupt* of all merciful feelings⟩
³**bankrupt** *transitive verb* (1588)
1 : to reduce to bankruptcy
2 : IMPOVERISH ⟨defections had *bankrupted* the party of its brainpower⟩
synonym see DEPLETE
bank·rupt·cy \ˈbaŋ-(ˌ)krəp(t)-sē\ *noun, plural* **-cies** (1700)
1 : the quality or state of being bankrupt
2 : utter failure or impoverishment
bank shot *noun* (1897)
1 : a shot in billiards and pool in which a player banks the cue ball or the object ball
2 : a shot in basketball played to rebound from the backboard into the basket
bank·sia \ˈbaŋ(k)-sē-ə\ *noun* [New Latin, genus name, from Sir Joseph *Banks*] (1788)
: any of a genus (*Banksia*) of Australian evergreen trees or shrubs of the protea family with alternate leathery leaves and flowers in dense cylindrical heads
bank·side \ˈbaŋk-ˌsīd\ *noun* (15th century)
: the slope of a bank especially of a stream
¹**ban·ner** \ˈba-nər\ *noun* [Middle English *banere*, from Old French, of Germanic origin; akin to Gothic *bandwo* sign; probably akin to Greek *phainein* to show — more at FANCY] (13th century)
1 a : a piece of cloth attached by one edge to a staff and used by a leader (as a monarch or feudal lord) as his standard **b :** ²FLAG 1 **:** an ensign displaying a distinctive or symbolic device or legend; *especially* **:** one presented as an award of honor or distinction
2 : a headline in large type running across a newspaper page
3 : a strip of cloth on which a sign is painted ⟨welcome *banners* stretched across the street⟩
4 : a name, slogan, or goal associated with a particular group or ideology ⟨the new *banner* is "community control" —F. M. Hechinger⟩ — often used with *under* ⟨every new administration arrives . . . under the *banner* of change —John Cogley⟩
²**banner** *adjective* (1840)
1 : prominent in support of a political party ⟨a *banner* Democratic county⟩
2 : distinguished from all others especially in excellence ⟨a *banner* year for business⟩
³**banner** *transitive verb* (1889)
1 : to furnish with a banner
2 : to print (as a news story) under a banner usually on the front page
¹**ban·ner·et** \ˈba-nə-rət, ˌba-nə-ˈret\ *noun, often capitalized* [Middle English *baneret*, from Old French, from *banere*] (14th century)
: a knight leading his vassals into the field under his own banner
²**banneret** *also* **ban·ner·ette** *noun* (14th century)
: a small banner
ban·ne·rol \ˈba-nə-ˌrōl\ *noun* (1548)
: BANDEROLE
bannister *variant of* BANISTER
ban·nock \ˈba-nək\ *noun* [Middle English *bannok*, from Old English *bannuc*] (before 12th century)
1 : a usually unleavened flat bread or biscuit made with oatmeal or barley meal
2 *chiefly New England* **:** CORN BREAD; *especially* **:** a thin cake baked on a griddle
banns \ˈbanz\ *noun plural* [plural of *bann*, from Middle English *bane, ban* proclamation, ban] (14th century)
: public announcement especially in church of a proposed marriage
¹**ban·quet** \ˈbaŋ-kwət, ˈban- *also* -ˌkwet\ *noun* [Middle French, from Old Italian *banchetto*, from diminutive of *banca* bench, bank] (15th century)

1 : a sumptuous feast; *especially* **:** an elaborate and often ceremonious meal for numerous people often in honor of a person ⟨a state *banquet*⟩
2 : a meal held in recognition of some occasion or achievement ⟨an awards *banquet*⟩
²**banquet** (circa 1500)
intransitive verb
: to partake of a banquet
transitive verb
: to treat with a banquet **:** FEAST
— **ban·quet·er** *noun*
banquet room *noun* (1837)
: a large room (as in a restaurant or hotel) suitable for banquets
ban·quette \baŋ-ˈket, ban-, *1b is also* ˈbaŋ-kət\ *noun* [French, from Middle French, from Old Provençal *banqueta*, diminutive of *banc* bench, of Germanic origin; akin to Old English *benc* bench] (1629)
1 a : a raised way along the inside of a parapet or trench for gunners or guns **b** *Southern* **:** SIDEWALK
2 a : a long upholstered bench **b :** a sofa having one roll-over arm **c :** a built-in upholstered bench along a wall
Ban·quo \ˈban-(ˌ)kwō, ˈban-\ *noun*
: a murdered Scottish thane in Shakespeare's *Macbeth* whose ghost appears to Macbeth
ban·shee \ˈban-(ˌ)shē, ban-ˈ\ *noun* [Irish *bean sídhe* & Scottish Gaelic *bean sìth*, literally, woman of fairyland] (1771)
: a female spirit in Gaelic folklore whose appearance or wailing warns a family that one of them will soon die
¹**ban·tam** \ˈban-təm\ *noun* [*Bantam*, former residency in Java] (1749)
1 : any of numerous small domestic fowls that are often miniatures of members of the standard breeds
2 : a person of diminutive stature and often combative disposition
²**bantam** *adjective* (1782)
1 : SMALL, DIMINUTIVE
2 : pertly combative
ban·tam·weight \-ˌwāt\ *noun* (1884)
: a boxer in a weight division having a maximum limit of 118 pounds for professionals and 119 pounds for amateurs — compare FEATHERWEIGHT, FLYWEIGHT
ban·teng \ˈbän-ˌteŋ\ *noun* [Malay of Indonesia, from Javanese *banténg*] (1817)
: a wild ox (*Bos javanicus* synonym *B. banteng*) of southeastern Asia sometimes domesticated for use as a draft animal or for its meat
¹**ban·ter** \ˈban-tər\ *verb* [origin unknown] (1676)
transitive verb
1 : to speak to or address in a witty and teasing manner
2 *archaic* **:** DELUDE
3 *chiefly Southern & Midland* **:** CHALLENGE
intransitive verb
: to speak or act playfully or wittily
— **ban·ter·er** \-tər-ər\ *noun*
— **ban·ter·ing·ly** \ˈban-tə-riŋ-lē\ *adverb*
²**banter** *noun* (1690)
: good-natured and usually witty and animated joking
bant·ling \ˈbant-liŋ\ *noun* [perhaps modification of German *Bänkling* bastard, from *Bank* bench, from Old High German — more at BENCH] (1593)
: a very young child
Ban·tu \ˈban-(ˌ)tü, ˈbän-\ *noun, plural* **Bantu** *or* **Bantus** (1862)
1 : a family of Niger-Congo languages spoken in central and southern Africa
2 : a member of any of a group of African peoples who speak Bantu languages
Ban·tu·stan \ˌban-tü-ˈstan, ˌbän-tü-ˈstän\ *noun* [*Bantu* + *-stan* land (as in *Hindustan*)] (1949)
: any of several all-black enclaves in the Republic of South Africa that have a limited degree of self-government

ban·yan \'ban-yən\ *noun* [earlier *banyan* Gujarati trader, from Portuguese *banean,* probably from Tamil *vāniyan* trader, from Sanskrit *vāṇija;* from a tree of the species in Iran under which such traders conducted business] (1634) **:** an East Indian fig tree (*Ficus benghalensis*) of the mulberry family with branches that send out shoots which grow down to the soil and root to form secondary trunks

ban·zai \(ₒ)bän-'zī, 'bän-,\ *noun* [Japanese] (1893) **:** a Japanese cheer or war cry

banzai attack *noun* (1944) **:** a mass attack by Japanese soldiers in World War II; *also* **:** an all-out usually desperate attack

banzai charge *noun* (1944)
1 : BANZAI ATTACK
2 : a determined often reckless act

bao·bab \'baù-,bab, 'bā-ə-\ *noun* [New Latin *bahobab*] (1640) **:** a broad-trunked Old World tropical tree (*Adansonia digitata*) of the silk-cotton family with an edible acid fruit resembling a gourd and bark used in making paper, cloth, and rope

bap \'bap\ *noun* [origin unknown] (circa 1575) *British* **:** a small bun or roll

bap·ti·sia \bap-'ti-zh(ē-)ə\ *noun* [New Latin, genus name, from Greek *baptisis* a dipping, from *baptein*] (circa 1868) **:** any of a genus (*Baptisia*) of North American leguminous plants having showy papilionaceous flowers similar in form to those of the pea plant

bap·tism \'bap-,ti-zəm, *especially Southern* 'bab-\ *noun* [Middle English *baptisme*] (14th century)
1 a : a Christian sacrament marked by ritual use of water and admitting the recipient to the Christian community **b :** a non-Christian rite using water for ritual purification **c** *Christian Science* **:** purification by or submergence in Spirit
2 : an act, experience, or ordeal by which one is purified, sanctified, initiated, or named
— **bap·tis·mal** \bap-'tiz-məl, *especially Southern* bab-\ *adjective*
— **bap·tis·mal·ly** \-mə-lē\ *adverb*

baptismal name *noun* (1869) **:** a name given at christening or confirmation

baptism of fire (1857)
1 : an introductory or initial experience that is a severe ordeal; *specifically* **:** a soldier's first exposure to enemy fire
2 : a spiritual baptism by a gift of the Holy Spirit — often used in allusion to Acts 2:3–4; Matthew 3:11 (Revised Standard Version)

bap·tist \'bap-tist, *especially Southern* 'bab-\ *noun* (13th century)
1 : one that baptizes
2 *capitalized* **:** a member or adherent of an evangelical Protestant denomination marked by congregational polity and baptism by immersion of believers only
— **Baptist** *adjective*

bap·tis·tery *or* **bap·tis·try** \'bap-tə-strē, *especially Southern* 'bab-\ *noun, plural* **-ter·ies** *or* **-tries** (14th century) **:** a part of a church or formerly a separate building used for baptism

bap·tize *also* **bap·tise** \bap-'tīz, 'bap-,, *especially Southern* bab- *or* 'bab-\ *verb* **bap·tized** *also* **bap·tised; bap·tiz·ing** *also* **bap·tis·ing** [Middle English, from Old French *baptiser,* from Late Latin *baptizare,* from Greek *baptizein* to dip, baptize, from *baptein* to dip, dye; akin to Old Norse *kvefja* to quench] (13th century)
transitive verb
1 : to administer baptism to
2 a : to purify or cleanse spiritually especially by a purging experience or ordeal **b :** INITIATE
3 : to give a name to (as at baptism) **:** CHRISTEN

intransitive verb **:** to administer baptism
— **bap·tiz·er** *noun*

¹bar \'bär\ *noun, often attributive* [Middle English *barre,* from Middle French] (12th century)
1 a : a straight piece (as of wood or metal) that is longer than it is wide and has any of various uses (as for a lever, support, barrier, or fastening) **b :** a solid piece or block of material that is usually considerably longer than it is wide ⟨a *bar* of gold⟩ ⟨candy *bar*⟩ **c :** a usually rigid piece (as of wood or metal) longer than it is wide that is used as a handle or support; *especially* **:** a handrail used by ballet dancers to maintain balance while exercising
2 : something that obstructs or prevents passage, progress, or action: as **a :** the destruction of an action or claim in law; *also* **:** a plea or objection that effects such destruction **b :** an intangible or nonphysical impediment **c :** a submerged or partly submerged bank (as of sand) along a shore or in a river often obstructing navigation
3 a (1) **:** the railing in a courtroom that encloses the place about the judge where prisoners are stationed or where the business of the court is transacted in civil cases (2) **:** COURT, TRIBUNAL (3) **:** a particular system of courts (4) **:** an authority or tribunal that hands down judgment **b** (1) **:** the barrier in the English Inns of Court that formerly separated the seats of the benchers or readers from the body of the hall occupied by the students (2) **:** the whole body of barristers or lawyers qualified to practice in the courts of any jurisdiction (3) **:** the profession of barrister or lawyer
4 : a straight stripe, band, or line much longer than it is wide: as **a :** one of two or more horizontal stripes on a heraldic shield **b :** a metal or embroidered strip worn on a usually military uniform especially to indicate rank (as of a company officer) or service
5 a : a counter at which food or especially alcoholic beverages are served **b :** BARROOM **c :** SHOP 2b
6 a : a vertical line across the musical staff before the initial measure accent **b :** MEASURE
7 : a lace and embroidery joining covered with buttonhole stitch for connecting various parts of the pattern in needlepoint lace and cutwork
— **behind bars :** in jail

²bar *transitive verb* **barred; bar·ring** (13th century)
1 a : to fasten with a bar **b :** to place bars across to prevent ingress or egress
2 : to mark with bars **:** STRIPE
3 a : to confine or shut in by or as if by bars **b :** to set aside **:** RULE OUT **c :** to keep out **:** EXCLUDE
4 a : to interpose legal objection to or to the claim of **b :** PREVENT, FORBID

³bar *preposition* (1714) **:** EXCEPT

⁴bar *noun* [German, from Greek *baros*] (1910) **:** a unit of pressure equal to one million dynes per square centimeter

bar- *or* **baro-** *combining form* [Greek *baros;* akin to Greek *barys* heavy — more at GRIEVE] **:** weight **:** pressure ⟨*barometer*⟩

Ba·rab·bas \bə-'ra-bəs\ *noun* [Greek, from Aramaic *Bar-abba*] **:** a Jewish prisoner according to Matthew, Mark, and John released in preference to Christ at the demand of the multitude

bar·a·thea \,bar-ə-'thē-ə\ *noun* [from *Barathea,* a trademark] (1862) **:** a fabric that has a broken rib weave and a pebbly texture and that is made of silk, worsted, or synthetic fiber or a combination of these

¹barb \'bärb\ *noun* [Middle English *barbe* barb, beard, from Middle French, from Latin *barba* — more at BEARD] (14th century)
1 : a medieval cloth headdress passing over or under the chin and covering the neck

2 a : a sharp projection extending backward (as from the point of an arrow or fishhook) and preventing easy extraction; *also* **:** a sharp projection with its point similarly oblique to something else **b :** a biting or pointedly critical remark or comment
3 : ²BARBEL
4 : any of the side branches of the shaft of a feather — see FEATHER illustration
5 : a plant hair or bristle ending in a hook

²barb *transitive verb* (1759) **:** to furnish with a barb

³barb *noun* [French *barbe,* from Italian *barbero,* from *barbero* of Barbary, from *Barberia* Barbary, coastal region in Africa] (1636) **:** any of a northern African breed of horses that are noted for speed and endurance and are related to Arabians

⁴barb *noun* (1967) *slang* **:** BARBITURATE

bar·bar·i·an \bär-'ber-ē-ən, -'bar-\ *adjective* [Latin *barbarus*] (14th century)
1 : of or relating to a land, culture, or people alien and usually believed to be inferior to another land, culture, or people
2 : lacking refinement, learning, or artistic or literary culture
— **barbarian** *noun*
— **bar·bar·i·an·ism** \-ē-ə-,ni-zəm\ *noun*

bar·bar·ic \bär-'bar-ik\ *adjective* (15th century)
1 a : of, relating to, or characteristic of barbarians **b :** possessing or characteristic of a cultural level more complex than primitive savagery but less sophisticated than advanced civilization
2 a : marked by a lack of restraint **:** WILD **b :** having a bizarre, primitive, or unsophisticated quality
3 : BARBAROUS 3 ◇
— **bar·bar·i·cal·ly** \-i-k(ə-)lē\ *adverb*

bar·ba·rism \'bär-bə-,ri-zəm\ *noun* (15th century)
1 a : a barbarian or barbarous social or intellectual condition **:** BACKWARDNESS **b :** the practice or display of barbarian acts, attitudes, or ideas
2 : an idea, act, or expression that in form or use offends against contemporary standards of good taste or acceptability

bar·bar·i·ty \bär-'bar-ə-tē\ *noun, plural* **-ties** (circa 1570)
1 : BARBARISM
2 a : barbarous cruelty **:** INHUMANITY **b :** an act or instance of such cruelty

bar·ba·ri·za·tion \,bär-bə-rə-'zā-shən\ *noun* (1822)

◇ WORD HISTORY
barbaric It is unfortunate that the ancient Greeks, in spite of their scientific curiosity and their distinction in the writing of history, left scant records of the languages spoken by peoples with whom they came into contact—languages now mostly lost forever to investigation. On the whole, the Greeks were not very interested in those who were not *Hellēnes,* "Greek-speakers." All non-Greek speakers were collectively *barbaroi,* a word that is onomatopoeic in origin, mimicking the babble-like sound of foreign speech to Greek ears. Especially after the Greeks' wars with the Persians, the *barbaroi* par excellence to the Greeks, the derivative *barbarikos* came to mean "violent" or "savage" in addition to simply "foreign." It is these senses we have inherited in the loanword *barbaric.*

\ə\ abut \ᵊ\ kitten \ər\ further \a\ ash \ā\ ace
\ä\ mop, mar \aù\ out \ch\ chin \e\ bet \ē\ easy
\g\ go \i\ hit \ī\ ice \j\ job \ŋ\ sing \ō\ go
\ò\ law \òi\ boy \th\ thin \t̲h̲\ the \ü\ loot \ù\ foot
\y\ yet \zh\ vision *see also* Guide to Pronunciation

: the act or process of barbarizing : the state of being barbarized

bar·ba·rize \'bär-bə-ˌrīz\ *verb* **-rized; -riz·ing** (1648)
transitive verb
: to make barbarian or barbarous
intransitive verb
: to become barbarous

bar·ba·rous \'bär-b(ə-)rəs\ *adjective* [Latin *barbarus*, from Greek *barbaros* foreign, ignorant] (15th century)
1 a : UNCIVILIZED **b** : lacking culture or refinement : PHILISTINE
2 : characterized by the occurrence of barbarisms
3 : mercilessly harsh or cruel
synonym see FIERCE
— **bar·ba·rous·ly** *adverb*
— **bar·ba·rous·ness** *noun*

Bar·ba·ry ape \'bär-b(ə-)rē-\ *noun* [*Barbary*, Africa] (1864)
: a tailless monkey (*Macaca sylvanus*) of northern Africa and Gibraltar

Barbary Coast *noun* (1880)
: a district or section of a city noted as a center of gambling, prostitution, and riotous nightlife

Barbary sheep *noun* (circa 1898)
: AOUDAD

barbe \'bärb\ *noun* [Middle English, from Middle French, literally, beard] (14th century)
: ¹BARB 1

¹bar·be·cue \'bär-bi-ˌkyü\ *transitive verb* **-cued; -cu·ing** (1690)
1 : to roast or broil on a rack over hot coals or on a revolving spit before or over a source of heat
2 : to cook in a highly seasoned vinegar sauce
— **bar·be·cu·er** *noun*

²barbecue *also* **bar·be·que** *noun* [American Spanish *barbacoa* framework for supporting meat over a fire, probably from Taino] (1709)
1 : a large animal (as a steer) roasted whole or split over an open fire or a fire in a pit; *also* : smaller pieces of barbecued meat
2 : a social gathering especially in the open air at which barbecued food is eaten
3 : an often portable fireplace over which meat and fish are roasted

barbed \'bärbd\ *adjective* (1611)
1 : having barbs
2 : characterized by pointed and biting criticism or sarcasm ⟨*barbed* witticisms⟩

barbed wire \'bärb(d)-'wīr, 'bäb(d)-\ *noun* (1881)
: twisted wires armed with barbs or sharp points — called also *barbwire*

¹bar·bel \'bär-bəl\ *noun* [Middle English, from Middle French, from (assumed) Vulgar Latin *barbellus*, diminutive of Latin *barbus* barbel, from *barba* beard — more at BEARD] (14th century)
: a European freshwater cyprinid fish (*Barbus barbus*) with four barbels on its upper jaw; *also* : any of various closely related fishes

²barbel *noun* [obsolete French, from Middle French, diminutive of *barbe* barb, beard] (1601)
: a slender tactile process on the lips of certain fishes (as catfishes)

bar·bell \'bär-ˌbel\ *noun* (1887)
: a bar with adjustable weighted disks attached to each end that is used for exercise and in weight lifting

¹bar·ber \'bär-bər\ *noun* [Middle English, from Middle French *barbeor*, from *barbe* beard — more at BARB] (14th century)
: one whose business is cutting and dressing hair, shaving and trimming beards, and performing related services

²barber *verb* **bar·bered; bar·ber·ing** \-b(ə-)riŋ\ (1606)
transitive verb
: to perform the services of a barber for
intransitive verb
: to perform the services of a barber

bar·ber·ry \'bär-ˌber-ē\ *noun* [Middle English *barbere*, from Middle French *barbarin*, from Arabic *barbārīs*] (14th century)
: any of a genus (*Berberis* of the family Berberidaceae, the barberry family) of shrubs usually having spines, yellow flowers, and oblong red berries

¹bar·ber·shop \'bär-bər-ˌshäp\ *noun* (1579)
: a barber's place of business

²barbershop *adjective* [from the old custom of men in barbershops forming quartets for impromptu singing of sentimental songs] (1910)
: of a style of unaccompanied group singing of popular songs usually marked by highly conventionalized close harmony

bar·bet \'bär-bət\ *noun* [probably from ¹*barb*] (1824)
: any of a family (Capitonidae) of nonpasserine tropical birds with a stout bill bearing bristles and usually swollen at the base

bar·bette \bär-'bet\ *noun* [French, diminutive of *barbe* headdress] (1772)
1 : a mound of earth or a protected platform from which guns fire over a parapet
2 : an armored structure protecting a gun turret on a warship

bar·bi·can \'bär-bi-kən\ *noun* [Middle English, from Middle French *barbacane*, from Medieval Latin *barbacana*] (13th century)
: an outer defensive work; *especially* : a tower at a gate or bridge

bar·bi·cel \'bär-bə-ˌsel\ *noun* [New Latin *barbicella*, diminutive of Latin *barba*] (1869)
: any of the small hook-bearing processes on a barbule of a feather — see FEATHER illustration

bar·bi·tal \'bär-bə-ˌtȯl\ *noun* [*barbit*uric + *-al* (as in *Veronal*, trademark for barbital)] (1919)
: a white crystalline addictive hypnotic $C_8H_{12}N_2O_3$ often administered in the form of its soluble sodium salt

bar·bi·tone \'bär-bə-ˌtōn\ *noun* [*barbit*uric + *-one*] (1914)
British : BARBITAL

bar·bi·tu·rate \bär-'bi-chə-rət, -ˌrāt; ˌbär-bə-'tyür-ət, -'tür-, -ˌāt\ *noun* (1928)
1 : a salt or ester of barbituric acid
2 : any of various derivatives of barbituric acid used especially as sedatives, hypnotics, and antispasmodics

bar·bi·tu·ric acid \ˌbär-bə-'t(y)ùr-ik-\ *noun* [part translation of German *Barbitursäure*, irregular from the name *Barbara* + International Scientific Vocabulary *ur*ic + German *Säure* acid] (1866)
: a synthetic crystalline acid $C_4H_4N_2O_3$ derived from pyrimidine

Bar·bi·zon \ˌbär-bə-'zōn, -'zän\ *adjective* [*Barbizon,* France] (1890)
: of, relating to, or being a school of mid-nineteenth century French landscape painters whose naturalistic canvases were based on direct observation of nature

bar·bule \'bär-(ˌ)byü(ə)l\ *noun* (1835)
: a minute barb; *especially* : one of the processes that fringe the barbs of a feather — see FEATHER illustration

barb·wire \'bärb-'wīr, 'bäb-\ *noun* (1880)
: BARBED WIRE

bar car *noun* (1945)
: CLUB CAR

bar·ca·role *or* **bar·ca·rolle** \'bär-kə-ˌrōl\ *noun* [French *barcarolle*, from Italian dialect (Venice) *barcarola*, from *barcarolo* gondolier, from *barca* bark, from Late Latin] (circa 1779)
1 : a Venetian boat song usually in ⁶/₈ or ¹²/₈ time characterized by the alternation of a strong and weak beat that suggests a rowing rhythm
2 : music imitating a barcarole

Bar·ce·lo·na chair \ˌbär-sə-'lō-nə-\ *noun* [*Barcelona,* Spain] (1970)
: an armless chair with leather-covered cushions on a stainless steel frame

bar·chan \(ˌ)bär-'kän, -'kän\ *noun* [Russian *barkhan*, from Kazakh] (1888)
: a moving crescent-shaped sand dune

Barcelona chair

bar chart *noun* (1914)
: BAR GRAPH

bar code *noun* (1963)
: a code consisting of a group of printed and variously patterned bars and spaces and sometimes numerals that is designed to be scanned and read into computer memory as identification for the object it labels

¹bard \'bärd\ *noun* [Middle English, from Scottish Gaelic & Irish] (15th century)
1 a : a tribal poet-singer skilled in composing and reciting verses on heroes and their deeds **b** : a composer, singer, or declaimer of epic or heroic verse
2 : POET
— **bard·ic** \'bär-dik\ *adjective*

²bard *or* **barde** \'bärd\ *noun* [Middle French *barde*, from Old Spanish *barda*, from Arabic *barda'ah*] (15th century)
: a piece of armor or ornament for a horse's neck, breast, or flank

³bard *transitive verb* (circa 1521)
1 : to furnish with bards
2 : to dress meat for cooking by covering with strips of fat

bard·ol·a·ter \bär-'dä-lə-tər\ *noun* [*Bard* (*of Avon*), epithet of Shakespeare + *-o-* + *-later*] (1903)
: a person who idolizes Shakespeare
— **bard·ol·a·try** \-lə-trē\ *noun*

Bar·do·li·no \ˌbär-dᵊl-'ē-(ˌ)nō\ *noun, plural* **-nos** [*Bardolino*, village on Lake Garda, Italy] (1934)
: a light red Italian wine

¹bare \'bar, 'ber\ *adjective* **bar·er; bar·est** [Middle English, from Old English *bær;* akin to Old High German *bar* naked, Lithuanian *basas* barefoot] (before 12th century)
1 a : lacking a natural, usual, or appropriate covering **b** (1) : lacking clothing (2) *obsolete* : BAREHEADED **c** : UNARMED
2 : open to view : EXPOSED
3 a : unfurnished or scantily supplied **b** : DESTITUTE ⟨*bare* of all safeguards⟩
4 a : having nothing left over or added ⟨the *bare* necessities of life⟩ **b** : MERE ⟨a *bare* two hours away⟩ **c** : devoid of amplification or adornment
5 *obsolete* : WORTHLESS ☆
— **bare·ness** *noun*

²bare *transitive verb* **bared; bar·ing** (before 12th century)
: to make or lay bare : UNCOVER

³bare *archaic past of* BEAR

bare·back \-ˌbak\ *or* **bare·backed** \-'bakt\ *adverb or adjective* (1562)
: on the bare back of a horse : without a saddle ⟨likes riding *bareback*⟩ ⟨*bareback* riding⟩

☆ SYNONYMS
Bare, naked, nude, bald, barren mean deprived of naturally or conventionally appropriate covering. BARE implies the removal of what is additional, superfluous, ornamental, or dispensable ⟨an apartment with *bare* walls⟩. NAKED suggests absence of protective or ornamental covering but may imply a state of nature, of destitution, or of defenselessness ⟨poor half-*naked* children⟩. NUDE applies especially to the unclothed human figure ⟨a *nude* model posing for art students⟩. BALD implies actual or seeming absence of natural covering and may suggest a conspicuous bareness ⟨a *bald* mountain peak⟩. BARREN often suggests aridity or impoverishment or sterility ⟨*barren* plains⟩.

bare·boat \-ˌbōt\ *noun* (circa 1949)
: a boat chartered without its crew

bare bones *noun plural* (1915)
: the barest essentials, facts, or elements
— **bare–bones** *adjective*

bare·faced \'bar-'fāst, 'ber-\ *adjective* (1590)
1 : having the face uncovered: **a** : having no whiskers : BEARDLESS **b** : wearing no mask
2 a : OPEN, UNCONCEALED **b** : lacking scruples
— **bare·faced·ly** \-'fā-sǝd-lē, -'fāst-lē\ *adverb*
— **bare·faced·ness** \-'fā-sǝd-nǝs, -'fās(t)-nǝs\ *noun*

bare·foot \-ˌfůt\ *or* **bare·foot·ed** \-'fů-tǝd\ *adverb or adjective* (before 12th century)
: with the feet bare ⟨went *barefoot* most of the summer⟩ ⟨*barefoot* boy, with cheek of tan —J. G. Whittier⟩

barefoot doctor *noun* (1971)
: an auxiliary medical worker trained to provide basic health care in rural areas of China

bare–hand·ed \'bar-'han-dǝd, 'ber-\ *adverb or adjective* (15th century)
1 : without gloves
2 : without tools or weapons ⟨fight an animal *bare-handed*⟩

bare·head·ed \-'he-dǝd\ *adverb or adjective* (14th century)
: without a covering for the head ⟨went *bareheaded* in the hot sun⟩ ⟨a *bareheaded* boy who had lost his cap⟩

bare–knuck·le \-'nǝ-kǝl\ *also* **bare–knuck·led** \-kǝld\ *adjective or adverb* (1903)
1 : not using boxing gloves ⟨champion *bare-knuckle* prizefighter of England —Dennis Craig⟩ ⟨when men fought *bare-knuckle*⟩
2 : having a fierce unrelenting character ⟨*bare-knuckle* politics⟩

bare·ly *adverb* (before 12th century)
1 : in a meager manner : PLAINLY ⟨a *barely* furnished room⟩
2 : SCARCELY, HARDLY ⟨*barely* enough money for lunch⟩

barf \'bärf\ *intransitive verb* [origin unknown] (1957)
: VOMIT

bar·fly \'bär-ˌflī\ *noun* (1910)
: a person who spends much time in bars

¹bar·gain \'bär-gǝn\ *noun, often attributive* (14th century)
1 : an agreement between parties settling what each gives or receives in a transaction between them or what course of action or policy each pursues in respect to the other
2 : something acquired by or as if by bargaining; *especially* : an advantageous purchase
3 : a transaction, situation, or event regarded in the light of its results
— **into the bargain** *also* **in the bargain** : BESIDES ⟨tastes good and is good for you, *into the bargain*⟩

²bargain *verb* [Middle English, from Middle French *bargaignier*, probably of Germanic origin; akin to Old English *borgian* to borrow — more at BURY] (14th century)
intransitive verb
1 : to negotiate over the terms of a purchase, agreement, or contract : HAGGLE
2 : to come to terms : AGREE
transitive verb
1 : to bring to a desired level by bargaining ⟨*bargain* a price down⟩
2 : to sell or dispose of by bargaining
— **bar·gain·er** *noun*
— **bargain for** : EXPECT ⟨more work than I *bargained for*⟩

bar·gain–base·ment \'bär-gǝn-'bās-mǝnt\ *adjective* (1948)
1 : of inferior quality or worth
2 : markedly inexpensive ⟨*bargain-basement* rates⟩

bargain basement *noun* (1899)
: a section of a store (as the basement) where merchandise is sold at reduced prices

¹barge \'bärj\ *noun* [Middle English, from Middle French, from Late Latin *barca*] (14th century)
: any of various boats: as **a** : a roomy usually flat-bottomed boat used chiefly for the transport of goods on inland waterways and usually propelled by towing **b** : a large motorboat supplied to the flag officer of a flagship **c** : a roomy pleasure boat; *especially* : a boat of state elegantly furnished and decorated

²barge *verb* **barged; barg·ing** (1649)
transitive verb
: to carry by barge
intransitive verb
1 : to move ponderously or clumsily
2 : to thrust oneself heedlessly or unceremoniously ⟨*barged* into the meeting⟩

barge·board \'bärj-ˌbōrd, -ˌbȯrd\ *noun* [origin unknown] (1833)
: an often ornamented board that conceals roof timbers projecting over gables

barg·ee \bär-'jē\ *noun* (1666)
British : BARGEMAN

bar·gel·lo \bär-'je-(ˌ)lō\ *noun* [the *Bargello*, museum in Florence, Italy; from the use of this stitch in the upholstery of 17th century chairs at the Bargello] (circa 1924)
: a needlework stitch that produces a zigzag pattern

barge·man \'bärj-mǝn\ *noun* (14th century)
: the master or a deckhand of a barge

bar graph *noun* (1924)
: a graphic means of quantitative comparison by rectangles with lengths proportional to the measure of the data or things being compared — called also **bar chart**

bar·hop \'bär-ˌhäp\ *intransitive verb* (1947)
: to visit and drink at a series of bars in the course of an evening

bar·ite \'bar-ˌīt, 'ber-\ *noun* [Greek *barytēs* weight, from *barys*] (1868)
: barium sulfate occurring as a mineral

¹bari·tone \'bar-ǝ-ˌtōn\ *noun* [French *baryton* or Italian *baritono*, from Greek *barytonos* deep sounding, from *barys* heavy + *tonos* tone — more at GRIEVE] (1609)
1 : a male singing voice of medium compass between bass and tenor; *also* : a person having this voice
2 : a member of a family of instruments having a range between tenor and bass; *especially* : the baritone saxhorn or baritone saxophone
— **bari·ton·al** \ˌbar-ǝ-'tō-nᵊl\ *adjective*

²baritone *adjective* (1729)
: relating to or having the range or part of a baritone

bar·i·um \'bar-ē-ǝm, 'ber-\ *noun* [New Latin, from *bar-*] (1808)
: a silver-white malleable toxic bivalent metallic element of the alkaline-earth group that occurs only in combination — see ELEMENT table

barium sulfate *noun* (1903)
: a colorless crystalline insoluble compound $BaSO_4$ that is used as a pigment and extender, as a filler, and as a substance opaque to X rays in medical photography of the alimentary canal

¹bark \'bärk\ *verb* [Middle English *berken*, from Old English *beorcan*; akin to Old Norse *berkja* to bark, Lithuanian *burgėti* to growl] (before 12th century)
intransitive verb
1 a : to make the characteristic short loud cry of a dog **b** : to make a noise resembling a bark
2 : to speak in a curt loud and usually angry tone : SNAP
transitive verb
1 : to utter in a curt loud usually angry tone
2 : to advertise by persistent outcry ⟨*barking* their wares⟩
— **bark up the wrong tree** : to proceed under a misapprehension; *also* : to misdirect one's efforts

²bark *noun* (before 12th century)

1 a : the sound made by a barking dog **b** : a similar sound
2 : a short sharp peremptory tone of speech or utterance
— **bark·less** \'bär-klǝs\ *adjective*

³bark *noun* [Middle English, from Old Norse *bark-*, *bȯrkr*; akin to Middle Dutch & Middle Low German *borke* bark] (14th century)
1 : the tough exterior covering of a woody root or stem; *specifically* : the tissues outside the cambium that include an inner layer especially of secondary phloem and an outer layer of periderm
2 : CINCHONA 2
— **bark·less** \'bär-klǝs\ *adjective*

⁴bark *transitive verb* (14th century)
1 : to treat with an infusion of tanbark
2 a : to strip the bark from **b** : to rub off or abrade the skin of

⁵bark *noun* [Middle English, from Middle French *barque*, from Old Provençal *barca*, from Late Latin] (15th century)
1 a : a small sailing ship **b** : a sailing ship of three or more masts with the aftmost mast fore-and-aft rigged and the others square-rigged
2 : a craft propelled by sails or oars

bark beetle *noun* (1862)
: any of numerous beetles (family Scolytidae) that bore under the bark of trees both as a larva and as an adult

bar·keep \'bär-ˌkēp\ *also* **bar·keep·er** \-ˌkē-pǝr\ *noun* (1712)
: BARTENDER

bar·ken·tine \'bär-kǝn-ˌtēn\ *noun* [⁵*bark* + -*entine*, alteration of -*antine* (as in *brigantine*)] (1693)
: a sailing ship of three or more masts with the foremost square-rigged and the others fore-and-aft rigged

¹bark·er \'bär-kǝr\ *noun* (14th century)
: one that barks; *especially* : a person who advertises by hawking at an entrance to a show

²barker *noun* (1611)
: one that removes or prepares bark

barking deer *noun* (1880)
: MUNTJAC

barky \'bär-kē\ *adjective* **bark·i·er; -est** (1590)
: covered with or resembling bark

bar·ley \'bär-lē\ *noun* [Middle English *barly*, from Old English *bærlic* of barley; akin to Old English *bere* barley, Latin *far* spelt] (before 12th century)
: a cereal grass (genus *Hordeum*, especially *H. vulgare*) having the flowers in dense spikes with long awns and three spikelets at each joint of the rachis; *also* : its seed used especially in malt beverages, breakfast foods, and stock feeds

bar·ley–bree \-ˌbrē\ *also* **bar·ley–broo** \-ˌbrü\ *noun* [*barley* + Scots *bree* or *broo* (bree)] (1724)
chiefly Scottish : WHISKY; *also* : MALT LIQUOR

bar·ley·corn \-ˌkȯrn\ *noun* (1500)
1 : a grain of barley
2 : an old unit of length equal to a third of an inch

bar·low \'bär-ˌlō\ *noun* [*Barlow*, family of 18th century English knife makers] (1884)
: a sturdy inexpensive jackknife

barm \'bärm\ *noun* [Middle English *berme*, from Old English *beorma*; akin to Latin *fermentum* yeast, *fervēre* to boil, Old Irish *berbaid* he boils] (before 12th century)
: yeast formed on fermenting malt liquors

bar·maid \'bär-ˌmād\ *noun* (circa 1658)
: a woman who serves liquor at a bar

bar·man \-mǝn\ *noun* (1837)
chiefly British : BARTENDER

\ǝ\ abut \ᵊ\ kitten \ǝr\ further \a\ ash \ā\ ace \ä\ mop, mar \aů\ out \ch\ chin \e\ bet \ē\ easy \g\ go \i\ hit \ī\ ice \j\ job \ŋ\ sing \ō\ go \ȯ\ law \ȯi\ boy \th\ thin \th\ the \ü\ loot \ů\ foot \y\ yet \zh\ vision *see also* Guide to Pronunciation

Bar·me·cid·al \ˌbär-mə-'sī-d°l\ *or* **Bar·me·cide** \'bär-mə-ˌsīd\ *adjective* [*Barmecide*, a wealthy Persian, who, in a tale of *The Arabian Nights' Entertainments,* invited a beggar to a feast of imaginary food] (1842)
: providing only the illusion of abundance ⟨a *Barmecidal* feast⟩

¹bar mitz·vah \bär-'mits-və\ *noun, often B&M capitalized* [Hebrew *bar miṣwāh,* literally, son of the (divine) law] (1816)
1 : a Jewish boy who reaches his 13th birthday and attains the age of religious duty and responsibility
2 : the initiatory ceremony recognizing a boy as a bar mitzvah

²bar mitzvah *transitive verb* **bar mitz·vahed; bar mitz·vah·ing** (1947)
: to administer the ceremony of bar mitzvah to

¹barmy \'bär-mē\ *adjective* **barm·i·er; -est** (15th century)
: full of froth or ferment

²barmy *adjective* **barm·i·er; -est** [alteration of *balmy*] (1892)
chiefly British **:** BALMY 2

barn \'bärn\ *noun* [Middle English *bern,* from Old English *bereærn,* from *bere* barley + *ærn* house, store] (before 12th century)
1 a : a usually large building for the storage of farm products or feed and usually for the housing of farm animals or farm equipment **b :** an unusually large and usually bare building ⟨a great *barn* of a hotel —W. A. White⟩
2 : a large building for the housing of a fleet of vehicles (as trolley cars or trucks) ◇
— **barn·like** \-ˌlīk\ *adjective*
— **barny** \'bär-nē\ *adjective*

Bar·na·bas \'bär-nə-bəs\ *noun* [Greek, from Aramaic *Barnebhū'āh*]
: a companion of the apostle Paul on his first missionary journey

bar·na·cle \'bär-ni-kəl\ *noun* [Middle English *barnakille,* alteration of *bernake, bernekke*] (15th century)
1 : BARNACLE GOOSE
2 [from a popular belief that the goose grew from the crustacean] **:** any of numerous marine crustaceans (subclass Cirripedia) with feathery appendages for gathering food that are free-swimming as larvae but permanently fixed (as to rocks, boat hulls, or whales) as adults
— **bar·na·cled** \-kəld\ *adjective*

barnacle 2:
1 peduncle, 2 cirri

barnacle goose *noun* (1768)
: a European goose (*Branta leucopsis*) that breeds in the arctic and is larger than the related brant

barn burner *noun* (circa 1960)
: one that arouses much interest or excitement ⟨the game should be a real *barn burner*⟩

barn dance *noun* (1831)
: an American social dance originally held in a barn and featuring several dance forms (as square dancing)

barn lot *noun* (1724)
chiefly Southern & Midland **:** BARNYARD

barn owl *noun* (1674)
: a widely distributed owl (*Tyto alba*) that has plumage mottled buff brown and gray above and chiefly white below, frequents barns and other buildings, and preys especially on rodents

barn raising *noun* (1856)
: a gathering for the purpose of erecting a barn
— compare ³BEE

barn·storm \'bärn-ˌstorm\ (1883)
intransitive verb
1 : to tour through rural districts staging usually theatrical performances

2 : to travel from place to place making brief stops (as in a political campaign or a promotional tour)
3 : to pilot one's airplane in sight-seeing flights with passengers or in exhibition stunts in an unscheduled course especially in rural districts
transitive verb
: to travel across while barnstorming
— **barn·storm·er** *noun*

barn swallow *noun* (1851)
: a swallow (*Hirundo rustica*) that is widespread in the northern hemisphere, has a deeply forked tail, and often nests in or near buildings

¹barn·yard \-ˌyärd\ *noun* (14th century)
: a usually fenced area adjoining a barn

²barnyard *adjective* (1927)
: SMUTTY, EARTHY, SCATOLOGICAL ⟨*barnyard* humor⟩

barnyard grass *noun* (1843)
: a coarse annual panicled grass (*Echinochloa crusgalli*) that has flowers borne on only one side of the raceme and is nearly cosmopolitan as a weed in cultivated ground

baro- — see BAR-

baro·gram \'bar-ə-ˌgram\ *noun* [International Scientific Vocabulary] (1884)
: a barographic tracing

baro·graph \-ˌgraf\ *noun* [International Scientific Vocabulary] (circa 1864)
: a recording barometer
— **baro·graph·ic** \ˌbar-ə-'gra-fik\ *adjective*

Ba·ro·lo \bä-'rō-(ˌ)lō, bə-\ *noun, plural* **-los** [*Barolo,* village in the Piedmont region, Italy] (1875)
: a dry red Italian wine

ba·rom·e·ter \bə-'rä-mə-tər\ *noun* (circa 1666)
1 : an instrument for determining the pressure of the atmosphere and hence for assisting in forecasting weather and for determining altitude
2 : one that indicates fluctuations (as in public opinion)
3 : STANDARD 4 ⟨a *barometer* to measure high school talent —Jeff Fellenzer⟩
— **baro·met·ric** \ˌbar-ə-'me-trik\ *adjective*
— **baro·met·ri·cal·ly** \-tri-k(ə-)lē\ *adverb*
— **ba·rom·e·try** \bə-'rä-mə-trē\ *noun*

barometric pressure *noun* (1827)
: the pressure of the atmosphere usually expressed in terms of the height of a column of mercury

bar·on \'bar-ən\ *noun* [Middle English, from Old French, of Germanic origin; akin to Old High German *baro* freeman] (13th century)
1 a : one of a class of tenants holding his rights and title by military or other honorable service directly from a feudal superior (as a king) **b :** a lord of the realm **:** NOBLE, PEER
2 a : a member of the lowest grade of the peerage in Great Britain **b :** a nobleman on the continent of Europe of varying rank **c :** a member of the lowest order of nobility in Japan
3 : a joint of meat consisting of two sirloins or loins and legs not cut apart at the backbone ⟨a *baron* of beef⟩
4 : a man of great power or influence in some field of activity ⟨cattle *baron*⟩

bar·on·age \-ə-nij\ *noun* (13th century)
: the whole body of barons or peers **:** NOBILITY 2

bar·on·ess \'bar-ə-nəs, -ˌnes, *US also* ˌbar-ə-'nes\ *noun* (15th century)
1 : the wife or widow of a baron
2 : a woman who holds a baronial title in her own right

bar·on·et \'bar-ə-nət, *US also* ˌbar-ə-'net\ *noun* (1614)
: the holder of a rank of honor below a baron and above a knight

bar·on·et·age \'bar-ə-nə-(ˌ)tij, ˌbar-ə-'ne-tij\ *noun* (1760)
1 : BARONETCY

2 : the whole body of baronets

bar·on·et·cy \'bar-ə-nət-sē, ˌbar-ə-'net-sē\ *noun* (1795)
: the rank of a baronet

ba·rong \bə-'roṅ, -'räṅ\ *noun* [of Austronesian origin; akin to Malay *parang* knife] (1898)
: a thick-backed thin-edged knife or sword used by the Moros

ba·ro·ni·al \bə-'rō-nē-əl\ *adjective* (1767)
1 : of or relating to a baron or the baronage
2 : STATELY, AMPLE ⟨a *baronial* room⟩

bar·ony \'bar-ə-nē\ *noun, plural* **-on·ies** (14th century)
1 : the domain, rank, or dignity of a baron
2 : a vast private landholding
3 : a field of activity under the sway of an individual or a special group

¹ba·roque \bə-'rōk, ba-, -'räk, -'rok\ *adjective, often capitalized* [French, from Middle French *barroque* irregularly shaped (of a pearl), from Portuguese *barroco* irregularly shaped pearl] (1765)
1 : of, relating to, or having the characteristics of a style of artistic expression prevalent especially in the 17th century that is marked generally by use of complex forms, bold ornamentation, and the juxtaposition of contrasting elements often conveying a sense of drama, movement, and tension
2 : characterized by grotesqueness, extravagance, complexity, or flamboyance
3 : irregularly shaped — used of gems ⟨a *baroque* pearl⟩
— **ba·roque·ly** *adverb*

²baroque *noun, often capitalized* (1877)
: the baroque style or the period in which it flourished

baro·re·cep·tor \ˌbar-ō-ri-'sep-tər\ *also* **baro·cep·tor** \'bar-ō-ˌsep-tər\ *noun* (1948)
: a neural receptor (as of the arterial walls) sensitive to changes in pressure

ba·rouche \bə-'rüsh\ *noun* [German *Barutsche,* from Italian *biroccio,* ultimately from Late Latin *birotus* two-wheeled, from Latin *bi- + rota* wheel — more at ROLL] (1801)
: a four-wheeled carriage with a driver's seat high in front, two double seats inside facing each other, and a folding top over the back seat

barque \'bärk\, **bar·quen·tine** \'bär-kən-ˌtēn\ *variant of* BARK, BARKENTINE

bar·quette \bär-'ket\ *noun* [French, diminutive of *barque* (ship)] (circa 1949)
: a small boat-shaped pastry shell

¹bar·rack \'bar-ək, -ik\ *noun* [French *baraque* hut, from Catalan *barraca*] (1686)
1 : a building or set of buildings used especially for lodging soldiers in garrison
2 a : a structure resembling a shed or barn that provides temporary housing **b :** housing characterized by extreme plainness or dreary uniformity — usually used in plural in all senses

◇ WORD HISTORY
barn Some English words that are monosyllabic today were obvious compound words to the Anglo-Saxons. Such a word is *barn,* from Old English *berern,* a compound of *bere, bære* "barley" and *ærn* "house, building." Neither *bere* nor *ærn* have left many direct descendants in Modern English, though in Scotland *bear* survived into the 20th century as a word for barley, and *ærn* "house, building" is akin to Old Norse *rann* "house," which figures in English *ransack.* Already in late Old English the compound *berern* was reduced to *bern,* which by the end of the Middle English period had become *barn.* In England, unlike the United States, a barn is still principally a place for storing fodder, so "barley-house" is not too inappropriate. English cows are typically housed and milked in a separate structure, the *cowhouse* or *cowshed.*

²**barrack** *transitive verb* (1701)
: to lodge in barracks

³**barrack** *verb* [origin unknown] (1887)
transitive verb
chiefly British : to shout at derisively or sarcastically
intransitive verb
1 *chiefly British* : ROOT, CHEER — usually used with *for*
2 *chiefly British* : JEER, SCOFF
— **bar·rack·er** *noun*

barracks bag *noun* (1938)
: a fabric bag for carrying personal equipment; *especially* : DUFFEL BAG

bar·ra·coon \ˌbar-ə-ˈkün\ *noun* [Spanish *barracón*, augmentative of *barraca* hut, from Catalan] (1848)
: an enclosure or barracks formerly used for temporary confinement of slaves or convicts — often used in plural

bar·ra·cou·ta \ˌbar-ə-ˈkü-tə\ *noun* [modification of American Spanish *barracuda*] (1835)
: a large elongate marine fish (*Thyrsites atun* of the family Gempylidae) used for food

bar·ra·cu·da \ˌbar-ə-ˈkü-də\ *noun, plural* **-da** *or* **-das** [American Spanish] (1678)
1 : any of a genus (*Sphyraena* of the family Sphyraenidae) of elongate predaceous often large fishes of warm seas that include fishes used for food as well as some forms regarded as toxic
2 : one that uses aggressive, selfish, and sometimes unethical methods to obtain a goal especially in business

¹**bar·rage** \ˈbär-ij\ *noun* [French, from *barrer* to bar, from *barre* bar] (1859)
: a dam placed in a watercourse to increase the depth of water or to divert it into a channel for navigation or irrigation

²**bar·rage** \bə-ˈräzh, -ˈräj\ *noun* [French (*tir de*) *barrage* barrier fire] (1916)
1 : artillery fire laid on a line close to friendly troops to screen and protect them
2 : a vigorous or rapid outpouring or projection of many things at once ⟨a *barrage* of protests⟩

³**bar·rage** \bə-ˈräzh, -ˈräj\ *transitive verb* **barraged; bar·rag·ing** (1918)
: to deliver a barrage against

barrage balloon *noun* (circa 1920)
: a small captive balloon used to support wires or nets as protection against air attacks

bar·ra·mun·di \ˌbar-ə-ˈmən-dē\ *also* **bar·ra·mun·da** \-də\ *noun* [probably from an Australian aboriginal language of Queensland] (1864)
: any of several Australian fishes (especially *Lates calcarifer* of the family Centropomidae) used for food

bar·ran·ca \bə-ˈraṇ-kə\ *or* **bar·ran·co** \-(ˌ)kō\ *noun, plural* **-cas** *or* **-cos** [Spanish] (circa 1691)
1 : a deep gully or arroyo with steep sides
2 : a steep bank or bluff

bar·ra·tor *also* **bar·ra·ter** \ˈbar-ə-tər\ *noun* (15th century)
: one who engages in barratry

bar·ra·try \ˈbar-ə-trē\ *noun, plural* **-tries** [Middle English *barratrie*, from Middle French *baraterie* deception, from *barater* to deceive, exchange] (15th century)
1 : the purchase or sale of office or preferment in church or state
2 : an unlawful act or fraudulent breach of duty on the part of a master of a ship or of the mariners to the injury of the owner of the ship or cargo
3 : the persistent incitement of litigation

Barr body \ˈbär-\ *noun* [Murray Llewellyn *Barr* (born 1908) Canadian anatomist] (1963)
: material of the inactivated X chromosome present in each of the female's somatic cells of most mammals used as a test of genetic femaleness (as in a fetus or an athlete) — called also *sex chromatin*

barre \ˈbär\ *noun* [French, from Medieval Latin *barra*] (1936)
: BAR 1c

barred \ˈbärd\ *adjective* (14th century)
: marked by or divided off by bars; *especially*
: having alternate bands of different color ⟨*barred* feather⟩

barred owl *noun* (1811)
: a large American owl (*Strix varia*) with brown eyes and bars of dark brown on the breast

¹**bar·rel** \ˈbar-əl\ *noun* [Middle English *barel*, from Middle French *baril*] (14th century)
1 : a round bulging vessel of greater length than breadth that is usually made of staves bound with hoops and has flat ends of equal diameter
2 a : the amount contained in a barrel; *especially* : the amount (as 31 gallons of fermented beverage or 42 gallons of petroleum) fixed for a certain commodity used as a unit of measure **b** : a great quantity
3 : a drum or cylindrical part: as **a** : the discharging tube of a gun **b** : the cylindrical metal box enclosing the mainspring of a timepiece **c** : the part of a fountain pen or of a pencil containing the ink or lead **d** : a cylindrical or tapering housing containing the optical components of a photographic-lens system and the iris diaphragm **e** : TUMBLING BARREL **f** : the fuel outlet from the carburetor on a gasoline engine
4 : the trunk of a quadruped
— **bar·reled** \-əld\ *adjective*
— **on the barrel** : asking for or granting no credit
— **over a barrel** : at a disadvantage : in an awkward position

²**barrel** *verb* **-reled** *or* **-relled; -rel·ing** *or* **-rel·ling** (15th century)
transitive verb
: to put or pack in a barrel
intransitive verb
: to move at a high speed or without hesitation

bar·rel·age \ˈbar-ə-lij\ *noun* (1890)
: amount (as of beer) in barrels

barrel cactus *noun* (1881)
: any of a genus (*Ferocactus*) of nearly globular deeply ribbed spiny cacti of Mexico and the adjacent U.S.

bar·rel–chest·ed \ˈbar-əl-ˌches-təd\ *adjective* (1926)
: having a large rounded chest

barrel cactus

barrel cuff *noun* (1926)
: an unfolded cuff (as on a shirt) usually fastened by a button

bar·rel·ful \ˈbar-əl-ˌfu̇l\ *noun, plural* **barrel·fuls** \-ˌfu̇lz\ *or* **bar·rels·ful** \-əlz-ˌfu̇l\ (14th century)
1 : as much or as many as a barrel will hold
2 : a large number or amount

bar·rel·head \-ˌhed\ *noun* (1840)
: the flat end of a barrel
— **on the barrelhead** : asking for or granting no credit ⟨paid cash *on the barrelhead*⟩

bar·rel·house \-ˌhau̇s\ *noun* (1883)
1 : a cheap drinking and usually dancing establishment
2 : a strident, uninhibited, and forcefully rhythmic style of jazz or blues

barrel organ *noun* (1772)
: an instrument for producing music by the action of a revolving cylinder studded with pegs on a series of valves that admit air from a bellows to a set of pipes

barrel racing *noun* (1972)
: a rodeo event for women in which a mounted rider makes a series of sharp turns around three barrels in a cloverleaf pattern

— **barrel race** *noun*
— **barrel racer** *noun*

barrel roll *noun* (circa 1920)
: an airplane maneuver in which a complete revolution about the longitudinal axis is made

barrel vault *noun* (1849)
: a semicylindrical vault
— **bar·rel–vault·ed** \-ˌvȯl-təd\ *adjective*

¹**bar·ren** \ˈbar-ən\ *adjective* [Middle English *bareine*, from Old French *baraine*] (13th century)
1 : not reproducing: as **a** : incapable of producing offspring — used especially of females or matings **b** : not yet or not recently pregnant **c** : habitually failing to fruit
2 : not productive: as **a** : producing little or no vegetation : DESOLATE ⟨*barren* deserts⟩ **b** : producing inferior crops ⟨*barren* soil⟩ **c** : unproductive of results or gain : FRUITLESS ⟨a *barren* scheme⟩
3 : DEVOID, LACKING — used with *of* ⟨*barren* of excitement⟩
4 : lacking interest, information, or charm
5 : DULL, UNRESPONSIVE
synonym see BARE
— **bar·ren·ly** *adverb*
— **bar·ren·ness** \-ə(n)-nəs\ *noun*

²**barren** *noun* (1651)
1 *plural* : an extent of usually level land having an inferior growth of trees or little vegetation
2 : a tract of barren land

bar·rette \bä-ˈret, bə-\ *noun* [French, diminutive of *barre* bar] (1901)
: a clip or bar for holding hair in place

¹**bar·ri·cade** \ˈbar-ə-ˌkād, ˌbar-ə-ˈ\ *transitive verb* **-cad·ed; -cad·ing** (1592)
1 : to block off or stop up with a barricade
2 : to prevent access to by means of a barricade

²**barricade** *noun* [French, from Middle French, from *barriquer* to barricade, from *barrique* barrel] (1642)
1 : an obstruction or rampart thrown up across a way or passage to check the advance of the enemy
2 : BARRIER 3, OBSTACLE
3 *plural* : a field of combat or dispute

bar·ri·ca·do \ˌbar-ə-ˈkā-(ˌ)dō\ *noun, plural* **-does** [modification of Middle French *barricade*] (1590)
archaic : BARRICADE
— **barricado** *transitive verb, archaic*

bar·ri·er \ˈbar-ē-ər\ *noun* [Middle English *barrere*, from Middle French *barriere*, from *barre*] (14th century)
1 a : something material that blocks or is intended to block passage ⟨highway *barriers*⟩ ⟨a *barrier* contraceptive⟩ **b** : a natural formation or structure that prevents or hinders movement or action ⟨geographic *barriers* to species dissemination⟩ ⟨*barrier* beaches⟩ ⟨drugs that cross the placental *barrier*⟩
2 *plural often capitalized* : a medieval war game in which combatants fight on foot with a fence or railing between them
3 : something immaterial that impedes or separates : OBSTACLE ⟨behavioral *barriers*⟩ ⟨trade *barriers*⟩ ⟨a *barrier* to honest communication⟩

barrier island *noun* (1943)
: a long broad sandy island lying parallel to a shore that is built up by the action of waves, currents, and winds and that protects the shore from the effects of the ocean

barrier reef *noun* (1805)
: a coral reef roughly parallel to a shore and separated from it by a lagoon

bar·ring \ˈbär-iŋ\ *preposition* (15th century)
: excluding by exception : EXCEPTING

bar·rio \'bär-ē-ˌō, 'bar-\ *noun, plural* **-ri·os** [Spanish, from Arabic *barrī* of the open country, from *barr* outside, open country] (1841) **1** : a ward, quarter, or district of a city or town in Spanish-speaking countries **2** : a Spanish-speaking quarter or neighborhood in a city or town in the U.S. especially in the Southwest

bar·ris·ter \'bar-ə-stər\ *noun* [Middle English *barrester,* from *barre* bar + *-ster* (as in *legister* lawyer)] (15th century) : a counsel admitted to plead at the bar and undertake the public trial of causes in an English superior court — compare SOLICITOR

bar·room \'bär-ˌrüm, -ˌrum\ *noun* (1797) : a room or establishment whose main feature is a bar for the sale of liquor

¹bar·row \'bar-(ˌ)ō\ *noun* [Middle English *bergh,* from Old English *beorg;* akin to Old High German *berg* mountain, Sanskrit *br̥hant* high] (before 12th century) **1** : MOUNTAIN, MOUND — used only in the names of hills in England **2** : a large mound of earth or stones over the remains of the dead : TUMULUS

²barrow *noun* [Middle English *barow,* from Old English *bearg;* akin to Old High German *barug* barrow] (before 12th century) : a male hog castrated before sexual maturity

³barrow *noun* [Middle English *barew,* from Old English *bearwe;* akin to Old English *beran* to carry — more at BEAR] (before 12th century) **1 a** : HANDBARROW **b** : WHEELBARROW **2** : a cart with a shallow box body, two wheels, and shafts for pushing it

barrow boy *noun* (1939) *British* : COSTERMONGER

bar sinister *noun* (1823) **1** : a heraldic charge held to be a mark of bastardy **2** : the fact or condition of being of illegitimate birth

bar·tend·er \'bär-ˌten-dər\ *noun* (1836) : one that serves liquor at a bar

¹bar·ter \'bär-tər\ *verb* [Middle English *bartren,* from Middle French *barater* to deceive, exchange] (15th century) *intransitive verb* : to trade by exchanging one commodity for another *transitive verb* : to trade or exchange by or as if by bartering — **bar·ter·er** \-tər-ər\ *noun*

²barter *noun* (15th century) **1** : the act or practice of carrying on trade by bartering **2** : the thing given in exchange in bartering

Bar·tho·lin's gland \'bär-thə-lənz-, 'bär-tᵊl-ənz-\ *noun* [Kaspar *Bartholin* (died 1738) Danish physician] (1901) : either of two oval racemose glands lying one to each side of the lower part of the vagina and secreting a lubricating mucus — compare COWPER'S GLAND

bar·ti·zan \'bär-tə-zən, ˌbär-tə-'zan\ *noun* [alteration of Middle English *bretasinge,* from *bretais* parapet — more at BRATTICE] (1808) : a small structure (as a turret) projecting from a building and serving especially for lookout or defense

Ba·ruch \bə-'rük, 'bär-ˌük\ *noun* [Late Latin, from Greek *Barouch,* from Hebrew *Bārūkh*] : a homiletic book included in the Roman Catholic canon of the Old Testament and in the Protestant Apocrypha — see BIBLE table

bar·ware \'bär-ˌwar, -ˌwer\ *noun* (1941) : glassware or utensils used in preparing and serving alcoholic beverages

bary·on \'bar-ē-ˌän\ *noun* [International Scientific Vocabulary *bary-* (from Greek *barys* heavy) + *²-on* — more at GRIEVE] (1953) : any of a group of elementary particles (as nucleons) that are subject to the strong force and are held to be a combination of three quarks

— bary·on·ic \ˌbar-ē-'ä-nik\ *adjective*

bar·yte \'bar-ˌīt, 'ber-\ *or* **ba·ry·tes** \bə-'rī-tēz\ *variant of* BARITE

bary·tone \'bar-ə-ˌtōn\ *variant of* BARITONE

bas·al \'bā-səl, -zəl\ *adjective* (1645) **1 a** : relating to, situated at, or forming the base **b** : arising from the base of a stem ⟨*basal* leaves⟩ **2 a** : of or relating to the foundation, base, or essence : FUNDAMENTAL **b** : of, relating to, or being essential for maintaining the fundamental vital activities of an organism : MINIMAL **c** : used for teaching beginners ⟨*basal* readers⟩ — **ba·sal·ly** *adverb*

basal body *noun* (1902) : a minute distinctively staining cell organelle found at the base of a flagellum or cilium and identical to a centriole in structure — called also *basal granule, kinetosome*

basal cell *noun* (circa 1903) : one of the innermost cells of the deeper epidermis of the skin

basal ganglion *noun* (circa 1889) : any of four deeply placed masses of gray matter (as the amygdala) in each cerebral hemisphere — called also *basal nucleus*

basal metabolic rate *noun* (1922) : the rate at which heat is given off by an organism at complete rest

basal metabolism *noun* (1913) : the turnover of energy in a fasting and resting organism using energy solely to maintain vital cellular activity, respiration, and circulation as measured by the basal metabolic rate

ba·salt \bə-'sȯlt, 'bā-ˌ\ *noun* [Latin *basaltes,* manuscript variant of *basanites* touchstone, from Greek *basanitēs* (*lithos*), from *basanos* touchstone, from Egyptian *bḫnw*] (1601) : a dark gray to black dense to fine-grained igneous rock that consists of basic plagioclase, augite, and usually magnetite — **ba·sal·tic** \bə-'sȯl-tik\ *adjective*

bas·cule \'bas-(ˌ)kyü(ə)l\ *noun* [French, seesaw] (1678) : an apparatus or structure (as a drawbridge) in which one end is counterbalanced by the other on the principle of the seesaw or by weights

¹base \'bās\ *noun, plural* **bas·es** \'bā-səz\ [Middle English, from Middle French, from Latin *basis,* from Greek, step, base, from *bainein* to go — more at COME] (13th century) **1 a** (1) : the lower part of a wall, pier, or column considered as a separate architectural feature (2) : the lower part of a complete architectural design **b** : the bottom of something considered as its support **c** : FOUNDATION : a side or face of a geometrical figure from which an altitude can be constructed; *especially* : one on which the figure stands (2) : the length of a base **d** : that part of a bodily organ by which it is attached to another more central structure of the organism **2 a** : a main ingredient ⟨paint having a latex *base*⟩ **b** : a supporting or carrying ingredient (as of a medicine) **3 a** : the fundamental part of something : GROUNDWORK, BASIS **b** : the economic factors on which in Marxist theory all legal, social, and political relations are formed **4** : the lower part of a heraldic field **5 a** : the starting point or line for an action or undertaking **b** : a baseline in surveying **c** : a center or area of operations: as (1) : the place from which a military force draws supplies (2) : a place where military operations begin (3) : a permanent military installation **d** (1) : a number (as 5 in $5^{6.44}$ or 5^7) that is raised to a power; *especially* : the number that when raised to a power equal to the logarithm of a

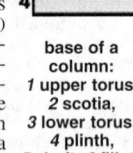

base of a
column:
1 upper torus,
2 scotia,
3 lower torus,
4 plinth,
5 shaft, *6* fillets

number yields the number itself ⟨the logarithm of 100 to the *base* 10 is 2 since $10^2 = 100$⟩ (2) : a number equal to the number of units in a given digit's place that for a given system of writing numbers is required to give the numeral 1 in the next higher place ⟨the decimal system uses a *base* of 10⟩; *also* : such a system of writing numbers using an indicated base ⟨convert from *base* 10 to *base* 2⟩ (3) : a number that is multiplied by a rate or of which a percentage or fraction is calculated ⟨to find the interest on $90 at 10% multiply the *base* 90 by .10⟩ **e** : ROOT 6 **6 a** : the starting place or goal in various games **b** : any one of the four stations at the corners of a baseball infield **c** : a point to be considered ⟨his opening remarks touched every *base*⟩ **7 a** : any of various typically water-soluble and bitter tasting compounds that in solution have a pH greater than 7, are capable of reacting with an acid to form a salt, and are molecules or ions able to take up a proton from an acid or able to give up an unshared pair of electrons to an acid **b** : any of the five purine or pyrimidine bases of DNA and RNA that include cytosine, guanine, adenine, thymine, and uracil **8** : a price level at which a security previously actively declining in price resists further price decline **9** : the part of a transformational grammar that consists of rules and a lexicon and generates the deep structures of a language — **based** \'bāst\ *adjective* — **base·less** \'bā-sləs\ *adjective* — **off base 1** : WRONG, MISTAKEN **2** : UNAWARES

²base *transitive verb* **based; bas·ing** (1587) **1** : to make, form, or serve as a base for **2** : to find a base or basis for — usually used with *on* or *upon*

³base *adjective* [Middle English *bas,* from Middle French, from Medieval Latin *bassus* short, low] (14th century) **1** *archaic* : of little height **2** *obsolete* : low in place or position **3** *obsolete* : BASS **4** *archaic* : BASEBORN **5 a** : resembling a villein : SERVILE ⟨a *base* tenant⟩ **b** : held by villenage ⟨*base* tenure⟩ **6 a** : being of comparatively low value and having relatively inferior properties (as lack of resistance to corrosion) ⟨a *base* metal such as iron⟩ — compare NOBLE **b** : containing a larger than usual proportion of base metals ⟨*base* silver denarii⟩ **7 a** : lacking or indicating the lack of higher qualities of mind or spirit : IGNOBLE **b** : lacking higher values : DEGRADING ⟨a drab *base* way of life⟩ ☆ — **base·ly** *adverb* — **base·ness** *noun*

base angle *noun* (circa 1949) : either of the angles of a triangle that have one side in common with the base

base·ball \'bās-ˌbȯl\ *noun, often attributive* (circa 1815) : a game played with a bat and ball between two teams of nine players each on a large field

having four bases that mark the course a runner must take to score; *also* **:** the ball used in this game

base·board \-ˌbōrd, -ˌbȯrd\ *noun* (1853)
: a board situated at or forming the base of something; *specifically* **:** a molding covering the joint of a wall and the adjoining floor

base·born \-'bȯrn\ *adjective* (1591)
1 : MEAN, IGNOBLE
2 a : of humble birth **b :** of illegitimate birth

base burner *noun* (1874)
: a stove in which the fuel is fed from a hopper as the lower layer is consumed

base exchange *noun* (circa 1956)
: a post exchange at a naval or air force base

base hit *noun* (1874)
: a hit in baseball that enables the batter to reach base safely without benefit of an error or fielder's choice

base·line \'bās-ˌlīn\ *noun, often attributive* (1750)
1 : a line serving as a basis; *especially* **:** one of known measure or position used (as in surveying or navigation) to calculate or locate something
2 a : either of the lines leading from home plate to first base and third base that are extended into the outfield as foul lines **b :** BASE PATH
3 : a boundary line at either end of a court (as in tennis or basketball)
4 : a set of critical observations or data used for comparison or as a control
5 : a starting point ⟨the *baseline* of this discussion⟩

base·lin·er \'bās-ˌlī-nər\ *noun* (circa 1929)
: a tennis player who stays on or near the baseline and seldom moves to the net

base·ment \'bā-smənt\ *noun* [probably from ¹*base*] (1730)
1 : the part of a building that is wholly or partly below ground level
2 : the ground floor facade or interior in Renaissance architecture
3 : the lowest or fundamental part of something; *specifically* **:** the rocks underlying stratified rocks
4 *chiefly New England* **:** a toilet or washroom especially in a school
— **base·ment·less** \-ləs\ *adjective*

basement membrane *noun* (1847)
: a thin membranous layer of connective tissue that separates a layer of epithelial cells from the underlying lamina propia

ba·sen·ji \bə-'sen-jē, -'zen-\ *noun* [probably from Lingala *basenji*, plural of *mosenji* native] (1933)
: any of a breed of small curly-tailed dogs of African origin that do not bark

base on balls (circa 1891)
: an advance to first base awarded a baseball player who during his turn at bat takes four pitches that are balls

base pair *noun* (1962)
: one of the pairs of chemical bases composed of a purine on one strand of DNA joined by hydrogen bonds to a pyrimidine on the other that hold together the two complementary strands much like the rungs of a ladder and include adenine linked to thymine or sometimes to uracil and guanine linked to cytosine

base path *noun* (1935)
: the area between the bases of a baseball field used by a base runner

base pay *noun* (1920)
: a rate or amount of pay for a standard work period, job, or position exclusive of additional payments or allowances

base runner *noun* (1867)
: a baseball player of the team at bat who is on base or is attempting to reach a base
— **base·run·ning** *noun*

bases *plural of* BASE *or of* BASIS

¹bash \'bash\ *verb* [origin unknown] (1750)

transitive verb
1 : to strike violently **:** HIT; *also* **:** to injure or damage by striking **:** SMASH — often used with *in*
2 : to attack physically or verbally ⟨media *bashing*⟩ ⟨celebrity *bashing*⟩
intransitive verb
: CRASH
— **bash·er** *noun*

²bash *noun* (1805)
1 : a forceful blow
2 : a festive social gathering **:** PARTY
3 : TRY, ATTEMPT ⟨have a *bash* at it⟩

ba·shaw \bə-'shò\ *variant of* PASHA

bash·ful \'bash-fəl\ *adjective* [obsolete *bash* (to be abashed)] (1548)
1 : socially shy or timid **:** DIFFIDENT, SELF-CONSCIOUS
2 : resulting from or typical of a bashful nature ⟨a *bashful* smile⟩
synonym see SHY
— **bash·ful·ly** \-fə-lē\ *adverb*
— **bash·ful·ness** \-fəl-nəs\ *noun*

¹ba·sic \'bā-sik *also* -zik\ *adjective* (1842)
1 : of, relating to, or forming the base or essence **:** FUNDAMENTAL
2 : constituting or serving as the basis or starting point
3 a : of, relating to, containing, or having the character of a chemical base **b :** having an alkaline reaction
4 : containing relatively little silica ⟨*basic* rocks⟩
5 : relating to, made by, used in, or being a process of making steel done in a furnace lined with basic material and under basic slag
— **ba·sic·i·ty** \bā-'si-sə-tē\ *noun*

²basic *noun* (1926)
1 : something that is basic **:** FUNDAMENTAL ⟨get back to *basics*⟩
2 : BASIC TRAINING

BA·SIC \'bā-sik\ *noun* [*Beginner's All-purpose Symbolic Instruction Code*] (1964)
: a simplified language for programming a computer

ba·si·cal·ly \'bā-si-k(ə-)lē *also* -zi-\ *adverb* (1903)
1 a : at a basic level **:** in fundamental disposition or nature ⟨*basically* correct⟩ ⟨*basically*, they are simple people⟩ **b :** for the most part ⟨they *basically* play zone defense⟩
2 : in a basic manner **:** SIMPLY ⟨live *basically*⟩

basic slag *noun* (1888)
: a slag low in silica and high in base-forming oxides that is used in the basic process of steelmaking and that is subsequently useful as a fertilizer

basic training *noun* (1943)
: the initial period of training of a military recruit

ba·sid·io·my·cete \bə-ˌsi-dē-ō-'mī-ˌsēt, -ˌmī-'sēt\ *noun* [ultimately from New Latin *basidium* + Greek *mykēt-*, *mykēs* fungus; akin to Greek *myxa* mucus — more at MUCUS] (1899)
: any of a large class (Basidiomycetes) or subdivision (Basidiomycotina) of higher fungi having septate hyphae, bearing spores on a basidium, and including rusts, smuts, mushrooms, and puffballs
— **ba·sid·io·my·ce·tous** \-dē-ō-ˌmī-'sē-təs\ *adjective*

ba·sid·io·spore \bə-'si-dē-ə-ˌspōr, -ˌspȯr\ *noun* [New Latin *basidium* + English *-o-* + *spore*] (1859)
: a spore produced by a basidium

ba·sid·i·um \bə-'si-dē-əm\ *noun, plural* **-ia** \-dē-ə\ [New Latin, from Latin *basis*] (1859)
: a structure on the fruiting body of a basidiomycete in which karyogamy occurs followed by meiosis to form usually four basidiospores

ba·si·fy \'bā-sə-ˌfī\ *transitive verb* **-fied; -fy·ing** (circa 1847)
: to convert into a base or make alkaline
— **ba·si·fi·ca·tion** \ˌbā-sə-fə-'kā-shən\ *noun*

ba·sil \'ba-zəl, 'bā-, -səl\ *noun* [Middle French *basile*, from Late Latin *basilicum*, from Greek *basilikon*, from neuter of *basilikos*] (15th century)
1 : any of several aromatic herbs (genus *Ocimum*) of the mint family; *especially* **:** SWEET BASIL
2 : the dried or fresh leaves of a basil used especially as a seasoning

bas·i·lar \'ba-zᵊl-ər, -sᵊl- *also* 'bā-\ *adjective* [Middle French *basilaire*, irregular from *base* base] (1541)
: of, relating to, or situated at the base

basilar membrane *noun* (1867)
: a membrane extending from the bony shelf of the cochlea to the outer wall and supporting the organ of Corti

Ba·sil·i·an \bə-'zi-lē-ən\ *noun* (1780)
: a member of the monastic order founded by Saint Basil in the 4th century in Cappadocia
— **Basilian** *adjective*

ba·sil·i·ca \bə-'si-li-kə *also* -'zi-\ *noun* [Latin, from Greek *basilikē*, from feminine of *basilikos* royal, from *basileus* king] (1541)
1 : an oblong building ending in a semicircular apse used in ancient Rome especially for a court of justice and place of public assembly
2 : an early Christian church building consisting of nave and aisles with clerestory and a large high transept from which an apse projects
3 : a Roman Catholic church given ceremonial privileges
— **ba·sil·i·can** \-kən\ *adjective*

bas·i·lisk \'ba-sə-ˌlisk, 'ba-zə-\ *noun* [Middle English, from Latin *basiliscus*, from Greek *basiliskos*, from diminutive of *basileus*] (14th century)
1 : a legendary reptile with fatal breath and glance
2 : any of several crested tropical American lizards (genus *Basiliscus*) related to the iguanas and noted for their ability to run on their hind legs
— **basilisk** *adjective*

ba·sin \'bā-sᵊn\ *noun* [Middle English, from Old French *bacin*, from Late Latin *bacchinon*] (13th century)
1 a : an open usually circular vessel with sloping or curving sides used typically for holding water for washing **b** *chiefly British* **:** a bowl used especially in cooking **c :** the quantity contained in a basin
2 a : a dock built in a tidal river or harbor **b :** an enclosed or partly enclosed water area
3 a : a large or small depression in the surface of the land or in the ocean floor **b :** the entire tract of country drained by a river and its tributaries **c :** a great depression in the surface of the lithosphere occupied by an ocean
4 : a broad area of the earth beneath which the strata dip usually from the sides toward the center
— **ba·sin·al** \-sᵊn-əl\ *adjective*
— **ba·sined** \-sᵊnd\ *adjective*
— **ba·sin·ful** \-ˌfùl\ *adjective*

bas·i·net \ˌba-sə-'net\ *noun* [Middle English *bacinet*, from Middle French, diminutive of Old French *bacin*] (14th century)
: a light often pointed steel helmet

ba·sip·e·tal \bā-'si-pə-tᵊl, -'zi-\ *adjective* [Latin *basis* + *petere* to go toward — more at FEATHER] (1869)
: proceeding from the apex toward the base or from above downward ⟨*basipetal* maturation of an inflorescence⟩
— **ba·sip·e·tal·ly** \-tᵊl-ē\ *adverb*

ba·sis \'bā-səs\ *noun, plural* **ba·ses** \-ˌsēz\ [Latin — more at BASE] (14th century)

1 : the bottom of something considered as its foundation
2 : the principal component of something
3 a : something on which something else is established or based **b :** an underlying condition or state of affairs ⟨hired on a trial *basis*⟩ ⟨on a first-name *basis*⟩
4 : the basic principle
5 : a set of linearly independent vectors in a vector space such that any vector in the vector space can be expressed as a linear combination of them with appropriately chosen coefficients

basis point *noun* (1967)
: one hundredth of one percent in the yield of an investment

bask \'bask\ *verb* [Middle English, probably from Old Norse *bathask*, reflexive of *batha* to bathe; akin to Old English *bæth* bath] (14th century)
intransitive verb
1 : to lie in or expose oneself to a pleasant warmth or atmosphere
2 : to take pleasure or derive enjoyment
transitive verb
obsolete **:** to warm by continued exposure to heat

bas·ket \'bas-kit, *British also* 'bäs-\ *noun* [Middle English, probably from (assumed) Old North French *baskot;* akin to Old French *baschoue* wooden vessel; both from Latin *bascauda* kind of basin, of Celtic origin; akin to Middle Irish *basc* necklace — more at FASCIA] (14th century)
1 a : a receptacle made of interwoven material (as osiers) **b :** any of various lightweight usually wood containers **c :** the quantity contained in a basket
2 : something that resembles a basket especially in shape or use
3 a : a net open at the bottom and suspended from a metal ring that constitutes the goal in basketball **b :** a field goal in basketball
4 a : an aggregate of values (as of selected currencies) the average of which serves as a monetary standard **b :** a selection of financial instruments (as equities, futures, or options) the values of which reflect market fluctuations
5 : a ring around the lower end of a ski pole that keeps the pole from sinking too deep in snow
— **bas·ket·like** \-,līk\ *adjective*

bas·ket·ball \-,bȯl\ *noun, often attributive* (1892)
: a usually indoor court game between two teams of usually five players each who score by tossing an inflated ball through a raised goal; *also* **:** the ball used in this game

basket case *noun* (1919)
1 : a person who has all four limbs amputated
2 : one that is completely incapacitated, inoperative, or worn out (as from nervous tension)

bas·ket·ful \'bas-kit-,fu̇l\ *noun, plural* **bas·ket·fuls** \-,fu̇lz\ *also* **bas·kets·ful** \-kits-,fu̇l\ (14th century)
: as much or as many as a basket will hold; *also* **:** a considerable quantity

basket hilt *noun* (circa 1550)
: a hilt with a basket-shaped guard to protect the hand
— **bas·ket–hilt·ed** \,bas-kit-'hil-təd\ *adjective*

Basket Maker *noun* (1897)
: any of three stages of an ancient culture of the plateau area of southwestern U.S.; *also* **:** a member of the people who produced the Basket Maker culture

basket–of–gold *noun* (1930)
: a European perennial herb (*Aurinia saxatilis* synonym *Alyssum saxatile*) widely cultivated for its grayish foliage and yellow flowers

bas·ket·ry \'bas-ki-trē\ *noun, plural* **-ries** (1851)
1 : BASKETWORK
2 : the art or craft of making baskets or objects woven like baskets

basket star *noun* (circa 1923)
: any of various brittle stars (suborder Euryalina) with slender complexly branched interlacing arms

basket weave *noun* (circa 1915)
: a textile weave resembling the checkered pattern of a plaited basket; *also* **:** something resembling this weave

bas·ket·work \'bas-kit-,wərk\ *noun* (1769)
: objects produced by basketry

bask·ing shark \'bas-kiŋ-\ *noun* (circa 1769)
: a large plankton-feeding shark (*Cetorhinus maximus*) that has an oil-rich liver and sometimes attains a length of 40 feet (12 meters)

bas·ma·ti rice \,bäz-'mä-tē- *also* ,baz-\ *noun* [Hindi *bāsmatī* kind of rice, literally, something fragrant] (1845)
: a cultivated aromatic long-grain rice of South Asian origin — called also *basmati*

bas mitz·vah \bäs-'mits-və\ *noun, often B&M capitalized* [Hebrew *bath miṣwāh*, literally, daughter of the (divine) law] (1952)
1 : a Jewish girl who at about 13 years of age assumes religious responsibilities
2 : the initiatory ceremony recognizing a girl as a bas mitzvah

ba·so·phil \'bā-sə-,fil, -zə-\ *or* **ba·so·phile** \-,fīl\ *noun* (circa 1890)
: a basophilic substance or structure; *especially* **:** a leukocyte containing basophilic granules that is similar in function to a mast cell

ba·so·phil·ia \,bā-sə-'fi-lē-ə, -zə-\ *noun* [New Latin] (1905)
1 : tendency to stain with basic dyes
2 : an abnormal condition in which some tissue element has increased basophilia

ba·so·phil·ic \-'fi-lik\ *adjective* [International Scientific Vocabulary *base* + *-o-* + *-philic*] (circa 1894)
: staining readily with basic stains

Ba·so·tho \bä-'sō-,tō, -'sü-,tü\ *noun plural* (1895)
: a Bantu-speaking people of Lesotho

Basque \'bask\ *noun* [French, from Middle French, from Latin *Vasco*] (1835)
1 : a member of a people inhabiting the western Pyrenees on the Bay of Biscay
2 : the language of the Basques of unknown relationship
3 *not capitalized* **:** a tight-fitting bodice for women
— **Basque** *adjective*

bas–re·lief \,bä-ri-'lēf, 'bä-ri-,\ *noun* [French, from *bas* low + *relief* raised work] (1667)
: sculptural relief in which the projection from the surrounding surface is slight and no part of the modeled form is undercut; *also* **:** sculpture executed in bas-relief

bas-relief

¹**bass** \'bas\ *noun, plural* **bass** *or* **bass·es** [Middle English *base, bærs*, from Old English *bærs;* akin to Old High German *bersich* perch] (before 12th century)
: any of numerous edible spiny-finned marine or freshwater fishes (especially families Centrarchidae, Serranidae, and Percichthyidae)

²**bass** \'bās\ *adjective* [Middle English *bas* base] (15th century)
1 : deep or grave in tone
2 a : of low pitch **b :** relating to or having the range or part of a bass

³**bass** \'bās\ *noun* (15th century)
1 a : the lowest voice part in a 4-part chorus **b :** the lower half of the whole vocal or instrumental tonal range — compare TREBLE **c :** the lowest adult male singing voice; *also* **:** a per-

son having this voice **d :** a member of a family of instruments having the lowest range; *especially* **:** DOUBLE BASS
2 : a deep or grave tone **:** a low-pitched sound

⁴**bass** \'bas\ *noun* [alteration of *bast*] (1691)
1 : BASSWOOD 1
2 : a coarse tough fiber from palms

bass clef *noun* (circa 1771)
1 : a clef placing the F below middle C on the fourth line of the staff
2 : the bass staff

bass drum *noun* (1804)
: a large drum having two heads and giving a booming sound of low indefinite pitch — see DRUM illustration

bas·set hound \'ba-sət\ *noun* [French *basset*, from Middle French, from *basset* short, from *bas* low — more at BASE] (1883)
: any of an old breed of short-legged hunting dogs of French origin having very long ears and crooked front legs — called also *bassett*

basset hound

bass fiddle *noun* (1951)
: DOUBLE BASS

bass horn *noun* (circa 1846)
: an obsolete wind instrument shaped like a bassoon but with a cup-shaped mouthpiece

bas·si·net \,ba-sə-'net\ *noun* [probably modification of French *barcelonnette*, diminutive of *berceau* cradle] (1854)
1 : a baby's basketlike bed (as of wickerwork or plastic) often with a hood over one end
2 : a perambulator that resembles a bassinet

bass·ist \'bā-sist\ *noun* (circa 1909)
: a person who plays an acoustic or electric bass

bas·so \'ba-(,)sō, 'bä-\ *noun, plural* **bassos** *or* **bas·si** \'bä-,sē\ [Italian, from Medieval Latin *bassus*, from *bassus* short, low] (circa 1724)
1 : a bass singer; *especially* **:** an operatic bass
2 : a low deep voice

bas·soon \bə-'sün, ba-\ *noun* [French *basson*, from Italian *bassone*, from *basso*] (1724)
: a double-reed woodwind instrument having a long U-shaped conical tube connected to the mouthpiece by a thin metal tube and a usual range two octaves lower than that of the oboe
— **bas·soon·ist** \-'sü-nist\ *noun*

bassoon

bas·so pro·fun·do \,ba-(,)sō-prə-'fən-(,)dō, ,bä-, -'fün-\ *noun, plural* **basso profundos** [Italian, literally, deep bass] (1860)
: a deep heavy bass voice with an exceptionally low range; *also* **:** a person having this voice

bas·so–re·lie·vo *also* **bas·so–ri·lie·vo** \,ba-(,)sō-ri-'lē-(,)vō, ,bä-(,)sō-rēl-'yā-(,)vō\ *noun* [Italian *bassorilievo*, from *basso* low + *rilievo* relief] (1644)
: BAS-RELIEF

bass viol *noun* (1590)
1 : VIOLA DA GAMBA
2 : DOUBLE BASS

bass·wood \'bas-,wu̇d\ *noun* (1670)
1 : any of several New World lindens; *especially* **:** LINDEN 1b
2 : the straight-grained white wood of a basswood

bast \'bast\ *noun* [Middle English, from Old English *bæst;* akin to Old High German & Old Norse *bast* bast] (before 12th century)
1 : PHLOEM
2 : BAST FIBER

¹bas·tard \'bas-tərd\ *noun* [Middle English, from Old French, probably of Germanic origin; akin to Old Frisian *bost* marriage, Old English *bindan* to bind] (14th century) **1 :** an illegitimate child **2 :** something that is spurious, irregular, inferior, or, or of questionable origin **3 a :** an offensive or disagreeable person — used as a generalized term of abuse **b :** MAN, FELLOW
— **bas·tard·ly** *adjective*

²bastard *adjective* (14th century) **1 :** ILLEGITIMATE **2 :** of mixed or ill-conceived origin ⟨known for coining *bastard* words⟩ **3 :** of abnormal shape or irregular size **4 :** of a kind similar to but inferior to or less typical than some standard ⟨*bastard* measles⟩ **5 :** lacking genuineness or authority **:** FALSE

bas·tard·ise *British variant of* BASTARDIZE

bas·tard·ize \'bas-tər-,dīz\ *transitive verb* **-ized; -iz·ing** (1587) **1 :** to reduce from a higher to a lower state or condition **:** DEBASE **2 :** to declare or prove to be a bastard **3 :** to modify especially by introducing discordant or disparate elements
— **bas·tard·i·za·tion** \,bas-tər-də-'zā-shən\ *noun*

bastard wing *noun* (1772) **:** ALULA

bas·tardy \'bas-tər-dē\ *noun, plural* **-tard·ies** (15th century) **1 :** the quality or state of being a bastard **:** ILLEGITIMACY **2 :** the begetting of an illegitimate child

¹baste \'bāst\ *transitive verb* **bast·ed; bast·ing** [Middle English, from Middle French *bastir,* of Germanic origin; akin to Old High German *besten* to patch, Old English *bæst* bast] (15th century) **:** to sew with long loose stitches in order to hold something in place temporarily
— **bas·ter** *noun*

²baste *transitive verb* **bast·ed; bast·ing** [Middle English *baisten*] (15th century) **:** to moisten (as meat) at intervals with a liquid (as melted butter, fat, or pan drippings) especially during cooking
— **bast·er** *noun*

³baste *transitive verb* **bast·ed; bast·ing** [probably from Old Norse *beysta;* akin to Old English *bēatan* to beat] (1533) **1 :** to beat severely or soundly **:** THRASH **2 :** to scold vigorously **:** BERATE

bast fiber *noun* (circa 1885) **:** a strong woody fiber obtained chiefly from the phloem of plants and used especially in cordage, matting, and fabrics

bas·tille *noun* \ba-'stē(ə)l\ [French *bastille,* from the *Bastille,* fortress in Paris, from Middle French *bastille,* modification of Old Provençal *bastida* fortified town, from *bastir* to build, of Germanic origin; akin to Old High German *besten* to patch] (1741) **:** PRISON, JAIL

Bastille Day *noun* (1920) **:** July 14 observed in France as a national holiday in commemoration of the fall of the Bastille in 1789

¹bas·ti·na·do \,bas-tə-'nā-(,)dō, -'nä-\ *or* **bas·ti·nade** \,bas-tə-'nād, -'näd\ *noun, plural* **-na·does** *or* **-nades** [Spanish *bastonada,* from *bastón* stick, from Late Latin *bastum*] (1572) **1 :** a blow with a stick or cudgel **2 a :** a beating especially with a stick **b :** a punishment consisting of beating the soles of the feet with a stick **3 :** STICK, CUDGEL

²bastinado *transitive verb* **-doed; -do·ing** (1599) **:** to subject to repeated blows

¹bast·ing \'bā-stiŋ\ *noun* (15th century) **1 :** the action of a sewer who bastes

2 a : the thread used in basting **b :** the stitching made by basting

²basting *noun* (1530) **1 :** the action of one that bastes food **2 :** the liquid used in basting

³basting *noun* (1590) **:** a severe beating

bas·tion \'bas-chən\ *noun* [Middle French, from Old Italian *bastione,* augmentative of *bastia* fortress, derivative from dialect form of *bastire* to build, of Germanic origin; akin to Old High German *besten* to patch] (1562) **1 :** a projecting part of a fortification **2 :** a fortified area or position **3 :** something that is considered a stronghold **:** BULWARK
— **bas·tioned** \-chənd\ *adjective*

Ba·su·to \bə-'sü-(,)tō\ *noun, plural* **Basuto** *or* **Basutos** (1835) **:** a member of the Basotho people

¹bat \'bat\ *noun* [Middle English, from Old English *batt*] (before 12th century) **1 :** a stout solid stick **:** CLUB **2 :** a sharp blow **:** STROKE **3 a :** a usually wooden implement used for hitting the ball in various games **b :** a paddle used in various games (as table tennis) **c :** the short whip used by a jockey **4 a :** BATSMAN **b :** a turn at batting — usually used in the phrase *at bat* **5 :** BATT **6** *British* **:** rate of speed **:** GAIT **7 :** BINGE
— **off one's own bat** *chiefly British* **:** through one's own efforts
— **off the bat** **:** without delay **:** IMMEDIATELY

²bat *verb* **bat·ted; bat·ting** (15th century) *transitive verb* **1 :** to strike or hit with or as if with a bat **2 a :** to advance (a base runner) by batting **b :** to have a batting average of **3 :** to discuss at length **:** consider in detail *intransitive verb* **1 a :** to strike or hit a ball with a bat **b :** to take one's turn at bat **2 :** to wander aimlessly

³bat *noun* [alteration of Middle English *bakke,* probably of Scandinavian origin; akin to Old Swedish *nattbakka* bat] (1580) **:** any of a widely distributed order (Chiroptera) of nocturnal usually frugivorous or insectivorous flying mammals that have wings formed from four elongated digits of the forelimb covered by a cutaneous membrane and that have adequate visual capabilities but often rely on echolocation

⁴bat *transitive verb* **bat·ted; bat·ting** [probably alteration of ²*bate*] (circa 1838) **:** to wink especially in surprise or emotion ⟨never *batted* an eye⟩; *also* **:** FLUTTER ⟨*batted* his eyelashes⟩

bat·boy \'bat-,bȯi\ *noun* (circa 1925) **:** a boy employed to look after the equipment (as bats) of a baseball team

¹batch \'bach\ *noun* [Middle English *bache;* akin to Old English *bacan* to bake] (15th century) **1 :** the quantity baked at one time **:** BAKING **2 a :** the quantity of material prepared or required for one operation; *specifically* **:** a mixture of raw materials ready for fusion into glass **b :** the quantity produced at one operation **c :** a group of jobs (as programs) which are submitted for processing on a computer and whose results are obtained at a later time ⟨*batch* processing⟩ — compare TIME-SHARING **3 :** a quantity (as of persons or things) considered as a group

²batch *transitive verb* (1876) **:** to bring together or process as a batch
— **batch·er** *noun*

³batch *variant of* BACH

¹bate \'bāt\ *verb* **bat·ed; bat·ing** [Middle English, short for *abaten* to abate] (14th century)

transitive verb **1 :** to reduce the force or intensity of **:** RESTRAIN ⟨with *bated* breath⟩ **2 :** to take away **:** DEDUCT **3** *archaic* **:** to lower especially in amount or estimation **4** *archaic* **:** BLUNT *intransitive verb obsolete* **:** DIMINISH, DECREASE

²bate *intransitive verb* **bat·ed; bat·ing** [Middle English, from Middle French *batre* to beat, from Latin *battuere*] (14th century) *of a falcon or hawk* **:** to attempt to fly off something (as a gauntlet) in fear

bat–eared fox \'bat-,ird-\ *noun* (1946) **:** a large-eared yellowish gray fox (*Otocyon megalotis*) that inhabits arid unforested areas of eastern and southern Africa

ba·teau \ba-'tō\ *noun, plural* **ba·teaux** \-'tō(z)\ [Canadian French, from French, from Old French *batel,* from Old English *bāt* boat — more at BOAT] (1711) **:** any of various small craft; *especially* **:** a flat-bottomed boat with raked bow and stern and flaring sides

Bates·ian \'bāt-sē-ən\ *adjective* [Henry Walter Bates (died 1892) English naturalist] (1896) **:** characterized by or being mimicry involving resemblance of an innocuous species to another that is protected from predators by repellent qualities (as unpalatability) ⟨*Batesian* mimic⟩

bat·fish \'bat-,fish\ *noun* (1873) **:** any of several fishes with winglike processes; *especially* **:** any of a family (Ogcocephalidae) of flattened pediculate fishes (as a common West Indian form *Ogcocephalus vespertilio*)

batfish

bat·fowl \-,faul\ *intransitive verb* (15th century) **:** to catch birds at night by blinding them with a light and knocking them down with a stick or netting them

¹bath \'bath, 'báth\ *noun, plural* **baths** \'bathz, 'baths, 'báthz, 'báths\ [Middle English, from Old English *bæth;* akin to Old High German *bad* bath, Old High German *bāen* to warm] (before 12th century) **1 :** a washing or soaking (as in water or steam) of all or part of the body **2 a :** water used for bathing **b** (1) **:** a contained liquid for a special purpose (2) **:** a receptacle holding the liquid **c** (1) **:** a medium for regulating the temperature of something placed in or on it (2) **:** a vessel containing this medium **3 a :** BATHROOM **b :** a building containing an apartment or a series of rooms designed for bathing **c :** SPA — usually used in plural **d** *British* **:** SWIMMING POOL — often used in plural **4 a :** the quality or state of being covered with a liquid **b :** FLOOD 3 **5 :** BATHTUB **6 :** a financial setback **:** LOSS ⟨took a *bath* in the market⟩

²bath (15th century) *transitive verb British* **:** to give a bath to *intransitive verb British* **:** to take a bath

³bath *noun* [Hebrew] (14th century)

: an ancient Hebrew liquid measure corresponding to the ephah of dry measure

bath chair \'bath-, 'bath-\ *noun, often B capitalized* [*Bath,* England] (1823)
: a hooded and sometimes glassed wheeled chair used especially by invalids; *broadly*
: WHEELCHAIR

¹bathe \'bāth\ *verb* **bathed; bath·ing** [Middle English, from Old English *bathian;* akin to Old English *bæth* bath] (before 12th century)
transitive verb
1 : MOISTEN, WET
2 : to wash in a liquid (as water)
3 : to apply water or a liquid medicament to
4 : to flow along the edge of **:** LAVE
5 : to suffuse with or as if with light
intransitive verb
1 : to take a bath
2 : to go swimming
3 : to become immersed or absorbed
— **bath·er** \'bā-thər\ *noun*

²bathe *noun* (1831)
1 *British* **:** ¹BATH 1
2 *British* **:** SWIM, DIP

ba·thet·ic \bə-'the-tik\ *adjective* [*bathos* + *-etic* (as in *pathetic*)] (circa 1864)
: characterized by bathos
— **ba·thet·i·cal·ly** \-ti-k(ə-)lē\ *adverb*

bath·house \'bath-,haus, 'bath-\ *noun* (1705)
1 : a building equipped for bathing
2 : a building containing dressing rooms for bathers

bathing beauty *noun* (1920)
: a woman in a bathing suit who is a contestant in a beauty contest

bathing suit *noun* (1873)
: SWIMSUIT

bath mat *noun* (1895)
: a usually washable mat used in a bathroom

bath·o·lith \'ba-thə-,lith\ *noun* [Greek *bathos* depth + International Scientific Vocabulary *-lith*] (circa 1900)
: a great mass of intruded igneous rock that for the most part stopped in its rise a considerable distance below the surface
— **bath·o·lith·ic** \,ba-thə-'li-thik\ *adjective*

ba·thos \'bā-,thäs\ *noun* [Greek, literally, depth] (1727)
1 a : the sudden appearance of the commonplace in otherwise elevated matter or style **b**
: ANTICLIMAX
2 : exceptional commonplaceness **:** TRITENESS
3 : insincere or overdone pathos **:** SENTIMENTALISM

bath·robe \'bath-,rōb, 'bath-\ *noun* (1902)
: a loose often absorbent robe worn before and after bathing or as a dressing gown

bath·room \-,rüm, -,rum\ *noun* (1780)
1 : a room containing a bathtub or shower and usually a sink and toilet
2 : LAVATORY 2

bath salts *noun plural* (1907)
: a usually colored crystalline compound for perfuming and softening bathwater

bath·tub \-,təb\ *noun* (1869)
: a usually fixed tub for bathing

bathtub gin *noun* (1930)
: a homemade spirit concocted from raw alcohol, water, essences, and essential oils

bath·wa·ter \'bath-,wo-tər, 'bath-, -,wä-tər\ *noun* (14th century)
: water for a bath

bathy- *combining form* [International Scientific Vocabulary, from Greek, from *bathys* deep]
1 : deep **:** depth ⟨*bathy*al⟩
2 : deep-sea ⟨*bathy*sphere⟩

bathy·al \'ba-thē-əl\ *adjective* (1921)
: of or relating to the ocean depths or floor usually from 600 to 6000 feet (180 to 1800 meters)

ba·thym·e·try \bə-'thi-mə-trē\ *noun, plural* **-tries** [International Scientific Vocabulary] (circa 1859)
: the measurement of water depth at various places in a body of water; *also* **:** the information derived from such measurements

— **bathy·met·ric** \,ba-thi-'me-trik\ *also* **bathy·met·ri·cal** \-tri-kəl\ *adjective*
— **bathy·met·ri·cal·ly** \-tri-k(ə-)lē\ *adverb*

bathy·pe·lag·ic \,ba-thi-pə-'la-jik\ *adjective* (circa 1900)
: of, relating to, or living in the ocean depths especially between 2000 and 12,000 feet (600 and 3600 meters)

bathy·scaphe \'ba-thi-,skaf, -,skāf\ *or* **bathy·scaph** \-,skaf\ *noun* [International Scientific Vocabulary *bathy-* + Greek *skaphē* light boat] (1947)
: a navigable submersible for deep-sea exploration having a spherical watertight cabin attached to its underside

bathy·sphere \-,sfir\ *noun* (1930)
: a strongly built steel diving sphere for deep-sea observation

bathy·ther·mo·graph \-'thər-mə-,graf\ *noun* (1938)
: an instrument designed to record water temperature as a function of depth

ba·tik \bə-'tēk, 'ba-tik\ *noun* [Javanese *batik*] (1880)
1 : a fabric printed by an Indonesian method of hand-printing textiles by coating with wax the parts not to be dyed; *also* **:** the method itself
2 : a design executed in batik

bat·ing \'bā-tin\ *preposition* (1647)
: with the exception of **:** EXCEPTING

ba·tiste \bə-'tēst, ba-\ *noun* [French] (1697)
: a fine soft sheer fabric of plain weave made of various fibers

bat·man \'bat-mən\ *noun* [French *bât* packsaddle] (1755)
: an orderly of a British military officer

bat mitz·vah \bät-'mits-və\ *often B&M capitalized, variant of* BAS MITZVAH

ba·ton \bə-'tän, ba-, -'tōⁿ *also* 'ba-tᵊn\ *noun* [French *bâton,* from Old French *baston,* from Late Latin *bastum* stick] (1520)
1 : CUDGEL, TRUNCHEON; *specifically* **:** BILLY CLUB
2 : a staff borne as a symbol of office
3 : a narrow heraldic bend
4 : a slender rod with which a leader directs a band or orchestra
5 : a hollow cylinder carried by each member of a relay team and passed to the succeeding runner
6 : a hollow metal rod with a weighted bulb at one or both ends that is flourished or twirled by a drum major or drum majorette

bat out *transitive verb* (1941)
: to compose especially in a casual, careless, or hurried manner

ba·tra·chi·an \bə-'trā-kē-ən\ *noun* [ultimately from Greek *batrachos* frog] (circa 1828)
: AMPHIBIAN 1; *especially* **:** FROG, TOAD
— **batrachian** *adjective*

bats \'bats\ *adjective* (1919)
: BATTY 2

bats·man \'bat-smən\ *noun* (1756)
: a batter especially in cricket

batt \'bat\ *noun* (1871)
: BATTING 2; *also* **:** an often square piece of batting

bat·tai·lous \'ba-tᵊl-əs\ *adjective* [Middle English *bataillous,* from Middle French *bataillos,* from *bataille* battle] (14th century)
archaic **:** ready for battle **:** WARLIKE

bat·ta·lia \bə-'tāl-yə, -'tal-\ *noun* [Italian *battaglia*] (1569)
1 *archaic* **:** order of battle
2 *obsolete* **:** a large body of men in battle array

bat·tal·ion \bə-'tal-yən\ *noun* [Middle French *bataillon,* from Old Italian *battaglione,* augmentative of *battaglia* company of soldiers, battle, from Late Latin *battalia* combat — more at BATTLE] (1579)
1 : a considerable body of troops organized to act together **:** ARMY

2 : a military unit composed of a headquarters and two or more companies, batteries, or similar units
3 : a large group

bat·teau *variant of* BATEAU

bat·te·ment \,bat-'mäⁿ\ *noun* [French, from *battre* to beat, from Latin *battuere*] (1830)
: a ballet movement in which the foot is extended in any direction usually followed by a beat against the supporting foot

¹bat·ten \'ba-tᵊn\ *verb* **bat·tened; bat·ten·ing** \'bat-niŋ, 'ba-tᵊn-iŋ\ [probably from Old Norse *batna* to improve; akin to Old English *betera* better] (1591)
intransitive verb
1 a : to grow fat **b :** to feed gluttonously
2 : to grow prosperous especially at the expense of another — usually used with *on*
transitive verb
: FATTEN

²batten *noun* [alteration of Middle English *batent, bataunt* finished board, from Middle French *batant,* from present participle of *battre*] (1658)
1 a *British* **:** a piece of lumber used especially for flooring **b :** a thin narrow strip of lumber used especially to seal or reinforce a joint
2 : a strip, bar, or support resembling or used similarly to a batten

³batten *verb* **bat·tened; bat·ten·ing** \'bat-niŋ, 'ba-tᵊn-iŋ\ (1663)
transitive verb
1 : to furnish with battens
2 : to fasten with or as if with battens — often used with *down*
intransitive verb
: to make one secure by or as if by battens ⟨*battening* down for the hurricane⟩

¹bat·ter \'ba-tər\ *verb* [Middle English *bateren,* probably frequentative of *batten* to bat, from *bat*] (14th century)
transitive verb
1 a : to beat with successive blows so as to bruise, shatter, or demolish **b :** BOMBARD
2 : to subject to strong, overwhelming, or repeated attack
3 : to wear or damage by hard usage or blows ⟨a *battered* old hat⟩
intransitive verb
: to strike heavily and repeatedly **:** BEAT
synonym see MAIM

²batter *noun* [Middle English *bater,* probably from *bateren*] (14th century)
1 a : a mixture consisting chiefly of flour, egg, and milk or water and being thin enough to pour or drop from a spoon **b :** a mixture (as of flour and egg) used as a coating for food (as chicken) that is to be fried
2 : an instance of battering

³batter *transitive verb* (1973)
: to coat (food) with batter for frying

⁴batter *noun* [origin unknown] (1743)
: a receding upward slope of the outer face of a structure

⁵batter *transitive verb* (circa 1882)
: to give a receding upward slope to (as a wall)

⁶batter *noun* (1773)
: one that bats; *especially* **:** the player whose turn it is to bat

battered child syndrome *noun* (1962)
: the complex of physical injuries sustained by a grossly abused child

bat·te·rie \,ba-tə-'rē\ *noun* [French, literally, beating — more at BATTERY] (1712)
: a ballet movement consisting of beating together the feet or calves of the legs during a leap

battering ram *noun* (1593)
1 : a military siege engine consisting of a large wooden beam with a head of iron used in ancient times to beat down the walls of a besieged place
2 : a heavy metal bar with handles used (as by firefighters) to batter down doors and walls

bat·tery \'ba-t(ə-)rē\ *noun, plural* **-ter·ies** [Middle French *batterie*, from Old French, from *battre* to beat, from Latin *battuere*] (1531)
1 a : the act of battering or beating **b :** an offensive touching or use of force on a person without the person's consent — compare ASSAULT 2a
2 a : a grouping of artillery pieces for tactical purposes **b :** the guns of a warship
3 : an artillery unit in the army equivalent to a company
4 a : a combination of apparatus for producing a single electrical effect **b :** a group of two or more cells connected together to furnish electric current; *also* **:** a single cell that furnishes electric current ⟨a flashlight *battery*⟩
5 a : a number of similar articles, items, or devices arranged, connected, or used together **:** SET, SERIES ⟨a *battery* of tests⟩ **b :** a usually impressive or imposing group **:** ARRAY
6 : the position of readiness of a gun for firing
7 : the pitcher and catcher of a baseball team
bat·ting \'ba-tiŋ\ *noun* (1773)
1 a : the action of one who bats **b :** the use of or ability with a bat
2 : layers or sheets of raw cotton or wool or of synthetic fibrous material used for lining quilts or for stuffing or packaging; *also* **:** a blanket of thermal insulation (as fiberglass)
batting average *noun* (1867)
1 : a ratio (as a rate per thousand) of base hits to official times at bat for a baseball player
2 : a record of achievement or accomplishment
¹bat·tle \'ba-t³l\ *noun, often attributive* [Middle English *batel*, from Old French *bataille* battle, fortifying tower, battalion, from Late Latin *battalia* combat, alteration of *battualia* fencing exercises, from Latin *battuere* to beat] (13th century)
1 *archaic* **:** BATTALION
2 : a combat between two persons
3 : a general encounter between armies, ships of war, or aircraft
4 : an extended contest, struggle, or controversy
²battle *verb* **bat·tled; bat·tling** \'bat-liŋ, 'ba-t³l-iŋ\ (14th century)
intransitive verb
1 : to engage in battle **:** FIGHT
2 : to contend with full strength, vigor, skill, or resources **:** STRUGGLE
transitive verb
1 : to fight against
2 : to force (as one's way) by battling
— bat·tler \-lər, 'ba-t³l-ər\ *noun*
³battle *transitive verb* **bat·tled; bat·tling** [Middle English *batailen*, from Middle French *bataillier* to fortify, from Old French, from *bataille*] (14th century)
archaic **:** to fortify with battlements
bat·tle–ax \'ba-t³l-,aks\ *noun* (14th century)
1 : a broadax formerly used as a weapon of war
2 : a sharp-tongued domineering usually older woman
battle cruiser *noun* (1911)
: a large heavily armed warship that is lighter, faster, and more maneuverable than a battleship
battle cry *noun* (1814)
: WAR CRY
battle fatigue *noun* (1945)
: COMBAT FATIGUE
— bat·tle–fa·tigued *adjective*
bat·tle·field \'ba-t³l-,fēld\ *noun* (1812)
1 : a place where a battle is fought
2 : an area of conflict
bat·tle·front \-,frənt\ *noun* (1914)
: the military sector in which actual combat takes place
bat·tle·ground \-,graùnd\ *noun* (1815)
: BATTLEFIELD
battle line (1814)
1 : a line along which a battle is fought

2 : a line defining the positions of opposing groups in a conflict or controversy — usually used in plural ⟨*battle lines* were drawn over economic policies⟩
bat·tle·ment \'ba-t³l-mənt\ *noun* [Middle English *batelment*, from Middle French *bataille*] (14th century)
: a parapet with open spaces that surmounts a wall and is used for defense or decoration
— bat·tle·ment·ed \-,men-təd\ *adjective*

battlement:
1 crenellations,
2 merlons,
3 machicolations

battle royal *noun, plural* **battles royal** *or* **battle royals** (1672)
1 a : a fight participated in by more than two combatants; *especially* **:** one in which the last man in the ring or on his feet is declared the winner **b :** a violent struggle
2 : a heated dispute
bat·tle·ship \'ba-t³l-,ship\ *noun* [short for *line-of-battle ship*] (1794)
: a warship of the largest and most heavily armed and armored class
bat·tle·wag·on \-,wa-gən\ *noun* (circa 1927)
: BATTLESHIP
bat·tu \ba-'tü, -'tyü\ *adjective* [French, from past participle of *battre* to beat] (1947)
of a ballet movement **:** performed with a striking together of the legs
bat·tue \ba-'tü, -'tyü\ *noun* [French, from *battre* to beat] (1816)
: the beating of woods and bushes to flush game; *also* **:** a hunt in which this procedure is used
bat·ty \'ba-tē\ *adjective* **bat·ti·er; -est** (1590)
1 : of, relating to, or resembling a bat
2 : mentally unstable **:** CRAZY
— bat·ti·ness *noun*
bau·ble \'bò-bəl, 'bä-\ *noun* [Middle English *babel*, from Middle French] (14th century)
1 : TRINKET
2 : a fool's scepter
3 : TRIFLE
Bau·cis \'bò-səs\ *noun* [Latin, from Greek *Baukis*]
: the wife of Philemon
baud \'bòd, 'bäd, *British* 'bòd\ *noun, plural* **baud** *also* **bauds** [*baud* (telegraphic transmission speed unit), from J. M. E. *Baudot* (died 1903) French inventor] (1931)
: a variable unit of data transmission speed (as one bit per second)
Bau·haus \'baù-,haùs\ *adjective* [German *Bauhaus*, literally, architecture house, school founded by Walter Gropius] (1923)
: of, relating to, or influenced by a school of design noted especially for a program that synthesized technology, craftsmanship, and design aesthetics
baulk *chiefly British variant of* BALK
Bau·mé \bō-'mā\ *adjective* [Antoine *Baumé*] (1877)
: being, calibrated in accordance with, or according to either of two arbitrary hydrometer scales for liquids lighter than water or for liquids heavier than water that indicate specific gravity in degrees
baum marten \'baùm-,mär-t³n\ *noun* [part translation of German *Baummarder*, from *Baum* tree + *Marder* marten] (1909)
: the pelt or fur of the European marten (*Martes martes*)
baux·ite \'bòk-,sīt, 'bäk-\ *noun* [French *bauxite*, from Les *Baux*, near Arles, France] (1861)
: an impure mixture of earthy hydrous aluminum oxides and hydroxides that is the principal source of aluminum
— baux·it·ic \bòk-'si-tik, bäk-\ *adjective*
Ba·var·i·an \bə-'ver-ē-ən, -'var-\ *noun* (1638)
1 : a native or inhabitant of Bavaria

2 : the High German dialect of southern Bavaria and Austria
— Bavarian *adjective*
Bavarian cream *noun* (circa 1879)
: flavored custard or pureed fruit combined with gelatin and whipped cream
baw·bee \'bò-,bē, bò-'\ *noun* [probably from Alexander Orrok, laird of Sille*bawbe* (flourished 1538) Scottish master of the mint] (1542)
1 : any of various Scottish coins of small value
2 : an English halfpenny
baw·cock \'bò-,käk\ *noun* [French *beau coq*, from *beau* fine + *coq* fellow, cock] (1599)
archaic **:** a fine fellow
bawd \'bòd\ *noun* [Middle English *bawde*] (14th century)
1 *obsolete* **:** PANDER
2 a : one who keeps a house of prostitution **:** MADAM **b :** PROSTITUTE
bawd·ry \'bò-drē\ *noun* [Middle English *bawderie*, from *bawde*] (15th century)
1 *obsolete* **:** UNCHASTITY
2 : suggestive, coarse, or obscene language
¹bawdy \'bò-dē\ *adjective* **bawd·i·er; -est** [*bawd*] (1513)
1 : OBSCENE, LEWD
2 : boisterously or humorously indecent
— bawd·i·ly \'bò-d³l-ē\ *adverb*
— bawd·i·ness \'bò-dē-nəs\ *noun*
²bawdy *noun* [probably from ¹*bawdy*] (1656)
: BAWDRY 2
bawdy house *noun* (1552)
: BORDELLO
¹bawl \'bòl\ *verb* [Middle English, to bark, probably of Scandinavian origin; akin to Icelandic *baula* to low] (1570)
intransitive verb
1 : to cry out loudly and unrestrainedly **:** YELL, BELLOW
2 : to cry loudly **:** WAIL
transitive verb
: to cry out at the top of one's voice
— bawl·er *noun*
²bawl *noun* (1792)
: a loud prolonged cry **:** OUTCRY
bawl out *transitive verb* (1905)
: to reprimand loudly or severely
¹bay \'bā\ *adjective* [Middle English, from Middle French *bai*, from Latin *badius;* akin to Old Irish *buide* yellow] (14th century)
: reddish brown ⟨a *bay* mare⟩
²bay *noun* (1535)
1 : a bay-colored animal; *specifically* **:** a horse with a bay-colored body and black mane, tail, and points — compare CHESTNUT 4, ¹SORREL 1
2 : a reddish brown
³bay *noun* [Middle English, from Middle French *baee* opening, from Old French, from feminine of *baé*, past participle of *baer* to gape, yawn — more at ABEYANCE] (14th century)
1 : a principal compartment of the walls, roof, or other part of a building or of the whole building
2 : a main division of a structure
3 : any of various compartments or sections used for a special purpose (as in an airplane, spacecraft, or service station) ⟨bomb *bay*⟩ ⟨cargo *bay*⟩
4 : BAY WINDOW 1
5 : a support or housing for electronic equipment
⁴bay *verb* [Middle English *baien, abaien*, from Old French *abaiier*, of imitative origin] (14th century)
intransitive verb
1 : to bark with prolonged tones
2 : to cry out **:** SHOUT

\ə\ abut \ᵊ\ kitten \ər\ further \a\ ash \ā\ ace
\ä\ mop, mar \aù\ out \ch\ chin \e\ bet \ē\ easy
\g\ go \i\ hit \ī\ ice \j\ job \ŋ\ sing \ō\ go
\ò\ law \òi\ boy \th\ thin \th\ the \ü\ loot \ù\ foot
\y\ yet \zh\ vision *see also* Guide to Pronunciation

transitive verb
1 : to bark at
2 : to bring to bay
3 : to pursue with barking
4 : to utter in deep prolonged tones
⁵**bay** *noun* (14th century)
1 : a baying of dogs
2 : the position of one unable to retreat and forced to face danger ⟨brought his quarry to *bay*⟩
3 : the position of one checked ⟨police kept the rioters at *bay*⟩
⁶**bay** *noun, often attributive* [Middle English *baye,* from Middle French *baie*] (14th century)
1 : an inlet of the sea or other body of water usually smaller than a gulf
2 : a small body of water set off from the main body
3 : any of various terrestrial formations resembling a bay of the sea
⁷**bay** *noun* [Middle English, berry, from Middle French *baie,* from Latin *baca*] (15th century)
1 a : the European laurel (*Laurus nobilis*) **b :** any of several shrubs or trees (as of the genera *Magnolia, Pimenta,* and *Gordonia*) resembling the laurel
2 a : a garland or crown especially of laurel given as a prize for victory or excellence **b :** HONOR, FAME — usually used in plural
ba·ya·dere \'bī-ə-,dir, -,der\ *noun* [French *bayadère* professional female dancer in India] (1856)
: a fabric with horizontal stripes in strongly contrasted colors
bay·ber·ry \'bā-,ber-ē\ *noun* (1687)
1 : any of several wax myrtles; *especially* **:** a hardy shrub (*Myrica pensylvanica*) of coastal eastern North America bearing dense clusters of small berries covered with grayish white wax
2 : the fruit of a bayberry
Bayes·ian \'bā-zē-ən, -zhən\ *adjective* (1961)
: being, relating to, or concerned with a theory (as of decision making or statistical inference) involving the application of Bayes' theorem and the use of probabilities based on prior knowledge and accumulated experience ⟨*Bayesian* probability models⟩
Bayes' theorem \'bāz-\ *noun* [Thomas *Bayes* (died 1761) English mathematician] (1939)
: a theorem about conditional probabilities: the probability that an event A occurs given that another event B has already occurred is equal to the probability that the event B occurs given that A has already occurred multiplied by the probability of occurrence of event A and divided by the probability of occurrence of event B
bay leaf *noun* (15th century)
: the dried leaf of the European laurel (*Laurus nobilis*) used in cooking
bay·man \'bā-mən, -,man\ *noun* (1641)
: a person and especially a fisherman who lives or works on or about a bay
¹**bay·o·net** \'bā-ə-nət, -,net, ,bā-ə-'net\ *noun* [French *baïonnette,* from *Bayonne,* France] (1704)
: a steel blade attached at the muzzle end of a shoulder arm (as a rifle) and used in hand-to-hand combat
²**bayonet** *verb* **-net·ed** *also* **-net·ted; -net·ing** *also* **-net·ting** (1858)
transitive verb
1 : to stab with a bayonet
2 : to compel or drive by or as if by the bayonet
intransitive verb
: to use a bayonet
bay·ou \'bī-(,)ü, -(,)ō\ *noun* [Louisiana French, from Choctaw *bayuk*] (1763)
1 : a creek, secondary watercourse, or minor river that is tributary to another body of water
2 : any of various usually marshy or sluggish bodies of water
bay rum *noun* (1840)

: a fragrant cosmetic and medicinal liquid distilled from the leaves of a West Indian bay tree (*Pimenta racemosa*) or usually prepared from essential oils, alcohol, and water
Bay Stat·er \'bā-,stā-tər\ *noun* (1845)
: a native or resident of Massachusetts — used as a nickname
bay window *noun* (15th century)
1 : a window or series of windows forming a bay in a room and projecting outward from the wall
2 : POTBELLY 1
ba·zaar \bə-'zär\ *noun* [Persian *bāzār*] (1612)
1 : an oriental market consisting of rows of shops or stalls selling miscellaneous goods
2 a : a place for the sale of goods **b :** DEPARTMENT STORE
3 : a fair for the sale of articles especially for charitable purposes
ba·zoo·ka \bə-'zü-kə\ *noun* [*bazooka* (a crude musical instrument made of pipes and a funnel)] (1943)
: a light portable antitank weapon consisting of an open-breech smoothbore firing tube that launches an armor-piercing rocket and is fired from the shoulder
BB \'bē-(,)bē\ *noun* (1874)
1 : a shot pellet 0.18 inch in diameter for use in a shotgun cartridge
2 : a shot pellet 0.175 inch in diameter for use in an air gun
BCD \,bē-(,)sē-'dē\ *noun* [*binary coded decimal*] (circa 1962)
: a computer code for representing alphanumeric information
B cell *noun* [*bone-marrow-derived cell*] (1968)
: any of the lymphocytes that have antibody molecules on the surface and comprise the antibody-secreting plasma cells when mature — called also *B lymphocyte; compare* T CELL
BCG vaccine \,bē-(,)sē-'jē-\ *noun* [*Bacillus Calmette-Guérin* (an attenuated strain of tubercle bacilli), from Albert *Calmette* (died 1933) and Camille *Guérin* (died 1961) French bacteriologists] (1927)
: a vaccine prepared from a living attenuated strain of tubercle bacilli and used to vaccinate human beings against tuberculosis — called also *BCG*
B complex *noun* (1934)
: VITAMIN B COMPLEX
BC soil \'bē-'sē-\ *noun* (circa 1938)
: a soil whose profile has only B horizons and C horizons
bdel·li·um \'de-lē-əm\ *noun* [Middle English, from Latin, from Greek *bdellion*] (14th century)
: a gum resin similar to myrrh obtained from various trees (genus *Commiphora*) of the East Indies and Africa
be \'bē\ *verb, past 1st & 3d singular* **was** \'wəz, 'wäz\; *2d singular* **were** \'wər\; *plural* **were;** *past subjunctive* **were;** *past participle* **been** \'bin, *chiefly British* 'bēn\; *present participle* **be·ing** \'bē-(i)ŋ\; *present 1st singular* **am** \əm, 'am\; *2d singular* **are** \'är, ər\; *3d singular* **is** \'iz, əz\ *plural* **are;** *present subjunctive* **be** [Middle English, from Old English *bēon;* akin to Old High German *bim* am, Latin *fui* I have been, *futurus* about to be, *fieri* to become, be done, Greek *phynai* to be born, be by nature, *phyein* to produce] (before 12th century)
intransitive verb
1 a : to equal in meaning **:** have the same connotation as **:** SYMBOLIZE ⟨God *is* love⟩ ⟨January *is* the first month⟩ ⟨let *x be* 10⟩ **b :** to have identity with ⟨the first person I met *was* my brother⟩ **c :** to constitute the same class as **d :** to have a specified qualification or characterization ⟨the leaves *are* green⟩ **e :** to belong to the class of ⟨the fish *is* a trout⟩ — used regularly in senses 1a through 1e as the copula of simple predication
2 a : to have an objective existence **:** have reality or actuality **:** LIVE ⟨I think, therefore I *am*⟩

⟨once upon a time there *was* a knight⟩ **b :** to have, maintain, or occupy a place, situation, or position ⟨the book *is* on the table⟩ **c :** to remain unmolested, undisturbed, or uninterrupted — used only in infinitive form ⟨let him *be*⟩ **d :** to take place **:** OCCUR ⟨the concert *was* last night⟩ **e :** to come or go ⟨has already *been* and gone⟩ ⟨has never *been* to the circus⟩ **f** *archaic* **:** BELONG, BEFALL
verbal auxiliary
1 — used with the past participle of transitive verbs as a passive-voice auxiliary ⟨the money *was* found⟩ ⟨the house *is being* built⟩
2 — used as the auxiliary of the present participle in progressive tenses expressing continuous action ⟨he *is* reading⟩ ⟨I have *been* sleeping⟩
3 — used with the past participle of some intransitive verbs as an auxiliary forming archaic perfect tenses ⟨Christ *is* risen from the dead —1 Corinthians 15:20 (Douay Version)⟩
4 — used with the infinitive with *to* to express futurity, arrangement in advance, or obligation ⟨I *am* to interview him today⟩ ⟨she *was* to become famous⟩
be- *prefix* [Middle English, from Old English *bi-, be-;* akin to Old English *bī* by, near — more at BY]
1 : on **:** around **:** over ⟨*be*daub⟩ ⟨*be*smear⟩
2 : to a great or greater degree **:** thoroughly ⟨*be*fuddle⟩ ⟨*be*rate⟩
3 : excessively **:** ostentatiously — in intensive verbs formed from simple verbs ⟨*be*deck⟩ and in adjectives based on adjectives ending in *-ed* ⟨*be*ribboned⟩
4 : about **:** to **:** at **:** upon **:** against **:** across ⟨*be*stride⟩ ⟨*be*speak⟩
5 : make **:** cause to be **:** treat as ⟨*be*little⟩ ⟨*be*fool⟩ ⟨*be*friend⟩
6 : call or dub especially excessively ⟨*be*doctor⟩
7 : affect, afflict, treat, provide, or cover with especially excessively ⟨*be*devil⟩ ⟨*be*fog⟩
¹**beach** \'bēch\ *noun* [origin unknown] (1535)
1 : shore pebbles **:** SHINGLE
2 a : a shore of a body of water covered by sand, gravel, or larger rock fragments **b :** a seashore area
²**beach** *transitive verb* (1840)
1 : to run or drive ashore
2 : to strand on or as if on a beach
beach ball *noun* (1940)
: a large inflated ball for use at the beach
beach·boy \-,bȯi\ *noun* (1941)
: a male beach attendant (as at a club or hotel)
beach buggy *noun* (1943)
: DUNE BUGGY
beach·comb·er \'bēch-,kō-mər\ *noun* (1840)
1 : a white man living as a drifter or loafer especially on the islands of the South Pacific
2 : a person who searches along a shore (as for salable refuse or for seashells)
— **beach·comb** \-,kōm\ *verb*
beach flea *noun* (1843)
: any of numerous amphipod crustaceans (family Talitridae) living on ocean beaches and leaping like fleas
beach·front \'bēch-,frənt\ *noun* (1921)
: a strip of land that fronts a beach
beach·go·er \-,gō-ər\ *noun* (1954)
: a person who frequently goes to the beach
beach grass *noun* (1681)
: any of several tough strongly rooted grasses that grow on exposed sandy shores; *especially* **:** any of a genus (*Ammophila*) of rhizomatous perennials widely planted to bind sandy slopes
beach·head \'bēch-,hed\ *noun* (1940)
1 : an area on a hostile shore occupied to secure further landing of troops and supplies
2 : FOOTHOLD
beach pea *noun* (1802)
: a wild pea (*Lathyrus japonicus* synonym *L. maritimus*) having tough roots and purple flowers that is found along sandy shores
beach plum *noun* (1784)

: a shrubby plum (*Prunus maritima*) having white flowers and growing along the northeastern coast of North America; *also* **:** its edible usually dark purple fruit that is used especially in preserves

beach·side \'bēch-,sīd\ *adjective* (1952)
: located at a beach

beach·wear \-,war, -,wer\ *noun* (1928)
: clothing for wear at a beach

beachy \'bē-chē\ *adjective* (1597)
: covered with pebbles or shingle

¹bea·con \'bē-kən\ *noun* [Middle English *beken*, from Old English *bēacen* sign; akin to Old High German *bouhhan* sign] (14th century)
1 : a signal fire commonly on a hill, tower, or pole
2 a : a lighthouse or other signal for guidance **b** : a radio transmitter emitting signals for guidance of aircraft
3 : a source of light or inspiration

²beacon (1821)
transitive verb
: to furnish with a beacon
intransitive verb
: to shine as a beacon

¹bead \'bēd\ *noun* [Middle English *bede* prayer, prayer bead, from Old English *bed*, *gebed* prayer; akin to Old English *biddan* to entreat, pray — more at BID] (before 12th century)
1 a *obsolete* : PRAYER — usually used in plural **b** *plural* : a series of prayers and meditations made with a rosary
2 : a small piece of material pierced for threading on a string or wire (as in a rosary)
3 *plural* **a** : ROSARY **b** : a necklace of beads or pearls
4 : a small ball-shaped body: as **a** : a drop of sweat or blood **b** : a bubble formed in or on a beverage **c** : a small metal knob on a firearm used as a front sight **d** : a blob or a line of weld metal
5 : a projecting rim, band, or molding ◇

²bead (1577)
transitive verb
1 : to furnish, adorn, or cover with beads or beading
2 : to string together like beads
intransitive verb
: to form into a bead

bead·ing *noun* (1845)
1 : a beaded molding
2 : material or a part or a piece consisting of a bead
3 : an openwork trimming
4 : BEADWORK

bea·dle \'bē-dᵊl\ *noun* [Middle English *bedel* messenger, from Old English *bydel*; akin to Old High German *butil* bailiff, Old English *bēodan* to command — more at BID] (1581)
: a minor parish official whose duties include ushering and preserving order at services and sometimes civil functions

bead·roll \'bēd-,rōl\ *noun* [from the reading in church of a list of names of persons for whom prayers are to be said] (1529)
1 : a list of names : CATALOG
2 : ROSARY

beads·man \'bēdz-mən\ *noun* (13th century)
archaic : one who prays for another

bead·work \'bēd-,wərk\ *noun* (1751)
1 : ornamental work in beads
2 : joinery beading

beady \'bē-dē\ *adjective* **bead·i·er; -est** (1826)
1 a : resembling beads **b** : small, round, and shiny with interest or greed ⟨*beady* eyes⟩
2 : marked by bubbles or beads ⟨a *beady* liquor⟩
— **bead·i·ly** \'bē-də-lē\ *adverb*

bea·gle \'bē-gəl\ *noun* [Middle English *begle*] (15th century)
: any of a breed of small short-legged smooth-coated often black, white, and tan hounds

beak \'bēk\ *noun* [Middle English *bec*, from Old French, from Latin *beccus*, of Gaulish origin] (13th century)
1 a : the bill of a bird; *especially* : a strong short broad bill **b** (1) : the elongated sucking mouth of some insects (as the true bugs) (2) : any of various rigid projecting mouth structures (as of a turtle) **c** : the human nose
2 : a pointed structure or formation: **a** : a metal-pointed beam projecting from the bow especially of an ancient galley for piercing an enemy ship **b** : the spout of a vessel **c** : a continuous slight architectural projection ending in an arris — see MOLDING illustration **d** : a process suggesting the beak of a bird
3 *chiefly British* **a** : MAGISTRATE **b** : HEADMASTER
— **beaked** \'bēkt\ *adjective*
— **beaky** \'bē-kē\ *adjective*

beagle

beaked whale *noun* (1877)
: any of a widely distributed family (Ziphiidae) of medium-sized toothed whales that have an elongated snout and a small dorsal fin

bea·ker \'bē-kər\ *noun* [Middle English *biker*, from Old Norse *bikarr*, probably from Old Saxon *bikeri*, from Medieval Latin *bicarium*] (14th century)
1 : a large drinking cup that has a wide mouth and is sometimes supported on a standard
2 : a deep widemouthed thin-walled vessel usually with a lip for pouring that is used especially in science laboratories

be–all and end–all \'bē-,ȯ-lən-'(d)en-,dȯl\ *noun* (1605)
1 : prime cause : essential element
2 : TOTALITY 1

¹beam \'bēm\ *noun* [Middle English *beem*, from Old English *bēam* tree, beam; akin to Old High German *boum* tree] (before 12th century)
1 a : a long piece of heavy often squared timber suitable for use in construction **b** : a wood or metal cylinder in a loom on which the warp is wound **c** : the part of a plow to which handles, standard, and coulter are attached **d** : the bar of a balance from which scales hang **e** : one of the principal horizontal supporting members (as of a building or ship) ⟨a steel *beam* supporting a floor⟩; *also* : BOOM, SPAR ⟨the *beam* of a crane⟩ **f** : the extreme width of a ship at the widest part **g** : an oscillating lever on a central axis receiving motion at one end from an engine piston rod and transmitting it at the other
2 a : a ray or shaft of light **b** : a collection of nearly parallel rays (as X rays) or a stream of particles (as electrons) **c** : a constant directional radio signal transmitted for the guidance of pilots; *also* : the course indicated by a radio beam
3 : the main stem of a deer's antler
4 : the width of the buttocks
— **on the beam 1** : following a guiding beam **2** : proceeding or operating correctly

²beam (15th century)
transitive verb
1 : to emit in beams or as a beam
2 : to support with beams
3 a : to aim and transmit (a broadcast) by directional antennas or by satellite **b** : to direct to a particular audience
intransitive verb
1 : to send out beams of light
2 : to smile with joy

beam–ends \'bēm-'en(d)z\ *noun plural* (1773)
: the ends of a ship's beams
— **on her beam–ends** : inclined so much on one side that the beams approach a vertical position

beam·ish \'bē-mish\ *adjective* (1870)
: beaming and bright with optimism, promise, or achievement
— **beam·ish·ly** *adverb*

beam splitter *noun* (1935)
: a mirror or prism or a combination of the two that is used to divide a beam of radiation into two or more parts

beamy \'bē-mē\ *adjective* (14th century)
1 : emitting beams of light : RADIANT
2 : broad in the beam ⟨a *beamy* cargo ship⟩

¹bean \'bēn\ *noun* [Middle English *bene*, from Old English *bēan*; akin to Old High German *bōna* bean] (before 12th century)
1 a : BROAD BEAN **b** : the seed of any of various erect or climbing leguminous plants (especially genera *Phaseolus, Dolichos,* and *Vigna*) other than the broad bean **c** : a plant bearing beans **d** : an immature bean pod used as a vegetable
2 a : a valueless item **b** *plural* : the least amount ⟨didn't know *beans* about it⟩
3 : any of various seeds or fruits that resemble beans or bean pods; *also* : a plant producing these
4 a *plural* : EXUBERANCE — used in the phrase *full of beans* **b** *plural* : NONSENSE, BUNKUM — used in the phrase *full of beans*
5 : HEAD, BRAIN
6 : a protuberance on the upper mandible of waterfowl — see DUCK illustration

²bean *transitive verb* (1910)
: to strike (a person) on the head with an object

bean·bag \'bēn-,bag\ *noun* (1871)
1 : a cloth bag partially filled typically with dried beans and used as a toy
2 : any of various pellet-filled bags used as furniture (as a chair) or household articles (as an ashtray base)

bean·ball \-,bȯl\ *noun* (circa 1905)
: a pitch thrown at a batter's head

bean counter *noun* (1975)
: a person involved in corporate financial decisions and especially one reluctant to spend money

bean curd *noun* (circa 1889)
: a soft vegetable cheese prepared by treating soybean milk with coagulants (as magnesium chloride or dilute acids) — called also *tofu*

bean·ery \'bēn-rē, 'bē-nə-\ *noun, plural* **-er·ies** (1887)
: RESTAURANT

bean·ie \'bē-nē\ *noun* (1940)
: a small round tight-fitting skullcap worn especially by schoolboys and college freshmen

\ə\ **abut** \ᵊ\ **kitten** \ər\ **further** \a\ **ash** \ā\ **ace**
\ä\ **mop, mar** \au̇\ **out** \ch\ **chin** \e\ **bet** \ē\ **easy**
\g\ **go** \i\ **hit** \ī\ **ice** \j\ **job** \ŋ\ **sing** \ō\ **go**
\ȯ\ **law** \ȯi\ **boy** \th\ **thin** \t̲h̲\ **the** \ü\ **loot** \u̇\ **foot**
\y\ **yet** \zh\ **vision** *see also* Guide to Pronunciation

beano \'bē-(,)nō\ *noun, plural* **beanos** [by alteration] (1935)
: BINGO
bean·pole \'bēn-,pō(ə)l\ *noun* (1798)
1 : a pole up which bean vines may climb
2 : a tall thin person
bean sprouts *noun plural* (1921)
: the sprouts of bean seeds especially of the mung bean used as a vegetable
¹**bear** \'bar, 'ber\ *noun, plural* **bears** *often attributive* [Middle English *bere,* from Old English *bera;* akin to Old English *brūn* brown — more at BROWN] (before 12th century)
1 *or plural* **bear** : any of a family (Ursidae of the order Carnivora) of large heavy mammals of America and Eurasia that have long shaggy hair, rudimentary tails, and plantigrade feet and feed largely on fruit and insects as well as on flesh
2 : a surly, uncouth, or shambling person
3 [probably from the proverb about *selling the bearskin before catching the bear*] : one that sells securities or commodities in expectation of a price decline — compare BULL
— **bear·like** \-,līk\ *adjective*
²**bear** *verb* **bore** \'bōr, 'bȯr\; **borne** \'bōrn, 'bȯrn\ *also* **born** \'bȯrn\; **bear·ing** [Middle English *beren* to carry, bring forth, from Old English *beran;* akin to Old High German *beran* to carry, Latin *ferre,* Greek *pherein*] (before 12th century)
transitive verb
1 a : to move while holding up and supporting **b** : to be equipped or furnished with **c** : BEHAVE, CONDUCT ⟨*bearing* himself well⟩ **d** : to have as a feature or characteristic **e** : to give as testimony ⟨*bear* false witness⟩ **f** : to have as an identification ⟨*bore* the name of John⟩ **g** : to hold in the mind **h** : DISSEMINATE **i** : LEAD, ESCORT **j** : RENDER, GIVE
2 a : to give birth to **b** : to produce as yield **c** (1) : to permit growth of (2) : CONTAIN ⟨oil-*bearing* shale⟩
3 a : to support the weight of : SUSTAIN **b** : to put up with especially without giving way ⟨couldn't *bear* the pain⟩ **c** : to call for as suitable or essential ⟨it *bears* watching⟩ **d** : to hold above, on top, or aloft **e** : to admit of : ALLOW **f** : ASSUME, ACCEPT
4 : THRUST, PRESS
intransitive verb
1 : to produce fruit : YIELD
2 a : to force one's way **b** : to extend in a direction indicated or implied **c** : to be situated : LIE **d** : to become directed **e** : to go or incline in an indicated direction
3 : to support a weight or strain — often used with *up*
4 a : to exert influence or force **b** : APPLY, PERTAIN ☆
— **bear a hand** : to join in and help out
— **bear arms 1** : to carry or possess arms **2** : to serve as a soldier
— **bear fruit** : to come to satisfying fruition, production, or development
— **bear in mind** : to think of especially as a warning : REMEMBER
— **bear with** : to be indulgent, patient, or forbearing with
bear·able \'bar-ə-bəl, 'ber-\ *adjective* (circa 1550)
: capable of being borne
— **bear·abil·i·ty** \,bar-ə-'bi-lə-tē, ,ber-\ *noun*
— **bear·ably** \-blē\ *adverb*
bear·bait·ing \'bar-,bā-tiŋ, 'ber-\ *noun* (14th century)
: the practice of setting dogs on a chained bear
bear·ber·ry \-,ber-ē\ *noun* (1625)
: a trailing evergreen plant (*Arctostaphylos uva-ursi*) of the heath family with astringent foliage and red berries
¹**beard** \'bird\ *noun* [Middle English *berd,* from Old English *beard;* akin to Old High German *bart* beard, Latin *barba*] (before 12th century)

1 : the hair that grows on a man's face often excluding the mustache
2 : a hairy or bristly appendage or tuft
3 : FRONT 7a
— **beard·ed** \'bir-dəd\ *adjective*
— **beard·ed·ness** *noun*
— **beard·less** \'bird-ləs\ *adjective*
²**beard** *transitive verb* (1525)
1 : to confront and oppose with boldness, resolution, and often effrontery : DEFY
2 : to furnish with a beard
bearded collie *noun* (1880)
: any of a breed of large working dogs of Scottish origin that have a long rough coat and drooping ears
bearded iris *noun* (1923)
: any of numerous wild or cultivated irises with a growth of short hairs on each fall
bearded seal *noun* (1913)
: a large arctic seal (*Erignathus barbatus*) with a tuft of long whiskers on each side of the muzzle
bear down (14th century)
transitive verb
: OVERCOME, OVERWHELM
intransitive verb
: to exert full strength and concentrated attention
— **bear down on 1** : EMPHASIZE **2** : to weigh heavily on : BURDEN
beard·tongue \'bird-,təŋ\ *noun* (1821)
: PENSTEMON
bear·er \'bar-ər, 'ber-\ *noun* (13th century)
: one that bears: as **a** : PORTER 1 **b** : a plant yielding fruit **c** : PALLBEARER **d** : one holding a check, draft, or other order for payment especially if marked payable to bearer
bear grass *noun* (1750)
: any of several plants (genera *Yucca, Nolina,* or *Xerophyllum*) of the lily or agave families chiefly of the southern and western U.S. with foliage resembling coarse blades of grass
bear hug *noun* (1921)
: a rough tight embrace
bear·ing *noun* (13th century)
1 : the manner in which one bears or comports oneself
2 a : the act, power, or time of bringing forth offspring or fruit **b** : a product of bearing : CROP
3 a : an object, surface, or point that supports **b** : a machine part in which another part (as a journal or pin) turns or slides
4 : a figure borne on a heraldic field
5 : PRESSURE, THRUST
6 a : the situation or horizontal direction of one point with respect to another or to the compass **b** : a determination of position **c** *plural* : comprehension of one's position, environment, or situation **d** : RELATION, CONNECTION; *also* : PURPORT
7 : the part of a structural member that rests on its supports ☆
bearing rein *noun* (1794)
: CHECKREIN 1
bear·ish \'bar-ish, 'ber-\ *adjective* (1744)
1 : resembling a bear in build or in roughness, gruffness, or surliness
2 a : marked by, tending to cause, or fearful of falling prices (as in a stock market) **b** : PESSIMISTIC
— **bear·ish·ly** *adverb*
— **bear·ish·ness** *noun*
bé·ar·naise sauce \'bā-är-,nāz-, -ər-; 'ber-\ *noun* [French *béarnaise,* feminine of *béarnais* of Béarn, France] (1877)
: a sauce of egg yolks and butter flavored with shallots, wine, vinegar, and seasonings
bear out *transitive verb* (15th century)
: CONFIRM, SUBSTANTIATE
bear·skin \'bar-,skin, 'ber-\ *noun* (1752)
: an article made of the skin of a bear; *especially* : a military hat made of the skin of a bear
bear up (13th century)
transitive verb

: SUPPORT, ENCOURAGE
intransitive verb
: to summon up courage, resolution, or strength ⟨*bearing up* under the strain⟩
beast \'bēst\ *noun* [Middle English *beste,* from Old French, from Latin *bestia*] (13th century)
1 a : a four-footed mammal as distinguished from a human being, a lower vertebrate, and an invertebrate **b** : a lower animal as distinguished from a human being **c** : an animal as distinguished from a plant **d** : an animal under human control
2 : a contemptible person
3 : something formidably difficult to control or deal with
beast epic *noun* (1889)
: a poem with epic conventions in which animals speak and act like human beings
beast fable *noun* (1865)
: a usually didactic prose or verse fable in which animals speak and act like human beings
beast·ie \'bē-stē\ *noun* (circa 1773)
: BEAST, ANIMAL, CRITTER
beas·tings *variant of* BEESTINGS
¹**beast·ly** \'bēst-lē\ *adjective* **beast·li·er; -est** (13th century)
1 : BESTIAL 1
2 : ABOMINABLE, DISAGREEABLE ⟨*beastly* weather⟩
— **beast·li·ness** *noun*
²**beastly** *adverb* (1865)
: VERY ⟨a *beastly* cold day⟩
beast of burden (1740)
: an animal employed to carry heavy loads or to perform other heavy work (as pulling a plow)
¹**beat** \'bēt\ *verb* **beat; beat·en** \'bē-t°n\ *or* **beat; beat·ing** [Middle English *beten,* from Old English *bēatan;* akin to Old High German *bōzan* to beat] (before 12th century)
transitive verb

☆ SYNONYMS

Bear, suffer, endure, abide, tolerate, stand mean to put up with something trying or painful. BEAR usually implies the power to sustain without flinching or breaking ⟨forced to *bear* a tragic loss⟩. SUFFER often suggests acceptance or passivity rather than courage or patience in bearing ⟨*suffering* many insults⟩. ENDURE implies continuing firm or resolute through trials and difficulties ⟨*endured* years of rejection⟩. ABIDE suggests acceptance without resistance or protest ⟨cannot *abide* their rudeness⟩. TOLERATE suggests overcoming or successfully controlling an impulse to resist, avoid, or resent something injurious or distasteful ⟨refused to *tolerate* such treatment⟩. STAND emphasizes more strongly the ability to bear without discomposure or flinching ⟨cannot *stand* teasing⟩.

Bearing, deportment, demeanor, mien, manner, carriage mean the outward manifestation of personality or attitude. BEARING is the most general of these words but now usually implies characteristic posture ⟨a woman of regal *bearing*⟩. DEPORTMENT suggests actions or behavior as formed by breeding or training ⟨your *deportment* was atrocious⟩. DEMEANOR suggests one's attitude toward others as expressed in outward behavior ⟨the haughty *demeanor* of the headwaiter⟩. MIEN is a literary term referring both to bearing and demeanor ⟨a *mien* of supreme self-satisfaction⟩. MANNER implies characteristic or customary way of moving and gesturing and addressing others ⟨the imperious *manner* of a man used to giving orders⟩. CARRIAGE applies chiefly to habitual posture in standing or walking ⟨the kind of *carriage* learned at boarding school⟩.

1 : to strike repeatedly: **a :** to hit repeatedly so as to inflict pain — often used with *up* **b :** to walk on : TREAD **c :** to strike directly against forcefully and repeatedly **:** dash against **d :** to flap or thrash at vigorously **e :** to strike at in order to rouse game; *also* **:** to range over in or as if in quest of game **f :** to mix by stirring **:** WHIP — often used with *up* **g :** to strike repeatedly in order to produce music or a signal ⟨*beat* a drum⟩

2 a : to drive or force by blows **b :** to pound into a powder, paste, or pulp **c :** to make by repeated treading or driving over **d** (1) **:** to dislodge by repeated hitting (2) **:** to lodge securely by repeated striking **e :** to shape by beating ⟨*beat* swords into plowshares⟩; *especially* **:** to flatten thin by blows **f :** to sound or express especially by drumbeat

3 : to cause to strike or flap repeatedly

4 a : OVERCOME, DEFEAT; *also* **:** SURPASS — often used with *out* **b :** to prevail despite ⟨*beat* the odds⟩ **c :** BEWILDER, BAFFLE **d** (1) **:** FATIGUE, EXHAUST (2) **:** to leave dispirited, irresolute, or hopeless **e :** CHEAT, SWINDLE

5 a (1) **:** to act ahead of usually so as to forestall (2) **:** to report a news item in advance of **b :** to come or arrive before **c :** CIRCUMVENT ⟨*beat* the system⟩ **d :** to outmaneuver (a defender) and get free **e :** to score against (a goalkeeper)

6 : to indicate by beating ⟨*beat* the tempo⟩
intransitive verb

1 a : to become forcefully impelled : DASH **b :** to glare or strike with oppressive intensity **c :** to sustain distracting activity **d :** to beat a drum

2 a (1) **:** PULSATE, THROB (2) **:** TICK **b :** to sound upon being struck

3 a : to strike repeated blows **b :** to strike the air : FLAP **c :** to strike cover in order to rouse game; *also* **:** to range or scour for or as if for game

4 : to progress with much difficulty

5 : to sail to windward by a series of tacks

— **beat·a·ble** \'bē-tə-bəl\ *adjective*
— **beat about the bush** *or* **beat around the bush :** to fail or refuse to come to the point in discourse
— **beat a retreat :** to leave in haste
— **beat it 1 :** to hurry away : SCRAM **2 :** HURRY, RUSH
— **beat one's brains out :** to try intently to resolve something difficult by thinking
— **beat the bushes :** to search thoroughly through all possible areas
— **beat the drum :** to proclaim as meritorious or significant **:** publicize vigorously
— **beat the rap :** to escape or evade the penalties connected with an accusation or charge
— **beat up on :** to attack physically or verbally

²**beat** *noun* (1615)
1 a : a single stroke or blow especially in a series; *also* **:** PULSATION, TICK **b :** a sound produced by or as if by beating **c :** a driving impact or force
2 : one swing of the pendulum or balance of a timepiece
3 a : a regularly traversed round ⟨the cop on the *beat*⟩ **b :** a group of news sources that a reporter covers regularly
4 a : a metrical or rhythmic stress in poetry or music or the rhythmic effect of these stresses **b :** the tempo indicated (as by a conductor) to a musical performer **c :** the pronounced rhythm that is the characteristic driving force in jazz or rock music; *also* **:** ²ROCK 2
5 a : one that excels ⟨I've never seen the *beat* of it⟩ **b :** the reporting of a news story ahead of competitors
6 : DEADBEAT
7 a : an act of beating to windward **b :** one of the reaches so traversed **:** TACK

8 : each of the pulsations of amplitude produced by the union of sound or radio waves or electric currents having different frequencies
9 : an accented stroke (as of one leg or foot against the other) in dancing
— **beat·less** \-ləs\ *adjective*

³**beat** *adjective* [Middle English *beten, bete*, from past participle of *beten*] (1832)
1 a : being in a state of exhaustion : EXHAUSTED **b :** sapped of resolution or morale
2 *often capitalized* **:** of, relating to, or being beatniks ⟨*beat* poets⟩

⁴**beat** *noun, often capitalized* (1957)
: BEATNIK

beat·en \'bē-tⁿn\ *adjective* (13th century)
1 : hammered into a desired shape
2 : much trodden and worn smooth; *also* **:** FAMILIAR ⟨a *beaten* path⟩
3 : being in a state of exhaustion : EXHAUSTED

beaten biscuit *noun* (1876)
: a biscuit whose dough is lightened by beating and folding

beat·er \'bē-tər\ *noun* (14th century)
1 : one that beats: as **a :** EGGBEATER **b :** a rotary blade attached to an electric mixer **c :** DRUMSTICK 1
2 : one that strikes cover to rouse game

be·atif·ic \bē-ə-'ti-fik\ *adjective* [Latin *beatificus* making happy, from *beatus* happy, from past participle of *beare* to bless; perhaps akin to Latin *bonus* good — more at BOUNTY] (1649)
1 : of, possessing, or imparting beatitude
2 : having a blissful appearance ⟨a *beatific* smile⟩
— **be·atif·i·cal·ly** \-fi-k(ə-)lē\ *adverb*

beatific vision *noun* (1639)
: the direct knowledge of God enjoyed by the blessed in heaven

be·at·i·fy \bē-'a-tə-,fī\ *transitive verb* **-fied; -fy·ing** [Middle French *beatifier*, from Late Latin *beatificare*, from Latin *beatus* + *facere* to make — more at DO] (1535)
1 : to make supremely happy
2 : to declare to have attained the blessedness of heaven and authorize the title "Blessed" and limited public religious honor
— **be·at·i·fi·ca·tion** \-,a-tə-fə-'kā-shən\ *noun*

beat·ing \'bē-tiŋ\ *noun* (13th century)
1 : an act of striking with repeated blows so as to injure or damage; *also* **:** the injury or damage thus inflicted
2 : PULSATION
3 : DEFEAT, SETBACK

beating reed *noun* (1879)
: a reed in a musical instrument that vibrates against the edges of an air opening (as in a clarinet or organ pipe) to which it is attached — compare FREE REED

be·at·i·tude \bē-'a-tə-,tüd, -,tyüd\ *noun* [Latin *beatitudo*, from *beatus*] (15th century)
1 a : a state of utmost bliss **b** — used as a title for a primate especially of an Eastern church
2 : any of the declarations made in the Sermon on the Mount (Matthew 5:3–12) beginning in the Authorized Version "Blessed are"

beat·nik \'bēt-nik\ *noun* [³*beat* + *-nik*] (1958)
: a person who rejects the mores of established society (as by dressing and behaving unconventionally) and indulges in exotic philosophizing and self-expression

beat off (15th century)
transitive verb
: REPEL
intransitive verb
: MASTURBATE — used of a male; usually considered vulgar

beat out *transitive verb* (1607)
1 : to make or perform by or as if by beating
2 : to mark or accompany by beating
3 : to turn (a routine ground ball) into a hit in baseball by fast running to first base

Be·a·trice \,bā-ä-'trē-(,)chā, 'bē-ə-trəs\ *noun* [Italian]

: a Florentine woman idealized in Dante's *Vita Nuova* and *Divina Commedia*

beat–up \'bēt-,əp, -'əp\ *adjective* (1946)
: DILAPIDATED, SHABBY

beau \'bō\ *noun, plural* **beaux** \'bōz\ *or* **beaus** [French, from *beau* beautiful, from Latin *bellus* pretty] (1684)
1 : DANDY 1
2 : BOYFRIEND 2

Beau Brum·mell \'bō-'brə-məl\ *noun* [nickname of G. B. *Brummell*] (1920)
: DANDY 1

beau·coup \'bō-(,)kü\ *adjective* [French] (1918)
slang **:** great in quantity or amount **:** MANY, MUCH ⟨spent *beaucoup* dollars⟩

Beau·fort scale \'bō-fərt-\ *noun* [Sir Francis *Beaufort*] (1858)
: a scale in which the force of the wind is indicated by numbers from 0 to 12
▶ The Beaufort scale table is on page 156.

beau geste \bō-'zhest\ *noun, plural* **beaux gestes** *or* **beau gestes** \bō-'zhest\ [French, literally, beautiful gesture] (1914)
1 : a graceful or magnanimous gesture
2 : an ingratiating conciliatory gesture

beau ide·al \,bō-ī-'dē(-ə)l, ,bō-ē-dā-'äl\ *noun, plural* **beau ideals** [French *beau idéal* ideal beauty] (1809)
: the perfect type or model

Beau·jo·lais \,bō-zhō-'lā, -zhə-\ *noun, plural* **Beaujolais** [French, from *Beaujolais*, region of eastern France] (1863)
: a light fruity red burgundy wine made from the Gamay grape

beau monde \bō-'mänd, -mōⁿd\ *noun, plural* **beau mondes** \-'män(d)z\ *or* **beaux mondes** \bō-mōⁿd\ [French, literally, fine world] (1673)
: the world of high society and fashion

¹**beaut** \'byüt\ *noun* (1896)
: BEAUTY 4

²**beaut** *adjective* (1918)
Australian & New Zealand **:** EXCELLENT 2

beau·te·ous \'byü-tē-əs\ *adjective* [Middle English, from *beaute*] (15th century)
: BEAUTIFUL
— **beau·te·ous·ly** *adverb*
— **beau·te·ous·ness** *noun*

beau·ti·cian \byü-'ti-shən\ *noun* [*beauty* + *-ician*] (1924)
: COSMETOLOGIST

beau·ti·ful \'byü-ti-fəl\ *adjective* (15th century)
1 : having qualities of beauty **:** exciting aesthetic pleasure
2 : generally pleasing **:** EXCELLENT ☆

\ə\ abut \ᵊ\ kitten \ər\ further \a\ ash \ā\ ace
\ä\ mop, mar \au̇\ out \ch\ chin \e\ bet \ē\ easy
\g\ go \i\ hit \ī\ ice \j\ job \ŋ\ sing \ō\ go
\ȯ\ law \ȯi\ boy \th\ thin \t̲h\ the \ü\ loot \u̇\ foot
\y\ yet \zh\ vision *see also* Guide to Pronunciation

BEAUFORT SCALE

BEAUFORT NUMBER	NAME	WIND SPEED		DESCRIPTION
		MPH	KPH	
0	calm	<1	<1	calm; smoke rises vertically
1	light air	1-3	1-5	direction of wind shown by smoke but not by wind vanes
2	light breeze	4-7	6-11	wind felt on face; leaves rustle; wind vane moves
3	gentle breeze	8-12	12-19	leaves and small twigs in constant motion; wind extends light flag
4	moderate breeze	13-18	20-28	wind raises dust and loose paper; small branches move
5	fresh breeze	19-24	29-38	small-leaved trees begin to sway; crested wavelets form on inland waters
6	strong breeze	25-31	39-49	large branches move; overhead wires whistle; umbrellas difficult to control
7	moderate gale *or* near gale	32-38	50-61	whole trees sway; walking against wind is difficult
8	fresh gale *or* gale	39-46	62-74	twigs break off trees; moving cars veer
9	strong gale	47-54	75-88	slight structural damage occurs; shingles may blow away
10	whole gale *or* storm	55-63	89-102	trees uprooted; considerable structural damage occurs
11	storm *or* violent storm	64-72	103-117	widespread damage occurs
12	hurricane*	>72	>117	widespread damage occurs

*The U.S. uses 74 statute mph as the speed criterion for a hurricane.

— **beau·ti·ful·ly** \-f(ə-)lē\ *adverb*
— **beau·ti·ful·ness** \-fəl-nəs\ *noun*
beautiful people *noun plural, often B&P capitalized* (1964)
: wealthy or famous people whose lifestyle is usually expensive and well-publicized
beau·ti·fy \'byü-tə-ˌfī\ *verb* **-fied; -fy·ing** (1526)
transitive verb
: to make beautiful or add beauty to
intransitive verb
: to grow beautiful
synonym see ADORN
— **beau·ti·fi·ca·tion** \byü-tə-fə-'kā-shən\ *noun*
— **beau·ti·fi·er** \'byü-tə-ˌfī(-ə)r\ *noun*
beau·ty \'byü-tē\ *noun, plural* **beauties** [Middle English *beaute,* from Old French *biauté,* from *bel, biau* beautiful, from Latin *bellus* pretty; akin to Latin *bonus* good — more at BOUNTY] (14th century)
1 : the quality or aggregate of qualities in a person or thing that gives pleasure to the senses or pleasurably exalts the mind or spirit **:** LOVELINESS
2 : a beautiful person or thing; *especially* **:** a beautiful woman
3 : a particularly graceful, ornamental, or excellent quality
4 : a brilliant, extreme, or egregious example or instance ⟨that mistake was a *beauty*⟩
5 : a quantum characteristic that accounts for the existence and lifetime of the upsilon particle; *also* **:** a particle having this characteristic
beauty bush *noun* (1926)

: a Chinese shrub (*Kolkwitzia amabilis*) of the honeysuckle family with pinkish flowers and bristly fruit
beauty contest *noun* (1899)
1 : an assemblage of girls or women at which judges select the most beautiful
2 : a presidential primary election in which the popular vote does not determine the number of convention delegates a candidate receives
beauty part *noun* (1951)
: the most desirable or beneficial aspect of something
beauty shop *noun* (1901)
: an establishment or department where hairdressing, facials, and manicures are done — called also *beauty parlor, beauty salon*
beauty spot *noun* (1657)
1 : ¹PATCH 2
2 : NEVUS
¹beaux arts \bō-'zär\ *noun plural* [French *beaux-arts*] (1821)
: FINE ARTS
²beaux arts *adjective, often B&A capitalized* [French *École des Beaux-Arts* School of Fine Arts, in Paris] (1924)
: characterized by the use of historic forms, rich decorative detail, and a tendency toward monumental conception in architecture
¹bea·ver \'bē-vər\ *noun, plural* **beavers** [Middle English *bever,* from Old English *beofor;* akin to Old High German *bibar* beaver, and probably to Old English *brūn* brown — more at BROWN] (before 12th century)
1 *or plural* **beaver a :** either of two large semiaquatic herbivorous rodents (*Castor canadensis* of North America and *C. fiber* of Eurasia) having webbed hind feet and a broad

flat scaly tail and constructing dams and partially submerged lodges **b :** the fur or pelt of the beaver
2 a : a hat made of beaver fur or a fabric imitation **b :** SILK HAT
3 : a heavy fabric of felted wool or of cotton napped on both sides
4 : the pudenda of a woman — usually considered vulgar
²beaver *noun* [Middle English *baviere,* from Middle French] (15th century)
1 : a piece of armor protecting the lower part of the face
2 : a helmet visor
³beaver *intransitive verb* (1946)
: to work energetically ⟨*beavering* away at the problem⟩
bea·ver·board \'bē-vər-ˌbōrd, -ˌbȯrd\ *noun* [from *Beaver Board,* a trademark] (1909)

B beaver 1

: a fiberboard used for partitions and ceilings
be·bop \'bē-ˌbäp\ *noun* [imitative] (1944)
: ³BOP 1
— **be·bop·per** *noun*
be·calm \bi-'kä(l)m, *New England also* -'kȧm\ *transitive verb* (1582)
1 a : to keep motionless by lack of wind **b :** to stop the progress of ⟨an industry *becalmed* by decreasing demand⟩
2 : to make calm **:** SOOTHE
be·cause \bi-'kȯz, -'kəz *also* -'kȯs\ *conjunction* [Middle English *because that, because,* from *by cause that*] (14th century)
1 : for the reason that **:** SINCE ⟨rested *because* he was tired⟩
2 : the fact that **:** THAT ⟨the reason I haven't been fired is *because* my boss hasn't got round to it yet —E. B. White⟩
because of *preposition* (14th century)
: by reason of **:** on account of
bé·cha·mel \ˌbā-shə-'mel\ *noun* [French *sauce béchamelle,* from Louis de *Béchamel* (died 1703) French courtier] (1796)
: a rich white sauce
be·chance \bi-'chan(t)s\ *verb* (1527)
archaic **:** BEFALL
bêche–de–mer \ˌbesh-də-'mer, ˌbäsh-\ *noun* [French, alteration of *biche de mer,* from Portuguese *bicho do mar,* literally, sea worm] (1783)
1 *plural* **bêche–de–mer** *or* **bêches–de–mer** \ˌbesh-də-, ˌbe-shəz-, ˌbäsh-\ **:** TREPANG
2 *B&M capitalized* **:** any of several English-based pidgins spoken on islands of the western Pacific
¹beck \'bek\ *noun* [Middle English *bek,* from Old Norse *bekkr;* akin to Old English *bæc* brook, Old High German *bah,* Lithuanian *bégti* to flee — more at PHOBIA] (14th century)
British **:** CREEK 2
²beck *transitive verb* [Middle English, alteration of *beknen*] (14th century)
archaic **:** BECKON
³beck *noun* (14th century)
1 *chiefly Scottish* **:** BOW, CURTSY
2 a : a beckoning gesture **b :** SUMMONS, BIDDING
— **at one's beck and call :** ready to obey one's command immediately
beck·et \'be-kət\ *noun* [origin unknown] (circa 1769)
: a device for holding something in place: as **a** : a grommet or a loop of rope with a knot at one end to catch in an eye at the other **b :** a ring of rope or metal **c :** a loop of rope (as for a handle)
beck·on \'be-kən\ *verb* **beck·oned; beck·on·ing** [Middle English *beknen,* from Old English *bīecnan,* from *bēacen* sign — more at BEACON] (before 12th century)
intransitive verb

1 : to summon or signal typically with a wave or nod
2 : to appear inviting **:** ATTRACT
transitive verb
: to beckon to
— **beckon** *noun*
be·cloud \bi-'klaùd\ *transitive verb* (1598)
1 : to obscure with or as if with a cloud
2 : to prevent clear perception or realization of **:** MUDDLE 〈prejudices that *becloud* his judgment〉
be·come \bi-'kəm\ *verb* **-came** \-'kām\; **-come; -com·ing** [Middle English, to come to, become, from Old English *becuman,* from *be-* + *cuman* to come] (before 12th century)
intransitive verb
1 a : to come into existence **b :** to come to be 〈*become* sick〉
2 : to undergo change or development
transitive verb
: to suit or be suitable to 〈seriousness *becoming* the occasion〉 〈her clothes *become* her〉
— **become of :** to happen to
be·com·ing \-'kə-miŋ\ *adjective* (15th century)
: SUITABLE, FITTING; *especially* **:** attractively suitable 〈*becoming* modesty〉
— **be·com·ing·ly** \-miŋ-lē\ *adverb*
¹**bed** \'bed\ *noun* [Middle English, from Old English *bedd;* akin to Old High German *betti* bed, Latin *fodere* to dig] (before 12th century)
1 a : a piece of furniture on or in which to lie and sleep **b** (1) **:** a place of sex relations (2) **:** marital relationship **c :** a place for sleeping **d :** SLEEP; *also* **:** a time for sleeping 〈took a walk before *bed*〉 **e** (1) **:** a mattress filled with soft material (2) **:** BEDSTEAD **f :** the equipment and services needed to care for one hospitalized patient or hotel guest
2 : a flat or level surface: as **a :** a plot of ground prepared for plants; *also* **:** the plants grown in such a plot **b :** the bottom of a body of water; *especially* **:** an area of sea bottom supporting a heavy growth of a particular organism 〈an oyster *bed*〉
3 : a supporting surface or structure **:** FOUNDATION
4 : LAYER, STRATUM
5 a : the place or material in which a block or brick is laid **b :** the lower surface of a brick, slate, or tile
6 : a mass or heap resembling a bed 〈a *bed* of ashes〉 〈served on a *bed* of lettuce〉
— **in bed :** in the act of sexual intercourse
²**bed** *verb* **bed·ded; bed·ding** (before 12th century)
intransitive verb
1 a : to find or make sleeping accommodations **b :** to go to bed
2 : to form a layer
3 : to lie flat or flush
transitive verb
1 a : to furnish with a bed or bedding **:** settle in sleeping quarters — often used with *down*
b : to put, take, or send to bed
2 a : EMBED **b :** to plant or arrange in beds **c :** BASE, ESTABLISH
3 a : to lay flat or in a layer **b :** to make a bed in or of
4 : to have sexual intercourse with — often used with *down*
be·dab·ble \bi-'da-bəl\ *transitive verb* (1590)
archaic **:** to wet or soil by dabbling
bed–and–breakfast *noun* (1910)
: an establishment (as an inn) offering lodging and breakfast
be·daub \bi-'dòb, -'däb\ *transitive verb* (1558)
1 : to daub over **:** BESMEAR
2 : to ornament with vulgar excess
be·daz·zle \bi-'da-zəl\ *transitive verb* (1596)
1 : to confuse by a strong light **:** DAZZLE
2 : to impress forcefully **:** ENCHANT
— **be·daz·zle·ment** \-mənt\ *noun*
bed board *noun* (1946)
: a stiff thin wide board inserted usually between a bedspring and mattress especially to

give support to one's back or to protect a mattress from sagging springs
bed·bug \'bed-,bəg\ *noun* (1808)
: a wingless bloodsucking bug (*Cimex lectularius*) sometimes infesting houses and especially beds and feeding on human blood
bed·cham·ber \-,chām-bər\ *noun* (14th century)
: BEDROOM
bed check *noun* (1927)
: a night inspection to check the presence of persons (as soldiers) required by regulations to be in bed or in quarters
bed·clothes \'bed-,klō(th)z\ *noun plural* (14th century)
: the covering (as sheets and blankets) used on a bed
bed·cov·er \-,kə-vər\ *also* **bed·cov·er·ing** \-,kə-v(ə-)riŋ\ *noun* (circa 1656)
1 : BEDSPREAD
2 : BEDCLOTHES — usually used in plural
bed·ded \'be-dəd\ *adjective* (1788)
: having a bed or beds of a specified kind or number — used in combination 〈a twin-*bedded* room〉
bed·der \'be-dər\ *noun* (1803)
1 : one that makes up beds
2 : a bedding plant
¹**bed·ding** \'be-diŋ\ *noun* [Middle English, from Old English, from *bedd*] (before 12th century)
1 : BEDCLOTHES
2 : a bottom layer **:** FOUNDATION
3 : material to provide a bed for livestock
4 : STRATIFICATION
²**bedding** *adjective* [from gerund of ²*bed*] (1856)
: suitable for planting in large groups in flower beds to produce a mass display 〈*bedding* plants〉
be·deck \bi-'dek\ *transitive verb* (circa 1566)
1 : to clothe with finery **:** DECK
2 : DECORATE 2
be·dev·il \bi-'de-vəl\ *transitive verb* (1574)
1 : to possess with or as if with a devil
2 : to cause distress **:** TROUBLE
3 : to change for the worse **:** SPOIL
4 : to confuse utterly **:** BEWILDER
— **be·dev·il·ment** \-mənt\ *noun*
be·dew \bi-'dü, -'dyü\ *transitive verb* (14th century)
: to wet with or as if with dew
bed·fast \'bed-,fast\ *adjective* (1560)
: BEDRIDDEN
bed·fel·low \-,fe-(,)lō\ *noun* (15th century)
1 : one who shares a bed with another
2 : ASSOCIATE, ALLY 〈political *bedfellows*〉
Bed·ford cord \'bed-fərd-\ *noun* [perhaps from New *Bedford,* Massachusetts] (1862)
: a clothing fabric with lengthwise ribs that resembles corduroy; *also* **:** the weave used in making this fabric
be·dight \bi-'dīt\ *transitive verb* **be·dight·ed** *or* **bedight; be·dight·ing** (14th century)
archaic **:** EQUIP, ARRAY
be·dim \bi-'dim\ *transitive verb* (1583)
1 : to make less bright
2 : to make indistinct **:** OBSCURE
Bed·i·vere \'be-də-,vir\ *noun*
: a knight of the Round Table
be·di·zen \bi-'dī-z³n, -'di-\ *transitive verb* (1661)
: to dress or adorn gaudily
— **be·di·zen·ment** \-mənt\ *noun*
bed·lam \'bed-ləm\ *noun* [*Bedlam,* popular name for the Hospital of Saint Mary of Bethlehem, London, an insane asylum, from Middle English *Bedlem* Bethlehem] (1522)
1 *obsolete* **:** MADMAN, LUNATIC
2 *often capitalized* **:** a lunatic asylum
3 : a place, scene, or state of uproar and confusion ◇
— **bedlam** *adjective*
bed·lam·ite \'bed-lə-,mīt\ *noun* (1589)
: MADMAN, LUNATIC
— **bedlamite** *adjective*

Bed·ling·ton terrier \'bed-liŋ-tən-\ *noun* [*Bedlington,* England] (1867)
: a swift lightly built terrier of English origin with a long narrow head, arched back, and usually curly coat — called also *Bedlington*
bed·mate \'bed-,māt\ *noun* (1583)
: one who shares one's bed; *especially* **:** a sexual partner
bed molding *noun* (1703)
: the molding of a cornice below the corona and above the frieze; *also* **:** a molding below a deep projection
bed of roses (1648)
: a place or situation of agreeable ease
bed·ou·in *or* **bed·u·in** \'be-də-wən\ *noun, plural* **bedouin** *or* **bedouins** *or* **beduin** *or* **beduins** *often capitalized* [Middle English *Bedoyne,* from Middle French *bedoïn,* from Arabic *badawī* desert dweller] (15th century)
: a nomadic Arab of the Arabian, Syrian, or North African deserts
bed·pan \'bed-,pan\ *noun* (1678)
: a shallow vessel used by a bedridden person for urination or defecation
bed·plate \-,plāt\ *noun* (1850)
: a plate or framing used as a support
bed·post \-,pōst\ *noun* (1598)
: the usually turned or carved post of a bed
be·drag·gle \bi-'dra-gəl\ *transitive verb* (1727)
: to wet thoroughly
be·drag·gled \bi-'dra-gəld\ *adjective* (1824)
1 : left wet and limp by or as if by rain
2 : soiled and stained by or as if by trailing in mud
3 : DILAPIDATED 〈*bedraggled* buildings〉
bed rest *noun* (1944)
: confinement of a sick person to bed
bed·rid·den \'bed-,ri-d³n\ *also* **bed·rid** \-,rid\ *adjective* [alteration of Middle English *bedrede, bedreden,* from Old English *bedreda,* from *bedreda* one confined to bed, from *bedd* bed + *-rida, -reda* from *rīdan* to ride] (before 12th century)
: confined (as by illness) to bed
¹**bed·rock** \-'räk, -,räk\ *noun* (1850)
1 : the solid rock underlying unconsolidated surface materials (as soil)
2 a : lowest point **:** NADIR **b :** BASIS
²**bed·rock** *adjective* (1896)
: solidly fundamental, basic, or reliable 〈traditional *bedrock* values〉 〈a *bedrock* constituency〉
bed·roll \-,rōl\ *noun* (1910)
: bedding rolled up for carrying
¹**bed·room** \-,rüm, -,rùm\ *noun* (1616)

◇ **WORD HISTORY**

bedlam In 1247 a house was founded in London for the religious order of St. Mary of Bethlehem. By 1330 this priory had become the Hospital of St. Mary of Bethlehem, and it was intended to serve the poor or homeless who where afflicted with any ailment. By 1405 the hospital, now under royal control, was being used, at least in part, as an asylum for the insane—the first such institution in England. Over time everyday speech telescoped *Bethlehem* into *Bedlam.* And over time Bedlam became proverbial for its wretched conditions and tumultuous commotion. By the latter part of the 17th century, the word *bedlam* had begun to be used generically for any lunatic asylum. At about the same time, the term was first applied metaphorically to a scene of wild uproar or confusion, its common meaning today.

\ə\ abut \ᵊ\ kitten \ər\ further \a\ ash \ā\ ace
\ä\ mop, mar \aù\ out \ch\ chin \e\ bet \ē\ easy
\g\ go \i\ hit \ī\ ice \j\ job \ŋ\ sing \ō\ go
\ò\ law \òi\ boy \th\ thin \t͟h\ the \ü\ loot \ù\ foot
\y\ yet \zh\ vision *see also* Guide to Pronunciation

: a room furnished with a bed and intended primarily for sleeping
— **bed·roomed** \-ˌrümd, -ˌrůmd\ *adjective*
²**bed·room** *adjective* (1915)
1 : dealing with, suggestive of, or inviting sexual relations ⟨a *bedroom* farce⟩ ⟨*bedroom* eyes⟩
2 : inhabited or used by commuters ⟨a *bedroom* community⟩
bed-sheet \'bed-ˌshēt\ *noun* (15th century)
: an oblong piece of usually cotton or linen cloth used as an article of bedding
¹**bed·side** \'bed-ˌsīd\ *noun* (14th century)
: the side of a bed : a place beside a bed
²**bedside** *adjective* (1837)
1 : of, relating to, or conducted at the bedside ⟨a *bedside* diagnosis⟩
2 : suitable for reading in bed ⟨a *bedside* book⟩
bedside manner *noun* (1869)
: the manner that a physician assumes toward patients
bed–sit·ter \'bed-ˌsi-tər\ *noun* [*bed-sit*ting room + *-er* (as in *fresher* freshman, *rugger* rugby)] (1927)
British : a one-room apartment serving as both bedroom and sitting room — called also *bed-sit, bed-sitting-room*
bed·sore \'bed-ˌsōr, -ˌsòr\ *noun* (1861)
: an ulceration of tissue deprived of adequate blood supply by prolonged pressure
bed·spread \-ˌspred\ *noun* (1845)
: a usually ornamental cloth cover for a bed
bed·spring \-ˌspriŋ\ *noun* (1897)
: a spring supporting a mattress
bed·stead \'bed-ˌsted\ *noun* [Middle English *bedstede,* from *bed + stede* stead, place — more at STEAD] (15th century)
: the framework of a bed
bed·straw \-ˌstrò\ *noun* [from its use for mattresses] (1527)
: any of a genus (*Galium*) of herbs of the madder family having squarish stems, whorled leaves, and small flowers
bed table *noun* (1811)
1 : an adjustable table used (as for eating or writing) by a person in bed
2 : a small table beside a bed
bed·time \-ˌtīm\ *noun* (13th century)
: a time for going to bed
bedtime story *noun* (1899)
: a story read or recounted to someone (as a child) at bedtime
be·du \'be-ˌdü\ *noun, plural* **bedu** *often capitalized* [Arabic *badw* Bedouins, literally, desert] (1912)
: BEDOUIN
bed warmer *noun* (1922)
: a covered pan containing hot coals used to warm a bed
bed–wet·ting \-ˌwe-tiŋ\ *noun* (1890)
: enuresis especially when occurring in bed during sleep
— **bed wetter** *noun*
¹**bee** \'bē\ *noun* [Middle English, from Old English *bēo;* akin to Old High German *bīa* bee, Old Irish *bech,* Lithuanian *bitis*] (before 12th century)
1 : HONEYBEE; *broadly* : any of numerous insects (superfamily Apoidea) that differ from the related wasps especially in the heavier hairier body and in having sucking as well as chewing mouthparts, that feed on pollen and nectar, and that store both and often also honey
2 : an eccentric notion : FANCY
— **bee·like** \-ˌlīk\ *adjective*
— **bee in one's bonnet** : ¹BEE 2
²**bee** *noun* (14th century)
: the letter *b*
³**bee** *noun* [perhaps from English dialect *been* help given by neighbors, from Middle English *bene* prayer, boon, from Old English *bēn* prayer — more at BOON] (1769)
: a gathering of people for a specific purpose ⟨quilting *bee*⟩

bee balm *noun* (1840)
1 : any of several monardas; *especially* : OSWEGO TEA
2 : LEMON BALM
bee·bee *variant of* BB
bee·bread \'bē-ˌbred\ *noun* (1657)
: bitter yellowish brown pollen stored up in honeycomb cells and used mixed with honey by bees as food
beech \'bēch\ *noun, plural* **beech·es** *or* **beech** [Middle English *beche,* from Old English *bēce;* akin to Old English *bōc* beech, Old High German *buohha,* Latin *fagus,* Greek *phēgos* oak] (before 12th century)
: any of a genus (*Fagus* of the family Fagaceae, the beech family) of hardwood trees with smooth gray bark and small edible nuts; *also* : its wood
— **beech·en** \'bē-chən\ *adjective*
beech·drops \'bēch-ˌdräps\ *noun plural but singular or plural in construction* (1815)
: a plant (*Epifagus virginiana*) of the broomrape family parasitic on the roots of beeches
beech·nut \-ˌnət\ *noun* (1739)
: the nut of the beech
bee–eat·er \'bē-ˌē-tər\ *noun* (1668)
: any of a family (Meropidae) of brightly colored slender-billed insectivorous chiefly tropical Old World birds
¹**beef** \'bēf\ *noun, plural* **beefs** \'bēfs\ *or* **beeves** \'bēvz\ [Middle English, from Old French *buef* ox, beef, from Latin *bov-, bos* head of cattle — more at COW] (14th century)
1 : the flesh of an adult domestic bovine (as a steer or cow) used as food
2 a : an ox, cow, or bull in a full-grown or nearly full-grown state; *especially* : a steer or cow fattened for food ⟨quality Texas *beeves*⟩ ⟨a herd of good *beef*⟩ **b** : a dressed carcass of a beef animal
3 : muscular flesh : BRAWN
4 *plural* **beefs** : COMPLAINT
²**beef** (1860)
transitive verb
: to add substance, strength, or power to — usually used with *up* ⟨money to *beef* up its staff of professional economists —John Fischer⟩
intransitive verb
: COMPLAIN
beef·a·lo \'bē-fə-ˌlō\ *noun, plural* **-a·los** *or* **-a·loes** [blend of ¹*beef* and *buffalo*] (1973)
: any of a breed of beef cattle developed in the U.S. that is genetically ⅜ North American bison and ⅝ domestic bovine
beef·cake \'bēf-ˌkāk\ *noun* (1949)
: a usually photographic display of muscular male physiques; *also* : men of the type featured in such a display — compare CHEESECAKE
beef cattle *noun plural* (1758)
: cattle developed primarily for the efficient production of meat and marked by capacity for rapid growth, heavy well-fleshed body, and stocky build
beef·eat·er \'bē-ˌfē-tər\ *noun, often capitalized* (1671)
: a yeoman of the guard of an English monarch

beef 2b: *A* wholesale cuts: *1* shank, *2* round with rump and shank cut off, *3* rump, *4* sirloin, *5* short loin, *6* flank, *7* rib, *8* chuck, *9* plate, *10* brisket, *11* shank; *B* retail cuts: *a* heel pot roast, *b* round steak, *c* rump roast, *d* sirloin steak, *e* pinbone steak, *f* short ribs, *g* porterhouse, *h* T-bone, *i* club steak, *j* flank steak, *k* rib roast, *l* blade rib roast, *m* plate, *n* brisket, *o* crosscut shank, *p* arm pot roast, *q* boneless neck, *r* blade roast

bee fly *noun* (1852)
: any of a family (Bombyliidae) of dipteran flies many of which resemble bees
beef·steak \'bēf-ˌstāk\ *noun* (1711)
: a steak of beef usually from the hindquarter
beefsteak tomato *noun* (1968)
: a very large globe-shaped red tomato with dense flesh
beef Stro·ga·noff \-'strò-gə-ˌnòf, -'strō-\ *noun* [Count Paul *Stroganoff,* 19th century Russian diplomat] (1932)
: beef sliced thin and cooked in a sour-cream sauce
beef Wel·ling·ton \-'we-liŋ-tən\ *noun* [probably from the name *Wellington*] (1965)
: a fillet of beef covered with pâté de foie gras and baked in a casing of pastry
beef·wood \'bēf-ˌwůd\ *noun* (1805)
1 : the hard heavy reddish wood of any of various chiefly tropical trees (as the Australian pine)
2 : AUSTRALIAN PINE
beefy \'bē-fē\ *adjective* **beef·i·er; -est** (1743)
1 a : heavily and powerfully built **b** : SUBSTANTIAL, STURDY
2 : full of beef
bee·hive \'bē-ˌhīv\ *noun* (14th century)
1 : HIVE 1
2 : something resembling a hive for bees: as **a** : a scene of crowded activity **b** : a woman's hairdo that is conical in shape
— **beehive** *adjective*
beehive oven *noun* (circa 1881)
: an arched oven used especially for baking food and formerly for coking coal
bee·keep·er \-ˌkē-pər\ *noun* (1817)
: a person who raises bees
— **bee·keep·ing** *noun*
¹**bee·line** \-ˌlīn\ *noun* [from the belief that nectar-laden bees return to their hives in a direct line] (1830)
: a straight direct course
²**beeline** *intransitive verb* (1940)
: to go quickly in a straight direct course
Beel·ze·bub \bē-'el-zi-ˌbəb, 'bēl-zi-, 'bel-\ *noun* [*Beelzebub,* prince of devils, from Latin, from Greek *Beelzeboub,* from Hebrew *Ba'al zĕbhübh,* a Philistine god, literally, lord of flies] (before 12th century)
1 : DEVIL
2 : a fallen angel in Milton's *Paradise Lost* ranking next to Satan
been *past participle of* BE
¹**beep** \'bēp\ *noun* [imitative] (1929)
: a short usually high-pitched sound (as from a horn or an electronic device) that serves as a signal or warning
²**beep** (1936)
intransitive verb
1 : to sound a horn
2 : to make a beep
transitive verb
: to cause (as a horn) to sound
beep·er \'bē-pər\ *noun* (1970)
: an electronic device that beeps to make contact with the person carrying it when it receives a special radio signal
beer \'bir\ *noun* [Middle English *ber,* from Old English *bēor;* akin to Old High German *bior* beer] (before 12th century)
1 : an alcoholic beverage usually made from malted cereal grain (as barley), flavored with hops, and brewed by slow fermentation
2 : a carbonated nonalcoholic or a fermented slightly alcoholic beverage with flavoring from roots or other plant parts ⟨birch *beer*⟩
3 : fermented mash
4 : a drink of beer
beer and skittles *noun plural but singular or plural in construction* (1857)
: a situation of agreeable ease ⟨won't be all *beer and skittles*⟩
beery \'bir-ē\ *adjective* **beer·i·er; -est** (1848)

1 : smelling or tasting of beer ⟨*beery* tavern⟩
2 : affected or caused by beer ⟨*beery* voices⟩

bees·tings \'bē-stiŋz\ *noun plural but singular or plural in construction* [Middle English *bestynge,* from Old English *bȳsting,* from *bēost* beestings; akin to Old High German *biost* beestings] (before 12th century)
: the colostrum especially of a cow

bee–stung \'bē-,stəŋ\ *adjective* (1933)
: having a red puffy appearance as if from being stung by a bee ⟨*bee-stung* lips⟩

bees·wax \'bēz-,waks\ *noun* (1676)
: WAX 1

beet \'bēt\ *noun* [Middle English *bete,* from Old English *bēte,* from Latin *beta*] (before 12th century)
: a biennial garden plant (*Beta vulgaris*) of the goosefoot family that has several cultivars (as Swiss chard and sugar beet) and possesses thick long-stalked edible leaves and swollen root used as a vegetable, as a source of sugar, or for forage; *also* **:** its root

beet armyworm *noun* (1902)
: an armyworm (*Spodoptera exigua*) that eats the foliage of beets, alfalfa, and vegetables

¹bee·tle \'bē-t³l\ *noun* [Middle English *betylle,* from Old English *bitula;* akin to *bītan* to bite] (before 12th century)
1 : any of an order (Coleoptera) of insects having four wings of which the outer pair are modified into stiff elytra that protect the inner pair when at rest
2 : any of various insects resembling a beetle

²beetle *intransitive verb* **bee·tled; bee·tling** \'bē-t³l-iŋ\ (circa 1919)
: to scurry like a beetle ⟨editors *beetled* around the office⟩

³beetle *noun* [Middle English *betel,* from Old English *bīetel;* akin to Old English *bēatan* to beat] (before 12th century)
1 : a heavy wooden hammering or ramming instrument
2 : a wooden pestle or bat for domestic tasks

⁴beetle *adjective* [Middle English *bitel-browed* having overhanging brows, probably from *betylle, bitel* beetle] (14th century)
: being prominent and overhanging ⟨*beetle* brows⟩

⁵beetle *intransitive verb* **bee·tled; bee·tling** \'bē-t³l-iŋ\ (1602)
: PROJECT, JUT ⟨to scale the *beetling* crags —R. L. Stevenson⟩

beet leafhopper *noun* (1919)
: a leafhopper (*Circulifer tenellus*) that transmits curly top virus to sugar beets and other garden plants

bee tree *noun* (1782)
: a hollow tree in which honeybees nest

beet·root \'bēt-,rüt\ *noun* (1579)
chiefly British **:** a beet grown for its edible usually red root; *also* **:** the root

beeves *plural of* BEEF

bee·yard \'bē-,yärd\ *noun* (15th century)
: APIARY

be·fall \bi-'fȯl\ *verb* **-fell** \-'fel\; **-fall·en** \-'fȯ-lən\ (13th century)
intransitive verb
: to happen especially as if by fate
transitive verb
: to happen to

be·fit \bi-'fit\ *transitive verb* **be·fit·ted; be·fit·ting** (15th century)
: to be proper or becoming to

be·fit·ting \-'fi-tiŋ\ *adjective* (1564)
1 : SUITABLE, APPROPRIATE
2 : PROPER, DECENT
— **be·fit·ting·ly** \-tiŋ-lē\ *adverb*

be·fog \bi-'fȯg, -'fäg\ *transitive verb* (1601)
1 : CONFUSE
2 : FOG, OBSCURE

be·fool \bi-'fül\ *transitive verb* (14th century)
1 : to make a fool of
2 : DELUDE, DECEIVE

¹be·fore \bi-'fȯr, -'fȯr\ *adverb or adjective* [Middle English, adverb & preposition, from

Old English *beforan,* from *be-* + *foran* before, from *fore*] (before 12th century)
1 : in advance **:** AHEAD ⟨marching on *before*⟩
2 : at an earlier time **:** PREVIOUSLY ⟨the night *before*⟩ ⟨knew her from *before*⟩

²before *preposition* (before 12th century)
1 a (1) : in front of (2) **:** in the presence of **b :** under the jurisdiction or consideration of ⟨the case *before* the court⟩ **c (1) :** at the disposal of (2) **:** in store for
2 : preceding in time **:** earlier than
3 : in a higher or more important position than ⟨put quantity *before* quality⟩

³before *conjunction* (13th century)
1 a (1) : earlier than the time that ⟨call me *before* you go⟩ **(2) :** sooner or quicker than ⟨I'll be done *before* you know it⟩ **(3) :** so that . . . do not ⟨get out of there *before* you get dirty⟩ **b :** until the time that ⟨miles to go *before* I sleep —Robert Frost⟩ **c (1) :** or else . . . not ⟨must be convicted *before* he can be removed from office⟩ **(2) :** or else ⟨get out of here *before* I call a cop⟩
2 : rather or sooner than ⟨would starve *before* he'd steal⟩

be·fore·hand \bi-'fōr-,hand, -'fȯr-\ *adverb or adjective* (13th century)
1 a : in anticipation **b :** in advance
2 : ahead of time **:** EARLY

be·fore·time \-,tīm\ *adverb* (14th century)
archaic **:** FORMERLY

be·foul \bi-'fau(ə)l\ *transitive verb* (before 12th century)
: to make foul with or as if with dirt

be·friend \bi-'frend\ *transitive verb* (1559)
: to act as a friend to

be·fud·dle \bi-'fə-d³l\ *transitive verb* (circa 1879)
1 : to muddle or stupefy with or as if with drink
2 : CONFUSE, PERPLEX
— **be·fud·dle·ment** \-mənt\ *noun*

beg \'beg\ *verb* **begged; beg·ging** [Middle English *beggen*] (13th century)
transitive verb
1 : to ask for as a charity
2 a : to ask earnestly for **:** ENTREAT **b :** to require as necessary or appropriate
3 a : EVADE, SIDESTEP ⟨*begged* the real problems⟩ **b :** to pass over or ignore by assuming to be established or settled ⟨*beg* the question⟩
intransitive verb
1 : to ask for alms
2 : to ask earnestly ⟨*begged* for mercy⟩ ☆

be·get \bi-'get\ *transitive verb* **-got** \-'gät\ *also* **-gat** \-'gat\; **-got·ten** \-'gä-t³n\ *or* **-got; -get·ting** [Middle English *begeten,* alteration of *beyeten,* from Old English *bigietan* — more at GET] (13th century)
1 : to procreate as the father **:** SIRE
2 : to produce especially as an effect or outgrowth
— **be·get·ter** *noun*

¹beg·gar \'be-gər\ *noun* [Middle English *beggere, beggare,* from *beggen* to beg + *-ere, -are* ²-er] (13th century)
1 : one that begs; *especially* **:** a person who lives by asking for gifts
2 : PAUPER
3 : FELLOW 4c

²beggar *transitive verb* **beg·gared; beg·gar·ing** \'be-gə-riŋ\ (15th century)
1 : to reduce to beggary
2 : to exceed the resources or abilities of **:** DEFY ⟨*beggars* description⟩

beg·gar·ly \'be-gər-lē\ *adjective* (1526)
1 : contemptibly mean, scant, petty, or paltry
2 : befitting or resembling a beggar; *especially* **:** marked by extreme poverty
— **beg·gar·li·ness** *noun*

beg·gar's–lice \'be-gərz-,līs\ *or* **beg·gar–lice** \-gər-,līs\ *noun plural but singular or plural in construction* (1837)
: any of various plants (as of the genera *Hackelia* and *Cynoglossum*) with prickly or adhesive fruits; *also* **:** one of these fruits

beg·gar–ticks *also* **beg·gar's–ticks** \-,tiks\ *noun plural but singular or plural in construction* (circa 1818)
1 : BUR MARIGOLD; *also* **:** its prickly achenes
2 : BEGGAR'S-LICE

beg·gar·weed \'be-gər-,wēd\ *noun* (circa 1809)
1 : any of various plants (as a knotgrass, spurrey, or dodder) that grow in waste ground
2 : any of several tick trefoils (genus *Desmodium*); *especially* **:** a West Indian forage plant (*D. tortuosum*) cultivated in the southern U.S.

beg·gary \'be-gə-rē\ *noun, plural* **-gar·ies** (14th century)
1 : POVERTY, PENURY
2 : the class of beggars
3 : the practice of begging

be·gin \bi-'gin\ *verb* **be·gan** \-'gan\; **be·gun** \-'gən\; **be·gin·ning** [Middle English *beginnen,* from Old English *beginnan;* akin to Old High German *biginnan* to begin, Old English *onginnan*] (before 12th century)
intransitive verb
1 : to do the first part of an action **:** go into the first part of a process **:** START
2 a : to come into existence **:** ARISE **b :** to have a starting point
3 : to do or succeed in the least degree ⟨I can't *begin* to tell you how pleased I am⟩
transitive verb
1 : to set about the activity of **:** START
2 a : to bring into being **:** FOUND **b :** ORIGINATE, INVENT ☆

☆ SYNONYMS

Beg, entreat, beseech, implore, supplicate, adjure, importune mean to ask urgently. BEG suggests earnestness or insistence especially in asking for a favor (children *begging* to stay up late). ENTREAT implies an effort to persuade or to overcome resistance (*entreated* him to change his mind). BESEECH implies great eagerness or anxiety (I *beseech* you to have mercy). IMPLORE adds to BESEECH a suggestion of greater urgency or anguished appeal (*implored* her not to leave him). SUPPLICATE suggests a posture of humility (with bowed heads they *supplicated* their Lord). ADJURE implies advising as well as pleading and suggests the invoking of something sacred (in God's name I *adjure* you to cease). IMPORTUNE suggests an annoying persistence in trying to break down resistance to a request (*importuning* viewers for contributions).

Begin, commence, start, initiate, inaugurate, usher in mean to take the first step in a course, process, or operation. BEGIN, START, and COMMENCE are often interchangeable. BEGIN, opposed to *end,* is the most general (*begin* a trip) (*began* dancing). START, opposed to *stop,* applies especially to first actions, steps, or stages (the work *started* slowly). COMMENCE can be more formal or bookish than BEGIN or START (*commence* firing) (*commenced* a conversation). INITIATE implies taking a first step in a process or series that is to continue (*initiated* diplomatic contacts). INAUGURATE suggests a beginning of some formality or notion of significance (the discovery of penicillin *inaugurated* a new era in medicine). USHER IN is somewhat less weighty than INAUGURATE (*ushered in* a period of economic decline).

\ə\ abut \ᵊ\ kitten \ər\ further \a\ ash \ā\ ace
\ä\ mop, mar \aù\ out \ch\ chin \e\ bet \ē\ easy
\g\ go \i\ hit \ī\ ice \j\ job \ŋ\ sing \ō\ go
\ȯ\ law \ȯi\ boy \th\ thin \t̲h̲\ the \ü\ loot \ù\ foot
\y\ yet \zh\ vision *see also* Guide to Pronunciation

— to begin with : as the first thing to be considered

be·gin·ner \bi-'gi-nər\ *noun* (14th century) **:** one that begins something; *especially* **:** an inexperienced person

¹be·gin·ning \bi-'gi-niŋ\ *noun* (12th century)
1 : the point at which something begins **:** START
2 : the first part
3 : ORIGIN, SOURCE
4 : a rudimentary stage or early period — usually used in plural

²beginning *adjective* (1576)
1 : just starting out ⟨a *beginning* writer⟩
2 a : being first or the first part ⟨the *beginning* chapters⟩ **b :** INTRODUCTORY ⟨*beginning* chemistry⟩

beginning rhyme *noun* (1913)
1 : rhyme at the beginning of successive lines of verse
2 : ALLITERATION

be·gird \bi-'gərd\ *transitive verb* **-gird·ed** *or* **-girt** \-'gərt\; **-girt·ing** (before 12th century)
1 : GIRD 1a
2 : SURROUND, ENCOMPASS

be·glam·our *also* **be·glam·or** \bi-'gla-mər\ *transitive verb* (1822) **:** to impress or deceive with glamour

beg off *intransitive verb* (1854) **:** to ask to be excused from something
— beg–off \'beg-ˌóf\ *noun*

be·gone \bi-'gòn *also* -'gän\ *intransitive verb* [Middle English, from *be gone* (imperative)] (14th century) **:** to go away **:** DEPART — used especially in the imperative

be·go·nia \bi-'gōn-yə\ *noun* [New Latin, from Michel *Bégon* (died 1710) French governor of Santo Domingo] (1751) **:** any of a large genus (*Begonia* of the family Begoniaceae, the begonia family) of tropical herbs and shrubs that have asymmetrical leaves and are widely cultivated as ornamentals

be·gor·ra \bi-'gór-ə, -'gär-\ *interjection* [euphemism for *by God*] (1839) *Irish* — used as a mild oath

be·grime \bi-'grīm\ *transitive verb* **be·grimed; be·grim·ing** (circa 1553)
1 : to make dirty with grime
2 : SULLY, CORRUPT

be·grudge \bi-'grəj\ *transitive verb* (14th century)
1 : to give or concede reluctantly or with displeasure
2 : to look upon with disapproval
— be·grudg·ing·ly \-'grə-jiŋ-lē\ *adverb*

be·guile \bi-'gī(ə)l\ *verb* **be·guiled; be·guil·ing** (13th century)
transitive verb
1 : to lead by deception
2 : HOODWINK
3 : to while away especially by some agreeable occupation; *also* **:** DIVERT 2
4 : to engage the interest of by or as if by guile
intransitive verb
: to deceive by wiles
synonym see DECEIVE
— be·guile·ment \-'gī(ə)l-mənt\ *noun*
— be·guil·er \-'gī-lər\ *noun*
— be·guil·ing·ly \-'gī-liŋ-lē\ *adverb*

be·guine \bi-'gēn\ *noun* [American French *béguine*, from French *béguin* flirtation] (1935) **:** a vigorous popular dance of the islands of Saint Lucia and Martinique that somewhat resembles the rumba

Be·guine \'bā-ˌgēn, ˌbā-'\ *noun* [Middle French] (15th century) **:** a member of one of various ascetic and philanthropic communities of women not under vows founded chiefly in the Netherlands in the 13th century

be·gum \'bā-gəm, 'bē-\ *noun* [Hindi *begam*] (1617) **:** a Muslim woman of high rank (as in India or Pakistan)

be·half \bi-'haf, -'håf\ *noun* [Middle English, from *by* + *half* half, side] (14th century) **:** INTEREST, BENEFIT; *also* **:** SUPPORT, DEFENSE ⟨argued in his *behalf*⟩ □
— on behalf of *or* **in behalf of :** in the interest of; *also* **:** as representative of

be·have \bi-'hāv\ *verb* **be·haved; be·hav·ing** [Middle English *behaven*, from *be-* + *haven* to have, hold] (15th century)
transitive verb
1 : to manage the actions of (oneself) in a particular way
2 : to conduct (oneself) in a proper manner
intransitive verb
1 : to act, function, or react in a particular way
2 : to conduct oneself properly ☆
— be·hav·er *noun*

be·hav·ior \bi-'hā-vyər\ *noun* [alteration of Middle English *behavour*, from *behaven*] (15th century)
1 a : the manner of conducting oneself **b :** anything that an organism does involving action and response to stimulation **c :** the response of an individual, group, or species to its environment
2 : the way in which someone behaves; *also* **:** an instance of such behavior
3 : the way in which something functions or operates
— be·hav·ior·al \-vyə-rəl\ *adjective*
— be·hav·ior·al·ly \-rə-lē\ *adverb*

behavioral science *noun* (1951) **:** a science (as psychology, sociology, or anthropology) that deals with human action and seeks to generalize about human behavior in society
— behavioral scientist *noun*

be·hav·ior·ism \bi-'hā-vyə-ˌri-zəm\ *noun* (1913) **:** a school of psychology that takes the objective evidence of behavior (as measured responses to stimuli) as the only concern of its research and the only basis of its theory without reference to conscious experience — compare INTROSPECTIONISM
— be·hav·ior·ist \-vyə-rist\ *adjective or noun*
— be·hav·ior·is·tic \-ˌhā-vyə-'ris-tik\ *adjective*

behavior therapy *noun* (1961) **:** psychotherapy that emphasizes the application of the principles of learning to substitute desirable responses and behavior patterns for undesirable ones — called also *behavior modification*

be·hav·iour *chiefly British variant of* BEHAVIOR

be·head \bi-'hed\ *transitive verb* (before 12th century) **:** to cut off the head of **:** DECAPITATE

be·he·moth \bi-'hē-məth, 'bē-ə-məth, -ˌmäth, -ˌmòth\ *noun, often attributive* [Middle English, from Late Latin, from Hebrew *běhēmōth*] (14th century)
1 *often capitalized* **:** a mighty animal described in Job 40:15–24 as an example of the power of God
2 : something of monstrous size or power

be·hest \bi-'hest\ *noun* [Middle English, promise, command, from Old English *behǣs* promise, from *behātan* to promise, from *be-* + *hātan* to command, promise — more at HIGHT] (12th century)
1 : an authoritative order **:** COMMAND
2 : an urgent prompting ⟨called at the *behest* of my friends⟩

¹be·hind \bi-'hīnd\ *adverb or adjective* [Middle English *behinde*, from Old English *behindan*, from *be-* + *hindan* from behind; akin to

Old English *hinder* behind — more at HIND] (before 12th century)
1 a : in the place or situation that is being or has been departed from ⟨stay *behind*⟩ **b :** in, to, or toward the back ⟨look *behind*⟩ ⟨came from *behind*⟩ **c :** later in time ⟨can spring be far *behind*⟩
2 a : in a secondary or inferior position **b :** in arrears ⟨*behind* in the rent⟩ **c :** SLOW
3 *archaic* **:** still to come

²behind *preposition* (before 12th century)
1 a : in or to a place or situation in back of or to the rear of ⟨look *behind* you⟩ ⟨put *behind* bars⟩ **b** — used as a function word to indicate something that screens an observer ⟨the sun went *behind* a cloud⟩ **c :** following in order ⟨marched *behind* the band⟩
2 — used as a function word to indicate backwardness, delay, or deficiency ⟨*behind* the times⟩ ⟨*behind* schedule⟩ ⟨lagged *behind* last year's sales⟩
3 a : in the background of ⟨the conditions *behind* the strike⟩ **b :** out of the mind or consideration of ⟨put our troubles *behind* us⟩ **c :** beyond in depth or time ⟨the story *behind* the story⟩ ⟨go back *behind* Saint Augustine⟩
4 a : in support of **:** on the side of ⟨solidly *behind* the candidate⟩ **b :** with the support of ⟨won 1–0 *behind* brilliant pitching⟩

³behind *noun* [¹*behind*] (circa 1830) **:** BUTTOCKS

be·hind·hand \bi-'hīnd-ˌhand\ *adjective* (1535)
1 : being in arrears
2 a : being in an inferior position **b :** being behind schedule

behind–the–scenes *adjective* (1711)
1 : being or working out of public view or in secret ⟨*behind-the-scenes* wrangling⟩ ⟨a *behind-the-scenes* player⟩
2 : revealing or reporting the hidden workings ⟨a *behind-the-scenes* account⟩ ⟨a *behind-the-scenes* glimpse⟩

be·hold \bi-'hōld\ *verb* **-held** \-'held\; **-holding** [Middle English, to keep, behold, from Old English *behealdan*, from *be-* + *healdan* to hold] (before 12th century)

☆ **SYNONYMS**
Behave, conduct, deport, comport, acquit mean to act or to cause oneself to do something in a certain way. BEHAVE may apply to the meeting of a standard of what is proper or decorous ⟨the children *behaved* in church⟩. CONDUCT implies action or behavior that shows the extent of one's power to control or direct oneself ⟨*conducted* herself with unfailing good humor⟩. DEPORT implies behaving so as to show how far one conforms to conventional rules of discipline or propriety ⟨the hero *deported* himself in accord with the code of chivalry⟩. COMPORT suggests conduct measured by what is expected or required of one in a certain class or position ⟨*comported* themselves as gentlemen⟩. ACQUIT applies to action under stress that deserves praise or meets expectations ⟨*acquitted* herself well in her first assignment⟩.

□ **USAGE**
behalf A body of opinion favors *in* with the "interest, benefit" sense of *behalf* and *on* with the "support, defense" sense. This distinction has been observed by some writers but overall has never had a sound basis in actual usage. In current British use, *on behalf* (*of*) has replaced *in behalf* (*of*); both are still used in American English, but the distinction is frequently not observed.

transitive verb
1 : to perceive through sight or apprehension **:** SEE
2 : to gaze upon **:** OBSERVE
intransitive verb
— used in the imperative especially to call attention
— **be·hold·er** *noun*
be·hold·en \bi-'hōl-dən\ *adjective* [Middle English, from past participle of *beholden*] (14th century)
: being under obligation for a favor or gift **:** INDEBTED ⟨I'm *beholden* to you⟩
be·hoof \bi-'hüf\ *noun* [Middle English *behof*, from Old English *behōf* profit, need; akin to Old English *hebban* to raise — more at HEAVE] (before 12th century)
: ADVANTAGE, PROFIT ⟨for his own *behoof*⟩
be·hoove \bi-'hüv\ *verb* **be·hooved; be·hoov·ing** [Middle English *behoven*, from Old English *behōfian*, from *behōf*] (before 12th century)
transitive verb
: to be necessary, proper, or advantageous for ⟨it *behooves* us to go⟩
intransitive verb
: to be necessary, fit, or proper
be·hove \bi-'hōv\ *chiefly British variant of* BEHOOVE
¹**beige** \'bāzh\ *noun* [French] (circa 1858)
1 : cloth made of natural undyed wool
2 a : a variable color averaging light grayish yellowish brown **b :** a pale to grayish yellow
— **beigy** \'bā-zhē\ *adjective*
²**beige** *adjective* (1879)
1 : of the color beige
2 : VANILLA 2, VAPID
bei·gnet \,bān-'yā, ,ben-\ *noun* [American French & French; American French, from French, from Middle French *bignet*, from *buyne* bump, bruise] (1835)
1 : FRITTER
2 : a light square doughnut
¹**be·ing** \'bē-(-i)ŋ\ *noun* (14th century)
1 a : the quality or state of having existence **b** (1) **:** something conceivable as existing (2) **:** something that actually exists (3) **:** the totality of existing things **c :** conscious existence **:** LIFE
2 : the qualities that constitute an existent thing **:** ESSENCE; *especially* **:** PERSONALITY
3 : a living thing; *especially* **:** PERSON
²**being** *adjective* [present participle of *be*] (14th century)
: PRESENT — used in the phrase *for the time being*
³**being** *conjunction* (1528)
chiefly dialect **:** SINCE, BECAUSE — usually used with *as, as how,* or *that* ⟩
Be·ja \'bā-jə\ *noun, plural* **Beja** (1819)
1 : a member of a pastoral people living between the Nile and the Red Sea
2 : the Cushitic language of the Beja people
be·je·sus *also* **be·jee·zus** \bi-'jē-zəs, -'jā-, -zəz\ *interjection* [alteration of *by Jesus*] (circa 1908)
— used as a mild oath; used as a noun for emphasis ⟨scares the *bejesus* out of me⟩
be·jew·eled *or* **be·jew·elled** \bi-'jü-əld, -'jüld *also* -'jú(ə)ld\ *adjective* (1557)
: ornamented with or as if with jewels
bel \'bel\ *noun* [Alexander Graham *Bell*] (1929)
: ten decibels
be·la·bor \bi-'lā-bər\ *transitive verb* (1596)
1 a : to attack verbally **b :** to beat soundly
2 : to explain or insist on excessively ⟨*belabor* the obvious⟩
be·la·bour *chiefly British variant of* BELABOR
be·lat·ed \bi-'lā-təd\ *adjective* [past participle of *belate* (to make late)] (1670)
1 : delayed beyond the usual time
2 : existing or appearing past the normal or proper time

— **be·lat·ed·ly** *adverb*
— **be·lat·ed·ness** *noun*
be·laud \bi-'lód\ *transitive verb* (circa 1849)
: to praise usually to excess
¹**be·lay** \bi-'lā\ *verb* [Middle English *beleggen* to beset, from Old English *belecgan*, from *be-* + *lecgan* to lay] (1548)
transitive verb
1 a : to secure (as a rope) by turns around a cleat, pin, or bitt **b :** to make fast
2 : STOP
3 a : to secure (a person) at the end of a rope **b :** to secure (a rope) to a person or object
intransitive verb
1 : to be made fast
2 : STOP, QUIT — used in the imperative ⟨*belay* there⟩
3 : to make a line fast by turns around a cleat, pin, or bitt
²**belay** *noun* (1908)
1 : the securing of a person or a safety rope to an anchor point (as during mountain climbing); *also* **:** a method of so securing a person or rope
2 : something (as a projection of rock) to which a person or rope is anchored
bel can·to \bel-'kän-(,)tō, -'kan-\ *noun* [Italian, literally, beautiful singing] (1894)
: operatic singing originating in 17th century and 18th century Italy and stressing ease, purity, and evenness of tone production and an agile and precise vocal technique
belch \'belch\ *verb* [Middle English, from Old English *bealcan*] (before 12th century)
intransitive verb
1 : to expel gas suddenly from the stomach through the mouth
2 : to erupt, explode, or detonate violently
3 : to issue forth spasmodically **:** GUSH
transitive verb
1 : to eject or emit violently
2 : to expel (gas) from the stomach suddenly **:** ERUCT
— **belch** *noun*
bel·dam *or* **bel·dame** \'bel-dəm\ *noun* [Middle English *beldam* grandmother, from Middle French *bel* beautiful + Middle English *dam*] (1580)
: an old woman
be·lea·guer \bi-'lē-gər\ *transitive verb* **-guered; -guer·ing** \-g(ə-)riŋ\ [Dutch *belegeren*, from *be-* (akin to Old English *be-*) + *leger* camp; akin to Old High German *legar* bed — more at LAIR] (1587)
1 : BESIEGE
2 : TROUBLE, HARASS ⟨*beleaguered* parents⟩
— **be·lea·guer·ment** \-mənt\ *noun*
bel·em·nite \'bel-əm-,nīt\ *noun* [New Latin *belemnites*, from Greek *belemnon* dart; akin to Greek *ballein* to throw — more at DEVIL] (1646)
: any of a genus (*Belemnites*) of extinct cephalopods that had bullet-shaped internal shells and were especially abundant in the Mesozoic era
bel·fry \'bel-frē\ *noun, plural* **belfries** [Middle English *belfrey*, alteration of *berfrey*, from Middle French *berfrei* bell tower, siege tower, of Germanic origin (akin to Middle High German *bërvrit* siege tower); akin to Old High German *bergan* to shelter and to Old English *frith* peace, refuge — more at BURY] (15th century)
1 : a bell tower; *especially* **:** one surmounting or attached to another structure
2 : a room or framework for enclosing a bell
3 : HEAD 2a ⟨batty in the *belfry*⟩ ◇
Bel·gae \'bel-,gī, -,jē\ *noun plural* [Latin, plural of *Belga*] (circa 1895)
: a people occupying parts of northern Gaul and Britain in Caesar's time
— **Bel·gic** \-jik\ *adjective*
Bel·gian \'bel-jən\ *noun* (circa 1623)
1 : a native or inhabitant of Belgium

2 : any of a breed of heavy muscular usually roan or chestnut draft horses developed in Belgium
— **Belgian** *adjective*
Belgian endive *noun* (1931)
: ENDIVE 2
Belgian hare *noun* (1900)
: any of a breed of slender chestnut-colored domestic rabbits
Belgian Ma·li·nois \-,ma-lən-'wä\ *noun* (1968)
: any of a breed of squarely built working dogs closely related to the Belgian sheepdog and having relatively short straight hair with a dense undercoat — called also *Malinois*
Belgian sheepdog *noun* (1929)
: any of a breed of hardy black dogs developed in Belgium especially for herding sheep
Belgian Ter·vu·ren \-(,)tər-'vyúr-ən, -ter-\ *noun* [*Tervuren*, commune in Brabant, Belgium] (1964)
: any of a breed of working dogs closely related to the Belgian sheepdog but having abundant long straight fawn-colored hair with black tips
Be·lial \'bē-lē-əl, 'bēl-yəl\ *noun* [Greek, from Hebrew *bĕlīya'al* worthlessness] (13th century)

□ USAGE
being If your own vocabulary does not include the conjunction *being* or its compound forms *being as, being as how,* and *being that,* you might well wonder at the wide coverage these terms receive in handbooks. The point that almost all of the handbooks miss is that this conjunction is dialectal. Like many words that have dwindled to regional use, *being* was once standard ⟨Sir John, you loiter here too long, *being* you are to take soldiers up in counties as you go —Shakespeare⟩ ⟨I am tired of Lives of Nelson, *being that* I never read any —Jane Austen⟩. *The Dictionary of American Regional English* reports that *being* and its compound forms still survive in the South, South Midland, and New England speech areas.

◇ WORD HISTORY
belfry In our day *belfry* means bell tower; the first syllable appears to be a perfect match with *bell*, whatever *-fry* might mean. But in fact *belfry* does not derive from *bell*, and the original meaning of its medieval French source was not "bell tower," but rather "siege tower." A siege tower was a wheeled wooden structure that was pushed up to the walls of a besieged castle to provide both shelter and a base of attack for the besiegers. A Middle High German word for such a tower was *bercvrit*, which appears to be a compound of the verb *bergen* "to protect, conceal, shelter" and *vride* "peace, refuge," the presumed sense of the compound being "that which affords refuge." The ancient Germanic language that had the greatest influence on early French was Frankish, and the Frankish counterpart to such a word would have been *bergfrithu*. This word would have emerged in Old French as *berfroi*, for which we have evidence from the mid-12th century. In some dialects, *berfroi* underwent alteration to *belfroi*, and it is from an Anglo-French form of this word that Middle English borrowed *belfrey*—hence Modern English *belfry*, with its illusory suggestion of *bell*.

\ə\ abut \ᵊ\ kitten \ər\ further \a\ ash \ā\ ace
\ä\ mop, mar \aú\ out \ch\ chin \e\ bet \ē\ easy
\g\ go \i\ hit \ī\ ice \j\ job \ŋ\ sing \ō\ go
\ó\ law \ói\ boy \th\ thin \ṯh\ the \ü\ loot \ú\ foot
\y\ yet \zh\ vision *see also* Guide to Pronunciation

1 — a biblical name of the devil or one of the fiends
2 : one of the fallen angels in Milton's *Paradise Lost*
be·lie \bi-'lī\ *transitive verb* **-lied; -ly·ing** (before 12th century)
1 a : to give a false impression of **b :** to present an appearance not in agreement with
2 a : to show (something) to be false or wrong **b :** to run counter to **:** CONTRADICT
3 : DISGUISE 3
— **be·li·er** \-'lī(-ə)r\ *noun*
be·lief \bə-'lēf\ *noun* [Middle English *beleave,* probably alteration of Old English *gelēafa,* from *ge-,* associative prefix + *lēafa;* akin to Old English *lȳfan*] (12th century)
1 : a state or habit of mind in which trust or confidence is placed in some person or thing
2 : something believed; *especially* **:** a tenet or body of tenets held by a group
3 : conviction of the truth of some statement or the reality of some being or phenomenon especially when based on examination of evidence ☆
be·liev·able \-'lē-və-bəl\ *adjective* (14th century)
: capable of being believed especially as within the range of known possibility or probability
— **be·liev·abil·i·ty** \-,lē-və-bə-'bil-ə-tē\ *noun*
— **be·liev·ably** \-'lē-və-blē\ *adverb*
be·lieve \bə-'lēv\ *verb* **be·lieved; be·liev·ing** [Middle English *beleven,* from Old English *belēfan,* from *be-* + *lȳfan, lēfan* to allow, believe; akin to Old High German *gilouben* to believe, Old English *lēof* dear — more at LOVE] (before 12th century)
intransitive verb
1 a : to have a firm religious faith **b :** to accept as true, genuine, or real ⟨ideals we *believe* in⟩ ⟨*believes* in ghosts⟩
2 : to have a firm conviction as to the goodness, efficacy, or ability of something ⟨*believe* in exercise⟩
3 : to hold an opinion **:** THINK ⟨I *believe* so⟩
transitive verb
1 a : to consider to be true or honest ⟨*believe* the reports⟩ ⟨you wouldn't *believe* how long it took⟩ **b :** to accept the word or evidence of ⟨I *believe* you⟩ ⟨couldn't *believe* my ears⟩
2 : to hold as an opinion **:** SUPPOSE ⟨I *believe* it will rain soon⟩
— **be·liev·er** *noun*
— **not believe :** to be astounded at ⟨I couldn't *believe* my luck⟩
be·like \bi-'līk\ *adverb* (circa 1533) *archaic*
: most likely **:** PROBABLY
be·lit·tle \bi-'li-tᵊl\ *transitive verb* **-lit·tled; -lit·tling** \-'li-tᵊl-iŋ, -'lit-liŋ\ (1797)
1 : to speak slightingly of **:** DISPARAGE ⟨*belittles* her efforts⟩
2 : to cause (a person or thing) to seem little or less
synonym see DECRY
— **be·lit·tle·ment** \-'li-tᵊl-mənt\ *noun*
— **be·lit·tler** \-'li-tᵊl-ər, -'lit-lər\ *noun*
be·live \bi-'līv\ *adverb* [Middle English *bilive* vigorously, from *by* + *live,* dative of *lif* life] (1594)
Scottish **:** in due time **:** BY AND BY
¹bell \'bel\ *noun* [Middle English *belle,* from Old English; perhaps akin to Old English *bellan* to roar — more at BELLOW] (before 12th century)
1 a : a hollow metallic device that gives off a reverberating sound when struck **b :** DOORBELL
2 a : the sounding of a bell as a signal **b :** a stroke of a bell (as on shipboard) to indicate the time; *also* **:** the time so indicated **c :** a half hour period of a watch on shipboard indicated by the strokes of a bell — see SHIP'S BELLS table below
3 : something having the form of a bell: as **a :** the corolla of a flower **b :** the part of the capital of a column between the abacus and neck

molding **c :** the flared end of a wind instrument
4 a : a percussion instrument consisting of metal bars or tubes that when struck give out tones resembling bells — usually used in plural **b :** GLOCKENSPIEL

SHIP'S BELLS

NO. OF BELLS	HOUR (A.M. OR P.M.)		
1	12:30	4:30	8:30
2	1:00	5:00	9:00
3	1:30	5:30	9:30
4	2:00	6:00	10:00
5	2:30	6:30	10:30
6	3:00	7:00	11:00
7	3:30	7:30	11:30
8	4:00	8:00	12:00

²bell (14th century)
transitive verb
1 : to provide with a bell
2 : to flare the end of (as a tube) into the shape of a bell
intransitive verb
: to take the form of a bell **:** FLARE
— **bell the cat :** to do a daring or risky deed
³bell *intransitive verb* [Middle English, from Old English *bellan*] (before 12th century)
: to make a resonant bellowing or baying sound ⟨the wild buck *bells* from ferny brake —Sir Walter Scott⟩
⁴bell *noun* (1862)
: BELLOW, ROAR
bel·la·don·na \,be-lə-'dä-nə\ *noun* [Italian, literally, beautiful lady] (1597)
1 : an Old World poisonous plant (*Atropa belladonna*) of the nightshade family having purple or green bell-shaped flowers, glossy black berries, and root and leaves that yield atropine — called also *deadly nightshade*
2 : a medicinal extract (as atropine) from the belladonna plant
belladonna lily *noun* (1734)
: AMARYLLIS
bell·bird \'bel-,bərd\ *noun* (1802)
: any of various birds (as of the genera *Procnias* and *Anthornis*) whose notes suggest the sound of a bell
bell–bot·toms \'bel-'bä-təmz\ *noun plural* (1898)
: pants with wide flaring bottoms
— **bell–bottom** *adjective*
bell·boy \'bel-,bȯi\ *noun* (1861)
: BELLHOP
bell buoy *noun* (1838)
: a buoy with a bell rung by the action of the waves
bell captain *noun* (1926)
: CAPTAIN 2c
bell curve *noun* [from the shape] (circa 1941)
: NORMAL CURVE
belle \'bel\ *noun* [French, from feminine of *beau* beautiful — more at BEAU] (1622)
: a popular and attractive girl or woman; *especially* **:** a girl or woman whose charm and beauty make her a favorite ⟨the *belle* of the ball⟩
Bel·leek \bə-'lēk\ *noun* [*Belleek,* town in Northern Ireland] (1869)
: a very thin translucent porcelain with a lustrous pearly glaze produced in Ireland — called also *Belleek china, Belleek ware*
belle epoque *or* **belle époque** \'bel-ā-'pȯk\ *noun, often B&E capitalized* [French, literally, beautiful age] (1954)
: a period of high artistic or cultural development; *especially* **:** such a period in fin de siècle France
Bel·ler·o·phon \bə-'ler-ə-fən, -,fän\ *noun* [Latin, from Greek *Bellerophōn*]
: a legendary Greek hero noted for killing the Chimera

belles let·tres \bel-'letrᵊ\ *noun plural but singular in construction* [French, literally, fine letters] (1710)
: literature that is an end in itself and not merely informative; *specifically* **:** light, entertaining, and often sophisticated literature
bel·le·trist \bel-'le-trist\ *noun* [*belles lettres*] (1816)
: a writer of belles lettres
— **bel·le·tris·tic** \,bel-lə-'tris-tik\ *adjective*
bell·flow·er \'bel-,flaú-(ə)r\ *noun* (1578)
: any of a genus (*Campanula* of the family Campanulaceae, the bellflower family) of widely cultivated herbs having alternate leaves and usually showy flowers
bell·hop \-,häp\ *noun* [short for *bell-hopper*] (1910)
: a hotel or club employee who escorts guests to rooms, assists them with luggage, and runs errands
bel·li·cose \'be-li-,kōs\ *adjective* [Middle English, from Latin *bellicosus,* from *bellicus* of war, from *bellum* war] (15th century)
: favoring or inclined to start quarrels or wars
synonym see BELLIGERENT
— **bel·li·cos·i·ty** \,be-li-'kä-sə-tē\ *noun*
bel·lied \'be-lēd\ *adjective* (15th century)
: having a belly of a specified kind — used in combination ⟨a big-*bellied* man⟩
bel·lig·er·ence \bə-'lij-rən(t)s, -'li-jə-\ *noun* (1814)
: an aggressive or truculent attitude, atmosphere, or disposition
bel·lig·er·en·cy \-rən(t)-sē\ *noun* (1863)
1 : the state of being at war or in conflict; *specifically* **:** the status of a legally recognized belligerent state or nation
2 : BELLIGERENCE
bel·lig·er·ent \-rənt\ *adjective* [modification of Latin *belligerant-, belligerans,* present participle of *belligerare* to wage war, from *belliger* waging war, from *bellum* + *gerere* to wage] (1577)
1 : waging war; *specifically* **:** belonging to or recognized as a state at war and protected by and subject to the laws of war
2 : inclined to or exhibiting assertiveness, hostility, or combativeness ☆
— **belligerent** *noun*
— **bel·lig·er·ent·ly** *adverb*
bell jar *noun* (circa 1859)

: a bell-shaped usually glass vessel designed to cover objects or to contain gases or a vacuum

bell·ly·ra \'bel-'lī-rə\ or **bell lyre** \-ˌlīr\ noun [lyra from Latin, lyre] (circa 1943)
: a glockenspiel mounted in a portable lyre-shaped frame and used especially in marching bands

bell jar

bell·man \'bel-mən\ noun (14th century)
1 : a man (as a town crier) who rings a bell
2 : BELLHOP

bell metal noun (1541)
: bronze that consists usually of three to four parts of copper to one of tin and that is used for making bells

Bel·lo·na \bə-'lō-nə\ noun [Latin]
: the Roman goddess of war

bel·low \'be-(ˌ)lō\ verb [Middle English belwen, from Old English bylgian; akin to Old English & Old High German bellan to roar] (before 12th century)
intransitive verb
1 : to make the loud deep hollow sound characteristic of a bull
2 : to shout in a deep voice
transitive verb
: BAWL ⟨bellows the orders⟩
— **bellow** noun

bel·lows \'be-(ˌ)lōz, -ləz\ noun plural but singular or plural in construction [Middle English belu, from Old English belg — more at BELLY] (before 12th century)
1 : an instrument or machine that by alternate expansion and contraction draws in air through a valve or orifice and expels it through a tube; also : any of various other blowers
2 : LUNGS
3 : the pleated expansible part in a camera; also : a metallic or plastic flexible and expansible vessel

bell pepper noun (1707)
: SWEET PEPPER

bell·pull \'bel-ˌpu̇l\ noun (1832)
: a handle or knob attached to a cord by which one rings a bell; also : the cord itself

bell push noun (1884)
: a button that is pushed to ring a bell

bells and whistles noun plural (1969)
: items or features that are useful or decorative but not essential : FRILLS

bell–shaped \'bel-ˌshāpt\ adjective (circa 1828)
1 : shaped like a bell
2 : relating to or being a normal curve or a normal distribution

Bell's palsy \'belz-\ noun [Sir Charles Bell (died 1842) Scottish anatomist] (circa 1860)
: paralysis of the facial nerve producing distortion on one side of the face

bell tower noun (1614)
: a tower that supports or shelters a bell

bell·weth·er \'bel-ˌwe-thər, -ˌwe-\ noun [Middle English, leading sheep of a flock, leader, from belle bell + wether; from the practice of belling the leader of a flock] (13th century)
: one that takes the lead or initiative : LEADER; also : an indicator of trends

bell·wort \'bel-ˌwərt, -ˌwȯrt\ noun (1784)
: any of a small genus (Uvularia) of herbs of the lily family with yellow drooping flowers

¹bel·ly \'be-lē\ noun, plural **bellies** [Middle English bely bellows, belly, from Old English belg bag, skin; akin to Old High German balg bag, skin, Old English blāwan to blow — more at BLOW] (before 12th century)
1 a : ABDOMEN 1; also : POTBELLY 1 **b** : the stomach and its adjuncts **c** : the undersurface of an animal's body; also : hide from this part **d** : WOMB, UTERUS
2 : an internal cavity : INTERIOR
3 : appetite for food

4 : a surface or object curved or rounded like a human belly
5 a : the enlarged fleshy body of a muscle **b** : the part of a sail that swells out when filled with wind
6 : GUT 1a(2)

²belly verb **bel·lied; bel·ly·ing** (1606)
transitive verb
: to cause to swell or fill out
intransitive verb
1 : SWELL, FILL
2 a : to slide or crawl on one's belly **b** : BELLY-LAND

¹bel·ly·ache \'be-lē-ˌāk\ noun (1552)
: pain in the abdomen and especially in the bowels : COLIC

²bellyache intransitive verb (1881)
: to complain whiningly or peevishly : find fault
— **bel·ly·ach·er** noun

bel·ly·band \'be-lē-ˌband\ noun (15th century)
: a band around or across the belly: as **a** : GIRTH 1 **b** : BAND 4b

belly button noun (circa 1877)
: the human navel

belly dance noun (1899)
: a usually solo dance emphasizing movements of the belly
— **belly dance** intransitive verb
— **belly dancer** noun

belly flop noun (1895)
: a dive (as into water or in coasting prone on a sled) in which the front of the body strikes flat against another surface — called also belly flopper
— **belly flop** intransitive verb

bel·ly·ful \'be-lē-ˌfu̇l\ noun (1535)
: an excessive amount ⟨a bellyful of advice⟩

bel·ly–land \-ˌland\ intransitive verb (1943)
: to land an airplane on its undersurface without use of landing gear
— **belly landing** noun

belly laugh noun (1921)
: a deep hearty laugh

bel·ly–up \-'əp\ adjective [from the floating position of a dead fish] (1939)
: hopelessly ruined or defeated; especially : BANKRUPT ⟨the business went belly-up⟩

belly up intransitive verb (1948)
: to move close or next to ⟨bellied up to the bar⟩

be·long \bi-'lȯŋ\ verb [Middle English belongen, from be- + longen to be suitable — more at LONG] (14th century)
intransitive verb
1 a : to be suitable, appropriate, or advantageous ⟨a dictionary belongs in every home⟩ **b** : to be in a proper situation ⟨a man of his ability belongs in teaching⟩
2 a : to be the property of a person or thing — used with to **b** : to be attached or bound by birth, allegiance, or dependency **c** : to be a member of a club, organization, or set
3 : to be an attribute, part, adjunct, or function of a person or thing ⟨nuts and bolts belong to a car⟩
4 : to be properly classified
verbal auxiliary
chiefly Southern & southern Midland : OUGHT, MUST

be·long·ing \-'lȯŋ-iŋ\ noun (1817)
1 : POSSESSION — usually used in plural
2 : close or intimate relationship ⟨a sense of belonging⟩
— **be·long·ing·ness** noun

Belo·rus·sian \ˌbe-lō-'rə-shən, ˌbye-\ noun (1943)
1 : a native or inhabitant of Belorussia (Belarus)
2 : the Slavic language of the Belorussians
— **Belorussian** adjective

be·loved \bi-'ləvd, -'lə-vəd\ adjective [Middle English, from past participle of beloven to love, from be- + loven to love] (14th century)
: dearly loved : dear to the heart
— **beloved** noun

¹be·low \bi-'lō\ adverb [Middle English bilooghe, from bi by + looghe ³low] (14th century)
1 : in or to a lower place
2 a : on earth **b** : in or to Hades or hell
3 : on or to a lower floor or deck
4 a : in, to, at, or by a lower rank or number **b** : below zero ⟨20 degrees below⟩
5 : lower on the same page or on a following page
6 : under the surface of the water

²below preposition (1575)
1 a : lower in place, rank, or value than : UNDER **b** : down river from **c** : south of
2 : inferior to (as in rank)
3 : not suitable to the rank of : BENEATH

³below noun (1697)
: something that is below

⁴below adjective (1916)
: written or discussed lower on the same page or on a following page

be·low·decks \bi-ˌlō-'deks; -'lō-ˌdeks\ adverb (1909)
: inside or into the superstructure of a boat
: down to a lower deck

be·low·ground \-'grau̇nd; -ˌgrau̇nd\ adjective (1928)
: being under the ground

Bel·shaz·zar \bel-'sha-zər\ noun [Hebrew Bēlshaṣṣar]
: a son of Nebuchadnezzar and king of Babylon

¹belt \'belt\ noun [Middle English, from Old English; akin to Old High German balz belt; both from Latin balteus belt] (before 12th century)
1 a : a strip of flexible material worn especially around the waist **b** : a similar article worn as a corset or for protection or safety or as a symbol of distinction
2 : a continuous band of tough flexible material for transmitting motion and power or conveying materials
3 : an area characterized by some distinctive feature (as of culture, habitation, geology, or life forms); especially : one suited to a particular crop ⟨the corn belt⟩
4 : BELTWAY
— **belt·ed** \'bel-təd\ adjective
— **belt·less** \'belt-ləs\ adjective
— **below the belt** : UNFAIR, UNFAIRLY
— **under one's belt** : in one's possession : as part of one's experience

²belt (14th century)
transitive verb
1 a : to encircle or fasten with a belt **b** : to strap on
2 a : to beat with or as if with a belt : THRASH **b** : STRIKE, HIT
3 : to mark with a band
4 : to sing in a forceful manner or style ⟨belting out popular songs⟩
intransitive verb
1 : to move or act in a speedy, vigorous, or violent manner
2 : to sing loudly
— **belt·er** \'bel-tər\ noun

³belt noun (1899)
1 : a jarring blow : WHACK
2 : DRINK ⟨a belt of gin⟩

Bel·tane \'bel-ˌtān, -tin\ noun [Middle English (Scots), 1st or 3rd of May, from Scottish Gaelic bealltain] (15th century)
: the Celtic May Day festival

belted kingfisher noun (1811)
: a North American kingfisher (Ceryle alcyon synonym Megaceryle alcyon) that is slate blue above and white below with a slate blue breast band and an additional chestnut-colored band in the female

belt·ing \'bel-tiŋ\ *noun* (1567)
1 : BELTS
2 : material for belts
belt-tight·en·ing \'belt-,tīt-niŋ, -,tī-t°n-iŋ\ *noun* (1937)
: a reduction in spending
belt up *intransitive verb* (1949)
British **:** SHUT UP
belt·way \'belt-,wā\ *noun* (circa 1952)
: a highway skirting an urban area — often used to refer specifically to the beltway around Washington D.C. especially as delimiting what is seen as an insular political and social world
be·lu·ga \bə-'lü-gə\ *noun* [Russian, from *belyĭ* white; akin to Greek *phalios* having a white spot — more at BALD] (1772)
1 a : a large white sturgeon (*Huso huso* synonym *Acipenser huso*) of the Black Sea, Caspian Sea, and their tributaries **b :** caviar processed from beluga roe
2 [Russian *belukha*, from *belyĭ*] **:** WHITE WHALE
bel·ve·dere \'bel-və-,dir\ *noun* [Italian, literally, beautiful view] (1593)
: a structure (as a cupola or a summerhouse) designed to command a view
be·ma \'bē-mə\ *noun* [Late Latin & Late Greek; Late Latin, from Late Greek *bēma*, from Greek, step, tribunal, from *bainein* to go — more at COME] (1683)
1 : the usually raised part of an Eastern church containing the altar
2 : a raised platform in a synagogue from which the Pentateuch and the Prophets are read
Bem·ba \'bem-bə\ *noun, plural* **Bemba** *or* **Bembas** (1940)
1 : a member of a primarily agricultural Bantu-speaking people of northeastern Zambia
2 : a Bantu language of the Bemba people
be·med·aled *or* **be·med·alled** \bi-'me-d°ld\ *adjective* (1880)
: wearing or decorated with medals
be·mire \bi-'mīr\ *transitive verb* (circa 1532)
1 : to soil with mud or dirt
2 : to drag through or sink in mire
be·moan \bi-'mōn\ *transitive verb* (before 12th century)
1 : to express deep grief or distress over
2 : to regard with displeasure, disapproval, or regret
synonym SEE DEPLORE
be·mock \bi-'mäk, -'mȯk\ *transitive verb* (1607)
archaic **:** MOCK
be·muse \bi-'myüz\ *transitive verb* (1735)
1 : to make confused **:** BEWILDER
2 : to occupy the attention of **:** ABSORB
— **be·mus·ed·ly** \-'myü-zəd-lē\ *adverb*
— **be·muse·ment** \-'myüz-mənt\ *noun*
¹ben \'ben\ *adverb* [Middle English, from Old English *binnan*, from *be-* + *innan* within, from within, from *in*] (before 12th century)
Scottish **:** WITHIN
²ben *preposition* (before 12th century)
Scottish **:** WITHIN
³ben *noun* (circa 1799)
Scottish **:** the inner room or parlor of a 2-room cottage
Bence–Jones protein \'ben(t)s-'jōnz-\ *noun* [Henry *Bence-Jones* (died 1873) English physician and chemist] (circa 1923)
: an immunoglobulin that is composed only of light chain polypeptides and that is found especially in the urine of persons affected with multiple myeloma
¹bench \'bench\ *noun* [Middle English, from Old English *benc*; akin to Old High German *bank* bench] (before 12th century)
1 a : a long seat for two or more persons **b :** a thwart in a boat **c** (1) **:** a seat on which the members of an athletic team await a turn or opportunity to play (2) **:** the reserve players on a team
2 a : the seat where a judge sits in court **b :** the place where justice is administered

: COURT **c :** the office or dignity of a judge **d :** the persons who sit as judges
3 a : the office or dignity of an official **b :** a seat for an official **c :** the officials occupying a bench
4 a : a long worktable; *also* **:** LABORATORY ⟨*bench* chemist⟩ ⟨*bench* test⟩ **b :** a table forming part of a machine
5 : TERRACE, SHELF: as **a :** a former wave-cut shore of a sea or lake or floodplain of a river **b :** a shelf or ridge formed in working an open excavation on more than one level
6 : a compartmented platform on which dogs or cats are kept at a show when not being judged
²bench (14th century)
transitive verb
1 : to furnish with benches
2 a : to seat on a bench **b** (1) **:** to remove from or keep out of a game (2) **:** to remove from the starting lineup
3 : to exhibit (dogs or cats) to the public on a bench
intransitive verb
: to form a bench by natural processes
bench·er \'ben-chər\ *noun* (15th century)
: one who sits on or presides at a bench
bench·land \'bench-,land\ *noun* (1857)
: BENCH 5a
bench·mark \'bench-,märk\ *noun* (circa 1842)
1 *usually* **bench mark :** a mark on a permanent object indicating elevation and serving as a reference in topographical surveys and tidal observations
2 a : a point of reference from which measurements may be made **b :** something that serves as a standard by which others may be measured or judged **c :** a standardized problem or test that serves as a basis for evaluation or comparison (as of computer system performance)
bench press *noun* (1973)
: a press in weight lifting performed by a lifter lying on a bench
— **bench–press** *transitive verb*
bench seat *noun* (1975)
: a seat in an automotive vehicle that extends the full width of the passenger section
bench·warm·er \'bench-,wȯr-mər\ *noun* (1892)
: a reserve player on an athletic team
bench warrant *noun* (1696)
: a warrant issued by a presiding judge or by a court against a person guilty of contempt or indicted for a crime
¹bend \'bend\ *verb* **bent** \'bent\; **bend·ing** [Middle English, from Old English *bendan*; akin to Old English *bend* fetter — more at BAND] (before 12th century)
transitive verb
1 : to constrain or strain to tension by curving ⟨*bend* a bow⟩
2 a : to turn or force from straight or even to curved or angular **b :** to force from a proper shape **c :** to force back to an original straight or even condition
3 : FASTEN ⟨*bend* a sail to its yard⟩
4 a : to cause to turn from a straight course **:** DEFLECT **b :** to guide or turn toward **:** DIRECT **c :** INCLINE, DISPOSE **d :** to adapt to one's purpose **:** DISTORT ⟨*bend* the rules⟩
5 : to direct strenuously or with interest **:** APPLY
6 : to make submissive **:** SUBDUE
intransitive verb
1 : to curve out of a straight line or position; *specifically* **:** to incline the body in token of submission
2 : to apply oneself vigorously ⟨*bending* to their work⟩
3 : INCLINE, TEND
4 : to make concessions **:** COMPROMISE
— **bend·a·ble** \'ben-də-bəl\ *adjective*
— **bend one's ear :** to talk to someone at length

²bend *noun* (15th century)
1 : the act or process of bending **:** the state of being bent
2 : something that is bent: as **a :** a curved part of a stream or road **b :** ¹WALE 2 — usually used in plural
3 *plural but singular or plural in construction* **:** a sometimes fatal disorder that is marked by neuralgic pains and paralysis, distress in breathing, and often collapse and that is caused by the release of gas bubbles (as of nitrogen) in tissue upon too rapid decrease in air pressure after a stay in a compressed atmosphere — usually used with *the;* called also *caisson disease, decompression sickness;* compare AEROEMBOLISM
— **around the bend :** MAD, CRAZY
³bend *noun* [Middle English, from Middle French *bende*, of Germanic origin; akin to Old High German *binta, bant* band — more at BAND] (15th century)
1 : a diagonal band that runs from the dexter chief to the sinister base on a heraldic shield — compare BEND SINISTER
2 [Middle English, band, from Old English *bend* fetter — more at BAND] **:** a knot by which one rope is fastened to another or to some object
ben·day \'ben-'dā\ *adjective, often capitalized* [*Benjamin Day* (died 1916) American printer] (1903)
: involving a process for adding shaded or tinted areas made up of dots for reproduction by line engraving
— **benday** *transitive verb*
bend·er \'ben-dər\ *noun* (15th century)
1 : one that bends
2 : SPREE
bend sinister *noun* (1612)
: a diagonal bend that runs from the sinister chief to the dexter base on a heraldic shield
bendy \'ben-dē\ *adjective* (1928)
: FLEXIBLE, PLIABLE ⟨a *bendy* mast⟩
¹be·neath \bi-'nēth\ *adverb* [Middle English *benethe*, from Old English *beneothan*, from *be-* + *neothan* below; akin to Old English *nithera* nether] (before 12th century)
1 : in or to a lower position **:** BELOW
2 : directly under **:** UNDERNEATH
²beneath *preposition* (before 12th century)
1 a : in or to a lower position than **:** BELOW **b :** directly under **c :** at the foot of
2 : not suitable to the rank of **:** unworthy of
3 : under the control, pressure, or influence of
4 : concealed by **:** under the guise of ⟨a warm heart *beneath* a gruff manner⟩
ben·e·dict \'be-nə-,dikt\ *noun* [alteration of *Benedick*, character in Shakespeare's *Much Ado about Nothing*] (1821)
: a newly married man who has long been a bachelor
Ben·e·dic·tine \,be-nə-'dik-tən, -,tēn\ *noun* (15th century)
: a monk or a nun of one of the congregations following the rule of Saint Benedict and devoted especially to scholarship and liturgical worship
— **Benedictine** *adjective*
bene·dic·tion \,be-nə-'dik-shən\ *noun* [Middle English *benediccioun*, from Late Latin *benediction-, benedictio*, from *benedicere* to bless, from Latin, to speak well of, from *bene* well (akin to Latin *bonus* good) + *dicere* to say — more at BOUNTY, DICTION] (15th century)
1 : the invocation of a blessing; *especially* **:** the short blessing with which public worship is concluded
2 : something that promotes goodness or wellbeing
3 *often capitalized* **:** a Roman Catholic or Anglo-Catholic devotion including the exposition of the eucharistic Host in the monstrance and the blessing of the people with it
4 : an expression of good wishes
bene·dic·to·ry \-'dik-t(ə-)rē\ *adjective* (1710)

: of or expressing benediction

Ben·e·dict's solution \'be-nə-,dik(t)s-\ *noun* [Stanley Rossiter *Benedict* (died 1936) American chemist] (1921)
: a blue solution containing a carbonate, citrate, and sulfate which yields a red, yellow, or orange precipitate upon warming with a sugar (as glucose) that is a reducing agent

Ben·e·dic·tus \,be-nə-'dik-təs\ *noun* [Late Latin, blessed, from past participle of *benedicere*; from its first word] (1552)
1 : a canticle from Luke 1:68 beginning "Blessed be the Lord God of Israel"
2 : a canticle from Matthew 21:9 beginning "Blessed is he that cometh in the name of the Lord"

ben·e·fac·tion \,be-nə-'fak-shən\ *noun* [Late Latin *benefaction-, benefactio,* from Latin *bene facere* to do good to, from *bene* + *facere* to do — more at DO] (circa 1662)
1 : the act of benefiting
2 : a benefit conferred; *especially* **:** a charitable donation

ben·e·fac·tor \'be-nə-,fak-tər\ *noun* (15th century)
: one that confers a benefit; *especially* **:** one that makes a gift or bequest

ben·e·fac·tress \'be-nə-,fak-tris\ *noun* (1711)
: a woman who is a benefactor

be·nef·ic \bə-'ne-fik\ *adjective* [Latin *beneficus,* from *bene* + *facere*] (1641)
: BENEFICENT

ben·e·fice \'be-nə-fəs\ *noun* [Middle English, from Middle French, from Medieval Latin *beneficium,* from Latin, favor, promotion, from *beneficus*] (14th century)
1 : an ecclesiastical office to which the revenue from an endowment is attached
2 : a feudal estate in lands **:** FIEF
— benefice *transitive verb*

be·nef·i·cence \bə-'ne-fə-sən(t)s\ *noun* [Latin *beneficentia,* from *beneficus*] (15th century)
1 : the quality or state of being beneficent
2 : BENEFACTION

be·nef·i·cent \-sənt\ *adjective* [back-formation from *beneficence*] (1616)
1 : doing or producing good; *especially* **:** performing acts of kindness and charity
2 : BENEFICIAL
— be·nef·i·cent·ly *adverb*

ben·e·fi·cial \,be-nə-'fi-shəl\ *adjective* [Latin *beneficium* favor, benefit] (15th century)
1 : conferring benefits **:** conducive to personal or social well-being
2 : receiving or entitling one to receive advantage, use, or benefit ⟨a *beneficial* legacy⟩
— ben·e·fi·cial·ly \-'fi-sh(ə-)lē\ *adverb*
— ben·e·fi·cial·ness *noun*

ben·e·fi·cia·ry \,be-nə-'fi-shē-,er-ē, -'fi-sh(ə-)rē\ *noun, plural* **-ries** (1662)
1 : one that benefits from something
2 a : the person designated to receive the income of a trust estate **b :** the person named (as in an insurance policy) to receive proceeds or benefits
— beneficiary *adjective*

ben·e·fi·ci·a·tion \,be-nə-,fi-shē-'ā-shən\ *noun* (circa 1881)
: the treatment of raw material (as iron ore) to improve physical or chemical properties especially in preparation for smelting
— ben·e·fi·ci·ate \-'fi-shē-,āt\ *transitive verb*

¹ben·e·fit \'be-nə-,fit\ *noun* [Middle English, from Anglo-French *benfet,* from Latin *bene factum,* from neuter of *bene factus,* past participle of *bene facere*] (14th century)
1 *archaic* **:** an act of kindness **:** BENEFACTION
2 a : something that promotes well-being **:** ADVANTAGE **b :** useful aid **:** HELP
3 a : financial help in time of sickness, old age, or unemployment **b :** a payment or service provided for under an annuity, pension plan, or insurance policy
4 : an entertainment or social event to raise funds for a person or cause

²benefit *verb* **-fit·ed** \-,fi-təd\ *also* **-fit·ted; -fit·ing** *also* **-fit·ting** (15th century)
transitive verb
: to be useful or profitable to
intransitive verb
: to receive benefit
— ben·e·fit·er \-,fi-tər\ *noun*

benefit of clergy (15th century)
1 : clerical exemption from trial in a civil court
2 : the ministration or sanction of the church

be·nev·o·lence \bə-'nev-lən(t)s, -'ne-və-\ *noun* (14th century)
1 : disposition to do good
2 a : an act of kindness **b :** a generous gift
3 : a compulsory levy by certain English kings with no other authority than the claim of prerogative

be·nev·o·lent \-lənt\ *adjective* [Middle English, from Latin *benevolent-, benevolens,* from *bene* + *volent-, volens,* present participle of *velle* to wish — more at WILL] (15th century)
1 a : marked by or disposed to doing good ⟨a *benevolent* donor⟩ **b :** organized for the purpose of doing good ⟨a *benevolent* society⟩
2 : marked by or suggestive of goodwill ⟨*benevolent* smiles⟩
— be·nev·o·lent·ly *adverb*
— be·nev·o·lent·ness *noun*

Ben·gali \ben-'gȯ-lē, beŋ-\ *noun* [Hindi *Baṅgālī,* from *Baṅgāl* Bengal] (1848)
1 : a native or resident of Bengal
2 : the modern Indo-Aryan language of Bengal
— Bengali *adjective*

ben·ga·line \'beŋ-gə-,lēn\ *noun* [French, from *Bengal*] (1884)
: a fabric with a crosswise rib made from textile fibers (as rayon, nylon, cotton, or wool) often in combination

Ben·gal light \'ben-,gȯl-, ,beŋ-, -,gäl-, -gəl-\ *noun* (1818)
: a usually blue light or flare used formerly especially for signaling and illumination

Bengal tiger *noun* (circa 1864)
: a tiger (*Panthera tigris tigris*) occurring especially in India

be·night·ed \bi-'nī-təd\ *adjective* (15th century)
1 : overtaken by darkness or night
2 : existing in a state of intellectual, moral, or social darkness **:** UNENLIGHTENED
— be·night·ed·ly *adverb*
— be·night·ed·ness *noun*

be·nign \bi-'nīn\ *adjective* [Middle English *benigne,* from Middle French, from Latin *benignus,* from *bene* + *gignere* to beget — more at KIN] (14th century)
1 : of a gentle disposition **:** GRACIOUS ⟨a *benign* teacher⟩
2 a : showing kindness and gentleness ⟨*benign* faces⟩ **b :** FAVORABLE, WHOLESOME ⟨a *benign* climate⟩
3 a : of a mild type or character that does not threaten health or life ⟨a *benign* tumor⟩ **b :** having no significant effect **:** HARMLESS ⟨environmentally *benign*⟩
— be·nig·ni·ty \-'nig-nə-tē\ *noun*
— be·nign·ly \-'nīn-lē\ *adverb*

be·nig·nan·cy \bi-'nig-nən(t)-sē\ *noun* (1876)
: benignant quality

be·nig·nant \-nənt\ *adjective* [*benign* + *-ant* (as in *malignant*)] (circa 1782)
1 : serenely mild and kindly **:** BENIGN
2 : FAVORABLE, BENEFICIAL ⟨a *benignant* power⟩
— be·nig·nant·ly *adverb*

benign neglect *noun* (1970)
: an attitude or policy of ignoring an often undesirable situation that one is perceived to be responsible for dealing with

ben·i·son \'be-nə-sən, -zən\ *noun* [Middle English *beneson,* from Middle French *beneiçon,*

from Late Latin *benediction-, benedictio*] (14th century)
: BLESSING, BENEDICTION

Ben·ja·min \'ben-jə-mən\ *noun* [Hebrew *Binyāmīn*]
: a son of Jacob and the traditional eponymous ancestor of one of the tribes of Israel

ben·ne *also* **bene** \'be-nē\ *noun* [of African origin; akin to Malinke *běne* sesame] (1769)
: SESAME 1

ben·ny \'be-nē\ *noun, plural* **bennies** [*Benzedrine* + *-ie*] (1949)
slang **:** a tablet of amphetamine taken as a stimulant

ben·o·myl \'be-nə-,mil\ *noun* [*benz- + -o- + methyl*] (1969)
: a derivative $C_{14}H_{18}N_4O_3$ of carbamate and benzimidazole used especially as a systemic agricultural fungicide

¹bent \'bent\ *noun* [Middle English, grassy place, bent grass, from Old English *beonot-*; akin to Old High German *binuz* rush] (14th century)
1 : unenclosed grassland
2 a (1) **:** a reedy grass (2) **:** a stalk of stiff coarse grass **b :** BENT GRASS

²bent *adjective* [Middle English, from past participle of *benden* to bend] (14th century)
1 : changed by bending out of an originally straight or even condition ⟨*bent* twigs⟩
2 : strongly inclined **:** DETERMINED ⟨was *bent* on going⟩
3 *slang* **a :** different from the normal or usual **b** *chiefly British* **:** DISHONEST, CORRUPT

³bent *noun* [irregular from ¹*bend*] (1586)
1 a : a strong inclination or interest **:** BIAS **b :** a special inclination or capacity **:** TALENT
2 : capacity of endurance
3 : a transverse framework (as in a bridge) to carry lateral as well as vertical loads
synonym see GIFT

bent grass *noun* (1778)
: any of a genus (*Agrostis*) of grasses including important chiefly perennial and rhizomatous pasture and lawn grasses with fine velvety or wiry herbage

Ben·tham·ism \'ben(t)-thə-,mi-zəm\ *noun* (1829)
: the utilitarian philosophy of Jeremy Bentham and his followers
— Ben·tham·ite \-,mīt\ *noun or adjective*

ben·thic \'ben(t)-thik\ *adjective* [*benthos*] (1902)
1 : of, relating to, or occurring at the bottom of a body of water
2 : of, relating to, or occurring in the depths of the ocean

ben·thon·ic \ben-'thä-nik\ *adjective* [irregular from *benthos*] (1897)
: BENTHIC

ben·thos \'ben-,thäs\ *noun* [New Latin, from Greek, depth, deep sea; akin to Greek *bathys* deep] (1891)
: organisms that live on or in the bottom of a body of water

ben·ton·ite \'ben-tⁿn-,īt\ *noun* [Fort *Benton,* Mont.] (1898)
: an absorptive and colloidal clay used especially as a sealing agent or carrier (as of drugs)
— ben·ton·it·ic \,ben-tⁿn-'i-tik\ *adjective*

ben tro·va·to \,ben-trō-'vä-(,)tō\ *adjective* [Italian, literally, well found] (1876)
: characteristic or appropriate even if not true ⟨the story is *ben trovato*⟩

bent·wood \'bent-,wu̇d\ *adjective* (1862)
: made of wood that is bent rather than cut into shape ⟨*bentwood* furniture⟩
— bentwood *noun*

\ə\ abut \ᵊ\ kitten \ər\ further \a\ ash \ā\ ace
\ä\ mop, mar \au̇\ out \ch\ chin \e\ bet \ē\ easy
\g\ go \i\ hit \ī\ ice \j\ job \ŋ\ sing \ō\ go
\ȯ\ law \ȯi\ boy \th\ thin \t͟h\ the \ü\ loot \u̇\ foot
\y\ yet \zh\ vision *see also* Guide to Pronunciation

be·numb \bi-'nəm\ *transitive verb* [Middle English *benomen,* from *benomen,* past participle of *benimen* to deprive, from Old English *beniman,* from *be-* + *niman* to take — more at NIMBLE] (14th century)
1 : to make inactive **:** DEADEN
2 : to make numb especially by cold
benz- *or* **benzo-** *combining form* [International Scientific Vocabulary, from *benzoin*]
: related to benzene or benzoic acid ⟨*benzophenone*⟩ ⟨*benzyl*⟩
benz·al·de·hyde \ben-'zal-də-ˌhīd\ *noun* [International Scientific Vocabulary] (1866)
: a colorless nontoxic aromatic liquid C_6H_5CHO found in essential oils (as in peach kernels) and used in flavoring and perfumery, in pharmaceuticals, and in synthesis of dyes
benz·an·thra·cene \ben-'zan(t)-thrə-ˌsēn\ *noun* [International Scientific Vocabulary] (1938)
: a crystalline feebly carcinogenic cyclic hydrocarbon $C_{18}H_{12}$ that is found in small amounts in coal tar
Ben·ze·drine \'ben-zə-ˌdrēn\ *trademark*
— used for amphetamine
ben·zene \'ben-ˌzēn, ben-'\ *noun* [International Scientific Vocabulary *benz-* + *-ene*] (circa 1872)
: a colorless volatile flammable toxic liquid aromatic hydrocarbon C_6H_6 used in organic synthesis, as a solvent, and as a motor fuel — called also *benzol*
— **ben·ze·noid** \'ben-zə-ˌnȯid\ *adjective*
benzene hexa·chlo·ride \-ˌhek-sə-'klȯr-ˌīd, -'klȯr-\ *noun* (1884)
: BHC
benzene ring *noun* (1877)
: a structural arrangement of atoms held to exist in benzene and other aromatic compounds and marked by six carbon atoms linked in a planar symmetrical hexagon with each carbon attached to hydrogen in benzene itself or to other atoms or groups in substituted benzenes — compare META- 4a, ORTH- 4b, PARA- 2b
ben·zi·dine \'ben-zə-ˌdēn\ *noun* [International Scientific Vocabulary *benz-* + *-idine*] (1878)
: a crystalline base $C_{12}H_{12}N_2$ prepared from nitrobenzene and used especially in making dyes
benz·imid·azole \ˌben-zi-mə-'da-ˌzōl, ˌbenzə-'mi-də-ˌzōl\ *noun* [International Scientific Vocabulary] (circa 1929)
: a crystalline base $C_7H_6N_2$ used especially to inhibit the growth of various viruses, parasitic worms, or fungi; *also* **:** one of its derivatives
ben·zine \'ben-ˌzēn, ben-'\ *noun* [German *Benzin,* from *benz-*] (1835)
: any of various volatile flammable petroleum distillates used especially as solvents or as motor fuels
ben·zo·a·py·rene \ˌben-zō-ˌā-'pīr-ˌēn, zō-ˌalfə-\ *noun* [*benz-* + *-a-,* denoting attachment of the benzene substituent at carbon atoms 1 and 2 of the pyrene molecule + *pyrene*] (1950)
: a yellow crystalline carcinogenic hydrocarbon $C_{20}H_{12}$ found in coal tar — *a* often italicized and placed in parentheses or brackets or between hyphens
ben·zo·ate \'ben-zə-ˌwāt\ *noun* (1806)
: a salt or ester of benzoic acid
ben·zo·caine \'ben-zə-ˌkān\ *noun* [International Scientific Vocabulary *benz-* + *-caine*] (1922)
: a white crystalline ester $C_9H_{11}NO_2$ used as a local anesthetic
ben·zo·di·az·e·pine \ˌben-zō-dī-'a-zə-ˌpēn\ *noun* [*benz-* + *di-* + *az-* + *-epine* (from *hepta-* + 2*-ine*)] (1934)
: any of a group of aromatic lipophilic amines (as diazepam and chlordiazepoxide) used especially as tranquilizers
ben·zo·fu·ran \ˌben-zō-'fyu̇r-ˌan, -fyu̇-'ran\ *noun* (1946)

: a compound C_8H_6O found in coal tar and polymerized with indene to form thermoplastic resins used especially in adhesives and printing inks
ben·zo·ic acid \ben-'zō-ik-\ *noun* [International Scientific Vocabulary, from *benzoin*] (1791)
: a white crystalline acid $C_7H_6O_2$ found naturally (as in benzoin or in cranberries) or made synthetically and used especially as a preservative of foods, in medicine, and in organic synthesis
ben·zo·in \'ben-zə-wən, -,wēn; -,zȯin\ *noun* [Middle French *benjoin,* from Catalan *benjuí,* from Arabic *lubān jāwi,* literally, frankincense of Java] (1562)
1 : a hard fragrant yellowish balsamic resin from trees (genus *Styrax*) of southeastern Asia used especially in medication, as a fixative in perfumes, and as incense
2 : a white crystalline hydroxy ketone $C_{14}H_{12}O_2$ made from benzaldehyde
ben·zol \'ben-ˌzȯl, -ˌzōl\ *noun* [German, from *benz-* + *-ol*] (1838)
: BENZENE; *also* **:** a mixture of benzene and other aromatic hydrocarbons
ben·zo·phe·none \ˌben-zō-fi-'nōn, -'fē-ˌnōn\ *noun* [International Scientific Vocabulary *benz-* + *phen-* + *-one*] (1885)
: a colorless crystalline ketone $C_{13}H_{10}O$ used chiefly in perfumery and sunscreens; *also* **:** a derivative of benzophenone
ben·zo·yl \'ben-zə-ˌwil, -ˌzȯil\ *noun* [German, from *Benzoësäure* benzoic acid + Greek *hylē* matter, literally, wood] (circa 1855)
: the radical C_6H_5CO of benzoic acid
benzoyl peroxide *noun* (1924)
: a white crystalline flammable compound $C_{14}H_{10}O_4$ used in bleaching and in medicine especially in the treatment of acne
ben·zyl \'ben-ˌzēl, -zəl\ *noun* [International Scientific Vocabulary *benz-* + *-yl*] (1869)
: a univalent radical $C_6H_5CH_2$ derived from toluene
— **ben·zyl·ic** \ben-'zi-lik\ *adjective*
Be·o·wulf \'bā-ə-ˌwu̇lf\ *noun*
: a legendary Geatish warrior and hero of the Old English poem *Beowulf*
be·paint \bi-'pānt\ *transitive verb* (circa 1555)
archaic **:** TINGE
be·queath \bi-'kwēth, -'kwēth\ *transitive verb* [Middle English *bequethen,* from Old English *becwethan,* from *be-* + *cwethan* to say — more at QUOTH] (before 12th century)
1 : to give or leave by will — used especially of personal property
2 : to hand down **:** TRANSMIT
— **be·queath·al** \-'kwē-thəl, -thəl\ *noun*
be·quest \bi-'kwest\ *noun* [Middle English, irregular from *bequethen*] (14th century)
1 : the act of bequeathing
2 : something bequeathed **:** LEGACY
be·rate \bi-'rāt\ *transitive verb* (1548)
: to scold or condemn vehemently and at length
synonym see SCOLD
Ber·ber \'bər-bər\ *noun* [Arabic *Barbar*] (1732)
1 : a member of any of various peoples living in northern Africa west of Tripoli
2 a : a branch of the Afro-Asiatic language family comprising languages spoken by various peoples of northern Africa and the Sahara (as the Tuaregs and the Kabyles) **b :** any one of the Berber languages
ber·ber·ine \'bər-bə-ˌrēn\ *noun* [German *Berberin,* from New Latin *berberis*] (circa 1847)
: a bitter crystalline yellow alkaloid $C_{20}H_{19}NO_5$ obtained from the roots of various plants (as barberry) and used as a tonic in medicine
ber·ber·is \'bər-bər-əs\ *noun* [New Latin, the genus including barberry, alteration of Medieval Latin *barberis* barberry, from Arabic *barbāris*] (circa 1868)
: BARBERRY

ber·ceuse \ber-'sœz, -'süz\ *noun, plural* **ber·ceuses** \-'sœz; -'süz, -'sü-zəz\ [French] (1876)
1 : LULLABY
2 : a musical composition usually in ⅛ time that resembles a lullaby
be·reave \bi-'rēv\ *transitive verb* **-reaved** *or* **-reft** \-'reft\; **-reav·ing** [Middle English *bereven,* from Old English *berēafian,* from *be-* + *rēafian* to rob — more at REAVE] (before 12th century)
1 : to deprive of something — usually used with *of* ⟨madam, you have *bereft* me of all words —Shakespeare⟩
2 : to take away (a valued or necessary possession) especially by force
¹**be·reaved** \bi-'rēvd\ *adjective* (1828)
: suffering the death of a loved one
²**bereaved** *noun, plural* **bereaved** (1943)
: one who is bereaved
be·reave·ment \bi-'rēv-mənt\ *noun* (circa 1731)
: the state or fact of being bereaved; *especially*
: the loss of a loved one by death
be·reft \-'reft\ *adjective* (1586)
1 a : deprived or robbed of the possession or use of something — usually used with *of* ⟨both players are instantly *bereft* of their poise —A. E. Wier⟩ **b :** lacking something needed, wanted, or expected — used with *of* ⟨the book is . . . completely *bereft* of an index — *Times Literary Supplement*⟩
2 : BEREAVED ⟨a *bereft* mother⟩
be·ret \bə-'rā\ *noun* [French *béret,* from Gascon *berret,* from Old Provençal, cap — more at BIRETTA] (1827)
: a visorless usually woolen cap with a tight headband and a soft full flat top
berg \'bərg\ *noun* (1823)
: ICEBERG
ber·ga·mot \'bər-gə-ˌmät\ *noun* [French *bergamote,* from Italian *bergamotta,* modification of Turkish *bey armudu,* literally, the bey's pear] (1696)
1 : a pear-shaped orange (*Citrus aurantium bergamia*) having a rind which yields an essential oil used in perfumery; *also* **:** this oil
2 : any of several mints (genus *Monarda*) — compare WILD BERGAMOT
be·rib·boned \bi-'ri-bənd\ *adjective* (1863)
: adorned with ribbons
beri·beri \ˌber-ē-'ber-ē\ *noun* [Sinhalese *bæribæri*] (1703)
: a deficiency disease marked by inflammatory or degenerative changes of the nerves, digestive system, and heart and caused by a lack of or inability to assimilate thiamine
Berke·le·ian *or* **Berke·ley·an** \'bär-klē-ən, 'bər-; bär-', ˌbər-'\ *adjective* (1842)
: of, relating to, or suggestive of Bishop Berkeley or his system of philosophical idealism
— **Berkeleian** *noun*
— **Berke·le·ian·ism** \-ə-ˌni-zəm\ *noun*
berke·li·um \'bər-klē-əm\ *noun* [New Latin, from *Berkeley,* Calif.] (1950)
: a radioactive metallic element produced by bombarding americium 241 with helium ions — see ELEMENT table
Berk·shire \'bərk-ˌshir, -shər\ *noun* [*Berkshire,* England] (1831)
: any of a breed of medium-sized black swine with white markings
berm \'bərm\ *noun* [French *berme,* from Dutch *berm* strip of ground along a dike; akin to Middle English *brimme* brim] (1729)
: a narrow shelf, path, or ledge typically at the top or bottom of a slope; *also* **:** a mound or wall of earth ⟨a landscaped *berm*⟩
Ber·mu·da bag \(ˌ)bər-ˈmyü-də-, *especially Southern* -'mü-də-\ *noun* [*Bermuda* islands, North Atlantic] (1979)
: a round or oval-shaped handbag with a wooden handle and removable cloth covers
Bermuda grass *noun* (1808)

: a creeping stoloniferous southern European grass (*Cynodon dactylon*) often used as a lawn and pasture grass

Bermuda rig *noun* (1853)
: a fore-and-aft rig marked by a triangular sail and a mast with an extreme rake

Ber·mu·das \(ˌ)bər-'myü-dəz, *especially Southern* -'mü-dəz\ *noun plural* (1961)
: BERMUDA SHORTS

Bermuda shorts *noun plural* (1951)
: knee-length walking shorts

Ber·nese mountain dog \'bər-ˌnēz-, -ˌnēs-\ *noun* [*Bern*, Switzerland] (1935)
: any of a breed of large powerful long-coated black dogs of Swiss origin that have tan and white markings and were developed as draft animals

Ber·noul·li's principle \bər-'nü-lēz-, ˌber-ˌnü-'lēz-\ *noun* [Daniel *Bernoulli* (died 1782) Swiss physicist] (1940)
: a principle in hydrodynamics: the pressure in a stream of fluid is reduced as the speed of the flow is increased

Ber·noul·li trial \bər-'nü-lē-, ˌber-ˌnü-'lē-\ *noun* [Jacques *Bernoulli* (died 1705) Swiss mathematician] (1951)
: one of the repetitions of a statistical experiment having two mutually exclusive outcomes with constant probability of occurrence

ber·ried \'ber-ēd\ *adjective* (1794)
1 : having or covered with berries ⟨*berried* shrub⟩
2 : bearing eggs ⟨a *berried* lobster⟩

¹ber·ry \'ber-ē\ *noun, plural* **berries** [Middle English *berye*, from Old English *berie;* akin to Old High German *beri* berry] (before 12th century)
1 a : a pulpy and usually edible fruit (as a strawberry, raspberry, or checkerberry) of small size irrespective of its structure **b** : a simple fruit (as a currant, grape, tomato, or banana) with a pulpy or fleshy pericarp **c** : the dry seed of some plants (as wheat)
2 : an egg of a fish or lobster

²berry *intransitive verb* **ber·ried; ber·ry·ing** (circa 1780)
1 : to bear or produce berries ⟨a *berrying* shrub⟩
2 : to gather or seek berries

ber·ry·like \'ber-ē-ˌlīk\ *adjective* (1864)
1 : resembling a berry especially in size or structure
2 : being small and rounded : COCCOID

ber·seem \(ˌ)bər-'sēm\ *noun* [Arabic *barsīm,* from Coptic *bersīm*] (circa 1902)
: a succulent clover (*Trifolium alexandrinum*) cultivated as a forage plant and green-manure crop especially in the alkaline soils of the Nile valley and in the southwestern U.S. — called also *Egyptian clover*

¹ber·serk \bə(r)-'sərk, -ˌbər-, -'zərk; 'bər-ˌ\ *or* **ber·serk·er** \-'sər-kər, -'zər-; 'bər-ˌ\ *noun* [Old Norse *berserkr,* from *bjǫrn* bear + *serkr* shirt] (1818)
1 : an ancient Scandinavian warrior frenzied in battle and held to be invulnerable
2 : one whose actions are recklessly defiant ◇

²berserk *adjective* (1851)
: FRENZIED, CRAZED — usually used in the phrase *go berserk* ⟨sinister ravings of an imagination gone *berserk* —John Gruen⟩
— **berserk** *adverb*
— **ber·serk·ly** *adverb*

¹berth \'bərth\ *noun* [probably from *²bear* + *-th*] (15th century)
1 a : sufficient distance for maneuvering a ship **b** : safe distance — used especially with *wide*
2 a : the place where a ship lies when at anchor or at a wharf **b** : a space for an automotive vehicle at rest ⟨a truck-loading *berth*⟩
3 : a place to sit or sleep especially on a ship or vehicle : ACCOMMODATION
4 a : a billet on a ship **b** : JOB, POSITION, PLACE ⟨a starting *berth* on the team⟩

²berth (1667)

transitive verb
1 : to bring into a berth
2 : to allot a berth to
intransitive verb
: to come into a berth

ber·tha \'bər-thə\ *noun* [French *berthe,* from *Berthe* (Bertha) (died 783) queen of the Franks] (1842)
: a wide round collar covering the shoulders

Ber·til·lon system \'bər-tᵊl-ˌän-, 'ber-tē-ˌyōⁿ-\ *noun* [Alphonse *Bertillon* (died 1914) French criminologist] (1896)
: a system of identification of persons by a description based on anthropometric measurements, photographs, and notation of data (as markings, color, and thumb line impressions)

ber·yl \'ber-əl\ *noun* [Middle English, from Middle French *beril,* from Latin *beryllus,* from Greek *bēryllos,* back-formation from *bēryllion* beryl, of Indo-Aryan origin; akin to Prakrit *verulia, veluriya* beryl] (13th century)
: a mineral consisting of a silicate of beryllium and aluminum of great hardness and occurring in green, bluish green, yellow, pink, or white hexagonal prisms

be·ryl·li·um \bə-'ri-lē-əm\ *noun* [New Latin, from Greek *bēryllion*] (circa 1847)
: a steel-gray light strong brittle toxic bivalent metallic element used chiefly as a hardening agent in alloys — see ELEMENT table

be·seech \bi-'sēch\ *verb* **-seeched** *or* **-sought** \-'sȯt\; **-seech·ing** [Middle English *besechen,* from *be-* + *sechen* to seek] (12th century)
transitive verb
1 : to beg for urgently or anxiously
2 : to request earnestly : IMPLORE
intransitive verb
: to make supplication
synonym see BEG
— **be·seech·ing·ly** \-'sē-chiŋ-lē\ *adverb*

be·seem \bi-'sēm\ (13th century)
intransitive verb
archaic : to be fitting or becoming
transitive verb
archaic : to be suitable to : BEFIT

be·set \bi-'set, bē-\ *transitive verb* **-set; -set·ting** [Middle English *besetten,* from Old English *besettan,* from *be-* + *settan* to set] (before 12th century)
1 : to set or stud with or as if with ornaments
2 : TROUBLE, HARASS ⟨inflation *besets* the economy⟩
3 a : to set upon : ASSAIL ⟨the settlers were *beset* by savages⟩ **b** : to hem in : SURROUND
— **be·set·ment** \-mənt\ *noun*

be·set·ting *adjective* (1795)
: constantly present or attacking : OBSESSIVE

be·shrew \bi-'shrü, bē-, *especially Southern* -'srü\ *transitive verb* (14th century)
archaic : CURSE

¹be·side \bi-'sīd\ *preposition* [Middle English, adverb & preposition, from Old English *be sīdan* at or to the side, from *be* at (from *bī*) + *sīdan,* dative & accusative of *sīde* side — more at BY] (13th century)
1 a : by the side of ⟨walk *beside* me⟩ **b** : in comparison with **c** : on a par with
2 : BESIDES
3 : not relevant to ⟨*beside* the point⟩
— **beside oneself** : in a state of extreme excitement

²beside *adverb* (14th century)
1 *archaic* : NEARBY
2 *archaic* : BESIDES

¹be·sides \bi-'sīdz\ *preposition* (14th century)
1 : OTHER THAN, EXCEPT
2 : together with

²besides *adverb* (1564)
1 : as well : ALSO
2 : MOREOVER, FURTHERMORE

³besides *adjective* (1954)
: ELSE

be·siege \bi-'sēj\ *transitive verb* **-sieged; -sieg·ing** (14th century)
1 : to surround with armed forces

2 a : to press with requests : IMPORTUNE **b** : to cause worry or distress to : BESET ⟨doubts *besieged* him⟩
— **be·sieg·er** *noun*

be·smear \bi-'smir\ *transitive verb* (before 12th century)
: SMEAR

be·smirch \bi-'smərch\ *transitive verb* (1599)
: SULLY, SOIL

be·som \'bē-zəm\ *noun* [Middle English *beseme,* from Old English *besma;* akin to Old High German *besmo* broom] (before 12th century)
: BROOM 2; *especially* : one made of twigs

besom pocket *noun* [origin unknown] (1966)
: a pocket with a welted slit opening

be·sot \bi-'sät\ *transitive verb* **be·sot·ted; be·sot·ting** [*be-* + *sot* (to stultify)] (1581)
1 : INFATUATE 2
2 : to make dull or stupid; *especially* : to muddle with drunkenness

be·spat·ter \bi-'spa-tər\ *transitive verb* (1640)
: SPATTER

be·speak \bi-'spēk\ *transitive verb* **-spoke** \-'spōk\; **-spo·ken** \-'spō-kən\; **-speak·ing** (1536)
1 : to hire, engage, or claim beforehand
2 : to speak to especially with formality : ADDRESS
3 : REQUEST ⟨*bespeak* a favor⟩
4 a : INDICATE, SIGNIFY ⟨her performance *bespeaks* considerable practice⟩ **b** : to show beforehand : FORETELL

be·spec·ta·cled \bi-'spek-(ˌ)ti-kəld\ *adjective* (1742)
: wearing spectacles

be·spoke \bi-'spōk\ *or* **be·spo·ken** \-'spō-kən\ *adjective* [past participle of *bespeak*] (1607)
1 a : CUSTOM-MADE **b** : dealing in or producing custom-made articles
2 *dialect* : ENGAGED

be·sprent \bi-'sprent\ *adjective* [Middle English *bespreynt,* from past participle of *besprengen* to besprinkle, from Old English *besprengan,* from *be-* + *sprengan* to scatter; akin to Old English *springan* to spring] (14th century)
archaic : sprinkled over

◇ **WORD HISTORY**
berserk During the 19th century, the word *berserk* made a rapid linguistic trip from literary use as a noun—arising out of antiquarian interest in medieval Scandinavia—to colloquial use as an adjective. In Old Norse sagas, a *berserkr* was a man experiencing a sort of ecstatic frenzy called *berserksgangr.* The 13th century Icelandic author Snorri Sturluson describes men seized by *berserksgangr* as going into battle without coats of mail and gnawing the rims of their shields. They supposedly had the strength of bears or oxen, and were invulnerable to iron or fire. The word *berserkr* is a compound of *ber-,* presumed to mean "bear," and *sarkr* "shirt." Originally the "bear-shirt" probably referred to a man dressed in a mask or garment representing a bear who entered a trancelike state in which he magically assumed powers associated with the animal. By the time the legend of the *berserkr* had made its way into Norse saga, it was this ecstatic frenzy—not bear paraphernalia—that characterized him and that is still dimly reflected in English *berserk.*

\ə\ abut \ᵊ\ kitten \ər\ further \a\ ash \ā\ ace
\ä\ mop, mar \aù\ out \ch\ chin \e\ bet \ē\ easy
\g\ go \i\ hit \ī\ ice \j\ job \ŋ\ sing \ō\ go
\ȯ\ law \ȯi\ boy \th\ thin \t͟h\ the \ü\ loot \ù\ foot
\y\ yet \zh\ vision *see also* Guide to Pronunciation

be·sprin·kle \bi-'spriŋ-kəl\ *transitive verb* [Middle English *besprengeln,* frequentative of *besprengen*] (15th century)
: SPRINKLE

Bes·sel function \'be-səl-\ *noun* [Friedrich W. *Bessel* (died 1846) Prussian astronomer] (1872)
: one of a class of transcendental functions expressible as infinite series and occurring in the solution of the differential equation

$$x^2 \frac{d^2y}{dx^2} + x \frac{dy}{dx} = (n^2 - x^2)y$$

Bes·se·mer converter \'be-sə-mər-\ *noun* (circa 1887)
: the furnace used in the Bessemer process

Bessemer process *noun* [Sir Henry *Bessemer*] (1875)
: a process of making steel from pig iron by burning out carbon and other impurities by means of a blast of air forced through the molten metal

¹best \'best\ *adjective, superlative of* GOOD [Middle English, from Old English *betst;* akin to Old English *bōt* remedy — more at BETTER] (before 12th century)
1 : excelling all others ⟨the *best* student⟩
2 : most productive of good or of advantage, utility, or satisfaction ⟨what is the *best* thing to do⟩
3 : MOST, LARGEST ⟨it rained for the *best* part of their vacation⟩

²best *adverb, superlative of* WELL (before 12th century)
1 : in the best way : to greatest advantage ⟨some things are *best* left unsaid⟩
2 : MOST ⟨those *best* able will provide needed support⟩

³best *noun, plural* **best** (before 12th century)
1 : the best state or part
2 : one that is best ⟨the *best* falls short⟩
3 : the greatest degree of good or excellence
4 : one's maximum effort ⟨do your *best*⟩
5 : best clothes ⟨Sunday *best*⟩
— **at best** : under the most favorable circumstances

⁴best *transitive verb* (1863)
: to get the better of : OUTDO

⁵best *verbal auxiliary* (1941)
: had best ⟨you *best* listen⟩

best–ball \'bes(t)-'bȯl\ *adjective* (1909)
: relating to or being a golf match in which one player competes against the best individual score of two or more players for each hole — compare FOUR-BALL

best boy *noun* (1937)
: the chief assistant to the gaffer in motion-picture or television production

best–case \'bes(t)-'kās\ *adjective* (1977)
: being, relating to, or based on a projection of future events that assumes only the best possible circumstances ⟨a *best-case* scenario⟩

¹be·stead *or* **be·sted** \bi-'sted\ *adjective* [Middle English *bested,* from *be-* + *sted,* past participle of *steden* to place, from *stede* place — more at STEAD] (14th century)
archaic : SITUATED

²bestead *transitive verb* **be·stead·ed; be·stead; be·stead·ing** [*be-* + *stead*] (1581)
1 *archaic* : HELP
2 *archaic* : to be useful to : AVAIL

bes·tial \'bes-chəl, 'besh-, 'bēs-, 'bēsh-\ *adjective* [Middle English, from Middle French, from Latin *bestialis,* from *bestia* beast] (14th century)
1 a : of or relating to beasts **b** : resembling a beast
2 a : lacking intelligence or reason **b** : marked by base or inhuman instincts or desires : BRUTAL
synonym *see* BRUTAL
— **bes·tial·ize** \-chə-,līz\ *transitive verb*
— **bes·tial·ly** \-chə-lē\ *adverb*

bes·ti·al·i·ty \,bes-chē-'a-lə-tē, ,besh-, ,bēs-, ,bēsh-\ *noun, plural* **-ties** (14th century)
1 : the condition or status of a lower animal
2 : display or gratification of bestial traits or impulses
3 : sexual relations between a human being and a lower animal

bes·ti·ary \'bes-chē-,er-ē, 'besh-, 'bēs-, 'bēsh-\ *noun, plural* **-ar·ies** [Medieval Latin *bestiarium,* from Latin, neuter of *bestiarius* of beasts, from *bestia*] (1840)
1 : a medieval allegorical or moralizing work on the appearance and habits of real or imaginary animals
2 : a collection of descriptions of real or imaginary animals

be·stir \bi-'stər\ *transitive verb* (14th century)
: to rouse to action : get going

best man *noun* (circa 1782)
: the principal groomsman at a wedding

be·stow \bi-'stō\ *transitive verb* [Middle English, from *be-* + *stowe* place — more at STOW] (14th century)
1 : to put to use : APPLY ⟨*bestowed* his spare time on study⟩
2 : to put in a particular or appropriate place : STOW
3 : to provide with quarters : PUT UP
4 : to convey as a gift — usually used with *on* or *upon*
synonym *see* GIVE
— **be·stow·al** \-'stō-əl\ *noun*

be·strew \bi-'strü\ *transitive verb* **-strewed; -strewed** *or* **-strewn** \-'strün\; **-strew·ing** (before 12th century)
1 : STREW
2 : to lie scattered over

be·stride \bi-'strīd\ *transitive verb* **-strode** \-'strōd\; **-strid·den** \-'stri-d⁰n\; **-strid·ing** \-'strī-diŋ\ (before 12th century)
1 : to ride, sit, or stand astride : STRADDLE
2 : to tower over : DOMINATE ⟨the bloated bureaucracy that *bestrides* us all —Edward Ney⟩
3 *archaic* : to stride across

best·sell·er \'bes(t)-'se-lər\ *noun* (1889)
: an article (as a book) whose sales are among the highest of its class
— **best·sell·er·dom** \-dəm\ *noun*
— **best·sell·ing** \-'se-liŋ\ *adjective*

¹bet \'bet\ *noun* [origin unknown] (1592)
1 a : something that is laid, staked, or pledged typically between two parties on the outcome of a contest or a contingent issue : WAGER **b** : the act of giving such a pledge
2 : something to wager on
3 : a choice made by consideration of probabilities ⟨your best *bet* is the back road⟩

²bet *verb* **bet** *also* **bet·ted; bet·ting** (1597) *transitive verb*
1 a : to stake on the outcome of an issue or the performance of a contestant **b** : to be able to be sure that — usually used in the expression *you bet* ⟨you *bet* I'll be there⟩
2 a : to maintain with or as if with a bet **b** : to make a bet with **c** : to make a bet on *intransitive verb*
: to lay a bet

¹be·ta \'bā-tə, *chiefly British* 'bē-\ *noun* [Middle English *betha,* from Latin *beta,* from Greek *bēta,* of Semitic origin; akin to Hebrew *bēth* beth] (14th century)
1 : the 2d letter of the Greek alphabet — see ALPHABET table
2 : BETA PARTICLE
3 : a measure of a stock's or a portfolio's volatility that is expressed numerically as deviation from the market's volatility taken as unity

²beta *adjective* (1899)
: second in position in the structure of an organic molecule from a particular group or atom ⟨*beta* substitution⟩ — often used in combination; symbol β

be·ta–ad·ren·er·gic \-,a-drə-'nər-jik\ *adjective* (1965)
: of, relating to, or being a beta-receptor ⟨*beta-adrenergic* blocking action⟩

be·ta–block·er \-,blä-kər\ *noun* (1968)
: any of a class of drugs (as propranolol) that slow heart action and increase coronary blood flow by blocking the activity of beta-receptors
— **be·ta–block·ing** \-kiŋ\ *adjective*

be·ta–car·o·tene \-'kar-ə-,tēn\ *noun* (1938)
: an isomer of carotene found in dark green and dark yellow vegetables and fruits

beta cell *noun* (1926)
: any of the insulin-secreting pancreatic cells in the islets of Langerhans

beta decay *noun* (1934)
: a radioactive nuclear transformation governed by the weak force in which a nucleon (as a neutron) changes into the other type of nucleon (as a proton) with the emission of an electron or positron and a neutrino and which results in a change in the atomic number of the nucleus of $+1$ or -1

be·ta–en·dor·phin \-en-'dȯr-fən\ *noun* (1977)
: an endorphin of the pituitary gland having a much greater analgesic potency than morphine

beta globulin *noun* [International Scientific Vocabulary] (1945)
: any of several globulins of plasma or serum that have at alkaline pH electrophoretic mobilities intermediate between those of the alpha globulins and gamma globulins

be·ta·ine \'bē-tə-,ēn\ *noun* [International Scientific Vocabulary, from Latin *beta* beet] (1879)
: a sweet crystalline quaternary ammonium salt $C_5H_{11}NO_2$ occurring especially in beet juice; *also* : its hydrate $C_5H_{13}NO_3$ or its hydrochloride $C_5H_{12}NO_2Cl$

be·take \bi-'tāk\ *transitive verb* **-took** \-'tȯk\; **-tak·en** \-'tā-kən\; **-tak·ing** (14th century)
1 *archaic* : COMMIT
2 : to cause (oneself) to go

be·ta–lac·ta·mase \-'lak-tə-,mās, -,māz\ *noun* [*lactam,* a cyclic amide (from International Scientific Vocabulary *lact-* + *am*ide) + *-ase*] (1965)
: PENICILLINASE

be·ta–ox·i·da·tion \'bā-tə-,äk-sə-'dā-shən\ *noun* (circa 1935)
: stepwise catabolism of fatty acids in which two-carbon fragments are successively removed from the carboxyl end of the chain

beta particle *noun* (1904)
: a high-speed electron; *specifically* : one emitted by a radioactive nucleus in beta decay

beta ray *noun* (1902)
1 : BETA PARTICLE
2 : a stream of beta particles — called also *beta radiation*

be·ta–re·cep·tor \'bā-tə-ri-'sep-tər\ *noun* (1948)
: any of a group of receptors postulated to exist on nerve cell membranes of the sympathetic nervous system to explain the specificity of certain adrenergic agents in affecting only some sympathetic activities (as vasodilation, increase in muscular contraction and beat of the heart, and relaxation of smooth muscle in the bronchi and intestine)

be·ta–thal·as·se·mia \-,tha-lə-'sē-mē-ə\ *noun* (1962)
: thalassemia in which the longer hemoglobin chain is affected and which comprises Cooley's anemia in the homozygous condition and a less severe thalassemia in the heterozygous condition

be·ta·tron \'bā-tə-,trän\ *noun* [International Scientific Vocabulary] (1941)
: an accelerator in which electrons are propelled by the inductive action of a rapidly varying magnetic field

beta wave *noun* (1936)
: an electrical rhythm of the brain with a frequency of 13 to 30 cycles per second that is associated with normal conscious waking experience — called also *beta, beta rhythm*

be·tel \'bē-t⁰l\ *noun* [Portuguese *bétele,* from Tamil *verrilai*] (1553)

: a climbing pepper (*Piper betle*) whose leaves are chewed together with betel nut and mineral lime as a stimulant masticatory especially by southeastern Asians

Be·tel·geuse \'bē-t°l-,jüs, 'be-, -,jüz\ *noun* [French *Bételgeuse,* from Arabic *bayt al-jawzā'* Gemini, literally, the house of the twins (confused with Orion & Betelgeuse)]
: a variable red giant star of the first magnitude near one shoulder of Orion

betel nut *noun* [from its being chewed with betel leaves] (1681)
: the astringent seed of the betel palm

betel palm *noun* (1875)
: an Asian pinnate-leaved palm (*Areca catechu*) that has an orange-colored drupe with an outer fibrous husk

bête noire \,bet-'nwär, ,bät-\ *noun, plural* **bêtes noires** \,bet-'nwär(z), ,bät-\ [French, literally, black beast] (1844)
: a person or thing strongly detested or avoided : BUGBEAR

beth \'bäth, 'bāt, 'bās\ *noun* [Hebrew *bēth,* from *bayith* house] (circa 1823)
: the 2d letter of the Hebrew alphabet — see ALPHABET table

beth·el \'be-thəl\ *noun* [Hebrew *bēth'ēl* house of God] (circa 1617)
1 : a hallowed spot
2 a : a chapel for Nonconformists **b** : a place of worship for seamen

be·think \bi-'think\ *transitive verb* **-thought** \-'thòt\; **-think·ing** (before 12th century)
1 a : REMEMBER, RECALL **b** : to cause (oneself) to be reminded
2 : to cause (oneself) to consider

be·tide \bi-'tīd\ (12th century)
intransitive verb
: to happen especially as if by fate
transitive verb
: to happen to : BEFALL — used chiefly in the phrase *woe betide* 〈woe *betide* our enemies〉

be·times \bi-'tīmz\ *adverb* (13th century)
1 : in good time : EARLY
2 *archaic* : in a short time : SPEEDILY
3 : at times : OCCASIONALLY

bê·tise \bā-'tēz\ *noun, plural* **bê·tises** \-'tēz\ [French] (1827)
1 : an act of foolishness or stupidity
2 : lack of good sense : STUPIDITY

be·to·ken \bi-'tō-kən\ *transitive verb* **-to·kened; -to·ken·ing** \-'tōk-niŋ, -'tō-kə-\ (15th century)
1 : to typify beforehand : PRESAGE
2 : to give evidence of : SHOW

be·tray \bi-'trā\ *verb* [Middle English, from *be-* + *trayen* to betray, from Old French *traïr,* from Latin *tradere* — more at TRAITOR] (13th century)
transitive verb
1 : to lead astray; *especially* : SEDUCE
2 : to deliver to an enemy by treachery
3 : to fail or desert especially in time of need
4 a : to reveal unintentionally **b** : SHOW, INDICATE **c** : to disclose in violation of confidence
intransitive verb
: to prove false
synonym see REVEAL
— **be·tray·al** \-'trā-(ə)l\ *noun*
— **be·tray·er** \-'trā-ər\ *noun*

be·troth \bi-'trōth, -'tròth\ *transitive verb* [Middle English, from *be-* + *trouthe* truth, troth] (14th century)
1 : to promise to marry
2 : to give in marriage

be·troth·al \-'trō-thəl, -'trò-, -thəl\ *noun* (1844)
1 : the act of betrothing or fact of being betrothed
2 : a mutual promise or contract for a future marriage

be·trothed \bi-'trōthd, -'tròtht\ *noun* (1588)
: the person to whom one is betrothed

bet·ta \'be-tə\ *noun* [New Latin] (1927)
: any of a genus (*Betta*) of small brilliantly colored long-finned freshwater fishes of southeastern Asia; *especially* : SIAMESE FIGHTING FISH

¹bet·ter \'be-tər\ *adjective, comparative of* GOOD [Middle English *bettre,* from Old English *betera;* akin to Old English *bōt* remedy, Sanskrit *bhadra* fortunate] (before 12th century)
1 : greater than half
2 : improved in health or mental attitude
3 : more attractive, favorable, or commendable
4 : more advantageous or effective
5 : improved in accuracy or performance

²better (before 12th century)
transitive verb
1 : to make better: as **a** : to make more tolerable or acceptable 〈trying to *better* the lot of slum dwellers〉 **b** : to make more complete or perfect 〈looked forward to *bettering* her acquaintance with the new neighbors〉
2 : to surpass in excellence : EXCEL
intransitive verb
: to become better
synonym see IMPROVE

³better *adverb, comparative of* WELL (12th century)
1 a : in a more excellent manner **b** : to greater advantage : PREFERABLY 〈some things are *better* left unsaid〉
2 a : to a higher or greater degree 〈he knows the story *better* than you do〉 **b** : MORE 〈it is *better* than nine miles to the next town〉

⁴better *noun* (12th century)
1 a : something better **b** : a superior especially in merit or rank
2 : ADVANTAGE, VICTORY 〈get the *better* of him〉

⁵better *verbal auxiliary* (1831)
: had better 〈you *better* hurry〉

bet·ter·ment \'be-tər-mənt\ *noun* (1598)
1 : a making or becoming better
2 : an improvement that adds to the value of a property or facility

better-off \,be-tə-'ròf\ *adjective* (circa 1859)
1 : being in comfortable economic circumstances 〈the *better-off* people live in the older section of town〉
2 : being in a more advantageous position

betting shop *noun* (1852)
British : a shop where bets are taken

bet·tor *or* **bet·ter** \'be-tər\ *noun* (1609)
: one that bets

¹be·tween \bi-'twēn\ *preposition* [Middle English *betwene,* preposition & adverb, from Old English *betwēonum,* from *be-* + *-twēonum* (dative plural) (akin to Gothic *tweihnai* two each); akin to Old English *twā* two] (before 12th century)
1 a : by the common action of : jointly engaging 〈shared the work *between* the two of them〉 〈talks *between* the three —*Time*〉 **b** : in common to : shared by 〈divided *between* his four grandchildren〉
2 a : in the time, space, or interval that separates **b** : in intermediate relation to
3 a : from one to another of 〈air service *between* Miami and Chicago〉 **b** : serving to connect or unite in a relationship 〈as difference, likeness, or proportion〉 〈a one-to-one correspondence *between* sets〉 **c** : setting apart 〈the line *between* fact and fancy〉
4 : in point of comparison of 〈not much to choose *between* the two coats〉
5 : in confidence restricted to 〈a secret *between* you and me〉 □

²between *adverb* (before 12th century)
: in an intermediate space or interval

be·tween·brain \-,brān\ *noun* (circa 1909)
: DIENCEPHALON

be·tween·ness \bi-'twēn-nəs\ *noun* (1892)
: the quality or state of being between two others in an ordered mathematical set

be·tween·times \bi-'twēn-,tīmz\ *adverb* (1907)

: at or during intervals

be·tween·whiles \-,hwīlz, -,wīlz\ *adverb* (1678)
: BETWEENTIMES

be·twixt \bi-'twikst\ *adverb or preposition* [Middle English, from Old English *betwux,* from *be-* + *-twux* (akin to Gothic *tweihnai*)] (before 12th century)
: BETWEEN

betwixt and between *adverb or adjective* (1832)

□ USAGE

between There is a persistent but unfounded notion that *between* can be used only of two items and that *among* must be used for more than two. *Between* has been used of more than two since Old English; it is especially appropriate to denote a one-to-one relationship, regardless of the number of items. It can be used when the number is unspecified 〈economic cooperation *between* nations〉, when more than two are enumerated 〈*between* you and me and the lamppost〉 〈partitioned *between* Austria, Prussia, and Russia —Nathaniel Benchley〉, and even when only one item is mentioned (but repetition is implied) 〈pausing *between* every sentence to rap the floor —George Eliot〉. *Among* is more appropriate where the emphasis is on distribution rather than individual relationships 〈discontent *among* the peasants〉. When *among* is automatically chosen for more than two, English idiom may be strained 〈a worthy book that nevertheless falls *among* many stools —John Simon〉 〈the author alternates *among* mod slang, clichés and quotes from literary giants —A. H. Johnston〉.

Grammarians and other commentators have been hard put to explain the occurrence of *I* where *me* would be expected as the proper form after this preposition: *between you and I*. The most common explanation put forward is hypercorrection—the use of an improper form in one expression on analogy with a proper use of the same form in another expression. In this instance it is supposed that many people taught to say "It is I" instead of "It is me" become intimidated by *me* and substitute *I* whenever they have a chance. On the surface of it, this seems to be a farfetched explanation, and another point against it is that the phrase can be found as early as the end of the 16th century, when there were no schoolteachers harping on "It is I" 〈an argument too deepe to be discussed *between you and I* —Thomas Deloney (1597)〉 〈all debts are cleared *between you and I* —Shakespeare, *The Merchant of Venice* (1600)〉. The most plausible explanation is that offered by the linguist Noam Chomsky, who in a 1986 book postulated that compound phrases like *you and I* are barriers to the assignment of case by verb or preposition, which means that pronouns may appear as nominative or objective or may even be reflexive—in our phrase, *I, me,* or *myself*. Chomsky's theory has the advantage of also accounting for other anomalies of pronoun case in compound subjects and objects of verbs. It is to be observed that the expected case—nominative in subject position, objective in object position—predominates, and that the others, while common, are much more likely to be found in speech than in writing.

\ə\ **abut** \°\ **kitten** \ər\ **further** \a\ **ash** \ā\ **ace**
\ä\ **mop, mar** \aù\ **out** \ch\ **chin** \e\ **bet** \ē\ **easy**
\g\ **go** \i\ **hit** \ī\ **ice** \j\ **job** \ŋ\ **sing** \ō\ **go**
\ò\ **law** \òi\ **boy** \th\ **thin** \t̶h̶\ **the** \ü\ **loot** \ù\ **foot**
\y\ **yet** \zh\ **vision** *see also* Guide to Pronunciation

: in a midway position **:** neither one thing nor the other

Beu·lah \'byü-lə\ *noun*
: an idyllic land near the end of life's journey in Bunyan's *Pilgrim's Progress*

beurre blanc \'bər-'blän\ *noun* [French, literally, white butter] (1931)
: a hot butter sauce (as for fish) flavored with vinegar or lemon juice

beurre ma·nié \-män-'yā\ *noun* [French, literally, handled butter] (1939)
: flour and butter kneaded together used as a thickener in sauces

beurre noir \-'nwär\ *noun* [French, literally, black butter] (1856)
: butter heated until brown or black and often flavored with vinegar or lemon juice

¹**bev·el** \'be-vəl\ *adjective* (circa 1600)
: OBLIQUE, BEVELED

²**bevel** *noun* [(assumed) Middle French, from Old French *baïf* with open mouth, from *baer* to yawn — more at ABEYANCE] (1610)

bevel 2

1 : an instrument consisting of two rules or arms jointed together and opening to any angle for drawing angles or adjusting surfaces to be cut at an angle
2 a : the angle that one surface or line makes with another when they are not at right angles **b :** the slant of such a surface or line
3 : the part of printing type extending from face to shoulder

³**bevel** *verb* **-eled** *or* **-elled; -el·ing** *or* **-el·ling** \'bev-liŋ, 'be-və-\ (1677)
transitive verb
: to cut or shape to a bevel
intransitive verb
: INCLINE, SLANT

bevel gear *noun* (1833)
: either of a pair of toothed wheels whose working surfaces are inclined to non-parallel axes

bev·er·age \'bev-rij, 'be-və-\ *noun*

bevel gears

[Middle English, from Middle French *bev-rage*, from *beivre* to drink, from Latin *bibere* — more at POTABLE] (14th century)
: a drinkable liquid

bevy \'be-vē\ *noun, plural* **bev·ies** [Middle English *bevey*] (15th century)
1 : a large group or collection ⟨a *bevy* of girls⟩
2 : a group of animals and especially quail together

be·wail \bi-'wā(ə)l\ *transitive verb* (14th century)
1 : to wail over
2 : to express deep sorrow for usually by wailing and lamentation ⟨wringing her hands and *bewailing* her fate⟩
synonym see DEPLORE

be·ware \bi-'war, -'wer\ *verb* [Middle English *been war*, from *been* to be + *war* careful — more at BE, WARE] (14th century)
intransitive verb
: to be on one's guard ⟨*beware* of the dog⟩
transitive verb
1 : to take care of ⟨*beware* your wallet⟩
2 : to be wary of ⟨we must . . . *beware* the exceedingly tenuous generalization —Matthew Lipman⟩

be·whis·kered \-'hwis-kərd, -'wis-\ *adjective* (1820)
: wearing whiskers

be·wigged \bi-'wigd\ *adjective* (1774)
: wearing a wig

be·wil·der \bi-'wil-dər\ *transitive verb* **-wildered; -wil·der·ing** \-d(ə-)riŋ\ (1684)
1 : to cause to lose one's bearings
2 : to perplex or confuse especially by a complexity, variety, or multitude of objects or considerations
synonym see PUZZLE
— **be·wil·dered·ly** *adverb*
— **be·wil·dered·ness** *noun*
— **be·wil·der·ing·ly** \-d(ə-)riŋ-lē\ *adverb*

be·wil·der·ment \-dər-mənt\ *noun* (1820)
1 : the quality or state of being bewildered
2 : a bewildering tangle or confusion

be·witch \bi-'wich\ (13th century)
transitive verb
1 a : to influence or affect especially injuriously by witchcraft **b :** to cast a spell over
2 : to attract as if by the power of witchcraft
: ENCHANT ⟨*bewitched* by her beauty⟩
intransitive verb
: to bewitch someone or something
— **be·witch·ery** \-'wi-ch(ə-)rē\ *noun*
— **be·witch·ing·ly** \-'wi-chiŋ-lē\ *adverb*

be·witch·ment \-'wich-mənt\ *noun* (1607)
1 a : the act or power of bewitching **b :** a spell that bewitches
2 : the state of being bewitched

be·wray \bi-'rā\ *transitive verb* [Middle English, from *be-* + *wreyen* to accuse, from Old English *wrēgan;* akin to Old High German *ruogen* to accuse] (13th century)
archaic **:** DIVULGE, BETRAY

bey \'bā\ *noun* [Turkish, gentleman, chief] (1595)
1 a : a provincial governor in the Ottoman Empire **b :** the former native ruler of Tunis or Tunisia
2 — used as a courtesy title in Turkey and Egypt

¹**be·yond** \bē-'änd\ *adverb* [Middle English, preposition & adverb, from Old English *begeondan*, from *be-* + *geondan* beyond, from *geond* yond — more at YOND] (before 12th century)
1 : on or to the farther side **:** FARTHER
2 : in addition **:** BESIDES

²**beyond** *preposition* (before 12th century)
1 : on or to the farther side of **:** at a greater distance than
2 a : out of the reach or sphere of **b :** in a degree or amount surpassing **c :** out of the comprehension of
3 : in addition to **:** BESIDES

³**beyond** *noun* (14th century)
1 : something that lies beyond
2 : something that lies outside the scope of ordinary experience; *specifically* **:** HEREAFTER

be·zant \'be-z'nt, bə-'zant\ *noun* [Middle English *besant*, from Old French, from Medieval Latin *Byzantius* Byzantine, from *Byzantium*, ancient name of Istanbul] (13th century)
1 : SOLIDUS 1
2 : a flat disk used in architectural ornament

be·zel \'bē-zəl, 'be-\ *noun* [probably from dialect form of French *biseau* bezel, from Middle French] (circa 1616)
1 : a rim that holds a transparent covering (as on a watch, clock, or headlight) or that is rotatable and has special markings (as on a watch)
2 : the oblique side or face of a cut gem; *specifically* **:** the upper faceted portion of a brilliant projecting from the setting
3 : a usually metal rim of a piece of jewelry in which an ornament (as a gem) is set

be·zique \bə-'zēk\ *noun* [French *bésique*] (1861)
: a card game similar to pinochle that is played with a pack of 64 cards

be·zoar \'bē-,zōr, -,zȯr\ *noun* [Middle French, from Medieval Latin, from Arabic dialect *bezuwār*, from Arabic *bāzahr*, from Persian *pād-zahr*, from *pād* protecting (against) + *zahr* poison] (1577)

: any of various calculi found chiefly in the gastrointestinal organs and formerly believed to possess magical properties — called also *bezoar stone*

B–girl *noun* [probably from *bar* + *girl*] (1936)
: a woman who entertains bar patrons and encourages them to spend freely

BHA \,bē-(,)ā-'chā\ *noun* [butylated hydroxyanisole] (1950)
: a phenolic antioxidant $C_{11}H_{16}O_2$ used especially to preserve fats and oils in food

Bha·ga·vad Gi·ta \,bä-gə-,väd-'gē-tə\ *noun* [Sanskrit *Bhagavadgītā*, literally, song of the blessed one (Krishna)] (circa 1785)
: a Hindu devotional work in poetic form

bhak·ti \'bək-tē\ *noun* [Sanskrit, literally, portion] (1832)
: devotion to a deity constituting a way to salvation in Hinduism

bhang \'baŋ, 'bäŋ\ *noun* [Hindi *bhāg*] (1563)
: HEMP 1a, c; *also* **:** the leaves and flowering tops of uncultivated hemp **:** CANNABIS — compare MARIJUANA, HASHISH

bhar·al \'bər-əl, 'bə-rəl\ *noun* [Hindi] (1838)
: a goatlike artiodactyl mammal (*Pseudois nayaur*) of the Himalayas and western China having a bluish-gray coat

BHC \,bē-,āch-'sē\ *noun* [benzene hexachloride] (1947)
1 : any of several stereoisomeric chlorine derivatives $C_6H_6Cl_6$ of cyclohexane in which the chlorine atoms are all attached to different carbon atoms
2 : LINDANE

Bhoj·puri \'bōj-,pu̇r-ē, 'bäj-, -pə-rē\ *noun* [Hindi *bhojpurī*, from *Bhojpur*, village in Bihar] (1901)
: an Indo-Aryan language spoken in western Bihar and eastern Uttar Pradesh, India

B horizon *noun* (1938)
: a subsurface soil layer that is immediately beneath the A horizon from which it obtains organic matter chiefly by illuviation and is usually distinguished by less weathering

BHT \,bē-,āch-'tē\ *noun* [butylated hydroxytoluene] (1961)
: a phenolic antioxidant $C_{15}H_{24}O$ used especially to preserve fats and oils in food, cosmetics, and pharmaceuticals

bi \'bī\ *noun or adjective* (circa 1965)
: BISEXUAL

¹**bi-** *prefix* [Middle English, from Latin — more at TWI-]
1 a : two ⟨*bilateral*⟩ **b :** coming or occurring every two ⟨*bicentennial*⟩ **c :** into two parts ⟨*bisect*⟩
2 a : twice **:** doubly **:** on both sides ⟨*biconvex*⟩ **b :** coming or occurring two times ⟨*biannual*⟩ — compare SEMI-
3 : between, involving, or affecting two (specified) symmetrical parts ⟨*bilabial*⟩
4 a : containing one (specified) constituent in double the proportion of the other constituent or in double the ordinary proportion ⟨*bicarbonate*⟩ **b :** DI- 2 ⟨*biphenyl*⟩ □

□ **USAGE**
bi- Many people are puzzled about *bimonthly* and *biweekly*, which are often ambiguous because they are formed from both senses 1b and 2b of *bi-*. This ambiguity has been in existence for nearly a century and a half and cannot be eliminated by the dictionary. The chief difficulty is that many users of these words assume that others know exactly what they mean, and they do not bother to make their context clear. So if you need *bimonthly* or *biweekly*, you should leave some clues in your context to the sense of *bi-* you mean. And if you need the meaning "twice a," you can substitute *semi-* for *bi-*. *Biannual* and *biennial* are usually differentiated.

BIBLE

OLD TESTAMENT		NEW TESTAMENT	PROTESTANT APOCRYPHA	JEWISH SCRIPTURE
ROMAN CATHOLIC CANON	PROTESTANT CANON	Matthew	1 & 2 Esdras	*Law*
Genesis	Genesis	Mark	Tobit	Genesis
Exodus	Exodus	Luke	Judith	Exodus
Leviticus	Leviticus	John	Additions to	Leviticus
Numbers	Numbers	Acts of the	Esther	Numbers
Deuteronomy	Deuteronomy	Apostles	Wisdom of	Deuteronomy
Joshua	Joshua	Romans	Solomon	*Prophets*
Judges	Judges	1 & 2	Ecclesiasticus	Joshua
Ruth	Ruth	Corinthians	or the Wisdom	Judges
1 & 2 Samuel	1 & 2 Samuel	Galatians	of Jesus Son	1 & 2 Samuel
1 & 2 Kings	1 & 2 Kings	Ephesians	of Sirach	1 & 2 Kings
1 & 2 Chronicles	1 & 2 Chronicles	Philippians	Baruch	Isaiah
Ezra	Ezra	Colossians	Prayer of	Jeremiah
Nehemiah	Nehemiah	1 & 2	Azariah and	Ezekiel
Tobit		Thessalonians	the Song of	Hosea
Judith		1 & 2 Timothy	the Three Holy	Joel
Esther	Esther	Titus	Children	Amos
Job	Job	Philemon	Susanna	Obadiah
Psalms	Psalms	Hebrews	Bel and the	Jonah
Proverbs	Proverbs	James	Dragon	Micah
Ecclesiastes	Ecclesiastes	1 & 2 Peter	The Prayer of	Nahum
Song of Songs	Song of Solomon	1, 2, 3 John	Manasses	Habakkuk
Wisdom		Jude	1 & 2 Maccabees	Zephaniah
Sirach		Revelation *or*		Haggai
Isaiah	Isaiah	Apocalypse		Zechariah
Jeremiah	Jeremiah			Malachi
Lamentations	Lamentations			*Hagiographa*
Baruch				Psalms
Ezekiel	Ezekiel			Proverbs
Daniel	Daniel			Job
Hosea	Hosea			Song of Songs
Joel	Joel			Ruth
Amos	Amos			Lamentations
Obadiah	Obadiah			Ecclesiastes
Jonah	Jonah			Esther
Micah	Micah			Daniel
Nahum	Nahum			Ezra
Habakkuk	Habakkuk			Nehemiah
Zephaniah	Zephaniah			1 & 2 Chronicles
Haggai	Haggai			
Zechariah	Zechariah			
Malachi	Malachi			
1 & 2 Maccabees				

²**bi-** *or* **bio-** *combining form* [Greek, from *bios* mode of life — more at QUICK]
: life **:** living organisms or tissue ⟨*bio*luminescence⟩

bi·aly \bē-'a-lē\ *noun, plural* **bialys** [Yiddish, short for *bialystoker,* from *bialystoker* of Bialystok, city in Poland] (1965)
: a flat breakfast roll that has a depressed center and is usually covered with onion flakes

bi·an·nu·al \(ˌ)bī-'an-yə(-wə)l\ *adjective* (1877)
: occurring twice a year; *sometimes* **:** BIENNIAL 1
usage see BI-
— **bi·an·nu·al·ly** *adverb*

¹**bi·as** \'bī-əs\ *noun* [Middle French *biais*] (1530)
1 : a line diagonal to the grain of a fabric; *especially* **:** a line at a 45° angle to the selvage often utilized in the cutting of garments for smoother fit
2 a : a peculiarity in the shape of a bowl that causes it to swerve when rolled on the green **b :** the tendency of a bowl to swerve; *also* **:** the impulse causing this tendency **c :** the swerve of the bowl
3 a : BENT, TENDENCY **b :** an inclination of temperament or outlook; *especially* **:** a personal and sometimes unreasoned judgment **:** PREJUDICE **c :** an instance of such prejudice **d** (1) **:** deviation of the expected value of a statistical estimate from the quantity it estimates (2) **:** systematic error introduced into sampling or testing by selecting or encouraging one outcome or answer over others

4 a : a voltage applied to a device (as a transistor control electrode) to establish a reference level for operation **b :** a high-frequency voltage combined with an audio signal to reduce distortion in tape recording
synonym see PREDILECTION
— **on the bias :** ASKEW, OBLIQUELY

²**bias** *adjective* (1551)
: DIAGONAL, SLANTING — used chiefly of fabrics and their cut
— **bi·as·ness** *noun*

³**bias** *adverb* (1575)
1 : DIAGONALLY ⟨cut cloth *bias*⟩
2 *obsolete* **:** AWRY

⁴**bias** *transitive verb* **bi·ased** *or* **bi·assed; bi·as·ing** *or* **bi·as·sing** (circa 1628)
1 : to give a settled and often prejudiced outlook to ⟨his background *biases* him against foreigners⟩
2 : to apply a slight negative or positive voltage to (as an electron-tube grid)
synonym see INCLINE

bi·as–belt·ed tire \'bī-əs-ˌbel-təd-\ *noun* (1968)
: a pneumatic tire with a belt (as of steel or fiberglass) around the tire under the tread and on top of the ply cords set diagonally to the center line of the tread

bi·ased *adjective* (1649)
1 : exhibiting or characterized by bias; *especially* **:** PREJUDICED
2 : tending to yield one outcome more frequently than others in a statistical experiment ⟨a *biased* coin⟩

3 : having an expected value different from the quantity or parameter estimated ⟨a *biased* estimate⟩

bi·as–ply tire \'bī-əs-ˌplī-\ *noun* (1968)
: a pneumatic tire having crossed layers of ply-cord set diagonally to the center line of the tread

bias tape *noun* (1926)
: a narrow strip of cloth cut on the bias, folded, and used for finishing or decorating clothing

bi·ath·lete \bī-'ath-ˌlēt\ *noun* [blend of *athlete* and *biathlon*] (1968)
: a competitor in a biathlon

bi·ath·lon \bī-'ath-lən, -ˌlän\ *noun* [¹*bi-* + *-athlon* (as in *decathlon*)] (1958)
: a composite athletic contest consisting of cross-country skiing and rifle sharpshooting

bi·ax·i·al \(ˌ)bī-'ak-sē-əl\ *adjective* (1854)
: having or relating to two axes or optic axes ⟨a *biaxial* crystal⟩
— **bi·ax·i·al·ly** \-ə-lē\ *adverb*

¹**bib** \'bib\ *verb* **bibbed; bib·bing** [Middle English *bibben*] (14th century)
: DRINK

²**bib** *noun* (1580)
1 : a cloth or plastic shield tied under the chin to protect the clothes
2 : the part of an apron or of overalls extending above the waist
3 : a patch of differently colored feathers or fur immediately below the bill or chin of a bird or mammal
— **bibbed** \'bibd\ *adjective*
— **bib·less** \'bib-ləs\ *adjective*

bib and tucker *noun* (1747)
: an outfit of clothing — usually used in the phrase *best bib and tucker*

bib·ber \'bi-bər\ *noun* (1536)
: a person who regularly drinks alcoholic beverages
— **bib·bery** \'bi-bə-rē\ *noun*

Bibb lettuce \'bib-\ *noun* [Major John *Bibb,* 19th century American grower] (1961)
: lettuce of a variety that has a small head and dark green color

bib·cock \'bib-ˌkäk\ *also* **bibb cock** *noun* (circa 1853)
: a faucet having a bent-down nozzle

bi·be·lot \'bē-bə-ˌlō\ *noun, plural* **bibelots** \-ˌlō(z)\ [French] (1873)
: a small household ornament or decorative object **:** TRINKET

bi·ble \'bī-bəl\ *noun* [Middle English, from Old French, from Medieval Latin *biblia,* from Greek, plural of *biblion* book, diminutive of *byblos* papyrus, book, from *Byblos,* ancient Phoenician city from which papyrus was exported] (14th century)
1 *capitalized* **a :** the sacred scriptures of Christians comprising the Old Testament and the New Testament **b :** the sacred scriptures of some other religion (as Judaism)
2 *obsolete* **:** BOOK
3 *capitalized* **:** a copy or an edition of the Bible
4 : a publication that is preeminent especially in authoritativeness or wide readership ⟨the fisherman's *bible*⟩ ⟨the *bible* of the entertainment industry⟩

Bible Belt *noun* (1925)
: an area chiefly in the southern U.S. believed to hold uncritical allegiance to the literal accuracy of the Bible; *broadly* **:** an area characterized by ardent religious fundamentalism

Bible paper *noun* (1903)
: INDIA PAPER 2

Bi·ble–thump·er \'bī-bəl-ˌthəm-pər\ *noun* (1937)

: an overzealous proponent of Christian fundamentalism
— **Bi·ble–thump·ing** \-piŋ\ *adjective*

bibli- *or* **biblio-** *combining form* [Middle French, from Latin, from Greek, from *biblion*] : book ⟨*bibli*ology⟩

bib·li·cal \'bi-bli-kəl\ *adjective* [Medieval Latin *biblicus,* from *biblia*] (circa 1775)
1 : of, relating to, or being in accord with the Bible
2 : suggestive of the Bible or Bible times
— **bib·li·cal·ly** \-k(ə-)lē\ *adverb*

bib·li·cism \'bi-blə-,si-zəm\ *noun, often capitalized* (1851)
: adherence to the letter of the Bible
— **bib·li·cist** \-lə-sist\ *noun, often capitalized*

bib·li·og·ra·pher \,bi-blē-'ä-grə-fər\ *noun* (1775)
1 : an expert in bibliography
2 : a compiler of bibliographies

bib·li·og·ra·phy \,bi-blē-'ä-grə-fē\ *noun, plural* **-phies** [probably from New Latin *bibliographia,* from Greek, the copying of books, from *bibli-* + *-graphia* -graphy] (1802)
1 : the history, identification, or description of writings or publications
2 a : a list often with descriptive or critical notes of writings relating to a particular subject, period, or author **b :** a list of works written by an author or printed by a publishing house
3 : the works or a list of the works referred to in a text or consulted by the author in its production
— **bib·lio·graph·ic** \,bi-blē-ə-'gra-fik\ *also* **bib·lio·graph·i·cal** \-fi-kəl\ *adjective*
— **bib·lio·graph·i·cal·ly** \-k(ə-)lē\ *adverb*

bib·li·o·la·ter \,bi-blē-'ä-lə-tər\ *noun* (1847)
1 : one having excessive reverence for the letter of the Bible
2 : one overly devoted to books
— **bib·li·ol·a·trous** \-'ä-lə-trəs\ *adjective*
— **bib·li·ol·a·try** \-trē\ *noun*

bib·li·ol·o·gy \,bi-blē-'ä-lə-jē\ *noun* (1806)
1 : the history and science of books as physical objects **:** BIBLIOGRAPHY
2 *often capitalized* **:** the study of the theological doctrine of the Bible

bib·lio·ma·nia \,bi-blē-ə-'mā-nē-ə, -nyə\ *noun* [French *bibliomanie,* from *bibli-* + *manie* mania, from Late Latin *mania*] (1734)
: extreme preoccupation with collecting books
— **bib·lio·ma·ni·ac** \-nē-,ak\ *noun or adjective*
— **bib·lio·ma·ni·a·cal** \-lē-ō-mə-'nī-ə-kəl\ *adjective*

bib·li·op·e·gy \,bi-blē-'ä-pə-jē\ *noun* [ultimately from Greek *bibli-* + *pēgnynai* to fasten together — more at PACT] (circa 1859)
: the art of binding books
— **bib·li·o·pe·gic** \,bi-blē-ə-'pe-jik, -'pē-\ *adjective*
— **bib·li·op·e·gist** \,bi-blē-'ä-pə-jist\ *noun*

bib·li·o·phile \'bi-blē-ə-,fīl\ *noun* [French, from *bibli-* + *-phile*] (1824)
: a lover of books especially for qualities of format; *also* : a book collector
— **bib·lio·phil·ic** \,bi-blē-ə-'fi-lik\ *adjective*
— **bib·li·oph·i·lism** \-'ä-fə-,li-zəm\ *noun*
— **bib·li·oph·i·ly** \-lē\ *noun*

bib·li·o·pole \'bi-blē-ə-,pōl\ *or* **bib·li·op·o·list** \,bi-blē-'ä-pə-list\ *noun* [Latin *bibliopola* bookseller, from Greek *bibliopōlēs,* from *bibli-* + *pōlein* to sell] (1775)
: a dealer especially in rare or curious books

bib·lio·the·ca \,bi-blē-ə-'thē-kə\ *noun, plural* **-cas** *or* **-cae** \-,sē, -,kē\ [Latin, from Greek *bibliothēkē,* from *bibli-* + *thēkē* case; akin to Greek *tithenai* to put, place — more at DO] (circa 1824)
1 : a collection of books
2 : a list of books
— **bib·lio·the·cal** \-'thē-kəl\ *adjective*

bib·lio·ther·a·py \,bi-blē-ə-'ther-ə-pē\ *noun* (1919)

: the use of reading materials for help in solving personal problems or for psychiatric therapy

bib·li·ot·ics \,bi-blē-'ä-tiks\ *noun plural but singular in construction* [*bibli-* + *¹-otic* + *-ics*] (1901)
: the study of handwriting, documents, and writing materials especially for determining genuineness or authorship
— **bib·li·ot·ic** \-tik\ *adjective*
— **bib·li·o·tist** \'bi-blē-ə-tist\ *noun*

bib·u·lous \'bi-byə-ləs\ *adjective* [Latin *bibulus,* from *bibere* to drink — more at POTABLE] (1675)
1 : highly absorbent
2 a : fond of alcoholic beverages **b :** of, relating to, or marked by the consumption of alcoholic beverages
— **bib·u·lous·ly** *adverb*
— **bib·u·lous·ness** *noun*

bi·cam·er·al \(,)bī-'kam-rəl, -'ka-mə-\ *adjective* [¹*bi-* + Late Latin *camera* chamber — more at CHAMBER] (1856)
: having, consisting of, or based on two legislative chambers ⟨a *bicameral* legislature⟩
— **bi·cam·er·al·ism** \-rə-,li-zəm\ *noun*

bi·carb \(,)bī-'kärb, 'bī-,\ *noun* (1922)
: SODIUM BICARBONATE

bi·car·bon·ate \(,)bī-'kär-bə-,nāt, -nət\ *noun* [International Scientific Vocabulary] (1819)
: an acid carbonate

bicarbonate of soda (circa 1887)
: SODIUM BICARBONATE

bi·cen·te·na·ry \,bī-(,)sen-'te-nə-rē, (,)bī-'sen-t³n-,er-ē, ,bī-(,)sen-'tē-nə-rē\ *noun* (1872)
: BICENTENNIAL
— **bicentenary** *adjective*

bi·cen·ten·ni·al \,bī-(,)sen-'te-nē-əl\ *noun* (1883)
: a 200th anniversary or its celebration
— **bicentennial** *adjective*

bi·ceps \'bī-,seps\ *noun, plural* **biceps** *also* **bi·ceps·es** [New Latin *bicipit-, biceps,* from Latin, two-headed, from *bi-* + *capit-, caput* head — more at HEAD] (1650)
: a muscle having two heads: as **a :** the large flexor muscle of the front of the upper arm **b :** the large flexor muscle of the back of the upper leg

biceps bra·chii \-'brā-kē-,ī, -kē-,ē\ *noun* [New Latin, literally, biceps of the arm] (circa 1860)
: BICEPS a

biceps fe·mo·ris \-'fe-mə-rəs\ *noun* [New Latin, literally, biceps of the femur] (circa 1860)
: BICEPS b

bi·chlo·ride of mercury \(,)bī-'klōr-,īd-, -'klȯr-\ [International Scientific Vocabulary] (1810)
: MERCURIC CHLORIDE

bi·chon fri·se \bē-,shōⁿ-frē-'zā\ *noun, plural* **bi·chons fri·ses** \-,shōⁿ-frē-'zā(z)\ [modification of French *bichon à poil frisé* curly-haired lapdog] (1966)
: any of a breed of small sturdy dogs of Mediterranean origin having a thick wavy white coat

bi·chro·mate \(,)bī-'krō-,māt, 'bī-krō-\ *noun* (1836)
: a dichromate especially of sodium or potassium
— **bi·chro·mat·ed** \-,mā-təd\ *adjective*

bi·chrome \'bī-,krōm\ *adjective* (1924)
: two-colored

bi·cip·i·tal \bī-'si-pə-t³l\ *adjective* (1646)
: of, relating to, or being a biceps

¹bick·er \'bi-kər\ *noun* [Middle English *biker*] (14th century)
1 : petulant quarreling **:** ALTERCATION
2 : a sound of or as if of bickering

²bicker *intransitive verb* **bick·ered; bick·er·ing** \'bi-k(ə-)riŋ\ (15th century)
1 : to engage in a petulant or petty quarrel
2 a : to move with a rapidly repeated noise ⟨a *bickering* stream⟩ **b :** QUIVER, FLICKER

— **bick·er·er** \-kə-rər\ *noun*

bi·coast·al \(,)bī-'kōs-təl\ *adjective* (1972)
: of or relating to or living or working on both the East and West coasts of the U.S.

bi·col·ored \'bī-,kə-lərd\ *or* **bi·col·or** \-lər\ *adjective* [Latin *bicolor,* from *bi-* + *color*] (circa 1843)
: two-colored
— **bicolor** *noun*

bi·com·po·nent \(,)bī-kəm-'pō-nənt, -käm-, -'käm-,\ *adjective* (1962)
: being a fiber made of two polymers having slightly different physical properties so that the fiber has a permanent crimp and fabrics made from it have inherent bulk and stretchability

bi·con·cave \(,)bī-(,)kän-'kāv, -'kän-,\ *adjective* (1833)
: concave on both sides
— **bi·con·cav·i·ty** \,bī-(,)kän-'ka-və-tē\ *noun*

bi·con·di·tion·al \,bī-kən-'dish-nəl, -'di-shə-\ *noun* (1940)
: a relation between two propositions that is true only when both propositions are simultaneously true or false

bi·con·vex \,bī-(,)kän-'veks, (,)bī-'kän-,\ *adjective* [International Scientific Vocabulary] (circa 1852)
: convex on both sides
— **bi·con·vex·i·ty** \,bī-kən-'vek-sə-tē, -(,)kän-\ *noun*

bi·corne \'bī-,kȯrn\ *noun* [French, from Latin *bicornis* two-horned, from *bi-* + *cornu* horn — more at HORN] (1936)
: COCKED HAT 2

bi·cul·tur·al \(,)bī-'kəl-chər-əl\ *adjective* (1940)
: of, relating to, or including two distinct cultures ⟨*bicultural* education⟩
— **bi·cul·tur·al·ism** \-ə-,li-zəm\ *noun*

¹bi·cus·pid \(,)bī-'kəs-pəd\ *adjective* [New Latin *bicuspid-, bicuspis,* from *bi-* + Latin *cuspid-, cuspis* point] (circa 1839)
: having or ending in two points ⟨*bicuspid* teeth⟩

²bicuspid *noun* (1852)
: a human premolar tooth — see TOOTH illustration

bicuspid valve *noun* (circa 1903)
: a cardiac valve consisting of two triangular flaps which allow only unidirectional blood flow from the left atrium to the ventricle — called also *mitral valve*

¹bi·cy·cle \'bī-si-kəl, -,si- *also* -,sī-\ *noun* [French, from *bi-* + *-cycle* (as in *tricycle*)] (1868)
: a vehicle with two wheels tandem, a steering handle, a saddle seat, and pedals by which it is propelled; *also* : a stationary exercise machine that resembles such a vehicle

²bicycle *intransitive verb* **bi·cy·cled; bi·cy·cling** \-k(ə-)liŋ\ (1869)
: to ride a bicycle
— **bi·cy·cler** \-klər\ *noun*
— **bi·cy·clist** \-klist\ *noun*

bi·cy·clic \(,)bī-'sī-klik, -'si-\ *adjective* [International Scientific Vocabulary] (circa 1909)
1 : consisting of or arranged in two cycles
2 : containing two usually fused rings in the structure of the molecule

¹bid \'bid\ *verb* **bade** \'bad, 'bād\ *or* **bid; bid·den** \'bi-d³n\ *or* **bid** *also* **bade; bid·ding** [partly from Middle English *bidden,* from Old English *biddan;* akin to Old High German *bitten* to entreat, and perhaps to Sanskrit *bādhate* he presses; partly from Middle English *beden* to offer, command, from Old English *bēodan;* akin to Old High German *biotan* to offer, Greek *pynthanesthai* to examine, Sanskrit *bodhi* enlightenment] (before 12th century) *transitive verb*
1 a *obsolete* **:** BESEECH, ENTREAT **b :** to issue an order to **:** TELL **c :** to request to come **:** INVITE
2 : to give expression to ⟨*bade* a tearful farewell⟩

3 a : OFFER — usually used in the phrase *to bid defiance* **b** *past and past participle* **bid** (1) **:** to offer (a price) whether for payment or acceptance (2) **:** to make a bid of or in (a suit at cards)
intransitive verb
: to make a bid
synonym see COMMAND
— **bid·der** *noun*
— **bid fair :** to seem likely
²**bid** *noun* (1788)
1 a : the act of one who bids **b :** a statement of what one will give or take for something; *especially* **:** an offer of a price **c :** something offered as a bid
2 : an opportunity to bid
3 : INVITATION
4 a : an announcement of what a cardplayer proposes to undertake **b :** the amount of such a bid **c :** a biddable bridge hand
5 : an attempt or effort to win, achieve, or attract ⟨a *bid* for reelection⟩
bid·da·ble \'bi-də-bəl\ *adjective* (circa 1768)
1 : easily led, taught, or controlled **:** DOCILE
2 : capable of being bid
— **bid·da·bil·i·ty** \ˌbi-də-'bi-lə-tē\ *noun*
— **bid·da·bly** \'bi-də-blē\ *adverb*
¹**bid·dy** \'bi-dē\ *noun, plural* **biddies** [perhaps imitative] (1601)
: HEN 1a; *also* **:** a young chicken
²**biddy** *noun, plural* **biddies** [diminutive of the name *Bridget*] (circa 1861)
1 : a hired girl or cleaning woman
2 : WOMAN; *especially* **:** an elderly woman — usually used disparagingly
bide \'bīd\ *verb* **bode** \'bōd\ *or* **bid·ed; bid·ed; bid·ing** [Middle English, from Old English *bīdan;* akin to Old High German *bītan* to wait, Latin *fidere* to trust, Greek *peithesthai* to believe] (before 12th century)
transitive verb
1 *past usually* **bided :** to wait for — used chiefly in the phrase *bide one's time*
2 *archaic* **:** WITHSTAND ⟨two men . . . might *bide* the winter storm —W. C. Bryant⟩
3 *chiefly dialect* **:** to put up with **:** TOLERATE
intransitive verb
1 : to continue in a state or condition
2 : to wait awhile **:** TARRY
3 : to continue in a place **:** SOJOURN
— **bid·er** *noun*
bi·det \bi-'dā\ *noun* [French, small horse, bidet, from Middle French, from *bider* to trot] (1766)
: a bathroom fixture used especially for bathing the external genitals and the posterior parts of the body
bi·di·a·lec·tal·ism \ˌbī-ˌdī-ə-'lek-tᵊl-ˌi-zəm\ *noun* (1958)
: facility in using two dialects of the same language; *also* **:** the teaching of Standard English to pupils who normally use a nonstandard dialect
— **bi·di·a·lec·tal** *adjective*
bi·di·rec·tion·al \ˌbī-də-'rek-shnəl, -dī-, -shə-nᵊl\ *adjective* (1928)
: involving, moving, or taking place in two usually opposite directions ⟨*bidirectional* flow⟩ ⟨*bidirectional* replication of DNA⟩
— **bi·di·rec·tion·al·ly** *adverb*
bi·don·ville \ˌbē-ˌdōⁿ-'vē(ə)l\ *noun* [French, from *bidon* metal can or drum + *ville* city] (1952)
: a settlement of jerry-built dwellings on the outskirts of a city (as in France or North Africa)
bid up *transitive verb* (1864)
: to raise the price of (as property at auction) by a succession of offers
Bie·der·mei·er \'bē-dər-ˌmī(-ə)r\ *adjective* [after Gottlieb *Biedermeier,* satirical name for an uninspired German bourgeois] (1905)
: of a style of unostentatious furniture and interior decoration popular especially with the middle class in early 19th century Germany
bi·en·ni·al \ˌ(ˌ)bī-'e-nē-əl\ *adjective* (1562)

1 : occurring every two years
2 : continuing or lasting for two years; *specifically* **:** growing vegetatively during the first year and fruiting and dying during the second
usage see BI-
— **biennial** *noun*
— **bi·en·ni·al·ly** \-ə-lē\ *adverb*
bi·en·ni·um \bī-'e-nē-əm\ *noun, plural* **-ni·ums** *or* **-nia** \-nē-ə\ [Latin, from *bi-* + *annus* year — more at ANNUAL] (1899)
: a period of two years
bier \'bir\ *noun* [Middle English *bere,* from Old English *bǣr;* akin to Old English *beran* to carry — more at BEAR] (before 12th century)
1 *archaic* **:** a framework for carrying
2 : a stand on which a corpse or coffin is placed; *also* **:** a coffin together with its stand
bi·face \'bī-ˌfās\ *noun* (1934)
: a bifacial stone tool
bi·fa·cial \(ˌ)bī-'fā-shəl\ *adjective* (circa 1847)
: having opposite sides or faces worked on to form an edge for cutting or scraping
— **bi·fa·cial·ly** *adverb*
biff \'bif\ *noun* [probably imitative] (circa 1889)
: WHACK, BLOW
— **biff** *transitive verb*
bi·fid \'bī-ˌfid, -fəd\ *adjective* [Latin *bifidus,* from *bi-* + *-fidus* -fid] (1661)
: divided into two equal lobes or parts by a median cleft ⟨a *bifid* leaf⟩
bi·fi·lar \(ˌ)bī-'fī-lər\ *adjective* [International Scientific Vocabulary *bi-* + Latin *filum* thread — more at FILE] (1846)
1 : involving two threads or wires ⟨*bifilar* suspension of a pendulum⟩
2 : involving a single thread or wire doubled back upon itself ⟨a *bifilar* resistor⟩
— **bi·fi·lar·ly** *adverb*
bi·fla·gel·late \(ˌ)bī-'fla-jə-lət, -ˌlāt; -flə-'je-lət\ *adjective* (1856)
: having two flagella ⟨*biflagellate* gametes⟩
¹**bi·fo·cal** \'bī-ˌfō-kəl\ *adjective* [International Scientific Vocabulary] (1888)
1 : having two focal lengths
2 : having one part that corrects for near vision and one for distant vision ⟨a *bifocal* eyeglass lens⟩
²**bifocal** *noun* (1899)
1 *plural* **:** eyeglasses with bifocal lenses
2 : a bifocal glass or lens
bi·func·tion·al \(ˌ)bī-'fəŋ(k)-shnəl, -shə-nᵊl\ *adjective* (1936)
: having two functions; *especially* **:** DIFUNCTIONAL
bi·fur·cate \'bī-(ˌ)fər-ˌkāt, bī-'fər-\ *verb* **-cat·ed; -cat·ing** [Medieval Latin *bifurcatus,* past participle of *bifurcare,* from Latin *bifurcus* two-pronged, from *bi-* + *furca* fork] (1615)
transitive verb
: to cause to divide into two branches or parts
intransitive verb
: to divide into two branches or parts
— **bi·fur·cate** \(ˌ)bī-'fər-kət, -ˌkāt; 'bī-(ˌ)fər-ˌkāt\ *adjective*
bi·fur·ca·tion \ˌbī-(ˌ)fər-'kā-shən\ *noun* (1615)
1 a : the point at which bifurcating occurs **b :** BRANCH
2 : the act of bifurcating **:** the state of being bifurcated
¹**big** \'big\ *adjective* **big·ger; big·gest** [Middle English, perhaps of Scandinavian origin; akin to Norwegian dialect *bugge* important man] (14th century)
1 a *obsolete* **:** of great strength **b :** of great force ⟨a *big* storm⟩
2 a : large or great in dimensions, bulk, or extent ⟨a *big* house⟩; *also* **:** large or great in quantity, number, or amount ⟨a *big* fleet⟩ **b :** operating on a large scale ⟨*big* government⟩ **c :** CAPITAL 1
3 a : PREGNANT; *especially* **:** nearly ready to give birth **b :** full to bursting **:** SWELLING ⟨*big* with rage⟩ **c** *of the voice* **:** full and resonant

4 a : CHIEF, PREEMINENT ⟨the *big* issue of the campaign⟩ **b :** outstandingly worthy or able ⟨a truly *big* man⟩ **c :** of great importance or significance ⟨the *big* moment⟩ **d :** IMPOSING, PRETENTIOUS; *also* **:** marked by or given to boasting ⟨*big* talk⟩ **e :** MAGNANIMOUS, GENEROUS ⟨was *big* about it⟩
5 : POPULAR ⟨soft drinks are very *big* in Mexico —Russ Leadabrand⟩
6 : full-bodied and flavorful — used of wine
— **big·ly** *adverb*
— **big·ness** *noun*
— **big on :** strongly favoring or liking; *also* **:** noted for ⟨she is *big on* blushing —Arnold Hano⟩
²**big** *adverb* (1807)
1 : in a loud or declamatory manner; *also* **:** in a boasting manner ⟨talk *big*⟩
2 a : to a large amount or extent ⟨won *big*⟩ ⟨lost *big*⟩ **b :** on a large scale ⟨think *big*⟩ ⟨worry *big*⟩
3 : HARD ⟨hits her forehand *big*⟩
³**big** *noun* (1965)
: an individual or organization of outstanding importance or power; *especially* **:** MAJOR LEAGUE — usually used in plural ⟨playing in the *bigs*⟩
big·a·mous \'bi-gə-məs\ *adjective* (1864)
1 : guilty of bigamy
2 : involving bigamy
— **big·a·mous·ly** *adverb*
big·a·my \'bi-gə-mē\ *noun* [Middle English *bigamie,* from Medieval Latin *bigamia,* from Latin *bi-* + Late Latin *-gamia* -gamy] (13th century)
: the act of entering into a marriage with one person while still legally married to another
— **big·a·mist** \-mist\ *noun*
bi·ga·rade \ˌbē-gä-'räd\ *noun* [French, from Provençal *bigarrado,* from *bigarra* to variegate] (1703)
1 : SOUR ORANGE
2 : a brown sauce flavored with the juice and grated rind of oranges
big band *noun* (1926)
: a band that is larger than a combo and that usually features a mixture of ensemble playing and solo improvisation typical of jazz or swing
big bang *noun* (1950)
: the cosmic explosion that marked the beginning of the universe according to the big bang theory
big bang theory *noun* (1955)
: a theory in astronomy: the universe originated billions of years ago in an explosion from a single point of nearly infinite energy density — compare STEADY STATE THEORY
big beat *noun, often both Bs capitalized* (1958)
: music (as rock) characterized by a heavy persistent beat
Big Ben \-'ben\ *noun* [Sir *Benjamin* Hall (died 1867) English Chief Commissioner of Works] (circa 1895)
1 : a large bell in the clock tower of the Houses of Parliament in London
2 : the tower that houses Big Ben; *also* **:** the clock in the tower
big boy *noun* (1926)
: BIG GUN — usually used in plural
big brother *noun* (1863)
1 : an older brother
2 : a man who befriends a delinquent or friendless boy
3 *both Bs capitalized* [*Big Brother,* personification of the power of the state in *1984* (1949) by George Orwell] **a :** the leader of an authoritarian state or movement **b :** an all-powerful government or organization monitoring and

\ə\ abut \ᵊ\ kitten \ər\ further \a\ ash \ā\ ace
\ä\ mop, mar \au̇\ out \ch\ chin \e\ bet \ē\ easy
\g\ go \i\ hit \ī\ ice \j\ job \ŋ\ sing \ō\ go
\ȯ\ law \ȯi\ boy \th\ thin \t͟h\ the \ü\ loot \u̇\ foot
\y\ yet \zh\ vision *see also* Guide to Pronunciation

directing people's actions ⟨data banks that tell *Big Brother* all about us —Herbert Brucker⟩

Big Broth·er·ism \'brə-thər-,i-zəm\ *noun* (1950)
: authoritarian attempts at complete control (as of a person or a nation)

big buck *noun* (1970)
: a large sum of money — usually used in plural; usually hyphenated when attributive

big business *noun* (1905)
1 : an economic group consisting of large profit-making corporations especially with regard to their influence on social or political policy
2 : a very profitable enterprise

big C *noun, often B capitalized* (1968)
: CANCER 2

big daddy *noun, often B&D capitalized* (1958)
: one preeminent especially by reason of power, size, or seniority : one representing paternalistic authority

big deal *noun* (1949)
: something of special importance — sometimes used ironically as an interjection

Big Dipper *noun*
: the seven principal stars in the constellation of Ursa Major

bi·gem·i·ny \bī-'je-mə-nē\ *noun* [*bigeminal* (double, paired), from Late Latin *bigeminus*, from *bi-* + *geminus* twin] (circa 1923)
: the state of having a pulse characterized by two beats close together with a pause following each pair of beats
— **bi·gem·i·nal** \-mə-n°l\ *adjective*

bi·ge·ner·ic \,bī-jə-'ner-ik\ *adjective* (1885)
: of, relating to, or involving two genera ⟨a *bigeneric* hybrid⟩

big·eye \'big-,ī\ *noun* (circa 1889)
: either of two small widely distributed reddish to silvery bony fishes (*Priacanthus cruentatus* and *P. arenatus* of the family Priacanthidae) of tropical seas

big·foot \'big-,fùt\ *noun, often capitalized* [from the size of the footprints ascribed to it] (1958)
: SASQUATCH

big game *noun* (1864)
1 : large animals sought or taken by hunting or fishing for sport
2 : an important objective especially when involving risk

big·ge·ty *or* **big·gi·ty** \'bi-gə-tē\ *adjective* [*big* + *-ety* (as in *persnickety*)] (1880)
1 *Southern & Midland* : CONCEITED, VAIN
2 *Southern & Midland* : rudely self-important : IMPUDENT ⟨never acted *biggety* in court, but she would bow her head only so low —Claude Brown⟩

big·gie \'bi-gē\ *noun* (circa 1931)
: one that is big

¹big·gin *or* **big·ging** \'bi-gən\ *noun* [Middle English *bigging*, from *biggen* to dwell, from Old Norse *byggja*; akin to Old English *bēon* to be] (14th century)
archaic : BUILDING

²biggin *noun* [Middle French *beguin*] (1530)
archaic : CAP: **a** : a child's cap **b** : NIGHTCAP

big·gish \'bi-gish\ *adjective* (circa 1626)
: somewhat big

big gun *noun* (1834)
: one having preeminent status or power in a field

big·head \'big-,hed\ *noun* (1805)
1 : any of several diseases of animals marked by swelling about the head
2 : an exaggerated opinion of one's importance — usually used with *the*
— **big·head·ed** \-'he-dəd\ *adjective*

big·heart·ed \-'här-təd\ *adjective* (1868)
: GENEROUS, CHARITABLE
— **big·heart·ed·ly** *adverb*
— **big·heart·ed·ness** *noun*

big·horn sheep \'big-,hȯrn-\ *noun* (1838)

: a usually gray-ish brown wild sheep (*Ovis canadensis*) of mountainous and desert regions of western North America — called also *big-horn*

big house *noun, often B&H capitalized* (1916)
slang : PENITENTIARY

bight \'bīt\ *noun* [Middle English, from Old English *byht* bend, bay; akin to Old English *būgan* to bend — more at BOW] (15th century)
1 : a bend in a coast forming an open bay; *also* : a bay formed by such a bend
2 : a slack part or loop in a rope

big league *noun* (1899)
1 : MAJOR LEAGUE
2 : BIG TIME 2 — often used in plural
— **big–league** *adjective*
— **big leaguer** *noun*

big lie *noun, sometimes B&L capitalized* (1946)
: a deliberate gross distortion of the truth used especially as a propaganda tactic

big–mouthed \'big-,maùthd, 'big-,maùtht, 'big-"\ *adjective* (1642)
1 : having a large mouth
2 : LOUDMOUTHED

big name *noun* (1932)
: a performer or personage of top rank in popular recognition
— **big–name** *adjective*

big·no·nia \big-'nō-nē-ə\ *noun* [New Latin, genus name, from J. P. *Bignon* (died 1743) French royal librarian] (1785)
: any of a genus (*Bignonia*) of American and Japanese woody vines of the trumpet-creeper family with compound leaves and tubular flowers

big·ot \'bi-gət\ *noun* [Middle French, hypocrite, bigot] (1661)
: a person obstinately or intolerantly devoted to his or her own opinions and prejudices
— **big·ot·ed** \-gə-təd\ *adjective*
— **big·ot·ed·ly** *adverb*

big·ot·ry \'bi-gə-trē\ *noun, plural* **-ries** (circa 1674)
1 : the state of mind of a bigot
2 : acts or beliefs characteristic of a bigot

big picture *noun, often B&P capitalized* (circa 1960)
: the entire perspective on a situation or issue — used with *the*

big shot *noun* (1929)
: a person of consequence or prominence

big stick *noun* (1904)
: threat especially of military or political intervention

big–tick·et \'big-'ti-kət\ *adjective* (1945)
: having a high price

big time *noun* (1910)
1 : a high-paying vaudeville circuit requiring only two performances a day
2 : the top rank of an activity or enterprise
— **big–time** *adjective*
— **big–tim·er** \-,tī-mər\ *noun*

big toe *noun* (circa 1887)
: the innermost and largest toe of the foot

big top *noun* (1895)
1 : the main tent of a circus
2 : CIRCUS 2a, b, c

big tree *noun* (1853)
: a California evergreen (*Sequoiadendron giganteum*) of the bald cypress family that sometimes exceeds 270 feet (about 82 meters) in height — called also *giant sequoia, sequoia*

big wheel *noun* (1942)

: BIGWIG, BIG SHOT

big·wig \'big-,wig\ *noun* (1703)
: an important person

Bi·ha·ri \bi-'här-ē\ *noun* (1882)
1 : a group of Indo-Aryan languages (as Bhojpuri) spoken in Bihar, India, and adjacent areas
2 a : a native or inhabitant of Bihar **b** : a Muslim born in Bihar who emigrated after the partition of India in 1947; *also* : a descendant of such a person

bi·jec·tion \(,)bī-'jek-shən\ *noun* [¹*bi-* + *-jection* (as in *injection*)] (1966)
: a mathematical function that is a one-to-one and onto mapping — compare INJECTION, SURJECTION
— **bi·jec·tive** \-'jek-tiv\ *adjective*

bi·jou \'bē-,zhü\ *noun, plural* **bijous** *or* **bijoux** \-,zhü(z)\ [French, from Breton *bizou* ring, from *biz* finger] (1668)
1 : a small dainty usually ornamental piece of delicate workmanship : JEWEL
2 : something delicate, elegant, or highly prized
— **bijou** *adjective*

bi·jou·te·rie \bi-'zhü-tə-(,)rē\ *noun* [French, from *bijou*] (1815)
: a collection of trinkets or ornaments : JEWELS; *also* : DECORATION

¹bike \'bīk\ *noun* [Middle English] (14th century)
1 *chiefly Scottish* : a nest of wild bees, wasps, or hornets
2 *chiefly Scottish* : a crowd or swarm of people

²bike *noun* [by shortening & alteration] (1882)
1 : BICYCLE
2 : MOTORCYCLE
3 : MOTORBIKE

³bike *intransitive verb* **biked; bik·ing** (1895)
: to ride a bike

bik·er \'bī-kər\ *noun* (1883)
1 : BICYCLIST
2 : MOTORCYCLIST; *especially* : one who is a member of an organized gang

bike·way \'bīk-,wā\ *noun* (1965)
: a thoroughfare for bicycles

bik·ie \'bī-kē\ *noun* [²*bike* + *-ie*] (1967)
: BIKER 2

bi·ki·ni \bə-'kē-nē\ *noun* [French, from *Bikini*, atoll of the Marshall islands] (1947)
1 a : a woman's scanty two-piece bathing suit **b** : a man's brief swimsuit
2 : a man's or woman's low-cut briefs ◇
— **bi·ki·nied** \-nēd\ *adjective*

¹bi·la·bi·al \(,)bī-'lā-bē-əl\ *adjective* [International Scientific Vocabulary] (1894)
of a consonant : produced with both lips

²bilabial *noun* (1899)
: a bilabial consonant

bi·la·bi·ate \-bē-ət\ *adjective* (1794)
: having two lips ⟨a *bilabiate* corolla⟩

bi·lat·er·al \(,)bī-'la-t(ə-)rəl\ *adjective* (1775)
1 : having two sides
2 : affecting reciprocally two nations or parties ⟨a *bilateral* treaty⟩ ⟨a *bilateral* trade agreement⟩
3 a : of, relating to, or affecting the right and left sides of the body or the right and left members of paired organs ⟨*bilateral* nephrectomy⟩ **b** : having bilateral symmetry
— **bi·lat·er·al·ism** \-t(ə-)rə-,li-zəm\ *noun*
— **bi·lat·er·al·ly** *adverb*

bilateral symmetry *noun* (1860)
: symmetry in which similar anatomical parts are arranged on opposite sides of a median axis so that only one plane can divide the individual into essentially identical halves

bi·lay·er \'bī-,lā-ər, -,lē(-ə)r\ *noun* (1963)
: a film or membrane with two molecular layers ⟨a *bilayer* of phospholipid molecules⟩
— **bilayer** *adjective*

bil·ber·ry \'bil-,ber-ē\ *noun* [*bil-* (probably of Scandinavian origin; akin to Danish *bølle* whortleberry) + *berry*] (1577)

bighorn sheep

: any of several ericaceous shrubs (genus *Vaccinium*) that resemble blueberries but have flowers which arise solitary or in very small clusters from axillary buds; *also* **:** its sweet edible fruit

¹bil·bo \'bil-(,)bō\ *noun, plural* **bilboes** [perhaps from *Bilboa,* Spain] (1557)
: a long bar of iron with sliding shackles used to confine the feet of prisoners especially on shipboard

²bilbo *or* **bil·boa** \'bil-(,)bō\ *noun, plural* **bilboes** *or* **bilboas** [*Bilboa, Bilbao,* Spain] (1565)
: SWORD

bil·dungs·ro·man \'bil-dúŋ(k)s-rō-,män, -dúŋz-\ *noun* [German, from *Bildung* education + *Roman* novel] (1910)
: a novel about the moral and psychological growth of the main character

bile \'bī(ə)l\ *noun* [Latin *bilis;* akin to Welsh *bustl* bile] (1547)
1 a : either of two humors associated in old physiology with irascibility and melancholy **b :** a yellow or greenish viscid alkaline fluid secreted by the liver and passed into the duodenum where it aids especially in the emulsification and absorption of fats
2 : inclination to anger

bile acid *noun* (circa 1881)
: any of several steroid acids (as cholic acid) of or derived from bile

bile duct *noun* (1774)
: a duct by which bile passes from the liver or gallbladder to the duodenum

bile salt *noun* (1881)
1 : a salt of bile acid
2 *plural* **:** a dry mixture of the principal salts of the gall of the ox used as a liver stimulant and as a laxative

¹bi·lev·el \'bī-'le-vəl\ *adjective* (1960)
1 : having two levels of freight or passenger space
2 : divided vertically into two ground-floor levels

²bi-level \'bī-,\ *noun* (1966)
: a bi-level house

¹bilge \'bilj\ *noun* [probably modification of Middle French *boulge, bouge* leather bag, curved part — more at BUDGET] (1513)
1 : the bulging part of a cask or barrel
2 a : the part of the underwater body of a ship between the flat of the bottom and the vertical topsides **b :** the lowest point of a ship's inner hull
3 : stale or worthless remarks or ideas

²bilge *intransitive verb* **bilged; bilg·ing** (1728)
: to become damaged in the bilge

bilge keel *noun* (1850)
: a projection like a fin extending from the hull near the turn of the bilge on either side to check rolling

bilge·wa·ter \'bilj-,wó-tər, -,wä-\ *noun* (1706)
: water that collects in the bilge of a ship

bil·har·zia \bil-'här-zē-ə; -'härt-sē-\ *noun* [New Latin, genus name, from Theodor *Bilharz* (died 1862) German zoologist] (circa 1881)
1 : SCHISTOSOMIASIS
2 : SCHISTOSOME
— **bil·har·zi·al** \-zē-əl\, -sē-\ *adjective*

bil·har·zi·a·sis \,bil-,här-'zī-ə-səs; -,härt-'sī-\ *noun, plural* **-a·ses** \-,sēz\ [New Latin] (circa 1900)
: SCHISTOSOMIASIS

bil·i·ary \'bi-lē-,er-ē\ *adjective* [French *biliare,* from Latin *bilis*] (1731)
: of, relating to, or conveying bile; *also* **:** affecting the bile-conveying structures

bi·lin·ear \(,)bī-'li-nē-ər\ *adjective* (1886)
: linear with respect to each of two mathematical variables; *specifically* **:** of or relating to an algebraic form each term of which involves one variable to the first degree from each of two sets of variables

bi·lin·gual \(,)bī-'liŋ-gwəl\ *also* -gyə-wəl\ *adjective* [Latin *bilinguis,* from *bi-* + *lingua* tongue — more at TONGUE] (1845)
1 : having or expressed in two languages
2 : using or able to use two languages especially with equal fluency
3 : of or relating to bilingual education
— **bilingual** *noun*
— **bi·lin·gual·ly** *adverb*

bilingual education *noun* (1972)
: education in an English-language school system in which minority students with little fluency in English are taught in their native language

bi·lin·gual·ism \-gwə-,li-zəm\ *noun* (1873)
: the ability to speak two languages **:** the frequent oral use of two languages

bil·ious \'bil-yəs\ *adjective* [Middle French *bilieux,* from Latin *biliosus,* from *bilis*] (1541)
1 a : of or relating to bile **b :** marked by or suffering from liver dysfunction and especially excessive secretion of bile **c :** appearing as if affected by a bilious disorder
2 : of or indicative of a peevish ill-natured disposition
— **bil·ious·ly** *adverb*
— **bil·ious·ness** *noun*

bil·i·ru·bin \,bi-li-'rü-bən, 'bi-li-,\ *noun* [Latin *bilis* + *ruber* red — more at RED] (1871)
: a reddish yellow water insoluble pigment occurring especially in bile and blood and causing jaundice if accumulated in excess

bil·i·ver·din \-'vər-d⁸n, -,vər-\ *noun* [Swedish, from Latin *bilis* + obsolete French *verd* green] (1845)
: a green pigment that occurs in bile and is an intermediate in the degradation of hemoglobin heme groups to bilirubin

¹bilk \'bilk\ *transitive verb* [perhaps alteration of ²*balk*] (1651)
1 : to block the free development of **:** FRUSTRATE ⟨fate *bilks* their hopes⟩
2 a : to cheat out of something valuable **:** DEFRAUD **b :** to evade payment of or to ⟨*bilks* his creditors⟩
3 : to slip away from **:** ELUDE ⟨*bilked* her pursuers⟩
— **bilk·er** *noun*

²bilk *noun* (1790)
: an untrustworthy tricky individual **:** CHEAT

¹bill \'bil\ *noun* [Middle English *bile,* from Old English; akin to Old English *bill*] (before 12th century)
1 : the jaws of a bird together with their horny covering
2 : a mouthpart (as the beak of a turtle) that resembles a bird's bill
3 : the point of an anchor fluke — see ANCHOR illustration
4 : the visor of a cap or hood

bill 1: *1* flamingo, *2* falcon, *3* pigeon, *4* thrush, *5* merganser, *6* toucan, *7* finch, *8* spoonbill, *9* pelican

²bill *intransitive verb* (1592)
1 : to touch and rub bill to bill
2 : to caress affectionately ⟨*billing* and cooing⟩

³bill *noun* [Middle English *bil,* from Old English *bill* sword; akin to Old High German *bill* pickax] (14th century)
1 : a weapon in use up to the 18th century that consists of a long staff ending in a hook-shaped blade
2 : BILLHOOK

⁴bill *noun* [Middle English, from Medieval Latin *billa* seal, alteration of *bulla,* from Latin, bubble, boss] (14th century)
1 : an itemized list or a statement of particulars (as a list of materials or of members of a ship's crew)
2 : a written document or note
3 *obsolete* **:** a formal petition
4 a : an itemized account of the separate cost of goods sold, services performed, or work done **:** INVOICE **b :** an amount expended or owed **c :** a statement of charges for food or drink **:** CHECK
5 a : a written or printed advertisement posted or otherwise distributed to announce an event of interest to the public; *especially* **:** an announcement of a theatrical entertainment **b :** a programmed presentation (as a motion picture, play, or concert)
6 : a draft of a law presented to a legislature for enactment; *also* **:** the law itself ⟨the GI *bill*⟩
7 : a declaration in writing stating a wrong a complainant has suffered from a defendant or stating a breach of law by some person ⟨a *bill* of complaint⟩
8 a : a piece of paper money **b :** an individual or commercial note ⟨*bills* receivable⟩ **c** *slang* **:** one hundred dollars
— **fill the bill** *or* **fit the bill :** to be exactly what is needed **:** be suitable

⁵bill *transitive verb* (14th century)
1 a : to enter in an accounting system **:** prepare a bill of (charges) **b :** to submit a bill of charges to **c :** to enter (as freight) in a waybill **d :** to issue a bill of lading to or for
2 : to announce (as a performance) especially by posters or placards
3 : ADVERTISE, PROMOTE ⟨the book is *billed* as a "report" —P. G. Altbach⟩
— **bill·able** *adjective*

bil·la·bong \'bi-lə-,bòŋ, -,bäŋ\ *noun* [Wiradhuri (Australian aboriginal language of central New South Wales) *bilabaŋ*] (1861)

◇ WORD HISTORY
bikini In July 1946 a joint U.S. Army-Navy task force detonated two thermonuclear bombs at Bikini, an atoll in the Marshall Islands. The second test, which was set off deep within the atoll's lagoon and propelled two million tons of water into an enormous cauliflower-shaped cloud over a mile high, remains one of the most enduring and terrifying images of our century. Nothing so characterizes the innocence of the early Atomic Age as the fact that the Bikini tests, which dominated news around the world from their announcement in June of 1946, became the vehicle for launching a titillating fashion statement. A French couturier, Jacques Heim, introduced an abbreviated two-piece bathing suit billed as the world's smallest and dubbed *l'atome,* "the atom." Another fashion designer, 49-year-old Louis Réard, created an even scantier suit, for which on June 20 he registered *bikini* as a French proprietary mark. The new sensation debuted at the opening of a Paris swimming pool on July 5, worn by a striptease dancer, Micheline Bernardini, whom Réard was forced to hire because Parisian couture models refused to wear the suit. By the time of Réard's death in 1984, this style with its bizarre link to atomic destruction accounted for a fifth of U.S. swimsuit sales, and French *bikini* had become an international word.

1 *Australian* **a :** a blind channel leading out from a river **b :** a usually dry streambed that is filled seasonally
2 *Australian* **:** a backwater forming a stagnant pool
¹bill·board \'bil-,bōrd, -,bȯrd\ *noun* (1851)
: a flat surface (as of a panel, wall, or fence) on which bills are posted; *specifically* **:** a large panel designed to carry outdoor advertising
²billboard *transitive verb* (1950)
: to promote by a conspicuous display on or as if on a billboard
bill-bug \'bil-,bəg\ *noun* [¹*bill* + *bug*] (1861)
: any of various weevils (as of the genus *Sphenophorus*) having larvae that eat the roots of cereal and other grasses
billed \'bild\ *adjective*
: having a bill of a specified kind — used in combination ⟨spoon-*billed*⟩
bill·er \'bi-lər\ *noun* (1920)
: one that bills; *especially* **:** one that makes out bills
¹bil·let \'bi-lət\ *noun* [Middle English *bylet*, from Middle French *billette*, diminutive of *bulle* document, from Medieval Latin *bulla*] (15th century)
1 *archaic* **:** a brief letter **:** NOTE
2 a : an official order directing that a member of a military force be provided with board and lodging (as in a private home) **b :** quarters assigned by or as if by a billet
3 : POSITION, JOB ⟨a lucrative *billet*⟩
²billet *transitive verb* (1594)
1 : to assign lodging to (as soldiers) by or as if by a billet
2 : to serve with a billet ⟨*billet* a householder⟩
³billet *noun* [Middle English *bylet*, from Middle French *billete*, diminutive of *bille* log, of Celtic origin; akin to Old Irish *bile* landmark tree] (15th century)
1 a : a chunky piece of wood (as for firewood) **b** *obsolete* **:** CUDGEL
2 a : a bar of metal **b :** a piece of semifinished iron or steel nearly square in section made by rolling an ingot or bloom **c :** a section of nonferrous metal ingot hot-worked by forging, rolling, or extrusion **d :** a nonferrous casting suitable for rolling or extrusion
bil·let-doux \,bi-lē-'dü, ,bi-(,)lā-\ *noun, plural* **bil·lets-doux** \-'dü(z)\ [French *billet doux*, literally, sweet letter] (1673)
: a love letter
bill·fish \'bil-,fish\ *noun* (1782)
: a fish with long slender jaws; *especially* **:** any of a family (Istiophoridae) including marlins, spearfishes, and sailfishes
bill·fold \-,fōld\ *noun* [short for earlier *bill-folder*] (1895)
: a folding pocketbook for paper money **:** WALLET
bill·hook \-,hu̇k\ *noun* (1611)
: a cutting or pruning tool with a hooked blade
bil·liard \'bil(l)-yərd\ *noun* (1580)
— used as an attributive form of *billiards* ⟨*billiard* ball⟩
bil·liards \-yərdz\ *noun plural but singular in construction* [Middle French *billard* billiard cue, billiards, from *bille*] (1580)
: any of several games played on an oblong table by driving small balls against one another or into pockets with a cue; *specifically* **:** a game in which one scores by causing a cue ball to hit in succession two object balls — compare POOL
bil·li–bi *also* **bil·ly–bi** \'bi-lē-,bē, ,bi-lē-'\ *noun* [French, alteration of *Billy B.*, perhaps from William B. Leeds, Jr. (died 1972) American industrialist] (1961)
: a soup of mussel stock, white wine, and cream served hot or cold
bill·ing \'bi-liŋ\ *noun* [⁵*bill*] (1875)
1 : advertising or public promotion (as of a product or personality); *also* **:** relative prominence of a name in such promotion ⟨got top *billing*⟩

2 : total amount of business or investments (as of an advertising agency) within a given period
bil·lings·gate \'bi-liŋz-,gāt, *British usually* -git\ *noun* [*Billingsgate*, old gate and fish market, London, England] (1652)
: coarsely abusive language ◇
synonym see ABUSE
bil·lion \'bi(l)-yən\ *noun* [French, from *bi-* + *-illion* (as in *million*)] (1834)
1 — see NUMBER table
2 : a very large number
— **billion** *adjective*
— **bil·lionth** \-yən(t)th\ *adjective or noun*
bil·lion·aire \,bi(l)-yə-'nar, -'ner, 'bi(l)-yə-,\ *noun* [*billion* + *-aire* (as in *millionaire*)] (1860)
: one whose wealth is estimated at a billion or more (as of dollars or pounds)
bill of exchange (1534)
: an unconditional written order from one person to another to pay a specified sum of money to a designated person
bill of fare (1636)
1 : MENU
2 : PROGRAM
bill of goods (1920)
1 : a consignment of merchandise
2 : something intentionally misrepresented **:** something passed off in a deception or fraud — often used in the phrase *sell a bill of goods*
bill of health (1644)
1 : a certificate given to the ship's master at the time of leaving port that indicates the state of health of a ship's company and of a port with regard to infectious diseases
2 : a usually favorable report following an examination or investigation ⟨gave the criticized textbook a clean *bill of health*⟩
bill of indictment (circa 1530)
: an indictment before it is found or ignored by the grand jury
bill of lading (1532)
: a receipt listing goods shipped that is signed by the agent of the owner of a ship or issued by a common carrier
bill of particulars (circa 1860)
: a detailed listing of charges or claims brought in a legal action or of a defendant's response or counterclaim
bill of rights *often B&R capitalized* (1798)
: a summary of fundamental rights and privileges guaranteed to a people against violation by the state — used especially of the first 10 amendments to the U.S. Constitution
bill of sale (1608)
: a formal instrument for the conveyance or transfer of title to goods and chattels
bil·lon \'bi-lən\ *noun* [French, from Middle French, from *bille* log — more at BILLET] (circa 1727)
1 : gold or silver heavily alloyed with a less valuable metal
2 : an alloy of silver containing more than 50 percent of copper by weight
¹bil·low \'bi-(,)lō\ *noun* [Old Norse *bylgja*; akin to Old High German *balg* bag — more at BELLY] (1552)
1 : WAVE; *especially* **:** a great wave or surge of water
2 : a rolling mass (as of flame or smoke) that resembles a high wave
— **bil·lowy** \'bi-lə-wē\ *adjective*
²billow (1597)
intransitive verb
1 : to rise or roll in waves or surges
2 : to bulge or swell out (as through action of the wind)
transitive verb
: to cause to billow
¹bil·ly \'bi-lē\ *noun, plural* **billies** [Scots *billy-pot* cooking utensil] (1839)
chiefly Australian & New Zealand **:** a metal or enamelware pail or pot with a lid and wire bail — called also *billycan*

²billy *noun, plural* **billies** [probably from the name *Billy*] (1848)
1 : BILLY CLUB
2 : BILLY GOAT
billy club *noun* [²*billy*] (1949)
: a heavy usually wooden club; *specifically* **:** a police officer's club
bil·ly·cock \'bi-lē-,käk\ *noun* [origin unknown] (1721)
British **:** DERBY 3
billy goat *noun* [from the name *Billy*] (1861)
: a male goat
bi·lobed \'bī-'lōbd\ *adjective* (1756)
: divided into two lobes ⟨a *bilobed* nucleus⟩
bi·lo·ca·tion \'bī-lō-,kā-shən\ *noun* (1858)
: the state of being or ability to be in two places at the same time
bil·tong \'bil-,töŋ, -,täŋ\ *noun* [Afrikaans, from *bil* rump + *tong* tongue] (1815)
chiefly South African **:** jerked meat
bi·man·u·al \(,)bī-'man-yə-wəl, -yəl\ *adjective* (circa 1889)
: done with or requiring the use of both hands
— **bi·man·u·al·ly** *adverb*
bim·bo \'bim-(,)bō\ *noun, plural* **bimbos** [perhaps from Italian *bimbo* baby] (1919)
1 *slang* **:** MAN, WOMAN — usually used disparagingly ⟨telling a thickheaded pitcher that the *bimbo* at the plate hasn't hit a curve in three seasons —Jay Stuller⟩ and especially of an attractive but empty-headed person ⟨we didn't want a blond *bimbo* in that role . . . we wanted her to be smart —Hugh Wilson⟩
2 *slang* **:** TRAMP 1c ⟨evidence of how her hubby's been cheating on her with various *bimbos* —Dan Greenburg⟩
bi·met·al \'bī-,me-t°l\ *adjective* (1924)
: BIMETALLIC
— **bimetal** *noun*
bi·me·tal·lic \,bī-mə-'ta-lik\ *adjective* (1876)
1 : relating to, based on, or using bimetallism
2 : composed of two different metals — often used of devices having a part in which two metals that expand differently are bonded together
— **bimetallic** *noun*
bi·met·al·lism \(,)bī-'me-t°l-,i-zəm\ *noun* [French *bimétallisme*, from *bi-* + *métal* metal] (1876)
: the use of two metals (as gold and silver) jointly as a monetary standard with both constituting legal tender at a predetermined ratio
— **bi·met·al·list** \-t°l-ist\ *noun*
— **bi·met·al·lis·tic** \,bī-,me-t°l-'is-tik\ *adjective*
bi·mil·le·na·ry \(,)bī-'mi-lə-,ner-ē, ,bī-mə-'le-nə-rē\ *or* **bi·mil·len·ni·al** \,bī-mə-'le-nē-əl\ *noun* (1850)
1 : a period of 2000 years

2 : a 2000th anniversary
— **bimillenary** *adjective*
bi·mod·al \(ˌ)bī-'mō-dᵊl\ *adjective* (1903)
: having or relating to two modes; *especially*
: having or occurring with two statistical modes
— **bi·mo·dal·i·ty** \ˌbī-mō-'da-lə-tē\ *noun*
bi·mo·lec·u·lar \ˌbī-mə-'le-kyə-lər\ *adjective* [International Scientific Vocabulary] (1899)
1 : relating to or formed from two molecules
2 : being two molecules thick ⟨*bimolecular* lipid layers⟩
— **bi·mo·lec·u·lar·ly** *adverb*
¹**bi·month·ly** \(ˌ)bī-'mən(t)th-lē\ *adjective* (1846)
1 : occurring every two months
2 : occurring twice a month **:** SEMIMONTHLY
usage see BI-
²**bimonthly** *adverb* (1864)
1 : once every two months
2 : twice a month
³**bimonthly** *noun* (circa 1890)
: a bimonthly publication
bi·mor·phe·mic \ˌbī-mòr-'fē-mik\ *adjective* (1942)
: consisting of two morphemes
¹**bin** \'bin\ *noun* [Middle English *binn,* from Old English] (before 12th century)
: a box, frame, crib, or enclosed place used for storage
²**bin** *transitive verb* **binned; bin·ning** (1841)
: to put into a bin
bin- *prefix* [Middle English, from Late Latin, from Latin *bini* two by two; akin to Old English *twinn* twofold — more at TWIN]
: ¹BI- ⟨*binaural*⟩
¹**bi·na·ry** \'bī-nə-rē, -ˌner-ē\ *noun, plural* **-ries** (15th century)
: something made of or based on two things or parts: as **a :** BINARY STAR **b :** a binary number system
²**binary** *adjective* [Late Latin *binarius,* from Latin *bini*] (1597)
1 : compounded or consisting of or marked by two things or parts
2 a : DUPLE — used of measure or rhythm **b :** having two musical subjects or two complementary sections
3 a : relating to, being, or belonging to a system of numbers having 2 as its base ⟨the *binary* digits 0 and 1⟩ **b :** involving a choice or condition of two alternatives (as on-off or yes-no)
4 a : composed of two chemical elements, an element and a radical that acts as an element, or two such radicals **b :** utilizing two harmless ingredients that upon combining form a lethal substance (as a gas) ⟨*binary* weapon⟩
5 : relating two logical or mathematical elements ⟨*binary* operation⟩
binary fission *noun* (1897)
: reproduction of a cell by division into two approximately equal parts ⟨the *binary fission* of protozoans⟩
binary star *noun* (circa 1847)
: a system of two stars that revolve around each other under their mutual gravitation — called also *binary system*
bi·na·tion·al \(ˌ)bī-'na-sh(ə-)nəl\ *adjective* (1888)
: of or relating to two nations ⟨a *binational* board of directors⟩
bin·au·ral \(ˌ)bī-'nòr-əl, (ˌ)bi-\ *adjective* [International Scientific Vocabulary] (1861)
1 : of, relating to, or involving two or both ears
2 : of, relating to, or constituting sound reproduction involving the use of two separated microphones and two transmission channels to achieve a stereophonic effect
— **bin·au·ral·ly** \-ə-lē\ *adverb*
¹**bind** \'bīnd\ *verb* **bound** \'baùnd\; **bind·ing** [Middle English, from Old English *bindan;* akin to Old High German *bintan* to bind, Greek *peisma* cable, Sanskrit *badhnāti* he binds] (before 12th century)

transitive verb
1 a : to make secure by tying **b :** to confine, restrain, or restrict at will with bonds **c :** to put under an obligation ⟨*binds* himself with an oath⟩ **d :** to constrain with legal authority
2 a : to wrap around with something so as to enclose or cover **b :** BANDAGE
3 : to fasten round about
4 : to tie together (as stocks of wheat)
5 a : to cause to stick together **b :** to take up and hold (as by chemical forces) **:** combine with
6 : CONSTIPATE
7 : to make a firm commitment for ⟨a handshake *binds* the deal⟩
8 : to protect, strengthen, or decorate by a band or binding
9 : to apply the parts of the cover to (a book)
10 : to set at work as an apprentice **:** INDENTURE
11 : to cause or bring about an emotional attachment
12 : to fasten together
intransitive verb
1 a : to form a cohesive mass **b :** to combine or be taken up especially by chemical action ⟨antibody *binds* to a specific antigen⟩
2 : to hamper free movement or natural action
3 : to become hindered from free operation
4 : to exert a restraining or compelling effect ⟨a promise that *binds*⟩
²**bind** *noun* (before 12th century)
1 a : something that binds **b :** the act of binding **:** the state of being bound **c :** a place where binding occurs
2 : TIE 3
3 : a position or situation in which one is hampered, constrained, or prevented from free movement or action
— **in a bind :** in trouble
bind·er \'bīn-dər\ *noun* (before 12th century)
1 : a person or machine that binds something (as books)
2 : something used in binding **b :** a usually detachable cover (as for holding sheets of paper)
3 : something (as tar or cement) that produces or promotes cohesion in loosely assembled substances
4 : a temporary insurance contract that provides coverage until the policy is issued
5 : something (as money) given in earnest; *also* **:** the agreement arrived at
bind·ery \'bīn-d(ə-)rē\ *noun, plural* **-er·ies** (1810)
: a place where books are bound
¹**bind·ing** \'bīn-diŋ\ *noun* (13th century)
1 : the action of one that binds
2 : a material or device used to bind: as **a :** the cover and materials that hold a book together **b :** a narrow fabric used to finish raw edges **c :** a set of ski fastenings for holding the boot firm on the ski
²**binding** *adjective* (14th century)
1 : that binds
2 : imposing an obligation
— **bind·ing·ly** \-diŋ-lē\ *adverb*
— **bind·ing·ness** *noun*
binding energy *noun* (1932)
: the energy required to break up a molecule, atom, or atomic nucleus completely into its constituent particles
bin·dle stiff \'bin-dᵊl-ˌstif\ *noun* [*bindle,* perhaps alteration of *bundle*] (1901)
: HOBO; *especially* **:** one who carries his clothes or bedding in a bundle
bind off *transitive verb* (circa 1939)
: to cast off in knitting
bind over *transitive verb* (1610)
: to put under a bond to do something (as to appear in court)
bind·weed \'bīnd-ˌwēd\ *noun* (1548)
: any of various twining plants (especially genus *Convolvulus* of the morning-glory family) that mat or interlace with plants among which they grow

bine \'bīn\ *noun* [alteration of ²*bind*] (1727)
: a twining stem or flexible shoot (as of the hop); *also* **:** a plant (as woodbine) whose shoots are bines
Bi·net–Si·mon scale \bi-ˌnā-sē-'mōⁿ-\ *noun* [Alfred *Binet* (died 1911) and Théodore *Simon* (died 1961) French psychologists] (1914)
: an intelligence test consisting originally of tasks graded from the level of the average 3-year-old to that of the average 12-year-old but later extended in range
¹**binge** \'binj\ *noun* [English dialect *binge* (to drink heavily)] (1854)
1 a : a drunken revel **:** SPREE **b :** an unrestrained and often excessive indulgence ⟨a buying *binge*⟩
2 : a social gathering **:** PARTY
²**binge** *intransitive verb* **binged; binge·ing** *or* **bing·ing** (1910)
: to go on a binge; *especially* **:** to go on an eating binge
— **bing·er** \'bin-jər\ *noun*
¹**bin·go** \'biŋ-(ˌ)gō\ *interjection* [alteration of *bing* (interjection suggestive of a ringing sound)] (1925)
1 — used to announce an unexpected event or instantaneous result
2 — used to announce a winning position in bingo
²**bingo** *noun, plural* **bingos** (1932)
: a game of chance played with cards having numbered squares corresponding to numbered balls drawn at random and won by covering five such squares in a row; *also* **:** a social gathering at which bingo is played
bin·na·cle \'bi-ni-kəl\ *noun* [alteration of Middle English *bitakle,* from Old Portuguese or Old Spanish; Old Portuguese *bitácola* & Old Spanish *bitácula,* from Latin *habitaculum* dwelling place, from *habitare* to inhabit — more at HABITATION] (1762)
: a housing for a ship's compass and a lamp
¹**bin·oc·u·lar** \bī-'nä-kyə-lər, bə-\ *adjective* (1738)
: of, relating to, using, or adapted to the use of both eyes ⟨*binocular* vision⟩
— **bin·oc·u·lar·i·ty** \(ˌ)bī-ˌnä-kyə-'lar-ə-tē, bə-\ *noun*
— **bin·oc·u·lar·ly** \bī-'nä-kyə-lər-lē, bə-\ *adverb*
²**bin·oc·u·lar** \bə-'nä-kyə-lər, bī-\ *noun* (1871)
1 : a binocular optical instrument
2 : a handheld optical instrument composed of two telescopes and a focusing device and usually having prisms to increase magnifying ability — usually used in plural
bi·no·mi·al \bī-'nō-mē-əl\ *noun* [New Latin *binomium,* from Medieval Latin, neuter of *binomius* having two names, alteration of Latin *binominis,* from *bi-* + *nomin-, nomen* name — more at NAME] (1557)
1 : a mathematical expression consisting of two terms connected by a plus sign or minus sign
2 : a biological species name consisting of two terms
— **binomial** *adjective*
— **bi·no·mi·al·ly** \-mē-ə-lē\ *adverb*
binomial coefficient *noun* (circa 1889)
: a coefficient of a term in the expansion of the binomial $(x + y)^n$ according to the binomial theorem
binomial distribution *noun* (1911)
: a probability function each of whose values gives the probability that an outcome with constant probability of occurrence in a statistical experiment will occur a given number of times in a succession of repetitions of the experiment
binomial nomenclature *noun* (1880)

\ə\ **abut** \ᵊ\ **kitten** \ər\ **further** \a\ **ash** \ā\ **ace**
\ä\ **mop, mar** \aù\ **out** \ch\ **chin** \e\ **bet** \ē\ **easy**
\g\ **go** \i\ **hit** \ī\ **ice** \j\ **job** \ŋ\ **sing** \ō\ **go**
\ò\ **law** \òi\ **boy** \th\ **thin** \t̲h̲\ **the** \ü\ **loot** \ù\ **foot**
\y\ **yet** \zh\ **vision** *see also* Guide to Pronunciation

: a system of nomenclature in which each species of animal or plant receives a name of two terms of which the first identifies the genus to which it belongs and the second the species itself

binomial theorem *noun* (1755)
: a theorem that specifies the expansion of a binomial of the form $(x + y)^n$ as the sum of $n + 1$ terms of which the general term is of the form

$$\frac{n!}{(n-k)!\,k!}\,x^{(n-k)}y^k$$

where k takes on values from 0 to n

bint \'bint\ *noun* [Arabic, girl, daughter] (1855) *British* : GIRL, WOMAN
bi·nu·cle·ate \(,)bī-'nü-klē-ət *also* -'nyü-\ *also* **bi·nu·cle·at·ed** \-klē-,ā-təd\ *adjective* (1881)
: having two cellular nuclei ⟨binucleate hepatocytes⟩
bio \'bī-(,)ō\ *noun, plural* **bi·os** (1947)
: a biography or biographical sketch
bio- — see BI-
bio·acous·tics \,bī-(,)ō-ə-'kü-stiks\ *noun plural but singular in construction* (1957)
: a branch of science concerned with the production of sound by and its effects on living systems
bio·ac·tive \,bī-ō-'ak-tiv\ *adjective* (1965)
: having an effect on a living organism ⟨bioactive molecules⟩
— **bio·ac·tiv·i·ty** \-ak-'ti-və-tē\ *noun*
bio·as·say \,bī-(,)ō-'a-,sā, -a-'sā\ *noun* (1912)
: determination of the relative strength of a substance (as a drug) by comparing its effect on a test organism with that of a standard preparation
— **bio·as·say** \-a-'sā, -'a-,sā\ *transitive verb*
bio·avail·abil·i·ty \-ə-,vā-lə-'bi-lə-tē\ *noun* (1971)
: the degree and rate at which a substance (as a drug) is absorbed into a living system or is made available at the site of physiological activity
— **bio·avail·able** \-'vā-lə-bəl\ *adjective*
bio·coe·no·sis *or* **bio·ce·no·sis** \,bī-ō-sə-'nō-səs\ *noun, plural* **-no·ses** \-,sēz\ [New Latin, from ²bi- + Greek *koinōsis* sharing, from *koinos* common] (1883)
: an ecological community especially when forming a self-regulating unit
bio·chem·i·cal \,bī-ō-'ke-mi-kəl\ *adjective* [International Scientific Vocabulary] (1851)
1 : of or relating to biochemistry
2 : characterized by, produced by, or involving chemical reactions in living organisms
— **biochemical** *noun*
— **bio·chem·i·cal·ly** \-k(ə-)lē\ *adverb*
biochemical oxygen demand *noun* (circa 1927)
: the oxygen used in meeting the metabolic needs of aerobic microorganisms in water rich in organic matter (as water polluted with sewage)
bio·chem·is·try \,bī-ō-'ke-mə-strē\ *noun* [International Scientific Vocabulary] (1881)
1 : chemistry that deals with the chemical compounds and processes occurring in organisms
2 : the chemical characteristics and reactions of a particular living system or biological substance (as chlorophyll) ⟨a change in the patient's *biochemistry*⟩
— **bio·chem·ist** \-mist\ *noun*
bio·chip \'bī-ō-,chip\ *noun* (1981)
: a hypothetical computer logic circuit or storage device in which the physical or chemical properties of large biological molecules (as proteins) are used to process information
bio·cid·al \,bī-ə-'sī-d°l\ *adjective* (1949)
: destructive to life
bio·cide \'bī-ə-,sīd\ *noun* (1947)

: a substance (as DDT) that is destructive to many different organisms
bio·cli·mat·ic \,bī-ō-klī-'ma-tik\ *adjective* (1918)
: of or relating to the relations of climate and living matter ⟨bioclimatic adaptations⟩
bio·com·pat·i·bil·i·ty \-kəm-,pa-tə-'bi-lə-tē\ *noun* (1971)
: compatibility with living tissue or a living system by not being toxic or injurious and not causing immunological rejection
— **bio·com·pat·i·ble** \-'pa-tə-bəl\ *adjective*
bio·con·trol \,bī-ō-kən-'trōl\ *noun* (1967)
: BIOLOGICAL CONTROL
bio·con·ver·sion \,bī-(,)ō-kən-'vər-zhən, -shən\ *noun* (1960)
: the conversion of organic materials (as wastes) into an energy source (as methane) by processes (as fermentation) involving living organisms
bio·de·grad·able \-di-'grā-də-bəl\ *adjective* (1961)
: capable of being broken down especially into innocuous products by the action of living things (as microorganisms) ⟨biodegradable trash bags⟩
— **bio·de·grad·abil·i·ty** \-,grā-də-'bi-lə-tē\ *noun*
— **bio·deg·ra·da·tion** \-,de-grə-'dā-shən\ *noun*
— **bio·de·grade** \-di-'grād\ *verb*
bio·de·te·ri·o·ra·tion \-di-,tir-ē-ə-'rā-shən\ *noun* (1953)
: the breakdown of materials by microbial action
bio·di·ver·si·ty \-də-'vər-sə-tē, -dī-\ *noun* (1986)
: biological diversity in an environment as indicated by numbers of different species of plants and animals
bio·dy·nam·ic \-dī-'na-mik, -dī-\ *adjective* (1939)
: of or relating to a system of farming that uses only organic materials for fertilizing and soil conditioning
bio·elec·tric \-i-'lek-trik\ *also* **bio·elec·tri·cal** \-tri-kəl\ *adjective* (1918)
: of or relating to electric phenomena in animals and plants
— **bio·elec·tric·i·ty** \-,lek-'tri-sə-tē, -'tris-tē\ *noun*
bio·en·er·get·ics \-,e-nər-'je-tiks\ *noun plural but singular in construction* (1912)
1 : the biology of energy transformations and energy exchanges (as in photosynthesis) within and between living things and their environments
2 : a system of physical and psychological therapy that is held to increase well-being by releasing blocked physical and psychic energy
— **bio·en·er·get·ic** \-'je-tik\ *adjective*
bio·en·gi·neer·ing \-,en-jə-'nir-iŋ\ *noun* (circa 1954)
: biological or medical application of engineering principles or engineering equipment; *broadly* : BIOTECHNOLOGY 1
— **bio·en·gi·neer** \-'nir\ *noun or transitive verb*
bio·eth·ics \-'e-thiks\ *noun plural but singular in construction* (1971)
: a discipline dealing with the ethical implications of biological research and applications especially in medicine
— **bio·eth·i·cal** \-'e-thi-kəl\ *adjective*
— **bio·eth·i·cist** \-'e-thə-sist\ *noun*
bio·feed·back \-'fēd-,bak\ *noun* (1970)
: the technique of making unconscious or involuntary bodily processes (as heartbeats or brain waves) perceptible to the senses (as by the use of an oscilloscope) in order to manipulate them by conscious mental control
bio·foul·ing \-'fau̇-liŋ\ *noun* (1943)
: the gradual accumulation of waterborne organisms (as bacteria and protozoa) on the surfaces of engineering structures in water that

contributes to corrosion of the structures and to a decrease in the efficiency of moving parts
bio·gas \'bī-ō-,gas\ *noun* (1974)
: a mixture of methane and carbon dioxide produced by the bacterial decomposition of organic wastes and used as a fuel
bio·gen·e·sis \,bī-ō-'je-nə-səs\ *noun* [New Latin] (1870)
1 : the development of life from preexisting life
2 : a supposed tendency for stages in the evolutionary history of a race to briefly recur during the development and differentiation of an individual of that race
3 : the synthesis of chemical compounds or structures in the living organism — compare BIOSYNTHESIS
— **bio·ge·net·ic** \-jə-'ne-tik\ *adjective*
— **bio·ge·net·i·cal·ly** \-ti-k(ə-)lē\ *adverb*
biogenetic law *noun* (1882)
: a theory of development much disputed in biology: an organism passes through successive stages resembling the series of ancestral types from which it has descended so that the ontogeny of the individual is a recapitulation of the phylogeny of the group
bio·gen·ic \-'je-nik\ *also* **bi·og·e·nous** \bī-'ä-jə-nəs\ *adjective* (1913)
: produced by living organisms ⟨biogenic methane formation⟩
bio·geo·chem·i·cal \-,jē-ə-'ke-mi-kəl\ *noun* (1938)
: of or relating to the partitioning and cycling of chemical elements and compounds between the living and nonliving parts of an ecosystem
— **bio·geo·chem·is·try** \-mə-strē\ *noun*
bio·ge·og·ra·phy \-jē-'ä-grə-fē\ *noun* [International Scientific Vocabulary] (1895)
: a science that deals with the geographical distribution of animals and plants
— **bio·ge·og·ra·pher** \-grə-fər\ *noun*
— **bio·geo·graph·ic** \-,jē-ə-'gra-fik\ *or* **bio·geo·graph·i·cal** \-fi-kəl\ *adjective*
bi·og·ra·phee \bī-,ä-grə-'fē *also* bē-\ *noun* (1841)
: a person about whom a biography is written
bi·og·ra·pher \-'ä-grə-fər\ *noun* (1715)
: a writer of a biography
bio·graph·i·cal \,bī-ə-'gra-fi-kəl\ *also* **bio·graph·ic** \-fik\ *adjective* (1738)
1 : of, relating to, or constituting biography
2 : consisting of biographies ⟨a *biographical* dictionary⟩
3 : relating to a list briefly identifying persons ⟨*biographical* notes⟩
— **bio·graph·i·cal·ly** \-fi-k(ə-)lē\ *adverb*
bi·og·ra·phy \bī-'ä-grə-fē *also* bē-\ *noun, plural* **-phies** [Late Greek *biographia*, from Greek *bi-* + *-graphia* -graphy] (1683)
1 : a usually written history of a person's life
2 : biographical writings as a whole
3 : an account of the life of something (as an animal, a coin, or a building)
bio·haz·ard \'bī-ō-,ha-zərd\ *noun* (1967)
: a biological agent or condition that constitutes a hazard to humans or the environment; *also* : a hazard posed by such an agent or condition
bi·o·log·ic \,bī-ə-'lä-jik\ *or* **bi·o·log·i·cal** \-ji-kəl\ *noun* (1921)
: a biological product used in medicine
biological *also* **biologic** *adjective* (1859)
1 : of or relating to biology or to life and living processes
2 : used in or produced by applied biology
3 : related by direct genetic relationship rather than by adoption or marriage ⟨*biological* parents⟩
— **bi·o·log·i·cal·ly** \-ji-k(ə-)lē\ *adverb*
biological clock *noun* (1955)
: an inherent timing mechanism that is inferred to exist in some living systems (as a cell) in order to explain various cyclical behaviors and physiological processes
biological control *noun* (1923)

: reduction in numbers or elimination of pest organisms by interference with their ecology (as by the introduction of parasites or diseases)

biological oxygen demand *noun* (1945)
: BIOCHEMICAL OXYGEN DEMAND

biological warfare *noun* (1946)
: warfare involving the use of living organisms (as disease germs) or their toxic products as weapons; *also* : warfare involving the use of herbicides

bi·ol·o·gism \bī-'ä-lə-,ji-zəm\ *noun* (1924)
: preoccupation with biological explanations in the analysis of social situations
— **bi·o·lo·gis·tic** \-,ä-lə-'jis-tik\ *adjective*

bi·ol·o·gy \bī-'ä-lə-jē\ *noun* [German *Biologie*, from *bi-* + *-logie* *-logy*] (1819)
1 : a branch of knowledge that deals with living organisms and vital processes
2 a : the plant and animal life of a region or environment **b** : the life processes especially of an organism or group; *broadly* : ECOLOGY
— **bi·o·lo·gist** \-jist\ *noun*

bio·lu·mi·nes·cence \,bī-ō-,lü-mə-'nes°n(t)s\ *noun* [International Scientific Vocabulary] (1916)
: the emission of light from living organisms; *also* : the light so produced
— **bio·lu·mi·nes·cent** \-s°nt\ *adjective*

bio·mass \'bī-ō-,mas\ *noun* (1934)
1 : the amount of living matter (as in a unit area or volume of habitat)
2 : plant materials and animal waste used especially as a source of fuel

bio·ma·te·ri·al \,bī-ō-mə-'tir-ē-əl\ *noun* (1966)
: material used for or suitable for use in prostheses that come in direct contact with living tissues

bio·math·e·mat·ics \-,ma-thə-'ma-tiks, -math-'ma-\ *noun plural but usually singular in construction* (1923)
: mathematics of special use in biology and medicine
— **bio·math·e·mat·i·cal** \-ti-kəl\ *adjective*
— **bio·math·e·ma·ti·cian** \-,math-mə-'ti-shən, -,ma-thə-\ *noun*

bi·ome \'bī-,ōm\ *noun* [²*bi-* + *-ome*] (1916)
: a major ecological community type (as tropical rain forest, grassland, or desert)

bio·me·chan·ics \'bī-ō-mə-'ka-niks\ *noun plural but singular or plural in construction* (circa 1933)
: the mechanics of biological and especially muscular activity (as in locomotion or exercise); *also* : the scientific study of this
— **bio·me·chan·i·cal** \-ni-kəl\ *adjective*
— **bio·me·chan·i·cal·ly** \-ni-k(ə-)lē\ *adverb*

bio·med·i·cal \,bī-ō-'me-di-kəl\ *adjective* (1955)
1 : of or relating to biomedicine
2 : of, relating to, or involving biological, medical, and physical science

bio·med·i·cine \-'me-də-sən, *British usually* -'med-sən\ *noun* (1947)
: medicine based on the application of the principles of the natural sciences and especially biology and biochemistry

bio·me·te·o·rol·o·gy \-,mē-tē-ə-'rä-lə-jē\ *noun* (1946)
: a science that deals with the relationship between living things and atmospheric phenomena
— **bio·me·te·o·ro·log·i·cal** \-rə-'lä-ji-kəl\ *adjective*

bi·om·e·try \bī-'ä-mə-trē\ *noun* [International Scientific Vocabulary] (1831)
: the statistical analysis of biological observations and phenomena
— **bio·met·ric** \,bī-ō-'me-trik\ *or* **bio·met·ri·cal** \-tri-kəl\ *adjective*
— **bio·me·tri·cian** \-me-'tri-shən\ *noun*
— **bio·met·rics** \-'me-triks\ *noun plural but singular or plural in construction*

bio·mol·e·cule \,bī-ō-'mä-li-,kyü(ə)l\ *noun* (1901)
: an organic molecule and especially a macromolecule in living organisms
— **bio·mo·lec·u·lar** \-mə-'le-kyə-lər\ *adjective*

bio·mor·phic \,bī-ō-'mòr-fik\ *adjective* (1895)
: resembling or suggesting the forms of living organisms ⟨*biomorphic* sculptures⟩ ⟨*biomorphic* images⟩

bi·on·ic \bī-'ä-nik\ *adjective* (1963)
1 : of or relating to bionics
2 : having normal biological capability or performance enhanced by or as if by electronic or electromechanical devices

bi·on·ics \bī-'ä-niks\ *noun plural but singular or plural in construction* [²*bi-* + *-onics* (as in *electronics*)] (1960)
: a science concerned with the application of data about the functioning of biological systems to the solution of engineering problems

bi·o·nom·ics \,bī-ə-'nä-miks\ *noun plural but singular or plural in construction* [*bionomic*, adjective, probably from French *bionomique*, from *bionomie* ecology, from *bi-* + *-nomie* *-nomy*] (1888)
: ECOLOGY
— **bi·o·nom·ic** \-mik\ *adjective*

bio·phys·ics \,bī-ō-'fi-ziks\ *noun plural but singular or plural in construction* (1892)
: a branch of science concerned with the application of physical principles and methods to biological problems
— **bio·phys·i·cal** \-zi-kəl\ *adjective*
— **bio·phys·i·cist** \-'fi-zə-sist, -'fiz-sist\ *noun*

bio·pic \'bī-(,)ō-,pik\ *noun* [²*bi-* + ¹*pic*] (1951)
: a biographical movie

bio·poly·mer \,bī-ō-'pä-lə-mər\ *noun* (1961)
: a polymeric substance (as a protein or polysaccharide) formed in a biological system

bi·op·sy \'bī-,äp-sē\ *noun, plural* **-sies** [International Scientific Vocabulary ²*bi-* + *-opsy* (as in *autopsy*)] (1895)
: the removal and examination of tissue, cells, or fluids from the living body
— **biopsy** *transitive verb*

bio·re·ac·tor \,bī-ō-rē-'ak-tər\ *noun* (1974)
: a device or apparatus in which living organisms and especially bacteria synthesize useful substances (as interferon) or break down harmful ones (as in sewage)

bio·rhythm \'bī-ō-,ri-thəm\ *noun* (1960)
: an inherent rhythm that appears to control or initiate various biological processes
— **bio·rhyth·mic** \-'rith-mik\ *adjective*

bio·safe·ty \,bī-ō-'sāf-tē\ *noun* (1977)
: safety with respect to the effects of biological research on humans and the environment

bio·sci·ence \-'sī-ən(t)s\ *noun* (1941)
: BIOLOGY 1; *also* : LIFE SCIENCE
— **bio·sci·en·tif·ic** \-,sī-ən-'ti-fik\ *adjective*
— **bio·sci·en·tist** \-'sī-ən-tist\ *noun*

bio·sen·sor \-'sen-,sòr, -'sen(t)-sər\ *noun* (1962)
: a device that is sensitive to a physical or chemical stimulus (as heat or an ion) and transmits information about a life process

-bi·o·sis *noun combining form, plural* **-bi·o·ses** [New Latin, from Greek *biōsis*, from *bioun* to live, from *bios* life — more at QUICK]
: mode of life ⟨para*biosis*⟩

bio·so·cial \,bī-ō-'sō-shəl\ *adjective* (1897)
: of, relating to, or concerned with the interaction of the biological aspects and social relationships of living organisms ⟨*biosocial* science⟩
— **bio·so·cial·ly** \-'sōsh-lē, -'sō-shə-\ *adverb*

bio·sphere \'bī-ə-,sfir\ *noun* (1899)
1 : the part of the world in which life can exist
2 : living beings together with their environment
— **bio·spher·ic** \,bī-ə-'sfir-ik, -'sfer-\ *adjective*

bio·sta·tis·tics \,bī-ō-stə-'tis-tiks\ *noun plural but singular in construction* (1950)
: statistics applied to the analysis of biological data
— **bio·sta·tis·ti·cal** \-ti-kəl\ *adjective*
— **bio·stat·is·ti·cian** \-,sta-tə-'sti-shən\ *noun*

bio·strati·graph·ic \-,stra-tə-'gra-fik\ *adjective* (1947)
: of or relating to the branch of paleontology dealing with the conditions and order of deposition of sedimentary rocks
— **bio·stra·tig·ra·phy** \-strə-'ti-grə-fē\ *noun*

bio·syn·the·sis \-'sin(t)-thə-səs\ *noun* [New Latin] (1930)
: the production of a chemical compound by a living organism
— **bio·syn·thet·ic** \-sin-'the-tik\ *adjective*
— **bio·syn·thet·i·cal·ly** \-ti-k(ə-)lē\ *adverb*

bio·sys·te·mat·ics \-,sis-tə-'ma-tiks\ *noun plural but singular or plural in construction* (1945)
: experimental taxonomy especially as based on cytogenetics and genetics
— **bio·sys·te·mat·ic** \-tik\ *adjective*
— **bio·sys·tem·atist** \-'sis-tə-mə-tist, -sis-'te-mə-\ *noun*

bi·o·ta \bī-'ō-tə\ *noun* [New Latin, from Greek *biotē* life; akin to Greek *bios*] (1901)
: the flora and fauna of a region

bio·tech \'bī-ō-,tek\ *noun* (1974)
: BIOTECHNOLOGY 1

bio·tech·ni·cal \,bī-ō-'tek-ni-kəl\ *adjective* (1938)
: of or relating to biotechnology

bio·tech·nol·o·gy \,bī-ō-tek-'nä-lə-jē\ *noun* (1941)
1 : applied biological science (as bioengineering or recombinant DNA technology)
2 : ERGONOMICS
— **bio·tech·no·log·i·cal** \-,tek-nə-'läj-i-kəl\ *adjective*
— **bio·tech·nol·o·gist** \-'nä-lə-jist\ *noun*

bio·te·lem·e·try \-tə-'le-mə-trē\ *noun* (1963)
: the remote detection and measurement of a human or animal function, activity, or condition
— **bio·tel·e·met·ric** \-,te-lə-'me-trik\ *adjective*

bi·ot·ic \bī-'ä-tik\ *adjective* [Greek *biōtikos*, from *bioun*] (1868)
: of or relating to life; *especially* : caused or produced by living beings ⟨*biotic* diversity⟩

-bi·ot·ic *adjective combining form* [probably from New Latin *-bioticus*, from Greek *biōtikos*]
: having a (specified) mode of life ⟨endo*biotic*⟩

biotic potential *noun* (1935)
: the inherent capacity of an organism or species to reproduce and survive

bi·o·tin \'bī-ə-tən\ *noun* [International Scientific Vocabulary, from Greek *biotos* life, sustenance; akin to Greek *bios*] (1936)
: a colorless crystalline growth vitamin $C_{10}H_{16}N_2O_3S$ of the vitamin B complex found especially in yeast, liver, and egg yolk

bi·o·tite \'bī-ə-,tīt\ *noun* [German *Biotit*, from Jean B. *Biot* (died 1862) French mathematician] (1862)
: a generally black or dark green form of mica that is a constituent of crystalline rocks and consists of a silicate of iron, magnesium, potassium, and aluminum
— **bi·o·tit·ic** \,bī-ə-'ti-tik\ *adjective*

bio·tope \'bī-ə-,tōp\ *noun* [²*bi-* + Greek *topos* place] (1927)

\ə\ abut \ᵊ\ kitten \ər\ further \a\ ash \ā\ ace
\ä\ mop, mar \aù\ out \ch\ chin \e\ bet \ē\ easy
\g\ go \i\ hit \ī\ ice \j\ job \ŋ\ sing \ō\ go
\ò\ law \òi\ boy \th\ thin \t͟h\ the \ü\ loot \ù\ foot
\y\ yet \zh\ vision *see also* Guide to Pronunciation

: a region uniform in environmental conditions and in its populations of animals and plants for which it is the habitat

bio·trans·for·ma·tion \'bī-ō-,tran(t)s-fər-'mā-shən, -,fȯr-\ *noun* (1955)
: the transformation of chemical compounds within a living system

bio·type \-,tīp\ *noun* [International Scientific Vocabulary] (1906)
: the organisms sharing a specified genotype; *also* : the genotype shared or its distinguishing peculiarity
— **bio·typ·ic** \,bī-ə-'ti-pik\ *adjective*

bi·pa·ren·tal \,bī-pə-'ren-t°l\ *adjective* (1900)
: of, relating to, involving, or derived from two parents
— **bi·pa·ren·tal·ly** \-t°l-ē\ *adverb*

bi·par·ti·san \(,)bī-'pär-tə-zən, -,san, -,zan, *chiefly British* ,bī-,pär-tə-'zan\ *adjective* (circa 1909)
: of, relating to, or involving members of two parties ⟨a *bipartisan* commission⟩
— **bi·par·ti·san·ism** \-zə-,ni-zəm, -sə-\ *noun*
— **bi·par·ti·san·ship** \-zən-,ship, -sən-\ *noun*

bi·par·tite \(,)bī-'pär-,tīt\ *adjective* [Latin *bipartitus*, past participle of *bipartire* to divide in two, from *bi-* + *partire* to divide, from *part-, pars* part] (1574)
1 a : being in two parts **b** : having a correspondent part for each of two parties ⟨a *bipartite* contract⟩ **c** : shared by two ⟨a *bipartite* treaty⟩
2 : divided into two parts almost to the base ⟨a *bipartite* leaf⟩
— **bi·par·tite·ly** *adverb*
— **bi·par·ti·tion** \,bī-(,)pär-'ti-shən\ *noun*

bi·ped \'bī-,ped\ *noun* [Latin *biped-, bipes*, from *bi-* + *ped-, pes* foot — more at FOOT] (1646)
: a two-footed animal
— **bi·ped·al** \(,)bī-'pe-d°l\ *adjective*
— **bi·ped·al·ly** \-ē\ *adverb*

bi·ped·al·ism \(,)bī-'pe-d°l-,i-zəm\ *noun* (1907)
: the condition of having two feet or of using only two feet for locomotion

bi·pe·dal·i·ty \,bī-pə-'da-lə-tē\ *noun* (1847)
: BIPEDALISM

bi·phas·ic \(,)bī-'fā-zik\ *adjective* (circa 1909)
: having two phases ⟨a *biphasic* immune response⟩

bi·phe·nyl \(,)bī-'fe-n°l, -'fē-\ *noun* [International Scientific Vocabulary] (circa 1923)
: a white crystalline hydrocarbon $C_6H_5 \cdot C_6H_5$ used especially as a heat-transfer medium

bi·pin·nate \-'pi-,nāt\ *adjective* (1794)
: twice pinnate
— **bi·pin·nate·ly** *adverb*

bi·plane \'bī-,plān\ *noun* (1874)
: an aircraft with two main supporting surfaces usually placed one above the other

bi·pod \'bī-,päd\ *noun* [*bi-* + *-pod* (as in *tripod*)] (1922)
: a two-legged support

bi·po·lar \(,)bī-'pō-lər\ *adjective* (1810)
1 : having or marked by two mutually repellent forces or diametrically opposed natures or views
2 a : having or involving the use of two poles or polarities **b** : relating to, being, or using a transistor in which both electrons and holes are utilized as charge carriers
3 : relating to, associated with, or occurring in both polar regions ⟨*bipolar* species of birds⟩
4 : characterized by the alternation of manic and depressive states ⟨a *bipolar* affective disorder⟩
— **bi·po·lar·i·ty** \,bī-pō-'lar-ə-tē\ *noun*
— **bi·po·lar·iza·tion** \(,)bī-,pō-lə-rə-'zā-shən\ *noun*
— **bi·po·lar·ize** \(,)bī-'pō-lə-,rīz\ *transitive verb*

bi·pro·pel·lant \,bī-prə-'pe-lənt\ *noun* (1947)

: a rocket propellant consisting of separate fuel and oxidizer that come together only in a combustion chamber

bi·pyr·a·mid \(,)bī-'pir-ə-mid\ *noun* (1897)
: a crystal consisting of two identical pyramids base to base
— **bi·py·ra·mi·dal** \-pə-'ra-mə-d°l\ *adjective*

bi·qua·drat·ic \,bī-kwä-'dra-tik\ *adjective or noun* (1668)
: QUARTIC

bi·ra·cial \(,)bī-'rā-shəl\ *adjective* (1922)
: of, relating to, or involving members of two races
— **bi·ra·cial·ism** \-shə-,li-zəm\ *noun*

bi·ra·di·al \(,)bī-'rā-dē-əl\ *adjective* (circa 1909)
: having both bilateral and radial symmetry

bi·ra·mous \(,)bī-'rā-məs\ *adjective* (1877)
: having two branches

¹birch \'bərch\ *noun* [Middle English, from Old English *beorc*; akin to Old High German *birka* birch, Old English *beorht* bright, and probably to Latin *fraxinus* ash tree — more at BRIGHT] (before 12th century)
1 : any of a genus (*Betula* of the family Betulaceae, the birch family) of monoecious deciduous usually short-lived trees or shrubs having simple petioled leaves and typically a layered membranous outer bark that peels readily
2 : the hard pale close-grained wood of a birch
3 : a birch rod or bundle of twigs for flogging
— **birch** *or* **birch·en** \'bər-chən\ *adjective*

²birch *transitive verb* (1830)
: to beat with or as if with a birch : WHIP

Birch·er \'bər-chər\ *noun* (1961)
: a member or adherent of the John Birch Society
— **Birch·ism** \'bər-,chi-zəm\ *noun*
— **Birch·ist** \-chist\ *or* **Birch·ite** \-,chīt\ *noun or adjective*

¹bird \'bərd\ *noun, often attributive* [Middle English, from Old English *bridd*] (before 12th century)
1 *archaic* : the young of a feathered vertebrate
2 : any of a class (Aves) of warm-blooded vertebrates distinguished by having the body more or less completely covered with feathers and the forelimbs modified as wings
3 : a game bird
4 : CLAY PIGEON
5 a : FELLOW **b** : a peculiar person **c** *chiefly British* : GIRL
6 : SHUTTLECOCK
7 *chiefly British* **a** : a hissing or jeering expressive of disapproval **b** : dismissal from employment
8 : a thin piece of meat rolled up with stuffing and cooked
9 : something (as an aircraft, rocket, or satellite) resembling a bird especially by flying or being aloft

10 : an obscene gesture of contempt made by pointing the middle finger upward while keeping the other fingers down — usually used with *the* — called also *finger*
— **bird·like** \-,līk\ *adjective*
— **for the birds** : WORTHLESS, RIDICULOUS

²bird *intransitive verb* (1918)
: to observe or identify wild birds in their natural environment

bird·bath \'bərd-,bath, -,båth\ *noun* (1895)
: a usually ornamental basin set up for birds to bathe in

bird·brain \-,brān\ *noun* (1943)
1 : a stupid person
2 : SCATTERBRAIN
— **bird·brained** \-,brānd\ *adjective*

bird·cage \-,kāj\ *noun* (15th century)
: a cage for confining birds

bird·call \-,kȯl\ *noun* (circa 1625)
1 : a device for imitating the cry of a bird
2 : the note or cry of a bird; *also* : a sound imitative of it

bird colonel *noun* [from the eagle serving as insignia for this rank] (circa 1947)
slang : COLONEL 1a

bird–dog \'bərd-,dȯg\ (1943)
intransitive verb
: to watch closely
transitive verb
: to seek out : FOLLOW, DETECT

bird dog *noun* (circa 1888)
1 : a gundog trained to hunt or retrieve birds
2 a : one (as a canvasser or talent scout) who seeks out something for another **b** : one who steals another's date

bird–dog·ging \-,dȯ-giŋ\ *noun* (circa 1941)
1 : the stealing of another's date (as at a party)
2 : the action of one that bird-dogs

bird·er \'bər-dər\ *noun* (15th century)
1 : a catcher or hunter of birds especially for market
2 : a person who birds

bird·house \'bərd-,haŭs\ *noun* (1870)
: an artificial nesting site for birds; *also* : AVIARY

¹bird·ie \'bər-dē\ *noun* (1792)
1 : a little bird
2 : a golf score of one stroke less than par on a hole — compare EAGLE

²birdie *transitive verb* **bird·ied; bird·ie·ing** (1948)
: to score a birdie on

bird·lime \'bərd-,līm\ *noun* (15th century)
1 : a sticky substance usually made from the bark of a holly (*Ilex aquifolium*) that is smeared on twigs to snare small birds
2 : something that ensnares
— **birdlime** *transitive verb*

bird louse *noun* (1826)
: BITING LOUSE

bird·man \'bərd-mən, *especially for 1 also* -,man\ *noun* (1697)
1 : a person who deals with birds
2 : a person who flies (as in an aircraft)

bird–of–paradise *noun* (circa 1894)
: an ornamental plant (*Strelitzia reginae* of the family Strelitziaceae) having scapes of orange or yellow and purple flowers with three sepals and three very irregular petals

bird of paradise (1638)
: any of numerous brilliantly colored plumed oscine birds (family Paradiseidae) of the New Guinea area

bird of passage (1728)
1 : a migratory bird
2 : a person who leads a wandering or unsettled life

bird of prey (14th century)
: a carnivorous bird (as a hawk, falcon, or vulture) that feeds wholly or chiefly on meat taken by hunting or on carrion

bird pepper *noun* (1696)
: a capsicum (*Capsicum annuum glabriusculum*) having very small oblong extremely pungent red fruits

bird·seed \'bərd-,sēd\ *noun* (1840)

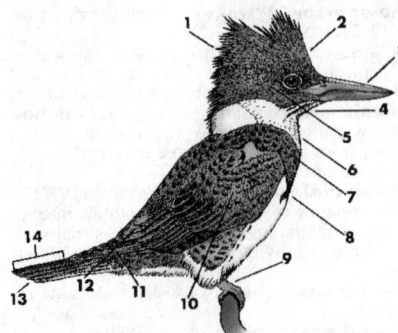

bird 2 (kingfisher): *1* crest, *2* crown, *3* bill, *4* throat, *5* auricular region, *6* breast, *7* scapulars, *8* abdomen, *9* tarsus, *10* upper wing coverts, *11* primaries, *12* secondaries, *13* rectrix, *14* tail

: a mixture of seeds (as of hemp, millet, and sunflowers) used for feeding caged and wild birds

¹bird's-eye \'bərd-ˌzī\ *noun* (1597)
1 : any of numerous plants with small bright-colored flowers; *especially* : a speedwell (*Veronica chamaedrys*)
2 a : an allover pattern for textiles consisting of a small diamond with a center dot **b** : a fabric woven with this pattern
3 : a small spot in wood surrounded with an ellipse of concentric fibers

²bird's-eye *adjective* (1665)
1 : marked with spots resembling birds' eyes
2 : having or involving a bird's-eye view ⟨*bird's-eye* perspective⟩ ⟨a *bird's-eye* survey of the topic⟩

bird's-eye view *noun* (1762)
1 : a view from a high angle as if seen by a bird in flight
2 : an overall or cursory look at something

bird's-foot trefoil \'bərdz-ˌfu̇t-\ *noun* (1833)
: a European legume (*Lotus corniculatus*) having claw-shaped pods and widely used especially in the U.S. as a forage and fodder plant or often planted along roadsides

bird's-foot violet *noun* (1839)
: a common violet (*Viola pedata*) of the eastern U.S. with deeply cleft leaves and pale blue to purple flattened flowers

bird's-nest fern \'bərdz-ˌnest-\ *noun* (1858)
: a large epiphytic spleenwort (*Asplenium nidus*) of tropical Asia and Polynesia that has large lance-shaped leaves and is often grown as a houseplant

bird's nest soup *noun* (1871)
: a soup made with the nests of small cave-nesting swifts (genus *Collocalia*) that build them using a glutinous secretion from their salivary glands

bird-song \'bərd-ˌsȯŋ\ *noun* (1896)
: the song of a bird

bird-watch \'bərd-ˌwäch\ *intransitive verb* [back-formation from *bird-watcher*] (1948)
: BIRD
— **bird-watch-er** \-ˌwä-chər\ *noun* (1905)
: BIRDER 2

bi-re-frin-gence \ˌbī-ri-ˈfrin-jən(t)s\ *noun* [International Scientific Vocabulary] (1898)
: the refraction of light in an anisotropic material (as calcite) in two slightly different directions to form two rays
— **bi-re-frin-gent** \-jənt\ *adjective*

bi-reme \'bī-ˌrēm\ *noun* [Latin *biremis*, from *bi-* + *remus* oar — more at ROW] (1662)
: a galley with two banks of oars used especially by the ancient Greeks and Phoenicians

bi-ret-ta \bə-ˈre-tə\ *noun* [Italian *berretta*, from Old Provençal *berret* cap, from Medieval Latin *birretum*, from Late Latin *birrus* cloak with a hood, perhaps of Celtic origin; akin to Middle Irish *berr* short] (1598)
: a square cap with three ridges on top worn by clergymen especially of the Roman Catholic Church

birk \'birk\ *noun* [Middle English *birch*, *birk*] (14th century)
chiefly Scottish : BIRCH

birk-ie \'bir-kē, 'bər-\ *noun* [origin unknown] (1724)
1 *Scottish* : a lively smart assertive person
2 *Scottish* : FELLOW, BOY

biretta

¹birl \'bər(-ə)l, *Scottish also* 'bir(-ə)l\ *intransitive verb* [Middle English from Old English *byrelian*; probably akin to Old English *beran* to carry — more at BEAR] (circa 1585)
chiefly Scottish : CAROUSE

²birl *verb* [perhaps imitative] (1790)
transitive verb
1 : SPIN

2 : to cause (a floating log) to rotate by treading
intransitive verb
: to progress by whirling
— **birl-er** \'bər-lər, 'bir-\ *noun*

Bi-ro \'bī-(ˌ)rō\ *trademark*
— used for a ballpoint pen

birr \'bər, 'bir\ *noun, plural* **birr** [Arabic] (circa 1978)
— see MONEY table

birse \'birs, 'bərs\ *noun* [(assumed) Middle English *birst*, from Old English *byrst* — more at BRISTLE] (before 12th century)
1 *chiefly Scottish* : a bristle or tuft of bristles
2 *chiefly Scottish* : ANGER

¹birth \'bərth\ *noun, often attributive* [Middle English, from Old Norse *byrth*; akin to Old English *beran*] (13th century)
1 a : the emergence of a new individual from the body of its parent **b** : the act or process of bringing forth young from the womb
2 : a state resulting from being born especially at a particular time or place ⟨a Southerner by *birth*⟩
3 a : LINEAGE, EXTRACTION ⟨marriage between equals in *birth*⟩ **b** : high or noble birth
4 a *archaic* : one that is born **b** : BEGINNING, START ⟨the *birth* of an idea⟩

²birth (1906)
transitive verb
1 *chiefly dialect* : to bring forth
2 : to give rise to : ORIGINATE
intransitive verb
: to bring forth a child or young

birth canal *noun* (1927)
: the channel formed by the cervix, vagina, and vulva through which the fetus passes during birth

birth certificate *noun* (1900)
: a copy of an official record of a person's date and place of birth and parentage

birth control *noun* (1914)
: control of the number of children born especially by preventing or lessening the frequency of conception : CONTRACEPTION

birth-day \'bərth-ˌdā\ *noun* (14th century)
1 a : the day of a person's birth **b** : a day of origin
2 : an anniversary of a birth ⟨her 21st *birthday*⟩

birthday suit *noun* (1753)
: unclothed skin : NAKEDNESS

birth defect *noun* (1971)
: a physical or biochemical defect that is present at birth and may be inherited or environmentally induced

birth-mark \'bərth-ˌmärk\ *noun* (1580)
: an unusual mark or blemish on the skin at birth : NEVUS

birth pang *noun* (circa 1887)
1 : one of the regularly recurrent pains that are characteristic of childbirth — usually used in plural
2 *plural* : disorder and distress incident especially to a major social change

birth-place \'bərth-ˌplās\ *noun* (1607)
: place of birth or origin

birth-rate \'bərth-ˌrāt\ *noun* (1859)
: the ratio between births and individuals in a specified population and time

birth-right \'bərth-ˌrīt\ *noun* (1535)
: a right, privilege, or possession to which a person is entitled by birth

birth-root \'bərth-ˌrüt, -ˌru̇t\ *noun* (1822)
: any of several trilliums with astringent roots used in folk medicine

birth-stone \'bərth-ˌstōn\ *noun* (1907)
: a gemstone associated symbolically with the month of one's birth

birth-wort \-ˌwərt, -ˌwȯrt\ *noun* (1551)
: any of several herbs or woody vines (genus *Aristolochia*) of the family Aristolochiaceae, the birthwort family) with aromatic roots used in folk medicine to aid childbirth

bis \'bis\ *adverb* [Latin, from Old Latin *dvis*; akin to Old High German *zwiro* twice, Latin *duo* two — more at TWO] (1819)
1 : AGAIN — used in music as a direction to repeat
2 : TWICE

Bi-sa-yan \bə-ˈsī-ən\ *noun* [Bisayan *Bisayâ*] (1951)
1 : a member of any of several peoples in the Visayan islands, Philippines
2 : the group of Austronesian languages of the Bisayans

bis-cuit \'bis-kət\ *noun, plural* **biscuits** *also* **biscuit** [Middle English *bisquite*, from Middle French *bescuit*, from (*pain*) *bescuit* twice-cooked bread] (14th century)
1 a : any of various hard or crisp dry baked products: as (1) *British* : CRACKER 4 (2) *British* : COOKIE **b** : a small quick bread made from dough that has been rolled out and cut or dropped from a spoon
2 : earthenware or porcelain after the first firing and before glazing
3 a : a light grayish yellowish brown **b** : a grayish yellow ◊

bi-sect \'bī-ˌsekt, bī-'\ *verb* [¹*bi-* + inter*sect*] (circa 1645)
transitive verb
: to divide into two usually equal parts
intransitive verb
: CROSS, INTERSECT
— **bi-sec-tion** \'bī-ˌsek-shən, bī-'\ *noun*
— **bi-sec-tion-al** \-shnəl, -shə-n°l\ *adjective*
— **bi-sec-tion-al-ly** *adverb*

bi-sec-tor \'bī-ˌsek-tər, bī-'\ *noun* (1864)
: one that bisects; *especially* : a straight line that bisects an angle or a line segment

bi-sex-u-al \(ˌ)bī-'sek-sh(ə-)wəl, -shəl\ *adjective* (1824)
1 a : possessing characters of both sexes : HERMAPHRODITIC **b** : sexually oriented toward both sexes
2 : of, relating to, or involving both sexes
— **bisexual** *noun*
— **bi-sex-u-al-i-ty** \ˌbī-ˌsek-shə-'wa-lə-tē\ *noun*
— **bi-sex-u-al-ly** \(ˌ)bī-'sek-sh(ə-)wə-lē, -sh(ə-)lē\ *adverb*

bish-op \'bi-shəp\ *noun* [Middle English *bisshop*, from Old English *bisceop*, from Late Latin *episcopus*, from Greek *episkopos*, literally, overseer, from *epi-* + *skeptesthai* to look — more at SPY] (before 12th century)
1 : one having spiritual or ecclesiastical supervision: as **a** : an Anglican, Eastern Orthodox, or Roman Catholic clergyman ranking above a

◊ WORD HISTORY
biscuit In earlier ages the preservation of food presented a greater problem than it does today, especially on long journeys. One approach was to preserve flat cakes of bread by baking them a second time in order to dry them out. In medieval French the result of this process was called *pain bescuit*, literally "twice-cooked bread." In the 14th century, the second element of this phrase was borrowed into English. The notion of cooking twice having been lost, *biscuit* came to be used to designate various hard or crisp, dry baked products. (This is the sense that now prevails in England, while Americans would say *cookie* or *cracker*.) Similarities in shape and size led to the use of *biscuit* as the name for a small quick bread made from dough that has been rolled out and cut, or dropped from a spoon.

\ə\ abut \ᵊ\ kitten \ər\ further \a\ ash \ā\ ace
\ä\ mop, mar \au̇\ out \ch\ chin \e\ bet \ē\ easy
\g\ go \i\ hit \ī\ ice \j\ job \ŋ\ sing \ō\ go
\ȯ\ law \ȯi\ boy \th\ thin \th̲\ the \ü\ loot \u̇\ foot
\y\ yet \zh\ vision *see also* Guide to Pronunciation

priest, having authority to ordain and confirm, and typically governing a diocese **b** : any of various Protestant clerical officials who superintend other clergy **c** : a Mormon high priest presiding over a ward or over all other bishops and over the Aaronic priesthood
2 : either of two pieces of each color in a set of chessmen having the power to move diagonally across any number of adjoining unoccupied squares
3 : mulled port wine flavored with roasted oranges and cloves

bish·op·ric \'bi-shə-(,)prik\ noun [Middle English bisshopriche, from Old English bisceoprīce, from bisceop + rīce kingdom — more at RICH] (before 12th century)
1 : DIOCESE
2 : the office of bishop
3 : the administrative body of a Mormon ward consisting of a bishop and two high priests as counselors

Bishops' Bible noun (1835)
: an officially commissioned English translation of the Bible published in 1568

bis·muth \'biz-məth\ noun [New Latin bismuthum, modification of German Wismut] (1668)
: a heavy brittle grayish white chiefly trivalent metallic element that is chemically like arsenic and antimony and that is used in alloys and pharmaceuticals — see ELEMENT table
— **bis·mu·thic** \biz-'mə-thik, -'myü-\ adjective

bi·son \'bī-sᵊn, -zᵊn\ noun, plural **bison** [Latin bisont-, bison, of Germanic origin; akin to Old High German wisant aurochs; akin to Old Prussian wissambrs aurochs] (1611)
: any of several large shaggy-maned usually gregarious recent or extinct bovine mammals (genus Bison) having a large head with short horns and heavy forequarters surmounted by a large fleshy hump: as **a** : WISENT **b** : BUFFALO 1c(1)
— **bi·son·tine** \-sᵊn-,tīn, -zᵊn-\ adjective

¹**bisque** \'bisk\ noun [French] (1647)
1 a : a thick cream soup made with shellfish or game **b** : a cream soup of pureed vegetables
2 : ice cream containing powdered nuts or macaroons

²**bisque** noun [French] (circa 1656)
: odds allowed an inferior player: as **a** : a point taken when desired in a set of tennis **b** : an extra turn in croquet **c** : one or more strokes off a golf score

³**bisque** noun [by shortening & alteration] (1664)
: BISCUIT 2; especially : unglazed china that is not to be glazed but is hard-fired and vitreous

bi·state \'bī-,stāt\ adjective (1928)
: of or relating to two states

bis·ter or **bis·tre** \'bis-tər\ noun [French bistre] (circa 1751)
1 : a yellowish brown to dark brown pigment used in art
2 : a grayish to yellowish brown
— **bis·tered** \-tərd\ adjective

bis·tort \'bis-,tȯrt, bis-\ noun [Middle French bistorte, from (assumed) Medieval Latin bistorta, from Latin bis + torta, feminine of tortus, past participle of torquēre to twist — more at TORTURE] (1578)
: any of several polygonums; especially : a European herb (Polygonum bistorta) or a related American plant (P. bistortoides) with twisted roots used as astringents

bis·tro \'bēs-(,)trō, 'bis-\ noun, plural **bistros** [French] (1921)
1 : a small or unpretentious restaurant
2 a : a small bar or tavern **b** : NIGHTCLUB
— **bis·tro·ic** \bēs-'trō-ik, bis-\ adjective

bi·sul·fate \(,)bī-'səl-,fāt\ noun (circa 1846)
: an acid sulfate

bi·sul·fide \-,fīd\ noun [International Scientific Vocabulary] (1863)
: DISULFIDE

bi·sul·fite \-,fīt\ noun [French, from bi- + sulfite] (circa 1846)
: an acid sulfite

bi–swing \'bī-'swiŋ\ adjective [¹bi- + swing; perhaps from the freedom of movement allowed by this jacket] (1968)
: made with a pleat or gusset at the back of the arms ⟨bi-swing jacket⟩

¹**bit** \'bit\ noun [Middle English bitt, from Old English bite act of biting; akin to Old English bītan] (14th century)
1 a (1) : the biting or cutting edge or part of a tool (2) : a replaceable part of a compound tool that actually performs the function (as drilling or boring) for which the whole tool is designed **b** plural : the jaws of tongs or pincers
2 : something bitten or held with the teeth: **a** : the usually steel part of a bridle inserted in the mouth of a horse **b** : the rimmed mouth end on the stem of a pipe or cigar holder
3 : something that curbs or restrains
4 : the part of a key that enters the lock and acts on the bolt and tumblers

²**bit** transitive verb **bit·ted; bit·ting** (1583)
1 a : to put a bit in the mouth of (a horse) **b** : to control as if with a bit
2 : to form a bit on (a key)

³**bit** noun [Middle English, from Old English bita; akin to Old English bītan] (before 12th century)
1 : a small quantity of food; especially : a small delicacy
2 a : a small piece or quantity of some material thing **b** (1) : a small coin (2) : a unit of value equal to ⅛ of a dollar ⟨four bits⟩
3 : something small or unimportant of its kind: as **a** : a brief period : WHILE **b** : an indefinite usually small degree, extent, or amount ⟨a bit of a rascal⟩ ⟨every bit as powerful⟩ **c** (1) : a small part usually with spoken lines in a theatrical performance (2) : a usually short theatrical routine ⟨a corny comedy bit⟩
4 : the aggregate of items, situations, or activities appropriate to a given style, genre, or role ⟨rejected the whole bit about love-marriage-motherhood —Vance Packard⟩
— **a bit** : SOMEWHAT, RATHER ⟨the play was a bit dull⟩
— **a bit much** : a little more than one wants to endure
— **bit by bit** : by degrees : LITTLE BY LITTLE

⁴**bit** noun [binary digit] (1948)
1 : a unit of computer information equivalent to the result of a choice between two alternatives (as yes or no, on or off)
2 : the physical representation of a bit by an electrical pulse, a magnetized spot, or a hole whose presence or absence indicates data

bi·tar·trate \(,)bī-'tär-,trāt\ noun [International Scientific Vocabulary] (1879)
: an acid tartrate

¹**bitch** \'bich\ noun [Middle English bicche, from Old English bicce] (before 12th century)
1 : the female of the dog or some other carnivorous mammals
2 a : a lewd or immoral woman **b** : a malicious, spiteful, or domineering woman — sometimes used as a generalized term of abuse
3 : something that is highly objectionable or unpleasant
4 : COMPLAINT

²**bitch** (1823)
transitive verb
1 : SPOIL, BOTCH ⟨I must have bitched up my life —Mavis Gallant⟩
2 : CHEAT, DOUBLECROSS
3 : to complain of or about
intransitive verb
: COMPLAIN

bitch·ery \'bi-chə-rē\ noun, plural **-er·ies** (1936)
: malicious, spiteful, or domineering behavior; also : an instance of such behavior

bitch goddess noun (1906)

: SUCCESS; especially : material or worldly success

bitchy \'bi-chē\ adjective **bitch·i·er; -est** (1937)
: characterized by malicious, spiteful, or arrogant behavior
— **bitch·i·ly** \'bi-chə-lē\ adverb
— **bitch·i·ness** \'bi-chē-nəs\ noun

¹**bite** \'bīt\ verb **bit** \'bit\; **bit·ten** \'bi-tᵊn\ also **bit; bit·ing** \'bī-tiŋ\ [Middle English, from Old English bītan; akin to Old High German bīzan to bite, Latin findere to split] (before 12th century)
transitive verb
1 a : to seize especially with teeth or jaws so as to enter, grip, or wound **b** : to wound, pierce, or sting especially with a fang or a proboscis
2 : to cut or pierce with or as if with an edged weapon
3 : to cause sharp pain or stinging discomfort to
4 : to take hold of
5 archaic : to take in : CHEAT
intransitive verb
1 : to bite or have the habit of biting something
2 of a weapon or tool : to cut, pierce, or take hold
3 : to cause irritation or smarting
4 : CORRODE
5 a of fish : to take a bait **b** : to respond so as to be caught (as by a trick)
6 : to take or maintain a firm hold
— **bit·er** \'bī-tər\ noun
— **bite off more than one can chew** : to undertake more than one can perform
— **bite the bullet** : to enter with resignation upon a difficult or distressing course of action
— **bite the dust 1** : to fall dead especially in battle **2** : to suffer humiliation or defeat
— **bite the hand that feeds one** : to injure a benefactor maliciously

²**bite** noun (15th century)
1 : the act or manner of biting
2 : FOOD: as **a** : the amount of food taken at a bite : MORSEL **b** : a small amount of food : SNACK
3 archaic **a** : CHEAT, TRICK **b** : SHARPER
4 : a wound made by biting
5 : the hold or grip by which friction is created or purchase is obtained
6 : a surface that creates friction or is brought into contact with another for the purpose of obtaining a hold
7 a : a keen incisive quality **b** : a sharp penetrating effect
8 : a single exposure of an etcher's plate to the corrosive action of acid
9 : an amount taken usually in one operation for one purpose : CUT

bite·wing \'bīt-,wiŋ\ noun (1938)
: a dental X-ray film designed to show the crowns of the upper and lower teeth simultaneously

bit·ing \'bī-tiŋ\ adjective (14th century)
: having the power to bite ⟨a biting wind⟩; especially : able to grip and impress deeply ⟨the report is biting in its intolerance of deceit⟩
— **bit·ing·ly** \-tiŋ-lē\ adverb

biting louse noun (1896)
: any of numerous wingless insects (order Mallophaga) that are parasitic especially on birds — called also bird louse

biting midge noun (1945)
: any of a family (Ceratopogonidae) of tiny biting dipteran flies of which some are vectors of filarial worms

bit·stock \'bit-,stäk\ noun (circa 1887)
: BRACE 3

bit·sy \'bit-sē\ adjective [itsy-bitsy] (1905)
: TINY

¹**bitt** \'bit\ noun [perhaps from Old Norse biti beam; akin to Old English bāt boat] (14th century)

1 : a post or pair of posts fixed on the deck of a ship for securing lines
2 : BOLLARD 1
²bitt *transitive verb* (1769)
: to make (a cable) fast about a bitt
¹bit·ter \'bi-tər\ *adjective* [Middle English, from Old English *biter;* akin to Old High German *bittar* bitter, Old English *bītan*] (before 12th century)
1 a : being or inducing the one of the four basic taste sensations that is peculiarly acrid, astringent, or disagreeable and suggestive of an infusion of hops — compare SALT. SOUR. SWEET **b** : distasteful or distressing to the mind : GALLING ⟨a *bitter* sense of shame⟩
2 : marked by intensity or severity: **a** : accompanied by severe pain or suffering ⟨a *bitter* death⟩ **b** : being relentlessly determined : VEHEMENT ⟨a *bitter* partisan⟩ **c** : exhibiting intense animosity ⟨*bitter* enemies⟩ **d** (1) : harshly reproachful ⟨*bitter* complaints⟩ (2) : marked by cynicism and rancor ⟨*bitter* contempt⟩ **e** : intensely unpleasant especially in coldness or rawness
3 : expressive of severe pain, grief, or regret ⟨*bitter* tears⟩
— **bit·ter·ish** \'bi-tə-rish\ *adjective*
— **bit·ter·ly** *adverb*
— **bit·ter·ness** *noun*
²bitter *noun* (before 12th century)
1 : bitter quality
2 a *plural* : a usually alcoholic solution of bitter and often aromatic plant products used especially in preparing mixed drinks or as a mild tonic **b** *British* : a very dry heavily hopped ale
³bitter *transitive verb* (12th century)
: to make bitter ⟨*bittered* ale⟩
⁴bitter *adverb* (1749)
: to a bitter degree ⟨it's *bitter* cold⟩
bitter almond *noun* (1632)
: an almond with a bitter taste that contains amygdalin; *also* : a tree (*Prunus dulcis amara*) producing bitter almonds
bit·ter·brush \'bi-tər-ˌbrəsh\ *noun* (1910)
: a much-branched silvery shrub (*Purshia tridentata*) of arid western North America that has 3-toothed leaves and yellow flowers and is valuable for forage
bitter cress *noun* (circa 1890)
: any of a genus (*Cardamine*) of cruciferous herbs that produce flat pods and wingless seeds
¹bitter end *noun* [probably from ²*bitter end*] (1849)
: the last extremity however painful or calamitous
— **bit·ter·end·er** \ˌbi-tər-'en-dər\ *noun*
²bitter end *noun* [*bitter* (a turn of cable around the bitts)] (circa 1862)
: the inboard end of a ship's anchoring cable
¹bit·tern \'bi-tərn\ *noun* [Middle English *bitoure,* from Middle French *butor,* from (assumed) Vulgar Latin *butitaurus,* from Latin *buteo* hawk + *taurus* bull] (1515)
: any of various small or medium-sized usually secretive herons (especially genera *Botaurus* and *Ixobrychus*)
²bittern *noun* [irregular from ¹*bitter*] (1682)
: the bitter water solution of salts that remains after sodium chloride has crystallized out of a brine
bit·ter·root \'bi-tə(r)-ˌrüt, -ˌrůt\ *noun* (1838)
: a succulent herb (*Lewisia rediviva*) of mountainous slopes of western North America that has starchy roots and pink or white flowers
¹bit·ter·sweet \'bi-tər-ˌswēt\ *noun* (14th century)
1 : something that is bittersweet; *especially* : pleasure alloyed with pain
2 a : a sprawling poisonous weedy nightshade (*Solanum dulcamara*) with purple flowers and oval reddish orange berries **b** : a North American woody climbing plant (*Celastrus scandens*) of the staff-tree family having clusters

of small greenish flowers succeeded by yellow capsules that open when ripe and disclose the scarlet aril
²bittersweet *adjective* (1611)
1 : being at once bitter and sweet; *especially* : pleasant but including or marked by elements of suffering or regret ⟨a *bittersweet* ballad⟩
2 : of or relating to a prepared chocolate containing little sugar
— **bit·ter·sweet·ly** *adverb*
— **bit·ter·sweet·ness** *noun*
bit·ter·weed \'bi-tər-ˌwēd\ *noun* (1819)
: any of several American plants containing a bitter substance: as **a** : HORSEWEED **b** : a sneezeweed (*Helenium amarum* synonym *H. tenuifolium*) **c** : an erect composite herb (*Hymenoxys odorata*) of the southwestern U.S. that has yellow terminal flowerheads and is poisonous to livestock
bit·tock \'bi-tək\ *noun* (circa 1802)
chiefly Scottish : a little bit
¹bit·ty \'bi-tē\ *adjective* (1892)
chiefly British : made up of or containing bits; *especially* : not cohesive or flowing
²bitty *adjective* (1905)
: SMALL, TINY ⟨a little *bitty* room⟩
bi·tu·men \bə-'tyü-mən, bī-, -'tü-, *especially British also* 'bit-yə-\ *noun* [Middle English *bithumen* mineral pitch, from Latin *bitumin-, bitumen*] (15th century)
1 : an asphalt of Asia Minor used in ancient times as a cement and mortar
2 : any of various mixtures of hydrocarbons (as tar) often together with their nonmetallic derivatives that occur naturally or are obtained as residues after heat-refining natural substances (as petroleum); *specifically* : such a mixture soluble in carbon disulfide
— **bi·tu·mi·ni·za·tion** \bə-ˌtyü-mə-nə-'zā-shən, bī-, -ˌtü-\ *noun*
— **bi·tu·mi·nize** \-'tyü-mə-ˌnīz, -'tü-\ *transitive verb*
bi·tu·mi·nous \bə-'tyü-mə-nəs, bī-, -'tü-\ *adjective* (1620)
1 : containing or impregnated with bitumen
2 : of or relating to bituminous coal
bituminous coal *noun* (1827)
: a coal that when heated yields considerable volatile bituminous matter — called also *soft coal*
bi·unique \ˌbī-yů-'nēk\ *adjective* (1941)
: being a correspondence between two sets that is one-to-one in both directions
— **bi·unique·ness** *noun*
¹bi·va·lent \(ˌ)bī-'vā-lənt, 'bī-və-\ *adjective* (1869)
1 : DIVALENT
2 : associated in pairs in synapsis
²bivalent *noun* (circa 1934)
: a pair of synaptic chromosomes
¹bi·valve \'bī-ˌvalv\ *adjective* (1661)
: having a shell composed of two valves
²bivalve *noun* (1683)
: an animal (as a clam) with a 2-valved shell
bi·var·i·ate \(ˌ)bī-'ver-ē-ət, -'var-\ *adjective* (1920)
: of, relating to, or involving two variables ⟨*bivariate* frequency distribution⟩
¹biv·ouac \'bi-və-ˌwak, 'biv-ˌwak\ *noun* [French, from Low German *biwacht,* from *bi* by + *wacht* guard] (circa 1702)
1 : a usually temporary encampment under little or no shelter
2 a : encampment usually for a night **b** : a temporary shelter or settlement
²bivouac *intransitive verb* **-ouacked; -ouack·ing** (1809)
: to make a bivouac : CAMP
¹bi·week·ly \(ˌ)bī-'wē-klē\ *adjective* (1832)
1 : occurring twice a week
2 : occurring every two weeks : FORTNIGHTLY
usage see BI-
— **biweekly** *adverb*
²biweekly *noun* (circa 1890)

1 : a publication issued every two weeks
2 : SEMIWEEKLY
bi·year·ly \(ˌ)bī-'yir-lē\ *adjective* (circa 1909)
1 : BIANNUAL 1
2 : BIENNIAL 1
biz \'biz\ *noun* (1862)
: BUSINESS
¹bi·zarre \bə-'zär\ *adjective* [French, from Italian *bizzarro*] (circa 1648)
: strikingly out of the ordinary: as **a** : odd, extravagant, or eccentric in style or mode **b** : involving sensational contrasts or incongruities
synonym see FANTASTIC
— **bi·zarre·ly** *adverb*
— **bi·zarre·ness** *noun*
²bizarre *noun* (circa 1753)
: a flower with atypical striped marking
bi·zar·re·rie \bi-ˌzär-ə-'rē\ *noun* [French] (1747)
1 : a bizarre quality
2 : something bizarre
bi·zon·al \(ˌ)bī-'zō-nᵊl\ *adjective* (1946)
: of or relating to the affairs of a zone governed or administered by two powers acting together
— **bi·zone** \'bī-ˌzōn\ *noun*
¹blab \'blab\ *noun* [Middle English *blabbe;* akin to Middle English *blaberen*] (14th century)
1 *archaic* : one that blabs : TATTLETALE
2 : idle or excessive talk : CHATTER
— **blab·by** \'bla-bē\ *adjective*
²blab *verb* **blabbed; blab·bing** (15th century)
intransitive verb
1 : to talk idly or thoughtlessly : PRATTLE
2 : to reveal a secret especially by indiscreet chatter
transitive verb
: to reveal especially without reserve or discretion ⟨*blabbed* the whole affair to the press⟩
¹blab·ber \'bla-bər\ *verb* **blab·bered; blab·ber·ing** \-b(ə-)riŋ\ [Middle English *blaberen*] (14th century)
intransitive verb
: to talk foolishly or excessively
transitive verb
: to say indiscreetly
²blabber *noun* (circa 1913)
: idle talk : BABBLE
³blabber *noun* [²*blab*] (1557)
: one that blabs
blab·ber·mouth \'bla-bər-ˌmaůth\ *noun* (1936)
: a person who talks too much; *especially* : TATTLETALE
¹black \'blak\ *adjective* [Middle English *blak,* from Old English *blæc;* akin to Old High German *blah* black, and probably to Latin *flagrare* to burn, Greek *phlegein*] (before 12th century)
1 a : of the color black **b** (1) : very dark in color ⟨his face was *black* with rage⟩ (2) : having a very deep or low register ⟨a bass with a *black* voice⟩ (3) : HEAVY, SERIOUS ⟨the play was a *black* intrigue⟩
2 a : having dark skin, hair, and eyes : SWARTHY ⟨the *black* Irish⟩ **b** (1) : *often capitalized* : of or relating to any of various population groups having dark pigmentation of the skin ⟨*black* Americans⟩ (2) : of or relating to the Afro-American people or their culture ⟨*black* literature⟩ ⟨a *black* college⟩ ⟨*black* pride⟩ ⟨*black* studies⟩ (3) : typical or representative of the most readily attended parts of black culture ⟨tried to play *blacker* jazz⟩
3 : dressed in black
4 : DIRTY, SOILED ⟨hands *black* with grime⟩

\ə\ abut \ᵊ\ kitten \ər\ further \a\ ash \ā\ ace \ä\ mop, mar \aů\ out \ch\ chin \e\ bet \ē\ easy \g\ go \i\ hit \ī\ ice \j\ job \ŋ\ sing \ō\ go \ȯ\ law \ȯi\ boy \th\ thin \th\ the \ü\ loot \ů\ foot \y\ yet \zh\ vision *see also* Guide to Pronunciation

5 a : characterized by the absence of light ⟨a *black* night⟩ **b :** reflecting or transmitting little or no light ⟨*black* water⟩ **c :** served without milk or cream ⟨*black* coffee⟩
6 a : thoroughly sinister or evil : WICKED ⟨a *black* deed⟩ **b :** indicative of condemnation or discredit ⟨got a *black* mark for being late⟩
7 : connected with or invoking the supernatural and especially the devil ⟨*black* magic⟩
8 a : very sad, gloomy, or calamitous ⟨*black* despair⟩ **b :** marked by the occurrence of disaster ⟨*black* Friday⟩
9 : characterized by hostility or angry discontent : SULLEN ⟨*black* resentment filled his heart⟩
10 *chiefly British* **:** subject to boycott by trade-union members as employing or favoring nonunion workers or as operating under conditions considered unfair by the trade union
11 a *of propaganda* **:** conducted so as to appear to originate within an enemy country and designed to weaken enemy morale **b :** characterized by or connected with the use of black propaganda ⟨*black* radio⟩
12 : characterized by grim, distorted, or grotesque satire ⟨*black* humor⟩
13 : of or relating to covert intelligence operations ⟨*black* government programs⟩
— **black·ish** \'bla-kish\ *adjective*
— **black·ly** *adverb*
— **black·ness** *noun*

²black *noun* (before 12th century)
1 : a black pigment or dye; *especially* **:** one consisting largely of carbon
2 : the achromatic color of least lightness characteristically perceived to belong to objects that neither reflect nor transmit light
3 : something that is black: as **a :** a black clothing ⟨looks good in *black*⟩ **b :** a black animal (as a horse)
4 a : a person belonging to any of various population groups having dark pigmentation of the skin **b :** AFRO-AMERICAN
5 : the pieces of a dark color in a board game for two players (as chess)
6 : total or nearly total absence of light ⟨the *black* of night⟩
7 : the condition of making a profit — usually used with *the* ⟨operating in the *black*⟩; compare RED

³black (13th century)
intransitive verb
: to become black
transitive verb
1 : to make black
2 *chiefly British* **:** to declare (as a business or industry) subject to boycott by trade-union members

black alder *noun* (1805)
: WINTERBERRY 1

black·a·moor \'bla-kə-ˌmür\ *noun* [irregular from *black* + *Moor*] (1547)
: a dark-skinned person; *especially* **:** BLACK 4a

black–and–blue \ˌbla-kən-'blü\ *adjective* (14th century)
: darkly discolored from blood effused by bruising

black–and–tan \-kən-'tan\ *adjective* (1850)
1 : having a predominantly black color pattern with deep red or rusty tan on the feet, breeching, and cheek patches, above the eyes, and inside the ears
2 : favoring or practicing proportional representation of whites and blacks in politics
3 : frequented by both blacks and whites ⟨a *black-and-tan* bar⟩

black and tan *noun* (1870)
1 : a black-and-tan animal (as a dog)
2 *chiefly British* **:** a drink consisting of a dark beer (as stout or porter) and ale or beer
3 *B&T capitalized* [from the color of his uniform] **:** a recruit enlisted in England in 1920–21 for service in the Royal Irish Constabulary against the armed movement for Irish independence

4 : a member of a black-and-tan political organization (as in the southern U.S.) — compare LILY-WHITE

black–and–tan coonhound *noun* (1948)
: any of a breed of strong vigorous coonhounds of American origin with black-and-tan markings

black–and–white \ˌbla-kən-'hwīt, -'wīt\ *adjective* (1612)
1 : being in writing or print
2 : partly black and partly white in color
3 : executed in dark pigment on a light background or in light pigment on a dark ground ⟨a *black-and-white* drawing⟩
4 : MONOCHROME 2a ⟨*black-and-white* film⟩ ⟨*black-and-white* television⟩
5 a : sharply divided into good and evil **b :** evaluating or viewing things as either all good or all bad ⟨*black-and-white* morality⟩ **c :** sharply defined : CLEAR-CUT ⟨the truth is not always *black-and-white*⟩

black and white *noun* (1599)
1 : WRITING, PRINT
2 : a drawing or print done in black and white or in monochrome
3 : monochrome reproduction of visual images (as by photography or television)

Black Angus *noun* (1948)
: ANGUS

black–a–vised \'bla-kə-ˌvīst\ *adjective* [*black* + French *à vis* as to face] (circa 1758)
: having a dark complexion

¹black·ball \'blak-ˌból\ *transitive verb* (1770)
1 : to vote against; *especially* **:** to exclude from membership by casting a negative vote
2 a : to exclude socially : OSTRACIZE **b :** BOYCOTT

²blackball *noun* (circa 1847)
1 : a small black ball for use as a negative vote in a ballot box
2 : an adverse vote especially against admitting someone to membership in an organization

black bass *noun* (1815)
: any of a genus (*Micropterus*) of freshwater sunfishes native to eastern and central North America and including the largemouth bass and smallmouth bass

black bean *noun* (1792)
1 : a black kidney bean commonly used in Latin American cuisine
2 : a black soybean commonly used in oriental cuisine

black bear *noun* (1781)
: the common American bear (*Ursus americanus*) ranging in color from brown or typical black to white

black bear

black beast *noun* (1926)
: BÊTE NOIRE

¹black belt \'blak-ˌbelt\ *noun* (1870)
1 : an area characterized by rich black soil
2 *often both Bs capitalized* **:** an area densely populated by blacks

²black belt *noun* (1954)
: one who holds the rating of expert in various arts of self-defense (as judo and karate); *also* **:** the rating itself

black·ber·ry \'blak-ˌber-ē\ *noun* (before 12th century)
1 : the usually black or dark purple juicy but seedy edible aggregate fruit of various brambles (genus *Rubus*) of the rose family
2 : a plant that bears blackberries

black bile *noun* (1797)
: a humor of medieval physiology believed to be secreted by the kidneys or spleen and to cause melancholy

black birch *noun* (1674)
: SWEET BIRCH

¹black·bird \'blak-ˌbərd\ *noun* (14th century)

1 : any of various birds of which the males are largely or entirely black: as **a :** a common thrush (*Turdus merula*) of Eurasia and northern Africa having an orange bill and eye rim **b :** any of several American birds (family Icteridae)
2 : a Pacific islander kidnapped for use as a plantation laborer

²blackbird *intransitive verb* (1894)
: to engage in the slave trade especially in the South Pacific

black·bird·er *noun* (1880)
1 : a person who blackbirds
2 : a ship used in blackbirding

black·board \'blak-ˌbórd, -ˌbórd\ *noun* (1823)
: a hard smooth usually dark surface used especially in a classroom for writing or drawing on with chalk

black·body \'blak-'bä-dē\ *noun* (1710)
: an ideal body or surface that completely absorbs all radiant energy falling upon it with no reflection and that radiates at all frequencies with a spectral energy distribution dependent on its absolute temperature

black book *noun* (1592)
: a book containing a blacklist

black box *noun* (circa 1945)
1 : a usually complicated electronic device that functions and is packaged as a unit and whose internal mechanism is usually hidden from or mysterious to the user; *broadly* **:** anything that has mysterious or unknown internal functions or mechanisms
2 : a crashworthy device in aircraft for recording cockpit conversations and flight data

black·cap \'blak-ˌkap\ *noun* (1678)
1 : any of several birds with black heads or crowns: as **a :** a small European warbler (*Sylvia atricapilla*) with a black crown **b :** CHICKADEE
2 : BLACK RASPBERRY

black–capped \-'kapt\ *adjective* (1781)
of a bird **:** having the top of the head black

black·cock \-ˌkäk\ *noun* (15th century)
chiefly British **:** BLACK GROUSE; *specifically* **:** the male black grouse

black cohosh *noun* (1828)
: a bugbane (*Cimicifuga racemosa*) of the eastern U.S.

black crappie *noun* (circa 1827)
: a silvery black-mottled sunfish (*Pomoxis nigromaculatus*) of the Mississippi drainage and eastern U.S. having seven or eight protruding spines on the dorsal fins

black–crowned night heron \'blak-ˌkraünd-\ *noun* (1844)
: a widely distributed night heron (*Nycticorax nycticorax*) having a black crown and back

black damp *noun* (1836)
: a carbon dioxide mixture occurring as a mine gas and incapable of supporting life or flame

black death *noun, often B&D capitalized* [from the black patches formed on the skin of its victims] (1780)
1 : PLAGUE 2b
2 : a severe epidemic of plague and especially bubonic plague that occurred in Asia and Europe in the 14th century

black diamond *noun* (1763)
1 : dense black hematite
2 *plural* **:** COAL 3a
3 : ³CARBONADO

black duck *noun* (1637)
: any of several ducks that are dark in color; *especially* **:** a common brown duck (*Anas rubripes*) of eastern North America

black dwarf *noun, plural* **black dwarfs** (1945)
: a very small star that emits no detectable light

black·en \'bla-kən\ *verb* **black·ened; black·en·ing** \'blak-niŋ, 'bla-kə-\ (14th century)
intransitive verb

: to become dark or black ⟨the sky *blackens*⟩
transitive verb
1 : to make black
2 : DEFAME, SULLY
— **black·en·er** \'blak-nər, 'bla-kə-\ *noun*
black·ened \-kənd\ *adjective* (1984)
: coated with a mixture of cayenne pepper and spices and cooked in a frying pan over extremely high heat ⟨*blackened* redfish⟩
Black English *noun* (1969)
: a nonstandard variety of English spoken by some American blacks — called also *Black English vernacular*
black·en·ing \'blak-niŋ, 'bla-kə-\ *noun* (circa 1909)
: BLACKING
black eye *noun* (1604)
1 : a discoloration of the skin around the eye from bruising
2 : a bad reputation
black–eyed pea \'blak-ˌīd-\ *noun* (1728)
: COWPEA
black–eyed Su·san \-'sü-z°n\ *noun* (1892)
: either of two North American coneflowers (*Rudbeckia hirta* and *R. serotina*) having flower heads with deep yellow to orange rays and dark conical disks
black·face \'blak-ˌfās\ *noun* (1869)
: makeup applied to a performer playing a black person especially in a minstrel show; *also* **:** a performer wearing such makeup
black·fish \-ˌfish\ *noun* (1754)
1 : any of numerous dark-colored fishes: as **a :** TAUTOG **b :** a small food fish (*Dallia pectoralis*) of Alaska and Siberia that is noted for its resistance to cold
2 : any of several small toothed whales (genus *Globicephala*) found in warm seas
black–flag \-'flag\ *transitive verb* (1963)
: to signal (a race-car driver) to go immediately to the pits
black flag *noun* (1720)
: a pirate's flag usually bearing a skull and crossbones
black·fly \'blak-ˌflī\ *noun, plural* **-flies** *or* **-fly** (1608)
: any of various small dark-colored insects; *especially* **:** any of a family (Simuliidae and especially genus *Simulium*) of bloodsucking dipteran flies whose larvae usually live in flowing streams
Black·foot \'blak-ˌfut\ *noun, plural* **Black·feet** *or* **Blackfoot** (1794)
1 : a member of an American Indian people of Montana, Alberta, and Saskatchewan
2 : the Algonquian language of the Blackfeet
black–foot·ed albatross \'blak-ˌfu-təd-\ *noun* (1839)
: an albatross (*Diomedea nigripes*) of the Pacific that is chiefly blackish with dusky bill and black feet and legs — called also *gooney*
black–footed ferret *noun* (1846)
: a rare weasel (*Mustela nigripes*) of western North American prairies having a yellowish coat, dark feet and facial mask, and a dark-tipped tail

black-footed ferret

black gold *noun* (1910)
: PETROLEUM
black grouse *noun* (1678)
: a large grouse (*Lyrurus tetrix*) of western Asia and Europe of which the male is black with white wing patches and the female is barred and mottled
¹black·guard \'bla-gərd, -ˌgärd; 'blak-ˌgärd\ *noun* (1535)
1 *obsolete* **:** the kitchen servants of a household
2 a : a rude or unscrupulous person **b :** a person who uses foul or abusive language

— **black·guard·ism** \-gər-ˌdi-zəm, -ˌgär-\ *noun*
— **black·guard·ly** \-gərd-lē, -ˌgärd\ *adjective or adverb*
²blackguard *transitive verb* (1823)
: to talk about or address in abusive terms
black gum *noun* (1709)
: a tupelo (*Nyssa sylvatica*) of the eastern U.S. with light and soft but tough wood
black hand *noun, often B&H capitalized* [*Black Hand*, a Sicilian and Italian-American secret society of the late 19th and 20th centuries] (1904)
: a lawless secret society engaged in criminal activities (as terrorism or extortion)
— **black·hand·er** \'blak-ˌhan-dər\ *noun*
black·head \'blak-ˌhed\ *noun* (circa 1837)
1 : a small plug of sebum blocking the duct of a sebaceous gland especially on the face
2 : a destructive disease of turkeys and related birds caused by a protozoan (*Histomonas meleagridis*) that invades the intestinal ceca and liver
3 : a larval clam or mussel attached to the skin or gills of a freshwater fish
black·heart \-ˌhärt\ *noun* (1909)
: a plant disease in which the central tissues blacken
black hole *noun* (1968)
1 : a hypothetical celestial object with a gravitational field so strong that light cannot escape from it which is believed to be created in the collapse of a very massive star
2 : something resembling a black hole: as **a :** something that consumes a resource continually ⟨a financial *black hole*⟩ **b :** an empty space **:** VOID
black ice *noun* (1961)
: a thin film of ice on paved surfaces (as roads) that is difficult to see
black·ing \'bla-kiŋ\ *noun* (1571)
: a substance (as a paste or polish) that is applied to an object to make it black
¹black·jack \-ˌjak\ *noun* (1591)
1 [*black* + *jack* (vessel)] **:** a tankard for beer or ale usually of tar-coated leather
2 : SPHALERITE
3 : a hand weapon typically consisting of a piece of leather-enclosed metal with a strap or springy shaft for a handle
4 : an often scrubby oak (*Quercus marilandica*) chiefly of the southeastern U.S. — called also *blackjack oak*
5 : a card game the object of which is to be dealt cards having a higher count than those of the dealer up to but not exceeding 21 — called also *twenty-one, vingt-et-un*
²blackjack *transitive verb* (1905)
1 : to strike with a blackjack
2 : to coerce with threats or pressure
black·land \'blak-ˌland\ *noun* (1583)
1 : a heavy sticky black soil such as that covering large areas in Texas
2 *plural* **:** a region of blackland
black·lead \'blak-ˌled\ *noun* (1583)
chiefly British **:** GRAPHITE 1
black·leg \'blak-ˌleg, -ˌlāg\ *noun* (circa 1722)
1 : a usually fatal toxemia especially of young cattle caused by a soil bacterium (*Clostridium chauvoei*)
2 : a cheating gambler **:** SWINDLER
3 *chiefly British* **:** a worker hostile to trade unionism or acting in opposition to union policies **:** SCAB
black letter *noun* (circa 1644)
: a heavy angular condensed typeface used especially by the earliest European printers and based on handwriting used chiefly in the 13th to 15th centuries; *also* **:** this style of handwriting

mnopqrstuv

black letter

black light *noun* (1927)

1 : invisible ultraviolet light
2 : a lamp that radiates black light
black·light trap \'blak-ˌlīt-\ *noun* (1961)
: a trap for insects that uses a form of black light perceptible to particular insects as an attractant
¹black·list \-ˌlist\ *noun* (circa 1619)
: a list of persons who are disapproved of or are to be punished or boycotted
²blacklist *transitive verb* (1718)
: to put on a blacklist
— **black·list·er** *noun*
black locust *noun* (1787)
: a tall tree (*Robinia pseudoacacia*) of eastern North America with pinnately compound leaves, drooping racemes of fragrant white flowers, and strong stiff wood
black lung *noun* (1837)
: pneumoconiosis caused by habitual inhalation of coal dust
black·mail \'blak-ˌmāl\ *noun* [*black* + ¹*mail*] (1552)
1 : a tribute anciently exacted on the Scottish border by freebooting chiefs for immunity from pillage
2 a : extortion or coercion by threats especially of public exposure or criminal prosecution **b :** the payment that is extorted
— **blackmail** *transitive verb*
— **black·mail·er** *noun*
Black Ma·ria \ˌblak-mə-'rī-ə\ *noun* (1847)
: PADDY WAGON
black–mar·ket (1943)
intransitive verb
: to buy or sell goods in the black market
transitive verb
: to sell in the black market
— **black marketer** *or* **black marke·teer** \-ˌmär-kə-'tir\ *noun*
black market *noun* (1931)
: illicit trade in goods or commodities in violation of official regulations; *also* **:** a place where such trade is carried on
Black Mass *noun* (1893)
: a travesty of the Christian mass ascribed to worshipers of Satan
Black Muslim *noun* (1960)
: a member of a chiefly black group that professes Islamic religious belief
black nationalist *noun, often B&N capitalized* (1963)
: a member of a group of militant blacks who advocate separatism from the whites and the formation of self-governing black communities
— **black nationalism** *noun, often B&N capitalized*
black·out \'blak-ˌaut\ *noun* (1913)
1 a : a turning off of the stage lighting to separate scenes in a play or end a play or skit; *also* **:** a skit that ends with a blackout **b :** a period of darkness enforced as a precaution against air raids **c :** a period of darkness (as in a city) caused by a failure of electrical power
2 : a transient dulling or loss of vision, consciousness, or memory ⟨an alcoholic *blackout*⟩
3 a : a wiping out **:** OBLITERATION **b :** a blotting out by censorship **:** SUPPRESSION ⟨a news *blackout*⟩
4 : a usually temporary loss of a radio signal
5 : the prohibition or restriction of the telecasting of a sports event
black out (1921)
intransitive verb
1 : to become enveloped in darkness

2 : to undergo a temporary loss of vision, consciousness, or memory
transitive verb
1 : to cause to black out ⟨*black out* the stage⟩
2 : to make inoperative (as by a power failure)
3 a : BLOT OUT, ERASE ⟨*blacked out* the event from his mind⟩ **b :** to suppress by censorship ⟨*black out* the news⟩
4 : to impose a blackout on

Black Panther *noun* (1965)
: a member of an organization of militant American blacks

black pepper *noun* (before 12th century)
: a spice that consists of the fruit of an East Indian plant (*Piper nigrum*) ground with the black husk still on

black·poll \'blak-ˌpōl\ *noun* (1783)
: a North American warbler (*Dendroica striata*) with the male having a black cap when in breeding plumage

black powder *noun* (circa 1909)
: an explosive mixture of potassium nitrate or sodium nitrate, charcoal, and sulfur used especially in fireworks and as a propellant in antique firearms — compare GUNPOWDER

black power *noun, often B&P capitalized* (1966)
: the mobilization of the political and economic power of American blacks especially to compel respect for their rights and improve their condition

black pudding *noun* (1568)
chiefly British **:** BLOOD SAUSAGE

black racer *noun* (1849)
: an American blacksnake (*Coluber constrictor constrictor*) common in the eastern U.S.

black raspberry *noun* (circa 1782)
: a raspberry (*Rubus occidentalis*) of eastern North America that has a purplish black fruit and is the source of several cultivated varieties — called also *blackcap*

black rhinoceros *noun* (1850)
: a rhinoceros (*Diceros bicornis*) of sub-Saharan Africa having a prehensile upper lip that protrudes in the middle — called also *black rhino*

Black Rod *noun* (circa 1607)
: the principal usher of the House of Lords

black rot *noun* (1849)
: a bacterial or fungal rot of plants marked by dark brown discoloration

black sheep *noun* (1792)
: a discreditable member of a respectable group

Black·shirt \'blak-ˌshərt\ *noun* (1922)
: a member of a fascist organization having a black shirt as a distinctive part of its uniform; *especially* **:** a member of the Italian Fascist party

black·smith \'blak-ˌsmith\ *noun* [from a distinction between black metal (iron) and white metal (tin)] (15th century)
: a smith who forges iron
— **black·smith·ing** \-ˌsmi-thiŋ\ *noun*

black smoker *noun* (1980)
: a vent in a geologically active region of the sea floor from which issues superheated water laden with minerals (as sulfide precipitates)

black·snake \-ˌsnāk\ *noun* (1634)
1 : any of several snakes that are largely black or very dark in color; *especially* **:** either of two harmless snakes (*Coluber constrictor* and *Elaphe obsoleta*) of the U.S.
2 : a long tapering braided whip of rawhide or leather

black spot *noun* (circa 1889)
: any of several bacterial or fungal diseases of plants characterized by black spots or blotches especially on the leaves

black·tail \'blak-ˌtāl\ *noun* (1828)
: BLACK-TAILED DEER

black–tailed deer \'blak-ˌtāl(d)-\ *noun* (1806)

: MULE DEER; *specifically* **:** one of a subspecies (*Odocoileus hemionus columbianus*) especially of British Columbia, Oregon, and Washington

black tea *noun* (1789)
: tea that is dark in color from complete fermentation of the leaf before firing

black·thorn \'blak-ˌthȯrn\ *noun* (14th century)
: a European spiny plum (*Prunus spinosa*) with hard wood and small white flowers

black–tie *adjective* (1933)
: characterized by or requiring the wearing of semiformal evening clothes consisting of a usually black tie and tuxedo for men and a formal dress for women ⟨a *black-tie* dinner⟩ — compare WHITE-TIE

black·top \'blak-ˌtäp\ *noun* (1931)
: a bituminous material used especially for surfacing roads; *also* **:** a surface paved with blacktop
— **blacktop** *transitive verb*

Blackwall hitch \'blak-ˌwȯl-\ *noun* [*Blackwall*, shipyard in London, England] (circa 1862)
: a hitch for securing a rope to a hook — see KNOT illustration

black walnut *noun* (1612)
: a walnut (*Juglans nigra*) of eastern North America with hard strong heavy dark brown wood and oily edible nuts; *also* **:** its wood or nut

black·wa·ter \'blak-ˌwȯ-tər, -ˌwä-\ *noun* (1800)
: any of several diseases (as blackwater fever) characterized by dark-colored urine

blackwater fever *noun* (1884)
: a febrile complication of repeated malarial attacks that is characterized especially by extensive kidney damage and urine discolored by heme from blood

black widow *noun* (1915)
: a venomous New World spider (*Latrodectus mactans*) the female of which is black with an hourglass-shaped red mark on the underside of the abdomen

black widow

black·wood \'blak-ˌwu̇d\ *noun* (1631)
: any of several hardwood trees (as the legumes *Acacia melanoxylon* and *Dalbergia latifolia*) or their dark-colored wood

blad·der \'bla-dər\ *noun* [Middle English, from Old English *blǣdre*; akin to Old High German *blātara* bladder, Old English *blāwan* to blow] (before 12th century)
1 a : a membranous sac in animals that serves as the receptacle of a liquid or contains gas; *especially* **:** URINARY BLADDER **b :** CYST 2b
2 : something (as the rubber bag inside a football) resembling a bladder
— **blad·der·like** \-ˌlīk\ *adjective*

bladder campion *noun* (1817)
: an Old World campion (*Silene vulgaris* synonym *S. cucubalus*) with an inflated calyx introduced into temperate North America

blad·der·nut \'bla-dər-ˌnət\ *noun* (1578)
: any of a genus (*Staphylea* of the family Staphyleaceae, the bladdernut family) of ornamental shrubs or small trees with panicles of small white flowers followed by inflated capsules; *also* **:** one of the capsules

bladder worm *noun* (1858)
: a bladderlike larval tapeworm (as a cysticercus)

blad·der·wort \'bla-dər-ˌwərt, -ˌwȯrt\ *noun* (circa 1815)

: any of a genus (*Utricularia* of the family Lentibulariaceae, the bladderwort family) of chiefly aquatic plants with leaves usually having insect-trapping bladders

bladder wrack *noun* (1810)
: a common rockweed (*Fucus vesiculosus*) used in preparing kelp and as a manure

blade \'blād\ *noun* [Middle English, from Old English *blæd*; akin to Old High German *blat* leaf, Latin *folium*, Greek *phyllon*, Old English *blōwan* to blossom — more at BLOW] (before 12th century)
1 a : LEAF 1a(1); *especially* **:** the leaf of an herb or a grass **b :** the flat expanded part of a leaf as distinguished from the petiole
2 : something resembling the blade of a leaf: as **a :** the broad flattened part of an oar or paddle **b :** an arm of a screw propeller, electric fan, or steam turbine **c :** the broad flat or concave part of a machine (as a bulldozer or snowplow) that comes into contact with the material to be moved **d :** a broad flat body part; *specifically* **:** SCAPULA — used chiefly in naming cuts of meat **e :** the flat portion of the tongue immediately behind the tip; *also* **:** this portion together with the tip
3 a : the cutting part of an implement **b** (1) **:** SWORD (2) **:** SWORDSMAN (3) **:** a dashing lively man **c :** the runner of an ice skate
— **blade·like** \-ˌlīk\ *adjective*

blad·ed \'blā-dəd\ *adjective* (1578)
: having blades — often used in combination ⟨five-*bladed* propeller⟩

blae \'blā\ *adjective* [Middle English *bla*, *blo*, from Old Norse *blār*; akin to Old High German *blāo* blue — more at BLUE] (13th century)
chiefly Scottish **:** dark blue or bluish gray

blae·ber·ry \'blā-ˌber-ē, -ˌb(ə-)rē\ *noun* (15th century)
chiefly Scottish **:** WHORTLEBERRY 1

¹blah \'blä\ *noun* [imitative] (1918)
1 *also* **blah–blah** \-ˌblä\ **:** silly or pretentious chatter or nonsense
2 *plural* [perhaps influenced in meaning by *blasé*] **:** a feeling of boredom, lethargy, or general dissatisfaction

²blah *adjective* (1923)
: lacking interest **:** MEDIOCRE ⟨a *blah* winter day⟩

blain \'blān\ *noun* [Middle English, from Old English *blegen*; akin to Middle Low German *bleine* blain, Old English *blāwan* to blow] (before 12th century)
: an inflammatory swelling or sore

blam·able \'blā-mə-bəl\ *adjective* (14th century)
: deserving blame **:** REPREHENSIBLE
synonym see BLAMEWORTHY
— **blam·ably** \-blē\ *adverb*

¹blame \'blām\ *transitive verb* **blamed; blam·ing** [Middle English, from Old French *blamer*, from Late Latin *blasphemare* to blaspheme, from Greek *blasphēmein*] (13th century)
1 : to find fault with **:** CENSURE ⟨the right to praise or *blame* a literary work⟩
2 a : to hold responsible ⟨they *blame* me for everything⟩ **b :** to place responsibility for ⟨*blames* it on me⟩ □
— **blam·er** *noun*
— **to blame :** at fault **:** RESPONSIBLE

²blame *noun* (13th century)
1 : an expression of disapproval or reproach **:** CENSURE
2 a : a state of being blameworthy **:** CULPABILITY **b** *archaic* **:** FAULT, SIN

□ **USAGE**
blame Use of *blame* in sense 2b with *on* has occasionally been disparaged as wrong. Such disparagement is without basis; *blame on* occurs as frequently as in carefully edited prose as *blame for*. Both forms are standard.

3 : responsibility for something believed to deserve censure ⟨they must share the *blame*⟩
— **blame·less** \-ləs\ *adjective*
— **blame·less·ly** *adverb*
— **blame·less·ness** *noun*
blame·ful \'blām-fəl\ *adjective* (14th century)
: BLAMABLE
— **blame·ful·ly** \-fə-lē\ *adverb*
blame·wor·thy \-,wər-t͟hē\ *adjective* (14th century)
: being at fault **:** deserving blame ☆
— **blame·wor·thi·ness** *noun*
blanc fixe \'blaŋk-'fiks\ *noun* [French, literally, fixed white] (1866)
: barium sulfate prepared as a heavy white powder and used especially as a filler in paper, rubber, and linoleum or as a pigment
blanch \'blanch\ *verb* [Middle English *blaunchen*, from Middle French *blanchir*, from Old French *blanche*, feminine of *blanc*, adjective, white — more at BLANK] (15th century)
transitive verb
: to take the color out of: as **a :** to bleach by excluding light ⟨*blanch* celery⟩ **b :** to scald or parboil in water or steam in order to remove the skin from, whiten, or stop enzymatic action in ⟨as food for freezing⟩ **c :** to make ashen or pale ⟨fear *blanches* the cheek⟩
intransitive verb
: to become white or pale
— **blanch·er** *noun*
blanc·mange \blə-'mänj, -'mänᵈzh\ *noun* [Middle English *blancmanger*, from Middle French *blanc manger*, literally, white food] (14th century)
: a usually sweetened and flavored dessert made from gelatinous or starchy ingredients and milk
bland \'bland\ *adjective* [Latin *blandus*] (1661)
1 a : smooth and soothing in manner or quality ⟨a *bland* smile⟩ **b :** exhibiting no personal concern or embarrassment **:** UNPERTURBED ⟨a *bland* confession of guilt⟩
2 a : not irritating, stimulating, or invigorating **:** SOOTHING **b :** DULL, INSIPID ⟨*bland* stories with little plot or action⟩
synonym *see* SUAVE
— **bland·ly** \'blan(d)-lē\ *adverb*
— **bland·ness** \'blan(d)-nəs\ *noun*
blan·dish \'blan-dish\ *verb* [Middle English, from Middle French *blandiss-*, stem of *blandir*, from Latin *blandiri*, from *blandus* mild, flattering] (14th century)
transitive verb
: to coax with flattery **:** CAJOLE
intransitive verb
: to act or speak in a flattering or coaxing manner
— **blan·dish·er** *noun*
blan·dish·ment \-dish-mənt\ *noun* (1591)
: something that tends to coax or cajole **:** ALLUREMENT — often used in plural
¹blank \'blaŋk\ *adjective* [Middle English, from Middle French *blanc* colorless, white, of Germanic origin; akin to Old High German *blanch* white; probably akin to Latin *flagrare* to burn — more at BLACK] (14th century)
1 *archaic* **:** COLORLESS
2 a : appearing or causing to appear dazed, confounded, or nonplussed ⟨stared in *blank* dismay⟩ **b :** EXPRESSIONLESS ⟨a *blank* stare⟩
3 a : devoid of covering or content; *especially* **:** free from writing or marks ⟨*blank* paper⟩ **b :** having spaces to be filled in **c :** lacking interest, variety, or change ⟨*blank* hours⟩
4 : ABSOLUTE, UNQUALIFIED ⟨a *blank* refusal⟩
5 : UNFINISHED; *especially* **:** having a plain or unbroken surface where an opening is usual ⟨a *blank* key⟩ ⟨a *blank* arch⟩
synonym *see* EMPTY
— **blank·ly** *adverb*
— **blank·ness** *noun*
²blank *noun* (1554)
1 *obsolete* **:** the bull's-eye of a target

2 a : an empty space (as on a paper) **b :** a paper with spaces for the entry of data ⟨an order *blank*⟩
3 a : a piece of material prepared to be made into something (as a key) by a further operation **b :** a cartridge loaded with propellant and a seal but no projectile
4 a : an empty or featureless place or space ⟨my mind was a *blank*⟩ **b :** a vacant or uneventful period ⟨a long *blank* in history⟩
5 : a dash substituting for an omitted word
³blank (circa 1765)
transitive verb
1 a : OBSCURE, OBLITERATE ⟨*blank* out a line⟩ **b :** to stop access to ⟨*blank* off a tunnel⟩
2 : to keep (an opposing team) from scoring ⟨were *blanked* for eight innings⟩
intransitive verb
1 : FADE — usually used with *out* ⟨the music *blanked* out⟩
2 : to become confused or abstracted — often used with *out* ⟨his mind *blanked* out momentarily⟩
blank check *noun* (1884)
1 : complete freedom of action or control **:** CARTE BLANCHE
2 : a signed check with the amount unspecified
¹blan·ket \'blaŋ-kət\ *noun* [Middle English, from Old French *blankete*, from *blanc*] (14th century)
1 a : a large usually oblong piece of woven fabric used as a bed covering **b :** a similar piece of fabric used as a body covering ⟨as for an animal⟩ ⟨a horse *blanket*⟩
2 : something that resembles a blanket ⟨a *blanket* of fog⟩ ⟨a *blanket* of gloom⟩
3 : a rubber or plastic sheet on the cylinder in an offset press that transfers the image to the surface being printed
— **blan·ket·like** \-,līk\ *adjective*
²blanket *transitive verb* (1605)
1 : to cover with or as if with a blanket ⟨new grass *blankets* the slope⟩
2 a : to cover so as to obscure, interrupt, suppress, or extinguish ⟨*blanket* a fire with foam⟩ **b :** to apply or cause to apply to uniformly despite wide separation or diversity among the elements included ⟨freight rates that *blanket* a region⟩ **c :** to cause to be included ⟨automatically *blanketed* into the insurance program⟩
³blanket *adjective* (1886)
1 : covering all members of a group or class ⟨a *blanket* wage increase⟩
2 : effective or applicable in all instances
blan·ket·flow·er \'blaŋ-kət-,flaù(-ə)r\ *noun* (1879)
: GAILLARDIA
blanket stitch *noun* (1880)
: a buttonhole stitch with spaces of variable width used on materials too thick to hem
— **blanket–stitch** *transitive verb*
blank verse *noun* (1588)
: unrhymed verse; *specifically* **:** unrhymed iambic pentameter verse

blanket stitch

blan·quette \blänᵀ-'ket\ *noun* [French, from Provençal *blanqueto*, from *blanc* white, of Germanic origin; akin to Old High German *blanch* white] (1727)
: a stew of light meat or seafood in a white sauce ⟨*blanquette* of veal⟩ ⟨*blanquette* of lobster⟩
¹blare \'blar, 'bler\ *verb* **blared; blar·ing** [Middle English *bleren*; akin to Middle Dutch *blēren* to shout] (15th century)
intransitive verb
: to sound loud and strident ⟨radios *blaring*⟩
transitive verb
1 : to sound or utter raucously ⟨sat *blaring* the car horn⟩
2 : to proclaim flamboyantly ⟨headlines *blared* his defeat⟩

²blare *noun* (1809)
1 : a loud strident noise
2 : dazzling often garish brilliance
3 : FLAMBOYANCE
blar·ney \'blär-nē\ *noun* [*Blarney stone*, a stone in Blarney Castle, near Cork, Ireland, held to bestow skill in flattery on those who kiss it] (1796)
1 : skillful flattery **:** BLANDISHMENT
2 : NONSENSE, HUMBUG ◇
— **blarney** *verb*
bla·sé \blä-'zā\ *also* **bla·se** *adjective* [French] (1819)
1 : apathetic to pleasure or excitement as a result of excessive indulgence or enjoyment **:** WORLD-WEARY
2 : SOPHISTICATED, WORLDLY-WISE
3 : UNCONCERNED
synonym *see* SOPHISTICATED
blas·pheme \blas-'fēm, 'blas-,\ *verb* **blas·phemed; blas·phem·ing** [Middle English *blasfemen*, from Late Latin *blasphemare* — more at BLAME] (14th century)
transitive verb
1 : to speak of or address with irreverence
2 : REVILE, ABUSE
intransitive verb
: to utter blasphemy
— **blas·phem·er** \-'fē-mər; 'blas-,fē-mər, -fə-mər\ *noun*
blas·phe·mous \'blas-fə-məs\ *adjective* (15th century)
: impiously irreverent **:** PROFANE
— **blas·phe·mous·ly** *adverb*
— **blas·phe·mous·ness** *noun*
blas·phe·my \'blas-fə-mē\ *noun, plural* **-mies** (13th century)

☆ SYNONYMS
Blameworthy, blamable, guilty, culpable mean deserving reproach or punishment. BLAMEWORTHY and BLAMABLE apply to any degree of reprehensibility ⟨conduct adjudged *blameworthy*⟩ ⟨an accident for which no one is *blamable*⟩. GUILTY implies responsibility for or consciousness of crime, sin, or, at the least, grave error or misdoing ⟨*guilty* of a breach of etiquette⟩. CULPABLE is weaker than *guilty* and is likely to connote malfeasance or errors of ignorance, omission, or negligence ⟨*culpable* neglect⟩.

◇ WORD HISTORY
blarney *Blarney* is the name of a town, a stream, and especially a castle, built in 1446, in County Cork, Ireland. Embedded in the southern wall of the castle's keep is a block of limestone, known as the Blarney Stone. Legend has it that anyone who manages to kiss the Blarney Stone (its position makes it not easily accessible) will be blessed with the gift of flattery or cajolery. The tradition of making a pilgrimage to the castle to kiss the Blarney Stone is supposedly based on a particular event in the castle's history. The story goes that in 1602 the lord of the castle contrived an endless series of plausible excuses and expressions of flattery to forestall a promised surrender of the castle to attacking English forces until help could arrive. The lack of historical evidence for the story has failed to stifle the claim that anyone who kisses the stone will acquire comparable persuasive powers.

1 a : the act of insulting or showing contempt or lack of reverence for God **b :** the act of claiming the attributes of deity
2 : irreverence toward something considered sacred or inviolable

¹blast \'blast\ *noun* [Middle English, from Old English *blǣst;* akin to Old High German *blāst* blast, *blāsan* to blow, Old English *blāwan* — more at BLOW] (before 12th century)
1 a : a violent gust of wind **b :** the effect or accompaniment (as sleet) of such a gust
2 : the sound produced by an impulsion of air through a wind instrument or whistle
3 : something resembling a gust of wind: as **a :** a stream of air or gas forced through a hole **b :** a vehement outburst **c :** the continuous blowing to which a charge of ore or metal is subjected in a blast furnace
4 a : a sudden pernicious influence or effect ⟨the *blast* of a huge epidemic⟩ **b :** a disease of plants that causes the foliage or flowers to wither
5 a : an explosion or violent detonation **b :** the violent effect produced in the vicinity of an explosion that consists of a wave of increased atmospheric pressure followed by a wave of decreased atmospheric pressure
6 : SPEED, CAPACITY, OPERATION ⟨go full *blast*⟩ ⟨in full *blast*⟩
7 : an enjoyably exciting experience, occasion, or event; *especially :* PARTY

²blast (14th century)
intransitive verb
1 : BLARE ⟨music *blasting* from the radio⟩
2 : to make a vigorous attack
3 a : to use an explosive **b :** SHOOT
4 : to hit a golf ball out of a sand trap with explosive force
transitive verb
1 a : to injure by or as if by the action of wind **b :** BLIGHT
2 a : to shatter by or as if by an explosive **b :** to remove, open, or form by or as if by an explosive **c :** SHOOT
3 : to attack vigorously
4 : to cause to blast off ⟨will *blast* themselves from the moon's surface⟩
5 : to hit vigorously and effectively
— **blast·er** *noun*

blast- *or* **blasto-** *combining form* [German, from Greek, from *blastos*]
: bud : budding : germ ⟨*blasto*disc⟩ ⟨*blast*ula⟩

-blast \,blast\ *noun combining form* [New Latin *-blastus,* from Greek *blastos* bud, shoot, from *blastanein* to bud, sprout]
: formative unit especially of living matter : germ : cell : cell layer ⟨epi*blast*⟩

blast·ed *adjective* (1552)
1 : damaged by or as if by an explosive, lightning, wind, or supernatural force ⟨upon this *blasted* heath —Shakespeare⟩ ⟨a *blasted* apple tree⟩
2 : DAMNED, DETESTABLE ⟨this *blasted* weather⟩

blas·te·ma \bla-'stē-mə\ *noun, plural* **-mas** *or* **-ma·ta** \-mə-tə\ [New Latin, from Greek *blastēma* offshoot, from *blastanein*] (circa 1823)
: a mass of living substance capable of growth and differentiation
— **blas·te·mal** \-məl\ *or* **blas·te·mat·ic** \,blas-tə-'ma-tik\ *adjective*

blast furnace *noun* (1706)
: a furnace in which combustion is forced by a current of air under pressure; *especially :* one for the reduction of iron ore

-blastic *adjective combining form* [International Scientific Vocabulary, from *-blast*]
: having (such or so many) buds, germs, cells, or cell layers ⟨diplo*blastic*⟩

blast·ie \'blas-tē\ *noun* [Scots *blast* to wither, from ²*blast*] (1787)
Scottish : an ugly little creature

blast·ment \'blas(t)-mənt\ *noun* (1602)
archaic : a blighting influence

blas·to·coel *or* **blas·to·coele** \'blas-tə-,sēl\ *noun* [International Scientific Vocabulary] (1877)
: the cavity of a blastula — see BLASTULA illustration
— **blas·to·coe·lic** \,blas-tə-'sē-lik\ *adjective*

blas·to·cyst \'blas-tə-,sist\ *noun* (circa 1881)
: the modified blastula of a placental mammal

blas·to·derm \-,dərm\ *noun* [German, from *blast-* + *-derm*] (circa 1843)
: a blastodisc after completion of cleavage and formation of the blastocoel

blas·to·der·mic vesicle \'blas-tə-,dər-mik-\ *noun* (circa 1860)
: BLASTOCYST

blas·to·disc \'blas-tə-,disk\ *noun* (circa 1881)
: the embryo-forming portion of an egg with discoidal cleavage usually appearing as a small disc on the upper surface of the yolk mass — see EGG illustration

blast·off \'blas-,tȯf\ *noun* (1951)
: a blasting off (as of a rocket)

blast off *intransitive verb* (1951)
: TAKE OFF 2d — used especially of rocket-propelled missiles and vehicles

blas·to·mere \'blas-tə-,mir\ *noun* [International Scientific Vocabulary] (1877)
: a cell produced during cleavage of a fertilized egg

blas·to·my·co·sis \,blas-tə-,mī-'kō-səs\ *noun* [New Latin, from *Blastomyces,* fungus genus, from *blast-* + Greek *mykēs* fungus; akin to Greek *myxa* mucus — more at MUCUS] (circa 1900)
: any of several fungal infections; *especially :* an infectious disease caused by a fungus (*Blastomyces dermtitides*) that affects especially the lungs and skin

blas·to·pore \'blas-tə-,pōr, -,pȯr\ *noun* (1880)
: the opening of the archenteron
— **blas·to·por·ic** \-'pȯr-ik, -'pȯr-\ *adjective*

blas·to·spore \'blas-tə-,spōr, -,spȯr\ *noun* [*blast-* + *spore*] (circa 1923)
: a fungal spore produced by budding

blas·tu·la \'blas-chə-lə\ *noun, plural* **-las** *or* **-lae** \-,lē\ [New Latin, from Greek *blastos*] (1887)
: an early metazoan embryo typically having the form of a hollow fluid-filled rounded cavity bounded by a single layer of cells — compare GASTRULA, MORULA
— **blas·tu·la·tion** \,blas-chə-'lā-shən\ *noun*

blat \'blat\ *verb* **blat·ted; blat·ting** [perhaps alteration of *bleat*] (1846)
intransitive verb
1 : to cry like a calf or sheep : BLEAT
2 a : to make a raucous noise **b :** BLAB
transitive verb
: to utter loudly or foolishly : BLURT
— **blat** *noun*

bla·tan·cy \'blā-tᵊn(t)-sē\ *noun, plural* **-cies** (1610)
1 : the quality or state of being blatant
2 : something that is blatant

bla·tant \'blā-tᵊnt\ *adjective* [perhaps from Latin *blatire* to chatter] (circa 1656)
1 : noisy especially in a vulgar or offensive manner : CLAMOROUS
2 : completely obvious, conspicuous, or obtrusive especially in a crass or offensive manner : BRAZEN
synonym see VOCIFEROUS
— **bla·tant·ly** *adverb*

blate \'blāt\ *adjective* [Middle English] (1535)
chiefly Scottish : TIMID, SHEEPISH

¹blath·er \'bla-thər\ *intransitive verb* **blath·ered; blath·er·ing** \-th(ə-)riŋ\ [Old Norse

section of blastula:
c blastocoel,
ma macromere,
mi micromere,
a animal pole,
v vegetal pole

blathra; akin to Middle High German *blōdern* to chatter] (1524)
: to talk foolishly at length — often used with *on*
— **blath·er·er** \-thər-ər\ *noun*

²blather *noun* (1719)
1 : voluble nonsensical or inconsequential talk or writing
2 : STIR, COMMOTION

blath·er·skite \'bla-thər-,skīt\ *noun* [*blather* + Scots dialect *skate* a contemptible person] (circa 1650)
1 : a person who blathers a lot
2 : NONSENSE, BLATHER

blat·ter \'bla-tər\ *intransitive verb* [perhaps from Latin *blaterare* to chatter] (circa 1555)
dialect : to talk noisily and fast

blaw \'blȯ\ *verb* **blawed; blawn** \'blȯn\; **blaw·ing** \'blȯ(-)iŋ\ [Middle English (northern dialect) *blawen,* from Old English *blāwan*] (before 12th century)
chiefly Scottish : BLOW

blax·ploi·ta·tion \,blak-(,)splȯi-'tā-shən\ *noun* [blend of *blax-* (alteration of *blacks*) and *exploitation*] (1972)
: the exploitation of blacks by producers of black-oriented films

¹blaze \'blāz\ *noun* [Middle English *blase,* from Old English *blǣse* torch] (before 12th century)
1 a : an intensely burning fire **b :** intense direct light often accompanied by heat ⟨the *blaze* of TV lights⟩ **c :** an active burning; *especially :* a sudden bursting forth of flame
2 : something that resembles the blaze of a fire: as **a :** a dazzling display ⟨a *blaze* of color⟩ **b :** a sudden outburst ⟨a *blaze* of fury⟩ **c** *plural :* HELL ⟨go to *blazes*⟩ ⟨as hot as *blazes*⟩

²blaze *intransitive verb* **blazed; blaz·ing** (13th century)
1 a : to burn brightly ⟨the sun *blazed* overhead⟩ **b :** to flare up : FLAME ⟨inflation *blazed* up⟩
2 : to be conspicuously brilliant or resplendent ⟨fields *blazing* with flowers⟩
3 : to shoot rapidly and repeatedly — usually used with *away*

³blaze *transitive verb* **blazed; blaz·ing** [Middle English *blasen,* from Middle Dutch *blāsen* to blow; akin to Old High German *blāst* blast] (1541)
: to make public or conspicuous

⁴blaze *noun* [German *Blas,* from Old High German *plas;* akin to Old English *blǣse*] (1639)
1 a : a usually white stripe down the center of the face of an animal **b :** a white or gray streak in the hair of the head
2 : a trail marker; *especially :* a mark made on a tree by chipping off a piece of the bark

⁵blaze *transitive verb* **blazed; blaz·ing** (1750)
1 : to mark (as a trail) with blazes
2 : to lead in some direction or activity ⟨*blaze* new trails in education⟩

blaz·er \'blā-zər\ *noun* (circa 1635)
1 : one that blazes
2 : a sports jacket often with notched collar and patch pockets

blaz·ing *adjective* (1596)
: of outstanding power, speed, heat, or intensity ⟨*blazing* eyes⟩ ⟨a *blazing* fastball⟩ ⟨*blazing* gunfire⟩
— **blaz·ing·ly** *adverb*

blazing star *noun* (15th century)
1 *archaic :* COMET
2 : any of various plants having conspicuous flower clusters or star-shaped flowers: as **a :** any of a genus (*Liatris*) of North American composite herbs with spikes of rosy-purple rayless flowers — called also *button snakeroot* **b :** any of several North American rough-

leaved herbs (genus *Mentzelia* of the family Losaceae)

¹bla·zon \'blā-zᵊn\ *noun* [Middle English *blason*, from Middle French] (14th century)
1 a : armorial bearings : COAT OF ARMS **b :** the proper description or representation of heraldic or armorial bearings
2 : ostentatious display
²blazon *transitive verb* **bla·zoned; bla·zon·ing** \'blāz-niŋ; 'blā-zᵊn-iŋ\ (1534)
1 : to publish widely : PROCLAIM
2 a : to describe (heraldic or armorial bearings) in technical terms **b :** to represent (armorial bearings) in drawing or engraving
3 a : DISPLAY **b :** DECK, ADORN ⟨the town was *blazoned* with flags⟩
— **bla·zon·er** \-nər; -zᵊn-ər\ *noun*
— **blazoning** *noun*
bla·zon·ry \'blā-zᵊn-rē\ *noun, plural* **-ries** (1622)
1 a : BLAZON 1b **b :** BLAZON 1a
2 : a dazzling display
¹bleach \'blēch\ *verb* [Middle English *blechen*, from Old English *blǣcean;* akin to Old English *blāc* pale; probably akin to Latin *flagrare* to burn — more at BLACK] (before 12th century)
transitive verb
1 : to remove color or stains from
2 : to make whiter or lighter especially by physical or chemical removal of color
intransitive verb
: to grow white or lose color
— **bleach·able** \'blē-chə-bəl\ *adjective*
²bleach *noun* (1887)
1 : the act or process of bleaching
2 : a preparation used in bleaching
3 : the degree of whiteness obtained by bleaching
bleach·er \'blē-chər\ *noun* (1550)
1 : one that bleaches or is used in bleaching
2 : a usually uncovered stand of tiered planks providing seating for spectators — usually used in plural
— **bleach·er·ite** \-chə-ˌrīt\ *noun*
bleaching powder *noun* (circa 1846)
: a white powder consisting chiefly of calcium hydroxide, calcium chloride, and calcium hypochlorite and used as a bleach, disinfectant, or deodorant
bleak \'blēk\ *adjective* [Middle English *bleke* pale; probably akin to Old English *blāc*] (1574)
1 : exposed and barren and often windswept
2 : COLD, RAW ⟨a *bleak* November evening⟩
3 a : lacking in warmth, life, or kindliness : GRIM **b :** not hopeful or encouraging : DEPRESSING ⟨a *bleak* outlook⟩ **c :** severely simple or austere
— **bleak·ish** \'blē-kish\ *adjective*
— **bleak·ly** *adverb*
— **bleak·ness** *noun*
¹blear \'blir\ *transitive verb* [Middle English *bleren*] (14th century)
1 : to make (the eyes) sore or watery
2 : DIM, BLUR
²blear *adjective* (14th century)
1 : dim with water or tears
2 : obscure to the view or imagination
blear–eyed \-ˌīd\ *adjective* (14th century)
: BLEARY-EYED
bleary \'blir-ē\ *adjective* (14th century)
1 *of the eyes or vision* **:** dull or dimmed especially from fatigue or sleep
2 : poorly outlined or defined : DIM
3 : tired to the point of exhaustion
— **blear·i·ly** \'blir-ə-lē\ *adverb*
— **blear·i·ness** \'blir-ē-nəs\ *noun*
bleary–eyed \-ˌīd\ *adjective* (circa 1927)
: having the eyes dimmed and watery (as from fatigue, drink, or emotion)
¹bleat \'blēt\ *verb* [*Northern also* 'blat, *Southern usually* 'blāt\ *verb* [Middle English *bleten*, from Old English *blǣtan;* akin to Latin *flēre* to

weep, Old English *bellan* to roar — more at BELLOW] (before 12th century)
intransitive verb
1 a : to utter the natural cry of a sheep or goat or a similar sound **b :** WHIMPER
2 a : to talk complainingly or with a whine **b :** BLATHER
transitive verb
: to utter in a bleating manner
— **bleat·er** *noun*
²bleat *noun* (circa 1505)
1 : the cry of a sheep or goat or a similar sound
2 : a feeble outcry, protest, or complaint
bleb \'bleb\ *noun* [perhaps alteration of *blob*] (1607)
1 : a small blister
2 : BUBBLE; *also* **:** a small particle
— **bleb·by** \'ble-bē\ *adjective*
¹bleed \'blēd\ *verb* **bled** \'bled\; **bleed·ing** [Middle English *bleden*, from Old English *blēdan*, from *blōd* blood] (before 12th century)
intransitive verb
1 a : to emit or lose blood **b :** to sacrifice one's blood especially in battle
2 : to feel anguish, pain, or sympathy ⟨a heart that *bleeds* at a friend's misfortune⟩
3 : to escape by oozing or flowing (as from a wound)
4 : to give up some constituent (as sap or dye) by exuding or diffusing it
5 a : to pay out or give money **b :** to have money extorted
6 : to be printed so as to run off one or more edges of the page after trimming
transitive verb
1 : to remove or draw blood from
2 : to get or extort money from especially over a prolonged period
3 : to draw sap from (a tree)
4 a : to extract or let out some or all of a contained substance from ⟨*bleed* a brake line⟩ **b :** to extract or cause to escape from a container **c :** to diminish gradually — usually used with *off* ⟨a pilot *bleeding* off airspeed⟩
5 : to cause (as a printed illustration) to bleed
— **bleed white :** to drain of blood or resources
²bleed *noun* (circa 1937)
: printed matter (as an illustration) that bleeds; *also* **:** the part of a bleed trimmed off
bleed·er *noun* (1803)
1 : one that bleeds; *especially* **:** HEMOPHILIAC
2 *British* **:** ROTTER; *also* **:** BLOKE
bleed·ing \'blē-diŋ, -dᵊn\ *adjective or adverb* (1858)
chiefly British **:** BLOODY — used as an intensive
bleeding heart *noun* (1691)
1 : a garden plant (*Dicentra spectabilis*) of the fumitory family with racemes of usually deep pink drooping heart-shaped flowers; *broadly* **:** any of several plants (genus *Dicentra*)
2 : a person who shows extravagant sympathy especially for an object of alleged persecution
¹bleep \'blēp\ *noun* [imitative] (1953)
: a short high-pitched sound (as from electronic equipment)
²bleep *transitive verb* (1968)
: BLIP
³bleep *interjection* (1970)
— used in place of an expletive
¹blem·ish \'ble-mish\ *transitive verb* [Middle English *blemisshen*, from Middle French *blesmiss-*, stem of *blesmir* to make pale, wound] (14th century)
: to spoil by a flaw
²blemish *noun* (1535)
: a noticeable imperfection; *especially* **:** one that seriously impairs appearance
¹blench \'blench\ *intransitive verb* [Middle English, to deceive, blench, from Old English *blencan* to deceive; akin to Old Norse *blekkja* to impose on] (13th century)

: to draw back or turn aside from lack of courage : FLINCH
synonym see RECOIL
²blench *verb* [alteration of *blanch*] (1813)
: BLEACH, WHITEN
¹blend \'blend\ *verb* **blend·ed** *also* **blent** \'blent\; **blend·ing** [Middle English, modification of Old Norse *blanda;* akin to Old English *blandan* to mix, Lithuanian *blandus* impure, cloudy] (14th century)
transitive verb
1 : MIX; *especially* **:** to combine or associate so that the separate constituents or the line of demarcation cannot be distinguished
2 : to prepare by thoroughly intermingling different varieties or grades
intransitive verb
1 a : to mingle intimately or unobtrusively **b :** to combine into an integrated whole
2 : to produce a harmonious effect
synonym see MIX
²blend *noun* (1883)
1 : something produced by blending: as **a :** a product prepared by blending **b :** a word (as *brunch*) produced by combining other words or parts of words
2 : a group of two or more consecutive consonants that begin a syllable
blende \'blend\ *noun* [German, from *blenden* to blind, from Old High German *blenten;* akin to Old English *blind*] (circa 1753)
: SPHALERITE
blended whiskey *noun* (1940)
: whiskey blended from two or more straight whiskeys or from whiskey and neutral spirits
blend·er \'blen-dər\ *noun* (circa 1798)
: one that blends; *especially* **:** an electric appliance for grinding or mixing ⟨a food *blender*⟩
blending inheritance *noun* (1922)
: the expression in offspring of phenotypic characters (as pink flower color from red and white parents) intermediate between those of the parents; *also* **:** inheritance in a now discarded theory in which the genetic material of offspring was held to be a uniform blend of that of the parents
blen·ny \'ble-nē\ *noun, plural* **blennies** [Latin *blennius*, a sea fish, from Greek *blennos*] (1774)
: any of numerous usually small and elongated marine fishes (especially families Blenniidae and Clinidae) including both scaled and scaleless forms
blephar- *or* **blepharo-** *combining form* [New Latin, from Greek, from *blepharon*]
1 : eyelid ⟨*blepharo*spasm⟩
2 : cilium ⟨*blepharo*plast⟩
bleph·a·ro·plast \'ble-fə-rō-ˌplast\ *noun* (1897)
: a basal body especially of a flagellated cell
bleph·a·ro·plas·ty \-ˌplas-tē\ *noun* (circa 1881)
: plastic surgery on the eyelid especially to remove fatty or excess tissue
bleph·a·ro·spasm \-ˌspa-zəm\ *noun* (1872)
: spasmodic winking from involuntary contraction of the orbicular muscle of the eyelids
bles·bok \'bles-ˌbäk\ *noun* [Afrikaans, from *bles* blaze + *bok* male antelope] (1824)
: a South African antelope (*Damaliscus dorcas*) having a large white patch down the center of the face
bless \'bles\ *transitive verb* **blessed** \'blest\ *also* **blest** \'blest\; **bless·ing** [Middle English, from Old English *blētsian*, from *blōd* blood; from the use of blood in consecration] (before 12th century)
1 : to hallow or consecrate by religious rite or word
2 : to hallow with the sign of the cross

3 : to invoke divine care for ⟨*bless* your heart⟩ **4 a :** PRAISE, GLORIFY ⟨*bless* his holy name⟩ **b :** to speak well of **:** APPROVE **5 :** to confer prosperity or happiness upon **6** *archaic* **:** PROTECT, PRESERVE **7 :** ENDOW, FAVOR ⟨*blessed* with athletic ability⟩

bless·ed \'ble-səd\ *also* **blest** \'blest\ *adjective* (before 12th century) **1 a :** held in reverence **:** VENERATED ⟨the *blessed* saints⟩ **b :** honored in worship **:** HALLOWED ⟨the *blessed* Trinity⟩ **c :** BEATIFIC ⟨a *blessed* visitation⟩ **2 :** of or enjoying happiness; *specifically* **:** enjoying the bliss of heaven — used as a title for a beatified person **3 :** bringing pleasure, contentment, or good fortune **4 :** — used as an intensive ⟨no one gave us a *blessed* penny —*Saturday Review*⟩ — **bless·ed·ly** *adverb* — **bless·ed·ness** *noun*

Bless·ed Sacrament \'ble-səd-\ *noun* (15th century) **:** the Communion elements; *specifically* **:** the consecrated host

bless·ing *noun* (before 12th century) **1 a :** the act or words of one that blesses **b :** APPROVAL, ENCOURAGEMENT **2 :** a thing conducive to happiness or welfare **3 :** grace said at a meal

bleth·er \'ble-thər\ *variant of* BLATHER

blew *past of* BLOW

¹blight \'blīt\ *noun* [origin unknown] (1611) **1 a :** a disease or injury of plants resulting in withering, cessation of growth, and death of parts without rotting **b :** an organism that causes blight **2 :** something that frustrates plans or hopes **3 :** something that impairs or destroys **4 :** a deteriorated condition ⟨urban *blight*⟩

²blight (1695) *transitive verb* **1 :** to affect (as a plant) with blight **2 :** to cause to deteriorate *intransitive verb* **:** to suffer from or become affected with blight

blight·er \'blī-tər\ *noun* (1822) **1 :** one that blights **2** *chiefly British* **a :** a disliked or contemptible person **b :** FELLOW, GUY

blimp \'blimp\ *noun* [imitative; perhaps from the sound made by striking the gas bag with the thumb] (1916) **1 :** a nonrigid airship **2** *capitalized* **:** COLONEL BLIMP

blimp·ish \'blim-pish\ *adjective, often capitalized* (1938) **:** of, relating to, or suggesting a Colonel Blimp — **blimp·ish·ly** *adverb* — **blimp·ish·ness** *noun*

blin \'blin\ *noun, plural* **bli·ni** \'blē-nē, 'bli-; blə-'nē\ *or* **bli·nis** \'blē-nēz, 'bli-; blə-'nēz\ [Russian] (1888) **:** a thin often buckwheat pancake usually filled (as with sour cream) and folded

¹blind \'blīnd\ *adjective* [Middle English, from Old English; akin to Old High German *blint* blind, Old English *blandan* to mix — more at BLEND] (before 12th century) **1 a (1) :** SIGHTLESS **(2) :** having less than ¹⁄₁₀ of normal vision in the more efficient eye when refractive defects are fully corrected by lenses **b :** of or relating to sightless persons **2 a :** unable or unwilling to discern or judge ⟨*blind* to a lover's faults⟩ **b :** UNQUESTIONING ⟨*blind* loyalty⟩ ⟨*blind* faith⟩ **3 a :** having no regard to rational discrimination, guidance, or restriction ⟨*blind* choice⟩ **b :** lacking a directing or controlling consciousness **c :** DRUNK **4 :** made or done without sight of certain objects or knowledge of certain facts that could serve for guidance ⟨a *blind* taste test⟩; *especially* **:** performed solely by the aid of instruments within an airplane ⟨a *blind* landing⟩

5 : DEFECTIVE: as **a :** lacking a growing point or producing leaves instead of flowers **b :** lacking a complete or legible address ⟨*blind* mail⟩ **6 a :** difficult to discern, make out, or discover **b :** hidden from sight **:** COVERED ⟨*blind* seam⟩ **7 :** having but one opening or outlet ⟨*blind* sockets⟩ **8 :** having no opening for light or passage **:** BLANK ⟨*blind* wall⟩ — **blind·ly** \'blīn(d)-lē\ *adverb* — **blind·ness** \'blīn(d)-nəs\ *noun*

²blind *transitive verb* (before 12th century) **1 a :** to make blind **b :** DAZZLE **2 a :** to withhold light from **b :** HIDE, CONCEAL — **blind·ing·ly** \'blīn-diŋ-lē\ *adverb*

³blind *noun* (1702) **1 :** something to hinder sight or keep out light: as **a :** a window shutter **b :** a roller window shade **c :** VENETIAN BLIND **d :** BLINDER **2 :** a place of concealment; *especially* **:** a concealing enclosure from which one may shoot game or observe wildlife **3 a :** something put forward for the purpose of misleading **:** SUBTERFUGE **b :** a person who acts as a decoy or distraction

⁴blind *adverb* (circa 1775) **1 :** BLINDLY: as **a :** to the point of insensibility ⟨*blind* drunk⟩ **b :** without seeing outside an airplane ⟨fly *blind*⟩ **2 :** — used as an intensive ⟨was robbed *blind*⟩

blind alley *noun* (1583) **:** a fruitless or mistaken course or direction

blind date *noun* (1925) **1 :** a date between two persons who have not previously met **2 :** either participant in a blind date

blind·er \'blīn-dər\ *noun* (1809) **1 :** either of two flaps on a horse's bridle to keep it from seeing objects at its sides **2** *plural* **:** a limitation or obstruction to sight or discernment

blind·fish \'blīn(d)-,fish\ *noun* (1843) **:** any of several small fishes with vestigial functionless eyes found usually in the waters of caves

¹blind·fold \-,fōld\ *transitive verb* [alteration of Middle English *blindfellen, blindfelden* to strike blind, blindfold, from *blind* + *fellen* to fell] (1599) **1 :** to cover the eyes of with or as if with a bandage **2 :** to hinder from seeing; *especially* **:** to keep from comprehension — **blindfold** *adjective*

²blindfold *noun* (1880) **1 :** a bandage for covering the eyes **2 :** something that obscures mental or physical vision

blind gut *noun* (15th century) **:** a digestive cavity open at only one end; *especially* **:** the cecum of the large intestine

blind·man's buff \'blīn(d)-'manz-\ *noun* (1600) **:** a group game in which a blindfolded player tries to catch and identify another player — called also *blindman's bluff*

blind pig *noun* (1887) **:** BLIND TIGER

blind·side \'blīn(d)-,sīd\ *transitive verb* (1968) **1 :** to hit unexpectedly from or as if from the blind side **2 :** to surprise unpleasantly

blind side *noun* (1606) **1 :** the side away from which one is looking **2 :** the side on which one that is blind in one eye cannot see

blind spot *noun* (1872) **1 a :** the nearly circular light-colored area at the back of the retina where the optic nerve enters the eyeball and which is not sensitive to light — called also *optic disk;* see EYE illustration **b :** a portion of a field that cannot be seen or inspected with available equipment

2 : an area in which one fails to exercise judgment or discrimination

blind tiger *noun* (1857) **:** a place that sells intoxicants illegally

blind trust *noun* (1969) **:** an arrangement in which the financial holdings of a person in an influential position (as a government official) are placed in the control of a fiduciary in order to avoid a possible conflict of interest

blind·worm \'blīnd-,wərm\ *noun* (15th century) **:** SLOWWORM

¹blink \'bliŋk\ *verb* [Middle English, to open one's eyes] (14th century) *intransitive verb* **1 a** *obsolete* **:** to look glancingly **:** PEEP **b :** to look with half-shut eyes **c :** to close and open the eyes involuntarily (as when dazzled) **2 :** to shine dimly or intermittently **3 a :** to look with too little concern **b :** to look with surprise or dismay *transitive verb* **1 a :** to cause to blink **b :** to remove (as tears) from the eye by blinking **2 :** to deny recognition to

²blink *noun* (1594) **1** *chiefly Scottish* **:** GLIMPSE, GLANCE **2 :** GLIMMER, SPARKLE **3 :** a usually involuntary shutting and opening of the eye **4 :** ICEBLINK — **on the blink :** in or into a disabled or useless condition

¹blink·er \'bliŋ-kər\ *noun* (1636) **1 :** one that blinks; *especially* **:** a light that flashes off and on (as for the directing of traffic or the coded signaling of messages) **2 a :** BLINDER 1 **b :** a cloth hood with shades projecting at the sides of the eye openings used on skittish racehorses — usually used in plural **3** *plural* **:** BLINDER 2

²blinker *transitive verb* (1865) **:** to put blinders on

blink·ered \'bliŋ-kərd\ *adjective* (1867) **1 :** limited in scope or understanding **:** NARROW-MINDED **2 :** fitted with blinders

blin·tze \'blin(t)-sə\ *or* **blintz** \'blin(t)s\ *noun* [Yiddish *blintse,* of Slavic origin; akin to Ukrainian *mlynets',* diminutive of *mlyn* pancake] (1903) **:** a thin usually wheat-flour pancake folded to form a casing and then sautéed or baked

¹blip \'blip\ *noun* [imitative] (1945) **1 :** a trace on an oscilloscope; *especially* **:** a spot on a radar screen **2 :** a short crisp sound **3 :** an interruption of the sound received in a radio or television program or occurring in a recording as a result of blipping **4 :** a transient sharp movement up or down (as of a quantity commonly shown on a graph)

²blip *transitive verb* **blipped; blip·ping** (1968) **:** to remove (recorded sound) from a recording so that there is an interruption of the sound in the reproduction ⟨a censor *blipped* the swearwords⟩

bliss \'blis\ *noun* [Middle English *blisse,* from Old English *bliss;* akin to Old English *blīthe* blithe] (before 12th century) **1 :** complete happiness **2 :** PARADISE, HEAVEN

blissed–out \'blist-'aút\ *adjective* (1973) **:** being in a state of bliss **:** ECSTATIC

bliss·ful \'blis-fəl\ *adjective* (12th century) **1 :** full of, marked by, or causing bliss **2 :** happily benighted ⟨*blissful* ignorance⟩ — **bliss·ful·ly** \-fə-lē\ *adverb* — **bliss·ful·ness** *noun*

¹blis·ter \'blis-tər\ *noun* [Middle English, modification of Old French or Middle Dutch;

Old French *blostre* leprous nodule, from Middle Dutch *bluyster* blister; akin to Old English *blǣst* blast] (14th century)
1 : an elevation of the epidermis containing watery liquid
2 : an enclosed raised spot (as in paint) resembling a blister
3 : an agent that causes blistering
4 : a disease of plants marked by large swollen patches on the leaves
5 : any of various structures that bulge out (as a gunner's compartment on a bomber)
— **blis·tery** \-t(ə-)rē\ *adjective*
²**blister** *verb* **blis·tered; blis·ter·ing** \-t(ə-)riŋ\ (15th century)
intransitive verb
: to become affected with a blister
transitive verb
1 : to raise a blister on
2 : LAMBASTE 2
blister beetle *noun* (1816)
: a beetle (as the Spanish fly) used medicinally dried and powdered to raise blisters on the skin; *broadly :* any of a family (Meloidae) of soft-bodied beetles
blister copper *noun* (1861)
: metallic copper of a black blistered surface that is the product of converting copper matte and is about 98.5 to 99.5 percent pure
blis·ter·ing *adjective* (1562)
: extremely intense or severe
— **blistering** *adverb*
— **blis·ter·ing·ly** \-t(ə-)riŋ-lē\ *adverb*
blister pack *noun* (1955)
: a package holding and displaying merchandise in a clear plastic case sealed to a sheet of cardboard
blister rust *noun* (1916)
: any of several diseases of pines that are caused by rust fungi (genus *Cronartium*) in the aecial stage and that affect the sapwood and inner bark and produce blisters externally
blithe \ˈblīth, ˈblīth\ *adjective* **blith·er; blith·est** [Middle English, from Old English *blīthe;* akin to Old High German *blīdi* joyous] (before 12th century)
1 : of a happy lighthearted character or disposition
2 : lacking due thought or consideration **:** CASUAL, HEEDLESS ⟨*blithe* unconcern⟩
synonym see MERRY
— **blithe·ly** *adverb*
blith·er \ˈbli-thər\ *intransitive verb or noun* [by alteration] (1868)
: BLATHER
blithe·some \ˈblīth-səm, ˈblīth-\ *adjective* (1724)
: GAY, MERRY
— **blithe·some·ly** *adverb*
blitz \ˈblits\ *noun* (circa 1939)
1 a : BLITZKRIEG 1 **b** (1) **:** an intensive aerial campaign (2) **:** AIR RAID
2 a : an intensive nonmilitary campaign **:** a sudden overwhelming bombardment ⟨an advertising *blitz*⟩ **b :** a rush of the passer by the defensive linebackers in football
— **blitz** *verb*
blitz·krieg \-ˌkrēg\ *noun* [German, from *Blitz* lightning + *Krieg* war] (1939)
1 : war conducted with great speed and force; *specifically :* a violent surprise offensive by massed air forces and mechanized ground forces in close coordination
2 : BLITZ 2a
bliz·zard \ˈbli-zərd\ *noun* [origin unknown] (1870)
1 : a long severe snowstorm
2 : an intensely strong cold wind filled with fine snow
3 : an overwhelming rush or deluge ⟨the *blizzard* of mail at Christmas⟩ ◆
— **bliz·zardy** \ˈbli-zər-dē\ *also* **bliz·zard·ly** \-ˌzərd-lē\ *adjective*
¹**bloat** \ˈblōt\ *adjective* [alteration of Middle English *blout*] (14th century)
: BLOATED, PUFFY

²**bloat** (1677)
transitive verb
1 : to make turgid or swollen
2 : to fill to capacity or overflowing
intransitive verb
: SWELL
³**bloat** *noun* (1860)
1 : one that is bloated
2 : a flatulent digestive disturbance of domestic animals and especially cattle marked by abdominal bloating
bloat·ed *adjective* (1711)
1 : being much larger than what is warranted ⟨a *bloated* estimate⟩
2 : obnoxiously vain
¹**bloat·er** \ˈblō-tər\ *noun* [obsolete *bloat* (to cure)] (1832)
: a large fat herring or mackerel lightly salted and briefly smoked
²**bloater** *noun* [²*bloat*] (1896)
: a small but common cisco (*Coregonus hoyi*) of the Great Lakes
¹**blob** \ˈbläb\ *noun* [Middle English] (15th century)
1 a : a small drop or lump of something viscid or thick **b :** a daub or spot of color
2 : something ill-defined or amorphous
²**blob** *transitive verb* **blobbed; blob·bing** (15th century)
: to mark with blobs **:** SPLOTCH
bloc \ˈbläk\ *noun* [French, literally, block] (1903)
1 a : a temporary combination of parties in a legislative assembly **b :** a group of legislators who act together for some common purpose irrespective of party lines
2 a : a combination of persons, groups, or nations forming a unit with a common interest or purpose **b :** a group of nations united by treaty or agreement for mutual support or joint action
¹**block** \ˈbläk\ *noun, often attributive* [Middle English *blok*, from Middle French *bloc*, from Middle Dutch *blok*; akin to Old High German *bloh* block] (14th century)
1 : a compact usually solid piece of substantial material especially when worked or altered to serve a particular purpose: as **a :** the piece of wood on which the neck of a person condemned to be beheaded is laid for execution **b :** a mold or form on which articles are shaped or displayed **c :** a hollow rectangular building unit usually of artificial material **d :** a lightweight usually cubical and solid wooden or plastic building toy that is usually provided in sets **e :** the casting that contains the cylinders of an internal-combustion engine
2 a : OBSTACLE **b :** an obstruction of an opponent's play in sports; *especially :* a halting or impeding of the progress or movement of an opponent in football by use of the body **c** (1) **:** interruption of normal physiological function (as of a tissue or organ); *especially :* HEART BLOCK (2) **:** local anesthesia (as by injection) produced by interruption of the flow of impulses along a nerve **d :** interruption or cessation especially of train of thought by competing thoughts or psychological suppression
3 *slang :* HEAD 1 ⟨threatened to knock his *block* off⟩
4 : a wooden or metal case enclosing one or more pulleys and having a hook, eye, or strap by which it may be attached
5 : a piece of material (as wood or linoleum) having on its surface a hand-cut design from which impressions are to be printed
6 a (1) **:** a usually rectangular space (as in a city) enclosed by streets and occupied by or intended for buildings (2) **:** the distance along one of the sides of such a block **b** (1) **:** a large building divided into separate functional units (2) **:** a line of row houses (3) **:** a distinctive part of a building or integrated group of buildings **c :** a short section of railroad track in the block system

7 : a platform from which property is sold at auction
8 a : a quantity, number, or section of things dealt with as a unit **b :** BLOC 2
— **on the block :** for sale
²**block** (1580)
transitive verb
1 a : to make unsuitable for passage or progress by obstruction **b** *archaic :* BLOCKADE **c :** to hinder the passage, progress, or accomplishment of by or as if by interposing an obstruction **d :** to shut off from view (forest canopy *blocking* the sun) **e :** to interfere usually legitimately with (as an opponent) in various games or sports **f :** to prevent normal functioning of **g :** to restrict the exchange of (as currency or checks)
2 : to mark or indicate the outline or chief lines of ⟨*block* out a design⟩ ⟨*block* in a sketched figure⟩
3 : to shape on, with, or as if with a block ⟨*block* a hat⟩
4 : to secure, support, or provide with a block
5 : to work out or chart the movements of (as stage performers) — often used with *out*
6 : to make (two or more lines of writing or type) flush at the left or at both left and right
intransitive verb
: to block an opponent in sports
synonym see HINDER
— **block·er** *noun*
¹**block·ade** \blä-ˈkād\ *transitive verb* **block·ad·ed; block·ad·ing** (1680)
1 : to subject to a blockade
2 : BLOCK, OBSTRUCT
— **block·ad·er** *noun*
²**blockade** *noun* (1693)
1 : the isolation by a warring nation of an enemy area (as a harbor) by troops or warships to prevent passage of persons or supplies; *broadly :* a restrictive measure designed to obstruct the commerce and communications of an unfriendly nation
2 : something that blocks
3 : interruption of normal physiological function (as transmission of nerve impulses) of a tissue or organ
block·ade–run·ner \-ˈkād-ˌrə-nər\ *noun* (1863)
: a ship or person that runs through a blockade

◇ WORD HISTORY
blizzard The word *blizzard*, when used in the meaning "severe snowstorm," first turned up in 19th century northwestern Iowa. Its earliest recorded appearance in printed form was in the April 23, 1870 issue of the *Northern Vindicator,* a newspaper published in the town of Estherville. Spelled *blizard*—the form *blizzard* appeared in the paper a week later—it was cautiously enclosed in quotation marks. *Blizzard* crops up again during the following years in several other newspapers of Iowa and neighboring states, and by 1888, when a March storm paralyzed the Eastern seaboard for days and took 400 lives, the word was well-known nationally. In other senses, however, *blizzard* existed decades earlier, and the ultimate origin of the word is unclear. The frontiersman and politician Davy Crockett used it on two occasions in the 1830s, once to mean a rifle blast, and once to refer figuratively to a blast of words. From a gun blast to a verbal blast to a wintry blast is a reasonable enough development, but evidence for *blizzard* is so scattered in time and place that it is difficult to draw any firm conclusions about the word's history.

\ə\ abut \ᵊ\ kitten \ər\ further \a\ ash \ā\ ace
\ä\ mop, mar \aú\ out \ch\ chin \e\ bet \ē\ easy
\g\ go \i\ hit \ī\ ice \j\ job \ŋ\ sing \ō\ go
\ó\ law \ói\ boy \th\ thin \th\ the \ü\ loot \ú\ foot
\y\ yet \zh\ vision *see also* Guide to Pronunciation

block·ade–run·ning \-,rə-niŋ\ *noun*
block·age \'blä-kij\ *noun* (1874)
: an act or instance of obstructing : the state of being blocked ⟨a *blockage* in a coronary artery⟩

block and tackle *noun* (1838)
: pulley blocks with associated rope or cable for hoisting or hauling

block·bust·er \'bläk-,bəs-tər\ *noun* (1942)
1 : a very large high-explosive bomb
2 : one that is notably effective, successful, large, or violent
3 : one who engages in blockbusting

block·bust·ing \-tiŋ\ *noun* (1954)
: profiteering by inducing property owners to sell hastily and often at a loss by appeals to fears of depressed values because of threatened minority encroachment and then reselling at inflated prices

block diagram *noun* (1944)
: a diagram (as of a system, process, or program) in which labeled figures (as rectangles) and interconnecting lines represent the relationship of parts

blocked \'bläkt\ *adjective* (1945)
: exhibiting or affected by a psychological block ⟨a *blocked* writer⟩

block grant *noun* (1900)
: an unrestricted federal grant

block·head \'bläk-,hed\ *noun* (1549)
: a stupid person

block·house \-,haús\ *noun* (1512)
1 a : a structure of heavy timbers formerly used for military defense with sides loopholed and pierced for gunfire and often with a projecting upper story **b** : a small easily defended building for protection from enemy fire

blockhouse 1a

2 : a building usually of reinforced concrete serving as an observation point for an operation likely to be accompanied by heat, blast, or radiation hazard

block·ish \'blä-kish\ *adjective* (1565)
: resembling a block

block letter *noun* (1908)
: an often hand-drawn simple capital letter composed of strokes of uniform thickness

block party *noun* (1941)
: an outdoor public party put on by the residents of a city block or neighborhood

block plane *noun* (circa 1884)
: a small plane made with the blade set at a lower pitch than other planes and used chiefly on end grains of wood

block system *noun* (1864)
: a system by which a railroad track is divided into short sections and trains are run by guidance signals

blocky \'blä-kē\ *adjective* **block·i·er; -est** (circa 1879)
1 : resembling a block in form : CHUNKY
2 : filled with or made up of blocks or patches

bloke \'blōk\ *noun* [origin unknown] (1851)
chiefly British : MAN, FELLOW

¹blond *or* **blonde** \'bländ\ *adjective* [Middle French *blond*, masculine, *blonde*, feminine] (15th century)
1 a : of a flaxen, golden, light auburn, or pale yellowish brown color ⟨*blond* hair⟩ **b** : of a pale white or rosy white color ⟨*blond* skin⟩ **c** : being a blond
2 a : of a light color **b** : of the color blond **c** : made light-colored by bleaching ⟨a table of *blond* walnut⟩
— **blond·ish** \'blän-dish\ *adjective*

²blond *or* **blonde** *noun* (1822)
1 : a person having blond hair and usually a light complexion and blue or gray eyes
2 : a light yellowish brown to dark grayish yellow

¹blood \'bləd\ *noun, often attributive* [Middle English, from Old English *blōd*; akin to Old High German *bluot* blood] (before 12th century)
1 a : the fluid that circulates in the heart, arteries, capillaries, and veins of a vertebrate animal carrying nourishment and oxygen to and bringing away waste products from all parts of the body **b** : a comparable fluid of an invertebrate **c** : a fluid resembling blood
2 : the shedding of blood; *also* : the taking of life
3 a : LIFEBLOOD; *broadly* : LIFE **b** : human stock or lineage; *especially* : royal lineage ⟨a prince of the *blood*⟩ **c** : relationship by descent from a common ancestor : KINSHIP **d** : persons related through common descent : KINDRED **e** (1) : honorable or high birth or descent (2) : descent from parents of recognized breed or pedigree
4 a : blood regarded as the seat of the emotions : TEMPER **b** *obsolete* : LUST **c** : a showy foppish man : RAKE
5 : PERSONNEL ⟨a company in need of new *blood*⟩
6 : a black American male — used especially among blacks

²blood *transitive verb* (1633)
1 *archaic* : BLEED 1
2 : to stain or wet with blood
3 : to expose (a hunting dog) to sight, scent, or taste of the blood of its prey
4 : to give experience to ⟨troops *blooded* in battle⟩

blood–and–guts \'blə-d°n-'gəts\ *adjective* (1937)
: marked by great vigor, violence, or fierceness ⟨*blood-and-guts* competition⟩

blood·bath \'bləd-,bath, -,báth\ *noun* (1867)
: a great slaughter

blood–brain barrier \'bləd-'brān-\ *noun* (1944)
: a barrier created by the modification of brain capillaries (as by reduction in fenestration and formation of tight cell-to-cell contacts) that prevents many substances from leaving the blood and crossing the capillary walls into the brain tissues

blood brother *noun* (1890)
1 : a brother by birth
2 : one of two men pledged to mutual loyalty by a ceremonial use of each other's blood
— **blood brotherhood** *noun*

blood cell *noun* (1846)
: a cell normally present in blood

blood count *noun* (circa 1900)
: the determination of the blood cells in a definite volume of blood; *also* : the number of cells so determined

blood·cur·dling \'bləd-,kərd-liŋ, -,kər-d°l-iŋ\ *adjective* (1904)
: arousing fright or horror ⟨*bloodcurdling* screams⟩

blood doping *noun* (1973)
: a technique for temporarily improving athletic performance in which oxygen-carrying red blood cells from blood previously withdrawn from an athlete are reinjected just before an event — called also *blood packing*

blood·ed \'blə-dəd\ *adjective* (1595)
1 : having blood of a specified kind — used in combination ⟨cold-*blooded*⟩
2 : being entirely or largely purebred ⟨a herd of *blooded* stock⟩

blood feud *noun* (1858)
: a feud between different clans or families

blood fluke *noun* (1872)
: SCHISTOSOME

blood group *noun* (1916)
: one of the classes (as those designated A, B, AB, or O) into which individuals or their blood can be separated on the basis of the presence or absence of specific antigens in the blood — called also *blood type*

blood·guilt \'bləd-,gilt\ *noun* (1593)
: guilt resulting from bloodshed

— **blood·guilt·i·ness** \-,gil-tē-nəs\ *noun*
— **blood·guilty** \-tē\ *adjective*

blood·hound \'bləd-,haúnd\ *noun* (14th century)
1 : any of a breed of large powerful hounds of European origin remarkable for acuteness of smell
2 : a person keen in pursuit

bloodhound 1

blood·less \'bləd-ləs\ *adjective* (before 12th century)
1 : deficient in or free from blood
2 : not accompanied by loss or shedding of blood ⟨a *bloodless* victory⟩
3 : lacking in spirit or vitality
4 : lacking in human feeling ⟨*bloodless* statistics⟩
— **blood·less·ly** *adverb*
— **blood·less·ness** *noun*

blood·let·ting \-,le-tiŋ\ *noun* (13th century)
1 : PHLEBOTOMY
2 : BLOODSHED
3 : elimination of personnel or resources

blood·line \-,līn\ *noun* (circa 1909)
: a sequence of direct ancestors especially in a pedigree; *also* : FAMILY, STRAIN

blood·mo·bile \-mō-,bēl\ *noun* (1948)
: an automotive vehicle staffed and equipped for collecting blood from donors

blood money *noun* (1535)
1 : money obtained at the cost of another's life
2 : money paid by a manslayer or members of his family, clan, or tribe to the next of kin of a person killed by him

blood orange *noun* (1855)
: a cultivated sweet orange having fruit with usually red pulp; *also* : its fruit

blood platelet *noun* (1898)
: one of the minute protoplasmic disks of vertebrate blood that assist in blood clotting

blood poisoning *noun* (1863)
: SEPTICEMIA

blood pressure *noun* (1874)
: pressure that is exerted by the blood upon the walls of the blood vessels and especially arteries and that varies with the muscular efficiency of the heart, the blood volume and viscosity, the age and health of the individual, and the state of the vascular wall

blood·red \'bləd-'red\ *adjective* (before 12th century)
: having the color of blood

blood·root \-,rüt, -,rút\ *noun* (1722)
: a plant (*Sanguinaria canadensis*) of the poppy family having a red root and sap and bearing a solitary lobed leaf and white flower in early spring — called also *sanguinaria*

blood sausage *noun* (1868)
: very dark sausage containing a large proportion of blood — called also *blood pudding*

blood serum *noun* (circa 1909)
: blood from which the fibrin and suspended material (as cells) have been removed

blood·shed \'bləd-,shed\ *noun* (15th century)
1 : the shedding of blood
2 : the taking of life : SLAUGHTER

blood·shot \-,shät\ *adjective* (1552)
of an eye : inflamed to redness

blood sport *noun* (1895)
: a sport or contest (as hunting or cockfighting) involving bloodshed

blood·stain \-,stān\ *noun* (1820)
: a discoloration caused by blood

blood·stained \-,stānd\ *adjective* (1596)
1 : stained with blood
2 : involved with slaughter ⟨a *bloodstained* chronicle of war⟩

blood·stock \-,stäk\ *noun* (1830)
: horses of Thoroughbred breeding

blood·stone \-ˌstōn\ noun (1551)
: a green chalcedony sprinkled with red spots resembling blood — called also *heliotrope*

blood·stream \-ˌstrēm\ noun (1873)
1 : the flowing blood in a circulatory system
2 : a mainstream of power or vitality ⟨introduce into the economic *bloodstream* a large amount of money —*Harper's*⟩

blood·suck·er \-ˌsə-kər\ noun (14th century)
1 : an animal that sucks blood; *especially* : LEECH
2 : a person who sponges or preys on another
— **blood·suck·ing** \-kiŋ\ adjective

blood sugar noun (1918)
: the glucose in the blood; *also* : its concentration (as in milligrams per 100 milliliters)

blood test noun (1912)
: a test of the blood; *especially* : a serologic test for the presence of substances indicative of disease (as syphilis) or disease-causing agents (as HIV)

blood·thirsty \ˈbləd-ˌthər-stē\ adjective (1535)
: eager for or marked by the shedding of blood, violence, or killing
— **blood·thirst·i·ly** \-stə-lē\ adverb
— **blood·thirst·i·ness** \-stē-nəs\ noun

blood·typ·ing \-ˌtī-piŋ\ noun (1926)
: the action or process of determining an individual's blood group

blood vessel noun (1694)
: any of the vessels through which blood circulates in the body

blood·worm \ˈbləd-ˌwərm\ noun (1714)
1 : any of various reddish annelid worms (as of genera *Glycera* or *Tubifex*) often used as bait
2 : any of several strongyle worms (genus *Strongylus*) that are parasitic in the large intestine of horses

¹bloody \ˈblə-dē\ adjective **blood·i·er; -est** (before 12th century)
1 a : containing or made up of blood **b** : of or contained in the blood
2 : smeared or stained with blood
3 : accompanied by or involving bloodshed; *especially* : marked by great slaughter
4 a : MURDEROUS **b** : MERCILESS, CRUEL
5 : BLOODRED
6 — used as an intensive; sometimes considered vulgar ☆
— **blood·i·ly** \ˈblə-dᵊl-ē\ adverb
— **blood·i·ness** \ˈblə-dē-nəs\ noun

²bloody transitive verb **blood·ied; bloody·ing** (1530)
: to make bloody or bloodred

³bloody adverb (1676)
— used as an intensive; sometimes considered vulgar

Bloody Mary noun, plural **Bloody Marys** [probably from *Bloody Mary,* appellation of Mary I of England] (1947)
: a cocktail consisting essentially of vodka and usually spiced tomato juice

bloody–mind·ed \ˌblə-dē-ˈmīn-dəd\ adjective (1584)
1 : inclined towards violence or bloodshed
2 *chiefly British* : stubbornly contrary or obstructive : CANTANKEROUS
— **bloody–mind·ed·ness** noun

bloody murder adverb (1925)
: in a loud and violent manner ⟨ran off, screaming *bloody murder*⟩; *also* : in vehement protest ⟨screaming *bloody murder* over the pay cut⟩

bloody shirt noun (1874)
: something intended to stir up or revive partisan animosity — usually used in the phrase *wave the bloody shirt*

¹bloom \ˈblüm\ noun [Middle English *blome* lump of metal, from Old English *blōma*] (before 12th century)
1 : a mass of wrought iron from the forge or puddling furnace
2 : a bar of iron or steel hammered or rolled from an ingot

²bloom noun [Middle English *blome,* from Old Norse *blōm;* akin to Old English *blōwan* to blossom — more at BLOW] (13th century)
1 a : FLOWER **b** : the flowering state ⟨the roses in *bloom*⟩ **c** : a period of flowering ⟨the spring *bloom*⟩ **d** : an excessive growth of plankton
2 a : a state or time of beauty, freshness, and vigor **b** : a state or time of high development or achievement ⟨a career in full *bloom*⟩
3 : a surface coating or appearance: as **a** : a delicate powdery coating on some fruits and leaves **b** : a rosy appearance of the cheeks; *broadly* : an outward evidence of freshness or healthy vigor **c** : a cloudiness on a film of varnish or lacquer **d** : a grayish discoloration on chocolate **e** : glare caused by an object reflecting too much light into a television camera

³bloom (13th century)
intransitive verb
1 a : to produce or yield flowers **b** : to support abundant plant life ⟨make the desert *bloom*⟩
2 a (1) : to mature into achievement of one's potential (2) : to flourish in youthful beauty, freshness or excellence **b** : to shine out : GLOW
3 : to appear or occur unexpectedly or in remarkable quantity or degree
4 : to become densely populated with microorganisms and especially plankton — used of bodies of water
transitive verb
1 *obsolete* : to cause to bloom
2 : to give bloom to

¹bloom·er \ˈblü-mər\ noun (circa 1736)
1 : a plant that blooms
2 : a person who reaches full competence or maturity
3 [*blooming*] : a stupid blunder

²bloo·mer \ˈblü-mər\ noun [Amelia *Bloomer*] (1851)
1 : a costume for women consisting of a skirt over long loose trousers gathered closely about the ankles
2 *plural* **a** : full loose trousers gathered at the knee formerly worn by women for athletics **b** : underpants of similar design worn chiefly by girls and women ◇

bloom·ing \ˈblü-mən, -miŋ\ adjective or adverb [probably euphemism for *bloody*] (1882)
chiefly British — used as a generalized intensive ⟨*blooming* fool⟩

bloomy \ˈblü-mē\ adjective (1593)
1 : full of bloom
2 : covered with bloom ⟨*bloomy* plums⟩
3 : showing freshness or vitality ⟨all the *bloomy* flush of life is fled —Oliver Goldsmith⟩

bloop \ˈblüp\ noun [back-formation from *blooper*] (1967)
: BLOOPER 1a
— **bloop** transitive verb

bloop·er \ˈblü-pər\ noun [*bloop* (an unpleasant sound)] (1937)
1 a : a fly ball hit barely beyond a baseball infield **b** : a high baseball pitch lobbed to the batter
2 : an embarrassing public blunder

¹blos·som \ˈblä-səm\ noun [Middle English *blosme,* from Old English *blōstm;* akin to Old English *blōwan*] (before 12th century)
1 a : the flower of a seed plant; *also* : the mass of such flowers on a single plant **b** : the state of bearing flowers
2 : a peak period or stage of development
— **blos·somy** \-sə-mē\ adjective

²blossom intransitive verb (before 12th century)
1 : BLOOM
2 a : to come into one's own : DEVELOP ⟨a *blossoming* talent⟩ **b** : to become evident : make an appearance

¹blot \ˈblät\ noun [Middle English] (14th century)
1 : a soiling or disfiguring mark : SPOT
2 : a mark of reproach : moral flaw

3 : a usually nitrocellulose sheet that contains spots of immobilized macromolecules (as of DNA, RNA, or protein) or their fragments and is used to identify specific components of the spots by applying a molecular probe (as a complementary nucleic acid or a radioactively labeled antibody)

²blot verb **blot·ted; blot·ting** (15th century)
transitive verb
1 : to spot, stain, or spatter with a discoloring substance
2 *obsolete* : MAR; *especially* : to stain with infamy
3 a : to dry (as writing) with an absorbing agent **b** : to remove with absorbing material ⟨*blotting* up spilled water⟩
intransitive verb
1 : to make a blot
2 : to become marked with a blot

³blot noun [origin unknown] (1595)
1 : a lone backgammon man exposed to capture
2 *archaic* : a weak or exposed point

¹blotch \ˈbläch\ transitive verb (1604)
: to mark or mar with blotches

²blotch noun [perhaps blend of ¹*blot* and ³*botch*] (1669)
1 : IMPERFECTION, BLEMISH
2 : a spot or mark (as of color or ink) especially when large or irregular
— **blotch·i·ly** \ˈblä-chə-lē\ adverb
— **blotchy** \ˈblä-chē\ adjective

☆ SYNONYMS

Bloody, sanguinary, gory mean affected by or involving the shedding of blood. BLOODY is applied especially to things that are actually covered with blood or are made up of blood ⟨*bloody* hands⟩. SANGUINARY applies especially to something attended by, or someone inclined to, bloodshed ⟨the Civil War was America's most *sanguinary* conflict⟩. GORY suggests a profusion of blood and slaughter ⟨exceptionally *gory,* even for a horror movie⟩.

◇ WORD HISTORY

bloomer *Bloomers* are named after a small-town feminist who unwittingly sparked a fashion revolution. A resident of Seneca Falls, New York—the site of a historic women's rights convention in 1848—Amelia Jenks Bloomer (1818–1894) was a feminist long before the cause was popular or the term even invented. A newspaper journalist already writing about various women's issues, she became involved with the right of women to liberate themselves from traditional clothing in 1849, when she defended the wearing of pantalets by the actress Fanny Kemble. The following year she rushed to the defense of visiting feminists who appeared in Seneca Falls wearing full Turkish pantaloons under a shortened skirt. Her articles attracted the attention of newspapers in New York City and elsewhere, and soon a fad of national proportions developed. Correspondents from all over solicited her for patterns and information about the new attire, which was first known in 1851 as the "Bloomer Costume" and immediately shortened to *bloomer* or *bloomers*. Bloomer herself wore the new attire exclusively for the next several years. Aided by their suitability for women's bicycling, bloomers remained fashionable for the rest of the 19th century.

\ə\ abut \ᵊ\ kitten \ər\ **further** \a\ ash \ā\ ace
\ä\ mop, mar \aů\ out \ch\ chin \e\ bet \ē\ **easy**
\g\ go \i\ hit \ī\ ice \j\ job \ŋ\ sing \ō\ go
\ȯ\ law \ȯi\ boy \th\ **thin** \t͟h\ **the** \ü\ loot \ů\ foot
\y\ yet \zh\ vision *see also* Guide to Pronunciation

blot out *transitive verb* (1530)
1 : to make obscure, insignificant, or inconsequential
2 : WIPE OUT, DESTROY
blot·ter \'blä-tər\ *noun* (1591)
1 : a piece of blotting paper
2 : a book in which entries (as of transactions or occurrences) are made temporarily pending their transfer to permanent record books ⟨police *blotter*⟩
blotting paper *noun* (15th century)
: a spongy unsized paper for absorbing ink
blot·to \'blä-(,)tō\ *adjective* [probably irregular from ²*blot*] (1917)
: DRUNK 1a
¹**blouse** \'blaüs *also* 'blaüz\ *noun, plural* **blous·es** \'blaü-səz, -zəz\ [French] (1828)
1 a : a long loose overgarment that resembles a shirt or smock and is worn especially by workmen, artists, and peasants **b** : the jacket of a uniform
2 : a usually loose-fitting garment especially for women that covers the body from the neck to the waist
— **blousy** \'blaü-sē, -zē\ *adjective*
²**blouse** \'blaüs, 'blaüz\ *verb* **bloused; blous·ing** (1904)
intransitive verb
: to fall in a fold ⟨coats that *blouse* above the hip⟩
transitive verb
: to cause to blouse ⟨trousers are *bloused* over the boots⟩
blou·son \'blaü-,sän, 'blü-,zän\ *noun* [French, from *blouse*] (1904)
: a garment (as a dress) having a close waistband with blousing of material over it
¹**blow** \'blō\ *verb* **blew** \'blü\; **blown** \'blōn\; **blow·ing** [Middle English, from Old English *blāwan;* akin to Old High German *blāen* to blow, Latin *flare,* Greek *phallos* penis] (before 12th century)
intransitive verb
1 *of air* : to move with speed or force
2 : to send forth a current of air or other gas
3 a : to make a sound by or as if by blowing **b** *of a wind instrument* : SOUND
4 a : BOAST **b** : to talk windily
5 a : PANT, GASP ⟨the horse *blew* heavily⟩ **b** *of a cetacean* : to eject moisture-laden air from the lungs through the blowhole
6 : to move or be carried by or as if by wind ⟨just *blew* into town⟩
7 *of an electric fuse* : to melt when overloaded — often used with *out*
8 *of a tire* : to release the contained air through a spontaneous rupture — usually used with *out*
transitive verb
1 a : to set (gas or vapor) in motion **b** : to act on with a current of gas or vapor
2 : to play or sound on (a wind instrument)
3 a : to spread by report **b** *past participle* **blowed** \'blōd\ : DAMN ⟨*blow* the expense⟩ ⟨I'm *blowed* if I know⟩
4 a : to drive with a current of gas or vapor **b** : to clear of contents by forcible passage of a current of air **c** : to project (a gesture or sound made with the mouth) by blowing ⟨*blew* him a kiss⟩
5 a : to distend with or as if with gas **b** : to produce or shape by the action of blown or injected air ⟨*blowing* bubbles⟩ ⟨*blowing* glass⟩
6 *of insects* : to deposit eggs or larvae on or in
7 : to shatter, burst, or destroy by explosion
8 a : to put out of breath with exertion **b** : to let (as a horse) pause to catch the breath
9 a : to expend (as money) extravagantly ⟨*blew* $50 on lunch⟩ **b** : to treat with unusual expenditure ⟨I'll *blow* you to a steak⟩
10 : to cause (a fuse) to blow
11 : to rupture by too much pressure ⟨*blew* a gasket⟩
12 : to foul up hopelessly ⟨*blew* her lines⟩ ⟨*blew* his chance⟩
13 : to leave hurriedly ⟨*blew* town⟩

14 : to propel with great force or speed ⟨*blew* a fastball by the batter⟩
— **blow hot and cold** : to be favorable at one moment and adverse the next
— **blow off steam** : to release pent-up emotions
— **blow one's cool** : to lose one's composure
— **blow one's cover** : to reveal one's real identity
— **blow one's mind** : to overwhelm one with wonder or bafflement
— **blow one's top** *or* **blow one's stack**
1 : to become violently angry **2** : to go crazy
— **blow smoke** : to speak idly, misleadingly, or boastfully
— **blow the whistle** : to call public or official attention to something (as a wrongdoing) kept secret — usually used with *on*
²**blow** *noun* (1660)
1 : a blowing of wind especially when strong or violent
2 : BRAG, BOASTING
3 : an act or instance of blowing
4 a : the time during which air is forced through molten metal to refine it **b** : the quantity of metal refined during that time
5 *slang* : COCAINE
³**blow** *intransitive verb* **blew** \'blü\; **blown** \'blōn\; **blow·ing** [Middle English, from Old English *blōwan;* akin to Old High German *bluoen* to bloom, Latin *florēre* to bloom, *flor-, flos* flower] (before 12th century)
: FLOWER, BLOOM
⁴**blow** *noun* (1710)
1 : BLOSSOMS
2 : ²BLOOM 1b ⟨lilacs in full *blow*⟩
⁵**blow** *noun* [Middle English (northern dialect) *blaw;* probably akin to Old High German *bliuwan* to beat] (15th century)
1 : a forcible stroke delivered with a part of the body or with an instrument
2 : a hostile act or state : COMBAT ⟨come to *blows*⟩
3 : a forcible or sudden act or effort : ASSAULT
4 : an unfortunate or calamitous happening ⟨failure to land the job came as a *blow*⟩
blow away *transitive verb* (1776)
1 : to kill by gunfire : shoot dead
2 : to dissipate or remove as if with a current of air ⟨their doubts were *blown away*⟩
3 : to impress very strongly and usually favorably
4 : to defeat soundly ⟨*blew* their rivals *away* in the first game⟩
blow·by \'blō-,bī\ *noun* (1926)
: leakage of combustion gases between a piston and the cylinder wall into the crankcase in an automobile
blow–by–blow \'blō-bī-'blō, -bə-\ *adjective* (1933)
: minutely detailed ⟨a *blow-by-blow* account⟩
blow·down \'blō-,daün\ *noun* (1895)
: an instance of trees being blown down by the wind; *also* : a tree blown down
blow–dried \'blō-,drīd\ *adjective* (1976)
: having blow-dried hair; *also* : being or appearing well-groomed but superficial or vacuous
blow–dry \-,drī\ (1966)
transitive verb
: to dry and usually style (hair) with a blow-dryer
intransitive verb
: to dry hair with a blow-dryer
— **blow–dry** *noun*
blow–dryer \-,drī-(-ə)r\ *noun* (1976)
: a handheld hair dryer
blow·er \'blō-(-ə)r\ *noun* (before 12th century)
1 : one that blows
2 : a device for producing a current of air or gas
3 : BRAGGART
4 *British* : TELEPHONE
blow·fish \'blō-,fish\ *noun* (circa 1893)
: PUFFER 2a

blow·fly \-,flī\ *noun* (1821)
: any of a family (Calliphoridae) of dipteran flies (as the bluebottle or screwworm) that deposit their eggs especially on meat or in wounds
blow·gun \-,gən\ *noun* (1864)
: a tube through which a projectile (as a dart) may be impelled by the force of the breath
blow·hard \-,härd\ *noun* (1857)
: BRAGGART
blow·hole \-,hōl\ *noun* (1691)
1 : a hole in metal caused by a bubble of gas captured during solidification
2 : a nostril in the top of the head of a cetacean and especially a whale
blow in *intransitive verb* (1895)
: to arrive casually or unexpectedly
blow job *noun* (1956)
: an act of fellatio — usually considered vulgar
blown \'blōn\ *adjective* [Middle English *blowen,* from past participle of *blowen* to blow] (14th century)
1 a : SWOLLEN **b** : affected with bloat
2 : being out of breath
blow off *transitive verb* (1987)
1 : to refuse to take notice of, honor, or deal with : IGNORE ⟨decided to *blow off* two billion viewers —Harry Homburg⟩
2 : to fail to attend or show up for ⟨*blew off* an official dinner⟩
blow·out \'blō-,aüt\ *noun* (1824)
1 : a festive social affair
2 : a bursting of a container (as a tire) by pressure of the contents on a weak spot
3 : an uncontrolled eruption of an oil or gas well
4 : an easy or one-sided victory
blow out (14th century)
transitive verb
1 : to extinguish by a gust
2 : to dissipate (itself) by blowing — used of storms
3 : to defeat easily
intransitive verb
1 : to become extinguished by a gust
2 : to erupt out of control — used of an oil or gas well
blow over *intransitive verb* (1617)
: to pass away without effect
blow·pipe \'blō-,pīp\ *noun* (1685)
1 : a small tubular instrument for directing a jet of air or other gas into a flame so as to concentrate and increase the heat
2 : BLOWGUN
3 : a tubular instrument used for revealing or cleaning a bodily cavity by forcing air into it
4 : a long metal tube on the end of which a glassmaker gathers a quantity of molten glass and through which he blows to expand and shape it
blow·sy *also* **blow·zy** \'blaü-zē\ *adjective* [English dialect *blowse, blowze* wench] (circa 1770)
1 : having a sloppy appearance or aspect : FROWSY
2 : being coarse and ruddy of complexion
blow·torch \'blō-,tórch\ *noun* (1897)
: a small burner having a device to intensify combustion by means of a blast of air or oxygen, usually including a fuel tank pressurized by a hand pump, and used especially in plumbing
blow·up \'blō-,əp\ *noun* (1807)
: a blowing up: as **a** : EXPLOSION **b** : an outburst of temper **c** : a photographic enlargement
blow up (1536)
transitive verb
1 : to build up or tout to an unreasonable extent ⟨advertisers *blowing up* their products⟩
2 : to rend apart, shatter, or destroy by explosion
3 : to fill up with a gas (as air) ⟨*blow up* a balloon⟩
4 : to make a photographic enlargement of

5 : to bring into existence by blowing of wind ⟨it may *blow up* a storm⟩
intransitive verb
1 a : EXPLODE **b** : to be disrupted or destroyed (as by explosion) **c** : to lose self-control; *especially* : to become violently angry
2 : to become or come into being by or as if by blowing of wind
3 a : to become filled with a gas (as air) **b** : to become expanded to unreasonable proportions
blow·y \'blō-ē\ *adjective* (1830)
1 : WINDY ⟨a *blowy* March day⟩
2 : readily blown about ⟨*blowy* desert sand⟩
BLT *noun* (1952)
: a bacon, lettuce, and tomato sandwich
blub \'bləb\ *intransitive verb* **blubbed; blub·bing** (1804)
chiefly British : BLUBBER
¹blub·ber \'blə-bər\ *verb* **blub·bered; blub·ber·ing** \'blə-b(ə-)riŋ\ [Middle English *blubren* to make a bubbling sound, from *bluber*] (15th century)
intransitive verb
: to weep noisily
transitive verb
1 : to swell, distort, or wet with weeping
2 : to utter while weeping
²blubber *noun* [Middle English *bluber* bubble, foam, probably of imitative origin] (15th century)
1 a : the fat of whales and other large marine mammals **b** : excessive fat on the body
2 : the action of blubbering
³blubber *adjective* (1667)
: puffed out : THICK ⟨*blubber* lips⟩
blub·bery \'blə-b(ə-)rē\ *adjective* (1791)
1 : having or characterized by blubber
2 : puffed out : THICK
blu·cher \'blü-chər *also* -kər\ *noun* [G. L. von *Blücher*] (1831)
: a shoe having the tongue and vamp cut in one piece and the quarters lapped over the vamp and laced together for closing
¹blud·geon \'blə-jən\ *noun* [origin unknown] (circa 1730)
1 : a short stick that usually has one thick or loaded end and is used as a weapon
2 : something used to attack or bully ⟨the *bludgeon* of satire⟩
²bludgeon *transitive verb* (1868)
1 : to hit with heavy impact
2 : to overcome by aggressive argument
blud·ger \'blə-jər\ *noun* [probably contraction of *bludgeoner* pimp, from ¹*bludgeon*] (1939)
chiefly Australian & New Zealand : LOAFER, SHIRKER
¹blue \'blü\ *adjective* **blu·er; blu·est** [Middle English, from Old French *blou*, of Germanic origin; akin to Old High German *blāo* blue; akin to Latin *flavus* yellow] (13th century)
1 : of the color blue
2 a : BLUISH **b** : discolored by or as if by bruising ⟨*blue* with cold⟩ **c** : bluish gray ⟨*blue* cat⟩
3 a : low in spirits : MELANCHOLY **b** : marked by low spirits : DEPRESSING ⟨a *blue* funk⟩ ⟨things looked *blue*⟩
4 : wearing blue
5 *of a woman* : LEARNED, INTELLECTUAL
6 : PURITANICAL
7 a : PROFANE, INDECENT ⟨*blue* movie⟩ **b** : OFF-COLOR, RISQUÉ ⟨*blue* jokes⟩
8 : of, relating to, or used in blues ⟨a *blue* song⟩
— **blue·ly** *adverb*
— **blue·ness** *noun*
— **blue in the face** : extremely exasperated
²blue *noun* (13th century)
1 : a color whose hue is that of the clear sky or that of the portion of the color spectrum lying between green and violet
2 a : a pigment or dye that colors blue **b** : BLUING
3 a : blue clothing or cloth **b** *plural* : a blue costume or uniform

4 a : a Union soldier in the Civil War **b** : the Union army
5 a (1) : SKY (2) : the far distance **b** : SEA
6 : a blue object
7 : BLUESTOCKING
8 : any of numerous small chiefly blue butterflies (family Lycaenidae)
9 : BLUEFISH
10 : BLUE CHEESE
— **out of the blue** : without advance notice : UNEXPECTEDLY ⟨the job offer came *out of the blue*⟩
³blue *verb* **blued; blue·ing** *or* **blu·ing** (1606)
transitive verb
: to make blue
intransitive verb
: to turn blue
blue baby *noun* (circa 1899)
: an infant with a bluish tint usually from a congenital heart defect in which mingling of venous and arterial blood occurs
blue·beard \'blü-ˌbird\ *noun, often capitalized* [*Bluebeard*, a fairy-tale character] (1822)
: a man who marries and kills one wife after another
blue·bell \-ˌbel\ *noun* (1578)
1 : any of various bellflowers; *especially* : HAREBELL
2 : any of various plants bearing blue bell-shaped flowers: as **a** : a European herb (*Endymion nonscriptus* synonym *Scilla nonscripta*) of the lily family having scapose racemes of drooping bell-shaped flowers — called also *wild hyacinth* **b** *plural* : a glabrous erect eastern U.S. herb (*Mertensia virginica*) of the borage family with entire leaves and showy blue flowers pink in the bud — called also *Virginia bluebells*
blue·ber·ry \'blü-ˌber-ē, -b(ə-)rē\ *noun* (1709)
: the edible blue or blackish berry of any of several plants (genus *Vaccinium*) of the heath family; *also* : a low or tall shrub producing these berries
blue·bird \-ˌbərd\ *noun* (1688)
: any of several small North American thrushes (genus *Sialia*) that are blue above and reddish brown or pale blue below
blue blood *noun* (1834)
1 \'blü-ˈbləd\ : membership in a noble or socially prominent family
2 \-ˌbləd\ : a member of a noble or socially prominent family
— **blue–blood·ed** \-ˈblə-dəd\ *adjective*
blue·bon·net \'blü-ˌbä-nət\ *noun* (1682)
1 a : a wide flat round cap of blue wool formerly worn in Scotland **b** : one that wears such a cap; *specifically* : SCOT
2 : either of two low-growing annual lupines (*Lupinus subcarnosus* or *Latin texensis*) of Texas with silky foliage and blue flowers
blue book *noun* (1836)
1 : a register especially of socially prominent persons
2 : a book of specialized information often published under government auspices
3 : a blue-covered booklet used for writing examinations
4 : a periodically issued price list (as of used cars)
blue·bot·tle \'blü-ˌbä-tᵊl\ *noun* (15th century)
1 : BACHELOR'S BUTTON
2 : any of several blowflies (genus *Calliphora*) that have the abdomen or the whole body iridescent blue in color and that make a loud buzzing noise in flight
blue catfish *noun* (1835)
: a large bluish catfish (*Ictalurus furcatus*) of the Mississippi valley that may weigh over 100 pounds (45 kilograms)
blue cheese *noun* (1925)
: cheese having veins of greenish blue mold
blue chip *noun* (1929)
1 a : a stock issue of high investment quality that usually pertains to a substantial well-established company and enjoys public confi-

dence in its worth and stability **b** : a consistently successful and profitable venture or enterprise
2 a : an outstandingly worthwhile or valuable property or asset **b** : an athlete rated as excellent or as an excellent prospect
— **blue–chip** *adjective*
blue–chip·per \'blü-ˌchi-pər\ *noun* (1968)
: BLUE CHIP 2b
blue·coat \'blü-ˌkōt\ *noun* (1593)
: a person who wears a blue coat: as **a** : a Union soldier during the Civil War **b** : POLICE OFFICER
blue cohosh *noun* (1821)
: a perennial herb (*Caulophyllum thalictroides*) of the barberry family that has greenish yellow or purplish flowers and large blue berrylike fruits
blue–col·lar \'blü-ˈkä-lər\ *adjective* (1946)
: of, relating to, or constituting the class of wage earners whose duties call for the wearing of work clothes or protective clothing — compare WHITE-COLLAR
blue crab *noun* (1883)
: a large bluish green edible crab (*Callinectes sapidus*) of the Atlantic and Gulf coasts

blue crab

blue curls *noun plural but singular or plural in construction* (1817)
: any of several mints (genus *Trichostema*) with irregular blue flowers
blue devils *noun plural* (1781)
: low spirits : DESPONDENCY
blue–eyed \'blü-ˌīd\ *adjective* (1610)
1 : having blue eyes
2 : performed by whites ⟨*blue-eyed* soul⟩; *also* : WHITE ⟨a *blue-eyed* soul singer⟩
blue–eyed grass *noun* (1784)
: any of several herbs (genus *Sisyrinchium*) of the iris family with grasslike foliage and blue flowers
blue·fin tuna \'blü-ˌfin-\ *noun* (1922)
: a very large tuna (*Thunnus thynnus*) that is an important food and game fish — called also *bluefin*
blue·fish \-ˌfish\ *noun* (circa 1622)
1 : an active food and game marine fish (*Pomatomus saltatrix*) that is bluish above with silvery sides
2 : any of various dark or bluish fishes (as the pollack)
blue flag *noun* (1784)
: a blue-flowered iris; *especially* : a common iris (*Iris versicolor*) of the eastern U.S. with a root formerly used medicinally
blue flu *noun* [from the color of a police uniform] (1970)
: a sick-out staged by police officers
blue·gill \'blü-ˌgil\ *noun* (1881)
: a common sunfish (*Lepomis macrochirus*) of the eastern and central U.S. sought for food and sport
blue·grass \-ˌgras\ *noun* (1751)
1 : any of several grasses (genus *Poa*) of which some have bluish green culms; *especially* : KENTUCKY BLUEGRASS
2 [from the *Blue Grass Boys*, performing group, from *Bluegrass state*, nickname of Kentucky] : country music played on unamplified stringed instruments (as banjo, fiddle, guitar, and mandolin) and characterized by free improvisation and close usually high-pitched harmony
blue–green alga \'blü-ˈgrēn-\ *noun* (1899)

: any of a group of photosynthetic microorganisms now usually classified as bacteria (division Cyanobacteria) or sometimes as plants (division Cyanophyta) — called also *blue-green bacterium, cyanobacterium*

blue gum *noun* (1799)
: any of several Australian trees (genus *Eucalyptus*) that yield valuable timber

blue heron *noun* (circa 1730)
: either of two herons with bluish or slaty plumage; *especially* : GREAT BLUE HERON

blue-jack-et \-ˌja-kət\ *noun* (1830)
: an enlisted man in the navy : SAILOR

blue jay \-ˌjā\ *noun* (1709)
: a crested bright blue North American jay (*Cyanocitta cristata*)

blue jeans *noun plural* (1901)
: pants usually made of blue denim
— **blue–jeaned** \-ˌjēnd\ *adjective*

blue law *noun* (1781)
1 : one of numerous extremely rigorous laws designed to regulate morals and conduct in colonial New England
2 : a statute regulating work, commerce, and amusements on Sundays

blue line *noun* (1937)
: either of two blue lines that divide an ice-hockey rink into three equal zones and that separate the offensive and defensive zones from the center-ice neutral zone

blue mold *noun* (1664)
: any of various fungi (genus *Penicillium*) that produce blue or blue-green surface growths

blue moon *noun* (1821)
: a very long period of time ⟨such people happen along only once in a *blue moon* — *Saturday Review*⟩

blue-nose \'blü-ˌnōz\ *noun* (1903)
: a person who advocates a rigorous moral code

blue note *noun* [from its frequent use in blues music] (1919)
: a variable microtonal lowering of the third, seventh, and occasionally fifth degrees of the major scale

blue–pen-cil \'blü-ˌpen(t)-səl\ *transitive verb* (1888)
: to edit especially by shortening or deletion
— **blue penciller** *noun*

blue pencil *noun* (1893)
: a writing instrument used for editing; *also*
: the act or practice of blue-penciling

blue pe-ter \-ˈpē-tər\ *noun* [probably from the name *Peter*] (1823)
: a blue signal flag with a white square in the center used to indicate that a merchant vessel is ready to sail

blue pike *noun* (1842)
: a grayish-blue walleye categorized as either a morph or a subspecies (*Stizostedion vitreum glaucum*)

blue plate *adjective* (1926)
: being a main course usually offered at a special price in a restaurant ⟨a *blue plate* luncheon⟩

blue-point \'blü-ˌpȯint\ *noun* [*Blue Point*, Long Island] (1789)
: a small oyster (*Crassostrea virginica*) typically from the south shore of Long Island

blue point \-ˌpȯint\ *adjective* (1944)
of a domestic cat : having a bluish cream body coat with dark gray points
— **blue point** *noun*

blue-print \-ˌprint\ *noun* (1886)
1 : a photographic print in white on a bright blue ground or blue on a white ground used especially for copying maps, mechanical drawings, and architects' plans
2 : something resembling a blueprint; *especially* : a detailed plan or program of action ⟨a *blueprint* for victory⟩
— **blueprint** *transitive verb*

blue racer *noun* (1886)
: a blue or greenish blue blacksnake (*Coluber constrictor* subspecies) occurring from Michigan and Wisconsin to Texas

blue–ribbon *adjective* (1926)
: of outstanding quality; *especially* : consisting of individuals selected for quality, reputation, or authority ⟨a *blue-ribbon* committee⟩ ⟨a *blue-ribbon* jury⟩

blue ribbon *noun* (1651)
1 : an honor or award gained for preeminence
2 : a blue ribbon awarded as an honor (as to the first-place winner in a competition)

blues \'blüz\ *noun plural but singular or plural in construction* [*blue devils*] (1741)
1 : low spirits : MELANCHOLY
2 : a song often of lamentation characterized by usually 12-bar phrases, 3-line stanzas in which the words of the second line usually repeat those of the first, and continual occurrence of blue notes in melody and harmony
3 : jazz or popular music using harmonic and phrase structures of blues

blue shark *noun* (circa 1672)
: a chiefly pelagic shark (*Prionace glauca*) found in all tropical and temperate seas that occasionally attacks humans

blue sheep *noun* (1911)
: BHARAL

blue-shift \'blü-ˌshift\ *noun* (1951)
: the displacement of the spectrum of an approaching celestial body toward shorter wavelengths
— **blue-shift-ed** *adjective*

blue–sky \'blü-'skī\ *adjective* (1906)
1 : having little or no value ⟨*blue-sky* stock⟩
2 : not grounded in the realities of the present : VISIONARY ⟨*blue-sky* thinking⟩

blue–sky law *noun* (1912)
: a law providing for the regulation of the sale of securities (as stock)

blues-man \'blüz-mən\ *noun* (1966)
: a man who plays or sings the blues

blue spruce *noun* (1884)
: a spruce (*Picea pungens*) of the Rocky Mountains having sharp usually bluish gray needles and often planted as an ornamental

blue-stem \'blü-ˌstem\ *noun* (circa 1862)
1 : a tall North American grass (*Andropogon gerardii* synonym *A. furcatus*) that has smooth bluish leaf sheaths and slender spikes borne in pairs or clusters and is used for hay and forage
2 : LITTLE BLUESTEM

blue-stock-ing \-ˌstä-kiŋ\ *noun* [*Bluestocking* society, 18th century literary clubs] (1790)
: a woman having intellectual or literary interests ◆

blue-stone \-ˌstōn\ *noun* (1709)
: a building stone of bluish gray color

blue streak *noun* (1830)
1 : something that moves very fast
2 : a constant stream of words ⟨talked a *blue streak*⟩

blues-y \'blü-zē\ *adjective* **blues-i-er; -est** (1946)
: resembling, characteristic of, or suited to the blues

blu-et \'blü-ət\ *noun* [probably from ¹*blue*] (circa 1821)
: a North American plant (*Hedyotis caerulea* synonym *Houstonia caerulea*) of the madder family having tufted stems and bluish or white flowers with yellow centers

blue-tick \-ˌtik\ *noun* (1945)
: any of a breed of tricolor coonhounds of American origin having the white areas of the coat heavily ticked with black

blue-tongue \'blü-ˌtəŋ\ *noun* (1863)
: a serious virus disease especially of sheep characterized by hyperemia, cyanosis, and punctate hemorrhages and by swelling and sloughing of the epithelium especially about the mouth and tongue

blue vitriol *noun* (1728)
: a hydrated copper sulfate $CuSO_4 \cdot 5H_2O$

blue water *noun* (1582)
: the open sea
— **blue-wa-ter** \'blü-ˌwȯ-tər, -ˌwä-\ *adjective*

blue-weed \'blü-ˌwēd\ *noun* (circa 1837)
1 : VIPER'S BUGLOSS
2 : a small weedy sunflower (*Helianthus ciliaris*) of the southwestern U.S. with blue-green or gray-green foliage

blue whale *noun* (1851)
: a very large baleen whale (*Balaenoptera musculus* synonym *Sibbaldus musculus*) that may reach a weight of 150 tons (135 metric tons) and a length of 100 feet (30 meters) and is generally considered the largest living animal

blue whale

bluey \'blü-ē\ *noun* [from the blue blanket commonly used to wrap the bundle] (1877) *Australian* : a swagman's bundle of personal effects; *also* : a bag of clothing carried in travel

¹**bluff** \'bləf\ *adjective* [obsolete Dutch *blaf* flat; akin to Middle Low German *blaff* smooth] (1627)
1 **a** : having a broad flattened front **b** : rising steeply with a broad flat or rounded front
2 : good-naturedly frank and outspoken ☆

☆ **SYNONYMS**

Bluff, blunt, brusque, curt, crusty, gruff mean abrupt and unceremonious in speech and manner. BLUFF connotes good-natured outspokenness and unconventionality ⟨a *bluff* manner⟩. BLUNT suggests directness of expression in disregard of others' feelings ⟨a *blunt* appraisal⟩. BRUSQUE applies to a sharpness or ungraciousness ⟨a *brusque* response⟩. CURT implies disconcerting shortness or rude conciseness ⟨a *curt* command⟩. CRUSTY suggests a harsh or surly manner sometimes concealing an inner kindliness ⟨a *crusty* exterior⟩. GRUFF suggests a hoarse or husky speech which may imply bad temper but more often implies embarrassment or shyness ⟨puts on a *gruff* pose⟩.

◇ **WORD HISTORY**

bluestocking The origin of *bluestocking* goes back to the mid-18th century, to a circle of English ladies who decided to replace their social evenings of cardplaying and idle chatter to which tradition had confined them, with more intellectual pursuits. Taking the literary salons of Paris as their model, they decided to hold discussions at which illustrious men of letters would be the honored guests. On one occasion, they invited the English botanist and sometime poet Benjamin Stillingfleet. A poor scholar who lacked fancy clothes, including the black silk stockings customarily worn to such high-society events, he felt obliged to decline the invitation, until he was assured that his everyday clothes, including his blue worsted stockings, would be quite acceptable. Thus attired, Stillingfleet became a popular fixture at the evening conversations and was dubbed "blue stockings." As it was then considered unseemly for women to aspire to learning, the circle presided over by Stillingfleet acquired the derisive nickname the "Blue Stocking Society." Rather defiantly, the members of the group embraced the intended put-down, adopting the name *Bluestocking*, or its French equivalent *Bas Bleu*. By the early 19th century, any woman with intellectual interests was called, often derogatorily still, a *bluestocking*.

— **bluff·ly** *adverb*
— **bluff·ness** *noun*
²bluff *noun* (1666)
: a high steep bank : CLIFF
³bluff *verb* [probably from Dutch *bluffen* to boast, play a kind of card game] (1839)
transitive verb
1 a : to deter or frighten by pretense or a mere show of strength **b :** DECEIVE **c :** FEIGN ⟨the catcher *bluffed* a throw to first⟩
2 : to deceive (an opponent) in cards by a bold bet on an inferior hand
intransitive verb
: to bluff someone : act deceptively
— **bluff·er** *noun*
⁴bluff *noun* (1845)
1 a : an act or instance of bluffing **b :** the practice of bluffing
2 : one who bluffs
blu·ing *or* **blue·ing** \'blü-iŋ\ *noun* (1669)
: a preparation used in laundering to counteract yellowing of white fabrics
blu·ish \'blü-ish\ *adjective* (14th century)
: somewhat blue : having a tinge of blue
— **blu·ish·ness** *noun*
¹blun·der \'blən-dər\ *verb* **blun·dered; blun·der·ing** \-d(ə-)riŋ\ [Middle English *blundren*] (14th century)
intransitive verb
1 : to move unsteadily or confusedly
2 : to make a mistake through stupidity, ignorance, or carelessness
transitive verb
1 : to utter stupidly, confusedly, or thoughtlessly
2 : to make a stupid, careless, or thoughtless mistake in
— **blun·der·er** \-dər-ər\ *noun*
— **blun·der·ing·ly** \-d(ə-)riŋ-lē\ *adverb*
²blunder *noun* (circa 1706)
: a gross error or mistake resulting usually from stupidity, ignorance, or carelessness
synonym SEE ERROR
blun·der·buss \'blən-dər-ˌbəs\ *noun* [by folk etymology from obsolete Dutch *donderbus*, from Dutch *donder* thunder + obsolete Dutch *bus* gun] (1654)
1 : a muzzle-loading firearm with a short barrel and flaring muzzle to facilitate loading

blunderbuss 1

2 : a blundering person
¹blunt \'blənt\ *adjective* [Middle English] (13th century)
1 a : slow or deficient in feeling : INSENSITIVE **b :** obtuse in understanding or discernment : DULL
2 : having an edge or point that is not sharp
3 a : abrupt in speech or manner **b :** being straight to the point : DIRECT
synonym SEE DULL, BLUFF
— **blunt·ly** *adverb*
— **blunt·ness** *noun*
²blunt (14th century)
transitive verb
: to make less sharp or definite
intransitive verb
: to become blunt
¹blur \'blər\ *noun* [perhaps akin to Middle English *bleren* to blear] (1548)
1 : a smear or stain that obscures
2 : something vaguely or indistinctly perceived; *especially* : something moving or occurring too quickly to be clearly perceived
²blur *verb* **blurred; blur·ring** (1581)
transitive verb
1 : to obscure or blemish by smearing
2 : SULLY
3 : to make dim, indistinct, or vague in outline or character
4 : to make cloudy or confused

intransitive verb
1 : to make blurs
2 : to become vague or indistinct
— **blur·ring·ly** \'blər-iŋ-lē\ *adverb*
¹blurb \'blərb\ *noun* [coined by Gelett Burgess] (1914)
: a short publicity notice (as on a book jacket)
◇
²blurb *transitive verb* (1915)
: to describe or praise in a blurb
blur·ry \'blər-ē\ *adjective* **blur·ri·er; -est** (1884)
: marked by blurring
— **blur·ri·ly** \'blər-ə-lē\ *adverb*
— **blur·ri·ness** \'blər-ē-nəs\ *noun*
blurt \'blərt\ *transitive verb* [probably imitative] (1573)
: to utter abruptly and impulsively — usually used with *out*
— **blurt·er** *noun*
¹blush \'bləsh\ *noun* [Middle English, probably from *blusshen*] (14th century)
1 : outward appearance : VIEW ⟨at first *blush*⟩
2 : a reddening of the face especially from shame, modesty, or confusion
3 : a red or rosy tint
— **blush·ful** \-fəl\ *adjective*
²blush *intransitive verb* [Middle English *blusshen*, from Old English *blyscan* to redden; akin to Old English *blȳsa* flame, Old High German *bluhhen* to burn brightly] (15th century)
1 : to become red in the face especially from shame, modesty, or confusion
2 : to feel shame or embarrassment
3 : to have a rosy or fresh color : BLOOM
— **blush·ing·ly** \'blə-shiŋ-lē\ *adverb*
blush·er \'blə-shər\ *noun* (1665)
1 : one that blushes
2 : a cosmetic applied to the face to give a usually pink color or to accent the cheekbones
blush wine *noun* (1985)
: any of various pinkish table wines
¹blus·ter \'bləs-tər\ *verb* **blus·tered; blus·ter·ing** \-t(ə-)riŋ\ [Middle English *blustren*, probably from Middle Low German *blüsteren*] (15th century)
intransitive verb
1 : to talk or act with noisy swaggering threats
2 a : to blow in stormy noisy gusts **b :** to be windy and boisterous
transitive verb
1 : to utter with noisy self-assertiveness
2 : to drive or force by blustering
— **blus·ter·er** \-tər-ər\ *noun*
— **blus·ter·ing·ly** \-t(ə-)riŋ-lē\ *adverb*
²bluster *noun* (1583)
1 : a violent boisterous blowing
2 : violent commotion
3 : loudly boastful or threatening speech
— **blus·ter·ous** \-t(ə-)rəs\ *adjective*
— **blus·tery** \-t(ə-)rē\ *adjective*
B lymphocyte *noun* (1971)
: B CELL
B movie *noun* (1948)
: a cheaply produced motion picture
boa \'bō-ə\ *noun* [Latin, a water snake] (14th century)
1 : a large snake (as the boa constrictor, anaconda, or python) that kills by constriction
2 : a long fluffy scarf of fur, feathers, or delicate fabric
boa constrictor *noun* (1809)
: a tropical American boa (*Constrictor constrictor* synonym *Boa constrictor*) that is light brown barred or mottled with darker brown and reaches a length of 10 feet (3 meters) or more; *broadly* : BOA 1
boar \'bōr, 'bȯr\ *noun* [Middle English *bor*, from Old English *bār*; akin to Old High German & Old Saxon *bēr* boar] (before 12th century)
1 a : an uncastrated male swine **b :** the male of any of several mammals (as a guinea pig or raccoon)
2 : WILD BOAR

— **boar·ish** \-ish\ *adjective*
¹board \'bōrd, 'bȯrd\ *noun* [Middle English *bord* piece of sawed lumber, border, ship's side, from Old English; akin to Old High German *bort* ship's side] (before 12th century)
1 *obsolete* : BORDER, EDGE
2 : the side of a ship
3 a : a piece of sawed lumber of little thickness and a length greatly exceeding its width **b** *plural* : STAGE 2a(2)
4 a *archaic* : TABLE 3a **b :** a table spread with a meal **c :** daily meals especially when furnished for pay **d :** a table at which a council or magistrates sit **e** (1) **:** a group of persons having managerial, supervisory, investigatory, or advisory powers ⟨*board* of directors⟩ ⟨*board* of examiners⟩ (2) **:** an examination given by an examining board — often used in plural ⟨pass the medical *boards*⟩ **f :** LEAGUE, ASSOCIATION **g** (1) **:** the exposed hands of all the players in a stud poker game (2) **:** an exposed dummy hand in bridge
5 a : a flat usually rectangular piece of material (as wood) designed for a special purpose: as (1) **:** SPRINGBOARD 1 (2) **:** SURFBOARD **b :** BACKBOARD; *also* : a rebound in basketball **c :** a surface, frame, or device for posting notices **d :** BLACKBOARD **e :** SWITCHBOARD
6 a : PAPERBOARD **b :** the stiff foundation piece for the side of a book cover
7 : a securities or commodities exchange
8 *plural* : the low wooden wall enclosing a hockey rink
9 : a sheet of insulating material carrying circuit elements and terminals so that it can be inserted in an electronic apparatus (as a computer)
— **board·like** \-ˌlīk\ *adjective*
— **across the board :** so as to include or affect all classes or categories ⟨cut spending *across the board*⟩; *also* : in all areas or respects ⟨considered an average player *across the board*⟩
— **on board :** ABOARD
²board (15th century)
transitive verb
1 *archaic* : to come up against or alongside (a ship) usually to attack
2 : ACCOST, ADDRESS

◇ **WORD HISTORY**
blurb The origin of the word *blurb* can be traced to a single individual and single occasion. At the annual dinner of the American Booksellers' Association in 1907 humorist Gelett Burgess was one of the guests. It was the custom at these dinners for the guest authors to present to the assembled company souvenir copies of their latest books. Seizing the occasion to satirize publishing's practice of plastering book jackets with effusive copy, Burgess prepared a mock-solemn commemorative jacket of his latest, placing on the front cover a doctored picture of a woman that he had lifted from a dental advertisement. He dubbed his creation Miss Belinda Blurb and appended a self-congratulatory text. Seven years later, Burgess defined *blurb* itself as "a flamboyant advertisement; an inspired testimonial On the 'jacket' of the 'latest' fiction, we find the blurb . . . attesting that this book is the 'sensation' of the year." Burgess's coinage filled a widely felt need, and the very sound of the word was suggestive of the "mush, gush and tosh" (in the words of one writer) that book publicists tend to favor.

\a\ abut \ᵊ\ kitten \ər\ further \a\ ash \ā\ ace
\ä\ mop, mar \au̇\ out \ch\ chin \e\ bet \ē\ easy
\g\ go \i\ hit \ī\ ice \j\ job \ŋ\ sing \ō\ go
\ȯ\ law \ȯi\ boy \th\ thin \t͟h\ the \ü\ loot \u̇\ foot
\y\ yet \zh\ vision *see also* Guide to Pronunciation

3 a : to go aboard (as a ship, train, airplane, or bus) **b :** to put aboard ⟨an airliner *boarding* passengers⟩ **4 :** to cover with boards ⟨*board* up a window⟩ **5 :** to provide with regular meals and often also lodging usually for compensation **6 :** to check with a board check *intransitive verb* **:** to take one's meals usually as a paying customer

board check *noun* (circa 1936) **:** a body check of an opposing player against the rink boards in ice hockey

board·er \'bȯr-dər, 'bȯr-\ *noun* (1530) **:** one that boards; *especially* **:** one that is provided with regular meals or regular meals and lodging

board foot *noun* (1896) **:** a unit of quantity for lumber equal to the volume of a board 12 × 12 × 1 inches — abbreviation **bd ft**

board game *noun* (1934) **:** a game of strategy (as checkers, chess, or backgammon) played by moving pieces on a board

board·ing·house \'bȯr-diŋ-,haůs, 'bȯr-\ *noun* (1728) **:** a lodging house at which meals are provided

boarding school *noun* (1677) **:** a school at which meals and lodging are provided

board·man \'bȯrd-,man, 'bȯrd-, *especially for* 2 -mən\ *noun* (circa 1923) **1 :** a member of a board **2 :** one who works at a board

board of trade (1780) **1** *B&T capitalized* **:** a British governmental department concerned with commerce and industry **2 :** a commodities exchange

board·room \'bȯrd-,rüm, 'bȯrd-, -,rům\ *noun* (1836) **:** a room that is designated for meetings of a board

board·sail·ing \-,sā-liŋ\ *noun* (1980) **:** WINDSURFING — **board·sail·or** \-,sā-lər\ *noun*

board·walk \-,wȯk\ *noun* (1872) **1 :** a walk constructed of planking **2 :** a walk constructed along a beach

boart \'bȯrt, 'bȯrt\ *variant of* BORT

¹boast \'bōst\ *noun* [Middle English *boost*] (14th century) **1 :** the act or an instance of boasting **:** BRAG **2 :** a cause for pride — **boast·ful** \'bōst-fəl\ *adjective* — **boast·ful·ly** \-fə-lē\ *adverb* — **boast·ful·ness** *noun*

²boast (14th century) *intransitive verb* **1 :** to puff oneself up in speech **:** speak vaingloriously **2** *archaic* **:** GLORY, EXULT *transitive verb* **1 :** to speak of or assert with excessive pride **2 a :** to possess and often call attention to (something that is a source of pride) ⟨*boasts* a new stadium⟩ **b :** HAVE, CONTAIN ⟨a room *boasting* no more than a desk and a chair⟩ ☆ — **boast·er** *noun*

³boast *transitive verb* [origin unknown] (1823) **:** to shape (stone) roughly in sculpture and stonecutting as a preliminary to finer work

¹boat \'bōt\ *noun* [Middle English *boot*, from Old English *bāt*; akin to Old Norse *beit* boat] (before 12th century) **1 a :** a small vessel for travel on water **b :** SHIP **2 :** a boat-shaped container, utensil, or device ⟨a gravy *boat*⟩ ⟨a laboratory *boat*⟩ — **boat·ful** \-,fůl\ *noun* — **boat·like** \-,līk\ *adjective* — **in the same boat :** in the same situation or predicament

²boat (1613) *transitive verb*

: to place in or bring into a boat *intransitive verb* **:** to go by boat

boat·build·er \-,bil-dər\ *noun* (1679) **:** one that builds boats — **boat·build·ing** \-,bil-diŋ\ *noun*

boat·er \'bō-tər\ *noun* (1605) **1 :** one who travels in a boat **2 :** a stiff hat usually made of braided straw with a brim, hatband, and flat crown

boat hook *noun* (circa 1611) **:** a pole-handled hook with a point or knob on the back used especially to pull or push a boat, raft, or log into place

boat·house \-,haůs\ *noun* (1722) **:** a building to house and protect boats

boat·load \'bōt-,lōd\ *noun* (1680) **1 :** a load that fills a boat **2 :** an indefinitely large number ⟨a *boatload* of money⟩

boat·man \'bōt-mən\ *noun* (14th century) **:** a man who works on, deals in, or operates boats

boat people *noun plural* (1977) **:** refugees fleeing by boat

boat·swain \'bō-sᵊn\ *noun* [Middle English *bootswein*, from *boot* boat + *swein* boy, servant — more at SWAIN] (14th century) **1 :** a petty officer on a merchant ship having charge of hull maintenance and related work **2 :** a naval warrant officer in charge of the hull and all related equipment

boat train *noun* (1884) **:** an express train for transporting passengers between a port and a city

boat·yard \'bōt-,yärd\ *noun* (1847) **:** a yard where boats are built, repaired, and stored and often sold or rented

¹bob \'bäb\ *verb* **bobbed; bob·bing** [Middle English *boben*] (13th century) *transitive verb* **1 :** to strike with a quick light blow **:** RAP **2 :** to move up and down in a short quick movement ⟨*bob* the head⟩ **3 :** to polish with a bob **:** BUFF *intransitive verb* **1 a :** to move up and down briefly or repeatedly ⟨a cork *bobbed* in the water⟩ **b :** to emerge, arise, or appear suddenly or unexpectedly ⟨the question *bobbed* up again⟩ **2 :** to nod or curtsy briefly **3 :** to try to seize a suspended or floating object with the teeth ⟨*bob* for apples⟩

²bob *noun* (1550) **1 a :** a short quick down-and-up motion **b** *Scottish* **:** any of several folk dances **2** *obsolete* **:** a blow or tap especially with the fist **3 a :** a modification of the order in change ringing **b :** a method of change ringing using a bob **4 :** a small polishing wheel of solid felt or leather with rounded edges

³bob *transitive verb* **bobbed; bob·bing** [Middle English *bobben*, from Middle French *bober*] (14th century) **1** *obsolete* **:** DECEIVE, CHEAT **2** *obsolete* **:** to take by fraud **:** FILCH

⁴bob *noun* [Middle English *bobbe*] (14th century) **1 a** (1) **:** BUNCH, CLUSTER (2) *Scottish* **:** NOSEGAY **b :** a knob, knot, twist, or curl especially of ribbons, yarn, or hair **c :** a short haircut on a woman or child **2 :** FLOAT 2a **3 :** a hanging ball or weight (as on a plumb line) **4 :** TRIFLE 1

⁵bob *transitive verb* **bobbed; bob·bing** (1675) **1 :** to cut shorter **:** CROP ⟨*bob* a horse's tail⟩ **2 :** to cut (hair) in the style of a bob

⁶bob *noun, plural* **bob** [perhaps from the name *Bob*] (1789) *slang British* **:** SHILLING

⁷bob *noun* (1856)

: BOBSLED

¹bob·ber \'bä-bər\ *noun* (1593) **:** one that bobs

²bobber *noun* (1904) **:** a person who rides or races on a bobsled

bob·bery \'bä-b(ə-)rē\ *noun, plural* **-ber·ies** [Hindi *bāp re*, literally, oh father!] (1803) **:** HUBBUB

bob·bin \'bä-bən\ *noun* [origin unknown] (1530) **1 a :** a cylinder or spindle on which yarn or thread is wound (as in a sewing machine) **b :** any of various small round devices on which threads are wound for working handmade lace **c :** a coil of insulated wire or the reel it is wound on **2 :** a cotton cord formerly used by dressmakers for piping

bob·bi·net \'bä-bə-,net\ *noun* [blend of *bobbin* and *net*] (1814) **:** a machine-made net of cotton, silk, or nylon usually with hexagonal mesh

¹bob·ble \'bä-bəl\ *verb* **bob·bled; bob·bling** \-b(ə-)liŋ\ [frequentative of ¹*bob*] (1812) **1 :** ¹BOB **2 :** FUMBLE

²bobble *noun* (1880) **1 :** a repeated bobbing movement **2 :** a small ball of fabric; *especially* **:** one in a series used on an edging ⟨curtains with *bobbles*⟩ **3 :** ERROR, MISTAKE; *especially* **:** a mishandling of the ball in baseball or football

bob·by \'bä-bē\ *noun, plural* **bobbies** [*Bobby*, nickname for *Robert*, after Sir *Robert* Peel, who organized the London police force] (1844) *British* **:** POLICE OFFICER

bobby pin *noun* [perhaps from ⁴*bob*] (1932) **:** a flat wire hairpin with prongs that press close together

bobby socks *or* **bobby sox** *noun plural* [perhaps from *bobby* pin] (1943) **:** girls' socks reaching above the ankle

bob·by–sox·er \-,säk-sər\ *noun* (1944) **:** an adolescent girl

bob·cat \'bäb-,kat\ *noun* [⁴*bob*; from the stubby tail] (1888) **:** a common North American lynx (*Lynx rufus*) variably reddish in base color with dark markings

bobcat

bo·beche \bō-'besh, -'bāsh\ *noun* [French *bobèche*] (circa 1897) **:** a usually glass collar on a candle socket to catch drippings or on a candlestick or chandelier to hold suspended glass prisms

bob·o·link \'bä-bə-,liŋk\ *noun* [imitative] (circa 1801)

☆ **SYNONYMS**
Boast, brag, vaunt, crow mean to express pride in oneself or one's accomplishments. BOAST often suggests ostentation and exaggeration ⟨*boasts* of every trivial success⟩, but it may imply a claiming with proper and justifiable pride ⟨the town *boasts* one of the best museums in the area⟩. BRAG suggests crudity and artlessness in glorifying oneself ⟨*bragging* of their exploits⟩. VAUNT usually connotes more pomp and bombast than BOAST and less crudity or naïveté than BRAG ⟨*vaunted* his country's military might⟩. CROW usually implies exultant boasting or bragging ⟨*crowed* after winning the championship⟩.

: an American migratory songbird (*Dolichonyx oryzivorus*) with the breeding male chiefly black

bob·sled \'bäb-ˌsled\ *noun* [perhaps from ⁴*bob*] (1839)
1 : a short sled usually used as one of a pair joined by a coupling
2 : a large usually metal sled used in racing and equipped with two pairs of runners in tandem, a long seat for two or more people, a steering wheel, and a hand brake
— **bobsled** *intransitive verb*
— **bob·sled·der** *noun*

bob·sled·ding \-ˌsle-diŋ\ *noun* (1883)
: the act, skill, or sport of riding or racing on a bobsled

bob·stay \'bäb-ˌstā\ *noun* [probably from ²*bob*] (1758)
: a stay to hold a ship's bowsprit down

bob·tail \'bäb-ˌtāl\ *noun* [⁴*bob*] (1605)
1 a : a bobbed tail **b** : a horse, dog, or cat with a bobbed or very short tail; *especially* : OLD ENGLISH SHEEPDOG
2 : something curtailed
— **bobtail** *or* **bob·tailed** \-ˌtāld\ *adjective*

bob veal \'bäb-\ *noun* [English dialect *bob* young calf] (1855)
: the veal of a very young or unborn calf

bob·white \'bäb-ˌhwīt, -ˌwīt\ *noun* [imitative] (1819)
: any of a genus (*Colinus*) of quail; *especially* : a popular game bird (*C. virginianus*) of the eastern and central U.S.

bo·cac·cio \bə-ˈkä-chē-ˌō, -chō\ *noun* [perhaps modification of Spanish *bocacha*, augmentative of *boca* mouth] (circa 1890)
: a large rockfish (*Sebastes paucispinis*) of the Pacific coast locally important as a market fish

boc·cie *or* **boc·ci** *or* **boc·ce** \'bä-chē\ *noun* [Italian *bocce*, plural of *boccia* ball, from (assumed) Vulgar Latin *bottia* boss] (1926)
: a game of Italian origin similar to lawn bowling played on a long narrow usually dirt court

bock \'bäk\ *noun* [German, short for *Bockbier*, by shortening & alteration from *Einbecker Bier*, literally, beer from Einbeck, from *Einbeck*, Germany] (1856)
: a heavy dark rich beer usually sold in the early spring

bod \'bäd\ *noun* (1933)
1 *British* : FELLOW, GUY
2 : BODY

bo·da·cious \bō-ˈdā-shəs\ *adjective* [probably blend of *bold* and *audacious*] (1845)
1 *Southern & Midland* : OUTRIGHT, UNMISTAKABLE
2 : REMARKABLE, NOTEWORTHY ⟨the *bodacious* 1974 comedy —*People*⟩
— **bo·da·cious·ly** *adverb*

¹bode \'bōd\ *transitive verb* **bod·ed; bod·ing** [Middle English, from Old English *bodian; akin to Old English *bēodan* to proclaim — more at BID] (before 12th century)
1 *archaic* : to announce beforehand : FORETELL
2 : to indicate by signs : PRESAGE ⟨this controversy . . . will *bode* ill for both of us —A. H. Lowe⟩

²bode *past of* BIDE

bo·de·ga \bō-ˈdā-gə\ *noun* [Spanish, from Latin *apotheca* storehouse — more at APOTHECARY] (1846)
1 : a storehouse for maturing wine
2 a : WINESHOP **b** (1) : ¹BAR 5a (2) : BARROOM
3 : a store specializing in Hispanic groceries

bode·ment \'bōd-mənt\ *noun* (1605)
1 : OMEN, FOREBODING
2 : PREDICTION, PROPHECY

bo·dhi·satt·va *or* **bod·dhi·satt·va** \ˌbō-di-ˈsət-və, -ˈsät-və\ *noun* [Sanskrit *bodhisattva* one whose essence is enlightenment, from *bodhi* enlightenment + *sattva* being — more at BID] (1828)
: a being that compassionately refrains from entering nirvana in order to save others and is worshiped as a deity in Mahayana Buddhism

bodh·ran \'bȯ-ˌrän, -rən\ *noun* [Irish *bodhrán*] (1972)
: an Irish goatskin drum

bod·ice \'bä-dəs\ *noun* [alteration of *bodies*, plural of ¹*body*] (circa 1567)
1 : the upper part of a woman's dress
2 *archaic* : CORSET, STAYS ◆

bodice ripper *noun* (1980)
: a historical or Gothic romance typically featuring scenes in which the heroine is subjected to sexual violence

bod·ied \'bä-dēd\ *adjective* (circa 1547)
: having a body of a specified kind — used in combination ⟨full-*bodied*⟩ ⟨glass-*bodied*⟩

bodi·less \'bä-di-ləs, 'bä-dºl-əs\ *adjective* (14th century)
: having no body

¹bodi·ly \'bä-dºl-ē\ *adjective* (14th century)
1 : having a body : PHYSICAL
2 : of or relating to the body ⟨*bodily* comfort⟩ ⟨*bodily* organs⟩

²bodily *adverb* (14th century)
1 : in the flesh
2 : as a whole : ALTOGETHER

bod·ing \'bō-diŋ\ *noun* (13th century)
: FOREBODING

bod·kin \'bäd-kən\ *noun* [Middle English *bodekin*] (14th century)
1 a : DAGGER, STILETTO **b** : a sharp slender instrument for making holes in cloth **c** : an ornamental hairpin shaped like a stiletto
2 : a blunt needle with a large eye for drawing tape or ribbon through a loop or hem

¹body \'bä-dē\ *noun, plural* **bod·ies** [Middle English, from Old English *bodig; akin to Old High German *boteh* corpse] (before 12th century)
1 a : the main part of a plant or animal body especially as distinguished from limbs and head : TRUNK **b** : the main, central, or principal part: as (1) : the nave of a church (2) : the bed or box of a vehicle on or in which the load is placed (3) : the enclosed or partly enclosed part of an automobile
2 a : the organized physical substance of an animal or plant either living or dead: as (1) : the material part or nature of a human being (2) : the dead organism : CORPSE **b** : a human being : PERSON
3 a : a mass of matter distinct from other masses ⟨a *body* of water⟩ ⟨a celestial *body*⟩ **b** : something that embodies or gives concrete reality to a thing; *also* : a sensible object in physical space **c** : AGGREGATE, QUANTITY ⟨a *body* of evidence⟩
4 a : the part of a garment covering the body or trunk **b** : the main part of a literary or journalistic work : TEXT 2b **c** : the sound box or pipe of a musical instrument
5 : a group of persons or things: as **a** : a fighting unit : FORCE **b** : a group of individuals organized for some purpose ⟨a legislative *body*⟩
6 a : fullness and richness of flavor (as of wine) **b** : VISCOSITY, CONSISTENCY — used especially of oils and grease **c** : compactness or firmness of texture **d** : fullness or resonance of a musical tone

²body *transitive verb* **bod·ied; body·ing** (15th century)
1 : to give form or shape to : EMBODY
2 : REPRESENT, SYMBOLIZE — usually used with *forth*

body bag *noun* (1954)
: a large zippered usually rubber bag in which a human corpse is placed especially for transportation

body blow *noun* (1792)
1 : a blow to the body
2 : a damaging or deeply felt blow ⟨an economic *body blow*⟩

body·build·ing \-ˌbil-diŋ\ *noun* (1904)
: the developing of the body through exercise and diet; *specifically* : the developing of the physique for competitive exhibition
— **body·build·er** *noun*

body cavity *noun* (1875)

: a cavity in an animal body; *specifically* : COELOM

body–cen·tered \'bä-dē-ˌsen-tərd\ *adjective* (1921)
: relating to or being a crystal space lattice in which each cubic unit cell has an atom at its center and at each vertex — compare FACE-CENTERED

body check *noun* (1892)
: a blocking of an opposing player with the body (as in ice hockey or lacrosse)
— **body-check** \'bä-dē-ˌchek\ *transitive verb*

body clock *noun* (1968)
: the internal mechanisms that schedule periodic bodily functions and activities — usually not used technically

body corporate *noun* (15th century)
: CORPORATION

body count *noun* (1967)
1 : a count of the bodies of killed enemy soldiers
2 : the number of persons involved in a particular activity

body English *noun* (1908)
: bodily motions made in a usually unconscious effort to influence the progress of a propelled object (as a ball)

body·guard \'bä-dē-ˌgärd\ *noun* (circa 1735)
: a usually armed attendant or group of attendants whose duty is to protect a person

body language *noun* (1926)
: the gestures, movements, and mannerisms by which a person or animal communicates with others

body louse *noun* (1575)
: a louse feeding primarily on the body; *especially* : a sucking louse (*Pediculus humanus humanus*) feeding on the body and living in the clothing of humans — called also *cootie*

body mechanics *noun plural but singular or plural in construction* (circa 1970)
: systematic exercises designed especially to develop coordination, endurance, and poise

body politic *noun* (15th century)
1 : a group of persons politically organized under a single governmental authority
2 *archaic* : CORPORATION 2
3 : a people considered as a collective unit

body shirt *noun* (1967)
1 : a close-fitting shirt or blouse
2 : a woman's close-fitting top made with a sewn-in or snapped crotch

body shop *noun* (1954)

◇ WORD HISTORY

bodice The word *bodice* was originally identical with *bodies*, the plural of *body*. In the 16th century, *body* was used for one half of a corsetlike undergarment worn originally by both women and men. The front and back halves together were called "a pair of bodies." In the 14th century, a tendency had begun to pronounce plural -*s* after a vowel sound as \z\, but in the 16th century this rule was not absolute. It was with the \s\ sound that *bodies* in "a pair of bodies" froze, as speakers lost the sense that *bodies* in reference to a corset had any connection with the plural of *body*. Like all other words ending in a vowel *body* came to form its plural exclusively with a final \z\ sound. By 1679 "a pair of bodies" was being spelled "a pair of bodice," and even when still spelled *bodies* it began to be used as a singular noun rather than a plural. By that time it frequently had its modern sense "the upper part of a woman's dress."

\ə\ abut \ᵊ\ kitten \ər\ **further** \a\ ash \ā\ ace
\ä\ mop, mar \au̇\ out \ch\ chin \e\ bet \ē\ easy
\g\ go \i\ hit \ī\ ice \j\ job \ŋ\ sing \ō\ go
\ȯ\ law \ȯi\ boy \th\ thin \t͟h\ the \ü\ loot \u̇\ foot
\y\ yet \zh\ vision *see also* Guide to Pronunciation

: a shop where automotive bodies are made or repaired

body snatcher *noun* (1812)
: one that steals corpses from graves

body stocking *noun* (1965)
: a sheer close-fitting one-piece garment for the torso that often has sleeves and legs

body·suit \'bä-dē-ˌsüt\ *noun* (1970)
: a close-fitting one-piece garment for the torso

body·surf \'bä-dē-ˌsərf\ *intransitive verb* (1943)
: to ride on a wave without a surfboard by planing on the chest and stomach
— **body·surf·er** *noun*

body wall *noun* (1888)
: the external surface of the animal body consisting of ectoderm and mesoderm and enclosing the body cavity

body·work \'bä-dē-ˌwərk\ *noun* (1908)
1 : a vehicle body
2 : the act or process of making or repairing vehicle bodies
3 : therapeutic touching or manipulation of the body by using specialized techniques

boehm·ite \'bā-ˌmīt, 'bə(r)-\ *noun* [German *Böhmit*, from J. *Böhm* (Boehm), 20th century German scientist] (circa 1929)
: a mineral consisting of an orthorhombic form of aluminum oxide and hydroxide AlO(OH) found in bauxite

Boer \'bōr, 'bȯr, 'bu̇r\ *noun* [Dutch, literally, farmer — more at BOOR] (1834)
: a South African of Dutch or Huguenot descent

¹boff \'bäf\ *transitive verb* [from *boff* blow, punch, perhaps imitative] (1937)
: to have sexual intercourse with — sometimes considered vulgar

²boff *or* **bof·fo** \'bä-(ˌ)fō\ *noun, plural* **boffs** *or* **boffos** [perhaps from *box office*] (1946)
1 : a hearty laugh
2 : a gag or line that produces a hearty laugh
3 : something that is conspicuously successful
: HIT

bof·fin \'bä-fən\ *noun* [origin unknown] (1945)
chiefly British : a scientific expert; *especially*
: one involved in technological research

bof·fo \'bä-(ˌ)fō\ *adjective* (1949)
: extremely successful : SENSATIONAL

bof·fo·la \bä-'fō-lə\ *noun* [irregular from *boff*] (1946)
: BOFF

Bo·fors gun \'bō-ˌfȯrz-, 'bü-\ *noun* [*Bofors*, munition works in Sweden] (1939)
: a double-barreled automatic antiaircraft gun

¹bog \'bäg, 'bȯg\ *noun* [Middle English (Scots), from Scottish Gaelic & Irish *bog-* (as in *bogluachair* bulrushes), from *bog* marshy, literally, soft, from Middle Irish *bocc*; probably akin to Old English *būgan* to bend — more at BOW] (14th century)
: wet spongy ground; *especially* : a poorly drained usually acid area rich in accumulated plant material, frequently surrounding a body of open water, and having a characteristic flora (as of sedges, heaths, and sphagnum)
— **bog·gy** \'bä-gē, 'bȯ-\ *adjective*

²bog *verb* **bogged; bog·ging** (1599)
transitive verb
: to cause to sink into or as if into a bog : IMPEDE, MIRE — usually used with *down*
intransitive verb
: to become impeded or stuck — usually used with *down*

bog asphodel *noun* (1857)
: either of two bog herbs (*Narthecium ossifragum* of Europe and *N. americanum* of the U.S.) of the lily family

¹bo·gey *also* **bo·gie** *or* **bo·gy** *noun, plural* **bogeys** *also* **bogies** [probably alteration of *bogle*] (1857)
1 \'bu̇-gē, 'bō-, 'bü-\ : SPECTER, PHANTOM
2 \'bō-gē *also* 'bu̇- *or* 'bü-\ : a source of fear, perplexity, or harassment

3 \'bō-gē\ **a** *chiefly British* : an average golfer's score used as a standard for a particular hole or course **b** : one stroke over par on a hole in golf
4 \'bō-gē\ : a numerical standard of performance set up as a mark to be aimed at in competition
5 \'bō-gē\ : an unidentified aircraft; *especially* : one not positively identified as friendly and so assumed to be hostile

²bo·gey \'bō-gē\ *transitive verb* **bo·geyed; bo·gey·ing** (1948)
: to shoot (a hole in golf) in one over par

bo·gey·man *also* **bo·gy·man** \'bu̇-gē-ˌman, 'bō-, 'bü-, 'bu̇-gər-\ *noun* (circa 1890)
1 : a monstrous imaginary figure used in threatening children
2 : a terrifying or dreaded person or thing
: BUGBEAR

bog·gle \'bä-gəl\ *verb* **bog·gled; bog·gling** \-g(ə-)liŋ\ [perhaps from *bogle*] (1598)
intransitive verb
1 : to start with fright or amazement : be overwhelmed ⟨the mind *boggles* at the research needed⟩
2 : to hesitate because of doubt, fear, or scruples
transitive verb
1 : MISHANDLE, BUNGLE
2 : to overwhelm with wonder or bewilderment
— **boggle** *noun*

bo·gie *also* **bo·gey** \'bō-gē\ *noun, plural* **bo·gies** *also* **bogeys** [origin unknown] (1835)
1 : a low strongly built cart
2 *chiefly British* : a swiveling railway truck **b** : the driving-wheel assembly consisting of the rear four wheels of a 6-wheel automotive truck
3 : a small supporting or aligning wheel (as on the inside perimeter of a tank tread)

bo·gle \'bō-gəl\ *also* **bog·gle** \'bä-gəl\ *noun* [origin unknown] (circa 1505)
dialect British : GOBLIN, SPECTER; *also* : an object of fear or loathing

Bo·go·mil *also* **Bo·go·mile** \ˌbə-gə-'mē(ə)l\ *noun* [Middle Greek *Bogomilos*, from *Bogomilos* Bogomil, 10th century Bulgarian priest, founder of the sect] (1841)
: a member of a medieval Bulgarian sect holding that God has two sons, the rebellious Satan and the obedient Jesus

bo·gus \'bō-gəs\ *adjective* [*bogus* (a machine for making counterfeit money)] (1825)
: not genuine : COUNTERFEIT, SHAM

bo·hea \bō-'hē\ *noun, often capitalized* [Chinese (Fujian) *Bú-î*, hills in China where it was grown] (1701)
: a black tea

bo·he·mia \bō-'hē-mē-ə\ *noun, often capitalized* [translation of French *bohème*] (1861)
: a community of bohemians : the world of bohemians

Bo·he·mi·an \-mē-ən\ *noun* (1603)
1 a : a native or inhabitant of Bohemia **b** : the group of Czech dialects used in Bohemia
2 *often not capitalized* **a** : VAGABOND, WANDERER; *especially* : GYPSY **b** : a person (as a writer or an artist) living an unconventional life usually in a colony with others
— **bohemian** *adjective, often capitalized*

Bohemian Brethren *noun plural* (circa 1862)
: a Christian body originating in Bohemia in 1467 and forming a parent body of the Moravian Church

bo·he·mi·an·ism \bō-'hē-mē-ə-ˌni-zəm\ *noun, often capitalized* (1861)
: the unconventional way of life of bohemians

Bohr effect \'bōr-, 'bȯr-\ *noun* [Christian *Bohr* (died 1911) Danish physiologist] (1939)
: the decrease in the oxygen affinity of a respiratory pigment (as hemoglobin) in response to decreased blood pH resulting from increased carbon dioxide concentration in the blood

Bohr theory *noun* [Niels *Bohr*] (1922)

: a theory in early quantum physics: an atom consists of a positively charged nucleus about which revolves one or more electrons of quantized energy

bo·hunk \'bō-ˌhəŋk\ *noun* [*Bohemian* + *Hunk* person of central European descent, by shortening & alteration of *Hungarian*] (circa 1903)
: a person of central European descent or birth — usually used disparagingly

¹boil \'bȯi(ə)l\ *verb* [Middle English, from Old French *boillir*, from Latin *bullire* to bubble, from *bulla* bubble] (13th century)
intransitive verb
1 a : to come to the boiling point **b** : to generate bubbles of vapor when heated — used of a liquid **c** : to cook in boiling water
2 : to become agitated like boiling water
: SEETHE
3 : to be moved, excited, or stirred up ⟨made his blood *boil*⟩
4 a : to rush headlong **b** : to burst forth
: ERUPT ⟨water *boiling* from a spring⟩
5 : to undergo the action of a boiling liquid
transitive verb
1 : to subject to the action of a boiling liquid
2 : to heat to the boiling point
3 : to form or separate (as sugar or salt) by boiling
— **boil·able** \'bȯi-lə-bəl\ *adjective*

²boil *noun* [Middle English, alteration of *bile*, from Old English *bӯl*; akin to Old High German *pūlla* bladder] (15th century)
: a localized swelling and inflammation of the skin resulting from infection in a skin gland, having a hard central core, and forming pus

³boil *noun* (15th century)
1 : the act or state of boiling
2 : a swirling upheaval (as of water)

boil down (1845)
transitive verb
1 : to reduce in bulk by boiling
2 : CONDENSE, SUMMARIZE ⟨*boil down* a report⟩
intransitive verb
1 : to undergo reduction in bulk by boiling
2 a : to be equivalent in summary : AMOUNT ⟨his speech *boiled down* to a plea for more money⟩ **b** : to reduce ultimately ⟨your choices *boil down* to three⟩

boil·er \'bȯi-lər\ *noun* (circa 1540)
1 : one that boils
2 a : a vessel used for boiling **b** : the part of a steam generator in which water is converted into steam and which consists usually of metal shells and tubes **c** : a tank in which water is heated or hot water is stored

boil·er·mak·er \'bȯi-lər-ˌmā-kər\ *noun* (1865)
1 : a worker who makes, assembles, or repairs boilers
2 : whiskey with a beer chaser

boil·er·plate \-ˌplāt\ *noun* (1897)
1 : syndicated material supplied especially to weekly newspapers in matrix or plate form
2 a : standardized text **b** : formulaic or hackneyed language ⟨bureaucratic *boilerplate*⟩

boiler room *noun* (1903)
1 : a room in which a boiler is located
2 : a room equipped with telephones used for making high-pressure usually fraudulent sales pitches

boil·er·suit \-ˌsüt\ *noun* (1928)
: COVERALL

¹boil·ing \'bȯi-liŋ\ *adjective* (14th century)
1 a : heated to the boiling point **b** : TORRID ⟨a *boiling* sun⟩
2 : intensely agitated ⟨a *boiling* sea⟩ ⟨boiling with anger⟩

²boiling *adverb* (1607)
: to an extreme degree : VERY ⟨*boiling* mad⟩ ⟨*boiling* hot⟩

boiling point *noun* (1773)
1 : the temperature at which a liquid boils
2 a : the point at which a person becomes uncontrollably angry **b** : the point of crisis
: HEAD 17b ⟨matters had reached the *boiling point*⟩

boil over *intransitive verb* (15th century)
1 : to overflow while boiling or during boiling
2 : to become so incensed as to lose one's temper

bois d'arc \'bō-,dä(r)k, *dialect also* 'bwä-, 'bȯr-\ *noun, plural* **bois d'arcs** *or* **bois d'arc** [American French, literally, bow wood] (1805)
: OSAGE ORANGE; *also* **:** its wood

bois·ter·ous \'bȯi-st(ə-)rəs\ *adjective* [Middle English *boistous* rough] (14th century)
1 *obsolete* **a :** COARSE **b :** DURABLE, STRONG **c :** MASSIVE
2 a : noisily turbulent **:** ROWDY **b :** marked by or expressive of exuberance and high spirits
3 : STORMY, TUMULTUOUS
synonym see VOCIFEROUS
— **bois·ter·ous·ly** *adverb*
— **bois·ter·ous·ness** *noun*

boîte \'bwät\ *noun* [French, literally, box] (1922)
: NIGHTCLUB

bok choy \'bäk-'chȯi\ *noun* [Chinese (Guangdong) *baahk-choi,* literally, white vegetable] (1938)
: a Chinese cabbage (*Brassica chinensis*) forming an open head with long white stalks and green leaves

Bok·mål \'bùk-,mȯl, 'bōk-\ *noun* [Norwegian, literally, book language] (1931)
: a literary form of Norwegian developed by the gradual reform of written Danish — compare NYNORSK

bo·la \'bō-lə\ *or* **bo·las** \-ləs\ *noun, plural* **bo·las** \-ləz\ *also* **bo·las·es** [American Spanish *bolas,* from Spanish *bola* ball] (1818)
: a cord with weights attached to the ends for throwing at and entangling an animal

¹bold \'bōld\ *adjective* [Middle English, from Old English *beald;* akin to Old High German *bald* bold] (before 12th century)
1 a : fearless before danger **:** INTREPID **b :** showing or requiring a fearless daring spirit ⟨a *bold* plan⟩
2 : IMPUDENT, PRESUMPTUOUS
3 *obsolete* **:** ASSURED, CONFIDENT
4 : SHEER, STEEP ⟨*bold* cliffs⟩
5 : ADVENTUROUS, FREE ⟨a *bold* thinker⟩
6 : standing out prominently
7 : being or set in boldface
— **bold·ly** \'bōl(d)-lē\ *adverb*
— **bold·ness** \'bōl(d)-nəs\ *noun*

²bold *noun* (circa 1871)
: BOLDFACE

bold·face \'bōl(d)-,fās\ *noun* (circa 1889)
: a heavy-faced type; *also* **:** printing in boldface

bold–faced \'bōl(d)-'fāst\ *adjective* (1591)
1 : bold in manner or conduct **:** IMPUDENT
2 *usually* **bold·faced :** being or set in boldface

bole \'bōl\ *noun* [Middle English, from Old Norse *bolr*] (14th century)
: TRUNK 1a

bo·le·ro \bə-'ler-(,)ō\ *noun, plural* **-ros** [Spanish] (1787)
1 : a Spanish dance characterized by sharp turns, stamping of the feet, and sudden pauses in a position with one arm arched over the head; *also* **:** music in ¾ time for a bolero
2 : a loose waist-length jacket open at the front

bo·lete \bō-'lēt\ *noun* [New Latin *Boletus*] (1914)
: any of a family (Boletaceae) of fleshy stalked pore fungi that usually grow on the ground in wooded areas; *especially* **:** BOLETUS

bo·le·tus \bō-'lē-təs\ *noun, plural* **-tus** *or* **-ti** \-'lē-,tī\ [New Latin, genus name, from Latin, mushroom] (1601)

bola

: any of a genus (*Boletus*) of boletes (as a cèpe) some of which are poisonous and others edible

bo·lide \'bō-,līd, -lid\ *noun* [French, from Latin *bolid-, bolis,* from Greek, from *bolē* throw, stroke] (1852)
: a large meteor **:** FIREBALL; *especially* **:** one that explodes

bo·li·var \bə-'lē-,vär, 'bä-lə-vər\ *noun, plural* **-va·res** \,bä-lə-'vär-,ās, ,bō-li-\ *or* **-vars** [American Spanish *bolívar,* from Simón *Bolívar*] (circa 1895)
— see MONEY table

bo·li·va·no \bə-,li-vē-'ä-(,)nō\ *noun, plural* **-nos** [American Spanish] (circa 1872)
— see MONEY table

boll \'bōl\ *noun* [Middle English] (15th century)
: the pod or capsule of a plant (as cotton)

bol·lard \'bä-lərd, *British also* -,lärd\ *noun* [perhaps from *bole*] (circa 1775)
1 : a post of metal or wood on a wharf around which to fasten mooring lines
2 : BITT 1
3 *chiefly British* **:** any of a series of short posts set at intervals to delimit an area (as a traffic island) or to exclude vehicles

bol·lix \'bä-liks\ *transitive verb* [alteration of *ballocks,* plural of *ballock* (testis), from Middle English, from Old English *bealluc* — more at BALL] (1937)
: to throw into disorder; *also* **:** BUNGLE — usually used with *up*
— **bollix** *noun*

boll weevil *noun* (1895)
: a grayish weevil (*Anthonomus grandis*) that infests the cotton plant and feeds on the squares and bolls

boll·worm \'bōl-,wərm\ *noun* (1847)
: CORN EARWORM; *also* **:** any of several other moths or their immature stages that feed on cotton bolls as larvae

bo·lo \'bō-(,)lō\ *noun, plural* **bolos** [Philippine Spanish] (circa 1900)
: a long heavy single-edged knife of Philippine origin used to cut vegetation and as a weapon

bo·lo·gna \bə-'lō-nē *also* -nyə, -nə\ *noun* [short for *Bologna* sausage, from *Bologna,* Italy] (1596)
: a large smoked sausage of beef, veal, and pork; *also* **:** a sausage made (as of turkey) to resemble bologna

bo·lom·e·ter \bō-'lä-mə-tər\ *noun* [Greek *bolē* stroke, beam of light (from *ballein* to throw) + English *-o-* + *-meter* — more at DEVIL] (1881)
: a very sensitive thermometer whose electrical resistance varies with temperature and which is used in the detection and measurement of feeble thermal radiation and is especially adapted to the study of infrared spectra
— **bo·lo·met·ric** \,bō-lə-'me-trik\ *adjective*
— **bo·lo·met·ri·cal·ly** \-tri-k(ə-)lē\ *adverb*

bo·lo·ney \bə-'lō-nē\ *variant of* BALONEY

bo·lo tie \'bō-lō-\ *or* **bo·la tie** \-lə-\ *noun* [probably from *bola*] (1964)
: a cord fastened around the neck with an ornamental clasp and worn as a necktie

Bol·she·vik \'bōl-shə-,vik, 'bäl-, -,vēk\ *noun, plural* **Bolsheviks** *also* **Bol·she·vi·ki** \,bōl-shə-'vi-kē, ,bōl-, ,bäl-, -'vē-kē\ [Russian *bol'shevik,* from *bol'shiĭ* greater] (1917)
1 : a member of the extremist wing of the Russian Social Democratic party that seized power in Russia by the Revolution of November 1917
2 : COMMUNIST 3
— **Bolshevik** *adjective*

Bol·she·vism \'bōl-shə-,vi-zəm, 'bōl-, 'bäl-\ *noun, often capitalized* (1917)
1 : the doctrine or program of the Bolsheviks advocating violent overthrow of capitalism
2 : Russian communism

Bol·she·vist \-vist\ *noun or adjective* (1917)
: BOLSHEVIK

bol·she·vize \-,vīz\ *transitive verb* **-vized; -viz·ing** (1919)
: to make Bolshevist
— **Bol·she·vi·za·tion** \,bōl-shə-və-'zā-shən, ,bōl-, ,bäl-\ *noun*

bol·shie *or* **bol·shy** \'bōl-shē, 'bōl-, 'bäl-\ *noun or adjective, often capitalized* [by shortening & alteration] (1918)
: BOLSHEVIK

¹bol·ster \'bōl-stər\ *noun* [Middle English, from Old English; akin to Old English *belg* bag — more at BELLY] (before 12th century)
1 : a long pillow or cushion
2 : a structural part designed to eliminate friction or provide support or bearing

²bolster *transitive verb* **bol·stered; bol·ster·ing** \-st(ə-)riŋ\ (1508)
1 : to support with or as if with a bolster **:** REINFORCE
2 : to give a boost to ⟨news that *bolstered* his spirits⟩
— **bol·ster·er** \-stər-ər\ *noun*

¹bolt \'bōlt\ *noun* [Middle English, from Old English; akin to Old High German *bolz* crossbow bolt, and perhaps to Lithuanian *beldėti* to beat] (before 12th century)
1 a : a shaft or missile designed to be shot from a crossbow or catapult; *especially* **:** a short stout usually blunt-headed arrow

bolt 4

b : a lightning stroke; *also* **:** THUNDERBOLT
2 a : a wood or metal bar or rod used to fasten a door **b :** the part of a lock that is shot or withdrawn by the key
3 : a roll of cloth or wallpaper of specified length
4 : a metal rod or pin for fastening objects together that usually has a head at one end and a screw thread at the other and is secured by a nut
5 a : a block of timber to be sawed or cut **b :** a short round section of a log
6 : a metal cylinder that drives the cartridge into the chamber of a firearm, locks the breech, and usually contains the firing pin and extractor

²bolt (13th century)
intransitive verb
1 : to move suddenly or nervously **:** START
2 : to move rapidly **:** DASH
3 a : to dart off or away **:** FLEE **b :** to break away from control or a set course
4 : to break away from or oppose one's previous affiliation (as with a political party or candidate)
5 : to produce seed prematurely
transitive verb
1 a *archaic* **:** SHOOT, DISCHARGE **b :** FLUSH, START ⟨*bolt* rabbits⟩
2 : to say impulsively **:** BLURT
3 : to secure with a bolt
4 : to attach or fasten with bolts
5 : to swallow hastily or without chewing
6 : to break away from or refuse to support (as a political party)

³bolt *adverb* (14th century)
1 : in an erect or straight-backed position **:** RIGIDLY ⟨sat *bolt* upright⟩
2 *archaic* **:** DIRECTLY, STRAIGHT

⁴bolt *noun* (1550)
: the act or an instance of bolting

⁵**bolt** *transitive verb* [Middle English *bulten*, from Old French *buleter*, modification of Middle High German *biuteln* to sift, from *biutel* bag, from Old High German *būtil*] (13th century)
1 : to sift (as flour) usually through fine-meshed cloth
2 *archaic* **:** SIFT 2
bolt–ac·tion \'bōlt-'ak-shən\ *adjective* (1896) *of a firearm* **:** loaded by means of a manually operated bolt
bolt·er \'bōl-tər\ *noun* (circa 1699)
: one that bolts: as **a :** a horse given to running away **b :** a voter who bolts from a political party
bolt–hole \'bōlt-,hōl\ *noun* (circa 1851) *chiefly British* **:** a place of escape or refuge
bolt·rope \'bōlt-,rōp\ *noun* (circa 1626)
: a strong rope stitched to the edges of a sail to strengthen it
bo·lus \'bō-ləs\ *noun* [Late Latin, from Greek *bōlos* lump] (1562)
: a rounded mass: as **a :** a large pill **b :** a soft mass of chewed food
¹**bomb** \'bäm\ *noun* [French *bombe*, from Italian *bomba*, probably from Latin *bombus* deep hollow sound, from Greek *bombos*, of imitative origin] (1684)
1 a : an explosive device fused to detonate under specified conditions **b :** ATOMIC BOMB; *also* **:** nuclear weapons in general — usually used with *the*
2 : a vessel for compressed gases: as **a :** a pressure vessel for conducting chemical experiments **b :** a container for an aerosol **:** SPRAY CAN
3 : a rounded mass of lava exploded from a volcano
4 : a lead-lined container for radioactive material
5 : FAILURE, FLOP ⟨the play was a *bomb*⟩
6 *British* **:** a large sum of money
7 *British* **:** a great success **:** HIT
8 : a long pass in football
²**bomb** (1688)
transitive verb
1 : to attack with or as if with bombs **:** BOMBARD
2 : to defeat decisively
intransitive verb
1 : to fall flat **:** FAIL
2 *slang* **:** to move rapidly ⟨*bombed* down the hill⟩
— **bomb·ing** *noun*
¹**bom·bard** \'bäm-,bärd\ *noun* [Middle English *bombarde*, from Middle French, probably from Latin *bombus*] (15th century)
: a late medieval cannon used to hurl large stones
²**bom·bard** \bäm-'bärd *also* bəm-\ *transitive verb* (1686)
1 : to attack especially with artillery or bombers
2 : to assail vigorously or persistently (as with questions)
3 : to subject to the impact of rapidly moving particles (as electrons)
synonym see ATTACK
— **bom·bard·ment** \-mənt\ *noun*
bom·bar·dier \,bäm-bə-'dir, -bər-\ *noun* (1560)
1 a *archaic* **:** ARTILLERYMAN **b :** a noncommissioned officer in the British artillery
2 : a bomber-crew member who releases the bombs
bom·bar·don \'bäm-bər-,dōn, bäm-'bär-dᵊn\ *noun* [French, from Italian *bombardone*] (1856)
1 : a bass tuba
2 : the bass member of the shawm family
bom·bast \'bäm-,bast\ *noun* [Middle English *bombast* cotton padding, from Middle French *bombace*, from Medieval Latin *bombac-, bombax* cotton, alteration of Latin *bombyc-, bom-*

byx silkworm, silk, from Greek *bombyk-, bombyx*] (1589)
: pretentious inflated speech or writing
bom·bas·tic \bäm-'bas-tik\ *adjective* (1704)
: marked by or given to bombast **:** POMPOUS, OVERBLOWN
— **bom·bas·ti·cal·ly** \-ti-k(ə-)lē\ *adverb*
bom·ba·zine \,bäm-bə-'zēn\ *noun* [Middle French *bombasin*, from Medieval Latin *bombacinum, bombycinum* silken texture, from Latin, neuter of *bombycinus* of silk, from *bombyc-, bombyx*] (1572)
1 : a twilled fabric with silk warp and worsted filling
2 : a silk fabric in twill weave dyed black
bombe \'bäm, 'bōⁿ(m)b\ *noun* [French, literally, bomb] (1892)
: a frozen dessert usually containing ice cream and formed in layers in a mold
bom·bé *or* **bom·be** \(,)bäm-'bā, (,)bōⁿ-\ *adjective* [French, from *bomber*] (1904)
: having outward curving lines — usually used of furniture
bombed \'bämd\ *adjective* (1959)
: affected by alcohol or drugs **:** DRUNK, HIGH
bomb·er \'bä-mər\ *noun* (1915)
1 : one that bombs; *specifically* **:** an airplane designed for bombing
2 : BOMBER JACKET
bomber jacket *noun* (1952)
: a zippered usually leather jacket with front pockets and knitted cuffs and waistband
bom·bi·nate \'bäm-bə-,nāt\ *intransitive verb* **-nat·ed; -nat·ing** [New Latin *bombinatus*, past participle of *bombinare*, alteration of Latin *bombilare*, from *bombus*] (1880)
: BUZZ, DRONE
— **bom·bi·na·tion** \,bäm-bə-'nā-shən\ *noun*
bomb·proof \'bäm-,prüf\ *adjective* (1702)
: safe from the force of bombs
bomb·shell \'bäm-,shel\ *noun* (1708)
1 : BOMB 1a
2 : one that is stunning, amazing, or devastating ⟨the book was a political *bombshell*⟩
bomb·sight \-,sīt\ *noun* (1917)
: a sighting device for aiming bombs
bo·na fide \'bō-nə-,fīd, 'bä-; ,bō-nə-'fī-dē, -'fī-də\ *adjective* [Latin, literally, in good faith] (1788)
1 : made in good faith without fraud or deceit ⟨a *bona fide* offer to buy a farm⟩
2 : made with earnest intent **:** SINCERE
3 : neither specious nor counterfeit **:** GENUINE
synonym see AUTHENTIC
bo·na fi·des \,bō-nə-'fī-,dēz, ÷'bō-nə-,fīdz\ *noun* [Latin, literally, good faith] (1798)
1 : good faith **:** SINCERITY
2 : the fact of being genuine — often plural in construction
3 : evidence of one's good faith or genuineness — often plural in construction
4 : evidence of one's qualifications or achievements — often plural in construction
bo·nan·za \bə-'nan-zə\ *noun* [Spanish, literally, calm sea, from Medieval Latin *bonacia*, alteration of Latin *malacia*, from Greek *malakia*, literally, softness, from *malakos* soft] (1844)
1 : an exceptionally large and rich mineral deposit (as of an ore, precious metal, or petroleum)
2 a : something that is very valuable, profitable, or rewarding ⟨a box-office *bonanza*⟩ **b :** an extremely large amount ⟨expected a *bonanza* of sympathy⟩
Bo·na·part·ism \'bō-nə-,pär-,ti-zəm\ *noun* (1815)
1 : support of the French emperors Napoleon I, Napoleon III, or their dynasty
2 : a political movement associated chiefly with authoritarian rule usually by a military leader ostensibly supported by a popular mandate
— **Bo·na·part·ist** \-,pär-tist\ *noun or adjective*

bon·bon \'bän-,bän\ *noun* [French, reduplication of *bon* good, from Latin *bonus* — more at BOUNTY] (1796)
: a candy with chocolate or fondant coating and fondant center that sometimes contains fruits and nuts
¹**bond** \'bänd\ *noun* [Middle English *band, bond* — more at BAND] (12th century)
1 : something that binds or restrains **:** FETTER
2 : a binding agreement **:** COVENANT
3 a : a band or cord used to tie something **b :** a material or device for binding **c :** an attractive force that holds together the atoms, ions, or groups of atoms in a molecule or crystal **d :** an adhesive, cementing material, or fusible ingredient that combines, unites, or strengthens
4 : a uniting or binding element or force **:** TIE ⟨the *bonds* of friendship⟩
5 a : an obligation made binding by a money forfeit; *also* **:** the amount of the money guarantee **b :** one who acts as bail or surety **c :** an interest-bearing certificate of public or private indebtedness **d :** an insurance agreement pledging surety for financial loss caused to another by the act or default of a third person or by some contingency over which the third person may have no control
6 : the systematic lapping of brick in a wall
7 : the state of goods made, stored, or transported under the care of bonded agencies until the duties or taxes on them are paid
8 : a 100-proof straight whiskey aged at least four years under government supervision before being bottled — called also *bonded whiskey*
9 : BOND PAPER
²**bond** (1677)
transitive verb
1 : to lap (as brick) for solidity of construction
2 a : to secure payment of duties and taxes on (goods) by giving a bond **b :** to convert into a debt secured by bonds **c :** to provide a bond for or cause to provide such a bond ⟨*bond* an employee⟩
3 a : to cause to adhere firmly **b :** to embed in a matrix **c :** to hold together in a molecule or crystal by chemical bonds
intransitive verb
: to hold together or solidify by or as if by means of a bond or binder **:** COHERE
— **bond·able** \'bän-də-bəl\ *adjective*
— **bond·er** *noun*
³**bond** *adjective* [Middle English *bonde*, from *bonde* peasant, serf, from Old English *bōnda* householder, from Old Norse *bōndi*] (14th century)
archaic **:** bound in slavery
bond·age \'bän-dij\ *noun* (14th century)
1 : the tenure or service of a villein, serf, or slave
2 : a state of being bound usually by compulsion (as of law or mastery): as **a :** CAPTIVITY, SERFDOM **b :** servitude or subjugation to a controlling person or force ⟨young people in *bondage* to drugs⟩
bond·ed \'bän-dəd\ *adjective* (1945)
: composed of two or more layers of the same or different fabrics held together by an adhesive ⟨*bonded* jersey⟩
bond·hold·er \'bänd-,hōl-dər\ *noun* (1823)
: one that holds a government or corporation bond
bond·ing *noun* (1976)
1 : the formation of a close personal relationship (as between a mother and child) especially through frequent or constant association
2 : the attaching of a material (as porcelain) to a tooth surface especially for cosmetic purposes
bond·maid \'bän(d)-,mād\ *noun* (1526)
archaic **:** a female bond servant
bond·man \'bän(d)-mən\ *noun* (13th century)
: SLAVE, SERF
bond paper *noun* (circa 1877)

: a durable paper originally used for documents

bond servant *noun* (15th century)
: one bound to service without wages; *also*
: SLAVE

¹**bonds·man** \'bän(d)z-mən\ *noun* (1713)
: one who assumes the responsibility of a bond : SURETY

²**bondsman** *noun* (1735)
: BONDMAN

bond·stone \'bän(d)-ˌstōn\ *noun* (circa 1845)
: a stone long enough to extend through the full thickness of a wall to bind it together

bond·wom·an \'bän-ˌdwu̇-mən\ *noun* (14th century)
: a female slave

¹**bone** \'bōn\ *noun, often attributive* [Middle English *bon,* from Old English *bān;* akin to Old High German & Old Norse *bein* bone, and perhaps to Old Irish *benaid* he hews] (before 12th century)
1 a : one of the hard parts of the skeleton of a vertebrate **b** : any of various hard animal substances or structures (as baleen or ivory) akin to or resembling bone **c** : the hard largely calcareous connective tissue of which the adult skeleton of most vertebrates is chiefly composed
2 a : ESSENCE, CORE ⟨cut costs to the *bone*⟩ ⟨a liberal to the *bone*⟩ **b** : the most deeply ingrained part : HEART — usually used in plural ⟨knew in his *bones* that it was wrong⟩
3 *plural* **a** (1) : SKELETON (2) : BODY ⟨rested my weary *bones*⟩ (3) : CORPSE ⟨inter a person's *bones*⟩ **b** : the basic design or framework (as of a play or novel)
4 : MATTER, SUBJECT ⟨a *bone* of contention⟩
5 a *plural* : thin bars of bone, ivory, or wood held in pairs between the fingers and used to produce musical rhythms **b** : a strip of whalebone or steel used to stiffen a corset or dress **c** *plural* : DICE
6 : something that is designed to placate : SOP
7 : a light beige
— **boned** \'bōnd\ *adjective*
— **bone·less** \'bōn-ləs\ *adjective*
— **bone to pick** : a matter to argue or complain about

²**bone** *verb* **boned; bon·ing** (15th century)
transitive verb
1 : to remove the bones from ⟨*bone* a fish⟩
2 : to provide (a garment) with stays
intransitive verb
: to study hard : GRIND ⟨*bone* through medical school⟩

³**bone** *adverb* (circa 1825)
: EXTREMELY, VERY ⟨*bone* tired⟩; *also* : TOTALLY

bone ash *noun* (1622)
: the white porous residue chiefly of tribasic calcium phosphate from bones calcined in air used especially in making pottery and glass and in cleaning jewelry

bone black *noun* (1815)
: the black residue chiefly of tribasic calcium phosphate and carbon from bones calcined in closed vessels used especially as a pigment or as a decolorizing adsorbent in sugar manufacturing — called also *bone char*

bone china *noun* (circa 1895)
: translucent white china made with bone ash or calcium phosphate and characterized by whiteness

bone–dry \'bōn-'drī\ *adjective* (circa 1825)
1 : very dry
2 : DRY 5

bone·fish \'bōn-ˌfish\ *noun* (1884)
1 : a slender silvery small-scaled fish (*Albula vulpes*) that is a notable sport and food fish of warm seas
2 : LADYFISH 2
— **bone·fish·ing** *noun*

¹**bone·head** \-ˌhed\ *noun* (1909)
: a stupid person : NUMSKULL
— **bone·head·ed** \-'he-dəd\ *adjective*
— **bone·head·ed·ness** *noun*

²**bonehead** *adjective* (1915)

: being a college course for students lacking fundamental skills ⟨teaches *bonehead* English⟩

bone·meal \'bōn-ˌmē(ə)l\ *noun* (1850)
: crushed or ground bone used especially as fertilizer or feed

bon·er \'bō-nər\ *noun* (circa 1899)
1 : one that bones
2 : HOWLER 2

bone·set \'bōn-ˌset\ *noun* (1764)
: any of several composite herbs (genus *Eupatorium*); *especially* : a perennial (*E. perfoliatum*) with opposite perfoliate leaves and white-rayed flower heads used in folk medicine

bone·set·ter \-ˌse-tər\ *noun* (15th century)
: a person who sets broken or dislocated bones usually without being a licensed physician

bone up *intransitive verb* (1887)
1 : to try to master necessary information quickly : CRAM ⟨*bone up* for the exam⟩
2 : to renew one's skill or refresh one's memory ⟨*boned up* on the speech just before giving it⟩

bone·yard \-ˌyärd\ *noun* (1866)
1 : CEMETERY
2 : a place where worn-out or damaged objects (as cars) are collected to await disposal

bon·fire \'bän-ˌfīr\ *noun* [Middle English *bonefire* a fire of bones, from *bon* bone + *fire*] (15th century)
: a large fire built in the open air

¹**bong** \'bäŋ, 'bȯŋ\ *noun* [imitative] (1860)
: the deep resonant sound especially of a bell
— **bong** *verb*

²**bong** *noun* [Thai *bhaung*³] (1971)
: a simple water pipe consisting of a bottle or vertical tube partially filled with a liquid (as water or liqueur) and a smaller offset tube ending in a bowl

¹**bon·go** \'bäŋ-(ˌ)gō, 'bȯŋ-\ *noun, plural* **bongos** *also* **bongoes** [American Spanish *bongó*] (1920)
: one of a pair of small connected drums of different sizes and pitches played with the hands
— **bon·go·ist** \-ˌgō-ist\ *noun*

²**bongo** *noun, plural* **bongo** *or* **bongos** [probably from Kele (Bantu language of Gabon)] (1861)
: an African antelope (*Tragelaphus euryceros* synonym *Boocerus euryceros*) that is chestnut-red with narrow white vertical stripes and is found in forests from Sierra Leone to Kenya

bon·ho·mie \ˌbä-nə-'mē, ˌbō-\ *noun* [French *bonhomie,* from *bonhomme* good-natured man, from *bon* good + *homme* man] (1779)
: good-natured easy friendliness
— **bon·ho·mous** \'bä-nə-məs\ *adjective*

bon·i·face \'bä-nə-fəs, -ˌfäs\ *noun* [*Boniface,* innkeeper in *The Beaux' Stratagem* (1707) by George Farquhar] (1803)
: the proprietor of a hotel, nightclub, or restaurant

bo·ni·to \bə-'nē-(ˌ)tō, -'nē-tə\ *noun, plural* **-tos** *or* **-to** [Spanish, from *bonito* pretty, diminutive of *bueno* good, from Latin *bonus*] (circa 1565)
: any of several scombroid fishes (especially genera *Sarda* and *Euthynnus*) intermediate between the smaller mackerels and the larger tunas

bon·kers \'bäŋ-kərz, 'bȯŋ-\ *adjective* [perhaps from *bonk* to hit, bang + *-ers* (as in *crackers*)] (circa 1948)
: CRAZY, MAD ⟨if I don't work, I go *bonkers* —Zoe Caldwell⟩
word history SEE NUTS

bon mot \bōⁿ-'mō\ *noun, plural* **bons mots** \bōⁿ-'mō(z)\ *or* **bon mots** \-'mō(z)\ [French, literally, good word] (circa 1730)
: a clever remark : WITTICISM

bonne \'bȯn\ *noun* [French, from feminine of *bon*] (1771)
: a French nursemaid or maidservant

¹**bon·net** \'bä-nət\ *noun* [Middle English *bonet,* from Middle French, probably of German-

ic origin; akin to Old Saxon *gibund* bundle, Old English *bindan* to bind] (14th century)
1 a (1) *chiefly Scottish* : a man's or boy's cap (2) : a brimless Scotch cap of seamless woolen fabric — compare TAM-O'-SHANTER **2 b** : a cloth or straw hat tied under the chin and worn by women and children
2 a *British* : an automobile hood **b** : a metal covering or cowl (as for a fireplace, valve chamber, or ventilator)

²**bonnet** *transitive verb* (1858)
: to provide with or dress in a bonnet

bon·ny *also* **bon·nie** \'bä-nē\ *adjective* **bon·ni·er; -est** [Middle English *bonie,* from Middle French *bon* good, from Latin *bonus*] (15th century)
chiefly British : ATTRACTIVE, FAIR; *also* : FINE, EXCELLENT
— **bon·ni·ly** \'bä-nə-lē\ *adverb*

bon·ny·clab·ber \'bä-nē-ˌkla-bər\ *noun* [Irish *bainne clabair,* from *bainne* milk + *clabair,* genitive of *clabar* sour thick milk] (1616)
Northern & Midland : CLABBER

bon·sai \(ˌ)bōn-'sī, 'bōn-ˌ, 'bän-ˌ, *also* 'bän-ˌzī\ *noun, plural* **bonsai** [Japanese, literally, tray planting] (1900)
: a potted plant (as a tree) dwarfed and trained to an artistic shape by special methods of culture; *also* : the art of growing such a plant

bon·spiel \'bän-ˌspēl\ *noun* [perhaps from Dutch *bond* league + *spel* game] (circa 1772)
: a match or tournament between curling clubs

bonsai

bon ton \(ˌ)bän-'tän, 'bän-ˌ\ *noun* [French, literally, good tone] (1747)
1 a : fashionable manner or style **b** : the fashionable or proper thing
2 : high society

bo·nus \'bō-nəs\ *noun* [Latin, literally, good — more at BOUNTY] (1773)
: something in addition to what is expected or strictly due: as **a** : money or an equivalent given in addition to an employee's usual compensation **b** : a premium (as of stock) given by a corporation to a purchaser of its securities, to a promoter, or to an employee **c** : a government payment to war veterans **d** : a sum in excess of salary given an athlete for signing with a team

bon vi·vant \ˌbän-vē-'vänt, ˌbōⁿ-vē-'väⁿ\ *noun, plural* **bons vivants** \ˌbän-vē-'vän(t)s, ˌbōⁿ-vē-'väⁿ(z)\ *or* **bon vivants** *same*\ [French, literally, good liver] (circa 1695)
: a person having cultivated, refined, and sociable tastes especially in respect to food and drink

bon voy·age \ˌbōⁿ-ˌvȯi-'äzh, ˌbän-; ˌbōⁿ-ˌvwī-'äzh, -ˌvwä-'yäzh\ *noun* [French, literally, good journey!] (15th century)
: FAREWELL — often used interjectionally

bony *also* **bon·ey** \'bō-nē\ *adjective* **bon·i·er; -est** (14th century)
1 a : consisting of bone **b** : resembling bone
2 a : full of bones ⟨a *bony* piece of fish⟩ **b** : having prominent bones ⟨a rugged *bony* face⟩
3 a : SKINNY, SCRAWNY **b** : BARREN, LEAN

bony fish *noun* (circa 1890)
: any of a major taxon (class Osteichthyes or superclass Teleostomi) comprising fishes (as a sturgeon, salmon, marlin, or ocean sunfish)

\ə\ abut \ᵊ\ kitten \ər\ **further** \a\ ash \ā\ ace \ä\ mop, mar \au̇\ out \ch\ chin \e\ bet \ē\ easy \g\ go \i\ hit \ī\ ice \j\ job \ŋ\ sing \ō\ go \ȯ\ law \ȯi\ boy \th\ thin \ṯẖ\ the \ü\ loot \u̇\ foot \y\ yet \zh\ vision *see also* Guide to Pronunciation

with a bony rather than a cartilaginous skeleton — called also *teleost;* compare CARTILAGINOUS FISH, JAWLESS FISH

bonze \'bänz\ *noun* [Middle French, from Portuguese *bonzo,* from Japanese *bonsō*] (1588) : a Buddhist monk

¹**boo** \'bü\ *interjection* [Middle English *bo*] (15th century) — used to express contempt or disapproval or to startle or frighten

²**boo** *noun, plural* **boos** (1575)
1 : a shout of disapproval or contempt
2 : any sound at all — usually used in negative constructions ⟨never said *boo*⟩

³**boo** (1884)
intransitive verb
: to deride especially by uttering *boo*
transitive verb
: to express disapproval of by booing ⟨the crowd *booed* the referee⟩

⁴**boo** *noun* [origin unknown] (circa 1959)
: MARIJUANA

¹**boob** \'büb\ *noun* [short for ¹booby] (1909)
1 : a stupid awkward person **:** SIMPLETON
2 : BOOR, PHILISTINE
— **boob·ish** \'bü-bish\ *adjective*

²**boob** *noun* [³boob] (1934)
British **:** MISTAKE, BLUNDER

³**boob** *intransitive verb* [¹boob] (1935)
British **:** GOOF 2

⁴**boob** *noun* [short for ²booby] (1945)
: BREAST — sometimes considered vulgar

boob·oi·sie \,büb-wä-'zē\ *noun* [blend of ¹boob and *bourgeoisie*] (1922)
: the general public regarded as consisting of boobs

boo–boo \'bü-(,)bü\ *noun, plural* **boo–boos** [probably baby-talk alteration of *boohoo,* imitation of the sound of weeping] (1953)
1 : a usually trivial injury (as a bruise or scratch) — used especially by or of a child
2 : MISTAKE, BLUNDER

boob tube *noun* (1966)
: TELEVISION — used with *the*

¹**boo·by** \'bü-bē\ *noun, plural* **boobies** [modification of Spanish *bobo,* from Latin *balbus* stammering, probably of imitative origin] (circa 1603)
1 : an awkward foolish person **:** DOPE
2 : any of several tropical seabirds (family Sulidae, especially genus *Sula*)

²**boo·by** \'bü-bē, 'bü-\ *noun, plural* **boobies** [alteration of *bubby*] (1934)
: BREAST — sometimes considered vulgar

booby hatch *noun* (1840)
1 : a raised framework with a sliding cover over a small hatch on a ship
2 : an insane asylum

booby prize *noun* (1889)
1 : an award for the poorest performance in a game or competition
2 : an acknowledgment of notable inferiority

booby trap *noun* (1850)
1 : a trap for the unwary or unsuspecting **:** PITFALL
2 : a concealed explosive device contrived to go off when some harmless-looking object is touched
— **boo·by–trap** *transitive verb*

boo·dle \'bü-d°l\ *noun* [Dutch *boedel* estate, lot, from Middle Dutch; akin to Old Norse *būth* booth] (1833)
1 : a collection or lot of persons **:** CABOODLE
2 a : bribe money **b :** a large amount especially of money

boog·er \'bu̇-gər, 'bü-\ *noun* [alteration of English dialect *buggard, boggart,* from ¹bug + *-ard*] (1866)
1 : BOGEYMAN
2 : a piece of dried nasal mucus

boo·gey·man \'bu̇-gē-,man, 'bü-\ *also* **boog·er·man** \'bu̇-gər-, 'bü-\ *noun* [by alteration] (circa 1850)
: BOGEYMAN

¹**boo·gie** \'bu̇-gē, 'bü-\ *noun* (1929)
1 : BOOGIE-WOOGIE

2 : earthy and strongly rhythmic rock music conducive to dancing; *also* **:** a period of or occasion for dancing to this music

²**boogie** *also* **boo·gy** *or* **boo·gey** \'bu̇-gē, 'bü-\ *intransitive verb* **boo·gied** *also* **boo·geyed; boo·gy·ing** *also* **boo·gey·ing** (1930)
1 : to dance to rock music; *also* **:** REVEL, PARTY
2 a : to move quickly **b :** to get going

boo·gie–woo·gie \,bu̇-gē-'wu̇-gē, ,bü-gē-'wü-gē\ *noun* [origin unknown] (1928)
: a percussive style of playing blues on the piano characterized by a steady rhythmic ground bass of eighth notes in quadruple time and a series of improvised melodic variations

¹**book** \'bu̇k\ *noun* [Middle English, from Old English *bōc;* akin to Old High German *buoh* book, Gothic *boka* letter] (before 12th century)
1 a : a set of written sheets of skin or paper or tablets of wood or ivory **b :** a set of written, printed, or blank sheets bound together into a volume **c :** a long written or printed literary composition **d :** a major division of a treatise or literary work **e :** a record of a business's financial transactions or financial condition — often used in plural ⟨the *books* show a profit⟩
2 *capitalized* **:** BIBLE 1
3 : something that yields knowledge or understanding ⟨the great *book* of nature⟩ ⟨her face was an open *book*⟩
4 a : the total available knowledge and experience that can be brought to bear on a task or problem ⟨tried every trick in the *book*⟩ ⟨the *book* on him is that he can't hit a curveball⟩ **b :** the standards or authority relevant in a situation ⟨run by the *book*⟩
5 a : all the charges that can be made against an accused person ⟨threw the *book* at him⟩ **b :** a position from which one must answer for certain acts **:** ACCOUNT ⟨bring criminals to *book*⟩
6 a : LIBRETTO **b :** the script of a play **c :** a book of arrangements for a musician or dance orchestra **:** musical repertory
7 : a packet of items bound together like a book ⟨a *book* of stamps⟩ ⟨a *book* of matches⟩
8 a : BOOKMAKER **b :** the bets registered by a bookmaker; *also* **:** the business or activity of giving odds and taking bets
9 : the number of tricks a cardplayer or side must win before any trick can have scoring value
— **book·ful** \'bu̇k-,fu̇l\ *noun*
— **in one's book :** in one's own opinion
— **in one's good books :** in favor with one
— **one for the book :** an act or occurrence worth noting
— **on the books :** on the records

²**book** *adjective* (13th century)
1 : derived from books and not from practical experience ⟨*book* learning⟩
2 : shown by books of account ⟨*book* assets⟩

³**book** (1807)
transitive verb
1 a : to register (as a name) for some future activity or condition (as to engage transportation or reserve lodgings) ⟨*booked* to sail on Monday⟩ **b :** to schedule engagements for ⟨*book* the band for a week⟩ **c :** to set aside time for **d :** to reserve in advance ⟨*book* two seats at the theater⟩ ⟨were all *booked* up⟩
2 a : to enter charges against in a police register **b** *chiefly British* **:** to charge (as a soccer player) with an infraction of the rules
intransitive verb
1 : to make a reservation ⟨*book* through your travel agent⟩
2 *chiefly British* **:** to register in a hotel — usually used with *in*
— **book·able** \'bu̇-kə-bəl\ *adjective, chiefly British*
— **book·er** *noun*

book·bind·ing \'bu̇k-,bīn-diŋ\ *noun* (1771)
1 : the art or trade of binding books

2 : the binding of a book
— **book·bind·er** \-,bīn-dər\ *noun*
— **book·bind·ery** \-d(ə-)rē\ *noun*

book·case \-,kās\ *noun* (1726)
: a piece of furniture consisting of shelves to hold books

book club *noun* (1905)
: an organization that ships selected books to members usually on a regular schedule and often at discount prices

book·end \-,end\ *noun* (1907)
: a support placed at the end of a row of books

book·ie \'bu̇-kē\ *noun* [by shortening & alteration] (1885)
: BOOKMAKER 2

book·ing \'bu̇-kiŋ\ *noun* (1881)
1 : the act of one that books
2 : an engagement or scheduled performance
3 : RESERVATION 1c

booking office *noun* (circa 1837)
chiefly British **:** a ticket office; *especially* **:** one in a railroad station

book·ish \'bu̇-kish\ *adjective* (1567)
1 a : of or relating to books **b :** fond of books and reading
2 a : inclined to rely on book knowledge **b** *of words* **:** literary and formal as opposed to colloquial and informal **c :** given to literary or scholarly pursuits; *also* **:** affectedly learned
— **book·ish·ly** *adverb*
— **book·ish·ness** *noun*

book·keep·er \'bu̇k-,kē-pər\ *noun* (1555)
: one who records the accounts or transactions of a business
— **book·keep·ing** \-piŋ\ *noun*

book·let \'bu̇k-lət\ *noun* (1859)
: a little book; *especially* **:** PAMPHLET

book louse *noun* (1867)
: any of various tiny usually wingless insects (order Psocoptera) that feed on organic matter; *especially* **:** an insect (as *Liposcelis divinatorius*) injurious especially to books

book lung *noun* (1879)
: a saccular breathing organ in many arachnids containing thin folds of membrane arranged like the leaves of a book

book·mak·er \'bu̇k-,mā-kər\ *noun* (1515)
1 : a printer, binder, or designer of books
2 : one who determines odds and receives and pays off bets
— **book·mak·ing** \-kiŋ\ *noun*

book·man \-mən\ *noun* (1583)
1 : one who has a love of books and especially of reading
2 : one who is involved in the writing, publishing, or selling of books

book·mark \-,märk\ *or* **book·mark·er** \-,mär-kər\ *noun* (1838)
: a marker for finding a place in a book

book·match \-,mach\ *transitive verb* (1942)
: to match the grains of (as two sheets of veneer) so that one sheet seems to be the mirrored image of the other

book·mo·bile \'bu̇k-mō-,bēl\ *noun* (1926)
: a truck that serves as a traveling library

Book of Common Prayer (1549)
: the service book of the Anglican Communion

book off *intransitive verb* (1971)
Canadian **:** to notify an employer that one is not reporting for work (as because of sickness)

book·plate \'bu̇k-,plāt\ *noun* (1791)
: a book owner's identification label that is usually pasted to the inside front cover of a book

book·sell·er \'bu̇k-,se-lər\ *noun* (15th century)
: one who sells books; *especially* **:** the proprietor of a bookstore
— **book·sell·ing** \-,se-liŋ\ *noun*

book·shelf \-,shelf\ *noun* (1818)
: an open shelf for holding books

book·shop \-,shäp\ *noun* (1862)
: BOOKSTORE

book·stall \-,stol\ *noun* (1800)
1 : a stall where books are sold

2 *chiefly British* : NEWSSTAND

book·store \-ˌstōr, -ˌstȯr\ *noun* (circa 1763) : a place of business where books are the main item offered for sale — called also *bookshop*

book value *noun* (1899) : the value of something as shown on book-keeping records as distinguished from market value: **a** : the value of an asset equal to cost less depreciation **b** : the value of a corporation's capital stock equal to its book value less its liabilities

book·worm \'bu̇k-ˌwərm\ *noun* (1592) : a person unusually devoted to reading and study

Bool·ean \'bü-lē-ən\ *adjective* [George *Boole* (died 1864) English mathematician] (1851) : of, relating to, or being a logical combinatorial system (as Boolean algebra) that represents symbolically relationships (as those implied by the logical operators AND, OR, and NOT) between entities (as sets, propositions, or on-off computer circuit elements) ⟨*Boolean* expression⟩ ⟨*Boolean* search strategy for information retrieval⟩

Boolean algebra *noun* (1889) : a set that is closed under two commutative binary operations and that can be described by any of various systems of postulates all of which can be deduced from the postulates that an identity element exists for each operation, that each operation is distributive over the other, and that for every element in the set there is another element which when combined with the first under one of the operations yields the identity element of the other operation

¹**boom** \'büm\ *verb* [imitative] (15th century) *intransitive verb* **1** : to make a deep hollow sound **2 a** : to increase in importance or esteem **b** : to experience a sudden rapid growth and expansion usually with an increase in prices ⟨business was *booming*⟩ **c** : to develop rapidly in population and importance ⟨California *boomed* when gold was discovered there⟩ *transitive verb* **1** : to cause to resound — often used with *out* ⟨his voice *booms* out the lyrics⟩ **2** : to cause a rapid growth or increase of : BOOST

²**boom** *noun* (circa 1500) **1** : a booming sound or cry **2** : a rapid expansion or increase: as **a** : a general movement in support of a candidate for office **b** : rapid settlement and development of a town or district **c** : a rapid widespread expansion of economic activity

³**boom** *noun* [Dutch, tree, beam; akin to Old High German *boum* tree — more at BEAM] (1627) **1** : a long spar used to extend the foot of a sail **2 a** : a chain cable or line of connected floating timbers extended across a river, lake, or harbor (as to obstruct passage or catch floating objects) **b** : a temporary floating barrier used to contain an oil spill **3 a** : a long beam projecting from the mast of a derrick to support or guide cargo **b** : a long more or less horizontal supporting arm or brace (as for holding a microphone or for supporting an antenna) **4** : a spar or outrigger connecting the tail surfaces and the main supporting structure of an aircraft

boom box *noun* (1981) : a large portable radio and often tape player with two attached speakers

boom·er *noun* (1880) **1** : one that booms **2** : one that joins a rush of settlers to a boom area **3** : a transient worker (as a bridge builder)

boo·mer·ang \'bü-mə-ˌraŋ\ *noun* [Dharuk (Australian aboriginal language of the Port Jackson area) *bumarin*] (1825) **1** : a bent or angular throwing club typically flat on one side and rounded on the other so

that it soars or curves in flight; *especially* : one designed to return near the thrower **2** : an act or utterance that backfires on its originator
— **boomerang** *intransitive verb*

boom·let \'büm-lət\ *noun* (1880) : a small boom; *specifically* : a sudden increase in business activity ⟨a stock market *boomlet*⟩

boom·town \'büm-ˌtau̇n\ *noun* (1896) : a town enjoying a business and population boom

boomy \'bü-mē\ *adjective* **boom·i·er; -est** (1888) **1** : of, relating to, or characterized by an economic boom **2** : having an excessive accentuation on the tones of lower pitch in reproduced sound

¹**boon** \'bün\ *noun* [Middle English, from Old Norse *bōn* petition; akin to Old English *bēn* prayer, *bannan* to summon — more at BAN] (12th century) **1** : BENEFIT, FAVOR; *especially* : one that is given in answer to a request **2** : a timely benefit : BLESSING

²**boon** *adjective* [Middle English *bon*, from Middle French, good — more at BONNY] (14th century) **1** *archaic* : FAVORABLE **2** : CONVIVIAL ⟨a *boon* companion⟩

boon·docks \'bün-ˌdäks\ *noun plural* [Tagalog *bundok* mountain] (circa 1909) **1** : rough country filled with dense brush **2** : a rural area : STICKS

boon·dog·gle \'bün-ˌdä-gəl, -ˌdȯ-\ *noun* [coined by Robert H. Link (died 1957) American scoutmaster] (1929) **1** : a braided cord worn by Boy Scouts as a neckerchief slide, hatband, or ornament **2** : a wasteful or impractical project or activity often involving graft ◇
— **boondoggle** *intransitive verb*
— **boon·dog·gler** \-g(ə-)lər\ *noun*

boon·ies \'bü-nēz\ *noun plural* (1956) *slang* : BOONDOCKS 2

boor \'bu̇r\ *noun* [Dutch *boer*; akin to Old English *būan* to dwell — more at BOWER] (1551) **1** : PEASANT **2** : a rude or insensitive person

boor·ish \'bu̇r-ish\ *adjective* (1562) : resembling or befitting a boor (as in crude insensitivity) ☆
— **boor·ish·ly** *adverb*
— **boor·ish·ness** *noun*

¹**boost** \'büst\ *verb* [origin unknown] (circa 1815) *transitive verb* **1** : to push or shove up from below **2** : INCREASE, RAISE ⟨plans to *boost* production⟩ ⟨an extra holiday to *boost* morale⟩ **3** : to promote the cause or interests of : PLUG ⟨a campaign to *boost* the new fashions⟩ **4** : to raise the voltage of or across (an electric circuit) **5** *slang* : STEAL, SHOPLIFT *intransitive verb* *slang* : SHOPLIFT
synonym see LIFT

²**boost** *noun* (1825) **1** : a push upward **2** : an act that brings help or encouragement : ASSIST **3** : an increase in amount

boost·er \'bü-stər\ *noun* (1890) : one that boosts: as **a** : an enthusiastic supporter **b** : an auxiliary device for increasing force, power, pressure, or effectiveness **c** *slang* : SHOPLIFTER **d** : a radio-frequency amplifier for a radio or television receiving set **e** : the first stage of a multistage rocket providing thrust for the launching and the initial part of the flight **f** : a substance that increases the effectiveness of a medicament; *especially* : BOOSTER SHOT

boost·er·ism \-stə-ˌri-zəm\ *noun* (circa 1913) : the activities and attitudes characteristic of boosters

booster shot *noun* (1944) : a supplementary dose of an immunizing agent — called also *booster, booster dose*

¹**boot** \'bu̇t\ *noun* [Middle English, from Old English *bōt* remedy; akin to Old English *betera* better] (before 12th century) **1** *archaic* : DELIVERANCE **2** *chiefly dialect* : something to equalize a trade **3** *obsolete* : AVAIL
— **to boot** : BESIDES

²**boot** *verb* (15th century) *archaic* : AVAIL, PROFIT

³**boot** *noun* [Middle English, from Middle French *bote*] (14th century) **1** : a fitted covering (as of leather or rubber) for the foot and usually reaching above the ankle **2** : an instrument of torture used to crush the leg and foot **3** : something that resembles or is likened to a boot; *especially* : an enclosing or protective casing or sheath (as for a rifle or over an electrical or mechanical connection) **4** : a navy or marine corps recruit undergoing basic training

☆ **SYNONYMS**

Boorish, churlish, loutish, clownish mean uncouth in manners or appearance. BOORISH implies rudeness of manner due to insensitiveness to others' feelings and unwillingness to be agreeable ⟨a drunk's *boorish* behavior⟩. CHURLISH suggests surliness, unresponsiveness, and ungraciousness ⟨*churlish* remarks⟩. LOUTISH implies bodily awkwardness together with stupidity ⟨a *loutish* oaf⟩. CLOWNISH suggests ill-bred awkwardness, ignorance or stupidity, ungainliness, and often a propensity for absurd antics ⟨an adolescent's *clownish* conduct⟩.

◇ **WORD HISTORY**

boondoggle *Boondoggle* is one of those colorful concoctions that, like *hornswoggle* or *sockdolager*, seem redolent of the 19th century American frontier. It is, in fact, a 20th century coinage, although there is an outdoorsy connection. At the World Jamboree of Scouts in England in 1929, Robert H. Link, usually identified as a scoutmaster from Rochester, N.Y., dubbed a plaited lanyard—a standard item of Boy Scout handicraft—a *boondoggle*. So designated, the lanyard was presented to the Prince of Wales at the Jamboree. Owing to the public nature of the presentation, the term spread through scouting circles. In the fall of 1929 the British magazine *Punch* discussed the word in a report on the presentation of a boondoggle to Lord Baden-Powell, the founder of the Boy Scouts. In 1935, during a municipal hearing in New York City, *boondoggle* was used by a government employee to describe the handicrafts, apparently of dubious value, that he was teaching to people on relief. The appearance of the word in news reports of the hearing did much to popularize it. Soon opponents of President Roosevelt's New Deal were using it to refer to any government project whose major or sole achievement was the expenditure of public funds.

\ə\ abut \ᵊ\ kitten \ər\ further \a\ ash \ā\ ace \ä\ mop, mar \au̇\ out \ch\ chin \e\ bet \ē\ easy \g\ go \i\ hit \ī\ ice \j\ job \ŋ\ sing \ō\ go \ȯ\ law \ȯi\ boy \th\ thin \t̲h̲\ the \ü\ loot \u̇\ foot \y\ yet \zh\ vision *see also* Guide to Pronunciation

5 *British* **:** an automobile trunk
6 a : a kick with the foot **b :** summary dismissal — used with *the* **c :** momentary pleasure or enjoyment **:** BANG ⟨got a big *boot* out of the joke⟩
7 : a sheath enclosing the inflorescence
⁴boot (15th century)
transitive verb
1 : to put boots on
2 a : KICK **b :** to eject or discharge summarily — often used with *out* ⟨was *booted* out of office⟩
3 : to make an error on (a grounder in baseball); *broadly* **:** BOTCH
4 : to ride (a horse) in a race ⟨*booted* home three winners⟩
5 [²*bootstrap*] **a :** to load (a program) into a computer from a disk **b :** to start or ready for use especially by booting a program ⟨*boot* a microcomputer⟩ — often used with *up*
intransitive verb
: to become loaded into a computer's memory from a disk (the program *boots* automatically)
— **boot·able** \'bü-tə-bəl\ *adjective*
⁵boot *noun* [¹*boot*] (1593)
archaic **:** BOOTY, PLUNDER
boot·black \'büt-ˌblak\ *noun* (1817)
: one who shines shoes
boot camp *noun* (circa 1942)
: a navy or marine corps camp for basic training
boot·ed \'bü-təd\ *adjective* (1552)
: wearing boots
boo·tee *or* **boo·tie** \bü-'tē, *of infants' footwear* 'bü-tē\ *noun* (1799)
: a usually ankle-length boot, slipper, or sock; *especially* **:** an infant's knitted or crocheted sock
Bo·ö·tes \bō-'ō-tēz\ *noun* [Latin (genitive *Boötis*), from Greek *Boōtēs*, literally, plowman, from *bous* head of cattle — more at COW]
: a northern constellation containing the bright star Arcturus
booth \'büth, *especially British* 'büth\ *noun, plural* **booths** \'büthz, 'büths\ [Middle English *bothe*, of Scandinavian origin; akin to Old Norse *būth* booth; akin to Old English *būan* to dwell — more at BOWER] (13th century)
1 : a temporary shelter for livestock or field workers
2 a : a stall or stand (as at a fair) for the sale or exhibition of goods **b** (1) **:** a small enclosure affording privacy for one person at a time ⟨a telephone *booth*⟩ ⟨polling *booth*⟩ (2) **:** a small enclosure that isolates its occupant especially from patrons or customers ⟨a ticket *booth*⟩ (3) **:** an isolated enclosure used in sound recording or in broadcasting ⟨a radio *booth*⟩ **c :** a restaurant seating arrangement consisting of a table between two high-back benches
boot·jack \'büt-ˌjak\ *noun* (circa 1841)
: a device (as with a V-shaped notch) used for pulling off boots
boot·lace \-ˌlās\ *noun* (circa 1887)
British **:** SHOELACE
¹boot·leg \-ˌleg, -ˌlāg\ *noun* (1634)
1 : the upper part of a boot
2 : something bootlegged; *specifically* **:** MOONSHINE
3 : a football play in which the quarterback fakes a handoff, hides the ball against his hip, and rolls out — compare DRAW 8
— **bootleg** *adjective*
²bootleg (1900)
transitive verb
1 a : to carry (alcoholic liquor) on one's person illegally **b :** to manufacture, sell, or transport for sale (alcoholic liquor) illegally

2 a : to produce, reproduce, or distribute illicitly or without authorization **b :** SMUGGLE
intransitive verb
1 : to engage in bootlegging
2 : to run a bootleg play in football
— **boot·leg·ger** *noun*
boot·less \'büt-ləs\ *adjective* (1559)
: USELESS, UNPROFITABLE
— **boot·less·ly** *adverb*
— **boot·less·ness** *noun*
boot·lick \-ˌlik\ (1845)
transitive verb
: to try to gain favor with through a servile or obsequious manner
intransitive verb
: to act obsequiously
— **boot·lick·er** *noun*
boots \'büts\ *noun plural but singular or plural in construction* [from plural of ³*boot*] (circa 1837)
British **:** a servant who shines shoes especially in a hotel
¹boot·strap \'büt-ˌstrap\ *noun* (1913)
1 *plural* **:** unaided efforts — often used in the phrase *by one's own bootstraps*
2 : a looped strap sewed at the side or the rear top of a boot to help in pulling it on
²bootstrap *adjective* (1926)
1 : designed to function independently of outside direction **:** capable of using one internal function or process to control another ⟨a *bootstrap* operation to load a computer⟩
2 : carried out with minimum resources or advantages **:** SELF-RELIANT ⟨the city recovered from the flood by the *bootstrap* method⟩
³bootstrap *transitive verb* (1951)
: to promote or develop by initiative and effort with little or no assistance ⟨*bootstrapped* herself to the top⟩
boo·ty \'bü-tē\ *noun, plural* **booties** [modification of Middle French *butin*, from Middle Low German *būte* exchange] (15th century)
1 : plunder taken (as in war); *especially* **:** plunder taken on land as distinguished from prizes taken at sea
2 : a rich gain or prize
synonym see SPOIL
¹booze \'büz\ *intransitive verb* **boozed; booz·ing** [Middle English *bousen*, from Middle Dutch *būsen*] (14th century)
: to drink intoxicating liquor especially to excess — often used in the phrase *booze it up*
²booze *noun* (14th century)
: intoxicating drink; *especially* **:** hard liquor
— **booz·i·ly** \-zə-lē\ *adverb*
— **boozy** \-zē\ *adjective*
booz·er \'bü-zər\ *noun* (circa 1819)
1 : a person who boozes **:** DRUNK
2 *British* **:** a drinking place **:** PUB
¹bop \'bäp\ *transitive verb* **bopped; bop·ping** [imitative] (1931)
: HIT, SOCK
²bop *noun* (1947)
: a blow (as with the fist or a club) that strikes a person
³bop *noun* [short for *bebop*] (1947)
1 : jazz characterized by harmonic complexity, convoluted melodic lines, and constant shifting of accent and often played at very rapid tempos
2 : JIVE 2
— **bop·per** *noun*
⁴bop *intransitive verb* **bopped; bop·ping** (1952)
1 : to go quickly or unceremoniously **:** POP ⟨*bop* into the corner store⟩ — often used with *off*
2 : to dance or shuffle along to or as if to bop music
bo·peep \(ˌ)bō-'pēp\ *noun* [¹*boo* + ³*peep*] (1528)
: PEEKABOO
bo·ra \'bōr-ə, 'bòr-\ *noun* [Italian, from Italian dialect (Trieste), from Latin *boreas*] (1864)
: a violent cold northerly wind of the Adriatic

bo·rac·ic acid \bə-'ras-ik-\ *noun* [Medieval Latin *borac-, borax* borax] (1801)
: BORIC ACID
bor·age \'bòr-ij, 'bär-\ *noun* [Middle English, from Old French *bourage*] (14th century)
: a coarse hairy blue-flowered European herb (*Borago officinalis* of the family Boraginaceae, the borage family) used medicinally and in salads
bo·rane \'bōr-ˌān, 'bòr-\ *noun* [International Scientific Vocabulary, from *boron*] (1916)
1 : a compound of boron and hydrogen; *specifically* **:** a compound BH_3 known only in the form of its derivatives
2 : a derivative of borane
bo·rate \-ˌāt\ *noun* (1816)
: a salt or ester of a boric acid
bo·rat·ed \-ˌā-təd\ *adjective* (circa 1901)
: mixed or impregnated with borax or boric acid
¹bo·rax \'bōr-ˌaks, 'bòr-, -əks\ *noun* [Middle English *boras*, from Middle French, from Medieval Latin *borac-, borax*, from Arabic *būraq*, from Persian *būrah*] (14th century)
: a white crystalline compound that consists of a hydrated sodium borate $Na_2B_4O_7 \cdot 10H_2O$, that occurs as a mineral or is prepared from other minerals, and that is used especially as a flux, cleansing agent, and water softener, as a preservative, and as a fireproofing agent
²borax *noun* [origin unknown] (1932)
: cheap shoddy merchandise
Bo·ra·zon \'bōr-ə-ˌzän, 'bòr-\ *trademark*
— used for a boron nitride abrasive
bor·bo·ryg·mus \ˌbòr-bə-'rig-məs\ *noun, plural* **-mi** \-ˌmī\ [New Latin, from Greek *borborygmos*, from *borboryzein* to rumble] (circa 1796)
: intestinal rumbling caused by moving gas
Bor·deaux \bòr-'dō\ *noun, plural* **Bordeaux** \-'dōz\ *often not capitalized* (circa 1570)
1 : white or red wine of the Bordeaux region of France
2 : CLARET 2
bor·deaux mixture \bòr-'dō-, 'bòr-ˌ\ *noun, often B capitalized* (1892)
: a fungicide made by reaction of copper sulfate, lime, and water
bor·de·laise sauce \ˌbòr-dᵊl-'āz-\ *noun, often B capitalized* [French *bordelaise*, feminine of *bordelais* of Bordeaux] (1902)
: a sauce consisting of stock thickened with roux and flavored typically with red wine and shallots
bor·del·lo \bòr-'de-(ˌ)lō\ *noun, plural* **-los** [Italian, from Old French *bordel*, from *borde* hut, of Germanic origin; akin to Old English *bord* board] (1593)
: a building in which prostitutes are available
¹bor·der \'bòr-dər\ *noun* [Middle English *bordure*, from Middle French, from Old French, from *border* to border, from *bort* border, of Germanic origin; akin to Old English *bord*] (14th century)
1 : an outer part or edge
2 : an ornamental design at the edge of a fabric or rug
3 : a narrow bed of planted ground along the edge of a garden or walk ⟨a *border* of tulips⟩
4 : BOUNDARY ⟨crossed the *border* into Italy⟩
5 : a plain or decorative margin around printed matter
— **bor·dered** \-dərd\ *adjective*
²border *verb* **bor·dered; bor·der·ing** \'bòr-d(ə-)riŋ\ (14th century)
transitive verb
1 : to put a border on
2 : to touch at the edge or boundary **:** BOUND ⟨*borders* the city on the south⟩
intransitive verb
1 : to lie on the border ⟨the U.S. *borders* on Canada⟩
2 : to approach the nature of a specified thing **:** VERGE ⟨*borders* on the ridiculous⟩
— **bor·der·er** \-dər-ər\ *noun*

bootjack

Border collie *noun* (1941)
: any of a breed of medium-sized sheepdogs of British origin noted for their herding abilities

bor·de·reau \ˌbȯr-də-'rō\ *noun, plural* **-reaux** \-'rō(z)\ [French, from Middle French *bordrel,* probably from *bord* border, from Old French *bort*] (circa 1858)
: a detailed note or memorandum of account; *especially* : one containing an enumeration of documents

bor·der·land \'bȯr-dər-ˌland\ *noun* (1813)
1 a : territory at or near a border **b** : FRINGE 3a ⟨lives on the *borderland* of society⟩
2 : a vague intermediate state or region ⟨the *borderland* between fantasy and reality⟩

¹**bor·der·line** \-ˌlīn\ *adjective* (1907)
1 : being in an intermediate position or state : not fully classifiable as one thing or its opposite; *especially* : not quite up to what is usual, standard, or expected ⟨*borderline* intelligence⟩
2 : situated at or near a border
— **borderline** *noun*

²**borderline** *adverb* (1925)
: ALMOST, NEARLY ⟨*borderline* tacky⟩ ⟨*borderline* suicidal⟩

Border terrier *noun* (1894)
: any of a breed of small terriers of British origin having a harsh dense coat and close undercoat

bor·dure \'bȯr-jər\ *noun* [Middle English] (14th century)
: a border on a heraldic shield

¹**bore** \'bȯr, 'bȯr\ *verb* **bored; bor·ing** [Middle English, from Old English *borian;* akin to Old High German *borōn* to bore, Latin *forare* to bore, *ferire* to strike] (before 12th century)
transitive verb
1 : to pierce with a turning or twisting movement of a tool
2 : to make (as a cylindrical hole) by boring or digging away material ⟨*bored* a tunnel⟩
intransitive verb
1 a : to make a hole by or as if by boring **b** : to sink a mine shaft or well
2 : to make one's way steadily especially against resistance ⟨we *bored* through the jostling crowd⟩

²**bore** *noun* (14th century)
1 a : a usually cylindrical hole made by or as if by boring **b** *chiefly Australian & New Zealand* : a borehole drilled especially to make an artesian well
2 a : the long usually cylindrical hollow part of something (as a tube or gun barrel) **b** : the inner surface of a hollow cylindrical object
3 : the size of a bore: as **a** : the interior diameter of a gun barrel; *specifically, chiefly British* : GAUGE 1a(2) **b** : the diameter of an engine cylinder

³**bore** *past of* BEAR

⁴**bore** *noun* [(assumed) Middle English *bore* wave, from Old Norse *bāra*] (1601)
: a tidal flood with a high abrupt front

⁵**bore** *noun* [origin unknown] (1766)
: one that causes boredom: as **a** : a tiresome person **b** : something that is devoid of interest

⁶**bore** *transitive verb* **bored; bor·ing** (1768)
: to cause to feel boredom

bo·re·al \'bȯr-ē-əl, 'bȯr-\ *adjective* [Middle English *boriall,* from Late Latin *borealis,* from Latin *boreas* north wind, north, from Greek, from *Boreas*] (15th century)
1 : of, relating to, or located in northern regions ⟨*boreal* waters⟩
2 : of, relating to, or comprising the northern biotic area characterized especially by dominance of coniferous forests

Bo·re·as \-ē-əs\ *noun* [Latin, from Greek]
1 : the Greek god of the north wind
2 : the north wind personified

bore·dom \'bȯr-dəm, 'bȯr-\ *noun* (1852)
: the state of being weary and restless through lack of interest

bo·reen \bȯr-'ēn, bȯr-\ *noun* [Irish *bóthrín,* diminutive of *bóthar* road] (1836)
Irish : a narrow country lane

bore·hole \'bȯr-ˌhōl, 'bȯr-\ *noun* (1708)
: a hole bored or drilled in the earth: as **a** : an exploratory well **b** *chiefly British* : a small-diameter well drilled especially to obtain water

bor·er \'bȯr-ər, 'bȯr-\ *noun* (14th century)
1 : a tool used for boring
2 a : SHIPWORM **b** : an insect that bores in the woody parts of plants

bore·scope \'bȯr-ˌskōp, 'bȯr-\ *noun* (1941)
: an optical device (as a prism or optical fiber) used to inspect an inaccessible space (as an engine cylinder)

boric acid *noun* [*boron*] (1869)
: a white crystalline acid H_3BO_3 obtained from its salts and used especially as a weak antiseptic and fire-retardant

bo·ride \'bȯr-ˌīd, 'bȯr-\ *noun* (1863)
: a binary compound of boron with a more electropositive element or radical

bor·ing \'bȯr-iŋ, 'bȯr-\ *adjective* (1840)
: causing boredom : TIRESOME
— **bor·ing·ly** \-iŋ-lē\ *adverb*
— **bor·ing·ness** *noun*

born \'bȯrn\ *adjective* [Middle English, from Old English *boren,* past participle of *beran* to carry — more at BEAR] (before 12th century)
1 a : brought forth by or as if by birth **b** : NATIVE — usually used in combination ⟨American-*born*⟩ **c** : deriving or resulting from — usually used in combination ⟨poverty-*born* crime⟩
2 a : having from birth specified qualities ⟨a *born* leader⟩ **b** : being in specified circumstances from birth ⟨nobly *born*⟩ ⟨*born* to wealth⟩
3 : destined from or as if from birth ⟨*born* to succeed⟩

born–again *adjective* [from the verse "Except a man be *born again,* he cannot see the Kingdom of God" (John 3:3 Authorized Version)] (1961)
1 : of, relating to, or being a usually Christian person who has made a renewed or confirmed commitment of faith especially after an intense religious experience
2 : having returned to or newly adopted an activity, a conviction, or a persona especially with a proselytizing zeal ⟨a *born-again* conservative⟩

¹**borne** \'bȯrn, 'bȯrn\ *past participle of* BEAR

²**borne** *adjective* [*borne*] (circa 1559)
: transported or transmitted by — used in combination ⟨soil*borne*⟩ ⟨air*borne*⟩

bor·ne·ol \'bȯr-nē-ˌȯl, -ˌōl\ *noun* [International Scientific Vocabulary, from *Borneo,* island of Indonesia] (1876)
: a crystalline cyclic alcohol $C_{10}H_{17}OH$ that occurs in two enantiomeric forms, is found in essential oils, and is used especially in perfumery

born·ite \'bȯr-ˌnīt\ *noun* [German *Bornit,* from Ignaz von *Born* (died 1791) Austrian mineralogist] (circa 1847)
: a brittle metallic-looking mineral that consists of a sulfide of copper and iron and is a valuable copper ore

boro- *combining form*
: boron ⟨*boro*silicate⟩

bo·ro·hy·dride \ˌbȯr-ō-'hī-ˌdrīd, ˌbȯr-\ *noun* (1940)
: the anion BH_4^- of boron and hydrogen that is used especially as a reducing agent and as a source of hydrogen atoms; *also* : any of various compounds (as of metals) containing the borohydride anion

bo·ron \'bȯr-ˌän, 'bȯr-\ *noun* [*borax* + *-on* (as in *carbon*)] (1812)
: a trivalent metalloid element found in nature only in combination and used in metallurgy and in composite structural materials — see ELEMENT table
— **bo·ron·ic** \bȯr-'ä-nik, bōr-\ *adjective*

boron carbide *noun* (circa 1909)
: a refractory shiny black crystalline compound B_4C that is one of the hardest known materials and is used especially in abrasives and as a structural reinforcing material

bo·ro·sil·i·cate \ˌbȯr-ō-'si-lə-ˌkāt, ˌbȯr-, -'si-li-kət\ *noun* [International Scientific Vocabulary] (1817)
1 : a silicate containing boron in the anion and occurring naturally
2 : BOROSILICATE GLASS

borosilicate glass *noun* (1933)
: a silicate glass that is composed of at least five percent oxide of boron and is used especially in heat-resistant glassware

bor·ough \'bər-(ˌ)ō, 'bə-(ˌ)rō\ *noun* [Middle English *burgh,* from Old English *burg* fortified town; akin to Old High German *burg* fortified place, and probably to Old English *beorg* hill — more at BARROW] (before 12th century)
1 a : a medieval fortified group of houses forming a town with special duties and privileges **b** : a town or urban constituency in Great Britain that sends a member to Parliament **c** : an urban area in Great Britain incorporated for purposes of self-government
2 a : a municipal corporation proper in some states (as New Jersey and Minnesota) corresponding to the incorporated town or village of the other states **b** : one of the five constituent political divisions of New York City
3 : a civil division of the state of Alaska corresponding to a county in most other states

borough English *noun* (14th century)
: a custom formerly existing in parts of England by which the lands of an intestate descended to the youngest son

borough hall *noun* (1939)
: the chief administrative building of a borough

bor·row \'bär-(ˌ)ō, 'bȯr-\ *verb* [Middle English *borwen,* from Old English *borgian;* akin to Old English *beorgan* to preserve — more at BURY] (before 12th century)
transitive verb
1 a : to receive with the implied or expressed intention of returning the same or an equivalent ⟨*borrow* a book⟩ ⟨*borrowed* a dollar⟩ **b** : to borrow (money) with the intention of returning the same plus interest
2 a : to appropriate for one's own use ⟨*borrow* a metaphor⟩ **b** : DERIVE, ADOPT
3 : to take (one) from a digit of the minuend in arithmetical subtraction in order to add as 10 to the digit holding the next lower place
4 : to adopt into one language from another
5 *dialect* : LEND
intransitive verb
: to borrow something
— **bor·row·er** \-ə-wər\ *noun*
— **borrow trouble** : to do something unnecessarily that may result in adverse reaction or repercussions

bor·rowed time *noun* (1898)
: an uncertain and usually uncontrolled postponement of something inevitable — used with *living on*

bor·row·ing \'bär-ə-wiŋ, 'bȯr-\ *noun* (circa 1630)
: something borrowed; *especially* : a word or phrase adopted from one language into another

borrow pit *noun* (1893)
: an excavated area where material has been dug for use as fill at another location

Bors \'bȯrz\ *noun* [Middle English, from Middle French *Bohort*]
: a knight of the Round Table and nephew of Lancelot

\ə\ abut \ᵊ\ kitten \ər\ further \a\ ash \ā\ ace
\ä\ mop, mar \au̇\ out \ch\ chin \e\ bet \ē\ easy
\g\ go \i\ hit \ī\ ice \j\ job \ŋ\ sing \ō\ go
\ȯ\ law \ȯi\ boy \th\ thin \t͟h\ the \ü\ loot \u̇\ foot
\y\ yet \zh\ vision *see also* Guide to Pronunciation

borscht *or* **borsch** \'bȯrsh(t)\ *noun* [Yiddish *borsht* & Ukrainian & Russian *borshch*] (1829)
: a soup made primarily of beets and served hot or cold often with sour cream

borscht belt *also* **borsch belt** *noun* (1938)
: BORSCHT CIRCUIT

borscht circuit *or* **borsch circuit** *noun*, often B&C capitalized [from the popularity of borscht on menus of the resorts] (1938)
: the theaters and nightclubs associated with the Jewish summer resorts in the Catskills

Bor·stal \'bȯr-st*ə*l\ *noun* [Borstal, English village where the first such institution was set up] (1907)
British : REFORMATORY

bort \'bȯrt\ *noun* [probably from Dutch *boort*] (1622)
: imperfectly crystallized diamond or diamond fragments used as an abrasive

bor·zoi \'bȯr-ˌzȯi\ *noun* [Russian *borzoĭ*, from *borzoĭ* swift] (1887)
: any of a breed of large long-haired dogs of greyhound type developed in Russia especially for pursuing wolves — called also *Russian wolfhound*

bos·cage *also* **bosk·age** \'bäs-kij\ *noun* [Middle English *boskage*, from Middle French *boscage*, from Old French, from *bois*, *bosc* forest, of Germanic origin; akin to Old High German *busk* forest, bush] (14th century)
: a growth of trees or shrubs : THICKET

bosh \'bäsh\ *noun* [Turkish *boş* empty] (1834)
: foolish talk or activity : NONSENSE — often used interjectionally

bosk *or* **bosque** \'bäsk\ *noun* [probably back-formation from *bosky*] (1814)
: a small wooded area

bosky \'bäs-kē\ *adjective* [English dialect *bosk* bush, from Middle English *bush, bosk*] (1593)
1 : having abundant trees or shrubs
2 : of or relating to a woods

bo·s'n *or* **bo'·s'n** *or* **bo·sun** *or* **bo'·sun** \'bō-s*ə*n\ *variant of* BOATSWAIN

¹**bos·om** \'bu̇-zəm *also* 'bü-\ *noun* [Middle English, from Old English *bōsm;* akin to Old High German *buosam* bosom] (before 12th century)
1 a : the human chest and especially the front part of the chest ⟨hugged the child to his *bosom*⟩ **b** : a woman's breasts regarded especially as a single feature ⟨a woman with an ample *bosom*⟩; *also* : BREAST
2 a : the chest conceived of as the seat of the emotions and intimate feelings ⟨a story you will take to your *bosom*⟩ **b** : the security and intimacy of or like that of being hugged to someone's bosom ⟨lived in the *bosom* of her family⟩
3 : the part of a garment that covers the chest or the breasts

²**bosom** *adjective* (1590)
: CLOSE, INTIMATE ⟨*bosom* friends⟩

³**bosom** *transitive verb* (1605)
1 : EMBRACE
2 : to enclose or carry in the bosom

bos·omed \-zəmd\ *adjective* (1603)
: having a bosom of a specified kind — used in combination ⟨full-*bosomed*⟩

bos·omy \'bu̇-zə-mē *also* 'bü-\ *adjective* (1860)
1 : swelling upward or outward ⟨*bosomy* hills⟩
2 : having prominent breasts

bo·son \'bō-ˌsän, -ˌzän\ *noun* [Satyendranath Bose (died 1974) Indian physicist + English ²-*on*] (1947)
: a particle (as a photon or meson) whose spin is zero or an integral number — compare FERMION

bos·quet \'bäs-kət\ *noun* [French, from Italian *boschetto*, diminutive of *bosco* forest, of Germanic origin; akin to Old High German *busk* forest, bush] (circa 1737)
: THICKET

¹**boss** \'bäs, 'bȯs\ *noun* [Middle English *boce*, from Middle French, from (assumed) Vulgar Latin *bottia*] (14th century)
1 a : a protuberant part or body ⟨a *boss* of granite⟩ ⟨a *boss* on an animal's horn⟩
b : a raised ornamentation : STUD **c** : an ornamental projecting block used in architecture
2 : a soft pad used in ceramics and glassmaking
3 : the hub of a propeller

boss 1c

²**boss** *transitive verb* (15th century)
1 : to ornament with bosses : EMBOSS
2 : to treat (as the surface of porcelain) with a boss

³**boss** *noun* [Dutch *baas* master] (1679)
1 : a person who exercises control or authority; *specifically* : one who directs or supervises workers
2 : a politician who controls votes in a party organization or dictates appointments or legislative measures ◇
— **boss·dom** \-dəm\ *noun*
— **boss·ism** \'bä-ˌsi-zəm, 'bȯ-\ *noun*

⁴**boss** \'bȯs\ *adjective* (1836)
slang : EXCELLENT, FIRST-RATE

⁵**boss** \'bȯs\ *transitive verb* (1856)
1 : to act as boss of
2 : to give usually arbitrary orders to — usually used with *around*

⁶**boss** \'bȯs, 'bäs\ *noun* [English dialect, young cow] (1790)
: COW, CALF

bos·sa no·va \ˌbä-sə-'nō-və\ *noun* [Portuguese, literally, new trend] (1962)
1 : popular music of Brazilian origin that is rhythmically related to the samba but with complex harmonies and improvised jazzlike passages
2 : a dance performed to bossa nova music

boss man *noun* (1934)
: ³BOSS

¹**bossy** \'bä-sē, 'bȯ-\ *adjective* (1543)
1 : marked by a swelling or roundness
2 : marked by bosses : STUDDED

²**bossy** \'bȯ-sē, 'bä-\ *noun, plural* **boss·ies** (1843)
: COW, CALF

³**bossy** \'bȯ-sē, 'bä-\ *adjective* **boss·i·er; -est** (1882)
: inclined to domineer : DICTATORIAL
— **boss·i·ness** *noun*

Bos·ton \'bȯs-tən\ *noun* [French, from *Boston*, Mass.] (1800)
1 : a variation of whist played with two decks of cards
2 [*Boston*, Mass.] : a dance somewhat like a waltz

Boston cream pie *noun* (circa 1933)
: a round cake that is split and filled with a custard or cream filling and usually frosted with chocolate

Boston fern *noun* (circa 1900)
: a luxuriant fern (*Nephrolepis exaltata bostoniensis*) often with drooping much-divided fronds

Boston ivy *noun* (circa 1900)
: a woody Asian vine (*Parthenocissus tricuspidata*) of the grape family typically having 3-lobed leaves

Boston rocker *noun* (1856)
: a wooden rocking chair with a high spindle back, a decorative top panel, and a seat and arms that curve down at the front

Boston terrier *noun* (1894)
: any of a breed of small smooth-coated terriers originating as a cross of the bulldog and bullterrier and being

Boston rocker

brindled or black with white markings — called also *Boston bull*

Bos·well \'bäz-ˌwel, -wəl\ *noun* [James Boswell] (1858)
: a person who records in detail the life of a usually famous contemporary
— **Bos·well·ian** \bäz-'we-lē-ən\ *adjective*
— **Bos·well·ize** \'bäz-wə-ˌlīz, -ˌwe-\ *verb*

bot *also* **bott** \'bät\ *noun* [Middle English; akin to Dutch lever*bot* liver fluke] (15th century)
: the larva of a botfly; *especially* : one infesting the horse

bo·ta \'bō-tə\ *noun* [Spanish, from Late Latin *buttis* cask] (1832)
: a leather bottle (as for wine)

bo·tan·i·ca \bə-'ta-ni-kə\ *noun* [American Spanish *botánica*, from feminine of Spanish *botánico* botanical] (1969)
: a shop that deals in herbs and charms used especially by adherents of Santeria

¹**bo·tan·i·cal** \bə-'ta-ni-kəl\ *adjective* [French *botanique*, from Greek *botanikos* of herbs, from *botanē* pasture, herb, from *boskein* to feed, graze; probably akin to Lithuanian *guotas* flock] (1658)
1 : of or relating to plants or botany
2 : derived from plants
3 : SPECIES ⟨*botanical* tulips⟩
— **bo·tan·i·cal·ly** \-k(ə-)lē\ *adverb*

²**botanical** *noun* (circa 1926)
: a plant part or extract used especially in skin and hair care products

botanical garden *noun* (1785)
: a garden often with greenhouses for the culture, study, and exhibition of special plants — called also *bo·tan·ic garden* \bə-'ta-nik-\

bot·an·ise *British variant of* BOTANIZE

bot·a·nist \'bä-t*ə*n-ist, 'bät-nist\ *noun* (circa 1682)
: a specialist in botany or in a branch of botany

bot·a·nize \-t*ə*n-ˌīz\ *verb* **-nized; -niz·ing** (1767)
intransitive verb
: to collect plants for botanical investigation; *also* : to study plants especially on a field trip
transitive verb
: to explore for botanical purposes

bot·a·ny \'bä-t*ə*n-ē, 'bät-nē\ *noun, plural* **-nies** [*botanic* botanical + ²-*y*] (1696)
1 : a branch of biology dealing with plant life
2 a : plant life **b** : the properties and life phenomena exhibited by a plant, plant type, or plant group
3 : a botanical treatise or study; *especially* : a particular system of botany

¹**botch** \'bäch\ *noun* [Middle English *boche*, from Old North French, from (assumed) Vulgar Latin *bottia* boss] (14th century)
: an inflammatory sore

²botch *transitive verb* [Middle English *bocchen*] (1530)
1 : to foul up hopelessly — often used with *up*
2 : to put together in a makeshift way
— **botch·er** *noun*
³botch *noun* (1605)
1 : something that is botched **:** MESS
2 : PATCHWORK, HODGEPODGE
— **botchy** \'bä-chē\ *adjective*
bot·fly \'bät-ˌflī\ *noun*
: any of various stout dipteran flies (family Oestridae) with larvae parasitic in cavities or tissues of various mammals including humans
¹both \'bōth\ *pronoun, plural in construction* [Middle English *bothe*, from Old Norse *bāthir*; akin to Old High German *beide* both] (12th century)
: the one as well as the other ⟨*both* of us⟩ ⟨we are *both* well⟩ ⟨$1000 fine or 30 days in jail, or *both*⟩
²both *conjunction* (12th century)
— used as a function word to indicate and stress the inclusion of each of two or more things specified by coordinated words, phrases, or clauses ⟨prized *both* for its beauty and for its utility⟩ ⟨he prayeth well, who loveth well *both* man and bird and beast —S. T. Coleridge⟩
³both *adjective* (13th century)
: being the two **:** affecting or involving the one and the other ⟨*both* feet⟩ ⟨*both* his eyes⟩ ⟨*both* these armies⟩
¹both·er \'bä-thər\ *verb* **both·ered; both·er·ing** \'bäth-riŋ, 'bä-thə-\ [origin unknown] (circa 1745)
transitive verb
1 : to annoy especially by petty provocation **:** IRK
2 : to intrude upon **:** PESTER
3 : to cause to be anxious or concerned — often used interjectionally
intransitive verb
1 : to become concerned
2 : to take pains **:** take the trouble
synonym see ANNOY
²bother *noun* (1834)
1 a : a state of petty discomfort, annoyance, or worry **b :** something that causes petty annoyance or worry
2 : FUSS
both·er·ation \ˌbä-thə-'rā-shən\ *noun* (1797)
1 : the act of bothering **:** the state of being bothered
2 : something that bothers — often used interjectionally
both·er·some \'bä-thər-səm\ *adjective* (1834)
: causing bother **:** VEXING
bo·thy \'bä-thē, 'bō-\ *noun* [Scots, probably from obsolete Scots *both* booth] (1771)
chiefly Scottish **:** HUT
bot·o·née *or* **bot·on·née** \ˌbä-tᵊn-'ā\ *adjective* [Middle French *botonné*] (15th century)
of a heraldic cross **:** having a cluster of three balls or knobs at the end of each arm — see CROSS illustration
bo tree \'bō-\ *noun* [Sinhalese *bō*, from Sanskrit *bodhi* enlightenment; from Buddha receiving enlightenment under this tree — more at BID] (1862)
: PIPAL
bot·ry·oi·dal \ˌbä-trē-'òi-dᵊl\ *adjective* [Greek *botryoeidēs*, from *botrys* bunch of grapes] (1816)
: having the form of a bunch of grapes ⟨*botryoidal* garnets⟩
bo·try·tis \bō-'trī-təs\ *noun* [New Latin, from Greek *botrys*] (1900)
: any of a genus (*Botrytis*) of imperfect fungi having botryoidal conidia and including several serious plant pathogens
¹bot·tle \'bä-tᵊl\ *noun, often attributive* [Middle English *botel*, from Middle French *bouteille*, from Medieval Latin *butticula*, di-

minutive of Late Latin *buttis* cask] (14th century)
1 a : a rigid or semirigid container typically of glass or plastic having a comparatively narrow neck or mouth and usually no handle **b :** a usually bottle-shaped container made of skin for storing a liquid
2 : the quantity held by a bottle
3 a : intoxicating drink **:** the practice of drinking **b :** liquid food (as milk) used in place of mother's milk
— **bot·tle·ful** \-ˌfùl\ *noun*
²bottle *transitive verb* **bot·tled; bot·tling** \'bä-tᵊl-iŋ, 'bät-liŋ\ (1600)
1 : to confine as if in a bottle **:** RESTRAIN — usually used with *up* ⟨*bottling* up their anger⟩
2 : to put into a bottle
— **bot·tler** \'bä-tᵊl-ər, 'bät-lər\ *noun*
bot·tle-brush \'bä-tᵊl-ˌbrəsh\ *noun* [from the shape of the flowers] (circa 1841)
: any of a genus (*Callistemon*) of Australian trees and shrubs of the myrtle family widely cultivated in warm regions especially for their spikes of brightly colored flowers
bottle club *noun* (1943)
: a club serving patrons previously purchased or reserved alcoholic drinks after normal legal closing hours
bottled gas *noun* (1930)
: gas under pressure in portable cylinders
bot·tle-feed \'bä-tᵊl-ˌfēd\ *transitive verb* **-fed; -feed·ing** (circa 1865)
: to feed (as an infant) with a bottle
bottle gourd *noun* (circa 1828)
: a common cultivated gourd (*Lagenaria siceraria*) with a variably shaped fruit that is sometimes used as a container
bottle green *noun* (1804)
: a dark green
¹bot·tle·neck \'bä-tᵊl-ˌnek\ *adjective* (1896)
: NARROW ⟨*bottleneck* harbors⟩
²bottleneck *noun* (1907)
1 a : a narrow route **b :** a point of traffic congestion
2 a : a condition or situation that retards or halts free movement and progress **b :** IMPASSE
3 : a style of guitar playing in which glissando effects are produced by sliding an object (as a knife blade or the neck of a bottle) along the strings
³bottleneck *transitive verb* (1933)
: to slow or halt by causing a bottleneck
bot·tle-nosed dolphin \'bä-tᵊl-ˌnōz-\ *noun* (circa 1909)
: a relatively small stout-bodied chiefly gray toothed whale (*Tursiops truncatus*) with a prominent beak and falcate dorsal fin
bottlenose dolphin *noun* (1940)
: BOTTLE-NOSED DOLPHIN
bot·tling \'bä-tᵊl-iŋ, 'bät-liŋ\ *noun* (1954)
: a beverage and especially a wine that is bottled at a particular time
¹bot·tom \'bä-təm\ *noun* [Middle English *botme*, from Old English *botm*; akin to Old High German *bodam* bottom, Latin *fundus*, Greek *pythmēn*] (before 12th century)
1 a : the underside of something **b :** a surface (as the seat of a chair) designed to support something resting on it **c :** the posterior end of the trunk **:** BUTTOCKS, RUMP
2 : the surface on which a body of water lies
3 a : the part of a ship's hull lying below the water **b :** BOAT, SHIP
4 a : the lowest part or place **b :** the remotest or inmost point **c :** the lowest or last place in point of precedence ⟨started work at the *bottom*⟩ **d :** the pants of pajamas — usually used in plural **e :** the last half of an inning of baseball **f :** the bass or baritone instruments of a band
5 : BOTTOMLAND — usually used in plural
6 : BASIS, SOURCE
7 : capacity (as of a horse) to endure strain

8 : a foundation color applied to textile fibers before dyeing
— **bot·tomed** \-təmd\ *adjective*
— **at bottom :** REALLY, BASICALLY
²bottom (1544)
transitive verb
1 : to furnish with a bottom
2 : to provide a foundation for
3 : to bring to the bottom
4 : to get to the bottom of **:** FATHOM
intransitive verb
1 : to become based
2 : to reach the bottom
3 : to reach a low point before rebounding — usually used with *out*
— **bot·tom·er** *noun*
³bottom *adjective* (1561)
1 : of, relating to, or situated at the bottom ⟨*bottom* rock⟩
2 : frequenting the bottom ⟨*bottom* fish⟩
3 : having a quantum characteristic that accounts for the existence and lifetime of upsilon particles and that has a value of zero for most known particles ⟨*bottom* quark⟩
bot·tom·land \'bä-təm-ˌland\ *noun* (1728)
: low-lying land along a watercourse
bot·tom·less \-ləs\ *adjective* (14th century)
1 : having no bottom ⟨a *bottomless* chair⟩
2 a : extremely deep **b :** impossible to comprehend **:** UNFATHOMABLE ⟨a *bottomless* mystery⟩ **c :** BOUNDLESS, UNLIMITED
3 a [from the absence of lower as well as upper garments] **:** NUDE ⟨*bottomless* dancers⟩ **b :** featuring nude entertainers
— **bot·tom·less·ly** *adverb*
— **bot·tom·less·ness** *noun*
bottom-line \'bä-təm-ˌlīn\ *adjective* (1972)
1 : concerned only with cost or profits
2 : PRAGMATIC, REALISTIC
bottom line *noun* (1967)
1 a : the essential or salient point **:** CRUX **b :** the primary or most important consideration
2 a : the line at the bottom of a financial report that shows the net profit or loss **b :** financial considerations (as cost or profit or loss) **c :** the final result **:** OUTCOME, UPSHOT
bot·tom·most \'bä-tə(m)-ˌmōst\ *adjective* (1861)
1 a : situated at the very bottom **:** LOWEST, DEEPEST **b :** LAST ⟨the *bottommost* part of the day —Alfred Kazin⟩
2 : most basic ⟨*bottommost* problems facing the world⟩
bottom round *noun* (1923)
: meat (as steak) from the outer part of a round of beef
bot·u·lin \'bä-chə-lən\ *noun* [probably from New Latin *botulinum*] (circa 1900)
: a neurotoxin formed by botulinum and causing botulism
bot·u·li·num \ˌbä-chə-'lī-nəm\ *also* **bot·u·li·nus** \-nəs\ *noun* [New Latin, from Latin *botulus* sausage] (1902)
: a spore-forming bacterium (*Clostridium botulinum*) that secretes botulin
— **bot·u·li·nal** \-'lī-nᵊl\ *adjective*
bot·u·lism \'bä-chə-ˌli-zəm\ *noun* (1887)
: an acute paralytic disease caused by botulin especially in food
bou·bou \'bü-ˌbü\ *noun* [French, from Malinke *bubu*] (1961)
: a long flowing garment worn in parts of Africa
bou·chée \bü-'shā\ *noun* [French, literally, mouthful, from Old French *buchiee*, from (assumed) Vulgar Latin *buccata*, from Latin *bucca* cheek, mouth] (1846)
: a small patty shell usually containing a creamed filling

\ə\ abut \ᵊ\ kitten \ər\ further \a\ ash \ā\ ace
\ä\ mop, mar \aù\ out \ch\ chin \e\ bet \ē\ easy
\g\ go \i\ hit \ī\ ice \j\ job \ŋ\ sing \ō\ go
\ò\ law \òi\ boy \th\ thin \th\ the \ü\ loot \ù\ foot
\y\ yet \zh\ vision *see also* Guide to Pronunciation

bou·clé *or* **bou·cle** \bü-'klā\ *noun* [French *bouclé* curly, from past participle of *boucler* to curl, from *bocle* buckle, curl] (1895)
1 : an uneven yarn of three plies one of which forms loops at intervals
2 : a fabric of bouclé yarn
bou·doir \'bü-ˌdwär, 'bù-, bü-', ˌbù-'\ *noun* [French, from *bouder* to pout] (1781)
: a woman's dressing room, bedroom, or private sitting room
bouf·fant \bü-'fänt, 'bü-ˌ\ *adjective* [French, from Middle French, from present participle of *bouffer* to puff] (1880)
: puffed out ⟨*bouffant* hairdos⟩ ⟨a *bouffant* veil⟩
bou·gain·vil·lea *also* **bou·gain·vil·laea** \ˌbü-gən-'vil-yə, ˌbō-, ˌbù-, -'vē-ə\ *noun* [New Latin, from Louis Antoine de *Bougainville*] (1881)
: any of a genus (*Bougainvillaea*) of the four-o'clock family of ornamental tropical American woody vines with brilliant purple or red floral bracts
bough \'baù\ *noun* [Middle English, shoulder, bough, from Old English *bōg*; akin to Old High German *buog* shoulder, Greek *pēchys* forearm] (before 12th century)
: a branch of a tree; *especially* **:** a main branch
— **boughed** \'baùd\ *adjective*
¹bought \'bȯt\ *past and past participle of* BUY
²bought *adjective* [past participle of *buy*] (1599)
: STORE 2 ⟨*bought* clothes⟩
bought·en \'bȯ-t°n\ *adjective* [*bought* + *-en* (as in *forgotten*)] (1793)
chiefly dialect **:** BOUGHT ⟨the only *boughten* carpet in the region —H. W. Thompson⟩
bou·gie \'bü-ˌzhē, -ˌjē\ *noun* [French, from *Bougie*, seaport in Algeria] (1755)
1 : a wax candle
2 a : a tapering cylindrical instrument for introduction into a tubular passage of the body **b :** SUPPOSITORY
bouil·la·baisse \ˌbü-yə-'bās, -'bāz, 'bü-yə-ˌ, -ˌbäz\ *noun* [French] (1855)
1 : a highly seasoned fish stew made with at least two kinds of fish
2 : POTPOURRI
bouil·lon \'bü(l)-ˌyän, 'bù(l)-; 'bùl-yən; 'bü-ˌyō°\ *noun* [French, from Old French *boillon*, from *boillir* to boil] (circa 1656)
: a clear seasoned soup made usually from lean beef; *broadly* **:** BROTH
bouillon cube *noun* (circa 1922)
: a cube of evaporated meat extract
boul·der \'bōl-dər\ *noun* [short for *boulder stone*, from Middle English *bulder ston*, part translation of a word of Scandinavian origin; akin to Swedish dialect *bullersten* large stone in a stream, from *buller* noise + *sten* stone] (1617)
: a detached and rounded or much-worn mass of rock
— **boul·dered** \-dərd\ *adjective*
— **boul·dery** \-d(ə-)rē\ *adjective*
¹bou·le \'bü-(ˌ)lē, bü-'lā\ *noun* [Greek *boulē*, literally, will, from *boulesthai* to wish] (1846)
: a legislative council of ancient Greece consisting first of an aristocratic advisory body and later of a representative senate
²boule \'bül\ *noun* [French, ball — more at BOWL] (1918)
: a pear-shaped synthetically formed mass (as of sapphire) with the atomic structure of a single crystal
bou·le·vard \'bù-lə-ˌvärd, 'bü- *also* 'bə-\ *noun* [French, modification of Middle Dutch *bolwerc* bulwark] (1769)
: a broad often landscaped thoroughfare ◇
bou·le·var·dier \ˌbù-lə-ˌvär-'dyā, ˌbü-, -'dir\ *noun* [French, from *boulevard*] (1879)
: a frequenter of the Parisian boulevards; *broadly* **:** MAN-ABOUT-TOWN
bou·le·ver·se·ment \bül-ver-sə-mä°\ *noun* [French] (1782)
1 : REVERSAL

2 : a violent disturbance **:** DISORDER
boulle \'bül, 'byü(ə)l\ *noun* [André Charles *Boulle* (died 1732) French cabinetmaker] (1823)
: inlaid decoration of tortoiseshell, yellow metal, and white metal in cabinetwork
¹bounce \'baùn(t)s\ *verb* **bounced; bounc·ing** [Middle English *bounsen*] (13th century)
transitive verb
1 *obsolete* **:** BEAT, BUMP
2 : to cause to rebound ⟨*bounce* a ball⟩
3 a : DISMISS, FIRE **b :** to expel precipitately from a place
4 : to issue (a check) drawn on an account with insufficient funds
5 : to present (as an idea) to another person to elicit comments or to gain approval — usually used with *off*
intransitive verb
1 : to rebound after striking a surface (as the ground)
2 : to recover from a blow or a defeat quickly — usually used with *back*
3 : to be returned by a bank because of insufficient funds in a checking account ⟨his checks *bounce*⟩
4 a : to leap suddenly **:** BOUND **b :** to walk with springing steps
5 : to hit a baseball so that it hits the ground before it reaches an infielder
²bounce *noun* (1523)
1 a : a sudden leap or bound **b :** REBOUND
2 : BLUSTER
3 : VERVE, LIVELINESS
bounc·er \'baùn(t)-sər\ *noun* (1865)
: one that bounces; *especially* **:** a person employed to restrain or eject disorderly persons
bounc·ing \-siŋ\ *adjective* (circa 1563)
1 : LIVELY, ANIMATED
2 : enjoying good health **:** ROBUST
— **bounc·ing·ly** \-siŋ-lē\ *adverb*
bouncing bet \-'bet\ *noun, often 2nd B capitalized* [from *Bet*, nickname for *Elizabeth*] (circa 1818)
: a European perennial herb (*Saponaria officinalis*) of the pink family that is widely naturalized in the U.S. and has pink or white flowers and leaves which yield a detergent when bruised
bouncy \'baùn(t)-sē\ *adjective* **bounc·i·er; -est** (1921)
1 : BUOYANT, EXUBERANT
2 : RESILIENT
3 : marked by or producing bounces
— **bounc·i·ly** \-sə-lē\ *adverb*
¹bound \'baùnd\ *adjective* [Middle English *boun*, from Old Norse *būinn*, past participle of *būa* to dwell, prepare; akin to Old High German *būan* to dwell — more at BOWER] (13th century)
1 *archaic* **:** READY
2 : intending to go **:** GOING ⟨*bound* for home⟩ ⟨college-*bound*⟩
²bound *noun* [Middle English, from Old French *bodne*, from Medieval Latin *bodina*] (13th century)
1 a : a limiting line **:** BOUNDARY — usually used in plural **b :** something that limits or restrains ⟨beyond the *bounds* of decency⟩
2 *usually plural* **a :** BORDERLAND **b :** the land within certain bounds
3 : a number greater than or equal to every number in a set (as the range of a function); *also* **:** a number less than or equal to every number in a set
³bound *past and past participle of* BIND
⁴bound *transitive verb* (14th century)
1 : to set limits or bounds to **:** CONFINE
2 : to form the boundary of **:** ENCLOSE
3 : to name the boundaries of
⁵bound *adjective* [Middle English *bounden*, from past participle of *binden* to bind] (14th century)
1 : placed under legal or moral restraint or obligation **:** OBLIGED ⟨duty-*bound*⟩

2 a : fastened by or as if by a band **:** CONFINED ⟨desk-*bound*⟩ **b :** very likely **:** SURE ⟨*bound* to rain soon⟩
3 : made costive **:** CONSTIPATED
4 *of a book* **:** secured to the covers by cords, tapes, or glue
5 : DETERMINED, RESOLVED
6 : held in chemical or physical combination
7 : always occurring in combination with another linguistic form ⟨*un-* in *unknown* and *-er* in *speaker* are *bound* forms⟩ — compare FREE 11d
⁶bound *noun* [Middle French *bond*, from *bondir* to leap, from (assumed) Vulgar Latin *bombitire* to hum, from Latin *bombus* deep hollow sound — more at BOMB] (circa 1553)
1 : LEAP, JUMP
2 : the action of rebounding **:** BOUNCE
⁷bound *intransitive verb* (1592)
1 : to move by leaping
2 : REBOUND, BOUNCE
bound·ary \'baùn-d(ə-)rē\ *noun, plural* **-aries** (1626)
: something (as a line, point, or plane) that indicates or fixes a limit or extent
boundary layer *noun* (1921)
: a region of retarded fluid near the surface of a body which moves through a fluid or past which a fluid moves
bound·ed·ness \'baùn-dəd-nəs\ *noun* (1674)
: the quality or state of being bounded
bound·en \'baùn-dən\ *adjective* [Middle English] (14th century)
1 *archaic* **:** being under obligation **:** BEHOLDEN
2 : made obligatory **:** BINDING ⟨our *bounden* duty⟩
bound·er \-dər\ *noun* (1505)
1 : one that bounds
2 : a man of objectionable social behavior **:** CAD
— **bound·er·ish** \-d(ə-)rish\ *adjective*
bound·less \'baùn(d)-ləs\ *adjective* (1592)
: having no boundaries **:** VAST
— **bound·less·ly** *adverb*
— **bound·less·ness** *noun*
bound up *adjective* (1611)
: closely involved or associated — usually used with *with*
boun·te·ous \'baùn-tē-əs\ *adjective* [Middle English *bountevous*, from Middle French *bontif* kind, from Old French, from *bonté*] (14th century)
1 : giving or disposed to give freely

◇ WORD HISTORY
boulevard The history of the word *boulevard* is actually a snippet of urban history in the West. In French, *boulevard* originally denoted the exterior rampart of a city wall. In the late Middle Ages, the dialects of French adjacent to the Netherlands had acquired the word from Middle Dutch *bolwerc*, and from the north of France it spread to other dialects. (Middle Dutch *bolwerc* is a compound of *bolle* "plank, beam" and *werc* "work, structure," alluding most likely to the use of wooden planks as supporting elements in earthworks; English *bulwark* is a direct borrowing of the same Middle Dutch word.) In 1675, the 14th century rampart of Charles V that had once formed the northern limit of Paris was razed and replaced by a wide tree-lined promenade, which contrasted pleasantly with the city's narrow streets. The same word *boulevard* that denoted the rampart was now applied to this promenade, and hence to similar avenues, which were created in 19th century Paris by demolishing existing buildings rather than old walls. As an English loanword, *boulevard* has been particularly successful in the United States; streets so named are now sometimes busy commercial thoroughfares or even highways, with no hint of the word's earlier applications.

2 : liberally bestowed
— **boun·te·ous·ly** *adverb*
— **boun·te·ous·ness** *noun*
boun·tied \'baùn-tēd\ *adjective* (1788)
1 : having the benefit of a bounty
2 : rewarded or rewardable by a bounty
boun·ti·ful \'baùn-ti-fəl\ *adjective* (1508)
1 : liberal in bestowing gifts or favors
2 : given or provided abundantly ⟨a *bountiful* harvest⟩
synonym see LIBERAL
— **boun·ti·ful·ly** \-f(ə-)lē\ *adverb*
— **boun·ti·ful·ness** \-fəl-nəs\ *noun*
boun·ty \'baùn-tē\ *noun, plural* **bounties** [Middle English *bounte* goodness, from Old French *bonté*, from Latin *bonitat-, bonitas,* from *bonus* good, from Old Latin *duenos;* akin to Sanskrit *duva* reverence, favor] (13th century)
1 : something that is given generously
2 : liberality in giving **:** GENEROSITY
3 : yield especially of a crop
4 : a reward, premium, or subsidy especially when offered or given by a government: as **a :** an extra allowance to induce entry into the armed services **b :** a grant to encourage an industry **c :** a payment to encourage the destruction of noxious animals **d :** a payment for the capture of or assistance in the capture of an outlaw
bounty hunter *noun* (1930)
1 : one that tracks down and captures outlaws for whom a reward is offered
2 : one that hunts predatory animals for the reward offered
bou·quet \bō-'kā, bü-\ *noun* [French, from Middle French, thicket, from Old North French *bosquet,* from Old French *bosc* forest — more at BOSCAGE] (circa 1718)
1 a : flowers picked and fastened together in a bunch **:** NOSEGAY **b :** MEDLEY ⟨*bouquet* of songs⟩
2 : COMPLIMENT
3 a : a distinctive and characteristic fragrance (as of wine) **b :** a subtle aroma or quality (as of an artistic performance)
bou·quet gar·ni \-gär-'nē\ *noun, plural* **bouquets gar·nis** \-'kā(z)-gär-'nē\ [French, literally, garnished bouquet] (circa 1852)
: an herb mixture that is either tied together or enclosed in a porous container and is cooked with a dish but removed before serving
bour·bon \'bùr-bən, 'bōr-, 'bòr-; *usually* 'bər- *in sense 3*\ *noun* [*Bourbon,* seigniory in France] (1600)
1 *capitalized* **:** a member of a French family founded in 1272 to which belong the rulers of France from 1589 to 1793 and from 1814 to 1830, of Spain from 1700 to 1808, from 1814 to 1868, from 1875 to 1931, and from 1975, of Naples from 1735 to 1805, and of the Two Sicilies from 1815 to 1860
2 [*Bourbon* (now Réunion), French island in the Indian Ocean] **:** a rose (*Rosa borboniana*) of compact upright growth with shining leaves, prickly branches, and clustered flowers
3 [*Bourbon* county, Kentucky] **:** a whiskey distilled from a mash made up of not less than 51 percent corn plus malt and rye — compare CORN WHISKEY
4 *often capitalized* **:** a person who clings obstinately to old social and political ideas; *specifically* **:** an extremely conservative member of the U.S. Democratic party usually from the South
— **bour·bon·ism** \-bə-,ni-zəm\ *noun, often capitalized*
bourg \'bùr(g)\ *noun* [Middle English, from Middle French, from Old French *borc,* from Latin *burgus* fortified place, of Germanic origin; akin to Old High German *burg* fortified place — more at BOROUGH] (12th century)
: TOWN, VILLAGE: as **a :** one neighboring a castle **b :** a market town

¹**bour·geois** \'bùrzh-,wä *also* 'bùzh- *or* 'bùzh- *or* bùrzh-\ *adjective* [Middle French, from Old French *borjois,* from *borc*] (circa 1565)
1 : of, relating to, or characteristic of the townsman or of the social middle class
2 : marked by a concern for material interests and respectability and a tendency toward mediocrity
3 : dominated by commercial and industrial interests **:** CAPITALISTIC
— **bour·geois·ifi·ca·tion** \,bù(r)zh-,wä-zə-fə-'kā-shən\ *noun*
— **bour·geois·ify** \bù(r)zh-'wä-zə-,fī\ *verb*
²**bourgeois** *noun, plural* **bourgeois** \-,wä(z), -'wä(z)\ (circa 1674)
1 a : BURGHER **b :** a middle-class person
2 : a person with social behavior and political views held to be influenced by private-property interest **:** CAPITALIST
3 *plural* **:** BOURGEOISIE
bour·geoise \'bùrzh-,wäz *also* 'bùzh- *or* 'bùzh- *or* bùrzh-\ *noun* [French, feminine of *bourgeois*] (1794)
: a woman of the middle class
bour·geoi·sie \,bù(r)zh-,wä-'zē\ *noun* [French, from *bourgeois*] (1707)
1 : MIDDLE CLASS
2 : a social order dominated by bourgeois
bour·geon \'bər-jən\ *variant of* BURGEON
bour·gui·gnonne \,bùr-gēn-'yòn\ *or* **bour·gui·gnon** \-'yōⁿ\ *adjective, often capitalized* [French, from *Bourgogne* Burgundy, region in France] (circa 1919)
: prepared or served in the manner of Burgundy (as with a sauce made with red wine) ⟨beef *bourguignonne*⟩
bourn *or* **bourne** \'bōrn, 'bòrn, 'bùrn\ *noun* [Middle English *burn, bourne* — more at BURN] (12th century)
: STREAM, BROOK
bourne *also* **bourn** *noun* [Middle French *bourne,* from Old French *bodne* — more at BOUND] (1523)
1 : BOUNDARY, LIMIT
2 : GOAL, DESTINATION
bour·rée \bù-'rā, 'bü-,\ *noun* [French] (1706)
1 : a 17th century French dance usually in quick duple time; *also* **:** a musical composition with the rhythm of this dance
2 : PAS DE BOURRÉE
bour·ride \bù-'rēd, bə-\ *noun* [French, from Provençal *bourrido,* alteration of *boulido* something boiled, from *bouli* to boil, from Latin *bullire* — more at BOIL] (circa 1919)
: a fish stew similar to bouillabaisse that is usually thickened with egg yolks and strongly flavored with garlic
bourse \'bùrs\ *noun* [Middle French, literally, purse, from Medieval Latin *bursa* — more at PURSE] (1597)
1 : EXCHANGE 5a; *specifically* **:** a European stock exchange
2 : a sale of numismatic or philatelic items on tables (as at a convention)
bouse *variant of* BOWSE
bou·stro·phe·don \,bü-strə-'fē-,dän, -d'n\ *noun* [Greek *boustrophēdon,* adverb, literally, turning like oxen in plowing, from *bous* ox, cow + *strephein* to turn — more at COW] (1699)
: the writing of alternate lines in opposite directions (as from left to right and from right to left)
— **boustrophedon** *adjective or adverb*
— **bou·stro·phe·don·ic** \-fē-'dä-nik\ *adjective*
bout \'baùt\ *noun* [English dialect, a trip going and returning in plowing, from Middle English *bought* bend] (1575)
: a spell of activity: as **a :** an athletic match (as of boxing) **b :** OUTBREAK, ATTACK ⟨a *bout* of lumbago⟩ **c :** SESSION
bou·tique \bü-'tēk\ *noun, often attributive* [French, shop, probably from Old Provençal *botica,* ultimately from Greek *apothēkē* storehouse — more at APOTHECARY] (1767)

1 a : a small fashionable specialty shop or business **b :** a small shop within a large department store
2 : a small company that offers highly specialized services ⟨an independent investment *boutique*⟩
bou·ton·niere \,bü-t'n-'ir, ,bü-tən-'yer\ *noun* [French *boutonnière* buttonhole, from Middle French, from *bouton* button] (circa 1867)
: a flower or bouquet worn in a buttonhole
Bou·vi·er des Flan·dres \,bü-vē-,ä-də-'flan-dərz, -'flänʺdrⁿ\ *noun* [French, literally, cowherd of Flanders] (1929)
: any of a breed of large powerfully built rough-coated dogs of Belgian origin used especially for herding and in guard work — called also *Bouvier*

Bouvier des Flandres

bou·zou·ki \bù-'zü-kē\ *noun, plural* **-kis** *also* **-kia** \-kē-ə\ [New Greek *mpouzouki*] (1952)
: a long-necked stringed instrument of Greek origin that resembles a mandolin
bo·vid \'bō-vid\ *noun* [New Latin *Bovidae,* from *Bov-, Bos,* type genus, from Latin *bov-, bos*] (1939)
: any of a family (Bovidae) of ruminants that have hollow unbranched permanently attached horns present in both sexes and that include antelopes, oxen, sheep, and goats
¹**bo·vine** \'bō-,vīn, -,vēn\ *adjective* [Late Latin *bovinus,* from Latin *bov-, bos* ox, cow — more at COW] (1817)
1 : of, relating to, or resembling bovines and especially the ox or cow
2 : having qualities (as placidity or dullness) characteristic of oxen or cows
— **bo·vine·ly** *adverb*
— **bo·vin·i·ty** \bō-'vi-nə-tē\ *noun*
²**bovine** *noun* (1865)
: any of a subfamily (Bovinae) of bovids including oxen, bison, buffalo, and their close relatives
¹**bow** \'baù\ *verb* [Middle English, from Old English *būgan;* akin to Old High German *biogan* to bend, Sanskrit *bhujati* he bends] (before 12th century)
intransitive verb
1 : to cease from competition or resistance **:** SUBMIT, YIELD ⟨refusing to *bow* to the inevitable —John O'Hara⟩; *also* **:** to suffer defeat ⟨*bowed* to the champion⟩
2 : to bend the head, body, or knee in reverence, submission, or shame
3 : to incline the head or body in salutation or assent or to acknowledge applause
transitive verb
1 : to cause to incline
2 : to incline (as the head) especially in respect or submission
3 : to crush with a heavy burden
4 a : to express by bowing **b :** to usher in or out with a bow
²**bow** *noun* (circa 1656)
: a bending of the head or body in respect, submission, assent, or salutation; *also* **:** a show of respect or submission
³**bow** \'bō\ *noun* [Middle English *bowe,* from Old English *boga;* akin to Old English *būgan*] (before 12th century)
1 a : something bent into a simple curve **:** BEND, ARCH **b :** RAINBOW

\ə\ abut	\ᵊ\ kitten	\ər\ further	\a\ ash	\ā\ ace	
\ä\ mop, mar	\aù\ out	\ch\ chin	\e\ bet	\ē\ easy	
\g\ go	\i\ hit	\ī\ ice	\j\ job	\ŋ\ sing	\ō\ go
\ò\ law	\òi\ boy	\th\ thin	\th̲\ the	\ü\ loot	\ù\ foot
\y\ yet	\zh\ vision	*see also* Guide to Pronunciation			

2 : a weapon that is made of a strip of flexible material (as wood) with a cord connecting the two ends and holding the strip bent and that is used to propel an arrow
3 : ARCHER
4 a : a metal ring or loop forming a handle (as of a key) **b :** a knot formed by doubling a ribbon or string into two or more loops **c :** BOW TIE **d :** a frame for the lenses of eyeglasses; *also* **:** the sidepiece of the frame passing over the ear
5 a : a wooden rod with horsehairs stretched from end to end used in playing an instrument of the viol or violin family **b :** a stroke of such a bow

⁴**bow** \'bō\ (before 12th century)
intransitive verb
1 : to bend into a curve
2 : to play a stringed musical instrument with a bow
transitive verb
1 : to cause to bend into a curve
2 : to play (a stringed instrument) with a bow

⁵**bow** \'baủ\ *noun* [Middle English *bowe, bowgh,* probably from Middle Dutch *boech* bow, shoulder; akin to Old English *bōg* bough] (15th century)
1 : the forward part of a ship
2 : ²BOWMAN

Bow bells \'bō-\ *noun plural* (1600)
: the bells of the Church of Saint Mary-le-Bow in London

bow·ler·ise *British variant of* BOWDLERIZE
bowd·ler·ize \'bōd-lə-,rīz, 'baủd-\ *transitive verb* **-ized; -iz·ing** [Thomas *Bowdler* (died 1825) English editor] (1836)
1 : to expurgate (as a book) by omitting or modifying parts considered vulgar
2 : to modify by abridging, simplifying, or distorting in style or content ◆
— **bowd·ler·iza·tion** \,bōd-lə-rə-'zā-shən, ,baủd-\ *noun*
— **bowd·ler·iz·er** *noun*

¹**bowed** \'baủd\ *adjective* [past participle of ¹*bow*] (14th century)
1 : bent downward and forward ⟨listened with *bowed* heads⟩
2 : having the back and head inclined
— **bowl·ful** \-,fùl\ *noun*

²**bowed** \'bōd\ *adjective* [partly from ³*bow* + *-ed;* partly from past participle of ⁴*bow*] (15th century)
: furnished with or shaped like a bow

bow·el \'baủ(-ə)l\ *noun* [Middle English, from Middle French *boel,* from Medieval Latin *botellus,* from Latin, diminutive of *botulus* sausage] (14th century)
1 : INTESTINE, GUT; *also* **:** one of the divisions of the intestines — usually used in plural except in medical use ⟨the large *bowel*⟩ ⟨move your *bowels*⟩
2 *archaic* **:** the seat of pity, tenderness, or courage — usually used in plural
3 *plural* **:** the interior parts; *especially* **:** the deep or remote parts ⟨*bowels* of the earth⟩
— **bow·el·less** \'baủ(-ə)l-ləs\ *adjective*

¹**bow·er** \'baủ(-ə)r\ *noun* [Middle English *bour* dwelling, from Old English *būr;* akin to Old English & Old High German *būan* to dwell, Old English *bēon* to be — more at BE] (before 12th century)
1 : an attractive dwelling or retreat
2 : a lady's private apartment in a medieval hall or castle
3 : a shelter (as in a garden) made with tree boughs or vines twined together **:** ARBOR
— **bow·ery** \-ē\ *adjective*

²**bower** *transitive verb* (1592)
: EMBOWER, ENCLOSE

³**bower** *noun* (1652)
: an anchor carried at the bow of a ship

bow·er·bird \'baủ(-ə)r-,bərd\ *noun* (1845)
: any of a family (Ptilonorhynchidae) of passerine birds of the Australian region in which the male builds a chamber or passage arched over with twigs and grasses, often adorned with

bright-colored objects, and used especially to attract the female

bow·ery \'baủ(-ə)r-ē\ *noun, plural* **-er·ies** [Dutch *bouwerij,* from *bouwer* farmer, from *bouwen* to till; akin to Old High German *būan* to dwell] (1650)
1 : a colonial Dutch plantation or farm
2 [*Bowery,* street in New York City] **:** a city district known for cheap bars and derelicts

bow·fin \'bō-,fin\ *noun* (1845)
: a predaceous dull-green iridescent North American freshwater fish (*Amia calva*) that is the only surviving member of an order (Amiiformes) dating back to the Jurassic

bow·front \-,frənt\ *adjective* (1925)
1 : having an outward curving front ⟨*bowfront* furniture⟩
2 : having a bow window in front ⟨*bowfront* houses⟩

bow·head whale \-,hed-\ *noun* (1887)
: a baleen whale (*Balaena mysticetus*) of arctic and subarctic seas — called also *bowhead*

bow·ie knife \'bü-ē, 'bō-\ *noun* [James *Bowie*] (1836)
: a stout single-edged hunting knife with part of the back edge curved concavely to a point and sharpened

bow·ing \'bō-iŋ\ *noun* (1838)
: the technique or manner of managing the bow in playing a stringed musical instrument

bow·knot \'bō-,nät\ *noun* (1547)
: a knot with decorative loops

¹**bowl** \'bōl\ *noun* [Middle English *bolle,* from Old English *bolla;* akin to Old High German *bolla* blister] (before 12th century)
1 : a concave usually hemispherical vessel often used for holding liquids; *especially* **:** a drinking vessel (as for wine)
2 : the contents of a bowl
3 : a bowl-shaped or concave part: as **a :** the hollow of a spoon or tobacco pipe **b :** the receptacle of a toilet
4 a : a natural formation or geographical region shaped like a bowl **b :** a bowl-shaped structure; *especially* **:** an athletic stadium
5 : a postseason football game between specially invited teams
— **bowled** \'bōld\ *adjective*
— **bowl·ful** \-,fùl\ *noun*

²**bowl** *noun* [Middle English *boule,* from Middle French, from Latin *bulla* bubble] (15th century)
1 a : a ball (as of lignum vitae) weighted or shaped to give it a bias when rolled in lawn bowling **b** *plural but singular in construction* **:** LAWN BOWLING
2 : a delivery of the ball in bowling
3 : a cylindrical roller or drum (as for a mechanical device)

³**bowl** (15th century)
intransitive verb
1 a : to participate in a game of bowling **b :** to roll a ball in bowling
2 : to travel smoothly and rapidly (as in a wheeled vehicle)
transitive verb
1 a : to roll (a ball) in bowling **b** (1) **:** to complete by bowling ⟨*bowl* a string⟩ (2) **:** to score by bowling ⟨*bowls* 150⟩
2 : to strike with a swiftly moving object
3 : to overwhelm with surprise

bowl·der *variant of* BOULDER

bow·leg \'bō-,leg, -,lāg, 'bō-'\ *noun* (circa 1864)
: a leg bowed outward at or below the knee
— **bow·legged** \'bō-,le-gəd, -,lā-; -,legd, -,lāgd\ *adjective*

¹**bowl·er** \'bō-lər\ *noun* (circa 1500)
: a person who bowls; *specifically* **:** the player that delivers the ball to the batsman in cricket

²**bowl·er** \'bō-lər\ *noun* [*Bowler,* 19th century family of English hatters] (1861)
: DERBY 3

bow·line \'bō-lən, -,līn\ *noun* [Middle English *bouline,* perhaps from *bowe* bow + *line*] (13th century)

1 : a rope used to keep the weather edge of a square sail taut forward
2 : a knot used to form a loop that neither slips nor jams — see KNOT illustration

bowl·ing \'bō-liŋ\ *noun* (1535)
: any of several games in which balls are rolled on a green or down an alley at an object or group of objects

bowl over *transitive verb* (1867)
1 : to take unawares
2 : ¹IMPRESS 2

¹**bow·man** \'bō-mən\ *noun* (13th century)
: ARCHER 1

²**bow·man** \'baủ-mən\ *noun* (1829)
: a boatman, oarsman, or paddler stationed in the front of a boat

Bow·man's capsule \'bō-mənz-\ *noun* [Sir William *Bowman* (died 1892) English surgeon] (circa 1860)
: a thin membranous double-walled capsule surrounding the glomerulus of a vertebrate nephron

bow out *intransitive verb* (1942)
: RETIRE, WITHDRAW

bow saw \'bō-\ *noun* (1677)
: a saw having a narrow blade held under tension by a light bow-shaped frame

bowse \'baủz\ *verb* **bowsed; bows·ing** [origin unknown] (1593)
transitive verb
: to haul by means of a tackle
intransitive verb
: to bowse something

bow shock \'baủ-\ *noun* (1950)
: the shock wave formed by the collision of a stellar wind with another medium (as the magnetosphere of a planet)

bow·sprit \'baủ-,sprit, *British usually* 'bō-\ *noun* [Middle English *bouspret,* probably from Middle Low German *bōchsprēt,* from *bōch* bow + *sprēt* pole] (13th century)
: a large spar projecting forward from the stem of a ship

bow·string \'bō-,striŋ\ *noun* (14th century)
: a waxed or sized cord joining the ends of a shooting bow

bowstring hemp *noun* (circa 1858)
: any of various Asian and African sansevierias; *also* **:** its soft tough leaf fiber used especially in cordage

bow tie \'bō-\ *noun* (1897)
: a short necktie tied in a bowknot

bow window \'bō-\ *noun* (1753)
: a usually curved bay window

◇ **WORD HISTORY**

bowdlerize Editors of books typically languish in obscurity, while authors bask in fame. Few editors have ever gained the public attention achieved by Thomas Bowdler (1754–1825). Born near Bath, England, and trained as a physician, Bowdler engaged in mostly nonmedical pursuits from the 1780s onward. His travels through Europe led to his first foray into publishing, a report warning English tourists against the uncleanliness of watering places in France. Expanding the scope of his interest in purification, he next tackled works of literature. His first effort was *The Family Shakespeare* (1818), the title page of which promised that "those words and expressions are omitted which cannot with propriety be read aloud in a family." Although Bowdler's edition met with adverse critical reaction, it pleased the 19th century public. Bowdler then went on to expurgate Gibbon's *History of the Decline and Fall of the Roman Empire* of all passages of "an irreligious or immoral tendency." A decade after his death Bowdler's name had become synonymous with censorship on moral grounds, and by 1836 *bowdlerize* was used to describe the expurgation of literary works.

bow·wow \'baù-,waù, baù-'\ *noun* [imitative] (1576)
1 : the bark of a dog; *also* : DOG
2 : noisy clamor
3 : arrogant dogmatic manner

bow·yer \'bō-yər\ *noun* [Middle English *bowyere*] (14th century)
: a person who makes shooting bows

¹box \'bäks\ *noun, plural* **box** *or* **box·es** [Middle English, from Old English, from Latin *buxus,* from Greek *pyxos*] (before 12th century)
: an evergreen shrub or small tree (genus *Buxus* of the family Buxaceae, the box family) with opposite entire leaves and capsular fruits; *especially* : a widely cultivated shrub (*B. sempervirens*) used for hedges, borders, and topiary figures

²box *noun* [Middle English, from Old English, from Late Latin *buxis,* from Greek *pyxis,* from *pyxos* box tree] (before 12th century)
1 : a rigid typically rectangular container with or without a cover ⟨a cigar *box*⟩: as **a** : an open cargo container of a vehicle **b** : COFFIN
2 : the contents of a box especially as a measure of quantity
3 : a box or boxlike container and its contents: as **a** *British* : a gift in a box **b** : an automobile transmission **c** : TELEVISION **d** : a signaling apparatus ⟨alarm *box*⟩ **e** : a usually self-contained piece of electronic equipment **f** : BOOM BOX
4 : an often small space, compartment, or enclosure: as **a** : an enclosed group of seats for spectators (as in a theater or stadium) **b** : a driver's seat on a carriage or coach **c** : a cell for holding mail **d** *British* : BOX STALL **e** : PENALTY BOX
5 : a usually rectangular space that is frequently outlined or demarcated on a surface: as **a** : any of six spaces on a baseball diamond where the batter, coaches, pitcher, and catcher stand **b** : a space on a page for printed matter or in which to make a mark
6 : PREDICAMENT, FIX
7 : a cubical building
— **box·ful** \-,fùl\ *noun*
— **box·like** \-,līk\ *adjective*

³box *transitive verb* (15th century)
1 : to enclose in or as if in a box
2 : to hem in (as an opponent) — usually used with *in, out,* or *up* ⟨*boxed* out the opposing tackle⟩

⁴box *noun* [Middle English] (14th century)
: a punch or slap especially on the ear

⁵box (1519)
transitive verb
1 : to hit (as the ears) with the hand
2 : to engage in boxing with
intransitive verb
: to fight with the fists : engage in boxing

⁶box *transitive verb* [probably from Spanish *bojar* to circumnavigate, from Catalan *vogir* to turn, from Latin *volvere* to roll — more at VOLUBLE] (1753)
: to name the 32 points of (the compass) in their order — used figuratively in the phrase *box the compass* to describe making a complete reversal

box·board \'bäks-,bōrd, -,bòrd\ *noun* (1841)
: paperboard used for making boxes and cartons

box camera *noun* (1902)
: a box-shaped camera with a simple lens and rotary shutter

¹box·car \'bäks-,kär\ *noun* (1856)
: a roofed freight car usually with sliding doors in the sides

²boxcar *adjective* [from the high numbers stenciled on the sides of boxcars] (1944)
: very large ⟨the judge awarded her a *boxcar* figure⟩

box coat *noun* (1822)
1 : a heavy overcoat formerly worn for driving
2 : a loose coat usually fitted at the shoulders

box elder *noun* (1787)

: a North American maple (*Acer negundo*) with compound leaves

¹box·er \'bäk-sər\ *noun* (1742)
1 : a person who engages in the sport of boxing
2 *plural* : SHORT 4b

²boxer *noun* (1871)
: one that makes boxes or packs things in boxes

³boxer *noun* [German, from English ¹*boxer*] (circa 1904)
: a compact medium-sized short-haired usually fawn or brindled dog of a breed originating in Germany

Box·er \'bäk-sər\ *noun* [approximate translation of Chinese (Beijing) *yìhé juǎn,* literally, righteous harmonious fist] (1899)
: a member of a Chinese secret society that in 1900 attempted by violence to drive foreigners out of China and to force Chinese converts to renounce Christianity

boxer shorts *noun plural* (1944)
: SHORT 4b

¹box·ing \'bäk-siŋ\ *noun* (1607)
1 : an act of enclosing in a box
2 : a boxlike enclosure : CASING
3 : material used for boxes and casings

²boxing *noun* (1711)
: the art of attack and defense with the fists practiced as a sport

Boxing Day *noun* (1833)
: the first weekday after Christmas observed as a legal holiday in parts of the Commonwealth and marked by the giving of Christmas boxes to service workers (as postal workers)

boxing glove *noun* (1875)
: one of a pair of leather mittens heavily padded on the back and worn in boxing

box kite *noun* (1897)
: a tailless kite consisting of two or more open-ended connected boxes

box kite

box lunch *noun* (1950)
: a lunch packed in a container (as a box)

box office *noun* (1786)
1 a : an office (as in a theater) where tickets of admission are sold **b** : income from ticket sales (as for a film)
2 : the ability or power (as of a show) to attract ticket buyers; *also* : something that enhances that ability ⟨any publicity is good *box office*⟩

box pleat *noun* (1883)
: a pleat made by forming two folded edges one facing right and the other left

box score *noun* [from its arrangement in a newspaper box] (1913)
: a printed score of a game (as baseball) giving the names and positions of the players and a record of the play arranged in tabular form; *broadly* : total count : SUMMARY

box seat *noun* (1849)
1 : ²BOX 4b
2 a : a seat in a box (as in a theater or grandstand) **b** : a position favorable for viewing something

box social *noun* (1928)
: a fund-raising affair at which box lunches are auctioned to the highest bidder

box spring *noun* (1895)
: a bedspring that consists of spiral springs attached to a foundation and enclosed in a cloth-covered frame

box stall *noun* (1885)
: an individual enclosure within a barn or stable in which an animal may move about freely without a restraining device

box·thorn \'bäks-,thòrn\ *noun* (1678)
: MATRIMONY VINE

box turtle *noun* (circa 1804)
: any of several North American land turtles (genus *Terrapene*) capable of withdrawing into its shell and closing it by hinged joints

in the lower half — called also *box tortoise*

box·wood \'bäks-,wùd\ *noun* (1652)
1 : the very close-grained heavy tough hard wood of the box (*Buxus*); *also* : a wood of similar properties
2 : a plant producing boxwood

box turtle

boxy \'bäk-sē\ *adjective* **box·i·er; -est** (circa 1861)
: resembling a box
— **box·i·ness** *noun*

boy \'bòi\ *noun, often attributive* [Middle English] (13th century)
1 : a male servant — sometimes taken to be offensive
2 a : a male child from birth to puberty **b** : SON **c** : an immature male : YOUTH **d** : SWEETHEART, BEAU
3 a : one native to a given place ⟨local *boy*⟩ **b** : FELLOW, PERSON ⟨the *boys* at the office⟩ **c** — used interjectionally to express intensity of feeling ⟨*boy,* what a game⟩
— **boy·hood** \-,hùd\ *noun*
— **boy·ish** \-ish\ *adjective*
— **boy·ish·ly** *adverb*
— **boy·ish·ness** *noun*

bo·yar *also* **bo·yard** \bō-'yär\ *noun* [Russian *boyarin*] (1591)
: a member of a Russian aristocratic order next in rank below the ruling princes until its abolition by Peter the Great

boy·chick \'bòi-,chik\ *noun* [American Yiddish *boytshik,* from English *boy* + Yiddish *-tshik,* diminutive suffix] (circa 1951)
: a young man : BOY

boy·cott \'bòi-,kät\ *transitive verb* [Charles C. Boycott (died 1897) English land agent in Ireland who was ostracized for refusing to reduce rents] (1880)
: to engage in a concerted refusal to have dealings with (as a person, store, or organization) usually to express disapproval or to force acceptance of certain conditions ◇

◇ WORD HISTORY

boycott In September 1880 the recently formed Irish National Land League, which grew out of unrest following an agricultural depression during the late 1870s, initiated a campaign against the eviction of tenants unable to pay their rents. Charles S. Boycott, a retired English army captain who rented a farm in County Mayo and worked as an agent for an absentee landlord, became the first victim of the Land League's campaign. When the landlord's tenants refused to pay their rents unless they received a 25 percent abatement, Boycott attempted to serve eviction notices. As a result, he was ostracized by the community, his laborers and servants quit, and the crops on his farm began to rot. His plight became well-known through press coverage and Boycott's own letters to *The Times* in London. A force of fifty volunteers from Ulster was raised and sent to Mayo to harvest his crops, guarded by nearly a thousand troops and police. The newly popular tactic of shunning a person to assert a grievance needed a name and Boycott's name was at hand. The Land League was banned by Parliament in 1881, but the word *boycott,* noun and verb, is still part of English.

\ə\ abut \ə\ kitten \ər\ further \a\ ash \ā\ ace
\ä\ mop, mar \aù\ out \ch\ chin \e\ bet \ē\ easy
\g\ go \i\ hit \ī\ ice \j\ job \ŋ\ sing \ō\ go
\ò\ law \òi\ boy \th\ thin \th\ the \ü\ loot \ù\ foot
\y\ yet \zh\ vision *see also* Guide to Pronunciation

— **boycott** *noun*

— **boy·cott·er** *noun*

boy·friend \'bȯi-ˌfrend\ *noun* (1896)
1 : a male friend
2 : a frequent or regular male companion of a girl or woman
3 : a male lover

Boyle's law \'bȯilz-\ *noun* [Robert *Boyle*] (circa 1860)
: a statement in physics: the volume of a gas at constant temperature varies inversely with the pressure exerted on it

boyo \'bȯi-(ˌ)ō\ *noun, plural* **boy·os** [*boy* + [1]*-o*] (circa 1870)
Irish **:** BOY, LAD

Boy Scout *noun* (1909)
1 : a member of any of various national scouting programs (as the Boy Scouts of America) for boys usually 11 to 17 years of age
2 : a person whose values or actions are characteristic of a Boy Scout

boy·sen·ber·ry \'bȯi-zᵊn-ˌber-ē, -sᵊn-, -zᵊm-\ *noun* [Rudolph *Boysen* (died 1950) American horticulturist + English *berry*] (1935)
: a large bramble fruit with a raspberry flavor; *also* **:** the trailing hybrid bramble yielding this fruit and developed by crossing several blackberries and raspberries

boy wonder *noun* (1946)
: a young man of noteworthy achievements

bo·zo \'bō-(ˌ)zō\ *noun, plural* **bozos** [origin unknown] (1920)
: a foolish or incompetent person

B picture *noun* (circa 1937)
: B MOVIE

bra \'brä\ *noun* (1936)
: BRASSIERE

— **bra·less** *adjective*

brab·ble \'bra-bəl\ *intransitive verb* **brab·bled; brab·bling** \-b(ə-)liŋ\ [perhaps from Middle Dutch *brabbelen*, of imitative origin] (circa 1530)
: SQUABBLE

— **brabble** *noun*

[1]**brace** \'brās\ *verb* **braced; brac·ing** [Middle English, from Middle French *bracier* to embrace, from *brace*] (14th century)
transitive verb
1 *archaic* **:** to fasten tightly **:** BIND
2 a : to prepare for use by making taut **b :** PREPARE, STEEL ⟨*brace* yourself for the shock⟩ **c :** INVIGORATE, FRESHEN
3 : to turn (a sail yard) by means of a brace
4 a : to furnish or support with a brace ⟨heavily *braced* against the wind⟩ **b :** to make stronger **:** REINFORCE
5 : to put or plant firmly ⟨*braces* his foot in the stirrup⟩
6 : to waylay especially with demands or questions
intransitive verb
1 : to take heart — used with *up*
2 : to get ready (as for an attack)

[2]**brace** *noun, plural* **brac·es** [Middle English, clasp, pair, from Middle French, two arms, from Latin *bracchia*, plural of *bracchium* arm, from Greek *brachiōn*, from comparative of *brachys* short — more at BRIEF] (14th century)
1 : something (as a clasp) that connects or fastens
2 *or plural* **brace :** two of a kind **:** PAIR ⟨several *brace* of quail⟩
3 : a crank-shaped instrument for turning a bit
4 : something that transmits, directs, resists, or supports weight or pressure: as **a :** a diagonal piece of structural material that serves to strengthen something (as a framework) **b :** a rope rove through a block at the end of a ship's yard to swing it horizontally **c** *plural* **:** SUSPENDERS **d :** an appliance for supporting a body part **e** *plural* **:** dental appliances used to exert pressure to straighten misaligned teeth

5 a : one of two marks { } used to connect words or items to be considered together **b :** one of these marks connecting two or more musical staffs carrying parts to be performed simultaneously **c :** BRACKET 3a
6 : a position of rigid attention
7 : something that arouses energy or strengthens morale

brace·let \'brās-lət\ *noun* [Middle English, from Middle French, diminutive of *bras* arm, from Latin *bracchium*] (15th century)
1 : an ornamental band or chain worn around the wrist
2 : something (as handcuffs) resembling a bracelet

[1]**bra·cer** \'brā-sər\ *noun* [Middle English, from Middle French *braciere*, from Old French, from *braz* arm, from Latin *bracchium*] (14th century)
: an arm or wrist protector especially for use by an archer

[2]**brac·er** \'brā-sər\ *noun* (1579)
1 : one that braces, binds, or makes firm
2 : a drink (as of liquor) taken as a stimulant

bra·ce·ro \brä-'ser-(ˌ)ō\ *noun, plural* **-ros** [Spanish, laborer, from *brazo* arm, from Latin *bracchium*] (1920)
: a Mexican laborer admitted to the U.S. especially for seasonal contract labor in agriculture — compare WETBACK

brace root *noun* (1892)
: PROP ROOT

brachi- *or* **brachio-** *combining form* [Latin *bracchium, brachium*]
1 : arm ⟨*brachi*al⟩
2 : brachial and ⟨*brachio*cephalic⟩

bra·chi·al \'brā-kē-əl\ *adjective* (1578)
: of, relating to, or situated in the arm or an armlike process ⟨the *brachial* artery of the upper arm⟩

brachial plexus *noun* (circa 1860)
: a network of nerves lying mostly in the armpit and supplying nerves to the chest, shoulder, and arm

bra·chi·ate \'brā-kē-ˌāt\ *intransitive verb* **-at·ed; -at·ing** (1932)
: to progress by swinging from one hold to another by the arms ⟨a *brachiating* gibbon⟩

— **bra·chi·a·tion** \ˌbrā-kē-'ā-shən\ *noun*

— **bra·chi·a·tor** \'brā-kē-ˌā-tər\ *noun*

bra·chio·ce·phal·ic artery \ˌbrā-kē-(ˌ)ō-sə-'fa-lik-\ *noun* (circa 1839)
: a short artery that arises from the arch of the aorta and divides into the carotid and subclavian arteries of the right side — called also *innominate artery*

brachiocephalic vein *noun* (circa 1852)
: either of two large veins that occur one on each side of the neck, receive blood from the head and neck, and unite to form the superior vena cava — called also *innominate vein*

bra·chio·pod \'brā-kē-ə-ˌpäd\ *noun* [ultimately from Latin *bracchium* + Greek *pod-, pous* foot — more at FOOT] (1836)
: any of a phylum (Brachiopoda) of marine invertebrates with bivalve shells within which is a pair of arms bearing tentacles by which a current of water is made to bring microscopic food to the mouth

— **brachiopod** *adjective*

brachy- *combining form* [Greek, from *brachys* — more at BRIEF]
: short ⟨*brachy*cephalic⟩

brachy·ce·phal·ic \ˌbra-ki-sə-'fa-lik\ *adjective* [New Latin *brachycephalus*, from Greek *brachy-* + *kephalē* head — more at CEPHALIC] (circa 1852)
: short-headed or broad-headed with a cephalic index of over 80

— **brachy·ceph·a·ly** \-'se-fə-lē\ *noun*

bra·chyp·ter·ous \bra-'kip-tə-rəs\ *adjective* [Greek *brachypteros*, from *brachy-* + *pteron* wing — more at FEATHER] (circa 1847)

: having rudimentary or abnormally small wings ⟨*brachypterous* insects⟩

brac·ing \'brā-siŋ\ *adjective* (1750)
: giving strength, vigor, or freshness ⟨a *bracing* breeze⟩

— **brac·ing·ly** *adverb*

bra·ci·o·la \ˌbrä-chē-'ō-lə, -'chō-lə\ *or* **bra·ci·o·le** \-'ō-ˌlā\ *noun* [Italian, literally, slice of meat roasted over coals, from *brace* live coals, probably of Germanic origin; akin to Swedish *brasa* fire] (circa 1945)
: a thin slice of meat wrapped around a seasoned filling and often cooked in wine

brack·en \'bra-kən\ *noun* [Middle English *braken*, probably of Scandinavian origin; akin to Old Swedish *brækne* fern] (14th century)
1 : a large coarse fern; *especially* **:** a nearly cosmopolitan brake (*Pteridium aquilinum*) found in most tropical and temperate regions
2 : a growth of brakes

[1]**brack·et** \'bra-kət\ *noun* [perhaps from Middle French *braguette* codpiece, from diminutive of *brague* breeches, from Old Provençal *braga*, from Latin *braca*, of Celtic origin — more at BREECH] (1580)
1 : an overhanging member that projects from a structure (as a wall) and is usually designed to support a vertical load or to strengthen an angle
2 : a fixture (as for holding a lamp) projecting from a wall or column
3 a : one of a pair of marks [] used in writing and printing to enclose matter or in mathematics and logic as signs of aggregation — called also *square bracket* **b :** one of the pair of marks ⟨ ⟩ used to enclose matter — called also *angle bracket* **c :** PARENTHESIS 3 **d :** BRACE 5b
4 : a section of a continuously numbered or graded series (as age ranges or income levels)

[2]**bracket** *transitive verb* (circa 1847)
1 a : to place within or as if within brackets ⟨editorial comments are *bracketed*⟩ ⟨news stories *bracketed* by commercials⟩ **b :** to eliminate from consideration ⟨*bracket* off politics⟩ **c :** to extend around so as to encompass **:** INCLUDE ⟨test pressures . . . which *bracket* virtually the entire range of passenger-car tire pressures —*Consumer Reports*⟩
2 : to furnish or fasten with brackets
3 : to put in the same category or group ⟨*bracketed* in a tie for third⟩
4 a : to get the range on (a target) by firing over and short ⟨there were mortar rounds *bracketing* the area —Ed Bradley⟩ **b :** to establish the limits of ⟨*bracketed* the problem neatly⟩ **c :** to take photographs at more than one exposure in order to ensure that the desired exposure is obtained

bracket creep *noun* (1980)
: movement into a higher tax bracket as a result of income rises intended to offset the effects of inflation

brack·et·ed *adjective* (1885)
of a serif **:** joined to the stroke by a curved line

bracket fungus *noun* (1899)
: a basidiomycete that forms shelflike sporophores

brack·ish \'bra-kish\ *adjective* [Dutch *brac* salty; akin to Middle Low German *brac* salty] (1538)
1 : somewhat salty ⟨*brackish* water⟩
2 a : not appealing to the taste ⟨*brackish* tea⟩ **b :** REPULSIVE

— **brack·ish·ness** *noun*

brac·o·nid \'bra-kə-(ˌ)nid\ *noun* [ultimately from Greek *brachys*] (circa 1893)
: any of a large family (Braconidae) of ichneumon flies

— **braconid** *adjective*

bract \'brakt\ *noun* [New Latin *bractea*, from Latin, thin metal plate] (1770)

1 : a leaf from the axil of which a flower or floral axis arises
2 : a leaf borne on a floral axis; *especially* : one subtending a flower or flower cluster
— **brac·te·al** \'brak-tē-əl\ *adjective*
— **brac·te·ate** \-tē-ət, -,āt\ *adjective*
— **bract·ed** \-təd\ *adjective*
brac·te·ole \'brak-tē-,ōl\ *noun* [New Latin *bracteola*, from Latin, diminutive of *bractea*] (circa 1828)
: a small bract especially on a floral axis
¹brad \'brad\ *noun* [Middle English, from Old Norse *broddr* spike; perhaps akin to Old English *byrst* bristle — more at BRISTLE] (13th century)
1 : a thin nail of the same thickness throughout but tapering in width and having a slight projection at the top of one side instead of a head
2 : a slender wire nail with a small barrel-shaped head
²brad *transitive verb* **brad·ded; brad·ding** (1794)
: to fasten with brads
brad·awl \'brad-,ȯl\ *noun* (1823)
: an awl with chisel edge used to make holes for brads or screws
brady- *combining form* [Greek *bradys*]
: slow ⟨*brady*kinin⟩
bra·dy·car·dia \,brā-di-'kär-dē-ə *also* ,bra-\ *noun* [New Latin] (circa 1890)
: relatively slow heart action — compare TACHYCARDIA
bra·dy·ki·nin \-'kī-nən\ *noun* (1949)
: a kinin that is formed locally in injured tissue, acts in vasodilation of small arterioles, is considered to play a part in inflammatory processes, and is composed of a chain of nine amino-acid residues
brae \'brā\ *noun* [Middle English *bra*, from Old Norse *brā* eyelid; akin to Old English *brǣw* eyebrow, and probably to Old English *bregdan* to move quickly — more at BRAID] (13th century)
chiefly Scottish : a hillside especially along a river
¹brag \'brag\ *noun* [Middle English] (14th century)
1 : a pompous or boastful statement
2 : arrogant talk or manner : COCKINESS
3 : BRAGGART
²brag *verb* **bragged; brag·ging** (14th century)
intransitive verb
: to talk boastfully : engage in self-glorification
transitive verb
: to assert boastfully
synonym see BOAST
— **brag·ger** \'brag-ər\ *noun*
— **brag·gy** \'bra-gē\ *adjective*
³brag *adjective* **brag·ger; brag·gest** (1836)
: FIRST-RATE
brag·ga·do·cio \,bra-gə-'dō-sē-,ō, -shē-, -chē-, -(,)shō, -(,)chō\ *noun, plural* **-cios** [*Braggadochio*, personification of boasting in *Faerie Queene* by Edmund Spenser] (1594)
1 : BRAGGART
2 a : empty boasting **b** : arrogant pretension : COCKINESS
brag·gart \'bra-gərt\ *noun* (circa 1577)
: a loud arrogant boaster
— **braggart** *adjective*
¹Brah·ma \'brä-mə\ *noun* [Sanskrit *brahman*] (1690)
1 : the creator god of the Hindu sacred triad — compare SIVA, VISHNU
2 : the ultimate ground of all being in Hinduism
²Brah·ma \'brä-mə, 'brä-, 'bra-\ *noun* (1938)
: BRAHMAN 2
Brah·man *or* **Brah·min** \'brä-mən; *2 is* 'brä-, 'brä-, 'bra-\ *noun* [Middle English *Bragman* inhabitant of India, from Latin *Bracmanus*, from Greek *Brachman*, from Sanskrit *brāh-maṇa* of the Brahman caste, from *brahman* Brahman] (15th century)

1 a : a Hindu of the highest caste traditionally assigned to the priesthood **b** : ¹BRAHMA 2
2 : any of an Indian breed of humped cattle : ZEBU; *especially* : a large vigorous heat-resistant and tick-resistant usually silvery gray animal developed in the southern U.S. from the zebu
3 *usually* **Brahmin** : a person of high social standing and cultivated intellect and taste ⟨Boston *Brahmins*⟩
— **Brah·man·ic** \brä-'ma-nik\ *or* **Brah·man·i·cal** \-ni-kəl\ *adjective*
Brah·man·ism \'brä-mə-,ni-zəm\ *noun* (1816)
: orthodox Hinduism adhering to the pantheism of the Vedas and to the ancient sacrifices and family ceremonies
¹braid \'brād\ *transitive verb* [Middle English *breyden* to move suddenly, snatch, plait, from Old English *bregdan;* akin to Old High German *brettan* to draw (a sword)] (before 12th century)
1 a : to make from braids ⟨*braid* a rug⟩ **b** : to form (three or more strands) into a braid
2 : to do up (the hair) by interweaving three or more strands
3 : MIX, INTERMINGLE ⟨*braid* fact with fiction⟩
4 : to ornament especially with ribbon or braid
— **braid·er** *noun*
²braid *noun* (1530)
1 a : a length of braided hair **b** : a cord or ribbon having usually three or more component strands forming a regular diagonal pattern down its length; *especially* : a narrow fabric of intertwined threads used especially for trimming
2 : high-ranking naval officers
braid·ed *adjective* (15th century)
1 a : made by intertwining three or more strands **b** : ornamented with braid
2 : forming an interlacing network of channels ⟨a *braided* river⟩
braid·ing \'brā-diŋ\ *noun* (15th century)
: something made of braided material
¹brail \'brā(ə)l\ *noun* [Middle English *brayle*, from Anglo-French *braiel*, from Old French, strap] (15th century)
1 : a rope fastened to the leech of a sail and used for hauling the sail up or in
2 : a dip net with which fish are hauled aboard a boat from a purse seine or trap
²brail *transitive verb* (1625)
1 : to take in (a sail) by the brails
2 : to hoist (fish) by means of a brail
braille \'brā(ə)l\ *noun, often capitalized* [Louis *Braille*] (1853)
: a system of writing for the blind that uses characters made up of raised dots ◇
— **braille** *transitive verb*
— **braill·ist** \'brā-list\ *noun*

	a	b	c	d	e	f	g	h	i	j
	1	2	3	4	5	6	7	8	9	0
	k	l	m	n	o	p	q	r	s	t
	u	v	w	x	y	z		Capital Sign	Numeral Sign	

braille alphabet

braille·writ·er \-,rī-tər\ *noun, often capitalized* (1942)
: a machine for writing braille
¹brain \'brān\ *noun* [Middle English, from Old English *brægen;* akin to Middle Low German *bregen* brain, and perhaps to Greek *brechmos* front part of the head] (before 12th century)
1 a : the portion of the vertebrate central nervous system that constitutes the organ of thought and neural coordination, includes all the higher nervous centers receiving stimuli from the sense organs and interpreting and

correlating them to formulate the motor impulses, is made up of neurons and supporting and nutritive structures, is enclosed within the skull, and is continuous with the spinal cord through the foramen magnum **b** : a nervous center in invertebrates comparable in position and function to the vertebrate brain
2 a (1) : INTELLECT, MIND ⟨has a clever *brain*⟩ (2) : intellectual endowment : INTELLIGENCE — often used in plural ⟨plenty of *brains* in that family⟩ **b** (1) : a very intelligent or intelligent person (2) : the chief planner of an organization or enterprise — usually used in plural
3 : something that performs the functions of a brain; *especially* : an automatic device (as a computer) for control or computation
²brain *transitive verb* (14th century)
1 : to kill by smashing the skull
2 : to hit on the head
brain·case \'brān-,kās\ *noun* (1741)
: the cranium enclosing the brain
brain·child \-,chīld\ *noun* (1631)
: a product of one's creative imagination
brain coral *noun* (circa 1711)
: a massive reef-building coral (as genus *Maeandra*) having the surface covered by ridges and furrows
brain death *noun* (1964)
: final cessation of activity in the central nervous system especially as indicated by a flat electroencephalogram for a predetermined length of time
— **brain–dead** *adjective*
brain drain *noun* (1963)
: the departure of educated or professional people from one country, economic sector, or field for another usually for better pay or living conditions
brained \'brānd\ *adjective* (15th century)
: having a brain of a specified kind — used in combination ⟨feather*brained*⟩
brain hormone *noun* (1957)
: a hormone that is secreted by neurosecretory cells of the insect brain and that stimulates the prothoracic glands to secrete ecdysone
brain·ish \'brā-nish\ *adjective* (circa 1530)

brain 1a: *1* cerebral hemisphere, *2* corpus callosum, *3* ventricle, *4* fornix, *5* thalamus, *6* pituitary gland, *7* pons, *8* medulla oblongata, *9* spinal cord, *10* cerebellum, *11* midbrain

◇ WORD HISTORY
braille The system of writing known as *braille* is named after its principal inventor, the Frenchman Louis Braille (1809–1852). Blinded at the age of three in an accident, Braille entered the Institution Nationale des Jeunes Aveugles (National Institute for Blind Children) in Paris in 1819. While there he became interested in a writing system developed by Charles Barbier in which messages were encoded in dots embossed on cardboard. Braille worked out an adaptation using a six-dot code and a simple instrument for producing the dots. He published treatises on his system in 1829 and 1837.

\ə\ **abut** \ᵊ\ **kitten** \ər\ **further** \a\ **ash** \ā\ **ace**
\ä\ **mop, mar** \aù\ **out** \ch\ **chin** \e\ **bet** \ē\ **easy**
\g\ **go** \i\ **hit** \ī\ **ice** \j\ **job** \ŋ\ **sing** \ō\ **go**
\ȯ\ **law** \ȯi\ **boy** \th\ **thin** \th̶\ **the** \ü\ **loot** \ù\ **foot**
\y\ **yet** \zh\ **vision** *see also* Guide to Pronunciation

archaic **:** IMPETUOUS, HOTHEADED ⟨and in this *brainish* apprehension kills the unseen good old man —Shakespeare⟩

brain·less \'brān-ləs\ *adjective* (15th century) **:** devoid of intelligence **:** STUPID
— **brain·less·ly** *adverb*
— **brain·less·ness** *noun*

brain·pan \'brān-,pan\ *noun* (14th century) **:** BRAINCASE

brain–pick·ing \-,pi-kiŋ\ *noun* (1954) **:** the act of gathering information from another's mind
— **brain–pick·er** \-kər\ *noun*

brain·pow·er \-,paů(-ə)r\ *noun* (1878)
1 : intellectual ability
2 : people with developed intellectual ability

brain·sick \-,sik\ *adjective* (15th century)
1 : mentally disordered
2 : arising from mental disorder ⟨a *brainsick* frenzy⟩
— **brain·sick·ly** *adverb*

brain stem *noun* (1879)
: the part of the brain composed of the mesencephalon, pons, and medulla oblongata and connecting the spinal cord with the forebrain and cerebrum

brain·storm \-,stȯrm\ *noun* (circa 1894)
1 : a violent transient fit of insanity
2 a : a sudden bright idea **b :** a harebrained idea

brain·storm·ing \-,stȯr-miŋ\ *noun* (circa 1955)
: a group problem-solving technique that involves the spontaneous contribution of ideas from all members of the group
— **brain·storm** *verb*
— **brain·storm·er** *noun*

brains trust *noun* (1934)
chiefly British **:** BRAIN TRUST

brain·teas·er \-,tē-zər\ *noun* (1923)
: something (as a puzzle) that demands mental effort and acuity for its solution

brain trust *noun* (1910)
: a group of official or unofficial advisers concerned especially with planning and strategy
— **brain trust·er** \-,trəs-tər\ *noun*

brain·wash·ing \'brān-,wȯ-shiŋ, -,wä-\ *noun* [translation of Chinese (Beijing) *xǐnǎo*] (1950)
1 : a forcible indoctrination to induce someone to give up basic political, social, or religious beliefs and attitudes and to accept contrasting regimented ideas
2 : persuasion by propaganda or salesmanship
— **brain·wash** *transitive verb*
— **brainwash** *noun*
— **brain·wash·er** *noun*

brain wave *noun* (1890)
1 : BRAINSTORM 2a
2 a : rhythmic fluctuations of voltage between parts of the brain resulting in the flow of an electric current **b :** a current produced by brain waves

brainy \'brā-nē\ *adjective* **brain·i·er; -est** (1874)
: having or showing a well-developed intellect **:** INTELLIGENT
— **brain·i·ness** *noun*

¹braise \'brāz\ *transitive verb* **braised; brais·ing** [French *braiser,* from *braise* live coals, from Old French *breze,* probably of Germanic origin; akin to Swedish *brasa* fire] (1797)
: to cook slowly in fat and little moisture in a closed pot

²braise *noun* (circa 1885)
: an item of braised food

¹brake \'brāk\ *archaic past of* BREAK

²brake *noun* [Middle English, fern, probably back-formation from *braken* bracken] (14th century)
: the common bracken fern (*Pteridium aquilinum*)

³brake *noun* [Middle English, from Middle Low German; akin to Old English *brecan* to break] (15th century)

1 : a toothed instrument or machine for separating out the fiber of flax or hemp by breaking up the woody parts
2 : a machine for bending, flanging, folding, and forming sheet metal

⁴brake *noun* [Middle English *-brake*] (1563)
: rough or marshy land overgrown usually with one kind of plant
— **braky** \'brā-kē\ *adjective*

⁵brake *noun* [perhaps from obsolete *brake* bridle] (circa 1782)
1 : a device for arresting or preventing the motion of a mechanism usually by means of friction
2 : something used to slow down or stop movement or activity ⟨use interest rates as a *brake* on spending⟩
— **brake·less** \'brā-kləs\ *adjective*

⁶brake *verb* **braked; brak·ing** (1868)
transitive verb
: to retard or stop by a brake
intransitive verb
1 : to operate or manage a brake; *especially* **:** to apply the brake on a vehicle
2 : to become checked by a brake

brake·man \'brāk-mən\ *noun* (1833)
1 : a freight or passenger train crew member who inspects the train and assists the conductor
2 : the end man on a bobsled team who operates the brake

bram·ble \'bram-bəl\ *noun* [Middle English *brembel,* from Old English *brēmel;* akin to Old English *brōm* broom] (before 12th century)
: any of a genus (*Rubus*) of usually prickly shrubs of the rose family including the raspberries and blackberries; *broadly* **:** a rough prickly shrub or vine
— **bram·bly** \-b(ə-)lē\ *adjective*

bran \'bran\ *noun* [Middle English, from Middle French] (14th century)
: the edible broken seed coats of cereal grain separated from the flour or meal by sifting or bolting

¹branch \'branch\ *noun, often attributive* [Middle English, from Middle French *branche,* from Late Latin *branca* paw] (14th century)
1 : a natural subdivision of a plant stem; *especially* **:** a secondary shoot or stem (as a bough) arising from a main axis (as of a tree)
2 : something that extends from or enters into a main body or source: as **a** (1) **:** a stream that flows into another usually larger stream **:** TRIBUTARY (2) *Southern & Midland* **:** CREEK 2 **b :** a side road or way **c :** a slender projection (as the tine of an antler) **d :** a distinctive part of a mathematical curve **e :** a part of a computer program executed as a result of a program decision
3 : a part of a complex body: as **a :** a division of a family descending from a particular ancestor **b :** an area of knowledge that may be considered apart from related areas ⟨pathology is a *branch* of medicine⟩ **c** (1) **:** a division of an organization (2) **:** a separate but dependent part of a central organization ⟨the neighborhood *branch* of the city library⟩ **d :** a language group less inclusive than a family ⟨the Germanic *branch* of the Indo-European language family⟩
— **branched** \'brancht\ *adjective*
— **branch·less** \'branch-ləs\ *adjective*
— **branchy** \'bran-chē\ *adjective*

²branch (14th century)
intransitive verb
1 : to put forth branches **:** RAMIFY
2 : to spring out (as from a main stem) **:** DIVERGE
3 : to be an outgrowth — used with *from* ⟨poetry that *branched* from religious prose⟩
4 : to extend activities — usually used with *out* ⟨the business is *branching* out⟩
5 : to follow one of two or more branches (as in a computer program)

transitive verb
1 : to ornament with designs of branches
2 : to divide up **:** SECTION

bran·chi·al \'braŋ-kē-əl\ *adjective* [Greek *branchia* gills] (1801)
: of, relating to, or supplying the gills or associated structures or their embryonic precursors

bran·chio·pod \'braŋ-kē-ə-,päd\ *noun* [ultimately from Greek *branchia* gills + *pod-, pous* foot — more at FOOT] (1836)
: any of a group (Branchiopoda) of small usually freshwater crustaceans (as fairy shrimp or water fleas) with usually many pairs of setae-bearing appendages
— **branchiopod** *adjective*

branch·let \'branch-lət\ *noun* (circa 1731)
: a small usually terminal branch

branch·line \-,līn\ *noun* (1846)
: a secondary line usually of a railroad

branch water *noun* [¹*branch* (creek)] (1835)
: plain water ⟨bourbon and *branch water*⟩

¹brand \'brand\ *noun* [Middle English, torch, sword, from Old English; akin to Old English *bærnan* to burn] (before 12th century)
1 a : a charred piece of wood **b :** FIREBRAND 1 **c :** something (as lightning) that resembles a firebrand
2 : SWORD
3 a (1) **:** a mark made by burning with a hot iron to attest manufacture or quality or to designate ownership (2) **:** a printed mark made for similar purposes **:** TRADEMARK **b** (1) **:** a mark put on criminals with a hot iron (2) **:** a mark of disgrace **:** STIGMA ⟨the *brand* of poverty⟩
4 a : a class of goods identified by name as the product of a single firm or manufacturer **:** MAKE **b :** a characteristic or distinctive kind ⟨a lively *brand* of theater⟩
5 : a tool used to produce a brand

²brand *transitive verb* (15th century)
1 : to mark with a brand
2 : to mark with disapproval **:** STIGMATIZE
3 : to impress indelibly ⟨*brand* the lesson on his mind⟩
— **brand·er** *noun*

brand·ed \'bran-dəd\ *adjective* (1897)
: having a brand name ⟨*branded* products⟩

¹bran·dish \'bran-dish\ *transitive verb* [Middle English *braundisshen,* from Middle French *brandiss-,* stem of *brandir,* from Old French, from *brand* sword, of Germanic origin; akin to Old English *brand*] (14th century)
1 : to shake or wave (as a weapon) menacingly
2 : to exhibit in an ostentatious or aggressive manner
synonym see SWING

²brandish *noun* (1599)
: an act or instance of brandishing

brand–name \'bran(d)-'nām\ *adjective* (1949)
1 : of or relating to a trade name ⟨*brand-name* products⟩
2 : having a reputation and a loyal following ⟨*brand-name* authors⟩

brand name *noun* (1922)
: TRADE NAME 1b

brand–new \-'nü, -'nyü\ *adjective* [¹*brand*] (circa 1570)
: conspicuously new and unused; *also* **:** recently introduced ⟨a *brand-new* executive officer⟩

¹bran·dy \'bran-dē\ *noun, plural* **brandies** [short for *brandywine,* from Dutch *brandewijn,* from Middle Dutch *brantwijn,* from *brant* distilled + *wijn* wine] (1657)
: an alcoholic beverage distilled from wine or fermented fruit juice

²brandy *transitive verb* **bran·died; bran·dy·ing** (circa 1848)
: to flavor, blend, or preserve with brandy

Bran·gus \'braŋ-gəs\ *trademark*
— used for polled solid black beef cattle of a breed developed from a Brahman-Angus cross

bran·ni·gan \'bra-ni-gən\ *noun* [probably from the name *Brannigan*] (1927)
1 : a drinking spree
2 : SQUABBLE

brant \\'brant\\ *noun, plural* **brant** *or* **brants** [Middle English *brand gos*] (14th century)
: any of several wild geese (especially genus *Branta*); *especially* **:** a small black-necked goose (*Branta bernicla*) about the size of a mallard

¹brash \\'brash\\ *adjective* [origin unknown] (1566)
1 : BRITTLE ⟨*brash* wood⟩
2 a : heedless of the consequences **:** AUDACIOUS ⟨the *brashest* bush pilot of them all⟩ **b :** done in haste without regard for consequences **:** RASH ⟨*brash* acts⟩
3 a : full of fresh raw vitality ⟨a *brash* frontier town⟩ **b :** uninhibitedly energetic or demonstrative **:** BUMPTIOUS ⟨a *brash* comedian⟩
4 a : lacking restraint and discernment **:** TACTLESS ⟨*brash* remarks⟩ **b :** aggressively self-assertive **:** IMPUDENT ⟨*brash* to the point of arrogance⟩
5 : piercingly sharp **:** HARSH ⟨a *brash* squeal of brakes⟩
6 : marked by vivid contrast **:** BOLD ⟨*brash* colors⟩
— **brash·ly** *adverb*
— **brash·ness** *noun*

²brash *noun* [obsolete English *brash* to breach a wall] (1787)
: a mass of fragments (as of ice)

brass \\'bras\\ *noun* [Middle English *bras*, from Old English *bræs*; akin to Middle Low German *bras* metal] (before 12th century)
1 : an alloy consisting essentially of copper and zinc in variable proportions
2 a : the brass instruments of an orchestra or band — often used in plural **b :** a usually brass memorial tablet **c :** bright metal fittings, utensils, or ornaments **d :** empty cartridge shells
3 : brazen self-assurance **:** GALL
4 *singular or plural in construction* **a :** high-ranking members of the military **b :** persons in high positions (as in a business or the government)
— **brass** *adjective*

bras·sard \\brə-'särd, 'bra-,\\ *noun* [French *brassard*, from Middle French *brassal*, from Old Italian *bracciale*, from *braccio* arm, from Latin *bracchium* — more at BRACE] (1830)
1 : armor for protecting the arm — see ARMOR illustration
2 : a cloth band worn around the upper arm usually bearing an identifying mark

brass band *noun* (1834)
: a band consisting chiefly or solely of brass and percussion instruments

brass-bound \\'bras-,baund, -'baund\\ *adjective* (1867)
1 : having trim made of brass or a metal resembling brass
2 a (1) **:** tradition-bound and opinionated (2) **:** making no concessions **:** INFLEXIBLE **b :** BRAZEN, PRESUMPTUOUS

brass collar Democrat *noun* (1951)
: a conservative Democrat especially in the south who votes the straight Democratic ticket

bras·se·rie \\,bras-'rē, ,bra-sə-\\ *noun* [French, literally, brewery, from Middle French *brasser* to brew, from Old French *bracier*, from (assumed) Vulgar Latin *braciare*, of Celtic origin; akin to Welsh *brag* malt] (1864)
: an informal usually French restaurant serving simple hearty food

brass hat *noun* [from the gold braid worn on the cap] (1893)
: a member of the brass

bras·si·ca \\'bra-si-kə\\ *noun* [New Latin, genus name, from Latin, cabbage] (1832)
: any of a large genus (*Brassica*) of Old World temperate zone herbs (as cabbages) of the mustard family with beaked cylindrical pods

bras·siere \\brə-'zir *also* ,bra-sē-'er\\ *noun* [obsolete French *brassière* bodice, from Old French *braciere* arm protector, from *bras* arm — more at BRACELET] (1911)
: a woman's undergarment to cover and support the breasts

brass instrument *noun* (1854)
: any of a group of wind instruments (as a French horn, trombone, trumpet, or tuba) that is usually characterized by a long cylindrical or conical metal tube commonly curved two or more times and ending in a flared bell, that produces tones by the vibrations of the player's lips against a usually cup-shaped mouthpiece, and that usually has valves or a slide by which the player may produce all the tones within the instrument's range

brass knuckles *noun plural but singular or plural in construction* (1855)
: KNUCKLE 4

brass ring *noun* (1950)
: a rich opportunity **:** PRIZE

brass tacks *noun plural* (1897)
: details of immediate practical importance — usually used in the phrase *get down to brass tacks*

brassy \\'bra-sē\\ *adjective* **brass·i·er; -est** (1576)
1 a : being shamelessly bold **b :** OBSTREPEROUS
2 : resembling brass especially in color
3 : resembling the sound of a brass instrument
— **brass·i·ly** \\'bra-sə-lē\\ *adverb*
— **brass·i·ness** \\'bra-sē-nəs\\ *noun*

brat \\'brat\\ *noun* [perhaps from English dialect *brat* (coarse garment)] (circa 1505)
1 a : CHILD; *specifically* **:** an ill-mannered annoying child **b :** an ill-mannered immature person
2 : the son or daughter of a career military person
— **brat·ti·ness** \\'bra-tē-nəs\\ *noun*
— **brat·tish** \\'bra-tish\\ *adjective*
— **brat·ty** \\-tē\\ *adjective*

brat·tice \\'bra-təs, 'bra-tish\\ *noun* [Middle English *bretais* parapet, from Old French *bretesche*, from Medieval Latin *breteschia*] (circa 1846)
: an often temporary partition of planks or cloth used especially to control mine ventilation
— **brattice** *transitive verb*

¹brat·tle \\'bra-tᵊl\\ *noun* [probably imitative] (circa 1500)
chiefly Scottish **:** CLATTER, SCAMPER

²brattle *intransitive verb* **brat·tled; brat·tling** (1513)
chiefly Scottish **:** to make a clattering or rattling sound

brat·wurst \\'brät-,)wərst *also* 'brat- *also* -,vu̇(r)st; *sometimes* -,vu̇sht\\ *noun* [German, from Old High German *brātwurst*, from *brāt* meat without waste + *wurst* sausage] (circa 1888)
: fresh pork sausage for frying

braun·schweig·er \\'braun-,shwī-gər, -,shvī- *also* 'brän-\\ *noun* [German *Braunschweiger* (*Wurst*), literally, Brunswick sausage] (1934)
: smoked liverwurst

bra·va \\'brä-(,)vä, brä-'vä\\ *noun* [Italian, feminine of *bravo*] (1803)
: BRAVO — used interjectionally in applauding a woman

bra·va·do \\brə-'vä-(,)dō\\ *noun, plural* **-does** *or* **-dos** [Middle French *bravade* & Old Spanish *bravata*, from Old Italian *bravata*, from *bravare* to challenge, show off, from *bravo*] (circa 1580)
1 a : blustering swaggering conduct **b :** a pretense of bravery
2 : the quality or state of being foolhardy

¹brave \\'brāv\\ *adjective* **brav·er; brav·est** [Middle French, from Old Italian & Old Spanish *bravo* courageous, wild, probably from Latin *barbarus* barbarous] (15th century)
1 : having courage **:** DAUNTLESS
2 : making a fine show **:** COLORFUL ⟨*brave* banners flying in the wind⟩
3 : EXCELLENT, SPLENDID ⟨the *brave* fire I soon had going —J. F. Dobie⟩

— **brave·ly** *adverb*

²brave *verb* **braved; brav·ing** (1546)
transitive verb
1 : to face or endure with courage
2 *obsolete* **:** to make showy
intransitive verb
archaic **:** to make a brave show
— **brav·er** *noun*

³brave *noun* (1590)
1 *archaic* **:** BRAVADO
2 : one who is brave; *specifically* **:** an American Indian warrior
3 *archaic* **:** BULLY, ASSASSIN

brave new world *noun* [from the dystopian novel *Brave New World* (1932) by Aldous Huxley] (1933)
: a future world, situation, or development; *also* **:** a recent development or recently changed situation

brav·ery \\'brāv-rē, 'brā-və-\\ *noun, plural* **-er·ies** (1548)
1 : the quality or state of being brave **:** COURAGE
2 a : fine clothes **b :** showy display

¹bra·vo \\'brä-(,)vō\\ *noun, plural* **bravos** *or* **bravoes** [Italian, from *bravo* brave] (1597)
: VILLAIN, DESPERADO; *especially* **:** a hired assassin

²bra·vo \\'brä-(,)vō, brä-'vō\\ *noun, plural* **bra·vos** (1761)
: a shout of approval — often used interjectionally in applauding a performance

³bra·vo *see* ²\\ *transitive verb* **bra·voed; bra·vo·ing** (1831)
: to applaud by shouts of *bravo*

Bra·vo \\'brä-(,)vō\\ (1952)
— a communications code word for the letter *b*

¹bra·vu·ra \\brə-'vyu̇r-ə, brä-, -'vu̇r-\\ *noun* [Italian, literally, bravery, from *bravare*] (1757)
1 : a musical passage requiring exceptional agility and technical skill in execution
2 : a florid brilliant style
3 : a show of daring or brilliance

²bravura *adjective* (1920)
1 : marked by an ostentatious display of skill
2 : ORNATE, SHOWY

braw \\'bró, 'brä\\ *adjective* [modification of Middle French *brave*] (circa 1565)
1 *chiefly Scottish* **:** GOOD, FINE
2 *chiefly Scottish* **:** well dressed

¹brawl \\'bról\\ *intransitive verb* [Middle English] (14th century)
1 : to quarrel or fight noisily **:** WRANGLE
2 : to make a loud confused noise
— **brawl·er** *noun*

²brawl *noun* (15th century)
1 : a noisy quarrel or fight
2 : a loud tumultuous noise

brawly \\'bró-lē\\ *adjective* **brawl·i·er; -est** (1940)
1 : inclined to brawl
2 : characterized by brawls or brawling

brawn \\'brón\\ *noun* [Middle English, from Middle French *braon* muscle, of Germanic origin; akin to Old English *brǣd* flesh] (13th century)
1 a *British* **:** the flesh of a boar **b :** HEADCHEESE
2 a : full strong muscles **b :** muscular strength

brawny \\'bró-nē\\ *adjective* **brawn·i·er; -est** (1599)
1 : MUSCULAR; *also* **:** STRONG, POWERFUL
2 : being swollen and hard ⟨a *brawny* infected foot⟩
— **brawn·i·ly** \\-nə-lē\\ *adverb*
— **brawn·i·ness** \\-nē-nəs\\ *noun*

\\ə\\ abut \\ᵊ\\ kitten \\ər\\ further \\a\\ ash \\ā\\ ace \\ä\\ mop, mar \\au̇\\ out \\ch\\ chin \\e\\ bet \\ē\\ easy \\g\\ go \\i\\ hit \\ī\\ ice \\j\\ job \\ŋ\\ sing \\ō\\ go \\ó\\ law \\ói\\ boy \\th\\ thin \\t͟h\\ the \\ü\\ loot \\u̇\\ foot \\y\\ yet \\zh\\ vision *see also* Guide to Pronunciation

¹bray \'brā\ *verb* [Middle English, from Middle French *braire* to cry, from (assumed) Vulgar Latin *bragere*, of Celtic origin; akin to Old Irish *braigid* he breaks wind] (14th century) *intransitive verb*
: to utter the characteristic loud harsh cry of a donkey; *also* **:** to utter a sound like a donkey's *transitive verb*
: to utter or play loudly, harshly, or discordantly
— **bray** *noun*

²bray *transitive verb* [Middle English, from Anglo-French *braier*, from Old French *breier*, of Germanic origin; akin to Old High German *brehhan* to break — more at BREAK] (14th century)
1 : to crush or grind fine ⟨*bray* seeds in a mortar⟩
2 : to spread thin ⟨*bray* printing ink⟩
bray·er \'brā-ər\ *noun* (1688)
: a printer's hand inking roller

¹braze \'brāz\ *transitive verb* **brazed; brazing** [irregular from *brass*] (1602)
archaic **:** HARDEN

²braze *transitive verb* **brazed; braz·ing** [French *braser*, from Old French, to burn, from *breze* hot coals — more at BRAISE] (1677)
: to solder with a nonferrous alloy that melts at a lower temperature than that of the metals being joined
— **braz·er** *noun*

¹bra·zen \'brā-z°n\ *adjective* [Middle English *brasen*, from Old English *bræsen*, from *bræs* brass] (before 12th century)
1 : made of brass
2 a : sounding harsh and loud like struck brass
b : of the color of polished brass
3 : marked by contemptuous boldness
— **bra·zen·ly** *adverb*
— **bra·zen·ness** \'brā-z°n-(n)əs\ *noun*

²brazen *transitive verb* **bra·zened; bra·zen·ing** \'brāz-niŋ, 'brā-z°n-iŋ\ (circa 1555)
: to face with defiance or impudence — usually used in the phrase *brazen it out*

bra·zen–faced \'brā-z°n-,fāst\ *adjective* (1571)
: marked by insolence and bold disrespect ⟨*brazen-faced* assertions⟩

¹bra·zier \'brā-zhər\ *noun* [Middle English *brasier*, from *bras* brass] (14th century)
: one that works in brass

²brazier *noun* [French *brasier*, from Old French, fire of hot coals, from *breze*] (circa 1690)
1 : a pan for holding burning coals
2 : a utensil in which food is exposed to heat through a wire grill

Bra·zil nut \brə-'zil-\ *noun* [Brazil, South America] (1830)
: a tall South American tree (*Bertholletia excelsa* of the family Lecythidaceae) that bears large globular capsules each containing several closely packed roughly triangular oily edible nuts; *also* **:** its nut

bra·zil·wood \brə-'zil-,wùd\ *noun* [Spanish *brasil*, from *brasa* live coals (from the wood's color), probably of Germanic origin; akin to Swedish *brasa* fire] (1559)
: the heavy wood of any of various tropical leguminous trees (especially genus *Caesalpinia*) that is used as red and purple dyewood and in cabinetwork

¹breach \'brēch\ *noun* [Middle English *breche*, from Old English *bræc* act of breaking; akin to Old English *brecan* to break] (before 12th century)
1 : infraction or violation of a law, obligation, tie, or standard
2 a : a broken, ruptured, or torn condition or area **b :** a gap (as in a wall) made by battering
3 a : a break in accustomed friendly relations **b :** a temporary gap in continuity **:** HIATUS
4 : a leap especially of a whale out of water

²breach (1547)
transitive verb
1 : to make a breach in
2 : BREAK, VIOLATE ⟨*breach* an agreement⟩
intransitive verb
: to leap out of water ⟨a whale *breaching*⟩

breach of promise (1590)
: violation of a promise especially to marry

¹bread \'bred\ *noun* [Middle English *breed*, from Old English *brēad*; akin to Old High German *brōt* bread, Old English *brēowan* to brew] (before 12th century)
1 : a usually baked and leavened food made of a mixture whose basic constituent is flour or meal
2 : FOOD, SUSTENANCE ⟨our daily *bread*⟩
3 a : LIVELIHOOD ⟨earns his *bread* as a laborer⟩ **b** *slang* **:** MONEY
— **bready** \'bre-dē\ *adjective*
— **bread upon the waters :** resources risked or charitable deeds performed without expectation of return

²bread *transitive verb* (1629)
: to cover with bread crumbs ⟨a *breaded* pork chop⟩

bread–and–butter *adjective* (circa 1837)
1 a : being as basic as the earning of one's livelihood ⟨*bread-and-butter* issues⟩ **b :** that can be depended on ⟨our *bread-and-butter* repertoire⟩
2 : sent or given as thanks for hospitality ⟨a *bread-and-butter* letter⟩

bread and butter *noun* (1732)
: a means of sustenance or livelihood

bread and circuses *noun plural* [translation of Latin *panis et circenses*] (1914)
: a palliative offered especially to avert potential discontent

bread·bas·ket \'bred-,bas-kət\ *noun* (1753)
1 *slang* **:** STOMACH
2 : a major cereal-producing region

¹bread·board \'bred-,bōrd, -,bòrd\ *noun* (1857)
1 : a board on which dough is kneaded or bread cut
2 : a board on which components are mounted for breadboarding

²breadboard *transitive verb* (1956)
: to make an experimental arrangement of (as an electronic circuit or a mechanical system) to test feasibility

bread·fruit \'bred-,früt\ *noun* (1697)
: a round starchy usually seedless fruit that resembles bread in color and texture when baked; *also* **:** a tall tropical evergreen tree (*Artocarpus altilis*) of the mulberry family that bears this fruit

bread·line \-,līn\ *noun* (1900)
: a line of people waiting to receive free food

bread mold *noun* (1914)
: any of various molds found especially on bread; *especially* **:** a rhizopus (*Rhizopus nigricans* synonym *R. stolonifer*)

bread·stuff \-,stəf\ *noun* (1793)
1 : a cereal product (as grain or flour)
2 : BREAD

breadth \'bretth, 'bredth, ÷'breth\ *noun* [obsolete English *brede* breadth (from Middle English, from Old English *brǣdu*, from *brād* broad) + -*th* (as in *length*)] (15th century)
1 : distance from side to side **:** WIDTH
2 : something of full width
3 a : comprehensive quality **:** SCOPE ⟨*breadth* of his learning⟩ **b :** liberality of views or taste ⟨*breadth* of mind⟩
— **breadth·wise** \-,wīz\ *adverb or adjective*

bread·win·ner \'bred-,wi-nər\ *noun* (1818)
1 : a means (as a tool or craft) of livelihood
2 : a member of a family whose wages supply its livelihood
— **bread·win·ning** \-,wi-niŋ\ *noun*

¹break \'brāk\ *verb* **broke** \'brōk\; **bro·ken** \'brō-kən\; **break·ing** [Middle English *breken*, from Old English *brecan*; akin to Old High German *brehhan* to break, Latin *frangere*] (before 12th century)
transitive verb
1 a : to separate into parts with suddenness or violence **:** FRACTURE ⟨*break* an arm⟩ **c :** RUPTURE ⟨*break* the skin⟩ **d :** to cut into and turn over the surface of ⟨*break* the soil⟩ **e :** to render inoperable ⟨*broke* his watch⟩
2 a : VIOLATE, TRANSGRESS ⟨*break* the law⟩ ⟨*break* a promise⟩ **b :** to invalidate (a will) by action at law
3 a *archaic* **:** to force entry into **b :** to burst and force a way through ⟨*break* the sound barrier⟩ ⟨*break* a racial barrier⟩ **c :** to escape by force from ⟨*break* jail⟩ **d :** to make or effect by cutting, forcing, or pressing through ⟨*break* a trail through the woods⟩
4 : to disrupt the order or compactness of ⟨*break* ranks⟩
5 : to make ineffective as a binding force ⟨*break* the spell⟩
6 a : to defeat utterly and end as an effective force **:** DESTROY **b :** to crush the spirit of **c :** to make tractable or submissive: as (1) *past participle often* **broke :** to train (an animal) to adjust to the service or convenience of humans ⟨a halter-*broke* horse⟩ (2) **:** INURE, ACCUSTOM **d :** to exhaust in health, strength, or capacity
7 a : to stop or bring to an end suddenly **:** HALT ⟨*break* a deadlock⟩ **b :** INTERRUPT, SUSPEND ⟨*break* the silence with a cry⟩ **c :** to open and bring about suspension of operation ⟨*break* an electric circuit⟩ **d :** to destroy unity or completeness of ⟨*break* a dining room set by buying a chair⟩ **e :** to change the appearance of uniformity of ⟨a dormer *breaks* the level roof⟩ **f :** to split the surface of ⟨fish *breaking* water⟩ **g :** to cause to discontinue a habit ⟨tried to *break* him of smoking⟩
8 a : to make known **:** TELL ⟨*break* the bad news gently⟩ **b :** to bring to attention or prominence initially ⟨radio stations *breaking* new musicians⟩ ⟨*break* a news story⟩
9 a : to ruin financially **b :** to reduce in rank
10 a : to split into smaller units, parts, or processes **:** DIVIDE **b** (1) **:** to give or get the equivalent of (a bill) in smaller denominations (2) **:** to use as the denomination in paying a bill ⟨didn't want to *break* a $20 bill⟩ — often used with *into, up,* or *down*
11 a : to check the speed, force, or intensity of ⟨the bushes will *break* his fall⟩ ⟨without *breaking* her stride⟩ **b :** to cause failure and discontinuance of (a strike) by measures outside bargaining processes
12 : to cause a sudden significant decrease in the price, value, or volume of ⟨news likely to *break* the market sharply⟩
13 a : EXCEED, SURPASS ⟨*break* the record⟩ **b :** to score less than (a specified total) ⟨golfer trying to *break* 90⟩ **c :** to win against (an opponent's service) in a racket game
14 : to open the action of (a breechloader)
15 a : to find an explanation or solution for **:** SOLVE ⟨the detective will *break* the case⟩ **b :** to discover the essentials of (a code or cipher system)
16 : to demonstrate the falsity of ⟨*break* an alibi⟩
17 : to ruin the prospects of ⟨could make or *break* her career⟩
18 : to produce visibly ⟨barely *breaks* a sweat⟩
intransitive verb
1 a : to escape with sudden forceful effort — often used with *out* ⟨*break* out of jail⟩ **b :** to come into being by or as if by bursting forth ⟨day was *breaking*⟩ **c :** to effect a penetration ⟨*break* through security lines⟩ **d :** to emerge through the surface of the water **e :** to start abruptly ⟨when the storm *broke*⟩ **f :** to become known or published ⟨when the news *broke*⟩ **g :** to make a sudden dash ⟨*break* for cover⟩ **h :** to separate after a clinch in boxing
2 a : to come apart or split into pieces **:** BURST, SHATTER **b :** to open spontaneously or by pressure from within ⟨his boil finally *broke*⟩ **c** *of a wave* **:** to curl over and fall apart in surf or foam

3 : to interrupt one's activity or occupation for a brief period ⟨*break* for lunch⟩
4 : to alter sharply in tone, pitch, or intensity ⟨a voice *breaking* with emotion⟩
5 : to become fair : CLEAR ⟨when the weather *breaks*⟩
6 : to make the opening shot of a game of pool
7 : to end a relationship, connection, or agreement — usually used with *with*
8 : to give way in disorderly retreat
9 a : to swerve suddenly **b :** to curve, drop, or rise sharply ⟨a pitch that *breaks* away from the batter⟩
10 a : to fail in health, strength, vitality, resolve, or control ⟨may *break* under questioning⟩ — often used with *down* **b :** to become inoperative because of damage, wear, or strain
11 : to fail to keep a prescribed gait — used of a horse
12 : to undergo a sudden significant decrease in price, value, or volume ⟨transportation stocks may *break* sharply⟩
13 : HAPPEN, DEVELOP ⟨for the team to succeed, everything has to *break* right⟩
14 : to win against an opponent's service in a racket game
15 a : to divide into classes, categories, or types — usually used with *into* and often with *down* ⟨the topic *breaks* down into three questions⟩ **b :** to fold, bend, lift, or come apart at a seam, groove, or joint **c :** *of cream* : to separate during churning into liquid and fat
— break a leg — used to wish good luck especially to a performer
— break bread : to dine together
— break camp : to pack up gear and leave a camp or campsite
— break cover *also* **break covert :** to start from a covert or lair
— break even : to achieve a balance; *especially* : to operate a business or enterprise without either loss or profit
— break ground 1 : to begin construction — usually used with *for* **2** *or* **break new ground :** to make or show discoveries : PIONEER
— break into 1 : to begin with or as if with a sudden throwing off of restraint ⟨*broke into* tears⟩ ⟨face *breaking into* a smile⟩ ⟨the horse *breaks into* a gallop⟩ **2 :** to make entry or entrance ⟨*broke into* the house⟩ ⟨*break into* show business⟩ **3 :** INTERRUPT ⟨*break into* a TV program with a news flash⟩
— break one's heart : to crush emotionally with sorrow
— break one's wrists : to turn the wrists as part of the swing of a club or bat
— break ranks *also* **break rank :** to differ in opinion or action from one's peers; often used with *with*
— break the back of : to subdue the main force of ⟨*break the back of* inflation⟩
— break the ice 1 : to make a beginning **2 :** to get through the first difficulties in starting a conversation or discussion
— break wind : to expel gas from the intestine
²break *noun* (14th century)
1 a : an act or action of breaking **b :** the opening shot in a game of pool or billiards
2 a : a condition produced by or as if by breaking : GAP ⟨a *break* in the clouds⟩ **b :** a gap in an otherwise continuous electric circuit
3 : the action or act of breaking in, out, or forth ⟨at *break* of day⟩ ⟨a jail *break*⟩
4 : a place or situation at which a break occurs; *especially* : the place at which a word is divided especially at the end of a line of print or writing
5 : an interruption in continuity ⟨a *break* in the weather⟩ as : **a :** a notable change of subject matter, attitude, or treatment **b** (1) : an abrupt, significant, or noteworthy change or interruption in a continuous process, trend, or surface

(2) : a respite from work, school, or duty ⟨coffee *break*⟩ ⟨spring *break*⟩ (3) : a planned interruption in a radio or television program ⟨a *break* for the commercial⟩ **c :** deviation of a pitched baseball from a straight line **d** *mining* : FAULT, DISLOCATION **e :** failure of a horse to maintain the prescribed gait **f :** an abrupt change in musical or vocal pitch or quality **g :** the action or an instance of breaking service in a racket game **h :** a usually solo instrumental passage in jazz, folk, or popular music
6 a : DASH, RUSH ⟨a base runner making a *break* for home⟩ **b :** FAST BREAK
7 : a sudden and abrupt decline of prices or values
8 a : the start of a race **b :** the act of separating after a clinch in boxing
9 a : a stroke of luck and especially of good luck ⟨a bad *break*⟩ ⟨got the *breaks*⟩ **b :** a favorable or opportune situation : CHANCE ⟨waiting for a big *break* in show business⟩ **c :** favorable consideration or treatment ⟨a tax *break*⟩ ⟨a *break* on the price⟩
10 a : a rupture in previously agreeable relations ⟨a *break* between the two countries⟩ **b :** an abrupt split or difference with something previously adhered to or followed ⟨a sharp *break* with tradition⟩
11 : BREAKDOWN 1c ⟨suffered a mental *break*⟩
break·able \'brā-kə-bəl\ *adjective* (1570)
: capable of being broken
— breakable *noun*
break·age \'brā-kij\ *noun* (1813)
1 a : the action or an instance of breaking **b :** a quantity broken
2 : loss due to things broken
¹break·away \'brā-kə-ˌwā\ *noun* (1881)
1 a : one that breaks away **b :** a departure from or rejection of (as a group or tradition)
2 a : a play (as in hockey) in which an offensive player breaks free of the defenders and rushes toward the goal **b :** a sudden acceleration by one or more bicyclists pulling away from the pack in a race
3 : an object made to shatter or collapse under pressure or impact
²breakaway *adjective* (1927)
1 : favoring independence from an affiliation : SECEDING ⟨a *breakaway* faction formed a new party⟩
2 : made to break, shatter, or bend easily ⟨*breakaway* road signs for highway safety⟩
break away *intransitive verb* (1535)
1 : to detach oneself especially from a group : get away
2 : to depart from former or accustomed ways
3 : to pull away with a burst of speed
break·bone fever \'brāk-ˌbōn-\ *noun* (circa 1860)
: DENGUE
break dancing *noun* [perhaps from ²*break* (solo passage)] (1983)
: dancing in which solo dancers perform acrobatics that involve touching various parts of the body (as the back or head) to the ground
— break-dance \'brāk-ˌdan(t)s\ *verb*
— break-danc·er \-ˌdan(t)-sər\ *noun*
break·down \'brāk-ˌdaůn\ *noun* (1832)
1 : the action or result of breaking down: as **a :** a failure to function : failure to progress or have effect : DISINTEGRATION ⟨a *breakdown* of negotiations⟩ **c :** a physical, mental, or nervous collapse **d :** the process of decomposing **e :** division into categories : CLASSIFICATION; *also* : an account analyzed into categories
2 : a fast shuffling dance; *also* : music for such a dance
break down (14th century)
transitive verb
1 a : to cause to fall or collapse by breaking or shattering **b :** to make ineffective ⟨*break down* legal barriers⟩
2 a : to divide into parts or categories **b :** to separate (as a chemical compound) into sim-

pler substances : DECOMPOSE **c :** to take apart especially for storage or shipment and for later reassembling
intransitive verb
1 a : to stop functioning because of breakage or wear **b :** to become inoperative or ineffective : FAIL ⟨negotiations *broke down*⟩
2 *of horses* : to tear or strain the tendons of the lower leg
3 a : to be susceptible to or undergo analysis or subdivision ⟨the statistics *break down* like this⟩ **b :** to undergo decomposition
synonym see ANALYZE
¹break·er \'brā-kər\ *noun* (12th century)
1 a : one that breaks **b :** a machine or plant for breaking rocks or coal **c** *chiefly British* : one who breaks up ships or cars for salvage
2 : a wave breaking into foam (as against the shore)
3 : a strip of fabric under the tread of a tire for extra protection of the carcass
²brea·ker \'brā-kər\ *noun* [by folk etymology from Spanish *barrica*] (1833)
: a small water cask
break·even \'brāk-ˌē-vən\ *noun* (1958)
: the point at which cost and income are equal and there is neither profit nor loss; *also* : a financial result reflecting neither profit nor loss
break–even \'brāk-ˌē-vən\ *adjective* (1931)
: having equal cost and income
break·fast \'brek-fəst\ *noun* (15th century)
1 : the first meal of the day especially when taken in the morning
2 : the food prepared for a breakfast ⟨eat your *breakfast*⟩
— breakfast *verb*
— break·fast·er *noun*
break·front \'brāk-ˌfrənt\ *noun* (1928)
: a large cabinet or bookcase whose center section projects beyond the flanking end sections
break–in \'brā-ˌkin\ *noun* (1856)
1 : the act or action of breaking in ⟨a rash of *break-ins* at the new apartment house⟩
2 : a performance or a series of performances serving as a trial run
breakfront
3 : an initial period of operation during which working parts begin to function efficiently
break in (circa 1552)
intransitive verb
1 : to enter a house or building by force
2 a : INTRUDE ⟨*break in* upon his privacy⟩ **b :** to interrupt a conversation
3 : to start in an activity or enterprise ⟨*breaking in* as a cub reporter⟩
transitive verb
1 : to accustom to a certain activity or occurrence ⟨*break in* the new clerk⟩
2 : to overcome the stiffness or newness of
breaking and entering *noun* (1797)
: the act of forcing or otherwise gaining unlawful passage into and entering another's building
breaking point *noun* (1908)
1 : the point at which a person gives way under stress
2 : the point at which a situation becomes critical
break·neck \'brāk-ˌnek\ *adjective* (1562)
: very fast or dangerous ⟨*breakneck* speed⟩
break off (14th century)

\ə\ abut \ᵊ\ kitten \ər\ further \a\ ash \ā\ ace
\ä\ mop, mar \aů\ out \ch\ chin \e\ bet \ē\ easy
\g\ go \i\ hit \ī\ ice \j\ job \ŋ\ sing \ō\ go
\ȯ\ law \ȯi\ boy \th\ thin \t̷h\ the \ü\ loot \ů\ foot
\y\ yet \zh\ vision *see also* Guide to Pronunciation

intransitive verb
: to stop abruptly ⟨*break off* in the middle of a sentence⟩
transitive verb
: DISCONTINUE ⟨*break off* diplomatic relations⟩
break·out \'brā-ˌkau̇t\ *noun* (1820)
: a violent or forceful break from a restraining condition or situation; *especially* **:** a military attack to break from encirclement
break out (before 12th century)
intransitive verb
1 : to develop or emerge with suddenness or force ⟨fire *broke out*⟩ ⟨a riot *broke out*⟩
2 a : to become covered ⟨*break out* in a sweat⟩ **b :** to become affected with a skin eruption
3 : to make a break from a restraining condition or situation ⟨*broke out* of a slump⟩
transitive verb
1 a : to make ready for action or use ⟨*break out* the tents and make camp⟩ **b :** to produce for consumption ⟨*break out* a bottle⟩
2 : to display flying and unfurled
3 : to separate from a mass of data ⟨*break out* newsstand sales⟩
break·through \'brāk-ˌthrü\ *noun, often attributive* (1918)
1 : an offensive thrust that penetrates and carries beyond a defensive line in warfare
2 : an act or instance of breaking through an obstruction
3 a : a sudden advance especially in knowledge or technique ⟨a medical *breakthrough*⟩ **b :** a person's first notable success
break through *intransitive verb* (1955)
: to make a breakthrough
break·up \'brā-ˌkəp\ *noun* (1794)
1 : an act or instance of breaking up
2 : the breaking, melting, and loosening of ice in the spring
break up (15th century)
intransitive verb
1 a : to cease to exist as a unified whole **:** DISPERSE ⟨their partnership *broke up*⟩ **b :** to end a romance
2 : to lose morale, composure, or resolution; *especially* **:** to become abandoned to laughter ⟨*breaks up* completely, laughing himself into a coughing fit —Gene Williams⟩
transitive verb
1 : to break into pieces
2 : to bring to an end ⟨*broke up* the fight⟩
3 : to do away with **:** DESTROY ⟨*break up* a monopoly⟩
4 : to disrupt the continuity or flow of ⟨*break up* a dull routine⟩
5 : DECOMPOSE ⟨*break up* a chemical⟩
6 : to cause to laugh heartily ⟨that joke *breaks* me up⟩
breakup value *noun* (1902)
: the value especially of shares of stock of a corporation liquidating its assets
break·wa·ter \'brāk-ˌwȯ-tər, -ˌwä-\ *noun* (circa 1769)
: an offshore structure (as a wall) protecting a harbor or beach from the force of waves
¹bream \'brim, 'brēm\ *noun, plural* **bream** *or* **breams** [Middle English *breme*, from Middle French, of Germanic origin; akin to Old High German *brahsima* bream, Middle High German *brehen* to shine] (14th century)
1 : a European freshwater cyprinid fish (*Abramis brama*); *broadly* **:** any of various related fishes
2 a : a porgy or related fish (family Sparidae) **b :** any of various freshwater sunfishes (*Lepomis* and related genera); *especially* **:** BLUEGILL
²bream \'brēm\ *transitive verb* [probably from Dutch *brem* furze] (1626)
: to clean (a ship's bottom) by heating and scraping
¹breast \'brest\ *noun* [Middle English *brest*, from Old English *brēost*; akin to Old High German *brust* breast, Old Irish *brú* belly, Russian *bryukho*] (before 12th century)
1 : either of the pair of mammary glands extending from the front of the chest in pubes-

cent and adult human females and some other mammals; *also* **:** either of the analogous but rudimentary organs of the male chest especially when enlarged
2 a : the fore or ventral part of the body between the neck and the abdomen **b :** the part of an article of clothing covering the breast
3 : the seat of emotion and thought **:** BOSOM
4 a : something (as a front, swelling, or curving part) resembling a breast **b :** FACE 6
— **breast·ed** \'bres-təd\ *adjective*
²breast *transitive verb* (1599)
1 : to contend with resolutely **:** CONFRONT ⟨*breasting* the waves⟩
2 *chiefly British* **:** CLIMB, ASCEND
3 : to thrust the chest against ⟨the sprinter *breasted* the tape⟩
breast–beat·ing \'bres(t)-ˌbē-tiŋ\ *noun* (1940)
: noisy demonstrative protestation (as of grief, anger, or self-recrimination)
breast·bone \'bres(t)-ˌbōn\ *noun* (before 12th century)
: STERNUM
breast drill *noun* (1865)
: a portable drill with a plate that is pressed by the breast in forcing the drill against the work
breast–feed \'brest-ˌfēd\ *transitive verb* (1903)
: to feed (a baby) from a mother's breast rather than from a bottle
breast·plate \'bres(t)-ˌplāt\ *noun* (14th century)
1 : a usually metal plate worn as defensive armor for the breast — see ARMOR illustration
2 : a vestment worn in ancient times by a Jewish high priest and set with 12 gems bearing the names of the tribes of Israel
3 : a piece against which a worker's breast is pressed in operating a tool (as a breast drill)
breast·stroke \'bres(t)-ˌstrōk\ *noun* (1867)
: a swimming stroke executed in a prone position by coordinating a kick in which the legs are brought forward with the knees together and the feet are turned outward and whipped back with a glide and a backward sweeping movement of the arms
— **breast·strok·er** \-ˌstrō-kər\ *noun*
breast·work \'brest-ˌwərk\ *noun* (1642)
: a temporary fortification
breath \'breth\ *noun* [Middle English *breth*, from Old English *brǣth*; akin to Old High German *brādam* breath, and perhaps to Old English *beorma* yeast — more at BARM] (before 12th century)
1 a : air filled with a fragrance or odor **b :** a slight indication **:** SUGGESTION ⟨the faintest *breath* of scandal⟩
2 a : the faculty of breathing ⟨recovering his *breath* after the race⟩ **b :** an act of breathing ⟨fought to the last *breath*⟩ **c :** opportunity or time to breathe **:** RESPITE
3 : a slight breeze
4 a : air inhaled and exhaled in breathing ⟨bad *breath*⟩ **b :** something (as moisture on a cold surface) produced by breath or breathing **c :** INHALATION
5 : a spoken sound **:** UTTERANCE
6 : SPIRIT, ANIMATION
— **in one breath** *or* **in the same breath :** almost simultaneously
— **out of breath :** breathing very rapidly (as from strenuous exercise)
breath·able \'brē-thə-bəl\ *adjective* (circa 1731)
1 : suitable for breathing ⟨*breathable* air⟩
2 : allowing air to pass through **:** POROUS ⟨a *breathable* synthetic fabric⟩
— **breath·abil·i·ty** \ˌbrē-thə-'bi-lə-tē\ *noun*
Breath·a·ly·zer \'bre-thə-ˌlī-zər\ *trademark*
— used for a device that is used to determine the alcohol content of a breath sample
breathe \'brēth\ *verb* **breathed; breath·ing** [Middle English *brethen*, from *breth*] (14th century)

intransitive verb
1 a : to draw air into and expel it from the lungs **:** RESPIRE; *broadly* **:** to take in oxygen and give out carbon dioxide through natural processes **b :** to inhale and exhale freely
2 : LIVE
3 *obsolete* **:** to emit a fragrance or aura **b :** to become perceptible **:** be expressed ⟨a personality that *breathes* and that distinguishes his work —Bennett Schiff⟩
4 : to pause and rest before continuing
5 : to blow softly
6 : to feel free of restraint ⟨needs room to *breathe*⟩
7 *of wine* **:** to develop flavor and bouquet by exposure to air
8 a : to permit passage of air or vapor ⟨a fabric that *breathes*⟩ **b** *of an internal-combustion engine* **:** to use air to support combustion
transitive verb
1 a : to send out by exhaling **b :** to instill by or as if by breathing ⟨*breathe* new life into the movement⟩
2 : to give rest from exertion to
3 : to take in in breathing ⟨*breathe* the scent of pines⟩
4 : to inhale and exhale ⟨*breathe* air⟩
5 a : UTTER, EXPRESS ⟨don't *breathe* a word of it to anyone⟩ **b :** to make manifest **:** EVINCE ⟨the novel *breathes* despair⟩
— **breathe down one's neck 1 :** to threaten especially in attack or pursuit **2 :** to keep one under close or constant surveillance ⟨parents always *breathing down his neck*⟩
— **breathe easily** *or* **breathe freely :** to enjoy relief (as from pressure or danger)
breathed \'bretht\ *adjective* (1555)
1 : having breath especially of a specified kind — usually used in combination ⟨sweet-*breathed*⟩
2 : VOICELESS 2
breath·er \'brē-thər\ *noun* (14th century)
1 : one that breathes
2 : a break in activity for rest or relief
3 : a small vent in an otherwise airtight enclosure
breath·ing \'brē-thiŋ\ *noun* (1746)
: either of the marks ' and ' used in writing Greek to indicate aspiration or its absence
breathing space *noun* (1650)
: some time in which to recover, get organized, or get going — called also *breathing room, breathing spell*
breath·less \'breth-ləs\ *adjective* (14th century)
1 a : not breathing **b :** DEAD
2 a : panting or gasping for breath **b :** leaving one breathless **:** very rapid or strenuous ⟨go at a *breathless* pace⟩ **c :** holding one's breath from emotion ⟨*breathless* in anticipation⟩ **d :** marked by or as if by a holding of one's breath **:** INTENSE, GRIPPING ⟨*breathless* tension⟩
3 : oppressive because of no fresh air or breeze
— **breath·less·ly** *adverb*
— **breath·less·ness** *noun*
breath·tak·ing \'breth-ˌtā-kiŋ\ *adjective* (1880)
1 : making one out of breath
2 a : EXCITING, THRILLING ⟨a *breathtaking* stock car race⟩ **b :** very great **:** ASTONISHING ⟨his *breathtaking* ignorance⟩
— **breath·tak·ing·ly** \-kiŋ-lē\ *adverb*
breathy \'bre-thē\ *adjective* **breath·i·er; -est** (1883)
: characterized or accompanied by or as if by the audible passage of breath
— **breath·i·ly** \-thə-lē\ *adverb*
— **breath·i·ness** \-thē-nəs\ *noun*
brec·cia \'bre-ch(ē-)ə\ *noun* [Italian] (1774)
: a rock consisting of sharp fragments embedded in a fine-grained matrix (as sand or clay)
brec·ci·ate \'bre-chē-ˌāt\ *transitive verb* **-at·ed; -at·ing** (1772)
1 : to form (rock) into breccia
2 : to break (rock) into fragments

— **brec·ci·a·tion** \,bre-chē-'ā-shən\ *noun*
brede \'brēd\ *noun* [variant of *braid*] (1640)
archaic : EMBROIDERY
bred–in–the–bone \'bre-d³n-thə-,bōn\ *adjective* (15th century)
1 : DEEP-ROOTED ⟨*bred-in-the-bone* honesty⟩
2 : INVETERATE ⟨a *bred-in-the-bone* gambler⟩
breech \'brēch\ *noun* [Middle English, breeches, from Old English *brēc*, plural of *brōc* leg covering; akin to Old High German *bruoh* breeches, Latin *brāca* pants] (before 12th century)
1 *plural* \'bri-chəz *also* 'brē-\ **a** : short pants covering the hips and thighs and fitting snugly at the lower edges at or just below the knee **b** : PANTS
2 a : the hind end of the body : BUTTOCKS **b** : BREECH PRESENTATION; *also* : a fetus that is presented breech first
3 : the part of a firearm at the rear of the barrel
word history see SILLY
breech·block \'brēch-,bläk\ *noun* (1881)
: the block in breech-loading firearms that closes the rear of the barrel against the force of the charge and prevents gases from escaping
breech·cloth \'brēch-,klȯth, 'brich-\ *noun* (1793)
: LOINCLOTH
breech·clout \-,klaut\ *noun* (1757)
: LOINCLOTH
breech·es buoy \'brē-chəz- *also* 'bri-\ *noun* (1880)
: a canvas seat in the form of breeches hung from a life buoy running on a hawser and used to haul persons from one ship to another or from ship to shore especially in rescue operations
breech·ing \'brē-chiŋ, 'bri-\ *noun* (circa 1524)
1 : the part of a harness that passes around the rump of a draft animal
2 : the short coarse wool on the rump and hind legs of a sheep or goat; *also* : the hair on the corresponding part of a dog
breech·load·er \'brēch-'lō-dər\ *noun* (1858)
: a firearm that loads at the breech
— **breech–load·ing** \-'lō-diŋ\ *adjective*
breech presentation *noun* (1811)
: presentation of the fetus in which the breech is the first part to appear at the uterine cervix
¹**breed** \'brēd\ *verb* bred \'bred\; **breed·ing** [Middle English *breden*, from Old English *brēdan*; akin to Old English *brōd* brood] (before 12th century)
transitive verb
1 : to produce (offspring) by hatching or gestation
2 a : BEGET 1 **b** : PRODUCE, ENGENDER ⟨despair often *breeds* violence⟩
3 : to propagate (plants or animals) sexually and usually under controlled conditions ⟨*bred* several strains of corn together to produce a superior variety⟩
4 a : BRING UP, NURTURE ⟨born and *bred* in the country⟩ **b** : to inculcate by training ⟨*breed* good manners into one's children⟩
5 a : ⁴MATE 3 **b** : to mate with : INSEMINATE **c** : IMPREGNATE 2
6 : to produce (a fissionable element) by bombarding a nonfissionable element with neutrons from a radioactive element
intransitive verb
1 a : to produce offspring by sexual union **b** : COPULATE, MATE
2 : to propagate animals or plants
²**breed** *noun* (1553)
1 : a group of animals or plants presumably related by descent from common ancestors and visibly similar in most characters; *especially* : such a group differentiated from the wild type under domestication
2 : a number of persons of the same stock
3 : CLASS, KIND ⟨a new *breed* of athlete⟩
breed·er \'brē-dər\ *noun* (1531)

: one that breeds: as **a** : an animal or plant kept for propagation **b** : one engaged in the breeding of a specified organism **c** : a nuclear reactor designed to produce more fissionable material than it uses as fuel — called also *breeder reactor*
breed·ing *noun* (14th century)
1 : the action or process of bearing or generating
2 : ANCESTRY
3 a *archaic* : EDUCATION ⟨she had her *breeding* at my father's charge —Shakespeare⟩ **b** : training in or observance of the proprieties
4 : the sexual propagation of plants or animals
breeding ground *noun* (1856)
1 : the place to which animals go to breed
2 : a place or set of circumstances suitable for or favorable to growth and development ⟨hurricane *breeding grounds*⟩
breeks \'brēks, 'briks\ *noun plural* [Middle English (northern dialect) *breke*, from Old English *brēc*] (14th century)
chiefly Scottish : BREECHES
¹**breeze** \'brēz\ *noun* [probably from Spanish *brisa* northeast wind] (1626)
1 a : a light gentle wind **b** : a wind of from 4 to 31 miles (6 to 50 kilometers) an hour
2 : something easily done : CINCH
— **breeze·less** \-ləs\ *adjective*
— **in a breeze** : EASILY
²**breeze** *intransitive verb* breezed; breez·ing (1907)
1 : to move swiftly and airily ⟨*breezed* past the protesters⟩
2 : to make progress quickly and easily ⟨*breezed* through the exam⟩ ⟨*breezed* to victory⟩
³**breeze** *noun* [probably modification of French *braise* cinders — more at BRAISE] (1726)
: residue from the making of coke or charcoal
breeze·way \'brēz-,wā\ *noun* (1931)
: a roofed often open passage connecting two buildings (as a house and garage) or halves of a building
breezy \'brē-zē\ *adjective* breez·i·er; -est (1718)
1 : swept by breezes
2 a : briskly informal **b** : AIRY, NONCHALANT
— **breez·i·ly** \-zə-lē\ *adverb*
— **breez·i·ness** \-zē-nəs\ *noun*
breg·ma \'breg-mə\ *noun, plural* -ma·ta \-mə-tə\ [New Latin *bregmat-, bregma*, from Late Latin, front part of the head, from Greek; akin to Greek *brechmos* front part of the head — more at BRAIN] (1578)
: the point of junction of the coronal and sagittal sutures of the skull
brems·strah·lung \'brem(p)-,shträ-lən\ *noun* [German, literally, decelerated radiation] (1939)
: the electromagnetic radiation produced by the sudden retardation of a charged particle in an intense electric field (as of an atomic nucleus); *also* : the process that produces such radiation
brent goose \'brent-\ *noun* (1570)
chiefly British : BRANT
breth·ren \'breth-rən\, 'bre-thə-, -thərn\ *plural of* BROTHER (before 12th century)
— used chiefly in formal or solemn address or in referring to the members of a profession, society, or sect
Brethren *noun plural* (1822)
: members of various sects originating chiefly in 18th century German Pietism; *especially* : DUNKERS
Bret·on \'bre-t³n\ *noun* [French, from Medieval Latin *Briton-, Brito*, from Latin, Briton] (1653)
1 : a native or inhabitant of Brittany
2 : the Celtic language of the Breton people
— **Breton** *adjective*
breve \'brēv, 'brev\ *noun* [Latin, neuter of *brevis* brief — more at BRIEF] (15th century)

1 : a note equivalent to two whole notes
2 : a curved mark ˘ used to indicate a short vowel or a short or unstressed syllable
¹**bre·vet** \bri-'vet, *chiefly British* 'bre-vit\ *noun* [Middle English, an official message, from Middle French, from Old French, diminutive of *brief* letter — more at BRIEF] (1689)
: a commission giving a military officer higher nominal rank than that for which pay is received
²**brevet** *transitive verb* **bre·vet·ted** *or* **brev·et·ed; bre·vet·ting** *or* **brev·et·ing** (1824)
: to confer rank upon by brevet
bre·via·ry \'brē-və-rē, -vyə-, -vē-,er-ē *also* 'bre-\ *noun, plural* -ries [Middle English *breviarie*, from Medieval Latin *breviarium*, from Latin, summary, from *brevis*] (15th century)
1 *often capitalized* **a** : a book containing the prayers, hymns, psalms, and readings for the canonical hours **b** : DIVINE OFFICE
2 [Latin *breviarium*] : a brief summary : ABRIDGMENT
brev·i·ty \'bre-və-tē\ *noun, plural* -ties [Latin *brevitas*, from *brevis*] (15th century)
: shortness of duration; *especially* : shortness or conciseness of expression
¹**brew** \'brü\ *verb* [Middle English, from Old English *brēowan*; akin to Latin *fervēre* to boil — more at BARM] (before 12th century)
transitive verb
1 : to prepare (as beer or ale) by steeping, boiling, and fermentation or by infusion and fermentation
2 a : to bring about : FOMENT ⟨*brew* trouble⟩ **b** : CONTRIVE, PLOT
3 : to prepare (as tea) by infusion in hot water
intransitive verb
1 : to brew beer or ale
2 : to be in the process of formation ⟨a storm is *brewing* in the east⟩
— **brew·er** \'brü-ər, 'brù(-ə)r\ *noun*
²**brew** *noun* (circa 1510)
1 a : a brewed beverage (as beer) **b** : a serving of a brewed beverage ⟨quaff a few *brews*⟩ **c** : something produced by or as if by brewing
2 : the process of brewing
brew·age \'brü-ij\ *noun* (1542)
: BREW 1a, 2
brewer's yeast *noun* (1871)
: a yeast used or suitable for use in brewing; *specifically* : the dried pulverized cells of such a yeast (*Saccharomyces cerevisiae*) used especially as a source of B-complex vitamins
brew·ery \'brü-ə-rē, 'brù(-ə)r-ē\ *noun, plural* -er·ies (1658)
: a plant where malt liquors are produced
¹**bri·ar** \'brī(-ə)r\ *variant of* BRIER
²**briar** \'brī(-ə)r\ *noun*
: a tobacco pipe made from the root or stem of a brier
bri·ard \brē-'är(d)\ *noun* [French, from *Brie*, district in France] (circa 1929)
: any of an old French breed of large long-coated sheepdogs
¹**bribe** \'brīb\ *noun* [Middle English, something stolen, from Middle French, bread given to a beggar] (15th century)
1 : money or favor given or promised in order to influence the judgment or conduct of a person in a position of trust
2 : something that serves to induce or influence
²**bribe** *verb* bribed; brib·ing (1528)
transitive verb
: to induce or influence by or as if by bribery
intransitive verb
: to practice bribery
— **brib·able** \'brī-bə-bəl\ *adjective*
— **brib·ee** \,brī-'bē\ *noun*

\ə\ **abut** \³\ **kitten** \ər\ **further** \a\ **ash** \ā\ **ace**
\ä\ **mop, mar** \aù\ **out** \ch\ **chin** \e\ **bet** \ē\ **easy**
\g\ **go** \i\ **hit** \ī\ **ice** \j\ **job** \ŋ\ **sing** \ō\ **go**
\ȯ\ **law** \ȯi\ **boy** \th\ **thin** \th\ **the** \ü\ **loot** \ù\ **foot**
\y\ **yet** \zh\ **vision** *see also* Guide to Pronunciation

— **brib·er** *noun*

brib·ery \'brī-b(ə-)rē\ *noun, plural* **-er·ies** (1549)
: the act or practice of giving or taking a bribe

bric-a-brac \'bri-kə-,brak\ *noun, plural* **bric-a-brac** [French *bric-à-brac*] (1840)
1 : a miscellaneous collection of small articles commonly of ornamental or sentimental value : CURIOS
2 : something suggesting bric-a-brac especially in extraneous decorative quality

¹**brick** \'brik\ *noun, often attributive* [Middle English *bryke*, from Middle French *brique*, from Middle Dutch *bricke*] (15th century)
1 *plural* **bricks** *or* **brick** : a handy-sized unit of building or paving material typically being rectangular and about 2¼ × 3¾ × 8 inches (57 × 95 × 203 millimeters) and of moist clay hardened by heat
2 : a good-hearted person
3 : a rectangular compressed mass (as of ice cream)
4 : a semisoft cheese with numerous small holes, smooth texture, and often mild flavor
5 : GAFFE, BLUNDER — used especially in the phrase *drop a brick*

²**brick** *transitive verb* (1592)
: to close, face, or pave with bricks — usually used with *up, in,* or *over*

brick·bat \'brik-,bat\ *noun* [*brick* + ¹*bat* (lump, fragment)] (circa 1587)
1 : a fragment of a hard material (as a brick); *especially* : one used as a missile
2 : an uncomplimentary remark

brick·field \-,fēld\ *noun* (1801)
British : BRICKYARD

brick·lay·er \'brik-,lā-ər, -,le(-ə)r\ *noun* (15th century)
: a person who lays brick
— **brick·lay·ing** \-,lā-iŋ\ *noun*

brick·le \'bri-kəl\ *adjective* [Middle English *brekyl*] (13th century)
dialect : BRITTLE

brick red *noun* (1810)
: a moderate reddish brown

brick·work \'brik-,wərk\ *noun* (1580)
: work of or with bricks and mortar

brick·yard \-,yärd\ *noun* (1731)
: a place where bricks are made

bri·co·lage \,brē-kō-'läzh, ,bri-\ *noun* [French, from *bricoler* to putter about] (1966)
: construction or something constructed by using whatever comes to hand

¹**brid·al** \'brī-dˀl\ *noun* [Middle English *bridale*, from Old English *brȳdealu*, from *brȳd* + *ealu* ale — more at ALE] (before 12th century)
: a marriage festival or ceremony ◇

²**bridal** *adjective* (13th century)
1 : of or relating to a bride or a wedding : NUPTIAL
2 : intended for a newly married couple ⟨a *bridal* suite⟩

bridal wreath *noun* (circa 1889)
: a spirea (*Spiraea prunifolia*) widely grown for its umbels of small white flowers borne in spring

bride \'brīd\ *noun* [Middle English, from Old English *brȳd*; akin to Old High German *brūt* bride] (before 12th century)
: a woman just married or about to be married

bride·groom \'brīd-,grüm, -,grum\ *noun* [Middle English (Scots) *brydegrome*, by folk etymology from Middle English *bridegome*, from Old English *brȳdguma*, from *brȳd* + *guma* man; akin to Old High German *brūtgomo* bridegroom — more at HOMAGE] (14th century)
: a man just married or about to be married

bride–price \'brīd-,prīs\ *noun* (1876)
: a payment given by or in behalf of a prospective husband to the bride's family in many cultures

brides·maid \'brīdz-,mād\ *noun* (1552)
1 : a woman attendant of a bride
2 : one that finishes just behind the winner

bride·well \'brīd-,wel, -wəl\ *noun* [*Bridewell*, London jail] (circa 1593)
: PRISON

¹**bridge** \'brij\ *noun* [Middle English *brigge*, from Old English *brycg*; akin to Old High German *brucka* bridge, Old Church Slavonic *brŭvŭno* beam] (before 12th century)
1 a : a structure carrying a pathway or roadway over a depression or obstacle **b** : a time, place, or means of connection or transition
2 : something resembling a bridge in form or function: as **a** : the upper bony part of the nose; *also* : the part of a pair of glasses that rests upon it **b** : a piece raising the strings of a musical instrument — see VIOLIN illustration **c** : the forward part of a ship's superstructure from which the ship is navigated **d** : GANTRY 2b **e** : the hand as a rest for a billiards or pool cue; *also* : a device used as a cue rest
3 a : a musical passage linking two sections of a composition **b** : a partial denture anchored to adjacent teeth **c** : a connection (as an atom or group of atoms) that joins two different parts of a molecule (as opposite sides of a ring)
4 : an electrical instrument or network for measuring or comparing resistances, inductances, capacitances, or impedances by comparing the ratio of two opposing voltages to a known ratio
— **bridge·less** \-ləs\ *adjective*

bridge 1a: *1* simple truss, *2* steel arch, *3* continuous truss, *4* cantilever, *5* suspension

²**bridge** *transitive verb* **bridged; bridg·ing** (before 12th century)
1 : to make a bridge over or across ⟨*bridge* the gap⟩; *also* : to join by a bridge
2 : to provide with a bridge
— **bridge·able** \'bri-jə-bəl\ *adjective*

³**bridge** *noun* [alteration of earlier *biritch*, of unknown origin] (circa 1897)
: any of various card games for usually four players in two partnerships that bid for the right to declare a trump suit, seek to win tricks equal to the final bid, and play with the hand of declarer's partner exposed and played by declarer; *especially* : CONTRACT BRIDGE

bridge·head \-,hed\ *noun* (1812)
1 a : a fortification protecting the end of a bridge nearest an enemy **b** : an area around the end of a bridge
2 : an advanced position seized in hostile territory

bridge·work \-,wərk\ *noun* (1883)
: dental bridges

¹**bri·dle** \'brī-dˀl\ *noun* [Middle English *bridel*, from Old English *brīdel*; akin to Old English *bregdan* to move quickly — more at BRAID] (before 12th century)
1 : the headgear with which a horse is governed and which carries a bit and reins
2 : a length of line or cable attached to two parts of something to spread the force of a pull; *especially* : rigging on a kite for attaching line
3 : CURB, RESTRAINT ⟨set a *bridle* on his power⟩

²**bridle** *verb* **bri·dled; bri·dling** \'brīd-liŋ, 'brī-dˀl-iŋ\ (before 12th century)
transitive verb
1 : to put a bridle on

2 : to restrain, check, or control with or as if with a bridle ⟨*bridle* your tongue⟩
intransitive verb
: to show hostility or resentment (as to an affront to one's pride or dignity) especially by drawing back the head and chin
synonym see RESTRAIN

bridle path *noun* (1811)
: a trail suitable for horseback riding

Brie \'brē\ *noun* [French, from *Brie*, district in France] (1876)
: a soft surface-ripened cheese with a whitish rind and a pale yellow interior

¹**brief** \'brēf\ *adjective* [Middle English *bref*, *breve*, from Middle French *brief*, from Latin *brevis*; akin to Old High German *murg* short, Greek *brachys*] (14th century)
1 : short in duration, extent, or length
2 a : CONCISE **b** : CURT, ABRUPT
— **brief·ness** *noun*

²**brief** *noun* [Middle English *bref*, from Middle French, from Medieval Latin *brevis*, from Late Latin, summary, from Latin *brevis*, adjective] (14th century)
1 : an official letter or mandate; *especially* : a papal letter less formal than a bull
2 a : a concise article **b** : SYNOPSIS, SUMMARY **c** : a concise statement of a client's case made out for the instruction of counsel in a trial at law
3 : an outline of an argument; *especially* : a formal outline especially in law that sets forth the main contentions with supporting statements or evidence
4 *plural* : short snug pants or underpants
— **in brief** : in a few words : BRIEFLY

³**brief** *transitive verb* (15th century)
1 : to make an abstract or abridgment of
2 a : to give final precise instructions to **b** : to coach thoroughly in advance **c** : to give essential information to
— **brief·er** *noun*

brief·case \'brēf-,kās\ *noun* (1917)
: a flat flexible case for carrying papers or books

brief·ing \'brē-fiŋ\ *noun* (1910)
: an act or instance of giving precise instructions or essential information

brief·less \'brē-fləs\ *adjective* (1824)
: having no legal clients

brief·ly \'brē-flē\ *adverb* (14th century)
1 a : in a brief way **b** : in brief
2 : for a short time

¹**bri·er** \'brī(-ə)r\ *noun* [Middle English *brere*, from Old English *brēr*] (before 12th century)

: a plant (as of the genera *Rosa, Rubus,* and *Smilax*) with a woody and thorny or prickly stem; *also* : a mass or twig of these
— **bri·ery** \'brī(-ə)r-ē\ *adjective*

²**brier** *noun* [French *bruyère* heath, from Middle French *bruiere,* from (assumed) Vulgar Latin *brucaria,* from Late Latin *brucus* heather, of Celtic origin; akin to Old Irish *froech* heather; akin to Greek *ereikē* heather] (1868)
: a heath (*Erica arborea*) of southern Europe whose roots and knotted stems are used for making briar tobacco pipes

¹**brig** \'brig\ *noun* [short for *brigantine*] (1712)
: a 2-masted square-rigged ship

²**brig** *noun* [probably from ¹*brig*] (1852)
1 : a place (as on a ship) for temporary confinement of offenders in the U.S. Navy
2 : GUARD-HOUSE, PRISON

brig

¹**bri·gade** \bri-'gād\ *noun* [French, from Italian *brigata,* from *brigare*] (1637)
1 a : a large body of troops **b** : a tactical and administrative unit composed of a headquarters, one or more units of infantry or armor, and supporting units
2 : a group of people organized for special activity

²**brigade** *transitive verb* **bri·gad·ed; bri·gad·ing** (1781)
: to form or unite into a brigade

brig·a·dier *noun* \,bri-gə-'dir\ [French, from *brigade*] (1678)
1 : an officer in the British army commanding a brigade and ranking immediately below a major general
2 : BRIGADIER GENERAL

brigadier general *noun* (1690)
: a commissioned officer in the army, air force, or marine corps who ranks above a colonel and whose insignia is one star

Brig·a·doon \,bri-gə-'dün\ *noun* [from *Brigadoon,* village in the musical *Brigadoon* (1947) by A. J. Lerner and F. Loewe] (1968)
: a place that is idyllic, unaffected by time, or remote from reality

brig·and \'bri-gənd\ *noun* [Middle English *brigaunt,* from Middle French *brigand,* from Old Italian *brigante,* from *brigare* to fight, from *briga* strife, of Celtic origin; akin to Old Irish *bríg* strength] (14th century)
: one who lives by plunder usually as a member of a band : BANDIT
— **brig·and·age** \-gən-dij\ *noun*

brig·an·dine \'bri-gən-,dēn\ *noun* [Middle English, from Middle French, from *brigand*] (15th century)
: medieval body armor of scales or plates

brig·an·tine \'bri-gən-,tēn\ *noun* [Middle French *brigantin,* from Old Italian *brigantino,* from *brigante*] (1525)
: a 2-masted sailing ship that is square-rigged except for a fore-and-aft mainsail

¹**bright** \'brīt\ *adjective* [Middle English, from Old English *beorht;* akin to Old High German *beraht* bright, Sanskrit *bhrājate* it shines] (before 12th century)
1 a : radiating or reflecting light : SHINING, SPARKLING ⟨*bright* lights⟩ ⟨*bright* eyes⟩ **b** : SUNNY ⟨a *bright* day⟩; *also* : radiant with happiness ⟨*bright* smiling faces⟩ ⟨*bright* moments⟩
2 : ILLUSTRIOUS, GLORIOUS ⟨*brightest* star of the opera⟩
3 : BEAUTIFUL
4 : of high saturation or brilliance ⟨*bright* colors⟩

5 a : LIVELY, CHEERFUL ⟨be *bright* and jovial among your guests —Shakespeare⟩ **b** : INTELLIGENT, CLEVER ⟨a *bright* idea⟩ ⟨*bright* children⟩
6 : AUSPICIOUS, PROMISING ⟨*bright* prospects for the future⟩ ☆
— **bright** *adverb*
— **bright·ly** *adverb*

²**bright** *noun* (1969)
: a bright color — usually used in plural ⟨rich earth tones and crisp *brights* —Patricia Peterson⟩

bright·en \'brī-t°n\ *verb* **bright·ened; bright·en·ing** \'brīt-niŋ, 'brī-t°n-iŋ\ (14th century)
intransitive verb
: to become bright or brighter
transitive verb
: to make bright or brighter
— **bright·en·er** \'brīt-nər, 'brī-t°n-ər\ *noun*

bright·ness *noun* (before 12th century)
1 a : the quality or state of being bright; *also* : an instance of such a quality or state **b** : LUMINANCE
2 : the attribute of light-source colors by which emitted light is ordered continuously from light to dark in correlation with its intensity — compare HUE 2c, ¹LIGHTNESS 2, SATURATION 4

Bright's disease \'brīts-\ *noun* [Richard *Bright* (died 1858) English physician] (1831)
: any of several kidney diseases marked especially by albumin in the urine

bright·work \'brīt-,wərk\ *noun* (1841)
: polished or plated metalwork

brill \'bril\ *noun, plural* **brill** [Middle English *brell*] (15th century)
: a European flatfish (*Scophthalmus rhombus* synonym *Bothus rhombus* of the family Bothidae); *broadly* : TURBOT

bril·liance \'bril-yən(t)s\ *noun* (1755)
: the quality or state of being brilliant

bril·lian·cy \-yən(t)-sē\ *noun, plural* **-cies** (1747)
1 : BRILLIANCE
2 : an instance of brilliance

¹**bril·liant** \'bril-yənt\ *adjective* [French *brillant,* present participle of *briller* to shine, from Italian *brillare*] (circa 1681)
1 : very bright : GLITTERING ⟨a *brilliant* light⟩
2 a : STRIKING, DISTINCTIVE ⟨a *brilliant* example⟩ **b** : distinguished by unusual mental keenness or alertness
synonym see BRIGHT
— **bril·liant·ly** *adverb*

²**brilliant** *noun* (1690)
: a gem (as a diamond) cut in a particular form with numerous facets so as to have special brilliance

bril·lian·tine \'bril-yən-,tēn\ *noun* (1873)
1 : a light lustrous fabric that is similar to alpaca and is woven usually with a cotton warp and mohair or worsted filling
2 : a preparation for making hair glossy

¹**brim** \'brim\ *noun* [Middle English *brimme;* akin to Middle High German *brem* edge] (13th century)
1 a (1) : an upper or outer margin : VERGE (2) *archaic* : the upper surface of a body of water **b** : the edge or rim of a hollow vessel, a natural depression, or a cavity
2 : the projecting rim of a hat
— **brim·less** \-ləs\ *adjective*

²**brim** *verb* **brimmed; brim·ming** (1611)
transitive verb
: to fill to the brim
intransitive verb
1 : to be or become full often to overflowing
2 : to reach or overflow a brim

brim·ful \'brim-'fúl, -,fúl\ *adjective* (circa 1530)
: full to the brim : ready to overflow

brimmed \'brimd\ *adjective* (1606)
: having a brim of a specified nature — used in combination ⟨a wide-*brimmed* hat⟩

brim·mer \'bri-mər\ *noun* (1663)

: a brimming cup or glass

brim·stone \'brim-,stōn\ *noun* [Middle English *brinston,* probably from *birnen* to burn + *ston* stone] (12th century)
: SULFUR

brind·ed \'brin-dəd\ *adjective* [Middle English *brended*] (15th century)
archaic : BRINDLED

brin·dle \'brin-d°l\ *noun* [*brindle,* adjective] (1696)
1 : a brindled color
2 : a brindled animal

brin·dled \-d°ld\ *or* **brindle** *adjective* [alteration of *brinded*] (1679)
: having obscure dark streaks or flecks on a gray or tawny ground

¹**brine** \'brīn\ *noun* [Middle English, from Old English *brȳne;* akin to Middle Dutch *brīne* brine] (before 12th century)
1 a : water saturated or strongly impregnated with common salt **b** : a strong saline solution (as of calcium chloride)
2 : the water of a sea or salt lake

²**brine** *transitive verb* **brined; brin·ing** (1552)
: to treat (as by steeping) with brine
— **brin·er** *noun*

Bri·nell hardness \brə-'nel-\ *noun* [Johann A. *Brinell* (died 1925) Swedish engineer] (1915)
: the hardness of a metal or alloy measured by hydraulically pressing a hard ball under a standard load into the specimen

Brinell hardness number *noun* (1915)
: a number expressing Brinell hardness and denoting the load applied in testing in kilograms divided by the spherical area of indentation produced in the specimen in square millimeters — called also *Brinell number*

brine shrimp *noun* (1836)
: any of a genus (*Artemia*) of branchiopod crustaceans that can exist in strongly saline environments

bring \'briŋ\ *verb* **brought** \'brót\; **bring·ing** \'briŋ-iŋ\ [Middle English, from Old English *bringan;* akin to Old High German *bringan* to bring, Welsh he*brwng* to accompany] (before 12th century)
transitive verb
1 a : to convey, lead, carry, or cause to come along with one toward the place from which the action is regarded **b** : to cause to be, act, or move in a special way: as (1) : ATTRACT ⟨her screams *brought* the neighbors⟩ (2) : PERSUADE, INDUCE (3) : FORCE, COMPEL (4) : to cause to come into a particular state or condition ⟨*bring* water to a boil⟩ **c** *dialect* : ESCORT, ACCOMPANY
2 : to cause to exist or occur: as **a** : to be the occasion of ⟨winter *brings* snow⟩ **b** : to result in **c** : INSTITUTE ⟨*bring* legal action⟩ **d** : ADDUCE ⟨*bring* an argument⟩
3 : PREFER ⟨*bring* charges⟩
4 : to procure in exchange : sell for

☆ **SYNONYMS**
Bright, brilliant, radiant, luminous, lustrous mean shining or glowing with light. BRIGHT implies emitting or reflecting a high degree of light. BRILLIANT implies intense often sparkling brightness. RADIANT stresses the emission or seeming emission of rays of light. LUMINOUS implies emission of steady, suffused, glowing light by reflection or in surrounding darkness. LUSTROUS stresses an even, rich light from a surface that reflects brightly without sparkling or glittering.

\ə\ abut \ᵊ\ kitten \ər\ further \a\ ash \ā\ ace
\ä\ mop, mar \aú\ out \ch\ chin \e\ bet \ē\ easy
\g\ go \i\ hit \ī\ ice \j\ job \ŋ\ sing \ō\ go
\ȯ\ law \ȯi\ boy \th\ thin \t̲h̲\ the \ü\ loot \ú\ foot
\y\ yet \zh\ vision *see also* Guide to Pronunciation

intransitive verb
chiefly Midland : YIELD, PRODUCE □
— **bring·er** *noun*
— **bring forth 1** : BEAR ⟨*brought forth* fruit⟩
2 : to give birth to : PRODUCE **3** : ADDUCE ⟨*bring forth* persuasive arguments⟩
— **bring forward 1** : to produce to view : INTRODUCE ⟨*brought* new evidence *forward*⟩
2 : to carry (a total) forward
— **bring home** : to make unmistakably clear
— **bring to account 1** : to bring to book
2 : REPRIMAND
— **bring to bear** : to use with effect ⟨*bring* pressure *to bear*⟩
— **bring to book** : to compel to give an account
— **bring to light** : DISCLOSE, REVEAL
— **bring to mind** : RECALL
— **bring to terms** : to compel to agree, assent, or submit
— **bring up the rear** : to come last or behind
bring about *transitive verb* (14th century)
: to cause to take place : EFFECT
bring around *transitive verb* (1862)
1 : to restore to consciousness : REVIVE
2 : PERSUADE
bring·down \'briŋ-ˌdaủn\ *noun* (circa 1944)
: COMEDOWN, LETDOWN
bring down *transitive verb* (14th century)
1 : to cause to fall by or as if by shooting
2 : to carry (a total) forward
— **bring down the house** : to win the enthusiastic approval of the audience
bring in *transitive verb* (14th century)
1 : INCLUDE, INTRODUCE
2 : to produce as profit or return ⟨each sale *brought in* $5⟩
3 : to enable (a base runner) to reach home plate by hitting the ball
4 : to report to a court ⟨the jury *brought in* a verdict⟩
5 a : to cause (as an oil well) to be productive **b** : to win tricks with the cards of (a long suit) in bridge
6 : EARN ⟨*brings in* a good salary⟩
bring off *transitive verb* (1606)
1 : to cause to escape : RESCUE
2 : to carry to a successful conclusion : ACHIEVE, ACCOMPLISH
bring on *transitive verb* (1602)
: to cause to appear or occur
bring out *transitive verb* (1605)
1 a : to make apparent **b** : to effectively develop (as a quality)
2 a : to present to the public **b** : to introduce formally to society
3 : UTTER
bring to *transitive verb* (1753)
1 : to cause (a boat) to lie to or come to a standstill
2 : to restore to consciousness : REVIVE
bring up (14th century)
transitive verb
1 : to bring (a person) to maturity through nurturing care and education
2 : to cause to stop suddenly
3 : to bring to attention : INTRODUCE
4 : VOMIT
intransitive verb
: to stop suddenly
brink \'briŋk\ *noun* [Middle English, of Scandinavian origin; akin to Old Norse *brekka* slope; akin to Middle Dutch *brink* grassland] (13th century)
1 : EDGE; *especially* : the edge at the top of a steep place
2 : a bank especially of a river
3 : the point of onset : VERGE ⟨on the *brink* of war⟩
4 : the threshold of danger
brink·man·ship \'briŋk-mən-ˌship\ *also*
brinks·man·ship \'briŋ(k)s-mən-\ *noun*
(1956)

: the art or practice of pushing a dangerous situation or confrontation to the limit of safety especially to force a desired outcome
word history see GAMESMANSHIP
briny \'brī-nē\ *adjective* **brin·i·er; -est** (1590)
: of, relating to, or resembling brine or the sea : SALTY
— **brin·i·ness** *noun*
brio \'brē-(ˌ)ō\ *noun* [Italian] (1734)
: enthusiastic vigor : VIVACITY, VERVE
bri·oche \brē-'ōsh, -'ȯsh\ *noun* [French, from Middle French dialect, from *brier* to knead, of Germanic origin; akin to Old High German *brehhan* to break — more at BREAK] (1826)
: light slightly sweet bread made with a rich yeast dough
bri·o·lette \ˌbrē-ə-'let\ *noun* [French] (1865)
: an oval or pear-shaped gemstone cut in triangular facets
bri·quette *or* **bri·quet** \bri-'ket\ *noun* [French *briquette,* diminutive of *brique* brick] (1883)
: a compacted often brick-shaped mass of usually fine material ⟨a charcoal *briquette*⟩
— **briquette** *transitive verb*
bri·sance \bri-'zän(t)s, -'zäⁿs\ *noun* [French, from *brisant,* present participle of *briser* to break, from Old French *brisier,* of Celtic origin; akin to Old Irish *brisid* he breaks; perhaps akin to Latin *fricare* to rub — more at FRICTION] (1915)
: the shattering or crushing effect of an explosive
— **bri·sant** \-'zänt, -'zäⁿ\ *adjective*
¹**brisk** \'brisk\ *adjective* [probably modification of Middle French *brusque*] (1560)
1 : keenly alert
2 a : pleasingly tangy ⟨*brisk* tea⟩ **b** : FRESH, INVIGORATING ⟨*brisk* weather⟩
3 : sharp in tone or manner
4 : ENERGETIC, QUICK ⟨a *brisk* pace⟩
— **brisk·ly** *adverb*
— **brisk·ness** *noun*
²**brisk** (1628)
transitive verb
: to make brisk
intransitive verb
: to become brisk — usually used with *up* ⟨business *brisked* up⟩
bris·ket \'bris-kət\ *noun* [Middle English *brusket;* akin to Old English *brēost* breast] (14th century)
: the breast or lower chest of a quadruped animal; *also* : a cut of beef from the brisket — see BEEF illustration
bris·ling \'briz-liŋ, 'bris-\ *noun* [Norwegian *brisling,* from Low German *bretling,* from *bret* broad; akin to Old English *brād* broad] (circa 1868)
: SPRAT 1a
¹**bris·tle** \'bri-səl\ *noun* [Middle English *bristil,* from *brust* bristle, from Old English *byrst;* akin to Old High German *burst* bristle, and perhaps to Latin *fastigium* top] (14th century)
: a short stiff coarse hair or filament
— **bris·tle·like** \'bri-sə(l)-ˌlīk\ *adjective*
²**bristle** *verb* **bris·tled; bris·tling** \'bris-liŋ, 'bri-sə-\ (15th century)
transitive verb
1 : to furnish with bristles
2 : to make bristly : RUFFLE
intransitive verb
1 a : to rise and stand stiffly erect ⟨quills *bristling*⟩ **b** : to raise the bristles (as in anger)
2 : to take on an aggressive attitude or appearance (as in response to a slight)
3 a : to be full of or covered with especially something suggestive of bristles ⟨roofs *bristled* with chimneys⟩ **b** : to be full of something specified ⟨book *bristles* with detail and irony —W. J. Broad⟩
bris·tle·cone pine \'bri-səl-ˌkōn\ *noun* (1894)

: either of two pines (*Pinus longaeva* and *P. aristata*) of the western U.S. that include the oldest living trees

bristlecone pine
bris·tle·tail \-ˌtāl\ *noun* (1706)
: any of an order (Thysanura) of wingless insects with two or three slender caudal bristles
bris·tly \'bris-lē, 'bri-sə-\ *adjective* **bris·tli·er; -est** (circa 1591)
1 a : consisting of or resembling bristles **b** : thickly set with bristles
2 : inclined to or exhibiting aggressiveness or anger
bris·tol board \'bris-t°l-\ *noun* [*Bristol,* England] (1809)
: a paperboard with a smooth surface suitable especially for artwork — called also *bristol*
Bristol fashion *adjective* [*Bristol,* England] (1823)
: being in good order : SHIPSHAPE
brit *also* **britt** \'brit\ *noun* [perhaps from Cornish *brȳthel* mackerel] (1851)
: minute marine animals (as crustaceans and pteropods) on which right whales feed
Brit \'brit\ *noun* (1901)
: BRITON 2
Bri·tan·nia metal \brə-'tan-yə-, -'ta-nē-ə-\ *noun* [*Britannia,* poetic name for Great Britain, from Latin] (1817)
: a silver-white alloy largely of tin, antimony, and copper that is similar to pewter
Bri·tan·nic \bri-'ta-nik\ *adjective* (1641)
: BRITISH
britch·es \'bri-chəz\ *noun plural* [alteration of *breeches*] (circa 1803)
: BREECHES, TROUSERS
Brith Mi·lah \'brit-mē-'lä, 'brith-, 'bris-, -'mē-(ˌ)lä\ *noun* [Late Hebrew *bĕrīth mīlāh* covenant of circumcision] (circa 1902)
: the Jewish rite of circumcision
Brit·i·cism \'bri-tə-ˌsi-zəm\ *noun* [*Brit*ish + *-icism* (as in *gallicism*)] (1868)
: a characteristic feature of British English

□ USAGE
bring Although almost every native speaker of English has mastered the directional complexities of *bring* and *take* before they are old enough for school, a surprisingly large number of usage commentators have felt it necessary to explain the distinction to adults. Their basic points are these: *bring* implies movement toward the speaker or writer, and *take* implies movement away. These are points well made, and they hold for all cases to which they apply. Unfortunately, they do not apply to all cases in the real world. There is a third point to be made that few commentators have noticed: either verb can be used when the point of view is irrelevant. This can be easily shown ⟨copies will be given to pupils to *bring* home to their parents —*N. Y. Times*⟩. The readers of the newspaper will not be misled by either *bring* or *take* in this sentence because they know the writer is neither a school administrator expecting the copies to be taken home nor a parent expecting them to be brought home. When the direction of movement does not matter to the reader or hearer, it need not matter to the writer or speaker. Either verb will do. Such cases are common and have been at least since Shakespeare's time. But *bring* and *take* are also used in a great many idiomatic phrases—*bring to bear, take to task*—in which the verbs are never interchanged.

Brit·ish \'bri-tish\ *noun* [Middle English *Brutische* of Britain, from Old English *Brettisc,* from *Brettas* Britons, of Celtic origin; akin to Welsh *Brython* Briton] (13th century)
1 a : the Celtic language of the ancient Britons **b :** BRITISH ENGLISH
2 *plural in construction* **:** the people of Great Britain or the Commonwealth
— **British** *adjective*
— **Brit·ish·ism** \'bri-ti-,shi-zəm\ *noun*
— **Brit·ish·ness** *noun*
British English *noun* (1869)
: the native language of most inhabitants of England; *especially* **:** English characteristic of England and clearly distinguishable from that used elsewhere (as in the U.S. or Australia)
Brit·ish·er \'bri-ti-shər\ *noun* (1829)
: BRITON 2
British thermal unit *noun* (1876)
: the quantity of heat required to raise the temperature of one pound of water one degree Fahrenheit at a specified temperature (as 39°F)
Brit·on \'bri-t°n\ *noun* [Middle English *Breton,* from Middle French & Latin; Middle French, from Latin *Britton-, Britto,* of Celtic origin; akin to Welsh *Brython*] (13th century)
1 : a member of one of the peoples inhabiting Britain prior to the Anglo-Saxon invasions
2 : a native or subject of Great Britain; *especially* **:** ENGLISHMAN
Brit·ta·ny \'bri-t°n-ē\ *noun, plural* **Brittanys** *also* **Brittanies** [*Brittany,* region in France] (1967)
: any of a breed of medium-sized pointing spaniels of French origin — called also *Brittany spaniel*
¹**brit·tle** \'bri-t°l\ *adjective* **brit·tler** \'brit-lər, 'bri-t°l-ər\; **brit·tlest** \-ləst, -t°l-əst\ [Middle English *britil;* akin to Old English *brēotan* to break, Old Norse *brjōta*] (14th century)
1 a : easily broken, cracked, or snapped ⟨*brittle* clay⟩ ⟨*brittle* glass⟩ **b :** easily disrupted, overthrown, or damaged **:** FRAIL ⟨a *brittle* friendship⟩
2 a : PERISHABLE, MORTAL **b :** TRANSITORY, EVANESCENT
3 : easily hurt or offended **:** SENSITIVE ⟨a *brittle* personality⟩
4 : SHARP ⟨*brittle* staccato of snare drums⟩
5 : lacking warmth, depth, or generosity of spirit **:** COLD ⟨a *brittle* selfish person⟩
6 : affected with or being a form of diabetes characterized by large and unpredictable fluctuations in blood glucose level
synonym see FRAGILE
— **brit·tle·ly** \'bri-t°l-(l)ē\ *adverb*
— **brit·tle·ness** \'bri-t°l-nəs\ *noun*
²**brittle** *noun* (1913)
: a candy made with caramelized sugar and nuts spread in thin sheets ⟨peanut *brittle*⟩
brittle star *noun* (1843)
: any of a subclass or class (Ophiuroidea) of echinoderms that have slender flexible arms distinct from the central disk
Brit·ton·ic \bri-'tä-nik\ *adjective* [Latin *Britton-, Britto* Briton] (1923)
: BRYTHONIC
Brix \'briks\ *adjective* (1897)
: of or relating to a Brix scale
Brix scale *noun* [Adolf F. *Brix* (died 1870) Austrian scientist] (1897)
: a hydrometer scale for sugar solutions so graduated that its readings at a specified temperature represent percentages by weight of sugar in the solution — called also *Brix*
bro \'brō\ *noun, plural* **bros** [by alteration] (1838)
1 : BROTHER 1
2 : SOUL BROTHER — often used informally as a term of address
¹**broach** \'brōch\ *noun* [Middle English *broche,* from Middle French, from (assumed) Vulgar Latin *brocca,* from Latin, feminine of *broccus* projecting] (13th century)
1 : BROOCH

2 : any of various pointed or tapered tools, implements, or parts: as **a :** a spit for roasting meat **b :** a tool for tapping casks **c :** a cutting tool for removing material from metal or plastic to shape an outside surface or a hole
²**broach** (15th century)
transitive verb
1 a : to pierce (as a cask) in order to draw the contents; *also* **:** to open for the first time **b :** to open up or break into (as a mine or stores)
2 : to shape or enlarge (a hole) with a broach
3 a : to make known for the first time **b :** to open up (a subject) for discussion
intransitive verb
: to break the surface from below
synonym see EXPRESS
— **broach·er** *noun*
³**broach** *intransitive verb* [perhaps from ²*broach*] (1705)
: to veer or yaw dangerously so as to lie broadside to the waves — often used with *to*
¹**broad** \'bròd\ *adjective* [Middle English *brood,* from Old English *brād;* akin to Old High German *breit* broad] (before 12th century)
1 a : having ample extent from side to side or between limits ⟨*broad* shoulders⟩ **b :** having a specified extension from side to side ⟨made the path 10 feet *broad*⟩
2 : extending far and wide **:** SPACIOUS ⟨the *broad* plains⟩
3 a : OPEN, FULL ⟨*broad* daylight⟩ **b :** PLAIN, OBVIOUS ⟨a *broad* hint⟩
4 : dialectal especially in pronunciation
5 : marked by lack of restraint, delicacy, or subtlety: **a** *obsolete* **:** OUTSPOKEN **b :** COARSE, RISQUÉ ⟨*broad* humor⟩
6 *of a vowel* **:** OPEN — used specifically of *a* pronounced as in *father*
7 a : LIBERAL, TOLERANT ⟨*broad* views⟩ **b :** widely applicable or applied **:** GENERAL
8 : relating to the main or essential points ⟨*broad* outlines⟩ ☆
— **broad·ly** *adverb*
— **broad·ness** *noun*
²**broad** *adverb* (before 12th century)
: in a broad manner **:** FULLY
³**broad** *noun* (1659)
1 *British* **:** an expansion of a river — often used in plural
2 *slang* **:** WOMAN
broad arrow *noun* (14th century)
1 : an arrow with a flat barbed head
2 *British* **:** a mark shaped like a broad arrow that identifies government property including clothing formerly worn by convicts
broad·ax *or* **broad·axe** \'brò-,daks\ *noun* (before 12th century)
: a large ax with a broad blade
broad·band \'bròd-,band\ *adjective* (1956)
1 : operating at, responsive to, or comprising a wide band of frequencies ⟨a *broadband* radio antenna⟩
2 : of, relating to, or being a communications network in which a frequency range is divided into multiple independent channels for simultaneous transmission of signals (as voice, data, or video)
broad bean *noun* (1783)
: the large flat edible seed of an Old World upright vetch (*Vicia faba*); *also* **:** this plant widely grown for its seeds and as fodder
broad–brush \'bròd-,brəsh\ *adjective* (1967)
: GENERAL, NONSPECIFIC
¹**broad·cast** \'bròd-,kast\ *adjective* (1767)
1 : cast or scattered in all directions
2 : made public by means of radio or television
3 : of or relating to radio or television broadcasting
²**broadcast** *verb* **broadcast** *also* **broadcast·ed; broad·cast·ing** (1813)
transitive verb
1 : to scatter or sow (as seed) broadcast
2 : to make widely known

3 : to transmit or make public by means of radio or television
intransitive verb
1 : to transmit a broadcast
2 : to speak or perform on a broadcast program
— **broad·cast·er** *noun*
³**broadcast** *adverb* (1814)
: to or over a broad area
⁴**broadcast** *noun* (1922)
1 : the act of transmitting sound or images by radio or television
2 : a single radio or television program
Broad Church *adjective* (1853)
: of or relating to a liberal party in the Anglican communion especially in the later 19th century
broad·cloth \'bròd-,klòth\ *noun* (15th century)
1 : a twilled napped woolen or worsted fabric with smooth lustrous face and dense texture
2 : a fabric usually of cotton, silk, or rayon made in plain and rib weaves with soft semigloss finish
broad·en \'brò-d°n\ *verb* **broad·ened; broad·en·ing** \'bròd-niŋ, 'brò-d°n-iŋ\ (1726)
transitive verb
: to make broader
intransitive verb
: to become broad
broad–gauge \'bròd-'gāj\ *or* **broad–gauged** \-'gājd\ *adjective* (1858)
1 : wide in area or scope ⟨a *broad-gauge* effort⟩
2 : comprehensive in outlook, range, or capability ⟨a *broad-gauge* statesman⟩
broad gauge *noun* (1844)
: a railroad gauge wider than standard gauge
broad jump *noun* (1872)
: LONG JUMP
— **broad jumper** *noun*
broad–leaved \-'lēvd\ *or* **broad–leaf** \-'lēf\ *also* **broad–leafed** \-'lēft\ *adjective* (1552)
1 : having broad leaves; *specifically* **:** having leaves that are not needles
2 : composed of broad-leaved plants ⟨*broad-leaved* forests⟩
¹**broad–loom** \-,lüm\ *adjective* (1925)
: woven on a wide loom; *also* **:** so woven in solid color
²**broadloom** *noun* (1926)
: a broadloom carpet
broad–mind·ed \'bròd-'mīn-dəd, -,mīn-\ *adjective* (1882)
1 : tolerant of varied views
2 : inclined to condone minor departures from conventional behavior
— **broad–mind·ed·ly** *adverb*
— **broad–mind·ed·ness** *noun*
broad·scale \-,skā(ə)l\ *adjective* (1939)
: broad in extent, range, or effect
broad·sheet \-,shēt\ *noun* (1705)
1 : BROADSIDE 1

☆ **SYNONYMS**
Broad, wide, deep mean having horizontal extent. BROAD and WIDE apply to a surface measured or viewed from side to side ⟨a *broad* avenue⟩. WIDE is more common when units of measurement are mentioned ⟨rugs eight feet *wide*⟩ or applied to unfilled space between limits ⟨a *wide* doorway⟩. BROAD is preferred when full horizontal extent is considered ⟨*broad* shoulders⟩. DEEP may indicate horizontal extent away from the observer or from a front or peripheral point ⟨a *deep* cupboard⟩ ⟨*deep* woods⟩.

\ə\ abut \°\ kitten \ər\ further \a\ ash \ā\ ace
\ä\ mop, mar \aù\ out \ch\ chin \e\ bet \ē\ easy
\g\ go \i\ hit \ī\ ice \j\ job \ŋ\ sing \ō\ go
\ò\ law \òi\ boy \th\ thin \tẖ\ the \ü\ loot \ù\ foot
\y\ yet \zh\ vision *see also* Guide to Pronunciation

2 *British* **:** a newspaper with full-size pages as distinguished from a tabloid

¹broad·side \-,sīd\ *noun* (1575)
1 a (1) **:** a sizable sheet of paper printed on one side (2) **:** a sheet printed on one or both sides and folded **b :** something (as a ballad) printed on a broadside
2 *archaic* **:** the side of a ship above the waterline
3 a : all the guns on one side of a ship; *also* **:** their simultaneous discharge **b :** a volley of abuse or denunciation
4 : a broad or unbroken surface

²broadside *adjective* (1646)
: directed or placed broadside ⟨a *broadside* attack⟩

³broadside *adverb* (1870)
1 a : with the side forward or toward a given point **:** SIDEWAYS ⟨turned *broadside*⟩ **b :** directly from the side ⟨the car was hit *broadside*⟩
2 : in one volley
3 : at random

⁴broadside *transitive verb* (1981)
: to hit broadside ⟨the car was *broadsided*⟩

broad–spectrum *adjective* (1952)
: effective against a wide range of organisms (as insects or bacteria) ⟨*broad-spectrum* antibiotic⟩

broad·sword \'brod-,sord, -,sord\ *noun* (before 12th century)
: a large heavy sword with a broad blade for cutting rather than thrusting

broad·tail \-,tāl\ *noun* (1892)
1 : KARAKUL 1
2 : the fur or skin of a very young or premature karakul lamb having a flat and wavy appearance resembling moiré silk

Broad·way \'brod-,wā, -'wā\ *noun* [*Broadway*, street in New York City] (1835)
: the New York commercial theater and amusement world; *specifically* **:** playhouses located in the area between the Avenue of the Americas and Ninth Avenue and from W. 41st Street to W. 53d Street
— **Broadway** *adjective*
— **Broad·way·ite** \-,īt\ *noun*

Brob·ding·nag·ian \,bräb-diŋ-'na-gē-ən, -dig-'na-\ *adjective* [*Brobdingnag*, imaginary land of giants in *Gulliver's Travels*, by Jonathan Swift] (1728)
: marked by tremendous size
— **Brobdingnagian** *noun*

bro·cade \brō-'kād\ *noun* [Spanish *brocado*, from Catalan *brocat*, from Italian *broccato*, from *broccare* to spur, brocade, from *brocco* small nail, from Latin *broccus* projecting] (1588)
1 : a rich oriental silk fabric with raised patterns in gold and silver
2 : a fabric characterized by raised designs
— **brocade** *transitive verb*
— **bro·cad·ed** *adjective*

Bro·ca's area \'brō-kəz-\ *noun* [Paul P. *Broca* (died 1880) French surgeon] (circa 1898)
: a brain center associated with the motor control of speech and usually located in the left side of the frontal lobe

broc·a·telle \,brä-kə-'tel\ *noun* [French, from Italian *broccatello*, diminutive of *broccato*] (1669)
: a stiff decorating fabric with patterns in high relief

broc·co·li \'brä-kə-lē, 'brä-klē\ *noun* [Italian, plural of *broccolo* flowering top of a cabbage, diminutive of *brocco* small nail, sprout] (1699)
1 *chiefly British* **:** a large hardy cauliflower
2 a : either of two garden vegetable plants closely related to the cabbage: (1) **:** one with a thick central stem and a compact head of dense usually green florets that is classified with the cauliflower (2) **:** one (*Brassica oleracea italica*) with slender stems and usually green or purple florets not arranged in a central head **b :** the stems and immature florets of broccoli used as food

broccoli rabe \-,räb\ *noun* [perhaps modification of Italian *broccoli di rapa*, literally, flowering tops of the turnip] (1976)
: a garden brassica (*Brassica rapa ruvo*) that is related to the turnip and produces edible leafy branching stalks and compact clusters of yellow florets — called also *broccoli raab* \-,räb, -,rab\, *rapini*

bro·chette \brō-'shet\ *noun* [French, from Old French *brochete*, from *broche* pointed tool — more at BROACH] (15th century)
: SKEWER; *also* **:** food broiled on a skewer

bro·chure \brō-'shur, *British especially* 'brō-,\ *noun* [French, from *brocher* to sew, from Middle French, to prick, from Old French *brochier*, from *broche*] (1748)
: PAMPHLET, BOOKLET; *especially* **:** one containing descriptive or advertising material

brock \'bräk\ *noun* [Middle English, from Old English *broc*, of Celtic origin; akin to Welsh *broch* badger] (before 12th century)
British **:** BADGER

brock·age \'brä-kij\ *noun* [English dialect *brock* rubbish + English -*age*] (1879)
: an imperfectly minted coin

brock·et \'brä-kət\ *noun* [Middle English *broket*, from Old North French *broquard*; akin to Old French *broche* tine of an antler, pointed tool — more at BROACH] (1837)
: any of several small deer (genus *Mazama*) of Central and South America with unbranched antlers

bro·gan \'brō-gən, -,gan; brō-'gan\ *noun* [Irish *brógán*, diminutive of *bróg*] (1835)
: a heavy shoe; *especially* **:** a coarse work shoe reaching to the ankle

¹brogue \'brōg\ *noun* [Irish *bróg* & Scottish Gaelic *bròg*, from Middle Irish *bróc*, probably from Old Norse *brók* leg covering; akin to Old English *brōc* leg covering — more at BREECH] (1586)
1 : a stout coarse shoe worn formerly in Ireland and the Scottish Highlands
2 : a heavy shoe often with a hobnailed sole **:** BROGAN
3 : a stout oxford shoe with perforations and usually a wing tip

²brogue *noun* [Irish *barróg* accent, speech impediment, literally, wrestling hold, tight grip] (1705)
: a dialect or regional pronunciation; *especially* **:** an Irish accent

broi·der \'broi-dər\ *transitive verb* [Middle English *broideren*, modification of Middle French *broder* — more at EMBROIDER] (14th century)
: EMBROIDER
— **broi·dery** \'broi-d(ə-)rē\ *noun*

¹broil \'broi(ə)l\ *verb* [Middle English, from Middle French *bruler* to burn, modification of Latin *ustulare* to singe, from *urere* to burn] (14th century)
transitive verb
: to cook by direct exposure to radiant heat **:** GRILL
intransitive verb
: to be subjected to great or oppressive heat ⟨*broiling* in the sun⟩

²broil *noun* (1583)
: the act or state of broiling

³broil *verb* [Middle English, from Middle French *brouiller* to mix, broil, from Old French *brooilier*, from *breu* broth, of Germanic origin; akin to Old High German *brod* broth — more at BROTH] (15th century)
intransitive verb
: BRAWL
transitive verb
: EMBROIL

⁴broil *noun* (1525)
: a noisy disturbance **:** TUMULT; *especially* **:** BRAWL ⟨a tavern row . . . widens into a general *broil* —J. R. Green⟩

broil·er \'broi-lər\ *noun* (14th century)
1 : one that broils

2 : a bird fit for broiling; *especially* **:** a young chicken of up to 2½ pounds (1.14 kilograms) dressed weight

¹broke \'brōk\ *past of* BREAK

²broke *adjective* [Middle English, alteration of *broken*] (1710)
: PENNILESS

bro·ken \'brō-kən\ *adjective* [Middle English, from Old English *brocen*, from past participle of *brecan* to break] (13th century)
1 : violently separated into parts **:** SHATTERED
2 : damaged or altered by breaking: as **a :** having undergone or been subjected to fracture ⟨a *broken* leg⟩ **b** *of land surfaces* **:** being irregular, interrupted, or full of obstacles **c :** violated by transgression ⟨a *broken* promise⟩ **d :** DISCONTINUOUS, INTERRUPTED **e :** disrupted by change **f** *of a flower* **:** having an irregular, streaked, or blotched pattern especially from virus infection
3 a : made weak or infirm **b :** subdued completely **:** CRUSHED ⟨a *broken* spirit⟩ **c :** BANKRUPT **d :** reduced in rank
4 a : cut off **:** DISCONNECTED **b :** imperfectly spoken or written ⟨*broken* English⟩
5 : not complete or full
6 : disunited by divorce, separation, or desertion of one parent ⟨children from *broken* homes⟩ ⟨a *broken* family⟩
— **bro·ken·ly** *adverb*
— **bro·ken·ness** \-kə(n)-nəs\ *noun*

broken–down *adjective* (1817)
: WORN-OUT, DEBILITATED

bro·ken–field \-,fēld\ *adjective* (1923)
: characterized by quick changes in direction to avoid widely scattered tacklers ⟨a halfback known for *broken-field* running⟩

bro·ken–heart·ed \-'här-təd\ *adjective* (1526)
: overcome by grief or despair

bro·ken–wind·ed \-'win-dəd\ *adjective* (1580)
: affected with or as if with heaves

bro·ker \'brō-kər\ *noun* [Middle English, negotiator, from Anglo-French *brocour*] (14th century)
1 : one who acts as an intermediary: as **a :** an agent who arranges marriages **b :** an agent who negotiates contracts of purchase and sale (as of real estate, commodities, or securities)
2 : POWER BROKER
— **broker** *verb*
— **bro·ker·ing** \'brō-k(ə-)riŋ\ *noun*

bro·ker·age \'brō-k(ə-)rij\ *noun* (15th century)
1 : the business or establishment of a broker
2 : a broker's fee or commission

bro·kered \-kərd\ *adjective* (1967)
: arranged or controlled by power brokers ⟨a *brokered* political convention⟩

bro·king \-kiŋ\ *noun* (1569)
chiefly British **:** the business of a broker **:** BROKERAGE

brol·ly \'brä-lē\ *noun, plural* **brollies** [by shortening & alteration] (circa 1874)
chiefly British **:** UMBRELLA

brom– *or* **bromo–** *combining form* [probably from French *brome*, from Greek *brōmos* bad smell]
: bromine ⟨*bromide*⟩

bro·mate \'brō-,māt\ *noun* (circa 1836)
: a salt of bromic acid

brome·grass \'brōm-,gras\ *noun* [New Latin *Bromus*, from Latin *bromos* oats, from Greek] (circa 1791)
: any of a large genus (*Bromus*) of tall grasses often having drooping spikelets

bro·me·lain \'brō-mə-lən, -,lān\ *also* **bro·me·lin** \'brō-mə-lən, brō-'mē-\ *noun* [*bromelain* by alteration of *bromelin*, from New Latin *Bromelia*] (1894)
: a protease obtained especially from the pineapple

bro·me·li·ad \brō-'mē-lē-,ad\ *noun* [New Latin *Bromelia*, genus of tropical American plants, from Olaf *Bromelius* (died 1705) Swedish botanist] (1866)

: any of a family (Bromeliaceae) of chiefly tropical American usually epiphytic herbaceous plants including the pineapple, Spanish moss, and various ornamentals

bro·mic acid \'brō-mik-\ *noun* (1828)
: an unstable strongly oxidizing acid $HBrO_3$ known only in solution or in the form of its salts

bro·mide \'brō-ˌmīd\ *noun* (1836)
1 : a binary compound of bromine with another element or a radical including some (as potassium bromide) used as sedatives
2 a : a commonplace or tiresome person **:** BORE **b :** a commonplace or hackneyed statement or notion

bro·mid·ic \brō-'mi-dik\ *adjective* (1906)
: lacking in originality **:** TRITE

bro·mi·nate \'brō-mə-ˌnāt\ *transitive verb* **-nat·ed; -nat·ing** (1873)
: to treat or cause to combine with bromine or a compound of bromine
— **bro·mi·na·tion** \ˌbrō-mə-'nā-shən\ *noun*

bro·mine \'brō-ˌmēn\ *noun* [French *brome* bromine + English ²-*ine*] (1827)
: a nonmetallic halogen element that is isolated as a deep red corrosive toxic volatile liquid of disagreeable odor — see ELEMENT table

bro·mo \'brō-(ˌ)mō\ *noun, plural* **bromos** [*brom-*] (1923)
: a dose of a proprietary effervescent headache remedy and antacid

bro·mo·crip·tine \ˌbrō-mō-'krip-ˌtēn, -tən\ *noun* [by shortening & alteration from *bromoergocryptine*, from *brom-* + *ergocryptine*, an ergot derivative, from *ergo-* + Greek *kryptos* hidden — more at CRYPT] (1975)
: a polypeptide ergot derivative $C_{32}H_{40}Br-N_5O_5$ that mimics the activity of dopamine in inhibiting prolactin secretion

bro·mo·ura·cil \ˌbrō-mō-'yùr-ə-ˌsil, -səl\ *noun* (1960)
: a mutagenic uracil derivative $C_4H_3N_2O_2Br$ that is an analogue of thymine and pairs readily with adenine and sometimes with guanine

brom·thy·mol blue \ˌbrōm-'thī-ˌmól-\ *noun* (1920)
: a dye derived from thymol that is an acid-base indicator — called also *bro·mo·thy·mol blue* \ˌbrō-mō-'thī-ˌmól-\

bronc \'bräṅk\ *noun* [short for *bronco*] (1893)
: an unbroken or imperfectly broken range horse of western North America; *broadly* **:** MUSTANG

bronch- *or* **broncho-** *combining form* [Late Latin, from Greek, from *bronchos* windpipe]
: bronchial tube **:** bronchial ⟨*bronch*itis⟩

bronchi- *or* **bronchio-** *combining form* [New Latin, from *bronchia*, plural, branches of the bronchi, from Late Latin, from Greek, diminutive of *bronchos*]
: bronchial tubes ⟨*bronchi*ectasis⟩

bron·chi·al \'bräŋ-kē-əl\ *adjective* (circa 1735)
: of or relating to the bronchi or their ramifications in the lungs
— **bron·chi·al·ly** \-kē-ə-lē\ *adverb*

bronchial asthma *noun* (circa 1881)
: asthma resulting from spasmodic contraction of bronchial muscles

bronchial tube *noun* (1847)
: a primary bronchus or any of its branches

bron·chi·ec·ta·sis \ˌbräŋ-kē-'ek-tə-səs\ *noun* [New Latin, from *bronchi-* + Greek *ektasis* extension — more at ATELECTASIS] (circa 1860)
: a chronic dilatation of bronchi or bronchioles

bron·chi·ole \'bräŋ-kē-ˌōl\ *noun* [New Latin *bronchiolum*, diminutive of *bronchia*] (circa 1860)
: a minute thin-walled branch of a bronchus
— **bron·chi·o·lar** \ˌbräŋ-kē-'ō-lər\ *adjective*

bron·chi·tis \brän-'kī-təs, bräŋ-\ *noun* [New Latin] (1808)
: acute or chronic inflammation of the bronchial tubes; *also* **:** a disease marked by this
— **bron·chit·ic** \-'ki-tik\ *adjective*

bron·cho·di·la·tor \ˌbrän-(ˌ)kō-dī-'lā-tər, -'dī-\ *noun* (1903)
: a drug that relaxes bronchial muscle resulting in expansion of the bronchial air passages
— **bronchodilator** *adjective*

bron·cho·gen·ic \ˌbrän-kə-'je-nik\ *adjective* (1927)
: of, relating to, or arising in or by way of the air passages of the lungs ⟨*bronchogenic* carcinoma⟩

bron·cho·pneu·mo·nia \ˌbrän-(ˌ)kō-nù-'mō-nyə, -nyù-\ *noun* [New Latin] (1858)
: pneumonia involving many relatively small areas of lung tissue

bron·cho·scope \'bräŋ-kə-ˌskōp\ *noun* [International Scientific Vocabulary] (1899)
: a tubular illuminated instrument used for inspecting or passing instruments into the bronchi
— **bron·cho·scop·ic** \ˌbräŋ-kə-'skä-pik\ *adjective*
— **bron·chos·co·pist** \brän-'käs-kə-pist, bräŋ-\ *noun*
— **bron·chos·co·py** \-pē\ *noun*

bron·cho·spasm \'bräŋ-kə-ˌspa-zəm\ *noun* (circa 1901)
: constriction of the air passages of the lung (as in asthma) by spasmodic contraction of the bronchial muscles
— **bron·cho·spas·tic** \ˌbräŋ-kə-'spas-tik\ *adjective*

bron·chus \'bräŋ-kəs\ *noun, plural* **bron·chi** \'bräŋ-ˌkī, -ˌkē\ [New Latin, from Greek *bronchos*] (circa 1706)
: either of the two primary divisions of the trachea that lead respectively into the right and the left lung; *broadly* **:** BRONCHIAL TUBE

bron·co *also* **bron·cho** \'bräŋ-(ˌ)kō\ *noun, plural* **broncos** *also* **bronchos** [Mexican Spanish, from Spanish, literally, rough, wild]
: BRONC

bron·co·bust·er \-ˌbəs-tər\ *noun* (1887)
: one who breaks wild horses to the saddle

bron·to·sau·rus \ˌbrän-tə-'sór-əs\ *also* **bron·to·saur** \'brän-tə-ˌsór\ *noun* [New Latin, from Greek *brontē* thunder + *sauros* lizard; akin to Greek *bremein* to roar] (1905)
: any of a genus (*Apatosaurus* synonym *Brontosaurus*) of large sauropod dinosaurs of the Jurassic — called also *apatosaurus* ◇

Bronx cheer \'bräŋ(k)s-\ *noun* [*Bronx*, borough of New York City] (1929)
: RASPBERRY 2

¹bronze \'bränz\ *transitive verb* **bronzed; bronz·ing** (1645)
: to give the appearance of bronze to ⟨a *bronzed* sculpture⟩; *also* **:** TAN 2
— **bronz·er** *noun*

²bronze *noun, often attributive* [French, from Italian *bronzo*] (1739)
1 a : an alloy of copper and tin and sometimes other elements **b :** any of various copper-base alloys with little or no tin
2 : a sculpture or artifact of bronze
3 : a moderate yellowish brown
— **bronzy** \'brän-zē\ *adjective*

Bronze Age *noun* (1865)
: the period of ancient human culture characterized by the use of bronze that began between 4000 and 3000 B.C. and ended with the advent of the Iron Age

Bronze Star Medal *noun* (1944)
: a U.S. military decoration awarded for heroic or meritorious service not involving aerial flights

bronz·ing *noun* (1868)
: a bronze coloring or discoloration (as of leaves)

brooch \'brōch *also* 'brüch\ *noun* [Middle English *broche* pointed tool, brooch — more at BROACH] (13th century)
: an ornament that is held by a pin or clasp and is worn at or near the neck

¹brood \'brüd\ *noun* [Middle English, from Old English *brōd*; akin to Old English *beorma* yeast — more at BARM] (before 12th century)
1 : the young of an animal or a family of young; *especially* **:** the young (as of a bird or insect) hatched or cared for at one time
2 : a group having a common nature or origin

²brood *adjective* (15th century)
: kept for breeding ⟨a *brood* flock⟩

³brood (15th century)
transitive verb
1 a : to sit on or incubate (eggs) **b :** to produce by or as if by incubation **:** HATCH
2 *of a bird* **:** to cover (young) with the wings
3 : to think anxiously or gloomily about **:** PONDER
intransitive verb
1 a *of a bird* **:** to brood eggs or young **b :** to sit quietly and thoughtfully **:** MEDITATE
2 : HOVER, LOOM
3 a : to dwell gloomily on a subject **:** WORRY **b :** to be in a state of depression
— **brood·ing·ly** \'brü-diŋ-lē\ *adverb*

brood·er \'brü-dər\ *noun* (1599)
1 : one that broods
2 : a heated structure used for raising young fowl

brood·mare \'brüd-ˌmar, -ˌmer\ *noun* (1821)
: a mare kept for breeding

broody \'brü-dē\ *adjective* (1523)
1 : being in a state of readiness to brood eggs that is characterized by cessation of laying and by marked changes in behavior and physiology ⟨a *broody* hen⟩
2 : given or conducive to introspection **:** CONTEMPLATIVE, MOODY
— **brood·i·ness** *noun*

¹brook \'brük\ *noun* [Middle English, from Old English *brōc*; akin to Old High German *bruoh* marshy ground] (before 12th century)
: CREEK 2

²brook *transitive verb* [Middle English *brouken* to use, enjoy, from Old English *brūcan*; akin to Old High German *brūhhan* to use, Latin *frui* to enjoy] (15th century)
: to stand for **:** TOLERATE ⟨he would *brook* no interference with his plans⟩

brook·ie \'brü-kē\ *noun* (1933)
: BROOK TROUT

brook·ite \'brü-ˌkīt\ *noun* [Henry J. *Brooke* (died 1857) English mineralogist] (1825)

◇ WORD HISTORY
brontosaurus Although it has been ousted in scientific nomenclature, the word *brontosaurus* is part of the vocabulary of all dinosaur aficionados. *Brontosaurus*—according to a literal translation of its Greek elements, "thunder lizard"—was the name given by American paleontologist Edward Drinker Cope (1840–97) to a genus of gigantic sauropods whose fossilized bones he had unearthed while affiliated with the U.S. Geological Survey in the 1870s. Unbeknownst to Cope, the same sauropod had already been discovered by his archrival, Othniel Charles Marsh (1831–99), who named the animal *Apatosaurus* "deceptive lizard." Not until the specimens were studied in museums years later was it discovered that *Brontosaurus* and *Apatosaurus* were one and the same. Biologists' rules of classification are strict and clear: the first name given to a new species is the correct one. By the time the mistake was discovered, however, *Brontosaurus* was firmly entrenched not just in scientific literature but in the public imagination as well.

\ə\ abut \ᵊ\ kitten \ər\ further \a\ ash \ā\ ace
\ä\ mop, mar \aù\ out \ch\ chin \e\ bet \ē\ easy
\g\ go \i\ hit \ī\ ice \j\ job \ŋ\ sing \ō\ go
\ó\ law \ói\ boy \th\ thin \th\ the \ü\ loot \ù\ foot
\y\ yet \zh\ vision *see also* Guide to Pronunciation

: titanium dioxide TiO_2 occurring as a mineral in orthorhombic crystals commonly translucent brown or opaque brown to black

brook·let \'brú-klət\ noun (1813)
: a small brook

Brook·lyn·ese \,brú-klə-'nēz, -'nēs\ noun [Brooklyn, borough of New York City] (1939)
: the vernacular speech of greater New York City and environs

brook trout noun (1836)
: the common speckled cold-water char (Salvelinus fontinalis) of North America

¹**broom** \'brüm, 'brum\ noun [Middle English, from Old English brōm; akin to Old High German brāmo bramble] (before 12th century)
1 : any of various leguminous shrubs (especially genera Cytisus and Genista) with long slender branches, small leaves, and usually showy yellow flowers; especially : SCOTCH BROOM
2 : a bundle of firm stiff twigs or fibers bound together on a long handle for sweeping and brushing

²**broom** transitive verb (1838)
1 : to sweep with or as if with a broom
2 : to finish (as a concrete surface) by means of a broom

broom·ball \-,ból\ noun (1933)
: a variation of ice hockey played on ice without skates and with brooms and a soccer ball used instead of sticks and a puck
— **broom·ball·er** \-,bó-lər\ noun

broom·corn \-,kórn\ noun (circa 1782)
: any of several tall cultivated sorghums having stiff-branched panicles used in brooms and brushes

broom·rape \-,rāp\ noun (1578)
: any of a genus (Orobanche of the family Orobanchaceae, the broomrape family) of herbs that have leaves modified to scales and that grow as parasites on the roots of other plants

broom·stick \-,stik\ noun (1683)
: the long thin handle of a broom

brose \'brōz\ noun [perhaps alteration of Scots bruis broth, from Middle English brewes, from Old French broez, nominative singular of broet, diminutive of breu broth — more at BROIL] (1515)
: a chiefly Scottish dish made with a boiling liquid and meal

broth \'bróth\ noun, plural **broths** \'bróths, 'bróthz\ [Middle English, from Old English; akin to Old High German brod broth, Old English brēowan to brew] (before 12th century)
1 : liquid in which meat, fish, cereal grains, or vegetables have been cooked : STOCK
2 : a fluid culture medium

broth·el \'brä-thəl, 'bró- also -thəl\ noun [Middle English, worthless fellow, prostitute, from brothen, past participle of brethen to waste away, go to ruin, from Old English brēothan to waste away; akin to Old English brēotan to break — more at BRITTLE] (circa 1593)
: BORDELLO

broth·er \'brə-thər\ noun, plural **brothers** also **breth·ren** \'breth-rən; 'bre-thə-rən, -thərn\ [Middle English, from Old English brōthor; akin to Old High German bruodor brother, Latin frater, Greek phratēr member of the same clan] (before 12th century)
1 : a male who has the same parents as another or one parent in common with another
2 : one related to another by common ties or interests
3 : a fellow member — used as a title for ministers in some evangelical denominations
4 : one of a type similar to another
5 a : KINSMAN **b** : one who shares with another a common national or racial origin; especially : SOUL BROTHER
6 a capitalized : a member of a congregation of men not in holy orders and usually in hospital or school work **b** : a member of a men's religious order who is not preparing for or is not ready for holy orders ⟨a lay brother⟩

broth·er·hood \'brə-thər-,húd\ noun [Middle English brotherhede, brotherhod, alteration of brotherrede, from Old English brōthorrǣden, from brōthor + rǣden condition — more at KINDRED] (14th century)
1 : the quality or state of being brothers
2 : FELLOWSHIP, ALLIANCE
3 : an association (as a labor union) for a particular purpose
4 : the whole body of persons engaged in a business or profession

broth·er–in–law \'brəth-rən-,ló, 'brə-thə-; 'brə-thərn-\ noun, plural **broth·ers–in–law** \'brə-thər-zən-\ (14th century)
1 : the brother of one's spouse
2 a : the husband of one's sister **b** : the husband of one's spouse's sister

broth·er·ly \'brə-thər-lē\ adjective (before 12th century)
1 : of or relating to brothers
2 : natural or becoming to brothers : AFFECTIONATE ⟨brotherly love⟩
— **broth·er·li·ness** noun
— **brotherly** adverb

brougham \'brü(-ə)m, 'brō(-ə)m\ noun [Henry Peter Brougham, Baron Brougham and Vaux (died 1868) Scottish jurist] (1851)
: a light closed horse-drawn carriage with the driver outside in front

brought past and past participle of BRING

brou·ha·ha \'brü-,hä-,hä, ,brü-,hä-'hä, brü-'hä-,hä\ noun [French] (1890)
: HUBBUB, UPROAR

¹**brow** \'braú\ noun [Middle English, from Old English brū; akin to Old Norse brūn eyebrow, Greek ophrys, Sanskrit bhrū] (before 12th century)
1 a : EYEBROW **b** : FOREHEAD
2 : the projecting upper part or margin of a steep place
3 : EXPRESSION, MIEN

²**brow** noun [perhaps from Danish or Swedish brother bridge; akin to Old English brycg bridge] (1867)
: GANGPLANK

brow·beat \'braú-,bēt\ transitive verb **-beat; -beat·en** \-'bē-t°n\ or **-beat; -beat·ing** (1581)
: to intimidate or disconcert by a stern manner or arrogant speech : BULLY
synonym see INTIMIDATE

browed \'braúd\ adjective (15th century)
: having brows of a specified nature — used in combination ⟨smooth-browed⟩

¹**brown** \'braún\ adjective [Middle English broun, from Old English brūn; akin to Old High German brūn brown, Greek phrynē toad] (before 12th century)
: of the color brown; especially : of dark or tanned complexion

²**brown** noun (13th century)
1 : any of a group of colors between red and yellow in hue, of medium to low lightness, and of moderate to low saturation
2 : a brown-skinned person
— **brown·ish** \'braú-nish\ adjective
— **browny** \-nē\ adjective

³**brown** (14th century)
intransitive verb
: to become brown
transitive verb
: to make brown

brown alga noun (circa 1899)
: any of a division (Phaeophyta) of variable mostly marine algae with chlorophyll masked by brown pigment

brown bagging noun (1959)
1 : the practice of carrying (as to work) one's lunch usually in a brown paper bag
2 : the practice of carrying a bottle of liquor into a restaurant or club where setups are available
— **brown–bag** \'braún-,bag\ verb or adjective
— **brown bagger** noun

brown bear noun (1805)

: any of several bears predominantly brown in color that are sometimes considered a single species (Ursus arctos) including the grizzly bear and that formerly inhabited western North America from the barrens of Alaska to northern Mexico and much of Europe and Asia but are now much restricted in range

brown Bet·ty \-'be-tē\ noun (1864)
: a baked pudding of apples, bread crumbs, and spices

brown bread \-,bred\ noun (14th century)
1 : bread made of whole wheat flour
2 : a dark brown steamed bread made usually of cornmeal, white or whole wheat flours, molasses, soda, and milk or water

brown coal noun (circa 1828)
: LIGNITE

brown dwarf noun (1978)
: a celestial object that is much smaller than a normal star and has insufficient mass for nuclear fusion to begin but that is hot enough to radiate energy especially at infrared wavelengths

brown earth noun (1932)
: any of a group of intrazonal soils developed in temperate humid regions under deciduous forests and characterized by a dark brown mull horizon that grades through lighter colored soil into parent material

brown–eyed Su·san \'braú-,nīd-'sü-z°n\ noun [brown-eyed + Susan (as in black-eyed Susan)] (1896)
: a dark-centered coneflower (Rudbeckia triloba) of eastern North America often having tripartite lower leaves

brown fat noun (1951)
: a mammalian heat-producing tissue occurring especially in human newborns and in hibernators — called also brown adipose tissue

Brown·ian motion \'braú-nē-ən-\ noun [Robert Brown (died 1858) Scottish botanist] (circa 1889)
: a random movement of microscopic particles suspended in liquids or gases resulting from the impact of molecules of the fluid surrounding the particles — called also Brownian movement

brown·ie \'braú-nē\ noun [¹brown] (circa 1500)
1 : a legendary good-natured elf that performs helpful services at night
2 capitalized : a member of a program of the Girl Scouts for girls in the first through third grades in school
3 : a small square or rectangle of rich usually chocolate cake often containing nuts

brownie point noun, often B capitalized (circa 1962)
: a credit regarded as earned especially by currying favor (as with a superior)

Brown·ing automatic rifle \'braú-niŋ-\ noun [John M. Browning (died 1926) American designer of firearms] (1920)
: a .30 caliber gas-operated air-cooled magazine-fed automatic rifle often provided with a rest for the barrel

Browning machine gun noun (1918)
: a .30 or .50 caliber recoil-operated air- or water-cooled machine gun fed by a cartridge belt

brown lung noun (1969)
: BYSSINOSIS

brown·nose \'braú(n)-,nōz\ transitive verb [from the implication that servility is equivalent to kissing the hinder parts of the person from whom advancement is sought] (circa 1939) slang
: to ingratiate oneself with : curry favor with
— **brownnose** noun
— **brown·nos·er** noun

brown–out \'braú-,naút\ noun [brown + blackout] (1942)
: a period of reduced voltage of electricity caused especially by high demand and resulting in subnormal illumination

brown pelican noun (1823)

: a pelican (*Pelecanus occidentalis*) of American coasts that has a brown body and a chiefly white or white with yellow head

brown rat *noun* (1826)
: a common domestic rat (*Rattus norvegicus*) that has been introduced worldwide — called also *Norway rat*

brown recluse spider *noun* (1964)
: a venomous spider (*Loxosceles reclusa*) of the U.S. that has a violin-shaped mark on the cephalothorax and produces a dangerous cytotoxin

brown rice *noun* (1916)
: hulled but unpolished rice that retains most of the bran layers, endosperm, and germ

brown rot *noun* (1894)
: a disease of stone fruits caused by fungi (genus *Monilinia*, especially *M. fructicola*)

brown sauce *noun* (1878)
: a sauce consisting typically of stock thickened with flour browned in fat

brown·shirt \'braun-ˌshərt\ *noun, often capitalized* (1932)
: NAZI; *especially* : STORM TROOPER

brown·stone \-ˌstōn\ *noun* (1858)
1 : a reddish brown sandstone used for building
2 : a dwelling faced with brownstone

brown study *noun* (1532)
: a state of serious absorption or abstraction

brown sugar *noun* (1704)
: soft brown sugar whose crystals are covered by a film of refined dark syrup

Brown Swiss *noun* (1902)
: any of a breed of large hardy brown dairy cattle originating in Switzerland

brown–tail moth \'braun-ˌtāl-\ *noun* (1782)
: a tussock moth (*Euproctis chrysorrhoea*) introduced in the U.S. and having larvae which feed on foliage and are irritating to the skin

brown trout *noun* (1886)
: a speckled European trout (*Salmo trutta*) widely introduced as a game fish

brow·ridge \'brau-ˌrij\ *noun* (1898)
: a prominence of the frontal bone above the eye caused by the projection of the frontal air sinuses

¹browse \'brauz\ *verb* **browsed; browsing** (15th century)
transitive verb
1 a : to consume as browse **b** : GRAZE
2 : to look over casually : SKIM
intransitive verb
1 a : to feed on or as if on browse **b** : GRAZE
2 a : to skim through a book reading at random passages that catch the eye **b** : to look over or through an aggregate of things casually especially in search of something of interest
— **brows·er** *noun*

²browse *noun* [probably modification of Middle French *brouts*, plural of *brout* sprout, from Old French *brost*, of Germanic origin; akin to Old Saxon *brustian* to sprout, and perhaps to Old English *brēost* breast] (1523)
1 : tender shoots, twigs, and leaves of trees and shrubs used by animals for food
2 : an act or instance of browsing

bru·cel·la \brü-'se-lə\ *noun, plural* **-cel·lae** \-'se-(ˌ)lē\ *or* **-cel·las** [New Latin, from Sir David *Bruce*] (1930)
: any of a genus (*Brucella*) of nonmotile pleomorphic bacteria that cause disease in humans and domestic animals

bru·cel·lo·sis \ˌbrü-sə-'lō-səs\ *noun, plural* **-lo·ses** \-ˌsēz\ [New Latin] (1930)
: infection with or disease caused by brucellae

bru·cine \'brü-ˌsēn\ *noun* [probably from French, from New Latin *Brucea* (genus name of *Brucea antidysenterica*, a shrub)] (1823)
: a poisonous alkaloid $C_{23}H_{26}N_2O_4$ found with strychnine especially in nux vomica

bru·in \'brü-ən\ *noun* [Middle Dutch, name of the bear in *Reynard the Fox*] (15th century)
: BEAR 1

¹bruise \'brüz\ *verb* **bruised; bruis·ing** [Middle English *brusen, brisen*, from Middle

French & Old English; Middle French *bruisier* to break, of Celtic origin; akin to Old Irish *bruid* he shatters; Old English *brȳsan* to bruise; akin to Old Irish *bruid*, Latin *frustum* piece] (14th century)
transitive verb
1 a *archaic* : DISABLE **b** : BATTER, DENT
2 : to inflict a bruise on : CONTUSE
3 : to break down (as leaves or berries) by pounding : CRUSH
4 : WOUND, INJURE; *especially* : to inflict psychological hurt on
intransitive verb
1 : to inflict a bruise
2 : to undergo bruising

²bruise *noun* (1541)
1 a : an injury involving rupture of small blood vessels and discoloration without a break in the overlying skin : CONTUSION **b** : a similar injury to plant tissue
2 : ABRASION, SCRATCH
3 : an injury especially to the feelings

bruis·er \'brü-zər\ *noun* (1744)
: a big husky man

¹bruit *noun* [Middle English, from Middle French, from Old French, noise] (15th century)
1 \'brüt\ *archaic* **a** : NOISE, DIN **b** : REPORT, RUMOR
2 \'brü-ē\ [French, literally, noise] : any of several generally abnormal sounds heard on auscultation

²bruit \'brüt\ *transitive verb* (15th century)
: to noise abroad : REPORT

bru·mal \'brü-məl\ *adjective* [Latin *brumalis*, from *bruma* winter] (1513)
archaic : indicative of or occurring in the winter

brum·by \'brəm-bē\ *noun, plural* **brumbies** [origin unknown] (1880)
Australian : a wild or unbroken horse

brume \'brüm\ *noun* [French, mist, winter, from Old Provençal *bruma*, from Latin, winter solstice, winter; akin to Latin *brevis* short — more at BRIEF] (1808)
: MIST, FOG
— **bru·mous** \'brü-məs\ *adjective*

brum·ma·gem \'brə-mi-jəm\ *adjective* [alteration of *Birmingham*, England, the source in the 17th century of counterfeit groats] (1637)
: SPURIOUS; *also* : cheaply showy : TAWDRY
— **brummagem** *noun*

brunch \'brənch\ *noun* [*breakfast* + *lunch*] (1896)
: a meal usually taken late in the morning that combines a late breakfast and an early lunch

¹bru·net *or* **bru·nette** \brü-'net\ *noun* (circa 1539)
: a person having brown or black hair and usually a relatively dark complexion

²brunet *or* **brunette** *adjective* [French *brunet*, masculine, *brunette*, feminine, brownish, from Old French, from *brun* brown, from Medieval Latin *brunus*, of Germanic origin; akin to Old High German *brūn* brown] (1752)
1 : being a brunet
2 : of a dark-brown or black color ⟨*brunet* hair⟩

Brun·hild \'brün-ˌhilt\ *noun* [German]
: a queen in Germanic legend won by Siegfried for Gunther

bru·ni·zem \'brü-nə-ˌzem\ *noun* [*bruni-* (from Medieval Latin *brunus* brown) + *-zem* earth (as in *chernozem*)] (1953)
: any of a zonal group of deep dark prairie soils developed from loess

Bruns·wick stew \'brənz-(ˌ)wik-\ *noun* [*Brunswick* county, Va.] (1856)
: a stew made of vegetables and usually two meats such as chicken and squirrel

brunt \'brənt\ *noun* [Middle English] (15th century)
1 : the principal force, shock, or stress (as of an attack)
2 : the greater part : BURDEN

¹brush \'brəsh\ *noun* [Middle English *brusch*, from Middle French *broce*] (14th century)
1 : BRUSHWOOD
2 a : scrub vegetation **b** : land covered with scrub vegetation

²brush *noun* [Middle English *brusshe*, from Middle French *broisse*, from Old French *broce*] (14th century)
1 : a device composed of bristles typically set into a handle and used especially for sweeping, smoothing, scrubbing, or painting
2 : something resembling a brush: as **a** : a bushy tail **b** : a feather tuft worn on a hat
3 : an electrical conductor that makes sliding contact between a stationary and a moving part (as of a generator or a motor)
4 a : an act of brushing **b** : a quick light touch or momentary contact in passing

³brush *transitive verb* (15th century)
1 a : to apply a brush to **b** : to apply with a brush
2 a : to remove with passing strokes (as of a brush) **b** : to dispose of in an offhand way : DISMISS ⟨*brushed* him off⟩
3 : to pass lightly over or across : touch gently against in passing
— **brush·er** *noun*

⁴brush *noun* [Middle English *brusche* rush, hostile collision, from *bruschen*] (14th century)
: a brief encounter or skirmish ⟨a *brush* with disaster⟩ ⟨a *brush* with the law⟩

⁵brush *intransitive verb* [Middle English *bruschen* to rush, from Middle French *brosser* to dash through underbrush, from *broce*] (1674)
: to move lightly or heedlessly ⟨*brushed* past the well-wishers waiting to greet him⟩

brush·abil·i·ty \ˌbrə-shə-'bi-lə-tē\ *noun* (1936)
: ease of application with a brush ⟨*brushability* of a paint⟩

brush·back \'brəsh-ˌbak\ *noun* (1954)
: a fastball intentionally thrown near the batter's head or body in baseball
— **brush back** *transitive verb*

brush border *noun* (1903)
: a stria of microvilli on the plasma membrane of an epithelial cell (as in a kidney tubule) that is specialized for absorption

brush cut *noun* (1945)
: CREW CUT

brush discharge *noun* (1849)
: a faintly luminous relatively slow electrical discharge having no spark

brushed \'brəsht\ *adjective* (1926)
1 : finished with a nap ⟨a *brushed* fabric⟩
2 : polished but not shiny ⟨*brushed* aluminum⟩

brush·fire \'brəsh-ˌfīr\ *adjective* [*brush fire* (a fire involving brush but not full-sized trees)] (1954)
: involving mobilization only on a small and local scale ⟨*brushfire* border wars⟩

brush·land \-ˌland\ *noun* (1853)
: an area covered with brush growth

brush·off \-ˌôf\ *noun* (1941)
: a quietly curt or disdainful dismissal

brush up (circa 1600)
transitive verb
1 : to improve or polish as if by brushing
2 : to renew one's skill in ⟨*brush up* your Spanish⟩
intransitive verb
: to refresh one's memory : renew one's skill ⟨*brush up* on math⟩
— **brush-up** \'brəsh-ˌəp\ *noun*

brush·wood \'brəsh-ˌwud\ *noun* (circa 1613)
1 : wood of small branches especially when cut or broken
2 : a thicket of shrubs and small trees

brush·work \-ˌwərk\ *noun* (1868)

\ə\ abut \ˀ\ kitten \ər\ further \a\ ash \ā\ ace
\ä\ mop, mar \au\ out \ch\ chin \e\ bet \ē\ easy
\g\ go \i\ hit \ī\ ice \j\ job \ŋ\ sing \ō\ go
\ô\ law \ȯi\ boy \th\ thin \th\ the \ü\ loot \u̇\ foot
\y\ yet \zh\ vision *see also* Guide to Pronunciation

: work done with a brush (as in painting); *especially* : the characteristic work of an artist using a brush

¹**brushy** \'brə-shē\ *adjective* **brush·i·er; -est** (1658)
: covered with or abounding in brush or brushwood ⟨*brushy* hills⟩ ⟨a *brushy* habitat⟩

²**brushy** *adjective* **brush·i·er; -est** (1673)
: SHAGGY, ROUGH ⟨a *brushy* moustache⟩

brusque *also* **brusk** \'brəsk\ *adjective* [French *brusque*, from Italian *brusco*, from Medieval Latin *bruscus* butcher's-broom (plant with bristly twigs)] (1651)
1 : markedly short and abrupt
2 : blunt in manner or speech often to the point of ungracious harshness
synonym see BLUFF
— **brusque·ly** *adverb*
— **brusque·ness** *noun*

brus·que·rie \,brəs-kə-'rē\ *noun* [French, from *brusque*] (1752)
: abruptness of manner

Brus·sels carpet \'brə-səlz-\ *noun* [*Brussels*, Belgium] (1799)
: a carpet made of colored worsted yarns first fixed in a foundation web of strong linen thread and then drawn up in loops to form the pattern

Brussels griffon *noun* (1904)
: any of a breed of short-faced compact rough- or smooth-coated toy dogs of Belgian origin — called also *griffon*

Brussels lace *noun* (1748)
1 : any of various fine needlepoint or bobbin laces with floral designs first made in or near Brussels
2 : a machine-made net of hexagonal mesh

Brussels griffon

brus·sels sprout \'brə-səl-\ *noun, often B capitalized* (1796)
1 *plural* : a plant (*Brassica oleracea gemmifera*) of the mustard family that bears small edible green heads on its stem
2 : any of the edible green heads borne on brussels sprouts — usually used in plural

brussels sprout 1

brut \'brüt, 'brūt\ *adjective* [French, literally, rough] (1891)
of champagne : very dry; *specifically* : being the driest made by the producer

bru·tal \'brü-t°l\ *adjective* [Middle English, from Middle French or Medieval Latin; Middle French, from Medieval Latin *brutalis*, from Latin *brutus*] (15th century)
1 *archaic* : typical of beasts : ANIMAL
2 : befitting a beast : as **a** : grossly ruthless or unfeeling ⟨a *brutal* slander⟩ **b** : CRUEL, COLDBLOODED ⟨a *brutal* attack⟩ **c** : HARSH, SEVERE ⟨*brutal* weather⟩ **d** : unpleasantly accurate and incisive ⟨the *brutal* truth⟩ ☆
— **bru·tal·ly** \-t°l-ē\ *adverb*

bru·tal·ise *British variant of* BRUTALIZE

bru·tal·i·ty \brü-'ta-lə-tē\ *noun, plural* **-ties** (1549)
1 : the quality or state of being brutal
2 : a brutal act or course of action

bru·tal·ize \'brü-t°l-,īz\ *transitive verb* **-ized; -iz·ing** (circa 1704)
1 : to make brutal, unfeeling, or inhuman ⟨people *brutalized* by poverty and disease⟩
2 : to treat brutally ⟨an accord not to *brutalize* prisoners of war⟩
— **bru·tal·iza·tion** \,brü-t°l-ə-'zā-shən\ *noun*

¹**brute** \'brüt\ *adjective* [Middle English, from Middle French *brut* rough, from Latin *brutus*

brutish, literally, heavy; akin to Latin *gravis* heavy — more at GRIEVE] (15th century)
1 : of or relating to beasts ⟨the ways of the *brute* world⟩
2 : INANIMATE 1a
3 : characteristic of an animal in quality, action, or instinct: as **a** : CRUEL, SAVAGE ⟨*brute* violence⟩ **b** : not working by reason ⟨*brute* instinct⟩
4 : purely physical ⟨*brute* strength⟩
5 : unrelievedly harsh ⟨*brute* facts⟩ ⟨*brute* necessity⟩

²**brute** *noun* (1611)
1 : BEAST
2 : a brutal person

brut·ish \'brü-tish\ *adjective* (1534)
1 : befitting beasts ⟨lived a short and *brutish* life as a slave⟩
2 a : strongly and grossly sensual ⟨*brutish* gluttony⟩ **b** : showing little intelligence or sensibility ⟨a *brutish* lack of understanding⟩
synonym see BRUTAL
— **brut·ish·ly** *adverb*
— **brut·ish·ness** *noun*

brux·ism \'brək-,si-zəm\ *noun* [irregular from Greek *brychein* to gnash the teeth + English *-ism*] (circa 1940)
: the habit of unconsciously gritting or grinding the teeth especially in situations of stress or during sleep

Bryn·hild \'brin-,hild\ *noun* [Old Norse *Brynhildr*]
: a Valkyrie who is waked from an enchanted sleep by Sigurd and later has him killed when he forgets her

bry·ol·o·gy \brī-'ä-lə-jē\ *noun* [Greek *bryon* moss (akin to Greek *bryein* to grow luxuriantly) + International Scientific Vocabulary *-logy*] (circa 1859)
1 : moss life or biology
2 : a branch of botany that deals with the bryophytes
— **bry·o·log·i·cal** \brī-ə-'lä-ji-kəl\ *adjective*
— **bry·ol·o·gist** \brī-'ä-lə-jist\ *noun*

bry·o·ny \'brī-ə-nē\ *noun, plural* **-nies** [Middle English, from Latin *bryonia*, from Greek *bryōnia;* akin to Greek *bryein*] (14th century)
: any of a genus (*Bryonia*) of tendril-bearing vines of the gourd family with large leaves and red or black fruit

bryo·phyl·lum \brī-ə-'fi-ləm\ *noun* [New Latin, from Greek *bryon* + *phyllon* leaf — more at BLADE] (circa 1868)
: any of various kalanchoes; *especially* : a succulent kalanchoe (*Kalanchoe pinnata*) often grown as a foliage plant that propagates new plants from its leaves

bryo·phyte \'brī-ə-,fīt\ *noun* [ultimately from Greek *bryon* + *phyton* plant; akin to Greek *phyein* to bring forth — more at BE] (1878)
: any of a division (Bryophyta) of nonflowering plants comprising the mosses, liverworts, and hornworts
— **bryo·phyt·ic** \,brī-ə-'fi-tik\ *adjective*

bryo·zo·an \,brī-ə-'zō-ən\ *noun* [New Latin *Bryozoa*, from Greek *bryon* + New Latin *-zoa*] (circa 1864)
: any of a phylum (Bryozoa) of aquatic mostly marine invertebrate animals that reproduce by budding and usually form permanently attached branched or mossy colonies
— **bryozoan** *adjective*

¹**Bry·thon·ic** \bri-'thä-nik\ *adjective* (1884)
: of, relating to, or characteristic of the division of the Celtic languages that includes Welsh, Cornish, and Breton

²**Brythonic** *noun* (1884)
: the Brythonic branch of the Celtic languages — see INDO-EUROPEAN LANGUAGES table

Bt \'bē-'tē\ *noun* [New Latin *Bacillus thuringiensis,* species name, literally, Thuringian bacillus] (1971)
: an insecticide composed of a bacterium (*Bacillus thuringiensis*) pathogenic especially for lepidopteran larvae; *also* : the bacterium itself

bub \'bəb\ *noun* [probably short for *bubby* little boy] (1839)
: FELLOW, BUDDY — used in informal address ⟨come on, *bub*, get moving⟩

¹**bub·ble** \'bə-bəl\ *noun, often attributive* [Middle English *bobel*] (14th century)
1 : a small globule typically hollow and light: as **a** : a small body of gas within a liquid **b** : a thin film of liquid inflated with air or gas **c** : a globule in a transparent solid **d** : something (as a plastic or inflatable structure) that is hemispherical or semicylindrical
2 a : something that lacks firmness, solidity, or reality **b** : a delusive scheme
3 : a sound like that of bubbling
4 : MAGNETIC BUBBLE

²**bubble** *verb* **bub·bled; bub·bling** \'bə-b(ə-)liŋ\ (15th century)
intransitive verb
1 a : to form or produce bubbles **b** : to rise in or as if in bubbles — usually used with *up*
2 : to flow with a gurgling sound ⟨a brook *bubbling* over rocks⟩
3 a : to become lively or effervescent ⟨*bubbling* with good humor⟩ **b** : to speak in a lively and fluent manner
transitive verb
1 : to utter (as words) effervescently
2 : to cause to bubble

bubble and squeak *noun* (circa 1785)
: a British dish consisting of usually leftover potatoes, greens (as cabbage), and sometimes meat fried together

bubble chamber *noun* (1953)
: a chamber of superheated liquid in which the path of an ionizing particle is made visible by a string of vapor bubbles

bub·ble·gum \'bə-bəl-,gəm\ *adjective* (1969)
: appealing to or characteristic of preteens or adolescents ⟨*bubblegum* music⟩

bubble gum *noun* (1937)
1 : a chewing gum that can be blown into large bubbles
2 *usually* **bub·ble·gum** \'bə-bəl-,gəm\ : rock music characterized by simple repetitive phrasings and intended especially for young teenagers

bub·ble·head \'bə-bəl-,hed\ *noun* (1949)
: a foolish or stupid person
— **bub·ble·head·ed** \-,he-dəd\ *adjective*

bubble memory *noun* (1969)
: a computer memory that uses magnetic bubbles to store information

bub·bler \'bə-b(ə-)lər\ *noun* (1914)
1 : a drinking fountain from which a stream of water bubbles upward
2 : one that bubbles

¹**bub·bly** \'bə-b(ə-)lē\ *adjective* **bub·bli·er; -est** (1599)
1 : full of bubbles : EFFERVESCENT ⟨a *bubbly* bottle of pop⟩
2 : full of or showing good spirits : LIVELY, EFFUSIVE
3 : resembling a bubble ⟨a *bubbly* dome⟩

²**bubbly** *noun* (1920)
: CHAMPAGNE

bub·by \'bə-bē\ *noun, plural* **bubbies** [probably of imitative origin] (1686)

: BREAST 1 — sometimes considered vulgar

bu·bo \'byü-(ˌ)bō, 'bü-\ *noun, plural* **buboes** [Medieval Latin *bubon-, bubo,* from Greek *boubōn*] (14th century)
: an inflammatory swelling of a lymph gland especially in the groin
— **bu·bon·ic** \byü-'bä-nik, bü-\ *adjective*

bubonic plague *noun* (1885)
: plague caused by a bacterium (*Yersinia pestis*) and characterized especially by the formation of buboes

buc·cal \'bə-kəl\ *adjective* [Latin *bucca* cheek] (circa 1771)
1 : of, relating to, near, involving, or supplying a cheek ⟨the *buccal* surface of a tooth⟩ ⟨the *buccal* branch of the facial nerve⟩
2 : of, relating to, involving, or lying in the mouth ⟨the *buccal* cavity⟩
— **buc·cal·ly** *adverb*

buc·ca·neer \ˌbə-kə-'nir\ *noun* [French *boucanier*] (circa 1690)
1 : any of the freebooters preying on Spanish ships and settlements especially in the West Indies in the 17th century; *broadly* **:** PIRATE
2 : an unscrupulous adventurer especially in politics or business ◇
— **buccaneer** *intransitive verb*
— **buc·ca·neer·ish** \-ish\ *adjective*

buc·ci·na·tor \'bək-sə-ˌnā-tər\ *noun* [New Latin, from Latin *bucinator* trumpeter, from *bucinare* to sound on the trumpet, from *bucina* trumpet, from *bov-, bos* cow + *canere* to sing, play — more at COW, CHANT] (1671)
: a thin broad muscle forming the wall of the cheek

¹buck \'bək\ *noun, plural* **bucks** [Middle English, from Old English *bucca* stag, he-goat; akin to Old High German *boc* he-goat, Middle Irish *bocc*] (before 12th century)
1 *or plural* **buck :** a male animal; *especially* **:** a male deer or antelope
2 a : a male human being **:** MAN **b :** a dashing fellow **:** DANDY
3 *or plural* **buck :** ANTELOPE
4 a : BUCKSKIN; *also* **:** an article (as a shoe) made of buckskin **b** (1) **:** DOLLAR 3b (2) **:** a sum of money especially to be gained ⟨make a quick *buck*⟩; *also* **:** MONEY — usually used in plural
5 [short for *sawbuck* sawhorse] **a :** a supporting rack or frame **b :** a short thick leather-covered block for gymnastic vaulting

²buck (1750)
transitive verb
1 a *archaic* **:** ¹BUTT **b :** OPPOSE, RESIST ⟨*bucking* the system⟩
2 : to throw (as a rider) by bucking
3 : to charge into (as the opponent's line in football)
4 a : to pass especially from one person to another **b :** to move or load (as heavy objects) especially with mechanical equipment
intransitive verb
1 *of a horse or mule* **:** to spring into the air with the back arched
2 : to charge against something (as an obstruction)
3 a : to move or react jerkily **b :** to refuse assent **:** BALK
4 : to strive for advancement sometimes without regard to ethical behavior ⟨*bucking* for a promotion⟩
— **buck·er** *noun*

³buck *noun* (circa 1877)
: an act or instance of bucking

⁴buck *noun* [short for earlier *buckhorn knife*] (1865)
1 : an object formerly used in poker to mark the next player to deal; *broadly* **:** a token used as a mark or reminder
2 : RESPONSIBILITY — used especially in the phrases *pass the buck* and *the buck stops here*

⁵buck *adjective* [probably from ¹*buck*] (1918)
: of the lowest grade within a military category ⟨*buck* private⟩

⁶buck *adverb* [origin unknown] (1928)

: STARK ⟨*buck* naked⟩

buck–and–wing \ˌbə-kⁿ-'wiŋ\ *noun* (1895)
: a solo tap dance with sharp foot accents, springs, leg flings, and heel clicks

buck·a·roo *also* **buck·er·oo** \ˌbə-kə-'rü, 'bə-kə-ˌ\ *noun, plural* **-aroos** *also* **-eroos** [by folk etymology from Spanish *vaquero,* from *vaca* cow, from Latin *vacca* — more at VACCINE] (1827)
1 : COWBOY
2 : BRONCOBUSTER

buck·bean \'bək-ˌbēn\ *noun* (1578)
: a plant (*Menyanthes trifoliata* of the family Menyanthaceae) growing in bogs and having racemes of white or purplish flowers

buck·board \-ˌbōrd, -ˌbȯrd\ *noun* [obsolete English *buck* body of a wagon + English *board*] (1839)
: a four-wheeled vehicle with a floor made of long springy boards

buckboard

¹buck·et \'bə-kət\ *noun* [Middle English, from Anglo-French *buket,* from Old English *būc* pitcher, belly; akin to Old High German *būh* belly] (13th century)
1 : a typically cylindrical vessel for catching, holding, or carrying liquids or solids
2 : something resembling a bucket: as **a :** the scoop of an excavating machine **b :** one of the receptacles on the rim of a waterwheel **c :** one of the cups of an endless-belt conveyor **d :** one of the vanes of a turbine rotor
3 : BUCKETFUL
4 : BUCKET SEAT
5 : BASKET 3b

²bucket (1649)
transitive verb
1 : to draw or lift in buckets
2 *British* **a :** to ride (a horse) hard **b :** to drive hurriedly or roughly
3 : to deal with in a bucket shop
intransitive verb
1 : HUSTLE, HURRY
2 a : to move about haphazardly or irresponsibly **b :** to move roughly or jerkily

bucket brigade *noun* (1911)
: a chain of persons acting to put out a fire by passing buckets of water from hand to hand

buck·et·ful \'bə-kət-ˌfu̇l\ *noun, plural* **bucketfuls** \-ˌfu̇lz\ *or* **buck·ets·ful** \-kəts-ˌfu̇l\ (circa 1563)
: as much as a bucket will hold; *broadly* **:** large quantity

bucket seat *noun* (1908)
: a low separate seat for one person (as in an automobile or an airplane)

bucket shop *noun* (1875)
1 : a saloon in which liquor was formerly sold from or dispensed in open containers (as buckets or pitchers)
2 a : a gambling establishment that formerly used market fluctuations (as in securities or commodities) as a basis for gaming **b :** a dishonest brokerage firm; *especially* **:** one that formerly failed to execute customers' margin orders in expectation of making a profit from market fluctuations adverse to the customers' interests

buck·eye \'bə-ˌkī\ *noun* (1763)
1 : a shrub or tree (genus *Aesculus*) of the horse-chestnut family; *also* **:** its large nutlike seed
2 *capitalized* **:** a native or resident of Ohio — used as a nickname

buck fever *noun* (1841)
: nervous excitement of an inexperienced hunter at the sight of game

¹buck·le \'bə-kəl\ *noun* [Middle English *bocle,* from Middle French, boss of a shield, buckle, from Latin *buccula,* diminutive of *bucca* cheek] (14th century)

1 : a fastening for two loose ends that is attached to one and holds the other by a catch
2 : an ornamental device that suggests a buckle
3 *archaic* **:** a crisp curl

²buckle *verb* **buck·led; buck·ling** \'bə-k(ə-)liŋ\ (14th century)
transitive verb
1 : to fasten with a buckle
2 : to prepare with vigor
3 : to cause to bend, give way, or crumple
intransitive verb
1 : to become fastened with a buckle
2 : to apply oneself with vigor ⟨*buckles* down to the job⟩
3 : to bend, heave, warp, or kink usually under the influence of some external agency ⟨wheat *buckling* in the wind⟩
4 : COLLAPSE ⟨the props *buckled* under the strain⟩
5 : to give way **:** YIELD ⟨he *buckled* under pressure⟩

³buckle *noun* (circa 1876)
1 : a product of buckling
2 : a coffee cake baked with berries and a crumbly topping ⟨blueberry *buckle*⟩

¹buck·ler \'bə-klər\ *noun* [Middle English *bocler,* from Middle French, shield with a boss, from *bocle*] (13th century)
1 a : a small round shield held by a handle at arm's length **b :** a shield worn on the left arm
2 : one that shields and protects

²buckler *transitive verb* (1590)
: to shield or defend with a buckler

buckle up *intransitive verb* (1976)
: to fasten one's seat belt

buck·min·ster·ful·ler·ene \'bək-(ˌ)min-stər-ˌfu̇-lə-ˌrēn\ *noun* [R. *Buckminster Fuller*] (1985)
: a spherical fullerene C_{60} that is an extremely stable form of pure carbon, consists of interconnected pentagons and hexagons suggestive of the geometry of a geodesic dome, and is believed to be a major constituent of soot

bucko \'bə-(ˌ)kō\ *noun, plural* **buck·oes** (1883)
1 : a person who is domineering and bullying **:** SWAGGERER

◇ WORD HISTORY

buccaneer The history of the word *buccaneer* begins not in the Caribbean, but rather on the coast of Brazil. The French Protestant missionary Jean de Léry, a member of a colonizing expedition to Guanabara Bay in 1556, wrote a detailed account of the Tupinambá Indians of that region and their customs. Léry describes their use of a raised wooden grill called by a word in their language that he rendered *boucan,* on which they would slowly cook meat, including limbs of their captured enemies. Most likely both this word and the culinary device were already familiar to French mariners, who during the previous half century had made many voyages to the Brazilian coast to collect brazilwood. In the 17th century, the word *boucan* surfaced again in the Caribbean, where the French had refocused their tropical American enterprises, and a new derivative *boucanier* now appeared, referring to Europeans, probably former mariners, who survived in the interior of the Antillean islands by hunting and smoking game and escaped livestock on a *boucan.* Some among these men returned to the sea as pirates, and the word *boucanier* continued to be applied to them in their new profession.

\ə\ **abut** \ᵊ\ **kitten** \ər\ **further** \a\ **ash** \ā\ **ace**
\ä\ **mop, mar** \au̇\ **out** \ch\ **chin** \e\ **bet** \ē\ **easy**
\g\ **go** \i\ **hit** \ī\ **ice** \j\ **job** \ŋ\ **sing** \ō\ **go**
\ȯ\ **law** \ȯi\ **boy** \th\ **thin** \t͟h\ **the** \ü\ **loot** \u̇\ **foot**
\y\ **yet** \zh\ **vision** *see also* Guide to Pronunciation

2 *chiefly Irish* **:** young fellow **:** LAD
buck passer *noun* (1920)
: a person who habitually passes the buck
— **buck–pass·ing** \'bək-ˌpa-siŋ\ *noun*
¹**buck·ram** \'bə-krəm\ *noun* [Middle English *bukeram,* from Old French *boquerant,* from Old Provençal *bocaran,* probably from *Bokhara,* city of central Asia] (15th century)
1 : a stiff-finished heavily sized fabric of cotton or linen used for interlinings in garments, for stiffening in millinery, and in bookbinding
2 *archaic* **:** STIFFNESS, RIGIDITY
²**buckram** *adjective* (circa 1589)
: suggesting buckram especially in stiffness
³**buckram** *transitive verb* (1783)
1 : to give strength or stiffness to (as with buckram)
2 *archaic* **:** to make pretentious
Buck Rogers \'bək-ˈrä-jərz\ *adjective* [*Buck Rogers,* hero of a science-fiction comic strip created by Phil Nowlan] (1941)
: marked by futuristic and high-tech qualities
: suggestive of science fiction
buck·saw \'bək-ˌsȯ\ *noun* (1856)
: a saw set in a usually H-shaped frame for sawing wood
buck·shee \'bək-(ˌ)shē, ˌbək-'\ *noun* [Hindi *bakhśīś,* from Persian *bakhshīsh* — more at BAKSHEESH] (circa 1760)
1 *British* **:** something extra obtained free; *especially* **:** extra rations
2 *British* **:** WINDFALL, GRATUITY
¹**buck·shot** \'bək-ˌshät\ *noun* (1775)
: lead shot that is from .24 to .33 inch (about 6.1 to 8.4 millimeters) in diameter
²**buckshot** *adjective* (1941)
: SCATTERSHOT
buck·skin \-ˌskin\ *noun, often attributive* (14th century)
1 a : the skin of a buck **b :** a soft pliable usually suede-finished leather
2 a *plural* **:** buckskin breeches **b** *archaic* **:** a person dressed in buckskin; *especially* **:** an early American backwoodsman
3 : a horse of a light yellowish dun color with black mane and tail
buck·skinned \-ˌskind\ *adjective* (1829)
: dressed in buckskin
buck·tail \-ˌtāl\ *noun* (1911)
: an angler's lure made typically of hairs from the tail of a deer
buck·thorn \-ˌthȯrn\ *noun* (1578)
1 : any of a genus (*Rhamnus* of the family Rhamnaceae, the buckthorn family) of often thorny trees or shrubs some of which yield purgatives or pigments
2 : a tree (*Bumelia lycioides*) of the sapodilla family of the southern U.S.
buck·tooth \-ˈtüth\ *noun* (1753)
: a large projecting front tooth
— **buck·toothed** \-ˈtütht\ *adjective*
buck up *verb* [²buck] (1844)
intransitive verb
: to become encouraged
transitive verb
1 : IMPROVE, SMARTEN
2 : to raise the morale of
buck·wheat \'bək-ˌhwēt, -ˌwēt\ *noun* [Dutch *boekweit,* from Middle Dutch *boecweit,* from *boec-* (akin to Old High German *buohha* beech tree) + *weit* wheat — more at BEECH] (1548)
1 : any of a genus (*Fagopyrum* of the family Polygonaceae, the buckwheat family) of herbs with alternate leaves, clusters of apetalous pinkish white flowers, and triangular seeds; *especially* **:** either of two plants (*F. esculentum* and *F. tartaricum*) cultivated for their edible seeds
2 : the seed of a buckwheat used as a cereal grain
bucky·ball \'bə-kē-ˌbȯl\ *noun* [R. *Buck*minster Fuller + ⁴-y] (1985)
: a molecule of buckminsterfullerene
bu·col·ic \byü-ˈkä-lik\ *adjective* [Latin *bucolicus,* from Greek *boukolikos,* from *boukolos*

cowherd, from *bous* head of cattle + *-kolos* (akin to Latin *colere* to cultivate) — more at COW, WHEEL] (circa 1609)
1 : of or relating to shepherds or herdsmen **:** PASTORAL
2 : relating to or typical of rural life ⟨picnicked in a pleasant *bucolic* setting⟩
— **bu·col·i·cal·ly** \-li-k(ə-)lē\ *adverb*
¹**bud** \'bəd\ *noun* [Middle English *budde*] (14th century)
1 : a small lateral or terminal protuberance on the stem of a plant that may develop into a flower, leaf, or shoot
2 : something not yet mature or at full development: as **a :** an incompletely opened flower **b :** CHILD, YOUTH **c :** an outgrowth of an organism that differentiates into a new individual **:** GEMMA; *also* **:** PRIMORDIUM
— **in the bud :** in an early stage of development ⟨nipped the rebellion *in the bud*⟩
²**bud** *verb* **bud·ded; bud·ding** (14th century)
intransitive verb
1 *of a plant* **a :** to set or put forth buds **b :** to commence growth from buds
2 : to grow or develop as if from a bud
3 : to reproduce asexually especially by the pinching off of a small part of the parent
transitive verb
1 : to produce or develop from buds
2 : to cause (as a plant) to bud
3 : to insert a bud from a plant of one kind into an opening in the bark of (a plant of another kind) usually in order to propagate a desired variety
— **bud·der** *noun*
Bud·dha \'bü-də, 'bu-\ *noun* [Sanskrit, enlightened; akin to Sanskrit *bodhi* enlightenment — more at BID] (1681)
1 : a person who has attained Buddhahood
2 : a representation of Gautama Buddha
Bud·dha·hood \-ˌhud\ *noun* (1837)
: a state of perfect enlightenment sought in Buddhism
Bud·dhism \'bü-ˌdi-zəm, 'bu-\ *noun* (1801)
: a religion of eastern and central Asia growing out of the teaching of Gautama Buddha that suffering is inherent in life and that one can be liberated from it by mental and moral self-purification
— **Bud·dhist** \'bü-dist, 'bu-\ *noun or adjective*
— **Bud·dhis·tic** \bü-ˈdis-tik, bu-\ *adjective*
bud·ding \'bə-diŋ\ *adjective* (1581)
: being in an early stage of development ⟨*budding* novelists⟩
bud·dle \'bə-dᵊl\ *noun* [origin unknown] (circa 1532)
: an apparatus on which crushed ore is concentrated by washing
bud·dle·ia \'bəd-lē-ə, ˌbəd-'lē-\ *noun* [New Latin, genus name, from Adam *Buddle* (died 1715) English botanist] (1791)
: any of a genus (*Buddleia* of the family Loganiaceae) of shrubs or trees of warm regions with showy terminal clusters of usually yellow or violet flowers
¹**bud·dy** \'bə-dē\ *noun, plural* **buddies** [probably baby talk alteration of *brother*] (1850)
1 a : COMPANION, PARTNER **b :** FRIEND 1
2 : FELLOW — used especially in informal address
²**buddy** *intransitive verb* **bud·died; bud·dy·ing** (1918)
: to become friendly — usually used with *up* or *with*
³**buddy** *adjective* (1976)
: featuring a friendship or partnership between the two main usually male characters ⟨a *buddy* movie⟩
bud·dy–bud·dy \ˌbə-dē-ˈbə-dē\ *adjective* (1951)
: familiarly friendly
buddy system *noun* (1942)

: an arrangement in which two individuals are paired (as for mutual safety in a hazardous situation)
¹**budge** \'bəj\ *noun* [Middle English *bugee,* from Anglo-French *bogee*] (14th century)
: a fur formerly prepared from lambskin dressed with the wool outward
²**budge** *verb* **budged; budg·ing** [Middle French *bouger,* from (assumed) Vulgar Latin *bullicare,* from Latin *bullire* to boil — more at BOIL] (1590)
intransitive verb
1 : MOVE, SHIFT ⟨the mule wouldn't *budge*⟩
2 : to give way **:** YIELD ⟨wouldn't *budge* on the issue⟩
transitive verb
: to cause to move or change
³**budge** *adjective* [origin unknown] (1634)
archaic **:** POMPOUS, SOLEMN
bud·ger·i·gar \'bə-jə-rē-ˌgär\ *noun* [modification of Yuwaalaraay (Australian aboriginal language of northern New South Wales) *gijirrigaa*] (1840)
: a small Australian parrot (*Melopsittacus undulatus*) usually light green with black and yellow markings in the wild but bred under domestication in many colors
¹**bud·get** \'bə-jət\ *noun* [Middle English *bowgett,* from Middle French *bougette,* diminutive of *bouge* leather bag, from Latin *bulga,* of Celtic origin; akin to Middle Irish *bolg* bag; akin to Old English *belg* bag — more at BELLY] (15th century)
1 *chiefly dialect* **:** a usually leather pouch, wallet, or pack; *also* **:** its contents
2 : STOCK, SUPPLY
3 : a quantity (as of energy or water) involved in, available for, or assignable to a particular situation; *also* **:** an account of gains and losses of such a quantity
4 a : a statement of the financial position of an administration for a definite period of time based on estimates of expenditures during the period and proposals for financing them **b :** a plan for the coordination of resources and expenditures **c :** the amount of money that is available for, required for, or assigned to a particular purpose ◊
— **bud·get·ary** \'bə-jə-ˌter-ē\ *adjective*
²**budget** (1618)
transitive verb
1 a : to put or allow for in a budget **b :** to require to adhere to a budget

◊ WORD HISTORY
budget Some loanwords have had a more successful career in the language that took them than in the one that gave them; on occasion this had led to reborrowing by the donor. Such a word is *budget,* borrowed from medieval French *bougette* "leather bag" and recorded in later Middle English as *bowgett.* The French word was a diminutive of *bouge* "travel bag, chest, sack." In French, both *bouge* and *bougette* became largely obsolete or historical in reference by the 18th century, at least in their original senses. Middle English *bowgett,* on the other hand, emerged in Early Modern English as *budget.* From its first sense "satchel," *budget* came to denote the contents of a satchel, especially a bundle of letters or papers—a semantic shift identical to that of ²*mail.* In the 18th century British Parliament, the Chancellor of the Exchequer was said "to open the budget" when he presented the government's estimates of revenues and expenditures for the following year. By the 19th century, any public or private estimation of a similar nature could be called a *budget.* The usefulness of this word and the influence of English parliamentary institutions led to the adoption of *budget* in a number of European languages, including French.

2 a : to allocate funds for in a budget ⟨*budget* a new hospital⟩ **b :** to plan or provide for the use of in detail ⟨*budgeting* manpower⟩
intransitive verb
: to put oneself on a budget ⟨*budgeting* for a vacation⟩
³budget *adjective* (1941)
: suitable for one on a budget **:** INEXPENSIVE
bud·ge·teer \ˌbə-jə-'tir\ *also* **bud·get·er** \'bə-jə-tər\ *noun* (circa 1845)
1 : one who prepares a budget
2 : one who is restricted to a budget
bud·gie \'bə-jē\ *noun* [by shortening and alteration] (1935)
: BUDGERIGAR
bud scale *noun* (circa 1880)
: one of the leaves resembling scales that form the sheath of a plant bud
bud·worm \'bəd-ˌwərm\ *noun* (1849)
: a moth larva that feeds on the buds of plants
— compare SPRUCE BUDWORM
¹buff \'bəf\ *noun* [Middle French *buffle* wild ox, from Old Italian *bufalo*] (1580)
1 : a garment (as a uniform) made of buff leather
2 : the state of being nude ⟨sunbathing in the *buff*⟩
3 a : a moderate orange yellow **b :** a light to moderate yellow
4 : a device having a soft absorbent surface (as of cloth) by which polishing material is applied
5 [earlier *buff* an enthusiast about going to fires; perhaps from the buff overcoats worn by volunteer firefighters in New York City *about* 1820] **:** FAN, ENTHUSIAST
²buff *adjective* (circa 1771)
: of the color buff
³buff *transitive verb* (1885)
1 : POLISH, SHINE ⟨waxed and *buffed* the floor⟩
2 : to give a velvety surface to (leather)
¹buf·fa·lo \'bə-fə-ˌlō\ *noun, plural* **-lo** *or* **-loes** *also* **-los** *often attributive* [Italian *bufalo* & Spanish *búfalo*, from Late Latin *bufalus*, alteration of Latin *bubalus*, from Greek *boubalos* African gazelle] (1562)
1 : any of several wild bovids: as **a :** WATER BUFFALO **b :** CAPE BUFFALO **c** (1) **:** any of a genus (*Bison*) of bovids; *especially* **:** a large shaggy-maned North American bovid (*B. bison*) that has short horns

buffalo 1c(1)

and heavy forequarters with a large muscular hump and that was formerly abundant on the central and western plains — compare WISENT (2) **:** the flesh of the buffalo used as food
2 : any of several suckers (genus *Ictiobus*) found mostly in the Mississippi valley — called also *buffalofish*
²buffalo *transitive verb* **-loed; -lo·ing** (circa 1896)
: BEWILDER, BAFFLE
buf·fa·lo·ber·ry \-ˌber-ē\ *noun* (1805)
: either of two western U.S. shrubs (*Shepherdia argentea* and *S. canadensis*) of the oleaster family with silvery foliage; *also* **:** their edible scarlet berry
buffalo gourd *noun* (circa 1928)
: a perennial cucurbit (*Cucurbita foetidissima*) of arid lands of the central and southwest U.S. and Mexico with a large starchy taproot and seeds rich in an oil suitable after processing for use in cooking or as fuel
buffalo grass *noun* (1784)

: a low-growing grass (*Buchloë dactyloides*) of former feeding grounds of the American buffalo; *also* **:** GRAMA
buffalo plaid *noun* (1979)
: a broad checkered plaid pattern usually of two colors
¹buff·er \'bə-fər\ *noun, often attributive* [*buff*, verb, to react like a soft body when struck] (1835)
1 : any of various devices or pieces of material for reducing shock or damage due to contact
2 : a means or device used as a cushion against the shock of fluctuations in business or financial activity
3 : something that serves as a protective barrier: as **a :** BUFFER STATE **b :** a person who shields another especially from annoying routine matters **c :** MEDIATOR 1
4 : a substance capable in solution of neutralizing both acids and bases and thereby maintaining the original acidity or basicity of the solution; *also* **:** a solution containing such a substance
5 : a temporary storage unit (as in a computer); *especially* **:** one that accepts information at one rate and delivers it at another
— **buff·ered** \-fərd\ *adjective*
²buffer *transitive verb* **buff·ered; buff·er·ing** \-f(ə-)riŋ\ (1894)
1 : to lessen the shock of **:** CUSHION
2 : to treat (as a solution or its acidity) with a buffer; *also* **:** to prepare (aspirin) with an antacid
3 : to collect (as data) in a buffer
³buffer *noun* (1854)
: one that buffs
buffer state *noun* (1883)
: a usually neutral state lying between two larger potentially rival powers
buffer zone *noun* (1908)
: a neutral area separating conflicting forces; *broadly* **:** an area designed to separate
¹buf·fet \'bə-fət\ *noun* [Middle English, from Old French, diminutive of *buffe* blow] (13th century)
1 : a blow especially with the hand
2 : something that strikes with telling force
²buffet (13th century)
transitive verb
1 : to strike sharply especially with the hand **:** CUFF
2 : to strike repeatedly **:** BATTER ⟨the waves *buffeted* the shore⟩
3 : to drive, force, move, or attack by or as if by repeated blows
intransitive verb
: to make one's way especially under difficult conditions
³buf·fet \(ˌ)bə-'fā, bü-', *British especially* 'bü-ˌ\ *noun* [French] (1718)
1 : SIDEBOARD
2 a : a counter for refreshments **b** *chiefly British* **:** a restaurant operated as a public convenience (as in a railway station) **c :** a meal set out on a buffet or table for ready access and informal service
⁴buf·fet *same as* ³\ *adjective* (1898)
: served informally (as from a buffet)
buffing wheel *noun* (circa 1889)
: a wheel covered with polishing material
buff leather *noun* (1580)
: a strong supple oil-tanned leather produced chiefly from cattle hides
buf·fle·head \'bə-fəl-ˌhed\ *noun* [archaic English *buffle* buffalo + English *head*] (1731)
: a small North American diving duck (*Bucephala albeola*)
buf·fo \'bü-(ˌ)fō\ *noun, plural* **buf·fi** \-(ˌ)fē\ *or* **buffos** [Italian, from *buffone*] (1764)
: CLOWN, BUFFOON; *specifically* **:** a male singer of comic roles in opera
buf·foon \(ˌ)bə-'fün\ *noun* [Middle French *bouffon*, from Old Italian *buffone*] (1585)
1 : a ludicrous figure **:** CLOWN

2 : a gross and usually ill-educated or stupid person
— **buf·foon·ish** \-'fü-nish\ *adjective*
buf·foon·ery \-'fü-nə-rē, -'fün-rē\ *noun, plural* **-er·ies** (1621)
: foolish or playful behavior or practice
¹bug \'bəg\ *noun* [Middle English *bugge* scarecrow; akin to Norwegian dialect *bugge* important man] (14th century)
obsolete **:** BOGEY, BUGBEAR
²bug *noun* [origin unknown] (1622)
1 a : an insect or other creeping or crawling invertebrate **b :** any of several insects commonly considered obnoxious: as (1) **:** BEDBUG (2) **:** COCKROACH (3) **:** HEAD LOUSE **c :** any of an order (Hemiptera and especially its suborder Heteroptera) of insects that have sucking mouthparts, forewings thickened at the base, and incomplete metamorphosis and are often economic pests — called also *true bug*
2 : an unexpected defect, fault, flaw, or imperfection
3 a : a germ or microorganism especially when causing disease **b :** an unspecified or nonspecific sickness usually presumed due to a bug
4 : a sudden enthusiasm
5 : ENTHUSIAST ⟨a camera *bug*⟩
6 : a prominent person
7 : a concealed listening device
8 [from its designation by an asterisk on race programs] **:** a weight allowance given apprentice jockeys
³bug *transitive verb* **bugged; bug·ging** (1949)
1 : BOTHER, ANNOY ⟨don't *bug* me with petty details⟩
2 : to plant a concealed microphone in
⁴bug *verb* **bugged; bug·ging** [probably from ²*bug*] (1877)
intransitive verb
of the eyes **:** PROTRUDE, BULGE — often used with *out*
transitive verb
: to cause to bug ⟨his eyes were *bugged* with horror⟩
bug·a·boo \'bə-gə-ˌbü\ *noun, plural* **-boos** [origin unknown] (1740)
1 : an imaginary object of fear
2 : BUGBEAR 2; *also* **:** something that causes fear or distress out of proportion to its importance
bug·bane \'bəg-ˌbān\ *noun* (1804)
: any of several perennial herbs (genus *Cimicifuga*) of the buttercup family; *especially* **:** BLACK COHOSH
bug·bear \-ˌbar, -ˌber\ *noun* (1581)
1 : an imaginary goblin or specter used to excite fear
2 a : an object or source of dread **b :** a continuing source of irritation **:** PROBLEM
bug·eye \-ˌī\ *noun* (1881)
: a small boat with a flat bottom, a centerboard, and two raked masts
bug-eyed \-ˌīd\ *adjective* (1922)
: having the eyes bulging (as with astonishment)
¹bug·ger \'bə-gər, 'bu̇-gər\ *noun* [Middle English *bougre* heretic, from Middle French, from Medieval Latin *Bulgarus*, literally, Bulgarian; from the association of Bulgaria with the Bogomils, who were accused of sodomy] (1555)
1 : SODOMITE
2 a : a worthless person **:** RASCAL **b :** FELLOW, CHAP
3 : a small or annoying thing ⟨put down my keys and now I can't find the *buggers*⟩
²bug·ger \'bə-gər\ *transitive verb* (1598)

1 : to commit sodomy with — usually considered vulgar
2 : DAMN
³bugger *noun* (1955)
: a person who plants electronic bugs
bugger all *noun* (circa 1937)
slang British **:** NOTHING
bugger off *intransitive verb* (1922)
slang British **:** LEAVE, DEPART
bug·gery \'bə-gə-rē\ *noun* (1514)
: SODOMY
¹bug·gy \'bə-gē\ *adjective* **bug·gi·er; -est**
(1714)
: infested with bugs
²buggy *noun, plural* **buggies** [origin unknown] (1773)
1 : a light one-horse carriage made with two wheels in England and with four wheels in the U.S.
2 : a small cart or truck for short transportations of heavy materials
3 : BABY CARRIAGE
¹bug·house \'bəg-,haus\ *adjective* (1895)
: mentally deranged **:** CRAZY
²bughouse *noun* (1902)
: an insane asylum
¹bu·gle \'byü-gəl\ *noun* [Middle English, from Old French, from Late Latin *bugula*] (13th century)
: any of a genus (*Ajuga*) of plants of the mint family; *especially* **:** a European annual (*A. reptans*) that has spikes of blue flowers and is naturalized in the U.S.
²bugle *noun* [Middle English, buffalo, instrument made of buffalo horn, bugle, from Middle French, from Latin *buculus*, diminutive of *bos* head of cattle — more at COW] (14th century)
: a valveless brass instrument that resembles a trumpet and is used especially for military calls

bugle

³bugle *intransitive verb* **bu·gled; bu·gling** \-g(ə-)liŋ\ (1884)
1 : to sound a bugle
2 : to utter the characteristic rutting call of the bull elk
⁴bugle *noun* [perhaps from ²*bugle*] (1579)
: a small cylindrical bead of glass or plastic used for trimming especially on women's clothing
bu·gler \'byü-glər\ *noun* (1838)
: a person who sounds a bugle
bu·gle·weed \'byü-gəl-,wēd\ *noun* (circa 1818)
1 : any of a genus (*Lycopus*) of mints; *especially* **:** one (*Latin virginicus*) that is mildly narcotic and astringent
2 : ¹BUGLE
bu·gloss \'byü-gläs, -,glós\ *noun* [Middle French *buglosse*, from Latin *buglossa*, irregular from Greek *bouglōssos*, from *bous* head of cattle + *glōssa* tongue — more at COW, GLOSS] (14th century)
: any of several coarse hairy plants (genera *Anchusa, Lycopsis,* and *Echium*) of the borage family — compare VIPER'S BUGLOSS
bug off *intransitive verb* [probably short for *bugger off*] (1971)
: LEAVE, DEPART — usually used as a command
buhl \'bül, 'byü(ə)l\ *variant of* BOULLE
buhr·stone \'bər-,stōn\ *noun* [probably from *burr + stone*] (1690)
1 : a siliceous rock used for millstones
2 : a millstone cut from buhrstone
¹build \'bild\ *verb* **built** \'bilt\; **build·ing**
[Middle English *bilden*, from Old English *byldan;* akin to Old English *būan* to dwell — more at BOWER] (before 12th century)

1 : to form by ordering and uniting materials by gradual means into a composite whole **:** CONSTRUCT
2 : to cause to be constructed
3 : to develop according to a systematic plan, by a definite process, or on a particular base
4 : INCREASE, ENLARGE
intransitive verb
1 : to engage in building
2 a : to progress toward a peak (as of intensity) ⟨*build* to a climax⟩ **b :** to develop in extent ⟨a crowd *building*⟩
— build a fire under : to stimulate to vigorous action
— build into : to make an integral part of ⟨*build* quality *into* the product⟩
— build on : to use as a foundation ⟨*building on* past experience⟩
²build *noun* (1667)
: form or mode of structure **:** MAKE; *especially* **:** bodily conformation of a person or lower animal
build·able \'bil-də-bəl\ *adjective* (1927)
: suitable for building ⟨*buildable* land⟩
build·ed *archaic past of* BUILD
build·er \'bil-dər\ *noun* (13th century)
1 : one that builds; *especially* **:** one that contracts to build and supervises building operations
2 : a substance added to or used with detergents to increase their cleansing action
build in *transitive verb* (1933)
: to make an integral part of something
build·ing \'bil-diŋ\ *noun* (14th century)
1 : a usually roofed and walled structure built for permanent use (as for a dwelling)
2 : the art or business of assembling materials into a structure
building block *noun* (1846)
: a unit of construction or composition
build·up \'bil-,dəp\ *noun* (1926)
1 : something produced by building up ⟨fluid *buildup* in the lungs⟩
2 : the act or process of building up
build up (1611)
transitive verb
1 : to develop gradually by increments ⟨*building up* endurance⟩ ⟨*built up* a library⟩
2 : to promote the health, strength, esteem, or reputation of
intransitive verb
: to accumulate or develop appreciably
— build·er-up·per \'bil-dər-'ə-pər\ *noun*
built \'bilt\ *adjective* (1621)
: formed as to physique or bodily contours ⟨slimly *built*⟩; *especially* **:** well or attractively formed
¹built-in \'bilt-'in\ *adjective* (1898)
1 : forming an integral part of a structure; *especially* **:** constructed as or in a recess in a wall
2 : INHERENT
²built-in \-,in\ *noun* (1930)
: a built-in piece of furniture
built-up \'bilt-'əp\ *adjective* (1829)
1 : made of several sections or layers fastened together
2 : covered with buildings
buird·ly \'bùr(d)-lē\ *adjective* [probably alteration of *burly*] (1773)
Scottish **:** STURDY
bulb \'bəlb\ *noun*
[Latin *bulbus,* from Greek *bolbos* bulbous plant] (circa 1601)
1 a : a resting stage of a plant (as the lily, onion, hyacinth, or tulip) that is usually formed underground and consists of a short stem base bearing one or more buds

bulb 1a: *1* hyacinth, *2* onion, *3* tulip, *4* lily

enclosed in overlapping membranous or fleshy leaves **b :** a fleshy structure (as a tuber or corm) resembling a bulb in appearance **c :** a plant having or developing from a bulb
2 : a bulb-shaped part; *specifically* **:** a glass envelope enclosing the light source of an electric lamp or such an envelope together with the light source it encloses
3 : a rounded or swollen anatomical structure
4 : a camera setting that indicates that the shutter can be opened by pressing on the release and closed by ending the pressure
— bulbed \'bəlbd\ *adjective*
bul·bar \'bəl-bər, -,bär\ *adjective* (1878)
: of or relating to a bulb; *specifically* **:** involving the medulla oblongata
bul·bil \'bəl-bəl, -,bil\ *noun* [French *bulbille,* diminutive of *bulbe* bulb, from Latin *bulbus*] (1831)
: BULBLET
bulb·let \'bəl-blət\ *noun* (1842)
: a small or secondary bulb; *especially* **:** an aerial deciduous bud produced in a leaf axil or replacing the flowers and capable when separated of producing a new plant
bul·bo·ure·thral gland \,bəl-(,)bō-yù-'rē-thrəl-\ *noun* [Latin *bulbus* bulb + English *urethral*] (circa 1903)
: COWPER'S GLAND
bul·bous \'bəl-bəs\ *adjective* (1578)
1 : having a bulb **:** growing from or bearing bulbs
2 : resembling a bulb especially in roundness ⟨a *bulbous* nose⟩
— bul·bous·ly *adverb*
bul·bul \'bùl-,bùl\ *noun* [Persian, from Arabic] (1665)
1 : a Persian songbird frequently mentioned in poetry that is probably a nightingale (*Erithacus megarhynchos*)
2 : any of a group of gregarious passerine birds (family Pycnonotidae) of Asia and Africa
Bul·gar \'bəl-,gär, 'bùl-\ *noun* [Medieval Latin *Bulgarus*] (1591)
: BULGARIAN
Bul·gar·i·an \,bəl-'gar-ē-ən, bùl-, -'ger-\ *noun* (1555)
1 : a native or inhabitant of Bulgaria
2 : the Slavic language of the Bulgarians
— Bulgarian *adjective*
¹bulge \'bəlj *also* 'bùlj\ *verb* **bulged; bulging** (15th century)
transitive verb
: to cause to bulge
intransitive verb
1 *archaic* **:** BILGE
2 a : to jut out **:** SWELL **b :** to bend outward **c :** to become swollen or protuberant
3 : to be filled to overflowing
²bulge *noun* [Middle French *boulge, bouge* leather bag, curved part — more at BUDGET] (1622)
1 : BILGE 1, 2
2 : a protuberant or swollen part or place
3 : ADVANTAGE, UPPER HAND
4 : sudden expansion
synonym see PROJECTION
— bulgy \'bəl-jē *also* 'bùl-\ *adjective*
bul·gur \'bəl-gər, 'bùl-\ *noun* [Turkish] (1926)
: parched cracked wheat
bu·lim·ia \bü-'lē-mē-ə, byü-, -'li-\ *noun* [New Latin, from Greek *boulimia* great hunger, from *bou-,* augmentative prefix (from *bous* head of cattle) + *limos* hunger — more at COW] (14th century)
1 : an abnormal and constant craving for food
2 : a serious eating disorder that occurs chiefly in females, is characterized by compulsive overeating usually followed by self-induced vomiting or laxative or diuretic abuse, and is often accompanied by guilt and depression
— bu·lim·ic \-'lē-mik, -'li-\ *adjective or noun*

¹**bulk** \'bəlk *also* 'bůlk\ *noun* [Middle English, heap, bulk, from Old Norse *bulki* cargo] (15th century)
1 a : spatial dimension : MAGNITUDE **b :** material that forms a mass in the intestine; *especially* : FIBER 1d
2 a : BODY; *especially* : a large or corpulent human body **b :** an organized structure especially when viewed primarily as a mass of material **c :** a ponderous shapeless mass
3 : the main or greater part ☆
— **in bulk 1 :** not divided into parts or packaged in separate units **2 :** in large quantities
²**bulk** (1540)
transitive verb
1 : to cause to swell or bulge : STUFF
2 : to gather into a mass or aggregate
intransitive verb
1 : SWELL, EXPAND
2 : to appear as a factor : LOOM ⟨a consideration that *bulks* large in everyone's thinking⟩
³**bulk** *adjective* (1693)
1 : being in bulk ⟨*bulk* cement⟩
2 : of or relating to materials in bulk
bulk·head \'bəlk-,hed, 'bəl-,ked\ *noun* [*bulk* structure projecting from a building + *head*] (15th century)
1 : an upright partition separating compartments
2 : a structure or partition to resist pressure or to shut off water, fire, or gas
3 : a retaining wall along a waterfront
4 : a projecting framework with a sloping door giving access to a cellar stairway or a shaft
bulk up (1981)
intransitive verb
: to gain weight especially by becoming more muscular
transitive verb
: to cause to bulk up
bulky \'bəl-kē *also* 'bůl-\ *adjective* **bulk·i·er; -est** (15th century)
1 a : having bulk **b** (1) : large of its kind (2) : CORPULENT
2 : having great volume in proportion to weight ⟨a *bulky* knit sweater⟩ ☆
— **bulk·i·ly** \-kə-lē\ *adverb*
— **bulk·i·ness** \-kē-nəs\ *noun*
¹**bull** \'bůl, 'bəl\ *noun* [Middle English *bule*, from Old English *bula*; akin to Old Norse *boli* bull] (before 12th century)
1 a : a male bovine; *especially* : an adult uncastrated male ox **b :** a usually adult male of various large animals (as elephants, whales, or seals)
2 : one who buys securities or commodities in expectation of a price rise or who acts to effect such a rise — compare BEAR
3 : one that resembles a bull (as in brawny physique)
4 : BULLDOG
5 *slang* : POLICE OFFICER, DETECTIVE
6 *capitalized* : TAURUS
²**bull** *adjective* (13th century)
1 a : of or relating to a bull **b :** MALE **c :** suggestive of a bull
2 : large of its kind
³**bull** (1884)
intransitive verb
: to advance forcefully
transitive verb
1 : to act on with violence
2 : FORCE ⟨*bulled* his way through the crowd⟩
⁴**bull** *noun* [Middle English *bulle*, from Medieval Latin *bulla*, from Latin, bubble, amulet] (14th century)
1 : a solemn papal letter sealed with a bulla or with a red-ink imprint of the device on the bulla
2 : EDICT, DECREE
⁵**bull** (1609)
transitive verb
slang : to fool especially by fast boastful talk
intransitive verb
slang : to engage in idle and boastful talk

⁶**bull** *noun* [perhaps from obsolete *bull* to mock] (1640)
1 : a grotesque blunder in language
2 *slang* : empty boastful talk
3 *slang* : NONSENSE 2
bul·la \'bů-lə\ *noun, plural* **bul·lae** \'bů-,lē, -,lī\ (14th century)
1 [Medieval Latin] **:** the round usually lead seal attached to a papal bull
2 [New Latin, from Latin] **:** a hollow thin-walled rounded bony prominence
3 : a large vesicle or blister
bul·lace \'bů-ləs\ *noun* [Middle English *bolace*, from Middle French *beloce*, from Medieval Latin *bolluca*] (14th century)
: a European plum (*Prunus domestica insititia*) with small ovoid fruit in clusters
bull-bait·ing \'bůl-,bā-tiŋ, 'bəl-\ *noun* (circa 1580)
: the former practice of baiting bulls with dogs
bull·bat \'bůl-,bat, 'bəl-\ *noun* (1838)
: NIGHTHAWK 1a
¹**bull·dog** \'bůl-,dòg *also* 'bəl-\ *noun* (circa 1500)
1 : any of a breed of compact muscular short-haired dogs having widely separated forelegs and an undershot lower jaw that were developed in England to fight bulls
2 : a handgun with a thick usually short barrel
3 : a proctor's attendant at an English university
²**bulldog** *adjective* (1855)
: suggestive of a bulldog ⟨*bulldog* tenacity⟩
³**bulldog** *transitive verb* (1907)
: to throw (a steer) by seizing the horns and twisting the neck
— **bull·dog·ger** *noun*
— **bull·dog·ging** *noun*
bull·doze \'bůl-,dōz *also* 'bəl-\ *verb* [perhaps from ¹*bull* + alteration of *dose*] (1876)
transitive verb
1 : to coerce or restrain by threats : BULLY
2 : to move, clear, gouge out, or level off by pushing with or as if with a bulldozer
3 : to force insensitively or ruthlessly ⟨*bulldozed* the program through the legislature⟩
intransitive verb
1 : to operate a bulldozer
2 : to force one's way like a bulldozer
synonym *see* INTIMIDATE
bull·doz·er \-,dō-zər\ *noun* (1876)
1 : one that bulldozes
2 : a tractor-driven machine usually having a broad blunt horizontal blade for moving earth (as in road building)
bull dyke *noun* (circa 1942)
: an aggressively masculine lesbian — often used disparagingly
bul·let \'bů-lət *also* 'bə-\ *noun, often attributive* [Middle French *boulette* small ball & *boulet* missile, diminutives of *boule* ball — more at BOWL] (1579)
1 : a round or elongated missile (as of lead) to be fired from a firearm; *broadly* : CARTRIDGE 1a
2 a : something resembling a bullet (as in curved form) **b :** a large dot placed in printed matter to call attention to a particular passage
3 : a very fast and accurately thrown ball
— **bul·let·ed** \-lə-təd\ *adjective*
— **bul·let-proof** \-,prüf\ *adjective*
¹**bul·le·tin** \'bů-lə-t⁽ə⁾n *also* 'bə-\ *noun* [French, from Middle French, from *bullette* seal, notice, diminutive of *bulle* seal, from Medieval Latin *bulla*] (1765)
1 : a brief public notice issuing usually from an authoritative source; *specifically* : a brief news item intended for immediate publication or broadcast
2 : PERIODICAL; *especially* : the organ of an institution or association
²**bulletin** *transitive verb* (1838)
: to make public by bulletin
bulletin board *noun* (1831)

1 : a board for posting notices (as at a school)
2 : a program on a computer system that allows users to read and write public notices and is accessed usually by modem
bullet train *noun* (1966)
: a high-speed passenger train especially of Japan
bull fiddle *noun* (1880)
: DOUBLE BASS
— **bull fiddler** *noun*
bull·fight \'bůl-,fīt *also* 'bəl-\ *noun* (1788)
: a spectacle in which men ceremonially fight with and in Hispanic tradition kill bulls in an arena for public entertainment
— **bull·fight·er** \-,fī-tər\ *noun*
bull·fight·ing \-tiŋ\ *noun* (circa 1753)
: the action involved in a bullfight
bull·finch \'bůl-,finch *also* 'bəl-\ *noun* (circa 1570)
: a European finch (*Pyrrhula pyrrhula*) having in the male rosy red underparts, blue-gray back, and black cap, chin, tail, and wings; *also* : any of several other finches
bull·frog \-,fròg, -,fräg\ *noun* (1698)
: a heavy-bodied deep-voiced frog (*Rana catesbeiana*) of the eastern U.S. and southern Canada that has been introduced elsewhere
bull·head \-,hed\ *noun* (15th century)
: any of various large-headed fishes (as a sculpin); *especially* : any of several common freshwater catfishes (genus *Ameiurus* sometimes included in the genus *Ictalurus*) of the U.S.
bull·head·ed \-'he-dəd\ *adjective* (1818)
: stupidly stubborn : HEADSTRONG
— **bull·head·ed·ly** *adverb*
— **bull·head·ed·ness** *noun*
bull·horn \-,hòrn\ *noun* (1942)
1 : a loudspeaker on a naval ship
2 : a handheld combined microphone and loudspeaker
bul·lion \'bůl-yən, -,yän\ *noun* [Middle English, from Anglo-French, mint] (14th century)
1 a : gold or silver considered as so much metal; *specifically* : uncoined gold or silver in bars or ingots **b :** metal in the mass ⟨lead *bullion*⟩
2 : lace, braid, or fringe of gold or silver threads
bull·ish \'bů-lish *also* 'bə-\ *adjective* (1566)
1 : suggestive of a bull (as in brawniness)
2 a : marked by, tending to cause, or hopeful of rising prices (as in a stock market) **b :** optimistic about something's or someone's prospects
— **bull·ish·ly** *adverb*
— **bull·ish·ness** *noun*
bull·mas·tiff \'bůl-'mas-təf *also* 'bəl-\ *noun* (1871)
: any of a breed of large powerful dogs developed by crossing bulldogs with mastiffs
Bull Moose *noun* [*bull moose*, emblem of the Progressive party of 1912] (1912)
: a follower of Theodore Roosevelt in the U.S. presidential campaign of 1912

☆ **SYNONYMS**
Bulk, mass, volume mean the aggregate that forms a body or unit. BULK implies an aggregate that is impressively large, heavy, or numerous ⟨the darkened *bulk* of the skyscrapers⟩. MASS suggests an aggregate made by piling together things of the same kind ⟨a *mass* of boulders⟩. VOLUME applies to an aggregate without shape or outline and capable of flowing or fluctuating ⟨a tremendous *volume* of water⟩.

\ə\ **abut** \ᵊ\ **kitten** \ər\ **further** \a\ **ash** \ā\ **ace**
\ä\ **mop, mar** \aů\ **out** \ch\ **chin** \e\ **bet** \ē\ **easy**
\g\ **go** \i\ **hit** \ī\ **ice** \j\ **job** \ŋ\ **sing** \ō\ **go**
\ò\ **law** \òi\ **boy** \th\ **thin** \t͟h\ **the** \ü\ **loot** \ů\ **foot**
\y\ **yet** \zh\ **vision** *see also* Guide to Pronunciation

Bull Moos·er \-'mü-sər\ *noun* (1912)
: BULL MOOSE

bull neck *noun* (1830)
: a thick short powerful neck
— **bull·necked** \'bùl-'nekt *also* 'bəl-\ *adjective*

bull·ock \'bù-lək *also* 'bə-\ *noun* (before 12th century)
1 : a young bull
2 : a castrated bull : STEER
— **bull·ocky** \-lə-kē\ *adjective*

bul·lous \'bù-ləs\ *adjective* (1833)
: resembling or characterized by bullae : VESICULAR ⟨*bullous* lesions⟩

bull pen *noun* (1809)
1 : a large cell where prisoners are detained until brought into court
2 a : a place on a baseball field where pitchers warm up before they start pitching **b** : the relief pitchers of a baseball team
3 : an open work area not divided into offices

bull·ring \'bùl-,riŋ\ *noun* (1802)
: an arena for bullfights

bull session *noun* [⁶*bull*] (1920)
: an informal discursive group discussion

bull's-eye \'bùl-,zī *also* 'bəl-\ *noun, plural* **bull's-eyes** (1825)
1 : a very hard globular candy
2 : a circular piece of glass with a lump in the middle formed at the end of a glassblower's pipe
3 a : the center of a target; *also* : something central or crucial **b** : a shot that hits the bull's-eye; *broadly* : something that precisely attains a desired end
4 : a simple lens of short focal distance; *also* : a lantern with such a lens

bull's-eye window *noun* (1926)
: a circular window; *also* : a window made up of glassblower's bull's-eyes

¹**bull·shit** \'bùl-,shit *also* 'bəl-\ *noun* [¹*bull* & ⁶*bull*] (circa 1915)
: NONSENSE; *especially* : foolish insolent talk
— usually considered vulgar

²**bullshit** (circa 1942)
intransitive verb
1 : to talk foolishly, boastfully, or idly — usually considered vulgar
2 : to engage in a discursive discussion — usually considered vulgar
transitive verb
: to talk nonsense to especially with the intention of deceiving or misleading — usually considered vulgar

bull·shot \-,shät\ *noun* (1964)
: a drink made of vodka and bouillon

bull snake *noun* (1784)
: any of several large harmless North American snakes (genus *Pituophis*) that feed chiefly on rodents — called also *gopher snake, pine snake*

bull·ter·ri·er \'bùl-'ter-ē-ər *also* 'bəl-\ *noun* [*bull*dog + *terrier*] (1848)
: any of a breed of short-haired terriers originated in England by crossing the bulldog with terriers

bull thistle *noun* (1863)
: a European thistle (*Cirsium vulgare*) with rather large heads and prickly leaves that is naturalized as a weed in the U.S.

bull tongue *noun* (1831)
: a wide blade attached to a cultivator or plow to stir the soil, kill weeds, or mark furrows

bull·whip \'bùl-,(h)wip *also* 'bəl-\ *noun* (1852)
: a rawhide whip with a very long plaited lash

¹**bul·ly** \'bù-lē, 'bə-\ *noun, plural* **bullies** [probably modification of Dutch *boel* lover, from Middle High German *buole*] (1538)
1 *archaic* **a** : SWEETHEART **b** : a fine chap
2 a : a blustering browbeating person; *especially* : one habitually cruel to others who are weaker **b** : PIMP
3 : a hired ruffian

²**bully** *adjective* (1681)
1 : EXCELLENT, FIRST-RATE — often used in interjectional expressions ⟨*bully* for you⟩

2 : resembling or characteristic of a bully

³**bully** *verb* **bul·lied; bul·ly·ing** (1710)
transitive verb
1 : to treat abusively
2 : to affect by means of force or coercion
intransitive verb
: to use browbeating language or behavior
: BLUSTER
synonym see INTIMIDATE

⁴**bully** *noun* [probably modification of French (*bœuf*) *bouli* boiled beef] (1753)
: pickled or canned usually corned beef

bul·ly·boy \'bù-lē-,bòi, 'bə-\ *noun* (1925)
: a swaggering tough

bully pulpit *noun* (1976)
: a prominent public position (as a political office) that provides an opportunity for expounding one's views; *also* : such an opportunity

bul·ly·rag \-,rag\ *transitive verb* [origin unknown] (circa 1790)
1 : to intimidate by bullying
2 : to vex by teasing : BADGER

bul·rush *also* **bull·rush** \'bùl-,rəsh\ *noun* [Middle English *bulrysche*] (15th century)
: any of several large rushes or sedges growing in wetlands: as **a** : any of a genus of annual or perennial sedges (*Scirpus*, especially *S. lacustris*) that bear solitary or much-clustered spikelets containing perfect flowers with a perianth of six bristles **b** *British* : either of two cattails (*Typha latifolia* and *T. angustifolia*) **c** : PAPYRUS

¹**bul·wark** \'bùl-(,)wərk, -,wòrk; 'bəl-(,)wərk; sense 3 *also* 'bə-,läk\ *noun* [Middle English *bulwerke*, from Middle Dutch *bolwerc*, from Middle High German *bole* plank + *werc* work] (15th century)
1 a : a solid wall-like structure raised for defense : RAMPART **b** : BREAKWATER, SEAWALL
2 : a strong support or protection
3 : the side of a ship above the upper deck — usually used in plural
word history see BOULEVARD

²**bulwark** *transitive verb* (15th century)
: to fortify or safeguard with a bulwark

¹**bum** \'bəm\ *noun* [Middle English *bom*] (14th century)
chiefly British : BUTTOCKS — sometimes considered vulgar

²**bum** *adjective* [perhaps from ⁴*bum*] (1859)
1 a : of poor quality or nature : INVALID, INFERIOR ⟨*bum* advice⟩ ⟨a *bum* check⟩ **b** : acutely disagreeable ⟨a *bum* trip⟩
2 : not functioning because of damage or injury : DISABLED ⟨a *bum* knee⟩

³**bum** *verb* **bummed; bum·ming** [probably back-formation from ¹*bummer*] (1863)
intransitive verb
1 : LOAF
2 : to spend time unemployed and often wandering — often used with *around*
transitive verb
: to obtain by begging : CADGE

⁴**bum** *noun* [probably short for *bummer*] (1864)
1 a : one who sponges off others and avoids work **b** : one who performs a function poorly ⟨called the umpire a *bum*⟩ **c** : one who devotes his time to a recreational activity ⟨a beach *bum*⟩ ⟨ski *bums*⟩
2 : VAGRANT, TRAMP
— **on the bum** : with no settled residence or means of support

⁵**bum** *noun* [probably from ³*bum*] (1871)
: a drinking spree : BENDER

bum·ber·shoot \'bəm-bər-,shüt\ *noun* [*bumber*- (alteration of *umbr*- in *umbrella*) + -*shoot* (alteration of -*chute* in *parachute*)] (circa 1896)
: UMBRELLA

¹**bum·ble** \'bəm-bəl\ *intransitive verb* **bumbled; bum·bling** \-b(ə-)liŋ\ [Middle English *bomblen* to boom, of imitative origin] (15th century)
1 : BUZZ

2 : DRONE, RUMBLE

²**bumble** *verb* **bumbled; bumbling** [perhaps alteration of *bungle*] (1532)
intransitive verb
1 : BLUNDER; *specifically* : to speak ineptly in a stuttering and faltering manner
2 : to proceed unsteadily : STUMBLE
transitive verb
: BUNGLE
— **bum·bler** \-b(ə-)lər\ *noun*
— **bum·bling·ly** \-b(ə-)liŋ-lē\ *adverb*

bum·ble·bee \'bəm-bəl-,bē\ *noun* (1530)
: any of numerous large robust hairy social bees (genus *Bombus*)

bum·boat \'bəm-,bōt\ *noun* [probably from Low German *bumboot,* from *bum* tree + *boot* boat] (1769)
: a boat that brings provisions and commodities for sale to larger ships in port or offshore

bumf *also* **bumph** \'bəm(p)f\ *noun* [from *bumf* toilet paper, short for *bumfodder,* from ¹*bum* + *fodder*] (circa 1889)
chiefly British : PAPERWORK

bummed \'bəmd\ *adjective* [probably back-formation from ²*bummer*] (1971)
: DISAPPOINTED, DEPRESSED — usually used with *out*

¹**bum·mer** \'bə-mər\ *noun* [probably modification of German *Bummler* loafer, from *bummeln* to dangle, loaf] (1855)
: one that bums

²**bummer** *noun* [²*bum* + ²-*er*] (1967)
1 : an unpleasant experience (as a bad reaction to a hallucinogenic drug)
2 : FAILURE, FLOP

¹**bump** \'bəmp\ *noun* [probably imitative of the sound of a blow] (1592)
1 : a relatively abrupt convexity or protuberance on a surface: as **a** : a swelling of tissue **b** : a cranial protuberance
2 a : a sudden forceful blow, impact, or jolt **b** : DEMOTION
3 : an act of thrusting the hips forward in an erotic manner

²**bump** (1611)
transitive verb
1 : to strike or knock with force or violence
2 : to collide with
3 a (1) : to dislodge with a jolt (2) : to subject to a scalar change ⟨rates being *bumped* up⟩ **b** : to oust usually by virtue of seniority or priority ⟨was *bumped* from the flight⟩
intransitive verb
1 : to knock against something with a forceful jolt
2 : to proceed in or as if in a series of bumps
3 : to encounter something that is an obstacle or hindrance ⟨*bumped* up against a chair⟩
— **bump into** : to encounter especially by chance

¹**bum·per** \'bəm-pər\ *noun* [probably from *bump* to bulge] (1676)
1 : a brimming cup or glass
2 : something unusually large

²**bumper** *adjective* (1885)
1 : unusually large ⟨a *bumper* crop⟩
2 : BANNER 2

³**bump·er** \'bəm-pər\ *noun* (1839)
1 : a device for absorbing shock or preventing damage (as in collision); *specifically* : a usually metal bar at either end of an automobile
2 : one that bumps

bumper car *noun* (1959)
: a small electric car made to be driven around in an enclosure and to be bumped into others (as at an amusement park)

bumper sticker *noun* (1967)
: a strip of adhesive paper or plastic bearing a printed message and designed to be stuck on a vehicle's bumper

bumper-to-bumper *adjective* (1951)
: marked by long closed lines of cars

¹**bump·kin** \'bəm(p)-kən\ *noun* [perhaps from Flemish *bommekijn* small cask, from Middle Dutch, from *bomme* cask] (1570)
: an awkward and unsophisticated rustic

— **bump·kin·ish** \-kə-nish\ *adjective*
— **bump·kin·ly** \-kən-lē\ *adjective*
²bump·kin *or* **bum·kin** \'bəm(p)-kən\ *noun* [probably from Flemish *boomken*, diminutive of *boom* tree] (circa 1632)
: a spar projecting from a ship especially at the stern
bump off *transitive verb* (1910)
: to murder casually or cold-bloodedly
bump·tious \'bəm(p)-shəs\ *adjective* [¹*bump* + *-tious* (as in *fractious*)] (1803)
: presumptuously, obtusely, and often noisily self-assertive : OBTRUSIVE
— **bump·tious·ly** *adverb*
— **bump·tious·ness** *noun*
bumpy \'bəm-pē\ *adjective* **bump·i·er; -est** (1865)
1 : having or covered with bumps 〈a *bumpy* road〉 〈*bumpy* skin〉
2 a : marked by bumps or jolts 〈a *bumpy* ride〉 **b** : marked by or full of difficulties 〈a *bumpy* relationship〉
— **bump·i·ly** \-pə-lē\ *adverb*
— **bump·i·ness** \-pē-nəs\ *noun*
bum's rush \'bəmz-\ *noun* (1922)
: forcible eviction or dismissal
¹bun \'bən\ *noun* [Middle English *bunne*] (14th century)
1 : a sweet or plain small bread; *especially* : a round roll
2 : a knot of hair shaped like a bun
3 *plural* : BUTTOCKS
²bun *noun* [perhaps from ¹*bun*] (1901)
: LOAD 4
Bu·na \'byü-nə, 'bü-\ *trademark*
— used for any of several rubbers made by polymerization or copolymerization of butadiene
¹bunch \'bənch\ *noun* [Middle English *bunche*] (14th century)
1 : PROTUBERANCE, SWELLING
2 a : a number of things of the same kind 〈a *bunch* of grapes〉 **b** : GROUP 2a 〈a *bunch* of friends〉 **c** : a considerable amount : LOT 〈a *bunch* of money〉
— **bunch·i·ly** \'bən-chə-lē\ *adverb*
— **bunchy** \-chē\ *adjective*
²bunch (14th century)
intransitive verb
1 : SWELL, PROTRUDE
2 : to form a group or cluster — often used with *up*
transitive verb
: to form into a bunch
bunch·ber·ry \'bənch-,ber-ē\ *noun* (1845)
: a creeping perennial herb (*Cornus canadensis*) of the dogwood family that has whorled leaves and white floral bracts and bears red berries in capitate cymes
bunch·grass \-,gras\ *noun* (1839)
: any of several grasses (as of the genus *Andropogon*) especially of the western U.S. that grow in tufts
bun·co *or* **bun·ko** \'bəŋ-(,)kō\ *noun, plural* **buncos** *or* **bunkos** [perhaps alteration of Spanish *banca* bench, banking, bank in gambling, from Italian — more at BANK] (1872)
: a swindling game or scheme
— **bunco** *transitive verb*
¹bund \'bənd\ *noun* [Hindi *band*, from Persian] (1810)
1 : an embankment used especially in India to control the flow of water
2 : an embanked thoroughfare along a river or the sea especially in the Far East
²bund \'bùnd, 'bənd, 'bùnt\ *noun, often capitalized* [Yiddish *bund* & German *Bund*, from Middle High German *bunt*; akin to Old English *byndel*] (1850)
: a political association: as **a** : a Jewish socialist organization founded in czarist Russia in 1897 **b** : a pro-Nazi German-American organization of the 1930s
— **bund·ist** \'bùn-dist, 'bən-\ *noun, often capitalized*

¹bun·dle \'bən-d°l\ *noun* [Middle English *bundel*, from Middle Dutch; akin to Old English *byndel* bundle, *bindan* to bind] (14th century)
1 a : a group of things fastened together for convenient handling **b** : PACKAGE, PARCEL **c** : a considerable number • LOT **d** : a sizable sum of money **e** : a person embodying a specified quality or characteristic 〈a *bundle* of energy〉
2 a : a small band of mostly parallel fibers (as of nerve or muscle) **b** : VASCULAR BUNDLE
²bundle *verb* **bun·dled; bun·dling** \'bən(d)-liŋ, 'bən-d°l-iŋ\ (circa 1628)
transitive verb
1 : to make into a bundle or package : WRAP
2 : to hustle or hurry unceremoniously 〈*bundled* the children off to school〉
3 : to include (a product or service) with a related product for sale at a single price 〈software is *bundled* with computer hardware〉
intransitive verb
1 : HURRY, HUSTLE
2 : to practice bundling
— **bun·dler** \-lər, -d°l-ər\ *noun*
bundle up (1918)
transitive verb
: to dress (someone) warmly
intransitive verb
: to dress warmly
bun·dling \'bən(d)-liŋ, 'bən-d°l-iŋ\ *noun* (1781)
: a former custom of an unmarried couple's occupying the same bed without undressing especially during courtship
¹bung \'bəŋ\ *noun* [Middle English, from Middle Dutch *bonne, bonghe*] (15th century)
1 : the stopper especially in the bunghole of a cask; *also* : BUNGHOLE
2 : the cecum or anus especially of a slaughtered animal
²bung *transitive verb* (1589)
1 : to plug with or as if with a bung
2 *British* : THROW, TOSS 〈*bung* a spanner into the works —P. G. Wodehouse〉
bun·ga·low \'bəŋ-gə-,lō\ *noun* [Hindi *baṅglā*, literally, (house) in the Bengal style] (1676)
: a usually one-storied house with a low-pitched roof
bun·gee cord \'bən-jē-\ *noun* [origin unknown] (1948)
: an elasticized cord used especially as a fastening or shock-absorbing device — called also *bungee*
bung·hole \'bəŋ-,hōl\ *noun* (1571)
: a hole for emptying or filling a cask
bun·gle \'bəŋ-gəl\ *verb* **bun·gled; bun·gling** \-g(ə-)liŋ\ [perhaps of Scandinavian origin; akin to Icelandic *banga* to hammer] (1549)
intransitive verb
: to act or work clumsily and awkwardly
transitive verb
: MISHANDLE, BOTCH
— **bungle** *noun*
— **bun·gler** \-g(ə-)lər\ *noun*
— **bun·gling·ly** \-g(ə-)liŋ-lē\ *adverb*
bun·gle·some \-gəl-səm\ *adjective* (circa 1889)
: AWKWARD, CLUMSY
bung up *transitive verb* (1951)
: BATTER
bun·ion \'bən-yən\ *noun* [probably alteration of *bunny* swelling] (circa 1718)
: an inflamed swelling of the small sac on the first joint of the big toe
¹bunk \'bəŋk\ *noun* [probably short for *bunker*] (1758)
1 a : BUNK BED **b** : a built-in bed (as on a ship) that is often one of a tier of berths **c** : a sleeping place
2 : a feeding trough for farm animals and especially cattle
²bunk (1840)
intransitive verb
: to occupy a bunk or bed : stay the night 〈*bunked* with a friend for the night〉

transitive verb
: to provide with a bunk or bed
³bunk *noun* (1900)
: BUNKUM, NONSENSE
⁴bunk *noun* [origin unknown] (circa 1870)
British : a hurried departure or escape — usually used in the phrase *do a bunk*
bunk bed *noun* (1924)
: one of two single beds usually placed one above the other
¹bun·ker \'bəŋ-kər\ *noun* [Scots *bonker* chest, box] (1839)
1 : a bin or compartment for storage; *especially* : one on shipboard for the ship's fuel
2 a : a protective embankment or dugout; *especially* : a fortified chamber mostly below ground often built of reinforced concrete and provided with embrasures **b** : a sand trap or embankment constituting a hazard on a golf course
— **bun·kered** \-kərd\ *adjective*
²bunker *verb* **bun·kered; bun·ker·ing** \-k(ə-)riŋ\ (1891)
intransitive verb
: to fill a ship's bunker with coal or oil
transitive verb
1 : to place or store in a bunker
2 : to hit (a golf ball or shot) into a bunker
bunker mentality *noun* (1976)
: a state of mind especially among members of a group that is characterized by chauvinistic defensiveness and self-righteous intolerance of criticism
bunk·house \'bəŋk-,haùs\ *noun* (1876)
: a rough simple building providing sleeping quarters
bun·kum *or* **bun·combe** \'bəŋ-kəm\ *noun* [*Buncombe* county, N.C.; from a remark made by its congressman, who defended an irrelevant speech by claiming that he was speaking to Buncombe] (1845)
: insincere or foolish talk : NONSENSE ◆
bun·ny \'bə-nē\ *noun, plural* **bunnies** [English dialect *bun* rabbit] (circa 1690)
1 : RABBIT; *especially* : a young rabbit
2 : a desirable young woman
Bun·ra·ku \bùn-'rä-(,)kü\ *noun* [Japanese] (1920)

◇ WORD HISTORY
bunkum The word *bunkum* or *buncombe* "nonsense" first occurs in 1828 in the phrase *talk to bunkum*, alluding to overly long congressional speeches given to a nearly empty chamber. According to a tale that has become part of American political folklore, this phrase originated around 1820, when Felix Walker (1753–1828), a U.S. Congressman who represented a district in North Carolina that included Buncombe County, persisted in delivering an exceptionally wearisome speech to the Sixteenth Congress, despite the objections of his impatient colleagues. In self-defense Walker explained that he had done what his constituents expected of him, which was "to make a speech for Buncombe." Whatever the veracity of this story, *bunkum* has remained thoroughly entrenched in American English. The noun *bunk*, recorded in 1893 in the sense "something fraudulent" and in 1900 alluding to nonsensical talk, is probably short for *bunkum*, though it has very likely been influenced by *bunco* (or *bunko*), a word that developed in the late 19th century in reference to rigged games of chance.

\ə\ **abut** \ᵊ\ **kitten** \ər\ **further** \a\ **ash** \ā\ **ace**
\ä\ **mop, mar** \aù\ **out** \ch\ **chin** \e\ **bet** \ē\ **easy**
\g\ **go** \i\ **hit** \ī\ **ice** \j\ **job** \ŋ\ **sing** \ō\ **go**
\ò\ **law** \òi\ **boy** \th\ **thin** \ṯẖ\ **the** \ü\ **loot** \ù\ **foot**
\y\ **yet** \zh\ **vision** *see also* Guide to Pronunciation

: Japanese puppet theater featuring large costumed wooden puppets, puppeteers who are onstage, and a chanter who speaks all the lines

Bun·sen burner \'bən(t)-sən-\ *noun* [Robert Welsh *Bunsen*] (circa 1888)
: a gas burner consisting typically of a straight tube with small holes at the bottom where air enters and mixes with the gas to produce an intensely hot blue flame

¹**bunt** \'bənt\ *noun* [perhaps from Low German, bundle, from Middle Low German; akin to Old English *byndel* bundle] (circa 1582)
1 a : the middle part of a square sail **b :** the part of a furled sail gathered up in a bunch at the center of the yard
2 : the bagging part of a fishing net

²**bunt** *verb* [alteration of *butt*] (1584)
transitive verb
1 : to strike or push with or as if with the head **:** BUTT
2 : to push or tap (a baseball) lightly without swinging the bat
intransitive verb
: to bunt a baseball
— **bunt·er** *noun*

³**bunt** *noun* (1767)
1 : an act or instance of bunting
2 : a bunted ball

⁴**bunt** *noun* [origin unknown] (circa 1790)
: a destructive covered smut of wheat caused by a fungus (*Tilletia foetida* or *T. caries*)

¹**bun·ting** \'bən-tiŋ\ *noun* [Middle English] (14th century)
: any of various stout-billed passerine birds (family Emberizidae) included with some of the finches — compare INDIGO BUNTING

²**bunting** *noun* [perhaps from English dialect *bunt* (to sift)] (1711)
1 : a lightweight loosely woven fabric used chiefly for flags and festive decorations
2 a : FLAGS **b :** decorations especially in the colors of the national flag

³**bunting** *noun* [term of endearment in the nursery rhyme "Bye, baby bunting"] (1922)
: an infant's hooded sleeping bag made of napped fabric

bunt·line \'bənt-,līn, -lən\ *noun* (1627)
: one of the lines attached to the foot of a square sail to haul the sail up to the yard for furling

Bun·yan·esque \,bən-yə-'nesk\ *adjective* (1888)
1 [John *Bunyan*] **:** of, relating to, or suggestive of the allegorical writings of John Bunyan
2 [Paul *Bunyan*, legendary giant lumberjack of U.S. & Canada] **a :** of, relating to, or suggestive of the tales of Paul Bunyan **b :** of fantastically large size

¹**buoy** \'bü-ē, 'böi\ *noun* [Middle English *boye*, probably from Middle Dutch *boeye*; akin to Old High German *bouhhan* sign — more at BEACON] (13th century)
1 : FLOAT 2; *especially* **:** a floating object moored to the bottom to mark a channel or something (as a shoal) lying under the water
2 : LIFE BUOY

²**buoy** (1596)
transitive verb
1 : to mark by or as if by a buoy
2 a : to keep afloat **b :** SUPPORT, UPLIFT ⟨an economy *buoyed* by the dramatic postwar growth of industry —*Time*⟩
3 : to raise the spirits of — usually used with *up* ⟨hope *buoys* him up⟩
intransitive verb
: FLOAT — usually used with *up*

buoy·ance \'böi-ən(t)s, 'bü-yən(t)s\ *noun* (1821)
: BUOYANCY

buoy·an·cy \'böi-ən(t)-sē, 'bü-yən(t)-\ *noun* (1713)

1 a : the tendency of a body to float or to rise when submerged in a fluid **b :** the power of a fluid to exert an upward force on a body placed in it; *also* **:** the upward force exerted
2 : the ability to recover quickly from depression or discouragement **:** RESILIENCE

buoy·ant \'böi-ənt, 'bü-yənt\ *adjective* (1578)
: having buoyancy: as **a :** capable of floating **b :** CHEERFUL, GAY **c :** capable of recovering **:** having positive indications ⟨a *buoyant* economy⟩
— **buoy·ant·ly** *adverb*

bup·pie \'bə-pē\ *noun* [¹*black* + *yuppie*] (1984)
: a college-educated black adult who is employed in a well-paying profession and who lives or works in or near a large city

bur *variant of* BURR

Bur·ber·ry \'bər-b(ə-)rē, 'bər-,ber-ē\ *trademark*
— used for various fabrics used especially for coats for outdoor wear

¹**bur·ble** \'bər-bəl\ *intransitive verb* **bur·bled; bur·bling** \-b(ə-)liŋ\ [Middle English] (14th century)
1 : BUBBLE
2 : BABBLE, PRATTLE
— **bur·bler** \-b(ə-)lər\ *noun*

²**burble** *noun* (1898)
1 : PRATTLE
2 : the breaking up of the streamline flow of air about a body (as an airplane wing)
— **bur·bly** \-b(ə-)lē\ *adjective*

bur·bot \'bər-bət\ *noun, plural* **burbot** *also* **burbots** [Middle English *borbot*, from Middle French *bourbotte*, from *bourbeter* to burrow in the mud] (14th century)
: a Holarctic freshwater fish (*Lota lota*) of the cod family having barbels on the nose and chin

burbs \'bərbz\ *noun plural* (1971)
: SUBURBS

¹**bur·den** \'bər-dᵊn\ *noun* [Middle English, from Old English *byrthen;* akin to Old English *beran* to carry — more at BEAR] (before 12th century)
1 a : something that is carried **:** LOAD **b :** DUTY, RESPONSIBILITY
2 : something oppressive or worrisome
3 a : the bearing of a load — usually used in the phrase *beast of burden* **b :** capacity for carrying cargo ⟨a ship of a hundred tons *burden*⟩
4 : the amount of a deleterious parasite, growth, or substance present in a human or animal body ⟨worm *burden*⟩ ⟨cancer *burden*⟩

²**burden** *transitive verb* **bur·dened; bur·den·ing** \'bərd-niŋ, 'bər-dᵊn-iŋ\ (1541)
: LOAD, OPPRESS ⟨I will not *burden* you with a lengthy account⟩

³**burden** *noun* [Middle English *burdoun*, from Middle French *bourdon* a drone bass, of imitative origin] (14th century)
1 *archaic* **:** a bass or accompanying part
2 a : CHORUS, REFRAIN **b :** a central topic **:** THEME

burden of proof (1593)
: the duty of proving a disputed assertion or charge

bur·den·some \'bər-dᵊn-səm\ *adjective* (1578)
: imposing or constituting a burden **:** OPPRESSIVE ⟨*burdensome* restrictions⟩
synonym see ONEROUS

bur·dock \'bər-,däk\ *noun* (15th century)
: any of a genus (*Arctium*) of coarse composite herbs bearing globular flower heads with prickly bracts

bu·reau \'byùr-(,)ō\ *noun, plural* **bureaus** *also* **bu·reaux** \-(,)ōz\ [French, desk, cloth covering for desks, from Old French *burel* woolen cloth, from (assumed) Old French *bure*, from Late Latin *burra* shaggy cloth] (1699)
1 a *British* **:** WRITING DESK; *especially* **:** one having drawers and a slant top **b :** a low chest of drawers for use in a bedroom

2 a : a specialized administrative unit; *especially* **:** a subdivision of an executive department of a government **b :** a branch of a newspaper, newsmagazine, or wire service in an important news center **c :** a usually commercial agency that serves as an intermediary especially for exchanging information or coordinating activities ⟨credit *bureau*⟩

bu·reau·cra·cy \byù-'rä-krə-sē\ *noun, plural* **-cies** [French *bureaucratie*, from *bureau* + *-cratie* -cracy] (1818)
1 a : a body of nonelective government officials **b :** an administrative policy-making group
2 : government characterized by specialization of functions, adherence to fixed rules, and a hierarchy of authority
3 : a system of administration marked by officialism, red tape, and proliferation

bu·reau·crat \'byùr-ə-,krat\ *noun* (1842)
: a member of a bureaucracy

bu·reau·crat·ese \,byùr-ə-(,)kra-'tēz, -'tēs\ *noun* (1949)
: a style of language held to be characteristic of bureaucrats and marked by the prevalence of abstractions, jargon, euphemisms, and circumlocutions

bu·reau·crat·ic \,byùr-ə-'kra-tik\ *adjective* (1836)
: of, relating to, or having the characteristics of a bureaucracy or a bureaucrat ⟨*bureaucratic* government⟩
— **bu·reau·crat·i·cal·ly** \-ti-k(ə-)lē\ *adverb*

bu·reau·cra·tise *British variant of* BUREAUCRATIZE

bu·reau·crat·ism \'byùr-ə-(,)kra-,ti-zəm\ *noun* (1880)
: a bureaucratic system **:** BUREAUCRACY

bu·reau·cra·tize \byù-'rä-krə-,tīz\ *transitive verb* **-tized; -tiz·ing** (1892)
: to make bureaucratic
— **bu·reau·cra·ti·za·tion** \-,rä-krə-tə-'zā-shən\ *noun*

bu·rette *or* **bu·ret** \byù-'ret\ *noun* [Middle French, cruet, from *buire* pitcher, perhaps of Germanic origin; akin to Old English *būr* storehouse, dwelling — more at BOWER] (1836)
: a graduated glass tube with a small aperture and stopcock for delivering measured quantities of liquid or for measuring the liquid or gas received or discharged

burg \'bərg\ *noun* [Old English — more at BOROUGH] (1753)
1 : an ancient or medieval fortress or walled town
2 [German *Burg*] **:** CITY, TOWN

bur·gage \'bər-gij\ *noun* [Middle English, property held by burgage tenure, from Middle French *bourgage*, from Old French, from *bourg, borc* town — more at BOURG] (15th century)
: a tenure by which real property in England and Scotland was held under the king or a lord for a yearly rent or for watching and warding

bur·gee \,bər-'jē, 'bər-,\ *noun* [perhaps from French dialect *bourgeais* shipowner] (1750)
1 : a swallow-tailed flag used especially by ships for signals or identification
2 : the usually triangular identifying flag of a yacht club

bur·geon \'bər-jən\ *intransitive verb* [Middle English *burjonen*, from *burjon* bud, from Old French, from (assumed) Vulgar Latin *burrion-, burrio*, from Late Latin *burra* fluff, shaggy cloth] (14th century)
1 a : to send forth new growth (as buds or branches) **:** SPROUT **b :** BLOOM
2 : to grow and expand rapidly **:** FLOURISH

bur·ger \'bər-gər\ *noun* (1939)
1 : HAMBURGER
2 : a sandwich similar to a hamburger — often used in combination ⟨tofu *burger*⟩

buoy 1

bur·gess \'bər-jəs\ *noun* [Middle English *burgeis,* from Old French *borjois,* from *borc*] (13th century)
1 a : a citizen of a British borough **b :** a representative of a borough, corporate town, or university in the British Parliament
2 : a representative in the popular branch of the legislature of colonial Maryland and Virginia

burgh \'bər-(ˌ)ō, 'bə-(ˌ)rō\ *noun* [Middle English — more at BOROUGH] (12th century)
: BOROUGH; *specifically* **:** an incorporated town in Scotland having local jurisdiction of certain services
— **burgh·al** \'bər-gəl\ *adjective*

bur·gher \'bər-gər\ *noun* (13th century)
1 : an inhabitant of a borough or a town
2 : a member of the middle class **:** a prosperous solid citizen

bur·glar \'bər-glər *also* -gə-lər\ *noun* [Anglo-French *burgler,* from Medieval Latin *burglator,* probably alteration of *burgator,* from *burgare* to commit burglary] (1541)
: one who commits burglary

bur·glar·ize \'bər-glə-ˌrīz *also* 'bər-gə-lə-\ *verb* **-ized; -iz·ing** (1871)
transitive verb
1 : to break into and steal from
2 : to commit burglary against
intransitive verb
: to commit burglary

bur·glar-proof \'bər-glər-ˌprüf\ *adjective* (1856)
: protected against or designed to afford protection against burglary

bur·glary \'bər-glə-rē *also* -gə-lə-rē *also* -gəl-rē\ *noun, plural* **-glar·ies** (circa 1523)
: the act of breaking and entering a dwelling at night to commit a felony (as theft); *broadly* **:** the entering of a building with the intent to commit a crime
— **bur·glar·i·ous** \ˌbər-'glar-ē-əs, -'gler-\ *adjective*
— **bur·glar·i·ous·ly** *adverb*

bur·gle \'bər-gəl\ *transitive verb* **bur·gled; bur·gling** \-g(ə-)liŋ\ [back-formation from *burglar*] (1870)
: BURGLARIZE

bur·go·mas·ter \'bər-gə-ˌmas-tər\ *noun* [part modification, part translation of Dutch *burgemeester,* from *burg* town + *meester* master] (1592)
: the chief magistrate of a town in some European countries **:** MAYOR

bur·go·net \'bər-gə-nət, ˌbər-gə-'net\ *noun* [modification of Middle French *bourguignotte*] (circa 1587)
: a helmet of either of two 16th century styles

bur·goo \'bər-ˌgü, (ˌ)bər-'\ *noun, plural* **bur·goos** [origin unknown] (1700)
1 : oatmeal gruel
2 : hardtack and molasses cooked together
3 a : a stew or thick soup of meat and vegetables originally served at outdoor gatherings **b :** a picnic at which burgoo is served

bur·gun·dy \'bər-gən-dē\ *noun, plural* **-dies** [*Burgundy,* region in France] (1668)
1 *often capitalized* **:** a red or white unblended wine from Burgundy; *also* **:** a blended red wine produced elsewhere (as California)
2 : a reddish purple color

buri·al \'ber-ē-əl *also* 'bər-\ *noun, often attributive* [Middle English *beriel, berial,* back-formation from *beriels* (taken as a plural), from Old English *byrgels;* akin to Old Saxon *burgisli* tomb, Old English *byrgan* to bury — more at BURY] (13th century)
1 : GRAVE, TOMB
2 : the act or process of burying

buri·er \'ber-ē-ər *also* 'bər-\ *noun* (before 12th century)
: one that buries

bu·rin \'byur-ən, 'bər-\ *noun* [French] (1662)
1 : an engraver's steel cutting tool having the blade ground obliquely to a sharp point
2 : a prehistoric flint tool with a beveled point

burke \'bərk\ *transitive verb* **burked; burk·ing** [from *burke* to suffocate, from William *Burke* (died 1829) Irish criminal executed for smothering victims to sell their bodies for dissection] (1840)
1 : to suppress quietly or indirectly ⟨*burke* an inquiry⟩
2 : BYPASS, AVOID ⟨*burke* an issue⟩

Bur·kitt's lymphoma \'bər-kəts-\ *also* **Bur·kitt lymphoma** \-kət-\ *noun* [Denis Parsons *Burkitt* (died 1993) British surgeon] (1963)
: a malignant lymphoma that occurs especially in children of central Africa and is associated with Epstein-Barr virus

burl \'bər(-ə)l\ *noun* [Middle English *burle,* from (assumed) Middle French *bourle* tuft of wool, from (assumed) Vulgar Latin *burrula,* diminutive of Late Latin *burra* shaggy cloth] (15th century)
1 : a knot or lump in thread or cloth
2 a : a hard woody often flattened hemispherical outgrowth on a tree **b :** veneer made from burls

bur·la·de·ro \ˌbür-lə-'der-(ˌ)ō, ˌbər-\ *noun, plural* **-ros** [Spanish, from *burlar* to make fun of, elude, from *burla* joke] (1938)
: a wooden shield near the wall in a bullring for bullfighters to take shelter behind if pursued

bur·lap \'bər-ˌlap\ *noun* [origin unknown] (circa 1696)
1 : a coarse heavy plain-woven fabric usually of jute or hemp used for bagging and wrapping and in furniture and linoleum manufacture
2 : a lightweight material resembling burlap used in interior decoration or for clothing

burled \'bər(-ə)ld\ *adjective* (1924)
: having a distorted grain due to burls

¹bur·lesque \(ˌ)bər-'lesk\ *noun* [*burlesque,* adjective, comic, droll, from French, from Italian *burlesco,* from *burla* joke, from Spanish] (1667)
1 : a literary or dramatic work that seeks to ridicule by means of grotesque exaggeration or comic imitation
2 : mockery usually by caricature
3 : theatrical entertainment of a broadly humorous often earthy character consisting of short turns, comic skits, and sometimes striptease acts
synonym see CARICATURE
— **burlesque** *adjective*
— **bur·lesque·ly** *adverb*

²burlesque *verb* **bur·lesqued; bur·lesqu·ing** (1676)
transitive verb
: to imitate in a humorous or derisive manner
: MOCK
intransitive verb
: to employ burlesque
— **bur·lesqu·er** *noun*

bur·ley \'bər-lē\ *noun, often capitalized* [probably from the name *Burley*] (1881)
: a thin-bodied air-cured tobacco grown mainly in Kentucky

bur·ly \'bər-lē\ *adjective* **bur·li·er; -est** [Middle English] (13th century)
1 : strongly and heavily built **:** HUSKY
2 : heartily direct and frank **:** BLUFF, FORTHRIGHT ⟨an evocative story less *burly* than the real thing but entertaining —E. A. Weeks⟩
— **bur·li·ly** \-lə-lē\ *adverb*
— **bur·li·ness** \-lē-nəs\ *noun*

bur marigold *noun* (circa 1818)
: any of a genus (*Bidens*) of coarse composite herbs with prickly flattened achenes that adhere to clothing

Bur·mese \ˌbər-'mēz, -'mēs\ *noun, plural* **Burmese** (1824)
1 : a native or inhabitant of Burma (Myanmar)
2 : the Tibeto-Burman language of the Burmese people
3 : any of a U.S.-developed breed of slender shorthaired cats having gold eyes and a usually dark brown coat

— **Burmese** *adjective*

¹burn \'bərn\ *noun* [Middle English, from Old English; akin to Old High German *brunno* spring of water] (before 12th century)
British **:** CREEK 2

²burn \'bərn\ *verb* **burned** \'bərnd, 'bərnt\ *or* **burnt** \'bərnt\; **burn·ing** [Middle English *birnen,* from Old English *byrnan,* intransitive verb, *bærnan,* transitive verb; akin to Old High German *brinnan* to burn] (before 12th century)
intransitive verb
1 a : to consume fuel and give off heat, light, and gases ⟨a small fire *burns* on the hearth⟩ **b :** to undergo combustion; *also* **:** to undergo nuclear fission or nuclear fusion **c :** to contain a fire ⟨a little stove *burning* in the corner⟩ **d :** to give off light **:** SHINE, GLOW ⟨a light *burning* in the window⟩
2 a : to be hot ⟨the *burning* sand⟩ **b :** to produce or undergo discomfort or pain ⟨ears *burning* from the cold⟩ **c :** to become emotionally excited or agitated: as (1) **:** to yearn ardently ⟨*burning* to tell the story⟩ (2) **:** to be or become very angry or disgusted ⟨the remark made him *burn*⟩
3 : to undergo alteration or destruction by the action of fire or heat ⟨the house *burned* down⟩ ⟨the potatoes *burned* to a crisp⟩ **b :** to die in the electric chair
4 : to force or make a way by or as if by burning ⟨her words *burned* into his heart⟩
5 : to receive sunburn ⟨she *burns* easily⟩
transitive verb
1 a : to cause to undergo combustion; *especially* **:** to destroy by fire ⟨*burned* the trash⟩ **b :** to use as fuel ⟨this furnace *burns* gas⟩ **c :** to use up ⟨CONSUME ⟨*burn* calories⟩
2 a : to transform by exposure to heat or fire ⟨*burn* clay to bricks⟩ **b :** to produce by burning ⟨*burned* a hole in his sleeve⟩
3 a : to injure or damage by or as if by exposure to fire, heat, or radiation **:** SCORCH ⟨*burned* his hand⟩ **b :** to execute by burning ⟨*burned* heretics at the stake⟩; *also* **:** ELECTROCUTE
4 a : IRRITATE, ANNOY — often used with *up* ⟨really *burns* me up⟩ **b :** to take advantage of: as (1) **:** DECEIVE, CHEAT — often used in passive (2) **:** OUTDO, BEAT ⟨*burned* the defense with a touchdown pass⟩
— **burn·able** \'bər-nə-bəl\ *adjective*
— **burn one's bridges** *also* **burn one's boats :** to cut off all means of retreat
— **burn one's ears :** to rebuke strongly
— **burn the candle at both ends :** to use one's resources or energies to excess
— **burn the midnight oil :** to work or study far into the night

³burn *noun* (1594)
1 : an act, process, instance, or result of burning: as **a :** injury or damage resulting from exposure to fire, heat, caustics, electricity, or certain radiations **b :** a burned area ⟨a *burn* on the tabletop⟩ **c :** an abrasion (as of the skin) having the appearance of a burn ⟨rope *burns*⟩ **d :** a burning sensation ⟨the *burn* of iodine on a cut⟩
2 : the firing of a spacecraft rocket engine in flight
3 : ANGER; *especially* **:** increasing fury — used chiefly in the phrase *slow burn*

burned–out \'bərn-'daut, 'bərnt-'aut\ *or* **burnt–out** \'bərnt-'aut\ *adjective* (1837)
: WORN-OUT; *also* **:** EXHAUSTED

burn·er \'bər-nər\ *noun* (14th century)
: one that burns; *especially* **:** the part of a fuel-burning or heat-producing device (as a furnace or stove) where the flame or heat is produced

bur·net \(ˌ)bər-'net, 'bər-nət\ *noun* [Middle English, from Middle French *burnete,* from *brun* brown — more at BRUNET] (14th century)

\ə\ abut \ᵊ\ kitten \ər\ further \a\ ash \ā\ ace
\ä\ mop, mar \au̇\ out \ch\ chin \e\ bet \ē\ easy
\g\ go \i\ hit \ī\ ice \j\ job \ŋ\ sing \ō\ go
\o̤\ law \o̤i\ boy \th\ thin \t̲h̲\ the \ü\ loot \u̇\ foot
\y\ yet \zh\ vision *see also* Guide to Pronunciation

: any of a genus (*Sanguisorba*) of herbs of the rose family with odd-pinnate stipulate leaves and spikes of apetalous flowers

burn–in \'bər-ˌnin\ *noun* (1966)
: the continuous operation of a device (as a computer) as a test for defects or failure prior to putting it to use

burn in *transitive verb* (circa 1939)
: to increase the density of (portions of a photographic print) during enlarging by giving extra exposure

burn·ing \'bər-niŋ\ *adjective* (before 12th century)
1 a : being on fire **b** : ARDENT, INTENSE ⟨*burning* enthusiasm⟩
2 a : affecting with or as if with heat ⟨a *burning* fever⟩ **b** : resembling that produced by a burn ⟨a *burning* sensation on the tongue⟩
3 : of fundamental importance : URGENT ⟨one of the *burning* issues of our time⟩
— **burn·ing·ly** \-niŋ-lē\ *adverb*

burning bush *noun* (1785)
: any of several plants associated with fire (as by redness): as **a** : ²WAHOO **b** : SUMMER CYPRESS

burning ghat *noun* (1877)
: a level space at the head of a ghat for cremation

¹bur·nish \'bər-nish\ *transitive verb* [Middle English *burnischen*, from Middle French *bruniss-*, stem of *brunir*, literally, to make brown, from *brun*] (14th century)
1 a : to make shiny or lustrous especially by rubbing **b** : POLISH 3
2 : to rub (a material) with a tool for compacting or smoothing or for turning an edge
— **bur·nish·er** *noun*
— **bur·nish·ing** *adjective or noun*

²burnish *noun* (circa 1647)
: LUSTER, GLOSS

burn off (circa 1925)
intransitive verb
: to be dissipated by the sun's warmth ⟨waiting for the fog to *burn off*⟩
transitive verb
: to cause to burn off

bur·noose *or* **bur·nous** \(ˌ)bər-'nüs\ *noun* [French *burnous*, from Arabic *burnus*] (1695)
: a one-piece hooded cloak worn by Arabs and Berbers
— **bur·noosed** \-'nüst\ *adjective*

burn·out \'bər-ˌnaut\ *noun* (1940)
1 : the cessation of operation of a jet or rocket engine; *also* : the point at which burnout occurs
2 a : exhaustion of physical or emotional strength or motivation usually as a result of prolonged stress or frustration **b** : a person suffering from burnout
3 : a person showing the results of drug abuse

burn out (1710)
transitive verb
1 : to drive out or destroy the property of by fire
2 : to cause to fail, wear out, or become exhausted especially from overwork or overuse
intransitive verb
: to suffer burnout

burn·sides \'bərn-ˌsīdz\ *noun plural* [Ambrose E. *Burnside*] (1875)
: SIDE-WHISKERS; *especially* : full muttonchop whiskers
word history *see* SIDEBURNS

¹burp \'bərp\ *noun* [imitative] (circa 1932)
: BELCH

²burp (circa 1932)
intransitive verb
: BELCH
transitive verb
: to help (a baby) expel gas from the stomach especially by patting or rubbing the back

burp gun *noun* (1944)
: a small submachine gun

¹burr \'bər\ *noun* [Middle English *burre*; akin to Old English *byrst* bristle — more at BRISTLE] (14th century)

1 *usually* **bur a** : a rough or prickly envelope of a fruit **b** : a plant that bears burs
2 a : something that sticks or clings ⟨a *burr* in the throat⟩ **b** : HANGER-ON
3 : an irregular rounded mass; *especially* : a tree burl
4 : a thin ridge or area of roughness produced in cutting or shaping metal
5 a : a trilled uvular \r\ as used by some speakers of English especially in northern England and in Scotland **b** : a tongue-point trill that is the usual Scottish \r\
6 a : a small rotary cutting tool **b** *usually* **bur** : a bit used on a dental drill
7 : a rough humming sound : WHIR
— **burred** \'bərd\ *adjective*

²burr (1798)
intransitive verb
1 : to speak with a burr
2 : to make a whirring sound
transitive verb
1 : to pronounce with a burr
2 a : to form into a projecting edge **b** : to remove burrs from
— **burr·er** *noun*

bur reed *noun* (1597)
: any of a genus (*Sparganium* of the family Sparganiaceae) of plants with globose fruits resembling burs

bur·ri·to \bə-'rē-(ˌ)tō\ *noun, plural* **-tos** [American Spanish, from Spanish, little donkey, diminutive of *burro*] (1934)
: a flour tortilla rolled or folded around a filling (as of meat, beans, or cheese) and usually baked

bur·ro \'bər-(ˌ)ō, 'bur-; 'bə-(ˌ)rō\ *noun, plural* **burros** [Spanish, irregular from *borrico*, from Late Latin *burricus* small horse] (1800)
: DONKEY; *especially* : a small one used as a pack animal

¹bur·row \'bər-(ˌ)ō; 'bə-(ˌ)rō\ *noun* [Middle English *borow*] (13th century)
: a hole or excavation in the ground made by an animal (as a rabbit) for shelter and habitation

²burrow (1602)
transitive verb
1 *archaic* : to hide in or as if in a burrow
2 a : to construct by tunneling **b** : to penetrate by means of a burrow
3 : to make a motion suggestive of burrowing with : NESTLE ⟨*burrows* her hand into mine⟩
intransitive verb
1 : to conceal oneself in or as if in a burrow
2 a : to make a burrow **b** : to progress by or as if by digging
3 : to make a motion suggestive of burrowing : SNUGGLE, NESTLE ⟨*burrowed* against his back for warmth⟩
— **bur·row·er** *noun*

burrstone *variant of* BUHRSTONE

bur·ry \'bər-ē\ *adjective* **bur·ri·er; -est** (15th century)
1 : containing burs
2 : PRICKLY
3 *of speech* : characterized by a burr

bur·sa \'bər-sə\ *noun, plural* **bur·sas** \-səz\ *or* **bur·sae** \-ˌsē, -ˌsī\ [New Latin, from Medieval Latin, bag, purse — more at PURSE] (1803)
: a bodily pouch or sac: as **a** : a small serous sac between a tendon and a bone **b** : BURSA OF FABRICIUS
— **bur·sal** \-səl\ *adjective*

bursa of Fa·bri·cius \-fə-'brē-sh(ē-)əs, -'bri-, -s(ē-)əs\ [Johan C. *Fabricius* (died 1808) Danish entomologist] (1945)
: a lymphoid organ that opens into the cloaca of birds and functions in B cell production

bur·sar \'bər-sər, -ˌsär\ *noun* [Medieval Latin *bursarius*, from *bursa*] (13th century)
: an officer of a monastery or college) in charge of funds : TREASURER

bur·sa·ry \'bər-sə-rē, 'bərs-rē\ *noun, plural* **-ries** [Medieval Latin *bursaria*, from *bursa*] (1695)

1 : the treasury of a college or monastery
2 *British* : a monetary grant to a needy student : SCHOLARSHIP

burse \'bərs\ *noun* [Middle French *bourse*, from Medieval Latin *bursa*] (15th century)
1 a : PURSE **b** : a square cloth case used to carry the corporal in a Communion service
2 *obsolete* : EXCHANGE, BOURSE

bur·si·tis \(ˌ)bər-'sī-təs\ *noun* [New Latin, from *bursa*] (1857)
: inflammation of a bursa especially of the shoulder or elbow

¹burst \'bərst\ *verb* **burst** *also* **burst·ed; burst·ing** [Middle English *bersten*, from Old English *berstan*; akin to Old High German *brestan* to burst] (before 12th century)
intransitive verb
1 : to break open, apart, or into pieces usually from impact or from pressure from within
2 a : to give way from an excess of emotion ⟨my heart will *burst*⟩ **b** : to give vent suddenly to a repressed emotion ⟨*burst* into tears⟩ ⟨*burst* out laughing⟩
3 a : to emerge or spring suddenly ⟨*burst* out of the house⟩ ⟨*burst* onto the scene⟩ **b** : LAUNCH, PLUNGE ⟨*burst* into song⟩
4 : to be filled to the breaking point ⟨*bursting* with excitement⟩ ⟨a crate *bursting* with fruit⟩
transitive verb
1 : to cause to burst
2 : to force open (as a door) by strong or vigorous action
3 : to produce by or as if by bursting
— **burst at the seams** : to be larger, fuller, or more crowded than could reasonably have been anticipated

²burst *noun* (1610)
1 a : a sudden outbreak; *especially* : a vehement outburst (as of emotion) **b** : EXPLOSION, ERUPTION **c** : a sudden intense effort ⟨a *burst* of speed⟩ **d** : the duration of fire in one engagement of the mechanism of an automatic firearm
2 : an act of bursting
3 : a result of bursting; *especially* : a visible puff accompanying the explosion of a shell

burst·er \'bərs-tər\ *noun* (1611)
1 : one that bursts
2 : the celestial source of an outburst of radiation (as X rays)

bur·then \'bər-thən\ *variant of* BURDEN

bur·weed \'bər-ˌwēd\ *noun* (circa 1783)
: any of various plants (as a cocklebur or burdock) having burry fruit

bury \'ber-ē *also* 'bər-\ *transitive verb* **buried; bury·ing** [Middle English *burien*, from Old English *byrgan*; akin to Old High German *bergan* to shelter, Russian *berech'* to spare] (before 12th century)
1 : to dispose of by depositing in or as if in the earth; *especially* : to inter with funeral ceremonies
2 a : to conceal by or as if by covering with earth **b** : to cover from view ⟨*buried* her face in her hands⟩
3 a : to have done with ⟨*burying* their differences⟩ **b** : to conceal in obscurity ⟨*buried* the retraction among the classified ads⟩ **c** : SUBMERGE, ENGROSS — usually used with *in* ⟨*buried* himself in his books⟩
4 : to put (a playing card) out of play by placing it in or under the dealer's pack
5 : to succeed emphatically or impressively in making (a shot) ⟨*bury* a jumper⟩
6 : to defeat overwhelmingly
synonym *see* HIDE
— **bury the hatchet** : to settle a disagreement : become reconciled

¹bus \'bəs\ *noun, plural* **bus·es** *or* **bus·ses** *often attributive* [short for *omnibus*] (circa 1909)
1 a : a large motor vehicle designed to carry passengers usually along a fixed route according to a schedule **b** : AUTOMOBILE
2 : a small hand truck

3 a : BUS BAR **b :** a set of parallel conductors in a computer system that forms a main transmission path

4 : a spacecraft or missile that carries one or more detachable devices (as warheads) ◆

²**bus** *verb* **bused** *or* **bussed; bus·ing** *or* **bus·sing** (circa 1909)
intransitive verb
1 : to travel by bus
2 : to work as a busboy
transitive verb
1 : to transport by bus
2 a : CLEAR 4d ⟨*bus* dishes⟩ **b :** to remove dirty dishes from ⟨*bus* tables⟩

bus bar *noun* (1893)
: a conductor or an assembly of conductors for collecting electric currents and distributing them to outgoing feeders

bus·boy \'bəs-ˌbȯi\ *noun* [*omnibus* busboy] (1913)
: a waiter's assistant; *specifically* **:** one who removes dirty dishes and resets tables in a restaurant

bus·by \'bəz-bē\ *noun, plural* **busbies** [probably from the name *Busby*] (1853)
1 : a military full-dress fur hat with a pendent bag on one side usually of the color of regimental facings
2 : the bearskin worn by British guardsmen — not used by the guardsmen themselves

¹**bush** \'bush\ *noun, often attributive* [Middle English; akin to Old High German *busc* forest] (14th century)
1 a : SHRUB; *especially* **:** a low densely branched shrub **b :** a close thicket of shrubs suggesting a single plant
2 : a large uncleared or sparsely settled area (as in Australia) usually scrub-covered or forested **:** WILDERNESS — usually used with *the*
3 a *archaic* **:** a bunch of ivy formerly hung outside a tavern to indicate wine for sale **b** *obsolete* **:** TAVERN **c :** ADVERTISING ⟨good wine needs no *bush* —Shakespeare⟩
4 : a bushy tuft or mass ⟨a *bush* of hair⟩; *especially* **:** ²BRUSH 2a
5 : MINOR LEAGUE — usually used in plural

²**bush** (15th century)
transitive verb
: to support, mark, or protect with bushes
intransitive verb
: to extend like a bush **:** resemble a bush

³**bush** *adjective* (1595)
1 : having a low-growing compact bushy habit — used especially of cultivated beans ⟨*bush* snap beans⟩
2 : serving, occurring in, or used in the bush ⟨*bush* planes⟩

⁴**bush** *noun* [Dutch *bus* bushing, box, from Middle Dutch *busse* box, from Late Latin *buxis* — more at BOX] (1566)
chiefly British **:** BUSHING

⁵**bush** *adjective* [short for *bush-league*] (1970)
: falling below acceptable standards **:** UNPROFESSIONAL ⟨*bush* behavior⟩

bush baby *noun* (1901)
: GALAGO

bush basil *noun* (1597)
: a sweet basil of a cultivar with small leaves

bush·buck \'bush-ˌbək\ *noun, plural* **bush·buck** *or* **bushbucks** [translation of Afrikaans *bosbok*] (1852)
: a small African striped antelope (*Tragelaphus scriptus*) especially of sub-Saharan forests that has spirally twisted horns

bush clover *noun* (circa 1818)
: any of several usually shrubby lespedezas

¹**bushed** \'busht\ *adjective* (14th century)
1 : covered with or as if with a bushy growth
2 *chiefly Australian* **a :** lost especially in the bush **b :** PERPLEXED 1, CONFUSED

3 : TIRED, EXHAUSTED

²**bushed** *adjective* (1907)
: having a bushing

¹**bush·el** \'bu-shəl\ *noun* [Middle English *busshel*, from Old French *boissel*, from (assumed) Old French *boisse* one sixth of a bushel, of Celtic origin; akin to Middle Irish *boss* breadth of the hand] (14th century)
1 : any of various units of dry capacity — see WEIGHT table
2 : a container holding a bushel
3 : a large quantity **:** LOTS ⟨makes *bushels* of money⟩

²**bushel** *verb* **bush·eled; bush·el·ing** \-sh(ə-)liŋ\ [probably from German *bosseln* to do poor work, to patch; akin to Old English *bēatan* to beat] (circa 1877)
: REPAIR, RENOVATE
— **bush·el·er** \-sh(ə-)lər\ *noun*

bush·fire \'bush-ˌfīr\ *noun* (1832)
Australian **:** an uncontrolled fire in a bush area

Bu·shi·do \'bu-shi-ˌdō, 'bü-\ *noun* [Japanese *bushidō*] (1898)
: a feudal-military Japanese code of chivalry valuing honor above life

bush·ing \'bu-shiŋ\ *noun* (1839)
1 : a usually removable cylindrical lining for an opening (as of a mechanical part) used to limit the size of the opening, resist abrasion, or serve as a guide
2 : an electrically insulating lining for a hole to protect a through conductor

bush jacket *noun* [from its use in rough country] (circa 1939)
: a long cotton jacket resembling a shirt and having four patch pockets and a belt

bush·land \'bush-ˌland\ *noun* (1827)
: ¹BUSH 2

bush–league *adjective* (1914)
: being of an inferior class or group of its kind

bush league *noun* (1909)
: MINOR LEAGUE
— **bush leaguer** *noun*

bush·man \'bush-mən\ *noun* (1785)
1 *capitalized* [modification of obsolete Afrikaans *boschjesman*, from *boschje* (diminutive of *bosch* forest) + Afrikaans *man*] **a :** a member of a group of short-statured peoples of southern Africa who traditionally live by hunting and foraging **b :** the Khoisan languages spoken by these people
2 a : WOODSMAN **b** *chiefly Australian* **:** a person who lives in the bush

bush·mas·ter \-ˌmas-tər\ *noun* (1826)
: a tropical American pit viper (*Lachesis mutus*) that is the largest New World venomous snake

bush·pig \-ˌpig\ *noun* (1840)
: a wild usually reddish to black pig (*Potamochoerus porcus*) of forests and scrubland of sub-Saharan Africa and Madagascar that has much facial hair, long pointed ears, and a light-colored mane along the top of the neck and back

bush pilot *noun* (1936)
: a pilot who flies a small plane into remote areas

bush·rang·er \-ˌrān-jər\ *noun* (1801)
1 *Australian* **:** an outlaw living in the bush
2 : FRONTIERSMAN, WOODSMAN
— **bush·rang·ing** \-jiŋ\ *noun*

bush shirt *noun* [from its use in rough country] (1909)
: a usually loose-fitting cotton shirt with patch pockets

bush·tit \-ˌtit\ *noun* (circa 1889)
: a small gray titmouse (*Psaltriparus minimus*) of western North America with light underparts that occurs in several geographic forms sometimes placed in separate species

bush·whack \'bush-ˌhwak, -ˌwak\ *verb* [back-formation from *bushwhacker*] (1866)

transitive verb
: AMBUSH; *broadly* **:** to attack suddenly **:** ASSAULT
intransitive verb
: to clear a path through thick woods especially by chopping down bushes and low branches
— **bush·whack·er** *noun*

bushy \'bu-shē\ *adjective* **bush·i·er; -est** (14th century)
1 : full of or overgrown with bushes
2 : resembling a bush; *especially* **:** being thick and spreading
— **bush·i·ly** \'bu-shə-lē\ *adverb*
— **bush·i·ness** \'bu-shē-nəs\ *noun*

busi·ness \'biz-nəs, -nəz, *Southern also* 'bid-\ *noun, often attributive* (14th century)
1 *archaic* **:** purposeful activity **:** BUSYNESS
2 a : ROLE, FUNCTION ⟨how the human mind went about its *business* of learning —H. A. Overstreet⟩ **b :** an immediate task or objective **:** MISSION ⟨what is your *business* here⟩ **c :** a particular field of endeavor ⟨the best in the *business*⟩
3 a : a usually commercial or mercantile activity engaged in as a means of livelihood **:** TRADE, LINE ⟨in the restaurant *business*⟩ **b :** a commercial or sometimes an industrial enterprise; *also* **:** such enterprises ⟨the *business* district⟩ **c :** usually economic dealings **:** PATRONAGE ⟨took their *business* elsewhere⟩
4 : AFFAIR, MATTER ⟨the whole *business* got out of hand⟩ ⟨*business* as usual⟩
5 : CREATION, CONCOCTION
6 : movement or action (as lighting a cigarette) by an actor intended especially to establish atmosphere, reveal character, or explain a situation — called also *stage business*
7 a : personal concern ⟨none of your *business*⟩ **b :** RIGHT ⟨you have no *business* speaking to me that way⟩
8 a : serious activity requiring time and effort and usually the avoidance of distractions ⟨got down to *business*⟩ ⟨she means *business*⟩ **b :** maximum effort
9 a : a damaging assault **b :** REBUKE, TONGUE-LASHING ⟨gave him the *business* for staying out so late⟩ **c :** DOUBLE CROSS

◇ **WORD HISTORY**
bus In 1828 a new era in public transportation dawned when horse-drawn boxes on wheels seating fourteen people on facing benches began to run regular routes in Paris. They were christened with the name *omnibus*, taken to be short for *voitures omnibus* "vehicles (open) to all"; *omnibus*, the dative of Latin *omnes* "everybody, all," summed up in one word their general accessibility. An earlier transport line of the same kind had operated in the city of Nantes, and according to one tradition the name *omnibus* occurred to the proprietors because the line terminated at the shop of a certain M. Omnes, who used the slogan *Omnes Omnibus*. In 1829 a horse-drawn line patterned after the French *omnibus* opened in London with the vehicles bearing the same name. By 1832 Londoners had clipped *omnibus* to *bus*. As the vehicles became self-propelled, first by steam and then by internal-combustion engines, the coinage *autobus* appeared, in English by 1899 and in French by 1907. *Bus* and *autobus* have since become international words, current over much of the world and in a number of languages.

busby 1

10 : a bowel movement — used especially of pets ☆

business administration *noun* (circa 1911)
: a program of studies in a college or university providing general knowledge of business principles and practices

business card *noun* (1840)
: a small card bearing information (as name and address) about a business or business representative

business cycle *noun* (1919)
: a cycle of economic activity usually consisting of recession, recovery, growth, and decline

business end *noun* (1878)
: the end with, from, or through which a thing's function is fulfilled ⟨the *business end* of a revolver⟩

busi·ness·like \'biz-nəs-,līk, -nəz-\ *adjective* (1791)
1 : exhibiting qualities believed to be advantageous in business
2 : SERIOUS, PURPOSEFUL

busi·ness·man \-,man, -mən\ *noun* (1826)
: a man who transacts business; *especially* **:** a business executive

busi·ness·peo·ple \-,pē-pəl\ *noun plural* (1865)
: persons active in business

busi·ness·per·son \-,pər-s°n\ *noun* (1974)
: a businessman or businesswoman

business suit *noun* (1870)
: a man's suit consisting of matching coat and trousers and sometimes a vest

busi·ness·wom·an \-,wŭ-mən\ *noun* (1844)
: a woman who transacts business; *especially* **:** a female business executive

bus·ing *or* **bus·sing** \'bə-siŋ\ *noun* (1923)
: the act of transporting by bus; *specifically* **:** the transporting of children to a school outside their residential area as a means of establishing racial balance in that school

busk·er \'bəs-kər\ *noun* [busk, probably from Italian *buscare* to procure, gain, from Spanish *buscar* to look for] (1857)
chiefly British **:** a person who entertains especially by playing music on the street
— **busk** \'bəsk\ *intransitive verb*

bus·kin \'bəs-kən\ *noun* [probably modification of Middle French *brozequin*] (1503)
1 : a laced boot reaching halfway or more to the knee
2 a : COTHURNUS 1 **b :** TRAGEDY; *especially* **:** tragedy resembling that of ancient Greek drama

bus·load \'bəs-,lōd\ *noun* (1938)
: a load that fills a bus ⟨*busloads* of tourists⟩

bus·man's holiday \'bəs-mənz-\ *noun* (1893)
: a holiday spent in following or observing the practice of one's usual occupation

buss \'bəs\ *noun* [perhaps alteration of Middle English *bassen* to kiss] (1570)
: KISS
— **buss** *transitive verb*

¹bust \'bəst\ *noun* [French *buste*, from Italian *busto*, from Latin *bustum* tomb] (1645)
1 : a sculptured representation of the upper part of the human figure including the head and neck and usually part of the shoulders and breast
2 : the upper part of the human torso between neck and waist; *especially* **:** the breasts of a woman

²bust *verb* **bust·ed** *also* **bust; bust·ing** [alteration of *burst*] (1806)
transitive verb
1 a : to break or smash especially with force; *also* **:** to make inoperative ⟨*busted* my watch⟩ **b :** to bring an end to **:** BREAK UP ⟨helped *bust* trusts —*Newsweek*⟩ — often used with *up* ⟨better not try to *bust* up his happy marriage —*Forbes*⟩ **c :** to ruin financially **d :** EXHAUST, WEAR OUT — used in phrases like *bust one's butt* to describe making a strenuous effort
2 : TAME ⟨bronco *busting*⟩

3 : DEMOTE
4 *slang* **a :** ARREST ⟨*busted* for carrying guns —Saul Gottlieb⟩ **b :** RAID ⟨*busted* the apartment⟩
5 : HIT, SLUG
intransitive verb
1 : to go broke
2 a : BURST ⟨laughing fit to *bust*⟩ **b :** BREAK DOWN
3 a : to lose at cards by exceeding a limit (as the count of 21 in blackjack) **b :** to fail to complete a straight or flush in poker

³bust *noun* (1840)
1 a : SPREE **b :** a hearty drinking session ⟨a beer *bust*⟩
2 a : a complete failure **:** FLOP **b :** a business depression
3 : PUNCH, SOCK
4 *slang* **a :** a police raid **b :** ARREST 2

⁴bust *or* **bust·ed** \'bəs-təd\ *adjective* (1837)
: BANKRUPT, BROKE ⟨go *bust*⟩

bus·tard \'bəs-tərd\ *noun* [Middle English, modification of Middle French *bistarde*, from Old Italian *bistarda*, from Latin *avis tarda*, literally, slow bird] (15th century)
: any of a family (Otididae) of large chiefly terrestrial Old World and Australian game birds

bust·er \'bəs-tər\ *noun* (1848)
1 *chiefly Australian* **:** a sudden violent wind often coming from the south
2 a : an unusually sturdy child **b** *often capitalized* **:** FELLOW — usually used as a noun of address ⟨hey *buster*, come here⟩
3 : one that breaks, breaks up, or eliminates something ⟨crime *busters*⟩: as **a :** PLOW **b** [short for *broncobuster*] **:** a person who breaks horses
4 : a bad fall

bus·tier \,büs-tē-'ā, ,bəs-, -'tyā\ *noun* [French, from *buste*] (1979)
: a tight-fitting often strapless top worn as a brassiere or outer garment

¹bus·tle \'bə-səl\ *intransitive verb* **bus·tled; bus·tling** \'bəs-liŋ, 'bə-sə-\ [probably alteration of obsolete *buskle* to prepare, frequentative of *busk*, from Old Norse *būask* to prepare oneself] (1580)
1 : to move briskly and often ostentatiously
2 : to be busily astir **:** TEEM
— **bustling** *adjective*
— **bus·tling·ly** \-liŋ-lē\ *adverb*

²bustle *noun* (1634)
: noisy, energetic, and often obtrusive activity ⟨the hustle and *bustle* of the big city⟩

³bustle *noun* [origin unknown] (1786)
: a pad or framework expanding and supporting the fullness and drapery of the back of a woman's skirt or dress; *also* **:** the drapery so supported

bust·line \'bəs(t)-,līn\ *noun* (1926)
1 : an arbitrary line encircling the fullest part of the bust
2 : body circumference at the bust

busty \'bəs-tē\ *adjective* **bust·i·er; -est** (1944)
: having a large bust

bu·sul·fan \byü-'səl-fən\ *noun* [butane + sulfonyl] (circa 1958)
: an antineoplastic agent $C_6H_{14}O_6S_2$ used in the treatment of chronic myelogenous leukemia

¹busy \'bi-zē\ *adjective* **busi·er; -est** [Middle English *bisy*, from Old English *bisig*; akin to Middle Dutch & Middle Low German *besich*] (before 12th century)
1 a : engaged in action **:** OCCUPIED **b :** being in use ⟨found the telephone *busy*⟩
2 : full of activity **:** BUSTLING ⟨a *busy* seaport⟩
3 : foolishly or intrusively active **:** MEDDLING
4 : full of distracting detail ⟨a *busy* design⟩ ☆
— **busi·ly** \'bi-zə-lē\ *adverb*
— **busy·ness** \'bi-zē-nəs\ *noun*

²busy *verb* **bus·ied; busy·ing** (before 12th century)
transitive verb

: to make busy **:** OCCUPY
intransitive verb
: BUSTLE ⟨small boats *busied* to and fro —Quentin Crewe⟩

busy·body \'bi-zē-,bä-dē\ *noun* (1526)
: an officious or inquisitive person

busy·work \-,wərk\ *noun* (1910)
: work that usually appears productive or of intrinsic value but actually only keeps one occupied

¹but \'bət\ *conjunction* [Middle English, from Old English *būtan*, preposition & conjugation, outside, without, except, except that; akin to Old High German *būzan* without, except; akin to Old English *be* by, *ūt* out — more at BY, OUT] (before 12th century)
1 a : except for the fact ⟨would have protested *but* that he was afraid⟩ **b :** THAT — used after a negative ⟨there is no doubt *but* he won⟩ **c :** without the concomitant that ⟨it never rains *but* it pours⟩ **d :** if not **:** UNLESS **e :** THAN ⟨no sooner started *but* it stopped⟩ — not often in formal use
2 a : on the contrary **:** on the other hand **:** NOTWITHSTANDING — used to connect coordinate elements ⟨he was called *but* he did not answer⟩ ⟨not peace *but* a sword⟩ **b :** YET ⟨poor *but* proud⟩ **c :** with the exception of — used before a word often taken to be the subject of a clause ⟨none *but* the brave deserves the fair —John Dryden⟩
— **but what :** that . . . not — used to indicate possibility or uncertainty ⟨I don't know *but what* I will go⟩

²but *preposition* (before 12th century)
1 a : with the exception of **:** BARRING ⟨no one there *but* me⟩ — compare ¹BUT 2c **b :** other than ⟨this letter is nothing *but* an insult⟩
2 *Scottish* **a :** WITHOUT, LACKING **b :** OUTSIDE

³but *adverb* (12th century)
1 : ONLY, MERELY ⟨he is *but* a child⟩
2 *Scottish* **:** OUTSIDE
3 : to the contrary ⟨who knows *but* that she may succeed⟩
4 — used as an intensive ⟨get there *but* fast⟩

⁴but *pronoun* (1556)
: that not **:** who not ⟨nobody *but* has his fault —Shakespeare⟩

⁵but *noun* [Scots *but*, adjective (outer)] (1724)

☆ SYNONYMS
Business, commerce, trade, industry, traffic mean activity concerned with the supplying and distribution of commodities. BUSINESS may be an inclusive term but specifically designates the activities of those engaged in the purchase or sale of commodities or in related financial transactions. COMMERCE and TRADE imply the exchange and transportation of commodities. INDUSTRY applies to the producing of commodities, especially by manufacturing or processing, usually on a large scale. TRAFFIC applies to the operation and functioning of public carriers of goods and persons. See in addition WORK.

Busy, industrious, diligent, assiduous, sedulous mean actively engaged or occupied. BUSY chiefly stresses activity as opposed to idleness or leisure ⟨too *busy* to spend time with the children⟩. INDUSTRIOUS implies characteristic or habitual devotion to work ⟨*industrious* employees⟩. DILIGENT suggests earnest application to some specific object or pursuit ⟨very *diligent* in her pursuit of a degree⟩. ASSIDUOUS stresses careful and unremitting application ⟨*assiduous* practice⟩. SEDULOUS implies painstaking and persevering application ⟨a *sedulous* investigation of the murder⟩.

Scottish **:** the kitchen or living quarters of a 2-room cottage

bu·ta·di·ene \ˌbyü-tə-'dī-ˌēn, -ˌdī-'\ *noun* [International Scientific Vocabulary *butane* + *di-* + *-ene*] (1900)
: a flammable gaseous open chain hydrocarbon C_4H_6 used in making synthetic rubbers

bu·tane \'byü-ˌtān\ *noun* [International Scientific Vocabulary *butyric* + *-ane*] (1875)
: either of two isomeric flammable gaseous alkanes C_4H_{10} obtained usually from petroleum or natural gas and used as fuels

bu·ta·nol \'byü-t³n-ˌȯl, -ˌōl\ *noun* (1894)
: either of two flammable four-carbon alcohols C_4H_9OH derived from normal butane

butch \'bu̇ch\ *adjective* [probably from *Butch,* male nickname] (1941)
1 : very masculine in appearance or manner
2 : playing the male role in a homosexual relationship

¹butch·er \'bu̇-chər\ *noun* [Middle English *bocher,* from Old French *bouchier,* from *bouc* he-goat, probably of Celtic origin; akin to Middle Irish *bocc* he-goat — more at BUCK] (13th century)
1 a : a person who slaughters animals or dresses their flesh **b :** a dealer in meat
2 : one that kills ruthlessly or brutally
3 : one that bungles or botches
4 : a vendor especially on trains or in theaters

²butcher *transitive verb* **butch·ered; butch·er·ing** \'bu̇ch-riŋ, 'bu̇-chə-\ (1562)
1 : to slaughter and dress for market ⟨*butcher* hogs⟩
2 : to kill in a barbarous manner
3 : BOTCH ⟨*butchered* the play⟩

butch·er·bird \'bu̇-chər-ˌbərd\ *noun* (1668)
: any of various shrikes

butcher block *noun* (1967)
: a block made with thick strips of usually laminated hardwood
— butcher-block *adjective*

butch·er·ly \'bu̇-chər-lē\ *adjective* (1513)
: resembling a butcher : SAVAGE

butcher paper *noun* (1944)
: heavy brown or white paper used especially for wrapping meats

butch·ery \'bu̇ch-rē, 'bu̇-chə-\ *noun, plural* **-er·ies** (14th century)
1 *chiefly British* **:** SLAUGHTERHOUSE
2 : the preparation of meat for sale
3 : cruel and ruthless slaughter of human beings
4 : BOTCH

bute \'byüt\ *noun* (1968)
: PHENYLBUTAZONE

bu·tene \'byü-ˌtēn\ *noun* [International Scientific Vocabulary *butyl* + *-ene*] (1885)
: a normal butylene

bu·teo \'byü-tē-ˌō\ *noun, plural* **-te·os** [New Latin, genus name, from Latin, a hawk] (1940)
: any of a genus (*Buteo*) of hawks with broad rounded wings, relatively short tails, and soaring flight

but for *preposition* (12th century)
: EXCEPT FOR

but·ler \'bət-lər\ *noun* [Middle English *buteler,* from Old French *bouteillier* bottle bearer, from *bouteille* bottle — more at BOTTLE] (13th century)
1 : a manservant having charge of the wines and liquors
2 : the chief male servant of a household who has charge of other employees, receives guests, directs the serving of meals, and performs various personal services

butler's pantry *noun* (1816)
: a service room between kitchen and dining room

¹butt \'bət\ *verb* [Middle English, from Old French *boter,* of Germanic origin; akin to Old High German *bōzan* to beat — more at BEAT] (13th century)

intransitive verb
: to thrust or push head foremost : strike with the head or horns
transitive verb
: to strike or shove with the head or horns

²butt *noun* (1647)
: a blow or thrust usually with the head or horns

³butt *noun* [Middle English, from Middle French *botte,* from Old Provençal *bota,* from Late Latin *buttis*] (14th century)
1 : a large cask especially for wine, beer, or water
2 : any of various units of liquid capacity; *especially* **:** a measure equal to 108 imperial gallons (491 liters)

⁴butt *noun* [Middle English, partly from Middle French *but* target, end, of Germanic origin; akin to Old Norse *būtr* log, Low German *butt* blunt; partly from Middle French *bute* backstop, from *but* target] (14th century)
1 a : a backstop (as a mound or bank) for catching missiles shot at a target **b :** TARGET **c** *plural* **:** RANGE 5c **d :** a blind for shooting birds
2 a *obsolete* **:** LIMIT, BOUND **b** *archaic* **:** GOAL ⟨here is my journey's end, here is my *butt* —Shakespeare⟩
3 : an object of abuse or ridicule : VICTIM ⟨the *butt* of all their jokes⟩

⁵butt *noun* [Middle English; probably akin to Middle English *buttock,* Low German *butt* blunt] (15th century)
1 : BUTTOCKS — often used as a euphemism for *ass* in idiomatic expressions ⟨get your *butt* over here⟩ ⟨kick *butt*⟩ ⟨saved our *butts*⟩
2 : the large or thicker end part of something: **a :** a lean upper cut of the pork shoulder **b :** the base of a plant from which the roots spring **c :** the thicker or handle end of a tool or weapon
3 : an unused remainder
4 : the part of a hide or skin corresponding to the animal's back and sides

⁶butt *verb* [partly from ⁴*butt,* partly from ⁵*butt*] (1785)
intransitive verb
: ABUT — used with *on* or *against*
transitive verb
1 : to place end to end or side to side without overlapping
2 : to trim or square off (as a log) at the end
3 : to reduce (as a cigarette) to a butt by stubbing or stamping

butte \'byüt\ *noun* [French, knoll, from Middle French *but*] (1805)
: an isolated hill or mountain with steep or precipitous sides usually having a smaller summit area than a mesa

¹but·ter \'bə-tər\ *noun* [Middle English, from Old English *butere,* from Latin *butyrum,* from Greek *boutyron,* from *bous* cow + *tyros* cheese; akin to Avestan *tūiri-* curds — more at COW] (before 12th century)
1 : a solid emulsion of fat globules, air, and water made by churning milk or cream and used as food
2 : a buttery substance: as **a :** any of various fatty oils remaining nearly solid at ordinary temperatures **b :** a creamy food spread; *especially* **:** one made of ground roasted nuts ⟨peanut *butter*⟩
3 : FLATTERY
— but·ter·less \-ləs\ *adjective*

²butter *transitive verb* (15th century)
: to spread with or as if with butter

but·ter-and-eggs \ˌbə-tər-³n-'egz, -'āgz\ *noun plural but singular or plural in construction* (1776)
: a common Eurasian perennial herb (*Linaria vulgaris*) of the snapdragon family that has showy yellow and orange flowers and is naturalized in much of North America — called also *toadflax*

but·ter·ball \'bə-tər-ˌbȯl\ *noun* (1813)
1 : BUFFLEHEAD
2 : a chubby person

butter bean *noun* (circa 1819)
1 : LIMA BEAN: as **a** *chiefly Southern & Midland* **:** a large dried lima bean **b :** SIEVA BEAN
2 : WAX BEAN
3 : a green shell bean especially as opposed to a snap bean

butter clam *noun* (1936)
: either of two clams (*Saxidomus nuttallii* and *S. giganteus*) of the Pacific coast of North America

but·ter·cup \'bə-tər-ˌkəp\ *noun* (1777)
: any of a genus (*Ranunculus* of the family Ranunculaceae, the buttercup family) of herbs with yellow or white flowers and alternate leaves

but·ter·fat \-ˌfat\ *noun* (1889)
: the natural fat of milk and chief constituent of butter consisting essentially of a mixture of glycerides (as those derived from butyric, capric, caproic, and caprylic acids)

but·ter·fin·gered \-ˌfiŋ-gərd\ *adjective* (1615)
: apt to let things fall or slip through the fingers : CARELESS
— but·ter·fin·gers \-gərz\ *noun plural but singular or plural in construction*

but·ter·fish \-ˌfish\ *noun* (1674)
: any of numerous bony fishes (especially family Stromateidae) with a slippery coating of mucus

¹but·ter·fly \-ˌflī\ *noun, often attributive* (before 12th century)
1 : any of numerous slender-bodied diurnal insects (order Lepidoptera) with broad often brightly colored wings
2 : something that resembles or suggests a butterfly; *especially* **:** a person chiefly occupied with the pursuit of pleasure
3 : a swimming stroke executed in a prone position by moving both arms in a circular motion while kicking both legs up and down
4 *plural* **:** a feeling of hollowness or queasiness caused especially by emotional or nervous tension or anxious anticipation

²butterfly *transitive verb* **-flied; -fly·ing** (1954)
: to split almost entirely and spread apart ⟨a *butterflied* steak⟩ ⟨*butterflied* shrimp⟩

butterfly bush *noun* (1924)
: BUDDLEIA

butterfly chair *noun* (1953)
: a chair for lounging consisting of a cloth sling supported by a frame of metal tubing or bars

but·ter·fly·er \'bə-tər-ˌflī(-ə)r\ *noun* (1967)
: a swimmer who specializes in the butterfly

butterfly chair

butterfly fish *noun* (1740)
1 : any of a family (Chaetodontidae) of small brilliantly colored spiny-finned fishes of tropical seas with a narrow deep body and scaled fins
2 : a small brown freshwater fish (*Pantodon buchholzi* of the family Pantodontidae) of western Africa that has elongate winglike pectoral fins

butterfly valve *noun* (1846)
1 : a valve consisting of two semicircular clappers hinged to a cross rib that permits fluid flow in only one direction
2 : a damper or valve in a pipe consisting of a disk turning on a diametral axis

butterfly weed *noun* (1816)
: an orange-flowered showy milkweed (*Asclepias tuberosa*) of eastern temperate North America

\ə\ abut \ᵊ\ kitten \ər\ further \a\ ash \ā\ ace
\ä\ mop, mar \au̇\ out \ch\ chin \e\ bet \ē\ easy
\g\ go \i\ hit \ī\ ice \j\ job \ŋ\ sing \ō\ go
\ȯ\ law \ȯi\ boy \th\ thin \t̲h̲\ the \ü\ loot \u̇\ foot
\y\ yet \zh\ vision *see also* Guide to Pronunciation

but·ter·milk \'bə-tər-,milk\ *noun* (15th century)
1 : the liquid left after butter has been churned from milk or cream
2 : cultured milk made by the addition of suitable bacteria to sweet milk

but·ter·nut \-,nət\ *noun* (1741)
1 : an eastern North American tree of the walnut family with sweet egg-shaped nuts and light brown wood — called also *white walnut*
2 a : a light yellowish brown **b** *plural* : homespun overalls dyed brown with a butternut extract **c** : a soldier or partisan of the Confederacy during the Civil War

butternut squash *noun* (1945)
: a smooth somewhat bottle-shaped buff-colored winter squash with usually orange flesh

but·ter·scotch \-,skäch\ *noun* (1855)
1 : a candy made from brown sugar, butter, corn syrup, and water; *also* : the flavor of such candy
2 : a moderate yellowish brown

butter up *transitive verb* (1819)
: to charm or beguile with lavish flattery or praise

but·ter·weed \'bə-tər-,wēd\ *noun* (circa 1845)
: any of several plants having yellow flowers or smooth soft foliage: as **a** : HORSEWEED 1 **b** : a North American groundsel (*Senecio glabellus*)

but·ter·wort \-,wərt, -,wȯrt\ *noun* (1597)
: any of a genus (*Pinguicula*) of herbs of the bladderwort family with fleshy leaves that produce a viscid secretion serving to capture and digest insects

¹but·tery \'bə-tə-rē, 'bə-trē\ *noun, plural* **-ter·ies** [Middle English *boterie*, from Middle French, from *botte* cask, butt — more at BUTT] (14th century)
1 : a storeroom for liquors
2 a *chiefly dialect* : PANTRY **b** : a room (as in an English college) stocking provisions for sale to students

²but·tery \'bə-tə-rē\ *adjective* (14th century)
1 a : having the qualities of butter **b** : containing or spread with butter
2 : marked by flattery

butt hinge *noun* (1815)
: a hinge usually mortised flush into the edge of a door and its jamb

butt in *intransitive verb* (1900)
: to meddle in the affairs of others : INTERFERE

butt·in·sky *also* **butt·in·ski** \bə-'din-skē\ *noun, plural* **-skies** [*butt in* + *-sky, -ski* (last element in Slavic surnames)] (1902)
: a person given to butting in : a troublesome meddler

butt joint *noun* (1823)
: a joint made by fastening the parts together end-to-end without overlap and often with reinforcement

but·tock \'bə-tək *also* -,täk\ *noun* [Middle English *buttok* — more at BUTT] (14th century)
1 : the back of a hip that forms one of the fleshy parts on which a person sits
2 *plural* **a** : the seat of the body **b** : RUMP

¹but·ton \'bə-t°n\ *noun, often attributive* [Middle English *boton*, from Middle French, from Old French, from *boter* to thrust — more at BUTT] (14th century)
1 a : a small knob or disk secured to an article (as of clothing) and used as a fastener by passing it through a buttonhole or loop **b** : a usually circular metal or plastic badge bearing a stamped design or printed slogan ⟨campaign *button*⟩
2 : something that resembles a button: as **a** : any of various parts or growths of a plant or of an animal: as (1) : an immature whole mushroom (2) : the terminal segment of a rattlesnake's rattle **b** : a small globule of metal remaining after fusion (as in assaying) **c** : a guard on the tip of a fencing foil

3 : PUSH BUTTON
4 : the point of the chin especially as a target for a knockout blow
— **but·ton·less** \-ləs\ *adjective*
— **on the button** : EXACTLY ⟨arrived at noon *on the button*⟩; *also* : exactly on target : on the nose ⟨the estimate was right *on the button*⟩

²button *verb* **but·toned; but·ton·ing** \'bət-niŋ, 'bə-t°n-iŋ\ (14th century)
transitive verb
1 : to furnish or decorate with buttons
2 a : to pass (a button) through a buttonhole or loop **b** : to close or fasten with buttons — often used with *up* ⟨*button* up your overcoat⟩
3 a : to close (the lips) to prevent speech ⟨*button* your lip⟩ **b** : to close or seal tightly — usually used with *up* ⟨*button* up the house for winter⟩
intransitive verb
: to have buttons for fastening ⟨this dress *buttons* at the back⟩
— **but·ton·er** \'bət-nər, 'bə-t°n-ər\ *noun*

but·ton·ball \'bə-t°n-,bȯl\ *noun* (1821)
: ²PLANE

but·ton·bush \-,bȯsh\ *noun* (1754)
: a North American shrub (*Cephalanthus occidentalis*) of the madder family with globular flower heads

¹but·ton–down \-,daȯn\ *adjective* (1934)
1 a *of a collar* : having the ends fastened to the garment with buttons **b** *of a garment* : having a button-down collar
2 *also* **but·toned–down** \-t°n-,daȯn\ : conservatively traditional or conventional; *especially* : adhering to conventional ideals in dress and behavior ⟨*button-down* businessmen⟩

²button–down *noun* (1952)
: a shirt with a button-down collar

but·toned–up \'bə-tən-'dəp\ *adjective* (1936)
: coldly reserved or standoffish

¹but·ton·hole \'bə-t°n-,hōl\ *noun* (1561)
1 : a slit or loop through which a button is passed
2 *chiefly British* : BOUTONNIERE

²buttonhole *transitive verb* (1828)
1 : to furnish with buttonholes
2 : to work with buttonhole stitch
— **but·ton·hol·er** \-,hō-lər\ *noun*

³buttonhole *transitive verb* [alteration of *buttonhold*] (1862)
: to detain in conversation by or as if by holding on to the outer garments of

buttonhole stitch *noun* (circa 1885)
: a closely worked loop stitch used to make a firm edge (as on a buttonhole)

but·ton·hook \'bə-t°n-,hȯk\ *noun* (1870)
1 : a hook for drawing small buttons through buttonholes
2 : an offensive play in football in which the pass receiver runs straight downfield and then abruptly cuts back toward the line of scrimmage
— **buttonhook** *intransitive verb*

button man *noun* [perhaps from *buttons* bellhop] (1966)
: a low-ranking member of a criminal underworld organization

button mushroom *noun* (1865)
: a small cultivated mushroom (*Agaricus bisporus* synonym *A. brunnescens*)

button quail *noun* (1885)
: any of a family (Turnicidae) of small terrestrial Old World birds that resemble quails and have only three toes on a foot with the hind toe being absent

button snakeroot *noun* (1775)
1 : BLAZING STAR 2a
2 : any of several usually prickly herbs (genus *Eryngium*) of the carrot family

but·ton·wood \'bə-t°n-,wȯd\ *noun* (1674)
: ²PLANE

¹but·tress \'bə-trəs\ *noun* [Middle English *butres*, from Middle French *bouterez*, from

Old French *boterez*, from *boter* — more at BUTT] (14th century)
1 : a projecting structure of masonry or wood for supporting or giving stability to a wall or building
2 : something that resembles a buttress: as **a** : a projecting part of a mountain or hill **b** : a horny protuberance on a horse's hoof at the heel — see HOOF illustration **c** : the broadened base of a tree trunk or a thickened vertical part of it
3 : something that supports or strengthens ⟨a *buttress* of the cause of peace⟩
— **but·tressed** \-trəst\ *adjective*

²buttress *transitive verb* (14th century)
: to furnish or shore up with a buttress; *also* : SUPPORT, STRENGTHEN ⟨arguments *buttressed* by solid facts⟩

butt shaft *noun* (1588)
: a target arrow without a barb

butt·stock \'bət-,stäk\ *noun* (circa 1909)
: the stock of a firearm in the rear of the breech mechanism

butt weld *noun* (circa 1864)
: a butt joint made by welding
— **butt–weld** *transitive verb*

but·ty \'bə-tē\ *noun, plural* **butties** [origin unknown] (circa 1790)
chiefly British : a fellow worker : CHUM, PARTNER

bu·tut \bü-'tüt\ *noun, plural* **bututs** *or* **butut** [Wolof] (1972)
— see *dalasi* at MONEY table

bu·tyl \'byü-t°l\ *noun* [International Scientific Vocabulary *butyric* + *-yl*] (1869)
: any of four isomeric univalent radicals C_4H_9 derived from butanes

butyl alcohol *noun* (circa 1871)
: any of four flammable alcohols C_4H_9OH (as butanol) used in organic synthesis and as solvents

bu·tyl·at·ed \'byü-t°l-,ā-təd\ *adjective* (1942)
: combined with the butyl group
— **bu·tyl·a·tion** \,byü-t°l-'ā-shən\ *noun*

butylated hy·droxy·an·i·sole \-,(,)hī-,dräk-sē-'a-nə-,sōl\ *noun* [*hydroxy* + *anise* + *-ole*] (1950)
: BHA

butylated hy·droxy·tol·u·ene \-'täl-yə-,wēn\ *noun* (1961)
: BHT

bu·tyl·ene \'byü-t°l-,ēn\ *noun* (1877)
: any of three isomeric hydrocarbons C_4H_8 of the ethylene series obtained usually by cracking petroleum

butyl rubber *noun* (1940)
: any of a class of synthetic rubbers that are made by copolymerizing isobutylene with a small amount usually of isoprene at low temperature

butyr- *or* **butyro-** *combining form* [International Scientific Vocabulary, from *butyric*]
: butyric ⟨*butyr*aldehyde⟩

bu·tyr·al·de·hyde \,byü-tə-'ral-də-,hīd\ *noun* [International Scientific Vocabulary] (circa 1885)
: either of two aldehydes C_4H_8O used especially in making synthetic resins

bu·ty·rate \'byü-tə-,rāt\ *noun* (1873)
: a salt or ester of butyric acid

bu·tyr·ic \byü-'tir-ik\ *adjective* [French *butyrique*, from Latin *butyrum* butter — more at BUTTER] (1854)
: relating to or producing butyric acid ⟨*butyric* fermentation⟩

butyric acid *noun* (1826)
: either of two isomeric fatty acids $C_4H_8O_2$; *especially* : an acid of unpleasant odor normally found in perspiration and rancid butter

bu·ty·ro·phe·none \,byü-tə-(,)rō-fə-'nōn\ *noun* [*butyr-* + *phen-* + *-one*] (1970)
: any of a class of neuroleptic drugs (as haloperidol) used especially in the treatment of schizophrenia

bux·om \'bək-səm\ *adjective* [Middle English *buxsum*, from (assumed) Old English *būhsum*;

akin to Old English *būgan* to bend — more at BOW] (12th century)
1 *obsolete* **a :** OBEDIENT, TRACTABLE **b :** offering little resistance : FLEXIBLE, PLIANT ⟨wing silently the *buxom* air —John Milton⟩
2 *archaic* **:** full of gaiety : BLITHE
3 : vigorously or healthily plump; *specifically* : full-bosomed
— **bux·om·ly** *adverb*
— **bux·om·ness** *noun*

¹buy \'bī\ *verb* **bought** \'bȯt\; **buy·ing** [Middle English *byen*, from Old English *bycgan*; akin to Gothic *bugjan* to buy] (before 12th century)
transitive verb
1 : to acquire possession, ownership, or rights to the use or services of by payment especially of money : PURCHASE
2 a : to obtain in exchange for something often at a sacrifice ⟨they *bought* peace with their freedom⟩ **b :** REDEEM 6
3 : BRIBE, HIRE
4 : to be the purchasing equivalent of ⟨the dollar *buys* less today than it used to⟩
5 : ACCEPT, BELIEVE ⟨I don't *buy* that hooey⟩
intransitive verb
: to make a purchase
— **buy·er** \'bī(-ə)r\ *noun*
— **buy it** *or* **buy the farm :** to get killed : DIE
— **buy time :** to delay an imminent action or decision : STALL

²buy *noun* (1879)
1 : something of value at a favorable price; *especially* **:** BARGAIN ⟨it's a real *buy* at that price⟩
2 : an act of buying : PURCHASE

buy·back \'bī-ˌbak\ *noun* (1974)
: the act or an instance of buying something back; *especially* **:** the repurchase by a corporation of shares of its own common stock on the open market

buyer's market *noun* (1926)
: a market in which goods are plentiful, buyers have a wide range of choice, and prices tend to be low — compare SELLER'S MARKET

buy off *transitive verb* (1629)
1 : to induce to refrain (as from prosecution) by a payment or other consideration
2 : to free (as from military service) by payment

buy·out \'bī-ˌaut\ *noun* (1971)
: an act or instance of buying out

buy out *transitive verb* (1644)
1 : to purchase the share or interest of
2 : to purchase the entire stock-in-trade and the goodwill of (a business)

buy up *transitive verb* (circa 1534)
1 : to buy freely or extensively
2 : to buy the entire available supply of

¹buzz \'bəz\ *verb* [Middle English *bussen*, of imitative origin] (14th century)
intransitive verb
1 : to make a low continuous humming sound like that of a bee
2 a : MURMUR, WHISPER **b :** to be filled with a confused murmur ⟨the room *buzzed* with excitement⟩
3 : to make a signal with a buzzer
4 : to go quickly : HURRY ⟨*buzzed* around town in a sports car⟩; *also* **:** SCRAM — usually used with *off*
transitive verb
1 : to utter covertly by or as if by whispering
2 : to cause to buzz
3 : to fly fast and close to ⟨planes *buzz* the crowd⟩
4 : to summon or signal with a buzzer
5 *dialect English* **:** to drink to the last drop ⟨get some more port whilst I *buzz* this bottle —W. M. Thackeray⟩

²buzz *noun* (1605)
1 : a persistent vibratory sound
2 a : RUMOR, GOSSIP **b :** a confused murmur **c :** a flurry of activity **d :** FAD, CRAZE
3 : a signal conveyed by buzzer; *specifically* **:** a telephone call

4 : HIGH 4

buz·zard \'bə-zərd\ *noun* [Middle English *busard*, from Old French, alteration of *buison*, from Latin *buteon, buteo* hawk] (14th century)
1 *chiefly British* **:** BUTEO
2 : any of various usually large birds of prey (as the turkey vulture)
3 : a contemptible or rapacious person

buzz bomb *noun* (1944)
: an unguided jet-propelled missile used by the Germans against England in World War II

buzz cut *noun* (1983)
: CREW CUT

buzz·er \'bə-zər\ *noun* (1606)
1 : one that buzzes; *specifically* **:** an electric signaling device that makes a buzzing sound
2 : the sound of a buzzer

buzz saw *noun* (1858)
: CIRCULAR SAW

buzz·word \'bəz-ˌwərd\ *noun* (1946)
1 : an important-sounding usually technical word or phrase often of little meaning used chiefly to impress laymen
2 : a voguish word or phrase — called also *buzz phrase*

BVD \ˌbē-(ˌ)vē-'dē\ *trademark*
— used for underwear

B vitamin *noun* (1920)
: any vitamin of the vitamin B complex

bwa·na \'bwä-nə\ *noun* [Swahili, from Arabic *abūna* our father] (1878)
: MASTER, BOSS

¹by \'bī, *before consonants also* bə\ *preposition* [Middle English, preposition & adverb, from Old English, preposition, *be, bī*; akin to Old High German *bī* by, near, Latin *ambi-* on both sides, around, Greek *amphi*] (before 12th century)
1 : in proximity to **:** NEAR ⟨standing *by* the window⟩
2 a : through or through the medium of **:** VIA ⟨enter *by* the door⟩ **b :** in the direction of **:** TOWARD ⟨north *by* east⟩ **c :** into the vicinity of and beyond **:** PAST ⟨went right *by* him⟩
3 a : during the course of ⟨studied *by* night⟩ **b :** not later than ⟨*by* 2 p.m.⟩
4 a : through the agency or instrumentality of ⟨*by* force⟩ **b :** born or begot of **c :** sired or borne by
5 : with the witness or sanction of ⟨swear *by* all that is holy⟩
6 a : in conformity with ⟨acted *by* the rules⟩ **b :** ACCORDING TO ⟨called her *by* name⟩
7 a : on behalf of ⟨did right *by* his children⟩ **b :** with respect to ⟨a lawyer *by* profession⟩
8 a : in or to the amount or extent of ⟨win *by* a nose⟩ **b** *chiefly Scottish* **:** in comparison with **:** BESIDE
9 — used as a function word to indicate successive units or increments ⟨little *by* little⟩ ⟨walk two *by* two⟩
10 — used as a function word in multiplication, in division, and in measurements ⟨divide *a* by *b*⟩ ⟨multiply 10 *by* 4⟩ ⟨a room 15 feet *by* 20 feet⟩
11 : in the opinion of ⟨okay *by* me⟩
— **by the by** *or* **by the bye :** INCIDENTALLY 2

²by \'bī\ *adverb* (before 12th century)
1 a : close at hand **:** NEAR **b :** at or to another's home ⟨stop *by*⟩
2 : PAST ⟨saw him go *by*⟩
3 : ASIDE, AWAY

³by *or* **bye** \'bī\ *adjective* (14th century)
1 : being off the main route **:** SIDE
2 : INCIDENTAL

⁴by *or* **bye** \'bī\ *noun, plural* **byes** \'bīz\ (1567)
: something of secondary importance : a side issue

⁵by *or* **bye** \'bī\ *interjection* [short for *goodbye*] (1709)
— used to express farewell; often used with following *now*

by-and-by \ˌbī-ən-'bī\ *noun* (1591)
: a future time or occasion

by and by *adverb* (1526)
: before long **:** SOON

by and large *adverb* (1706)
: on the whole **:** in general

by-blow \'bī-ˌblō\ *noun* (1594)
1 : an indirect blow
2 : an illegitimate child

bye \'bī\ *noun* [alteration of ²*by*] (1883)
: the position of a participant in a tournament who advances to the next round without playing

¹bye-bye *or* **by-by** \'bī-ˌbī, bī-'bī\ *interjection* [baby-talk reduplication of *goodbye*] (circa 1736)
— used to express farewell

²bye-bye *or* **by-by** \'bī-ˌbī\ *adverb* (1917)
: out especially for a walk or ride — used with the verb *go*

³bye-bye *or* **by-by** \'bī-ˌbī\ *noun* (1867)
: BED, SLEEP ⟨lie down . . . and go to *bye-bye* —Rudyard Kipling⟩

⁴bye-bye *or* **by-by** \'bī-ˌbī\ *adverb* (1920)
: to bed or sleep — used with the verb *go*

by-elec·tion *also* **bye-election** \'bī-ə-ˌlek-shən\ *noun* (1880)
: a special election held between regular elections in order to fill a vacancy

by·gone \'bī-ˌgȯn *also* -ˌgän\ *adjective* (15th century)
: gone by **:** PAST; *especially* **:** OUTMODED
— **bygone** *noun*

by·law *or* **bye·law** \'bī-ˌlȯ\ *noun* [Middle English *bilawe*, probably from (assumed) Old Norse *bȳlog*, from Old Norse *bȳr* town + *log* law] (14th century)
1 : a rule adopted by an organization chiefly for the government of its members and the regulation of its affairs
2 : a local ordinance

¹by·line \'bī-ˌlīn\ *noun* (1916)
1 : a secondary line **:** SIDELINE
2 : a line at the beginning of a news story, magazine article, or book giving the writer's name

²byline *transitive verb* (1938)
: to write (an article) under a byline
— **by·lin·er** \-ˌlī-nər\ *noun*

by·name \'bī-ˌnām\ *noun* (14th century)
1 : a secondary name
2 : NICKNAME

¹by·pass \'bī-ˌpas\ *noun* (1848)
1 : a passage to one side; *especially* **:** a deflected route usually around a town
2 a : a channel carrying a fluid around a part and back to the main stream **b** (1) **:** SHUNT 1b (2) **:** SHUNT 1c; *also* **:** a surgical procedure for the establishment of a shunt ⟨have a coronary *bypass*⟩

²bypass *transitive verb* (1886)
1 a : to avoid by means of a bypass **b :** to cause to follow a bypass
2 a : to neglect or ignore usually intentionally **b :** CIRCUMVENT

by·past \'bī-ˌpast\ *adjective* (15th century)
: BYGONE

by·path \-ˌpath, -ˌpath\ *noun* (14th century)
: BYWAY

by·play \-ˌplā\ *noun* (1812)
: action engaged in on the side while the main action proceeds (as during a dramatic production)

by-prod·uct \-ˌprä-(ˌ)dəkt\ *noun* (1857)
1 : something produced in a usually industrial or biological process in addition to the principal product
2 : a secondary and sometimes unexpected or unintended result ⟨unpleasant *by-products* of civilization⟩

byre \'bīr\ *noun* [Middle English, from Old English *bȳre*; akin to Old English *būr* dwelling

— more at BOWER] (before 12th century)
chiefly British **:** a cow barn

by·road \'bī-ˌrōd\ *noun* (1673)
: BYWAY

bys·si·no·sis \ˌbi-sə-'nō-səs\ *noun, plural* **-no·ses** \-ˌsēz\ [New Latin, from Latin *byssinus* of fine linen, from Greek *byssinos,* from *byssos*] (1881)
: an occupational respiratory disease associated with inhalation of cotton, flax, or hemp dust and characterized initially by chest tightness, shortness of breath, and cough and eventually by irreversible lung disease

bys·sus \'bi-səs\ *noun, plural* **bys·sus·es** *or* **bys·si** \-ˌsī, -ˌ(ˌ)sē\ [Middle English *bissus,* from Latin *byssus,* from Greek *byssos* flax, of Semitic origin; akin to Hebrew *būṣ* linen cloth] (14th century)
1 : a fine probably linen cloth of ancient times
2 [New Latin, from Latin] **:** a tuft of long tough filaments by which some bivalve mollusks (as mussels) adhere to a surface

by·stand·er \'bī-ˌstan-dər\ *noun* (circa 1619)
: one present but not taking part in a situation or event **:** a chance spectator

by·street \-ˌstrēt\ *noun* (1672)
: a street off a main thoroughfare

byte \'bīt\ *noun* [perhaps alteration of ²*bite*] (1959)
: a group of eight binary digits processed as a unit by a computer and used especially to represent an alphanumeric character — compare WORD 2c

by·way \'bī-ˌwā\ *noun* (14th century)
1 : a little traveled side road
2 : a secondary or little known aspect or field ⟨meandering more and more in the fascinating *byways* of learning —*Times Literary Supplement*⟩

by·word \-ˌwərd\ *noun* (before 12th century)
1 : a proverbial saying **:** PROVERB
2 a : one that personifies a type **b :** one that is noteworthy or notorious
3 : EPITHET
4 : a frequently used word or phrase

by–your–leave \ˌbī-yər-'lēv\ *noun* (1914)
: a request for permission ⟨imposed . . . without so much as a *by-your-leave* —J. L. Granatstein⟩

¹**Byz·an·tine** \'bi-zᵊn-ˌtēn, 'bī-, -ˌtīn; bə-'zan-ˌ, bī-\ *adjective* (1794)
1 : of, relating to, or characteristic of the ancient city of Byzantium
2 : of, relating to, or having the characteristics of a style of architecture developed in the Byzantine Empire especially in the 5th and 6th centuries featuring the dome carried on pendentives over a square and incrustation with marble veneering and with colored mosaics on grounds of gold
3 : of or relating to the churches using a traditional Greek rite and subject to Eastern canon law
4 *often not capitalized* **a :** of, relating to, or characterized by a devious and usually surreptitious manner of operation ⟨a *Byzantine* power struggle⟩ **b :** intricately involved **:** LABYRINTHINE ⟨rules of *Byzantine* complexity⟩

²**Byzantine** *noun* (1836)
: a native or inhabitant of Byzantium

Byz·an·tin·ist \bi-'zan-ti-nist, bī-\ *noun* (1892)
: a student of Byzantine culture

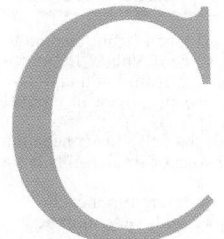

C *is the third letter of the English alphabet and of most alphabets closely related to that of English. It came through the Latin from the Etruscan and there from the Greek, which took it from the Phoenician; it has the alphabetic position, but not the pronunciation, of Greek* gamma *and Phoenician* gimel. *In Phoenician and Greek,* C *represented the sound of g in* go. *Etruscan assigned* C *the value of* k, *since its speakers did not use the g sound. Latin, on the other hand, had both sound values, and so the Romans invented a new letter* G *for the value g, while keeping* C *for the value k.* C *retains the k pronunciation in modern English before* a, o, u, *or a consonant other than* h, *and has taken on the pronunciation of* s *before* e, i, *or* y. *The small form of* c *emerged through a simple reduction in the size of the capital form.*

c \'sē\ *noun, plural* **c's** *or* **cs** \'sēz\ *often capitalized, often attributive*
1 a : the 3rd letter of the English alphabet **b** : a graphic representation of this letter **c** : a speech counterpart of orthographic *c*
2 a : one hundred — see NUMBER table **b** *slang* : a sum of $100
3 : the keynote of a C-major scale
4 : a graphic device for reproducing the letter *c*
5 : one designated *c* especially as the 3rd in order or class
6 a : a grade rating a student's work as fair or mediocre in quality **b** : one graded or rated with a C
7 : something shaped like the letter C
8 : a structured programming language designed to produce a compact and efficient translation of a program into machine language
ca' \'kò, 'kä\ *Scottish variant of* CALL
¹cab \'kab, 'käb\ *noun* [Hebrew *qabh*] (1535)
: an ancient Hebrew unit of capacity equal to about two quarts (2.2 liters)
²cab \'kab\ *noun* [short for *cabriolet*] (1827)
1 a (1) : CABRIOLET (2) : a similar light closed carriage (as a hansom) **b** : a carriage for hire
2 : TAXICAB
3 [short for *cabin*] **a** : the part of a locomotive that houses the engineer and operating controls **b** : a comparable shelter (as on a truck) housing operating controls
¹ca·bal \kə-'bäl, -'bal\ *noun* [French *cabale* cabala, intrigue, cabal, from Medieval Latin *cabbala* cabala, from Late Hebrew *qabbālāh*, literally, received (lore)] (1614)
: the artifices and intrigues of a group of persons secretly united to bring about an overturn or usurpation especially in public affairs; *also* : a group engaged in such artifices and intrigues
synonym see PLOT
²cabal *intransitive verb* **ca·balled; ca·bal·ling** (1680)
: to unite in or form a cabal
ca·ba·la *or* **cab·ba·la** *or* **cab·ba·lah** \kə-'bä-lə, 'ka-bə-lə\ *noun, often capitalized* [Medieval Latin *cabbala*] (1521)
1 : a medieval and modern system of Jewish theosophy, mysticism, and thaumaturgy marked by belief in creation through emanation and a cipher method of interpreting Scripture
2 a : a traditional, esoteric, occult, or secret matter **b** : esoteric doctrine or mysterious art
— **cab·a·lism** \'ka-bə-,li-zəm, 'ka-\ *noun*
— **cab·a·lis·tic** \,kä-bə-'lis-tik, ,ka-\ *adjective*
ca·ba·let·ta \,ka-bə-'le-tə, ,kä-\ *noun* [Italian] (1842)
1 : an operatic song in simple popular style characterized by a uniform rhythm

2 : the lively bravura concluding section of an extended aria or duet
¹ca·ba·list \kə-'bä-list, 'ka-bə-\ *noun* (circa 1533)
1 *often capitalized* : a student, interpreter, or devotee of the Jewish cabala
2 : one skilled in esoteric doctrine or mysterious art
²cab·al·ist \kə-'ba-list, -'bä-\ *noun* (1569)
: a member of a cabal
ca·bal·le·ro \,ka-bə-'ler-(,)ō, -bə(l)-'yer-\ *noun, plural* **-ros** [Spanish, from Late Latin *caballarius* hostler — more at CAVALIER] (1749)
1 : KNIGHT, CAVALIER
2 *chiefly Southwest* : HORSEMAN
ca·bana \kə-'ban-yə, -'ba-nə\ *noun* [Spanish *cabaña*, literally, hut, from Medieval Latin *capanna*] (1890)
1 : a shelter resembling a cabin usually with an open side facing a beach or swimming pool
2 : a lightweight structure with living facilities
cab·a·ret \,ka-bə-'rā, 'ka-bə-,\ *noun* [French, from Old North French] (1655)
1 *archaic* : a shop selling wines and liquors
2 a : a restaurant serving liquor and providing entertainment (as by singers or dancers) : NIGHTCLUB **b** : the show provided at a cabaret
¹cab·bage \'ka-bij\ *noun, often attributive* [Middle English *caboche*, from Old North French, head] (15th century)
1 : a leafy garden plant (*Brassica oleracea capitata*) of European origin with a short stem and a dense globular head of usually green leaves that is used as a vegetable
2 *slang* : PAPER MONEY, BANKNOTES ◆
²cabbage *noun* [perhaps by folk etymology from Middle French *cabas* cheating, theft] (1663)
British : pieces of cloth left in cutting out garments and traditionally kept by tailors as perquisites
³cabbage *transitive verb* **cab·baged; cab·bag·ing** (1712)
: STEAL, FILCH
cabbage butterfly *noun* (1816)
: any of several largely white butterflies (family Pieridae) whose green larvae are cabbageworms; *especially* : a small cosmopolitan butterfly (*Pieris rapae* synonym *Artogeia rapae*) that is a pest on cabbage — called also *cabbage white*
cabbage looper *noun* (circa 1902)
: a noctuid moth (*Trichoplusia ni*) having pale green white-striped larvae that feed on cruciferous plants (as the cabbage)
cabbage palm *noun* (circa 1784)

cabbage butterfly: *1* larva, *2* adult

: a palm with terminal buds eaten as a vegetable
cabbage palmetto *noun* (1802)
: a cabbage palm (*Sabal palmetto*) with fan-shaped leaves that is native to coastal southeastern U.S. and the Bahamas
cabbage rose *noun* (1795)
: a fragrant garden rose (*Rosa centifolia*) with upright branches and large pink flowers
cab·bage·worm \'ka-bij-,wərm\ *noun* (1688)
: an insect larva (as of a cabbage butterfly) that feeds on cabbages
cab·bie *or* **cab·by** \'ka-bē\ *noun, plural* **cabbies** (1859)
: CABDRIVER
cab·driv·er \'kab-,drī-vər\ *noun* (1830)
: a driver of a cab
ca·ber \'kā-bər, 'kä-\ *noun* [Scottish Gaelic *cabar*] (1505)
: POLE; *especially* : a young tree trunk used for tossing as a trial of strength in a Scottish sport
cab·er·net sau·vi·gnon \,ka-bər-'nā-sō-vē-'nyō"\ *noun, often C&S capitalized* [French] (1941)
: a dry red wine made from a single widely cultivated variety of black grape — called also *cabernet*
¹cab·in \'ka-bən\ *noun* [Middle English *cabane*, from Middle French, from Old Provençal *cabana* hut, from Medieval Latin *capanna*] (14th century)
1 a (1) : a private room on a ship or boat (2) : a compartment below deck on a boat used for living accommodations **b** : the passenger or cargo compartment of a vehicle (as an airplane or automobile) **c** : the crew compartment of an exploratory vehicle (as a spacecraft)
2 : a small one-story dwelling usually of simple construction
3 *chiefly British* : CAB 3
²cabin (1586)
intransitive verb
: to live in or as if in a cabin
transitive verb
: CONFINE
cabin boy *noun* (1726)
: a boy working as servant on a ship
cabin car *noun* (1879)
: CABOOSE
cabin class *noun* (1929)
: a class of accommodations on a passenger ship superior to tourist class and inferior to first class

◇ WORD HISTORY

cabbage Old French *caboce* was a jocular word for "head," probably similar in this respect to the English word *noggin*. The form of the word in the dialects of Normandy and Picardy was *caboche*, which spread to the French of the Paris region and retains some currency in Modern French. The origin of *caboce* and *caboche* is not entirely clear, though the second syllable appears to be *boce* "boss, protuberance." While *caboche* has remained limited to very colloquial uses in French, the medieval French word found its way into later Middle English in the sense "head of cabbage." In English it has become the everyday word for the vegetable that the French call *chou*. Middle English *caboche* emerged as *cabage* in Early Modern English, through the same change of a final \ch\ sound to \j\ in an unstressed syllable that is evident in *knowledge* (Middle English *knowleche*) and *sausage* (Middle English *sawsiche*).

\ə\ **abut** \ᵊ\ **kitten** \ər\ **further** \a\ **ash** \ā\ **ace**
\ä\ **mop, mar** \aú\ **out** \ch\ **chin** \e\ **bet** \ē\ **easy**
\g\ **go** \i\ **hit** \ī\ **ice** \j\ **job** \ŋ\ **sing** \ō\ **go**
\ò\ **law** \òi\ **boy** \th\ **thin** \ṯẖ\ **the** \ü\ **loot** \ú\ **foot**
\y\ **yet** \zh\ **vision** *see also* Guide to Pronunciation

cabin cruiser noun (1921)
: CRUISER 1b

¹**cab·i·net** \'kab-nit, 'ka-bə-\ noun [Middle French, small room, diminutive of Old North French cabine gambling house] (circa 1550)
1 a : a case or cupboard usually having doors and shelves **b :** a collection of specimens especially of biological or numismatic interest **c :** CONSOLE 4a **d :** a chamber having temperature and humidity controls and used especially for incubating biological samples
2 a archaic **:** a small room providing seclusion **b :** a small exhibition room in a museum
3 a archaic (1) **:** the private room serving as council chamber of the chief councillors or ministers of a sovereign (2) **:** the consultations and actions of these councillors **b** (1) often capitalized **:** a body of advisers of a head of state (2) **:** a similar advisory council of a governor of a state or a mayor **c** British **:** a meeting of a cabinet

²**cabinet** adjective (1631)
1 : of or relating to a governmental cabinet
2 : suitable by reason of size for a small room or by reason of attractiveness or perfection for preservation and display in a cabinet
3 a : used or adapted for cabinetmaking **b :** done or used by a cabinetmaker

cab·i·net·mak·er \-,mā-kər\ noun (1681)
: a skilled woodworker who makes fine furniture
— **cab·i·net·mak·ing** \-,mā-kiŋ\ noun

cab·i·net·ry \'kab-ni-trē, 'ka-bə-\ noun (1926)
: CABINETWORK; also : CABINETS ⟨kitchen cabinetry⟩

cab·i·net·work \-,wərk\ noun (1732)
: finished woodwork made by a cabinetmaker

cabin fever noun (1918)
: extreme irritability and restlessness from living in isolation or a confined indoor area for a prolonged time

¹**ca·ble** \'kā-bəl\ noun, often attributive [Middle English, from Old North French, from Medieval Latin capulum lasso, from Latin capere to take — more at HEAVE] (13th century)
1 a : a strong rope especially of 10 inches (25 centimeters) or more in circumference **b :** a cable-laid rope **c :** a wire rope or metal chain of great tensile strength **d :** a wire or wire rope by which force is exerted to control or operate a mechanism
2 : CABLE LENGTH
3 a : an assembly of electrical conductors insulated from each other but laid up together usually by being twisted around a central core **b :** CABLEGRAM; also : a radio message or telegram
4 : something resembling or fashioned like a cable ⟨a fiber-optic cable⟩
5 : CABLE TELEVISION

²**cable** verb **ca·bled; ca·bling** \'kā-b(ə-)liŋ\ (circa 1500)
transitive verb
1 : to fasten with or as if with a cable
2 : to provide with cables
3 : to telegraph by submarine cable
4 : to make into a cable or into a form resembling a cable
intransitive verb
: to communicate by a submarine cable

cable car noun (1887)
: a vehicle moved by an endless cable: **a :** one suspended from an overhead cable **b :** one that moves along tracks

ca·ble·gram \'kā-bəl-,gram\ noun (1868)
: a message sent by a submarine telegraph cable

ca·ble-laid \'kā-bəl-'lād\ adjective (1723)
: composed of three ropes laid together left-handed with each containing three strands twisted together

cable length noun (1555)
: a maritime unit of length variously reckoned as 100 fathoms, 120 fathoms, or 608 feet

cable television noun (1965)

: a system of television reception in which signals from distant stations are picked up by a master antenna and sent by cable to the individual receivers of paying subscribers — called also cable TV

ca·ble·way \'kā-bəl-,wā\ noun (1899)
: a suspended cable used as a track along which carriers can be pulled

cab·man \'kab-mən\ noun (1834)
: CABDRIVER

cab·o·chon \'ka-bə-,shän\ noun [Middle French, diminutive of Old North French caboche head] (1578)
: a gem or bead cut in convex form and highly polished but not faceted; also : this style of cutting
— **cabochon** adverb

ca·boo·dle \kə-'bü-dᵊl\ noun [probably from ca- (intensive prefix) + boodle] (circa 1848)
: COLLECTION, LOT ⟨sell the whole caboodle⟩

ca·boose \kə-'büs\ noun [probably from Dutch kabuis, from Middle Low German kabūse] (1769)
1 : a ship's galley
2 : a freight-train car attached usually to the rear mainly for the use of the train crew
3 : one that follows or brings up the rear

cab·o·tage \'ka-bə-,täzh\ noun [French, from caboter to sail along the coast] (1831)
1 : trade or transport in coastal waters or airspace or between two points within a country
2 : the right to engage in cabotage

ca·bret·ta \kə-'bre-tə\ noun [modification of Portuguese and Spanish cabra goat] (1926)
: a light soft leather from skins of hairy sheep

ca·bril·la \kə-'brē-ə, -'bri-lə\ noun [Spanish, diminutive of cabra goat, from Latin capra she-goat, feminine of caper he-goat — more at CAPRIOLE] (1859)
: any of various sea basses (especially of the genera Epinephelus and Paralabrax) of the Mediterranean, the California coast, and the warmer parts of the western Atlantic

cab·ri·ole \'ka-brē-,ōl\ noun [French, caper] (1797)
1 : a ballet leap in which one leg is extended in midair and the other struck against it
2 : a curved furniture leg ending in an ornamental foot

cab·ri·o·let \,ka-brē-ə-'lā\ noun [French, from diminutive of cabriole caper, alteration of Middle French capriole] (1763)
1 : a light 2-wheeled one-horse carriage with a folding leather hood, a large apron, and upward-curving shafts
2 : a convertible coupe

cab·stand \'kab-,stand\ noun (1848)
: a place where cabs await hire

cac- or **caco-** combining form [New Latin, from Greek kak-, kako-, from kakos bad]
: bad ⟨cacography⟩

ca' can·ny \kȯ-'ka-nē\ noun [Scots, verb, to proceed cautiously, from ca' (call) + canny careful] (1886)
British : SLOWDOWN
— **ca' canny** intransitive verb, British

ca·cao \kə-'kaů, kə-'kā-(,)ō\ noun, plural **ca·caos** [Spanish, from Nahuatl cacahuatl cacao beans] (1555)
1 : the dried partly fermented fatty seeds of a South American evergreen tree (Theobroma cacao of the family Sterculiaceae) that are used in making cocoa, chocolate, and cocoa butter — called also cacao bean, cocoa bean
2 : a tree having small yellowish flowers followed by fleshy pods with many seeds that bears cacao

cacao butter variant of COCOA BUTTER

cac·cia·to·re \,kä-chə-'tȯr-ē, -'tȯr-\ adjective [Italian, from cacciatore hunter] (1942)
: cooked with tomatoes and herbs and sometimes wine ⟨chicken cacciatore⟩

cach·a·lot \'ka-shə-,lät, -,lō\ noun [French] (1747)
: SPERM WHALE

¹**cache** \'kash\ noun [French, from cacher to press, hide, from (assumed) Vulgar Latin coacticare to press together, from Latin coactare to compel, frequentative of cogere to compel — more at COGENT] (1797)
1 a : a hiding place especially for concealing and preserving provisions or implements **b :** a secure place of storage
2 : something hidden or stored in a cache
3 : a computer memory with very short access time used for storage of frequently used instructions or data — called also cache memory

²**cache** transitive verb **cached; cach·ing** (1805)
: to place, hide, or store in a cache

ca·chec·tic \kə-'kek-tik, ka-\ adjective [French cachectique, from Latin cachecticus, from Greek kachektikos, from kak- + echein] (1634)
: affected by cachexia

cache·pot \'kash-,pät, 'kash-,pō, 'ka-shə-\ noun [French, from cacher to hide + pot pot] (1872)
: an ornamental receptacle to hold and usually to conceal a flowerpot

ca·chet \ka-'shā\ noun [French, from cacher] (circa 1639)
1 a : a seal used especially as a mark of official approval **b :** an indication of approval carrying great prestige
2 a : a characteristic feature or quality conferring prestige **b :** PRESTIGE ⟨being rich . . . doesn't have the cachet it used to —Truman Capote⟩
3 : a medicinal preparation for swallowing consisting of a case usually of rice-flour paste enclosing a medicine
4 a : a design or inscription on an envelope to commemorate a postal or philatelic event **b :** an advertisement forming part of a postage meter impression **c :** a motto or slogan included in a postal cancellation

ca·chex·ia \kə-'kek-sē-ə, ka-\ noun [Late Latin cachexia, from Greek kachexia bad condition, from kak- cac- + hexis condition, from echein to have, be disposed — more at SCHEME] (1541)
: general physical wasting and malnutrition usually associated with chronic disease

cach·in·nate \'ka-kə-,nāt\ intransitive verb **-nat·ed; -nat·ing** [Latin cachinnatus, past participle of cachinnare, of imitative origin] (1824)
: to laugh loudly or immoderately
— **cach·in·na·tion** \,ka-kə-'nā-shən\ noun

ca·chou \ka-'shü, 'ka-,\ noun [French, from Portuguese cachu, from Malayalam kāccu] (circa 1879)
: a pill or pastille used to sweeten the breath

ca·cique \kə-'sēk\ noun [Spanish, from Taino, chief] (1555)
1 : a native Indian chief in areas dominated primarily by a Spanish culture
2 : a local political boss in Spain and Latin America
— **ca·ciqu·ism** \-'sē-,ki-zəm\ noun

cack·le \'ka-kəl\ intransitive verb **cack·led; cack·ling** \-k(ə-)liŋ\ [Middle English cakelen, of imitative origin] (13th century)
1 : to make the sharp broken noise or cry characteristic of a hen especially after laying
2 : to laugh especially in a harsh or sharp manner
3 : CHATTER
— **cackle** noun
— **cack·ler** \-k(ə-)lər\ noun

caco·de·mon \,ka-kə-'dē-mən\ noun [Greek kakodaimōn, from kak- cac- + daimōn spirit] (1594)
: DEMON
— **caco·de·mon·ic** \-di-'mä-nik\ adjective

cacodylic acid \,ka-kə-'di-lik-\ noun [German Kakodyl the radical As(CH₃)₂, from Greek kakōdēs foul-smelling, from kak- +

-*ōdēs* (akin to Greek *ozein* to smell) — more at ODOR] (1850)
: a toxic crystalline compound of arsenic $C_2H_7AsO_2$ used especially as an herbicide

ca·co·ë·thes \,ka-kə-'wē-(,)thēz\ *noun* [Latin, from Greek *kakoēthes* wickedness, from neuter of *kakoēthēs* malignant, from *kak-* cac- + *ēthos* character — more at SIB] (circa 1587)
: an insatiable desire : MANIA

ca·cog·ra·phy \ka-'kä-grə-fē\ *noun* (1580)
1 : bad spelling — compare ORTHOGRAPHY
2 : bad handwriting — compare CALLIGRAPHY
— **caco·graph·i·cal** \,ka-kə-'gra-fi-kəl\ *adjective*

cac·o·mis·tle \'ka-kə-,mi-səl, ,ka-kə-'mis(t)-lē\ *noun* [Mexican Spanish, from Nahuatl *tlahcomiztli,* from *tlahco* half + *miztli* mountain lion] (1869)
: RINGTAIL 2

ca·coph·o·nous \ka-'kä-fə-nəs, -'kò- *also* -'ka-\ *adjective* [Greek *kakophōnos,* from *kak-* + *phōnē* voice, sound — more at BAN] (1797)
: marked by cacophony : harsh-sounding
— **ca·coph·o·nous·ly** *adverb*

ca·coph·o·ny \-nē\ *noun, plural* **-nies** (circa 1656)
: harsh or discordant sound : DISSONANCE 2; *specifically* **:** harshness in the sound of words or phrases

cac·tus \'kak-təs\ *noun, plural* **cac·ti** \-,tī, -(,)tē\ *or* **cac·tus·es** *also* **cactus** [New Latin, genus name, from Latin, cardoon, from Greek *kaktos*] (1767)
: any of a family (Cactaceae, the cactus family) of plants that have succulent stems and branches with scales or spines instead of leaves and are found especially in dry areas (as deserts)

ca·cu·mi·nal \ka-'kyü-mə-n°l, kə-\ *adjective* [International Scientific Vocabulary, from Latin *cacumin-, cacumen* top, point] (1862)
: RETROFLEX 2

cad \'kad\ *noun* [English dialect, unskilled assistant, short for Scots *caddie*] (1833)
1 : an omnibus conductor
2 : a man who acts with deliberate disregard for another's feelings or rights

ca·das·tral \kə-'das-trəl\ *adjective* (1858)
1 : of or relating to a cadastre
2 : showing or recording property boundaries, subdivision lines, buildings, and related details
— **ca·das·tral·ly** \-trə-lē\ *adverb*

ca·das·tre \kə-'das-tər\ *noun* [French, from Italian *catastro,* from Old Italian *catastico,* from Late Greek *katastichon* notebook, from Greek *kata* by + *stichos* row, line — more at CATA-, DISTICH] (1804)
: an official register of the quantity, value, and ownership of real estate used in apportioning taxes

ca·dav·er \kə-'da-vər\ *noun* [Latin, from *cadere* to fall] (circa 1500)
: a dead body; *especially* **:** one intended for dissection
— **ca·dav·er·ic** \-'da-vrik, -'da-və-\ *adjective*

ca·dav·er·ine \kə-'da-və-,rēn\ *noun* (1887)
: a syrupy colorless poisonous ptomaine $C_5H_{14}N_2$ formed by decarboxylation of lysine especially in putrefaction of flesh

ca·dav·er·ous \kə-'da-v-rəs, -'da-vər-əs\ *adjective* (1627)
1 a : of or relating to a corpse **b :** suggestive of corpses or tombs
2 a : PALLID, LIVID **b :** GAUNT, EMACIATED
— **ca·dav·er·ous·ly** *adverb*

cad·die *or* **cad·dy** \'ka-dē\ *noun, plural* **caddies** [French *cadet* military cadet] (circa 1730)
1 *Scottish* **:** one that waits about for odd jobs
2 a : one who assists a golfer especially by carrying the clubs **b :** a wheeled device for conveying things not readily carried by hand
— **caddie** *or* **caddy** *intransitive verb*

1cad·dis *also* **cad·dice** \'ka-dəs\ *noun* [Middle English *cadas* cotton wool, probably from Middle French *cadaz,* from Old Provençal *cadarz*] (1530)
: worsted yarn; *specifically* **:** a worsted ribbon or binding formerly used for garters and girdles

2caddis *noun* (1651)
: CADDISWORM

caddis fly *noun* (1787)
: any of an order (Trichoptera) of insects with four membranous wings, vestigial mouthparts, slender many-jointed antennae, and aquatic larvae — compare CADDISWORM

cad·dish \'ka-dish\ *adjective* (1868)
: of, relating to, or resembling a cad
— **cad·dish·ly** *adverb*
— **cad·dish·ness** *noun*

cad·dis·worm \'ka-dəs-,wərm\ *noun* [probably alteration of obsolete *codworm;* from the case or tube in which it lives] (1622)
: the larva of a caddis fly that lives in and carries around a silken case covered with bits of debris

Cad·do \'ka-(,)dō\ *noun, plural* **Caddo** *or* **Caddos** (1805)
: a member of a group of American Indian peoples of Louisiana, Arkansas, and eastern Texas

cad·dy \'ka-dē\ *noun, plural* **caddies** [Malay *kati* catty] (1792)
1 : a small box, can, or chest used especially to keep tea in
2 : a container or device for storing or holding objects when they are not in use

cade \'kād\ *adjective* [English dialect *cade* pet lamb, from Middle English *cad*] (1551)
: left by its mother and reared by hand **:** PET ⟨a *cade* lamb⟩

-cade *noun combining form* [*cavalcade*]
: procession ⟨motor*cade*⟩

ca·delle \kə-'del\ *noun* [French, from Provençal *cadello,* from Latin *catella,* feminine of *catellus* little dog, diminutive of *catulus* young animal] (circa 1861)
: a small cosmopolitan black beetle (*Tenebroides mauritanicus*) destructive to stored grain

ca·dence \'kā-d°n(t)s\ *noun* [Middle English, from Old Italian *cadenza,* from *cadere* to fall, from Latin — more at CHANCE] (14th century)
1 a : a rhythmic sequence or flow of sounds in language **b :** the beat, time, or measure of rhythmical motion or activity
2 a : a falling inflection of the voice **b :** a concluding and usually falling strain; *specifically* **:** a musical chord sequence moving to a harmonic close or point of rest and giving the sense of harmonic completion
3 : the modulated and rhythmic recurrence of a sound especially in nature
— **ca·denced** \-d°n(t)st\ *adjective*
— **ca·den·tial** \kā-'den(t)-shəl\ *adjective*

ca·den·cy \'kā-d°n(t)-sē\ *noun, plural* **-cies** (1627)
: CADENCE

ca·dent \'kā-d°nt\ *adjective* [Latin *cadent-, cadens,* present participle of *cadere*] (1605)
1 *archaic* **:** being in the process of falling ⟨with *cadent* tears fret channels in her cheeks —Shakespeare⟩
2 : having rhythmic cadence

ca·den·za \kə-'den-zə\ *noun* [Italian, cadence, cadenza] (1836)
1 : a parenthetical flourish in an aria or other solo piece commonly just before a final or other important cadence
2 : a technically brilliant sometimes improvised solo passage toward the close of a concerto

3 : an exceptionally brilliant part of an artistic work

cade oil \'kād-\ *noun* [*cade* juniper, from Middle French, from Old Provençal, from Medieval Latin *catanus*] (1880)
: JUNIPER TAR

ca·det \kə-'det\ *noun, often attributive* [French, from Gascon *capdet* chief, from Late Latin *capitellum,* diminutive of Latin *capit-, caput* head — more at HEAD] (1610)
1 a : a younger brother or son **b :** youngest son **c :** a younger branch of a family or a member of it
2 : one in training for a military or naval commission; *especially* **:** a student in a service academy
3 *slang* **:** PIMP ◇
— **ca·det·ship** \-,ship\ *noun*

Ca·dette \kə-'det\ *noun* [from *cadet*] (1963)
: a member of a program of the Girl Scouts for girls in the sixth through ninth grades in school

cadge \'kaj\ *verb* **cadged; cadg·ing** [back-formation from Scots *cadger* carrier, huckster, from Middle English *cadgear*] (circa 1812)
: BEG, SPONGE
— **cadg·er** *noun*

cad·mi·um \'kad-mē-əm\ *noun* [New Latin, from Latin *cadmia* zinc oxide, from Greek *kadmeia,* literally, Theban (earth), from feminine of *kadmeios* Theban, from *Kadmos;* from the occurrence of its ores together with zinc oxide] (1822)
: a bluish white malleable ductile toxic bivalent metallic element used especially in protective platings and in bearing metals — see ELEMENT table

cadmium sulfide *noun* (circa 1893)
: a yellow-brown poisonous salt CdS used especially in electronic parts, in photoelectric cells, and in medicine

Cad·mus \'kad-məs\ *noun* [Latin, from Greek *Kadmos*]
: the legendary founder of Thebes

cad·re \'ka-,drā, 'kä-, -,drē; *especially British* 'kä-də(r), 'kä-, -,drə\ *noun* [French, from Italian *quadro,* from Latin *quadrum* square — more at QUARREL] (1830)

◇ **WORD HISTORY**
cadet Until relatively recent times, most inhabitants of France south of an irregular line running from the Gironde to the Alps spoke Occitan (or, to use a more traditional name, Provençal), a Romance language quite different from French. Usually considered a dialect of Occitan is Gascon, spoken in southwestern France, though it is so distinct from the rest of Occitan that it is practically an independent language itself. One Gascon contribution to the lexicon of French, and through French to English, is *cadet,* from 15th century Gascon *capdet* "chief, captain." The younger sons of noble Gascon families served as officers in the 15th century French army and retained the Gascon word *capdet* as a name for their rank, but the socially conscious French took the word as marking genealogical rather than military status, so *capdet* was borrowed in the sense "younger son." Reduced to *cadet,* the word was used additionally in the 16th century for a young gentleman who served as a common soldier to learn the military profession—hence, ultimately, the English use of *cadet* to denote a student in a service academy. *Cadet* entered English in the 17th century.

\ə\ abut \ᵊ\ kitten \ər\ further \a\ ash \ā\ ace
\ä\ mop, mar \au̇\ out \ch\ chin \e\ bet \ē\ easy
\g\ go \i\ hit \ī\ ice \j\ job \ŋ\ sing \ō\ go
\ȯ\ law \ȯi\ boy \th\ thin \th\ the \ü\ loot \u̇\ foot
\y\ yet \zh\ vision *see also* Guide to Pronunciation

caddisworm

1 : FRAME, FRAMEWORK
2 : a nucleus or core group especially of trained personnel able to assume control and to train others; *broadly* **:** a group of people having some unifying relationship ⟨a *cadre* of lawyers⟩
3 : a cell of indoctrinated leaders active in promoting the interests of a revolutionary party
4 : a member of a cadre

ca·du·ceus \kə-'dü-sē-əs, -'dyü-, -shəs\ *noun*, *plural* **-cei** \-sē-ˌī\ [Latin, modification of Greek *karykeion*, from *karyx, kēryx* herald; akin to Sanskrit *kāru* singer] (1588)
1 : the symbolic staff of a herald; *specifically* **:** a representation of a staff with two entwined snakes and two wings at the top
2 : an insignia bearing a caduceus and symbolizing a physician

ca·du·ci·ty \kə-'dü-sə-tē, -'dyü-\ *noun* [French *caducité*, from *caduc* transitory, from Latin *caducus*] (1769)
1 : SENILITY
2 : the quality of being transitory or perishable

ca·du·cous \kə-'dü-kəs, -'dyü-\ *adjective* [Latin *caducus* tending to fall, transitory, from *cadere* to fall — more at CHANCE] (1808)
: falling off easily or before the usual time — used especially of floral organs

cae·cal, cae·cum *variant of* CECAL, CECUM

cae·ci·lian \si-'sil-yən, -'sēl-, -'si-lē-ən\ *noun* [ultimately from Latin *caecilia* slowworm, from *caecus* blind] (circa 1879)
: any of an order (Gymnophiona) of chiefly tropical burrowing amphibians resembling worms
— **caecilian** *adjective*

Caer·phil·ly \kär-'fi-lē\ *noun* [*Caerphilly*, urban district in Wales] (circa 1893)
: a mild white friable cheese of Welsh origin

Cae·sar \'sē-zər\ *noun* [Gaius Julius *Caesar*] (1567)
1 : any of the Roman emperors succeeding Augustus Caesar — used as a title
2 a : *often not capitalized* **:** a powerful ruler: (1) **:** EMPEROR (2) **:** AUTOCRAT, DICTATOR **b** [from the reference in Matthew 22:21] **:** the civil power **:** a temporal ruler
— **Cae·sar·e·an** *or* **Cae·sar·i·an** \si-'zar-ē-ən, -zer-\ *adjective*

cae·sar·e·an *also* **cae·sar·i·an** *variant of* CESAREAN

Cae·sar·ism \'sē-zə-ˌri-zəm\ *noun* (1857)
: imperial authority or system **:** political absolutism **:** DICTATORSHIP
— **Cae·sar·ist** \-zə-rist\ *noun*

Caesar salad *noun* [*Caesar*'s, restaurant in Tijuana, Mexico] (1950)
: a tossed salad usually made of romaine, garlic, anchovies, and croutons and dressed with olive oil, coddled egg, lemon juice, and grated cheese

cae·si·um *chiefly British variant of* CESIUM

caes·pi·tose \'ses-pə-ˌtōs\ *adjective* [New Latin *caespitosus*, from Latin *caespit-, caespes* turf] (1830)
1 : growing in clusters or tufts
2 : forming a dense turf

cae·su·ra \si-'zyür-ə, -'zhür-\ *noun*, *plural* **-suras** *or* **-su·rae** \-'zyür-(ˌ)ē, -'zhür-\ [Late Latin, from Latin, act of cutting, from *caedere* to cut] (1556)
1 *in modern prosody* **:** a usually rhetorical break in the flow of sound in the middle of a line of verse
2 *Greek & Latin prosody* **:** a break in the flow of sound in a verse caused by the ending of a word within a foot
3 : BREAK, INTERRUPTION
4 : a pause marking a rhythmic point of division in a melody
— **cae·su·ral** \-'zyür-əl, -'zhür-\ *adjective*

ca·fé *also* **ca·fe** \ka-'fā, kə-\ *noun*, *often attributive* [French *café* coffee, café, from Turkish *kahve* — more at COFFEE] (1802)

1 : a usually small and informal establishment serving various refreshments (as coffee); *broadly* **:** RESTAURANT
2 : BARROOM
3 : CABARET, NIGHTCLUB

ca·fé au lait \(ˌ)ka-ˌfā-ō-'lā\ *noun* [French, coffee with milk] (1763)
1 : coffee with usually hot milk in about equal parts
2 : the color of coffee with milk

ca·fé noir \-'nwär\ *noun* [French, black coffee] (1841)
: coffee without milk or cream; *also* **:** DEMITASSE

café society *noun* (1937)
: society of persons who are regular patrons of fashionable cafés

¹caf·e·te·ria \ˌka-fə-'tir-ē-ə\ *noun* [American Spanish *cafetería* coffeehouse, from *cafetera* coffee maker, from French *cafetière*, from *café*] (1894)
: a restaurant in which the customers serve themselves or are served at a counter and take the food to tables to eat ◇

²cafeteria *adjective* (1951)
: providing a selection from which a choice may be made ⟨*cafeteria* benefit plan⟩ ⟨a *cafeteria* curriculum⟩

caf·e·to·ri·um \-'tōr-ē-əm, -'tòr-\ *noun* [blend of *cafeteria* and *auditorium*] (1952)
: a large room (as in a school building) designed for use both as a cafeteria and an auditorium

caff \'kaf\ *noun* (1931)
British **:** CAFÉ 1

caf·feine \ka-'fēn, 'ka-ˌ\ *noun* [German *Kaffein*, from *Kaffee* coffee, from French *café*] (circa 1823)
: a bitter alkaloid $C_8H_{10}N_4O_2$ found especially in coffee, tea, and kola nuts and used medicinally as a stimulant and diuretic

caf·fe lat·te \ˌkä-(ˌ)fā-'lä-(ˌ)tā\ *noun* [Italian *caffelatte*, short for *caffè e latte* coffee and milk] (1927)
: espresso mixed with hot or steamed milk

caf·tan \'kaf-(ˌ)tan\ *noun* [Russian *kaftan*, from Turkish, from Persian *qaftān*] (1591)
: a usually cotton or silk ankle-length garment with long sleeves that is common throughout the Levant

¹cage \'kāj\ *noun* [Middle English, from Old French, from Latin *cavea* cavity, cage, from *cavus* hollow — more at CAVE] (13th century)
1 : a box or enclosure having some openwork for confining or carrying animals (as birds)
2 a : a barred cell for confining prisoners **b :** a fenced area for prisoners of war
3 : a framework serving as support ⟨the steel *cage* of a skyscraper⟩
4 a : an enclosure resembling a cage in form or purpose ⟨a cashier's *cage*⟩ **b :** an arrangement of atoms or molecules so bonded as to enclose a space in which another atom or ion (as of a metal) can reside
5 a : a screen placed behind home plate to stop baseballs during batting practice **b :** a goal consisting of posts or a frame with a net attached (as in ice hockey)
6 : a large building containing an area for practicing outdoor sports and often adapted for indoor events
— **cage·ful** \-ˌfu̇l\ *noun*

²cage *transitive verb* **caged; cag·ing** (1577)
1 : to confine or keep in or as if in a cage
2 : to drive (as a puck) into a cage and score a goal

cage·ling \'kāj-liŋ\ *noun* (1859)
: a caged bird

ca·gey *also* **ca·gy** \'kā-jē\ *adjective* **ca·gi·er; -est** [origin unknown] (circa 1893)
1 : hesitant about committing oneself
2 a : wary of being trapped or deceived **:** SHREWD ⟨a *cagey* consumer⟩ **b :** marked by cleverness ⟨a *cagey* reply⟩
— **ca·gi·ly** \-jə-lē\ *adverb*

— **ca·gi·ness** *also* **ca·gey·ness** \-jē-nəs\ *noun*

ca·hier \kä-'yā, kī-'ā\ *noun* [French, from Middle French *quaer, caier* quire — more at QUIRE] (1789)
: a report or memorial concerning policy especially of a parliamentary body

ca·hoot \kə-'hüt\ *noun* [perhaps from French *cahute* cabin, hut] (1829)
: PARTNERSHIP, LEAGUE — usually used in plural ⟨they're in *cahoots*⟩

ca·how \kə-'hau̇\ *noun* [imitative] (1615)
: a dark-colored petrel (*Pterodroma cahow*) formerly abundant in Bermuda but now nearly extinct

cai·man \'kā-mən; kā-'man, kī-\ *noun* [Spanish *caimán*, probably from Carib *caymán*] (1577)
: any of several Central and South American crocodilians (genera *Caiman, Melanosuchus*, and *Paleosuchus*) similar to alligators

Cain \'kān\ *noun* [Hebrew *Qayin*]
: the brother and murderer of Abel

-caine *noun combining form* [German *-kain*, from *kokain* cocaine]
: synthetic alkaloid anesthetic ⟨*procaine*⟩

ca·ique \kä-'ēk, 'kīk\ *noun* [French, from Turkish *kayık*] (1625)
1 : a light skiff used on the Bosporus
2 : a Levantine sailing vessel

caird \'kerd\ *noun* [Scottish Gaelic *ceard* craftsman; akin to Greek *kerdos* profit] (1663)
Scottish **:** a traveling tinker; *also* **:** TRAMP, GYPSY

cairn \'karn, 'kern\ *noun* [Middle English (Scots) *carne*, from Scottish Gaelic *carn*; akin to Old Irish & Welsh *carn* cairn] (15th century)
: a heap of stones piled up as a memorial or as a landmark
— **cairned** \'karnd, 'kernd\ *adjective*

cairn·gorm \'karn-ˌgo̅rm, 'kern-\ *noun* [*Cairngorm*, mountain in Scotland] (1794)
: a yellow or smoky-brown crystalline quartz

cairn terrier *noun* [from its use in hunting among cairns] (1910)
: any of a breed of small compactly built hard-coated terriers of Scottish origin

cais·son \'kā-ˌsän, -sᵊn, *British also* kə-'sün\ *noun* [French, from Middle French, from Old

◇ WORD HISTORY

cafeteria Although American English *cafeteria* is in all likelihood borrowed from Spanish, and within Spanish its derivational pathway from *café* "coffee" is fairly straightforward, the details of the word's passage from one language to the other are murky. Early evidence for Spanish *cafetería* is slim; the word was current in Cuba in the 19th century, but it referred to a shop that sold ground coffee, not a restaurant. During the early decades of the century, the heyday of the self-service restaurant, dictionary etymologists believed that both the word and the institution originated in southern California. Evidence for the word first surfaces, however, not on the West Coast, but in Chicago, where a "Cafetiria Catering Company" operated four downtown restaurants—presumably self-service style—in 1895. (There are some indications that self-service restaurants grew out of the World's Columbian Exposition held in Chicago in 1893.) During the 1920s and '30s in the U.S., coinages based on *cafeteria* proliferated: there were marketerias, gaseterias, and washeterias, usually having some self-service feature. These have faded since World War II, while the cafeteria itself has survived mainly in schools, hospitals, and other domains of institutional food service—pushed off America's street corners by the fast-food restaurant.

Provençal, from *caissa* chest, from Latin *capsa* — more at CASE] (circa 1702)
1 a : a chest to hold ammunition **b :** a usually 2-wheeled vehicle for artillery ammunition attachable to a horse-drawn limber; *also* : a limber with its attached caisson

caisson 1b

2 a : a watertight chamber used in construction work under water or as a foundation **b :** a hollow floating box or a boat used as a floodgate for a dock or basin
3 : COFFER 3
caisson disease *noun* (1873)
: ²BEND 3
cai·tiff \'kā-təf\ *adjective* [Middle English *caitif*, from Old North French, captive, vile, from Latin *captivus* captive] (14th century)
: being base, cowardly, or despicable
— **caitiff** *noun*
caj·e·put \'ka-jə-pət, -ˌpùt\ *noun* [Malay *kayu putih*, from *kayu* wood, tree + *putih* white] (1832)
: an Australian and southeast Asian tree (*Melaleuca quinquenervia* synonym *M. leucadendron*) of the myrtle family that yields a pungent medicinal oil and has been introduced into Florida
ca·jole \kə-'jōl\ *transitive verb* **ca·joled; ca·jol·ing** [French *cajoler*] (1645)
1 : to persuade with flattery or gentle urging especially in the face of reluctance : COAX ⟨had to *cajole* them into going⟩
2 : to deceive with soothing words or false promises
— **ca·jole·ment** \-'jōl-mənt\ *noun*
— **ca·jol·er** *noun*
— **ca·jol·ery** \-'jō-lə-rē\ *noun*
¹Ca·jun *also* **Ca·jan** \'kā-jən\ *noun* [alteration of *Acadian*] (1868)
: a Louisianian descended from French-speaking immigrants from Acadia
²Cajun *adjective* (1885)
1 : of, relating to, or characteristic of the Cajuns
2 : of, relating to, or prepared in a style of cooking originating among the Cajuns and characterized by the use of hot seasonings (as cayenne pepper)
¹cake \'kāk\ *noun* [Middle English, from Old Norse *kaka;* akin to Old High German *kuocho* cake] (13th century)
1 a : a breadlike food made from a dough or batter that is usually fried or baked in small flat shapes and is often unleavened **b :** a sweet baked food made from a dough or thick batter usually containing flour and sugar and often shortening, eggs, and a raising agent (as baking powder) **c :** a flattened usually round mass of food that is baked or fried ⟨a fish *cake*⟩
2 a : a block of compacted or congealed matter ⟨a *cake* of ice⟩ **b :** a hard or brittle layer or deposit
— **cak·ey** \'kā-kē\ *adjective*
²cake *verb* **caked; cak·ing** (1607)
transitive verb
1 : ENCRUST ⟨*caked* with dust⟩
2 : to fill (a space) with a packed mass
intransitive verb
: to form or harden into a mass
cake·walk \'kāk-ˌwòk\ *noun* (1879)
1 : a black American entertainment having a cake as prize for the most accomplished steps and figures in walking
2 : a stage dance developed from walking steps and figures typically involving a high prance with backward tilt
3 a : a one-sided contest **b :** an easy task
— **cakewalk** *intransitive verb*
— **cake·walk·er** *noun*

Cal·a·bar bean \'ka-lə-ˌbär-\ *noun* [*Calabar*, Nigeria] (circa 1876)
: the dark brown highly poisonous seed of a tropical African woody vine (*Physostigma venenosum*) that is used as a source of physostigmine and as an ordeal poison in native witchcraft trials
cal·a·bash \'ka-lə-ˌbash\ *noun* [French & Spanish; French *calebasse* gourd, from Spanish *calabaza*] (1596)
1 : a tropical American tree (*Crescentia cujete*) of the trumpet-creeper family; *also* : its hard globose fruit
2 : GOURD; *especially* : one whose hard shell is used for a utensil
3 : a utensil (as a bottle or dipper) made from the shell of a calabash
cal·a·boose \'ka-lə-ˌbüs\ *noun* [Spanish *calabozo* dungeon] (1792)
: JAIL; *especially* : a local jail
ca·la·di·um \kə-'lā-dē-əm\ *noun* [New Latin, genus name, from Malay *kĕladi*, an aroid plant] (circa 1845)
: any of a genus (*Caladium*, especially *C. bicolor*) of tropical American plants of the arum family widely cultivated for their showy variably colored leaves
cal·a·man·der \'ka-lə-ˌman-dər, ˌka-lə-'-\ *noun* [probably from Dutch *kalamanderhout* calamander wood] (1804)
: the hazel-brown black-striped wood of a southeast Asian tree (genus *Diospyros*, especially *D. quaesita*) that is used in furniture manufacturing
cal·a·mari \ˌkä-lə-'mär-ē, 'ka-lə-ˌmer-ē\ *noun* [Italian, plural of *calamaro, calamaio*, from Medieval Latin *calamarium* ink pot, from Latin *calamus;* from the inky substance the squid secretes] (circa 1961)
: squid used as food
cal·a·mary \'ka-lə-ˌmer-ē\ *noun, plural* **-mar·ies** [Medieval Latin *calamarium*] (1567)
: SQUID
cal·a·mine \'ka-lə-ˌmīn, -mən\ *noun* [Middle English *calamyn* ore of zinc, from Medieval Latin *calamina*, alteration of Latin *cadmia* — more at CADMIUM] (15th century)
: a mixture of zinc oxide with a small amount of ferric oxide used in lotions, liniments, and ointments
cal·a·mint \'ka-lə-ˌmint\ *noun* [Middle English *calament*, from Old French, from Medieval Latin *calamentum*, from Greek *kalaminthē*] (14th century)
: any of a genus (*Satureja*, especially *S. calamintha*) of mints
cal·a·mite \'ka-lə-ˌmīt\ *noun* [New Latin *Calamites*, genus of fossil plants, from Latin *calamus*] (1837)
: a Paleozoic fossil plant (especially genus *Calamites*) resembling a giant horsetail
ca·lam·i·tous \kə-'la-mə-təs\ *adjective* (1545)
: being, causing, or accompanied by calamity
— **ca·lam·i·tous·ly** *adverb*
ca·lam·i·ty \kə-'la-mə-tē\ *noun, plural* **-ties** [Middle English *calamytee*, from Middle French *calamité*, from Latin *calamitat-, calamitas;* perhaps akin to Latin *clades* destruction] (15th century)
1 : a state of deep distress or misery caused by major misfortune or loss
2 : an extraordinarily grave event marked by great loss and lasting distress and affliction
cal·a·mon·din \ˌka-lə-'män-dən\ *noun* [Tagalog *kalamundíng*] (circa 1928)
: a small hybrid citrus tree (*Citrofortunella mitis* synonym *Citrus mitis*); *also* : its tart fruit
cal·a·mus \'ka-lə-məs\ *noun, plural* **-mi** \-ˌmī, -ˌmē\ [Latin, reed, reed pen, from Greek *kalamos* — more at HAULM] (14th century)
1 a : SWEET FLAG **b :** the aromatic peeled and dried rhizome of the sweet flag that is the source of a carcinogenic essential oil
2 : the hollow basal portion of a feather below the vane : QUILL

ca·lash \kə-'lash\ *noun* [French *calèche*, from German *Kalesche*, from Czech *kolesa* wheels, carriage; akin to Greek *kyklos* wheel — more at WHEEL] (1679)
1 a : a light small-wheeled 4-passenger carriage with a folding top **b :** CALÈCHE 1b
2 : a large hood worn by women in the 18th century
calc- *or* **calci-** *combining form* [Latin *calc-, calx* lime — more at CHALK]
: calcium : calcium salt ⟨*calcic*⟩ ⟨*calcify*⟩
cal·ca·ne·al \kal-'kā-nē-əl\ *adjective* (circa 1849)
: relating to the heel or calcaneus
cal·ca·ne·um \-nē-əm\ *noun, plural* **-nea** \-nē-ə\ [Latin, heel — more at CALK] (circa 1751)
: CALCANEUS
cal·ca·ne·us \-nē-əs\ *noun, plural* **-nei** \-nē-ˌī\ [Late Latin, heel, alteration of Latin *calcaneum*] (circa 1925)
: a tarsal bone that in humans is the great bone of the heel
cal·car·e·ous \kal-'kar-ē-əs, -'ker-\ *adjective* [Latin *calcarius* of lime, from *calc-, calx*] (1677)
1 a : resembling calcite or calcium carbonate especially in hardness **b :** consisting of or containing calcium carbonate; *also* : containing calcium
2 : growing on limestone or in soil impregnated with lime
— **cal·car·e·ous·ly** *adverb*
calces *plural of* CALX
cal·cic \'kal-sik\ *adjective* (1871)
: derived from or containing calcium or lime : rich in calcium
cal·ci·cole \'kal-sə-ˌkōl\ *noun* [French, calcicolous, from *calc-* + *-cole* -colous] (1882)
: a plant normally growing on calcareous soils
— **cal·cic·o·lous** \kal-'si-kə-ləs\ *adjective*
cal·cif·er·ol \kal-'si-fə-ˌròl, -ˌrōl\ *noun* [*calciferous* + ergo*sterol*] (1931)
: an alcohol $C_{28}H_{43}OH$ usually prepared by irradiation of ergosterol and used as a dietary supplement in nutrition and medicinally in the control of rickets and related disorders — called also *vitamin D₂*
cal·cif·er·ous \kal-'si-f(ə-)rəs\ *adjective* (1799)
: producing or containing calcium carbonate
cal·cif·ic \kal-'si-fik\ *adjective* [*calcify*] (1861)
: involving or caused by calcification ⟨*calcific* lesions⟩
cal·ci·fuge \'kal-sə-ˌfyüj\ *noun* [French, calcifugous, from *calc-* + Latin *fugere* to flee — more at FUGITIVE] (1926)
: a plant not normally growing on calcareous soils
— **calcifuge** *also* **cal·cif·u·gous** \kal-'si-fyə-gəs\ *adjective*
cal·ci·fy \'kal-sə-ˌfī\ *verb* **-fied; -fy·ing** (1854)
transitive verb
1 : to make calcareous by deposit of calcium salts
2 : to make inflexible or unchangeable
intransitive verb
1 : to become calcareous
2 : to become inflexible and changeless : HARDEN
— **cal·ci·fi·ca·tion** \ˌkal-sə-fə-'kā-shən\ *noun*
cal·ci·mine \'kal-sə-ˌmīn\ *noun* [alteration of *kalsomine*, of unknown origin] (circa 1859)
: a white or tinted wash of glue, whiting or zinc white, and water that is used especially on plastered surfaces
— **calcimine** *transitive verb*

cal·ci·na·tion \ˌkal-sə-'nā-shən\ *noun* (14th century)
: the act or process of calcining : the state of being calcined

¹**cal·cine** \kal-'sīn, 'kal-ˌ\ *verb* **cal·cined; cal·cin·ing** [Middle English *calcenen*, from Medieval Latin *calcinare*, from Late Latin *calcina* lime, from Latin *calc-, calx*] (14th century)
transitive verb
: to heat (as inorganic materials) to a high temperature but without fusing in order to drive off volatile matter or to effect changes (as oxidation or pulverization)
intransitive verb
: to undergo calcination

²**cal·cine** \'kal-ˌsīn\ *noun* (circa 1909)
: a product (as a metal oxide) of calcination or roasting

cal·ci·no·sis \ˌkal-sə-'nō-səs\ *noun, plural* **-no·ses** \-ˌsēz\ [New Latin, irregular (influenced by International Scientific Vocabulary *calcine*) from *calc-* + *-osis*] (circa 1929)
: the abnormal deposition of calcium salts in a part or tissue of the body

cal·cite \'kal-ˌsīt\ *noun* (1849)
: a mineral $CaCO_3$ consisting of calcium carbonate crystallized in hexagonal form and including common limestone, chalk, and marble
— compare ARAGONITE
— **cal·cit·ic** \kal-'si-tik\ *adjective*

cal·ci·to·nin \ˌkal-sə-'tō-nən\ *noun* [*calci-* + *-tonin* (as in *serotonin*)] (1961)
: a polypeptide hormone especially from the thyroid gland that tends to lower the level of calcium in the blood plasma — called also *thyrocalcitonin*

cal·ci·um \'kal-sē-əm\ *noun, often attributive* [New Latin, from Latin *calc-, calx* lime] (1808)
: a silver-white bivalent metallic element of the alkaline-earth group occurring only in combination — see ELEMENT table

calcium carbide *noun* (circa 1888)
: a usually dark gray crystalline compound CaC_2 used especially for the generation of acetylene and for making calcium cyanamide

calcium carbonate *noun* (1873)
: a compound $CaCO_3$ found in nature as calcite and aragonite and in plant ashes, bones, and shells and used in making lime and portland cement and as a gastric antacid

calcium channel blocker *noun* (1982)
: any of a class of drugs that prevent or slow the influx of calcium ions into smooth muscle cells and are used to treat some forms of angina pectoris and some cardiac arrhythmias

calcium chloride *noun* (circa 1885)
: a white deliquescent salt $CaCl_2$ used in its anhydrous state as a drying and dehumidifying agent and in a hydrated state for controlling dust and ice on roads

calcium cyanamide *noun* (circa 1893)
: a compound $CaCN_2$ used as a fertilizer and a weed killer and as a source of other nitrogen compounds

calcium gluconate *noun* (1884)
: a white powdery salt $CaC_{12}H_{22}O_{14}$ used especially to supplement bodily calcium stores

calcium hydroxide *noun* (circa 1889)
: a white crystalline strong alkali $Ca(OH)_2$ that is used especially to make mortar and plaster and to soften water

calcium hypochlorite *noun* (circa 1889)
: a white powder $CaCl_2O_2$ used especially as a bleaching agent and disinfectant

calcium oxalate *noun* (1919)
: a crystalline salt CaC_2O_4 normally deposited in many plant cells and in animals sometimes excreted in urine or retained in the form of urinary calculi

calcium oxide *noun* (circa 1885)
: a caustic solid CaO that is white when pure and that is the chief constituent of lime

calcium phosphate *noun* (1869)
: any of various phosphates of calcium: as **a** : the phosphate $CaH_4P_2O_8$ used as a fertilizer and in baking powder **b** : the phosphate $CaHPO_4$ used in pharmaceutical preparations and animal feeds **c** : the phosphate $Ca_3P_2O_8$ used as a fertilizer **d** : the naturally occurring phosphate $Ca_5(F,Cl,OH,½CO_3)(PO_4)_3$ that contains other elements or radicals and is the chief constituent of phosphate rock, bones, and teeth

calcium silicate *noun* (circa 1888)
: any of several silicates of calcium used especially in construction materials (as portland cement)

calcium sulfate *noun* (circa 1885)
: a white salt $CaSO_4$ that occurs especially as anhydrite, gypsum, and plaster of paris and that in hydrated form is used as a building material and in anhydrous form is used as a drying agent

cal·cu·la·ble \'kal-kyə-lə-bəl\ *adjective* (circa 1734)
1 : subject to or ascertainable by calculation
2 : that may be counted on : DEPENDABLE

cal·cu·late \'kal-kyə-ˌlāt\ *verb* **-lat·ed; -lat·ing** [Latin *calculatus*, past participle of *calculare*, from *calculus* pebble (used in reckoning), perhaps irregular diminutive of *calc-, calx* lime — more at CHALK] (1570)
transitive verb
1 a : to determine by mathematical processes **b** : to reckon by exercise of practical judgment : ESTIMATE **c** : to solve or probe the meaning of : FIGURE OUT ⟨trying to *calculate* his expression —Hugh MacLennan⟩
2 : to design or adapt for a purpose
3 a : to judge to be true or probable **b** : INTEND ⟨I *calculate* to do it or perish in the attempt —Mark Twain⟩
intransitive verb
1 a : to make a calculation **b** : to forecast consequences
2 : COUNT, RELY

cal·cu·lat·ed \-ˌlā-təd\ *adjective* (1722)
1 : APT, LIKELY
2 a : worked out by mathematical calculation **b** : engaged in, undertaken, or displayed after reckoning or estimating the statistical probability of success or failure ⟨a *calculated* risk⟩
3 a : planned or contrived to accomplish a purpose **b** : DELIBERATE, INTENDED
— **cal·cu·lat·ed·ly** *adverb*
— **cal·cu·lat·ed·ness** *noun*

cal·cu·lat·ing \-ˌlā-tiŋ\ *adjective* (1710)
1 : making calculations ⟨*calculating* machine⟩
2 : marked by prudent analysis or by shrewd consideration of self-interest : SCHEMING
— **cal·cu·lat·ing·ly** \-tiŋ-lē\ *adverb*

cal·cu·la·tion \ˌkal-kyə-'lā-shən\ *noun* (14th century)
1 a : the process or an act of calculating **b** : the result of an act of calculating
2 a : studied care in analyzing or planning **b** : cold heartless planning to promote self-interest
— **cal·cu·la·tion·al** \-'lāsh-nəl, -'lā-shə-nᵊl\ *adjective*

cal·cu·la·tor \'kal-kyə-ˌlā-tər\ *noun* (14th century)
: one that calculates: as **a** : a usually electronic device for performing mathematical calculations **b** : a person who operates a calculator

cal·cu·lous \'kal-kyə-ləs\ *adjective* (1605)
: caused or characterized by a calculus or calculi

cal·cu·lus \-ləs\ *noun, plural* **-li** \-ˌlī, -ˌlē\ *also* **-lus·es** [Latin, stone (used in reckoning)] (1666)
1 a : a method of computation or calculation in a special notation (as of logic or symbolic logic) **b** : the mathematical methods comprising differential and integral calculus
2 : CALCULATION
3 a : a concretion usually of mineral salts around organic material found especially in hollow organs or ducts **b** : TARTAR 2

4 : a system or arrangement of intricate or interrelated parts ◇

calculus of variations (1837)
: a branch of mathematics concerned with applying the methods of calculus to finding the maxima and minima of a function which depends for its values on another function or a curve

cal·de·ra \kal-'der-ə, kȯl-, -'dir-\ *noun* [Spanish, literally, caldron, from Late Latin *caldaria* — more at CAULDRON] (1691)
: a volcanic crater that has a diameter many times that of the vent and is formed by collapse of the central part of a volcano or by explosions of extraordinary violence

cal·dron *variant of* CAULDRON

ca·lèche *or* **ca·leche** \kə-'lesh, -'lash\ *noun* [French *calèche* — more at CALASH] (1666)
1 a : CALASH 1a **b** : a 2-wheeled horse-drawn vehicle with a driver's seat on the splashboard used in Quebec
2 : CALASH 2

cal·e·fac·to·ry \ˌka-lə-'fak-t(ə-)rē\ *noun, plural* **-ries** [Medieval Latin *calefactorium*, from Latin *calefacere* to warm — more at CHAFE] (circa 1681)
: a monastery room warmed and used as a sitting room

¹**cal·en·dar** \'ka-lən-dər\ *noun* [Middle English *calender*, from Anglo-French or Medieval Latin; Anglo-French *calender*, from Medieval Latin *kalendarium*, from Latin, moneylender's account book, from *kalendae* calends] (13th century)
1 : a system for fixing the beginning, length, and divisions of the civil year and arranging days and longer divisions of time (as weeks and months) in a definite order — see MONTH table
2 : a tabular register of days according to a system usually covering one year and referring the days of each month to the days of the week
3 : an orderly list: as **a** : a list of cases to be tried in court **b** : a list of bills or other items reported out of committee for consideration by a legislative assembly **c** : a list or schedule of planned events or activities giving dates and details
4 *British* : a university catalog

²**calendar** *transitive verb* **-dared; -dar·ing** \-d(ə-)riŋ\ (15th century)
: to enter in a calendar

calendar year *noun* (circa 1909)
1 : a period of a year beginning and ending with the dates that are conventionally accepted as marking the beginning and end of a numbered year
2 : a period of time equal in length to that of the year in the calendar conventionally in use

¹**cal·en·der** \'ka-lən-dər\ *transitive verb* **-dered; -der·ing** \-d(ə-)riŋ\ [Middle French *calandrer*, from *calandre* machine for calendering, from (assumed) Vulgar Latin *colendra*

◇ WORD HISTORY
calculus In Latin *calculus* meant "pebble." Because the Romans used pebbles to do addition and subtraction on a counting board, the word became associated with computation, and the phrase *ponere calculos*, literally, "to place pebbles" meant figuratively "to perform a computation." Latin and Late Latin derivatives from *calculus* include *calculator* "person versed in arithmetic" and *calculare* "to reckon" (hence English *calculate*). *Calculus* itself has been borrowed into English as a medical term to refer to concretions of matter in the body such as kidney and bladder stones—a sense first found in Medieval Latin and a straightforward extension of the meaning "pebble"—and to refer to systems of mathematical computations such as differential and integral calculus.

cylinder, modification of Greek *kylindros* — more at CYLINDER] (1513)
: to press (as cloth, rubber, or paper) between rollers or plates in order to smooth and glaze or to thin into sheets
— **cal·en·der·er** \-dər-ər\ *noun*

²calender *noun* (1688)
: a machine for calendering something

³calender *noun* [Persian *qalandar,* from Arabic, from Persian *kalandar* uncouth man] (1621)
: a member of a Sufic order of wandering mendicant dervishes

ca·len·dri·cal \kə-'len-dri-kəl, ka-\ *also* **ca·len·dric** \-drik\ *adjective* (circa 1843)
: of, relating to, characteristic of, or used in a calendar

ca·lends \'ka-lən(d)z, 'kā-\ *noun plural but singular or plural in construction* [Middle English *kalendes,* from Latin *kalendae, calendae*] (14th century)
: the first day of the ancient Roman month from which days were counted backward to the ides

ca·len·du·la \kə-'len-jə-lə, -dyù-lə\ *noun* [New Latin, genus name, from Medieval Latin, from Latin *calendae* calends] (1789)
: any of a small genus (*Calendula*) of yellow-rayed composite herbs of temperate regions

cal·en·ture \'ka-lən-,chúr\ *noun* [Spanish *calentura,* from *calentar* to heat, from Latin *calent-, calens,* present participle of *calēre* to be warm — more at LEE] (1593)
: a fever formerly supposed to affect sailors in the tropics

¹calf \'kaf, 'kàf, *dialect also* 'kàf\ *noun, plural* **calves** \'kavz, 'kàvz, 'kàvz\ *also* **calfs** *often attributive* [Middle English, from Old English *cealf;* akin to Old High German *kalb* calf] (before 12th century)
1 a : the young of the domestic cow; *also* **:** that of a closely related mammal (as a bison) **b :** the young of various large animals (as the elephant or whale)
2 *plural* **calfs :** the hide of the domestic calf; *especially* **:** CALFSKIN
3 : an awkward or silly youth
— **calf-like** \'kaf-,līk, 'kàf-, *dialect also* 'kàf-\ *adjective*
— **in calf :** PREGNANT — used of a cow

²calf *noun, plural* **calves** \'kavz, 'kàvz\ [Middle English, from Old Norse *kālfi*] (14th century)
: the fleshy back part of the leg below the knee

calf-love \-,ləv\ *noun* (1823)
: PUPPY LOVE

calf's-foot jelly \'kavz-,fút-, 'kafs-, 'kàvz-, 'kàfs- *also* 'kàvz-\ *noun* (1775)
: jelly made from gelatin obtained by boiling calves' feet

calf·skin \'kaf-,skin, 'kàf- *also* 'kàf-\ *noun* (15th century)
: leather made of the skin of a calf

Cal·gon \'kal-,gän\ *trademark*
— used for a water softener

Cal·i·ban \'ka-lə-,ban\ *noun*
: a savage and deformed slave in Shakespeare's *The Tempest*

cal·i·ber *or* **cal·i·bre** \'ka-lə-bər, *British also* kə-'lē-\ *noun* [Middle French *calibre,* from Old Italian *calibro,* from Arabic *qālib* shoemaker's last] (1567)
1 a : degree of mental capacity or moral quality **b :** degree of excellence or importance
2 a : the diameter of a bullet or other projectile **b :** the diameter of a bore of a gun usually expressed in hundredths or thousandths of an inch and typically written as a decimal fraction (.32 *caliber*)
3 : the diameter of a round body; *especially* **:** the internal diameter of a hollow cylinder

cal·i·brate \'ka-lə-,brāt\ *transitive verb* **-brat·ed; -brat·ing** (circa 1864)
1 : to ascertain the caliber of (as a thermometer tube)

2 : to determine, rectify, or mark the graduations of (as a thermometer tube)
3 : to standardize (as a measuring instrument) by determining the deviation from a standard so as to ascertain the proper correction factors
4 : to adjust precisely for a particular function
— **cal·i·bra·tor** \-,brā-tər\ *noun*

cal·i·bra·tion \,ka-lə-'brā-shən\ *noun* (circa 1859)
1 : the act or process of calibrating **:** the state of being calibrated
2 : a set of graduations to indicate values or positions — usually used in plural (*calibrations* on a gauge)

ca·li·che \kə-'lē-chē\ *noun* [American Spanish, from Spanish, flake of lime, from *cal* lime, from Latin *calx* — more at CHALK] (circa 1858)
1 : the nitrate-bearing gravel or rock of the sodium nitrate deposits of Chile and Peru
2 : a crust of calcium carbonate that forms on the stony soil of arid regions

cal·i·co \'ka-li-,kō\ *noun, plural* **-coes** *or* **-cos** [*Calicut,* India] (1578)
1 a : cotton cloth imported from India **b** *British* **:** a plain white cotton fabric that is heavier than muslin **c :** any of various cheap cotton fabrics with figured patterns
2 : a blotched or spotted animal; *especially* **:** one that is predominantly white with red and black patches
— **calico** *adjective*

calico bass *noun* (circa 1882)
: BLACK CRAPPIE

calico bush *noun* (1814)
: MOUNTAIN LAUREL

Cal·i·for·nia condor \,ka-lə-'fòr-nyə-\ *noun* [*California,* state of U.S.] (circa 1889)
: a large nearly extinct vulture (*Gymnogyps californianus*) found most recently in the mountains of southern California that is related to the condor of South America

California condor

California laurel *noun* (1871)
: an evergreen Pacific coast tree (*Umbellularia californica*) of the laurel family with small umbellate flowers

California poppy *noun* (1891)
: any of a genus (*Eschscholzia*) of herbs of the poppy family; *especially* **:** one (*E. californica*) widely cultivated for its usually yellow or orange flowers

Cal·i·for·nio \,ka-lə-'fòr-nē-,ō\ *noun, plural* **-nios** [Spanish, from *California*] (1923)
: one of the original Spanish colonists of California or their descendants

cal·i·for·ni·um \,ka-lə-'fòr-nē-əm\ *noun* [New Latin, from *California,* U.S.] (1950)
: a radioactive element discovered by bombarding curium 242 with alpha particles — see ELEMENT table

ca·lig·i·nous \kə-'li-jə-nəs\ *adjective* [Middle French or Latin; Middle French *caligineux,* from Latin *caliginosus,* from *caligin-, caligo* darkness] (1548)
: MISTY, DARK

¹cal·i·per \'ka-lə-pər\ *noun* [alteration of *caliber*] (1588)
1 a : any of various measuring instruments having two usually adjustable arms, legs, or jaws used especially to measure diameter or thickness — usually used in plural (a pair of *calipers*) **b :** a device consisting of two plates lined with a frictional material that press

against the sides of a rotating wheel or disc in certain brake systems
2 : thickness especially of paper, paperboard, or a tree

²caliper *transitive verb* **-pered; -per·ing** \-p(ə-)riŋ\ (1876)
: to measure by or as if by calipers

ca·liph *or* **ca·lif** \'kā-ləf, 'ka-ləf\ *noun* [Middle English *caliphe,* from Middle French *calife,* from Arabic *khalīfah* successor] (14th century)
: a successor of Muhammad as temporal and spiritual head of Islam — used as a title
— **ca·liph·al** \-lə-fəl\ *adjective*

ca·liph·ate \-lə-,fāt, -fət\ *noun* (1614)
: the office or dominion of a caliph

cal·is·then·ic \,ka-ləs-'the-nik\ *adjective* (1827)
: of or relating to calisthenics

cal·is·then·ics \-niks\ *noun plural but singular or plural in construction* [Greek *kalos* beautiful + *sthenos* strength] (1827)
1 : systematic rhythmic bodily exercises performed usually without apparatus
2 *usually singular in construction* **:** the art or practice of calisthenics

ca·lix \'kā-liks, 'ka-\ *noun, plural* **ca·li·ces** \'kā-lə-,sēz, 'ka-\ [Latin *calic-, calix* — more at CHALICE] (1698)
: CUP

¹calk \'kòk\, **calk·er** \'kò-kər\ *variant of* CAULK, CAULKER

²calk \'kòk\ *noun* [probably alteration of *calkin,* from Middle English *kakun,* from Middle Dutch or Old North French; Middle Dutch *calcoen* horse's hoof, from Old North French *calcain* heel, from Latin *calcaneum,* from *calc-, calx* heel] (1587)
: a tapered piece projecting downward on the shoe of a horse to prevent slipping; *also* **:** a similar device worn on the sole of a shoe

³calk *transitive verb* (1624)
1 : to furnish with calks
2 : to wound with a calk

¹call \'kòl\ *verb* [Middle English, from Old Norse *kalla;* akin to Old English *hildecalla* battle herald, Old High German *kallōn* to talk loudly, Old Church Slavonic *glasŭ* voice] (before 12th century)
intransitive verb
1 a : to speak in a loud distinct voice so as to be heard at a distance **:** SHOUT (*call* for help) **b :** to make a request or demand (*call* for an investigation) **c** *of an animal* **:** to utter a characteristic note or cry **d :** to get or try to get into communication by telephone — often used with *up* **e :** to make a demand in card games (as for a particular card or for a show of hands) **f :** to give the calls for a square dance
2 : to make a brief visit (*called* to pay his respects) (*called* on a friend)
transitive verb
1 a (1) **:** to utter in a loud distinct voice — often used with *out* (*call* out a number) (2) **:** to announce or read loudly or authoritatively (*call* the roll) (*call* off a row of figures) **b** (1) **:** to command or request to come or be present (*called* to testify) (2) **:** to cause to come **:** BRING (*calls* to mind an old saying) **c :** to summon to a particular activity, employment, or office (was *called* to active duty) **d :** to invite or command to meet **:** CONVOKE (*call* a meeting) **e :** to rouse from sleep or summon to get up **f** (1) **:** to give the order for **:** bring into action (*call* a strike against the company) (*call* a pitchout) (2) **:** to manage by giving the signals or orders (that catcher *calls* a good game)

\ə\ abut \ᵊ\ kitten \ər\ further \a\ ash \ā\ ace \ä\ mop, mar \aù\ out \ch\ chin \e\ bet \ē\ easy \g\ go \i\ hit \ī\ ice \j\ job \ŋ\ sing \ō\ go \ò\ law \òi\ boy \th\ thin \t͟h\ the \ü\ loot \ù\ foot \y\ yet \zh\ vision *see also* Guide to Pronunciation

g (1) **:** to make a demand in bridge for (a card or suit) (2) **:** to require (a player) to show the hand in poker by making an equal bet (3) **:** to challenge to make good on a statement (4) **:** to charge with or censure for an offense ⟨deserves to be *called* on that⟩ **h :** to attract (as game) by imitating the characteristic cry **i :** to halt (as a baseball game) because of unsuitable conditions **j :** to rule on the status of (as a pitched ball or a player's action) ⟨*call* balls and strikes⟩ ⟨*call* a base runner safe⟩ **k :** to give the calls for (a square dance) — often used with *off* **l** (1) **:** to demand payment of especially by formal notice ⟨*call* a loan⟩ (2) **:** demand presentation of (as a bond or option) for redemption **m** (1) **:** to get or try to get in communication with by telephone (2) **:** to generate signals for (a telephone number) in order to reach the party to whom the number is assigned ⟨*call* 911⟩ (3) **:** to make a signal to in order to transmit a message ⟨*call* the flagship⟩ **2 a :** to speak of or address by a specified name **:** give a name to ⟨*call* her Kitty⟩ **b** (1) **:** to regard or characterize as of a certain kind **:** CONSIDER ⟨can hardly be *called* generous⟩ (2) **:** to estimate or consider for purposes of an estimate or for convenience ⟨*call* it an even dollar⟩ **c** (1) **:** to describe correctly in advance of or without knowledge of the event **:** PREDICT (2) **:** to name or specify in advance ⟨*call* the toss of a coin⟩ **3 :** to temporarily transfer control of computer processing to (as a subroutine or procedure)
synonym see SUMMON
— **call a spade a spade :** to speak frankly
— **call for 1 :** to call (as at one's house) to get ⟨I'll *call for* you after dinner⟩ **2 :** to require as necessary or appropriate ⟨the job *calls for* typing skills⟩ ⟨the design *calls for* three windows⟩
— **call forth :** ELICIT, EVOKE ⟨these events *call forth* great emotions⟩
— **call in question** or **call into question :** to cast doubt upon
— **call it a day :** to stop for the remainder of the day or for the present whatever one has been doing
— **call it quits :** to call it a day **:** QUIT
— **call names :** to address or speak of a person or thing contemptuously or offensively
— **call on 1 :** to call upon **2 :** to elicit a response from (as a student) ⟨the teacher *called on* her first⟩
— **call one's bluff :** to challenge in order to expose an empty pretense or threat
— **call the shots :** to be in charge or control **:** determine the policy or procedure
— **call the tune :** to call the shots
— **call time :** to ask for or grant a time-out
— **call to account :** to hold responsible **:** REPRIMAND
— **call upon 1 :** REQUIRE, OBLIGE ⟨may be *called upon* to do several jobs⟩ **2 :** to make a demand on **:** depend on ⟨universities are *called upon* to produce trained professionals⟩

²call *noun* (14th century)
1 a : an act of calling with the voice **:** SHOUT **b :** an imitation of the cry of a bird or other animal made to attract it **c :** an instrument used for calling ⟨a duck *call*⟩ **d :** the cry of an animal (as a bird)
2 a : a request or command to come or assemble **b :** a summons or signal on a drum, bugle, or pipe **c :** admission to the bar as a barrister **d :** an invitation to become the minister of a church or to accept a professional appointment **e :** a divine vocation or strong inner prompting to a particular course of action **f :** a summoning of actors to rehearsal ⟨the *call* is for 11 o'clock⟩ **g :** the attraction or appeal of a particular activity, condition, or place ⟨the *call* of the wild⟩ **h :** an order specifying the number of men to be inducted into the armed services during a specified period **i :** the selection of a play in football

3 a : DEMAND, CLAIM **b :** NEED, JUSTIFICATION **c :** a demand for payment of money **d :** an option to buy a specified amount of a security (as stock) or commodity (as wheat) at a fixed price at or within a specified time — compare PUT 2 **e :** an instance of asking for something **:** REQUEST ⟨many *calls* for Christmas stories⟩
4 : ROLL CALL
5 : a short usually formal visit
6 : the name or thing called ⟨the *call* was heads⟩
7 : the act of calling in a card game
8 : the act of calling on the telephone
9 : a direction or a succession of directions for a square dance rhythmically called to the dancers
10 : a decision or ruling made by an official of a sports contest; *also* **:** DECISION 1 ⟨a tough *call* to make⟩
11 : a temporary transfer of control of computer processing to a particular set of instructions (as a subroutine or procedure)
— **at call** or **on call 1 a :** available for use **:** at the service of ⟨thousands of men *at his call*⟩ **b :** ready to respond to a summons or command ⟨a doctor *on call*⟩ **2 :** subject to demand for payment or return without previous notice ⟨money lent *at call*⟩
— **within call :** within hearing or reach of a summons **:** subject to summons

call·a·ble \'kȯ-lə-bəl\ *adjective* (1826)
: capable of being called; *specifically* **:** subject to a demand for presentation for payment ⟨*callable* bond⟩

cal·la lily \'ka-lə-\ *noun* [New Latin, genus name, modification of Greek *kallaia* rooster's wattles] (1870)
: any of several herbs (genus *Zantedeschia*) of the arum family; *especially* **:** a house or greenhouse plant (*Z. aethiopica*) with a white showy spathe and yellow spadix — called also *calla*

cal·la·loo \ˌka-lə-'lü, ˌka-lə-\ *noun* [American Spanish *calalú* plant of the genus *Xanthosoma* whose leaves are used as greens] (1892)
: a soup or stew made with greens, onions, and crabmeat

cal·lant \'ka-lənt, 'kä-\ *noun* [Dutch or Old North French; Dutch *kalant* customer, fellow, from Old North French *calland* customer, from Latin *calent-, calens,* present participle of *calēre* to be warm — more at LEE] (circa 1592)
chiefly Scottish **:** BOY, LAD

call·back \'kȯl-ˌbak\ *noun* (1926)
1 : a return call
2 a : RECALL 5 **b :** a recall of an employee to work after a layoff **c :** a second or additional audition for a theatrical part

call–board \-ˌbōrd, -ˌbȯrd\ *noun* (1886)
: BULLETIN BOARD 1

call box *noun* (1885)
1 *British* **:** a public telephone booth
2 : a telephone usually located on the side of a road for reporting emergencies (as fires or automobile breakdowns)

call·boy \'kȯl-ˌbȯi\ *noun* (1794)
: BELLHOP, PAGE

call down *transitive verb* (1810)
1 : to cause or entreat to descend ⟨*call down* a blessing⟩
2 : REPRIMAND ⟨*called* me *down* for being late⟩

called strike *noun* (1887)
: a pitched baseball not struck at by the batter that passes through the strike zone

¹cal·ler \'kä-lər\ *adjective* [Middle English *callour*] (14th century)
1 *Scottish* **:** FRESH
2 *Scottish* **:** COOL

²call·er \'kȯ-lər\ *noun* (15th century)
: one that calls

cal·let \'ka-lət\ *noun* [perhaps from Middle French *caillette* frivolous person, from *Caillette* (flourished 1500) French court fool] (15th century)
chiefly Scottish **:** PROSTITUTE

call girl *noun* (circa 1940)
: a prostitute with whom an appointment may be made by telephone

call house *noun* (1929)
: a house or apartment where call girls may be procured

cal·lig·ra·pher \kə-'li-grə-fər\ *noun* (1753)
1 : a professional copyist or engrosser
2 : one who writes a beautiful hand
3 : PENMAN ⟨a fair *calligrapher*⟩

cal·lig·ra·phist \-fist\ *noun* (1816)
: CALLIGRAPHER

cal·lig·ra·phy \-fē\ *noun* [French or Greek; French *calligraphie,* from Greek *kalligraphia,* from *kalli-* beautiful (from *kallos* beauty) + *-graphia* -graphy] (1604)
1 a : artistic, stylized, or elegant handwriting or lettering **b :** the art of producing such writing
2 : PENMANSHIP
3 : an ornamental line in drawing or painting
— **cal·li·graph·ic** \ˌka-lə-'gra-fik\ *adjective*
— **cal·li·graph·i·cal·ly** \-fi-k(ə-)lē\ *adverb*

call–in \'kȯl-ˌin\ *adjective* (1967)
: allowing listeners to engage in broadcast telephone conversations with the host or a guest ⟨a *call-in* show⟩

call in (1597)
transitive verb
1 : to order to return or to be returned: as **a :** to withdraw from an advanced position ⟨*call in* the outposts⟩ **b :** to withdraw from circulation ⟨*call in* bank notes and issue new ones⟩
2 : to summon to one's aid or for consultation ⟨*call in* a mediator⟩
3 : to deliver (a message) by telephone ⟨*call in* an order for pizza⟩
intransitive verb
: to communicate with a person by telephone
— **call in sick :** to report by telephone that one will be absent because of illness

call·ing \'kȯ-liŋ\ *noun* (14th century)
1 : a strong inner impulse toward a particular course of action especially when accompanied by conviction of divine influence
2 : the vocation or profession in which one customarily engages
3 : the characteristic cry of a female cat in heat; *also* **:** the period of heat
synonym see WORK

calling card *noun* (1896)
1 : VISITING CARD
2 : a sign or evidence that someone or something is or has been present; *broadly* **:** an identifying mark

cal·li·ope \kə-'lī-ə-(ˌ)pē, in sense 2 also 'ka-lē-ˌōp\ *noun* [Latin, from Greek *Kalliopē*]
1 *capitalized* **:** the Greek Muse of heroic poetry
2 : a keyboard musical instrument resembling an organ and consisting of a series of whistles sounded by steam or compressed air

cal·li·per *chiefly British variant of* CALIPER

cal·li·pyg·ian \ˌka-lə-'pi-j(ē-)ən\ *or* **cal·li·py·gous** \-'pī-gəs\ *adjective* [Greek *kallipygos,* from *kalli-* + *pygē* buttocks] (circa 1800)
: having shapely buttocks

Cal·lis·to \kə-'lis-(ˌ)tō\ *noun* [Latin, from Greek *Kallistō*]
: a nymph loved by Zeus, changed into a she-bear by Hera, and subsequently changed into the Great Bear constellation

cal·li·thump \'ka-lə-ˌthəmp\ *noun* [back-formation from *callithumpian,* adjective, alteration of English dialect *gallithumpian* disturber of order at elections in 18th century] (1856)
: a noisy boisterous band or parade
— **cal·li·thump·ian** \ˌka-lə-'thəm-pē-ən\ *adjective*

call letters *noun plural* (1913)
: CALL SIGN

call loan *noun* (1852)
: a loan payable at the discretion of the borrower or on demand of the lender

call number *noun* (1876)

: a combination of characters assigned to a library book to indicate its place on a shelf
call off *transitive verb* (1633)
1 : to draw away **:** DIVERT ⟨her attention was *called off* by a new arrival⟩
2 : CANCEL ⟨*call* the trip *off*⟩
call of nature (1763)
: the need to urinate or defecate
cal·los·i·ty \ka-'lä-sə-tē, kə-\ *noun, plural* **-ties** (1578)
1 : the quality or state of being callous: as **a :** marked or abnormal hardness and thickness **b :** lack of feeling or capacity for emotion
2 : CALLUS 1
¹cal·lous \'ka-ləs\ *adjective* [Middle French *calleux*, from Latin *callosus*, from *callum, callus* callous skin] (15th century)
1 a : being hardened and thickened **b :** having calluses
2 a : feeling no emotion **b :** feeling no sympathy for others
— **cal·lous·ly** *adverb*
— **cal·lous·ness** *noun*
²callous *transitive verb* (1834)
: to make callous
call out *transitive verb* (15th century)
1 : to summon into action ⟨*call out* troops⟩
2 : to challenge to a duel
3 : to order on strike ⟨*call out* the workers⟩
cal·low \'ka-(,)lō\ *adjective* [Middle English *calu* bald, from Old English; akin to Old High German *kalo* bald, Old Church Slavonic *golŭ* bare] (1580)
: lacking adult sophistication **:** IMMATURE ⟨*callow* youth⟩
— **cal·low·ness** \'ka-lō-nəs, -lə-nəs\ *noun*
call sign *noun* (1919)
: the combination of identifying letters or letters and numbers assigned to an operator, office, activity, or station for use in communication (as in the address of a message sent by radio)
call slip *noun* (1881)
: a form filled out by a library patron for a desired book
call to quarters (circa 1918)
: a bugle call usually shortly before taps that summons soldiers to their quarters
call-up \'kȯ-,ləp\ *noun* (1940)
: an order to report for military service
call up *transitive verb* (1632)
1 : to bring to mind **:** EVOKE
2 : to summon before an authority
3 : to summon together (as for a united effort) ⟨*call up* all his forces for the attack⟩
4 : to summon for active military duty
5 : to bring forward for consideration or action
6 : to retrieve from the memory of a computer especially for display and user interaction
¹cal·lus \'ka-ləs\ *noun* [Latin] (1563)
1 : a thickening of or a hard thickened area on skin or bark
2 : a mass of exudate and connective tissue that forms around a break in a bone and is converted into bone in healing
3 : soft tissue that forms over a wounded or cut plant surface
²callus (1864)
intransitive verb
: to form callus
transitive verb
: to cause callus to form on
call-waiting *noun* (1986)
: a telephone service that signals (as by a click) to the user when an incoming call is received during a call in progress
¹calm \'käm, 'kälm, 'kam, 'kȯ(l)m, *New England also* 'kȧm\ *noun* [Middle English *calme*, from Middle French, from Old Italian *calma*, from Late Latin *cauma* heat, from Greek *kauma*, from *kaiein* to burn] (14th century)
1 a : a period or condition of freedom from storms, high winds, or rough activity of water

b : complete absence of wind or presence of wind having a speed no greater than one mile (1.6 kilometers) per hour — see BEAUFORT SCALE table
2 : a state of tranquillity
²calm (14th century)
intransitive verb
: to become calm — usually used with *down*
transitive verb
: to make calm — often used with *down*
³calm *adjective* (14th century)
1 : marked by calm **:** STILL ⟨a *calm* sea⟩
2 : free from agitation, excitement, or disturbance ⟨a *calm* manner⟩ ☆
— **calm·ly** *adverb*
— **calm·ness** *noun*
calm·ative \'kä-mə-tiv, 'käl-, *also* 'kä-, 'kȯ(l)-, 'ka-\ *noun or adjective* [²calm + -ative (as in *sedative*)] (1870)
: SEDATIVE
cal·mod·u·lin \(,)kal-'mä-jə-lin, -dyu̇-lin\ *noun* [calcium + modulate + ¹-in] (1979)
: a calcium-binding protein that regulates cellular metabolic processes (as the contraction of muscle fibers) by modifying the activity of calcium-sensitive enzymes
ca·ló \kə-'lō\ *noun* [Spanish, argot, speech of Spanish Gypsies, from Romany *kalo* Gypsy, literally, black, from Sanskrit *kāla*] (circa 1948)
: any of several Spanish argots; *especially* **:** an argot used by Chicano youths in cities of the U.S. Southwest
cal·o·mel \'ka-lə-məl, -,mel\ *noun* [probably from (assumed) New Latin *calomelas*, from Greek *kalos* beautiful + *melas* black — more at MELAN-] (1676)
: a white tasteless compound Hg_2Cl_2 used especially as a fungicide and insecticide and occasionally in medicine as a purgative — called also *mercurous chloride*
¹ca·lo·ric \kə-'lȯr-ik, -'lȯr-\ *noun* [French *calorique*, from Latin *calor*] (1792)
1 : a supposed form of matter formerly held responsible for the phenomena of heat and combustion
2 *archaic* **:** HEAT
²caloric *adjective* (circa 1828)
1 : of or relating to heat
2 : of or relating to calories
— **ca·lo·ri·cal·ly** \kə-'lȯr-i-k(ə-)lē, -'lȯr-\ *adverb*
cal·o·rie *also* **cal·o·ry** \'ka-lə-rē, 'kal-rē\ *noun, plural* **-ries** [French *calorie*, from Latin *calor* heat, from *calēre* to be warm — more at LEE] (1866)
1 a : the amount of heat required at a pressure of one atmosphere to raise the temperature of one gram of water one degree Celsius that is equal to about 4.19 joules — called also *gram calorie, small calorie*; abbreviation *cal* **b :** the amount of heat required to raise the temperature of one kilogram of water one degree Celsius **:** 1000 gram calories or 3.968 Btu — called also *large calorie*; abbreviation *Cal*
2 a : a unit equivalent to the large calorie expressing heat-producing or energy-producing value in food when oxidized in the body **b :** an amount of food having an energy-producing value of one large calorie
cal·o·rif·ic \,ka-lə-'ri-fik\ *adjective* [French or Latin; French *calorifique*, from Latin *calorificus*, from *calor*] (1812)
1 : CALORIC
2 : of or relating to heat production
cal·o·rim·e·ter \,ka-lə-'ri-mə-tər\ *noun* [International Scientific Vocabulary, from Latin *calor*] (1794)
: any of several apparatuses for measuring quantities of absorbed or evolved heat or for determining specific heats
— **ca·lo·ri·met·ric** \,ka-lə-rə-'me-trik; kə-,lȯr-ə-, -,lȯr-\ *adjective*
— **ca·lo·ri·met·ri·cal·ly** \-tri-k(ə-)lē\ *adverb*
— **cal·o·rim·e·try** \,ka-lə-'ri-mə-trē\ *noun*

ca·lotte \kə-'lät\ *noun* [French] (1632)
: SKULLCAP 1; *especially* **:** ZUCCHETTO
cal·o·type \'ka-lə-,tīp\ *noun* [Greek *kalos* beautiful + *-type* (as in *daguerreotype*)] (1845)
: a photographic process by which a large number of prints could be produced from a paper negative; *also* **:** a positive print so made
cal·pac *or* **cal·pack** \'kal-,pak, kal-'\ *noun* [Turkish *kalpak*] (1598)
: a high-crowned cap worn in Turkey, Iran, and neighboring countries
calque \'kalk\ *noun* [French, literally, copy, from *calquer* to trace, from Italian *calcare* to trample, trace, from Latin, to trample — more at CAULK] (1937)
: LOAN TRANSLATION
cal·trop \'kal-trəp, 'kȯl-\ *also* **cal·throp** \-thrəp\ *noun* [Middle English *caltrappe*, alteration of *calketrappe* star thistle, from Old English *calcatrippe*, from Medieval Latin *calcatrippa*] (15th century)
1 a *plural but singular or plural in construction* **:** STAR THISTLE 1 **b :** PUNCTURE VINE; *also* **:** any of various related herbs (genera *Tribulus* and *Kallstroemia*) of the same family (Zygophyllaceae, the caltrop family)
2 : a device with four metal points so arranged that when any three are on the ground the fourth projects upward as a hazard to the hooves of horses or to pneumatic tires
cal·u·met \'kal-yə-,met, -mət\ *noun* [American French, from French dialect, pipe stem, from Late Latin *calamellus*, diminutive of Latin *calamus* reed — more at CALAMUS] (1673)
: a highly ornamented ceremonial pipe of the American Indians

calumet

ca·lum·ni·ate \kə-'ləm-nē-,āt\ *transitive verb* **-at·ed; -at·ing** (1554)
1 : to utter maliciously false statements, charges, or imputations about
2 : to injure the reputation of by calumny
synonym see MALIGN
— **ca·lum·ni·a·tion** \-,ləm-nē-'ā-shən\ *noun*
— **ca·lum·ni·a·tor** \-'ləm-nē-,ā-tər\ *noun*
cal·um·ny \'ka-ləm-nē *also* 'kal-yəm-\ *noun, plural* **-nies** [Middle French & Latin; Middle French *calomnie*, from Latin *calumnia*, from *calvi* to deceive; perhaps akin to Old English *hōlian* to slander, Greek *kēlein* to beguile] (15th century)

\ə\ abut \ᵊ\ kitten \ər\ further \a\ ash \ā\ ace
\ä\ mop, mar \au̇\ out \ch\ chin \e\ bet \ē\ easy
\g\ go \i\ hit \ī\ ice \j\ job \ŋ\ sing \ō\ go
\ȯ\ law \ȯi\ boy \th\ thin \t̲h̲\ the \ü\ loot \u̇\ foot
\y\ yet \zh\ vision *see also* Guide to Pronunciation

1 : a misrepresentation intended to blacken another's reputation
2 : the act of uttering false charges or misrepresentations maliciously calculated to damage another's reputation
— **ca·lum·ni·ous** \kə-'ləm-nē-əs\ *adjective*
— **ca·lum·ni·ous·ly** *adverb*
cal·u·tron \'kal-yə-,trän\ *noun* [*Cal*ifornia *U*niversity cyclo*tron*] (1945)
: an electromagnetic apparatus for separating isotopes according to their masses
cal·va·dos \,kal-və-'dōs, ,käl-\ *noun, often capitalized* [French, from *Calvados*, department in Normandy, France] (1906)
: an applejack made in Calvados
cal·var·i·um \kal-'var-ē-əm, -'ver-\ *noun, plural* -**ia** \-ē-ə\ [New Latin, from Latin *calvaria* skull, from *calvus* bald; probably akin to Sanskrit *kulva* bald] (14th century)
: the portion of a skull including the braincase and excluding the lower jaw or lower jaw and facial portion
cal·va·ry \'kal-v(ə-)rē\ *noun, plural* -**ries** [*Calvary*, the hill near Jerusalem where Jesus was crucified] (1738)
1 : an open-air representation of the crucifixion of Jesus
2 : an experience of usually intense mental suffering
Calvary cross *noun* (1826)
: a Latin cross usually mounted on three steps — see CROSS illustration
calve \'kav, 'kàv\ *verb* **calved; calv·ing** [Middle English, from Old English *cealfian*, from *cealf* calf] (before 12th century)
intransitive verb
1 : to give birth to a calf; *also* : to produce offspring
2 *of an ice mass* **:** to separate or break so that a part becomes detached
transitive verb
1 : to produce by birth
2 *of an ice mass* **:** to let become detached
calves *plural of* CALF
Cal·vin cycle \'kal-vən-\ *noun* [Melvin *Calvin*] (1957)
: the cycle of enzyme-catalyzed dark reactions of photosynthesis that occurs in the chloroplasts of plants and in many bacteria and that involves the fixation of carbon dioxide and the formation of a six-carbon sugar
Cal·vin·ism \'kal-və-,ni-zəm\ *noun* [John *Calvin*] (circa 1570)
: the theological system of Calvin and his followers marked by strong emphasis on the sovereignty of God, the depravity of mankind, and the doctrine of predestination
— **Cal·vin·ist** \-və-nist\ *noun or adjective*
— **Cal·vin·is·tic** \,kal-və-'nis-tik\ *adjective*
— **Cal·vin·is·ti·cal·ly** \-ti-k(ə-)lē\ *adverb*
calx \'kalks\ *noun, plural* **calx·es** *or* **cal·ces** \'kal-,sēz\ [Middle English *cals*, from Latin *calx* lime — more at CHALK] (15th century)
: the crumbly residue left when a metal or mineral has been subjected to calcination or combustion
¹ca·lyp·so \kə-'lip-(,)sō\ *noun* [Latin, from Greek *Kalypsō*]
1 *capitalized* : a sea nymph in Homer's *Odyssey* who keeps Odysseus seven years on the island of Ogygia
2 *plural* **calypsos** [New Latin, genus name, probably from Latin] : a bulbous bog orchid (*Calypso bulbosa*) of northern regions bearing a single white to purple flower
²calypso *noun, plural* -**sos** *or* -**soes** [origin unknown] (1934)
: a style of music originating in the West Indies, marked by lively duple meter, and having lyrics that are often improvised and usually satirize local personalities and events; *also* : a song in this style
— **ca·lyp·so·ni·an** \kə-,lip-'sō-nē-ən, ,ka-(,)lip-\ *noun or adjective*

ca·lyp·tra \kə-'lip-trə\ *noun* [New Latin, from Greek *kalyptra* veil, from *kalyptein* to cover — more at HELL] (circa 1753)
: a hoodlike structure in a plant; *especially* : haploid tissue forming a membranous hood over the capsule in a moss
ca·lyx \'kā-liks *also* 'ka-\ *noun, plural* **ca·lyx·es** *or* **ca·ly·ces** \'kā-lə-,sēz *also* 'ka-\ [Latin *calyc-, calyx*, from Greek *kalyx* — more at CHALICE] (1693)
1 : the usually green outer whorl of a flower consisting of sepals
2 : a cuplike animal structure (as the body wall of a crinoid or a division of the kidney pelvis)
cal·zo·ne \kal-'zōn, -'zō-nē, -'zō-nā; käl-'zō-nā\ *noun, plural* **calzone** *or* **calzones** [Italian, from *calzone* (singular of *calzoni* pants), augmentative of *calza* stocking, from Medieval Latin *calcea*, from Latin *calceus* shoe, from *calc-, calx* heel] (circa 1950)
: a baked or fried turnover of pizza dough stuffed with various fillings usually including cheese
cam \'kam\ *noun* [perhaps from French *came*, from German *Kamm*, literally, comb, from Old High German *kamb*] (1777)
: a rotating or sliding piece in a mechanical linkage used especially in transforming rotary motion into linear motion or vice versa
ca·ma·ra·de·rie \,käm-'rä-d(ə-)rē, ,kam-, ,kä-mə-, ,ka-, -'ra-\ *noun* [French, from *camarade* comrade] (1840)
: a spirit of friendly good-fellowship
cam·a·ril·la \,ka-mə-'ri-lə, -'rē-ə\ *noun* [Spanish, literally, small room] (1839)
: a group of unofficial often secret and scheming advisers; *also* : CABAL
cam·as *also* **cam·ass** \'ka-məs\ *noun* [Chinook Jargon *kamass*] (1805)
: any of a genus (*Camassia* especially *C. quamash*) of plants of the lily family chiefly of the western U.S. with edible bulbs — compare DEATH CAMAS
¹cam·ber \'kam-bər\ *verb* **cam·bered; cam·ber·ing** \-b(ə-)riŋ\ [French *cambrer*, from Middle French *cambre* curved, from Latin *camur*] (1627)
intransitive verb
: to curve upward in the middle
transitive verb
1 : to arch slightly
2 : to impart camber to
²camber *noun* (1823)
1 : a slight convexity, arching, or curvature (as of a beam, deck, or road)
2 : the convexity of the curve of an airfoil from the leading edge to the trailing edge
3 : a setting of the wheels of an automotive vehicle closer together at the bottom than at the top
cam·bi·um \'kam-bē-əm\ *noun, plural* -**bi·ums** *or* -**bia** \-bē-ə\ [New Latin, from Medieval Latin, exchange, from Latin *cambire* to exchange — more at CHANGE] (1671)
: a thin formative layer between the xylem and phloem of most vascular plants that gives rise to new cells and is responsible for secondary growth
— **cam·bi·al** \-bē-əl\ *adjective*
Cam·bo·di·an \kam-'bō-dē-ən\ *noun* (1770)
1 : a native or inhabitant of Cambodia
2 : KHMER 2
— **Cambodian** *adjective*
Cam·bri·an \'kam-brē-ən, 'käm-\ *adjective* [Medieval Latin *Cambria* Wales, from Middle Welsh *Cymry* Wales, Welshmen] (circa 1656)
1 : WELSH
2 : of, relating to, or being the earliest geologic period of the Paleozoic era or the corresponding system of rocks marked by fossils of every great animal type except the vertebrates — see GEOLOGIC TIME table
— **Cambrian** *noun*

cam·bric \'kām-brik\ *noun* [obsolete Flemish *Kameryk* Cambrai, city of France] (1530)
1 : a fine thin white linen fabric
2 : a cotton fabric that resembles cambric
cambric tea *noun* (1888)
: a hot drink of water, milk, sugar, and often a small amount of tea
cam·cord·er \'kam-,kòr-dər\ *noun* [*cam*era + re*corder*] (1982)
: a small portable combined video camera and videocassette recorder
¹came *past of* COME
²came \'kām\ *noun* [origin unknown] (1688)
: a slender grooved lead rod used to hold together panes of glass especially in a stained-glass window
cam·el \'ka-məl\ *noun* [Middle English, from Old English & Old North French, from Latin *camelus*, from Greek *kamēlos*, of Semitic origin; akin to Hebrew *gāmāl* camel] (before 12th century)
1 : either of two large ruminant mammals (genus *Camelus*) used as draft and saddle animals in desert regions especially of Africa and Asia: **a :** the one-humped camel (*C. dromedarius*) extant only as a domestic or feral animal — called also *dromedary* **b :** the two-humped camel (*C. bactrianus* synonym *C. ferus*) of Chinese Turkestan and Mongolia — called also *Bactrian camel*
2 : a watertight structure used especially to lift submerged ships
3 : a light yellowish brown

camel 1: *1* dromedary, *2* Bactrian camel

cam·el·back \'kam-əl-,bak\ *noun* (1860)
: the back of a camel
cam·el·eer \,ka-mə-'lir\ *noun* (1808)
: a camel driver
camel hair *also* **camel's hair** *noun* (14th century)
1 : the hair of the camel or a substitute for it (as hair from squirrels' tails)
2 : cloth made of camel hair or a mixture of camel hair and wool usually light tan and of soft silky texture
ca·mel·lia \kə-'mēl-yə\ *noun* [New Latin *Camellia*, from *Camellus* (Georg Josef Kamel (died 1706) Moravian Jesuit missionary)] (circa 1753)
: any of a genus (*Camellia*) of shrubs or trees of the tea family; *especially* : an ornamental greenhouse shrub (*C. japonica*) with glossy leaves and roselike flowers
ca·mel·o·pard \kə-'me-lə-,pärd\ *noun* [Late Latin *camelopardus*, alteration of Latin *camelopardalis*, from Greek *kamēlopardalis*, from *kamēlos* + *pardalis* leopard] (14th century)
1 *archaic* : GIRAFFE
2 *capitalized* : CAMELOPARDALIS
Ca·mel·o·par·da·lis \kə-,me-lə-'pär-d°l-əs\ *noun* [Latin (genitive *Camelopardalis*), cameloopard]
: a northern constellation between Cassiopeia and Ursa Major
Cam·e·lot \'ka-mə-,lät\ *noun*
1 : the site of King Arthur's palace and court
2 : a time, place, or atmosphere of idyllic happiness
Cam·em·bert \'ka-məm-,ber\ *noun* [French, from *Camembert*, Normandy, France] (1878)
: a soft surface-ripened cheese with a thin grayish white rind and a yellow interior
cam·eo \'ka-mē-,ō\ *noun, plural* -**eos** [Middle English *camew*, from Middle French *camau, kamaheu*] (15th century)
1 a : a gem carved in relief; *especially* : a small piece of sculpture on a stone or shell cut

in relief in one layer with another contrasting layer serving as background **b :** a small medallion with a profiled head in relief
2 : a carving or sculpture made in the manner of a cameo
3 : a usually brief literary or filmic piece that brings into delicate or sharp relief the character of a person, place, or event
4 : a small theatrical role usually performed by a well-known actor and often limited to a single scene; *broadly :* any brief appearance
— **cameo** *adjective*
— **cameo** *transitive verb*

cam·era \'kam-rə, 'ka-mər-ə\ *noun* [Late Latin, room — more at CHAMBER] (1712)
1 : the treasury department of the papal curia
2 a : CAMERA OBSCURA **b :** a device that consists of a lightproof chamber with an aperture fitted with a lens and a shutter through which the image of an object is projected onto a surface for recording (as on film) or for translation into electrical impulses (as for television broadcast)
— **on camera :** before a live television camera

cam·era lu·ci·da \-'lü-sə-də\ *noun* [New Latin, literally, light chamber] (1831)
: an instrument that by means of a prism or mirrors and often a microscope causes a virtual image of an object to appear as if projected upon a plane surface so that an outline may be traced

cam·era·man \-,man, -mən\ *noun* (1908)
: a person who operates a camera (as for motion pictures or television)

cam·era ob·scu·ra \-əb-'skyur-ə\ *noun* [New Latin, literally, dark chamber] (1725)
: a darkened enclosure having an aperture usually provided with a lens through which light from external objects enters to form an image of the objects on the opposite surface

cam·era·per·son \-,pər-s°n\ *noun* (1976)
: a cameraman or camerawoman

cam·era·wom·an \-,wu̇-mən\ *noun* (1971)
: a woman who operates a camera

cam·er·len·go \,ka-mər-'leŋ-(,)gō\ *noun, plural* **-gos** [Italian *camarlingo*] (1625)
: a cardinal who heads the Apostolic Camera

ca·mion \kä-'myōⁿ\ *noun* [French] (1911)
: MOTORTRUCK; *also :* BUS

cam·i·sa·do \,ka-mə-'sä-(,)dō, -'sä-\ *noun, plural* **-does** [probably from obsolete Spanish *camisada*] (1548)
archaic : an attack by night

ca·mise \kə-'mēz, -'mēs\ *noun* [Arabic *qamīṣ*, perhaps from Late Latin *camisia*] (1812)
: a light loose long-sleeved shirt, gown, or tunic

cam·i·sole \'ka-mə-,sōl\ *noun* [French, from Provençal *camisolla*, diminutive of *camisa* shirt, from Late Latin *camisia*] (1795)
1 : a short negligee jacket for women
2 : a short sleeveless garment for women

cam·let \'kam-lət\ *noun* [Middle English *cameloit*, from Middle French *camelot*, from Arabic *khamlat* woolen plush] (15th century)
1 a : a medieval Asian fabric of camel hair or angora wool **b :** a European fabric of silk and wool **c :** a fine lustrous woolen
2 : a garment made of camlet

camomile *variant of* CHAMOMILE

ca·mor·ra \kə-'mȯr-ə, -'mär-\ *noun* [Italian] (1865)
: a group of persons united for dishonest or dishonorable ends; *especially :* a secret organization formed about 1820 at Naples, Italy

ca·mor·ris·ta \,kä-mȯ-'rē-stə\ *noun, plural* **-ti** \-(,)stē\ [Italian, from *camorra*] (1897)
: a member of a camorra

¹cam·ou·flage \'ka-mə-,fläzh, -,fläj\ *noun* [French, from *camoufler* to disguise] (1917)
1 : the disguising especially of military equipment or installations with paint, nets, or foliage; *also :* the disguise so applied

2 a : concealment by means of disguise **b :** behavior or artifice designed to deceive or hide
— **cam·ou·flag·ic** \,ka-mə-'flä-zhik, -jik\ *adjective*

²camouflage *verb* **-flaged; -flag·ing** (1917)
transitive verb
: to conceal or disguise by camouflage
intransitive verb
: to practice camouflage
— **cam·ou·flage·able** \'ka-mə-,flä-zhə-bəl, -jə-bəl\ *adjective*

³camouflage *adjective* (1945)
: made in colors or patterns typical of camouflage ⟨a *camouflage* jacket⟩

¹camp \'kamp\ *noun, often attributive* [Middle French, probably from Old North French or Old Provençal, from Latin *campus* plain, field] (1528)
1 a : a place usually away from urban areas where tents or simple buildings (as cabins) are erected for shelter or for temporary residence (as for laborers, prisoners, or vacationers) ⟨migrant labor *camp*⟩ **b :** a group of tents, cabins, or huts ⟨fishing *camps* along the river⟩ **c :** a settlement newly sprung up in a lumbering or mining region **d :** a place usually in the country for recreation or instruction during the summer ⟨goes to *camp* every July⟩ ⟨computer *camp*⟩ ⟨football *camp*⟩
2 a : a body of persons encamped **b** (1) **:** a group of persons; *especially :* a group engaged in promoting or defending a theory, doctrine, position, or person (2) **:** an ideological position
3 : military service or life

²camp (1543)
intransitive verb
1 : to make camp or occupy a camp
2 : to live temporarily in a camp or outdoors — often used with *out*
3 : to take up one's quarters **:** LODGE
4 : to take up one's position **:** settle down
transitive verb
: to put into a camp; *also :* ACCOMMODATE

³camp *noun* [origin unknown] (circa 1909)
1 : exaggerated effeminate mannerisms exhibited especially by homosexuals
2 : a homosexual displaying camp
3 : something so outrageously artificial, affected, inappropriate, or out-of-date as to be considered amusing
4 : something self-consciously exaggerated or theatrical
— **camp·i·ly** \'kam-pə-lē\ *adverb*
— **camp·i·ness** \-pē-nəs\ *noun*
— **campy** \'kam-pē\ *adjective*

⁴camp *adjective* (1909)
: of, relating to, being, or displaying camp ⟨*camp* send-ups of the songs of the fifties and sixties —John Elsom⟩

⁵camp *intransitive verb* (1925)
: to engage in camp **:** exhibit the qualities of camp ⟨he . . . was *camping*, hands on hips, with a quick eye to notice every man who passed by —R. M. McAlmon⟩

¹cam·paign \(,)kam-'pān\ *noun* [French *campagne*, probably from Italian *campagna* level country, campaign, from Late Latin *campania* level country, from Latin, the level country around Naples] (circa 1656)
1 : a connected series of military operations forming a distinct phase of a war
2 : a connected series of operations designed to bring about a particular result ⟨election *campaign*⟩

²campaign *intransitive verb* (1701)
: to go on, engage in, or conduct a campaign
— **cam·paign·er** *noun*

cam·pa·ni·le \,kam-pə-'nē-lē, ,käm-, -(,)lā, *especially US structures also* -'nē(ə)l\ *noun, plural* **-ni·les** *or* **-ni·li** \-'nē-lē\ [Italian, from *campana* bell, from Late Latin] (1640)
: a usually freestanding bell tower

cam·pa·nol·o·gist \,kam-pə-'nä-lə-jist\ *noun* (1857)

: one that practices or is skilled in campanology

cam·pa·nol·o·gy \-jē\ *noun* [New Latin *campanologia*, from Late Latin *campana* + New Latin *-o- + -logia* -logy] (circa 1823)
: the art of bell ringing

cam·pan·u·la \kam-'pan-yə-lə\ *noun* [New Latin, diminutive of Late Latin *campana*] (1664)
: any of a genus (*Campanula*) of bellflowers

cam·pan·u·late \-lət, -,lāt\ *adjective* [New Latin *campanula* bell-shaped part, diminutive of Late Latin *campana*] (1668)
: shaped like a bell ⟨*campanulate* flower⟩

Camp·bell·ite \'ka-mə-,līt *also* 'kam-bə-\ *noun* [Alexander *Campbell*] (1830)
: DISCIPLE 2 — often taken to be offensive

camp·craft \'kamp-,kraft\ *noun* (circa 1893)
: skill and practice in the activities relating to camping

camp·er \'kam-pər\ *noun* (1856)
1 : one that camps
2 : a portable dwelling (as a specially equipped trailer or automotive vehicle) for use during casual travel and camping

cam·pe·si·no \,kam-pə-'sē-(,)nō\ *noun, plural* **-nos** [Spanish, from *campo* field, country, from Latin *campus* field] (1898)
: a native of a Latin-American rural area; *especially :* a Latin-American Indian farmer or farm laborer

cam·pes·tral \kam-'pes-trəl\ *adjective* [Latin *campestr-, campester*, from *campus*] (circa 1750)
: of or relating to fields or open country **:** RURAL

camp·fire \'kamp-,fīr\ *noun* (1675)
: a fire built outdoors (as at a camp or a picnic)

Camp Fire girl *noun* [from *Camp Fire Girls*, Inc., former name of Camp Fire, Inc.] (1912)
: a girl who is a member of a national organization of young people from ages 5 to 18

camp follower *noun* (1810)
1 : a civilian who follows a military unit to attend or exploit military personnel; *specifically* **:** PROSTITUTE
2 : a disciple or follower who is not of the main body of members or adherents; *especially :* a politician who joins the party or movement solely for personal gain

camp·ground \'kamp-,graund\ *noun* (1805)
: the area or place (as a field or grove) used for a camp, for camping, or for a camp meeting

cam·phene \'kam-,fēn\ *noun* (circa 1847)
: any of several terpenes related to camphor; *especially :* a colorless crystalline terpene $C_{10}H_{16}$ used in insecticides

cam·phor \'kam(p)-fər\ *noun* [Middle English *caumfre*, from Anglo-French, from Medieval Latin *camphora*, from Arabic *kāfūr*, from Malay *kapur*] (14th century)
: a tough gummy volatile aromatic crystalline compound $C_{10}H_{16}O$ obtained especially from the wood and bark of the camphor tree and used as a liniment and mild topical analgesic in medicine, as a plasticizer, and as an insect repellent; *also :* any of several similar compounds (as some terpene alcohols and ketones)
— **cam·pho·ra·ceous** \,kam(p)-fə-'rā-shəs\ *adjective*

cam·phor·ate \'kam(p)-fə-,rāt\ *transitive verb* **-at·ed; -at·ing** (1641)
: to impregnate or treat with camphor

camphor tree *noun* (1607)
: a large Asian evergreen tree (*Cinnamomum camphora*) of the laurel family grown in warm regions

cam·pi·on \'kam-pē-ən\ *noun* [probably from obsolete *campion* (champion)] (1576)
: any of various plants (genera *Lychnis* and *Silene*) of the pink family

camp meeting *noun* (1803)
: a series of evangelistic meetings usually held outdoors and attended by persons who often camp nearby

cam·po \'kam-(ˌ)pō, 'käm-\ *noun, plural* **campos** [American Spanish, from Spanish, field, from Latin *campus*] (1863)
: a grassland plain in South America with scattered perennial herbs

camp·o·ree \ˌkam-pə-'rē\ *noun* [*camp* + jam-*boree*] (1927)
: a gathering of Boy Scouts or Girl Scouts from a given geographic area

camp shirt *noun* (1979)
: a woman's shirt having a notched collar and often patch pockets

camp·site \'kamp-ˌsīt\ *noun* (1910)
: a place suitable for or used as the site of a camp

cam·pus \'kam-pəs\ *noun, often attributive* [Latin, plain] (1774)
1 : the grounds and buildings of a university, college, or school
2 : a university, college, or school viewed as an academic, social, or spiritual entity
3 : grounds that resemble a campus ⟨hospital *campus*⟩ ⟨landscaped corporate *campus*⟩

cam·pylo·bac·ter \ˌkam-pi-lō-'bak-tər, kam-ˌpi-lə-\ *noun* [New Latin, from Greek *kampylos* bent + New Latin *bacterium*; akin to Greek *kampē* bend — more at GAMBIT] (1964)
: any of a genus (*Campylobacter*) of spirally curved motile gram-negative rod-shaped bacteria of which some are pathogenic in domestic animals and humans

cam·py·lot·ro·pous \ˌkam-pi-'lä-trə-pəs\ *adjective* [Greek *kampylos* + International Scientific Vocabulary *-tropous* -tropous] (1835)
: having the ovule curved

cam·shaft \'kam-ˌshaft\ *noun* (circa 1877)
: a shaft to which a cam is fastened or of which a cam forms an integral part

cam wheel *noun* (circa 1853)
: a wheel set or shaped to act as a cam

¹can \kən, 'kan\ *verb, past* **could** \kəd, 'kud\ *pres singular & plural* **can** [Middle English (1st & 3d singular present indicative), from Old English; akin to Old High German *kan* (1st & 3d singular present indicative) know, am able, Old English *cnāwan* to know — more at KNOW] (before 12th century)
transitive verb
1 *obsolete* : KNOW, UNDERSTAND
2 *archaic* : to be able to do, make, or accomplish
intransitive verb
archaic : to have knowledge or skill
verbal auxiliary
1 a : know how to ⟨she *can* read⟩ **b** : be physically or mentally able to ⟨he *can* lift 200 pounds⟩ **c** — used to indicate possibility ⟨do you think he *can* still be alive⟩ ⟨those things *can* happen⟩; sometimes used interchangeably with *may* **d** : be permitted by conscience or feeling to ⟨*can* hardly blame her⟩ **e** : be made possible or probable by circumstances to ⟨he *can* hardly have meant that⟩ **f** : be inherently able or designed to ⟨everything that money *can* buy⟩ **g** : be logically or axiologically able to ⟨2 + 2 *can* also be written 3 + 1⟩ **h** : be enabled by law, agreement, or custom to
2 : have permission to — used interchangeably with *may* ⟨you *can* go now if you like⟩ □

²can \'kan\ *noun* [Middle English *canne*, from Old English; akin to Old High German *channa*] (before 12th century)
1 : a usually cylindrical receptacle: **a** : a vessel for holding liquids; *specifically* : a drinking vessel **b** : a usually metal typically cylindrical receptacle usually with an open top, often with a removable cover, and sometimes with a spout or side handles (as for holding milk or trash) **c** : a container (as of tinplate) in which products (as perishable foods) are hermetically sealed for preservation until use **d** : a jar for packing or preserving fruit or vegetables
2 : JAIL
3 a : TOILET **b** : BATHROOM 1
4 : BUTTOCKS
5 : DESTROYER 2
6 *slang* : an ounce of marijuana
— **can·ful** \'kan-ˌful\ *noun*
— **in the can** *of a film or videotape* : completed and ready for release

³can \'kan\ *transitive verb* **canned; canning** (1861)
1 a : to put in a can : preserve by sealing in airtight cans or jars **b** : to hit (a golf shot) into the cup **c** : to hit (a shot) in basketball
2 : to discharge from employment
3 *slang* : to put a stop or end to
— **can·ner** *noun*

Ca·naan·ite \'kā-nə-ˌnīt\ *noun* [Greek *Kananitēs*, from *Kanaan* Canaan, from Hebrew *Kena'an*] (1535)
: a member of a Semitic people inhabiting ancient Palestine and Phoenicia from about 3000 B.C.
— **Canaanite** *adjective*

Can·a·da balsam \'kan-ə-də-\ *noun* [Canada, country in North America] (1811)
: a viscid yellowish to greenish oleoresin exudate of the balsam fir (*Abies balsmea*) that solidifies to a transparent mass and is used as a transparent cement especially in microscopy

Canada Day *noun* (1950)
: July 1 observed as a legal holiday in commemoration of the proclamation of dominion status in 1867

Canada goose *noun* (1731)
: the common wild goose (*Branta canadensis*) of North America that is chiefly gray and brownish with black head and neck and a white patch running from the sides of the head under the throat

Canada goose

Canada thistle *noun* (1799)
: a European thistle (*Cirsium arvense*) with pinkish purple or white flowers naturalized as a weed in North America

Ca·na·di·an \kə-'nā-dē-ən\ *noun* (1568)
: a native or inhabitant of Canada
— **Canadian** *adjective*

Canadian bacon *noun* (circa 1934)
: bacon cut from the loin that has little fat and is cut into round or oblong slices

Canadian football *noun* (1944)
: a game resembling American football that is played on a turfed field between two teams of 12 players each

Canadian French *noun* (1816)
: the language of the French Canadians

Canadian lynx *or* **Canada lynx** *noun* (1840)
: LYNX c

ca·naille \kə-'nī, -'nä(ə)l\ *noun* [French, from Italian *canaglia*, from *cane* dog, from Latin *canis* — more at HOUND] (1661)
1 : RABBLE, RIFFRAFF
2 : PROLETARIAN

¹ca·nal \kə-'nal\ *noun* [Middle English, from Latin *canalis* pipe, channel, from *canna* reed — more at CANE] (15th century)
1 : a tubular anatomical passage or channel : DUCT
2 : CHANNEL, WATERCOURSE
3 : an artificial waterway for navigation or for draining or irrigating land
4 : any of various faint narrow lines on the planet Mars seen through telescopes and once thought by some to be canals built by Martians

²canal *transitive verb* **-nalled** *or* **-naled; -nal·ling** *or* **-nal·ing** (1819)
: to construct a canal through or across

can·a·lic·u·lus \ˌka-nə-'li-kyə-ləs\ *noun, plural* **-li** \-ˌlī, -ˌlē\ [Latin, diminutive of *canalis*] (1854)
: a minute canal in a bodily structure
— **can·a·lic·u·lar** \-lər\ *adjective*

can·a·li·za·tion \ˌka-nᵊl-ə-'zā-shən\ *noun* (1844)
1 : an act or instance of canalizing
2 : a system of channels

can·a·lize \'ka-nᵊl-ˌīz\ *verb* **-lized; -liz·ing** (1860)
transitive verb
1 a : to provide with a canal or channel **b** : to make into or similar to a canal
2 : to provide with an outlet; *especially* : to direct into preferred channels
intransitive verb
1 : to flow in or into a channel
2 : to establish new channels

can·a·pé \'ka-nə-pē, -ˌpā\ *noun* [French, literally, sofa, from Medieval Latin *canopeum, canapeum* mosquito net — more at CANOPY] (1890)
: an appetizer consisting of a piece of bread or toast or a cracker topped with a savory spread (as caviar or cheese) — compare HORS D'OEUVRE ◇

ca·nard \kə-'närd *also* -'när\ *noun* [French, literally, duck; in sense 1, from Middle French *vendre des canards à moitié* to cheat, literally, to half-sell ducks] (circa 1859)

1 : a false or unfounded report or story; *especially* **:** a fabricated report
2 : an airplane with horizontal stabilizing and control surfaces in front of supporting surfaces; *also* **:** a small airfoil in front of the wing of an aircraft that increases the aircraft's stability ◇

ca·nary \kə-'ner-ē\ *noun, plural* **ca·nar·ies** [Middle French *canarie*, from Old Spanish *canario*, from *Islas Canarias* Canary Islands] (1592)
1 : a lively 16th century court dance
2 : a Canary Islands usually sweet wine similar to Madeira
3 : a small finch (*Serinus canarius*) of the Canary Islands that is usually greenish to yellow and is kept as a cage bird and singer
4 *slang* **:** INFORMER 2

canary seed *noun* (1597)
: seed of a Canary Islands grass (*Phalaris canariensis*) used as food for cage birds

canary yellow *noun* (circa 1865)
: a light to moderate or vivid yellow

ca·nas·ta \kə-'nas-tə\ *noun* [Spanish, literally, basket] (1948)
1 : a form of rummy using two full decks in which players or partnerships try to meld groups of three or more cards of the same rank and score bonuses for 7-card melds
2 : a meld of seven cards of the same rank in canasta

can·can \'kan-,kan\ *noun* [French] (1848)
: a woman's dance of French origin characterized by high kicking usually while holding up the front of a full ruffled skirt

¹can·cel \'kan(t)-səl\ *verb* **-celed** *or* **-celled; -cel·ing** *or* **-cel·ling** \-s(ə-)liŋ\ [Middle English *cancellen*, from Middle French *canceller*, from Late Latin *cancellare*, from Latin, to make like a lattice, from *cancelli* (plural), diminutive of *cancer* lattice, probably alteration of *carcer* prison] (14th century)
transitive verb
1 a : to destroy the force, effectiveness, or validity of **:** ANNUL ⟨*cancel* a magazine subscription⟩ ⟨a *canceled* check⟩ **b :** to bring to nothingness **:** DESTROY **c :** to match in force or effect **:** OFFSET — often used with *out* ⟨his irritability *canceled* out his natural kindness —Osbert Sitwell⟩ **d :** to call off usually without expectation of conducting or performing at a later time ⟨*cancel* a football game⟩
2 a : to mark or strike out for deletion **b :** OMIT, DELETE
3 a : to remove (a common divisor) from numerator and denominator **b :** to remove (equivalents) on opposite sides of an equation or account
4 : to deface (a postage or revenue stamp) especially with a set of ink lines so as to invalidate for reuse
intransitive verb
: to neutralize each other's strength or effect **:** COUNTERBALANCE
— **can·cel·able** *or* **can·cel·la·ble** \-s(ə-)lə-bəl\ *adjective*
— **can·cel·er** *or* **can·cel·ler** \-s(ə-)lər\ *noun*

²cancel *noun* (1806)
1 : CANCELLATION
2 a : a deleted part or passage **b** (1) **:** a leaf containing matter to be deleted (2) **:** a new leaf or slip substituted for matter already printed

can·cel·la·tion *also* **can·cel·ation** \,kan(t)-sə-'lā-shən\ *noun* (1535)
1 : the act or an instance of canceling
2 : a released accommodation
3 : a mark made to cancel something (as a postage stamp)

can·cel·lous \kan-'se-ləs, 'kan(t)-sə-ləs\ *adjective* [New Latin *cancelli* intersecting osseous plates and bars in cancellous bone, from Latin, lattice] (circa 1839)
of bone **:** having a porous structure

can·cer \'kan(t)-sər\ *noun* [Middle English, from Latin (genitive *Cancri*), literally, crab; akin to Greek *karkinos* crab, cancer]
1 *capitalized* **a :** a northern zodiacal constellation between Gemini and Leo **b** (1) **:** the 4th sign of the zodiac in astrology — see ZODIAC table (2) **:** one born under the sign of Cancer
2 [Latin, crab, cancer] **a :** a malignant tumor of potentially unlimited growth that expands locally by invasion and systemically by metastasis **b :** an abnormal bodily state marked by such tumors
3 : something evil or malignant that spreads destructively ⟨the *cancer* of hidden resentment —*Irish Digest*⟩
4 a : an enlarged tumorlike plant growth (as that of crown gall) **b :** a plant disease marked by such growths
word history see RANKLE
— **can·cer·ous** \'kan(t)s-rəs, 'kan(t)-sə-\ *adjective*
— **can·cer·ous·ly** *adverb*

Can·cer·ian \kan-'ser-ē-ən, -'sir-\ *noun* (1911)
: CANCER 1b(2)

can·de·la \kan-'dē-lə, -'de-, -'dā-; 'kan-də-lə\ *noun* [Latin, candle] (1949)
: the base unit of luminous intensity in the International System of Units that is equal to the luminous intensity in a given direction of a source which emits monochromatic radiation of frequency 540×10^{12} hertz and has a radiant intensity in that direction of $1/683$ watt per unit solid angle — called also *candle*; abbreviation *cd*

can·de·la·bra \,kan-də-'lä-brə *sometimes* -'la-\ *noun* [alteration of Latin *candelabrum*, from *candela*] (1815)
: a branched candlestick or lamp with several lights

can·de·la·brum \-brəm\ *noun, plural* **-bra** \-brə\ *also* **-brums** [Latin] (1811)
: CANDELABRA

can·dent \'kan-dənt\ *adjective* [Latin *candent-, candens*, present participle of *candēre*] (1577)
: glowing from or as if from great heat

can·des·cence \kan-'de-s⁼n(t)s\ *noun* (circa 1864)
: a candescent state **:** glowing whiteness

can·des·cent \-s⁼nt\ *adjective* [Latin *candescent-, candescens*, present participle of *candescere*, inchoative of *candēre*] (1824)
: glowing or dazzling from or as if from great heat

can·did \'kan-dəd\ *adjective* [French & Latin; French *candide*, from Latin *candidus* bright, white, from *candēre* to shine, glow; akin to Welsh *can* white, Sanskrit *candati* it shines] (1630)
1 : WHITE ⟨*candid* flames⟩
2 : free from bias, prejudice, or malice **:** FAIR ⟨a *candid* observer⟩
3 a : marked by honest sincere expression **b :** indicating or suggesting sincere honesty and absence of deception **c :** disposed to criticize severely **:** BLUNT
4 : relating to photography of subjects acting naturally or spontaneously without being posed
synonym see FRANK
— **can·did·ly** *adverb*
— **can·did·ness** *noun*

can·di·da \'kan-də-də\ *noun* [New Latin, genus name, from feminine of *candidus*] (1939)
: any of a genus (*Candida*) of parasitic imperfect fungi that resemble yeasts and occur especially in the mouth, vagina, and intestinal tract and that are usually benign but can become pathogenic; *especially* **:** one (*C. albicans*) causing thrush

can·di·da·cy \'kan-də-də-sē, 'ka-nə-\ *noun, plural* **-cies** (1864)
: the state of being a candidate

can·di·date \'kan-də-,dāt, 'ka-nə-, -dət\ *noun* [Latin *candidatus*, from *candidatus* clothed in white, from *candidus* white; from the white toga worn by candidates for office in ancient Rome] (1600)
1 a : one that aspires to or is nominated or qualified for an office, membership, or award **b :** one likely or suited to undergo or be chosen for something specified ⟨a *candidate* for surgery⟩
2 : a student in the process of meeting final requirements for a degree ◇

can·di·da·ture \'kan-də-də-,chúr, 'ka-nə-, -chər\ *noun* (1851)
chiefly British **:** CANDIDACY

candid camera *noun* (1929)
: a camera used to record subjects in a natural, spontaneous, or unposed manner; *also* **:** something likened to a camera used in such a manner
— **candid–camera** *adjective*

can·di·di·a·sis \,kan-də-'dī-ə-səs\ *noun, plural* **-a·ses** \-,sēz\ [New Latin] (1951)
: infection with or disease caused by a candida — called also *moniliasis*

can·died \'kan-dēd\ *adjective* (circa 1606)
1 : encrusted or coated with sugar
2 : baked with sugar or syrup until translucent

¹can·dle \'kan-d⁼l\ *noun* [Middle English *candel*, from Old English, from Latin *candela*, from *candēre*] (before 12th century)
1 : a usually molded or dipped mass of wax or tallow containing a wick that may be burned (as to give light, heat, or scent or for celebration or votive purposes)
2 : something resembling a candle in shape or use ⟨a sulfur *candle* for fumigating⟩

candelabra

WORD HISTORY

canard In 16th century France, *vendre des canards à moitié*, which means literally "to half-sell ducks," was a colorful way of saying "to cheat." Unfortunately, no one knows just what was meant by this expression; it probably alludes to an incident in some story widely known at the time that has not survived. At any rate, *canard* in the sense of "duck" came to stand for any hoax, especially a made-up report. And French *canard*, in this sense, was borrowed into English.

candidate A person campaigning for public office in ancient Rome traditionally wore a toga that had been whitened with chalk when he greeted voters in the Forum. Whatever the original significance of the whitening might have been, it apparently came to be regarded as a form of electioneering, and according to the historian Livy it was banned by the Senate as early as 432 B.C. As with later curbs on soliciting votes, however, the ban was habitually disregarded, and office seekers wore white togas for some time after the Caesars had replaced the Roman Republic. The Latin word for an office seeker was *candidatus*, from an adjective of the same form meaning "wearing white," itself a derivative of *candidus* "white, bright." In the 16th and 17th centuries, the word *candidatus* was borrowed into French (as *candidat*), German (as *Kandidat*), and English, denoting aspirants either to a political office or to some academic degree.

\ə\ abut \ᵊ\ kitten \ər\ further \a\ ash \ā\ ace
\ä\ mop, mar \aù\ out \ch\ chin \e\ bet \ē\ easy
\g\ go \i\ hit \ī\ ice \j\ job \ŋ\ sing \ō\ go
\ò\ law \òi\ boy \th\ thin \t͟h\ the \ü\ loot \ù\ foot
\y\ yet \zh\ vision *see also* Guide to Pronunciation

3 : required effort, expense, or trouble — usually used in the phrase *not worth the candle*
4 : CANDELA

²candle *transitive verb* **can·dled; can·dling** \'kan(d)-liŋ, 'kan-d°l-iŋ\ (1879)
: to examine by holding between the eye and a light; *especially* **:** to test (eggs) in this way for staleness, blood clots, fertility, and growth
— **can·dler** \'kan(d)-lər, 'kan-d°l-ər\ *noun*

can·dle·ber·ry \'kan-d°l-,ber-ē\ *noun* (circa 1730)
: a wax myrtle (*Myrica cerifera*); *also* **:** a bayberry (*Myrica pensylvanica*)

can·dle·fish \-,fish\ *noun* (1881)
: EULACHON

can·dle·hold·er \-,hōl-dər\ *noun* (1932)
: CANDLESTICK

can·dle·light \'kan-d°l-,(l)īt\ *noun* (before 12th century)
1 a : the light of a candle **b :** a soft artificial light
2 : the time for lighting candles **:** TWILIGHT

can·dle·light·er \-,(l)ī-tər\ *noun* (15th century)
1 : one who lights the candles for a ceremony
2 : a long-handled implement with a taper and a snuffer that is used for the ceremonial lighting and extinguishing of candles

can·dle·lit \-,(l)it\ *or* **can·dle·light·ed** \-,(l)ī-təd\ *adjective* (1917)
: illuminated by candlelight ⟨a *candlelit* dinner⟩

Can·dle·mas \'kan-d°l-məs\ *noun* [Middle English *candelmasse*, from Old English *candelmæsse*, from *candel* + *mæsse* mass, feast; from the candles blessed and carried in celebration of the feast] (before 12th century)
: February 2 observed as a church festival in commemoration of the presentation of Christ in the temple and the purification of the Virgin Mary

can·dle·nut \-,nət\ *noun* (circa 1836)
: the oily seed of a tropical tree (*Aleurites moluccana*) of the spurge family used locally to make candles and commercially as a source of oil; *also* **:** this tree

can·dle·pin \-,pin\ *noun* (1901)
1 : a slender bowling pin tapering toward top and bottom
2 *plural but singular in construction* **:** a bowling game using candlepins and a smaller ball than that used in tenpins

can·dle·pow·er \-,pau̇-(ə)r\ *noun* (1877)
: luminous intensity expressed in candelas; *also* **:** CANDELA

can·dle·snuff·er \-,snə-fər\ *noun* (1552)
: an implement for snuffing candles that consists of a small hollow cone attached to a handle

can·dle·stick \-,stik\ *noun* (before 12th century)
: a holder with a socket for a candle

can·dle·wick \-,wik\ *noun* (before 12th century)
1 : the wick of a candle
2 : a soft cotton embroidery yarn; *also* **:** embroidery made with this yarn usually in tufts

can·dle·wood \-,wu̇d\ *noun* (1712)
1 : any of several trees or shrubs (as ocotillo) chiefly of resinous character
2 : slivers of resinous wood burned for light

can–do \'kan-'dü\ *adjective* (1945)
: characterized by eager willingness to accept and meet challenges ⟨a *can-do* attitude⟩

can·dor \'kan-dər, -,dȯr\ *noun* [French & Latin; French *candeur*, from Latin *candor*, from *candēre* — more at CANDID] (14th century)
1 a : WHITENESS, BRILLIANCE **b** *obsolete* **:** unstained purity
2 : freedom from prejudice or malice **:** FAIRNESS
3 *archaic* **:** KINDLINESS
4 : unreserved, honest, or sincere expression **:** FORTHRIGHTNESS ⟨the *candor* with which he

acknowledged a weakness in his own case —Aldous Huxley⟩

can·dour \'kan-dər\ *chiefly British variant of* CANDOR

¹can·dy \'kan-dē\ *noun, plural* **candies** [Middle English *sugre candy*, part translation of Middle French *sucre candi*, part translation of Old Italian *zucchero candi*, from *zucchero* sugar + Arabic *qandī* candied, from *qand* cane sugar] (15th century)
1 : crystallized sugar formed by boiling down sugar syrup
2 a : a confection made with sugar and often flavoring and filling **b :** a piece of such confection
— **candy** *adjective*

²candy *verb* **can·died; can·dy·ing** (1533)
transitive verb
1 : to encrust in or coat with sugar; *specifically* **:** to cook (as fruit or fruit peel) in a heavy syrup until glazed
2 : to make attractive **:** SWEETEN
3 : to crystallize into sugar
intransitive verb
: to become coated or encrusted with sugar crystals **:** become crystallized into sugar

candy floss *noun* (1951)
1 *British* **:** COTTON CANDY
2 *usually* **candyfloss** *British* **:** something attractive but insubstantial

candy striper *noun* [from the striped uniform worn suggesting the stripes on some sticks of candy] (1963)
: a teenage volunteer worker at a hospital

can·dy·tuft \'kan-dē-,təft\ *noun* [*Candy*, alteration of *Candia* Crete, Greek island + English *tuft*] (1664)
: any of a genus (*Iberis*) of plants of the mustard family cultivated for their white, pink, or purple flowers

¹cane \'kān\ *noun* [Middle English, from Middle French *cane*, from Old Provençal *cana*, from Latin *canna*, from Greek *kanna*, of Semitic origin; akin to Arabic *qanāh* hollow stick, reed] (14th century)
1 a (1) **:** a hollow or pithy and usually slender and flexible jointed stem (as of a reed) (2) **:** any of various slender woody stems; *especially* **:** an elongated flowering or fruiting stem (as of a rose) usually arising directly from the ground **b :** any of various tall woody grasses or reeds: as (1) **:** any of a genus (*Arundinaria*) of coarse grasses (2) **:** SUGARCANE (3) **:** SORGHUM
2 : cane dressed for use: as **a :** a cane walking stick; *broadly* **:** WALKING STICK **b :** a cane or rod for flogging **c :** RATTAN; *especially* **:** split rattan for wickerwork or basketwork
3 : a tiny glass rod used in decorative glasswork (as in millefiori and paperweights)

²cane *transitive verb* **caned; can·ing** (circa 1667)
1 : to beat with a cane ⟨he sat in a professor's chair and *caned* sophomores for blowing spitballs —H. L. Mencken⟩
2 : to weave or furnish with cane ⟨*cane* the seat of a chair⟩

cane·brake \'kān-,brāk\ *noun* (1769)
: a thicket of cane

can·er \'kā-nər\ *noun* (1868)
: one that canes chairs

ca·nes·cent \kə-'ne-s°nt, ka-\ *adjective* [Latin *canescent-, canescens*, present participle of *canescere*, inchoative of *canēre* to be gray, be white, from *canus* white, hoary — more at HARE] (circa 1828)
: growing white, whitish, or hoary; *especially* **:** having a fine grayish white pubescence ⟨*canescent* leaves⟩

cane sugar *noun* (1841)
: sugar from sugarcane

cane·ware \'kān-,war, -,wer\ *noun* [from its color] (1878)
: a buff or yellowish stoneware

ca·nic·o·la fever \kə-'ni-kə-lə-\ *noun* [New Latin *canicola*, from Latin *canis* dog + *-cola* inhabitant — more at HOUND, -COLOUS] (1943)
: an acute disease in humans and dogs characterized by gastroenteritis and mild jaundice and caused by a spirochete (*Leptospira canicola*)

ca·nic·u·lar \kə-'ni-kyə-lər\ *adjective* [Middle English *caniculer* of the star Sirius, from Late Latin *canicularis*, from Latin *Canicula* Sirius, diminutive of *canis*] (12th century)
: of or relating to the dog days

ca·nid \'ka-nəd, 'kā-\ *noun* [New Latin *Canidae*, from *Canis*, type genus, from Latin *canis*] (circa 1889)
: any of a family (Canidae) of carnivorous animals that includes the wolves, jackals, foxes, coyote, and the domestic dog

¹ca·nine \'kā-,nīn, *British also* 'ka-\ *noun* (15th century)
1 [Middle English, from Latin (*dens*) *caninus* canine tooth] **:** a conical pointed tooth; *especially* **:** one situated between the lateral incisor and the first premolar — see TOOTH illustration
2 : CANID; *also* **:** DOG 1a

²canine *adjective* [Latin *caninus*, from *canis* dog — more at HOUND] (1607)
1 : of or resembling that of a dog ⟨*canine* loyalty⟩
2 : of or relating to dogs or to the family (Canidae) including the canids

Ca·nis Ma·jor \,kā-nəs-'mā-jər, ,ka-\ *noun* [Latin (genitive *Canis Majoris*), literally, greater dog]
: a constellation to the southeast of Orion containing Sirius

Canis Mi·nor \-'mī-nər\ *noun* [Latin (genitive *Canis Minoris*), literally, lesser dog]
: a constellation to the east of Orion containing Procyon

can·is·ter *also* **can·nis·ter** \'ka-nə-stər\ *noun* [Latin *canistrum* basket, from Greek *kanastron* wicker basket, from *kanna* reed — more at CANE] (1711)
1 : an often cylindrical container for holding a usually specified object or substance ⟨a film *canister*⟩
2 : encased shot for close-range artillery fire
3 : a perforated metal box for gas masks with material to adsorb, filter, or detoxify airborne poisons and irritants

¹can·ker \'kaŋ-kər\ *noun* [Middle English, from Old North French *cancre*, from Latin *cancer* crab, cancer] (13th century)
1 a (1) **:** an erosive or spreading sore (2) **:** an area of necrosis in a plant; *also* **:** a plant disease characterized by cankers **b :** any of various disorders of animals marked by chronic inflammatory changes
2 *archaic* **:** a caterpillar destructive to plants
3 *chiefly dialect* **:** RUST 1
4 : a source of corruption or debasement
5 *chiefly dialect* **:** DOG ROSE
— **can·ker·ous** \'kaŋ-k(ə-)rəs\ *adjective*

²canker *verb* **can·kered; can·ker·ing** \'kaŋ-k(ə-)riŋ\ (14th century)
transitive verb
1 *obsolete* **:** to infect with a spreading sore
2 : to corrupt the spirit of
intransitive verb
1 : to become infested with canker
2 : to become corrupted

canker sore *noun* (circa 1909)
: a small painful ulcer especially of the mouth

can·ker·worm \'kaŋ-kər-,wərm\ *noun* (1530)
: either of two geometrid moths (*Alsophila pometaria* and *Paleacrita vernata*) and especially their larvae which are serious pests of fruit and shade trees

can·na \'ka-nə\ *noun* [New Latin, genus name, from Latin, reed — more at CANE] (1664)
: any of a genus (*Canna* of the family Cannaceae) of tropical herbs with simple stems, large leaves, and a terminal raceme of irregular flowers

can·na·bi·noid \kə-'na-bə-ˌnȯid\ *noun* [Latin *cannabis* + [1]-*in* + [1]-*oid*] (1970)
: any of various chemical constituents (as THC or cannabinol) of cannabis or marijuana

can·na·bi·nol \-ˌnȯl, -ˌnōl\ *noun* [Latin *cannabis* + [1]-*in* + [1]-*ol*] (1896)
: a physiologically inactive crystalline cannabinoid $C_{21}H_{26}O_2$

can·na·bis \'ka-nə-bəs\ *noun* [Latin, hemp, from Greek *kannabis;* akin to Old English *hænep* hemp] (1783)
1 : HEMP 1a
2 : any of the preparations (as marijuana or hashish) or chemicals (as THC) that are derived from the hemp and are psychoactive

canned \'kand\ *adjective* (1904)
1 a : prepared or recorded in advance; *especially* **:** prepared in standardized form for nonspecific use or wide distribution ⟨*canned* laughter⟩ ⟨*canned* music⟩ ⟨*canned* speeches⟩ **b :** lacking originality or individuality as if mass-produced ⟨*canned* sales pitch⟩
2 *slang* **:** DRUNK 1a

can·nel coal \'ka-nᵊl-\ *noun* [probably from English dialect *cannel* candle, from Middle English *candel*] (1610)
: a bituminous coal containing much volatile matter that burns brightly

can·nel·lo·ni \ˌka-nə-'lō-nē\ *noun plural but singular or plural in construction* [Italian, plural of *cannellone,* augmentative of *cannello* segment of cane stalk, from *canna*] (1906)
: boiled tube-shaped or rolled pasta filled with a meat, fish, cheese, or vegetable mixture and baked in a sauce

can·nery \'ka-nə-rē\ *noun, plural* **-ner·ies** (1870)
: a factory for the canning of foods

can·ni·bal \'ka-nə-bəl\ *noun* [New Latin *Canibalis* Carib, from Spanish *Caníbal,* from Taino *Caniba,* of Cariban origin; akin to Carib *kariʔna* Carib, person] (1553)
: one that eats the flesh of its own kind ◇

can·ni·bal·ise *British variant of* CANNIBALIZE

can·ni·bal·ism \'ka-nə-bə-ˌli-zəm\ *noun* (1796)
1 : the usually ritualistic eating of human flesh by a human being
2 : the eating of the flesh of an animal by another animal of the same kind
3 : an act of cannibalizing something
— **can·ni·bal·is·tic** \ˌka-nə-bə-'lis-tik\ *adjective*

can·ni·bal·ize \'ka-nə-bə-ˌlīz\ *verb* **-ized; -iz·ing** (1943)
transitive verb
1 a : to take salvageable parts from (as a disabled machine) for use in building or repairing another machine **b :** to make use of (a part taken from one thing) in building or repairing something else
2 : to deprive of an essential part or element in creating or sustaining another facility or enterprise ⟨the energy system has begun *cannibalizing* the economic system it is supposed to fuel —Barry Commoner⟩
3 : to use or draw on material of (as another writer or an earlier work) ⟨a volume . . . that not only *cannibalizes* previous publications but is intended itself to be *cannibalized* —R. M. Adams⟩
4 : to take (sales) away from an existing product by selling or being sold as a similar but new product usually from the same manufacturer; *also* **:** to affect (as an existing product) adversely by cannibalizing sales
intransitive verb
1 : to practice cannibalism
2 : to cannibalize one unit for the sake of another of the same kind
— **can·ni·bal·i·za·tion** \ˌka-nə-bə-lə-'zā-shən\ *noun*

can·ni·kin \'ka-ni-kən\ *noun* [probably from obsolete Dutch *kanneken,* from Middle Dutch *canneken,* diminutive of *canne* can; akin to Old English *canne* can] (1570)
: a small can or drinking vessel

can·no·li \kə-'nō-lē, ka-\ *noun plural but singular or plural in construction* [Italian, plural of *cannolo* small tube, diminutive of *canna*] (1943)
: a deep-fried tube of pastry filled with sweetened and flavored ricotta cheese

[1]can·non \'ka-nən\ *noun, plural* **cannons** *or* **cannon** [Middle French *canon,* from Italian *cannone,* literally, large tube, augmentative of *canna* reed, tube, from Latin, cane, reed — more at CANE] (15th century)
1 *plural usually* **cannon a :** a large heavy gun usually mounted on a carriage **b :** a heavy-caliber automatic aircraft gun firing explosive shells
2 *or* **can·on :** the projecting part of a bell by which it is hung **:** EAR
3 : the part of the leg in which the cannon bone is found

[2]cannon (1691)
intransitive verb
: to discharge cannon
transitive verb
: CANNONADE

[1]can·non·ade \ˌka-nə-'nād\ *noun* (1562)
1 : a heavy fire of artillery
2 : an attack (as with words) likened to artillery **:** BOMBARDMENT

[2]cannonade *verb* **-ad·ed; -ad·ing** (circa 1670)
transitive verb
: to attack with or as if with artillery
intransitive verb
: to deliver artillery fire

[1]can·non·ball \'ka-nən-ˌbȯl\ *noun* (1663)
1 : a usually round solid missile made for firing from a cannon
2 : a jump into water made with the arms holding the knees tight against the chest
3 : a hard flat tennis service
4 : an express train

[2]cannonball *intransitive verb* (1951)
: to travel with great speed

cannon bone *noun* [French *canon,* literally, cannon] (1834)
: a bone in hoofed mammals that extends from the knee or hock to the fetlock

can·non·eer \ˌka-nə-'nir\ *noun* (1562)
: an artillery gunner

cannon fodder *noun* (circa 1891)
: soldiers regarded or treated as expendable in battle

can·non·ry \'ka-nən-rē\ *noun, plural* **-ries** (circa 1840)
: a battery of cannons or cannon fire

can·not \'ka-(ˌ)nät; kə-'nät, ka-'\ (15th century)
: can not
— **cannot but** *or* **cannot help but** *also* **cannot help :** to be unable to do otherwise than

can·nu·la \'kan-yə-lə\ *noun, plural* **-las** *or* **-lae** \-ˌlē, -ˌlī\ [New Latin, from Latin, diminutive of *canna* reed — more at CANE] (1684)
: a small tube for insertion into a body cavity or into a duct or vessel

can·nu·lar \'kan-yə-lər\ *adjective* (1823)
: TUBULAR

[1]can·ny \'ka-nē\ *adjective* **can·ni·er; -est** [[1]*can*] (1596)
1 : CLEVER, SHREWD; *also* **:** PRUDENT
2 *chiefly Scottish* **a :** CAREFUL, STEADY; *also* **:** RESTRAINED **b :** QUIET, SNUG ⟨then *canny,* in some cozy place, they close the day —Robert Burns⟩
— **can·ni·ly** \'ka-nᵊl-ē\ *adverb*
— **can·ni·ness** \'ka-nē-nəs\ *noun*

[2]canny *adverb* (circa 1796)
Scottish **:** in a canny manner **:** CAREFULLY

[1]ca·noe \kə-'nü\ *noun* [French, from New Latin *canoa,* from Spanish, from Arawakan, of Cariban origin; akin to Carib *kana:wa* canoe] (1555)
: a light narrow boat with both ends sharp that is usually propelled by paddling

[2]canoe *verb* **ca·noed; ca·noe·ing** (1794)
transitive verb
: to transport in a canoe; *also* **:** to travel by canoe down (a river)
intransitive verb
: to go or travel in a canoe
— **ca·noe·able** \-ə-bəl\ *adjective*
— **ca·noe·ist** *noun*

can of worms (1962)
: PANDORA'S BOX

ca·no·la \kə-'nō-lə\ *noun* [*Can*ada *o*il—*l*ow *a*cid] (1979)
1 : a rape plant of an improved variety having seeds that are low in erucic acid and are the source of canola oil
2 : CANOLA OIL

canola oil *noun* (1986)
: an edible vegetable oil obtained from the seeds of canola that is high in monounsaturated fatty acids

[1]can·on \'ka-nən\ *noun* [Middle English, from Old English, from Late Latin, from Latin, ruler, rule, model, standard, from Greek *kanōn*] (before 12th century)
1 a : a regulation or dogma decreed by a church council **b :** a provision of canon law
2 [Middle English, probably from Old French, from Late Latin, from Latin, model] **:** the most solemn and unvarying part of the Mass including the consecration of the bread and wine
3 [Middle English, from Late Latin, from Latin, standard] **a :** an authoritative list of books accepted as Holy Scripture **b :** the authentic works of a writer **c :** a sanctioned or accepted group or body of related works ⟨the *canon* of great literature⟩
4 a : an accepted principle or rule **b :** a criterion or standard of judgment **c :** a body of principles, rules, standards, or norms
5 [Late Greek *kanōn,* from Greek, model] **:** a contrapuntal musical composition in two or more voice parts in which the melody is imitated exactly and completely by the successive voices though not always at the same pitch
synonym see LAW

[2]canon *noun* [Middle English *canoun,* from Anglo-French *canunie,* from Late Latin *canonicus* one living under a rule, from Latin, according to rule, from Greek *kanonikos,* from *kanōn*] (13th century)

◇ WORD HISTORY
cannibal On Christopher Columbus's first voyage to the New World, the mainly Arawakan-speaking peoples whom he encountered in Cuba and Hispaniola told him about a people living to their east, who periodically raided them and whom they greatly feared. In his log Columbus recorded a number of phonetically similar names for this people, including *canibales* and *caribes.* The Spanish court historian Petrus Martyr wrote a Latin account of Columbus's discoveries, first printed in 1516, that used these two words and widely disseminated them throughout Europe. In Petrus Martyr's words, "the inhabitants of these lands assert that the *Canibales* or *Caribes* are eaters of human flesh." Subsequently, the meaning of the two words diverged. *Caribes* was applied to the Carib-speaking peoples of the Lesser Antilles and northern South America who were so feared by the Arawakans; it is also ultimately the base of the word *Caribbean. Canibales,* on the other hand, passed into English as *cannibal* and became a generic word for any creature that eats the flesh of its own kind.

\ə\ **abut** \ᵊ\ **kitten** \ər\ **further** \a\ **ash** \ā\ **ace**
\ä\ **mop, mar** \aù\ **out** \ch\ **chin** \e\ **bet** \ē\ **easy**
\g\ **go** \i\ **hit** \ī\ **ice** \j\ **job** \ŋ\ **sing** \ō\ **go**
\ȯ\ **law** \ȯi\ **boy** \th\ **thin** \ṯẖ\ **the** \ü\ **loot** \ù\ **foot**
\y\ **yet** \zh\ **vision** *see also* Guide to Pronunciation

1 : a clergyman belonging to the chapter or the staff of a cathedral or collegiate church
2 : CANON REGULAR

ca·ñon \'kan-yən\ *variant of* CANYON

can·on·ess \'ka-nə-nəs\ *noun* (1682)
1 : a woman living in community under a religious rule but not under a perpetual vow
2 : a member of a Roman Catholic congregation of women corresponding to canons regular

ca·non·ic \kə-'nä-nik\ *adjective* (15th century)
1 : CANONICAL
2 : of or relating to musical canon

ca·non·i·cal \-ni-kəl\ *adjective* (15th century)
1 : of, relating to, or forming a canon
2 : conforming to a general rule or acceptable procedure : ORTHODOX
3 : of or relating to a clergyman who is a canon
4 : reduced to the canonical form ⟨a *canonical* matrix⟩
— **ca·non·i·cal·ly** \-k(ə-)lē\ *adverb*

canonical form *noun* (1851)
: the simplest form of something; *specifically*
: the form of a square matrix that has zero elements everywhere except along the principal diagonal

canonical hour *noun* (15th century)
1 : a time of day canonically appointed for an office of devotion
2 : one of the daily offices of devotion that compose the Divine Office and include matins with lauds, prime, terce, sext, none, vespers, and compline

ca·non·i·cals \kə-'nä-ni-kəlz\ *noun plural* (1748)
: the vestments prescribed by canon for an officiating clergyman

can·on·ic·i·ty \,ka-nə-'ni-sə-tē\ *noun* (1797)
: the quality or state of being canonical

can·on·ist \'ka-nə-nist\ *noun* (1542)
: a specialist in canon law

can·on·ize \'ka-nə-,nīz\ *transitive verb* **can·on·ized** \-,nīzd\; *in* "Hamlet" *usually* kə-'nä-,nīzd\; **can·on·iz·ing** [Middle English, from Medieval Latin *canonizare*, from Late Latin *canon* catalog of saints, from Latin, standard] (14th century)
1 : to declare (a deceased person) an officially recognized saint
2 : to make canonical
3 : to sanction by ecclesiastical authority
4 : to attribute authoritative sanction or approval to
5 : to treat as illustrious, preeminent, or sacred
— **can·on·i·za·tion** \,ka-nə-nə-'zā-shən\ *noun*

canon law *noun* (1552)
: the usually codified law governing a church

canon lawyer *noun* (circa 1859)
: CANONIST

canon regular *noun, plural* **canons regular** (14th century)
: a member of one of several Roman Catholic religious institutes of regular priests living in community under a usually Augustinian rule

can·on·ry \'ka-nən-rē\ *noun, plural* **-ries** (15th century)
: the office of a canon; *also* : the endowment that financially supports a canon

ca·no·pic jar \kə-'nō-pik-, -'nä-\ *noun* [*Canopus,* Egypt] (1893)
: a jar in which the ancient Egyptians preserved the viscera of a deceased person usually for burial with the mummy

Ca·no·pus \kə-'nō-pəs\ *noun* [Latin, from Greek *Kanōpos*] **:** a star of the first magnitude in the constellation Carina not visible north of 37° latitude

¹can·o·py \'ka-nə-pē\ *noun, plural* **-pies** [Middle En-

canopic jar

glish *canope,* from Medieval Latin *canopeum* mosquito net, from Latin *conopeum,* from Greek *kōnōpion,* from *kōnōps* mosquito] (14th century)
1 a : a cloth covering suspended over a bed **b :** a cover (as of cloth) fixed or carried above a person of high rank or a sacred object : BALDACHIN **c :** a protective covering: as (1) : the uppermost spreading branchy layer of a forest (2) : AWNING, MARQUEE
2 : an ornamental rooflike structure
3 a : the transparent enclosure over an airplane cockpit **b :** the fabric part of a parachute that catches the air
word history see CANAPÉ

²canopy *transitive verb* **-pied; -py·ing** (1599)
: to cover with or as if with a canopy

ca·no·rous \kə-'nōr-əs, -'nòr-; 'ka-nə-rəs\ *adjective* [Latin *canorus,* from *canor* melody, from *canere* to sing — more at CHANT] (1646)
: pleasant sounding : MELODIOUS
— **ca·no·rous·ly** *adverb*
— **ca·no·rous·ness** *noun*

canst \kən(t)st, 'kan(t)st\ *archaic present 2d singular of* CAN

¹cant \'kant\ *adjective* [Middle English, probably from (assumed) Middle Low German *kant*] (14th century)
dialect English : LIVELY, LUSTY

²cant (circa 1543)
transitive verb
1 : to give a cant or oblique edge to : BEVEL
2 : to set at an angle : TILT
3 *chiefly British* : to throw with a lurch
intransitive verb
1 : to pitch to one side : LEAN
2 : SLOPE

³cant *noun* [Middle English *cante* edge, probably from Middle Dutch or Old North French; Middle Dutch, edge, corner, from Old North French, edge, from Latin *canthus, cantus* iron tire, perhaps of Celtic origin; akin to Welsh *cant* rim; perhaps akin to Greek *kanthos* corner of the eye] (1603)
1 *obsolete* : CORNER, NICHE
2 : an external angle (as of a building)
3 : a log with one or more squared sides
4 a : an oblique or slanting surface **b :** INCLINATION, SLOPE

⁴cant *adjective* (1663)
1 : having canted corners or sides
2 : INCLINED 2

⁵cant *intransitive verb* [probably from Old North French *canter* to tell, literally, to sing, from Latin *cantare* — more at CHANT] (1567)
1 : to talk or beg in a whining or singsong manner
2 : to speak in cant or jargon
3 : to talk hypocritically

⁶cant *noun* (1640)
1 : affected singsong or whining speech
2 a : the private language of the underworld **b** *obsolete* : the phraseology peculiar to a religious class or sect **c** : JARGON 2
3 : a set or stock phrase
4 : the expression or repetition of conventional or trite opinions or sentiments; *especially* : the insincere use of pious words

can't \'kant, 'kànt, 'känt, *especially Southern* 'kānt\ (circa 1652)
: can not

Can·tab \'kan-,tab\ *noun* [by shortening] (1750)
: CANTABRIGIAN

can·ta·bi·le \kän-'tä-bi-,lā, -lē\ *adverb or adjective* [Italian, from Late Latin *cantabilis* worthy to be sung, from *cantare*] (circa 1724)
: in a singing manner — often used as a direction in music

Can·ta·brig·i·an \,kan-tə-'bri-j(ē-)ən\ *noun* [Medieval Latin *Cantabrigia* Cambridge] (circa 1540)
1 : a student or graduate of Cambridge University

2 : a native or resident of Cambridge, Mass.
— **Cantabrigian** *adjective*

can·ta·la \kan-'tä-lə\ *noun* [New Latin, specific epithet of *Agave cantala,* perhaps from Sanskrit *kaṇṭala* babul, from *kaṇṭa* thorn] (1911)
: a hard fiber produced from the leaves of an agave (*Agave cantala*)

can·ta·loupe *also* **can·ta·loup** \'kan-t³l-,ōp *also* -,üp\ *noun* [*Cantalupo,* former papal villa near Rome, Italy] (1739)
1 : a muskmelon (*Cucumis melo reticulatus*) having a rind with netted tracery and reddish orange flesh
2 : any of several muskmelons resembling the cantaloupe; *broadly* : MUSKMELON

can·tan·ker·ous \kan-'taŋ-k(ə-)rəs, kən-\ *adjective* [perhaps irregular from obsolete *contack* (contention)] (1772)
: difficult or irritating to deal with
— **can·tan·ker·ous·ly** *adverb*
— **can·tan·ker·ous·ness** *noun*

can·ta·ta \kən-'tä-tə\ *noun* [Italian, from Latin, from feminine of *cantatus,* past participle of *cantare*] (1724)
: a composition for one or more voices usually comprising solos, duets, recitatives, and choruses and sung to an instrumental accompaniment

can·ta·trice \,kän-tə-'trē-(,)chā, ,kän-tə-'trēs\ *noun, plural* **-trices** \-'trē-(,)chāz, -'trēs, -'trē-səz\ *or* **-tri·ci** \,kän-tə-'trē-(,)chē\ [Italian & French, from Italian, from Late Latin *cantatric-, cantatrix,* feminine of Latin *cantator* singer, from *cantare*] (1803)
: a woman who is a singer; *especially* : an opera singer

cant dog *noun* [³*cant*] (1850)
: PEAVEY

can·teen \kan-'tēn\ *noun* [French *cantine* bottle case, sutler's shop, from Italian *cantina* wine cellar, probably from *canto* corner, from Latin *canthus* iron tire — more at CANT] (1737)
1 a : a portable chest with compartments for carrying bottles or for cooking and eating utensils **b :** a flask for carrying liquids (as on a hike) **c :** MESS KIT **d** *British* : a chest for storing flatware
2 a : a bar at a military post or camp **b :** a general store at a military post : EXCHANGE **c :** an establishment that serves as an informal social club (as for soldiers or a community's teenagers) **d :** a small cafeteria or snack bar

¹cant·er \'kan-tər\ *noun* (1609)
: one that uses cant: as **a :** BEGGAR, VAGABOND **b :** a user of professional or religious cant

²can·ter \'kan-tər\ *verb* [short for obsolete *canterbury,* noun (canter), from *Canterbury,* England; from the supposed gait of pilgrims riding to Canterbury] (1706)
intransitive verb
1 : to move at or as if at a canter : LOPE
2 : to ride a horse at a canter ◇

◇ WORD HISTORY

canter In the Middle Ages, the town of Canterbury in southwest England became a popular pilgrimage site after the canonization of Thomas à Becket, who was murdered in Canterbury cathedral in 1170. A classic of medieval literature, Geoffrey Chaucer's *Canterbury Tales,* used a pilgrimage to the town as the frame for a set of stories told by a group of fictional pilgrims in the course of their journey. In the 17th century, the word *canterbury* was applied to a horse's gait that is slower and smoother than a gallop, allegedly because pilgrims traveling to Canterbury on horseback rode at that gait, though by this date the era of such pilgrimages had long passed and was largely remembered through Chaucer. In reference to a horse's gait, *canterbury* came to be used as a verb and was then shortened to *canter.*

transitive verb
: to cause to go at a canter
³can·ter *noun* (1755)
1 : a 3-beat gait resembling but smoother and slower than the gallop
2 : a ride at a canter
Can·ter·bury bell \'kan-tə(r)-,ber-ē-, -,b(ə-)rē-\ *noun* [*Canterbury*, England] (1578)
: any of several bellflowers (as *Campanula medium*) cultivated for their showy flowers
can·thar·i·din \kan-'thar-ə-d°n, -'ther-\ *noun* (1819)
: a bitter crystalline compound $C_{10}H_{12}O_4$ that is the active blister-producing ingredient of cantharides
can·tha·ris \'kan(t)-thə-rəs\ *noun, plural* **can·thar·i·des** \kan-'thar-ə-,dēz\ [Middle English & Latin; Middle English *cantharide*, from Latin *cantharid-, cantharis*, from Greek *kantharid-, kantharis*] (14th century)
1 : SPANISH FLY 1
2 *plural but singular or plural in construction* **:** a preparation of dried beetles (as Spanish flies) used in medicine as a counterirritant and formerly as an aphrodisiac
can·tha·xan·thin \,kan(t)-thə-'zan-,thin\ *noun* [International Scientific Vocabulary *cantha-* (from New Latin *Cantharellus cinnabarinus*, mushroom species from which it was obtained) + *xanth-* + ¹-*in*] (circa 1951)
: a carotenoid $C_{40}H_{52}O_2$ used especially as a color additive for food
cant hook *noun* [³*cant*] (circa 1848)
: a lumberman's lever that has a pivoting hooked arm and a blunt often toothed metal cap at one end — compare PEAVEY
can·thus \'kan(t)-thəs\ *noun, plural* **can·thi** \'kan-,thī, -,thē\ [Late Latin, from Greek *kanthos* — more at CANT] (1646)
: either of the angles formed by the meeting of an eye's upper and lower eyelids
can·ti·cle \'kan-ti-kəl\ *noun* [Middle English, from Latin *canticulum*, diminutive of *canticum* song, from *cantus*, past participle of *canere*] (13th century)
: SONG; *specifically* **:** one of several liturgical songs (as the Magnificat) taken from the Bible
Canticle of Canticles (circa 1934)
: SONG OF SOLOMON
Canticles *noun plural but singular in construction* (15th century)
: SONG OF SOLOMON
can·ti·le·na \,kan-tə-'lā-nə, -'lē-\ *noun* [Italian, from Latin, song, from *cantus*] (circa 1740)
: a vocal or instrumental passage of sustained lyricism
¹can·ti·le·ver \'kan-tə-,lē-vər, -,le-\ *noun* [perhaps from ³*cant* + -*i-* + *lever*] (1667)
: a projecting beam or member supported at only one end: as **a :** a bracket-shaped member supporting a balcony or a cornice **b :** either of the two beams or trusses that project from piers toward each other and that when joined directly or by a suspended connecting member form a span of a cantilever bridge — see BRIDGE illustration
²cantilever (1902)
transitive verb
1 : to support by a cantilever ⟨a *cantilevered* shelf⟩
2 : to build as a cantilever
intransitive verb
: to project as a cantilever
can·til·late \'kan-t°l-,āt\ *transitive verb* **-lated; -lat·ing** [Latin *cantilatus*, past participle of *cantilare* to sing, perhaps from *cantilena*] (circa 1828)
: to recite with musical tones
— can·til·la·tion \,kan-t°l-'ā-shən\ *noun*
can·ti·na \kan-'tē-nə\ *noun* [American Spanish, from Spanish, canteen, from Italian, wine cellar — more at CANTEEN] (1844)
1 *Southwest* **:** a pouch or bag at the pommel of a saddle
2 *Southwest* **:** a small barroom **:** SALOON

cant·ing \'kan-tiŋ\ *adjective* [⁵*cant*] (1663)
: affectedly pious or righteous
can·tle \'kan-t°l\ *noun* [Middle English *cantel*, from Old North French, diminutive of *can* edge, corner — more at CANT] (14th century)
1 : a segment cut off or out of something **:** PART, PORTION
2 : the upward projecting rear part of a saddle
can·to \'kan-(,)tō\ *noun, plural* **cantos** [Italian, from Latin *cantus* song, from *canere* to sing — more at CHANT] (1590)
: one of the major divisions of a long poem
¹can·ton \'kan-t°n, -,tän\ *noun* [Middle French, from Italian *cantone*, from *canto* corner, from Latin *canthus* iron tire — more at CANT] (1522)
: a small territorial division of a country: as **a :** one of the states of the Swiss confederation **b :** a division of a French arrondissement
²canton *noun* [Middle French, from Old Provençal, from *cant* edge, corner, from Latin *canthus*] (1572)
1 *obsolete* **:** DIVISION, SECTION
2 : the top inner quarter of a flag
3 : the dexter chief region of a heraldic field
— can·ton·al \'kan-t°n-əl, kan-'tä-n°l\ *adjective*
Can·ton·ese \,kan-t°n-'ēz, -'ēs\ *noun, plural* **Cantonese** (1857)
1 : a native or inhabitant of Canton, China
2 : the dialect of Chinese spoken in and around Canton
3 : a style of Chinese cooking that is typically based on mild spices
— Cantonese *adjective*
can·ton flannel \'kan-,tän-, -t°n-\ *noun, often C capitalized* [*Canton*, China] (circa 1879)
: FLANNEL 1c
can·ton·ment \kan-'tōn-mənt, -'tän- *also* -'tün-\ *noun* (1756)
1 : usually temporary quarters for troops
2 : a permanent military station in India
Can·ton ware \'kan-,tän-\ *noun* (circa 1902)
: ceramic ware exported from China especially during the 18th and 19th centuries by way of Canton and including blue-and-white and enameled porcelain and various ornamented stonewares
can·tor \'kan-tər\ *noun* [Latin, singer, from *canere* to sing] (1538)
1 : a choir leader **:** PRECENTOR
2 : a synagogue official who sings or chants liturgical music and leads the congregation in prayer
— can·to·ri·al \kan-'tōr-ē-əl, -'tór-\ *adjective*
can·trip \'kan-trəp\ *noun* [probably alteration of *caltrop*] (1719)
1 *chiefly Scottish* **:** a witch's trick **:** SPELL
2 *chiefly British* **:** HOCUS-POCUS 2
can·tus \'kan-təs\ *noun, plural* **can·tus** \'kan-təs, 'kan-,tüs\ (1590)
1 : CANTUS FIRMUS
2 : the principal melody or voice
cantus fir·mus \-'fir-məs, -'fər-\ *noun* [Medieval Latin, literally, fixed song] (1847)
1 : the plainsong or simple Gregorian melody originally sung in unison and prescribed as to form and use by ecclesiastical tradition
2 : a melodic theme or subject; *especially* **:** one for contrapuntal treatment
canty \'kan-tē\ *adjective* [¹*cant*] (1720)
dialect British **:** CHEERFUL, SPRIGHTLY
Ca·nuck \kə-'nək *sometimes* -'nùk\ *noun* [origin unknown] (1835)
: a Canadian and especially a French Canadian
¹can·vas *also* **can·vass** \'kan-vəs\ *noun* [Middle English *canevas*, from Old North French, from (assumed) Vulgar Latin *cannabaceus* hempen, from Latin *cannabis* hemp — more at CANNABIS] (13th century)
1 : a firm closely woven cloth usually of linen, hemp, or cotton used for clothing and formerly much used for tents and sails
2 : a set of sails **:** SAIL

3 : a piece of canvas used for a particular purpose
4 : TENT; *also* **:** a group of tents
5 a : a piece of cloth backed or framed as a surface for a painting; *also* **:** the painting on such a surface **b :** the background, setting, or scope of an historical or fictional account or narrative
6 : a coarse cloth so woven as to form regular meshes for working with the needle
7 : the canvas-covered floor of a boxing or wrestling ring
— can·vas·like \-vəs-,līk\ *adjective*
²canvas *transitive verb* **-vased** *or* **-vassed; -vas·ing** *or* **-vass·ing** (1556)
: to cover, line, or furnish with canvas
can·vas·back \'kan-vəs-,bak\ *noun* (1782)
: a North American wild duck (*Aythya valisineria*) that has a reddish brown head, black breast, and whitish body and is characterized especially by the elongate sloping profile of the bill and head
¹can·vass *also* **can·vas** \'kan-vəs\ (1508)
transitive verb
1 *obsolete* **:** to toss in a canvas sheet in sport or punishment
2 a : to examine in detail; *specifically* **:** to examine (votes) officially for authenticity **b :** DISCUSS, DEBATE
3 : to go through (a district) or go to (persons) in order to solicit orders or political support or to determine opinions or sentiments
intransitive verb
: to seek orders or votes **:** SOLICIT
— can·vass·er *or* **can·vas·er** *noun*
²canvass *also* **canvas** *noun* (circa 1611)
: the act or an instance of canvassing; *especially* **:** a personal solicitation of votes or survey of public opinion
can·yon \'kan-yən\ *noun* [American Spanish *cañón*, probably alteration of obsolete Spanish *callón*, augmentative of *calle* street, from Latin *callis* footpath] (1837)
: a deep narrow valley with steep sides and often with a stream flowing through it
can·zo·ne \kan-'zō-nē, känt-'sō-(,)nā\ *noun, plural* **-nes** \-nēz, -(,)nāz\ *or* **-ni** \-nē\ [Italian, from Latin *cantion-, cantio* song, from *canere* to sing — more at CHANT] (1589)
1 : a medieval Italian or Provençal lyric poem
2 : the musical setting of a canzone
can·zo·net \,kan-zə-'net\ *noun* [Italian *canzonetta*, diminutive of *canzone*] (1588)
1 : a light usually strophic song
2 : a part-song resembling but less elaborate than a madrigal
caou·tchouc \'kaù-,chùk, -,chük, -,chü\ *noun* [French, from obsolete Spanish *cauchuc* (now *caucho*), from Quechua *kawchu*] (1775)
: ¹RUBBER 2a
¹cap \'kap\ *noun, often attributive* [Middle English *cappe*, from Old English *cæppe*, from Late Latin *cappa* head covering, cloak] (before 12th century)
1 a : a head covering especially with a visor and no brim **b :** a distinctive head covering emblematic of a position or office: as (1) **:** a cardinal's biretta (2) **:** MORTARBOARD
2 : a natural cover or top: as **a :** an overlying rock layer that is usually hard to penetrate **b** (1) **:** PILEUS (2) **:** CALYPTRA **c :** the top of a bird's head or a patch of distinctively colored feathers in this area
3 a : something that serves as a cover or protection especially for a tip, knob, or end ⟨a bottle *cap*⟩ **b :** a fitting for closing the end of a tube (as a water pipe or electric conduit) **c** *British* **:** CERVICAL CAP
4 : an overlaying or covering structure

\ə\ abut \ᵊ\ kitten \ər\ further \a\ ash \ā\ ace
\ä\ mop, mar \aù\ out \ch\ chin \e\ bet \ē\ easy
\g\ go \i\ hit \ī\ ice \j\ job \ŋ\ sing \ō\ go
\ò\ law \ói\ boy \th\ thin \th\ the \ü\ loot \ù\ foot
\y\ yet \zh\ vision *see also* Guide to Pronunciation

5 : a paper or metal container holding an explosive charge (as for a toy pistol)
6 : an upper limit (as on expenditures) : CEILING
7 : the symbol ∩ indicating the intersection of two sets — compare CUP 9
8 : a cluster of molecules or chemical groups bound to one end or a region of a cell, virus, or molecule
— cap in hand : in a respectful, humble, or sometimes fearful manner

²cap *verb* **capped; cap·ping** (15th century)
transitive verb
1 a : to provide or protect with a cap **b :** to give a cap to as a symbol of honor, rank, or achievement
2 : to form a cap over : CROWN ⟨the mountains were *capped* with mist —John Buchan⟩
3 a : to follow with something more noticeable or more significant : OUTDO **b :** CLIMAX
4 : to form a chemical cap on
intransitive verb
: to form or produce a chemical cap

ca·pa·bil·i·ty \ˌkā-pə-ˈbi-lə-tē\ *noun, plural* **-ties** (1587)
1 : the quality or state of being capable; *also* **:** ABILITY
2 : a feature or faculty capable of development **:** POTENTIALITY
3 : the facility or potential for an indicated use or deployment ⟨the *capability* of a metal to be fused⟩ ⟨nuclear *capability*⟩

ca·pa·ble \ˈkā-pə-bəl, *in rapid speech* ˈkāp-bəl\ *adjective* [Middle French or Late Latin; Middle French *capable*, from Late Latin *capabilis*, irregular from Latin *capere* to take — more at HEAVE] (1579)
1 : SUSCEPTIBLE ⟨a remark *capable* of being misunderstood⟩
2 *obsolete* **:** COMPREHENSIVE
3 : having attributes (as physical or mental power) required for performance or accomplishment ⟨is *capable* of intense concentration⟩
4 : having traits conducive to or features permitting ⟨this woman is *capable* of murder by violence —Robert Graves⟩ ⟨an outer coat of light color *capable* of reflecting solar heat —*Current Biography*⟩
5 : having legal right to own, enjoy, or perform
6 : having general efficiency and ability
— ca·pa·ble·ness \ˈkā-pə-bəl-nəs\ *noun*
— ca·pa·bly \-pə-blē\ *adverb*

ca·pa·cious \kə-ˈpā-shəs\ *adjective* [Latin *capac-, capax* capacious, capable, from Latin *capere*] (1614)
: containing or capable of containing a great deal
synonym see SPACIOUS
— ca·pa·cious·ly *adverb*
— ca·pa·cious·ness *noun*

ca·pac·i·tance \kə-ˈpa-sə-tən(t)s\ *noun* [*capacity*] (1893)
1 a : the property of an electric nonconductor that permits the storage of energy as a result of the separation of charge that occurs when opposite surfaces of the nonconductor are maintained at a difference of potential **b :** the measure of this property that is equal to the ratio of the charge on either surface to the potential difference between the surfaces
2 : a part of a circuit or network that possesses capacitance
— ca·pac·i·tive \-ˈpa-sə-tiv\ *adjective*
— ca·pac·i·tive·ly *adverb*

ca·pac·i·tate \kə-ˈpa-sə-ˌtāt\ *transitive verb* **-tat·ed; -tat·ing** (1657)
1 *archaic* **:** to make capable
2 : to cause (sperm) to undergo capacitation

ca·pac·i·ta·tion \kə-ˌpa-sə-ˈtā-shən\ *noun* (1951)
: the change undergone by sperm in the female reproductive tract that enables them to penetrate and fertilize an egg

ca·pac·i·tor \kə-ˈpa-sə-tər\ *noun* (1925)

: a device giving capacitance and usually consisting of conducting plates or foils separated by thin layers of dielectric (as air or mica) with the plates on opposite sides of the dielectric layers oppositely charged by a source of voltage and the electrical energy of the charged system stored in the polarized dielectric

¹ca·pac·i·ty \kə-ˈpa-sə-tē, -ˈpas-tē\ *noun, plural* **-ties** [Middle English *capacite*, from Middle French *capacité*, from Latin *capacitat-, capacitas*, from *capac-, capax*] (15th century)
1 : legal competency or fitness
2 a : the potential or suitability for holding, storing, or accommodating **b :** the maximum amount or number that can be contained or accommodated ⟨a jug with a one-gallon *capacity*⟩ ⟨the auditorium was filled to *capacity*⟩ — see METRIC SYSTEM table, WEIGHT table
3 a : an individual's mental or physical ability **:** APTITUDE, SKILL **b :** the faculty or potential for treating, experiencing, or appreciating ⟨*capacity* for love⟩
4 : DUTY, POSITION, ROLE ⟨will be happy to serve in any *capacity*⟩
5 : the facility or power to produce, perform, or deploy **:** CAPABILITY ⟨a plan to double the factory's *capacity*⟩; *also* **:** maximum output ⟨industries running at three-quarter *capacity*⟩
6 a : CAPACITANCE **b :** the quantity of electricity that a battery can deliver under specified conditions

²capacity *adjective* (1897)
: equaling maximum capacity ⟨a *capacity* crowd⟩

cap·a·pie *or* **cap·à·pie** \ˌka-pə-ˈpē, -ˈpā\ *adverb* [Middle French (*de*) *cap a pé* from head to foot] (1523)
: from head to foot ⟨armed *cap-a-pie* for battle⟩

¹ca·par·i·son \kə-ˈpar-ə-sən\ *noun* [Middle French *caparaçon*, from Old Spanish *caparazón*] (1579)
1 a : an ornamental covering for a horse **b :** decorative trappings and harness
2 : rich clothing **:** ADORNMENT

²caparison *transitive verb* (1594)
: to provide with or as if with a rich ornamental covering **:** ADORN

¹cape \ˈkāp\ *noun, often attributive* [Middle English *cap*, from Middle French, from Old Provençal, from Latin *caput* head — more at HEAD] (14th century)
1 : a point or extension of land jutting out into water as a peninsula or as a projecting point
2 *often capitalized* **:** CAPE COD COTTAGE

²cape *noun* [probably from Spanish *capa* cloak, from Late Latin *cappa* head covering, cloak] (circa 1578)
1 : a sleeveless outer garment or part of a garment that fits closely at the neck and hangs loosely over the shoulders
2 : the short feathers covering the shoulders of a fowl — see DUCK illustration

Cape buffalo \ˈkāp-\ *noun* [*Cape* of Good Hope, Africa] (circa 1890)
: the large reddish brown to black wild buffalo (*Syncerus caffer*) of sub-Saharan Africa — called also *African buffalo*

Cape Cod cottage \(ˈ)kāp-ˈkäd-\ *noun* [*Cape Cod,* Mass.] (1916)
: a compact rectangular dwelling of one or one-and-a-half stories usually with a central chimney and steep gable roof

Cape gooseberry *noun* (1833)
: any of several ground-cherries (especially *Physalis peruviana*) bearing edible acid berries; *also* **:** its berry

Cape Horn·er \ˌkāp-ˈhȯr-nər\ *noun* (1840)
: a ship that voyages around Cape Horn

cape·let \ˈkāp-lət\ *noun* (1912)
: a small cape usually covering the shoulders

cap·e·lin \ˈka-p(ə-)lən\ *noun* [Canadian French *capelan*, from French, codfish, from Old Provençal, chaplain, codfish, from Medi-

eval Latin *cappellanus* chaplain — more at CHAPLAIN] (1620)
: a small northern sea fish (*Mallotus villosus*) related to the smelts

Ca·pel·la \kə-ˈpe-lə\ *noun* [Latin, literally, she-goat, from *caper* he-goat — more at CAPRIOLE]
: a star of the first magnitude in Auriga

¹ca·per \ˈkā-pər\ *noun* [back-formation from earlier *capers* (taken as a plural), from Middle English *caperis*, from Latin *capparis*, from Greek *kapparis*] (14th century)
1 : any of a genus (*Capparis* of the family Capparidaceae, the caper family) of low prickly shrubs of the Mediterranean region; *especially* **:** one (*C. spinosa*) cultivated for its buds
2 : one of the greenish flower buds or young berries of the caper pickled and used as a seasoning or garnish

²caper *intransitive verb* **ca·pered; ca·per·ing** \-p(ə-)riŋ\ [probably by shortening & alteration from *capriole*] (1588)
: to leap or prance about in a playful manner

³caper *noun* (1592)
1 : a frolicsome leap
2 : a capricious escapade **:** PRANK
3 : an illegal or questionable act; *especially* **:** THEFT

cap·er·cail·lie \ˌka-pər-ˈkā-lē, -ˈkāl-yē\ *or* **cap·er·cail·zie** \-ˈkāl-zē\ *noun, plural* **-caillie** *or* **-cailzies** *also* **-caillies** *or* **-cailzie** [Scottish Gaelic *capalcoille*, literally, horse of the woods] (1536)
: the largest Old World grouse (*Tetrao urogallus*)

cape·skin \ˈkāp-ˌskin\ *noun* [*Cape* of Good Hope, Africa] (1919)
: a light flexible leather made from sheepskins with the natural grain retained and used especially for gloves and garments

Ca·pe·tian \kə-ˈpē-shən\ *adjective* [Hugh *Capet*] (1836)
: of or relating to the French royal house that ruled from 987 to 1328
— Capetian *noun*

cape·work \ˈkāp-ˌwərk\ *noun* (1926)
: the art of the bullfighter in working a bull with the cape

cap·ful \ˈkap-ˌfu̇l\ *noun* (1873)
: as much as a cap will hold ⟨a *capful* of detergent⟩

capful of wind (1719)
: a sudden light breeze

ca·pi·as \ˈkā-pē-əs\ *noun* [Middle English, from Latin, literally, you should seize, from *capere* to take — more at HEAVE] (15th century)
: an arrest warrant

cap·il·lar·i·ty \ˌka-pə-ˈlar-ə-tē\ *noun, plural* **-ties** (1830)
1 : the property or state of being capillary
2 : the action by which the surface of a liquid where it is in contact with a solid (as in a capillary tube) is elevated or depressed depending on the relative attraction of the molecules of the liquid for each other and for those of the solid

¹cap·il·lary \ˈka-pə-ˌler-ē, *British usually* kə-ˈpi-lə-rē\ *adjective* [French or Latin; French *capillaire*, from Latin *capillaris*, from *capillus* hair] (14th century)
1 a : resembling a hair especially in slender elongated form ⟨*capillary* leaves⟩ **b :** having a very small bore ⟨a *capillary* tube⟩
2 : involving, held by, or resulting from surface tension ⟨*capillary* water in the soil⟩
3 : of or relating to capillaries or capillarity

²capillary *noun, plural* **-lar·ies** (1667)
: a capillary tube; *especially* **:** any of the smallest blood vessels connecting arterioles with venules and forming networks throughout the body

capillary attraction *noun* (1813)
: the force of adhesion between a solid and a liquid in capillarity

¹**cap·i·tal** \'ka-pə-t³l, 'kap-t³l\ *noun* [Middle English *capitale*, modification of Old North French *capitel*, from Late Latin *capitellum* small head, top of column, diminutive of Latin *capit-, caput* head — more at HEAD] (13th century)
: the uppermost member of a column or pilaster crowning the shaft and taking the weight of the entablature — see COLUMN illustration

²**capital** *adjective* [Middle English, from Latin *capitalis*, from *capit-, caput*] (14th century)
1 *of a letter* : of or conforming to the series A, B, C, etc. rather than a, b, c, etc.
2 a : punishable by death ⟨a *capital* crime⟩ **b** : involving execution ⟨*capital* punishment⟩ **c** : most serious ⟨a *capital* error⟩
3 a : chief in importance or influence ⟨*capital* ships⟩ ⟨the *capital* importance of criticism in the work of creation itself —T. S. Eliot⟩ **b** : being the seat of government
4 : of or relating to capital; *especially* : relating to or being assets that add to the long-term net worth of a corporation ⟨*capital* improvements⟩
5 : EXCELLENT ⟨a *capital* book⟩

³**capital** *noun* [French or Italian; French, from Italian *capitale*, from *capitale*, adjective, chief, principal, from Latin *capitalis*] (circa 1639)
1 a (1) : a stock of accumulated goods especially at a specified time and in contrast to income received during a specified period; *also* : the value of these accumulated goods (2) : accumulated goods devoted to the production of other goods (3) : accumulated possessions calculated to bring in income **b** (1) : net worth (2) : CAPITAL STOCK **c** : persons holding capital **d** : ADVANTAGE, GAIN ⟨make *capital* of the situation⟩
2 [²*capital*] **a** : a capital letter; *especially* : an initial capital letter **b** : a letter belonging to a style of alphabet modeled on the style customarily used in inscriptions
3 [²*capital*] **a** : a city serving as a seat of government **b** : a city preeminent in some special activity ⟨the fashion *capital*⟩

capital gain *noun* (1921)
: the increase in value of an asset (as stock or real estate) between the time it is bought and the time it is sold

capital goods *noun plural* (1896)
: ³CAPITAL 1a(1), 1a(2)

capital–intensive *adjective* (1959)
: having a high capital cost per unit of output; *especially* : requiring greater expenditure in the form of capital than of labor

cap·i·tal·ise *British variant of* CAPITALIZE

cap·i·tal·ism \'ka-pə-t³l-,iz-əm, 'kap-t³l-, *British also* kə-'pi-t³l-\ *noun* (1877)
: an economic system characterized by private or corporate ownership of capital goods, by investments that are determined by private decision, and by prices, production, and the distribution of goods that are determined mainly by competition in a free market

¹**cap·i·tal·ist** \-ist\ *noun* (1792)
1 : a person who has capital especially invested in business; *broadly* : a person of wealth : PLUTOCRAT
2 : a person who favors capitalism

²**capitalist** *or* **cap·i·tal·is·tic** \,ka-pə-t³l-'is-tik, ,kap-t³l-, *British also* kə-,pi-t³l-\ *adjective* (1845)
1 : owning capital ⟨the *capitalist* class⟩
2 a : practicing or advocating capitalism ⟨*capitalist* nations⟩ **b** : marked by capitalism ⟨*capitalist* period of history⟩
— **cap·i·tal·is·ti·cal·ly** \-ti-k(ə-)lē\ *adverb*

cap·i·tal·i·za·tion \,ka-pə-t³l-ə-'zā-shən, ,kap-t³l-, *British also* kə-,pi-t³l-\ *noun* (1860)
1 a : the act or process of capitalizing **b** : a sum resulting from a process of capitalizing **c** : the total liabilities of a business including both ownership capital and borrowed capital **d**

: the total par value or the stated value of no-par issues of authorized capital stock
2 : the use of a capital letter in writing or printing

cap·i·tal·ize \'ka-pə-t³l-,īz, 'kap-t³l-, *British also* kə-'pi-t³l-\ *verb* **-ized; -iz·ing** (1764)
transitive verb
1 : to write or print with an initial capital or in capitals
2 a : to convert into capital ⟨*capitalize* the company's reserve fund⟩ **b** : to treat as capital rather than as an expense
3 a : to compute the present value of (an income extended over a period of time) **b** : to convert (a periodic payment) into an equivalent capital sum ⟨*capitalized* annuities⟩
4 : to supply capital for
intransitive verb
: to gain by turning something to advantage : PROFIT ⟨*capitalize* on an opponent's mistake⟩

cap·i·tal·ly \'ka-pə-t³l-ē, 'kap-t³l-\ *adverb* (1619)
1 : in a manner involving capital punishment
2 : in a capital manner : EXCELLENTLY

capital stock *noun* (1709)
1 : the outstanding shares of a joint-stock company considered as an aggregate
2 : CAPITALIZATION 1d
3 : the ownership element of a corporation divided into shares and represented by certificates

cap·i·tate \'ka-pə-,tāt\ *adjective* [Latin *capitatus* headed, from *capit-, caput* head] (1661)
1 : forming a head
2 : abruptly enlarged and globose

cap·i·ta·tion \,ka-pə-'tā-shən\ *noun* [Late Latin *capitation-, capitatio* poll tax, from Latin *capit-, caput*] (1641)
1 : a direct uniform tax imposed on each head or person : POLL TAX
2 : a uniform per capita payment or fee

cap·i·tol \'ka-pə-t³l, 'kap-t³l\ *noun* [Latin *Capitolium*, temple of Jupiter at Rome on the Capitoline hill] (1699)
1 a : a building in which a state legislative body meets **b** : a group of buildings in which the functions of state government are carried out
2 *capitalized* : the building in which the U.S. Congress meets at Washington

Capitol Hill *noun* [*Capitol Hill*, Washington, site of the U.S. Capitol] (1943)
: the legislative branch of the U.S. government

Cap·i·to·line \'ka-pə-t³l-,īn, *British usually* kə-'pi-tə-,līn\ *adjective* [Latin *capitolinus*, from *Capitolium*] (1667)
: of or relating to the smallest of the seven hills of ancient Rome, the temple on it, or the gods worshiped there

ca·pit·u·lar \kə-'pi-chə-lər\ *adjective* [Medieval Latin *capitularis*, from *capitulum*] (circa 1525)
: of or relating to an ecclesiastical chapter

ca·pit·u·lary \-,ler-ē\ *noun, plural* **-lar·ies** [Medieval Latin *capitulare*, literally, document divided into sections, from Late Latin *capitulum* section, chapter — more at CHAPTER] (1650)
: a civil or ecclesiastical ordinance; *also* : a collection of ordinances

ca·pit·u·late \kə-'pi-chə-,lāt\ *intransitive verb* **-lat·ed; -lat·ing** [Medieval Latin *capitulatus*, past participle of *capitulare* to distinguish by heads or chapters, from Late Latin *capitulum*] (1537)
1 *archaic* : PARLEY, NEGOTIATE
2 a : to surrender often after negotiation of terms **b** : to cease resisting : ACQUIESCE
synonym see YIELD

ca·pit·u·la·tion \kə-,pi-chə-'lā-shən\ *noun* (1535)
1 : a set of terms or articles constituting an agreement between governments
2 a : the act of surrendering or yielding **b** : the terms of surrender

ca·pit·u·lum \kə-'pi-chə-ləm\ *noun, plural* **-la** \-lə\ [New Latin, from Latin, small head — more at CHAPTER] (circa 1755)
1 : a rounded protuberance of an anatomical part (as a bone)
2 : a racemose inflorescence (as of the buttonbush) with the axis shortened and dilated to form a rounded or flattened cluster of sessile flowers — see INFLORESCENCE illustration

Cap·lets \'ka-pləts\ *trademark*
— used for capsule-shaped medicinal tablets

¹**ca·po** \'kā-(,)pō\ *noun, plural* **capos** [short for *capotasto*, from Italian, literally, head of fingerboard] (1926)
: a movable bar attached to the fingerboard of a fretted instrument to uniformly raise the pitch of all the strings

²**ca·po** \'kä-(,)pō, 'ka-\ *noun, plural* **capos** [Italian, head, chief, from Latin *caput*] (circa 1959)
: the head of a branch of a crime syndicate

ca·pon \'kā-,pän, -pən\ *noun* [Middle English, from Old English *capūn*, probably from Old North French *capon*, from Latin *capon-, capo;* akin to Lithuanian *kapoti* to mince, Greek *koptein* to cut] (before 12th century)
: a castrated male chicken

ca·po·na·ta \,kä-pə-'nä-tə\ *noun* [Italian, from Italian dialect (Sicily) *capunata*, perhaps from *capuni* capon, from Latin *capon-, capo*] (1951)
: a relish of chopped eggplant and assorted vegetables

ca·pote \kə-'pōt\ *noun* [French, from *cape* cloak, from Late Latin *cappa*] (1799)
: a usually long and hooded cloak or overcoat

cap·pel·let·ti \,ka-pə-'le-tē\ *noun plural but singular or plural in construction* [Italian, plural of *cappelletto*, diminutive of *cappello* hat, from Medieval Latin *cappellus* cap, diminutive of Late Latin *cappa* head covering — more at CAP] (1945)
: pasta in the form of little peaked hats filled with a savory mixture

cap·per \'ka-pər\ *noun* (1587)
1 : one that caps: as **a** : a device that fits caps on bottles **b** : FINALE, CLIMAX, CLINCHER
2 : a lure or decoy especially in an illicit or questionable activity : SHILL

cap·ping \'ka-piŋ\ *noun* (14th century)
: something that caps

cap·puc·ci·no \,ka-pə-'chē-(,)nō, ,kä-pù-\ *noun* [Italian, literally, Capuchin; from the likeness of its color to that of a Capuchin's habit] (1948)
: espresso coffee mixed with frothed hot milk or cream and often flavored with cinnamon

cap·ric acid \'ka-prik-\ *noun* [International Scientific Vocabulary, from Latin *capr-, caper* goat; from its odor — more at CAPRIOLE] (1836)
: a fatty acid $C_{10}H_{20}O_2$ found in fats and oils and used in flavors and perfumes

ca·pric·cio \kə-'prē-ch(ē-,)ō\ *noun, plural* **-cios** [Italian] (1601)
1 : FANCY, WHIMSY
2 : CAPER, PRANK
3 : an instrumental piece in free form usually lively in tempo and brilliant in style

ca·price \kə-'prēs\ *noun* [French, from Italian *capriccio* caprice, shudder, from *capo* head (from Latin *caput*) + *riccio* hedgehog, from Latin *ericius* — more at HEAD, URCHIN] (1667)
1 a : a sudden, impulsive, and seemingly unmotivated notion or action **b** : a sudden usually unpredictable condition, change, or series of changes ⟨the *caprices* of the weather⟩
2 : a disposition to do things impulsively

\ə\ abut \³\ kitten \ər\ further \a\ ash \ā\ ace
\ä\ mop, mar \aù\ out \ch\ chin \e\ bet \ē\ easy
\g\ go \i\ hit \ī\ ice \j\ job \ŋ\ sing \ō\ go
\ò\ law \òi\ boy \th\ thin \t̲h̲\ the \ü\ loot \ù\ foot
\y\ yet \zh\ vision *see also* Guide to Pronunciation

3 : CAPRICCIO 3 ☆

ca·pri·cious \kə-'pri-shəs, -'prē-\ *adjective* (1601)
: governed or characterized by caprice **:** IMPULSIVE, UNPREDICTABLE
synonym see INCONSTANT
— **ca·pri·cious·ly** *adverb*
— **ca·pri·cious·ness** *noun*

Cap·ri·corn \'ka-pri-ˌkȯrn\ *noun* [Middle English *Capricorne*, from Latin *Capricornus* (genitive *Capricorni*), from *caper* goat + *cornu* horn — more at HORN]
1 : a southern zodiacal constellation between Sagittarius and Aquarius
2 a : the 10th sign of the zodiac in astrology — see ZODIAC table **b :** one born under the sign of Capricorn

cap·ri·fi·ca·tion \ˌka-prə-fə-'kā-shən\ *noun* [Latin *caprification-, caprificatio*, from *caprificare* to pollinate by caprification, from *caprificus*] (1601)
: artificial pollination of figs that usually bear only pistillate flowers by hanging male flowering branches of the caprifig in the trees to facilitate pollen transfer by a wasp

cap·ri·fig \'ka-prə-ˌfig\ *noun* [Middle English *caprifige*, part translation of Latin *caprificus*, from *capr-, caper* goat + *ficus* fig — more at FIG] (15th century)
: a wild fig (*Ficus carica sylvestris*) of southern Europe and Asia Minor used for caprification of the edible fig; *also* **:** its fruit

cap·rine \'ka-ˌprīn\ *adjective* [Latin *caprinus*, from *capr-, caper*] (15th century)
: of, relating to, or being a goat ⟨*caprine* serum⟩ ⟨the *caprine* family⟩

cap·ri·ole \'ka-prē-ˌōl\ *noun* [Middle French or Old Italian; Middle French *capriole*, from Old Italian *capriola*, from *capriolo* roebuck, from Latin *capreolus* goat, roebuck, from *capr-, caper* he-goat; akin to Old English *hæfer* goat, Greek *kapros* wild boar] (1594)
1 : a playful leap **:** CAPER
2 *of a trained horse* **:** a vertical leap with a backward kick of the hind legs at the height of the leap
— **capriole** *intransitive verb*

ca·pri pants \kə-'prē-\ *noun plural, often C capitalized* [*Capri*, Italy] (circa 1956)
: close-fitting women's pants that end above the ankle — called also *capris*

cap·rock \'kap-ˌräk\ *noun* (1867)
: CAP 2a

ca·pro·ic acid \kə-'prō-ik-\ *noun* [International Scientific Vocabulary, from Latin *capr-, caper*] (circa 1847)
: a liquid fatty acid $C_6H_{12}O_2$ that is found as a glycerol ester in fats and oils or made synthetically and used in pharmaceuticals and flavors

cap·ro·lac·tam \ˌka-prō-'lak-ˌtam\ *noun* [*caproic* acid + *lactone* + *amide*] (1944)
: a white crystalline cyclic amide $C_6H_{11}NO$ used especially in making one type of nylon

ca·pryl·ic acid \kə-'pri-lik-\ *noun* [International Scientific Vocabulary *capryl*, a radical contained in it] (1845)
: a fatty acid $C_8H_{16}O_2$ of rancid odor occurring in fats and oils and used in perfumes

cap·sa·i·cin \kap-'sā-ə-sən\ *noun* [irregular from New Latin *Capsicum*] (circa 1890)
: a colorless irritant phenolic amide $C_{18}H_{27}NO_3$ that is found in various capsicums and that gives hot peppers their hotness

Cap·si·an \'kap-sē-ən\ *adjective* [French *capsien*, from Latin *Capsa* Gafsa, Tunisia] (1915)
: of or relating to a Paleolithic culture of northern Africa and southern Europe

cap·si·cum \'kap-si-kəm\ *noun* [New Latin, perhaps from Latin *capsa*] (1588)
1 : any of a genus (*Capsicum*) of tropical herbs and shrubs of the nightshade family widely cultivated for their many-seeded usually fleshy-walled berries — called also *pepper*

2 : the dried ripe fruit of some capsicums (as *C. frutescens*) used as a gastric and intestinal stimulant

cap·sid \'kap-səd\ *noun* [French *capside*, from Latin *capsa* case + French *-ide* ²*-id*] (1960)
: the outer protein shell of a virus particle

cap·size \'kap-ˌsīz, kap-'\ *verb* **cap·sized;** **cap·siz·ing** [perhaps from Spanish *capuzar* or Catalan *cabussar* to thrust (the head) under-water] (1788)
transitive verb
: to cause to overturn ⟨*capsize* a canoe⟩
intransitive verb
: to become upset or overturned **:** TURN OVER ⟨the canoe *capsized*⟩

cap sleeve *noun* (1926)
: a very short sleeve (as on a dress) that hangs over the edge of the shoulder without extending along the underside of the arm

cap·stan \'kap-stən, -ˌstan\ *noun* [Middle English, probably from Middle French *cabestant*] (14th century)
1 : a machine for moving or raising heavy weights that consists of a vertical drum which can be rotated and around which cable is turned
2 : a rotating shaft that drives tape at a constant speed in a recorder

cap·stone \'kap-ˌstōn\ *noun* [¹*cap*] (14th century)
1 : a coping stone **:** COPING
2 : the high point **:** crowning achievement

cap·su·lar \'kap-sə-lər\ *adjective* (circa 1730)
1 : of, relating to, or resembling a capsule
2 : CAPSULATED

cap·su·lat·ed \-ˌlā-təd\ *adjective* (1668)
: enclosed in a capsule

¹cap·sule \'kap-səl, -(ˌ)sül *also* -ˌsyü(ə)l\ *noun* [French, from Latin *capsula*, diminutive of *capsa* box — more at CASE] (circa 1693)
1 a : a membrane or sac enclosing a body part **b :** either of two layers of white matter in the cerebrum
2 : a closed receptacle containing spores or seeds: as **a :** a dry dehiscent usually many-seeded fruit composed of two or more carpels **b :** the spore case of a moss
3 : a shell usually of gelatin for packaging something (as a drug or vitamins); *also* **:** a usually medicinal or nutritional preparation for oral use consisting of the shell and its contents
4 : an often polysaccharide envelope surrounding a microorganism
5 : an extremely brief condensation **:** OUTLINE, SURVEY
6 a : a compact often sealed and detachable container or compartment **b :** a small pressurized compartment or vehicle (as for space flight or emergency escape)

²capsule *transitive verb* **cap·suled;** **cap·sul·ing** (1859)
1 : to equip with or enclose in a capsule
2 : to condense into or devise in a compact form

³capsule *adjective* (1938)
1 : extremely brief
2 : small and very compact

cap·sul·ize \'kap-sə-ˌlīz\ *transitive verb* **-ized; -iz·ing** (1945)
: CAPSULE

¹cap·tain \'kap-tən *also* 'kap-ᵊm\ *noun* [Middle English *capitane*, from Middle French *capitain*, from Late Latin *capitaneus*, adjective & noun, chief, from Latin *capit-, caput* head — more at HEAD] (14th century)
1 a (1) **:** a military leader **:** the commander of a unit or a body of troops (2) **:** a subordinate officer commanding under a sovereign or general (3) **:** a commissioned officer in the army, air force, or marine corps ranking above a first lieutenant and below a major **b :** a naval officer who is master or commander of a ship; *especially* **:** a commissioned officer in the navy ranking above a commander and below a commodore and in the coast guard ranking above a

commander and below a rear admiral **c :** a senior pilot who commands the crew of an airplane **d :** an officer in a police department or fire department in charge of a unit (as a precinct or company) and usually ranking above a lieutenant and below a chief
2 : one who leads or supervises: as **a :** a leader of a sports team or side **b :** HEADWAITER **c :** a person in charge of hotel bellhops — called also *bell captain*
3 : a person of importance or influence in a field ⟨*captains* of industry⟩
— **cap·tain·cy** \'kap-tən-sē\ *noun*
— **cap·tain·ship** \-ˌship\ *noun*

²captain *transitive verb* (1598)
: to be captain of **:** LEAD ⟨*captained* the football team⟩

captain's chair *noun* (1946)
: an armchair with a saddle seat and a low curved back with vertical spindles

captain's mast *noun* (1941)
: MAST 3

cap·tan \'kap-ˌtan\ *noun* [short for *mercaptan*] (1952)
: a fungicide $C_9H_8Cl_3NO_2S$ used on agricultural crops

¹cap·tion \'kap-shən\ *noun* [Middle English *capcioun*, from Latin *caption-, captio* act of taking, from *capere* to take — more at HEAVE] (1670)
1 : the part of a legal document that shows where, when, and by what authority it was taken, found, or executed
2 a : the heading especially of an article or document **:** TITLE **b :** the explanatory comment or designation accompanying a pictorial illustration **c :** a motion-picture subtitle
— **cap·tion·less** \-ləs\ *adjective*

²caption *transitive verb* **cap·tioned; cap·tion·ing** \-sh(ə-)niŋ\ (1901)
: to furnish with a caption

cap·tious \'kap-shəs\ *adjective* [Middle English *capcious*, from Middle French or Latin; Middle French *captieux*, from Latin *captiosus*, from *captio*] (14th century)
1 : marked by an often ill-natured inclination to stress faults and raise objections
2 : calculated to confuse, entrap, or entangle in argument
synonym see CRITICAL
— **cap·tious·ly** *adverb*
— **cap·tious·ness** *noun*

cap·ti·vate \'kap-tə-ˌvāt\ *transitive verb* **-vat·ed; -vat·ing** (circa 1555)
1 *archaic* **:** SEIZE, CAPTURE
2 : to influence and dominate by some special charm, art, or trait and with an irresistible appeal
synonym see ATTRACT
— **cap·ti·va·tion** \ˌkap-tə-'vā-shən\ *noun*
— **cap·ti·va·tor** \'kap-tə-ˌvā-tər\ *noun*

cap·tive \'kap-tiv\ *adjective* [Middle English, from Latin *captivus*, from *captus*, past participle of *capere*] (14th century)
1 a : taken and held as or as if a prisoner of war **b :** kept within bounds **:** CONFINED
2 : held under control of another but having the appearance of independence; *especially* **:** owned or controlled by another concern and

operated for its needs rather than for an open market ⟨a *captive* mine⟩

3 : being such involuntarily because of a situation that makes free choice or departure difficult ⟨the airline passengers were a *captive* audience⟩

— **captive** *noun*

cap·tiv·i·ty \kap-'ti-və-tē\ *noun* (14th century)
1 : the state of being captive ⟨some birds thrive in *captivity*⟩
2 *obsolete* **:** a group of captives

cap·to·pril \'kap-tə-ˌpril\ *noun* [mer*captan* + *-o-* + *proline* + *-il*, alteration of *-yl*] (1978)
: an antihypertensive drug $C_9H_{15}NO_3S$ that is an ACE inhibitor

cap·tor \'kap-tər, -ˌtȯr\ *noun* [Late Latin, from Latin *capere*] (circa 1688)
: one that has captured a person or thing

¹cap·ture \'kap-chər, -shər\ *noun* [Middle French, from Latin *captura*, from *captus*] (circa 1542)
1 : an act or instance of capturing: as **a :** an act of catching, winning, or gaining control by force, stratagem, or guile **b :** a move in a board game (as chess or checkers) that gains an opponent's piece **c :** the absorption by an atom, nucleus, or particle of a subatomic particle that often results in subsequent emission of radiation or in fission **d :** the act of recording in a permanent file ⟨data *capture*⟩
2 : one that has been taken (as a prize ship)

²capture *transitive verb* **cap·tured; cap·tur·ing** \'kap-chə-riŋ, 'kap-shriŋ\ (1795)
1 a : to take captive; *also* **:** to gain control of especially by force ⟨*capture* a city⟩ **b :** to gain or win especially through effort ⟨*captured* 60% of the vote⟩
2 : to emphasize, represent, or preserve (as a scene, mood, or quality) in a more or less permanent form ⟨at any such moment as a photograph might *capture* —C. E. Montague⟩
3 : to captivate and hold the interest of
4 : to take according to the rules of a game
5 : to bring about the capture of (a subatomic particle)
6 : to record in a permanent file (as in a computer)
synonym see CATCH

capture the flag *noun* (circa 1925)
: a game in which players on each of two teams seek to capture the other team's flag and return it to their side without being captured and imprisoned

ca·puche \kə-'püch, -'püsh\ *noun* [Middle French, from Italian *cappuccio*, from *cappa* cloak, from Late Latin] (circa 1600)
: HOOD; *especially* **:** the cowl of a Capuchin friar

ca·pu·chin \'ka-pyə-shən, -pə-, *especially for 3 also* kə-'pyü-, -'pü-\ *noun* [Middle French, from Old Italian *cappuccino*, from *cappuccio*; from his cowl] (1589)
1 *capitalized* **:** a member of the Order of Friars Minor Capuchin forming since 1529 an austere branch of the first order of Saint Francis of Assisi engaged in missionary work and preaching
2 : a hooded cloak for women
3 : any of a genus (*Cebus*) of South American monkeys; *especially* **:** one (*C. capucinus*) with the hair on its crown resembling a monk's cowl

Cap·u·let \'ka-pyə-lət\ *noun*
: the family of Juliet in Shakespeare's *Romeo and Juliet*

cap·y·bara \ˌka-pi-'bar-ə, -'bär-\ *noun* [Portuguese *capibara*, from Tupi] (1774)
: a tailless largely aquatic South American rodent (*Hydrochaerus hydrochaeris*) often exceeding four feet (1.2 meters) in length

car \'kär, *dialect also* 'kȯr, 'kyär\ *noun* [Middle English *carre*, from Anglo-French, from Latin *carra*, plural of *carrum*, alteration of *carrus*, of Celtic origin; akin to Old Irish & Middle Welsh *carr* vehicle; akin to Latin *currere* to run] (14th century)

1 : a vehicle moving on wheels: as **a** *archaic* **:** CARRIAGE, CHARIOT **b :** a vehicle designed to move on rails (as of a railroad) **c :** AUTOMOBILE
2 : the passenger compartment of an elevator
3 : the part of an airship or balloon that carries the passengers and cargo

ca·ra·bao \ˌkar-ə-'baů, ˌkär-\ *noun, plural* **-bao** *or* **-baos** [Philippine Spanish, from Bisayan of Samar and Leyte *karabáw*] (1900)
: WATER BUFFALO

ca·ra·bid \'kar-ə-bəd, kə-'ra-bəd\ *noun* [ultimately from Greek *karabos* horned beetle] (1880)
: GROUND BEETLE

car·a·bi·neer *or* **car·a·bi·nier** \ˌkar-ə-bə-'nir\ *noun* [French *carabinier*, from *carabine* carbine] (1672)
: a cavalry soldier armed with a carbine

car·a·bi·ner \ˌkar-ə-'bē-nər\ *noun* [German *Karabiner*, short for *Karabinerhaken*, literally, carabineer's hook] (1920)
: an oblong metal ring with one spring-hinged side that is used especially in mountain climbing as a connector and to hold a freely running rope

carabiner

ca·ra·bi·ne·ro \ˌkar-ə-bə-'ner-(ˌ)ō, ˌkär-\ *noun, plural* **-ros** [Spanish, from *carabina* carbine, from French *carabine*] (1845)
1 : a member of a Spanish national police force serving especially as frontier guards
2 : a customs or coast guard officer in the Philippines

ca·ra·bi·nie·re \ˌkar-ə-bən-'yer-(ˌ)ā, ˌkär-\ *noun, plural* **-nie·ri** \-'yer-ē\ [Italian, from French *carabinier*] (1847)
: a member of the Italian national police force

car·a·cal \'kar-ə-ˌkal\ *noun* [French, from Turkish *karakulak*, from *kara* black + *kulak* ear] (1760)
: a long-legged reddish brown nocturnal cat (*Felis caracal* synonym *Lynx caracal*) of savannas in Africa and parts of Asia that has long pointed ears with a tuft of black hairs at the tip

ca·ra·ca·ra \ˌkar-ə-'kär-ə, -ə-kə-'rä\ *noun* [Spanish *caracara* & Portuguese *caracará*, from Tupi *caracará*] (1838)
: any of various large long-legged mostly South American hawks classified with the falcons

car·a·cole \'kar-ə-ˌkōl\ *noun* [French, from Spanish *caracol* snail, spiral stair, caracole] (1614)
: a half turn to right or left executed by a mounted horse
— **caracole** *verb*

car·a·cul \'kar-ə-kəl\ *noun* [alteration of *karakul*] (1894)
: the pelt of a karakul lamb after the curl begins to loosen

ca·rafe \kə-'raf, -'räf\ *noun* [French, from Italian *caraffa*, from Arabic *gharrāfah*] (1786)
: a bottle with a flaring lip used to hold beverages and especially wine

car·am·bo·la \ˌkar-əm-'bō-lə\ *noun* [Portuguese, from Marathi *karambal*, from Sanskrit *karmaphala*] (1598)
1 : a five-angled green to yellow tropical fruit of star-shaped cross section — called also *starfruit*
2 : a tropical tree (*Averrhoa carambola*) of the wood-sorrel family widely cultivated for carambolas

car·a·mel \'kär-məl; 'kar-ə-məl, -ˌmel\ *noun* [French, from Spanish *caramelo*, from Portuguese, icicle, caramel, from Late Latin *calamellus* small reed — more at SHAWM] (1725)
1 : an amorphous brittle brown and somewhat bitter substance obtained by heating sugar and used as a coloring and flavoring agent

2 : a firm chewy usually caramel-flavored candy

car·a·mel·ise *British variant of* CARAMELIZE

car·a·mel·ize \-mə-ˌlīz\ *verb* **-ized; -iz·ing** (1842)
transitive verb
: to change (as sugar) into caramel
intransitive verb
: to change to caramel

ca·ran·gid \kə-'ran-jəd, -'raŋ-gəd\ *adjective* [ultimately from French *carangue* shad, horse mackerel, from Spanish *caranga*] (1931)
: of or relating to a large family (Carangidae of the order Perciformes) of marine spiny-finned bony fishes including important food fishes
— **carangid** *noun*

car·a·pace \'kar-ə-ˌpās\ *noun* [French, from Spanish *carapacho*] (1836)
1 : a bony or chitinous case or shield covering the back or part of the back of an animal (as a turtle or crab)
2 : a protective, decorative, or disguising shell ⟨the *carapace* of reserve he built around himself —M. M. Mintz⟩

¹carat *variant of* KARAT

²car·at \'kar-ət\ *noun* [Middle English, from Middle French, from Italian *carato*, from Arabic *qīrāṭ* bean pod, a small weight, from Greek *keration* carob bean, a small weight, from diminutive of *kerat-, keras* horn — more at HORN] (1555)
: a unit of weight for precious stones equal to 200 milligrams

¹car·a·van \'kar-ə-ˌvan\ *noun* [Italian *caravana*, from Persian *kārwān*] (1588)
1 a : a company of travelers on a journey through desert or hostile regions; *also* **:** a train of pack animals **b :** a group of vehicles traveling together in a file
2 a : a covered wagon or motor vehicle equipped as traveling living quarters **b** *British* **:** TRAILER 3b

²caravan *intransitive verb* **-vanned** *or* **-vaned; -van·ning** *or* **-van·ing** (1885)
: to travel in a caravan

car·a·van·ner *or* **car·a·van·er** \-ˌva-nər\ *noun* (1909)
1 : one that travels in a caravan
2 *British* **:** one who goes camping with a trailer

car·a·van·sa·ry \ˌkar-ə-'van(t)-sə-rē\ *or* **car·a·van·se·rai** \-sə-ˌrī\ *noun, plural* **-ries** *or* **-rais** *or* **-rai** [Persian *kārwānsarāī*, from *kārwān* caravan + *sarāī* palace, inn] (1599)
1 : an inn surrounding a court in eastern countries where caravans rest at night
2 : HOTEL, INN

car·a·vel \'kar-ə-ˌvel, -vəl\ *noun* [Middle French *caravelle*, from Old Portuguese *caravela*] (1527)
: any of several sailing ships; *specifically* **:** a small 15th and 16th century ship that has broad bows, high narrow poop, and usually three masts with lateen or both square and lateen sails

car·a·way \'kar-ə-ˌwā\ *noun* [Middle English, probably from Medieval Latin *carvi*, from Arabic *karawyā*, from Greek *karon*] (13th century)

caravel

1 : a biennial usually white-flowered aromatic herb (*Carum carvi*) of the carrot family
2 : the pungent fruit of the caraway used in seasoning and medicine — called also *caraway seed*

¹carb \'kärb\ *noun* (circa 1942)
slang **:** CARBURETOR

²carb \'kärb\ *or* **car·bo** \'kär-(,)bō\ *noun* (1965)
: CARBOHYDRATE; *also* **:** a high-carbohydrate food — usually used in plural

carb- *or* **carbo-** *combining form* [French, from *carbone*]
: carbon : carbonic : carbonyl : carboxyl ⟨*carbide*⟩ ⟨*carbo*hydrate⟩

car·ba·chol \'kär-bə-ˌkȯl, -ˌkōl\ *noun* [*carbamic acid + choline*] (circa 1940)
: a synthetic parasympathomimetic drug $C_6H_{15}ClN_2O_2$ that is used in veterinary medicine and topically in glaucoma

car·ba·mate \'kär-bə-ˌmāt, kär-'ba-ˌmāt\ *noun* (1888)
: a salt or ester of carbamic acid; *especially*
: one that is a synthetic organic insecticide

car·bam·ic acid \(ˌ)kär-'ba-mik-\ *noun* [International Scientific Vocabulary *carbam*ide + ¹*-ic*] (1869)
: an acid CH_3NO_2 known in the form of salts and esters that is a half amide of carbonic acid

car·bam·ide \'kär-bə-ˌmīd, kär-'ba-məd\ *noun* [International Scientific Vocabulary *carb-* + *amide*] (1865)
: UREA

carb·am·i·no \ˌkär-bə-'mē-(ˌ)nō\ *adjective* (1922)
: relating to any carbamic acid derivative formed by reaction of carbon dioxide with an amino acid or a protein (as hemoglobin)

carb·an·ion \kär-'ba-ˌnī-ən, -ˌnī-ˌän\ *noun* (1933)
: an organic ion carrying a negative charge on a carbon atom — compare CARBONIUM ION

car·barn \'kär-ˌbärn\ *noun* (1880)
: a building that houses the cars of a street railway or the buses of a bus system

car·ba·ryl \'kär-bə-ˌril\ *noun* [*carb*amate + *aryl*] (1963)
: a carbamate insecticide $C_{12}H_{11}NO_2$ effective especially against numerous crop, forage, and forest pests

car·ba·zole \'kär-bə-ˌzōl\ *noun* [International Scientific Vocabulary *carb-* + *az-* + *-ole*] (1887)
: a crystalline slightly basic cyclic compound $C_{12}H_9N$ found in anthracene and used in making dyes

car·bide \'kär-ˌbīd\ *noun* [International Scientific Vocabulary] (circa 1865)
1 : a binary compound of carbon with a more electropositive element; *especially* **:** CALCIUM CARBIDE
2 : a very hard material made of carbon and one or more heavy metals

car·bine \'kär-ˌbēn, -ˌbīn\ *noun* [French *carabine*, from Middle French *carabin* carabineer] (1605)
1 : a short-barreled lightweight firearm originally used by cavalry
2 : a light short-barreled repeating rifle that is used as a supplementary military arm or for hunting in dense brush

car·bi·nol \'kär-bə-ˌnȯl, -ˌnōl\ *noun* [International Scientific Vocabulary, from obsolete German *Karbin* methyl, from German *karb-* carb-] (circa 1885)
: METHANOL; *also* **:** an alcohol derived from it

car·bo·cy·clic \ˌkär-bō-'sī-klik, -'si-\ *adjective* [International Scientific Vocabulary] (1899)
: being or having an organic ring composed of carbon atoms

car·bo·hy·drase \ˌkär-bō-'hī-ˌdrās, -bə-, -ˌdrāz\ *noun* [International Scientific Vocabulary] (1910)

: any of a group of enzymes (as amylase) that promote hydrolysis or synthesis of a carbohydrate (as a disaccharide)

car·bo·hy·drate \-ˌdrāt, -drət\ *noun* (circa 1869)
: any of various neutral compounds of carbon, hydrogen, and oxygen (as sugars, starches, and celluloses) most of which are formed by green plants and which constitute a major class of animal foods

car·bol·ic \kär-'bä-lik\ *noun* (1884)
: PHENOL 1

carbolic acid *noun* [International Scientific Vocabulary *carb-* + Latin *oleum* oil — more at OIL] (circa 1859)
: PHENOL 1

car bomb *noun* (1973)
: an explosive device concealed in an automobile for use as a weapon of terrorism

car·bon \'kär-bən\ *noun, often attributive* [French *carbone*, from Latin *carbon-, carbo* ember, charcoal] (1789)
1 : a nonmetallic chiefly tetravalent element found native (as in the diamond and graphite) or as a constituent of coal, petroleum, and asphalt, of limestone and other carbonates, and of organic compounds or obtained artificially in varying degrees of purity especially as carbon black, lampblack, activated carbon, charcoal, and coke — see ELEMENT table
2 : a carbon rod used in an arc lamp
3 a : a sheet of carbon paper **b :** CARBON COPY

car·bo·na·ceous \ˌkär-bə-'nā-shəs\ *adjective* (1791)
1 : rich in carbon
2 : relating to, containing, or composed of carbon

¹car·bo·na·do \ˌkär-bə-'nā-(ˌ)dō, -'nä-\ *noun, plural* **-dos** *or* **-does** [Spanish *carbonada*] (1586)
archaic **:** a piece of meat scored before grilling

²carbonado *transitive verb* (1599)
1 *archaic* **:** to make a carbonado of
2 *archaic* **:** CUT, SLASH

³carbonado *noun, plural* **-dos** [Portuguese, literally, carbonated] (1853)
: an impure opaque dark-colored fine-grained aggregate of diamond particles valuable for its superior toughness

car·bo·nara \ˌkär-bə-'när-ə\ *noun* [Italian dialect (*alla*) *carbonara*, literally, in the manner of a charcoal maker] (1963)
: a dish of hot pasta into which other ingredients (as eggs, bacon or ham, and grated cheese) have been mixed — often used as a postpositive modifier ⟨spaghetti *carbonara*⟩

¹car·bon·ate \'kär-bə-ˌnāt, -nət\ *noun* (1794)
: a salt or ester of carbonic acid

²car·bon·ate \-ˌnāt\ *transitive verb* **-at·ed; -at·ing** (1805)
1 : to convert into a carbonate
2 : to combine or impregnate with carbon dioxide ⟨*carbonated* beverages⟩
— car·bon·ation \ˌkär-bə-'nā-shən\ *noun*

carbon black *noun* (circa 1889)
: any of various colloidal black substances consisting wholly or principally of carbon obtained usually as soot and used especially in tires and as pigments

carbon copy *noun* (1895)
1 : a copy made by carbon paper
2 : DUPLICATE

carbon cycle *noun* (1912)
1 : the cycle of carbon in the earth's ecosystems in which carbon dioxide is fixed by photosynthetic organisms to form organic nutrients and is ultimately restored to the inorganic state by respiration and protoplasmic decay
2 : a cycle of thermonuclear reactions in which four hydrogen atoms synthesize into a helium atom by the catalytic action of carbon with the release of nuclear energy and which is held to be the source of most of the energy radiated by the sun and stars

carbon dating *noun* (1951)

: the determination of the age of old material (as an archaeological or paleontological specimen) by means of the content of carbon 14
— carbon–date \'kär-bən-'dāt\ *transitive verb*

carbon dioxide *noun* (1873)
: a heavy colorless gas CO_2 that does not support combustion, dissolves in water to form carbonic acid, is formed especially in animal respiration and in the decay or combustion of animal and vegetable matter, is absorbed from the air by plants in photosynthesis, and is used in the carbonation of beverages

carbon disulfide *noun* (1869)
: a colorless flammable poisonous liquid CS_2 used as a solvent for rubber and as an insect fumigant — called also *carbon bisulfide*

carbon fiber *noun* (1960)
: a very strong lightweight synthetic fiber made especially by carbonizing acrylic fiber at high temperatures

carbon 14 \see FOURTEEN\ *noun* (1936)
: a heavy radioactive isotope of carbon of mass number 14 used especially in tracer studies and in dating archaeological and geological materials

car·bon·ic \kär-'bä-nik\ *adjective* (1791)
: of, relating to, or derived from carbon, carbonic acid, or carbon dioxide

carbonic acid *noun* (1791)
: a weak dibasic acid H_2CO_3 known only in solution that reacts with bases to form carbonates

carbonic acid gas *noun* (circa 1880)
: CARBON DIOXIDE

carbonic an·hy·drase \-an-'hī-ˌdrās, -ˌdrāz\ *noun* [*anhydrous* + *-ase;* from its promotion of dehydration] (1932)
: a zinc-containing enzyme that occurs in living tissues (as red blood cells) and aids carbon-dioxide transport from the tissues and its release from the blood in the lungs by catalyzing the reversible hydration of carbon dioxide to carbonic acid

car·bon·if·er·ous \ˌkär-bə-'ni-f(ə-)rəs\ *adjective* (1799)
1 : producing or containing carbon or coal
2 *capitalized* **:** of, relating to, or being the period of the Paleozoic era between the Devonian and the Permian or the corresponding system of rocks that includes coal beds — see GEOLOGIC TIME table
— Carboniferous *noun*

car·bo·ni·um ion \kär-'bō-nē-əm-\ *noun* [*carb-* + *-onium*] (1942)
: an organic ion carrying a positive charge on a carbon atom — compare CARBANION

car·bon·iza·tion \ˌkär-bə-nə-'zā-shən\ *noun* (1804)
: the process of carbonizing; *especially* **:** DESTRUCTIVE DISTILLATION

car·bon·ize \'kär-bə-ˌnīz\ *verb* **-ized; -iz·ing** (1806)
transitive verb
1 : to convert into carbon or a carbonic residue
2 : CARBURIZE 1
intransitive verb
: to become carbonized : CHAR

car·bon·less \'kär-bən-ləs\ *adjective* (1850)
1 : being without carbon
2 : being or composed of paper that makes multiple copies without intervening layers of carbon paper ⟨*carbonless* forms⟩

carbon monoxide *noun* (1873)
: a colorless odorless very toxic gas CO that burns to carbon dioxide with a blue flame and is formed as a product of the incomplete combustion of carbon

car·bon·nade *also* **car·bo·nade** \ˌkär-bə-'näd\ *noun* [French, literally, dish of grilled meat, from Italian *carbonata*, from *carbone* charcoal, coal, from Latin *carbon-, carbo*] (1877)
: a beef stew cooked in beer

carbon paper *noun* (1895)
: a thin paper faced with a waxy pigmented coating so that when placed between two sheets of paper the pressure of writing or typing on the top sheet causes transfer of pigment to the bottom sheet

carbon steel *noun* (1903)
: a strong hard steel that derives its physical properties from the presence of carbon and is used in hand tools and kitchen utensils

carbon tetrachloride *noun* (1866)
: a colorless nonflammable toxic liquid CCl₄ that has an odor resembling that of chloroform and is used as a solvent and a refrigerant

carbon 13 \-thir-'tēn, -'thir-ˌtēn\ *noun* (1939)
: an isotope of carbon of mass number 13 that constitutes about ¹⁄₇₀ of natural carbon and is used as a tracer especially in spectroscopy utilizing nuclear magnetic resonance

carbon 12 \-'twelv\ *noun* (1946)
: an isotope of carbon of mass number 12 that is the most abundant carbon isotope and is used as a standard for measurements of atomic weight

car·bon·yl \'kär-bə-ˌnil, -ˌnēl\ *noun* (1869)
1 : an organic functional group −CO− occurring in aldehydes, ketones, carboxylic acids, esters, and their derivatives
2 : a coordination complex involving the neutral radical CO ⟨chromium *carbonyl*⟩
— **car·bon·yl·ic** \ˌkär-bə-'ni-lik\ *adjective*

car·bon·yl·a·tion \(ˌ)kär-ˌbä-nə-'lā-shən\ *noun* (1946)
: the synthesis of a carbonyl compound especially by a reaction involving carbon monoxide

Car·bo·run·dum \ˌkär-bə-'rən-dəm\ *trademark*
— used for various abrasives

carboxy- *or* **carbox-** *combining form*
: carboxyl ⟨*carboxy*peptidase⟩

car·box·yl \kär-'bäk-səl\ *noun* [International Scientific Vocabulary] (1869)
: a univalent radical COOH typical of organic acids — called also *carboxyl group*
— **car·box·yl·ic** \ˌkär-(ˌ)bäk-'si-lik\ *adjective*

car·box·yl·ase \kär-'bäk-sə-ˌlās, -ˌlāz\ *noun* [International Scientific Vocabulary] (1911)
: an enzyme that catalyzes decarboxylation or carboxylation

¹car·box·yl·ate \-ˌlāt, -lət\ *noun* (1927)
: a salt or ester of a carboxylic acid

²car·box·yl·ate \-ˌlāt\ *transitive verb* **-at·ed; -at·ing** (circa 1928)
: to introduce carboxyl or carbon dioxide into (a compound) with formation of a carboxylic acid
— **car·box·yl·a·tion** \(ˌ)kär-ˌbäk-sə-'lā-shən\ *noun*

carboxylic acid *noun* (1902)
: an organic acid (as acetic acid) containing one or more carboxyl groups

car·boxy·meth·yl·cel·lu·lose \kär-ˌbäk-sē-ˌme-thəl-'sel-yə-ˌlōs, -ˌlōz\ *noun* (1947)
: an acid ether derivative of cellulose that in the form of its sodium salt is used as a thickening, emulsifying, and stabilizing agent and as a bulk laxative in medicine

car·boxy·pep·ti·dase \-'pep-tə-ˌdās, -ˌdāz\ *noun* (1937)
: an enzyme that hydrolyzes peptides and especially polypeptides by splitting off sequentially the amino acids at the end of the peptide chain which contain free carboxyl groups

car·boy \'kär-ˌbȯi\ *noun* [Persian *qarāba*, from Arabic *qarrābah* demijohn] (1753)
: a large container for liquids

car·bun·cle \'kär-ˌbən-kəl\ *noun* [Middle English, from Old French, from Latin *carbunculus* small coal, carbuncle, diminutive of *carbon-, carbo* charcoal, ember] (13th century)
1 a *obsolete* **:** any of several red precious stones **b :** the garnet cut cabochon

2 : a painful local purulent inflammation of the skin and deeper tissues with multiple openings for the discharge of pus and usually necrosis and sloughing of dead tissue
— **car·bun·cled** \-kəld\ *adjective*
— **car·bun·cu·lar** \kär-'bəŋ-kyə-lər\ *adjective*

car·bu·ret·ed \'kär-bə-ˌrā-təd, -byə-\, *especially by chemists* \-ˌre-təd\ *adjective* [back-formation from *carburetor*] (1972)
: equipped with a carburetor ⟨a *carbureted* engine⟩

car·bu·re·tion \ˌkär-bə-'rā-shən, -byə-\ *noun* [*carburet* to combine chemically with carbon, from obsolete *carburet* carbide] (1896)
: the process of mixing (as in a carburetor) the vapor of a flammable hydrocarbon (as gasoline) with air to form an explosive mixture especially for use in an internal-combustion engine

car·bu·re·tor \'kär-bə-ˌrā-tər, -byə-\ *noun* (1896)
: an apparatus for supplying an internal combustion engine with an explosive mixture of vaporized fuel and air

car·bu·ret·tor *also* **car·bu·ret·ter** \ˌkär-byə-'re-tər, 'kär-byə-ˌ\ *chiefly British variant of* CARBURETOR

car·bu·rise *British variant of* CARBURIZE

car·bu·rize \'kär-bə-ˌrīz, -byə-\ *transitive verb* **-rized; -riz·ing** [obsolete *carburet* carbide] (circa 1889)
: to combine or impregnate (as metal) with carbon
— **car·bu·ri·za·tion** \ˌkär-bə-rə-'zā-shən, -byə-\ *noun*

car·ca·net \'kär-kə-nət\ *noun* [Middle French *carcan*] (circa 1530)
archaic **:** an ornamental necklace, chain, collar, or headband

car·case \'kär-kəs\ *British variant of* CARCASS

car·cass \'kär-kəs\ *noun* [Middle English *carcays*, from Middle French *carcasse*, from Old French *carcois*] (14th century)
1 : a dead body **:** CORPSE; *especially* **:** the dressed body of a meat animal
2 : the living, material, or physical body
3 : the decaying or worthless remains of a structure ⟨the *carcass* of an abandoned automobile⟩
4 : the underlying structure or frame of something (as of a piece of furniture)

carcin- *or* **carcino-** *combining form* [Greek *karkin-, karkino-*, from *karkinos* ulcerous sore, literally, crab — more at CANCER]
: tumor **:** cancer ⟨*carcino*genic⟩

car·ci·no·em·bry·on·ic antigen \ˌkär-sᵊn-ō-ˌem-brē-'ä-nik-\ *noun* (1967)
: a glycoprotein present in fetal gut tissues during the first two trimesters of pregnancy and in peripheral blood of patients with some forms of cancer

car·cin·o·gen \kär-'si-nə-jən, 'kär-sᵊn-ə-ˌjen\ *noun* (1853)
: a substance or agent producing or inciting cancer
— **car·ci·no·gen·ic** \ˌkär-sᵊn-ō-'je-nik\ *adjective*
— **car·ci·no·ge·nic·i·ty** \-jə-'ni-sə-tē\ *noun*

car·ci·no·gen·e·sis \ˌkär-sᵊn-ō-'je-nə-sis\ *noun* (circa 1923)
: the production of cancer

car·ci·noid \'kär-sᵊn-ˌȯid\ *noun* (1925)
: a benign or malignant tumor arising especially from the mucosa of the gastrointestinal tract

car·ci·no·ma \ˌkär-sᵊn-'ō-mə\ *noun, plural* **-mas** *or* **-ma·ta** \-mə-tə\ [Latin, from Greek *karkinōma* cancer, from *karkinos*] (circa 1751)
: a malignant tumor of epithelial origin
— **car·ci·no·ma·tous** \-'ō-mə-təs\ *adjective*

car·ci·no·ma·to·sis \-ˌō-mə-'tō-səs\ *noun* [New Latin, from Latin *carcinomat-, carcinoma*] (1903)

: a condition in which multiple carcinomas develop simultaneously usually after dissemination from a primary source

car·ci·no·sar·co·ma \ˌkär-sᵊn-ō-(ˌ)sär-'kō-mə\ *noun, plural* **-mas** *or* **-ma·ta** \-mə-tə\ (circa 1919)
: a malignant tumor combining elements of carcinoma and sarcoma

car coat *noun* (1958)
: a three-quarter-length overcoat

¹card \'kärd\ *transitive verb* (14th century)
: to cleanse, disentangle, and collect together (as fibers) by the use of cards preparatory to spinning
— **card·er** *noun*

²card *noun* [Middle English *carde*, from Middle French *carde*, from Late Latin *cardus* thistle, from Latin *carduus* — more at CHARD] (15th century)
1 : an instrument or machine for carding fibers that consists usually of bent wire teeth set closely in rows in a thick piece of leather fastened to a back
2 : an implement for raising a nap on cloth

³card *noun* [Middle English *carde*, modification of Middle French *carte*, probably from Old Italian *carta*, literally, leaf of paper, from Latin *charta* leaf of papyrus, from Greek *chartēs*] (15th century)
1 : PLAYING CARD
2 *plural but singular or plural in construction*
a : a game played with cards **b :** card playing
3 : something compared to a valuable playing card in one's hand
4 : a usually clownishly amusing person **:** WAG
5 : COMPASS CARD
6 a : a flat stiff usually small and rectangular piece of material (as paper, paperboard, or plastic) usually bearing information: as (1) **:** POSTCARD (2) **:** VISITING CARD (3) **:** CREDIT CARD (4) **:** one bearing a picture (as of a baseball player) on one side and usually statistical data on the other (5) **:** one on which computer information is stored (as in the form of punched holes or magnetic encoding) (6) **:** one bearing electronic circuit components for insertion into a larger electronic device (as a computer) **b :** PROGRAM; *especially* **:** a sports program **c** (1) **:** a wine list (2) **:** MENU **d :** GREETING CARD ⟨a birthday *card*⟩
— **in the cards** *also* **on the cards :** INEVITABLE

⁴card *transitive verb* (1884)
1 : to place or fasten on or by means of a card
2 : to provide with a card
3 : to list or record on a card
4 : SCORE
5 : to ask for identification (as in a bar)

car·da·mom \'kär-də-məm, -ˌmäm\ *noun* [Latin *cardamomum*, from Greek *kardamōmon*, blend of *kardamon* peppergrass and *amōmon*, an Indian spice plant] (1553)
: the aromatic capsular fruit of an East Indian herb (*Elettaria cardamomum*) of the ginger family with seeds used as a spice or condiment and in medicine; *also* **:** this plant

¹card·board \'kärd-ˌbȯrd, -ˌbȯrd\ *noun* (1848)
: PAPERBOARD

²cardboard *adjective* (1893)
1 a : made of or as if of cardboard **b :** FLAT, TWO-DIMENSIONAL
2 : UNREAL, STEREOTYPED ⟨a play with *cardboard* characters⟩

card–car·ry·ing \'kärd-ˌkar-ē-iŋ\ *adjective* [from the assumption that such a person carries an identification card] (1948)
1 : being a full-fledged member especially of a Communist party
2 : being strongly identified with a group (as of people with a common interest) ⟨*card-*

\ə\ **abut** \ᵊ\ **kitten** \ər\ **further** \a\ **ash** \ā\ **ace**
\ä\ **mop, mar** \au̇\ **out** \ch\ **chin** \e\ **bet** \ē\ **easy**
\g\ **go** \i\ **hit** \ī\ **ice** \j\ **job** \ŋ\ **sing** \ō\ **go**
\ȯ\ **law** \ȯi\ **boy** \th\ **thin** \ṯh\ **the** \ü\ **loot** \u̇\ **foot**
\y\ **yet** \zh\ **vision** *see also* Guide to Pronunciation

carrying members of the ecology movement
—Richard Neuhaus⟩

card catalog *noun* (1854)
: a catalog (as of books) in which the entries are arranged systematically on cards

card·hold·er \'kärd-ˌhōl-dər\ *noun* (1909)
: one who possesses a card and especially a credit card

cardi- *or* **cardio-** *combining form* [Greek *kardi-, kardio-,* from *kardia* — more at HEART]
: heart : cardiac : cardiac and ⟨*cardio*gram⟩ ⟨*cardio*vascular⟩

car·dia \'kär-dē-ə\ *noun, plural* **-di·ae** \-dē-ˌē\ *or* **-dias** [New Latin, from Greek *kardia* heart, upper orifice of the stomach] (1782)
: the opening of the esophagus into the stomach; *also* : the part of the stomach adjoining this opening

-cardia *noun combining form* [New Latin, from Greek *kardia*]
: heart action or location (of a specified type) ⟨tachy*cardia*⟩

¹car·di·ac \'kär-dē-ˌak\ *adjective* [Latin *cardiacus,* from Greek *kardiakos,* from *kardia*] (1601)
1 a : of, relating to, situated near, or acting on the heart **b** : of or relating to the cardia of the stomach
2 : of, relating to, or affected with heart disease

²cardiac *noun* (circa 1929)
: a person with heart disease

cardiac muscle *noun* (circa 1881)
: the principal muscle tissue of the vertebrate heart made up of striated fibers that appear to be separated from each other under the electron microscope but that function in long-term rhythmic contraction as if in protoplasmic continuity

car·di·gan \'kär-di-gən\ *noun* [James Thomas Brudenell, 7th Earl of *Cardigan* (died 1868) English soldier] (1868)
: a usually collarless sweater or jacket that opens the full length of the center front ◇

Cardigan Welsh corgi *noun* [*Cardigan,* former county in Wales] (1935)
: a Welsh corgi with rounded ears, slightly bowed forelegs, and long tail — called also *Cardigan;* see WELSH CORGI illustration

¹car·di·nal \'kärd-nəl, 'kär-dᵊn-əl\ *noun* [Middle English, from Medieval Latin *cardinalis,* from Late Latin *cardinalis,* adjective] (12th century)
1 : a high ecclesiastical official of the Roman Catholic Church who ranks next below the pope and is appointed by him to assist him as a member of the college of cardinals
2 : CARDINAL NUMBER — usually used in plural
3 : a woman's short hooded cloak originally of scarlet cloth
4 [from its color, resembling that of the cardinal's robes] : a crested finch (*Cardinalis cardinalis*) of the eastern U.S. and adjacent Canada, the southwestern U.S., and Mexico to Belize which has a black face and heavy red bill in both sexes and is nearly completely red in the male
— **car·di·nal·ship** \-ˌship\ *noun*

²cardinal *adjective* [Middle English, from Late Latin *cardinalis,* from Latin, serving as a hinge, from *cardin-, cardo* hinge] (14th century)
: of basic importance : MAIN, CHIEF, PRIMARY
synonym see ESSENTIAL
— **car·di·nal·ly** *adverb*

car·di·nal·ate \'kärd-nə-lət, 'kär-dᵊn-ə-let, -ˌlāt\ *noun* (1645)
: the office, rank, or dignity of a cardinal

cardinal flower *noun* (1698)
: a North American lobelia (*Lobelia cardinalis*) that bears a spike of brilliant red flowers

car·di·nal·i·ty \ˌkär-dᵊn-'a-lə-tē\ *noun, plural* **-ties** [¹*cardinal* + *-ity*] (1935)
: the number of elements in a given mathematical set

cardinal number *noun* (1591)
1 : a number (as 1, 5, 15) that is used in simple counting and that indicates how many elements there are in an assemblage — see NUMBER table
2 : the property that a mathematical set has in common with all sets that can be put in one-to-one correspondence with it

cardinal point *noun* (1755)
: one of the four principal compass points north, south, east, and west

cardinal virtue *noun* (14th century)
1 : one of the four classically defined natural virtues prudence, justice, temperance, or fortitude
2 : a quality designated as a major virtue

car·dio·gen·ic \ˌkär-dē-ō-'je-nik\ *adjective* (circa 1923)
: originating in the heart : caused by a cardiac condition ⟨*cardiogenic* shock⟩

car·dio·gram \'kär-dē-ə-ˌgram\ *noun* [International Scientific Vocabulary] (1876)
: the curve or tracing made by a cardiograph

car·dio·graph \-ˌgraf\ *noun* [International Scientific Vocabulary] (1870)
: an instrument that registers graphically movements of the heart
— **car·dio·graph·ic** \ˌkär-dē-ə-'gra-fik\ *adjective*
— **car·di·og·ra·phy** \ˌkär-dē-'ä-grə-fē\ *noun*

car·di·oid \'kär-dē-ˌȯid\ *noun* (1753)
: a heart-shaped curve that is traced by a point on the circumference of a circle rolling completely around an equal fixed circle and has the general equation $\rho = a(1 + \cos \theta)$ in polar coordinates

cardioid: *ABP* fixed circle; *PCD* first position of rolling circle; *P* tracing point; P_1, P_2, P_3, P_4 various positions of *P*; $P_1M_1, P_2M_2, P_3M_3, P_4M_4$ various positions of *PM*

car·di·ol·o·gy \ˌkär-dē-'ä-lə-jē\ *noun* [International Scientific Vocabulary] (1847)
: the study of the heart and its action and diseases
— **car·di·o·log·i·cal** \-dē-ə-'lä-ji-kəl\ *adjective*
— **car·di·ol·o·gist** \-dē-'ä-lə-jist\ *noun*

car·dio·my·op·a·thy \ˌkär-dē-ō-(ˌ)mī-'ä-pə-thē\ *noun, plural* **-thies** (1961)
: a typically chronic disorder of heart muscle that may involve hypertrophy and obstructive damage to the heart

car·di·op·a·thy \ˌkär-dē-'ä-pə-thē\ *noun, plural* **-thies** (1885)
: any disease of the heart

car·dio·pul·mo·nary \ˌkär-dē-ō-'pul-mə-ˌner-ē, -'pəl-\ *adjective* (circa 1881)
: of or relating to the heart and lungs

cardiopulmonary resuscitation *noun* (1972)
: a procedure designed to restore normal breathing after cardiac arrest that includes the clearance of air passages to the lungs, mouth-to-mouth method of artificial respiration, and heart massage by the exertion of pressure on the chest

car·dio·re·spi·ra·to·ry \ˌkär-dē-ō-'res-p(ə-)rə-ˌtȯr-ē, -ri-'spī-rə-, -ˌtȯr-\ *adjective* (1892)
: of or relating to the heart and the respiratory system

car·dio·tho·rac·ic \-thə-'ra-sik\ *adjective* (1962)
: relating to or involving the heart and chest

car·dio·ton·ic \-'tä-nik\ *adjective* (1927)
: tending to increase the tonus of heart muscle
— **cardiotonic** *noun*

car·dio·vas·cu·lar \-'vas-kyə-lər\ *adjective* [International Scientific Vocabulary] (1879)
: of, relating to, or involving the heart and blood vessels

-cardium *noun combining form, plural* **-cardia** [New Latin, from Greek *kardia*]
: heart ⟨epi*cardium*⟩

car·doon \kär-'dün\ *noun* [French *cardon,* from Late Latin *cardon-, cardo* thistle, from *cardus,* from Latin *carduus* thistle, cardoon] (1611)
: a large perennial plant (*Cynara cardunculus*) related to the artichoke and cultivated for its edible root and petioles; *also* : the root and petioles

card·play·er \'kärd-ˌplā-ər\ *noun* (1589)
: one that plays cards

card·sharp·er \-ˌshär-pər\ *or* **card·sharp** \-ˌshärp\ *noun* (1859)
: one who habitually cheats at cards

¹care \'ker, 'kar\ *noun* [Middle English, from Old English *caru;* akin to Old High German *kara* lament, Latin *garrire* to chatter] (before 12th century)
1 : suffering of mind : GRIEF
2 a : a disquieted state of mixed uncertainty, apprehension, and responsibility **b** : a cause for such anxiety
3 a : painstaking or watchful attention **b** : MAINTENANCE ⟨floor-*care* products⟩
4 : regard coming from desire or esteem
5 : CHARGE, SUPERVISION ⟨under a doctor's *care*⟩
6 : a person or thing that is an object of attention, anxiety, or solicitude ☆

²care *verb* **cared; car·ing** (before 12th century)
intransitive verb
1 a : to feel trouble or anxiety **b** : to feel interest or concern ⟨*care* about freedom⟩
2 : to give care ⟨*care* for the sick⟩
3 a : to have a liking, fondness, or taste ⟨don't *care* for your attitude⟩ **b** : to have an inclination ⟨would you *care* for some pie⟩
transitive verb
1 : to be concerned about or to the extent of
2 : WISH ⟨if you *care* to go⟩ □
— **car·er** *noun*
— **care less** : not to care — used positively and negatively with the same meaning ⟨I could *care* less what happens⟩ ⟨I couldn't *care* less what happens⟩

¹ca·reen \kə-'rēn\ *verb* [from *carine* side of a ship, from Middle French, submerged part of a

hull, from Latin *carina* hull, half of a nutshell; perhaps akin to Greek *karyon* nut] (circa 1583)
transitive verb
1 : to put (a ship or boat) on a beach especially in order to clean, caulk, or repair the hull
2 : to cause to heel over
intransitive verb
1 a : to careen a boat **b :** to undergo this process
2 : to heel over
3 : to sway from side to side **:** LURCH ⟨a *careening* carriage being pulled wildly . . . by a team of runaway horses —J. P. Getty⟩
4 : CAREER

²careen *noun* (1712)
archaic **:** the act or process of careening **:** the state of being careened

¹ca·reer \kə-ˈrir\ *noun* [Middle French *carrière*, from Old Provençal *carriera* street, from Medieval Latin *carraria* road for vehicles, from Latin *carrus* car] (1580)
1 a : speed in a course ⟨ran at full *career*⟩ **b :** COURSE, PASSAGE
2 : ENCOUNTER, CHARGE
3 : a field for or pursuit of consecutive progressive achievement especially in public, professional, or business life ⟨Washington's *career* as a soldier⟩
4 : a profession for which one trains and which is undertaken as a permanent calling ⟨a *career* diplomat⟩

²career *intransitive verb* (1647)
: to go at top speed especially in a headlong manner ⟨a car *careered* off the road⟩

ca·reer·ism \-ˌi-zəm\ *noun* (1933)
: the policy or practice of advancing one's career often at the cost of one's integrity
— **ca·reer·ist** \-ist\ *noun*

care·free \ˈker-ˌfrē, ˈkar-\ *adjective* (1795)
: free from care: as **a :** having no worries or troubles **b :** IRRESPONSIBLE ⟨is *carefree* with his money⟩

care·ful \-fəl\ *adjective* **care·ful·ler; care·ful·lest** (before 12th century)
1 *archaic* **a :** SOLICITOUS, ANXIOUS **b :** filling with care or solicitude
2 : exercising or taking care
3 a : marked by attentive concern and solicitude **b :** marked by wary caution or prudence ⟨be very *careful* with knives⟩ **c :** marked by painstaking effort to avoid errors or omissions — often used of or an infinitive ⟨*careful* of money⟩ ⟨*careful* to adjust the machine⟩ ☆
— **care·ful·ly** \-f(ə-)lē\ *adverb*
— **care·ful·ness** \-fəl-nəs\ *noun*

care·giv·er \-ˌgi-vər\ *noun* (1975)
: a person who provides direct care (as for children or the chronically ill)
— **care·giv·ing** \-ˌgi-viŋ\ *noun*

care·less \-ləs\ *adjective* (before 12th century)
1 a : free from care **:** UNTROUBLED ⟨*careless* days⟩ **b :** INDIFFERENT, UNCONCERNED ⟨*careless* of the consequences⟩
2 : not taking care
3 : not showing or receiving care: **a :** NEGLIGENT, SLOVENLY ⟨*careless* writing⟩ **b :** UNSTUDIED, SPONTANEOUS ⟨*careless* grace⟩ **c** *obsolete* **:** UNVALUED, DISREGARDED
— **care·less·ly** *adverb*
— **care·less·ness** *noun*

¹ca·ress \kə-ˈres\ *noun* [French *caresse*, from Italian *carezza*, from *caro* dear, from Latin *carus* — more at CHARITY] (circa 1611)
1 : an act or expression of kindness or affection **:** ENDEARMENT
2 a : a light stroking, rubbing, or patting **b :** KISS
— **ca·res·sive** \-ˈre-siv\ *adjective*
— **ca·res·sive·ly** *adverb*

²caress *transitive verb* (1658)
1 : to treat with tokens of fondness, affection, or kindness **:** CHERISH

2 a : to touch or stroke lightly in a loving or endearing manner **b :** to touch or affect as if with a caress ⟨echoes that *caress* the ear⟩
— **ca·ress·er** *noun*
— **ca·ress·ing·ly** \kə-ˈre-siŋ-lē\ *adverb*

car·et \ˈkar-ət\ *noun* [Latin, there is lacking, from *carēre* to lack, be without] (1681)
: a wedge-shaped mark made on written or printed matter to indicate the place where something is to be inserted

care·tak·er \ˈker-ˌtā-kər, ˈkar-\ *noun* (1858)
1 : one that gives physical or emotional care and support ⟨served as *caretaker* to the younger children⟩
2 : one that takes care of the house or land of an owner who may be absent
3 : one temporarily fulfilling the function of office ⟨a *caretaker* government⟩
— **care·take** \-ˌtāk\ *verb*
— **care·tak·ing** *noun*

care·worn \-ˌwōrn, -ˌwȯrn\ *adjective* (1828)
: showing the effect of grief or anxiety ⟨a *careworn* face⟩

car·fare \ˈkär-ˌfar, -ˌfer\ *noun* (1870)
: passenger fare (as on a bus)

car·ful \ˈkär-ˌfu̇l\ *noun* (1832)
: as much or as many as a car will hold

car·go \ˈkär-(ˌ)gō\ *noun, plural* **cargoes** *or* **cargos** [Spanish, load, charge, from *cargar* to load, from Late Latin *carricare* — more at CHARGE] (1657)
: the goods or merchandise conveyed in a ship, airplane, or vehicle **:** FREIGHT

cargo cult *noun* (1949)
: any of various Melanesian religious groups characterized by the belief that material wealth (as money or manufactured goods) can be obtained through ritual worship

cargo pocket *noun* (1974)
: a large pocket usually with a flap and a pleat

car·hop \ˈkär-ˌhäp\ *noun* [*car* + *-hop* (as in *bellhop*)] (1937)
: one who serves customers at a drive-in restaurant

Car·ib \ˈkar-əb\ *noun* [New Latin *Caribes* (plural), from Spanish *Caribe*, of Cariban origin — more at CANNIBAL] (1555)
1 : a member of an Indian people of northern South America and the Lesser Antilles
2 : the language of the Caribs

Ca·ri·ban \ˈkar-ə-bən, kə-ˈrē-bən\ *noun* (1901)
1 : a member of a group of Indian peoples of South America and the Lesser Antilles
2 : the language family comprising the languages of the Cariban peoples

Ca·rib·be·an \ˌkar-ə-ˈbē-ən, kə-ˈri-bē-ən\ *adjective* [New Latin *Caribbaeus*, from *Caribes*] (1777)
: of or relating to the Caribs, the eastern and southern West Indies, or the Caribbean Sea □

ca·ri·be \kə-ˈrē-bē\ *noun* [American Spanish, from Spanish, Carib, cannibal] (1868)
: PIRANHA

car·i·bou \ˈkar-ə-ˌbü\ *noun, plural* **-bou** *or* **-bous** [Canadian French, from Micmac *ɣalipu*] (circa 1665)
: a large gregarious deer (*Rangifer tarandus*) of Holarctic taiga and tundra that usually has palmate antlers in both sexes — used especially for one of the New World; called also *reindeer*

caribou

¹car·i·ca·ture
\ˈkar-i-kə-ˌchu̇r, -ˌchər, -ˌtyu̇r, -ˌtu̇r\ *noun* [Italian *caricatura*, literally, act of loading, from

caricare to load, from Late Latin *carricare*] (1712)
1 : exaggeration by means of often ludicrous distortion of parts or characteristics
2 : a representation especially in literature or art that has the qualities of caricature

\ə\ **abut** \ᵊ\ **kitten** \ər\ **further** \a\ **ash** \ā\ **ace** \ä\ **mop, mar** \au̇\ **out** \ch\ **chin** \e\ **bet** \ē\ **easy** \g\ **go** \i\ **hit** \ī\ **ice** \j\ **job** \ŋ\ **sing** \ō\ **go** \ȯ\ **law** \ȯi\ **boy** \th\ **thin** \t̲h̲\ **the** \ü\ **loot** \u̇\ **foot** \y\ **yet** \zh\ **vision** *see also* Guide to Pronunciation

3 : a distortion so gross as to seem like caricature ☆
— **car·i·ca·tur·al** \,kar-i-kə-'chu̇r-əl, -'chər-, -'tyu̇r-, -'tu̇r-\ *adjective*
— **car·i·ca·tur·ist** \'kar-i-kə-,chu̇r-ist, -,chər-, -,tyu̇r-, -,tu̇r-\ *noun*
²**caricature** *transitive verb* **-tured; -tur·ing** (circa 1771)
: to make or draw a caricature of **:** represent in caricature ⟨the portrait *caricatured* its subject⟩
car·ies \'kar-ēz, 'ker-\ *noun, plural* **caries** [Latin, decay; akin to Old Irish ara-*chrinn* it decays] (1634)
: a progressive destruction of bone or tooth; *especially* **:** tooth decay
car·il·lon \'kar-ə-,län, -lən; 'kar-ē-,än, -,ōn; kə-'ril-yən\ *noun* [French, alteration of Old French *quarregnon*, modification of Late Latin *quaternion-, quaternio* set of four — more at QUATERNION] (1775)
1 a : a set of fixed chromatically tuned bells sounded by hammers controlled from a keyboard **b :** an electronic instrument imitating a carillon
2 : a composition for the carillon
car·il·lon·neur \,kar-ə-lə-'nər, ,kar-ē-ə-'nər, kə-,ril-yə-'nər\ *noun* [French, from *carillon*] (1772)
: a carillon player
ca·ri·na \kə-'rī-nə, -'rē-\ *noun, plural* **-ri·nas** *or* **-ri·nae** \-'rī-,nē, -'rē-,nī\ [New Latin, from Latin, hull, keel — more at CAREEN] (circa 1704)
1 : a keel-shaped anatomical part, ridge, or process
2 *capitalized* **:** a constellation in the southern hemisphere lying near the Southern Cross
car·i·nate \'kar-ə-,nāt, -nət\ *or* **car·i·nat·ed** \-,nā-təd\ *adjective* (1781)
: having or shaped like a keel or carina
ca·ri·o·ca \,kar-ē-'ō-kə\ *noun* [Brazilian Portuguese] (1830)
1 *capitalized* **:** a native or resident of Rio de Janeiro
2 a : a variation of the samba **b :** the music for this dance
car·i·o·gen·ic \,kar-ē-ə-'je-nik, ,ker-, -'jē-\ *adjective* [caries + -o- + -genic] (1930)
: producing or promoting the development of tooth decay ⟨*cariogenic* foods⟩
car·i·ous \'kar-ē-əs, 'ker-\ *adjective* [Latin *cariosus*, from *caries*] (1676)
: affected with caries
car·jack·ing \'kär-,ja-kiŋ\ *noun* [car + hijack + -ing] (1991)
: the theft of an automobile from its driver by force or intimidation
— **car·jack·er** *noun*
cark·ing \'kär-kiŋ\ *adjective* [Middle English, from *carken*, literally, to load, burden, from Old North French *carquier*, from Late Latin *carricare*] (circa 1565)
: BURDENSOME, ANNOYING
carl *or* **carle** \'kär(-ə)l\ *noun* [Middle English, from Old English -*carl*, from Old Norse *karl* man, carl — more at CHURL] (before 12th century)
1 : a man of the common people
2 *chiefly dialect* **:** CHURL, BOOR
car·line *or* **car·lin** \'kär-lən\ *noun* [Middle English *kerling*, from Old Norse, from *karl* man] (14th century)
chiefly Scottish **:** WOMAN; *especially* **:** an old woman
Car·list \'kär-list\ *noun* [Spanish *carlista*, from Don *Carlos*] (1830)
: a supporter of Don Carlos or his successors as having rightful title to the Spanish throne
— **Carlist** *adjective*
car·load \'kär-,lōd, -,lōd\ *noun* (1854)
1 : a load that fills a car
2 : the minimum number of tons required for shipping at carload rates
carload rate *noun* (1906)
: a rate for large shipments lower than that

quoted for less-than-carload lots of the same class
Car·lo·vin·gian \,kär-lə-'vin-j(ē-)ən\ *adjective* [French *carlovingien*, from Medieval Latin *Carlus* Charles + French -*ovingien* (as in *mérovingien* Merovingian)] (1781)
: CAROLINGIAN
car·ma·gnole \'kär-mən-,yōl\ *noun* [French] (1793)
1 : a lively song popular at the time of the first French Revolution
2 : a street dance in a meandering course to the tune of the carmagnole
car·mak·er \'kär-,mā-kər\ *noun* (1954)
: an automobile manufacturer
Car·mel·ite \'kär-mə-,līt\ *noun* [Middle English, from Medieval Latin *carmelita*, from *Carmel* Mount Carmel, Palestine] (15th century)
: a member of the Roman Catholic mendicant Order of Our Lady of Mount Carmel founded in the 12th century
— **Carmelite** *adjective*
car·mi·na·tive \kär-'mi-nə-tiv, 'kär-mə-,nā-\ *adjective* [French *carminatif*, from Latin *carminatus*, past participle of *carminare* to card, from (assumed) Latin *carmin-, carmen* card, from Latin *carrere* to card; akin to Lithuanian *karšti* to card] (15th century)
: expelling gas from the alimentary canal so as to relieve colic or griping
— **carminative** *noun*
car·mine \'kär-mən, -,mīn\ *noun* [French *carmin*, from Medieval Latin *carminium*, irregular from Arabic *qirmiz* kermes + Latin *minium* cinnabar] (1712)
1 : a rich crimson or scarlet lake made from cochineal
2 : a vivid red
car·nage \'kär-nij\ *noun* [French, from Medieval Latin *carnaticum* tribute consisting of animals or meat, from Latin *carn-, caro*] (circa 1656)
1 : the flesh of slain animals or men
2 : great and bloody slaughter (as in battle)
car·nal \'kär-n³l\ *adjective* [Middle English, from Old North French or Late Latin; Old North French, from Late Latin *carnalis*, from Latin *carn-, caro* flesh; akin to Greek *keirein* to cut — more at SHEAR] (14th century)
1 a : relating to or given to crude bodily pleasures and appetites **b :** marked by sexuality
2 : BODILY, CORPOREAL
3 a : TEMPORAL **b :** WORLDLY ☆
— **car·nal·i·ty** \kär-'na-lə-tē\ *noun*
— **car·nal·ly** \'kär-n³l-ē\ *adverb*
car·nal·lite \'kär-n³l-,īt\ *noun* [German *Carnallit*, from Rudolf von *Carnall* (died 1874) German mining engineer] (1876)
: a mineral consisting of hydrous potassium-magnesium chloride that is an important source of potassium
car·nas·si·al \kär-'na-sē-əl\ *adjective* [French *carnassier* carnivorous, ultimately from Latin *carn-, caro*] (circa 1852)
: of, relating to, or being teeth of a carnivore often larger and longer than adjacent teeth and adapted for cutting rather than tearing
— **carnassial** *noun*
car·na·tion \kär-'nā-shən\ *noun* [Middle French, from Old Italian *carnagione*, from *carne* flesh, from Latin *carn-, caro*] (circa 1535)
1 a (1) **:** the variable color of human flesh (2) **:** a pale to grayish yellow **b :** a moderate red
2 : a plant of any of numerous often cultivated and usually double-flowered varieties or subspecies of an Old World pink (*Dianthus caryophyllus*) originally flesh-colored but now found in many color variations
car·nau·ba \kär-'nȯ-bə, -'naù-; ,kär-nə-'ü-bə\ *noun* [Portuguese] (1866)
: a fan-leaved palm (*Copernicia prunifera* synonym *C. cerifera*) of Brazil that has an edible root and yields a useful leaf fiber and carnauba wax

carnauba wax *noun* (1854)
: a hard brittle high-melting wax obtained from the leaves of the carnauba palm and used chiefly in polishes
car·ne·lian \kär-'nēl-yən\ *noun* [alteration of *cornelian*, from Middle English *corneline*, from Middle French, perhaps from *cornelle* cornel] (1695)
: a hard tough chalcedony that has a reddish color and is used in jewelry
car·ni·tine \'kär-nə-,tēn\ *noun* [International Scientific Vocabulary, from Latin *carn-, caro*] (circa 1922)
: a quaternary ammonium compound C_7H_{15}-NO_3 that is present especially in vertebrate muscle and is involved in the transfer of fatty acids across mitochondrial membranes
car·ni·val \'kär-nə-vəl\ *noun* [Italian *carnevale*, alteration of earlier *carnelevare*, literally, removal of meat, from *carne* flesh (from Latin *carn-, caro*) + *levare* to remove, from Latin, to raise] (1549)
1 : a season or festival of merrymaking before Lent
2 a : an instance of merrymaking, feasting, or masquerading **b :** an instance of riotous excess ⟨a *carnival* of violence⟩
3 a : a traveling enterprise offering amusements **b :** an organized program of entertainment or exhibition **:** FESTIVAL ⟨a winter *carnival*⟩ ◆
car·niv·o·ra \kär-'ni-və-rə\ *noun plural* [Latin, neuter plural of *carnivorus*] (1830)
: carnivorous mammals
car·ni·vore \'kär-nə-,vȯr, -,vȯr\ *noun* [ultimately from Latin *carnivorus*] (1840)
1 : a carnivorous animal; *especially* **:** any of an order (Carnivora) of flesh-eating mammals
2 : a carnivorous plant
car·niv·o·rous \kär-'ni-v(ə-)rəs\ *adjective* [Latin *carnivorus*, from *carn-, caro* + -*vorus* -vorous] (1592)
1 : subsisting or feeding on animal tissues
2 *of a plant* **:** subsisting on nutrients obtained from the breakdown of animal protoplasm
3 : of or relating to the carnivores
4 : RAPACIOUS
— **car·niv·o·rous·ly** *adverb*
— **car·niv·o·rous·ness** *noun*

☆ **SYNONYMS**
Caricature, burlesque, parody, travesty mean a comic or grotesque imitation. CARICATURE implies ludicrous exaggeration of the characteristic features of a subject ⟨*caricatures* of politicians in cartoons⟩. BURLESQUE implies mockery especially through giving a serious or lofty subject a frivolous treatment ⟨a nightclub *burlesque* of a trial in court⟩. PARODY applies especially to treatment of a trivial or ludicrous subject in the exactly imitated style of a well-known author or work ⟨a witty *parody* of a popular novel⟩. TRAVESTY implies that the subject remains unchanged but that the style is extravagant or absurd ⟨this production is a *travesty* of the opera⟩.

Carnal, fleshly, sensual, animal mean having a relation to the body. CARNAL may mean only this but more often connotes derogatorily an action or manifestation of a person's lower nature ⟨a slave to *carnal* desires⟩. FLESHLY is less derogatory than CARNAL ⟨a saint who had experienced *fleshly* temptations⟩. SENSUAL may apply to any gratification of a bodily desire or pleasure but commonly implies sexual appetite with absence of the spiritual or intellectual ⟨fleshpots providing *sensual* delights⟩. ANIMAL stresses the physical as distinguished from the rational nature of a person ⟨led a mindless *animal* existence⟩.

car·no·tite \'kär-nə-ˌtīt\ *noun* [French, from M. A. *Carnot* (died 1920) French inspector general of mines] (1899)
: a mineral consisting of a hydrous radioactive vanadate of uranium and potassium that is a source of radium and uranium

car·ny *or* **car·ney** *or* **car·nie** \'kär-nē\ *noun, plural* **carnies** *or* **carneys** *often attributive* (circa 1933)
1 : CARNIVAL 3a
2 : a person who works with a carnival

car·ob \'kar-əb\ *noun* [Middle French *carobe,* from Medieval Latin *carrubium,* from Arabic *kharrūbah*] (1548)
1 : a Mediterranean evergreen leguminous tree (*Ceratonia siliqua*) with racemose red flowers
2 : a carob pod or its sweet pulp having a flavor similar to that of chocolate

ca·roche \kə-'rōch, -'rōsh\ *noun* [Middle French *carroche,* from Old Italian *carroccio,* augmentative of *carro* car, from Latin *carrus*] (1591)
: a luxurious horse-drawn carriage

¹car·ol \'kar-əl\ *noun* [Middle English *carole,* from Middle French, modification of Late Latin *choraula* choral song, from Latin, choral accompanist, from Greek *choraulēs,* from *choros* chorus + *aulein* to play a reed instrument, from *aulos,* a reed instrument — more at ALVEOLUS] (14th century)
1 : an old round dance with singing
2 : a song of joy or mirth ⟨the *carol* of a bird —Lord Byron⟩
3 : a popular song or ballad of religious joy ◊

²carol *verb* **-oled** *or* **-olled; -ol·ing** *or* **-ol·ling** (14th century)
intransitive verb
1 : to sing especially in a joyful manner
2 : to sing carols; *specifically* : to go about outdoors in a group singing Christmas carols
transitive verb
1 : to praise in or as if in song
2 : to sing especially in a cheerful manner : WARBLE
— **car·ol·er** *or* **car·ol·ler** \-ə-lər\ *noun*

Car·o·line \'kar-ə-ˌlīn, -lən\ *or* **Car·o·le·an** \ˌkar-ə-'lē-ən\ *adjective* [New Latin *carolinus,* from Medieval Latin *Carolus* Charles] (1652)
: of or relating to Charles — used especially with reference to Charles I and Charles II of England

Car·o·lin·gi·an \ˌkar-ə-'lin-j(ē-)ən\ *adjective* [French *carolingien,* from Medieval Latin *Karolingi* Carolingians, from *Karolus* Charlemagne + *-ingi* (as in *Merovingi* Merovingians)] (1881)
: of or relating to a Frankish dynasty dating from about A.D. 613 and including among its members the rulers of France from 751 to 987, of Germany from 752 to 911, and of Italy from 774 to 961
— **Carolingian** *noun*

¹car·om \'kar-əm\ *noun* [by shortening & alteration from obsolete *carambole,* from Spanish *carambola*] (1779)
1 a : a shot in billiards in which the cue ball strikes each of two object balls **b** : a shot in pool in which an object ball strikes another ball before falling into a pocket — compare COMBINATION SHOT
2 : a rebounding especially at an angle

²carom *intransitive verb* (1860)
1 : to strike and rebound : GLANCE ⟨the car *caromed* off a tree⟩
2 : to make a carom
3 : to proceed by or as if by caroms

car·o·tene \'kar-ə-ˌtēn\ *noun* [International Scientific Vocabulary, from Late Latin *carota* carrot] (1861)
: any of several orange or red crystalline hydrocarbon pigments $C_{40}H_{56}$ that occur in the chromoplasts of plants and in the fatty tissues of plant-eating animals and are convertible to vitamin A

ca·rot·en·oid *also* **ca·rot·in·oid** \kə-'rä-t-ᵊn-ˌȯid\ *noun* (1911)

: any of various usually yellow to red pigments (as carotenes) found widely in plants and animals and characterized chemically by a long aliphatic polyene chain composed of eight isoprene units
— **carotenoid** *adjective*

ca·rot·id \kə-'rä-təd\ *adjective* [French or Greek; French *carotide,* from Greek *karōtides* carotid arteries, from *karoun* to stupefy; akin to Greek *kara* head — more at CEREBRAL] (1543)
: of, relating to, or being the chief artery or pair of arteries that pass up the neck and supply the head
— **carotid** *noun*

carotid body *noun* (1940)
: a small body of vascular tissue that adjoins the carotid sinus, functions as a chemoreceptor sensitive to change in the oxygen content of blood, and mediates reflex changes in respiratory activity

carotid sinus *noun* (circa 1923)
: a small but richly innervated arterial enlargement that is located near the point in the neck where either carotid artery divides to form its main branches and that functions in the regulation of heart rate and blood pressure

ca·rous·al \kə-'rau̇-zəl\ *noun* (1765)
: CAROUSE 2

¹ca·rouse \kə-'rau̇z\ *noun* [Middle French *carrousse,* from *carous,* adverb, all out (in *boire carous* to empty the cup), from German *gar aus*] (1559)
1 *archaic* : a large draft of liquor : TOAST
2 : a drunken revel

²carouse *verb* **ca·roused; ca·rous·ing** (1567)
intransitive verb
1 : to drink liquor deeply or freely
2 : to take part in a carouse : engage in dissolute behavior
transitive verb
obsolete : to drink up : QUAFF
— **ca·rous·er** *noun*

car·ou·sel \ˌkar-ə-'sel *also* -'zel; 'kar-ə-ˌ\ *noun* [French *carrousel,* from Italian *carosello*] (1650)
1 : a tournament or exhibition in which horsemen execute evolutions
2 a : MERRY-GO-ROUND **b** : a circular conveyer ⟨the luggage *carousel* at the airport⟩ **c** : a revolving case used for storage or display

¹carp \'kärp\ *intransitive verb* [Middle English, of Scandinavian origin; akin to Icelandic *karpa* to dispute] (14th century)
: to find fault or complain querulously
— **carp·er** *noun*

²carp *noun* (1904)
: COMPLAINT

³carp *noun, plural* **carp** *or* **carps** [Middle English *carpe,* from Middle French, from Late Latin *carpa,* probably of Germanic origin; akin to Old High German *karpfo* carp] (15th century)
1 : a large variable Asian soft-finned freshwater cyprinid fish (*Cyprinus carpio*) of sluggish waters that is often raised for food and has been widely introduced into U.S. waters; *also* : any of various related fishes
2 : a fish (as the European sea bream) resembling a carp

carp- *or* **carpo-** *combining form* [French & New Latin, from Greek *karp-, karpo-,* from *karpos* — more at HARVEST]
: fruit ⟨*carpo*gonium⟩

-carp *noun combining form* [New Latin *-carpium,* from Greek *-karpion,* from *karpos*]
: part of a fruit ⟨meso*carp*⟩ : fruit ⟨schizo*carp*⟩

car·pac·cio \kär-'pä-ch(ē-)ō\ *noun* [Vittore *Carpaccio;* from the prominent use of red in his painting] (1969)
: thinly sliced raw meat or fish served with a sauce — often used as a postpositive modifier ⟨beef *carpaccio*⟩

¹car·pal \'kär-pəl\ *adjective* [New Latin *carpalis,* from *carpus*] (1743)
: relating to the carpus

²carpal *noun* (1855)
: a carpal element or bone

carpal tunnel syndrome *noun* (1954)
: a condition caused by compression of a nerve where it passes through the wrist into the hand and characterized especially by weakness, pain, and disturbances of sensation in the hand

car park *noun* (1926)
chiefly British : PARKING LOT

car·pe di·em \ˌkär-pe-'dē-ˌem, -'dī-, -əm\ *noun* [Latin, literally, pluck the day] (1817)
: the enjoyment of the pleasures of the moment without concern for the future

car·pel \'kär-pəl\ *noun* [New Latin *carpellum,* from Greek *karpos* fruit] (1835)
: one of the ovule-bearing structures in an angiosperm that comprises the innermost whorl of a flower — compare PISTIL
— **car·pel·lary** \-pə-ˌler-ē\ *adjective*
— **car·pel·late** \-ˌlāt, -lət\ *adjective*

¹car·pen·ter \'kär-pən-tər, 'kärp-ᵊm-tər\ *noun* [Middle English, from Old North French *carpentier,* from Latin *carpentarius* carriage maker, from *carpentum* carriage, of Celtic origin; akin to Old Irish *carpat* chariot, *carr* vehicle — more at CAR] (14th century)
: a worker who builds or repairs wooden structures or their structural parts

◊ WORD HISTORY

carnival In Roman Catholic countries, Lent has traditionally been a period of abstinence from meat, and the days immediately before Lent a time of unrestrained indulgence and merrymaking that ended on the eve of Ash Wednesday. A pattern common to a number of European languages was to apply the name for the very beginning of Lent, the end of meat-eating, to the preceding festive period. In Italian dialects, the word for this period was a compound formed from descendants of Latin *carn-* "meat" and any of several verbs marking removal or cessation. Examples of such compounds are Tuscan *carnasciale,* ultimately from Latin *carn-* plus *laxare* "to let go," and, in the dialect of the area around Rome, *carnevale,* ultimately from Latin *carn-* plus *levare* "to raise, remove." The splendor of pre-Lenten festivities held in Rome during the Renaissance led to the adoption of *carnevale* into other languages of Europe in the 16th century, including French and English.

carol In medieval England and France, the word *carole* referred to a courtly dance that could be either processional or circular, one in which the musical accompaniment was provided by the dancers' own singing. The original choreography of such dances has not survived, nor are there any extant musical or literary texts from the 14th century or earlier that are explicitly given this name. It appears, though, that the leader of the dance sang verses to which the other dancers responded with a refrain. In any event, the Middle English word *carole* is applied in the 15th century to a kind of popular song with a refrain that both begins the song and is repeated after each stanza. Because these songs were often about events of the Nativity, the word *carol* has become closely associated with the Christmas season. Now it may refer not only to traditional compositions of medieval date but also to comparatively modern stanzaic hymns such as "Joy to the World" or "Hark the Herald Angels Sing."

\ə\ abut \ᵊ\ kitten \ər\ further \a\ ash \ā\ ace \ä\ mop, mar \au̇\ out \ch\ chin \e\ bet \ē\ easy \g\ go \i\ hit \ī\ ice \j\ job \ŋ\ sing \ō\ go \ȯ\ law \ȯi\ boy \th\ thin \th\ the \ü\ loot \u̇\ foot \y\ yet \zh\ vision *see also* Guide to Pronunciation

²**carpenter** *verb* **-tered; -ter·ing** \-t(ə-)riŋ\ (circa 1815)
intransitive verb
: to follow the trade of a carpenter 〈*carpentered* when he was young〉
transitive verb
1 : to make by or as if by carpentry
2 : to put together often in a mechanical manner 〈*carpentered* many television scripts〉

carpenter ant *noun* (1883)
: an ant (especially genus *Camponotus*) that gnaws galleries especially in dead or decayed wood

carpenter bee *noun* (1838)
: any of various solitary bees (genera *Xylocopa* and *Ceratina*) that nest in wood

car·pen·try \-trē\ *noun* (14th century)
1 : the art or trade of a carpenter; *specifically* : the art of shaping and assembling structural woodwork
2 : timberwork constructed by a carpenter
3 : the form or manner of putting together the parts (as of a literary or musical composition)

car·pet \ˈkär-pət\ *noun* [Middle English, from Middle French *carpite*, from Old Italian *carpita*, from *carpire* to pluck, modification of Latin *carpere* to pluck — more at HARVEST] (15th century)
1 : a heavy often tufted fabric used as a floor covering; *also* : a floor covering made of this fabric
2 : a surface resembling or suggesting a carpet
— **carpet** *transitive verb*
— **on the carpet** : before an authority for censure or reproof

¹**car·pet·bag** \-ˌbag\ *noun* (1830)
: a traveler's bag made of carpet and widely used in the U.S. in the 19th century

²**carpetbag** *or* **car·pet·bag·ging** \-ˌba-giŋ\ *adjective* (1870)
: of, relating to, or characteristic of carpetbaggers 〈a *carpetbag* government〉

car·pet·bag·ger \-ˌba-gər\ *noun* [from their carrying all their belongings in carpetbags] (1868)
1 : a Northerner in the South after the American Civil War usually seeking private gain under the reconstruction governments
2 : OUTSIDER; *especially* : a nonresident or new resident who meddles in politics
— **car·pet·bag·gery** \-ˌba-g(ə-)rē\ *noun*

carpetbag steak *noun* (1958)
: a thick piece of steak in which a pocket is cut and stuffed (as with oysters)

carpet beetle *noun* (1889)
: any of several small dermestid beetles (genera *Anthrenus* and *Attagenus*) whose larvae are destructive especially to woolen goods

carpet bombing *noun* (1944)
: the dropping of large numbers of bombs so as to cause uniform devastation over a given area
— **carpet bomb** *verb*

car·pet·ing \ˈkär-pə-tiŋ\ *noun* (1758)
: material for carpets; *also* : CARPETS

car·pet·weed \ˈkär-pət-ˌwēd\ *noun* (1784)
: a North American mat-forming weed (*Mollugo verticillata* of the family Aizoaceae, the carpetweed family)

-carpic *adjective combining form* [probably from New Latin *-carpicus*, from Greek *karpos* fruit]
: -CARPOUS 〈mono*carpic*〉

carp·ing \ˈkär-piŋ\ *adjective* (1581)
: marked by or inclined to querulous and often perverse criticism
synonym see CRITICAL
— **carp·ing·ly** \-piŋ-lē\ *adverb*

car·po·go·ni·um \ˌkär-pə-ˈgō-nē-əm\ *noun*, *plural* **-nia** \-nē-ə\ [New Latin] (1882)
: the flask-shaped egg-bearing portion of the female reproductive branch in some thallophytes (as red algae)
— **car·po·go·ni·al** \-nē-əl\ *adjective*

car·pool \ˈkär-ˌpü(ə)l\ *intransitive verb* (1962)
: to participate in a car pool
— **car·pool·er** *noun*

car pool *noun* (1942)
: an arrangement in which a group of people commute together by car; *also* : the group entering into such an arrangement

car·po·phore \ˈkär-pə-ˌfōr, -ˌfȯr\ *noun* [probably from New Latin *carpophorum*, from *carp-* + *-phorum* -phore] (circa 1859)
1 : the stalk of a fungal fruiting body; *also* : the entire fruiting body
2 : a slender prolongation of a floral axis from which the carpels are suspended

car·port \ˈkär-ˌpōrt, -ˌpȯrt\ *noun* (1939)
: an open-sided automobile shelter by the side of a building

car·po·spore \ˈkär-pə-ˌspōr, -ˌspȯr\ *noun* (1881)
: a diploid spore of a red alga

-carpous *adjective combining form* [New Latin *-carpus*, from Greek *-karpos*, from *karpos* fruit — more at HARVEST]
: having (such) fruit or (so many) fruits 〈syn*carpous*〉
— **-carpy** *noun combining form*

car·pus \ˈkär-pəs\ *noun*, *plural* **car·pi** \-ˌpī, -ˌpē\ [New Latin, from Greek *karpos* — more at WHARF] (1679)
1 : WRIST 1
2 : the bones of the wrist

carr \ˈkä(r)\ *noun* [Middle English *ker*, of Scandinavian origin; akin to Old Norse *kjarr* underbrush] (14th century)
chiefly British : ¹FEN

car·rack \ˈkar-ək, -ik\ *noun* [Middle English *carrake*, from Middle French *caraque*, from Old Spanish *carraca*, from Arabic *qarāqīr*, plural of *qurqūr* merchant ship] (14th century)
: a beamy sailing ship especially of the 15th and 16th centuries

car·ra·geen *also* **car·ra·gheen** \ˈkar-ə-ˌgēn\ *noun* [*Carragheen*, near Waterford, Ireland] (1829)
1 : IRISH MOSS 2
2 : CARRAGEENAN

car·ra·geen·an *or* **car·ra·geen·in** \ˌkar-ə-ˈgē-nən\ *noun* [*carrageen* + ³*-an* or ¹*-in*] (circa 1889)
: a colloid extracted from various red algae and especially Irish moss and used especially as a stabilizing or thickening agent

car·re·four \ˌkar-ə-ˈfür\ *noun* [Middle French, from Late Latin *quadrifurcum*, neuter of *quadrifurcus* having four forks, from Latin *quadri-* + *furca* fork] (15th century)
1 : CROSSROADS
2 : SQUARE, PLAZA 〈the farmers . . . preferred the open *carrefour* for their transactions —Thomas Hardy〉

car·rel \ˈkar-əl\ *noun* [alteration of Middle English *caroll*, from Medieval Latin *carola*, perhaps from *carola* round dance, something circular, from Late Latin *choraula* choral song — more at CAROL] (1593)
: a table that is often partitioned or enclosed and is used for individual study especially in a library

car·riage \ˈkar-ij\ *noun* [Middle English *cariage*, from Old North French, from *carier* to transport in a vehicle — more at CARRY] (14th century)
1 : the act of carrying
2 a *archaic* : DEPORTMENT **b** : manner of bearing the body : POSTURE
3 *archaic* : MANAGEMENT
4 *chiefly British* : the price or expense of carrying
5 *obsolete* : BURDEN, LOAD
6 a : a wheeled vehicle; *especially* : a horse-drawn vehicle designed for private use and comfort **b** *British* : a railway passenger coach
7 : a wheeled support carrying a burden
8 *obsolete* : IMPORT, SENSE
9 *obsolete* : a hanger for a sword
10 : a movable part of a machine for supporting some other movable object or part 〈a typewriter *carriage*〉
synonym see BEARING

carriage trade *noun* (circa 1909)
: trade from well-to-do or upper-class people; *also* : well-to-do people

car·riage·way \ˈkar-ij-ˌwā\ *noun* (1800)
British : a road used by vehicular traffic : HIGHWAY

car·rick bend \ˈkar-ik-\ *noun* [probably from obsolete English *carrick* carrack, from Middle English *carrake*, *carryk*] (1819)
: a knot used to join the ends of two large ropes — see KNOT illustration

car·ri·er \ˈkar-ē-ər\ *noun* (14th century)
1 : one that carries : BEARER, MESSENGER
2 a : an individual or organization engaged in transporting passengers or goods for hire **b** : a transportation line carrying mail between post offices **c** : a postal employee who delivers or collects mail **d** : one that delivers newspapers **e** : an entity (as a hole or an electron) capable of carrying an electric charge
3 a : a container for carrying **b** : a device or machine that carries : CONVEYER
4 : AIRCRAFT CARRIER
5 a : a bearer and transmitter of a causative agent of an infectious disease; *especially* : one who carries the causative agent of a disease (as typhoid fever) systemically but is immune to it **b** : an individual (as one heterozygous for a recessive) having a specified gene that is not expressed or only weakly expressed in its phenotype
6 a : a usually inactive accessory substance : VEHICLE 〈a *carrier* for a drug or an insecticide〉 **b** : a substance (as a catalyst) by whose agency some element or group is transferred from one compound to another
7 a : an electromagnetic wave or alternating current whose modulations are used as signals in radio, telephonic, or telegraphic transmission **b** : a telecommunication company
8 : an organization acting as an insurer

carrier pigeon *noun* (1647)
1 : a pigeon used to carry messages; *especially* : HOMING PIGEON
2 : any of a breed of large long-bodied show pigeons

car·ri·on \ˈkar-ē-ən\ *noun* [Middle English *caroine*, from Anglo-French, from (assumed) Vulgar Latin *caronia*, irregular from Latin *carn-*, *caro* flesh — more at CARNAL] (14th century)
: dead and putrefying flesh; *also* : flesh unfit for food

carrion crow *noun* (1528)
: a uniformly black crow (*Corvus corone corone*) occurring in much of western Europe

car·ron·ade \ˌkar-ə-ˈnād\ *noun* [*Carron*, Scotland] (1779)
: a short-barreled gun of the late 18th and 19th centuries that fired large shot at short range and was used especially on warships

car·rot \ˈkar-ət\ *noun* [Middle French *carotte*, from Late Latin *carota*, from Greek *karōton*] (1533)
1 : a biennial herb (*Daucus carota* of the family Umbelliferae, the carrot family) with a usually orange spindle-shaped edible root; *also* : its root
2 : a reward or advantage offered especially as an inducement

car·rot-and-stick \ˌkar-ət-°n-ˈstik\ *adjective* [from the traditional alternatives of driving a donkey on by either holding out a carrot or whipping it with a stick] (1951)
: characterized by the use of both reward and punishment to induce cooperation 〈*carrot-and-stick* foreign policy〉

car·rot·top \ˈkar-ə(t)-ˌtäp\ *noun* (circa 1902)
: REDHEAD 1
— **car·rot·topped** \-ˌtäpt\ *adjective*

car·roty \ˈkar-ə-tē\ *adjective* (1696)
: resembling carrots in color 〈*carroty* hair〉

car·rou·sel *variant of* CAROUSEL

¹**car·ry** \ˈkar-ē, ˈker-\ *verb* **car·ried; car·ry·ing** [Middle English *carien*, from Old North French *carier* to transport in a vehicle, from

car vehicle, from Latin *carrus* — more at CAR] (14th century)
transitive verb

1 : to move while supporting **:** TRANSPORT ⟨her legs refused to *carry* her further —Ellen Glasgow⟩
2 : to convey by direct communication ⟨*carry* tales about a friend⟩
3 *chiefly dialect* **:** CONDUCT, ESCORT
4 : to influence by mental or emotional appeal **:** SWAY
5 : to get possession or control of **:** CAPTURE ⟨*carried* off the prize⟩
6 : to transfer from one place (as a column) to another ⟨*carry* a number in adding⟩
7 : to contain and direct the course of ⟨the drain *carries* sewage⟩
8 a : to wear or have on one's person **b :** to bear upon or within one ⟨is *carrying* an unborn child⟩
9 a : to have or bear especially as a mark, attribute, or property ⟨*carry* a scar⟩ **b :** IMPLY, INVOLVE ⟨the crime *carried* a heavy penalty⟩
10 : to hold or comport (as one's person) in a specified manner
11 : to sustain the weight or burden of ⟨pillars *carry* an arch⟩
12 : to bear as a crop
13 : to sing with reasonable correctness of pitch ⟨*carry* a tune⟩
14 a : to keep in stock for sale **b :** to provide sustenance for ⟨land *carrying* 10 head of cattle⟩ **c :** to have or maintain on a list or record ⟨*carry* a person on a payroll⟩
15 : to be chiefly or solely responsible for the success, effectiveness, or continuation of ⟨a player capable of *carrying* a team⟩
16 : to prolong in space, time, or degree ⟨*carry* a principle too far⟩
17 a : to gain victory for; *especially* **:** to secure the adoption or passage of **b :** to win a majority of votes in (as a legislative body or a state)
18 : to present for public consumption ⟨newspapers *carry* weather reports⟩ ⟨channel 9 will *carry* the game⟩
19 a : to bear the charges of holding or having (as stocks or merchandise) from one time to another **b :** to keep on one's books as a debtor ⟨a merchant *carries* a customer⟩
20 : to hold to and follow after (as a scent)
21 : to hoist and maintain (a sail) in use
22 : to pass over (as a hazard) at a single stroke in golf ⟨*carry* a bunker⟩
23 : to propel and control (a puck or ball) along a playing surface
intransitive verb
1 : to act as a bearer
2 a : to reach or penetrate to a distance ⟨voices *carry* well⟩ ⟨fly balls don't *carry* well in cold air⟩ **b :** to convey itself to a reader or audience
3 : to undergo or admit of carriage in a specified way
4 *of a hunting dog* **:** to keep and follow the scent
5 : to win adoption ⟨the motion *carried* by a vote of 71–25⟩
— carry a torch *or* **carry the torch 1 :** CRUSADE **2 :** to be in love especially without reciprocation **:** cherish a longing or devotion ⟨still *carrying a torch* for a former lover⟩
— carry the ball : to perform or assume the chief role **:** bear the major portion of work or responsibility
— carry the day : WIN, PREVAIL

²**carry** *noun, plural* **car·ries** (1858)
1 : carrying power; *especially* **:** the range of a gun or projectile or of a struck or thrown ball
2 a : PORTAGE **b :** the act or method of carrying ⟨fireman's *carry*⟩ **c :** the act of rushing with the ball in football ⟨averaged four yards per *carry*⟩
3 : the position assumed by a color-bearer with the flag or guidon held in position for marching

4 : a quantity that is transferred in addition from one number place to the adjacent one of higher place value

car·ry·all \'kar-ē-ˌȯl, 'ker-\ *noun* (1714)
1 [by folk etymology from French *carriole*, from Old Provençal *carriola*, ultimately from Latin *carrus* car] **a :** a light covered carriage for four or more persons **b :** a passenger automobile used as a small bus
2 [¹*carry* + ³*all*] **:** a capacious bag or carrying case

carry away *transitive verb* (1570)
1 : to arouse to a high and often excessive degree of emotion or enthusiasm
2 : CARRY OFF !

car·ry·back \'kar-ē-ˌbak, 'ker-\ *noun* (1942)
: a loss sustained or a portion of a credit not used in a given period that may be deducted from taxable income of a prior period

car·ry·cot \-ˌkät\ *noun* (1943)
British **:** a portable bed for an infant

car·ry·for·ward \'kar-ē-'fȯr-wərd, 'ker-, -ˌfȯr-, *Southern also* -'fär-, -ˌfär-\ *noun* (1898)
: CARRYOVER

carrying capacity *noun* (1921)
: the population (as of deer) that an area will support without undergoing deterioration

carrying charge *noun* (1914)
1 : expense incident to ownership or use of property
2 : a charge added to the price of merchandise sold on the installment plan

car·ry·ing-on \ˌkar-ē-iŋ-'ȯn, ˌker-, -'än\ *noun, plural* **carryings-on** (1663)
: foolish, excited, or improper behavior; *also* **:** an instance of such behavior

carry off *transitive verb* (circa 1680)
1 : to cause the death of ⟨the plague *carried off* thousands⟩
2 : to perform or manage successfully **:** BRING OFF ⟨tried to look suave but couldn't *carry it off*⟩

¹**car·ry·on** \'kar-ē-ˌȯn, 'ker-, -ˌän\ *noun* (1890)
1 *British* **:** CARRYING-ON
2 : a piece of luggage suitable for being carried aboard an airplane by a passenger

²**carry-on** *adjective* (1967)
: carried or suitable for being carried aboard ⟨*carry-on* baggage⟩

carry on (1644)
transitive verb
: to continue doing, pursuing, or operating ⟨*carry on* research⟩ ⟨*carried on* the business⟩
intransitive verb
1 : to behave or speak in a foolish, excited, or improper manner ⟨embarrassed by the way he *carries on*⟩
2 : to continue especially in spite of hindrance or discouragement

car·ry·out \'kar-ē-ˌaut, 'ker-\ *noun* (1964)
1 : prepared food packaged to be consumed away from its place of sale
2 : an establishment selling carryout
— carryout *adjective*

carry out *transitive verb* (1605)
1 : to put into execution ⟨*carry out* a plan⟩
2 : to bring to a successful issue **:** COMPLETE, ACCOMPLISH ⟨you will be paid when you have *carried out* the assignment⟩
3 : to continue to an end or stopping point

car·ry·over \'kar-ē-ˌō-vər, 'ker-\ *noun* (1894)
1 : the act or process of carrying over
2 : something retained or carried over

carry over (1745)
transitive verb
1 a : to transfer (an amount) to the next column, page, or book relating to the same account **b :** to hold over (as goods) for another time or season
2 : to deduct (a loss or an unused credit) from taxable income of a later period
intransitive verb
: to persist from one stage or sphere of activity to another

carry through (1605)
transitive verb

: CARRY OUT
intransitive verb
: PERSIST, SURVIVE ⟨feelings that *carry through* to the present⟩

car·sick \'kär-ˌsik\ *adjective* (1908)
: affected with motion sickness especially in an automobile
— car sickness *noun*

¹**cart** \'kärt\ *noun* [Middle English, probably from Old Norse *kartr;* akin to Old English *cræt* cart] (13th century)
1 : a heavy usually horse-drawn 2-wheeled vehicle used for farming or transporting freight
2 : a lightweight 2-wheeled vehicle drawn by a horse, pony, or dog
3 : a small wheeled vehicle

²**cart** *transitive verb* (14th century)
1 : to carry or convey in or as if in a cart ⟨buses to *cart* the kids to and from school —L. S. Gannett⟩
2 : to take or drag away without ceremony or by force — usually used with *off* ⟨they *carted* him off to jail⟩
— cart·er *noun*

cart·age \'kär-tij\ *noun* (15th century)
: the action of or rate charged for carting

carte blanche \'kärt-'bläⁿsh, -'blänch\ *noun, plural* **cartes blanches** \'kärt(s)-\ [French, literally, blank document] (1754)
: full discretionary power ⟨was given *carte blanche* to furnish the house⟩

carte du jour \ˌkärt-də-'zhùr\ *noun, plural* **cartes du jour** \ˌkärt(s)-\ [French, literally, card of the day] (1936)
: MENU

car·tel \kär-'tel\ *noun* [French, letter of defiance, from Old Italian *cartello*, literally, placard, from *carta* leaf of paper — more at CARD] (1692)
1 : a written agreement between belligerent nations
2 : a combination of independent commercial or industrial enterprises designed to limit competition or fix prices
3 : a combination of political groups for common action ◇

◇ WORD HISTORY
cartel The Italian word *carta* "paper," descended from Latin *charta* "sheet of papyrus," is related to English *card*, *chart*, and *charter*, all likewise from Romance descendants of the Latin word. From *carta*, Italian derived a masculine noun *cartello*, which meant originally "public notice, poster," and then "written challenge to a duel, letter of defiance." In the latter senses the word was borrowed into French as *cartel* and from French into English. During the 17th century, *cartel* became current in several European languages as a designation for a written agreement between warring nations regulating the exchange of prisoners. In addition to this sense, German *Kartell* in the late 19th century came to stand first for an agreement between political parties in the Reichstag (the national legislature), and then for a compact between commercial enterprises to control market conditions and fix prices. Italian *cartello* and English and French *cartel* all borrowed this sense from German. Government antitrust laws in the U.S. and other countries ban such commercial compacts, though *cartel* is now often applied to international organizations that fix prices, such as the Organization of Petroleum Exporting Countries (OPEC).

\ə\ **abut** \ᵊ\ **kitten** \ər\ **further** \a\ **ash** \ā\ **ace**
\ä\ **mop, mar** \aù\ **out** \ch\ **chin** \e\ **bet** \ē\ **easy**
\g\ **go** \i\ **hit** \ī\ **ice** \j\ **job** \ŋ\ **sing** \ō\ **go**
\ȯ\ **law** \ȯi\ **boy** \th\ **thin** \t͟h\ **the** \ü\ **loot** \ù\ **foot**
\y\ **yet** \zh\ **vision** *see also* Guide to Pronunciation

car·tel·ise *British variant of* CARTELIZE

car·tel·ize \'kär-tə-ˌlīz\ *transitive verb* **-ized; -iz·ing** (1915)
: to bring under the control of a cartel
— **car·tel·i·za·tion** \ˌkär-tə-lə-'zā-shən\ *noun*

Car·te·sian \kär-'tē-zhən\ *adjective* [New Latin *cartesianus,* from *Cartesius* Descartes] (1656)
: of or relating to René Descartes or his philosophy ◆
— **Cartesian** *noun*
— **Car·te·sian·ism** \-zhə-ˌni-zəm\ *noun*

Cartesian coordinate *noun* (circa 1888)
1 : either of two coordinates that locate a point on a plane and measure its distance from either of two intersecting straight-line axes along a line parallel to the other axis
2 : any of three coordinates that locate a point in space and measure its distance from any of three intersecting coordinate planes measured parallel to that one of three straight-line axes that is the intersection of the other two planes

Cartesian plane *noun* (1960)
: a plane whose points are labeled with Cartesian coordinates

Cartesian product *noun* (1958)
: a set that is constructed from two given sets and comprises all pairs of elements such that the first element of the pair is from the first set and the second is from the second set

Car·thu·sian \kär-'thü-zhən, -'thyü-\ *noun* [Medieval Latin *Cartusiensis,* from *Cartusia* Chartreuse, motherhouse of the Carthusian order, near Grenoble, France] (1526)
: a member of an ascetic contemplative religious order founded by Saint Bruno in 1084
— **Carthusian** *adjective*

car·ti·lage \'kär-tᵊl-ij, 'kärt-lij\ *noun* [Latin *cartilagin-, cartilago*] (15th century)
1 : a usually translucent somewhat elastic tissue that composes most of the skeleton of vertebrate embryos and except for a small number of structures (as some joints, respiratory passages, and the external ear) is replaced by bone during ossification in the higher vertebrates
2 : a part or structure composed of cartilage

car·ti·lag·i·nous \ˌkär-tə-'la-jə-nəs\ *adjective* (14th century)
: composed of, relating to, or resembling cartilage

cartilaginous fish *noun* (1695)
: any of a class (Chondrichthyes) of fishes (as a shark, ray, or chimaera) having the skeleton wholly or largely composed of cartilage — compare BONY FISH, JAWLESS FISH

cart·load \'kärt-ˌlōd, -ˌlōd\ *noun* (14th century)
: as much as a cart will hold

car·tog·ra·pher \kär-'tä-grə-fər\ *noun* (circa 1847)
: one that makes maps

car·tog·ra·phy \-fē\ *noun* [French *cartographie,* from *carte* card, map + *-graphie* -graphy — more at CARD] (circa 1847)
: the science or art of making maps
— **car·to·graph·ic** \ˌkär-tə-'gra-fik\ *also* **car·to·graph·i·cal** \-fi-kəl\ *adjective*
— **car·to·graph·i·cal·ly** \-fi-k(ə-)lē\ *adverb*

¹car·ton \'kär-tᵊn\ *noun* [French, from Italian *cartone* pasteboard] (circa 1859)
: a box or container usually made of paperboard and often of corrugated paperboard

²carton (1921)
transitive verb
: to pack or enclose in a carton
intransitive verb
: to shape cartons from paperboard sheets

car·toon \kär-'tün\ *noun, often attributive* [Italian *cartone* pasteboard, cartoon, augmentative of *carta* leaf of paper — more at CARD] (1671)

1 : a preparatory design, drawing, or painting (as for a fresco)
2 a : a drawing intended as satire, caricature, or humor ⟨a political *cartoon*⟩ **b** : COMIC STRIP
3 : ANIMATED CARTOON
4 : a ludicrously simplistic, unrealistic, or one-dimensional portrayal or version ⟨the film's villain is an entertaining *cartoon*⟩
— **cartoon** *verb*
— **car·toon·ing** *noun*
— **car·toon·ish** \-'tü-nish\ *adjective*
— **car·toon·ish·ly** *adverb*
— **car·toon·ist** \-'tü-nist\ *noun*
— **car·toon·like** \-'tün-ˌlīk\ *adjective*
— **car·toony** \-'tü-nē\ *adjective*

car·top \'kär-ˌtäp\ *adjective* (1946)
: suitable in size and weight for carrying on top of an automobile ⟨a *cartop* fishing boat⟩
— **car·top·per** \-ˌtä-pər\ *noun*

car·touche *also* **car·touch** \kär-'tüsh\ *noun* [French *cartouche,* from Italian *cartoccio,* from *carta*] (1611)
1 : a gun cartridge with a paper case
2 : an ornate or ornamental frame
3 : an oval or oblong figure (as on ancient Egyptian monuments) enclosing a sovereign's name

car·tridge \'kär-trij, *dialect* 'ka-trij\ *noun* [alteration of earlier *cartage,* modification of Middle French *cartouche*] (1579)
: a case or container that holds a substance, device, or material which is difficult, troublesome, or awkward to handle and that usually can be easily changed: as **a** : a tube (as of metal) containing a complete charge for a firearm and usually an initiating device (as a primer) **b** : a case containing an explosive charge for blasting **c** : an often cylindrical container for insertion into a larger mechanism or apparatus **d** : CASSETTE 2 **e** : a small case that contains a phonograph needle and transducer and is attached to a tonearm **f** : a case containing a reel of magnetic tape arranged for insertion into a recorder or player **g** : a removable case containing a magnetic tape or one or more disks and used as a computer storage medium **h** : a case for holding printed circuit chips containing a computer program ⟨a video-game *cartridge*⟩

cartridge belt *noun* (1874)
1 : a belt having a series of loops for holding cartridges
2 : a belt worn around the waist and designed for carrying various attachable equipment (as a cartridge case, canteen, or compass)

car·tu·lary \'kär-chə-ˌler-ē\ *noun, plural* **-lar·ies** [Medieval Latin *chartularium,* from *chartula* charter — more at CHARTER] (1541)
: a collection of charters; *especially* : a book holding copies of the charters and title deeds of an estate

¹cart·wheel \'kärt-ˌhwēl, -ˌwēl\ *noun* (1855)
1 : a large coin (as a silver dollar)
2 : a lateral handspring with arms and legs extended

²cartwheel *intransitive verb* (1917)
: to move like a turning wheel; *specifically* : to perform cartwheels
— **cart·wheel·er** *noun*

car·un·cle \'kar-ˌəŋ-kəl, kə-'rəŋ-\ *noun* [obsolete French *caruncule,* from Latin *caruncula* little piece of flesh, diminutive of *caro* flesh — more at CARNAL] (1615)
1 : a naked fleshy outgrowth (as a bird's wattle)
2 : an outgrowth on a seed adjacent to the micropyle

car·va·crol \'kär-və-ˌkrȯl, -ˌkrōl\ *noun* [International Scientific Vocabulary, from New Latin *carvi* (specific epithet of *Carum carvi* caraway) + Latin *acr-, acer* sharp — more at CARAWAY, EDGE] (1854)
: a liquid phenol $C_{10}H_{14}O$ found in essential oils of various mints (as thyme) and used as a fungicide and disinfectant

carve \'kärv\ *verb* **carved; carv·ing** [Middle English *kerven,* from Old English *ceorfan;* akin to Old High German *kerban* to notch, Greek *graphein* to scratch, write] (before 12th century)
transitive verb
1 : to cut with care or precision ⟨*carved* fretwork⟩
2 : to make or get by or as if by cutting — often used with *out* ⟨*carve* out a career⟩
3 : to cut into pieces or slices ⟨*carved* the turkey⟩
intransitive verb
1 : to cut up and serve meat
2 : to work as a sculptor or engraver
— **carv·er** *noun*

car·vel–built \'kär-vəl-ˌbilt, -ˌvel-\ *adjective* [probably from Dutch *karveel-,* from *karveel* caravel, from Middle French *carvelle*] (1798)
: built with the planks meeting flush at the seams

carv·en \'kär-vən\ *adjective* (14th century)
: wrought or ornamented by carving

carv·ing \'kär-viŋ\ *noun* (13th century)
1 : the act or art of one who carves
2 : a carved object, design, or figure

car wash *noun* (1956)
: an area or structure equipped with facilities for washing automobiles

cary- *or* **caryo-** — see KARY-

cary·at·id \ˌkar-ē-'a-təd, 'kar-ē-ə-ˌtid\ *noun, plural* **-ids** *or* **-i·des** \ˌkar-ē-'a-tə-ˌdēz\ [Latin *caryatides,* plural, from Greek *karyatides* priestesses of Artemis at Caryae, caryatids, from *Karyai* Caryae in Laconia] (1563)
: a draped female figure supporting an entablature

cary·op·sis \ˌkar-ē-'äp-səs\ *noun, plural* **-op·ses** \-ˌsēz\ *also* **-si·des** \-sə-ˌdēz\ [New Latin] (1830)
: a small one-seeded dry indehiscent fruit (as of Indian corn or wheat) in which the fruit and seed fuse in a single grain

ca·sa \'kä-sə\ *noun* [Spanish & Italian, from Latin, cottage] (1844)
chiefly Southwest : DWELLING

ca·sa·ba \kə-'sä-bə\ *noun* [*Kasaba* (now Turgutlu), Turkey] (1889)
: any of several winter melons with yellow rind and sweet flesh

Ca·sa·no·va \ˌka-zə-'nō-və, ˌka-sə-\ *noun* [Giacomo Girolamo *Casanova*] (1888)
1 : LOVER; *especially* : a man who is a promiscuous and unscrupulous lover

Cas·bah \'kaz-ˌbä, 'käz-\ *noun* [French, from Arabic dialect *qaṣbah*] (1944)
1 : a North African castle or fortress
2 : the native section of a North African city

cas·ca·bel \'kas-kə-ˌbel\ *noun* [Spanish, literally, small bell] (1639)
1 : a projection behind the breech of a muzzle-loading cannon

caryatid

◇ WORD HISTORY
Cartesian That the derivative adjective for the French philosopher and mathematician René Descartes should be *Cartesian* might seem puzzling at first. The explanation lies in the fact that Descartes lived and wrote in the 17th century, when Latin was the international language of science and letters. Descartes' name was Latinized as Renatus Cartesius, and so *Cartesian* became the word for things relating to him and his work.

2 : a small hollow perforated spherical bell enclosing a loose pellet

¹cas·cade \\(ˌ)kas-'kād\ *noun* [French, from Italian *cascata,* from *cascare* to fall, from (assumed) Vulgar Latin *casicare,* from Latin *casus* fall] (1641)
1 : a steep usually small fall of water; *especially* **:** one of a series
2 a : something arranged or occurring in a series or in a succession of stages so that each stage derives from or acts upon the product of the preceding ⟨blood clotting involves a biochemical *cascade*⟩ **b :** a fall of material (as lace) that hangs in a zigzag line
3 : something falling or rushing forth in quantity ⟨a *cascade* of sound⟩ ⟨a *cascade* of events⟩

²cascade *verb* **cas·cad·ed; cas·cad·ing** (1702)
intransitive verb
: to fall, pour, or rush in or as if in a cascade
transitive verb
1 : to cause to fall like a cascade
2 : to connect in a cascade arrangement

cas·cara \kas-'skar-ə\ *noun* [Spanish *cáscara* husk, bark, probably from *cascar* to crack, break, from (assumed) Vulgar Latin *quassicare* to shake, from Latin *quassare* — more at QUASH] (1879)
1 : CASCARA BUCKTHORN
2 : CASCARA SAGRADA

cascara buckthorn *noun* (circa 1900)
: a buckthorn (*Rhamnus purshiana*) of the Pacific coast of the U.S. yielding cascara sagrada

cascara sa·gra·da \-sə-'grä-də\ *noun* [American Spanish *cáscara sagrada,* literally, sacred bark] (1885)
: the dried bark of cascara buckthorn used as a laxative

cas·ca·ril·la \ˌkas-kə-'ri-lə, -'rē-ə\ *noun* [Spanish, diminutive of *cáscara*] (1686)
: the aromatic bark of a West Indian shrub (*Croton eluteria*) of the spurge family used for making incense and as a tonic; *also* **:** this shrub

¹case \'kās\ *noun* [Middle English *cas,* from Old French, from Latin *casus* fall, chance, from *cadere* to fall — more at CHANCE] (13th century)
1 a : a set of circumstances or conditions ⟨is the statement true in all three *cases*⟩ **b** (1) **:** a situation requiring investigation or action (as by the police) (2) **:** the object of investigation or consideration
2 : CONDITION; *specifically* **:** condition of body or mind
3 [Middle English *cas,* from Middle French, from Latin *casus,* translation of Greek *ptōsis,* literally, fall] **a :** an inflectional form of a noun, pronoun, or adjective indicating its grammatical relation to other words **b :** such a relation whether indicated by inflection or not
4 : what actually exists or happens **:** FACT
5 a : a suit or action in law or equity **b** (1) **:** the evidence supporting a conclusion or judgment (2) **:** ARGUMENT; *especially* **:** a convincing argument
6 a : an instance of disease or injury; *also* **:** PATIENT **b :** an instance that directs attention to a situation or exhibits it in action **:** EXAMPLE **c :** a peculiar person **:** CHARACTER
7 : oneself considered as an object of harassment ⟨get off my *case*⟩
synonym see INSTANCE
— in any case : without regard to or in spite of other considerations **:** whatever else is done or is the case ⟨war is inevitable *in any case*⟩ ⟨*in any case* the report will be made public next month⟩
— in case : as a precaution ⟨took an umbrella, just *in case*⟩
— in case of : in the event of ⟨*in case of* trouble, yell⟩

²case *noun* [Middle English *cas,* from Old North French *casse,* from Latin *capsa* chest, case, probably from *capere* to take — more at HEAVE] (14th century)
1 a : a box or receptacle for holding something **b :** a box together with its contents **c :** SET; *specifically* **:** PAIR
2 a : an outer covering or housing ⟨a pastry *case*⟩ **b :** a tube into which the components of a round of ammunition are loaded
3 : a divided tray for holding printing type
4 : the frame of a door or window **:** CASING

³case *transitive verb* **cased; cas·ing** (1575)
1 : to enclose in or cover with or as if with a case **:** ENCASE
2 : to line (as a well) with supporting material (as metal pipe)
3 : to inspect or study especially with intent to rob

ca·se·ation \ˌkā-sē-'ā-shən\ *noun* [Latin *caseus* cheese] (1866)
: necrosis with conversion of damaged tissue into a soft cheesy substance
— ca·se·ate \'kā-sē-ˌāt\ *intransitive verb*

case-bear·er \'kās-ˌbar-ər, -ˌber-\ *noun* (circa 1889)
: an insect larva that forms a protective case (as of silk)

case·book \-ˌbuk\ *noun* (1762)
1 : a book containing records of illustrative cases that is used for reference and instruction (as in law or medicine)
2 : a compilation of primary and secondary documents relating to a central topic together with scholarly comment, exercises, and study aids that is designed to serve as a sourcebook for short papers (as in a writing course) or as a point of departure for a research paper

cased glass \'kāst-\ *noun* (1849)
: glass consisting of two or more fused layers of different colors often decorated by cutting so that the inner layers show through — called also *case glass*

case goods *noun plural* (1922)
1 : furniture (as bureaus or bookcases) that provides interior storage space; *also* **:** dining-room and bedroom furniture sold as sets
2 : products often sold by the case

case-hard·en \'kās-ˌhär-d°n\ *transitive verb* (1677)
1 : to harden (a ferrous alloy) so that the surface layer is harder than the interior
2 : to make callous or insensible
— case-hard·ened *adjective*

case history *noun* (1894)
: a record of history, environment, and relevant details of a case especially for use in analysis or illustration

ca·sein \'kā-ˌsēn, kā-'\ *noun* [probably from French *caséine,* from Latin *caseus*] (1841)
: a phosphoprotein of milk: as **a :** one that is precipitated from milk by heating with an acid or by the action of lactic acid in souring and is used in making paints and adhesives **b :** one that is produced when milk is curdled by rennet, is the chief constituent of cheese, and is used in making plastics

ca·sein·ate \kā-'sē-ˌnāt, 'kā-si-ˌnāt\ *noun* (1904)
: a compound of casein with a metal (as calcium or sodium)

case in point (1965)
: an illustrative, relevant, or pertinent case

case knife *noun* (1704)
1 : SHEATH KNIFE
2 : a table knife

case law *noun* (1861)
: law established by judicial decision in cases

case·load \'kās-ˌlōd\ *noun* (1938)
: the number of cases handled (as by a court or clinic) usually in a particular period

case·mate \'kās-ˌmāt\ *noun* [Middle French, from Old Italian *casamatta*] (1575)
: a fortified position or chamber or an armored enclosure on a warship from which guns are fired through embrasures

case·ment \'kās-mənt\ *noun* [Middle English, hollow molding, probably from Old North French *encassement* frame, from *encasser* to enchase, frame, from *en-* + *casse*] (15th century)
: a window sash that opens on hinges at the side; *also* **:** a window with such a sash

ca·se·ous \'kā-sē-əs\ *adjective* [Latin *caseus* cheese] (1661)
: marked by caseation; *also* **:** CHEESY

ca·sern *or* **ca·serne** \kə-'zərn\ *noun* [French *caserne*] (1696)
: a military barracks in a garrison town

case study *noun* (1875)
1 : an intensive analysis of an individual unit (as a person or community) stressing developmental factors in relation to environment
2 : CASE HISTORY

case system *noun* (circa 1889)
: a system of teaching law in which instruction is chiefly on the basis of leading or selected cases as primary authorities instead of from textbooks

case·work \'kās-ˌwərk\ *noun* (1886)
: social work involving direct consideration of the problems, needs, and adjustments of the individual case (as a person or family)
— case·work·er \-ˌwər-kər\ *noun*

¹cash \'kash\ *noun* [modification of Middle French or Old Italian; Middle French *casse* money box, from Old Italian *cassa,* from Latin *capsa* chest — more at CASE] (1596)
1 : ready money
2 : money or its equivalent (as a check) paid for goods or services at the time of purchase or delivery
— cash·less \-ləs\ *adjective*

²cash *adjective* (1622)
: being a method of accounting that includes as income only what has been received in cash and as expenses only those paid in cash

³cash *transitive verb* (1811)
1 : to pay or obtain cash for ⟨*cash* a check⟩
2 : to lead and win a bridge trick with (a card that is the highest remaining card of its suit)
— cash·able \'ka-shə-bəl\ *adjective*

⁴cash *noun, plural* **cash** [Portuguese *caixa,* from Tamil *kācu,* a small copper coin, from Sanskrit *karṣa,* a weight of gold or silver] (1598)
1 : any of various coins of small value in China and southern India; *especially* **:** a Chinese coin with a square hole in the center
2 : a unit of value equivalent to one cash

¹cash–and–car·ry \ˌka-sh°n-'kar-ē, -'ker-\ *adjective* (1917)
: sold or provided for cash and usually without delivery service

²cash–and–carry *noun* (1921)
: the policy of selling on a cash-and-carry basis

cash bar *noun* (1968)
: a bar (as at a reception) at which drinks are sold — compare OPEN BAR

cash·book \'kash-ˌbuk\ *noun* (1622)
: a book in which record is kept of all cash receipts and disbursements

cash cow *noun* (1979)
: a consistently profitable business, property, or product whose profits are used to finance a company's investments in other areas

cash crop *noun* (1868)
: a readily salable crop (as cotton or tobacco) produced or gathered primarily for market

cash discount *noun* (1917)
: a discount granted in consideration of immediate payment or payment within a prescribed time

cash·ew \'ka-(ˌ)shü, kə-'shü\ *noun* [Portuguese *acajú, cajú,* from Tupi *acajú*] (1598)

: a tropical American tree (*Anacardium occidentale* of the family Anacardiaceae, the cashew family) grown for a phenolic oil and the edible kernel of its nut and for a gum from its stem; *also* : CASHEW NUT

cashew nut *noun* (1796)
: the kidney-shaped kernel of the fruit of the cashew that is edible when roasted

cash flow *noun* (1954)
1 : a measure of an organization's liquidity that usually consists of net income after taxes plus noncash charges (as depreciation) against income
2 : a flow of cash; *especially* : one that provides solvency

¹**ca·shier** \ka-'shir, kə-\ *transitive verb* [Dutch *casseren*, from Middle French *casser* to discharge, annul — more at QUASH] (1592)
1 : to dismiss from service; *especially* : to dismiss dishonorably
2 : REJECT, DISCARD

²**cash·ier** \(ˌ)ka-'shir\ *noun* [Dutch or Middle French; Dutch *kassier*, from Middle French *cassier*, from *casse* money box] (1596)
: one that has charge of money: as **a** : a high officer in a bank or trust company responsible for moneys received and expended **b** : one who collects and records payments

cashier's check *noun* (1867)
: a check drawn by a bank on its own funds and signed by the cashier

cash in (1888)
transitive verb
: to obtain cash for ⟨*cashed in* the bonds⟩
intransitive verb
1 a : to retire from a gambling game **b** : to settle accounts and withdraw from an involvement (as a business deal)
2 : to obtain advantage or financial profit — often used with *on* ⟨*cash in* on a best-seller⟩

cash·mere \'kazh-ˌmir, 'kash-\ *noun* [*Cashmere* (Kashmir)] (1684)
1 : fine wool from the undercoat of the cashmere goat; *also* : a yarn of this wool
2 : a soft twilled fabric made originally from cashmere

cashmere goat *noun* (circa 1890)
: an Indian goat raised especially for its undercoat of fine soft wool that constitutes the cashmere wool of commerce

cash register *noun* (1879)
: a business machine that usually has a money drawer, indicates the amount of each sale, and records the amount of money received and often automatically makes change

cas·ing \'kā-siŋ\ *noun* (1791)
1 : something that encases : material for encasing: as **a** : an enclosing frame especially around a door or window opening **b** : a metal pipe used to case a well **c** : ⁴TIRE 2 **d** : a membranous case for processed meat
2 : a space formed between two parallel lines of stitching through at least two layers of cloth into which something (as a rod or string) may be inserted

ca·si·no \kə-'sē-(ˌ)nō\ *noun, plural* **-nos** [Italian, from *casa* house, from Latin, cottage] (1744)
1 : a building or room used for social amusements; *specifically* : one used for gambling
2 *also* **cas·si·no** : a card game in which cards are won by matching or combining cards in a hand with those exposed on the table
3 : SUMMERHOUSE 2

ca·si·ta \kə-'sē-tə\ *noun* [Spanish, diminutive of *casa*] (1923)
: a small house

cask \'kask\ *noun* [Middle English *caske*, perhaps from Middle French *casque* helmet, from Spanish *casco* potsherd, skull, helmet] (15th century)
1 : a barrel-shaped vessel of staves, headings, and hoops usually for liquids

2 : a cask and its contents; *also* : the quantity contained in a cask

cas·ket \'kas-kət\ *noun* [Middle English, perhaps modification of Middle French *cassette*] (15th century)
1 : a small chest or box (as for jewels)
2 : a usually fancy coffin
— **casket** *transitive verb*

casque \'kask\ *noun* [Middle French — more at CASK] (1580)
1 : a piece of armor for the head : HELMET
2 : an anatomic structure suggestive of a helmet

Cas·san·dra \kə-'san-drə, -'sän-\ *noun* [Latin, from Greek *Kassandra*]
1 : a daughter of Priam endowed with the gift of prophecy but fated never to be believed
2 : one that predicts misfortune or disaster

cas·sa·va \kə-'sä-və\ *noun* [Spanish *cazabe* cassava bread, from Taino *caçábi*] (1555)
: any of several plants (genus *Manihot* and especially *M. esculenta*) of the spurge family grown in the tropics for their fleshy edible rootstocks which yield a nutritious starch; *also* : the rootstock

cas·se·role \'ka-sə-ˌrōl *also* 'ka-zə-\ *noun* [French, saucepan, from Middle French, diminutive of *casse* ladle, dripping pan, from Old Provençal *cassa*, probably ultimately from Greek *kyathos* ladle] (1708)
1 : a dish in which food may be baked and served
2 : food cooked and served in a casserole
3 : a deep round usually porcelain dish with a handle used for heating substances in the laboratory

cas·sette *also* **ca·sette** \kə-'set, ka-\ *noun* [French, from Middle French, diminutive of Old North French *casse* case] (1793)
1 : CASKET 1
2 : a usually flat case or container that is used especially in a device or machine, that holds something which is difficult, troublesome, or awkward to handle, and that can be easily loaded or unloaded: as **a** : a lightproof magazine for holding film or plates for use in a camera **b** : a plastic cartridge containing magnetic tape with the tape on one reel passing to the other

cas·sia \'ka-shə\ *noun* [Middle English, from Old English, from Latin, from Greek *kassia*, of Semitic origin; akin to Hebrew *qěṣî'āh* cassia] (before 12th century)
1 : a coarse cinnamon bark (as from *Cinnamomum cassia*)
2 : any of a genus (*Cassia*) of leguminous herbs, shrubs, and trees of warm regions

cas·si·mere \'ka-zə-ˌmir, 'ka-sə-\ *noun* [obsolete *Cassimere* (Kashmir)] (1774)
: a closely woven smooth twilled usually wool fabric (as for suits)

Cas·si·ni division \kə-'sē-nē-\ *noun* [Gian Domenico *Cassini* (died 1712) Italian astronomer] (circa 1909)
: the dark region between the two brightest rings of Saturn — called also *Cassini's division*

Cas·si·o·pe·ia \ˌka-sē-ə-'pē-ə\ *noun* [Latin, from Greek *Kassiopeia*]
1 : the wife of King Cepheus who gives birth to Andromeda and is later changed into a constellation
2 [Latin (genitive *Cassiopeiae*), from Greek *Kassiopeia*] : a northern constellation between Andromeda and Cepheus

cas·sis \kə-'sēs\ *noun* [French, literally, black currants, perhaps from Latin *cassia*] (1899)
: a liqueur made from black currants

cas·sit·er·ite \kə-'si-tə-ˌrīt\ *noun* [French *cassitérite*, from Greek *kassiteros* tin] (1858)
: a brown or black mineral that consists of tin dioxide and is the chief source of metallic tin

cas·sock \'ka-sək\ *noun* [Middle French *casaque*] (1631)
: a close-fitting ankle-length garment worn especially in Roman Catholic and Anglican

churches by the clergy and by laymen assisting in services

cas·sou·let \ˌka-sə-'lā\ *noun* [French, from Provençal, literally, earthenware dish, diminutive of *cassolo* dish, diminutive of *casso* ladle, from Old Provençal *cassa*] (circa 1929)
: a casserole of white beans baked with herbs and meat (as pork, lamb, and goose or duck)

cassock

cas·so·wary \'ka-sə-ˌwer-ē\ *noun, plural* **-war·ies** [Malay *kěsuari*, from an Austronesian language of the Moluccas] (1611)
: any of a genus (*Casuarius*) of large ratite birds chiefly of New Guinea and northern Australia that have a horny casque on the head and are closely related to the emu

¹**cast** \'kast\ *verb* **cast**; **cast·ing** [Middle English, from Old Norse *kasta*; akin to Old Norse *kǫs* heap] (13th century)
transitive verb
1 a : to cause to move or send forth by throwing ⟨*cast* a fishing lure⟩ ⟨*cast* dice⟩ **b** : DIRECT ⟨*cast* a glance⟩ **c** (1) : to put forth ⟨the fire *casts* a warm glow⟩ (2) : to place as if by throwing ⟨*cast* doubt on their reliability⟩ **d** : to deposit (a ballot) formally **e** (1) : to throw off or away ⟨the horse *cast* a shoe⟩ (2) : to get rid of : DISCARD ⟨*cast* off all restraint⟩ (3) : SHED, MOLT (4) : to bring forth; *especially* : to give birth to prematurely **f** : to throw to the ground especially in wrestling **g** : to build by throwing up earth
2 a (1) : to perform arithmetical operations on : ADD (2) : to calculate by means of astrology **b** *archaic* : DECIDE, INTEND
3 a : to dispose or arrange into parts or into a suitable form or order **b** (1) : to assign the parts of (a dramatic production) to actors (2) : to assign (as an actor) to a role or part
4 a : to give a shape to (a substance) by pouring in liquid or plastic form into a mold and letting harden without pressure ⟨*cast* steel⟩ **b** : to form by this process
5 : TURN ⟨*cast* the scale slightly⟩
6 : to make (a knot or stitch) by looping or catching up
7 : TWIST, WARP ⟨a beam *cast* by age⟩
intransitive verb
1 : to throw something; *specifically* : to throw out a lure with a fishing rod
2 *dialect British* : VOMIT
3 *dialect English* : to bear fruit : YIELD
4 a : to perform addition **b** *obsolete* : ESTIMATE, CONJECTURE
5 : WARP
6 : to range over land in search of a trail — used of hunting dogs or trackers
7 : VEER
synonym see DISCARD, THROW
— **cast·abil·i·ty** \ˌkas-tə-'bi-lə-tē\ *noun*
— **cast·able** \'kas-tə-bəl\ *adjective*
— **cast lots** : to draw lots to determine a matter by chance

²**cast** *noun* (14th century)
1 a : an act of casting **b** : something that happens as a result of chance **c** : a throw of dice **d** : a throw of a line (as a fishing line) or net
2 a : the form in which a thing is constructed **b** (1) : the set of actors in a dramatic production (2) : a set (as in a narrative) of characters or persons **c** : the arrangement of draperies in a painting
3 : the distance to which a thing can be thrown; *specifically* : the distance a bow can shoot
4 a : a turning of the eye in a particular direction; *also* : EXPRESSION ⟨this freakish, elfish *cast* came into the child's eye —Nathaniel Hawthorne⟩ **b** : a slight strabismus
5 : something that is thrown or the quantity thrown; *especially, British* : the leader of a fishing line

6 a : something that is formed by casting in a mold or form: as (1) **:** a reproduction (as of a statue) in metal or plaster **:** CASTING (2) **:** a fossil reproduction of the details of a natural object by mineral infiltration **b :** an impression taken from an object with a liquid or plastic substance **:** MOLD **c :** a rigid dressing of gauze impregnated with plaster of paris for immobilizing a diseased or broken part
7 : FORECAST, CONJECTURE
8 a : an overspread of a color or modification of the appearance of a substance by a trace of some added hue **:** SHADE ⟨gray with a greenish *cast*⟩ **b :** TINGE, SUGGESTION
9 a : a ride on one's way in a vehicle **:** LIFT **b** *Scottish* **:** HELP, ASSISTANCE
10 a : SHAPE, APPEARANCE ⟨the delicate *cast* of her features⟩ **b :** characteristic quality ⟨his father's conservative *cast* of mind⟩
11 : something that is shed, ejected, or thrown out or off: as **a :** the excrement of an earthworm **b :** a mass of soft matter formed in cavities of diseased organs and discharged from the body **c :** the skin of an insect
12 : the ranging in search of a trail by a dog, hunting pack, or tracker

cast about (1575)
intransitive verb
: to look around **:** SEEK ⟨*cast about* for a seat⟩
transitive verb
: to lay plans concerning **:** CONTRIVE ⟨*cast about* how he was to go⟩
cas·ta·net \,kas-tə-'net\ *noun* [Spanish *castañeta,* from *castaña* chestnut, from Latin *castanea* — more at CHESTNUT] (circa 1647)
: a percussion instrument used especially by dancers that consists of two small shells of hard wood, ivory, or plastic usually fastened to the thumb and clicked together by the other fingers — usually used in plural

castanets

cast around *intransitive verb* (1946)
: CAST ABOUT
cast·away \'kas-tə-,wā\ *adjective* (1534)
1 : thrown away **:** REJECTED
2 a : cast adrift or ashore as a survivor of a shipwreck **b :** thrown out or left without friends or resources
— **castaway** *noun*
cast down *adjective* (14th century)
: DOWNCAST
caste \'kast *also* 'käst\ *noun* [Portuguese *casta,* literally, race, lineage, from feminine of *casto* pure, chaste, from Latin *castus*] (1613)
1 : one of the hereditary social classes in Hinduism that restrict the occupation of their members and their association with the members of other castes
2 a : a division of society based on differences of wealth, inherited rank or privilege, profession, or occupation **b :** the position conferred by caste standing **:** PRESTIGE
3 : a system of rigid social stratification characterized by hereditary status, endogamy, and social barriers sanctioned by custom, law, or religion
4 : a specialized form (as the worker of an ant or bee) of a polymorphic social insect that carries out a particular function in the colony
— **caste·ism** \'kas-,ti-zəm\ *noun*
cas·tel·lan \'kas-tə-lən\ *noun* [Middle English *castelleyn,* from Old North French *castelain,* from Latin *castellanus* occupant of a castle, from *castellanus* of a castle, from *castellum* castle] (14th century)
: a governor or warden of a castle or fort
cas·tel·lat·ed \'kas-tə-,lā-təd\ *adjective* [Medieval Latin *castellatus,* past participle of *castellare* to fortify, from Latin *castellum*] (1679)
1 : having battlements like a castle
2 : having or supporting a castle

cast·er \'kas-tər\ *noun* (14th century)
1 : one that casts; *especially* **:** a machine that casts type
2 *or* **cas·tor** \-tər\ **a :** a usually silver table vessel with a perforated top for sprinkling a seasoning (as sugar or spice) **b :** a usually revolving metal stand bearing condiment containers (as cruets, mustard pot, and often shakers) for table use **:** a cruet stand
3 : any of a set of wheels or rotating balls mounted in a swivel frame and used for the support and movement of furniture, trucks, and portable equipment
4 : the slight usually backward tilt of the upper end of the kingbolt of an automobile for giving directional stability to the front wheels
cas·ti·gate \'kas-tə-,gāt\ *transitive verb* **-gat·ed; -gat·ing** [Latin *castigatus,* past participle of *castigare* — more at CHASTEN] (1607)
: to subject to severe punishment, reproof, or criticism
synonym see PUNISH
— **cas·ti·ga·tion** \,kas-tə-'gā-shən\ *noun*
— **cas·ti·ga·tor** \'kas-tə-,gā-tər\ *noun*
cas·tile soap \(,)kas-'tēl-\ *noun, often C* capitalized [Middle English *castell sope,* from *Castell* Castile] (15th century)
: a fine hard bland soap made from olive oil and sodium hydroxide; *also* **:** any of various similar soaps
Cas·til·ian \ka-'stil-yən\ *noun* (1796)
1 : a native or inhabitant of Castile; *broadly* **:** SPANIARD
2 a : the dialect of Castile **b :** the official and literary language of Spain based on this dialect
— **Castilian** *adjective*
cast·ing *noun* (14th century)
1 : something (as excrement) that is cast out or off
2 : the act of one that casts: as **a :** the throwing of a fishing line by means of a rod and reel **b :** the assignment of parts and duties to actors or performers
3 : something cast in a mold
casting director *noun* (1922)
: a person who supervises the casting of dramatic productions (as films and plays)
casting vote *noun* (1678)
: a deciding vote cast by a presiding officer to break a tie
cast–iron *adjective* (1692)
1 : made of cast iron
2 : resembling cast iron: as **a :** capable of withstanding great strain ⟨a *cast-iron* stomach⟩ **b :** not admitting change, adaptation, or exception **:** RIGID ⟨a *cast-iron* will⟩
cast iron *noun* (1664)
: a commercial alloy of iron, carbon, and silicon that is cast in a mold and is hard, brittle, nonmalleable, and incapable of being hammer-welded but more easily fusible than steel
¹cas·tle \'ka-səl\ *noun* [Middle English *castel,* from Old English, from Old North French, from Latin *castellum* fortress, castle, diminutive of *castrum* fortified place; perhaps akin to Latin *castrare* to castrate] (before 12th century)
1 a : a large fortified building or set of buildings **b :** a massive or imposing house
2 : a retreat safe against intrusion or invasion
3 : ³ROOK
²castle *verb* **cas·tled; cas·tling** \'kas(ə-)liŋ\ (1587)
transitive verb
1 : to establish in a castle
2 : to move (the chess king) in castling
intransitive verb
: to move a chess king two squares toward a rook and in the same move the rook to the square next past the king
cas·tled \'ka-səld\ *adjective* (1789)
: CASTELLATED
castle in the air (1580)
: an impractical project **:** DAYDREAM — called also *castle in Spain*

cast–off \'kas-,tòf\ *adjective* (1746)
: thrown away or aside
— **cast–off** *noun*
cast off (1602)
transitive verb
1 : LOOSE ⟨*cast off* a hunting dog⟩
2 : UNFASTEN ⟨*cast off* a boat⟩
3 : to remove (a stitch) from a knitting needle in such a way as to prevent unraveling
intransitive verb
1 : to unfasten or untie a boat or a line
2 : to turn one's partner in a square dance and pass around the outside of the set and back
3 : to finish a knitted fabric by casting off all stitches
cast on *transitive verb* (1840)
: to place (stitches) on a knitting needle for beginning or enlarging knitted work
cas·tor \'kas-tər\ *noun* [Middle English, from Latin, from Greek *kastōr,* from *Kastōr* Castor] (14th century)
1 : BEAVER 1a
2 : CASTOREUM
3 : a beaver hat
Cas·tor \'kas-tər\ *noun* [Latin, from Greek *Kastōr*]
1 : one of the Dioscuri
2 : the more northern of the two bright stars in Gemini
castor bean *noun* (1819)
: the very poisonous seed of the castor-oil plant; *also* **:** CASTOR-OIL PLANT
cas·to·re·um \ka-'stōr-ē-əm, -'stòr-\ *noun* [Middle English *castorium,* from Latin *castoreum,* from *castor*] (14th century)
: a bitter strong-smelling creamy orange-brown substance that consists of the dried perineal glands of the beaver and their secretion and is used especially by perfumers — called also *castor*
castor oil *noun* [probably from its former use as a substitute for castoreum in medicine] (1746)
: a pale viscous fatty oil from castor beans used especially as a cathartic and as a lubricant and plasticizer
castor–oil plant *noun* (1836)
: a tropical Old World herb (*Ricinus communis*) widely grown as an ornamental or for its oil-rich castor beans
castor sugar *or* **caster sugar** *noun* [*caster*] (1855)
chiefly British **:** finely granulated white sugar
cast out *transitive verb* (13th century)
: to drive out **:** EXPEL
cas·trate \'kas-,trāt\ *transitive verb* **cas·trat·ed; cas·trat·ing** [Latin *castratus,* past participle of *castrare;* akin to Greek *keazein* to split, Sanskrit *śasati* he slaughters] (1609)
1 a : to deprive of the testes **:** GELD **b :** to deprive of the ovaries **:** SPAY
2 : to render impotent or deprive of vitality especially by psychological means
— **castrate** *noun*
— **cas·tra·tion** \kas-'trā-shən\ *noun*
— **cas·tra·tor** \-,trā-tər\ *noun*
— **cas·tra·to·ry** \'kas-trə-,tòr-ē, -,tòr-\ *adjective*
cas·tra·to \ka-'strä-(,)tō, kə-\ *noun, plural* **-ti** \-tē\ [Italian, from past participle of *castrare* to castrate, from Latin] (1763)
: a singer castrated before puberty to preserve the soprano or contralto range of his voice
Cas·tro·ism \'kas-(,)trō-,i-zəm\ *noun* (1960)
: the political, economic, and social principles and policies of Fidel Castro
— **Cas·tro·ite** \-,īt\ *noun*
¹ca·su·al \'kazh-wəl, 'ka-zhə-wəl, 'ka-zhəl\ *adjective* [Middle English, from Middle French & Late Latin; Middle French *casuel,*

from Late Latin *casualis,* from Latin *casus*
fall, chance — more at CASE] (14th century)
1 : subject to, resulting from, or occurring by
chance
2 a : occurring without regularity **:** OCCASION-
AL **b :** employed for irregular periods
3 a : feeling or showing little concern **:** NON-
CHALANT **b** (1) **:** INFORMAL, NATURAL (2) **:** de-
signed for informal use
synonym see ACCIDENTAL, RANDOM
— **ca·su·al·ly** *adverb*
— **ca·su·al·ness** *noun*
²**casual** *noun* (circa 1852)
1 : a casual or migratory worker
2 : an officer or enlisted man awaiting assign-
ment or transportation to a unit
ca·su·al·ty \'ka-zhəl-tē, 'kazh-wəl-, 'ka-zhə-
wəl-\ *noun, plural* **-ties** (15th century)
1 *archaic* **:** CHANCE, FORTUNE ⟨losses that befall
them by mere *casualty* —Sir Walter Raleigh⟩
2 : serious or fatal accident **:** DISASTER
3 a : a military person lost through death,
wounds, injury, sickness, internment, or cap-
ture or through being missing in action **b :** a
person or thing injured, lost, or destroyed
: VICTIM ⟨the ex-senator was a *casualty* of the
last election⟩
casual water *noun* (1899)
: a temporary accumulation of water not form-
ing a regular hazard of a golf course
ca·su·a·ri·na \,ka-zhə-(wə-)'rē-nə\ *noun*
[New Latin, genus name, from Malay (*pohon*)
kĕsuari, literally, cassowary tree; from the re-
semblance of its twigs to cassowary feathers]
(1806)
: any of a genus (*Casuarina* of the family Ca-
suarinaceae) of dicotyledonous chiefly Austra-
lian trees which have whorls of scalelike
leaves and jointed stems resembling horsetails
and some of which yield a heavy hard wood
ca·su·ist \'ka-zhü-ist, 'kazh-wist\ *noun* [prob-
ably from Spanish *casuista,* from Latin *casus*
fall, chance — more at CASE] (1609)
: one skilled in or given to casuistry
— **ca·su·is·tic** \,ka-zhə-'wis-tik\ *or* **ca·su·
is·ti·cal** \-ti-kəl\ *adjective*
ca·su·ist·ry \'kazh-wə-strē, 'ka-zhə-\ *noun,*
plural **-ries** (1725)
1 : a resolving of specific cases of conscience,
duty, or conduct through interpretation of ethi-
cal principles or religious doctrine
2 : specious argument **:** RATIONALIZATION
ca·sus bel·li \'kä-səs-'be-,lē, 'kä-səs-'be-,lī\
noun, plural **ca·sus belli** \'kä-,süs-, 'kä-
,süs-\ [New Latin, occasion of war] (1849)
: an event or action that justifies or allegedly
justifies a war or conflict
¹**cat** \'kat\ *noun, often attributive* [Middle En-
glish, from Old English *catt,* probably from
Late Latin *cattus, catta* cat] (before 12th cen-
tury)
1 a : a carnivorous mammal (*Felis catus*) long
domesticated as a pet and for catching rats and
mice **b :** any of a family (Felidae) of carnivo-
rous usually solitary and nocturnal mammals
(as the domestic cat, lion, tiger, leopard, jag-
uar, cougar, wildcat, lynx, and cheetah)
2 : a malicious woman
3 : a strong tackle used to hoist an anchor to
the cathead of a ship
4 a : CATBOAT **b :** CATAMARAN
5 : CAT-O'-NINE-TAILS
6 : CATFISH
7 a : a player or devotee of jazz **b :** GUY
²**cat** *verb* **cat·ted; cat·ting** (1769)
transitive verb
: to bring (an anchor) up to the cathead
intransitive verb
: to search for a sexual mate — often used
with *around*
Cat \'kat\ *trademark*
— used for a Caterpillar tractor
cata- *or* **cat-** *or* **cath-** *prefix* [Greek *kata-,*
kat-, kath-, from *kata* down, in accordance
with, by; akin to Old Welsh *cant* with, Hittite
katta]

: down ⟨*cation*⟩ ⟨*cathode*⟩
ca·tab·o·lism \kə-'ta-bə-,li-zəm\ *noun* [Greek
katabolē throwing down, from *kataballein* to
throw down, from *kata-* + *ballein* to throw —
more at DEVIL] (1876)
: destructive metabolism involving the release
of energy and resulting in the breakdown of
complex materials within the organism —
compare ANABOLISM
— **cat·a·bol·ic** \,ka-tə-'bä-lik\ *adjective*
— **cat·a·bol·i·cal·ly** \-li-k(ə-)lē\ *adverb*
ca·tab·o·lite \-,līt\ *noun* (circa 1909)
: a product of catabolism
ca·tab·o·lize \-,līz\ *verb* **-lized; -liz·ing**
(circa 1926)
transitive verb
: to subject to catabolism
intransitive verb
: to undergo catabolism
cat·a·chre·sis \,ka-tə-'krē-səs\ *noun, plural*
-chre·ses \-,sēz\ [Latin, from Greek *kata-
chrēsis* misuse, from *katachrēsthai* to use up,
misuse, from *kata-* + *chrēsthai* to use] (1553)
1 : use of the wrong word for the context
2 : use of a forced and especially paradoxical
figure of speech (as *blind mouths*)
— **cat·a·chres·tic** \-'kres-tik\ *or* **cat·a·
chres·ti·cal** \-ti-kəl\ *adjective*
— **cat·a·chres·ti·cal·ly** \-ti-k(ə-)lē\ *ad-
verb*
cat·a·clysm \'ka-tə-,kli-zəm\ *noun* [French
cataclysme, from Latin *cataclysmos,* from
Greek *kataklysmos,* from *katakizein* to inun-
date, from *kata-* + *klyzein* to wash — more at
CLYSTER] (1637)
1 : FLOOD, DELUGE
2 : CATASTROPHE 3a
3 : a momentous and violent event marked by
overwhelming upheaval and demolition;
broadly **:** an event that brings great changes
— **cat·a·clys·mal** \,ka-tə-'kliz-məl\ *or*
cat·a·clys·mic \-mik\ *adjective*
— **cat·a·clys·mi·cal·ly** \-mi-k(ə-)lē\ *ad-
verb*
cat·a·comb \'ka-tə-,kōm\ *noun* [Middle
French *catacombe,* probably from Old Italian
catacomba, from Late Latin *catacumbae,* plu-
ral] (15th century)
1 : a subterranean cemetery of galleries with
recesses for tombs — usually used in plural
2 : something resembling a catacomb: as **a**
: an underground passageway or group of pas-
sageways **b :** a complex set of interrelated
things (the endless *catacombs* of formal edu-
cation —Kingman Brewster, Jr.)
cata·di·op·tric \,ka-tə-dī-'äp-trik\ *adjective*
(1723)
: belonging to, produced by, or involving both
the reflection and the refraction of light
ca·tad·ro·mous \kə-'ta-drə-məs\ *adjective*
[probably from New Latin *catadromus,* from
cata- + *-dromus* -dromous] (1880)
: living in fresh water and going to the sea to
spawn ⟨*catadromous* eels⟩ — compare ANAD-
ROMOUS
cat·a·falque \'ka-tə-,fo(l)k, -,falk\ *noun* [Ital-
ian *catafalco,* from (assumed) Vulgar Latin
catafalicum scaffold, from *cata-* + Latin *fala*
siege tower] (1641)
1 : an ornamental structure sometimes used in
funerals for the lying in state of the body
2 : a pall-covered coffin-shaped structure used
at requiem masses celebrated after burial
Cat·a·lan \'ka-tə-lən, -,lan\ *noun* [Spanish
catalán] (15th century)
1 : a native or inhabitant of Catalonia
2 : the Romance language of Catalonia, Valen-
cia, Andorra, and the Balearic islands
— **Catalan** *adjective*
cat·a·lase \'ka-tə-,lās, -,lāz\ *noun* [*catalysis*]
(1901)
: a red crystalline enzyme that consists of a
protein complex with hematin groups and cat-
alyzes the decomposition of hydrogen perox-
ide into water and oxygen
— **cat·a·lat·ic** \,ka-tə-'la-tik\ *adjective*

cat·a·lec·tic \,ka-tə-'lek-tik\ *adjective* [Late
Latin *catalecticus,* from Greek *katalēktikos,*
from *katalēgein* to leave off, from *kata-* +
lēgein to stop — more at SLACK] (1589)
: lacking a syllable at the end or ending in an
incomplete foot
— **catalectic** *noun*
cat·a·lep·sy \'ka-tə-,lep-sē\ *noun, plural*
-sies [Middle English *catalempsi,* from Me-
dieval Latin *catalepsia,* from Late Latin *cata-
lepsis,* from Greek *katalēpsis,* literally, act of
seizing, from *katalambanein* to seize, from
kata- + *lambanein* to take — more at LATCH]
(14th century)
: a condition of suspended animation and loss
of voluntary motion in which the limbs remain
in whatever position they are placed
— **cat·a·lep·tic** \,ka-tə-'lep-tik\ *adjective*
or noun
— **cat·a·lep·ti·cal·ly** \-ti-k(ə-)lē\ *adverb*
cat·a·lex·is \,ka-tə-'lek-səs\ *noun, plural*
-lex·es \-,sēz\ [New Latin, from Greek *kata-
lēxis* close, cadence, from *katalēgein*] (1830)
: omission or incompleteness usually in the
last foot of a line in metrical verse
¹**cat·a·log** *or* **cat·a·logue** \'ka-tə-,log, -,läg\
noun [Middle English *cateloge,* from Middle
French *catalogue,* from Late Latin *catalogus,*
from Greek *katalogos,* from *katalegein* to list,
enumerate, from *kata-* + *legein* to gather,
speak — more at LEGEND] (15th century)
1 : LIST, REGISTER
2 a : a complete enumeration of items ar-
ranged systematically with descriptive details
b : a pamphlet or book that contains such a list
c : material in such a list
²**catalog** *or* **catalogue** *verb* **-loged** *or*
-logued; -log·ing *or* **-logu·ing** (1598)
transitive verb
1 : to make a catalog of
2 a : to enter in a catalog **b :** to classify (as
books or information) descriptively
intransitive verb
1 : to make or work on a catalog
2 : to become listed in a catalog at a specified
price (this stamp *catalogs* at $2)
— **cat·a·log·er** *or* **cat·a·logu·er** *noun*
catalogue rai·son·né \-,rā-z°n-'ā\ *noun,*
plural **cat·a·logues rai·son·nés** \-,log(z)-
,rā-z°n-'ā\ [French, literally, reasoned catalog]
(1784)
: a systematic annotated catalog; *especially* **:** a
critical bibliography
ca·tal·pa \kə-'tal-pə, -'tol-\ *noun* [Creek
kataḷpa, from *iká* head + *taḷpa* wing] (circa
1730)
: any of a genus (*Catalpa*) of American and
Asian trees of the trumpet-creeper family with
pale showy flowers in terminal clusters
ca·tal·y·sis \kə-'ta-lə-səs\ *noun, plural* **-y·
ses** \-,sēz\ [Greek *katalysis* dissolution, from
katalyein to dissolve, from *kata-* + *lyein* to
dissolve, release — more at LOSE] (1836)
1 : a modification and especially increase in
the rate of a chemical reaction induced by ma-
terial unchanged chemically at the end of the
reaction
2 : a reaction between two or more persons or
forces precipitated by a separate agent (a rep-
resentative list of questions . . . valuable for
the *catalysis* of class discussions —B. S. Mey-
er & D. B. Anderson)
cat·a·lyst \'ka-t°l-əst\ *noun* (1902)
1 : a substance (as an enzyme) that enables a
chemical reaction to proceed at a usually fast-
er rate or under different conditions (as at a
lower temperature) than otherwise possible
2 : an agent that provokes or speeds signifi-
cant change or action
cat·a·lyt·ic \,ka-tə-'li-tik\ *adjective* (1836)
: causing, involving, or relating to catalysis
— **cat·a·lyt·i·cal·ly** \-'li-ti-k(ə-)lē\ *adverb*
catalytic converter *noun* (1964)

: an automobile exhaust-system component containing a catalyst that causes decomposition of harmful gases into mostly harmless products (as water and carbon dioxide)

catalytic cracker *noun* (1947)
: the unit in a petroleum refinery in which cracking is carried out in the presence of a catalyst

cat·a·lyze \'ka-tə-ˌlīz\ *transitive verb* **-lyzed; -lyz·ing** (1902)
1 : to bring about the catalysis of (a chemical reaction)
2 : BRING ABOUT, INSPIRE
3 : to alter significantly by catalysis ⟨innovations in basic chemical theory that have *catalyzed* the field —*Newsweek*⟩
— **cat·a·lyz·er** *noun*

cat·a·ma·ran \ˌka-tə-mə-ˈran, ˈka-tə-mə-ˌran\ *noun* [Tamil *kaṭṭumaram*, from *kaṭṭu* to tie + *maram* tree, wood] (1673)
: a vessel (as a sailboat) with twin hulls and usually a deck or superstructure connecting the hulls

cat·a·me·nia \ˌka-tə-ˈmē-nē-ə\ *noun plural* [New Latin, from Greek *katamēnia*, from neuter plural of *katamēnios* monthly, from *kata* by + *mēn* month — more at CATA-, MOON] (1750)
: MENSES
— **cat·a·me·ni·al** \-nē-əl\ *adjective*

cat·a·mite \'ka-tə-ˌmīt\ *noun* [Latin *catamitus*, from *Catamitus* Ganymede, from Etruscan *Catmite*, from Greek *Ganymēdēs*] (1593)
: a boy kept by a pederast

cat·a·mount \'ka-tə-ˌmaůnt\ *noun* [short for *cat-a-mountain*] (1664)
: any of various wild cats: as **a :** COUGAR **b :** LYNX

cat–a–moun·tain \ˌka-tə-ˈmaůn-t°n\ *noun* [Middle English *cat of the mountaine*] (15th century)
: any of various wild cats

cat and mouse *noun* (1887)
: behavior like that of a cat with a mouse: as **a** : the act of toying with or tormenting something before destroying it **b** : a contrived action involving constant pursuit, near captures, and repeated escapes ⟨played a game of *cat and mouse* with the police⟩; *broadly* : an evasive action

ca·taph·o·ra \kə-ˈta-fə-rə\ *noun* [*cata-* + *anaphora*] (1976)
: the use of a grammatical substitute (as a pronoun) that has the same reference as a following word or phrase

cat·a·pho·re·sis \ˌka-tə-fə-ˈrē-səs\ *noun, plural* **-re·ses** \-ˌsēz\ [New Latin] (1889)
: ELECTROPHORESIS
— **cat·a·pho·ret·ic** \-ˈre-tik\ *adjective*
— **cat·a·pho·ret·i·cal·ly** \-ti-k(ə-)lē\ *adverb*

cat·a·phor·ic \ˌka-tə-ˈfȯr-ik\ *adjective* (1968)
: of or relating to cataphora; *especially* : being a word or phrase (as a pronoun) that takes its reference from a following word or phrase (as *her* in *before her Jane saw nothing but desert*)
— compare ANAPHORIC

cat·a·plasm \'ka-tə-ˌpla-zəm\ *noun* [Middle French *cataplasme*, from Latin *cataplasma*, from Greek *kataplasma*, from *kataplassein* to plaster over, from *kata-* + *plassein* to mold — more at PLASTER] (1541)
: POULTICE

cat·a·plexy \'ka-tə-ˌplek-sē\ *noun, plural* **-plex·ies** \-ˌsēz\ [German *Kataplexie*, from Greek *kataplēxis*, from *kataplēssein* to strike down, terrify, from *kata-* + *plēssein* to strike — more at PLAINT] (1883)
: sudden loss of muscle power following a strong emotional stimulus

¹cat·a·pult \'ka-tə-ˌpəlt, -ˌpůlt\ *noun* [Middle French or Latin; Middle French *catapulte*, from Latin *catapulta*, from Greek *katapaltēs*, from *kata-* + *pallein* to hurl] (1577)
1 : an ancient military device for hurling missiles

2 : a device for launching an airplane at flying speed (as from an aircraft carrier)

catapult 1

²catapult (1848)
transitive verb
: to throw or launch by or as if by a catapult
intransitive verb
: to become catapulted

cat·a·ract \'ka-tə-ˌrakt\ *noun* [Latin *cataracta* waterfall, portcullis, from Greek *kataraktēs*, from *katarassein* to dash down, from *kata-* + *arassein* to strike, dash] (14th century)
1 [Middle English, from Middle French or Medieval Latin; Middle French *cataracte*, from Medieval Latin *cataracta*, from Latin, portcullis] : a clouding of the lens of the eye or of its surrounding transparent membrane that obstructs the passage of light
2 a *obsolete* : WATERSPOUT **b** : WATERFALL; *especially* : a large one over a precipice **c** : steep rapids in a river **d** : DOWNPOUR, FLOOD ⟨*cataracts* of rain⟩ ⟨*cataracts* of information⟩
— **cat·a·rac·tous** \ˌka-tə-ˈrak-təs\ *adjective*

ca·tarrh \kə-ˈtär\ *noun* [Middle French or Late Latin; Middle French *catarrhe*, from Late Latin *catarrhus*, from Greek *katarrhous*, from *katarrhein* to flow down, from *kata-* + *rhein* to flow — more at STREAM] (15th century)
: inflammation of a mucous membrane; *especially* : one chronically affecting the human nose and air passages
— **ca·tarrh·al** \-əl\ *adjective*
— **ca·tarrh·al·ly** \-ə-lē\ *adverb*

cat·ar·rhine \'ka-tə-ˌrīn\ *adjective* [New Latin *Catarrhina*, from Greek *katarrhina*, neuter plural of *katarrhin* hook-nosed, from *kata-* + *rhin-, rhis* nose] (1863)
: of, relating to, or being any of a division (Catarrhina) of primates comprising the Old World monkeys, higher apes, and hominids that have the nostrils close together and directed downward, 32 teeth, and the tail when present never prehensile
— **catarrhine** *noun*

ca·tas·tro·phe \kə-ˈtas-trə-(ˌ)fē\ *noun* [Greek *katastrophē*, from *katastrephein* to overturn, from *kata-* + *strephein* to turn] (1540)
1 : the final event of the dramatic action especially of a tragedy
2 : a momentous tragic event ranging from extreme misfortune to utter overthrow or ruin
3 a : a violent and sudden change in a feature of the earth **b** : a violent usually destructive natural event (as a supernova)
4 : utter failure : FIASCO ◇
— **cat·a·stroph·ic** \ˌka-tə-ˈsträ-fik\ *adjective*
— **cat·a·stroph·i·cal·ly** \-fi-k(ə-)lē\ *adverb*

catastrophe theory *noun* (1976)
: mathematical theory and conjecture that uses topology to explain events (as an earthquake or a stock market crash) characterized by major abrupt changes

ca·tas·tro·phism \kə-ˈtas-trə-ˌfi-zəm\ *noun* (1869)
: a geological doctrine that changes in the earth's crust have in the past been brought about suddenly by physical forces operating in ways that cannot be observed today — compare UNIFORMITARIANISM
— **ca·tas·tro·phist** \-fist\ *noun*

cat·a·to·nia \ˌka-tə-ˈtō-nē-ə\ *noun* [New Latin, from German *Katatonie*, from *kata-* cata- + New Latin *-tonia*] (circa 1891)

: catatonic schizophrenia

cat·a·ton·ic \-ˈtä-nik\ *adjective* (1904)
1 : of, relating to, being, resembling, or affected by schizophrenia characterized especially by a marked psychomotor disturbance that may involve stupor or mutism, negativism, rigidity, purposeless excitement, and inappropriate or bizarre posturing
2 : characterized by a marked lack of movement, activity, or expression
— **catatonic** *noun*
— **cat·a·ton·i·cal·ly** \-ni-k(ə-)lē\ *adverb*

Ca·taw·ba \kə-ˈtȯ-bə\ *noun* (1715)
1 *plural* **Catawba** *or* **Catawbas** : a member of an American Indian people of North Carolina and South Carolina
2 : the language of the Catawba people
3 : any of various wines produced from a pale red native American grape

cat·bird \'kat-ˌbərd\ *noun* (1709)
: an American songbird (*Dumetella carolinensis*) that is dark gray in color with a black cap and reddish coverts under the tail and is related to the mockingbird

catbird seat *noun* (1942)
: a position of great prominence or advantage

cat·boat \'kat-ˌbōt\ *noun* (1878)
: a sailboat having a cat rig and usually a centerboard and being of light draft and broad beam

cat·bri·er \-ˌbrī(-ə)r\ *noun* (1839)
: any of a genus (*Smilax*) of dioecious often prickly climbing plants of the lily family

catboat

cat burglar *noun* (1907)
: a burglar who is adept at entering and leaving the burglarized place without attracting notice

cat·call \-ˌkȯl\ *noun* (1749)
: a loud or raucous cry made especially to express disapproval (as at a sports event)
— **catcall** *verb*

¹catch \'kach, 'kech\ *verb* **caught** \'kȯt *also* 'kät\; **catch·ing** [Middle English *cacchen*, from Old North French *cachier* to hunt, from (assumed) Vulgar Latin *captiare*, alteration of Latin *captare* to chase, frequentative of *capere* to take — more at HEAVE] (13th century)
transitive verb

◇ WORD HISTORY

catastrophe The Greek noun *katastrophē* meant "end, conclusion," especially one not desired; as a derivative of the verb *katastrephein* "to overturn, ruin, undo," it might more literally be translated "undoing." The word aptly fit the finale of a classical tragedy, which normally ended with the complete ruin of the central character. English *catastrophe*, borrowed from Greek in the 16th century, first denoted the donouement of a play, comic or tragic. Later its scope was extended beyond drama to any kind of final event in a series, though usually an event of an unhappy nature, better matching the original sense of the Greek word. Since the 18th century, the meaning "unfortunate event" has prevailed over "conclusion," so that *catastrophe* is now nearly synonymous with *disaster*.

\ə\ abut \ə\ kitten \ər\ further \a\ ash \ā\ ace \ä\ mop, mar \aů\ out \ch\ chin \e\ bet \ē\ easy \g\ go \i\ hit \ī\ ice \j\ job \ŋ\ sing \ō\ go \ȯ\ law \ȯi\ boy \th\ thin \t̲h̲\ the \ü\ loot \ů\ foot \y\ yet \zh\ vision *see also* Guide to Pronunciation

1 a : to capture or seize especially after pursuit **b :** to take or entangle in or as if in a snare **c :** DECEIVE **d :** to discover unexpectedly **:** FIND ⟨*caught* in the act⟩ **e :** to check (oneself) suddenly or momentarily **f :** to become suddenly aware of ⟨*caught* me looking at him⟩
2 a : to take hold of **:** SEIZE **b :** to affect suddenly **c :** INTERCEPT **d :** to avail oneself of **:** TAKE **e :** to obtain through effort **:** GET **f :** to get entangled ⟨*catch* a sleeve on a nail⟩
3 : to become affected by: as **a :** CONTRACT ⟨*catch* a cold⟩ **b :** to respond sympathetically to the point of being imbued with ⟨*catch* the spirit of an occasion⟩ **c :** to be struck by **d :** to be subjected to **:** RECEIVE ⟨*catch* hell⟩
4 a : to seize and hold firmly **b :** FASTEN
5 : to take or get usually momentarily or quickly ⟨*catch* a glimpse of a friend⟩ ⟨*catch* a nap⟩
6 a : OVERTAKE **b :** to get aboard in time ⟨*catch* the bus⟩
7 : to attract and hold **:** ARREST, ENGAGE ⟨*caught* my attention⟩ ⟨*caught* her eye⟩
8 : to make contact with **:** STRIKE
9 a : to grasp by the senses or the mind ⟨you *catch* what I mean?⟩ ⟨didn't *catch* the name⟩ **b :** to apprehend and fix by artistic means
10 a : SEE, WATCH ⟨*catch* a game on TV⟩ **b :** to listen to
11 : to serve as a catcher for in baseball
12 : to meet with socially ⟨*catch* you later⟩
intransitive verb
1 : to grasp hastily or try to grasp
2 : to become caught
3 : to catch fire
4 *of a crop* **:** to come up and become established
5 : to play the position of catcher on a baseball team
6 : KICK OVER ☆
— **catch·able** \'ka-chə-bəl, 'ke-\ *adjective*
— **catch a crab :** to fail to raise an oar clear of the water on recovery of a stroke
— **catch dead :** willing to be publicly exposed — used in negative constructions ⟨wouldn't be *caught dead* in that shirt⟩
— **catch fire 1 :** to become ignited **2 :** to become fired with enthusiasm **3 :** to increase greatly in scope, popularity, interest, or effectiveness ⟨this stock has not *caught fire*—yet —*Forbes*⟩
— **catch it :** to incur blame, reprimand, or punishment
— **catch one's breath :** to rest long enough to restore normal breathing; *broadly* **:** to rest after a period of intense activity
²**catch** *noun* (15th century)
1 : something caught; *especially* **:** the total quantity caught at one time ⟨a large *catch* of fish⟩
2 a : the act, action, or fact of catching **b :** a game in which a ball is thrown and caught
3 : something that checks or holds immovable ⟨a safety *catch*⟩
4 : one worth catching especially as a spouse
5 : a round for three or more unaccompanied usually male voices often with suggestive or obscene lyrics
6 : FRAGMENT, SNATCH
7 : a concealed difficulty or complication ⟨there must be a *catch*⟩
8 : the germination of a field crop to such an extent that replanting is unnecessary
catch·all \'ka-ˌchȯl, 'ke-\ *noun, often attributive* (1838)
: something that holds or includes odds and ends or a wide variety of things
catch–as–catch–can *adjective* (1764)
: using any available means or method **:** UNPLANNED ⟨a *catch-as-catch-can* existence begging and running errands —*Time*⟩
catch·er \'ka-chər, 'ke-\ *noun* (15th century)
: one that catches; *specifically* **:** a baseball player positioned behind home plate
catch·fly \'kach-ˌflī, 'kech-\ *noun* (1597)

: any of various plants (as of the genera *Lychnis* and *Silene*) of the pink family often with viscid stems
catch·ing *adjective* (1590)
1 : INFECTIOUS, CONTAGIOUS ⟨the flu is *catching*⟩ ⟨his spirit is *catching*⟩
2 : CATCHY, ALLURING
catch·ment \'kach-mənt, 'kech-\ *noun* (1847)
1 : something that catches water; *also* **:** the amount of water caught
2 : the action of catching water
catchment area *noun* (1940)
: the geographical area served by an institution
catch on *intransitive verb* (1883)
1 : to become aware **:** LEARN; *also* **:** UNDERSTAND ⟨didn't *catch on* to what was going on⟩
2 : to become popular ⟨this idea has already *caught on*⟩
catch out *transitive verb* (1816)
: to detect in error or wrongdoing ⟨delighting to *catch out* his literary victims in error —John Clive⟩
catch·pen·ny \'kach-ˌpe-nē, 'kech-\ *adjective* (1748)
: using sensationalism or cheapness for appeal ⟨a *catchpenny* newspaper⟩
catch·phrase \-ˌfrāz\ *noun* (circa 1850)
: an expression that has caught on and is used repeatedly
catch·pole *or* **catch·poll** \-ˌpōl\ *noun* [Middle English *cacchepol*, from Old English *cæcepol*, from (assumed) Old North French *cachepol*, literally, chicken chaser, from Old North French *cachier* + *pol* chicken, from Latin *pullus* — more at CATCH, PULLET] (before 12th century)
: a sheriff's deputy; *especially* **:** one who makes arrests for failure to pay a debt
catch–22 \-ˌtwen-tē-'tü\ *noun, plural* **catch–22's** *or* **catch–22s** *often capitalized* [from *Catch-22*, paradoxical rule in the novel *Catch-22* (1961) by Joseph Heller] (1961)
1 : a problematic situation for which the only solution is denied by a circumstance inherent in the problem or by a rule ⟨the show-business *catch-22*—no work unless you have an agent, no agent unless you've worked —Mary Murphy⟩; *also* **:** the circumstance or rule that denies a solution
2 a : an illogical, unreasonable, or senseless situation **b :** a measure or policy whose effect is the opposite of what was intended **c :** a situation presenting two equally undesirable alternatives
3 : a hidden difficulty or means of entrapment **:** CATCH
catch–up \'ke-chəp, 'ka-; 'kat-səp\ *variant of* KETCHUP
¹**catch–up** \'kach-ˌəp, 'kech-\ *adjective* (1945)
: intended to catch up to a theoretical norm or a competitor's accomplishments
²**catch–up** *noun* (1948)
: the act or fact of catching up or trying to catch up (as with a norm or competitor) ⟨had to play *catch-up*⟩; *also* **:** an increase intended to achieve catch-up
catch up (14th century)
transitive verb
1 a : to pick up often abruptly ⟨the thief *caught* the purse *up* and ran⟩ **b :** ENSNARE, ENTANGLE ⟨education has been *caught up* in a stultifying mythology —N. M. Pusey⟩ **c :** ENTHRALL ⟨the . . . public was *caught up* in the car's magic —D. A. Jedlicka⟩
2 : to provide with the latest information ⟨*catch* me *up* on the news⟩
intransitive verb
1 a : to travel fast enough to overtake an advance party **b :** to reach a state of parity or of being able to cope ⟨kids left behind in preschool may never *catch up*⟩
2 : to bring about arrest for illicit activities ⟨the police *caught up* with the thieves⟩

3 a : to complete or compensate for something belatedly ⟨*catch up* on lost sleep⟩ **b :** to acquire belated information ⟨*catch up* on the news⟩
catch·word \'kach-ˌwərd, 'kech-\ *noun* (circa 1736)
1 a : a word under the right-hand side of the last line on a book page that repeats the first word on the following page **b :** GUIDE WORD
2 : a word or expression repeated until it becomes representative of a party, school, or point of view
catchy \'ka-chē, 'ke-chē\ *adjective* **catch·i·er; -est** (1831)
1 : tending to catch the interest or attention ⟨a *catchy* title⟩
2 : FITFUL, IRREGULAR ⟨*catchy* breathing⟩
3 : TRICKY ⟨a *catchy* question⟩
cat-claw \'kat-ˌklȯ\ *noun* (1898)
: a yellow-flowered spiny acacia (*Acacia greggi*) of the southwestern U.S. and Mexico
cat distemper *noun* (circa 1950)
: PANLEUKOPENIA
cate \'kāt\ *noun* [Middle English, article of purchased food, short for *acate*, from Old North French *acat* purchase, from *acater* to buy, from (assumed) Vulgar Latin *accaptare*, from Latin *acceptare* to accept] (15th century)
archaic **:** a dainty or choice food
cat·e·che·sis \ˌka-tə-'kē-səs\ *noun, plural* **-che·ses** \-ˌsēz\ [Late Latin, from Greek *katēchēsis*, from *katēchein* to teach] (1753)
: oral instruction of catechumens
— **cat·e·chet·i·cal** \-'ke-ti-kəl\ *adjective*
cat·e·chin \'ka-tə-, *noun* [International Scientific Vocabulary *catechu* + ¹-*in*] (1853)
: a crystalline compound $C_{15}H_{14}O_6$ or its derivatives related chemically to the flavones and used in dyeing and tanning
cat·e·chism \'ka-tə-ˌki-zəm\ *noun* (1502)
1 : oral instruction
2 : a manual for catechizing; *specifically* **:** a summary of religious doctrine often in the form of questions and answers
3 a : a set of formal questions put as a test **b :** something resembling a catechism especially in being a rote response or formulaic statement
— **cat·e·chis·mal** \ˌka-tə-'kiz-məl\ *adjective*
— **cat·e·chis·tic** \-'kis-tik\ *adjective*
cat·e·chist \'ka-tə-kist\ *noun* (circa 1563)
: one that catechizes: as **a :** a teacher of catechumens **b :** a native in a missionary district who does Christian teaching
cat·e·chize \'ka-tə-ˌkīz\ *transitive verb* **-chized; -chiz·ing** [Late Latin *catechizare*, from Greek *katēchein* to teach, literally, to din into, from *kata-* cata- + *ēchein* to resound, from *ēchē* sound — more at ECHO] (15th century)
1 : to instruct systematically especially by questions, answers, and explanations and cor-

rections; *specifically* **:** to give religious instruction in such a manner
2 : to question systematically or searchingly
— **cat·e·chi·za·tion** \,ka-ti-kə-'zā-shən\ *noun*
— **cat·e·chiz·er** \'ka-tə-,kī-zər\ *noun*
cat·e·chol \'ka-tə-,kȯl, -,kōl\ *noun* (1880)
1 : CATECHIN
2 : PYROCATECHOL
cat·e·chol·amine \,ka-tə-'kō-lə-,mēn, -'kȯ-\ *noun* (1954)
: any of various amines (as epinephrine, norepinephrine, and dopamine) that function as hormones or neurotransmitters or both
cat·e·chol·amin·er·gic \-,kō-lə-mē-'nər-jik, -,kȯ-, -mi-\ *adjective* (1970)
: involving, liberating, or mediated by catecholamine
cat·e·chu \'ka-tə-,chü, -,shü\ *noun* [probably modification of Malay *kachu*, of Dravidian origin; akin to Tamil & Kannada *kācu* catechu] (1683)
: any of several dry, earthy, or resinous astringent substances obtained from tropical plants of Asia: as **a :** an extract of the heartwood of an East Indian acacia (*Acacia catechu*) **b :** GAMBIER
cat·e·chu·men \,ka-tə-'kyü-mən\ *noun* [Middle English *cathecumyn*, from Middle French *cathecumine*, from Late Latin *catechumenus*, from Greek *katēchoumenos*, present passive participle of *katēchein*] (15th century)
1 : a convert to Christianity receiving training in doctrine and discipline before baptism
2 : one receiving instruction in the basic doctrines of Christianity before admission to communicant membership in a church
cat·e·gor·i·cal \,ka-tə-'gȯr-i-kəl, -'gär-\ *also* **cat·e·gor·ic** \-ik\ *adjective* [Late Latin *categoricus*, from Greek *katēgorikos*, from *katēgoria*] (1588)
1 : ABSOLUTE, UNQUALIFIED ⟨a *categorical* denial⟩
2 a : of, relating to, or constituting a category **b :** involving, according with, or considered with respect to specific categories
— **cat·e·gor·i·cal·ly** \-i-k(ə-)lē\ *adverb*
categorical imperative *noun* (1827)
: a moral obligation or command that is unconditionally and universally binding
cat·e·go·rise *British variant of* CATEGORIZE
cat·e·go·rize \'ka-ti-gə-,rīz\ *transitive verb* **-rized; -riz·ing** (1705)
: to put into a category **:** CLASSIFY
— **cat·e·go·ri·za·tion** \,ka-ti-gə-rə-'zā-shən\ *noun*
cat·e·go·ry \'ka-tə-,gȯr-ē, -,gȯr-\ *noun, plural* **-ries** [Late Latin *categoria*, from Greek *katēgoria* predication, category, from *katēgorein* to accuse, affirm, predicate, from *kata-* + *agora* public assembly, from *ageirein* to gather] (1588)
1 : any of several fundamental and distinct classes to which entities or concepts belong
2 : a division within a system of classification
ca·te·na \kə-'tē-nə\ *noun, plural* **-nae** \-(,)nē\ *or* **-nas** [Medieval Latin, from Latin, chain] (1641)
: a connected series of related things
cat·e·nary \'ka-tə-,ner-ē, *especially British* kə-'tē-nə-rē\ *noun, plural* **-nar·ies** [New Latin *catenaria*, from Latin, feminine of *catenarius* of a chain, from *catena*] (1788)
1 : the curve assumed by a cord of uniform density and cross section that is perfectly flexible but not capable of being stretched and that hangs freely from two fixed points
2 : something in the form of a catenary
— **catenary** *adjective*
cat·e·nate \'ka-tə-,nāt\ *transitive verb* **-nat·ed; -nat·ing** [Latin *catenatus*, past participle of *catenare*, from *catena*] (circa 1623)
: to connect in a series **:** LINK
— **cat·e·na·tion** \,ka-tə-'nā-shən\ *noun*
ca·ter \'kā-tər\ *verb* [obsolete *cater* buyer of provisions, from Middle English *catour*, short

for *acatour*, from Anglo-French, from Old North French *acater* to buy — more at CATE] (1600)
intransitive verb
1 : to provide a supply of food
2 : to supply what is required or desired ⟨*catering* to middle-class tastes⟩
transitive verb
: to provide food and service for ⟨*catered* the banquet⟩
— **ca·ter·er** \-tər-ər\ *noun*
cat·er·an \'ka-tə-rən\ *noun* [Middle English *ketharan*, probably from Scottish Gaelic *ceathairneach* freebooter, robber] (14th century)
: a former military irregular or brigand of the Scottish Highlands
cat·er·cor·ner \'ka-tē-,kȯr-nər, 'ka-tə-, 'ki-tē-\ *also* **cat·er·cor·nered** \-nərd\ *adverb or adjective* [obsolete *cater* four + *corner*] (1838)
: in a diagonal or oblique position **:** on a diagonal or oblique line ⟨the house stood *catercorner* across the square⟩
ca·ter–cous·in \'kā-tər-,kə-z°n\ *noun* [perhaps from obsolete *cater* buyer of provisions] (1519)
: an intimate friend
cat·er·pil·lar \'ka-tə(r)-,pi-lər\ *noun, often attributive* [Middle English *catyrpel*, from Old North French *catepelose*, literally, hairy cat] (15th century)
: the elongated wormlike larva of a butterfly or moth; *also* **:** any of various similar larvae ◇
Caterpillar *trademark*
— used for a tractor made for use on rough or soft ground and moved on two endless metal belts
cat·er·waul \'ka-tər-,wȯl\ *intransitive verb* [Middle English *caterwawen*] (14th century)
1 : to make a harsh cry
2 : to quarrel noisily
— **caterwaul** *noun*
cat·fac·ing \'kat-,fā-sin\ *noun* (1940)
: a disfigurement or malformation of fruit suggesting a cat's face in appearance
cat·fight \-,fīt\ *noun* (1919)
: an intense fight or argument between two women
cat·fish \-,fish\ *noun* (1612)
: any of an order (Siluriformes) of chiefly freshwater stout-bodied scaleless bony fishes having long tactile barbels

catfish

cat·gut \-,gət\ *noun* (1599)
: a tough cord made usually from sheep intestines
cath- — see CATA-
Cath·ar \'ka-,thär\ *noun, plural* **Cath·a·ri** \'ka-thə-,rī, -,rē\ *or* **Cathars** [Late Latin *cathari* (plural), from Late Greek *katharoi*, from Greek, plural of *katharos* pure] (1637)
: a member of one of various ascetic and dualistic Christian sects especially of the later Middle Ages teaching that matter is evil and professing faith in an angelic Christ who did not really undergo human birth or death
— **Cath·a·rism** \'ka-thə-,ri-zəm\ *noun*
— **Cath·a·rist** \-rist\ *or* **Cath·a·ris·tic** \,ka-thə-'ris-tik\ *adjective*
ca·thar·sis \kə-'thär-səs\ *noun, plural* **ca·thar·ses** \-,sēz\ [New Latin, from Greek *katharsis*, from *kathairein* to cleanse, purge, from *katharos*] (circa 1775)
1 : PURGATION
2 a : purification or purgation of the emotions (as pity and fear) primarily through art **b :** a purification or purgation that brings about spiritual renewal or release from tension

3 : elimination of a complex by bringing it to consciousness and affording it expression
¹ca·thar·tic \kə-'thär-tik\ *adjective* [Late Latin or Greek; Late Latin *catharticus*, from Greek *kathartikos*, from *kathairein*] (1612)
: of, relating to, or producing catharsis
²cathartic *noun* (1651)
: a cathartic medicine **:** PURGATIVE
cat·head \'kat-,hed\ *noun* (1626)
: a projecting piece of timber or iron near the bow of a ship to which the anchor is hoisted and secured
ca·thect \kə-'thekt, ka-\ *transitive verb* [back-formation from *cathectic*] (1925)
: to invest with mental or emotional energy
ca·thec·tic \kə-'thek-tik, ka-\ *adjective* [New Latin *cathexis*] (1927)
: of, relating to, or invested with mental or emotional energy
ca·the·dra \kə-'thē-drə\ *noun* [Latin, chair — more at CHAIR] (circa 1797)
: a bishop's official throne
¹ca·the·dral \kə-'thē-drəl\ *adjective* (14th century)
1 : of, relating to, or containing a cathedra
2 : emanating from a chair of authority
3 : suggestive of a cathedral
²cathedral *noun* (1587)
1 : a church that is the official seat of a diocesan bishop
2 : something that resembles or suggests a cathedral
ca·thep·sin \kə-'thep-sən\ *noun* [Greek *kathepsein* to digest (from *kata-* cata- + *hepsein* to boil) + English ²-*in*] (1929)
: any of several intracellular proteases of animal tissue that aid in autolysis
Cath·er·ine wheel \'ka-th(ə-)rin-\ *noun* [Saint *Catherine* of Alexandria (died about 307) Christian martyr] (1584)
1 : a wheel with spikes projecting from the rim
2 : PINWHEEL 1
3 : CARTWHEEL 2
cath·e·ter \'ka-thə-tər, 'kath-tər\ *noun* [Late Latin, from Greek *kathetēr*, from *kathienai* to send down, from *kata-* cata- + *hienai* to send — more at JET] (1601)
: a tubular medical device for insertion into canals, vessels, passageways, or body cavities usually to permit injection or withdrawal of fluids or to keep a passage open
cath·e·ter·i·za·tion \,ka-thə-tə-rə-'zā-shən, ,kath-tə-rə-\ *noun* (circa 1852)
: the use of or introduction of a catheter (as in or into the bladder, trachea, or heart)

◇ WORD HISTORY
caterpillar *Caterpillar,* our common word for a butterfly or moth larva, first appeared in a 15th century English-Latin dictionary as *catirpel.* It was presumably altered from the medieval form of a word which emerges in the modern French dialect of Normandy as *catepeleuse* or *carpeleuse* and which then meant literally "hairy cat." (Similar applications of a name for a furry animal to fuzzy larvae are English *woolly bear* and French *chenille* "caterpillar," descended from Latin *canicula* "little dog.") In the 16th century, *caterpil* is replaced by *catirpiller,* probably influenced by the now obsolete word *piller* "pillager, looter," a not inappropriate association in view of the destructive habits of some insects. The spelling *caterpillar,* which much less appropriately suggests *pillar,* was adopted by the 18th century lexicographer Samuel Johnson and has since remained standard.

\ə\ abut \ᵊ\ kitten \ər\ further \a\ ash \ā\ ace
\ä\ mop, mar \au̇\ out \ch\ chin \e\ bet \ē\ easy
\g\ go \i\ hit \ī\ ice \j\ job \ŋ\ sing \ō\ go
\ȯ\ law \ȯi\ boy \th\ thin \th\ the \ü\ loot \u̇\ foot
\y\ yet \zh\ vision *see also* Guide to Pronunciation

— **cath·e·ter·ize** \\'ka-thə-tə-ˌrīz, 'kath-tə-\\ *transitive verb*

ca·thex·is \\kə-'thek-səs, ka-\\ *noun, plural* **ca·thex·es** \\-ˌsēz\\ [New Latin (intended as translation of German *Besetzung*), from Greek *kathexis* holding, from *katechein* to hold fast, occupy, from *kata-* + *echein* to have, hold — more at SCHEME] (1922)
: investment of mental or emotional energy in a person, object, or idea

cath·ode \\'ka-ˌthōd\\ *noun* [Greek *kathodos* way down, from *kata-* + *hodos* way] (1834)
1 : the electrode of an electrochemical cell at which reduction occurs **a** : the negative terminal of an electrolytic cell **b** : the positive terminal of a galvanic cell
2 : the electron-emitting electrode of an electron tube — compare ANODE
— **cath·od·al** \\'ka-ˌthō-dᵊl\\ *adjective*
— **cath·od·al·ly** *adverb*
— **ca·thod·ic** \\ka-'thä-dik, -'thō-\\ *adjective*
— **ca·thod·i·cal·ly** \\-di-k(ə-)lē\\ *adverb*

cathode ray *noun* (1880)
1 *plural* : the high-speed electrons emitted in a stream from the heated cathode of a vacuum tube
2 : a stream of electrons emitted from the cathode of a vacuum tube — usually used in plural

cathode–ray tube *noun* (1905)
: a vacuum tube in which a beam of electrons is projected on a fluorescent screen to produce a luminous spot at a point on the screen determined by the effect on the electron beam of a variable magnetic field within the tube

cathodic protection *noun* (1930)
: the prevention of electrolytic corrosion of a usually metallic structure (as a pipeline) by causing it to act as the cathode rather than as the anode of an electrochemical cell

cath·o·lic \\'kath-lik, 'ka-thə-\\ *adjective* [Middle French & Late Latin; Middle French *catholique*, from Late Latin *catholicus*, from Greek *katholikos* universal, general, from *katholou* in general, from *kata* by + *holos* whole — more at CATA-, SAFE] (14th century)
1 a *often capitalized* : of, relating to, or forming the church universal **b** *often capitalized* : of, relating to, or forming the ancient undivided Christian church or a church claiming historical continuity from it **c** *capitalized* : ROMAN CATHOLIC
2 : COMPREHENSIVE, UNIVERSAL; *especially* : broad in sympathies, tastes, or interests
— **ca·thol·i·cal·ly** \\kə-'thä-li-k(ə-)lē\\ *adverb*
— **ca·thol·i·cize** \\-'thä-lə-ˌsīz\\ *verb*

Cath·o·lic \\'kath-lik, 'ka-thə-\\ *noun* (15th century)
1 : a person who belongs to the universal Christian church
2 : a member of a Catholic church; *especially* : ROMAN CATHOLIC

Catholic Apostolic *adjective* (1888)
: of or relating to a Christian sect founded in 19th century England in anticipation of Christ's second coming

ca·thol·i·cate \\kə-'thȯ-lə-ˌkāt, -kət\\ *noun* (1850)
: the jurisdiction of a catholicos

Catholic Epistles *noun plural* (1582)
: the five New Testament letters including James, I and II Peter, I John, and Jude addressed to the early Christian churches at large

Ca·thol·i·cism \\kə-'thä-lə-ˌsi-zəm\\ *noun* (circa 1617)
1 : ROMAN CATHOLICISM
2 : the faith, practice, or system of Catholic Christianity

cath·o·lic·i·ty \\ˌka-thə-'li-sə-tē, ˌkath-'li-\\ *noun, plural* **-ties** (1704)
1 *capitalized* : the character of being in conformity with a Catholic church

2 a : liberality of sentiments or views ⟨*catholicity* of viewpoint —W. V. O'Connor⟩ **b** : UNIVERSALITY **c** : comprehensive range ⟨*catholicity* of topics⟩

ca·thol·i·con \\kə-'thä-lə-ˌkän\\ *noun* [Middle English, from Medieval Latin, from Greek *katholikon*, neuter of *katholikos*] (15th century)
: CURE-ALL, PANACEA

ca·thol·i·cos \\kə-'thȯ-li-ˌkȯs\\ *noun, plural* **-i·cos·es** \\-kȯ-səz\\ *or* **-i·coi** \\-'thȯ-lə-ˌkȯi\\ *often capitalized* [Late Greek *katholikos*, from Greek, general] (1878)
: a primate of certain Eastern churches and especially of the Armenian or of the Nestorian church

cat·house \\'kat-ˌhau̇s\\ *noun* (1931)
: BORDELLO

cat·ion \\'kat-ˌī-ən, 'ka-(ˌ)tī-ən\\ *noun* [Greek *kation*, neuter of *kation*, present participle of *katienai* to go down, from *kata-* cata- + *ienai* to go — more at ISSUE] (1834)
: the ion in an electrolyzed solution that migrates to the cathode; *broadly* : a positively charged ion

cat·ion·ic \\ˌkat-(ˌ)ī-'ä-nik, ˌka-(ˌ)tī-\\ *adjective* (circa 1920)
1 : of, relating to, or being a cation
2 : characterized by an active and especially surface-active cation ⟨a *cationic* dye⟩
— **cat·ion·i·cal·ly** \\-ni-k(ə-)lē\\ *adverb*

cat·kin \\'kat-kən\\ *noun* [from its resemblance to a cat's tail] (1578)
: a spicate inflorescence (as of the willow, birch, or oak) bearing scaly bracts and unisexual usually apetalous flowers — called also *ament*

cat·like \\'kat-ˌlīk\\ *adjective* (1600)
: resembling a cat; *especially* : STEALTHY ⟨with *catlike* tread, upon our prey we steal —W. S. Gilbert⟩

cat·mint \\-ˌmint\\ *noun* (13th century)
: CATNIP

cat·nap \\-ˌnap\\ *noun* (1823)
: a very short light nap
— **catnap** *intransitive verb*

cat·nap·per *also* **cat·nap·er** \\'kat-ˌna-pər\\ *noun* [¹*cat* + *-napper* (as in *kidnapper*)] (1942)
: one that steals cats usually to sell them for research

cat·nip \\-ˌnip\\ *noun* [¹*cat* + obsolete *nep* catnip, from Middle English, from Old English *nepte*, from Latin *nepeta*] (1712)
1 : a strong-scented mint (*Nepeta cataria*) that has whorls of small pale flowers in terminal spikes and contains a substance attractive to cats
2 : something very attractive

cat-o'-nine-tails \\ˌka-tə-'nīn-ˌtālz\\ *noun, plural* **cat-o'-nine-tails** [from the resemblance of its scars to the scratches of a cat] (1665)
: a whip made of usually nine knotted lines or cords fastened to a handle

ca·top·tric \\kə-'täp-trik\\ *adjective* [Greek *katoptrikos*, from *katoptron* mirror, from *katopsesthai* to be going to observe, from *kata-* + *opsesthai* to be going to see — more at OPTIC] (circa 1774)
: being or using a mirror to focus light

cat rig *noun* (1867)
: a rig consisting of a single mast far forward carrying a single large sail extended by a boom
— **cat-rigged** \\'kat-'rigd\\ *adjective*

cats and dogs *adverb* (1738)
: in great quantities : very hard ⟨it was raining *cats and dogs*⟩

CAT scan \\'kat-\\ *noun* [computerized *axial tomography*] (1975)
: an image made by computed tomography
— **CAT scanning** *noun*

CAT scanner *noun* (1975)

: a medical instrument consisting of integrated X-ray and computing equipment and used for computed tomography

cat's cradle *noun* (1768)

cat's cradle 1
1 : a game in which a string looped in a pattern like a cradle on the fingers of one person's hands is transferred to the hands of another so as to form a different figure
2 : something that is intricate, complicated, or elaborate ⟨a *cat's cradle* of red tape⟩

cat scratch disease *noun* (1952)
: an illness characterized by swelling of the lymph glands, fever, and chills and assumed to be caused by a bacterium transmitted especially by a cat scratch — called also *cat scratch fever*

cat's-eye \\'kat-ˌsī\\ *noun, plural* **cat's-eyes** (circa 1599)
1 : any of various gems (as a chrysoberyl or a chalcedony) exhibiting opalescent reflections from within
2 : a marble with eyelike concentric circles

cat's meow *noun* (1926)
: a highly admired person or thing

cat's-paw \\'kats-ˌpȯ\\ *noun, plural* **cat's-paws** (circa 1769)
1 : a light air that ruffles the surface of the water in irregular patches during a calm
2 [from the fable of the monkey that used a cat's paw to draw chestnuts from the fire] : one used by another as a tool : DUPE
3 : a hitch formed with two eyes for attaching a line to a hook — see KNOT illustration

cat·sup *variant of* KETCHUP

cat·tail \\'kat-ˌtāl\\ *noun* (1548)
: any of a genus (*Typha* of the family Typhaceae, the cattail family) of tall reedy marsh plants with brown furry fruiting spikes; *especially* : a plant (*Typha latifolia*) with long flat leaves used especially for making mats and chair seats

cat·tery \\'ka-tə-rē\\ *noun, plural* **-ter·ies** (circa 1843)
: an establishment for the breeding and boarding of cats

cat·tle \\'ka-tᵊl\\ *noun plural* [Middle English *catel*, from Old North French, personal property, from Medieval Latin *capitale*, from Latin, neuter of *capitalis* of the head — more at CAPITAL] (14th century)
1 : domesticated quadrupeds held as property or raised for use; *specifically* : bovine animals on a farm or ranch
2 : human beings especially en masse

cattle call *noun* (1952)
: a mass audition (as of actors)

cattle egret *noun* (circa 1899)
: a small Old World white egret (*Bubulcus ibis*) introduced into the New World and having a yellow bill and in the breeding season buff on the crown, breast, and back

cattle grub *noun* (1926)
: either of two warble flies (genus *Hypoderma*) especially in the larval stage: **a** : COMMON CATTLE GRUB **b** : a related warble fly (*H. bovis*)

cat·tle·man \\-mən, -ˌman\\ *noun* (1864)
: one who tends or raises cattle

cattle tick *noun* (1869)
: either of two ixodid ticks (*Boophilus annulatus* and *B. microplus*) that infest cattle and transmit the protozoan which causes Texas fever

cat·tle·ya \\'kat-lē-ə; kat-'lā-ə, -'lē-\\ *noun* [New Latin, from William *Cattley* (died 1832) English patron of botany] (1828)
: any of a genus (*Cattleya*) of tropical American epiphytic orchids with showy hooded flowers

¹cat·ty \\'ka-tē\\ *noun, plural* **catties** [Malay *kati*] (1598)

: any of various units of weight of China and southeast Asia varying around 1⅓ pounds (about 600 grams); *also* **:** a standard Chinese unit equal to 1.1023 pounds (500 grams)

²**catty** *adjective* **cat·ti·er; -est** (1886)
1 : resembling a cat; *especially* **:** slyly spiteful **:** MALICIOUS
2 : of or relating to a cat
— **cat·ti·ly** \'ka-t°l-ē\ *adverb*
— **cat·ti·ness** \-tē-nəs\ *noun*

cat·ty–cor·ner *or* **cat·ty–cor·nered** *variant of* CATERCORNER

cat·walk \'kat-,wȯk\ *noun* (1885)
: a narrow walkway (as along a bridge)

Cau·ca·sian \kȯ-'kā-zhən, kä- *also* -'ka-zhən\ *adjective* (1807)
1 : of or relating to the Caucasus or its inhabitants
2 a : of or relating to the white race of humankind as classified according to physical features **b :** of or relating to the white race as defined by law specifically as composed of persons of European, North African, or southwest Asian ancestry
— **Caucasian** *noun*
— **Cau·ca·soid** \'kȯ-kə-,sȯid\ *adjective or noun*

Cau·chy sequence \kō-'shē-, 'kō-shē-\ *noun* [Augustin-Louis *Cauchy* (died 1857) French mathematician] (circa 1949)
: a sequence of elements in a metric space such that for any positive number no matter how small there exists a term in the sequence for which the distance between any two terms beyond this term is less than the arbitrarily small number

¹**cau·cus** \'kȯ-kəs\ *noun* [origin unknown] (1763)
: a closed meeting of a group of persons belonging to the same political party or faction usually to select candidates or to decide on policy; *also* **:** a group of people united to promote an agreed-upon cause

²**caucus** *intransitive verb* (1788)
: to meet in or hold a caucus

cau·dad \'kȯ-,dad\ *adverb* [Latin *cauda*] (1889)
: toward the tail or posterior end

cau·dal \'kȯ-d°l\ *adjective* [New Latin *caudalis*, from Latin *cauda* tail] (1661)
1 : of, relating to, or being a tail
2 : situated in or directed toward the hind part of the body
— **cau·dal·ly** \-d°l-ē\ *adverb*

cau·date \'kȯ-,dāt\ *adjective* (1600)
: having a tail or a taillike appendage

caudate nucleus *noun* (circa 1903)
: the most medial of the four basal ganglia in each cerebral hemisphere — called also *caudate*

cau·dex \'kȯ-,deks\ *noun, plural* **cau·di·ces** \'kȯ-də-,sēz\ *or* **cau·dex·es** [Latin, tree trunk or stem] (circa 1797)
1 : the stem of a palm or tree fern
2 : the woody base of a perennial plant

cau·di·llis·mo \,kaú-thē-'yēz-(,)mō, -thēl-'yēz-\ *noun* [Spanish, from *caudillo*] (1927)
: the doctrine or practice of a caudillo

cau·di·llo \kaú-'thē-(,)yō, -'thēl-(,)yō\ *noun, plural* **-llos** [Spanish, from Late Latin *capitellum* small head — more at CADET] (1852)
: a Spanish or Latin-American military dictator

cau·dle \'kȯ-d°l\ *noun* [Middle English *caudel*, from Old North French, from *caut* warm, from Latin *calidus* — more at CAULDRON] (14th century)
: a drink (as for invalids) usually of warm ale or wine mixed with bread or gruel, eggs, sugar, and spices

¹**caught** \'kȯt\ *past and past participle of* CATCH

²**caught** *adjective* (1858)
: PREGNANT — often used in the phrase *get caught*

caul \'kȯl\ *noun* [Middle English *calle*, from Middle French *cale*] (14th century)
1 : the large fatty omentum covering the intestines (as of a cow, sheep, or pig)
2 : the inner fetal membrane of higher vertebrates especially when covering the head at birth

caul·dron \'kȯl-drən\ *noun* [Middle English, alteration of *cauderon*, from Old North French, diminutive of *caudiere*, from Late Latin *caldaria*, from feminine of Latin *caldarius* used for hot water, from *calidus* warm, from *calēre* to be warm — more at LEE] (14th century)
1 : a large kettle or boiler
2 : something resembling a boiling cauldron ⟨a *cauldron* of intense emotions⟩

cau·li·flow·er \'kȯ-li-,flaú(-ə)r, 'kä-\ *noun, often attributive* [Italian *cavolfiore*, from *cavolo* cabbage (from Late Latin *caulus*, from Latin *caulis* stem, cabbage) + *fiore* flower, from Latin *flor-, flos* — more at COLE, BLOW] (1597)
: a garden plant (*Brassica oleracea botrytis*) related to the cabbage and grown for its compact edible head of usually white undeveloped flowers; *also* **:** its flower cluster used as a vegetable

cauliflower ear *noun* (1909)
: an ear deformed from injury and excessive growth of reparative tissue

cau·li·flow·er·et \,kȯ-li-,flaú(-ə)-'ret, ,kä-\ *noun* (1946)
: a bite-size piece of cauliflower

cau·line \'kȯ-,līn\ *adjective* [probably from New Latin *caulinus*, from Latin *caulis*] (1756)
: of, relating to, or growing on a stem and especially on the upper part

¹**caulk** \'kȯk\ *transitive verb* [Middle English *caulken*, from Old North French *cauquer* to trample, from Latin *calcare*, from *calc-, calx* heel] (15th century)
: to stop up and make tight against leakage (as a boat or its seams, the cracks in a window frame, or the joints of a pipe)
— **caulk·er** *noun*

²**caulk** *also* **caulk·ing** \'kȯ-kiŋ\ *noun* (1954)
: material used to caulk

³**caulk** *variant of* ²CALK

caus·al \'kȯ-zəl\ *adjective* (circa 1530)
1 : expressing or indicating cause **:** CAUSATIVE ⟨a *causal* clause introduced by *since*⟩
2 : of, relating to, or constituting a cause ⟨the *causal* agent of a disease⟩
3 : involving causation or a cause ⟨the relationship . . . was not one of *causal* antecedence so much as one of analogous growth —H. O. Taylor⟩
4 : arising from a cause ⟨a *causal* development⟩
— **caus·al·ly** \-zə-lē\ *adverb*

cau·sal·gia \kȯ-'zal-j(ē-)ə, -'sal-\ *noun* [New Latin, from Greek *kausos* fever (from *kaiein* to burn) + New Latin *-algia*] (1872)
: a constant usually burning pain resulting from injury to a peripheral nerve
— **cau·sal·gic** \-jik\ *adjective*

cau·sal·i·ty \kȯ-'za-lə-tē\ *noun, plural* **-ties** (1603)
1 : a causal quality or agency
2 : the relation between a cause and its effect or between regularly correlated events or phenomena

cau·sa·tion \kȯ-'zā-shən\ *noun* (1615)
1 a : the act or process of causing **b :** the act or agency which produces an effect
2 : CAUSALITY

caus·a·tive \'kȯ-zə-tiv\ *adjective* (15th century)
1 : effective or operating as a cause or agent ⟨*causative* bacteria of cholera⟩
2 : expressing causation; *specifically* **:** being a linguistic form that indicates that the subject causes an act to be performed or a condition to come into being
— **causative** *noun*
— **caus·a·tive·ly** *adverb*

¹**cause** \'kȯz\ *noun* [Middle English, from Old French, from Latin *causa*] (13th century)
1 a : a reason for an action or condition **:** MOTIVE **b :** something that brings about an effect or a result **c :** a person or thing that is the occasion of an action or state; *especially* **:** an agent that brings something about **d :** sufficient reason ⟨discharged for *cause*⟩
2 a : a ground of legal action **b :** CASE
3 : a matter or question to be decided
4 a : a principle or movement militantly defended or supported **b :** a charitable undertaking ⟨for a good *cause*⟩
— **cause·less** \-ləs\ *adjective*

²**cause** *transitive verb* **caused; caus·ing** (14th century)
1 : to serve as a cause or occasion of **:** MAKE
2 : to effect by command, authority, or force
— **caus·er** *noun*

'**cause** \'kȯz, 'kəz\ *conjunction* (15th century)
: BECAUSE

cause cé·lè·bre *also* **cause ce·le·bre** \,kȯz-sə-'leb, -'le-brə, ,kȯz-, -'lebr°\ *noun, plural* **causes cé·lè·bres** *also* **causes celebres** *same*\ [French, literally, celebrated case] (1763)
1 : a legal case that excites widespread interest
2 : a notorious person, thing, incident, or episode

cau·se·rie \,kȯz-'rē, ,kō-zə-\ *noun* [French, from *causer* to chat, from Latin *causari* to plead, discuss, from *causa*] (1827)
1 : an informal conversation **:** CHAT
2 : a short informal essay

cause·way \'kȯz-,wā\ *noun* [Middle English *cauciwey*, from *cauci* + *wey* way] (15th century)
1 : a raised way across wet ground or water
2 : HIGHWAY; *especially* **:** one of ancient Roman construction in Britain
— **causeway** *transitive verb*

cau·sey \'kȯ-zē\ *noun, plural* **causeys** [Middle English *cauci*, from Old North French *caucie*, from Medieval Latin *calciata* paved highway, probably from Latin *calc-, calx* limestone — more at CHALK] (14th century)
1 : CAUSEWAY 1
2 *obsolete* **:** CAUSEWAY 2

¹**caus·tic** \'kȯs-tik\ *adjective* [Latin *causticus*, from Greek *kaustikos*, from *kaiein* to burn] (14th century)
1 : capable of destroying or eating away by chemical action **:** CORROSIVE
2 : marked by incisive sarcasm
3 : relating to or being the surface or curve of a caustic ☆
— **caus·ti·cal·ly** \-ti-k(ə-)lē\ *adverb*
— **caus·tic·i·ty** \kȯ-'sti-sə-tē\ *noun*

²**caustic** *noun* (15th century)
1 : a caustic agent: as **a :** a substance that burns or destroys organic tissue by chemical action **b :** SODIUM HYDROXIDE
2 : the envelope of rays emanating from a point and reflected or refracted by a curved surface

caustic potash *noun* (1869)
: POTASSIUM HYDROXIDE

☆ **SYNONYMS**
Caustic, mordant, acrid, scathing mean stingingly incisive. CAUSTIC suggests a biting wit ⟨*caustic* comments⟩. MORDANT suggests a wit that is used with deadly effectiveness ⟨*mordant* reviews of the play⟩. ACRID implies bitterness and often malevolence ⟨*acrid* invective⟩. SCATHING implies indignant attacks delivered with fierce severity ⟨a *scathing* satire⟩.

\ə\ abut \°\ kitten \ər\ further \a\ ash \ā\ ace
\ä\ mop, mar \aú\ out \ch\ chin \e\ bet \ē\ easy
\g\ go \i\ hit \ī\ ice \j\ job \ŋ\ sing \ō\ go
\ȯ\ law \ȯi\ boy \th\ thin \th\ the \ü\ loot \ú\ foot
\y\ yet \zh\ vision *see also* Guide to Pronunciation

caustic soda *noun* (1876)
: SODIUM HYDROXIDE

cau·ter·ize \'kȯ-tə-ˌrīz\ *transitive verb* **-ized; -iz·ing** (14th century)
1 : to sear with a cautery or caustic
2 : to make insensible : DEADEN ⟨must oust the feeling, or *cauterize* it —Robert Craft⟩
— **cau·ter·iza·tion** \ˌkȯ-tə-rə-'zā-shən\ *noun*

cau·tery \'kȯ-tə-rē\ *noun, plural* **-ter·ies** [Latin *cauterium*, from Greek *kautērion* branding iron, from *kaiein*] (14th century)
1 : the act or effect of cauterizing : CAUTERIZATION
2 : an agent (as a hot iron or caustic) used to burn, sear, or destroy tissue

¹cau·tion \'kȯ-shən\ *noun* [Latin *caution-, cautio* precaution, from *cavēre* to be on one's guard — more at HEAR] (1596)
1 : WARNING, ADMONISHMENT
2 : PRECAUTION
3 : prudent forethought to minimize risk
4 : one that astonishes or commands attention ⟨some shoes you see . . . these days are a *caution* —*Esquire*⟩
— **cau·tion·ary** \-shə-ˌner-ē\ *adjective*

²caution *transitive verb* **cau·tioned; cau·tion·ing** \'kȯ-sh(ə-)niŋ\ (1683)
: to advise caution to

cau·tious \'kȯ-shəs\ *adjective* (circa 1640)
: marked by or given to caution ☆
— **cau·tious·ly** *adverb*
— **cau·tious·ness** *noun*

cav·al·cade \ˌka-vəl-'kād, 'ka-vəl-ˌ\ *noun* [French, ride on horseback, from Old Italian *cavalcata*, from *cavalcare* to go on horseback, from Late Latin *caballicare*, from Latin *caballus* horse; akin to Greek *kaballeion* horse, Middle Irish *capall* workhorse] (1644)
1 a : a procession of riders or carriages **b** : a procession of vehicles or ships
2 : a dramatic sequence or procession : SERIES

¹cav·a·lier \ˌka-və-'lir\ *noun* [Middle French, from Old Italian *cavaliere*, from Old Provençal *cavalier*, from Late Latin *caballarius* horseman, from Latin *caballus*] (1589)
1 : a gentleman trained in arms and horsemanship
2 : a mounted soldier : KNIGHT
3 *capitalized* : an adherent of Charles I of England
4 : GALLANT

²cavalier *adjective* (circa 1641)
1 : DEBONAIR
2 : marked by or given to offhand and often disdainful dismissal of important matters
3 a *capitalized* : of or relating to the party of Charles I of England in his struggles with the Puritans and Parliament **b** : ARISTOCRATIC **c** *capitalized* : of or relating to the English Cavalier poets of the mid-17th century
— **ca·va·lier·ism** \-ˌi-zəm\ *noun*
— **cav·a·lier·ly** *adverb*

cavalier King Charles spaniel \-'chär(-ə)lz-\ *noun* [¹*cavalier* + *King Charles spaniel*, a breed of toy spaniel, from *Charles* II of England] (1969)
: any of a breed of toy spaniels with a tapered muzzle and a long silky coat

ca·val·la \kə-'va-lə\ *noun, plural* **-la** *or* **-las** [Spanish *caballa*, a fish, from Late Latin, mare, feminine of Latin *caballus*] (1624)
1 *also* **ca·val·ly** \-'va-lē\ : any of various carangid fishes (especially genus *Caranx*)
2 : CERO

cav·a·let·ti *also* **cav·a·let·ti** \ˌka-və-'le-tē\ *noun plural but singular or plural in construction* [Italian, plural of *cavalletto* trestle, diminutive of *cavallo* horse, from Latin *caballus*] (1950)
: a series of timber jumps that are adjustable in height for schooling horses

cav·al·ry \'ka-vəl-rē, ÷'kal-və-rē\ *noun, plural* **-ries** [Italian *cavalleria* cavalry, chivalry, from *cavaliere*] (1546)

1 a : an army component mounted on horseback **b** : an army component moving in motor vehicles or helicopters and assigned to combat missions that require great mobility
2 : HORSEMEN ⟨a thousand *cavalry* in flight⟩

cav·al·ry·man \-rē-mən, -ˌman\ *noun* (1860)
: a cavalry soldier

cavalry twill *noun* (1942)
: TRICOTINE

cav·a·ti·na \ˌka-və-'tē-nə, ˌkä-\ *noun* [Italian, from *cavata* production of sound from an instrument, extraction, from *cavare* to dig out, from Latin, to make hollow, from *cavus*] (1813)
1 : an operatic solo simpler and briefer than an aria
2 : a songlike instrumental piece or movement

¹cave \'kāv\ *noun* [Middle English, from Old French, from Latin *cava*, from *cavus* hollow; akin to Greek *koilos* hollow, and probably to Greek *kyein* to be pregnant — more at CYME] (13th century)
1 : a natural underground chamber or series of chambers open to the surface
2 : a usually underground chamber for storage ⟨a wine *cave*⟩; *also* : the articles stored there

²cave *verb* **caved; cav·ing** (15th century)
transitive verb
: to form a cave in or under : HOLLOW, UNDERMINE
intransitive verb
: to explore caves especially as a sport or hobby
— **cav·er** \'kā-vər\ *noun*

³cave \'kāv\ *verb* **caved; cav·ing** [probably alteration of *calve*] (1513)
intransitive verb
1 : to fall in or down especially from being undermined — usually used with *in*
2 : to cease to resist : SUBMIT — usually used with *in*
transitive verb
: to cause to fall or collapse — usually used with *in*

ca·ve·at \'ka-vē-ˌät, -ˌat; 'kä-vē-ˌät; 'kä-vē-ˌat\ *noun* [Latin, let him beware, from *cavēre* — more at HEAR] (1533)
1 a : a warning enjoining one from certain acts or practices **b** : an explanation to prevent misinterpretation
2 : a legal warning to a judicial officer to suspend a proceeding until the opposition has a hearing

caveat emp·tor \-'em(p)-tər, -ˌtȯr\ *noun* [New Latin, let the buyer beware] (1523)
: a principle in commerce: without a warranty the buyer takes the risk

cave dweller *noun* (1865)
1 : one (as a prehistoric man) that dwells in a cave
2 : one that lives in a city apartment building

cave–in \'kā-ˌvin\ *noun* (1860)
1 : the action of caving in
2 : a place where earth has caved in

cave·man \'kāv-ˌman\ *noun* (1865)
1 : a cave dweller especially of the Stone Age
2 : a man who acts in a rough or crude manner

¹cav·ern \'ka-vərn *also* -vrən\ *noun* [Middle English *caverne*, from Middle French, from Latin *caverna*, from *cavus*] (14th century)
: CAVE; *especially* : one of large or indefinite extent

²cavern *transitive verb* (circa 1630)
1 : to place in or as if in a cavern
2 : to form a cavern of : HOLLOW — used with *out*

cav·er·nic·o·lous \ˌka-vər-'ni-kə-ləs\ *adjective* (circa 1889)
: inhabiting caves

cav·ern·ous \'ka-vər-nəs\ *adjective* (15th century)
1 a : having caverns or cavities **b** *of animal tissue* : composed largely of vascular sinuses and capable of dilating with blood to bring about the erection of a body part
2 : constituting or suggesting a cavern

— **cav·ern·ous·ly** *adverb*

ca·vet·to \kə-'ve-(ˌ)tō, kä-\ *noun, plural* **-ti** \-tē\ [Italian, from *cavo* hollow, from Latin *cavus*] (1664)
: a concave molding having a curve that approximates a quarter circle — see MOLDING illustration

cav·i·ar *or* **cav·i·are** \'ka-vē-ˌär *also* 'kä-\ *noun* [earlier *cavery, caviarie*, from obsolete Italian *caviari*, plural of *caviaro*, from Turkish *havyar*] (circa 1560)
1 : processed salted roe of large fish (as sturgeon)
2 : something considered too delicate or lofty for mass appreciation — usually used in the phrase *caviar to the general*
3 : something considered the best of its kind ⟨the *caviar* of porcelain⟩

cav·il \'ka-vəl\ *verb* **-iled** *or* **-illed; -il·ing** *or* **-il·ling** \'ka-və-liŋ, 'kav-liŋ\ [Latin *cavillari* to jest, cavil, from *cavilla* raillery; akin to Latin *calvi* to deceive — more at CALUMNY] (1542)
intransitive verb
: to raise trivial and frivolous objection
transitive verb
: to raise trivial objections to
— **cavil** *noun*
— **cav·il·er** *or* **cav·il·ler** \'ka-və-lər, 'kav-lər\ *noun*

cav·ing \'kā-viŋ\ *noun* (1932)
: the sport of exploring caves : SPELUNKING

cav·i·tary \'ka-və-ˌter-ē\ *adjective* (1835)
: of, relating to, or characterized by bodily cavitation ⟨*cavitary* tuberculosis⟩ ⟨*cavitary* lesions⟩

cav·i·tate \'ka-və-ˌtāt\ *verb* **-tat·ed; -tat·ing** (1909)
intransitive verb
: to form cavities or bubbles
transitive verb
: to cavitate in

cav·i·ta·tion \ˌka-və-'tā-shən\ *noun* [*cavity* + *-ation*] (1895)
: the process of cavitating: as **a** : the formation of partial vacuums in a liquid by a swiftly moving solid body (as a propeller) or by high-intensity sound waves; *also* : the pitting and wearing away of solid surfaces (as of metal or concrete) as a result of the collapse of these vacuums in surrounding liquid **b** : the formation of cavities in an organ or tissue especially in disease

cav·i·ty \'ka-və-tē\ *noun, plural* **-ties** [Middle French *cavité*, from Late Latin *cavitas*, from Latin *cavus*] (1541)
1 : an unfilled space within a mass; *especially* : a hollowed-out space
2 : an area of decay in a tooth : CARIES

ca·vort \kə-'vȯrt\ *intransitive verb* [perhaps alteration of *curvet*] (1794)
1 : PRANCE
2 : to engage in extravagant behavior

ca·vy \'kā-vē\ *noun, plural* **cavies** [New Latin *Cavia*, genus name, from obsolete Portuguese *çavía* (now *savía*), from Tupi *sawiya* rat] (1796)

☆ SYNONYMS
Cautious, circumspect, wary, chary mean prudently watchful and discreet in the face of danger or risk. CAUTIOUS implies the exercise of forethought usually prompted by fear of danger ⟨a *cautious* driver⟩. CIRCUMSPECT suggests less fear and stresses the surveying of all possible consequences before acting or deciding ⟨*circumspect* in his business dealings⟩. WARY emphasizes suspiciousness and alertness in watching for danger and cunning in escaping it ⟨keeps a *wary* eye on the competition⟩. CHARY implies a cautious reluctance to give, act, or speak freely ⟨*chary* of signing papers without having read them first⟩.

: any of several short-tailed rough-haired South American rodents (family Caviidae); *especially* **:** GUINEA PIG

caw \'kȯ\ *intransitive verb* [imitative] (1589)
: to utter the harsh raucous natural call of the crow or a similar cry
— **caw** *noun*

cay \'kē, 'kā\ *noun* [Spanish *cayo* — more at KEY] (1707)
: a low island or reef of sand or coral

cay·enne pepper \(,)kī-'en-, (,)kā-; 'kī-,, 'kā-,\ *noun* [by folk etymology from earlier *cayan*, modification of Tupi *kyinha*] (1756)
1 : a pungent condiment consisting of the ground dried fruits or seeds of hot peppers
2 : HOT PEPPER; *especially* **:** a cultivated pepper with very long twisted pungent red fruits
3 : the fruit of a cayenne pepper

cay·man *variant of* CAIMAN

Ca·yu·ga \kā-'yü-gə, kī-\ *noun, plural* **Cayuga** *or* **Cayugas** (1744)
1 : a member of an American Indian people of New York
2 : the Iroquoian language of the Cayuga people

Cay·use \'kī-,yüs, kī-'\ *noun, plural* **Cayuse** *or* **Cayuses** (1825)
1 : a member of an American Indian people of Oregon and Washington
2 *plural cayuses, not capitalized, West* **:** a native range horse

CB \,sē-'bē\ *noun* (1959)
: CITIZENS BAND; *also* **:** the radio transmitting and receiving set used for citizens-band communications

CBer \(,)sē-'bē-ər, -'bir\ *noun* (1959)
: one that operates a CB radio

CCD \,sē-(,)sē-'dē\ *noun* (1973)
: CHARGE-COUPLED DEVICE

C-clamp \'sē-,klamp\ *noun* (1926)
: a C-shaped general-purpose clamp

C clef *noun* (1596)
: a movable clef indicating middle C by its placement on one of the lines of the staff

CD \,sē-'dē\ *noun* (1979)
: COMPACT DISC

CD4 \,sē-(,)dē-'fȯr, -'fȯr\ *noun* [cluster of *d*ifferentiation] (1985)
: a large glycoprotein that is found on the surface of T4 cells and is the receptor for HIV

cDNA \'sē-,dē-(,)en-'ā, ,sē-\ *noun* [complementary] (1973)
: a strand of DNA that is complementary to a given messenger RNA and that serves as a template for production of the messenger RNA in the presence of reverse transcriptase

CD-ROM \,sē-,dē-'räm\ *noun* [compact *d*isc *r*ead-*o*nly *m*emory] (1983)
: a compact disc containing data that can be read by a computer

ce·a·no·thus \,sē-ə-'nō-thəs\ *noun* [New Latin, from Greek *keanōthos*, a thistle] (1785)
: any of a genus (*Ceanothus*) of American vines, shrubs, and small trees of the buckthorn family having the calyx disk adherent to the ovary

¹cease \'sēs\ *verb* **ceased; ceas·ing** [Middle English *cesen*, from Middle French *cesser*, from Latin *cessare* to hold back, be remiss, frequentative of *cedere*] (14th century)
transitive verb
: to cause to come to an end especially gradually **:** no longer continue
intransitive verb
1 a : to come to an end **b :** to bring an activity or action to an end **:** DISCONTINUE
2 *obsolete* **:** to become extinct **:** DIE OUT
synonym see STOP

²cease *noun* (14th century)
: CESSATION — usually used with *without*

cease and desist order *noun* (1926)
: an order from an administrative agency to refrain from a method of competition or a labor practice found by the agency to be unfair

cease-fire \'sēs-'fīr\ *noun* (1859)
1 : a military order to cease firing

2 : a suspension of active hostilities

cease·less \'sēs-ləs\ *adjective* (1586)
: continuing without cease **:** CONSTANT
— **cease·less·ly** *adverb*
— **cease·less·ness** *noun*

ce·cro·pia moth \si-'krō-pē-ə-\ *noun* [New Latin *cecropia*, from Latin, feminine of *Cecropius* Athenian, from Greek *Kekropios*, from *Kekrops* Cecrops, legendary king of Athens] (1885)
: a large North American saturniid moth (*Hyalophora cecropia*) that is brown with red, white, and black markings

ce·cum \'sē-kəm\ *noun, plural* **ce·ca** \-kə\ [New Latin, from Latin *intestinum caecum*, literally, blind intestine] (circa 1721)
: a cavity open at one end (as the blind end of a duct); *especially* **:** the blind pouch at the beginning of the large intestine into which the ileum opens from one side and which is continuous with the colon
— **ce·cal** \-kəl\ *adjective*
— **ce·cal·ly** \-kə-lē\ *adverb*

ce·dar \'sē-dər\ *noun* [Middle English *cedre*, from Old French, from Latin *cedrus*, from Greek *kedros*] (14th century)
1 a : any of a genus (*Cedrus*) of usually tall coniferous trees (as the cedar of Lebanon or the deodar) of the pine family noted for their fragrant durable wood **b :** any of numerous coniferous trees (as of the genera *Juniperus*, *Chamaecyparis*, or *Thuja*) that resemble the true cedars especially in the fragrance and durability of their wood
2 : the wood of a cedar

ce·dar-ap·ple rust \'sē-dər-'a-pəl-\ *noun* (1946)
: a gall-producing disease especially of the apple caused by a rust fungus (*Gymnosporangium juniperi-virginianae*) that completes the first part of its life cycle on the common red cedar (*Juniperus virginiana*) and the second on the leaves and fruit of the apple

ce·dar·bird \-,bərd\ *noun* (1883)
: CEDAR WAXWING

ce·darn \'sē-dərn\ *adjective* (1634)
archaic **:** made or suggestive of cedar

cedar of Leb·a·non \-'leb-nän, -'le-bə-, -nən\ (14th century)
: a long-lived cedar (*Cedrus libani*) native to Asia Minor with short fascicled leaves and erect cones

cedar waxwing *noun* (circa 1844)
: a brown gregarious American waxwing (*Bombycilla cedrorum*) with a yellow band on the tip of the tail and a pale yellow belly

ce·dar·wood \'sē-dər-,wùd\ *noun* (14th century)
: the wood of a cedar that is especially repellent to insects

cede \'sēd\ *transitive verb* **ced·ed; ced·ing** [French or Latin; French *céder*, from Latin *cedere* to go, withdraw, yield] (1754)
1 : to yield or grant typically by treaty
2 : ASSIGN, TRANSFER
— **ced·er** *noun*

ce·di \'sā-dē\ *noun* [Twi *sedi* cowry] (1965)
— see MONEY table

ce·dil·la \si-'di-lə\ *noun* [Spanish, the obsolete letter ç (actually a medieval form of the letter z), cedilla, from diminutive of *ceda, zeda* the letter z, from Late Latin *zeta* — more at ZED] (1599)
: the diacritical mark ̧ placed under a letter (as ç in French) to indicate an alteration or modification of its usual phonetic value (as in the French word *façade*)

cee \'sē\ *noun* (1542)
: the letter c

cei·ba \'sā-bə\ *noun* [Spanish] (1790)
1 : a massive tropical tree (*Ceiba pentandra*) of the silk-cotton family with large pods filled with seeds invested with a silky floss that yields the fiber kapok
2 : KAPOK

ceil \'sē(ə)l\ *transitive verb* [Middle English *celen*, from Medieval Latin *celare, caelare*, perhaps from Latin *caelare* to carve, from *caelum* chisel; akin to Latin *caedere* to cut] (15th century)
1 : to furnish (as a wooden ship) with a lining
2 : to finish with a ceiling

ceil·ing \'sē-lin\ *noun* [Middle English *celing*, from *celen*] (1535)
1 a : the overhead inside lining of a room **b :** material used to ceil a wall or roof of a room
2 : something thought of as an overhanging shelter or a lofty canopy ⟨a *ceiling* of stars⟩
3 a : the height above the ground from which prominent objects on the ground can be seen and identified **b :** the height above the ground of the base of the lowest layer of clouds when over half of the sky is obscured
4 a : ABSOLUTE CEILING **b :** SERVICE CEILING
5 : an upper usually prescribed limit ⟨a *ceiling* on prices, rents, and wages⟩
— **ceil·inged** \-lind\ *adjective*

ceil·om·e·ter \sē-'lä-mə-tər\ *noun* [*ceil*ing + -*o*- + -*meter*] (1943)
: a photoelectric instrument for determining by triangulation the height of the cloud ceiling above the earth

cein·ture \saⁿ(n)-'tyùr, -'tùr, 'san-chər\ *noun* [Middle English *seynture*, from Middle French *ceinture*, from Latin *cinctura* — more at CINCTURE] (15th century)
: a belt or sash for the waist

cel *also* **cell** \'sel\ *noun* [short for *celluloid*] (1938)
: a transparent sheet of celluloid on which objects are drawn or painted in the making of animated cartoons

cel·a·don \'se-lə-,dän, -lə-dᵊn\ *noun* [French *céladon*] (circa 1768)
1 : a grayish yellow green
2 : a ceramic glaze originated in China that is greenish in color; *also* **:** an article with a celadon glaze

cel·an·dine \'se-lən-,dīn, -,dēn\ *noun* [Middle English *celidoine*, from Middle French, from Latin *chelidonia*, from feminine of *chelidonius* of the swallow, from Greek *chelidonios*, from *chelidon-, chelidōn* swallow] (12th century)
1 : a yellow-flowered Eurasian biennial herb (*Chelidonium majus*) of the poppy family naturalized in the eastern U.S.
2 : LESSER CELANDINE

-cele *noun combining form* [Middle French, from Latin, from Greek *kēlē*; akin to Old English *hēala* hernia]
: tumor **:** hernia ⟨varico*cele*⟩

ce·leb \sə-'leb\ *noun* (circa 1912)
: CELEBRITY 2

cel·e·brant \'se-lə-brənt\ *noun* (1839)
: one who celebrates; *specifically* **:** the priest officiating at the Eucharist

cel·e·brate \'se-lə-,brāt\ *verb* **-brat·ed; -brat·ing** [Latin *celebratus*, past participle of *celebrare* to frequent, celebrate, from *celebr-, celeber* much frequented, famous; perhaps akin to Latin *celer* swift] (15th century)
transitive verb
1 : to perform (a sacrament or solemn ceremony) publicly and with appropriate rites ⟨*celebrate* the mass⟩
2 a : to honor (as a holiday) by solemn ceremonies or by refraining from ordinary business **b :** to mark (as an anniversary) by festivities or other deviation from routine
3 : to hold up or play up for public notice ⟨her poetry *celebrates* the glory of nature⟩
intransitive verb
1 : to observe a holiday, perform a religious ceremony, or take part in a festival

\ə\ abut \ᵊ\ kitten \ər\ further \a\ ash \ā\ ace
\ä\ mop, mar \aù\ out \ch\ chin \e\ bet \ē\ easy
\g\ go \i\ hit \ī\ ice \j\ job \ŋ\ sing \ō\ go
\ȯ\ law \ȯi\ boy \th\ thin \t͟h\ the \ü\ loot \ù\ foot
\y\ yet \zh\ vision *see also* Guide to Pronunciation

2 : to observe a notable occasion with festivities
synonym see KEEP
— **cel·e·bra·tion** \,se-lə-'brā-shən\ noun
— **cel·e·bra·tor** \'se-lə-,brā-tər\ noun
— **cel·e·bra·to·ry** \-brə-,tōr-ē, -,tór-; ,se-lə-'brā-\ adjective
cel·e·brat·ed adjective (circa 1669)
: widely known and often referred to
synonym see FAMOUS
— **cel·e·brat·ed·ness** noun
ce·leb·ri·ty \sə-'le-brə-tē\ noun, plural **-ties** (14th century)
1 : the state of being celebrated
2 : a celebrated person
ce·le·ri·ac \sə-'ler-ē-,ak, -'lir-\ noun [irregular from celery] (1743)
: a celery (Apium graveolens rapaceum) grown for its knobby edible root — called also celery root
ce·ler·i·ty \sə-'ler-ə-tē\ noun [Middle English celerite, from Middle French, from Latin celeritat-, celeritas, from celer swift — more at HOLD] (15th century)
: rapidity of motion or action
cel·ery \'se-lə-rē, 'sel-rē\ noun, plural **-er·ies** [obsolete French celeris, from Italian dialect seleri, plural of selero, modification of Late Latin selinon, from Greek] (1664)
: a European herb (Apium graveolens) of the carrot family; specifically : one of a cultivated variety (A. graveolens dulce) with leafstalks eaten raw or cooked
celery cabbage noun (1930)
: CHINESE CABBAGE b
ce·les·ta \sə-'les-tə, chə-\ or **ce·leste** \sə-'lest, chə-\ noun [French célesta, alteration of céleste, literally, heavenly, from Latin caelestis] (1899)
: a keyboard instrument with hammers that strike steel plates producing a tone similar to that of a glockenspiel
¹**ce·les·tial** \sə-'les-chəl, -'lesh-, -'les-tē-əl\ adjective [Middle English, from Middle French, from Latin caelestis celestial, from caelum sky] (14th century)
1 : of, relating to, or suggesting heaven or divinity
2 : of or relating to the sky or visible heavens 〈the sun, moon, and stars are celestial bodies〉
3 a : ETHEREAL, OTHERWORLDLY **b :** OLYMPIAN, SUPREME
4 capitalized [Celestial Empire, old name for China] : of or relating to China or the Chinese
— **ce·les·tial·ly** \-chə-lē, -tē-ə-lē\ adverb
²**celestial** noun (1573)
1 : a heavenly or mythical being
2 capitalized : CHINESE 1a
celestial equator noun (1875)
: the great circle on the celestial sphere midway between the celestial poles
celestial globe noun (circa 1771)
: a globe depicting the celestial bodies
celestial hierarchy noun (1883)
: a traditional hierarchy of angels ranked from lowest to highest into the following nine orders: angels, archangels, principalities, powers, virtues, dominions, thrones, cherubim, and seraphim
celestial marriage noun (1919)
: a special order of Mormon marriage solemnized in a Mormon temple and held to be binding for a future life as well as the present one
celestial navigation noun (1939)
: navigation by observation of the positions of celestial bodies
celestial pole noun (1868)
: either of the two points on the celestial sphere around which the diurnal rotation of the stars appears to take place
celestial sphere noun (1879)
: an imaginary sphere of infinite radius against which the celestial bodies appear to be projected and of which the apparent dome of the visible sky forms half

ce·les·tite \'se-ləs-,tīt, sə-'les-,tīt\ noun [German Zölestin, from Latin caelestis] (1854)
: a usually white mineral consisting of the sulfate of strontium
ce·li·ac \'sē-lē-,ak\ adjective [Latin coeliacus, from Greek koiliakos, from koilia cavity, from koilos hollow — more at CAVE] (1662)
: of or relating to the abdominal cavity
celiac disease noun (1911)
: a chronic nutritional disorder especially in young children that is characterized by defective digestion and utilization of fats and often by abdominal distention, diarrhea, and fatty stools
cel·i·ba·cy \'se-lə-bə-sē\ noun (1663)
1 : the state of not being married
2 a : abstention from sexual intercourse **b** : abstention by vow from marriage
cel·i·bate \'se-lə-bət\ noun [Latin caelibatus, from caelib-, caelebs unmarried] (circa 1847)
: a person who lives in celibacy
— **celibate** adjective
cell \'sel\ noun [Middle English, from Old English, religious house and Old French celle hermit's cell, from Latin cella small room; akin to Latin celare to conceal — more at HELL] (12th century)
1 : a small religious house dependent on a monastery or convent
2 a : a one-room dwelling occupied by a solitary person (as a hermit) **b :** a single room (as in a convent or prison) usually for one person
3 : a small compartment, cavity, or bounded space: as **a :** one of the compartments of a honeycomb **b :** a membranous area bounded by veins in the wing of an insect
4 : a small usually microscopic mass of protoplasm bounded externally by a semipermeable membrane, usually including one or more nuclei and various other organelles with their products, capable alone or interacting with other cells of performing all the fundamental functions of life, and forming the smallest structural unit of living matter capable of functioning independently
5 a (1) **:** a receptacle (as a cup or jar) containing electrodes and an electrolyte either for generating electricity by chemical action or for use in electrolysis (2) **:** FUEL CELL **b :** a single unit in a device for converting radiant energy into electrical energy or for varying the intensity of an electrical current in accordance with radiation
6 : a unit in a statistical array (as a spreadsheet) formed by the intersection of a column and a row
7 : the basic and usually smallest unit of an organization or movement 〈a communist cell〉
8 : a portion of the atmosphere that behaves as a unit
9 : any of the small sections of a geographic area of a cellular telephone system

cell 4 (schematic): A plant, B animal; 1 cell wall, 2 middle lamella, 3 plasma membrane, 4 mitochondrion, 5 vacuole, 6 Golgi apparatus, 7 cytoplasm, 8 nuclear membrane, 9 nucleolus, 10 nucleus, 11 chromatin, 12 endoplasmic reticulum with associated ribosomes, 13 chloroplast, 14 centriole, 15 lysosome

¹**cel·lar** \'se-lər\ noun [Middle English celer, from Anglo-French, from Latin cellarium storeroom, from cella] (13th century)
1 a : BASEMENT; also : a covered excavation **b** : the lowest grade or rank; especially : the lowest place in the standings (as of an athletic league)
2 : a stock of wines
²**cellar** transitive verb (1677)
: to put into a cellar (as for storage)
cel·lar·age \'se-lə-rij\ noun (1602)
: cellar space especially for storage
cel·lar·er \'se-lər-ər\ noun [Middle English celerer, from Old French, from Late Latin cellarius, from Latin cellarium] (13th century)
: an official (as in a monastery) in charge of provisions
cel·lar·ette or **cel·lar·et** \,se-lə-'ret\ noun (circa 1807)
: a case or sideboard for holding bottles of wine or liquor
cell body noun (1878)
: the nucleus-containing central part of a neuron exclusive of its axons and dendrites
cell cycle noun (1961)
: the complete series of events from one cell division to the next — compare G_1 PHASE, G_2 PHASE, M PHASE, S PHASE
cell division noun (1882)
: the process by which cells multiply involving both nuclear and cytoplasmic division — compare MEIOSIS, MITOSIS
celled \'seld\ adjective
: having (such or so many) cells — used in combination 〈single-celled organisms〉
cell–me·di·at·ed \'sel-'mē-dē-,ā-təd\ adjective (1967)
: relating to or being the part of immunity or the immune response that is mediated primarily by T cells
cell membrane noun (1870)
: PLASMA MEMBRANE
cel·lo \'che-(,)lō\ noun, plural **cello** also **cel·li** \-lē\ [short for violoncello] (circa 1876)
: the bass member of the violin family tuned an octave below the viola
— **cel·list** \'che-list\ noun
cel·lo·bi·ose \,se-lə-'bī-,ōs, -,ōz\ noun [International Scientific Vocabulary cellulose + -o- + biose disaccharide, from ¹bi- + ²-ose] (1902)
: a faintly sweet disaccharide $C_{12}H_{22}O_{11}$ obtained by partial hydrolysis of cellulose
cel·loi·din \se-'lói-dᵊn\ noun [cellulose + ¹-oid + ¹-in] (1883)
: a purified pyroxylin used chiefly in microscopy
cel·lo·phane \'se-lə-,fān\ noun [French, from cellulose + -phane (as in diaphane diaphanous, from Medieval Latin diaphanus)] (1912)
: regenerated cellulose in thin transparent sheets used especially for packaging
cell plate noun (1882)
: a disk formed in the phragmoplast of a dividing plant cell that eventually forms the middle lamella of the wall between the daughter cells
cell sap noun (circa 1889)
1 : the liquid contents of a plant cell vacuole
2 : CYTOSOL
cell theory noun (circa 1890)
: a theory in biology that includes one or both of the statements that the cell is the fundamental structural and functional unit of living matter and that the organism is composed of autonomous cells with its properties being the sum of those of its cells
cel·lu·lar \'sel-yə-lər\ adjective [New Latin cellularis, from cellula living cell, from Latin, diminutive of cella small room] (circa 1739)
1 : of, relating to, or consisting of cells
2 : containing cavities : having a porous texture 〈cellular rocks〉
3 : of, relating to, or being a radiotelephone

system in which a geographical area (as a city) is divided into small sections each served by a transmitter of limited range so that any available radio channel can be used in different parts of the area simultaneously
— **cel·lu·lar·i·ty** \,sel-yə-'lar-ə-tē\ *noun*
cel·lu·lase \'sel-yə-,lās, -,lāz\ *noun* [International Scientific Vocabulary] (1903)
: an enzyme that hydrolyzes cellulose
cel·lule \'sel-(,)yü(ə)l\ *noun* [Latin *cellula*] (circa 1693)
: a small cell
cel·lu·lite \'sel-yə-,līt, -,lēt\ *noun* [French, literally, accumulation of subcutaneous fat, cellulitis, from *cellule* cell + *-ite* -itis] (1968)
: lumpy fat found in the thighs, hips, and buttocks of some women
cel·lu·li·tis \,sel-yə-'lī-təs\ *noun* [New Latin, from *cellula*] (1861)
: diffuse and especially subcutaneous inflammation of connective tissue
cel·lu·loid \'sel-yə-,loid\ *noun* [from *Celluloid,* a trademark] (1871)
1 : a tough flammable thermoplastic composed essentially of cellulose nitrate and camphor
2 : a motion-picture film ⟨a work . . . making its third appearance on *celluloid* —John McCarten⟩
— **celluloid** *adjective*
cel·lu·lo·lyt·ic \,sel-yə-lō-'li-tik\ *adjective* [*cellul*ose + *-o-* + *-lytic*] (1943)
: hydrolyzing or having the capacity to hydrolyze cellulose
cel·lu·lose \'sel-yə-,lōs, -,lōz\ *noun* [French, from *cellule* living cell, from New Latin *cellula*] (1848)
: a polysaccharide $(C_6H_{10}O_5)x$ of glucose units that constitutes the chief part of the cell walls of plants, occurs naturally in such fibrous products as cotton and kapok, and is the raw material of many manufactured goods (as paper, rayon, and cellophane)
cellulose acetate *noun* (1895)
: any of several compounds insoluble in water that are formed especially by the action of acetic acid, anhydride of acetic acid, and sulfuric acid on cellulose and are used for making textile fibers, packaging sheets, photographic films, and varnishes
cellulose nitrate *noun* (1880)
: NITROCELLULOSE
cel·lu·los·ic \,sel-yə-'lō-sik, -zik\ *adjective* (1881)
: of, relating to, or made from cellulose
— **cellulosic** *noun*
cell wall *noun* (circa 1849)
: the usually rigid nonliving permeable wall that surrounds the plasma membrane and encloses and supports the cells of most plants, bacteria, fungi, and algae — see CELL illustration
Cel·si·us \'sel-sē-əs, -shəs\ *adjective* [Anders *Celsius*] (circa 1850)
: relating to, conforming to, or having the international thermometric scale on which the interval between the triple point of water and the boiling point of water is divided into 99.99 degrees with 0.01° representing the triple point and 100° the boiling point ⟨10° *Celsius*⟩ — abbreviation *C;* compare CENTIGRADE ◇
celt \'selt\ *noun* [Late Latin *celtis* chisel] (1715)
: a prehistoric stone or metal implement shaped like a chisel or ax head
Celt \'kelt, 'selt\ *noun* [Latin *Celtae,* plural, from Greek *Keltoi*] (1550)
1 : a member of a division of the early Indo-European peoples distributed from the British Isles and Spain to Asia Minor
2 : a modern Gael, Highland Scot, Irishman, Welshman, Cornishman, or Breton
¹**Celt·ic** \'kel-tik, 'sel-\ *adjective* (1590)
: of, relating to, or characteristic of the Celts or their languages

²**Celtic** *noun* (1739)
: a group of Indo-European languages usually subdivided into Brythonic and Goidelic and now largely confined to Brittany, Wales, western Ireland, and the Scottish Highlands — see INDO-EUROPEAN LANGUAGES table
Celtic cross *noun* (1873)
: a cross having essentially the form of a Latin cross with a ring about the intersection of the crossbar and upright shaft — see CROSS illustration
Celt·i·cist \'kel-tə-sist, 'sel-\ *noun* (1912)
: a specialist in Celtic languages or cultures
cem·ba·lo \'chem-bə-,lō\ *noun, plural* **-ba·li** \-(,)lē\ *or* **-balos** [Italian] (circa 1801)
: HARPSICHORD
¹**ce·ment** \si-'ment *also* 'sē-ment\ *noun* [Middle English *sement,* from Middle French *ciment,* from Latin *caementum* stone chips used in making mortar, from *caedere* to cut] (14th century)
1 a : a powder of alumina, silica, lime, iron oxide, and magnesium oxide burned together in a kiln and finely pulverized and used as an ingredient of mortar and concrete; *also* : any mixture used for a similar purpose **b** : CONCRETE
2 : a binding element or agency: as **a** : a substance to make objects adhere to each other **b** : something serving to unite firmly ⟨justice is the *cement* that holds a political community together —R. M. Hutchins⟩
3 : CEMENTUM
4 : a plastic composition made especially of zinc or silica for filling dental cavities
5 : the fine-grained groundmass or glass of a porphyry
²**cement** (14th century)
transitive verb
1 : to unite or make firm by or as if by cement
2 : to overlay with concrete
intransitive verb
: to become cemented
— **ce·ment·er** *noun*
ce·men·ta·tion \,sē-,men-'tā-shən\ *noun* (1594)
1 : a process of surrounding a solid with a powder and heating the whole so that the solid is changed by chemical combination with the powder
2 : the act or process of cementing : the state of being cemented
ce·ment·ite \si-'men-,tīt\ *noun* [¹*cement*] (1888)
: a hard brittle iron carbide Fe_3C that occurs in steel, cast iron, and iron-carbon alloys
ce·men·ti·tious \,sē-,men-'ti-shəs\ *adjective* (circa 1828)
: having the properties of cement
ce·men·tum \si-'men-təm\ *noun* [New Latin, from Latin *caementum*] (1842)
: a specialized external bony layer covering the dentin of the part of a tooth normally within the gum — see TOOTH illustration
cem·e·tery \'se-mə-,ter-ē\ *noun, plural* **-ter·ies** [Middle English *cimitery,* from Middle French *cimitere,* from Late Latin *coemeterium,* from Greek *koimētērion* sleeping chamber, burial place, from *koiman* to put to sleep; akin to Greek *keisthai* to lie, Sanskrit *śete* he lies] (15th century)
: a burial ground
cen·a·cle \'se-ni-kəl\ *noun* [Late Latin *cenaculum* the room where Christ and his disciples had the Last Supper, from Latin, top story, probably from *cena* dinner] (1889)
: a retreat house; *especially* : one for Roman Catholic women directed by nuns of the Society of Our Lady of the Cenacle
-cene *adjective combining form* [Greek *kainos* new, recent — more at RECENT]
: recent — in names of geologic periods ⟨Eo*cene*⟩
cen·o·bite \'se-nə-,bīt, *especially British* 'sē-\ *noun* [Late Latin *coenobita,* from *coenobium* monastery, from Late Greek *koinobion,* ulti-

mately from Greek *koin-* coen- + *bios* life — more at QUICK] (circa 1500)
: a member of a religious group living together in a monastic community
— **cen·o·bit·ic** \,se-nə-'bi-tik, ,sē-\ *adjective*
ce·no·spe·cies \'sē-nə-,spē-(,)shēz, 'se-, -(,)sēz\ *noun* [*coen-* + *species*] (1922)
: a group of related biological taxonomic units capable by reason of closely related genotypes of essentially free gene interchange
ceno·taph \'se-nə-,taf, -,täf\ *noun* [French *cénotaphe,* from Latin *cenotaphium,* from Greek *kenotaphion,* from *kenos* empty + *taphos* tomb] (1603)
: a tomb or a monument erected in honor of a person or group of persons whose remains are elsewhere
ce·no·te \si-'nō-tē\ *noun* [Mexican Spanish, from Yucatec *ts'onot*] (1841)
: a deep sinkhole in limestone with a pool at the bottom that is found especially in Yucatán
Ce·no·zo·ic \,sē-nə-'zō-ik, ,se-\ *adjective* [Greek *kainos* + English *-zoic*] (1854)
: of, relating to, or being an era of geological history that extends from the beginning of the Tertiary period to the present time and is marked by a rapid evolution of mammals and birds and of angiosperms and especially grasses and by little change in the invertebrates; *also* : relating to the corresponding system of rocks — see GEOLOGIC TIME table
— **Cenozoic** *noun*
cense \'sen(t)s\ *transitive verb* **censed; cens·ing** [Middle English, probably short for *encensen* to incense, from Middle French *encenser,* from Late Latin *incensare,* from *incensum* incense] (14th century)
: to perfume especially with a censer
cen·ser \'sen(t)-sər\ *noun* (13th century)
: a vessel for burning incense; *especially* : a covered incense burner swung on chains in a religious ritual
¹**cen·sor** \'sen(t)-sər\ *noun* [Latin, from *censēre* to give as one's opinion, assess; perhaps akin to Sanskrit *śaṁsati* he praises] (1531)
1 : one of two magistrates of early Rome acting as census takers, assessors, and inspectors of morals and conduct
2 : one who supervises conduct and morals: as **a** : an official who examines materials (as publications or films) for objectionable matter **b** : an official (as in time of war) who reads communications (as letters) and deletes material considered sensitive or harmful

censer

◇ **WORD HISTORY**
Celsius The Celsius scale is named after the Swedish astronomer Anders Celsius (1701–44), whose astronomical work is now largely forgotten. Although he was not the first to propose a temperature metric of 100 degrees, Celsius' observations on the usefulness of the freezing and boiling points of water as thermometric constants, published in 1742, were influential. Celsius chose 0° as the boiling point and 100° as the freezing point, but in 1747 the Swedes reversed the order. The Swedish 100-degree system gained widespread scientific acceptance in the 19th century.

\ə\ abut \ᵊ\ kitten \ər\ further \a\ ash \ā\ ace \ä\ mop, mar \aù\ out \ch\ chin \e\ bet \ē\ easy \g\ go \i\ hit \ī\ ice \j\ job \ŋ\ sing \ō\ go \ò\ law \òi\ boy \th\ thin \t͟h\ the \ü\ loot \ù\ foot \y\ yet \zh\ vision *see also* Guide to Pronunciation

3 : a hypothetical psychic agency that represses unacceptable notions before they reach consciousness
— **cen·so·ri·al** \sen-ˈsōr-ē-əl, -ˈsȯr-\ adjective

²**censor** transitive verb **cen·sored; cen·sor·ing** \ˈsen(t)-sə-riŋ, ˈsen(t)s-riŋ\ (1882)
: to examine in order to suppress or delete anything considered objectionable

cen·so·ri·ous \sen-ˈsōr-ē-əs, -ˈsȯr-\ adjective [Latin censorius of a censor, from censor] (1536)
: marked by or given to censure
synonym see CRITICAL
— **cen·so·ri·ous·ly** adverb
— **cen·so·ri·ous·ness** noun

cen·sor·ship \ˈsen(t)-sər-ˌship\ noun (circa 1591)
1 a : the institution, system, or practice of censoring **b :** the actions or practices of censors; especially **:** censorial control exercised repressively
2 : the office, power, or term of a Roman censor
3 : exclusion from consciousness by the psychic censor

cen·sur·able \ˈsen(t)-sh(ə-)rə-bəl\ adjective (1634)
: deserving or open to censure

¹**cen·sure** \ˈsen(t)-shər\ noun [Latin censura, from censēre] (14th century)
1 : a judgment involving condemnation
2 archaic **:** OPINION, JUDGMENT
3 : the act of blaming or condemning sternly
4 : an official reprimand

²**censure** transitive verb **cen·sured; cen·sur·ing** \ˈsen(t)-sh(ə-)riŋ\ (1587)
1 obsolete **:** ESTIMATE, JUDGE
2 : to find fault with and criticize as blameworthy
synonym see CRITICIZE
— **cen·sur·er** \ˈsen(t)-shər-ər\ noun

cen·sus \ˈsen(t)-səs\ noun [Latin, from censēre] (1634)
1 : a count of the population and a property evaluation in early Rome
2 : a usually complete enumeration of a population; specifically **:** a periodic governmental enumeration of population
3 : COUNT, TALLY
— **census** transitive verb

cent \ˈsent\ noun [Middle French, hundred, from Latin centum — more at HUNDRED] (1782)
1 : a monetary unit equal to ¹⁄₁₀₀ of a basic unit of value — see birr, dollar, gulden, leone, lilangeni, lira, pound, rand, rupee, shilling at MONEY table
2 : a coin, token, or note representing one cent
3 : the fen of the People's Republic of China

cen·tal \ˈsen-tᵊl\ noun [Latin centum + English -al (as in quintal)] (1870)
chiefly British **:** HUNDREDWEIGHT 1

cen·taur \ˈsen-ˌtȯr\ noun [Middle English, from Latin Centaurus, from Greek Kentauros] (14th century)
: any of a race of creatures fabled to be half man and half horse and to live in the mountains of Thessaly

cen·tau·rea \sen-ˈtȯr-ē-ə\ noun [New Latin, genus name, from Medieval Latin] (circa 1829)
: any of a large genus (Centaurea) of composite herbs (as knapweed) including several cultivated for their showy heads of tubular florets

Cen·tau·rus \-ˈtȯr-əs\ noun [Latin (genitive Centauri)]
: a southern constellation between the Southern Cross and Hydra

cen·tau·ry \ˈsen-ˌtȯr-ē\ noun, plural **-ries** [Middle English centaure, from Middle French centaurée, from Medieval Latin centaurea, from Latin centaureum, from Greek kentaureion, from Kentauros] (14th century)

1 : any of a genus (Centaurium) of low herbs of the gentian family; especially **:** an Old World herb (C. umbellatum) formerly used as a tonic
2 : an herb (Sabatia angularis) of the eastern U.S. closely related to centaury

¹**cen·ta·vo** \sen-ˈtä-(ˌ)vō\ noun, plural **-vos** [Spanish, literally, hundredth, from ciento hundred, from Latin centum] (1883)
— see boliviano, colón, cordoba, lempira, peso, quetzal, sol, sucre at MONEY table

²**cen·ta·vo** \-ˈtä-(ˌ)vü, -(ˌ)vō\ noun, plural **-vos** [Portuguese, from Spanish] (1920)
— see escudo, metical at MONEY table

cen·te·nar·i·an \ˌsen-tə-ˈner-ē-ən\ noun (circa 1841)
: one that is 100 years old or older
— **centenarian** adjective

cen·te·na·ry \sen-ˈte-nə-rē, ˈsen-tə-ˌner-ē, especially British sen-ˈtē-nə-rē\ noun, plural **-ries** [Late Latin centenarium, from Latin centenarius of a hundred, from centeni one hundred each, from centum hundred — more at HUNDRED] (1788)
: CENTENNIAL
— **centenary** adjective

cen·ten·ni·al \sen-ˈte-nē-əl\ noun [Latin centum + English -ennial (as in biennial)] (1876)
: a 100th anniversary or its celebration
— **centennial** adjective
— **cen·ten·ni·al·ly** \-ə-lē\ adverb

¹**cen·ter** \ˈsen-tər, ˈse-nər\ noun [Middle English centre, from Middle French, from Latin centrum, from Greek kentron sharp point, center of a circle, from kentein to prick; probably akin to Old High German hantag pointed] (14th century)
1 a : the point around which a circle or sphere is described; broadly **:** a point that is related to a geometrical figure in such a way that for any point on the figure there is another point on the figure such that a straight line joining the two points is bisected by the original point — called also center of symmetry **b :** the center of the circle inscribed in a regular polygon
2 a : a point, area, person, or thing that is most important or pivotal in relation to an indicated activity, interest, or condition ⟨a railroad center⟩ ⟨the center of the controversy⟩ **b :** a source from which something originates ⟨a propaganda center⟩ **c :** a group of nerve cells having a common function ⟨respiratory center⟩ **d :** a region of concentrated population ⟨an urban center⟩ **e :** a facility providing a place for a particular activity or service ⟨a day-care center⟩
3 a : the middle part (as of the forehead or a stage) **b** often capitalized (1) **:** a grouping of political figures holding moderate views especially between those of conservatives and liberals (2) **:** the views of such politicians (3) **:** the adherents of such views
4 a : a player occupying a middle position on a team: as (1) **:** the football player in the middle of a line who passes the ball between his legs to a back to start a down (2) **:** the usually tallest player on a basketball team who usually plays near the basket **b :** CENTER FIELD
5 a : either of two tapered rods which support work in a lathe or grinding machine and about or with which the work revolves **b :** a conical recess in the end of work (as a shaft) for receiving such a center
— **cen·ter·less** \-ləs\ adjective

²**center** verb **cen·tered; cen·ter·ing** \ˈsen-t(ə-)riŋ, ˈse-nər-iŋ\ (1610)
transitive verb
1 : to place or fix at or around a center or central area or position ⟨center the picture on the wall⟩
2 : to give a central focus or basis ⟨centers her hopes on her son⟩ ⟨the plot was centered on espionage⟩
3 : to adjust (as lenses) so that the axes coincide

4 a : to pass (a ball or puck) from either side toward the middle of the playing area **b :** to hand or pass (a football) backward between one's legs to a back to start a down
intransitive verb
: to have a specified center **:** FOCUS □

cen·ter·board \ˈsen-tər-ˌbȯrd, ˈse-nər-, -ˌbȯrd\ noun (1867)
: a retractable keel used especially in sailboats

cen·tered \ˈsen-tərd, ˈse-nərd\ adjective (circa 1893)
1 : having a center — often used in combination ⟨a dark-centered coneflower⟩
2 : having a center of curvature — often used in combination ⟨a 3-centered arch⟩
3 : emotionally stable and secure
— **cen·tered·ness** \-nəs\ noun

center field noun (1857)
1 : the position of the player for defending center field
2 : the part of the baseball outfield between right and left field
— **center fielder** noun

cen·ter·fold \ˈsen-tər-ˌfōld, ˈse-nər-\ noun (1952)
1 : a foldout that is the center spread of a magazine
2 : a picture (as of a nude) on a centerfold; also **:** a model featured in such a picture

cen·ter·line \-ˈlīn, -ˌlīn\ noun (1807)
: a real or imaginary line that is equidistant from the surface or sides of something

center of curvature (circa 1856)
: the center of the circle whose center lies on the concave side of a curve on the normal to a given point of the curve and whose radius is equal to the radius of curvature at that point

center of gravity (1659)
1 : CENTER OF MASS
2 : the point at which the entire weight of a body may be considered as concentrated so that if supported at this point the body would remain in equilibrium in any position
3 : CENTER 2a

center of mass (1879)
: the point in a body or system of bodies at which the whole mass may be considered as concentrated

cen·ter·piece \-ˌpēs\ noun (1803)
1 : an object occupying a central position; especially **:** an adornment in the center of a table
2 : one that is of central importance or interest in a larger whole

center punch noun (1879)
: a hand punch consisting of a short steel bar with a hardened conical point at one end used for marking the centers of holes to be drilled

center stage noun (1954)
1 : the central part of a theatrical stage
2 : a central or highly prominent position
— **center stage** adjective or adverb

cen·tes·i·mal \sen-ˈte-sə-məl\ adjective [Latin centesimus hundredth, from centum] (1809)
: marked by or relating to division into hundredths

¹**cen·tes·i·mo** \chen-ˈte-zə-ˌmō\ noun, plural **-mi** \-(ˌ)mē\ [Italian] (1851)

□ USAGE
center The intransitive verb center is most commonly used with the prepositions in, on, at, and around. At appears to be favored in mathematical contexts; the others are found in a broad range of contexts. Center around, a standard idiom, has often been objected to as illogical. The logic on which the objections are based is irrelevant, since center around is an idiom and idioms have their own logic. Center on is currently more common in edited prose, and revolve around and similar verbs are available if you want to avoid center around.

— see *lira* at MONEY table

²cen·tes·i·mo \sen-'te-sə-,mō\ *noun, plural* **-mos** [Spanish *centésimo*] (circa 1883)
— see *balboa, peso* at MONEY table

centi- *combining form* [French & Latin; French, hundredth, from Latin, hundred, from *centum* — more at HUNDRED]
1 : hundred ⟨*centi*pede⟩
2 : hundredth part ⟨*centi*meter⟩

cen·ti·grade \'sen-tə-,grād, 'sän-\ *adjective* [French, from Latin *centi*- hundred + French *grade*] (1801)
: relating to, conforming to, or having a thermometric scale on which the interval between the freezing point of water and the boiling point of water is divided into 100 degrees with 0° representing the freezing point and 100° the boiling point ⟨10° *centigrade*⟩ — abbreviation *C;* compare CELSIUS

cen·ti·gram \-,gram\ *noun* (1801)
— see METRIC SYSTEM table

cen·ti·li·ter \'sen-ti-,lē-tər, 'sän-\ *noun* (1801)
— see METRIC SYSTEM table

cen·til·lion \sen-'til-yən\ *noun, often attributive* [Latin *centum* + English *-illion* (as in *million*)] (circa 1889)
— see NUMBER table

cen·time \'sän-,tēm, 'sen-\ *noun* [French, from *cent* hundred, from Latin *centum*] (1801)
— see *dinar, dirham, franc, gourde* at MONEY table

cen·ti·me·ter \'sen-tə-,mē-tər, 'sän-\ *noun* (1801)
— see METRIC SYSTEM table

centimeter–gram–second *adjective* (1875)
: of, relating to, or being a system of units based on the centimeter as the unit of length, the gram as the unit of mass, and the second as the unit of time — abbreviation *cgs*

cen·ti·mo \'sen-tə-,mō\ *noun, plural* **-mos** [Spanish *céntimo*] (1899)
— see *bolivar, colon, dobra, guarani, peseta* at MONEY table

cen·ti·mor·gan \'sen-tə-,mȯr-gən, 'sän-\ *noun* (1919)
: a genetic unit equivalent to $\frac{1}{100}$ of a morgan

cen·ti·pede \'sen-tə-,pēd\ *noun* [Latin *centipeda*, from *centi*- + *ped-, pes* foot — more at FOOT] (1601)
: any of a class (Chilopoda) of long flattened many-segmented predaceous arthropods with each segment bearing one pair of legs of which the foremost pair is modified into poison fangs

cent·ner \'sent-nər\ *noun* [probably from Low German] (1683)
: any of various units of weight used especially in Europe and usually equal to about 110 pounds (about 50 kilograms)

cen·to \'sen-(,)tō\ *noun, plural* **cen·to·nes** \sen-'tō-(,)nēz\ [Late Latin, from Latin, patchwork garment; perhaps akin to Sanskrit *kanthā* patched garment] (1605)
: a literary work made up of parts from other works

centr- *or* **centri-** *or* **centro-** *combining form* [Greek *kentr-, kentro-*, from *kentron* center — more at CENTER]
: center ⟨*centr*ifugal⟩ ⟨*centr*oid⟩

centra *plural of* CENTRUM

¹cen·tral \'sen-trəl\ *adjective* [Latin *centralis*, from *centrum* center] (1647)
1 : containing or constituting a center
2 : of cardinal importance : ESSENTIAL, PRINCIPAL ⟨the *central* character of the novel⟩
3 a : situated at, in, or near the center **b** : easily accessible from outlying districts ⟨a *central* location for the new theater⟩
4 a : centrally placed and superseding separate scattered units ⟨*central* heating⟩ **b** : controlling or directing local or branch activities ⟨the *central* committee⟩
5 : holding to a middle between extremes : MODERATE

6 : of, relating to, or comprising the brain and spinal cord; *also* : originating within the central nervous system ⟨*central* deafness⟩
— **cen·tral·ly** \-trə-lē\ *adverb*

²central *noun* (1889)
1 : a telephone exchange or operator
2 : a central office or bureau usually controlling others ⟨weather *central*⟩

central angle *noun* (1904)
: an angle formed by two radii of a circle

central bank *noun* (1922)
: a national bank that operates to establish monetary and fiscal policy and to control the money supply and interest rate
— **central banker** *noun*

central casting *noun* (1957)
: the department of a movie studio responsible for casting actors — usually used figuratively ⟨a politician right out of *central casting*⟩

central city *noun* (1950)
: a city that constitutes the densely populated center of a metropolitan area

cen·tral·ise *British variant of* CENTRALIZE

cen·tral·ism \'sen-trə-,li-zəm\ *noun* (1831)
: the concentration of power and control in the central authority of an organization (as a political or educational system) — compare FEDERALISM
— **cen·tral·ist** \-list\ *noun or adjective*
— **cen·tral·is·tic** \,sen-trə-'lis-tik\ *adjective*

cen·tral·i·ty \sen-'tra-lə-tē\ *noun, plural* **-ties** (1647)
1 : the quality or state of being central
2 : central situation
3 : tendency to remain in or at the center

cen·tral·ize \'sen-trə-,līz\ *verb* **-ized; -iz·ing** (1800)
intransitive verb
: to form a center : cluster around a center
transitive verb
1 : to bring to a center : CONSOLIDATE ⟨*centralize* all the data in one file⟩
2 : to concentrate by placing power and authority in a center or central organization
— **cen·tral·i·za·tion** \,sen-trə-lə-'zā-shən\ *noun*
— **cen·tral·iz·er** \'sen-trə-,lī-zər\ *noun*

central limit theorem *noun* (1951)
: any of several fundamental theorems of probability and statistics that state the conditions under which the distribution of a sum of independent random variables is approximated by the normal distribution; *especially* : one which is much applied in sampling and which states that the distribution of a mean of a sample from a population with finite variance is approximated by the normal distribution as the number in the sample becomes large

central nervous system *noun* (circa 1907)
: the part of the nervous system which in vertebrates consists of the brain and spinal cord, to which sensory impulses are transmitted and from which motor impulses pass out, and which coordinates the activity of the entire nervous system — compare AUTONOMIC NERVOUS SYSTEM

central processing unit *noun* (1961)
: PROCESSOR 2a(2) — abbreviation *cpu*

central tendency *noun* (circa 1928)
: the degree of clustering of the values of a statistical distribution that is usually measured by the arithmetic mean, mode, or median

central time *noun, often C capitalized* (1883)
: the time of the 6th time zone west of Greenwich that includes the central U.S. — see TIME ZONE illustration

cen·tre *chiefly British variant of* CENTER

cen·tric \'sen-trik\ *adjective* [Greek *kentrikos* of the center, from *kentron*] (circa 1590)
1 : located in or at a center : CENTRAL ⟨a *centric* point⟩
2 : concentrated about or directed to a center ⟨a *centric* activity⟩
3 : of, relating to, or having a centromere

4 : of, relating to, or resembling an order (Centrales) of radially symmetrical diatoms
— **cen·tri·cal·ly** \-tri-k(ə-)lē\ *adverb*
— **cen·tric·i·ty** \sen-'tri-sə-tē\ *noun*

-centric *adjective combining form* [Medieval Latin *-centricus*, from Latin *centrum* center]
1 : having (such) a center or (such or so many) centers ⟨poly*centric*⟩
2 : having (something specified) as its center ⟨helio*centric*⟩

¹cen·trif·u·gal \sen-'tri-fyə-gəl, -'tri-fi-, *especially British* ,sen-tri-'fyü-gəl\ *adjective* [New Latin *centrifugus*, from *centr-* + Latin *fugere* to flee — more at FUGITIVE] (circa 1721)
1 : proceeding or acting in a direction away from a center or axis
2 : using or acting by centrifugal force ⟨a *centrifugal* pump⟩
3 : EFFERENT
4 : tending away from centralization : SEPARATIST ⟨*centrifugal* tendencies in modern society⟩
— **cen·trif·u·gal·ly** \-gə-lē\ *adverb*

²centrifugal *noun* (1866)
: a centrifugal machine or a drum in such a machine

centrifugal force *noun* (circa 1721)
1 : the force that tends to impel a thing or parts of a thing outward from a center of rotation
2 : the force that an object moving along a circular path exerts on the body constraining the object and that acts outwardly away from the center of rotation ⟨a stone whirled on a string exerts *centrifugal force* on the string⟩

cen·tri·fu·ga·tion \,sen-trə-fyü-'gā-shən, -f(y)ə-\ *noun* (1903)
: the process of centrifuging

¹cen·tri·fuge \'sen-trə-,fyüj\ *noun* [French, from *centrifuge* centrifugal, from New Latin *centrifugus*] (1887)
: a machine using centrifugal force for separating substances of different densities, for removing moisture, or for simulating gravitational effects

²centrifuge *transitive verb* **-fuged; -fug·ing** (circa 1895)
: to subject to centrifugal action especially in a centrifuge

cen·tri·ole \'sen-trē-,ōl\ *noun* [German *Zentriol*, from *Zentrum* center] (circa 1896)
: one of a pair of cellular organelles that occur especially in animals, are adjacent to the nucleus, function in the formation of the spindle apparatus during cell division, and consist of a cylinder with nine microtubules arranged peripherally in a circle — see CELL illustration

cen·trip·e·tal \sen-'tri-pə-t°l\ *adjective* [New Latin *centripetus*, from *centr-* + Latin *petere* to go to, seek — more at FEATHER] (1709)
1 : proceeding or acting in a direction toward a center or axis
2 : AFFERENT
3 : tending toward centralization : UNIFYING
— **cen·trip·e·tal·ly** \-t°l-ē\ *adverb*

centripetal force *noun* (1709)
: the force that is necessary to keep an object moving in a circular path and that is directed inward toward the center of rotation ⟨a string on the end of which a stone is whirled about exerts *centripetal force* on the stone⟩

cen·trist \'sen-trist\ *noun* (1872)
1 *often capitalized* : a member of a center party
2 : one who holds moderate views
— **cen·trism** \-,tri-zəm\ *noun*
— **centrist** *adjective*

cen·troid \'sen-,trȯid\ *noun* (1882)
1 : CENTER OF MASS

\ə\ abut	\ᵊ\ kitten	\ər\ further	\a\ ash	\ā\ ace	
\ä\ mop, mar		\au̇\ out	\ch\ chin	\e\ bet	\ē\ easy
\g\ go	\i\ hit	\ī\ ice	\j\ job	\ŋ\ sing	\ō\ go
\ȯ\ law	\ȯi\ boy	\th\ thin	\t͟h\ the	\ü\ loot	\u̇\ foot
\y\ yet	\zh\ vision	*see also* Guide to Pronunciation			

2 : a point whose coordinates are the averages of the corresponding coordinates of a given set of points and which for a given planar or three-dimensional figure (as a triangle or sphere) corresponds to the center of mass of a thin plate of uniform thickness and consistency or a body of uniform consistency having the same boundary

cen·tro·mere \'sen-trə-ˌmir\ *noun* [International Scientific Vocabulary] (circa 1925)
: the point or region on a chromosome to which the spindle attaches during mitosis and meiosis
— **cen·tro·mer·ic** \ˌsen-trə-'mir-ik, -'mer-\ *adjective*

cen·tro·some \'sen-trə-ˌsōm\ *noun* [International Scientific Vocabulary] (1889)
1 : CENTRIOLE
2 : the centriole-containing region of clear cytoplasm adjacent to the cell nucleus

cen·tro·sym·met·ric \ˌsen-trə-sə-'me-trik\ *adjective* (circa 1909)
: symmetric with respect to a central point ⟨*centrosymmetric* molecules⟩ ⟨a *centrosymmetric* curve⟩

cen·trum \'sen-trəm\ *noun, plural* **centrums** *or* **cen·tra** \-trə\ [Latin — more at CENTER] (1854)
1 : CENTER
2 : the body of a vertebra ventral to the neural arch

cen·tum \'ken-təm, -ˌtùm\ *adjective* [Latin, hundred; from the fact that its initial sound (a velar stop) is the representative of an Indo-European palatal stop — more at HUNDRED] (1901)
: of, relating to, or constituting an Indo-European language group in which the palatal stops did not in prehistoric times become palatal or alveolar fricatives — compare SATEM

cen·tu·ri·on \sen-'chùr-ē-ən, -'tyùr-, -'tùr-\ *noun* [Middle English, from Middle French & Latin; Middle French, from Latin *centurion-, centurio*, from *centuria*] (13th century)
: an officer commanding a Roman century

cen·tu·ry \'sen(t)-sh(ə-)rē\ *noun, plural* **-ries** [Latin *centuria*, irregular from *centum* hundred] (1533)
1 : a subdivision of the Roman legion
2 : a group, sequence, or series of 100 like things
3 : a period of 100 years especially of the Christian era or of the preceding period of human history
4 : a race over a hundred units (as yards or miles)

century plant *noun* (1764)
: a Mexican agave (*Agave americana*) that takes many years to mature, flowers only once, and then dies

CEO \ˌsē-(ˌ)ē-'ō\ *noun* [chief executive officer] (1975)
: the executive with the chief decision-making authority in an organization or business

ceorl \'chā-ˌòrl\ *noun* [Old English — more at CHURL] (before 12th century)
: a freeman of the lowest rank in Anglo-Saxon England

cèpe *or* **cepe** \'sēp, sep\ *also* **cep** \'sep\ *noun* [French, from Gascon *cep* tree trunk, mushroom, from Latin *cippus* stake, post] (1865)
: a wild edible boletus mushroom (especially *Boletus edulis*)

cephal- *or* **cephalo-** *combining form* [Latin, from Greek *kephal-, kephalo-*, from *kephalē*]
: head ⟨*cephala*d⟩ ⟨*cephalo*pod⟩

ceph·a·lad \'se-fə-ˌlad\ *adverb* (1887)
: toward the head or anterior end of the body

ceph·a·lex·in \ˌse-fə-'lek-sən\ *noun* [*cepha*losporin + *-ex-* (of unknown origin) + [1]-*in*] (1967)
: a semisynthetic cephalosporin $C_{16}H_{17}N_3O_4S$ with a spectrum of antibiotic activity similar to the penicillins

ce·phal·ic \sə-'fa-lik\ *adjective* [Middle French *céphalique*, from Latin *cephalicus,*

from Greek *kephalikos*, from *kephalē* head; akin to Old High German *gebal* skull, Old Norse *gafl* gable, Tocharian A *śpāl* head] (1599)
1 : of or relating to the head
2 : directed toward or situated on or in or near the head
— **ce·phal·i·cal·ly** \-li-k(ə-)lē\ *adverb*

cephalic index *noun* (1866)
: the ratio multiplied by 100 of the maximum breadth from side to side of the head to its maximum length from front to back in living individuals — compare CRANIAL INDEX

ceph·a·lin \'ke-fə-lən, 'se-\ *noun* [International Scientific Vocabulary] (circa 1899)
: PHOSPHATIDYLETHANOLAMINE

ceph·a·li·za·tion \ˌse-fə-lə-'zā-shən\ *noun* (1864)
: a tendency in the evolution of organisms to concentrate the sensory and neural organs in an anterior head

ceph·a·lom·e·try \ˌse-fə-'lä-mə-trē\ *noun* [International Scientific Vocabulary] (circa 1889)
: the science of measuring the head in living individuals — compare CRANIOMETRY
— **ceph·a·lo·met·ric** \-lō-'me-trik\ *adjective*

ceph·a·lo·pod \'se-fə-lə-ˌpäd\ *noun* [ultimately from *cephal-* + Greek *pod-, pous* foot — more at FOOT] (1826)
: any of a class (Cephalopoda) of marine mollusks including the squids, cuttlefishes, and octopuses that move by expelling water from a tubular siphon under the head and that have a group of muscular usually sucker-bearing arms around the front of the head, highly developed eyes, and usually a sac containing ink which is ejected for defense or concealment
— **cephalopod** *adjective*

ceph·a·lor·i·dine \ˌse-fə-'lòr-ə-ˌdēn, -'lär-\ *noun* [probably from *cephalo*sporin + *-idine*] (1965)
: a semisynthetic broad-spectrum antibiotic $C_{19}H_{17}N_3O_4S_2$ derived from cephalosporin

ceph·a·lo·spo·rin \ˌse-fə-lə-'spòr-ən, -'spór-\ *noun* [*Cephalosporium*, genus of fungi + [1]-*in*] (1951)
: any of several antibiotics produced by an imperfect fungus (genus *Cephalosporium*)

ceph·a·lo·thin \'se-fə-lə-thən, -ˌthin\ *noun* [*cephalo*sporin + *thi-* + [1]-*in*] (1962)
: a semisynthetic broad-spectrum antibiotic derived from cephalosporin and used as the sodium salt $C_{16}H_{15}N_2NaO_6S_2$

ceph·a·lo·tho·rax \ˌse-fə-lə-'thōr-ˌaks, -'thòr-\ *noun* [International Scientific Vocabulary] (1835)
: the united head and thorax of an arachnid or higher crustacean

Ce·phe·id \'se-f(ē-)id, 'sē-\ *noun* [International Scientific Vocabulary, from *Cepheus*] (circa 1903)
: any of a class of pulsating stars whose very regular light variations are related directly to their intrinsic luminosities and whose apparent luminosities are used to estimate distances in astronomy

Ce·pheus \'sē-ˌfyüs; 'sē-fē-əs, 'se-\ *noun* [Latin (genitive *Cephei*), from Greek *Kēpheus*]
: a constellation between Cygnus and the north pole

¹ce·ram·ic \sə-'ra-mik, *especially British* kə-\ *adjective* [Greek *keramikos*, from *keramos* potter's clay, pottery] (1850)
: of or relating to the manufacture of any product (as earthenware, porcelain, or brick) made essentially from a nonmetallic mineral (as clay) by firing at a high temperature; *also* : of or relating to such a product

²ceramic *noun* (1859)
1 *plural but singular in construction* **:** the art or process of making ceramic articles
2 : a product of ceramic manufacture

ce·ra·mist \sə-'ra-mist, 'ser-ə\ *or* **ce·ram·i·cist** \sə-'ra-mə-sist\ *noun* (1855)

: one who engages in ceramics

ce·ras·tes \sə-'ras-(ˌ)tēz\ *noun* [Middle English, from Latin, from Greek *kerastēs*, literally, horned, from *keras* horn] (14th century)
: a venomous viper (*Cerastes cornutus*) of the Near East having a horny process over each eye — called also *horned viper*

ce·rate \'sir-ˌāt\ *noun* [Middle English, from Latin *ceratum* wax salve, from *cera* wax — more at CERUMEN] (15th century)
: an unctuous preparation for external use consisting of wax or resin or spermaceti mixed with oil, lard, and medicinal ingredients

ce·ra·top·sian \ˌsər-ə-'täp-sē-ən\ *noun* [New Latin *Ceratopsia*, from *Ceratops*, a genus, from Greek *kerat-, keras* horn + *ōps* facehorn, eye] (1909)
: any of a suborder (Ceratopsia) of ornithischian dinosaurs of the Late Cretaceous having horns, a sharp horny beak, and a bony frill projecting backward from the skull
— **ceratopsian** *adjective*

Cer·ber·us \'sər-b(ə-)rəs\ *noun* [Latin, from Greek *Kerberos*]
: a 3-headed dog that in Greek mythology guards the entrance to Hades
— **Cer·ber·e·an** \ˌsər-bə-'rē-ən\ *adjective*

-cercal *adjective combining form* [French *-cerque*, from Greek *kerkos* tail]
: -tailed ⟨homo*cercal*⟩

cer·car·ia \(ˌ)sər-'kar-ē-ə, -'ker-\ *noun, plural* **-i·ae** \-ē-ˌē\ [New Latin, from Greek *kerkos*] (circa 1871)
: a usually tadpole-shaped larval trematode worm that develops in a molluscan host from a redia
— **cer·car·i·al** \-ē-əl\ *adjective*

cer·cus \'sər-kəs\ *noun, plural* **cer·ci** \'sər-ˌsī, -ˌkī\ [New Latin, from Greek *kerkos*] (1826)
: either of a pair of simple or segmented appendages at the posterior end of various arthropods that usually act as sensory organs

¹cere \'sir\ *transitive verb* **cered; cer·ing** [Middle English, to wax, from Middle French *cirer*, from Latin *cerare*, from *cera*] (15th century)
: to wrap in or as if in a cerecloth

²cere *noun* [Middle English *sere*, from Middle French *cere*, from Medieval Latin *cera*, from Latin, wax] (15th century)
: a usually waxy protuberance or enlarged area at the base of the bill of a bird

¹ce·re·al \'sir-ē-əl\ *adjective* [French or Latin; French *céréale*, from Latin *cerealis* of Ceres, of grain, from *Ceres*] (1818)
: relating to grain or to the plants that produce it; *also* : made of grain

²cereal *noun* (1832)
1 : a plant (as a grass) yielding starchy grain suitable for food; *also* : its grain
2 : a prepared foodstuff of grain

cereal leaf beetle *noun* (1962)
: a small reddish brown black-headed Old World chrysomelid beetle (*Oulema melanopus*) that feeds on cereal grasses and is a serious threat to U.S. grain crops

cer·e·bel·lum \ˌser-ə-'be-ləm\ *noun, plural* **-bellums** *or* **-bel·la** \-'be-lə\ [Medieval Latin, from Latin, diminutive of *cerebrum*] (1543)
: a large dorsally projecting part of the brain concerned especially with the coordination of muscles and the maintenance of bodily equilibrium, situated between the brain stem and the back of the cerebrum, and formed in humans of two lateral lobes and a median lobe — see BRAIN illustration
— **cer·e·bel·lar** \-'be-lər\ *adjective*

cerebr- *or* **cerebro-** *combining form* [*cerebrum*]
1 : brain **:** cerebrum ⟨*cerebr*ation⟩
2 : cerebral and ⟨*cerebro*spinal⟩

ce·re·bral \sə-'rē-brəl, 'ser-ə-\ *adjective* [French *cérébral*, from Latin *cerebrum* brain; akin to Old High German *hirni* brain, Greek

kara head, *keras* horn, Sanskrit *śiras* head — more at HORN] (1816)
1 a : of or relating to the brain or the intellect **b :** of, relating to, or being the cerebrum
2 a : appealing to intellectual appreciation ⟨*cerebral* drama⟩ **b :** primarily intellectual in nature ⟨a *cerebral* society⟩
— **ce·re·bral·ly** \-brə-lē\ *adverb*

cerebral cortex *noun* (1926)
: the surface layer of gray matter of the cerebrum that functions chiefly in coordination of sensory and motor information

cerebral hemisphere *noun* (1816)
: either of the two hollow convoluted lateral halves of the cerebrum — see BRAIN illustration

cerebral palsy *noun* (1889)
: a disability resulting from damage to the brain before, during, or shortly after birth and outwardly manifested by muscular incoordination and speech disturbances — compare SPASTIC PARALYSIS
— **cerebral–palsied** *adjective*

cer·e·brate \'ser-ə-,brāt\ *intransitive verb* **-brat·ed; -brat·ing** [back-formation from *cerebration,* from *cerebrum*] (1915)
: to use the mind **:** THINK
— **cer·e·bra·tion** \,ser-ə-'brā-shən\ *noun*

ce·re·bro·side \'ser-ə-brə-,sīd, sə-'rē-\ *noun* [*cerebrose* galactose] (1883)
: any of various lipids found especially in nerve tissue

ce·re·bro·spi·nal \sə-,rē-brō-'spī-nᵊl, ,ser-ə-brō-\ *adjective* (1826)
: of or relating to the brain and spinal cord or to these together with the cranial and spinal nerves that innervate voluntary muscles

cerebrospinal fluid *noun* (circa 1889)
: a liquid that is comparable to serum, is secreted from the blood into the lateral ventricles of the brain, and serves chiefly to maintain uniform pressure within the brain and spinal cord

cerebrospinal meningitis *noun* (1889)
: inflammation of the meninges of both brain and spinal cord; *specifically* **:** an infectious epidemic and often fatal meningitis caused by the meningococcus

ce·re·bro·vas·cu·lar \sə-,rē-brō-'vas-kyə-lər, ,ser-ə-brō-\ *adjective* (1935)
: of or involving the cerebrum and the blood vessels supplying it

ce·re·brum \sə-'rē-brəm, 'ser-ə-brəm\ *noun, plural* **-brums** *or* **-bra** \-brə\ [Latin] (1615)
1 : BRAIN 1a
2 : an enlarged anterior or upper part of the brain; *especially* **:** the expanded anterior portion of the brain that in higher mammals overlies the rest of the brain, consists of cerebral hemispheres and connecting structures, and is considered to be the seat of conscious mental processes **:** TELENCEPHALON

cere·cloth \'sir-,klȯth\ *noun* [alteration of earlier *cered cloth* (waxed cloth)] (1553)
: cloth treated with melted wax or gummy matter and formerly used especially for wrapping a dead body

cere·ment \'ser-ə-mənt, 'sir-mənt\ *noun* (1602)
: a shroud for the dead; *especially* **:** CERECLOTH — usually used in plural

¹cer·e·mo·ni·al \,ser-ə-'mō-nē-əl\ *adjective* (14th century)
: marked by, involved in, or belonging to ceremony **:** stressing careful attention to form and detail ☆
— **cer·e·mo·ni·al·ism** \-ə-,li-zəm\ *noun*
— **cer·e·mo·ni·al·ist** \-ə-list\ *noun*
— **cer·e·mo·ni·al·ly** \-ə-lē\ *adverb*

²ceremonial *noun* (14th century)
: a ceremonial act, action, or system

cer·e·mo·ni·ous \,ser-ə-'mō-nē-əs\ *adjective* (1553)
1 : devoted to forms and ceremony **:** PUNCTILIOUS
2 : of, relating to, or constituting a ceremony

3 : according to formal usage or prescribed procedures
4 : marked by ceremony
synonym see CEREMONIAL
— **cer·e·mo·ni·ous·ly** *adverb*
— **cer·e·mo·ni·ous·ness** *noun*

cer·e·mo·ny \'ser-ə-,mō-nē\ *noun, plural* **-nies** [Middle English *ceremonie,* from Middle French *cérémonie,* from Latin *caerimonia*] (14th century)
1 : a formal act or series of acts prescribed by ritual, protocol, or convention ⟨the marriage *ceremony*⟩
2 a : a conventional act of politeness or etiquette ⟨the *ceremony* of introduction⟩ **b :** an action performed only formally with no deep significance **c :** a routine action performed with elaborate pomp
3 a : prescribed procedures **:** USAGES ⟨the *ceremony* attending an inauguration⟩ **b :** observance of an established code of civility or politeness ⟨opened the door without *ceremony* and strode in⟩

Ce·ren·kov radiation \chə-'ren-kȯf-, chər-'yen-\ *noun* [P. A. *Cherenkov*] (1939)
: light produced by charged particles (as electrons) traversing a transparent medium at a speed greater than that of light in the same medium — called also *Cerenkov light*

Ce·res \'sir-(,)ēz\ *noun* [Latin]
: the Roman goddess of agriculture — compare DEMETER

ce·re·us \'sir-ē-əs\ *noun* [New Latin, genus name, from Latin, wax candle, from *cera* wax — more at CERUMEN] (1730)
: any of various cacti (as of the genus *Cereus*) of the western U.S. and tropical America

ce·ric \'sir-ik, 'ser-\ *adjective* (circa 1879)
: of, relating to, or containing cerium especially with a valence of four

ce·rise \sə-'rēs, -'rēz\ *noun* [French, literally, cherry, from Late Latin *ceresia* — more at CHERRY] (1844)
: a moderate red

ce·ri·um \'sir-ē-əm\ *noun* [New Latin, from *Ceres*] (1804)
: a malleable ductile metallic element that is the most abundant of the rare-earth group — see ELEMENT table

cer·met \'sər-,met\ *noun* [*ceramic* + *metal*] (1948)
: a composite structural material of a heat-resistant compound (as titanium carbide) and a metal (as nickel) used especially for turbine blades

cero \'ser-(,)ō\ *noun, plural* **cero** *or* **ceros** [modification of Spanish *sierra* saw, cero] (1884)
: either of two large food and sport fishes (*Scomberomorus regalis* and *S. cavalla* of the warmer parts of the western Atlantic

ce·rous \'sir-əs\ *adjective* (circa 1872)
: of, relating to, or containing cerium especially with a valence of three

¹cer·tain \'sər-tᵊn\ *adjective* [Middle English, from Old French, from (assumed) Vulgar Latin *certanus,* from Latin *certus,* from past participle of *cernere* to sift, discern, decide; akin to Greek *krinein* to separate, decide, judge, Old Irish *criathar* sieve] (13th century)
1 : FIXED, SETTLED ⟨a *certain* percentage of the profit⟩
2 : of a specific but unspecified character, quantity, or degree ⟨the house has a *certain* charm⟩
3 a : DEPENDABLE, RELIABLE ⟨a *certain* remedy for the disease⟩ **b :** known or proved to be true **:** INDISPUTABLE ⟨it is *certain* that we exist⟩
4 a : INEVITABLE ⟨the *certain* advance of age⟩ **b :** incapable of failing **:** DESTINED — used with a following infinitive ⟨she is *certain* to do well⟩
5 : assured in mind and action
synonym see SURE
— **for certain :** as a certainty **:** ASSUREDLY

²certain *pronoun, plural in construction* (15th century)
: certain ones

cer·tain·ly \-lē\ *adverb* (14th century)
1 : in a manner that is certain **:** with certainty
2 : it is certain that **:** ASSUREDLY

cer·tain·ty \'sər-tᵊn-tē\ *noun, plural* **-ties** (14th century)
1 : something that is certain
2 : the quality or state of being certain especially on the basis of evidence ☆

cer·tes \'sər-tēz, 'sərts\ *adverb* [Middle English, from Old French, from *cert* certain, from Latin *certus*] (13th century)
archaic **:** in truth **:** CERTAINLY

¹cer·tif·i·cate \(,)sər-'ti-fi-kət\ *noun* [Middle English *certificat,* from Middle French, from Medieval Latin *certificatum,* from Late Latin, neuter of *certificatus,* past participle of *certificare* to certify] (15th century)
1 : a document containing a certified statement especially as to the truth of something; *specifically* **:** a document certifying that one has fulfilled the requirements of and may practice in a field
2 : something serving the same end as a certificate
3 : a document evidencing ownership or debt ⟨a *certificate* of deposit⟩

²cer·tif·i·cate \-'ti-fə-,kāt\ *transitive verb* **-cat·ed; -cat·ing** (1883)
: to testify to or authorize by a certificate; *especially* **:** to recognize as having met special qualifications (as of a governmental agency or professional board) within a field
— **cer·tif·i·ca·to·ry** \-'ti-fi-kə-,tȯr-ē, -,tȯr-\ *adjective*

cer·ti·fi·ca·tion \,sər-tə-fə-'kā-shən\ *noun* (15th century)
1 : the act of certifying **:** the state of being certified
2 : a certified statement

certification mark *noun* (1947)

☆ **SYNONYMS**
Ceremonial, ceremonious, formal, conventional mean marked by attention to or adhering strictly to prescribed forms. CEREMONIAL and CEREMONIOUS both imply strict attention to what is prescribed by custom or by ritual, but CEREMONIAL applies to things that are associated with ceremonies ⟨a *ceremonial* offering⟩, CEREMONIOUS to persons given to ceremony or to acts attended by ceremony ⟨made his *ceremonious* entrance⟩. FORMAL applies both to things prescribed by and to persons obedient to custom and may suggest stiff, restrained, or old-fashioned behavior ⟨a *formal* report⟩ ⟨the headmaster's *formal* manner⟩. CONVENTIONAL implies accord with general custom and usage ⟨*conventional* courtesy⟩ and may suggest a stodgy lack of originality or independence ⟨*conventional* fiction⟩.

Certainty, certitude, conviction mean a state of being free from doubt. CERTAINTY and CERTITUDE are very close; CERTAINTY may stress the existence of objective proof ⟨claims that cannot be confirmed with scientific *certainty*⟩, while CERTITUDE may emphasize a faith in something not needing or not capable of proof ⟨believes with *certitude* in an afterlife⟩. CONVICTION applies especially to belief strongly held by an individual ⟨holds firm *convictions* on every issue⟩.

\ə\ abut \ᵊ\ kitten \ər\ further \a\ ash \ā\ ace
\ä\ mop, mar \au̇\ out \ch\ chin \e\ bet \ē\ easy
\g\ go \i\ hit \ī\ ice \j\ job \ŋ\ sing \ō\ go
\ȯ\ law \ȯi\ boy \th\ thin \t̲h̲\ the \ü\ loot \u̇\ foot
\y\ yet \zh\ vision *see also* Guide to Pronunciation

: a mark or device used to identify a product or service that has been certified to conform to a particular set of standards

certified mail *noun* (1955)
: first class mail for which proof of delivery is secured but no indemnity value is claimed

certified milk *noun* (1899)
: milk produced in dairies that operate under the rules and regulations of an authorized medical milk commission

certified public accountant *noun* (1896)
: an accountant who has met the requirements of a state law and has been granted a certificate

cer·ti·fy \'sər-tə-ˌfī\ *transitive verb* **-fied; -fy·ing** [Middle English *certifien,* from Middle French *certifier,* from Late Latin *certificare,* from Latin *certus* certain — more at CERTAIN] (14th century)
1 : to attest authoritatively: as **a** : CONFIRM **b** : to present in formal communication **c** : to attest as being true or as represented or as meeting a standard **d** : to attest officially to the insanity of
2 : to inform with certainty : ASSURE
3 : to guarantee (a personal check) as to signature and amount by so indicating on the face
4 : CERTIFICATE, LICENSE ☆
— **cer·ti·fi·able** \-ˌfī-ə-bəl\ *adjective*
— **cer·ti·fi·ably** \-blē\ *adverb*
— **cer·ti·fi·er** \-ˌfī(-ə)r\ *noun* See in addition APPROVE.

cer·tio·ra·ri \ˌsər-sh(ē-)ə-'rar-ē, -'rär-ē\ *noun* [Middle English, from Latin, literally, to be informed; from the use of the word in the writ] (15th century)
: a writ of superior court to call up the records of an inferior court or a body acting in a quasi-judicial capacity

cer·ti·tude \'sər-tə-ˌtüd *also* -ˌtyüd\ *noun* [Middle English, from Late Latin *certitudo,* from Latin *certus*] (15th century)
1 : the state of being or feeling certain
2 : certainty of act or event
synonym see CERTAINTY

ce·ru·le·an \sə-'rü-lē-ən\ *adjective* [Latin *caeruleus* dark blue] (1667)
: resembling the blue of the sky

ce·ru·lo·plas·min \sə-ˌrü-lō-'plaz-mən\ *noun* [International Scientific Vocabulary *cerulo-* (from Latin *caeruleus*) + *plasma* + 1*-in*] (circa 1952)
: a blue copper-binding serum alpha globulin with enzymatic activity

ce·ru·men \sə-'rü-mən\ *noun* [New Latin, irregular from Latin *cera* wax; akin to Greek *kēros* wax] (1741)
: the yellow waxy secretion from the glands of the external ear — called also *earwax*
— **ce·ru·mi·nous** \-mə-nəs\ *adjective*

ce·ruse \sə-'rüs, 'sir-ˌüs\ *noun* [Middle English, from Middle French *céruse,* from Latin *cerussa*] (14th century)
1 : white lead as a pigment
2 : a cosmetic containing white lead

ce·rus·site \sə-'rə-ˌsīt\ *noun* [German *Zerussit,* from Latin *cerussa*] (1850)
: a mineral that consists of lead carbonate occurring in colorless transparent crystals and also in massive form and is a source of white lead

cer·ve·lat \'sər-və-ˌlat, -ˌlä\ *noun* [obsolete French (now *cervelas*)] (1613)
: smoked sausage made from a combination of pork and beef

cer·vi·cal \'sər-vi-kəl\ *adjective* (1681)
: of or relating to a neck or cervix

cervical cap *noun* (1923)
: a contraceptive device in the form of a thimble-shaped molded cap that fits over the uterine cervix and blocks sperm from entering the uterus

cer·vi·ci·tis \ˌsər-və-'sī-təs\ *noun* [New Latin] (1889)
: inflammation of the uterine cervix

cer·vine \'sər-ˌvīn\ *adjective* [Latin *cervinus* of a deer, from *cervus* stag, deer — more at HART] (circa 1828)
: of, relating to, or resembling deer

cer·vix \'sər-viks\ *noun, plural* **cer·vi·ces** \'sər-və-ˌsēz, (ˌ)sər-'vī-(ˌ)sēz\ *or* **cer·vix·es** [Latin *cervic-, cervix*] (15th century)
1 : NECK; *especially* : the back part of the neck
2 : a constricted portion of an organ or part; *especially* : the narrow outer end of the uterus

ce·sar·e·an *also* **ce·sar·i·an** \si-'zar-ē-ən, -'zer-\ *noun* (circa 1903)
: CESAREAN SECTION
— **cesarean** *also* **cesarian** *adjective*

cesarean section *also* **cesarian section** *noun* [from the belief that Julius Caesar was born this way] (1615)
: surgical incision of the walls of the abdomen and uterus for delivery of offspring ◇

ce·si·um \'sē-zē-əm *also* -zhē-\ *noun* [New Latin, from Latin *caesius* bluish gray] (1861)
: a silver-white soft ductile element of the alkali metal group that is the most electropositive element known and that is used especially in photoelectric cells — see ELEMENT table

cesium 133 *noun* (1966)
: an isotope of cesium used especially in atomic clocks and one of whose atomic transitions is used as a scientific time standard

cess \'ses\ *noun* [probably short for *success*] (1830)
chiefly Irish : LUCK — usually used in the phrase *bad cess to you*

ces·sa·tion \se-'sā-shən\ *noun* [Middle English *cessacioun,* from Middle French *cessation,* from Latin *cessation-, cessatio* delay, idleness, from *cessare* to delay, be idle — more at CEASE] (14th century)
: a temporary or final ceasing (as of action)
: STOP

ces·sion \'se-shən\ *noun* [Middle English, from Middle French, from Latin *cession-, cessio,* from *cedere* to withdraw — more at CEDE] (15th century)
: a yielding to another : CONCESSION

cess·pit \'ses-ˌpit\ *noun* [*cesspool* + *pit*] (1777)
: a pit for the disposal of refuse (as sewage)

cess·pool \-ˌpü(ə)l\ *noun* [by folk etymology from Middle English *suspiral* vent, cesspool, from Middle French *souspirail* ventilator, from *souspirer* to sigh, from Latin *suspirare,* literally, to draw a long breath — more at SUSPIRE] (1782)
: an underground reservoir for liquid waste (as household sewage)

ces·ta \'ses-tə\ *noun* [Spanish, literally, basket, from Latin *cista* box, basket] (circa 1902)
: a narrow curved wicker basket used to catch and propel the ball in jai alai

ces·tode \'ses-ˌtōd\ *noun* [New Latin *Cestoda,* taxonomic group comprising tapeworms, ultimately from Greek *kestos* girdle] (circa 1890)
: TAPEWORM
— **cestode** *adjective*

1**ces·tus** \'ses-təs\ *noun, plural* **ces·ti** \-ˌtī\ [Latin, girdle, belt, from Greek *kestos,* from *kestos* stitched, from *kentein* to prick — more at CENTER] (1557)
: a woman's belt; *especially* : a symbolic one worn by a bride

cesta

2**cestus** *noun* [Latin *cestus, caestus*] (circa 1720)
: a hand covering of leather bands often loaded with lead or iron and used by boxers in ancient Rome

ce·su·ra *variant of* CAESURA

ce·ta·cean \si-'tā-shən\ *noun* [ultimately from Latin *cetus* whale, from Greek *kētos*] (1836)

: any of an order (Cetacea) of aquatic mostly marine mammals that include the whales, dolphins, porpoises, and related forms and that have a torpedo-shaped nearly hairless body, paddle-shaped forelimbs but no hind limbs, one or two nares opening externally at the top of the head, and a horizontally flattened tail used for locomotion
— **cetacean** *adjective*
— **ce·ta·ceous** \-shəs\ *adjective*

ce·tane \'sē-ˌtān\ *noun* [from *cetyl,* the radical $C_{16}H_{33}$] (1871)
: a colorless oily hydrocarbon $C_{16}H_{34}$ found in petroleum

cetane number *noun* (1935)
: a measure of the ignition value of a diesel fuel that represents the percentage by volume of cetane in a mixture of liquid methylnaphthalene that gives the same ignition lag as the oil being tested — called also *cetane rating;* compare OCTANE NUMBER

ce·te·ris pa·ri·bus \'kā-tər-əs-'par-ə-bəs, 'ke-, 'se-\ *adverb* [New Latin, other things being equal] (1601)
: if all other relevant things, factors, or elements remain unaltered

ce·tol·o·gy \sē-'tä-lə-jē\ *noun* [Latin *cetus* whale] (circa 1828)
: a branch of zoology dealing with the cetaceans
— **ce·tol·o·gist** \-jist\ *noun*

Ce·tus \'sē-təs\ *noun* [Latin (genitive *Ceti*), literally, whale]
: an equatorial constellation south of Pisces and Aries

☆ **SYNONYMS**
Certify, attest, witness, vouch mean to testify to the truth or genuineness of something. CERTIFY usually applies to a written statement, especially one carrying a signature or seal 〈*certified* that the candidate had met all requirements〉. ATTEST applies to oral or written testimony usually from experts or witnesses 〈*attested* to the authenticity of the document〉. WITNESS applies to the subscribing of one's own name to a document as evidence of its genuineness 〈*witnessed* the signing of the will〉. VOUCH applies to one who testifies as a competent authority or a reliable person 〈willing to *vouch* for her integrity〉.

◇ **WORD HISTORY**
cesarean section The name *Caesar* is a cognomen, a nickname given to one member of a Roman clan and borne by his descendants as a kind of surname. No one knows who the original Caesar was, but his descendants within his clan, the Julii, continued to use his cognomen and formed a major branch of the clan. According to a legend related by the Roman naturalist Pliny, the first Caesar was so called because he was cut from the womb of his mother (*a caeso matris utero*), *Caesar* supposedly being a derivative of the verb *caedere* "to cut." This etymology is dubious, but the name *Caesar* has continued to be associated with surgery to remove a child that cannot be delivered naturally. In recent centuries, it has been widely believed that the most famous bearer of the cognomen, the politician and general Gaius Julius Caesar (100–44 B.C.), was delivered by cesarean section, but there is no authority for this notion in ancient sources. Moreover, Julius Caesar's mother lived long after his birth, an unlikely outcome if she had undergone such an operation, which few women could have survived in those days.

ce·tyl alcohol \'sē-t⁺l-\ *noun* [International Scientific Vocabulary *cet-* (from Latin *cetus* whale) + *-yl;* from its occurrence in spermaceti] (1873)
: a waxy crystalline alcohol $C_{16}H_{34}O$ obtained by the saponification of spermaceti or the hydrogenation of palmitic acid and used especially in pharmaceutical and cosmetic preparations and in making detergents

ce·vi·che \sə-'vē-(ˌ)chā, -chē\ *variant of* SEVICHE

Cha·blis \sha-'blē, shə-, shä-; 'sha-(ˌ)blē\ *noun, plural* **Cha·blis** \-'blēz, -(ˌ)blēz\ [French, from *Chablis,* town in France] (1668)
1 : a dry sharp white burgundy wine
2 : a semidry soft white California wine

cha–cha \'chä-(ˌ)chä\ *noun* [American Spanish *cha-cha-cha*] (1954)
: a fast rhythmic ballroom dance of Latin-American origin with a basic pattern of three steps and a shuffle

chac·ma baboon \'chäk-mə-\ *noun* [Khoikhoi] (circa 1909)
: a large dusky baboon (*Papio ursinus*) of southern African savannas — called also *chacma*

cha·conne \shä-'kòn, sha-, -'kän, -'kən\ *noun* [French & Spanish; French *chaconne,* from Spanish *chacona*] (1685)
1 : an old Spanish dance tune of Latin American origin
2 : a musical composition in moderate triple time typically consisting of variations on a repeated succession of chords

chad \'chad\ *noun* [origin unknown] (1947)
: small pieces of paper or cardboard produced in punching paper tape or data cards; *also* **:** a piece of chad
— **chad·less** \-ləs\ *adjective*

Chad·ic \'cha-dik\ *or* **Chad** \'chad\ *noun* (circa 1950)
: a subfamily of the Afro-Asiatic language family comprising numerous languages of northern Nigeria, northern Cameroon, and Chad
— **Chadic** *adjective*

cha·dor \'chə-dər, 'chä-\ *noun* [Hindi & Persian; Hindi *caddar,* from Persian *chaddar, chādar*] (1614)
: a large cloth worn as a combination head covering, veil, and shawl usually by Muslim women especially in Iran

chae·ta \'kē-tə\ *noun, plural* **chae·tae** \'kē-ˌtē\ [New Latin, from Greek *chaitē* long flowing hair] (circa 1866)
: BRISTLE, SETA
— **chae·tal** \'kē-t⁺l\ *adjective*

chae·to·gnath \'kē-ˌtäg-ˌnath, -tə(g)-\ *noun* [New Latin *Chaetognatha,* class or phylum name, ultimately from Greek *chaitē* + *gnathos* jaw — more at -GNATHOUS] (circa 1889)
: ARROWWORM
— **chaetognath** *adjective*

¹chafe \'chāf\ *verb* **chafed; chaf·ing** [Middle English *chaufen* to warm, from Middle French *chaufer,* from (assumed) Vulgar Latin *calfare,* alteration of Latin *calefacere,* from *calēre* to be warm + *facere* to make — more at LEE, DO] (14th century)
transitive verb
1 : IRRITATE, VEX
2 : to warm by rubbing especially with the hands
3 a : to rub so as to wear away : ABRADE ⟨the boat *chafed* its sides against the dock⟩ **b :** to make sore by or as if by rubbing
intransitive verb
1 : to feel irritation or discontent : FRET ⟨*chafes* at his restrictive desk job⟩
2 : to rub and thereby cause wear or irritation

²chafe *noun* (1551)
1 : a state of vexation : RAGE
2 : injury or wear caused by friction; *also* **:** FRICTION, RUBBING

cha·fer \'chā-fər\ *noun* [Middle English *cheaffer,* from Old English *ceafor;* probably akin to Old English *ceafl* jowl — more at JOWL] (before 12th century)
: any of various scarab beetles (as a cockchafer) that feed on leaves and flowers and whose larvae feed on plant roots

¹chaff \'chaf\ *noun* [Middle English *chaf,* from Old English *ceaf;* akin to Old High German *cheva* husk] (before 12th century)
1 : the seed coverings and other debris separated from the seed in threshing grain
2 : something comparatively worthless
3 : the scales borne on the receptacle among the florets in the heads of many composite plants
4 : material (as strips of foil or clusters of fine wires) ejected into the air for reflecting radar waves (as for confusing an enemy's radar detection or for tracking a descending spacecraft)
— **chaffy** \'cha-fē\ *adjective*

²chaff *noun* [probably from ¹*chaff*] (1821)
: light jesting talk : BANTER

³chaff (1827)
transitive verb
: to tease good-naturedly
intransitive verb
: JEST, BANTER

¹chaf·fer \'cha-fər\ *noun* [Middle English *chaffare,* from *chep* trade + *fare* journey — more at CHEAP, FARE] (13th century)
archaic **:** a haggling about price

²chaffer *verb* **chaf·fered; chaf·fer·ing** \'cha-f(ə-)riŋ\ (14th century)
intransitive verb
1 : HAGGLE
2 *British* **:** to exchange small talk : CHATTER
transitive verb
1 : EXCHANGE, BARTER
2 : to bargain for
— **chaf·fer·er** \-fər-ər\ *noun*

chaf·finch \'cha-(ˌ)finch\ *noun* [Middle English, from Old English *ceaffinc,* from *ceaf* + *finc* finch] (before 12th century)
: a common European finch (*Fringilla coelebs*) of which the male has a pinkish-brown breast

chaf·ing dish \'chā-fiŋ-\ *noun* [Middle English *chafing,* present participle of *chaufen, chafen* to warm] (15th century)
: a utensil for cooking or keeping food warm at the table

Cha·gas' disease \'shä-gəs-, -gə-ˌsəz-\ *noun* [Carlos *Chagas* (died 1934) Brazilian physician] (1912)
: a tropical American disease that is caused by a trypanosome (*Trypanosoma cruzi*) and is marked by prolonged high fever, edema, and enlargement of the spleen, liver, and lymph nodes

¹cha·grin \shə-'grin\ *noun* [French, from *chagrin* sad] (circa 1681)
: disquietude or distress of mind caused by humiliation, disappointment, or failure

²chagrin *transitive verb* **cha·grined** \-'grind\; **cha·grin·ing** \-'gri-niŋ\ (1733)
: to vex or unsettle by disappointing or humiliating

¹chain \'chān\ *noun, often attributive* [Middle English *cheyne,* from Middle French *chaeine,* from Latin *catena*] (14th century)
1 a : a series of usually metal links or rings connected to or fitted into one another and used for various purposes (as support, restraint, transmission of mechanical power, or measurement) **b :** a series of links used or worn as an ornament or insignia **c** (1) **:** a measuring instrument of 100 links used in surveying (2) **:** a unit of length equal to 66 feet (20 meters)
2 : something that confines, restrains, or secures
3 a : a series of things linked, connected, or associated together ⟨a *chain* of events⟩ **b :** a group of enterprises or institutions of the same kind or function usually under a single owner-ship, management, or control ⟨fast-food *chains*⟩ **c :** a number of atoms or chemical groups united like links in a chain

²chain *transitive verb* (14th century)
1 : to obstruct or protect by a chain
2 : to fasten, bind, or connect with or as if with a chain; *also* **:** FETTER

chai·né \shā-'nā\ *noun* [French, from past participle of *chaîner* to chain] (1897)
: a series of short usually fast turns by which a ballet dancer moves across the stage

chain gang *noun* (1834)
: a gang of convicts chained together especially as an outside working party

chain letter *noun* (1905)
: a letter sent to several persons with a request that each send copies of the letter to an equal number of persons

chain–link fence *noun* (circa 1927)
: a fence of heavy steel wire woven to form a diamond-shaped mesh

chain mail *noun* (1822)
: flexible armor of interlinked metal rings

chain of command *noun* (1898)
: a series of executive positions in order of authority ⟨a military *chain of command*⟩

chain pickerel *noun* [from the markings resembling chains on the sides] (1887)
: a large greenish black pickerel (*Esox niger*) with dark markings along the sides that is common in quiet waters of eastern North America

chain reaction *noun* (circa 1902)
1 a : a series of events so related to each other that each one initiates the next **b :** a number of events triggered by the same initial event
2 : a self-sustaining chemical or nuclear reaction yielding energy or products that cause further reactions of the same kind
— **chain–re·act** \'chān-rē-'akt\ *intransitive verb*

chain rule *noun* (circa 1847)
: a mathematical rule concerning the differentiation of a function of a function (as $f[u(x)]$) by which under suitable conditions of continuity and differentiability one function is differentiated with respect to the second function considered as an independent variable and then the second function is differentiated with respect to its independent variable

chain saw *noun* (1944)
: a portable power saw that has teeth linked together to form an endless chain
— **chain·saw** \'chān-ˌsò\ *transitive verb*

chain–smoke \'chān-'smōk\ (1930)
intransitive verb
: to smoke especially cigarettes continually
transitive verb
: to smoke (as cigarettes) almost without interruption
— **chain–smok·er** \-ˌsmō-kər\ *noun*

chain stitch *noun* (1820)
1 : an ornamental stitch like chain links
2 : a machine stitch forming a chain on the underside of the work

chain store *noun* (1910)
: one of numerous usually retail stores having the same ownership and selling the same lines of goods

chain·wheel \'chān-ˌhwēl, -ˌwēl\ *noun* (1845)
: SPROCKET 1

¹chair \'cher, 'char\ *noun* [Middle English *chaiere,* from Old French, from Latin *cathedra,* from Greek *kathedra,* from *kata-* cata- + *hedra* seat — more at SIT] (13th century)
1 a : a seat typically having four legs and a back for one person **b :** ELECTRIC CHAIR — used with *the*

\ə\ abut \⁺\ kitten \ər\ further \a\ ash \ā\ ace
\ä\ mop, mar \aú\ out \ch\ chin \e\ bet \ē\ easy
\g\ go \i\ hit \ī\ ice \j\ job \ŋ\ sing \ō\ go
\ò\ law \òi\ boy \th\ thin \th̶\ the \ü\ loot \ú\ foot
\y\ yet \zh\ vision *see also* Guide to Pronunciation

2 a : an official seat or a seat of authority, state, or dignity **b :** an office or position of authority or dignity **c :** PROFESSORSHIP ⟨holds a university *chair*⟩ **d :** CHAIRMAN 1
3 : a sedan chair
4 : a position of employment usually of one occupying a chair or desk; *specifically* **:** the position of a player in an orchestra or band
5 : any of various devices that hold up or support
usage see CHAIRMAN
²**chair** *transitive verb* (1552)
1 : to install in office
2 *chiefly British* **:** to carry on the shoulders in acclaim ⟨we *chaired* you through the market place —A. E. Housman⟩
3 : to preside as chairman of
chair car *noun* (1880)
1 : a railroad car having pairs of chairs with individually adjustable backs on each side of the aisle
2 : PARLOR CAR
chair·lift \'cher-,lift, 'char-\ *noun* (1940)
: a motor-driven conveyor consisting of a series of seats suspended from a cable and used for transporting skiers or sightseers up or down a long slope or mountainside
¹**chair·man** \-mən\ *noun* (1650)
1 a : the presiding officer of a meeting or an organization or committee **b :** the administrative officer of a department of instruction (as in a college)
2 : a carrier of a sedan chair ▢
— **chair·man·ship** \-,ship\ *noun*
²**chairman** *transitive verb* -**maned** *or* -**manned; -man·ing** *or* -**man·ning** (1888)
: CHAIR 3
chair·per·son \-,pər-s°n\ *noun* (1971)
: CHAIRMAN 1
usage see CHAIRMAN
chair·wom·an \-,wu̇-mən\ *noun* (1685)
: a woman who acts as chairman
usage see CHAIRMAN
chaise \'shāz\ *noun* [French, chair, chaise, alteration of Old French *chaiere*] (1701)
1 : any of various light horse-drawn vehicles: as **a :** a two-wheeled carriage for one or two persons with a folding top **b :** POST CHAISE
2 : CHAISE LONGUE
chaise longue \'shāz-'lȯŋ\ *noun, plural* **chaise longues** *also* **chaises longues** \'shāz-'lȯŋ(z)\ [French, literally, long chair] (1800)
: a long reclining chair
chaise lounge \'shāz-'lau̇nj, 'chās-\ *noun* [by folk etymology from French *chaise longue*] (circa 1906)
: CHAISE LONGUE
chak·ra \'chä-krə, 'shä-, 'chə-\ *noun* [Sanskrit *cakra*, literally, wheel — more at WHEEL] (1888)
: any of several points of physical or spiritual energy in the human body according to yoga philosophy
cha·la·za \kə-'lā-zə, -'la-\ *noun, plural* -**zae** \-,zē\ *or* -**zas** [New Latin, from Greek, hailstone] (circa 1704)
1 : either of two spiral bands in the white of a bird's egg that extend from the yolk and attach to opposite ends of the lining membrane — see EGG illustration
2 : the basal part of a plant ovule where the nucellus is fused to the surrounding integument and to which the funiculus is usually attached
— **cha·la·zal** \-'lā-zəl, -'la-\ *adjective*
Chal·ce·do·ni·an \,kal-sə-'dō-nē-ən\ *adjective* (1788)
: of or relating to Chalcedon or the ecumenical council held there in A.D. 451 declaring Monophysitism heretical
— **Chalcedonian** *noun*
chal·ce·do·ny \kal-'se-d°n-ē, chal-; 'kal-sə-,dō-nē, 'chal-, -,dä-\ *noun, plural* -**nies** [Middle English *calcedonie*, a precious stone, from

Late Latin *chalcedonius,* from Greek *Chalkē·dōn* Chalcedon] (13th century)
: a translucent quartz that is commonly pale blue or gray with nearly waxlike luster
— **chal·ce·don·ic** \,kal-sə-'dä-nik\ *adjective*
chal·cid \'kal-səd\ *noun* [ultimately from Greek *chalkos* copper, bronze] (1893)
: any of a large superfamily (Chalcidoidea) of mostly minute hymenopterous insects parasitic in the larval state on the larvae or pupae of other insects
— **chalcid** *adjective*
chal·co·cite \'kal-kə-,sīt\ *noun* [alteration of *chalcosine,* from French, irregular from Greek *chalkos*] (1868)
: a black or gray lustrous metallic mineral that consists of a sulfide of copper and is an important copper ore
chal·co·gen \'kal-kə-jən\ *noun* [International Scientific Vocabulary *chalk-* bronze, ore (from Greek *chalkos*) + *-gen;* from the occurrence of oxygen and sulfur in many ores] (circa 1961)
: any of the elements oxygen, sulfur, selenium, and tellurium
chal·co·gen·ide \-jə-,nīd\ *noun* (1945)
: a binary compound of a chalcogen with a more electropositive element or radical
chal·co·py·rite \,kal-kə-'pī-,rīt\ *noun* [New Latin *chalcopyrites,* from Greek *chalkos* + Latin *pyrites*] (1835)
: a yellow mineral consisting of copper-iron sulfide and constituting an important ore of copper
Chal·da·ic \kal-'dā-ik, kȯl-, käl-\ *adjective or noun* (1662)
: CHALDEAN
Chal·de·an \kal-'dē-ən, kȯl-, käl-\ *noun* [Latin *Chaldaeus* Chaldean, astrologer, from Greek *Chaldaios,* from *Chaldaia* Chaldea, region of ancient Babylonia] (1581)
1 a : a member of an ancient Semitic people that became dominant in Babylonia **b :** the Semitic language of the Chaldeans
2 : a person versed in the occult arts
— **Chaldean** *adjective*
Chal·dee \'kal-,dē, 'kȯl-, 'käl-\ *noun* [Middle English *Caldey,* probably from Middle French *chaldée,* from Latin *Chaldaeus*] (14th century)
1 : CHALDEAN 1a
2 : the Aramaic vernacular that was the original language of some parts of the Bible
chal·dron \'chȯl-drən, 'chäl-\ *noun* [Middle French *chauderon,* from *chaudere* pot, from Late Latin *caldaria* — more at CAULDRON] (1615)
: any of various old units of measure varying from 32 to 72 imperial bushels
cha·let \sha-'lā, 'sha-(,)lā\ *noun* [French] (1782)
1 : a remote herdsman's hut in the Alps
2 a : a Swiss dwelling with unconcealed structural members and a wide overhang at the front and sides **b :** a cottage or house in chalet style

chalet 2a

chal·ice \'cha-ləs\ *noun* [Middle English, from Anglo-French, from Latin *calic-, calix;* akin to Greek *kalyx* calyx] (14th century)
1 : a drinking cup **:** GOBLET; *especially* **:** the eucharistic cup
2 : the cup-shaped interior of a flower
¹**chalk** \'chȯk\ *noun* [Middle English, from Old English *cealc,* from Latin *calc-, calx* lime; akin to Greek *chalix* pebble] (before 12th century)
1 a : a soft white, gray, or buff limestone composed chiefly of the shells of foraminifers **b :** chalk or a material resembling chalk especially when used in the form of a crayon

2 a : a mark made with chalk **b** *British* **:** a point scored in a game
— **chalky** \'chȯ-kē\ *adjective*
²**chalk** (1580)
transitive verb
1 : to write or draw with chalk
2 : to rub or mark with chalk
3 a : to delineate roughly **:** SKETCH ⟨*chalk* out a plan of attack⟩ **b :** to set down or add up with or as if with chalk **:** RECORD — usually used with *up* ⟨*chalk* up a victory⟩
intransitive verb
: to become chalky
chalk·board \'chȯk-,bȯrd, -,bȯrd\ *noun* (1936)
: BLACKBOARD
chalk talk \'chȯk-,tȯk\ *noun* (1881)
: a talk or lecture illustrated at a blackboard
chalk up *transitive verb* (1826)
1 : ASCRIBE, CREDIT
2 : ATTAIN, ACHIEVE ⟨*chalk up* a record score for the season⟩
chal·lah *also* **chal·la** \'kä-lə, 'hä-\ *noun* [Yiddish *khale,* from Hebrew *ḥallāh*] (1927)
: egg-rich yeast-leavened bread that is usually braided or twisted before baking and is traditionally eaten by Jews on the Sabbath and holidays
¹**chal·lenge** \'cha-lənj\ *verb* **chal·lenged; chal·leng·ing** [Middle English *chalengen* to accuse, from Old French *chalengier,* from Latin *calumniari* to accuse falsely, from *calumnia* calumny] (13th century)
transitive verb
1 : to demand as due or deserved **:** REQUIRE ⟨an event that *challenges* explanation⟩
2 : to order to halt and prove identity ⟨the sentry *challenged* the stranger⟩
3 : to dispute especially as being unjust, invalid, or outmoded **:** IMPUGN ⟨new data that *challenges* old assumptions⟩
4 : to question formally the legality or legal qualifications of
5 a : to confront or defy boldly **:** DARE **b :** to call out to duel or combat **c :** to invite into competition
6 : to arouse or stimulate especially by presenting with difficulties
7 : to administer a physiological and especially an immunologic challenge to (an organism or cell)
intransitive verb
1 : to make or present a challenge

▢ USAGE
chairman *Chairman, chair, chairperson,* and *chairwoman* are available alternative terms for a presiding or administrative officer. *Chair* has been disparaged by some as an ugly creation of the women's liberation movement. On the contrary, it is a standard parliamentary term and has been in use since the second half of the 17th century. *Chairperson,* a much more recent coinage, gained rapid acceptance in spite of strong initial opposition especially from usage commentators and newspaper editors; it is now nearly as frequent as *chairman.* Our most recent evidence shows some current variation in use. *Chairman* is preferred in reference to a corporate office, regardless of the sex of the officer. *Chairman, chairperson,* and *chairwoman* are all commonly used in reference to political and social functions. *Chairman* and *chairperson* are common with reference to academic office, but *chairwoman* is not. *Chairman* and *chairperson* are applied to both men and women; when a name is mentioned with *chairperson,* it is slightly more likely to be a woman than a man. *Chair* differs from the rest in that, while it is commonly used as a title and in parliamentary rules, it is much less frequent in running context.

2 : to take legal exception
— **chal·leng·er** *noun*

²**challenge** *noun* (14th century)
1 a : a summons that is often threatening, provocative, stimulating, or inciting; *specifically* **:** a summons to a duel to answer an affront **b :** an invitation to compete in a sport
2 a : a calling to account or into question **:** PROTEST **b :** an exception taken to a juror before he is sworn **c :** a sentry's command to halt and prove identity **d :** a questioning of the right or validity of a vote or voter
3 : a stimulating task or problem ⟨looking for new *challenges*⟩
4 : the process of provoking or testing physiological activity by exposure to a specific substance; *especially* **:** a test of immunity by exposure to an antigen

chal·leng·ing \-lən-jiŋ\ *adjective* (1842)
1 : arousing competitive interest, thought, or action ⟨a *challenging* course of study⟩
2 : invitingly provocative **:** FASCINATING ⟨a *challenging* personality⟩
— **chal·leng·ing·ly** \-jiŋ-lē\ *adverb*

chal·lis \'sha-lē\ *noun, plural* **chal·lises** \'sha-lēz\ [probably from the name *Challis*] (circa 1837)
: a lightweight soft clothing fabric made of cotton, wool, or synthetic yarns

cha·lone \'kā-,lōn, 'ka-\ *noun* [Greek *chalōn*, present participle of *chalan* to slacken] (1914)
: an internal secretion that is held to inhibit mitosis in a specific tissue — compare HORMONE

¹**cha·ly·be·ate** \kə-'lē-bē-ət, -'li-\ *adjective* [probably from New Latin *chalybeatus*, irregular from Latin *chalybs* steel, from Greek *chalyb-, chalyps*, from *Chalybes*, ancient people in Asia Minor] (1634)
: impregnated with salts of iron; *also* **:** having a taste due to iron ⟨*chalybeate* springs⟩

²**chalybeate** *noun* (1667)
: a chalybeate liquid or medicine

cham \'kam\ *variant of* KHAN

cham·ae·phyte \'ka-mi-,fīt\ *noun* [Greek *chamai* on the ground + English *-phyte* — more at HUMBLE] (1913)
: a perennial plant that bears its perennating buds just above the surface of the soil

¹**cham·ber** \'chām-bər\ *noun* [Middle English *chambre*, from Old French, from Late Latin *camera*, from Latin, arched roof, from Greek *kamara* vault] (13th century)
1 : ROOM; *especially* **:** BEDROOM
2 : a natural or artificial enclosed space or cavity
3 a : a hall for the meetings of a deliberative, legislative, or judicial body ⟨the senate *chamber*⟩ **b :** a room where a judge transacts business — usually used in plural **c :** the reception room of a person of rank or authority
4 a : a legislative or judicial body; *especially* **:** either of the houses of a bicameral legislature **b :** a voluntary board or council
5 a : the part of the bore of a gun that holds the charge **b :** a compartment in the cartridge cylinder of a revolver
— **cham·bered** \-bərd\ *adjective*

²**chamber** *transitive verb* **cham·bered; cham·ber·ing** \-b(ə-)riŋ\ (1575)
1 : to place in or as if in a chamber **:** HOUSE
2 : to serve as a chamber for; *especially* **:** to accommodate in the chamber of a firearm

³**chamber** *adjective* (1706)
: being, relating to, or performing chamber music

chambered nautilus *noun* (1858)
: NAUTILUS 1

cham·ber·lain \'chām-bər-lən\ *noun* [Middle English, from Old French *chamberlayn*, of Germanic origin; akin to Old High German *chamarling* chamberlain, from *chamara* chamber, from Late Latin *camera*] (13th century)
1 : an attendant on a sovereign or lord in his bedchamber

2 a : a chief officer in the household of a king or nobleman **b :** TREASURER
3 : an often honorary papal attendant; *specifically* **:** a priest having a rank of honor below domestic prelate

cham·ber·maid \-,mād\ *noun* (1587)
: a maid who makes beds and does general cleaning of bedrooms (as in a hotel)

chamber music *noun* (circa 1789)
: music and especially instrumental ensemble music intended for performance in a private room or small auditorium and usually having one performer for each part

chamber of commerce (1797)
: an association of businessmen to promote commercial and industrial interests in the community

chamber of horrors (1849)
: a place in which macabre or horrible objects are exhibited; *also* **:** a collection of such exhibits

chamber orchestra *noun* (circa 1927)
: a small orchestra usually with one player for each part

chamber pot *noun* (1540)
: a bedroom vessel for urination and defecation

cham·bray \'sham-,brā, -brē\ *noun* [irregular from *Cambrai*, France] (1814)
: a lightweight clothing fabric with colored warp and white filling yarns

cha·me·leon \kə-'mēl-yən\ *noun, often attributive* [Middle English *camelion*, from Middle French, from Latin *chamaeleon*, from Greek *chamaileōn*, from *chamai* on the ground + *leōn* lion — more at HUMBLE] (14th century)
1 : any of a family (Chamaeleontidae) of chiefly arboreal Old World lizards with prehensile tail, independently movable eyeballs, and unusual ability to change the color of the skin
2 a : a person given to often expedient or facile change in ideas or character **b :** one that is subject to quick or frequent change especially in appearance
3 : AMERICAN CHAMELEON
— **cha·me·le·on·ic** \-,mē-lē-'ä-nik\ *adjective*
— **cha·me·leon·like** \-,līk\ *adjective*

¹**cham·fer** \'cham(p)-fər, 'cham-pər\ *transitive verb* **cham·fered; cham·fer·ing** \-f(ə-)riŋ, -p(ə-)riŋ\ [back-formation from *chamfering*, alteration of Middle French *chanfreint*, from past participle of *chanfraindre* to bevel, from *chant* edge (from Latin *canthus* iron tire) + *fraindre* to break, from Latin *frangere* — more at CANT, BREAK] (circa 1573)
1 : to cut a furrow in (as a column) **:** GROOVE
2 : to make a chamfer on **:** BEVEL

²**chamfer** *noun* (circa 1847)
: a beveled edge

cham·fron \'sham-frən, 'cham-\ *noun* [Middle English *shamfron*, from Middle French *chanfrein*] (15th century)
: the headpiece of a horse's bard

cham·ois \'sha-mē, *sense 1 also* sham-'wä\ *noun, plural* **cham·ois** *also* **cham·oix** *sense 1* 'sha-mē(z) *or* sham-'wä(z), *senses 2 & 3* 'sha-mēz\ [Middle French, from Late Latin *camox*] (1560)
1 : a small goatlike antelope (*Rupicapra rupicapra*) of mountainous regions from southern Europe to the Caucasus
2 *also* **cham·my** *or* **sham·my** \'sha-mē\ **:** a soft pliant leather prepared from the skin of the chamois or from sheepskin
3 : a cotton fabric made in imitation of chamois leather

cham·o·mile \'ka-mə-,mīl, -,mēl\ *noun* [Middle English *camemille*, from Medieval Latin *camomilla*, modification of Latin *chamaemelon*, from Greek *chamaimēlon*, from *chamai + mēlon* apple] (13th century)
1 : a composite herb (*Chamaemelum nobile* synonym *Anthemis nobilis*) of Europe and

North Africa with strong-scented foliage and flower heads that contain a bitter medicinal substance
2 : any of several composite plants (genera *Matricaria* and *Anthemis*) related to chamomile; *especially* **:** a Eurasian herb (*M. recutita* synonym *M. chamomilla*) naturalized in North America

chamomile

¹**champ** \'champ, 'chämp, 'chómp\ *verb* [perhaps imitative] (14th century)
transitive verb
1 : CHOMP
2 : MASH, TRAMPLE
intransitive verb
1 : to make biting or gnashing movements
2 : to show impatience of delay or restraint — usually used in the phrase *champing at the bit* ⟨he was *champing* at the bit to begin⟩

²**champ** \'champ\ *noun* (1868)
: CHAMPION

cham·pac *or* **cham·pak** \'cham-,pak, 'chəm-(,)pək\ *noun* [Hindi & Sanskrit; Hindi *campak*, from Sanskrit *campaka*] (circa 1770)
: an Asian tree (*Michelia champaca*) of the magnolia family with yellow flowers

cham·pagne \sham-'pān\ *noun* [French, from *Champagne*, France] (1664)
1 : a white sparkling wine made in the old province of Champagne, France; *also* **:** a similar wine made elsewhere
2 : a pale orange yellow to light grayish yellowish brown

cham·paign \sham-'pān\ *noun* [Middle English *champaine*, from Middle French *champagne*, from Late Latin *campania* — more at CAMPAIGN] (15th century)
1 : an expanse of level open country **:** PLAIN
2 *archaic* **:** BATTLEFIELD
— **champaign** *adjective*

cham·pers \'sham-pərz\ *noun plural but singular in construction* [by alteration] (1955)
British **:** CHAMPAGNE 1

cham·per·ty \'cham-pər-tē\ *noun* [Middle English *champartie*, from Middle French *champart* field rent, from *champ* field (from Latin *campus*) + *part* portion — more at PART] (15th century)
: a proceeding by which a person not a party in a suit bargains to aid in or carry on its prosecution or defense in consideration of a share of the matter in suit
— **cham·per·tous** \-pər-təs\ *adjective*

cham·pi·gnon \(,)sham-pē-'nyōn, (,)shäm-, -'nyōⁿ; sham-'pin-yən, cham-\ *noun* [French, from Middle French, alteration of *champigneul*, ultimately from Late Latin *campania*] (1670)
: an edible fungus; *especially* **:** MEADOW MUSHROOM

¹**cham·pi·on** \'cham-pē-ən\ *noun* [Middle English, from Old French, from Medieval Latin *campion-, campio*, of West Germanic origin; akin to Old English *cempa* warrior] (13th century)
1 : WARRIOR, FIGHTER
2 : a militant advocate or defender ⟨a *champion* of civil rights⟩
3 : one that does battle for another's rights or honor ⟨God will raise me up a *champion* —Sir Walter Scott⟩
4 : a winner of first prize or first place in competition; *also* **:** one who shows marked superiority ⟨a *champion* at selling⟩

²**champion** *transitive verb* (1605)
1 *archaic* **:** CHALLENGE, DEFY

\ə\ **abut** \ᵊ\ **kitten** \ər\ **further** \a\ **ash** \ā\ **ace**
\ä\ **mop, mar** \aú\ **out** \ch\ **chin** \e\ **bet** \ē\ **easy**
\g\ **go** \i\ **hit** \ī\ **ice** \j\ **job** \ŋ\ **sing** \ō\ **go**
\ò\ **law** \òi\ **boy** \th\ **thin** \t̪h\ **the** \ü\ **loot** \ù\ **foot**
\y\ **yet** \zh\ **vision** *see also* Guide to Pronunciation

2 : to protect or fight for as a champion
3 : to act as militant supporter of **:** UPHOLD, AD-VOCATE ⟨always *champions* the cause of the underdog⟩
synonym see SUPPORT

cham·pi·on·ship \-ˌship\ *noun* (1825)
1 : designation as champion
2 : the act of championing **:** DEFENSE ⟨his *championship* of freedom of speech⟩
3 : a contest held to determine a champion

champ·le·vé \ˌshäⁿl(-ə)-ˈvā\ *adjective* [French] (1856)
: of, relating to, or being a style of enamel decoration in which the enamel is applied and fired in cells depressed (as by incising) into a metal background — compare CLOISONNÉ
— **champlevé** *noun*

¹chance \ˈchan(t)s\ *noun* [Middle English, from Old French, from (assumed) Vulgar Latin *cadentia* fall, from Latin *cadent-, cadens*, present participle of *cadere* to fall; perhaps akin to Sanskrit *śad-* to fall off] (14th century)
1 a : something that happens unpredictably without discernible human intention or observable cause **b :** the assumed impersonal purposeless determiner of unaccountable happenings **:** LUCK **c :** the fortuitous or incalculable element in existence **:** CONTINGENCY
2 : a situation favoring some purpose **:** OPPORTUNITY ⟨needed a *chance* to relax⟩
3 : a fielding opportunity in baseball
4 a : the possibility of a particular outcome in an uncertain situation; *also* **:** the degree of likelihood of such an outcome ⟨a small *chance* of success⟩ **b** *plural* **:** the more likely indications ⟨*chances* are he's already gone⟩
5 a : RISK ⟨not taking any *chances*⟩ **b :** a raffle ticket
— **chance** *adjective*
— **by chance :** in the haphazard course of events ⟨they met *by chance*⟩

²chance *verb* **chanced; chanc·ing** (14th century)
intransitive verb
1 a : to take place or come about by chance **:** HAPPEN **b :** to be found by chance **c :** to have the good or bad luck ⟨we *chanced* to meet⟩
2 : to come or light by chance
transitive verb
1 : to leave the outcome of to chance
2 : to accept the hazard of **:** RISK
— **chance one's arm** *British* **:** to take a risk

chance·ful \ˈchan(t)s-fəl\ *adjective* (1594)
1 *archaic* **:** CASUAL
2 : EVENTFUL

chan·cel \ˈchan(t)-səl\ *noun* [Middle English, from Middle French, from Late Latin *cancellus* lattice, from Latin *cancelli*; from the latticework enclosing it — more at CANCEL] (14th century)
: the part of a church containing the altar and seats for the clergy and choir

chan·cel·lery *or* **chan·cel·lory** \ˈchan(t)-s(ə)lə-rē, -səl-rē\ *noun, plural* **-ler·ies** *or* **-lor·ies** (14th century)
1 a : the position, court, or department of a chancellor **b :** the building or room where a chancellor has his office
2 : the office of secretary of the court of a person high in authority
3 : the office or staff of an embassy or consulate

chan·cel·lor \ˈchan(t)-s(ə)-lər\ *noun* [Middle English *chanceler*, from Old French *chancelier*, from Late Latin *cancellarius* doorkeeper, secretary, from *cancellus*] (14th century)
1 a : the secretary of a nobleman, prince, or king **b :** the lord chancellor of Great Britain **c** *British* **:** the chief secretary of an embassy **d :** a Roman Catholic priest heading the office in which diocesan business is transacted and recorded

2 a : the titular head of a British university **b** (1) **:** a university president (2) **:** the chief executive officer in some state systems of higher education
3 a : a lay legal officer or adviser of an Anglican diocese **b :** a judge in a court of chancery or equity in various states of the U.S.
4 : the chief minister of state in some European countries
— **chan·cel·lor·ship** \-ˌship\ *noun*

chancellor of the exchequer *often* C&E *capitalized* (1672)
: a member of the British cabinet in charge of the public income and expenditure

chance–med·ley \ˈchan(t)s-ˈmed-lē\ *noun* [Anglo-French *chance medlée* mingled chance] (15th century)
1 : accidental homicide not entirely without fault of the killer but without evil intent
2 : haphazard action **:** CONFUSION

chan·cery \ˈchan(t)-sə-rē, ˈchan(t)s-rē\ *noun, plural* **-cer·ies** [Middle English *chancerie*, alteration of *chancellerie* chancellery, from Old French *chancelier*] (14th century)
1 a *capitalized* **:** a high court of equity in England and Wales with common-law functions and jurisdiction over causes in equity **b :** a court of equity in the American judicial system **c :** the principles and practice of judicial equity
2 : a record office for public archives or those of ecclesiastical, legal, or diplomatic proceedings
3 a : a chancellor's court or office or the building in which it is located **b :** the office in which the business of a Roman Catholic diocese is transacted and recorded **c :** the office of an embassy **:** CHANCELLERY 3
— **in chancery 1 :** in litigation in a court of chancery; *also* **:** under the superintendence of the lord chancellor ⟨a ward *in chancery*⟩ **2 :** in a hopeless predicament

chan·cre \ˈshaŋ-kər\ *noun* [French, from Latin *cancer*] (circa 1605)
: a primary sore or ulcer at the site of entry of a pathogen (as in tularemia); *especially* **:** the initial lesion of syphilis
— **chan·crous** \-k(ə-)rəs\ *adjective*

chan·croid \ˈshaŋ-ˌkròid\ *noun* (1861)
: a venereal disease caused by a hemophilic bacterium (*Hemophilus ducreyi*) and characterized by chancres unlike those of syphilis in lacking firm indurated margins — called also *soft chancre*
— **chan·croi·dal** \shaŋ-ˈkròi-dᵊl\ *adjective*

chancy \ˈchan(t)-sē\ *adjective* **chanc·i·er; -est** (1513)
1 *Scottish* **:** bringing good luck **:** AUSPICIOUS
2 : uncertain in outcome or prospect **:** RISKY
3 : occurring by chance **:** HAPHAZARD
— **chanc·i·ness** *noun*

chan·de·lier \ˌshan-də-ˈlir\ *noun* [French, literally, candlestick, modification of Latin *candelabrum*] (1736)
: a branched often ornate lighting fixture suspended from a ceiling
— **chan·de·liered** \-ˈlird\ *adjective*

chan·delle \shan-ˈdel, shäⁿ-\ *noun* [French, literally, candle] (1918)
: an abrupt climbing turn of an airplane in which the momentum of the plane is used to attain a higher rate of climb
— **chandelle** *intransitive verb*

chandelier

chan·dler \ˈchan(d)-lər\ *noun* [Middle English *chandeler*, from Middle French *chandelier*, from Old French, from *chandelle* candle, from Latin *candela*] (14th century)
1 : a maker or seller of tallow or wax candles and usually soap

2 : a retail dealer in provisions and supplies or equipment of a specified kind ⟨a yacht *chandler*⟩

chan·dlery \-lə-rē\ *noun, plural* **-dler·ies** (15th century)
1 : a place where candles are kept
2 : the business of a chandler
3 : the commodities sold by a chandler

¹change \ˈchānj\ *verb* **changed; chang·ing** [Middle English, from Old French *changier*, from Latin *cambiare* to exchange, probably of Celtic origin; akin to Old Irish *camm* crooked] (13th century)
transitive verb
1 a : to make different in some particular **:** ALTER ⟨never bothered to *change* the will⟩ **b :** to make radically different **:** TRANSFORM ⟨can't *change* human nature⟩ **c :** to give a different position, course, or direction to
2 a : to replace with another ⟨let's *change* the subject⟩ **b :** to make a shift from one to another **:** SWITCH ⟨always *changes* sides in an argument⟩ **c :** to exchange for an equivalent sum or comparable item **d :** to undergo a modification of ⟨foliage *changing* color⟩ **e :** to put fresh clothes or covering on ⟨*change* a bed⟩
intransitive verb
1 : to become different ⟨her mood *changes* every hour⟩
2 *of the moon* **:** to pass from one phase to another
3 : to shift one's means of conveyance **:** TRANSFER ⟨on the bus trip he had to *change* twice⟩
4 *of the voice* **:** to shift to lower register **:** BREAK
5 : to undergo transformation, transition, or substitution ⟨winter *changed* to spring⟩
6 : to put on different clothes
7 : EXCHANGE, SWITCH ⟨neither liked his seat so they *changed* with each other⟩ ☆
— **chang·er** *noun*
— **change hands :** to pass from the possession of one owner to that of another ⟨money *changes hands* many times⟩

²change *noun* (13th century)
1 : the act, process, or result of changing: as **a :** ALTERATION ⟨a *change* in the weather⟩ **b :** TRANSFORMATION ⟨a time of vast social *change*⟩ ⟨going through *changes*⟩ **c :** SUBSTITUTION ⟨a *change* of scenery⟩ **d :** the passage of the moon from one monthly revolution to another; *also* **:** the passage of the moon from one phase to another
2 : a fresh set of clothes
3 *British* **:** EXCHANGE 5a
4 a : money in small denominations received in exchange for an equivalent sum in larger denominations **b :** money returned when a payment exceeds the amount due **c :** coins especially of low denominations ⟨a pocketful of *change*⟩ **d :** a negligible additional amount ⟨only six minutes and *change* left in the game⟩
5 : an order in which a set of bells is struck in change ringing
6 : CHANGE-UP

☆ SYNONYMS
Change, alter, vary, modify mean to make or become different. CHANGE implies making either an essential difference often amounting to a loss of original identity or a substitution of one thing for another ⟨*changed* the shirt for a larger size⟩. ALTER implies a difference in some particular respect without suggesting loss of identity ⟨slightly *altered* the original design⟩. VARY stresses a breaking away from sameness, duplication, or exact repetition ⟨*vary* your daily routine⟩. MODIFY suggests a difference that limits, restricts, or adapts to a new purpose ⟨*modified* the building for use by the handicapped⟩.

change·able \'chān-jə-bəl\ *adjective* (13th century)
: capable of change: as **a** : able or apt to vary ⟨*changeable* weather⟩ **b** : subject to change : ALTERABLE **c** : FICKLE **d** : IRIDESCENT
— **change·abil·i·ty** \,chān-jə-'bi-lə-tē\ *noun*
— **change·able·ness** \'chān-jə-bəl-nəs\ *noun*
— **change·ably** \-blē\ *adverb*
change·ful \'chānj-fəl\ *adjective* (1591)
: notably variable : UNCERTAIN
— **change·ful·ly** \-fə-lē\ *adverb*
— **change·ful·ness** *noun*
change·less \'chānj-ləs\ *adjective* (1580)
: marked by the absence of change : CONSTANT
— **change·less·ly** *adverb*
— **change·less·ness** *noun*
change·ling \'chānj-liŋ\ *noun* (1537)
1 *archaic* : TURNCOAT
2 : a child secretly exchanged for another in infancy
3 *archaic* : IMBECILE
— **changeling** *adjective*
change off *intransitive verb* (1873)
1 : to alternate with another at doing an act
2 : to alternate between two different acts or instruments or between an action and a rest period
change of heart (circa 1828)
: a reversal in position or attitude
change of life (1834)
: ²CLIMACTERIC 2
change of pace (1912)
1 : CHANGE-UP
2 : an interruption of continuity by a shift to a different activity
change·over \'chān-,jō-vər\ *noun* (1907)
1 : CONVERSION, TRANSITION
2 : a pause in a tennis match during which the players change sides of the court
change ringing *noun* (1872)
: the art or practice of ringing a set of tuned bells (as in the bell tower of a church) in continually varying order
change–up \'chān-,jəp\ *noun* (1949)
: a slow pitch in baseball thrown with the same motion as a fastball in order to deceive the batter
¹chan·nel \'cha-nᵊl\ *noun* [Middle English *chanel*, from Middle French, from Latin *canalis* channel — more at CANAL] (14th century)
1 a : the bed where a natural stream of water runs **b** : the deeper part of a river, harbor, or strait **c** : a strait or narrow sea between two close landmasses **d** : a means of communication or expression: as (1) : a path along which information (as data or music) in the form of an electrical signal passes (2) *plural* : a fixed or official course of communication ⟨went through established military *channels* with his grievances⟩ **e** : a way, course, or direction of thought or action ⟨new *channels* of exploration⟩ **f** : a band of frequencies of sufficient width for a single radio or television communication **g** : CHANNELER
2 a : a usually tubular enclosed passage : CONDUIT **b** : a passage created in a selectively permeable membrane by a conformational change in membrane proteins
3 : a long gutter, groove, or furrow
4 : a metal bar of flattened U-shaped section
²channel *transitive verb* **-neled** *or* **-nelled; -nel·ing** *or* **-nel·ling** (15th century)
1 a : to form, cut, or wear a channel in **b** : to make a groove in ⟨*channel* a chair leg⟩
2 : to convey or direct into or through a channel ⟨*channel* his energy into constructive activities⟩
3 : to serve as a channeler or intermediary for
³channel *noun* [alteration of *chainwale*, from ¹*chain* + ¹*wale*] (1769)
: one of the flat ledges of heavy plank or metal bolted edgewise to the outside of a ship to increase the spread of the shrouds
channel bass *noun* (1887)

: a large coppery drum (*Sciaenops ocellatus*) chiefly of the Atlantic coast of North America that has a black spot at the base of the tail and is an important game and food fish — called also *red drum, redfish*
channel catfish *noun* (1820)
: a large black-spotted catfish (*Ictalurus punctatus*) that is an important freshwater food fish of the U.S. and Canada — called also *channel cat*
chan·nel·er \'cha-nᵊl-ər\ *noun* (1987)
: a person who conveys thoughts or energy from a source believed to be outside the person's body or conscious mind; *specifically* : one who speaks for nonphysical beings or spirits
chan·nel·ize \'cha-nᵊl-,īz\ *transitive verb* **-ized; -iz·ing** (1609)
1 : CHANNEL 1, 2
2 : to straighten by means of a channel ⟨*channelize* a stream⟩
— **chan·nel·i·za·tion** \,cha-nᵊl-ə-'zā-shən\ *noun*
channel surfing *noun* (1990)
: the act or practice of scanning through television programs usually by use of a remote control to find something of interest
— **channel surf** *intransitive verb*
— **channel surfer** *noun*
chan·son \shäⁿ-'sōⁿ\ *noun, plural* **chansons** \-'sōⁿ(z)\ [French, from Latin *cantion-, cantio*, from *canere*] (1602)
: SONG; *specifically* : a music-hall or cabaret song
chanson de geste \-də-'zhest\ *noun, plural* **chansons de geste** *same*\ [French, literally, song of heroic deeds] (1868)
: any of several Old French epic poems of the 11th to the 13th centuries
chan·son·nier \,shäⁿ-sō-'nyā\ *noun* [French, from *chanson*] (1887)
: a writer or singer of chansons; *especially* : a cabaret singer
¹chant \'chant\ *verb* [Middle English *chaunten*, from Middle French *chanter*, from Latin *cantare*, frequentative of *canere* to sing; akin to Old English *hana* rooster, Old Irish *canid* he sings] (14th century)
intransitive verb
1 : to make melodic sounds with the voice; *especially* : to sing a chant
2 : to recite in a monotonous repetitive tone
transitive verb
1 : to utter as in chanting
2 : to celebrate or praise in song or chant
²chant *noun* (1671)
1 : SONG
2 a : PLAINSONG **b** : a rhythmic monotonous utterance or song **c** : a composition for chanting
chant·er \'chan-tər\ *noun* (14th century)
1 : one that chants: **a** : CHORISTER **b** : CANTOR
2 : the chief singer in a chantry
3 : the reed pipe of a bagpipe with finger holes on which the melody is played
chan·te·relle \,shan-tə-'rel, ,shän-\ *noun* [French] (1775)
: a fragrant edible mushroom (*Cantharellus cibarius*) of rich yellow color
chan·teuse \shan-'tüz, shäⁿ-'tə(r)z\ *noun, plural* **chan·teuses** \-'tüz, -'tü-zəz, -'tə(r)z, -'tə(r)-zəz\ [French, feminine of *chanteur* singer, from *chanter*] (1888)
: a woman who is a concert or nightclub singer
chan·tey *or* **chan·ty** \'shan-tē, 'chan-\ *noun, plural* **chanteys** *or* **chanties** [modification of French *chanter*] (1856)
: a song sung by sailors in rhythm with their work
chan·ti·cleer \,chan-tə-'klir, ,shan-\ *noun* [Middle English *Chantecleer*, rooster in verse narratives, from Old French *Chantecler*, rooster in the *Roman de Renart*] (14th century)
: ROOSTER

Chan·til·ly lace \shan-'ti-lē-\ *noun* [*Chantilly*, France] (1848)
: a delicate silk, linen, or synthetic lace having a six-sided mesh ground and a floral or scrolled design — called also *Chantilly*
chan·try \'chan-trē\ *noun, plural* **chantries** [Middle English *chanterie*, from Middle French, singing, from *chanter*] (14th century)
1 : an endowment for the chanting of masses commonly for the founder
2 : a chapel endowed by a chantry
Cha·nu·kah \'kä-nə-kə, 'hä-\ *variant of* HANUKKAH
cha·os \'kā-,äs\ *noun* [Latin, from Greek — more at GUM] (15th century)
1 *obsolete* : CHASM, ABYSS
2 a *often capitalized* : a state of things in which chance is supreme; *especially* : the confused unorganized state of primordial matter before the creation of distinct forms — compare COSMOS **b** : the inherent unpredictability in the behavior of a natural system (as the atmosphere, boiling water, or the beating heart)
3 a : a state of utter confusion **b** : a confused mass or mixture ⟨a *chaos* of television antennas⟩
— **cha·ot·ic** \kā-'ä-tik\ *adjective*
— **cha·ot·i·cal·ly** \-ti-k(ə-)lē\ *adverb*
¹chap \'chap\ *noun* (14th century)
: a crack in or a sore roughening of the skin caused by exposure to wind or cold
²chap *verb* **chapped; chap·ping** [Middle English *chappen*; akin to Middle Dutch *cappen* to cut down] (15th century)
intransitive verb
: to open in cracks, slits, or chinks; *also* : to become cracked, roughened, or reddened especially by the action of wind or cold ⟨hands often *chap* in winter⟩
transitive verb
: to cause to chap ⟨wind-*chapped* lips⟩
³chap \'chäp, 'chap\ *noun* [origin unknown] (1555)
1 a : the fleshy covering of a jaw; *also* : JAW — usually used in plural ⟨a wolf's *chaps*⟩
2 : the forepart of the face — usually used in plural
⁴chap *noun* [short for *chapman*] (1716)
1 : FELLOW 4c
2 *Southern & Midland* : BABY, CHILD
chap·a·ra·jos *or* **chap·a·re·jos** \,sha-pə-'rä-(,)ōs, -'rä-\ *noun plural* [modification of Mexican Spanish *chaparreras*, from *chaparro*] (1887)
: CHAPS
chap·ar·ral \,sha-pə-'ral, -'rel\ *noun* [Spanish, from *chaparro* dwarf evergreen oak, from Basque *txapar*] (1845)
1 : a thicket of dwarf evergreen oaks; *broadly* : a dense impenetrable thicket of shrubs or dwarf trees
2 : an ecological community composed of shrubby plants adapted to dry summers and moist winters that occurs especially in southern California
chaparral cock *noun* (1853)
: ROADRUNNER — called also *chaparral bird*
cha·pa·ti *also* **chap·pa·ti** \chə-'pä-tē\ *noun, plural* **chapatis** *also* **chappatis** [Hindi *capātī*] (1810)
: a round flat unleavened bread of India that is usually made of whole wheat flour and cooked on a griddle
chap·book \'chap-,bùk\ *noun* [*chap*man + *book*] (1798)
: a small book containing ballads, poems, tales, or tracts

\ə\ abut \ᵊ\ kitten \ər\ further \a\ ash \ä\ ace
\ä\ mop, mar \aù\ out \ch\ chin \e\ bet \ē\ easy
\g\ go \i\ hit \ī\ ice \j\ job \ŋ\ sing \ō\ go
\ò\ law \òi\ boy \th\ thin \th\ the \ü\ loot \ù\ foot
\y\ yet \zh\ vision *see also* Guide to Pronunciation

chape \'chāp, 'chap\ *noun* [Middle English, scabbard, from Middle French, cape, from Late Latin *cappa*] (14th century)
: the metal mounting or trimming of a scabbard or sheath

cha·peau \sha-'pō, shə-\ *noun, plural* **cha·peaus** \-'pōz\ *or* **cha·peaux** \-'pō(z)\ [Middle French, from Old French *chapel* — more at CHAPLET] (1523)
: HAT

chap·el \'cha-pəl\ *noun* [Middle English, from Old French *chapele*, from Medieval Latin *cappella*, from diminutive of Late Latin *cappa* cloak; from the cloak of Saint Martin of Tours preserved as a sacred relic in a chapel built for that purpose] (13th century)
1 : a subordinate or private place of worship: as **a** : a place of worship serving a residence or institution **b** : a small house of worship usually associated with a main church **c** : a room or recess in a church for meditation and prayer or small religious services
2 : a place of worship used by a Christian group other than an established church
3 : a choir of singers belonging to a chapel
4 : a chapel service or assembly at a school or college
5 : an association of the employees in a printing office
6 a : FUNERAL HOME **b** : a room for funeral services in a funeral home ◇

chapel of ease (1538)
: a chapel or dependent church built to accommodate an expanding parish

¹**chap·er·on** *or* **chap·er·one** \'sha-pə-,rōn\ *noun* [French *chaperon*, literally, hood, from Middle French, head covering, from *chape*] (1720)
1 : a person (as a matron) who for propriety accompanies one or more young unmarried women in public or in mixed company
2 : an older person who accompanies young people at a social gathering to ensure proper behavior; *broadly* : one delegated to ensure proper behavior

²**chaperon** *or* **chaperone** *verb* **-oned; -on·ing** (1796)
transitive verb
1 : ESCORT
2 : to act as chaperon to or for
intransitive verb
: to act as a chaperon
— **chap·er·on·age** \-,rō-nij\ *noun*

chap·fall·en \'chap-,fȯ-lən, 'chäp-\ *adjective* (1598)
1 : having the lower jaw hanging loosely
2 : cast down in spirit : DEPRESSED

chap·i·ter \'cha-pə-tər\ *noun* [Middle English *chapitre*, from Middle French, alteration of Old French *chapitle*, from Latin *capitulum*, literally, little head] (15th century)
: the capital of a column

chap·lain \'cha-plən\ *noun* [Middle English *chapelain*, from Old French, from Medieval Latin *cappellanus*, from *cappella*] (14th century)
1 : a clergyman in charge of a chapel
2 : a clergyman officially attached to a branch of the military, to an institution, or to a family or court
3 : a person chosen to conduct religious exercises (as at a meeting of a club or society)
4 : a clergyman appointed to assist a bishop (as at a liturgical function)
— **chap·lain·cy** \-sē\ *noun*

chap·let \'chap-lət\ *noun* [Middle English *chapelet*, from Middle French, from Old French, diminutive of *chapel* hat, garland, from Medieval Latin *cappellus* head covering, from Late Latin *cappa*] (14th century)
1 : a wreath to be worn on the head
2 a : a string of beads **b** : a part of a rosary comprising five decades
3 : a small molding carved with small decorative forms
— **chap·let·ed** \-lə-təd\ *adjective*

chap·man \'chap-mən\ *noun* [Middle English, from Old English *cēapman*, from *cēap* trade + *man* — more at CHEAP] (before 12th century)
1 *archaic* : MERCHANT, TRADER
2 *British* : PEDDLER

chaps \'shaps, 'chaps\ *noun plural* [modification of Mexican Spanish *chaparreras*] (1844)
: leather leggings joined by a belt or lacing, often having flared outer flaps, and worn over the trousers (as by western ranch hands)

chaps

chap·ter \'chap-tər\ *noun* [Middle English *chapitre*, from Old French, from Late Latin *capitulum* division of a book & Medieval Latin, meeting place of canons, from Latin, diminutive of *capit-, caput* head — more at HEAD] (13th century)
1 a : a main division of a book **b** : something resembling a chapter in being a significant specified unit ⟨a new *chapter* in my life⟩
2 a : a regular meeting of the canons of a cathedral or collegiate church or of the members of a religious house **b** : the body of canons of a cathedral or collegiate church
3 : a local branch of an organization

chapter and verse *noun* (1628)
1 : the exact reference or source of information or justification for an assertion ⟨clinched their arguments by citing *chapter and verse* —J. M. Burns⟩
2 : full precise information or detail ⟨can give *chapter and verse* on the effects of diverting defense spending —Horace Sutton⟩
— **chapter and verse** *adverb*

¹**char** \'chär\ *noun, plural* **char** *or* **chars** [origin unknown] (1662)
: any of a genus (*Salvelinus*) of small-scaled trouts with light-colored spots

²**char** *verb* **charred; char·ring** [*charcoal*] (1679)
transitive verb
1 : to convert to charcoal or carbon usually by heat : BURN
2 : to burn slightly or partly : SCORCH ⟨the fire *charred* the beams⟩
intransitive verb
: to become charred

³**char** *noun* (1879)
: a charred substance : CHARCOAL; *specifically* : a combustible residue remaining after the destructive distillation of coal

⁴**char** *intransitive verb* **charred; char·ring** [*charwoman*] (1732)
: to work as a cleaning woman

⁵**char** *noun* [by shortening] (1906)
British : CHARWOMAN

char·a·banc \'shar-ə-,baŋ, -,bän\ *noun* [French *char à bancs*, literally, wagon with benches] (1914)
British : a sight-seeing motor coach

char·a·cin \'kar-ə-sən\ *noun* [ultimately from Greek *charak-, charax* pointed stake, a fish] (1882)
: any of a family (Characidae) of usually small brightly colored tropical freshwater fishes that includes many aquarium fishes
— **characin** *adjective*

¹**char·ac·ter** \'kar-ik-tər\ *noun* [Middle English *caracter*, from Middle French *caractère*, from Latin *character* mark, distinctive quality, from Greek *charaktēr*, from *charassein* to scratch, engrave; perhaps akin to Lithuanian *žeyti* to scratch] (14th century)
1 a : a conventionalized graphic device placed on an object as an indication of ownership, origin, or relationship **b** : a graphic symbol (as a hieroglyph or alphabet letter) used in writing or printing **c** : a magical or astrological emblem **d** : ALPHABET **e** (1) : WRITING, PRINTING (2) : style of writing or printing (3) : CIPHER **f** : a symbol (as a letter or number) that repre-

sents information; *also* : a representation of such a character that may be accepted by a computer
2 a : one of the attributes or features that make up and distinguish an individual **b** (1) : a feature used to separate distinguishable things into categories; *also* : a group or kind so separated ⟨advertising of a very primitive *character*⟩ (2) : the detectable expression of the action of a gene or group of genes (3) : the aggregate of distinctive qualities characteristic of a breed, strain, or type ⟨a wine of great *character*⟩ **c** : the complex of mental and ethical traits marking and often individualizing a person, group, or nation **d** : main or essential nature especially as strongly marked and serving to distinguish ⟨excess sewage gradually changed the *character* of the lake⟩
3 : POSITION, CAPACITY ⟨his *character* as a town official⟩
4 : REFERENCE 4b
5 : REPUTATION
6 : moral excellence and firmness ⟨a man of sound *character*⟩
7 a : a person marked by notable or conspicuous traits ⟨quite a *character*⟩ **b** : one of the persons of a drama or novel **c** : the personality or part which an actor recreates **d** : characterization especially in drama or fiction **e** : PERSON, INDIVIDUAL ⟨some *character* just stole her purse⟩
8 : a short literary sketch of the qualities of a social type
synonym see DISPOSITION, QUALITY, TYPE
— **char·ac·ter·less** \-ləs\ *adjective*
— **in character** : in accord with a person's usual qualities or traits
— **out of character** : not in accord with a person's usual qualities or traits

²**character** *transitive verb* (1591)
1 *archaic* : ENGRAVE, INSCRIBE
2 a *archaic* : REPRESENT, PORTRAY **b** : CHARACTERIZE

³**character** *adjective* (1893)
1 : capable of portraying an unusual or eccentric personality often markedly different from the player ⟨a *character* actor⟩
2 : requiring the qualities of a character actor ⟨a *character* role⟩

character assassination *noun* (1949)
: the slandering of a person usually with the intention of destroying public confidence in that person

char·ac·ter·ful \'kar-ik-tər-fəl\ *adjective* (1901)
1 : markedly expressive of character ⟨a *characterful* face⟩

◇ WORD HISTORY
chapel One harsh winter while he was a youthful soldier in the Roman army, St. Martin of Tours (ca. 316–397) is said to have divided his military cloak in half with his sword, giving one part to a naked pauper at the gate of Amiens and keeping the other part for himself. After his death, a cloak supposedly belonging to the saint, to which his demonstration of charity gave special significance, was preserved as a relic by Frankish kings. In early Medieval Latin documents, St. Martin's cloak was referred to as *capella* or *cappella*, a diminutive of Late Latin *cappa*, also meaning "cloak." The meaning of *capella* was eventually expanded to include not only the cloak, but the entire royal treasury of saints' relics, and then the rooms in the royal palace set aside for private worship, where the relics were kept. By the early 9th century, *capella* could refer to any private place of worship. *Chapelle*, the vernacular form of *capella* in the medieval French of the Paris region, is first attested about 1100, and it had been borrowed into English by the early 13th century.

2 : marked by character ⟨a *characterful* decision⟩

¹char·ac·ter·is·tic \,kar-ik-tə-'ris-tik\ *noun* (1664)
1 : a distinguishing trait, quality, or property
2 : the integral part of a common logarithm
3 : the smallest positive integer *n* which for an operation in a ring or field yields 0 when any element is used *n* times with the operation
²characteristic *adjective* (1665)
: revealing, distinguishing, or typical of an individual character ☆
— **char·ac·ter·is·ti·cal·ly** \-ti-k(ə-)lē\ *adverb*

characteristic equation *noun* (circa 1925)
: an equation in which the characteristic polynomial of a matrix is set equal to 0

characteristic polynomial *noun* (circa 1957)
: the determinant of a square matrix in which an arbitrary variable (as *x*) is subtracted from each of the elements along the principal diagonal

characteristic root *noun* (circa 1957)
: EIGENVALUE

characteristic value *noun* (1956)
: EIGENVALUE

characteristic vector *noun* (1957)
: EIGENVECTOR

char·ac·ter·iza·tion \,kar-ik-t(ə-)rə-'zā-shən\ *noun* (1814)
: the act of characterizing; *especially* **:** the artistic representation (as in fiction or drama) of human character or motives

char·ac·ter·ize \'kar-ik-tə-,rīz\ *transitive verb* **-ized; -iz·ing** (1633)
1 : to describe the character or quality of ⟨*characterizes* him as ambitious⟩
2 : to be a characteristic of **:** DISTINGUISH ⟨an era *characterized* by greed⟩

char·ac·ter·olog·i·cal \,kar-ik-t(ə-)rə-'lä-ji-kəl\ *adjective* [*characterology* study of character] (1916)
: of, relating to, or based on character or the study of character including its development and its differences in different individuals
— **char·ac·ter·olog·i·cal·ly** \-'lä-ji-k(ə-)lē\ *adverb*

character witness *noun* (1952)
: a person who gives evidence in a legal action concerning the reputation, conduct, and moral nature of a party

char·ac·tery \'kar-ik-t(ə-)rē, kə-'rak-\ *noun, plural* **-ter·ies** (1598)
: a system of written letters or symbols used in the expression of thought

cha·rade \shə-'rād, -'räd\ *noun* [French, from Provençal *charrado* chat, from *charrá* to chat, chatter] (1776)
1 : a word represented in riddling verse or by picture, tableau, or dramatic action
2 *plural* **:** a game in which some of the players try to guess a word or phrase from the actions of another player who may not speak
3 : an empty or deceptive act or pretense ⟨his concern was a *charade*⟩

cha·ras \'chär-əs\ *noun* [Hindi *caras*] (circa 1860)
: HASHISH

char·broil \'chär-,brȯi(ə)l\ *transitive verb* (1968)
: to broil on a rack over hot charcoal
— **char·broil·er** \-,brȯi-lər\ *noun*

¹char·coal \'chär-,kōl\ *noun* [Middle English *charcole*] (14th century)
1 : a dark or black porous carbon prepared from vegetable or animal substances (as from wood by charring in a kiln from which air is excluded)
2 a : a piece or pencil of fine charcoal used in drawing **b :** a charcoal drawing
3 : a dark gray
²charcoal *transitive verb* (1965)
: CHARBROIL

char·cu·te·rie \(,)shär-,kü-tə-'rē\ *noun* [French, literally, pork-butcher's shop, from

Middle French *chaircuiterie*, from *chaircutier* pork butcher, from *chair cuite* cooked meat] (circa 1858)
: a delicatessen specializing in dressed meats and meat dishes; *also* **:** the products sold in such a shop

chard \'chärd\ *noun* [modification of French *carde*, from Provençal *cardo*, from Latin *carduus* thistle, cardoon] (1664)
: SWISS CHARD

char·don·nay \,shär-d°n-'ā\ *noun, often capitalized* [French] (circa 1941)
: a dry white table wine of Chablis type

chare \'char, 'cher\ *or* **char** \'chär\ *noun* [Middle English *char* turn, piece of work, from Old English *cierr;* akin to Old English *cierran* to turn] (before 12th century)
: CHORE

¹charge \'chärj\ *noun* [Middle English, from Old French, from *chargier*] (13th century)
1 a *obsolete* **:** a material load or weight **b :** a figure borne on a heraldic field
2 a : the quantity that an apparatus is intended to receive and fitted to hold **b :** a store or accumulation of impelling force ⟨the deeply emotional *charge* of the drama⟩ **c :** a definite quantity of electricity; *especially* **:** an excess or deficiency of electrons in a body **d :** THRILL, KICK ⟨got a *charge* out of the game⟩
3 a : OBLIGATION, REQUIREMENT **b :** MANAGEMENT, SUPERVISION ⟨has *charge* of the home office⟩ **c :** the ecclesiastical jurisdiction (as a parish) committed to a clergyman **d :** a person or thing committed to the care of another
4 a : INSTRUCTION, COMMAND **b :** instruction in points of law given by a court to a jury
5 a : EXPENSE, COST ⟨gave the banquet at his own *charge*⟩ **b :** the price demanded for something ⟨no admission *charge*⟩ **c :** a debit to an account ⟨the purchase was a *charge*⟩ **d :** the record of a loan (as of a book from a library) **e** *British* **:** an interest in property granted as security for a loan
6 a : a formal assertion of illegality ⟨a *charge* of murder⟩ **b :** a statement of complaint or hostile criticism ⟨denied the *charges* of nepotism that were leveled against him⟩
7 : a violent rush forward (as to attack)
— **in charge :** having control or custody of something ⟨he is *in charge* of the training program⟩

²charge *verb* **charged; charg·ing** [Middle English, from Old French *chargier*, from Late Latin *carricare*, from Latin *carrus* wheeled vehicle — more at CAR] (14th century)
transitive verb
1 a *archaic* **:** to lay or put a load on or in **:** LOAD **b** (1) **:** to place a charge (as of powder) in (2) **:** to load or fill to capacity **c** (1) **:** to restore the active materials in (a storage battery) by the passage of a direct current through in the opposite direction to that of discharge (2) **:** to give an electric charge to ⟨*charge* a capacitor⟩ **d** (1) **:** to assume as a heraldic bearing (2) **:** to place a heraldic bearing on **e :** to fill or furnish fully ⟨the music is *charged* with excitement⟩
2 a : to impose a task or responsibility on ⟨*charge* him with the job of finding a new meeting place⟩ **b :** to command, instruct, or exhort with authority ⟨I *charge* you not to go⟩ **c** *of a judge* **:** to give a charge to (a jury)
3 a : to make an assertion against especially by ascribing guilt or blame ⟨*charges* him with armed robbery⟩ ⟨they were *charged* as being instigators⟩ **b :** to place the guilt or blame for ⟨*charge* her failure to negligence⟩ **c :** to assert as an accusation ⟨*charges* that he distorted the data⟩
4 a : to bring (a weapon) into position for attack **:** LEVEL ⟨*charge* a lance⟩ **b :** to rush against **:** ATTACK; *also* **:** to rush into (an opponent) usually illegally in various sports
5 a (1) **:** to impose a financial burden on ⟨*charge* his estate with debts incurred⟩ (2) **:** to

impose or record as financial obligation ⟨*charge* debts to an estate⟩ **b** (1) **:** to fix or ask as fee or payment ⟨*charges* $50 for an office visit⟩ (2) **:** to ask payment of (a person) ⟨*charge* a client for expenses⟩ **c :** to record (an item) as an expense, debt, obligation, or liability ⟨*charged* a new sofa⟩
intransitive verb
1 : to rush forward in or as if in assault **:** ATTACK; *also* **:** to charge an opponent in sports
2 : to ask or set a price ⟨do you *charge* for this service?⟩
3 : to charge an item to an account ⟨*charge* now, pay later⟩
synonym see COMMAND

charge·able \'chär-jə-bəl\ *adjective* (14th century)
1 *archaic* **:** financially burdensome **:** EXPENSIVE
2 : liable to be charged: as **a :** liable to be accused or held responsible **b :** suitable to be charged to a particular account **c :** qualified to be made a charge on the county or parish

charge account *noun* (1903)
: a customer's account with a creditor (as a merchant) to which the purchase of goods is charged

charge card *noun* (1950)
: CREDIT CARD

charge–coupled device *noun* (1971)
: a semiconductor device that is used especially as an optical sensor and that stores charge and transfers it sequentially to an amplifier and detector — called also *CCD*

charged \'chärjd\ *adjective* (1934)
1 : possessing or showing strong emotion ⟨attacked the author in a highly *charged* review⟩
2 : capable of arousing strong emotion ⟨a politically *charged* subject⟩

char·gé d'af·faires \(,)shär-,zhä-də-'far, -'fer\ *noun, plural* **char·gés d'affaires** \-,zhä-də-, -,zhäz-də-\ [French, literally, one charged with affairs] (1767)
1 : a subordinate diplomat who substitutes for an absent ambassador or minister
2 : a diplomat inferior in rank to an ambassador or minister who heads a mission when no ambassador or minister is assigned

charge·hand \'chärj-,hand\ *noun* (1916)
British **:** FOREMAN

charge off *transitive verb* (circa 1923)
: to treat as a loss or expense
— **charge–off** \'chärj-,ȯf\ *noun*

charge of quarters (circa 1918)
: an enlisted man designated to handle administrative matters in his unit especially after duty hours — abbreviation *CQ*

☆ **SYNONYMS**
Characteristic, individual, peculiar, distinctive mean indicating a special quality or identity. CHARACTERISTIC applies to something that distinguishes or identifies a person or thing or class ⟨responded with her *characteristic* wit⟩. INDIVIDUAL stresses qualities that distinguish one from all other members of the same kind or class ⟨a highly *individual* writing style⟩. PECULIAR applies to qualities possessed only by a particular individual or class or kind and stresses rarity or uniqueness ⟨an eccentricity that is *peculiar* to the British⟩. DISTINCTIVE indicates qualities distinguishing and uncommon and often superior or praiseworthy ⟨a *distinctive* aura of grace and elegance⟩.

¹char·ger \'chär-jər\ *noun* [Middle English *chargeour*; akin to Middle English *chargen* to charge] (14th century)
: a large flat dish or platter

²charg·er *noun* (1539)
1 : one that charges: as **a** : an appliance for holding or inserting a charge of powder or shot in a gun **b** : a cartridge clip **c** : a device for charging storage batteries
2 : a horse for battle or parade

char·i·ness \'char-ē-nəs, 'cher-\ *noun* (1571)
1 : the quality or state of being chary : CAUTION
2 : carefully preserved state : INTEGRITY

¹char·i·ot \'char-ē-ət\ *noun* [Middle English, from Middle French, from Old French, from *char* wheeled vehicle, from Latin *carrus* — more at CAR] (14th century)
1 : a light four-wheeled pleasure or state carriage
2 : a two-wheeled horse-drawn battle car of ancient times used also in processions and races

²chariot (1550)
intransitive verb
: to drive or ride in or as if in a chariot
transitive verb
: to carry in or as if in a chariot

char·i·ot·eer \,char-ē-ə-'tir\ *noun* (14th century)
1 : one who drives a chariot
2 *capitalized* : AURIGA

cha·ris·ma \kə-'riz-mə\ *also* **char·ism** \'kar-,i-zəm\ *noun, plural* **cha·ris·ma·ta** \kə-'riz-mə-tə, ,kär-iz-'mä-tə\ *also* **charisms** [Greek *charisma* favor, gift, from *charizesthai* to favor, from *charis* grace; akin to Greek *chairein* to rejoice — more at YEARN] (circa 1641)
1 : an extraordinary power (as of healing) given a Christian by the Holy Spirit for the good of the church
2 a : a personal magic of leadership arousing special popular loyalty or enthusiasm for a public figure (as a political leader) **b** : a special magnetic charm or appeal ⟨the *charisma* of a popular actor⟩

¹char·is·mat·ic \,kar-əz-'ma-tik\ *adjective* [*charisma*] (circa 1868)
1 : of, relating to, or constituting charisma
2 : having, exhibiting, or based on charisma ⟨*charismatic* sects⟩ ⟨*charismatic* leader⟩

²charismatic *noun* (1951)
: a member of a charismatic religious group or movement

char·i·ta·ble \'char-ə-tə-bəl\ *adjective* (14th century)
1 : full of love for and goodwill toward others : BENEVOLENT
2 a : liberal in benefactions to the needy : GENEROUS **b** : of or relating to charity ⟨*charitable* institutions⟩
3 : merciful or kind in judging others : LENIENT
— **char·i·ta·ble·ness** *noun*
— **char·i·ta·bly** \-blē\ *adverb*

char·i·ty \'char-ə-tē\ *noun, plural* **-ties** [Middle English *charite*, from Old French *charité*, from Late Latin *caritat-, caritas* Christian love, from Latin, dearness, from *carus* dear; akin to Old Irish *carae* friend, Sanskrit *kāma* love] (13th century)
1 : benevolent goodwill toward or love of humanity
2 a : generosity and helpfulness especially toward the needy or suffering; *also* : aid given to those in need **b** : an institution engaged in relief of the poor **c** : public provision for the relief of the needy
3 a : a gift for public benevolent purposes **b** : an institution (as a hospital) founded by such a gift
4 : lenient judgment of others
synonym see MERCY

cha·ri·va·ri \,shi-və-'rē, 'shi-və-,\ *noun* [French, perhaps from Late Latin *caribaria* headache, from Greek *karēbaria*, from *kara*,

karē head + *barys* heavy — more at CEREBRAL, GRIEVE] (circa 1681)
: SHIVAREE

char·la·tan \'shär-lə-tən\ *noun* [Italian *ciarlatano*, alteration of *cerretano*, literally, inhabitant of Cerreto, from *Cerreto*, Italy] (1618)
1 : QUACK 2 ⟨*charlatans* killing their patients with empirical procedures⟩
2 : one making usually showy pretenses to knowledge or ability : FRAUD, FAKER ◇
— **char·la·tan·ism** \-tə-,ni-zəm\ *noun*
— **char·la·tan·ry** \-rē\ *noun*

Charles's Wain \'chärlz-'wān, ,chärl-zəz-\ *noun* [*Charlemagne*]
: BIG DIPPER

Charles·ton \'chärl-stən\ *noun* [Charleston, S. C.] (1925)
: a lively ballroom dance in which the knees are twisted in and out and the heels are swung sharply outward on each step

char·ley horse \'chär-lē-,hŏrs\ *noun* [from *Charley*, nickname for *Charles*] (1888)
: a muscular pain, cramping, or stiffness especially of the quadriceps that results from a strain or bruise

char·lie *also* **char·ley** \'chär-lē\ *noun, often capitalized* [from the name *Charlie*] (circa 1946)
British : FOOL

Char·lie \'chär-lē\ [from the name *Charlie*] (1946)
— a communications code word for the letter *c*

char·lock \'chär-,läk, -lək\ *noun* [Middle English *cherlok*, from Old English *cerlic*] (before 12th century)
: a mustard (*Brassica kaber*) that is a common weed in grainfields — called also *wild mustard*

char·lotte \'shär-lət\ *noun* [French] (1796)
: a dessert consisting of a filling (as of fruit, whipped cream, or custard) layered with or placed in a mold lined with strips of bread, ladyfingers, or biscuits

char·lotte russe \'shär-lət-'rüs\ *noun* [French, literally, Russian charlotte] (circa 1845)
: a charlotte made with sponge cake or ladyfingers and a whipped-cream or custard-gelatin filling

¹charm \'chärm\ *noun* [Middle English *charme*, from Middle French, from Latin *carmen* song, from *canere* to sing — more at CHANT] (14th century)
1 a : the chanting or reciting of a magic spell : INCANTATION **b** : a practice or expression believed to have magic power
2 : something worn about the person to ward off evil or ensure good fortune : AMULET
3 a : a trait that fascinates, allures, or delights **b** : a physical grace or attraction — used in plural **c** : compelling attractiveness ⟨the island possessed great *charm*⟩
4 : a small ornament worn on a bracelet or chain
5 : a quantum characteristic of subatomic particles that accounts for the unexpectedly long lifetime of the J/psi particle, explains difficulties in the theory of the weak force, is conserved in interactions involving electromagnetism or the strong force, and has a value of zero for most known particles
— **charm·less** \-ləs\ *adjective*

²charm (14th century)
transitive verb
1 a : to affect by or as if by magic : COMPEL **b** : to please, soothe, or delight by compelling attraction ⟨*charms* customers with his suave manner⟩
2 : to endow with or as if with supernatural powers by means of charms; *also* : to protect by or as if by spells, charms, or supernatural influences
3 : to control (an animal) typically by charms ⟨*charm* a snake⟩
intransitive verb

1 : to practice magic and enchantment
2 : to have the effect of a charm : FASCINATE
synonym see ATTRACT
— **charm·er** \'chär-mər\ *noun*

charmed \'chärmd\ *adjective* (1964)
: having the quantum characteristic of charm ⟨a *charmed* antiquark⟩

charmed circle *noun* (1898)
: a group marked by exclusiveness

char·meuse \(,)shär-'müz, -'müs, -'myüz, -'mə(r)z\ *noun* [French, feminine of *charmeuse* charmer, from *charmer* to charm] (1907)
: a fine semilustrous crepe in satin weave

charm·ing \'chär-miŋ\ *adjective* (1663)
: extremely pleasing or delightful : ENTRANCING
— **charm·ing·ly** \-miŋ-lē\ *adverb*

char·nel \'chär-nᵊl\ *noun* [Middle English, from Middle French, from Medieval Latin *carnale*, from Late Latin, neuter of *carnalis* of the flesh — more at CARNAL] (14th century)
: a building or chamber in which bodies or bones are deposited — called also *charnel house*
— **charnel** *adjective*

Cha·ro·lais \,shar-ə-'lā\ *noun* [Charolais, district in eastern France] (1893)
: any of a breed of large white cattle developed in France and used primarily for beef and crossbreeding

Char·on \'kar-ən, 'ker-, -än\ *noun* [Latin, from Greek *Charōn*]
: a son of Erebus who in Greek mythology ferries the souls of the dead over the Styx

char·poy \'chär-,pŏi\ *noun, plural* **charpoys** [Hindi *cārpāī*] (1845)
: a bed used especially in India consisting of a frame strung with tapes or light rope

charr \'chär\ *variant of* ¹CHAR

¹chart \'chärt\ *noun* [Middle French *charte*, from Latin *charta* piece of papyrus, document — more at CARD] (1571)
1 : MAP: as **a** : an outline map exhibiting something (as climatic or magnetic variations) in its geographical aspects **b** : a map for the use of navigators
2 a : a sheet giving information in tabular form **b** : GRAPH **c** : DIAGRAM **d** : a sheet of paper ruled and graduated for use in a recording instrument **e** : a listing by rank (as of sales) — usually used in plural ⟨number one on the *charts* —Tim Cahill⟩
3 : a musical arrangement; *also* : a part in such an arrangement

²chart (1842)
transitive verb
1 : to lay out a plan for
2 : to make a map or chart of

◇ WORD HISTORY
charlatan There was a wide gap in medieval Italy between the handful of learned physicians who had studied medicine at the great schools of Salerno or Bologna and the average peasant who knew only simple folk remedies. This gap was filled by a large group of pretenders to medical skills, who would perform surgery on demand and traveled from one market town to another advertising cures of dubious efficacy. For reasons now osbcure, the region of Umbria in central Italy was particularly noted as the home of itinerant medicine-peddlers, and the Italian word *cerretano*, which literally meant an inhabitant of Cerreto, a town in eastern Umbria, became an epithet for a quack physician. *Cerretano* was blended with the verb *ciarlare* "to chatter," alluding to the patter of the medicine seller, to form *ciarlatano*, in use by the end of the 15th century. *Ciarlatano* was borrowed into French as *charlatan* and hence into English, where it was in use by the early 17th century.

intransitive verb
: to be ranked on a chart ⟨the song *charted* for three months⟩

¹char·ter \'chär-tər\ *noun* [Middle English *chartre*, from Old French, from Medieval Latin *chartula*, from Latin, diminutive of *charta*] (13th century)
1 : a written instrument or contract (as a deed) executed in due form
2 a : a grant or guarantee of rights, franchises, or privileges from the sovereign power of a state or country **b :** a written instrument that creates and defines the franchises of a city, educational institution, or corporation **c :** CONSTITUTION
3 : a written instrument from the authorities of a society creating a lodge or branch
4 : a special privilege, immunity, or exemption
5 : a mercantile lease of a ship or some principal part of it
6 : a charter travel arrangement

²charter *transitive verb* (15th century)
1 a : to establish, enable, or convey by charter **b** *British* **:** CERTIFY ⟨a *chartered* mechanical engineer⟩
2 : to hire, rent, or lease for usually exclusive and temporary use ⟨*chartered* a boat for deep-sea fishing⟩
synonym see HIRE
— **char·ter·er** \-tər-ər\ *noun*

³charter *adjective* (1922)
: of, relating to, or being a travel arrangement in which transportation (as a bus or plane) is hired by and for one specific group of people ⟨a *charter* flight⟩

chartered accountant *noun* (1855)
British **:** a member of a chartered institute of accountants

charter member *noun* (circa 1909)
: an original member of a group (as a society or corporation)
— **charter membership** *noun*

Char·tism \'chär-ˌti-zəm\ *noun* [Medieval Latin *charta* charter, from Latin, document] (1839)
: the principles and practices of a body of 19th century English political reformers advocating better social and industrial conditions for the working classes
— **Char·tist** \'chär-tist\ *noun or adjective*

chart·ist \'chär-tist\ *noun* (1919)
1 : an analyst of market action whose predictions of market courses are based on study of graphic presentations of past market performance
2 : CARTOGRAPHER

char·treuse \shär-'trüz, -'trüs\ *noun* [*Chartreuse*] (1884)
: a variable color averaging a brilliant yellow green

Chartreuse *trademark*
— used for a usually green or yellow liqueur

char·tu·lary \'kär-chə-ˌler-ē\ *noun, plural* **-lar·ies** [Medieval Latin *chartularium*] (1571)
: CARTULARY

char·wom·an \'chär-ˌwu̇-mən\ *noun* [*chare* + *woman*] (1596)
: a cleaning woman especially in a large building

chary \'char-ē, 'cher-\ *adjective* **chari·er;** **-est** [Middle English, sorrowful, dear, from Old English *cearig* sorrowful, from *caru* sorrow — more at CARE] (15th century)
1 *archaic* **:** DEAR, TREASURED
2 : discreetly cautious: as **a :** hesitant and vigilant about dangers and risks **b :** slow to grant, accept, or expend ⟨a person very *chary* of compliments⟩
synonym see CAUTIOUS
— **chari·ly** \'char-ə-lē, 'cher-\ *adverb*

Cha·ryb·dis \kə-'rib-dəs *also* shə- *or* chə-\ *noun* [Latin, from Greek]

: a whirlpool off the coast of Sicily personified in Greek mythology as a female monster — compare SCYLLA

¹chase \'chās\ *noun* (13th century)
1 a : the hunting of wild animals — used with *the* **b :** the act of chasing **:** PURSUIT **c :** an earnest or frenzied seeking after something desired
2 : something pursued **:** QUARRY
3 : a tract of unenclosed land used as a game preserve
4 : STEEPLECHASE 1
5 : a sequence (as in a movie) in which the characters pursue one another

²chase *verb* **chased; chas·ing** [Middle English, from Middle French *chasser*, from (assumed) Vulgar Latin *captiare* — more at CATCH] (14th century)
transitive verb
1 a : to follow rapidly **:** PURSUE **b :** HUNT **c :** to follow regularly or persistently with the intention of attracting or alluring
2 *obsolete* **:** HARASS
3 : to seek out — often used with *down* ⟨detectives *chasing* down clues⟩
4 : to cause to depart or flee **:** DRIVE ⟨*chase* the dog out of the garden⟩
5 : to cause the removal of (a baseball pitcher) by a batting rally
intransitive verb
1 : to chase an animal, person, or thing ⟨*chase* after material possessions⟩
2 : RUSH, HASTEN ⟨*chased* all over town looking for a place to stay⟩ ☆

³chase *transitive verb* **chased; chas·ing** [Middle English *chassen*, modification of Middle French *enchasser* to set] (15th century)
1 a : to ornament (metal) by indenting with a hammer and tools without a cutting edge **b :** to make by such indentation **c :** to set with gems
2 a : GROOVE, INDENT **b :** to cut (a thread) with a chaser

⁴chase *noun* [French *chas* eye of a needle, from Late Latin *capsus* enclosed space, alteration of Latin *capsa* box — more at CASE] (1611)
1 : GROOVE, FURROW
2 : the bore of a cannon
3 a : TRENCH **b :** a channel (as in a wall) for something to lie in or pass through

⁵chase *noun* [probably from French *châsse* frame, reliquary, from Middle French *chasse*, from Latin *capsa*] (1612)
: a rectangular steel or iron frame in which letterpress matter is locked (as for printing)

¹chas·er \'chā-sər\ *noun* (13th century)
1 : one that chases
2 : a mild drink (as beer) taken after hard liquor

²chaser *noun* (1707)
1 : a skilled worker who produces ornamental chasing
2 : a tool for cutting screw threads

Cha·sid *or* **Chas·sid** \'ha-səd, 'kä-\ *noun, plural* **Cha·si·dim** *or* **Chas·si·dim** \'ha-sə-dəm, kä-'sē-\ *variant of* HASID

chasm \'ka-zəm\ *noun* [Latin *chasma*, from Greek; akin to Latin *hiare* to yawn — more at YAWN] (1596)
1 : a deep cleft in the surface of a planet (as the earth) **:** GORGE
2 : a marked division, separation, or difference ⟨a political *chasm* between the two countries⟩

¹chas·sé \sha-'sā\ *intransitive verb* **chas·séd; chas·sé·ing** (1803)
1 : to make a chassé
2 : SASHAY

²chassé *noun* [French, from past participle of *chasser* to chase] (1828)
: a sliding dance step resembling the galop

chasse·pot \'shas-ˌpō, 'sha-sə-\ *noun* [French, from Antoine A. *Chassepot* (died 1905) French inventor] (1869)
: a bolt-action rifle firing a paper cartridge

chas·seur \sha-'sər\ *noun* [French, from Middle French *chasser*] (1795)
1 : HUNTER, HUNTSMAN
2 : one of a body of light cavalry or infantry trained for rapid maneuvering
3 : a liveried attendant **:** FOOTMAN

chas·sis \'cha-sē, 'sha-sē *also* 'cha-səs\ *noun, plural* **chas·sis** \-sēz\ [French *châssis*, from Middle French *chaciz*, from *chasse*] (circa 1864)
: the supporting frame of a structure (as an automobile or television); *also* **:** the frame and working parts (as of an automobile or electronic device) exclusive of the body or housing

chaste \'chāst\ *adjective* **chast·er; chast·est** [Middle English, from Old French, from Latin *castus* pure] (13th century)
1 : innocent of unlawful sexual intercourse
2 : CELIBATE
3 : pure in thought and act **:** MODEST
4 a : severely simple in design or execution **:** AUSTERE ⟨*chaste* classicism⟩ **b :** CLEAN, SPOTLESS ☆
— **chaste·ly** *adverb*
— **chaste·ness** \'chās(t)-nəs\ *noun*

chas·ten \'chā-sᵊn\ *transitive verb* **chastened; chas·ten·ing** \'chās-niŋ, 'chā-sᵊn-iŋ\ [alteration of obsolete English *chaste* to chasten, from Middle English, from Old French *chastier*, from Latin *castigare*, from *castus* + *-igare* (from *agere* to drive) — more at ACTIVE] (13th century)
1 : to correct by punishment or suffering **:** DISCIPLINE; *also* **:** PURIFY
2 a : to prune (as a work or style of art) of excess, pretense, or falsity **:** REFINE **b :** to cause to be more humble or restrained **:** SUBDUE
synonym see PUNISH
— **chas·ten·er** \'chās-nər, 'chā-sᵊn-ər\ *noun*

chas·tise \(ˌ)chas-'tīz\ *transitive verb* **chas·tised; chas·tis·ing** [Middle English *chastisen*, alteration of *chasten*] (14th century)
1 : to inflict punishment on (as by whipping)
2 : to censure severely **:** CASTIGATE

☆ **SYNONYMS**

Chase, pursue, follow, trail mean to go after or on the track of something or someone. CHASE implies going swiftly after and trying to overtake something fleeing or running ⟨a dog *chasing* a cat⟩. PURSUE suggests a continuing effort to overtake, reach, or attain ⟨*pursued* the criminal through narrow streets⟩. FOLLOW puts less emphasis upon speed or intent to overtake ⟨friends *followed* me home in their car⟩. TRAIL may stress a following of tracks or traces rather than a visible object ⟨*trail* deer⟩ ⟨*trailed* a suspect across the country⟩.

Chaste, pure, modest, decent mean free from all taint of what is lewd or salacious. CHASTE primarily implies a refraining from acts or even thoughts or desires that are not virginal or not sanctioned by marriage vows ⟨they maintained *chaste* relations⟩. PURE differs from CHASTE in implying innocence and absence of temptation rather than control of one's impulses and actions ⟨the *pure* of heart⟩. MODEST and DECENT apply especially to deportment and dress as outward signs of inward chastity or purity ⟨preferred more *modest* swimsuits⟩ ⟨*decent* people didn't go to such movies⟩.

\ə\ abut \ᵊ\ kitten \ər\ further \a\ ash \ā\ ace
\ä\ mop, mar \au̇\ out \ch\ chin \e\ bet \ē\ easy
\g\ go \i\ hit \ī\ ice \j\ job \ŋ\ sing \ō\ go
\ȯ\ law \ȯi\ boy \th\ thin \t͟h\ the \ü\ loot \u̇\ foot
\y\ yet \zh\ vision *see also* Guide to Pronunciation

3 *archaic* : CHASTEN 2
synonym see PUNISH
— **chas·tise·ment** \(ˌ)chas-ˈtīz-mənt *also* ˈchas-təz-\ *noun*
— **chas·tis·er** \(ˌ)chas-ˈtī-zər\ *noun*
chas·ti·ty \ˈchas-tə-tē\ *noun* (13th century)
1 : the quality or state of being chaste: as **a** : abstention from unlawful sexual intercourse **b** : abstention from all sexual intercourse **c** : purity in conduct and intention **d** : restraint and simplicity in design or expression
2 : personal integrity
chastity belt *noun* (1931)
: a belt device (as of medieval times) designed to prevent sexual intercourse on the part of the woman wearing it
cha·su·ble \ˈcha-zə-bəl, -zhə-, -sə-\ *noun* [Middle French, from Late Latin *casubla* hooded garment] (14th century)
: a sleeveless outer vestment worn by the officiating priest at mass

chasuble: *1* Gothic, *2* fiddleback

¹chat \ˈchat\ *verb* **chat·ted; chat·ting** [Middle English *chatten*, short for *chatteren*] (15th century) *intransitive verb*
1 : CHATTER, PRATTLE
2 : to talk in an informal or familiar manner *transitive verb*
chiefly British : to talk to; *especially* : to talk lightly, glibly, or flirtatiously with — often used with *up*
²chat *noun* (1530)
1 : idle small talk : CHATTER
2 : light familiar talk; *especially* : CONVERSATION
3 [imitative] : any of several songbirds (as of the genera *Saxicola, Granatellus,* or *Icteria*)
châ·teau \sha-ˈtō\ *noun, plural* **châ·teaus** \-ˈtōz\ *or* **châ·teaux** \-ˈtō(z)\ [French, from Latin *castellum* castle] (1739)
1 : a feudal castle or fortress in France
2 : a large country house : MANSION
3 : a French vineyard estate
cha·teau·bri·and \(ˌ)sha-ˌtō-brē-ˈäⁿ\ *noun, often capitalized* [François René de *Chateaubriand*] (1877)
: a large tenderloin steak usually grilled or broiled and served with a sauce (as béarnaise)
chat·e·lain \ˈsha-tᵊl-ˌän\ *noun* [Middle French *châtelain,* from Latin *castellanus* occupant of a castle] (15th century)
: CASTELLAN
chat·e·laine \ˈsha-tᵊl-ˌän\ *noun* [French *châtelaine,* feminine of *châtelain*] (1845)
1 a : the wife of a castellan : the mistress of a château **b** : the mistress of a household or of a large establishment
2 : a clasp or hook for a watch, purse, or bunch of keys
cha·toy·ance \shə-ˈtȯi-ən(t)s\ *noun* (1910)
: CHATOYANCY
cha·toy·an·cy \-ən(t)-sē\ *noun* (1894)
: the quality or state of being chatoyant
¹cha·toy·ant \shə-ˈtȯi-ənt\ *adjective* [French, from present participle of *chatoyer* to shine like a cat's eyes] (1816)
: having a changeable luster or color with an undulating narrow band of white light ⟨a *chatoyant* gem⟩
²chatoyant *noun* (circa 1828)
: a chatoyant gem
chat show *noun* (1969)
British : TALK SHOW
chat·tel \ˈcha-tᵊl\ *noun* [Middle English *chatel* property, from Middle French, from Medieval Latin *capitale* — more at CATTLE] (14th century)

1 : an item of tangible movable or immovable property except real estate, freehold, and things (as buildings) connected with real property
2 : SLAVE, BONDSMAN
¹chat·ter \ˈcha-tər\ *verb* [Middle English *chatteren,* of imitative origin] (13th century) *intransitive verb*
1 : to utter rapid short sounds suggestive of language but inarticulate and indistinct ⟨squirrels *chattered* angrily⟩ ⟨a *chattering* stream⟩
2 : to talk idly, incessantly, or fast : JABBER
3 a : to click repeatedly or uncontrollably ⟨teeth *chattering* with cold⟩ ⟨machine guns *chattering*⟩ **b** : to vibrate rapidly especially as a consequence of repeated sticking and slipping ⟨*chattering* brakes⟩ *transitive verb*
: to utter rapidly, idly, or indistinctly
— **chat·ter·er** *noun*
²chatter *noun* (13th century)
1 : the action or sound of chattering
2 : idle talk : PRATTLE
chat·ter·box \ˈcha-tər-ˌbäks\ *noun* (1774)
: one who engages in much idle talk
chatter mark *noun* (1888)
1 : a fine undulation formed on the surface of work by a chattering tool
2 : one of a series of short curved cracks on a glaciated rock surface transverse to the glacial striae
chat·ty \ˈcha-tē\ *adjective* **chat·ti·er; -est** (circa 1762)
1 : fond of chatting : TALKATIVE ⟨a *chatty* neighbor⟩
2 : having the style and manner of light familiar conversation ⟨a *chatty* letter⟩
— **chat·ti·ly** \ˈcha-tᵊl-ē\ *adverb*
— **chat·ti·ness** \ˈcha-tē-nəs\ *noun*
¹chauf·feur \ˈshō-fər, shō-ˈ\ *noun* [French, literally, stoker, from *chauffer* to heat, from Middle French *chaufer* — more at CHAFE] (1899)
1 : a person employed to drive a motor vehicle
2 : one that transports others by operating a motor vehicle ◆
²chauffeur *verb* **chauf·feured; chauf·feur·ing** \ˈshō-f(ə-)riŋ, shō-ˈfər-iŋ\ (1917) *intransitive verb*
: to do the work of a chauffeur *transitive verb*
1 : to transport in the manner of a chauffeur ⟨*chauffeurs* the children to school⟩
2 : to operate (as an automobile) as chauffeur
chaul·moo·gra \chȯl-ˈmü-grə\ *noun* [Bengali *cālmugrā*] (circa 1815)
: any of several East Indian trees (family Flacourtiaceae) that yield an acrid oil used especially formerly in treating leprosy and skin diseases
chaunt \ˈchȯnt, ˈchänt\, **chaunt·er** *variant of* CHANT, CHANTER
chaus·sure \shō-ˈsᵫr\ *noun, plural* **chaussures** \same\ [Middle English *chaucer,* from Middle French, from *chaussure,* from *chausser* to put on footwear, from Latin *calceare,* from *calceus* shoe — more at CALZONE] (14th century)
1 : FOOTGEAR
2 *plural* : SHOES
chau·tau·qua \shə-ˈtȯ-kwə\ *noun, often capitalized* [*Chautauqua* Lake] (1873)
: an institution that flourished in the late 19th and early 20th centuries providing popular education combined with entertainment in the form of lectures, concerts, and plays often presented outdoors or in a tent
chau·vin·ism \ˈshō-və-ˌni-zəm\ *noun* [French *chauvinisme,* from Nicolas *Chauvin,* character noted for his excessive patriotism and devotion to Napoleon in Théodore and Hippolyte Cogniard's play *La Cocarde tricolore* (1831)] (1870)
1 : excessive or blind patriotism — compare JINGOISM

2 : undue partiality or attachment to a group or place to which one belongs or has belonged
3 : an attitude of superiority toward members of the opposite sex; *also* : behavior expressive of such an attitude
— **chau·vin·ist** \-və-nist\ *noun or adjective*
— **chau·vin·is·tic** \ˌshō-və-ˈnis-tik\ *adjective*
— **chau·vin·is·ti·cal·ly** \-ti-k(ə-)lē\ *adverb*
¹chaw \ˈchȯ\ *verb* [by alteration] (1506)
: CHEW
²chaw *noun* (1709)
: a chew especially of tobacco
chaw·ba·con \ˈchȯ-ˌbā-kən\ *noun* [¹*chaw* + *bacon*] (1537)
: BUMPKIN, HICK
cha·yo·te \chī-ˈyō-tē, chē-, -(ˌ)tä\ *noun* [Spanish, from Nahuatl *chayohtli*] (1887)
: the pear-shaped fruit of a West Indian annual vine (*Sechium edule*) of the gourd family that is widely cultivated as a vegetable; *also* : the plant — called also *mirliton*
¹cheap \ˈchēp\ *noun* [Middle English *chep,* from Old English *cēap* trade; akin to Old High German *kouf* trade; both from Latin *caupo* tradesman] (before 12th century)
obsolete : BARGAIN
— **on the cheap** : at minimum expense
: CHEAPLY
²cheap *adjective* (1509)
1 a : purchasable below the going price or the real value **b** : charging or obtainable at a low price **c** : depreciated in value (as by currency inflation) ⟨*cheap* dollars⟩
2 : gained with little effort ⟨a *cheap* victory⟩
3 a : of inferior quality or worth : TAWDRY, SLEAZY **b** : contemptible because of lack of any fine, lofty, or redeeming qualities **c** : STINGY
4 a : yielding small satisfaction **b** : paying or able to pay less than going prices
5 *of money* : obtainable at a low rate of interest
— **cheap** *adverb*
— **cheap·ish** \ˈchē-pish\ *adjective*
— **cheap·ish·ly** *adverb*
— **cheap·ly** \ˈchē-plē\ *adverb*
— **cheap·ness** *noun*
cheap·en \ˈchē-pən\ *verb* **cheap·ened; cheap·en·ing** \ˈchēp-niŋ, ˈchē-pə-\ (1574) *transitive verb*
1 [obsolete English *cheap* to price, bid for] *archaic* **a** : to ask the price of **b** : to bid or bargain for
2 a : to make cheap in price or value **b** : to lower in general esteem **c** : to make tawdry, vulgar, or inferior *intransitive verb*
: to become cheap
cheap·ie \ˈchē-pē\ *noun* (circa 1898)
: one that is cheap; *especially* : an inexpensively produced motion picture

◇ WORD HISTORY
chauffeur *Chauffeur* in French means literally "stoker," a person who maintains the fire that powers the steam engine of a locomotive or ship. In the 1890s, *chauffeur* also began to be used for the driver of an automobile, who in effect stoked the engine mechanically with the accelerator. Earlier, the compound *chauffeur-mécanicien* "stoker-engineer" was applied to someone who both stoked an engine and ran it, and it is possible that *chauffeur* in the sense "driver" is actually short for *chauffeur-mécanicien*. In any case, the French word has had a successful career in a number of other European languages, from Spanish *chófer* to Russian *shofyor,* usually denoting a professional driver of a motor vehicle. In English, *chauffeur* often refers to someone who is hired to drive a passenger car.

— **cheapie** *adjective*
¹cheap·jack \'chēp-ˌjak\ *noun* [*cheap* + the name *Jack*] (1851)
1 : a haggling huckster
2 : a dealer in cheap merchandise
²cheapjack *adjective* (1865)
1 : being inferior, cheap, or worthless ⟨*cheapjack* movie companies⟩
2 : unscrupulously opportunistic ⟨*cheapjack* speculators⟩
cheapo \'chē-(ˌ)pō\ *adjective* (1972)
: CHEAP
cheap shot *noun* (1971)
1 : an act of deliberate roughness against a defenseless opponent especially in a contact sport
2 : a critical statement that takes unfair advantage of a known weakness of the target
cheap·skate \'chēp-ˌskāt\ *noun* (1896)
: a miserly or stingy person; *especially* **:** one who tries to avoid paying a fair share of costs or expenses
¹cheat \'chēt\ (1590)
transitive verb
1 : to deprive of something valuable by the use of deceit or fraud
2 : to influence or lead by deceit, trick, or artifice
3 : to elude or thwart by or as if by outwitting ⟨*cheat* death⟩
intransitive verb
1 a : to practice fraud or trickery **b :** to violate rules dishonestly (as at cards or on an examination)
2 : to be sexually unfaithful — usually used with *on* ☆
— **cheat·er** *noun*
²cheat *noun* [earlier *cheat* forfeited property, from Middle English *chet* escheat, short for *eschete* — more at ESCHEAT] (1631)
1 : the act or an instance of fraudulently deceiving **:** DECEPTION, FRAUD
2 : one that cheats **:** PRETENDER, DECEIVER
3 : any of several grasses; *especially* **:** the common chess (*Bromus secalinus*)
4 : the obtaining of property from another by an intentional active distortion of the truth
¹check \'chek\ *noun* [Middle English *chek*, from Middle French *eschec*, from Arabic *shāh*, from Persian, literally, king; akin to Greek *ktasthai* to acquire, Sanskrit *kṣatra* dominion] (15th century)
1 : exposure of a chess king to an attack from which he must be protected or moved to safety
2 a : a sudden stoppage of a forward course or progress **:** ARREST **b :** a checking of an opposing player (as in ice hockey)
3 : a sudden pause or break in a progression
4 *archaic* **:** REPRIMAND, REBUKE
5 : one that arrests, limits, or restrains **:** RESTRAINT ⟨against all *checks*, rebukes, and manners, I must advance —Shakespeare⟩
6 a : a standard for testing and evaluation **:** CRITERION **b :** EXAMINATION **c :** INSPECTION, INVESTIGATION ⟨a loyalty *check* on government employees⟩ **d :** the act of testing or verifying; *also* **:** the sample or unit used for testing or verifying
7 : a written order directing a bank to pay money as instructed **:** DRAFT
8 a : a ticket or token showing ownership or identity or indicating payment made ⟨a baggage *check*⟩ **b :** a counter in various games **c :** a slip indicating the amount due **:** BILL
9 [Middle English *chek*, short for *cheker* checker] **a :** a pattern in squares that resembles a checkerboard **b :** a fabric woven or printed with such a design
10 : a mark typically √ placed beside an item to show it has been noted, examined, or verified
11 : CRACK, BREAK
— **check·less** \'che-kləs\ *adjective*
— **in check :** under restraint or control
²check (14th century)
transitive verb

1 : to put (a chess king) in check
2 *chiefly dialect* **:** REBUKE, REPRIMAND
3 a : to slow or bring to a stop **:** BRAKE ⟨hastily *checked* the impulse⟩ **b :** to block the progress of (as a hockey player)
4 a : to restrain or diminish the action or force of **:** CONTROL **b :** to slack or ease off and then belay again (as a rope)
5 a : to compare with a source, original, or authority **:** VERIFY **b :** to inspect, examine, or look at appraisingly — usually used with *out* or *over* ⟨*checking* out new cars⟩ **c :** to mark with a check as examined, verified, or satisfactory — often used with *off* ⟨*checked* off each item⟩
6 a : to consign (as luggage) to a common carrier from which one has purchased a passenger ticket ⟨*checked* our bags before boarding⟩ **b :** to ship or accept for shipment under such a consignment
7 : to mark into squares **:** CHECKER
8 : to leave or accept for safekeeping in a checkroom
9 : to make checks or chinks **:** cause to crack ⟨the sun *checks* timber⟩
intransitive verb
1 a *of a dog* **:** to stop in a chase especially when scent is lost **b :** to halt through caution, uncertainty, or fear **:** STOP
2 a : to investigate conditions ⟨*checked* on the passengers' safety⟩ **b :** to prove to be consistent or truthful ⟨the description *checks* with the photograph⟩ — often used with *out* ⟨the story *checked* out⟩
3 : to draw a check on a bank
4 : to waive the right to initiate the betting in a round of poker
5 : CRACK, SPLIT
synonym see RESTRAIN
— **check into 1 :** to check in at ⟨*check into* a hotel⟩ **2 :** INVESTIGATE
— **check up on :** INVESTIGATE
check·able *adjective* (1877)
1 : capable of being checked ⟨a *checkable* story⟩
2 : held in or being a bank account on which checks can be drawn ⟨*checkable* deposits⟩
check·book \'chek-ˌbuk\ *noun* (circa 1846)
: a book containing blank checks to be drawn on a bank
checkbook journalism *noun* (1975)
: the practice of paying someone for a news story and especially for granting an interview
¹check·er \'che-kər\ *noun* [Middle English *cheker*, from Middle French *eschequier*, from *eschec*] (14th century)
1 *archaic* **:** CHESSBOARD
2 : a square or spot resembling the markings of a checkerboard
3 [singular of *checkers*] **:** a piece in checkers
²checker *transitive verb* **check·ered; check·er·ing** \'che-k(ə-)riŋ\ (15th century)
1 a : to variegate with different colors or shades **b :** to vary with contrasting elements or situations ⟨had a *checkered* career⟩
2 : to mark into squares
³checker *noun* (1535)
1 : one that checks ⟨a fact *checker*⟩ ⟨spelling *checker*⟩
2 : an employee who checks out purchases in a self-service store
check·er·ber·ry \'che-kər-ˌber-ē\ *noun* [*checker* wild service tree + *berry*] (1776)
1 : the spicy red berrylike fruit of an American wintergreen (*Gaultheria procumbens*)
2 : a plant producing checkerberries
check·er·board \-ˌbȯrd, -ˌbȯrd\ *noun* (1775)
1 : a board used in various games (as checkers) with usually 64 squares in 2 alternating colors
2 : something that has a pattern or arrangement like a checkerboard
check·ers \'che-kərz\ *noun plural but singular in construction* (1712)
: a checkerboard game for 2 players each with 12 pieces

check–in \'che-ˌkin\ *noun* (1927)
: an act or instance of checking in
check in (1918)
intransitive verb
1 : to register at a hotel
2 : to report one's presence or arrival ⟨*check in* at a convention⟩
transitive verb
: to satisfy all requirements in returning ⟨*check in* the equipment after using⟩
checking account *noun* (circa 1909)
: a bank account against which the depositor can draw checks
check·list \'chek-ˌlist\ *noun* (1853)
: a list of things to be checked or done ⟨a pilot's *checklist* before takeoff⟩; *also* **:** a comprehensive list ⟨a *checklist* of bird species⟩
check mark *noun* (1917)
: CHECK 10
— **check·mark** *transitive verb*
¹check·mate \'chek-ˌmāt\ *transitive verb* [Middle English *chekmaten*, from *chekmate*, interjection used to announce checkmate, from Middle French *eschec mat*, from Arabic *shāh māt*, from Persian, literally, the king is left unable to escape] (14th century)
1 : to arrest, thwart, or counter completely
2 : to check (a chess opponent's king) so that escape is impossible
²checkmate *noun* (15th century)
1 a : the act of checkmating **b :** the situation of a checkmated king
2 : a complete check
check·off \'che-ˌkȯf\ *noun* (1911)
1 a : the deduction of union dues from a worker's paycheck by the employer **b :** designation on an income tax return of a small amount of money to be applied to a special fund (as for financing political campaigns)
2 : AUTOMATIC 2
check off (1839)
transitive verb
1 : to eliminate from further consideration
2 : to deduct (union dues) from a worker's paycheck
intransitive verb
: to change a play at the line of scrimmage in football by calling an automatic
check·out \'che-ˌkaut\ *noun* (1933)
1 : the action or an instance of checking out
2 : the time at which a lodger must vacate a room (as in a hotel) or be charged for retaining it
3 : a counter or area in a store where goods are checked out
4 a : the action of examining and testing something for performance, suitability, or readiness **b :** the action of familiarizing oneself with the operation of a mechanical thing (as an airplane)
check out (1921)
intransitive verb

☆ SYNONYMS
Cheat, cozen, defraud, swindle mean to get something by dishonesty or deception. CHEAT suggests using trickery that escapes observation ⟨*cheated* me out of a dollar⟩. COZEN implies artful persuading or flattering to attain a thing or a purpose ⟨always able to *cozen* her grandfather out of a few dollars⟩. DEFRAUD stresses depriving one of his or her rights and usually connotes deliberate perversion of the truth ⟨*defrauded* of her inheritance by an unscrupulous lawyer⟩. SWINDLE implies large-scale cheating by misrepresentation or abuse of confidence ⟨*swindled* of their savings by con artists⟩.

\ə\ abut \ᵊ\ kitten \ər\ **further** \a\ ash \ā\ ace \ä\ mop, mar \au̇\ **out** \ch\ chin \e\ bet \ē\ **easy** \g\ go \i\ hit \ī\ ice \j\ job \ŋ\ sing \ō\ law \ȯi\ boy \th\ **thin** \th̲\ **the** \ü\ loot \u̇\ **foot** \y\ yet \zh\ vision *see also* Guide to Pronunciation

: to vacate and pay for one's lodging (as at a hotel)
transitive verb
1 : to satisfy all requirements in taking away ⟨*checked out* a library book⟩
2 a : to itemize and total the cost of and receive payment for (outgoing merchandise) especially in a self-service store **b :** to have the cost totaled and pay for (purchases) at a checkout

check·point \'chek-,point\ *noun* (1926)
: a point at which a check is performed ⟨vehicles were inspected at various *checkpoints*⟩

check·rein \-,rān\ *noun* (circa 1809)
1 : a short rein looped over a hook on the saddle of a harness to prevent a horse from lowering its head
2 : a branch rein connecting the driving rein of one horse of a pair with the bit of the other

check·room \-,rüm, -,rùm\ *noun* (1900)
: a room at which baggage, parcels, or clothing is checked

check·up \'che-,kəp\ *noun* (1921)
: EXAMINATION; *especially* **:** a general physical examination

check valve *noun* (circa 1877)
: a valve that permits flow in one direction only

ched·dar \'che-dər\ *noun, often capitalized* [*Cheddar*, England] (circa 1661)
: a hard white, yellow, or orange smooth-textured cheese with a flavor that ranges from mild to strong as the cheese matures — called also *cheddar cheese*

che·der \'kä-dər, 'ke-\ *variant of* HEDER

chee·cha·ko \chē-'chä-(,)kō, -'chò- *also* -'cha-\ *noun, plural* **-kos** [Chinook Jargon, from *chee* new (from Lower Chinook *čxi* right away) + *chako* come, from Nootka *čokʷaʾ* come, imperative] (1897)
: TENDERFOOT 1 — used chiefly in Alaska

¹cheek \'chēk\ *noun* [Middle English *cheke*, from Old English *cēace*; akin to Middle Low German *kāke* jawbone] (before 12th century)
1 : the fleshy side of the face below the eye and above and to the side of the mouth; *broadly* **:** the lateral aspect of the head
2 : something suggestive of the human cheek in position or form; *especially* **:** one of two laterally paired parts
3 : insolent boldness and self-assurance
4 : BUTTOCK 1
synonym see TEMERITY
— **cheek·ful** \-,fúl\ *noun*

²cheek *transitive verb* (1840)
chiefly British **:** to speak rudely or impudently to

cheek·bone \'chēk-,bōn\ *noun* (circa 1775)
: the prominence below the eye that is formed by the zygomatic bone; *also* **:** ZYGOMATIC BONE

cheek by jowl *adverb* (1577)
: SIDE BY SIDE

cheeked \'chēkt\ *adjective* (1592)
: having cheeks of a specified nature — used in combination ⟨rosy-*cheeked*⟩

cheek tooth *noun* (14th century)
: any of the molar or premolar teeth

cheeky \'chē-kē\ *adjective* **cheek·i·er; -est** (1859)
: having or showing cheek **:** IMPUDENT
— **cheek·i·ly** \-kə-lē\ *adverb*
— **cheek·i·ness** \-kē-nəs\ *noun*

cheep \'chēp\ *intransitive verb* [imitative] (1513)
1 : to utter faint shrill sounds **:** PEEP
2 : to utter a single word or sound
— **cheep** *noun*

¹cheer \'chir\ *noun* [Middle English *chere* face, cheer, from Old French, face, from Medieval Latin *cara*, probably from Greek *kara* head, face — more at CEREBRAL] (13th century)
1 a *obsolete* **:** FACE **b** *archaic* **:** facial expression
2 : state of mind or heart **:** SPIRIT ⟨be of good *cheer* —Matthew 9:2 (Authorized Version)⟩

3 : lightness of mind and feeling **:** ANIMATION, GAIETY
4 : hospitable entertainment **:** WELCOME
5 : food and drink for a feast **:** FARE
6 : something that gladdens ⟨words of *cheer*⟩
7 : a shout of applause or encouragement

²cheer (14th century)
transitive verb
1 a : to instill with hope or courage **:** COMFORT — usually used with *up* **b :** to make glad or happy — usually used with *up*
2 : to urge on or encourage especially by shouts ⟨*cheered* the team on⟩
3 : to applaud with shouts
intransitive verb
1 *obsolete* **:** to be mentally or emotionally disposed
2 : to grow or be cheerful **:** REJOICE — usually used with *up*
3 : to utter a shout of applause or triumph
— **cheer·er** *noun*

cheer·ful \'chir-fəl\ *adjective* (15th century)
1 a : full of good spirits **:** MERRY **b :** UNGRUDGING ⟨*cheerful* obedience⟩
2 : conducive to cheer **:** likely to dispel gloom or worry ⟨sunny *cheerful* room⟩
— **cheer·ful·ly** \-f(ə-)lē\ *adverb*
— **cheer·ful·ness** \-fəl-nəs\ *noun*

cheer·io \,chir-ē-'ō\ *interjection* [*cheery* + *-o*] (1910)
chiefly British — usually used as a farewell and sometimes as a greeting or toast

cheer·lead·er \'chir-,lē-dər\ *noun* (1903)
: one that calls for and directs organized cheering (as at a football game)
— **cheer·lead** \-,lēd\ *transitive verb*

cheer·less \-ləs\ *adjective* (1579)
: lacking qualities that cheer **:** BLEAK, JOYLESS ⟨a *cheerless* room⟩
— **cheer·less·ly** *adverb*
— **cheer·less·ness** *noun*

cheers \'chirz\ *interjection* (1919)
— used as a toast

cheery \'chir-ē\ *adjective* **cheer·i·er; -est** (15th century)
1 : marked by cheerfulness or good spirits
2 : causing or suggesting cheerfulness
— **cheer·i·ly** \'chir-ə-lē\ *adverb*
— **cheer·i·ness** \'chir-ē-nəs\ *noun*

¹cheese \'chēz\ *noun, often attributive* [Middle English *chese*, from Old English *cēse*, from Latin *caseus* cheese] (before 12th century)
1 a : a food consisting of the coagulated, compressed, and usually ripened curd of milk separated from the whey **b :** an often cylindrical cake of this food
2 : something resembling cheese in shape or consistency

²cheese *transitive verb* **cheesed; cheesing** [origin unknown] (circa 1811)
: to put an end to **:** STOP
— **cheese it** — used in the imperative as a warning of danger ⟨*cheese it*, the cops⟩

³cheese *noun* [perhaps from Urdu *chīz* thing] (1920)
slang **:** someone important

cheese·burg·er \'chēz-,bər-gər\ *noun* [*cheese* + ham*burger*] (circa 1938)
: a hamburger topped with a slice of cheese

cheese·cake \-,kāk\ *noun* (15th century)
1 : a dessert consisting of a creamy filling usually containing cheese baked in a pastry or pressed-crumb shell
2 : a photographic display of shapely and scantily clothed female figures — compare BEEFCAKE

cheese·cloth \-,klòth\ *noun* [from its use in the making of cheese] (14th century)
: a very lightweight unsized cotton gauze

cheese·par·ing \-,par-in, -,per-\ *noun* (1597)
1 : something worthless or insignificant
2 : miserly economizing
— **cheeseparing** *adjective*

cheesy \'chē-zē\ *adjective* **chees·i·er; -est** (14th century)

1 a : resembling or suggesting cheese especially in consistency or odor **b :** containing cheese
2 : SHABBY 3c, CHEAP
— **chees·i·ness** *noun*

chee·tah \'chē-tə\ *noun, plural* **cheetahs** *also* **cheetah** [Hindi *cītā* leopard, from Sanskrit *citraka*, from *citra* bright, variegated; akin to Old High German *heitar* bright — more at -HOOD] (1610)
: a long-legged spotted swift-moving African and formerly Asian cat (*Acinonyx jubatus*) about the size of a small leopard that has blunt nonretractile claws and is often trained to run down game

cheetah

chef \'shef\ *noun* [French, short for *chef de cuisine* head of the kitchen] (1826)
1 : a skilled cook who manages the kitchen (as of a restaurant)
2 : COOK
— **chef** *intransitive verb*
— **chef·dom** \-dəm\ *noun*

chef d'oeu·vre \shā-dœvrᵊ, (,)shā-'də(r)v\ *noun, plural* **chefs d'oeuvre** \-'də(r)v(z)\ [French *chef-d'oeuvre*, literally, leading work] (1619)
: a masterpiece especially in art or literature

che·la \'kē-lə\ *noun, plural* **che·lae** \-(,)lē\ [New Latin, from Greek *chēlē* claw] (1646)
: a pincerlike organ or claw borne by a limb of a crustacean or arachnid

¹che·late \'kē-,lāt *also* 'chē-\ *adjective* (1826)
1 : resembling or having chelae
2 : of, relating to, or being a chelate

²chelate *verb* **che·lat·ed; che·lat·ing** (1922)
transitive verb
: to combine with (a metal) so as to form a chelate ring
intransitive verb
: to react so as to form a chelate ring
— **che·lat·able** \-,lā-tə-bəl\ *adjective*
— **che·la·tion** \kē-'lā-shən *also* chē-\ *noun*
— **che·la·tor** \-,lā-tər\ *noun*

³chelate *noun* (1943)
: a compound having a ring structure that usually contains a metal ion held by coordinate bonds

che·lic·era \ki-'li-sə-rə\ *noun, plural* **-er·ae** \-,rē\ [New Latin, from French *chélicère*, from Greek *chēlē* + *keras* horn — more at HORN] (1835)
: one of the anterior pair of appendages of an arachnid often specialized as fangs
— **che·lic·er·al** \-sə-rəl\ *adjective*

che·li·ped \'kē-lə-,ped\ *noun* [Greek *chēlē* claw + English *-i-* + *-ped*] (1869)
: one of the pair of legs that bears the large chelae in decapod crustaceans

Chel·le·an *or* **Chel·li·an** \'she-lē-ən\ *adjective* [French *chelléen*, from *Chelles*, France] (1893)
: ABBEVILLIAN

che·lo·ni·an \ki-'lō-nē-ən\ *noun* [Greek *che-lōnē* tortoise] (1828)
: TURTLE
— **chelonian** *adjective*

chem- *or* **chemo-** *also* **chemi-** *combining form* [New Latin, from Late Greek *chēmeia* alchemy — more at ALCHEMY]
1 : chemical ⟨*chemo*taxis⟩
2 : chemically ⟨*chemi*sorb⟩

chem·ic \'ke-mik\ *adjective* [New Latin *chimicus* alchemist, from Medieval Latin *alchimicus*, from *alchymia* alchemy] (1576)
1 *archaic* **:** ALCHEMIC
2 : CHEMICAL

¹chem·i·cal \'ke-mi-kəl\ *adjective* (1576)

1 : of, relating to, used in, or produced by chemistry
2 a : acting or operated or produced by chemicals **b :** detectable by chemical means
— **chem·i·cal·ly** \-mi-k(ə-)lē\ *adverb*
²**chemical** *noun* (1747)
: a substance obtained by a chemical process or used for producing a chemical effect
chemical engineering *noun* (1888)
: engineering dealing with the industrial application of chemistry
chemical warfare *noun* (1917)
: tactical warfare using incendiary mixtures, smokes, or irritant, burning, poisonous, or asphyxiating gases
chemical weapon *noun* (1980)
: a weapon used in chemical warfare
chemi·lu·mi·nes·cence \ˌke-mē-ˌlü-mə-'ne-sᵊn(t)s, ˌkē-\ *noun* [International Scientific Vocabulary] (1889)
: luminescence (as bioluminescence) due to chemical reaction
— **chemi·lu·mi·nes·cent** \-'ne-sᵊnt\ *adjective*
che·min de fer \shə-ˌman-də-'fer\ *noun, plural* **che·mins de fer** \same\ [French, literally, railroad] (1891)
: a card game in which two hands are dealt, any number of players may bet against the dealer, and the winning hand is the one that comes closer to but does not exceed a count of nine on two or three cards
chemi·os·mot·ic \ˌke-mē-äz-'mä-tik, ˌkē-\ *adjective* (1966)
: relating to or being a hypothesis that seeks to explain the mechanism of ATP formation in oxidative phosphorylation by mitochondria and chloroplasts without recourse to the formation of high-energy intermediates by postulating the formation of an energy gradient of hydrogen ions across the organelle membranes that results in the reversible movement of hydrogen ions to the outside and is generated by electron transport or the activity of electron carriers
che·mise \shə-'mēz, *sometimes* -'mēs\ *noun* [Middle English, from Old French, shirt, from Late Latin *camisia*] (13th century)
1 : a woman's one-piece undergarment
2 : a loose straight-hanging dress
chem·i·sette \ˌshe-mi-'zet\ *noun* [French, diminutive of *chemise*] (1807)
: a woman's garment; *especially* **:** one (as of lace) to fill the open front of a dress
chem·i·sorb \'ke-mi-ˌsȯrb, 'kē-, -ˌzȯrb\ *transitive verb* [chem- + -sorb (as in *adsorb*)] (1935)
: to take up and hold usually irreversibly by chemical forces
— **chem·i·sorp·tion** \ˌke-mi-'sȯrp-shən, ˌkē-, -'zȯrp-\ *noun*
chem·ist \'ke-mist\ *noun* [New Latin *chimista*, short for Medieval Latin *alchimista*] (1562)
1 a *obsolete* **:** ALCHEMIST **b :** one trained in chemistry
2 *British* **:** PHARMACIST
chem·is·try \'ke-mə-strē\ *noun, plural* **-tries** (1646)
1 : a science that deals with the composition, structure, and properties of substances and with the transformations that they undergo
2 a : the composition and chemical properties of a substance ⟨the *chemistry* of iron⟩ **b :** chemical processes and phenomena (as of an organism) ⟨blood *chemistry*⟩
3 : a strong mutual attraction, attachment, or sympathy ⟨they have a special *chemistry*⟩
che·mo \'kē-(ˌ)mō\ *noun* (1982)
: CHEMOTHERAPY
che·mo·au·to·tro·phic \ˌkē-mō-ˌȯ-tə-'trō-fik *also* ˌkē-\ *adjective* (1945)
: being autotrophic and oxidizing an inorganic compound as a source of energy ⟨*chemoautotrophic* bacteria⟩

— **che·mo·au·tot·ro·phy** \-ȯ-'tä-trə-fē\ *noun*
che·mo·pro·phy·lax·is \-ˌprō-fə-'lak-səs *also* -ˌprä-fə-\ *noun* (1936)
: the prevention of infectious disease by the use of chemical agents
— **che·mo·pro·phy·lac·tic** \-'lak-tik\ *adjective*
che·mo·re·cep·tion \-ri-'sep-shən\ *noun* [International Scientific Vocabulary] (1919)
: the physiological reception of chemical stimuli
— **che·mo·re·cep·tive** \-'sep-tiv\ *adjective*
che·mo·re·cep·tor \-ri-'sep-tər\ *noun* [International Scientific Vocabulary] (1906)
: a sense organ (as a taste bud) responding to chemical stimuli
che·mo·sur·gery \ˌkē-mō-'sərj-rē, -'sər-jə-rē\ *noun* (circa 1944)
: chemical removal of diseased or unwanted tissue
— **che·mo·sur·gi·cal** \-'sər-ji-kəl\ *adjective*
che·mo·syn·the·sis \-'sin(t)-thə-səs\ *noun* [New Latin] (1901)
: synthesis of organic compounds (as in living cells) by energy derived from chemical reactions
— **che·mo·syn·thet·ic** \-sin-'the-tik\ *adjective*
che·mo·tac·tic \-'tak-tik\ *adjective* (1893)
: involving, inducing, or exhibiting chemotaxis
— **che·mo·tac·ti·cal·ly** \-ti-k(ə-)lē\ *adverb*
che·mo·tax·is \-'tak-səs\ *noun* [New Latin] (circa 1887)
: orientation or movement of an organism or cell in relation to chemical agents
che·mo·tax·on·o·my \-(ˌ)tak-'sä-nə-mē\ *noun* (1963)
: the classification of plants and animals based on similarities and differences in biochemical composition
— **che·mo·tax·o·nom·ic** \-ˌtak-sə-'nä-mik\ *adjective*
— **che·mo·tax·on·o·mist** \-(ˌ)tak-'sä-nə-mist\ *noun*
che·mo·ther·a·peu·tic \-ˌther-ə-'pyü-tik\ *adjective* (1907)
: of, relating to, or used in chemotherapy
— **chemotherapeutic** *noun*
— **che·mo·ther·a·peu·ti·cal·ly** \-ti-k(ə-)lē\ *adverb*
che·mo·ther·a·py \-'ther-ə-pē\ *noun* [International Scientific Vocabulary] (1910)
: the use of chemical agents in the treatment or control of disease or mental illness
— **che·mo·ther·a·pist** \-pist\ *noun*
che·mot·ro·pism \ki-'mä-trə-ˌpi-zəm, ke-\ *noun* [International Scientific Vocabulary] (1897)
: orientation of cells or organisms in relation to chemical stimuli
che·nille \shə-'nē(ə)l\ *noun* [French, literally, caterpillar, from Latin *canicula*, diminutive of *canis* dog; from its hairy appearance — more at HOUND] (circa 1739)
1 : a wool, cotton, silk, or rayon yarn with protruding pile; *also* **:** a pile-face fabric with a filling of this yarn
2 : an imitation of chenille yarn or fabric
che·no·pod \'kē-nə-ˌpäd, 'ke-\ *noun* [ultimately from Greek *chēn* goose + *podion*, diminutive of *pod-*, *pous* foot — more at GOOSE, FOOT] (1555)
: any plant of the goosefoot family
cheong·sam \'chȯŋ-ˌsäm\ *noun* [Chinese (Guangdong) *chèuhng-sāam*, literally, long gown] (1952)
: an oriental dress with a slit skirt and a mandarin collar
cheque \'chek\ *chiefly British variant of* ¹CHECK 7

che·quer \'che-kər\ *chiefly British variant of* CHECKER
cher·i·moya \ˌcher-ə-'mȯi-ə, ˌchir-\ *noun* [Spanish *chirimoya*] (1736)
: a round, oblong, or heart-shaped fruit with a pitted rind that is borne by a widely cultivated tropical American tree (*Annona cherimola*) of the custard-apple family; *also* **:** this tree
cher·ish \'cher-ish\ *transitive verb* [Middle English *cherisshen*, from Middle French *cheriss-*, stem of *cherir* to cherish, from Old French, from *chier* dear, from Latin *carus* — more at CHARITY] (14th century)
1 a : to hold dear **:** feel or show affection for **b :** to keep or cultivate with care and affection
2 : to entertain or harbor in the mind deeply and resolutely ⟨still *cherishes* that memory⟩
synonym SEE APPRECIATE
— **cher·ish·able** \-i-shə-bəl\ *adjective*
— **cher·ish·er** \-i-shər\ *noun*
cher·no·zem \ˌcher-nə-'zyȯm, -'zem\ *noun* [Russian, from *chёrnyĭ* black + *zemlya* earth] (1841)
: any of a group of dark-colored zonal soils with a deep rich humus horizon found in regions (as the grasslands of central North America) of temperate to cool climate
— **cher·no·zem·ic** \-'zyȯ-mik, -'ze-\ *adjective*
Cher·o·kee \'cher-ə-(ˌ)kē\ *noun, plural* **Cherokee** *or* **Cherokees** [probably from Creek *tciloki* people of a different speech] (1674)
1 : a member of an American Indian people originally of Tennessee and North Carolina
2 : the language of the Cherokee people
Cherokee rose *noun* (1823)
: a Chinese climbing rose (*Rosa laevigata*) with a fragrant white blossom
che·root \shə-'rüt, chə-\ *noun* [Tamil *curuttu*, literally, roll] (circa 1679)
: a cigar cut square at both ends
cher·ry \'cher-ē\ *noun, plural* **cherries** [Middle English *chery*, from Old North French *cherise* (taken as a plural), from Late Latin *ceresia*, from Latin *cerasus* cherry tree, from Greek *kerasos*] (14th century)
1 a : any of numerous trees and shrubs (genus *Prunus*) of the rose family that bear pale yellow to deep red or blackish smooth-skinned drupes enclosing a smooth seed and that include some cultivated for their fruits or ornamental flowers — compare SWEET CHERRY **b :** the fruit of a cherry **c :** the wood of a cherry
2 : a variable color averaging a moderate red
3 a : HYMEN **b :** VIRGINITY
word history SEE SHERRY
— **cher·ry·like** \-ˌlīk\ *adjective*
cherry bomb *noun* (1953)
: a powerful globular red firecracker
cherry picker *noun* (circa 1944)
: a traveling crane equipped for holding a passenger at the end of the boom
cher·ry·stone \'cher-ē-ˌstōn\ *noun* (1880)
: a small quahog
cherry tomato *noun* (1847)
: a small globose red or orange tomato borne in long dense clusters; *also* **:** a plant (*Lycopersicon lypersicum cerasiforme*) bearing cherry tomatoes
chert \'chərt, 'chat\ *noun* [origin unknown] (1679)
: a rock resembling flint and consisting essentially of a large amount of fibrous chalcedony with smaller amounts of cryptocrystalline quartz and amorphous silica
— **cherty** \'chər-tē, 'cha-\ *adjective*
cher·ub \'cher-əb\ *noun, plural usually* **cher·u·bim** \'cher-ə-ˌbim, 'ker- *also* 'cher-yə-\ [Latin, from Greek *cheroub*, from Hebrew *kĕrūbh*] (13th century)

\ə\ abut \ᵊ\ kitten \ər\ further \a\ ash \ā\ ace
\ä\ mop, mar \au̇\ out \ch\ chin \e\ bet \ē\ easy
\g\ go \i\ hit \ī\ ice \j\ job \ŋ\ sing \ō\ go
\ȯ\ law \ȯi\ boy \th\ thin \th̲\ the \ü\ loot \u̇\ foot
\y\ yet \zh\ vision *see also* Guide to Pronunciation

1 *plural* **:** an order of angels — see CELESTIAL HIERARCHY
2 *plural usually* **cherubs a :** a beautiful usually winged child in painting and sculpture **b :** an innocent-looking usually chubby and rosy person
— **che·ru·bic** \chə-'rü-bik *also* 'cher-ə-\ *adjective*
— **che·ru·bi·cal·ly** \-bi-k(ə-)lē\ *adverb*
— **cher·ub·like** \'cher-əb-,līk\ *adjective*
cher·vil \'chər-vəl\ *noun* [Middle English *cherville*, from Old English *cerfille*, from Latin *caerefolium*, modification of (assumed) Greek *chairephyllon*, from *chairein* to rejoice + *phyllon* leaf — more at YEARN, BLADE] (before 12th century)
: an aromatic herb (*Anthriscus cerefolium*) of the carrot family with divided leaves that are often used in soups and salads; *also* **:** any of several related plants
Ches·a·peake Bay retriever \'che-sə-,pēk-'bā-\ *noun* (1891)
: any of a breed of large brown sporting dogs developed in Maryland and having a dense oily water-shedding coat
Chesh·ire cat \'che-shər-\ *noun* [*Cheshire*, England] (1866)
: a broadly grinning cat in Lewis Carroll's *Alice's Adventures in Wonderland*
Cheshire cheese *noun* (1597)
: a cheese similar to cheddar made chiefly in Cheshire, England
¹chess \'ches\ *noun* [Middle English *ches*, from Middle French *esches*, accusative plural of *eschec* check at chess — more at CHECK] (14th century)
: a game for 2 players each of whom moves 16 pieces according to fixed rules across a checkerboard and tries to checkmate the opponent's king

chessboard with chess pieces arranged as at the beginning of a game

²chess *noun* [origin unknown] (1736)
: a weedy annual bromegrass (*Bromus secalinus*) widely distributed as a weed especially in grain; *broadly* **:** any of several weedy bromegrasses
chess·board \'ches-,bōrd, -,bȯrd\ *noun* (15th century)
: a checkerboard used in the game of chess
chess·man \-,man, -mən\ *noun* (15th century)
: any of the pieces used in chess
chess pie *noun* [perhaps alteration of *chest*] (1932)
: a pie or tart with a filling made especially of eggs, butter, and sugar
chest \'chest\ *noun* [Middle English, from Old English *cest, cist* chest, box, from Latin *cista*, from Greek *kistē* basket, hamper] (before 12th century)
1 a : a container for storage or shipping; *especially* **:** a box with a lid used especially for the safekeeping of belongings **b :** a cupboard used especially for the storing of medicines or first-aid supplies
2 : the place where money of a public institution is kept **:** TREASURY; *also* **:** the fund so kept
3 a : THORAX; *especially* **:** the human thorax ⟨a pain in the *chest*⟩ **b :** BREAST 2a ⟨a hairy *chest*⟩
— **chest·ful** \-,fu̇l\ *noun*
chest·ed \'ches-təd\ *adjective* (1662)
: having a chest of a specified kind — used in combination ⟨flat-*chested*⟩
ches·ter·field \'ches-tər-,fēld\ *noun* [from a 19th century Earl of *Chesterfield*] (1852)
1 : a single-breasted or double-breasted semifitted overcoat with velvet collar

2 : a davenport usually with upright armrests
Ches·ter White \'ches-tər-\ *noun* [*Chester* County, Pa.] (1856)
: any of a breed of large white swine
¹chest·nut \'ches(t)-(,)nət\ *noun* [Middle English *chasteine, chesten* chestnut tree, from Middle French *chastaigne*, from Latin *castanea*, from Greek *kastanea*] (14th century)
1 a : any of a genus (*Castanea*) of trees or shrubs of the beech family; *especially* **:** an American tree (*C. dentata*) that was formerly a dominant or codominant member of many deciduous forests of the eastern U.S. but has now been largely eliminated by the chestnut blight and seldom grows beyond the shrub or sapling stage **b :** the edible nut of a chestnut **c :** the wood of a chestnut
2 : a grayish to reddish brown
3 : HORSE CHESTNUT
4 : a chestnut-colored animal; *specifically* **:** a horse having a body color of any shade of pure or reddish brown with mane, tail, and points of the same or a lighter shade — compare ²BAY 1, ¹SORREL 1
5 : a callosity on the inner side of the leg of the horse — see HORSE illustration
6 a : an old joke or story **b :** something (as a musical piece or a saying) repeated to the point of staleness
²chestnut *adjective* (1555)
1 : of the color chestnut
2 : of, relating to, or resembling a chestnut
chestnut blight *noun* (circa 1909)
: a destructive disease of the American chestnut marked by cankers of the bark and cambium and caused by an imported fungus (*Endothia parasitica* synonym *Cryphonectria parasitica*)
chestnut oak *noun* (1703)
: any of several oaks having oblong to lanceolate leaves with crenate or serrate edges: as
a : CHINQUAPIN OAK **b :** a medium-sized oak (*Quercus prinus*) of eastern North America with large acorns and leaves that are shiny yellow-green above and paler below
chest of drawers (1649)
: a piece of furniture designed to contain a set of drawers (as for holding clothing)
chesty \'ches-tē\ *adjective* **chest·i·er; -est** (1899)
1 : proudly or arrogantly self-assertive
2 : marked by a large or well-developed chest
chet·rum \'chē-trəm, 'che-\ *noun, plural* **chetrums** *or* **chetrum** [Tibetan] (1973)
— see *ngultrum* at MONEY table
che·val–de–frise \shə-,val-də-'frēz\ *noun, plural* **che·vaux–de–frise** \shə-,vō-\ [French, literally, horse from Friesland] (1668)
1 : a defense consisting of a timber or an iron barrel covered with projecting spikes and often strung with barbed wire
2 : a protecting line (as of spikes) on top of a wall — usually used in plural
che·val glass \shə-'val-\ *noun* [French *cheval* horse, support] (1828)
: a full-length mirror in a frame in which it may be tilted
che·va·lier \,she-və-'lir, *especially for 1b & 2 also* shə-'val-,yā\ *noun* [Middle English, from Middle French, from Late Latin *caballarius* horseman — more at CAVALIER] (14th century)
1 a : CAVALIER 2 **b :** a member of any of various orders of knighthood or of merit (as the Legion of Honor)
2 a : a member of the lowest rank of French nobility **b :** a cadet of the French nobility
3 : a chivalrous man
che·ve·lure \shəv-lŭr\ *noun* [French, from Late Latin *capillatura*, from Latin *capillatus* having long hair, from *capillus* hair] (15th century)
: a head of hair
chev·i·ot \'she-vē-ət, *especially British* 'che-\ *noun, often capitalized* (1815)

1 : any of a breed of hardy hornless relatively small sheep that are a source of quality mutton and have their origin in the Cheviot hills
2 a : a fabric of cheviot wool **b :** a heavy rough napped plain or twill fabric of coarse wool or worsted **c :** a sturdy soft-finished plain or twill cotton shirting
chèvre \'shev(r³), 'shev-rə\ *noun* [French, literally, goat, from Old French *chievre*, from Latin *capra* she-goat, from *caper* he-goat — more at CAPRIOLE] (1950)
: GOAT CHEESE
chev·ron \'shev-rən\ *noun* [Middle English, from Middle French, rafter, chevron, from (assumed) Vulgar Latin *caprion-, caprio* rafter; akin to Latin *caper* goat] (14th century)
: a figure, pattern, or object having the shape of a V or an inverted V: as **a** *or* **chev·er·on** \'shev-rən, 'she-və-\ **:** a heraldic charge consisting of two diagonal stripes meeting at an angle usually with the point up **b :** a sleeve badge that usually consists of one or more chevron-shaped stripes that indicates the wearer's rank and service (as in the armed forces)

chevrons b: *1* marine staff sergeant, *2* air force staff sergeant, *3* army staff sergeant

¹chew \'chü\ *verb* [Middle English *chewen*, from Old English *cēowan*; akin to Old High German *kiuwan* to chew, Russian *zhevat'*] (before 12th century)
transitive verb
: to crush, grind, or gnaw (as food) with or as if with the teeth **:** MASTICATE
intransitive verb
: to chew something; *specifically* **:** to chew tobacco
— **chew·able** \-ə-bəl\ *adjective*
— **chew·er** *noun*
— **chewy** \'chü-ē\ *adjective*
— **chew the rag** *or* **chew the fat** *slang*
: to make friendly familiar conversation **:** CHAT
²chew *noun* (13th century)
1 : the act of chewing
2 : something for chewing
chewing gum *noun* (1850)
: a sweetened and flavored insoluble plastic material (as a preparation of chicle) used for chewing
che·wink \chi-'wiŋk\ *noun* [imitative] (1793)
: TOWHEE 1
chew out *transitive verb* (1943)
: REPRIMAND, BAWL OUT
chew over *transitive verb* (1939)
: to meditate on **:** think about reflectively
Chey·enne \shī-'an, -'en\ *noun, plural* **Cheyenne** *or* **Cheyennes** [Canadian French, from Dakota *šahíyena*] (1778)
1 : a member of an American Indian people of the western plains of the U.S.
2 : the Algonquian language of the Cheyenne people
chez \'shā\ *preposition* [French, from Latin *casae*, locative of *casa* cottage] (1740)
: at or in the home or business place of
chi \'kī, 'kē\ *noun* [Greek *chei, chi*] (15th century)
: the 22nd letter of the Greek alphabet — see ALPHABET table
Chi·a·ni·na \,kē-ə-'nē-nə\ *noun, plural* **Chianina** *or* **Chianinas** [Italian, from feminine of *chianino* of the *Chiani* River valley, Italy] (1914)
: any of a breed of tall white cattle of Italian origin noted especially for producing lean meat
Chi·an·ti \kē-'än-tē, -'an-\ *noun* [Italian, from the *Chianti* region, Italy] (1833)
: a dry usually red wine from the Tuscany region of Italy; *also* **:** a similar wine made elsewhere

chiar·oscu·rist \kē-,är-ə-'skyùr-ist, kē-,ar-, -'skùr-\ *noun* (circa 1798)
: an artist who specializes in chiaroscuro

chiar·oscu·ro \-'skyùr-(,)ō, -'skùr-\ *noun, plural* **-ros** [Italian, from *chiaro* clear, light + *oscuro* obscure, dark] (1686)
1 : pictorial representation in terms of light and shade without regard to color
2 a : the arrangement or treatment of light and dark parts in a pictorial work of art **b :** the interplay or contrast of dissimilar qualities (as of mood or character)
3 : a 16th century woodcut technique involving the use of several blocks to print different tones of the same color; *also* **:** a print made by this technique
4 : the interplay of light and shadow on or as if on a surface
5 : the quality of being veiled or partly in shadow

chi·asm \'kī-,a-z°m, 'kē-\ *noun* [New Latin *chiasma*] (1870)
: CHIASMA 1

chi·as·ma \kī-'az-mə, kē-\ *noun, plural* **-ma·ta** \-mə-tə\ [New Latin, X-shaped configuration, from Greek, crosspiece, from *chiazein* to mark with a chi, from *chi* (x)] (1839)
1 : an anatomical intersection or decussation — compare OPTIC CHIASMA
2 : a cross-shaped configuration of paired chromatids visible in the diplotene of meiotic prophase and considered the cytological equivalent of genetic crossing-over
— **chi·as·mat·ic** \,kī-əz-'ma-tik, ,kē-\ *adjective*

chi·as·mus \kī-'az-məs, kē-\ *noun* [New Latin, from Greek *chiasmos*, from *chiazein* to mark with a chi] (1871)
: an inverted relationship between the syntactic elements of parallel phrases (as in Goldsmith's *to stop too fearful, and too faint to go*)

chiaus \'chaùs, 'chaùsh\ *noun* [Turkish *çavuş*] (1595)
: a Turkish messenger or sergeant

Chib·cha \'chib-(,)chä\ *noun, plural* **Chib·cha** *or* **Chibchas** [Spanish] (1814)
1 : a member of an Indian people of central Colombia
2 : the extinct language of the Chibcha people

Chib·chan \-chən\ *adjective* (1902)
: of, relating to, or constituting a language family of Colombia and Central America

chi·bouk *or* **chi·bouque** \chə-'bük, shə-\ *noun* [French *chibouque*, from Turkish *çubuk*] (1813)
: a long-stemmed Turkish tobacco pipe with a clay bowl

¹chic \'shēk\ *noun* [French] (1856)
1 : smart elegance and sophistication especially of dress or manner **:** STYLE ⟨wears her clothes with superb *chic*⟩
2 : a distinctive mode of dress or manner associated with a fashionable lifestyle, ideology, or pursuit

²chic *adjective* (1865)
1 : cleverly stylish **:** SMART ⟨the woman who is *chic* adapts fashion to her own personality —Elizabeth L. Post⟩
2 : currently fashionable ⟨a *chic* restaurant⟩
— **chic·ly** *adverb*
— **chic·ness** *noun*

Chi·ca·na \chi-'kä-nə *also* shi-\ *noun* [Mexican Spanish, feminine of *chicano*] (1967)
: an American woman or girl of Mexican descent
— **Chicana** *adjective*

¹chi·cane \shi-'kän, chi-\ *verb* **chi·caned; chi·can·ing** [French *chicaner*, from Middle French, to quibble, prevent justice] (circa 1672)
intransitive verb
: to use chicanery ⟨a wretch he had taught to lie and *chicane* —George Meredith⟩
transitive verb
: TRICK, CHEAT

²chicane *noun* (1686)
1 : CHICANERY
2 a : an obstacle on a racecourse **b :** a series of tight turns in opposite directions in an otherwise straight stretch of a road-racing course
3 : the absence of trumps in a hand of cards

chi·ca·nery \-'kän-rē, -'kä-nə-\ *noun, plural* **-ner·ies** (1609)
1 : deception by artful subterfuge or sophistry **:** TRICKERY
2 : a piece of sharp practice (as at law) **:** TRICK

Chi·ca·no \chi-'kä-(,)nō *also* shi-\ *noun, plural* **-nos** [Mexican Spanish, alteration of Spanish *mexicano* Mexican] (1947)
: an American of Mexican descent
— **Chicano** *adjective*

¹chi·chi \'shē-(,)shē *also* 'chē-(,)chē\ *noun* [French] (1908)
1 : frilly or elaborate ornamentation
2 : AFFECTATION, PRECIOSITY
3 : CHIC

²chichi *adjective* (1926)
1 : elaborately ornamented **:** SHOWY, FRILLY ⟨a *chichi* dress⟩
2 : ARTY, PRECIOUS ⟨*chichi* poetry⟩
3 : CHIC, FASHIONABLE ⟨a *chichi* nightclub⟩

chick \'chik\ *noun* [Middle English *chyke*, alteration of *chiken*] (15th century)
1 a : a domestic chicken; *especially* **:** one newly hatched **b :** the young of any bird
2 : CHILD
3 *slang* **:** a young woman

chick·a·dee \'chi-kə-(,)dē\ *noun* [imitative] (1838)
: any of several crestless American titmice (genus *Parus*) usually with the crown of the head sharply demarked and darker than the body

chick·a·ree \'chi-kə-,rē\ *noun* [imitative] (1829)
: RED SQUIRREL; *also* **:** a related squirrel (*Tamiasciurus douglasii*) of forests from southwestern British Columbia to central California

Chick·a·saw \'chi-kə-,sò\ *noun, plural* **Chickasaw** *or* **Chickasaws** (1674)
1 : a member of an American Indian people of Mississippi and Alabama
2 : a dialect of Choctaw spoken by the Chickasaw

¹chick·en \'chi-k°n, *sometimes* -k°ŋ\ *noun* [Middle English *chiken*, from Old English *cicen* young chicken; akin to Old English *cocc* cock] (14th century)
1 a : the common domestic fowl (*Gallus gallus*) especially when young; *also* **:** its flesh used as food — compare JUNGLE FOWL **b :** any of various birds or their young
2 : a young woman
3 a : COWARD **b :** any of various contests in which the participants risk personal safety in order to see which one will give up first
4 [short for *chickenshit*] *slang* **:** petty details
5 : a young male homosexual

²chicken *adjective* (1941)
1 a : SCARED **b :** TIMID, COWARDLY
2 *slang* **a :** insistent on petty details of duty or discipline **b :** PETTY, UNIMPORTANT

³chicken *intransitive verb* **chick·ened; chick·en·ing** \'chi-k°n-iŋ, 'chik-niŋ\ (1943)
: to lose one's nerve — usually used with *out* ⟨seemed to exhibit courage, manliness, and conviction when others *chickened* out —J. R. Seeley⟩

chicken–and–egg *adjective* [from the proverbial question "which came first, the chicken or the egg?"] (1959)
: of, relating to, or being a cause-and-effect dilemma

chicken colonel *noun* [from the eagle serving as insignia of the rank] (1947)
slang **:** COLONEL 1a

chicken feed *noun* (1836)
slang **:** a paltry sum (as in profits or wages)

chick·en–fried steak \'chi-k°n-'frīd-\ *noun* (1952)
: steak coated with batter, fried, and served with gravy

chicken hawk *noun* (1827)
: a hawk that preys or is believed to prey on chickens

chick·en·heart·ed \'chi-kən-,här-təd\ *adjective* (1681)
: TIMID, COWARDLY

chick·en–liv·ered \-,li-vərd\ *adjective* (1872)
: FAINTHEARTED, COWARDLY

chicken pox *noun* (circa 1738)
: an acute contagious disease especially of children marked by low-grade fever and formation of vesicles and caused by a herpesvirus — compare HERPES ZOSTER

¹chick·en·shit \'chi-k°n-,shit\ *noun* (1947)
1 : the petty details of a duty or discipline — usually considered vulgar
2 : COWARD, CHICKEN — usually considered vulgar

²chickenshit *adjective* (1951)
1 : PETTY, INSIGNIFICANT — usually considered vulgar
2 : lacking courage, manliness, or effectiveness — usually considered vulgar

chicken snake *noun* (1709)
: RAT SNAKE

chicken wire *noun* [from its use for making enclosures for chickens] (circa 1904)
: a light galvanized wire netting of hexagonal mesh

chick·pea \'chik-,pē\ *noun* [alteration of *chich pea*, from Middle English *chiche*, from Middle French, from Latin *cicer*] (circa 1722)
: an Asian leguminous herb (*Cicer arietinum*) cultivated for its short pods with one or two seeds; *also* **:** its seed

chick·weed \-,wēd\ *noun* (14th century)
: any of various low-growing small-leaved weedy plants of the pink family (especially genera *Cerastium* and *Stellaria*); *especially* **:** a cosmopolitan weed (*Stelleria media*) naturalized in the U.S. from Eurasia

chi·cle \'chi-kəl, 'chi-klē\ *noun* [American Spanish, from Nahuatl *tzictli*] (circa 1889)
: a gum from the latex of the sapodilla used as the chief ingredient of chewing gum

chic·o·ry *also* **chick·o·ry** \'chi-k(ə-)rē\ *noun, plural* **-ries** [Middle English *cicoree*, from Middle French *cichorée, chicorée*, from Latin *cichoreum*, from Greek *kichoreia*] (15th century)
1 : a thick-rooted usually blue-flowered European perennial composite herb (*Cichorium intybus*) widely grown for its roots and as a salad plant — compare ENDIVE 2, RADICCHIO
2 : the dried ground roasted root of chicory used to flavor or adulterate coffee

chide \'chīd\ *verb* **chid** \'chid\ *or* **chid·ed** \'chī-dəd\; **chid** *or* **chid·den** \'chi-d°n\ *or* **chided; chid·ing** \'chī-diŋ\ [Middle English, from Old English *cīdan* to quarrel, chide, from *cīd* strife] (before 12th century)
intransitive verb
: to speak out in angry or displeased rebuke
transitive verb
: to voice disapproval to **:** reproach in a usually mild and constructive manner **:** SCOLD
synonym *see* REPROVE

¹chief \'chēf\ *adjective* (14th century)
1 : accorded highest rank or office ⟨*chief* librarian⟩
2 : of greatest importance or influence ⟨the *chief* reasons⟩

²chief *adverb* (14th century)
archaic **:** CHIEFLY

³chief *noun* [Middle English, from Middle French, head, chief, from Latin *caput* head — more at HEAD] (15th century)

\ə\ abut \°\ kitten \ər\ further \a\ ash \ā\ ace
\ä\ mop, mar \aù\ out \ch\ chin \e\ bet \ē\ easy
\g\ go \i\ hit \ī\ ice \j\ job \ŋ\ sing \ō\ go
\ò\ law \òi\ boy \th\ thin \th\ the \ü\ loot \ù\ foot
\y\ yet \zh\ vision *see also* Guide to Pronunciation

1 : the upper part of a heraldic field
2 : the head of a body of persons or an organization **:** LEADER ⟨*chief* of police⟩
3 : the principal or most valuable part
— **chief·dom** \-dəm\ *noun*
— **chief·ship** \-,ship\ *noun*
— **in chief :** in the chief position or place
— often used in titles ⟨commander *in chief*⟩

chief executive *noun* (1833)
: a principal executive officer: as **a :** the president of a republic **b :** the governor of a state

chief justice *noun* (1534)
: the presiding or principal judge of a court of justice

¹**chief·ly** \'chē-flē\ *adverb* (14th century)
1 : most importantly **:** PRINCIPALLY, ESPECIALLY
2 : for the most part **:** MOSTLY, MAINLY

²**chiefly** *adjective* (1870)
: of or relating to a chief ⟨*chiefly* duties⟩

chief master sergeant *noun* (1959)
: a noncommissioned officer in the air force ranking above a senior master sergeant

chief master sergeant of the air force (circa 1961)
: the ranking noncommissioned officer in the air force serving as adviser to the chief of staff

chief of naval operations (1915)
: the commanding officer of the navy and a member of the Joint Chiefs of Staff

chief of staff (circa 1881)
1 : the ranking officer of a staff in the armed forces serving as principal adviser to a commander
2 : the commanding officer of the army or air force and a member of the Joint Chiefs of Staff

chief of state (1950)
: the formal head of a national state as distinguished from the head of the government

chief petty officer *noun* (circa 1887)
: an enlisted man in the navy or coast guard ranking above a petty officer first class and below a senior chief petty officer

chief·tain \'chēf-tən\ *noun* [Middle English *chieftaine*, from Middle French *chevetain*, from Late Latin *capitaneus* chief — more at CAPTAIN] (14th century)
: a chief especially of a band, tribe, or clan
— **chief·tain·ship** \-,ship\ *noun*

chief·tain·cy \-sē\ *noun, plural* **-cies** (1788)
1 : the rank, dignity, office, or rule of a chieftain
2 : a region or a people ruled by a chief **:** CHIEFDOM

chief warrant officer *noun* (1956)
: a warrant officer of senior rank in the armed forces; *also* **:** a commissioned officer in the navy or coast guard ranking below an ensign

chiel \'chē(ə)l\ *or* **chield** \'chē(ə)ld\ *noun* [Middle English (Scots) *cheld*, alteration of Middle English *child* child] (1728)
chiefly Scottish **:** FELLOW, LAD

chiff·chaff \'chif-,chaf\ *noun* [imitative] (1780)
: a small grayish European warbler (*Phylloscopus collybita*)

¹**chif·fon** \shi-'fän, 'shi-,\ *noun* [French, literally, rag, from *chiffe* old rag, alteration of Middle French *chipe*, from Middle English *chip* chip] (1765)
1 : an ornamental addition (as a knot of ribbons) to a woman's dress
2 : a sheer fabric especially of silk

²**chiffon** *adjective* (1903)
1 : resembling chiffon in sheerness or softness
2 : having a light delicate texture achieved usually by adding whipped egg whites or whipped gelatin ⟨lemon *chiffon* pie⟩

chif·fo·nade \,shi-fə-'näd, -'näd\ *noun* [French *chiffonnade*, from *chiffonner* to crumple, from *chiffon*] (1877)
: shredded or finely cut vegetables used especially as a garnish

chif·fo·nier \,shi-fə-'nir\ *noun* [French *chiffonier*, from *chiffon*] (1765)

: a high narrow chest of drawers

chif·fo·robe \'shi-fə-,rōb\ *noun* [*chiffo*nier + ward*robe*] (1908)
: a combination of wardrobe and chest of drawers

chig·ger \'chi-gər, 'ji-\ *noun* (1756)
1 : CHIGOE 1
2 [alteration of ²*jigger*] **:** a 6-legged mite larva (family Trombiculidae) that sucks the blood of vertebrates and causes intense irritation

chifforobe

chi·gnon \'shēn-,yän *also* -,yòn\ *noun* [French, from Middle French *chaignon* chain, collar, nape] (1783)
: a knot of hair that is worn at the back of the head and especially at the nape of the neck

chi·goe \'chi-(,)gō, 'chē-\ *noun* [Carib *chico*] (1691)
1 : a tropical flea (*Tunga penetrans*) of which the fertile female causes great discomfort by burrowing under the skin
2 : CHIGGER 2

Chi·hua·hua \chə-'wä-(,)wä, shə-, -wə\ *noun* [Mexican Spanish, from *Chihuahua*, Mexico] (1858)
: any of a breed of very small round-headed dogs that occur in short-coated and long-coated varieties

chil·blain \'chil-,blān\ *noun* [¹*chill*] (1547)
: an inflammatory swelling or sore caused by exposure (as of the feet or hands) to cold

Chihuahua

child \'chī(ə)ld\ *noun, plural* **chil·dren** \'chil-drən, -dərn\ *often attributive* [Middle English, from Old English *cild*; akin to Gothic *kilthei* womb, and perhaps to Sanskrit *jaṭhara* belly] (before 12th century)
1 a : an unborn or recently born person **b** *dialect* **:** a female infant
2 a : a young person especially between infancy and youth **b :** a childlike or childish person **c :** a person not yet of age
3 *usually* **childe** \'chī(ə)ld\ *archaic* **:** a youth of noble birth
4 a : a son or daughter of human parents **b :** DESCENDANT
5 : one strongly influenced by another or by a place or state of affairs
6 : PRODUCT, RESULT ⟨barbed wire . . . is truly a *child* of the plains —W. P. Webb⟩
— **child·less** \'chī(ə)l(d)-ləs\ *adjective*
— **child·less·ness** *noun*
— **with child :** PREGNANT

child·bear·ing \'chīl(d)-,bar-iŋ, -,ber-\ *adjective* (14th century)
: of or relating to the process of conceiving, being pregnant with, and giving birth to children ⟨women of *childbearing* age⟩
— **childbearing** *noun*

child·bed \-,bed\ *noun* (13th century)
: the condition of a woman in childbirth

childbed fever *noun* (1928)
: PUERPERAL FEVER

child·birth \'chīl(d)-,bərth\ *noun* (15th century)
: PARTURITION

child·hood \'chīld-,hùd\ *noun* (before 12th century)
1 : the state or period of being a child
2 : the early period in the development of something

child·ish \'chīl-dish\ *adjective* (before 12th century)

1 : of, relating to, or befitting a child or childhood
2 a : marked by or suggestive of immaturity and lack of poise ⟨a *childish* spiteful remark⟩ **b :** lacking complexity **:** SIMPLE ⟨it's a *childish* device, but it works⟩ **c :** deteriorated with age especially in mind **:** SENILE
— **child·ish·ly** *adverb*
— **child·ish·ness** *noun*

child·like \'chī(ə)l(d)-,līk\ *adjective* (1586)
: of, relating to, or resembling a child or childhood; *especially* **:** marked by innocence, trust, and ingenuousness
— **child·like·ness** *noun*

child·ly \'chī(ə)l(d)-lē\ *adjective* (before 12th century)
: CHILDLIKE

child·proof \'chīl(d)-,prüf\ *adjective* (1956)
: designed to prevent tampering or opening by children ⟨*childproof* pill bottles⟩

child's play *noun* (14th century)
1 : an extremely simple task or act
2 : something that is insignificant ⟨his injury was *child's play* compared with the damage he inflicted⟩

Chile saltpeter \'chi-lē-, 'chē-(,)lā-\ *noun* [*Chile*, South America] (circa 1909)
: sodium nitrate especially occurring naturally (as in caliche)

chili *or* **chile** *or* **chil·li** \'chi-lē\ *noun, plural* **chil·ies** *or* **chil·es** *or* **chil·lies** [Spanish *chile*, from Nahuatl *chīlli*] (1604)
1 a : HOT PEPPER **b** *usually* chilli, *chiefly British* **:** a pepper whether hot or sweet
2 a : a thick sauce of meat and chilies **b :** CHILI CON CARNE

chil·i·ad \'ki-lē-,ad, -əd\ *noun* [Late Latin *chiliad-, chilias*, from Greek, from *chilioi* thousand] (1598)
1 : a group of 1000
2 : MILLENNIUM 2a

chil·i·asm \'ki-lē-,a-zᵊm\ *noun* [New Latin *chiliasmus*, from Late Latin *chiliastes* one that believes in chiliasm, from *chilias*] (1610)
: MILLENARIANISM
— **chil·i·ast** \-lē-,ast, -lē-əst\ *noun*
— **chil·i·as·tic** \,ki-lē-'as-tik\ *adjective*

chili con car·ne \,chi-lē-,kän-'kär-nē, -kən-\ *noun* [American Spanish *chile con carne* chili with meat] (1857)
: a spiced stew of ground beef and minced chilies or chili powder usually with beans

chili dog *noun* (1969)
: a hot dog topped with chili

chili powder *noun* (1938)
: a condiment made with chilies ground to a powder

chili sauce *noun* (1880)
: a spiced tomato sauce usually made with red and green peppers

¹**chill** \'chil\ *noun* [Middle English *chile* chill, frost, from Old English *ciele*; akin to Old English *ceald* cold] (before 12th century)
1 a : a sensation of cold accompanied by shivering **b :** a disagreeable sensation of coldness
2 : a moderate but disagreeable degree of cold
3 : a check to enthusiasm or warmth of feeling ⟨felt the *chill* of his opponent's stare⟩

²**chill** *adjective* (14th century)
1 a : moderately cold **b :** COLD, RAW
2 : affected by cold ⟨*chill* travelers⟩
3 : DISTANT, FORMAL ⟨a *chill* reception⟩
4 : DEPRESSING, DISPIRITING ⟨*chill* penury —Thomas Gray⟩
— **chill·ness** *noun*

³**chill** (14th century)
intransitive verb
1 a : to become cold **b :** to shiver or quake with or as if with cold
2 : to become taken with a chill
transitive verb
1 a : to make cold or chilly **b :** to make cool especially without freezing
2 : to affect as if with cold **:** DISPIRIT, DISCOURAGE ⟨were *chilled* by the drab austerity —William Attwood⟩

— **chill·ing·ly** \'chi-liŋ-lē\ *adverb*

chill·er \'chi-lər\ *noun* (1798)
1 : one that chills
2 : an eerie or frightening story of murder, violence, or the supernatural

chill factor *noun* (1965)
: WINDCHILL

chill out *intransitive verb* (1983) *slang*
: to calm down **:** go easy **:** RELAX — often used in the imperative

chil·lum \'chi-ləm\ *noun* [Hindi *cilam*, from Persian *chilam*] (1781)
1 : the part of a water pipe that contains the substance (as tobacco or hashish) which is smoked; *also* **:** a quantity of a substance thus smoked
2 : a funnel-shaped clay pipe for smoking

chilly \'chi-lē\ *adjective* **chill·i·er; -est** (1570)
1 : noticeably cold **:** CHILLING
2 : unpleasantly affected by cold
3 : lacking warmth of feeling
4 : tending to arouse fear or apprehension ⟨*chilly* suspicions⟩
— **chill·i·ly** \'chi-lə-lē\ *adverb*
— **chill·i·ness** \'chi-lē-nəs\ *noun*

¹chi·mae·ra \kī-'mir-ə, kə-\ *variant of* CHIMERA

²chimaera *noun* [New Latin, genus name, from Latin, chimera] (1804)
: any of a family (Chimaeridae) of marine cartilaginous fishes with a tapering or threadlike tail and usually no anal fin

chi·mae·ric, chi·mae·rism *British variant of* CHIMERIC, CHIMERISM

¹chime \'chīm\ *noun* [Middle English *chimbe*, from Old English *cimb-*; akin to Middle Dutch *kimme* edge of a cask] (14th century)
: the edge or rim of a cask or drum

²chime *verb* **chimed; chim·ing** (14th century)
intransitive verb
1 a : to make a musical and especially a harmonious sound **b :** to make the sounds of a chime
2 : to be or act in accord ⟨the music and the mood *chimed* well together⟩
transitive verb
1 : to cause to sound musically by striking
2 : to produce by chiming
3 : to call or indicate by chiming ⟨the clock *chimed* midnight⟩
4 : to utter repetitively **:** DIN 2
— **chim·er** *noun*

³chime *noun* [Middle English, cymbal, from Middle French *chimbe*, from Old French, from Latin *cymbalum* cymbal] (15th century)
1 : an apparatus for chiming a bell or set of bells
2 a : a musically tuned set of bells **b :** one of a set of objects giving a bell-like sound when struck
3 a : the sound of a set of bells — usually used in plural **b :** a musical sound suggesting that of bells
4 : ACCORD, HARMONY ⟨such happy *chime* of fact and theory —Henry Maudsley⟩

chime in (1681)
intransitive verb
1 : to combine harmoniously ⟨the artist's illustrations *chime in* perfectly with the text —*Book Production*⟩
2 : to break into a conversation or discussion especially to express an opinion
transitive verb
: to remark while chiming in

chi·me·ra \kī-'mir-ə, kə-\ *noun* [Latin *chimaera*, from Greek *chimaira* she-goat, chimera; akin to Old Norse *gymbr* yearling ewe, Greek *cheimōn* winter — more at HIBERNATE]
1 a *cap* **:** a fire-breathing she-monster in Greek mythology having a lion's head, a goat's body, and a serpent's tail **b :** an imaginary monster compounded of incongruous parts

2 : an illusion or fabrication of the mind; *especially* **:** an unrealizable dream ⟨a fancy, a *chimera* in my brain, troubles me in my prayer —John Donne⟩
3 : an individual, organ, or part consisting of tissues of diverse genetic constitution

chi·mere \shə-'mir, chə-\ *noun* [Middle English *chimer, chemeyr*] (14th century)
: a loose sleeveless robe worn by Anglican bishops over the rochet

chi·me·ric \kī-'mir-ik, kə-, -'mer-\ *adjective* (1973)
: relating to, derived from, or being a genetic chimera or its genetic material ⟨a *chimeric* cat⟩

chi·me·ri·cal \kī-'mer-i-kəl, kə-, -'mir-\ *also* **chi·me·ric** \-ik\ *adjective* [*chimera*] (1638)
1 : existing only as the product of unchecked imagination **:** fantastically visionary or improbable
2 : given to fantastic schemes
synonym see IMAGINARY
— **chi·me·ri·cal·ly** \-i-k(ə-)lē\ *adverb*

chi·me·rism \kī-'mir-,i-zəm, kə-; 'kī-mə-,ri-\ *noun* (1961)
: the state of being a genetic chimera

chi·mi·chan·ga \,chi-mē-'chän-gə\ *noun* [Mexican Spanish, trinket] (1982)
: a tortilla wrapped around a filling (as of meat) and deep-fried

chim·ney \'chim-nē\ *noun, plural* **chimneys** [Middle English, from Middle French *cheminée*, from Late Latin *caminata*, from Latin *caminus* furnace, fireplace, from Greek *kaminos*; perhaps akin to Greek *kamara* vault] (14th century)
1 *dialect* **:** FIREPLACE, HEARTH
2 : a vertical structure incorporated into a building and enclosing a flue or flues that carry off smoke; *especially* **:** the part of such a structure extending above a roof
3 : SMOKESTACK
4 : a tube usually of glass placed around a flame (as of a lamp)
5 : something resembling a chimney: as **a :** a narrow cleft in rock **b :** a tall column of rock on the ocean floor that is formed by the precipitation of minerals from superheated water issuing from a vent in the earth's crust and rising through the column of rock
— **chim·ney·like** \-,līk\ *adjective*

chim·ney·piece \'chim-nē-,pēs\ *noun* (1680)
: an ornamental construction over and around a fireplace that includes the mantel

chimney pot *noun* (circa 1806)
: a usually earthenware pipe placed at the top of a chimney

chimney sweep *noun* (1727)
: a person whose occupation is cleaning soot from chimney flues — called also *chimney sweeper*

chimney swift *noun* (1849)
: a small sooty-gray swift (*Chaetura pelagica*) with long narrow wings that often builds its nest inside an unused chimney — called also *chimney swallow*

chimp \'chimp *sometimes* 'shimp\ *noun* (1877)
: CHIMPANZEE

chim·pan·zee \(,)chim-,pan-'zē, -pən-'zē, -'pan-zē *sometimes* (,)shim-\ *noun* [Kongo dialect *chimpenzi*] (1738)
: an anthropoid ape (*Pan troglodytes*) of equatorial Africa that is smaller and more arboreal than the gorilla — compare PYGMY CHIMPANZEE

¹chin \'chin\ *noun* [Middle English, from Old English *cinn*; akin to Old High German *kinni* chin, Latin *gena* cheek, Greek *genys* jaw, cheek] (before 12th century)

chimpanzee

1 : the lower portion of the face lying below the lower lip and including the prominence of the lower jaw
2 : the surface beneath or between the branches of the lower jaw
— **chin·less** \-ləs\ *adjective*

²chin *verb* **chinned; chin·ning** (1869)
transitive verb
1 : to bring to or hold with the chin ⟨*chin* a violin⟩
2 : to raise (oneself) while hanging by the hands until the chin is level with the support
intransitive verb
slang **:** to talk idly

chi·na \'chī-nə\ *noun* [Persian *chīnī* Chinese porcelain] (1579)
1 : PORCELAIN; *also* **:** vitreous porcelain wares (as dishes, vases, or ornaments) for domestic use
2 : earthenware or porcelain tableware

China aster *noun* (1794)
: a common annual garden aster (*Callistephus chinensis*) native to northern China that occurs in many showy forms

chi·na·ber·ry \'chī-nə-,ber-ē, *Southern also* 'chä-nē-,ber-ē\ *noun* (1890)
: a small Asian tree (*Melia azedarach*) of the mahogany family naturalized in the southern U.S. where it is widely planted for shade or ornament

china clay *noun* (1840)
: KAOLIN

china closet *noun* (1771)
: a cabinet or cupboard for the storage or display of household china

Chi·na·man \'chī-nə-mən\ *noun* (1849)
: a native of China **:** CHINESE — often taken to be offensive

China rose *noun* (circa 1731)
: any of numerous garden roses derived from a shrubby Chinese rose (*Rosa chinensis*)

China Syndrome *noun* [from the notion that the molten reactor contents could theoretically sink through the earth to reach China] (1970)
: MELTDOWN 1

Chi·na·town \'chī-nə-,taün\ *noun* (1857)
: the Chinese quarter of a city

China tree *noun* (1819)
: CHINABERRY

chi·na·ware \'chī-nə-,war, -,wer\ *noun* (1634)
: tableware made of china

chin·bone \'chin-,bōn\ *noun* (before 12th century)
: MANDIBLE; *especially* **:** the median anterior part of the human mandible

chinch \'chinch\ *noun* [Spanish *chinche*, from Latin *cimic-, cimex*] (1616)
: BEDBUG

chinch bug *noun* (1785)
: a small black-and-white bug (*Blissus leucopterus*) very destructive to cereal grasses

chin·che·rin·chee \,chin-chə-ri(n)-'chē, ,chiŋ-kə-\ *noun, plural* **chincherinchee** *or* **chincherinchees** [Afrikaans *tjienkerientjee*] (1904)
: a southern African perennial bulbous herb (*Ornithogalum thyrsoides*) of the lily family with spikes of white to golden-yellow blossoms

chin·chil·la \chin-'chi-lə\ *noun* [Spanish] (1604)
1 : either of two small South American rodents (*Chinchilla laniger* and *C. brevicaudata*) of the high Andes that are the size of large squirrels, have very soft pearly gray fur, and are extensively bred in captivity; *also* **:** the fur of a chinchilla

chinchilla

\ə\ **abut** \ᵊ\ **kitten** \ər\ **further** \a\ **ash** \ā\ **ace**
\ä\ **mop, mar** \aù\ **out** \ch\ **chin** \e\ **bet** \ē\ **easy**
\g\ **go** \i\ **hit** \ī\ **ice** \j\ **job** \ŋ\ **sing** \ō\ **go**
\ò\ **law** \òi\ **boy** \th\ **thin** \t͟h\ **the** \ü\ **loot** \ù\ **foot**
\y\ **yet** \zh\ **vision** *see also* Guide to Pronunciation

2 : a heavy twilled woolen coating

¹chine \'chīn\ *noun* [Middle English, from Middle French *eschine*, of Germanic origin; akin to Old High German *scina* shinbone, needle — more at SHIN] (14th century)
1 : BACKBONE, SPINE; *also* **:** a cut of meat including all or part of the backbone
2 : the intersection of the bottom and the sides of a flat or V-bottomed boat

²chine *transitive verb* **chined; chin·ing** (circa 1611)
: to cut through the backbone of (as in butchering)

Chi·nese \chī-'nēz, -'nēs\ *noun, plural* **Chinese** (1606)
1 a : a native or inhabitant of China **b :** a person of Chinese descent
2 : a group of related languages used by the people of China that are often mutually unintelligible in their spoken form but share a single system of writing and that constitute a branch of the Sino-Tibetan language family; *especially* **:** MANDARIN
— **Chinese** *adjective*

Chinese boxes *noun plural* (1829)
1 : a set of boxes graduated in size so that each fits into the next larger one
2 : something that resembles a set of Chinese boxes especially in complexity

Chinese cabbage *noun* (1842)
: either of two Asian brassicas now grown in the U.S. and widely used as greens: **a :** BOK CHOY **b :** one (*Brassica rapa pekinensis*) that forms elongate more or less solid cylindrical heads and has pale green or cream-colored leaves

Chinese checkers *noun plural but singular or plural in construction* (1938)
: a game in which each player seeks to be the first to transfer a set of marbles from a home point to the opposite point of a pitted 6-pointed star by single moves or jumps

Chinese chestnut *noun* (circa 1909)
: an Asian chestnut (*Castanea mollissima*) that is resistant to chestnut blight

Chinese copy *noun* (1920)
: an exact imitation or duplicate that includes defects as well as desired qualities

Chinese crested *noun* (1976)
: any of a breed of hairless or coated dogs with a plumed tail and a crest of hair on the head

Chinese gooseberry *noun* (1925)
: a subtropical vine (*Actinidia chinensis* of the family Actinidiaceae) that bears kiwifruit; *also* **:** KIWIFRUIT

Chinese lantern *noun* (1825)
: a collapsible translucent covering for a light

Chinese parsley *noun* (circa 1953)
: CILANTRO

Chinese puzzle *noun* (circa 1815)
1 : an intricate or ingenious puzzle
2 : something intricate and obscure

Chinese restaurant syndrome *noun* (1968)
: a group of symptoms (as numbness of the neck, arms, and back with headache, dizziness, and palpitations) that is held to affect susceptible persons eating food and especially Chinese food heavily seasoned with monosodium glutamate

chinese shar–pei *noun* (1975)
: SHAR-PEI

Chinese wall *noun* [*Chinese Wall*, a defensive wall built in the 3d century B.C. between China and Mongolia] (1900)
: a strong barrier; *especially* **:** a serious obstacle to understanding

Chinese white *noun* (circa 1884)
: ZINC WHITE

Ching *or* **Ch'ing** \'chiŋ\ *noun* [Chinese (Beijing) *Qīng*] (1795)
: a Manchu dynasty in China dated 1644–1912 and the last imperial dynasty

¹chink \'chiŋk\ *noun* [probably alteration of Middle English *chine* crack, fissure] (1535)
1 : a small cleft, slit, or fissure ⟨a *chink* in the curtain⟩
2 : a weak spot that may leave one vulnerable
3 : a narrow beam of light shining through a chink

²chink *transitive verb* (1748)
: to fill the chinks of (as by caulking) ⟨*chink* a log cabin⟩

³chink *noun* [imitative] (1573)
1 *archaic* **:** COIN, MONEY
2 : a short sharp sound

⁴chink (1589)
intransitive verb
: to make a slight sharp metallic sound
transitive verb
: to cause to make a chink

Chink \'chiŋk\ *noun or adjective* [perhaps alteration of *Chinese*] (1887)
: CHINESE — usually taken to be offensive

chi·no \'chē-(,)nō, 'shē-\ *noun, plural* **chinos** [origin unknown] (1943)
1 : a usually khaki cotton or synthetic-fiber twill of the type used for military uniforms
2 *plural* **:** an article of clothing made of chino

chi·noi·se·rie \shēn-'wäz-rē, -'wä-zə-; ,shēn-,wäz-'rē, -,wä-zə-\ *noun* [French, from *chinois* Chinese, from *Chine* China] (1883)
: a style in art (as in decoration) reflecting Chinese qualities or motifs; *also* **:** an object or decoration in this style

Chi·nook \shə-'nuk, chə-, -'nük\ *noun, plural* **Chinook** *or* **Chinooks** [Lower Chehalis (Salishan language of western Washington) *činúk*, name of a Chinook village] (1805)
1 : a member of an American Indian people of the north shore of the Columbia River at its mouth
2 : a Chinookan language of the Chinook and other nearby peoples
3 *often not capitalized* **a :** a warm moist southwest wind of the coast from Oregon northward **b :** a warm dry wind that descends the eastern slopes of the Rocky Mountains
4 *not capitalized* **:** CHINOOK SALMON

Chi·nook·an \-'nu̇-kən, -'nü-\ *noun* (circa 1890)
: an American Indian language family of Washington and Oregon
— **Chinookan** *adjective*

Chinook jargon *noun, often J capitalized* (1840)
: a pidgin language based on Chinook and other Indian languages, French, and English and formerly used as a lingua franca in the northwestern U.S. and on the Pacific coast of Canada and Alaska

chinook salmon *noun* (1851)
: a large commercially important Pacific salmon (*Oncorhynchus tshawytscha*) with red flesh that occurs in the northern Pacific Ocean — called also *king salmon*

chin·qua·pin *or* **chin·ka·pin** \'chiŋ-ki-,pin\ *noun* [probably modification of Virginia Algonquian *chechinquamin* chinquapin nut] (1612)
1 : the edible nut of a chinquapin
2 : any of several trees (genera *Castanea* and *Castanopsis*); *especially* **:** a dwarf chestnut (*Castanea pumila*) of the U.S.

chinquapin oak *noun* (1785)
: either of two chestnut oaks (*Quercus muhlenbergii* and *Q. prinoides*) of the eastern U.S.

chintz \'chints\ *noun* [earlier *chints*, plural of *chint*, from Hindi *chīṭ*] (1614)
1 : a printed calico from India
2 : a usually glazed printed cotton fabric

chintzy \'chin(t)-sē\ *adjective* **chintz·i·er; -est** (1851)
1 : decorated with or as if with chintz
2 a : GAUDY, CHEAP ⟨*chintzy* toys⟩ **b :** STINGY

chin–up \'chi-(,)nəp\ *noun* (1954)
: the act or an instance of chinning oneself especially as a conditioning exercise

chin–wag \'chin-,wag\ *noun* (1879)
slang **:** CONVERSATION, CHAT

chi·o·no·doxa \,kī-ə-nō-'däk-sə, kī-,ä-nə-\ *noun* [New Latin, genus name, from Greek *chion-, chiōn* snow (akin to Greek *cheimōn* winter) + *doxa* glory — more at HIBERNATE, DOXOLOGY] (1879)
: GLORY-OF-THE-SNOW

¹chip \'chip\ *noun* [Middle English; akin to Old English *-cippian*] (14th century)
1 a : a small usually thin and flat piece (as of wood or stone) cut, struck, or flaked off **b** (1) **:** a small thin slice of food; *especially* **:** POTATO CHIP (2) **:** FRENCH FRY
2 : something small, worthless, or trivial
3 a : one of the counters used as a token for money in poker and other games **b** *plural* **:** MONEY — used especially in the phrase *in the chips* **c :** something valuable that can be used for advantage in negotiation or trade ⟨a bargaining *chip*⟩
4 : a piece of dried dung — usually used in combination ⟨cow *chip*⟩
5 : a flaw left after a chip is removed
6 a : INTEGRATED CIRCUIT **b :** a small wafer of semiconductor material that forms the base for an integrated circuit
7 : CHIP SHOT
— **chip off the old block :** a child that resembles his or her parent
— **chip on one's shoulder :** a challenging or belligerent attitude

²chip *verb* **chipped; chip·ping** [Middle English *chippen*, from Old English *-cippian* (as in *forcippian* to cut off); akin to Old English *cipp* beam, Old High German *chipfa* stave] (15th century)
transitive verb
1 a : to cut or hew with an edged tool **b** (1) **:** to cut or break (a small piece) from something (2) **:** to cut or break a fragment from (3) **:** to cut into chips ⟨*chip* a tree stump⟩
2 *British* **:** CHAFF, BANTER
3 : to hit (a return in tennis) with backspin
intransitive verb
1 : to break off in small pieces
2 : to play a chip shot

chip·board \'chip-,bȯrd, -,bȯrd\ *noun* (1919)
: a paperboard usually made entirely from wastepaper

chip in (1861)
intransitive verb
1 : CONTRIBUTE ⟨everyone *chipped in* for the gift⟩
2 *chiefly British* **:** CHIME IN 2
transitive verb
: CONTRIBUTE

chip·munk \'chip-,məŋk\ *noun* [alteration of earlier *chitmunk*, probably from Ojibwa *ačitamoˀnˀ* red squirrel] (1832)
: any of a genus (*Tamias*) of small striped North American and Asian rodents of the squirrel family

chipped beef \'chip(t)-\ *noun* (1859)
: smoked dried beef sliced thin

Chip·pen·dale \'chi-pən-,dāl\ *adjective* [Thomas *Chippendale*] (1876)
: of or relating to an 18th century English furniture style characterized by graceful outline and often ornate rococo ornamentation

¹chip·per \'chi-pər\ *noun* (1513)
: one that chips

²chipper *adjective* [perhaps alteration of English dialect *kipper* (lively)] (1838)
: SPRIGHTLY

Chip·pe·wa \'chi-pə-,wȯ, -,wä, -,wā, -wə\ *noun, plural* **Chippewa** *or* **Chippewas** (1671)
: OJIBWA

chipping sparrow \'chi-piŋ-\ *noun* [*chip* to cheep] (1791)
: a small gray-breasted North American sparrow (*Spizella passerina*) with a black line through the eye, a white line above it, and in breeding plumage a reddish patch on the top of the head

chip·py \'chi-pē\ *adjective* **chip·pi·er; -est** [*chip* on one's shoulder] (1898)

: aggressively belligerent ⟨a *chippy* hockey player⟩; *also* **:** marked by much fighting ⟨a *chippy* game⟩

chip shot *noun* (1909)
: a short usually low approach shot in golf that lofts the ball to the green and allows it to roll

chir- *or* **chiro-** *combining form* [Latin, from Greek *cheir-*, *cheiro-*, from *cheir*; akin to Hittite *keššar* hand]
: hand ⟨*chiropractic*⟩

chi·ral \'kī-rəl\ *adjective* [*chir-* + [1]*-al*] (1894)
: of or relating to a molecule that is not superimposable on its mirror image
— **chi·ral·i·ty** \kī-'ra-lə-tē, kə-\ *noun*

chiral center *noun* (1970)
: an atom especially in an organic molecule that has four different atoms or groups attached to it

Chi–Rho \'kī-'rō, 'kē-\ *noun, plural* **Chi-Rhos** [*chi* + *rho*] (1868)
: a Christian monogram and symbol formed from the first two letters X and P of the Greek word for *Christ* — called also *Christogram*

Chir·i·ca·hua \,chir-ə-'kä-wə\ *noun, plural* **Chiricahua** *or* **Chiricahuas** (1885)
: a member of an Apache people of Arizona

chir·i·moya *variant of* CHERIMOYA

chirk \'chərk\ *verb* [Middle English *charken*, *chirken* to creak, chirp, from Old English *cearcian* to creak; akin to Old English *cracian* to crack] (1843)
: CHEER ⟨play with her and *chirk* her up a little —Harriet B. Stowe⟩

chi·rog·ra·phy \kī-'rä-grə-fē\ *noun* (1654)
1 : HANDWRITING, PENMANSHIP
2 : CALLIGRAPHY 1
— **chi·rog·ra·pher** \-fər\ *noun*
— **chi·ro·graph·ic** \,kī-rə-'gra-fik\ *or* **chi·ro·graph·i·cal** \-fi-kəl\ *adjective*

chi·ro·man·cy \'kī-rə-,man(t)-sē\ *noun* [probably from Middle French *chiromancie*, from Medieval Latin *chiromantia*, from Greek *cheir-* chir- + *-manteia* -mancy] (circa 1528)
: PALMISTRY
— **chi·ro·man·cer** \-,man(t)-sər\ *noun*

chi·ron·o·mid \kī-'rä-nə-məd\ *noun* [ultimately from Greek *cheironomos* one who gestures with his hands] (1915)
: any of a family (Chironomidae) of midges that lack piercing mouthparts
— **chironomid** *adjective*

chi·rop·o·dy \kə-'rä-pə-dē, shə- *also* kī-\ *noun* [*chir-* + *pod-*; from its original concern with both hands and feet] (1886)
: PODIATRY
— **chi·rop·o·dist** \-dist\ *noun*

chi·ro·prac·tic \'kī-rə-,prak-tik, ,kī-rə-'\ *noun* [*chir-* + Greek *praktikos* practical, operative — more at PRACTICAL] (1898)
: a system of therapy which holds that disease results from a lack of normal nerve function and which employs manipulation and specific adjustment of body structures (as the spinal column)
— **chi·ro·prac·tor** \-tər\ *noun*

chi·rop·ter·an \kī-'räp-tə-rən\ *noun* [ultimately from Greek *cheir* hand + *pteron* wing — more at FEATHER] (1835)
: [3]BAT

chirp \'chərp\ *noun* [imitative] (circa 1755)
: the characteristic short sharp sound especially of a small bird or insect
— **chirp** *intransitive verb*

chirpy \'chər-pē\ *adjective* **chirp·i·er; -est** (1837)
1 : cheerfully lively ⟨a *chirpy* manner⟩
2 a : making chirps **b :** suggestive of chirping ⟨a *chirpy* voice⟩
— **chirp·i·ly** \-pə-lē\ *adverb*

chirr \'chər\ *noun* [imitative] (circa 1600)
: the short vibrant or trilled sound characteristic of an insect (as a grasshopper or cicada)
— **chirr** *intransitive verb*

chir·rup \'chər-əp, 'chir-\ *noun* [imitative] (1788)
: CHIRP

— chirrup *intransitive verb*

chir·rupy \'chər-ə-pē, 'chir-\ *adjective* (1874)
: CHIRPY

chi·rur·geon \kī-'rər-jən\ *noun* [Middle English *cirurgian*, from Old French *cirurgien*, from *cirurgie* surgery] (13th century)
archaic **:** SURGEON

¹chis·el \'chi-zᵊl\ *noun* [Middle English, from Old North French, from (assumed) Vulgar Latin *cisellum*, alteration of *caesellum*, from Latin *caesus*, past participle of *caedere* to cut] (14th century)
: a metal tool with a sharpened edge at one end used to chip, carve, or cut into a solid material (as wood, stone, or metal)

²chisel *verb* **-eled** *or* **-elled; -el·ing** *or* **-el·ling** \'chi-zᵊl-iŋ, 'chiz-liŋ\ (1509)
transitive verb
1 : to cut or work with or as if with a chisel
2 : to employ shrewd or unfair practices on in order to obtain one's end; *also* **:** to obtain by such practices ⟨*chisel* a job⟩
intransitive verb
1 : to work with or as if with a chisel
2 a : to employ shrewd or unfair practices **b :** to thrust oneself **:** INTRUDE ⟨*chisel* in on a racket⟩
— **chis·el·er** *or* **chis·el·ler** \'chi-zᵊl-ər, 'chiz-lər\ *noun*

chis·eled *or* **chis·elled** \'chi-zᵊld\ *adjective* (1821)
: formed or crafted as if with a chisel ⟨*chiseled* good looks⟩ ⟨a *chiseled* essay⟩

chi–square \'kī-,skwär, -'skwär\ *noun, often attributive* (circa 1934)
: a statistic that is a sum of terms each of which is a quotient obtained by dividing the square of the difference between the observed and theoretical values of a quantity by the theoretical value

chi–square distribution *noun* (circa 1956)
: a probability density function that gives the distribution of the sum of the squares of a number of independent random variables each with a normal distribution with zero mean and unit variance, that has the property that the sum of two or more random variables with such a distribution also has one, and that is widely used in testing statistical hypotheses especially about the theoretical and observed values of a quantity and about population variances and standard deviations

¹chit \'chit\ *noun* [Middle English *chitte* kitten, cub] (circa 1624)
1 : CHILD
2 : a pert young woman

²chit *noun* [Hindi *ciṭṭhī*] (1757)
1 : a short letter or note; *especially* **:** a signed voucher of a small debt (as for food)
2 : a small slip of paper with writing on it

chit·chat \'chit-,chat\ *noun* [reduplication of *chat*] (1710)
: SMALL TALK, GOSSIP
— **chitchat** *intransitive verb*

chi·tin \'kī-tᵊn\ *noun* [French *chitine*, from Greek *chitōn*] (circa 1839)
: a horny polysaccharide that forms part of the hard outer integument especially of insects, arachnids, and crustaceans
— **chi·tin·ous** \'kī-tᵊn-əs, 'kīt-nəs\ *adjective*

chi·ton \'kī-tᵊn, 'kī-,tän\ *noun* [New Latin, genus name, from Greek *chitōn* tunic, of Semitic origin; akin to Hebrew *kuttōneth* tunic] (1816)
1 : any of a class (Polyplacophora) of elongated bilaterally symmetrical marine mollusks with a dorsal shell of calcareous plates
2 [Greek *chitōn*] **:** the basic garment of ancient Greece worn usually knee-length by men and full-length by women

chit·ter \'chi-tər\ *intransitive verb* [Middle English *chiteren*, probably of imitative origin] (13th century)
: TWITTER, CHIRP; *also* **:** CHATTER

chit·ter·lings *or* **chit·lins** \'chit-lənz\ *noun plural* [Middle English *chiterling*] (13th century)

: the intestines of hogs especially when prepared as food

chi·val·ric \shə-'val-rik\ *adjective* (1797)
: relating to chivalry **:** CHIVALROUS

chiv·al·rous \'shi-vəl-rəs\ *adjective* (14th century)
1 : VALIANT
2 : of, relating to, or characteristic of chivalry and knight-errantry
3 a : marked by honor, generosity, and courtesy **b :** marked by gracious courtesy and high-minded consideration especially to women
synonym see CIVIL
— **chiv·al·rous·ly** *adverb*
— **chiv·al·rous·ness** *noun*

chiv·al·ry \'shi-vəl-rē\ *noun, plural* **-ries** [Middle English *chivalrie*, from Middle French *chevalerie*, from *chevalier* knight — more at CHEVALIER] (14th century)
1 : mounted men-at-arms
2 *archaic* **a :** martial valor **b :** knightly skill
3 : gallant or distinguished gentlemen
4 : the system, spirit, or customs of medieval knighthood
5 : the qualities of the ideal knight **:** chivalrous conduct

chive \'chīv\ *noun* [Middle English, from Old North French, from Latin *cepa* onion] (14th century)
: a perennial plant (*Allium schoenoprasum*) related to the onion and having slender leaves used as a seasoning — usually used in plural

chivy *or* **chiv·vy** \'chi-vē\ *noun* **chiv·ied** *or* **chiv·vied; chivy·ing** *or* **chiv·vy·ing** [*chivy*, noun (chase, hunt), probably from English dialect *Chevy Chase* chase, confusion, from the name of a ballad describing the battle of Otterburn (1388)] (1918)
1 : to tease or annoy with persistent petty attacks
2 : to move or obtain by small maneuvers
synonym see BAIT

chla·myd·ia \klə-'mi-dē-ə\ *noun, plural* **-i·ae** \-dē-,ē\ [New Latin, from Greek *chlamyd-*, *chlamys*] (1966)
1 : any of a genus (*Chlamydia*, family Chlamydiaceae) of spherical gram-negative intracellular bacteria; *especially* **:** one (*C. trachomatis*) that causes or is associated with various diseases of the eye and urogenital tract including trachoma, lymphogranuloma venereum, cervicitis, and some forms of urethritis
2 : a disease or infection caused by chlamydiae
— **chla·myd·i·al** \-dē-əl\ *adjective*

chla·mydo·spore \klə-'mi-də-,spōr, -,spȯr\ *noun* [Latin *chlamyd-*, *chlamys* + International Scientific Vocabulary *spore*] (1884)
: a thick-walled usually resting fungal spore

chla·mys \'kla-məs, 'klā-\ *noun, plural* **chla·mys·es** *or* **chla·my·des** \-mə-,dēz\ [Latin *chlamyd-*, *chlamys*, from Greek] (1699)
: a short oblong mantle worn by young men of ancient Greece

Chloe \'klō-ē\ *noun* [Latin, from Greek *Chloē*]
: a lover of Daphnis in a Greek pastoral romance

chlor- *or* **chloro-** *combining form* [New Latin, from Greek, from *chlōros* greenish yellow — more at YELLOW]
1 : green ⟨*chlor*ine⟩ ⟨*chlor*osis⟩
2 : chlorine **:** containing chlorine ⟨*chlor*oprene⟩

chlamys

\ə\ abut \ᵊ\ kitten \ər\ further \a\ ash \ā\ ace
\ä\ mop, mar \au̇\ out \ch\ chin \e\ bet \ē\ easy
\g\ go \i\ hit \ī\ ice \j\ job \ŋ\ sing \ō\ go
\ȯ\ law \ȯi\ boy \th\ thin \t͟h\ the \ü\ loot \u̇\ foot
\y\ yet \zh\ vision *see also* Guide to Pronunciation

chlor·ac·ne \klō-'rak-nē, klȯ-\ *noun* (circa 1928)
: a skin eruption resembling acne and resulting from exposure to chlorine or its compounds

chlo·ral \'klȯr-əl, 'klȯr-\ *noun* [French, from *chlor-* + *al*cool alcohol] (1838)
1 : a pungent colorless oily aldehyde CCl_3CHO used in making DDT and chloral hydrate
2 : CHLORAL HYDRATE

chloral hydrate *noun* (1874)
: a bitter white crystalline drug $C_2H_3Cl_3O_2$ used as a hypnotic and sedative or in knockout drops

chlo·ral·ose \'klȯr-ə-,lōs, 'klȯr-, -,lōz\ *noun* (1893)
: a bitter crystalline compound $C_8H_{11}Cl_3O_6$ used especially to anesthetize animals
— **chlo·ral·osed** \-,lōst, -,lōzd\ *adjective*

chlo·ra·mine \'klȯr-ə-,mēn, 'klȯr-\ *noun* [International Scientific Vocabulary] (1893)
: any of various compounds containing nitrogen and chlorine

chlor·am·phen·i·col \,klȯr-,am-'fe-ni-,kȯl, ,klȯr-, -,kōl\ *noun* [*chlor-* + *am*ide + *phen-* + *nitr-* + *glyc*ol] (1949)
: a broad-spectrum antibiotic $C_{11}H_{12}Cl_2N_2O_5$ isolated from cultures of a soil actinomycete (*Streptomyces venezuelae*) or prepared synthetically

chlo·rate \'klȯr-,āt, 'klȯr-\ *noun* (1823)
: a salt containing the anion ClO_3^- ⟨*chlorate* of potassium⟩

chlor·dane \'klȯr-,dān\ *noun* [*chlor-* + *in*dane (C_9H_{10})] (1947)
: a highly chlorinated viscous volatile liquid insecticide $C_{10}H_6Cl_8$

chlor·di·az·epox·ide \,klȯr-dī-,a-zə-'päk-,sīd, ,klȯr-\ *noun* [*chlor-* + *di-* + *az-* + *ep*oxide] (1961)
: a benzodiazepine $C_{16}H_{14}ClN_3O$ related to diazepam and used in the form of its hydrochloride especially as a tranquilizer and in the treatment of alcoholism

chlo·rel·la \klə-'re-lə\ *noun* [New Latin, genus name, from Greek *chlōros*] (1904)
: any of a genus (*Chlorella*) of unicellular green algae

chlor·en·chy·ma \klȯr-'eŋ-kə-mə, klȯr-\ *noun* (1894)
: chlorophyll-containing parenchyma of plants

chlo·ride \'klȯr-,īd, 'klȯr-\ *noun* [German *Chlorid*, from *chlor-* + *-id* -ide] (1812)
1 : a compound of chlorine with another element or group; *especially* : a salt or ester of hydrochloric acid
2 : a univalent anion consisting of one atom of chlorine

chloride of lime (1826)
: BLEACHING POWDER

chlo·ri·nate \'klȯr-ə-,nāt, 'klȯr-\ *transitive verb* **-nat·ed; -nat·ing** (1856)
: to treat or combine with chlorine or a chlorine compound
— **chlo·ri·na·tion** \,klȯr-ə-'nā-shən, ,klȯr-\ *noun*
— **chlo·ri·na·tor** \'klȯr-ə-,nā-tər, 'klȯr-\ *noun*

chlorinated lime *noun* (1876)
: BLEACHING POWDER

chlo·rine \'klȯr-,ēn, 'klȯr-, -ən\ *noun* (1810)
: a halogen element that is isolated as a heavy greenish yellow gas of pungent odor and is used especially as a bleach, oxidizing agent, and disinfectant in water purification — see ELEMENT table

chlo·rin·i·ty \klō-'ri-nə-tē, klȯ-\ *noun* (circa 1931)
: a measure of the concentration of halides in one kilogram of seawater

¹chlo·rite \'klȯr-,īt, 'klȯr-\ *noun* [German *Chlorit*, from Latin *chloritis*, a green stone, from Greek *chlōritis*, from *chlōros*] (1794)
: any of a group of monoclinic usually green minerals associated with and resembling the micas

— **chlo·rit·ic** \klō-'ri-tik, klȯ-\ *adjective*

²chlorite *noun* [probably from French, from *chlor-*] (1853)
: a salt containing the anion ClO_2^- ⟨*chlorite* of sodium⟩

chloro- — see CHLOR-

chlo·ro·ben·zene \,klȯr-ō-'ben-,zēn, ,klȯr-, -ben-\ *noun* [International Scientific Vocabulary] (circa 1889)
: a colorless flammable volatile toxic liquid C_6H_5Cl used in organic synthesis (as of DDT) and as a solvent

chlo·ro·fluo·ro·car·bon \,klȯr-ō-,flȯr-ō-'kär-bən, ,klȯr-, -,flu̇r-, -,flȯr-\ *noun* (1949)
: any of several simple gaseous compounds that contain carbon, chlorine, fluorine, and sometimes hydrogen, that are used as refrigerants, cleaning solvents, and aerosol propellants and in the manufacture of plastic foams, and that are suspected to be a major cause of stratospheric ozone depletion — abbreviation CFC

chlo·ro·fluo·ro·meth·ane \-'me-,thān, *British usually* -'mē-\ *noun* (1965)
: a chlorofluorocarbon derived from methane

¹chlo·ro·form \'klȯr-ə-,fȯrm, 'klȯr-\ *noun* [French *chloroforme*, from *chlor-* + *formyle* formyl; from its having been regarded as a trichloride of this group] (1838)
: a colorless volatile heavy toxic liquid $CHCl_3$ with an ether odor used especially as a solvent or as a veterinary anesthetic

²chloroform *transitive verb* (1848)
: to treat with or as if with chloroform especially so as to produce anesthesia, insensibility, or death

chlo·ro·gen·ic acid \,klȯr-ə-'je-nik-, ,klȯr-\ *noun* (circa 1889)
: a crystalline acid $C_{16}H_{18}O_9$ occurring in various plant parts (as coffee beans)

chlo·ro·hy·drin \,klȯr-ə-'hī-drən, ,klȯr-\ *noun* [International Scientific Vocabulary *chlor-* + *hydr-* + *¹-in*] (circa 1890)
: any of various organic compounds derived from diols or polyhydroxy alcohols by substitution of chlorine for part of the hydroxyl groups

Chlo·ro·my·ce·tin \,klȯr-ō-mī-'sē-t³n, ,klȯr-\ *trademark*
— used for chloramphenicol

chlo·ro·phyll \'klȯr-ə-,fil, 'klȯr-, -fəl\ *noun* [French *chlorophylle*, from *chlor-* + Greek *phyllon* leaf — more at BLADE] (1819)
1 : the green photosynthetic pigment found chiefly in the chloroplasts of plants and occurring especially as a blue-black ester $C_{55}H_{72}MgN_4O_5$ or a dark green ester $C_{55}H_{70}MgN_4O_6$ — called also respectively *chlorophyll a, chlorophyll b*
2 : a waxy green chlorophyll-containing substance extracted from green plants and used as a coloring agent or deodorant
— **chlo·ro·phyl·lous** \,klȯr-ə-'fi-ləs, ,klȯr-\ *adjective*

chlo·ro·pic·rin \klȯr-ə-'pi-krən, ,klȯr-\ *noun* [German *Chlorpikrin*, from *chlor-* + Greek *pikros* sharp — more at PAINT] (circa 1889)
: a colorless liquid CCl_3NO_2 that causes tears and vomiting and is used especially as a soil fumigant

chlo·ro·plast \'klȯr-ə-,plast, 'klȯr-\ *noun* [International Scientific Vocabulary] (1887)
: a plastid that contains chlorophyll and is the site of photosynthesis — see CELL illustration
— **chlo·ro·plas·tic** \,klȯr-ə-'plas-tik, ,klȯr-\ *adjective*

chlo·ro·prene \-,prēn\ *noun* [*chlor-* + *iso*prene] (1931)
: a colorless liquid C_4H_5Cl used especially in making neoprene by polymerization

chlo·ro·quine \'klȯr-ə-,kwēn, 'klȯr-\ *noun* [*chlor-* + *qu*inoline] (1946)
: an antimalarial drug $C_{18}H_{26}ClN_3$ administered as the bitter crystalline diphosphate

chlo·ro·sis \klə-'rō-səs\ *noun* (1678)
1 : an iron-deficiency anemia especially of adolescent girls that may impart a greenish tint to the skin — called also *greensickness*
2 : a diseased condition in green plants marked by yellowing or blanching
— **chlo·rot·ic** \-'rä-tik\ *adjective*

chlo·ro·thi·a·zide \,klȯr-ō-'thī-ə-,zīd, ,klȯr-, -zəd\ *noun* (1957)
: a thiazide diuretic $C_7H_6ClN_3O_4S_2$ used especially to treat edema and to increase the effectiveness of antihypertensive drugs

chlor·prom·a·zine \klȯr-'prä-mə-,zēn, ,klȯr-\ *noun* [*chlor-* + *propyl* + *methyl* + *azine*] (1952)
: a phenothiazine $C_{17}H_{19}ClN_2S$ used as a tranquilizer especially in the form of its hydrochloride to suppress the more flagrant symptoms of psychotic disorders (as in schizophrenia)

chlor·prop·amide \-'prä-pə-,mīd, -'prō-\ *noun* [*chlor-* + *prop*ane + *amide*] (1960)
: a sulfonylurea drug $C_{10}H_{13}ClN_2O_3S$ used orally to reduce blood sugar in the treatment of mild diabetes

chlor·tet·ra·cy·cline \,klȯr-,te-trə-'sī-,klēn, ,klȯr-\ *noun* (1953)
: a yellow crystalline broad-spectrum antibiotic $C_{22}H_{23}ClN_2O_8$ that is produced by a soil actinomycete (*Streptomyces aureofaciens*) and is sometimes used in animal feeds to stimulate growth

cho·ano·cyte \kō-'a-nə-,sīt\ *noun* [International Scientific Vocabulary *choan-* funnel-shaped (from Greek *choanē* funnel) + *-cyte*] (1888)
: COLLAR CELL

¹chock \'chäk\ *noun* [origin unknown] (1769)
1 : a wedge or block for steadying a body (as a cask) and holding it motionless, for filling in an unwanted space, or for blocking the movement of a wheel
2 : a heavy metal casting (as on the bow or stern of a ship) with two short horn-shaped arms curving inward between which ropes or hawsers may pass for mooring or towing

²chock *adverb* (1834)
: as close or as completely as possible

³chock *transitive verb* (1854)
: to stop or make fast with or as if with chocks

¹chock·a·block \'chä-kə-,bläk\ *adverb* (1850)
: CHOCK ⟨*chockablock* full⟩

²chockablock *adjective* (circa 1890)
1 : brought close together
2 : very full

chock-full *or* **chock·ful** \'chək-'fu̇l, 'chäk-, -,fu̇l\ *adjective* [Middle English *chokkefull*, probably from *choken* to choke + *full*] (15th century)
: full to the limit

choc·o·hol·ic \,chä-kə-'hȯ-lik, ,chȯ-, -'hä-\ *noun* [*chocolate* + *-oholic* (as in *alcoholic*)] (1968)
: a person who craves or compulsively consumes chocolate

choc·o·late \'chä-k(ə-)lət, 'chȯ-\ *noun* [Spanish, from Nahuatl *chocolātl*] (1604)
1 : a beverage made by mixing chocolate with water or milk
2 : a food prepared from ground roasted cacao beans
3 : a small candy with a center (as a fondant) and a chocolate coating
4 : a brownish gray
— **chocolate** *adjective*

chocolate-box *adjective* [from the pictures formerly commonly seen on boxes of chocolates] (1901)
: superficially pretty or sentimental

choc·o·la·tier \,chä-k(ə-)lə-'tir, ,chȯ-\ *noun* [French, from *chocolat* chocolate] (1888)
: a maker or seller of chocolate candy

choc·o·laty *or* **choc·o·lat·ey** \'chä-k(ə-)lə-tē, 'chȯ-\ *adjective* (1926)
: made of or like chocolate; *also* : having a rich chocolate flavor

Choc·taw \'chäk-(ˌ)tò\ *noun, plural* **Choc·taw** *or* **Choctaws** [Choctaw *čahta*] (1722)
1 : a member of an American Indian people of Mississippi, Alabama, and Louisiana
2 : the language of the Choctaw and Chickasaw people

¹choice \'chȯis\ *noun* [Middle English *chois*, from Old French, from *choisir* to choose, of Germanic origin; akin to Old High German *kiosan* to choose — more at CHOOSE] (13th century)
1 : the act of choosing **:** SELECTION
2 : power of choosing **:** OPTION
3 a : the best part **:** CREAM **b :** a person or thing chosen
4 : a sufficient number and variety to choose among
5 : care in selecting
6 : a grade of meat between prime and good
— **of choice :** to be preferred ☆

²choice *adjective* **choic·er; choic·est** (14th century)
1 : worthy of being chosen
2 : selected with care
3 a : of high quality **b :** of a grade between prime and good ⟨*choice* meat⟩ ☆
— **choice·ly** *adverb*
— **choice·ness** *noun*

¹choir \'kwī-(ə)r\ *noun* [Middle English *quer*, from Middle French *cuer*, from Medieval Latin *chorus*, from Latin, chorus — more at CHORUS] (14th century)
1 : an organized company of singers (as in a church service)
2 : a group of instruments of the same class ⟨a brass *choir*⟩
3 : an organized group of persons or things
4 : a division of angels
5 : the part of a church occupied by the singers or by the clergy; *also* **:** the part of a church where the services are performed
6 : a group organized for ensemble speaking

²choir *intransitive verb* (1596)
: to sing or sound in chorus or concert

choir·boy \'kwī-(ə)r-ˌbȯi\ *noun* (1837)
: a boy member of a choir

choir loft *noun* (1929)
: a gallery occupied by a church choir

choir·mas·ter \-ˌmas-tər\ *noun* (1860)
: the director of a choir (as in a church)

¹choke \'chōk\ *verb* **choked; chok·ing** [Middle English, alteration of *achoken*, from Old English *ācēocian*, from *ā-*, perfective prefix + *cēoce, cēace* jaw, cheek — more at ABIDE, CHEEK] (14th century)
transitive verb
1 : to check normal breathing of by compressing or obstructing the trachea or by poisoning or adulterating available air
2 a : to check the growth, development, or activity of ⟨the flowers were *choked* by the weeds⟩ **b :** to obstruct by filling up or clogging ⟨leaves *choked* the drain⟩ **c :** to fill completely **:** JAM ⟨roads *choked* with traffic⟩
3 : to enrich the fuel mixture of (a motor) by partially shutting off the air intake of the carburetor
4 : to grip (as a baseball bat) some distance from the end of the handle
intransitive verb
1 : to become choked in breathing
2 a : to become obstructed or checked **b :** to become or feel constricted in the throat (as from strong emotion) — usually used with *up* ⟨*choked* up and couldn't finish the speech⟩
3 : to shorten one's grip especially on the handle of a bat — usually used with *up*
4 : to lose one's composure and fail to perform effectively in a critical situation

²choke *noun* (1736)
1 : the filamentous inedible center of an artichoke head; *broadly* **:** an artichoke head
2 : something that obstructs passage or flow: as **a :** a valve for choking a gasoline engine **b :** a constriction in an outlet (as of an oil well) that restricts flow **c :** REACTOR 2 **d :** a constriction (as a narrowing of the barrel or an attachment) at the muzzle of a shotgun that serves to limit the spread of shot
3 : the act of choking

choke·ber·ry \-ˌber-ē\ *noun* (1778)
: a small berrylike astringent fruit; *also* **:** any of a genus (*Aronia*) of shrubs of the rose family bearing chokeberries

choke chain *noun* (1955)
: a collar that may be tightened as a noose and that is used especially in training and controlling powerful or stubborn dogs — called also *choke collar*

choke·cher·ry \'chōk-ˌcher-ē\ *noun* (1784)
: an American wild cherry (*Prunus virginiana*) with bitter or astringent red to black edible fruit; *also* **:** this fruit

choke coil *noun* (circa 1896)
: REACTOR 2

choke off *transitive verb* (1818)
: to bring to a stop or an end as if by choking

choke point *noun* (1944)
: a strategic narrow route providing passage through or to another region

chok·er \'chō-kər\ *noun* (circa 1552)
1 : one that chokes
2 : something (as a collar or necklace) worn closely about the throat or neck

chok·ing \'chō-kiŋ\ *adjective* (1562)
1 : producing the feeling of strangulation ⟨a *choking* cloud of smog⟩
2 : indistinct in utterance — used especially of a person's voice ⟨a low *choking* laugh⟩
— **chok·ing·ly** \-kiŋ-lē\ *adverb*

choky \'chō-kē\ *adjective* (1579)
: tending to cause choking or to become choked

chol- *or* **chole-** *or* **cholo-** *combining form* [Greek *chol-, cholē-, cholo-,* from *cholē, cholos* — more at GALL]
: bile **:** gall ⟨*cholate*⟩

chol·an·gi·og·ra·phy \kə-ˌlan-jē-'ä-grə-fē, (ˌ)kō-\ *noun* (1936)
: radiographic visualization of the bile ducts after injection of a radiopaque substance
— **chol·an·gio·graph·ic** \-jē-ə-'gra-fik\ *adjective*
— **chol·an·gio·gram** \-'lan-jē-ə-ˌgram\ *noun*

cho·late \'kō-ˌlāt\ *noun* (circa 1846)
: a salt or ester of cholic acid

cho·le·cal·cif·er·ol \ˌkō-lə-(ˌ)kal-'si-fə-ˌrȯl, -ˌrōl\ *noun* [International Scientific Vocabulary] (1955)
: a sterol $C_{27}H_{43}OH$ that is a natural form of vitamin D found especially in fish, egg yolks, and fish-liver oils and is formed in the skin on exposure to sunlight or ultraviolet rays — called also *vitamin D₃*

cho·le·cys·tec·to·my \-(ˌ)sis-'tek-tə-mē\ *noun, plural* **-mies** [New Latin *cholecystis* gallbladder (from *chol-* + Greek *kystis* bladder) + International Scientific Vocabulary *-ectomy* — more at CYST] (1885)
: surgical excision of the gallbladder
— **cho·le·cys·tec·to·mized** \-ˌmīzd\ *adjective*

cho·le·cys·ti·tis \-(ˌ)sis-'tī-təs\ *noun* [New Latin, from *cholecystis*] (1866)
: inflammation of the gallbladder

cho·le·cys·to·ki·nin \-ˌsis-tə-'kī-nən\ *noun* [New Latin *cholecystis* + English *-o-* + *kinin*] (circa 1929)
: a hormone secreted especially by the duodenal mucosa that regulates the emptying of the gallbladder and secretion of enzymes by the pancreas and that has been found in the brain — called also *cholecystokinin-pancreozymin, pancreozymin*

cho·le·li·thi·a·sis \ˌkō-lə-li-'thī-ə-səs\ *noun* [New Latin] (circa 1860)
: production of gallstones; *also* **:** the resulting abnormal condition

cho·ler \'kä-lər, 'kō-\ *noun* [Middle English *coler*, from Middle French *colere*, from Latin *cholera* cholera, from Greek] (14th century)
1 a *archaic* **:** YELLOW BILE **b** *obsolete* **:** BILE 1a
2 *obsolete* **:** the quality or state of being bilious
3 : ready disposition to irritation **:** IRASCIBILITY; *also* **:** ANGER

chol·era \'kä-lə-rə\ *noun* [Latin] (1601)
: any of several diseases of humans and domestic animals usually marked by severe gastrointestinal symptoms; *especially* **:** an acute diarrheal disease caused by an enterotoxin produced by a comma-shaped gram-negative bacillus (*Vibrio cholerae* synonym *V. comma*) when it is present in large numbers in the proximal part of the human small intestine ◇

☆ SYNONYMS

Choice, option, alternative, preference, selection, election mean the act or opportunity of choosing or the thing chosen. CHOICE suggests the opportunity or privilege of choosing freely ⟨freedom of *choice*⟩. OPTION implies a power to choose that is specifically granted or guaranteed ⟨the *option* of paying now or later⟩. ALTERNATIVE implies a necessity to choose one and reject another possibility ⟨equally attractive *alternatives*⟩. PREFERENCE suggests the guidance of choice by one's judgment or predilections ⟨a *preference* for cool weather⟩. SELECTION implies a wide range of choice ⟨a varied *selection* of furniture⟩. ELECTION implies an end or purpose which requires exercise of judgment ⟨a tax return forces certain *elections* on you⟩.

Choice, exquisite, elegant, rare, delicate, dainty mean having qualities that appeal to a cultivated taste. CHOICE stresses preeminence in quality or kind ⟨*choice* fabric⟩. EXQUISITE implies a perfection in workmanship or design that appeals only to very sensitive taste ⟨an *exquisite* gold bracelet⟩. ELEGANT applies to what is rich and luxurious but restrained by good taste ⟨a sumptuous but *elegant* dining room⟩. RARE suggests an uncommon excellence ⟨*rare* beauty⟩. DELICATE implies exquisiteness, subtlety, and fragility ⟨*delicate* craftsmanship⟩. DAINTY sometimes carries an additional suggestion of smallness and of appeal to the eye or palate ⟨*dainty* sandwiches⟩.

◇ WORD HISTORY

cholera The word *cholera* now usually denotes Asiatic cholera, a still dreaded disease that typically assumes epidemic proportions when a concentrated population, such as that of a city or refugee camp, draws its drinking water from a source contaminated by fecal matter. Nineteeth-century medicine also recognized other forms of cholera ("summer cholera" or "European cholera") that manifested the same symptoms—vomiting and diarrhea—but in milder form. The antiquity of severe gastrointestinal disorders is evidenced by the word *cholera* itself, which is part of the medical vocabulary inherited by us from the ancient Greeks. Classical authors were divided on whether the Greek word was a derivative of *cholē* "bile" or *cholades* "intestines." In Late Latin, *cholera*, by association with Greek *cholē*, was used in the sense "bile." Through the medieval theory of humors, one of which was yellow bile (the fiery humor), it gave us English *choler* and *choleric*. See in addition HUMOR.

\ə\ abut \ᵊ\ kitten \ər\ further \a\ ash \ā\ ace
\ä\ mop, mar \au̇\ out \ch\ chin \e\ bet \ē\ easy
\g\ go \i\ hit \ī\ ice \j\ job \ŋ\ sing \ō\ go
\ȯ\ law \ȯi\ boy \th\ thin \t̷h\ the \ü\ loot \u̇\ foot
\y\ yet \zh\ vision *see also* Guide to Pronunciation

chol·era mor·bus \-'mòr-bəs, *dialect* -'mä(r)-; *dialect* 'kä-lē-\ *noun* [New Latin, literally, the disease cholera] (1673) : gastrointestinal illness characterized by griping, diarrhea, and sometimes vomiting — not used technically

cho·ler·ic \'kä-lə-rik, kə-'ler-ik\ *adjective* (1583)
1 : easily moved to often unreasonable or excessive anger **:** hot-tempered
2 : ANGRY, IRATE
— **cho·ler·i·cal·ly** \-ri-k(ə-)lē, -i-k(ə-)lē\ *adverb*

cho·le·sta·sis \ˌkō-lə-'stā-səs\ *noun, plural* **-sta·ses** \-ˌsēz\ [New Latin] (circa 1935) : a checking or failure of bile flow
— **cho·le·stat·ic** \-'sta-tik\ *adjective*

cho·le·ster·ic \ˌkō-lə-'ster-ik, kə-'les-tə-rik\ *adjective* [*cholesteric* relating to cholesterol, from French *cholesterique*] (1942) : of, relating to, or being the phase of a liquid crystal characterized by arrangement of molecules in layers with the long molecular axes parallel to one another in the plane of each layer and incrementally displaced in successive layers to give helical stacking — compare NEMATIC, SMECTIC

cho·les·ter·ol \kə-'les-tə-ˌrōl, -ˌròl\ *noun* [International Scientific Vocabulary, from *chol-* + Greek *stereos* solid] (1894) : a steroid alcohol $C_{27}H_{45}OH$ that is present in animal cells and body fluids, regulates membrane fluidity, and functions as a precursor molecule in various metabolic pathways and as a constituent of LDL may cause arteriosclerosis

cho·le·styr·amine \(ˌ)kō-ˌles-tə-'ra-ˌmēn, kə-; ˌkō-lə-'stir-ə-ˌmēn\ *noun* [*chol-* + *styrene* + *amine*] (circa 1962) : a strongly basic synthetic resin that forms insoluble complexes with bile acids and has been used to lower cholesterol levels in hypercholesterolemic patients

cho·lic acid \'kō-lik-\ *noun* [Greek *cholikos* bilious, from *cholē*] (1846) : a crystalline bile acid $C_{24}H_{40}O_5$

cho·line \'kō-ˌlēn\ *noun* [International Scientific Vocabulary] (circa 1871) : a base $C_5H_{15}NO_2$ that occurs as a component of phospholipids especially in animals, is a precursor of acetylcholine, and is essential to liver function

cho·lin·er·gic \ˌkō-lə-'nər-jik\ *adjective* [International Scientific Vocabulary] (1934)
1 : liberating, activated by, or involving acetylcholine ⟨*cholinergic* nerve fiber⟩ ⟨*cholinergic* functions⟩
2 : resembling acetylcholine especially in physiologic action ⟨a *cholinergic* drug⟩
— **cho·lin·er·gi·cal·ly** \-ji-k(ə-)lē\ *adverb*

cho·lin·es·ter·ase \ˌkō-lə-'nes-tə-ˌrās, -ˌrāz\ *noun* (1932)
1 : ACETYLCHOLINESTERASE
2 : an enzyme that hydrolyzes choline esters and that is found especially in blood plasma — called also *pseudocholinesterase*

chol·la \'chòi-yə\ *noun* [Mexican Spanish, from Spanish, head] (1846) : any of numerous shrubby opuntias chiefly of the southwestern U.S. and Mexico that have needlelike spines partly enclosed in a papery sheath and cylindrical joints

chomp \'chämp, 'chòmp\ *verb* [alteration of *champ*] (circa 1847)
intransitive verb **:** to chew or bite on something
transitive verb **:** to chew or bite on

chon \'chän\ *noun, plural* **chon** [Korean *chŏn*] — see *won* at MONEY table

cholla

chon·drio·some \'kän-drē-ə-ˌsōm\ *noun* [Greek *chondrion,* diminutive of *chondros* grain + International Scientific Vocabulary *-some*] (1910) : MITOCHONDRION

chon·drite \'kän-ˌdrīt\ *noun* [International Scientific Vocabulary, from Greek *chondros*] (1883) : a meteoric stone characterized by the presence of chondrules
— **chon·drit·ic** \kän-'dri-tik\ *adjective*

chon·dro·cra·ni·um \ˌkän-drō-'krā-nē-əm\ *noun* [Greek *chondros* grain, cartilage] (1875) : the cartilaginous parts of an embryonic cranium; *also* **:** the part of the adult skull derived therefrom

chon·droi·tin \kän-'dròi-tʲn, -'drō-ə-tʲn\ *noun* [International Scientific Vocabulary *chondroit*ic acid, an acid found in cartilage + 1*-in*] (1895) : a mucopolysaccharide occurring in sulfated form in various animal tissues (as cartilage)

chon·drule \'kän-(ˌ)drül\ *noun* [Greek *chondros* grain] (circa 1889) : a rounded granule of cosmic origin often found embedded in meteoric stones and sometimes free in marine sediments

chook \'chùk\ *noun* [imitative] (1880) *Australian & New Zealand* **:** CHICKEN 1

choose \'chüz\ *verb* **chose** \'chōz\; **cho·sen** \'chō-zʲn\; **choos·ing** \'chü-ziŋ\ [Middle English *chosen,* from Old English *cēosan;* akin to Old High German *kiosan* to choose, Latin *gustare* to taste] (before 12th century)
transitive verb
1 a : to select freely and after consideration ⟨*choose* a career⟩ **b :** to decide on especially by vote **:** ELECT ⟨*chose* her as captain⟩
2 a : to have a preference for ⟨*choose* one car over another⟩ **b :** DECIDE ⟨*chose* to go by train⟩
intransitive verb
1 : to make a selection
2 : to take an alternative — used after *cannot* and usually followed by *but* ⟨when earth is so kind, men cannot *choose* but be happy —J. A. Froude⟩
— **choos·er** \'chü-zər\ *noun*

choose up (1910)
transitive verb **:** to form (sides) especially for a game by having opposing captains choose their players
intransitive verb **:** to form sides for a game ⟨let's *choose up* and play ball⟩

choosy *or* **choos·ey** \'chü-zē\ *adjective* **choos·i·er; -est** (1862) **:** fastidiously selective **:** PARTICULAR

¹chop \'chäp\ *verb* **chopped; chop·ping** [Middle English *chappen, choppen* — more at CHAP] (14th century)
transitive verb
1 a : to cut into or sever usually by repeated blows of a sharp instrument **b :** to cut into pieces — often used with *up* **c :** to weed and thin out (young cotton) **d :** to cut as if by chopping ⟨*chop* prices⟩ ⟨a bridge *chops* the lake in two⟩
2 : to strike (as a ball) with a short quick downward stroke
3 : to subject to the action of a chopper ⟨*chop* a beam of light⟩
intransitive verb
1 : to make a quick stroke or repeated strokes with or as if with a sharp instrument (as an ax)
2 *archaic* **:** to move or act suddenly or violently

²chop *noun* (14th century)
1 a : a forceful usually slanting blow with or as if with an ax or cleaver **b :** a sharp downward blow or stroke
2 : a small cut of meat often including part of a rib — see LAMB illustration
3 : a mark made by or as if by chopping
4 : material that has been chopped up

5 a : a short abrupt motion (as of a wave) **b :** a stretch of choppy sea
6 : CHOPPER 6
7 *chiefly British* **:** AX 3

³chop *intransitive verb* **chopped; chop·ping** [Middle English *chappen, choppen* to barter, from Old English *cēapian*] (1540)
1 : to change direction
2 : to veer with or as if with wind
— **chop logic :** to argue with sophistical reasoning and minute distinctions

⁴chop *noun* [Hindi *chāp* stamp] (1614)
1 a : a seal or official stamp or its impression **b :** a license validated by a seal
2 a : a mark on goods or coins to indicate nature or quality **b :** a kind, brand, or lot of goods bearing the same chop **c :** QUALITY, GRADE ⟨of the first *chop*⟩

chop–chop \'chäp-'chäp, 'chäp-\ *adverb* [Chinese Pidgin English, reduplication of *chop* fast] (1834) **:** without delay **:** QUICKLY

chop–fall·en \'chäp-ˌfò-lən\ *variant of* CHAPFALLEN

chop–house \'chäp-ˌhaùs\ *noun* (circa 1690) **:** RESTAURANT

cho·pine \shä-'pēn, chä-\ *noun* [Middle French *chapin,* from Old Spanish] (1577) : a woman's shoe of the 16th and 17th centuries with a very high sole designed to increase stature and protect the feet from mud and dirt

chop·log·ic \'chäp-ˌlä-jik\ *noun* [obsolete *chop* to exchange, trade, from Middle English *choppen* to barter] (1533) : involved and often specious argumentation
— **choplogic** *adjective*

chop mark *noun* (1949) : an indentation made on a coin to attest weight, silver content, or legality
— **chop–marked** \'chäp-ˌmärkt\ *adjective*

chopped liver *noun* (1980) *slang* **:** one that is insignificant or not worth considering

¹chop·per \'chä-pər\ *noun* (1552)
1 : one that chops
2 *plural, slang* **:** TEETH
3 : a device that interrupts an electric current or a beam of radiation (as light) at short regular intervals
4 : MACHINE GUN
5 : HELICOPTER
6 : a high-bouncing batted baseball
7 : a customized motorcycle

²chopper *verb* (1955) **:** HELICOPTER

chop·pi·ness \'chä-pē-nəs\ *noun* (1881) : the quality or state of being choppy

chopping block *noun* (1703) : a wooden block on which material (as meat, wood, or vegetables) is cut, split, or diced

¹chop·py \'chä-pē\ *adjective* **chop·pi·er; -est** [²*chop*] (1605)
1 : being roughened **:** CHAPPED
2 : rough with small waves
3 a : interrupted by ups and downs ⟨*choppy* country⟩ **b :** JERKY ⟨short *choppy* strides⟩ **c :** DISCONNECTED ⟨*choppy* writing⟩
— **chop·pi·ly** \'chä-pə-lē\ *adverb*

²choppy *adjective* **chop·pi·er; -est** [³*chop*] (1865) **:** CHANGEABLE, VARIABLE ⟨a *choppy* wind⟩

chops \'chäps\ *noun plural* [alteration of ³*chap*] (1589)
1 : JAW
2 a : MOUTH **b :** the fleshy covering of the jaws ⟨a dog licking its *chops*⟩
3 *slang* **:** EMBOUCHURE; *broadly* **:** the technical facility of a musical performer

chop shop *noun* (1977) **:** a place where stolen automobiles are stripped of salable parts

chop·stick \'chäp-ˌstik\ *noun* [Chinese Pidgin English *chop* fast + English *stick*] (1699)

: one of a pair of slender sticks held between thumb and fingers and used chiefly in oriental countries to lift food to the mouth

chop su·ey \chäp-ˈsü-ē\ *noun, plural* **chop sueys** [Chinese (Guangdong) *jaahp-seui* odds and ends, from *jaahp* miscellaneous + *seui* bits] (1888)

: a dish prepared chiefly from bean sprouts, bamboo shoots, water chestnuts, onions, mushrooms, and meat or fish and served with rice and soy sauce

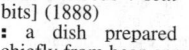

chopsticks

cho·ra·gus \kə-ˈrā-gəs\ *or* **cho·re·gus** \-ˈrē-, -ˈrā-\ *noun* [Latin & Greek; Latin *choragus*, from Greek *choragos, chorēgos*, from *choros* chorus + *agein* to lead — more at AGENT] (1625)

1 : the leader of a chorus or choir; *broadly* : the leader of any group or movement
2 : a leader of a dramatic chorus in ancient Greece
— **cho·rag·ic** \-ˈra-jik\ *adjective*

cho·ral \ˈkōr-əl, ˈkȯr-\ *adjective* [French or Medieval Latin; French *choral*, from Medieval Latin *choralis*, from Latin *chorus*] (1587)

1 : of or relating to a chorus or choir ⟨a *choral* group⟩
2 : sung or designed for singing by a choir ⟨a *choral* arrangement⟩
— **cho·ral·ly** \-ə-lē\ *adverb*

cho·rale \kə-ˈral, -ˈräl\ *noun* [German *Choral*, short for *Choralgesang* choral song] (1841)

1 : a hymn or psalm sung to a traditional or composed melody in church; *also* : a harmonization of a chorale melody ⟨a Bach *chorale*⟩
2 : CHORUS, CHOIR

chorale prelude *noun* (circa 1924)
: a composition usually for organ based on a chorale

¹**chord** \ˈkȯrd\ *noun* [alteration of Middle English *cord*, short for *accord*] (1608)
: three or more musical tones sounded simultaneously

²**chord** (14th century)
intransitive verb
1 : ACCORD
2 : to play chords especially on a stringed instrument
transitive verb
1 : to make chords on
2 : HARMONIZE

³**chord** *noun* [alteration of ¹*cord*] (1543)
1 : CORD 3a
2 : a straight line segment joining and included between two points on a circle; *broadly* : a straight line joining two points on a curve
3 : an individual emotion or disposition ⟨struck a responsive *chord*⟩
4 : either of the two outside members of a truss connected and braced by the web members
5 : the straight line distance joining the leading and trailing edges of an airfoil

chord·al \ˈkȯr-dᵊl\ *adjective* (1848)
1 : of, relating to, or suggesting a chord
2 : relating to music characterized more by harmony than by counterpoint

chor·da·meso·derm \ˌkȯr-də-ˈme-zə-ˌdərm *also* -ˈme-sə-\ *noun* [New Latin *chorda* cord + English *mesoderm*] (1939)
: the portion of the embryonic mesoderm that forms notochord and related structures and induces the formation of neural structures
— **chor·da·meso·der·mal** \-ˌme-zə-ˈdər-məl, -ˌme-sə-\ *adjective*

chor·date \ˈkȯr-ˌdāt, -dət\ *noun* [ultimately from Latin *chorda* cord] (1897)
: any of a phylum (Chordata) of animals having at least at some stage of development a

notochord, dorsally situated central nervous system, and gill clefts and including the vertebrates, lancelets, and tunicates
— **chordate** *adjective*

chore \ˈchōr, ˈchȯr\ *noun* [alteration of *chare*] (1746)
1 *plural* : the regular or daily light work of a household or farm
2 : a routine task or job
3 : a difficult or disagreeable task
synonym see TASK

cho·rea \kə-ˈrē-ə\ *noun* [New Latin, from Latin, dance, from Greek *choreia*, from *choros* chorus] (1804)
: a nervous disorder (as of humans or dogs) marked by spasmodic movements of limbs and facial muscles and by incoordination
— **cho·re·ic** \-ˈrē-ik\ *adjective*

cho·re·i·form \kə-ˈrē-ə-ˌfȯrm\ *adjective* [International Scientific Vocabulary] (circa 1899)
: resembling chorea ⟨*choreiform* convulsions⟩

cho·reo·graph \ˈkȯr-ē-ə-ˌgraf, ˈkȯr-\ (1943)
transitive verb
1 : to compose the choreography of
2 : to arrange or direct the movements, progress, or details of
intransitive verb
: to engage in choreography
— **cho·re·og·ra·pher** \ˌkȯr-ē-ˈä-grə-fər, ˌkȯr-\ *noun*

cho·re·og·ra·phy \ˌkȯr-ē-ˈä-grə-fē, ˌkȯr-\ *noun, plural* **-phies** [French *chorégraphie*, from Greek *choreia* + French *-graphie* -graphy] (circa 1789)
1 : the art of symbolically representing dancing
2 a : the composition and arrangement of dances especially for ballet **b** : a composition created by this art
3 : something resembling choreography ⟨a snail-paced *choreography* of delicate high diplomacy —Wolfgang Saxon⟩
— **cho·reo·graph·ic** \ˌkȯr-ē-ə-ˈgra-fik, ˌkȯr-\ *adjective*
— **cho·reo·graph·i·cal·ly** \-fi-k(ə-)lē\ *adverb*

cho·ric \ˈkȯr-ik, ˈkȯr-, ˈkär-\ *adjective* (1830)
: of, relating to, or being in the style of a chorus and especially a Greek chorus

cho·rine \ˈkȯr-ˌēn, ˈkȯr-\ *noun* [*chorus* + *-ine*, feminine noun suffix (as in *Pauline*)] (1922)
: CHORUS GIRL

cho·rio·al·lan·to·is \ˌkȯr-ē-(ˌ)ō-ə-ˈlan-tə-wəs, ˌkȯr-\ *noun* [New Latin, from Greek *chorion* + New Latin *allantois*] (1933)
: a vascular fetal membrane composed of the fused chorion and adjacent wall of the allantois that in the hen's egg is used as a living culture medium for viruses and for tissues — called also *chorioallantoic membrane*
— **cho·rio·al·lan·to·ic** \-ˌa-lən-ˈtō-ik\ *adjective*

cho·rio·car·ci·no·ma \-ˌkär-sᵊn-ˈō-mə\ *noun* [New Latin, from *chorion* + *carcinoma*] (1901)
: a malignant tumor developing in the uterus from the trophoblast and rarely in the testes from a neoplasm

cho·ri·on \ˈkōr-ē-ˌän, ˈkȯr-\ *noun* [New Latin, from Greek] (1545)
: the highly vascular outer embryonic membrane of reptiles, birds, and mammals that in placental mammals is associated with the allantois in the formation of the placenta

cho·ri·on·ic \ˌkōr-ē-ˈä-nik, ˌkȯr-\ *adjective* (1892)
1 : of, relating to, or being part of the chorion ⟨*chorionic* villi⟩
2 : secreted or produced by chorionic or related tissue (as in the placenta or a choriocarcinoma) ⟨human *chorionic* gonadotropin⟩

cho·ris·ter \ˈkȯr-ə-stər, ˈkȯr-, ˈkär-\ *noun* [Middle English *querister*, from Anglo-French *cueristre*, from Medieval Latin *chorista*, from Latin *chorus*] (14th century)
1 : a singer in a choir; *specifically* : CHOIRBOY

2 : the leader of a church choir

cho·ri·zo \chə-ˈrē-(ˌ)zō, -(ˌ)sō\ *noun, plural* **-zos** [Spanish] (1846)
: a pork sausage highly seasoned especially with chili powder and garlic

C horizon *noun* (1935)
: the soil layer lying beneath the B horizon and consisting essentially of more or less weathered parent rock

cho·rog·ra·phy \kə-ˈrä-grə-fē\ *noun* [Latin *chorographia*, from Greek *chōrographia*, from *chōros* place + *-graphia* -graphy] (1559)
1 : the art of describing or mapping a region or district
2 : a description or map of a region; *also* : the physical conformation and features of such a region
— **cho·rog·ra·pher** \-grə-fər\ *noun*
— **cho·ro·graph·ic** \ˌkȯr-ə-ˈgra-fik, ˌkär-\ *adjective*

cho·roid \ˈkōr-ˌȯid, ˈkȯr-\ *also* **cho·ri·oid** \ˈkōr-ē-ˌȯid, ˈkȯr-\ *noun* [New Latin *choroides* resembling the chorion, from Greek *chorioeidēs*, from *chorion* chorion] (1683)
: a vascular membrane containing large branched pigmented cells that lies between the retina and the sclera of the vertebrate eye — called also *choroid coat*; see EYE illustration
— **choroid** *or* **cho·roi·dal** \kə-ˈrȯi-dᵊl\ *adjective*

chor·tle \ˈchȯr-tᵊl\ *verb* **chor·tled; chor·tling** \ˈchȯrt-liŋ, ˈchȯr-tᵊl-iŋ\ [probably blend of *chuckle* and *snort*] (1872)
intransitive verb
1 : to sing or chant exultantly ⟨he *chortled* in his joy —Lewis Carroll⟩
2 : to laugh or chuckle especially in satisfaction or exultation
transitive verb
: to say or sing with a chortling intonation
— **chortle** *noun*
— **chor·tler** \ˈchȯrt-lər, ˈchȯr-tᵊl-ər\ *noun*

¹**cho·rus** \ˈkōr-əs, ˈkȯr-\ *noun* [Latin, ring dance, chorus, from Greek *choros*] (1586)
1 a : a company of singers and dancers in Athenian drama participating in or commenting on the action; *also* : a similar company in later plays **b** : a character in Elizabethan drama who speaks the prologue and epilogue and comments on the action **c** : an organized company of singers who sing in concert : CHOIR; *especially* : a body of singers who sing the choral parts of a work (as in opera) **d** : a group of dancers and singers supporting the featured players in a musical comedy or revue
2 a : a part of a song or hymn recurring at intervals **b** : the part of a drama sung or spoken by the chorus **c** : a composition to be sung by a number of voices in concert **d** : the main part of a popular song; *also* : a jazz variation on a melodic theme
3 a : something performed, sung, or uttered simultaneously or unanimously by a number of persons or animals ⟨a *chorus* of boos⟩ ⟨that eternal *chorus* of: "Are we there yet?" from the back seat —Sheila More⟩ **b** : sounds so uttered ⟨visitors are taken to the woods by car to hear the mournful *choruses* of howling wolves —Bob Gaines⟩
— **in chorus** : in unison

²**chorus** *transitive verb* (1826)
: to sing or utter in chorus

chorus boy *noun* (1943)
: a young man who sings or dances in the chorus of a theatrical production (as a musical or revue)

chorus girl *noun* (1894)

\ə\ abut	\ᵊ\ kitten	\ər\ further	\a\ ash	\ā\ ace	
\ä\ mop, mar	\au̇\ out	\ch\ chin	\e\ bet	\ē\ easy	
\g\ go	\i\ hit	\ī\ ice	\j\ job	\ŋ\ sing	\ō\ go
\ȯ\ law	\ȯi\ boy	\th\ thin	\t̲h\ the	\ü\ loot	\u̇\ foot
\y\ yet	\zh\ vision	*see also* Guide to Pronunciation			

: a young woman who sings or dances in the chorus of a theatrical production (as a musical or revue)

¹chose *past of* CHOOSE

²chose \'shōz\ *noun* [French, from Latin *causa* cause, reason] (1670)
: a piece of personal property : THING

¹cho·sen \'chō-z°n\ *noun, plural* **chosen** (13th century)
: one who is the object of choice or of divine favor : an elect person

²chosen *adjective* [Middle English, from past participle of *chosen* to choose] (14th century)
1 : ELECT
2 : selected or marked for favor or special privilege ⟨a *chosen* few⟩

Chou \'jō\ *noun* [Chinese (Beijing) *Zhōu*] (1771)
: a Chinese dynasty traditionally dated 1122 to about 256 B.C. and marked by the development of the philosophical schools of Confucius, Mencius, Lao-tzu, and Mo Ti

chough \'chəf\ *noun* [Middle English] (13th century)
: either of two Old World birds (*Pyrrhocorax pyrrhocorax* and *P. graculus*) that are related to the crows and have red legs and glossy blue-black plumage

¹chouse \'chaùs\ *transitive verb* **choused; chous·ing** [perhaps from Turkish *çavuş* doorkeeper, messenger] (1708)
: CHEAT, TRICK

²chouse *transitive verb* **choused; chous·ing** [origin unknown] (1904)
West : to drive or herd roughly

¹chow \'chaù\ *noun* [short for *chowchow*] (1856)
: FOOD, VICTUALS

²chow *intransitive verb* (1917)
: EAT — often used with *down*

³chow *noun* [by shortening] (1889)
: CHOW CHOW

chow-chow \'chaù-ˌchaù\ *noun* [Chinese Pidgin English *chowchow* food] (1850)
1 : a Chinese preserve of ginger, fruits, and peels in heavy syrup
2 : a relish of chopped mixed pickles in mustard sauce

chow chow \'chaù-ˌchaù\ *noun, often both Cs capitalized* [perhaps from *chow-chow* Chinese person, from Chinese Pidgin English *chowchow* food] (1886)
: any of a breed of heavy-coated blocky dogs of Chinese origin having a broad head and muzzle, a distinctive blue-black tongue and black-lined mouth, and either a long dense coat with a full ruff or a short smooth coat — called also *chow*

chow chow

¹chow·der \'chaù-dər\ *transitive verb* (1732)
: to make chowder of

²chowder *noun* [French *chaudière* kettle, contents of a kettle, from Late Latin *caldaria* — more at CAULDRON] (1751)
: a soup or stew of seafood (as clams or fish) usually made with milk or tomatoes, salt pork, onions, and other vegetables (as potatoes); *also* : a soup resembling chowder ⟨corn *chowder*⟩

chow·der·head \-ˌhed\ *noun* [alteration of dialect *jolterhead* blockhead] (1833)
: DOLT, BLOCKHEAD
— **chow·der·head·ed** \'chaù-dər-ˌhe-dəd\ *adjective*

chow·hound \'chaù-ˌhaùnd\ *noun* (1942)
: one fond of eating

chow line *noun* (1919)
: a line of people waiting to be served food

chow mein \'chaù-'mān\ *noun* [Chinese (Guangdong) *cháau-mihn* fried noodles] (1903)
: a seasoned stew of shredded or diced meat, mushrooms, and vegetables that is usually served with fried noodles

chres·tom·a·thy \kre-'stä-mə-thē\ *noun, plural* **-thies** [New Latin *chrestomathia*, from Greek *chrēstomatheia*, from *chrēstos* useful + *manthanein* to learn — more at MATHEMATICAL] (1832)
1 : a selection of passages compiled as an aid to learning a language
2 : a volume of selected passages or stories of an author

chrism \'kri-zəm\ *noun* [Middle English *crisme*, from Old English *crisma*, from Late Latin *chrisma*, from Greek, ointment, from *chriein* to anoint] (before 12th century)
: consecrated oil used in Greek and Latin churches especially in baptism, chrismation, confirmation, and ordination

chris·ma·tion \kriz-'mā-shən\ *noun* [Medieval Latin *chrismation-, chrismatio* anointment with chrism, from Late Latin *chrismare* to anoint with chrism, from *chrisma*] (1642)
: a confirmatory sacrament of the Eastern Orthodox Church in which a baptized member is anointed with chrism

chris·mon \'kriz-ˌmän\ *noun, plural* **chris·ma** \-mə\ *or* **chrismons** [Medieval Latin, from Latin *Christus* Christ + Late Latin *monogramma* monogram] (1872)
: CHI-RHO

chris·om \'kri-zəm\ *noun* [Middle English *crisom*, short for *crisom cloth*, from *crisom* chrism + *cloth*] (13th century)
: a white cloth or robe put on a person at baptism as a symbol of innocence

chrisom child *noun* (1593)
: a child that dies in its first month

Christ \'krīst\ *noun* [Middle English *Crist*, from Old English, from Latin *Christus*, from Greek *Christos*, literally, anointed, from *chriein*] (before 12th century)
1 : MESSIAH
2 : JESUS
3 : an ideal type of humanity
4 *Christian Science* : the ideal truth that comes as a divine manifestation of God to destroy incarnate error
— **Christ·like** \-ˌlīk\ *adjective*
— **Christ·ly** \-lē\ *adjective*

chris·ten \'kri-s°n\ *transitive verb* **christened; chris·ten·ing** \'kris-niŋ, 'kri-s°n-iŋ\ [Middle English *cristnen*, from Old English *cristnian*, from *cristen* Christian, from Latin *christianus*] (before 12th century)
1 a : BAPTIZE **b** : to name at baptism
2 : to name or dedicate (as a ship) by a ceremony suggestive of baptism
3 : NAME
4 : to use for the first time

Chris·ten·dom \'kri-s°n-dəm\ *noun* [Middle English *cristendom*, from Old English *cristendōm*, from *cristen*] (before 12th century)
1 : CHRISTIANITY 1
2 : the part of the world in which Christianity prevails

chris·ten·ing *noun* (14th century)
: the ceremony of baptizing and naming a child

¹Chris·tian \'kris-chən, 'krish-\ *noun* [Latin *christianus*, adjective & noun, from Greek *christianos*, from *Christos*] (1526)
1 a : one who professes belief in the teachings of Jesus Christ **b** (1) : DISCIPLE 2 (2) : a member of one of the Churches of Christ separating from the Disciples of Christ in 1906 (3) : a member of the Christian denomination having part in the union of the United Church of Christ concluded in 1961
2 : the hero in Bunyan's *Pilgrim's Progress*

²Christian *adjective* (1553)

1 a : of or relating to Christianity ⟨*Christian* scriptures⟩ **b** : based on or conforming with Christianity ⟨*Christian* ethics⟩
2 a : of or relating to a Christian ⟨*Christian* responsibilities⟩ **b** : professing Christianity ⟨a *Christian* affirmation⟩
3 : commendably decent or generous ⟨has a very *Christian* concern for others⟩
— **Chris·tian·ly** *adjective or adverb*

Christian Brother *noun* (1883)
: a member of the Roman Catholic institute of Brothers of the Christian Schools founded by Saint John Baptist de la Salle in France in 1684 and dedicated to education

Christian era *noun* (1657)
: the period dating from the birth of Christ

chris·ti·a·nia \ˌkris-chē-'a-nē-ə, ˌkrish-, ˌkris-tē-, -'ä-nē-ə\ *noun* [*Christiania*, former name of Oslo, Norway] (1905)
: CHRISTIE

Chris·tian·i·ty \ˌkris-chē-'a-nə-tē, ˌkrish-, -'cha-nə-, ˌkris-tē-'a-\ *noun* (14th century)
1 : the religion derived from Jesus Christ, based on the Bible as sacred scripture, and professed by Eastern, Roman Catholic, and Protestant bodies
2 : conformity to the Christian religion
3 : CHRISTENDOM 2

Chris·tian·ize \'kris-chə-ˌnīz, 'krish-\ *transitive verb* **-ized; -iz·ing** (1593)
: to make Christian
— **Chris·tian·i·za·tion** \ˌkris-chə-nə-'zā-shən, ˌkrish-\ *noun*
— **Chris·tian·iz·er** \'kris-chə-ˌnī-zər, 'krish-\

Christian name *noun* (1549)
: GIVEN NAME

Christian Science *noun* (circa 1867)
: a religion founded by Mary Baker Eddy in 1866 that was organized under the official name of the Church of Christ, Scientist, that derives its teachings from the Scriptures as understood by its adherents, and that includes a practice of spiritual healing based on the teaching that cause and effect are mental and that sin, sickness, and death will be destroyed by a full understanding of the divine principle of Jesus's teaching and healing
— **Christian Scientist** *noun*

chris·tie *or* **chris·ty** \'kris-tē\ *noun, plural* **christies** [by shortening & alteration from *christiania*] (1925)
: a skiing turn used for altering the direction of hill descent or for stopping and executed usually at high speed by shifting the body weight forward and skidding into a turn with parallel skis

Christ·mas \'kris-məs\ *noun, often attributive* [Middle English *Christemasse*, from Old English *Cristes mæsse*, literally, Christ's mass] (before 12th century)
1 : a Christian feast on December 25 or among some Eastern Orthodox on January 7 that commemorates the birth of Christ and is usually observed as a legal holiday
2 : CHRISTMASTIDE
— **Christ·mas·sy** *or* **Christ·masy** \-mə-sē\ *adjective*

Christmas cactus *noun* [from its annual blooming around Christmastime] (circa 1900)
: a branching Brazilian cactus (*Schlumbergera truncata* synonym *Zygocactus truncatus*) with flat stems, joints with margins having one to several blunt teeth, and showy usually red, pink, white, or violet zygomorphic flowers — called also *crab cactus*

Christmas card *noun* (1883)
: a greeting card sent at Christmas

Christmas club *noun* (circa 1925)
: a savings account in which regular deposits are made throughout the year to provide money for Christmas shopping

Christmas fern *noun* (1878)
: a North American evergreen fern (*Polystichum acrostichoides*)

Christmas rose *noun* (1688)

: a European evergreen herb (*Helleborus niger*) of the buttercup family that has usually white flowers produced in winter

Christ·mas·tide \'kris-məs-,tīd\ *noun* (1626)
: the festival season from Christmas Eve till after New Year's Day or especially in England till Epiphany

Christ·mas·time \-,tīm\ *noun* (1837)
: the Christmas season

Christmas tree *noun* (1835)
1 : a usually evergreen tree decorated at Christmas
2 : an oil-well control device consisting of an assembly of fittings placed at the top of the well

Chris·to·cen·tric \,kris-tə-'sen-trik, ,krīs-\ *adjective* [Greek *Christos* Christ + English *-centric*] (1873)
: centering theologically on Christ

Chris·to·gram \'kris-tə-,gram, 'krīs-\ *noun* [Greek *Christos* + English *-gram*] (1900)
: a graphic symbol of Christ; *especially* **:** CHI-RHO

Chris·tol·o·gy \kris-'tä-lə-jē, krīs-\ *noun, plural* **-gies** [Greek *Christos* + English *-logy*] (1673)
: theological interpretation of the person and work of Christ
— **Chris·to·log·i·cal** \,kris-tə-'lä-ji-kəl, 'krīs-\ *adjective*

Christ's–thorn \'krīs(ts)-'thórn\ *or* **Christ–thorn** \'krīs(t)-\ *noun* (1562)
: any of several prickly or thorny shrubs (as the shrub *Paliurus spina-christi* or the jujube *Ziziphus jujuba*)

chrom- *or* **chromo-** *combining form* [International Scientific Vocabulary, from Greek *chrōma* color]
1 : chromium ⟨*chromize*⟩
2 a : color **:** colored ⟨*chromo*lithograph⟩ **b :** pigment ⟨*chromo*gen⟩

chro·ma \'krō-mə\ *noun* [Greek *chrōma*] (circa 1889)
1 : SATURATION 4a
2 : a quality of color combining hue and saturation

chro·maf·fin \'krō-mə-fən\ *adjective* [International Scientific Vocabulary *chrom-* + Latin *affinis* bordering on, related — more at AFFINITY] (1903)
: staining deeply with chromium salts ⟨*chromaffin* cells of the adrenal medulla⟩

chromat- *or* **chromato-** *combining form* [Greek *chrōmat-*, *chrōma*]
1 : color ⟨*chromat*id⟩
2 : chromatin ⟨*chromato*lysis⟩

chro·mate \'krō-,māt\ *noun* [French, from Greek *chrōma*] (1819)
: a salt of chromic acid

¹chro·mat·ic \krō-'ma-tik\ *noun* (1708)
: ACCIDENTAL 2

²chromatic *adjective* [Greek *chrōmatikos*, from *chrōmat-*, *chrōma* skin, color, modified tone; akin to Greek *chrōs* color] (circa 1798)
1 a : of or relating to color or color phenomena or sensations **b :** highly colored
2 : of or relating to chrome
3 a : of, relating to, or giving all the tones of the chromatic scale **b :** characterized by frequent use of accidentals
— **chro·mat·i·cal·ly** \-ti-k(ə-)lē\ *adverb*
— **chro·mat·i·cism** \-'ma-tə-,si-zəm\ *noun*

chromatic aberration *noun* (1831)
: aberration caused by the differences in refraction of the colored rays of the spectrum

chro·ma·tic·i·ty \,krō-mə-'ti-sə-tē\ *noun* (1922)
: the quality of color characterized by its dominant or complementary wavelength and purity taken together

chro·mat·ics \krō-'ma-tiks\ *noun plural but singular in construction* (circa 1790)
: the branch of colorimetry that deals with hue and saturation

chromatic scale *noun* (circa 1789)
: a musical scale consisting entirely of half steps

chro·ma·tid \'krō-mə-təd\ *noun* (1900)
: one of the usually paired and parallel strands of a duplicated chromosome joined by a single centromere

chro·ma·tin \'krō-mə-tən\ *noun* (1882)
: a complex of nucleic acid and basic proteins (as histone) in eukaryotic cells that is usually dispersed in the interphase nucleus and condensed into chromosomes in mitosis and meiosis — compare EUCHROMATIN, HETEROCHROMATIN; see CELL illustration
— **chro·ma·tin·ic** \,krō-mə-'ti-nik\ *adjective*

chro·mato·gram \krō-'ma-tə-,gram, krə-\ *noun* (1922)
1 : the pattern formed on the adsorbent medium by the layers of components separated by chromatography
2 : a time-based graphic record (as of concentration of eluted materials) of a chromatographic separation

chro·mato·graph \krō-'ma-tə-,graf, krə-\ *noun* (1946)
: an instrument for performing chromatographic separations and producing chromatograms
— **chromatograph** *verb*
— **chro·ma·tog·ra·pher** \,krō-mə-'tä-grə-fər\ *noun*

chro·ma·tog·ra·phy \,krō-mə-'tä-grə-fē\ *noun* (1937)
: a process in which a chemical mixture carried by a liquid or gas is separated into components as a result of differential distribution of the solutes as they flow around or over a stationary liquid or solid phase
— **chro·mato·graph·ic** \,krō-,ma-tə-'gra-fik, krə-\ *adjective*
— **chro·mato·graph·i·cal·ly** \-fi-k(ə-)lē\ *adverb*

chro·ma·tol·y·sis \,krō-mə-'tä-lə-səs\ *noun* [New Latin] (1901)
: the dissolution and breaking up of chromophil material (as chromatin) of a cell and especially a nerve cell
— **chro·mato·lyt·ic** \,krō-,ma-tə-'li-tik, krə-\ *adjective*

chro·mato·phore \krō-'ma-tə-,fōr, krə-, -,fòr\ *noun* [International Scientific Vocabulary] (circa 1859)
1 : a pigment-bearing cell; *especially* **:** one of the cells of an animal integument capable of causing integumentary color changes by expanding or contracting
2 : the organelle of photosynthesis in blue-green algae and photosynthetic bacteria; *broadly* **:** CHROMOPLAST, CHLOROPLAST

¹chrome \'krōm\ *noun* [French, from Greek *chrōma*] (1800)
1 a : CHROMIUM **b :** a chromium pigment
2 : something plated with an alloy of chromium

²chrome *transitive verb* **chromed; chroming** (1876)
1 : to treat with a compound of chromium (as in dyeing)
2 : CHROMIZE

-chrome \,krōm\ *noun combining form or adjective combining form* [Medieval Latin *-chromat-*, *-chroma* colored thing, from Greek *chrōmat-*, *chrōma*]
1 : colored thing ⟨helio*chrome*⟩
2 : coloring matter ⟨uro*chrome*⟩

chrome green *noun* (circa 1859)
: any of various brilliant green pigments containing or consisting of chromium compounds

chrome yellow *noun* (1819)
: a yellow pigment consisting essentially of neutral lead chromate $PbCrO_4$

chro·mic \'krō-mik\ *adjective* (circa 1828)
: of, relating to, or derived from chromium especially with a valence of three

chromic acid *noun* (1800)

: an acid H_2CrO_4 analogous to sulfuric acid but known only in solution and especially in the form of its salts

chro·mi·nance \'krō-mə-nən(t)s\ *noun* [*chrom-* + lum*inance*] (1952)
: the difference between a color and a chosen reference color of the same luminous intensity in color television

chro·mite \'krō-,mīt\ *noun* [German *Chromit*, from *chrom-*] (1840)
1 : a mineral that consists of an oxide of iron and chromium
2 : an oxide of bivalent chromium

chro·mi·um \'krō-mē-əm\ *noun* [New Latin, from French *chrome*] (1807)
: a blue-white metallic element found naturally only in combination and used especially in alloys and in electroplating — see ELEMENT table

chro·mize \'krō-,mīz\ *transitive verb* **chromized; chro·miz·ing** (1939)
: to treat (metal) with chromium in order to form a protective surface alloy

chro·mo \'krō-(,)mō\ *noun, plural* **chromos** (1869)
: CHROMOLITHOGRAPH

chro·mo·cen·ter \'krō-mə-,sen-tər\ *noun* (1926)
: a densely staining aggregation of heterochromatic regions in the nucleus of some cells

chro·mo·dy·nam·ics \,krō-mə-dī-'na-miks\ *noun plural but singular in construction* (1976)
: QUANTUM CHROMODYNAMICS

chro·mo·gen \'krō-mə-jən\ *noun* [International Scientific Vocabulary] (1858)
1 : a precursor of a biochemical pigment
2 : a pigment-producing microorganism

chro·mo·gen·ic \,krō-mə-'je-nik\ *adjective* (1884)
1 : of or relating to a chromogen
2 : being a process of photographic film development in which silver halides activate precursors of chemical dyes that form the final image while the silver is removed; *also* **:** being a film developed by this process

chro·mo·litho·graph \,krō-mə-'li-thə-,graf\ *noun* (1860)
: a picture printed in colors from a series of lithographic stones or plates
— **chromolithograph** *transitive verb*
— **chro·mo·litho·graph·ic** \-,li-thə-'gra-fik\ *adjective*
— **chro·mo·li·thog·raph·er** \-li-'thä-grə-fər\ *noun*
— **chro·mo·li·thog·ra·phy** \-grə-fē\ *noun*

chro·mo·mere \'krō-mə-,mir\ *noun* [International Scientific Vocabulary] (1896)
: one of the small bead-shaped and heavily staining masses of coiled chromatin that are linearly arranged along the chromosome
— **chro·mo·mer·ic** \,krō-mə-'mer-ik, -'mir-\ *adjective*

chro·mo·ne·ma \,krō-mə-'nē-mə\ *noun, plural* **-ne·ma·ta** \-'nē-mə-tə\ [New Latin, from *chrom-* + Greek *nēmat-*, *nēma* thread — more at NEMAT-] (circa 1925)
: the coiled filamentous core of a chromatid
— **chro·mo·ne·mat·ic** \-ni-'ma-tik\ *adjective*

chro·mo·phil \'krō-mə-,fil\ *adjective* [International Scientific Vocabulary] (1899)
: staining readily with dyes

chro·mo·phobe \-,fōb\ *adjective* (circa 1909)
: resisting staining with dyes

chro·mo·phore \'krō-mə-,fōr, -,fòr\ *noun* [International Scientific Vocabulary] (1879)
: a chemical group (as an azo group) that absorbs light at a specific frequency and so im-

\ə\ abut \ᵊ\ kitten \ər\ further \a\ ash \ā\ ace
\ä\ mop, mar \aú\ out \ch\ chin \e\ bet \ē\ easy
\g\ go \i\ hit \ī\ ice \j\ job \ŋ\ sing \ō\ go
\ò\ law \òi\ boy \th\ thin \th̲\ the \ü\ loot \ù\ foot
\y\ yet \zh\ vision *see also* Guide to Pronunciation

parts color to a molecule; *also* **:** a colored chemical compound
— **chro·mo·phor·ic** \‚krō-mə-'fòr-ik, -'fär-\ *adjective*
chro·mo·plast \'krō-mə-‚plast\ *noun* [International Scientific Vocabulary] (1900)
: a colored plastid usually containing red or yellow pigment (as carotene)
chro·mo·pro·tein \‚kro-mə-'prō-‚tēn, -'prō-tē-ən\ *noun* (1924)
: any of various proteins (as hemoglobins, carotenoids, or flavoproteins) having a pigment as a prosthetic group
chro·mo·some \'krō-mə-‚sōm, -‚zōm\ *noun* [International Scientific Vocabulary] (1889)
: one of the linear or sometimes circular DNA-containing bodies of viruses, prokaryotic organisms, and the cell nucleus of eukaryotic organisms that contain most or all of the genes of the individual — compare CHROMATIN
— **chro·mo·som·al** \‚krō-mə-'sō-məl, -'zō-\ *adjective*
— **chro·mo·som·al·ly** \-mə-lē\ *adverb*
chromosome number *noun* (1910)
: the usually constant number of chromosomes characteristic of a particular kind of animal or plant
chro·mo·sphere \'krō-mə-‚sfir\ *noun* (1868)
: the region of the atmosphere of a star (as the sun) between the star's photosphere and its corona
— **chro·mo·spher·ic** \‚krō-mə-'sfir-ik, -'sfer-\ *adjective*
chro·mous \'krō-məs\ *adjective* (1840)
: of, relating to, or derived from chromium especially with a valence of two
chron- *or* **chrono-** *combining form* [Greek, from *chronos*]
: time ⟨*chrono*gram⟩
chron·ax·ie *also* **chron·axy** \'krō-‚nak-sē, 'krä-\ *noun* [French *chronaxie*, from *chron-* + Greek *axia* value, from *axios* worthy — more at AXIOM] (1917)
: the minimum time required for excitation of a structure (as a nerve cell) by a constant electric current of twice the threshold voltage
chron·ic \'krä-nik\ *adjective* [French *chronique*, from Greek *chronikos* of time, from *chronos*] (1601)
1 a : marked by long duration or frequent recurrence **:** not acute ⟨*chronic* indigestion⟩ ⟨*chronic* experiments⟩ **b :** suffering from a chronic disease ⟨the special needs of *chronic* patients⟩
2 a : always present or encountered; *especially* **:** constantly vexing, weakening, or troubling ⟨*chronic* petty warfare⟩ **b :** being such habitually ⟨a *chronic* grumbler⟩
synonym see INVETERATE
— **chronic** *noun*
— **chron·i·cal·ly** \-ni-k(ə-)lē\ *adverb*
— **chro·nic·i·ty** \krä-'ni-sə-tē, krō-\ *noun*
¹**chron·i·cle** \'krä-ni-kəl\ *noun* [Middle English *cronicle*, from Anglo-French, alteration of Old French *chronique*, from Latin *chronica*, from Greek *chronika*, from neuter plural of *chronikos*] (14th century)
1 : a usually continuous historical account of events arranged in order of time without analysis or interpretation
2 : NARRATIVE
²**chronicle** *transitive verb* **-cled; -cling** \-k(ə-)liŋ\ (15th century)
1 : to record in or as if in a chronicle
2 : LIST, DESCRIBE
— **chron·i·cler** \-k(ə-)lər\ *noun*
chronicle play *noun* (1902)
: a play with a theme from history consisting usually of rather loosely connected episodes chronologically arranged
Chron·i·cles \'krä-ni-kəlz\ *noun plural but singular in construction*
: either of two historical books of canonical Jewish and Christian Scripture — called also *Paralipomenon;* see BIBLE table

chro·no·bi·ol·o·gy \‚krä-nō-bī-'ä-lə-jē, ‚krō-\ *noun* (1972)
: the study of biological rhythms
— **chro·no·bi·o·log·ic** \-bī-ə-'lä-jik\ *or* **chro·no·bi·o·log·i·cal** \-ji-kəl\ *adjective*
— **chro·no·bi·o·lo·gist** \-bī-'ä-lə-jist\ *noun*
chro·no·gram \'krä-nə-‚gram, 'krō-\ *noun* (1621)
: an inscription, sentence, or phrase in which certain letters express a date or epoch
chro·no·graph \'krä-nə-‚graf, 'krō-\ *noun* (1868)
: an instrument for measuring and recording time intervals: as **a :** an instrument having a revolving drum on which a stylus makes marks **b :** STOPWATCH; *also* **:** a watch incorporating the functions of a stopwatch **c :** an instrument for measuring the time of flight of projectiles
— **chro·no·graph·ic** \‚krä-nə-'gra-fik, ‚krō-\ *adjective*
— **chro·nog·ra·phy** \krə-'nä-grə-fē\ *noun*
chro·nol·o·ger \krə-'nä-lə-jər\ *noun* (circa 1572)
: CHRONOLOGIST
chro·no·log·i·cal \‚krä-nə-'lä-ji-kəl, ‚krō-\ *also* **chro·no·log·ic** \-jik\ *adjective* (1614)
: of, relating to, or arranged in or according to the order of time ⟨*chronological* tables of American history⟩; *also* **:** reckoned in units of time ⟨*chronological* age⟩
— **chro·no·log·i·cal·ly** \-ji-k(ə-)lē\ *adverb*
chro·nol·o·gist \krə-'nä-lə-jist\ *noun* (1611)
: an expert in chronology
chro·nol·o·gy \-jē\ *noun, plural* **-gies** [New Latin *chronologia*, from *chron-* + *-logia* -logy] (1593)
1 : the science that deals with measuring time by regular divisions and that assigns to events their proper dates
2 : a chronological table, list, or account
3 : an arrangement (as of events) in order of occurrence ⟨reconstruct the *chronology* of the trip⟩
chro·nom·e·ter \krə-'nä-mə-tər\ *noun* (circa 1735)
: TIMEPIECE; *especially* **:** one designed to keep time with great accuracy
chro·no·met·ric \‚krä-nə-'me-trik, ‚krō-\ *also* **chro·no·met·ri·cal** \-tri-kəl\ *adjective* (1830)
: of or relating to a chronometer or chronometry
— **chro·no·met·ri·cal·ly** \-tri-k(ə-)lē\ *adverb*
chro·nom·e·try \krə-'nä-mə-trē\ *noun* (1833)
: the measuring of time
chro·no·ther·a·py \‚krä-nō-'ther-ə-pē, ‚krō-\ *noun* (1973)
: treatment of a sleep disorder (as insomnia) by changing sleeping and waking times in an attempt to reset the patient's biological clock
chrys- *or* **chryso-** *combining form* [Greek, from *chrysos*]
: gold **:** yellow ⟨*chrys*arobin⟩
chrys·a·lid \'kri-sə-ləd\ *noun* (1777)
: CHRYSALIS
— **chrysalid** *adjective*
chrys·a·lis \'kri-sə-ləs\ *noun, plural* **chry·sal·i·des** \kri-'sa-lə-‚dēz\ *or* **chrys·a·lis·es** [Latin *chrysallid-, chrysallis* gold-colored pupa of butterflies, from Greek, from *chrysos* gold, of Semitic origin; akin to Hebrew *ḥārūṣ* gold] (1601)
1 : a pupa of a butterfly; *broadly* **:** an insect pupa
2 : a protecting covering **:** a sheltered state or stage of being or growth ⟨a budding writer could not emerge from his *chrysalis* too soon —William Du Bois⟩
chry·san·the·mum \kri-'san(t)-thə-məm *also* -'zan(t)-\ *noun* [Latin, from Greek *chrysanthemon*, from *chrys-* + *anthemon* flower; akin to Greek *anthos* flower] (1551)

1 : any of various composite plants (genus *Chrysanthemum*) including weeds, ornamentals grown for their brightly colored often double flower heads, and others important as sources of medicinals and insecticides
2 : a flower head of an ornamental chrysanthemum

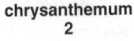
chrysanthemum 2

chrys·a·ro·bin \‚kri-sə-'rō-bən\ *noun* [*chrys-* + ar*aroba*, powder found in the wood of a Brazilian tree (*Andira araroba*) + ¹*-in*] (1887)
: a powder derived from the wood of a tropical tree used to treat skin diseases
Chry·se·is \krī-'sē-əs\ *noun* [Latin, from Greek *Chrysēis*]
: a daughter of a priest of Apollo in the *Iliad* narrative taken at Troy by Agamemnon but later restored to her father
chryso·ber·yl \'kri-sə-‚ber-əl\ *noun* [Latin *chrysoberyllus*, from Greek *chrysoberyllos*, from *chrys-* + *bēryllos* beryl] (1661)
1 *obsolete* **:** a yellowish beryl
2 : a usually yellow or pale green mineral consisting of beryllium aluminum oxide with a little iron and sometimes used as a gem
chrys·o·lite \'kri-sə-‚līt\ *noun* [Middle English *crisolite*, from Middle French, from Latin *chrysolithos*, from Greek, from *chrys-* + *-lithos* -lite] (13th century)
: OLIVINE
chrys·o·me·lid \‚kri-sə-'me-ləd, -'mē-\ *noun* [ultimately from Greek *chrysomēlolonthē* golden cockchafer] (circa 1904)
: any of a large family (Chrysomelidae) of small, usually oval and smooth, shining, and brightly colored beetles (as the Colorado potato beetle)
— **chrysomelid** *adjective*
chryso·phyte \'kri-sə-‚fīt\ *noun* [ultimately from Greek *chrysos* + *phyton* plant — more at PHYT-] (1959)
: GOLDEN-BROWN ALGA
chrys·o·prase \'kri-sə-‚prāz\ *noun* [alteration of Middle English *crisopace*, from Old French, from Latin *chrysoprasus*, from Greek *chrysoprasos*, from *chrys-* + *prason* leek; akin to Latin *porrum* leek] (1646)
: an apple-green chalcedony valued as a gem
chrys·o·tile \-‚tīl\ *noun* [German *Chrysotil*, from *chrys-* + *-til* fiber, from Greek *tillein* to pluck] (1850)
: a mineral consisting of a fibrous silky serpentine and constituting a kind of asbestos
chthon·ic \'thä-nik\ *also* **chtho·ni·an** \'thō-nē-ən\ *adjective* [Greek *chthon-, chthōn* earth — more at HUMBLE] (1882)
: of or relating to the underworld **:** INFERNAL ⟨*chthonic* deities⟩
chub \'chəb\ *noun, plural* **chub** *or* **chubs** [Middle English *chubbe*] (15th century)
1 : any of numerous freshwater cyprinid fishes (as of the genera *Gila* and *Nocomis*)
2 : any of several marine or freshwater fishes that are not cyprinids
chub·bi·ly \'chə-bə-lē\ *adverb* (1909)
: in the manner of one that is chubby
chub·by \'chə-bē\ *adjective* **chub·bi·er; -est** [*chub*] (1722)
: PLUMP ⟨a *chubby* boy⟩
— **chub·bi·ness** \'chə-bē-nəs\ *noun*
¹**chuck** \'chək\ *verb* [Middle English *chukken*, of imitative origin] (14th century)
: CLUCK
²**chuck** *noun* [perhaps from *chuck* chicken] (1595)
— used as an endearment
³**chuck** *transitive verb* [origin unknown] (1583)
1 : PAT, TAP
2 a : TOSS **b :** DISCARD ⟨*chucked* his old shirt⟩ **c :** DISMISS, OUST — used especially with *out* ⟨was *chucked* out of office⟩

3 : to have done with ⟨*chucked* his job⟩ ⟨*chuck* it all and retire⟩

⁴chuck *noun* (1611)
1 : a pat or nudge under the chin
2 : an abrupt movement or toss

⁵chuck *noun* [English dialect *chuck* lump] (1723)
1 : a cut of beef that includes most of the neck, the parts about the shoulder blade, and those about the first three ribs — see BEEF illustration
2 *chiefly West* **:** FOOD
3 : an attachment for holding a workpiece or tool in a machine (as a drill or lathe)

chuck·hole \'chǝk-ˌhōl\ *noun* [perhaps from ³*chuck* + *hole*] (1836)
: a hole or rut in a road **:** POTHOLE

chuck·le \'chǝ-kᵊl\ *intransitive verb* **chuck·led; chuck·ling** [probably frequentative of ¹*chuck*] (1803)
1 : to laugh inwardly or quietly
2 : to make a continuous gentle sound resembling suppressed mirth ⟨the clear bright water *chuckled* over gravel —B. A. Williams⟩
— **chuckle** *noun*
— **chuck·le·some** \-sǝm\ *adjective*
— **chuck·ling·ly** \-iŋ-lē\ *adverb*

chuck·le·head \'chǝ-kᵊl-ˌhed\ *noun* [*chuckle* lumpish + *head*] (1748)
: BLOCKHEAD
— **chuck·le·head·ed** \-ˌhe-dǝd\ *adjective*

chuck wagon *noun* [⁵*chuck*] (1890)
: a wagon carrying supplies and provisions for cooking (as on a ranch)

chuck·wal·la \'chǝk-ˌwä-lǝ\ *or* **chuck·a·wal·la** \'chǝ-kǝ-ˌwä-lǝ\ *noun* [American Spanish *chacahuala*, from Cahuilla (Uto-Aztecan language of southeast California) *čáxwal*] (1893)
: a large herbivorous lizard (*Sauromalus obesus* of the family Iguanidae) of desert regions of the southwestern U.S.

chuckwalla

chuck–will's–wid·ow \ˌchǝk-ˌwilz-'wi-(ˌ)dō\ *noun* [imitative] (1791)
: a nightjar (*Caprimulgus carolinensis*) of the southern U.S.

¹chuff \'chǝf\ *noun* [Middle English *chuffe*] (15th century)
: BOOR, CHURL

²chuff *intransitive verb* [imitative] (1914)
: to produce noisy exhaust or exhalations
: proceed or operate with chuffs ⟨the *chuffing* and snorting of switch engines —Paul Gallico⟩

³chuff *noun* (1915)
: the sound of noisy exhaust or exhalations

chuffed \'chǝft\ *adjective* [English dialect *chuff* pleased, puffed with fat] (1957)
British **:** PROUD, SATISFIED

chuf·fy \'chǝ-fē\ *adjective* **chuf·fi·er; -est** [English dialect *chuff* puffed with fat] (1611)
: FAT, CHUBBY

¹chug \'chǝg\ *noun* [imitative] (1866)
: a dull explosive sound made by or as if by a laboring engine

²chug *intransitive verb* **chugged; chug·ging** (1896)
: to move or go with or as if with chugs ⟨a locomotive *chugging* along⟩
— **chug·ger** *noun*

³chug *transitive verb* **chugged; chug·ging** (circa 1968)
: CHUGALUG

chug·a·lug \'chǝ-gǝ-ˌlǝg\ *verb* **-lugged; -lug·ging** [imitative] (1956)
transitive verb
: to drink a container of (as beer) without pause; *also* **:** GUZZLE

intransitive verb
: to drink a container (as of beer) without pause

chu·kar \'chǝ-kǝr *also* chǝ-'kär\ *noun* [Hindi *cakor*] (1814)
: a grayish brown Eurasian partridge (*Alectoris chukar*) introduced as a game bird into arid mountainous regions of the western U.S.
— called also *chukar partridge*

chuk·ka \'chǝ-kǝ\ *noun* [*chukka*, alteration of *chukker*; from a similar polo player's boot] (1948)
: a usually ankle-length leather boot with two or three pairs of eyelets or a buckle and strap

chuk·ker \'chǝ-kǝr\ *also* **chuk·ka** \'chǝ-kǝ\ *noun* [Hindi *cakkar* circular course, from Sanskrit *cakra* wheel, circle — more at WHEEL] (1898)
: a playing period of a polo game

¹chum \'chǝm\ *noun* [perhaps by shortening & alteration from *chamber fellow* roommate] (1684)
: a close friend **:** PAL
— **chum·ship** \-ˌship\ *noun*

²chum *intransitive verb* **chummed; chum·ming** (1730)
1 : to room together
2 a : to be a close friend **b :** to show affable friendliness

³chum *noun* [origin unknown] (1857)
: animal or vegetable matter (as chopped fish or corn) thrown overboard to attract fish

⁴chum *verb* **chummed; chum·ming** (1857)
transitive verb
: to attract with chum
intransitive verb
: to throw chum overboard to attract fish

⁵chum *noun* [Chinook Jargon *cǝm* spotted, striped, from Lower Chinook *c̓ǝm* variegated] (1902)
: CHUM SALMON

Chu·mash \'chü-ˌmash\ *noun* (1891)
: a member of an American Indian people of southwestern California

chum·my \'chǝ-mē\ *adjective* **chum·mi·er; -est** (1884)
: INTIMATE, SOCIABLE
— **chum·mi·ly** \'chǝ-mǝ-lē\ *adverb*
— **chum·mi·ness** \'chǝ-mē-nǝs\ *noun*

chump \'chǝmp\ *noun* [perhaps blend of *chunk* and *lump*] (1883)
: FOOL, DUPE

chump change *noun* (circa 1968)
: a relatively small or insignificant amount of money

chum salmon *noun* [⁵*chum*] (1907)
: a salmon (*Oncorhynchus keta*) of the northern Pacific — called also *chum*

¹chunk \'chǝŋk\ *noun* [perhaps alteration of *chuck* short piece of wood] (1691)
1 : a short thick piece or lump (as of wood or coal)
2 : a large noteworthy quantity ⟨bet a sizable *chunk* of money on the race⟩
3 : a strong thickset horse usually smaller than a draft horse

²chunk *intransitive verb* [imitative] (1890)
: to make a dull plunging or explosive sound ⟨the rhythmic *chunking* of thrown quoits —John Updike⟩

chunky \'chǝŋ-kē\ *adjective* **chunk·i·er; -est** (1751)
1 : short and thick or broad; *especially* **:** STOCKY
2 : filled with chunks ⟨*chunky* peanut butter⟩
— **chunk·i·ly** \-kǝ-lē\ *adverb*

chun·ter \'chǝn-tǝr\ *intransitive verb* [probably of imitative origin] (1599)
British **:** to talk in a low inarticulate way
: MUTTER

¹church \'chǝrch\ *noun* [Middle English *chirche*, from Old English *cirice*, ultimately from Late Greek *kyriakon*, from Greek, neuter of *kyriakos* of the lord, from *kyrios* lord, mas-

ter; akin to Sanskrit *śūra* hero, warrior] (before 12th century)
1 : a building for public and especially Christian worship
2 : the clergy or officialdom of a religious body
3 : a body or organization of religious believers: as **a :** the whole body of Christians **b :** DENOMINATION **c :** CONGREGATION
4 : a public divine worship ⟨goes to *church* every Sunday⟩
5 : the clerical profession ⟨considered the *church* as a possible career⟩

²church *adjective* (before 12th century)
1 : of or relating to a church ⟨*church* government⟩
2 *chiefly British* **:** of or relating to the established church

³church *transitive verb* (14th century)
: to bring to church to receive one of its rites

churched \'chǝrcht\ *adjective* (14th century)
: affiliated with a church

church father *noun* (1856)
: FATHER 4

church·go·er \'chǝrch-ˌgō(-ǝ)r\ *noun* (1687)
: one who habitually attends church
— **church·go·ing** \-ˌgō-iŋ, -ˌgȯ(-)iŋ\ *adjective or noun*

church·i·an·i·ty \ˌchǝr-chē-'a-nǝ-tē\ *noun* [*church* + *-ianity* (as in *Christianity*)] (1837)
: the usually excessive or sectarian attachment to the practices and interests of a particular church

church·ing *noun* (15th century)
: the administration or reception of a rite of the church; *specifically* **:** a ceremony in some churches by which women after childbirth are received in the church with prayers, blessings, and thanksgiving

church key *noun* (circa 1953)
: an implement with a triangular pointed head at one end for piercing the tops of cans and often with a rounded head at the other end for opening bottles

church·less \'chǝrch-lǝs\ *adjective* (1641)
: not affiliated with a church

church·ly \'chǝrch-lē\ *adjective* (before 12th century)
1 : of or relating to a church
2 : suitable to or suggestive of a church
3 : adhering to a church
4 : CHURCHY 1
— **church·li·ness** *noun*

church·man \'chǝrch-mǝn\ *noun* (14th century)
1 : CLERGYMAN
2 : a member of a church

church·man·ship \-mǝn-ˌship\ *noun* (circa 1680)
: the attitude, belief, or practice of a churchman

church mode *noun* (circa 1864)
: one of eight scales prevalent in medieval music each utilizing a different pattern of intervals and beginning on a different tone

Church of England (1534)
: the established episcopal church of England

church register *noun* (1846)
: a parish register of baptisms, marriages, and deaths

church school *noun* (1862)
1 : a school providing a general education but supported by a particular church in contrast to a public school or a nondenominational private school
2 : an organization of officers, teachers, and pupils for purposes of moral and religious education under the supervision of a local church

Church Slavonic *noun* (1850)
: any of several Slavic literary and liturgical languages that continue Old Church Slavonic

but vary regionally under influence of vernacular languages

church·war·den \'chərch-,wȯr-d°n\ *noun* (15th century)
1 : one of two lay parish officers in Anglican churches with responsibility especially for parish property and alms
2 : a long-stemmed clay pipe

church·wom·an \-,wu̇-mən\ *noun* (1722)
: a woman who is a member of a church

churchy \'chər-chē\ *adjective* (1843)
1 : marked by strict conformity or zealous adherence to the forms or beliefs of a church
2 : of or suggestive of a church or church services

church·yard \'chərch-,yärd\ *noun* (12th century)
: a yard that belongs to a church and is often used as a burial ground

churl \'chər(-ə)l\ *noun* [Middle English, from Old English *ceorl* man, ceorl; akin to Old Norse *karl* man, husband] (before 12th century)
1 : CEORL
2 : a medieval peasant
3 : RUSTIC, COUNTRYMAN
4 a : a rude ill-bred person **b :** a stingy morose person

churl·ish \'chər-lish\ *adjective* (before 12th century)
1 : of, resembling, or characteristic of a churl
: VULGAR
2 : marked by a lack of civility or graciousness **:** SURLY
3 : difficult to work with or deal with **:** INTRACTABLE ⟨*churlish* soil⟩
synonym see BOORISH
— **churl·ish·ly** *adverb*
— **churl·ish·ness** *noun*

¹churn \'chərn\ *noun* [Middle English *chyrne*, from Old English *cyrin*; akin to Old Norse *kjarni* churn] (before 12th century)
: a vessel for making butter in which milk or cream is agitated in order to separate the oily globules from the watery medium

²churn (15th century)
transitive verb
1 : to agitate (milk or cream) in a churn in order to make butter
2 a : to stir or agitate violently ⟨an old sternwheeler *churning* the muddy river⟩ **b :** to make (as foam) by so doing
3 : to make (the account of a client) excessively active by frequent purchases and sales primarily in order to generate commissions
intransitive verb
1 : to work a churn
2 a : to produce or be in violent motion **b :** to proceed by means of rotating members (as wheels)

churn out *transitive verb* (1912)
: to produce mechanically or copiously **:** GRIND OUT ⟨the usual pap which has been *churned out* about this superstar —W. S. Murphy⟩

churr \'chər\ *intransitive verb* [imitative] (1555)
: to make a vibrant or whirring noise like that made by some insects (as the cockchafer) or some birds (as the partridge)
— **churr** *noun*

chur·ri·gue·resque \,chu̇r-i-gə-'resk\ *adjective*, *often capitalized* [Spanish *churrigueresco*, from José *Churriguera* (died 1725) Spanish architect] (1845)
: of or relating to a Spanish baroque architectural style characterized by elaborate surface decoration or its Latin-American adaptation

¹chute \'shüt\ *noun* [French, from Old French, from *cheoir* to fall, from Latin *cadere* — more at CHANCE] (1805)
1 a : FALL 6b **b :** a quick descent (as in a river)
: RAPID
2 : an inclined plane, sloping channel, or passage down or through which things may pass
: SLIDE
3 : PARACHUTE

²chute *verb* **chut·ed; chut·ing** (1884)
transitive verb
: to convey by a chute
intransitive verb
1 : to go in or as if in a chute
2 : to utilize a chute (as by passing ore down it)

chut·ist \'shü-tist\ *noun* (1920)
: PARACHUTIST

chut·ney \'chət-nē\ *noun*, *plural* **chutneys** [Hindi *caṭnī*] (1813)
: a thick sauce of Indian origin that contains fruits, vinegar, sugar, and spices and is used as a condiment

chutz·pah *also* **chutz·pa** \'hu̇t-spə, 'ku̇t-, -(,)spä\ *noun* [Yiddish *khutspe*, from Late Hebrew *ḥuṣpāh*] (1892)
: supreme self-confidence **:** NERVE, GALL
synonym see TEMERITY

chyle \'kī(ə)l\ *noun* [Late Latin *chylus*, from Greek *chylos* juice, chyle; akin to Greek *chein* to pour — more at FOUND] (1541)
: lymph that is milky from emulsified fats, characteristically present in the lacteals, and most apparent during intestinal absorption of fats
— **chy·lous** \'kī-ləs\ *adjective*

chy·lo·mi·cron \,kī-lō-'mī-,krän\ *noun* [Greek *chylos* + *mikron*, neuter of *mikros* small — more at MICRO-] (1921)
: a microscopic lipid particle common in the blood during fat digestion and assimilation

chyme \'kīm\ *noun* [New Latin *chymus*, from Late Latin, chyle, from Greek *chymos* juice; akin to Greek *chein*] (1607)
: the semifluid mass of partly digested food expelled by the stomach into the duodenum

chy·mo·tryp·sin \,kī-mō-'trip-sən\ *noun* [*chyme* + *-o-* + *trypsin*] (1933)
: a protease that hydrolyzes peptide bonds and is formed in the intestine from chymotrypsinogen
— **chy·mo·tryp·tic** \-tik\ *adjective*

chy·mo·tryp·sin·o·gen \-,trip-'si-nə-jən\ *noun* (1933)
: a zymogen that is secreted by the pancreas and is converted by trypsin to chymotrypsin

ciao \'chau̇\ *interjection* [Italian, from Italian dialect, literally, (I am your) slave, from Medieval Latin *sclavus* — more at SLAVE] (1929)
— used conventionally as an utterance at meeting or parting

ci·bo·ri·um \sə-'bȯr-ē-əm, -'bȯr-\ *noun*, *plural* **-ria** \-ē-ə\ [Medieval Latin, from Latin, cup, from Greek *kibōrion*] (1651)
1 : a goblet-shaped vessel for holding eucharistic bread
2 : BALDACHIN; *specifically* **:** a freestanding vaulted canopy supported by four columns over a high altar

ci·ca·da \sə-'kā-də, -'kä-; sī-'kā-\ *noun*, *plural* **-das** *also* **-dae** \-'kā-(,)dē, -'kä-\ [New Latin, genus name, from Latin, cicada] (14th century)
: any of a family (Cicadidae) of homopterous insects which have a stout body, wide blunt head, and large transparent wings and the males of which produce a loud buzzing noise usually by stridulation

ci·ca·la \sə-'kä-lə\ *noun* [Italian, from Medieval Latin, alteration of Latin *cicada*] (1820)
: CICADA

cic·a·tri·cial \,si-kə-'tri-shəl\ *adjective* (1881)
: of or relating to a cicatrix

cic·a·trix \'si-kə-,triks, sə-'kā-triks\ *noun*, *plural* **cic·a·tri·ces** \,si-kə-'trī-(,)sēz, sə-'kā-trə-,sēz\ [Latin *cicatric-, cicatrix*] (1641)
1 : a scar resulting from formation and contraction of fibrous tissue in a wound
2 : a mark resembling a scar especially when caused by the previous attachment of an organ or part (as a leaf)

cic·a·tri·za·tion \,si-kə-trə-'zā-shən\ *noun* (15th century)
: scar formation at the site of a healing wound
— **cic·a·trize** \'si-kə-,trīz\ *transitive verb*

ci·ce·ro·ne \,si-sə-'rō-nē, ,chē-chə-\ *noun*, *plural* **-ni** \-(,)nē\ [Italian, from *Cicerone* Cicero] (1726)
: a guide who conducts sightseers

cich·lid \'si-kləd\ *noun* [ultimately from Greek *kichlē* thrush, a kind of wrasse; perhaps akin to Greek *chelidōn* swallow] (1884)
: any of a family (Cichlidae) of mostly tropical spiny-finned usually freshwater fishes including several kept in tropical aquariums
— **cichlid** *adjective*

ci·cis·beo \,chē-chəz-'bā-(,)ō\ *noun*, *plural* **-bei** \-'bā-,ē\ [Italian] (1718)
: LOVER, GALLANT
— **ci·cis·be·ism** \-'bā-,i-zəm\ *noun*

-cidal *adjective combining form* [Late Latin *-cidalis*, from Latin *-cida*]
: killing : having power to kill ⟨insecti*cidal*⟩

-cide *noun combining form* [Middle French, from Latin *-cida*, from *caedere* to cut, kill]
1 : killer ⟨insecti*cide*⟩
2 [Middle French, from Latin *-cidium*, from *caedere*] **:** killing ⟨sui*cide*⟩

ci·der \'sī-dər\ *noun* [Middle English *sidre*, from Middle French, from Late Latin *sicera* strong drink, from Greek *sikera*, from Hebrew *shēkhār*] (13th century)
1 : fermented apple juice often made sparkling by carbonation or fermentation in a sealed container
2 : the expressed juice of fruit (as apples) used as a beverage or for making other products (as applejack)

cider vinegar *noun* (1851)
: vinegar made from fermented cider

ci·de·vant \,sē-də-'väⁿ\ *adjective* [French, literally, formerly] (1790)
: FORMER

ci·gar \si-'gär\ *noun* [Spanish *cigarro*] (1730)
: a small roll of tobacco leaf for smoking

cig·a·rette *also* **cig·a·ret** \,si-gə-'ret, 'si-gə-,\ *noun* [French *cigarette*, diminutive of *cigare* cigar, from Spanish *cigarro*] (1835)
: a slender roll of cut tobacco enclosed in paper and meant to be smoked; *also* **:** a similar roll of another substance (as marijuana)

cig·a·ril·lo \,si-gə-'ri-(,)lō, -'re-(,)yō\ *noun*, *plural* **-los** [Spanish *cigarrillo* cigarette, diminutive of *cigarro* cigar] (1832)
1 : a very small cigar
2 : a cigarette wrapped in tobacco rather than paper

ci·gua·te·ra \,sē-gwə-'ter-ə, ,si-\ *noun* [American Spanish, from *ciguato* person ill with ciguatera, perhaps from *cigua* sea snail] (1862)
: poisoning caused by the ingestion of various normally edible tropical fish in whose flesh a toxic substance has accumulated

ci·lan·tro \si-'län-(,)trō, -'lan-\ *noun* [Spanish, coriander, from Medieval Latin *celiandrum*, alteration of Latin *coriandrum* — more at CORIANDER] (1903)
: leaves of coriander used as a flavoring or garnish; *also* **:** CORIANDER 1

cil·i·ary \'si-lē-,er-ē\ *adjective* (1691)
1 : of or relating to cilia
2 : of, relating to, or being the annular suspension of the lens of the eye

cil·i·ate \'si-lē-ət, -lē-,āt\ *noun* (1916)
: any of a phylum or subphylum (Ciliophora) of ciliated protozoans (as paramecia)

cil·i·at·ed \'si-lē-,ā-təd\ *or* **cil·i·ate** \-lē-ət, -lē-,āt\ *adjective* (1753)
: possessing cilia ⟨*ciliated* epithelial cells⟩ ⟨leaves with *ciliate* petioles⟩
— **cil·i·a·tion** \,si-lē-'ā-shən\ *noun*

cil·i·um \'si-lē-əm\ *noun*, *plural* **cil·ia** \-lē-ə\ [New Latin, from Latin, eyelid; akin to Latin *celare* to conceal — more at HELL] (1794)
1 : a minute short hairlike process often forming part of a fringe; *especially* **:** one on a cell that is capable of lashing movement and serves especially in free unicellular organisms to produce locomotion or in higher forms a current of fluid

2 : EYELASH

ci·met·i·dine \sī-'me-tə-ˌdēn\ *noun* [*ci-* (alteration of *cyan-*) + *me*thyl + *-idine*] (1975) **:** a histamine analogue $C_{10}H_{16}N_6S$ used especially in the treatment of duodenal ulcers

¹Cim·me·ri·an \sə-'mir-ē-ən\ *adjective* (1580) **:** very dark or gloomy ⟨under ebon shades . . . in dark *Cimmerian* desert ever dwell —John Milton⟩

²Cimmerian *noun* [Latin *Cimmerii,* a mythical people, from Greek *Kimmerioi*] (1584) **:** any of a mythical people described by Homer as dwelling in a remote realm of mist and gloom

¹cinch \'sinch\ *noun* [Spanish *cincha,* from Latin *cingula* girdle, girth, from *cingere*] (1859)
1 : a girth for a pack or saddle
2 : a tight grip
3 a : a thing done with ease **b :** a certainty to happen

²cinch (1866)
transitive verb
1 : to put a cinch on
2 : to make certain **:** ASSURE
intransitive verb
: to tighten the cinch — often used with *up*

cin·cho·na \sin-'kō-nə, sin-'chō-\ *noun* [New Latin, genus name, from the countess of *Chinchón* (died 1641) wife of the Peruvian viceroy] (1786)
1 : any of a genus (*Cinchona*) of South American trees and shrubs of the madder family
2 : the dried bark of a cinchona (as *C. ledgeriana*) containing alkaloids (as quinine) and formerly used as a specific in malaria

cin·cho·nine \'siŋ-kə-ˌnēn, 'sin-chə-\ *noun* (1825)
: a bitter white crystalline alkaloid $C_{19}H_{22}N_2O$ found especially in cinchona bark and used like quinine

cin·cho·nism \'siŋ-kə-ˌni-zəm, 'sin-chə-\ *noun* (1857)
: a disorder due to excessive or prolonged use of cinchona or its alkaloids and marked by temporary deafness, ringing in the ears, headache, dizziness, and rash

cinc·ture \'siŋ(k)-chər\ *noun* [Latin *cinctura* girdle, from *cinctus,* past participle of *cingere* to gird; probably akin to Sanskrit *kāñcī* girdle] (1600)
1 : the act of encircling
2 a : an encircling area **b :** GIRDLE, BELT; *especially* **:** a cord or sash of cloth worn around an ecclesiastical vestment (as an alb) or the habit of a religious

cin·der \'sin-dər\ *noun* [Middle English *sinder,* from Old English; akin to Old High German *sintar* dross, slag, Serbo-Croatian *sedra* calcium carbonate] (before 12th century)
1 : the slag from a metal furnace **:** DROSS
2 a *plural* **:** ASHES **b :** a fragment of ash
3 a : a partly burned combustible in which fire is extinct **b :** a hot coal without flame **c :** a partly burned coal capable of further burning without flame
4 : a fragment of lava from an erupting volcano
— **cin·dery** \-d(ə-)rē\ *adjective*

cinder block *noun* (1926)
: a hollow rectangular building block made of cement and coal cinders

cinder cone *noun* (1849)
: a conical hill formed by the accumulation of volcanic debris around a vent

Cin·der·el·la \ˌsin-də-'re-lə\ *noun* [after *Cinderella,* fairy-tale heroine who is used as a drudge by her stepmother but ends up married to a prince] (1840)
: one resembling the fairy-tale Cinderella: as **a :** one suffering undeserved neglect **b :** one suddenly lifted from obscurity to honor or significance

cine \'si-nē\ *noun* [probably from French *ciné,* short for *cinéma* cinema] (1920)
: MOTION PICTURE

cine·ast \'si-nē-ˌast, -nē-əst\ *or* **cine·aste** \-ˌast\ *or* **ciné·aste** \-ˌast\ *noun* [French *cinéaste,* from *ciné* + *-aste* (as in *enthousiaste* enthusiast)] (1926)
: a devotee of motion pictures; *also* **:** MOVIEMAKER

cin·e·ma \'si-nə-mə, *British also* -ˌmä\ *noun* [short for *cinematograph*] (1909)
1 a : MOTION PICTURE — usually used attributively **b :** a motion-picture theater
2 a : MOVIES; *especially* **:** the film industry **b :** the art or technique of making motion pictures

cin·e·ma·go·er \-ˌgō(-ə)r\ *noun* (1920)
: MOVIEGOER

cin·e·ma·theque \ˌsi-nə-mə-'tek\ *noun* [French *cinémathèque* film library, from *cinéma* + *-thèque* (as in *bibliothèque* library)] (1966)
: a small movie house specializing in avant-garde films

cin·e·mat·ic \ˌsi-nə-'ma-tik\ *adjective* (1916)
1 : of, relating to, suggestive of, or suitable for motion pictures or the filming of motion pictures ⟨*cinematic* principles and techniques⟩
2 : filmed and presented as a motion picture ⟨*cinematic* fantasies⟩
— **cin·e·mat·i·cal·ly** \-'ma-ti-k(ə-)lē\ *adverb*

cin·e·ma·tize \'si-nə-mə-ˌtīz\ *transitive verb* **-tized; -tiz·ing** (1916)
: to make a motion picture of (as a novel) **:** adapt for motion pictures

cin·e·mat·o·graph \ˌsi-nə-'ma-tə-ˌgraf\ *noun* [French *cinématographe,* from Greek *kinēmat-, kinēma* movement (from *kinein* to move) + French *-o-* + *-graphe* -graph — more at -KINESIS] (1896)
chiefly British **:** a motion-picture camera, projector, theater, or show

cin·e·ma·tog·ra·pher \ˌsi-nə-mə-'tä-grə-fər\ *noun* (1897)
1 : a motion-picture cameraman
2 : a motion-picture projectionist

cin·e·ma·tog·ra·phy \ˌsi-nə-mə-'tä-grə-fē\ *noun* (1897)
: the art or science of motion-picture photography
— **cin·e·mat·o·graph·ic** \-ˌma-tə-'gra-fik\ *adjective*
— **cin·e·mat·o·graph·i·cal·ly** \-fi-k(ə-)lē\ *adverb*

ci·ne·ma ve·ri·té \'si-nə-mə-ˌver-i-'tā; si-nā-'mä-ve-rē-'tā\ *noun* [French *cinéma-vérité,* literally, cinema-truth, translation of Russian *kinopravda*] (1963)
: the art or technique of filming a motion picture so as to convey candid realism

cin·e·ole \'si-nē-ˌōl\ *noun* [International Scientific Vocabulary, by transposition from New Latin *oleum cinae* wormseed oil] (1885)
: a liquid $C_{10}H_{18}O$ with a camphor odor contained in many essential oils (as of eucalyptus) and used especially as an expectorant and flavoring agent — called also *eucalyptol*

cin·er·ar·ia \ˌsi-nə-'rer-ē-ə, -'rar-\ *noun* [New Latin, from Latin, feminine of *cinerarius* of ashes, from *ciner-, cinis* ashes — more at INCINERATE] (1597)
: any of several garden or potted plants derived from a perennial composite herb (*Senecio cruentus*) of the Canary Islands and having heart-shaped leaves and clusters of bright flower heads

cin·er·ar·i·um \-ē-əm\ *noun, plural* **-ia** \-ē-ə\ [Latin, from *ciner-, cinis*] (1880)
: a place to receive the ashes of the cremated dead
— **cin·er·ary** \'si-nə-ˌrer-ē\ *adjective*

ci·ne·re·ous \sə-'nir-ē-əs\ *adjective* [Latin *cinereus,* from *ciner-, cinis*] (1661)
1 : gray tinged with black
2 : resembling or consisting of ashes

cin·er·in \'si-nə-rən\ *noun* [Latin *ciner-, cinis*] (1948)
: either of two oily liquid esters $C_{20}H_{28}O_3$ and

$C_{21}H_{28}O_5$ occurring especially in the flowers of pyrethrum and possessing insecticidal properties

cin·gu·lum \'siŋ-gyə-ləm\ *noun, plural* **-la** \-lə\ [New Latin, from Latin, girdle, from *cingere* to gird — more at CINCTURE] (1845)
: an anatomical band or encircling ridge
— **cin·gu·late** \-lət\ *adjective*

cin·na·bar \'si-nə-ˌbär\ *noun* [Middle English *cynabare,* from Middle French & Latin; Middle French *cenobre,* from Latin *cinnabaris,* from Greek *kinnabari,* of non-Indo-European origin; akin to Arabic *zinjafr* cinnabar] (14th century)
1 : artificial red mercuric sulfide used especially as a pigment
2 : native red mercuric sulfide HgS that is the only important ore of mercury
— **cin·na·bar·ine** \-bə-ˌrīn, -ˌbär-in\ *adjective*

cinnabar moth *noun* (circa 1893)
: a European moth (*Tyria jacobeae*) that has been introduced into the western U.S. in attempts to control the tansy ragwort on which its larvae feed — called also *cinnabar*

cin·nam·ic acid \sə-'na-mik-\ *noun* [French *cinnamique* of cinnamon, from *cinname* cinnamon, from Latin *cinnamomum*] (circa 1864)
: a white crystalline odorless acid $C_9H_8O_2$ found especially in cinnamon oil and storax

cin·na·mon \'si-nə-mən\ *noun, often attributive* [Middle English *cynamone,* from Latin *cinnamomum, cinnamon,* from Greek *kinnamōmon, kinnamon,* of non-Indo-European origin; akin to Hebrew *qinnāmōn* cinnamon] (14th century)
1 a : any of several Asian trees (genus *Cinnamomum*) of the laurel family **b :** an aromatic spice prepared from the dried inner bark of a cinnamon (especially *C. zeylanicum*); *also* **:** the bark
2 : a light yellowish brown

cinnamon fern *noun* (1818)
: a large fern (*Osmunda cinnamomea*) with cinnamon-colored spore-bearing fronds shorter than and separate from the green foliage fronds

cinnamon stone *noun* (1805)
: ESSONITE

cin·quain \'siŋ-ˌkān, 'saŋ-\ *noun* [French, from *cinq* five, from Latin *quinque* — more at FIVE] (1882)
: a 5-line stanza

cin·que·cen·tist \ˌchiŋ-kwi-'chen-tist\ *noun* (1871)
: an Italian of the cinquecento; *especially* **:** a poet or artist of this period

cin·que·cen·to \ˌchiŋ-kwi-'chen-(ˌ)tō\ *noun* [Italian, literally, five hundred, from *cinque* five (from Latin *quinque*) + *cento* hundred, from Latin *centum* — more at HUNDRED] (1760)
: the 16th century especially in Italian art and literature

cinque·foil \'siŋk-ˌfȯil, 'saŋk-\ *noun* [Middle English *sink foil,* from Middle French *cincfoille,* from Latin *quinquefolium,* from *quinque* five + *folium* leaf — more at BLADE] (14th century)
1 : any of a genus (*Potentilla*) of herbs and shrubs of the rose family with 5-lobed leaves and 5-petaled flowers — called also *potentilla*
2 : a design enclosed by five joined foils

cinquefoil 2

ciop·pi·no \chə-'pē-(ˌ)nō\ *noun* [perhaps from Italian dialect] (1936)
: a dish of fish and shellfish cooked usually with tomatoes, wine, spices, and herbs

¹ci·pher \\'sī-fər\\ *noun, often attributive* [Middle English, from Middle French *cifre*, from Medieval Latin *cifra*, from Arabic *ṣifr* empty, cipher, zero] (14th century)
1 a : ZERO 1a **b :** one that has no weight, worth, or influence **:** NONENTITY
2 a : a method of transforming a text in order to conceal its meaning — compare CODE 3b **b :** a message in code
3 : ARABIC NUMERAL
4 : a combination of symbolic letters; *especially* **:** the interwoven initials of a name

²cipher *verb* **ci·phered; ci·pher·ing** \\-f(ə-)riŋ\\ (circa 1530)
intransitive verb
: to use figures in a mathematical process
transitive verb
1 : ENCIPHER
2 : to compute arithmetically

ci·pher·text \\'sī-fər-ˌtekst\\ *noun* (1939)
: the enciphered form of a text or of its elements — compare PLAINTEXT

cir·ca \\'sər-kə\\ *preposition* [Latin, from *circum* around — more at CIRCUM-] (1861)
: at, in, or of approximately — used especially with dates ⟨born *circa* 1600⟩

cir·ca·di·an \\sər-'kā-dē-ən\\ *adjective* [Latin *circa* about + *dies* day + English *²-an* — more at DEITY] (1959)
: being, having, characterized by, or occurring in approximately 24-hour periods or cycles (as of biological activity or function) ⟨*circadian* rhythms in activity⟩

Cir·cas·sian \\(ˌ)sər-'ka-sh(ē-)ən\\ *noun* [*Circassia*, region of the Caucasus] (1555)
1 : a member of a group of peoples of the northwestern Caucasus
2 : the language of the Circassian peoples
— Circassian *adjective*

Circassian walnut *noun* (1914)
: the light brown irregularly black-veined wood of the English walnut much used for veneer and cabinetwork

Cir·ce \\'sər-(ˌ)sē\\ *noun* [Latin, from Greek *Kirkē*]
: a sorceress who changes Odysseus' men into swine but is forced by Odysseus to change them back

cir·ci·nate \\'sər-sⁿn-ˌāt\\ *adjective* [Latin *circinatus*, past participle of *circinare* to round, from *circinus* pair of compasses, from *circus*] (1830)
: ROUNDED, COILED; *especially* **:** rolled in the form of a flat coil with the apex as a center ⟨*circinate* fern fronds unfolding⟩
— cir·ci·nate·ly *adverb*

¹cir·cle \\'sər-kəl\\ *noun, often attributive* [Middle English *cercle*, from Old French, from Latin *circulus*, diminutive of *circus* circle, circus, from or akin to Greek *krikos, kirkos* ring; akin to Old English *hring* ring — more at RING] (14th century)
1 a : RING, HALO **b :** a closed plane curve every point of which is equidistant from a fixed point within the curve **c :** the plane surface bounded by such a curve
2 : the orbit of a celestial body
3 : something in the form of a circle or section of a circle: as **a :** DIADEM **b :** an instrument of astronomical observation the graduated limb of which consists of an entire circle **c :** a balcony or tier of seats in a theater **d :** a circle formed on the surface of a sphere by the intersection of a plane that passes through it

circle 1b: *AB* diameter; *C* center; *CD, CA, CB* radii; *EKF* arc on chord *EF; EFKL* (area) segment on chord *EF; ACD* (area) sector; *GH* secant; *TPM* tangent at point *P; EKFBPDA* circumference

⟨*circle* of latitude⟩ **e :** ROTARY 2
4 : an area of action or influence **:** REALM
5 a : CYCLE, ROUND ⟨the wheel has come full *circle*⟩ **b :** fallacious reasoning in which something to be demonstrated is covertly assumed
6 : a group of persons sharing a common interest or revolving about a common center ⟨the sewing *circle* of her church⟩ ⟨family *circle*⟩ ⟨the gossip of court *circles*⟩
7 : a territorial or administrative division or district
8 : a curving side street

²circle *verb* **cir·cled; cir·cling** \\-k(ə-)liŋ\\ (14th century)
transitive verb
1 : to enclose in or as if in a circle
2 : to move or revolve around
intransitive verb
1 a : to move in or as if in a circle **b :** CIRCULATE
2 : to describe or extend in a circle
— cir·cler \\-k(ə-)lər\\ *noun*

circle graph *noun* (1928)
: PIE CHART

cir·clet \\'sər-klət\\ *noun* (15th century)
: a little circle; *especially* **:** a circular ornament

¹cir·cuit \\'sər-kət\\ *noun, often attributive* [Middle English, from Middle French *circuite*, from Latin *circuitus*, from *circumire, circuire* to go around, from *circum-* + *ire* to go — more at ISSUE] (14th century)
1 a : a usually circular line encompassing an area **b :** the space enclosed within such a line
2 a : a course around a periphery **b :** a circuitous or indirect route
3 a : a regular tour (as by a traveling judge or preacher) around an assigned district or territory **b :** the route traveled **c :** a group of church congregations ministered to by one pastor
4 a : the complete path of an electric current including usually the source of electric energy **b :** an assemblage of electronic elements **:** HOOKUP **c :** a two-way communication path between points (as in a computer)
5 a : an association of similar groups **:** LEAGUE **b :** a number or series of public outlets (as theaters, radio shows, or arenas) offering the same kind of presentation **c :** a number of similar social gatherings ⟨cocktail *circuit*⟩
— cir·cuit·al \\-kə-tⁿl\\ *adjective*

²circuit (15th century)
transitive verb
: to make a circuit about
intransitive verb
: to make a circuit

circuit board *noun* (1948)
: BOARD 9

circuit breaker *noun* (1872)
: a switch that automatically interrupts an electric circuit under an infrequent abnormal condition

circuit court *noun* (1708)
: a court that sits at two or more places within one judicial district

circuit judge *noun* (1801)
: a judge who holds a circuit court

cir·cu·i·tous \\(ˌ)sər-'kyü-ə-təs\\ *adjective* [perhaps from Medieval Latin *circuitosus*, from Latin *circuitus*] (1664)
1 : having a circular or winding course ⟨a *circuitous* route⟩
2 : not being forthright or direct in language or action
— cir·cu·i·tous·ly *adverb*
— cir·cu·i·tous·ness *noun*

circuit rider *noun* (1837)
: a clergyman assigned to a circuit especially in a rural area

cir·cuit·ry \\'sər-kə-trē\\ *noun, plural* **-ries** (1946)
1 : the detailed plan or arrangement of an electric circuit
2 : the components of an electric circuit

cir·cu·i·ty \\(ˌ)sər-'kyü-ə-tē\\ *noun, plural* **-ities** [*circuitous*] (circa 1626)
: lack of straightforwardness **:** INDIRECTION

¹cir·cu·lar \\'sər-kyə-lər\\ *adjective* [Middle English *circuler*, from Middle French, from Late Latin *circularis*, from Latin *circulus* circle] (15th century)
1 a : having the form of a circle **:** ROUND **b :** moving in or describing a circle or spiral
2 a : of or relating to a circle or its mathematical properties ⟨a *circular* arc⟩ **b :** having a circular base or bases ⟨a *circular* cylinder⟩
3 : CIRCUITOUS, INDIRECT
4 : marked by or moving in a cycle
5 : being or involving reasoning that uses in the argument or proof a conclusion to be proved or one of its unproved consequences
6 : intended for circulation
— cir·cu·lar·i·ty \\ˌsər-kyə-'lar-ə-tē\\ *noun*
— cir·cu·lar·ly \\'sər-kyə-lər-lē\\ *adverb*
— cir·cu·lar·ness *noun*

²circular *noun* (1789)
: a paper (as a leaflet) intended for wide distribution

circular dichroism *noun* (circa 1961)
1 : the property (as of an optically active medium) of unequal absorption of right and left plane-polarized light so that the emergent light is elliptically polarized
2 : a spectroscopic technique that makes use of circular dichroism

circular file *noun* (1967)
: WASTEBASKET

circular function *noun* (1884)
: TRIGONOMETRIC FUNCTION

cir·cu·lar·ise *British variant of* CIRCULARIZE

cir·cu·lar·ize \\'sər-kyə-lə-ˌrīz\\ *transitive verb* **-ized; -iz·ing** (1848)
1 a : to send circulars to **b :** to poll by questionnaire
2 : PUBLICIZE
— cir·cu·lar·i·za·tion \\ˌsər-kyə-lər-ə-'zā-shən\\ *noun*

circular saw *noun* (1817)
: a power saw with a circular cutting blade; *also* **:** the blade itself

cir·cu·late \\'sər-kyə-ˌlāt\\ *verb* **-lat·ed; -lat·ing** [Latin *circulatus*, past participle of *circulare*, from *circulus*] (circa 1650)
intransitive verb
1 : to move in a circle, circuit, or orbit; *especially* **:** to follow a course that returns to the starting point ⟨blood *circulates* through the body⟩
2 : to pass from person to person or place to place: as **a :** to flow without obstruction **b :** to become well-known or widespread ⟨rumors *circulated* through the town⟩ **c :** to go from group to group at a social gathering **d :** to come into the hands of readers; *specifically* **:** to become sold or distributed
transitive verb
: to cause to circulate
— cir·cu·lat·able \\-ˌlā-tə-bəl\\ *adjective*
— cir·cu·la·tive \\-ˌlā-tiv\\ *adjective*
— cir·cu·la·tor \\-ˌlā-tər\\ *noun*

circulating decimal *noun* (1768)
: REPEATING DECIMAL

cir·cu·la·tion \\ˌsər-kyə-'lā-shən\\ *noun* (1654)
1 : orderly movement through a circuit; *especially* **:** the movement of blood through the vessels of the body induced by the pumping action of the heart
2 : FLOW
3 a : passage or transmission from person to person or place to place; *especially* **:** the interchange of currency ⟨coins in *circulation*⟩ **b :** the extent of dissemination: as (1) **:** the average number of copies of a publication sold over a given period (2) **:** the total number of items borrowed from a library

cir·cu·la·to·ry \\'sər-kyə-lə-ˌtōr-ē, -ˌtor-\\ *adjective* (1605)
: of or relating to circulation or the circulatory system ⟨*circulatory* failure⟩

circulatory system *noun* (1862)

: the system of blood, blood vessels, lymphatics, and heart concerned with the circulation of the blood and lymph

circum- *prefix* [Old French or Latin; Old French, from Latin, from *circum*, from *circus* circle — more at CIRCLE]
: around : about ⟨*circum*polar⟩

cir·cum·am·bi·ent \ˌsər-kəm-'am-bē-ənt\ *adjective* [Late Latin *circumambient-, circumambiens,* present participle of *circumambire* to surround in a circle, from Latin *circum-* + *ambire* to go around — more at AMBIENT] (1633)
: being on all sides : ENCOMPASSING
— **cir·cum·am·bi·ent·ly** *adverb*

cir·cum·am·bu·late \-'am-byə-ˌlāt\ *transitive verb* **-lat·ed; -lat·ing** [Late Latin *circumambulatus,* past participle of *circumambulare,* from Latin *circum-* + *ambulare* to walk] (circa 1656)
: to circle on foot especially ritualistically
— **cir·cum·am·bu·la·tion** \-ˌam-byə-'lā-shən\ *noun*

cir·cum·cen·ter \'sər-kəm-ˌsen-tər\ *noun* (circa 1889)
: the point at which the perpendicular bisectors of the sides of a triangle intersect and which is equidistant from the three vertices

cir·cum·cir·cle \ˌsər-kəl\ *noun* (1885)
: a circle which passes through all the vertices of a polygon (as a triangle)

cir·cum·cise \'sər-kəm-ˌsīz\ *transitive verb* **-cised; -cis·ing** [Middle English, from Latin *circumcisus,* past participle of *circumcidere,* from *circum-* + *caedere* to cut] (13th century)
: to cut off the prepuce of (a male) or the clitoris of (a female)
— **cir·cum·cis·er** *noun*

cir·cum·ci·sion \ˌsər-kəm-'si-zhən, 'sər-kəm-ˌ\ *noun* (12th century)
1 a : the act of circumcising; *especially* : a Jewish rite performed on male infants as a sign of inclusion in the Jewish religious community **b** : the condition of being circumcised **2** *capitalized* : January 1 observed as a church festival in commemoration of the circumcision of Jesus

cir·cum·fer·ence \sə(r)-'kəm(p)-fərn(t)s, -f(ə-)rən(t)s\ *noun* [Middle English, from Middle French, from Latin *circumferentia,* from *circumferre* to carry around, from *circum-* + *ferre* to carry — more at BEAR] (14th century)
1 : the perimeter of a circle **2** : the external boundary or surface of a figure or object : PERIPHERY
— **cir·cum·fer·en·tial** \-ˌkəm(p)-fə-'ren(t)-shəl\ *adjective*

¹cir·cum·flex \'sər-kəm-ˌfleks\ *adjective* [Latin *circumflexus,* past participle of *circumflectere* to bend around, mark with a circumflex, from *circum-* + *flectere* to bend] (circa 1577)
1 : characterized by the pitch, quantity, or quality indicated by a circumflex **2** : marked with a circumflex

²circumflex *noun* (1609)
: a mark ^, ˆ, or ~ originally used in Greek over long vowels to indicate a rising-falling tone and in other languages to mark length, contraction, or a particular vowel quality

cir·cum·flu·ent \(ˌ)sər-'kəm-flü-ənt\ *adjective* [from Latin *circumfluent-, circumfluens,* present participle of *circumfluere* to flow around, from *circum-* + *fluere* to flow — more at FLUID] (1577)
: flowing round or surrounding in the manner of a fluid
— **cir·cum·flu·ous** \(ˌ)sər-'kəm-flü-əs\ *adjective*

cir·cum·fuse \ˌsər-kəm-'fyüz\ *transitive verb* **-fused; -fus·ing** [Latin *circumfusus,* past participle of *circumfundere* to pour around, from *circum-* + *fundere* to pour — more at FOUND] (1605)
: SURROUND, ENVELOP
— **cir·cum·fu·sion** \-'fyü-zhən\ *noun*

cir·cum·ja·cent \ˌsər-kəm-'jā-sᵉnt\ *adjective* [Latin *circumjacent-, circumjacens,* present

participle of *circumjacēre* to lie around, from *circum-* + *jacēre* to lie — more at ADJACENT] (15th century)
: lying adjacent on all sides : SURROUNDING

cir·cum·lo·cu·tion \ˌsər-kəm-lō-'kyü-shən\ *noun* [Latin *circumlocution-, circumlocutio,* from *circum-* + *locutio* speech, from *loqui* to speak] (15th century)
1 : the use of an unnecessarily large number of words to express an idea **2** : evasion in speech
— **cir·cum·loc·u·to·ry** \-'lä-kyə-ˌtōr-ē, -ˌtōr-\ *adjective*

cir·cum·lu·nar \ˌsər-kəm-'lü-nər\ *adjective* (circa 1909)
: revolving about or surrounding the moon

cir·cum·nav·i·gate \-'na-və-ˌgāt\ *transitive verb* [Latin *circumnavigatus,* past participle of *circumnavigare* to sail around, from *circum-* + *navigare* to navigate] (1634)
: to go completely around (as the earth) especially by water; *also* : to go around instead of through : BYPASS ⟨*circumnavigate* a congested area⟩
— **cir·cum·nav·i·ga·tion** \-ˌna-və-'gā-shən\ *noun*
— **cir·cum·nav·i·ga·tor** \-'na-və-ˌgā-tər\ *noun*

cir·cum·po·lar \ˌsər-kəm-'pō-lər\ *adjective* (1686)
1 : continually visible above the horizon ⟨a *circumpolar* star⟩ **2** : surrounding or found in the vicinity of a terrestrial pole

cir·cum·scis·sile \-'si-səl, -ˌsīl\ *adjective* [Latin *circumscissus,* past participle of *circumscindere* to tear around, from *circum-* + *scindere* to cut, split — more at SHED] (1835)
: dehiscing by fissure around the capsule of the fruit

cir·cum·scribe \'sər-kəm-ˌskrīb\ *transitive verb* [Latin *circumscribere,* from *circum-* + *scribere* to write, draw — more at SCRIBE] (1835)
1 a : to constrict the range or activity of definitely and clearly **b** : to define or mark off carefully **2 a** : to draw a line around **b** : to surround by or as if by a boundary **3** : to construct or be constructed around (a geometrical figure) so as to touch as many points as possible
synonym see LIMIT

cir·cum·scrip·tion \ˌsər-kəm-'skrip-shən\ *noun* [Latin *circumscription-, circumscriptio,* from *circumscribere*] (1531)
1 : the act of circumscribing : the state of being circumscribed: as **a** : DEFINITION, DELIMITATION **b** : LIMITATION **2** : something that circumscribes: as **a** : LIMIT, BOUNDARY **b** : RESTRICTION **3** : a circumscribed area or district

cir·cum·spect \'sər-kəm-ˌspekt\ *adjective* [Middle English, from Middle French or Latin; Middle French *circonspect,* from Latin *circumspectus,* from past participle of *circumspicere* to look around, be cautious, from *circum-* + *specere* to look — more at SPY] (15th century)
: careful to consider all circumstances and possible consequences : PRUDENT
synonym see CAUTIOUS
— **cir·cum·spec·tion** \ˌsər-kəm-'spek-shən\ *noun*
— **cir·cum·spect·ly** \'sər-kəm-ˌspek(t)-lē\ *adverb*

cir·cum·stance \'sər-kəm-ˌstan(t)s, -stən(t)s\ *noun* [Middle English, from Old French, from Latin *circumstantia,* from *circumstant-, circumstans,* present participle of *circumstare* to stand around, from *circum-* + *stare* to stand — more at STAND] (13th century)
1 a : a condition, fact, or event accompanying, conditioning, or determining another : an essential or inevitable concomitant ⟨the weather is a *circumstance* to be taken into consider-

ation⟩ **b** : a subordinate or accessory fact or detail ⟨cost is a minor *circumstance* in this case⟩ **c** : a piece of evidence that indicates the probability or improbability of an event (as a crime) ⟨the *circumstance* of the missing weapon told against him⟩ ⟨the *circumstances* suggest murder⟩
2 a : the sum of essential and environmental factors (as of an event or situation) ⟨constant and rapid change in economic *circumstance* —G. M. Trevelyan⟩ **b** : state of affairs : EVENTUALITY ⟨open rebellion was a rare *circumstance*⟩ — often used in plural ⟨a victim of *circumstances*⟩ **c** *plural* : situation with regard to wealth ⟨he was in easy *circumstances*⟩ **3** : attendant formalities and ceremonial ⟨pride, pomp, and *circumstance* of glorious war —Shakespeare⟩ **4** : an event that constitutes a detail (as of a narrative or course of events) ⟨considering each *circumstance* in turn⟩
synonym see OCCURRENCE

cir·cum·stanced \ˌstan(t)st, -stən(t)st\ *adjective* (circa 1611)
: placed in particular circumstances especially in regard to property or income

cir·cum·stan·tial \ˌsər-kəm-'stan(t)-shəl\ *adjective* (1600)
1 : belonging to, consisting in, or dependent on circumstances **2** : pertinent but not essential : INCIDENTAL **3** : marked by careful attention to detail : abounding in factual details ⟨a *circumstantial* account of the fight⟩ **4** : CEREMONIAL ☆
— **cir·cum·stan·ti·al·i·ty** \-ˌstan(t)-shē-'a-lə-tē\ *noun*
— **cir·cum·stan·tial·ly** \-'stan(t)-sh(ə-)lē\ *adverb*

circumstantial evidence *noun* (1736)
: evidence that tends to prove a fact by proving other events or circumstances which afford a basis for a reasonable inference of the occurrence of the fact at issue

cir·cum·stan·ti·ate \ˌsər-kəm-'stan(t)-shē-ˌāt\ *transitive verb* **-at·ed; -at·ing** (circa 1652)
: to supply with circumstantial evidence or support

cir·cum·stel·lar \ˌsər-kəm-'ste-lər\ *adjective* (1951)
: surrounding or occurring in the vicinity of a star

¹cir·cum·val·late \-'va-ˌlāt\ *transitive verb* **-lat·ed; -lat·ing** [Latin *circumvallatus,* past participle of *circumvallare* to surround with siege works, from *circum-* + *vallum* rampart — more at WALL] (circa 1798)
: to surround by or as if by a rampart
— **cir·cum·val·la·tion** \-ˌva-'lā-shən\ *noun*

²cir·cum·val·late \-'va-ˌlāt, -'va-lət\ *adjective* (circa 1852)

☆ **SYNONYMS**

Circumstantial, minute, particular, detailed mean dealing with a matter fully and usually point by point. CIRCUMSTANTIAL implies fullness of detail that fixes something described in time and space ⟨a *circumstantial* account of our visit⟩. MINUTE implies close and searching attention to the smallest details ⟨a *minute* examination of a fossil⟩. PARTICULAR implies a precise attention to every detail ⟨a *particular* description of the scene of the crime⟩. DETAILED stresses abundance or completeness of detail ⟨a *detailed* analysis of the event⟩.

\ə\ abut \ᵊ\ kitten \ər\ further \a\ ash \ā\ ace
\ä\ mop, mar \aú\ out \ch\ chin \e\ bet \ē\ easy
\g\ go \i\ hit \ī\ ice \j\ job \ŋ\ sing \ō\ go
\ò\ law \òi\ boy \th\ thin \th\ the \ü\ loot \ú\ foot
\y\ yet \zh\ vision *see also* Guide to Pronunciation

: being any of approximately 12 large papillae near the back of the tongue each of which is surrounded with a marginal sulcus and supplied with taste buds responsive especially to bitter flavors

cir·cum·vent \ˌsər-kˈəm-'vent\ *transitive verb* [Latin *circumventus*, past participle of *circumvenire*, from *circum-* + *venire* to come — more at COME] (1539)
1 a : to hem in **b :** to make a circuit around
2 : to manage to get around especially by ingenuity or stratagem ⟨the setup *circumvented* the red tape —Lynne McTaggart⟩
— **cir·cum·ven·tion** \-'ven(t)-shən\ *noun*
cir·cum·vo·lu·tion \ˌsər-ˌkəm-və-'lü-shən, ˌsər-kˈəm-vō-\ *noun* [Middle English *circumvolucioun*, from Medieval Latin *circumvolution-*, *circumvolutio*, from Latin *circumvolvere* to revolve, from *circum-* + *volvere* to roll — more at VOLUBLE] (15th century)
: an act or instance of turning around an axis
cir·cus \'sər-kəs\ *noun, often attributive* [Latin, circle, circus — more at CIRCLE] (14th century)
1 a : a large arena enclosed by tiers of seats on three or all four sides and used especially for sports or spectacles (as athletic contests, exhibitions of horsemanship, or in ancient times chariot racing) **b :** a public spectacle
2 a : an arena often covered by a tent and used for variety shows usually including feats of physical skill, wild animal acts, and performances by clowns **b :** a circus performance **c :** the physical plant, livestock, and personnel of such a circus **d :** something suggestive of a circus (as in frenzied activity, sensationalism, theatricality, or razzle-dazzle)
3 a *obsolete* **:** CIRCLE, RING **b** *British* **:** a usually circular area at an intersection of streets
— **cir·cusy** \-kə-sē\ *adjective*
circus catch *noun* (1893)
: a catch (as in baseball or football) requiring an extraordinary or spectacular effort
ci·ré *also* **ci·re** \sə-'rā, sē-\ *noun* [French, from past participle of *cirer* to wax, from *cire* wax, from Latin *cera* — more at CERUMEN] (1921)
1 : a highly glazed finish for fabrics usually achieved by applying wax to the fabric
2 : a fabric or garment with a ciré finish
cirque \'sərk\ *noun* [French, from Latin *circus*] (1601)
1 *archaic* **:** CIRCUS
2 : CIRCLE, CIRCLET
3 : a deep steep-walled basin on a mountain usually forming the blunt end of a valley
cir·rho·sis \sə-'rō-səs\ *noun, plural* **-rho·ses** \-ˌsēz\ [New Latin, from Greek *kirrhos* orange-colored; akin to Old English *hār* gray — more at HOAR] (circa 1847)

cirque 3

: widespread disruption of normal liver structure by fibrosis and the formation of regenerative nodules that is caused by any of various chronic progressive conditions affecting the liver (as long term alcohol abuse or hepatitis)
— **cir·rhot·ic** \-'rä-tik\ *adjective or noun*
cirro- *combining form* [New Latin *cirrus*]
: cirrus ⟨*cirro*stratus⟩
cir·ro·cu·mu·lus \ˌsir-ō-'kyü-myə-ləs\ *noun* [New Latin] (circa 1803)
: a cloud form of small white rounded masses at a high altitude usually in regular groupings forming a mackerel sky — see CLOUD illustration
cir·ro·stra·tus \ˌsir-ō-'strā-təs, -'stra-\ *noun* [New Latin] (circa 1803)
: a fairly uniform layer of high stratus darker than cirrus — see CLOUD illustration
cir·rus \'sir-əs\ *noun, plural* **cir·ri** \'sir-ˌī\ [New Latin, from Latin, curl] (1708)
1 : TENDRIL

2 : a slender usually flexible animal appendage: as **a :** an arm of a barnacle **b :** a filament of a crinoid **c :** a fused group of cilia functioning like a limb on some protozoans **d :** the male copulatory organ of various invertebrate animals
3 : a wispy white cloud usually of minute ice crystals formed at altitudes of 20,000 to 40,000 feet (6,000 to 12,000 meters) — see CLOUD illustration
cis \'sis\ *adjective* [Latin, literally, on this side] (1888)
: characterized by having certain atoms or groups of atoms on the same side of the longitudinal axis of a double bond or of the plane of a ring in a molecule
cis- *prefix* [Latin, from *cis* — more at HE]
1 : on this side ⟨*cis*lunar⟩
2 *usually italic* **:** cis ⟨*cis*-dichloroethylene⟩ — compare TRANS- 2b
cis·al·pine \(ˌ)sis-'al-ˌpīn\ *adjective* (1542)
: situated on the south side of the Alps ⟨*Cisalpine* Gaul⟩ — compare TRANSALPINE
cis·co \'sis-(ˌ)kō\ *noun, plural* **ciscoes** [short for Canadian French *ciscoette*] (1848)
: any of various whitefishes (genus *Coregonus*); *especially* **:** LAKE HERRING
cis·lu·nar \(ˌ)sis-'lü-nər\ *adjective* (circa 1877)
: lying between the earth and the moon or the moon's orbit ⟨*cislunar* space⟩
cis·plat·in \(ˌ)sis-'pla-tᵊn\ *noun* [*cis-* + *platinum*] (1977)
: a platinum-containing antineoplastic drug $Cl_2H_6N_2Pt$ used especially in the treatment of testicular and ovarian tumors and advanced bladder cancer
cis–plat·i·num \-'plat-nəm, -'pla-tᵊn-əm\ *noun* (1977)
: CISPLATIN
cissy *British variant of* SISSY
cist \'sist, 'kist\ *noun* [Welsh, chest, from Latin *cista*] (1804)
: a neolithic or Bronze Age burial chamber typically lined with stone
Cis·ter·cian \sis-'tər-shən\ *noun* [Medieval Latin *Cistercium* Cîteaux] (1611)
: a member of a monastic order founded by Saint Robert of Molesme in 1098 at Cîteaux, France, under Benedictine rule
— **Cistercian** *adjective*
cis·tern \'sis-tərn\ *noun* [Middle English, from Old French *cisterne*, from Latin *cisterna*, from *cista* box, chest — more at CHEST] (13th century)
1 : an artificial reservoir (as an underground tank) for storing liquids and especially water (as rainwater)
2 : a large usually silver vessel formerly used (as in cooling wine) at the dining table
3 : a fluid-containing sac or cavity in an organism
cis·ter·na \sis-'tər-nə\ *noun, plural* **-nae** \-ˌnē\ [New Latin, from Latin, reservoir] (circa 1860)
: CISTERN 3: as **a :** one of the large spaces under the arachnoid membrane **b :** one of the interconnected flattened vesicles comprising the part of the endoplasmic reticulum that is studded with ribosomes
— **cis·ter·nal** \-nəl\ *adjective*
cis·tron \'sis-ˌträn\ *noun* [*cis-* + *trans-* + ²*-on*] (1957)
: a segment of DNA that is equivalent to a gene and that specifies a single functional unit (as a protein or enzyme)
— **cis·tron·ic** \sis-'trä-nik\ *adjective*
cit·a·del \'si-tə-dᵊl, -ˌdel\ *noun* [Middle French *citadelle*, from Old Italian *cittadella*, diminutive of *cittade* city, from Medieval Latin *civitat-*, *civitas* — more at CITY] (1562)
1 : a fortress that commands a city
2 : STRONGHOLD
ci·ta·tion \sī-'tā-shən\ *noun* (13th century)
1 : an official summons to appear (as before a court)

2 a : an act of quoting; *especially* **:** the citing of a previously settled case at law **b :** EXCERPT, QUOTE
3 : MENTION: as **a :** a formal statement of the achievements of a person receiving an academic honor **b :** specific reference in a military dispatch to meritorious performance of duty
synonym see ENCOMIUM
— **ci·ta·tion·al** \-shnəl, -shə-nᵊl\ *adjective*
cite \'sīt\ *transitive verb* **cit·ed; cit·ing** [Middle French *citer* to cite, summon, from Latin *citare* to put in motion, rouse, summon, from frequentative of *ciēre* to stir, move — more at -KINESIS] (15th century)
1 : to call upon officially or authoritatively to appear (as before a court)
2 : to quote by way of example, authority, or proof
3 a : to refer to; *especially* **:** to mention formally in commendation or praise **b :** to name in a citation
4 : to bring forward or call to another's attention especially as an example, proof, or precedent
synonym see SUMMON
— **cit·able** \'sī-tə-bəl\ *adjective*
cith·a·ra \'si-thə-rə, 'ki-\ *variant of* KITHARA
cith·er \'si-thər, -thər\ *noun* [French *cithare*, from Latin *cithara* kithara, from Greek *kithara*] (1606)
: CITTERN
cit·ied \'si-tēd\ *adjective* (1612)
: occupied by cities
cit·i·fied \'si-ti-ˌfīd\ *adjective* (1828)
: of, relating to, or characteristic of a sophisticated urban style of living — often used disparagingly
cit·i·fy \-ˌfī\ *transitive verb* **-fied; -fy·ing** (1828)
: URBANIZE
— **cit·i·fi·ca·tion** \ˌsi-tə-fi-'kā-shən\ *noun*
cit·i·zen \'si-tə-zən *also* -sən\ *noun* [Middle English *citizein*, from Anglo-French *citezein*, alteration of Old French *citeien*, from *cité* city] (14th century)
1 : an inhabitant of a city or town; *especially* **:** one entitled to the rights and privileges of a freeman
2 a : a member of a state **b :** a native or naturalized person who owes allegiance to a government and is entitled to protection from it
3 : a civilian as distinguished from a specialized servant of the state ☆
— **cit·i·zen·ly** \-zən-lē *also* -sən-\ *adjective*
cit·i·zen·ess \-zə-nəs *also* -sə-\ *noun* (1796)
: a female citizen
cit·i·zen·ry \-zən-rē *also* -sən-\ *noun, plural* **-ries** (1819)
: a whole body of citizens
citizen's arrest *noun* (1941)
: an arrest made not by a law officer but by a citizen who derives authority from the fact of being a citizen
citizens band *noun* (1948)
: a range of radio-wave frequencies that in the U.S. is allocated officially for private radio communications
cit·i·zen·ship \'si-tə-zən-ˌship\ *noun* (1611)

1 : the status of being a citizen
2 a : membership in a community (as a college) **b :** the quality of an individual's response to membership in a community

citr- *or* **citri-** *or* **citro-** *combining form* [New Latin, from *Citrus*, genus name]
1 : citrus ⟨*citri*culture⟩
2 : citric acid ⟨*citr*ate⟩

cit·ral \'si-,tral\ *noun* [International Scientific Vocabulary] (1891)
: an unsaturated liquid isomeric aldehyde $C_{10}H_{16}O$ of many essential oils that has a strong lemon odor and is used especially in perfumery and as a flavoring

cit·rate \'si-,trāt\ *noun* [International Scientific Vocabulary] (1794)
: a salt or ester of citric acid

cit·ric acid \'si-trik-\ *noun* [International Scientific Vocabulary] (1813)
: a tricarboxylic acid $C_6H_8O_7$ occurring in cellular metabolism, obtained especially from lemon and lime juices or by fermentation of sugars, and used as a flavoring

citric acid cycle *noun* (1942)
: KREBS CYCLE

cit·ri·cul·ture \'si-trə-,kəl-chər\ *noun* (1916)
: the cultivation of citrus fruits
— **cit·ri·cul·tur·ist** \,si-trə-'kəl-ch(ə-)rist\ *noun*

¹cit·rine \'si-,trīn\ *adjective* [Middle English, from Middle French *citrin*, from Medieval Latin *citrinus*, from Latin *citrus* citron tree] (14th century)
: resembling a citron or lemon especially in color

²ci·trine \si-'trēn\ *noun* (1748)
: a semiprecious yellow stone resembling topaz formed by heating a black quartz in order to change its color

ci·tri·nin \si-'trī-nən\ *noun* [New Latin *citrinum*, specific epithet of *Penicillium citrinum*] (1931)
: a toxic antibiotic $C_{13}H_{14}O_5$ that is produced especially by a penicillium (*Penicillium citrinum*) and an aspergillus (*Aspergillus niveus*) and is effective against some gram-positive bacteria

cit·ron \'si-trən\ *noun* [Middle English, from Middle French, modification of Latin *citrus*] (15th century)
1 a : a citrus fruit resembling a lemon but larger with little pulp and a very thick rind **b :** a small shrubby tree (*Citrus medica*) that produces citrons and is cultivated in tropical regions **c :** the preserved rind of the citron used especially in cakes and puddings
2 : a small hard-fleshed watermelon used especially in pickles and preserves

cit·ro·nel·la \,si-trə-'ne-lə\ *noun* [New Latin, from French *citronnelle* lemon balm, from *citron*] (circa 1858)
: a fragrant grass (*Cymbopogon nardus*) of southern Asia that yields an oil used in perfumery and as an insect repellent; *also* **:** its oil

cit·ro·nel·lal \-'ne-,lal\ *noun* [International Scientific Vocabulary, from New Latin *citronella*] (1893)
: a lemon-odored aldehyde $C_{10}H_{18}O$ that is derived especially from citronella oil and is used in perfumery and as an insect repellent

cit·ro·nel·lol \-'ne-,lȯl, -,lōl\ *noun* [International Scientific Vocabulary, from New Latin *citronella*] (1872)
: an unsaturated liquid alcohol $C_{10}H_{20}O$ with a roselike odor that is found in two optically active forms in many essential oils (as rose oil) and is used in perfumery and soaps

ci·trov·o·rum factor \sə-'trä-və-rəm-\ *noun* [New Latin *citrovorum*, specific epithet of *Leuconostoc citrovorum*, bacterium that requires this form of folic acid] (1948)
: a metabolically active form of folic acid that has been used in cancer therapy to protect normal cells against methotrexate

cit·rul·line \'si-trə-,lēn\ *noun* [International Scientific Vocabulary, from New Latin *Citrullus*, genus name of the watermelon] (1930)
: a crystalline amino acid $C_6H_{13}N_3O_3$ formed especially as an intermediate in the conversion of ornithine to arginine in the living system

cit·rus \'si-trəs\ *noun, plural* **citrus** *or* **cit·rus·es** *often attributive* [New Latin, genus name, from Latin] (1825)
: any of a group of often thorny trees and shrubs (*Citrus* and related genera) of the rue family grown in warm regions for their edible fruit (as the orange or lemon) with firm usually thick rind and pulpy flesh; *also* **:** the fruit
— **cit·rusy** \'si-trə-sē\ *adjective*

citrus canker *noun* (1916)
: a destructive disease of citrus caused by a bacterium (*Xanthomonas campestris citri*) that produces lesions on the leaves, twigs, and fruits

citrus red mite *noun* (1935)
: a relatively large mite (*Panonychus citri*) that is a destructive pest on the foliage of citrus

cit·tern \'si-tərn\ *also* **cith·ern** \'si-thərn, -,thərn\ *or* **cith·ren** \'si-thrən\ *noun* [blend of *cither* and *gittern*] (1566)
: a Renaissance stringed instrument like a guitar with a flat pear-shaped body

city \'si-tē\ *noun, plural* **cit·ies** *often attributive* [Middle English *citie* large or small town, from Old French *cité*, from Medieval Latin *civitat-, civitas*, from Latin, citizenship, state, city of Rome, from *civis* citizen — more at HIND] (13th century)
1 a : an inhabited place of greater size, population, or importance than a town or village **b :** an incorporated British town usually of major size or importance having the status of an episcopal see **c** *capitalized* **(1) :** the financial district of London **(2) :** the influential financial interests of the British economy **d :** a usually large or important municipality in the U.S. governed under a charter granted by the state **e :** an incorporated municipal unit of the highest class in Canada
2 : CITY-STATE
3 : the people of a city
4 *slang* — used with a preceding adjective or noun naming an abundant or quintessential feature or quality ⟨the movie was shoot-out *city*⟩

city clerk *noun* (1919)
: a public officer charged with recording the official proceedings and vital statistics of a city

city council *noun* (1789)
: the legislative body of a city

city editor *noun* (1834)
: a newspaper editor usually in charge of local news and staff assignments

city father *noun* (1845)
: a member (as an alderman or councilman) of the governing body of a city

city hall *noun* (1675)
1 : the chief administrative building of a city
2 a : municipal government **b :** city officialdom or bureaucracy ⟨you can't fight *city hall*⟩

city manager *noun* (1913)
: an official employed by an elected council to direct the administration of a city government

city planning *noun* (1912)
: the drawing up of an organized arrangement (as of streets, parks, and business and residential areas) of a city
— **city planner** *noun*

city room *noun* (1919)
: the department where local news is handled in a newspaper editorial office

city·scape \'si-tē-,skāp\ *noun* (1856)
1 : a city viewed as a scene
2 : an artistic representation of a city

city slicker *noun* (1924)
: SLICKER 2b

city-state \'si-tē-,stāt *also* -'stāt\ *noun* (1893)
: an autonomous state consisting of a city and surrounding territory

city·wide \'si-tē-,wīd\ *adjective* (1961)
: including all parts of a city

civ·et \'si-vət\ *noun* [Middle French *civette*, from Old Italian *zibetto*, from Arabic *zabād* civet perfume] (1532)

civet

1 : any of various Old World carnivorous mammals (family Viverridae) with long bodies, short legs, and a usually long tail
2 : a thick yellowish musky-odored substance found in a pouch near the sexual organs of the civet (especially genera *Civettictis, Viverra,* and *Viverricula*) and used in perfume

civet cat *noun* (1607)
1 : CIVET 1
2 : RINGTAIL 2
3 : any of the small spotted skunks (genus *Spilogale*) of western North America

civ·ic \'si-vik\ *adjective* [Latin *civicus*, from *civis* citizen] (circa 1656)
: of or relating to a citizen, a city, citizenship, or civil affairs
— **civ·i·cal·ly** \'si-vi-k(ə-)lē\ *adverb*

civ·ic-mind·ed \,si-vik-'mīn-dəd\ *adjective* (1947)
: disposed to look after civic needs and interests
— **civ·ic-mind·ed·ness** *noun*

civ·ics \'si-viks\ *noun plural but singular or plural in construction* (1886)
: a social science dealing with the rights and duties of citizens

civ·il \'si-vəl\ *adjective* [Middle English, from Middle French, from Latin *civilis*, from *civis*] (14th century)
1 a : of or relating to citizens **b :** of or relating to the state or its citizenry
2 a : CIVILIZED ⟨*civil* society⟩ **b :** adequate in courtesy and politeness **:** MANNERLY
3 a : of, relating to, or based on civil law **b :** relating to private rights and to remedies sought by action or suit distinct from criminal proceedings **c :** established by law
4 : of, relating to, or involving the general public, their activities, needs, or ways, or civic affairs as distinguished from special (as military or religious) affairs
5 *of time* **:** based on the mean sun and legally recognized for use in ordinary affairs ☆

☆ **SYNONYMS**
Civil, polite, courteous, gallant, chivalrous mean observant of the forms required by good breeding. CIVIL often suggests little more than the avoidance of overt rudeness ⟨owed the questioner a *civil* reply⟩. POLITE commonly implies polish of speech and manners and sometimes suggests an absence of cordiality ⟨if you can't be pleasant, at least be *polite*⟩. COURTEOUS implies more actively considerate or dignified politeness ⟨clerks who were unfailingly *courteous* to customers⟩. GALLANT and CHIVALROUS imply courteous attentiveness especially to women. GALLANT suggests spirited and dashing behavior and ornate expressions of courtesy ⟨a *gallant* suitor of the old school⟩. CHIVALROUS suggests high-minded and self-sacrificing behavior ⟨a *chivalrous* display of duty⟩.

\ə\ abut \ᵊ\ kitten \ər\ further \a\ ash \ā\ ace
\ä\ mop, mar \au̇\ out \ch\ chin \e\ bet \ē\ easy
\g\ go \i\ hit \ī\ ice \j\ job \ŋ\ sing \ō\ go
\ȯ\ law \ȯi\ boy \th\ thin \th̲\ the \ü\ loot \u̇\ foot
\y\ yet \zh\ vision *see also* Guide to Pronunciation

civil death *noun* (1767)
: the status of a living person equivalent in its legal consequences to natural death; *specifically* : deprivation of civil rights

civil defense *noun* (1939)
: the system of protective measures and emergency relief activities conducted by civilians in case of hostile attack, sabotage, or natural disaster

civil disobedience *noun* (1866)
: refusal to obey governmental demands or commands especially as a nonviolent and usually collective means of forcing concessions from the government

civil engineer *noun* (circa 1792)
: an engineer whose training or occupation is in the design and construction especially of public works (as roads or harbors)
— **civil engineering** *noun*

ci·vil·ian \sə-'vil-yən *also* -'vi-yən\ *noun* (14th century)
1 : a specialist in Roman or modern civil law
2 a : one not on active duty in a military, police, or fire-fighting force **b** : OUTSIDER 1
— **civilian** *adjective*

ci·vil·ian·ize \-yə-,nīz\ *transitive verb* **-ized; -iz·ing** (1870)
: to convert from military to civilian status or control
— **ci·vil·ian·i·za·tion** \-,vil-yə-nə-'zā-shən\ *noun*

civ·i·li·sa·tion, civ·i·lise *chiefly British variant of* CIVILIZATION, CIVILIZE

ci·vil·i·ty \sə-'vi-lə-tē\ *noun, plural* **-ties** (1533)
1 *archaic* : training in the humanities
2 a : COURTESY, POLITENESS **b** : a polite act or expression

civ·i·li·za·tion \,si-və-lə-'zā-shən\ *noun* (1772)
1 a : a relatively high level of cultural and technological development; *specifically* : the stage of cultural development at which writing and the keeping of written records is attained **b** : the culture characteristic of a particular time or place
2 : the process of becoming civilized
3 a : refinement of thought, manners, or taste **b** : a situation of urban comfort
— **civ·i·li·za·tion·al** \-shnəl, -shə-n°l\ *adjective*

civ·i·lize \'si-və-,līz\ *verb* **-lized; -liz·ing** (1601)
transitive verb
1 : to cause to develop out of a primitive state; *especially* : to bring to a technically advanced and rationally ordered stage of cultural development
2 a : EDUCATE, REFINE **b** : SOCIALIZE 1
intransitive verb
: to acquire the customs and amenities of a civil community
— **civ·i·liz·er** *noun*

civilized *adjective* (1611)
: characteristic of a state of civilization ⟨*civilized* society⟩; *especially* : characterized by taste, refinement, or restraint ⟨a *civilized* way to spend the evening⟩

civil law *noun, often C&L capitalized* (14th century)
1 : Roman law especially as set forth in the Justinian code
2 : the body of private law developed from Roman law and used in Louisiana and in many countries outside the English-speaking world
3 : the law established by a nation or state for its own jurisdiction
4 : the law of civil or private rights

civil liberty *noun* (1644)
: freedom from arbitrary governmental interference (as with the right of free speech) specifically by denial of governmental power and in the U.S. especially as guaranteed by the Bill of Rights — usually used in plural

— **civil libertarian** *noun or adjective*

civ·il·ly \'si-və(l)-lē\ *adverb* (15th century)
1 : in terms of civil rights, law, or matters ⟨*civilly* dead⟩
2 : in a civil manner : POLITELY

civil marriage *noun* (circa 1889)
: a marriage performed by a magistrate

civil rights *noun plural* (1721)
: the nonpolitical rights of a citizen; *especially* : the rights of personal liberty guaranteed to U.S. citizens by the 13th and 14th amendments to the Constitution and by acts of Congress

civil servant *noun* (1800)
1 : a member of a civil service
2 : a member of the administrative staff of an international agency (as the United Nations)

civil service *noun* (circa 1785)
: the administrative service of a government or international agency exclusive of the armed forces; *especially* : one in which appointments are determined by competitive examination

civil war *noun* (15th century)
: a war between opposing groups of citizens of the same country

Civ·i·tan \'si-və-,tan\ *noun* [*Civitan (Club)*] (1926)
: a member of a major national and international service club

civ·vy *also* **civ·ie** \'si-vē\ *noun, plural* **civ·vies** *also* **civies** (circa 1889)
1 *plural* : civilian clothes as distinguished from a particular uniform (as of the military)
2 : CIVILIAN

civvy street *noun, often C&S capitalized* (1943)
British : civilian life

¹clab·ber \'kla-bər\ *noun* [short for *bonnyclabber*] (1634)
chiefly dialect : sour milk that has thickened or curdled

²clabber *intransitive verb* (circa 1879)
chiefly dialect : CURDLE

clach·an \'kla-kən\ *noun* [Middle English, from Scottish Gaelic] (15th century)
Scottish & Irish : HAMLET

¹clack \'klak\ *verb* [Middle English, of imitative origin] (13th century)
intransitive verb
1 : CHATTER, PRATTLE
2 : to make an abrupt striking sound or series of sounds
3 *of fowl* : CACKLE, CLUCK
transitive verb
1 : to cause to make a clatter
2 : to produce with a chattering sound; *specifically* : BLAB
— **clack·er** *noun*

²clack *noun* (15th century)
1 a : rapid continuous talk : CHATTER **b** : TONGUE
2 *archaic* : an object (as a valve) that produces clapping or rattling noises usually in regular rapid sequence
3 : a sound of clacking ⟨the *clack* of a typewriter⟩

Clac·to·ni·an \klak-'tō-nē-ən\ *adjective* [*Clacton*-on-Sea, England] (1932)
: of or relating to a Lower Paleolithic culture usually characterized by stone flakes with a half cone at the point of striking

¹clad \'klad\ *past and past participle of* CLOTHE

²clad *adjective* [Middle English, past participle of *clothen* to clothe] (14th century)
1 : being covered or clothed ⟨ivy-*clad* buildings⟩
2 *of a coin* : consisting of outer layers of one metal bonded to a core of a different metal

³clad *transitive verb* **clad; clad·ding** (1939)
: SHEATHE, FACE; *specifically* : to cover (a metal) with another metal by bonding

⁴clad *noun* (1941)
1 a : a composite material formed by cladding **b** : a clad coin

2 : CLADDING; *specifically* : the outer layer of a clad coin

clad- *or* **clado-** *combining form* [New Latin, from Greek *klad-, klado-*, from *klados* branch, shoot of a tree; akin to Old English *holt* woods — more at HOLT]
: slip : sprout ⟨*cladophyll*⟩

clad·ding \'kla-diŋ\ *noun* (1936)
: something that covers or overlays; *specifically* : metal coating bonded to a metal core

clade \'klād\ *noun* [Greek *klados*] (1911)
: a group of biological taxa (as species) that includes all descendants of one common ancestor

cla·dis·tics \klə-'dis-tiks, kla-\ *noun plural but singular in construction* (1965)
: a system of biological taxonomy that defines taxa uniquely by shared characteristics not found in ancestral groups and uses inferred evolutionary relationships to arrange taxa in a branching hierarchy such that all members of a given taxon have the same ancestors
— **cla·dist** \'kla-dist\ *noun*
— **cla·dis·tic** \-'dis-tik\ *adjective*
— **cla·dis·ti·cal·ly** \-ti-k(ə-)lē\ *adverb*

cla·doc·er·an \klə-'dä-sə-rən\ *noun* [New Latin *Cladocera*, from *clad-* + Greek *keras* horn — more at HORN] (1909)
: any of an order (Cladocera) of minute chiefly freshwater branchiopod crustaceans that includes the water fleas

clad·ode \'kla-,dōd\ *noun* [New Latin *cladodium*, from Greek *klados*] (1870)
: CLADOPHYLL
— **cla·do·di·al** \kla-'dō-dē-əl\ *adjective*

clad·o·gen·e·sis \,kla-də-'je-nə-səs\ *noun* (1953)
: evolutionary change characterized by treelike branching of taxa — compare ANAGENESIS
— **clad·o·ge·net·ic** \,kla-dō-jə-'ne-tik\ *adjective*
— **clad·o·ge·net·i·cal·ly** \-ti-k(ə-)lē\ *adverb*

clad·o·gram \'kla-də-,gram\ *noun* (1966)
: a branching diagrammatic tree used in cladistic classification to illustrate phylogenetic relationships

clad·o·phyll \'kla-də-,fil\ *noun* (1879)
: a flattened photosynthetic branch assuming the form of and closely resembling an ordinary foliage leaf

¹claim \'klām\ *transitive verb* [Middle English, from Middle French *clamer*, from Latin *clamare* to cry out, shout; akin to Latin *calare* to call — more at LOW] (14th century)
1 a : to ask for especially as a right ⟨*claimed* the inheritance⟩ **b** : to call for : REQUIRE ⟨this matter *claims* our attention⟩ **c** : TAKE 16b ⟨the accident *claimed* her life⟩
2 : to take as the rightful owner ⟨went to *claim* their bags at the station⟩
3 a : to assert in the face of possible contradiction : MAINTAIN ⟨*claimed* that he'd been cheated⟩ **b** : to claim to have ⟨organization . . . which *claims* 11,000 . . . members —*Rolling Stone*⟩ **c** : to assert to be rightfully one's own ⟨*claimed* responsibility for the attack⟩
synonym see DEMAND
— **claim·able** \'klā-mə-bəl\ *adjective*

²claim *noun* (14th century)
1 : a demand for something due or believed to be due ⟨insurance *claim*⟩
2 a : a right to something; *specifically* : a title to a debt, privilege, or other thing in the possession of another **b** : an assertion open to challenge ⟨a *claim* of authenticity⟩
3 : something that is claimed; *especially* : a tract of land staked out

claim·ant \'klā-mənt\ *noun* (15th century)
: one that asserts a right or title ⟨a *claimant* to an estate⟩

claim·er \'klā-mər\ *noun* (15th century)
1 : one that claims

2 : a horse running in a claiming race

claiming race *noun* (1935)
: a horse race in which each entry is offered for sale at a specified price that must be deposited before the race

clair·au·di·ence \klar-'ȯ-dē-ən(t)s, kler-, -'ä-\ *noun* [*clair-* (as in *clairvoyance*) + *audience* (act of hearing)] (1864)
: the power or faculty of hearing something not present to the ear but regarded as having objective reality
— **clair·au·di·ent** \-ənt\ *adjective*
— **clair·au·di·ent·ly** *adverb*

clair·voy·ance \klar-'vȯi-ən(t)s, kler-\ *noun* (1840)
1 : the power or faculty of discerning objects not present to the senses
2 : ability to perceive matters beyond the range of ordinary perception : PENETRATION

¹clair·voy·ant \-ənt\ *adjective* [French, from *clair* clear (from Latin *clarus*) + *voyant*, present participle of *voir* to see, from Latin *vidēre* — more at WIT] (1671)
1 : unusually perceptive : DISCERNING
2 : of or relating to clairvoyance
— **clair·voy·ant·ly** *adverb*

²clairvoyant *noun* (1851)
: one having the power of clairvoyance

¹clam \'klam\ *noun* [Middle English, from Old English *clamm* bond, fetter; akin to Old High German *klamma* constriction, Latin *glomus* ball] (before 12th century)
: CLAMP, CLASP

²clam *noun, often attributive* [¹*clam*; from the clamping action of the shells] (circa 1520)
1 a : any of numerous edible marine bivalve mollusks living in sand or mud **b :** a freshwater mussel
2 : a stolid or closemouthed person
3 : CLAMSHELL
4 : DOLLAR 3

³clam *intransitive verb* **clammed; clam·ming** (1636)
: to gather clams especially by digging
— **clam·mer** \'kla-mər\ *noun*

cla·mant \'klā-mənt, 'kla-\ *adjective* [Latin *clamant-, clamans*, present participle of *clamare* to cry out] (1639)
1 : CLAMOROUS, BLATANT
2 : demanding attention : URGENT
— **cla·mant·ly** *adverb*

clam·bake \'klam-,bāk\ *noun* (1835)
1 a : an outdoor party; *especially* **:** a seashore outing where food is usually cooked on heated rocks covered by seaweed **b :** the food served at a clambake
2 : a gathering characterized by noisy sociability; *especially* **:** a political rally

clam·ber \'klam-bər, 'kla-mər\ *intransitive verb* **clam·bered; clam·ber·ing** \'klamb(ə-)riŋ, 'klam-riŋ, 'kla-mər-iŋ\ [Middle English *clambren;* akin to Old English *climban* to climb] (14th century)
: to climb awkwardly (as by scrambling) ⟨*clambered* over the rocks⟩
— **clam·ber·er** \-bər-ər, -mər-ər\ *noun*

clam·my \'kla-mē\ *adjective* **clam·mi·er; -est** [Middle English, probably from *clammen* to smear, stick, from Old English *clǣman;* akin to Old English *clǣg* clay] (14th century)
1 : being damp, soft, sticky, and usually cool ⟨a *clammy* and intensely cold mist —Charles Dickens⟩
2 : lacking normal human warmth ⟨the *clammy* atmosphere of an institution⟩
— **clam·mi·ly** \'kla-mə-lē\ *adverb*
— **clam·mi·ness** \'kla-mē-nəs\ *noun*

¹clam·or \'kla-mər\ *noun* [Middle English,

from Middle French *clamour*, from Latin *clamor*, from *clamare* to cry out — more at CLAIM] (14th century)
1 a : noisy shouting **b :** a loud continuous noise
2 : insistent public expression (as of support or protest) ⟨a *clamor* against increased taxes⟩

²clamor *verb* **clam·ored; clam·or·ing** \'klam-riŋ, 'kla-mər-iŋ\ (14th century)
intransitive verb
1 : to make a din
2 : to become loudly insistent ⟨*clamored* for his impeachment⟩
transitive verb
1 : to utter or proclaim insistently and noisily
2 : to influence by means of clamor

³clamor *transitive verb* [origin unknown] (1611)
obsolete **:** SILENCE

clam·or·ous \'klam-rəs, 'kla-mər-əs\ *adjective* (15th century)
1 : marked by confused din or outcry : TUMULTUOUS ⟨the busy *clamorous* market⟩
2 : noisily insistent
synonym see VOCIFEROUS
— **clam·or·ous·ly** *adverb*
— **clam·or·ous·ness** *noun*

clam·our \'kla-mər\ *chiefly British variant of* CLAMOR

¹clamp \'klamp\ *noun* [Middle English, probably from (assumed) Middle Dutch *klampe;* akin to Old English *clamm* bond, fetter — more at CLAM] (14th century)
1 : a device designed to bind or constrict or to press two or more parts together so as to hold them firmly
2 : any of various instruments or appliances having parts brought together for holding or compressing something

²clamp *transitive verb* (circa 1696)
1 : to fasten with or as if with a clamp
2 a : to place by decree : IMPOSE — often used with *on* ⟨*clamped* on a curfew after the riots⟩ **b :** to hold tightly

clamp·down \'klamp-,daún\ *noun* (1940)
: the act or action of making regulations and restrictions more stringent ⟨a *clampdown* on charge accounts, bank loans, and other inflationary influences —*Time*⟩

clamp down *intransitive verb* (1940)
: to impose restrictions ⟨the police are *clamping down* on speeders⟩

clams casino *noun plural but singular or plural in construction, often 2d C capitalized* (1952)
: clams on the half shell usually topped with green pepper and baked or broiled

clam·shell \'klam-,shel\ *noun* (circa 1520)
1 : the shell of a clam
2 a : a bucket or grapple (as on a dredge) having two hinged jaws **b :** an excavating machine having a clamshell **c :** either of a pair of doors (as in an airplane tail) that open out and away from each other

clam up *intransitive verb* (1916)
: to become silent

clam worm *noun* (1885)
: any of several large burrowing polychaete worms often used as bait

clan \'klan\ *noun* [Middle English, from Scottish Gaelic *clann* offspring, clan, from Old Irish *cland* plant, offspring, from Latin *planta* plant] (15th century)
1 a : a Celtic group especially in the Scottish Highlands comprising a number of households whose heads claim descent from a common ancestor **b :** a group of people tracing descent from a common ancestor
2 : a group united by a common interest or common characteristics

clan·des·tine \klan-'des-tən *also* -,tīn *or* -,tēn *or* 'klan-dəs-\ *adjective* [Middle French or Latin; Middle French *clandestin*, from Latin *clan-*

destinus, from *clam* secretly; akin to Latin *celare* to hide — more at HELL] (1566)
: marked by, held in, or conducted with secrecy : SURREPTITIOUS
synonym see SECRET
— **clan·des·tine·ly** *adverb*
— **clan·des·tine·ness** *noun*
— **clan·des·tin·i·ty** \,klan-də-'sti-nə-tē, -des-'ti-\ *noun*

¹clang \'klaŋ\ *verb* [Latin *clangere;* akin to Greek *klazein* to scream, bark, Old English *hliehhan* to laugh] (1576)
intransitive verb
1 a : to make a loud metallic ringing sound ⟨anvils *clanged*⟩ **b :** to go with a clang
2 : to utter the characteristic harsh cry of a bird
transitive verb
: to cause to clang ⟨*clang* a bell⟩

²clang *noun* (1596)
1 : a loud ringing metallic sound ⟨the *clang* of a fire alarm⟩
2 : a harsh cry of a bird (as a crane or goose)

clang·er \'klaŋ-ər\ *noun* (1948)
British **:** a conspicuous blunder — often used in the phrase *drop a clanger*

¹clan·gor \'klaŋ-ər *also* -gər\ *noun* [Latin *clangor*, from *clangere*] (1593)
: a resounding clang or medley of clangs ⟨the *clangor* of hammers⟩
— **clan·gor·ous** \-(g)ə-rəs\ *adjective*
— **clan·gor·ous·ly** *adverb*

²clangor *intransitive verb* (1837)
: to make a clangor

clan·gour \'klaŋ-ər, -gər\ *chiefly British variant of* CLANGOR

¹clank \'klaŋk\ *verb* [probably imitative] (1656)
intransitive verb
1 : to make a clank or series of clanks ⟨the radiator hissed and *clanked*⟩
2 : to go with or as if with a clank ⟨tanks *clanking* through the streets⟩
transitive verb
: to cause to clank
— **clank·ing·ly** \'klaŋ-kiŋ-lē\ *adverb*

²clank *noun* (1656)
: a sharp brief metallic ringing sound

clan·nish \'kla-nish\ *adjective* (1776)
1 : of or relating to a clan
2 : tending to associate only with a select group of similar background or status
— **clan·nish·ly** *adverb*
— **clan·nish·ness** *noun*

clans·man \'klanz-mən\ *noun* (1810)
: a member of a clan

¹clap \'klap\ *verb* **clapped** *also* **clapt; clap·ping** [Middle English *clappen*, from Old English *clæppan* to throb; akin to Old High German *klaphōn* to beat] (14th century)
transitive verb
1 : to strike (as two flat hard surfaces) together so as to produce a sharp percussive noise
2 a : to strike (the hands) together repeatedly usually in applause **b :** APPLAUD
3 : to strike with the flat of the hand in a friendly way ⟨*clapped* his friend on the shoulder⟩
4 : to place, put, or set especially energetically ⟨*clap* him into jail⟩ ⟨since I first *clapped* eyes on it⟩
5 : to improvise hastily
intransitive verb
1 : to produce a percussive sound; *especially* **:** SLAM
2 : to go abruptly or briskly
3 : APPLAUD

²clap *noun* (13th century)
1 : a device that makes a clapping noise

clam 1a: *a* incurrent orifice, *b* siphon, *c* excurrent orifice, *d* mantle, *e* shell, *f* foot

\ə\ abut	\ᵊ\ kitten	\ər\ further	\a\ ash	\ā\ ace	
\ä\ mop, mar	\aú\ out	\ch\ chin	\e\ bet	\ē\ easy	
\g\ go	\i\ hit	\ī\ ice	\j\ job	\ŋ\ sing	\ō\ go
\ȯ\ law	\ȯi\ boy	\th\ thin	\t͟h\ the	\ü\ loot	\ú\ foot
\y\ yet	\zh\ vision	*see also* Guide to Pronunciation			

2 *obsolete* **:** a sudden stroke of fortune and especially ill fortune
3 : a loud percussive noise; *specifically* **:** a sudden crash of thunder
4 a : a sudden blow **b :** a friendly slap
5 : the sound of clapping hands; *especially* **:** APPLAUSE
³clap *noun* [Middle French *clapoir* bubo] (1587)
: GONORRHEA — often used with *the*
clap·board \'kla-bərd; 'kla(p)-ˌbȯrd, -ˌbȯrd\ *noun* [part translation of Dutch *klaphout* stave wood] (circa 1520)
1 *archaic* **:** a size of board for making staves and wainscoting
2 : a narrow board usually thicker at one edge than the other used for siding
3 \'klap-ˌbȯrd, -ˌbȯrd\ **:** a pair of hinged boards one of which has a slate with data identifying a piece of film and which are banged together in front of a motion-picture camera at the start of a take to facilitate editing — called also *clapper board*
— clapboard *transitive verb*
clapped–out \ˌklapt-'aut\ *adjective* (1946)
British **:** WORN-OUT; *also* **:** TIRED
clap·per \'kla-pər\ *noun* (14th century)
: one that claps: as **a :** the tongue of a bell **b :** a mechanical device that makes noise especially by the banging of one part against another **c :** a person who applauds
clap·per·claw \'kla-pər-ˌklȯ\ *transitive verb* [perhaps from *clapper* + *claw* (verb)] (1590)
1 *dialect English* **:** to claw with the nails
2 *dialect English* **:** SCOLD, REVILE
¹clap·trap \'klap-ˌtrap\ *noun* [²*clap;* from its attempt to win applause] (1799)
: pretentious nonsense **:** TRASH
²claptrap *adjective* (1815)
: characterized by or suggestive of claptrap; *especially* **:** of a cheap showy nature ⟨*claptrap* sentiment⟩
claque \'klak\ *noun* [French, from *claquer* to clap, of imitative origin] (1864)
1 : a group hired to applaud at a performance
2 : a group of sycophants
cla·queur \kla-'kər\ *noun* [French, from *claquer* to clap] (1837)
: a member of a claque
clar·et \'klar-ət\ *noun* [Middle English, from Middle French (*vin*) *claret* clear wine, from *claret* clear, from *cler* clear] (1707)
1 : a red Bordeaux wine; *also* **:** a similar wine produced elsewhere
2 : a dark purplish red
— claret *adjective*
clar·i·fy \'klar-ə-ˌfī\ *verb* **-fied; -fy·ing** [Middle English *clarifien,* from Middle French *clarifier,* from Late Latin *clarificare,* from Latin *clarus* clear — more at CLEAR] (14th century)
transitive verb
1 : to make (as a liquid) clear or pure usually by freeing from suspended matter
2 : to free of confusion
3 : to make understandable
intransitive verb
: to become clear
— clar·i·fi·ca·tion \ˌklar-ə-fə-'kā-shən\ *noun*
— clar·i·fi·er \'klar-ə-ˌfī-(-ə)r\ *noun*
clar·i·net \ˌklar-ə-'net, 'klar-ə-nət\ *noun* [French *clarinette,* probably ultimately from Medieval Latin *clarion-, clario*] (1796)
: a single-reed woodwind instrument having a cylindrical tube with a moderately flared bell and a usual range from D below middle C upward for 3½ octaves
— clar·i·net·ist *or* **clar·i·net·tist** \ˌklar-ə-'ne-tist\ *noun*
¹clar·i·on \'klar-ē-ən\ *noun* [Middle English, from Middle French & Medieval Latin; Middle French *clairon,* from Medieval Latin *clarion-, clario,* from Latin *clarus*] (14th century)

1 : a medieval trumpet with clear shrill tones
2 : the sound of or as if of a clarion
²clarion *adjective* (1841)
: brilliantly clear ⟨her *clarion* top notes⟩; *also* **:** loud and clear ⟨a *clarion* call to action⟩
clar·i·ty \'klar-ə-tē\ *noun* [Middle English *clarite,* from Latin *claritat-, claritas,* from *clarus*] (1616)
: the quality or state of being clear **:** LUCIDITY
clark·ia \'klär-kē-ə\ *noun* [New Latin, from William *Clark*] (1827)
: any of a genus (*Clarkia*) of showy annual herbs of the evening-primrose family that are native to the Pacific slope of North America and southwestern South America
cla·ro \'klär-(ˌ)ō\ *noun, plural* **claros** [Spanish, from *claro* light, from Latin *clarus*] (1891)
: a light-colored usually mild cigar
clary \'klar-ē, 'kler-\ *noun, plural* **clar·ies** [Middle English *clarie,* from Middle French *sclaree,* from Medieval Latin *sclareia*] (14th century)
: an aromatic mint (*Salvia sclarea*) of southern Europe that is widely cultivated especially as an ornamental
¹clash \'klash\ *verb* [imitative] (circa 1500)
intransitive verb
1 : to make a clash ⟨cymbals *clashed*⟩
2 : to come into conflict ⟨where ignorant armies *clash* by night —Matthew Arnold⟩; *also* **:** to be incompatible ⟨the colors *clashed*⟩
transitive verb
: to cause to clash
— clash·er *noun*
²clash *noun* (1513)
1 : a noisy usually metallic sound of collision
2 a : a hostile encounter **:** SKIRMISH **b :** a sharp conflict ⟨a *clash* of opinions⟩
¹clasp \'klasp\ *noun* [Middle English *claspe*] (14th century)
1 a : a device (as a hook) for holding objects or parts together **b :** a device (as a bar) attached to a military medal to indicate an additional award of the medal or the action or service for which it was awarded
2 : a holding or enveloping with or as if with the hands or arms
²clasp *transitive verb* (14th century)
1 : to fasten with or as if with a clasp ⟨a robe *clasped* with a brooch⟩
2 : to enclose and hold with the arms; *specifically* **:** EMBRACE
3 : to seize with or as if with the hand **:** GRASP
clasp·er \'klas-pər\ *noun* (circa 1847)
: a male copulatory structure: **a :** one of a pair of external anal processes of an insect that are used to grasp a female **b :** one of a pair of organs that are extensions of the pelvic fins of cartilaginous fishes
clasp knife *noun* (circa 1755)
: POCKETKNIFE; *especially* **:** a large one-bladed folding knife having a catch to hold the blade open
¹class \'klas\ *noun, often attributive* [French *classe,* from Latin *classis* group called to military service, fleet, class; perhaps akin to Latin *calare* to call — more at LOW] (1602)
1 a : a body of students meeting regularly to study the same subject **b :** the period during which such a body meets **c :** a course of instruction **d :** a body of students or alumni whose year of graduation is the same
2 a : a group sharing the same economic or social status ⟨the working *class*⟩ **b :** social rank; *especially* **:** high social rank **c :** high quality **:** ELEGANCE
3 : a group, set, or kind sharing common attributes: as **a :** a major category in biological taxonomy ranking above the order and below the phylum or division **b :** a collection of adjacent and discrete or continuous values of a random variable **c :** SET 21
4 : a division or rating based on grade or quality

5 : the best of its kind ⟨the *class* of the league⟩
²class *transitive verb* (1705)
: CLASSIFY
class act *noun* (1976)
: an example of outstanding quality or prestige
class action *noun* (1952)
: a legal action undertaken by one or more plaintiffs on behalf of themselves and all other persons having an identical interest in the alleged wrong
class–conscious *adjective* (1903)
1 : actively aware of one's common status with others in a particular economic or social level of society
2 : believing in class struggle
— class consciousness *noun*
¹clas·sic \'kla-sik\ *adjective* [French or Latin; French *classique,* from Latin *classicus* of the highest class of Roman citizens, of the first rank, from *classis*] (circa 1604)
1 a : serving as a standard of excellence **:** of recognized value **b :** TRADITIONAL, ENDURING **c :** characterized by simple tailored lines in fashion year after year ⟨a *classic* suit⟩
2 : of or relating to the ancient Greeks and Romans or their culture **:** CLASSICAL
3 a : historically memorable **b :** noted because of special literary or historical associations ⟨Paris is the *classic* refuge of expatriates⟩
4 a : AUTHENTIC, AUTHORITATIVE **b :** TYPICAL ⟨a *classic* example of chicanery⟩
5 *capitalized* **:** of or relating to the period of highest development of Mesoamerican and especially Mayan culture about A.D. 300–900
²classic *noun* (1711)
1 : a literary work of ancient Greece or Rome
2 a : a work of enduring excellence; *also* **:** its author **b :** an authoritative source
3 : a typical or perfect example
4 : a traditional event ⟨a football *classic*⟩
clas·si·cal \'kla-si-kəl\ *adjective* [Latin *classicus*] (1599)
1 : STANDARD, CLASSIC
2 a : of or relating to the ancient Greek and Roman world and especially to its literature, art, architecture, or ideals **b :** versed in the classics
3 a : of or relating to music of the late 18th and early 19th centuries characterized by an emphasis on balance, clarity, and moderation **b :** of, relating to, or being music in the educated European tradition that includes such forms as art song, chamber music, opera, and symphony as distinguished from folk or popular music or jazz
4 a : AUTHORITATIVE, TRADITIONAL **b** (1) **:** of or relating to a form or system considered of first significance in earlier times ⟨*classical* Mendelian genetics⟩ (2) **:** not involving relativity, wave mechanics, or quantum theory ⟨*classical* physics⟩ **c :** conforming to a pattern of usage sanctioned by a body of literature rather than by everyday speech
5 : concerned with or giving instruction in the humanities, the fine arts, and the broad aspects of science ⟨a *classical* curriculum⟩
classical conditioning *noun* (1949)
: conditioning in which the conditioned stimulus (as the sound of a bell) is paired with and precedes the unconditioned stimulus (as the sight of food) until the conditioned stimulus alone is sufficient to elicit the response (as salivation in a dog) — compare OPERANT CONDITIONING
clas·si·cal·i·ty \ˌkla-sə-'ka-lə-tē\ *noun* (1819)
1 : the quality or state of being classic
2 : classical scholarship
clas·si·cal·ly \'kla-si-k(ə-)lē\ *adverb* (1772)
1 : in a classic or classical manner ⟨*classically* exact forms of the dance⟩ ⟨*classically* trained⟩
2 a : in classic or traditional circumstances **:** TYPICALLY ⟨*classically,* the whole fish is stuffed⟩ **b :** as a classic example ⟨*classically* bad writing⟩

clas·si·cism \'kla-sə-ˌsi-zəm\ *noun* (1830)
1 a : the principles or style embodied in the literature, art, or architecture of ancient Greece and Rome **b :** classical scholarship **c :** a classical idiom or expression
2 : adherence to traditional standards (as of simplicity, restraint, and proportion) that are universally and enduringly valid
clas·si·cist \-sist\ *noun* (1830)
1 : an advocate or follower of classicism
2 : a classical scholar
— **clas·si·cis·tic** \ˌkla-sə-'sis-tik\ *adjective*
clas·si·cize \'kla-sə-ˌsīz\ *verb* **-cized; -ciz·ing** (1854)
transitive verb
: to make classic or classical
intransitive verb
: to follow classic style
clas·si·co \'kla-si-(ˌ)kō\ *adjective* [Italian, from Latin *classicus*] (1968)
: produced in a delimited area of Italy known for its standards of quality ⟨Chianti *classico*⟩
clas·si·fi·ca·tion \ˌkla-sə-fə-'kā-shən\ *noun* (1790)
1 : the act or process of classifying
2 a : systematic arrangement in groups or categories according to established criteria; *specifically* **:** TAXONOMY **b :** CLASS, CATEGORY
— **clas·si·fi·ca·to·ry** \'kla-sə-fi-kə-ˌtōr-ē, kla-'si-fə-, -ˌtōr-; ˌkla-sə-fə-ˌkā-tə-rē\ *adjective*
clas·si·fied \'kla-sə-ˌfīd\ *adjective* (1889)
1 : divided into classes or placed in a class ⟨*classified* ads⟩
2 : withheld from general circulation for reasons of national security ⟨*classified* information⟩
clas·si·fi·er \'kla-sə-ˌfī(-ə)r\ *noun* (1819)
1 : one that classifies; *specifically* **:** a machine for sorting out the constituents of a substance (as ore)
2 : a word or morpheme used with numerals or with nouns designating countable or measurable objects
clas·si·fy \'kla-sə-ˌfī\ *transitive verb* **-fied; -fy·ing** (1799)
1 : to arrange in classes ⟨*classifying* books according to subject matter⟩
2 : to assign (as a document) to a category
— **clas·si·fi·able** \ˌkla-sə-'fī-ə-bəl\ *adjective*
class interval *noun* (1929)
: CLASS 3b; *also* **:** its numerical width
clas·sis \'kla-sis\ *noun, plural* **clas·ses** \'kla-ˌsēz\ [New Latin, from Latin, class] (1593)
1 : a governing body in some Reformed churches (as in the former Reformed Church in the U.S.) corresponding to a presbytery
2 : the district governed by a classis
class·ism \'kla-ˌsi-zəm\ *noun* (1842)
: prejudice or discrimination based on class
— **class·ist** \'kla-sist\ *adjective*
class·less \'klas-ləs\ *adjective* (1878)
1 : belonging to no particular social class
2 : free from distinctions of social class ⟨a *classless* society⟩
— **class·less·ness** *noun*
class·mate \-ˌmāt\ *noun* (1713)
: a member of the same class in a school or college
class·room \-ˌrüm, -ˌrùm\ *noun* (1870)
: a place where classes meet
classy \'kla-sē\ *adjective* **class·i·er; -est** (1891)
: ELEGANT, STYLISH ⟨a *classy* clientele⟩; *also* **:** notably superior ⟨a *classy* outfielder⟩
— **class·i·ness** *noun*
clast \'klast\ *noun* [Greek *klastos* broken, from *klan* to break; perhaps akin to Latin *clades* disaster] (1952)
: a fragment of rock
clas·tic \'klas-tik\ *adjective* [International Scientific Vocabulary] (1877)
: made up of fragments of preexisting rocks ⟨a *clastic* sediment⟩

— **clastic** *noun*
clath·rate \'kla-ˌthrāt\ *adjective* [Latin *clathratus*, furnished with a lattice, from *clathri* (plural) lattice, from Greek *klēithron* bar, from *kleiein* to close — more at CLAVICLE] (1906)
: relating to or being a compound formed by the inclusion of molecules of one kind in cavities of the crystal lattice of another
— **clathrate** *noun*
¹clat·ter \'kla-tər\ *verb* [Middle English *clatren*, from (assumed) Old English *clatrian*; of imitative origin] (13th century)
intransitive verb
1 : to make a rattling sound ⟨the dishes *clattered* on the shelf⟩
2 : to talk noisily or rapidly
3 : to move or go with a clatter ⟨*clattered* down the stairs⟩
transitive verb
: to cause to clatter
— **clat·ter·er** \-tər-ər\ *noun*
— **clat·ter·ing·ly** \'kla-tə-riṇ-lē\ *adverb*
²clatter *noun* (14th century)
1 : a rattling sound (as of hard bodies striking together) ⟨the *clatter* of pots and pans⟩
2 : COMMOTION ⟨the midday *clatter* of the business district⟩
3 : noisy chatter
clat·tery \'kla-tə-rē\ *adjective*
clau·di·ca·tion \ˌklò-də-'kā-shən\ *noun* [Latin *claudication-, claudicatio*, from *claudicare* to limp, from *claudus* lame] (15th century)
: the quality or state of being lame : LIMPING
claus·al \'klò-zəl\ *adjective* (1904)
: relating to or of the nature of a clause
clause \'klòz\ *noun* [Middle English, from Old French, from Medieval Latin *clausa* close of a rhetorical period, from Latin, feminine of *clausus*, past participle of *claudere* to close — more at CLOSE] (13th century)
1 : a group of words containing a subject and predicate and functioning as a member of a complex or compound sentence
2 : a separate section of a discourse or writing; *specifically* **:** a distinct article in a formal document
claus·tral \'klòs-trəl\ *adjective* [Middle English, from Medieval Latin *claustralis*, from *claustrum* cloister, from Latin, bar, bolt, confining space, from *claudere*] (15th century)
: CLOISTRAL
claus·tro·pho·bia \ˌklòs-trə-'fō-bē-ə\ *noun* [New Latin, from Latin *claustrum* + New Latin *-phobia*] (1879)
: abnormal dread of being in closed or narrow spaces
— **claus·tro·phobe** \'klòs-trə-ˌfōb\ *noun*
claus·tro·pho·bic \ˌklòs-trə-'fō-bik\ *adjective* (circa 1889)
1 : affected with or inclined to claustrophobia
2 : inducing or suggesting claustrophobia
— **claus·tro·pho·bi·cal·ly** \-bi-k(ə-)lē\ *adverb*
claus·trum \'klòs-trəm, 'klaùs-\ *noun, plural* **claus·tra** \-trə\ [New Latin, from Latin, bar] (1848)
: the one of the four basal ganglia in each cerebral hemisphere that consists of a thin lamina of gray matter separated from the lenticular nucleus by a layer of white matter
cla·vate \'klā-ˌvāt\ *adjective* [New Latin *clavatus*, from Latin *clava* club, from *clavus* nail, knot in wood] (1813)
: gradually thickening near the distal end
: shaped like a club
¹clave *past of* CLEAVE
²clave \'klä-(ˌ)vā, 'kläv\ *noun* [American Spanish, from Spanish, keystone, clef, from Latin *clavis*] (1928)
: one of a pair of cylindrical hardwood sticks that are used as a percussion instrument
cla·ver \'klā-vər\ *intransitive verb* [probably of Celtic origin; akin to Scottish Gaelic *clabaire* babbler] (circa 1605)
chiefly Scottish **:** PRATE, GOSSIP
— **claver** *noun, chiefly Scottish*

clav·i·chord \'kla-və-ˌkòrd\ *noun* [Medieval Latin *clavichordium*, from Latin *clavis* key + *chorda* string — more at CORD] (15th century)
: an early keyboard instrument having strings struck by tangents attached directly to the key ends
— **clav·i·chord·ist** \-ˌkòr-dist\ *noun*
clav·i·cle \'kla-vi-kəl\ *noun* [French *clavicule*, from New Latin *clavicula*, from Latin, diminutive of Latin *clavis*; akin to Greek *kleid-, kleis* key, *kleiein* to close] (1615)
: a bone of the vertebrate pectoral girdle typically serving to link the scapula and sternum — called also collarbone
— **cla·vic·u·lar** \kla-'vi-kyə-lər, klə-\ *adjective*
cla·vier \klə-'vir; 'klā-vē-ər, 'kla-\ *noun* [French, from Old French, key bearer, from Latin *clavis*] (1708)
1 : the keyboard of a musical instrument
2 [German *Klavier*, from French *clavier*] **:** an early keyboard instrument
— **cla·vier·ist** \klə-'vir-ist; 'klā-vē-ə-rist, 'kla-\ *noun*
— **cla·vier·is·tic** \klə-ˌvi-'ris-tik; ˌklā-vē-ə-'ris-tik, ˌkla-\ *adjective*
¹claw \'klò\ *noun, often attributive* [Middle English *clawe*, from Old English *clawu* hoof, claw; akin to Old Norse *klō* claw, and probably to Old English *cliewen* ball — more at CLEW] (before 12th century)
1 : a sharp usually slender and curved nail on the toe of an animal
2 : any of various sharp curved processes especially at the end of a limb (as of an insect); *also* **:** a limb ending in such a process
3 : one of the pincerlike organs terminating some limbs of various arthropods (as a lobster or scorpion)
4 : something that resembles a claw; *specifically* **:** the forked end of a tool (as a hammer)
— **clawed** \'klòd\ *adjective*
— **claw·like** \-ˌlīk\ *adjective*
²claw (before 12th century)
transitive verb
: to rake, seize, dig, or progress with or as if with claws
intransitive verb
: to scrape, scratch, dig, or pull with or as if with claws
claw back *transitive verb* (1953)
chiefly British **:** to get back (as money) by strenuous or forceful means (as taxation)
— **claw–back** \'klò-ˌbak\ *noun*
claw–ham·mer \'klò-ˌha-mər\ *adjective* (1964)
: of or relating to a style of banjo playing using the thumb and one or more fingers picking or strumming in a downward direction
claw hammer *noun* (circa 1769)
1 : a hammer with one end of the head forked for pulling out nails
2 : TAILCOAT
clay \'klā\ *noun, often attributive* [Middle English, from Old English *clǣg*; akin to Old High German *klīwa* bran, Latin *gluten* glue, Middle Greek *glia*] (before 12th century)
1 a : an earthy material that is plastic when moist but hard when fired, that is composed mainly of fine particles of hydrous aluminum silicates and other minerals, and that is used for brick, tile, and pottery; *specifically* **:** soil composed chiefly of this material having particles less than a specified size **b :** EARTH, MUD
2 a : a substance that resembles clay in plasticity and is used for modeling **b :** the human body as distinguished from the spirit **c :** fundamental nature or character ⟨the common *clay*⟩

\ə\ abut \ᵊ\ kitten \ər\ further \a\ ash \ā\ ace
\ä\ mop, mar \aù\ out \ch\ chin \e\ bet \ē\ easy
\g\ go \i\ hit \ī\ ice \j\ job \ṇ\ sing \ō\ go
\ò\ law \òi\ boy \th\ thin \t̲h̲\ the \ü\ loot \ù\ foot
\y\ yet \zh\ vision *see also* Guide to Pronunciation

3 : CLAY COURT
— **clay·ey** \'klā-ē\ *adjective*
— **clay·ish** \'klā-ish\ *adjective*
— **clay·like** \-,līk\ *adjective*

clay·bank \'klā-,baŋk\ *noun* (1851)
: a horse of yellowish color

clay court *noun* (1885)
: a tennis court with a clay surface or a synthetic surface that resembles clay

clay loam *noun* (circa 1889)
: a loam containing from 20 to 30 percent clay

clay mineral *noun* (1947)
: any of a group of hydrous silicates of aluminum and sometimes other metals formed chiefly in weathering processes and occurring especially in clay and shale

clay·more \'klā-,mōr, -,mȯr\ *noun* [Scottish Gaelic *claidheamh mór,* literally, great sword] (1772)
: a large 2-edged sword formerly used by Scottish Highlanders; *also* : their basket-hilted broadsword

claymore mine *noun* [perhaps from *claymore*] (1961)
: a usually electrically fired land mine that contains steel fragments which are discharged in a predetermined direction

clay·pan \-,pan\ *noun* (1837)
1 : hardpan consisting mainly of clay
2 *Australian* : a shallow depression in which water collects after rain

clay pigeon *noun* (1888)
: a saucer-shaped target usually made of baked clay or limestone and pitch and thrown from a trap in skeet and trapshooting

clay·ware \'klā-,war, -,wer\ *noun* (1896)
: articles made of fired clay

¹clean \'klēn\ *adjective* [Middle English *clene,* from Old English *clǣne;* akin to Old High German *kleini* delicate, dainty] (before 12th century)
1 a : free from dirt or pollution ⟨changed to *clean* clothes⟩ ⟨*clean* solar energy⟩ **b** : free from contamination or disease **c** : free or relatively free from radioactivity ⟨a *clean* atomic explosion⟩
2 a : UNADULTERATED, PURE ⟨the *clean* thrill of one's first flight⟩ **b** *of a precious stone* : having no interior flaws visible **c** : free from growth that hinders tillage
3 a : free from moral corruption or sinister connections of any kind ⟨a candidate with a *clean* record⟩ **b** : free from offensive treatment of sexual subjects and from the use of obscenity ⟨a *clean* joke⟩ **c** : observing the rules : FAIR ⟨a *clean* fight⟩
4 : ceremonially or spiritually pure ⟨and all who are *clean* may eat flesh —Leviticus 7:19 (Revised Standard Version)⟩
5 a : THOROUGH, COMPLETE ⟨a *clean* break with the past⟩ **b** : deftly executed : SKILLFUL ⟨*clean* ballet technique⟩ **c** : hit beyond the reach of an opponent ⟨a *clean* single to center⟩
6 a : relatively free from error or blemish : CLEAR; *specifically* : LEGIBLE ⟨*clean* copy⟩ **b** : UNENCUMBERED ⟨*clean* bill of sale⟩
7 a : characterized by clarity and precision : TRIM ⟨a *clean* prose style⟩ ⟨architecture with *clean* almost austere lines⟩ **b** : EVEN, SMOOTH ⟨a *clean* edge⟩ ⟨a sharp blow causing a *clean* break⟩ **c** : free from impedances to smooth flow (as of water or air) ⟨a *clean* airplane⟩ ⟨a ship with a *clean* bottom⟩
8 a : EMPTY ⟨the ship returned with a *clean* hold⟩ **b** : free from drug addiction **c** *slang* : having no contraband (as weapons or drugs) in one's possession
9 : habitually neat
— **clean·ness** \'klēn-nəs\ *noun*

²clean *adverb* (before 12th century)
1 a : so as to clean ⟨a new broom sweeps *clean*⟩ **b** : in a clean manner ⟨play the game *clean*⟩
2 : all the way : COMPLETELY ⟨the bullet went *clean* through his arm⟩

³clean (15th century)
transitive verb
1 a : to make clean: as (1) : to rid of dirt, impurities, or extraneous matter (2) : to rid of corruption ⟨vowing to *clean* up city hall⟩ **b** : REMOVE, ERADICATE — usually used with *up* or *off* ⟨*clean* up that mess⟩
2 a : STRIP, EMPTY ⟨a tree *cleaned* of fruit⟩ **b** : to remove the entrails from ⟨*clean* fish⟩ **c** : to deprive of money or possessions — often used with *out* ⟨they *cleaned* him out completely⟩
intransitive verb
: to undergo or perform a process of cleaning ⟨*clean* up before dinner⟩
— **clean·abil·i·ty** \,klē-nə-'bi-lə-tē\ *noun*
— **clean·able** \'klē-nə-bəl\ *adjective*
— **clean house 1** : to clean a house and its furniture **2** : to make sweeping reforms or changes (as of personnel)
— **clean one's clock** : to beat one badly in a fight or competition
— **clean up one's act** : to behave in a more acceptable manner

⁴clean *noun* (circa 1889)
: an act of cleaning dirt especially from the surface of something

clean and jerk *noun* (1939)
: a lift in weight lifting in which the weight is raised to shoulder height, held momentarily, and then quickly thrust overhead usually with a lunge or a spring from the legs — compare PRESS, SNATCH

clean-cut \'klēn-'kət\ *adjective* (1843)
1 : cut so that the surface or edge is smooth and even
2 : sharply defined
3 : of wholesome appearance

clean·er \'klē-nər\ *noun* (circa 1792)
1 a : one whose work is cleaning **b** : DRY CLEANER
2 : a preparation for cleaning
3 : an implement or machine for cleaning

clean-hand·ed \'klēn-'han-dəd\ *adjective* (1728)
: innocent of wrongdoing

clean–limbed \'klēn-'limd\ *adjective* (15th century)
: well proportioned : TRIM ⟨*clean-limbed* youths⟩

¹clean·ly \'klēn-lē\ *adverb* (13th century)
: in a clean manner

²clean·ly \'klen-lē\ *adjective* **clean·li·er; -est** (circa 1500)
1 : careful to keep clean : FASTIDIOUS
2 : habitually kept clean
— **clean·li·ness** *noun*

clean room \'klēn-,rüm, -,rùm\ *noun* (1963)
: a room for the manufacture or assembly of objects (as precision parts) that is maintained at a high level of cleanliness by special means

cleanse \'klenz\ *verb* **cleansed; cleans·ing** [Middle English *clensen,* from Old English *clǣnsian* to purify, from *clǣne* clean] (before 12th century)
: CLEAN; *especially* : to rid of impurities by or as if by washing

cleans·er \'klen-zər\ *noun* (before 12th century)
1 : one that cleanses
2 : a preparation (as a scouring powder or a skin cream) used for cleaning

¹clean·up \'klē-,nəp\ *noun* (1872)
1 : an act or instance of cleaning
2 : an exceptionally large profit : KILLING

²cleanup *adjective* (1937)
: being in the fourth position in the batting order of a baseball team ⟨a *cleanup* hitter⟩
— **cleanup** *adverb*

clean up *intransitive verb* (1920)
: to make a spectacular profit in a business enterprise or a killing in speculation or gambling

¹clear \'klir\ *adjective* [Middle English *clere,* from Old French *cler,* from Latin *clarus* clear, bright; akin to Latin *calare* to call — more at LOW] (13th century)
1 a : BRIGHT, LUMINOUS **b** : CLOUDLESS; *specifically* : less than one-tenth covered ⟨a *clear* sky⟩ **c** : free from mist, haze, or dust ⟨a *clear* day⟩ **d** : UNTROUBLED, SERENE ⟨a *clear* gaze⟩
2 : CLEAN, PURE: as **a** : free from blemishes **b** : easily seen through : TRANSPARENT **c** : free from abnormal sounds on auscultation
3 a : easily heard **b** : easily visible : PLAIN **c** : free from obscurity or ambiguity : easily understood : UNMISTAKABLE
4 a : capable of sharp discernment : KEEN **b** : free from doubt : SURE
5 : free from guile or guilt : INNOCENT
6 : unhampered by restriction or limitation: as **a** : unencumbered by debts or charges **b** : NET ⟨a *clear* profit⟩ **c** : UNQUALIFIED, ABSOLUTE **d** : free from obstruction **e** : emptied of contents or cargo **f** : free from entanglement **g** : BARE, DENUDED ☆ ☆
— **clear·ness** *noun*

²clear *adverb* (14th century)
1 : in a clear manner ⟨to cry loud and *clear*⟩
2 : all the way ⟨drove *clear* across the state⟩

³clear (14th century)
transitive verb
1 a : to make clear or translucent **b** : to free from pollution or cloudiness
2 : to free from accusation or blame : EXONERATE, VINDICATE ⟨the opportunity to *clear* himself⟩
3 a : to give insight to : ENLIGHTEN **b** : to make intelligible : EXPLAIN ⟨*clear* up the mystery⟩
4 a : to free from what obstructs or is unneeded: as (1) : OPEN 1b ⟨*clear* a path⟩ (2) : to remove unwanted growth or items from ⟨*clear* the land of timber⟩ (3) : to rid or make a rasping noise as if ridding (the throat) of phlegm (4) : to erase stored or displayed data from (as a computer or calculator) **b** : to empty of occupants ⟨*clear* the room⟩ **c** : DISENTANGLE ⟨*clear* a fishing line⟩ **d** : to remove from an area or place ⟨*clear* the dishes from the table⟩ **e** : TRANSMIT, DISPATCH
5 a : to submit for approval ⟨*clear* it with me first⟩ **b** : AUTHORIZE, APPROVE ⟨*cleared* the article for publication⟩: as (1) : to certify as trustworthy ⟨*clear* a person for classified information⟩ (2) : to permit (an aircraft) to proceed usually with a specified action
6 a : to free from obligation or encumbrance **b** : SETTLE, DISCHARGE ⟨*clear* an account⟩ **c** (1) : to free (a ship or shipment) by payment of duties or harbor fees (2) : to pass through (customs) **d** : to gain without deduction : NET ⟨*clear* a profit⟩ **e** : to put through a clearinghouse

☆ SYNONYMS
Clear, transparent, translucent, limpid mean capable of being seen through. CLEAR implies absence of cloudiness, haziness, or muddiness ⟨*clear* water⟩. TRANSPARENT implies being so clear that objects can be seen distinctly ⟨a *transparent* sheet of film⟩. TRANSLUCENT implies the passage of light but not a clear view of what lies beyond ⟨*translucent* frosted glass⟩. LIMPID suggests the soft clearness of pure water ⟨her eyes were *limpid* pools of blue⟩.

Clear, perspicuous, lucid mean quickly and easily understood. CLEAR implies freedom from obscurity, ambiguity, or undue complexity ⟨*clear* instructions⟩. PERSPICUOUS applies to a style that is simple and elegant as well as clear ⟨a *perspicuous* style⟩. LUCID suggests a clear logical coherence and evident order of arrangement ⟨a *lucid* explanation⟩. See in addition EVIDENT.

7 a : to go over, under, or by without touching **b :** PASS ⟨the bill *cleared* the legislature⟩
intransitive verb
1 a : to become clear ⟨it *cleared* up quickly after the rain⟩ **b :** to go away **:** VANISH ⟨the symptoms *cleared* gradually⟩ **c :** SELL
2 a : to obtain permission to discharge cargo **b :** to conform to regulations or pay requisite fees prior to leaving port
3 : to pass through a clearinghouse
4 : to go to an authority (as for approval) before becoming effective
— **clear·able** \'klir-ə-bəl\ *adjective*
— **clear·er** \'klir-ər\ *noun*
— **clear the air** *also* **clear the atmosphere :** to remove elements of hostility, tension, confusion, or uncertainty ⟨had a long meeting to *clear the air*⟩
— **clear the decks :** to make sweeping preparations for action
⁴clear *noun* (1674)
1 : a clear space or part
2 : a high arcing shot over an opponent's head in badminton
— **in the clear 1 :** in inside measurement **2 :** free from guilt or suspicion **3 :** in plaintext **:** not in code or cipher ⟨a message sent *in the clear*⟩

clear–air turbulence *noun* (1955)
: sudden severe turbulence occurring in cloudless regions that causes violent jarring or buffeting of aircraft
clear·ance \'klir-ən(t)s\ *noun* (1540)
1 : an act or process of clearing: as **a :** the removal of buildings from an area (as a city slum) **b :** the act of clearing a ship at the customhouse; *also* **:** the papers showing that a ship has cleared **c :** the offsetting of checks and other claims among banks through a clearinghouse **d :** certification as clear of objection **:** AUTHORIZATION ⟨security *clearance*⟩ **e :** a sale to clear out stock **f :** authorization for an aircraft to proceed especially with a specified action ⟨*clearance* to land⟩
2 : the distance by which one object clears another or the clear space between them
3 : the volume of blood or plasma that could be freed of a specified constituent in a specified time (usually one minute) by its excretion into the urine through the kidneys — called also *renal clearance*
¹clear–cut \'klir-'kət\ *adjective* (1855)
1 : sharply outlined **:** DISTINCT
2 : free from ambiguity or uncertainty **:** UNAMBIGUOUS
²clear–cut \-'kət\ *noun* (circa 1958)
: an area of forest which has been clear-cut; *also* **:** CLEAR-CUTTING
clear–cut·ting \-'kə-tiŋ\ *noun* (1922)
: removal of all the trees in a stand of timber
— **clear–cut** *verb*
clear–eyed \'klir-'īd\ *adjective* (1530)
: CLEAR-SIGHTED
clear·head·ed \-'he-dəd\ *adjective* (1709)
1 : having a clear understanding **:** PERCEPTIVE
2 : able to think clearly
— **clear·head·ed·ly** *adverb*
— **clear·head·ed·ness** *noun*
clear·ing \'klir-iŋ\ *noun* (14th century)
1 : the act or process of making or becoming clear
2 : a tract of land cleared of wood and brush
3 a : a method of exchanging and offsetting commercial papers or accounts with cash settlement only of the balances due after the clearing **b** *plural* **:** the gross amount of balances so adjusted
clear·ing·house \-,haùs\ *noun* (1832)
1 : an establishment maintained by banks for settling mutual claims and accounts
2 : a central agency for the collection, classification, and distribution especially of information; *broadly* **:** an informal channel for distributing information or assistance
clear·ly \'klir-lē\ *adverb* (14th century)
1 : in a clear manner ⟨speaking *clearly*⟩

2 : it is clear ⟨*clearly*, a new approach is needed⟩
usage see HOPEFULLY
clear out (1792)
intransitive verb
: DEPART
transitive verb
: to drive out or away usually forcibly
clear–sight·ed \'klir-,sī-təd\ *adjective* (1586)
1 : having clear vision
2 : DISCERNING
— **clear–sight·ed·ly** *adverb*
— **clear–sight·ed·ness** *noun*
clear·sto·ry *variant of* CLERESTORY
clear·wing \-,wiŋ\ *noun* (1868)
: a moth (as of the families Aegeriidae or Sphingidae) having the wings largely transparent and devoid of scales
¹cleat \'klēt\ *noun* [Middle English *clete* wedge, from (assumed) Old English *clēat*; akin to Middle High German *klōz* lump — more at CLOUT] (14th century)
1 a : a wedge-shaped piece fastened to or projecting from something and serving as a support or check **b :** a wooden or metal fitting usually with two projecting horns around which a rope may be made fast
2 a : a strip fastened across something to give strength or hold in position **b** (1) **:** a projecting piece (as on the bottom of a shoe) that furnishes a grip (2) *plural* **:** shoes equipped with cleats
²cleat *transitive verb* (1794)
1 : to secure to or by a cleat
2 : to provide with a cleat
cleav·able \'klē-və-bəl\ *adjective* (circa 1864)
: capable of being split
cleav·age \'klē-vij\ *noun* (1816)
1 a : the quality of a crystallized substance or rock of splitting along definite planes; *also* **:** the occurrence of such splitting **b :** a fragment (as of a diamond) obtained by splitting
2 : the action of cleaving **:** the state of being cleft
3 : the series of synchronized mitotic cell divisions of the fertilized egg that results in the formation of the blastomeres and changes the single-celled zygote into a multicellular embryo; *also* **:** one of these cell divisions
4 : the splitting of a molecule into simpler molecules
5 : the depression between a woman's breasts especially when made visible by the wearing of a low-cut dress
¹cleave \'klēv\ *intransitive verb* **cleaved** \'klēvd\ *or* **clove** \'klōv\ *also* **clave** \'klāv\; **cleaved; cleav·ing** [Middle English *clevien*, from Old English *clifian;* akin to Old High German *kleben* to stick] (before 12th century)
: to adhere firmly and closely or loyally and unwaveringly
synonym see STICK
²cleave *verb* **cleaved** \'klēvd\ *also* **cleft** \'kleft\ *or* **clove** \'klōv\; **cleaved** *also* **cleft** *or* **clo·ven** \'klō-vən\; **cleav·ing** [Middle English *cleven*, from Old English *clēofan;* akin to Old Norse *kljūfa* to split, Latin *glubere* to peel, Greek *glyphein* to carve] (before 12th century)
transitive verb
1 : to divide by or as if by a cutting blow **:** SPLIT
2 : to separate into distinct parts and especially into groups having divergent views
3 : to subject to chemical cleavage ⟨a protein *cleaved* by an enzyme⟩
intransitive verb
1 : to split especially along the grain
2 : to penetrate or pass through something by or as if by cutting
synonym see TEAR
cleav·er \'klē-vər\ *noun* (15th century)
1 : one that cleaves; *especially* **:** a butcher's implement for cutting animal carcasses into joints or pieces

2 : a prehistoric stone tool having a sharp edge at one end
cleav·ers \'klē-vərz\ *noun plural but singular or plural in construction* [Middle English *clivre*, alteration of Old English *clife* burdock, cleavers; akin to Old English *clifian*] (14th century)
: an annual bedstraw (*Galium aparine*) that has numerous stalked white flowers, stems covered with curved prickles, and whorls of bristle-tipped leaves; *also* **:** any of several related plants
cleek \'klēk\ *noun* [Middle English (northern) *cleke*, from *cleken* to clutch] (15th century)
chiefly Scottish **:** a large hook (as for a pot over a fire)
clef \'klef\ *noun* [French, literally, key, from Latin *clavis* — more at CLAVICLE] (circa 1577)
: a sign placed at the beginning of a musical staff to determine the pitch of the notes
¹cleft \'kleft\ *noun* [Middle English *clift*, from Old English *geclyft;* akin to Old English *clēofan* to cleave] (14th century)
1 : a space or opening made by or as if by splitting **:** FISSURE
2 : a usually V-shaped indented formation **:** a hollow between ridges or protuberances ⟨the anal *cleft* of the human body⟩
²cleft *adjective* [Middle English, from past participle of *cleven*] (14th century)
: partially split or divided; *specifically* **:** divided about halfway to the midrib ⟨a *cleft* leaf⟩

clef: *1* treble clef, *2* bass clef

cleft lip *noun* (circa 1946)
: HARELIP
cleft palate *noun* (1847)
: congenital fissure of the roof of the mouth
clei·do·ic \klī-'dō-ik\ *adjective* [Greek *kleidoun* to fasten, lock in, from *kleid-, kleis* key — more at CLAVICLE] (1931)
of an egg **:** enclosed in a relatively impervious shell which reduces free exchange with the environment
cleis·tog·a·mous \klī-'stä-gə-məs\ *also* **cleis·to·gam·ic** \,klī-stə-'ga-mik\ *adjective* [Greek *kleistos* closed (from *kleiein* to close) + International Scientific Vocabulary *-gamous* — more at CLAVICLE] (1874)
: characterized by or being small inconspicuous closed self-pollinating flowers additional to and often more fruitful than showier ones on the same plant ⟨violets are *cleistogamous*⟩
— **cleis·tog·a·mous·ly** \klī-'stä-gə-məs-lē\ *adverb*
— **cleis·tog·a·my** \-'stä-gə-mē\ *noun*
clem·a·tis \'kle-mə-təs; kli-'ma-təs, -'mā-, -'mä-\ *noun* [New Latin, genus name, from Latin, from Greek *klēmatis* brushwood, clematis, from *klēmat-, klēma* twig, from *klan* to break — more at CLAST] (1578)
: any of a genus (*Clematis*) of vines or herbs of the buttercup family having three leaflets on each leaf and usually white, red, pink, or purple flowers
clem·en·cy \'kle-mən(t)-sē\ *noun, plural* **-cies** (15th century)
1 a : disposition to be merciful and especially to moderate the severity of punishment due **b :** an act or instance of leniency
2 : pleasant mildness of weather
synonym see MERCY
clem·ent \'kle-mənt\ *adjective* [Middle English, from Latin *clement-, clemens*] (15th century)

1 : inclined to be merciful **:** LENIENT ⟨a *clement* judge⟩
2 : MILD ⟨*clement* weather for November⟩
— **clem·ent·ly** *adverb*

clench \'klench\ *transitive verb* [Middle English, from Old English *-clencan*; akin to Old English *clingan* to cling] (13th century)
1 : CLINCH 2
2 : to hold fast **:** CLUTCH ⟨*clenched* the arms of the chair⟩
3 : to set or close tightly ⟨*clench* one's teeth⟩ ⟨*clench* one's fists⟩
— **clench** *noun*

clepe \'klep\ *transitive verb* **cleped** \'klept\; **yclept** \i-'klept\ *also* **cleped** *or* **ycleped** \i-'klept\; **clep·ing** \'kle-piŋ\ [Middle English, from Old English *clipian* to speak, call; akin to Old Frisian *kleppa* to ring] (before 12th century)
archaic **:** NAME, CALL

clep·sy·dra \'klep-sə-drə\ *noun, plural* **-dras** *or* **-drae** \-,drē, -,drī\ [Latin, from Greek *klepsydra*, from *kleptein* to steal + *hydōr* water — more at KLEPT-, WATER] (1646)
: WATER CLOCK

clere·sto·ry \'klir-,stōr-ē, -,stor-, -st(ə-)rē\ *noun* [Middle English, from *clere* clear + *story*] (15th century)
1 : an outside wall of a room or building that rises above an adjoining roof and contains windows
2 : GALLERY

clerestory 1

cler·gy \'klər-jē\ *noun, plural* **cler·gies** [Middle English *clergie*, from Old French, from *clerc* clergyman] (13th century)
1 : a group ordained to perform pastoral or sacerdotal functions in a Christian church
2 : the official or sacerdotal class of a non-Christian religion

cler·gy·man \-mən\ *noun* (1577)
: a member of the clergy

cler·gy·wom·an \-,wu̇-mən\ *noun* (1673)
: a woman who is a member of the clergy

cler·ic \'kler-ik\ *noun* [Late Latin *clericus*] (1621)
: a member of the clergy

¹cler·i·cal \'kler-i-kəl\ *adjective* (1592)
1 : of, relating to, or characteristic of the clergy
2 : of or relating to a clerk
— **cler·i·cal·ly** \-i-k(ə-)lē\ *adverb*

²clerical *noun* (1605)
1 : a member of the clergy
2 : CLERICALIST
3 : CLERK
4 *plural* **:** clerical garments

clerical collar *noun* (1948)
: a narrow stiffly upright white collar worn buttoned at the back of the neck by members of the clergy

cler·i·cal·ism \'kler-i-kə-,li-zəm\ *noun* (1864)
: a policy of maintaining or increasing the power of a religious hierarchy

cler·i·cal·ist \-list\ *noun* (1881)
: one that favors maintained or increased ecclesiastical power and influence

cler·i·hew \'kler-i-,hyü\ *noun* [Edmund *Clerihew* Bentley (died 1956) English writer] (1928)
: a light verse quatrain rhyming *aabb* and usually dealing with a person named in the initial rhyme

cler·i·sy \'kler-ə-sē\ *noun* [German *Klerisei* clergy, from Medieval Latin *clericia*, from Late Latin *clericus* cleric] (1818)

: INTELLIGENTSIA

¹clerk \'klərk, *British usually* 'klärk\ *noun* [Middle English, from Old French *clerc* & Old English *cleric, clerc*, both from Late Latin *clericus*, from Late Greek *klērikos*, from Greek *klēros* lot, inheritance (in allusion to Deuteronomy 18:2), stick of wood; akin to Greek *klan* to break — more at CLAST] (before 12th century)
1 : CLERIC
2 *archaic* **:** SCHOLAR
3 a : an official responsible (as to a government agency) for correspondence, records, and accounts and vested with specified powers or authority (as to issue writs or other processes as ordered by a court) ⟨city *clerk*⟩ **b :** one employed to keep records or accounts or to perform general office work **c :** one who works at a sales or service counter
— **clerk·ship** \-,ship\ *noun*

²clerk *intransitive verb* (1551)
: to act or work as a clerk

clerk·ly \'klər-klē, *British usually* 'klär-\ *adjective* (15th century)
1 : of, relating to, or characteristic of a clerk
2 *archaic* **:** SCHOLARLY
— **clerkly** *adverb*

Cleve·land bay \'klēv-lənd-\ *noun* [*Cleveland*, district in Yorkshire, England] (1796)
: a large strong horse of a breed of English origin that is uniformly bay with black legs, mane, and tail

clev·er \'kle-vər\ *adjective* [Middle English *cliver*, perhaps of Scandinavian origin; akin to Danish dialect *kløver* alert, skillful] (circa 1595)
1 a : skillful or adroit in using the hands or body **:** NIMBLE **b :** mentally quick and resourceful but often lacking in depth and soundness
2 : marked by wit or ingenuity
3 *dialect* **a :** GOOD **b :** easy to use or handle ☆
— **clev·er·ish** \-v(ə-)rish\ *adjective*
— **clev·er·ly** \-vər-lē\ *adverb*
— **clev·er·ness** \-vər-nəs\ *noun*

clev·is \'kle-vəs\ *noun* [earlier *clevi*, perhaps of Scandinavian origin; akin to Old Norse *kljufa* to split — more at CLEAVE] (1592)
: SHACKLE 3

¹clew \'klü\ *noun* [Middle English *clewe*, from Old English *cliewen*; akin to Old High German *kliuwa* ball, Sanskrit *glau* lump] (before 12th century)
1 : a ball of thread, yarn, or cord
2 : CLUE
3 a : a lower corner or only the after corner of a sail **b :** a metal loop attached to the lower corner of a sail **c** *plural* **:** a combination of lines by which a hammock is suspended

²clew *transitive verb* (15th century)
1 : to roll into a ball
2 : CLUE
3 : to haul (a sail) up or down by ropes through the clews

cli·ché *also* **cli·che** \klē-'shā, 'klē-,, kli-'\ *noun* [French, literally, printer's stereotype, from past participle of *clicher* to stereotype, of imitative origin] (1892)
1 : a trite phrase or expression; *also* **:** the idea expressed by it
2 : a hackneyed theme, characterization, or situation
3 : something (as a menu item) that has become overly familiar or commonplace ◇
— **cliché** *adjective*

cli·chéd \-'shād\ *adjective* (1928)
1 : marked by or abounding in clichés
2 : HACKNEYED

¹click \'klik\ *verb* [probably imitative] (1581)
transitive verb
: to strike, move, or produce with a click ⟨*clicked* his heels together⟩
intransitive verb
1 : to make a click
2 a : to fit or agree exactly **b :** to fit together

c : to hit it off ⟨they did not *click* as friends⟩ **c :** to function smoothly **d :** SUCCEED ⟨a movie that *clicks*⟩

²click *noun* (1611)
1 a : a slight sharp noise **b :** a speech sound in some languages made by enclosing air between two stop articulations of the tongue, enlarging the enclosure to rarefy the air, and suddenly opening the enclosure
2 : DETENT

click beetle *noun* (circa 1864)
: any of a family (Elateridae) of beetles able to right themselves with a click when inverted by flexing the articulation between the prothorax and mesothorax

click stop *noun* (1950)
: a turnable control device (as for a camera diaphragm opening) that engages with a definite click at specific settings

cli·ent \'klī-ənt\ *noun* [Middle English, from Middle French & Latin; Middle French *client*, from Latin *client-, cliens*; perhaps akin to Latin *clinare* to lean — more at LEAN] (14th century)
1 : one that is under the protection of another **:** DEPENDENT
2 a : a person who engages the professional advice or services of another ⟨a lawyer's *clients*⟩ **b :** CUSTOMER ⟨hotel *clients*⟩ **c :** a person served by or utilizing the services of a social agency ⟨a welfare *client*⟩
3 : CLIENT STATE
— **cli·ent·age** \-ən-tij\ *noun*
— **cli·en·tal** \klī-'en-t³l, 'klī-ən-\ *adjective*
— **cli·ent·less** \'klī-ənt-ləs\ *adjective*

cli·en·tele \,klī-ən-'tel, ,klē-ən- *also* ,klē-,än-\ *noun* [French *clientèle*, from Latin *clientela*, from *client-, cliens*] (circa 1587)
: a body of clients ⟨a shop that caters to an exclusive *clientele*⟩

client state *noun* (1918)
: a country that is economically, politically, or militarily dependent on another country

cliff \'klif\ *noun* [Middle English *clif*, from Old English; akin to Old High German *klep*] (before 12th century)
: a very steep, vertical, or overhanging face of rock, earth, or ice **:** PRECIPICE

☆ **SYNONYMS**
Clever, adroit, cunning, ingenious
mean having or showing practical wit or skill in contriving. CLEVER stresses physical or mental quickness, deftness, or great aptitude ⟨a person *clever* with horses⟩. ADROIT often implies a skillful use of expedients to achieve one's purpose in spite of difficulties ⟨an *adroit* negotiator⟩. CUNNING implies great skill in constructing or creating ⟨a filmmaker *cunning* in his use of special effects⟩. INGENIOUS suggests the power of inventing or discovering a new way of accomplishing something ⟨an *ingenious* software engineer⟩. See in addition INTELLIGENT.

◇ **WORD HISTORY**
cliché *Cliché* is the French word for a stereotype, a duplicate printing plate cast from a mold or a matrix of composed type. The production of such plates became standard in 19th century printing to save wear on type and permit longer press runs. Passing from printers' jargon to the world of letters, *cliché* was applied to a turn of phrase or metaphor that through repeated use loses its effectiveness and becomes the mark of unimaginative writing. The word *stereotype* itself, from French *stéréotype*, has undergone a similar shift in sense, and now usually refers to a conventional mental image of a person or thing that is passed about without critical reappraisal.

— **cliffy** \'kli-fē\ *adjective*
cliff dweller *noun* (1881)
 1 *often C&D capitalized* **a :** a member of a prehistoric American Indian people of the southwestern U.S. who built their homes on rock ledges or in the natural recesses of canyon walls and cliffs **b :** a member of any cliff-dwelling people
 2 : a resident of a large usually metropolitan apartment building
— **cliff dwelling** *noun*
cliff–hang \'klif-,haŋ\ *intransitive verb* [back-formation from *cliff-hanger*] (1946)
 : to await the outcome of a suspenseful situation
cliff–hang·er \-,haŋ-ər\ *noun* (circa 1937)
 1 : an adventure serial or melodrama; *especially* : one presented in installments each ending in suspense
 2 : a contest whose outcome is in doubt up to the very end; *broadly* : a suspenseful situation
— **cliff–hang·ing** \-iŋ\ *adjective*
cliff swallow *noun* (1825)
 : a colonial swallow (*Petrochelidon pyrrhonota*) of the New World with a pale buff rump and dark throat patch that builds mud nests like jugs especially under eaves and on cliffs
¹cli·mac·ter·ic \klī-'mak-t(ə-)rik, ,klī-,mak-'ter-ik, -'tir-\ *adjective* [Latin *climactericus*, from Greek *klimaktērikos*, from *klimaktēr* critical point, literally, rung of a ladder, from *klimak-, klimax* ladder] (1582)
 1 : constituting or relating to a climacteric
 2 : CRITICAL, CRUCIAL
²climacteric *noun* (circa 1630)
 1 : a major turning point or critical stage
 2 : MENOPAUSE; *also* : a corresponding period in the male usually occurring with less well-defined physiological and psychological changes
 3 : the marked and sudden rise in the respiratory rate of fruit just prior to full ripening
cli·mac·tic \klī-'mak-tik, klə-\ *adjective* (1872)
 : of, relating to, or constituting a climax
— **cli·mac·ti·cal·ly** \-ti-k(ə-)lē\ *adverb*
cli·mate \'klī-mət\ *noun* [Middle English *climat*, from Middle French, from Late Latin *climat-, clima*, from Greek *klimat-, klima* inclination, latitude, climate, from *klinein* to lean — more at LEAN] (14th century)
 1 : a region of the earth having specified climatic conditions
 2 a : the average course or condition of the weather at a place usually over a period of years as exhibited by temperature, wind velocity, and precipitation **b :** the prevailing set of conditions (as of temperature and humidity) indoors ⟨a *climate*-controlled office⟩
 3 : the prevailing influence or environmental conditions characterizing a group or period : ATMOSPHERE ⟨a *climate* of fear⟩
cli·mat·ic \klī-'ma-tik, klə-\ *adjective* (circa 1828)
 1 : of or relating to climate
 2 : resulting from or influenced by the climate rather than the soil ⟨forests that had reverted to the *climatic* type⟩ — compare EDAPHIC 2
— **cli·mat·i·cal·ly** \-ti-k(ə-)lē\ *adverb*
climatic climax *noun* (circa 1928)
 : the one of the ecological climaxes possible in a particular climatic area whose stability is directly due to the influence of climate — compare EDAPHIC CLIMAX
cli·ma·tol·o·gy \,klī-mə-'tä-lə-jē\ *noun* (1843)
 : the science that deals with climates and their phenomena
— **cli·ma·to·log·i·cal** \,klī-mə-tə-'lä-ji-kəl\ *adjective*
— **cli·ma·to·log·i·cal·ly** \-k(ə-)lē\ *adverb*
— **cli·ma·tol·o·gist** \-mə-'tä-lə-jist\ *noun*
¹cli·max \'klī-,maks\ *noun* [Latin, from Greek *klimax* ladder, from *klinein* to lean] (circa 1550)

 1 : a figure of speech in which a series of phrases or sentences is arranged in ascending order of rhetorical forcefulness
 2 a : the highest point : CULMINATION **b :** the point of highest dramatic tension or a major turning point in the action (as of a play) **c :** ORGASM **d :** MENOPAUSE
 3 : a relatively stable ecological stage or community especially of plants that is achieved through successful adjustment to an environment; *especially* : the final stage in ecological succession
 synonym see SUMMIT
— **cli·max·less** *adjective*
²climax (1835)
 transitive verb
 : to bring to a climax ⟨*climaxed* his boxing career with a knockout⟩
 intransitive verb
 : to come to a climax ⟨a riot *climaxing* in the destruction of several houses⟩
¹climb \'klīm\ *verb* [Middle English, from Old English *climban*; probably akin to Old English *clifian* to adhere — more at CLEAVE] (before 12th century)
 intransitive verb
 1 a : to go upward with gradual or continuous progress : RISE, ASCEND **b :** to increase gradually **c :** to slope upward
 2 a : to go upward or raise oneself especially by grasping or clutching with the hands ⟨*climbed* upon her father's knee⟩ **b** *of a plant* : to ascend in growth (as by twining)
 3 : to go about or down usually by grasping or holding with the hands ⟨*climb* down the ladder⟩
 4 : to get into or out of clothing usually with some haste or effort ⟨the firemen *climbed* into their clothes⟩
 transitive verb
 1 : to go upward on or along, to the top of, or over ⟨*climb* a hill⟩
 2 : to draw or pull oneself up, over, or to the top of by using hands and feet ⟨children *climbing* the tree⟩
 3 : to grow up or over
— **climb·able** \'klī-mə-bəl\ *adjective*
²climb *noun* (circa 1587)
 1 : a place where climbing is necessary to progress
 2 : the act or an instance of climbing : RISE, ASCENT
climb·er \'klī-mər\ *noun* (15th century)
 1 a : one that climbs or helps in climbing **b :** a vine or twining plant (as a rose or sweet pea) that readily grows up a support or over other plants
 2 : one who attempts to gain a superior social or business position
climbing iron *noun* (1857)
 : a steel framework with spikes attached that may be affixed to one's boots for climbing (as a pole or tree)
clime \'klīm\ *noun* [Late Latin *clima*] (14th century)
 : CLIMATE ⟨traveled to warmer *climes*⟩
-clinal *adjective combining form* [International Scientific Vocabulary, from Greek *klinein* to lean — more at LEAN]
 : sloping ⟨iso*clinal*⟩
¹clinch \'klinch\ *verb* [probably alteration of *clench*] (1542)
 transitive verb
 1 : CLENCH 3
 2 a : to turn over or flatten the protruding pointed end of (a driven nail); *also* : to treat (as a screw, bolt, or rivet) in a similar way **b :** to fasten in this way
 3 a : to make final or irrefutable : SETTLE ⟨that *clinched* the argument⟩ **b :** to secure conclusively : WIN
 intransitive verb
 1 : to hold an opponent (as in boxing) at close quarters with one or both arms

 2 : to hold fast or firmly
— **clinch·ing·ly** \'klin-chiŋ-lē\ *adverb*
²clinch *noun* (1659)
 1 : a fastening by means of a clinched nail, rivet, or bolt; *also* : the clinched part of a nail, rivet, or bolt
 2 *archaic* **:** PUN
 3 : an act or instance of clinching in boxing
 4 : EMBRACE
clinch·er \'klin-chər\ *noun* (1737)
 : one that clinches: as **a :** a decisive fact, argument, act, or remark ⟨the expense was the *clincher* that persuaded us to give up the enterprise⟩ **b :** a tire with flanged beads fitting into the wheel rim
cline \'klīn\ *noun* [Greek *klinein*] (1938)
 : a gradient of morphological or physiological change in a group of related organisms usually along a line of environmental or geographic transition
— **clin·al** \'klī-nᵊl\ *adjective*
— **clin·al·ly** \-nᵊl-ē\ *adverb*
-cline *noun combining form* [back-formation from *-clinal*]
 : slope ⟨mono*cline*⟩
¹cling \'kliŋ\ *intransitive verb* **clung** \'kləŋ\; **cling·ing** [Middle English, from Old English *clingan*; akin to Old High German *klunga* tangled ball of thread] (before 12th century)
 1 a : to hold together **b :** to adhere as if glued firmly **c :** to hold or hold on tightly or tenaciously
 2 a : to have a strong emotional attachment or dependence **b :** to remain or linger as if resisting complete dissipation or dispersal ⟨the odor *clung* to the room for hours⟩
 synonym see STICK
— **cling·er** \'kliŋ-ər\ *noun*
— **clingy** \'kliŋ-ē\ *adjective*
²cling *noun* (circa 1625)
 : an act or instance of clinging : ADHERENCE
cling·stone \'kliŋ-,stōn\ *noun* (1705)
 : any of various stone fruits (as some peaches or plums) with flesh that adheres strongly to the pit
clin·ic \'kli-nik\ *noun* [French *clinique*, from Greek *klinikē* medical practice at the sickbed, from feminine of *klinikos* of a bed, from *klinē* bed, from *klinein* to lean, recline — more at LEAN] (circa 1843)
 1 : a class of medical instruction in which patients are examined and discussed
 2 : a group meeting devoted to the analysis and solution of concrete problems or to the acquiring of specific skills or knowledge ⟨writing *clinics*⟩ ⟨golf *clinics*⟩
 3 a : a facility (as of a hospital) for diagnosis and treatment of outpatients **b :** a group practice in which several physicians work cooperatively
-clinic *adjective combining form* [International Scientific Vocabulary, from Greek *klinein*]
 1 : inclining : dipping
 2 : having (so many) oblique intersections of the axes ⟨mono*clinic*⟩ ⟨tri*clinic*⟩
clin·i·cal \'kli-ni-kəl\ *adjective* (circa 1780)
 1 : of, relating to, or conducted in or as if in a clinic: as **a :** involving direct observation of the patient **b :** diagnosable by or based on clinical observation
 2 : analytical or coolly dispassionate ⟨a *clinical* attitude⟩
— **clin·i·cal·ly** \-k(ə-)lē\ *adverb*
clinical thermometer *noun* (1878)
 : a thermometer for measuring body temperature that has a constriction in the tube where the column of liquid breaks when the temperature drops from its maximum and that continues to indicate the maximum temperature by

the part of the column above the constriction until reset by shaking

cli·ni·cian \kli-'ni-shən\ *noun* (1875)
1 : a person qualified in the clinical practice of medicine, psychiatry, or psychology as distinguished from one specializing in laboratory or research techniques or in theory
2 : a person who conducts a clinic

clin·i·co·path·o·log·ic \,kli-ni-(,)kō-,pa-thə-'lä-jik\ *or* **clin·i·co·path·o·log·i·cal** \-'lä-ji-kəl\ *adjective* [*clinical*] (1898)
: relating to or concerned both with the signs and symptoms directly observable by the physician and with the results of laboratory examination
— **clin·i·co·path·o·log·i·cal·ly** \-ji-k(ə-)lē\ *adverb*

¹clink \'kliŋk\ *verb* [Middle English, of imitative origin] (14th century)
intransitive verb
: to give out a slight sharp short metallic sound
transitive verb
: to cause to clink

²clink *noun* (15th century)
: a clinking sound

³clink *noun* [probably from *Clink*, a prison in Southwark, London, England] (1515)
1 *slang* : a prison cell
2 *slang* : JAIL, PRISON

¹clin·ker \'kliŋ-kər\ *noun* [alteration of earlier *klincard* a hard yellowish Dutch brick] (1641)
1 : a brick that has been burned too much in the kiln
2 : stony matter fused together : SLAG

²clink·er \'kliŋ-kər\ *noun* [¹*clink*] (1733)
1 *British* : something first-rate
2 a : a wrong note **b** : a serious mistake or error : BONER **c** : an utter failure : FLOP **d** : something of poor quality

clink·er–built \-,bilt\ *adjective* [*clinker*, noun, clinch] (1769)
: having the external planks or plates overlapping like the clapboards on a house ⟨a *clinker‑built* boat⟩

clink·ety–clank \'kliŋ-kə-tē-'klaŋk\ *noun* [imitative] (1901)
: a repeated usually rhythmic clanking sound ⟨the *clinkety-clank* of a loose tire chain⟩

cli·nom·e·ter \klī-'nä-mə-tər\ *noun* [Greek *klinein* to lean] (1811)
: any of various instruments for measuring angles of elevation or inclination

-clinous *adjective combining form* [probably from New Latin *-clinus*, from Greek *klinē* bed — more at CLINIC]
: having the androecium and gynoecium in a (single or different) flower or (two separate) flowers ⟨di*clinous*⟩

¹clin·quant \'kliŋ-kənt, klaⁿ-'käⁿ\ *adjective* [Middle French, from present participle of *clinquer* to glitter, literally, to clink, of imitative origin] (1591)
: glittering with gold or tinsel

²clinquant *noun* [French, from *clinquant*, adjective] (1682)
: TINSEL

clin·to·nia \klin-'tō-nē-ə\ *noun* [New Latin, genus name, from DeWitt *Clinton*] (1843)
: any of a genus (*Clintonia*) of herbs of the lily family with yellow or white flowers

Clio \'klī-(,)ō, 'klē-\ *noun* [Latin, from Greek *Kleiō*]
1 : the Greek Muse of history
2 *plural* **Cli·os** : a statuette awarded annually by a professional organization for notable achievement in radio and television commercials

clio·met·rics \,klī-ə-'me-triks\ *noun plural but singular in construction* [*Clio* + *-metrics* (as in *econometrics*)] (1966)
: the application of methods developed in other fields (as economics, statistics, and data processing) to the study of history
— **clio·met·ric** \-trik\ *adjective*
— **clio·met·ri·cian** \-me-'tri-shən\ *noun*

¹clip \'klip\ *transitive verb* **clipped; clip·ping** [Middle English *clippen*, from Old English *clyppan*; akin to Old High German *kläftra* fathom, Lithuanian *globti* to embrace] (before 12th century)
1 : ENCOMPASS
2 a : to hold in a tight grip : CLUTCH **b** : to clasp or fasten with a clip

²clip *noun* (15th century)
1 : any of various devices that grip, clasp, or hook
2 : a device to hold cartridges for charging the magazines of some rifles; *also* : a magazine from which ammunition is fed into the chamber of a firearm
3 : a piece of jewelry held in position by a clip

³clip *verb* **clipped; clip·ping** [Middle English *clippen*, from Old Norse *klippa*] (13th century)
transitive verb
1 a : to cut or cut off with or as if with shears ⟨*clip* a dog's hair⟩ ⟨*clip* an hour off traveling time⟩ **b** : to cut off the distal or outer part of **c** (1) : ³EXCISE (2) : to cut items out of (as a newspaper)
2 a : CURTAIL, DIMINISH **b** : to abbreviate in speech or writing
3 : HIT, PUNCH
4 : to illegally block (an opposing player) in football
5 : to take money from unfairly or dishonestly especially by overcharging ⟨the nightclub *clipped* the tourist for $200⟩
intransitive verb
1 : to clip something
2 : to travel or pass rapidly
3 : to clip an opposing player in football

⁴clip *noun* (15th century)
1 a *plural, Scottish* : SHEARS **b** : a 2-bladed instrument for cutting especially the nails
2 : something that is clipped: as **a** : the product of a single shearing (as of sheep) **b** : a crop of wool of a sheep, a flock, or a region **c** : a section of filmed or videotaped material **d** : a clipping especially from a newspaper
3 : an act of clipping
4 : a sharp blow
5 : RATE 4a ⟨continues at a brisk *clip*⟩
6 : a single instance or occasion : TIME ⟨he charged $10 a *clip*⟩ — often used in the phrase *at a clip* ⟨trained 1000 workers at a *clip*⟩

clip·board \'klip-,bōrd, -,bȯrd\ *noun* (1896)
: a small writing board with a clip at the top for holding papers

clip–clop \'klip-,kläp\ *noun* [imitative] (1884)
: the sound made by or as if by a horse walking on a hard surface
— **clip–clop** *intransitive verb*

clip joint *noun* (1933)
1 *slang* : a place of public entertainment (as a nightclub) that makes a practice of defrauding patrons (as by overcharging)
2 *slang* : a business that makes a practice of overcharging

clip–on \'kli-,pȯn, -,pän\ *adjective* (1909)
: of or relating to something that attaches with a clip ⟨a *clip-on* tie⟩ ⟨*clip-on* earrings⟩
— **clip–on** *noun*

clip·per \'kli-pər\ *noun* (14th century)
1 : one that clips something
2 : an implement for clipping especially hair, fingernails, or toenails — usually used in plural
3 a : one that moves swiftly **b** : a fast sailing ship; *especially* : one with long slender lines, an overhanging bow, tall masts, and a large sail area

clip·ping \'kli-piŋ\ *noun* (15th century)
: something that is clipped off or out of something; *especially* : an item clipped from a publication

clip·sheet \'klip-,shēt\ *noun* (1926)
: a sheet of newspaper material issued by an organization for clipping and reprinting

clique \'klēk, 'klik\ *noun* [French] (1711)

: a narrow exclusive circle or group of persons; *especially* : one held together by common interests, views, or purposes
— **cliqu·ey** *also* **cliquy** \'klē-kē, 'kli-\ *adjective*
— **cliqu·ish** \'kli-kish\ *adjective*
— **cliqu·ish·ly** *adverb*
— **cliqu·ish·ness** *noun*

cli·tel·lum \klī-'te-ləm\ *noun, plural* **-la** \-lə\ [New Latin, modification of Latin *clitellae* packsaddle] (1839)
: a thickened glandular section of the body wall of some annelids that secretes a viscid sac in which the eggs are deposited

clit·ic \'kli-tik\ *noun* [en*clitic* or pro*clitic*] (1946)
: a word that is treated in pronunciation as forming a part of a neighboring word and that is often unaccented or contracted

clit·o·ri·dec·to·my \,kli-tə-ri-'dek-tə-mē\ *also* **clit·o·rec·to·my** \,kli-tə-'rek-tə-mē\ *noun, plural* **-mies** (1866)
: excision of all or part of the clitoris

clit·o·ris \'kli-tə-rəs, kli-'tȯr-əs\ *noun, plural* **clit·o·ri·des** \kli-'tȯr-ə-,dēz\ [New Latin, from Greek *kleitoris*] (1615)
: a small erectile organ at the anterior or ventral part of the vulva homologous to the penis
— **clit·o·ral** \'kli-tə-rəl\ *or* **clit·or·ic** \kli-'tȯr-ik, -'tär-\ *adjective*

clo·a·ca \klō-'ā-kə\ *noun, plural* **-a·cae** \-,kē, -,sē\ [Latin; akin to Greek *klyzein* to wash — more at CLYSTER] (1599)
1 : ³SEWER
2 [New Latin, from Latin] : the common chamber into which the intestinal, urinary, and generative canals discharge in birds, reptiles, amphibians, and many fishes; *also* : a comparable chamber of an invertebrate
— **clo·a·cal** \-'ā-kəl\ *adjective*

¹cloak \'klōk\ *noun* [Middle English *cloke*, from Old North French *cloque* bell, cloak, from Medieval Latin *clocca* bell; from its shape] (13th century)
1 : a loose outer garment
2 : something that conceals : PRETENSE, DISGUISE

²cloak *transitive verb* (1509)
: to cover or hide with or as if with a cloak
synonym see DISGUISE

cloak–and–dagger *adjective* (1860)
: dealing in or suggestive of melodramatic intrigue and action usually involving secret agents and espionage
— **cloak–and–dagger** *noun*

cloak·room \'klōk-,rüm, -,rȯm\ *noun* (circa 1852)
1 a : a room in which outdoor clothing may be placed during one's stay **b** : a room or cubicle where garments, parcels, and luggage may be checked for temporary safekeeping
2 : an anteroom of a legislative chamber where members may relax and confer with colleagues
3 *British* : LAVATORY 2

¹clob·ber \'klä-bər\ *noun* [origin unknown] (1879)
slang British : CLOTHES 1

²clobber *transitive verb* **clob·bered; clob·ber·ing** \-b(ə-)riŋ\ [origin unknown] (circa 1943)
1 : to pound mercilessly; *also* : to hit with force : SMASH
2 : to defeat overwhelmingly

clo·chard \klō-'shär\ *noun* [French, from *clocher* to limp, from (assumed) Vulgar Latin *cloppicare*, from Late Latin *cloppus* lame] (1937)
: TRAMP, VAGRANT

cloche \'klōsh\ *noun* [French, literally, bell, from Medieval Latin *clocca*] (1882)
1 : a transparent plant cover used outdoors especially for protection against cold
2 : a woman's small close-fitting hat usually with deep rounded crown and very narrow brim

¹clock \'kläk\ *noun, often attributive* [Middle English *clok,* from Middle Dutch *clocke* bell, clock, from Old North French or Medieval Latin; Old North French *cloque* bell, from Medieval Latin *clocca,* of Celtic origin; akin to Middle Irish *clocc* bell] (14th century)
1 : a device other than a watch for indicating or measuring time commonly by means of hands moving on a dial; *broadly* **:** any periodic system by which time is measured
2 : a registering device usually with a dial; *specifically* **:** ODOMETER
3 : TIME CLOCK
4 : a synchronizing device (as in a computer) that produces pulses at regular intervals
5 : BIOLOGICAL CLOCK
— around the clock *also* **round the clock 1 :** continuously for 24 hours **:** day and night without cessation **2 :** without relaxation and heedless of time
— kill the clock *or* **run out the clock :** to use up as much as possible of the playing time remaining in a game (as football) while retaining possession of the ball or puck especially to protect a lead
²clock (1883)
transitive verb
1 : to time with a stopwatch or by an electric timing device
2 : to register on a mechanical recording device ⟨wind velocities were *clocked* at 80 miles per hour⟩
3 : to hit hard
4 *chiefly British* **:** ATTAIN, REALIZE — usually used with *up* ⟨just *clocked* up a million . . . paperback sales —*Punch*⟩
intransitive verb
: to register on a time sheet or time clock **:** PUNCH — used with *in, out, on, off* ⟨he *clocked* in late⟩
— clock·er *noun*
³clock *noun* [perhaps from ¹*clock*] (1530)
: an ornamental figure on the ankle or side of a stocking or sock
clock·like \'kläk-,līk\ *adjective* (circa 1770)
: unusually regular, undeviating, and precise ⟨does his job with *clocklike* efficiency⟩
clock radio *noun* (1949)
: a combination clock and radio device in which the clock can be set to turn on the radio at a designated time
clock–watch·er \-,wä-chər\ *noun* (1911)
: a person (as a worker or student) who keeps close watch on the passage of time
— clock–watch·ing \-chiŋ\ *noun*
clock·wise \'kläk-,wīz\ *adverb* (1888)
: in the direction in which the hands of a clock rotate as viewed from in front or as if standing on a clock face
— clockwise *adjective*
clock·work \-,wərk\ *noun* (1628)
1 : the inner workings of something
2 : the machinery (as springs and a train of gears) that run a clock; *also* **:** a similar mechanism running a mechanical device (as a toy)
3 : the precision, regularity, or absence of variation associated with a clock or clockwork ⟨a *clockwork* operation⟩ ⟨the planning went like *clockwork*⟩
clod \'kläd\ *noun* [Middle English *clodde,* from Old English *clod-* (in *clodhamer* fieldfare)] (15th century)
1 a : a lump or mass especially of earth or clay **b :** SOIL, EARTH
2 : OAF, DOLT
— clod·dish \'klä-dish\ *adjective*
— clod·dish·ness *noun*
— clod·dy \'klä-dē\ *adjective*
clod·hop·per \'kläd-,hä-pər\ *noun* (1721)
1 : a clumsy and uncouth rustic
2 : a large heavy work shoe or boot
clod·hop·ping \-,hä-piŋ\ *adjective* (1843)
: BOORISH, RUDE
clod·poll *or* **clod·pole** \'kläd-,pōl\ *noun* (1601)

: BLOCKHEAD
clo·fi·brate \klō-'fī-,brāt, -'fi-\ *noun* [perhaps from *chlor-* + *fibr-* + ¹*-ate*] (1964)
: a compound $C_{12}H_{15}ClO_3$ used especially to lower abnormally high concentrations of fats and cholesterol in the blood
¹clog \'kläg, 'klȯg\ *noun* [Middle English *clogge* short thick piece of wood] (14th century)
1 a : a weight attached especially to an animal to hinder motion **b :** something that shackles or impedes **:** ENCUMBRANCE
2 : a shoe, sandal, or overshoe having a thick typically wooden sole
²clog *verb* **clogged; clog·ging** (1526)
transitive verb
1 a : to impede with a clog **:** HINDER **b :** to halt or retard the progress, operation, or growth of **:** ENCUMBER ⟨restraints that have been *clogging* the market —T. W. Arnold⟩
2 : to fill beyond capacity **:** OVERLOAD ⟨cars *clogged* the main street⟩ ⟨a speech *clogged* with clichés⟩
intransitive verb
1 : to become filled with extraneous matter
2 : to unite in a mass **:** CLOT
3 : to dance a clog dance
synonym *see* HAMPER
— clog·ger \'klä-gər, 'klȯ-\ *noun*
clog dance *noun* (1869)
: a dance in which the performer wears clogs and beats out a clattering rhythm on the floor
— clog dancer *noun*
— clog dancing *noun*
cloi·son·né *also* **cloi·son·ne** \,klȯi-zə-'nā, ,klwä-\ *adjective* [French, from past participle of *cloisonner* to partition] (1863)
: of, relating to, or being a style of enamel decoration in which the enamel is applied and fired in raised cells (as of soldered wires) on a usually metal background — compare CHAMPLEVÉ
— cloisonné *noun*
¹clois·ter \'klȯi-stər\ *noun* [Middle English *cloistre,* from Old French, from Medieval Latin *claustrum,* from Latin, bar, bolt, from *claudere* to close — more at CLOSE] (13th century)
1 a : a monastic establishment **b :** an area within a monastery or convent to which the religious are normally restricted **c :** monastic life **d :** a place or state of seclusion

cloister 2

2 : a covered passage on the side of a court usually having one side walled and the other an open arcade or colonnade
²cloister *transitive verb* **clois·tered; clois·ter·ing** \-st(ə-)riŋ\ (1581)
1 : to seclude from the world in or as if in a cloister ⟨a scientist who *cloisters* herself in a laboratory⟩
2 : to surround with a cloister ⟨*cloistered* gardens⟩
clois·tered \'klȯi-stərd\ *adjective* (1581)
1 : being or living in or as if in a cloister
2 : providing shelter from contact with the outside world ⟨the *cloistered* atmosphere of a small college⟩
clois·tral \'klȯi-strəl\ *adjective* (1605)
: of, relating to, or suggestive of a cloister
clois·tress \'klȯi-strəs\ *noun* (1601)
obsolete **:** NUN
clo·mi·phene \'klō-mə-,fēn\ *noun* [*chlor-* + *amine* + *-phene* (from *phenyl*)] (1963)
: a synthetic drug $C_{26}H_{28}ClNO$ used in the form of its citrate to induce ovulation
clomp \'klämp, 'klȯmp, 'kləmp\ *intransitive verb* [by alteration] (1829)

: CLUMP 1
¹clone \'klōn\ *noun* [Greek *klōn* twig, slip; akin to Greek *klan* to break — more at CLAST] (1903)
1 a : the aggregate of the asexually produced progeny of an individual; *also* **:** a group of replicas of all or part of a macromolecule (as DNA or an antibody) **b :** an individual grown from a single somatic cell of its parent and genetically identical to it
2 : one that appears to be a copy of an original form ⟨a *clone* of a personal computer⟩
— clon·al \'klō-n°l\ *adjective*
— clon·al·ly \-n°l-ē\ *adverb*
²clone *verb* **cloned; clon·ing** (circa 1948)
transitive verb
1 : to propagate a clone from
2 : to make a copy of
intransitive verb
: to produce a clone
clo·ni·dine \'klä-nə-,dēn, 'klō-, -,dīn\ *noun* [*chlor-* + *aniline* + *imide* + ²*-ine*] (1970)
: an antihypertensive drug $C_9H_9Cl_2N_3$ used to treat essential hypertension, to prevent migraine headache, and to diminish withdrawal symptoms
clonk \'kläŋk, 'klȯŋk\ *verb* [imitative] (1930)
intransitive verb
: to make a dull hollow thumping sound
transitive verb
: to cause to clonk
— clonk *noun*
clo·nus \'klō-nəs\ *noun* [New Latin, from Greek *klonos* agitation — more at HOLD] (1817)
: a rapid succession of alternating contractions and partial relaxations of a muscle occurring in some nervous diseases
— clon·ic \'klä-nik\ *adjective*
— clo·nic·i·ty \klō-'ni-sə-tē, klä-\ *noun*
cloot \'klüt\ *noun* [probably of Scandinavian origin; akin to Old Norse *klō* claw — more at CLAW] (1725)
1 *Scottish* **:** a cloven hoof
2 *plural, capitalized, Scottish* **:** CLOOTIE
Cloot·ie \'klü-tē\ *noun* [diminutive of *cloot*] *chiefly Scottish* — used as a name of the devil
clop \'kläp\ *noun* [imitative] (1899)
: a sound made by or as if by a hoof or wooden shoe against the pavement
— clop *intransitive verb*
clop–clop \'kläp-,kläp\ *noun* (1901)
: a sound of rhythmically repeated clops
— clop–clop *intransitive verb*
clo·que *also* **clo·qué** \klō-'kā, 'klō-,\ *noun* [French *cloqué,* from past participle of *cloquer* to become blistered, from French dialect (Picard) *cloque* bell, bubble, from Medieval Latin *clocca* bell — more at CLOCK] (1936)
1 : a fabric with an embossed design
2 : a fabric especially of piqué with small woven figures
¹close \'klōz\ *verb* **closed; clos·ing** [Middle English, from Old French *clos-,* stem of *clore,* from Latin *claudere* to shut, close; perhaps akin to Greek *kleiein* to close — more at CLAVICLE] (13th century)
transitive verb
1 a : to move so as to bar passage through something ⟨*close* the gate⟩ **b :** to block against entry or passage ⟨*close* a street⟩ **c :** to deny access to ⟨the city *closed* the beach⟩ **d :** SCREEN, EXCLUDE ⟨*close* a view⟩ **e :** to suspend or stop the operations of ⟨*close* school⟩ — often used with *down*
2 *archaic* **:** ENCLOSE, CONTAIN
3 a : to bring to an end or period ⟨*close* an account⟩ **b :** to conclude discussion or negotiation about ⟨the question is *closed*⟩; *also* **:** to

consummate by performing something previously agreed ⟨*close* a transfer of real estate title⟩ **c :** to terminate access to (a computer file) **4 a :** to bring or bind together the parts or edges of ⟨a *closed* book⟩ **b :** to fill up (as an opening) **c :** to make complete by circling or enveloping or by making continuous ⟨*close* a circuit⟩ **d :** to reduce to nil ⟨*closed* the distance to the lead racer⟩
intransitive verb
1 a : to contract, fold, swing, or slide so as to leave no opening ⟨the door *closed* quietly⟩ **b :** to cease operation ⟨the factory *closed* down⟩ ⟨the stores *close* at 9 p.m.⟩
2 a : to draw near ⟨the ship was *closing* with the island⟩ **b :** to engage in a struggle at close quarters **:** GRAPPLE ⟨*close* with the enemy⟩
3 a : to come together **:** MEET **b :** to draw the free foot up to the supporting foot in dancing
4 : to enter into or complete an agreement
5 : to come to an end or period
6 : to reduce a gap ⟨*closed* to within two points⟩ ☆
— **clos·able** *or* **close·able** \'klō-zə-bəl\ *adjective*
— **clos·er** *noun*
— **close one's doors 1 :** to refuse admission ⟨the nation *closed its doors* to immigrants⟩ **2 :** to go out of business
— **close one's eyes to :** to ignore deliberately
— **close ranks :** to unite in a concerted stand especially to meet a challenge
— **close the door :** to be uncompromisingly obstructive ⟨*closed the door* to further negotiation⟩

²close \'klōz\ *noun* (14th century)
1 a : a coming or bringing to a conclusion ⟨at the *close* of the party⟩ **b :** a conclusion or end in time or existence **:** CESSATION ⟨the decade drew to a *close*⟩ **c :** the concluding passage (as of a speech or play)
2 : the conclusion of a musical strain or period **:** CADENCE
3 *archaic* **:** a hostile encounter
4 : the movement of the free foot in dancing toward or into contact with the supporting foot

³close \'klōs, U.S. also 'klōz\ *noun* [Middle English *clos*, literally, enclosure, from Old French *clos*, from Latin *clausum*, from neuter of *clausus*, past participle] (13th century)
1 a : an enclosed area **b** *chiefly British* **:** the precinct of a cathedral
2 *chiefly British* **a :** a narrow passage leading from a street to a court and the houses within or to the common stairway of tenements **b :** a road closed at one end

⁴close \'klōs\ *adjective* **clos·er; clos·est** [Middle English *clos*, from Middle French, from Latin *clausus*, past participle of *claudere*] (14th century)
1 : having no openings **:** CLOSED
2 a : confined or carefully guarded ⟨*close* arrest⟩ **b** (1) *of a vowel* **:** HIGH 13 (2) **:** formed with the tongue in a higher position than for the other vowel of a pair
3 : restricted to a privileged class
4 a : SECLUDED, SECRET **b :** SECRETIVE ⟨she could tell us something if she would . . . but she was as *close* as wax —A. Conan Doyle⟩
5 : STRICT, RIGOROUS ⟨keep *close* watch⟩
6 : hot and stuffy
7 : not generous in giving or spending **:** TIGHT
8 : having little space between items or units ⟨a *close* weave⟩
9 a : fitting tightly or exactly **b :** very short or near to the surface ⟨a *close* haircut⟩
10 : being near in time, space, effect, or degree
11 : INTIMATE, FAMILIAR
12 a : ACCURATE, PRECISE ⟨a *close* study⟩ **b :** marked by fidelity to an original ⟨a *close* copy of an old master⟩ **c :** TERSE, COMPACT
13 : decided or won by a narrow margin ⟨a *close* baseball game⟩
14 : difficult to obtain ⟨money is *close*⟩

15 *of punctuation* **:** characterized by liberal use especially of commas
synonym see STINGY
— **close·ly** *adverb*
— **close·ness** *noun*
— **close to home :** within one's personal interests so that one is strongly affected ⟨the speaker's remarks hit *close to home*⟩
— **close to the vest :** in a reserved or cautious manner

⁵close \'klōs\ *adverb* (15th century)
: in a close position or manner
close call \'klōs-\ *noun* (1881)
: a narrow escape
close corporation \'klōs-\ *noun* (circa 1902)
: a corporation whose stock is not publicly traded but held by a few persons (as those in management)
close–cropped \'klōs-,kräpt\ *adjective* (circa 1893)
1 : clipped short
2 : having the hair clipped short
closed \'klōzd\ *adjective* (13th century)
1 a : not open **b :** ENCLOSED **c :** composed entirely of closed tubes or vessels ⟨a *closed* circulatory system⟩
2 a : forming a self-contained unit allowing no additions ⟨*closed* association⟩ **b** (1) **:** traced by a moving point that returns to an arbitrary starting point ⟨*closed* curve⟩; *also* **:** so formed that every plane section is a closed curve ⟨*closed* surface⟩ (2) **:** characterized by mathematical elements that when subjected to an operation produce only elements of the same set ⟨the set of whole numbers is *closed* under addition and multiplication⟩ (3) **:** containing all the limit points of every possible subset ⟨a *closed* interval contains its endpoints⟩ **c :** characterized by continuous return and reuse of the working substance ⟨a *closed* cooling system⟩ **d** *of a racecourse* **:** having the same starting and finishing point
3 a : confined to a few ⟨*closed* membership⟩ **b :** excluding participation of outsiders or witnesses **:** conducted in strict secrecy **c :** rigidly excluding outside influence ⟨a *closed* mind⟩
4 : ending in a consonant ⟨*closed* syllable⟩
closed book *noun* (1913)
: something beyond comprehension **:** ENIGMA
closed–cap·tioned \'klōz(d)-'kap-shənd\ *adjective* (1980)
of a television program **:** broadcast with captions that appear only on the screen of a receiver equipped with a decoder
closed–cir·cuit \-'sər-kət\ *adjective* (1949)
: used in, shown on, or being a television installation in which the signal is transmitted by wire to a limited number of receivers
closed corporation *noun* (1924)
: CLOSE CORPORATION
closed couplet *noun* (1910)
: a rhymed couplet in which the sense is complete
closed–door \'klōz(d)-'dōr, -'dȯr\ *adjective* (1950)
: barring public and press ⟨a *closed-door* session of the investigating committee⟩
closed–end \'klōzd-'end\ *adjective* (circa 1938)
: having a fixed capitalization of shares that are traded on the market at prices determined by the operation of the law of supply and demand ⟨a *closed-end* investment company⟩ — compare OPEN-END
closed loop *noun* (1951)
: an automatic control system for an operation or process in which feedback in a closed path or group of paths acts to maintain output at a desired level
closed·down \'klōz-,daůn\ *noun* (1889)
: an instance of suspending or stopping operations
closed shop *noun* (1904)
: an establishment in which the employer by agreement hires only union members in good standing

closed stance *noun* (circa 1934)
: a stance (as in golf) in which the forward foot is closer to the line of play than the back foot — compare OPEN STANCE
close–fist·ed \'klōs-,fis-təd\ *adjective* (1608)
: STINGY, TIGHTFISTED
close–grained \-,grānd\ *adjective* (1754)
: having a compacted smooth texture; *especially* **:** having narrow annual rings or small wood elements
close–hauled \-'hȯld\ *adjective* (1769)
: having the sails set for sailing as nearly against the wind as the vessel will go
close–in \'klōs-'in\ *adjective* (1945)
: near a center of activity and especially a city ⟨*close-in* suburbs⟩
close in \'klōz-\ (14th century)
transitive verb
1 : to encircle closely and isolate
2 : to enshroud to such an extent as to preclude entrance or exit ⟨the airport was *closed in* by the storm⟩
intransitive verb
1 : to gather in close all around with an oppressing or isolating effect ⟨despair *closed in* on her⟩
2 : to approach to close quarters especially for an attack, raid, or arrest ⟨the police *closed in*⟩
3 : to grow dark ⟨the short November day was already *closing in* —Ellen Glasgow⟩
close–knit \'klōs-'nit\ *adjective* (1926)
: bound together by intimate social or cultural ties or by close economic or political ties ⟨*close-knit* families⟩
closely held *adjective* (1946)
: having most stock shares and voting rights in the hands of a few ⟨a *closely held* business⟩
close–mouthed \'klōs-'maůthd, -'maůtht\ *adjective* (1881)
: cautious in speaking **:** UNCOMMUNICATIVE; *also* **:** SECRETIVE
close order *noun* (circa 1797)
: an arrangement of troops in a typical marching formation
close·out \'klō-,zaůt\ *noun* (1925)
1 : a clearing out by a sale usually at reduced prices of the whole remaining stock (as of a business)
2 : an article offered or bought at a closeout
close out \'klōz-\ (14th century)
transitive verb
1 a : EXCLUDE **b :** PRECLUDE ⟨*close out* his chances⟩
2 a : to dispose of a whole stock of by sale **b :** to dispose of (a business) **c :** SELL ⟨*closed out* his share of the business⟩ **d :** to put (an account) in order for disposal or transfer
3 a : to bring to an often rapid or abrupt conclusion **b :** to discontinue operation of
intransitive verb
1 : to sell out a business
2 : to buy or sell securities or commodities in order to terminate an account

☆ **SYNONYMS**
Close, end, conclude, finish, complete, terminate mean to bring or come to a stopping point or limit. CLOSE usually implies that something has been in some way open as well as unfinished ⟨*close* a debate⟩. END conveys a strong sense of finality ⟨*ended* his life⟩. CONCLUDE may imply a formal closing (as of a meeting) ⟨the service *concluded* with a blessing⟩. FINISH may stress completion of a final step in a process ⟨after it is painted, the house will be *finished*⟩. COMPLETE implies the removal of all deficiencies or a successful finishing of what has been undertaken ⟨the resolving of this last issue *completes* the agreement⟩. TERMINATE implies the setting of a limit in time or space ⟨your employment *terminates* after three months⟩.

close quarters \'klōs-\ *noun plural* (1809)
: immediate contact or close range ⟨fought at *close quarters*⟩
close shave \'klōs-, 'klōsh-\ *noun* (1834)
: a narrow escape
close-stool \'klōs-,stül\ *noun* (15th century)
: a stool holding a chamber pot
¹clos·et \'klä-zət, 'klò-\ *noun* [Middle English, from Middle French, diminutive of *clos* enclosure — more at CLOSE] (14th century)
1 a : an apartment or small room for privacy **b** : a monarch's or official's private chamber
2 : a cabinet or recess for especially china, household utensils, or clothing
3 : a place of retreat or privacy
4 : WATER CLOSET
5 : a state or condition of secrecy, privacy, or obscurity ⟨came out of the *closet*⟩
— **clos·et·ful** \-,fùl\ *noun*
²closet *transitive verb* (1595)
1 : to shut up in or as if in a closet
2 : to take into a closet for a secret interview
³closet *adjective* (circa 1615)
1 : closely private
2 : working in or suited to the closet as the place of seclusion or study : THEORETICAL
3 : being so in private ⟨a *closet* racist⟩
closet drama *noun* (1922)
: drama suited primarily for reading rather than production
closet queen *noun* (1967)
: one who secretly engages in homosexual activities while leading an ostensibly heterosexual life — often used disparagingly
¹close–up \'klō-,səp\ *noun* (1913)
1 : a photograph or movie shot taken at close range
2 : an intimate view or examination of something
²close–up \,klō-'səp\ *adverb or adjective* (1926)
: at close range
clos·ing \'klō-ziŋ\ *noun* (1596)
1 : a concluding part (as of a speech)
2 : a closable gap (as in an article of clothing)
3 : a meeting of parties to a real-estate deal for formally transferring title
clos·trid·i·um \klä-'stri-dē-əm\ *noun, plural* **-ia** \-dē-ə\ [New Latin, genus name, from Greek *klōstēr* spindle, from *klōthein* to spin] (1884)
: any of a genus (*Clostridium*) of spore-forming mostly anaerobic soil or intestinal bacteria — compare BOTULINUM
— **clos·trid·i·al** \-dē-əl\ *adjective*
clo·sure \'klō-zhər\ *noun* [Middle English, from Middle French, from Latin *clausura*, from *clausus*, past participle of *claudere* to close — more at CLOSE] (14th century)
1 *archaic* **:** means of enclosing : ENCLOSURE
2 : an act of closing : the condition of being closed ⟨*closure* of the eyelids⟩
3 : something that closes ⟨pocket with zipper *closure*⟩
4 [translation of French *clôture*] : CLOTURE
5 : the property that a number system or a set has when it is mathematically closed under an operation
6 : a set that contains a given set together with all the limit points of the given set
¹clot \'klät\ *noun* [Middle English, from Old English *clott;* akin to Middle High German *klōz* lump, ball — more at CLOUT] (before 12th century)
1 : a portion of a substance cleaving together in a thick nondescript mass (as of clay or gum)
2 a : a roundish viscous lump formed by coagulation of a portion of liquid or by melting
b : a coagulated mass produced by clotting of blood
3 *British* **:** BLOCKHEAD
4 : CLUSTER, GROUP ⟨a *clot* of spectators⟩
²clot *verb* **clot·ted; clot·ting** (15th century)
intransitive verb
1 : to become a clot : form clots

2 : to undergo a sequence of complex chemical and physical reactions that results in conversion of fluid blood into a coagulated mass : COAGULATE
transitive verb
1 : to cause to form into or as if into a clot
2 : to fill with clots
cloth \'klòth\ *noun, plural* **cloths** \'klòthz, 'klòths\ *often attributive* [Middle English, from Old English *clāth* cloth, garment; akin to Middle High German *kleit* garment] (before 12th century)
1 a : a pliable material made usually by weaving, felting, or knitting natural or synthetic fibers and filaments **b :** a similar material (as of glass)
2 : a piece of cloth adapted for a particular purpose; *especially* : TABLECLOTH
3 a : a distinctive dress of a profession or calling **b :** the dress of the clergy; *also* : CLERGY
cloth·bound \-,baùnd\ *adjective* (1860)
of a book **:** bound in stiff boards covered with cloth
clothe \'klōth\ *transitive verb* **clothed** *or* **clad** \'klad\; **cloth·ing** [Middle English, from Old English *clāthian*, from *clāth*] (before 12th century)
1 a : to cover with or as if with cloth or clothing : DRESS **b :** to provide with clothes
2 : to express or enhance by suitably significant language : COUCH ⟨treaties *clothed* in stately phraseology⟩
3 : to endow especially with power or a quality
clothes \'klōz *also* 'klōthz\ *noun plural, often attributive* [Middle English, from Old English *clāthas*, plural of *clāth*] (before 12th century)
1 : CLOTHING
2 : BEDCLOTHES
3 : all the cloth articles of personal and household use that can be washed
clothes·horse \-,hòrs\ *noun* (1775)
1 : a frame on which to hang clothes
2 : a conspicuously dressy person
¹clothes·line \-,līn\ *noun* (1830)
: a line (as of cord) on which clothes may be hung to dry
²clothesline *transitive verb* (1964)
: to knock down (a football player) by catching by the neck with an outstretched arm
clothes moth *noun* (1753)
: any of several small yellowish or buff-colored moths (especially *Tinea pellionella* and *Tineola bisselliella* of the family Tineidae) whose larvae eat wool, fur, or feathers
clothes·peg \'klōz-,peg *also* 'klōthz-\ *noun* (1825)
British **:** CLOTHESPIN
clothes·pin \-,pin\ *noun* (1846)
: a forked piece of wood or plastic or a small spring clamp used for fastening clothes on a clothesline
clothes·press \-,pres\ *noun* (1713)
: a receptacle for clothes
cloth·ier \'klōth-yər, 'klō-thē-ər\ *noun* [Middle English, alteration of *clother*, from *cloth*] (14th century)
: one who makes or sells clothing
cloth·ing \'klō-thiŋ\ *noun* (13th century)
: garments in general; *also* : COVERING
cloth yard *noun* (15th century)
: a yard especially for measuring cloth; *specifically* : a unit of 37 inches equal to the Scottish ell and used also as a length for arrows
clotted cream *noun* (1878)
: a thick cream made chiefly in England by slowly heating whole milk on which the cream has been allowed to rise and then skimming the cooled cream from the top — called also *Devonshire cream*
clo·ture \'klō-chər\ *noun* [French *clôture*, literally, closure, alteration of Middle French *closure*] (1871)
: the closing or limitation of debate in a legislative body especially by calling for a vote
— **cloture** *transitive verb*

¹cloud \'klaùd\ *noun, often attributive* [Middle English, rock, cloud, from Old English *clūd;* perhaps akin to Greek *gloutos* buttock] (14th century)
1 : a visible mass of particles of condensed vapor (as water or ice) suspended in the atmosphere of a planet (as the earth) or moon
2 : something resembling or suggesting a cloud: as **a :** a light filmy, puffy, or billowy mass seeming to float in the air ⟨a *cloud* of blond hair⟩ ⟨a ship under a *cloud* of sail⟩ **b** (1) : a usually visible mass of minute particles suspended in the air or a gas (2) : an aggregation of usually obscuring matter especially in interstellar space (3) : an aggregate of charged particles (as electrons) **c :** a great crowd or multitude : SWARM ⟨*clouds* of mosquitoes⟩
3 : something that has a dark, lowering, or threatening aspect ⟨*clouds* of war⟩ ⟨a *cloud* of suspicion⟩
4 : something that obscures or blemishes ⟨a *cloud* of ambiguity⟩
5 : a dark or opaque vein or spot (as in marble or a precious stone)
²cloud (1562)
intransitive verb
1 : to grow cloudy — usually used with *over* or *up* ⟨*clouded* over before the storm⟩
2 a *of facial features* **:** to become troubled, apprehensive, or distressed in appearance **b :** to become blurry, dubious, or ominous — often used with *over*
3 : to billow up in the form of a cloud
transitive verb
1 a : to envelop or hide with or as if with a cloud ⟨smog *clouded* our view⟩ **b :** to make opaque especially by condensation of moisture **c :** to make murky especially with smoke or mist
2 : to make unclear or confused ⟨*cloud* the issue⟩
3 : TAINT, SULLY ⟨a *clouded* reputation⟩
4 : to cast gloom over
cloud·ber·ry \'klaùd-,ber-ē\ *noun* (1597)
: a creeping herbaceous raspberry (*Rubus chamaemorus*) of north temperate regions; *also* : its pale amber-colored edible fruit
cloud·burst \-,bərst\ *noun* (1869)
1 : a sudden copious rainfall
2 : DELUGE 2
cloud chamber *noun* (1897)
: a vessel containing air saturated with water vapor whose sudden expansion reveals the passage of an ionizing particle by a trail of visible droplets
cloud–cuck·oo–land \,klaùd-'kü-(,)kü-,land, -'kù-\ *noun* [translation of Greek *nephelokokkygia*] (1899)
: a realm of fantasy or of whimsical or foolish behavior
cloud·ed leopard \'klaù-dəd-\ *noun* (1910)
: a medium-sized cat (*Neofelis nebulosa*) that occurs from Nepal to southeast China and Indonesia and is grayish to yellowish with dark-er irregular rings, ovals, and rosettes
cloud forest *noun* (1922)
: a wet tropical mountain forest at an altitude

cloud 1: *1* cirrus,
2 cirrostratus,
3 cirrocumulus,
4 altostratus,
5 altocumulus,
6 stratocumulus,
7 nimbostratus,
8 cumulus,
9 cumulonimbus,
10 stratus

usually between 3000 and 8000 feet (1000 and 2500 meters) that is characterized by a profusion of epiphytes and the presence of clouds even in the dry season

cloud·land \'klaùd-,land\ *noun* (1817)
1 : the region of the clouds
2 : the realm of visionary speculation or poetic imagination

cloud·less \-ləs\ *adjective* (14th century)
: free from clouds : CLEAR
— **cloud·less·ly** *adverb*
— **cloud·less·ness** *noun*

cloud·let \'klaùd-lət\ *noun* (1788)
: a small cloud

cloud nine *noun* (1959)
: a feeling of well-being or elation — usually used with *on*

cloud·scape \'klaùd-,skāp\ *noun* (1880)
: a view or pictorial representation of a cloud formation

cloud street *noun* (1943)
: a row of cumulus clouds

cloudy \'klaù-dē\ *adjective* **cloud·i·er; -est** (14th century)
1 : of, relating to, or resembling cloud
2 : darkened by gloom or anxiety
3 a : overcast with clouds **b** : having a cloudy sky
4 : obscure in meaning ⟨*cloudy* issues⟩; *also* : uncertain as to fact or outcome ⟨a *cloudy* future⟩
5 : dimmed or dulled as if by clouds ⟨a *cloudy* mirror⟩
6 : uneven in color or texture
7 : having visible material in suspension : MURKY
— **cloud·i·ly** \'klaù-dᵊl-ē\ *adverb*
— **cloud·i·ness** \'klaù-dē-nəs\ *noun*

¹clout \'klaùt\ *noun* [Middle English, from Old English *clūt*; akin to Middle High German *klōz* lump, Russian *gluda*] (before 12th century)
1 *dialect chiefly British* : a piece of cloth or leather : RAG
2 : a blow especially with the hand; *also* : a hard hit in baseball
3 : a white cloth on a stake or frame used as a target in archery
4 : PULL, INFLUENCE ⟨political *clout*⟩

²clout *transitive verb* (14th century)
1 : to cover or patch with a clout
2 : to hit forcefully

¹clove \'klōv\ *noun* [Middle English, from Old English *clufu*; akin to Old English *clēofan* to cleave] (before 12th century)
: one of the small bulbs (as in garlic) developed in the axils of the scales of a large bulb

²clove *past of* CLEAVE

³clove \'klōv\ *noun* [alteration of Middle English *clowe*, from Old French *clou (de girofle)*, literally, nail of clove, from Latin *clavus* nail] (13th century)
: the dried flower bud of a tropical tree (*Syzygium aromaticum* synonym *Eugenia aromatica*) of the myrtle family that is used as a spice and is the source of an oil; *also* : this tree

clove hitch \'klōv-\ *noun* [Middle English *cloven, clove* divided, from past participle of *clevien* to cleave] (circa 1769)
: a knot securing a rope temporarily to an object (as a post or spar) and consisting of a turn around the object, over the standing part, around the object again, and under the last turn — see KNOT illustration

clo·ven \'klō-vən\ *past participle of* CLEAVE

cloven foot *noun* (13th century)
: CLOVEN HOOF
— **clo·ven–foot·ed** \'klō-vən-,fù-təd\ *adjective*

cloven hoof *noun* (1870)
1 : a foot (as of a sheep) divided into two parts at its distal extremity
2 [from the traditional representation of Satan as cloven-hoofed] : the sign of devilish character

— **clo·ven–hoofed** \'klō-vən-,hùft, -,hüft, -,hùvd, -,hüvd\ *adjective*

clove pink *noun* (circa 1855)
: CARNATION 2

clo·ver \'klō-vər\ *noun* [Middle English, from Old English *clāfre*; akin to Old High German *klēo* clover] (before 12th century)
1 : any of a genus (*Trifolium*) of low leguminous herbs having trifoliolate leaves and flowers in dense heads and including many that are valuable for forage and attractive to bees
2 : any of various leguminous plants (as of the genera *Melilotus, Lespedeza,* or *Medicago*) other than the clovers (genus *Trifolium*)
— **in clover** *or* **in the clover** : in prosperity or in pleasant circumstances

¹clo·ver·leaf \-,lēf\ *adjective* (1917)
: resembling a clover leaf in shape

²cloverleaf *noun, plural* **-leafs** \-,lēfs\ *or* **-leaves** \-,lēvz\ (1931)
: an interchange between two major highways that allows traffic to change from one to the other without requiring any left turns or crossings and that from above resembles a four-leaf clover

cloverleaf

Clo·vis \'klō-vəs\ *adjective* [*Clovis,* New Mexico] (1956)
: of or relating to a widely distributed prehistoric culture of North America characterized by leaf-shaped flint projectile points having fluted sides

¹clown \'klaùn\ *noun* [probably of Low German origin; akin to Frisian *klönne* clumsy fellow, Old English *clyne* lump of metal] (1563)
1 : FARMER, COUNTRYMAN
2 : a rude ill-bred person : BOOR
3 a : a fool, jester, or comedian in an entertainment (as a play); *specifically* : a grotesquely dressed comedy performer in a circus **b** : a person who habitually plays the buffoon : JOKER 1b

²clown *intransitive verb* (1599)
: to act as or like a clown

clown·ery \'klaù-nə-rē\ *noun, plural* **-er·ies** (1589)
: clownish behavior or an instance of clownishness : BUFFOONERY

clown·ish \'klaù-nish\ *adjective* (circa 1570)
: resembling or befitting a clown (as in ignorance and lack of sophistication)
synonym see BOORISH
— **clown·ish·ly** *adverb*
— **clown·ish·ness** *noun*

clox·a·cil·lin \,kläk-sə-'si-lən\ *noun* [chlor- + oxacillin] (1963)
: a semisynthetic oral penicillin $C_{19}H_{17}ClN_3NaO_5S$ effective especially against staphylococci which secrete penicillinase

cloy \'klòi\ *verb* [alteration of Middle English *acloien* to lame, from Middle French *encloer* to drive in a nail, from Medieval Latin *inclavare*, from Latin *in* + *clavus* nail] (1528)
transitive verb
: to surfeit with an excess usually of something originally pleasing
intransitive verb
: to cause surfeit
synonym see SATIATE

cloy·ing \'klòi-iŋ, 'klòin\ *adjective* (1594)
: disgusting or distasteful by reason of excess ⟨*cloying* sweetness⟩; *also* : excessively sweet or sentimental ⟨a *cloying* romantic comedy⟩
— **cloy·ing·ly** *adverb*

cloze \'klōz\ *adjective* [by shortening & alteration from *closure*] (1953)
: of, relating to, or being a test of reading

comprehension that involves having the person being tested supply words which have been systematically deleted from a text

¹club \'kləb\ *noun, often attributive* [Middle English *clubbe*, from Old Norse *klubba*; akin to Old High German *kolbo* club] (13th century)
1 a : a heavy usually tapering staff especially of wood wielded as a weapon **b** : a stick or bat used to hit a ball in any of various games **c** : something resembling a club
2 a : a playing card marked with a stylized figure of a black clover **b** *plural but singular or plural in construction* : the suit comprising cards marked with clubs
3 a : an association of persons for some common object usually jointly supported and meeting periodically; *also* : a group identified by some common characteristic ⟨nations in the nuclear *club*⟩ **b** : the meeting place of a club **c** : an association of persons participating in a plan by which they agree to make regular payments or purchases in order to secure some advantage **d** : NIGHTCLUB **e** : an athletic association or team
— **club·bish** \'klə-bish\ *adjective*

²club *verb* **clubbed; club·bing** (1593)
transitive verb
1 a : to beat or strike with or as if with a club **b** : to gather into a club-shaped mass ⟨*clubbed* her hair⟩
2 a : to unite or combine for a common cause **b** : to contribute to a common fund
intransitive verb
1 : to unite : COMBINE
2 : to pay a share of a common expense

club·ba·ble *also* **club·able** \'klə-bə-bəl\ *adjective* (1783)
: SOCIABLE

clubbed \'kləbd\ *adjective* (14th century)
: shaped like a club ⟨*clubbed* antennae⟩

club·ber \'klə-bər\ *noun* (1633)
: a member of a club

club·by \'klə-bē\ *adjective* **club·bi·er; -est** (1859)
: characteristic of a club or club members: as **a** : displaying friendliness especially to other members of the same social group : SOCIABLE **b** : open only to qualified or approved persons : SELECT, ELITE
— **club·bi·ness** *noun*

club car *noun* (1886)
: a railroad passenger car with facilities for serving refreshments and drinks — called also *bar car, lounge car*

club chair *noun* (1919)
: a deep low thickly upholstered easy chair often with rather low back and heavy sides and arms

club cheese *noun* (1916)
: a process cheese made by grinding cheddar and other cheeses usually with added condiments and seasoning

club·foot \'kləb-,fùt\ *noun* (1538)
: a misshapen foot twisted out of position from birth; *also* : this deformity
— **club·foot·ed** \-,fù-təd\ *adjective*

club fungus *noun* (1899)
: any of a family (Clavariaceae) of basidiomycetes with a simple or branched often club-shaped sporophore

club·house \'kləb-,haùs\ *noun* (1818)
1 : a house occupied by a club or used for club activities
2 : locker rooms used by an athletic team

club·man \'kləb-mən, -,man\ *noun* (1851)
: a usually wealthy man given to club life

club moss *noun* (1597)
: any of an order (Lycopodiales) of primitive vascular plants (as ground pine) often with the sporangia borne in club-shaped strobili

club·root \'kləb-,rüt, -,rùt\ *noun* (1846)
: a disease of cruciferous plants and especially of cabbage caused by a slime mold (*Plasmodiophora brassicae*) producing swellings or distortions of the root

club sandwich *noun* (1903)
: a sandwich of three slices of bread with two layers of meat (as turkey) and lettuce, tomato, and mayonnaise

club soda *noun* (1942)
: SODA WATER 2a

club steak *noun* (1915)
: a small steak cut from the end of the short loin — see BEEF illustration

¹cluck \'klək\ *verb* [imitative] (15th century)
intransitive verb
1 : to make a cluck
2 : to make a clicking sound with the tongue
3 : to express interest or concern ⟨critics *clucked* over the new developments⟩
transitive verb
1 : to call with a cluck
2 : to express with interest or concern

²cluck *noun* (1703)
1 : the characteristic sound made by a hen especially in calling her chicks
2 : a stupid or naive person

¹clue \'klü\ *noun* [alteration of *clew*] (1596)
: something that guides through an intricate procedure or maze of difficulties; *specifically* **:** a piece of evidence that leads one toward the solution of a problem ◆

²clue *transitive verb* **clued; clue·ing** *or* **clu·ing** (1663)
1 : to provide with a clue
2 : to give reliable information to ⟨*clue* me in on how it happened⟩

clue·less \'klü-ləs\ *adjective* (1862)
1 : providing no clue
2 : completely or hopelessly bewildered, unaware, ignorant, or foolish

clum·ber spaniel \'kləm-bər-\ *noun, often C capitalized* [*Clumber*, estate in Nottinghamshire, England] (1883)
: any of a breed of large massive heavyset spaniels with a dense silky largely white coat

¹clump \'kləmp\ *noun* [probably from Low German *klump*] (circa 1586)
1 : a group of things clustered together ⟨a *clump* of bushes⟩
2 : a compact mass
3 : a heavy tramping sound
— **clumpy** \'kləm-pē\ *adjective*

²clump (1665)
intransitive verb
1 : to walk or move clumsily and noisily
2 : to form clumps
transitive verb
: to arrange in or cause to form clumps ⟨the serum *clumps* the bacteria⟩

clum·sy \'kləm-zē\ *adjective* **clum·si·er; -est** [probably from obsolete English *clumse* benumbed with cold] (circa 1598)
1 a : lacking dexterity, nimbleness, or grace ⟨*clumsy* fingers⟩ **b :** lacking tact or subtlety ⟨a *clumsy* joke⟩
2 : awkward or inefficient in use or construction **:** UNWIELDY
synonym see AWKWARD
— **clum·si·ly** \-zə-lē\ *adverb*
— **clum·si·ness** \-zē-nəs\ *noun*

clung *past and past participle of* CLING

¹clunk \'kləŋk\ *verb* [imitative] (circa 1796)
intransitive verb
1 : to make a clunk
2 : to hit something with a clunk
transitive verb
: to strike or hit with a clunk

²clunk *noun* (1823)
1 : a blow or the sound of a blow **:** THUMP
2 : a dull or stupid person

clunk·er \'kləŋ-kər\ *noun* (1943)
1 : an old or badly working piece of machinery; *especially* **:** a dilapidated automobile
2 : someone or something notably unsuccessful

clunky \'kləŋ-kē\ *adjective* **clunk·i·er; -est** (1968)
: clumsy in style, form, or execution ⟨a *clunky* thriller⟩ ⟨*clunky* earrings⟩

clu·pe·id \'klü-pē-əd\ *noun* [ultimately from Latin *clupea*, a small river fish] (1880)
: any of a large family (Clupeidae) of soft-finned bony fishes (as herrings) that have a laterally compressed body and a forked tail and usually occur in schools
— **clupeid** *adjective*

¹clus·ter \'kləs-tər\ *noun* [Middle English, from Old English *clyster*; akin to Old English *clott* clot] (before 12th century)
: a number of similar individuals that occur together: as **a :** two or more consecutive consonants or vowels in a segment of speech **b :** a group of buildings and especially houses built close together on a sizable tract in order to preserve open spaces larger than the individual yard for common recreation **c :** an aggregation of stars or galaxies that appear close together in the sky and are gravitationally associated
— **clus·tery** \-t(ə-)rē\ *adjective*

²cluster *verb* **clus·tered; clus·ter·ing** \-t(ə-)riŋ\ (14th century)
transitive verb
1 : to collect into a cluster ⟨*cluster* the tents together⟩
2 : to furnish with clusters
intransitive verb
: to grow, assemble, or occur in a cluster

cluster analysis *noun* (1948)
: a statistical classification technique for discovering whether the individuals of a population fall into different groups by making quantitative comparisons of multiple characteristics

cluster bomb *noun* (1967)
: an aircraft-dropped canister of small fragmentation bombs

cluster headache *noun* (1953)
: a headache that is characterized by severe pain in the eye or temple and tends to recur in a series of attacks

¹clutch \'kləch\ *verb* [Middle English *cluc-chen*, from Old English *clyccan*] (before 12th century)
transitive verb
1 : to grasp or hold with or as if with the hand or claws usually strongly, tightly, or suddenly
2 *obsolete* **:** CLENCH
intransitive verb
1 : to seek to grasp and hold
2 : to operate an automobile clutch
synonym see TAKE

²clutch *noun* (13th century)
1 a : the claws or a hand in the act of grasping or seizing firmly **b :** an often cruel or unrelenting control, power, or possession ⟨the fell *clutch* of circumstance —W. E. Henley⟩ **c :** the act of grasping, holding, or restraining
2 a : a coupling used to connect and disconnect a driving and a driven part of a mechanism **b :** a lever (as a pedal) operating such a clutch
3 : a tight or critical situation **:** PINCH ⟨come through in the *clutch*⟩
4 : CLUTCH BAG

³clutch *adjective* (1944)
1 : made or done in a crucial situation ⟨a *clutch* hit⟩
2 : successful in a crucial situation ⟨a *clutch* pitcher⟩

⁴clutch *noun* [alteration of dialect English *cletch* hatching, brood] (1721)
1 : a nest of eggs or a brood of chicks
2 : GROUP, BUNCH

clutch bag *noun* (1949)
: a woman's small usually strapless handbag

¹clut·ter \'klə-tər\ *verb* [Middle English *clotteren* to clot, from *clot*] (1556)
intransitive verb
chiefly dialect **:** to run in disorder
transitive verb
: to fill or cover with scattered or disordered things that impede movement or reduce effectiveness — often used with *up*

²clutter *noun* (1649)
1 a : a crowded or confused mass or collection **b :** things that clutter a place

2 : interfering radar echoes caused by reflection from objects (as on the ground) other than the target
3 *chiefly dialect* **:** DISTURBANCE, HUBBUB

Clyde \'klīd\ *noun* (1894)
: CLYDESDALE

Clydes·dale \'klīdz-,dāl\ *noun* (1786)
: a heavy draft horse with feathering on the legs of a breed originally from Clydesdale, Scotland

clyp·e·us \'kli-pē-əs\ *noun, plural* **clyp·ei** \-pē-,ī, -pē-,ē\ [New Latin, from Latin, round shield] (1834)
: a plate on the anterior median aspect of an insect's head

clys·ter \'klis-tər\ *noun* [Middle English, from Middle French or Latin; Middle French *clistere*, from Latin *clyster*, from Greek *klystēr*, from *klyzein* to wash out; akin to Welsh *clir* pure, Old English *hlūtor* clean] (14th century)
: ENEMA

Cly·tem·nes·tra \,klī-təm-'nes-trə\ *noun* [Latin, from Greek *Klytaimnēstra*]
: the wife and murderess of Agamemnon

cni·dar·i·an \nī-'dar-ē-ən, -'der-\ *noun* [ultimately from New Latin *cnida* nematocyst, from Greek *knidē* nettle] (circa 1909)
: COELENTERATE
— **cnidarian** *adjective*

co- *prefix* [Middle English, from Latin, from *com-*; akin to Old English *ge-*, perfective and collective prefix, Old Irish *com-* with]
1 : with **:** together **:** joint **:** jointly ⟨*coexist*⟩ ⟨*coheir*⟩
2 : in or to the same degree ⟨*coextensive*⟩
3 a : one that is associated in an action with another **:** fellow **:** partner ⟨*coauthor*⟩ ⟨*coworker*⟩ **b :** having a usually lesser share in duty or responsibility **:** alternate **:** deputy ⟨*copilot*⟩
4 : of, relating to, or constituting the complement of an angle ⟨*cosine*⟩ ⟨*codeclination*⟩

co·act	co·chair·per·son
co·ac·tive	co·chair·wom·an
co·ac·tor	co·cham·pi·on
co·ad·min·is·tra·tion	co·com·pos·er
co·an·chor	co·con·spir·a·tor
co·au·thor	co·coun·sel
co·au·thor·ship	co·cre·ate
co·cap·tain	co·cre·ator
co·cat·a·lyst	co·cul·ti·vate
co·chair	co·cul·ti·va·tion
co·chair·man	co·cul·ture

◇ WORD HISTORY
clue *Clue* was originally a variant spelling of *clew*, meaning "ball of thread or yarn." Our usual modern sense of *clue* and *clew*, "guide to the solution of a mystery," is the metaphorical application of a motif in myth and folklore, the ball of thread that helps in finding one's way out of a maze. Of stories containing such a motif, the best-known is the Greek myth of Theseus and Ariadne. Ariadne, daughter of King Minos of Crete, gives the Athenian hero Theseus a ball of thread and instructs him to unravel it as he searches the Labyrinth of King Minos for the monstrous Minotaur. Theseus follows Adriadne's instructions, and after killing the Minotaur, he retraces his steps out of the maze by rewinding the thread. The old literal "ball of thread" sense of *clew* and *clue* is now little used, though *clew* in the nautical sense "corner of a sail" (if it is indeed the same word and not of independent origin) is still current in the language of yachtsmen.

\ə\ **abut** \ᵊ\ **kitten** \ər\ **further** \a\ **ash** \ā\ **ace**
\ä\ **mop, mar** \au̇\ **out** \ch\ **chin** \e\ **bet** \ē\ **easy**
\g\ **go** \i\ **hit** \ī\ **ice** \j\ **job** \ŋ\ **sing** \ō\ **go**
\ȯ\ **law** \ȯi\ **boy** \th\ **thin** \t̷h\ **the** \ü\ **loot** \u̇\ **foot**
\y\ **yet** \zh\ **vision** *see also* Guide to Pronunciation

co·cu·ra·tor
co·de·fen·dant
co·de·sign
co·de·vel·op
co·de·vel·op·er
co·di·rect
co·di·rec·tion
co·di·rec·tor
co·dis·cov·er
co·dis·cov·er·er
co·drive
co·driv·er
co·ed·it
co·ed·i·tor
co·eter·nal
co·ex·ec·u·tor
co·fa·vor·ite
co·fea·ture
co·fi·nance
co·found
co·found·er
co·head
co·heir
co·heir·ess
co·hold·er
co·host
co·host·ess
co·in·vent
co·in·ven·tor
co·in·ves·ti·ga·tor
co·in·ves·tor
co·join
co·lead
co·lead·er
co·man·age
co·man·age·ment
co·man·ag·er
co·mem·ber
co·nom·i·nee
co·oc·cur
co·oc·cur·rence

co·oc·cur·rent
co·of·fi·cial
co·or·ga·niz·er
co·own
co·own·er
co·own·er·ship
co·part·ner
co·part·ner·ship
co·pre·sent
co·pres·i·dent
co·prince
co·prin·ci·pal
co·pris·on·er
co·pro·cess·ing
co·pro·duce
co·pro·duc·er
co·pro·duc·tion
co·pro·mot·er
co·pro·pri·etor
co·pros·per·i·ty
co·pub·lish
co·pub·lish·er
co·re·cip·i·ent
co·re·search·er
co·res·i·dent
co·res·i·den·tial
co·rul·er
co·script
co·spon·sor
co·spon·sor·ship
co·star
co·sur·fac·tant
co·ten·ant
co·trans·duce
co·trans·duc·tion
co·trans·port
co·trust·ee
co·win·ner
co·work·er
co·write

co·ac·er·vate \kō-'a-sər-ˌvāt\ noun [Latin coacervatus, past participle of coacervare to heap up, from co- + acervus heap] (1929)
: an aggregate of colloidal droplets held together by electrostatic attractive forces
— **co·ac·er·vate** \-ˌa-sər-vət\ adjective
— **co·ac·er·va·tion** \(ˌ)kō-ˌa-sər-'vā-shən\ noun

¹**coach** \'kōch\ noun, often attributive [Middle English coche, from Middle French, from German Kutsche, from Hungarian kocsi (szekér), literally, wagon from Kocs, Hungary] (1556)
1 a : a large usually closed four-wheeled horse-drawn carriage having doors in the sides and an elevated seat in front for the driver **b :** a railroad passenger car intended primarily for day travel **c :** BUS 1a **d :** TRAILER 3b **e :** a two-door enclosed automobile **f :** a class of passenger air transportation at a lower fare than first class
2 [from the concept that the tutor conveys the student through his examinations] **a :** a private tutor **b :** one who instructs or trains a performer or a team of performers; specifically : one who instructs players in the fundamentals of a competitive sport and directs team strategy ⟨football coach⟩

²**coach** (1630)
intransitive verb
1 : to go in a coach
2 : to instruct, direct, or prompt as a coach
transitive verb
1 : to train intensively (as by instruction and demonstration) ⟨coach pupils⟩
2 : to act as coach of ⟨coach tennis⟩ ⟨coach a team⟩
— **coach·able** \'kō-chə-bəl\ adjective
— **coach·er** noun

coach dog noun (1840)
: DALMATIAN

coach·man \'kōch-mən\ noun (1579)
: a man who drives a coach or carriage

coach·work \-ˌwərk\ noun (1906)
: an automobile body : BODYWORK

co·ac·tion \-'ak-shən\ noun (1625)
1 : joint action
2 : the interaction between individuals or kinds (as species) in an ecological community

co·adapt·ed \ˌkō-ə-'dap-təd\ adjective (1836)
: mutually adapted especially by natural selection ⟨coadapted gene complexes⟩
— **co·ad·ap·ta·tion** \ˌkō-ˌa-ˌdap-'tā-shən, -dəp-\ noun

co·ad·ju·tor \ˌkō-ə-'jü-tər, kō-'a-jə-tər\ noun [Middle English coadjutour, from Middle French coadjuteur, from Late Latin coadjutor, from Latin co- + adjutor helper, from adjuvare to help — more at AID] (15th century)
1 : one who works together with another : ASSISTANT
2 : a bishop assisting a diocesan bishop and often having the right of succession
— **coadjutor** adjective

co·ad·ju·trix \ˌkō-ə-'jü-triks, kō-'a-jə-(ˌ)triks\ noun, plural **co·ad·ju·tri·ces** \ˌkō-ə-'jü-trə-ˌsēz, (ˌ)kō-ˌa-jə-'trī-(ˌ)sēz\ [New Latin, feminine of coadjutor] (1646)
: a female coadjutor

co·ag·u·lant \kō-'a-gyə-lənt\ noun (1770)
: something that produces coagulation

co·ag·u·lase \kō-'a-gyə-ˌlās, -ˌlāz\ noun (1914)
: any of several enzymes that cause coagulation (as of blood)

¹**co·ag·u·late** \-lət, -ˌlāt\ adjective (14th century)
archaic : being clotted or congealed

²**co·ag·u·late** \-ˌlāt\ verb **-lat·ed; -lat·ing** [Latin coagulatus, past participle of coagulare to curdle, from coagulum curdling agent, from cogere to drive together — more at COGENT] (15th century)
transitive verb
1 : to cause to become viscous or thickened into a coherent mass : CURDLE, CLOT
2 : to gather together or form into a mass or group
intransitive verb
: to become coagulated
— **co·ag·u·la·bil·i·ty** \kō-ˌa-gyə-lə-'bi-lə-tē\ noun
— **co·ag·u·la·ble** \-'a-gyə-lə-bəl\ adjective
— **co·ag·u·la·tion** \-'lā-shən\ noun

co·ag·u·lum \kō-'a-gyə-ləm\ noun, plural **-u·la** \-lə\ or **-ulums** [Latin] (1658)
: a coagulated mass or substance : CLOT

¹**coal** \'kōl\ noun, often attributive [Middle English col, from Old English; akin to Old High German & Old Norse kol burning ember, Middle Irish gúal coal] (before 12th century)
1 : a piece of glowing carbon or charred wood : EMBER
2 : CHARCOAL 1
3 a : a black or brownish black solid combustible substance formed by the partial decomposition of vegetable matter without free access of air and under the influence of moisture and often increased pressure and temperature that is widely used as a natural fuel **b** plural, British : pieces or a quantity of the fuel broken up for burning

²**coal** (1602)
transitive verb
1 : to burn to charcoal : CHAR
2 : to supply with coal
intransitive verb
: to take in coal

co·a·lesce \ˌkō-ə-'les\ verb **co·a·lesced; co·a·lesc·ing** [Latin coalescere, from co- + alescere to grow — more at OLD] (circa 1656)
intransitive verb
1 : to grow together
2 a : to unite into a whole : FUSE ⟨separate townships have coalesced into a single, sprawling colony —Donald Gould⟩ **b :** to unite for a common end : join forces ⟨people with different points of view coalesce into opposing factions —I. L. Horowitz⟩
3 : to arise from the combination of distinct elements ⟨an organized and a popular resis-

tance immediately coalesced —C. C. Menges⟩
transitive verb
: to cause to unite ⟨sometimes a book coalesces a public into a mass market —Walter Meade⟩
synonym see MIX
— **co·a·les·cence** \-'le-s°n(t)s\ noun
— **co·a·les·cent** \-s°nt\ adjective

coal·field \'kōl-ˌfēld\ noun (1813)
: a region rich in coal deposits

coal·fish \-ˌfish\ noun (1603)
: any of several blackish or dark-backed fishes (as a pollack, cobia, or sablefish)

coal gas noun (1809)
: gas made from coal: as **a :** the mixture of gases thrown off by burning coal **b :** gas made by carbonizing bituminous coal in retorts and used for heating and lighting

coal·hole \'kōl-ˌhōl\ noun (circa 1662)
1 British : a compartment for storing coal
2 : a hole for coal (as an opening in a sidewalk leading to a coal bin)

coal·i·fi·ca·tion \ˌkō-lə-fə-'kā-shən\ noun (1911)
: a process in which vegetable matter becomes converted into coal of increasingly higher rank with anthracite as the final product
— **coal·i·fy** \'kō-lə-ˌfī\ transitive verb

co·a·li·tion \ˌkō-ə-'li-shən\ noun [French, from Latin coalescere] (1612)
1 a : the act of coalescing : UNION **b :** a body formed by the coalescing of originally distinct elements : COMBINATION
2 : a temporary alliance of distinct parties, persons, or states for joint action
— **co·a·li·tion·ist** \-'li-sh(ə-)nist\ noun

coal measures noun plural (1832)
: beds of coal with the associated rocks

coal oil noun (1858)
1 : petroleum or a refined oil prepared from it
2 : KEROSENE

coal seam noun (1849)
: a bed of coal usually thick enough to be profitably mined

coal tar noun (1785)
: tar obtained by distillation of bituminous coal and used especially in making dyes and drugs

coam·ing \'kō-min\ noun [probably irregular from comb] (1611)
: a raised frame (as around a hatchway in the deck of a ship) to keep out water

co·apt \kō-'apt\ transitive verb [Late Latin coaptare, from Latin co- + aptus fastened, fit — more at APT] (1570)
: to fit together and make fast
— **co·ap·ta·tion** \(ˌ)kō-ˌap-'tā-shən\ noun

co·arc·ta·tion \(ˌ)kō-ˌärk-'tā-shən\ noun (1545)
: a stricture or narrowing especially of a canal or vessel (as the aorta)

coarse \'kōrs, 'kȯrs\ adjective **coars·er; coars·est** [Middle English cors, perhaps from course, noun] (14th century)
1 : of ordinary or inferior quality or value : COMMON
2 a (1) : composed of relatively large parts or particles ⟨coarse sand⟩ (2) : loose or rough in texture ⟨coarse cloth⟩ **b :** adjusted or designed for heavy, fast, or less delicate work ⟨a coarse saw with large teeth⟩ **c :** not precise or detailed with respect to adjustment or discrimination
3 : crude or unrefined in taste, manners, or language
4 : harsh, raucous, or rough in tone
5 chiefly British : of or relating to coarse fish ⟨coarse fishing⟩ ☆
— **coarse·ly** adverb
— **coarse·ness** noun

coarse fish noun (1886)
1 chiefly British : a freshwater fish other than a salmonid
2 : ROUGH FISH

coarse–grained \'kōrs-ˌgrānd, 'kȯrs-\ adjective (circa 1774)

1 : having a coarse grain
2 : CRUDE

coars·en \'kȯr-sᵊn, 'kȯr-\ *verb* **coars·ened; coars·en·ing** (1805)
transitive verb
: to make coarse
intransitive verb
: to become coarse

¹coast \'kōst\ *noun* [Middle English *cost,* from Middle French *coste,* from Latin *costa* rib, side; akin to Old Church Slavonic *kostĭ* bone] (14th century)
1 : the land near a shore **:** SEASHORE
2 *obsolete* **:** BORDER, FRONTIER
3 a : a hill or slope suited to coasting **b :** a slide down a slope (as on a sled)
4 *often capitalized* **:** the Pacific coast of the U.S.
5 : the immediate area of view — used in the phrase *the coast is clear*
— **coast·al** \'kōs-t⁰l\ *adjective*
— **coast·wise** \'kōst-ˌwīz\ *adverb or adjective*
— **from coast to coast :** across an entire nation or continent

²coast (14th century)
transitive verb
1 *obsolete* **:** to move along or past the side of **:** SKIRT
2 : to sail along the shore of
intransitive verb
1 a *archaic* **:** to travel on land along a coast or along or past the side of something **b :** to sail along the shore
2 a : to slide, run, or glide downhill by the force of gravity **b :** to move along without or as if without further application of propulsive power (as by momentum or gravity) **c :** to proceed easily without special application of effort or concern ⟨*coasted* through school⟩

coast·er \'kōs-tər\ *noun* (1574)
1 : one that coasts: as **a :** a person engaged in coastal traffic or commerce **b :** a ship sailing along a coast or engaged in trade between ports of the same country
2 : a resident of a seacoast
3 a : a tray or decanter stand usually of silver and sometimes on wheels **b :** a shallow container or a plate or mat to protect a surface
4 a : a small vehicle (as a sled or wagon) used in coasting **b :** ROLLER COASTER

coaster brake *noun* (1899)
: a brake in the hub of the rear wheel of a bicycle operated by reverse pressure on the pedals

coaster wagon *noun* (1911)
: a child's toy wagon often used for coasting

coast guard *noun* (1833)
1 : a military or naval force employed in guarding a coast or responsible for the safety, order, and operation of maritime traffic in neighboring waters
2 *usually* **coast·guard** *chiefly British* **:** COASTGUARDSMAN

coast·guards·man \'kōs(t)-ˌgärdz-mən\ *or* **coast·guard·man** \-ˌgärd-mən\ *noun* (circa 1891)
: a member of a coast guard

coast·land \-ˌland\ *noun* (1852)
: land bordering the sea

coast·line \-ˌlīn\ *noun* (circa 1859)
1 : a line that forms the boundary between the land and the ocean or a lake
2 : the outline of a coast

coast redwood *noun* (circa 1897)
: REDWOOD 3a

coast–to–coast \'kōs-tə-'kōst\ *adjective* (1911)
: extending or airing across an entire nation or continent

coast·ward \'kōs-twərd\ *or* **coast·wards** \-twərdz\ *adverb* (1853)
: toward the coast
— **coastward** *adjective*

¹coat \'kōt\ *noun, often attributive* [Middle English *cote,* from Middle French, of Germanic origin; akin to Old High German *kozza* coarse wool mantle] (14th century)
1 a : an outer garment worn on the upper body and varying in length and style according to fashion and use **b :** something resembling a coat
2 : the external growth on an animal
3 : a layer of one substance covering another ⟨a *coat* of paint⟩
— **coat·ed** \'kō-təd\ *adjective*
— **coat·less** *adjective*

²coat *transitive verb* (14th century)
1 : to cover with a coat
2 : to cover or spread with a finishing, protecting, or enclosing layer
— **coat·er** *noun*

coat·dress \'kōt-ˌdres\ *noun* (1854)
: a dress styled like a coat usually with a front buttoning from neckline to hemline

coat hanger *noun* (1895)
: a device which is shaped like the outline of a person's shoulders and over which garments may be hung

co·a·ti \kə-'wä-tē, kwä-'tē\ *noun* [Portuguese *coatí,* from Tupi] (1676)
: either of two tropical American mammals (*Nasua nasua* and *N. nelsoni*) related to the raccoon but with a longer body and tail and a long flexible snout

co·a·ti·mun·di \kə-ˌwä-ti-'mən-dē, ˌkwä-, -'mùn-\ *noun* [Tupi] (1676)
: COATI

coati

coat·ing \'kō-tiŋ\ *noun* (1768)
1 : cloth for coats
2 : COAT, COVERING

coat of arms [Middle English *cote of armes,* translation of Middle French *cote d'armes*] (14th century)
1 : a tabard or surcoat embroidered with armorial bearings
2 a : the particular heraldic bearings (as of a person) usually depicted on an escutcheon often with accompanying adjuncts (as a crest, motto, and supporters) **b :** a similar symbolic emblem

coat of mail (15th century)
: a garment of metal scales or chain mail worn as armor

coat·rack \'kōt-ˌrak\ *noun* (1915)
: a stand or rack fitted with pegs, hooks, or hangers and used for the temporary storage of garments

coat·room \-ˌrüm, -ˌrùm\ *noun* (1870)
: CLOAKROOM

coat·tail \'kōt-ˌtāl\ *noun* (circa 1600)
1 : the rear flap of a man's coat
2 *plural* **:** the skirts of a dress coat, cutaway, or frock coat
3 *plural* **:** the influence or pulling power of a popular movement or candidate ⟨congressmen riding into office on the president's *coattails*⟩

¹coax \'kōks\ *transitive verb* [earlier *cokes,* from *cokes* simpleton] (1589)
1 *obsolete* **:** FONDLE, PET
2 : to influence or gently urge by caressing or flattering **:** WHEEDLE
3 : to draw, gain, or persuade by means of gentle urging or flattery
4 : to manipulate with great perseverance and usually with considerable effort toward a desired state or activity ⟨*coax* a fire to burn⟩

²co·ax \'kō-ˌaks\ *noun* (1949)
: COAXIAL CABLE

co·ax·i·al \(ˌ)kō-'ak-sē-əl\ *adjective* (1881)
1 : having coincident axes

2 : mounted on concentric shafts
— **co·ax·i·al·ly** \-sē-ə-lē\ *adverb*

coaxial cable *noun* (1936)
: a transmission line that consists of a tube of electrically conducting material surrounding a central conductor held in place by insulators and that is used to transmit telegraph, telephone, and television signals of high frequency — called also *coax cable*

cob \'käb\ *noun* [Middle English *cobbe* leader] (15th century)
1 : a male swan
2 *dialect English* **:** a rounded mass, lump, or heap
3 : a crudely struck old Spanish coin of irregular shape
4 : CORNCOB 1
5 : a stocky short-legged riding horse
— **cob·by** \'kä-bē\ *adjective*

co·bal·a·min \kō-'ba-lə-mən\ *noun* [*cobalt* + *vitamin*] (1956)
: VITAMIN B₁₂

co·balt \'kō-ˌbȯlt\ *noun* [German *Kobalt,* alteration of *Kobold,* literally, goblin, from Middle High German *kobolt;* from its occurrence in silver ore, believed to be due to goblins] (1683)
1 : a tough lustrous silver-white magnetic metallic element that is related to and occurs with iron and nickel and is used especially in alloys — see ELEMENT table
2 : COBALT BLUE 2 ◇

\ə\ abut \ᵊ\ kitten \ər\ further \a\ ash \ā\ ace
\ä\ mop, mar \aù\ out \ch\ chin \e\ bet \ē\ easy
\g\ go \i\ hit \ī\ ice \j\ job \ŋ\ sing \ō\ go
\ȯ\ law \ȯi\ boy \th\ thin \t͟h\ the \ü\ loot \ù\ foot
\y\ yet \zh\ vision *see also* Guide to Pronunciation

cobalt blue *noun* (1835)
1 : a greenish blue pigment consisting essentially of cobalt oxide and alumina
2 : a strong greenish blue

cobalt chloride *noun* (1885)
: a chloride of cobalt; *especially* : the dichloride $CoCl_2$ that is blue when dehydrated, turns red in the presence of moisture, and is used to indicate humidity

co·bal·tic \kō-'bȯl-tik\ *adjective* (1782)
: of, relating to, or containing cobalt especially with a valence of three

co·balt·ite \'kō-,bȯl-,tīt, kō-'\ *or* **co·balt·ine** \-,tēn\ *noun* [*cobaltite*, alteration of *cobaltine*, from French, from *cobalt*] (1868)
: a mineral consisting of a grayish to silver-white cobalt sulfur arsenide used in making smalt

co·bal·tous \kō-'bȯl-təs\ *adjective* (1863)
: of, relating to, or containing cobalt especially with a valence of two

cobalt 60 *noun* (1946)
: a heavy radioactive isotope of cobalt of the mass number 60 produced in nuclear reactors and used as a source of gamma rays (as for radiotherapy)

cob·ber \'kȯ-bər\ *noun* [origin unknown] (1893)
Australian & New Zealand : BUDDY

¹**cob·ble** \'kä-bəl\ *transitive verb* **cob·bled; cob·bling** \-b(ə-)liŋ\ [Middle English *coblen*, perhaps back-formation from *cobelere* cobbler] (15th century)
1 *chiefly British* : to mend or patch coarsely
2 : REPAIR, MAKE ⟨*cobble* shoes⟩
3 : to make or put together roughly or hastily — often used with *together* or *up*

²**cobble** *noun* (1600)
1 : COBBLESTONE
2 *plural, chiefly British* : lump coal about the size of small cobblestones

cobbled *adjective* (1853)
: paved with cobblestones

cob·bler \'kä-blər\ *noun* [Middle English *cobelere*] (13th century)
1 : a mender or maker of shoes and often of other leather goods
2 *archaic* : a clumsy workman
3 : a tall iced drink consisting usually of wine, rum, or whiskey and sugar garnished with mint or a slice of lemon or orange
4 : a deep-dish fruit dessert with a thick top crust

cob·ble·stone \'kä-bəl-,stōn\ *noun* [Middle English, from *cobble-* (probably from *cob*) + *stone*] (15th century)
: a naturally rounded stone larger than a pebble and smaller than a boulder; *especially* : such a stone used in paving a street or in construction
— **cob·ble·stoned** \-,stōnd\ *adjective*

cob·by \'kä-bē\ *adjective* **cob·bi·er; -est** (1883)
: STOCKY ⟨a *cobby* horse⟩

co·bel·lig·er·ent \,kō-bə-'lij-rənt, -'li-jə-\ *noun* (1813)
: a country fighting with another power against a common enemy
— **cobelligerent** *adjective*

co·bia \'kō-bē-ə\ *noun* [origin unknown] (circa 1873)
: a large bony fish (*Rachycentron canadum* of the family Rachycentridae) of warm seas that is a food and sport fish

co·ble \'kō-bəl\ *noun* [Middle English] (14th century)
: a flat-bottomed boat propelled chiefly by oars and used in Scotland and northern England especially for fishing

cob·nut \'käb-,nət\ *noun* (1580)
: the fruit of a European hazel (*Corylus avellana grandis*); *also* : the plant bearing this fruit

CO·BOL *or* **Co·bol** \'kō-,bȯl\ *noun* [common business oriented *l*anguage] (1960)
: a computer programming language designed for business applications

co·bra \'kō-brə\ *noun* [Portuguese *cobra (de capello)*, literally, hooded snake, from Latin *colubra* snake] (1802)
: any of several venomous Asian and African elapid snakes (genera *Naja* and *Ophiophagus*) that when excited expand the skin of the neck into a hood by movement of the anterior ribs; *also* : any of several related African snakes

cob·web \'käb-,web\ *noun* [Middle English *coppeweb*, from *coppe* spider (from Old English *ātorcoppe*) + *web*; akin to Middle Dutch *coppe* spider] (14th century)
1 a : the network spread by a spider : SPIDERWEB **b** : tangles of the silken threads of a cobweb usually covered with accumulated dirt and dust
2 : something that entangles, obscures, or confuses ⟨a *cobweb* of law and politics⟩
— **cob·webbed** \-,webd\ *adjective*
— **cob·web·by** \-,we-bē\ *adjective*

co·ca \'kō-kə\ *noun* [Spanish, from Quechua *kuka*] (1577)
1 : any of several South American shrubs (genus *Erythroxylon*, family Erythroxylaceae); *especially* : one (*E. coca*) that is the primary source of cocaine
2 : dried leaves of a coca (especially *Erythroxylon coca*) containing alkaloids including cocaine

co·caine \kō-'kā, 'kō-\ *noun* (1874)
: a bitter crystalline alkaloid $C_{17}H_{21}NO_4$ obtained from coca leaves that is used medically as a topical anesthetic and illicitly for its euphoric effects and that may result in a compulsive psychological need

co·cain·ize \kō-'kā-,nīz\ *transitive verb* **-ized; -iz·ing** (1887)
: to treat or anesthetize with cocaine
— **co·cain·i·za·tion** \-,kā-nə-'zā-shən\ *noun*

co·car·box·yl·ase \,kō-kär-'bäk-sə-,lās, -,lāz\ *noun* (1932)
: a coenzyme $C_{12}H_{19}ClN_4O_7P_2S \cdot H_2O$ that is a pyrophosphate of thiamine and is important in metabolic reactions (as decarboxylation in the Krebs cycle)

co·car·cin·o·gen \,kō-kär-'si-nə-jən, kō-'kär-sⁿ-ə-,jen\ *noun* (1938)
: an agent that aggravates the carcinogenic effects of another substance
— **co·car·cin·o·gen·ic** \,kō-,kär-sⁿ-ō-'je-nik\ *adjective*

coc·cid \'käk-səd\ *noun* [New Latin *Coccus*, genus of scales, from Greek *kokkos* grain, kermes] (circa 1889)
: SCALE INSECT

coc·cid·i·oi·do·my·co·sis \(,)käk-,si-dē-,ȯi-dō-(,)mī-'kō-səs\ *noun* [New Latin, from *Coccidioides*, genus of fungi (from *coccidium*) + *mycosis*] (1937)
: a disease especially of humans and domestic animals caused by a fungus (*Coccidioides immitis*) and marked especially by fever and pulmonary symptoms

coc·cid·i·o·sis \(,)käk-,si-dē-'ō-səs\ *noun*, *plural* **-o·ses** \-,sēz\ [New Latin] (1892)
: infestation with or disease caused by coccidia

coc·cid·i·um \käk-'si-dē-əm\ *noun*, *plural* **-ia** \-dē-ə\ [New Latin, diminutive of *coccus*] (circa 1879)
: any of an order (Coccidia) of protozoans usually parasitic in the digestive epithelium of vertebrates

coc·coid \'kä-,kȯid\ *adjective* (1893)
: of, relating to, or resembling a coccus : GLOBULAR 1a(1)
— **coccoid** *noun*

coc·cus \'kä-kəs\ *noun*, *plural* **coc·ci** \'kä-,kī, -,kē; 'käk-,sī, -,sē\ [New Latin, from Greek *kokkos*] (1888)
: a spherical bacterium
— **coc·cal** \'kä-kəl\ *adjective*

-coc·cus *noun combining form*, *plural* **-coc·ci** [New Latin]
: berry-shaped microorganism ⟨micro*coccus*⟩

coc·cy·ge·al \käk-'si-j(ē-)əl\ *adjective* [Medieval Latin *coccygeus* of the coccyx, from Greek *kokkyk-*, *kokkyx*] (1836)
: of or relating to the coccyx

coc·cyx \'käk-siks\ *noun*, *plural* **coc·cy·ges** \'käk-sə-,jēz\ *also* **coc·cyx·es** \'käk-sik-səz\ [New Latin, from Greek *kokkyx* cuckoo, coccyx; from its resemblance to a cuckoo's beak] (1615)
: a small bone that articulates with the sacrum and that usually consists of four fused vertebrae which form the terminus of the spinal column in humans and tailless apes

Co·chin \'kō-chin\ *noun* [Cochin China, part of French Indochina] (1853)
: any of an Asian breed of large domestic fowl with thick plumage, small wings and tail, and densely feathered legs and feet — called also *Cochin China*

co·chi·neal \'kä-chə-,nēl, 'kō-\ *noun* [Middle French & Spanish; Middle French *cochenille*, from Old Spanish *cochinilla* cochineal insect] (1582)
1 : a red dye consisting of the dried bodies of female cochineal insects
2 : COCHINEAL INSECT

cochineal insect *noun* (1801)
: a small red cactus-feeding scale insect (*Dactylopius coccus*) the females of which are the source of cochineal

co·chlea \'kō-klē-ə, 'kä-klē-\ *noun*, *plural* **co·chle·as** *or* **co·chle·ae** \-klē-,ē, -,ī\ [New Latin, from Latin, snail, snail shell, from Greek *kochlias*, from *kochlos* snail; probably akin to Greek *konchē* mussel] (1688)
: a division of the bony labyrinth of the inner ear of higher vertebrates that is usually coiled like a snail shell and is the seat of the hearing organ — see EAR illustration
— **co·chle·ar** \'kō-klē-ər, 'kä-\ *adjective*

¹**cock** \'käk\ *noun* [Middle English *cok*, from Old English *cocc*, of imitative origin] (before 12th century)
1 a : the adult male of the domestic fowl (*Gallus gallus*) **b** : the male of birds other than the domestic fowl **c** : WOODCOCK **d** *archaic* : the crowing of a cock; *also* : COCKCROW **e** : WEATHERCOCK
2 : a device (as a faucet or valve) for regulating the flow of a liquid
3 a : a chief person : LEADER **b** : a person of spirit and often of a certain swagger or arrogance
4 a : the hammer in the lock of a firearm **b** : the cocked position of the hammer
5 : PENIS — usually considered vulgar
— **cock of the walk** : one that dominates a group or situation especially overbearingly

²**cock** (1575)
intransitive verb
1 : STRUT, SWAGGER
2 : to turn, tip, or stick up
3 : to position the hammer of a firearm for firing
transitive verb
1 a : to draw the hammer of (a firearm) back and set for firing; *also* : to set (the trigger) for firing **b** : to draw or bend back in preparation for throwing or hitting **c** : to set a mechanism (as a camera shutter) for tripping
2 a : to set erect **b** : to turn, tip, or tilt usually to one side
3 : to turn up (as a hat brim)
— **cock a snook** *also* **cock snooks** : to thumb the nose

³**cock** *noun* (1717)
: TILT, SLANT ⟨*cock* of the head⟩

⁴**cock** *noun* [Middle English *cok*, of Scandinavian origin] (14th century)
: a small pile (as of hay)

⁵**cock** *transitive verb* (14th century)
: to put (as hay) into cocks

cock·ade \kä-'kād\ *noun* [modification of

French *cocarde*, from feminine of *cocard* vain, from *coq* cock, from Old French *coc*, of imitative origin] (1709)
: an ornament (as a rosette) usually worn on a hat as a badge
— **cock·ad·ed** \-'kä-dəd\ *adjective*

cock–a–hoop \ˌkä-kə-'hüp, -'hup\ *adjective* [from the phrase *to set cock a hoop* to be festive] (1663)
1 : triumphantly boastful **:** EXULTING
2 : AWRY

Cock·aigne \kä-'kān\ *noun* [Middle English *cokaygne*, from Middle French (*pais de*) *cocaigne* land of plenty] (13th century)
: an imaginary land of great luxury and ease

cock–a–leek·ie \ˌkä-ki-'lē-kē\ *noun* [alteration of *cockie* (diminutive of [1]*cock*) + *leekie*, diminutive of *leek*] (1737)
: a soup made of chicken and leeks

cock·a·lo·rum \ˌkä-kə-'lōr-əm, -'lor-\ *noun*, *plural* **-rums** [probably modification of obsolete Flemish *kockeloeren* to crow, of imitative origin] (circa 1715)
1 : a boastful and self-important person
2 : LEAPFROG
3 : boastful talk

cock·a·ma·my *or* **cock·a·ma·mie** \ˌkä-kə-'mā-mē\ *adjective* [perhaps alteration of *decalcomania*] (1960)
: RIDICULOUS, INCREDIBLE ⟨of all the *cockamamy* excuses I ever heard —Leo Rosten⟩

cock–and–bull story \ˈkä-kən-'bul-\ *noun* (1795)
: an incredible story told as true

cock·a·poo \'kä-kə-ˌpü\ *noun* [alteration of *cocker* (*spaniel*) + *poo*dle] (1970)
: a dog that is a cross between a cocker spaniel and a poodle

cock·a·tiel \'käk-ə-ˌtē(ə)l\ *noun* [Dutch *kaketielje*, from Portuguese *cacatilha*, from *catua* cockatoo] (1877)
: a crested small gray Australian parrot (*Nymphicus hollandicus*) with a yellow head

cock·a·too \'kä-kə-ˌtü\ *noun*, *plural* **-toos** [Dutch *kaketoe*, from Malay *kakatua*] (1634)
: any of various large noisy chiefly Australasian crested parrots (family Cacatuidae and especially genus *Cacatua*)

cock·a·trice \'kä-kə-trəs, -ˌtrīs\ *noun* [Middle English *cocatrice*, from Middle French *cocatris* ichneumon, cockatrice, from Medieval Latin *cocatric-*, *cocatrix* ichneumon] (14th century)
: a legendary serpent that is hatched by a reptile from a cock's egg and that has a deadly glance

cockatoo

cock·boat \'käk-ˌbōt\ *noun* (15th century)
: a small boat; *especially* **:** one used as a tender to a larger boat

cock·cha·fer \'käk-ˌchā-fər\ *noun* [[1]*cock* + *chafer*] (1712)
: a large European beetle (*Melolontha melolontha*) destructive to vegetation as an adult and to roots as a larva; *also* **:** any of various related beetles

cock·crow \'käk-ˌkrō\ *noun* (13th century)
: DAWN

cocked hat \'käkt-\ *noun* (1673)
1 : a hat with brim turned up to give a 3-cornered appearance
2 : a hat with brim turned up on two sides and worn either front to back or sideways

[1]**cock·er** \'kä-kər\ *transitive verb* [Middle English *cokeren*] (15th century)
: INDULGE, PAMPER

[2]**cocker** *noun* (1689)
: a keeper or handler of fighting cocks

[3]**cocker** *noun* (circa 1811)
: COCKER SPANIEL

cock·er·el \'kä-k(ə-)rəl\ *noun* [Middle English *cokerelle*, from Middle French dialect *kokerel*, diminutive of Old French *coc*] (15th century)
: a young male of the domestic fowl (*Gallus gallus*)

cock·er spaniel \'kä-kər-\ *noun* [*cocking* woodcock hunting] (1840)
1 : ENGLISH COCKER SPANIEL
2 : any of a breed of spaniels developed in the U.S. from the English cocker spaniel that are smaller in size and have a shorter muzzle and longer thicker coat

cock·eye \'käk-'ī, -ˌī\ *noun* (circa 1825)
: a squinting eye

cock·eyed \'käk-ˌīd\ *adjective* (1821)
1 : having a cockeye
2 a : ASKEW, AWRY **b :** slightly crazy **:** TOPSYTURVY ⟨a *cockeyed* scheme⟩ **c :** DRUNK 1a
— **cock·eyed·ly** \-ˌīd-lē\ *adverb*
— **cock·eyed·ness** \-ˌīd-nəs\ *noun*

cock·fight \'käk-ˌfīt\ *noun* (circa 1566)
: a contest in which gamecocks usually fitted with metal spurs are pitted against each other
— **cock·fight·ing** \-ˌfī-tiŋ\ *adjective or noun*

cock·horse \'käk-ˌhors\ *noun* [perhaps from *cock*, adjective, (male) + *horse*] (circa 1541)
: ROCKING HORSE

[1]**cock·le** \'kä-kəl\ *noun* [Middle English, from Old English *coccel*] (before 12th century)
: any of several weedy plants of the pink family; *especially* **:** CORN COCKLE

[2]**cockle** *noun* [Middle English *cokille*, from Middle French *coquille* shell, modification of Latin *conchylia*, plural of *conchylium*, from Greek *konchylion*, from *konchē* conch] (14th century)
1 : any of various chiefly marine bivalve mollusks (family Cardiidae) having a shell with convex radially ribbed valves; *especially* **:** a common edible European bivalve (*Cerastoderma edule* synonym *Cardium edule*)
2 : COCKLESHELL

[3]**cockle** *noun* [Middle English *kokell*, ultimately from Middle French *coquillé* wavy or rounded like a shell, from *coquille*] (15th century)
: PUCKER, WRINKLE
— **cockle** *verb*

cock·le·bur \'kä-kəl-ˌbər, 'kə-\ *noun* (1804)
: any of a genus (*Xanthium*) of prickly-fruited composite plants; *also* **:** one of its stiff-spined fruits

cock·le·shell \'kä-kəl-ˌshel\ *noun* (15th century)
1 a : the shell or one of the shell valves of a cockle **b :** a shell (as a scallop shell) suggesting a cockleshell
2 : a light flimsy boat

cockles of the heart [perhaps from [2]*cockle*] (1671)
: the core of one's being
— usually used in the phrase *warm the cockles of the heart*

cockleshell 1a

cock·loft \'käk-ˌloft\ *noun* [probably from [1]*cock*] (1589)
: a small garret

cock·ney \'käk-nē\ *noun*, *plural* **cockneys** [Middle English *cokeney*, literally, cocks' egg, from *coken* (genitive plural of *cok* cock) + *ey* egg, from Old English *æg*] (14th century)
1 obsolete a : a spoiled child **b :** a squeamish woman
2 often capitalized a : a native of London and especially of the East End of London **b :** the dialect of London or of the East End of London
— **cockney** *adjective*
— **cock·ney·fy** \'käk-ni-ˌfī\ *transitive verb*
— **cock·ney·ish** \-nē-ish\ *adjective*

— **cock·ney·ism** \-ˌi-zəm\ *noun*

cock·pit \'käk-ˌpit\ *noun* (1587)
1 a : a pit or enclosure for cockfights **b :** a place noted for especially bloody, violent, or long-continued conflict
2 obsolete : the pit of a theater
3 : a compartment in a sailing warship used as quarters for junior officers and for treatment of the wounded in an engagement
4 : a space or compartment in a usually small vehicle (as a boat, airplane, or automobile) from which it is steered, piloted, or driven — see AIRPLANE illustration

cock·roach \'käk-ˌrōch\ *noun* [by folk etymology from Spanish *cucaracha* cockroach, from *cuca* caterpillar] (1623)
: any of an order or suborder (Blattodea synonym Blattaria) of chiefly nocturnal insects including some that are domestic pests

cocks·comb \'käks-ˌkōm\ *noun* (1542)
1 : COXCOMB
2 : a garden plant (*Celosia cristata*) of the amaranth family grown for its flowers

cocks·foot \'käks-ˌfut\ *noun* (1697)
: ORCHARD GRASS

cock·shut \'käk-ˌshət\ *noun* [from the time poultry are shut in to rest] (1598)
dialect English **:** evening twilight

cock·shy \-ˌshī\ *noun*, *plural* **cockshies** [[1]*cock* + *shy*, noun] (1836)
1 a : a throw at an object set up as a mark **b :** a mark or target so set up
2 : an object or person taken as a butt (as of criticism)

cock·suck·er \-ˌsə-kər\ *noun* (circa 1891)
: one who performs fellatio — usually considered obscene; often used as a generalized term of abuse

cock·sure \'käk-'shur\ *adjective* [probably from [1]*cock* + *sure*] (1672)
1 : feeling perfect assurance sometimes on inadequate grounds
2 : marked by overconfidence or presumptuousness **:** COCKY
synonym see SURE
— **cock·sure·ly** *adverb*
— **cock·sure·ness** *noun*

[1]**cock·tail** \'käk-ˌtāl\ *noun* [probably from [1]*cock* + *tail*] (1806)
1 a : an iced drink of wine or distilled liquor mixed with flavoring ingredients **b :** something resembling or suggesting such a drink **c :** a solution of agents taken or used together especially for medical treatment or diagnosis
2 : an appetizer served as a first course at a meal

[2]**cocktail** *adjective* (1865)
1 : of, relating to, or set aside for cocktails ⟨a *cocktail* hour⟩
2 : designed for semiformal wear ⟨*cocktail* dress⟩

[3]**cocktail** *noun* [[1]*cock* + *tail*] (1808)
: a horse with its tail docked

cocktail glass *noun* (1907)
: a bell-shaped drinking glass usually having a foot and stem and holding about three ounces (90 milliliters)

cocktail lounge *noun* (1939)
: a public room (as in a hotel, club, or restaurant) where cocktails and other drinks are served

cocktail party *noun* (1928)
: an informal or semiformal party or gathering at which cocktails are served

cocktail table *noun* (1946)
: COFFEE TABLE

cock–up \'kä-ˌkəp\ *noun* (circa 1948)
British **:** MESS 3b

cocky \'kä-kē\ *adjective* **cock·i·er; -est** (1768)

1 : boldly or brashly self-confident
2 : JAUNTY
— **cock·i·ly** \'kä-kə-lē\ adverb
— **cock·i·ness** \'kä-kē-nəs\ noun

co·co \'kō-(,)kō\ noun, plural **cocos** [Spanish coco & Portuguese côco bogeyman, grimace, coconut] (1555)
: the coconut palm; also **:** its fruit

co·coa \'kō-(,)kō\ noun [modification of Spanish cacao] (1788)
1 a : powdered ground roasted cacao beans from which a portion of the fat has been removed **b :** a beverage prepared by heating cocoa with water or milk
2 : CACAO 2
3 : a medium brown color

cocoa bean noun (1855)
: CACAO 1

cocoa butter noun (1872)
: a pale vegetable fat with a low melting point obtained from cacao beans

co·co·nut \'kō-kə-(,)nət\ noun (1613)
1 : the drupaceous fruit of the coconut palm whose outer fibrous husk yields coir and whose nut contains thick edible meat and coconut milk
2 : the edible meat of the coconut

coconut crab noun (circa 1889)
: a large edible coconut-eating burrowing land crab (Birgus latro) widely distributed about islands of the tropical Indian and Pacific Oceans

coconut oil noun (1838)
: a fatty oil or semisolid fat extracted from fresh coconuts and used especially in making soaps and food products

coconut palm noun (1852)
: a tall pinnate-leaved coconut-bearing palm (Cocos nucifera) that grows along tropical coasts

¹**co·coon** \kə-'kün\ noun [French cocon, from Provençal coucoun, from coco shell, probably from Latin coccum kermes (thought to be a gall or berry), from Greek kokkos berry, kermes] (1699)
1 a : an envelope often largely of silk which an insect larva forms about itself and in which it passes the pupa stage **b :** any of various other protective coverings produced by animals
2 a : a covering suggesting a cocoon **b :** a protective covering placed or sprayed over military or naval equipment in storage

²**cocoon** transitive verb (1881)
: to wrap or envelop in or as if in a cocoon

co·coon·ing \-'kü-niŋ\ noun (1987)
: the practice of spending leisure time at home in preference to going out

co·cotte \kò-kót\ noun, plural **cocottes** \-kót(s)\ [French] (1867)
1 : PROSTITUTE
2 : a shallow individual baking dish usually with one or two handles

co·co·yam \'kō-(,)kō-yam\ noun [probably coco + yam] (1922)
1 : TARO
2 : YAUTIA

co·cur·ric·u·lar \,kō-kə-'ri-kyə-lər\ adjective (1949)
: being outside of but usually complementing the regular curriculum

cod \'käd\ noun, plural **cod** also **cods** [Middle English] (14th century)
1 : any of various bottom-dwelling fishes (family Gadidae, the cod family) that usually occur in cold marine waters and often have barbels and three dorsal fins: as **a :** one (Gadus morhua) of the North Atlantic that is an important food fish **b :** one (Gadus macrocephalus) of the Pacific Ocean
2 : any of various bony fishes resembling the true cods

co·da \'kō-də\ noun [Italian, literally, tail, from Latin cauda] (circa 1753)
1 a : a concluding musical section that is formally distinct from the main structure **b :** a concluding part of a literary or dramatic work

2 : something that serves to round out, conclude, or summarize yet has its own interest

cod·dle \'kä-dᵊl\ transitive verb **cod·dled; cod·dling** \'käd-liŋ, 'kä-dᵊl-iŋ\ [perhaps from caudle] (1598)
1 : to cook (as eggs) in liquid slowly and gently just below the boiling point
2 : to treat with extreme care **:** PAMPER
— **cod·dler** \'käd-lər, 'kä-dᵊl-ər\ noun

¹**code** \'kōd\ noun [Middle English, from Middle French, from Latin caudex, codex trunk of a tree, document formed originally from wooden tablets] (14th century)
1 : a systematic statement of a body of law; especially **:** one given statutory force
2 : a system of principles or rules (moral code)
3 a : a system of signals or symbols for communication **b :** a system of symbols (as letters or numbers) used to represent assigned and often secret meanings
4 : GENETIC CODE
5 : a set of instructions for a computer
— **code·less** \-ləs\ adjective

²**code** verb **cod·ed; cod·ing** (1815)
transitive verb
: to put in or into the form or symbols of a code
intransitive verb
: to specify the genetic code (a gene that codes for a protein)
— **cod·able** \'kō-də-bəl\ adjective
— **cod·er** noun

code·book noun (1884)
: a book containing an alphabetical list of words or expressions with their code equivalents

co·deine \'kō-,dēn\ noun [French codéine, from Greek kōdeia poppyhead] (1881)
: a morphine derivative $C_{18}H_{21}NO_3 \cdot H_2O$ that is found in opium, is weaker in action than morphine, and is used especially in cough remedies

code name noun (1919)
: a designation having a secret meaning
— **code–name** \'kōd-,nām\ transitive verb

co·de·pen·dence \,kō-di-'pen-dən(t)s\ noun (1989)
: CODEPENDENCY

co·de·pen·den·cy \-dən(t)-sē\ noun (1987)
: a psychological condition or a relationship in which a person is controlled or manipulated by another who is affected with a pathological condition (as an addiction to alcohol or heroin)
— **co·de·pen·dent** \-dənt\ noun or adjective

co·de·ter·mi·na·tion \,kō-di-,tər-mə-'nā-shən\ noun (1949)
: the participation of labor with management in determining business policy

code word noun (1884)
1 : CODE NAME
2 : EUPHEMISM

co·dex \'kō-,deks\ noun, plural **co·di·ces** \'kō-də-,sēz, 'kä-\ [Latin] (1670)
: a manuscript book especially of Scripture, classics, or ancient annals

cod·fish \'käd-,fish\ noun (14th century)
: COD; also **:** its flesh used as food

cod·ger \'kä-jər\ noun [probably alteration of cadger] (1756)
: an often mildly eccentric and usually elderly fellow (old codger)

cod·i·cil \'kä-də-səl, -,sil\ noun [Middle French codicille, from Latin codicillus, diminutive of codic-, codex] (15th century)
1 : a legal instrument made to modify an earlier will
2 : APPENDIX, SUPPLEMENT
— **cod·i·cil·la·ry** \,kä-də-'si-lə-rē\ adjective

co·di·col·o·gy \,kō-də-'kä-lə-jē, ,kä-\ noun [Latin codic-, codex + -o- + English -logy] (1953)
: the study of manuscripts as cultural artifacts for historical purposes

— **co·di·co·log·i·cal** \-kə-'lä-ji-kəl\ adjective

cod·i·fy \'kä-də-,fī, 'kō-\ transitive verb **-fied; -fy·ing** (circa 1800)
1 : to reduce to a code
2 a : SYSTEMATIZE **b :** CLASSIFY
— **cod·i·fi·abil·i·ty** \,kä-də-,fī-ə-'bi-lə-tē, ,kō-\ noun
— **cod·i·fi·ca·tion** \-fə-'kā-shən\ noun

¹**cod·ling** \'käd-liŋ\ noun (13th century)
1 : a young cod
2 : any of several hakes (especially genus Urophycis)

²**cod·ling** \'käd-liŋ\ or **cod·lin** \-lən\ noun [alteration of Middle English querdlyng] (15th century)
: a small immature apple; also **:** any of several elongated greenish English cooking apples

codling moth noun (1747)
: a small tortricid moth (Cydia pomonella) having larvae that live in apples, pears, quinces, and English walnuts

cod–liver oil noun (1783)
: an oil obtained from the liver of the cod and closely related fishes and used as a source of vitamins A and D

co·dom·i·nant \,kō-'dä-mə-nənt, -'däm-nənt\ adjective (circa 1900)
1 a : forming part of the main canopy of a forest (codominant trees) **b :** sharing in the controlling influence of a biotic community
2 : being fully expressed in the heterozygous condition (codominant alleles)
— **codominant** noun

co·don \'kō-,dän\ noun [¹code + ²-on] (1963)
: a specific sequence of three consecutive nucleotides that is part of the genetic code and that specifies a particular amino acid in a protein or starts or stops protein synthesis

cod·piece \'käd-,pēs\ noun [Middle English codpese, from cod bag, scrotum (from Old English codd) + pese piece] (15th century)
: a flap or bag concealing an opening in the front of men's breeches especially in the 15th and 16th centuries

cods·wal·lop \'kädz-,wä-ləp, 'kädz-\ noun [origin unknown] (1963)
British **:** NONSENSE

¹**co·ed** \'kō-(,)ed\ adjective (1889)
1 : of or relating to a coed
2 : of or relating to coeducation
3 : open to or used by both men and women

²**coed** noun [short for coeducational student] (circa 1893)
: a student and especially a female student in a coeducational institution

co·edi·tion \,kō-ə-'di-shən\ noun (1964)
: an edition of a book published simultaneously by more than one publisher usually in different countries and in different languages

co·ed·u·ca·tion \(,)kō-,e-jə-'kā-shən\ noun (1852)
: the education of students of both sexes at the same institution
— **co·ed·u·ca·tion·al** \-shnəl, -shə-nᵊl\ adjective
— **co·ed·u·ca·tion·al·ly** adverb

co·ef·fi·cient \,kō-ə-'fi-shənt\ noun [New Latin coefficient-, coefficiens, from Latin co- + efficient-, efficiens efficient] (circa 1715)
1 : any of the factors of a product considered in relation to a specific factor; especially **:** a constant factor of a term as distinguished from a variable
2 a : a number that serves as a measure of some property or characteristic (as of a substance, device, or process) (coefficient of expansion of a metal) **b :** MEASURE

coefficient of correlation (1896)
: CORRELATION COEFFICIENT

coefficient of viscosity (1866)
: VISCOSITY 3

coe·la·canth \'sē-lə-,kan(t)th\ noun [ultimately from Greek koilos hollow + akantha spine — more at CAVE] (1857)

: any of an order (Coelacanthiformes) of lobe-finned fishes known chiefly from Paleozoic and Mesozoic fossils

coelacanth

-coele or **-coel** noun combining form [probably from New Latin *-coela*, from neuter plural of *-coelus* hollow, concave, from Greek *-koilos*, from *koilos*]
: cavity : chamber : ventricle ⟨blasto*coel*⟩ ⟨entero*coele*⟩

coe·len·ter·ate \si-'len-tə-,rāt, -rət\ noun [ultimately from Greek *koilos* + *enteron* intestine — more at INTER-] (1872)
: any of a phylum (Cnidaria synonym Coelenterata) of radially symmetrical invertebrate animals including the corals, sea anemones, jellyfishes, and hydroids — called also *cnidarian*
— **coelenterate** adjective

coe·len·ter·on \-,rän, -rən\ noun, plural **-tera** \-rə\ [New Latin, from Greek *koilos* + *enteron*] (1893)
: the internal cavity of a coelenterate

coe·li·ac \'sē-lē-,ak\ variant of CELIAC

coe·lom \'sē-ləm\ noun, plural **coeloms** or **coe·lo·ma·ta** \si-'lō-mə-tə\ [German, from Greek *koilōma* cavity, from *koilos*] (1878)
: the usually epithelium-lined space between the body wall and the digestive tract of metazoans above the lower worms
— **coe·lo·mate** \'sē-lə-,māt\ adjective or noun
— **coe·lo·mic** \si-'lä-mik, -'lō-\ adjective

coen- or **coeno-** combining form [New Latin, from Greek *koin-, koino-*, from *koinos*]
: common : general ⟨*coeno*cyte⟩

coe·no·bite \'sē-nə-,bīt\ variant of CENOBITE

coe·no·cyte \'sē-nə-,sīt\ noun [International Scientific Vocabulary] (1897)
1 a : a multinucleate mass of protoplasm resulting from repeated nuclear division unaccompanied by cell fission **b** : an organism consisting of such a structure
2 : SYNCYTIUM 1
— **coe·no·cyt·ic** \,sē-nə-'si-tik\ adjective

coe·nu·rus \si-'nùr-əs, -'nyùr-\ noun, plural **-nu·ri** \-,ī\ [New Latin, from *coen-* + Greek *oura* tail] (1876)
: a complex tapeworm larva consisting of a sac from the inner wall of which numerous scolices develop

co·en·zyme \(,)kō-'en-,zīm\ noun (1908)
: a thermostable nonprotein compound that forms the active portion of an enzyme system after combination with an apoenzyme
— **co·en·zy·mat·ic** \(,)kō-,en-zə-'ma-tik, -(,)zī-\ adjective
— **co·en·zy·mat·i·cal·ly** \-ti-k(ə-)lē\ adverb

coenzyme A noun (1949)
: a coenzyme $C_{21}H_{36}N_7O_{16}P_3S$ that occurs in all living cells and is essential to the metabolism of carbohydrates, fats, and some amino acids — compare ACETYL COENZYME A

coenzyme Q noun (1958)
: UBIQUINONE

co·equal \(,)kō-'ē-kwəl\ adjective (14th century)
: equal with one another
— **coequal** noun
— **co·equal·i·ty** \,kō-ē-'kwä-lə-tē\ noun
— **co·equal·ly** \(,)kō-'ē-kwə-lē\ adverb

co·erce \kō-'ərs\ transitive verb **co·erced; co·erc·ing** [Latin *coercēre*, from *co-* + *arcēre* to shut up, enclose — more at ARK] (15th century)
1 : to restrain or dominate by force ⟨religion in the past has tried to *coerce* the irreligious —W. R. Inge⟩
2 : to compel to an act or choice
3 : to bring about by force or threat ⟨*coerce*

the compliance of the rest of the community —Scott Buchanan⟩
synonym see FORCE
— **co·erc·ible** \-'ər-sə-bəl\ adjective

co·er·cion \-'ər-zhən, -shən\ noun (15th century)
: the act, process, or power of coercing

co·er·cive \-'ər-siv\ adjective (circa 1600)
: serving or intended to coerce
— **co·er·cive·ly** adverb
— **co·er·cive·ness** noun

coercive force noun (1827)
: the opposing magnetic intensity that must be applied to a magnetized material to remove the residual magnetism

co·er·civ·i·ty \,kō-,ər-'si-və-tē\ noun (1898)
: the property of a material determined by the value of the coercive force when the material has been magnetized to saturation

co·e·ta·ne·ous \,kō-ə-'tā-nē-əs\ adjective [Latin *coaetaneus*, from *co-* + *aetas* age — more at AGE] (1608)
: COEVAL

co·eval \kō-'ē-vəl\ adjective [Latin *coaevus*, from *co-* + *aevum* age, lifetime — more at AYE] (circa 1662)
: of the same or equal age, antiquity, or duration
synonym see CONTEMPORARY
— **coeval** noun
— **co·e·val·i·ty** \,kō-(,)ē-'va-lə-tē\ noun

co·evo·lu·tion \,kō-,e-və-'lü-shən also -,ē-və-\ noun (1965)
: evolution involving successive changes in two or more ecologically interdependent species (as of a plant and its pollinators) that affect their interactions
— **co·evo·lu·tion·ary** \-shə-,ner-ē\ adjective
— **co·evolve** \,kō-i-'välv, -'vólv\ intransitive verb

co·ex·ist \,kō-ig-'zist\ intransitive verb (1667)
1 : to exist together or at the same time
2 : to live in peace with each other especially as a matter of policy
— **co·ex·is·tence** \-'zis-tən(t)s\ noun
— **co·ex·is·tent** \-tənt\ adjective

co·ex·ten·sive \,kō-ik-'sten(t)-siv\ adjective (1771)
: having the same spatial or temporal scope or boundaries
— **co·ex·ten·sive·ly** adverb

co·fac·tor \'kō-,fak-tər\ noun (circa 1909)
1 : the signed minor of an element of a square matrix or of a determinant with the sign positive if the sum of the column number and row number of the element is even and with the sign negative if it is odd
2 : a substance that acts with another substance to bring about certain effects; *especially* : COENZYME

cof·fee \'kó-fē, 'kä-\ noun, often attributive [Italian & Turkish; Italian *caffè*, from Turkish *kahve*, from Arabic *qahwa*] (1598)
1 a : a beverage made by percolation, infusion, or decoction from the roasted and ground seeds of the coffee plant **b** : any of several Old World tropical plants (genus *Coffea* and especially *C. arabica* and *C. canephora*) of the madder family that are widely cultivated in warm regions for their seeds from which coffee is prepared **c** : coffee seeds especially roasted and often ground — compare ARABICA, ROBUSTA **d** : a dehydrated product made from brewed coffee ⟨instant *coffee*⟩; *also* : a beverage made from this
2 : a cup of coffee ⟨two *coffees*⟩
3 : COFFEE HOUR

coffee 1b

coffee break noun (1951)
: a short period for rest and refreshments

coffee cake noun (1879)
: a sweet rich bread often with added fruit, nuts, and spices that is sometimes glazed after baking

coffee hour noun (1952)
1 : a usually fixed occasion of informal meeting and chatting at which refreshments are served
2 : COFFEE BREAK

cof·fee·house \-,haùs\ noun (1612)
: an establishment that sells coffee and usually other refreshments and that commonly serves as an informal club for its regular customers

coffee klatch also **cof·fee–klatsch** \-,klach, -,kläch, -,klạch\ noun [part translation of German *Kaffeeklatsch*] (1895)
: KAFFEEKLATSCH

cof·fee·mak·er \-,mā-kər\ noun (1930)
: a utensil or appliance in which coffee is brewed

coffee mill noun (1691)
: a mill for grinding coffee beans

cof·fee·pot \-,pät\ noun (1704)
: a pot for brewing and serving coffee

coffee ring noun (1924)
: coffee cake in the shape of a ring

coffee roll noun (1945)
: a sweet roll

coffee room noun (1712)
: a room where refreshments are served

coffee royal noun (1921)
: a drink of black coffee and a liquor

coffee shop noun (1836)
: a small restaurant

coffee–table adjective (1962)
: of, relating to, or being an article (as a book or magazine) intended for display (as on a coffee table)

coffee table noun (1877)
: a low table customarily placed in front of a sofa — called also *cocktail table*

coffee tree noun (1741)
1 : a tree (as *arabica*) that produces coffee
2 : KENTUCKY COFFEE TREE

¹cof·fer \'kó-fər, 'kä-\ noun [Middle English *coffre*, from Old French, from Latin *cophinus* basket, from Greek *kophinos*] (13th century)
1 : CHEST, BOX; *especially* : STRONGBOX
2 : TREASURY — usually used in plural
3 : a recessed panel in a vault, ceiling, or soffit

²coffer transitive verb (14th century)
1 : to store or hoard up in a coffer
2 : to form (as a ceiling) with recessed panels

cof·fer·dam \-,dam\ noun (1736)
1 : a watertight enclosure from which water is pumped to expose the bottom of a body of water and permit construction (as of a pier)
2 : a watertight structure for making repairs below the waterline of a ship

¹cof·fin \'kó-fən\ noun [Middle English, basket, receptacle, from Middle French *cofin*, from Latin *cophinus*] (1525)
: a box or chest for burying a corpse

²coffin transitive verb (1564)
: to enclose in or as if in a coffin

coffin bone noun (circa 1720)
: the principal bone enclosed within the hoof of a horse — called also *pedal bone*

coffin corner noun (1940)
: one of the corners formed by a goal line and a sideline on a football field into which a punt is often aimed so that it may go out of bounds close to the defender's goal line

coffin nail noun (1888)
slang : CIGARETTE

cof·fle \'kó-fəl, 'kä-\ noun [Arabic *qāfila* caravan] (1799)

\ə\ abut	\ə\ kitten	\ər\ further	\a\ ash	\ā\ ace	
\ä\ mop, mar	\au\ out	\ch\ chin	\e\ bet	\ē\ easy	
\g\ go	\i\ hit	\ī\ ice	\j\ job	\ŋ\ sing	\ō\ go
\ó\ law	\ói\ boy	\th\ thin	\th\ the	\ü\ loot	\ù\ foot
\y\ yet	\zh\ vision	see also Guide to Pronunciation			

: a train of slaves or animals fastened together

co·func·tion \'kō-ˌfəŋ(k)-shən\ *noun* (1909)
: a trigonometric function whose value for the complement of an angle is equal to the value of a given trigonometric function of the angle itself ⟨the sine is the *cofunction* of the cosine⟩

¹**cog** \'käg\ *noun* [Middle English *cogge*, of Scandinavian origin; akin to Norwegian *kug* cog] (13th century)
1 : a tooth on the rim of a wheel or gear
2 : a subordinate but vital person or part
— **cogged** \'kägd\ *adjective*

²**cog** *verb* **cogged; cog·ging** [obsolete *cog* a trick] (1532)
intransitive verb
1 *obsolete* : to cheat in throwing dice
2 *obsolete* : DECEIVE
3 *obsolete* : to use venal flattery
transitive verb
1 : to direct the fall of (dice) fraudulently
2 *obsolete* : WHEEDLE

³**cog** *transitive verb* **cogged; cog·ging** [probably alteration of *cock* to cog] (1823)
: to connect (as timbers or joists) by means of mortises and tenons

⁴**cog** *noun* (circa 1858)
: a tenon on a beam or timber

co·gen·cy \'kō-jən(t)-sē\ *noun* (1667)
: the quality or state of being cogent

co·gen·er·a·tion \ˌkō-ˌje-nə-'rā-shən\ *noun* (1978)
: the production of electricity using waste heat (as in steam) from an industrial process or the use of steam from electric power generation as a source of heat
— **co·gen·er·a·tor** \-'je-nə-ˌrā-tər\ *noun*

co·gent \'kō-jənt\ *adjective* [Latin *cogent-, cogens*, present participle of *cogere* to drive together, collect, from *co- + agere* to drive — more at AGENT] (1659)
1 : having power to compel or constrain ⟨*cogent* forces⟩
2 a : appealing forcibly to the mind or reason : CONVINCING ⟨*cogent* evidence⟩ **b** : PERTINENT, RELEVANT ⟨a *cogent* analysis of a problem⟩
synonym see VALID
— **co·gent·ly** *adverb*

cog·i·ta·ble \'kä-jə-tə-bəl\ *adjective* (15th century)
: CONCEIVABLE, THINKABLE

cog·i·tate \'kä-jə-ˌtāt\ *verb* **-tat·ed; -tat·ing** [Latin *cogitatus*, past participle of *cogitare* to think, think about, from *co- + agitare* to drive, agitate] (circa 1587)
transitive verb
: to ponder or meditate on usually intently
intransitive verb
: to meditate deeply or intently
synonym see THINK

cog·i·ta·tion \ˌkä-jə-'tā-shən\ *noun* (13th century)
1 a : the act of cogitating : MEDITATION **b** : the capacity to think or reflect
2 : a single thought

cog·i·ta·tive \'kä-jə-ˌtā-tiv\ *adjective* (15th century)
1 : of or relating to cogitation
2 : capable of or given to cogitation

co·gi·to \'kä-gi-ˌtō, 'kō-, 'kä-ji-\ *noun* [New Latin *cogito, ergo sum*, literally, I think, therefore I am, principle stated by René Descartes] (1838)
1 : the philosophic principle that one's existence is demonstrated by the fact that one thinks
2 : the intellectual processes of the self or ego

co·gnac \'kōn-ˌyak *also* 'kòn- *or* 'kän-\ *noun* [French, from *Cognac*, France] (1755)
: a brandy from the departments of Charente and Charente-Maritime distilled from white wine

¹**cog·nate** \'käg-ˌnāt\ *adjective* [Latin *cognatus*, from *co- + gnatus, natus*, past participle of *nasci* to be born; akin to Latin *gignere* to beget — more at KIN] (circa 1645)

1 : of the same or similar nature : generically alike
2 : related by blood; *also* : related on the mother's side
3 a : related by descent from the same ancestral language **b** *of a word or morpheme* : related by derivation, borrowing, or descent **c** *of a substantive* : related to a verb usually by derivation and serving as its object to reinforce the meaning
— **cog·nate·ly** *adverb*

²**cognate** *noun* (1754)
: one that is cognate with another

cog·na·tion \käg-'nā-shən\ *noun* (14th century)
: cognate relationship

cog·ni·tion \käg-'ni-shən\ *noun* [Middle English *cognicioun*, from Latin *cognition-, cognitio*, from *cognoscere* to become acquainted with, know, from *co- + gnoscere* to come to know — more at KNOW] (15th century)
: the act or process of knowing including both awareness and judgment; *also* : a product of this act
— **cog·ni·tion·al** \-'nish-nəl, -'ni-shə-nᵊl\ *adjective*

cog·ni·tive \'käg-nə-tiv\ *adjective* (1586)
1 : of, relating to, or involving cognition ⟨the *cognitive* elements of perception —C. H. Hamburg⟩
2 : based on or capable of being reduced to empirical factual knowledge
— **cog·ni·tive·ly** *adverb*

cognitive dissonance *noun* (1957)
: psychological conflict resulting from incongruous beliefs and attitudes held simultaneously

cognitive science *noun* (1976)
: an interdisciplinary science that draws on many fields (as psychology, artificial intelligence, linguistics, and philosophy) in developing theories about human perception, thinking, and learning

cog·ni·za·ble \'käg-nə-zə-bəl, käg-'nī-\ *adjective* (1678)
1 : capable of being known
2 : capable of being judicially heard and determined
— **cog·ni·za·bly** \-blē\ *adverb*

cog·ni·zance \'käg-nə-zən(t)s\ *noun* [Middle English *conisaunce*, from Middle French *conoissance*, from *conoistre* to know, from Latin *cognoscere*] (14th century)
1 : a distinguishing mark or emblem (as a heraldic bearing)
2 a : KNOWLEDGE, AWARENESS ⟨had no *cognizance* of the situation⟩ **b** : NOTICE, ACKNOWLEDGMENT ⟨take *cognizance* of their achievement⟩
3 : JURISDICTION, RESPONSIBILITY

cog·ni·zant \-zənt\ *adjective* (1820)
: knowledgeable of something especially through personal experience; *also* : MINDFUL
synonym see AWARE

cog·nize \käg-'nīz, 'käg-ˌ\ *transitive verb* **cog·nized; cog·niz·ing** [back-formation from *cognizance*] (circa 1837)
: KNOW, UNDERSTAND
— **cog·niz·er** *noun*

cog·no·men \käg-'nō-mən, 'käg-nə-\ *noun*, *plural* **cognomens** *or* **cog·no·mi·na** \käg-'nä-mə-nə, -'nō-\ [Latin, irregular from *co- + nomen* name — more at NAME] (1809)
1 : SURNAME; *especially* : the third of usually three names borne by a male citizen of ancient Rome
2 : NAME; *especially* : a distinguishing nickname or epithet
— **cog·nom·i·nal** \käg-'nä-mə-nᵊl\ *adjective*

cog·no·scen·te \ˌkän-yə-'shen-tē, ˌkäg-nə-, -'sen-\ *noun*, *plural* **-scen·ti** \-tē\ [obsolete Italian (now *conoscente*), from *cognoscente*, adjective, wise, from Latin *cognoscent-, cognoscens*, present participle of *cognoscere*] (1776)

: a person who is especially knowledgeable in a subject : CONNOISSEUR

cog·nos·ci·ble \käg-'nä-sə-bəl\ *adjective* [Late Latin *cognoscibilis*, from Latin *cognoscere*] (circa 1644)
: COGNIZABLE, KNOWABLE

co·gon \kō-'gōn\ *noun* [Spanish *cogón*, from Tagalog & Bisayan *kugon*] (1898)
: any of several coarse tall grasses (genus *Imperata*) used especially in the Philippines for thatching

cog railway *noun* (1896)
: a steep mountain railroad that has a rail with cogs engaged by a cogwheel on the locomotive to ensure traction

cog·wheel \'käg-ˌhwēl, -ˌwēl\ *noun* (14th century)
: a wheel with cogs : GEAR 6a(2)

co·hab·it \(ˌ)kō-'ha-bət\ *intransitive verb* [Late Latin *cohabitare*, from Latin *co- + habitare* to inhabit, from frequentative of *habēre* to have — more at GIVE] (circa 1530)
1 : to live together as or as if a married couple
2 a : to live together or in company ⟨buffaloes *cohabiting* with crossbred cows —*Biological Abstracts*⟩ **b** : to exist together ⟨two strains in his philosophy . . . *cohabit* in each of his major works —Justus Buchler⟩
— **co·hab·i·tant** \-bə-tənt\ *noun*
— **co·hab·i·ta·tion** \(ˌ)kō-ˌha-bə-'tā-shən\ *noun*

co·here \kō-'hir\ *verb* **co·hered; co·her·ing** [Latin *cohaerēre*, from *co- + haerēre* to stick] (1598)
intransitive verb
1 a : to hold together firmly as parts of the same mass; *broadly* : STICK, ADHERE **b** : to display cohesion of plant parts
2 : to hold together as a mass of parts that cohere
3 a : to become united in principles, relationships, or interests **b** : to be logically or aesthetically consistent
transitive verb
: to cause (parts or components) to cohere
synonym see STICK

co·her·ence \kō-'hir-ən(t)s, -'her-\ *noun* (1580)
1 : the quality or state of cohering: as **a** : systematic or logical connection or consistency **b** : integration of diverse elements, relationships, or values
2 : the property of being coherent

co·her·en·cy \kō-'hir-ən(t)-sē, -'her-\ *noun*, *plural* **-cies** (1630)
: COHERENCE

co·her·ent \-ənt\ *adjective* [Middle French or Latin; Middle French *cohérent*, from Latin *cohaerent-, cohaerens*, present participle of *cohaerēre*] (circa 1555)
1 a : logically or aesthetically ordered or integrated : CONSISTENT ⟨*coherent* style⟩ ⟨a *coherent* argument⟩ **b** : having clarity or intelligibility : UNDERSTANDABLE ⟨a *coherent* person⟩ ⟨a *coherent* passage⟩
2 : having the quality of cohering; *especially* : COHESIVE, COORDINATED ⟨a *coherent* plan for action⟩
3 a : relating to or composed of waves having a constant difference in phase ⟨*coherent* light⟩ **b** : producing coherent light ⟨a *coherent* source⟩
— **co·her·ent·ly** *adverb*

co·her·er \kō-'hir-ər\ *noun* (1894)
: a radio detector in which an imperfectly conducting contact between pieces of conductive material loosely resting against each other is materially improved in conductance by the passage of high-frequency current

co·he·sion \kō-'hē-zhən\ *noun* [Latin *cohaesus*, past participle of *cohaerēre*] (1660)
1 : the act or state of sticking together tightly; *especially* : UNITY ⟨the lack of *cohesion* in the Party —*Times Literary Supplement*⟩
2 : union between similar plant parts or organs

3 : molecular attraction by which the particles of a body are united throughout the mass
— **co·he·sion·less** \-ləs\ *adjective*
co·he·sive \kō-'hē-siv, -ziv\ *adjective* (circa 1731)
: exhibiting or producing cohesion or coherence ⟨a *cohesive* social unit⟩ ⟨*cohesive* soils⟩
— **co·he·sive·ly** *adverb*
— **co·he·sive·ness** *noun*
co·ho \'kō-(,)hō\ *noun, plural* **cohos** *or* **coho** [Halkomelem (Salishan language of southwest British Columbia) kʷáxʷəθ] (1869)
: a rather small Pacific salmon (*Oncorhynchus kisutch*) that has light-colored flesh and is native to both coasts of the North Pacific and is stocked in the Great Lakes
co·ho·mol·o·gy \(,)kō-hō-'mä-lə-jē\ *noun* (circa 1959)
: a part of the theory of topology in which groups are used to study the properties of topological spaces and which is related in a complementary way to homology theory — called also *cohomology theory*
— **co·ho·mo·log·i·cal** \-,hō-mə-'lä-ji-kəl, -,hä-\ *adjective*
co·hort \'kō-,hòrt\ *noun* [Middle French & Latin; Middle French *cohorte*, from Latin *cohort-, cohors* — more at COURT] (15th century)
1 a : one of 10 divisions of an ancient Roman legion **b :** a group of warriors or soldiers **c :** BAND, GROUP **d :** a group of individuals having a statistical factor (as age or class membership) in common in a demographic study ⟨a *cohort* of premedical students⟩
2 : COMPANION, COLLEAGUE ⟨a few of their . . . *cohorts* decided to form a company —Burt Hochberg⟩ □
co·hosh \'kō-,häsh\ *noun* [Eastern Abenaki kkʷàhas] (1789)
: any of several American medicinal or poisonous plants: as **a :** BLACK COHOSH **b :** BLUE COHOSH **c :** BANEBERRY
¹coif \'kòif, *in sense 2 also* 'kwäf\ *noun* [Middle English *coife*, from Middle French, from Late Latin *cofea*] (14th century)
1 : a close-fitting cap: as **a :** a hoodlike cap worn under a veil by nuns **b :** a protective usually metal skullcap formerly worn under a hood of mail **c :** a white cap formerly worn by English lawyers and especially by serjeants-at-law; *also* **:** the order or rank of a serjeant-at-law
2 : COIFFURE
²coif \'kòif, 'kwäf\ *transitive verb* **coiffed** *or* **coifed; coif·fing** *or* **coif·ing** (15th century)
1 : to cover or dress with or as if with a coif
2 : to arrange (hair) by brushing, combing, or curling
coif·feur \kwä-'fər\ *noun* [French, from *coiffer*] (1847)
: a man who is a hairdresser
coif·feuse \kwä-'fə(r)z, -'fyüz, -'füz\ *noun* [French, feminine of *coiffeur*] (1870)
: a woman who is a hairdresser
coif·fure \kwä-'fyùr\ *noun* [French, from *coiffer* to cover with a coif, arrange (hair), from *coife*] (circa 1631)
: a style or manner of arranging the hair
coif·fured \-'fyùrd\ *adjective* (1907)
1 : being dressed ⟨beautifully *coiffured* hair⟩
2 : having the hair brushed, combed, and curled ⟨stylishly *coiffured* women⟩
coign of van·tage \,kòi-nə-'van-tij\ [*coign*, earlier spelling of ¹*coin* (corner)] (1605)
: an advantageous position
¹coil \'kòi(ə)l\ *noun* [origin unknown] (1567)
1 : TURMOIL
2 : TROUBLE; *also* **:** everyday cares and worries ⟨when we have shuffled off this mortal *coil* —Shakespeare⟩
²coil *verb* [French *coillir, cuillir* to gather — more at CULL] (1611)
transitive verb

1 : to wind into rings or spirals
2 : to roll or twist into a shape resembling a coil
intransitive verb
1 : to move in a circular or spiral course
2 : to form or lie in a coil
— **coil·abil·i·ty** \,kòi-lə-'bi-lə-tē\ *noun*
³coil *noun* (1627)
1 a (1) **:** a series of loops (2) **:** SPIRAL **b :** a single loop of such a coil
2 a : a number of turns of wire wound around a core (as of iron) to create a magnetic field for an electromagnet or an induction coil **b :** INDUCTION COIL
3 : a series of connected pipes in rows, layers, or windings
4 : a roll of postage stamps; *also* **:** a stamp from such a roll
¹coin \'kòin\ *noun* [Middle English, from Middle French, wedge, corner, from Latin *cuneus* wedge] (14th century)
1 *archaic* **a :** CORNER, CORNERSTONE, QUOIN **:** WEDGE
2 a : a usually flat piece of metal issued by governmental authority as money **b :** metal money **c :** something resembling a coin especially in shape
3 : something used as if it were money (as in verbal or intellectual exchange) ⟨perhaps wisecracks . . . are respectable literary *coin* in the U.S. —*Times Literary Supplement*⟩ ⟨would repay him with the full *coin* of his mind —Ian Fleming⟩
4 : something having two different and usually opposing sides — usually used in the phrase *the other side of the coin*
5 : MONEY ⟨I'm in it for the *coin* —Sinclair Lewis⟩
²coin *transitive verb* (14th century)
1 a : to make (a coin) especially by stamping **:** MINT **b :** to convert (metal) into coins
2 : CREATE, INVENT ⟨*coin* a phrase⟩
— **coin·er** \'kòi-nər\ *noun*
— **coin money :** to get rich quickly
³coin *adjective* (circa 1566)
1 : of or relating to coins
2 : operated by coins
coin·age \'kòi-nij\ *noun* (14th century)
1 : the act or process of coining
2 a : COINS **b :** something (as a word) made up or invented
co·in·cide \,kō-ən-'sīd, 'kō-ən-,\ *intransitive verb* **-cid·ed; -cid·ing** [Medieval Latin *coincidere*, from Latin *co- + incidere* to fall on, from *in- + cadere* to fall — more at CHANCE] (1719)
1 a : to occupy the same place in space or time **b :** to occupy exactly corresponding or equivalent positions on a scale or in a series
2 : to correspond in nature, character, or function
3 : to be in accord or agreement **:** CONCUR
synonym see AGREE
co·in·ci·dence \kō-'in(t)-sə-dən(t)s, -sə-,den(t)s\ *noun* (1605)
1 : the act or condition of coinciding **:** CORRESPONDENCE
2 : the occurrence of events that happen at the same time by accident but seem to have some connection; *also* **:** any of these occurrences
co·in·ci·dent \-sə-dənt, -,dent\ *adjective* [French *coincident*, from Medieval Latin *coincident-, coincidens*, present participle of *coincidere*] (circa 1587)
1 : of similar nature **:** HARMONIOUS ⟨a theory *coincident* with the facts⟩
2 : occupying the same space or time ⟨*coincident* events⟩
synonym see CONTEMPORARY
— **co·in·ci·dent·ly** \-sə-dənt-lē, -,dent-; (,)kō-,in(t)-sə-'dent-lē\ *adverb*
co·in·ci·den·tal \(,)kō-,in(t)-sə-'dent-ᵊl\ *adjective* (circa 1800)
1 : resulting from a coincidence
2 : occurring or existing at the same time

— **co·in·ci·den·tal·ly** \-'dent-lē, -'den-t°l-ē\ *adverb*
coin–op \'kòin-,näp\ *noun* (1961)
: a self-service laundry where the machines are operated by coins
co·in·sur·ance \,kō-ən-'shùr-ən(t)s *also* -'in-,\ *noun* (circa 1889)
1 : joint assumption of risk (as by two underwriters) with another
2 : insurance (as fire insurance) in which the insured is obligated to maintain coverage on a risk at a stipulated percentage of its total value or in the event of loss suffer a penalty in proportion to the deficiency
co·in·sure \,kō-ən-'shùr\ *transitive verb* (circa 1899)
: to insure jointly
— **co·in·sur·er** *noun*
coir \'kòi(-ə)r\ *noun* [Tamil *kayiru* rope] (1582)
: a stiff coarse fiber from the outer husk of a coconut
cois·trel \'kòi-strəl\ *noun* [Middle French *coustillier* soldier carrying a short sword, from *coustille* short sword, from Latin *cultellus* knife — more at CUTLASS] (1581)
archaic **:** a mean fellow **:** VARLET
co·i·tion \kō-'i-shən\ *noun* [Late Latin, from Latin *coition-, coitio* a coming together, from *coire* to come together, from *co- + ire* to go — more at ISSUE] (1615)
: COITUS
— **co·i·tion·al** \-'ish-nəl, -'i-shə-nᵊl\ *adjective*
co·i·tus \'kō-ə-təs, kō-'ē-, 'kòi-təs\ *noun* [Latin, from *coire*] (1855)
: physical union of male and female genitalia accompanied by rhythmic movements usually leading to the ejaculation of semen from the

□ **USAGE**
cohort Sense 2 is an American development with a curious history. The first extension of the meaning of *cohort* was from the Roman army to other armies ⟨the Assyrian came down like the wolf on the fold, and his *cohorts* were gleaming in purple and gold —Lord Byron⟩. Then the word was extended to any group or band ⟨Harry, with a loyal *cohort* of adherents, forcibly barred his entrance —S. N. Behrman⟩. This sense could also be used in the plural ⟨Dr. Mossadegh and his *cohorts* nationalized the British-owned oil concession in southern Iran —*N. Y. Times*⟩. On reflection, it would seem clear that these cohorts are large and probably organized bands, but the word can easily be read as meaning "followers." Some uses could seem even more ambiguous ⟨as Carrie Nation and her *cohorts* swarmed forward and pounded the panels —Herbert Asbury⟩. Here evidently a mob scene is being described, a far cry from the disciplined Roman army units. And again *cohorts* can readily be interpreted as "friends, followers." It is presumably from uses like these that our sense 2 developed ⟨formulated a second constitution which virtually restricted the suffrage to the freedmen and their white *cohorts* —*Dictionary of American History*⟩ ⟨had left, accompanied by two of his *cohorts* —Mary McCarthy⟩. Sense 2 was becoming established in the 1940s, and ten years or so later some critics began to notice it disapprovingly. Disapproval came too late, though, for by then the sense was well established as standard—at least in American English—and it is standard now.

penis into the female reproductive tract; *also*
: INTERCOURSE 3 — compare ORGASM
— **co·i·tal** \-t³l\ *adjective*
— **co·i·tal·ly** \-t³l-ē\ *adverb*
coitus in·ter·rup·tus \-,in-tə-'rəp-təs\ *noun*
[New Latin, interrupted coitus] (1900)
: coitus in which the penis is withdrawn prior
to ejaculation to prevent the deposit of sperm
into the vagina
¹**coke** \'kōk\ *noun* [perhaps from dialect *coke,
colk* core, from Middle English; akin to Swedish *kälk* pith] (1669)
: the residue of coal left after destructive distillation and used as fuel; *also* **:** a similar residue left by other materials (as petroleum) distilled to dryness
²**coke** *verb* **coked; cok·ing** (1763)
transitive verb
: to change into coke
intransitive verb
: to become coke or like coke
³**coke** *noun* [by shortening & alteration] (circa 1903)
: COCAINE
Coke \'kōk\ *trademark*
— used for a cola drink
coke·head \'kō-ked, 'kōk-,hed\ *noun* (circa 1927)
: a person who uses cocaine compulsively
col \'käl\ *noun* [French, from Middle French, neck, from Latin *collum*] (1853)
: SADDLE 3
¹**col-** — see COM-
²**col-** *or* **coli-** *or* **colo-** *combining form* [New Latin, from Latin *colon*]
1 : colon ⟨*colitis*⟩ ⟨*colostomy*⟩
2 [New Latin *Escherichia coli*, species of colon bacillus] **:** colon bacillus ⟨*coliform*⟩
¹**cola** *plural of* COLON
²**co·la** \'kō-lə\ *noun* [from *Coca-Cola,* a trademark] (1920)
: a carbonated soft drink colored usually with caramel and flavored usually with extracts from kola nuts
col·an·der \'käl-ən-dər, 'kəl-\ *noun* [Middle English *colyndore,* probably modification of Old Provençal *colador,* from Medieval Latin *colatorium,* from Latin *colare* to sieve, from *colum* sieve] (14th century)
: a perforated utensil for washing or draining food
co·lat·i·tude \(,)kō-'la-tə-,tüd, -,tyüd\ *noun* (1790)
: the complement of the latitude
Col·by \'kōl-bē\ *noun* [probably from the name *Colby*] (1942)
: a moist mild cheese similar to cheddar
col·can·non \käl-'ka-nən\ *noun* [Irish *cál ceannan,* literally, white-headed cabbage] (circa 1785)
: potatoes and cabbage boiled and mashed together with butter and seasoning
col·chi·cine \'käl-chə-,sēn, 'käl-kə-\ *noun* (circa 1847)
: a poisonous alkaloid $C_{22}H_{25}NO_6$ that inhibits mitosis, is extracted from the corms or seeds of the autumn crocus (*Colchicum autumnale*), and is used especially in the treatment of gout and to produce polyploidy in plants
col·chi·cum \'käl-chi-kəm, 'käl-ki-\ *noun* [New Latin, genus name, from Latin, a kind of plant with a poisonous root, from Greek *kolchikon,* literally, product of Colchis] (1597)
1 : any of a genus (*Colchicum*) of Old World corm-producing herbs of the lily family with flowers that resemble crocuses
2 : the dried corm or dried seeds of autumn crocus containing colchicine, possessing emetic, diuretic, and cathartic action, and used to treat gout
¹**cold** \'kōld\ *adjective* [Middle English, from Old English *ceald, cald;* akin to Old High German *kalt* cold, Latin *gelu* frost, *gelare* to freeze] (before 12th century)
1 a : having or being a temperature that is uncomfortably low for humans ⟨it is *cold* outside

today⟩ **b :** having a relatively low temperature or one lower than normal or expected ⟨the bath water has gotten *cold*⟩ **c :** not heated: as **(1)** *of food* **:** served without heating especially after initial cooking or processing ⟨*cold* cereal⟩ ⟨*cold* roast beef⟩ **(2) :** served chilled or with ice ⟨a *cold* drink⟩ **(3) :** involving processing without the use of heat ⟨*cold* working of steel⟩
2 a : marked by a lack of the warmth of normal human emotion, friendliness, or compassion ⟨got a *cold* reception⟩; *also* **:** not moved to enthusiasm ⟨the movie leaves me *cold*⟩ **b :** not colored or affected by personal feeling or bias **:** DETACHED, INDIFFERENT ⟨*cold* chronicles recorded by an outsider —Andrew Sarris⟩; *also* **:** IMPERSONAL, OBJECTIVE ⟨*cold* facts⟩ ⟨*cold* reality⟩ **c :** marked by sure familiarity **:** PAT ⟨had her lines *cold* weeks before opening night⟩
3 : conveying the impression of being cold: as **a :** DEPRESSING, GLOOMY ⟨*cold* gray skies⟩ **b :** COOL 6a
4 a : marked by the loss of normal body heat ⟨*cold* hands⟩; *especially* **:** DEAD **b :** giving the appearance of being dead **:** UNCONSCIOUS ⟨passed out *cold*⟩
5 a : having lost freshness or vividness **:** STALE ⟨dogs trying to pick up a *cold* scent⟩ **b :** far off the mark **:** not close to finding or solving — used especially in children's games **c :** marked by poor or unlucky performance ⟨the team's shooting turned *cold* in the second half⟩ **d :** not prepared or suitably warmed up
— **cold·ish** \'kōl-dish\ *adjective*
— **cold·ly** \'kōl(d)-lē\ *adverb*
— **cold·ness** \'kōl(d)-nəs\ *noun*
— **in cold blood :** with premeditation **:** DELIBERATELY
²**cold** *noun* (13th century)
1 : bodily sensation produced by loss or lack of heat
2 : a condition of low temperature; *especially* **:** cold weather
3 : a bodily disorder popularly associated with chilling; *specifically* **:** COMMON COLD
— **out in the cold :** deprived of benefits given others ⟨the plan benefits management but leaves labor *out in the cold*⟩
³**cold** *adverb* (1889)
1 : with utter finality **:** ABSOLUTELY, COMPLETELY ⟨turned down *cold*⟩; *also* **:** ABRUPTLY ⟨stopped them *cold*⟩
2 a : without introduction or advance notice **b :** without preparation or warm-up
cold-blood·ed \'kōl(d)-'blə-dəd\ *adjective* (1595)
1 a : done or acting without consideration, compunction, or clemency ⟨*cold-blooded* murder⟩ **b :** MATTER-OF-FACT, EMOTIONLESS ⟨a *cold-blooded* assessment⟩
2 : having cold blood; *specifically* **:** having a body temperature not internally regulated but approximating that of the environment
3 *or* **cold-blood** \-'bləd\ **:** of mixed or inferior breeding
4 : noticeably sensitive to cold
— **cold-blood·ed·ly** *adverb*
— **cold-blood·ed·ness** *noun*
cold call *noun* (1966)
: a telephone call soliciting business made directly to a potential customer without prior contact or without a lead
— **cold-call** *verb*
cold cash *noun* (1925)
: money in hand
cold chisel *noun* (1699)
: a chisel made of tool steel of a strength, shape, and temper suitable for chipping or cutting cold metal
cold·cock \'kōl(d)-'käk, ,kōl(d)-\ *transitive verb* [perhaps ²*cock*] (circa 1927)
: to knock unconscious
cold comfort *noun* (14th century)
: quite limited sympathy, consolation, or encouragement

cold cream *noun* (1709)
: a soothing and cleansing cosmetic
cold cuts *noun plural* (1945)
: sliced assorted cold cooked meats
cold duck *noun* [translation of German *Kalte Ente*] (1969)
: a beverage that consists of a blend of sparkling burgundy and champagne
cold-eyed \'kōl-'dīd, -,dīd\ *adjective* (1950)
: cold in manner or appearance; *especially* **:** coolly dispassionate ⟨*cold-eyed* analysis⟩
cold feet *noun plural* (1893)
: apprehension or doubt strong enough to prevent a planned course of action
cold fish *noun* (1924)
: a cold aloof person
cold frame *noun* (1851)
: a usually glass- or plastic-covered frame without artificial heat used to protect plants and seedlings outdoors

cold frame

cold front *noun* (1921)
: an advancing edge of a cold air mass
cold-heart·ed \'kōld-'här-təd\ *adjective* (1606)
: marked by lack of sympathy, interest, or sensitivity
— **cold-heart·ed·ly** *adverb*
— **cold-heart·ed·ness** *noun*
cold shoulder *noun* (1816)
: intentionally cold or unsympathetic treatment
— **cold-shoulder** *transitive verb*
cold sore *noun* (circa 1889)
: a group of blisters appearing about or within the mouth and caused by a herpes simplex virus
cold storage *noun* (1877)
1 : storage (as of food) in a cold place for preservation
2 : a condition of being held or continued without being acted on **:** ABEYANCE
cold store *noun* (1895)
: a building for cold storage
cold sweat *noun* (1706)
: concurrent perspiration and chill usually associated with fear, pain, or shock
¹**cold turkey** *noun* (1921)
1 : abrupt complete cessation of the use of an addictive drug; *also* **:** the symptoms experienced by a person undergoing withdrawal from a drug
2 : unrelieved blunt language or procedure
3 : a cold aloof person
— **cold turkey** *transitive verb*
²**cold turkey** *adverb* (1941)
: without a period of gradual adjustment, adaptation, or withdrawal **:** all at once ⟨quit smoking *cold turkey*⟩
cold type *noun* (1949)
: composition or typesetting (as photocomposition) done without the casting of metal; *specifically* **:** such composition produced directly on paper by a typewriter mechanism
cold war *noun* (1945)
1 : a conflict over ideological differences carried on by methods short of sustained overt military action and usually without breaking off diplomatic relations; *specifically, often C&W capitalized* **:** the ideological conflict between the U.S. and the U.S.S.R — compare HOT WAR
2 : a condition of rivalry, mistrust, and often open hostility short of violence especially between power groups (as labor and management)
cold warrior *noun* (1949)
: one that supports or is engaged in a cold war
cold-water *adjective* (1942)
: having only running water without heat or utility services provided ⟨a *cold-water* flat⟩

cold water *noun* (1808)
: depreciation of something as being ill-advised, unwarranted, or worthless ⟨threw *cold water* on our hopes⟩

cold wave *noun* (1876)
1 : an unusually large and rapid drop in temperature over a short period of time (as 24 hours)
2 : a permanent wave set by a chemical preparation without the use of heat

cole \'kōl\ *noun* [Middle English, from Old English *cāl*, from Latin *caulis* stem, cabbage; akin to Greek *kaulos* stem, Latvian *kauls*] (before 12th century)
: any of several brassicas; *especially* : any of various crop plants (as broccoli, kale, brussels sprouts, cabbage, cauliflower, and kohlrabi) derived from the same wild ancestor (*Brassica oleracea*)

cole·man·ite \'kōl-mə-ˌnīt\ *noun* [William T. *Coleman* (died 1893) American businessman and mine owner] (1884)
: a mineral consisting of a hydrous calcium borate occurring in brilliant colorless or white massive monoclinic crystals

co·le·op·tera \ˌkō-lē-'äp-tə-rə\ *noun plural* [New Latin, ultimately from Greek *koleon* sheath + *pteron* wing — more at FEATHER] (1873)
: insects that are beetles
— **co·le·op·ter·ist** \-tə-rist\ *noun*
— **co·le·op·ter·ous** \-tə-rəs\ *adjective*

co·le·op·ter·an \-tə-rən\ *noun* (circa 1847)
: ¹BEETLE 1
— **coleopteran** *adjective*

co·le·op·tile \-'äp-tᵊl\ *noun* [New Latin *coleoptilum*, from Greek *koleon* + *ptilon* down; akin to Greek *pteron*] (circa 1866)
: the first leaf of a monocotyledon forming a protective sheath about the plumule

co·le·o·rhi·za \ˌkō-lē-ə-'rī-zə\ *noun, plural* **-zae** \-ˌzē\ [New Latin, from Greek *koleon* + New Latin *-rhiza*] (circa 1866)
: the sheath investing the hypocotyl in some monocotyledonous plants through which the roots burst

cole·slaw \'kōl-ˌslò\ *noun* [Dutch *koolsla*, from *kool* cabbage + *sla* salad] (1794)
: a salad made of raw sliced or chopped cabbage

co·le·us \'kō-lē-əs\ *noun* [New Latin, genus name, from Greek *koleos, koleon* sheath] (1885)
: any of a large genus (*Coleus*) of herbs of the mint family

cole·wort \'kōl-ˌwərt, -ˌwórt\ *noun* (14th century)
: COLE; *especially* : one (as kale) that forms no head

coli- — see COL-

¹col·ic \'kä-lik\ *noun* [Middle English, from Middle French *colique*, from Late Latin *colicus* colicky, from Greek *kōlikos*, from *kōlon*, alteration of *kolon* colon] (15th century)
: a paroxysm of acute abdominal pain localized in a hollow organ and often caused by spasm, obstruction, or twisting

²colic *adjective* (15th century)
: of or relating to colic : COLICKY ⟨*colic* crying⟩

³co·lic \'kō-lik, 'kä-\ *adjective* (1615)
: of or relating to the colon ⟨*colic* lymph nodes⟩

co·li·cin \'kō-lə-sən\ *also* **co·li·cine** \-ˌsēn\ *noun* [French *colicine*, from *col-* + *-cine* (as in *streptomycine* streptomycin)] (1946)
: any of various antibacterial substances that are produced by strains of intestinal bacteria (as of *Escherichia coli*) having a specific plasmid and that often act to inhibit macromolecular synthesis in related strains

col·icky \'kä-li-kē\ *adjective* (1742)
1 : relating to or associated with colic ⟨*colicky* pain⟩
2 : suffering from colic ⟨*colicky* babies⟩

col·ic·root \'kä-lik-ˌrüt, -ˌrut\ *noun* (1833)
: any of several plants having roots used in folk medicine to treat colic; *especially* : either of two bitter herbs (*Aletris farinosa* and *A. aurea*) of the lily family

co·li·form \'kō-lə-ˌform, 'kä-\ *adjective* (1906)
: relating to, resembling, or being the colon bacillus
— **coliform** *noun*

co·lin·ear \(ˌ)kō-'li-nē-ər\ *adjective* (1927)
1 : COLLINEAR
2 : having corresponding parts arranged in the same linear order ⟨a gene and the protein it determines are *colinear*⟩
— **co·lin·ear·i·ty** \(ˌ)kō-ˌli-nē-'ar-ə-tē\ *noun*

co·li·phage \'kō-lə-ˌfāj, -ˌfäzh\ *noun* (1944)
: any bacteriophage active against the colon bacillus

col·i·se·um \ˌkä-lə-'sē-əm\ *noun* [Medieval Latin *Colosseum, Colisseum*] (circa 1715)
1 *capitalized* : COLOSSEUM 1
2 : a large sports stadium or building designed like the Colosseum for public entertainments

co·lis·tin \kə-'lis-tən, kō-\ *noun* [New Latin *colistinus*, specific epithet of the bacterium producing it] (1951)
: a polymyxin produced by a bacterium (*Bacillus polymyxa* variety *colistinus*) from Japanese soil

co·li·tis \kō-'lī-təs, kə-\ *noun* (circa 1860)
: inflammation of the colon

coll- *or* **collo-** *combining form* [New Latin, from Greek *koll-, kollo-*, from *kolla* — more at PROTOCOL]
1 : glue ⟨*coll*enchyma⟩
2 : colloid ⟨*collo*type⟩

col·lab·o·rate \kə-'la-bə-ˌrāt\ *intransitive verb* **-rat·ed; -rat·ing** [Late Latin *collaboratus*, past participle of *collaborare* to labor together, from Latin *com-* + *laborare* to labor] (1871)
1 : to work jointly with others or together especially in an intellectual endeavor
2 : to cooperate with or willingly assist an enemy of one's country and especially an occupying force
3 : to cooperate with an agency or instrumentality with which one is not immediately connected
— **col·lab·o·ra·tion** \-ˌla-bə-'rā-shən\ *noun*
— **col·lab·o·ra·tive** \-'la-bə-ˌrā-tiv, -b(ə-)rə-\ *adjective or noun*
— **col·lab·o·ra·tive·ly** \-lē\ *adverb*
— **col·lab·o·ra·tor** \-'la-bə-ˌrā-tər\ *noun*

col·lab·o·ra·tion·ism \kə-ˌla-bə-'rā-shə-ˌni-zəm\ *noun* (1923)
: the advocacy or practice of collaboration with an enemy
— **col·lab·o·ra·tion·ist** \-sh(ə-)nist\ *adjective or noun*

col·lage \kə-'läzh, kò-, kō-\ *noun* [French, literally, gluing, from *coller* to glue, from *colle* glue, from (assumed) Vulgar Latin *colla*, from Greek *kolla*] (1919)
1 : an artistic composition made of various materials (as paper, cloth, or wood) glued on a surface
2 : the art of making collages
3 : an assembly of diverse fragments ⟨a *collage* of ideas⟩
4 : a work (as a film) having disparate scenes in rapid succession without transitions
— **collage** *transitive verb*
— **col·lag·ist** \-'lä-zhist\ *noun*

col·la·gen \'kä-lə-jən\ *noun* [Greek *kolla* + International Scientific Vocabulary *-gen*] (circa 1865)
: an insoluble fibrous protein that occurs in vertebrates as the chief constituent of connective tissue fibrils and in bones and yields gelatin and glue on prolonged heating with water
— **col·lag·e·nous** \kə-'la-jə-nəs\ *adjective*

col·la·ge·nase \kə-'la-jə-ˌnās, 'kä-lə-jə-, -ˌnāz\ *noun* (1926)
: any of a group of proteolytic enzymes that decompose collagen and gelatin

¹col·lapse \kə-'laps\ *verb* **col·lapsed; col-**

laps·ing [Latin *collapsus*, past participle of *collabi*, from *com-* + *labi* to fall, slide — more at SLEEP] (1732)
intransitive verb
1 : to fall or shrink together abruptly and completely **:** fall into a jumbled or flattened mass through the force of external pressure ⟨a blood vessel that *collapsed*⟩
2 : to break down completely **:** DISINTEGRATE ⟨his case had *collapsed* in a mass of legal wreckage —Erle Stanley Gardner⟩
3 : to cave or fall in or give way
4 : to suddenly lose force, significance, effectiveness, or worth
5 : to break down in vital energy, stamina, or self-control through exhaustion or disease; *especially* : to fall helpless or unconscious
6 : to fold down into a more compact shape ⟨a chair that *collapses*⟩
transitive verb
: to cause to collapse
— **col·laps·ibil·i·ty** \-ˌlap-sə-'bi-lə-tē\ *noun*
— **col·laps·ible** \-'lap-sə-bəl\ *adjective*

²collapse *noun* (1801)
1 a : a breakdown in vital energy, strength, or stamina **b :** a state of extreme prostration and physical depression (as from circulatory failure or great loss of body fluids) **c :** an airless state of all or part of a lung originating spontaneously or induced surgically
2 : the act or action of collapsing ⟨the cutting of many tent ropes, the *collapse* of the canvas —Rudyard Kipling⟩
3 : a sudden failure **:** BREAKDOWN, RUIN
4 : a sudden loss of force, value, or effect ⟨the *collapse* of respect for ancient law and custom —L. S. B. Leakey⟩

¹col·lar \'kä-lər\ *noun* [Middle English *coler*, from Old French, from Latin *collare*, from *collum* neck; akin to Old English *heals* neck, and probably to Old English *hwēol* wheel — more at WHEEL] (14th century)
1 : a band, strip, or chain worn around the neck: as **a :** a band that serves to finish or decorate the neckline of a garment **b :** a short necklace **c :** a band placed about the neck of an animal **d :** a part of the harness of draft animals fitted over the shoulders and taking strain when a load is drawn **e :** an indication of control **:** a token of subservience **f :** a protective or supportive device (as a brace or cast) worn around the neck **g :** CLERICAL COLLAR
2 : something resembling a collar in shape or use (as a ring or round flange to restrain motion or hold something in place)
3 : any of various animal structures or markings similar to a collar
4 : an act of collaring **:** ARREST, CAPTURE
— **col·lared** \-lərd\ *adjective*
— **col·lar·less** \-lər-ləs\ *adjective*

²collar *transitive verb* (1613)
1 a : to seize by the collar or neck **b :** ARREST, GRAB **c :** to get control of **:** PREEMPT ⟨we can *collar* nearly the whole of this market —Roald Dahl⟩ **d :** to stop and detain in unwilling conversation
2 : to put a collar on

col·lar·bone \'kä-lər-ˌbōn\ *noun* (15th century)
: CLAVICLE

collar cell *noun* (circa 1889)
: a flagellated endodermal cell that lines the cavity of a sponge and has a contractile protoplasmic cup surrounding the flagellum — called also *choanocyte*

col·lard \'kä-lərd\ *noun* [alteration of *colewort*] (1755)

\ə\ abut \ᵊ\ kitten \ər\ further \a\ ash \ā\ ace
\ä\ mop, mar \au̇\ out \ch\ chin \e\ bet \ē\ easy
\g\ go \i\ hit \ī\ ice \j\ job \ŋ\ sing \ō\ go
\ò\ law \òi\ boy \th\ thin \t͟h\ the \ü\ loot \u̇\ foot
\y\ yet \zh\ vision *see also* Guide to Pronunciation

: a stalked smooth-leaved kale — usually used in plural

col·late \kə-'lāt, kä-, kō-; 'kä-ˌ, 'kō-\ *transitive verb* **col·lat·ed; col·lat·ing** [back-formation from *collation*] (1612)
1 a : to compare critically **b :** to collect, compare carefully in order to verify, and often to integrate or arrange in order
2 [Latin *collatus,* past participle] **:** to institute (a cleric) to a benefice
3 a : to verify the order of (printed sheets) **b :** to assemble in proper order; *especially* **:** to assemble (as printed sheets) in order for binding
synonym *see* COMPARE
— **col·la·tor** \-'lā-tər, -ˌlā-\ *noun*

¹col·lat·er·al \kə-'la-t(ə-)rəl\ *adjective* [Middle English, probably from Middle French, from Medieval Latin *collateralis,* from Latin *com-* + *lateralis* lateral] (14th century)
1 a : accompanying as secondary or subordinate **:** CONCOMITANT ⟨digress into *collateral* matters⟩ **b :** INDIRECT **c :** serving to support or reinforce **:** ANCILLARY
2 : belonging to the same ancestral stock but not in a direct line of descent — compare LINEAL 3a
3 : parallel, coordinate, or corresponding in position, order, time, or significance ⟨*collateral* states like Athens and Sparta⟩
4 a : of, relating to, or being collateral used as security (as for payment of a debt or performance of a contract) **b :** secured by collateral
— **col·lat·er·al·i·ty** \-ˌla-tə-'ra-lə-tē\ *noun*
— **col·lat·er·al·ly** \-'la-t(ə-)rə-lē\ *adverb*

²collateral *noun* (1691)
1 : a collateral relative
2 : property (as securities) pledged by a borrower to protect the interests of the lender
3 : a branch of a bodily part (as a vein)

col·lat·er·al·ize \kə-'la-t(ə-)rə-ˌlīz\ *transitive verb* **-ized; -iz·ing** (1941)
1 : to make (a loan) secure with collateral
2 : to use (as securities) for collateral

col·la·tion \kə-'lā-shən, kä-, kō-\ *noun* (14th century)
1 [Middle English, from Medieval Latin *collation-, collatio,* from Late Latin, conference, from Latin, bringing together, comparison, from *conferre* (past participle *collatus*) to bring together — more at CONFER, TOLERATE]
a : a light meal allowed on fast days in place of lunch or supper **b :** a light meal
2 [Middle English, from Latin *collation-, collatio*] **:** the act, process, or result of collating

col·league \'kä-(ˌ)lēg\ *noun* [Middle French *collegue,* from Latin *collega,* from *com-* + *legare* to depute — more at LEGATE] (circa 1533)
: an associate in a profession or in a civil or ecclesiastical office
— **col·league·ship** \-ˌship\ *noun*

¹col·lect \'kä-likt *also* -ˌlekt\ *noun* [Middle English *collecte,* from Old French, from Medieval Latin *collecta* (short for *oratio ad collectam* prayer upon assembly), from Late Latin, assembly, from Latin, assemblage, from feminine of *collectus*] (13th century)
1 : a short prayer comprising an invocation, petition, and conclusion; *specifically, often capitalized* **:** one preceding the eucharistic Epistle and varying with the day
2 : COLLECTION

²col·lect \kə-'lekt\ *verb* [Latin *collectus,* past participle of *colligere* to collect, from *com-* + *legere* to gather — more at LEGEND] (1563)
transitive verb
1 a : to bring together into one body or place **b :** to gather or exact from a number of persons or sources ⟨*collect* taxes⟩
2 : INFER, DEDUCE
3 : to gain or regain control of ⟨*collect* his thoughts⟩
4 : to claim as due and receive payment for
5 : to get and bring with one; *specifically*

: PICK UP ⟨went to *collect* her at the train station⟩
intransitive verb
1 : to come together in a band, group, or mass **:** GATHER
2 a : to collect objects **b :** to receive payment ⟨*collecting* on the insurance⟩
synonym *see* GATHER

³col·lect \kə-'lekt\ *adverb or adjective* (1893)
: to be paid for by the receiver

col·lec·ta·nea \ˌkä-ˌlek-'tā-nē-ə\ *noun plural* [Latin, neuter plural of *collectaneus* collected, from *collectus,* past participle] (1791)
: collected writings; *also* **:** literary items forming a collection

col·lect·ed \kə-'lek-təd\ *adjective* (1610)
1 : possessed of calmness and composure often through concentrated effort
2 : gathered together ⟨the *collected* works of Scott⟩
3 *of a horse's gait* **:** performed slowly and restrainedly with the animal's center of gravity toward the hindquarters — compare EXTENDED
synonym *see* COOL
— **col·lect·ed·ly** *adverb*
— **col·lect·ed·ness** *noun*

¹col·lect·ible *or* **col·lect·able** \kə-'lek-tə-bəl\ *adjective* (1660)
1 : suitable for being collected
2 : due for present payment **:** PAYABLE

²collectible *or* **collectable** *noun* (1953)
: an object that is collected by fanciers; *especially* **:** one other than such traditionally collectible items as art, stamps, coins, and antiques

col·lec·tion \kə-'lek-shən\ *noun* (14th century)
1 : the act or process of collecting
2 a : something collected; *especially* **:** an accumulation of objects gathered for study, comparison, or exhibition or as a hobby **b :** GROUP, AGGREGATE **c :** a set of apparel designed for sale usually in a particular season

¹col·lec·tive \kə-'lek-tiv\ *adjective* (15th century)
1 : denoting a number of persons or things considered as one group or whole ⟨*flock* is a *collective* word⟩
2 a : formed by collecting **:** AGGREGATED **b** *of a fruit* **:** MULTIPLE
3 a : of, relating to, or being a group of individuals **b :** involving all members of a group as distinct from its individuals
4 : marked by similarity among or with the members of a group
5 : collectivized or characterized by collectivism
6 : shared or assumed by all members of the group ⟨*collective* responsibility⟩
— **col·lec·tive·ly** *adverb*

²collective *noun* (1655)
1 : a collective body **:** GROUP
2 : a cooperative unit or organization; *specifically* **:** COLLECTIVE FARM

collective bargaining *noun* (1891)
: negotiation between an employer and a labor union usually on wages, hours, and working conditions

collective farm *noun* (1925)
: a farm especially in a communist country formed from many small holdings collected into a single unit for joint operation under governmental supervision

collective mark *noun* (1938)
: a trademark or a service mark of a group (as a cooperative association)

collective security *noun* (1934)
: the maintenance by common action of the security of all members of an association of nations

collective unconscious *noun* (1917)
: the genetically determined part of the unconscious that especially in the psychoanalytic theory of C. G. Jung occurs in all the members of a people or race

col·lec·tiv·ise *chiefly British variant of* COLLECTIVIZE

col·lec·tiv·ism \kə-'lek-ti-ˌvi-zəm\ *noun* (1857)
: a political or economic theory advocating collective control especially over production and distribution; *also* **:** a system marked by such control
— **col·lec·tiv·ist** \-vist\ *adjective or noun*
— **col·lec·tiv·is·tic** \-ˌlek-ti-'vis-tik\ *adjective*
— **col·lec·tiv·is·ti·cal·ly** \-ti-k(ə-)lē\ *adverb*

col·lec·tiv·i·ty \kə-ˌlek-'ti-və-tē, ˌkä-\ *noun, plural* **-ties** (1862)
1 : the quality or state of being collective
2 : a collective whole; *especially* **:** the people as a body

col·lec·tiv·ize \kə-'lek-ti-ˌvīz\ *transitive verb* **-ized; -iz·ing** (1893)
: to organize by collectivism
— **col·lec·tiv·i·za·tion** \kə-ˌlek-ti-və-'zā-shən\ *noun*

col·lec·tor \kə-'lek-tər\ *noun* (14th century)
: one that collects: as **a :** an official who collects funds or moneys **b :** a person who makes a collection ⟨stamp *collector*⟩ **c :** an object or device that collects ⟨the statuette was a dust *collector*⟩ **d :** SOLAR COLLECTOR
— **col·lec·tor·ship** \-ˌship\ *noun*

collector's item *noun* (1932)
: an item whose rarity or excellence makes it especially worth collecting; *broadly* **:** COLLECTIBLE

col·leen \kä-'lēn, 'kä-ˌ\ *noun* [Irish *cailín*] (1828)
: an Irish girl

col·lege \'kä-lij\ *noun, often attributive* [Middle English, from Middle French, from Latin *collegium* society, from *collega* colleague — more at COLLEAGUE] (14th century)
1 : a body of clergy living together and supported by a foundation
2 : a building used for an educational or religious purpose
3 a : a self-governing constituent body of a university offering living quarters and instruction but not granting degrees ⟨Balliol and Magdalen *Colleges* at Oxford⟩ **b :** a preparatory or high school **c :** an independent institution of higher learning offering a course of general studies leading to a bachelor's degree **d :** a part of a university offering a specialized group of courses **e :** an institution offering instruction usually in a professional, vocational, or technical field ⟨business *college*⟩
4 : COMPANY, GROUP; *specifically* **:** an organized body of persons engaged in a common pursuit or having common interests or duties
5 a : a group of persons considered by law to be a unit **b :** a body of electors — compare ELECTORAL COLLEGE
6 : the faculty, students, or administration of a college

College Board *service mark*
— used for administration of tests of aptitude and achievement considered by some colleges in determining admission and placement of students

college try *noun* [from the phrase "give it the old *college try*"] (1947)
: a zealous all-out effort

col·le·gial \kə-'lē-j(ē-)əl, *especially for 2a also* -'lē-gē-əl\ *adjective* (14th century)
1 : COLLEGIATE 2
2 a : marked by power or authority vested equally in each of a number of colleagues **b :** characterized by equal sharing of authority especially by Roman Catholic bishops
3 : marked by camaraderie among colleagues
— **col·le·gial·ly** *adverb*

col·le·gi·al·i·ty \-ˌlē-jē-'a-lə-tē, -ˌlē-gē-\ *noun* (1887)
: the relationship of colleagues; *specifically* **:** the participation of bishops in the govern-

ment of the Roman Catholic Church in collaboration with the pope

col·le·gian \kə-'lē-j(ē-)ən\ *noun* (15th century)
: a student or recent graduate of a college

col·le·giate \kə-'lē-jət, -jē-ət\ *adjective* [Medieval Latin *collegiatus*, from Latin *collegium*] (15th century)
1 : of or relating to a collegiate church
2 : of, relating to, or comprising a college
3 : COLLEGIAL 2
4 : designed for or characteristic of college students
— **col·le·giate·ly** *adverb*

collegiate church *noun* (15th century)
1 : a church other than a cathedral that has a chapter of canons
2 : a church or corporate group of churches under the joint pastorate of two or more ministers

col·le·gi·um \kə-'le-gē-əm, -'lā-\ *noun, plural* **-gia** \-gē-ə\ *or* **-giums** [modification of Russian *kollegiya*, from Latin *collegium*] (1917)
: a group in which each member has approximately equal power and authority

col·lem·bo·lan \kə-'lem-bə-lən\ *noun* [ultimately from *coll-* + Greek *embolos* wedge, stopper — more at EMBOLUS] (1873)
: SPRINGTAIL
— **collembolan** *or* **col·lem·bo·lous** \-ləs\ *adjective*

col·len·chy·ma \kə-'len-kə-mə, kä-\ *noun* [New Latin] (1857)
: a plant tissue that consists of living usually elongated cells with unevenly thickened walls and acts as support especially in areas of primary growth — compare SCLERENCHYMA
— **col·len·chy·ma·tous** \ˌkä-lən-'ki-mə-təs, -'kī-\ *adjective*

col·let \'kä-lət\ *noun* [Middle French, diminutive of *col* collar, from Latin *collum* neck — more at COLLAR] (1528)
: a metal band, collar, ferrule, or flange: as **a** : a casing or socket for holding a tool (as a drill bit) **b** : a circle or flange in which a gem is set

col·le·te·ri·al gland \ˌkä-lə-'tir-ē-əl-, -'ter-\ *noun* [New Latin *colleterium* colleterial gland, irregular from Greek *kollan* to glue — more at PROTOCOL] (1870)
: a gland in female insects that secretes a cement by which the eggs are glued together or attached to an external object

col·lide \kə-'līd\ *intransitive verb* **col·lid·ed; col·lid·ing** [Latin *collidere*, from *com-* + *laedere* to injure by striking] (1700)
1 : to come together with solid or direct impact
2 : CLASH

col·lid·er \kə-'lī-dər\ *noun* (1980)
: a particle accelerator in which two beams of particles moving in opposite directions are made to collide

col·lie \'kä-lē\ *noun* [probably from English dialect *colly* black] (circa 1651)
: any of a breed of large dogs developed in Scotland that occur in rough-coated and smooth-coated varieties

col·lier \'käl-yər\ *noun* [Middle English *colier*, from *col* coal] (13th century)
1 : one that produces charcoal

collie

2 : a coal miner
3 : a ship for transporting coal

col·liery \'käl-yə-rē\ *noun, plural* **-lier·ies** (1635)
: a coal mine and its connected buildings

col·lie-shang·ie \'kä-lē-ˌshaŋ-ē, 'kə-\ *noun* [perhaps from *collie* + *shang* kind of meal] (1737)
Scottish : SQUABBLE, BRAWL

col·li·gate \'kä-lə-ˌgāt\ *verb* **-gat·ed; -gat·ing** [Latin *colligatus*, past participle of *colligare*, from *com-* + *ligare* to tie — more at LIGATURE] (1545)
transitive verb
1 : to bind, unite, or group together
2 : to subsume (isolated facts) under a general concept
intransitive verb
: to be or become a member of a group or unit
— **col·li·ga·tion** \ˌkä-lə-'gā-shən\ *noun*

col·li·ga·tive \'kä-lə-ˌgā-tiv, kə-'li-gə-\ *adjective* (1901)
: depending on the number of particles (as molecules) and not on the nature of the particles (pressure is a *colligative* property)

col·li·mate \'kä-lə-ˌmāt\ *transitive verb* **-mat·ed; -mat·ing** [Latin *collimatus*, past participle of *collimare*, manuscript variant of *collineare* to make straight, from *com-* + *linea* line] (1878)
: to make (as light rays) parallel
— **col·li·ma·tion** \ˌkä-lə-'mā-shən\ *noun*

col·li·ma·tor \'kä-lə-ˌmā-tər\ *noun* (1865)
1 : a device for producing a beam of parallel rays (as of light) or for forming an infinitely distant virtual image that can be viewed without parallax
2 : a device for obtaining a beam (as of particles) of limited cross section

col·lin·ear \kə-'li-nē-ər, kä-\ *adjective* [International Scientific Vocabulary] (1863)
1 : lying on or passing through the same straight line
2 : having axes lying end to end in a straight line (*collinear* antenna elements)
— **col·lin·ear·i·ty** \ˌli-nē-'ar-ə-tē\ *noun*

col·lins \'kä-lənz\ *noun* [probably from the name *Collins*] (circa 1887)
: a tall iced drink of soda water, sugar, lemon or lime juice, and liquor (as gin)

col·li·sion \kə-'li-zhən\ *noun* [Middle English, from Latin *collision-, collisio*, from *collidere*] (15th century)
1 : an act or instance of colliding : CLASH
2 : an encounter between particles (as atoms or molecules) resulting in exchange or transformation of energy
— **col·li·sion·al** \-'lizh-nəl, -'li-zhə-nᵊl\ *adjective*
— **col·li·sion·al·ly** *adverb*

collision course *noun* (1944)
: a course (as of moving bodies or antithetical philosophies) that will result in collision or conflict if continued unaltered

collo- — see COLL-

col·lo·cate \'kä-lə-ˌkāt\ *verb* **-cat·ed; -cat·ing** [Latin *collocatus*, past participle of *collocare*, from *com-* + *locare* to place, from *locus* place — more at STALL] (1513)
transitive verb
: to set or arrange in a place or position; *especially* : to set side by side
intransitive verb
: to occur in conjunction with something

col·lo·ca·tion \ˌkä-lə-'kā-shən\ *noun* (1605)
: the act or result of placing or arranging together; *specifically* : a noticeable arrangement or conjoining of linguistic elements (as words)
— **col·lo·ca·tion·al** \-shnəl, -shə-nᵊl\ *adjective*

col·lo·di·on \kə-'lō-dē-ən\ *noun* [modification of New Latin *collodium*, from Greek *kollōdēs* glutinous, from *kolla* glue — more at PROTOCOL] (1851)

: a viscous solution of pyroxylin used especially as a coating for wounds or for photographic films

col·logue \kə-'lōg\ *intransitive verb* **col·logued; col·logu·ing** [origin unknown] (1646)
1 *dialect* : INTRIGUE, CONSPIRE
2 : to talk privately : CONFER

col·loid \'kä-ˌlóid\ *noun* [International Scientific Vocabulary *coll-* + *-oid*] (circa 1852)
1 : a gelatinous or mucinous substance found in tissues in disease (as in the thyroid) or normally
2 a : a substance that consists of particles dispersed throughout another substance which are too small for resolution with an ordinary light microscope but are incapable of passing through a semipermeable membrane **b** : a mixture consisting of a colloid together with the medium in which it is dispersed (smoke is a *colloid*)
— **col·loi·dal** \kə-'lói-dᵊl, kä-\ *adjective*
— **col·loi·dal·ly** *adverb*

col·lop \'kä-ləp\ *noun* [Middle English] (14th century)
1 : a small piece or slice especially of meat
2 : a fold of fat flesh

col·lo·qui·al \kə-'lō-kwē-əl\ *adjective* (1751)
1 : of or relating to conversation : CONVERSATIONAL
2 a : used in or characteristic of familiar and informal conversation; *also* : unacceptably informal **b** : using conversational style
— **colloquial** *noun*
— **col·lo·qui·al·i·ty** \-ˌlō-kwē-'a-lə-tē\ *noun*
— **col·lo·qui·al·ly** \-'lō-kwē-ə-lē\ *adverb*

col·lo·qui·al·ism \-'lō-kwē-ə-ˌli-zəm\ *noun* (1810)
1 a : a colloquial expression **b** : a local or regional dialect expression
2 : colloquial style

col·lo·quist \'kä-lə-kwist\ *noun* (1792)
: SPEAKER

col·lo·qui·um \kə-'lō-kwē-əm\ *noun, plural* **-qui·ums** *or* **-quia** \-kwē-ə\ [Latin, colloquy] (1844)
: a usually academic meeting at which specialists deliver addresses on a topic or on related topics and then answer questions relating to them

col·lo·quy \'kä-lə-kwē\ *noun, plural* **-quies** [Latin *colloquium*, from *colloqui* to converse, from *com-* + *loqui* to speak] (15th century)
1 : CONVERSATION, DIALOGUE
2 : a high-level serious discussion : CONFERENCE

col·lo·type \'kä-lə-ˌtīp\ *noun* [International Scientific Vocabulary] (1883)
1 : a photomechanical process for making prints directly from a hardened film of gelatin or other colloid that has ink-receptive and ink-repellent parts
2 : a print made by collotype

col·lude \kə-'lüd\ *intransitive verb* **col·lud·ed; col·lud·ing** [Latin *colludere*, from *com-* + *ludere* to play, from *ludus* game — more at LUDICROUS] (1535)
: CONSPIRE, PLOT

col·lu·sion \kə-'lü-zhən\ *noun* [Middle English, from Middle French, from Latin *collusion-, collusio*, from *colludere*] (14th century)
: secret agreement or cooperation especially for an illegal or deceitful purpose
— **col·lu·sive** \-'lü-siv, -ziv\ *adjective*
— **col·lu·sive·ly** *adverb*

col·lu·vi·um \kə-'lü-vē-əm\ *noun, plural* **-via** \-vē-ə\ *or* **-vi·ums** [New Latin, from Medieval Latin, offscourings, alteration of Latin

colluvies, from *colluere* to wash, from *com-* + *lavere* to wash — more at LYE] (circa 1936)
: rock detritus and soil accumulated at the foot of a slope
— **col·lu·vi·al** \-vē-əl\ *adjective*
col·ly \'kä-lē\ *transitive verb* **col·lied; col·ly·ing** [alteration of Middle English *colwen,* from (assumed) Old English *colgian,* from Old English *col* coal] (1590)
dialect chiefly British : to blacken with or as if with soot
col·lyr·i·um \kə-'lir-ē-əm\ *noun, plural* **-ia** \-ē-ə\ *or* **-i·ums** [Middle English *collirium,* from Latin *collyrium,* from Greek *kollyrion* pessary, eye salve, from diminutive of *kollyra* roll of bread] (14th century)
: EYEWASH 1
col·ly·wob·bles \'kä-lē-,wä-bəlz\ *noun plural but singular or plural in construction* [perhaps by folk etymology from New Latin *cholera morbus,* literally, the disease cholera] (circa 1823)
: BELLYACHE
colo- — see COL-
col·o·bus monkey \'kä-lə-bəs-\ *noun* [New Latin *colobus,* from Greek *kolobos* docked, mutilated, from *kolos* docked; probably akin to Greek *klan* to break — more at CLAST] (1889)
: any of various long-tailed African monkeys (genus *Colobus* and related genera) — called also *colobus*
co·lo·cate \(,)kō-'lō-,kāt, -lō-'kāt\ *transitive verb* (1965)
: to locate together; *especially* : to place two or more units close together so as to share common facilities
col·o·cynth \'kä-lə-,sin(t)th\ *noun* [Latin *colocynthis,* from Greek *kolokynthis*] (1543)
: a Mediterranean and African herbaceous vine (*Citrullus colocynthis*) related to the watermelon; *also* : its spongy fruit from which a powerful cathartic is prepared
co·log·a·rithm \(,)kō-'lò-gə-,ri-thəm, -'lä-\ *noun* (1881)
: the logarithm of the reciprocal of a number
co·logne \kə-'lōn\ *noun* [*Cologne,* Germany] (1814)
1 : a perfumed liquid composed of alcohol and fragrant oils
2 : a cream or paste of cologne sometimes formed into a semisolid stick
— **co·logned** \-'lōnd\ *adjective*
¹**co·lon** \'kō-lən\ *noun, plural* **colons** *or* **co·la** \-lə\ [Middle English, from Latin, from Greek *kolon*] (14th century)
: the part of the large intestine that extends from the cecum to the rectum
— **co·lon·ic** \kō-'lä-nik, kə-\ *adjective*
²**colon** *noun, plural* **colons** *or* **co·la** \-lə\ [Latin, part of a poem, from Greek *kōlon* limb, part of a strophe] (circa 1550)
1 *plural* **cola** : a rhythmical unit of an utterance; *specifically, in Greek or Latin verse* : a system or series of from two to not more than six feet having a principal accent and forming part of a line
2 *plural* **colons** **a** : a punctuation mark : used chiefly to direct attention to matter (as a list, explanation, or quotation) that follows **b** : the sign : used between the parts of a numerical expression of time in hours and minutes (as in 1:15) or in hours, minutes, and seconds (as in 8:25:30), in a bibliographical reference (as in *Nation* 130:20), in a ratio where it is usually read as "to" (as in 4:1 read "four to one"), or in a proportion where it is usually read as "is to" or when doubled as "as" (as in 2:1::8:4 read "two is to one as eight is to four")
³**co·lon** \kò-'lōn, kə-'lōn\ *noun* [French, from Latin *colonus*] (1888)
: a colonial farmer or plantation owner
co·lón *also* **co·lone** \kə-'lōn\ *noun, plural* **co·lo·nes** \-'lō-,nās\ [Spanish *colón,* from

Cristóbal *Colón* Christopher Columbus] (1916)
— see MONEY table
colon bacillus *noun* (circa 1909)
: any of various bacilli (especially genera *Escherichia* and *Aerobacter*) that are normally commensal in vertebrate intestines; *especially* : one (*E. coli*) used extensively in genetic research
col·o·nel \'kər-nᵊl\ *noun* [alteration of *coronel,* from Middle French, modification of Old Italian *colonnello* column of soldiers, colonel, diminutive of *colonna* column, from Latin *columna*] (1548)
1 a : a commissioned officer in the army, air force, or marine corps ranking above a lieutenant colonel and below a brigadier general **b** : LIEUTENANT COLONEL
2 : a minor titular official of a state especially in southern or midland U.S. — used as an honorific title ◊
— **col·o·nel·cy** \-nᵊl-sē\ *noun*
Colonel Blimp \-'blimp\ *noun* [*Colonel Blimp,* cartoon character created by David Low] (1937)
: a pompous person with out-of-date or ultraconservative views; *broadly* : REACTIONARY
— **Colonel Blimp·ism** \-'blim-,pi-zəm\ *noun*
¹**co·lo·nial** \kə-'lō-nē-əl, -nyəl\ *adjective* (1776)
1 : of, relating to, or characteristic of a colony
2 *often capitalized* : of or relating to the original 13 colonies forming the United States: **a** : made or prevailing in America during the colonial period ⟨*colonial* architecture⟩ **b** : adapted from or reminiscent of an American colonial mode of design ⟨*colonial* furniture⟩
3 : forming or existing in a colony ⟨*colonial* organisms⟩
4 : possessing or composed of colonies ⟨a *colonial* empire⟩
— **co·lo·nial·ize** \-nē-ə-,līz, -nyə-,līz\ *transitive verb*
— **co·lo·nial·ly** *adverb*
— **co·lo·nial·ness** *noun*
²**colonial** *noun* (1798)
1 : a member or inhabitant of a colony
2 a : a product made for use in a colony **b** : a product (as a house) exhibiting colonial style
co·lo·nial·ism \kə-'lō-nē-ə-,li-zəm, -nyə-,li-\ *noun* (1853)
1 : the quality or state of being colonial
2 : something characteristic of a colony
3 a : control by one power over a dependent area or people **b** : a policy advocating or based on such control
— **co·lo·nial·ist** \-list\ *noun or adjective*
— **co·lo·nial·is·tic** \-,lō-nē-ə-'lis-tik, -nyə-'lis-\ *adjective*
¹**co·lon·ic** \kō-'lä-nik, kə-\ *adjective* (circa 1885)
: of or relating to the colon of the intestine
²**colonic** *noun* (1939)
: irrigation of the colon : ENEMA
col·o·ni·sa·tion, col·o·nise *British variant of* COLONIZATION, COLONIZE
col·o·nist \'kä-lə-nist\ *noun* (1701)
1 : a member or inhabitant of a colony
2 : one that colonizes or settles in a new country
col·o·ni·za·tion \,kä-lə-nə-'zā-shən\ *noun* (1770)
: an act or instance of colonizing
— **col·o·ni·za·tion·ist** \-sh(ə-)nist\ *noun*
col·o·nize \'kä-lə-,nīz\ *verb* **-nized; -niz·ing** (1622)
transitive verb
1 a : to establish a colony in or on or of **b** : to establish in a colony
2 : to send illegal or irregularly qualified voters into ⟨*colonizing* doubtful districts⟩
3 : to infiltrate with usually subversive militants for propaganda and strategy reasons ⟨*colonize* industries⟩

intransitive verb
: to make or establish a colony : SETTLE
— **col·o·niz·er** *noun*
col·on·nade \,kä-lə-'nād\ *noun* [French, from Italian *colonnato,* from *colonna* column] (1718)
: a series of columns set at regular intervals and usually supporting the base of a roof structure
— **col·on·nad·ed** \-'nā-dəd\ *adjective*
co·lo·nus \kə-'lō-nəs\ *noun, plural* **-ni** \-,nī, -(,)nē\ [Latin, literally, farmer] (1888)
: a free-born serf in the later Roman Empire who could sometimes own property but who was bound to the land and obliged to pay a rent usually in produce
col·o·ny \'kä-lə-nē\ *noun, plural* **-nies** [Middle English *colonie,* from Middle French & Latin; Middle French, from Latin *colonia,* from *colonus* farmer, colonist, from *colere* to cultivate — more at WHEEL] (14th century)
1 a : a body of people living in a new territory but retaining ties with the parent state **b** : the territory inhabited by such a body
2 : a distinguishable localized population within a species ⟨*colony* of termites⟩
3 a : a circumscribed mass of microorganisms usually growing in or on a solid medium **b** : the aggregation of zooids of a compound animal
4 a : a group of individuals or things with common characteristics or interests situated in close association ⟨an artist *colony*⟩ **b** : the section occupied by such a group
5 : a group of persons institutionalized away from others ⟨a leper *colony*⟩ ⟨a penal *colony*⟩; *also* : the land or buildings occupied by such a group
colony–stimulating factor *noun* (1969)
: any of several glycoproteins that promote the differentiation of stem cells especially into blood granulocytes and macrophages and that stimulate their proliferation into colonies in culture
col·o·phon \'kä-lə-fən, -,fän\ *noun* [Latin, from Greek *kolophōn* summit, finishing touch; perhaps akin to Latin *culmen* top — more at HILL] (1774)
1 : an inscription placed at the end of a book or manuscript usually with facts relative to its production
2 : an identifying device used by a printer or a publisher
co·lo·pho·ny \kə-'lä-fə-nē, 'kä-lə-,fō-\ *noun, plural* **-nies** [Middle English *colophonie,* ultimately from Greek *Kolophōn* Colophon, an Ionian city] (14th century)
: ROSIN
¹**col·or** \'kə-lər\ *noun, often attributive* [Middle English *colour,* from Old French, from Latin

◊ **WORD HISTORY**
colonel The pronunciation of *colonel* as if it were spelled *kernel* is one of the more striking oddities of the English vocabulary. The source of this discrepancy was not sheer contrariness, for at one time a spelling *coronel* existed to match the pronunciation with \r\ and a pronunciation \'kəl-nᵊl\ existed to match the spelling *colonel.* For a time both forms competed, with *colonel* holding the ground long enough for this spelling to become standard. Later the pronunciation with \r\ made a resurgence and finally won the day, but a corresponding spelling change to *r* never took place. Both *coronel* and *colonel* were borrowed from 16th century French; the French form *coronel* resulted from a phonetic change called dissimilation, by which one of two identical or similar sounds in the same word changes to a contrasting sound. In this case the first \l\ became \r\.

color; akin to Latin *celare* to conceal — more at HELL] (13th century)
1 a : a phenomenon of light (as red, brown, pink, or gray) or visual perception that enables one to differentiate otherwise identical objects **b :** the aspect of objects and light sources that may be described in terms of hue, lightness, and saturation for objects and hue, brightness, and saturation for light sources **c :** a hue as contrasted with black, white, or gray
2 a : an outward often deceptive show : APPEARANCE ⟨his story has the *color* of truth⟩ **b :** a legal claim to or appearance of a right, authority, or office **c :** a pretense offered as justification : PRETEXT ⟨she could have drawn from the Versailles treaty the *color* of legality for any action she chose —*Yale Review*⟩ **d :** an appearance of authenticity : PLAUSIBILITY ⟨lending *color* to this notion⟩
3 : complexion tint: **a :** the tint characteristic of good health **b :** BLUSH
4 : vividness or variety of effects of language **b :** LOCAL COLOR
5 a : an identifying badge, pennant, or flag — usually used in plural ⟨a ship sailing under Swedish *colors*⟩ **b :** colored clothing distinguishing one as a member of a particular group or representative of a particular person or thing — usually used in plural ⟨a jockey wearing the *colors* of the stable⟩
6 a *plural* **:** position as to a question or course of action : STAND ⟨the USSR changed neither its *colors* nor its stripes during all of this —Norman Mailer⟩ **b :** CHARACTER, NATURE — usually used in plural ⟨showed himself in his true *colors*⟩
7 a : the use or combination of colors **b :** two or more hues employed in a medium of presentation ⟨movies in *color*⟩ ⟨*color* television⟩
8 *plural* **a :** a naval or nautical salute to a flag being hoisted or lowered **b :** ARMED FORCES
9 : VITALITY, INTEREST ⟨the play had a good deal of *color* to it⟩
10 : something used to give color : PIGMENT
11 : tonal quality in music ⟨the *color* and richness of the cello⟩
12 : skin pigmentation especially other than white characteristic of race ⟨a person of *color*⟩
13 : a small particle of gold in a gold miner's pan after washing
14 : analysis of game action or strategy, statistics and background information on participants, and often anecdotes provided by a sportscaster to give variety and interest to the broadcast of a game or contest
15 : a hypothetical property of quarks that differentiates each type into three forms having a distinct role in binding quarks together
— **col·or·ism** \-lə-ˌri-zəm\ *noun*

²color (14th century)
transitive verb
1 a : to give color to **b :** to change the color of (as by dyeing, staining, or painting)
2 : to change as if by dyeing or painting: as **a :** MISREPRESENT, DISTORT **b :** GLOSS, EXCUSE ⟨*color* a lie⟩ **c :** INFLUENCE ⟨the lives of most of us have been *colored* by politics —Christine Weston⟩
3 : CHARACTERIZE, LABEL ⟨call it progress; *color* it inevitable with shades of job security —C. E. Price⟩
intransitive verb
: to take on color; *specifically* **:** BLUSH
— **col·or·er** \ˈkə-lər-ər\ *noun*

col·or·able \ˈkə-lə-rə-bəl, ˈkəl-rə-\ *adjective* (14th century)
1 : seemingly valid or genuine
2 : intended to deceive : COUNTERFEIT
— **col·or·ably** \-blē\ *adverb*

Col·o·ra·do blue spruce \ˌkä-lə-la-'ra-dō-, -'rä-\ *noun* [*Colorado,* state of the U.S.] (1897)
: BLUE SPRUCE

Colorado potato beetle *noun* (1868)
: a black-and-yellow striped beetle (*Leptinotarsa decemlineata*) that feeds on the leaves of the potato — called also *potato beetle, potato bug*

col·or·ant \ˈkə-lə-rənt\ *noun* (1884)
: a substance used for coloring a material : DYE, PIGMENT

col·or·a·tion \ˌkə-lə-'rā-shən\ *noun* (1617)
1 a : the state of being colored ⟨the dark *coloration* of his skin⟩ **b :** use or choice of colors (as by an artist) **c :** arrangement of colors ⟨the *coloration* of a butterfly's wing⟩
2 a : characteristic quality ⟨the newspapers . . . took on the former *coloration* of the magazine —L. B. Seltzer⟩ **b :** aspect suggesting an attitude : PERSUASION ⟨the chameleon talent for taking on the intellectual *coloration* of whatever idea he happened to fasten onto —Budd Schulberg⟩
3 : subtle variation of intensity or quality of tone ⟨a wide range of *coloration* from the orchestra⟩

Colorado potato beetle

col·or·a·tu·ra \ˌkə-lə-rə-'tùr-ə, -'tyùr-\ *noun* [obsolete Italian, literally, coloring, from Late Latin, from Latin *coloratus,* past participle of *colorare* to color, from *color*] (circa 1740)
1 : elaborate embellishment in vocal music; *broadly* **:** music with ornate figuration
2 : a soprano with a light agile voice specializing in coloratura

color bar *noun* (1913)
: a barrier preventing colored persons from participating with whites in various activities — called also *color line*

col·or·bear·er \ˈkə-lər-ˌbar-ər, -ˌber-\ *noun* (circa 1891)
: one that carries a color or standard especially in a military parade or drill

col·or–blind \-ˌblīnd\ *adjective* (1854)
1 : affected with partial or total inability to distinguish one or more chromatic colors
2 : INSENSITIVE, OBLIVIOUS
3 : not recognizing differences of race ⟨tried to get the welfare establishment . . . to abandon its *color-blind* policy —D. P. Moynihan⟩; *especially* **:** free from racial prejudice ⟨a white man with an invisible black skin in a *color-blind* community —James Farmer⟩
— **color blindness** *noun*

col·or·bred \-ˌbred\ *adjective* (1948)
: selectively bred for the development of particular colors ⟨pure *colorbred* dogs⟩

co·lo·rec·tal \ˌkō-lō-'rek-t⁽ə⁾l\ *adjective* (1962)
: relating to or affecting the colon and rectum ⟨*colorectal* cancer⟩

¹col·ored \ˈkə-lərd\ *adjective* (14th century)
1 : having color
2 a : COLORFUL **b :** marked by exaggeration or bias
3 a : of a race other than the white; *especially* **:** BLACK 2b — sometimes taken to be offensive **b :** of mixed race — sometimes taken to be offensive
4 : of or relating to colored persons — sometimes taken to be offensive

²colored *noun, plural* **colored** *or* **coloreds** *often capitalized* (1916)
: a colored person — sometimes taken to be offensive

col·or·fast \ˈkə-lər-ˌfast\ *adjective* (1926)
: having color that retains its original hue without fading or running
— **col·or·fast·ness** \-ˌfas(t)-nəs\ *noun*

col·or–field \-ˌfē(ə)ld\ *noun, often attributive* (1964)
: abstract painting in which color is emphasized and form and surface are correspondingly de-emphasized

color filter *noun* (1900)
: FILTER 3b

col·or·ful \ˈkə-lər-fəl\ *adjective* (1889)

1 : having striking colors
2 : full of variety or interest
— **col·or·ful·ly** \-f(ə-)lē\ *adverb*
— **col·or·ful·ness** \-fəl-nəs\ *noun*

color guard *noun* (circa 1823)
: an honor guard for the colors of an organization

col·or·if·ic \ˌkə-lə-'ri-fik\ *adjective* (1676)
: capable of communicating color

col·or·im·e·ter \ˌkə-lə-'ri-mə-tər\ *noun* [International Scientific Vocabulary] (circa 1872)
: an instrument or device for determining and specifying colors; *specifically* **:** one used for chemical analysis by comparison of a liquid's color with standard colors
— **col·or·i·met·ric** \ˌkə-lə-rə-'me-trik\ *adjective*
— **col·or·i·met·ri·cal·ly** \-tri-k(ə-)lē\ *adverb*
— **col·or·im·e·try** \ˌkə-lə-'ri-mə-trē\ *noun*

col·or·ing \ˈkə-lə-riŋ\ *noun* (14th century)
1 a : the act of applying colors **b :** something that produces color or color effects **c** (1) **:** the effect produced by applying or combining colors (2) **:** natural color (3) **:** COMPLEXION, COLORATION **d :** change of appearance (as by adding color)
2 : INFLUENCE, BIAS
3 : COLOR 4
4 : TIMBRE, QUALITY

col·or·ist \ˈkə-lə-rist\ *noun* (1686)
: one that colors or deals with color
— **col·or·is·tic** \ˌkə-lə-'ris-tik\ *adjective*
— **col·or·is·ti·cal·ly** \-ti-k(ə-)lē\ *adverb*

col·or·ize \ˈkə-lə-ˌrīz\ *transitive verb* **-ized; -iz·ing** (1979)
: to add color to (a black-and-white film) by means of a computer
— **col·or·i·za·tion** \ˌkə-lə-rə-'zā-shən\ *noun*

col·or·less \ˈkə-lər-ləs\ *adjective* (14th century)
: lacking color: as **a :** PALLID, BLANCHED **b :** DULL, UNINTERESTING
— **col·or·less·ly** *adverb*
— **col·or·less·ness** *noun*

col·or·man \-ˌman\ *noun* (1973)
: a sportscaster who provides color

color phase *noun* (1927)
1 : a seasonally variant pelage color
2 a : a genetic variation manifested by the occurrence of a skin or pelage color unlike the wild type of the animal group in which it appears **b :** an individual marked by such a variant

col·or·point shorthair \ˈkə-lər-ˌpȯint-\ *noun* (1974)
: any of a breed of domestic cats of Siamese type and coat pattern but occurring in different colors — called also *colorpoint*

color temperature *noun* (1916)
: the temperature at which a blackbody emits radiant energy competent to evoke a color the same as that evoked by radiant energy from a given source (as a lamp)

color wheel *noun* (circa 1893)
: a circular diagram of the spectrum used to show the relationships between the colors

co·los·sal \kə-'lä-səl\ *adjective* (1712)
1 : of, relating to, or resembling a colossus
2 : of a bulk, extent, power, or effect approaching or suggesting the stupendous or incredible
3 : of an exceptional or astonishing degree
synonym see ENORMOUS
— **co·los·sal·ly** \-sə-lē\ *adverb*

col·os·se·um \ˌkä-lə-'sē-əm\ *noun* [Medieval Latin, from Latin, neuter of *colosseus* colossal, from *colossus*] (circa 1715)

\ə\ abut \ᵊ\ kitten \ər\ further \a\ ash \ā\ ace
\ä\ mop, mar \aú\ out \ch\ chin \e\ bet \ē\ easy
\g\ go \i\ hit \ī\ ice \j\ job \ŋ\ sing \ō\ go
\ò\ law \òi\ boy \th\ thin \th\ the \ü\ loot \ù\ foot
\y\ yet \zh\ vision *see also* Guide to Pronunciation

1 *capitalized* **:** an amphitheater built in Rome in the first century A.D.
2 : COLISEUM 2

Co·los·sians \kə-'lä-shənz *also* -shē-ənz, -sē-\ *noun plural but singular in construction*
: a letter written by Saint Paul to the Christians of Colossae and included as a book in the New Testament — see BIBLE table

co·los·sus \kə-'lä-səs\ *noun, plural* **co·los·si** \-'lä-ˌsī\ [Latin, from Greek *kolossos*] (14th century)
1 : a statue of gigantic size and proportions
2 : one that resembles a colossus in size or scope

co·los·to·my \kə-'läs-tə-mē\ *noun, plural* **-mies** [International Scientific Vocabulary ²*col-* + *-stomy*] (1888)
: surgical formation of an artificial anus

co·los·trum \kə-'läs-trəm\ *noun* [Latin, beestings] (1577)
: milk secreted for a few days after parturition and characterized by high protein and antibody content
— **co·los·tral** \-trəl\ *adjective*

col·our \'kə-lər\ *chiefly British variant of* COLOR

-colous *adjective combining form* [Latin *-cola* inhabitant; akin to Latin *colere* to inhabit — more at WHEEL]
: living or growing in or on ⟨areni*colous*⟩

col·por·tage \'käl-ˌpōr-tij, -ˌpòr-; ˌkäl-pōr-'täzh, -ˌpòr-\ *noun* (circa 1846)
: a colporteur's work

col·por·teur \'käl-ˌpōr-tər, -ˌpòr-; ˌkäl-pōr-'tər, -ˌpòr-\ *noun* [French, alteration of Middle French *comporteur*, from *comporter* to bear, peddle] (1796)
: a peddler of religious books

colt \'kōlt\ *noun* [Middle English, from Old English; akin to Swedish dialect *kult* half-grown pig] (before 12th century)
1 a : FOAL **b :** a young male horse that is either sexually immature or has not attained an arbitrarily designated age
2 : a young untried person

colt·ish \'kōl-tish\ *adjective* (14th century)
1 a : not subjected to discipline **b :** FRISKY, PLAYFUL
2 : of, relating to, or resembling a colt
— **colt·ish·ly** *adverb*
— **colt·ish·ness** *noun*

colts·foot \'kōlts-ˌfùt\ *noun, plural* **colts·foots** (14th century)
: any of various plants with large rounded leaves resembling the foot of a colt; *especially* **:** a perennial composite herb (*Tussilago farfara*) with yellow flower heads appearing before the leaves

col·u·brid \'käl-yə-brəd, 'kä-lə-\ *noun* [ultimately from Latin *colubra* snake] (1887)
: any of a large cosmopolitan family (Colubridae) of chiefly nonvenomous snakes
— **colubrid** *adjective*

col·u·brine \-ˌbrīn\ *adjective* (circa 1528)
1 : of, relating to, or resembling a snake
2 : of or relating to colubrids **:** COLUBRID

co·lu·go \kə-'lü-ˌgō\ *noun, plural* **-gos** [perhaps from a language of the Philippines] (circa 1890)
: FLYING LEMUR

col·um·bar·i·um \ˌkä-ləm-'bar-ē-əm, -'ber-\ *noun, plural* **-ia** \-ē-ə\ [Latin, literally, dovecote, from *columba* dove] (1846)
1 : a structure of vaults lined with recesses for cinerary urns
2 : a recess in a columbarium

Co·lum·bia \kə-'ləm-bē-ə\ *noun* [New Latin, from Christopher *Columbus*] (1775)
: the United States

Co·lum·bi·an \-bē-ən\ *adjective* (1757)
: of or relating to the United States or to Christopher Columbus

col·um·bine \'kä-ləm-ˌbīn\ *noun* [Middle English, from Medieval Latin *columbina*, from Latin, feminine of *columbinus* like a dove, from *columba* dove; akin to Old High German

holuntar elder tree, Greek *kolymbos* a small grebe, *kelainos* black] (14th century)
: any of a genus (*Aquilegia*) of plants of the buttercup family with irregular showy spurred flowers: as **a :** a red-flowered plant (*A. canadensis*) of eastern North America **b :** a blue-flowered plant (*A. caerulea*) of the Rocky Mountains

Col·um·bine \-ˌbīn, -ˌbēn\ *noun* [Italian *Colombina*]
: the saucy sweetheart of Harlequin in comedy and pantomime

columbine a

co·lum·bite \kə-'ləm-ˌbīt, 'kä-ləm-\ *noun* [New Latin *columbium*] (1805)
: a black mineral consisting mostly of iron and niobium

co·lum·bi·um \kə-'ləm-bē-əm\ *noun* [New Latin, from *Columbia*] (1801)
: NIOBIUM

Co·lum·bus Day \kə-'ləm-bəs-\ *noun* (1893)
1 : October 12 formerly observed as a legal holiday in many states of the U.S. in commemoration of the landing of Columbus in the Bahamas in 1492
2 : the second Monday in October observed as a legal holiday in many states of the U.S.

col·u·mel·la \ˌkäl-yə-'me-lə\ *noun, plural* **-mel·lae** \-'me-(ˌ)lē, -ˌlī\ [New Latin, from Latin, diminutive of *columna*] (circa 1755)
1 : the central column or axis of a spiral univalve shell
2 : the axis of the capsule in mosses and in some liverworts
3 a : the bony or partly cartilaginous rod connecting the tympanic membrane with the internal ear in birds and in many reptiles and amphibians **b :** the bony central axis of the cochlea
4 : the central sterile portion of the sporangium in various fungi (*Mucor* and related genera)
— **col·u·mel·lar** \-'me-lər\ *adjective*

col·umn \'kä-ləm *also* 'käl-yəm\ *noun* [Middle English *columne*, from Middle French *colomne*, from Latin *columna*, from *columen* top; akin to Latin *collis* hill — more at HILL] (15th century)
1 a : a vertical arrangement of items printed or written on a page **b :** one of two or more vertical sections of a printed page separated by a rule or blank space **c :** an accumulation arranged vertically **:** STACK **d :** one in a usually regular series of newspaper or magazine articles ⟨gossip *column*⟩
2 : a supporting pillar; *especially* **:** one consisting of a usually round shaft, a capital, and a base
3 a : something resembling a column in form, position, or function ⟨a *column* of water⟩ **b :** a tube or cylinder in which a chromatographic separation takes place
4 : a long row (as of soldiers)
5 : one of the vertical lines of elements of a determinant or matrix
— **col·umned** \-ləmd, -yəmd\ *adjective*

co·lum·nar \kə-'ləm-nər\ *adjective* (1728)
1 : of, relating to, resembling, or characterized by columns
2 : of, relating to, being, or composed of tall

Labels on figure: CORNICE, FRIEZE, ARCHITRAVE, CAPITAL, ENTABLATURE, SHAFT, COLUMN, BASE, PEDESTAL

narrow somewhat cylindrical or prismatic epithelial cells

co·lum·ni·a·tion \kə-ˌləm-nē-'ā-shən\ *noun* [probably from *intercolumniation*] (1664)
: the employment or the arrangement of columns in a structure

col·um·nist \'kä-ləm-nist, -lə-mist *also* 'käl-yəm-nist, -yə-mist\ *noun* (1920)
: one who writes a newspaper or magazine column
— **col·um·nis·tic** \ˌkä-ləm-'nis-tik *also* ˌkäl-yəm-\ *adjective*

col·za \'käl-zə, 'kōl-\ *noun* [French, from Dutch *koolzaad*, from Middle Dutch *coolsaet*, from *coole* cabbage + *saet* seed] (1712)
1 : any of several coles; *especially* **:** one (as rape) producing seed used as a source of oil
2 : RAPESEED

com- *or* **col-** *or* **con-** *prefix* [Middle English, from Old French, from Latin, with, together, thoroughly — more at CO-]
: with **:** together — usually *com-* before *b*, *p*, or *m* ⟨*com*mingle⟩, *col-* before *l* ⟨*col*linear⟩, and *con-* before other sounds ⟨*con*centrate⟩

¹co·ma \'kō-mə\ *noun* [New Latin, from Greek *kōma* deep sleep] (1646)
1 : a state of profound unconsciousness caused by disease, injury, or poison
2 : a state of mental or physical sluggishness **:** TORPOR

²coma *noun, plural* **co·mae** \-ˌmē, -ˌmī\ [Latin, hair, from Greek *komē*] (1669)
1 : a tufted bunch (as of branches, bracts, or seed hairs)
2 : the head of a comet usually containing a nucleus
3 : an optical aberration in which the image of a point source is a comet-shaped blur
— **co·mat·ic** \kō-'ma-tik\ *adjective*

Co·ma Ber·e·ni·ces \'kō-mə-ˌber-ə-'nī-(ˌ)sēz\ *noun* [Latin (genitive *Comae Berenices*), literally, Berenice's hair]
: a constellation north of Virgo and between Boötes and Leo

co·mak·er \(ˌ)kō-'mā-kər\ *noun* (circa 1934)
: one that participates in an agreement; *specifically* **:** one who stands to meet a financial obligation in the event of the maker's default

Co·man·che \kə-'man-chē\ *noun, plural* **Comanche** *or* **Comanches** [American Spanish, from Southern Paiute *kimmancin^wi* Shoshones, strangers] (1806)
1 : a member of an American Indian people ranging from Wyoming and Nebraska south into New Mexico and northwestern Texas
2 : the Uto-Aztecan language of the Comanche people

co·mate \(ˌ)kō-'māt, 'kō-ˌ\ *noun* (1576)
: COMPANION

co·ma·tose \'kō-mə-ˌtōs, 'kä-\ *adjective* [French *comateux*, from Greek *kōmat-, kōma*] (1755)
1 : of, resembling, or affected with coma
2 : characterized by lethargic inertness **:** TORPID ⟨a *comatose* economy⟩

¹comb \'kōm\ *noun* [Middle English, from Old English *camb;* akin to Old High German *kamb* comb, Greek *gomphos* tooth] (before 12th century)
1 a : a toothed instrument used especially for adjusting, cleaning, or confining hair **b :** a structure resembling such a comb; *especially* **:** any of several toothed devices used in handling or ordering textile fibers **c :** CURRYCOMB
2 a : a fleshy crest on the head of the domestic fowl and other gallinaceous birds **b :** something (as the ridge of a roof) resembling the comb of a cock
3 : HONEYCOMB
— **combed** \'kōmd\ *adjective*
— **comb·like** \'kōm-ˌlīk\ *adjective*

²comb (14th century)
transitive verb

1 : to draw a comb through for the purpose of arranging or cleaning
2 : to pass across with a scraping or raking action
3 a : to eliminate (as with a comb) by a thorough going-over **b :** to search or examine systematically
4 : to use in a combing action
intransitive verb
1 *of a wave or its crest* **:** to roll over or break into foam
2 : to make a thorough search ⟨*comb* through the classified ads⟩

¹**com·bat** \'käm-ˌbat\ *noun* (1546)
1 : a fight or contest between individuals or groups
2 : CONFLICT, CONTROVERSY
3 : active fighting in a war : ACTION ⟨casualties suffered in *combat*⟩

²**com·bat** \kəm-'bat, 'käm-ˌ\ *verb* **-bat·ed** *or* **-bat·ted; -bat·ing** *or* **-bat·ting** [Middle French *combattre,* from (assumed) Vulgar Latin *combattere,* from Latin *com-* + *battuere* to beat] (1564)
intransitive verb
: to engage in combat : FIGHT
transitive verb
1 : to fight with : BATTLE
2 : to struggle against; *especially* **:** to strive to reduce or eliminate ⟨*combat* pollution⟩
synonym see OPPOSE

³**com·bat** \'käm-ˌbat\ *adjective* (1825)
1 : relating to combat ⟨*combat* missions⟩
2 : designed or destined for combat ⟨*combat* boots⟩ ⟨*combat* troops⟩

com·bat·ant \kəm-'ba-t°nt *also* 'käm-bə-tənt\ *noun* (15th century)
: one that is engaged in or ready to engage in combat
— **combatant** *adjective*

combat fatigue *noun* (1943)
: a traumatic psychoneurotic reaction or an acute psychotic reaction occurring under conditions (as wartime combat) that cause intense stress — called also *battle fatigue*

com·bat·ive \kəm-'ba-tiv\ *adjective* (circa 1834)
: marked by eagerness to fight or contend
— **com·bat·ive·ly** *adverb*
— **com·bat·ive·ness** *noun*

combe \'küm, 'kōm\ *noun* [Middle English *coumbe, cumbe,* from Old English *cumb,* of Celtic origin; akin to Welsh *cwm* valley] (before 12th century)
1 *British* **:** a deep narrow valley
2 *British* **:** a valley or basin on the flank of a hill

comb·er \'kō-mər\ *noun* (circa 1682)
1 : one that combs
2 : a long curling wave of the sea

com·bi·na·tion \ˌkäm-bə-'nā-shən\ *noun, often attributive* (14th century)
1 a : a result or product of combining; *especially* **:** an alliance of individuals, corporations, or states united to achieve a social, political, or economic end **b :** two or more persons working as a team
2 : an ordered sequence: as **a :** a sequence of letters or numbers chosen in setting a lock; *also* **:** the mechanism operating or moved by the sequence **b :** a rapid sequence of punches in boxing **c :** any subset of a set considered without regard to order within the subset
3 : any of various one-piece undergarments for the upper and lower parts of the body — usually used in plural
4 : an instrument designed to perform two or more tasks
5 a : the act or process of combining; *especially* **:** that of uniting to form a chemical compound **b :** the quality or state of being combined
— **com·bi·na·tion·al** \-shnəl, -shə-n°l\ *adjective*

combination shot *noun* (circa 1909)
: a shot in pool in which a ball is pocketed by an object ball

com·bi·na·tive \'käm-bə-ˌnā-tiv, kəm-'bī-nə-\ *adjective* (1855)
1 : tending or able to combine
2 : resulting from combination

com·bi·na·to·ri·al \ˌkäm-bə-nə-'tōr-ē-əl, kəm-ˌbī-nə-, -(ˌ)bi-, -'tȯr-\ *adjective* (1818)
1 : of, relating to, or involving combinations
2 : of or relating to the arrangement of, operation on, and selection of discrete mathematical elements belonging to finite sets or making up geometric configurations
— **com·bi·na·to·ri·al·ly** \-ē-ə-lē\ *adverb*

com·bi·na·tor·ics \-'tȯr-iks, -'tär-\ *noun plural but singular in construction* (1951)
: combinatorial mathematics

com·bi·na·to·ry \kəm-'bī-nə-ˌtōr-ē, -ˌtȯr-\ *adjective* (1647)
: COMBINATIVE

¹**com·bine** \kəm-'bīn\ *verb* **com·bined; com·bin·ing** [Middle English, from Middle French *combiner,* from Late Latin *combinare,* from Latin *com-* + *bini* two by two — more at BIN-] (15th century)
transitive verb
1 a : to bring into such close relationship as to obscure individual characters **:** MERGE **b :** to cause to unite into a chemical compound **c :** to unite into a single number or expression ⟨*combine* fractions and simplify⟩
2 : INTERMIX, BLEND
3 : to possess in combination
intransitive verb
1 a : to become one **b :** to unite to form a chemical compound
2 : to act together
synonym see JOIN
— **com·bin·able** \-'bī-nə-bəl\ *adjective*
— **com·bin·er** *noun*

²**com·bine** \'käm-ˌbīn\ *noun* (1886)
1 : a combination especially of business or political interests
2 : a harvesting machine that heads, threshes, and cleans grain while moving over a field

³**com·bine** \'käm-ˌbīn\ *verb* **com·bined; com·bin·ing** (1926)
transitive verb
: to harvest with a combine
intransitive verb
: to combine a crop

comb·ing \'kō-miŋ\ *variant of* COAMING

comb·ings \'kō-miŋz\ *noun plural* (1656)
: loose hair removed by a comb

combing wool *noun* (1757)
: long-staple strong-fibered wool found suitable for combing and used especially in the manufacture of worsteds

combining form *noun* (1884)
: a linguistic form that occurs only in compounds or derivatives and can be distinguished descriptively from an affix by its ability to occur as one immediate constituent of a form whose only other immediate constituent is an affix (as *cephal-* in *cephalic*) or by its being an allomorph of a morpheme having another allomorph that may occur alone or can be distinguished historically from an affix by the fact that it is borrowed from another language in which it is descriptively a word or a combining form

comb jelly *noun* (circa 1889)
: CTENOPHORE

com·bo \'käm-(ˌ)bō\ *noun, plural* **combos** [*combination* + ¹*-o*] (1924)
1 : a usually small jazz or dance band
2 : COMBINATION

com·bust \kəm-'bəst\ *verb* [Latin *combustus,* past participle of *comburere* to burn up, irregular from *com-* + *urere* to burn — more at EMBER] (15th century)
: BURN

com·bus·ti·ble \kəm-'bəs-tə-bəl\ *adjective* (1529)
1 : capable of combustion
2 : easily excited
— **com·bus·ti·bil·i·ty** \-ˌbəs-tə-'bi-lə-tē\ *noun*

— **combustible** *noun*
— **com·bus·ti·bly** \-'bəs-tə-blē\ *adverb*

com·bus·tion \kəm-'bəs-chən\ *noun* (15th century)
1 : an act or instance of burning
2 : a usually rapid chemical process (as oxidation) that produces heat and usually light; *also* **:** a slower oxidation (as in the body)
3 : violent agitation : TUMULT
— **com·bus·tive** \-'bəs-tiv\ *adjective*

com·bus·tor \-'bəs-tər\ *noun* (1945)
: a chamber (as in a gas turbine or a jet engine) in which combustion occurs — called also *combustion chamber*

¹**come** \'kəm\ *verb* **came** \'kām\; **come; com·ing** \'kə-miŋ\ [Middle English, from Old English *cuman;* akin to Old High German *queman* to come, Latin *venire,* Greek *bainein* to walk, go] (before 12th century)
intransitive verb
1 a : to move toward something : APPROACH ⟨*come* here⟩ **b :** to move or journey to a vicinity with a specified purpose ⟨*come* see us⟩ ⟨*come* and see what's going on⟩ **c** (1) **:** to reach a particular station in a series ⟨now we *come* to the section on health⟩ (2) **:** to arrive in due course ⟨the time has *come*⟩ **d** (1) **:** to approach in kind or quality ⟨this *comes* near perfection⟩ (2) **:** to reach a condition or conclusion ⟨*came* to regard him as a friend⟩ ⟨*come* to think of it, you may be right⟩ **e** (1) **:** to advance toward accomplishment ⟨learning new ways doesn't *come* easy⟩ ⟨the job is *coming* nicely⟩ (2) **:** to advance in a particular manner ⟨*come* running when I call⟩ (3) **:** to advance, rise, or improve in rank or condition ⟨has *come* a long way⟩ **f :** to get along : FARE — often used with *along* ⟨*came* to her ankles⟩ **g :** EXTEND ⟨her dress *came* to her ankles⟩
2 a (1) **:** to arrive at a particular place, end, result, or conclusion ⟨*come* to his senses⟩ ⟨*come* untied⟩ (2) **:** AMOUNT ⟨the taxes on it *come* to more than it's worth⟩ **b** (1) **:** to appear to the mind ⟨the answer *came* to them⟩ (2) **:** to appear on a scene **:** make an appearance ⟨children *come* equipped to learn any language⟩ **c** (1) **:** HAPPEN, OCCUR ⟨no harm will *come* to you⟩ (2) **:** to come to pass **:** take place — used in the subjunctive with inverted subject and verb to express the particular time or occasion ⟨*come* spring the days will be longer⟩ **d :** ORIGINATE, ARISE ⟨wine *comes* from grapes⟩ ⟨*come* of sturdy stock⟩ **e :** to enter or assume a condition ⟨artillery *came* into action⟩ **f :** to fall within a field of view or a range of application ⟨this *comes* within the terms of the treaty⟩ **g :** to issue forth ⟨a sob *came* from her throat⟩ **h :** to take form ⟨churn till the butter *comes*⟩ **i :** to be available ⟨this model comes in several sizes⟩ ⟨as good as they *come*⟩ **j :** to experience orgasm — often considered vulgar
3 : to fall to a person in a division or inheritance of property
4 *obsolete* **:** to become moved favorably : RELENT
5 : to turn out to be ⟨good clothes *come* high⟩
6 : BECOME ⟨a dream that *came* true⟩
transitive verb
1 : to approach or be near (an age) ⟨a child *coming* eight years old⟩
2 : to take on the aspect of ⟨*come* the stern parent⟩
— **come a cropper :** to fail completely
— **come clean :** to tell the whole story **:** CONFESS
— **come into :** to acquire as a possession or achievement ⟨*come into* a fortune⟩
— **come into one's own :** to achieve one's potential; *also* **:** to gain recognition

\ə\ abut \ˌ°\ kitten \ər\ further \a\ ash \ā\ ace \ä\ mop, mar \au̇\ out \ch\ chin \e\ bet \ē\ easy \g\ go \i\ hit \ī\ ice \j\ job \ŋ\ sing \ō\ go \o̊\ law \o̊i\ boy \th\ thin \th̲\ the \ü\ loot \u̇\ foot \y\ yet \zh\ vision *see also* Guide to Pronunciation

— **come of age** : to reach maturity

— **come off it** : to cease foolish or pretentious talk or behavior

— **come over** : to seize suddenly and strangely ⟨what's *come over* you⟩

— **come to** : to be a question of ⟨when it *comes to* pitching horseshoes, he's the champ⟩

— **come to grips with** : to meet or deal with firmly, frankly, or straightforwardly ⟨*come to grips with* the unemployment problem⟩

— **come to oneself** : to get hold of oneself : regain self-control

— **come to pass** : HAPPEN

— **come to terms 1** : to reach an agreement — often used with *with* **2** : to become adjusted especially emotionally or intellectually — usually used with *with* ⟨*come to terms* with modern life⟩

²**come** *noun* (1923)
1 : SEMEN — often considered vulgar
2 : ORGASM — often considered vulgar

come about *intransitive verb* (14th century)
1 : HAPPEN
2 : to change direction ⟨the wind has *come about* into the north⟩
3 : to shift to a new tack

come across *intransitive verb* (1910)
1 : to give over or furnish something demanded; *especially* : to pay over money
2 : to produce an impression ⟨*comes across* as a good speaker⟩
3 : COME THROUGH 2

come along *intransitive verb* (1694)
1 : to accompany someone who leads the way ⟨asked me to *come along* on the trip⟩
2 : to make progress ⟨work is *coming along* well⟩
3 : to make an appearance ⟨won't just marry the first man that *comes along*⟩

come around *intransitive verb* (1934)
1 : COME ROUND
2 : MENSTRUATE

come·back \'kəm-ˌbak\ *noun* (1889)
1 a : a sharp or witty reply : RETORT **b** : a cause for complaint
2 : a return to a former position or condition (as of success or prosperity) : RECOVERY, REVIVAL ⟨staging his ultimate *comeback* from self-imposed exile —Howard Mandel⟩

come back *intransitive verb* (1850)
1 : to return to life or vitality
2 : to return to memory ⟨it's all *coming back* to me now⟩
3 : REPLY, RETORT
4 : to regain a former favorable condition or position

come by (1863)
intransitive verb
: to make a visit
transitive verb
: to get possession of : ACQUIRE ⟨a good job is hard to *come by*⟩

co·me·di·an \kə-'mē-dē-ən\ *noun* (1581)
1 *archaic* **a** : a writer of comedies **b** : an actor who plays comic roles
2 : a comical individual; *specifically* : a professional entertainer who uses any of various physical or verbal means to be amusing

co·me·dic \-'mē-dik\ *adjective* (1639)
1 : of or relating to comedy
2 : COMICAL 2

— **co·me·dic·al·ly** \-di-k(ə-)lē\ *adverb*

co·me·di·enne \-ˌmē-dē-'en\ *noun* [French *comédienne*, feminine of *comédien* comedian, from *comédie*] (circa 1859)
: a woman who is a comedian

come·do \'kä-mə-ˌdō\ *noun, plural* **come·do·nes** \ˌkä-mə-'dō-(ˌ)nēz\ [New Latin, from Latin, glutton, from *comedere* to eat — more at COMESTIBLE] (1866)
: BLACKHEAD 1

come·down \'kəm-ˌdau̇n\ *noun* (1840)
: a descent in rank or dignity

come down *intransitive verb* (1711)
1 a : to pass by tradition ⟨a story that has

come down from medieval times⟩ **b** : to pass from a usually high source ⟨word *came down* that the strike was over⟩
2 a : to reduce itself : AMOUNT ⟨it *comes down* to this⟩ **b** : to deal with a subject directly ⟨when you *come down* to it, we all depend on others⟩
3 : to lose or fall in estate or condition ⟨has *come down* in the world⟩
4 : to place oneself in opposition ⟨*came down* hard on gambling⟩
5 : to become ill ⟨*came down* with measles⟩
6 : COME OUT 2

com·e·dy \'kä-mə-dē\ *noun, plural* **-dies** [Middle English, from Middle French *comedie*, from Latin *comoedia*, from Greek *kōmōidia*, from *kōmos* revel + *aeidein* to sing — more at ODE] (14th century)
1 a : a medieval narrative that ends happily ⟨Dante's Divine *Comedy*⟩ **b** : a literary work written in a comic style or treating a comic theme
2 a : a drama of light and amusing character and typically with a happy ending **b** : the genre of dramatic literature dealing with the comic or with the serious in a light or satirical manner — compare TRAGEDY
3 : a ludicrous or farcical event or series of events
4 a : the comic element ⟨the *comedy* of many life situations⟩ **b** : humorous entertainment ⟨nightclub *comedy*⟩

comedy drama *noun* (1885)
: serious drama that is interspersed with comedy

comedy of manners (1822)
: comedy that satirically portrays the manners and fashions of a particular class or set

come–hith·er \(ˌ)kəm-'hi-thər, (ˌ)kə-'mi-\ *adjective* (1925)
: sexually provocative ⟨that *come-hither* look in your eyes⟩

come in *intransitive verb* (14th century)
1 a : to arrive on a scene ⟨new models *coming in*⟩ **b** : to become available ⟨data began *coming in*⟩
2 : to place among those finishing ⟨*came in* last⟩
3 a : to function in an indicated manner ⟨*come in* handy⟩ **b** *of a telecommunications signal* : to be received ⟨*came in* loud and clear⟩
4 : to assume a role or function ⟨that's where you *come in*⟩
5 : to attain maturity, fruitfulness, or production

— **come in for** : to become subject to ⟨*coming in for* increasing criticism⟩

come·ly \'kəm-lē *also* 'kōm- *or* 'käm-\ *adjective* **come·li·er; -est** [Middle English *comly*, alteration of Old English *cȳmlic* glorious, from *cȳme* lively, fine; akin to Old High German *kūmig* weak] (13th century)
1 : pleasurably conforming to notions of good appearance, suitability, or proportion
2 : having a pleasing appearance : not homely or plain
synonym see BEAUTIFUL

— **come·li·ness** *noun*

come off (1596)
intransitive verb
1 a : to acquit oneself : FARE ⟨*came off* well in the contest⟩ **b** : APPEAR, SEEM
2 : SUCCEED ⟨a television series that never *came off* —TV Guide⟩
3 : HAPPEN, OCCUR
transitive verb
: to have recently completed or recovered from ⟨*coming off* a good year⟩ ⟨*coming off* an injury⟩

come–on \'kə-ˌmȯn, -ˌmän\ *noun* (1902)
1 : something (as an advertising promotion) intended to entice or allure
2 : a usually sexual advance

come on *intransitive verb* (15th century)

1 a : to advance by degrees ⟨darkness *came on*⟩ **b** : to begin by degrees ⟨rain *came on* toward noon⟩
2 a : PLEASE — used in cajoling or pleading **b** — used interjectionally to express astonishment, incredulity, or recognition of a put-on
3 : to project an indicated personal image ⟨*comes on* as a conservative⟩
4 : to show sexual interest in someone; *also* : to make sexual advances ⟨tried to *come on* to her⟩

come out *intransitive verb* (13th century)
1 a : to come into public view : make a public appearance ⟨a new magazine has *come out*⟩ **b** : to become evident ⟨his pride *came out* in his refusal to accept help⟩
2 : to declare oneself especially in public utterance ⟨*came out* in favor of the proposal⟩
3 : to turn out in an outcome : end up ⟨everything *came out* all right⟩
4 : to make a debut
5 : to openly declare one's homosexuality

— **com·ing–out** \ˌkə-miŋ-'au̇t\ *adjective*

— **come out with 1** : to give expression to ⟨*came out with* a new proposal⟩ **2** : PUBLISH

come–out·er \(ˌ)kə-'mau̇-tər\ *noun* (1840)
1 : a person who withdraws from something established (as a religious body)
2 : a person who advocates political reform

come over *intransitive verb* (1576)
1 a : to change from one side (as of a controversy) to the other **b** : to visit casually : DROP IN ⟨*come over* whenever you like⟩
2 *British* : BECOME

com·er \'kə-mər\ *noun* (14th century)
1 : one that comes or arrives ⟨all *comers*⟩
2 : one making rapid progress or showing promise

come round *intransitive verb* (1818)
1 : to change direction
2 : to return to a former condition; *especially* : COME TO 1
3 : to accede to a particular opinion or course of action ⟨knew you'd *come round* to our side eventually⟩

¹**co·mes·ti·ble** \kə-'mes-tə-bəl\ *adjective* [Middle French, from Medieval Latin *comestibilis*, from Latin *comestus*, past participle of *comedere* to eat, from *com-* + *edere* to eat — more at EAT] (15th century)
: EDIBLE

²**comestible** *noun* (1837)
: FOOD — usually used in plural

com·et \'kä-mət\ *noun* [Middle English *comete*, from Old English *cometa*, from Latin, from Greek *komētēs*, literally, long-haired, from *koman* to wear long hair, from *komē* hair] (before 12th century)
: a celestial body that consists of a fuzzy head usually surrounding a bright nucleus, that has a usually highly eccentric orbit, and that often when in the part of its orbit near the sun develops a long tail which points away from the sun

— **com·e·tary** \-mə-ˌter-ē\ *adjective*
— **co·met·ic** \kə-'me-tik, kä-\ *adjective*

come through *intransitive verb* (1914)
1 : to do what is needed or expected ⟨*came through* in the clutch⟩
2 : to become communicated

come to *intransitive verb* (circa 1572)
1 : to recover consciousness
2 a : to bring a ship's head nearer the wind : LUFF **b** : to come to anchor or to a stop

come up *intransitive verb* (14th century)
1 : RISE 6
2 : to come near : make an approach ⟨*came up* and introduced himself⟩
3 : to rise in rank or status ⟨an officer who *came up* from the ranks⟩
4 a : to come to attention or consideration ⟨the question never *came up*⟩ **b** : to occur in the course of time ⟨any problem that may *come up*⟩
5 : to turn out to be ⟨the coin *came up* tails⟩

— **come up with** : to produce especially in

dealing with a problem or challenge ⟨came up with a solution⟩

come·up·pance \(ˌ)kə-'mə-pən(t)s\ *noun* [*come up* + *-ance*] (1859)
: a deserved rebuke or penalty : DESERTS

com·fit \'kəm(p)-fət, 'käm(p)-\ *noun* [Middle English *confit*, from Middle French, from past participle of *confire* to prepare, from Latin *conficere*, from *com-* + *facere* to make — more at DO] (14th century)
: a candy consisting of a piece of fruit, a root (as licorice), a nut, or a seed coated and preserved with sugar

¹com·fort \'kəm(p)-fərt\ *transitive verb* [Middle English, from Old French *conforter*, from Late Latin *confortare* to strengthen greatly, from Latin *com-* + *fortis* strong] (13th century)
1 : to give strength and hope to : CHEER
2 : to ease the grief or trouble of : CONSOLE
— **com·fort·ing·ly** \-fər-tiŋ-lē\ *adverb*

²comfort *noun* (13th century)
1 : strengthening aid : **a** : ASSISTANCE, SUPPORT ⟨accused of giving aid and *comfort* to the enemy⟩ **b** : consolation in time of trouble or worry : SOLACE
2 a : a feeling of relief or encouragement **b** : contented well-being
3 : a satisfying or enjoyable experience
4 : one that gives or brings comfort ⟨all the *comforts* of home⟩
— **com·fort·less** \-ləs\ *adjective*

com·fort·able \'kəm(p)(f)-tə(r)-bəl, 'kəm(p)-fə(r)-tə-bəl, 'kəm(p)-fər-tə-bəl\ *adjective* (1769)
1 a : affording or enjoying contentment and security ⟨a *comfortable* income⟩ **b** : affording or enjoying physical comfort ⟨a *comfortable* chair⟩ ⟨was too *comfortable* to move⟩
2 a : free from vexation or doubt ⟨*comfortable* assumptions⟩ **b** : free from stress or tension ⟨a *comfortable* routine⟩ ☆
— **com·fort·able·ness** *noun*
— **com·fort·ably** \-blē\ *adverb*

com·fort·er \'kəm(p)-fə(r)-tər\ *noun* (14th century)
1 a *capitalized* : HOLY SPIRIT **b** : one that gives comfort
2 a : a long narrow usually knitted neck scarf **b** : a thick bed covering made of two layers of cloth containing a filling (as down)

comfort station *noun* (circa 1913)
: REST ROOM

com·frey \'kəm(p)-frē\ *noun, plural* **comfreys** [Middle English *cumfirie*, from Old French, from Latin *conferva* a water plant, from *confervēre* to grow together (of bones), from *com-* + *fervēre* to boil — more at BARM] (13th century)
: any of a genus (*Symphytum*) of perennial herbs of the borage family with coarse hairy entire leaves and flowers in one-sided racemes

com·fy \'kəm(p)-fē\ *adjective* [by shortening & alteration] (1829)
: COMFORTABLE

¹com·ic \'kä-mik\ *adjective* [Latin *comicus*, from Greek *kōmikos*, from *kōmos* revel] (1576)
1 : of, relating to, or marked by comedy
2 : causing laughter or amusement : FUNNY
3 : of or relating to comic strips
synonym see LAUGHABLE

²comic *noun* (1581)
1 : COMEDIAN
2 : the comic element
3 a : COMIC STRIP **b** : COMIC BOOK **c** *plural* : the part of a newspaper devoted to comic strips

com·i·cal \'kä-mi-kəl\ *adjective* (15th century)
1 *obsolete* : of or relating to comedy
2 : causing laughter especially because of a startlingly or unexpectedly humorous impact
synonym see LAUGHABLE
— **com·i·cal·i·ty** \ˌkä-mi-'ka-lə-tē\ *noun*
— **com·i·cal·ly** \'kä-mi-k(ə-)lē\ *adverb*

comic book *noun* (1941)
: a magazine containing sequences of comic strips

comic–opera *adjective* (1906)
: not to be taken seriously ⟨a *comic-opera* regime⟩

comic opera *noun* (1762)
: opera of a humorous character with a happy ending and usually some spoken dialogue

comic relief *noun* (1875)
: a relief from the emotional tension of a drama that is provided by the interposition of a comic episode or element

comic strip *noun* (1920)
: a group of cartoons in narrative sequence

¹com·ing \'kə-miŋ\ *noun* (13th century)
: an act or instance of arriving

²coming *adjective* (15th century)
1 : immediately due in sequence or development ⟨in the *coming* year⟩
2 : gaining importance

co·min·gle \kə-'miŋ-gəl\ *transitive verb* (1602)
: COMMINGLE

coming–of–age *noun* (1916)
: the attainment of prominence, respectability, recognition, or maturity

Com·in·tern \'kä-mən-ˌtərn\ *noun* [Russian *Komintern*, from *Kom*munisticheskiĭ *Intern*atsional'nyĭ Communist International] (1923)
: the Communist International established in 1919 and dissolved in 1943

co·mi·tia \kə-'mi-sh(ē-)ə\ *noun, plural* **comitia** [Latin, plural of *comitium*, from *com-* + *-it-* (akin to *ire* to go) — more at ISSUE] (1600)
: any of several public assemblies of the people in ancient Rome for legislative, judicial, and electoral purposes
— **co·mi·tial** \-'mi-shəl\ *adjective*

co·mi·ty \'kä-mə-tē, 'kō-\ *noun, plural* **-ties** [Latin *comitat-, comitas*, from *comis* courteous, probably from Old Latin *cosmis* (akin to *com-* + *-smis* (akin to Sanskrit *smayate* he smiles) — more at SMILE] (1543)
1 a : friendly social atmosphere : social harmony ⟨group activities promoting *comity*⟩ **b** : a loose widespread community based on common social institutions ⟨the *comity* of civilization⟩ **c** : COMITY OF NATIONS **d** : the informal and voluntary recognition by courts of one jurisdiction of the laws and judicial decisions of another
2 : avoidance of proselytizing members of another religious denomination

comity of nations (1862)
1 : the courtesy and friendship of nations marked especially by mutual recognition of executive, legislative, and judicial acts
2 : the group of nations practicing international comity

com·ma \'kä-mə\ *noun* [Late Latin, from Latin, part of a sentence, from Greek *komma* segment, clause, from *koptein* to cut — more at CAPON] (1554)
1 : a punctuation mark , used especially as a mark of separation within the sentence
2 : PAUSE, INTERVAL
3 : any of several nymphalid butterflies (genus *Polygonia*) with a silvery comma-shaped mark on the underside of the hind wings

comma fault *noun* (circa 1934)
: COMMA SPLICE

¹com·mand \kə-'mand\ *verb* [Middle English *comanden*, from Middle French *comander*, from (assumed) Vulgar Latin *commandare*, alteration of Latin *commendare* to commit to one's charge — more at COMMEND] (14th century)
transitive verb
1 : to direct authoritatively : ORDER
2 : to exercise a dominating influence over : have command of: as **a** : to have at one's immediate disposal **b** : to demand or receive as one's due ⟨*commands* a high fee⟩ **c** : to overlook or dominate from or as if from a strategic

position **d** : to have military command of as senior officer
3 *obsolete* : to order or request to be given
intransitive verb
1 : to have or exercise direct authority : GOVERN
2 : to give orders
3 : to be commander
4 : to dominate as if from an elevated place ☆
— **com·mand·able** \-'man-də-bəl\ *adjective*

²command *noun* (15th century)
1 a : an order given **b** : a signal that actuates a device (as a control mechanism in a spacecraft or one step in a computer); *also* : the activation of a device by means of such a signal
2 a : the ability to control : MASTERY **b** : the authority or right to command ⟨the officer in *command*⟩ **c** (1) : the power to dominate (2) : scope of vision **d** : facility in use ⟨a good *command* of French⟩
3 : the act of commanding
4 : the personnel, area, or organization under a commander; *specifically* : a unit of the U.S. Air Force higher than an air force
5 : a position of highest usually military authority
synonym see POWER

³command *adjective* (1826)
: done on command or request ⟨a *command* performance⟩

com·man·dant \'kä-mən-ˌdänt, -ˌdant\ *noun* (1687)
: COMMANDING OFFICER

☆ **SYNONYMS**
Comfortable, cozy, snug, easy, restful mean enjoying or providing a position of contentment and security. COMFORTABLE applies to anything that encourages serenity, well-being, or complacency as well as physical ease ⟨started feeling *comfortable* in our new surroundings⟩. COZY suggests warmth, shelter, assured ease, and friendliness ⟨a *cozy* neighborhood coffee shop⟩. SNUG suggests having just enough space for comfort and safety but no more ⟨a *snug* little cottage⟩. EASY implies relief from or absence of anything likely to cause physical or mental discomfort or constraint ⟨living in *easy* circumstances⟩. RESTFUL applies to whatever induces or contributes to rest or relaxation ⟨a quiet *restful* vacation⟩.

Command, order, bid, enjoin, direct, instruct, charge mean to issue orders. COMMAND and ORDER imply authority and usually some degree of formality and impersonality. COMMAND stresses official exercise of authority ⟨a general *commanding* troops⟩. ORDER may suggest peremptory or arbitrary exercise ⟨*ordered* his employees about like slaves⟩. BID suggests giving orders peremptorily (as to children or servants) ⟨she *bade* him be seated⟩. ENJOIN implies giving an order or direction authoritatively and urgently and often with admonition or solicitude ⟨a sign *enjoining* patrons to be quiet⟩. DIRECT and INSTRUCT both connote expectation of obedience and usually concern specific points of procedure or method. INSTRUCT sometimes implying greater explicitness or formality ⟨*directed* her assistant to hold all calls⟩ ⟨the judge *instructed* the jury to ignore the remark⟩. CHARGE adds to ENJOIN an implication of imposing as a duty or responsibility ⟨*charged* by the President with a secret mission⟩.

\ə\ abut \ᵊ\ kitten \ər\ further \a\ ash \ā\ ace
\ä\ mop, mar \au̇\ out \ch\ chin \e\ bet \ē\ easy
\g\ go \i\ hit \ī\ ice \j\ job \ŋ\ sing \ō\ go
\ȯ\ law \ȯi\ boy \th\ thin \t̲h\ the \ü\ loot \u̇\ foot
\y\ yet \zh\ vision *see also* Guide to Pronunciation

command car *noun* (1941)
: an open armored car designed especially for military reconnaissance and capable of traveling over rough terrain

com·man·deer \ˌkä-mən-'dir\ *transitive verb* [Afrikaans *kommandeer,* from French *commander* to command, from Old French *comander*] (1881)
1 a : to compel to perform military service **b :** to seize for military purposes
2 : to take arbitrary or forcible possession of

com·mand·er \kə-'man-dər\ *noun* (14th century)
1 : one in an official position of command or control: as **a :** COMMANDING OFFICER **b :** the presiding officer of a society or organization
2 : a commissioned officer in the navy or coast guard ranking above a lieutenant commander and below a captain
— **com·mand·er·ship** \-ˌship\ *noun*

commander in chief (1654)
: one who holds the supreme command of an armed force

com·mand·ery \kə-'man-d(ə-)rē\ *noun, plural* **-er·ies** (15th century)
1 : a district under the control of a commander of an order of knights
2 : an assembly or lodge in a secret order

com·mand·ing \kə-'man-diŋ\ *adjective* (1591)
1 : drawing attention or priority ⟨a *commanding* presence⟩
2 : difficult to overcome ⟨a *commanding* lead⟩
— **com·mand·ing·ly** \-diŋ-lē\ *adverb*

commanding officer *noun* (1720)
: an officer in command; *especially* : an officer in the armed forces in command of an organization or installation

com·mand·ment \kə-'man(d)-mənt\ *noun* (13th century)
1 : the act or power of commanding
2 : something that is commanded; *especially* : one of the biblical Ten Commandments

command module *noun* (1962)
: a space vehicle module designed to carry the crew, the chief communication equipment, and the equipment for reentry

com·man·do \kə-'man-(ˌ)dō\ *noun, plural* **-dos** *or* **-does** [Afrikaans *kommando,* from Dutch *commando* command, from Spanish *comando,* from *comandar* to command, from Late Latin *commandare*] (1884)
1 *South African* **a :** a military unit or command of the Boers **b :** a raiding expedition
2 a : a military unit trained and organized as shock troops especially for hit-and-run raids into enemy territory **b :** a member of such a unit

command post *noun* (circa 1918)
: a post at which the commander of a unit in the field receives orders and exercises command

command sergeant major *noun* (1967)
: a noncommissioned officer in the army ranking above a first sergeant

comma splice *noun* (1924)
: the careless or unjustified use of a comma between coordinate main clauses not connected by a conjunction (as in "nobody goes there anymore, it's boring")

com·me·dia del·l'ar·te \kə-ˌmā-dē-ə-(ˌ)del-'är-tē, kə-ˌme-\ *noun* [Italian, literally, comedy of art] (1877)
: Italian comedy of the 16th to 18th centuries improvised from standardized situations and stock characters

comme il faut \ˌkə-mē(l)-'fō\ *adjective* [French, literally, as it should be] (1756)
: conforming to accepted standards : PROPER

com·mem·o·rate \kə-'me-mə-ˌrāt\ *transitive verb* **-rat·ed; -rat·ing** [Latin *commemoratus,* past participle of *commemorare,* from *com-* + *memorare* to remind of, from *memor* mindful — more at MEMORY] (1599)
1 : to call to remembrance

2 : to mark by some ceremony or observation : OBSERVE
3 : to serve as a memorial of ⟨a plaque that *commemorates* the battle⟩
synonym see KEEP
— **com·mem·o·ra·tor** \-ˌrā-tər\ *noun*

com·mem·o·ra·tion \kə-ˌme-mə-'rā-shən\ *noun* (14th century)
1 : the act of commemorating
2 : something that commemorates

com·mem·o·ra·tive \kə-'mem-rə-tiv, -'me-mə-; -'me-mə-ˌrā-tiv\ *adjective* (1612)
: intended as a commemoration; *especially* : issued in limited quantities for a relatively short period in commemoration of a person, place, or event ⟨a *commemorative* stamp⟩
— **commemorative** *noun*
— **com·mem·o·ra·tive·ly** *adverb*

com·mence \kə-'men(t)s\ *verb* **com·menced; com·menc·ing** [Middle English *comencen,* from Middle French *comencer,* from (assumed) Vulgar Latin *cominitiare,* from Latin *com-* + Late Latin *initiare* to begin, from Latin, to initiate] (14th century)
transitive verb
: to enter upon : BEGIN ⟨*commence* proceedings⟩
intransitive verb
1 : to have or make a beginning : START
2 *chiefly British* : to begin to be or to act as
3 *chiefly British* : to take a degree at a university
synonym see BEGIN
— **com·menc·er** *noun*

com·mence·ment \kəm-'men(t)s-mənt\ *noun* (13th century)
1 : an act, instance, or time of commencing
2 a : the ceremonies or the day for conferring degrees or diplomas **b :** the period of activities at this time

com·mend \kə-'mend\ *verb* [Middle English, from Latin *commendare,* from *com-* + *mandare* to entrust — more at MANDATE] (14th century)
transitive verb
1 : to entrust for care or preservation
2 : to recommend as worthy of confidence or notice
3 : to mention with approbation : PRAISE
intransitive verb
: to commend or serve as a commendation of something
— **com·mend·able** \-'men-də-bəl\ *adjective*
— **com·mend·ably** \-blē\ *adverb*
— **com·mend·er** *noun*

com·men·da·tion \ˌkä-mən-'dā-shən, -ˌmen-\ *noun* (14th century)
1 a : an act of commending **b :** something (as a formal citation) that commends
2 *archaic* : COMPLIMENT

com·men·da·to·ry \kə-'men-də-ˌtōr-ē, -ˌtòr-\ *adjective* (1555)
: serving to commend

com·men·sal \kə-'men(t)-səl\ *adjective* [Middle English, from Medieval Latin *commensalis,* from Latin *com-* + Late Latin *mensalis* of the table, from Latin *mensa* table] (1877)
: of, relating to, or living in a state of commensalism
— **commensal** *noun*
— **com·men·sal·ly** \-sə-lē\ *adverb*

com·men·sal·ism \-sə-ˌli-zəm\ *noun* (1870)
: a relation between two kinds of organisms in which one obtains food or other benefits from the other without damaging or benefiting it

com·men·su·ra·ble \kə-'men(t)s-rə-bəl, -'men(t)sh-; -'men(t)-sə-, -shə-\ *adjective* (1557)
1 : having a common measure; *specifically* : divisible by a common unit an integral number of times
2 : COMMENSURATE 2
— **com·men·su·ra·bil·i·ty** \-ˌmen(t)s-rə-'bi-lə-tē, -ˌmen(t)sh-; -ˌmen(t)-sə-, -shə-\ *noun*

com·men·su·ra·bly \-'men(t)s-rə-blē, -'men(t)sh-; -'men(t)-sə-, -shə-\ *adverb*

com·men·su·rate \kə-'men(t)s-rət, -'men(t)sh-; -'men(t)-sə-, -shə-\ *adjective* [Late Latin *commensuratus,* from Latin *com-* + Late Latin *mensuratus,* past participle of *mensurare* to measure, from neuter of *commensus,* from Latin *mensura* measure — more at MEASURE] (1641)
1 : equal in measure or extent : COEXTENSIVE ⟨lived a life *commensurate* with the early years of the republic⟩
2 : corresponding in size, extent, amount, or degree : PROPORTIONATE ⟨was given a job *commensurate* with her abilities⟩
3 : COMMENSURABLE 1
— **com·men·su·rate·ly** *adverb*
— **com·men·su·ra·tion** \-ˌmen(t)-sə-'rā-shən, -sha-\ *noun*

¹**com·ment** \'kä-ˌment\ *noun* [Middle English, from Late Latin *commentum,* from Latin, invention, from neuter of *commentus,* past participle of *comminisci* to invent, from *com-* + *-minisci* (akin to *ment-, mens* mind) — more at MIND] (14th century)
1 : COMMENTARY
2 : a note explaining, illustrating, or criticizing the meaning of a writing
3 a : an observation or remark expressing an opinion or attitude **b :** a judgment expressed indirectly

²**comment** (15th century)
transitive verb
: to make a comment on ⟨the discovery . . . is hardly *commented* by the press —*Nation*⟩
intransitive verb
: to explain or interpret something by comment ⟨*commenting* on recent developments⟩

com·men·tary \'kä-mən-ˌter-ē\ *noun, plural* **-tar·ies** (15th century)
1 a : an explanatory treatise — usually used in plural **b :** a record of events usually written by a participant — usually used in plural
2 a : a systematic series of explanations or interpretations (as of a writing) **b :** COMMENT 2
3 a : something that serves for illustration or explanation ⟨the dark, airless apartments and sunless factories . . . are a sad *commentary* upon our civilization —H. A. Overstreet⟩ **b :** an expression of opinion

com·men·tate \'kä-mən-ˌtāt\ *verb* **-tat·ed; -tat·ing** [back-formation from *commentator*] (1794)
transitive verb
: to give a commentary on
intransitive verb
: to comment in a usually expository or interpretive manner; *also* : to act as a commentator

com·men·ta·tor \-ˌtā-tər\ *noun* (14th century)
: one who gives a commentary; *especially* : one who reports and discusses news on radio or television

¹**com·merce** \'kä-(ˌ)mərs\ *noun* [Middle French, from Latin *commercium,* from *com-* + *merc-, merx* merchandise] (1537)
1 : social intercourse : interchange of ideas, opinions, or sentiments
2 : the exchange or buying and selling of commodities on a large scale involving transportation from place to place
3 : SEXUAL INTERCOURSE
synonym see BUSINESS

²**com·merce** \'kä-(ˌ)mərs, kə-'mərs\ *intransitive verb* **com·merced; com·merc·ing** (1596)
archaic : COMMUNE

¹**com·mer·cial** \kə-'mər-shəl\ *adjective* (1598)
1 a (1) : occupied with or engaged in commerce or work intended for commerce ⟨a *commercial* artist⟩ (2) : of or relating to commerce ⟨*commercial* regulations⟩ (3) : characteristic of commerce ⟨*commercial* weights⟩ (4) : suitable, adequate, or prepared for commerce ⟨found oil in *commercial* quantities⟩ **b** (1) : being of an average or inferior quality ⟨*commercial* oxalic

acid⟩ ⟨show-quality versus *commercial* cattle⟩ (2) **:** producing artistic work of low standards for quick market success
2 a : viewed with regard to profit ⟨a *commercial* success⟩ **b :** designed for a large market
3 : emphasizing skills and subjects useful in business
4 : supported by advertisers ⟨*commercial* TV⟩
— **com·mer·ci·al·i·ty** \kə-ˌmər-shē-'a-lə-tē\ *noun*
— **com·mer·cial·ly** \-'mər-sh(ə-)lē\ *adverb*
²**commercial** *noun* (1935)
: an advertisement broadcast on radio or television

commercial bank *noun* (1910)
: a bank organized chiefly to handle the everyday financial transactions of businesses (as through demand deposit accounts and short-term commercial loans)
com·mer·cial·ise *British variant of* COMMERCIALIZE
com·mer·cial·ism \kə-'mər-shə-ˌli-zəm\ *noun* (1849)
1 : commercial spirit, institutions, or methods
2 : excessive emphasis on profit
— **com·mer·cial·ist** \-'mər-sh(ə-)list\ *noun*
— **com·mer·cial·is·tic** \-ˌmər-shə-'lis-tik\ *adjective*
com·mer·cial·ize \kə-'mər-shə-ˌlīz\ *transitive verb* **-ized; -iz·ing** (1830)
1 a : to manage on a business basis for profit **b :** to develop commerce in
2 : to exploit for profit ⟨*commercialize* Christmas⟩
3 : to debase in quality for more profit
— **com·mer·cial·i·za·tion** \-ˌmər-sh(ə-)lə-'zā-shən\ *noun*
commercial paper *noun* (1836)
: short-term unsecured discounted paper usually sold by one company to another for immediate cash needs
commercial traveler *noun* (1807)
: TRAVELING SALESMAN
com·mie \'kä-mē\ *noun, often capitalized* [by shortening & alteration] (1940)
: COMMUNIST
com·mi·na·tion \ˌkä-mə-'nā-shən\ *noun* [Middle English, from Middle French or Latin; Middle French, from Latin *commination-, comminatio,* from *comminari* to threaten, from *com-* + *minari* to threaten — more at MOUNT] (15th century)
: DENUNCIATION
— **com·mi·na·to·ry** \'kä-mə-nə-ˌtōr-ē, -ˌtòr-; kə-'mi-nə-, -'mī-\ *adjective*
com·min·gle \kə-'miŋ-gəl, kä-\ (circa 1626) *transitive verb*
1 : to blend thoroughly into a harmonious whole
2 : to combine (funds or properties) into a common fund or stock
intransitive verb
: to become commingled
synonym *see* MIX
com·mi·nute \'kä-mə-ˌnüt, -ˌnyüt\ *transitive verb* **-nut·ed; -nut·ing** [Latin *comminutus,* past participle of *comminuere,* from *com-* + *minuere* to lessen — more at MINOR] (1626)
: to reduce to minute particles **:** PULVERIZE
— **com·mi·nu·tion** \ˌkä-mə-'nü-shən, -'nyü-\ *noun*
com·mis·er·ate \kə-'mi-zə-ˌrāt\ *verb* **-at·ed; -at·ing** [Latin *commiseratus,* past participle of *commiserari,* from *com-* + *miserari* to pity, from *miser* wretched] (1599)
intransitive verb
: to feel or express sympathy **:** CONDOLE ⟨*commiserates* with them on their loss⟩
transitive verb
: to feel or express sorrow or compassion for
— **com·mis·er·at·ing·ly** *adverb*
— **com·mis·er·a·tion** \-ˌmi-zə-'rā-shən\ *noun*
— **com·mis·er·a·tive** \-'mi-zə-ˌrā-tiv\ *adjective*

com·mis·sar \'kä-mə-ˌsär\ *noun* [Russian *komissar,* from German *Kommissar,* from Medieval Latin *commissarius*] (1918)
1 a : a Communist party official assigned to a military unit to teach party principles and policies and to ensure party loyalty **b :** one that attempts to control public opinion or its expression
2 : the head of a government department in the U.S.S.R. until 1946
— **com·mis·sar·i·al** \ˌkä-mə-'sär-ē-əl, -'ser-\ *adjective*
com·mis·sar·i·at \ˌkä-mə-'ser-ē-ət, -'sar-, *especially for 3* -'sär-\ *noun* [New Latin *commissariatus,* from Medieval Latin *commissarius*] (1779)
1 : a system for supplying an army with food
2 : food supplies
3 [Russian *komissariat,* from German *Kommissariat,* from New Latin *commissariatus*] **:** a government department in the U.S.S.R. until 1946
4 : a board of commissioners
com·mis·sary \'kä-mə-ˌser-ē\ *noun, plural* **-sar·ies** [Middle English *commissarie,* from Medieval Latin *commissarius,* from Latin *commissus,* past participle of *committere*] (14th century)
1 : one delegated by a superior to execute a duty or an office
2 a : a store for equipment and provisions; *especially* **:** a supermarket for military personnel **b :** food supplies **c :** a lunchroom especially in a motion-picture studio
¹**com·mis·sion** \kə-'mi-shən\ *noun* [Middle English, from Middle French, from Latin *commission-, commissio* act of bringing together, from *committere*] (14th century)
1 a : a formal written warrant granting the power to perform various acts or duties **b :** a certificate conferring military rank and authority; *also* **:** the rank and authority so conferred
2 : an authorization or command to act in a prescribed manner or to perform prescribed acts **:** CHARGE
3 a : authority to act for, in behalf of, or in place of another **b :** a task or matter entrusted to one as an agent for another
4 a : a group of persons directed to perform some duty **b :** a government agency having administrative, legislative, or judicial powers **c :** a city council having legislative and executive functions
5 : an act of committing something
6 : a fee paid to an agent or employee for transacting a piece of business or performing a service; *especially* **:** a percentage of the money received from a total paid to the agent responsible for the business
7 : an act of entrusting or giving authority
— **in commission** *or* **into commission**
1 : under the authority of commissioners **2** *of a ship* **:** ready for active service **3 :** in use or in condition for use
— **on commission :** with commission serving as partial or full pay for work done
— **out of commission 1 :** out of active service or use **2 :** out of working order
²**commission** *transitive verb* **-mis·sioned; -mis·sion·ing** \-'mi-sh(ə-)niŋ\ (circa 1661)
1 : to furnish with a commission: as **a :** to confer a formal commission on ⟨was *commissioned* lieutenant⟩ **b :** to appoint or assign to a task or function ⟨was *commissioned* to do the biography⟩
2 : to order to be made ⟨*commissioned* a portrait⟩
3 : to put (a ship) in commission
com·mis·sion·aire \kə-ˌmi-shə-'nar, -'ner\ *noun* [French *commissionnaire,* from *commission*] (1641)
chiefly British **:** a uniformed attendant
commissioned officer *noun* (15th century)

: an officer of the armed forces holding by a commission a rank of second lieutenant or ensign or above
com·mis·sion·er \kə-'mi-sh(ə-)nər\ *noun* (15th century)
: a person with a commission: as **a :** a member of a commission **b :** the representative of the governmental authority in a district, province, or other unit often having both judicial and administrative powers **c :** the officer in charge of a department or bureau of the public service **d :** the administrative head of a professional sport
— **com·mis·sion·er·ship** \-ˌship\ *noun*
commission merchant *noun* (1796)
: BROKER 1b
commission plan *noun* (1919)
: a method of municipal government under which a small elective commission exercises both executive and legislative powers and each commissioner directly administers one or more municipal departments
com·mis·sure \'kä-mə-ˌshùr\ *noun* [Middle English, from Middle French or Latin; Middle French, from Latin *commissura* a joining, from *commissus,* past participle] (15th century)
1 : a point or line of union or junction especially between two anatomical parts (as adjacent heart valves)
2 : a connecting band of nerve tissue in the brain or spinal cord
— **com·mis·sur·al** \ˌkä-mə-'shùr-əl\ *adjective*
com·mit \kə-'mit\ *verb* **com·mit·ted; com·mit·ting** [Middle English *committen,* from Latin *committere* to connect, entrust, from *com-* + *mittere* to send] (14th century)
transitive verb
1 a : to put into charge or trust **:** ENTRUST **b :** to place in a prison or mental institution **c :** to consign or record for preservation ⟨*commit* it to memory⟩ **d :** to put into a place for disposal or safekeeping **e :** to refer (as a legislative bill) to a committee for consideration and report
2 : to carry into action deliberately **:** PERPETRATE ⟨*commit* a crime⟩
3 a : OBLIGATE, BIND **b :** to pledge or assign to some particular course or use ⟨*commit* all troops to the attack⟩ **c :** to reveal the views of ⟨refused to *commit* himself on the issue⟩
intransitive verb
1 *obsolete* **:** to perpetrate an offense
2 : to obligate or pledge oneself ☆
— **com·mit·ta·ble** \-'mi-tə-bəl\ *adjective*

☆ **SYNONYMS**
Commit, entrust, confide, consign, relegate mean to assign to a person or place for a definite purpose. COMMIT may express the general idea of delivering into another's charge or the special sense of transferring to a superior power or to a special place of custody (*committed* the felon to prison). ENTRUST implies committing with trust and confidence (the president is *entrusted* with broad powers). CONFIDE implies entrusting with great assurance or reliance (*confided* complete control of my affairs to my attorney). CONSIGN suggests removing from one's control with formality or finality (*consigned* the damaging notes to the fire). RELEGATE implies a consigning to a particular class or sphere often with a suggestion of getting rid of (*relegated* to an obscure position in the company).

\ə\ **abut** \ᵊ\ **kitten** \ər\ **further** \a\ **ash** \ā\ **ace**
\ä\ **mop, mar** \aù\ **out** \ch\ **chin** \e\ **bet** \ē\ **easy**
\g\ **go** \i\ **hit** \ī\ **ice** \j\ **job** \ŋ\ **sing** \ō\ **go**
\ò\ **law** \òi\ **boy** \th\ **thin** \t͟h\ **the** \ü\ **loot** \ù\ **foot**
\y\ **yet** \zh\ **vision** *see also* Guide to Pronunciation

com·mit·ment \kə-'mit-mənt\ noun (1621)
1 a : an act of committing to a charge or trust: as (1) **:** a consignment to a penal or mental institution (2) **:** an act of referring a matter to a legislative committee **b :** MITTIMUS
2 a : an agreement or pledge to do something in the future; *especially* **:** an engagement to assume a financial obligation at a future date **b :** something pledged **c :** the state or an instance of being obligated or emotionally impelled ⟨a *commitment* to a cause⟩
com·mit·tal \kə-'mi-t³l\ noun (1818)
: COMMITMENT, CONSIGNMENT
com·mit·tee \kə-'mi-tē, *sense 1 also* ˌkä-mi-'tē\ noun (15th century)
1 *archaic* **:** a person to whom a charge or trust is committed
2 a : a body of persons delegated to consider, investigate, take action on, or report on some matter; *especially* **:** a group of fellow legislators chosen by a legislative body to give consideration to legislative matters **b :** a self-constituted organization for the promotion of a common object
com·mit·tee·man \kə-'mi-tē-mən, -ˌman\ noun (1654)
1 : a member of a committee
2 : a party leader of a ward or precinct
committee of the whole (1775)
: the whole membership of a legislative house sitting as a committee and operating under informal rules
com·mit·tee·wom·an \-ˌwu̇-mən\ noun (1853)
1 : a woman who is a member of a committee
2 : a woman who is a party leader of a ward or precinct
com·mix \kə-'miks, kä-\ verb [back-formation from Middle English *comixt* blended, from Latin *commixtus*, past participle of *commiscēre* to mix together, from *com-* + *miscēre* to mix — more at MIX] (15th century)
transitive verb
: MINGLE, BLEND
intransitive verb
: to become mingled or blended
com·mix·ture \-chər\ noun [Latin *commixtura*, from *commixtus*] (1592)
1 : the act or process of mixing **:** the state of being mixed
2 : COMPOUND, MIXTURE
com·mode \kə-'mōd\ noun [French, from *commode*, adjective, suitable, convenient, from Latin *commodus*, from *com-* + *modus* measure — more at METE] (1688)
1 : a woman's ornate cap popular in the late 17th and early 18th centuries
2 a : a low chest of drawers **b :** a movable washstand with a cupboard underneath **c :** a boxlike structure holding a chamber pot under an open seat; *also* **:** CHAMBER POT **d :** TOILET 3b
com·mod·i·fy \kə-'mä-də-ˌfī\ transitive verb **-fied; -fy·ing** (1982)
: to turn (as an intrinsic value or a work of art) into a commodity
— **com·mod·i·fi·ca·tion** \-ˌmä-də-fə-'kā-shən\ noun
com·mo·di·ous \kə-'mō-dē-əs\ adjective [Middle English, useful, from Middle French *commodieux*, from Medieval Latin *commodiosus*, irregular from Latin *commodum* convenience, from neuter of *commodus*] (15th century)
1 : comfortably or conveniently spacious **:** ROOMY ⟨a *commodious* closet⟩
2 *archaic* **:** HANDY, SERVICEABLE
synonym see SPACIOUS
— **com·mo·di·ous·ly** adverb
— **com·mo·di·ous·ness** noun
com·mod·i·ty \kə-'mä-də-tē\ noun, plural

-ties [Middle English *commoditee*, from Middle French *commodité*, from Latin *commoditat-*, *commoditas*, from *commodus*] (15th century)
1 : an economic good: as **a :** a product of agriculture or mining **b :** an article of commerce especially when delivered for shipment ⟨*commodities* futures⟩ **c :** a mass-produced unspecialized product ⟨*commodity* chemicals⟩ ⟨*commodity* memory chips⟩
2 a : something useful or valued ⟨that valuable *commodity* patience⟩ **b :** CONVENIENCE, ADVANTAGE
3 *obsolete* **:** QUANTITY, LOT
com·mo·dore \'kä-mə-ˌdȯr, -ˌdȯr\ noun [probably modification of Dutch *commandeur* commander, from French, from Old French *comandeor*, from *comander* to command] (1695)
1 a : a captain in the navy in command of a squadron **b :** a commissioned officer in the navy formerly ranking above captain and below rear admiral and having an insignia of one star
2 : the ranking officer commanding a body of merchant ships
3 : the chief officer of a yacht club or boating association
¹com·mon \'kä-mən\ adjective [Middle English *commun*, from Old French, from Latin *communis* — more at MEAN] (13th century)
1 a : of or relating to a community at large **:** PUBLIC ⟨work for the *common* good⟩ **b :** known to the community ⟨*common* nuisances⟩
2 a : belonging to or shared by two or more individuals or things or by all members of a group ⟨a *common* friend⟩ ⟨buried in a *common* grave⟩ **b :** belonging equally to two or more mathematical entities ⟨triangles with a *common* base⟩ **c :** having two or more branches ⟨*common* carotid artery⟩
3 a : occurring or appearing frequently **:** FAMILIAR ⟨a *common* sight⟩ **b :** of the best known kind **c :** VERNACULAR 2 ⟨*common* names⟩
4 a : WIDESPREAD, GENERAL ⟨*common* knowledge⟩ **b :** characterized by a lack of privilege or special status ⟨*common* people⟩ **c :** just satisfying accustomed criteria **:** ELEMENTARY ⟨*common* decency⟩
5 a : falling below ordinary standards **:** SECOND-RATE **b :** lacking refinement **:** COARSE
6 : denoting nominal relations by a single linguistic form that in a more highly inflected language might be denoted by two or more different forms ⟨*common* gender⟩ ⟨*common* case⟩
7 : of, relating to, or being common stock ☆
— **com·mon·ly** adverb
— **com·mon·ness** \-mən-nəs\ noun
²common noun (14th century)
1 *plural* **:** the common people
2 *plural but singular in construction* **:** a dining hall
3 *plural but singular or plural in construction, often capitalized* **a :** the political group or estate comprising the commoners **b :** the parliamentary representatives of the commoners **c :** HOUSE OF COMMONS
4 : the legal right of taking a profit in another's land in common with the owner or others
5 : a piece of land subject to common use: as **a :** undivided land used especially for pasture **b :** a public open area in a municipality
6 a : a religious service suitable for any of various festivals **b :** ORDINARY 2
7 : COMMON STOCK
— **in common :** shared together
com·mon·age \'kä-mə-nij\ noun (1649)
1 : community land
2 : COMMONALTY 1a(2)
com·mon·al·i·ty \ˌkä-mə-'na-lə-tē\ noun, plural **-ties** [Middle English *communalite* commonwealth, alteration of *communalte*] (1582)
1 : the common people

2 a : possession of common features or attributes **:** COMMONNESS **b :** a common feature or attribute
com·mon·al·ty \'kä-mə-n³l-tē\ noun, plural **-ties** [Middle English *communalte*, from Middle French *comunalté*, from *comunal* communal] (14th century)
1 a (1) **:** the common people (2) **:** the political estate formed by the common people **b :** a usage or practice common to members of a group
2 : a general group or body
common carrier noun (15th century)
: a business or agency that is available to the public for transportation of persons, goods, or messages
common cattle grub noun (1947)
: a cattle grub (*Hypoderma lineatum*) which is found throughout the U.S. and whose larva is particularly destructive to cattle
common cold noun (1786)
: an acute virus disease of the upper respiratory tract marked by inflammation of the mucous membranes of the nose, throat, eyes, and eustachian tubes and by a watery then purulent discharge
common denominator noun (1594)
1 : a common multiple of the denominators of a number of fractions
2 : a common trait or theme
common difference noun (circa 1891)
: the difference between two consecutive terms of an arithmetic progression
common divisor noun (circa 1847)
: a number or expression that divides two or more numbers or expressions without remainder — called also *common factor*
com·mon·er \'kä-mə-nər\ noun (14th century)
1 a : one of the common people **b :** one who is not of noble rank
2 : a student (as at Oxford) who pays for his own board
Common Era noun (circa 1889)
: CHRISTIAN ERA
common fraction noun (circa 1897)
: a fraction in which the numerator and denominator are both integers and are separated by a horizontal or slanted line — compare DECIMAL FRACTION
common ground noun (1874)
: a basis of mutual interest or agreement
common–law adjective (1848)
1 : of, relating to, or based on the common law
2 : relating to or based on a common-law marriage
common law noun (14th century)
: the body of law developed in England prima-

commode 1

rily from judicial decisions based on custom and precedent, unwritten in statute or code, and constituting the basis of the English legal system and of the system in all of the U.S. except Louisiana

common–law marriage *noun* (1900)
1 : a marriage recognized in some jurisdictions and based on the parties' agreement to consider themselves married and sometimes also on their cohabitation
2 : the cohabitation of a couple even when it does not constitute a legal marriage

common logarithm *noun* (circa 1903)
: a logarithm whose base is 10

common market *noun* (1952)
: an economic association (as of nations) formed to remove trade barriers among its members

common measure *noun* (1922)
: a meter consisting chiefly of iambic lines of 7 accents each arranged in rhymed pairs usually printed in 4-line stanzas — called also *common meter*

common multiple *noun* (circa 1890)
: a multiple of each of two or more numbers or expressions ⟨90 is a *common multiple* of 6 and 10⟩

common noun *noun* (circa 1864)
: a noun that may occur with limiting modifiers (as *a* or *an, some, every,* and *my*) and that designates any one of a class of beings or things

common or garden *adjective* (1892)
chiefly British **:** ORDINARY

¹**com·mon·place** \'kä-mən-ˌplās\ *noun* [translation of Latin *locus communis* widely applicable argument, translation of Greek *koinos topos*] (1561)
1 *archaic* **:** a striking passage entered in a commonplace book
2 a : an obvious or trite comment **:** TRUISM **b :** something commonly found

²**commonplace** *adjective* (1609)
: commonly found **:** ORDINARY, UNREMARKABLE
— **com·mon·place·ness** *noun*

commonplace book *noun* (1578)
: a book of memorabilia

common pleas *noun plural* (1531)
1 *singular in construction* **:** COURT OF COMMON PLEAS
2 a : actions over which the English crown did not exercise exclusive jurisdiction **b :** civil actions between English subjects

common ratio *noun* (1875)
: the ratio of each term of a geometric progression to the term preceding it

common room *noun* (1683)
1 : a lounge available to all members of a residential community
2 : a room in a college for faculty use

common salt *noun* (1676)
: SALT 1a

common school *noun* (circa 1657)
: a free public school

common sense *noun* (1535)
1 : the unreflective opinions of ordinary people
2 : sound and prudent but often unsophisticated judgment
synonym see SENSE
— **com·mon·sense** \'kä-mən-'sen(t)s\ *adjective*
— **com·mon·sen·si·ble** \-'sen(t)-sə-bəl\ *adjective*
— **com·mon·sen·si·cal** \-'sen(t)-si-kəl\ *adjective*
— **com·mon·sen·si·cal·ly** \-si-k(ə-)lē\ *adverb*

common situs picketing *noun* (1965)
: the picketing of an entire construction site by a trade union having a grievance with only a single subcontractor working there

common stock *noun* (1888)
: capital stock other than preferred stock

common time *noun* (1674)

: a musical meter marked by four beats per measure with the quarter note receiving a single beat

common touch *noun* (1944)
: the gift of appealing to or arousing the sympathetic interest of the common people

com·mon·weal \'kä-mən-ˌwēl\ *noun* (14th century)
1 *archaic* **:** COMMONWEALTH
2 : the general welfare

com·mon·wealth \-ˌwelth *also* -ˌweltth\ *noun* (15th century)
1 *archaic* **:** COMMONWEAL 2
2 : a nation, state, or other political unit: as **a :** one founded on law and united by compact or tacit agreement of the people for the common good **b :** one in which supreme authority is vested in the people **c :** REPUBLIC
3 *capitalized* **a :** the English state from the death of Charles I in 1649 to the Restoration in 1660 **b :** PROTECTORATE 1b
4 : a state of the U.S. — used officially of Kentucky, Massachusetts, Pennsylvania, and Virginia
5 *capitalized* **:** a federal union of constituent states — used officially of Australia
6 *often capitalized* **:** an association of self-governing autonomous states more or less loosely associated in a common allegiance (as to the British crown)
7 *often capitalized* **:** a political unit having local autonomy but voluntarily united with the U.S. — used officially of Puerto Rico and of the Northern Mariana Islands

Commonwealth Day *noun* (1959)
: May 24 observed in parts of the Commonwealth of Nations as the anniversary of Queen Victoria's birthday

common year *noun* (circa 1909)
: a calendar year containing no intercalary period

com·mo·tion \kə-'mō-shən\ *noun* [Middle English, from Middle French, from Latin *commotion-, commotio,* from *commovēre*] (15th century)
1 : a condition of civil unrest or insurrection
2 : steady or recurrent motion
3 : mental excitement or confusion
4 a : an agitated disturbance **:** TO-DO **b :** noisy confusion **:** AGITATION

com·move \kə-'müv, kä-\ *transitive verb* **com·moved; com·mov·ing** [Middle English *commoeven,* from Middle French *commuev-,* present stem of *commovoir,* from Latin *commovēre,* from *com-* + *movēre* to move] (14th century)
1 : to move violently **:** AGITATE
2 : to rouse intense feeling in **:** excite to passion

com·mu·nal \kə-'myü-nᵊl, 'käm-yə-nᵊl\ *adjective* [French, from Late Latin *communalis,* from Latin *communis*] (1811)
1 : of or relating to one or more communes
2 : of or relating to a community
3 a : characterized by collective ownership and use of property **b :** participated in, shared, or used in common by members of a group or community
4 : of, relating to, or based on racial or cultural groups
— **com·mu·nal·ize** \kə-'myü-nᵊl-ˌīz, 'käm-yə-\ *transitive verb*
— **com·mu·nal·ly** *adverb*

com·mu·nal·ism \-nᵊl-ˌi-zəm\ *noun* (1871)
1 : social organization on a communal basis
2 : loyalty to a sociopolitical grouping based on religious or ethnic affiliation
— **com·mu·nal·ist** \-nᵊl-ist\ *noun or adjective*

com·mu·nal·i·ty \ˌkäm-yù-'na-lə-tē\ *noun, plural* **-ties** (1901)
1 : communal state or character
2 : a feeling of group solidarity

com·mu·nard \ˌkäm-yù-'när(d)\ *noun* [French] (1874)

1 *capitalized* **:** one who supported or participated in the Commune of Paris in 1871
2 : a person who lives in a commune

¹**com·mune** \kə-'myün\ *verb* **com·muned; com·mun·ing** [Middle English, to converse, administer Communion, from Middle French *comunier* to converse, administer or receive Communion, from Late Latin *communicare,* from Latin] (15th century)
transitive verb
obsolete **:** TALK OVER, DISCUSS ⟨have more to *commune* —Shakespeare⟩
intransitive verb
1 : to receive Communion
2 : to communicate intimately ⟨*commune* with nature⟩

²**com·mune** \'käm-ˌyün; kə-'myün, kä-\ *noun* [French, alteration of Middle French *comugne,* from Medieval Latin *communia,* from Latin, neuter plural of *communis*] (1673)
1 : the smallest administrative district of many countries especially in Europe
2 : COMMONALTY 1a
3 : COMMUNITY: as **a :** a medieval usually municipal corporation **b** (1) **:** MIR (2) **:** an often rural community organized on a communal basis

com·mu·ni·ca·ble \kə-'myü-ni-kə-bəl\ *adjective* (1534)
1 : capable of being communicated **:** TRANSMITTABLE ⟨*communicable* disease⟩
2 : COMMUNICATIVE
— **com·mu·ni·ca·bil·i·ty** \-ˌmyü-ni-kə-'bi-lə-tē\ *noun*
— **com·mu·ni·ca·ble·ness** \-'myü-ni-kə-bəl-nəs\ *noun*
— **com·mu·ni·ca·bly** \-blē\ *adverb*

com·mu·ni·cant \-'myü-ni-kənt\ *noun* (1552)
1 : a church member entitled to receive Communion; *broadly* **:** a member of a fellowship
2 : one that communicates; *specifically* **:** INFORMANT
— **communicant** *adjective*

com·mu·ni·cate \kə-'myü-nə-ˌkāt\ *verb* **-cat·ed; -cat·ing** [Latin *communicatus,* past participle of *communicare* to impart, participate, from *communis* common — more at MEAN] (1526)
transitive verb
1 *archaic* **:** SHARE
2 a : to convey knowledge of or information about **:** make known ⟨*communicate* a story⟩ **b :** to reveal by clear signs ⟨his fear *communicated* itself to his friends⟩
3 : to cause to pass from one to another ⟨some diseases are easily *communicated*⟩
intransitive verb
1 : to receive Communion
2 : to transmit information, thought, or feeling so that it is satisfactorily received or understood
3 : to open into each other **:** CONNECT ⟨the rooms *communicate*⟩
— **com·mu·ni·ca·tee** \-ˌmyü-ni-kə-'tē\ *noun*
— **com·mu·ni·ca·tor** \-'myü-nə-ˌkā-tər\ *noun*

com·mu·ni·ca·tion \kə-ˌmyü-nə-'kā-shən\ *noun* (14th century)
1 : an act or instance of transmitting
2 a : information communicated **b :** a verbal or written message
3 a : a process by which information is exchanged between individuals through a common system of symbols, signs, or behavior ⟨the function of pheromones in insect *communication*⟩; *also* **:** exchange of information **b :** personal rapport ⟨a lack of *communication* between old and young persons⟩
4 *plural* **a :** a system (as of telephones) for

\ə\ abut \ᵊ\ kitten \ər\ further \a\ ash \ā\ ace
\ä\ mop, mar \aù\ out \ch\ chin \e\ bet \ē\ easy
\g\ go \i\ hit \ī\ ice \j\ job \ŋ\ sing \ō\ go
\ò\ law \òi\ boy \th\ thin \t̲h̲\ the \ü\ loot \ú\ foot
\y\ yet \zh\ vision *see also* Guide to Pronunciation

communicating **b :** a system of routes for moving troops, supplies, and vehicles **c :** personnel engaged in communicating
5 *plural but singular or plural in construction* **a :** a technique for expressing ideas effectively (as in speech) **b :** the technology of the transmission of information (as by print or telecommunication)
— **com·mu·ni·ca·tion·al** \-shnəl, -shə-nᵊl\ *adjective*
com·mu·ni·ca·tive \kə-'myü-nə-ˌkā-tiv, -ni-kə-tiv\ *adjective* (14th century)
1 : tending to communicate **:** TALKATIVE
2 : of or relating to communication
— **com·mu·ni·ca·tive·ly** *adverb*
— **com·mu·ni·ca·tive·ness** *noun*
com·mu·ni·ca·to·ry \kə-'myü-ni-kə-ˌtōr-ē, -ˌtòr-\ *adjective* (1646)
1 : designed to communicate information ⟨*communicatory* letters⟩
2 : COMMUNICATIVE 2
com·mu·nion \kə-'myü-nyən\ *noun* [Middle English, from Latin *communion-, communio* mutual participation, from *communis*] (14th century)
1 : an act or instance of sharing
2 a *capitalized* **:** a Christian sacrament in which consecrated bread and wine are consumed as memorials of Christ's death or as symbols for the realization of a spiritual union between Christ and communicant or as the body and blood of Christ **b :** the act of receiving Communion **c** *capitalized* **:** the part of a Communion service in which the sacrament is received
3 : intimate fellowship or rapport **:** COMMUNICATION
4 : a body of Christians having a common faith and discipline ⟨the Anglican *communion*⟩
com·mu·ni·qué \kə-'myü-nə-ˌkā, -ˌmyü-nə-'\ *noun* [French, from past participle of *communiquer* to communicate, from Latin *communicare*] (1852)
: BULLETIN 1
com·mu·nise *British variant of* COMMUNIZE
com·mu·nism \'käm-yə-ˌni-zəm\ *noun* [French *communisme,* from *commun* common] (1840)
1 a : a theory advocating elimination of private property **b :** a system in which goods are owned in common and are available to all as needed
2 *capitalized* **a :** a doctrine based on revolutionary Marxian socialism and Marxism-Leninism that was the official ideology of the U.S.S.R. **b :** a totalitarian system of government in which a single authoritarian party controls state-owned means of production **c :** a final stage of society in Marxist theory in which the state has withered away and economic goods are distributed equitably **d :** communist systems collectively
com·mu·nist \'käm-yə-nist\ *noun* (1840)
1 : an adherent or advocate of communism
2 *capitalized* **:** COMMUNARD
3 a *capitalized* **:** a member of a Communist party or movement **b** *often capitalized* **:** an adherent or advocate of a Communist government, party, or movement
4 *often capitalized* **:** one held to engage in leftwing, subversive, or revolutionary activities
— **communist** *adjective, often capitalized*
— **com·mu·nis·tic** \ˌkäm-yə-'nis-tik\ *adjective, often capitalized*
— **com·mu·nis·ti·cal·ly** \-ti-k(ə-)lē\ *adverb*
com·mu·ni·tar·i·an \kə-ˌmyü-nə-'ter-ē-ən\ *adjective* (circa 1909)
: of or relating to social organization in small cooperative partially collectivist communities
— **communitarian** *noun*
— **com·mu·ni·tar·i·an·ism** \-ē-ə-ˌni-zəm\ *noun*
com·mu·ni·ty \kə-'myü-nə-tē\ *noun, plural* **-ties** *often attributive* [Middle English *comunete,* from Middle French *comuneté,* from Lat-

in *communitat-, communitas,* from *communis*] (14th century)
1 : a unified body of individuals: as **a :** STATE, COMMONWEALTH **b :** the people with common interests living in a particular area; *broadly* **:** the area itself ⟨the problems of a large *community*⟩ **c :** an interacting population of various kinds of individuals (as species) in a common location **d :** a group of people with a common characteristic or interest living together within a larger society ⟨a *community* of retired persons⟩ **e :** a group linked by a common policy **f :** a body of persons or nations having a common history or common social, economic, and political interests ⟨the international *community*⟩ **g :** a body of persons of common and especially professional interests scattered through a larger society ⟨the academic *community*⟩
2 : society at large
3 a : joint ownership or participation ⟨*community* of goods⟩ **b :** common character **:** LIKENESS ⟨*community* of interests⟩ **c :** social activity **:** FELLOWSHIP **d :** a social state or condition
community antenna television *noun* (1953)
: CABLE TELEVISION
community center *noun* (1915)
: a building or group of buildings for a community's educational and recreational activities
community chest *noun* (1919)
: a general fund accumulated from individual subscriptions to defray demands on a community for charity and social welfare
community college *noun* (1948)
: a 2-year government-supported college that offers an associate degree
community property *noun* (circa 1925)
: property held jointly by husband and wife
com·mu·nize \'käm-yə-ˌnīz\ *transitive verb* **-nized; -niz·ing** [back-formation from *communization*] (1888)
1 a : to make common **b :** to make into state-owned property
2 : to subject to Communist principles of organization
— **com·mu·ni·za·tion** \ˌkäm-yə-nə-'zā-shən\ *noun*
com·mu·tate \'käm-yə-ˌtāt\ *transitive verb* **-tat·ed; -tat·ing** [back-formation from *commutation*] (1893)
: to reverse every other half cycle of (an alternating current) so as to form a unidirectional current
com·mu·ta·tion \ˌkäm-yə-'tā-shən\ *noun* [Middle English, from Middle French, from Latin *commutation-, commutatio,* from *commutare*] (15th century)
1 : EXCHANGE, TRADE
2 : REPLACEMENT; *specifically* **:** a substitution of one form of payment or charge for another
3 : a change of a legal penalty or punishment to a lesser one
4 : an act or process of commuting
5 : the action of commutating
commutation ticket *noun* (1848)
: a transportation ticket sold for a fixed number of trips over the same route during a limited period
com·mu·ta·tive \kə-'myü-tə-tiv, 'käm-yə-ˌtā-tiv\ *adjective* (1612)
1 : of, relating to, or showing commutation
2 : of, relating to, having, or being the property that a given mathematical operation and set have when the result obtained using any two elements of the set with the operation does not differ with the order in which the elements are used ⟨a *commutative* group⟩ ⟨addition of the positive integers is *commutative*⟩
com·mu·ta·tiv·i·ty \kə-ˌmyü-tə-'ti-və-tē, ˌkäm-yə-tə-\ *noun* (1929)
: the property of being commutative ⟨the *commutativity* of a mathematical operation⟩
com·mu·ta·tor \'käm-yə-ˌtā-tər\ *noun* (1880)
1 : a series of bars or segments so connected

to armature coils of a generator or motor that rotation of the armature will in conjunction with fixed brushes result in unidirectional current output in the case of a generator and in the reversal of the current into the coils in the case of a motor
2 : an element of a mathematical group that when used to multiply the product of two given elements either on the right side or on the left side but not necessarily on both sides yields the product of the two given elements in reverse order
¹com·mute \kə-'myüt\ *verb* **com·mut·ed; com·mut·ing** [Latin *commutare* to change, exchange, from *com-* + *mutare* to change — more at MUTABLE] (15th century)
transitive verb
1 a : CHANGE, ALTER **b :** to give in exchange for another **:** EXCHANGE
2 : to convert (as a payment) into another form
3 : to exchange (a penalty) for another less severe
4 : COMMUTATE
intransitive verb
1 : MAKE UP, COMPENSATE
2 : to pay in gross
3 : to travel back and forth regularly (as between a suburb and a city)
4 : to yield the same mathematical result regardless of order — used of two elements undergoing an operation or of two operations on elements
— **com·mut·able** \-'myü-tə-bəl\ *adjective*
²commute *noun* (1954)
1 : an act or an instance of commuting
2 : the distance covered in commuting
com·mut·er \kə-'myü-tər\ *noun* (circa 1859)
1 : a person who commutes (as between a suburb and a city)
2 : a small airline that carries passengers relatively short distances on a regular schedule
co·mo·no·mer \(ˌ)kō-'mä-nə-mər, -'mō-\ *noun* [*co-* + *monomer*] (1945)
: one of the constituents of a copolymer
¹comp \'kämp\ *noun* [short for *complimentary*] (1887)
: a complimentary ticket; *broadly* **:** something provided free of charge
²comp \'kəmp, 'kämp\ *intransitive verb* [short for *accompany*] (1949)
: to punctuate and support a jazz solo with irregularly spaced chords
¹com·pact \kəm-'pakt, käm-', 'käm-ˌ\ *adjective* [Middle English, firmly put together, from Latin *compactus,* from past participle of *compingere* to put together, from *com-* + *pangere* to fasten — more at PACT] (14th century)
1 : predominantly formed or filled **:** COMPOSED, MADE
2 a : having a dense structure or parts or units closely packed or joined ⟨a *compact* woolen⟩ ⟨*compact* bone⟩ **b :** not diffuse or verbose ⟨a *compact* statement⟩ **c :** occupying a small volume by reason of efficient use of space ⟨a *compact* camera⟩ ⟨a *compact* formation of troops⟩ **d :** short-bodied, solid, and without excess flesh
3 : being a topological space and especially a metric space with the property that for any collection of open sets which contains it there is a subset of the collection with a finite number of elements which also contains it
— **com·pact·ly** \-'pak(t)-lē, -ˌpak(t)-\ *adverb*
— **com·pact·ness** \-'pak(t)-nəs, -ˌpak(t)-\ *noun*
²compact (15th century)
transitive verb
1 : to make up by connecting or combining **:** COMPOSE
2 a : to knit or draw together **:** COMBINE **b :** to press together **:** COMPRESS
intransitive verb
: to become compacted

— **com·pact·ible** \-'pak-tə-bəl, -,pak-\ *adjective*

— **com·pac·tor** *also* **com·pact·er** \-'pak-tər, -,pak-\ *noun*

³**com·pact** \'käm-,pakt\ *noun* (1601)
: something that is compact or compacted: **a** : a small cosmetic case (as for compressed powder) **b** : an automobile smaller than an intermediate but larger than a subcompact

⁴**com·pact** \'käm-,pakt\ *noun* [Latin *compactum,* from neuter of *compactus,* past participle of *compacisci* to make an agreement, from *com-* + *pacisci* to contract — more at PACT] (1591)
: an agreement or covenant between two or more parties

com·pact disc \'käm-,pakt-\ *noun* (1979)
: a small plastic optical disc usually containing recorded music or computer data

com·pac·tion \kəm-'pak-shən, käm-\ *noun* (14th century)
: the act or process of compacting : the state of being compacted

¹**com·pan·ion** \kəm-'pan-yən\ *noun* [Middle English *compainoun,* from Old French *compagnon,* from Late Latin *companion-, companio,* from Latin *com-* + *panis* bread, food — more at FOOD] (13th century)
1 : one that accompanies another : COMRADE, ASSOCIATE; *also* : one that keeps company with another
2 *obsolete* : RASCAL
3 a : one that is closely connected with something similar **b** : one employed to live with and serve another ◆

²**companion** (1622)
transitive verb
: ACCOMPANY
intransitive verb
: to keep company

³**companion** *noun* [by folk etymology from Dutch *kampanje* poop deck] (1762)
1 : a hood covering at the top of a companion-way
2 : COMPANIONWAY

com·pan·ion·able \kəm-'pan-yə-nə-bəl\ *adjective* (14th century)
: marked by, conducive to, or suggestive of companionship : SOCIABLE
— **com·pan·ion·abil·i·ty** \-,pan-yə-nə-'bi-lə-tē\ *noun*
— **com·pan·ion·able·ness** *noun*
— **com·pan·ion·ably** \-'pan-yə-nə-blē\ *adverb*

com·pan·ion·ate \kəm-'pan-yə-nət\ *adjective* (1926)
: relating to or having the manner of companions; *specifically* : harmoniously or suitably accompanying

companion cell *noun* (1887)
: a living nucleated cell that is closely associated in origin, position, and probably function with a cell making up part of a sieve tube of a vascular plant

companion piece *noun* (1844)
: a work (as of literature) that is associated with and complements another

com·pan·ion·ship \kəm-'pan-yən-,ship\ *noun* (1548)
: the fellowship existing among companions : COMPANY

com·pan·ion·way \-yən-,wā\ *noun* [³companion] (1840)
: a ship's stairway from one deck to another

¹**com·pa·ny** \'kəmp-nē, 'käm-pə-\ *noun, plural* **-nies** *often attributive* [Middle English *companie,* from Old French *compagnie,* from *compain* companion, from Late Latin *companio*] (13th century)
1 a : association with another : FELLOWSHIP ⟨enjoy a person's *company*⟩ **b** : COMPANIONS, ASSOCIATES ⟨know a person by the *company* she keeps⟩ **c** : VISITORS, GUESTS ⟨having *company* for dinner⟩

2 a : a group of persons or things ⟨a *company* of horsemen⟩ **b** : a body of soldiers; *especially* : a unit (as of infantry) consisting usually of a headquarters and two or more platoons **c** : an organization of performing artists **d** : the officers and crew of a ship **e** : a fire-fighting unit
3 a : a chartered commercial organization or medieval trade guild **b** : an association of persons for carrying on a commercial or industrial enterprise **c** : those members of a partnership firm whose names do not appear in the firm name ⟨John Doe and *Company*⟩

²**company** *verb* **-nied; -ny·ing** (14th century)
transitive verb
: ACCOMPANY ⟨may . . . fair winds *company* your safe return —John Masefield⟩
intransitive verb
: ASSOCIATE

company man *noun* (circa 1921)
: a worker who acquiesces in company policy without complaint

company officer *noun* (1844)
: a commissioned officer in the army, air force, or marine corps of the rank of captain, first lieutenant, or second lieutenant — called also *company grade officer*; compare FIELD OFFICER, GENERAL OFFICER

company town *noun* (1927)
: a community that is dependent on one firm for all or most of the necessary services or functions of town life (as employment, housing, and stores)

company union *noun* (1917)
: an unaffiliated labor union of the employees of a single firm; *especially* : one dominated by the employer

com·pa·ra·bil·i·ty \,käm-p(ə-)rə-'bi-lə-tē, ÷kəm-,par-ə-\ *noun* (1843)
: the quality or state of being comparable

com·pa·ra·ble \'käm-p(ə-)rə-bəl, ÷kəm-'par-ə-bəl\ *adjective* (15th century)
1 : capable of or suitable for comparison
2 : SIMILAR, LIKE ⟨fabrics of *comparable* quality⟩
— **com·pa·ra·ble·ness** *noun*
— **com·pa·ra·bly** \-blē\ *adverb*

comparable worth *noun* (1983)
: the concept that women and men should receive equal pay for jobs calling for comparable skill and responsibility

com·pa·ra·tist \kəm-'par-ə-tist\ *noun* [*comparative* + *-ist*] (1933)
: one that uses a comparative method (as in the study of literature)

¹**com·par·a·tive** \kəm-'par-ə-tiv\ *adjective* (15th century)
1 : of, relating to, or constituting the degree of comparison in a language that denotes increase in the quality, quantity, or relation expressed by an adjective or adverb
2 : considered as if in comparison to something else as a standard not quite attained : RELATIVE ⟨a *comparative* stranger⟩
3 : characterized by systematic comparison especially of likenesses and dissimilarities ⟨*comparative* anatomy⟩
— **com·par·a·tive·ly** *adverb*
— **com·par·a·tive·ness** *noun*

²**comparative** *noun* (15th century)
1 a : one that compares with another especially on equal footing : RIVAL **b** : one that makes witty or mocking comparisons
2 : the comparative degree or form in a language

com·par·a·tiv·ist \kəm-'par-ə-ti-vist\ *noun* (1887)
: COMPARATIST

com·par·a·tor \kəm-'par-ə-tər\ *noun* (1883)
: a device for comparing something with a similar thing or with a standard measure

¹**com·pare** \kəm-'par, -'per\ *verb* **compared; com·par·ing** [Middle English, from Middle French *comparer,* from Latin *comparare* to couple, compare, from *compar* like, from *com-* + *par* equal] (14th century)

transitive verb
1 : to represent as similar : LIKEN ⟨shall I *compare* thee to a summer's day? —Shakespeare⟩
2 a : to examine the character or qualities of especially in order to discover resemblances or differences ⟨*compare* your responses with the answers⟩ **b** : to view in relation to ⟨tall *compared* to me⟩
3 : to inflect or modify (an adjective or adverb) according to the degrees of comparison
intransitive verb
1 : to bear being compared
2 : to make comparisons
3 : to be equal or alike ⟨nothing *compares* to you⟩ ☆ □

²**compare** *noun* (1589)
: the possibility of comparing ⟨beauty beyond *compare*⟩; *also* : something with which to be compared ⟨a city without *compare*⟩

☆ SYNONYMS

Compare, contrast, collate mean to set side by side in order to show differences and likenesses. COMPARE implies an aim of showing relative values or excellences by bringing out characteristic qualities whether similar or divergent ⟨*compared* the convention facilities of the two cities⟩. CONTRAST implies an emphasis on differences ⟨*contrasted* the computerized system with the old filing cards⟩. COLLATE implies minute and critical inspection in order to note points of agreement or divergence ⟨data from districts around the country will be *collated*⟩.

□ USAGE

compare A great many authors of handbooks and other commentators are eager to point out the difference between *compare to* and *compare with.* Their basic rule is easy enough: use *to* with *transitive verb* sense 1 and use *with* with *transitive verb* sense 2a. But in the less tidy world of actual usage these rules state only broad tendencies: more writers use *to* than *with* for sense 1; somewhat more writers use *with* than *to* for sense 2a. When *compared* is used as a detached participle, *to* and *with* are used with about equal frequency ⟨you always seemed so firm to me *compared* to myself —E. B. White⟩ ⟨*compared* with the fables, my own work is insignificant —Marianne Moore⟩. Sense 2b is unnoticed by the commentators, who probably include it within 2a; it takes either *to* or *with.* Intransitive senses use both prepositions.

◇ WORD HISTORY

companion *Companion* descends ultimately from Late Latin *companio,* formed from Latin *com-* "with" and *panis* "bread," and so literally means "a person with whom one shares bread, a messmate." The word in all likelihood arose in the soldier's Latin of the declining Roman Empire and is a loan translation from a word in an early Germanic language such as Gothic *gahlaiba,* formed from *ga-* "with" and *hlaifs* "bread." The Roman army of that time recruited many troops from the Goths and other Germanic peoples who lived on the borders of the Empire. In the 4th century A.D. translation of the Bible into Gothic, *gahlaifa* renders Greek *synstratiōtēs,* literally, "fellow-soldier."

\ə\ abut \ᵊ\ kitten \ər\ further \a\ ash \ā\ ace \ä\ mop, mar \aú\ out \ch\ chin \e\ bet \ē\ easy \g\ go \i\ hit \ī\ ice \j\ job \ŋ\ sing \ō\ go \ò\ law \òi\ boy \th\ thin \t͟h\ the \ü\ loot \ù\ foot \y\ yet \zh\ vision *see also* Guide to Pronunciation

com·par·i·son \kəm-'par-ə-sən\ *noun* [Middle English, from Middle French *comparaison*, from Latin *comparation-, comparatio*, from *comparare*] (14th century)
1 : the act or process of comparing: as **a :** the representing of one thing or person as similar to or like another **b :** an examination of two or more items to establish similarities and dissimilarities
2 : identity of features **:** SIMILARITY ⟨several points of *comparison* between the two⟩
3 : the modification of an adjective or adverb to denote different levels of quality, quantity, or relation

comparison shop *intransitive verb* (1970)
: to compare prices (as of competing brands) in order to find the best value

¹com·part·ment \kəm-'pärt-mənt\ *noun* [Middle French *compartiment*, from Italian *compartimento*, from *compartire* to mark out in parts, from Late Latin *compartiri* to share out, from Latin *com-* + *partiri* to share, from *part-, pars* part, share] (circa 1578)
1 : a separate division or section
2 : one of the parts into which an enclosed space is divided
— **com·part·men·tal** \kəm-,pärt-'men-t³l, ,käm-\ *adjective*

²com·part·ment \-,ment, -mənt\ *transitive verb* (1918)
: COMPARTMENTALIZE

com·part·men·tal·ise *British variant of* COMPARTMENTALIZE

com·part·men·tal·ize \kəm-,pärt-'men-t³l-,īz, ,käm-\ *transitive verb* **-ized; -iz·ing** (1925)
: to separate into isolated compartments or categories
— **com·part·men·tal·i·za·tion** \-,men-t³l-ə-'zā-shən\ *noun*

com·part·men·ta·tion \kəm-,pärt-mən-'tā-shən, -,men-\ *noun* (1926)
: division into separate sections or units

¹com·pass \'kəm-pəs *also* 'käm-\ *transitive verb* [Middle English, from Old French *compasser* to measure, from (assumed) Vulgar Latin *compassare* to pace off, from Latin *com-* + *passus* pace] (14th century)
1 : to devise or contrive often with craft or skill
2 : ENCOMPASS
3 a : BRING ABOUT, ACHIEVE **b :** to get into one's possession or power **:** OBTAIN
4 : COMPREHEND
— **com·pass·able** \-pə-sə-bəl\ *adjective*

²compass *noun* (14th century)
1 a : BOUNDARY, CIRCUMFERENCE ⟨within the *compass* of the city walls⟩ **b :** a circumscribed space ⟨within the narrow *compass* of 21 pages —V. L. Parrington⟩ **c :** RANGE, SCOPE ⟨the *compass* of a voice⟩
2 : a curved or roundabout course ⟨a *compass* of seven days' journey —2 Kings 3:9 (Authorized Version)⟩
3 a : a device for determining directions by means of a magnetic needle or group of needles turning freely on a pivot and pointing to the magnetic north **b :** any of various nonmagnetic devices that indicate direction **c :** an instrument for describing circles or transferring measurements that consists of two pointed branches joined at the top by a pivot — usually used in plural; called also *pair of compasses*
4 : DIRECTION 6c
synonym see RANGE

³compass *adjective* (1523)
: forming a curve **:** CURVED ⟨a *compass* timber⟩

compass card *noun* (circa 1859)
: the circular card attached to the needles of a mariner's compass on which are marked the

32 points of the compass and the 360° of the circle

com·pas·sion \kəm-'pa-shən\ *noun* [Middle English, from Middle French or Late Latin; Middle French, from Late Latin *compassion-, compassio*, from *compati* to sympathize, from Latin *com-* + *pati* to bear, suffer — more at PATIENT] (14th century)
: sympathetic consciousness of others' distress together with a desire to alleviate it
synonym see PITY
— **com·pas·sion·less** \-ləs\ *adjective*

¹com·pas·sion·ate \kəm-'pa-sh(ə-)nət\ *adjective* (1587)
1 : having or showing compassion **:** SYMPATHETIC
2 : granted because of unusual distressing circumstances affecting an individual — used of some military privileges (as leave)
— **com·pas·sion·ate·ly** *adverb*
— **com·pas·sion·ate·ness** *noun*

²com·pas·sion·ate \-'pa-shə-,nāt\ *transitive verb* **-at·ed; -at·ing** (1592)
: PITY

compass plant *noun* (1848)
: a coarse yellow-flowered composite plant (*Silphium laciniatum*) with large pinnatifid leaves that occurs in prairies and along roadsides and railroad tracks of the central U.S.

compass rose *noun* (circa 1891)
: a circle graduated to degrees or quarters and printed on a chart to show direction

com·pat·i·ble \kəm-'pa-tə-bəl\ *adjective* [Middle English, from Middle French, from Medieval Latin *compatibilis*, literally, sympathetic, from Late Latin *compati*] (15th century)
1 : capable of existing together in harmony ⟨*compatible* theories⟩
2 : capable of cross-fertilizing freely or uniting vegetatively
3 : capable of forming a homogeneous mixture that neither separates nor is altered by chemical interaction
4 : capable of being used in transfusion or grafting without immunological reaction (as agglutination or tissue rejection)
5 : designed to work with another device or system without modification; *especially* **:** being a computer designed to operate in the same manner and use the same software as another computer
— **com·pat·i·bil·i·ty** \-,pa-tə-'bi-lə-tē\ *noun*
— **compatible** *noun*
— **com·pat·i·ble·ness** \-'pa-tə-bəl-nəs\ *noun*
— **com·pat·i·bly** \-blē\ *adverb*

com·pa·tri·ot \kəm-'pā-trē-ət, käm-, -trē-,ät, *chiefly British* -'pa-\ *noun* [French *compatriote*, from Late Latin *compatriota*, from Latin *com-* + Late Latin *patriota* fellow countryman — more at PATRIOT] (1611)
1 : a person born, residing, or holding citizenship in the same country as another
2 : COMPEER, COLLEAGUE
— **com·pa·tri·ot·ic** \kəm-,pā-trē-'ä-tik, ,käm-, *chiefly British* -,pa-\ *adjective*

¹com·peer \'käm-,pir, käm-', kəm-'\ *noun* [Middle English, from Old French *compere*, literally, godfather, from Medieval Latin *compater*, from Latin *com-* + *pater* father — more at FATHER] (13th century)
: COMPANION

²compeer *noun* [Middle English *compere*, from Old French, from Latin *compar*,

from *compar*, adjective, like — more at COMPARE] (15th century)
: EQUAL, PEER
— **compeer** *transitive verb, obsolete*

com·pel \kəm-'pel\ *transitive verb* **com·pelled; com·pel·ling** [Middle English *compellen*, from Middle French *compellir*, from Latin *compellere*, from *com-* + *pellere* to drive — more at FELT] (14th century)
1 : to drive or urge forcefully or irresistibly
2 : to cause to do or occur by overwhelming pressure
3 *archaic* **:** to drive together
synonym see FORCE
— **com·pel·la·ble** \-'pe-lə-bəl\ *adjective*

com·pel·la·tion \,käm-pə-'lā-shən, -,pe-\ *noun* [Latin *compellation-, compellatio*, from *compellare* to address, from *com-* + *-pellare* (as in *appellare* to accost, appeal to)] (1603)
1 : an act or action of addressing someone
2 : APPELLATION 1

com·pel·ling \kəm-'pe-liŋ\ *adjective* (1606)
: that compels: as **a :** FORCEFUL ⟨a *compelling* personality⟩ **b :** demanding attention ⟨for *compelling* reasons⟩ **c :** CONVINCING ⟨no *compelling* evidence⟩
— **com·pel·ling·ly** *adverb*

com·pend \'käm-,pend\ *noun* [Medieval Latin *compendium*] (1596)
: COMPENDIUM

com·pen·di·ous \kəm-'pen-dē-əs\ *adjective* (14th century)
: marked by brief expression of a comprehensive matter **:** concise and comprehensive; *also* **:** COMPREHENSIVE ☐
synonym see CONCISE
— **com·pen·di·ous·ly** *adverb*
— **com·pen·di·ous·ness** *noun*

com·pen·di·um \kəm-'pen-dē-əm\ *noun, plural* **-di·ums** *or* **-dia** \-dē-ə\ [Medieval Latin, from Latin, saving, shortcut, from *compendere* to weigh together, from *com-* + *pendere* to weigh — more at PENDANT] (1589)
1 : a brief summary of a larger work or of a field of knowledge **:** ABSTRACT
2 a : a list of a number of items **b :** COLLECTION, COMPILATION

com·pen·sa·ble \kəm-'pen(t)-sə-bəl\ *adjective* (1661)

compass card

compass 3a

: that is to be or can be compensated ⟨a *compensable* job-related injury⟩
— **com·pen·sa·bil·i·ty** \kəm-ˌpen(t)-sə-'bi-lə-tē, ˌkäm-\ *noun*

com·pen·sate \'käm-pən-ˌsāt, -ˌpen-\ *verb* **-sat·ed; -sat·ing** [Latin *compensatus*, past participle of *compensare*, frequentative of *compendere*] (1646)
transitive verb
1 : to be equivalent to **:** COUNTERBALANCE
2 : to make an appropriate and usually counterbalancing payment to
3 a : to provide with means of counteracting variation **b :** to neutralize the effect of (variations)
intransitive verb
1 : to supply an equivalent — used with *for*
2 : to offset an error, defect, or undesired effect
3 : to undergo or engage in psychological or physiological compensation
synonym see PAY
— **com·pen·sa·tive** \'käm-pən-ˌsā-tiv, -ˌpen-; kəm-'pen(t)-sə-\ *adjective*
— **com·pen·sa·tor** \'käm-pən-ˌsā-tər, -ˌpen-\ *noun*
— **com·pen·sa·to·ry** \kəm-'pen(t)-sə-ˌtōr-ē, -ˌtōr-\ *adjective*

com·pen·sa·tion \ˌkäm-pən-'sā-shən, -ˌpen-\ *noun* (14th century)
1 a : the act of compensating **:** the state of being compensated **b :** correction of an organic defect or loss by hypertrophy or by increased functioning of another organ or unimpaired parts of the same organ **c :** a psychological mechanism by which feelings of inferiority, frustration, or failure in one field are counterbalanced by achievement in another
2 a (1) **:** something that constitutes an equivalent or recompense ⟨age has its *compensations*⟩ (2) **:** payment to unemployed or injured workers or their dependents **b :** PAYMENT, REMUNERATION
— **com·pen·sa·tion·al** \-shnəl, -shə-nᵊl\ *adjective*

compensatory education *noun* (1965)
: educational programs intended to make up for experiences (as cultural) lacked by disadvantaged children

¹com·pere *or* **com·père** \'käm-ˌper\ *noun* [French *compère*, literally, godfather — more at COMPEER] (1914)
chiefly British **:** the master of ceremonies of an entertainment (as a television program)

²compere *or* **compère** *verb* **com·pered** *or* **com·pèred; com·per·ing** *or* **com·pèr·ing** (1933)
transitive verb
chiefly British **:** to act as compere for
intransitive verb
chiefly British **:** to act as a compere

com·pete \kəm-'pēt\ *intransitive verb* **com·pet·ed; com·pet·ing** [Late Latin *competere* to seek together, from Latin, to come together, agree, be suitable, from *com-* + *petere* to go to, seek — more at FEATHER] (1620)
: to strive consciously or unconsciously for an objective (as position, profit, or a prize) **:** be in a state of rivalry

com·pe·tence \'käm-pə-tən(t)s\ *noun* (1632)
1 : a sufficiency of means for the necessities and conveniences of life ⟨provided his family with a comfortable *competence* —Rex Ingamells⟩
2 : the quality or state of being competent: as **a :** the properties of an embryonic field that enable it to respond in a characteristic manner to an organizer **b :** readiness of bacteria to undergo genetic transformation
3 : the knowledge that enables a person to speak and understand a language — compare PERFORMANCE

com·pe·ten·cy \-pə-tən(t)-sē\ *noun, plural* **-cies** (1596)
: COMPETENCE

com·pe·tent \'käm-pə-tənt\ *adjective* [Middle English, suitable, from Middle French & Latin; Middle French, from Latin *competent-, competens*, from present participle of *competere*] (15th century)
1 : proper or rightly pertinent
2 : having requisite or adequate ability or qualities **:** FIT ⟨a *competent* teacher⟩ ⟨a *competent* piece of work⟩
3 : legally qualified or adequate ⟨a *competent* witness⟩
4 : having the capacity to function or develop in a particular way; *specifically* **:** having the capacity to respond (as by producing an antibody) to an antigenic determinant ⟨immunologically *competent* cells⟩
synonym see SUFFICIENT
— **com·pe·tent·ly** *adverb*

com·pe·ti·tion \ˌkäm-pə-'ti-shən\ *noun* [Late Latin *competition-, competitio*, from Latin *competere*] (1605)
1 : the act or process of competing **:** RIVALRY: as **a :** the effort of two or more parties acting independently to secure the business of a third party by offering the most favorable terms **b :** active demand by two or more organisms or kinds of organisms for some environmental resource in short supply
2 : a contest between rivals; *also* **:** one's competitors ⟨faced tough *competition*⟩

com·pet·i·tive \kəm-'pe-tə-tiv\ *adjective* (1829)
1 : relating to, characterized by, or based on competition ⟨*competitive* sports⟩
2 : inclined, desiring, or suited to compete ⟨a *competitive* personality⟩ ⟨salary benefits must be *competitive* —M. S. Eisenhower⟩
3 : depending for effectiveness on the relative concentration of two or more substances ⟨*competitive* inhibition of an enzyme⟩
— **com·pet·i·tive·ly** *adverb*
— **com·pet·i·tive·ness** *noun*

com·pet·i·tor \kəm-'pe-tə-tər\ *noun* (1534)
: one that competes: as **a :** RIVAL **b :** one selling or buying goods or services in the same market as another **c :** an organism that lives in competition with another

com·pi·la·tion \ˌkäm-pə-'lā-shən *also* -ˌpī-\ *noun* (15th century)
1 : the act or process of compiling
2 : something compiled

com·pile \kəm-'pī(ə)l\ *transitive verb* **com·piled; com·pil·ing** [Middle English, from Middle French *compiler*, from Latin *compilare* to plunder] (14th century)
1 : to compose out of materials from other documents
2 : to collect and edit into a volume
3 : to run (as a program) through a compiler
4 : to build up gradually ⟨*compiled* a record of four wins and two losses⟩

com·pil·er \kəm-'pī-lər\ *noun* (14th century)
1 : one that compiles
2 : a computer program that translates an entire set of instructions written in a higher-level symbolic language (as Pascal) into machine language before the instructions can be executed

com·pla·cence \kəm-'plā-sᵊn(t)s\ *noun* (15th century)
1 : calm or secure satisfaction with oneself or one's lot **:** SELF-SATISFACTION
2 *obsolete* **:** COMPLAISANCE
3 : UNCONCERN

com·pla·cen·cy \-sᵊn(t)-sē\ *noun, plural* **-cies** (1650)
1 : COMPLACENCE; *especially* **:** self-satisfaction accompanied by unawareness of actual dangers or deficiencies
2 : an instance of complacency

com·pla·cent \kəm-'plā-sᵊnt\ *adjective* [Latin *complacent-, complacens*, present participle of *complacēre* to please greatly, from *com-* + *placēre* to please — more at PLEASE] (1767)
1 : SELF-SATISFIED ⟨a *complacent* smile⟩
2 : COMPLAISANT 1

3 : UNCONCERNED
— **com·pla·cent·ly** *adverb*

com·plain \kəm-'plān\ *intransitive verb* [Middle English *compleynen*, from Middle French *complaindre*, from (assumed) Vulgar Latin *complangere*, from Latin *com-* + *plangere* to lament — more at PLAINT] (14th century)
1 : to express grief, pain, or discontent
2 : to make a formal accusation or charge
— **com·plain·er** *noun*
— **com·plain·ing·ly** \-'plā-niŋ-lē\ *adverb*

com·plain·ant \kəm-'plā-nənt\ *noun* (15th century)
: the party who makes the complaint in a legal action or proceeding

com·plaint \kəm-'plānt\ *noun* [Middle English *compleynte*, from Middle French *complainte*, from Old French, from *complaindre*] (14th century)
1 : expression of grief, pain, or dissatisfaction
2 a : something that is the cause or subject of protest or outcry **b :** a bodily ailment or disease
3 : a formal allegation against a party

com·plai·sance \kəm-'plā-sᵊn(t)s, -zᵊn(t)s; ˌkäm-plā-'zan(t)s, -plə-, -'zän(t)s\ *noun* (1651)
: disposition to please or comply **:** AFFABILITY

com·plai·sant \-sᵊnt, -zᵊnt, -'zant, -'zänt\ *adjective* [French, from Middle French, from present participle of *complaire* to gratify, acquiesce, from Latin *complacēre*] (1647)
1 : marked by an inclination to please or oblige
2 : tending to consent to others' wishes
synonym see AMIABLE
— **com·plai·sant·ly** *adverb*

com·pleat \kəm-'plēt\ *adjective* [archaic variant of *complete* in *The Compleat Angler* (1653) by Izaak Walton] (1526)
: COMPLETE 3

com·plect·ed \kəm-'plek-təd\ *adjective* [irregular from *complexion*] (1806)
: having a specified facial complexion ⟨a tall, thin man, fairly dark *complected* —E. J. Kahn⟩ □

¹com·ple·ment \'käm-plə-mənt\ *noun* [Middle English, from Latin *complementum*, from *complēre* to fill up, complete, from *com-* + *plēre* to fill — more at FULL] (14th century)
1 a : something that fills up, completes, or makes perfect **b :** the quantity or number required to make a thing complete ⟨the usual *complement* of eyes and ears —Francis Parkman⟩; *especially* **:** the whole force or personnel of a ship **c :** one of two mutually completing parts **:** COUNTERPART
2 a : the angle or arc that when added to a given angle or arc equals a right angle in measure **b :** the set of all elements that do not belong to a given set and are contained in a particular mathematical set containing the given

\ə\ **abut** \ᵊ\ **kitten** \ər\ **further** \a\ **ash** \ā\ **ace** \ä\ **mop, mar** \aů\ **out** \ch\ **chin** \e\ **bet** \ē\ **easy** \g\ **go** \i\ **hit** \ī\ **ice** \j\ **job** \ŋ\ **sing** \ō\ **go** \ȯ\ **law** \ȯi\ **boy** \th\ **thin** \t̲h̲\ **the** \ü\ **loot** \ů\ **foot** \y\ **yet** \zh\ **vision** *see also* Guide to Pronunciation

set **c** : a number that when added to another number of the same sign yields zero if the significant digit farthest to the left is discarded — used especially in assembly language programming **3** : the musical interval required with a given interval to complete the octave **4** : an added word or expression by which a predication is made complete (as *president* in "they elected him president" and *beautiful* in "he thought her beautiful") **5** : the thermolabile group of proteins in normal blood serum and plasma that in combination with antibodies causes the destruction especially of particulate antigens (as bacteria and foreign blood corpuscles)

²**com·ple·ment** \-,ment\ (1602) *intransitive verb* *obsolete* : to exchange formal courtesies *transitive verb* **1** : to be complementary to **2** *obsolete* : COMPLIMENT

com·ple·men·tal \,käm-plə-'men-t³l\ *adjective* (1597) **1** : relating to or being a complement **2** *obsolete* : CEREMONIOUS, COMPLIMENTARY

com·ple·men·tar·i·ty \,käm-plə-(,)men-'tar-ə-tē, -mən-\ *noun* (1911) : the quality or state of being complementary

com·ple·men·ta·ry \,käm-plə-'men-t(ə-)rē\ *adjective* (1829) **1** : relating to or constituting one of a pair of contrasting colors that produce a neutral color when combined in suitable proportions **2** : serving to fill out or complete **3** : mutually supplying each other's lack **4** : being complements of each other (*complementary* acute angles) **5** : characterized by the capacity for precise pairing of purine and pyrimidine bases between strands of DNA and sometimes RNA such that the structure of one strand determines the other
— **com·ple·men·ta·ri·ly** \-'men-t(ə-)rə-lē, -(,)men-'ter-ə-lē\ *adverb*
— **com·ple·men·ta·ri·ness** \-'men-t(ə-)rē-nəs\ *noun*
— **complementary** *noun*

com·ple·men·ta·tion \,käm-plə-(,)men-'tā-shən, -mən-\ *noun* (1942) **1** : the operation of determining the complement of a mathematical set **2** : production of normal phenotype in an individual heterozygous for two closely related mutations with one on each homologous chromosome and at a slightly different position

complement fixation *noun* (1906) : the process of binding serum complement to the product formed by the union of an antibody and the antigen for which it is specific that occurs when complement is added to a suitable mixture of such an antibody and antigen

complement–fixation test *noun* (1911) : a diagnostic test for the presence of a particular antibody in the serum of a patient that involves inactivation of the complement in the serum, addition of measured amounts of the antigen for which the antibody is specific and of foreign complement, and detection of the presence or absence of complement fixation by the addition of a suitable indicator system
— compare WASSERMANN TEST

com·ple·men·ti·zer \'käm-plə-mən-,tī-zər, -(,)men-\ *noun* (1965) : a function word or morpheme that combines with a clause or verbal phrase to form a subordinate clause

complement 2a: *ACB* right angle, *ACD* complement of *DCB* (and vice versa), *AD* complement of *DB* (and vice versa)

¹**com·plete** \kəm-'plēt\ *adjective* **com·plet·er; -est** [Middle English *complet*, from Middle French, from Latin *completus*, from past participle of *complēre*] (14th century) **1 a** : having all necessary parts, elements, or steps (*complete* diet) **b** : having all four sets of floral organs **c** *of a subject or predicate* : including modifiers, complements, or objects **2** : brought to an end : CONCLUDED (a *complete* period of time) **3** : highly proficient (a *complete* artist) **4 a** : fully carried out : THOROUGH (a *complete* renovation) **b** : TOTAL, ABSOLUTE (*complete* silence) **5** *of insect metamorphosis* : characterized by the occurrence of a pupal stage between the motile immature stages and the adult — compare INCOMPLETE 1b **6** *of a metric space* : having the property that every Cauchy sequence of elements converges to a limit in the space
synonym see FULL
— **com·plete·ly** *adverb*
— **com·plete·ness** *noun*
— **com·ple·tive** \-'plē-tiv\ *adjective*
— **complete with** : made complete by the inclusion of (a birthday cake *complete with* candles)

²**complete** *transitive verb* **com·plet·ed; com·plet·ing** (15th century) **1** : to bring to an end and especially into a perfected state (*complete* a painting) **2 a** : to make whole or perfect (its song *completes* the charm of this bird) **b** : to mark the end of (a rousing chorus *completes* the show) **c** : EXECUTE, FULFILL (*complete* a contract) **3** : to carry out (a forward pass) successfully
synonym see CLOSE

complete fertilizer *noun* (1900) : a fertilizer that contains the three chief plant nutrients nitrogen, phosphoric acid, and potash

com·ple·tion \kəm-'plē-shən\ *noun* (1657) **1** : the act or process of completing **2** : the quality or state of being complete **3** : a completed forward pass in football

¹**com·plex** \'käm-,pleks\ *noun* [Late Latin *complexus* totality, from Latin, embrace, from *complecti*] (1643) **1** : a whole made up of complicated or interrelated parts (a *complex* of university buildings) (a *complex* of welfare programs) (the military-industrial *complex*) **2 a** : a group of culture traits relating to a single activity (as hunting), process (as use of flint), or culture unit **b** (1) : a group of repressed desires and memories that exerts a dominating influence upon the personality (2) : an exaggerated reaction to a subject or situation **c** : a group of obviously related units of which the degree and nature of the relationship is imperfectly known **3** : a chemical association of two or more species (as ions or molecules) joined usually by weak electrostatic bonds rather than covalent bonds

²**com·plex** \käm-'pleks, kəm-', 'käm-,\ *adjective* [Latin *complexus*, past participle of *complecti* to embrace, comprise (a multitude of objects), from *com-* + *plectere* to braid — more at PLY] (circa 1652) **1 a** : composed of two or more parts : COMPOSITE **b** (1) *of a word* : having a bound form as one or more of its immediate constituents (*unmanly* is a *complex* word) (2) *of a sentence* : consisting of a main clause and one or more subordinate clauses **2** : hard to separate, analyze, or solve **3** : of, concerned with, being, or containing complex numbers (a *complex* root) (*complex* analysis) ☆
— **com·plex·ly** *adverb*
— **com·plex·ness** *noun*

³**com·plex** \same as ²\ *transitive verb* (1658) **1** : to make complex or into a complex

2 : CHELATE
— **com·plex·a·tion** \,käm-,plek-'sā-shən, kəm-\ *noun*

complex fraction *noun* (1827) : a fraction with a fraction or mixed number in the numerator or denominator or both — compare SIMPLE FRACTION

com·plex·i·fy \käm-'plek-sə-,fī, kəm-\ *verb* **-fied; -fy·ing** (1830) *transitive verb* : to make complex *intransitive verb* : to become complex

com·plex·ion \kəm-'plek-shən\ *noun* [Middle English, from Middle French, from Medieval Latin *complexion-, complexio*, from Latin, combination, from *complecti*] (14th century) **1** : the combination of the hot, cold, moist, and dry qualities held in medieval physiology to determine the quality of a body **2 a** : an individual complex of ways of thinking or feeling **b** : a complex of attitudes and inclinations **3** : the hue or appearance of the skin and especially of the face (a dark *complexion*) **4** : overall aspect or character (by changing the *complexion* of the legislative branch —Trevor Armbrister)
— **com·plex·ion·al** \-shnəl, -shə-n³l\ *adjective*
— **com·plex·ioned** \-shənd\ *adjective*

com·plex·i·ty \käm-'plek-sə-tē, käm-\ *noun, plural* **-ties** (1685) **1** : the quality or state of being complex **2** : something complex

complex number *noun* (1860) : a number of the form $a + b\sqrt{-1}$ where a and b are real numbers

complex plane *noun* (circa 1909) : a plane whose points are identified by means of complex numbers; *especially* : ARGAND DIAGRAM

com·pli·ance \kəm-'plī-ən(t)s\ *noun* (1647) **1 a** : the act or process of complying to a desire, demand, or proposal or to coercion **b** : conformity in fulfilling official requirements **2** : a disposition to yield to others **3** : the ability of an object to yield elastically when a force is applied : FLEXIBILITY

com·pli·an·cy \-ən(t)-sē\ *noun* (1643) : COMPLIANCE

com·pli·ant \-ənt\ *adjective* (1642) : ready or disposed to comply : SUBMISSIVE
— **com·pli·ant·ly** *adverb*

com·pli·ca·cy \'käm-pli-kə-sē\ *noun, plural* **-cies** [²complicate] (circa 1828) **1** : the quality or state of being complicated **2** : something that is complicated

¹**com·pli·cate** \'käm-plə-,kāt\ *transitive verb* **-cat·ed; -cat·ing** (1621) **1** : to combine especially in an involved or inextricable manner **2** : to make complex or difficult **3** : INVOLVE; *especially* : to cause to be more

complex or severe ⟨a virus disease *complicated* by bacterial infection⟩

²**com·pli·cate** \-pli-kət\ *adjective* [Latin *complicatus*, past participle of *complicare* to fold together, from *com-* + *plicare* to fold — more at PLY] (1638)
1 : COMPLEX, INTRICATE
2 : CONDUPLICATE

com·pli·cat·ed \'käm-plə-ˌkā-təd\ *adjective* (1656)
1 : consisting of parts intricately combined
2 : difficult to analyze, understand, or explain
synonym see COMPLEX
— **com·pli·cat·ed·ly** *adverb*
— **com·pli·cat·ed·ness** *noun*

com·pli·ca·tion \ˌkäm-plə-'kā-shən\ *noun* (15th century)
1 a : COMPLEXITY, INTRICACY; *especially* **:** a situation or a detail of character complicating the main thread of a plot **b :** a making difficult, involved, or intricate **c :** a complex or intricate feature or element **d :** a difficult factor or issue often appearing unexpectedly and changing existing plans, methods, or attitudes
2 : a secondary disease or condition developing in the course of a primary disease or condition

com·plice \'käm-pləs, 'kəm-\ *noun* [Middle English, from Middle French, from Late Latin *complic-, complex,* from Latin, closely connected, from *complicare*] (15th century)
archaic **:** ASSOCIATE

com·plic·it \kəm-'pli-sət\ *adjective* (1973)
: having complicity

com·plic·it·ous \-'pli-sə-təs\ *adjective* (1860)
: COMPLICIT

com·plic·i·ty \kəm-'pli-s(ə-)tē\ *noun, plural* **-ties** (circa 1656)
1 : association or participation in or as if in a wrongful act
2 : an instance of complicity

com·pli·er \-'plī(-ə)r\ *noun* (1660)
: one that complies

¹**com·pli·ment** \'käm-plə-mənt\ *noun* [French, from Italian *complimento,* from Spanish *cumplimiento,* from *cumplir* to be courteous — more at COMPLY] (1654)
1 a : an expression of esteem, respect, affection, or admiration; *especially* **:** an admiring remark **b :** formal and respectful recognition **:** HONOR
2 *plural* **:** best wishes **:** REGARDS ⟨accept my *compliments*⟩ ⟨*compliments* of the season⟩

²**com·pli·ment** \-ˌment\ *transitive verb* (1735)
1 : to pay a compliment to
2 : to present with a token of esteem

com·pli·men·ta·ry \ˌkäm-plə-'men-t(ə-)rē\ *adjective* (1716)
1 a : expressing or containing a compliment **b :** FAVORABLE ⟨the novel received *complimentary* reviews⟩
2 : given free as a courtesy or favor ⟨*complimentary* tickets⟩
— **com·pli·men·ta·ri·ly** \-'men-t(ə-)rə-lē, -(ˌ)men-'ter-ə-lē\ *adverb*

complimentary close *noun* (1919)
: the words (as *sincerely yours*) that conventionally come immediately before the signature of a letter and express the sender's regard for the receiver — called also *complimentary closing*

com·pline \'käm-plən, -ˌplīn\ *noun, often capitalized* [Middle English *compline, complie,* from Old French *complie,* modification of Late Latin *completa,* from Latin, feminine of *completus* complete] (13th century)
: the seventh and last of the canonical hours

¹**com·plot** \'käm-ˌplät\ *noun* [Middle French *complot* crowd, plot] (1577)
archaic **:** PLOT, CONSPIRACY

²**com·plot** \kəm-'plät, käm-\ *verb* (1579)
archaic **:** PLOT

com·ply \kəm-'plī\ *intransitive verb* **com·plied; com·ply·ing** [Italian *complire,* from Spanish *cumplir* to complete, perform what is

due, be courteous, modification of Latin *complēre* to complete] (1602)
1 *obsolete* **:** to be ceremoniously courteous
2 : to conform or adapt one's actions to another's wishes, to a rule, or to necessity

com·po \'käm-(ˌ)pō\ *noun, plural* **compos** [short for *composition*] (1823)
: any of various composition materials

¹**com·po·nent** \käm-'pō-nənt, 'käm-ˌ, käm-'\ *noun* [Latin *component-, componens,* present participle of *componere* to put together — more at COMPOUND] (1645)
1 : a constituent part **:** INGREDIENT
2 a : any one of the vector terms added to form a vector sum or resultant **b :** a coordinate of a vector; *also* **:** either member of an ordered pair of numbers
synonym see ELEMENT
— **com·po·nen·tial** \ˌkäm-pə-'nen(t)-shəl\ *adjective*

²**component** *adjective* (1664)
: serving or helping to constitute **:** CONSTITUENT

¹**com·port** \kəm-'pōrt, -'pȯrt\ *verb* [Middle French *comporter* to bear, conduct, from Latin *comportare* to bring together, from *com-* + *portare* to carry — more at FARE] (1589)
intransitive verb
: to be fitting **:** ACCORD ⟨actions that *comport* with policy⟩
transitive verb
: BEHAVE; *especially* **:** to behave in a manner conformable to what is right, proper, or expected ⟨*comported* himself well in the crisis⟩
synonym see BEHAVE
— **com·port·ment** \-mənt\ *noun*

²**com·port** \'käm-ˌpōrt, -ˌpȯrt\ *noun* (1771)
: COMPOTE 2

com·pose \kəm-'pōz\ *verb* **com·posed; com·pos·ing** [Middle English, from Middle French *composer,* from Latin *componere* (perfect indicative *composui*) — more at COMPOUND] (15th century)
transitive verb
1 a : to form by putting together **:** FASHION ⟨a committee *composed* of three representatives —*Current Biography*⟩ **b :** to form the substance of **:** CONSTITUTE ⟨*composed* of many ingredients⟩ **c :** to produce (as columns or pages of type) by composition
2 a : to create by mental or artistic labor **:** PRODUCE ⟨*compose* a sonnet⟩ **b** (1) **:** to formulate and write (a piece of music) (2) **:** to compose music for
3 : to deal with or act on so as to reduce to a minimum ⟨*compose* their differences⟩
4 : to arrange in proper or orderly form
5 : to free from agitation **:** CALM, SETTLE ⟨*composed* himself⟩
intransitive verb
: to practice composition

com·posed \-'pōzd\ *adjective* (1607)
: free from agitation **:** CALM; *especially* **:** SELF-POSSESSED
synonym see COOL
— **com·pos·ed·ly** \-'pō-zəd-lē\ *adverb*
— **com·pos·ed·ness** \-'pō-zəd-nəs\ *noun*

com·pos·er \kəm-'pō-zər\ *noun* (1597)
: one that composes; *especially* **:** a person who writes music

composing room *noun* (1737)
: the department in a printing office where typesetting and related operations are performed

composing stick *noun* (1679)
: a tray with an adjustable slide that a compositor holds in one hand and sets type into with the other

¹**com·pos·ite** \käm-'pä-zət, kəm-', *especially British* 'käm-pə-zit/ *adjective* [Latin *com-*

composing stick

positus, past participle of *componere*] (1563)
1 : made up of distinct parts: as **a** *capitalized* **:** relating to or being a modification of the Corinthian order combining angular Ionic volutes with the acanthus-circled bell of the Corinthian **b :** of or relating to a very large family (Compositae) of dicotyledonous herbs, shrubs, and trees often considered to be the most highly evolved plants and characterized by florets arranged in dense heads that resemble single flowers **c :** factorable into two or more prime factors other than 1 and itself ⟨8 is a positive *composite* integer⟩
2 : combining the typical or essential characteristics of individuals making up a group ⟨the *composite* man called the Poet —Richard Poirier⟩
3 : *of a statistical hypothesis* **:** specifying a range of values for one or more statistical parameters — compare SIMPLE 10
— **com·pos·ite·ly** *adverb*

²**composite** *noun* (1656)
1 : something composite **:** COMPOUND
2 : a composite plant
3 : COMPOSITE FUNCTION
4 : a solid material which is composed of two or more substances having different physical characteristics and in which each substance retains its identity while contributing desirable properties to the whole; *especially* **:** a structural material made of plastic within which a fibrous material (as silicon carbide) is embedded

³**composite** *transitive verb* **-it·ed; -it·ing** (1923)
: to make composite or into something composite ⟨*composited* four soil samples⟩

composite function *noun* (1965)
: a function whose values are found from two given functions by applying one function to an independent variable and then applying the second function to the result and whose domain consists of those values of the independent variable for which the result yielded by the first function lies in the domain of the second

com·po·si·tion \ˌkäm-pə-'zi-shən\ *noun* [Middle English *composicioun,* from Middle French *composition,* from Latin *composition-, compositio,* from *componere*] (14th century)
1 a : the act or process of composing; *specifically* **:** arrangement into specific proportion or relation and especially into artistic form **b** (1) **:** the arrangement of type for printing ⟨hand *composition*⟩ (2) **:** the production of type or typographic characters (as in photocomposition) arranged for printing
2 a : the manner in which something is composed **b :** general makeup ⟨the changing ethnic *composition* of the city —Leonard Buder⟩ **c :** the qualitative and quantitative makeup of a chemical compound
3 : mutual settlement or agreement
4 : a product of mixing or combining various elements or ingredients
5 : an intellectual creation: as **a :** a piece of writing; *especially* **:** a school exercise in the form of a brief essay **b :** a written piece of music especially of considerable size and complexity
6 : the quality or state of being compound
7 : the operation of forming a composite function; *also* **:** COMPOSITE FUNCTION
— **com·po·si·tion·al** \-'zish-nəl, -'zi-shə-nᵊl\ *adjective*
— **com·po·si·tion·al·ly** *adverb*

com·pos·i·tor \käm-'pä-zə-tər\ *noun* (1569)
: one who sets type

com·pos men·tis \'käm-pəs-'men-təs\ *adjective* [Latin, literally, having mastery of one's mind] (1616)
: of sound mind, memory, and understanding

¹**com·post** \'käm-,pōst, *especially British* -,päst\ *noun* [Middle French, from Medieval Latin *compostum*, from Latin, neuter of *compositus, compostus*, past participle of *componere*] (1587)
1 : a mixture that consists largely of decayed organic matter and is used for fertilizing and conditioning land
2 : MIXTURE, COMPOUND

²**compost** *transitive verb* (1829)
: to convert (as plant debris) to compost

com·po·sure \kəm-'pō-zhər\ *noun* (1647)
: a calmness or repose especially of mind, bearing, or appearance : SELF-POSSESSION
synonym see EQUANIMITY

com·pote \'käm-,pōt\ *noun* [French, from Old French *composte*, from Latin *composta*, feminine of *compostus*, past participle] (1693)
1 : a dessert of fruit cooked in syrup
2 : a bowl of glass, porcelain, or metal usually with a base and stem from which compotes, fruits, nuts, or sweets are served

¹**com·pound** \käm-'paund, kəm-', 'käm-\ *verb* [Middle English *compounen*, from Middle French *compondre*, from Latin *componere*, from *com-* + *ponere* to put — more at POSITION] (14th century)
transitive verb
1 : to put together (parts) so as to form a whole : COMBINE 〈*compound* ingredients〉
2 : to form by combining parts 〈*compound* a medicine〉
3 a : to settle amicably : adjust by agreement **b** : to agree for a consideration not to prosecute (an offense) 〈*compound* a felony〉
4 a : to pay (interest) on both the accrued interest and the principal **b** : to add to : AUGMENT 〈we *compounded* our error in later policy —Robert Lekachman〉
intransitive verb
1 : to become joined in a compound
2 : to come to terms of agreement
— **com·pound·able** \-'paun-də-bəl, -,paun-\ *adjective*
— **com·pound·er** *noun*

²**com·pound** \'käm-,paund, käm-', kəm-\ *adjective* [Middle English *compouned*, past participle of *compounen*] (14th century)
1 : composed of or resulting from union of separate elements, ingredients, or parts: as **a** : composed of united similar elements especially of a kind usually independent 〈a *compound* plant ovary〉 **b** : having the blade divided to the midrib and forming two or more leaflets on a common axis 〈a *compound* leaf〉
2 : involving or used in a combination
3 a *of a word* : constituting a compound **b** *of a sentence* : having two or more main clauses

³**com·pound** \'käm-,paund\ *noun* (1530)
1 a : a word consisting of components that are words (as *rowboat, high school, devil-may-care*) **b** : a word (as *anthropology, kilocycle, builder*) consisting of any of various combinations of words, combining forms, or affixes
2 : something formed by a union of elements or parts; *especially* : a distinct substance formed by chemical union of two or more ingredients in definite proportion by weight

⁴**com·pound** \'käm-,paund\ *noun* [by folk etymology from Malay *kampung* group of buildings, village] (1679)
: a fenced or walled-in area containing a group of buildings and especially residences

compound–complex *adjective* (1923)
of a sentence : having two or more main clauses and one or more subordinate clauses

compound eye *noun* (1836)
: an eye (as of an insect) made up of many separate visual units

compound fracture *noun* (1543)
: a bone fracture resulting in an open wound through which bone fragments usually protrude

compound interest *noun* (1660)
: interest computed on the sum of an original principal and accrued interest

compound microscope *noun* (circa 1859)
: a microscope consisting of an objective and an eyepiece mounted in a drawtube

compound number *noun* (15th century)
: a number (as 2 feet 5 in.) involving different denominations or more than one unit

com·pra·dor *or* **com·pra·dore** \,käm-prə-'dōr, -'dȯr\ *noun* [Portuguese *comprador*, literally, buyer] (1840)
1 : a Chinese agent engaged by a foreign establishment in China to have charge of its Chinese employees and to act as an intermediary in business affairs
2 : INTERMEDIARY

com·pre·hend \,käm-pri-'hend\ *transitive verb* [Middle English, from Latin *comprehendere*, from *com-* + *prehendere* to grasp — more at GET] (14th century)
1 : to grasp the nature, significance, or meaning of
2 : to contain or hold within a total scope, significance, or amount 〈philosophy's scope *comprehends* the truth of everything which man may understand —H. O. Taylor〉
3 : to include by construction or implication 〈does not prudence *comprehend* all the virtues? —Thomas B. Silver〉
synonym see UNDERSTAND, INCLUDE
— **com·pre·hend·ible** \-'hen-də-bəl\ *adjective*

com·pre·hen·si·ble \-'hen(t)-sə-bəl\ *adjective* (1598)
: capable of being comprehended : INTELLIGIBLE
— **com·pre·hen·si·bil·i·ty** \-,hen(t)-sə-'bi-lə-tē\ *noun*
— **com·pre·hen·si·ble·ness** \-'hen(t)-sə-bəl-nəs\ *noun*
— **com·pre·hen·si·bly** \-blē\ *adverb*

com·pre·hen·sion \,käm-pri-'hen(t)-shən\ *noun* [Middle French & Latin; Middle French, from Latin *comprehension-, comprehensio*, from *comprehendere* to understand, comprise] (15th century)
1 a : the act or action of grasping with the intellect : UNDERSTANDING **b** : knowledge gained by comprehending **c** : the capacity for understanding fully
2 a : the act or process of comprising **b** : the faculty or capability of including : COMPREHENSIVENESS
3 : CONNOTATION 3

com·pre·hen·sive \-'hen(t)-siv\ *adjective* (1614)
1 : covering completely or broadly : INCLUSIVE 〈*comprehensive* examinations〉 〈*comprehensive* insurance〉
2 : having or exhibiting wide mental grasp 〈*comprehensive* knowledge〉
— **com·pre·hen·sive·ly** *adverb*
— **com·pre·hen·sive·ness** *noun*

¹**com·press** \kəm-'pres\ *verb* [Middle English, from Late Latin *compressare* to press hard, frequentative of Latin *comprimere* to compress, from *com-* + *premere* to press — more at PRESS] (14th century)
transitive verb
1 : to press or squeeze together
2 : to reduce in size or volume as if by squeezing
intransitive verb
: to undergo compression
synonym see CONTRACT

²**com·press** \'käm-,pres\ *noun* [Middle French *compresse*, from *compresser* to compress, from Late Latin *compressare*] (1599)
1 : a folded cloth or pad applied so as to press upon a body part

2 : a machine for compressing

com·pressed \kəm-'prest *also* 'käm-,\ *adjective* (14th century)
1 : pressed together : reduced in size or volume (as by pressure)
2 : flattened as though subjected to compression: **a** : flattened laterally 〈petioles *compressed*〉 **b** : narrow from side to side and deep in a dorsoventral direction
— **com·pressed·ly** \kəm-'prest-lē, -'presəd-lē\ *adverb*

compressed air *noun* (1669)
: air under pressure greater than that of the atmosphere

com·press·ible \kəm-'pre-sə-bəl\ *adjective* (circa 1691)
: capable of being compressed
— **com·press·ibil·i·ty** \-,pre-sə-'bi-lə-tē\ *noun*

com·pres·sion \kəm-'pre-shən\ *noun* (15th century)
1 a : the act, process, or result of compressing **b** : the state of being compressed
2 : the process of compressing the fuel mixture in a cylinder of an internal combustion engine (as in an automobile)
3 : a much compressed fossil plant
— **com·pres·sion·al** \-'presh-nəl, -'pre-shə-n°l\ *adjective*

compressional wave *noun* (1887)
: a longitudinal wave (as a sound wave) propagated by the elastic compression of the medium — called also *compression wave*

com·pres·sive \kəm-'pre-siv\ *adjective* (1572)
1 : of or relating to compression
2 : tending to compress
— **com·pres·sive·ly** *adverb*

com·pres·sor \-'pre-sər\ *noun* (1839)
: one that compresses: as **a** : a muscle that compresses a part **b** : a machine that compresses gases

com·prise \kəm-'prīz\ *transitive verb* **com·prised; com·pris·ing** [Middle English, from Middle French *compris*, past participle of *comprendre*, from Latin *comprehendere*] (15th century)
1 : to include especially within a particular scope 〈civilization as Lenin used the term would then certainly have *comprised* the changes that are now associated with our minds with "developed" rather than "developing" states —*Times Literary Supplement*〉
2 : to be made up of 〈a vast installation, *comprising* fifty buildings —Jane Jacobs〉
3 : COMPOSE, CONSTITUTE 〈a misconception as to what *comprises* a literary generation —William Styron〉 〈about 8 percent of our military forces are *comprised* of women —Jimmy Carter〉 □

¹**com·pro·mise** \'käm-prə-,mīz\ *noun* [Middle English, mutual promise to abide by an arbiter's decision, from Middle French *compromis*, from Latin *compromissum*, from neuter of *compromissus*, past participle of *compromittere* to promise mutually, from *com-* + *promittere* to promise — more at PROMISE] (15th century)
1 a : settlement of differences by arbitration or by consent reached by mutual concessions **b** : something intermediate between or blending qualities of two different things
2 : a concession to something derogatory or prejudicial 〈a *compromise* of principles〉

²**compromise** *verb* **-mised; -mis·ing** (1598)
transitive verb
1 *obsolete* : to bind by mutual agreement
2 : to adjust or settle by mutual concessions
3 a : to expose to suspicion, discredit, or mischief **b** : to reveal or expose to an unauthorized person and especially to an enemy 〈confidential information was *compromised*〉 **c** : to cause the impairment of 〈a *compromised* immune system〉 〈a seriously *compromised* patient〉

intransitive verb
1 a : to come to agreement by mutual concession **b :** to find or follow a way between extremes
2 : to make a shameful or disreputable concession ⟨wouldn't *compromise* with their principles⟩
— **com·pro·mis·er** *noun*

compt \'kaůnt, 'käm(p)t\ *archaic variant of* COUNT

comp·trol·ler \kən-'trō-lər, 'käm(p)-,käm(p)-'\ *noun* [Middle English, alteration of *conterroller* controller] (15th century)
1 : a royal-household official who examines and supervises expenditures
2 : a public official who audits government accounts and sometimes certifies expenditures
3 : CONTROLLER 1c
— **comp·trol·ler·ship** \-,ship\ *noun*

com·pul·sion \kəm-'pəl-shən\ *noun* [Middle English, from Middle French or Late Latin; Middle French, from Late Latin *compulsion-, compulsio,* from Latin *compellere* to compel] (15th century)
1 a : an act of compelling **:** the state of being compelled **b :** a force that compels
2 : an irresistible impulse to perform an irrational act

com·pul·sive \-'pəl-siv\ *adjective* (1588)
1 : having power to compel
2 : of, relating to, caused by, or suggestive of psychological compulsion or obsession ⟨*compulsive* actions⟩
— **com·pul·sive·ly** *adverb*
— **com·pul·sive·ness** *noun*
— **com·pul·siv·i·ty** \kəm-,pəl-'si-və-tē, ,käm-\ *noun*

com·pul·so·ry \kəm-'pəls-rē, -'pəl-sə-\ *adjective* (1581)
1 : MANDATORY, ENFORCED
2 : COERCIVE, COMPELLING
— **com·pul·so·ri·ly** \-rə-lē\ *adverb*

com·punc·tion \kəm-'pəŋ(k)-shən\ *noun* [Middle English *compunccioun,* from Middle French *componction,* from Late Latin *compunction-, compunctio,* from Latin *compungere* to prick hard, sting, from *com- + pungere* to prick — more at PUNGENT] (14th century)
1 a : anxiety arising from awareness of guilt ⟨*compunctions* of conscience⟩ **b :** distress of mind over an anticipated action or result ⟨showed no *compunction* in planning devilish engines of . . . destruction —Havelock Ellis⟩
2 : a twinge of misgiving **:** SCRUPLE ⟨cheated without *compunction*⟩ ◇
synonym see PENITENCE, QUALM
— **com·punc·tious** \-shəs\ *adjective*

com·pur·ga·tion \,käm-(,)pər-'gä-shən\ *noun* [Late Latin *compurgation-, compurgatio,* from Latin *compurgare* to clear completely, from *com- + purgare* to purge] (circa 1658)
: the clearing of an accused person by oaths of others who swear to the veracity or innocence of the accused

com·pur·ga·tor \'käm-(,)pər-,gä-tər\ *noun* (1533)
: one that under oath vouches for the character or conduct of an accused person

com·put·able \kəm-'pyü-tə-bəl\ *adjective* (1646)
: capable of being computed
— **com·put·abil·i·ty** \-,pyü-tə-'bi-lə-tē\ *noun*

com·pu·ta·tion \,käm-pyù-'tā-shən\ *noun* (15th century)
1 a : the act or action of computing **:** CALCULATION **b :** the use or operation of a computer
2 : a system of reckoning
3 : an amount computed
— **com·pu·ta·tion·al** \-shnəl, -shə-n°l\ *adjective*
— **com·pu·ta·tion·al·ly** *adverb*

com·pute \kəm-'pyüt\ *verb* **com·put·ed; com·put·ing** [Latin *computare* — more at COUNT] (1616)

transitive verb
: to determine especially by mathematical means ⟨*compute* your income tax⟩; *also* **:** to determine or calculate by means of a computer
intransitive verb
1 : to make calculation **:** RECKON
2 : to use a computer

computed tomography *noun* (1975)
: radiography in which a three-dimensional image of a body structure is constructed by computer from a series of plane cross-sectional images made along an axis — called also *computed axial tomography, computerized axial tomography, computerized tomography*

com·put·er \kəm-'pyü-tər\ *noun, often attributive* (1646)
: one that computes; *specifically* **:** a programmable electronic device that can store, retrieve, and process data
— **com·put·er·dom** \-dəm\ *noun*
— **com·put·er·less** \-ləs\ *adjective*
— **com·put·er·like** \-,līk\ *adjective*

com·put·er·ese \-,pyü-tə-'rēz, -'rēs\ *noun* (circa 1960)
: jargon used by computer technologists

com·put·er·ise *chiefly British variant of* COMPUTERIZE

com·put·er·ist \kəm-'pyü-tə-rist\ *noun* (1973)
: a person who uses or operates a computer

com·put·er·ize \kəm-'pyü-tə-,rīz\ *transitive verb* **-ized; -iz·ing** (1957)
1 : to carry out, control, or produce by means of a computer
2 : to equip with computers
3 a : to store in a computer **b :** to put in a form that a computer can use
— **com·put·er·iz·able** \-,pyü-tə-'rī-zə-bəl\ *adjective*
— **com·put·er·i·za·tion** \-,pyü-tə-rə-'zā-shən\ *noun*

com·put·er·nik \kəm-'pyü-tər-,nik\ *noun* (1968)
: a computer enthusiast or expert

com·put·er·phobe \-,fōb\ *noun* (1976)
: a person who experiences anxiety about computers and especially about their use
— **com·put·er·pho·bia** \-,pyü-tər-'fō-bē-ə\ *noun*
— **com·put·er·pho·bic** \-'fō-bik\ *adjective*

com·rade \'käm-,rad, -rəd, *especially British* -,rād\ *noun* [Middle French *camarade* group sleeping in one room, roommate, companion, from Old Spanish *camarada,* from *cámara* room, from Late Latin *camera, camara* — more at CHAMBER] (1544)
1 a : an intimate friend or associate **:** COMPANION **b :** a fellow soldier
2 [from its use as a form of address by communists] **:** COMMUNIST ◇
— **com·rade·li·ness** \-lē-nəs\ *noun*
— **com·rade·ly** *adjective*
— **com·rade·ship** \-,ship\ *noun*

com·rad·ery \'käm-,ra-d(ə-)rē, -rə-drē, -,rä-d(ə-)rē\ *noun* (1879)
: CAMARADERIE

Comsat \'käm-,sat\ *service mark*
— used for communications services involving an artificial satellite

Com·stock·ery \'käm-,stä-kə-rē *also* 'kəm-\ *noun* [Anthony *Comstock* + English *-ery*] (1905)
1 : strict censorship of materials considered obscene
2 : censorious opposition to alleged immorality (as in literature)

Com·stock·ian \käm-'stä-kē-ən *also* ,kəm-\ *adjective* (1921)
: of or relating to Comstockery

com·symp \'käm-,simp\ *noun* [*communist* + *symp*athizer] (circa 1961)
: a person sympathetic to communist causes
— usually used disparagingly

Comt·ian *or* **Comt·ean** \'käm(p)-tē-ən, 'kō� ^n(n)-tē-\ *adjective* (1846)
: of or relating to Auguste Comte or his doctrines
— **Comt·ism** \'käm(p)-,ti-zəm, 'kō^n(n)-\ *noun*
— **Comt·ist** \'käm(p)-tist, 'kō^n(n)-\ *adjective or noun*

¹con \'kän\ *transitive verb* **conned; con·ning** [Middle English *connen* to know, learn, study, alteration of *cunnen* to know, infinitive of *can* — more at CAN] (13th century)
1 : to commit to memory
2 : to study or examine closely

²con *variant of* CONN

³con *adverb* [Middle English, short for *contra*] (15th century)
: on the negative side **:** in opposition ⟨so much has been written pro and *con*⟩

⁴con *noun* (1589)
1 : an argument or evidence in opposition
2 : the negative position or one holding it ⟨an appraisal of the pros and *cons*⟩

□ USAGE
comprise Although it has been in use since the late 18th century, sense 3 is still attacked as wrong. Why it has been singled out is not clear, but until comparatively recent times it was found chiefly in scientific or technical writing rather than belles lettres. Our current evidence shows a slight shift in usage: sense 3 is somewhat more frequent in recent literary use than the earlier senses. You should be aware, however, that if you use sense 3 you may be subject to criticism for doing so, and you may want to choose a safer synonym such as *compose* or *make up.*

◇ WORD HISTORY
compunction When we express the hope that someone doing, or about to do, wrong will feel some compunction—or will experience a sting of conscience—we may not realize that both expressions embody the same metaphor. *Compunction* derives ultimately from the Latin verb *compungere* "to prick hard" or "to sting." Because some people seem not to experience even a momentary twinge of guilt, *compunction* is often used in negative constructions, as "acted without compunction."

comrade In classical Latin, *camara* or *camera* denoted a vaulted ceiling or roof. By the time of the Latin Church Fathers, the word meant simply "room, chamber," and was inherited by most of the Romance languages, ultimately yielding English *chamber* (through French *chambre*). Through scientific writing in New Latin, English has also acquired *camera lucida, camera obscura,* and the word *camera* itself. In Spanish, the outcome of the Latin word was *cámara*; a 16th century derivative of *cámara* was *camarada* "group of soldiers quartered in a room" and hence "fellow-soldier, companion." Spanish *camarada* was borrowed into French as *camarade,* and from French into Elizabethan English as both *camerade* and *comerade.* The form with *-o-* probably arose by association with the Latin prefix *com-* "together."

\ə\ abut \ᵊ\ kitten \ər\ further \a\ ash \ā\ ace
\ä\ mop, mar \aů\ out \ch\ chin \e\ bet \ē\ easy
\g\ go \i\ hit \ī\ ice \j\ job \ŋ\ sing \ō\ go
\ò\ law \òi\ boy \th\ thin \t͟h\ the \ü\ loot \ů\ foot
\y\ yet \zh\ vision *see also* Guide to Pronunciation

⁵con adjective [by shortening] (1889)
: CONFIDENCE

⁶con transitive verb **conned; con·ning** (1896)
1 : SWINDLE
2 : MANIPULATE 2b
3 : PERSUADE, CAJOLE

⁷con noun (1901)
: something (as a ruse) used deceptively to gain another's confidence; also : a confidence game : SWINDLE

⁸con noun [by shortening] (1893)
: CONVICT

⁹con noun [short for consumption] (1915)
slang : a destructive disease of the lungs; especially : TUBERCULOSIS

con- — see COM-

con amo·re \ˌkän-ə-ˈmōr-ē, ˌkōn-ə-ˈmōr-(ˌ)ā, -ˈmȯr-\ adverb [Italian] (1739)
1 : with love, devotion, or zest
2 : in a tender manner — used as a direction in music

con ani·ma \kän-ˈä-nə-ˌmä, kōn-ˈä-ni-\ adverb [Italian, literally, with spirit] (circa 1906)
: in a spirited manner — used as a direction in music

co·na·tion \kō-ˈnā-shən\ noun [Latin conation-, conatio act of attempting, from conari to attempt — more at DEACON] (circa 1837)
: an inclination (as an instinct, a drive, a wish, or a craving) to act purposefully : IMPULSE 3
— **co·na·tive** \ˈkō-nə-tiv, ˈkä-, ˈkō-ˌnā-\ adjective

con brio \kän-ˈbrē-(ˌ)ō, kōn-\ adverb [Italian, literally, with vigor] (circa 1889)
: in a vigorous or brisk manner — used as a direction in music

con·ca·nav·a·lin \ˌkän-kə-ˈna-və-lən\ noun [com- + canavalin, a noncrystalline globulin found in the jack bean, from New Latin Canavalia, genus name of the jack bean] (1917)
: either of two crystalline globulins occurring in the jack bean; especially : one that is a potent hemagglutinin

¹con·cat·e·nate \kän-ˈka-tə-nət, kən-\ adjective [Middle English, from Late Latin concatenatus, past participle of concatenare to link together, from Latin com- + catena chain] (15th century)
: linked together

²concatenate \-ˌnāt\ transitive verb **-nat·ed; -nat·ing** (1598)
: to link together in a series or chain
— **con·cat·e·na·tion** \(ˌ)kän-ˌka-tə-ˈnā-shən, kən-\ noun

¹con·cave \kän-ˈkāv, ˈkän-ˌ\ adjective [Middle English, from Middle French, from Latin concavus, from com- + cavus hollow — more at CAVE] (15th century)
1 : hollowed or rounded inward like the inside of a bowl
2 : arched in : curving in — used of the side of a curve or surface on which neighboring normals to the curve or surface converge and on which lies the chord joining two neighboring points of the curve or surface

²con·cave \ˈkän-ˌkāv\ noun (1552)
: a concave line or surface

con·cav·i·ty \kän-ˈka-və-tē\ noun, plural **-ties** (15th century)
1 : a concave line, surface, or space : HOLLOW
2 : the quality or state of being concave

con·ca·vo–con·vex \kän-ˌkā-vō-kän-ˈveks; ˈkän-, kōn-\ adjective (1676)
1 : concave on one side and convex on the other
2 : having the concave side curved more than the convex ⟨a concavo-convex lens⟩

con·ceal \kən-ˈsē(ə)l\ transitive verb [Middle English concelen, from Middle French conceler, from Latin concelare to hide, from com- + celare to hide — more at HELL] (14th century)

1 : to prevent disclosure or recognition of
2 : to place out of sight
synonym see HIDE
— **con·ceal·able** \-ˈsē-lə-bəl\ adjective
— **con·ceal·er** \-ˈsē-lər\ noun
— **con·ceal·ing·ly** \-ˈsē-liŋ-lē\ adverb
— **con·ceal·ment** \-ˈsē(ə)l-mənt\ noun

con·cede \kən-ˈsēd\ verb **con·ced·ed; con·ced·ing** [French or Latin; French concéder, from Latin concedere, from com- + cedere to yield] (1632)
transitive verb
1 : to grant as a right or privilege
2 a : to accept as true, valid, or accurate ⟨the right of the state to tax is generally conceded⟩
b : to acknowledge grudgingly or hesitantly
intransitive verb
: to make concession : YIELD
synonym see GRANT
— **con·ced·ed·ly** \-ˈsē-dəd-lē\ adverb
— **con·ced·er** noun

¹con·ceit \kən-ˈsēt\ noun [Middle English, from conceiven] (14th century)
1 a (1) : a result of mental activity : THOUGHT (2) : individual opinion **b** : favorable opinion; especially : excessive appreciation of one's own worth or virtue
2 : a fancy article
3 a : a fanciful idea **b** : an elaborate or strained metaphor **c** : use or presence of such conceits in poetry **d** : an organizing theme or concept ⟨found his conceit for the film early —Peter Wilkinson⟩

²conceit transitive verb (1557)
1 obsolete : CONCEIVE, UNDERSTAND
2 chiefly dialect : IMAGINE
3 dialect British : to take a fancy to

con·ceit·ed \-ˈsē-təd\ adjective [¹conceit] (1593)
1 : ingeniously contrived : FANCIFUL
2 : having an excessively high opinion of oneself
— **con·ceit·ed·ly** adverb
— **con·ceit·ed·ness** noun

con·ceiv·able \kən-ˈsē-və-bəl\ adjective (15th century)
: capable of being conceived : IMAGINABLE
— **con·ceiv·abil·i·ty** \kən-ˌsē-və-ˈbi-lə-tē\ noun
— **con·ceiv·able·ness** \-ˈsē-və-bəl-nəs\ noun

con·ceiv·ably \-blē\ adverb (1625)
1 : in a conceivable manner
2 : it may be conceived : POSSIBLY

con·ceive \kən-ˈsēv\ verb **con·ceived; con·ceiv·ing** [Middle English, from Middle French conceivre, from Latin concipere to take in, conceive, from com- + capere to take — more at HEAVE] (14th century)
transitive verb
1 a : to become pregnant with (young) **b** : to cause to begin : ORIGINATE
2 a : to take into one's mind ⟨conceive a prejudice⟩ **b** : to form a conception of : IMAGINE
3 : to apprehend by reason or imagination : UNDERSTAND
4 : to be of the opinion
intransitive verb
1 : to become pregnant
2 : to have a conception — usually used with of ⟨conceives of death as emptiness⟩
synonym see THINK
— **con·ceiv·er** noun

con·cel·e·brant \kən-ˈse-lə-brənt, kän-\ noun (circa 1931)
: one that concelebrates a Eucharist or Mass

con·cel·e·brate \kən-ˈse-lə-ˌbrāt, kän-\ verb [Medieval Latin concelebratus, past participle of concelebrare, from Latin, to frequent, celebrate, from com- + celebrare to celebrate] (1879)
transitive verb
: to participate in (a Eucharist) as a joint celebrant who recites the canon in unison with other celebrants

intransitive verb
: to participate as a celebrant in a concelebrated Eucharist
— **con·cel·e·bra·tion** \(ˌ)kän-ˌse-lə-ˈbrā-shən, kən-\ noun

con·cent \kən-ˈsent\ noun [Latin concentus, from concinere to sing together, from com- + canere to sing — more at CHANT] (1585)
archaic : HARMONY

con·cen·ter \kən-ˈsen-tər, kän-\ verb [French concentrer, from com- + centre center] (1598)
transitive verb
: to draw or direct to a common center : CONCENTRATE
intransitive verb
: to come to a common center

¹con·cen·trate \ˈkän(t)-sən-ˌtrāt, -ˌsen-\ verb **-trat·ed; -trat·ing** [com- + Latin centrum center] (1646)
transitive verb
1 a : to bring or direct toward a common center or objective : FOCUS **b** : to gather into one body, mass, or force ⟨power was concentrated in a few able hands⟩ **c** : to accumulate (a toxic substance) in bodily tissues ⟨fish concentrate mercury⟩
2 a : to make less dilute ⟨concentrate syrup⟩ **b** : to express or exhibit in condensed form
intransitive verb
1 : to draw toward or meet in a common center
2 : GATHER, COLLECT
3 : to concentrate one's powers, efforts, or attention ⟨concentrate on a problem⟩
— **con·cen·trat·ed·ly** \-ˌtrā-təd-lē; ˌkän(t)-sən-ˈtrā-\ adverb
— **con·cen·tra·tive** \-ˌtrā-tiv\ adjective

²concentrate noun (1883)
1 : something concentrated: as **a** : a mineral-rich product obtained after an initial processing of ore **b** : a food reduced in bulk by elimination of fluid ⟨orange juice concentrate⟩
2 : a feedstuff (as grains) relatively rich in digestible nutrients — compare FIBER

con·cen·tra·tion \ˌkän(t)-sən-ˈtrā-shən, -ˌsen-\ noun (1634)
1 a : the act or process of concentrating; the state of being concentrated; especially : direction of attention to a single object **b** : MAJOR 4a
2 : a concentrated mass or thing
3 : the amount of a component in a given area or volume

concentration camp noun (1901)
: a camp where persons (as prisoners of war, political prisoners, or refugees) are detained or confined

con·cen·tra·tor \ˈkän(t)-sən-ˌtrā-tər\ noun (1833)
: one that concentrates: as **a** : an industrial plant that produces concentrates from ores **b** : a mirror or group of mirrors that focus sunlight for use as an energy source **c** : a device in a computer network that collects data from separate low-volume transmission channels and retransmits it over a single high-volume channel

con·cen·tric \kən-ˈsen-trik, ˌkän-\ adjective [Medieval Latin concentricus, from Latin com- + centrum center] (14th century)
1 : having a common center ⟨concentric circles⟩
2 : having a common axis : COAXIAL
— **con·cen·tri·cal·ly** \-tri-k(ə-)lē\ adverb
— **con·cen·tric·i·ty** \ˌkän-ˌsen-ˈtri-sə-tē\ noun

con·cept \ˈkän-ˌsept\ noun [Latin conceptum, neuter of conceptus, past participle of concipere to conceive — more at CONCEIVE] (1556)
1 : something conceived in the mind : THOUGHT, NOTION
2 : an abstract or generic idea generalized from particular instances
synonym see IDEA

con·cep·ta·cle \kən-ˈsep-ti-kəl\ noun [New Latin conceptaculum, from Latin, receptacle,

from *conceptus,* past participle of *concipere* to take in] (1835)
: an external cavity containing reproductive cells in algae (as of the genus *Fucus*)

con·cep·tion \kən-'sep-shən\ *noun* [Middle English *concepcioun,* from Old French *conception,* from Latin *conception-, conceptio,* from *concipere*] (14th century)
1 a (1) **:** the act of becoming pregnant **:** the state of being conceived (2) **:** EMBRYO, FETUS **b** **:** BEGINNING ⟨joy had the like *conception* in our eyes —Shakespeare⟩
2 a **:** the capacity, function, or process of forming or understanding ideas or abstractions or their symbols **b** **:** a general idea **:** CONCEPT **c** **:** a complex product of abstract or reflective thinking **d** **:** the sum of a person's ideas and beliefs concerning something
3 **:** the originating of something in the mind
synonym see IDEA
— **con·cep·tion·al** \-shnəl, -shə-nᵊl\ *adjective*
— **con·cep·tive** \-'sep-tiv\ *adjective*

con·cep·tu·al \kən-'sep-chə-wəl, kän-, -chəl, -shwəl\ *adjective* [Medieval Latin *conceptualis* of thought, from Late Latin *conceptus* act of conceiving, thought, from Latin *concipere*] (circa 1834)
: of, relating to, or consisting of concepts
— **con·cep·tu·al·i·ty** \-,sep-chə-'wa-lə-tē, -shə-\ *noun*
— **con·cep·tu·al·ly** *adverb*

conceptual art *noun* (circa 1969)
: an art form in which the artist's intent is to convey a concept rather than to create an art object
— **conceptual artist** *noun*

con·cep·tu·al·ise *British variant of* CONCEPTUALIZE

con·cep·tu·al·ism \-'sep-chə-wə-,li-zəm, -chə-,li-, -shwə-,li-\ *noun* (circa 1838)
: a theory in philosophy intermediate between realism and nominalism that universals exist in the mind as concepts of discourse or as predicates which may be properly affirmed of reality
— **con·cep·tu·al·is·tic** \-,sep-chə-wə-'lis-tik, -chə-'lis-, -shwə-'lis-\ *adjective*
— **con·cep·tu·al·is·ti·cal·ly** \-ti-k(ə-)lē\ *adverb*

con·cep·tu·al·ist \-'sep-chə-wə-list, -chə-list, -shwə-list\ *noun* (1785)
: an adherent to the tenets of conceptualism or of conceptual art

con·cep·tu·al·ize \-'sep-chə-wə-,līz, -chə-,līz, -shwə-,līz\ *transitive verb* **-ized; -iz·ing** (1878)
: to form a concept of; *especially* **:** to interpret conceptually
— **con·cep·tu·al·i·za·tion** \-,sep-chə-wə-lə-'zā-shən, -chə-lə-, -shwə-lə-\ *noun*
— **con·cep·tu·al·iz·er** \-'sep-chə-wə-,lī-zər, chə-,lī-, -shwə-,lī-\ *noun*

con·cep·tus \kən-'sep-təs\ *noun* [Latin, one conceived, from past participle of *concipere* to conceive] (circa 1860)
: a fertilized egg, embryo, or fetus

¹con·cern \kən-'sərn\ *verb* [Middle English, from Middle French & Medieval Latin; Middle French *concerner,* from Medieval Latin *concernere,* from Late Latin, to sift together, mingle, from Latin *com-* + *cernere* to sift — more at CERTAIN] (15th century)
transitive verb
1 a **:** to relate to **:** be about ⟨the novel *concerns* three soldiers⟩ **b** **:** to bear on
2 **:** to have an influence on **:** INVOLVE; *also* **:** to be the business or affair of ⟨the problem *concerns* us all⟩
3 **:** to be a care, trouble, or distress to ⟨her ill health *concerns* me⟩
4 **:** ENGAGE, OCCUPY ⟨he *concerns* himself with trivia⟩
intransitive verb
obsolete **:** to be of importance **:** MATTER

²concern *noun* (1655)

1 a **:** marked interest or regard usually arising through a personal tie or relationship **b** **:** an uneasy state of blended interest, uncertainty, and apprehension
2 **:** something that relates or belongs to one **:** AFFAIR
3 **:** matter for consideration
4 **:** an organization or establishment for business or manufacture
5 **:** CONTRIVANCE, GADGET
synonym see CARE

concerned *adjective* (1656)
1 a **:** ANXIOUS, WORRIED ⟨*concerned* for their safety⟩ **b** **:** INTERESTED ⟨*concerned* to prove the point⟩
2 a **:** interestedly engaged ⟨*concerned* with books and music⟩ **b** **:** culpably involved **:** IMPLICATED ⟨arrested all *concerned*⟩

concerning *preposition* (15th century)
: relating to **:** REGARDING

con·cern·ment \kən-'sərn-mənt\ *noun* (1610)
1 **:** something in which one is concerned
2 **:** IMPORTANCE, CONSEQUENCE
3 *archaic* **:** INVOLVEMENT, PARTICIPATION
4 **:** SOLICITUDE, ANXIETY

¹con·cert \'kän(t)-sərt, 'kän-,sərt\ *noun* [French, from Italian *concerto,* from *concertare*] (1674)
1 *obsolete* **:** musical harmony **:** CONCORD
2 a **:** agreement in design or plan **:** union formed by mutual communication of opinion and views **b** **:** a concerted action ⟨the sacrifice was hailed with a *concert* of praise⟩
3 **:** a public performance (as of music or dancing)
— **concert** *adjective*
— **in concert** **:** TOGETHER

²con·cert \kən-'sərt\ *verb* [Middle French *concerter,* from Old Italian *concertare,* perhaps from *com-* + *certo* certain, decided, from Latin *certus* — more at CERTAIN] (1694)
transitive verb
1 **:** to settle or adjust by conferring and reaching an agreement ⟨*concerted* their differences⟩
2 **:** to make a plan for ⟨*concert* measures for aiding the poor⟩
intransitive verb
: to act in harmony or conjunction

con·cert·ed \kən-'sər-təd\ *adjective* (1716)
1 a **:** mutually contrived or agreed on ⟨a *concerted* effort⟩ **b** **:** performed in unison ⟨*concerted* artillery fire⟩
2 **:** arranged in parts for several voices or instruments
— **con·cert·ed·ly** *adverb*
— **con·cert·ed·ness** *noun*

con·cert·go·er \'kän(t)-sərt-,gō(-ə)r, 'kän-,sərt-\ *noun* (1855)
: one who frequently attends concerts
— **con·cert·go·ing** \-,gō-iŋ, -,gò(-)iŋ\ *noun or adjective*

concert grand *noun* (circa 1891)
: a grand piano of the largest size adapted in volume, timbre, and brilliance of tone to concert use

con·cer·ti·na \,kän(t)-sər-'tē-nə\ *noun* [probably from *¹concert* + Italian *-ina,* diminutive suffix] (1837)
1 **:** a musical instrument of the accordion family
2 **:** a coiled barbed wire for use as an obstacle — called also *concertina wire*

con·cer·ti·no \,kän-chər-'tē-(,)nō\ *noun, plural* **-nos** [Italian, diminutive of *concerto*] (circa 1801)
1 **:** the solo instruments in a concerto grosso
2 **:** a short concerto

con·cert·ize \'kän(t)-sər-,tīz\ *intransitive verb* **-ized; -iz·ing** (1883)

concertina 1

: to perform professionally in concerts

con·cert·mas·ter \'kän(t)-sərt-,mas-tər\ *or* **con·cert·meis·ter** \-,mī-stər\ *noun* [German *Konzertmeister,* from *Konzert* concert + *Meister* master] (circa 1889)
: the leader of the first violins of an orchestra and by custom usually the assistant to the conductor

con·cer·to \kən-'cher-(,)tō *also* -'chər-\ *noun, plural* **-ti** \-(,)tē\ *or* **-tos** [Italian, from *concerto* concert] (1730)
: a piece for one or more soloists and orchestra with three contrasting movements

concerto gros·so \-'grō-(,)sō, -'grò-\ *noun, plural* **concerti gros·si** \-(,)sē\ [Italian, literally, big concerto] (1724)
: a baroque orchestral composition featuring a small group of solo instruments contrasting with the full orchestra

concert pitch *noun* (1767)
1 **:** INTERNATIONAL PITCH
2 **:** a high state of fitness, tension, or readiness

con·ces·sion \kən-'se-shən\ *noun* [Middle English, from Middle French or Latin; Middle French, from Latin *concession-, concessio,* from *concedere* to concede] (15th century)
1 a **:** the act or an instance of conceding **b** **:** the admitting of a point claimed in argument
2 **:** something conceded: **a** **:** ACKNOWLEDGMENT, ADMISSION **b** **:** GRANT **c** (1) **:** a grant of land or property especially by a government in return for services or for a particular use (2) **:** a right to undertake and profit by a specified activity (3) **:** a lease of a portion of premises for a particular purpose; *also* **:** the portion leased or the activities carried on
— **con·ces·sion·al** \-'sesh-nəl, -'se-shə-nᵊl\ *adjective*
— **con·ces·sion·ary** \-'se-shə-,ner-ē\ *adjective*

con·ces·sion·aire \kən-,se-shə-'nar, -'ner\ *noun* [French *concessionnaire,* from *concession*] (1862)
: the owner or operator of a concession; *especially* **:** one that operates a refreshment stand at a recreational center

con·ces·sion·er \kən-'se-sh(ə-)nər\ *noun* (circa 1891)
: CONCESSIONAIRE

con·ces·sive \kən-'se-siv\ *adjective* (1711)
1 **:** denoting concession ⟨a *concessive* clause⟩
2 **:** making for or being a concession
— **con·ces·sive·ly** *adverb*

conch \'käŋk, 'känch, 'kòŋk\ *noun, plural* **conchs** \'käŋks, 'kòŋks\ *or* **conches** \'kän-chəz\ [Middle English, from Latin *concha* mussel, mussel shell, from Greek *konchē;* akin to Sanskrit *śaṅkha* conch shell] (15th century)
1 **:** any of various large spiral-shelled marine gastropod mollusks (as of the genus *Strombus*); *also* **:** its shell used especially for cameos
2 *often capitalized* **:** a native or resident of the Florida Keys
3 **:** CONCHA 2

con·cha \'kän-kə\ *noun, plural* **con·chae** \-,kē, -,kī\ [Italian & Latin; Italian *conca* semidome, apse, from Late Latin *concha,* from Latin, shell] (circa 1639)
1 a **:** the plain semidome of an apse **b** **:** APSE
2 **:** something shaped like a shell; *especially* **:** the largest and deepest concavity of the external ear
— **con·chal** \-kəl\ *adjective*

conch 1

con·choi·dal \kän-'kȯi-dᵊl, kän-\ *adjective* [Greek *konchoeidēs* like a mussel, from *konchē*] (1666)
: having elevations or depressions shaped like the inside surface of a bivalve shell
— **con·choi·dal·ly** \-dᵊl-ē\ *adverb*

con·chol·o·gy \kän-'kä-lə-jē\ *noun* [Greek *konchē*] (1776)
1 : a branch of zoology that deals with shells
2 : a treatise on shells
— **con·chol·o·gist** \-jist\ *noun*

con·cierge \kōⁿ-'syerzh\ *noun, plural* **con·cierges** \-'syerzh, -'syer-zhəz\ [French, from Old French, probably from (assumed) Vulgar Latin *conservius*, alteration of Latin *conservus* fellow slave, from *com-* + *servus* slave] (circa 1697)
1 : a resident in an apartment building especially in France who serves as doorkeeper, landlord's representative, and janitor
2 : a usually multilingual hotel staff member who handles luggage and mail, makes reservations, and arranges tours

con·cil·i·ar \kən-'si-lē-ər\ *adjective* [Latin *concilium* council] (circa 1677)
: of, relating to, or issued by a council
— **con·cil·i·ar·ly** *adverb*

con·cil·i·ate \kən-'si-lē-ˌāt\ *verb* **-at·ed; -at·ing** [Latin *conciliatus*, past participle of *conciliare* to assemble, unite, win over, from *concilium* assembly, council — more at COUNCIL] (1545)
transitive verb
1 : to gain (as goodwill) by pleasing acts
2 : to make compatible : RECONCILE
3 : APPEASE
intransitive verb
: to become friendly or agreeable
synonym see PACIFY
— **con·cil·i·a·tion** \-ˌsi-lē-'ā-shən\ *noun*
— **con·cil·i·a·tive** \-'si-lē-ˌā-tiv\ *adjective*
— **con·cil·i·a·tor** \-ˌā-tər\ *noun*
— **con·cil·ia·to·ry** \-'sil-yə-ˌtȯr-ē, -'si-lē-ə-, -ˌtȯr-\ *adjective*

con·cin·ni·ty \kən-'si-nə-tē\ *noun, plural* **-ties** [Latin *concinnitas*, from *concinnus* skillfully put together] (1531)
: harmony or elegance of design especially of literary style in adaptation of parts to a whole or to each other

con·cise \kən-'sīs\ *adjective* [Latin *concisus*, from past participle of *concidere* to cut up, from *com-* + *caedere* to cut, strike] (circa 1590)
1 : marked by brevity of expression or statement : free from all elaboration and superfluous detail
2 : cut short : BRIEF ☆
— **con·cise·ly** *adverb*
— **con·cise·ness** *noun*

con·ci·sion \kən-'si-zhən\ *noun* [Middle English, from Latin *concision-, concisio*, from *concidere*] (14th century)
1 *archaic* : a cutting up or off
2 : the quality or state of being concise

con·clave \'kän-ˌklāv\ *noun* [Middle English, from Middle French or Medieval Latin; Middle French, from Medieval Latin, from Latin, room that can be locked up, from *com-* + *clavis* key — more at CLAVICLE] (1524)
1 : a private meeting or secret assembly; *especially* : a meeting of Roman Catholic cardinals secluded continuously while choosing a pope
2 : a gathering of a group or association

con·clude \kən-'klüd\ *verb* **con·clud·ed; con·clud·ing** [Middle English, from Latin *concludere* to shut up, end, infer, from *com-* + *claudere* to shut — more at CLOSE] (14th century)
transitive verb
1 *obsolete* : to shut up : ENCLOSE
2 : to bring to an end especially in a particular way or with a particular action ⟨*conclude* a meeting with a prayer⟩

3 a : to reach as a logically necessary end by reasoning : infer on the basis of evidence ⟨*concluded* that her argument was sound⟩ **b** : to make a decision about : DECIDE ⟨*concluded* he would wait a little longer⟩ **c** : to come to an agreement on : EFFECT ⟨*conclude* a sale⟩
4 : to bring about as a result : COMPLETE
intransitive verb
1 : END
2 a : to form a final judgment **b** : to reach a decision or agreement
synonym see CLOSE, INFER
— **con·clud·er** *noun*

con·clu·sion \kən-'klü-zhən\ *noun* [Middle English, from Middle French, from Latin *conclusion-, conclusio*, from *concludere*] (14th century)
1 a : a reasoned judgment : INFERENCE **b** : the necessary consequence of two or more propositions taken as premises; *especially* : the inferred proposition of a syllogism
2 : the last part of something: as **a** : RESULT, OUTCOME **b** *plural* : trial of strength or skill — used in the phrase *try conclusions* **c** : a final summation **d** : the final decision in a law case **e** : the final part of a pleading in law
3 : an act or instance of concluding

con·clu·sion·ary \kən-'klü-zhə-ˌner-ē\ *adjective* (1948)
: CONCLUSORY

con·clu·sive \-'klü-siv, -ziv\ *adjective* (1536)
1 : of, relating to, or being a conclusion
2 : putting an end to debate or question especially by reason of irrefutability ☆
— **con·clu·sive·ly** *adverb*
— **con·clu·sive·ness** *noun*

con·clu·so·ry \kən-'klüs-rē, -'klü-sə-\ *adjective* (1923)
: consisting of or relating to a conclusion or assertion for which no supporting evidence is offered ⟨*conclusory* allegations⟩

con·coct \kən-'käkt, kän-\ *transitive verb* [Latin *concoctus*, past participle of *concoquere* to cook together, from *com-* + *coquere* to cook — more at COOK] (1675)
1 : to prepare by combining raw materials
2 : DEVISE, FABRICATE
— **con·coct·er** *noun*
— **con·coc·tion** \-'käk-shən\ *noun*
— **con·coc·tive** \-'käk-tiv\ *adjective*

con·com·i·tance \kən-'kä-mə-tən(t)s, kän-\ *noun* (circa 1535)
: ACCOMPANIMENT; *especially* : a conjunction that is regular and is marked by correlative variation of accompanying elements

¹con·com·i·tant \-mə-tənt\ *adjective* [Latin *concomitant-, concomitans*, present participle of *concomitari* to accompany, from *com-* + *comitari* to accompany, from *comit-, comes* companion — more at COUNT] (1607)
: accompanying especially in a subordinate or incidental way
— **con·com·i·tant·ly** *adverb*

²concomitant *noun* (1621)
: something that accompanies or is collaterally connected with something else : ACCOMPANIMENT

con·cord \'kän-ˌkȯrd, 'kän-\ *noun* [Middle English, from Middle French *concorde*, from Latin *concordia*, from *concord-, concors* agreeing, from *com-* + *cord-, cor* heart — more at HEART] (14th century)
1 a : a state of agreement : HARMONY **b** : a simultaneous occurrence of two or more musical tones that produces an impression of agreeableness or resolution on a listener — compare DISCORD
2 : agreement by stipulation, compact, or covenant
3 : grammatical agreement

con·cor·dance \kən-'kȯr-dᵊn(t)s, kän-\ *noun* [Middle English, from Middle French, from Medieval Latin *concordantia*, from Latin *concordant-, concordans*, present participle of

concordare to agree, from *concord-, concors*] (14th century)
1 : an alphabetical index of the principal words in a book or the works of an author with their immediate contexts
2 : CONCORD, AGREEMENT

con·cor·dant \-dᵊnt\ *adjective* [Middle English, from Middle French, from Latin *concordant-, concordans*] (15th century)
: CONSONANT, AGREEING
— **con·cor·dant·ly** *adverb*

con·cor·dat \kən-'kȯr-ˌdat\ *noun* [French, from Medieval Latin *concordatum*, from Latin, neuter of *concordatus*, past participle of *concordare*] (1616)
: COMPACT, COVENANT; *specifically* : an agreement between a pope and a sovereign or government for the regulation of ecclesiastical matters

con·cours d'e·le·gance \(ˌ)kōⁿ-ˌkŭr-dā-lā-'gäⁿs\ *noun* [French *concours d'élégance*, literally, competition of elegance] (1950)
: a show or contest of vehicles and accessories in which the entries are judged chiefly on excellence of appearance and turnout

con·course \'kän-ˌkȯrs, 'kän-, -ˌkȯrs\ *noun* [Middle English, from Middle French & Latin; Middle French *concours*, from Latin *concursus*, from *concurrere* to run together — more at CONCUR] (14th century)
1 : an act or process of coming together and merging
2 : a meeting produced by voluntary or spontaneous coming together
3 a : an open space where roads or paths meet **b** : an open space or hall (as in a railroad terminal) where crowds gather

con·cres·cence \kən-'kre-sᵊn(t)s, kän-\ *noun* [Latin *concrescentia*, from *concrescent-, concrescens*, present participle of *concrescere* to grow together, from *com-* + *crescere* to grow — more at CRESCENT] (1614)
1 : increase by the addition of particles
2 : a growing together : COALESCENCE; *especially* : convergence and fusion of the lateral lips of the blastopore to form the primordium of an embryo

☆ SYNONYMS
Concise, terse, succinct, laconic, summary, pithy, compendious mean very brief in statement or expression. CONCISE suggests the removal of all that is superfluous or elaborative ⟨a *concise* description⟩. TERSE implies pointed conciseness ⟨a *terse* reply⟩. SUCCINCT implies the greatest possible compression ⟨a *succinct* letter of resignation⟩. LACONIC implies brevity to the point of seeming rude, indifferent, or mysterious ⟨an aloof and *laconic* stranger⟩. SUMMARY suggests the statement of main points with no elaboration or explanation ⟨a *summary* listing of the year's main events⟩. PITHY adds to SUCCINCT or TERSE the implication of richness of meaning or substance ⟨a comedy sharpened by *pithy* one-liners⟩. COMPENDIOUS applies to what is at once full in scope and brief and concise in treatment ⟨a *compendious* dictionary⟩.

Conclusive, decisive, determinative, definitive mean bringing to an end. CONCLUSIVE applies to reasoning or logical proof that puts an end to debate or questioning ⟨*conclusive* evidence⟩. DECISIVE may apply to something that ends a controversy, a contest, or any uncertainty ⟨a *decisive* battle⟩. DETERMINATIVE adds an implication of giving a fixed character or direction ⟨the *determinative* factor in the court's decision⟩. DEFINITIVE applies to what is put forth as final and permanent ⟨the *definitive* biography⟩.

— **con·cres·cent** \-s°nt\ *adjective*

¹**con·crete** \(ˌ)kän-ˈkrēt, ˈkän-ˌ, kən-ˈ\ *adjective* [Middle English, from Latin *concretus*, from past participle of *concrescere*] (14th century)
1 : naming a real thing or class of things ⟨the word *poem* is *concrete*, *poetry* is abstract⟩
2 : formed by coalition of particles into one solid mass
3 a : characterized by or belonging to immediate experience of actual things or events **b :** SPECIFIC, PARTICULAR **c :** REAL, TANGIBLE
4 : relating to or made of concrete
— **con·crete·ly** *adverb*
— **con·crete·ness** *noun*

²**con·crete** \ˈkän-ˌkrēt, kän-ˈ\ *verb* **con·cret·ed; con·cret·ing** (1590)
transitive verb
1 a : to form into a solid mass **:** SOLIDIFY **b :** COMBINE, BLEND
2 : to make actual or real **:** cause to take on the qualities of reality
3 : to cover with, form of, or set in concrete
intransitive verb
: to become concreted

³**con·crete** \ˈkän-ˌkrēt, (ˌ)kän-ˈ\ *noun* (1656)
1 : a mass formed by concretion or coalescence of separate particles of matter in one body
2 : a hard strong building material made by mixing a cementing material (as portland cement) and a mineral aggregate (as sand and gravel) with sufficient water to cause the cement to set and bind the entire mass
3 : a waxy essence of flowers prepared by extraction and evaporation and used in perfumery

concrete music *noun* (1953)
: MUSIQUE CONCRÈTE

concrete poetry *noun* (1958)
: poetry in which the poet's intent is conveyed by the graphic patterns of letters, words, or symbols rather than by the conventional arrangement of words

con·cre·tion \kän-ˈkrē-shən, kən-\ *noun* (1541)
1 : something concreted: as **a :** a hard usually inorganic mass (as a bezoar or tophus) formed in a living body **b :** a mass of mineral matter found generally in rock of a composition different from its own and produced by deposition from aqueous solution in the rock
2 : the act or process of concreting **:** the state of being concreted ⟨*concretion* of ideas in an hypothesis⟩
— **con·cre·tion·ary** \-shə-ˌner-ē\ *adjective*

con·cret·ism \kän-ˈkrē-ˌti-zəm, ˈkän-ˌ\ *noun* (1865)
: representation of abstract things as concrete; *especially* **:** the theory or practice of concrete poetry
— **con·cret·ist** \-ˈkrē-tist, -ˌkrē-\ *noun*

con·cret·ize \-ˌtīz\ *verb* **-ized; -iz·ing** (1884)
transitive verb
: to make concrete, specific, or definite ⟨tried to *concretize* his ideas⟩
intransitive verb
: to become concrete
— **con·cret·i·za·tion** \(ˌ)kän-ˌkrē-tə-ˈzā-shən\ *noun*

con·cu·bi·nage \kän-ˈkyü-bə-nij, kən-\ *noun* (14th century)
1 : cohabitation of persons not legally married
2 : the state of being a concubine

con·cu·bine \ˈkän-kyu̇-ˌbīn, ˈkän-\ *noun* [Middle English, from Middle French, from Latin *concubina*, from *com-* + *cubare* to lie] (14th century)
: a woman with whom a man cohabits without being married: as **a :** one having a recognized social status in a household below that of a wife **b :** MISTRESS 4a

con·cu·pis·cence \kän-ˈkyü-pə-sən(t)s,

kən-\ *noun* [Middle English, from Middle French, from Late Latin *concupiscentia*, from Latin *concupiscent-, concupiscens*, present participle of *concupiscere* to desire ardently, from *com-* + *cupere* to desire] (14th century)
: strong desire; *especially* **:** sexual desire
— **con·cu·pis·cent** \-sənt\ *adjective*

con·cu·pis·ci·ble \-ˈkyü-pə-sə-bəl\ *adjective* [Middle English, from Middle French or Late Latin; Middle French, from Late Latin *concupiscibilis*, from Latin *concupiscere*] (14th century)
: LUSTFUL, DESIROUS

con·cur \kən-ˈkər, kän-\ *intransitive verb* **con·curred; con·cur·ring** [Middle English *concurren*, from Latin *concurrere*, from *com-* + *currere* to run — more at CAR] (15th century)
1 : to act together to a common end or single effect
2 a : APPROVE ⟨*concur* in a statement⟩ **b :** to express agreement ⟨*concur* with an opinion⟩
3 *obsolete* **:** to come together **:** MEET
4 : to happen together **:** COINCIDE
synonym see AGREE

con·cur·rence \-ˈkər-ən(t)s, -ˈkə-rən(t)s\ *noun* (15th century)
1 a : the simultaneous occurrence of events or circumstances **b :** the meeting of concurrent lines in a point
2 a : agreement or union in action **:** COOPERATION **b** (1) **:** agreement in opinion or design (2) **:** CONSENT
3 : a coincidence of equal powers in law

con·cur·ren·cy \-ən(t)-sē, -rən(t)-sē\ *noun* (1597)
: CONCURRENCE

con·cur·rent \-ˈkər-ənt, -ˈkə-rənt\ *adjective* [Middle English, from Middle French & Latin; Middle French, from Latin *concurrent-, concurrens*, present participle of *concurrere*] (14th century)
1 : operating or occurring at the same time
2 a : running parallel **b :** CONVERGENT; *specifically* **:** meeting or intersecting in a point
3 : acting in conjunction
4 : exercised over the same matter or area by two different authorities ⟨*concurrent* jurisdiction⟩
— **concurrent** *noun*
— **con·cur·rent·ly** *adverb*

concurrent resolution *noun* (1802)
: a resolution passed by both houses of a legislative body that lacks the force of law

con·cuss \kən-ˈkəs\ *transitive verb* [Latin *concussus*, past participle] (1597)
: to affect with or as if with concussion

con·cus·sion \kən-ˈkə-shən\ *noun* [Middle English *concussioun*, from Middle French or Latin; Middle French *concussion*, from Latin *concussion-, concussio*, from *concutere* to shake violently, from *com-* + *quatere* to shake] (14th century)
1 a : a stunning, damaging, or shattering effect from a hard blow; *especially* **:** a jarring injury of the brain resulting in disturbance of cerebral function **b :** a hard blow or collision
2 : AGITATION, SHAKING
— **con·cus·sive** \-ˈkə-siv\ *adjective*

con·demn \kən-ˈdem\ *transitive verb* [Middle English, from Middle French *condemner*, from Latin *condemnare*, from *com-* + *damnare* to condemn — more at DAMN] (14th century)
1 : to declare to be reprehensible, wrong, or evil usually after weighing evidence and without reservation
2 a : to pronounce guilty **:** CONVICT **b :** SENTENCE, DOOM
3 : to adjudge unfit for use or consumption
4 : to declare convertible to public use under the right of eminent domain
synonym see CRITICIZE
— **con·demn·able** \-ˈdem-nə-bəl, -ˈde-mə-\ *adjective*

— **con·dem·na·to·ry** \-ˈdem-nə-ˌtōr-ē, -ˈde-mə-, -ˌtȯr-\ *adjective*
— **con·demn·er** \-ˈde-mər\ *or* **con·dem·nor** \kən-ˈde-mər; kən-ˌdem-ˈnȯr, ˌkän-\ *noun*

con·dem·na·tion \ˌkän-ˌdem-ˈnā-shən, -dəm-\ *noun* (14th century)
1 : CENSURE, BLAME
2 : the act of judicially condemning
3 : the state of being condemned
4 : a reason for condemning

con·den·sate \ˈkän-dən-ˌsāt, -ˌden-; kən-ˈden-\ *noun* (1889)
: a product of condensation; *especially* **:** a liquid obtained by condensation of a gas or vapor ⟨steam *condensate*⟩

con·den·sa·tion \ˌkän-ˌden-ˈsā-shən, -dən-\ *noun* (1603)
1 : the act or process of condensing: as **a :** a chemical reaction involving union between molecules often with elimination of a simple molecule (as water) to form a new more complex compound of often greater molecular weight **b :** the conversion of a substance (as water) from the vapor state to a denser liquid or solid state usually initiated by a reduction in temperature of the vapor **c :** compression of a written or spoken work into more concise form
2 : the quality or state of being condensed
3 : a product of condensing
— **con·den·sa·tion·al** \-shnəl, -shə-nᵊl\ *adjective*

con·dense \kən-ˈden(t)s\ *verb* **con·densed; con·dens·ing** [Middle English, from Middle French *condenser*, from Latin *condensare*, from *com-* + *densare* to make dense, from *densus* dense] (15th century)
transitive verb
: to make denser or more compact; *especially* **:** to subject to condensation
intransitive verb
: to undergo condensation
synonym see CONTRACT
— **con·dens·able** *also* **con·dens·ible** \-ˈden(t)-sə-bəl\ *adjective*

condensed *adjective* (15th century)
: reduced to a more compact or dense form; *also* **:** having a face narrower than that of a standard typeface

condensed milk *noun* (1863)
: evaporated milk with sugar added

con·dens·er \kən-ˈden(t)-sər\ *noun* (1686)
1 : one that condenses: as **a :** a lens or mirror used to concentrate light on an object **b :** an apparatus in which gas or vapor is condensed
2 : CAPACITOR

con·de·scend \ˌkän-di-ˈsend\ *intransitive verb* [Middle English, from Middle French *condescendre*, from Late Latin *condescendere*, from Latin *com-* + *descendere* to descend] (14th century)
1 a : to descend to a less formal or dignified level **:** UNBEND **b :** to waive the privileges of rank
2 : to assume an air of superiority

con·de·scen·dence \-ˈsen-dən(t)s\ *noun* (1638)
: CONDESCENSION

condescending *adjective* (1707)
: showing or characterized by condescension **:** PATRONIZING
— **con·de·scend·ing·ly** \-ˈsen-diŋ-lē\ *adverb*

con·de·scen·sion \ˌkän-di-ˈsen(t)-shən\ *noun* [Late Latin *condescension-, condescensio*, from *condescendere*] (1647)
1 : voluntary descent from one's rank or dignity in relations with an inferior

2 : patronizing attitude or behavior

con·dign \kən-'dīn, 'kän-,\ *adjective* [Middle English *condigne,* from Middle French, from Latin *condignus* very worthy, from *com-* + *dignus* worthy — more at DECENT] (15th century)
: DESERVED, APPROPRIATE ⟨*condign* punishment⟩
— **con·dign·ly** *adverb*

con·di·ment \'kän-də-mənt\ *noun* [Middle English, from Middle French, from Latin *condimentum,* from *condire* to season] (15th century)
: something used to enhance the flavor of food; *especially* **:** a pungent seasoning
— **con·di·men·tal** \,kän-də-'men-t°l\ *adjective*

¹con·di·tion \kən-'di-shən\ *noun* [Middle English *condicion,* from Middle French, from Latin *condicion-, condicio* terms of agreement, condition, from *condicere* to agree, from *com-* + *dicere* to say, determine — more at DICTION] (14th century)
1 a : a premise upon which the fulfillment of an agreement depends **:** STIPULATION **b** *obsolete* **:** COVENANT **c :** a provision making the effect of a legal instrument contingent upon an uncertain event; *also* **:** the event itself
2 : something essential to the appearance or occurrence of something else **:** PREREQUISITE: as **a :** an environmental requirement ⟨available oxygen is an essential *condition* for animal life⟩ **b :** the subordinate clause of a conditional sentence
3 a : a restricting or modifying factor **:** QUALIFICATION **b :** an unsatisfactory academic grade that may be raised by doing additional work
4 a : a state of being **b :** social status **:** RANK **c :** a usually defective state of health ⟨a serious heart *condition*⟩ **d :** a state of physical fitness or readiness for use ⟨the car was in good *condition*⟩ ⟨exercising to get into *condition*⟩ **e** *plural* **:** attendant circumstances
5 a *obsolete* **:** temper of mind **b** *obsolete* **:** TRAIT **c** *plural, archaic* **:** MANNERS, WAYS

²condition *verb* **con·di·tioned; con·di·tion·ing** \-'di-sh(ə-)niŋ\ (15th century)
intransitive verb
archaic **:** to make stipulations
transitive verb
1 : to agree by stipulating
2 : to make conditional
3 a : to put into a proper state for work or use **b :** AIR-CONDITION
4 : to give a grade of condition to
5 a : to adapt, modify, or mold so as to conform to an environing culture **b :** to modify so that an act or response previously associated with one stimulus becomes associated with another
— **con·di·tion·able** \-sh(ə-)nə-bəl\ *adjective*
— **con·di·tion·er** \-sh(ə-)nər\ *noun*

¹con·di·tion·al \kən-'dish-nəl, -'di-shə-n°l\ *adjective* (14th century)
1 : subject to, implying, or dependent upon a condition ⟨a *conditional* promise⟩
2 : expressing, containing, or implying a supposition ⟨the *conditional* clause *if he speaks*⟩
3 a : true only for certain values of the variables or symbols involved ⟨*conditional* equations⟩ **b :** stating the case when one or more random variables are fixed or one or more events are known ⟨*conditional* frequency distribution⟩
4 a : CONDITIONED 2 ⟨*conditional* reflex⟩ ⟨*conditional* response⟩ **b :** established by conditioning as the stimulus eliciting a conditional response
— **con·di·tion·al·i·ty** \-,di-shə-'na-lə-tē\ *noun*
— **con·di·tion·al·ly** \-'dish-nə-lē, -'di-shə-n°l-ē\ *adverb*

²conditional *noun* (1828)
1 : a conditional word, clause, verb form, or morpheme

2 : IMPLICATION 2b
conditional probability *noun* (1961)
: the probability that a given event will occur if it is certain that another event has taken place or will take place
conditioned *adjective* (1537)
1 : brought or put into a specified state
2 : determined or established by conditioning
con·do \'kän-(,)dō\ *noun* (1964)
: CONDOMINIUM 3
con·dole \kən-'dōl\ *verb* **con·doled; con·dol·ing** [Late Latin *condolēre,* from Latin *com-* + *dolēre* to feel pain] (1590)
intransitive verb
1 *obsolete* **:** GRIEVE
2 : to express sympathetic sorrow
transitive verb
archaic **:** LAMENT, GRIEVE
— **con·do·la·to·ry** \-'dō-lə-,tōr-ē, -,tȯr-\ *adjective*
con·do·lence \kən-'dō-lən(t)s *also* 'kän-də-\ *noun* (1603)
1 : sympathy with another in sorrow
2 : an expression of sympathy
synonym see PITY
con·dom \'kän-dəm, 'kȯn-, *dialect* -drəm\ *noun* [origin unknown] (circa 1706)
: a sheath commonly of rubber worn over the penis (as to prevent conception or venereal infection during coitus); *also* **:** a similar device inserted into the vagina
con·do·min·i·um \,kän-də-'mi-nē-əm\ *noun, plural* **-ums** [New Latin, from Latin *com-* + *dominium* domain] (circa 1714)
1 a : joint dominion; *especially* **:** joint sovereignty by two or more nations **b :** a government operating under joint rule
2 : a politically dependent territory under condominium
3 a : individual ownership of a unit in a multiunit structure (as an apartment building) or on land owned in common (as a town house complex); *also* **:** a unit so owned **b :** a building containing condominiums ◊
con·do·na·tion \,kän-də-'nā-shən, -dō-\ *noun* (1625)
: implied pardon of an offense by treating the offender as if it had not been committed
con·done \kən-'dōn\ *transitive verb* **con·doned; con·don·ing** [Latin *condonare* to absolve, from *com-* + *donare* to give — more at DONATION] (1857)
: to pardon or overlook voluntarily; *especially* **:** to treat as if trivial, harmless, or of no importance ⟨*condone* corruption in politics⟩
synonym see EXCUSE
— **con·don·able** \-'dō-nə-bəl\ *adjective*
— **con·don·er** *noun*
con·dor \'kän-dər, -,dȯr\ *noun* [Spanish *cóndor,* from Quechua *kuntur*] (1604)
1 a : a very large American vulture (*Vultur gryphus*) of the high Andes having the head and neck bare and the plumage dull black with a downy white neck ruff and white patches on the wings **b :** CALIFORNIA CONDOR
2 *plural* **condors** *or* **con·do·res** \kən-'dȯr-ās, -'dȯr-\ **:** a coin (as the centesimo of Chile) bearing the picture of a condor
con·dot·tie·re \,kän-də-'tyer-ē, ,kän-,dä-tē-'er-\ *noun, plural* **-tie·ri** \-ē\ [Italian, from *condotta* troop of mercenaries, from feminine of *condotto,* past participle of *condurre* to conduct, hire, from Latin *conducere*] (1794)
1 : a leader of a band of mercenaries common in Europe between the 14th and 16th centuries; *also* **:** a member of such a band
2 : a mercenary soldier
con·duce \kən-'düs, -'dyüs\ *intransitive verb* **con·duced; con·duc·ing** [Middle English, to conduct, from Latin *conducere* to conduct, conduce, from *com-* + *ducere* to lead — more at TOW] (1586)
: to lead or tend to a particular and usually desirable result **:** CONTRIBUTE

con·du·cive \-'dü-siv, -'dyü-\ *adjective* (1646)
: tending to promote or assist ⟨an atmosphere *conducive* to education⟩
— **con·du·cive·ness** *noun*
¹con·duct \'kän-(,)dəkt\ *noun* [Middle English, alteration of *conduit,* from Middle French, act of leading, escort, from Medieval Latin *conductus,* from Latin *conducere*] (15th century)
1 *obsolete* **:** ESCORT, GUIDE
2 : the act, manner, or process of carrying on **:** MANAGEMENT
3 : a mode or standard of personal behavior especially as based on moral principles
²con·duct \kən-'dəkt *also* 'kän-,dəkt\ (15th century)
transitive verb
1 : to bring by or as if by leading **:** GUIDE ⟨*conduct* tourists through a museum⟩
2 a : to lead from a position of command ⟨*conduct* a siege⟩ ⟨*conduct* a class⟩ **b :** to direct or take part in the operation or management of ⟨*conduct* an experiment⟩ ⟨*conduct* a business⟩ ⟨*conduct* an investigation⟩ **c :** to direct the performance of ⟨*conduct* an orchestra⟩ ⟨*conduct* an opera⟩
3 a : to convey in a channel **b :** to act as a medium for conveying or transmitting
4 : to cause (oneself) to act or behave in a particular and especially in a controlled manner
intransitive verb
1 *of a road or passage* **:** to show the way **:** LEAD
2 a : to act as leader or director **b :** to have the quality of transmitting light, heat, sound, or electricity ☆
— **con·duct·ibil·i·ty** \kən-,dək-tə-'bi-lə-tē\ *noun*
— **con·duct·ible** \-'dək-tə-bəl\ *adjective*
con·duc·tance \kən-'dək-tən(t)s\ *noun* (1885)
1 : conducting power
2 : the readiness with which a conductor transmits an electric current expressed as the reciprocal of electrical resistance
con·duc·tion \kən-'dək-shən\ *noun* (1534)
1 : the act of conducting or conveying
2 a : transmission through or by means of a conductor; *also* **:** the transfer of heat through matter by communication of kinetic energy from particle to particle with no net displacement of the particles — compare CONVECTION, RADIATION **b :** CONDUCTIVITY
3 : the transmission of excitation through living tissue and especially nervous tissue

◊ **WORD HISTORY**
condominium The word *condominium* was coined by European jurists in the 17th century and used in Latin treatises on international law to refer to dual sovereignty exercised by two countries over the same territory; in this sense it was borrowed into English by the early 18th century. Probably the best-known such condominium historically was the joint British and Egyptian rule of the Sudan in Africa, which began in 1899 and ended in 1956 with Sudanese independence. *Condominium* was probably introduced into U.S. real estate terminology in 1961, when the federal government first insured mortgage loans for individually owned units in apartment buildings. Three years earlier condominium mortgages had received U.S. government sanction in Puerto Rico, where the concept of joint ownership of land combined with individual ownership of living space had most likely spread from South America. In the 1960s and 1970s, *condominium* became a common word across the U.S. as state after state passed enabling legislation setting up guidelines for this type of ownership.

conduction band *noun* (1953)
: the range of permissible energy values that allow an electron of an atom to dissociate from the atom and become a free charge carrier — compare VALENCE BAND

con·duc·tive \kən-'dək-tiv\ *adjective* (1528)
: having conductivity : relating to conduction (as of electricity)

con·duc·tiv·i·ty \ˌkän-ˌdək-'ti-və-tē, kən-\ *noun, plural* **-ties** (1837)
: the quality or power of conducting or transmitting: as **a** : the reciprocal of electrical resistivity **b** : the quality of living matter responsible for the transmission of and progressive reaction to stimuli

con·duc·to·met·ric *also* **con·duc·ti·met·ric** \kən-ˌdək-tə-'me-trik\ *adjective* (circa 1926)
1 : of or relating to the measurement of conductivity
2 : being or relating to titration based on determination of changes in the electrical conductivity of the solution

con·duc·tor \kən-'dək-tər\ *noun* (15th century)
: one that conducts: as **a** : GUIDE **b** : a collector of fares in a public conveyance **c** : the leader of a musical ensemble **d** (1) : a material or object that permits an electric current to flow easily — compare INSULATOR, SEMICONDUCTOR (2) : a material capable of transmitting another form of energy (as heat or sound)
— **con·duc·to·ri·al** \ˌkän-ˌdək-'tōr-ē-əl, kən-, -'tòr-\ *adjective*

con·duc·tress \kən-'dək-trəs\ *noun* (1624)
: a woman who is a conductor

con·duit \'kän-ˌdü-ət, -ˌdyü- *also* -dwət, -dət\ *noun* [Middle English — more at CONDUCT] (14th century)
1 : a natural or artificial channel through which something (as a fluid) is conveyed
2 *archaic* : FOUNTAIN
3 : a pipe, tube, or tile for protecting electric wires or cables
4 : a means of transmitting or distributing ⟨a *conduit* for illicit payments⟩ ⟨a *conduit* of information⟩

con·du·pli·cate \(ˌ)kän-'dü-pli-kət, -'dyü-\ *adjective* [Latin *conduplicatus*, past participle of *conduplicare* to double, from *com-* + *duplic-*, *duplex* double — more at DUPLEX] (1777)
: folded lengthwise ⟨*conduplicate* petals in the bud⟩

con·dy·lar \'kän-də-lər\ *adjective* (1876)
: of or relating to a condyle

con·dyle \'kän-ˌdīl *also* -dᵊl\ *noun* [French & Latin; French, from Latin *condylus* knuckle, from Greek *kondylos*] (1634)
: an articular prominence of a bone; *especially* : one resembling a pair of knuckles
— **con·dy·loid** \-də-ˌlȯid\ *adjective*

con·dy·lo·ma \ˌkän-də-'lō-mə\ *noun, plural* **-ma·ta** \-mə-tə\ *also* **-mas** [New Latin, from Greek *kondylōma*, from *kondylos*] (circa 1526)
: a warty growth on the skin or adjoining mucous membrane usually near the anus and genital organs
— **con·dy·lo·ma·tous** \-mə-təs\ *adjective*

¹cone \'kōn\ *noun* [Middle French or Latin; Middle French, from Latin *conus*, from Greek *kōnos*] (1545)
1 a : a solid generated by rotating a right triangle about one of its legs — called also *right circular cone* **b** : a solid bounded by a circular or other closed plane base and the surface formed by line segments joining every point of the boundary of the base to a common vertex — see VOLUME table **c** : a surface traced by a moving straight line passing through a fixed vertex
2 a : a mass of ovule-bearing or pollen-bearing scales or bracts in trees of the pine family or in cycads that are arranged usually

on a somewhat elongated axis **b** : any of several flower or fruit clusters suggesting a cone
3 : something that resembles a cone in shape: as **a** : any of the conical photosensitive receptor cells of the vertebrate retina that function in color vision — compare ROD 3 **b** : any of a family (Conidae) of tropical marine gastropod mollusks that inject their prey with a potent toxin **c** : the apex of a volcano **d** : a crisp usually cone-shaped wafer for holding ice cream

cone 2a: *1* Sitka spruce, *2* cryptomeria, *3* big tree, *4* white spruce, *5* redwood, *6* lodgepole pine, *7* Douglas fir, *8* bald cypress, *9* jack pine

²cone *transitive verb* **coned; con·ing** (circa 1859)
1 : to make cone-shaped
2 : to bevel like the slanting surface of a cone ⟨*cone* a tire⟩

cone·flow·er \'kōn-ˌflau̇(-ə)r\ *noun* (circa 1818)
: any of several composite plants having cone-shaped flower disks; *especially* : RUDBECKIA

cone·nose \'kōn-ˌnōz\ *noun* (circa 1891)
: any of various large bloodsucking bugs and especially some assassin bugs (genus *Triatoma*) including some capable of inflicting painful bites — called also *kissing bug*

con es·pres·sio·ne \ˌkän-ˌes-(ˌ)pre-sē-'ō-nē, ˌkōn-, -'ō-(ˌ)nā\ *adverb* [Italian, literally, with expression] (circa 1891)
: with feeling — used as a direction in music

Con·es·to·ga wagon \ˌkä-nə-'stō-gə-\ *noun* [*Conestoga*, Pa.] (1717)
: a broad-wheeled covered wagon drawn usually by six horses and used especially for transporting freight across the prairies — called also *Conestoga*

co·ney \'kō-nē, *1 likely* 'kə-nē\ *noun, plural* **co·neys** [Middle English *conies*, plural, from Old French *conis*, plural of *conil*, from Latin *cuniculus*] (12th century)
1 a : rabbit fur **b** (1) : RABBIT; *especially* : the European rabbit (*Oryctolagus cuniculus*) (2) : PIKA **c** : HYRAX
2 *archaic* : DUPE
3 : any of several fishes; *especially* : a dusky black-spotted reddish-finned grouper (*Epinephelus fulvus*) of the tropical Atlantic

con·fab \kən-'fab, 'kän-ˌ\ *intransitive verb* **con·fabbed; con·fab·bing** (1741)
: CONFABULATE
— **con·fab** \'kän-ˌfab, kən-'\ *noun*

con·fab·u·late \kən-'fa-byə-ˌlāt\ *intransitive verb* **-lat·ed; -lat·ing** [Latin *confabulatus*, past participle of *confabulari*, from *com-* + *fabulari* to talk, from *fabula* story — more at FABLE] (circa 1604)
1 : CHAT
2 : to hold a discussion : CONFER
3 : to fill in gaps in memory by fabrication
— **con·fab·u·la·tion** \kən-ˌfa-byə-'lā-shən\ *noun*
— **con·fab·u·la·tor** \kən-'fa-byə-ˌlā-tər\ *noun*
— **con·fab·u·la·to·ry** \-lə-ˌtōr-ē, -ˌtȯr-\ *adjective*

con·fect \kən-'fekt\ *transitive verb* [Middle English, from Latin *confectus*, past participle of *conficere* to prepare — more at COMFIT] (14th century)
1 : to put together from varied material

2 a : PREPARE **b** : PRESERVE
— **con·fect** \'kän-\ *noun*

con·fec·tion \kən-'fek-shən\ *noun* (15th century)
1 : the act or process of confecting
2 : something confected: as **a** : a fancy dish or sweetmeat; *also* : a sweet food **b** : a medicinal preparation usually made with sugar, syrup, or honey **c** : a piece of fine craftsmanship

con·fec·tion·ary \-shə-ˌner-ē\ *noun, plural* **-ar·ies** (1605)
1 *archaic* : CONFECTIONER
2 : CONFECTIONERY 3
3 : SWEETS
— **confectionary** *adjective*

con·fec·tion·er \-sh(ə-)nər\ *noun* (1591)
: a manufacturer of or dealer in confections

confectioners' sugar *noun* (circa 1889)
: a refined finely powdered sugar

con·fec·tion·ery \-shə-ˌner-ē\ *noun, plural* **-er·ies** (1769)
1 : sweet foods (as candy or pastry)
2 : the confectioner's art or business
3 : a confectioner's shop

con·fed·er·a·cy \kən-'fe-d(ə-)rə-sē\ *noun, plural* **-cies** (14th century)
1 : a league or compact for mutual support or common action : ALLIANCE
2 : a combination of persons for unlawful purposes : CONSPIRACY
3 : the body formed by persons, states, or nations united by a league; *specifically, capitalized* : the 11 southern states seceding from the U.S. in 1860 and 1861

con·fed·er·al \-d(ə-)rəl\ *adjective* (1782)
: of or relating to a confederation

¹con·fed·er·ate \kən-'fe-d(ə-)rət\ *adjective* [Middle English *confederat*, from Late Latin *confoederatus*, past participle of *confoederare* to unite by a league, from Latin *com-* + *foeder-*, *foedus* compact — more at FEDERAL] (14th century)
1 : united in a league : ALLIED
2 *capitalized* : of or relating to the Confederate States of America

²confederate *noun* (15th century)
1 : ALLY, ACCOMPLICE
2 *capitalized* : an adherent of the Confederate States of America or their cause

³con·fed·er·ate \-'fe-də-ˌrāt\ *verb* **-at·ed; -at·ing** (1531)
transitive verb
: to unite in a confederacy
intransitive verb
: to band together
— **con·fed·er·a·tive** \-'fe-d(ə-)rə-tiv, -də-ˌrā-\ *adjective*

Confederate Memorial Day *noun* (1899)
: any of several days appointed for the commemoration of servicemen of the Confederacy

\ə\ abut \ᵊ\ kitten \ər\ further \a\ ash \ā\ ace
\ä\ mop, mar \au̇\ out \ch\ chin \e\ bet \ē\ easy
\g\ go \i\ hit \ī\ ice \j\ job \ŋ\ sing \ō\ go
\ȯ\ law \ȯi\ boy \th\ thin \th\ the \ü\ loot \u̇\ foot
\y\ yet \zh\ vision *see also* Guide to Pronunciation

con·fed·er·a·tion \kən-ˌfe-də-ˈrā-shən\ *noun* (15th century)
1 : an act of confederating **:** a state of being confederated **:** ALLIANCE
2 : LEAGUE

con·fer \kən-ˈfər\ *verb* **con·ferred; con·fer·ring** [Latin *conferre* to bring together, from *com-* + *ferre* to carry — more at BEAR] (1570)
transitive verb
1 : to bestow from or as if from a position of superiority ⟨*conferred* an honorary degree on her⟩ ⟨knowing how to read was a gift *conferred* with manhood —Murray Kempton⟩
2 : to give (as a property or characteristic) to someone or something ⟨a reputation for power will *confer* power —John Spanier⟩
intransitive verb
: to compare views or take counsel **:** CONSULT
synonym see GIVE
— **con·fer·ment** \-ˈfər-mənt\ *noun*
— **con·fer·ra·ble** \-ˈfər-ə-bəl\ *adjective*
— **con·fer·ral** \-ˈfər-əl\ *noun*
— **con·fer·rer** \-ˈfər-ər\ *noun*

con·fer·ee \ˌkän-fə-ˈrē\ *noun* (1771)
: one taking part in a conference

con·fer·ence \ˈkän-f(ə-)rən(t)s, -fərn(t)s, *for 2 usually* kən-ˈfər-ən(t)s\ *noun* (1527)
1 a : a meeting of two or more persons for discussing matters of common concern **b :** a usually formal interchange of views **:** CONSULTATION **c :** a meeting of members of the two branches of a legislature to adjust differences **d :** CAUCUS
2 *also* **con·fer·rence** \kən-ˈfər-ən(t)s\ **:** BESTOWAL, CONFERMENT
3 a : a representative assembly or administrative organization of a religious denomination **b :** a territorial division of a religious denomination
4 : an association of athletic teams
— **con·fer·en·tial** \ˌkän-fə-ˈren(t)-shəl\ *adjective*

conference call *noun* (1941)
: a telephone call by which a caller can speak with several people at the same time

con·fer·enc·ing \ˈkän-f(ə-)rən(t)-siŋ, -fərn(t)-\ *noun* (1865)
: the holding of conferences especially by means of an electronic communications system ⟨computer *conferencing*⟩

con·fess \kən-ˈfes\ *verb* [Middle English, from Middle French *confesser*, from Old French, from *confes* having confessed, from Latin *confessus*, past participle of *confitēri* to confess, from *com-* + *fatēri* to confess; akin to Latin *fari* to speak — more at BAN] (14th century)
transitive verb
1 : to tell or make known (as something wrong or damaging to oneself) **:** ADMIT
2 a : to acknowledge (sin) to God or to a priest **b :** to receive the confession of (a penitent)
3 : to declare faith in or adherence to **:** PROFESS
4 : to give evidence of
intransitive verb
1 a : to disclose one's faults; *specifically* **:** to unburden one's sins or the state of one's conscience to God or to a priest **b :** to hear a confession
2 : ADMIT, OWN
synonym see ACKNOWLEDGE
— **con·fess·able** \-ˈfe-sə-bəl\ *adjective*

con·fess·ed·ly \-ˈfe-səd-lē, -ˈfest-lē\ *adverb* (1640)
: by confession

con·fes·sion \kən-ˈfe-shən\ *noun* (14th century)
1 : an act of confessing; *especially* **:** a disclosure of one's sins in the sacrament of reconciliation
2 : a statement of what is confessed: as **a :** a written acknowledgment of guilt by a party accused of an offense **b :** a formal statement of religious beliefs **:** CREED
3 : an organized religious body having a common creed

¹con·fes·sion·al \-ˈfesh-nəl, -ˈfe-shə-nᵊl\ *noun* (1727)
1 : a place where a priest hears confessions
2 : the practice of confessing to a priest

²confessional *adjective* (1817)
1 : of, relating to, or being a confession especially of faith
2 : of, relating to, or being intimately autobiographical ⟨*confessional* fiction⟩
— **con·fes·sion·al·ism** \-nə-ˌli-zəm\ *noun*
— **con·fes·sion·al·ist** \-list\ *noun*
— **con·fes·sion·al·ly** \-nə-lē, -nᵊl-ē\ *adverb*

con·fes·sor \kən-ˈfe-sər, *1 & 3 also* ˈkän-ˌfe-sər, *3 also* ˈkän-fə-ˌsȯr\ *noun* (12th century)
1 : one who gives heroic evidence of faith but does not suffer martyrdom
2 : one that confesses
3 a : a priest who hears confessions **b :** a priest who is one's regular spiritual guide

con·fet·ti \kən-ˈfe-tē\ *noun* [Italian, plural of *confetto* sweetmeat, from Medieval Latin *confectum*, from Latin, neuter of *confectus*, past participle of *conficere* to prepare — more at COMFIT] (1815)
: small bits or streamers of brightly colored paper made for throwing (as at weddings)

con·fi·dant \ˈkän-fə-ˌdänt *also* -ˌdant, -dənt\ *noun* [French *confident*, from Italian *confidente*, from *confidente* confident, trustworthy, from Latin *confident-, confidens*] (1646)
: one to whom secrets are entrusted; *especially* **:** INTIMATE

con·fi·dante *same as* CONFIDANT\ *noun* [French *confidente*, feminine of *confident*] (1696)
: CONFIDANT; *especially* **:** one who is a woman

con·fide \kən-ˈfīd\ *verb* **con·fid·ed; con·fid·ing** [Middle English, from Middle French or Latin; Middle French *confider*, from Latin *confidere*, from *com-* + *fidere* to trust — more at BIDE] (15th century)
intransitive verb
1 : to have confidence **:** TRUST
2 : to show confidence by imparting secrets
transitive verb
1 : to tell confidentially
2 : to give to the care or protection of another **:** ENTRUST
synonym see COMMIT
— **con·fid·er** *noun*

¹con·fi·dence \ˈkän-fə-dən(t)s, -ˌden(t)s\ *noun* (14th century)
1 a : a feeling or consciousness of one's powers or of reliance on one's circumstances ⟨had perfect *confidence* in her ability to succeed⟩ ⟨met the risk with brash *confidence*⟩ **b :** faith or belief that one will act in a right, proper, or effective way ⟨have *confidence* in a leader⟩
2 : the quality or state of being certain **:** CERTITUDE ⟨they had every *confidence* of success⟩
3 a : a relation of trust or intimacy ⟨took his friend into his *confidence*⟩ **b :** reliance on another's discretion ⟨their story was told in strictest *confidence*⟩ **c :** support especially in a legislative body ⟨vote of *confidence*⟩
4 : a communication made in confidence **:** SECRET ☆

²confidence *adjective* (1849)
: of, relating to, or adept at swindling by false promises ⟨a *confidence* game⟩ ⟨a *confidence* man⟩

confidence interval *noun* (1934)
: a group of continuous or discrete adjacent values that is used to estimate a statistical parameter (as a mean or variance) and that tends to include the true value of the parameter a predetermined proportion of the time if the process of finding the group of values is repeated a number of times

confidence limits *noun plural* (1939)
: the end points of a confidence interval

con·fi·dent \ˈkän-fə-dənt, -ˌdent\ *adjective* [Latin *confident-, confidens*, from present participle of *confidere*] (1576)
1 : characterized by assurance; *especially* **:** SELF-RELIANT
2 *obsolete* **:** TRUSTFUL, CONFIDING
3 a : full of conviction **:** CERTAIN **b :** COCKSURE
— **con·fi·dent·ly** *adverb*

con·fi·den·tial \ˌkän-fə-ˈden(t)-shəl\ *adjective* (1759)
1 : marked by intimacy or willingness to confide ⟨a *confidential* tone⟩
2 : PRIVATE, SECRET ⟨*confidential* information⟩
3 : entrusted with confidences ⟨*confidential* clerk⟩
4 : containing information whose unauthorized disclosure could be prejudicial to the national interest — compare SECRET, TOP SECRET
— **con·fi·den·ti·al·i·ty** \-ˌden(t)-shē-ˈa-lə-tē\ *noun*
— **con·fi·den·tial·ly** \-ˈden(t)-sh(ə-)lē\ *adverb*

con·fid·ing \kən-ˈfī-diŋ\ *adjective* (1829)
: tending to confide **:** TRUSTFUL
— **con·fid·ing·ly** \-diŋ-lē\ *adverb*
— **con·fid·ing·ness** *noun*

con·fig·u·ra·tion \kən-ˌfi-gyə-ˈrā-shən, ˌkän-, -gə-\ *noun* [Late Latin *configuration-, configuratio* similar formation, from Latin *configurare* to form from or after, from *com-* + *figurare* to form, from *figura* figure] (1646)
1 a : relative arrangement of parts or elements: as (1) **:** SHAPE (2) **:** contour of land ⟨*configuration* of the mountains⟩ (3) **:** functional arrangement ⟨a small business computer system in its simplest *configuration*⟩ **b :** something (as a figure, contour, pattern, or apparatus) that results from a particular arrangement of parts or components **c :** the stable structural makeup of a chemical compound especially with reference to the space relations of the constituent atoms
2 : GESTALT ⟨personality *configuration*⟩
— **con·fig·u·ra·tion·al** \-shnəl, -shə-nᵊl\ *adjective*
— **con·fig·u·ra·tion·al·ly** *adverb*
— **con·fig·u·ra·tive** \-ˈfi-gyə-rə-tiv, -ˈfi-gə-\ *adjective*

con·fig·ure \kən-ˈfi-gyər, *especially British* -ˈfi-gər\ *transitive verb* **-ured; -ur·ing** (1677)
: to set up for operation especially in a particular way ⟨a fighter plane *configured* for the Malaysian air force⟩

¹con·fine \ˈkän-ˌfīn *also* kən-ˈ\ *noun* [Middle English, from Middle French or Latin; Middle French *confines*, plural, from Latin *confine* border, from neuter of *confinis* adjacent, from *com-* + *finis* end] (15th century)
1 *plural* **a :** something (as borders or walls) that encloses ⟨outside the *confines* of the office or hospital —W. A. Nolen⟩; *also* **:** something that restrains ⟨escape from the *confines*

of soot and clutter —E. S. Muskie⟩ **b :** SCOPE 3 ⟨work within the *confines* of a small group —Frank Newman⟩
2 a *archaic* **:** RESTRICTION **b** *obsolete* **:** PRISON
²**con·fine** \kən-'fīn\ *verb* **con·fined; con·fin·ing** (1523)
intransitive verb
archaic **:** BORDER
transitive verb
1 a : to hold within a location **b :** IMPRISON
2 : to keep within limits ⟨will *confine* my remarks to one subject⟩
synonym see LIMIT
— **con·fin·er** *noun*
con·fined \kən-'fīnd\ *adjective* (1772)
: undergoing childbirth
con·fine·ment \kən-'fīn-mənt\ *noun* (1646)
: an act of confining **:** the state of being confined ⟨solitary *confinement*⟩; *especially* **:** LY-ING-IN
con·firm \kən-'fərm\ *transitive verb* [Middle English, from Old French *confirmer*, from Latin *confirmare*, from *com-* + *firmare* to make firm, from *firmus* firm] (13th century)
1 : to give approval to **:** RATIFY
2 : to make firm or firmer **:** STRENGTHEN
3 : to administer the rite of confirmation to
4 : to give new assurance of the validity of **:** remove doubt about by authoritative act or indisputable fact ☆
— **con·firm·abil·i·ty** \-ˌfər-mə-'bi-lə-tē\ *noun*
— **con·firm·able** \-'fər-mə-bəl\ *adjective*
con·fir·mand \ˌkän-fər-'mand\ *noun* [Latin *confirmandus,* gerundive of *confirmare*] (1884)
: a candidate for religious confirmation
con·fir·ma·tion \ˌkän-fər-'mā-shən\ *noun* (14th century)
1 : an act or process of confirming: as **a** (1) **:** a Christian rite conferring the gift of the Holy Spirit and among Protestants full church membership (2) **:** a ceremony especially of Reform Judaism confirming youths in their faith **b :** the ratification of an executive act by a legislative body
2 a : confirming proof **:** CORROBORATION **b :** the process of supporting a statement by evidence
— **con·fir·ma·tion·al** \-shnəl, -shə-n'l\ *adjective*
con·fir·ma·to·ry \kən-'fər-mə-ˌtōr-ē, -ˌtòr-\ *adjective* (1636)
: serving to confirm **:** CORROBORATIVE
con·firmed \kən-'fərmd\ *adjective* (14th century)
1 a : marked by long continuance and likely to persist ⟨a *confirmed* habit⟩ **b :** fixed in habit and unlikely to change ⟨a *confirmed* do-gooder⟩
2 : having received the rite of confirmation
synonym see INVETERATE
— **con·firm·ed·ly** \-'fər-məd-lē\ *adverb*
— **con·firmed·ness** \-'fər-məd-nəs, -'fərm(d)-nəs\ *noun*
con·fis·ca·ble \kən-'fis-kə-bəl\ *adjective* (circa 1736)
: liable to confiscation
con·fis·cat·able \'kän-fə-ˌskā-tə-bəl\ *adjective* (1863)
: CONFISCABLE
¹**con·fis·cate** \'kän-fə-ˌskāt, kən-'fis-kət\ *adjective* [Latin *confiscatus,* past participle of *confiscare* to confiscate, from *com-* + *fiscus* treasury] (circa 1533)
1 : appropriated by the government **:** FORFEIT-ED
2 : deprived of property by confiscation
²**con·fis·cate** \'kän-fə-ˌskāt\ *transitive verb* **-cat·ed; -cat·ing** (1552)
1 : to seize as forfeited to the public treasury
2 : to seize by or as if by authority
— **con·fis·ca·tion** \ˌkän-fə-'skā-shən\ *noun*
— **con·fis·ca·tor** \'kän-fə-ˌskā-tər\ *noun*
— **con·fis·ca·to·ry** \kən-'fis-kə-ˌtōr-ē, -ˌtòr-\ *adjective*

con·fit \kōⁿ-'fē, kòn-, kän-\ *noun* [French, from Old French, preparation, preserves, from past participle of *confire* to prepare — more at COMFIT] (1951)
: meat (as goose, duck, or pork) that has been cooked and preserved in its own fat
con·fi·te·or \kən-'fē-tē-ˌòr, -ər\ *noun* [Middle English, from Latin, literally, I confess, from the opening words — more at CONFESS] (13th century)
: a liturgical form in which sinfulness is acknowledged and intercession for God's mercy requested
con·fi·ture \'kän-fə-ˌchùr, -ˌtyùr, -ˌtùr\ *noun* [French, from Middle French, from *confit*] (1802)
: preserved or candied fruit **:** JAM
con·fla·grant \kən-'flā-grənt\ *adjective* [Latin *conflagrant-, conflagrans,* present participle of *conflagrare* to burn, from *com-* + *flagrare* to burn — more at BLACK] (circa 1656)
: BURNING, BLAZING
con·fla·gra·tion \ˌkän-flə-'grā-shən\ *noun* [Latin *conflagration-, conflagratio,* from *conflagrare*] (circa 1656)
1 : FIRE; *especially* **:** a large disastrous fire
2 : CONFLICT, WAR
con·flate \kən-'flāt\ *transitive verb* **con·flat·ed; con·flat·ing** [Latin *conflatus,* past participle of *conflare* to blow together, fuse, from *com-* + *flare* to blow — more at BLOW] (1610)
1 a : to bring together **:** FUSE **b :** CONFUSE
2 : to combine (as two readings of a text) into a composite whole
con·fla·tion \-'flā-shən\ *noun* (15th century)
: BLEND, FUSION; *especially* **:** a composite reading or text
¹**con·flict** \'kän-ˌflikt\ *noun* [Middle English, from Latin *conflictus* act of striking together, from *confligere* to strike together, from *com-* + *fligere* to strike — more at PROFLIGATE] (15th century)
1 : FIGHT, BATTLE, WAR
2 a : competitive or opposing action of incompatibles **:** antagonistic state or action (as of divergent ideas, interests, or persons) **b :** mental struggle resulting from incompatible or opposing needs, drives, wishes, or external or internal demands
3 : the opposition of persons or forces that gives rise to the dramatic action in a drama or fiction
synonym see DISCORD
— **con·flict·ful** \'kän-ˌflikt-fəl\ *adjective*
— **con·flic·tu·al** \kän-'flik-chə-wəl, kən-, -chəl, -shwəl\ *adjective*
²**con·flict** \kōⁿ-'flikt, 'kän-ˌ\ *intransitive verb* (15th century)
1 *archaic* **:** to contend in warfare
2 : to show antagonism or irreconcilability
— **con·flic·tion** \kən-'flik-shən, kän-\ *noun*
— **con·flic·tive** \kən-'flik-tiv, 'kän-ˌ\ *adjective*
con·flict·ed \kən-'flik-təd\ *adjective* (1967)
: having or experiencing an emotional conflict ⟨this unhappy and *conflicted* modern woman —John Updike⟩
conflicting *adjective* (1607)
: being in conflict, collision, or opposition **:** IN-COMPATIBLE
— **con·flict·ing·ly** \-'flik-tiŋ-lē, -ˌflik-\ *adverb*
conflict of interest (1951)
: a conflict between the private interests and the official responsibilities of a person in a position of trust
con·flu·ence \'kän-ˌflü-ən(t)s, kən-\ *noun* (15th century)
1 : a coming or flowing together, meeting, or gathering at one point ⟨a happy *confluence* of weather and scenery⟩
2 a : the flowing together of two or more streams **b :** the place of meeting of two streams **c :** the combined stream formed by conjunction

¹**con·flu·ent** \-ənt\ *adjective* [Latin *confluent-, confluens,* present participle of *confluere* to flow together, from *com-* + *fluere* to flow — more at FLUID] (15th century)
1 : flowing or coming together; *also* **:** run together ⟨*confluent* pustules⟩
2 : characterized by confluent lesions ⟨*confluent* smallpox⟩
²**confluent** *noun* (1850)
: a confluent stream; *broadly* **:** TRIBUTARY
con·flux \'kän-ˌfləks\ *noun* [Medieval Latin *confluxus,* from Latin *confluere*] (1606)
: CONFLUENCE
con·fo·cal \(ˌ)kän-'fō-kəl\ *adjective* (1867)
: having the same foci ⟨*confocal* ellipses⟩ ⟨*confocal* lenses⟩
— **con·fo·cal·ly** \-kə-lē\ *adverb*
con·form \kən-'fòrm\ *verb* [Middle English, from Middle French *conformer,* from Latin *conformare,* from *com-* + *formare* to form, from *forma* form] (14th century)
transitive verb
: to give the same shape, outline, or contour to **:** bring into harmony or accord ⟨*conform* furrows to the slope of the land⟩
intransitive verb
1 : to be similar or identical; *also* **:** to be in agreement or harmony — used with *to* or *with*
2 a : to be obedient or compliant — usually used with *to* **b :** to act in accordance with prevailing standards or customs
synonym see ADAPT
— **con·form·er** *noun*
— **con·form·ism** \-'fòr-ˌmi-zəm\ *noun*
— **con·form·ist** \-mist\ *noun or adjective*
con·form·able \kən-'fòr-mə-bəl\ *adjective* (15th century)
1 : corresponding in form or character **:** SIMI-LAR — usually used with *to*
2 : SUBMISSIVE, COMPLIANT
3 : following in unbroken sequence — used of geologic strata formed under uniform conditions
— **con·form·ably** \-blē\ *adverb*
con·for·mal \kən-'fòr-məl, (ˌ)kän-\ *adjective* [Late Latin *conformalis* having the same shape, from Latin *com-* + *formalis* formal, from *forma*] (1893)
1 : leaving the size of the angle between corresponding curves unchanged ⟨*conformal* transformation⟩
2 *of a map* **:** representing small areas in their true shape
con·for·mance \kən-'fòr-mən(t)s\ *noun* (1606)

☆ **SYNONYMS**
Confirm, corroborate, substantiate, verify, authenticate, validate mean to attest to the truth or validity of something. CONFIRM implies the removing of doubts by an authoritative statement or indisputable fact ⟨*confirmed* the reports⟩. CORROBORATE suggests the strengthening of what is already partly established ⟨witnesses *corroborated* his story⟩. SUBSTANTIATE implies the offering of evidence that sustains the contention ⟨the claims have yet to be *substantiated*⟩. VERIFY implies the establishing of correspondence of actual facts or details with those proposed or guessed at ⟨all statements of fact in the article have been *verified*⟩. AUTHENTICATE implies establishing genuineness by adducing legal or official documents or expert opinion ⟨handwriting experts *authenticated* the diaries⟩. VALIDATE implies establishing validity by authoritative affirmation or by factual proof ⟨*validated* the hypothesis by experiments⟩.

\ə\ abut \ᵊ\ kitten \ər\ further \a\ ash \ā\ ace
\ä\ mop, mar \aù\ out \ch\ chin \e\ bet \ē\ easy
\g\ go \i\ hit \ī\ ice \j\ job \ŋ\ sing \ō\ go
\ò\ law \òi\ boy \th\ thin \th\ the \ü\ loot \ù\ foot
\y\ yet \zh\ vision *see also* Guide to Pronunciation

: CONFORMITY

con·for·ma·tion \ˌkän-(ˌ)fȯr-'mā-shən, -fər-\ *noun* (1511)
1 : the act of conforming or producing conformity : ADAPTATION
2 : formation of something by appropriate arrangement of parts or elements : an assembling into a whole ⟨the gradual *conformation* of the embryo⟩
3 a : correspondence especially to a model or plan **b :** STRUCTURE **c :** the shape or proportionate dimensions especially of an animal **d :** any of the spatial arrangements of a molecule that can be obtained by rotation of the atoms about a single bond
— con·for·ma·tion·al \-shnəl, -shə-nᵊl\ *adjective*

con·for·mi·ty \kən-'fȯr-mə-tē\ *noun, plural* **-ties** (15th century)
1 : correspondence in form, manner, or character : AGREEMENT ⟨behaved in *conformity* with her beliefs⟩
2 : an act or instance of conforming
3 : action in accordance with some specified standard or authority ⟨*conformity* to social custom⟩

con·found \kən-'fau̇nd, kän-\ *transitive verb* [Middle English, from Middle French *confondre*, from Latin *confundere* to pour together, confuse, from *com-* + *fundere* to pour — more at FOUND] (14th century)
1 a *archaic* **:** to bring to ruin : DESTROY **b :** BAFFLE, FRUSTRATE ⟨conferences . . . are not for accomplishment but to *confound* knavish tricks —J. K. Galbraith⟩
2 *obsolete* **:** CONSUME, WASTE
3 a : to put to shame : DISCOMFIT ⟨a performance that *confounded* the critics⟩ **b :** REFUTE ⟨sought to *confound* his arguments⟩
4 : DAMN
5 : to throw (a person) into confusion or perplexity
6 a : to fail to discern differences between : mix up **b :** to increase the confusion of
synonym see PUZZLE
— con·found·er \-'fau̇n-dər\ *noun*
— con·found·ing·ly \-diŋ-lē\ *adverb*

con·found·ed \kən-'fau̇n-dəd, (ˌ)kän-', 'kän-,\ *adjective* (14th century)
1 : CONFUSED, PERPLEXED
2 : DAMNED
— con·found·ed·ly *adverb*

con·fra·ter·ni·ty \ˌkän-frə-'tər-nə-tē\ *noun* [Middle English *confraternite*, from Middle French *confraternité*, from Medieval Latin *confraternitat-, confraternitas*, from *confrater* fellow, brother, from Latin *com-* + *frater* brother — more at BROTHER] (15th century)
1 : a society devoted especially to a religious or charitable cause
2 : fraternal union

con·frere *also* **con·frère** \'kän-ˌfrer, kōⁿ-ˌ, kän-', kōⁿ-', kən-\ *noun* [Middle English, from Middle French, translation of Medieval Latin *confrater*] (15th century)
: COLLEAGUE, COMRADE

con·front \kən-'frənt\ *transitive verb* [Middle French *confronter* to border on, confront, from Medieval Latin *confrontare* to bound, from Latin *com-* + *front-, frons* forehead, front] (circa 1568)
1 : to face especially in challenge : OPPOSE
2 a : to cause to meet : bring face-to-face ⟨*confront* a reader with statistics⟩ **b :** to meet face-to-face : ENCOUNTER ⟨*confronted* the possibility of failure⟩
— con·front·al \-'frən-tᵊl\ *noun*
— con·front·er *noun*
con·fron·ta·tion \ˌkän-(ˌ)frən-'tā-shən\ *noun* (1632)
: the act of confronting : the state of being confronted: as **a :** a face-to-face meeting **b :** the clashing of forces or ideas : CONFLICT **c :** COMPARISON ⟨the flashbacks bring into meaningful *confrontation* present and past, near and far —R. J. Clements⟩

— con·fron·ta·tion·al \-shnəl, -shə-nᵊl\ *adjective*
— con·fron·ta·tion·ist \-sh(ə-)nist\ *noun or adjective*

Con·fu·cian \kən-'fyü-shən\ *adjective* (1837)
: of or relating to the Chinese philosopher Confucius or his teachings or followers
— Confucian *noun*
— Con·fu·cian·ism \-shə-ˌni-zəm\ *noun*
— Con·fu·cian·ist \-nist\ *noun or adjective*

con·fuse \kən-'fyüz\ *transitive verb* **con·fused; con·fus·ing** [back-formation from Middle English *confused* perplexed, from Middle French *confus*, from Latin *confusus*, past participle of *confundere*] (14th century)
1 *archaic* **:** to bring to ruin
2 a : to make embarrassed : ABASH **b :** to disturb in mind or purpose : THROW OFF
3 a : to make indistinct : BLUR ⟨stop *confusing* the issue⟩ **b :** to mix indiscriminately : JUMBLE **c :** to fail to differentiate from an often similar or related other ⟨*confuse* money with comfort⟩
— con·fus·ing·ly \-'fyü-ziŋ-lē\ *adverb*

con·fused \-'fyüzd\ *adjective* (14th century)
1 : being perplexed or disconcerted ⟨the *confused* students⟩
2 : INDISTINGUISHABLE ⟨a zigzag, crisscross, *confused* trail —Harry Hervey⟩
3 : being disordered or mixed up ⟨a contradictory and often *confused* story⟩
— con·fused·ly \-'fyü-zəd-lē, -'fyüzd-\ *adverb*
— con·fused·ness \-'fyü-zəd-nəs, -'fyüz(d)-\ *noun*

con·fu·sion \kən-'fyü-zhən\ *noun* (14th century)
1 : an act or instance of confusing
2 a : the quality or state of being confused **b :** a confused mass or mixture ⟨a *confusion* of voices⟩
— con·fu·sion·al \-'fyüzh-nəl, -'fyü-zhə-nᵊl\ *adjective*

con·fu·ta·tion \ˌkän-fyu̇-'tā-shən\ *noun* (15th century)
1 : the act or process of confuting : REFUTATION
2 : something (as an argument or statement) that confutes
— con·fu·ta·tive \kən-'fyü-tə-tiv\ *adjective*

con·fute \kən-'fyüt\ *transitive verb* **con·fut·ed; con·fut·ing** [Latin *confutare* to check, silence] (1529)
1 : to overwhelm in argument : refute conclusively ⟨Elijah . . . *confuted* the prophets of Baal —G. B. Shaw⟩
2 *obsolete* **:** CONFOUND
— con·fut·er *noun*

con·ga \'käŋ-gə\ *noun* [American Spanish, probably from feminine of *congo* Negro, from *Congo*, region in Africa] (1935)
1 : a Cuban dance of African origin involving three steps followed by a kick and performed by a group usually in single file
2 : a tall barrel-shaped or tapering drum of Afro-Cuban origin that is played with the hands

conga line *noun* (1947)
: SNAKE DANCE 2

con·gé \kōⁿ-'zhä, 'kän-ˌzhä\ *noun* [French, from Latin *commeatus* going back and forth, leave, from *commeare* to go back and forth, from *com-* + *meare* to go — more at PERMEATE] (1702)
1 a : a formal permission to depart **b :** DISMISSAL
2 : a ceremonious bow
3 : FAREWELL
4 : an architectural molding of concave profile — see MOLDING illustration

conga 2

con·geal \kən-'jē(ə)l\ *verb* [Middle English *congelen*, from Middle French *congeler*, from Latin *congelare*, from *com-* + *gelare* to freeze — more at COLD] (14th century)
transitive verb
1 : to change from a fluid to a solid state by or as if by cold
2 : to make viscid or curdled : COAGULATE
3 : to make rigid, fixed, or immobile
intransitive verb
: to become congealed : SOLIDIFY
— con·geal·ment \-mənt\ *noun*

con·gee \'kän-(ˌ)jē, -(ˌ)zhē\ *noun* (14th century)
: CONGÉ

con·ge·la·tion \ˌkän-jə-'lā-shən\ *noun* (15th century)
: the process or result of congealing

con·ge·ner \'kän-jə-nər, kən-'jē-\ *noun* [Latin, of the same kind, from *com-* + *gener-, genus* kind — more at KIN] (circa 1736)
1 : a member of the same taxonomic genus as another plant or animal
2 : a person or thing resembling another in nature or action ⟨the New England private schools and their *congeners* west of the Alleghenies —Oliver La Farge⟩
— con·ge·ner·ic \ˌkän-jə-'ner-ik\ *adjective*
— con·ge·ner·ous \kən-'jē-nə-rəs, -'je-nə-, (ˌ)kän-\ *adjective*

con·ge·nial \kən-'jē-nē-əl, -'jēn-yəl\ *adjective* [*com-* + *genius*] (circa 1625)
1 : having the same nature, disposition, or tastes : KINDRED
2 a : existing or associated together harmoniously **b :** PLEASANT; *especially* **:** agreeably suited to one's nature, tastes, or outlook **c :** SOCIABLE, GENIAL
— con·ge·ni·al·i·ty \-ˌjē-nē-'a-lə-tē, -ˌjēn-'ya-\ *noun*
— con·ge·nial·ly \-'jē-nē-ə-lē, -'jēn-yə-\ *adverb*

con·gen·i·tal \kən-'je-nə-tᵊl, kän-\ *adjective* [Latin *congenitus*, from *com-* + *genitus*, past participle of *gignere* to bring forth — more at KIN] (1796)
1 a : existing at or dating from birth ⟨*congenital* deafness⟩ **b :** constituting an essential characteristic : INHERENT ⟨*congenital* fear of snakes⟩ **c :** acquired during development in the uterus and not through heredity ⟨*congenital* syphilis⟩
2 : being such by nature ⟨*congenital* liar⟩
synonym see INNATE
— con·gen·i·tal·ly \-tᵊl-ē\ *adverb*

con·ger eel \'käŋ-gər-\ *noun* [Middle English *congre*, from Old French, from Latin *congr-, conger*, probably from Greek *gongros*] (1602)
: a large strictly marine scaleless eel (*Conger oceanicus*) of the Atlantic; *broadly* **:** any of various related eels (family Congridae)

con·ge·ries \'kän-jə-(ˌ)rēz\ *noun, plural* **congeries** *same*\ [Latin, from *congerere*] (circa 1619)
: AGGREGATION, COLLECTION

con·gest \kən-'jest\ *verb* [Latin *congestus*, past participle of *congerere* to bring together, from *com-* + *gerere* to bear] (1758)
transitive verb
1 : to cause an excessive fullness of the blood vessels of (as an organ)
2 : CLOG ⟨traffic *congested* the highways⟩
3 : to concentrate in a small or narrow space
intransitive verb
: to become congested
— con·ges·tion \-'jes-chən, -'jesh-\ *noun*
— con·ges·tive \-'jes-tiv\ *adjective*

congestive heart failure *noun* (1930)
: heart failure in which the heart is unable to maintain an adequate circulation of blood in the bodily tissues or to pump out the venous blood returned to it by the veins

con·glo·bate \kän-'glō-ˌbāt, kən-\ *transitive verb* **-bat·ed; -bat·ing** [Latin *conglobatus*, past participle of *conglobare*, from *com-* + *globus* globe] (1635)

: to form into a round compact mass
— **con·glo·bate** \-bət, -ˌbāt\ *adjective*
— **con·glo·ba·tion** \ˌkän-(ˌ)glō-'bā-shən\ *noun*

con·globe \kän-'glōb, kən-\ *transitive verb* **con·globed; con·glob·ing** (1535)
: CONGLOBATE

¹**con·glom·er·ate** \kən-'gläm-rət, -'glä-mə-\ *adjective* [Latin *conglomeratus,* past participle of *conglomerare* to roll together, from *com-* + *glomerare* to wind into a ball, from *glomer-, glomus* ball — more at CLAM] (1572)
: made up of parts from various sources or of various kinds

²**con·glom·er·ate** \-'glä-mə-ˌrāt\ *verb* **-at·ed; -at·ing** (1642)
intransitive verb
: to gather into a mass or coherent whole ⟨numbers of dull people *conglomerated* round her —Virginia Woolf⟩
transitive verb
: ACCUMULATE
— **con·glom·er·a·tive** \-'gläm-rə-tiv, -'glä-mə-; -mə-ˌrā-\ *adjective*
— **con·glom·er·a·tor** \-'glä-mə-ˌrā-tər\ *noun*

³**con·glom·er·ate** \-'gläm-rət, -'glä-mə-\ *noun* (1818)
1 : a composite mass or mixture; *especially* : rock composed of rounded fragments varying from small pebbles to large boulders in a cement (as of hardened clay)
2 : a widely diversified corporation
— **con·glom·er·at·ic** \kən-ˌglä-mə-'ra-tik, ˌkän-\ *adjective*

con·glom·er·a·teur \kən-ˌglä-mə-rə-'tər, -'tyür, -'tür\ *noun* [³*conglomerate* + *-eur* (as in *entrepreneur*)] (1969)
: a person who forms or heads a conglomerate
: CONGLOMERATOR

con·glom·er·a·tion \kən-ˌglä-mə-'rā-shən, ˌkän-\ *noun* (1626)
1 : the act of conglomerating : the state of being conglomerated
2 : something conglomerated : a mixed mass or collection

con·glu·ti·nate \kən-'glü-t²n-ˌāt, kän-\ *verb* **-nat·ed; -nat·ing** [Latin *conglutinatus,* past participle of *conglutinare* to glue together, from *com-* + *glutin-, gluten* glue — more at GLUTEN] (1546)
transitive verb
: to unite by or as if by a glutinous substance
intransitive verb
: to become conglutinated ⟨blood platelets *conglutinate* in blood clotting⟩
— **con·glu·ti·na·tion** \kən-ˌglü-t²n-'ā-shən, kän-\ *noun*

Congo red *noun* [*Congo,* territory in Africa] (1885)
: an azo dye $C_{32}H_{22}N_6Na_2O_6S_2$ that is red in alkaline and blue in acid solution and that is used especially as an indicator and as a biological stain

con·gou \'käŋ-(ˌ)gō, -(ˌ)gü\ *noun* [probably from Chinese (Xiamen) *kong-hu* pains taken] (1725)
: a black tea from China

con·grat·u·late \kən-'gra-chə-ˌlāt, -'gra-jə-\ *transitive verb* **-lat·ed; -lat·ing** [Latin *gratulatus,* past participle of *congratulari* to wish joy, from *com-* + *gratulari* to wish joy, from *gratus* pleasing — more at GRACE] (1539)
1 *archaic* : to express sympathetic pleasure at (an event)
2 : to express vicarious pleasure to (a person) on the occasion of success or good fortune; *also* : to feel pleased with ⟨*congratulating* herself for a job well done⟩
3 *obsolete* : SALUTE, GREET
— **con·grat·u·la·tor** \-ˌlā-tər\ *noun*
— **con·grat·u·la·to·ry** \-lə-ˌtōr-ē, -ˌtor-\ *adjective*

con·grat·u·la·tion \kən-ˌgra-chə-'lā-shən, -ˌgra-jə-\ *noun* (15th century)

1 : the act of congratulating
2 : a congratulatory expression — usually used in plural

con·gre·gant \'käŋ-gri-gənt\ *noun* (1886)
: one that congregates; *specifically* : a member of a congregation

¹**con·gre·gate** \-ˌgāt\ *verb* **-gat·ed; -gat·ing** [Middle English, from Latin *congregatus,* past participle of *congregare,* from *com-* + *greg-, grex* flock] (15th century)
transitive verb
: to collect into a group or crowd : ASSEMBLE
intransitive verb
: to come together into a group, crowd, or assembly
synonym see GATHER
— **con·gre·ga·tor** \-ˌgā-tər\ *noun*

²**con·gre·gate** \-gət\ *adjective* (1900)
: providing or being group services or facilities designed especially for elderly persons requiring supportive services ⟨*congregate* housing⟩

con·gre·ga·tion \ˌkäŋ-gri-'gā-shən\ *noun* (14th century)
1 a : an assembly of persons : GATHERING; *especially* : an assembly of persons met for worship and religious instruction **b** : a religious community: as (1) : an organized body of believers in a particular locality (2) : a Roman Catholic religious institute with only simple vows (3) : a group of monasteries forming an independent subdivision of an order
2 : the act or an instance of congregating or bringing together : the state of being congregated
3 : a body of cardinals and officials forming an administrative division of the papal curia

con·gre·ga·tion·al \-shnəl, -shə-n²l\ *adjective* (1639)
1 : of or relating to a congregation
2 *capitalized* : of or relating to a body of Protestant churches deriving from the English Independents of the 17th century and affirming the essential importance and the autonomy of the local congregation
3 : of or relating to church government placing final authority in the assembly of the local congregation
— **con·gre·ga·tion·al·ism** \-shnə-ˌli-zəm, -shə-n²l-ˌi-\ *noun, often capitalized*
— **con·gre·ga·tion·al·ist** \-shnə-list, -shə-n²l-ist\ *noun or adjective, often capitalized*

con·gress \'käŋ-grəs *also* -rəs, *British usually* 'käŋ-ˌgres\ *noun* [Latin *congressus,* from *congredi* to come together, from *com-* + *gradi* to go — more at GRADE] (1528)
1 a : the act or action of coming together and meeting **b** : COITUS
2 : a formal meeting of delegates for discussion and usually action on some question
3 : the supreme legislative body of a nation and especially of a republic
4 : an association usually made up of delegates from constituent organizations
5 : a single meeting or session of a group
— **con·gres·sio·nal** \kən-'gresh-nəl, käŋ-, -'gre-shə-n²l\ *adjective*
— **con·gres·sio·nal·ly** *adverb*

congressional district *noun* (1812)
: a territorial division of a state from which a member of the U.S. House of Representatives is elected

Congressional Medal *noun* (1910)
: MEDAL OF HONOR

con·gress·man \'käŋ-(g)rəs-mən\ *noun* (1780)
: a member of a congress; *especially* : a member of the U.S. House of Representatives

con·gress·peo·ple \-(g)rəs-ˌpē-pəl\ *noun plural* (1973)
: congressmen or congresswomen

con·gress·per·son \-(g)rəs-ˌpər-sən\ *noun* (1972)
: a congressman or congresswoman

con·gress·wom·an \-(g)rəs-ˌwü-mən\ *noun* (1917)
: a female member of a congress; *especially* : a female member of the U.S. House of Representatives

con·gru·ence \kən-'grü-ən(t)s, 'käŋ-grü-ən(t)s\ *noun* (1533)
1 : the quality or state of agreeing, coinciding, or being congruent
2 : a statement that two numbers or geometric figures are congruent

con·gru·en·cy \-ən(t)-sē\ *noun, plural* **-cies** (15th century)
: CONGRUENCE

con·gru·ent \kən-'grü-ənt, 'käŋ-grü-ənt\ *adjective* [Middle English, from Latin *congruent-, congruens,* present participle of *congruere*] (15th century)
1 : CONGRUOUS
2 : superposable so as to be coincident throughout
3 : having the difference divisible by a given modulus ⟨12 is *congruent* to 2 (modulo 5) since $12-2=2\cdot5$⟩
— **con·gru·ent·ly** *adverb*

con·gru·i·ty \kən-'grü-ə-tē, kän-\ *noun, plural* **-ties** (14th century)
1 : the quality or state of being congruent or congruous
2 : a point of agreement

con·gru·ous \'käŋ-grü-əs\ *adjective* [Latin *congruus,* from *congruere* to come together, agree] (1599)
1 a : being in agreement, harmony, or correspondence **b** : conforming to the circumstances or requirements of a situation : APPROPRIATE ⟨a *congruous* room to work in —G. B. Shaw⟩
2 : marked or enhanced by harmonious agreement among constituent elements ⟨a *congruous* theme⟩
— **con·gru·ous·ly** *adverb*
— **con·gru·ous·ness** *noun*

¹**con·ic** \'kä-nik\ *adjective* (1570)
1 : of or relating to a cone
2 : CONICAL
— **co·nic·i·ty** \kō-'ni-sə-tē\ *noun*

²**conic** *noun* (1879)
: CONIC SECTION

con·i·cal \'kä-ni-kəl\ *adjective* (1570)
: resembling a cone especially in shape
— **con·i·cal·ly** \-k(ə-)lē\ *adverb*

conic section *noun* (1664)
1 : a plane curve, line, pair of intersecting lines, or point that is the intersection of or bounds the intersection of a plane and a cone with two nappes
2 : a curve generated by a point which always

conic section 1: *1* straight lines, *2* circle, *3* ellipse, *4* parabola, *5* hyperbola

moves so that the ratio of its distance from a fixed point to its distance from a fixed line is constant

co·nid·i·o·phore \kə-'ni-dē-ə-ˌfōr, -ˌfor\ *noun* [New Latin *conidium* + International Scientific Vocabulary *-phore*] (1874)
: a structure that bears conidia; *specifically* : a specialized hyphal branch of some fungi that produces conidia usually by the successive cutting off of parts of the sporophore through the growth of septa

co·nid·i·um \kə-'ni-dē-əm\ *noun, plural* **-ia** \-dē-ə\ [New Latin, from Greek *konis* dust — more at INCINERATE] (1856)
: an asexual spore produced on a conidiophore
— **co·nid·i·al** \-dē-əl\ *adjective*

\ə\ abut \²\ kitten \ər\ further \a\ ash \ā\ ace
\ä\ mop, mar \au̇\ out \ch\ chin \e\ bet \ē\ easy
\g\ go \i\ hit \ī\ ice \j\ job \ŋ\ sing \ō\ go
\ȯ\ law \ȯi\ boy \th\ thin \th\ the \ü\ loot \u̇\ foot
\y\ yet \zh\ vision *see also* Guide to Pronunciation

co·ni·fer \'kä-nə-fər *also* 'kō-\ *noun* [ultimately from Latin *conifer* cone-bearing, from *conus* cone + *-fer*] (circa 1841)
: any of an order (Coniferales) of mostly evergreen trees and shrubs including forms (as pines) with true cones and others (as yews) with an arillate fruit
— **co·nif·er·ous** \kō-'ni-f(ə-)rəs, kə-\ *adjective*

co·ni·ine \'kō-nē-,ēn\ *noun* [German *Koniin*, from Late Latin *conium* hemlock, from Greek *kōneion*] (1831)
: a poisonous alkaloid $C_8H_{17}N$ found in poison hemlock (*Conium maculatum*)

con·jec·tur·al \kən-'jek-chə-rəl, -'jek-shrəl\ *adjective* (1553)
1 : of the nature of or involving or based on conjecture
2 : given to conjectures
— **con·jec·tur·al·ly** *adverb*

¹con·jec·ture \kən-'jek-chər\ *noun* [Middle English, from Middle French or Latin; Middle French, from Latin *conjectura*, from *conjectus*, past participle of *conicere*, literally, to throw together, from *com-* + *jacere* to throw — more at JET] (14th century)
1 *obsolete* **a** : interpretation of omens **b** : SUPPOSITION
2 a : inference from defective or presumptive evidence **b** : a conclusion deduced by surmise or guesswork **c** : a proposition (as in mathematics) before it has been proved or disproved

²conjecture *verb* **-tured; -tur·ing** \-'jek-chə-riŋ, -'jek-shriŋ\ (15th century)
transitive verb
1 : to arrive at by conjecture
2 : to make conjectures as to
intransitive verb
: to form conjectures
— **con·jec·tur·er** \-'jek-chər-ər\ *noun*

con·join \kən-'jöin, kän-\ *verb* [Middle English, from Middle French *conjoindre*, from Latin *conjungere*, from *com-* + *jungere* to join — more at YOKE] (14th century)
transitive verb
: to join together (as separate entities) for a common purpose
intransitive verb
: to join together for a common purpose

con·joined \-'jöind\ *adjective* (1570)
: being, coming, or brought together so as to meet, touch, or overlap ⟨*conjoined* heads on a coin⟩

con·joint \-'jöint\ *adjective* [Middle English, from Middle French, past participle of *conjoindre*] (1725)
1 : UNITED, CONJOINED
2 : related to, made up of, or carried on by two or more in combination : JOINT
— **con·joint·ly** *adverb*

con·ju·gal \'kän-ji-gəl *also* kən-'jü-\ *adjective* [Middle French or Latin; Middle French, from Latin *conjugalis*, from *conjug-, conjux* husband, wife, from *conjungere* to join, unite in marriage] (1545)
: of or relating to the married state or to married persons and their relations : CONNUBIAL
— **con·ju·gal·i·ty** \,kän-ji-'ga-lə-tē, -jü-\ *noun*
— **con·ju·gal·ly** \'kän-ji-gə-lē *also* kən-'jü-\ *adverb*

conjugal rights *noun plural* (circa 1891)
: the sexual rights or privileges implied by and involved in the marriage relationship : the right of sexual intercourse between husband and wife

con·ju·gant \'kän-ji-gənt\ *noun* (1910)
: either of a pair of conjugating gametes or organisms

¹con·ju·gate \'kän-ji-gət, -jə-,gāt\ *adjective* [Middle English *conjugat*, from Latin *conjugatus*, past participle of *conjugare* to unite, from *com-* + *jugare* to join, from *jugum* yoke — more at YOKE] (15th century)
1 a : joined together especially in pairs : COUPLED **b** : acting or operating as if joined

2 a : having features in common but opposite or inverse in some particular **b** : relating to or being conjugate complex numbers ⟨complex roots occurring in *conjugate* pairs⟩
3 *of an acid or base* : related by the difference of a proton ⟨the acid NH_4 and the base NH_3 are *conjugate* to each other⟩
4 : having the same derivation and therefore usually some likeness in meaning ⟨*conjugate* words⟩
5 *of two leaves of a book* : forming a single piece
— **con·ju·gate·ly** *adverb*
— **con·ju·gate·ness** *noun*

²con·ju·gate \-jə-,gāt\ *verb* **-gat·ed; -gat·ing** (1530)
transitive verb
1 : to give in prescribed order the various inflectional forms of — used especially of a verb
2 : to join together
intransitive verb
1 : to become joined together
2 a : to pair and fuse in conjugation **b** : to pair in synapsis

³conjugate *same as* ¹\ *noun* (circa 1586)
1 : something conjugate : a product of conjugating
2 : CONJUGATE COMPLEX NUMBER
3 : an element of a mathematical group that is equal to a given element of the group multiplied on the right by another element and on the left by the inverse of the latter element

conjugate complex number *noun* (circa 1909)
: one of two complex numbers differing only in the sign of the imaginary part

con·ju·gat·ed \-,gā-təd\ *adjective* (1882)
1 : formed by the union of two compounds or united with another compound ⟨*conjugated* bile acids⟩
2 : relating to or containing a system of two double bonds separated by a single bond ⟨*conjugated* fatty acids⟩

conjugated protein *noun* (circa 1909)
: a compound of a protein with a nonprotein ⟨hemoglobin is a *conjugated protein*⟩ — compare SIMPLE PROTEIN

con·ju·ga·tion \,kän-jə-'gā-shən\ *noun* (15th century)
1 a : a schematic arrangement of the inflectional forms of a verb **b** : verb inflection **c** : a class of verbs having the same type of inflectional forms ⟨the weak *conjugation*⟩ **d** : a set of the simple or derivative inflectional forms of a verb especially in Sanskrit or the Semitic languages ⟨the causative *conjugation*⟩
2 : the act of conjugating : the state of being conjugated
3 a : fusion of usually similar gametes with ultimate union of their nuclei that among lower thallophytes replaces the typical fertilization of higher forms **b** : temporary cytoplasmic union with exchange of nuclear material that is the usual sexual process in ciliated protozoans **c** : the one-way transfer of DNA between bacteria in cellular contact
— **con·ju·ga·tion·al** \-shnəl, -shə-nᵊl\ *adjective*
— **con·ju·ga·tion·al·ly** *adverb*

¹con·junct \kən-'jəŋ(k)t, kän-\ *adjective* [Middle English, from Latin *conjunctus*, past participle of *conjungere*] (15th century)
1 : UNITED, JOINED
2 : JOINT
3 : relating to melodic progression by intervals of no more than a major second — compare DISJUNCT

²con·junct \'kän-,jəŋ(k)t\ *noun* (1667)
1 : something joined or associated with another; *specifically* : one of the components of a conjunction
2 : an adverb or adverbial (as *so, in addition, however, secondly*) that indicates the speaker's or writer's assessment of the connection between linguistic units (as clauses)

con·junc·tion \kən-'jəŋ(k)-shən\ *noun* (14th century)
1 : the act or an instance of conjoining : the state of being conjoined : CONJUNCTION
2 : occurrence together in time or space : CONCURRENCE
3 a : the apparent meeting or passing of two or more celestial bodies in the same degree of the zodiac **b** : a configuration in which two celestial bodies have their least apparent separation
4 : an uninflected linguistic form that joins together sentences, clauses, phrases, or words
5 : a complex sentence in logic true if and only if each of its components is true
— **con·junc·tion·al** \-shnəl, -shə-nᵊl\ *adjective*
— **con·junc·tion·al·ly** *adverb*

con·junc·ti·va \,kän-,jəŋ(k)-'tī-və, kən-\ *noun, plural* **-vas** *or* **-vae** \-(,)vē\ [New Latin, from Late Latin, feminine of *conjunctivus* conjoining, from Latin *conjunctus*] (14th century)
: the mucous membrane that lines the inner surface of the eyelids and is continued over the forepart of the eyeball — see EYE illustration
— **con·junc·ti·val** \-vəl\ *adjective*

con·junc·tive \kən-'jəŋ(k)-tiv\ *adjective* (1581)
1 : CONNECTIVE
2 : CONJUNCT, CONJOINED
3 : being or functioning like a conjunction
4 : COPULATIVE 1a
— **conjunctive** *noun*
— **con·junc·tive·ly** *adverb*

con·junc·ti·vi·tis \kən-,jəŋ(k)-ti-'vī-təs\ *noun* (1835)
: inflammation of the conjunctiva

con·junc·ture \kən-'jəŋ(k)-chər\ *noun* (1605)
1 : CONJUNCTION, UNION
2 : a combination of circumstances or events usually producing a crisis : JUNCTURE

con·ju·ra·tion \,kän-jù-'rā-shən, ,kən-\ *noun* (14th century)
1 : the act or process of conjuring : INCANTATION
2 : an expression or trick used in conjuring
3 : a solemn appeal : ADJURATION

con·jure *verb transitive 2 & verb intransitive senses* 'kän-jər *also* 'kən-; *verb transitive 1* kən-'jùr\ *verb* **con·jured; con·jur·ing** \'känj-riŋ, 'kän-jə-, 'kənj-; 'kən-jə-; kən-'jùr-iŋ\ [Middle English, from Old French *conjurer*, from Latin *conjurare* to swear together, from *com-* + *jurare* to swear — more at JURY] (13th century)
transitive verb
1 : to charge or entreat earnestly or solemnly
2 a : to summon by or as if by invocation or incantation **b** (1) : to affect or effect by or as if by magic (2) : IMAGINE, CONTRIVE — often used with *up* ⟨we *conjure* up our own metaphors for our own needs —R. J. Kaufmann⟩ (3) : to bring to mind ⟨words that *conjure* pleasant images⟩
intransitive verb
1 a : to summon a devil or spirit by invocation or incantation **b** : to practice magical arts
2 : to use a conjurer's tricks : JUGGLE

con·jur·er *or* **con·ju·ror** \'kän-jər-ər, 'kən-\ *noun* (14th century)
1 : one that practices magic arts : WIZARD
2 : one that performs feats of sleight of hand and illusion : MAGICIAN, JUGGLER

¹conk \'käŋk, 'köŋk\ *transitive verb* [English slang *conk* head] (1821)
: to hit especially on the head : KNOCK OUT

²conk *noun* [probably alteration of *conch*] (1851)
: the visible fruiting body of a bracket fungus; *also* : decay caused by such a fungus
— **conky** \'kän-kē, 'köŋ-\ *adjective*

³conk *intransitive verb* [probably imitative] (1918)

1 : BREAK DOWN; *especially* **:** STALL — usually used with *out* ⟨the motor suddenly *conked* out⟩ **2 a :** FAINT **b :** to go to sleep — usually used with *off* or *out* ⟨*conked* out for a while after lunch⟩ **c :** DIE ⟨I caught pneumonia. I almost *conked* —Truman Capote⟩

⁴**conk** *transitive verb* [probably by shortening & alteration from *congolene* preparation used for straightening hair] (1950)
: to straighten out (hair) usually by the use of chemicals

⁵**conk** *noun* (1965)
: a hairstyle in which the hair is straightened out and flattened down or lightly waved — called also *process*

conk·er \'käŋ-kər\ *noun* [*conch* + ²*-er*, from the original use of a snail shell on a string in the game] (circa 1886)
1 : a horse chestnut especially when used in conkers
2 *plural* **:** a game in which each player swings a horse chestnut on a string to try to break one held by the opponent

con mo·to \kän-'mō-(,)tō, kōn-\ *adverb* [Italian] (circa 1854)
: with movement **:** in a spirited manner — used as a direction in music

¹**conn** \'kän\ *transitive verb* [alteration of Middle English *condien* to conduct, from Middle French *conduire*, from Latin *conducere* — more at CONDUCE] (1626)
: to conduct or direct the steering of (as a ship)

²**conn** *noun* (1825)
: the control exercised by one who conns a ship

con·nate \kä-'nāt, 'kä-,\ *adjective* [Late Latin *connatus*, past participle of *connasci* to be born together, from Latin *com-* + *nasci* to be born — more at NATION] (1641)
1 : AKIN, CONGENIAL
2 : INNATE, INBORN
3 : congenitally or firmly united ⟨*connate* leaves⟩
4 : born or originated together
5 : entrapped in sediments at the time of their deposition ⟨*connate* water⟩
— **con·nate·ly** *adverb*

con·nat·u·ral \kä-'nach-rəl, kə-, -'na-chə-\ *adjective* [Medieval Latin *connaturalis*, from Latin *com-* + *naturalis* natural] (1592)
1 : connected by nature **:** INBORN
2 : of the same nature
— **con·nat·u·ral·i·ty** \-,na-chə-'ra-lə-tē\ *noun*
— **con·nat·u·ral·ly** \-'nach-rə-lē, -'na-chə-\ *adverb*

con·nect \kə-'nekt\ *verb* [Middle English, from Latin *conectere, connectere*, from *com-* + *nectere* to bind] (15th century)
intransitive verb
1 : to become joined ⟨the two rooms *connect* by a hallway⟩ ⟨ideas that *connect* easily to form a theory⟩
2 : to make a successful hit, shot, or throw ⟨*connected* for a home run⟩ ⟨*connected* on 60 percent of his shots —*N.Y. Times*⟩
3 : to have or establish a rapport ⟨tried to *connect* with the younger generation⟩
transitive verb
1 : to join or fasten together usually by something intervening
2 : to place or establish in relationship
synonym see JOIN
— **con·nect·able** *also* **con·nect·ible** \-'nek-tə-bəl\ *adjective*
— **con·nec·tor** *also* **con·nect·er** \-'nek-tər\ *noun*

connected *adjective* (1712)
1 : joined or linked together
2 : having the parts or elements logically linked together ⟨presented a thoroughly *connected* view of the problem⟩
3 : related by blood or marriage
4 : having social, professional, or commercial relationships ⟨a well-*connected* lawyer⟩

5 *of a set* **:** having the property that any two of its points can be joined by a line completely contained in the set; *also* **:** incapable of being separated into two or more closed disjoint subsets
— **con·nect·ed·ly** *adverb*
— **con·nect·ed·ness** *noun*

connecting rod *noun* (1839)
: a rod that transmits motion from a reciprocating part of a machine (as a piston) to a rotating part or vice versa

con·nec·tion \kə-'nek-shən\ *noun* [Latin *connexion-, connexio*, from *conectere*] (14th century)
1 : the act of connecting **:** the state of being connected: as **a :** causal or logical relation or sequence ⟨the *connection* between two ideas⟩ **b** (1) **:** contextual relation or association ⟨in this *connection* the word has a different meaning⟩ (2) **:** relationship in fact ⟨wanted in *connection* with a robbery⟩ **c :** a relation of personal intimacy (as of family ties) **d :** COHERENCE, CONTINUITY
2 a : something that connects **:** LINK ⟨a loose *connection* in the wiring⟩ **b :** a means of communication or transport
3 : a person connected with another especially by marriage, kinship, or common interest ⟨has powerful *connections*⟩
4 : a political, social, professional, or commercial relationship: as **a :** POSITION, JOB **b :** an arrangement to execute orders or advance interests of another ⟨a firm's foreign *connections*⟩ **c :** a source of contraband (as illegal drugs)
5 : a set of persons associated together: as **a :** DENOMINATION **b :** CLAN
— **con·nec·tion·al** \-shnəl, -shə-n°l\ *adjective*

¹**con·nec·tive** \kə-'nek-tiv\ *adjective* (circa 1660)
: serving to connect
— **con·nec·tive·ly** *adverb*

²**connective** *noun* (1751)
: something that connects: as **a :** a linguistic form that connects words or word groups **b :** the tissue connecting the pollen sacs of an anther **c :** a logical term (as *or, if-then, and, not*) or symbol for it that relates propositions in such a way that the truth or falsity of the resulting statement is determined by the truth or falsity of the components

connective tissue *noun* (1846)
: a tissue of mesodermal origin rich in intercellular substance or interlacing processes with little tendency for the cells to come together in sheets or masses; *specifically* **:** connective tissue of stellate or spindle-shaped cells with interlacing processes that pervades, supports, and binds together other tissues and forms ligaments, tendons, and aponeuroses

con·nec·tiv·i·ty \(,)kä-,nek-'ti-və-tē, kə-\ *noun, plural* **-ties** (1893)
: the quality or state of being connective or connected ⟨*connectivity* of a surface⟩; *especially* **:** the ability to connect to or communicate with another computer or computer system

Con·ne·ma·ra \,kä-nə-'mär-ə, ,kó-\ *noun* [*Connemara*, Ireland] (circa 1952)
: any of a breed of rugged ponies developed in Ireland

con·nex·ion \kə-'nek-shən\ *chiefly British variant of* CONNECTION

conning tower \'kä-niŋ-\ *noun* (1886)
: a raised structure on the deck of a submarine used especially formerly for navigation and attack direction

con·nip·tion \kə-'nip-shən\ *noun* [origin unknown] (1833)
: a fit of rage, hysteria, or alarm ⟨went into *conniptions*⟩

con·niv·ance \kə-'nī-vən(t)s\ *noun* (1593)
: the act of conniving; *especially* **:** knowledge of and active or passive consent to wrongdoing

con·nive \kə-'nīv\ *intransitive verb* **con·nived; con·niv·ing**
[French or Latin; French *conniver*, from Latin *connivēre* to close the eyes, connive, from *com-* + *-nivēre* (akin to *nictare* to wink); akin to Old English & Old High German *hnīgan* to bow] (1601)

conning tower

1 : to pretend ignorance of or fail to take action against something one ought to oppose
2 a : to be indulgent or in secret sympathy **:** WINK **b :** to cooperate secretly or have a secret understanding
3 : CONSPIRE, INTRIGUE
— **con·niv·er** *noun*

con·ni·vent \-'nī-vənt\ *adjective* [Latin *conivent-, conivens*, present participle of *conivēre*] (1757)
: converging but not fused ⟨*connivent* stamens⟩

con·nois·seur \,kä-nə-'sər *also* -'sùr\ *noun* [obsolete French (now *connaisseur*), from Old French *connoisseor*, from *connoistre* to know, from Latin *cognoscere* — more at COGNITION] (1714)
1 : EXPERT; *especially* **:** one who understands the details, technique, or principles of an art and is competent to act as a critical judge
2 : one who enjoys with discrimination and appreciation of subtleties ⟨a *connoisseur* of fine wines⟩
— **con·nois·seur·ship** \-,ship\ *noun*

con·no·ta·tion \,kä-nə-'tā-shən\ *noun* (1532)
1 a : the suggesting of a meaning by a word apart from the thing it explicitly names or describes **b :** something suggested by a word or thing **:** IMPLICATION ⟨the *connotations* of comfort that surrounded that old chair⟩
2 : the signification of something ⟨that abuse of logic which consists in moving counters about as if they were known entities with a fixed *connotation* —W. R. Inge⟩
3 : an essential property or group of properties of a thing named by a term in logic — compare DENOTATION
— **con·no·ta·tion·al** \-shnəl, -shə-n°l\ *adjective*

con·no·ta·tive \'kä-nə-,tā-tiv, kə-'nō-tə-tiv\ *adjective* (1614)
1 : connoting or tending to connote
2 : relating to connotation
— **con·no·ta·tive·ly** *adverb*

con·note \kə-'nōt, kä-\ *transitive verb* **con·not·ed; con·not·ing** [Medieval Latin *connotare*, from Latin *com-* + *notare* to note] (1665)
1 : to be associated with or inseparable from as a consequence or concomitant ⟨the remorse so often *connoted* by guilt⟩
2 a : to convey in addition to exact explicit meaning ⟨all the misery that poverty *connotes*⟩ **b :** to imply as a logical connotation

con·nu·bi·al \kə-'nü-bē-əl, -'nyü-\ *adjective* [Latin *conubialis*, from *conubium, connubium* marriage, from *com-* + *nubere* to marry — more at NUPTIAL] (circa 1656)
: of or relating to the married state **:** CONJUGAL
— **con·nu·bi·al·ism** \-bē-ə-,li-zəm\ *noun*
— **con·nu·bi·al·i·ty** \-,nü-bē-'a-lə-tē, -,nyü-\ *noun*

— **con·nu·bi·al·ly** \-'nü-bē-ə-lē, -'nyü-\ *adverb*

co·no·dont \'kō-nə-,dänt, 'kä-\ *noun* [International Scientific Vocabulary *con-* (from Greek *kōnos* cone) + *-odont*] (1859)
: a Paleozoic toothlike fossil that is probably the remains of an extinct marine invertebrate

co·noid \'kō-,nóid\ *or* **co·noi·dal** \kō-'nói-d²l\ *adjective* (1668)
: shaped like or nearly like a cone ⟨*conoid* shells⟩ ⟨*conoid* pottery⟩
— **conoid** *noun*

con·quer \'käŋ-kər\ *verb* **con·quered; con·quer·ing** \-k(ə-)riŋ\ [Middle English, to acquire, conquer, from Old French *conquerre*, from (assumed) Vulgar Latin *conquaerere*, alteration of Latin *conquirere* to search for, collect, from *com-* + *quaerere* to ask, search] (14th century)
transitive verb
1 : to gain or acquire by force of arms : SUBJUGATE
2 : to overcome by force of arms : VANQUISH
3 : to gain mastery over or win by overcoming obstacles or opposition ⟨*conquered* the mountain⟩
4 : to overcome by mental or moral power : SURMOUNT ⟨*conquered* her fear⟩
intransitive verb
: to be victorious ☆
— **con·quer·or** \-kər-ər\ *noun*

con·quest \'kän-,kwest, 'käŋ-; 'käŋ-kwəst\ *noun* [Middle English, from Middle French, from (assumed) Vulgar Latin *conquaesitus*, alteration of Latin *conquisitus*, past participle of *conquirere*] (14th century)
1 : the act or process of conquering
2 a : something conquered; *especially* : territory appropriated in war **b** : a person whose favor or hand has been won

con·qui·an \'kän-kē-ən\ *noun* [Mexican Spanish *conquián* — more at COONCAN] (circa 1911)
: a card game for two played with 40 cards from which all games of rummy developed

con·quis·ta·dor \kän-'kēs-tə-,dor, kən- *also* -'kwis-, -'kis-\ *noun, plural* **con·quis·ta·do·res** \(,)kän-,kēs-tə-'dor-ēz, -'dor-,ās, kən-; (,)kän-,kwis-, -,kis-\ *or* **con·quis·ta·dors** [Spanish, ultimately from Latin *conquirere*] (1830)
: one that conquers; *specifically* : a leader in the Spanish conquest of America and especially of Mexico and Peru in the 16th century

con·san·guine \kän-'saŋ-gwən, kən-\ *adjective* (1610)
: CONSANGUINEOUS

con·san·guin·e·ous \,kän-,san-'gwi-nē-əs, -,saŋ-\ *adjective* [Latin *consanguineus*, from *com-* + *sanguin-, sanguis* blood] (1601)
: of the same blood or origin; *specifically* : descended from the same ancestor
— **con·san·guin·e·ous·ly** *adverb*

con·san·guin·i·ty \-'gwi-nə-tē\ *noun, plural* **-ties** (14th century)
1 : the quality or state of being consanguineous
2 : a close relation or connection

con·science \'kän(t)-shən(t)s\ *noun* [Middle English, from Old French, from Latin *conscientia*, from *conscient-, consciens*, present participle of *conscire* to be conscious, be conscious of guilt, from *com-* + *scire* to know — more at SCIENCE] (13th century)
1 a : the sense or consciousness of the moral goodness or blameworthiness of one's own conduct, intentions, or character together with a feeling of obligation to do right or be good **b** : a faculty, power, or principle enjoining good acts **c** : the part of the superego in psychoanalysis that transmits commands and admonitions to the ego
2 *archaic* : CONSCIOUSNESS
3 : conformity to the dictates of conscience : CONSCIENTIOUSNESS

4 : sensitive regard for fairness or justice : SCRUPLE
— **con·science·less** \-ləs\ *adjective*
— **in all conscience** *or* **in conscience**
: in all fairness

conscience money *noun* (1848)
: money paid usually anonymously to relieve the conscience by restoring what has been wrongfully acquired

con·sci·en·tious \,kän(t)-shē-'en(t)-shəs\ *adjective* (1611)
1 : governed by or conforming to the dictates of conscience : SCRUPULOUS ⟨a *conscientious* public servant⟩
2 : METICULOUS, CAREFUL ⟨a *conscientious* listener⟩
synonym see UPRIGHT
— **con·sci·en·tious·ly** *adverb*
— **con·sci·en·tious·ness** *noun*

conscientious objection *noun* (1916)
: objection on moral or religious grounds (as to service in the armed forces or to bearing arms)

conscientious objector *noun* (1899)
: a person who refuses to serve in the armed forces or bear arms on moral or religious grounds

con·scio·na·ble \'kän(t)-sh(ə-)nə-bəl\ *adjective* [irregular from *conscience*] (1549)
: CONSCIENTIOUS

¹con·scious \'kän(t)-shəs\ *adjective* [Latin *conscius*, from *com-* + *scire* to know] (1592)
1 : perceiving, apprehending, or noticing with a degree of controlled thought or observation
2 *archaic* : sharing another's knowledge or awareness of an inward state or outward fact
3 : personally felt ⟨*conscious* guilt⟩
4 : capable of or marked by thought, will, design, or perception
5 : SELF-CONSCIOUS
6 : having mental faculties undulled by sleep, faintness, or stupor : AWAKE ⟨became *conscious* after the anesthesia wore off⟩
7 : done or acting with critical awareness ⟨a *conscious* effort to do better⟩
8 a : likely to notice, consider, or appraise ⟨a bargain-*conscious* shopper⟩ **b** : being concerned or interested ⟨a budget-*conscious* businessman⟩ **c** : marked by strong feelings or notions ⟨a race-*conscious* society⟩
synonym see AWARE
— **con·scious·ly** *adverb*

²conscious *noun* (1919)
: CONSCIOUSNESS 5

con·scious·ness \-nəs\ *noun* (1632)
1 a : the quality or state of being aware especially of something within oneself **b** : the state or fact of being conscious of an external object, state, or fact **c** : AWARENESS; *especially* : concern for some social or political cause
2 : the state of being characterized by sensation, emotion, volition, and thought : MIND
3 : the totality of conscious states of an individual
4 : the normal state of conscious life ⟨regained *consciousness*⟩
5 : the upper level of mental life of which the person is aware as contrasted with unconscious processes

consciousness–raising *noun* (1971)
: an increasing of concerned awareness especially of some social or political issue

con·scribe \kən-'skrīb\ *transitive verb* **con·scribed; con·scrib·ing** [Latin *conscribere*] (1613)
1 : LIMIT, CIRCUMSCRIBE ⟨ill-health . . . *conscribed* the force of his intentions —*Times Literary Supplement*⟩
2 : to enlist forcibly : CONSCRIPT

¹con·script \'kän-,skript\ *noun* (1800)
: a conscripted person (as a military recruit)

²con·script \kən-'skript\ *transitive verb* (1813)
: to enroll into service by compulsion : DRAFT ⟨was *conscripted* into the army⟩

³con·script \'kän-,skript\ *adjective* [alteration of French *conscrit*, from Latin *conscriptus*, past participle of *conscribere* to enroll, enlist, from *com-* + *scribere* to write — more at SCRIBE] (1823)
1 : enrolled into service by compulsion : DRAFTED
2 : made up of conscripted persons

con·scrip·tion \kən-'skrip-shən\ *noun* (1800)
: compulsory enrollment of persons especially for military service : DRAFT

¹con·se·crate \'kän(t)-sə-,krāt\ *adjective* (14th century)
: dedicated to a sacred purpose

²consecrate *transitive verb* **-crat·ed; -crat·ing** [Middle English, from Latin *consecratus*, past participle of *consecrare*, from *com-* + *sacrare* to consecrate — more at SACRED] (14th century)
1 : to induct (a person) into a permanent office with a religious rite; *especially* : to ordain to the office of bishop
2 a : to make or declare sacred; *especially* : to devote irrevocably to the worship of God by a solemn ceremony **b** : to effect the liturgical transubstantiation of (eucharistic bread and wine) **c** : to devote to a purpose with or as if with deep solemnity or dedication
3 : to make inviolable or venerable ⟨principles *consecrated* by the weight of history⟩
synonym see DEVOTE
— **con·se·cra·tive** \-,krā-tiv\ *adjective*
— **con·se·cra·tor** \-,krā-tər\ *noun*
— **con·se·cra·to·ry** \'kän(t)-si-krə-,tōr-ē, -,tòr-, -,krā-tə-rē\ *adjective*

con·se·cra·tion \,kän(t)-sə-'krā-shən\ *noun* (14th century)
1 : the act or ceremony of consecrating
2 : the state of being consecrated
3 *capitalized* : the part of a Communion rite in which the bread and wine are consecrated

con·se·cu·tion \,kän(t)-si-'kyü-shən\ *noun* [Latin *consecution-, consecutio*, from *consequi* to follow along — more at CONSEQUENT] (1651)
: SEQUENCE

con·sec·u·tive \kən-'se-kyə-tiv, -kə-tiv\ *adjective* (1611)
: following one after the other in order : SUCCESSIVE
— **con·sec·u·tive·ly** *adverb*
— **con·sec·u·tive·ness** *noun*

con·sen·su·al \kən-'sen(t)-sh(ə-)wəl, -shəl\ *adjective* [Latin *consensus* + English *-al*] (1754)
1 a : existing or made by mutual consent without an act of writing ⟨a *consensual* contract⟩ **b** : involving or based on mutual consent ⟨*consensual* acts⟩
2 : relating to or being the constrictive pupillary response of an eye that is covered when the other eye is exposed to light

☆ **SYNONYMS**
Conquer, vanquish, defeat, subdue, reduce, overcome, overthrow mean to get the better of by force or strategy. CONQUER implies gaining mastery of ⟨Caesar *conquered* Gaul⟩. VANQUISH implies a complete overpowering ⟨*vanquished* the enemy and ended the war⟩. DEFEAT does not imply the finality or completeness of VANQUISH which it otherwise equals ⟨the Confederates *defeated* the Union forces at Manassas⟩. SUBDUE implies a defeating and suppression ⟨*subdued* the native tribes after years of fighting⟩. REDUCE implies a forcing to capitulate or surrender ⟨the city was *reduced* after a month-long siege⟩. OVERCOME suggests getting the better of with difficulty or after hard struggle ⟨*overcame* a host of bureaucratic roadblocks⟩. OVERTHROW stresses the bringing down or destruction of existing power ⟨violently *overthrew* the old regime⟩.

— **con·sen·su·al·ly** *adverb*

con·sen·sus \kən-'sen(t)-səs\ *noun, often attributive* [Latin, from *consentire*] (1858) **1 a :** general agreement : UNANIMITY ⟨the *consensus* of their opinion, based on reports . . . from the border —John Hersey⟩ **b :** the judgment arrived at by most of those concerned ⟨the *consensus* was to go ahead⟩ **2 :** group solidarity in sentiment and belief □

¹**con·sent** \kən-'sent\ *intransitive verb* [Middle English, from Latin *consentire*, from *com-* + *sentire* to feel — more at SENSE] (13th century) **1 :** to give assent or approval : AGREE **2** *archaic* **:** to be in concord in opinion or sentiment

synonym see ASSENT

— **con·sent·ing·ly** \-'sen-tiŋ-lē\ *adverb*

²**consent** *noun* (14th century) **1 :** compliance in or approval of what is done or proposed by another : ACQUIESCENCE ⟨he shall have power, by and with the advice and *consent* of the Senate, to make treaties —*U.S. Constitution*⟩ **2 :** agreement as to action or opinion; *specifically* **:** voluntary agreement by a people to organize a civil society and give authority to the government

— **con·sent·er** *noun*

con·sen·ta·ne·ous \ˌkän(t)-sən-'tā-nē-əs, ˌkän-ˌsen-\ *adjective* [Latin *consentaneus*, from *consentire* to agree] (1625) **1 :** expressing agreement : SUITED **2 :** done or made by the consent of all

— **con·sen·ta·ne·ous·ly** *adverb*

consent decree *noun* (1904) **:** a judicial decree that sanctions a voluntary agreement between parties in dispute

con·se·quence \'kän(t)-sə-ˌkwen(t)s, -si-kwən(t)s\ *noun* (14th century) **1 :** a conclusion derived through logic : INFERENCE **2 :** something produced by a cause or necessarily following from a set of conditions **3 a :** importance with respect to power to produce an effect : MOMENT **b :** social importance **4 :** the appearance of importance; *especially* **:** SELF-IMPORTANCE

synonym see IMPORTANCE

— **in consequence :** as a result : CONSEQUENTLY

¹**con·se·quent** \-kwənt, -ˌkwent\ *noun* (14th century) **1 a :** DEDUCTION 2b **b :** the conclusion of a conditional sentence **2 :** the second term of a ratio

²**consequent** *adjective* [Middle English, from Middle French, from Latin *consequent-, consequens*, present participle of *consequi* to follow along, from *com-* + *sequi* to follow — more at SUE] (15th century) **1 :** following as a result or effect ⟨her new job and *consequent* relocation⟩ **2 :** observing logical sequence : RATIONAL

con·se·quen·tial \ˌkän(t)-sə-'kwen(t)-shəl\ *adjective* (1626) **1 :** of the nature of a secondary result : INDIRECT **2 :** CONSEQUENT **3 :** having significant consequences : IMPORTANT ⟨a grave and *consequential* event⟩ **4 :** SELF-IMPORTANT

— **con·se·quen·ti·al·i·ty** \-ˌkwen(t)-shē-'a-lə-tē\ *noun*

— **con·se·quen·tial·ly** \-'kwen(t)-sh(ə-)lē\ *adverb*

— **con·se·quen·tial·ness** \-'kwen(t)-shəl-nəs\ *noun*

con·se·quent·ly \'kän(t)-sə-ˌkwent-lē, -si-kwənt-\ *adverb* (15th century) **:** as a result : in view of the foregoing : ACCORDINGLY

con·ser·van·cy \kən-'sər-vən(t)-sē\ *noun, plural* **-cies** [alteration of obsolete *conservacy* conservation, from Anglo-French *conser-*

vacie, from Medieval Latin *conservatia*, from Latin *conservare*] (1755) **1** *British* **:** a board regulating fisheries and navigation in a river or port **2 a :** CONSERVATION **b :** an organization or area designated to conserve and protect natural resources

con·ser·va·tion \ˌkän(t)-sər-'vā-shən\ *noun* [Middle English, from Middle French, from Latin *conservation-, conservatio*, from *conservare*] (14th century) **1 :** a careful preservation and protection of something; *especially* **:** planned management of a natural resource to prevent exploitation, destruction, or neglect **2 :** the preservation of a physical quantity during transformations or reactions

— **con·ser·va·tion·al** \-shnəl, -shə-nᵊl\ *adjective*

con·ser·va·tion·ist \-sh(ə-)nist\ *noun* (1870) **:** a person who advocates conservation especially of natural resources

conservation of charge (1949) **:** a principle in physics: the total electric charge of an isolated system remains constant irrespective of whatever internal changes may take place

conservation of energy (1853) **:** a principle in physics: the total energy of an isolated system remains constant irrespective of whatever internal changes may take place with energy disappearing in one form reappearing in another

conservation of mass (1884) **:** a principle in classical physics: the total mass of any material system is neither increased nor diminished by reactions between the parts — called also *conservation of matter*

con·ser·va·tism \kən-'sər-və-ˌti-zəm\ *noun* (1835) **1** *capitalized* **a :** the principles and policies of a Conservative party **b :** the Conservative party **2 a :** disposition in politics to preserve what is established **b :** a political philosophy based on tradition and social stability, stressing established institutions, and preferring gradual development to abrupt change **3 :** the tendency to prefer an existing or traditional situation to change

¹**con·ser·va·tive** \kən-'sər-və-tiv\ *adjective* (14th century) **1 :** PRESERVATIVE **2 a :** of or relating to a philosophy of conservatism **b** *capitalized* **:** of or constituting a political party professing the principles of conservatism: as (1) **:** of or constituting a party of the United Kingdom advocating support of established institutions (2) **:** PROGRESSIVE CONSERVATIVE **3 a :** tending or disposed to maintain existing views, conditions, or institutions : TRADITIONAL **b :** marked by moderation or caution ⟨a *conservative* estimate⟩ **c :** marked by or relating to traditional norms of taste, elegance, style, or manners ⟨a *conservative* suit⟩ **4 :** of or relating to Conservative Judaism

— **con·ser·va·tive·ly** *adverb*

— **con·ser·va·tive·ness** *noun*

²**conservative** *noun* (1831) **1 a :** an adherent or advocate of political conservatism **b** *capitalized* **:** a member or supporter of a conservative political party **2 a :** one who adheres to traditional methods or views **b :** a cautious or discreet person

Conservative Judaism *noun* (1946) **:** Judaism as practiced especially among some U.S. Jews with adherence to the Torah and Talmud but with allowance for some departures in keeping with differing times and circumstances — compare ORTHODOX JUDAISM, REFORM JUDAISM

con·ser·va·tize \-ˌtīz\ *verb* **-tized; -tiz·ing** (1849) *intransitive verb* **:** to grow conservative

transitive verb **:** to make conservative

con·ser·va·toire \kən-'sər-və-ˌtwär\ *noun* [French, from Italian *conservatorio*] (1845) **:** CONSERVATORY 2

con·ser·va·tor \kən-'sər-və-tər, -və-ˌtȯr; 'kän(t)-sər-ˌvā-tər\ *noun* (15th century) **1 a :** one that preserves from injury or violation : PROTECTOR **b :** one that is responsible for the care, restoration, and repair of archival or museum articles **2 :** a person, official, or institution designated to take over and protect the interests of an incompetent **3 :** an official charged with the protection of something affecting public welfare and interests

— **con·ser·va·to·ri·al** \kən-ˌsər-və-'tȯr-ē-əl, (ˌ)kän-, -'tȯr-\ *adjective*

— **con·ser·va·tor·ship** \kən-'sər-və-tər-ˌship, -və-ˌtȯr-; 'kän(t)-sər-ˌvā-tər-\ *noun*

con·ser·va·to·ry \kən-'sər-və-ˌtȯr-ē, -ˌtȯr-\ *noun, plural* **-ries** (1664) **1 :** a greenhouse for growing or displaying plants **2** [Italian *conservatorio* home for foundlings, music school, from Latin *conservare*] **:** a school specializing in one of the fine arts ⟨a music *conservatory*⟩

¹**con·serve** \kən-'sərv\ *transitive verb* **con·served; con·serv·ing** [Middle English, from Middle French *conserver*, from Latin *conservare*, from *com-* + *servare* to keep, guard, observe; akin to Avestan *haurvaiti* he guards] (14th century) **1 :** to keep in a safe or sound state ⟨he *conserved* his inheritance⟩; *especially* **:** to avoid wasteful or destructive use of ⟨*conserve* natural resources⟩ **2 :** to preserve with sugar **3 :** to maintain (a quantity) constant during a process of chemical, physical, or evolutionary change

— **con·serv·er** *noun*

²**con·serve** \'kän-ˌsərv\ *noun* (15th century) **1 :** SWEETMEAT; *especially* **:** a candied fruit **2 :** PRESERVE; *specifically* **:** one prepared from a mixture of fruits

con·sid·er \kən-'si-dər\ *verb* **con·sid·ered; con·sid·er·ing** \-d(ə-)riŋ\ [Middle English, from Middle French *considerer*, from Latin *considerare* to observe, think about, from *com-* + *sider-, sidus* star] (14th century) *transitive verb* **1 :** to think about carefully: as **a :** to think of especially with regard to taking some action ⟨is *considering* you for the job⟩ ⟨*considered* moving to the city⟩ **b :** to take into account ⟨defendant's age must be *considered*⟩ **2 :** to regard or treat in an attentive or kindly way ⟨he *considered* her every wish⟩ **3 :** to gaze on steadily or reflectively **4 :** to come to judge or classify ⟨*consider* thrift essential⟩ **5 :** REGARD ⟨his works are well *considered* abroad⟩ **6 :** SUPPOSE

\ə\ abut \ᵊ\ kitten \ər\ **further** \a\ **ash** \ā\ **ace** \ä\ **mop, mar** \au̇\ **out** \ch\ **chin** \e\ **bet** \ē\ **easy** \g\ **go** \i\ **hit** \ī\ **ice** \j\ **job** \ŋ\ **sing** \ō\ **go** \ȯ\ **law** \ȯi\ **boy** \th\ **thin** \t͟h\ **the** \ü\ **loot** \u̇\ **foot** \y\ **yet** \zh\ **vision** *see also* Guide to Pronunciation

intransitive verb
: REFLECT, DELIBERATE ⟨paused a moment to *consider*⟩ ☆

¹**con·sid·er·able** \-'si-dər(-ə)-bəl, -'si-drə-bəl\ *adjective* (circa 1619)
1 : worth consideration : SIGNIFICANT
2 : large in extent or degree ⟨a *considerable* number⟩
— **con·sid·er·ably** \-blē\ *adverb*

²**considerable** *noun* (1685)
: a considerable amount, degree, or extent

con·sid·er·ate \kən-'si-d(ə-)rət\ *adjective* (1572)
1 : marked by or given to careful consideration : CIRCUMSPECT
2 : thoughtful of the rights and feelings of others
— **con·sid·er·ate·ly** *adverb*
— **con·sid·er·ate·ness** *noun*

con·sid·er·ation \kən-si-də-'rā-shən\ *noun* (14th century)
1 : continuous and careful thought ⟨after long *consideration* he agreed to their requests⟩
2 a : a matter weighed or taken into account when formulating an opinion or plan ⟨economic *considerations* forced her to leave college⟩ **b** : a taking into account
3 : thoughtful and sympathetic regard
4 : an opinion obtained by reflection
5 : ESTEEM, REGARD ⟨the family built themselves a large, ugly villa . . . and became people of *consideration* —V. S. Pritchett⟩
6 a : RECOMPENSE, PAYMENT **b** : the inducement to a contract or other legal transaction; *specifically* : an act or forbearance or the promise thereof done or given by one party in return for the act or promise of another
— **in consideration of** : as payment or recompense for ⟨a small fee *in consideration of* many kind services⟩

con·sid·ered \kən-'si-dərd\ *adjective* (circa 1677)
1 : matured by extended deliberative thought ⟨a *considered* opinion⟩
2 : viewed with respect or esteem

¹**con·sid·er·ing** \-d(ə-)riŋ\ *preposition* (14th century)
: in view of : taking into account ⟨he did well *considering* his limitations⟩

²**considering** *conjunction* (15th century)
: INASMUCH AS ⟨*considering* he was new at the job, he did quite well⟩

con·sig·li·e·re \kōn-(,)sil-'ye-re, -'yer-ē\ kän-(,)si-glē-'ye-rā, -rē, -'yer\ *noun, plural* **-ri** \-rē\ [Italian, from *consiglio* advice, counsel, from Latin *consilium* — more at COUNSEL] (1615)
: COUNSELOR, ADVISER ⟨*consigliere* of a Mafia family⟩

con·sign \kən-'sīn\ *verb* [Middle French *consigner*, from Latin *consignare*, from *com-* + *signum* sign, mark, seal — more at SIGN] (1528)
transitive verb
1 : to give over to another's care
2 : to give, transfer, or deliver into the hands or control of another; *also* : to commit especially to a final destination or fate ⟨a writer *consigned* to oblivion⟩
3 : to send or address to an agent to be cared for or sold
intransitive verb
obsolete : AGREE, SUBMIT
synonym *see* COMMIT
— **con·sign·able** \-'sī-nə-bəl\ *adjective*
— **con·sig·na·tion** \,kän-,sī-'nā-shən, ,kän-(,)sig-\ *noun*
— **con·sign·or** \,kän-,sī-'nòr, kən-\ *noun*

con·sign·ee \,kän(t)-sə-'nē, ,kän-,sī-, kən-,sī-\ *noun* (1789)
: one to whom something is consigned or shipped

¹**con·sign·ment** \kən-'sīn-mənt\ *noun* (circa 1668)
1 : the act or process of consigning
2 : something consigned especially in a single shipment

— **on consignment** : shipped to a dealer who pays only for what he sells and who may return what is unsold ⟨goods shipped *on consignment*⟩

²**consignment** *adjective* (1913)
: of, relating to, or received as goods on consignment ⟨a *consignment* sale⟩

¹**con·sist** \kən-'sist\ *intransitive verb* [Middle French & Latin; Middle French *consister*, from Latin *consistere*, literally, to stop, stand still, from *com-* + *sistere* to take a stand; akin to Latin *stare* to stand — more at STAND] (1526)
1 : LIE, RESIDE — usually used with *in* ⟨liberty *consists* in the absence of obstructions —A. E. Housman⟩
2 *archaic* **a** : EXIST, BE **b** : to be capable of existing
3 : to be composed or made up — usually used with *of* ⟨breakfast *consisted* of cereal, milk, and fruit⟩
4 : to be consistent ⟨it *consists* with the facts⟩

²**con·sist** \'kän-,sist\ *noun* (1898)
: makeup or composition (as of coal sizes or a railroad train) by classes, types, or grades and arrangement

con·sis·tence \kən-'sis-tən(t)s\ *noun* (1601)
: CONSISTENCY

con·sis·ten·cy \kən-'sis-tən(t)-sē\ *noun, plural* **-cies** (1594)
1 a *archaic* : condition of adhering together : firmness of material substance **b** : firmness of constitution or character : PERSISTENCY
2 : degree of firmness, density, viscosity, or resistance to movement or separation of constituent particles ⟨boil the juice to the *consistency* of a thick syrup⟩
3 a : agreement or harmony of parts or features to one another or a whole : CORRESPONDENCE; *specifically* : ability to be asserted together without contradiction **b** : harmony of conduct or practice with profession ⟨followed her own advice with *consistency*⟩

con·sis·tent \kən-'sis-tənt\ *adjective* [Latin *consistent-, consistens*, present participle of *consistere*] (1647)
1 *archaic* : possessing firmness or coherence
2 a : marked by harmony, regularity, or steady continuity : free from variation or contradiction ⟨a *consistent* style in painting⟩ **b** : COMPATIBLE — usually used with *with* **c** : showing steady conformity to character, profession, belief, or custom ⟨a *consistent* patriot⟩
3 : tending to be arbitrarily close to the true value of the parameter estimated as the sample becomes large ⟨a *consistent* statistical estimator⟩
— **con·sis·tent·ly** \-lē\ *adverb*

con·sis·to·ry \kən-'sis-t(ə-)rē\ *noun, plural* **-ries** [Middle English *consistorie*, from Middle French, from Medieval Latin & Late Latin; Medieval Latin *consistorium* church tribunal, from Late Latin, imperial council, from Latin *consistere*] (14th century)
1 : a solemn assembly : COUNCIL
2 : a church tribunal or governing body: as **a** : a solemn meeting of Roman Catholic cardinals convoked and presided over by the pope **b** : a church session in some Reformed churches
3 : the organization that confers the degrees of the Ancient and Accepted Scottish Rite of Freemasonry usually from the 19th to the 32d inclusive; *also* : a meeting of such an organization
— **con·sis·to·ri·al** \,kän-si-'stōr-ē-əl, -'stòr-\ *adjective*

con·so·ci·ate \kən-'sō-sē-,āt, -shē-,āt\ *verb* **-at·ed; -at·ing** [Latin *consociatus*, past participle of *consociare*, from *com-* + *socius* companion — more at SOCIAL] (1566)
transitive verb
: to bring into association

intransitive verb
: to associate especially in fellowship or partnership

con·so·ci·a·tion \-,sō-sē-'ā-shən, -shē-\ *noun* (1593)
1 : association in fellowship or alliance
2 : an association of churches or religious societies
3 : an ecological community with a single dominant species
— **con·so·ci·a·tion·al** \-shnəl, -shə-nᵊl\ *adjective*

con·so·la·tion \,kän(t)-sə-'lā-shən\ *noun* (14th century)
1 : the act or an instance of consoling : the state of being consoled : COMFORT
2 : something that consoles; *specifically* : a contest held for those who have lost early in a tournament ⟨the losers met in a *consolation* game⟩
— **con·so·la·to·ry** \kən-'sō-lə-,tōr-ē, -'sä-, -,tòr-\ *adjective*

consolation prize *noun* (1886)
: a prize given to a runner-up or a loser in a contest

¹**con·sole** \'kän-,sōl\ *noun* [French] (1664)
1 : an architectural member projecting from a wall to form a bracket or from a keystone for ornament
2 : CONSOLE TABLE
3 a : an upright case which houses the keyboards and controlling mechanisms of an organ and from which the organ is played **b** : a combination of readouts or displays and an input device (as a keyboard or switches) by which an operator can monitor and interact with a system (as a computer or dubber)
4 a : a cabinet (as for a radio or television set) designed to rest directly on the floor **b** : a small storage cabinet between bucket seats in an automobile

²**con·sole** \kən-'sōl\ *transitive verb* **con·soled; con·sol·ing** [French *consoler*, from Latin *consolari*, from *com-* + *solari* to console] (1693)
: to alleviate the grief, sense of loss, or trouble of : COMFORT ⟨*console* a widow⟩
— **con·sol·ing·ly** \-'sō-liŋ-lē\ *adverb*

console table *noun* (1813)
: a table fixed to a wall with its top supported by consoles or front legs; *broadly* : a table designed to fit against a wall

console table

con·sol·i·date \kən-'sä-lə-,dāt\ *verb* **-dat·ed; -dat·ing** [Latin *consolidatus*, past participle of *consolidare* to make solid, from *com-* + *solidus* solid] (circa 1512)
transitive verb
1 : to join together into one whole : UNITE ⟨*consolidate* several small school districts⟩
2 : to make firm or secure : STRENGTHEN ⟨*consolidate* their hold on first place⟩

☆ **SYNONYMS**
Consider, study, contemplate, weigh mean to think about in order to arrive at a judgment or decision. CONSIDER may suggest giving thought to in order to reach a suitable conclusion, opinion, or decision ⟨refused even to *consider* my proposal⟩. STUDY implies sustained purposeful concentration and attention to details and minutiae ⟨*study* the plan closely⟩. CONTEMPLATE stresses focusing one's thoughts on something but does not imply coming to a conclusion or decision ⟨*contemplate* the consequences of refusing⟩. WEIGH implies attempting to reach the truth or arrive at a decision by balancing conflicting claims or evidence ⟨*weigh* the pros and cons of the case⟩.

3 : to form into a compact mass
intransitive verb
: to become consolidated; *specifically* **:** MERGE ⟨the two companies *consolidated*⟩
— **con·sol·i·da·tor** \-ˌdā-tər\ *noun*
consolidated school *noun* (1911)
: a public school formed by merging other schools
con·sol·i·da·tion \kən-ˌsä-lə-'dā-shən\ *noun* (15th century)
1 : the act or process of consolidating **:** the state of being consolidated
2 : the process of uniting **:** the quality or state of being united; *specifically* **:** the unification of two or more corporations by dissolution of existing ones and creation of a single new corporation
3 : pathological alteration of lung tissue from an aerated condition to one of solid consistency
con·som·mé \ˌkän(t)-sə-'mā\ *noun* [French, from past participle of *consommer* to complete, boil down, from Latin *consummare* to complete — more at CONSUMMATE] (1815)
: clear soup made from well-seasoned stock
con·so·nance \'kän(t)-s(ə-)nən(t)s\ *noun* (15th century)
1 : harmony or agreement among components
2 a : correspondence or recurrence of sounds especially in words; *specifically* **:** recurrence or repetition of consonants especially at the end of stressed syllables without the similar correspondence of vowels (as in the final sounds of "stroke" and "luck") **b :** CONCORD 1b
c : SYMPATHETIC VIBRATION, RESONANCE
con·so·nan·cy \-s(ə-)nən(t)-sē\ *noun, plural* **-cies** (14th century)
: CONSONANCE 1
¹con·so·nant \'kän(t)-s(ə-)nənt\ *adjective* [Middle French, from Latin *consonant-, consonans,* present participle of *consonare* to sound together, agree, from *com- + sonare* to sound — more at SOUND] (15th century)
1 : being in agreement or harmony **:** free from elements making for discord
2 : marked by musical consonances
3 : having similar sounds ⟨*consonant* words⟩
4 : relating to or exhibiting consonance **:** RESONANT
— **con·so·nant·ly** *adverb*
²consonant *noun* [Middle English, from Latin *consonant-, consonans,* from present participle of *consonare*] (14th century)
: one of a class of speech sounds (as \p\, \g\, \n\, \l\, \s\, \r\) characterized by constriction or closure at one or more points in the breath channel; *also* **:** a letter representing a consonant — usually used in English of any letter except *a, e, i, o,* and *u*
con·so·nan·tal \ˌkän(t)-sə-'nan-tᵊl\ *adjective* (1795)
: relating to, being, or marked by a consonant or group of consonants
consonant shift *noun* (1888)
: a set of regular changes in consonant articulation in the history of a language or dialect: **a :** such a set affecting the Indo-European stops and distinguishing the Germanic languages from the other Indo-European languages — compare GRIMM'S LAW **b :** such a set affecting the Germanic stops and distinguishing High German from the other Germanic languages
¹con·sort \'kän-ˌsȯrt\ *noun* [Middle English, from Middle French, from Latin *consort-, consors* partner, sharer, from *com- + sort-, sors* lot, share — more at SERIES] (15th century)
1 : ASSOCIATE
2 : a ship accompanying another
3 : SPOUSE — compare PRINCE CONSORT
²consort *noun* [Middle French *consorte,* from *consort*] (1584)
1 : GROUP, ASSEMBLY ⟨a *consort* of specialists⟩
2 : CONJUNCTION, ASSOCIATION ⟨he ruled in *consort* with his father⟩

3 a : a group of singers or instrumentalists performing together **b :** a set of musical instruments of the same family
³con·sort \kən-'sȯrt, kän-', 'kän-,\ (1588)
transitive verb
1 : UNITE, ASSOCIATE
2 *obsolete* **:** ESCORT
intransitive verb
1 : to keep company ⟨*consorting* with criminals⟩
2 *obsolete* **:** to make harmony **:** PLAY
3 : ACCORD, HARMONIZE ⟨the illustrations *consort* admirably with the text —*Times Literary Supplement*⟩
con·sor·tium \kən-'sȯr-sh(ē-)əm, -'sȯr-tē-əm\ *noun, plural* **-sor·tia** \-'sȯr-sh(ē-)ə, -'sȯr-tē-ə\ *also* **-sortiums** [Latin, fellowship, from *consort-, consors*] (1829)
1 : an agreement, combination, or group (as of companies) formed to undertake an enterprise beyond the resources of any one member
2 : ASSOCIATION, SOCIETY
3 : the legal right of one spouse to the company, affection, and assistance of and to sexual relations with the other
con·spe·cif·ic \ˌkän(t)-spi-'si-fik\ *adjective* (1859)
: of the same species
— **conspecific** *noun*
con·spec·tus \kən-'spek-təs\ *noun* [Latin, from *conspectus,* from *conspicere*] (circa 1837)
1 : a usually brief survey or summary (as of an extensive subject) often providing an overall view
2 : OUTLINE, SYNOPSIS
con·spi·cu·i·ty \ˌkän(t)-spə-'kyü-ə-tē\ *noun* (1601)
: the quality or state of being conspicuous **:** CONSPICUOUSNESS
con·spic·u·ous \kən-'spi-kyə-wəs\ *adjective* [Latin *conspicuus,* from *conspicere* to get sight of, from *com- + specere* to look — more at SPY] (1545)
1 : obvious to the eye or mind
2 : attracting attention **:** STRIKING
3 : marked by a noticeable violation of good taste
synonym see NOTICEABLE
— **con·spic·u·ous·ly** *adverb*
— **con·spic·u·ous·ness** \-nəs\ *noun*
conspicuous consumption *noun* (1899)
: lavish or wasteful spending thought to enhance social prestige
con·spir·a·cy \kən-'spir-ə-sē\ *noun, plural* **-cies** [Middle English *conspiracie,* from Latin *conspirare*] (14th century)
1 : the act of conspiring together
2 a : an agreement among conspirators **b :** a group of conspirators
synonym see PLOT
conspiracy of silence (1865)
: a secret agreement to keep silent about an occurrence, situation, or subject especially in order to promote or protect selfish interests
con·spi·ra·tion \ˌkän(t)-spə-'rā-shən, ˌkän-(ˌ)spi-'rā-\ *noun* (14th century)
1 : the act or action of plotting or secretly combining
2 : a joint effort toward a particular end
— **con·spi·ra·tion·al** \-shnəl, -shə-nᵊl\ *adjective*
con·spir·a·tor \kən-'spir-ə-tər\ *noun* (15th century)
: one that conspires **:** PLOTTER
con·spir·a·to·ri·al \kən-ˌspir-ə-'tȯr-ē-əl, -'tȯr-\ *adjective* (1855)
: of, relating to, or suggestive of a conspiracy
— **con·spir·a·to·ri·al·ly** \-ē-ə-lē\ *adverb*
con·spire \kən-'spīr\ *verb* **con·spired; con·spir·ing** [Middle English, from Middle French *conspirer,* from Latin *conspirare* to be in harmony, conspire, from *com- + spirare* to breathe] (14th century)
transitive verb
: PLOT, CONTRIVE

intransitive verb
1 a : to join in a secret agreement to do an unlawful or wrongful act or an act which becomes unlawful as a result of the secret agreement **b :** SCHEME
2 : to act in harmony toward a common end ⟨circumstances *conspired* to defeat his efforts⟩
con spi·ri·to \kän-'spir-ə-ˌtō, kōn-\ *adverb* [Italian] (circa 1891)
: with spirit or animation — used as a direction in music
con·sta·ble \'kän(t)-stə-bəl, 'kən(t)-\ *noun* [Middle English *conestable,* from Old French, from Late Latin *comes stabuli,* literally, officer of the stable] (13th century)
1 : a high officer of a medieval royal or noble household
2 : the warden or governor of a royal castle or a fortified town
3 a : a public officer usually of a town or township responsible for keeping the peace and for minor judicial duties **b** *British* **:** POLICE OFFICER; *especially* **:** one ranking below sergeant ◇
¹con·stab·u·lary \kən-'sta-byə-ˌler-ē\ *adjective* (1824)
: of or relating to a constable or constabulary
²constabulary *noun, plural* **-lar·ies** (1837)
1 : the organized body of constables of a particular district or country
2 : an armed police force organized on military lines but distinct from the regular army
con·stan·cy \'kän(t)-stən(t)-sē\ *noun, plural* **-cies** (14th century)
1 a : steadfastness of mind under duress **:** FORTITUDE **b :** FIDELITY, LOYALTY
2 : a state of being constant or unchanging
¹con·stant \'kän(t)-stənt\ *adjective* [Middle English, from Middle French, from Latin *constant-, constans,* from present participle of *constare* to stand firm, be consistent, from *com- + stare* to stand — more at STAND] (14th century)
1 : marked by firm steadfast resolution or faithfulness **:** exhibiting constancy of mind or attachment
2 : INVARIABLE, UNIFORM
3 : continually occurring or recurring **:** REGULAR
synonym see FAITHFUL, CONTINUAL
— **con·stant·ly** *adverb*
²constant *noun* (1832)

◇ WORD HISTORY
constable In the late Roman Empire, *comes stabuli,* literally, "count of the stable," became the title of various high-ranking civil and military officers whose duties extended far beyond the care of the imperial horses. (A word whose history shows a similar broadening of meaning is *marshal.*) Shrunk in early Medieval Latin to *constabulum,* it appears in Old French as *conestable,* which under the Capetian rulers of France could denote the sovereign's chief executive officer, the commander of an army, or the governor of a royal castle or domain. *Conestable* became the designation for the same functionaries in England after the Norman Conquest. In the 13th century, it was also applied to lower-ranking officers of the king's peace in English shires and towns. With the gradual reshaping of the constabulary in recent centuries into a police force, *constable* in Britain has now become virtually synonymous with "police officer." See in addition MARSHAL.

\ə\ abut \ᵊ\ kitten \ər\ further \a\ ash \ā\ ace
\ä\ mop, mar \au̇\ out \ch\ chin \e\ bet \ē\ easy
\g\ go \i\ hit \ī\ ice \j\ job \ŋ\ sing \ō\ go
\ȯ\ law \ȯi\ boy \th\ thin \t͟h\ the \ü\ loot \u̇\ foot
\y\ yet \zh\ vision *see also* Guide to Pronunciation

: something invariable or unchanging: as **a** : a number that has a fixed value in a given situation or universally or that is characteristic of some substance or instrument **b** : a number that is assumed not to change value in a given mathematical discussion **c** : a term in logic with a fixed designation

con·stan·tan \'kän(t)-stən-,tan\ *noun* [from the fact that its resistance remains constant under change of temperature] (1903)
: an alloy of copper and nickel used for electrical resistors and in thermocouples

con·sta·tive \kən-'stā-tiv, 'kän-stə-tiv\ *adjective* [*constate* to assert positively, from French *constater*, from Latin *constat* it is certain, 3d singular present indicative of *constare*] (1901)
1 : of, relating to, or being a verbal form that expresses past completed action
2 : being or relating to an utterance (as an assertion, question, or command) that is capable of being judged true or false
— **constative** *noun*

con·stel·late \'kän(t)-stə-,lāt\ *verb* **-lat·ed; -lat·ing** (1643)
transitive verb
1 : to unite in a cluster
2 : to set or adorn with or as if with constellations
intransitive verb
: CLUSTER

con·stel·la·tion \,kän(t)-stə-'lā-shən\ *noun* [Middle English *constellacioun*, from Middle French *constellation*, from Late Latin *constellation-*, *constellatio*, from Latin *com-* + *stella* star — more at STAR] (14th century)
1 : the configuration of stars especially at one's birth
2 : any of 88 arbitrary configurations of stars or an area of the celestial sphere covering one of these configurations
3 : an assemblage, collection, or gathering of usually related persons, qualities, or things ⟨a *constellation* of . . . relatives, friends, and hangers-on —Brendan Gill⟩
4 : PATTERN, ARRANGEMENT ⟨taking advantage of the shifting *constellation* of power throughout the known world —H. D. Lasswell⟩
— **con·stel·la·to·ry** \kən-'ste-lə-,tōr-ē, -,tȯr-\ *adjective*

con·ster·nate \'kän(t)-stər-,nāt\ *transitive verb* **-nat·ed; -nat·ing** (1651)
: to fill with consternation

con·ster·na·tion \,kän(t)-stər-'nā-shən\ *noun* [French or Latin; French, from Latin *consternation-*, *consternatio*, from *consternare* to throw into confusion, from *com-* + *-sternare*, probably from *sternere* to spread, strike down — more at STREW] (circa 1611)
: amazement or dismay that hinders or throws into confusion ⟨the two . . . stared at each other in *consternation*, and neither knew what to do —Pearl Buck⟩

con·sti·pate \'kän(t)-stə-,pāt\ *transitive verb* **-pat·ed; -pat·ing** [Medieval Latin *constipatus*, past participle of *constipare*, from Latin, to crowd together, from *com-* + *stipare* to pack tight — more at STIFF] (1533)
1 : to cause constipation in
2 : to make immobile, inactive, or dull : STULTIFY ⟨so much clutter . . . will tend to *constipate* the novel's working order —*Times Literary Supplement*⟩

con·sti·pat·ed \-,pā-təd\ *adjective* (1547)
1 : affected with constipation
2 : stilted or stodgy in appearance, expression, or action

con·sti·pa·tion \,kän(t)-stə-'pā-shən\ *noun* (15th century)
1 : abnormally delayed or infrequent passage of usually dry hardened feces
2 : STULTIFICATION

con·stit·u·en·cy \kən-'stich-wən(t)-sē, -'sti-chə-\ *noun, plural* **-cies** (1831)
1 a : a body of citizens entitled to elect a representative (as to a legislative or executive po-

sition) **b** : the residents in an electoral district
c : an electoral district
2 a : a group or body that patronizes, supports, or offers representation ⟨creating . . . a grass-roots *constituency* for continuing the project —Fred Reed⟩ **b** : the people involved in or served by an organization (as a business or institution) ⟨regards its corporate customers as its prime *constituency* —Andrew Hacker⟩

¹con·stit·u·ent \-wənt\ *noun* [French *constituant*, from Middle French, from present participle of *constituer* to constitute, from Latin *constituere*] (1622)
1 : one who authorizes another to act as agent : PRINCIPAL
2 : a member of a constituency
3 : an essential part : COMPONENT, ELEMENT
4 : a structural unit of a definable syntactic, semantic, or phonological category that consists of one or more linguistic elements (as words, morphemes, or features) and that can occur as a component of a larger construction
synonym see ELEMENT

²constituent *adjective* [Latin *constituent-*, *constituens*, present participle of *constituere*] (1660)
1 : serving to form, compose, or make up a unit or whole : COMPONENT
2 : having the power to create a government or frame or amend a constitution ⟨a *constituent* assembly⟩
— **con·stit·u·ent·ly** *adverb*

con·sti·tute \'kän(t)-stə-,tüt, -,tyüt\ *transitive verb* **-tut·ed; -tut·ing** [Middle English, from Latin *constitutus*, past participle of *constituere* to set up, constitute, from *com-* + *statuere* to set — more at STATUTE] (15th century)
1 : to appoint to an office, function, or dignity
2 : SET UP, ESTABLISH: as **a** : ENACT **b** : FOUND **c** (1) : to give due or lawful form to (2) : to legally process
3 : MAKE UP, FORM, COMPOSE ⟨12 months *constitute* a year⟩ ⟨high school dropouts who *constitute* a major problem in large city slums —J. B. Conant⟩

con·sti·tu·tion \,kän(t)-stə-'tü-shən, -'tyü-\ *noun* (14th century)
1 : an established law or custom : ORDINANCE
2 a : the physical makeup of the individual comprising inherited qualities modified by environment **b** : the structure, composition, physical makeup, or nature of something
3 : the act of establishing, making, or setting up
4 : the mode in which a state or society is organized; *especially* : the manner in which sovereign power is distributed
5 a : the basic principles and laws of a nation, state, or social group that determine the powers and duties of the government and guarantee certain rights to the people in it **b** : a written instrument embodying the rules of a political or social organization
— **con·sti·tu·tion·less** \-ləs\ *adjective*

¹con·sti·tu·tion·al \-shnəl, -shə-n°l\ *adjective* (1682)
1 : relating to, inherent in, or affecting the constitution of body or mind
2 : of, relating to, or entering into the fundamental makeup of something : ESSENTIAL
3 : being in accordance with or authorized by the constitution of a state or society ⟨a *constitutional* government⟩
4 : regulated by or ruling according to a constitution ⟨a *constitutional* monarchy⟩
5 : of or relating to a constitution
6 : loyal to or supporting an established constitution or form of government

²constitutional *noun* (1829)
: a walk taken for one's health

con·sti·tu·tion·al·ism \-sh(ə-)nə-,li-zəm\ *noun* (1832)
: adherence to or government according to constitutional principles; *also* : a constitutional system of government
— **con·sti·tu·tion·al·ist** \-list\ *noun*

con·sti·tu·tion·al·i·ty \-,tü-shə-'na-lə-tē, -,tyü-\ *noun* (1787)
: the quality or state of being constitutional; *especially* : accordance with the provisions of a constitution ⟨questioned the *constitutionality* of the law⟩

con·sti·tu·tion·al·ize \-'tü-shnə-,līz, -shə-n°l-,īz\ *transitive verb* **-ized; -iz·ing** (1831)
: to provide with a constitution : organize along constitutional principles
— **con·sti·tu·tion·al·i·za·tion** \-,tü-shnə-lə-'zā-shən, -shə-n°l-ə-\ *noun*

con·sti·tu·tion·al·ly \-'tü-shnə-lē, -'tyü-, -shə-n°l-ē\ *adverb* (1742)
1 a : in accordance with one's constitution ⟨*constitutionally* unable to grasp subtleties⟩ **b** : in structure, composition, or constitution ⟨despite repeated heatings the material remained *constitutionally* the same⟩
2 : in accordance with a political constitution ⟨was not *constitutionally* eligible to fill the office⟩

con·sti·tu·tive \'kän(t)-stə-,tü-tiv, -,tyü-; kən-'sti-chə-tiv\ *adjective* (1592)
1 : having the power to enact or establish : CONSTRUCTIVE
2 : CONSTITUENT, ESSENTIAL
3 : relating to or dependent on constitution ⟨a *constitutive* property of all electrolytes⟩
— **con·sti·tu·tive·ly** *adverb*

con·strain \kən-'strān\ *transitive verb* [Middle English, from Middle French *constraindre*, from Latin *constringere* to constrict, constrain, from *com-* + *stringere* to draw tight — more at STRAIN] (14th century)
1 a : to force by imposed stricture, restriction, or limitation **b** : to restrict the motion of (a mechanical body) to a particular mode
2 : COMPRESS; *also* : to clasp tightly
3 : to secure by or as if by bonds : CONFINE; *broadly* : LIMIT
4 : to force or produce in an unnatural or strained manner ⟨a *constrained* smile⟩
5 : to hold back by or as if by force ⟨*constraining* my mind not to wander from the task —Charles Dickens⟩
synonym see FORCE
— **con·strained·ly** \-'strā-nəd-lē, -'strānd-lē\ *adverb*

con·straint \kən-'strānt\ *noun* [Middle English, from Middle French *constrainte*, from *constraindre*] (15th century)
1 a : the act of constraining **b** : the state of being checked, restricted, or compelled to avoid or perform some action ⟨the *constraint* and monotony of a monastic life —Matthew Arnold⟩ **c** : a constraining condition, agency, or force : CHECK ⟨put legal *constraints* on the board's activities⟩
2 a : repression of one's own feelings, behavior, or actions **b** : a sense of being constrained : EMBARRASSMENT

con·strict \kən-'strikt\ *verb* [Latin *constrictus*, past participle of *constringere*] (1732)
transitive verb
1 a : to make narrow or draw together **b** : COMPRESS, SQUEEZE ⟨*constrict* a nerve⟩
2 : to stultify, stop, or cause to falter : INHIBIT
intransitive verb
: to become constricted
synonym see CONTRACT
— **con·stric·tive** \-'strik-tiv\ *adjective*

con·stric·tion \-'strik-shən\ *noun* (15th century)
1 : an act or product of constricting
2 : the quality or state of being constricted
3 : something that constricts

con·stric·tor \-'strik-tər\ *noun* (1735)
1 : a muscle that contracts a cavity or orifice or compresses an organ
2 : a snake (as a boa *constrictor*) that kills prey by compression in its coils
3 : one that constricts

con·stringe \kən-'strinj\ *transitive verb* **con·stringed; con·string·ing** [Latin *constringere*] (1604)

1 : to cause to shrink ⟨cold *constringes* the pores⟩
2 : CONSTRICT
— **con·strin·gent** \-'strin-jənt\ *adjective*

¹**con·struct** \kən-'strəkt\ *transitive verb* [Latin *constructus*, past participle of *construere*, from *com-* + *struere* to build — more at STRUCTURE] (1663)
1 : to make or form by combining or arranging parts or elements **:** BUILD; *also* **:** CONTRIVE, DEVISE
2 : to draw (a geometrical figure) with suitable instruments and under specified conditions
3 : to set in logical order
— **con·struct·ible** \-'strək-tə-bəl\ *adjective*
— **con·struc·tor** \-tər\ *noun*

²**con·struct** \'kän-,strəkt\ *noun* (1933)
1 : something constructed by the mind: as **a** **:** a theoretical entity ⟨the deductive study of abstract *constructs* —Daniel J. Boorstin⟩ **b :** a working hypothesis or concept ⟨a point of view which made "abroad" singularly containable as a literary *construct* —Jonathan Raban⟩ **c :** a product of mental invention ⟨the novel . . . a verbal *construct* in which invented human characters appear —Anthony Burgess⟩
2 : something produced by human effort ⟨the East bloc was always an unnatural *construct* —Walter Isaacson⟩

con·struc·tion \kən-'strək-shən\ *noun* (14th century)
1 : the act or result of construing, interpreting, or explaining
2 a : the process, art, or manner of constructing something; *also* **:** a thing constructed **b :** the construction industry ⟨working in *construction*⟩
3 : the arrangement and connection of words or groups of words in a sentence **:** syntactical arrangement
4 : a sculpture that is put together out of separate pieces of often disparate materials
— **con·struc·tion·al** \-shnəl, -shə-n°l\ *adjective*
— **con·struc·tion·al·ly** *adverb*

con·struc·tion·ist \-sh(ə-)nist\ *noun* (1838)
: one who construes a legal document (as the U.S. Constitution) in a specific way ⟨a strict *constructionist*⟩

construction paper *noun* (circa 1924)
: a thick groundwood paper available in many colors and used especially for school artwork

con·struc·tive \kən-'strək-tiv\ *adjective* (circa 1680)
1 : declared such by judicial construction or interpretation ⟨*constructive* fraud⟩
2 : of or relating to construction or creation
3 : promoting improvement or development ⟨*constructive* criticism⟩
— **con·struc·tive·ly** *adverb*
— **con·struc·tive·ness** *noun*

con·struc·tiv·ism \kän-'strək-ti-,vi-zəm\ *noun, often capitalized* (1925)
: a nonobjective art movement originating in Russia and concerned with formal organization of planes and expression of volume in terms of modern industrial materials (as glass and plastic)
— **con·struc·tiv·ist** \-vist\ *adjective or noun, often capitalized*

¹**con·strue** \kən-'strü\ *verb* **con·strued; con·stru·ing** [Middle English, from Late Latin *construere*, from Latin, to construct] (14th century)
transitive verb
1 : to analyze the arrangement and connection of words in (a sentence or sentence part)
2 : to understand or explain the sense or intention of usually in a particular way or with respect to a given set of circumstances ⟨*construed* my actions as hostile⟩
intransitive verb
: to construe a sentence or sentence part especially in connection with translating
— **con·stru·able** \-'strü-ə-bəl\ *adjective*

²**con·strue** \'kän-,strü\ *noun* (1844)
: an act or the result of construing especially by piecemeal translation

con·sub·stan·tial \,kän(t)-səb-'stan(t)-shəl\ *adjective* [Late Latin *consubstantialis*, from Latin *com-* + *substantia* substance] (14th century)
: of the same substance

con·sub·stan·ti·a·tion \,kän(t)-səb-,stan(t)-shē-'ā-shən\ *noun* (1597)
: the actual substantial presence and combination of the body and blood of Christ with the eucharistic bread and wine according to a teaching associated with Martin Luther — compare TRANSUBSTANTIATION

con·sue·tude \'kän(t)-swi-,tüd, kən-'sü-ə-, -,tyüd\ *noun* [Middle English, from Latin *consuetudo* — more at CUSTOM] (14th century)
: social usage **:** CUSTOM
— **con·sue·tu·di·nary** \,kän(t)-swi-'tü-də-,ner-ē, kən-,sü-ə-, -'tyü-\ *adjective*

con·sul \'kän(t)-səl\ *noun* [Middle English, from Latin; perhaps akin to Latin *consulere* to consult] (14th century)
1 a : either of two annually elected chief magistrates of the Roman republic **b :** one of three chief magistrates of the French republic from 1799 to 1804
2 : an official appointed by a government to reside in a foreign country to represent the commercial interests of citizens of the appointing country
— **con·sul·ar** \-s(ə-)lər\ *adjective*
— **con·sul·ship** \-səl-,ship\ *noun*

con·sul·ate \-s(ə-)lət\ *noun* (14th century)
1 : a government by consuls
2 : the office, term of office, or jurisdiction of a consul
3 : the residence or official premises of a consul

consulate general *noun, plural* **consulates general** (1883)
: the residence, office, or jurisdiction of a consul general

consul general *noun, plural* **consuls general** (1753)
: a consul of the first rank stationed in an important place or having jurisdiction in several places or over several consuls

¹**con·sult** \kən-'səlt\ *verb* [Middle French or Latin; Middle French *consulter*, from Latin *consultare*, frequentative of *consulere* to deliberate, counsel, consult] (1527)
transitive verb
1 : to have regard to **:** CONSIDER
2 a : to ask the advice or opinion of ⟨*consult* a doctor⟩ **b :** to refer to ⟨*consult* a dictionary⟩
intransitive verb
1 : to consult an individual
2 : to deliberate together **:** CONFER
3 : to serve as a consultant
— **con·sult·er** *noun*

²**con·sult** \kən-'səlt, 'kän-,\ *noun* (1560)
: CONSULTATION

con·sul·tan·cy \kən-'səl-t°n(t)-sē\ *noun, plural* **-cies** (1955)
1 : CONSULTATION
2 : an agency that provides consulting services
3 : the position of a consultant

con·sul·tant \kən-'səl-t°nt\ *noun* (1697)
1 : one who consults another
2 : one who gives professional advice or services **:** EXPERT
— **con·sul·tant·ship** \-,ship\ *noun*

con·sul·ta·tion \,kän(t)-səl-'tā-shən\ *noun* (15th century)
1 : COUNCIL, CONFERENCE; *specifically* **:** a deliberation between physicians on a case or its treatment
2 : the act of consulting or conferring

con·sul·ta·tive \kən-'səl-tə-tiv, 'kän(t)-səl-,tā-tiv\ *adjective* (1583)
: of, relating to, or intended for consultation **:** ADVISORY ⟨*consultative* committee⟩

con·sult·ing \kən-'səl-tiŋ\ *adjective* (1801)

1 : providing professional or expert advice ⟨a *consulting* architect⟩
2 : of or relating to consultation or a consultant ⟨the *consulting* room of a psychiatrist⟩

con·sul·tive \kən-'səl-tiv\ *adjective* (1616)
: CONSULTATIVE

con·sul·tor \kən-'səl-tər\ *noun* (1611)
: one that consults or advises; *especially* **:** an adviser to a Roman Catholic bishop, provincial, or sacred congregation

¹**con·sum·able** \kən-'sü-mə-bəl\ *adjective* (1641)
: capable of being consumed

²**consumable** *noun* (1802)
: something (as food or fuel) that is consumable — usually used in plural

con·sume \kən-'süm\ *verb* **con·sumed; con·sum·ing** [Middle English, from Middle French or Latin; Middle French *consumer*, from Latin *consumere*, from *com-* + *sumere* to take up, take, from *sub-* up + *emere* to take — more at SUB-, REDEEM] (14th century)
transitive verb
1 : to do away with completely **:** DESTROY ⟨fire *consumed* several buildings⟩
2 a : to spend wastefully **:** SQUANDER **b :** USE UP ⟨writing *consumed* much of his time⟩
3 : to eat or drink especially in great quantity ⟨*consumed* several kegs of beer⟩
4 : to engage fully **:** ENGROSS ⟨*consumed* with curiosity⟩
intransitive verb
1 : to waste or burn away **:** PERISH
2 : to utilize economic goods

con·sum·ed·ly \-'sü-məd-lē\ *adverb* (1707)
: as if consumed **:** EXCESSIVELY

con·sum·er \kən-'sü-mər\ *noun, often attributive* (15th century)
: one that consumes: as **a :** one that utilizes economic goods **b :** an organism requiring complex organic compounds for food which it obtains by preying on other organisms or by eating particles of organic matter — compare PRODUCER 4
— **con·sum·er·ship** \-,ship\ *noun*

consumer credit *noun* (1927)
: credit granted to an individual especially to finance the purchase of consumer goods or to defray personal expenses

consumer goods *noun plural* (1890)
: goods that directly satisfy human wants

con·sum·er·ism \kən-'sü-mə-,ri-zəm\ *noun* (1944)
1 : the promotion of the consumer's interests
2 : the theory that an increasing consumption of goods is economically desirable; *also* **:** a preoccupation with and an inclination toward the buying of consumer goods
— **con·sum·er·ist** \-rist\ *noun*
— **con·sum·er·is·tic** \kən-,sü-mə-'ris-tik\ *adjective*

consumer price index *noun* (1948)
: an index measuring the change in the cost of typical wage-earner purchases of goods and services expressed as a percentage of the cost of these same goods and services in some base period — called also *cost-of-living index*

con·sum·ing \kən-'sü-miŋ\ *adjective* (1920)
: deeply felt **:** ARDENT ⟨a *consuming* interest⟩; *also* **:** ENGROSSING

¹**con·sum·mate** \'kän(t)-sə-mət, kən-'sə-mət\ *adjective* [Middle English *consummat* fulfilled, from Latin *consummatus*, past participle of *consummare* to sum up, finish, from *com-* + *summa* sum] (1527)
1 : complete in every detail **:** PERFECT
2 : extremely skilled and accomplished ⟨a *consummate* liar⟩
3 : of the highest degree ⟨*consummate* skill⟩ ⟨*consummate* cruelty⟩

\ə\ abut \ᵊ\ kitten \ər\ further \a\ ash \ā\ ace
\ä\ mop, mar \au̇\ out \ch\ chin \e\ bet \ē\ easy
\g\ go \i\ hit \ī\ ice \j\ job \ŋ\ sing \ō\ go
\ȯ\ law \ȯi\ boy \th\ thin \th\ the \ü\ loot \u̇\ foot
\y\ yet \zh\ vision *see also* Guide to Pronunciation

— **con·sum·mate·ly** *adverb*

²**con·sum·mate** \'kän(t)-sə-ˌmāt\ *verb* **-mat·ed; -mat·ing** (1530)
transitive verb
1 a : FINISH, COMPLETE ⟨*consummate* a business deal⟩ **b :** to make perfect **c :** ACHIEVE
2 : to make (marital union) complete by sexual intercourse ⟨*consummate* a marriage⟩
intransitive verb
: to become perfected
— **con·sum·ma·tive** \'kän(t)-sə-ˌmā-tiv, kən-'sə-mə-tiv\ *adjective*
— **con·sum·ma·tor** \'kän(t)-sə-ˌmāt-ər\ *noun*

con·sum·ma·tion \ˌkän-sə-'mā-shən\ *noun* (14th century)
1 : the act of consummating ⟨the *consummation* of a contract by mutual signature⟩; *specifically* **:** the consummating of a marriage
2 : the ultimate end **:** FINISH

con·sum·ma·to·ry \kən-'sə-mə-ˌtōr-ē, -ˌtȯr-\ *adjective* (1648)
1 : of or relating to consummation **:** CONCLUDING
2 : of, relating to, or being a response or act (as eating or copulating) that terminates a period of usually goal-directed behavior

con·sump·tion \kən-'səm(p)-shən\ *noun* [Middle English *consumpcioun*, from Latin *consumption-, consumptio,* from *consumere*] (14th century)
1 a : a progressive wasting away of the body especially from pulmonary tuberculosis **b :** TUBERCULOSIS
2 : the act or process of consuming
3 : the utilization of economic goods in the satisfaction of wants or in the process of production resulting chiefly in their destruction, deterioration, or transformation

¹**con·sump·tive** \-'səm(p)-tiv\ *adjective* (1664)
1 : tending to consume
2 : of, relating to, or affected with consumption
— **con·sump·tive·ly** *adverb*

²**consumptive** *noun* (1666)
: a person affected with consumption

¹**con·tact** \'kän-ˌtakt\ *noun* [French or Latin; French, from Latin *contactus,* from *contingere* to have contact with — more at CONTINGENT] (1626)
1 a : union or junction of surfaces **b :** the apparent touching or mutual tangency of the limbs of two celestial bodies or of the disk of one body with the shadow of another during an eclipse, transit, or occultation **c** (1) **:** the junction of two electrical conductors through which a current passes (2) **:** a special part made for such a junction
2 a : ASSOCIATION, RELATIONSHIP **b :** CONNECTION, COMMUNICATION **c :** an establishing of communication with someone or an observing or receiving of a significant signal from a person or object ⟨radar *contact* with Mars⟩
3 : a person serving as a go-between, messenger, connection, or source of special information ⟨business *contacts*⟩
4 : CONTACT LENS

²**con·tact** \'kän-ˌtakt, kən-'\ (1834)
intransitive verb
: to make contact
transitive verb
1 : to bring into contact
2 a : to enter or be in contact with **:** JOIN **b :** to get in communication with ⟨*contact* your local dealer⟩ □

³**con·tact** \'kän-ˌtakt\ *adjective* (1859)
: maintaining, involving, or activated or caused by contact ⟨*contact* poisons⟩ ⟨*contact* sports⟩

contact binary *noun* (1952)
: a binary star system in which the two stars are close enough together for material to pass between them

contact hitter *noun* (1982)
: a hitter in baseball who seldom strikes out

contact inhibition *noun* (1965)
: cessation of cellular undulating movements upon contact with other cells with accompanying cessation of cell growth and division

contact language *noun* (1950)
: PIDGIN

contact lens *noun* (1888)
: a thin lens designed to fit over the cornea and usually worn to correct defects in vision

contact print *noun* (1890)
: a photographic print made with the negative in contact with the sensitized paper, plate, or film

con·ta·gion \kən-'tā-jən\ *noun* [Middle English, from Middle French & Latin; Middle French, from Latin *contagion-, contagio,* from *contingere* to have contact with, pollute] (14th century)
1 a : a contagious disease **b :** the transmission of a disease by direct or indirect contact **c :** a disease-producing agent (as a virus)
2 a : POISON **b :** contagious influence, quality, or nature **c :** corrupting influence or contact
3 a : rapid communication of an influence (as a doctrine or emotional state) **b :** an influence that spreads rapidly

con·ta·gious \-jəs\ *adjective* (14th century)
1 : communicable by contact **:** CATCHING ⟨*contagious* diseases⟩
2 : bearing contagion
3 : used for contagious diseases ⟨a *contagious* ward⟩
4 : exciting similar emotions or conduct in others ⟨*contagious* enthusiasm⟩
— **con·ta·gious·ly** *adverb*
— **con·ta·gious·ness** *noun*

contagious abortion *noun* (1910)
: a contagious or infectious disease (as a brucellosis) of domestic animals characterized by abortion

con·ta·gium \kən-'tā-j(ē-)əm\ *noun, plural* **-gia** \-j(ē-)ə\ [Latin, contagion, from *contingere*] (1870)
: a virus or living organism capable of causing a communicable disease

con·tain \kən-'tān\ *verb* [Middle English *conteinen,* from Old French *contenir,* from Latin *continēre* to hold together, hold in, contain, from *com-* + *tenēre* to hold — more at THIN] (14th century)
transitive verb
1 : to keep within limits: as **a :** RESTRAIN, CONTROL **b :** CHECK, HALT **c :** to follow successfully a policy of containment toward **d :** to prevent (as an enemy or opponent) from advancing or from making a successful attack
2 a : to have within **:** HOLD **b :** COMPRISE, INCLUDE
3 a : to be divisible by usually without a remainder **b :** ENCLOSE, BOUND
intransitive verb
: to restrain oneself ☆
— **con·tain·able** \-'tā-nə-bəl\ *adjective*

contained *adjective* (1653)
: RESTRAINED; *also* **:** CALM

con·tain·er \kən-'tā-nər\ *noun* (15th century)
: one that contains; *especially* **:** a receptacle (as a box or jar) for holding goods
— **con·tain·er·less** \-ləs\ *adjective*

con·tain·er·board \-ˌbōrd, -ˌbȯrd\ *noun* (circa 1924)
: corrugated or solid paperboard used for making containers

con·tain·er·i·sa·tion, **con·tain·er·ise**
British variant of CONTAINERIZATION, CONTAINERIZE

con·tain·er·i·za·tion \kən-ˌtā-nə-rə-'zā-shən\ *noun* (1956)
: a shipping method in which a large amount of material (as merchandise) is packaged into large standardized containers

con·tain·er·ize \kən-'tā-nə-ˌrīz\ *transitive verb* **-ized; -iz·ing** (1956)
1 : to ship by containerization
2 : to pack in containers

con·tain·er·port \-nər-ˌpōrt, -ˌpȯrt\ *noun* (1970)
: a shipping port specially equipped to handle containerized cargo

con·tain·er·ship \-nər-ˌship\ *noun* (1966)
: a ship specially designed or equipped for carrying containerized cargo

con·tain·ment \kən-'tān-mənt\ *noun* (1655)
1 : the act, process, or means of containing
2 : the policy, process, or result of preventing the expansion of a hostile power or ideology

con·tam·i·nant \kən-'ta-mə-nənt\ *noun* (1922)
: something that contaminates

con·tam·i·nate \kən-'ta-mə-ˌnāt\ *transitive verb* **-nat·ed; -nat·ing** [Middle English, from Latin *contaminatus,* past participle of *contaminare;* akin to Latin *contagio* contagion] (15th century)
1 a : to soil, stain, corrupt, or infect by contact or association ⟨bacteria *contaminated* the wound⟩ **b :** to make inferior or impure by admixture ⟨iron *contaminated* with phosphorus⟩
2 : to make unfit for use by the introduction of unwholesome or undesirable elements ☆
— **con·tam·i·na·tive** \-ˌnā-tiv\ *adjective*
— **con·tam·i·na·tor** \-ˌnā-tər\ *noun*

con·tam·i·na·tion \kən-ˌta-mə-'nā-shən\ *noun* (15th century)
1 : a process of contaminating **:** a state of being contaminated
2 : CONTAMINANT

conte \'kōⁿ(n)t\ *noun* [French] (1891)
: a usually short tale of adventure

con·temn \kən-'tem\ *transitive verb* [Middle English *contempnen,* from Middle French *contempner,* from Latin *contemnere,* from *com-* + *temnere* to despise] (15th century)
: to view or treat with contempt **:** SCORN
synonym *see* DESPISE
— **con·tem·ner** *also* **con·tem·nor** \-'tem-nər, -'te-mər\ *noun*

☆ SYNONYMS
Contain, hold, accommodate mean to have or be capable of having within. CONTAIN implies the actual presence of a specified substance or quantity within something ⟨the can *contains* a quart of oil⟩. HOLD implies the capacity of containing or the usual or permanent function of containing or keeping ⟨the bookcase will *hold* all my textbooks⟩. ACCOMMODATE stresses holding without crowding or inconvenience ⟨the hall can *accommodate* 500 people⟩.

Contaminate, taint, pollute, defile mean to make impure or unclean. CONTAMINATE implies intrusion of or contact with dirt or foulness from an outside source ⟨water *contaminated* by industrial wastes⟩. TAINT stresses the loss of purity or cleanliness that follows contamination ⟨*tainted* meat⟩ ⟨a politician's *tainted* reputation⟩. POLLUTE, sometimes interchangeable with *contaminate,* distinctively may imply that the process which begins with contamination is complete and that what was pure or clean has been made foul, poisoned, or filthy ⟨the *polluted* waters of the river⟩. DEFILE implies befouling of what could or should have been kept clean and pure or held sacred and commonly suggests violation or desecration ⟨*defile* a hero's memory with slanderous innuendo⟩.

□ USAGE
contact The use of *contact* as a verb, especially in sense 2b, is accepted as standard by almost all commentators except those who write college handbooks.

con·tem·plate \'kän-təm-ˌplāt, -ˌtem-\ *verb* **-plat·ed; -plat·ing** [Latin *contemplatus,* past participle of *contemplari,* from *com-* + *templum* space marked out for observation of auguries — more at TEMPLE] (1537) *transitive verb*
1 : to view or consider with continued attention **:** meditate on
2 : to view as contingent or probable or as an end or intention *intransitive verb*
: PONDER, MEDITATE
synonym see CONSIDER
— **con·tem·pla·tor** \-ˌplā-tər\ *noun*
con·tem·pla·tion \ˌkän-təm-ˈplā-shən, -ˌtem-\ *noun* (13th century)
1 a : concentration on spiritual things as a form of private devotion **b :** a state of mystical awareness of God's being
2 : an act of considering with attention **:** STUDY
3 : the act of regarding steadily
4 : INTENTION, EXPECTATION
¹con·tem·pla·tive \kən-ˈtem-plə-tiv; 'kän-təm-ˌplā-, -ˌtem-\ *adjective* (14th century)
: marked by or given to contemplation; *specifically* **:** of or relating to a religious order devoted to prayer and penance
— **con·tem·pla·tive·ly** *adverb*
— **con·tem·pla·tive·ness** *noun*
²contemplative *noun* (14th century)
: a person who practices contemplation
con·tem·po·ra·ne·i·ty \kən-ˌtem-p(ə-)rə-'nē-ə-tē, -'nā-\ *noun* (1772)
: the quality or state of being contemporaneous or contemporary
con·tem·po·ra·ne·ous \kən-ˌtem-pə-'rā-nē-əs\ *adjective* [Latin *contemporaneus,* from *com-* + *tempor-, tempus* time] (circa 1656)
: existing, occurring, or originating during the same time
synonym see CONTEMPORARY
— **con·tem·po·ra·ne·ous·ly** *adverb*
— **con·tem·po·ra·ne·ous·ness** *noun*
¹con·tem·po·rary \kən-ˈtem-pə-ˌrer-ē\ *adjective* [*com-* + Latin *tempor-, tempus*] (1631)
1 : happening, existing, living, or coming into being during the same period of time
2 a : SIMULTANEOUS **b :** marked by characteristics of the present period **:** MODERN, CURRENT ☆
— **con·tem·po·rar·i·ly** \-ˌtem-pə-'rer-ə-lē\ *adverb*
²contemporary *noun, plural* **-rar·ies** (1646)
1 : one that is contemporary with another
2 : one of the same or nearly the same age as another
con·tem·po·rize \kən-'tem-pə-ˌrīz\ *transitive verb* **-rized; -riz·ing** (1646)
: to make contemporary
con·tempt \kən-'tem(p)t\ *noun* [Middle English, from Latin *contemptus,* from *contemnere*] (14th century)
1 a : the act of despising **:** the state of mind of one who despises **:** DISDAIN **b :** lack of respect or reverence for something
2 : the state of being despised
3 : willful disobedience to or open disrespect of a court, judge, or legislative body 〈*contempt* of court〉
con·tempt·ible \kən-'tem(p)-tə-bəl\ *adjective* (14th century)
1 : worthy of contempt
2 *obsolete* **:** SCORNFUL, CONTEMPTUOUS ☆
— **con·tempt·i·bil·i·ty** \-ˌtem(p)-tə-'bi-lə-tē\ *noun*
— **con·tempt·ible·ness** *noun*
— **con·tempt·ibly** \-'tem(p)-tə-blē\ *adverb*
con·temp·tu·ous \kən-'tem(p)-chə-wəs, -chəs, -shwəs\ *adjective* [Latin *contemptus*] (1595)
: manifesting, feeling, or expressing contempt
— **con·temp·tu·ous·ly** *adverb*
— **con·temp·tu·ous·ness** *noun*
con·tend \kən-'tend\ *verb* [Middle English, from Middle French or Latin; Middle French

contendre, from Latin *contendere,* from *com-* + *tendere* to stretch — more at THIN] (15th century)
intransitive verb
1 : to strive or vie in contest or rivalry or against difficulties **:** STRUGGLE
2 : to strive in debate **:** ARGUE
transitive verb
1 : MAINTAIN, ASSERT 〈*contended* that he was right〉
2 : to struggle for **:** CONTEST
con·tend·er \-'ten-dər\ *noun* (1547)
: one that contends; *especially* **:** a competitor for a championship or high honor 〈a heavyweight title *contender*〉
¹con·tent \kən-'tent\ *adjective* [Middle English, from Middle French, from Latin *contentus,* from past participle of *continēre* to hold in, contain — more at CONTAIN] (15th century)
: CONTENTED, SATISFIED
²content *transitive verb* (15th century)
1 : to appease the desires of
2 : to limit (oneself) in requirements, desires, or actions
³content *noun* (1579)
: CONTENTMENT 〈ate to his heart's *content*〉
⁴con·tent \'kän-ˌtent\ *noun* [Middle English, from Latin *contentus,* past participle of *continēre* to contain] (15th century)
1 a : something contained — usually used in plural 〈the jar's *contents*〉 〈the drawer's *contents*〉 **b :** the topics or matter treated in a written work 〈table of *contents*〉
2 a : SUBSTANCE, GIST **b :** MEANING, SIGNIFICANCE **c :** the events, physical detail, and information in a work of art — compare FORM 10b
3 a : the matter dealt with in a field of study **b :** a part, element, or complex of parts
4 : the amount of specified material contained **:** PROPORTION
content analysis *noun* (1945)
: analysis of the manifest and latent content of a body of communicated material (as a book or film) through a classification, tabulation, and evaluation of its key symbols and themes in order to ascertain its meaning and probable effect
con·tent·ed \kən-'ten-təd\ *adjective* (1526)
: feeling or manifesting satisfaction with one's possessions, status, or situation 〈a *contented* smile〉
— **con·tent·ed·ly** *adverb*
— **con·tent·ed·ness** *noun*
con·ten·tion \kən-'ten(t)-shən\ *noun* [Middle English *contencioun,* from Middle French, from Latin *contention-, contentio,* from *contendere*] (14th century)
1 : an act or instance of contending
2 : a point advanced or maintained in a debate or argument
3 : RIVALRY, COMPETITION
synonym see DISCORD
con·ten·tious \kən-'ten(t)-shəs\ *adjective* (15th century)
1 : likely to cause contention 〈a *contentious* argument〉
2 : exhibiting an often perverse and wearisome tendency to quarrels and disputes 〈a man of a most *contentious* nature〉
synonym see BELLIGERENT
— **con·ten·tious·ly** *adverb*
— **con·ten·tious·ness** *noun*
con·tent·ment \kən-'tent-mənt\ *noun* (15th century)
1 : the quality or state of being contented
2 : something that contents
con·tent word \'kän-ˌtent-\ *noun* (1940)
: a word that primarily expresses lexical meaning — compare FUNCTION WORD
con·ter·mi·nous \kən-'tər-mə-nəs, kän-\ *adjective* [Latin *conterminus,* from *com-* + *terminus* boundary — more at TERM] (1631)
1 : having a common boundary
2 : COTERMINOUS

3 : enclosed within one common boundary 〈the 48 *conterminous* states〉
— **con·ter·mi·nous·ly** *adverb*
¹con·test \kən-'test, 'kän-\ *verb* [Middle French *contester,* from Latin *contestari* (*litem*) to bring an action at law, from *contestari* to call to witness, from *com-* + *testis* witness — more at TESTAMENT] (1603)
intransitive verb
: STRIVE, VIE
transitive verb
: to make the subject of dispute, contention, or litigation; *especially* **:** DISPUTE, CHALLENGE
— **con·test·able** \-'tes-tə-bəl\ *adjective*
— **con·test·er** *noun*
²con·test \'kän-ˌtest\ *noun* (1647)
1 : a struggle for superiority or victory **:** COMPETITION
2 : a competition in which each contestant performs without direct contact with or interference from his competitors
con·tes·tant \kən-'tes-tənt *also* 'kän-\ *noun* (1665)
1 : one that participates in a contest
2 : one that contests an award or decision
con·tes·ta·tion \ˌkän-ˌtes-'tā-shən\ *noun* (1580)
: CONTROVERSY, DEBATE
con·text \'kän-ˌtekst\ *noun* [Middle English, weaving together of words, from Latin *contextus* connection of words, coherence, from *contexere* to weave together, from *com-* + *texere* to weave — more at TECHNICAL] (circa 1568)
1 : the parts of a discourse that surround a word or passage and can throw light on its meaning
2 : the interrelated conditions in which something exists or occurs **:** ENVIRONMENT, SETTING
— **con·text·less** \-ˌtekst-ləs\ *adjective*

☆ **SYNONYMS**
Contemporary, contemporaneous, coeval, synchronous, simultaneous, coincident mean existing or occurring at the same time. CONTEMPORARY is likely to apply to people and what relates to them 〈Abraham Lincoln was *contemporary* with Charles Darwin〉. CONTEMPORANEOUS applies to events 〈*contemporaneous* accounts of the kidnapping〉. COEVAL refers usually to periods, ages, eras, eons 〈two stars thought to be *coeval*〉. SYNCHRONOUS implies exact correspondence in time and especially in periodic intervals 〈*synchronous* timepieces〉. SIMULTANEOUS implies correspondence in a moment of time 〈the two shots were *simultaneous*〉. COINCIDENT is applied to events and may be used in order to avoid implication of causal relationship 〈the end of World War II was *coincident* with a great vintage year〉.

Contemptible, despicable, pitiable, sorry, scurvy mean arousing or deserving scorn. CONTEMPTIBLE may imply any quality provoking scorn or a low standing in any scale of values 〈a *contemptible* liar〉. DESPICABLE may imply utter worthlessness and usually suggests arousing an attitude of moral indignation 〈a *despicable* crime〉. PITIABLE applies to what inspires mixed contempt and pity 〈a *pitiable* attempt at tragedy〉. SORRY may stress pitiable inadequacy or may suggest wretchedness or sordidness 〈this rattletrap is a *sorry* excuse for a car〉. SCURVY adds to DESPICABLE an implication of arousing disgust 〈a *scurvy* crew of hangers-on〉.

— **con·tex·tu·al** \kän-'teks-chə-wəl, kən-, -chəl\ *adjective*
— **con·tex·tu·al·ly** *adverb*
con·text–free \'kän-ˌtekst-'frē\ *adjective* (1964)
: of, relating to, or being a grammar or language based on rules that describe a change in a string without reference to elements outside of the string; *also* : being such a rule
con·tex·tu·al·ize \kən-'teks-chə-wə-ˌlīz, -chə-ˌlīz\ *transitive verb* **-ized; -iz·ing** (1934)
: to place (as a word or activity) in a context
con·tex·ture \kən-'teks-chər, 'kän-ˌ, kän-'\ *noun* [French, from Latin *contextus*, past participle of *contexere*] (1603)
1 : the act, process, or manner of weaving parts into a whole; *also* : a structure so formed ⟨a *contexture* of lies⟩
2 : CONTEXT
con·ti·gu·i·ty \ˌkän-tə-'gyü-ə-tē\ *noun, plural* **-ties** (1612)
: the quality or state of being contiguous : PROXIMITY
con·tig·u·ous \kən-'ti-gyə-wəs\ *adjective* [Latin *contiguus*, from *contingere* to have contact with — more at CONTINGENT] (circa 1609)
1 : being in actual contact : touching along a boundary or at a point
2 *of angles* : ADJACENT 2
3 : next or near in time or sequence
4 : touching or connected throughout in an unbroken sequence ⟨*contiguous* row houses⟩
synonym see ADJACENT
— **con·tig·u·ous·ly** *adverb*
— **con·tig·u·ous·ness** *noun*
con·ti·nence \'kän-tᵊn-ən(t)s\ *noun* (14th century)
1 : SELF-RESTRAINT; *especially* : a refraining from sexual intercourse
2 : the ability to retain a bodily discharge voluntarily ⟨fecal *continence*⟩
¹**con·ti·nent** \'kän-tᵊn-ənt\ *adjective* [Middle English, from Middle French, from Latin *continent-, continens*, from present participle of *continēre* to hold in — more at CONTAIN] (14th century)
1 : exercising continence
2 *obsolete* : RESTRICTIVE
— **con·ti·nent·ly** *adverb*
²**con·ti·nent** \'kän-tᵊn-ənt, 'känt-nənt\ *noun* [in senses 1 & 2, from Latin *continent-, continens*, present participle of *continēre*, to hold together, contain; in senses 3 & 4, from Latin *continent-, continens* continuous mass of land, mainland, from *continent-, continens*, present participle] (1541)
1 *archaic* : CONTAINER, CONFINES
2 *archaic* : EPITOME
3 : MAINLAND
4 a : one of the six or seven great divisions of land on the globe **b** *capitalized* : the continent of Europe — used with *the*
¹**con·ti·nen·tal** \ˌkän-tᵊn-'en-tᵊl\ *adjective* (1760)
1 a : of, relating to, or characteristic of a continent ⟨*continental* waters⟩; *specifically, often capitalized* : of or relating to the continent of Europe excluding the British Isles **b** *often capitalized* : of, relating to, or being a cuisine derived from the classic dishes of Europe and especially France
2 a *often capitalized* : of or relating to the colonies later forming the U.S. ⟨*Continental* Congress⟩ **b** : being the part of the U.S. on the North American continent; *also* : being the part of the U.S. comprising the lower 48 states
— **con·ti·nen·tal·ly** \-tᵊl-ē\ *adverb*
²**continental** *noun* (1777)
1 a *often capitalized* : an American soldier of the Revolution in the Continental army **b** (1) : a piece of Continental paper currency (2) : the least bit ⟨not worth a *continental*⟩
2 : an inhabitant of a continent and especially the continent of Europe
continental breakfast *noun, often C capitalized* (1911)

: a light breakfast (as of rolls or toast and coffee)
continental drift *noun* (1926)
: a hypothetical slow movement of the continents on a deep-seated viscous zone within the earth — compare PLATE TECTONICS
continental shelf *noun* (1892)
: a shallow submarine plain of varying width forming a border to a continent and typically ending in a steep slope to the oceanic abyss
continental slope *noun* (1900)
: the usually steep slope from a continental shelf to the ocean floor
con·tin·gence \kən-'tin-jən(t)s\ *noun* (circa 1530)
1 : CONTINGENCY
2 : TANGENCY
con·tin·gen·cy \kən-'tin-jən(t)-sē\ *noun, plural* **-cies** (1561)
1 : the quality or state of being contingent
2 : a contingent event or condition: as **a** : an event (as an emergency) that may but is not certain to occur ⟨trying to provide for every *contingency*⟩ **b** : something liable to happen as an adjunct to or result of something else
synonym see JUNCTURE
contingency fee *noun* (1945)
: a fee for services (as of a lawyer) paid upon successful completion of the services and usually calculated as a percentage of the gain realized for the client — called also *contingent fee*
contingency table *noun* (circa 1947)
: a table of data in which the row entries tabulate the data according to one variable and the column entries tabulate it according to another variable and which is used especially in the study of the correlation between variables
¹**con·tin·gent** \kən-'tin-jənt\ *adjective* [Middle English, from Middle French, from Latin *contingent-, contingens*, present participle of *contingere* to have contact with, befall, from *com-* + *tangere* to touch — more at TANGENT] (14th century)
1 : likely but not certain to happen : POSSIBLE
2 : not logically necessary; *especially* : EMPIRICAL
3 a : happening by chance or unforeseen causes **b** : subject to chance or unseen effects : UNPREDICTABLE **c** : intended for use in circumstances not completely foreseen
4 : dependent on or conditioned by something else
5 : not necessitated : determined by free choice
synonym see ACCIDENTAL
— **con·tin·gent·ly** *adverb*
²**contingent** *noun* (1548)
1 : something contingent : CONTINGENCY
2 : a representative group : DELEGATION, DETACHMENT
con·tin·u·al \kən-'tin-yü-əl, -yəl\ *adjective* [Middle English, from Middle French, from Latin *continuus* continuous] (14th century)
1 : continuing indefinitely in time without interruption ⟨*continual* fear⟩
2 : recurring in steady usually rapid succession ⟨a history of *continual* invasions⟩ ☆
— **con·tin·u·al·ly** *adverb*
con·tin·u·ance \kən-'tin-yü-ən(t)s\ *noun* (14th century)
1 : CONTINUATION
2 : the extent of continuing : DURATION
3 : the quality of enduring : PERMANENCE
4 : an adjournment of a court case to a future day
con·tin·u·ant \-yü-ənt\ *noun* (1861)
1 : something that continues or serves as a continuation
2 : a speech sound (as a fricative or vowel) that is produced without a complete closure of the breath passage — compare STOP
— **continuant** *adjective*
con·tin·u·ate *adjective* (1555)
obsolete : CONTINUOUS, UNINTERRUPTED

con·tin·u·a·tion \kən-ˌtin-yə-'wā-shən\ *noun* (14th century)
1 : the act or fact of continuing in or the prolongation of a state or activity
2 : resumption after an interruption
3 : something that continues, increases, or adds
con·tin·u·a·tive \kən-'tin-yə-ˌwā-tiv, -wə-tiv\ *adjective* (1684)
: expressing continuity or continuation (as of an idea or action)
con·tin·u·a·tor \-ˌwā-tər\ *noun* (1646)
: one that continues
con·tin·ue \kən-'tin-(ˌ)yü\ *verb* **-tin·ued; -tinu·ing** [Middle English, from Middle French *continuer*, from Latin *continuare*, from *continuus*] (14th century)
intransitive verb
1 : to maintain without interruption a condition, course, or action
2 : to remain in existence : ENDURE
3 : to remain in a place or condition : STAY
4 : to resume an activity after interruption
transitive verb
1 a : KEEP UP, MAINTAIN ⟨*continues* walking⟩ **b** : to keep going or add to : PROLONG; *also* : to resume after intermission
2 : to cause to continue
3 : to allow to remain in a place or condition : RETAIN
4 : to postpone (a legal proceeding) by a continuance ☆
— **con·tinu·er** \-yü-ər\ *noun*
continued *adjective* (15th century)
1 : lasting or extending without interruption ⟨*continued* success⟩
2 : resumed after interruption ⟨a *continued* story⟩
continued fraction *noun* (circa 1856)
: a fraction whose numerator is an integer and whose denominator is an integer plus a fraction whose numerator is an integer and whose denominator is an integer plus a fraction and so on
continuing *adjective* (14th century)

☆ SYNONYMS
Continual, continuous, constant, incessant, perpetual, perennial mean characterized by continued occurrence or recurrence. CONTINUAL often implies a close prolonged succession or recurrence ⟨*continual* showers the whole weekend⟩. CONTINUOUS usually implies an uninterrupted flow or spatial extension ⟨football's oldest *continuous* rivalry⟩. CONSTANT implies uniform or persistent occurrence or recurrence ⟨lived in *constant* pain⟩. INCESSANT implies ceaseless or uninterrupted activity ⟨annoyed by the *incessant* quarreling⟩. PERPETUAL suggests unfailing repetition or lasting duration ⟨a land of *perpetual* snowfall⟩. PERENNIAL implies enduring existence often through constant renewal ⟨a *perennial* source of controversy⟩.

Continue, last, endure, abide, persist mean to exist or last over a period of time or indefinitely. CONTINUE applies to a process going on without ending ⟨the search for peace will *continue*⟩. LAST, especially when unqualified, may stress existing beyond what is normal or expected ⟨buy shoes that will *last*⟩. ENDURE adds an implication of resisting destructive forces or agencies ⟨in spite of everything, her faith *endured*⟩. ABIDE implies stable and constant existing especially as opposed to mutability ⟨a love that *abides* through 40 years of marriage⟩. PERSIST suggests outlasting the normal or appointed time and often connotes obstinacy or doggedness ⟨the sense of guilt *persisted*⟩.

1 : CONTINUOUS, CONSTANT ⟨*continuing* poverty⟩
2 : needing no renewal **:** ENDURING ⟨*continuing* fame⟩
— **con·tin·u·ing·ly** *adverb*
continuing education *noun* (1954)
: formal courses of study for adult part-time students
con·ti·nu·i·ty \ˌkän-tᵊn-ˈü-ə-tē, -ˈyü-\ *noun, plural* **-ties** (15th century)
1 a : uninterrupted connection, succession, or union **b :** uninterrupted duration or continuation especially without essential change
2 : something that has, exhibits, or provides continuity: as **a :** a script or scenario in the performing arts **b :** transitional spoken or musical matter especially for a radio or television program **c :** the story and dialogue of a comic strip
3 : the property of being mathematically continuous
con·tin·uo \kən-ˈtin-yə-ˌwō, -ˈti-nə-\ *noun, plural* **-u·os** [Italian, from *continuo* continuous, from Latin *continuus*] (1724)
: a bass part (as for a keyboard or stringed instrument) used especially in baroque ensemble music and consisting of a succession of bass notes with figures that indicate the required chords — called also *figured bass, thoroughbass*
con·tin·u·ous \kən-ˈtin-yü-əs\ *adjective* [Latin *continuus*, from *continēre* to hold together — more at CONTAIN] (1673)
1 : marked by uninterrupted extension in space, time, or sequence
2 *of a function* **:** having the property that the absolute value of the numerical difference between the value at a given point and the value at any point in a neighborhood of the given point can be made as close to zero as desired by choosing the neighborhood small enough
synonym see CONTINUAL
— **con·tin·u·ous·ly** *adverb*
— **con·tin·u·ous·ness** *noun*
con·tin·u·um \kən-ˈtin-yü-əm\ *noun, plural* **-ua** \-yü-ə\ *also* **-ums** [Latin, neuter of *continuus*] (1646)
1 : a coherent whole characterized as a collection, sequence, or progression of values or elements varying by minute degrees (“good” and “bad” . . . stand at opposite ends of a *continuum* —Wayne Shumaker⟩
2 : the set of real numbers including both the rationals and the irrationals; *broadly* **:** a compact set which cannot be separated into two sets neither of which contains a limit point of the other
con·tort \kən-ˈtȯrt\ *verb* [Middle English, from Latin *contortus*, past participle of *contorquēre*, from *com-* + *torquēre* to twist — more at TORTURE] (15th century)
transitive verb
: to twist in a violent manner ⟨features *contorted* with fury⟩
intransitive verb
: to twist into or as if into a strained shape or expression
synonym see DEFORM
— **con·tor·tion** \-ˈtȯr-shən\ *noun*
— **con·tor·tive** \-ˈtȯr-tiv\ *adjective*
con·tor·tion·ist \kən-ˈtȯr-sh(ə-)nist\ *noun* (1859)
: one who contorts; *specifically* **:** an acrobat able to twist the body into unusual postures
— **con·tor·tion·is·tic** \-ˌtȯr-shə-ˈnis-tik\ *adjective*
¹con·tour \ˈkän-ˌtu̇r\ *noun* [French, from Italian *contorno*, from *contornare* to round off, from Medieval Latin, to turn around, from Latin *com-* + *tornare* to turn on a lathe — more at TURN] (1662)
1 : an outline especially of a curving or irregular figure **:** SHAPE; *also* **:** the line representing this outline
2 : the general form or structure of something **:** CHARACTERISTIC — often used in plural

⟨*contours* of a melody⟩ ⟨to delineate the tortured psychological *contours* of the tribal past —B. J. Phillips⟩
3 : a usually meaningful change in intonation in speech
synonym see OUTLINE
²contour *adjective* (1844)
1 : following contour lines or forming furrows or ridges along them ⟨*contour* flooding⟩ ⟨*contour* farming⟩
2 : made to fit the contour of something ⟨a *contour* couch⟩ ⟨*contour* sheets⟩
³contour *transitive verb* (1871)
1 a : to shape the contour of **b :** to shape so as to fit contours
2 : to construct (as a road) in conformity to a contour
contour feather *noun* (1867)
: one of the medium-sized feathers that form the general covering of a bird and determine the external contour
contour line *noun* (1844)
: a line (as on a map) connecting the points on a land surface that have the same elevation
contour map *noun* (1862)
: a map having contour lines

contour map

¹con·tra \ˈkän-trə\ *preposition* [Latin] (15th century)
1 : AGAINST — used chiefly in the phrase *pro and contra*
2 : in opposition or contrast to — used before a proper name
²con·tra \ˈkän-trə, ˈkōn-, -ˌträ\ *noun* [American Spanish, short for *contra-revolucionario* counterrevolutionary] (1981)
: a member of a guerrilla group opposed to the Sandinista government in Nicaragua
contra- *prefix* [Middle English, from Latin, from *contra* against, opposite — more at COUNTER]
1 : against **:** contrary **:** contrasting ⟨*contra*distinction⟩
2 : pitched below normal bass ⟨*contra*octave⟩
con·tra·band \ˈkän-trə-ˌband\ *noun* [Italian *contrabbando*, from Medieval Latin *contrabannum*, from *contra-* + *bannum*, *bannum* decree, of Germanic origin; akin to Old High German *bannan* to command — more at BAN] (circa 1529)
1 : illegal or prohibited traffic in goods **:** SMUGGLING
2 : goods or merchandise whose importation, exportation, or possession is forbidden; *also* **:** smuggled goods
3 : a slave who during the Civil War escaped to or was brought within the Union lines
— **contraband** *adjective*
con·tra·band·ist \-ˌban-dist\ *noun* (circa 1818)
: SMUGGLER
con·tra·bass \ˈkän-trə-ˌbās\ *noun* [Italian *contrabbasso*, from *contra-* + *basso* bass] (circa 1611)
: DOUBLE BASS
— **con·tra·bass·ist** \-ˌbā-sist\ *noun*
con·tra·bas·soon \ˌkän-trə-bə-ˈsün, -ba-\ *noun* (1891)
: a double-reed woodwind instrument having a range an octave lower than that of the bassoon — called also *double bassoon*
con·tra·cep·tion \ˌkän-trə-ˈsep-shən\ *noun* [*contra-* + conception] (1886)
: deliberate prevention of conception or impregnation
— **con·tra·cep·tive** \-ˈsep-tiv\ *adjective or noun*
¹con·tract \ˈkän-ˌtrakt\ *noun* [Middle English, from Latin *contractus*, from *contrahere* to draw together, make a contract, reduce in size, from *com-* + *trahere* to draw] (14th century)
1 a : a binding agreement between two or more persons or parties; *especially* **:** one legal-

ly enforceable **b :** a business arrangement for the supply of goods or services at a fixed price ⟨make parts on *contract*⟩ **c :** the act of marriage or an agreement to marry
2 : a document describing the terms of a contract
3 : the final bid to win a specified number of tricks in bridge
4 : an order or arrangement for a hired assassin to kill someone
²con·tract *verb transitive* 2a & *verb intransitive 1 usually* ˈkän-ˌtrakt, *others usually* kən-ˈ\ *verb* [Middle English, from Middle French or Latin; Middle French *contracter* to agree upon, from Latin *contractus*] (14th century)
transitive verb
1 a : to bring on oneself especially inadvertently **:** INCUR ⟨*contracting* debts⟩ **b :** to become affected with ⟨*contract* pneumonia⟩
2 a : to establish or undertake by contract **b :** BETROTH; *also* **:** to establish (a marriage) formally **c** (1) **:** to hire by contract (2) **:** to purchase (as goods or services) on a contract basis — often used with *out*
3 a : LIMIT, RESTRICT **b :** KNIT, WRINKLE ⟨frown *contracted* his brow⟩ **c :** to draw together **:** CONCENTRATE
4 : to reduce to smaller size by or as if by squeezing or forcing together
5 : to shorten (as a word) by omitting one or more sounds or letters
intransitive verb
1 : to make a contract
2 : to draw together so as to become diminished in size ⟨metal *contracts* on cooling⟩; *also* **:** to become less in compass, duration, or length ⟨muscle *contracts* in tetanus⟩ ☆
— **con·tract·ibil·i·ty** \kən-ˌtrak-tə-ˈbi-lə-tē, ˌkän-\ *noun*
— **con·tract·ible** \kən-ˈtrak-tə-bəl, ˈkän-ˌ\ *adjective*
contract bridge \ˈkän-ˌtrakt-\ *noun* (1924)
: a bridge game distinguished by the fact that overtricks do not count toward game or slam bonuses
con·trac·tile \kən-ˈtrak-tᵊl, -ˌtīl\ *adjective* (circa 1706)
: having or concerned with the power or property of contracting ⟨*contractile* proteins of muscle fibrils⟩
— **con·trac·til·i·ty** \ˌkän-ˌtrak-ˈti-lə-tē\ *noun*
contractile vacuole *noun* (1877)

\ə\ abut \ᵊ\ kitten \ər\ **further** \a\ **ash** \ā\ **ace**
\ä\ mop, mar \au̇\ out \ch\ **chin** \e\ **bet** \ē\ **easy**
\g\ **go** \i\ **hit** \ī\ **ice** \j\ **job** \ŋ\ **sing** \ō\ **go**
\ȯ\ **law** \ȯi\ **boy** \th\ **thin** \t̲h̲\ **the** \ü\ **loot** \u̇\ **foot**
\y\ **yet** \zh\ **vision** *see also* Guide to Pronunciation

: a vacuole in a unicellular organism that contracts regularly to discharge fluid from the body

con·trac·tion \kən-ˈtrak-shən\ *noun* (15th century)
1 a : the action or process of contracting : the state of being contracted **b** : the shortening and thickening of a functioning muscle or muscle fiber **c** : a reduction in business activity or growth
2 : a shortening of a word, syllable, or word group by omission of a sound or letter; *also* : a form produced by such shortening
— **con·trac·tion·al** \-shnəl, -shə-nᵊl\ *adjective*
— **con·trac·tive** \kən-ˈtrak-tiv, ˈkän-,\ *adjective*
— **con·trac·tion·ary** \kən-ˈtrak-shə-,ner-ē\ *adjective*

con·trac·tor \1 usually ˈkän-,trak-tər, 2 usually kən-ˈ\ *noun* (1548)
1 : one that contracts or is party to a contract: as **a** : one that contracts to perform work or provide supplies **b** : one that contracts to erect buildings
2 : something (as a muscle) that contracts or shortens

con·trac·tu·al \kən-ˈtrak-chə-wəl, -chəl, -shwəl\ *adjective* (1861)
: of, relating to, or constituting a contract
— **con·trac·tu·al·ly** *adverb*

con·trac·ture \kən-ˈtrak-chər\ *noun* (1601)
: a permanent shortening (as of muscle, tendon, or scar tissue) producing deformity or distortion

con·tra·dict \,kän-trə-ˈdikt\ *transitive verb* [Latin *contradictus*, past participle of *contradicere*, from *contra-* + *dicere* to say, speak — more at DICTION] (circa 1576)
1 : to assert the contrary of : take issue with
2 : to imply the opposite or a denial of ⟨your actions *contradict* your words⟩
synonym *see* DENY
— **con·tra·dict·able** \-ˈdik-tə-bəl\ *adjective*
— **con·tra·dic·tor** \-ˈdik-tər\ *noun*

con·tra·dic·tion \,kän-trə-ˈdik-shən\ *noun* (14th century)
1 : act or an instance of contradicting
2 a : a proposition, statement, or phrase that asserts or implies both the truth and falsity of something **b** : a statement or phrase whose parts contradict each other ⟨a round square is a *contradiction* in terms⟩
3 a : logical incongruity **b** : a situation in which inherent factors, actions, or propositions are inconsistent or contrary to one another

con·tra·dic·tious \-shəs\ *adjective* (1604)
1 : CONTRADICTORY, OPPOSITE
2 : given to or marked by contradiction : CONTRARY

¹con·tra·dic·to·ry \,kän-trə-ˈdik-t(ə-)rē\ *noun, plural* **-ries** (14th century)
: a proposition so related to another that if either of the two is true the other is false and if either is false the other must be true

²contradictory *adjective* (1534)
: involving, causing, or constituting a contradiction
synonym *see* OPPOSITE
— **con·tra·dic·to·ri·ly** \-t(ə-)rə-lē\ *adverb*
— **con·tra·dic·to·ri·ness** \-t(ə-)rē-nəs\ *noun*

con·tra·dis·tinc·tion \,kän-trə-dis-ˈtiŋ(k)-shən\ *noun* (1647)
: distinction by means of contrast ⟨painting in *contradistinction* to sculpture⟩
— **con·tra·dis·tinc·tive** \-ˈtiŋ(k)-tiv\ *adjective*
— **con·tra·dis·tinc·tive·ly** *adverb*

con·tra·dis·tin·guish \-ˈtiŋ-gwish\ *transitive verb* (1622)
: to distinguish by contrasting qualities

con·trail \ˈkän-,trāl\ *noun* [*condensation trail*] (1943)

: streaks of condensed water vapor created in the air by an airplane or rocket at high altitudes

con·tra·in·di·cate \,kän-trə-ˈin-də-,kāt\ *transitive verb* (1666)
: to make (a treatment or procedure) inadvisable

con·tra·in·di·ca·tion \-,in-də-ˈkā-shən\ *noun* (1623)
: something (as a symptom or condition) that makes a particular treatment or procedure inadvisable

con·tra·lat·er·al \-ˈla-t(ə-)rəl\ *adjective* [International Scientific Vocabulary] (1882)
: occurring on or acting in conjunction with a part on the opposite side of the body

con·tral·to \kən-ˈtral-(,)tō\ *noun, plural* **-tos** [Italian, from *contra-* + *alto*] (1730)
1 a : a singing voice having a range between tenor and mezzo-soprano **b** : a person having this voice
2 : the part sung by a contralto

con·tra·oc·tave \,kän-trə-ˈäk-tiv, -təv, -,tāv\ *noun* (circa 1891)
: the musical octave that begins on the third C below middle C — see PITCH illustration

con·tra·po·si·tion \-pə-ˈzi-shən\ *noun* [Late Latin *contrapositon-, contrapositio*, from Latin *contraponere* to place opposite, from *contra-* + *ponere* to place — more at POSITION] (1551)
: the relationship between two propositions when the subject and predicate of one are respectively the negation of the predicate and the negation of the subject of the other

con·tra·pos·i·tive \-ˈpä-zə-tiv, -ˈpäz-tiv\ *noun* (1870)
: a proposition resulting from an operation of immediate inference in which the terms of a given proposition are permuted and negated ⟨"all not-*P* is not-*S* " is the *contrapositive* of "all *S* is *P* "⟩

con·trap·tion \kən-ˈtrap-shən\ *noun* [perhaps blend of *contrivance, trap,* and *invention*] (circa 1825)
: DEVICE, GADGET

con·tra·pun·tal \,kän-trə-ˈpən-tᵊl\ *adjective* [Italian *contrappunto* counterpoint, from Medieval Latin *contrapunctus* — more at COUNTERPOINT] (1845)
1 : POLYPHONIC
2 : of, relating to, or marked by counterpoint
— **con·tra·pun·tal·ly** \-tᵊl-ē\ *adverb*

con·tra·pun·tist \-ˈpən-tist\ *noun* (1776)
: one who writes counterpoint

con·trar·i·an \kən-ˈtrer-ē-ən, kän-\ *noun* (1657)
: a person who takes a contrary position or attitude; *specifically* : an investor who buys shares of stock when most others are selling and sells when others are buying
— **contrarian** *adjective*

con·tra·ri·ety \,kän-trə-ˈrī-ə-tē\ *noun, plural* **-eties** [Middle English *contrariete*, from Middle French *contrarieté*, from Late Latin *contrarietat-, contrarietas*, from Latin *contrarius* contrary] (14th century)
1 : the quality or state of being contrary
2 : something contrary

con·trar·i·ous \kən-ˈtrer-ē-əs, kän-\ *adjective* (13th century)
: PERVERSE, ANTAGONISTIC

con·trari·wise \ˈkän-,trer-ē-,wīz, kən-ˈ\ *adverb* (14th century)
1 : on the contrary
2 : VICE VERSA
3 : in a contrary manner

¹con·trary \ˈkän-,trer-ē\ *noun, plural* **-traries** (13th century)
1 : a fact or condition incompatible with another : OPPOSITE — usually used with *the*
2 : one of a pair of opposites
3 a : a proposition so related to another that though both may be false they cannot both be true — compare SUBCONTRARY **b** : either of

two terms (as *good* and *evil*) that cannot both be affirmed of the same subject
— **by contraries** *obsolete* : in a manner opposite to what is logical or expected
— **on the contrary** : just the opposite
— **to the contrary 1** : on the contrary **2** : NOTWITHSTANDING

²con·trary \ˈkän-,trer-ē, 4 often kən-ˈtrer-ē\ *adjective* [Middle English *contrarie*, from Middle French *contraire*, from Latin *contrarius*, from *contra* opposite] (14th century)
1 : being so different as to be at opposite extremes : OPPOSITE ⟨come to the *contrary* conclusion⟩ ⟨went off in *contrary* directions⟩; *also* : being opposite to or in conflict with each other ⟨*contrary* viewpoints⟩
2 : being not in conformity with what is usual or expected ⟨actions *contrary* to company policy⟩ ⟨*contrary* evidence⟩
3 : UNFAVORABLE — used of wind or weather
4 : temperamentally unwilling to accept control or advice ☆
— **con·trari·ly** \-,trer-ə-lē, -ˈtrer-\ *adverb*
— **con·trari·ness** \-,trer-ē-nəs, -ˈtrer-\ *noun*

³contrary *same as* ²\ *adverb* (15th century)
: CONTRARIWISE, CONTRARILY

contrary to *preposition* (14th century)
: in conflict with : DESPITE ⟨*contrary to* orders, he set out alone⟩

¹con·trast \kən-ˈtrast, ˈkän-,\ *verb* [French *contraster*, from Middle French, to oppose, resist, alteration of *contrester*, from (assumed) Vulgar Latin *contrastare*, from Latin *contra-* + *stare* to stand — more at STAND] (1695)
transitive verb
: to set off in contrast : compare or appraise in respect to differences ⟨*contrast* European and American manners⟩ — often used with *to* or *with* ⟨*contrasting* her with other women —Victoria Sackville-West⟩
intransitive verb
: to form a contrast
synonym *see* COMPARE
— **con·trast·able** \-ˈtras-tə-bəl, -,tras-\ *adjective*

²con·trast \ˈkän-,trast\ *noun* (1711)
1 a : juxtaposition of dissimilar elements (as color, tone, or emotion) in a work of art **b** : degree of difference between the lightest and darkest parts of a picture
2 a : the difference or degree of difference between things having similar or comparable natures ⟨the *contrast* between the two forms of government⟩ **b** : comparison of similar objects to set off their dissimilar qualities : the state of being so compared ⟨the enforced simplicity in this diary . . . is in *contrast* to the intensity of his former life —*Times Literary Supplement*⟩
3 : a person or thing that exhibits differences when compared with another

con·tras·tive \kən-ˈtras-tiv, ˈkän-,\ *adjective* (1841)
: forming or consisting of a contrast
— **con·tras·tive·ly** *adverb*

con·trasty \ˈkän-,tras-tē\ *adjective* (1891)

☆ **SYNONYMS**
Contrary, perverse, restive, balky, wayward mean inclined to resist authority or control. CONTRARY implies a temperamental unwillingness to accept orders or advice ⟨a *contrary* child⟩. PERVERSE may imply wrongheaded, determined, or cranky opposition to what is reasonable or normal ⟨a *perverse*, intractable critic⟩. RESTIVE suggests unwillingness or inability to submit to discipline or follow orders ⟨tired soldiers growing *restive*⟩. BALKY suggests a refusing to proceed in a desired direction or course of action ⟨a *balky* witness⟩. WAYWARD suggests strong-willed capriciousness and irregularity in behavior ⟨a school for *wayward* youths⟩. See in addition OPPOSITE.

: having or producing in photography great contrast between highlights and shadows

con·tra·vene \ˌkän-trə-'vēn\ *transitive verb* **-vened; -ven·ing** [Middle French or Late Latin; Middle French *contrevenir,* from Late Latin *contravenire,* from Latin *contra-* + *venire* to come — more at COME] (1567)
1 : to go or act contrary to : VIOLATE ⟨*contra- vene* a law⟩
2 : to oppose in argument : CONTRADICT ⟨*con- travene* a proposition⟩
synonym see DENY
— **con·tra·ven·er** *noun*

con·tra·ven·tion \ˌkän-trə-'ven(t)-shən\ *noun* [Middle French, from Late Latin *contravenire*] (1579)
: the act of contravening : VIOLATION

con·tre·danse \'kän-trə-ˌdan(t)s, kōⁿ-trə- däⁿs\ *or* **con·tra dance** \'kän-trə-ˌdan(t)s\ *noun* [French *contredanse,* by folk etymology from English *country-dance*] (1803)
1 : a folk dance in which couples face each other in two lines or in a square
2 : a piece of music for a contredanse

con·tre·temps \'kän-trə-ˌtäⁿ, kōⁿ-trə-täⁿ\ *noun, plural* **con·tre·temps** \-(ˌ)täⁿ(z)\ [French, from *contre-* counter- + *temps* time, from Latin *tempus*] (1769)
: an inopportune or embarrassing occurrence or situation

con·trib·ute \kən-'tri-byət, -(ˌ)byüt *also & es- pecially before* -ed *or* -ing 'tri-bət; *chiefly British also* 'kän-trə-ˌbyüt\ *verb* **-ut·ed; -ut·ing** [Latin *contributus,* past participle of *con- tribuere,* from *com-* + *tribuere* to grant — more at TRIBUTE] (1530)
transitive verb
1 : to give or supply in common with others
2 : to supply (as an article) for a publication
intransitive verb
1 a : to give a part to a common fund or store **b** : to play a significant part in bringing about an end or result
2 : to submit articles to a publication
— **con·trib·u·tor** \-byə-tər, -bə-, -ˌbyü-\ *noun*

con·tri·bu·tion \ˌkän-trə-'byü-shən\ *noun* (14th century)
1 : a payment (as a levy or tax) imposed by military, civil, or ecclesiastical authorities usu- ally for a special or extraordinary purpose
2 : the act of contributing; *also* : the thing contributed
— **con·trib·u·tive** \kən-'tri-byə-tiv\ *adjec- tive*
— **con·trib·u·tive·ly** *adverb*

con·trib·u·to·ry \kən-'tri-byə-ˌtōr-ē, -ˌtȯr-\ *adjective* (15th century)
1 a : subject to a levy of supplies, money, or men **b** : contributing to a common fund or en- terprise
2 : of, relating to, or forming a contribution

con·trite \'kän-ˌtrīt, kən-'\ *adjective* [Middle English *contrit,* from Middle French, from Medieval Latin *contritus,* from Latin, past par- ticiple of *conterere* to grind, bruise, from *com- + terere* to rub — more at THROW] (14th cen- tury)
1 : grieving and penitent for sin or shortcom- ing
2 : proceeding from contrition ⟨*contrite* sighs⟩
— **con·trite·ly** *adverb*
— **con·trite·ness** *noun*

con·tri·tion \kən-'tri-shən\ *noun* (14th centu- ry)
: the state of being contrite : REPENTANCE
synonym see PENITENCE

con·triv·ance \kən-'trī-vən(t)s\ *noun* (circa 1628)
1 a : a thing contrived; *especially* : a mechan- ical device **b** : an artificial arrangement or de- velopment
2 : the act or faculty of contriving : the state of being contrived

con·trive \kən-'trīv\ *verb* **con·trived; con- triv·ing** [Middle English *controven, con-*

treven, from Middle French *controver,* from Medieval Latin *contropare* to compare, from Latin *com-* + (assumed) Vulgar Latin *tropare* to compose, find — more at TROUBADOR] (14th century)
transitive verb
1 a : DEVISE, PLAN ⟨*contrive* ways of handling the situation⟩ **b** : to form or create in an artis- tic or ingenious manner ⟨*contrived* household utensils from stone⟩
2 : to bring about by stratagem or with diffi- culty : MANAGE
intransitive verb
: to make schemes
— **con·triv·er** *noun*

contrived *adjective* (15th century)
: ARTIFICIAL, LABORED

¹con·trol \kən-'trōl\ *transitive verb* **con- trolled; con·trol·ling** [Middle English *con- trollen,* from Middle French *contreroller,* from *contrerolle* copy of an account, audit, from Medieval Latin *contrarotulus,* from Latin *contra-* + Medieval Latin *rotulus* roll — more at ROLL] (15th century)
1 a *archaic* : to check, test, or verify by evi- dence or experiments **b** : to incorporate suit- able controls in ⟨a *controlled* experiment⟩
2 a : to exercise restraining or directing influ- ence over : REGULATE **b** : to have power over : RULE **c** : to reduce the incidence or severity of especially to innocuous levels ⟨*control* an insect population⟩ ⟨*control* a disease⟩
synonym see CONDUCT
— **con·trol·la·bil·i·ty** \-ˌtrō-lə-'bi-lə-tē\ *noun*
— **con·trol·la·ble** \-'trō-lə-bəl\ *adjective*
— **con·trol·ment** \-'trōl-mənt\ *noun*

²control *noun, often attributive* (1590)
1 a : an act or instance of controlling; *also* : power or authority to guide or manage **b** : skill in the use of a tool, instrument, tech- nique, or artistic medium **c** : the regulation of economic activity especially by government directive — usually used in plural ⟨price *con- trols*⟩
2 : RESTRAINT, RESERVE
3 : one that controls: as **a** (1) : an experiment in which the subjects are treated as in a paral- lel experiment except for omission of the pro- cedure or agent under test and which is used as a standard of comparison in judging experi- mental effects — called also *control experi- ment* (2) : one (as an organism, culture, or group) that is part of a control **b** : a device or mechanism used to regulate or guide the oper- ation of a machine, apparatus, or system **c** : an organization that directs a spaceflight ⟨mission *control*⟩ **d** : a personality or spirit believed to actuate the utterances or performances of a spiritualist medium
synonym see POWER

con·trolled \kən-'trōld\ *adjective* (1586)
1 : RESTRAINED
2 : regulated by law with regard to possession and use ⟨*controlled* drugs⟩

con·trol·ler \kən-'trō-lər, 'kän-ˌ\ *noun* [Middle English *contreroller,* from Middle French *con- trerolleur,* from *contrerolle*] (15th century)
1 a : COMPTROLLER 1 **b** : COMPTROLLER 2 **c** : the chief accounting officer of a business en- terprise or an institution (as a college)
2 a : one that controls or has power or author- ity to control ⟨air traffic *controller*⟩ **b** : CON- TROL 3b
— **con·trol·ler·ship** \-ˌship\ *noun*

controlling interest *noun* (circa 1924)
: sufficient stock ownership in a corporation to exert control over policy

control surface *noun* (1917)
: a movable airfoil designed to change the atti- tude of an aircraft

con·tro·ver·sial \ˌkän-trə-'vər-shəl, -'vər-sē- əl\ *adjective* (1583)
1 : of, relating to, or arousing controversy
2 : given to controversy : DISPUTATIOUS

— **con·tro·ver·sial·ism** \-shə-ˌli-zəm, -sē- ə-ˌ\ *noun*
— **con·tro·ver·sial·ist** \-list\ *noun*
— **con·tro·ver·sial·ly** *adverb*

con·tro·ver·sy \'kän-trə-ˌvər-sē, *British also* kən-'trä-vər-sē\ *noun, plural* **-sies** [Middle English *controversie,* from Latin *controversia,* from *controversus* disputable, literally, turned against, from *contro-* (akin to *contra-*) + *ver- sus,* past participle of *vertere* to turn — more at WORTH] (14th century)
1 : a discussion marked especially by the ex- pression of opposing views : DISPUTE
2 : QUARREL, STRIFE

con·tro·vert \'kän-trə-ˌvərt, ˌkän-trə-'\ *verb* [*controversy*] (1609)
transitive verb
: to dispute or oppose by reasoning ⟨*controvert* a point in a discussion⟩
intransitive verb
: to engage in controversy
— **con·tro·vert·er** \-ˌvər-tər, -'vər-\ *noun*
— **con·tro·vert·ible** \-tə-bəl\ *adjective*

con·tu·ma·cious \ˌkän-tü-'mā-shəs, -tyü-', -chə-\ *adjective* (circa 1600)
: stubbornly disobedient : REBELLIOUS
— **con·tu·ma·cious·ly** *adverb*

con·tu·ma·cy \kən-'tü-mə-sē, -'tyü-; 'kän-tü- , -tyü-, -chə-\ *noun* [Middle English *contuma- cie,* from Latin *contumacia,* from *contumac-, contumax* rebellious] (13th century)
: stubborn resistance to authority; *specifically* : willful contempt of court

con·tu·me·li·ous \ˌkän-tü-'mē-lē-əs, -tyü-', -chə-\ *adjective* (15th century)
: insolently abusive and humiliating
— **con·tu·me·li·ous·ly** *adverb*

con·tume·ly \'kän-tü-mə-lē, kən-, -'tyü-; 'kän- tü-,mē-lē, -tyü-,, -chə-,; *in "Hamlet"* 'kän- (ˌ)tyüm-lē *or* 'kän-chəm-\ *noun, plural* **-lies** [Middle English *contumelie,* from Middle French, from Latin *contumelia*] (14th century)
: harsh language or treatment arising from haughtiness and contempt; *also* : an instance of such language or treatment

con·tu·sion \kən-'tü-zhən, -'tyü-\ *noun* [Mid- dle English *conteschown,* from Middle French *contusion,* from Latin *contusion-, contusio,* from *contundere* to pound, bruise, from *com- + tundere* to beat; akin to Gothic *stautan* to strike, Sanskrit *tudati* he pushes] (15th centu- ry)
: injury to tissue usually without laceration : BRUISE 1a
— **con·tuse** \-'tüz, -'tyüz\ *transitive verb*

co·nun·drum \kə-'nən-drəm\ *noun* [origin un- known] (1645)
1 : a riddle whose answer is or involves a pun
2 a : a question or problem having only a con- jectural answer **b** : an intricate and difficult problem

con·ur·ba·tion \ˌkä-(ˌ)nər-'bā-shən\ *noun* [*com-* + Latin *urb-, urbs* city] (1915)
: an aggregation or continuous network of ur- ban communities

co·nus ar·te·ri·o·sus \'kō-nəs-är-ˌtir-ē- 'ō-səs\ *noun, plural* **co·ni ar·te·ri·o·si** \-ˌnī- är-ˌtir-ē-'ō-ˌsī\ [New Latin, literally, arterial cone] (circa 1860)
1 : a conical prolongation of the right ventricle in mammals from which the pulmonary arter- ies emerge — called also *conus*
2 : a prolongation of the ventricle of amphibi- ans and some fishes that has a spiral valve separating venous blood going to the respira- tory arteries from blood going to the aorta and systemic arteries

con·va·lesce \ˌkän-və-'les\ *intransitive verb* **-lesced; -lesc·ing** [Latin *convalescere,* from *com-* + *valescere* to grow strong, from

valēre to be strong, be well — more at
WIELD] (15th century)
: to recover health and strength gradually after
sickness or weakness
— **con·va·les·cence** \-'le-s⁰n(t)s\ *noun*
— **con·va·les·cent** \-s⁰nt\ *adjective or
noun*
con·vect \kən-'vekt\ *verb* [back-formation
from *convection*] (1881)
intransitive verb
: to transfer heat by convection
transitive verb
: to circulate (as air) by convection
— **con·vec·tive** \-'vek-tiv\ *adjective*
con·vec·tion \kən-'vek-shən\ *noun* [Late Lat-
in *convection-, convectio,* from Latin *conve-
here* to bring together, from *com-* + *vehere* to
carry — more at WAY] (circa 1623)
1 : the action or process of conveying
2 a : the circulatory motion that occurs in a
fluid at a nonuniform temperature owing to
the variation of its density and the action of
gravity **b :** the transfer of heat by convection
— compare CONDUCTION, RADIATION
— **con·vec·tion·al** \-shnəl, -shə-n⁰l\ *adjec-
tive*
convection oven *noun* (1973)
: an oven having a fan that circulates hot air
uniformly and continuously around food
con·vec·tor \-'vek-tər\ *noun* (1907)
: a heating unit in which air heated by contact
with a heating device (as a radiator or a tube
with fins) in a casing circulates by convection
con·vene \kən-'vēn\ *verb* **con·vened; con-
ven·ing** [Middle English, from Middle
French *convenir* to come together, from Latin
convenire] (15th century)
intransitive verb
: to come together in a body
transitive verb
1 : to summon before a tribunal
2 : to cause to assemble
synonym see SUMMON
— **con·ven·er** *or* **con·ve·nor** \-'vē-nər\
noun
¹**con·ve·nience** \kən-'vēn-yən(t)s\ *noun*
(14th century)
1 : fitness or suitability for performing an ac-
tion or fulfilling a requirement
2 a : something (as an appliance, device, or
service) conducive to comfort or ease **b** *chiefly
British* **:** TOILET 3
3 : a suitable or convenient time ⟨at your *con-
venience*⟩
4 : freedom from discomfort **:** EASE
²**convenience** *adjective* (1917)
: designed for quick and easy preparation or
use ⟨*convenience* foods⟩
convenience store *noun* (1965)
: a small often franchised market that is open
long hours
con·ve·nien·cy \-yən(t)-sē\ *noun* (1601)
archaic **:** CONVENIENCE
con·ve·nient \kən-'vēn-yənt\ *adjective* [Mid-
dle English, from Latin *convenient-, conve-
niens,* from present participle of *convenire* to
come together, be suitable, from *com-* + *ve-
nire* to come — more at COME] (14th century)
1 *obsolete* **:** SUITABLE, PROPER
2 a : suited to personal comfort or to easy per-
formance **b :** suited to a particular situation **c**
: affording accommodation or advantage
3 : being near at hand **:** HANDY
— **con·ve·nient·ly** *adverb*
¹**con·vent** \'kän-vənt, -ˌvent\ *noun* [Middle
English *covent,* from Old French, from Medi-
eval Latin *conventus,* from Latin, assembly,
from *convenire*] (13th century)
: a local community or house of a religious or-
der or congregation; *especially* **:** an establish-
ment of nuns
²**con·vent** \kən-'vent\ *verb* [Latin *conventus,*
past participle of *convenire*] (1514)
obsolete **:** CONVENE

con·ven·ti·cle \kən-'ven-ti-kəl\ *noun* [Middle
English, from Latin *conventiculum,* diminutive
of *conventus* assembly] (14th century)
1 : ASSEMBLY, MEETING
2 : an assembly of an irregular or unlawful
character
3 : an assembly for religious worship; *espe-
cially* **:** a secret meeting for worship not sanc-
tioned by law
4 : MEETINGHOUSE
— **con·ven·ti·cler** \-k(ə-)lər\ *noun*
con·ven·tion \kən-'ven(t)-shən\ *noun* [Middle
English, from Middle French or Latin; Middle
French, from Latin *convention-, conventio,*
from *convenire*] (15th century)
1 a : AGREEMENT, CONTRACT **b :** an agreement
between states for regulation of matters affect-
ing all of them **c :** a compact between oppos-
ing commanders especially concerning prison-
er exchange or armistice **d :** a general
agreement about basic principles or proce-
dures; *also* **:** a principle or procedure accepted
as true or correct by convention
2 a : the summoning or convening of an as-
sembly **b :** an assembly of persons met for a
common purpose; *especially* **:** a meeting of the
delegates of a political party for the purpose of
formulating a platform and selecting candi-
dates for office **c :** the usually state or national
organization of a religious denomination
3 a : usage or custom especially in social mat-
ters **b :** a rule of conduct or behavior **c :** a
practice in bidding or playing that conveys in-
formation between partners in a card game (as
bridge) **d :** an established technique, practice,
or device (as in literature or the theater)
con·ven·tion·al \kən-'vench-nəl, -'ven(t)-
shə-n⁰l\ *adjective* (15th century)
1 : formed by agreement or compact
2 a : according with, sanctioned by, or based
on convention **b :** lacking originality or indi-
viduality **:** TRITE **c** (1) **:** ORDINARY, COMMON-
PLACE (2) **:** NONNUCLEAR 1 ⟨*conventional* war-
fare⟩
3 a : according with a mode of artistic repre-
sentation that simplifies or provides symbols
or substitutes for natural forms **b :** of tradi-
tional design
4 : of, resembling, or relating to a convention,
assembly, or public meeting
synonym see CEREMONIAL
— **con·ven·tion·al·ism** \-nə-ˌli-zəm, -n⁰l-
ˌi-zəm\ *noun*
— **con·ven·tion·al·ist** \-list\ *noun or ad-
jective*
— **con·ven·tion·al·i·za·tion** \-ˌvench-nə-
lə-'zā-shən, -ˌven(t)-shə-n⁰l-ə-'zā-\ *noun*
— **con·ven·tion·al·ize** \-'vench-nə-ˌlīz,
-'ven(t)-shə-n⁰l-ˌīz\ *transitive verb*
— **con·ven·tion·al·ly** *adverb*
con·ven·tion·al·i·ty \-ˌven(t)-shə-'na-lə-tē\
noun, plural **-ties** (circa 1834)
1 : a conventional usage, practice, or thing
2 : the quality or state of being conventional;
especially **:** adherence to conventions
con·ven·tion·eer \kən-ˌven(t)-shə-'nir\ *noun*
(1926)
: a person attending a convention
¹**con·ven·tu·al** \kən-'ven-chə-wəl, kän-,
-'vench-wəl\ *adjective* [Middle English, from
Middle French or Medieval Latin; Middle
French, from Medieval Latin *conventualis,*
from *conventus* convent] (15th century)
1 : of, relating to, or befitting a convent or
monastic life **:** MONASTIC
2 *capitalized* **:** of or relating to the Conventu-
als
— **con·ven·tu·al·ly** *adverb*
²**conventual** *noun* (1533)
1 *capitalized* **:** a member of the Order of Fri-
ars Minor Conventual forming a branch of the
first order of Saint Francis of Assisi under a
mitigated rule
2 : a member of a conventual community
con·verge \kən-'vərj\ *verb* **con·verged;
con·verg·ing** [Late Latin *convergere,* from

Latin *com-* + *vergere* to bend, incline —
more at WRENCH] (1691)
intransitive verb
1 : to tend or move toward one point or one
another **:** come together **:** MEET
2 : to come together and unite in a common
interest or focus
3 : to approach a limit as the number of terms
increases without limit
transitive verb
: to cause to converge
con·ver·gence \kən-'vər-jən(t)s\ *noun* (1713)
1 : the act of converging and especially mov-
ing toward union or uniformity; *especially*
: coordinated movement of the two eyes so
that the image of a single point is formed on
corresponding retinal areas
2 : the state or property of being convergent
3 : independent development of similar char-
acters (as of bodily structure or cultural traits)
often associated with similarity of habits or
environment
con·ver·gen·cy \-jən(t)-sē\ *noun* (1709)
: CONVERGENCE
con·ver·gent \-jənt\ *adjective* (circa 1751)
1 : tending to move toward one point or to ap-
proach each other **:** CONVERGING ⟨*convergent*
lines⟩
2 : exhibiting convergence in form, function,
or development ⟨*convergent* evolution⟩
3 a *of an improper integral* **:** having a value
that is a real number **b :** characterized by hav-
ing the *n*th term or the sum of the first *n* terms
approach a finite limit ⟨a *convergent* se-
quence⟩ ⟨a *convergent* series⟩
converging lens *noun* (1860)
: a lens that causes parallel rays (as of light) to
come to a focus
con·vers·able \kən-'vər-sə-bəl\ *adjective*
(circa 1631)
1 *archaic* **:** relating to or suitable for social in-
teraction
2 : pleasant and easy to converse with
con·ver·sance \kən-'vər-s⁰n(t)s *also* 'kän-
vər-sən(t)s\ *noun* (1609)
: the quality or state of being conversant
con·ver·san·cy \-s⁰n(t)-sē, -sən(t)-\ *noun*
(1798)
: CONVERSANCE
con·ver·sant \kən-'vər-s⁰nt *also* 'kän-vər-
sənt\ *adjective* (14th century)
1 *archaic* **:** having frequent or familiar associ-
ation
2 *archaic* **:** CONCERNED, OCCUPIED
3 : having knowledge or experience — used
with *with*
con·ver·sa·tion \ˌkän-vər-'sā-shən\ *noun*
[Middle English *conversacioun,* from Middle
French *conversation,* from Latin *conversa-
tion-, conversatio,* from *conversari* to asso-
ciate with, frequentative of *convertere* to turn
around] (14th century)
1 *obsolete* **:** CONDUCT, BEHAVIOR
2 a (1) **:** oral exchange of sentiments, observa-
tions, opinions, or ideas (2) **:** an instance of
such exchange **:** TALK **b :** an informal discus-
sion of an issue by representatives of govern-
ments, institutions, or groups **c :** an exchange
similar to conversation
— **con·ver·sa·tion·al** \-shnəl, -shə-n⁰l\
adjective
— **con·ver·sa·tion·al·ly** *adverb*
con·ver·sa·tion·al·ist \-shnə-list, -shə-n⁰l-
ist\ *noun* (1836)
: one who converses a great deal or who ex-
cels in conversation
conversation piece *noun* (1712)
1 : a painting of a group of persons in their
customary surroundings
2 : something (as a novel or unusual object)
that stimulates conversation
con·ver·sa·zi·o·ne \ˌkän-vər-ˌsät-sē-'ō-nē,
ˌkōn-\ *noun, plural* **-o·nes** *or* **-o·ni** \-'ō-(ˌ)nē\
[Italian, literally, conversation, from Latin
conversation-, conversatio] (1739)

: a meeting for conversation especially about art, literature, or science

¹con·verse \'kän-,vərs\ *noun* (15th century)
1 *obsolete* : social interaction
2 : CONVERSATION

²con·verse \kən-'vərs\ *intransitive verb* **con·versed; con·vers·ing** [Middle English, to live (with), from Middle French *converser*, from Latin *conversari*] (1586)
1 *archaic* **a** : to become occupied or engaged **b** : to have acquaintance or familiarity
2 a : to exchange thoughts and opinions in speech : TALK **b** : to carry on an exchange similar to a conversation (as with a computer)
— **con·vers·er** \-'vər-sər\ *noun*

³con·verse \'kän-,vərs\ *noun* [Latin *conversus,* past participle of *convertere*] (1570)
: something reversed in order, relation, or action: as **a** : a theorem formed by interchanging the hypothesis and conclusion of a given theorem **b** : a proposition obtained by interchange of the subject and predicate of a given proposition 〈"no *P* is *S*" is the *converse* of "no *S* is *P*"〉

⁴con·verse \kən-'vərs, 'kän-,\ *adjective* (1794)
1 : reversed in order, relation, or action
2 : being a logical or mathematical converse 〈the *converse* theorem〉
— **con·verse·ly** *adverb*

con·ver·sion \kən-'vər-zhən, -shən\ *noun* [Middle English, from Middle French, from Latin *conversion-, conversio,* from *convertere*] (14th century)
1 : the act of converting : the process of being converted — compare GENE CONVERSION
2 : an experience associated with a definite and decisive adoption of religion
3 a : the operation of finding a converse in logic or mathematics **b** : reduction of a mathematical expression by clearing of fractions
4 : a successful try for point or free throw
5 : something converted from one use to another
— **con·ver·sion·al** \-'vərzh-nəl; -'vər-zhə-, -'vər-shnəl, -shə-nºl\ *adjective*

conversion reaction *noun* (1945)
: a psychoneurosis in which bodily symptoms (as paralysis of the limbs) appear without physical basis — called also *conversion hysteria*

¹con·vert \kən-'vərt\ *verb* [Middle English, from Middle French *convertir,* from Latin *convertere* to turn around, transform, convert, from *com-* + *vertere* to turn — more at WORTH] (14th century)
transitive verb
1 a : to bring over from one belief, view, or party to another **b** : to bring about a religious conversion in
2 a : to alter the physical or chemical nature or properties of especially in manufacturing **b** (1) : to change from one form or function to another (2) : to alter for more effective utilization (3) : to appropriate without right **c** : to exchange for an equivalent
3 *obsolete* : TURN
4 : to subject to logical conversion
5 a : to make a goal after receiving (a pass) from a teammate **b** : to score on (as a try for point or free throw) **c** : to make (a spare) in bowling
intransitive verb
1 : to undergo conversion
2 : to make good on a try for point, field goal, or free throw
synonym see TRANSFORM

²con·vert \'kän-,vərt\ *noun* (1561)
: one that is converted

con·vert·er \kən-'vər-tər\ *noun* (1533)
: one that converts: as **a** : the furnace used in the Bessemer process **b** *or* **con·ver·tor** \-'vər-tər\ : a device employing mechanical rotation for changing electrical energy from one form to another (as from direct current to alternating current or vice versa); *also* : a radio

device for converting one frequency to another **c** : a device for adapting a television or radio receiver to receive channels or frequencies for which it was not originally designed 〈a cable *converter*〉 〈FM *converter*〉 **d** : a device that accepts data in one form and converts it to another 〈analog-digital *converter*〉 **e** : CATALYTIC CONVERTER

¹con·vert·ible \kən-'vər-tə-bəl\ *adjective* (14th century)
1 : capable of being converted
2 : having a top that may be lowered or removed 〈*convertible* coupe〉
3 : capable of being exchanged for a specified equivalent (as another currency or security) 〈a bond *convertible* to 12 shares of common stock〉
— **con·vert·ibil·i·ty** \-,vər-tə-'bi-lə-tē\ *noun*
— **con·vert·ible·ness** \-'vər-tə-bəl-nəs\ *noun*
— **con·vert·ibly** \-blē\ *adverb*

²convertible *noun* (1615)
: something convertible; *especially* : a convertible automobile

con·verti·plane *also* **con·verta·plane** \kən-'vər-tə-,plän\ *noun* (1949)
: an aircraft that takes off and lands like a helicopter and is convertible to a fixed-wing configuration for forward flight

con·vex \kän-'veks; 'kän-,, kən-'\ *adjective* [Middle French or Latin; Middle French *convexe,* from Latin *convexus* vaulted, concave, convex, from *com-* + *-vexus;* perhaps akin to Latin *vehere* to carry — more at WAY] (1571)
1 a : curved or rounded like the exterior of a sphere or circle **b** : being a continuous function or part of a continuous function with the property that a line joining any two points on its graph lies on or above the graph
2 a *of a set of points* : containing all points in a line joining any two constituent points **b** *of a geometric figure* : comprising a convex set when combined with its interior 〈a *convex* polygon〉

con·vex·i·ty \kən-'vek-sət-ē, kän-\ *noun, plural* **-ties** (1599)
1 : the quality or state of being convex
2 : a convex surface or part

con·vexo–con·cave \kən-,vek-(,)sō-kän-'kāv, kän-,vek-, -'käv\ *adjective* (1693)
1 : CONCAVO-CONVEX
2 : having the convex side of greater curvature than the concave

con·vey \kən-'vā\ *transitive verb* **con·veyed; con·vey·ing** [Middle English, from Middle French *conveier* to accompany, escort, from (assumed) Vulgar Latin *conviare,* from Latin *com-* + *via* way — more at WAY] (14th century)
1 *obsolete* : LEAD, CONDUCT
2 a : to bear from one place to another; *especially* : to move in a continuous stream or mass **b** : to impart or communicate by statement, suggestion, gesture, or appearance **c** (1) *archaic* : STEAL (2) *obsolete* : to carry away secretly **d** : to transfer or deliver to another especially by a sealed writing **e** : to cause to pass from one place or person to another

con·vey·ance \kən-'vā-ən(t)s\ *noun* (15th century)
1 : the action of conveying
2 : a means or way of conveying: as **a** : an instrument by which title to property is conveyed **b** : a means of transport : VEHICLE

con·vey·anc·er \-ən(t)-sər\ *noun* (1650)
: one whose business is conveyancing

con·vey·anc·ing \-ən(t)-siŋ\ *noun* (1714)
: the act or business of drawing deeds, leases, or other writings for transferring the title to property

con·vey·or *also* **con·vey·er** \kən-'vā-ər\ *noun* (circa 1514)
: one that conveys: as **a** : a person who transfers property **b** *usually* conveyor : a mechanical apparatus for moving articles or bulk mate-

rial from place to place (as by an endless moving belt or a chain of receptacles)

con·vey·or·ise *British variant of* CONVEYORIZE

con·vey·or·ize \-ə-,rīz\ *transitive verb* **-ized; -iz·ing** (1941)
: to equip with a conveyor
— **con·vey·or·i·za·tion** \-,vā-ə-rə-'zā-shən\ *noun*

¹con·vict \kən-'vikt\ *adjective* (14th century)
archaic
: having been convicted

²con·vict \kən-'vikt\ *transitive verb* [Middle English, from Latin *convictus,* past participle of *convincere* to refute, convict] (14th century)
1 : to find or prove to be guilty
2 : to convince of error or sinfulness

³con·vict \'kän-,vikt\ *noun* (15th century)
1 : a person convicted of and under sentence for a crime
2 : a person serving a usually long prison sentence

con·vic·tion \kən-'vik-shən\ *noun* (15th century)
1 : the act or process of convicting of a crime especially in a court of law
2 a : the act of convincing a person of error or of compelling the admission of a truth **b** : the state of being convinced of error or compelled to admit the truth
3 a : a strong persuasion or belief **b** : the state of being convinced
synonym see CERTAINTY, OPINION

con·vince \kən-'vin(t)s\ *transitive verb* **con·vinced; con·vinc·ing** [Latin *convincere* to refute, convict, prove, from *com-* + *vincere* to conquer — more at VICTOR] (1530)
1 *obsolete* **a** : to overcome by argument **b** : OVERPOWER, OVERCOME
2 *obsolete* : DEMONSTRATE, PROVE
3 : to bring (as by argument) to belief, consent, or a course of action : PERSUADE 〈*convinced* himself that she was all right —William Faulkner〉 〈something I could never *convince* him to read —John Lahr〉
— **con·vinc·er** *noun*

con·vinc·ing \kən-'vin(t)-siŋ\ *adjective* (1624)
1 : satisfying or assuring by argument or proof 〈a *convincing* test of a new product〉
2 : having power to convince of the truth, rightness, or reality of something : PLAUSIBLE 〈told a *convincing* story〉
synonym see VALID
— **con·vinc·ing·ly** \-siŋ-lē\ *adverb*
— **con·vinc·ing·ness** *noun*

con·viv·ial \kən-'viv-yəl, -'vi-vē-əl\ *adjective* [Late Latin *convivialis,* from Latin *convivium* banquet, from *com-* + *vivere* to live — more at QUICK] (circa 1668)
: relating to, occupied with, or fond of feasting, drinking, and good company
— **con·viv·i·al·i·ty** \-,vi-vē-'a-lə-tē\ *noun*
— **con·viv·ial·ly** \-'viv-yə-lē, -'vi-vē-ə-lē\ *adverb*

con·vo·ca·tion \,kän-və-'kā-shən\ *noun* [Middle English, from Middle French, from Latin *convocation-, convocatio,* from *convocare*] (14th century)
1 a : an assembly of persons convoked **b** (1) : an assembly of bishops and representative clergy of the Church of England (2) : a consultative assembly of clergy and lay delegates from one part of an Episcopal diocese; *also* : a territorial division of an Episcopal diocese **c** : a ceremonial assembly of members of a college or university
2 : the act or process of convoking
— **con·vo·ca·tion·al** \-shnəl, -shə-nºl\ *adjective*

con·voke \kən-'vōk\ *transitive verb* **con·voked; con·vok·ing** [Middle French *convoquer*, from Latin *convocare*, from *com-* + *vocare* to call, from *voc-, vox* voice — more at VOICE] (1598)
: to call together to a meeting
synonym see SUMMON

con·vo·lute \'kän-və-,lüt\ *verb* **-lut·ed; -lut·ing** [Latin *convolutus*, past participle of *convolvere*] (1698)
: TWIST, COIL

con·vo·lut·ed \-,lü-təd\ *adjective* (1766)
1 : having convolutions
2 : INVOLVED, INTRICATE

convoluted tubule *noun* (1923)
: all or part of the coiled sections of a nephron: **a** : PROXIMAL CONVOLUTED TUBULE **b** : DISTAL CONVOLUTED TUBULE

con·vo·lu·tion \,kän-və-'lü-shən\ *noun* (1545)
1 : a form or shape that is folded in curved or tortuous windings
2 : one of the irregular ridges on the surface of the brain and especially of the cerebrum of higher mammals
3 : a complication or intricacy of form, design, or structure

con·volve \kən-'välv, -'vȯlv *also* -'väv *or* -'vȯv\ *verb* **con·volved; con·volv·ing** [Latin *convolvere*, from *com-* + *volvere* to roll — more at VOLUBLE] (1650)
transitive verb
: to roll together : WRITHE
intransitive verb
: to roll together or circulate involvedly

con·vol·vu·lus \kən-'väl-vyə-ləs, -'vȯl- *also* -'väv-yə- *or* -'vȯv-yə-\ *noun, plural* **-lus·es** *or* **-li** \-,lī, -,lī, -,lē\ [New Latin, from Latin *convolvere*] (1548)
: any of a genus (*Convolvulus*) of erect, trailing, or twining herbs and shrubs of the morning-glory family

¹con·voy \'kän-,vȯi, kən-'\ *transitive verb* [Middle English, from Middle French *conveier, convoier* — more at CONVEY] (14th century)
: ACCOMPANY; *especially* : to escort for protection

²con·voy \'kän-,vȯi\ *noun* (1523)
1 : one that convoys; *especially* : a protective escort (as for ships)
2 : the act of convoying
3 : a group convoyed or organized for convenience or protection in moving

con·vul·sant \kən-'vəl-sənt\ *adjective* (1875)
: causing convulsions : CONVULSIVE 1a
— **convulsant** *noun*

con·vulse \kən-'vəls\ *verb* **con·vulsed; con·vuls·ing** [Latin *convulsus*, past participle of *convellere* to pluck up, convulse, from *com-* + *vellere* to pluck — more at VULNERABLE] (1643)
transitive verb
: to shake or agitate violently; *especially* : to shake with or as if with irregular spasms
intransitive verb
: to become affected with convulsions
synonym see SHAKE

con·vul·sion \kən-'vəl-shən\ *noun* (1547)
1 : an abnormal violent and involuntary contraction or series of contractions of the muscles
2 a : a violent disturbance **b** : an uncontrolled fit : PAROXYSM
— **con·vul·sion·ary** \-shə-,ner-ē\ *adjective*

con·vul·sive \kən-'vəl-siv\ *adjective* (1615)
1 a : constituting or producing a convulsion **b** : attended or affected with convulsions
2 : resembling a convulsion in being violent, sudden, frantic, or spasmodic
synonym see FITFUL
— **con·vul·sive·ly** *adverb*
— **con·vul·sive·ness** *noun*

cony *variant of* CONEY

coo \'kü\ *intransitive verb* [imitative] (1670)
1 : to make the low soft cry of a dove or pigeon or a similar sound

2 : to talk fondly, amorously, or appreciatively ⟨an album that will be *cooed* over by condescending classical music critics —Ellen Sander⟩
— **coo** *noun*

¹cook \'kůk\ *noun* [Middle English, from Old English *cōc*, from Latin *coquus*, from *coquere* to cook; akin to Old English *āfigen* fried, Greek *pessein* to cook] (before 12th century)
1 : a person who prepares food for eating
2 : a technical or industrial process comparable to cooking food; *also* : a substance so processed

²cook (14th century)
intransitive verb
1 : to prepare food for eating by means of heat
2 : to undergo the action of being cooked ⟨the rice is *cooking* now⟩
3 : OCCUR, HAPPEN ⟨find out what was *cooking* in the committee⟩
4 : to perform, do, or proceed well ⟨the jazz quartet was *cooking* along⟩ ⟨the party *cooked* right through the night⟩
transitive verb
1 : CONCOCT, FABRICATE — usually used with *up* ⟨*cooked* up a scheme⟩
2 : to prepare for eating by a heating process
3 : FALSIFY, DOCTOR ⟨*cooked* the books with phony spending cuts and accounting gimmickry —Colleen O'Connor⟩
4 : to subject to the action of heat or fire
— **cook·able** \'ků-kə-bəl\ *adjective*
— **cook one's goose** : to ruin one irretrievably

¹cook·book \-,bůk\ *noun* (1809)
: a book of cooking directions and recipes; *broadly* : a book of detailed instructions

²cookbook *adjective* (1944)
: involving or using step-by-step procedures whose rationale is usually not explained ⟨a *cookbook* approach⟩

cook cheese *noun* (1941)
: an unripened cheese made from curd that has been cooked to a soft consistency — called also *cooked cheese*

cook·er \'ků-kər\ *noun* (1869)
: one that cooks: as **a** : a utensil, device, or apparatus for cooking **b** : a person who tends a cooking process : COOK **c** *British* : STOVE

cook·ery \'ků-k(ə-)rē\ *noun, plural* **-er·ies** (14th century)
1 : the art or practice of cooking
2 : an establishment for cooking

cookery book *noun* (1639)
chiefly British : COOKBOOK

cook·house \'kůk-,haůs\ *noun* (1795)
: a building for cooking

cook·ie *or* **cooky** \'ků-kē\ *noun, plural* **cook·ies** [Dutch *koekje*, diminutive of *koek* cake] (1703)
1 : a small flat or slightly raised cake
2 a : an attractive woman ⟨a buxom French *cookie* who haunts the . . . colony's one night spot —*Newsweek*⟩ **b** : PERSON, GUY ⟨a tough *cookie*⟩

cookie–cutter *adjective* (1963)
: marked by lack of originality or distinction ⟨*cookie-cutter* shopping malls⟩

cookie cutter *noun* (1903)
: a device used to cut rolled cookie dough into shapes before baking

cookie sheet *noun* (1926)
: a flat rectangle of metal with at least one rolled edge used especially for the baking of cookies or biscuits

cooking *adjective* (circa 1813)
: suitable for or used in cooking ⟨*cooking* apples⟩

cook–off \'kůk-,ȯf, -,äf\ *noun* (1937)
: a cooking competition

cook off *intransitive verb* (1945)
of a cartridge : to fire as a result of overheating

cook·out \'kůk-,aůt\ *noun* (1947)
: an outing at which a meal is cooked and served in the open; *also* : the meal cooked

cook·shack \-,shak\ *noun* (1909)
: a shack used for cooking

cook·shop \-,shäp\ *noun* (circa 1552)
: a shop supplying or serving cooked food

Cook's tour \'kůks-\ *noun* [Thomas Cook & Son, English travel agency] (circa 1909)
: a rapid or cursory survey or review

cook·stove \'kůk-,stōv\ *noun* (1824)
: a stove for cooking

cook·top \'kůk-,täp\ *noun* (1948)
1 : the flat top of a range
2 : a built-in cabinet-top cooking apparatus containing usually four heating units

cook·ware \'kůk-,war, -,wer\ *noun* (1953)
: utensils used in cooking

¹cool \'kül\ *adjective* [Middle English *col*, from Old English *cōl*; akin to Old High German *kuoli* cool, Old English *ceald* cold — more at COLD] (before 12th century)
1 : moderately cold : lacking in warmth
2 a : marked by steady dispassionate calmness and self-control ⟨a *cool* and calculating administrator —*Current Biography*⟩ **b** : lacking ardor or friendliness ⟨a *cool* impersonal manner⟩ **c** *of jazz* : marked by restrained emotion and the frequent use of counterpoint **d** : free from tensions or violence ⟨meeting with minority groups in an attempt to keep the city *cool*⟩
3 — used as an intensive ⟨a *cool* million dollars⟩
4 : marked by deliberate effrontery or lack of due respect or discretion ⟨a *cool* reply⟩
5 : facilitating or suggesting relief from heat ⟨a *cool* dress⟩
6 a *of a color* : producing an impression of being cool; *specifically* : of a hue in the range violet through blue to green **b** *of a musical tone* : relatively lacking in timbre or resonance
7 *slang* **a** : very good : EXCELLENT; *also* : ALL RIGHT **b** : FASHIONABLE 1 ☆
— **cool·ish** \'kü-lish\ *adjective*
— **cool·ly** *also* **cooly** \'kü(l)-lē\ *adverb*
— **cool·ness** \'kül-nəs\ *noun*

²cool (before 12th century)
intransitive verb
1 : to become cool : lose heat or warmth ⟨placed the pie in the window to *cool*⟩ — sometimes used with *off* or *down*
2 : to lose ardor or passion ⟨his anger *cooled*⟩
transitive verb
1 : to make cool : impart a feeling of coolness to ⟨*cooled* the room with a fan⟩ — often used with *off* or *down* ⟨a swim *cooled* us off a little⟩
2 a : to moderate the heat, excitement, or force of : CALM ⟨*cooled* her growing anger⟩ **b** : to slow or lessen the growth or activity of — usually used with *off* or *down* ⟨wants to *cool* off the economy without freezing it —*Newsweek*⟩

— cool it : to calm down **:** go easy ⟨the word went out to the young to *cool it* —W. M. Young⟩

— cool one's heels : to wait or be kept waiting for a long time especially from or as if from disdain or discourtesy

³**cool** *noun* (15th century)
1 : a cool time, place, or situation ⟨the *cool* of the evening⟩
2 a : absence of excitement or emotional involvement **:** DETACHMENT ⟨must surrender his fine *cool* and enter the closed crazy world of suicide —Wilfrid Sheed⟩ **b :** POISE, COMPOSURE ⟨press questions . . . seemed to rattle him and he lost his *cool* —*New Republic*⟩

⁴**cool** *adverb* (1951)
: in a casual and nonchalant manner ⟨play it *cool*⟩

cool·ant \'kü-lənt\ *noun* (1926)
: a usually fluid cooling agent

cool·down \'kül-ˌdaůn\ *noun* (1980)
: the act or an instance of allowing physiological activity to return to normal gradually after strenuous exercise by engaging in less strenuous exercise

cool·er \'kü-lər\ *noun* (1575)
1 : one that cools: as **a :** a container for cooling liquids **b :** REFRIGERATOR
2 : LOCKUP, JAIL; *especially* **:** a cell for violent or unmanageable prisoners
3 : an iced drink usually with an alcoholic beverage as a base

Coo·ley's anemia \'kü-lēz-\ *noun* [Thomas B. *Cooley* (died 1945) American pediatrician] (circa 1935)
: a severe thalassemic anemia that is associated with the presence of microcytes, enlargement of the liver and spleen, increase in the erythroid bone marrow, and jaundice and that occurs especially in children of Mediterranean parents

cool·head·ed \'kül-ˌhe-dəd\ *adjective* (1777)
: not easily excited

coo·lie \'kü-lē\ *noun* [Hindi *kulī*] (1638)
: an unskilled laborer or porter usually in or from the Far East hired for low or subsistence wages

coolie hat *noun* (1924)
: a conical-shaped usually straw hat worn especially to protect the head from the heat of the sun

cool·ing–off \'kü-liŋ-ˈòf\ *adjective* (1926)
: designed to allow passions to cool or to permit negotiation between parties ⟨a *cooling-off* period⟩

cooling tower *noun* (1901)
: a structure over which circulated water is trickled to reduce its temperature by partial evaporation

coombe *or* **coomb** \'küm\ *variant of* COMBE

coon \'kün\ *noun* (1742)
1 : RACCOON
2 : BLACK 4 — usually taken to be offensive

coon·can \'kün-ˌkan\ *noun* [by folk etymology from Mexican Spanish *conquián* conquian, from Spanish *¿con quién?* with whom?] (1889)
: a game of rummy played with two packs including two jokers

coon cat *noun* (1901)
: MAINE COON

coon cheese \'kün-\ *noun* [probably from *coon* (black person); from the color of the coating] (1953)
: a sharp cheddar cheese that has been cured at higher than usual temperature and humidity and that is usually coated with black wax

coon·hound \'kün-ˌhaůnd\ *noun* (1920)
: a sporting dog trained to hunt raccoons; *especially* **:** BLACK-AND-TAN COONHOUND

coon's age *noun* (1844)
: a long while ⟨best fried chicken I've tasted for a *coon's age* —Sinclair Lewis⟩

coon·skin \'kün-ˌskin\ *noun* (1818)
1 : the skin or pelt of the raccoon

2 : an article (as a cap or coat) made of coonskin

coon·tie \'kün-tē\ *noun* [Creek (Florida dialect) *kuntí*] (1791)
: any of several tropical American woody plants (genus *Zamia*) of the cycad family whose roots and stems yield a starchy foodstuff — called also *arrowroot*

¹**coop** \'küp, 'kůp\ *noun* [Middle English *cupe*; akin to Old English *cȳpe* basket] (14th century)
1 : a cage or small enclosure (as for poultry); *also* **:** a small building for housing poultry
2 a : a confined area **b :** JAIL

²**coop** *transitive verb* (1583)
1 : to confine in a restricted and often crowded area — usually used with *up*
2 : to place or keep in a coop **:** PEN — often used with *up*

co–op \'kō-ˌäp, kō-'\ *noun* (1869)
: COOPERATIVE

¹**coo·per** \'kü-pər, 'ků-\ *noun* [Middle English *couper, cowper,* from Middle Dutch *cūper* (from *cūpe* cask) or Middle Low German *kūper,* from *kūpe* cask; Middle Dutch *cūpe* & Middle Low German *kūpe,* from Latin *cupa;* akin to Greek *kypellon* cup — more at HIVE] (14th century)
: one that makes or repairs wooden casks or tubs

²**cooper** *verb* **coo·pered; coo·per·ing** \'kü-p(ə-)riŋ, 'ků-\ (1742)
transitive verb
: to work as a cooper on
intransitive verb
: to work at or do coopering

coo·per·age \'kü-p(ə-)rij, 'ků-\ *noun* (1705)
1 : a cooper's work or products
2 : a cooper's place of business

co·op·er·ate \kō-'ä-pə-ˌrāt\ *intransitive verb* [Late Latin *cooperatus,* past participle of *cooperari,* from Latin *co-* + *operari* to work — more at OPERATE] (1582)
1 : to act or work with another or others **:** act together
2 : to associate with another or others for mutual benefit

— co·op·er·a·tor \-ˌrā-tər\ *noun*

co·op·er·a·tion \(ˌ)kō-ˌä-pə-'rā-shən\ *noun* (14th century)
1 : the action of cooperating **:** common effort
2 : association of persons for common benefit

— co·op·er·a·tion·ist \-sh(ə-)nist\ *noun*

¹**co·op·er·a·tive** \kō-'ä-p(ə-)rə-tiv, -'ä-pə-ˌrā-\ *adjective* (1603)
1 a : marked by cooperation ⟨*cooperative* efforts⟩ **b :** marked by a willingness and ability to work with others ⟨*cooperative* neighbors⟩
2 : of, relating to, or organized as a cooperative
3 : relating to or comprising a program of combined liberal arts and technical studies at different schools

— co·op·er·a·tive·ly *adverb*
— co·op·er·a·tive·ness *noun*

²**cooperative** *noun* (1883)
: an enterprise or organization owned by and operated for the benefit of those using its services

Coo·per's hawk \'kü-pərz-, 'ků-\ *noun* [William *Cooper* (died 1864) American naturalist] (1828)
: an American hawk (*Accipiter cooperii*) that is larger than the similarly colored sharp-shinned hawk and has a more rounded tail

co–opt \kō-'äpt\ *transitive verb* [Latin *cooptare,* from *co-* + *optare* to choose] (1651)
1 a : to choose or elect as a member **b :** to appoint as a colleague or assistant
2 a : to take into a group (as a faction, movement, or culture) ⟨the students are *co-opted* by a system they serve even in their struggle against it —A. C. Danto⟩ **b :** TAKE OVER, APPROPRIATE

— co–op·ta·tion \ˌkō-ˌäp-'tā-shən\ *noun*
— co–op·ta·tive \kō-'äp-tə-tiv\ *adjective*

— co–op·tion \-'äp-shən\ *noun*
— co–op·tive \-'äp-tiv\ *adjective*

¹**co·or·di·nate** \kō-'órd-nət; -'ór-d⁰n-ət, -də-ˌnāt\ *adjective* [probably back-formation from *coordination*] (1641)
1 a : equal in rank, quality, or significance **b :** being of equal rank in a sentence ⟨*coordinate* clauses⟩
2 : relating to or marked by coordination
3 a : being a university that awards degrees to men and women taught usually by the same faculty but attending separate classes often on separate campuses **b :** being one of the colleges and especially the women's branch of a coordinate university
4 : of, relating to, or being a system of indexing by two or more terms so that documents may be retrieved through the intersection of index terms

— co·or·di·nate·ly *adverb*
— co·or·di·nate·ness *noun*

²**co·or·di·nate** \kō-'ór-d⁰n-ˌāt\ *verb* **-nat·ed; -nat·ing** (1665)
transitive verb
1 : to put in the same order or rank
2 : to bring into a common action, movement, or condition **:** HARMONIZE
3 : to attach so as to form a coordination complex
intransitive verb
1 : to be or become coordinate especially so as to act together in a smooth concerted way
2 : to combine by means of a coordinate bond

— co·or·di·na·tive \kō-'órd-nə-tiv; -'ór-d⁰n-ə-tiv, -də-ˌnā-\ *adjective*
— co·or·di·na·tor \-'ór-də-ˌnā-tər\ *noun*

³**co·or·di·nate** *same as* ¹\ *noun* (circa 1823)
1 a : any of a set of numbers used in specifying the location of a point on a line, on a surface, or in space **b :** any one of a set of variables used in specifying the state of a substance or the motion of a particle or momentum
2 : one who is of equal rank, authority, or importance with another
3 *plural* **:** articles (as of clothing) designed to be used together and to attain their effect through pleasing contrast (as of color, material, or texture)

coordinate bond *noun* (1947)
: a covalent bond that consists of a pair of electrons supplied by only one of the two atoms it joins

co·or·di·nat·ed \-'ór-də-ˌnā-təd\ *adjective* (1939)
: able to use more than one set of muscle movements to a single end ⟨a well-*coordinated* athlete⟩

Coordinated Universal Time *noun* (1969)
: the international standard of time that is kept by atomic clocks around the world — abbreviation *UTC*

coordinate geometry *noun* (1855)
: ANALYTIC GEOMETRY

coordinating conjunction *noun* (1916)
: a conjunction that joins together words or word groups of equal grammatical rank

co·or·di·na·tion \(ˌ)kō-ˌór-də-'nā-shən\ *noun* [Late Latin *coordination-, coordinatio,* from Latin *co-* + *ordination-, ordinatio* arrangement, from *ordinare* to arrange — more at ORDAIN] (circa 1643)
1 : the act or action of coordinating
2 : the harmonious functioning of parts for effective results

coordination complex *noun* (1951)
: a compound or ion with a central usually metallic atom or ion combined by coordinate bonds with a definite number of surrounding

\ə\ abut	\⁰\ kitten	\ər\ further	\a\ ash	\ā\ ace	
\ä\ mop, mar	\aů\ out	\ch\ chin	\e\ bet	\ē\ easy	
\g\ go	\i\ hit	\ī\ ice	\j\ job	\ŋ\ sing	\ō\ go
\ò\ law	\òi\ boy	\th\ thin	\t͟h\ the	\ü\ loot	\ů\ foot
\y\ yet	\zh\ vision		*see also* Guide to Pronunciation		

ions, groups, or molecules — called also *co-ordination compound*

coordination number *noun* (1908)
1 : the number of attachments to the central atom in a coordination complex
2 : a number used in specifying the spatial arrangement of the constituent groups of crystals

coot \'küt\ *noun* [Middle English *coote;* akin to Dutch *koet* coot] (15th century)
1 : any of various sluggish slow-flying slaty-black birds (genus *Fulica*) of the rail family that somewhat resemble ducks and have lobed toes and the upper mandible prolonged on the forehead as a horny frontal shield
2 : any of several North American scoters
3 : a harmless simple person; *broadly* **:** FELLOW 4c

coo·ter \'kü-tər *also* 'ku̇-tə\ *noun* [of African origin; akin to Bambara & Malinke *kuta* turtle] (1832)
chiefly Southern **:** any of several turtles (genus *Pseudemys* and especially *P. concinna*) especially of the southern and eastern U.S.

coo·tie \'kü-tē\ *noun* [perhaps modification of Malay *kutu*] (1917)
: BODY LOUSE

¹cop \'käp\ *noun* [Middle English, from Old English *copp*] (before 12th century)
1 *dialect chiefly English* **:** TOP, CREST
2 : a cylindrical or conical mass of thread, yarn, or roving wound on a quill or tube; *also* **:** a quill or tube upon which it is wound

²cop *transitive verb* **copped; cop·ping** [perhaps from Dutch *kapen* to steal, from Frisian *kāpia* to take away; akin to Old High German *kouf* trade — more at CHEAP] (1704)
1 *slang* **:** to get hold of **:** CATCH, CAPTURE; *also* **:** PURCHASE
2 *slang* **:** STEAL, SWIPE
— **cop a plea :** to plead guilty to a lesser charge in order to avoid standing trial for a more serious one; *broadly* **:** to admit fault and plead for mercy

³cop *noun* [short for ³*copper*] (1859)
: POLICE OFFICER

co·pa·cet·ic *or* **co·pe·set·ic** *also* **co·pa·set·ic** \,kō-pə-'se-tik\ *adjective* [origin unknown] (1919)
: very satisfactory

co·pai·ba \kō-'pī-bə, -'pā-\ *noun* [Spanish & Portuguese; Spanish, from Portuguese *copaíba*, from Tupi] (1712)
: a stimulant oleoresin obtained from several pinnate-leaved South American leguminous trees (genus *Copaifera*); *also* **:** one of these trees

co·pal \'kō-pəl, -,pal; kō-'pal\ *noun* [Spanish, from Nahuatl *copalli* resin] (1577)
: a recent or fossil resin from various tropical trees

co·par·ce·nary \kō-'pär-s°n-,er-ē\ *noun, plural* **-nar·ies** (circa 1504)
1 : joint heirship
2 : joint ownership

co·par·ce·ner \-'pärs-nər, -'pär-s°n-ər\ *noun* (15th century)
: a joint heir

co·pay·ment \'kō-,pā-mənt, ,kō-'\ *noun* (1975)
: a relatively small fixed fee required by a health insurer (as an HMO) to be paid by the patient at the time of each office visit, outpatient service, or filling of a prescription

¹cope \'kōp\ *noun* [Middle English, from Old English *-cāp*, from Late Latin *cappa* head covering] (13th century)
1 : a long enveloping ecclesiastical vestment
2 a : something resembling a cope (as by concealing or covering) ⟨the dark sky's starry *cope* —P. B. Shelley⟩ **b :** COPING

²cope *transitive verb* **coped; cop·ing** (14th century)
: to cover or furnish with a cope

³cope *verb* **coped; cop·ing** [Middle English *copen, coupen,* from Middle French *couper* to strike, cut, from Old French, from *coup* blow,

from Late Latin *colpus,* alteration of Latin *colaphus,* from Greek *kolaphos* buffet] (14th century)
intransitive verb
1 *obsolete* **:** STRIKE, FIGHT
2 a : to maintain a contest or combat usually on even terms or with success — used with *with* **b :** to deal with and attempt to overcome problems and difficulties — often used with *with*
3 *archaic* **:** MEET, ENCOUNTER
transitive verb
1 *obsolete* **:** to meet in combat
2 *obsolete* **:** to come in contact with
3 *obsolete* **:** MATCH

⁴cope *transitive verb* **coped; cop·ing** [probably from French *couper* to cut] (circa 1901)
1 : to shape (a structural member) to fit a coping or fit with the shape of another member
2 : NOTCH

co·peck *variant of* KOPECK

co·pe·pod \'kō-pə-,päd\ *noun* [ultimately from Greek *kōpē* oar, handle + *pod-, pous* foot; probably akin to Latin *capere* to take — more at HEAVE, FOOT] (1836)
: any of a large subclass (Copepoda) of usually minute freshwater and marine crustaceans
— **copepod** *adjective*

cop·er \'kō-pər\ *noun* [English dialect *cope* to trade] (1825)
British **:** a horse dealer; *especially* **:** a dishonest one

Co·per·ni·can \kə-'pər-ni-kən, kō-\ *adjective* [Nicolaus *Copernicus*] (1667)
1 : of or relating to Copernicus or the belief that the earth rotates daily on its axis and the planets revolve in orbits around the sun
2 : of radical or major importance or degree ⟨effected a *Copernican* revolution in philosophy —*Times Literary Supplement*⟩
— **Copernican** *noun*
— **Co·per·ni·can·ism** \-kə-,ni-zəm\ *noun*

cope·stone \'kōp-,stōn\ *noun* (1567)
1 : a stone forming a coping
2 : a finishing touch **:** CROWN

cop·i·er \'kä-pē-ər\ *noun* (1597)
: one that copies; *specifically* **:** a machine for making copies of graphic matter (as printing, drawings, or pictures)

co·pi·lot \'kō-,pī-lət\ *noun* (1927)
: a qualified pilot who assists or relieves the pilot but is not in command

cop·ing \'kō-piŋ\ *noun* (1601)
: the covering course of a wall usually with a sloping top

coping saw \'kō-piŋ-\ *noun* [from present participle of ⁴*cope*] (1925)
: a handsaw with a very narrow blade held under tension in a U-shaped frame and used especially for cutting curves in wood

coping saw

cop·ing·stone \'kō-piŋ-,stōn\ *noun* (1778)
chiefly British **:** COPESTONE

co·pi·ous \'kō-pē-əs\ *adjective* [Middle English, from Latin *copiosus,* from *copia* abundance, from *co-* + *ops* wealth — more at OPULENT] (14th century)
1 a : yielding something abundantly ⟨a *copious* harvest⟩ ⟨*copious* springs⟩ **b :** plentiful in number ⟨*copious* references to other writers⟩
2 a : full of thought, information, or matter **b :** profuse or exuberant in words, expression, or style ⟨a *copious* talker⟩
3 : present in large quantity **:** taking place on a large scale ⟨*copious* weeping⟩ ⟨*copious* food and drink⟩
synonym see PLENTIFUL
— **co·pi·ous·ly** *adverb*
— **co·pi·ous·ness** *noun*

co·pla·nar \(,)kō-'plā-nər, -,när\ *adjective* (1862)
: lying or acting in the same plane

— **co·pla·nar·i·ty** \,kō-plā-'nar-ə-tē\ *noun*

co·pol·y·mer \(,)kō-'pä-lə-mər\ *noun* (1936)
: a product of copolymerization
— **co·pol·y·mer·ic** \,kō-,pä-lə-'mer-ik\ *adjective*

co·po·ly·mer·i·za·tion \kō-pə-,li-mə-rə-'zā-shən, ,kō-,pä-lə-mə-\ *noun* (1936)
: the polymerization of two substances (as different monomers) together
— **co·po·ly·mer·ize** \,kō-pə-'li-mə-,rīz, ,kō-'pä-lə-mə-\ *verb*

cop–out \'käp-,au̇t\ *noun* (circa 1942)
1 : the act or an instance of copping out
2 : an excuse or means for copping out **:** PRETEXT
3 : a person who cops out

cop out *intransitive verb* (circa 1961)
1 : to back out of (as of an unwanted responsibility) ⟨*cop out* on jury duty⟩
2 : to avoid or neglect problems, responsibilities, or commitments ⟨accused the mayor of *copping out* on the issue of homelessness⟩

¹cop·per \'kä-pər\ *noun, often attributive* [Middle English *coper,* from Old English, from Late Latin *cuprum* copper, from Latin (*aes*) *Cyprium,* literally, Cyprian metal] (before 12th century)
1 : a common reddish metallic element that is ductile and malleable and is one of the best conductors of heat and electricity — see ELEMENT table
2 : a coin or token made of copper or bronze
3 *chiefly British* **:** a large boiler (as for cooking)
4 : any of a subfamily (Lycaeninae of the family Lycaenidae) of small butterflies with usually copper-colored wings

²copper *transitive verb* **cop·pered; cop·per·ing** \'kä-p(ə-)riŋ\ (1530)
: to coat or sheathe with or as if with copper

³copper *noun* [²*cop*] (1846)
: POLICE OFFICER

cop·per·as \'kä-p(ə-)rəs\ *noun* [Middle English *coperas,* from Old French *couperose,* from Medieval Latin *cuprosa,* probably from *aqua cuprosa,* literally, copper water, from Late Latin *cuprum*] (14th century)
: a green hydrated ferrous sulfate $FeSO_4 \cdot 7H_2O$ used especially in making inks and pigments

cop·per·head \'kä-pər-,hed\ *noun* (1775)
1 : a common pit viper (*Agkistrodon contortrix*) of the eastern and central U.S. usually having a copper-colored head and often a reddish brown hourglass pattern on the body

copperhead 1

2 : a person in the northern states who sympathized with the South during the Civil War

cop·per·plate \'kä-pər-,plāt\ *noun* (1663)
1 : an engraved or etched copper printing plate; *also* **:** a print made from such a plate
2 : a neat script handwriting based on engraved models

copper pyrites *noun* (1776)
: CHALCOPYRITE

cop·per·smith \'kä-pər-,smith\ *noun* (14th century)
: a worker in copper

copper sulfate *noun* (circa 1893)
: a sulfate of copper; *especially* **:** the normal sulfate that is white in the anhydrous form but blue in the crystalline hydrous form $CuSO_4 \cdot 5H_2O$ and that is often used as an algicide and fungicide

cop·pery \'kä-p(ə-)rē\ *adjective* (circa 1775)
: resembling or suggesting copper; *especially* **:** having the reddish to brownish orange color of copper ⟨*coppery* leaves⟩

¹**cop·pice** \'kä-pəs\ *noun* [Middle French *copeiz*, from *couper* to cut — more at COPE] (1534)
1 : a thicket, grove, or growth of small trees
2 : forest originating mainly from shoots or root suckers rather than seed
²**coppice** *verb* **cop·piced; cop·pic·ing** (1538)
transitive verb
: to cut back so as to regrow in the form of a coppice
intransitive verb
: to form a coppice; *specifically, of a tree* : to sprout freely from the base
copr- *or* **copro-** *combining form* [New Latin, from Greek *kopr-, kopro-,* from *kopros* akin to Sanskrit *śakṛt* dung]
: dung : feces ⟨*copro*lite⟩
co·pra \'kō-prə *also* 'kä-\ *noun* [Portuguese, from Malayalam *koppara*] (1584)
: dried coconut meat yielding coconut oil
co·pro·ces·sor \(,)kō-'prä-se-sər, -'prō-\ *noun* (1980)
: an extra processor in a computer that is designed to perform specialized tasks (as mathematical calculations)
co·prod·uct \(,)kō-'prä-(,)dəkt\ *noun* (1942)
: BY-PRODUCT 1
cop·ro·lite \'kä-prə-,līt\ *noun* (1829)
: fossilized excrement
— **cop·ro·lit·ic** \,kä-prə-'li-tik\ *adjective*
co·proph·a·gous \kə-'prä-fə-gəs\ *adjective* [Greek *koprophagos,* from *kopr-* + *-phagos* -phagous] (1826)
: feeding on dung
— **co·proph·a·gy** \-fə-jē\ *noun*
cop·ro·phil·ia \,kä-prə-'fi-lē-ə\ *noun* [New Latin] (1923)
: marked interest in excrement; *especially* : the use of feces or filth for sexual excitement
— **cop·ro·phil·i·ac** \-lē-,ak\ *noun*
cop·roph·i·lous \kə-'prä-fə-ləs\ *adjective* (circa 1900)
: growing or living on dung ⟨*coprophilous* fungi⟩
copse \'käps\ *noun* [by alteration] (1578)
: COPPICE 1
Copt \'käpt\ *noun* [Arabic *qubṭ* Copts, from Coptic *gyptios* Egyptian, from Greek *Aigyptios*] (1615)
1 : a member of the traditional Monophysite Christian church originating and centering in Egypt
2 : a member of a people descended from the ancient Egyptians
cop·ter \'käp-tər\ *noun* (1943)
: HELICOPTER
¹**Cop·tic** \'käp-tik\ *adjective* (1677)
: of or relating to the Copts, their liturgical language, or their church
²**Coptic** *noun* (1711)
: an Afro-Asiatic language descended from ancient Egyptian and used as the liturgical language of the Coptic church
cop·u·la \'kä-pyə-lə\ *noun* [Latin, bond — more at COUPLE] (1619)
: something that connects: as **a** : the connecting link between subject and predicate of a proposition **b** : LINKING VERB
cop·u·late \'kä-pyə-,lāt\ *intransitive verb* **-lat·ed; -lat·ing** [Latin *copulatus,* past participle of *copulare* to join, from *copula*] (1632)
: to engage in sexual intercourse
— **cop·u·la·tion** \,kä-pyə-'lā-shən\ *noun*
— **cop·u·la·to·ry** \'kä-pyə-lə-,tōr-ē, -,tòr-\ *adjective*
¹**cop·u·la·tive** \'kä-pyə-lə-tiv, -,lā-\ *adjective* (14th century)
1 a : joining together coordinate words or word groups and expressing addition of their meanings ⟨a *copulative* conjunction⟩ **b** : functioning as a copula
2 : relating to or serving for copulation
²**copulative** *noun* (1530)
: a copulative word

¹**copy** \'kä-pē\ *noun, plural* **cop·ies** [Middle English *copie,* from Middle French, from Medieval Latin *copia,* from Latin, abundance — more at COPIOUS] (14th century)
1 : an imitation, transcript, or reproduction of an original work (as a letter, a painting, a table, or a dress)
2 : one of a series of especially mechanical reproductions of an original impression; *also* : an individual example of such a reproduction
3 *archaic* : something to be imitated : MODEL
4 a : matter to be set especially for printing **b** : something considered printable or newsworthy — used without an article ⟨remarks that make good *copy*⟩ —Norman Cousins **c** : text especially of an advertisement
synonym see REPRODUCTION
²**copy** *verb* **cop·ied; copy·ing** (14th century)
transitive verb
1 : to make a copy of
2 : to model oneself on
intransitive verb
1 : to make a copy
2 : to undergo copying ⟨the document did not *copy* well⟩ ☆
copy·book \'kä-pē-,bůk\ *noun* (1588)
: a book formerly used in teaching penmanship and containing models for imitation
copy·boy \-,bòi\ *noun* (1888)
: one who carries copy and runs errands
¹**copy·cat** \-,kat\ *noun, often attributive* (1896)
1 : one who imitates or adopts the behavior or practices of another
2 : an imitative act or product ⟨*copycat* board games⟩
²**copycat** *verb* **copy·cat·ted; copy·cat·ting** (1926)
intransitive verb
: to act as a copycat
transitive verb
: IMITATE
copy·desk \-,desk\ *noun* (1921)
: the desk at which newspaper copy is edited
copy editor *noun* (1899)
: an editor who prepares copy for the printer; *also* : one who edits and headlines newspaper copy
— **copy·ed·it** \'kä-pē-,e-dət\ *transitive verb*
copy·hold \'kä-pē-,hōld\ *noun* (15th century)
1 : a former tenure of land in England and Ireland by right of being recorded in the court of the manor
2 : an estate held by copyhold
copy·hold·er \-,hōl-dər\ *noun* (1874)
1 : a device for holding copy especially for a typesetter
2 : one who reads copy for a proofreader
copy·ist \'kä-pē-ist\ *noun* (1699)
1 : one who makes copies
2 : IMITATOR
copy·read·er \-,rē-dər\ *noun* (1892)
: COPY EDITOR
— **copy·read** \-,rēd\ *transitive verb*
¹**copy·right** \-,rīt\ *noun* (1735)
: the exclusive legal right to reproduce, publish, and sell the matter and form (as of a literary, musical, or artistic work)
²**copyright** *transitive verb* (circa 1806)
: to secure a copyright on
— **copy·right·able** \-,rī-tə-bəl\ *adjective*
³**copyright** *adjective* (1870)
: secured by copyright
copy·writ·er \'kä-pē-,rī-tər\ *noun* (1911)
: a writer of advertising or publicity copy
coq au vin \,kök-ō-'va[n], ,käk-ō-\ *noun* [French, cock with wine] (circa 1938)
: chicken cooked in usually red wine
¹**co·quet** *noun* [French, diminutive of *coq* cock] (1691)
1 \kō-'ket, -'kā\ : a man who indulges in coquetry
2 \-'ket\ : COQUETTE
²**co·quet** \kō-'ket\ *adjective* (1697)
: characteristic of a coquette : COQUETTISH

³**co·quet** *or* **co·quette** \-'ket\ *intransitive verb* **co·quet·ted; co·quet·ting** (1701)
1 : to play the coquette : FLIRT
2 : to deal with something playfully rather than seriously
synonym see TRIFLE
co·que·try \'kō-kə-trē, kō-'ke-trē\ *noun, plural* **-tries** (circa 1656)
: a flirtatious act or attitude
co·quette \kō-'ket\ *noun* [French, feminine of *coquet*] (circa 1611)
: a woman who endeavors without sincere affection to gain the attention and admiration of men
— **co·quett·ish** \-'ke-tish\ *adjective*
— **co·quett·ish·ly** *adverb*
— **co·quett·ish·ness** *noun*
co·qui·na \kō-'kē-nə\ *noun* [Spanish, probably diminutive of *coca* head, alteration of *coco* bogeyman, coconut] (1837)
1 : a soft whitish limestone formed of broken shells and corals cemented together and used for building
2 : a small clam (*Donax variabilis*) used for broth or chowder and occurring in the intertidal zone of sandy Atlantic beaches from Delaware to the Gulf of Mexico
cor \'kòr\ *noun* [Middle English, from Late Latin *corus,* from Hebrew *kōr*] (14th century)
: an ancient Hebrew and Phoenician unit of measure of capacity
cor·a·cle \'kòr-ə-kəl, 'kär-\ *noun* [Welsh *corwgl*] (circa 1547)
: a small boat used in Britain from ancient times and made of a frame (as of wicker) covered usually with hide or tarpaulin
cor·a·coid \'kòr-ə-,kòid, 'kär-\ *adjective* [New Latin *coracoides,* from Greek *korakoeidēs,* literally, like a raven, from *korak-, korax* raven — more at RAVEN] (1741)
: of, relating to, or being a process of the scapula in most mammals or a well-developed cartilage bone of many lower vertebrates that extends from the scapula to or toward the sternum
— **coracoid** *noun*
cor·al \'kòr-əl, 'kär-\ *noun* [Middle English, from Middle French, from Latin *corallium,* from Greek *korallion*] (14th century)
1 a : the calcareous or horny skeletal deposit produced by anthozoan or rarely hydrozoan polyps; *especially* : a richly red precious coral secreted by a gorgonian (genus *Corallium*) **b** : a polyp or polyp colony together with its membranes and skeleton
2 : a piece of coral and especially of red coral
3 a : a bright reddish ovary (as of a lobster or scallop) **b** : a deep pink
— **coral** *adjective*
— **cor·al·loid** \-ə-,lòid\ *adjective*

☆ **SYNONYMS**
Copy, imitate, mimic, ape, mock mean to make something so that it resembles an existing thing. COPY suggests duplicating an original as nearly as possible ⟨*copied* the painting and sold the fake as an original⟩. IMITATE suggests following a model or a pattern but may allow for some variation ⟨*imitate* a poet's style⟩. MIMIC implies a close copying (as of voice or mannerism) often for fun, ridicule, or lifelike imitation ⟨pupils *mimicking* their teacher⟩. APE may suggest presumptuous, slavish, or inept imitating of a superior original ⟨American fashion designers *aped* their European colleagues⟩. MOCK usually implies imitation with derision ⟨*mocking* a vain man's pompous manner⟩.

\ə\ abut \ə'\ kitten \ər\ further \a\ ash \ā\ ace
\ä\ mop, mar \au̇\ out \ch\ chin \e\ bet \ē\ easy
\g\ go \i\ hit \ī\ ice \j\ job \ŋ\ sing \ō\ go
\ò\ law \òi\ boy \th\ thin \th\ the \ü\ loot \u̇\ foot
\y\ yet \zh\ vision *see also* Guide to Pronunciation

cor·al·bells \'kȯr-əl-ˌbelz, 'kär-\ *noun plural but singular or plural in construction* (circa 1900)
: a perennial alumroot (*Heuchera sanguinea*) widely cultivated for its feathery spikes of tiny bright red campanulate flowers

cor·al·ber·ry \-ˌber-ē\ *noun* (circa 1859)
: an American dwarf shrub (*Symphoricarpos orbiculatus*) that bears clusters of small flowers succeeded by red berries

¹cor·al·line \'kȯr-ə-ˌlīn, 'kär-\ *noun* (1543)
1 : a coralline red alga
2 : a bryozoan or hydroid that resembles a coral

²coralline *adjective* [Middle French, from feminine of *corallin* coral-like, from Late Latin *corallinus*, from Latin *corallium*] (circa 1633)
1 : of, relating to, or resembling coral
2 : of, relating to, or being any of a family (Corallinaceae) of calcareous red algae

coral snake *noun* (circa 1772)
1 : any of several venomous chiefly tropical New World elapid snakes (genus *Micrurus*) brilliantly banded in red, black, and yellow or white that include two (*M. fulvius* and *M. euryxanthus*) ranging northward into the southern U.S.
2 : any of several harmless snakes resembling the coral snakes

co·ran·to \kə-'ran-(ˌ)tō\ *noun, plural* **-tos** *or* **-toes** [modification of French *courante*] (1564)
: COURANTE

cor·ban \'kȯr-ˌban\ *noun* [Hebrew *qorbān* offering] (14th century)
: a sacrifice or offering to God among the ancient Hebrews

cor·beil *or* **cor·beille** \'kȯr-bəl, kȯr-'bā\ *noun* [French *corbeille*, literally, basket, from Late Latin *corbicula*] (circa 1734)
: a sculptured basket of flowers or fruit as an architectural decoration

¹cor·bel \'kȯr-bəl\ *noun* [Middle English, from Middle French, from diminutive of *corp* raven, from Latin *corvus* — more at RAVEN] (15th century)
: an architectural member that projects from within a wall and supports a weight; *especially* : one that is stepped upward and outward from a vertical surface

²corbel *transitive verb* **-beled** *or* **-belled**; **-bel·ing** *or* **-bel·ling** (1843)
: to furnish with or make into a corbel

corbeling *noun* (1548)
1 : corbel work
2 : the construction of a corbel

cor·bic·u·la \kȯr-'bi-kyə-lə\ *noun, plural* **-lae** \-(ˌ)lē, -ˌlī\ [Late Latin, diminutive of Latin *corbis* basket] (1816)
: POLLEN BASKET

cor·bie \'kȯr-bē\ *noun* [Middle English, modification of Middle French *corbin*, from Latin *corvinus* of a raven — more at CORVINE] (15th century)
chiefly Scottish : CARRION CROW; *also* : RAVEN

cor·bi·na \kȯr-'bē-nə\ *noun* [Mexican Spanish, from Spanish *corvina*, a marine fish (*Argyrosomus regius*), from feminine of *corvino* of a raven, from Latin *corvinus*] (1901)
: a coastal marine croaker (*Menticirrhus undulatus*) favored by surf casters along the California coast

¹cord \'kȯrd\ *noun* [Middle English, from Middle French *corde*, from Latin *chorda* string, from Greek *chordē* — more at YARN] (14th century)
1 a : a long slender flexible material usually consisting of several strands (as of thread or yarn) woven or twisted together **b** : the hangman's rope
2 : a moral, spiritual, or emotional bond
3 a : an anatomical structure (as a nerve or the umbilical cord) resembling a cord **b** : a small flexible insulated electrical cable having a

plug at one or both ends used to connect a lamp or other appliance with a receptacle
4 : a unit of wood cut for fuel equal to a stack 4 x 4 x 8 feet or 128 cubic feet
5 a : a rib like a cord on a textile **b** (1) : a fabric made with such ribs or a garment made of such a fabric (2) *plural* : trousers made of such a fabric

²cord *transitive verb* (15th century)
1 : to furnish, bind, or connect with a cord
2 : to pile up (wood) in cords
— **cord·er** *noun*

cord·age \'kȯr-dij\ *noun* (1598)
1 : ropes or cords; *especially* : the ropes in the rigging of a ship
2 : the number of cords (as of wood) on a given area

cor·date \'kȯr-ˌdāt\ *adjective* [New Latin *cordatus*, from Latin *cord-, cor*] (1769)
: shaped like a heart ⟨a *cordate* leaf⟩ — see LEAF illustration
— **cor·date·ly** *adverb*

cord·ed \'kȯr-dəd\ *adjective* (14th century)
1 a : made of or provided with cords or ridges; *specifically* : muscled in ridges **b** *of a muscle* : TENSE, TAUT
2 : bound, fastened, or wound about with cords
3 : striped or ribbed with or as if with cord : TWILLED

cord·grass \'kȯrd-ˌgras\ *noun* (1857)
: any of a genus (*Spartina*) of chiefly saltmarsh grasses of coastal regions of Europe, northern Africa, and the New World that have stiff culms and panicled spikelets

¹cor·dial \'kȯr-jəl\ *adjective* [Middle English, from Medieval Latin *cordialis*, from Latin *cord-, cor* heart — more at HEART] (14th century)
1 *obsolete* : of or relating to the heart : VITAL
2 : tending to revive, cheer, or invigorate
3 a : sincerely or deeply felt ⟨a *cordial* dislike for each other⟩ **b** : warmly and genially affable ⟨*cordial* relations⟩
synonym see GRACIOUS
— **cor·dial·ly** \'kȯrj-lē, 'kȯr-jə-\ *adverb*
— **cor·dial·ness** \'kȯr-jəl-nəs\ *noun*

²cordial *noun* (14th century)
1 : a stimulating medicine or drink
2 : LIQUEUR

cor·dial·i·ty \ˌkȯr-jē-'a-lə-tē, kȯr-'ja- *also* kȯr-'dya-\ *noun* (1611)
: sincere affection and kindness : cordial regard

cordia pulmonalia *plural of* COR PULMONALE

cor·di·er·ite \'kȯr-dē-ə-ˌrīt\ *noun* [French, from Pierre L. A. *Cordier* (died 1861) French geologist] (circa 1814)
: a blue mineral of vitreous luster and strong dichroism that consists of a silicate of aluminum, iron, and magnesium

cor·di·form \'kȯr-də-ˌfȯrm\ *adjective* [French *cordiforme*, from Latin *cord-, cor* + French *-iforme* -iform] (1828)
: shaped like a heart ⟨a *cordiform* sea-urchin shell⟩

cor·dil·le·ra \ˌkȯr-d°l-'yer-ə, -də-'ler- *also* kȯr-'di-lə-rə\ *noun* [Spanish] (1704)
: a system of mountain ranges often consisting of a number of more or less parallel chains
— **cor·dil·le·ran** \-'yer-ən, -'ler-, -'di-lə-rən\ *adjective*

cord·ite \'kȯr-ˌdīt\ *noun* (1889)
: a smokeless powder composed of nitroglycerin, guncotton, and a petroleum substance usually gelatinized by addition of acetone and pressed into cords resembling brown twine

cord·less \'kȯr-dləs\ *adjective* (1906)
: having no cord; *especially* : powered by a battery ⟨*cordless* tools⟩

cor·do·ba \'kȯr-də-bə, -və\ *noun* [Spanish *córdoba*, from Francisco Fernández de *Córdoba* (died 1526) Spanish explorer] (1913)
— see MONEY table

¹cor·don \'kȯr-d°n, -ˌdän\ *noun* [French, diminutive of *corde* cord] (15th century)

1 a : an ornamental cord or ribbon **b** : STRINGCOURSE
2 a : a line of troops or of military posts enclosing an area to prevent passage **b** : a line of persons or objects around a person or place ⟨a *cordon* of police⟩
3 : an espalier especially of a fruit tree trained as a single horizontal shoot or two diverging horizontal shoots in a single line

²cordon *transitive verb* (1561)
: to form a protective or restrictive cordon around — usually used with *off*

cor·don sa·ni·taire \ˌkȯr-ˌdōⁿ-sà-nē-'ter\ *noun* [French, literally, sanitary cordon (quarantine line)] (1920)
: a protective barrier (as of buffer states) against a potentially aggressive nation or a dangerous influence (as an ideology)

¹cor·do·van \'kȯr-də-vən\ *adjective* [Old Spanish *cordovano*, from *Córdova* (now *Córdoba*), Spain] (1591)
1 *capitalized* : of or relating to Córdoba and especially Córdoba, Spain
2 : made of cordovan leather

²cordovan *noun* (circa 1625)
1 : a soft fine-grained colored leather
2 : dense nonporous leather tanned from the inner layer of horsehide

¹cor·du·roy \'kȯr-də-ˌrȯi\ *noun, plural* **-roys** [origin unknown] (circa 1791)
1 a *plural* : trousers of corduroy fabric **b** : a durable usually cotton pile fabric with vertical ribs or wales
2 : logs laid side by side transversely to make a road surface

²corduroy *transitive verb* **-royed**; **-roy·ing** (1854)
: to build (a road) of logs laid side by side transversely; *also* : to build a corduroy road across

cord·wain \'kȯrd-ˌwān\ *noun* [Middle English *cordwane*, from Middle French *cordoan*, from Old Spanish *cordovano, cordován*] (14th century) *archaic*
: cordovan leather

cord·wain·er \-ˌwā-nər\ *noun* (14th century)
1 *archaic* : a worker in cordovan leather
2 : SHOEMAKER
— **cord·wain·ery** \-ˌwā-nə-rē\ *noun*

cord·wood \'kȯrd-ˌwùd\ *noun* (circa 1639)
: wood piled or sold in cords

¹core \'kȯr, 'kȯr\ *noun, often attributive* [Middle English] (14th century)
1 : a central and often foundational part usually distinct from the enveloping part by a difference in nature ⟨*core* of the city⟩: as **a** : the usually inedible central part of some fruits (as a pineapple); *especially* : the papery or leathery carpels composing the ripened ovary in a pome fruit **b** : the portion of a foundry mold that shapes the interior of a hollow casting **c** : a vertical space (as for elevator shafts, stairways, or plumbing apparatus) in a multistory building **d** (1) : a mass of iron serving to concentrate and intensify the magnetic field resulting from a current in a surrounding coil (2) : a tiny doughnut-shaped piece of magnetic material (as ferrite) used in computer memories (3) : a computer memory consisting of an array of cores strung on fine wires; *broadly* : the internal memory of a computer **e** : the central part of a celestial body (as the earth or sun) usually having different physical properties from the surrounding parts **f** : a nodule of stone (as flint or obsidian) from which flakes have been struck for making implements **g** : the conducting wire with its insulation in an electric cable **h** : an arrangement of a course of studies that combines under basic topics material from subjects conventionally separated and aims to provide a common background for all students ⟨*core* curriculum⟩ **i** : the place in a nuclear reactor where fission occurs
2 a : a basic, essential, or enduring part (as of an individual, a class, or an entity) ⟨the staff had a *core* of experts⟩ ⟨the *core* of her beliefs⟩

b : the essential meaning **:** GIST ⟨the *core* of the argument⟩ **c :** the inmost or most intimate part ⟨honest to the *core*⟩
3 : a part (as a thin cylinder of material) removed from the interior of a mass especially to determine composition
²**core** *transitive verb* **cored; cor·ing** (15th century)
: to remove a core from
— cor·er *noun*
³**core** *noun* [perhaps alteration of Middle English *chore* chorus, company, perhaps from Latin *chorus*] (1622)
chiefly Scottish **:** a group of people
core city *noun* (1965)
: INNER CITY
cored \'kōrd, 'kȯrd\ *adjective* (1945)
: having a core of a specified kind — usually used in combination
co·re·li·gion·ist \ˌkō-ri-'lij-nist, -'li-jə-\ *noun* (1826)
: a person of the same religion
co·re·mi·um \kə-'rē-mē-əm\ *noun, plural* **-mia** \-mē-ə\ [New Latin, from Greek *korēma* broom, from *korein* to sweep] (1929)
: a fruiting body characteristic of some fungi (as the one causing Dutch elm disease) that consists of a sterile stalk of parallel or fascicled hyphae and a terminal fertile or spore-bearing head
co·re·op·sis \ˌkȯr-ē-'äp-səs, ˌkȯr-\ *noun, plural* **coreopsis** [New Latin, genus name, from Greek *koris* bedbug + New Latin *-opsis;* akin to Greek *keirein* to cut — more at SHEAR] (circa 1753)
: any of a genus (*Coreopsis*) of widely cultivated composite herbs with showy flower heads and pinnately lobed or dissected leaves
co·re·pres·sor \ˌkō-ri-'pre-sər\ *noun* (1963)
: a substance that activates a particular genetic repressor by combining with it
co·req·ui·site \kō-'re-kwə-zət\ *noun* (circa 1948)
: a formal course of study required to be taken simultaneously with another
co·re·spon·dent \ˌkō-ri-'spän-dənt\ *noun* (1857)
: a person named as guilty of adultery with the defendant in a divorce suit
corf \'kȯrf\ *noun, plural* **corves** \'kȯrvz\ [Middle English, basket, from Middle Dutch *corf* or Middle Low German *korf,* from Latin *corbis* basket] (1653)
British **:** a basket, tub, or truck used in a mine
cor·gi \'kȯr-gē\ *noun, plural* **corgis** [Welsh, from *cor* dwarf + *ci* dog; akin to Old Irish *cú* dog, Old English *hund* — more at HOUND] (1926)
1 : CARDIGAN WELSH CORGI
2 : PEMBROKE WELSH CORGI
co·ri·a·ceous \ˌkōr-ē-'ā-shəs, ˌkȯr-\ *adjective* [Late Latin *coriaceus* — more at CUIRASS] (1674)
: resembling leather ⟨*coriaceous* foliage⟩
co·ri·an·der \'kȯr-ē-ˌan-dər, ˌkȯr-ē-', 'kȯr-, ˌkȯr-\ *noun* [Middle English *coriandre,* from Old French, from Latin *coriandrum,* from Greek *koriandron, koriannon*] (14th century)
1 : an Old World herb (*Coriandrum sativum*) of the carrot family with aromatic fruits
2 : the ripened dried fruit of coriander used as a flavoring — called also *coriander seed*
¹**Co·rin·thi·an** \kə-'rin(t)-thē-ən\ *noun* (1526)
1 : a native or resident of Corinth, Greece
2 : a merry profligate man
²**Corinthian** *adjective* (1594)
1 : of, relating to, or characteristic of Corinth or Corinthians
2 : of or relating to the lightest and most ornate of the three ancient Greek architectural orders distinguished especially by its large capitals decorated with carved acanthus leaves — see ORDER illustration
Co·rin·thi·ans \-thē-ənz\ *noun plural but singular in construction*

: either of two letters written by Saint Paul to the Christians of Corinth and included as books in the New Testament — see BIBLE table
Co·ri·o·lis effect \ˌkōr-ē-'ō-ləs-, ˌkȯr-\ *noun* (circa 1946)
: the apparent deflection of a moving object that is the result of the Coriolis force
Coriolis force *noun* [Gaspard G. *Coriolis* (died 1843) French civil engineer] (1923)
: an apparent force that as a result of the earth's rotation deflects moving objects (as projectiles or air currents) to the right in the northern hemisphere and to the left in the southern hemisphere
co·ri·um \'kōr-ē-əm, 'kȯr-\ *noun, plural* **co·ria** \-ē-ə\ [New Latin, from Latin, leather — more at CUIRASS] (1836)
: DERMIS
¹**cork** \'kȯrk\ *noun* [Middle English, cork, bark, probably from Arabic *qurq,* from Latin *cortic-, cortex* bark — more at CUIRASS] (14th century)
1 a : the elastic tough outer tissue of the cork oak that is used especially for stoppers and insulation **b :** PHELLEM
2 : a usually cork stopper for a bottle or jug
3 : a fishing float
²**cork** *transitive verb* (1535)
1 : to furnish or fit with cork or a cork
2 : to stop up with a cork
3 : to blacken with burnt cork
cork·age \'kȯr-kij\ *noun* (1838)
: a charge (as by a restaurant) for opening a bottle of wine bought elsewhere
cork·board \'kȯrk-ˌbōrd, -ˌbȯrd\ *noun* (circa 1893)
: a heat-insulating material made of compressed granulated cork; *also* **:** a bulletin board made with this material
cork cambium *noun* (1878)
: PHELLOGEN
corked \'kȯrkt\ *adjective* (1830)
: CORKY 2
cork·er \'kȯr-kər\ *noun* (1881)
1 : one that corks containers (as bottles)
2 : one that is excellent or remarkable
cork·ing \'kȯr-kiŋ\ *adjective or adverb* (1895)
: extremely fine — often used as an intensive especially before *good* ⟨had a *corking* good time⟩
cork oak *noun* (1873)
: an oak (*Quercus suber*) of southern Europe and northern Africa that is the source of the cork of commerce
¹**cork·screw** \'kȯrk-ˌskrü\ *noun* (1720)
: a device for drawing corks from bottles that has a pointed spiral piece of metal turned by a handle
²**corkscrew** *adjective* (1815)
: resembling a corkscrew **:** SPIRAL
³**corkscrew** (1837)
transitive verb
1 : WIND
2 : to draw out with difficulty
3 : to twist into a spiral
intransitive verb
: to move in a winding course
cork·wood \'kȯrk-ˌwu̇d\ *noun* (1756)
: any of several trees having light or corky wood; *especially* **:** a small or shrubby tree (*Leitneria floridana*) of the southeastern U.S. that has extremely light soft wood
corky \'kȯr-kē\ *adjective* **cork·i·er; -est** (1756)
1 : resembling cork
2 : having an unpleasant odor and taste (as from a tainted cork) ⟨*corky* wine⟩
— cork·i·ness \-kē-nəs\ *noun*
corm \'kȯrm\ *noun* [New Latin *cormus,* from Greek *kormos* tree trunk, from *keirein* to cut — more at SHEAR] (1830)
: a rounded thick modified underground stem base bearing membranous or scaly leaves and buds and acting as a vegetative reproductive structure — compare BULB, TUBER

corm·el \'kȯr-məl, kȯr-'mel\ *noun* [diminutive of *corm*] (circa 1900)
: a small or secondary corm produced by a larger corm
cor·mo·rant \'kȯrm-rənt, 'kȯr-mə-, 'kȯr-mə-ˌrant\ *noun* [Middle English *cormeraunt,* from Middle French *cormorant,* from Old French *cormareng,* from *corp* raven + *marenc* of the sea, from Latin *marinus* — more at CORBEL, MARINE] (14th century)

cormorant

1 : any of a family (Phalacrocoracidae) of dark-colored web-footed water birds that have a long neck, hooked bill, and distensible throat pouch
2 : a gluttonous, greedy, or rapacious person
¹**corn** \'kȯrn\ *noun, often attributive* [Middle English, from Old English; akin to Old High German & Old Norse *korn* grain, Latin *granum*] (before 12th century)
1 *chiefly dialect* **:** a small hard particle **:** GRAIN
2 : a small hard seed
3 a : the seeds of a cereal grass and especially of the important cereal crop of a particular region (as wheat in Britain, oats in Scotland and Ireland, and Indian corn in the New World and Australia) **b :** the kernels of sweet corn served as a vegetable while still soft and milky
4 : a plant that produces corn
5 : CORN WHISKEY
6 a : something (as writing, music, or acting) that is corny **b :** the quality or state of being corny **:** CORNINESS
²**corn** *transitive verb* (1560)
1 : to form into grains **:** GRANULATE
2 a : to preserve or season with salt in grains **b :** to cure or preserve in brine containing preservatives and often seasonings ⟨*corned* beef⟩
3 : to feed with corn ⟨*corn* the horses⟩
³**corn** *noun* [Middle English *corne,* from Middle French, horn, corner, from Latin *cornu* horn, point — more at HORN] (15th century)
: a local hardening and thickening of epidermis (as on a toe)
¹**corn·ball** \'kȯrn-ˌbȯl\ *noun* (circa 1949)
: an unsophisticated person; *also* **:** something corny
²**cornball** *adjective* (1951)
: CORNY
corn borer *noun* (1919)
: any of several insects that bore in maize: as **a :** EUROPEAN CORN BORER **b :** SOUTHWESTERN CORN BORER
corn bread *noun* (1750)
: bread made with cornmeal
corn chip *noun* (1950)
: a piece of a dry crisp snack food prepared from a seasoned cornmeal batter
corn·cob \'kȯrn-ˌkäb\ *noun* (1793)
1 : the axis on which the kernels of Indian corn are arranged
2 : an ear of Indian corn
corncob pipe *noun* (1832)
: a tobacco pipe with a bowl made of a corncob
corn cockle *noun* (1713)
: an annual hairy weed (*Agrostemma githago*) of the pink family with purplish red flowers that is found in grainfields
corn·crake \'kȯrn-ˌkrāk\ *noun* (15th century)
: a common Eurasian short-billed rail (*Crex crex*) that frequents grainfields

corn·crib \-ˌkrib\ noun (1681)
: a crib for storing ears of Indian corn

corn dodger noun (1834)
chiefly Southern & Midland : a cake of corn bread that is fried, baked, or boiled as a dumpling

corn dog noun (1967)
: a frankfurter dipped in cornmeal batter, fried, and served on a stick

cor·nea \ˈkȯr-nē-ə\ noun [Middle English, from Medieval Latin, from Latin, feminine of *corneus* horny, from *cornu*] (14th century)
: the transparent part of the coat of the eyeball that covers the iris and pupil and admits light to the interior — see EYE illustration
— **cor·ne·al** \-əl\ adjective

corn ear·worm \-ˈir-ˌwərm\ noun (1802)
: a noctuid moth (*Heliothis zea*) whose large striped yellow-headed larva is especially destructive to Indian corn, tomatoes, tobacco, and cotton bolls

cor·nel \ˈkȯr-nᵊl, -ˌnel\ noun [ultimately from Latin *cornus* cornel cherry tree; akin to Greek *kranon* cornel cherry tree] (1551)
: any of various shrubs or trees (genus *Cornus*) of the dogwood family with very hard wood and perfect flowers; *specifically* : DOGWOOD

cor·ne·lian \kȯr-ˈnēl-yən\ noun (15th century)
: CARNELIAN

cor·ne·ous \ˈkȯr-nē-əs\ adjective [Latin *corneus*] (1646)
: of a horny texture

¹cor·ner \ˈkȯr-nər\ noun [Middle English, from Old French *cornere*, from *corne* horn, corner] (13th century)
1 a : the point where converging lines, edges, or sides meet : ANGLE **b** : the place of intersection of two streets or roads **c** : a piece designed to form, mark, or protect a corner
2 : the angular part or space between meeting lines, edges, or borders near the vertex of the angle ⟨the southwest *corner* of the state⟩ ⟨the *corners* of the tablecloth⟩: as **a** : the area of a playing field or court near the intersection of the sideline and the goal line or baseline **b** (1) : either of the four angles of a boxing ring; *especially* : the area in which a boxer rests or is worked on by his seconds during periods between rounds (2) : a group of supporters, well-wishers, or adherents associated especially with a contestant **c** : the side of home plate nearest to or farthest from a batter ⟨a fast ball over the outside *corner*⟩ **d** : CORNER KICK **e** (1) : the outside of a football formation (2) : CORNERBACK
3 a : a private, secret, or remote place ⟨a quiet *corner* of New England⟩ ⟨to every *corner* of the earth⟩ ⟨dark *corners* of the mind⟩ **b** : a difficult or embarrassing situation : a position from which escape or retreat is difficult or impossible ⟨was backed into a *corner*⟩
4 : control or ownership of enough of the available supply of a commodity or security especially to permit manipulation of the price
5 : a point at which significant change occurs — often used in the phrase *turn the corner*
— **cor·nered** \-nərd\ adjective
— **around the corner** : at hand : IMMINENT ⟨good times are just *around the corner*⟩

²corner adjective (13th century)
1 : situated at a corner ⟨the *corner* drugstore⟩
2 : used or fitted for use in or on a corner ⟨a *corner* table⟩

³corner (1824)
transitive verb
1 a : to drive into a corner ⟨the animal is dangerous when *cornered*⟩ **b** : to catch and hold the attention of especially to force an interview
2 : to get a corner on ⟨*corner* the market⟩
intransitive verb
1 : to meet or converge at a corner or angle
2 : to turn a corner ⟨the car *corners* well⟩

cor·ner·back \ˈkȯr-nər-ˌbak\ noun (1955)

: a defensive halfback in football who defends the flank

corner kick noun (1882)
: a free kick from a corner of a soccer field awarded to an attacker when a defender plays the ball out-of-bounds over the end line

cor·ner·man \ˈkȯr-nər-ˌman\ noun (1957)
1 : one who plays in or near the corner: as **a** : CORNERBACK **b** : a basketball forward
2 : a boxer's second

cor·ner·stone \-ˌstōn\ noun (13th century)
1 : a stone forming a part of a corner or angle in a wall; *specifically* : such a stone laid at a formal ceremony
2 : a basic element : FOUNDATION ⟨a *cornerstone* of foreign policy⟩

cor·ner·ways \-ˌwāz\ adverb (1922)
: DIAGONALLY

cor·ner·wise \-ˌwīz\ adverb (15th century)
: DIAGONALLY

cor·net \kȯr-ˈnet, *British usually* ˈkȯr-nit\ noun [Middle English, from Middle French, from diminutive of *corn* horn, from Latin *cornu*] (14th century)
1 : a valved brass instrument resembling a trumpet in design and range but having a shorter partly conical tube and less brilliant tone
2 : something shaped like a cone: as **a** : a piece of paper twisted for use as a container **b** : a cone-shaped pastry shell that is often filled with whipped cream **c** *British* : an ice-cream cone
— **cor·net·ist** or **cor·net·tist** \kȯr-ˈne-tist, ˈkȯr-ni-\ noun

corn–fed \ˈkȯrn-ˌfed\ adjective (14th century)
1 : fed or fattened on grain (as corn) ⟨*corn-fed* hogs⟩
2 : looking well-fed : PLUMP
3 : rustically wholesome or corny

corn·field \-ˌfēld\ noun (14th century)
: a field in which corn is grown

corn·flakes \-ˌflāks\ noun plural (1907)
: toasted flakes made from the coarse meal of hulled corn for use as a breakfast cereal

corn flour (1791)
British : CORNSTARCH

corn·flow·er \ˈkȯrn-ˌflau̇(-ə)r\ noun (1527)
1 : CORN COCKLE
2 : BACHELOR'S BUTTON

cornflower blue noun (1907)
: a moderate purplish blue

Corn·husk·er \ˈkȯrn-ˌhəs-kər\ noun (circa 1948)
: a native or resident of Nebraska — used as a nickname

corn·husk·ing \-ˌhəs-kiŋ\ noun (1692)
: a social gathering especially of farm families to husk corn

¹cor·nice \ˈkȯr-nəs, -nish\ noun [Middle French, from Italian, frame, cornice, from Latin *cornic-, cornix* crow; akin to Greek *korax* raven — more at RAVEN] (1563)
1 a : the molded and projecting horizontal member that crowns an architectural composition **b** : a top course that crowns a wall
2 : a decorative band of metal or wood used to conceal curtain fixtures
3 : an overhanging mass of snow, ice, or rock usually on a ridge

c cornice 1a

²cornice transitive verb **cor·niced; cor·nic·ing** (1744)
: to furnish or crown with a cornice

cor·niche \kȯr-ˈnēsh\ noun [French *cornice, corniche*, literally, cornice, from Italian *cornice*] (1837)
: a road built along a coast and especially along the face of a cliff

cor·nic·u·late cartilage \kȯr-ˈni-kyə-lət-\ noun [Latin *corniculatus* horned, from *corniculum*, diminutive of *cornu* horn] (circa 1909)

: a small nodule of yellow elastic cartilage articulating with the apex of the arytenoid

cor·ni·fi·ca·tion \ˌkȯr-nə-fə-ˈkā-shən\ noun [Latin *cornu* horn] (circa 1843)
1 : conversion into horn or a horny substance or tissue
2 : the conversion of the vaginal epithelium from the columnar to the squamous type

¹Cor·nish \ˈkȯr-nish\ adjective [Middle English *Cornysshe*, from *Cornwaile* Cornwall, England] (14th century)
: of, relating to, or characteristic of Cornwall, Cornishmen, or Cornish

²Cornish noun (1547)
1 : a Celtic language of Cornwall extinct since the late 18th century
2 : any of an English breed of domestic fowls much used in crossbreeding for meat production

Cor·nish·man \-mən\ noun (15th century)
: a native or resident of Cornwall, England

Corn Law noun (1766)
: one of a series of laws in force in Great Britain before 1846 prohibiting or discouraging the importation of grain

corn leaf aphid noun (circa 1939)
: a dusky greenish or brownish aphid (*Rhopalosiphum maidis*) that feeds on the flowers and foliage of various commercially important grasses (as Indian corn)

corn·meal \ˈkȯrn-ˌmēl\ noun (1749)
: meal ground from corn

corn oil noun (1900)
: a yellow fatty oil obtained from the germ of Indian corn kernels and used chiefly as salad oil, in soft soap, and in margarine

corn·pone \ˈkȯrn-ˌpōn\ adjective (1972)
: DOWN-HOME, COUNTRIFIED ⟨*cornpone* humor⟩

corn pone noun (1859)
Southern & Midland : corn bread often made without milk or eggs and baked or fried

corn poppy noun (circa 1859)
: an annual red-flowered Eurasian poppy (*Papaver rhoeas*) common in fields and cultivated in several varieties

corn rootworm noun (1892)
: any of several chrysomelid beetles (genus *Diabrotica*) whose root-eating larvae are pests especially of corn

corn·row \ˈkȯrn-ˌrō\ noun (1946)
1 : a section of hair which is braided usually flat to the scalp
2 : a hairstyle in which the hair is divided into cornrow sections arranged in rows
— **cornrow** verb

cornrow 2

corn salad noun [from its occurrence as a weed in fields of grain] (1597)
: any of several herbs (genus *Valerianella*) of the valerian family; *especially* : a low European herb (*V. locusta* synonym *V. olitoria*) that is widely cultivated as a salad plant and potherb

corn silk noun (1861)
: the silky styles on an ear of Indian corn

corn snow noun (1935)
: granular snow formed by alternate thawing and freezing

corn·stalk \ˈkȯrn-ˌstȯk\ noun (1645)
: a stalk of Indian corn

corn·starch \-ˌstärch\ noun (1853)
: starch made from corn and used in foods as a thickening agent, in making corn syrup and sugars, and in the manufacture of adhesives and sizes for paper and textiles

corn sugar noun (1850)
: DEXTROSE

corn syrup noun (1903)
: a syrup containing dextrins, maltose, and dextrose that is obtained by partial hydrolysis of cornstarch

cor·nu \'kȯr-(,)nü, -(,)nyü\ *noun, plural* **cor·nua** \-nü-ə, -nyü-\ [Latin] (1691)
: a horn-shaped anatomical part (as of the uterus)
— **cor·nu·al** \-nü-əl, -nyü-\ *adjective*

cor·nu·co·pia \,kȯr-nə-'kō-pē-ə, -nyə-\ *noun* [Late Latin, from Latin *cornu copiae* horn of plenty] (1508)
1 : a curved goat's horn overflowing with fruit and ears of grain that is used as a decorative motif emblematic of abundance
2 : an inexhaustible store : ABUNDANCE
3 : a receptacle shaped like a horn or cone
— **cor·nu·co·pi·an** \-pē-ən\ *adjective*

cornucopia 1

cor·nu·to \kȯr-'nü-(,)tō, -'nyü-\ *noun, plural* **-tos** [Italian, from Latin *cornutus* having horns, from *cornu*] (1598)
: CUCKOLD

corn whiskey *noun* (1780)
: whiskey distilled from a mash made up of not less than 80 percent corn — compare BOURBON

¹corny \'kȯr-nē\ *adjective* **corn·i·er; -est** (14th century)
1 *archaic* : tasting strongly of malt
2 : of or relating to corn
3 : mawkishly old-fashioned : tiresomely simple and sentimental
— **corn·i·ly** \'kȯr-nᵊl-ē\ *adverb*
— **corn·i·ness** \'kȯr-nē-nəs\ *noun*

²corny *adjective* **corn·i·er; -est** (1707)
: relating to or having corns on the feet

cor·o·dy \'kȯr-ə-dē, 'kär-\ *noun, plural* **-dies** [Middle English *corrodie*, from Medieval Latin *corrodium*] (15th century)
: an allowance of provisions for maintenance dispensed as a charity

co·rol·la \kə-'rä-lə, -'rō-\ *noun* [New Latin, from Latin, diminutive of *corona*] (circa 1753)
: the part of a flower that consists of the separate or fused petals and constitutes the inner whorl of the perianth
— **co·rol·late** \kə-'rä-lət; 'kȯr-ə-,lāt, 'kär-\ *adjective*

cor·ol·lary \'kȯr-ə-,ler-ē, 'kär-, *British* kə-'rä-lə-rē\ *noun, plural* **-lar·ies** [Middle English *corolarie*, from Late Latin *corollarium*, from Latin, money paid for a garland, gratuity, from *corolla*] (14th century)
1 : a proposition inferred immediately from a proved proposition with little or no additional proof
2 a : something that naturally follows : RESULT **b** : something that incidentally or naturally accompanies or parallels
— **corollary** *adjective*

cor·o·man·del \,kȯr-ə-'man-dᵊl, ,kär-\ *noun* [*Coromandel* coast region, India] (1845)
: CALAMANDER

coromandel screen *noun, often C capitalized* (1926)
: a Chinese lacquered folding screen

co·ro·na \kə-'rō-nə\ *noun* [Latin, garland, crown, cornice — more at CROWN] (1563)
1 : the projecting part of a classic cornice
2 a : a usually colored circle often seen around and close to a luminous body (as the sun or moon) caused by diffraction produced by suspended droplets or occasionally particles of dust **b** : the tenuous outermost part of the atmosphere of a star (as the sun) **c** : a circle of light made by the apparent convergence of the

a corona 2e

streamers of the aurora borealis **d** : the upper portion of a bodily part (as a tooth or the skull) **e** : an appendage or series of united appendages on the inner side of the corolla in some flowers (as the daffodil, jonquil, or milkweed) **f** : a faint glow adjacent to the surface of an electrical conductor at high voltage
3 [from *La Corona*, a trademark] : a long cigar having the sides straight to the end to be lit and being roundly blunt at the other end

Corona Aus·tra·lis \-ȯ-'strä-ləs, -ä-\ *noun* [New Latin (genitive *Coronae Australis*), literally, southern crown]
: a southern constellation adjoining Sagittarius on the south

Corona Bo·re·al·is \-,bȯr-ē-'a-ləs, -,bȯr-\ *noun* [New Latin (genitive *Coronae Borealis*), literally, northern crown]
: a northern constellation between Hercules and Boötes

cor·o·nach \'kȯr-ə-nək, 'kär-\ *noun* [Scottish Gaelic *corranach* & Irish *coránach*] (1530)
: a funeral dirge sung or played on the bagpipes in Scotland and Ireland

co·ro·na·graph *also* **co·ro·no·graph** \kə-'rō-nə-,graf\ *noun* (1885)
: a telescope for observation of the sun's corona

¹cor·o·nal *also* **cor·o·nel** \'kȯr-ə-nᵊl, 'kär-\ *noun* [Middle English *coronal*, from Anglo-French, from Latin *coronalis* of a crown, from *corona*] (14th century)
: a circlet for the head usually implying rank or dignity

²co·ro·nal \'kȯr-ə-nᵊl, 'kär-; kə-'rō-\ *adjective* (14th century)
1 a : lying in the direction of the coronal suture **b** : of or relating to the frontal plane that passes through the long axis of the body
2 : of or relating to a corona or crown

coronal suture *noun* (1615)
: a suture extending across the skull between the parietal and frontal bones

co·ro·na ra·di·a·ta \kə-'rō-nə-,rā-dē-'ä-tə, -'ä-tə\ *noun, plural* **co·ro·nae ra·di·a·tae** \-(,)nē-,rā-dē-'ä-(,)tē, -'ä-(,)tē\ [New Latin, literally, crown with rays] (1892)
: the zone of small follicular cells immediately surrounding the ovum in the graafian follicle and accompanying the ovum on its discharge from the follicle

¹cor·o·nary \'kȯr-ə-,ner-ē, 'kär-\ *adjective* (1610)
1 : of, relating to, resembling, or being a crown or coronal
2 : of, relating to, or being the coronary arteries or veins of the heart; *broadly* : of or relating to the heart

²coronary *noun, plural* **-nar·ies** (1893)
1 a : CORONARY ARTERY **b** : CORONARY VEIN
2 : CORONARY THROMBOSIS; *broadly* : HEART ATTACK

coronary artery *noun* (1741)
: either of two arteries that arise one from the left and one from the right side of the aorta immediately above the semilunar valves and supply the tissues of the heart itself

coronary occlusion *noun* (1946)
: the partial or complete blocking (as by a thrombus, by spasm, or by sclerosis) of a coronary artery

coronary sinus *noun* (1831)
: a venous channel that is derived from the sinus venosus, is continuous with the largest of the cardiac veins, receives most of the blood from the walls of the heart, and empties into the right atrium

coronary thrombosis *noun* (1926)
: the blocking of a coronary artery of the heart by a thrombus

coronary vein *noun* (circa 1828)
: any of several veins that drain the tissues of the heart and empty into the coronary sinus

co·ro·nate \'kȯr-ə-,nāt, 'kär-\ *transitive verb* **-nat·ed; -nat·ing** [Latin *coronatus*, past participle of *coronare* to crown, from *corona*] (circa 1623)
: CROWN 1a

cor·o·na·tion \,kȯr-ə-'nā-shən, ,kär-\ *noun* [Middle English *coronacion*, from Middle French *coronation*, from *coroner* to crown] (14th century)
: the act or occasion of crowning; *also* : accession to the highest office

cor·o·ner \'kȯr-ə-nər, 'kär-\ *noun* [Middle English, an officer of the crown, from Anglo-French, from Old French *corone* crown, from Latin *corona*] (circa 1630)
: a public officer whose principal duty is to inquire by an inquest into the cause of any death which there is reason to suppose is not due to natural causes

cor·o·net \,kȯr-ə-'net, ,kär-\ *noun* [Middle French *coronette*, from Old French *coronete*, from *corone*] (15th century)
1 : a small or lesser crown usually signifying a rank below that of a sovereign
2 : an ornamental wreath or band for the head usually for wear by women on formal occasions
3 : the lower part of a horse's pastern where the horn terminates in skin — see HORSE illustration

co·ro·tate \(,)kō-'rō-,tāt\ *intransitive verb* (1962)
: to rotate in conjunction with or at the same rate as another rotating body
— **co·ro·ta·tion** \,kō-rō-'tā-shən\ *noun*

corpora *plural of* CORPUS

¹cor·po·ral \'kȯr-p(ə-)rəl\ *noun* [Middle English, from Middle French, from Medieval Latin *corporale*, from Latin, neuter of *corporalis; from the doctrine that the bread of the Eucharist becomes or represents the body of Christ] (14th century)
: a linen cloth on which the eucharistic elements are placed

²corporal *adjective* [Middle English, from Middle French, from Latin *corporalis*, from *corpor-, corpus* body — more at MIDRIFF] (14th century)
1 *obsolete* : CORPOREAL, PHYSICAL
2 : of, relating to, or affecting the body ⟨*corporal* punishment⟩
— **cor·po·ral·ly** \-p(ə-)rə-lē\ *adverb*

³corporal *noun* [Middle French, lowest noncommissioned officer, alteration of *caporal*, from Old Italian *caporale*, from *capo* head, from Latin *caput* — more at HEAD] (1579)
: a noncommissioned officer ranking in the army above a private first class and below a sergeant and in the marine corps above a lance corporal and below a sergeant

cor·po·ral·i·ty \,kȯr-pə-'ra-lə-tē\ *noun, plural* **-ties** (14th century)
: the quality or state of being or having a body or a material or physical existence

corporal's guard *noun* (1844)
1 : the small detachment commanded by a corporal
2 : a small group

cor·po·rate \'kȯr-p(ə-)rət\ *adjective* [Latin *corporatus*, past participle of *corporare* to make into a body, from *corpor-, corpus*] (1512)
1 a : formed into an association and endowed by law with the rights and liabilities of an individual : INCORPORATED **b** : of or relating to a corporation ⟨a plan to reorganize the *corporate* structure⟩
2 : of, relating to, or formed into a unified body of individuals ⟨human law arises by the *corporate* action of a people —G. H. Sabine⟩

3 : CORPORATIVE 2
— **cor·po·rate·ly** *adverb*
cor·po·ra·tion \ˌkȯr-pə-ˈrā-shən\ *noun* (15th century)
1 a *obsolete* : a group of merchants or traders united in a trade guild **b** : the municipal authorities of a town or city
2 : a body formed and authorized by law to act as a single person although constituted by one or more persons and legally endowed with various rights and duties including the capacity of succession
3 : an association of employers and employees in a basic industry or of members of a profession organized as an organ of political representation in a corporative state
4 : POTBELLY 1
cor·po·rat·ism \ˈkȯr-p(ə-)rə-ˌti-zəm\ *noun* (1890)
: the organization of a society into industrial and professional corporations serving as organs of political representation and exercising some control over persons and activities within their jurisdiction
— **cor·po·rat·ist** \-p(ə-)rə-tist\ *adjective*
cor·po·ra·tive \ˈkȯr-pə-ˌrā-tiv, -p(ə-)rə-\ *adjective* (1833)
1 : of or relating to a corporation
2 : of or relating to corporatism ⟨a *corporative* state⟩
cor·po·ra·tiv·ism \ˈkȯr-pə-ˌrā-ti-ˌvi-zəm, -p(ə-)rə-\ *noun* (1930)
: CORPORATISM
cor·po·ra·tor \ˈkȯr-pə-ˌrā-tər\ *noun* (1784)
: a corporation organizer, member, or stockholder
cor·po·re·al \kȯr-ˈpōr-ē-əl, -ˈpȯr-\ *adjective* [Latin *corporeus* of the body, from *corpor-, corpus*] (15th century)
1 : having, consisting of, or relating to a physical material body: as **a** : not spiritual **b** : not immaterial or intangible : SUBSTANTIAL
2 *archaic* : CORPORAL
synonym see MATERIAL
— **cor·po·re·al·ly** \-ē-ə-lē\ *adverb*
— **cor·po·re·al·ness** *noun*
cor·po·re·al·i·ty \(ˌ)kȯr-ˌpōr-ē-ˈa-lə-tē, -ˌpȯr-\ *noun, plural* **-ties** (1651)
: corporeal existence
cor·po·re·i·ty \ˌkȯr-pə-ˈrē-ə-tē, -ˈrā-\ *noun, plural* **-ties** (1621)
: the quality or state of having or being a body : MATERIALITY
cor·po·sant \ˈkȯr-pə-ˌsant, -ˌzant\ *noun* [Portuguese *corpo-santo,* literally, holy body] (1655)
: SAINT ELMO'S FIRE
corps \ˈkōr, ˈkȯr\ *noun, plural* **corps** \ˈkōrz, ˈkȯrz\ [French, from Latin *corpus* body] (1711)
1 a : an organized subdivision of the military establishment ⟨Marine *Corps*⟩ ⟨Signal *Corps*⟩ **b** : a tactical unit usually consisting of two or more divisions and auxiliary arms and services
2 : a group of persons associated together or acting under common direction; *especially* : a body of persons having a common activity or occupation ⟨the press *corps*⟩
3 : CORPS DE BALLET
corps de bal·let \ˌkōr-də-(ˌ)ba-ˈlā, ˌkȯr-\ *noun, plural* **corps de ballet** *same or* ˌkȯrz-də-, ˌkȯrz-\ [French] (1826)
: the ensemble of a ballet company
corps d'elite \ˌkōr-dā-ˈlēt, ˌkȯr-\ *noun, plural* **corps d'elite** *same or* ˌkȯrz-dā-, ˌkȯrz-\ [French *corps d'élite*] (1884)
1 : a body of picked troops
2 : a group of the best people in a category
corpse \ˈkȯrps\ *noun* [Middle English *corps,* from Middle French, from Latin *corpus*] (13th century)
1 *obsolete* : a human or animal body whether living or dead
2 a : a dead body especially of a human being **b** : the remains of something discarded or defunct ⟨the *corpses* of rusting cars⟩

corps·man \ˈkōr(z)-mən, ˈkȯr(z)-\ *noun* (1901)
1 : an enlisted man trained to give first aid and minor medical treatment
2 : a member of a government-sponsored service corps
cor·pu·lence \ˈkȯr-pyə-lən(t)s\ *noun* (1581)
: the state of being corpulent
cor·pu·len·cy \-lən(t)-sē\ *noun, plural* **-cies** (1577)
: CORPULENCE
cor·pu·lent \-lənt\ *adjective* [Middle English, from Latin *corpulentus,* from *corpus*] (14th century)
: having a large bulky body : OBESE
— **cor·pu·lent·ly** *adverb*
cor pul·mo·na·le \ˌkȯr-ˌpu̇l-mə-ˈnä-lē, -ˌpäl-, -ˈna-\ *noun, plural* **cor·dia pul·mo·na·lia** \ˈkȯr-dē-ə-ˌpu̇l-mə-ˈnä-lē-ə, -ˌpäl-, -ˈna-\ [New Latin, literally, pulmonary heart] (1857)
: disease of the heart characterized by hypertrophy and dilatation of the right ventricle and secondary to disease of the lungs or their blood vessels
cor·pus \ˈkȯr-pəs\ *noun, plural* **cor·po·ra** \-p(ə-)rə\ [Middle English, from Latin] (15th century)
1 : the body of a human or animal especially when dead
2 a : the main part or body of a bodily structure or organ ⟨the *corpus* of the uterus⟩ **b** : the main body or corporeal substance of a thing; *specifically* : the principal of a fund or estate as distinct from income or interest
3 a : all the writings or works of a particular kind or on a particular subject; *especially* : the complete works of an author **b** : a collection or body of knowledge or evidence; *especially* : a collection of recorded utterances used as a basis for the descriptive analysis of a language
corpus al·la·tum \-ə-ˈlā-təm, -ˈlä-\ *noun, plural* **corpora al·la·ta** \-ˈlā-tə, -ˈlä-tə\ [New Latin, literally, applied body] (1947)
: one of a pair of separate or fused bodies in many insects that are sometimes closely associated with the corpora cardiaca and that secrete hormones (as juvenile hormone)
corpus cal·lo·sum \-ka-ˈlō-səm\ *noun, plural* **corpora cal·lo·sa** \-sə\ [New Latin, literally, callous body] (1706)
: the great band of commissural fibers uniting the cerebral hemispheres of higher mammals including humans — see BRAIN illustration
corpus car·di·a·cum \-kär-ˈdī-ə-kəm\ *noun, plural* **corpora car·di·a·ca** \-ə-kə\ [New Latin, literally, cardiac body] (1960)
: one of a pair of separate or fused bodies of nervous tissue in many insects that lie posterior to the brain and dorsal to the esophagus and that function in the storage and secretion of brain hormone
Cor·pus Chris·ti \ˈkȯr-pəs-ˈkris-tē\ *noun* [Middle English, from Medieval Latin, literally, body of Christ] (14th century)
: the Thursday after Trinity observed as a Roman Catholic festival in honor of the Eucharist
cor·pus·cle \ˈkȯr-(ˌ)pə-səl\ *noun* [Latin *corpusculum,* diminutive of *corpus*] (1660)
1 : a minute particle
2 a : a living cell; *especially* : one (as a red or white blood cell or a cell in cartilage or bone) not aggregated into continuous tissues **b** : any of various small circumscribed multicellular bodies
— **cor·pus·cu·lar** \kȯr-ˈpəs-kyə-lər\ *adjective*
cor·pus de·lic·ti \ˈkȯr-pəs-di-ˈlik-ˌtī, -(ˌ)tē\ *noun, plural* **corpora delicti** [New Latin, literally, body of the crime] (1832)
1 : the substantial and fundamental fact necessary to prove the commission of a crime
2 : the material substance (as the body of the victim of a murder) upon which a crime has been committed

corpus lu·te·um \-ˈlü-tē-əm\ *noun, plural* **corpora lu·tea** \-tē-ə\ [New Latin, literally, yellowish body] (1788)
: a yellowish mass of progesterone-secreting endocrine tissue that forms immediately after ovulation from the ruptured graafian follicle in the mammalian ovary
corpus stri·a·tum \-(ˌ)strī-ˈā-təm\ *noun, plural* **corpora stri·a·ta** \-ˈā-tə\ [New Latin, literally, striated body] (1851)
: either of a pair of masses of nervous tissue within the brain that contain two large nuclei of gray matter separated by sheets of white matter
cor·rade \kə-ˈrād\ *verb* **cor·rad·ed; cor·rad·ing** [Latin *corradere* to scrape together, from *com-* + *radere* to scrape — more at RODENT] (1646)
transitive verb
: to wear away by abrasion
intransitive verb
: to crumble away through abrasion
— **cor·ra·sion** \-ˈrā-zhən\ *noun*
— **cor·ra·sive** \-ˈrā-siv, -ziv\ *adjective*
¹**cor·ral** \kə-ˈral, -ˈrel\ *noun* [Spanish, from (assumed) Vulgar Latin *currale* enclosure for vehicles, from Latin *currus* cart, from *currere* to run — more at CAR] (1582)
1 : a pen or enclosure for confining or capturing livestock
2 : an enclosure made with wagons for defense of an encampment
²**corral** *transitive verb* **cor·ralled; cor·ral·ling** (1847)
1 : to enclose in a corral
2 : to arrange (wagons) so as to form a corral
3 : COLLECT, GATHER ⟨*corralling* votes for the upcoming election⟩
¹**cor·rect** \kə-ˈrekt\ *transitive verb* [Middle English, from Latin *correctus,* past participle of *corrigere,* from *com-* + *regere* to lead straight — more at RIGHT] (14th century)
1 a : to make or set right **b** : COUNTERACT, NEUTRALIZE **c** : to alter or adjust so as to bring to some standard or required condition ⟨*correct* a lens for spherical aberration⟩
2 a : to punish (as a child) with a view to reforming or improving **b** : to point out usually for amendment the errors or faults of ⟨spent the day *correcting* tests⟩ ☆
— **cor·rect·able** \-ˈrek-tə-bəl\ *adjective*
— **cor·rec·tor** \-ˈrek-tər\ *noun*
²**correct** *adjective* [Middle English, corrected, from Latin *correctus,* from past participle of *corrigere*] (1676)
1 : conforming to an approved or conventional standard

2 : conforming to or agreeing with fact, logic, or known truth
3 : conforming to a set figure ⟨enclosed the *correct* return postage⟩ ☆
— **cor·rect·ly** \kə-'rek(t)-lē\ *adverb*
— **cor·rect·ness** \-'rek(t)-nəs\ *noun*
corrected time *noun* (circa 1891)
: a boat's elapsed time less its time allowance in yacht racing
cor·rec·tion \kə-'rek-shən\ *noun* (14th century)
1 : the action or an instance of correcting: as **a** : AMENDMENT, RECTIFICATION **b :** REBUKE, PUNISHMENT **c :** a bringing into conformity with a standard **d :** NEUTRALIZATION, COUNTERACTION ⟨*correction* of acidity⟩
2 : a decline in market price or business activity following and counteracting a rise
3 a : something substituted in place of what is wrong ⟨marking *corrections* on the students' papers⟩ **b :** a quantity applied by way of correcting (as for adjustment of an instrument)
4 : the treatment and rehabilitation of offenders through a program involving penal custody, parole, and probation; *also* : the administration of such treatment as a matter of public policy — usually used in plural
— **cor·rec·tion·al** \-shnəl, -shə-n°l\ *adjective*
cor·rec·ti·tude \kə-'rek-tə-ˌtüd, -ˌtyüd\ *noun* [blend of *correct* and *rectitude*] (1893)
: correctness or propriety of conduct
cor·rec·tive \kə-'rek-tiv\ *adjective* (1531)
: intended to correct ⟨*corrective* lenses⟩ ⟨*corrective* punishment⟩
— **corrective** *noun*
— **cor·rec·tive·ly** *adverb*
¹**cor·re·late** \'kȯr-ə-lət, 'kär-, -ˌlāt\ *noun* [back-formation from *correlation*] (1643)
1 : either of two things so related that one directly implies or is complementary to the other (as husband and wife)
2 : a phenomenon (as brain activity) that accompanies another phenomenon (as behavior), is usually parallel to it (as in form, type, development, or distribution), and is related in some way to it
— **correlate** *adjective*
²**cor·re·late** \-ˌlāt\ *verb* **-lat·ed; -lat·ing** (circa 1742)
intransitive verb
: to bear reciprocal or mutual relations : CORRESPOND
transitive verb
1 a : to establish a mutual or reciprocal relation between ⟨*correlate* activities in the lab and the field⟩ **b :** to show correlation or a causal relationship between
2 : to present or set forth so as to show relationship ⟨he *correlates* the findings of the scientists, the psychologists, and the mystics —Eugene Exman⟩
— **cor·re·lat·able** \-ˌlā-tə-bəl\ *adjective*
— **cor·re·lat·or** \-ˌlā-tər\ *noun*
cor·re·la·tion \ˌkȯr-ə-'lā-shən, ˌkär-\ *noun* [Medieval Latin *correlation-, correlatio,* from Latin *com-* + *relation-, relatio* relation] (1561)
1 : the state or relation of being correlated; *specifically* : a relation existing between phenomena or things or between mathematical or statistical variables which tend to vary, be associated, or occur together in a way not expected on the basis of chance alone ⟨the obviously high positive *correlation* between scholastic aptitude and college entrance —J. B. Conant⟩
2 : the act of correlating
— **cor·re·la·tion·al** \-shnəl, -shə-n°l\ *adjective*
correlation coefficient *noun* (circa 1909)
: a number or function that indicates the degree of correlation between two sets of data or between two random variables and that is equal to their covariance divided by the product of their standard deviations
cor·rel·a·tive \kə-'re-lə-tiv\ *adjective* (1530)

1 : naturally related : CORRESPONDING
2 : reciprocally related
3 : regularly used together but typically not adjacent ⟨the *correlative* conjunctions *either . . . or*⟩
— **correlative** *noun*
— **cor·rel·a·tive·ly** *adverb*
cor·re·spond \ˌkȯr-ə-'spänd, ˌkär-\ *intransitive verb* [Middle French or Medieval Latin; Middle French *correspondre,* from Medieval Latin *correspondēre,* from Latin *com-* + *respondēre* to respond] (1529)
1 a : to be in conformity or agreement ⟨the ideal failed . . . to *correspond* with the reality —James Sutherland⟩ **b :** to compare closely : MATCH — usually used with *to* or *with* **c :** to be equivalent or parallel
2 : to communicate with a person by exchange of letters
cor·re·spon·dence \-'spän-dən(t)s\ *noun* (15th century)
1 a : the agreement of things with one another **b :** a particular similarity **c :** a relation between sets in which each member of one set is associated with one or more members of the other — compare FUNCTION 5a
2 a : communication by letters; *also* : the letters exchanged **b :** the news, information, or opinion contributed by a correspondent to a newspaper or periodical
correspondence course *noun* (1902)
: a course offered by a correspondence school
correspondence school *noun* (1889)
: a school that teaches nonresident students by mailing them lessons and exercises which upon completion are returned to the school for grading
cor·re·spon·den·cy \ˌkȯr-ə-'spän-dən(t)-sē, ˌkär-\ *noun, plural* **-cies** (1589)
: CORRESPONDENCE
¹**cor·re·spon·dent** \ˌkȯr-ə-'spän-dənt, ˌkär-\ *adjective* [Middle English, from Middle French or Medieval Latin; Middle French, from Medieval Latin *correspondent-, correspondens,* present participle of *correspondēre*] (15th century)
1 : CORRESPONDING
2 : FITTING, CONFORMING — used with *with* or *to* ⟨the outcome was entirely *correspondent* with my wishes⟩
²**correspondent** *noun* (circa 1630)
1 a : one who communicates with another by letter **b :** one who has regular commercial relations with another **c :** one who contributes news or commentary to a publication (as a newspaper) or a radio or television network often from a distant place ⟨a war *correspondent*⟩
2 : something that corresponds
corresponding *adjective* (1579)
1 a : having or participating in the same relationship (as kind, degree, position, correspondence, or function) especially with regard to the same or like wholes (as geometric figures or sets) ⟨*corresponding* parts of similar triangles⟩ **b :** RELATED, ACCOMPANYING ⟨all rights carry with them *corresponding* responsibilities —W. P. Paepcke⟩
2 a : charged with the duty of writing letters ⟨*corresponding* secretary⟩ **b :** participating or serving at a distance and by mail ⟨a *corresponding* member of the society⟩
— **cor·re·spond·ing·ly** \-'spän-diŋ-lē\ *adverb*
corresponding angles *noun plural* (circa 1804)
: any pair of angles each of which is on the same side of one of two lines cut by a transversal and on the same side of the transversal
cor·re·spon·sive \ˌkȯr-ə-'spän(t)-siv, ˌkär-\ *adjective* (1606)
: mutually responsive
cor·ri·da \kȯ-'rē-thə\ *noun* [Spanish, literally, act of running] (1898)
: BULLFIGHT

cor·ri·dor \'kȯr-ə-dər, 'kär-, -ˌdȯr\ *noun* [Middle French, from Old Italian *corridore,* from *correre* to run, from Latin *currere* — more at CAR] (1814)
1 : a passageway (as in a hotel) into which compartments or rooms open
2 : a usually narrow passageway or route: as **a :** a narrow strip of land through foreign-held territory **b :** a restricted lane for air traffic
3 : a densely populated strip of land including two or more major cities ⟨the Northeast *corridor* stretching from Washington into New England —S. D. Browne⟩
cor·rie \'kȯr-ē, 'kär-ē\ *noun* [Scottish Gaelic *coire,* literally, kettle] (1795)
: CIRQUE 3
Cor·rie·dale \-ˌdāl\ *noun* [*Corriedale,* ranch in New Zealand] (1902)
: any of a dual-purpose breed of rather large usually hornless sheep developed in New Zealand
cor·ri·gen·dum \ˌkȯr-ə-'jen-dəm, ˌkär-\ *noun, plural* **-da** \-də\ [Latin, neuter of *corrigendus,* gerundive of *corrigere* to correct] (circa 1850)
: an error in a printed work discovered after printing and shown with its correction on a separate sheet
cor·ri·gi·ble \'kȯr-ə-jə-bəl, 'kär-\ *adjective* [Middle English, from Middle French, from Medieval Latin *corrigibilis,* from Latin *corrigere*] (15th century)
: capable of being set right : REPARABLE ⟨a *corrigible* defect⟩
— **cor·ri·gi·bil·i·ty** \ˌkȯr-ə-jə-'bi-lə-tē, ˌkär-\ *noun*
cor·ri·val \kə-'rī-vəl, kȯ-, kō-\ *noun* [Middle French, from Latin *corrivalis,* from *com-* + *rivalis* rival] (1579)
: RIVAL, COMPETITOR
— **corrival** *adjective*
cor·rob·o·rant \kə-'rä-bə-rənt\ *adjective* (1626) *archaic*
: having an invigorating effect — used of a medicine
cor·rob·o·rate \kə-'rä-bə-ˌrāt\ *transitive verb* **-rat·ed; -rat·ing** [Latin *corroboratus,* past participle of *corroborare,* from *com-* + *robor-, robur* strength] (1530)
: to support with evidence or authority : make more certain
synonym see CONFIRM
— **cor·rob·o·ra·tion** \-ˌrä-bə-'rā-shən\ *noun*
— **cor·rob·o·ra·tive** \-'rä-bə-ˌrā-tiv, -'rä-b(ə-)rə-\ *adjective*
— **cor·rob·o·ra·tor** \-'rä-bə-ˌrā-tər\ *noun*
— **cor·rob·o·ra·to·ry** \-'rä-b(ə-)rə-ˌtȯr-ē, -ˌtȯr-\ *adjective*

☆ **SYNONYMS**
Correct, accurate, exact, precise, nice, right mean conforming to fact, standard, or truth. CORRECT usually implies freedom from fault or error ⟨*correct* answers⟩ ⟨socially *correct* dress⟩. ACCURATE implies fidelity to fact or truth attained by exercise of care ⟨an *accurate* description⟩. EXACT stresses a very strict agreement with fact, standard, or truth ⟨*exact* measurements⟩. PRECISE adds to EXACT an emphasis on sharpness of definition or delimitation ⟨*precise* calibration⟩. NICE stresses great precision and delicacy of adjustment or discrimination ⟨makes *nice* distinctions⟩. RIGHT is close to CORRECT but has a stronger positive emphasis on conformity to fact or truth rather than mere absence of error or fault ⟨the *right* thing to do⟩.

\ə\ **abut** \°\ **kitten** \ər\ **further** \a\ **ash** \ā\ **ace**
\ä\ **mop, mar** \aú\ **out** \ch\ **chin** \e\ **bet** \ē\ **easy**
\g\ **go** \i\ **hit** \ī\ **ice** \j\ **job** \ŋ\ **sing** \ō\ **go**
\ȯ\ **law** \ȯi\ **boy** \th\ **thin** \t̲h̲\ **the** \ü\ **loot** \ú\ **foot**
\y\ **yet** \zh\ **vision** *see also* Guide to Pronunciation

cor·rob·o·ree \kə-'rä-bə-rē, -'rä-\ *noun* [Dharuk (Australian aboriginal language of the Port Jackson area) *garaabara*] (1811)
1 : a nocturnal festivity with songs and symbolic dances by which the Australian aborigines celebrate events of importance
2 *Australian* **a :** a noisy festivity **b :** TUMULT
cor·rode \kə-'rōd\ *verb* **cor·rod·ed; cor·rod·ing** [Middle English, from Latin *corrodere* to gnaw to pieces, from *com-* + *rodere* to gnaw — more at RODENT] (14th century)
transitive verb
1 : to eat away by degrees as if by gnawing; *especially* **:** to wear away gradually usually by chemical action (the metal was *corroded* beyond repair)
2 : to weaken or destroy gradually **:** UNDERMINE (manners and miserliness that *corrode* the human spirit —Bernard DeVoto)
intransitive verb
: to undergo corrosion
— **cor·rod·ible** \-'rō-də-bəl\ *adjective*
cor·ro·dy *variant of* CORODY
cor·ro·sion \kə-'rō-zhən\ *noun* [Middle English, from Late Latin *corrosion-, corrosio* act of gnawing, from Latin *corrodere*] (14th century)
1 : the action, process, or effect of corroding
2 : a product of corroding
cor·ro·sive \-'rō-siv, -ziv\ *adjective* (14th century)
1 : tending or having the power to corrode (*corrosive* acids) (*corrosive* action) (the *corrosive* effects of alcoholism)
2 : bitingly sarcastic (*corrosive* satire)
— **corrosive** *noun*
— **cor·ro·sive·ly** *adverb*
— **cor·ro·sive·ness** *noun*
corrosive sublimate *noun* (circa 1751)
: MERCURIC CHLORIDE
cor·ru·gate \'kór-ə-,gāt, 'kär-\ *verb* **-gat·ed; -gat·ing** [Latin *corrugatus*, past participle of *corrugare*, from *com-* + *ruga* wrinkle; probably akin to Lithuanian *raukas* wrinkle — more at ROUGH] (1620)
transitive verb
: to form or shape into wrinkles or folds or into alternating ridges and grooves **:** FURROW
intransitive verb
: to become corrugated
corrugated *adjective* (1590)
: having corrugations (*corrugated* paper); *also* **:** made of corrugated material (as paperboard) (*corrugated* boxes)
cor·ru·ga·tion \,kór-ə-'gā-shən, ,kär-\ *noun* (1528)
1 : the act of corrugating
2 : a ridge or groove of a surface that has been corrugated
¹cor·rupt \kə-'rəpt\ *verb* [Middle English, from Latin *corruptus*, past participle of *corrumpere*, from *com-* + *rumpere* to break — more at REAVE] (14th century)
transitive verb
1 a : to change from good to bad in morals, manners, or actions; *also* **:** BRIBE **b :** to degrade with unsound principles or moral values
2 : ROT, SPOIL
3 : to subject (a person) to corruption of blood
4 : to alter from the original or correct form or version
intransitive verb
1 a : to become tainted or rotten **b :** to become morally debased
2 : to cause disintegration or ruin
synonym see DEBASE
— **cor·rupt·er** *also* **cor·rup·tor** \-'rəp-tər\ *noun*
— **cor·rupt·ibil·i·ty** \-,rəp-tə-'bi-lə-tē\ *noun*
— **cor·rupt·ible** \-'rəp-tə-bəl\ *adjective*
— **cor·rupt·ibly** \-blē\ *adverb*
²corrupt *adjective* [Middle English, from Middle French or Latin; Middle French, from Latin *corruptus*] (14th century)

1 a : morally degenerate and perverted **:** DEPRAVED **b :** characterized by improper conduct (as bribery or the selling of favors) (*corrupt* judges)
2 : PUTRID, TAINTED
3 : adulterated or debased by change from an original or correct condition
synonym *see* VICIOUS
— **cor·rupt·ly** \-'rəp(t)-lē\ *adverb*
— **cor·rupt·ness** \-'rəp(t)-nəs\ *noun*
cor·rup·tion \kə-'rəp-shən\ *noun* (14th century)
1 a : impairment of integrity, virtue, or moral principle **:** DEPRAVITY **b :** DECAY, DECOMPOSITION **c :** inducement to wrong by improper or unlawful means (as bribery) **d :** a departure from the original or from what is pure or correct
2 *archaic* **:** an agency or influence that corrupts
3 *chiefly dialect* **:** PUS
cor·rup·tion·ist \-sh(ə-)nist\ *noun* (1810)
: one who practices or defends corruption especially in politics
corruption of blood (1563)
: the effect of an attainder which bars a person from inheriting, retaining, or transmitting any estate, rank, or title
cor·rup·tive \kə-'rəp-tiv\ *adjective* (15th century)
: producing or tending to produce corruption
— **cor·rup·tive·ly** *adverb*
cor·sage \kór-'säzh, -'säj, 'kór-,\ *noun* [French, bust, bodice, from Old French, bust, from *cors* body, from Latin *corpus*] (1843)
1 : the waist or bodice of a dress
2 : an arrangement of flowers worn as a fashion accessory
cor·sair \'kór-,sar, -,ser; kór-'\ *noun* [Middle French & Old Italian; Middle French *corsaire* pirate, from Old Provençal *corsari*, from Old Italian *corsaro*, from Medieval Latin *cursarius*, from Latin *cursus* course — more at COURSE] (1549)
: PIRATE; *especially* **:** a privateer of the Barbary Coast
corse \'kórs\ *noun* [Middle English *cors*, from Middle French] (13th century)
archaic **:** CORPSE
corse·let \for 1 'kór-slət, for 2 ,kór-sə-'let\ *noun* (1563)
1 *or* **cors·let** [Middle French, diminutive of *cors* body, bodice] **:** a piece of armor covering the trunk
2 *or* **cor·se·lette** [from *Corselette*, a trademark] **:** an undergarment combining girdle and brassiere
¹cor·set \'kór-sət\ *noun* [Middle English, from Old French, diminutive of *cors*] (13th century)
1 : a usually close-fitting and often laced medieval jacket
2 : a woman's close-fitting boned supporting undergarment that is often hooked and laced and that extends from above or beneath the bust or from the waist to below the hips and has garters attached
²corset *transitive verb* (circa 1847)
1 : to dress in or fit with a corset
2 : to restrict closely **:** control rigidly
cor·se·tiere \,kór-sə-'tir, -'tyer\ *noun* [French *corsetière*, feminine of *corsetier*, from *corset*] (1848)
: one who makes, fits, or sells corsets, girdles, or brassieres
cor·tege *also* **cor·tège** \kór-'tezh, 'kór-,\ *noun* [French *cortège*, from Italian *corteggio*, from *corteggiare* to court, from *corte* court, from Latin *cohort-, cohors* enclosure — more at COURT] (1648)
1 : a train of attendants **:** RETINUE
2 : PROCESSION; *especially* **:** a funeral procession
cor·tex \'kór-,teks\ *noun, plural* **cor·ti·ces** \'kór-tə-,sēz\ *or* **cor·tex·es** [Latin *cortic-, cortex* bark — more at CUIRASS] (1677)

1 a : the outer or superficial part of an organ or bodily structure (as the kidney, adrenal gland, or a hair); *especially* **:** the outer layer of gray matter of the cerebrum and cerebellum **b :** the outer part of some organisms (as paramecia)
2 : a plant bark or rind (as cinchona) used medicinally
3 a : the typically parenchymatous layer of tissue external to the vascular tissue and internal to the corky or epidermal tissues of a green plant; *broadly* **:** all tissues external to the xylem **b :** an outer or investing layer of various algae, lichens, or fungi
cor·ti·cal \'kór-ti-kəl\ *adjective* (1671)
1 : of, relating to, or consisting of cortex
2 : involving or resulting from the action or condition of the cerebral cortex
— **cor·ti·cal·ly** \-k(ə-)lē\ *adverb*
cortico- *combining form*
: cortex (*cortico*tropin)
cor·ti·coid \'kór-ti-,kóid\ *noun* (1941)
: CORTICOSTEROID
— **corticoid** *adjective*
cor·ti·co·ste·roid \,kór-ti-kō-'stir-,óid *also* -'ster-\ *noun* (1944)
: any of various adrenal-cortex steroids (as corticosterone, cortisone, and aldosterone) used medically especially as anti-inflammatory agents
cor·ti·co·ste·rone \,kór-tə-'käs-tə-,rōn, -ti-kō-stə-'; ,kór-ti-kō-'stir-,ōn, -'ster-\ *noun* (1937)
: a colorless crystalline corticosteroid $C_{21}H_{30}O_4$ that is important in protein and carbohydrate metabolism
cor·ti·co·tro·pin \,kór-ti-kō-'trō-pən\ *also* **cor·ti·co·tro·phin** \-fən\ *noun* (1946)
: ACTH; *also* **:** a preparation of ACTH that is used especially in the treatment of rheumatoid arthritis and rheumatic fever
cor·tin \'kór-tⁿn\ *noun* (1928)
: the active principle of the adrenal cortex
cor·ti·sol \'kór-tə-,sól, -,zól, -,sōl, -,zōl\ *noun* [*cortis*one + ¹-*ol*] (1951)
: HYDROCORTISONE
cor·ti·sone \-,sōn, -,zōn\ *noun* [alteration of *corticosterone*] (1949)
: a glucocorticoid $C_{21}H_{28}O_5$ of the adrenal cortex used especially in the treatment of rheumatoid arthritis
co·run·dum \kə-'rən-dəm\ *noun* [Tamil *kuruntam*; akin to Sanskrit *kuruvinda* ruby] (1804)
: a very hard mineral that consists of aluminum oxide and occurs in massive form and as variously colored crystals (as ruby and sapphire), that can be synthesized, and that is used as an abrasive
co·rus·cant \kə-'rəs-kənt\ *adjective* (15th century)
: SHINING, GLITTERING
cor·us·cate \'kór-ə-,skāt, 'kär-\ *intransitive verb* **-cat·ed; -cat·ing** [Latin *coruscatus*, past participle of *coruscare* to flash] (1705)
1 : to give off or reflect light in bright beams or flashes **:** SPARKLE
2 : to be brilliant or showy in technique or style
cor·us·ca·tion \,kór-ə-'skā-shən, ,kär-\ *noun* (15th century)
1 : GLITTER, SPARKLE
2 : a flash of wit
cor·vée \'kór-,vā, kór-'\ *noun* [Middle English *corvee*, from Middle French, from Medieval Latin *corrogata*, from Latin, feminine of *corrogatus*, past participle of *corrogare* to collect, requisition, from *com-* + *rogare* to ask — more at RIGHT] (14th century)
1 : unpaid labor (as toward constructing roads) due from a feudal vassal to his lord
2 : labor exacted in lieu of taxes by public authorities especially for highway construction or repair
corves *plural of* CORF

cor·vette \kȯr-'vet\ *noun* [French, from Middle French, probably from Middle Dutch *corf,* a kind of ship, literally, basket — more at CORF] (1636)
1 : a warship ranking in the old sailing navies next below a frigate
2 : a highly maneuverable armed escort ship that is smaller than a destroyer

cor·vi·na \kȯr-'vē-nə\ *variant of* CORBINA

cor·vine \'kȯr-,vīn\ *adjective* [Latin *corvinus,* from *corvus* raven — more at RAVEN] (circa 1656)
: of or relating to the crows **:** resembling a crow

Cor·vus \'kȯr-vəs\ *noun* [Latin (genitive *Corvi*), literally, raven]
: a small constellation adjoining Virgo on the south

Cor·y·bant \'kȯr-ə-,bant, 'kär-\ *noun, plural* **Cor·y·bants** \-,ban(t)s\ *or* **Cor·y·ban·tes** \,kȯr-ə-'ban-tēz, ,kär-\ [Middle French *Corybante,* from Latin *Corybas,* from Greek *Korybas*] (14th century)
: one of the attendants or priests of Cybele noted for wildly emotional processions and rites

cor·y·ban·tic \,kȯr-ē-'ban-tik, ,kär-\ *adjective* (1642)
: like or in the spirit of a Corybant; *especially* **:** WILD, FRENZIED

co·ryd·a·lis \kə-'ri-dᵊl-əs\ *noun* [New Latin, genus name, from Greek *korydallis* crested lark (*Galerida cristata*), from *korydos* crested lark] (1818)
: any of a large genus (*Corydalis*) of chiefly temperate herbs of the fumitory family with racemose irregular flowers and dissected leaves

cor·ymb \'kȯr-,im(b), 'kär-, -əm(b)\ *noun, plural* **corymbs** \-,imz, -əmz\ [French *corymbe,* from Latin *corymbus* cluster of fruit or flowers, from Greek *korymbos*] (1776)
: a flat-topped inflorescence; *specifically* **:** one in which the flower stalks arise at different levels on the main axis and reach about the same height and in which the outer flowers open first and the inflorescence is indeterminate
— **cor·ymbed** \-,imd, -əmd\ *adjective*
— **cor·ym·bose** \-əm-,bōs\ *adjective*
— **cor·ym·bose·ly** *adverb*

corymb

co·ry·ne·bac·te·ri·um \,kȯr-ə-(,)nē-bak-'tir-ē-əm, kə-,ri-nə-\ *noun* [New Latin, from Greek *korynē* club] (1909)
: any of a large genus (*Corynebacterium*) of usually gram-positive nonmotile bacteria that occur as irregular or branching rods and include numerous important animal and plant parasites
— **co·ry·ne·bac·te·ri·al** \-ē-əl\ *adjective*

co·ryn·e·form \kə-'ri-nə-,fȯrm\ *adjective* (1952)
: being or resembling corynebacteria

cor·y·phae·us \,kȯr-ə-'fē-əs, ,kär-\ *noun, plural* **-phaei** \-'fē-,ī\ [Latin, leader, from Greek *koryphaios,* from *koryphē* summit] (1610)
1 : the leader of a party or school of thought
2 : the leader of a chorus

co·ry·phée \,kȯr-i-'fā\ *noun* [French, from Latin *coryphaeus*] (1828)
: a ballet dancer who dances in a small group instead of in the corps de ballet or as a soloist

co·ry·za \kə-'rī-zə\ *noun* [Late Latin, from Greek *koryza* nasal mucus; akin to Old English *hrot* nasal mucus, Sanskrit *kardama* mud] (1634)
: an acute inflammatory contagious disease involving the upper respiratory tract; *especially* **:** COMMON COLD
— **co·ry·zal** \-zəl\ *adjective*

co·se·cant \(,)kō-'sē-,kant, -kənt\ *noun* [New Latin *cosecant-, cosecans,* from *co-* + *secant-, secans* secant] (circa 1706)
1 : a trigonometric function that for an acute angle is the ratio between the hypotenuse of a right triangle of which the angle is considered part and the leg opposite the angle
2 : a trigonometric function csc θ that is the reciprocal of the sine for all real numbers θ for which the sine is not zero and that is exactly equal to the cosecant of an angle of measure θ in radians

co·set \'kō-,set\ *noun* (1910)
: a subset of a mathematical group that consists of all the products obtained by multiplying either on the right or the left a fixed element of the group by each of the elements of a given subgroup

¹cosh \'käsh\ *noun* [perhaps from Romany *kaš, kašt* stick, piece of wood] (1869)
chiefly British **:** a weighted weapon similar to a blackjack

²cosh *transitive verb* (1896)
chiefly British **:** to strike or assault with or as if with a cosh

co·sig·na·to·ry \(,)kō-'sig-nə-,tōr-ē, -,tȯr-\ *noun* (1865)
: a joint signer

co·sign·er \'kō-,sī-nər\ *noun* (circa 1903)
: COSIGNATORY; *especially* **:** a joint signer of a promissory note
— **co·sign** \'kō-,sīn\ *verb*

co·sine \'kō-,sīn\ *noun* [New Latin *cosinus,* from *co-* + Medieval Latin *sinus* sine] (1635)
1 : a trigonometric function that for an acute angle is the ratio between the leg adjacent to the angle when it is considered part of a right triangle and the hypotenuse
2 : a trigonometric function cos θ that for all real numbers θ is given by the sum of the alternating series

$$\cos\theta = 1 - \frac{\theta^2}{2!} + \frac{\theta^4}{4!} - \frac{\theta^6}{6!} + \frac{\theta^8}{8!} - \cdots$$

and that is exactly equal to the cosine of an angle of measure θ in radians

cos lettuce \'käs-, 'kȯs-\ *noun* [*Kos, Cos,* Greek island] (1699)
: ROMAINE

¹cos·met·ic \käz-'me-tik\ *adjective* [Greek *kosmētikos* skilled in adornment, from *kosmein* to arrange, adorn, from *kosmos* order] (1650)
1 : of, relating to, or making for beauty especially of the complexion **:** BEAUTIFYING ⟨*cosmetic* salves⟩
2 : done or made for the sake of appearance: as **a :** correcting defects especially of the face ⟨*cosmetic* surgery⟩ **b :** DECORATIVE, ORNAMENTAL **c :** not substantive **:** SUPERFICIAL ⟨*cosmetic* changes⟩
3 : visually appealing
— **cos·met·i·cal·ly** \-ti-k(ə-)lē\ *adverb*

²cosmetic *noun* (1650)
: something that is cosmetic: as **a :** a cosmetic preparation for external use **b** *plural* **:** superficial features ⟨a poem without rhetorical *cosmetics* —Guy Davenport⟩

cosmetic case *noun* (1948)
: a small piece of luggage especially for cosmetics

cos·me·ti·cian \,käz-mə-'ti-shən\ *noun* (1924)
: a person who is professionally trained in the use of cosmetics

cos·met·i·cize \käz-'me-tə-,sīz\ *transitive verb* **-cized; -ciz·ing** (1824)
: to make (something unpleasant or ugly) superficially attractive

cos·me·tol·o·gist \,käz-mə-'tä-lə-jist\ *noun* (1926)
: a person who gives beauty treatments (as to skin and hair) — called also *beautician*

cos·me·tol·o·gy \-jē\ *noun* [French *cosmétologie,* from *cosmétique* cosmetic (from English *cosmetic*) + *-logie* -logy] (1926)
: the cosmetic treatment of the skin, hair, and nails

cos·mic \'käz-mik\ *also* **cos·mi·cal** \-mi-kəl\ *adjective* [Greek *kosmikos,* from *kosmos* order, universe] (1685)
1 : of or relating to the cosmos, the extraterrestrial vastness, or the universe in contrast to the earth alone
2 : characterized by greatness especially in extent, intensity, or comprehensiveness ⟨a *cosmic* thinker⟩ ⟨*cosmic* boredom⟩
— **cos·mi·cal·ly** \-mi-k(ə-)lē\ *adverb*

cosmic background radiation *noun* (circa 1976)
: BACKGROUND RADIATION

cosmic dust *noun* (1881)
: very fine particles of solid matter found in any part of the universe

cosmic noise *noun* (1947)
: unidentified celestial radio-frequency radiation; *especially* **:** such radiation originating from outside the Milky Way

cosmic ray *noun* (1925)
: a stream of atomic nuclei of extremely penetrating character that enter the earth's atmosphere from outer space at speeds approaching that of light

cosmic string *noun* (1984)
: any of a class of hypothetical supermassive astronomical objects that are extremely thin but are millions of light years long and that are postulated to have formed very early in the history of the universe

cos·mo·chem·is·try \,käz-mō-'ke-mə-strē\ *noun* [Greek *kosmos* universe] (1940)
: a branch of chemistry that deals with the chemical composition of and changes in the universe
— **cos·mo·chem·i·cal** \-'ke-mi-kəl\ *adjective*
— **cos·mo·chem·ist** \-mist\ *noun*

cos·mo·gen·ic \,käz-mə-'je-nik\ *adjective* [*cosmic ray* + *-o-* + *-genic*] (1962)
: produced by the action of cosmic rays ⟨*cosmogenic* carbon 14⟩

cos·mog·o·ny \käz-'mä-gə-nē\ *noun, plural* **-nies** [New Latin *cosmogonia,* from Greek *kosmogonia,* from *kosmos* + *gonos* offspring; akin to Greek *genos* race — more at KIN] (1766)
1 : the creation or origin of the world or universe
2 : a theory of the origin of the universe
— **cos·mo·gon·ic** \,käz-mə-'gä-nik\ *or* **cos·mo·gon·i·cal** \-ni-kəl\ *adjective*
— **cos·mog·o·nist** \käz-'mä-gə-nist\ *noun*

cos·mog·ra·phy \käz-'mä-grə-fē\ *noun, plural* **-phies** [Middle English *cosmographie,* from Late Latin *cosmographia,* from Greek *kosmographia,* from *kosmos* + *-graphia* -graphy] (14th century)
1 : a general description of the world or of the universe
2 : the science that deals with the constitution of the whole order of nature
— **cos·mog·ra·pher** \-fər\ *noun*
— **cos·mo·graph·ic** \,käz-mə-'gra-fik\ *or* **cos·mo·graph·i·cal** \-fi-kəl\ *adjective*

Cos·mo·line \'käz-mə-,lēn\ *trademark*
— used for petroleum jelly

cos·mol·o·gy \käz-'mä-lə-jē\ *noun, plural* **-gies** [New Latin *cosmologia,* from Greek *kosmos* + New Latin *-logia* -logy] (circa 1656)
1 a : a branch of metaphysics that deals with the nature of the universe **b :** a theory or doctrine describing the natural order of the universe

2 : a branch of astronomy that deals with the origin, structure, and space-time relationships of the universe; *also* **:** a theory dealing with these matters
— **cos·mo·log·i·cal** \,käz-mə-'lä-ji-kəl\ *adjective*
— **cos·mo·log·i·cal·ly** \-ji-k(ə-)lē\ *adverb*
— **cos·mol·o·gist** \käz-'mä-lə-jist\ *noun*
cos·mo·naut \'käz-mə-,nȯt, -,nät\ *noun* [Russian *kosmonavt*, from Greek *kosmos* + Russian *-navt* (as in *aeronavt* aeronaut)] (1959)
: an astronaut of the Soviet or Russian space program
cos·mop·o·lis \käz-'mä-pə-ləs\ *noun* [New Latin, back-formation from *cosmopolites*] (1849)
: a cosmopolitan city
¹**cos·mo·pol·i·tan** \,käz-mə-'pä-lə-t³n\ *noun* (circa 1645)
: COSMOPOLITE
²**cosmopolitan** *adjective* (1844)
1 : having worldwide rather than limited or provincial scope or bearing
2 : having wide international sophistication **:** WORLDLY
3 : composed of persons, constituents, or elements from all or many parts of the world
4 : found in most parts of the world and under varied ecological conditions ⟨a *cosmopolitan* herb⟩
— **cos·mo·pol·i·tan·ism** \-tə-,ni-zəm\ *noun*
cos·mop·o·lite \käz-'mä-pə-,līt\ *noun* [New Latin *cosmopolites*, from Greek *kosmopolitēs*, from *kosmos* + *politēs* citizen] (circa 1618)
: a cosmopolitan person or organism
— **cos·mo·po·li·tism** \käz-'mä-pə-,lī-,ti-zəm, -lə-,ti-; ,käz-mə-'pä-lə-,ti-\ *noun*
cos·mos \'käz-məs, *1 & 2 also* -,mōs, -,mäs\ *noun* [Greek *kosmos*] (1650)
1 a (1) **:** an orderly harmonious systematic universe — compare CHAOS (2) **:** ORDER, HARMONY **b :** UNIVERSE 1
2 : a complex orderly self-inclusive system
3 *plural* **cosmos** \-məs, -,mȯz\ *also* **cosmos·es** \-mə-səz\ [New Latin, genus name, from Greek *kosmos*] **:** any of a genus (*Cosmos*) of tropical American composite herbs; *especially* **:** a widely cultivated tall annual (*C. bipinnatus*) with yellow or red disks and showy ray flowers
cos·sack \'kä-,sak, -sək\ *noun, often capitalized* [Polish & Ukrainian *kozak*, of Turkic origin; akin to Volga Tatar *kazak* free person] (1589)
: a member of a group of frontiersmen of southern Russia organized as cavalry in the czarist army
¹**cos·set** \'kä-sət\ *noun* [origin unknown] (1579)
: a pet lamb; *broadly* **:** PET
²**cosset** *transitive verb* (1659)
: to treat as a pet **:** PAMPER
¹**cost** \'kȯst\ *noun* (13th century)
1 a : the amount or equivalent paid or charged for something **:** PRICE **b :** the outlay or expenditure (as of effort or sacrifice) made to achieve an object
2 : loss or penalty incurred especially in gaining something
3 *plural* **:** expenses incurred in litigation; *especially* **:** those given by the law or the court to the prevailing party against the losing party
— **cost·less** \-ləs\ *adjective*
— **cost·less·ly** *adverb*
²**cost** *verb* **cost; cost·ing** [Middle English, from Middle French *coster*, from Latin *constare* to stand firm, cost — more at CONSTANT] (14th century)
intransitive verb
1 : to require expenditure or payment ⟨the best goods *cost* more⟩
2 : to require effort, suffering, or loss
transitive verb
1 : to have a price of

2 : to cause to pay, suffer, or lose something ⟨frequent absences *cost* him his job⟩
3 *past* **cost·ed :** to estimate or set the cost of — often used with *out*
cos·ta \'käs-tə\ *noun, plural* **cos·tae** \-(,)tē, -,tī\ [Latin — more at COAST] (circa 1864)
1 : ¹RIB 1a
2 : a part (as the midrib of a leaf or the anterior vein of an insect wing) that resembles a rib
— **cos·tal** \-t³l\ *adjective*
cost accountant *noun* (1918)
: a specialist in cost accounting
cost accounting *noun* (1913)
: the systematic recording and analysis of the costs of material, labor, and overhead incident to production
cos·tard \'käs-tərd\ *noun* [Middle English] (13th century)
1 : any of several large English cooking apples
2 *archaic* **:** NODDLE, PATE
cost–ben·e·fit \'kȯs(t)-'be-nə-,fit\ *adjective* (1928)
: of, relating to, or being economic analysis that assigns a numerical value to the cost-effectiveness of an operation, procedure, or program
cost–ef·fec·tive \'kȯst-ə-'fek-tiv, -,fek-\ *adjective* (1967)
: economical in terms of tangible benefits produced by money spent ⟨*cost-effective* measures to combat poverty⟩
— **cost–ef·fec·tive·ness** *noun*
cost–ef·fi·cient \-i-'fi-shənt, -,fi-\ *adjective* (1979)
: COST-EFFECTIVE
cos·ter \'käs-tər\ *noun* (1851)
British **:** COSTERMONGER
cos·ter·mon·ger \-,mən-gər, -,mäŋ-\ *noun* [*costard* + *monger*] (1514)
British **:** a hawker of fruit or vegetables
cos·tive \'käs-tiv, 'kȯs-\ *adjective* [Middle English, from Middle French *costivé*, past participle of *costiver* to constipate, from Latin *constipare*] (14th century)
1 a : affected with constipation **b :** causing constipation
2 : slow in action or expression
3 : NIGGARDLY, STINGY
— **cos·tive·ly** *adverb*
— **cos·tive·ness** *noun*
cost·ly \'kȯs(t)-lē\ *adjective* **cost·li·er; -est** (14th century)
1 a : commanding a high price especially because of intrinsic worth ⟨*costly* gems⟩ **b :** RICH, SPLENDID
2 : made or done at heavy expense or sacrifice ⟨a *costly* mistake⟩
— **cost·li·ness** *noun*
cost·mary \'kȯst-,mer-ē, 'käst-\ *noun, plural* **-mar·ies** [Middle English *costmarie*, from *coste* costmary (from Old English *cost*, from Latin *costum*, from Greek *kostos*, a fragrant root) + *Marie* the Virgin Mary] (14th century)
: an aromatic composite herb (*Chrysanthemum balsamita*) used as a potherb and in flavoring
cost of living (1896)
: the cost of purchasing those goods and services which are included in an accepted standard level of consumption
cost–of–living index *noun* (1913)
: CONSUMER PRICE INDEX
cost–plus \'kȯs(t)-'pləs\ *adjective* (1918)
1 : paid on the basis of a fixed fee or a percentage added to actual cost ⟨a *cost-plus* contract⟩
2 : of or relating to a cost-plus contract
cost–push \'kȯs(t)-,pu̇sh\ *noun* (1951)
: an increase or upward trend in production costs (as wages) that tends to result in increased consumer prices irrespective of the level of demand — compare DEMAND-PULL
— **cost–push** *adjective*
cos·trel \'käs-trəl\ *noun* [Middle English, from Middle French *costerel*, from *costier* at

the side, from *coste* rib, side — more at COAST] (14th century)
: a flat usually earthenware container for liquids with loops through which a belt or cord may be passed for easy carrying — called also *pilgrim bottle*
¹**cos·tume** \'käs-,tüm, -,tyüm *also* -təm *or* -,chüm\ *noun* [French, from Italian, custom, dress, from Latin *consuetudin-, consuetudo* custom — more at CUSTOM] (1715)
1 : the prevailing fashion in coiffure, jewelry, and apparel of a period, country, or class
2 : an outfit worn to create the appearance characteristic of a particular period, person, place, or thing ⟨Halloween *costumes*⟩
3 : a person's ensemble of outer garments; *especially* **:** a woman's ensemble of dress with coat or jacket
— **cos·tum·ey** *adjective*
²**cos·tume** \käs-'tüm, -'tyüm *also* -'chüm; *or* 'käs-, *or* -təm\ *transitive verb* **cos·tumed; cos·tum·ing** (1823)
1 : to provide with a costume
2 : to design costumes for ⟨*costume* a play⟩
³**costume** ⟨*same as* ¹⟩ *adjective* (1884)
1 : characterized by the use of costumes ⟨a *costume* ball⟩ ⟨a *costume* drama⟩
2 : suitable for enhancing the effect of a particular costume ⟨a *costume* handbag⟩
costume jewelry *noun* (1933)
: jewelry designed for wear with current fashions and usually made of inexpensive materials
cos·tum·er \'käs-,tü-mər, -,tyü- *also* -,chü-; käs-'\ *noun* (circa 1859)
1 : one that deals in or makes costumes
2 : an upright stand with hooks or pegs on which to hang clothes
cos·tum·ery \-mə-rē\ *noun* (1838)
1 : articles of costume
2 : the art of costuming
cos·tu·mi·er \käs-'tü-mē-,ā, -'tyü-, -mē-ər\ *noun* [French] (1831)
chiefly British **:** COSTUMER 1
co·sy \'kō-zē\ *variant of* COZY
¹**cot** \'kät\ *noun* [Middle English, from Old English; akin to Old Norse *kot* small hut] (before 12th century)
1 : a small house
2 : COVER, SHEATH; *especially* **:** STALL 4
²**cot** *noun* [Hindi *khāṭ* bedstead, from Sanskrit *khaṭvā*, perhaps of Dravidian origin; akin to Tamil *kaṭṭil* bedstead] (1634)
1 : a small usually collapsible bed often of fabric stretched on a frame
2 *British* **:** CRIB 2b
co·tan·gent \(,)kō-'tan-jənt, 'kō-,\ *noun* [New Latin *cotangent-, cotangens*, from *co-* + *tangent-, tangens* tangent] (1635)
1 : a trigonometric function that for an acute angle is the ratio between the leg adjacent to the angle when it is considered part of a right triangle and the leg opposite
2 : a trigonometric function cot θ that is equal to the cosine divided by the sine for all real numbers θ for which the sine is not equal to zero and is exactly equal to the cotangent of an angle of measure θ in radians
¹**cote** \'kōt, 'kät\ *noun* [Middle English, from Old English] (before 12th century)
1 *dialect English* **:** ¹COT 1
2 : a shed or coop for small domestic animals and especially pigeons
²**cote** \'kōt\ *transitive verb* [probably from Middle French *cotoyer*] (1555)
obsolete **:** to pass by
co·te·rie \'kō-tə-(,)rē, ,kō-tə-'\ *noun* [French, from Middle French, tenants, from Old French *cotier* cotter, of Germanic origin; akin to Old English *cot* hut] (1738)
: an intimate and often exclusive group of persons with a unifying common interest or purpose
co·ter·mi·nous \(,)kō-'tər-mə-nəs\ *adjective* [alteration of *conterminous*] (1799)

1 : having the same or coincident boundaries ⟨*coterminous* states⟩
2 : coextensive in scope or duration ⟨an experience of life *coterminous* with the years of his father —Elizabeth Hardwick⟩
— **co·ter·mi·nous·ly** *adverb*

co·thur·nus \kō-'thər-nəs\ *noun, plural* **-ni** \-ˌnī, -ˌ)nē\ [Latin, from Greek *kothornos*] (1606)
1 : a high thick-soled laced boot worn by actors in Greek and Roman tragic drama — called also *co·thurn* \'kō-ˌthərn, kō-'\
2 : the dignified somewhat stilted style of ancient tragedy

co·tid·al \(ˌ)kō-'tī-dᵊl\ *adjective* (1833)
: indicating equality in the tides or a coincidence in the time of high or low tide

co·til·lion \kō-'til-yən, kə-\ *also* **co·til·lon** \kō-'til-yən, kə-, kȯ-tē-(y)ōⁿ\ *noun* [French *cotillon*, literally, petticoat, from Old French, from *cote* coat] (1766)
1 : a ballroom dance for couples that resembles the quadrille
2 : an elaborate dance with frequent changing of partners carried out under the leadership of one couple at formal balls
3 : a formal ball

co·to·ne·as·ter \kə-'tō-nē-ˌas-tər, 'kä-tᵊn-ˌēs-\ *noun* [New Latin, genus name, from Latin *cotoneum* quince + New Latin *-aster*] (1796)
: any of a genus (*Cotoneaster*) of Old World flowering shrubs of the rose family

cot·quean \'kät-ˌkwēn\ *noun* [¹*cot* + *quean*] (1547)
1 *archaic* **:** a coarse masculine woman
2 *archaic* **:** a man who busies himself with women's work or affairs

Cots·wold \'kät-ˌswōld, -swəld\ *noun* [*Cotswold* Hills, England] (circa 1658)
: any of an English breed of large long-wooled sheep

cot·ta \'kä-tə\ *noun* [Medieval Latin, of Germanic origin; akin to Old High German *kozza* coarse mantle — more at COAT] (1848)
: a waist-length surplice

cot·tage \'kä-tij\ *noun* [Middle English *cotage*, from (assumed) Anglo-French, from Middle English *cot* — more at COT] (14th century)
1 : the dwelling of a farm laborer or small farmer
2 : a usually small frame one-family house
3 : a small detached dwelling unit at an institution
4 : a usually small house for vacation use
— **cot·tag·ey** \-ti-jē\ *adjective*

cottage cheese *noun* (1848)
: a bland soft white cheese made from the curds of skim milk — called also *Dutch cheese, pot cheese, smearcase*

cottage curtains *noun plural* (1943)
: a double set of upper and lower straight-hanging window curtains

cottage industry *noun* (1921)
1 : an industry whose labor force consists of family units or individuals working at home with their own equipment
2 : a small and often informally organized industry

cottage pie *noun* (1791)
: a shepherd's pie made especially with beef

cottage pudding *noun* (circa 1854)
: plain cake covered with a hot sweet sauce

cot·tag·er \'kä-ti-jər\ *noun* (1550)
: a person who lives in a cottage

cottage tulip *noun* (1928)
: any of various tall late-flowering tulips

cot·tar *or* **cot·ter** \'kä-tər\ *noun* [Middle English *cottar*, from Medieval Latin *cotarius*, from Middle English *cot*] (14th century)
: a peasant or farm laborer who occupies a cottage and sometimes cultivates a small holding of land usually in return for services

cot·ter \'kä-tər\ *noun* [origin unknown] (14th century)

1 : a wedge-shaped or tapered piece used to fasten together parts of a structure
2 : COTTER PIN
— **cot·tered** \-tərd\ *adjective*
— **cot·ter·less** \-tər-ləs\ *adjective*

cotter pin *noun* (1881)
: a half-round metal strip bent into a pin whose ends can be flared after insertion through a slot or hole

¹cot·ton \'kä-tᵊn\ *noun, often attributive* [Middle English *coton*, from Middle French, from Arabic *quṭun*] (14th century)
1 a : a soft usually white fibrous substance composed of the hairs surrounding the seeds of various erect freely branching tropical plants (genus *Gossypium*) of the mallow family **b :** a plant producing cotton; *especially* **:** one grown for its cotton **c :** a crop of cotton
2 a : fabric made of cotton **b :** yarn spun from cotton
3 : a downy cottony substance produced by various plants (as the cottonwood)

cotton: *1* flowering branch; *2* fruit, unopened; *3* fruit, partly opened

²cotton *intransitive verb* **cot·toned; cot·ton·ing** \'kät-niŋ, 'ka-tᵊn-iŋ\ (1605)
1 : to take a liking — used with *to* ⟨*cottons* to people easily⟩
2 : to come to understand — used with *to* or *on to* ⟨*cottoned* on to the fact that our children work furiously —H. M. McLuhan⟩

cotton candy *noun* (1926)
1 : a candy made of spun sugar
2 : something attractive but insubstantial

cotton gin *noun* (1796)
: a machine that separates the seeds, hulls, and foreign material from cotton

cotton grass *noun* (1597)
: any of a genus (*Eriophorum*) of sedges with tufted spikes

cot·ton·mouth \'kä-tᵊn-ˌmaùth\ *noun* [from the white interior of its mouth] (1832)
: WATER MOCCASIN

cottonmouth moccasin *noun* (1879)
: WATER MOCCASIN

cot·ton–pick·ing \'kä-tᵊn-ˌpi-kiŋ, -ˌpi-kən\ *adjective* (circa 1952)
1 : DAMNED — used as a generalized expression of disapproval ⟨a *cotton-picking* hypocrite⟩
2 : DAMNED — used as an intensive ⟨out of his *cotton-picking* mind —Irving Kristol⟩

cot·ton·seed \'kä-tᵊn-ˌsēd\ *noun* (1774)
: the seed of the cotton plant

cottonseed oil *noun* (1833)
: a pale yellow semidrying fatty oil that is obtained from the cottonseed and is used chiefly in salad and cooking oils and after hydrogenation in shortenings and margarine

cotton stainer *noun* (1856)
: any of several bugs (genus *Dysdercus*) that damage and stain the lint of developing cotton; *especially* **:** a red and brown bug (*D. suturellus*) that attacks cotton in the southern U.S.

cot·ton·tail \'kä-tᵊn-ˌtāl\ *noun* (1869)
: any of several rather small North American rabbits (genus *Sylvilagus*) sandy to grayish brown in color with a white-tufted underside of the tail

cot·ton·weed \-ˌwēd\ *noun* (1562)
: any of various weedy plants (as cudweed) with hoary pubescence or cottony seeds

cot·ton·wood \-ˌwùd\ *noun* (1802)
: any of several poplars having seeds with cottony hairs; *especially* **:** one (*Populus del-*

toides) of the eastern and central U.S. often cultivated for its rapid growth and luxuriant foliage

cotton wool *noun* (14th century)
: raw cotton; *especially* **:** cotton batting

cot·tony \'kät-nē, 'kä-tᵊn-ē\ *adjective* (1578)
: resembling cotton in appearance or character: as **a :** covered with hairs or pubescence **b :** SOFT

cot·tony–cush·ion scale \-'kù-shən-\ *noun* (1886)
: a scale insect (*Icerya purchasi*) introduced into the U.S. from Australia that infests citrus and other plants

-cotyl *noun combining form* [*cotyledon*]
: cotyledon ⟨hypo*cotyl*⟩

cot·y·le·don \ˌkä-tə-'lē-dᵊn\ *noun* [New Latin, from Greek *kotylēdōn* cup-shaped hollow, from *kotylē* cup, anything hollow] (1540)
1 : a lobule of the mammalian placenta
2 : the first leaf or one of the first pair or whorl of leaves developed by the embryo of a seed plant or of some lower plants (as ferns) — see PLUMULE illustration
— **cot·y·le·don·ary** \-'lē-də-ˌner-ē\ *adjective*

co·ty·lo·saur \'kä-tᵊl-ō-ˌsȯr, kə-'ti-lə-\ *noun* [ultimately from Greek *kotylē* + *sauros* lizard] (circa 1909)
: any of an order (Cotylosauria) of extinct primitive reptiles with short legs and massive bodies that were probably the earliest truly terrestrial vertebrate animals

¹couch \'kaùch\ *verb* [Middle English, from Middle French *coucher*, from Latin *collocare* to set in place — more at COLLOCATE] (14th century)
transitive verb
1 : to lay (oneself) down for rest or sleep
2 : to embroider (a design) by laying down a thread and fastening it with small stitches at regular intervals
3 : to place or hold level and pointed forward ready for use
4 : to phrase or express in a specified manner ⟨the comments were *couched* in strong terms⟩
5 : to treat (a cataract) by displacing the lens of the eye into the vitreous humor
intransitive verb
1 : to lie down or recline for sleep or rest
2 : to lie in ambush

²couch *noun* [Middle English *couche* bed, from Middle French, from *coucher*] (14th century)
1 a : an article of furniture for sitting or reclining **b :** a couch on which a patient reclines when undergoing psychoanalysis
2 : the den of an animal (as an otter)
— **on the couch :** receiving psychiatric treatment

couch·ant \'kaù-chənt\ *adjective* [Middle English, from Middle French, from present participle of *coucher*] (15th century)
: lying down especially with the head up ⟨a heraldic lion *couchant*⟩

couch grass \'kaùch-, 'küch-\ *noun* [alteration of *quitch*] (1578)
1 : QUACK GRASS
2 : any of several grasses that resemble quack grass in spreading by creeping rhizomes

couch potato *noun* (1982)
: a lazy and inactive person; *especially* **:** one who spends a great deal of time watching television

cou·dé \kü-'dā\ *adjective* [French *coudé* bent like an elbow, from *coude* elbow, from Latin *cubitum*] (circa 1889)
: of, relating to, or being a telescope constructed so that the light is reflected along the polar axis to come to a focus at a point where the

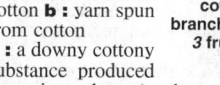

\ə\ **abut** \ᵊ\ **kitten** \ər\ **further** \a\ **ash** \ā\ **ace**
\ä\ **mop, mar** \aù\ **out** \ch\ **chin** \e\ **bet** \ē\ **easy**
\g\ **go** \i\ **hit** \ī\ **ice** \j\ **job** \ŋ\ **sing** \ō\ **go**
\ȯ\ **law** \ȯi\ **boy** \th\ **thin** \th̷\ **the** \ü\ **loot** \ù\ **foot**
\y\ **yet** \zh\ **vision** *see also* Guide to Pronunciation

holder for a photographic plate or a spectrograph may be mounted

cou·gar \'kü-gər *also* -ˌgär\ *noun, plural* **cougars** *also* **cougar** [French *couguar*, modification of New Latin *cuguacuarana*, from Tupi *siwasuarána*, from *siwasú* deer + *-rana* resembling] (1774)
: a large powerful tawny brown cat (*Felis concolor*) formerly widespread in the Americas but now reduced in number or extinct in many areas — called also *catamount, mountain lion, panther, puma*

cougar

¹**cough** \'kof\ *verb* [Middle English, from (assumed) Old English *cohhian;* akin to Middle High German *kūchen* to breathe heavily] (14th century)
intransitive verb
1 : to expel air from the lungs suddenly with an explosive noise
2 : to make a noise like that of coughing
transitive verb
: to expel by coughing — often used with *up* ⟨*cough* up mucus⟩

²**cough** *noun* (14th century)
1 : a condition marked by repeated or frequent coughing
2 : an act or sound of coughing

cough drop *noun* (1831)
: a lozenge or troche used to relieve coughing

cough syrup *noun* (1877)
: any of various sweet usually medicated liquids used to relieve coughing

cough up *transitive verb* (1894)
: HAND OVER, DELIVER ⟨*cough up* the money⟩

could \kəd, 'kud\ [Middle English *couthe, coude,* from Old English *cūthe;* akin to Old High German *konda* could] *past of* CAN
— used in auxiliary function in the past ⟨we found we *could* go⟩, in the past conditional ⟨we said we would go if we *could*⟩, and as an alternative to *can* suggesting less force or certainty or as a polite form in the present ⟨if you *could* come we would be pleased⟩

could·est \'ku-dəst\ *archaic past 2d singular of* CAN

couldn't \'ku-d²nt, -d²n, *dialect also* 'kut-²n(t) *or* 'kunt\ (1646)
: could not

couldst \kədst, 'kudst, kətst, 'kutst\ *archaic past 2d singular of* CAN

cou·lee \'kü-lē\ *noun* [Canadian French *coulée,* from French, flowing, flow of lava, from *couler* to flow, from Old French, from Latin *colare* to strain, from *colum* sieve] (1807)
1 a : a small stream **b :** a dry streambed **c :** a usually small or shallow ravine **:** GULLY
2 : a thick sheet or stream of lava

cou·lis \kü-'lē\ *noun* [French, from Old French *coleïs,* from *coleïs, coleïz* flowing] (1978)
: a thick sauce made with pureed vegetable or fruit and often used as a garnish

cou·lisse \kü-'lēs, -'lis\ *noun* [French, from Old French *coulice* portcullis, from feminine of *coleïz* flowing, sliding, from *couler*] (1819)
1 a : a side scene of a stage; *also* **:** the space between the side scenes **b :** a backstage area **c :** HALLWAY
2 : a piece of timber having a groove in which something glides

cou·loir \kül-'wär\ *noun* [French, literally, passage, from *couler*] (1822)
: a steep mountainside gorge

¹**cou·lomb** \'kü-ˌläm, -ˌlōm\ *noun* [Charles A. de *Coulomb*] (1881)
: the practical meter-kilogram-second unit of electric charge equal to the quantity of electricity transferred by a current of one ampere in one second

²**coulomb** *or* **cou·lom·bic** \kü-'läm-bik, -'lōm-, -'lä-mik, -'lō-\ *adjective* (1930)
: of, relating to, or being the electrostatic force of attraction or repulsion between charged particles

Cou·lomb's law \'kü-ˌlämz-, -ˌlōmz-\ *noun* (1854)
: a statement in physics: the force of attraction or repulsion acting along a straight line between two electric charges is directly proportional to the product of the charges and inversely to the square of the distance between them

cou·lo·me·ter \kü-'lä-mə-tər, 'kü-lə-ˌmē-tər\ *noun* [alteration of *coulombmeter,* from *coulomb* + *-meter*] (circa 1889)
: an instrument of chemical analysis that determines the amount of a substance released in electrolysis by measurement of the quantity of electricity used
— **cou·lo·met·ric** \ˌkü-lə-'me-trik\ *adjective*
— **cou·lo·met·ri·cal·ly** \-tri-k(ə-)lē\ *adverb*
— **cou·lom·e·try** \kü-'lä-mə-trē\ *noun*

coul·ter \'kōl-tər\ *noun* [Middle English *colter,* from Old English *culter* & Old French *coltre,* both from Latin *culter* plowshare; akin to Greek *skallein* to hoe — more at SHELL] (before 12th century)
: a cutting tool (as a knife or sharp disc) that is attached to the beam of a plow, makes a vertical cut in the surface, and permits clean separation and effective covering of the soil and materials being turned under

cou·ma·rin \'kü-mə-rən\ *noun* [French *coumarine,* from *coumarou* tonka bean tree, from Spanish or Portuguese; Spanish *cumarú,* from Portuguese, from Tupi *kumarú*] (1830)
: a toxic white crystalline lactone $C_9H_6O_2$ with an odor of new-mown hay found in plants or made synthetically and used especially in perfumery; *also* **:** a derivative of this compound

¹**coun·cil** \'kaun(t)-səl\ *noun* [Middle English *counceil,* from Old French *concile,* from Latin *concilium,* from *com-* + *calare* to call — more at LOW] (12th century)
1 : an assembly or meeting for consultation, advice, or discussion
2 : a group elected or appointed as an advisory or legislative body
3 a : a usually administrative body **b :** an executive body whose members are equal in power and authority **c :** a governing body of delegates from local units of a federation
4 : deliberation in a council
5 a : a federation of or a central body uniting a group of organizations **b :** a local chapter of an organization **c :** CLUB, SOCIETY

²**council** *adjective* (14th century)
1 : used for councils especially by or with North American Indians ⟨a *council* ground⟩
2 *British* **:** built, maintained, or operated by a local governing agency ⟨*council* housing⟩ ⟨*council* flats⟩

coun·cil·lor *or* **coun·cil·or** \'kaun(t)-s(ə-)lər\ *noun* (15th century)
: a member of a council
— **coun·cil·lor·ship** \-ˌship\ *noun*

coun·cil·man \'kaun(t)-səl-mən\ *noun* (1659)
: a member of a council (as of a town or city)
— **coun·cil·man·ic** \ˌkaun(t)-səl-'ma-nik\ *adjective*

council of ministers *often C&M capitalized* (circa 1909)
: CABINET 3b

coun·cil·wom·an \'kaun(t)-səl-ˌwu-mən\ *noun* (circa 1928)
: a woman who is a member of a council

¹**coun·sel** \'kaun(t)-səl\ *noun* [Middle English *conseil,* from Old French, from Latin *consilium,* from *consulere* to consult] (13th century)
1 a : advice given especially as a result of consultation **b :** a policy or plan of action or behavior

2 : DELIBERATION, CONSULTATION
3 a *archaic* **:** PURPOSE **b :** guarded thoughts or intentions
4 a *plural* **counsel** (1) **:** a lawyer engaged in the trial or management of a case in court (2) **:** a lawyer appointed to advise and represent in legal matters an individual client or a corporate and especially a public body **b :** CONSULTANT 2

²**counsel** *verb* **-seled** *or* **-selled; -sel·ing** *or* **-sel·ling** \-s(ə-)liŋ\ (14th century)
transitive verb
: ADVISE ⟨*counseled* them to avoid rash actions —George Orwell⟩
intransitive verb
: CONSULT ⟨*counseled* with her husband⟩

coun·sel·ee \ˌkaun(t)-sə-'lē\ *noun* (1923)
: one who is being counseled

counseling *or* **counselling** *noun* (1927)
: professional guidance of the individual by utilizing psychological methods especially in collecting case history data, using various techniques of the personal interview, and testing interests and aptitudes

coun·sel·or *or* **coun·sel·lor** \'kaun(t)-s(ə-)lər\ *noun* (13th century)
1 : a person who gives advice or counseling ⟨marriage *counselor*⟩
2 : LAWYER; *specifically* **:** one that gives advice in law and manages cases for clients in court
3 : one who has supervisory duties at a summer camp
— **coun·sel·or·ship** \-ˌship\ *noun*

counselor–at–law *noun, plural* **counselors–at–law** (1617)
: COUNSELOR 2

¹**count** \'kaunt, *dialect* 'kyaunt\ *verb* [Middle English, from Middle French *conter, compter,* from Latin *computare,* from *com-* + *putare* to consider] (14th century)
transitive verb
1 a : to indicate or name by units or groups so as to find the total number of units involved **:** NUMBER **b :** to name the numbers in order up to and including ⟨*count* ten⟩ **c :** to include in a tallying and reckoning ⟨about 100 present, *counting* children⟩ **d :** to call aloud (beats or time units) ⟨*count* cadence⟩ ⟨*count* eighth notes⟩
2 a : CONSIDER, ACCOUNT ⟨*count* oneself lucky⟩ **b :** to record as of an opinion or persuasion ⟨*count* me as uncommitted⟩
3 : to include or exclude by or as if by counting ⟨*count* me in⟩
intransitive verb
1 a : to recite or indicate the numbers in order by units or groups ⟨*count* by fives⟩ **b :** to count the units in a group
2 : to rely or depend on someone or something ⟨*counted* on his parents to help with the expenses⟩
3 : ADD, TOTAL ⟨it *counts* up to a sizable amount⟩
4 : to have value or significance ⟨these are the people who really *count*⟩
— **count heads** *or* **count noses :** to count the number present
— **count on :** to look forward to as certain **:** ANTICIPATE ⟨*counted on* winning⟩

²**count** *noun* (14th century)
1 a : the action or process of counting **b :** a total obtained by counting **:** TALLY
2 *archaic* **a :** RECKONING, ACCOUNT **b :** CONSIDERATION, ESTIMATION
3 a : ALLEGATION, CHARGE; *specifically* **:** one separately stating the cause of action or prosecution in a legal declaration or indictment ⟨guilty on all *counts*⟩ **b :** a specific point under consideration **:** ISSUE
4 : the total number of individual things in a given unit or sample obtained by counting all or a subsample of them ⟨bacteria *count*⟩
5 a : the calling off of the seconds from one to ten when a boxer has been knocked down **b**

: the number of balls and strikes charged to a baseball batter during one turn ⟨the *count* stood at 3 and 2⟩ **c** : SCORE ⟨tied the *count* with a minute to play⟩

6 : a measurement of the thickness or fineness of yarn by determining the number of hanks or yards per pound it produces

³**count** *noun* [Middle English, from Middle French *comte*, from Late Latin *comit-*, *comes*, from Latin, companion, one of the imperial court, from *com-* + *ire* to go — more at IS-SUE] (15th century)

: a European nobleman whose rank corresponds to that of a British earl

count·able \'kaun-tə-bəl\ *adjective* (1581)

: capable of being counted; *especially* : DENU-MERABLE ⟨a *countable* set⟩

— **count·abil·i·ty** \ˌkaun-tə-'bi-lə-tē\ *noun*

— **count·ably** \'kaun-tə-blē\ *adverb*

count·down \'kaunt-ˌdaun\ *noun* (circa 1952)

: an audible backward counting in fixed units (as seconds) from an arbitrary starting number to mark the time remaining before an event; *also* : preparations carried on during such a count

— **count down** \-'daun\ *intransitive verb*

¹**coun·te·nance** \'kaunt-ᵊn-ən(t)s, 'kaunt-nən(t)s\ *noun* [Middle English, from Middle French *contenance*, from Medieval Latin *continentia*, from Latin, restraint, from *continent-*, *continens*, present participle of *continēre* to hold together — more at CON-TAIN] (13th century)

1 *obsolete* : BEARING, DEMEANOR

2 a : calm expression **b** : mental composure **c** : LOOK, EXPRESSION

3 *archaic* **a** : ASPECT, SEMBLANCE **b** : PRETENSE

4 : FACE, VISAGE; *especially* : the face as an indication of mood, emotion, or character

5 : bearing or expression that offers approval or sanction : moral support

²**countenance** *transitive verb* **-nanced; -nanc·ing** (1568)

: to extend approval or toleration to : SANCTION

— **coun·te·nanc·er** *noun*

¹**count·er** \'kaun-tər\ *noun* [Middle English *countour*, from Middle French *comptouer*, from Medieval Latin *computatorium* computing place, from Latin *computare*] (14th century)

1 : a piece (as of metal or plastic) used in reckoning or in games

2 : something of value in bargaining : ASSET

3 : a level surface (as a table, shelf or display case) over which transactions are conducted or food is served or on which goods are displayed or work is conducted ⟨jewelry *counter*⟩ ⟨a lunch *counter*⟩

— **over the counter 1** : in or through a broker's office rather than through a stock exchange ⟨stock bought *over the counter*⟩ **2** : without a prescription ⟨drugs available *over the counter*⟩

— **under the counter** : by surreptitious means : in an illicit and private manner

²**count·er** \'kaun-tər\ *noun* [Middle English, from Middle French *conteor*, from *compter* to count] (14th century)

: one that counts; *especially* : a device for indicating a number or amount

³**coun·ter** *verb* **coun·tered; coun·ter·ing** \'kaun-t(ə-)riŋ\ [Middle English *countren*, from Middle French *contre* against, opposite, from Latin *contra;* akin to Latin *com-* with, together — more at CO-] (14th century)

transitive verb

1 a : to act in opposition to : OPPOSE **b** : OFF-SET, NULLIFY ⟨tried to *counter* the trend toward depersonalization⟩

2 : to adduce in answer ⟨we *countered* that our warnings had been ignored⟩

intransitive verb

: to meet attacks or arguments with defensive or retaliatory steps

⁴**coun·ter** *adverb* [Middle English *contre*, from Middle French] (15th century)

1 : in an opposite or wrong direction

2 : to or toward a different or opposite direction, result, or effect ⟨values that run *counter* to those of society⟩

⁵**coun·ter** *noun* (15th century)

1 : CONTRARY, OPPOSITE

2 : the after portion of a boat from the waterline to the extreme outward swell or stern overhang

3 a : the act of making an attack while parrying one (as in boxing or fencing); *also* : a blow thus given in boxing **b** : an agency or force that offsets : CHECK

4 : a stiffener to give permanent form to a boot or shoe upper around the heel

5 : an area within the face of a letter wholly or partly enclosed by strokes

6 : a football play in which the ballcarrier goes in a direction opposite to the movement of the play

⁶**coun·ter** *adjective* (1596)

1 : marked by or tending toward or in an opposite direction or effect

2 : given to or marked by opposition, hostility, or antipathy

3 : situated or lying opposite ⟨the *counter* side⟩

4 : recalling or ordering back by a superseding contrary order : COUNTERMANDING ⟨*counter* orders from the colonel⟩

counter- *prefix* [Middle English *contre-*, from Middle French, from *contre*]

1 a : contrary : opposite ⟨*counter*clockwise⟩ ⟨*counter*march⟩ **b** : opposing : retaliatory ⟨*counter*force⟩ ⟨*counter*offensive⟩

2 : complementary : corresponding ⟨*counter*weight⟩ ⟨*counter*part⟩

3 : duplicate : substitute ⟨*counter*foil⟩

coun·ter·ac·cu·sa·tion
coun·ter·ad·ap·ta·tion
coun·ter·ad·ver·tis·ing
coun·ter·agent
coun·ter·ag·gres·sion
coun·ter·ar·gue
coun·ter·ar·gu·ment
coun·ter·as·sault
coun·ter·at·tack
coun·ter·at·tack·er
coun·ter·bid
coun·ter·blast
coun·ter·block·ade
coun·ter·blow
coun·ter·cam·paign
coun·ter·charge
coun·ter·com·mer·cial
coun·ter·com·plaint
coun·ter·con·spir·a·cy
coun·ter·con·ven·tion
coun·ter·coun·ter·mea·sure
coun·ter·coup
coun·ter·crit·i·cism
coun·ter·cry
coun·ter·de·mand
coun·ter·dem·on·strate
coun·ter·dem·on·stra·tion
coun·ter·dem·on·stra·tor
coun·ter·de·ploy·ment
coun·ter·ed·u·ca·tion·al
coun·ter·ef·fort
coun·ter·ev·i·dence
coun·ter·fire
coun·ter·force

coun·ter·gov·ern·ment
coun·ter·hy·poth·e·sis
coun·ter·im·age
coun·ter·in·cen·tive
coun·ter·in·fla·tion
coun·ter·in·fla·tion·ary
coun·ter·in·flu·ence
coun·ter·in·stance
coun·ter·in·sti·tu·tion
coun·ter·in·ter·pre·ta·tion
coun·ter·memo
coun·ter·mo·bi·li·za·tion
coun·ter·move
coun·ter·move·ment
coun·ter·myth
coun·ter·or·der
coun·ter·pe·ti·tion
coun·ter·pick·et
coun·ter·play
coun·ter·play·er
coun·ter·ploy
coun·ter·pow·er
coun·ter·pres·sure
coun·ter·pro·ject
coun·ter·pro·pa·gan·da
coun·ter·pro·test
coun·ter·ques·tion
coun·ter·raid
coun·ter·ral·ly
coun·ter·re·ac·tion
coun·ter·re·form
coun·ter·re·form·er
coun·ter·re·sponse
coun·ter·re·tal·i·a·tion
coun·ter·sci·en·tif·ic
coun·ter·shot
coun·ter·snip·er
coun·ter·spell

coun·ter·state
coun·ter·state·ment
coun·ter·step
coun·ter·strat·e·gist
coun·ter·strat·e·gy
coun·ter·stream
coun·ter·strike
coun·ter·stroke
coun·ter·style
coun·ter·sue
coun·ter·sug·ges·tion
coun·ter·suit

coun·ter·sur·veil·lance
coun·ter·tac·tics
coun·ter·ten·den·cy
coun·ter·ter·ror
coun·ter·ter·ror·ism
coun·ter·ter·ror·ist
coun·ter·threat
coun·ter·thrust
coun·ter·tra·di·tion
coun·ter·trend
coun·ter·vi·o·lence
coun·ter·world

coun·ter·act \ˌkaun-tə-'rakt\ *transitive verb* (1678)

: to make ineffective or restrain or neutralize the usually ill effects of by an opposite force

— **coun·ter·ac·tion** \-'rak-shən\ *noun*

— **coun·ter·ac·tive** \-'rak-tiv\ *adjective*

¹**coun·ter·bal·ance** \'kaun-tər-ˌba-lən(t)s, ˌkaun-tər-'\ *noun* (1611)

1 : a weight that balances another

2 : a force or influence that offsets or checks an opposing force

²**counterbalance** \ˌkaun-tər-', 'kaun-tər-ˌ\ *transitive verb* (1611)

1 : to oppose or balance with an equal weight or force

2 : to equip with counterbalances

coun·ter·change \'kaun-tər-ˌchānj\ *transitive verb* (circa 1604)

1 : INTERCHANGE, TRANSPOSE

2 : CHECKER 1a

¹**coun·ter·check** \-ˌchek\ *noun* (1559)

: a check or restraint often operating against something that is itself a check

²**countercheck** *transitive verb* (1587)

1 : CHECK, COUNTERACT

2 : to check a second time for verification

counter check *noun* (1856)

: a check obtainable at a bank usually to be cashed only at the bank by the drawer

¹**coun·ter·claim** \'kaun-tər-ˌklām\ *noun* (1784)

: an opposing claim; *especially* : a claim brought by a defendant against a plaintiff in a legal action

²**counterclaim** (1881)

intransitive verb

: to enter or plead a counterclaim

transitive verb

: to ask in a counterclaim

coun·ter·clock·wise \ˌkaun-tər-'kläk-ˌwīz\ *adverb* (1888)

: in a direction opposite to that in which the hands of a clock rotate as viewed from in front

— **counterclockwise** *adjective*

coun·ter·con·di·tion·ing \-kən-'di-sh(ə-)niŋ\ *noun* (1962)

: conditioning in order to replace an undesirable response (as fear) to a stimulus (as an engagement in public speaking) by a favorable one

coun·ter·cul·ture \'kaun-tər-ˌkəl-chər\ *noun* (1968)

: a culture with values and mores that run counter to those of established society

— **coun·ter·cul·tur·al** \ˌkaun-tər-'kəlch-rəl, -'kəl-chə-\ *adjective*

— **coun·ter·cul·tur·al·ism** \-rə-ˌli-zəm\ *noun*

— **coun·ter·cul·tur·ist** \-rist\ *noun*

¹**coun·ter·cur·rent** \'kaun-tər-ˌkər-ənt, -ˌkə-rənt\ *noun* (1684)

: a current flowing in a direction opposite that of another current

²**countercurrent** \ˌkaun-tər-'\ *adjective* (1799)

1 : flowing in an opposite direction

2 : involving flow of materials in opposite directions ⟨*countercurrent* dialysis⟩
— **coun·ter·cur·rent·ly** *adverb*

coun·ter·cy·cli·cal \-'sī-kli-kəl, -'si-\ *adjective* (1944)
: calculated to check excessive developments in a business cycle : COMPENSATORY ⟨*counter-cyclical* budget policies⟩
— **coun·ter·cy·cli·cal·ly** \-k(ə-)lē\ *adverb*

coun·ter·es·pi·o·nage \,kaùn-tər-'es-pē-ə-,näzh, -,nij, *Canadian also* -,nazh; -,es-pē-ə-'näzh; -ə-'spē-ə-nij\ *noun* (1899)
: the activity concerned with detecting and thwarting enemy espionage

coun·ter·ex·am·ple \'kaùn-tər-ig-,zam-pəl\ *noun* (1957)
: an example that disproves a proposition or theory

coun·ter·fac·tu·al \,kaùn-tər-'fak-chə-wəl, -chəl, -shwəl\ *adjective* (1946)
: contrary to fact ⟨*counterfactual* assumptions⟩

¹coun·ter·feit \'kaùnt-ər-,fit\ *noun* [Middle English *countrefet*, from Middle French *contrefait*, from past participle of *contrefaire* to imitate, from *contre-* + *faire* to make, from Latin *facere* — more at DO] (14th century)
1 : made in imitation of something else with intent to deceive : FORGED ⟨*counterfeit* money⟩
2 a : INSINCERE, FEIGNED ⟨*counterfeit* sympathy⟩ **b :** IMITATION ⟨*counterfeit* Georgian houses⟩

²counterfeit (14th century)
transitive verb
: to imitate or feign especially with intent to deceive; *also* : to make a fraudulent replica of ⟨*counterfeiting* $20 bills⟩
intransitive verb
1 : to try to deceive by pretense or dissembling
2 : to engage in counterfeiting something of value
synonym see ASSUME
— **coun·ter·feit·er** *noun*

³counterfeit *noun* (15th century)
1 : something counterfeit : FORGERY
2 : something likely to be mistaken for something of higher value ⟨pity was a *counterfeit* of love —Harry Hervey⟩
synonym see IMPOSTURE

coun·ter·flow \'kaùn-tər-,flō\ *noun* (1870)
: the flow of a fluid in opposite directions (as in an apparatus)

coun·ter·foil \-,fòil\ *noun* (1706)
: a detachable stub (as on a check or ticket) usually serving as a record or receipt

coun·ter·guer·ril·la *also* **coun·ter·gue·ril·la** \,kaùn-tər-gə-'ri-lə, -gi-, -gyi-, -ge-\ *noun* (1901)
: a guerrilla who is trained to thwart enemy guerrilla operations

coun·ter·in·sur·gen·cy \,kaùn-tər-in-'sər-jən(t)-sē\ *noun* (1962)
: organized military activity designed to combat insurgency
— **coun·ter·in·sur·gent** \-jənt\ *noun*

coun·ter·in·tel·li·gence \,kaùn-tər-in-'te-lə-jən(t)s\ *noun* (1940)
: organized activity of an intelligence service designed to block an enemy's sources of information, to deceive the enemy, to prevent sabotage, and to gather political and military information

coun·ter·in·tu·i·tive \-in-'tü-ə-tiv, -'tyü-\ *adjective* (1955)
: contrary to what one would intuitively expect
— **coun·ter·in·tu·i·tive·ly** \-lē\ *adverb*

coun·ter·ion \'kaùn-tər-,ī-ən, -,än\ *noun* (1940)
: an ion having a charge opposite to that of the substance with which it is associated

coun·ter·ir·ri·tant \,kaùn-tər-'ir-ə-tənt\ *noun* (1854)

1 : an agent applied locally to produce superficial inflammation with the object of reducing inflammation in deeper adjacent structures
2 : an irritation or discomfort that diverts attention from another
— **counterirritant** *adjective*

count·er·man \'kaùn-tər-,man, -mən\ *noun* (1853)
: one who tends a counter

¹coun·ter·mand \'kaùn-tər-,mand, ,kaùn-tər-'\ *transitive verb* [Middle English *countermaunden*, from Middle French *contremander*, from *contre-* counter- + *mander* to command, from Latin *mandare* — more at MANDATE] (15th century)
1 : to revoke (a command) by a contrary order
2 : to recall or order back by a superseding contrary order ⟨*countermand* reinforcements⟩

²coun·ter·mand \'kaùn-tər-,mand\ *noun* (1548)
1 : a contrary order
2 : the revocation of an order or command

coun·ter·march \'kaùn-tər-,märch\ *noun* (1598)
1 : a marching back; *specifically* : a movement in marching by which a unit of troops reverses direction while marching but keeps the same order
2 : a march (as of political demonstrators) designed to counter the effect of another march
— **countermarch** *intransitive verb*

coun·ter·mea·sure \-,me-zhər, -,mā-\ *noun* (1923)
: an action or device designed to negate or offset another; *especially* : a military system or device intended to thwart a sensing mechanism (as radar) ⟨electronic *countermeasures*⟩

coun·ter·mel·o·dy \-,me-lə-dē\ *noun* (1926)
: a secondary melody that is sounded simultaneously with the principal one

coun·ter·mine \-,mīn\ *noun* (1548)
: a tunnel for intercepting an enemy mine

coun·ter·of·fen·sive \'kaùn-tər-ə-,fen(t)-siv\ *noun* (1909)
: a large-scale military offensive undertaken by a force previously on the defensive

coun·ter·of·fer \-,ò-fər, -,ä-fər\ *noun* (1788)
: a return offer made by one who has rejected an offer

coun·ter·pane \'kaùn-tər-,pān\ *noun* [alteration of Middle English *countrepointe*, modification of Middle French *coute pointe*, literally, embroidered quilt] (15th century)
: BEDSPREAD

coun·ter·part \-,pärt\ *noun* (15th century)
1 : one of two corresponding copies of a legal instrument : DUPLICATE
2 a : a thing that fits another perfectly **b** : something that completes : COMPLEMENT
3 a : one remarkably similar to another **b** : one having the same function or characteristics as another ⟨college presidents and their *counterparts* in business⟩

coun·ter·plan \'kaùn-tər-,plan\ *noun* (1788)
1 : a plan designed to counter another plan
2 : an alternate or substitute plan

coun·ter·plea \-,plē\ *noun* (1523)
: a replication to a legal plea

¹coun·ter·plot \-,plät\ *noun* (circa 1611)
: a plot designed to thwart an opponent's plot

²counterplot *transitive verb* (1662)
: to intrigue against : foil with a plot

¹coun·ter·point \'kaùn-tər-,pòint\ *noun* [Middle French *contrepoint*, from Medieval Latin *contrapunctus*, from Latin *contra-* counter- + Medieval Latin *punctus* musical note, melody, from Latin, act of pricking, from *pungere* to prick — more at PUNGENT] (15th century)
1 a : one or more independent melodies added above or below a given melody **b** : the combination of two or more independent melodies into a single harmonic texture in which each retains its linear character : POLYPHONY

2 a : a complementing or contrasting item : OPPOSITE **b** : use of contrast or interplay of elements in a work of art (as a drama)

²counterpoint *transitive verb* (1875)
1 : to compose or arrange in counterpoint
2 : to set off or emphasize by juxtaposition : set in contrast ⟨*counterpoints* the public and the private man —Tom Bishop⟩

¹coun·ter·poise \-,pòiz\ *transitive verb* [Middle English *countrepesen*, from Middle French *contrepeser*, from *contre-* + *peser* to weigh — more at POISE] (14th century)
: COUNTERBALANCE

²counterpoise *noun* (15th century)
1 : COUNTERBALANCE
2 : an equivalent power or force acting in opposition
3 : a state of balance

coun·ter·pose \,kaùn-tər-'pōz\ *transitive verb* [*counter-* + *-pose* (as in *compose*)] (1594)
: to place in opposition, contrast, or equilibrium ⟨*counterpose* a positive view to the negative assessment⟩

coun·ter·pro·duc·tive \-prə-'dək-tiv\ *adjective* (1959)
: tending to hinder the attainment of a desired goal ⟨violence as a means to achieve an end is *counterproductive* —W. E. Brock (born 1930)⟩

coun·ter·pro·gram·ming \,kaùn-tər-'prō-,gra-miŋ, -grə-\ *noun* (circa 1966)
: the scheduling of programs by television networks so as to attract audiences away from simultaneously telecast programs of competitors

coun·ter·pro·pos·al \'kaùn-tər-prə-,pō-zəl\ *noun* (1885)
: a return proposal made by one who has rejected a proposal

coun·ter·punch \'kaùn-tər-,pənch\ *noun* (1942)
: a counter in boxing; *also* : a countering blow or attack
— **counterpunch** *intransitive verb*
— **coun·ter·punch·er** \-,pən-chər\ *noun*

coun·ter·ref·or·ma·tion \,kaùn-tə(r)-,re-fər-'mā-shən\ *noun* (1840)
1 *usually* **Counter–Reformation :** the reform movement in the Roman Catholic Church following the Reformation
2 : a reformation designed to counter the effects of a previous reformation

coun·ter·rev·o·lu·tion \-,re-və-'lü-shən\ *noun* (1793)
1 : a revolution directed toward overthrowing a government or social system established by a previous revolution
2 : a movement to counteract revolutionary trends
— **coun·ter·rev·o·lu·tion·ary** \-shə-,ner-ē\ *adjective or noun*

coun·ter·shad·ing \'kaùn-tər-,shā-diŋ\ *noun* (1896)
: cryptic coloration of an animal with parts normally in shadow being light and parts normally illuminated being dark thereby reducing shadows and contours

coun·ter·sign \-,sīn\ *noun* (1591)
1 : a signature attesting the authenticity of a document already signed by another
2 : a sign given in reply to another; *specifically* : a military secret signal that must be given by one wishing to pass a guard
— **countersign** *transitive verb*
— **coun·ter·sig·na·ture** \,kaùn-tər-'sig-nə-,chùr, -chər, -,tyùr, -,tùr\ *noun*

¹coun·ter·sink \'kaùn-tər-,siŋk\ *transitive verb* **-sunk** \-,səŋk\; **-sink·ing** (1816)
1 : to make a countersink on
2 : to set the head of (as a screw) at or below the surface

²countersink *noun* (1816)
1 : a bit or drill for making a funnel-shaped enlargement at the outer end of a drilled hole
2 : the enlargement made by a countersink

coun·ter·spy \'kaùn-tər-,spī\ *noun* (1939)
: a spy engaged in counterespionage

coun·ter·stain \-ˌstān\
transitive verb (1895)
: to stain (as a microscopy specimen) so as to color parts (as the cytoplasm of cells) not colored by another stain (as a nuclear stain)
— **counterstain** *noun*

countersink

coun·ter·ten·or \-ˌte-nər\ *noun* [Middle English *countretenour,* from Middle French *contreteneur,* from *contre-* + *teneur* tenor] (15th century)
: a tenor with an unusually high range (as an alto range)

coun·ter·top \-ˌtäp\ *noun* [¹*counter* + ¹*top*] (1897)
: the flat working surface on top of waist-level kitchen cabinets

coun·ter·trade \-ˌtrād\ *noun* (1978)
: a form of international trade in which purchases made by an importing nation are linked to offsetting purchases made by the exporting nation

coun·ter·trans·fer·ence \ˌkaun-tər-(ˌ)tran(t)s-ˈfər-ən(t)s, -ˈtran(t)s-(ˌ)\ *noun* (1920)
1 : psychological transference especially by a psychotherapist during the course of treatment; *especially* : the psychotherapist's reactions to the patient's transference
2 : the complex of feelings of a psychotherapist toward the patient

coun·ter·vail \ˌkaun-tər-ˈvā(ə)l\ *verb* [Middle English *countrevailen,* from Middle French *contrevaloir,* from *contre-* counter- + *valoir* to be worth, from Latin *valēre* — more at WIELD] (14th century)
transitive verb
1 : to compensate for
2 *archaic* : EQUAL, MATCH
3 : to exert force against : COUNTERACT
intransitive verb
: to exert force against an opposing and often bad or harmful force or influence

coun·ter·view \ˈkaun-tər-ˌvyü\ *noun* (1590)
1 *archaic* : CONFRONTATION
2 : an opposite point of view

coun·ter·weight \-ˌwāt\ *noun* (1693)
: an equivalent weight or force : COUNTERBALANCE
— **counterweight** *transitive verb*

count·ess \ˈkaun-təs\ *noun* (12th century)
1 : the wife or widow of an earl or count
2 : a woman who holds in her own right the rank of earl or count

coun·ti·an \ˈkaun-tē-ən\ *noun* (15th century)
: a native or resident of a usually specified county

count·ing·house \ˈkaun-tiŋ-ˌhaus\ *noun* (15th century)
: a building, room, or office used for keeping books and transacting business

counting number *noun* (circa 1965)
: NATURAL NUMBER

counting room *noun* (1712)
: COUNTINGHOUSE

count·less \ˈkaunt-ləs\ *adjective* (1588)
: too numerous to be counted : MYRIAD, MANY
— **count·less·ly** *adverb*

count noun *noun* (1952)
: a noun (as *bean* or *sheet*) that forms a plural and is used with a numeral, with words such as *many* or *few,* or with the indefinite article *a* or *an* — compare MASS NOUN

count palatine *noun* (1539)
1 a : a count of the Holy Roman Empire having imperial powers in his own domain **b** : a high judicial official in the Holy Roman Empire
2 : the proprietor of a county palatine in England or Ireland

coun·tri·fied *also* **coun·try·fied** \ˈkən-tri-ˌfīd\ *adjective* [*country* + *-fied* (as in *glorified*)] (1653)
1 : RURAL, RUSTIC
2 : UNSOPHISTICATED

3 : played or sung in the manner of country music ⟨*countrified* rock⟩

¹**coun·try** \ˈkən-trē\ *noun, plural* **countries** [Middle English *contree,* from Old French *contrée,* from Medieval Latin *contrata,* from Latin *contra* against, on the opposite side] (13th century)
1 : an indefinite usually extended expanse of land : REGION
2 a : the land of a person's birth, residence, or citizenship **b** : a political state or nation or its territory
3 a : the people of a state or district : POPULACE **b** : JURY **c** : ELECTORATE 2
4 : rural as distinguished from urban areas
5 : COUNTRY MUSIC ◇
— **coun·try·ish** \-trē-ish\ *adjective*

²**country** *adjective* (14th century)
1 : of, relating to, or characteristic of the country
2 a : of or relating to a decorative style associated with life in the country ⟨an English country look⟩; *also* : possessing a style of rustic simplicity ⟨*country* furniture⟩ **b** : prepared or processed with farm supplies and procedures ⟨*country* ham⟩
3 : of, relating to, suitable for, or featuring country music ⟨*country* singers⟩

country and western *noun* (1960)
: COUNTRY MUSIC — usually hyphenated in attributive use

country club *noun* (1867)
: a suburban club for social life and recreation; *especially* : one having a golf course — usually hyphenated in attributive use

coun·try–dance \ˈkən-trē-ˌdan(t)s\ *noun* (1579)
: any of various native English dances in which partners face each other especially in rows

country gentleman *noun* (1632)
1 : a well-to-do country resident : an owner of a country estate
2 : one of the English landed gentry

country house *noun* (14th century)
: a house and especially a mansion in the country

coun·try·man \ˈkən-trē-mən, *3 often* -ˌman\ *noun* (14th century)
1 : an inhabitant or native of a specified country
2 : COMPATRIOT
3 : one living in the country or marked by country ways : RUSTIC

country mile *noun* (1950)
: a long distance

country music *noun* (1952)
: music derived from or imitating the folk style of the Southern U.S. or of the Western cowboy

country rock *noun* (1968)
: ROCKABILLY

coun·try·seat \ˌkən-trē-ˈsēt\ *noun* (1583)
: a house or estate in the country

coun·try·side \ˈkən-trē-ˌsīd\ *noun* (1727)
1 : a rural area
2 : the inhabitants of a countryside

coun·try·wide \ˈkən-trē-ˈwīd\ *adjective* (1915)
: extending throughout a country

coun·try·wom·an \ˈkən-trē-ˌwu-mən\ *noun* (15th century)
1 : a woman compatriot
2 : a woman resident of the country

¹**coun·ty** \ˈkaun-tē\ *noun, plural* **counties** [Middle English *counte,* from Middle French *conté,* from Medieval Latin *comitatus,* from Late Latin, office of a count, from *comit-, comes* count — more at COUNT] (14th century)
1 : the domain of a count
2 a : one of the territorial divisions of England and Wales and formerly also of Scotland and Northern Ireland constituting the chief units for administrative, judicial, and political pur-

poses **b** (1) : the people of a county (2) *British* : the gentry of a county
3 : the largest territorial division for local government within a state of the U.S.
4 : the largest local administrative unit in various countries
— **county** *adjective*

²**county** *noun, plural* **counties** [modification of Middle French *comte*] (1550)
archaic : ³COUNT

county agent *noun* (1705)
: a consultant employed jointly by federal and state governments to provide information about agriculture and home economics

county court *noun* (1639)
: a court in some states that has a designated jurisdiction usually both civil and criminal within the limits of a county

county fair *noun* (1856)
: a fair usually held annually at a set location in a county especially to exhibit local agricultural products and livestock

county palatine *noun* (15th century)
: the territory of a count palatine

county seat *noun* (1803)
: a town that is the seat of county administration

county town *noun* (1670)
chiefly British : COUNTY SEAT

¹**coup** \ˈküp\ *verb* [Middle English, to strike, from Middle French *couper* — more at COPE] (circa 1572)
chiefly Scottish : OVERTURN, UPSET

²**coup** \ˈkü\ *noun, plural* **coups** \ˈküz\ [French, blow, stroke — more at COPE] (1791)
1 : a brilliant, sudden, and usually highly successful stroke or act
2 : COUP D'ÉTAT

coup de grâce *or* **coup de grace** \ˌkü-də-ˈgräs\ *noun, plural* **coups de grâce** *or* **coups de grace** \ˌkü-də-\ [French *coup de grâce,* literally, stroke of mercy] (1699)
1 : a death blow or shot administered to end the suffering of one mortally wounded
2 : a decisive finishing blow, act, or event

coup de main \-ˈmaⁿ\ *noun, plural* **coups de main** \ˌkü-də-\ [French, literally, hand stroke] (1758)
: a sudden attack in force

coup d'état *or* **coup d'etat** \ˌkü-(ˌ)dā-ˈtä, ˈkü-(ˌ)dā-, -də-\ *noun, plural* **coups d'état** *or* **coups d'etat** \-ˈtä(z), -ˌtä(z)\ [French, literally, stroke of state] (1646)
: a sudden decisive exercise of force in politics; *especially* : the violent overthrow or alteration of an existing government by a small group

coup de thé·â·tre *or* **coup de the·a·tre** \ˌkü-də-tā-ˈätrᵊ\ *noun, plural* **coups de thé·âtre** *or* **coups de theatre** \ˌkü-də-\

◇ WORD HISTORY
country In Latin the adverb and preposition *contra* means "against" or "on the opposite side." The spoken Latin from which the Romance languages descend formed the derivative *contrata,* which literally meant "that which is situated on the opposite side." But in the Romance words, such as Old Italian *contrata* and Old French *contree,* the attested sense is invariably "environs," "area of land," or "region." Borrowed from French as *contree* in the 13th century, English *country* has had a rich development in its adopted home, acquiring significant new senses, such as "populace" and "rural as opposed to urban areas," that are not shared by Modern French *contrée.*

\ə\ abut \ᵊ\ kitten \ər\ further \a\ ash \ā\ ace
\ä\ mop, mar \au\ out \ch\ chin \e\ bet \ē\ easy
\g\ go \i\ hit \ī\ ice \j\ job \ŋ\ sing \ō\ go
\o\ law \oi\ boy \th\ thin \th\ the \ü\ loot \u\ foot
\y\ yet \zh\ vision *see also* Guide to Pronunciation

[French *coup de théâtre,* literally, stroke of theater] (1747)
1 : a sudden sensational turn in a play; *also* **:** a sudden dramatic effect or turn of events
2 : a theatrical success
coup d'oeil \kü-'də(r), -'dəi\ *noun, plural* **coups d'oeil** *same*\ [French, literally, stroke of the eye] (1739)
: a brief survey **:** GLANCE
cou·pé *or* **coupe** \kü-'pā, *2 often* 'küp\ *noun* [French *coupé,* from past participle of *couper* to cut, strike] (1834)
1 : a four-wheeled closed horse-drawn carriage for two persons inside with an outside seat for the driver in front
2 *usually* **coupe :** a 2-door automobile often seating only two persons; *also* **:** one with a tight-spaced rear seat — compare SEDAN
¹cou·ple \'kə-pəl\ *"couple of" is often* ,kə-plə(v)\ *noun* [Middle English, pair, bond, from Old French *cople,* from Latin *copula* bond, from *co-* + *apere* to fasten — more at APT] (13th century)
1 a : a man and woman married, engaged, or otherwise paired **b :** two persons paired together
2 : PAIR, BRACE
3 : something that joins or links two things together: as **a :** two equal and opposite forces that act along parallel lines **b :** a pair of substances that in contact with an electrolyte participate in a transfer of electrons which causes an electric current to flow
4 : an indefinite small number **:** FEW ⟨a *couple* of days ago⟩ □
²cou·ple \'kə-pəl\ *verb* **cou·pled; cou·pling** \-p(ə-)liŋ\ (13th century)
transitive verb
1 a : to connect for consideration together **b :** to join for combined effect
2 a : to fasten together **:** LINK **b :** to bring (two electric circuits) into such close proximity as to permit mutual influence
3 : to join in marriage or sexual union
intransitive verb
1 : to unite in sexual union
2 : JOIN
3 : to unite chemically
³couple *adjective* (1924)
: TWO; *also* **:** FEW — used with *a* ⟨a *couple* drinks⟩ □
cou·ple·ment \'kə-pəl-mənt\ *noun* [Middle French, from *coupler* to join, from Latin *copulare,* from *copula*] (1548)
archaic **:** the act or result of coupling
cou·pler \'kə-p(ə-)lər\ *noun* (1552)
1 : one that couples
2 : a contrivance on a keyboard instrument by which keyboards or keys are connected to play together
cou·plet \'kə-plət\ *noun* [Middle French, diminutive of *cople*] (1580)
1 : two successive lines of verse forming a unit marked usually by rhythmic correspondence, rhyme, or the inclusion of a self-contained utterance **:** DISTICH
2 : COUPLE
3 : one of the musical episodes alternating with the main theme (as in a rondo)
cou·pling \'kə-pliŋ (*usual for 2*), -pə-liŋ\ *noun* (14th century)
1 : the act of bringing or coming together **:** PAIRING; *specifically* **:** sexual union
2 : a device that serves to connect the ends of adjacent parts or objects
3 : the joining of or the part of the body that joins the hindquarters to the forequarters of a quadruped
4 : a means of electric connection of two electric circuits by having a part common to both
cou·pon \'kü-,pän, 'kyü-\ *noun* [French, from Old French, piece, from *couper* to cut — more at COPE] (1822)
1 : a statement of due interest to be cut from a bearer bond when payable and presented for payment; *also* **:** the interest rate of a coupon

2 : a form surrendered in order to obtain an article, service, or accommodation: as **a :** one of a series of attached tickets or certificates often to be detached and presented as needed **b :** a ticket or form authorizing purchases of rationed commodities **c :** a certificate or similar evidence of a purchase redeemable in premiums **d :** a part of a printed advertisement to be cut off to use as an order blank or inquiry form or to obtain a discount on merchandise □
cou·pon·ing \'kü-,pä-niŋ, 'kyü-\ *noun* (1954)
: the distribution or redemption of coupons
cour·age \'kər-ij, 'kə-rij\ *noun* [Middle English *corage,* from Old French, from *cuer* heart, from Latin *cor* — more at HEART] (14th century)
: mental or moral strength to venture, persevere, and withstand danger, fear, or difficulty ☆
cou·ra·geous \kə-'rā-jəs\ *adjective* (14th century)
: having or characterized by courage **:** BRAVE
— **cou·ra·geous·ly** *adverb*
— **cou·ra·geous·ness** *noun*
cou·rante \kù-'ränt, -'rant\ *noun* [Middle French, from *courir* to run, from Latin *currere*] (1586)
1 : a dance of Italian origin marked by quick running steps
2 : music in quick triple time or in a mixture of ³/₂ and ⁶/₄ time
cou·reur de bois \kù-,rər-də-'bwä\ *noun, plural* **coureurs de bois** *same*\ [Canadian French, literally, woods runner] (1700)
: a French or métis trapper of North America and especially of Canada
cour·gette \kùr-'zhet\ *noun* [French, diminutive of *courge* gourd, from Latin *cucurbita*] (1931)
chiefly British **:** ZUCCHINI
cou·ri·er \'kùr-ē-ər, 'kər-ē-, 'kə-rē-\ *noun* [Middle French *courrier,* from Old Italian *corriere,* from *correre* to run, from Latin *currere*] (1579)
1 : MESSENGER: as **a :** a member of a diplomatic service entrusted with bearing messages **b** (1) **:** an espionage agent transferring secret information (2) **:** a runner of contraband **c :** a member of the armed services whose duties include carrying mail, information, or supplies
2 : a traveler's paid attendant; *especially* **:** a tourists' guide employed by a travel agency
¹course \'kōrs, 'kòrs\ *noun* [Middle English, from Old French, from Latin *cursus,* from *currere* to run — more at CAR] (14th century)
1 : the act or action of moving in a path from point to point
2 : the path over which something moves or extends: as **a :** RACECOURSE **b** (1) **:** the direction of travel of a vehicle (as a ship or airplane) usually measured as a clockwise angle from north; *also* **:** the projected path of travel (2) **:** a point of the compass **c :** WATERCOURSE **d :** GOLF COURSE
3 a : accustomed procedure or normal action ⟨the law taking its *course*⟩ **b :** a chosen manner of conducting oneself **:** way of acting ⟨our wisest *course* is to retreat⟩ **c** (1) **:** progression through a development or period or a series of acts or events (2) **:** LIFE HISTORY, CAREER
4 : an ordered process or succession: as **a :** a number of lectures or other matter dealing with a subject ⟨a premed *course*⟩ **b :** a series of such courses constituting a curriculum **b :** a series of doses or medications administered over a designated period
5 a : a part of a meal served at one time **b :** LAYER; *especially* **:** a continuous level range of brick or masonry throughout a wall **c :** the lowest sail on a square-rigged mast
— **in due course :** after a normal passage of time **:** in the expected or allotted time
— **of course 1 :** following the ordinary way or procedure **2 :** as might be expected
²course *verb* **coursed; cours·ing** (15th century)

transitive verb
1 : to follow close upon **:** PURSUE

2 a : to hunt or pursue (game) with hounds **b** : to cause (dogs) to run (as after game) **3 :** to run or move swiftly through or over : TRAVERSE ⟨jets *coursed* the area daily⟩ *intransitive verb* : to run or pass rapidly along or as if along an indicated path ⟨blood *coursing* through the veins⟩

course of study (1781) **1 :** CURRICULUM **2 :** COURSE 4a

¹cours·er \'kōr-sər, 'kȯr-\ *noun* [Middle English, from Middle French *coursier,* from Old French *course* course, run] (14th century) : a swift or spirited horse : CHARGER

²courser *noun* (1600) **1 :** a dog for coursing **2 :** one that courses : HUNTSMAN **3 :** any of various Old World birds (subfamily Cursoriinae of the family Glareolidae) noted for their speed in running

course·ware \'kōrs-ˌwar, 'kȯrs-, -ˌwer\ *noun* (1972) : educational software

coursing *noun* (1538) **1 :** the pursuit of running game with dogs that follow by sight instead of by scent **2 :** the act of one that courses

¹court \'kōrt, 'kȯrt\ *noun, often attributive* [Middle English, from Old French, from Latin *cohort-, cohors* enclosure, group, retinue, cohort, from *co-* + *-hort-, -hors* (akin to *hortus* garden) — more at YARD] (12th century) **1 a :** the residence or establishment of a sovereign or similar dignitary **b :** a sovereign's formal assembly of councillors and officers **c :** the sovereign and officers and advisers who are the governing power **d :** the family and retinue of a sovereign **e :** a reception held by a sovereign **2 a** (1) **:** a manor house or large building surrounded by usually enclosed grounds (2) **:** MOTEL **b :** an open space enclosed wholly or partly by buildings or circumscribed by a single building **c :** a quadrangular space walled or marked off for playing one of various games with a ball (as lawn tennis, handball, or basketball); *also* : a division of such a court **d :** a wide alley with only one opening onto a street **3 a :** an official assembly for the transaction of judicial business **b :** a session of such a court ⟨*court* is now adjourned⟩ **c :** a place (as a chamber) for the administration of justice **d :** a judge or judges in session; *also* : a faculty or agency of judgment or evaluation ⟨rest our case in the *court* of world opinion —L. H. Marks⟩ **4 a :** an assembly or board with legislative or administrative powers **b :** PARLIAMENT, LEGISLATURE **5 :** conduct or attention intended to win favor or dispel hostility : HOMAGE ⟨pay *court* to the king⟩

²court (1571) *transitive verb* **1 a :** to seek to gain or achieve **b** (1) **:** ALLURE, TEMPT (2) **:** to act so as to invite or provoke ⟨*courts* disaster⟩ **2 a :** to seek the affections of; *especially* : to seek to win a pledge of marriage from **b** *of an animal* **:** to perform actions in order to attract for mating **3 a :** to seek to attract (as by solicitous attention or offers of advantages) ⟨college teams *courting* high school basketball stars⟩ **b :** to seek an alliance with *intransitive verb* **1 :** to engage in social activities leading to engagement and marriage **2** *of an animal* **:** to engage in activity leading to mating

court bouil·lon \'ku̇r-(ˌ)bü-'yȯⁿ, -(ˌ)bwē-, 'kōr-, 'kȯr-\ *noun* [French *court-bouillon,* literally, short bouillon] (1723) : a liquid made usually with water, white wine, vegetables, and seasonings and used to poach fish

cour·te·ous \'kər-tē-əs, *British also* 'kȯr-\ *adjective* [Middle English *corteis,* from Old French, from *court*] (13th century) **1 :** marked by polished manners, gallantry, or ceremonial usage of a court **2 :** marked by respect for and consideration of others **synonym** see CIVIL — **cour·te·ous·ly** *adverb* — **cour·te·ous·ness** *noun*

cour·te·san \'kōr-tə-zən, 'kȯr-, -ˌzan *also* 'kər-, -ˌzän; *especially British* ˌkȯr-tə-'zan\ *noun* [Middle French *courtisane,* from northern Italian dialect form of Italian *cortigiana* woman courtier, feminine of *cortigiano* courtier, from *corte* court, from Latin *cohort-, cohors*] (1533) : a prostitute with a courtly, wealthy, or upper-class clientele

¹cour·te·sy \'kər-tə-sē, *British also* 'kȯr-\ *noun, plural* **-sies** [Middle English *corteisie,* from Old French, from *corteis*] (13th century) **1 a :** courteous behavior **b :** a courteous act or expression **2 a :** general allowance despite facts : INDULGENCE ⟨hills called mountains by *courtesy* only⟩ **b :** consideration, cooperation, and generosity in providing (as a gift or privilege); *also* : AGENCY, MEANS — used chiefly in the phrases *through the courtesy of* or *by courtesy of* or sometimes simply *courtesy of*

²courtesy *adjective* (1613) : granted, provided, or performed as a courtesy or by way of courtesy ⟨made a *courtesy* call on the ambassador⟩

courtesy card *noun* (1934) : a card entitling its holder to some special privilege

courtesy title *noun* (1865) **1 :** a title (as "Lord" added to the Christian name of a peer's younger son) used in addressing certain lineal relatives of British peers **2 :** a title (as "Professor" for any teacher) taken by the user and commonly accepted without consideration of official right

court·house \'kōrt-ˌhau̇s, 'kȯrt-\ *noun* (15th century) **1 a :** a building in which courts of law are regularly held **b :** the principal building in which county offices are housed **2 :** COUNTY SEAT

cour·tier \'kōr-tē-ər, 'kȯr-; 'kōrt-yər, 'kȯrt-; 'kōr-chər, 'kȯr-\ *noun* (14th century) **1 :** one in attendance at a royal court **2 :** one who practices flattery

¹court·ly \'kōrt-lē, 'kȯrt-\ *adjective* **court·li·er; -est** (15th century) **1 a :** of a quality befitting the court : ELEGANT **b :** insincerely flattering **2 :** favoring the policy or party of the court — **court·li·ness** *noun*

²courtly *adverb* (circa 1592) : in a courtly manner : POLITELY

courtly love *noun* (1896) : a late medieval conventionalized code prescribing conduct and emotions of ladies and their lovers

¹court–mar·tial \'kōrt-ˌmär-shəl, 'kȯrt-, -'mär-\ *noun, plural* **courts–martial** *also* **court–martials** (1651) **1 :** a court consisting of commissioned officers and in some instances enlisted personnel for the trial of members of the armed forces or others within its jurisdiction **2 :** a trial by court-martial

²court–martial *transitive verb* **–mar·tialed** *also* **–mar·tialled; –mar·tial·ing** *also* **–mar·tial·ling** \-ˌmär-sh(ə-)liŋ, -'mär-\ (1859) : to subject to trial by court-martial

court of appeals *often C&A capitalized* (1777)
: a court hearing appeals from the decisions of lower courts — called also *court of appeal*

court of claims (1691) : a court that has jurisdiction over claims (as against a government)

court of common pleas (1687) **1 :** a former English superior court having civil jurisdiction **2 :** an intermediate court in some American states that usually has civil and criminal jurisdiction

court of domestic relations (1926) : a court that has jurisdiction and often special advisory powers over family disputes involving the rights and duties of husband, wife, parent, or child especially in matters affecting the support, custody, and welfare of children

court of honor (1687) : a tribunal (as a military court) for investigating questions of personal honor

court of inquiry (1757) : a military court that inquires into and reports on some military matter (as an officer's questionable conduct)

court of law (14th century) : a court that hears cases and decides them on the basis of statutes or the common law

court of record (15th century) : a court whose acts and proceedings are kept on permanent record

Court of St. James's \-sənt-'jāmz, -'jām-zəz, -ˌsānt-\ [from *Saint James's* Palace, London, former seat of the British court] (1848) : the British court

court of sessions (circa 1889) : any of various state criminal courts of record

court order *noun* (1650) : an order issuing from a competent court that requires a party to do or abstain from doing a specified act

court plaster *noun* [from its use for beauty spots by ladies at royal courts] (1772) : an adhesive plaster especially of silk coated with isinglass and glycerin

court reporter *noun* (1894) : a stenographer who records and transcribes a verbatim report of all proceedings in a court of law

court·room \'kōrt-ˌrüm, 'kȯrt-, -ˌru̇m\ *noun* (1677) : a room in which a court of law is held

court·ship \-ˌship\ *noun* (1596) : the act, process, or period of courting

court·side \-ˌsīd\ *noun* (1969) : the area at the edge of a court (as for tennis or basketball)

court tennis *noun* (circa 1890) : a game played with a ball and racket in an enclosed court divided by a net

court·yard \'kōrt-ˌyärd, 'kȯrt-\ *noun* (1552) : a court or enclosure adjacent to a building (as a house or palace)

cous·cous \'küs-ˌküs\ *noun* [French *couscous, couscoussou,* from Arabic *kuskus, kuskusū*] (1759) : a North African dish of steamed semolina usually served with meat or vegetables; *also* : the semolina itself

cous·in \'kə-zən\ *noun* [Middle English *cosin,* from Old French, from Latin *consobrinus,* from *com-* + *sobrinus* second cousin, from *soror* sister — more at SISTER] (13th century) **1 a :** a child of one's uncle or aunt **b :** a relative descended from one's grandparent or more remote ancestor by two or more steps and in a different line **c :** KINSMAN, RELATIVE ⟨a distant *cousin*⟩ **2 :** one associated with or related to another : COUNTERPART

\ə\ **abut** \ᵊ\ **kitten** \ər\ **further** \a\ **ash** \ā\ **ace** \ä\ **mop, mar** \au̇\ **out** \ch\ **chin** \e\ **bet** \ē\ **easy** \g\ **go** \i\ **hit** \ī\ **ice** \j\ **job** \ŋ\ **sing** \ō\ **go** \ȯ\ **law** \ȯi\ **boy** \th\ **thin** \ṯẖ\ **the** \ü\ **loot** \u̇\ **foot** \y\ **yet** \zh\ **vision** *see also* Guide to Pronunciation

3 — used as a title by a sovereign in addressing a nobleman
4 : a person of a race or people ethnically or culturally related ⟨our English *cousins*⟩
— **cous·in·hood** \-ˌhů̇d\ *noun*
— **cous·in·ly** *adjective*
— **cous·in·ship** \-ˌship\ *noun*
cous·in·age \'kə-zə-nij\ *noun* (14th century)
1 : relationship of cousins : KINSHIP
2 : a collection of cousins : KINFOLK
cous·in-ger·man \ˌkə-zən-'jər-mən\ *noun*, *plural* **cous·ins-ger·man** \-zənz-\ [Middle English *cosin germain*, from Middle French, from Old French, from *cosin* + *germain* german] (14th century)
: COUSIN 1a
Cousin Jack \ˌkə-zən-'jak\ *noun* (1890)
: CORNISHMAN; *especially* **:** a Cornish miner
¹couth \'küth\ *adjective* [back-formation from *uncouth*] (1896)
: SOPHISTICATED, POLISHED
²couth *noun* (1956)
: POLISH, REFINEMENT ⟨I expected kindness and gentility . . . but there is such a thing as too much *couth* —S. J. Perelman⟩
couth·ie \'kü-thē\ *adjective* [Middle English *couth* familiar, from Old English *cūth* — more at UNCOUTH] (1719)
chiefly Scottish **:** PLEASANT, KINDLY
cou·ture \kü-'tůr, -'tēr\ *noun* [French, from Old French *cousture* sewing, from (assumed) Vulgar Latin *consutura*, from Latin *consutus*, past participle of *consuere* to sew together, from *com-* + *suere* to sew — more at SEW] (1908)
1 : the business of designing, making, and selling fashionable custom-made women's clothing
2 : the designers and establishments engaged in couture
3 : the clothes created by couture
cou·tu·ri·er \kü-'tůr-ē-ər, -ē-ˌā\ *noun* [French, dressmaker, from Old French *cousturier* tailor's assistant, from *couture*] (1899)
: an establishment engaged in couture; *also* **:** the proprietor of or designer for such an establishment
cou·tu·ri·ere \kü-'tůr-ē-ər, -ē-ˌer\ *noun* [French *couturière*, from Old French *cousturiere*, feminine of *cousturier*] (1818)
: a woman who is a couturier
cou·vade \kü-'väd\ *noun* [French, from Middle French, cowardly inactivity, from *cover* to sit on, brood over — more at COVEY] (1865)
: a custom in some cultures in which when a child is born the father takes to bed as if bearing the child and submits himself to fasting, purification, or taboos
co·va·lence \ˌkō-'vā-lən(t)s, 'kō-ˌ\ *noun* (1919)
: valence characterized by the sharing of electrons
co·va·len·cy \-lən(t)-sē\ *noun* (1919)
: COVALENCE
co·va·lent \ˌkō-'vā-lənt, 'kō-ˌ\ *adjective* (circa 1926)
: of, relating to, or characterized by covalent bonds
— **co·va·lent·ly** \-lē\ *adverb*
covalent bond *noun* (1939)
: a chemical bond formed between atoms by the sharing of electrons
co·vari·ance \ˌkō-'ver-ē-ən(t)s, -'var-; 'kō-ˌ\ *noun* (1931)
1 : the expected value of the product of the deviations of two random variables from their respective means
2 : the arithmetic mean of the products of the deviations of corresponding values of two quantitative variables from their respective means
co·vari·ant \-ənt\ *adjective* [International Scientific Vocabulary] (1893)
: varying with something else so as to preserve certain mathematical interrelations

co·vari·a·tion \ˌkō-ˌver-ē-'ā-shən, -ˌvar-\ *noun* (1906)
: correlated variation of two or more variables
¹cove \'kōv\ *noun* [Middle English, den, from Old English *cofa*; akin to Old High German *chubisi* hut] (before 12th century)
1 : a recessed place : CONCAVITY: as **a :** an architectural member with a concave cross section **b :** a trough for concealed lighting at the upper part of a wall
2 : a small sheltered inlet or bay
3 a : a deep recess or small valley in the side of a mountain **b :** a level area sheltered by hills or mountains
²cove *transitive verb* **coved; cov·ing** (1756)
: to make in a hollow concave form
³cove *noun* [Romany *kova* thing, person] (1567)
British **:** MAN, FELLOW
co·vel·lite \kō-'ve-ˌlīt, 'kō-və-\ *also* **co·vel·line** \-ˌlēn\ *noun* [French *covelline*, from Niccolò *Covelli* (died 1829) Italian chemist] (1850)
: a native copper sulfide
co·ven \'kə-vən *also* 'kō-\ *noun* [Middle English *covin* band, from Middle French, from Medieval Latin *convenium* agreement, from Latin *convenire* to agree — more at CONVENIENT] (circa 1520)
1 : a collection of individuals with similar interests or activities ⟨a *coven* of intellectuals⟩
2 : an assembly or band of usually 13 witches
¹cov·e·nant \'kəv-nənt, 'kə-və-nənt\ *noun* [Middle English, from Middle French, from present participle of *covenir* to agree, from Latin *convenire*] (14th century)
1 : a usually formal, solemn, and binding agreement : COMPACT
2 a : a written agreement or promise usually under seal between two or more parties especially for the performance of some action **b :** the common-law action to recover damages for breach of a contract
— **cov·e·nan·tal** \ˌkə-və-'nan-t°l\ *adjective*
²cov·e·nant \-nənt, -ˌnant\ (14th century)
transitive verb
: to promise by a covenant : PLEDGE
intransitive verb
: to enter into a covenant : CONTRACT
cov·e·nan·tee \ˌkə-və-ˌnan-'tē, -nən-\ *noun* (1649)
: the person to whom a promise in the form of a covenant is made
cov·e·nant·er \'kə-və-ˌnan-tər, *1 also* ˌkə-və-'\ *noun* (1638)
1 *capitalized* **:** a signer or adherent of the Scottish National Covenant of 1638
2 : one that makes a covenant
cov·e·nan·tor \'kə-və-ˌnan-tər; ˌkə-və-ˌnan-'tòr, -nən\ *noun* (1649)
: a party bound by a covenant
Cov·en·try \'kə-vən-trē *also* 'kä-\ *noun* [*Coventry*, England] (1765)
: a state of ostracism or exclusion ⟨sent to *Coventry*⟩
¹cov·er \'kə-vər\ *verb* **cov·ered; cov·er·ing** \'kəv-riŋ, 'kə-və-\ [Middle English, from Old French *covrir*, from Latin *cooperire*, from *co-* + *operire* to close, cover] (13th century)
transitive verb
1 a : to guard from attack **b** (1) **:** to have within the range of one's guns : COMMAND (2) **:** to hold within range of an aimed firearm **c** (1) **:** to afford protection or security to **:** INSURE (2) **:** to afford protection against or compensation for **d** (1) **:** to guard (an opponent) in order to obstruct a play (2) **:** to be in position to receive a throw to (a base in baseball) **e** (1) **:** to make provision for (a demand or charge) by means of a reserve or deposit ⟨your balance is insufficient to *cover* the check⟩ (2) **:** to maintain a check on especially by patrolling (3) **:** to protect by contrivance or expedient
2 a : to hide from sight or knowledge : CONCEAL ⟨*cover* up a scandal⟩ **b :** to lie over : ENVELOP
3 : to lay or spread something over : OVERLAY

4 a : to spread over **b :** to appear here and there on the surface of
5 : to place or set a cover or covering over
6 a : to copulate with (a female animal) ⟨a horse *covers* a mare⟩ **b :** to sit on and incubate (eggs)
7 : to invest with a large or excessive amount of something ⟨*covered* herself with glory⟩
8 : to play a higher-ranking card on (a previously played card)
9 : to have sufficient scope to include or take into account : COMPRISE
10 : to deal with : TREAT
11 a : to have as one's territory or field of activity ⟨one sales rep *covers* the whole state⟩ **b :** to report news about
12 : to pass over : TRAVERSE
13 : to place one's stake in equal jeopardy with in a bet
14 : to buy securities or commodities for delivery against (an earlier short sale)
15 : to record a cover of (a song)
intransitive verb
1 : to conceal something illicit, blameworthy, or embarrassing from notice — usually used with *up*
2 : to act as a substitute or replacement during an absence
— **cov·er·able** \'kəv-rə-bəl, 'kə-və-\ *adjective*
— **co·ver·er** \'kə-vər-ər\ *noun*
— **cover one's tracks :** to conceal traces in order to elude pursuers
— **cover the ground** *or* **cover ground** **:** to deal with a subject or assignment in a particular manner ⟨the new book *covers* a lot of ground⟩
²cover *noun, often attributive* (14th century)
1 : something that protects, shelters, or guards: as **a :** natural shelter for an animal; *also* **:** the factors that provide such shelter **b** (1) **:** a position or situation affording protection from enemy fire (2) **:** the protection offered by airplanes in tactical support of a military operation **c** *British* **:** COVERAGE 1a, b, 2a
2 : something that is placed over or about another thing: **a :** LID, TOP **b :** a binding or case for a book or the analogous part of a magazine; *also* **:** the front or back of such a binding **c :** an overlay or outer layer especially for protection ⟨a mattress *cover*⟩ **d :** a tablecloth and the other table accessories **e :** COVER CHARGE **f :** ROOF **g :** a cloth used on a bed **h :** something (as vegetation or snow) that covers the ground **i :** the extent to which clouds obscure the sky
3 a : something that conceals or obscures ⟨under *cover* of darkness⟩ **b :** a masking device : PRETEXT ⟨the project was a *cover* for intelligence operations⟩
4 : an envelope or wrapper for mail
5 : one who substitutes for another during an absence
6 : a recording of a song previously recorded usually by another performer
— **cov·er·less** \'kə-vər-ləs\ *adjective*
— **under cover 1 :** in an envelope or wrapper **2 :** under concealment : in secret
cov·er·age \'kəv-rij, 'kə-və-\ *noun* (1912)
1 : something that covers: as **a :** inclusion within the scope of an insurance policy or protective plan : INSURANCE **b :** the amount available to meet liabilities **c :** inclusion within the scope of discussion or reporting ⟨the news *coverage* of the trial⟩
2 : the total group covered : SCOPE: as **a :** all the risks covered by the terms of an insurance contract **b :** the number or percentage of persons reached by a communications medium
3 : the act or fact of covering
cov·er·all \'kə-və-ˌròl\ *noun* (1824)
: a one-piece outer garment worn to protect other garments — usually used in plural
— **cov·er·alled** \-ˌròld\ *adjective*
cov·er-all \'kə-və-ˌròl\ *adjective* (1895)
: COMPREHENSIVE ⟨*cover-all* provisions⟩

cover charge *noun* (1921)
: a charge made by a restaurant or nightclub in addition to the charge for food and drink

cover crop *noun* (1899)
: a crop planted to prevent soil erosion and to provide humus

covered bridge *noun* (1809)
: a bridge that has its roadway protected by a roof and enclosing sides

covered smut *noun* (1900)
: a smut disease of grains in which the spore masses are held together by the persistent grain membrane and glumes

covered wagon *noun* (1745)
: a wagon with a canvas top supported by bowed strips of wood or metal

cover girl *noun* (1915)
: an attractive young woman whose picture appears on a magazine cover

cover glass *noun* (1881)
: a piece of very thin glass used to cover material on a glass microscope slide

¹cov·er·ing \'kəv-riŋ, 'kə-və-\ *noun* (14th century)
: something that covers or conceals

²covering *adjective* (1887)
: containing explanation of or additional information about an accompanying communication ⟨a *covering* letter⟩

cov·er·let \'kə-vər-lət, -(,)lid\ *noun* [Middle English, alteration of *coverlite*, from Anglo-French *coverelyth*, from Old French *covrir* + literally bed, from Latin *lectus* — more at LIE] (14th century)
: BEDSPREAD
word history *see* CURFEW

cov·er·slip \'kə-vər-,slip\ *noun* (1875)
: COVER GLASS

cover story *noun* (1948)
: a story accompanying a magazine-cover illustration

¹co·vert \'kō-(,)vərt, kō-'; 'kə-vərt\ *adjective* [Middle English, from Middle French, past participle of *covrir* to cover] (14th century)
1 : not openly shown, engaged in, or avowed : VEILED ⟨a *covert* alliance⟩
2 : covered over : SHELTERED
synonym *see* SECRET
— **co·vert·ly** *adverb*
— **co·vert·ness** *noun*

²co·vert \'kə-vərt, 'kō-vərt *also* 'kə-vər\ *noun* (14th century)
1 a : hiding place : SHELTER **b** : a thicket affording cover for game **c** : a masking or concealing device
2 : a feather covering the bases of the quills of the wings and tail of a bird — see BIRD illustration
3 : a firm durable twilled sometimes waterproofed cloth usually of mixed-color yarns

cov·er·ture \'kə-vər-,chùr, -chər, -,tyùr, -,tùr\ *noun* (13th century)
1 a : COVERING **b** : SHELTER
2 : the status a woman acquires upon marriage under common law

cov·er-up \'kə-və-,rəp\ *noun* (1927)
1 : a device or stratagem for masking or concealing ⟨his garrulousness is a *cover-up* for insecurity⟩; *also* : a usually concerted effort to keep an illegal or unethical act or situation from being made public
2 : a loose outer garment

cov·et \'kə-vət\ *verb* [Middle English *coveiten*, from Old French *coveitier*, from *coveitié* desire, modification of Latin *cupiditat-, cupiditas*, from *cupidus* desirous, from *cupere* to desire] (14th century)
transitive verb
1 : to wish for enviously
2 : to desire (what belongs to another) inordinately or culpably
intransitive verb
: to feel inordinate desire for what belongs to another
synonym *see* DESIRE
— **cov·et·able** \-və-tə-bəl\ *adjective*

— **cov·et·er** \-tər\ *noun*
— **cov·et·ing·ly** \-tiŋ-lē\ *adverb*
cov·et·ous \'kə-və-təs\ *adjective* (13th century)
1 : marked by inordinate desire for wealth or possessions or for another's possessions
2 : having a craving for possession ⟨*covetous* of power⟩ ☆
— **cov·et·ous·ly** *adverb*
— **cov·et·ous·ness** *noun*

cov·ey \'kə-vē\ *noun, plural* **coveys** [Middle English, from Middle French *covee*, from Old French, from *cover* to sit on, brood over, from Latin *cubare* to lie] (14th century)
1 : a mature bird or pair of birds with a brood of young; *also* : a small flock
2 : COMPANY, GROUP

¹cow \'kaù\ *noun* [Middle English *cou*, from Old English *cū*; akin to Old High German *kuo* cow, Latin *bos* head of cattle, Greek *bous*, Sanskrit *go*] (before 12th century)
1 a : the mature female of cattle (genus *Bos*) **b** : the mature female of various usually large animals (as an elephant, whale, or moose)
2 : a domestic bovine animal regardless of sex or age
— **cowy** \-ē\ *adjective*

cow 1: *1* hoof, *2* pastern, *3* dewclaw, *4* switch, *5* hock, *6* rear udder, *7* flank, *8* thigh, *9* tail, *10* pinbone, *11* tail head, *12* thurl, *13* hip, *14* barrel, *15* ribs, *16* crops, *17* withers, *18* heart girth, *19* neck, *20* horn, *21* poll, *22* forehead, *23* bridge of nose, *24* muzzle, *25* jaw, *26* throat, *27* point of shoulder, *28* dewlap, *29* point of elbow, *30* brisket, *31* chest floor, *32* knee, *33* milk well, *34* milk vein, *35* fore udder, *36* teats, *37* rump, *38* loin

²cow *transitive verb* [probably of Scandinavian origin; akin to Danish *kue* to subdue] (1605)
: to destroy the resolve or courage of ⟨the party that Stalin had *cowed* —*World Press Review*⟩; *also* : to bring to a state or an action by intimidation — used with *into* ⟨like too many Asian armies, adept at *cowing* a population into feeding them —Edward Lansdale⟩
synonym *see* INTIMIDATE
— **cowed·ly** \'kaù(-ə)d-lē\ *adverb*

cow·ard \'kaù(-ə)rd\ *noun* [Middle English, from Old French *coart*, from *coe* tail, from Latin *cauda*] (13th century)
: one who shows disgraceful fear or timidity ◇
— **coward** *adjective*

cow·ard·ice \'kaù(-ə)r-dəs, *dialect* -(,)dīs\ *noun* [Middle English *cowardise*, from Middle French *coardise*, from *coart*] (14th century)
: lack of courage or resolution

¹cow·ard·ly \-lē\ *adverb* (14th century)
: in a cowardly manner

²cowardly *adjective* (1551)
: being, resembling, or befitting a coward ⟨a *cowardly* retreat⟩ ☆
— **cow·ard·li·ness** *noun*

cow·bane \'kaù-,bān\ *noun* (1776)
: any of several poisonous plants (as a water hemlock) of the carrot family

cow·bell \-,bel\ *noun* (1652)

: a bell hung around the neck of a cow to make a sound by which the cow can be located

cow·ber·ry \-,ber-ē\ *noun* (1800)
: MOUNTAIN CRANBERRY; *also* : its fruit

cow·bird \-,bərd\ *noun* (1810)
: a small North American blackbird (*Molothrus ater*) that lays its eggs in the nests of other birds

cow·boy \-,bòi\ *noun* (1623)
1 : one who tends cattle or horses; *especially* : a usually mounted cattle-ranch hand
2 : a rodeo performer

cowboy boot *noun* (1895)
: a boot made with a high arch, a high Cuban heel, and usually fancy stitching

cowboy hat *noun* (1895)
: a wide-brimmed hat with a large soft crown — called also *ten-gallon hat*

cow·catch·er \'kaù-,ka-chər, -,ke-\ *noun* (1838)
: an inclined frame on the front of a railroad locomotive for throwing obstacles off the track

cow college *noun* (circa 1915)
1 : a college that specializes in agriculture

☆ SYNONYMS
Covetous, greedy, acquisitive, grasping, avaricious mean having or showing a strong desire for especially material possessions. COVETOUS implies inordinate desire often for another's possessions (*covetous* of his brother's country estate). GREEDY stresses lack of restraint and often of discrimination in desire (*greedy* for status symbols). ACQUISITIVE implies both eagerness to possess and ability to acquire and keep (an eagerly *acquisitive* mind). GRASPING adds to COVETOUS and GREEDY an implication of selfishness and often suggests unfair or ruthless means (a hard *grasping* trader who cheated the natives). AVARICIOUS implies obsessive acquisitiveness especially of money and strongly suggests stinginess (an *avaricious* miser).

Cowardly, pusillanimous, craven, dastardly mean having or showing a lack of courage. COWARDLY implies a weak or ignoble lack of courage (a *cowardly* failure to stand up for principle). PUSILLANIMOUS suggests a contemptible lack of courage (the *pusillanimous* fear of a future full of possibility). CRAVEN suggests extreme defeatism and complete lack of resistance (secretly despised her own *craven* yes-men). DASTARDLY often implies behavior that is both cowardly and treacherous or skulking or outrageous (a *dastardly* attack on unarmed civilians).

◇ WORD HISTORY
coward A frightened animal may draw its tail between its hind legs—or it may simply turn tail and run. If the fleeing animal has a white tail, as does the hare, the flash of white can leave a keen impression. But fear can be found in humans as well as animals, and armies have their tail ends also. A traditional belief holds that it is in the tail end of an advancing army that one is most likely to find the cowards lurking. Although it is not known whether the original reference was to the tail of an army or an animal, it is certain that the Old French word *cuart* or *coart*, the source of our word *coward*, comes from *coe* or *coue*, meaning "tail."

\ä\ mop, mar \aù\ out \ch\ chin \e\ bet \ē\ easy
\g\ go \i\ hit \ī\ ice \j\ job \ŋ\ sing \ō\ go
\ò\ law \òi\ boy \th\ thin \th\ the \ü\ loot \ù\ foot
\y\ yet \zh\ vision *see also* Guide to Pronunciation

2 : a provincial college or university that lacks culture, sophistication, and tradition

cow·er \'kaù(-ə)r\ *intransitive verb* [Middle English *couren*, of Scandinavian origin; akin to Old Norse *kura* to cower] (14th century) : to shrink away or crouch especially for shelter from something that menaces, domineers, or dismays
synonym see FAWN

cow·fish \'kaù-ˌfish\ *noun* (1870) : any of various small bright-colored fishes (family Ostraciidae) with hornlike projections over the eyes

cow·girl \-ˌgər(-ə)l\ *noun* (1884)
1 : a girl or woman who tends cattle or horses
2 : a girl or woman who is a rodeo performer

cow·hage *also* **cow·age** \'kaù-ij\ *noun* [Hindi *kavãc*] (1640) : a tropical leguminous woody vine (*Mucuna pruriens*) with crooked pods covered with barbed hairs that cause severe itching; *also* : these hairs formerly used as a vermifuge

cow·hand \'kaù-ˌhand\ *noun* (1852) : COWBOY 1

cow·herd \-ˌhərd\ *noun* (before 12th century) : one who tends cows

¹cow·hide \-ˌhīd\ *noun* (14th century)
1 : the hide of a cow; *also* : leather made from this hide
2 : a coarse whip of rawhide or braided leather

²cowhide *transitive verb* **cow·hid·ed; cow·hid·ing** (1794) : to flog with a cowhide whip

cow horse *noun* (1853) : COW PONY

¹cowl \'kaù(ə)l\ *noun* [Middle English *cowle*, from Old English *cugele*, from Late Latin *cuculla* monk's hood, from Latin *cucullus* hood] (before 12th century)
1 a : a hood or long hooded cloak especially of a monk **b** : a draped neckline on a woman's garment
2 a : a chimney covering designed to improve the draft **b** : the top portion of the front part of an automobile body forward of the two front doors to which are attached the windshield and instrument board **c** : COWLING

²cowl *transitive verb* (1536) : to cover with or as if with a cowl

cow·lick \'kaù-ˌlik\ *noun* (1598) : a lock or tuft of hair growing in a different direction from the rest of the hair

cowl·ing \'kaù-liŋ\ *noun* (1917) : a removable metal covering that houses the engine and sometimes a part of the fuselage or nacelle of an airplane; *also* : a metal cover for an engine

cowl·staff \'kōl-ˌstaf, 'kaù(ə)l-, 'kül-\ *noun* [Middle English *cuvelstaff*, from *cuvel* vessel (from Old English *cȳfel*, from Old North French *cuvele* small vat) + ¹*staff*] (13th century)
archaic : a staff from which a vessel is suspended and carried between two persons

cow·man \'kaù-mən, -ˌman\ *noun* (1677)
1 : COWHERD, COWBOY
2 : a cattle owner or rancher

cow parsnip *noun* (1548) : a tall perennial North American plant (*Heracleum lanatum*) of the carrot family with large compound leaves and broad umbels of white or purplish flowers; *also* : a related Eurasian plant (*H. sphondylium*) naturalized in the U.S.

cow·pat \'kaù-ˌpat\ *noun* (1937) : a dropping of cow dung

cow·pea \'kaù-ˌpē\ *noun* (1776) : a sprawling leguminous herb (*Vigna unguiculata* synonym *V. sinensis*) related to the bean and widely cultivated in the southern U.S. especially for forage and green manure; *also* : its edible seed — called also *black-eyed pea*

Cow·per's gland \'kaù-pərz-, 'kü-, 'kù-\ *noun* [William *Cowper* (died 1709) English surgeon] (1738) : either of two small glands lying on either side of the male urethra below the prostate gland and discharging a secretion into the semen — called also *bulbourethral gland;* compare BARTHOLIN'S GLAND

cow·poke \'kaù-ˌpōk\ *noun* (circa 1881) : COWBOY 1

cow pony *noun* (1874) : a strong and agile saddle horse trained for herding cattle

cow·pox \'kaù-ˌpäks\ *noun* (1798) : a mild eruptive disease of the cow that when communicated to humans protects against smallpox

cow·punch·er \-ˌpən-chər\ *noun* (1878) : COWBOY 1

cow·rie *or* **cow·ry** \'kaù-rē\ *noun, plural* **cowries** [Hindi *kaurī*] (1662) : any of various marine gastropods (family Cypraeidae) that are widely distributed in warm seas and have glossy and often brightly colored shells; *also* : the shell of a cowrie

cow·shed \'kaù-ˌshed\ *noun* (1835) : a shed for the housing of cows

cow·slip \'kaù-ˌslip\ *noun* [Middle English *cowslyppe*, from Old English *cūslyppe*, literally, cow dung, from *cū* cow + *slypa, slyppe* paste] (before 12th century)
1 : a common European primrose (*Primula veris*) with fragrant yellow flowers
2 : MARSH MARIGOLD

cow town *noun* (1885)
1 : a town or city that serves as a market center or shipping point for cattle
2 : a small unsophisticated town within a cattle-raising area

¹cox \'käks\ *noun* (1869) : COXSWAIN

²cox *verb* (1881) : COXSWAIN

coxa \'käk-sə\ *noun, plural* **cox·ae** \-ˌsē, -ˌsī\ [Latin, hip; akin to Old High German *hāhsina* hock, Sanskrit *kakṣa* armpit] (1826) : the basal segment of a limb of various arthropods (as an insect)
— **cox·al** \-səl\ *adjective*

cox·comb \'käk-ˌskōm\ *noun* [Middle English *cokkes comb*, literally, cock's comb] (1573)
1 a *obsolete* : a jester's cap adorned with a strip of red **b** *archaic* : PATE, HEAD
2 a *obsolete* : FOOL **b** : a conceited foolish person : FOP
— **cox·comb·i·cal** \käk-'skō-mi-kəl, -'skä-\ *adjective*

cox·comb·ry \'käk-skəm-rē, -ˌskōm-\ *noun, plural* **-ries** (1608) : behavior that is characteristic of a coxcomb : FOPPERY

Cox·sack·ie virus \(ˌ)käk-'sa-kē-\ *noun* [*Coxsackie*, N.Y.] (1949) : any of several enteroviruses associated with human diseases (as meningitis)

¹cox·swain \'käk-sən, -ˌswān\ *noun* [Middle English *cokswayne*, from *cok* cockboat + *swain* servant] (15th century)
1 : a sailor who has charge of a ship's boat and its crew and who usually steers
2 : a steersman of a racing shell who usually directs the rowers

²coxswain (1928)
transitive verb
: to direct as coxswain
intransitive verb
: to act as coxswain

¹coy \'kói\ *adjective* [Middle English, quiet, shy, from Middle French *coi* calm, from Latin *quietus* quiet] (14th century)
1 a : shrinking from contact or familiarity **b** : marked by cute, coquettish, or artful playfulness
2 : showing reluctance to make a definite commitment
synonym see SHY
— **coy·ly** *adverb*
— **coy·ness** *noun*

²coy (1583)

transitive verb
obsolete : CARESS
intransitive verb
archaic : to act coyly

coy·dog \'kói-ˌdòg\ *noun* [*coyote* + *dog*] (1950) : a hybrid between a coyote and a feral dog

coy·ote \'kī-ˌōt, kī-'ō-tē\ *noun, plural* **coyotes** *or* **coyote** [Mexican Spanish, from Nahuatl *coyōtl*] (1759)
1 : a buff-gray to reddish gray North American canid (*Canis latrans*) closely related to but smaller than the wolf
2 : one who smuggles immigrants into the U.S.

coyote 1

coy·o·til·lo \ˌkī-ə-'ti-(ˌ)lō, ˌkói-ə-, -'tē-(ˌ)yō\ *noun* [Mexican Spanish, diminutive of *coyote*] (circa 1892) : a shrub (*Karwinskia humboldtiana*) of the buckthorn family of the southwestern U.S. and Mexico having poisonous berries

coy·pu \'kói-(ˌ)pü, kói-'\ *noun* [American Spanish *coipú*, from Araucanian *coipu*] (1793) : NUTRIA

coz \'käz\ *noun* [by shortening & alteration] (1559) : COUSIN

coz·en \'kə-zən\ *transitive verb* **coz·ened; coz·en·ing** \'kəz-niŋ, 'kə-zə-\ [perhaps from obsolete Italian *cozzonare*, from Italian *cozzone* horse trader, from Latin *cocion-, cocio* trader] (1573)
1 : to deceive, win over, or induce to do something by artful coaxing and wheedling or shrewd trickery
2 : to gain by cozening someone ⟨*cozened* his supper out of the old couple⟩
synonym see CHEAT
— **coz·en·er** \'kəz-nər, 'kə-zə-\ *noun*

coz·en·age \'kaz-nij, 'kə-zə-\ *noun* (1583)
1 : the art or practice of cozening : FRAUD
2 : an act or an instance of cozening

¹co·zy \'kō-zē\ *adjective* **co·zi·er; -est** [probably of Scandinavian origin; akin to Norwegian *kose*lig cozy] (1709)
1 : enjoying or affording warmth and ease : SNUG
2 a : marked by the intimacy of the family or a close group **b** : marked by or suggesting close association or connivance ⟨a *cozy* agreement⟩
3 : marked by a discreet and cautious attitude or procedure
synonym see COMFORTABLE
— **co·zi·ly** \-zə-lē\ *adverb*
— **co·zi·ness** \-zē-nəs\ *noun*

²cozy *noun, plural* **co·zies** (1863) : a padded covering especially for a teapot to keep the contents hot

³cozy *adverb* (1946) : in a cautious manner ⟨play it *cozy* and wait for the other team to make a mistake —Bobby Dodd⟩

cozy up *intransitive verb* (1937) : to attain or try to attain familiarity, friendship, or intimacy : ingratiate oneself ⟨*cozying up* to the boss⟩

¹crab \'krab\ *noun, often attributive* [Middle English *crabbe*, from Old English *crabba;* akin to Old High German *krebiz* crab, Old English *ceorfan* to carve — more at CARVE] (before 12th century)
1 : any of numerous chiefly marine broadly built decapod crustaceans: **a** : any of a group (Brachyura) with a short broad usually flattened carapace, a small abdomen that curls forward beneath the body, short antennae, and the anterior pair of limbs modified as grasping pincers **b** : any of various crustaceans of a

group (Anomura) resembling true crabs in the more or less reduced condition of the abdomen
2 *capitalized* **:** CANCER 1
3 *plural* **:** infestation with crab lice
4 : the angular difference between an aircraft's course and the heading necessary to make that course in the presence of a crosswind
²**crab** *verb* **crabbed; crab·bing** (1918)
transitive verb
1 : to cause to move sideways or in an indirect or diagonal manner; *specifically* **:** to head (an airplane) into a crosswind to counteract drift
2 : to subject to crabbing
intransitive verb
1 a (1) **:** to move sideways indirectly or diagonally (2) **:** to crab an airplane **b :** to scuttle or scurry sideways
2 : to fish for crabs
— **crab·ber** *noun*
³**crab** *noun* [Middle English *crabbe,* perhaps from *crabbe* ¹crab] (14th century)
: CRAB APPLE
⁴**crab** *noun* (1580)
: an ill-tempered person **:** CROSSPATCH
⁵**crab** *verb* **crabbed; crab·bing** [Middle English *crabben,* probably back-formation from *crabbed*] (1662)
transitive verb
1 : to make sullen **:** SOUR ⟨old age has *crabbed* his nature⟩
2 : to complain about peevishly
3 : SPOIL, RUIN
intransitive verb
: CARP, GROUSE ⟨always *crabs* about the weather⟩
— **crab·ber** *noun*
crab apple *noun* [³*crab*] (1712)
: any of various wild or cultivated trees (genus *Malus*) that are cultivars or relatives of the cultivated apple and that produce small sour fruit; *also* **:** the fruit
crab·bed \'kra-bəd\ *adjective* [Middle English, partly from *crabbe* ¹crab, partly from *crabbe* crab apple] (14th century)
1 : marked by a forbidding moroseness
2 : difficult to read or understand ⟨*crabbed* handwriting⟩
synonym see SULLEN
— **crab·bed·ness** *noun*
crab·by \'kra-bē\ *adjective* **crab·bi·er; -est** [⁴*crab*] (1776)
: CROSS, ILL-NATURED
crab cactus *noun* (1900)
: CHRISTMAS CACTUS
crab·grass \'krab-,gras\ *noun* (1743)
: a grass (especially *Digitaria sanguinalis*) that has creeping or decumbent stems which root freely at the nodes and that is often a pest in turf or cultivated lands
crab louse *noun* (1547)
: a sucking louse (*Phthirus pubis*) infesting the pubic region of the human body
crab·meat \'krab-,mēt\ *noun* (1876)
: the edible part of a crab
crab·stick \-,stik\ *noun* (1703)
1 : a stick, cane, or cudgel of crab apple tree wood
2 : a crabbed ill-natured person
crab·wise \-,wīz\ *adverb* (1898)
1 : SIDEWAYS
2 : in a sidling or cautiously indirect manner
¹**crack** \'krak\ *verb* [Middle English *crakken,* from Old English *cracian;* akin to Old High German *chrahhōn* to resound] (before 12th century)
intransitive verb
1 : to make a very sharp explosive sound ⟨the whip *cracks* through the air⟩
2 : to break, split, or snap apart
3 : FAIL: **a :** to lose control or effectiveness under pressure — often used with *up* **b :** to fail in tone ⟨his voice *cracked*⟩
4 : to go or travel at good speed — usually used with *on* ⟨the steamboat *cracked* on⟩
transitive verb

1 a : to break so that fissures appear on the surface ⟨*crack* a mirror⟩ **b :** to break with a sudden sharp sound ⟨*crack* nuts⟩
2 : to tell especially suddenly or strikingly ⟨*crack* a joke⟩
3 : to strike with a sharp noise **:** RAP ⟨then *cracks* him over the head⟩ ⟨*cracked* a two-run homer in the fifth —*N.Y. Times*⟩
4 a (1) **:** to open (as a bottle) for drinking (2) **:** to open (a book) for studying **b :** to puzzle out and expose, solve, or reveal the mystery of ⟨*crack* a code⟩ **c :** to break into ⟨*crack* a safe⟩ **d :** to open slightly ⟨*crack* the throttle⟩ **e :** to break through (as a barrier) so as to gain acceptance or recognition
5 a : to impair seriously or irreparably **:** WRECK ⟨*crack* a car up⟩ **b :** to destroy the tone of (a voice) **c :** DISORDER, CRAZE **d :** to interrupt sharply or abruptly ⟨the criticism *cracked* our complacency⟩
6 : to cause to make a sharp noise ⟨*cracks* his knuckles⟩
7 a (1) **:** to subject (hydrocarbons) to cracking (2) **:** to produce by cracking ⟨*cracked* gasoline⟩ **b :** to break up (chemical compounds) into simpler compounds by means of heat
²**crack** *noun* (14th century)
1 a : a loud roll or peal ⟨a *crack* of thunder⟩ **b :** a sudden sharp noise ⟨the *crack* of rifle fire⟩
2 : a sharp witty remark **:** QUIP
3 a : a narrow break **:** FISSURE ⟨a *crack* in the ice⟩ **b :** a narrow opening ⟨leave the door open a *crack*⟩
4 a : a weakness or flaw caused by decay, age, or deficiency **:** UNSOUNDNESS **b :** a broken tone of the voice **c :** CRACKPOT
5 : MOMENT, INSTANT ⟨the *crack* of dawn⟩
6 : HOUSEBREAKING, BURGLARY
7 : a sharp resounding blow ⟨gave him a *crack* on the head⟩
8 : ATTEMPT, TRY ⟨her first *crack* at writing a novel⟩
9 : highly purified cocaine in small chips used illicitly usually for smoking
³**crack** *adjective* (1793)
: of superior excellence or ability ⟨a *crack* marksman⟩
crack·back \'krak-,bak\ *noun* (1967)
: a blind-side block on a defensive back in football by a pass receiver who starts downfield and then cuts back to the middle of the line
crack·brain \-,brān\ *noun* (circa 1570)
: an erratic person **:** CRACKPOT
— **crack·brained** \-'brānd\ *adjective*
crack·down \-,daùn\ *noun* (1935)
: an act or instance of cracking down
crack down *intransitive verb* (1939)
: to take positive regulatory or disciplinary action
cracked \'krakt\ *adjective* (1503)
1 a : broken (as by a sharp blow) so that the surface is fissured ⟨*cracked* china⟩ **b :** broken into coarse particles ⟨*cracked* wheat⟩ **c :** marked by harshness, dissonance, or failure to sustain a tone ⟨a *cracked* voice⟩
2 : mentally disturbed **:** CRAZY
crack·er \'kra-kər\ *noun* (15th century)
1 *chiefly dialect* **:** a bragging liar **:** BOASTER
2 : something that makes a cracking or snapping noise: as **a :** FIRECRACKER **b :** the snapping end of a whiplash **:** SNAPPER **c :** a paper holder for a party favor that pops when the ends are pulled sharply
3 *plural* **:** NUTCRACKER
4 : a dry thin crispy baked bread product that may be leavened or unleavened
5 a : a poor usually Southern white — usually used disparagingly **b** *capitalized* **:** a native or resident of Florida or Georgia — used as a nickname
6 : the equipment in which cracking (as of petroleum) is carried out
crack·er-bar·rel \-,bar-əl\ *adjective* [from the cracker barrel in country stores around

which customers lounged for informal conversation] (1916)
: suggestive of the friendly homespun character of a country store ⟨a *cracker-barrel* philosopher⟩
crack·er·jack \'kra-kər-,jak\ *also* **crack·a·jack** \-kə-,jak\ *noun* [probably alteration of ³*crack* + *jack* (man)] (1895)
: a person or thing of marked excellence
— **crackerjack** *adjective*
Cracker Jack *trademark*
— used for a candied popcorn confection
crack·ers \'kra-kərz\ *adjective* [probably *cracked* + *-ers* (as in *starkers*)] (1928)
: CRAZY
word history see NUTS
¹**crack·ing** \'kra-kiŋ\ *adjective* (1830)
: very impressive or effective **:** GREAT
²**cracking** *adverb* (1903)
: VERY, EXTREMELY ⟨a *cracking* good book⟩
³**cracking** *noun* (1868)
: a process in which relatively heavy hydrocarbons are broken up by heat into lighter products (as gasoline)
¹**crack·le** \'kra-kəl\ *verb* **crack·led; crack·ling** \-k(ə-)liŋ\ [frequentative of ¹*crack*] (circa 1560)
intransitive verb
1 a : to make small sharp sudden repeated noises ⟨the fire *crackles* on the hearth⟩ **b :** to show animation **:** SPARKLE ⟨the essays *crackle* with wit⟩
2 : CRAZE 3
transitive verb
: to crush or crack with snapping noises
²**crackle** *noun* (1833)
1 a : the noise of repeated small cracks or reports **b :** SPARKLE, EFFERVESCENCE
2 : a network of fine cracks on an otherwise smooth surface
crack·le·ware \'kra-kəl-,war, -,wer\ *noun* (1881)
: ceramic ware with a decorative crazed glaze
crack·ling *noun* (1599)
1 \'kra-k(ə)liŋ\ **:** a series of small sharp noises ⟨the *crackling* of frozen snow as we walk⟩
2 \'kra-klən, -kliŋ\ **:** the crisp residue left after the rendering of lard from fat or the frying or roasting of the skin (as of pork) — usually used in plural
crack·ly \'kra-k(ə-)lē\ *adjective* (1859)
: inclined to crackle **:** CRISP
crack·nel \'krak-nᵊl\ *noun* [Middle English *krakenelle*] (14th century)
1 : a hard brittle biscuit
2 : CRACKLING 2 — usually used in plural
crack·pot \'krak-,pät\ *noun* (1883)
: one given to eccentric or lunatic notions
— **crackpot** *adjective*
cracks·man \'krak-smən\ *noun* (circa 1812)
: BURGLAR; *also* **:** SAFECRACKER
crack-up \'krak-,əp\ *noun* (circa 1926)
1 : CRASH, WRECK ⟨an automobile *crack-up*⟩
2 a : a mental collapse **:** NERVOUS BREAKDOWN ⟨his wife's death brought on his *crack-up*⟩ **b :** COLLAPSE, BREAKDOWN
crack up (1829)
transitive verb
1 : PRAISE, TOUT 4 ⟨wasn't all that it was *cracked up* to be⟩
2 : to cause to laugh out loud ⟨that joke really *cracks* him *up*⟩
intransitive verb
1 : to smash up a vehicle (as by losing control) ⟨*cracked up* on a curve⟩
2 : to laugh out loud
-cracy *noun combining form* [Middle French & Late Latin; Middle French *-cratie,* from Late Latin *-cratia,* from Greek *-kratia,* from *kratos* strength, power — more at HARD]

\ə\ abut \ᵊ\ kitten \ər\ further \a\ ash \ā\ ace
\ä\ mop, mar \aù\ out \ch\ chin \e\ bet \ē\ easy
\g\ go \i\ hit \ī\ ice \j\ job \ŋ\ sing \ō\ go
\ò\ law \òi\ boy \th\ thin \th\ the \ü\ loot \ù\ foot
\y\ yet \zh\ vision *see also* Guide to Pronunciation

1 : form of government; *also* **:** state having such a form ⟨mono*cracy*⟩
2 : social or political class (as of powerful persons) ⟨mob*ocracy*⟩
3 : theory of social organization ⟨techno*cracy*⟩

¹**cra·dle** \'krā-dᵊl\ *noun* [Middle English *cradel,* from Old English *cradol;* perhaps akin to Old High German *kratto* basket, Sanskrit *grantha* knot] (before 12th century)
1 a : a bed or cot for a baby usually on rockers or pivots **b :** a framework or support suggestive of a baby's cradle : as (1) **:** a framework of bars and rods (2) **:** the support for a telephone receiver or handset **c :** an implement with rods like fingers attached to a scythe and used formerly for harvesting grain **d :** a frame to keep the bedclothes from contact with an injured part of the body
2 a : the earliest period of life **:** INFANCY ⟨from the *cradle* to the grave⟩ **b :** a place of origin ⟨the *cradle* of civilization⟩
3 : a rocking device used in panning for gold

²**cradle** *verb* **cra·dled; cra·dling** \'krād-liŋ, 'krā-dᵊl-iŋ\ (15th century)
transitive verb
1 a : to place or keep in or as if in a cradle **b :** SHELTER, REAR **c :** to support protectively or intimately ⟨*cradling* the injured man's head in her arms⟩
2 : to cut (grain) with a cradle scythe
3 : to place, raise, support, or transport on a cradle
intransitive verb
obsolete **:** to rest in or as if in a cradle

cradle cap *noun* (circa 1890)
: a seborrheic condition in infants that usually affects the scalp and is characterized by greasy gray or dark brown adherent scaly crusts

cra·dle·song \'krā-dᵊl-,soṅ\ *noun* (14th century)
: LULLABY

¹**craft** \'kraft\ *noun* [Middle English, strength, skill, from Old English *cræft;* akin to Old High German *kraft* strength] (before 12th century)
1 : skill in planning, making, or executing **:** DEXTERITY
2 : an occupation or trade requiring manual dexterity or artistic skill ⟨the carpenter's *craft*⟩ ⟨the *craft* of writing plays⟩ ⟨*crafts* such as pottery, carpentry, and sewing⟩
3 : skill in deceiving to gain an end ⟨used *craft* and guile to close the deal⟩
4 : the members of a trade or trade association
5 *plural usually* **craft a :** a boat especially of small size **b :** AIRCRAFT **c :** SPACECRAFT
synonym see ART

²**craft** *transitive verb* (15th century)
: to make or produce with care, skill, or ingenuity ⟨is *crafting* a new sculpture⟩ ⟨a carefully *crafted* story⟩

crafts·man \'kraf(t)s-mən\ *noun* (13th century)
1 : a worker who practices a trade or handicraft
2 : one who creates or performs with skill or dexterity especially in the manual arts ⟨jewelry made by European *craftsmen*⟩
— **crafts·man·like** \-,līk\ *adjective*
— **crafts·man·ly** \-lē\ *adjective*
— **crafts·man·ship** \-,ship\ *noun*

crafts·peo·ple \-,pē-pəl\ *noun plural* (1953)
: workers who practice a trade or craft

crafts·per·son \-,pər-sᵊn\ *noun* (1920)
: a craftsman or craftswoman

crafts·wom·an \'kraf(t)s-,wù-mən\ *noun* (1886)
1 : a woman artisan
2 : a woman who is skilled in a craft

craft union *noun* (1922)
: a labor union with membership limited to workers of the same craft — compare INDUSTRIAL UNION

crafty \'kraf-tē\ *adjective* **craft·i·er; -est** (before 12th century)
1 *dialect chiefly British* **:** SKILLFUL, CLEVER

2 a : adept in the use of subtlety and cunning **b :** marked by subtlety and guile ⟨a *crafty* scheme⟩
synonym see SLY
— **craft·i·ly** \'kraf-tə-lē\ *adverb*
— **craft·i·ness** \-tē-nəs\ *noun*

¹**crag** \'krag\ *noun* [Middle English, of Celtic origin; akin to Welsh *craig* rock] (14th century)
1 : a steep rugged rock or cliff
2 *archaic* **:** a sharp detached fragment of rock
— **crag·ged** \'kra-gəd\ *adjective*

²**crag** *noun* [Middle English, from Middle Dutch *crāghe;* akin to Old English *cræga* throat — more at CRAW] (14th century)
chiefly Scottish **:** NECK, THROAT

crag·gy \'kra-gē\ *adjective* **crag·gi·er; -est** (15th century)
1 : full of crags ⟨*craggy* slopes⟩
2 : ROUGH, RUGGED ⟨a *craggy* face⟩
— **crag·gi·ly** \'kra-gə-lē\ *adverb*
— **crag·gi·ness** \'kra-gē-nəs\ *noun*

crags·man \'kragz-mən\ *noun* (1816)
: one that is expert in climbing crags or cliffs

crake \'krāk\ *noun* [Middle English, probably from Old Norse *krāka* crow or *krākr* raven; akin to Old English *crāwan* to crow] (14th century)
1 : any of various rails; *especially* **:** a short-billed rail (as the corncrake)
2 : the corncrake's cry

¹**cram** \'kram\ *verb* **crammed; cram·ming** [Middle English *crammen,* from Old English *crammian;* akin to Old Norse *kremja* to squeeze] (before 12th century)
transitive verb
1 : to pack tight **:** JAM ⟨*cram* a suitcase with clothes⟩
2 a : to fill with food to satiety **:** STUFF **b :** to eat voraciously **:** BOLT ⟨the child *crams* her food⟩
3 : to thrust in or as if in a rough or forceful manner ⟨*crammed* the letters into his pocket⟩
4 : to prepare hastily for an examination ⟨*cram* the students for the test⟩
intransitive verb
1 : to eat greedily or to satiety **:** STUFF
2 : to study hastily for an imminent examination
— **cram·mer** *noun*

²**cram** *noun* (1810)
1 : a compressed multitude or crowd **:** CRUSH
2 : last-minute study for an examination

cram·bo \'kram-(,)bō\ *noun, plural* **cram·boes** [alteration of earlier *crambe,* from Latin, cabbage, from Greek *krambē*] (1660)
: a game in which one player gives a word or line of verse to be matched in rhyme by other players

cram·oi·sie *or* **cram·oi·sy** \'kra-,mȯi-zē, 'kra-mə-zē\ *noun, plural* **-sies** [Middle English *crammassy,* from Middle French *cramoisi,* from *cramoisi* crimson] (15th century)
: crimson cloth

¹**cramp** \'kramp\ *noun* [Middle English *crampe,* from Middle French, of Germanic origin; akin to Middle Dutch *crampe;* akin to Old High German *krampf* bent] (14th century)
1 : a painful involuntary spasmodic contraction of a muscle
2 : a temporary paralysis of muscles from overuse — compare WRITER'S CRAMP
3 a : sharp abdominal pain — usually used in plural **b :** persistent and often intense though dull lower abdominal pain associated with dysmenorrhea — usually used in plural

²**cramp** *noun* [Middle English *crampe,* from Middle Dutch] (15th century)
1 a : a usually iron device bent at the ends and used to hold timbers or blocks of stone together **b :** CLAMP
2 a : something that confines **:** SHACKLE **b :** the state of being confined

³**cramp** (15th century)
transitive verb

1 : to affect with or as if with a cramp or cramps
2 a : CONFINE, RESTRAIN ⟨was *cramped* in the tiny apartment⟩ **b :** to restrain from free expression — used especially in the phrase *cramp one's style*
3 : to turn (the front wheels of a vehicle) to right or left
4 : to fasten or hold with a cramp
intransitive verb
: to suffer from cramps

⁴**cramp** *adjective* (1674)
1 : hard to understand or figure out ⟨*cramp* law terms⟩ ⟨*cramp* handwriting⟩
2 : being cramped ⟨a *cramp* corner⟩

cram·pon \'kram-,pän\ *noun* [Middle English, from Middle French *crampon,* of Germanic origin; akin to Middle Dutch *crampe*] (15th century)
1 : a hooked clutch or dog for raising heavy objects — usually used in plural
2 : a climbing iron used especially on ice and snow in mountaineering — usually used in plural

crampon 2

cran·ber·ry \'kran-,ber-ē, -b(ə-)rē\ *noun* [part translation of Low German *kraanbere,* from *kraan* crane + *bere* berry] (1647)
1 : the red acid berry produced by some plants (as *Vaccinium oxycoccos* and *V. macrocarpon*) of the heath family; *also* **:** a plant producing these
2 : any of various plants with a fruit that resembles a cranberry

cranberry bush *noun* (1778)
: a shrubby or arborescent viburnum (*Viburnum opulus*) of North America and Europe with prominently 3-lobed leaves and red fruit

cranch \'kränch\ *variant of* CRAUNCH

¹**crane** \'krān\ *noun* [Middle English *cran,* from Old English; akin to Old High German *krano* crane, Greek *geranos,* Latin *grus*] (before 12th century)
1 : any of a family (Gruidae of the order Gruiformes) of tall wading birds superficially resembling the herons but structurally more nearly related to the rails
2 : any of several herons
3 : an often horizontal projection swinging about a vertical axis: as **a** **:** a machine for raising, shifting, and lowering heavy weights by means of a projecting swinging arm or with the hoisting apparatus supported on an overhead track **b :** an iron arm in a fireplace for supporting kettles **c :** a boom for holding a motion-picture or television camera

crane 1

²**crane** *verb* **craned; cran·ing** (1570)
transitive verb
1 : to raise or lift by or as if by a crane
2 : to stretch (as the neck) toward an object of attention ⟨*craning* her neck to get a better view⟩
intransitive verb
1 : to stretch one's neck toward an object of attention ⟨I *craned* out of the window of my compartment —Webb Waldron⟩
2 : HESITATE

crane fly *noun* (1658)
: any of a family (Tipulidae) of long-legged slender dipteran flies that resemble large mosquitoes but do not bite

cranes·bill \'krānz-,bil\ *noun* (1548)
: GERANIUM 1

crani- *or* **cranio-** *combining form* [Medieval Latin *cranium*]
: cranium ⟨*crani*ate⟩ : cranial and ⟨*cranio*sacral⟩

cra·ni·al \'krā-nē-əl\ *adjective* (1800)
1 : of or relating to the skull or cranium
2 : CEPHALIC
— **cra·ni·al·ly** \-ə-lē\ *adverb*

cranial index *noun* (1868)
: the ratio multiplied by 100 of the maximum breadth of the bare skull to its maximum length from front to back

cranial nerve *noun* (1840)
: any of the nerves that arise in pairs from the lower surface of the brain one on each side and pass through openings in the skull to the periphery of the body and that comprise 12 pairs in reptiles, birds, and mammals and usually 10 in fishes and amphibians

cra·ni·ate \'krā-nē-ət, -,āt\ *adjective* (1879)
: having a cranium
— **craniate** *noun*

cra·nio·ce·re·bral \,krā-nē-ō-sə-'rē-brəl, -'ser-ə-\ *adjective* (circa 1903)
: involving both cranium and brain ⟨*craniocerebral* injury⟩

cra·nio·fa·cial \-'fā-shəl\ *adjective* (circa 1859)
: of, relating to, or involving both the cranium and the face

cra·ni·ol·o·gy \,krā-nē-'ä-lə-jē\ *noun* [probably from German *Kraniologie*, from *kraniocrani-* + *-logie* -logy] (1851)
: a science dealing with variations in size, shape, and proportions of skulls among human races

cra·ni·om·e·try \-'ä-mə-trē\ *noun* [International Scientific Vocabulary] (circa 1828)
: a science dealing with cranial measurement — compare CEPHALOMETRY

cra·nio·sa·cral \,krā-nē-ō-'sa-krəl, -'sā-\ *adjective* (circa 1923)
: PARASYMPATHETIC

cra·ni·ot·o·my \,krā-nē-'ä-tə-mē\ *noun* [International Scientific Vocabulary] (1855)
: surgical opening of the skull

cra·ni·um \'krā-nē-əm\ *noun, plural* **-ni·ums** *or* **-nia** \-nē-ə\ [Medieval Latin, from Greek *kranion*; akin to Greek *kara* head — more at CEREBRAL] (15th century)
: SKULL; *specifically* : the part that encloses the brain : BRAINCASE

¹crank \'kraŋk\ *noun* [Middle English *cranke*, from Old English *cranc-* (as in *crancstæf*, a weaving instrument); probably akin to Middle High German *krank* weak, sick — more at CRINGE] (13th century)
1 : a bent part of an axle or shaft or an arm keyed at right angles to the end of a shaft by which circular motion is imparted to or received from the shaft or by which reciprocating motion is changed into circular motion or vice versa
2 a *archaic* : BEND **b** : a twist or turn of speech : CONCEIT — used especially in the phrase *quips and cranks* **c** (1) : CAPRICE, CROTCHET (2) : an annoyingly eccentric person; *also* : one that is overly enthusiastic about a particular subject or activity **d** : a bad-tempered person : GROUCH
3 : CRYSTAL 7
— **crank·ish** \'kraŋ-kish\ *adjective*

²crank (1592)
intransitive verb
1 : to move with a winding course : ZIGZAG
2 a : to turn a crank **b** : to get started by or as if by the turning of a crank **c** : to gain speed, momentum, or intensity — usually used with *up* ⟨the campaign is *cranking* up⟩
transitive verb

1 : to move or operate by or as if by a crank ⟨*crank* the window down⟩
2 a : to cause to start (as an automobile) **b** : to rotate the shaft (as a crankshaft) of especially with a starter ⟨*crank* over an engine⟩ **c** : to use in trying to start an engine ⟨*crank* the starter⟩
3 a : to start as if by use of a crank — usually used with *up* ⟨*crank* up an atom smasher⟩ **b** : TURN UP 2 — usually used with *up* ⟨*crank* up the volume⟩

³crank *adjective* (1924)
: of, relating to, or being a cranky or eccentric person; *also* : made or sent by such a person ⟨*crank* calls⟩ ⟨a *crank* letter⟩

⁴crank *adjective* [Middle English *cranke*, of unknown origin] (15th century)
1 *chiefly dialect* : MERRY, HIGH-SPIRITED
2 *chiefly dialect* : COCKY, CONFIDENT

⁵crank *adjective* [short for *crank-sided* (easily tipped)] (circa 1649)
of a boat : easily tipped by an external force

crank·case \'kraŋk-,kās\ *noun* (circa 1878)
: the housing of a crankshaft

crank out *transitive verb* (1956)
: to produce especially in a mechanical manner

crank·pin \'kraŋk-,pin\ *noun* (1839)
: the cylindrical piece which forms the handle of a crank or to which a connecting rod is attached

crank·shaft \'kraŋk-,shaft\ *noun* (1854)
1 : a shaft driven by or driving a crank
2 : a shaft consisting of a series of cranks and crankpins to which the connecting rods of an engine are attached

¹cranky \'kraŋ-kē\ *adjective* **crank·i·er; -est** [¹*crank*] (1821)
1 a : given to fretful fussiness : readily angered when opposed : CROTCHETY **b** : marked by eccentricity
2 : full of twists and turns : TORTUOUS ⟨a *cranky* road⟩
3 : working erratically : UNPREDICTABLE ⟨a *cranky* old tractor⟩
4 *dialect* : CRAZY, IMBECILE
— **crank·i·ly** \-kə-lē\ *adverb*
— **crank·i·ness** \-kē-nəs\ *noun*

²cranky *adjective* (1841) *of a boat*
: ⁵CRANK

cran·nog \'kra-,nòg, kra-'nōg\ *noun* [Scottish Gaelic *crannag* & Irish *crannóg*] (1608)
: an artificial fortified island constructed in a lake or marsh originally in prehistoric Ireland and Scotland

cran·ny \'kra-nē\ *noun, plural* **crannies** [Middle English *crany*, from Middle French *cren, cran* notch] (15th century)
1 : a small break or slit : CREVICE
2 : an obscure nook or corner
— **cran·nied** \-nēd\ *adjective*

cran·reuch \'kran-,rúk\ *noun* [probably modification of Scottish Gaelic *crannreotha*] (1682)
Scottish : HOARFROST, RIME

¹crap \'krap\ *intransitive verb* **crapped; crap·ping** (1846)
: DEFECATE — usually considered vulgar

²crap *noun* [Middle English *crappe* chaff, residue from rendered fat, perhaps from Old French *crappe* chaff, residue, from Medieval Latin *crappa*] (circa 1897)
1 a : EXCREMENT — usually considered vulgar **b** : the act of defecating — usually considered vulgar
2 : NONSENSE, RUBBISH; *also* : STUFF 4b — sometimes considered vulgar

³crap *noun* [singular of *craps*] (1885)
1 — used as an attributive form of *craps* ⟨*crap* game⟩ ⟨*crap* table⟩
2 : a throw of 2, 3, or 12 in the game of craps losing the shooter his bet unless he has a point — called also *craps*; compare NATURAL

⁴crap *intransitive verb* **crapped; crap·ping** (circa 1930)
1 : to throw a crap

2 : to throw a seven while trying to make a point — usually used with *out*

¹crape \'krāp\ *noun* [alteration of French *crêpe*, from Middle French *crespe*, from *crespe* curly, from Latin *crispus* — more at CRISP] (1633)
1 : CREPE
2 : a band of crepe worn on a hat or sleeve as a sign of mourning

²crape *transitive verb* **craped; crap·ing** (1815)
: to cover or shroud with or as if with crape

³crape *transitive verb* **craped; crap·ing** [French *crêper*, from Latin *crispare*, from *crispus*] (1774)
: to make (the hair) curly

crape myrtle *noun* (1850)
: an Asian shrub (*Lagerstroemia indica*) of the loosestrife family widely grown in warm regions for its flowers

crap·per \'kra-pər\ *noun* [¹*crap*] (circa 1932)
: TOILET — usually considered vulgar

crap·pie \'krä-pē\ *noun* [Canadian French *crapet*] (circa 1827)
1 : BLACK CRAPPIE
2 : WHITE CRAPPIE

crap·py \'kra-pē\ *adjective* **crap·pi·er; -est** (1846)
slang : markedly inferior in quality : LOUSY

craps \'kraps\ *noun plural but singular or plural in construction* [Louisiana French, from French *crabs, craps*, from English *crabs* lowest throw at hazard, from plural of ¹*crab*] (1843)
1 : a gambling game played with two dice
2 : ³CRAP 2

crap·shoot \'krap-,shüt\ *noun* (1971)
: something (as a business venture) that has an unpredictable outcome

crap·shoot·er \'krap-,shü-tər\ *noun* (1895)
: one who plays craps

crap·u·lous \'kra-pyə-ləs\ *adjective* [Late Latin *crapulosus*, from Latin *crapula* intoxication, from Greek *kraipalē*] (1536)
1 : marked by intemperance especially in eating or drinking
2 : sick from excessive indulgence in liquor

¹crash \'krash\ *verb* [Middle English *crasschen*] (15th century)
transitive verb
1 a : to break violently and noisily : SMASH **b** : to damage (an airplane) in landing
2 a : to cause to make a loud noise ⟨*crash* the cymbals together⟩ **b** : to force (as one's way) through with loud crashing noises
3 : to enter or attend without invitation or without paying ⟨*crash* the party⟩
intransitive verb
1 a : to break or go to pieces with or as if with violence and noise **b** : to fall, land, or hit with destructive force **c** : to decline suddenly and steeply **d** *of a computer system or program* : to suffer a sudden major failure usually with attendant loss of data
2 : to make a smashing noise ⟨thunder *crashing* overhead⟩
3 : to move or force one's way with or as if with a crash ⟨*crashes* into the room⟩
4 *slang* : to experience the aftereffects (as dysphoria or depression) of drug intoxication
5 *slang* : to go to bed or fall asleep; *also* : to reside temporarily : STAY ⟨*crashing* with friends for a few days⟩
— **crash·er** *noun*

²crash *noun* (circa 1580)
1 : a loud sound (as of things smashing) ⟨a *crash* of thunder⟩
2 a : a breaking to pieces by or as if by collision **b** : an instance of crashing ⟨a plane *crash*⟩ ⟨a system *crash*⟩

\ə\ abut \ᵊ\ kitten \ər\ further \a\ ash \ā\ ace
\ä\ mop, mar \aú\ out \ch\ chin \e\ bet \ē\ easy
\g\ go \i\ hit \ī\ ice \j\ job \ŋ\ sing \ō\ go
\ò\ law \òi\ boy \th\ thin \t͟h\ the \ü\ loot \ù\ foot
\y\ yet \zh\ vision *see also* Guide to Pronunciation

3 : a sudden decline (as of a population) or failure (as of a business) ⟨a stockmarket *crash*⟩
4 *slang* **:** the process of crashing after drug intoxication
³**crash** *adjective* (1945)
: marked by a concerted effort and effected in the shortest possible time ⟨a *crash* program⟩
⁴**crash** *noun* [probably from Russian *krashenina* colored linen] (1812)
: a coarse fabric used for draperies, toweling, and clothing and for strengthening joints of cased-in books
crash dive *noun* (1918)
: a dive made by a submarine in the least possible time
— **crash–dive** *intransitive verb*
crash helmet *noun* (circa 1918)
: a helmet that is worn (as by motorcyclists) as protection for the head in the event of an accident
crash·ing \'kra-shin\ *adjective* (1924)
1 : UTTER, ABSOLUTE ⟨a *crashing* bore⟩
2 : SUPERLATIVE ⟨a *crashing* effect⟩
— **crash·ing·ly** \-lē\ *adverb*
crash–land \'krash-'land\ (1941)
transitive verb
: to land (an airplane or spacecraft) under emergency conditions usually with damage to the craft
intransitive verb
: to crash-land an airplane or spacecraft
— **crash landing** *noun*
crash pad *noun* (1939)
1 : protective padding (as on the inside of an automobile or a tank)
2 : a place to stay temporarily
crash·wor·thy \'krash-,wər-thē\ *adjective* (1966)
: resistant to the effects of collision ⟨*crashworthy* cars⟩
— **crash·wor·thi·ness** *noun*
crass \'kras\ *adjective* [Latin *crassus* thick, gross] (1653)
1 a : GROSS 6a; *especially* **:** having or indicating such grossness of mind as precludes delicacy and discrimination **b :** being beneath one's dignity ⟨*crass* concerns of daily life⟩ **c** — used as a pejorative intensifier ⟨*crass* flattery⟩ ⟨*crass* propaganda⟩
2 : guided by or indicative of base or materialistic values ⟨*crass* commercialism⟩ ⟨*crass* measures of success⟩
synonym see STUPID
— **crass·ly** *adverb*
— **crass·ness** *noun*
cras·si·tude \'kra-sə-,tüd, -,tyüd\ *noun* (1679)
: the quality or state of being crass **:** GROSSNESS; *also* **:** an instance of grossness
-crat *noun combining form* [French *-crate*, back-formation from *-cratie* *-cracy*]
1 : advocate or partisan of a (specified) theory of government ⟨theo*crat*⟩
2 : member of a (specified) dominant class ⟨pluto*crat*⟩
— **-cratic** *adjective combining form*
cratch \'krach\ *noun* [Middle English *cracche*, from Old French *creche* manger — more at CRÈCHE] (13th century)
1 *archaic* **:** MANGER
2 : a crib or rack especially for fodder; *also* **:** FRAME
¹**crate** \'krāt\ *noun* [Middle English, from Latin *cratis*] (15th century)
1 : an open box of wooden slats or a usually wooden protective case or framework for shipping
2 : JALOPY
²**crate** *transitive verb* **crat·ed; crat·ing** (1871)
: to pack in a crate
¹**cra·ter** \'krā-tər\ *noun* [Latin, mixing bowl, crater, from Greek *kratēr*, from *kerannynai* to mix; akin to Sanskrit *śrīṇāti* he mixes] (1613)

1 \'krā-tər\ **a :** the bowl-shaped depression around the orifice of a volcano **b :** a depression formed by the impact of a meteorite **c :** a hole in the ground made by the explosion of a bomb or shell **d :** an eroded lesion **e :** a dimple in a painted surface
2 \'krā-tər, krä-'ter\ **:** KRATER
— **cra·ter·like** \'krā-tər-,līk\ *adjective*
²**crater** (1884)
intransitive verb
: to exhibit or form craters
transitive verb
: to form craters in
cra·ter·let \'krā-tər-lət\ *noun* (1881)
: a small crater
C ration *noun* (1942)
: a canned field ration of the U.S. Army
cra·ton \'krā-,tän, 'krā-\ *noun* [German *Kraton*, modification of Greek *kratos* strength — more at HARD] (1944)
: a stable relatively immobile area of the earth's crust that forms the nuclear mass of a continent or the central basin of an ocean
— **cra·ton·ic** \krə-'tä-nik, krā-, kra-\ *adjective*
craunch \'kronch, 'kränch\ *verb* [probably imitative] (1631)
: CRUNCH
— **craunch** *noun*
cra·vat \krə-'vat\ *noun* [French *cravate*, from *Crabate*, *Cravate* Croatian] (circa 1656)
1 : a band or scarf worn around the neck
2 : NECKTIE
crave \'krāv\ *verb* **craved; crav·ing** [Middle English, from Old English *crafian*; akin to Old Norse *krefja* to crave, demand] (before 12th century)
transitive verb
1 : to ask for earnestly **:** BEG, DEMAND ⟨*crave* a pardon for neglect⟩
2 a : to want greatly **:** NEED ⟨*craves* drugs⟩ **b :** to yearn for ⟨*crave* a vanished youth⟩
intransitive verb
: to have a strong or inward desire ⟨*craves* after affection⟩
synonym see DESIRE
— **crav·er** *noun*
cra·ven \'krā-vən\ *adjective* [Middle English *cravant*] (13th century)
1 *archaic* **:** DEFEATED, VANQUISHED
2 : lacking the least bit of courage **:** contemptibly fainthearted
synonym see COWARDLY
— **craven** *noun*
— **cra·ven·ly** *adverb*
— **cra·ven·ness** \-vən-nəs\ *noun*
crav·ing \'krā-viŋ\ *noun* (1633)
: an intense, urgent, or abnormal desire or longing
craw \'kro\ *noun* [Middle English *crawe*, from (assumed) Old English *cræga*; perhaps akin to Latin *vorare* to devour — more at VORACIOUS] (14th century)
1 : the crop of a bird or insect
2 : the stomach especially of a lower animal
craw·dad \'kro-,dad\ *noun* [alteration of *crawfish*] (circa 1905)
: CRAYFISH 1 — used chiefly west of the Appalachians
¹**craw·fish** \'kro-,fish\ *noun* [by folk etymology from Middle English *crevis*, *kraveys*] (1624)
1 : CRAYFISH 1
2 : SPINY LOBSTER
²**crawfish** *intransitive verb* (1842)
: to retreat from a position **:** back out
¹**crawl** \'krol\ *verb* [Middle English, from Old Norse *krafla*] (14th century)
intransitive verb
1 : to move slowly in a prone position without or as if without the use of limbs ⟨the snake *crawled* into its hole⟩
2 : to move or progress slowly or laboriously ⟨traffic *crawls* along at 10 miles an hour⟩
3 : to advance by guile or servility ⟨*crawling* into favor by toadying to his boss⟩

4 : to spread by extending stems or tendrils
5 a : to be alive or swarming with or as if with creeping things ⟨a kitchen *crawling* with ants⟩ **b :** to have the sensation of insects creeping over one ⟨the story made her flesh *crawl*⟩
6 : to fail to stay evenly spread — used of paint, varnish, or glaze
transitive verb
1 : to move upon in or as if in a creeping manner
2 : to reprove harshly ⟨they got no good right to *crawl* me for what I wrote —Marjorie K. Rawlings⟩
²**crawl** *noun* (1818)
1 a : the act or action of crawling **b :** slow or laborious progress **c** *chiefly British* **:** a going from one pub to another
2 : a prone speed swimming stroke consisting of alternating overarm strokes and a flutter kick
3 : lettering that moves vertically or horizontally across a television or motion-picture screen to give information (as performer credits or news bulletins)
crawl·er \'kro-lər\ *noun* (circa 1629)
1 : one that crawls
2 : a vehicle (as a crane) that travels on endless chain belts
crawl space *noun* (1946)
: a shallow unfinished space beneath the first floor or under the roof of a building especially for access to plumbing or wiring
crawl·way \'krol-,wā\ *noun* (1909)
: a low passageway (as in a cave) that can be traversed only by crawling
crawly \'kro-lē\ *adjective* (1857)
1 : CREEPY 1
2 : marked by crawling or slow motion ⟨*crawly* creatures⟩
cray·fish \'krā-,fish\ *noun* [by folk etymology from Middle English *crevis*, from Middle French *crevice*, of Germanic origin; akin to Old High German *krebiz* crab — more at CRAB] (14th century)
1 : any of numerous freshwater decapod crustaceans (superfamily Astacoidea) resembling the lobster but usually much smaller
2 : SPINY LOBSTER
¹**cray·on** \'krā-,än, -ən *also* 'kran\ *noun* [French, crayon, pencil, from diminutive of *craie* chalk, from Latin *creta*] (1644)
1 : a stick of white or colored chalk or of colored wax used for writing or drawing
2 : a crayon drawing

crayfish 1

²**crayon** *transitive verb* (1662)
: to draw with a crayon
— **cray·on·ist** \'krā-ə-nist\ *noun*
¹**craze** \'krāz\ *verb* **crazed; craz·ing** [Middle English *crasen* to crush, craze, of Scandinavian origin; akin to Old Swedish *krasa* to crush] (14th century)
transitive verb
1 *obsolete* **:** BREAK, SHATTER
2 : to produce minute cracks on the surface or glaze of
3 : to make insane or as if insane ⟨*crazed* by pain and fear⟩
intransitive verb
1 *archaic* **:** SHATTER, BREAK
2 : to become insane
3 : to develop a mesh of fine cracks
²**craze** *noun* (1813)
1 : an exaggerated and often transient enthusiasm **:** MANIA
2 : a crack in a surface or coating (as of glaze or enamel)
synonym see FASHION
¹**cra·zy** \'krā-zē\ *adjective* **cra·zi·er; -est** (1583)

1 a : full of cracks or flaws **:** UNSOUND **b :** CROOKED, ASKEW
2 a : MAD, INSANE **b** (1) **:** IMPRACTICAL (2) **:** ERRATIC **c :** being out of the ordinary **:** UNUSUAL ⟨a taste for *crazy* hats⟩
3 a : distracted with desire or excitement ⟨a thrill-*crazy* mob⟩ **b :** absurdly fond **:** INFATUATED ⟨he's *crazy* about the girl⟩ **c :** passionately preoccupied **:** OBSESSED ⟨*crazy* about boats⟩
— **cra·zi·ly** \-zə-lē\ *adverb*
— **cra·zi·ness** \-zē-nəs\ *noun*
— **like crazy :** to an extreme degree ⟨everyone dancing *like crazy*⟩
²**crazy** *noun, plural* **cra·zies** (1867)
: one who is or acts crazy; *especially* **:** such a one associated with a radical or extremist political cause
crazy bone *noun* (1876)
: FUNNY BONE
crazy quilt *noun* (1886)
1 : a patchwork quilt without a design
2 : JUMBLE, HODGEPODGE ⟨a *crazy quilt* of regulations⟩
cra·zy·weed \'krā-zē-ˌwēd\ *noun* (circa 1889)
: LOCOWEED
C-re·ac·tive protein \'sē-rē-'ak-tiv-\ *noun* [*C-polysaccharide*, a polysaccharide found in the cell wall of pneumococci and precipitated by this protein, from *carbohydrate*] (1955)
: a protein present in blood serum in various abnormal states (as inflammation or neoplasia)
¹**creak** \'krēk\ *intransitive verb* [Middle English *creken* to croak, of imitative origin] (1583)
: to make a prolonged grating or squeaking sound often as a result of being worn-out; *also* **:** to proceed slowly with or as if with creaking wheels ⟨the story *creaks* along to a dull conclusion⟩
²**creak** *noun* (1605)
: a rasping or grating noise
creaky \'krē-kē\ *adjective* **creak·i·er; -est** (1834)
1 : marked by creaking **:** SQUEAKY ⟨*creaky* shoes⟩
2 : showing signs of deterioration or decrepitude ⟨a *creaky* old house⟩ ⟨a *creaky* economy⟩
— **creak·i·ly** \-kə-lē\ *adverb*
— **creak·i·ness** \-nəs\ *noun*
¹**cream** \'krēm\ *noun, often attributive* [Middle English *creime, creme*, from Middle French *craime, cresme*, from Late Latin *cramum*, of Celtic origin; akin to Welsh *cramen* scab, crust] (14th century)
1 : the yellowish part of milk containing from 18 to about 40 percent butterfat
2 a : a food prepared with cream **b :** something having the consistency of cream; *especially* **:** a usually emulsified medicinal or cosmetic preparation
3 : the choicest part **:** BEST ⟨the *cream* of the crop⟩
4 : CREAMER 1
5 a : a pale yellow **b :** a cream-colored animal
— **cream·i·ly** \'krē-mə-lē\ *adverb*
— **cream·i·ness** \-mē-nəs\ *noun*
— **creamy** \-mē\ *adjective*
²**cream** (1596)
intransitive verb
1 : to form cream or a surface layer like the cream on standing milk
2 : to break into or cause something to break into a creamy froth; *also* **:** to move like froth
transitive verb
1 a : SKIM 1c **b :** to remove (something choice) from an aggregate ⟨she has *creamed* off her favorite stories from her earlier books —*Times Literary Supplement*⟩
2 : to furnish, prepare, or treat with cream; *also* **:** to dress with a cream sauce
3 a : to beat into a creamy froth **b :** to work or blend to the consistency of cream ⟨*cream* butter and sugar together⟩ **c :** to cause to form a surface layer of or like cream

4 a : to defeat decisively ⟨was *creamed* in the first round⟩ **b :** WRECK ⟨*creamed* the car on the turnpike⟩
cream cheese *noun* (1583)
: a mild soft unripened cheese made from whole sweet milk enriched with cream
cream·cups \'krēm-ˌkəps\ *noun plural but singular or plural in construction* (1888)
: a California annual (*Platystemon californicus*) of the poppy family
cream·er \'krē-mər\ *noun* (1858)
1 : a small vessel for serving cream
2 : a nondairy product used as a substitute for cream (as in coffee)
cream·ery \'krēm-rē, 'krē-mə-\ *noun, plural* **-er·ies** (1872)
: an establishment where butter and cheese are made or where milk and cream are prepared or sold
cream of tartar (1662)
: a white crystalline salt $C_4H_5KO_6$ used especially in baking powder and in certain treatments of metals
cream puff *noun* (1880)
1 : a round shell of light pastry filled with whipped cream or a cream filling
2 : an ineffectual person
3 : something trifling, inconsiderable, or easily dealt with
4 : a usually used motor vehicle that is in especially good condition
cream soda *noun* (1854)
: a carbonated soft drink flavored with vanilla
cream·ware \'krēm-ˌwar, -ˌwer\ *noun* (1780)
: earthenware having a cream-colored glaze
¹**crease** \'krēs\ *noun* [probably alteration of earlier *creaste*, from Middle English *creste* crest] (1578)
1 : a line, mark, or ridge made by or as if by folding a pliable substance
2 : a specially marked area in various sports; *especially* **:** an area surrounding or in front of a goal (as in lacrosse or hockey)
— **crease·less** \-ləs\ *adjective*
²**crease** *verb* **creased; creas·ing** (1588)
transitive verb
1 : to make a crease in or on **:** WRINKLE ⟨a smile *creased* her face⟩
2 : to wound slightly especially by grazing
intransitive verb
: to become creased
— **creas·er** *noun*
¹**cre·ate** \krē-'āt, 'krē-ˌ\ *verb* **cre·at·ed; cre·at·ing** [Middle English, from Latin *creatus*, past participle of *creare*; akin to Latin *crescere* to grow — more at CRESCENT] (14th century)
transitive verb
1 : to bring into existence ⟨God *created* the heaven and the earth —Genesis 1:1 (Authorized Version)⟩
2 a : to invest with a new form, office, or rank ⟨was *created* a lieutenant⟩ **b :** to produce or bring about by a course of action or behavior ⟨her arrival *created* a terrible fuss⟩ ⟨*create* new jobs⟩
3 : CAUSE, OCCASION ⟨famine *creates* high food prices⟩
4 a : to produce through imaginative skill ⟨*create* a painting⟩ **b :** DESIGN ⟨*creates* dresses⟩
intransitive verb
: to make or bring into existence something new
²**create** *adjective* (15th century)
archaic **:** CREATED
cre·a·tine \'krē-ə-ˌtēn, -tᵊn\ *noun* [French *créatine*, from Greek *kreat-, kreas* flesh — more at RAW] (1840)
: a white crystalline nitrogenous substance $C_4H_9N_3O_2$ found especially in the muscles of vertebrates either free or as phosphocreatine
creatine phosphate *noun* (1945)
: PHOSPHOCREATINE
cre·at·i·nine \krē-'a-tᵊn-ˌēn, -ən\ *noun* [German *Kreatinin*, from *Kreatin* creatine] (1851)

: a white crystalline strongly basic compound $C_4H_7N_3O$ formed from creatine and found especially in muscle, blood, and urine
cre·a·tion \krē-'ā-shən\ *noun* (14th century)
1 : the act of creating; *especially* **:** the act of bringing the world into ordered existence
2 : the act of making, inventing, or producing: as **a :** the act of investing with a new rank or office **b :** the first representation of a dramatic role
3 : something that is created: as **a :** WORLD **b :** creatures singly or in aggregate **c :** an original work of art **d :** a new usually striking article of clothing
cre·a·tion·ism \-shə-ˌni-zəm\ *noun* (1880)
: a doctrine or theory holding that matter, the various forms of life, and the world were created by God out of nothing and usually in the way described in Genesis — compare EVOLUTION 4b
— **cre·a·tion·ist** \-shə-nist\ *noun or adjective*
creation science *noun* (1979)
: CREATIONISM; *also* **:** scientific evidence or arguments put forth in support of creationism
cre·a·tive \krē-'ā-tiv, 'krē-ˌ\ *adjective* (1678)
1 : marked by the ability or power to create **:** given to creating ⟨the *creative* impulse⟩
2 : having the quality of something created rather than imitated **:** IMAGINATIVE ⟨the *creative* arts⟩
3 : managed so as to get around legal or conventional limits ⟨*creative* financing⟩; *also* **:** deceptively arranged so as to conceal or defraud ⟨*creative* accounting⟩
— **cre·a·tive·ly** *adverb*
— **cre·a·tive·ness** *noun*
creative evolution *noun* (1909)
: evolution that is a creative product of a vital force rather than a spontaneous process explicable in terms of scientific laws — compare EMERGENT EVOLUTION
cre·a·tiv·i·ty \ˌkrē-(ˌ)ā-'ti-və-tē, ˌkrē-ə-\ *noun* (1875)
1 : the quality of being creative
2 : the ability to create
cre·a·tor \krē-'ā-tər\ *noun* (13th century)
: one that creates usually by bringing something new or original into being; *especially*, *capitalized* **:** GOD 1
crea·ture \'krē-chər\ *noun* [Middle English, from Old French, from Late Latin *creatura*, from Latin *creatus*, past participle of *creare*] (14th century)
1 : something created either animate or inanimate: as **a :** a lower animal; *especially* **:** a farm animal **b :** a human being **c :** a being of anomalous or uncertain aspect or nature ⟨*creatures* of fantasy⟩
2 : one that is the servile dependent or tool of another **:** INSTRUMENT
— **crea·tur·al** \'krē-chə-rəl\ *adjective*
— **crea·ture·hood** \'krē-chər-ˌhùd\ *noun*
— **crea·ture·li·ness** \-lē-nəs\ *noun*
— **crea·ture·ly** \-lē\ *adjective*
creature comfort *noun* (1659)
: something (as food, warmth, or special accommodations) that gives bodily comfort
crèche \'kresh, 'krāsh\ *noun* [French, from Old French *creche* manger, crib, of Germanic origin; akin to Old High German *krippa* manger — more at CRIB] (1792)
1 : a representation of the Nativity scene
2 : DAY NURSERY
3 : a foundling hospital
cre·dence \'krē-dᵊn(t)s\ *noun* [Middle English, from Middle French or Medieval Latin;

\ə\ abut \ᵊ\ kitten \ər\ further \a\ ash \ā\ ace
\ä\ mop, mar \aù\ out \ch\ chin \e\ bet \ē\ easy
\g\ go \i\ hit \ī\ ice \j\ job \ŋ\ sing \ō\ go
\ò\ law \òi\ boy \th\ thin \th\ the \ü\ loot \ù\ foot
\y\ yet \zh\ vision *see also* Guide to Pronunciation

Middle French, from Medieval Latin *credentia*, from Latin *credent-, credens,* present participle of *credere* to believe, trust — more at CREED] (14th century)

1 a : mental acceptance as true or real ⟨give *credence* to gossip⟩ **b :** CREDIBILITY 1 ⟨lends *credence* to the theory⟩
2 : CREDENTIALS — used in the phrase *letters of credence*
3 [Middle French, from Old Italian *credenza*] **:** a Renaissance sideboard used chiefly for valuable plate
4 : a small table where the bread and wine rest before consecration
synonym see BELIEF

cre·dent \'krē-dᵊnt\ *adjective* [Latin *credent-, credens,* present participle] (1602)
1 *archaic* **:** giving credence **:** CONFIDING
2 *obsolete* **:** CREDIBLE

¹cre·den·tial \kri-'den(t)-shəl\ *adjective* (15th century)
: warranting credit or confidence — used chiefly in the phrase *credential letters*

²credential *noun* (circa 1674)
1 : something that gives a title to credit or confidence
2 *plural* **:** testimonials showing that a person is entitled to credit or has a right to exercise official power
3 : CERTIFICATE, DIPLOMA

³credential *transitive verb* **-tialed** *also* **-tialled; -tial·ing** *also* **-tial·ling** (1888)
: to furnish with credentials ⟨to *credential* adequate academic performance —K. Patricia Cross⟩

cre·den·tial·ism \-chə-,li-zəm\ *noun* (1967)
: undue emphasis on credentials (as college degrees) as prerequisites to employment

cre·den·za \kri-'den-zə\ *noun* [Italian, literally, belief, confidence, from Medieval Latin *credentia*] (1880)
1 : CREDENCE 3
2 : a sideboard, buffet, or bookcase patterned after a Renaissance credence; *especially* **:** one without legs ◆

cred·i·bil·i·ty \,kre-də-'bi-lə-tē\ *noun* (1594)
1 : the quality or power of inspiring belief ⟨an account lacking in *credibility*⟩
2 : capacity for belief ⟨strains her reader's *credibility* —*Times Literary Supplement*⟩

credibility gap *noun* (1966)
1 a : lack of trust ⟨a *credibility gap* between generations⟩ **b :** lack of believability ⟨a *credibility gap* created by contradictory official statements —Samuel Ellenport⟩
2 : DISCREPANCY ⟨the *credibility gap* between the professed ideals . . . and their actual practices —Jeanne L. Noble⟩

cred·i·ble \'kre-də-bəl\ *adjective* [Middle English, from Latin *credibilis,* from *credere*] (14th century)
1 : offering reasonable grounds for being believed ⟨a *credible* account of an accident⟩ ⟨*credible* witnesses⟩
2 : of sufficient capability to be militarily effective ⟨a *credible* deterrent⟩ ⟨*credible* forces⟩
— **cred·i·bly** \-də-blē\ *adverb*

¹cred·it \'kre-dit\ *noun* [Middle French, from Old Italian *credito,* from Latin *creditum* something entrusted to another, loan, from neuter of *creditus,* past participle of *credere* to believe, entrust — more at CREED] (1537)
1 : reliance on the truth or reality of something ⟨gave *credit* to everything he said⟩
2 a : the balance in a person's favor in an account **b :** an amount or sum placed at a person's disposal by a bank **c :** time given for payment for goods or services sold on trust ⟨long-term *credit*⟩ **d** (1) **:** an entry on the right-hand side of an account constituting an addition to a revenue, net worth, or liability account (2) **:** a deduction from an expense or asset account **e :** any one of or the sum of the items entered on the right-hand side of an account **f :** a deduction from an amount otherwise due

3 a : influence or power derived from enjoying the confidence of another or others **b :** good name **:** ESTEEM; *also* **:** financial or commercial trustworthiness
4 *archaic* **:** CREDIBILITY
5 : a source of honor ⟨a *credit* to the school⟩
6 a : something that gains or adds to reputation or esteem **:** HONOR ⟨took no *credit* for his kindly act⟩ **b :** RECOGNITION, ACKNOWLEDGMENT ⟨quite willing to accept undeserved *credit*⟩
7 : recognition by name of a person contributing to a performance (as a film or telecast) ⟨the opening *credits*⟩
8 a : recognition by a school or college that a student has fulfilled a requirement leading to a degree **b :** CREDIT HOUR
synonym see BELIEF, INFLUENCE

²credit *transitive verb* [partly from ¹*credit;* partly from Latin *creditus,* past participle] (1541)
1 : to supply goods on credit to
2 : to trust in the truth of **:** BELIEVE
3 *archaic* **:** to bring credit or honor upon
4 a : to enter upon the credit side of an account **b :** to place an amount to the credit of ⟨*credit* his account with ten dollars⟩
5 a : to consider usually favorably as the source, agent, or performer of an action or the possessor of a trait ⟨*credits* him with an excellent sense of humor⟩ **b :** to attribute to some person ⟨they *credit* the invention to him⟩
synonym see ASCRIBE

cred·it·able \'kre-di-tə-bəl\ *adjective* (1526)
1 : worthy of belief
2 : sufficiently good to bring esteem or praise
3 : worthy of commercial credit
4 : capable of being assigned
— **cred·it·abil·i·ty** \,kre-di-tə-'bi-lə-tē\ *noun*
— **cred·it·able·ness** \'kre-di-tə-bəl-nəs\ *noun*
— **cred·it·ably** \-blē\ *adverb*

credit card *noun* (1888)
: a card authorizing purchases on credit

credit hour *noun* (circa 1927)
: the unit of measuring educational credit usually based on the number of classroom hours per week throughout a term

credit line *noun* (1914)
1 : a line, note, or name that acknowledges the source of an item (as a news dispatch or television program)
2 : LINE OF CREDIT

cred·i·tor \'kre-di-tər, -,tȯr\ *noun* (15th century)
: one to whom a debt is owed; *especially* **:** a person to whom money or goods are due

credit union *noun* (1881)
: a cooperative association that makes small loans to its members at low interest rates

cred·it·wor·thy \'kre-dit-,wər-thē\ *adjective* (1924)
: financially sound enough to justify the extension of credit
— **cred·it·wor·thi·ness** *noun*

cre·do \'krē-(,)dō, 'krā-\ *noun, plural* **credos** [Middle English, from Latin, I believe] (12th century)
: CREED

cre·du·li·ty \kri-'dü-lə-tē, -'dyü-\ *noun* (15th century)
: readiness or willingness to believe especially on slight or uncertain evidence

cred·u·lous \'kre-jə-ləs\ *adjective* [Latin *credulus,* from *credere*] (1576)
1 : ready to believe especially on slight or uncertain evidence
2 : proceeding from credulity
— **cred·u·lous·ly** *adverb*
— **cred·u·lous·ness** *noun*

Cree \'krē\ *noun, plural* **Cree** *or* **Crees** [Canadian French *Cris,* plural, short for *Cristinaux,* from Ojibwa dialect *kiristino*ˈ, singular, member of a band living south of James Bay] (1744)

1 : a member of an American Indian people of Quebec, Ontario, Manitoba, and Saskatchewan
2 : the Algonquian language of the Cree people

creed \'krēd\ *noun* [Middle English *crede,* from Old English *crēda,* from Latin *credo* (first word of the Apostles' and Nicene Creeds), from *credere* to believe, trust, entrust; akin to Old Irish *cretid* he believes, Sanskrit *śrad-dadhāti*] (before 12th century)
1 : a brief authoritative formula of religious belief
2 : a set of fundamental beliefs; *also* **:** a guiding principle
— **creed·al** *or* **cre·dal** \'krē-dᵊl\ *adjective*

creek \'krēk, 'krik\ *noun* [Middle English *crike, creke,* from Old Norse *-kriki* bend] (13th century)
1 *chiefly British* **:** a small inlet or bay narrower and extending farther inland than a cove
2 : a natural stream of water normally smaller than and often tributary to a river
3 *archaic* **:** a narrow or winding passage
— **up the creek :** in a difficult or perplexing situation

Creek \'krēk\ *noun* (1725)
1 : an American Indian confederacy of peoples chiefly of Muskogean stock of Alabama, Georgia, and Florida
2 : a member of any of the Creek peoples
3 : the Muskogean language of the Creek Indians

¹creel \'krē(ə)l\ *noun* [Middle English *creille, crele*] (14th century)
1 : a wicker basket (as for carrying newly caught fish)
2 : a bar with skewers for holding bobbins in a spinning machine

²creel *transitive verb* (1844)
: to put (caught fish) in a creel

¹creep \'krēp\ *intransitive verb* **crept** \'krept\; **creep·ing** [Middle English *crepen,* from Old English *crēopan;* akin to Old Norse *krjūpa* to creep] (before 12th century)
1 a : to move along with the body prone and close to the ground **b :** to move slowly on hands and knees
2 a : to go very slowly ⟨the hours *crept* by⟩ **b :** to go timidly or cautiously so as to escape notice ⟨she *crept* away from the festive scene⟩ **c :** to enter or advance gradually so as to be almost unnoticed ⟨age *creeps* up on us⟩ ⟨a note of irritation *crept* into her voice⟩
3 : to have the sensation of being covered with creeping things ⟨the thought made his flesh *creep*⟩
4 *of a plant* **:** to spread or grow over a surface rooting at intervals or clinging with tendrils, stems, or aerial roots
5 a : to slip or gradually shift position **b :** to change shape permanently from prolonged stress or exposure to high temperatures

²creep *noun* (1818)

◇ WORD HISTORY
credenza In Italian *credenza* literally means "belief" or "confidence," the latter being just what a member of a royal or noble household needed to have in his food and drink during the Middle Ages and Renaissance. Being poisoned by one's enemies, employees, or even one's own family was an ever-present danger during those times. As a result, it became customary for royalty and noblemen to have a servant taste their food and drink after it had left the kitchen and just before it was served. The tasting was accomplished at a dining room sideboard reserved for the purpose. If the servant survived the tasting, the master had every reason to believe that he would also. The name for the sideboard became *credenza* in Italian. Sideboards and buffets of Italian Renaissance style are still called credenzas.

1 : a movement of or like creeping ⟨traffic moving at a *creep*⟩
2 : a distressing sensation like that caused by the creeping of insects over one's flesh; *especially* **:** a feeling of apprehension or horror — usually used in plural with *the* ⟨that gives me the *creeps*⟩
3 : a feed trough or enclosure that young animals can enter while adults are excluded
4 : the slow change of dimensions of an object from prolonged exposure to high temperature or stress
5 : an unpleasant or obnoxious person

creep·age \'krē-pij\ *noun* (1903)
: gradual movement **:** CREEP

creep·er \'krē-pər\ *noun* (before 12th century)
1 : one that creeps: as **a :** a creeping plant **b :** a bird (as of the family Certhiidae) that creeps about on trees or bushes searching for insects **c :** a creeping insect or reptile
2 : any of various devices used for creeping: as **a :** a fixture with iron points worn on the shoe to prevent slipping **b :** a low wheeled platform for supporting the body when working under an automobile
3 : a usually one-piece garment for a child at the crawling age

creep·ing \'krē-piŋ\ *adjective* (14th century)
: developing or advancing by slow imperceptible degrees ⟨a period of *creeping* inflation⟩

creeping eruption *noun* (1926)
: a skin disorder marked by a spreading red line of eruption and caused especially by larvae (as of hookworms not normally parasitic in humans) burrowing beneath the human skin

creepy \'krē-pē\ *adjective* **creep·i·er; -est** (1883)
1 : producing a nervous shivery apprehension ⟨*creepy* things were crawling over us⟩ ⟨a *creepy* horror story⟩
2 : of, relating to, or being a creep **:** annoyingly unpleasant
— **creep·i·ly** \-pə-lē\ *adverb*
— **creep·i·ness** \-pē-nəs\ *noun*

creese *variant of* KRIS

cre·mains \kri-'mānz\ *noun plural* [blend of *cremated* and *remains*] (1947)
: the ashes of a cremated human body

cre·mate \'krē-,māt, kri-'\ *transitive verb* **cre·mat·ed; cre·mat·ing** [Latin *crematus*, past participle of *cremare* to burn up, cremate] (1874)
: to reduce (as a dead body) to ashes by burning
— **cre·ma·tion** \kri-'mā-shən\ *noun*

cre·ma·to·ri·um \,krē-mə-'tōr-ē-əm, ,krē-, -'tòr-\ *noun, plural* **-ri·ums** *or* **-ria** \-ē-ə\ (1880)
: CREMATORY

cre·ma·to·ry \'krē-mə-,tōr-ē, 'krē-, -,tòr-\ *noun, plural* **-ries** (1876)
: a furnace for cremating; *also* **:** an establishment containing such a furnace
— **crematory** *adjective*

crème *or* **creme** \'krem *also* 'krēm *or* 'krām\ *noun, plural* **crèmes** *or* **cremes** \'krem(z), 'krēmz\ [French, from Old French *cresme* — more at CREAM] (circa 1821)
1 : a sweet liqueur
2 : cream or a preparation made with or resembling cream used in cooking
3 : CREAM 2b

crème an·glaise \,äŋ-'glāz, -aŋ-, -äⁿ-'glez\ *noun* [French, literally, English cream] (1975)
: a vanilla-flavored custard sauce usually served with desserts

crème brû·lée \-brü-'lā, -brü-\ *noun* [French, literally, scorched cream] (1886)
: a rich custard topped with caramelized sugar

crème car·a·mel \-kár-ə-'mel, *or see* CARA-MEL\ *noun* [French, literally, caramel cream] (1906)
: a custard that has been baked with caramel sauce

crème de ca·cao \'krem-də-'kō-(,)kō; ,krem-də-kə-'kaù, -kə-'kā-(,)ō\ *noun* [French, literally, cream of cacao] (1904)
: a sweet brown or colorless liqueur flavored with cacao beans and vanilla

crème de la crème \'krem-də-lä-'krem, -lə-\ *noun* [French, literally, cream of the cream] (1848)
: the very best

crème de menthe \'krem-də-'men(t)th, 'krēm-, -'mint, 'krem-də-'mänt\ *noun* [French, literally, cream of mint] (1901)
: a sweet green or colorless mint-flavored liqueur

crème fraîche *or* **crème fraiche** \'krem-'fresh *also* 'krēm- *or* 'krām-\ *noun* [French, literally, fresh cream] (1950)
: heavy cream thickened and slightly soured with buttermilk and often served on fruit

cre·nate \'krē-,nāt\ *or* **cre·nat·ed** \-,nā-təd\ *adjective* [New Latin *crenatus*, from Medieval Latin *crena* notch] (1794)
: having the margin or surface cut into rounded scallops ⟨a *crenate* leaf⟩

cre·na·tion \kri-'nā-shən\ *noun* (1846)
1 a : a crenate formation; *especially* **:** one of the rounded projections on an edge (as of a coin) **b :** the quality or state of being crenate
2 : shrinkage of red blood cells resulting in crenate margins

cren·el·lat·ed *or* **cren·el·at·ed** \'kre-nᵊl-,ā-təd\ *adjective* [French *créneler* to furnish with embrasures, from Old French *querneler*, from *kernel, crenel* embrasure, diminutive of *cren* notch, from *crener* to notch; akin to Medieval Latin *crena*] (circa 1823)
: having crenellations

cren·el·la·tion *also* **cren·el·a·tion** \,kre-nᵊl-'ā-shən\ *noun* (1849)
1 : BATTLEMENT
2 : any of the embrasures alternating with merlons in a battlement — see BATTLEMENT illustration

cren·u·lat·ed \'kren-yə-,lā-təd\ *or* **cren·u·late** \-lət, -,lāt\ *adjective* [New Latin *crenulatus*, from *crenula*, diminutive of Medieval Latin *crena*] (1794)
: having an irregularly wavy or serrate outline ⟨a *crenulated* shoreline⟩
— **cren·u·la·tion** \,kren-yə-'lā-shən\ *noun*

cre·ole \'krē-,ōl\ *adjective* (1748)
1 *often capitalized* **:** of or relating to Creoles or their language
2 *often capitalized* **:** relating to or being highly seasoned food typically prepared with rice, okra, tomatoes, and peppers ⟨shrimp *creole*⟩

Cre·ole \'krē-,ōl\ *noun* [French *créole*, from Spanish *criollo*, from Portuguese *crioulo* white person born in the colonies] (1737)
1 : a person of European descent born especially in the West Indies or Spanish America
2 : a white person descended from early French or Spanish settlers of the U.S. Gulf states and preserving their speech and culture
3 : a person of mixed French or Spanish and black descent speaking a dialect of French or Spanish
4 a : a language evolved from pidginized French that is spoken by blacks in southern Louisiana **b :** HAITIAN **c** *not capitalized* **:** a language that has evolved from a pidgin but serves as the native language of a speech community

cre·ol·ise *British variant of* CREOLIZE

cre·ol·ize \'krē-ə-,līz, 'krē-,ō-\ *transitive verb* **-ized; -iz·ing** (circa 1932)
: to cause (a pidginized language) to become a creole in a speech community
— **cre·ol·i·za·tion** \,krē-ə-lə-'zā-shən, ,krē-(,)ō-\ *noun*

¹cre·o·sote \'krē-ə-,sōt\ *noun* [German *Kreosot*, from Greek *kreas* flesh + *sōtēr* preserver, from *sōzein* to preserve, from *sōs* safe (probably akin to Sanskrit *tavīti* he is strong); from its antiseptic properties — more at RAW] (1835)

1 : a clear or yellowish flammable oily liquid mixture of phenolic compounds obtained by the distillation of wood tar especially from beech wood
2 : a brownish oily liquid consisting chiefly of aromatic hydrocarbons obtained by distillation of coal tar and used especially as a wood preservative
3 : a dark brown or black flammable tar deposited from especially wood smoke on the walls of a chimney

²creosote *transitive verb* **-sot·ed; -sot·ing** (1846)
: to treat with creosote

creosote bush *noun* (1846)
: a resinous desert shrub (*Larrea tridentata*) of the caltrop family found in the southwestern U.S. and Mexico

crepe *or* **crêpe** \'krāp\ *noun* [French *crêpe* — more at CRAPE] (1797)
1 : a light crinkled fabric woven of any of various fibers
2 : CRAPE 2
3 : crude rubber in the form of nearly white to brown crinkled sheets used especially for shoe soles ⟨*crepe*-soled shoes⟩
4 : a small very thin pancake
— **crepe** *adjective*
— **crep·ey** *or* **crepy** \'krā-pē\ *adjective*

crepe de chine *or* **crêpe de chine** \,krāp-də-'shēn\ *noun, often 2d C capitalized* [French *crêpe de Chine*, literally, China crepe] (1872)
: a soft fine or sheer clothing crepe especially of silk

crepe myrtle *or* **crêpe myrtle** *noun* (1916)
: CRAPE MYRTLE

crepe paper *noun* (1897)
: paper with a crinkled or puckered texture

crêpe su·zette \,krāp-sù-'zet\ *noun, plural* **crêpes suzette** \,krāp(s)-sù-'zet\ *or* **crêpe suzettes** \,krāp-sù-'zets\ *often S capitalized* [French *crêpe Suzette*, probably from *Suzette*, nickname of Suzanne Reichenberg (died 1924) French actress] (1922)
: a thin folded or rolled pancake in a hot orange-butter sauce that is sprinkled with a liqueur (as cognac or curaçao) and set ablaze for serving

crep·i·tant \'kre-pə-tənt\ *adjective* (1855)
: having or making a crackling sound ⟨*crepitant* sounds in breathing⟩

crep·i·tate \'kre-pə-,tāt\ *intransitive verb* **-tat·ed; -tat·ing** [Latin *crepitatus*, past participle of *crepitare* to crackle, frequentative of *crepare* to rattle, crack] (circa 1828)
: to make a crackling sound **:** CRACKLE
— **crep·i·ta·tion** \,kre-pə-'tā-shən\ *noun*

cre·pon \'krā-,pän\ *noun* [French, from *crêpe*] (circa 1864)
: a heavy crepe fabric with lengthwise crinkles

crept *past and past participle of* CREEP

cre·pus·cu·lar \kri-'pəs-kyə-lər\ *adjective* (1668)
1 : of, relating to, or resembling twilight **:** DIM
2 : active in the twilight ⟨*crepuscular* insects⟩

cre·pus·cule \kri-'pəs-(,)kyü(ə)l\ *or* **cre·pus·cle** \-'pə-səl\ *noun* [Latin *crepusculum*, from *creper* dusky] (14th century)
: TWILIGHT

¹cre·scen·do \krə-'shen-(,)dō\ *noun, plural* **-dos** *or* **-does** *also* **-di** \-dē\ [Italian, from *crescendo*, adjective, increasing, gerund of *crescere* to grow, increase, from Latin] (1776)
1 a : a gradual increase; *specifically* **:** a gradual increase in volume of a musical passage **b :** the peak of a gradual increase **:** CLIMAX ⟨complaints about stifling smog conditions reach a *crescendo* —*Down Beat*⟩

\ə\ abut \ᵊ\ kitten \ər\ further \a\ ash \ā\ ace
\ä\ mop, mar \aù\ out \ch\ chin \e\ bet \ē\ easy
\g\ go \i\ hit \ī\ ice \j\ job \ŋ\ sing \ō\ go
\ò\ law \òi\ boy \th\ thin \t͟h\ the \ü\ loot \ù\ foot
\y\ yet \zh\ vision *see also* Guide to Pronunciation

2 : a crescendo musical passage □
— **crescendo** *intransitive verb*

²**crescendo** *adverb or adjective* (1859)
: with an increase in volume — used as a direction in music

mark indicating crescendo 2

¹**cres·cent** \'kre-s°nt\ *noun* [Middle English *cressant*, from Middle French *creissant*, from present participle of *creistre* to grow, increase, from Latin *crescere*; akin to Old High German *hirsi* millet, Lithuanian *šerti* to feed, Greek *koros* boy] (15th century)
1 a : the moon at any stage between new moon and first quarter and between last quarter and the succeeding new moon when less than half of the illuminated hemisphere is visible **b** : the figure of the moon at such a stage defined by a convex and a concave edge **2** : something shaped like a crescent
— **cres·cen·tic** \kre-'sen-tik, krə-\ *adjective*

²**crescent** *adjective* [Latin *crescent-, crescens,* present participle of *crescere*] (1574)
: marked by an increase

Cres·cent \'kre-s°nt\ *trademark*
— used for an adjustable open-end wrench

cres·cive \'kre-siv\ *adjective* [Latin *crescere* to grow] (1566)
: marked by gradual spontaneous development
— **cres·cive·ly** *adverb*

cre·sol \'krē-ˌsȯl, -ˌsōl\ *noun* [International Scientific Vocabulary, irregular from *creosote*] (circa 1869)
: any of three poisonous colorless crystalline or liquid isomeric phenols C_7H_8O

cress \'kres\ *noun* [Middle English *cresse,* from Old English *cærse, cressa;* akin to Old High German *kressa* cress] (before 12th century)
: any of numerous crucifers (especially genera *Lepidium* and *Nasturtium*) with moderately pungent leaves used especially in salads

cres·set \'kre-sət\ *noun* [Middle English, from Middle French, from Old French *craisset,* from *craisse* grease — more at GREASE] (14th century)
: an iron vessel or basket used for holding an illuminant (as oil) and mounted as a torch or suspended as a lantern

Cres·si·da \'kre-sə-də\ *noun*
: a Trojan woman of medieval legend who pledges herself to Troilus but while a captive of the Greeks gives herself to Diomedes

¹**crest** \'krest\ *noun* [Middle English *creste,* from Middle French, from Latin *crista;* probably akin to Latin *crinis* hair] (14th century)
1 a : a showy tuft or process on the head of an animal and especially a bird — see BIRD illustration **b** : the plume or identifying emblem worn on a knight's helmet; *also* : the top of a helmet **c** (1) : a heraldic representation of the crest (2) : a heraldic device depicted above the escutcheon but not upon a helmet (3) : COAT OF ARMS 2a **d** : a ridge or prominence on a part of an animal body **2** : something suggesting a crest especially in being an upper prominence, edge, or limit: as **a** : PEAK; *especially* : the top line of a mountain or hill **b** : the ridge of a roof **c** : the top of a wave **3 a** : a high point of an action or process and especially of one that is rhythmic **b** : CLIMAX, CULMINATION ⟨at the *crest* of his fame⟩
— **crest·al** \'kres-t°l\ *adjective*
— **crest·less** \-ləs\ *adjective*

²**crest** (15th century)
transitive verb
1 : to furnish with a crest; *also* : CROWN **2** : to reach the crest of ⟨*crested* the hill and looked around⟩
intransitive verb
: to rise to a crest ⟨waves *cresting* in the storm⟩

crest·ed \'kres-təd\ *adjective* (14th century)
: having a crest ⟨a *crested* bird⟩

crested wheatgrass *noun* (1923)
: either of two Eurasian grasses (*Agropyron cristatum* or *A. sibericum* synonym *A. desertorum*) that are grown in the U.S. for forage and for erosion control

crest·fall·en \'krest-ˌfȯ-lən\ *adjective* (1589)
1 : having a drooping crest or hanging head **2** : feeling shame or humiliation : DEJECTED
— **crest·fall·en·ly** *adverb*
— **crest·fall·en·ness** \-lən-nəs\ *noun*

crest·ing \'kres-tiŋ\ *noun* (1908)
: a decorative edging or railing (as on pottery or furniture)

cre·syl \'kre-səl, 'krē-ˌsil\ *noun* [International Scientific Vocabulary *cresol* + *-yl*] (circa 1872)
: TOLYL

Cre·ta·ceous \kri-'tā-shəs\ *adjective* [Latin *cretaceus* resembling chalk, from *creta* chalk] (1832)
: of, relating to, or being the last period of the Mesozoic era characterized by continued dominance of reptiles, emergent dominance of angiosperms, diversification of mammals, and the extinction of many types of organisms at the close of the period; *also* : of, relating to, or being the corresponding system of rocks — see GEOLOGIC TIME table
— **Cretaceous** *noun*

cre·tin \'krē-t°n\ *noun* [French *crétin,* from French dialect *cretin,* literally, wretch, innocent victim, from Latin *christianus* Christian] (1779)
1 : one afflicted with cretinism **2** : a stupid, vulgar, or insensitive person : CLOD, LOUT ◇
— **cre·tin·ous** \-t°n-əs\ *adjective*

cre·tin·ism \-t°n-ˌi-zəm\ *noun* (1801)
: a usually congenital abnormal condition marked by physical stunting and mental retardation and caused by severe hypothyroidism

cre·tonne \'krē-ˌtän, kri-'\ *noun* [French, from *Creton,* Normandy] (1870)
: a strong cotton or linen cloth used especially for curtains and upholstery

Creutz·feldt–Ja·kob disease *also* **Creutz·feld–Ja·cob disease** \'krȯits-ˌfelt-'yä-(ˌ)kōb-\ *noun* [Hans G. *Creutzfeldt* (died 1964) German psychiatrist and Alfons M. *Jakob* (died 1931) German psychiatrist] (1963)
: a rare progressive fatal encephalopathy caused by a slow virus and marked by development of porous brain tissue, premature dementia in middle age, and gradual loss of muscular coordination

cre·val·le \kri-'va-lē\ *noun* [by alteration] (1879)
: CAVALLA 1; *especially* : JACK CREVALLE

cre·vasse \kri-'vas\ *noun* [French, from Old French *crevace*] (1813)
1 : a breach in a levee **2** : a deep crevice or fissure (as in a glacier or the earth)

crev·ice \'kre-vəs\ *noun* [Middle English, from Middle French *crevace,* from Old French, from *crever* to break, from Latin *crepare* to crack] (14th century)
: a narrow opening resulting from a split or crack (as in a cliff) : FISSURE

¹**crew** \'krü\ *chiefly British past of* CROW

²**crew** \'krü\ *noun* [Middle English *crue,* literally, reinforcement, from Middle French *creue* increase, from *creistre* to grow — more at CRESCENT] (15th century)
1 *archaic* : a band or force of armed men **2** : a group of people associated together in a common activity or by common traits or interests **3 a** : a company of people working on one job or under one foreman or operating a machine **b** : the whole company belonging to a ship sometimes including the officers and master; *also* : one who assists the skipper of a sailboat

c : the persons who have duties on an aircraft in flight **d** : the rowers and coxswain of a racing shell; *also* : ROWING
— **crew·less** \-ləs\ *adjective*

³**crew** (1935)
intransitive verb
: to act as a member of a crew
transitive verb
: to serve as a crew member on (as a ship or aircraft)

crew cut *noun* (1942)
: a very short haircut usually for men or boys in which the hair resembles the bristle surface of a brush

crew·el \'krü-əl\ *noun* [Middle English *crule*] (15th century)
1 : slackly twisted worsted yarn used for embroidery **2** : CREWELWORK

crew·el·work \-ˌwərk\ *noun* (1863)
: embroidery work with crewel

crew·man \'krü-mən\ *noun* (circa 1927)
: a member of a crew

crew·mate \-ˌmāt\ *noun* (1938)
: a fellow crewman

crew neck *noun* [from the sweaters with this neckline worn by oarsmen] (1940)
1 : a round collarless neckline **2** *usually* **crew·neck** \'krü-ˌnek\ : a sweater with a crew neck

crew sock *noun* (1948)
: a short bulky usually ribbed sock

¹**crib** \'krib\ *noun* [Middle English, from Old English *cribb;* akin to Old High German *krippa* manger, and perhaps to Greek *griphos* reed basket] (before 12th century)
1 : a manger for feeding animals **2** : an enclosure especially of framework: as **a** : a stall for a stabled animal **b** : a small child's bedstead with high enclosing usually slatted sides **c** : any of various devices resembling a crate or framework in structure **d** : a building for storage : BIN

3 a : a small narrow room or dwelling **:** HUT, SHACK **b :** a room or shack used for prostitution
4 : the cards discarded in cribbage for the dealer to use in scoring
5 a : a small theft **b :** PLAGIARISM **c :** a literal translation; *especially* **:** PONY 3 **d :** a summary and key to understanding a literary work **e :** something used for cheating in an examination
6 : CRÈCHE 1

²**crib** *verb* **cribbed; crib·bing** (1605)
transitive verb
1 : CONFINE, CRAMP
2 : to provide with or put into a crib; *especially* **:** to line or support with a framework of timber
3 : PILFER, STEAL; *especially* **:** PLAGIARIZE
intransitive verb
1 a : STEAL, PLAGIARIZE **b :** to use a crib **:** CHEAT
2 : to have the vice of cribbing
— **crib·ber** *noun*
crib·bage \'kri-bij\ *noun* [¹*crib*] (1630)
: a card game for two players in which each player tries to form various counting combinations of cards
crib·bing \'kri-biŋ\ *noun* (1841)
1 : material for use in making a crib
2 : a vice of horses in which they gnaw (as at the manger) while slobbering and salivating
crib biting *noun* (1831)
: CRIBBING 2
crib death *noun* (1965)
: SUDDEN INFANT DEATH SYNDROME
crib·ri·form \'kri-brə-₁fȯrm\ *adjective* [Latin *cribrum* sieve; akin to Latin *cernere* to sift — more at CERTAIN] (1741)
: pierced with small holes
cri·ce·tid \krī-'sē-təd, -'se-\ *noun* [ultimately from New Latin *Cricetus,* genus name, of Slavic origin; akin to Czech *křeček* hamster] (1960)
: any of a family (Cricetidae) of small rodents including the hamsters
— **cricetid** *adjective*
¹**crick** \'krik\ *noun* [Middle English *cryk*] (15th century)
: a painful spasmodic condition of muscles (as of the neck or back)
²**crick** *transitive verb* (1884)
1 : to cause a crick in (as the neck)
2 : to turn or twist (as the head) especially into a strained position
¹**crick·et** \'kri-kət\ *noun* [Middle English *criket,* from Middle French *criquet,* of imitative origin] (14th century)
1 : any of a family (Gryllidae) of leaping orthopteran insects noted for the

cricket 1

chirping notes produced by the male by rubbing together specially modified parts of the forewings
2 : a low wooden footstool
3 : a small metal toy or signaling device that makes a sharp click or snap when pressed
²**cricket** *noun* [Middle French *criquet* goal stake in a bowling game] (1598)
1 : a game played with a ball and bat by two sides of usually 11 players each on a large field centering upon two wickets each defended by a batsman
2 : fair and honorable behavior ⟨it wasn't *cricket* for her to break her contract —Gerry Nadel⟩
³**cricket** *intransitive verb* (circa 1809)
: to play the game of cricket
— **crick·et·er** *noun*
cri·coid \'krī-₁kȯid\ *adjective* [New Latin *cricoides,* from Greek *krikoeidēs* ring-shaped, from *krikos* ring — more at CIRCLE] (1746)

: of, relating to, or being a cartilage of the larynx with which arytenoid cartilages articulate
cri de coeur \krē-də-'kər\ *noun, plural* **cris de coeur** *same*\ [French, literally, cry from the heart] (1904)
: a passionate outcry (as of appeal or protest)
cri·er \'krī(-ə)r\ *noun* (14th century)
: one that cries: **a :** an officer who proclaims the orders of a court **b :** TOWN CRIER
cri·key \'krī-kē\ *or* **crick·ey** \'kri-kē\ *interjection* [euphemism for *Christ*] (1838)
— used as a mild oath
crime \'krīm\ *noun* [Middle English, from Middle French, from Latin *crimen* accusation, reproach, crime; probably akin to Latin *cernere* to sift, determine] (14th century)
1 : an act or the commission of an act that is forbidden or the omission of a duty that is commanded by a public law and that makes the offender liable to punishment by that law; *especially* **:** a gross violation of law
2 : a grave offense especially against morality
3 : criminal activity ⟨efforts to fight *crime*⟩
4 : something reprehensible, foolish, or disgraceful ⟨it's a *crime* to waste good food⟩
synonym see OFFENSE
— **crime·less** \-ləs\ *adjective*
crime against humanity (1945)
: atrocity (as extermination or enslavement) that is directed especially against an entire population or part of a population on specious grounds and without regard to individual guilt or responsibility even on such grounds
crime against nature (1828)
: SODOMY
¹**crim·i·nal** \'kri-mə-n°l, 'krim-nəl\ *adjective* [Middle English, from Middle French or Late Latin; Middle French *criminel,* from Late Latin *criminalis,* from Latin *crimin- crimen* crime] (15th century)
1 : relating to, involving, or being a crime ⟨*criminal* neglect⟩
2 : relating to crime or to the prosecution of suspects in a crime ⟨*criminal* statistics⟩ ⟨brought *criminal* action⟩
3 : guilty of crime; *also* **:** of or befitting a criminal ⟨a *criminal* mind⟩
4 : DISGRACEFUL
— **crim·i·nal·ly** *adverb*
²**criminal** *noun* (circa 1626)
1 : one who has committed a crime
2 : a person who has been convicted of a crime
criminal conversation *noun* (1768)
: adultery considered as a tort
criminal court *noun* (1678)
: a court that has jurisdiction to try and punish offenders against criminal law
crim·i·nal·is·tics \₁kri-mə-n°l-'is-tiks, ₁krim-nə-'lis-\ *noun plural but singular in construction* (1943)
: application of scientific techniques in collecting and analyzing physical evidence in criminal cases
crim·i·nal·i·ty \₁kri-mə-'na-lə-tē\ *noun* (1611)
1 : the quality or state of being criminal
2 : criminal activity ⟨urban *criminality*⟩
crim·i·nal·ize \'kri-mə-n°l-₁īz, 'krim-nə-₁līz\ *transitive verb* **-ized; -iz·ing** (circa 1956)
: to make illegal **:** OUTLAW; *also* **:** to turn into or treat as a criminal
— **crim·i·nal·i·za·tion** \₁kri-mə-n°l-ə-'zā-shən, ₁krim-nə-lə-₁zā-\ *noun*
criminal law *noun* (1864)
: the law of crimes and their punishments
criminal lawyer *noun* (1869)
: a lawyer who specializes in criminal law; *especially* **:** a lawyer who represents defendants in criminal cases
crim·i·nate \'kri-mə-₁nāt\ *transitive verb* **-nat·ed; -nat·ing** [Latin *criminatus,* past participle of *criminari,* from *crimin-, crimen* accusation] (1645)
: INCRIMINATE
— **crim·i·na·tion** \₁kri-mə-'nā-shən\ *noun*

crim·i·nol·o·gy \₁kri-mə-'nä-lə-jē\ *noun* [Italian *criminologia,* from Latin *crimin-, crimen* + Italian *-o- + -logia* -logy] (1890)
: the scientific study of crime as a social phenomenon, of criminals, and of penal treatment
— **crim·i·no·log·i·cal** \-mə-n°l-'ä-ji-kəl\ *adjective*
— **crim·i·no·log·i·cal·ly** \-k(ə-)lē\ *adverb*
— **crim·i·nol·o·gist** \₁kri-mə-'nä-lə-jist\ *noun*
crim·i·nous \'kri-mə-nəs\ *adjective* (15th century)
: CRIMINAL
¹**crimp** \'krimp\ *transitive verb* [Dutch or Low German *krimpen* to shrivel; akin to Middle Dutch *crampe* hook, cramp] (1712)
1 : to cause to become wavy, bent, or pinched: as **a :** to form (leather) into a desired shape **b :** to give (synthetic fibers) a curl or wave like that of natural fibers **c :** to pinch or press together (as the margins of a pie crust) in order to seal
2 : to be an inhibiting or restraining influence on **:** CRAMP ⟨sales had been *crimped* by credit controls —*Time*⟩
— **crimp·er** \'krim-pər\ *noun*
²**crimp** *noun* (1863)
1 : something produced by or as if by crimping: as **a :** a section of hair artificially waved or curled **b :** a succession of waves (as in wool fiber) **c :** a bend or crease formed in something
2 : something that cramps or inhibits **:** RESTRAINT, CURB
³**crimp** *noun* [perhaps from ¹*crimp*] (1758)
: a person who entraps or forces men into shipping or into enlisting in an army or navy
⁴**crimp** *transitive verb* (1812)
: to trap into military or sea service **:** IMPRESS
crimpy \'krim-pē\ *adjective* **crimp·i·er; -est** (1888)
: FRIZZY
¹**crim·son** \'krim-zən\ *noun* [Middle English *crimsin,* from Old Spanish *cremesín,* from Arabic *qirmizī,* from *qirmiz* kermes] (15th century)
: any of several deep purplish reds
²**crimson** *adjective* (15th century)
: of the color crimson
³**crimson** (1601)
transitive verb
: to make crimson
intransitive verb
: to become crimson; *especially* **:** BLUSH
¹**cringe** \'krinj\ *intransitive verb* **cringed; cring·ing** [Middle English *crengen;* akin to Old English *cringan* to yield, Middle High German *krank* weak] (13th century)
1 : to draw in or contract one's muscles involuntarily (as from cold or pain)
2 : to shrink in fear or servility
3 : to behave in an excessively humble or servile way
synonym see FAWN
— **cring·er** *noun*
²**cringe** *noun* (1597)
: a cringing act; *specifically* **:** a servile bow
crin·gle \'krin-gəl\ *noun* [Low German *kringel,* diminutive of *kring* ring] (1627)
: a loop or grommet at the corner of a sail to which a line is attached
¹**crin·kle** \'krin-kəl\ *verb* **crin·kled; crin·kling** \-k(ə-)liŋ\ [Middle English *crynkelen;* akin to Old English *cringan* to yield] (14th century)
intransitive verb
1 a : to form many short bends or ripples **b :** WRINKLE

\ə\ abut \ᵊ\ kitten \ər\ further \a\ ash \ā\ ace
\ä\ mop, mar \au̇\ out \ch\ chin \e\ bet \ē\ easy
\g\ go \i\ hit \ī\ ice \j\ job \ŋ\ sing \ō\ go
\o̊\ law \o̊i\ boy \th\ thin \th\ the \ü\ loot \u̇\ foot
\y\ yet \zh\ vision *see also* Guide to Pronunciation

2 : to give forth a thin crackling sound **:** RUSTLE ⟨*crinkling* silks⟩
transitive verb
: to cause to crinkle **:** make crinkles in
²**crinkle** *noun* (1596)
1 : WRINKLE, CORRUGATION, PUCKER
2 : any of several plant diseases marked by crinkling of leaves
— **crin·kly** \-k(ə-)lē\ *adjective*
cri·noid \'krī-ˌnȯid\ *noun* [ultimately from Greek *krinon* lily] (1847)
: any of a large class (Crinoidea) of echinoderms usually having a somewhat cup-shaped body with five or more feathery arms
— **crinoid** *adjective*
crin·o·line \'kri-nᵊl-ən\ *noun* [French, from Italian *crinolino,* from *crino* horsehair (from Latin *crinis* hair) + *lino* flax, linen, from Latin *linum* — more at CREST] (1830)
1 : an open-weave fabric of horsehair or cotton that is usually stiffened and used especially for interlinings and millinery
2 : a full stiff skirt or underskirt made of crinoline; *also* **:** HOOPSKIRT
— **crinoline** *or* **crin·o·lined** \-ənd\ *adjective*
cri·o·llo \krē-'ōl-(ˌ)yō, -'ō-(ˌ)yō\ *noun, plural* **-llos** [Spanish — more at CREOLE] (1604)
1 a : a person of pure Spanish descent born in Spanish America **b :** a person born and usually raised in a Spanish-American country
2 : a domestic animal of a breed or strain developed in Latin America; *especially, often capitalized* **:** a hardy muscular pony of a breed originally developed in Argentina
— **criollo** *adjective*
cripes \'krīps\ *interjection* [euphemism for *Christ*] (1910)
— used as a mild oath
¹**crip·ple** \'kri-pəl\ *noun* [Middle English *cripel,* from Old English *crypel;* akin to Old English *crēopan* to creep — more at CREEP] (before 12th century)
1 a : a lame or partly disabled person or animal — sometimes taken to be offensive **b :** one that is disabled or deficient in a specified manner ⟨a social *cripple*⟩
2 : something flawed or imperfect
²**cripple** *adjective* (13th century)
: being a cripple **:** LAME
³**cripple** *transitive verb* **crip·pled; crip·pling** \-p(ə-)liŋ\ (14th century)
1 : to deprive of the use of a limb and especially a leg
2 : to deprive of capability for service or of strength, efficiency, or wholeness
synonym see MAIM, WEAKEN
— **crip·pler** \-p(ə-)lər\ *noun*
— **crip·pling·ly** \-p(ə-)liŋ-lē\ *adverb*
cri·sis \'krī-səs\ *noun, plural* **cri·ses** \'krī-ˌsēz\ [Middle English, from Latin, from Greek *krisis,* literally, decision, from *krinein* to decide — more at CERTAIN] (15th century)
1 a : the turning point for better or worse in an acute disease or fever **b :** a paroxysmal attack of pain, distress, or disordered function **c :** an emotionally significant event or radical change of status in a person's life ⟨a midlife *crisis*⟩
2 : the decisive moment (as in a literary plot)
3 a : an unstable or crucial time or state of affairs in which a decisive change is impending; *especially* **:** one with the distinct possibility of a highly undesirable outcome ⟨a financial *crisis*⟩ **b :** a situation that has reached a critical phase ⟨the environmental *crisis*⟩
synonym see JUNCTURE
¹**crisp** \'krisp\ *adjective* [Middle English, from Old English, from Latin *crispus;* akin to Welsh *crych* curly] (before 12th century)
1 : CURLY, WAVY; *also* **:** having close stiff or wiry curls or waves
2 a : easily crumbled **:** BRITTLE **b :** being desirably firm and fresh ⟨*crisp* lettuce⟩
3 a : being sharp, clean-cut, and clear ⟨a *crisp* illustration⟩; *also* **:** concise and to the point ⟨a

crisp reply⟩ **b :** noticeably neat ⟨*crisp* new clothes⟩ **c :** BRISK, LIVELY ⟨a *crisp* tale of intrigue⟩ ⟨*crisp* musical tempi⟩ **d :** FROSTY, SNAPPY ⟨*crisp* winter weather⟩; *also* **:** FRESH, INVIGORATING ⟨*crisp* autumn air⟩ ⟨a *crisp* white wine⟩
synonym see FRAGILE
— **crisp·ly** *adverb*
— **crisp·ness** *noun*
²**crisp** (14th century)
transitive verb
1 : CURL, CRIMP
2 : to cause to ripple **:** WRINKLE
3 : to make or keep crisp
intransitive verb
1 : CURL
2 : RIPPLE
3 : to become crisp
³**crisp** *noun* (14th century)
1 a : something crisp or brittle ⟨burned to a *crisp*⟩ **b** *chiefly British* **:** POTATO CHIP — usually used in plural
2 : a baked dessert of fruit with crumb topping ⟨apple *crisp*⟩
crisp·bread \'krisp-ˌbred\ *noun* (circa 1927)
: a plain dry unsweetened cracker made from crushed grain (as wheat or rye)
crisp·en \'kris-pən\ (1943)
transitive verb
: to make crisp
intransitive verb
: to become crisp
crisp·er \'kris-pər\ *noun* (1835)
: one that crisps; *specifically* **:** a closed container in a refrigerator intended to prevent loss of moisture from fresh produce
crispy \'kris-pē\ *adjective* **crisp·i·er; -est** (14th century)
: CRISP
— **crisp·i·ness** *noun*
¹**criss·cross** \'kris-ˌkrȯs\ *verb* [obsolete *christcross, crisscross* mark of a cross] (1818)
transitive verb
1 : to mark with intersecting lines
2 : to pass back and forth through or over
intransitive verb
: to go or pass back and forth
²**crisscross** *adjective* (1846)
: marked or characterized by crisscrossing
— **crisscross** *adverb*
³**crisscross** *noun* (1876)
1 : a crisscross pattern **:** NETWORK
2 : the state of being at cross-purposes; *also* **:** a confused state
cris·ta \'kris-tə\ *noun, plural* **cris·tae** \-ˌtē, -ˌtī\ [New Latin, from Latin, crest — more at CREST] (1959)
: any of the inwardly projecting folds of the inner membrane of a mitochondrion
cri·te·ri·on \krī-'tir-ē-ən *also* krə-\ *noun, plural* **-ria** \-ē-ə\ *also* **-ri·ons** [Greek *kritērion,* from *krinein* to judge, decide — more at CERTAIN] (1622)
1 : a standard on which a judgment or decision may be based
2 : a characterizing mark or trait
synonym see STANDARD □
cri·te·ri·um \krī-'tir-ē-əm, krē-ter-'yȯm\ *noun* [French *critérium* competition, literally, criterion, from Late Latin *criterium,* from Greek *kritērion*] (1970)
: a bicycle race of a specified number of laps on a closed course over public roads closed to normal traffic
¹**crit·ic** \'kri-tik\ *noun* [Latin *criticus,* from Greek *kritikos,* from *kritikos* able to discern or judge, from *krinein*] (1588)
1 a : one who expresses a reasoned opinion on any matter especially involving a judgment of its value, truth, righteousness, beauty, or technique **b :** one who engages often professionally in the analysis, evaluation, or appreciation of works of art or artistic performances
2 : one given to harsh or captious judgment
²**critic** *noun* [Greek *kritikē* art of the critic, from feminine of *kritikos*] (1656)
1 *archaic* **:** CRITICISM

2 *archaic* **:** CRITIQUE
crit·i·cal \'kri-ti-kəl\ *adjective* (1547)
1 a : of, relating to, or being a turning point or specially important juncture ⟨*critical* phase⟩: as (1) **:** relating to or being the stage of a disease at which an abrupt change for better or worse may be expected; *also* **:** being or relating to an illness or condition involving danger of death ⟨*critical* care⟩ (2) **:** relating to or being a state in which a measurement or point at which some quality, property, or phenomenon suffers a definite change ⟨*critical* temperature⟩ **b :** CRUCIAL, DECISIVE ⟨*critical* test⟩ **c :** INDISPENSABLE, VITAL ⟨a *critical* waterfowl habitat⟩ ⟨a component *critical* to the operation of a machine⟩ **d :** being in or approaching a state of crisis ⟨a *critical* shortage⟩ ⟨a *critical* situation⟩
2 a : inclined to criticize severely and unfavorably **b :** consisting of or involving criticism ⟨*critical* writings⟩; *also* **:** of or relating to the judgment of critics ⟨the play was a *critical* success⟩ **c :** exercising or involving careful judgment or judicious evaluation **d :** including variant readings and scholarly emendations ⟨a *critical* edition⟩
3 : characterized by risk or uncertainty
4 a : of sufficient size to sustain a chain reaction — used of a mass of fissionable material **b :** sustaining a chain reaction — used of a nuclear reactor ☆
— **crit·i·cal·i·ty** \ˌkri-tə-'ka-lə-tē\ *noun*
— **crit·i·cal·ly** \'kri-ti-k(ə-)lē\ *adverb*
— **crit·i·cal·ness** \-kəl-nəs\ *noun*
critical angle *noun* (1873)
: the least angle of incidence at which total reflection takes place
critical mass *noun* (1964)
: a size, number, or amount large enough to produce a particular result ⟨the *critical mass* of activity needed for a retail store⟩

critical angle: *AOB, AO'B', AO"B"* angles of incidence; *AOC* refracted ray; *AO"C"* totally reflected ray; *AO'B'* critical angle

critical point *noun* (circa 1889)
: a point on the graph of a function where the derivative is zero or infinite
critical region *noun* (1951)
: the set of outcomes of a statistical test for which the null hypothesis is to be rejected
critical value *noun* (circa 1909)
: the value of an independent variable corresponding to a critical point of a function
crit·ic·as·ter \'kri-ti-ˌkas-tər\ *noun* (1684)
: an inferior or petty critic
crit·i·cise *British variant of* CRITICIZE
crit·i·cism \'kri-tə-ˌsi-zəm\ *noun* (1607)
1 a : the act of criticizing usually unfavorably **b** : a critical observation or remark **c** : CRITIQUE
2 : the art of evaluating or analyzing works of art or literature
3 : the scientific investigation of literary documents (as the Bible) in regard to such matters as origin, text, composition, or history
crit·i·cize \'kri-tə-ˌsīz\ *verb* **-cized; -ciz·ing** (1649)
intransitive verb
: to act as a critic
transitive verb
1 : to consider the merits and demerits of and judge accordingly : EVALUATE
2 : to find fault with : point out the faults of ☆
— **crit·i·ciz·able** \-ˌsī-zə-bəl\ *adjective*
— **crit·i·ciz·er** *noun*
¹cri·tique \krə-'tēk, kri-\ *noun* [alteration of ²*critic*] (1702)
: an act of criticizing; *especially* : a critical estimate or discussion
²critique *transitive verb* **cri·tiqued; cri·tiqu·ing** (1751)
: REVIEW, CRITICIZE
crit·ter \'kri-tər\ *noun* [by alteration] (1815)
: CREATURE
¹croak \'krōk\ *verb* [Middle English *croken*, of imitative origin] (15th century)
intransitive verb
1 a : to make a deep harsh sound **b** : to speak in a hoarse throaty voice
2 : GRUMBLE 1
3 *slang* : DIE
transitive verb
1 : to utter in a hoarse raucous voice
2 *slang* : KILL
²croak *noun* (1561)
: a hoarse harsh cry or sound
— **croaky** \'krō-kē\ *adjective*
croak·er \'krō-kər\ *noun* (1651)
1 : an animal that croaks
2 : any of various fishes (especially family Sciaenidae) that produce croaking or grunting noises
3 *slang* : DOCTOR
Croat \'krō-ˌat *also* 'krō-(-ə)t\ *noun* [New Latin *Croata*, from Serbo-Croatian *Hrvat*] (circa 1702)
: CROATIAN
Cro·atian \krō-'ā-shən\ *noun* (1555)
1 : a native or inhabitant of Croatia
2 : a south Slavic language spoken by the Croatian people and distinct from Serbian chiefly in its use of the Latin alphabet
— **Croatian** *adjective*
croc \'kräk\ *noun* (1884)
: CROCODILE
¹cro·chet \krō-'shā\ *noun* [French, hook, crochet, from Middle French, diminutive of *croche* hook, of Scandinavian origin; akin to Old Norse *krōkr* hook] (1846)
: needlework consisting of the interlocking of looped stitches formed with a single thread and a hooked needle
²crochet (1858)
transitive verb
: to make of crochet ⟨*crocheted* a doily⟩
intransitive verb
: to work with crochet
— **cro·chet·er** \-'shā-ər\ *noun*
cro·cid·o·lite \krō-'si-dᵊl-ˌīt\ *noun* [German *Krokydolith*, from Greek *krokyd-, krokys* nap

on cloth (akin to Greek *krekein* to weave) + German *-lith* -lite — more at REEL] (1835)
: a lavender-blue or light green mineral of the amphibole group that occurs in silky fibers and in massive form and is a type of asbestos — compare TIGEREYE
¹crock \'kräk\ *noun* [Middle English, from Old English *crocc*; akin to Middle High German *krūche* crock] (before 12th century)
1 : a thick earthenware pot or jar
2 [from its formation on cooking pots] *dialect* : SOOT, SMUT
3 : coloring matter that rubs off from cloth or dyed leather
4 : BUNKUM — usually used with *a*
²crock (1594)
transitive verb
1 : to put or preserve in a crock
2 *dialect* : to soil with crock : SMUDGE
intransitive verb
: to transfer color (as when rubbed or washed) ⟨a suede that will not *crock*⟩
³crock *noun* [Middle English *crok*, probably of Scandinavian origin; akin to Norwegian dialect *krokje* crock] (1528)
1 : one that is broken-down, disabled, or impaired
2 : a complaining medical patient whose illness is largely imaginary or psychosomatic
⁴crock (1896)
transitive verb
: to cause to become disabled
intransitive verb
: BREAK DOWN
crocked \'kräkt\ *adjective* (circa 1927)
: DRUNK
crock·ery \'krä-k(ə-)rē\ *noun* (circa 1755)
: EARTHENWARE
crock·et \'krä-kət\ *noun* [Middle English *croket*, from Old North French *croquet* crook, diminutive of *croc* hook, of Scandinavian origin; akin to Old Norse *krōkr* hook] (1673)
: an ornament usually in the form of curved and bent foliage used on the edge of a gable or spire
— **crock·et·ed** \-kə-təd\ *adjective*
Crock–Pot \'kräk-ˌpät\ *trademark*
— used for an electric cooking pot
croc·o·dile \'krä-kə-ˌdīl\ *noun* [Middle English & Latin; Middle English *cocodrille*, from Middle French, from Medieval Latin *cocodrillus*, alteration of Latin *crocodilus*, from Greek *krokodilos* lizard, crocodile, from *krokē* shingle, pebble + *drilos* worm; akin to Sanskrit *śarkara* pebble] (1684)

crocodile 1a

1 a : any of several large carnivorous thick-skinned long-bodied aquatic reptiles (family Crocodilidae) of tropical and subtropical waters; *broadly* : CROCODILIAN **b** : the skin or hide of a crocodile
2 *chiefly British* : a line of people (as schoolchildren) usually walking in pairs
crocodile bird *noun* (1868)
: an African bird (*Pluvianus aegyptius*) that is related to the pratincoles and lights on the crocodile and eats its insect parasites
crocodile tears *noun plural* (1563)
: false or affected tears; *also* : hypocritical sorrow
croc·o·dil·ian \ˌkrä-kə-'di-lē-ən, -'dil-yən\ *noun* (1837)
: any of an order (Crocodylia) of reptiles including the crocodiles, alligators, caimans, gavials, and related extinct forms
— **crocodilian** *adjective*
cro·cus \'krō-kəs\ *noun, plural* **cro·cus·es** [Middle English, the saffron plant, from Latin, from Greek *krokos*, of Semitic origin; akin to Akkadian *kurkānū* saffron] (14th century)
1 a *plural also* **crocus** *or* **cro·ci** \-ˌkē, -ˌkī, -ˌsī\ : any of a large genus (*Crocus*) of herbs

of the iris family developing from corms and having solitary long-tubed flowers and slender linear leaves **b** : SAFFRON 1a
2 : a dark red ferric oxide used for polishing metals
Croe·sus \'krē-səs\ *noun* [*Croesus,* king of Lydia, famed for his wealth] (1650)
: a very rich man
croft \'kröft\ *noun* [Middle English, from Old English; akin to Middle Dutch *krocht* hill] (before 12th century)
1 *chiefly British* : a small enclosed field usually adjoining a house
2 *chiefly British* : a small farm worked by a tenant
— **croft·er** \'kröf-tər\ *noun, chiefly British*
crois·sant \krə-'sänt, krə-; krwä-'säⁿ\ *noun, plural* **croissants** \-'sänt(s), -'säⁿ(z)\ [French, literally, crescent, from Middle French *creissant*] (1899)
: a flaky rich crescent-shaped roll
Croix de Guerre \ˌkrwä-di-'ger\ *noun* [French, literally, war cross] (1915)
: a French military decoration awarded for gallant action in war
cro·ker sack \'krō-kər-\ *noun* [alteration of *crocus sack, crocus bag,* of unknown origin] (1895)
chiefly Southern : a sack of a coarse material (as burlap)
Cro–Ma·gnon \krō-'mag-nən, -'man-yən\ *noun* [*Cro-Magnon,* a cave near Les Eyzies, France] (1869)
: a tall erect race of hominids of the Upper Paleolithic known from skeletal remains found chiefly in southern France and classified as the same species (*Homo sapiens*) as present day humans
crom·lech \'kräm-ˌlek\ *noun* [Welsh, literally, bent stone] (1695)
1 : DOLMEN
2 : a circle of monoliths usually enclosing a dolmen or mound
crone \'krōn\ *noun* [Middle English, from Old North French *carogne,* literally, carrion, from (assumed) Vulgar Latin *caronia* — more at CARRION] (14th century)
: a withered old woman
Cro·nus \'krō-nəs, 'krä-\ *noun* [Latin, from Greek *Kronos*]
: a Titan dethroned by his son Zeus
cro·ny \'krō-nē\ *noun, plural* **cronies** [perhaps from Greek *chronios* long-lasting, from *chronos* time] (1663)
: a close friend especially of long standing : PAL
cro·ny·ism \-nē-ˌi-zəm\ *noun* (1840)

\ə\ abut \ᵊ\ kitten \ər\ further \a\ ash \ā\ ace
\ä\ mop, mar \au̇\ out \ch\ chin \e\ bet \ē\ easy
\g\ go \i\ hit \ī\ ice \j\ job \ŋ\ sing \ō\ go
\ȯ\ law \ȯi\ boy \th\ thin \t͟h\ the \ü\ loot \u̇\ foot
\y\ yet \zh\ vision *see also* Guide to Pronunciation

: partiality to cronies especially as evidenced in the appointment of political hangers-on to office without regard to their qualifications

¹**crook** \'krùk\ (12th century)
transitive verb
: BEND
intransitive verb
: CURVE, WIND

²**crook** *noun* [Middle English *crok,* from Old Norse *krōkr* hook] (13th century)
1 : an implement having a bent or hooked form: as **a** : POTHOOK **b** (1) : a shepherd's staff (2) : CROSIER 1
2 : a part of something that is hook-shaped, curved, or bent ⟨the *crook* of an umbrella handle⟩
3 : BEND, CURVE
4 : a person who engages in fraudulent or criminal practices

³**crook** *adjective* [probably short for *crooked*] (1898)
Australian & New Zealand : not right: **a** : UNSATISFACTORY **b** : DISHONEST, CROOKED **c** : IRRITABLE, ANGRY — used especially in the phrase *go crook* **d** : ILL, UNWELL

crook·back \'krùk-,bak\ *noun* (1508)
1 *obsolete* : a crooked back
2 *obsolete* : HUNCHBACK
— **crook·backed** \-'bakt\ *adjective*

crook·ed \'krù-kəd\ *adjective* (13th century)
1 : not straight ⟨a *crooked* road⟩ ⟨your tie is *crooked*⟩
2 : DISHONEST ⟨a *crooked* election⟩ ⟨*crooked* politicians⟩
— **crook·ed·ly** *adverb*
— **crook·ed·ness** *noun*

crook·ery \'krù-kə-rē\ *noun* (1927)
: crooked dealings or practices

crook·neck \'krùk-,nek\ *noun* (1784)
: a squash with a long recurved neck

croon \'krün\ *verb* [Middle English *croynen,* from Middle Dutch *cronen;* akin to Old High German *crōnen* to chatter] (15th century)
intransitive verb
1 *chiefly Scottish* : BELLOW, BOOM
2 : to sing or speak in a gentle murmuring manner; *especially* : to sing in a soft intimate manner adapted to amplifying systems
transitive verb
: to sing (as a popular song or a lullaby) in a crooning manner
— **croon** *noun*

croon·er \'krü-nər\ *noun* (1930)
: one that croons; *especially* : a singer of popular songs

¹**crop** \'kräp\ *noun* [Middle English, craw, head of a plant, yield of a field, from Old English *cropp* craw, head of a plant; akin to Old High German *kropf* goiter, craw] (before 12th century)
1 : a pouched enlargement of the gullet of many birds that serves as a receptacle for food and for its preliminary maceration; *also* : an enlargement of the gullet of another animal (as an insect)
2 a (1) : a plant or animal or plant or animal product that can be grown and harvested extensively for profit or subsistence ⟨an apple *crop*⟩ ⟨a *crop* of wool⟩ (2) : the total yearly production from a specified area **b** : the product or yield of something formed together ⟨the ice *crop*⟩ **c** : a batch or lot of something produced during a particular cycle ⟨the current *crop* of films⟩ **d** : COLLECTION ⟨a *crop* of lies⟩
3 : the stock or handle of a whip; *also* : a riding whip with a short straight stock and a loop
4 [²*crop*] **a** : the part of the chine of a quadruped (as a domestic cow) lying immediately behind the withers — usually used in plural; see COW illustration **b** : an earmark on an animal; *especially* : one made by a straight cut squarely removing the upper part of the ear **c** : a close cut of the hair

²**crop** *verb* **cropped; crop·ping** (13th century)

transitive verb
1 a : to remove the upper or outer parts of ⟨*crop* a hedge⟩ ⟨*crop* a dog's ears⟩ **b** : HARVEST ⟨*crop* trout⟩ **c** : to cut off short : TRIM ⟨*crop* a photograph⟩
2 : to cause (land) to bear a crop ⟨will *crop* another 40 acres⟩; *also* : to grow as a crop
intransitive verb
1 : to feed by cropping something
2 : to yield or make a crop
3 : to appear unexpectedly or casually ⟨problems *crop* up daily⟩

crop duster *noun* (1939)
: a person who sprays crops with fungicidal or insecticidal dusts from an airplane; *also* : the airplane used for such spraying

crop–eared \'kräp-,ird\ *adjective* (1530)
: having the ears cropped

crop·land \-,land\ *noun* (1846)
: land that is suited to or used for crops

¹**crop·per** \'krä-pər\ *noun* (15th century)
1 : one that crops
2 : one that raises crops; *specifically* : SHARECROPPER

²**cropper** *noun* [probably from English dialect *crop* neck, from ¹*crop*] (1858)
1 : a severe fall
2 : a sudden or violent failure or collapse

crop rotation *noun* (1909)
: the practice of growing different crops in succession on the same land chiefly to preserve the productive capacity of the soil

cro·quet \krō-'kā\ *noun* [French dialect, hockey stick, from Old North French, crook — more at CROCKET] (1858)
1 : a game in which players using mallets drive wooden balls through a series of wickets set out on a lawn
2 : the act of driving away an opponent's croquet ball by striking one's own ball placed against it
— **croquet** *transitive verb*

cro·quette \krō-'ket\ *noun* [French, from *croquer* to crunch, of imitative origin] (1706)
: a small often rounded mass consisting usually of minced meat, fish, or vegetable coated with egg and bread crumbs and deep-fried

cro·qui·gnole \'krō-kə-,nōl *also* -kən-,yōl\ *noun* [French, light blow, fillip] (1932)
: a method used in waving the hair by winding it on curlers from the ends of the hair toward the scalp

cro·quis \krō-'kē\ *noun, plural* **cro·quis** \-'kē(z)\ [French, from *croquer* to sketch, rough out, literally, to crunch] (1805)
: a rough draft : SKETCH

crore \'krōr, 'ròr\ *noun, plural* **crores** *also* **crore** [Hindi *karoṛ*] (1609)
: a unit of value equal to ten million rupees or 100 lakhs

cro·sier \'krō-zhər\ *noun* [Middle English *crocer* crosier bearer, from Middle French *crossier,* from *crosse* crosier, of Germanic origin; akin to Old English *crycc* crutch — more at CRUTCH] (1500)
1 : a staff resembling a shepherd's crook carried by bishops and abbots as a symbol of office
2 : a plant structure with a coiled end

¹**cross** \'kròs\ *noun* [Middle English, from Old English, from Old Norse or Old Irish; Old Norse *kross,* from Old Irish *cros,* from Latin *cruc-, crux*] (before 12th century)
1 a : a structure consisting of an upright with a transverse beam used especially by the ancient Romans for execution **b** *often capitalized* : the cross on which Jesus was crucified
2 a : CRUCIFIXION **b** : an affliction that tries one's virtue, steadfastness, or patience
3 : a cruciform sign made to invoke the blessing of Christ especially by touching the forehead, breast, and shoulders
4 a : a device composed of an upright bar traversed by a horizontal one; *specifically* : one used as a Christian symbol **b** *capitalized* : the Christian religion

5 : a structure (as a monument) shaped like or surmounted by a cross
6 : a figure or mark formed by two intersecting lines crossing at their midpoints; *specifically* : such a mark used as a signature
7 : a cruciform badge, emblem, or decoration
8 : the intersection of two ways or lines : CROSSING
9 : ANNOYANCE, THWARTING ⟨a *cross* in love⟩
10 a : an act of crossing dissimilar individuals **b** : a crossbred individual or kind **c** : one that combines characteristics of two different types or individuals
11 a : a fraudulent or dishonest contest **b** : dishonest or illegal practices — used especially in the phrase *on the cross*
12 : a movement from one part of a theater stage to another
13 : a hook thrown over the opponent's lead in boxing
14 : a security transaction in which a broker acts for both buyer and seller (as in the placing of a large lot of common stock) — called also *cross-trade*

cross 4a: *1* Latin, *2* Calvary, *3* patriarchal, *4* papal, *5* Lorraine, *6* Greek, *7* Celtic, *8* Maltese, *9* Saint Andrew's, *10* tau, *11* pommée, *12* botonée, *13* fleury, *14* avellan, *15* moline, *16* formée, *17* fourchée, *18* crosslet, *19* quadrate, *20* potent

²**cross** (14th century)
transitive verb
1 a : to lie or be situated across **b** : INTERSECT
2 : to make the sign of the cross upon or over
3 : to cancel by marking a cross on or drawing a line through : strike out ⟨*cross* names off a list⟩
4 : to place or fold crosswise one over the other ⟨*cross* the arms⟩
5 a (1) : to run counter to : OPPOSE (2) : to deny the validity of : CONTRADICT **b** : to confront in a troublesome manner : OBSTRUCT (1) : to spoil completely : DISRUPT — used with *up* ⟨his failure to appear *crossed* up the whole program⟩ (2) : to turn against : BETRAY ⟨*crossed* me up on the deal⟩
6 a : to extend across or over : TRAVERSE ⟨a highway *crossing* the entire state⟩ **b** : REACH, ATTAIN ⟨only two *crossed* the finish line⟩ **c** : to go from one side of to the other ⟨*cross* a street⟩ ⟨*crosses* racial barriers⟩
7 a : to draw a line across **b** : to mark or figure with lines : STREAK
8 : to cause (an animal or plant) to interbreed with one of a different kind : HYBRIDIZE
9 : to meet and pass on the way ⟨our letters must have *crossed* each other⟩
10 : to occur to ⟨it never *crossed* my mind⟩
11 : to carry or take across something ⟨*crossed* the children at the intersection⟩
intransitive verb

1 a : to move, pass, or extend across something ⟨*crossed* through France⟩ ⟨*crossed* over to the other side of the river⟩ **b :** to move or pass from one character, condition, or allegiance to another — used with *over* **2 :** to lie or be athwart each other **3 :** to meet in passing especially from opposite directions **4 :** INTERBREED, HYBRIDIZE — **cross·er** *noun* — **cross swords :** to engage in a dispute

³**cross** *adjective* (14th century) **1 a :** lying across or athwart **b :** moving across ⟨*cross* traffic⟩ **2 a :** running counter : OPPOSITE **b :** mutually opposed ⟨*cross* purposes⟩ **3 :** involving mutual interchange : RECIPROCAL **4 :** marked by typically transitory bad temper **5 :** extending over or treating several groups or classes ⟨a *cross* sample from 25 colleges⟩ **6 :** CROSSBRED, HYBRID — **cross·ly** *adverb* — **cross·ness** *noun*

⁴**cross** *preposition* (1551) **:** ACROSS

⁵**cross** *adverb* (1577) **:** not parallel : CRISSCROSS, CROSSWISE

cross·abil·i·ty \ˌkrȯ-sə-'bi-lə-tē\ *noun* (1916) **:** the ability of different species or varieties to cross with each other

cross·able \'krȯ-sə-bəl\ *adjective* (1865) **:** capable of being crossed

cross action *noun* (circa 1859) **:** a legal action in which the defendant in an existing action files a suit against the plaintiff on the same subject matter : COUNTERSUIT

cross·band·ing \'krȯs-ˌban-diŋ\ *noun* (1904) **:** a veneer border (as on furniture) with its grain at right angles to the grain of the adjacent wood — **cross·band·ed** \-ˌban-dəd\ *adjective*

cross·bar \'krȯs-ˌbär\ *noun* (1562) **:** a transverse bar or stripe

cross·bear·er \'krȯs-ˌbar-ər, -ˌber-\ *noun* (1568) **:** CRUCIFER 1

cross·bill \-ˌbil\ *noun* (circa 1672) **:** any of a small genus (*Loxia*) of finches with strongly curved mandibles that cross each other

cross·bones \-ˌbōnz\ *noun plural* (1798) **:** two leg or arm bones placed or depicted crosswise — compare SKULL AND CROSSBONES

cross·bow \-ˌbō\ *noun* (15th century) **:** a weapon for discharging quarrels and stones that consists chiefly of a short bow mounted crosswise near the end of a stock

crossbow

cross·bow·man \-mən\ *noun* (circa 1500) **:** a person (as a soldier or a hunter) whose weapon is a crossbow

cross·bred \'krȯs-'bred\ *adjective* (1856) **:** produced by crossbreeding : HYBRID — **cross·bred** \-ˌbred\ *noun*

¹**cross·breed** \'krȯs-ˌbrēd, -'brēd\ *verb* **-bred** \-ˌbred, -'bred\; **-breed·ing** (1675) *transitive verb* **:** HYBRIDIZE, CROSS; *especially* **:** to cross (two varieties or breeds) within the same species *intransitive verb* **:** to engage in or undergo hybridization

²**cross·breed** \-ˌbrēd\ *noun* (1774) **:** HYBRID

¹**cross–check** \-ˌchek\ *transitive verb* (circa 1930) **1 :** to obstruct in ice hockey or lacrosse by thrusting one's stick held in both hands across an opponent's face or body

2 : to check (as data or reports) from various angles or sources to determine validity or accuracy

²**cross–check** *noun* (1937) **:** an act or instance of cross-checking

cross–claim \-ˌklām\ *noun* (1952) **:** a claim against a party on the same side of a legal action

¹**cross–coun·try** \'krȯs-'kən-trē, -ˌkən-\ *adjective* (1767) **1 :** extending or moving across a country ⟨a *cross-country* concert tour⟩ **2 :** proceeding over countryside (as across fields and through woods) and not by roads **3 :** of or relating to racing or skiing over the countryside instead of over a track or run — **cross–country** *adverb*

²**cross–country** *noun* (1925) **:** cross-country racing or skiing

cross·court \'krȯs-'kȯrt, -'kȯrt\ *adverb or adjective* (1915) **:** to or toward the opposite side of a court (as in tennis or basketball)

cross–cul·tur·al \'krȯs-'kəlch-rəl, -'kəl-chə-\ *adjective* (circa 1942) **:** dealing with or offering comparison between two or more different cultures or cultural areas — **cross–cul·tur·al·ly** \-rə-lē\ *adverb*

cross·cur·rent \'krȯs-ˌkər-ənt, -ˌkə-rənt\ *noun* (1598) **1 :** a current running counter to the general forward direction **2 :** a conflicting tendency — usually used in plural ⟨political *crosscurrents*⟩

¹**cross–cut** \'krȯs-ˌkət, -'kət\ *transitive verb* (1590) **1 :** to cut, go, or move across or through **2 :** to cut with a crosscut saw **3 :** to subject (as movie scenes) to crosscutting

²**crosscut** *adjective* (1645) **1 :** made or used for cutting transversely ⟨a saw with *crosscut* teeth⟩ **2 :** cut across or transversely ⟨a *crosscut* incision⟩

³**cross–cut** \'krȯs-ˌkət\ *noun* (1789) **1 :** something that cuts across or through; *specifically* **:** a mine working driven horizontally and at right angles to an adit, drift, or level **2 :** CROSS SECTION **3 :** CROSSCUT SAW **4 :** an instance of crosscutting (as in a movie)

crosscut saw *noun* (1645) **:** a saw designed chiefly to cut across the grain of wood — compare RIPSAW

cross–cut·ting \'krȯs-ˌkə-tiŋ\ *noun* (1930) **:** a technique especially in filmmaking of interweaving bits of two or more separate scenes

cross–dress·ing \'krȯs-ˌdre-siŋ\ *noun* (1911) **:** the wearing of clothes designed for the opposite sex — **cross–dress** *intransitive verb* — **cross–dress·er** *noun*

crosse \'krȯs\ *noun* [French, literally, crosier — more at CROSIER] (1867) **:** a stick with a small net at one end that is used in lacrosse

cross–ex·am·i·na·tion \'krȯs-ig-ˌza-mə-'nā-shən\ *noun* (1824) **:** the examination of a witness who has already testified in order to check or discredit the witness's testimony, knowledge, or credibility — compare DIRECT EXAMINATION — **cross–ex·am·ine** \-ig-'za-mən\ *transitive verb* — **cross–ex·am·in·er** \-'zam-nər, -'za-mə-\ *noun*

cross–eye \'krȯ-ˌsī\ *noun* (1826) **1 :** strabismus in which the eye turns inward toward the nose **2** *plural* **:** eyes affected with cross-eye — **cross–eyed** \-ˌsīd\ *adjective*

cross–fer·tile \'krȯs-'fər-t°l, -ˌfər-\ *adjective* (1929) **:** fertile in a cross or capable of cross-fertilization

cross–fer·til·i·za·tion \-ˌfər-t°l-ə-'zā-shən\ *noun* (1876) **1 a :** fertilization in which the gametes are produced by separate individuals or sometimes by individuals of different kinds **b :** CROSS-POLLINATION **2 :** interchange or interaction (as between different ideas, cultures, or categories) especially of a broadening or productive nature

cross–fer·til·ize \-'fər-t°l-ˌīz\ (1876) *transitive verb* **:** to accomplish cross-fertilization of *intransitive verb* **:** to undergo cross-fertilization

cross–file \-'fī(ə)l\ (1949) *intransitive verb* **:** to register as a candidate in the primary elections of more than one political party *transitive verb* **:** to register (a person) as a candidate for more than one party

cross fire *noun* (circa 1859) **1 a :** firing (as in combat) from two or more points so that the lines of fire cross **b :** a situation wherein the forces of opposing factions meet, cross, or clash ⟨caught in a political *cross fire*⟩ **2 :** rapid or heated exchange of words

cross–grained \'krȯs-ˌgrānd\ *adjective* (1647) **1 :** difficult to deal with **2 :** having the grain or fibers running diagonally, transversely, or irregularly

cross–hair \-ˌhar, -ˌher\ *noun* (circa 1884) **:** a fine wire or thread in the focus of the eyepiece of an optical instrument used as a reference line in the field or for marking the instrumental axis

cross·hatch \'krȯs-ˌhach\ *transitive verb* (1822) **:** to mark with two series of parallel lines that intersect — **crosshatch** *noun* — **cross–hatch·ing** *noun*

cross–head \-ˌhed\ *noun* (1827) **1 :** a metal block to which one end of a piston rod is secured **2 :** a heading centered usually between portions of text

cross–in·dex \'krȯs-'in-ˌdeks\ *transitive verb* (1892) **1 :** to index (an item) under a second or under more than one heading **2 :** to supply (as a book) with a cross-referenced index — **cross–index** *noun*

cross·ing \'krȯ-siŋ\ *noun* (1575) **1 :** the act or action of crossing: as **a :** a traversing or traveling across **b :** an opposing, blocking, or thwarting especially in an unfair or dishonest manner **2 a :** a place or structure (as on a street or over a river) where pedestrians or vehicles cross; *especially* **:** CROSSWALK **b :** the place in a cruciform church where the transept crosses the nave **c :** a place where a railroad track crosses a street

cross·ing–over \ˌkrȯ-siŋ-'ō-vər\ *noun* (1912) **:** an interchange of genes or segments between homologous chromosomes

cross–legged \'krȯs-ˌle-gəd, -ˌlā-; -ˌlegd, -ˌlāgd\ *adverb or adjective* (circa 1530) **1 :** with legs crossed and knees spread wide apart **2 :** with one leg placed over and across the other

cross·let \'krȯs-lət\ *noun* (15th century) **:** a small cross usually with crossed arms; *especially* **:** one used as a heraldic bearing — see CROSS illustration

cross·lin·guis·tic \-liŋ-'gwis-tik\ *adjective* (1954)
: of or relating to languages of different families and types; *especially* : relating to the comparison of different languages
— **cross·lin·guis·ti·cal·ly** \-ti-k(ə-)lē\ *adverb*

cross–link \'kròs-,liŋk\ *noun* (1936)
: a crosswise connecting part (as an atom or group) that connects parallel chains in a complex chemical molecule (as a polymer)
— **cross–link** *verb*

cross–link·age \'kròs-'liŋ-kij\ *noun* (1937)
: the process of forming cross-links; *also* : CROSS-LINK

cross multiply *intransitive verb* (1951)
: to find the two products obtained by multiplying the numerator of each of two fractions by the denominator of the other
— **cross multiplication** *noun*

cross–na·tion·al \'kròs-'nash-nəl, -'na-shə-nʰl\ *adjective* (1965)
: of or relating to two or more nations

cross of Lor·raine \-lə-'rān, -lò-\ [*Lorraine*, France] (circa 1889)
: a cross with two crossbars the lower one of which is longer than the upper one — see CROSS illustration

cross·sop·ter·yg·ian \,krò-,säp-tə-'ri-j(ē-)ən\ *noun* [New Latin *Crossopterygii*, subclass name, from Greek *krossoi* fringe + *pterygion*, diminutive of *pteryg-*, *pteryx* wing; akin to Greek *pteron* wing — more at FEATHER] (1861)
: any of a subclass (Crossopterygii) of fishes (as a coelacanth) that have paired fins suggesting limbs, that may be ancestral to the terrestrial vertebrates, and that are mostly extinct — called also *lobe-fin*
— **crossopterygian** *adjective*

¹cross·over \'kròs-,ō-vər\ *noun* (1884)
1 : CROSSING 2a
2 : an instance or product of genetic crossing-over
3 : a voter registered as a member of one political party who votes in the primary of the other party
4 : a broadening of the popular appeal of an artist (as a musician) or an artist's work that is often the result of a change of the artist's medium or style; *also* : an artist or artistic work that has achieved a crossover
5 : an instance of breaking into another category ⟨trying to make the *crossover* to serious acting —Michael Neill⟩

²crossover *adjective* (1893)
1 : having two pieces that cross especially one over the other ⟨a *crossover* vest⟩
2 : CRITICAL 1 ⟨the *crossover* point⟩

cross–own·er·ship \-'ō-nər-,ship\ *noun* (1969)
: single ownership of two or more related businesses (as a newspaper and a television station) that allows the owner to control competition

cross·patch \'kròs-,pach\ *noun* [³*cross* + ³*patch*] (circa 1700)
: GROUCH 2

cross·piece \'kròs-,pēs\ *noun* (1607)
: a horizontal member (as of a structure)

cross·pol·li·nate \'kròs-'pä-lə-,nāt\ *transitive verb* (circa 1900)
: to subject to cross-pollination

cross–pol·li·na·tion \,kròs-,pä-lə-'nā-shən\ *noun* (1882)
1 : the transfer of pollen from one flower to the stigma of another
2 : CROSS-FERTILIZATION 2

cross product *noun* (1929)
1 : VECTOR PRODUCT
2 : either of the two products obtained by multiplying the two means or the two extremes of a proportion

cross–pur·pose \'kròs-'pər-pəs\ *noun* (1681)
: a purpose usually unintentionally contrary to another purpose of oneself or of someone or something else — usually used in plural ⟨the two were always working at *cross-purposes*⟩

cross–ques·tion \'kròs-'kwes-chən, -'kwesh-\ *noun* (circa 1694)
: a question asked in cross-examination
— **cross–question** *transitive verb*

cross–re·ac·tion \,kròs-rē-'ak-shən\ *noun* (1946)
: reaction of one antigen with antibodies developed against another antigen
— **cross–re·act** \-rē-'akt\ *intransitive verb*
— **cross–re·ac·tive** \-'ak-tiv\ *adjective*
— **cross–re·ac·tiv·i·ty** \-(,)rē-,ak-'ti-və-tē\ *noun*

cross–re·fer \,kròs-ri-'fər\ (1879)
transitive verb
: to refer (a reader) by a notation or direction from one place to another (as in a book, list, or catalog)
intransitive verb
: to make a cross-reference

¹cross–ref·er·ence \'kròs-'re-fərn(t)s, -'re-f(ə-)rən(t)s\ *noun* (1834)
: a notation or direction at one place (as in a book or filing system) to pertinent information at another place

²cross–reference *transitive verb* (1902)
: to supply with cross-references

cross–re·sis·tance \,kròs-ri-'zis-tən(t)s\ *noun* (1946)
: tolerance (as of an insect population) to a normally toxic substance (as an insecticide) that is acquired not as a result of direct exposure but by exposure to a related substance

cross·road \'kròs-,rōd *also* -'rōd\ *noun* (1719)
1 : a road that crosses a main road or runs cross-country between main roads
2 *usually plural but singular or plural in construction* **a** : the place of intersection of two or more roads **b** (1) : a small community located at such a crossroads (2) : a central meeting place **c** : a crucial point especially where a decision must be made

cross–ruff \'kròs-,rəf, -'rəf\ *noun* (1862)
: a series of plays in a card game (as bridge) in which partners alternately trump different suits and lead to each other for that purpose
— **crossruff** *verb*

cross section *noun* (1835)
1 a : a cutting or piece of something cut off at right angles to an axis; *also* : a representation of such a cutting **b** : SECTION 3b
2 : a measure of the probability of an encounter between particles such as will result in a specified effect (as scattering or capture)
3 : a composite representation typifying the constituents of a thing in their relations
— **cross–section** *transitive verb*
— **cross–sec·tion·al** \'kròs-'sek-shnəl, -shə-nʰl\ *adjective*

cross–stitch \'kró(s)-,stich\ *noun* (circa 1710)
1 : a needlework stitch that forms an X
2 : work having cross-stitch
— **cross–stitch** *verb*

cross talk *noun* (1887)
: unwanted signals in a communication channel (as in a telephone, radio, or computer) caused by transference of energy from another circuit (as by leakage or coupling)

cross–tol·er·ance \'kròs-'täl-rən(t)s, -'tä-lə-\ *noun* (circa 1923)
: tolerance or resistance to a drug that develops through continued use of another drug with similar pharmacological action

cross·town \'kròs-'taùn\ *adjective* (1886)
1 : situated at opposite points of a town
2 : extending or running across a town ⟨a *crosstown* street⟩ ⟨a *crosstown* bus⟩

cross–trade \'kròs-,trād\ *noun* (circa 1923)
: CROSS 14

cross·trees \-(,)trēz\ *noun plural* (1626)
: two horizontal crosspieces of timber or metal supported by trestletrees at a masthead that spread the upper shrouds in order to support the mast

cross vault *noun* (1850)
: a vault formed by the intersection of two or more simple vaults — called also *cross vaulting*

cross·walk \'kròs-,wòk\ *noun* (1744)
: a specially paved or marked path for pedestrians crossing a street or road

cross·way \-,wā\ *noun* (14th century)
: CROSSROAD — often used in plural

cross·ways \-,wāz\ *adverb* (1564)
: CROSSWISE, DIAGONALLY

cross·wind \-,wind\ *noun* (1677)
: a wind blowing in a direction not parallel to a course (as of an airplane)

¹cross·wise \-,wīz\ *adverb* (14th century)
1 *archaic* : in the form of a cross
2 : so as to cross something : ACROSS ⟨logs laid *crosswise*⟩

²crosswise *adjective* (1903)
: TRANSVERSE, CROSSING

cross·word \'kròs-,wərd\ *noun* (1914)
: a puzzle in which words are filled into a pattern of numbered squares in answer to correspondingly numbered clues and in such a way that the words read across and down

crotch \'kräch\ *noun* [probably alteration of ¹*crutch*] (1573)
1 : a pole with a forked end used especially as a prop
2 : an angle formed by the parting of two legs, branches, or members
— **crotched** \'krächt\ *adjective*

crotch·et \'krä-chət\ *noun* [Middle English *crochet*, from Middle French — more at CROCHET] (14th century)
1 *obsolete* **a** : a small hook or hooked instrument **b** : BROOCH
2 a : a highly individual and usually eccentric opinion or preference **b** : a peculiar trick or device
3 : QUARTER NOTE
synonym see CAPRICE

crotch·ety \'krä-chə-tē\ *adjective* (1825)
1 : given to crotchets : subject to whims, crankiness, or ill temper ⟨a *crotchety* old man⟩
2 : full of or arising from crotchets
— **crotch·et·i·ness** \-tē-nəs\ *noun*

cro·ton \'krō-tʰn\ *noun* [New Latin, genus name, from Greek *krotōn* castor-oil plant] (1751)
1 : any of a genus (*Croton*) of herbs, shrubs, and trees of the spurge family: as **a** : one (*C. eluteria*) of the Bahamas yielding cascarilla bark **b** : an Asian plant (*C. tiglium*) yielding croton oil
2 : any of a genus (*Codiaeum*) of shrubs and trees related to the crotons

Cro·ton bug \'krō-tʰn-\ *noun* [*Croton* River, N.Y., used as a water supply for New York City] (1877)
: GERMAN COCKROACH

croton oil *noun* (circa 1831)
: a viscid acrid fixed oil from an Asian croton (*Croton tiglium*) formerly used as a drastic cathartic but now used especially in pharmacological experiments as an irritant

crouch \'kraùch\ *verb* [Middle English] (14th century)
intransitive verb
1 a : to lower the body stance especially by bending the legs ⟨a sprinter *crouched* ready to go⟩ **b** : to lie close to the ground with the legs bent ⟨a pair of cats, *crouching* on the brink of a fight —Aldous Huxley⟩
2 : to bend or bow servilely : CRINGE
transitive verb
: to bow submissively in humility or fear : BEND
— **crouch** *noun*

¹croup \'krüp\ *noun* [Middle English *croupe*, from Old French, of Germanic origin; akin to Old High German *kropf* craw — more at CROP] (14th century)
: the rump of a quadruped

²croup *noun* [English dialect *croup* to cry hoarsely, cough, probably of imitative origin] (1765)

: a spasmodic laryngitis especially of infants marked by episodes of difficult breathing and hoarse metallic cough
— **croup·ous** \'krü-pəs\ *adjective*
— **croupy** \-pē\ *adjective*

crou·pi·er \'krü-pē-ər, -pē-,ā\ *noun* [French, literally, rider on the croup of a horse, from *croupe* croup] (1709)
: an employee of a gambling casino who collects and pays bets and assists at the gaming tables

crouse \'krüs\ *adjective* [Middle English] (15th century)
chiefly Scottish : BRISK, LIVELY

crous·tade \krü-'städ\ *noun* [French, probably from Italian *crostata* tart, from *crosta* pastry shell, crust, from Latin *crusta* — more at CRUST] (circa 1845)
: a crisp shell (as of toast or puff pastry) in which to serve food

crou·ton \'krü-,tän, krü-'\ *noun* [French *croûton*, diminutive of *croûte* crust, from Middle French *crouste*, from Old French, from Latin *crusta*] (1806)
: a small cube of toasted or crisply fried bread

¹crow \'krō\ *noun* [Middle English *crowe*, from Old English *crāwe*; akin to Old High German *krāwa* crow, Old English *crāwan* to crow] (before 12th century)
1 : any of various large usually entirely glossy black passerine birds (family Corvidae and especially genus *Corvus*)
2 *capitalized* **a** : a member of an American Indian people of the region between the Platte and Yellowstone rivers **b** : the language of the Crow people
3 *capitalized* : CORVUS
— **as the crow flies** : in a straight line

²crow *verb* **crowed** \'krōd\ *also in sense 1 chiefly British* **crew** \'krü\; **crow·ing** [Middle English, from Old English *crāwan*] (before 12th century)
intransitive verb
1 : to make the loud shrill sound characteristic of a cock
2 : to utter a sound expressive of pleasure
3 a : to exult gloatingly especially over the distress of another **b** : to brag exultantly or blatantly
transitive verb
: to say with self-satisfaction
synonym see BOAST

³crow *noun* (13th century)
1 : the cry of the cock
2 : a triumphant cry

crow·bar \'krō-,bär\ *noun* (1748)
: an iron or steel bar that is usually wedge-shaped at the working end for use as a pry or lever
— **crowbar** *transitive verb*

crow·ber·ry \'krō-,ber-ē\ *noun* (1597)
1 : an evergreen subshrub (*Empetrum nigrum* of the family Empetraceae) of arctic and alpine regions with an insipid black berry
2 : the fruit of a crowberry

¹crowd \'kraüd\ *verb* [Middle English *crouden*, from Old English *crūdan*; akin to Middle High German *kroten* to crowd, Old English *crod* multitude, Middle Irish *gruth* curds] (before 12th century)
intransitive verb
1 a : to press on : HURRY **b** : to press close
2 : to collect in numbers
transitive verb
1 a : to fill by pressing or thronging together **b** : to press, force, or thrust into a small space
2 : PUSH, FORCE — often used with *off* or *out*
3 a : to urge on **b** : to put on (sail) in excess of the usual for greater speed
4 : to put pressure on ⟨don't *crowd* me, I'll pay⟩
5 : THRONG, JOSTLE
6 : to press or stand close to

²crowd *noun* (1567)
1 : a large number of persons especially when collected together : THRONG

2 a : the great body of the people : POPULACE **b** : most of one's peers ⟨follow the *crowd*⟩
3 : a large number of things close together
4 : a group of people having something (as a habit, interest, or occupation) in common ⟨in with the wrong *crowd*⟩ ☆

³crowd \'kraüd, 'krüd\ *noun* [Middle English *crowde*, from Middle Welsh *crwth*] (14th century)
1 : an ancient Celtic stringed instrument that is plucked or bowed — called also *crwth*
2 *dialect English* : VIOLIN

crowd 1

crowd·ed·ness \'kraü-dəd-nəs\ *noun* (1823)
: the quality or state of being crowded

crow·die \'kraü-dē\ *noun* [alteration of *crud* curd] (1820)
: a Scottish cottage cheese that is partially cooked

crow·foot \'krō-,fút\ *noun, plural* **crow·feet** \-,fēt\ (14th century)
1 *plural usually* **crow·foots** : any of numerous plants having leaves with cleft lobes; *especially* : BUTTERCUP
2 : CROW'S-FOOT 1 — usually used in plural

crow·keep·er \'krō-,kē-pər\ *noun* (1562)
dialect English : a person employed to scare off crows

¹crown \'kraün\ *noun, often attributive* [Middle English *coroune, crowne*, from Old French *corone*, from Latin *corona* wreath, crown, from Greek *korōnē* culmination, something curved like a crow's beak, literally, crow; akin to Latin *cornix* crow, Greek *korax* raven — more at RAVEN] (12th century)
1 : a reward of victory or mark of honor; *especially* : the title representing the championship in a sport
2 : a royal or imperial headdress or cap of sovereignty : DIADEM
3 : the highest part: as **a** : the topmost part of the skull or head **b** : the summit of a mountain **c** : the head of foliage of a tree or shrub **d** : the part of a hat or other headgear covering the crown of the head **e** : the part of a tooth external to the gum or an artificial substitute for this — see TOOTH illustration
4 : a wreath, band, or circular ornament for the head
5 a : something resembling a wreath or crown **b** : the knurled cap on top of a watch stem
6 *often capitalized* **a** (1) : imperial or regal power : SOVEREIGNTY (2) : the government under a constitutional monarchy **b** : MONARCH
7 : something that imparts splendor, honor, or finish : CULMINATION
8 a : any of several old gold coins with a crown as part of the device **b** : an old usually silver British coin worth five shillings
9 a : KORUNA **b** : KRONA **c** : KRONE
10 a : the region of a seed plant at which stem and root merge **b** : the thick arching end of the shank of an anchor where the arms join it — see ANCHOR illustration
— **crowned** \'kraünd\ *adjective*
— **crown·less** \-ləs\ *adjective*

²crown *verb* [Middle English *corounen*, from Old French *coroner*, from Latin *coronare*, from *corona*] (12th century)
transitive verb
1 a : to place a crown or wreath on the head of; *specifically* : to invest with regal dignity and power **b** : to recognize officially as ⟨they *crowned* her athlete of the year⟩
2 : to bestow something on as a mark of honor or recompense : ADORN
3 : SURMOUNT, TOP; *especially* : to top (a checker) with a checker to make a king
4 : to bring to a successful conclusion : CLIMAX

5 : to provide with something like a crown: as **a** : to fill so that the surface forms a crown **b** : to put an artificial crown on (a tooth)
6 : to hit on the head
intransitive verb
of a forest fire : to burn rapidly through the tops of trees

crown colony *noun, often both Cs capitalized* (1845)
: a colony of the Commonwealth over which the Crown retains some control

crown court *noun* (1827)
: a court in England and Wales that exercises jurisdiction over matters formerly heard by the quarter sessions and criminal matters formerly heard by the courts of assize

crow·ner \'krü-nər, 'kraü-\ *noun* [Middle English, alteration of *coroner*] (14th century)
dialect chiefly English : CORONER

crown·et \'kraü-nət\ *noun* (15th century)
archaic : CORONET

crown gall *noun* (1900)
: a disease that affects many species of plants and is caused by a bacterium (*Agrobacterium tumefaciens*) which forms tumorous enlargements just below the ground on the stem

crown glass *noun* (1706)
1 : a glass blown and whirled into the form of a disk with a center lump left by the worker's rod
2 : alkali-lime silicate optical glass having relatively low index of refraction and low dispersion value

crown jewel *noun* (1649)
1 *plural* : the jewels (as crown and scepter) belonging to a sovereign's regalia
2 : the most attractive or valuable one of a collection or group

crown land *noun* (circa 1625)
1 : land belonging to the crown and yielding revenues that the reigning sovereign is entitled to
2 : public land in some British dominions or colonies

crown of thorns (1964)
: a starfish (*Acanthaster planci*) of the Pacific region that is covered with long spines and is destructive to the coral of coral reefs — called also *crown-of-thorns starfish*

crown prince *noun* (1791)
: a male heir apparent to a crown or throne

crown princess *noun* (1863)
1 : the wife of a crown prince
2 : a female heir apparent or heir presumptive to a crown or throne

crown roast *noun* (circa 1909)
: a fancy roast of lamb, veal, or pork made from the rib portions of two loins skewered together at the ends to form a circle

crown rust *noun* (circa 1899)

☆ **SYNONYMS**
Crowd, throng, crush, mob, horde mean an assembled multitude usually of people. CROWD implies a close gathering and pressing together ⟨a small *crowd* gathered⟩. THRONG strongly suggests movement and pushing ⟨a *throng* of reporters⟩. CRUSH emphasizes the compactness of the group, the difficulty of individual movement, and the attendant discomfort ⟨a *crush* of fans⟩. MOB implies a disorderly crowd with the potential for violence ⟨an angry *mob* outside the jail⟩. HORDE suggests a rushing or tumultuous crowd ⟨a *horde* of shoppers⟩.

\ə\ abut \ᵊ\ kitten \ər\ further \a\ ash \ā\ ace
\ä\ mop, mar \aú\ out \ch\ chin \e\ bet \ē\ easy
\g\ go \i\ hit \ī\ ice \j\ job \ŋ\ sing \ō\ go
\ò\ law \ói\ boy \th\ thin \th\ the \ü\ loot \ú\ foot
\y\ yet \zh\ vision *see also* Guide to Pronunciation

: a leaf rust of oats and other grasses that is caused by a fungus (*Puccinia coronata*) and is characterized by rounded light-orange uredinia and buried telia

crown vetch *noun* (circa 1900)
: a European leguminous herb (*Coronilla varia*) that is naturalized in the eastern U.S. and has umbels of pink-and-white flowers and sharp-angled pods

crow's–foot \'krōz-ˌfut\ *noun, plural* **crow's–feet** \-ˌfēt\ (14th century)
1 : a wrinkle extending from the outer corner of the eye — usually used in plural
2 : CROWFOOT 1

crow's nest *noun* (1818)
: a partly enclosed platform high on a ship's mast for use as a lookout; *also* **:** a similar lookout (as for traffic control)

crow·step \'krō-ˌstep\ *noun* (1822)
: any of a series of steps at the top of a gable wall
— **crow·stepped** \-ˌstept\ *adjective*

cro·zier *variant of* CROSIER

CRT \ˌsē-(ˌ)är-'tē\ *noun, plural* **CRTs** *or* **CRT's** (circa 1945)
: CATHODE-RAY TUBE; *also* **:** a display device incorporating a cathode-ray tube

cruces *plural of* CRUX

cru·cial \'krü-shəl\ *adjective* [French, from Latin *cruc-, crux* cross] (1706)
1 *archaic* **:** CRUCIFORM
2 a : important or essential as resolving a crisis **:** DECISIVE ⟨a *crucial* step⟩ **b :** marked by final determination of a doubtful issue ⟨the *crucial* game of a series⟩ **c :** IMPORTANT, SIGNIFICANT ⟨what use we make of them will be the *crucial* question —Stanley Kubrick⟩
synonym *see* ACUTE

cru·cial·ly \'krü-sh(ə-)lē\ *adverb* (1879)
1 : in a crucial manner
2 : very importantly

cru·cian carp \'krü-shən-\ *noun* [modification of Low German *karuse*, from Middle Low German *karusse*, perhaps of Baltic origin; akin to Lithuanian *karušis* carp] (1836)
: a European carp (*Carassius carassius*) — called also *crucian*

cru·ci·ate \'krü-shē-ˌāt\ *adjective* [New Latin *cruciatus*, from Latin *cruc-, crux*] (1826)
: cross-shaped **:** CRUCIFORM

cru·ci·ble \'krü-sə-bəl\ *noun* [Middle English *corusible*, from Medieval Latin *crucibulum* earthen pot for melting metals] (15th century)
1 : a vessel of a very refractory material (as porcelain) used for melting and calcining a substance that requires a high degree of heat
2 : a severe test
3 : a place or situation in which concentrated forces interact to cause or influence change or development ⟨conditioned by having grown up within the *crucible* of Chinatown —Tom Wolfe⟩

crucible steel *noun* (circa 1879)
: hard cast steel made in pots that are lifted from the furnace before the metal is poured into molds

cru·ci·fer \'krü-sə-fər\ *noun* [Late Latin, from Latin *cruc-, crux* + *-fer*] (1574)
1 : one who carries a cross especially at the head of an ecclesiastical procession
2 : any of a family (Cruciferae) of plants including the cabbage, turnip, and mustard
— **cru·cif·er·ous** \krü-'si-f(ə-)rəs\ *adjective*

cru·ci·fix \'krü-sə-ˌfiks\ *noun* [Middle English, from Late Latin *crucifixus* the crucified Christ, from *crucifixus*, past participle of *crucifigere* to crucify, from Latin *cruc-, crux* + *figere* to fasten — more at FIX] (13th century)
: a representation of Christ on the cross

cru·ci·fix·ion \ˌkrü-sə-'fik-shən\ *noun* (15th century)
1 a *capitalized* **:** the crucifying of Christ **b** **:** the act of crucifying
2 : extreme and painful punishment, affliction, or suffering

cru·ci·form \'krü-sə-ˌform\ *adjective* [Latin *cruc-, crux* + English *-form*] (1661)
: forming or arranged in a cross
— **cruciform** *noun*

cru·ci·fy \'krü-sə-ˌfī\ *transitive verb* **-fied; -fy·ing** [Middle English *crucifien*, from Old French *crucifier*, from Late Latin *crucifigere*] (14th century)
1 : to put to death by nailing or binding the wrists or hands and feet to a cross
2 : to destroy the power of **:** MORTIFY ⟨*crucify* the flesh⟩
3 a : to treat cruelly **:** TORMENT **b :** PILLORY 2

cruck \'krək\ *noun* [probably from dialect form of ²*crook* (curved timber)] (1888)
: one of a pair of curved timbers forming a principal support of a roof in primitive English house construction

¹crud \'krəd\ *noun* [Middle English *curd, crudd*] (14th century)
1 *dialect* **:** CURD
2 a : a deposit or incrustation of filth, grease, or refuse **b :** something disagreeable or disgusting **:** RUBBISH **c** *slang* **:** a despicable or contemptible person
3 : a usually ill-defined or imperfectly identified bodily disorder
— **crud·dy** \'krə-dē\ *adjective*

²crud *verb* **crud·ded; crud·ding** (14th century)
dialect **:** ²CURD

¹crude \'krüd\ *adjective* **crud·er; crud·est** [Middle English, from Latin *crudus* raw, crude, undigested — more at RAW] (14th century)
1 : existing in a natural state and unaltered by cooking or processing ⟨*crude* oil⟩
2 *archaic* **:** UNRIPE, IMMATURE
3 : marked by the primitive, gross, or elemental or by uncultivated simplicity or vulgarity ⟨a *crude* stereotype⟩
4 : rough or inexpert in plan or execution ⟨a *crude* shelter⟩
5 : lacking a covering, glossing, or concealing element **:** OBVIOUS ⟨*crude* facts⟩
6 : tabulated without being broken down into classes ⟨the *crude* death rate⟩
synonym *see* RUDE
— **crude·ly** *adverb*
— **crude·ness** *noun*

²crude *noun* (1904)
: a substance in its natural unprocessed state; *especially* **:** unrefined petroleum

cru·di·tés \ˌkrē-dē-'tā, ˌkrü-di-'tā\ *noun plural* [French, from plural of *crudité* rawness, from Latin *cruditas* indigestion, from *crudus*] (1960)
: pieces of raw vegetables (as celery or carrot sticks) served as an hors d'oeuvre often with a dip

cru·di·ty \'krü-də-tē\ *noun, plural* **-ties** (1547)
1 : the quality or state of being crude
2 : something that is crude

cru·el \'krü-(ə)l\ *adjective* **cru·el·er** *or* **cru·el·ler; cru·el·est** *or* **cru·el·lest** [Middle English, from Old French, from Latin *crudelis*, from *crudus*] (14th century)
1 : disposed to inflict pain or suffering **:** devoid of humane feelings
2 a : causing or conducive to injury, grief, or pain ⟨a *cruel* joke⟩ **b :** unrelieved by leniency
synonym *see* FIERCE
— **cru·el·ly** \'krü-(ə)lē\ *adverb*
— **cru·el·ness** *noun*

cru·el·ty \'krü-(ə)l-tē\ *noun, plural* **-ties** [Middle English *cruelte*, from Old French *crueltë*, from Latin *crudelitat-, crudelitas*, from *crudelis*] (13th century)
1 : the quality or state of being cruel
2 a : a cruel action **b :** inhuman treatment
3 : marital conduct held (as in a divorce action) to endanger life or health or to cause mental suffering or fear

cru·et \'krü-ət\ *noun* [Middle English, from Anglo-French, diminutive of Old French *crue*,

of Germanic origin; akin to Old English *crūce*] (14th century)
1 : a vessel to hold wine or water for the Eucharist
2 : a usually glass bottle used to hold a condiment (as oil or vinegar) for use at the table

¹cruise \'krüz\ *verb* **cruised; cruis·ing** [Dutch *kruisen* to make a cross, cruise, from Middle Dutch *crucen*, from *crūce* cross, from Latin *cruc-, crux*] (1651)
intransitive verb
1 : to sail about touching at a series of ports
2 : to move or proceed speedily, smoothly, or effortlessly ⟨I'll *cruise* over to her house to see if she's home⟩
3 : to travel without destination or purpose
4 a : to go about the streets at random but on the lookout for possible developments ⟨the cabdriver *cruised* for an hour before being hailed⟩ **b :** to search (as in public places) for a sexual partner
5 a *of an airplane* **:** to fly at the most efficient operating speed **b** *of an automobile* **:** to travel at a speed suitable for being maintained for a long distance
transitive verb
1 : to cruise over or about
2 : to inspect (as land) with reference to possible lumber yield
3 a : to search in (a public place) for a sexual partner **b :** to approach and suggest sexual relations to

²cruise *noun* (circa 1706)
: an act or an instance of cruising; *especially* **:** a tour by ship

cruise control *noun* (1968)
1 : an electronic device in an automobile that controls the throttle so as to maintain a constant speed
2 : a relaxed and seemingly automatic pace that is easily maintained

cruise missile *noun* (1959)
: a guided missile that has a terrain-following radar system and that flies at moderate speed and low altitude

cruis·er \'krü-zər\ *noun* (1695)
1 : a vehicle that cruises: as **a :** SQUAD CAR **b :** a powerboat with facilities (as a cabin and plumbing) necessary for living aboard — called also *cabin cruiser*
2 : a large fast moderately armored and gunned warship usually of 6000 to 15,000 tons displacement
3 : a person who cruises

crul·ler \'krə-lər\ *noun* [Dutch *krulle*, a twisted cake, from *krul* curly, from Middle Dutch *crul* — more at CURL] (1818)
1 : a small sweet cake in the form of a twisted strip fried in deep fat
2 *Northern & Midland* **:** an unraised doughnut

¹crumb \'krəm\ *noun* [Middle English *crumme*, from Old English *cruma*; akin to Middle High German *krume* crumb] (before 12th century)
1 a : a small fragment especially of something baked (as bread) **b :** a porous aggregate of soil particles
2 : BIT ⟨a *crumb* of good news⟩
3 : the soft part of bread
4 *slang* **:** a worthless person

²crumb *transitive verb* (14th century)
1 : to break into crumbs
2 : to cover or thicken with crumbs
3 : to remove crumbs from ⟨*crumb* a table⟩

¹crum·ble \'krəm-bəl\ *verb* **crum·bled; crum·bling** \-b(ə-)liŋ\ [alteration of Middle English *kremelen*, frequentative of Old English *gecrymian* to crumble, from *cruma*] (1570)
transitive verb
: to break into small pieces
intransitive verb
1 : to fall into small pieces **:** DISINTEGRATE
2 : to break down completely **:** COLLAPSE ⟨marriages *crumble*⟩

²crumble *noun* (1820)

1 : something crumbled : fine debris

2 : CRISP 2

crum·blings \'krəm-b(ə-)liŋz\ *noun plural* (1660)
: crumbled particles : CRUMBS

crum·bly \-b(ə-)lē\ *adjective* **crum·bli·er; -est** (1523)
: easily crumbled : FRIABLE ⟨*crumbly* soil⟩
— **crum·bli·ness** *noun*

crumb structure *noun* (circa 1906)
: a soil condition suitable for farming in which the soil particles are aggregated into crumbs

crumhorn *variant of* KRUMMHORN

crum·mie *or* **crum·my** \'krə-mē\ *noun, plural* **crummies** [Scots *crumb* crooked, from Middle English, from Old English] (1724)
chiefly Scottish : COW; *especially* : one with crumpled horns

crum·my *also* **crumby** \'krə-mē\ *adjective* **crum·mi·er** *also* **crumb·i·er; -est** [Middle English *crumme*] (1567)
1 *obsolete* : CRUMBLY
2 a : MISERABLE, FILTHY **b** : CHEAP, WORTHLESS
— **crum·mi·ness** *noun*

¹crump \'krəmp\ *intransitive verb* [imitative] (1646)
1 : CRUNCH
2 : to explode heavily

²crump *noun* (1914)
1 : a crunching sound
2 : SHELL, BOMB

³crump *adjective* [perhaps alteration of *crimp* friable] (1787)
chiefly Scottish : BRITTLE

crum·pet \'krəm-pət\ *noun* [perhaps from Middle English *crompid* (*cake*) wafer, literally, curled-up cake, from *crumped*, past participle of *crumpen* to curl up, from *crump*, *crumb* crooked, from Old English *crumb*; akin to Old High German *krump* crooked] (1769)
: a small round unsweetened bread cooked on a griddle and usually split and toasted before serving

¹crum·ple \'krəm-pəl\ *verb* **crum·pled; crum·pling** \-p(ə-)liŋ\ [Middle English *crumplen*, frequentative of Middle English *crumpen*] (14th century)
transitive verb
1 : to press, bend, or crush out of shape : RUMPLE
2 : to cause to collapse
intransitive verb
1 : to become crumpled
2 : COLLAPSE

²crumple *noun* (15th century)
: a wrinkle or crease made by crumpling
— **crum·ply** \'krəm-p(ə-)lē\ *adjective*

¹crunch \'krənch\ *verb* [alteration of *craunch*] (1814)
intransitive verb
1 : to chew or press with a crushing noise
2 : to make one's way with a crushing noise
transitive verb
1 : to chew, press, or grind with a crunching sound
2 : PROCESS; *especially* : to perform mathematical computations on ⟨*crunch* numbers⟩
— **crunch·able** \'krən-chə-bəl\ *adjective*

²crunch *noun* (1836)
1 : an act of crunching
2 : a sound made by crunching
3 : a tight or critical situation: as **a** : a critical point in the buildup of pressure between opposing elements : SHOWDOWN **b** : a severe economic squeeze (as on credit) **c** : SHORTAGE ⟨an energy *crunch*⟩

crunch·er \'krən-chər\ *noun* (1946)
1 : one that crunches
2 : a finishing blow

crunchy \'krən-chē\ *adjective* **crunch·i·er; -est** (1913)
: making a crunching sound when chewed or pressed
— **crunch·i·ly** \-chə-lē\ *adverb*
— **crunch·i·ness** \-chē-nəs\ *noun*

crup·per \'krə-pər, 'krü-\ *noun* [Middle English *cruper*, from Old French *crupiere*, from *croupe* hindquarters — more at CROUP] (14th century)
1 : a leather loop passing under a horse's tail and buckled to the saddle
2 : ¹CROUP; *broadly* : BUTTOCKS

cru·ral \'krúr-əl\ *adjective* [Latin *crur-, crus* leg] (1599)
: of or relating to the thigh or leg; *specifically* : FEMORAL ⟨*crural* artery⟩

crus \'krüs, 'krəs\ *noun, plural* **cru·ra** \'krúr-ə\ [Latin *crur-, crus*] (circa 1751)
: any of various anatomical parts that resemble a leg or a pair of legs

¹cru·sade \krü-'sād\ *noun* [blend of Middle French *croisade* & Spanish *cruzada*; both ultimately from Latin *cruc-, crux* cross] (circa 1708)
1 *capitalized* : any of the military expeditions undertaken by Christian powers in the 11th, 12th, and 13th centuries to win the Holy Land from the Muslims
2 : a remedial enterprise undertaken with zeal and enthusiasm ◇

²crusade *intransitive verb* **cru·sad·ed; cru·sad·ing** (1732)
: to engage in a crusade
— **cru·sad·er** *noun*

cru·sa·do \krü-'sā-(,)dō\ *also* **cru·za·do** \-'zä-(,)dō, -(,)dü\ *noun, plural* **-does** *or* **-dos** [Portuguese *cruzado*, literally, marked with a cross] (1544)
: an old gold or silver coin of Portugal having a cross on the reverse

cruse \'krüz, 'krüs\ *noun* [Middle English; akin to Old English *crūse* pitcher] (13th century)
: a small vessel (as a jar or pot) for holding a liquid (as water or oil)

¹crush \'krəsh\ *verb* [Middle English *crusshen*, from Middle French *cruisir*, of Germanic origin; akin to Middle Low German *krossen* to crush] (15th century)
transitive verb
1 a : to squeeze or force by pressure so as to alter or destroy structure **b** : to squeeze together into a mass
2 : HUG, EMBRACE
3 : to reduce to particles by pounding or grinding
4 a : to suppress or overwhelm as if by pressure or weight **b** : to oppress or burden grievously **c** : to subdue completely
5 : CROWD, PUSH
6 *archaic* : DRINK
intransitive verb
1 *obsolete* : CRASH
2 : to become crushed
3 : to advance with or as if with crushing
— **crush·able** \'krə-shə-bəl\ *adjective*
— **crush·er** *noun*
— **crush·ing·ly** *adverb*

²crush *noun* (1599)
1 : an act of crushing
2 : the quantity of material crushed
3 a : a crowding together (as of people) **b** : CROWD, MOB; *especially* : a crowd of people pressing against one another
4 : an intense and usually passing infatuation ⟨have a *crush* on someone⟩; *also* : the object of infatuation
synonym see CROWD
— **crush·proof** \-,prüf\ *adjective*

crust \'krəst\ *noun* [Middle English, from Latin *crusta*; akin to Old English *hrūse* earth, Greek *kryos* icy cold, *krystallos* ice, crystal] (14th century)
1 a : the hardened exterior or surface part of bread **b** : a piece of this or of bread grown dry or hard
2 : the pastry cover of a pie

3 : a hard or brittle external coat or covering: as **a** : a hard surface layer (as of soil or snow) **b** : the outer part of a planet, moon, or asteroid composed essentially of crystalline rocks **c** : a deposit built up on the interior surface of a wine bottle during long aging **d** : an encrusting deposit of dried secretions or exudate; *especially* : SCAB
4 : GALL, NERVE
— **crust** *verb*
— **crust·al** \'krəs-t°l\ *adjective*
— **crust·less** \'krəs(t)-ləs\ *adjective*

crus·ta·cea \,krəs-'tā-sh(ē-)ə\ *noun plural* [New Latin, group name, from neuter plural of *crustaceus*] (1814)
: arthropods that are crustaceans

crus·ta·cean \,krəs-'tā-shən\ *noun* (1835)
: any of a large class (Crustacea) of mostly aquatic mandibulate arthropods that have a chitinous or calcareous and chitinous exoskeleton, a pair of often much modified appendages on each segment, and two pairs of antennae and that include the lobsters, shrimps, crabs, wood lice, water fleas, and barnacles
— **crustacean** *adjective*

crus·ta·ceous \-shəs\ *adjective* [New Latin *crustaceus*, from Latin *crusta* crust, shell] (circa 1656)
: of, relating to, having, or forming a crust or shell; *especially* : CRUSTOSE

crus·tose \'krəs-,tōs\ *adjective* [Latin *crustosus* crusted, from *crusta*] (circa 1879)
: having a thallus adhering closely to a substrate (as of rock, bark, or soil) ⟨*crustose* lichens⟩ — compare FOLIOSE, FRUTICOSE

crusty \'krəs-tē\ *adjective* **crust·i·er; -est** (14th century)
1 : having or being a crust
2 : giving an effect of surly incivility in address or disposition
synonym see BLUFF
— **crust·i·ly** \-tə-lē\ *adverb*
— **crust·i·ness** \-tē-nəs\ *noun*

¹crutch \'krəch\ *noun* [Middle English *crucche*, from Old English *crycc*; akin to Old High German *krucka* crutch] (before 12th century)
1 a : a support typically fitting under the armpit for use by the disabled in walking **b** : PROP, STAY
2 : a forked leg rest constituting the pommel of a sidesaddle
3 : the crotch of a human being or an animal

◇ WORD HISTORY
crusade In 1095 when Palestinian lands sacred to Christians were held by Muslims, Pope Urban II convoked a council at Clermont-Ferrand in France and exhorted the assembly to go forth and reclaim the Holy Sepulcher and other venerated sites from the infidels. Those who responded to the call wore on their breasts crosses of cloth to identify themselves as soldiers in Christ's army. These crosses would provide the name for their enterprise and succeeding invasions of the Holy Land in following centuries. Medieval French words for such a holy war against infidels were *croisement*, *croiserie*, *croisée*, and *croisade*, all derivatives of *crois* "cross." The last word, *croisade*, was formed under the influence of Old Provençal *crozata* and Spanish *cruzada*, likewise formed from words meaning "cross." English borrowed both French *croisade* and Spanish *cruzada*, blending the two to produce *crusade* in the 18th century, long after the crusades themselves had ceased.

4 : a forked support
²crutch *transitive verb* (1681)
: to support on crutches **:** prop up
crux \'krəks, 'krúks\ *noun, plural* **crux·es**
also **cru·ces** \'krü-,sēz\ [Latin *cruc-, crux*
cross, torture] (1718)
1 : a puzzling or difficult problem **:** an un-
solved question
2 : an essential point requiring resolution or
resolving an outcome ⟨the *crux* of the prob-
lem⟩
3 : a main or central feature (as of an argu-
ment)
cru·za·do \krü-'zä-(,)dō, -(,)dü\ *noun, plural*
-dos [Portuguese] (1986)
: the basic monetary unit of Brazil 1986–90
Cru·zan \krü-'zan\ *noun* [(assumed) American
Spanish *cruzano,* from *Santa Cruz* Saint
Croix] (1958)
: a native or inhabitant of Saint Croix
— **Cruzan** *adjective*
cru·zei·ro \krü-'zer-(,)ō, -(,)ü\ *noun, plural*
-ros [Portuguese] (1927)
: the basic monetary unit of Brazil 1942–85
and 1991–93
crwth \'krüth\ *noun* [Welsh] (circa 1837)
: ³CROWD 1
¹cry \'krī\ *verb* **cried; cry·ing** [Middle En-
glish *crien,* from Old French *crier,* from Latin
quiritare to make a public outcry, perhaps
from *Quirit-, Quiris,* name for the Roman cit-
izen] (13th century)
transitive verb
1 : to utter loudly **:** SHOUT
2 *archaic* **:** BEG, BESEECH
3 : to proclaim publicly **:** ADVERTISE ⟨*cry* their
wares⟩
intransitive verb
1 : to call loudly **:** SHOUT
2 : to shed tears often noisily **:** WEEP, SOB
3 : to utter a characteristic sound or call
4 : to require or suggest strongly a remedy or
disposition ⟨a hundred things which *cry* out
for planning —Roger Burlingame⟩
— **cry havoc :** to sound an alarm
— **cry over spilled milk :** to express vain
regrets for what cannot be recovered or un-
done
— **cry wolf :** to give alarm unnecessarily
²cry *noun, plural* **cries** (13th century)
1 : an instance of crying: as **a :** an inarticulate
utterance of distress, rage, or pain **b** *obsolete*
: OUTCRY, CLAMOR
2 a *obsolete* **:** PROCLAMATION **b** *plural, Scottish*
: BANNS
3 : ENTREATY, APPEAL
4 : a loud shout
5 : WATCHWORD, SLOGAN
6 a : common report **b :** a general opinion
7 : the public voice raised in protest or ap-
proval
8 : a fit of weeping
9 : the characteristic sound or call of an ani-
mal
10 a : a pack of hounds **b :** PURSUIT — used
in the phrase *in full cry*
11 : DISTANCE — usually used in the phrase *a
far cry*
cry- *or* **cryo-** *combining form* [German *kryo-,*
from Greek, from *kryos* — more at CRUST]
: cold **:** freezing ⟨cryonics⟩ ⟨cryogen⟩
cry·ba·by \'krī-,bā-bē\ *noun* (1851)
: one who cries or complains easily or often
cry down *transitive verb* (1598)
: DISPARAGE, DEPRECIATE
cry·ing \'krī-iŋ\ *adjective* (1607)
1 : calling for notice ⟨a *crying* need⟩
2 : NOTORIOUS, HEINOUS ⟨a *crying* shame⟩
cryo·bi·ol·o·gy \,krī-ō-bī-'ä-lə-jē\ *noun*
(1960)
: the study of the effects of extremely low
temperature on biological systems
— **cryo·bi·o·log·i·cal** \-,bī-ə-'lä-ji-kəl\ *ad-
jective*
— **cryo·bi·ol·o·gist** \-bī-'ä-lə-jist\ *noun*
cry off (1928)

transitive verb
: to call off (as a bargain)
intransitive verb
chiefly British **:** to beg off
cryo·gen \'krī-ə-jən\ *noun* (1875)
: a substance for obtaining low temperatures
: REFRIGERANT — called also *cryogenic*
cryo·gen·ic \,krī-ə-'je-nik\ *adjective* (1896)
1 a : of or relating to the production of very
low temperatures **b :** being or relating to very
low temperatures
2 a : requiring or involving the use of a cryo-
genic temperature **b :** requiring cryogenic stor-
age **c :** suitable for storage of a cryogenic sub-
stance
— **cryo·gen·i·cal·ly** \-ni-k(ə-)lē\ *adverb*
cryo·gen·ics \-niks\ *noun plural but singular
in construction* (circa 1934)
: a branch of physics that deals with the pro-
duction and effects of very low temperatures
cryo·lite \'krī-ə-,līt\ *noun* (1801)
: a mineral consisting of a fluoride of sodium
and aluminum found in Greenland usually in
white cleavable masses and used as a source
of aluminum
cry·on·ics \krī-'ä-niks\ *noun plural but usual-
ly singular in construction* [*cry-* + *-onics* (as
in *electronics*)] (1967)
: the practice of freezing a dead diseased hu-
man in hopes of restoring life at some future
time when a cure for the disease has been de-
veloped
— **cry·on·ic** \-nik\ *adjective*
cryo·phil·ic \,krī-ə-'fi-lik\ *adjective* (1942)
: thriving at low temperatures
cryo·pres·er·va·tion \,krī-ō-,pre-zər-'vā-
shən\ *noun* (1968)
: preservation (as of cells) by subjection to ex-
tremely low temperatures
— **cryo·pre·serve** \,krī-ō-pri-'zərv, 'krī-ō-
pri-,\ *transitive verb*
cryo·probe \'krī-ə-,prōb\ *noun* (1965)
: a blunt chilled instrument used to freeze tis-
sues in cryosurgery
cryo·pro·tec·tive \,krī-ō-prə-'tek-tiv\ *adjec-
tive* (1967)
: serving to protect from freezing ⟨an extracel-
lular *cryoprotective* agent⟩
— **cryo·pro·tec·tant** \-'tek-tənt\ *noun or
adjective*
cryo·scope \'krī-ə-,skōp\ *noun* (1920)
: an instrument for determining freezing points
cry·os·co·py \krī-'äs-kə-pē\ *noun* [Interna-
tional Scientific Vocabulary] (circa 1900)
: the determination of the lowered freezing
points produced in liquid by dissolved sub-
stances in order to determine molecular
weights of solutes and various properties of
solutions
— **cryo·scop·ic** \,krī-ə-'skä-pik\ *adjective*
cryo·stat \'krī-ə-,stat\ *noun* [International Sci-
entific Vocabulary] (1913)
: an apparatus for maintaining a constant low
temperature especially below 0°C
— **cryo·stat·ic** \,krī-ə-'sta-tik\ *adjective*
cryo·sur·gery \,krī-ō-'sərj-rē, -'sər-jə-\ *noun*
(1962)
: surgery in which the tissue to be treated or
operated on is frozen (as by liquid nitrogen)
— **cryo·sur·geon** \-'sər-jən\ *noun*
— **cryo·sur·gi·cal** \-ji-kəl\ *adjective*
cryo·ther·a·py \-'ther-ə-pē\ *noun* (1926)
: the therapeutic use of cold
crypt \'kript\ *noun* [Latin *crypta,* from Greek
kryptē, from feminine of *kryptos* hidden, from
kryptein to hide; perhaps akin to Lithuanian
krauti to pile up] (1789)
1 a : a chamber (as a vault) wholly or partly
underground; *especially* **:** a vault under the
main floor of a church **b :** a chamber in a
mausoleum
2 a : an anatomical pit or depression **b :** a
simple tubular gland
crypt- *or* **crypto-** *combining form* [New Lat-
in, from Greek *kryptos*]
1 : hidden **:** covered ⟨*crypto*genic⟩

2 : CRYPTOGRAPHIC ⟨*crypt*analysis⟩
crypt·anal·y·sis \,krip-tə-'na-lə-səs\ *noun*
(1923)
1 : the solving of cryptograms or cryptograph-
ic systems
2 : the theory of solving cryptograms or cryp-
tographic systems **:** the art of devising meth-
ods for this
— **crypt·an·a·lyt·ic** \,krip-,ta-nºl-'i-tik\
also **crypt·an·a·lyt·i·cal** \-ti-kəl\ *adjective*
crypt·an·a·lyst \krip-'ta-nºl-ist\ *noun* (1921)
: a specialist in cryptanalysis
cryp·ta·rithm \'krip-tə-,ri-thəm\ *noun* [*crypt-
+ -arithm* (as in *logarithm*)] (1943)
: an arithmetic problem in which letters have
been substituted for numbers and which is
solved by finding all possible pairings of dig-
its with letters that produce a numerically cor-
rect answer
cryp·tic \'krip-tik\ *adjective* [Late Latin *cryp-
ticus,* from Greek *kryptikos,* from *kryptos*]
(circa 1638)
1 : SECRET, OCCULT
2 a : having or seeming to have a hidden or
ambiguous meaning **:** MYSTERIOUS ⟨*cryptic*
messages⟩ **b :** marked by an often perplexing
brevity ⟨*cryptic* marginal notes⟩
3 : serving to conceal ⟨*cryptic* coloration in
animals⟩; *also* **:** exhibiting cryptic coloration
⟨*cryptic* animals⟩
4 : UNRECOGNIZED ⟨a *cryptic* infection⟩
5 : employing cipher or code
synonym see OBSCURE
— **cryp·ti·cal·ly** \-ti-k(ə-)lē\ *adverb*
¹cryp·to \'krip-(,)tō\ *noun, plural* **cryptos**
[*crypt-*] (1946)
: a person who adheres or belongs secretly to a
party, sect, or other group
²crypto *adjective* (1952)
1 : CRYPTOGRAPHIC
2 : not openly avowed or declared — often
used in combination ⟨*crypto*-fascist⟩
cryp·to·coc·co·sis \,krip-tə-(,)kä-'kō-səs\
noun, plural **-co·ses** \-(,)sēz\ [New Latin]
(1938)
: an infectious disease that is caused by a fun-
gus (*Cryptococcus neoformans*) and is charac-
terized by the production of nodular lesions or
abscesses in the lungs, subcutaneous tissues,
joints, and especially the brain and meninges
cryp·to·coc·cus \-'kä-kəs\ *noun, plural*
-coc·ci \-'käk-,sī, -,sē, -'kä-,kī, -,kē\ [New
Latin] (circa 1902)
: any of a genus (*Cryptococcus*) of budding
imperfect fungi that resemble yeasts and in-
clude a number of saprophytes and a few seri-
ous pathogens
— **cryp·to·coc·cal** \-'kä-kəl\ *adjective*
cryp·to·crys·tal·line \,krip-tō-'kris-tə-lən\
adjective [International Scientific Vocabulary]
(1862)
: having a crystalline structure so fine that no
distinct particles are recognizable under the
microscope ⟨*cryptocrystalline* quartz⟩
cryp·to·gam \'krip-tə-,gam\ *noun* [ultimately
from Greek *kryptos* + *-gamia* -gamy] (1847)
: a plant (as a fern, moss, alga, or fungus) re-
producing by spores and not producing flow-
ers or seed
— **cryp·to·gam·ic** \,krip-tə-'ga-mik\ *or*
cryp·tog·a·mous \krip-'tä-gə-məs\ *adjec-
tive*
cryp·to·gen·ic \,krip-tə-'je-nik\ *adjective*
(1908)
: of obscure or unknown origin ⟨a *cryptogenic*
disease⟩
cryp·to·gram \'krip-tə-,gram\ *noun* [French
cryptogramme, from *crypt-* + *-gramme* -gram]
(1880)
1 : a communication in cipher or code
2 : a figure or representation having a hidden
significance
cryp·to·graph \'krip-tə-,graf\ *noun* (1849)
: CRYPTOGRAM
cryp·tog·ra·pher \krip-'tä-grə-fər\ *noun*
(1641)

: a specialist in cryptography: as **a** : a clerk who enciphers and deciphers messages **b** : one who devises cryptographic methods or systems **c** : CRYPTANALYST

cryp·to·graph·ic \ˌkrip-tə-ˈgra-fik\ *adjective* (1824)
: of, relating to, or using cryptography
— **cryp·to·graph·i·cal·ly** \-fi-k(ə-)lē\ *adverb*

cryp·tog·ra·phy \krip-ˈtä-grə-fē\ *noun* [New Latin *cryptographia,* from *crypt-* + *-graphia* -graphy] (1658)
1 : secret writing
2 : the enciphering and deciphering of messages in secret code or cipher
3 : CRYPTANALYSIS

cryp·tol·o·gy \krip-ˈtä-lə-jē\ *noun* (1935)
: the scientific study of cryptography and cryptanalysis
— **cryp·to·log·i·cal** \ˌkrip-tə-ˈlä-ji-kəl\ *or* **cryp·to·log·ic** \-jik\ *adjective*
— **cryp·tol·o·gist** \krip-ˈtä-lə-jist\ *noun*

cryp·to·me·ria \ˌkrip-tə-ˈmir-ē-ə\ *noun* [New Latin, genus name, from *crypt-* + Greek *meros* part — more at MERIT] (1841)
: an evergreen tree (*Cryptomeria japonica*) of the pine family that is a valuable timber tree of Japan

cryp·to·nym \ˈkrip-tə-ˌnim\ *noun* (1876)
: a secret name

cryp·tor·chid \krip-ˈtȯr-kəd\ *noun* [New Latin *cryptorchid-, cryptorchis,* from *crypt-* + *orchid-, orchis* testicle, from Greek *orchis* — more at ORCHIS] (1874)
: one affected with cryptorchidism
— **cryptorchid** *adjective*

crypt·or·chi·dism \-kə-ˌdi-zəm\ *or* **crypt·or·chism** \-ˌki-zəm\ *noun* (circa 1882)
: a condition in which one or both testes fail to descend normally

cryp·to·zo·ol·o·gy \ˌkrip-tə-zō-ˈä-lə-jē, -zə-ˈwä-\ *noun* (1969)
: the study of the lore concerning legendary animals (as Sasquatch) especially in order to evaluate the possibility of their existence
— **cryp·to·zo·ol·o·gist** \-ˈä-lə-jist, -ˈwä-\ *noun*

¹crys·tal \ˈkris-t°l\ *noun* [Middle English *cristal,* from Old French, from Latin *crystallum,* from Greek *krystallos* — more at CRUST] (13th century)
1 : quartz that is transparent or nearly so and that is either colorless or only slightly tinged
2 : something resembling crystal in transparency and colorlessness
3 : a body that is formed by the solidification of a chemical element, a compound, or a mixture and has a regularly repeating internal arrangement of its atoms and often external plane faces
4 : a clear colorless glass of superior quality; *also* : objects or ware of such glass
5 : the glass or transparent plastic cover over a watch or clock dial
6 : a crystalline material used in electronics as a frequency-determining element or for rectification
7 : powdered methamphetamine

²crystal *adjective* (14th century)
1 : consisting of or resembling crystal : CLEAR, LUCID
2 : relating to or using a crystal ⟨a *crystal* radio receiver⟩

crystal ball *noun* (1855)
1 : a sphere especially of quartz crystal traditionally used by fortune-tellers
2 : a means or method of predicting future events

crystal gazing *noun* (1889)
1 : the art or practice of concentrating on a glass or crystal globe with the aim of inducing a psychic state in which divination can be performed
2 : the attempt to predict future events or make difficult judgments especially without adequate data

— **crystal gazer** *noun*

crystall- *or* **crystallo-** *combining form* [Greek *krystallos*]
: crystal ⟨*crystallo*graphy⟩

crys·tal·line \ˈkris-tə-lən *also* -ˌlīn, -ˌlēn\ *adjective* [Middle English *cristallin,* from Middle French & Latin; Middle French, from Latin *crystallinus,* from Greek *krystallinos,* from *krystallos*] (15th century)
1 : resembling crystal: as **a** : strikingly clear or sparkling ⟨*crystalline* air⟩ ⟨a *crystalline* lake⟩ **b** : CLEAR-CUT
2 : made of crystal : composed of crystals
3 : constituting or relating to a crystal
— **crys·tal·lin·i·ty** \ˌkris-tə-ˈli-nə-tē\ *noun*

crystalline lens *noun* (1794)
: the lens of the eye in vertebrates

crys·tal·lise *British variant of* CRYSTALLIZE

crys·tal·lite \ˈkris-tə-ˌlīt\ *noun* [German *Kristallit,* from Greek *krystallos*] (1805)
1 a : a minute mineral form (as in glassy volcanic rocks) that marks the beginning of crystallization **b** : a single grain in a polycrystalline substance
2 : MICELLE

crys·tal·lize *also* **crys·tal·ize** \ˈkris-tə-ˌlīz\ *verb* **-lized; -liz·ing** (1598)
transitive verb
1 : to cause to form crystals or assume crystalline form
2 : to cause to take a definite form ⟨tried to *crystallize* his thoughts⟩
3 : to coat with crystals especially of sugar ⟨*crystallize* grapes⟩
intransitive verb
: to become crystallized
— **crys·tal·liz·able** \-ˌlī-zə-bəl, ˌkris-tə-ˈ\ *adjective*
— **crys·tal·li·za·tion** \ˌkris-tə-li-ˈzā-shən\ *noun*
— **crys·tal·liz·er** *noun*

crys·tal·lo·graph·ic \ˌkris-tə-lə-ˈgra-fik\ *adjective* (1804)
: of or relating to crystals or crystallography
— **crys·tal·lo·graph·i·cal·ly** \-fi-k(ə-)lē\ *adverb*

crys·tal·log·ra·phy \ˌkris-tə-ˈlä-grə-fē\ *noun* (1802)
: a science that deals with the forms and structures of crystals
— **crys·tal·log·ra·pher** \-fər\ *noun*

crys·tal·loid \ˈkris-tə-ˌlȯid\ *noun* (1861)
: a substance that forms a true solution and is capable of being crystallized
— **crystalloid** *or* **crys·tal·loi·dal** \ˌkris-tə-ˈlȯi-d°l\ *adjective*

crystal pleat *noun* (1976)
: any of a series of narrow sharply pressed pleats all turned in one direction
— **crystal pleated** *adjective*

crystal violet *noun* (circa 1893)
: a triphenylmethane dye found in gentian violet

cry up *transitive verb* (1593)
: to praise publicly in order to enhance in value or repute

CS \ˌsē-ˈes\ *noun* [Ben B. *C*orson (born 1896) and Roger W. *S*taughton (died 1957) American chemists] (1960)
: a potent tear gas used especially for riot control

C–sec·tion \ˈsē-ˌsek-shən\ *noun* (1973)
: CESAREAN SECTION

cte·noid \ˈte-ˌnȯid, ˈtē-\ *adjective* [International Scientific Vocabulary, from Greek *ktenoeidēs,* from *kten-, kteis* comb — more at PECTINATE] (1872)
: having the margin toothed ⟨*ctenoid* scale⟩; *also* : having or consisting of ctenoid scales ⟨*ctenoid* fishes⟩

cteno·phore \ˈte-nə-ˌfōr, -ˌfȯr\ *noun* [ultimately from Greek *kten-, kteis* + *pherein* to carry — more at BEAR] (circa 1882)
: any of a phylum (Ctenophora) of marine animals superficially resembling jellyfishes but having biradial symmetry and swimming by

means of eight meridional bands of transverse ciliated plates — called also *comb jelly*
— **cte·noph·o·ran** \tə-ˈnä-fə-rən\ *noun or adjective*

CT scan \ˌsē-ˈtē-\ *noun* [computerized *t*omography] (1974)
: CAT SCAN
— **CT scanner** *noun*

C–type \ˈsē-ˌtīp\ *adjective* (1967)
: relating to or being any of the oncornaviruses in which the structure containing the nucleic acid is spherical and centrally located ⟨*C-type* virus particles⟩

cua·dri·lla \kwä-ˈdrē-yə, -ˈdrēl-\ *noun* [Spanish, diminutive of *cuadra* square, from Latin *quadra*] (1893)
: the team assisting the matador in the bullring

cub \ˈkəb\ *noun* [origin unknown] (1530)
1 a : a young carnivorous mammal (as a bear, fox, or lion) **b** : a young shark
2 : a young person
3 : APPRENTICE; *especially* : an inexperienced newspaper reporter

cub·age \ˈkyü-bij\ *noun* (1840)
: cubic content, volume, or displacement

Cu·ban heel \ˈkyü-bən-\ *noun* [*Cuba,* West Indies] (1908)
: a broad medium-high heel with a moderately curved back

cu·ba·ture \ˈkyü-bə-ˌchu̇r, -ˌchər, -ˌtyu̇r, -ˌtu̇r\ *noun* [*cube* + *-ature* (as in *quadrature*)] (1679)
: the process of determining the volume of a solid

cub·by \ˈkə-bē\ *noun, plural* **cubbies** [obsolete English *cub* pen, from Dutch *kub* fish basket; akin to Old English *cofa* den] (circa 1859)
: CUBBYHOLE

cub·by·hole \ˈkə-bē-ˌhōl\ *noun* (circa 1842)
: a small snug place (as for hiding or storage); *also* : a cramped space

¹cube \ˈkyüb\ *noun* [Latin *cubus,* from Greek *kybos* die, cube] (1551)
1 a : the regular solid of six equal square sides — see VOLUME table **b** : something shaped like a cube ⟨ice *cube*⟩
2 : the product got by taking a number three times as a factor

²cube *adjective* (1570)
: raised to the third power

³cube *transitive verb* **cubed; cub·ing** (1588)
1 : to raise to the third power
2 : to form into a cube
3 : to cut partly through (a steak) in a checkered pattern to increase tenderness by breaking the fibers
— **cub·er** *noun*

⁴cu·be *or* **cu·bé** \ˈkyü-ˌbā, kyü-ˈ\ *noun* [American Spanish *cubé*] (1924)
: any of several tropical American plants (genus *Lonchocarpus*) furnishing rotenone

cu·beb \ˈkyü-ˌbeb\ *noun* [Middle French *cubebe,* from Old French, from Medieval Latin *cubeba,* from Arabic *kubābah*] (14th century)
: the dried unripe berry of a tropical shrub (*Piper cubeba*) of the pepper family that is crushed and smoked in cigarettes for catarrh

cube root *noun* (circa 1696)
: a number whose cube is a given number

cube steak *noun* (1930)
: a thin slice of beef that has been cubed

¹cu·bic \ˈkyü-bik\ *adjective* (15th century)
1 : having the form of a cube : CUBICAL
2 a : relating to the cube considered as a crystal form **b** : ISOMETRIC 1
3 a : THREE-DIMENSIONAL **b** : being the volume of a cube whose edge is a specified unit ⟨*cubic* inch⟩

\ə\ abut \ᵊ\ kitten \ər\ further \a\ ash \ā\ ace \ä\ mop, mar \au̇\ out \ch\ chin \e\ bet \ē\ easy \g\ go \i\ hit \ī\ ice \j\ job \ŋ\ sing \ō\ go \ȯ\ law \ȯi\ boy \th\ thin \t͟h\ the \ü\ loot \u̇\ foot \y\ yet \zh\ vision *see also* Guide to Pronunciation

4 : of third degree, order, or power ⟨a *cubic* polynomial⟩

²cubic *noun* (1799)
: a cubic curve, equation, or polynomial

cu·bi·cal \'kyü-bi-kəl\ *adjective* (15th century)
1 : CUBIC; *especially* **:** shaped like a cube
2 : relating to volume
— **cu·bi·cal·ly** \-k(ə-)lē\ *adverb*

cubic equation *noun* (circa 1751)
: a polynomial equation in which the highest sum of exponents of variables in any term is three

cu·bi·cle \'kyü-bi-kəl\ *noun* [Latin *cubiculum,* from *cubare* to lie, recline] (15th century)
1 : a sleeping compartment partitioned off from a large room
2 : a small partitioned space; *especially* **:** CARREL

cubic measure *noun* (1660)
: a unit (as cubic inch or cubic centimeter) for measuring volume — see METRIC SYSTEM table, WEIGHT table

cub·ism \'kyü-ˌbi-zəm\ *noun, often capitalized* (1911)
: a style of art that stresses abstract structure at the expense of other pictorial elements especially by displaying several aspects of the same object simultaneously and by fragmenting the form of depicted objects
— **cub·ist** \-bist\ *noun or adjective, often capitalized*
— **cu·bis·tic** \kyü-'bis-tik\ *adjective*

cu·bit \'kyü-bət\ *noun* [Middle English, from Latin *cubitum* elbow, cubit] (14th century)
: any of various ancient units of length based on the length of the forearm from the elbow to the tip of the middle finger and usually equal to about 18 inches (45.7 centimeters)

¹cu·boid \'kyü-ˌbȯid\ *adjective* (circa 1828)
1 : approximately cubical in shape
2 : relating to or being the cuboid

²cuboid *noun* (1839)
: the outermost bone in the distal row of tarsal bones of many higher vertebrates

cu·boi·dal \kyü-'bȯi-dᵊl\ *adjective* (1803)
1 : somewhat cubical
2 : composed of nearly cubical elements ⟨*cuboidal* epithelium⟩

Cub Scout *noun* (circa 1935)
: a member of the scouting program of the Boy Scouts for boys in the first through fifth grades in school

cuck·ing stool \'kə-kiŋ-\ *noun* [Middle English *cucking stol,* literally, defecating chair] (12th century)
: a chair formerly used for punishing offenders (as dishonest tradesmen) by public exposure or ducking in water

cuck·old \'kə-kəld, -(ˌ)kōld\ *noun* [Middle English *cokewold*] (13th century)
: a man whose wife is unfaithful
— **cuckold** *transitive verb*

cuck·old·ry \-kəl-drē\ *noun* (1529)
1 : the practice of making cuckolds
2 : the state of being a cuckold

¹cuck·oo \'kü-(ˌ)kü, 'kù-\ *noun, plural* **cuck·oos** [Middle English *cuccu,* of imitative origin] (13th century)
1 : a largely grayish brown European bird (*Cuculus canorus*) that is a parasite given to laying its eggs in the nests of other birds which hatch them and rear the offspring; *broadly* **:** any of a large family (Cuculidae of the order Cuculiformes) to which this bird belongs
2 : the call of the cuckoo
3 : a silly or slightly crackbrained person

cuckoo 1

²cuckoo *transitive verb* (1648)
: to repeat monotonously as a cuckoo does its call

³cuckoo *adjective* (1627)
1 : of, relating to, or resembling the cuckoo
2 : deficient in sense or intelligence **:** SILLY

cuckoo clock *noun* (1789)
: a wall or shelf clock that announces the hours by sounds resembling a cuckoo's call

cuck·oo·flow·er \'kü-(ˌ)kü-ˌflaù(-ə)r, 'kù-\ *noun* (1578)
1 : a bitter cress (*Cardamine pratensis*) of Eurasia and North America
2 : RAGGED ROBIN

cuck·oo·pint \-ˌpint\ *noun* [Middle English *cuccupintel,* from *cuccu* + *pintel* pintle] (1551)
: a European arum (*Arum maculatum*) with erect spathe and short purple spadix

cuckoo spit *noun* (1592)
1 : a frothy secretion exuded on plants by the nymphs of spittle insects
2 : SPITTLEBUG

cu·cul·late \'kyü-kə-ˌlāt, kyü-'kə-lət\ *adjective* [Medieval Latin *cucullatus,* from Latin *cucullus* hood] (1794)
: having the shape of a hood ⟨a *cucullate* leaf⟩

cu·cum·ber \'kyü-(ˌ)kəm-bər\ *noun* [Middle English, from Middle French *cocombre,* from Latin *cucumer-, cucumis*] (14th century)
: the fruit of a vine (*Cucumis sativus*) of the gourd family cultivated as a garden vegetable; *also* **:** this vine

cucumber mosaic *noun* (1916)
: a virus disease especially of cucumbers that is transmitted chiefly by an aphid and produces mottled foliage and often pale warty fruits

cucumber tree *noun* (circa 1782)
: a magnolia (*Magnolia acuminata*) of the eastern U.S. having fruit resembling a small cucumber

cu·cur·bit \kyü-'kər-bət\ *noun* [Middle English *cucurbite,* from Middle French, from Latin *cucurbita* gourd] (14th century)
1 : a vessel or flask for distillation used with or forming part of an alembic
2 : a plant of the gourd family

cud \'kəd, *chiefly Southern* 'kùd\ *noun* [Middle English *cudde,* from Old English *cwudu;* akin to Old High German *kuti* glue, Sanskrit *jatu* gum] (before 12th century)
1 : food brought up into the mouth by a ruminating animal from its first stomach to be chewed again
2 : ²QUID

cud·bear \'kəd-ˌbar, -ˌber\ *noun* [irregular from Dr. *Cuthbert* Gordon, 18th century Scottish chemist] (1764)
: a reddish coloring matter from lichens

¹cud·dle \'kə-dᵊl\ *verb* **cud·dled; cud·dling** \'kəd-liŋ, 'kə-dᵊl-iŋ\ [origin unknown] (1520)
transitive verb
: to hold close for warmth or comfort or in affection
intransitive verb
: to lie close or snug **:** NESTLE, SNUGGLE
— **cud·dler** \'kəd-lər, 'kə-dᵊl-ər\ *noun*

²cuddle *noun* (1825)
: a close embrace

cud·dle·some \'kə-dᵊl-səm\ *adjective* (1876)
: CUDDLY

cud·dly \'kəd-lē, 'kə-dᵊl-ē\ *adjective* **cud·dli·er; -est** (1863)
: fit for or inviting cuddling

¹cud·dy \'kə-dē\ *noun, plural* **cuddies** [origin unknown] (1660)
1 : a usually small cabin or shelter (as on a sailboat)
2 : a small room or cupboard

²cud·dy *or* **cud·die** \'kù-dē, 'kə-\ *noun, plural* **cuddies** [perhaps from *Cuddy,* nickname for *Cuthbert*] (circa 1715)
1 *dialect British* **:** DONKEY
2 *dialect British* **:** BLOCKHEAD

¹cud·gel \'kə-jəl\ *noun* [Middle English *kuggel,* from Old English *cycgel;* perhaps akin to Middle High German *kugele* ball] (before 12th century)

: a short heavy club

²cudgel *transitive verb* **-geled** *or* **-gelled; -gel·ing** *or* **-gel·ling** \'kəj-liŋ, 'kə-jə-\ (1596)
: to beat with or as if with a cudgel
— **cudgel one's brains :** to think hard (as for a solution to a problem)

cud·weed \'kəd-ˌwēd, *chiefly Southern* 'kùd- *or* 'küd-\ *noun* (1548)
: any of several composite plants (as of the genus *Gnaphalium*) with silky or woolly foliage

¹cue \'kyü\ *noun* [Middle English *cu* half a farthing (spelled form of *q,* abbreviation for Latin *quadrans* quarter of an as)] (circa 1755)
: the letter *q*

²cue *noun* [probably from *qu,* abbreviation (used as a direction in actors' copies of plays) of Latin *quando* when] (1553)
1 a : a signal (as a word, phrase, or bit of stage business) to a performer to begin a specific speech or action **b :** something serving a comparable purpose **:** HINT
2 : a feature indicating the nature of something perceived
3 *archaic* **:** the part one has to perform in or as if in a play
4 *archaic* **:** MOOD, HUMOR

³cue *transitive verb* **cued; cu·ing** *or* **cue·ing** (1922)
1 : to give a cue to **:** PROMPT
2 : to insert into a continuous performance ⟨*cue* in sound effects⟩

⁴cue *noun* [French *queue,* literally, tail, from Latin *cauda*] (circa 1749)
1 a : a leather-tipped tapering rod for striking the cue ball (as in billiards and pool) **b :** a long-handled instrument with a concave head for shoving disks in shuffleboard
2 : QUEUE 2

⁵cue *verb* **cued; cu·ing** *or* **cue·ing** (circa 1784)
transitive verb
1 : QUEUE
2 : to strike with a cue
intransitive verb
1 : QUEUE
2 : to use a cue

cue ball *noun* (1881)
: the ball a player strikes with the cue in billiards and pool

cues·ta \'kwes-tə\ *noun* [Spanish, from Latin *costa* side, rib — more at COAST] (1818)
: a hill or ridge with a steep face on one side and a gentle slope on the other

¹cuff \'kəf\ *noun* [Middle English *coffe, cuffe* mitten] (1522)
1 : something (as a part of a sleeve or glove) encircling the wrist
2 : the turned-back hem of a trouser leg
3 a : HANDCUFF — usually used in plural **b :** a usually wide metal band worn as a bracelet
4 : an inflatable band that is wrapped around an extremity to control the flow of blood through the part when recording blood pressure with a sphygmomanometer
— **cuff·less** \'kə-fləs\ *adjective*
— **off the cuff :** without preparation **:** AD LIB
— **on the cuff :** on credit

²cuff *transitive verb* (1693)
1 : to furnish with a cuff
2 : HANDCUFF

³cuff *verb* [perhaps from obsolete English, glove, from Middle English] (1530)
transitive verb
: to strike especially with or as if with the palm of the hand **:** BUFFET
intransitive verb
: FIGHT, SCUFFLE

⁴cuff *noun* (1570)
: a blow with the hand especially when open **:** SLAP

cuff link *noun* (1897)
: a usually ornamental device consisting of two parts joined by a shank, chain, or bar for

passing through buttonholes to fasten shirt cuffs — usually used in plural

cui bo·no \'kwē-'bō-(,)nō\ *noun* [Latin, to whose advantage?] (1604)
1 : a principle that probable responsibility for an act or event lies with one having something to gain
2 : usefulness or utility as a principle in estimating the value of an act or policy

cui·rass \kwi-'ras, kyù-\ *noun* [Middle English *curas,* from Middle French *curasse,* from Late Latin *coreacea,* feminine of *coreaceus* leathern, from Latin *corium* skin, leather; akin to Old English *heortha* deerskin, Latin *cortex* bark, Greek *keirein* to cut — more at SHEAR] (15th century)
1 : a piece of armor covering the body from neck to waist; *also* **:** the breastplate of such a piece
2 : something (as bony plates covering an animal) resembling a cuirass
— cui·rassed *adjective*

cui·ras·sier \,kwir-ə-'sir, ,kyùr-\ *noun* (1625)
: a mounted soldier wearing a cuirass

Cui·se·naire rod \,kwē-zə-'nar-, -'ner-\ *noun* [from *Cuisenaire,* a trademark] (1954)
: any of a set of colored rods usually of 1 centimeter cross section and of 10 lengths from 1 to 10 centimeters that are used for teaching number concepts and the basic operations of arithmetic

cui·sine \kwi-'zēn, kwē-\ *noun* [French, literally, kitchen, from Late Latin *coquina* — more at KITCHEN] (1786)
: manner of preparing food **:** style of cooking; *also* **:** the food prepared

cuisse \'kwis\ *also* **cuish** \'kwish\ *noun* [Middle English *cusseis,* plural, from Middle French *cuissaux,* plural of *cuissel,* from *cuisse* thigh, from Latin *coxa* hip — more at COXA] (15th century)
: a piece of plate armor for the front of the thigh — see ARMOR illustration

cuke \'kyük\ *noun* (1903)
: CUCUMBER

cul–de–sac \'kəl-di-,sak, 'kúl-; ,kəl-di-', ,kúl-\ *noun, plural* **culs–de–sac** \'kəl(z)-, 'kúl(z)-, ,kəl(z)-, ,kúl(z)-\ *also* **cul–de–sacs** \-,saks, -'saks\ [French, literally, bottom of the bag] (1738)
1 : a blind diverticulum or pouch
2 : a street or passage closed at one end
3 : BLIND ALLEY

cu·let \'kyü-lət, 'kə-lət\ *noun* [French, from diminutive of *cul* backside, from Latin *culus;* akin to Old Irish *cúl* back] (1678)
1 : the small flat facet at the bottom of a brilliant parallel to the table
2 : plate armor covering the buttocks

cu·lex \'kyü-,leks\ *noun* [New Latin, from Latin, gnat; akin to Old Irish *cuil* fly] (15th century)
: any of a large cosmopolitan genus (*Culex*) of mosquitoes that includes the common house mosquito (*C. pipiens*) of Europe and North America
— cu·li·cine \'kyü-lə-,sīn\ *adjective or noun*

cu·li·nar·i·an \,kə-lə-'ner-ē-ən, ,kyü-\ *noun* (1949)
: COOK, CHEF

cu·li·nary \'kə-lə-,ner-ē, 'kyü-\ *adjective* [Latin *culinarius,* from *culina* kitchen — more at KILN] (1638)
: of or relating to the kitchen or cookery
— cu·li·nar·i·ly \,kə-lə-'ner-ə-lē, ,kyü-\ *adverb*

¹cull \'kəl\ *transitive verb* [Middle English, from Middle French *cuillir,* from Latin *colligere* to bind together — more at COLLECT] (13th century)
1 : to select from a group **:** CHOOSE ⟨*culled* the best passages from the poet's work⟩
2 : to identify and remove the culls from
— cull·er *noun*

²cull *noun* (1809)
: something rejected especially as being inferior or worthless ⟨how to separate good-looking pecans from *culls* —*Washington Post*⟩

cul·len·der \'kə-lən-dər\ *variant of* COLANDER

cul·let \'kə-lət\ *noun* [perhaps from French *cueillette* act of gathering, from Latin *collecta,* from feminine of *collectus,* past participle of *colligere*] (1817)
: broken or refuse glass usually added to new material to facilitate melting in making glass

cul·lion \'kə-lyən\ *noun* [Middle English *coillon* testicle, from Middle French, from (assumed) Vulgar Latin *coleon-, coleo,* from Latin *coleus* scrotum] (1575) *archaic*
: a mean or base fellow

¹cul·ly \'kə-lē\ *noun, plural* **cullies** [perhaps alteration of *cullion*] (1664)
: one easily tricked or imposed on **:** DUPE

²cully *transitive verb* **cul·lied; cul·ly·ing** (1676)
archaic **:** CHEAT, DECEIVE

¹culm \'kəlm\ *noun* [Middle English] (14th century)
: refuse coal screenings **:** SLACK

²culm *noun* [Latin *culmus* stalk — more at HAULM] (circa 1657)
: a monocotyledonous stem (as of a grass or sedge)

cul·mi·nant \'kəl-mə-nənt\ *adjective* (1605)
1 : being at greatest altitude or on the meridian
2 : fully developed

cul·mi·nate \'kəl-mə-,nāt\ *verb* **-nat·ed; -nat·ing** [Medieval Latin *culminatus,* past participle of *culminare,* from Late Latin, to crown, from Latin *culmin-, culmen* top — more at HILL] (1647)
intransitive verb
1 *of a celestial body* **:** to reach its highest altitude; *also* **:** to be directly overhead
2 a : to rise to or form a summit **b :** to reach the highest or a climactic or decisive point
transitive verb
: to bring to a head or to the highest point

cul·mi·na·tion \,kəl-mə-'nā-shən\ *noun* (1633)
1 : the action of culminating
2 : culminating position **:** CLIMAX
synonym see SUMMIT

cu·lotte \'kü-,lät, 'kyü-; kü-'lät, kyü-'\ *noun* [French, breeches, from diminutive of *cul* backside — more at CULET] (1911)
: a divided skirt; *also* **:** a garment having a divided skirt — often used in plural

cul·pa·ble \'kəl-pə-bəl\ *adjective* [Middle English *coupable,* from Middle French, from Latin *culpabilis,* from *culpare* to blame, from *culpa* guilt] (14th century)
1 *archaic* **:** GUILTY, CRIMINAL
2 : meriting condemnation or blame especially as wrong or harmful ⟨*culpable* negligence⟩
synonym see BLAMEWORTHY
— cul·pa·bil·i·ty \,kəl-pə-'bi-lə-tē\ *noun*
— cul·pa·ble·ness \'kəl-pə-bəl-nəs\ *noun*
— cul·pa·bly \-blē\ *adverb*

cul·prit \'kəl-prət, -,prit\ *noun* [Anglo-French *cul.* (abbreviation of *culpable* guilty) + *prest, prit* ready (i.e., to prove it), from Latin *praestus* — more at PRESTO] (1678)
1 : one accused of or charged with a crime
2 : one guilty of a crime or a fault
3 : the source or cause of a problem

cult \'kəlt\ *noun, often attributive* [French & Latin; French *culte,* from Latin *cultus* care, adoration, from *colere* to cultivate — more at WHEEL] (1617)
1 : formal religious veneration **:** WORSHIP
2 : a system of religious beliefs and ritual; *also* **:** its body of adherents
3 : a religion regarded as unorthodox or spurious; *also* **:** its body of adherents
4 : a system for the cure of disease based on dogma set forth by its promulgator ⟨health *cults*⟩

5 a : great devotion to a person, idea, object, movement, or work (as a film or book); *especially* **:** such devotion regarded as a literary or intellectual fad **b :** a usually small group of people characterized by such devotion
— cul·tic \'kəl-tik\ *adjective*
— cult·ish \-tish\ *adjective*
— cult·ish·ly \-lē\ *adverb*
— cult·ish·ness \-nəs\ *noun*
— cult·ism \'kəl-,ti-zəm\ *noun*
— cult·ist \'kəl-tist\ *noun*
— cult·like \-,līk\ *adjective*

cultch *also* **culch** \'kəlch\ *noun* [perhaps from a French dialect form of French *couche* couch] (1667)
1 : material (as oyster shells) laid down on oyster grounds to furnish points of attachment for the spat
2 *chiefly New England* **:** CLUTTER, TRASH

cul·ti·gen \'kəl-tə-jən\ *noun* [*culti*vated + *-gen*] (1924)
1 : a cultivated or domestic organism of a variety or species for which a wild ancestor is unknown
2 : CULTIVAR

cul·ti·va·ble \'kəl-tə-və-bəl\ *adjective* (1682)
: capable of being cultivated
— cul·ti·va·bil·i·ty \,kəl-tə-və-'bi-lə-tē\ *noun*

cul·ti·var \'kəl-tə-,vär, -,ver, -,var\ *noun* [*culti*vated + *var*iety] (1923)
: an organism of a kind originating and persistent under cultivation

cul·ti·vate \'kəl-tə-,vāt\ *transitive verb* **-vat·ed; -vat·ing** [Medieval Latin *cultivatus,* past participle of *cultivare,* from *cultivus* cultivable, from Latin *cultus,* past participle of *colere*] (circa 1655)
1 : to prepare or prepare and use for the raising of crops; *also* **:** to loosen or break up the soil about (growing plants)
2 a : to foster the growth of ⟨*cultivate* vegetables⟩ **b :** CULTURE 2a **c :** to improve by labor, care, or study ⟨*cultivate* the mind⟩
3 : FURTHER, ENCOURAGE ⟨*cultivate* the arts⟩
4 : to seek the society of **:** make friends with
— cul·ti·vat·able \-,vā-tə-bəl\ *adjective*

cultivated *adjective* (1665)
: REFINED, EDUCATED ⟨*cultivated* speech⟩ ⟨*cultivated* tastes⟩

cul·ti·va·tion \,kəl-tə-'vā-shən\ *noun* (circa 1716)
1 : CULTURE, REFINEMENT
2 : the act or art of cultivating or tilling

cul·ti·va·tor \'kəl-tə-,vā-tər\ *noun* (1665)
: one that cultivates; *especially* **:** an implement for loosening the soil while crops are growing

cul·tur·al \'kəlch-rəl, 'kəl-chə-\ *adjective* (circa 1864)
1 : of or relating to culture or culturing
2 : concerned with the fostering of plant or animal growth
— cul·tur·al·ly \-rə-lē\ *adverb*

cultural anthropology *noun* (1933)
: anthropology that deals with human culture especially with respect to social structure, language, law, politics, religion, magic, art, and technology — compare PHYSICAL ANTHROPOLOGY
— cultural anthropologist *noun*

cul·tur·a·ti \,kəl-chə-'rä-(,)tē\ *noun plural* [¹*culture* + *-ati* (as in *literati*)] (1964)
: people intensely interested in cultural affairs

¹cul·ture \'kəl-chər\ *noun* [Middle English, from Middle French, from Latin *cultura,* from *cultus,* past participle] (15th century)
1 : CULTIVATION, TILLAGE
2 : the act of developing the intellectual and moral faculties especially by education
3 : expert care and training ⟨beauty *culture*⟩

\ə\ **abut** \ᵊ\ **kitten** \ər\ **further** \a\ **ash** \ā\ **ace**
\ä\ **mop, mar** \aù\ **out** \ch\ **chin** \e\ **bet** \ē\ **easy**
\g\ **go** \i\ **hit** \ī\ **ice** \j\ **job** \ŋ\ **sing** \ō\ **go**
\ò\ **law** \òi\ **boy** \th\ **thin** \ṭh\ **the** \ü\ **loot** \ù\ **foot**
\y\ **yet** \zh\ **vision** *see also* Guide to Pronunciation

4 a : enlightenment and excellence of taste acquired by intellectual and æsthetic training **b :** acquaintance with and taste in fine arts, humanities, and broad aspects of science as distinguished from vocational and technical skills **5 a :** the integrated pattern of human knowledge, belief, and behavior that depends upon man's capacity for learning and transmitting knowledge to succeeding generations **b :** the customary beliefs, social forms, and material traits of a racial, religious, or social group **c :** the set of shared attitudes, values, goals, and practices that characterizes a company or corporation **6 :** cultivation of living material in prepared nutrient media; *also* **:** a product of such cultivation

²**culture** *transitive verb* **cul·tured; cul·tur·ing** \'kəlch-riŋ, 'kəl-chə-\ (1510)
1 : CULTIVATE
2 a : to grow in a prepared medium **b :** to start a culture from

cultured *adjective* (circa 1746)
1 : CULTIVATED
2 : produced under artificial conditions ⟨*cultured* viruses⟩ ⟨*cultured* pearls⟩

culture shock *noun* (circa 1940)
: a sense of confusion and uncertainty sometimes with feelings of anxiety that may affect people exposed to an alien culture or environment without adequate preparation

cul·tus \'kəl-təs\ *noun* [Latin, adoration] (1640)
: CULT

cul·ver \'kəl-vər, 'kul-\ *noun* [Middle English, from Old English *culfer,* from (assumed) Vulgar Latin *columbra,* from Latin *columbula,* diminutive of Latin *columba* dove — more at COLUMBINE] (before 12th century)
: PIGEON

cul·ver·in \'kəl-və-rən\ *noun* [Middle English, from Middle French *couleuvrine,* from *couleuvre* snake, from Latin *colubra*] (15th century)
: an early firearm: **a :** a rude musket **b :** a long cannon (as an 18-pounder) of the 16th and 17th centuries

cul·vert \'kəl-vərt\ *noun* [origin unknown] (1773)
1 : a transverse drain
2 : a conduit for a culvert
3 : a bridge over a culvert

cum \'kum, 'kəm\ *conjunction* [Latin, with; akin to Latin *com-* — more at CO-] (circa 1873)
: along with being **:** AND — used to form usually hyphenated phrases ⟨a credible mining camp elder-*cum*-publican —G. B. Shaw⟩ ⟨Christian and Christian-*cum*-voodoo churches —David Binder⟩

¹**cum·ber** \'kəm-bər\ *transitive verb* **cum·bered; cum·ber·ing** \-b(ə-)riŋ\ [Middle English *combren,* perhaps from Old French *combrer* to prevent, from (assumed) Old French *combre* abatis] (14th century)
1 *archaic* **:** TROUBLE, HARASS
2 a : to hinder or encumber by being in the way ⟨*cumbered* with heavy clothing⟩ **b :** to clutter up ⟨rocks *cumbering* the yard⟩

²**cumber** *noun* (14th century)
: something that cumbers; *especially* **:** HINDRANCE

cum·ber·some \'kəm-bər-səm\ *adjective* (1535)
1 *dialect* **:** BURDENSOME, TROUBLESOME
2 : unwieldy because of heaviness and bulk
3 : slow-moving **:** PONDEROUS
synonym see HEAVY
— **cum·ber·some·ly** *adverb*
— **cum·ber·some·ness** *noun*

cum·brous \'kəm-b(ə-)rəs\ *adjective* (15th century)
: CUMBERSOME
synonym see HEAVY
— **cum·brous·ly** *adverb*
— **cum·brous·ness** *noun*

cum·in \'kə-mən, 'kyü-\ *noun* [Middle English, from Old English *cymen,* from Latin *cyminum,* from Greek *kyminon,* of Semitic origin; akin to Akkadian *kamūnu* cumin] (before 12th century)
: a low plant (*Cuminum cyminum*) of the carrot family long cultivated for its aromatic seeds; *also* **:** the fruit or seed of cumin used as a spice

cum lau·de \kùm-'laù-də, -dē; ˌkəm-'lò-dē\ *adverb or adjective* [New Latin, with praise] (1893)
: with distinction ⟨graduated *cum laude*⟩ — compare MAGNA CUM LAUDE, SUMMA CUM LAUDE

cum·mer·bund \'kə-mər-ˌbənd, 'kəm-bər-\ *also* **cum·ber·bund** \'kəm-bər-\ *noun* [Hindi *kamarband,* from Persian, from *kamar* waist + *band* band] (1616)
: a broad waistband usually worn in place of a vest with men's dress clothes and adapted in various styles of women's clothes

cum·shaw \'kəm-ˌshò\ *noun* [Chinese (Xiamen) *kam siā* grateful thanks] (1839)
: PRESENT, GRATUITY

cumul- *or* **cumuli-** *or* **cumulo-** *combining form* [New Latin, from Latin *cumulus*]
: cumulus and ⟨*cumulo*nimbus⟩

cu·mu·late \'kyü-myə-ˌlāt\ *verb* **-lat·ed; -lat·ing** [Latin *cumulatus,* past participle of *cumulare,* from *cumulus* mass] (1534)
transitive verb
1 : to gather or pile in a heap
2 : to combine into one
3 : to build up by addition of new material
intransitive verb
: to become massed
— **cu·mu·late** \-lət, -ˌlāt\ *adjective*
— **cu·mu·la·tion** \ˌkyü-myə-'lā-shən\ *noun*

cu·mu·la·tive \'kyü-my lə-tiv, -ˌlā-\ *adjective* (1605)
1 a : made up of accumulated parts **b :** increasing by successive additions
2 a : tending to prove the same point ⟨*cumulative* evidence⟩ **b :** additional rather than repeated ⟨*cumulative* legacy⟩
3 a : taking effect upon completion of another penal sentence ⟨*cumulative* sentence⟩ **b :** increasing in severity with repetition of the offense ⟨*cumulative* penalty⟩
4 : formed by the addition of new material of the same kind ⟨*cumulative* book index⟩
5 : summing or integrating overall data or values of a random variable less than or less than or equal to a specified value ⟨*cumulative* normal distribution⟩ ⟨*cumulative* frequency distribution⟩
— **cu·mu·la·tive·ly** *adverb*
— **cu·mu·la·tive·ness** *noun*

cumulative distribution function *noun* (circa 1965)
: DISTRIBUTION FUNCTION

cu·mu·li·form \'kyü-myə-lə-ˌfòrm\ *adjective* (1885)
: of the form of a cumulus

cu·mu·lo·nim·bus \-'nim-bəs\ *noun* [New Latin] (1887)
: cumulus cloud often spread out in the shape of an anvil extending to great heights — see CLOUD illustration

cu·mu·lous \'kyü-myə-ləs\ *adjective* (1815)
: resembling cumulus

cu·mu·lus \-ləs\ *noun, plural* **-li** \-ˌlī, -ˌlē\ [Latin] (1659)
1 : HEAP, ACCUMULATION
2 [New Latin, from Latin] **:** a massy cloud form having a flat base and rounded outlines often piled up like a mountain — see CLOUD illustration

cunc·ta·tion \ˌkəŋ(k)-'tā-shən\ *noun* [Latin *cunctation-, cunctatio,* from *cunctari* to hesitate; akin to Sanskrit *śaṅkate* he wavers, Old English *hangian* to hang] (1585)
: DELAY
— **cunc·ta·tive** \'keŋ(k)-ˌtā-tiv, -tə-tiv\ *adjective*

cu·ne·ate \'kyü-nē-ˌāt, -ət\ *adjective* [Latin *cuneatus,* from *cuneus* wedge] (1810)
: narrowly triangular with the acute angle toward the base — see LEAF illustration

¹**cu·ne·i·form** \kyü-'nē-ə-ˌfòrm, 'kyü-n(ē-)ə-\ *adjective* [probably from French *cunéiforme,* from Middle French, from Latin *cuneus* + Middle French *-iforme* -iform] (1677)
1 : having the shape of a wedge
2 : composed of or written in wedge-shaped characters ⟨*cuneiform* syllabary⟩

²**cuneiform** *noun* (1808)
1 : a cuneiform part; *specifically* **:** a cuneiform bone or cartilage
2 : cuneiform writing

cuneiform 2

cun·ner \'kə-nər\ *noun* [origin unknown] (1602)
: either of two wrasses: **a :** a European wrasse (*Crenilabrus melops*) **b :** a wrasse (*Tautogolabrus adspersus*) common along the northeastern U.S. and adjacent Canadian coast

cun·ni·lin·gus \ˌkə-ni-'liŋ-gəs\ *also* **cun·ni·linc·tus** \-'liŋ(k)-təs\ *noun* [*cunnilingus,* New Latin, from Latin, one who licks the vulva, from *cunnus* vulva + *lingere* to lick; *cunnilinctus,* New Latin, from Latin *cunnus* + *linctus,* act of licking, from *lingere* — more at LICK] (1887)
: oral stimulation of the vulva or clitoris

¹**cun·ning** \'kə-niŋ\ *adjective* [Middle English, from present participle of *can* know] (14th century)
1 : dexterous or crafty in the use of special resources (as skill or knowledge) or in attaining an end ⟨a *cunning* plotter⟩
2 : displaying keen insight ⟨a *cunning* observation⟩
3 : characterized by wiliness and trickery ⟨*cunning* schemes⟩
4 : prettily appealing **:** CUTE
synonym see CLEVER, SLY
— **cun·ning·ly** \-niŋ-lē\ *adverb*
— **cun·ning·ness** *noun*

²**cunning** *noun* (14th century)
1 *obsolete* **a :** KNOWLEDGE, LEARNING **b :** magic art
2 : dexterous skill and subtlety (as in inventing, devising, or executing) ⟨high-ribbed vault . . . with perfect *cunning* framed —William Wordsworth⟩
3 : CRAFT, SLYNESS
synonym see ART

cunt \'kənt\ *noun* [Middle English *cunte;* akin to Middle Low German *kunte* female pudenda] (14th century)
1 : the female pudenda; *also* **:** coitus with a woman — usually considered obscene
2 : WOMAN 1a — usually used disparagingly; usually considered obscene

¹**cup** \'kəp\ *noun* [Middle English *cuppe,* from Old English, from Late Latin *cuppa* cup, alteration of Latin *cupa* tub — more at HIVE] (before 12th century)
1 : an open usually bowl-shaped drinking vessel
2 a : a drinking vessel and its contents **b :** the consecrated wine of the Communion
3 : something that falls to one's lot
4 : an ornamental cup offered as a prize (as in a championship)
5 a : something resembling a cup **b :** a cup-shaped plant organ **c :** an athletic supporter reinforced usually with plastic to provide extra protection to the wearer **d :** either of two parts of a brassiere that are shaped like and fit over the breasts **e :** the metal case inside a hole in golf; *also* **:** the hole itself
6 : a usually iced beverage resembling punch but served from a pitcher rather than a bowl
7 : a half pint **:** eight fluid ounces
8 : a food served in a cup-shaped usually footed vessel ⟨fruit *cup*⟩

9 : the symbol ∪ indicating the union of two sets — compare CAP 7
— **cup·like** \-‚līk\ adjective
— **in one's cups** : DRUNK

²cup transitive verb **cupped; cup·ping** (14th century)
1 : to treat by cupping
2 a : to curve into the shape of a cup ⟨*cupped* his hands around his mouth⟩ **b** : to place in or as if in a cup

cup·bear·er \'kəp-‚bar-ər, -‚ber-\ noun (15th century)
: one who has the duty of filling and handing around the cups in which wine is served

cup·board \'kə-bərd\ noun (1530)
: a closet with shelves where dishes, utensils, or food is kept; also : a small closet

cup·cake \'kəp-‚kāk\ noun (1828)
: a small cake baked in a cuplike mold

¹cu·pel \kyü-'pel, 'kyü-pəl\ noun [French *coupelle*, diminutive of *coupe* cup, from Late Latin *cuppa*] (1605)
: a small shallow porous cup especially of bone ash used in assaying to separate precious metals from lead

²cupel transitive verb **-pelled** or **-peled; -pel·ling** or **-pel·ing** (1644)
: to refine by means of a cupel
— **cu·pel·ler** noun

cu·pel·la·tion \‚kyü-pə-'lā-shən, -‚pe-\ noun (circa 1691)
: refinement (as of gold or silver) in a cupel by exposure to high temperature in a blast of air by which the lead, copper, tin, and other unwanted metals are oxidized and partly sink into the porous cupel

cup·ful \'kəp-‚fùl\ noun, plural **cup·fuls** \-‚fùlz\ also **cups·ful** \'kəps-‚fùl\ (12th century)
1 : as much as a cup will hold
2 : CUP 7
usage see ²-FUL

cup fungus noun (circa 1905)
: any of an order (Pezizales) of mostly saprophytic fungi with a fleshy or horny apothecium that is often colored and is typically shaped like a cup, saucer, or disk

Cu·pid \'kyü-pəd\ noun [Latin *Cupido*]
1 : the Roman god of erotic love — compare EROS
2 not capitalized : a figure that represents Cupid as a naked usually winged boy often holding a bow and arrow
word history see EROTIC

cu·pid·i·ty \kyü-'pi-də-tē\ noun, plural **-ties** [Middle English *cupidite*, from Middle French *cupidité*, from Latin *cupiditat-, cupiditas* — more at COVET] (15th century)
1 : inordinate desire for wealth : AVARICE, GREED
2 : strong desire : LUST

Cupid's bow noun (1858)
: a bow that consists of two convex curves usually with recurved ends

cup of tea (1932)
1 : something one likes or excels in ⟨I see already that storytelling isn't my *cup of tea* —John Barth⟩; also : a person suited to one's taste
2 : a thing to be reckoned with : MATTER ⟨poltergeists are a different *cup of tea* —D. B. W. Lewis⟩

cu·po·la \'kyü-pə-lə, ÷-‚lō\ noun [Italian, from Latin *cupula*, diminutive of *cupa* tub] (1549)
1 a : a rounded vault resting on a usually circular base and forming a roof or a ceiling **b** : a small structure built on top of a roof
2 : a vertical cylindrical furnace for melting iron in the foundry that has tuyeres and tapping spouts near the bottom
3 : a raised observation post in the roof of a railroad caboose
— **cu·po·laed** \-ləd, ÷-‚lōd\ adjective

cup·pa \'kə-pə\ noun [short for *cuppa tea*, pronunciation spelling of *cup of tea*] (1934)
chiefly British : a cup of tea

cup·ping noun (14th century)
: an operation of drawing blood to the surface of the body by use of a glass vessel evacuated by heat

cup·py \'kə-pē\ adjective **cup·pi·er; -est** (1882)
1 : resembling a cup
2 : full of small depressions ⟨a *cuppy* racetrack⟩

cupr- or **cupri-** or **cupro-** combining form [Late Latin *cuprum* — more at COPPER]
1 : copper ⟨*cupri*ferous⟩
2 : copper and ⟨*cupro*nickel⟩

cu·pric \'kyü-prik, 'kü-\ adjective (1799)
: of, relating to, or containing copper with a valence of two

cu·prif·er·ous \kyü-'pri-f(ə-)rəs, kü-\ adjective (1784)
: containing copper

cu·prite \'kyü-‚prīt, 'kü-\ noun [German *Kuprit*, from Late Latin *cuprum*] (circa 1850)
: a mineral consisting of copper oxide and constituting an ore of copper

cu·pro·nick·el \‚kyü-prō-'ni-kəl, ‚kü-\ noun (1900)
: an alloy of copper and nickel; especially : one containing about 70 percent copper and 30 percent nickel

cu·prous \'kyü-prəs, 'kü-\ adjective (1669)
: of, relating to, or containing copper with a valence of one

cu·pu·late \'kyü-pyə-‚lāt, -lət\ adjective (1835)
: shaped like, having, or bearing a cupule

cu·pule \'kyü-(‚)pyü(ə)l\ noun [New Latin *cupula*, from Late Latin, diminutive of Latin *cupa* tub — more at HIVE] (1826)
: a cup-shaped anatomical structure: as **a** : an involucre characteristic of the oak in which the bracts are indurated and coherent **b** : an outer integument partially enclosing the seed of some seed ferns

cur \'kər\ noun [Middle English, short for *curdogge*, from (assumed) Middle English *curren* to growl (perhaps from Old Norse *kurra* to grumble) + Middle English *dogge* dog] (13th century)
1 : a mongrel or inferior dog
2 : a surly or cowardly fellow

cur·able \'kyùr-ə-bəl\ adjective (14th century)
: capable of being cured
— **cur·abil·i·ty** \‚kyùr-ə-'bi-lə-tē\ noun
— **cur·able·ness** \'kyùr-ə-bəl-nəs\ noun
— **cur·ably** \-blē\ adverb

cu·ra·çao \'kyùr-ə-‚sō, -‚saù, 'kùr-; ‚k(y)ùr-ə-'\ also **cu·ra·çoa** \same, or ‚kyùr-ə-'sō-ə\ noun [Dutch *curaçao*, from *Curaçao*, Netherlands Antilles] (1813)
: a liqueur flavored with the dried peel of the sour orange

cu·ra·cy \'kyùr-ə-sē\ noun, plural **-cies** (1682)
: the office or term of office of a curate

cu·ra·re also **cu·ra·ri** \kyü-'rär-ē, kù-\ noun [Portuguese & Spanish *curare*, from Carib *kurari*] (1777)
: a dried aqueous extract especially of a vine (as *Strychnos toxifera* of the family Loganiaceae or *Chondodendron tomentosum* of the family Menispermaceae) used by South American Indians to poison arrow tips and in medicine to produce muscular relaxation

cu·ra·rine \-'rär-ən, -‚ēn\ noun (circa 1872)
: any of several alkaloids from curare

cu·ra·rize \-'rär-‚īz\ transitive verb **-rized; -riz·ing** (1875)
: to treat with curare
— **cu·ra·ri·za·tion** \-‚rär-ə-'zā-shən\ noun

cu·ras·sow \'kyùr-ə-‚sō, 'kùr-\ noun [alteration of *Curaçao*] (1685)
: any of several large arboreal game birds (family Cracidae, especially genus *Crax*) of South and Central America related to the domestic fowls

¹cu·rate \'kyùr-ət also 'kyùr-‚āt\ noun [Middle English, from Medieval Latin *curatus*, from *cura* cure of souls, from Latin, care] (14th century)
1 : a clergyman in charge of a parish
2 : a clergyman serving as assistant (as to a rector) in a parish

²cu·rate \'kyùr-‚āt, kyù-'rāt\ transitive verb **cu·rat·ed; cu·rat·ing** (1909)
: to act as curator of

curate's egg noun [from the story of a curate who was given a stale egg by his bishop and declared that parts of it were excellent] (1905) *British* : something with both good and bad parts or qualities

cu·ra·tive \'kyùr-ə-tiv\ adjective (15th century)
: relating to or used in the cure of diseases
: tending to cure
— **curative** noun
— **cu·ra·tive·ly** adverb

cu·ra·tor \'kyùr-‚ā-tər, kyù-'rā-, 'kyùr-ə-\ noun [Latin, from *curatus*, past participle of *curare* to care, from *cura* care] (1632)
: one that has the care and superintendence of something; especially : one in charge of a museum, zoo, or other place of exhibit
— **cu·ra·to·ri·al** \‚kyùr-ə-'tōr-ē-əl, -'tòr-\ adjective
— **cu·ra·tor·ship** \'kyùr-‚ā-tər-‚ship, kyù-'rā-, 'kyùr-ə-\ noun

¹curb \'kərb\ noun [Middle French *courbe* curve, curved piece of wood or iron, from *courbe* curved, from Latin *curvus*] (15th century)
1 : a bit that exerts severe pressure on a horse's jaws; also : the chain or strap attached to it
2 : an enclosing frame, border, or edging
3 : CHECK, RESTRAINT ⟨a price *curb*⟩
4 : a raised edge or margin to strengthen or confine
5 : an edging (as of concrete) built along a street to form part of a gutter
6 [from the fact that it originally transacted its business on the street] : a market for trading in securities not listed on a stock exchange

²curb transitive verb (1530)
1 : to furnish with a curb
2 : to check or control with or as if with a curb ⟨trying to *curb* her curiosity⟩
3 : to lead (a dog) to a suitable place (as a gutter) for defecation
synonym see RESTRAIN

curb·ing \'kər-biŋ\ noun (1838)
1 : the material for a curb
2 : CURB

curb service noun (1931)
: service extended (as by a restaurant) to persons sitting in parked automobiles

curb·side \'kərb-‚sīd\ noun (1946)
1 : the side of a pavement bordered by a curb
2 : SIDEWALK

¹curb·stone \-‚stōn\ noun (1791)
: a stone or edging of concrete forming a curb

²curbstone adjective (1848)
1 : operating on the street without maintaining an office ⟨a *curbstone* broker⟩
2 : not having the benefit of training or experience ⟨a *curbstone* critic⟩

curb weight noun (1949)
: the weight of an automobile with standard equipment and fuel, oil, and coolant

curch \'kərch\ noun [Middle English] (14th century)
Scottish : KERCHIEF 1

cur·cu·lio \(‚)kər-'kyü-lē-‚ō\ noun, plural **-li·os** [Latin, grain weevil] (1756)

\ə\ abut \ᵊ\ kitten \ər\ further \a\ ash \ā\ ace
\ä\ mop, mar \aù\ out \ch\ chin \e\ bet \ē\ easy
\g\ go \i\ hit \ī\ ice \j\ job \ŋ\ sing \ō\ go
\ò\ law \òi\ boy \th\ thin \th\ the \ü\ loot \ù\ foot
\y\ yet \zh\ vision *see also* Guide to Pronunciation

: any of various weevils; *especially* : one that injures fruit

¹curd \'kərd\ *noun* [Middle English *crud*; probably akin to Old English *crūdan* to press — more at CROWD] (15th century)
1 : the thick casein-rich part of coagulated milk
2 : something suggesting the curd of milk
— **curdy** \'kər-dē\ *adjective*

²curd *verb* (15th century)
: COAGULATE, CURDLE

cur·dle \'kər-d°l\ *verb* **cur·dled; cur·dling** \'kərd-liŋ, 'kər-d°l-iŋ\ [frequentative of ²*curd*] (1590)
intransitive verb
1 : to form curds; *also* : to congeal as if by forming curds ⟨a scream *curdled* in her throat⟩
2 : to go bad or wrong : SPOIL
transitive verb
1 : to cause curds to form in
2 : SPOIL, SOUR

¹cure \'kyur\ *noun* [Middle English, from Old French, from Medieval Latin & Latin; Medieval Latin *cura*, cure of souls, from Latin, care] (14th century)
1 a : spiritual charge : CARE **b** : pastoral charge of a parish
2 a : recovery or relief from a disease **b** : something (as a drug or treatment) that cures a disease **c** : a course or period of treatment ⟨take the *cure* for alcoholism⟩ **d** : SPA
3 : a complete or permanent solution or remedy ⟨seeking a *cure* for unemployment⟩
4 : a process or method of curing
— **cure·less** \-ləs\ *adjective*

²cure *verb* **cured; cur·ing** (14th century)
transitive verb
1 a : to restore to health, soundness, or normality **b** : to bring about recovery from
2 a : to deal with in a way that eliminates or rectifies ⟨his small size, which time would *cure* for him —William Faulkner⟩ **b** : to free from something objectionable or harmful
3 : to prepare or alter especially by chemical or physical processing for keeping or use
intransitive verb
1 a : to undergo a curing process **b** : SET 11
2 : to effect a cure
— **cur·er** *noun*

cu·ré \kyu-'rā, 'kyur-,ā\ *noun* [French, from Old French, from Medieval Latin *curatus* — more at CURATE] (1655)
: a parish priest

cure–all \'kyur-,ȯl\ *noun* (1821)
: a remedy for all ills : PANACEA

cu·ret·tage \,kyur-ə-'täzh\ *noun* (1897)
: a surgical scraping or cleaning by means of a curette

¹cu·rette *also* **cu·ret** \kyu-'ret\ *noun* [French *curette*, from *curer* to cure, from Latin *curare*, from *cura*] (1753)
: a surgical instrument that has a scoop, ring, or loop at the tip and is used in performing curettage

²curette *also* **curet** *transitive verb* **cu·rett·ed; cu·rett·ing** (1888)
: to perform curettage on
— **cu·rette·ment** \kyu-'ret-mənt\ *noun*

cur·few \'kər-,fyü\ *noun* [Middle English, from Middle French *covrefeu*, signal given to bank the hearth fire, curfew, from *covrir* to cover + *feu* fire, from Latin *focus* hearth] (14th century)
1 : the sounding of a bell at evening ⟨the *Curfew* tolls the knell of parting day —Thomas Gray⟩
2 a : a regulation enjoining the withdrawal of usually specified persons (as juveniles or military personnel) from the streets or the closing of business establishments or places of assembly at a stated hour **b** : a signal to announce the beginning of a curfew **c** : the hour at which a curfew becomes effective **d** : the period during which a curfew is in effect ◆

cu·ria \'kyur-ē-ə, 'kur-\ *noun, plural* **cu·ri·ae** \'kyur-ē-,ē, 'kur-ē-,ī\ [Latin, perhaps from *co- + vir* man — more at VIRILE] (1600)
1 a : a division of the ancient Roman people comprising several gentes of a tribe **b** : the place of assembly of one of these divisions
2 a : the court of a medieval king **b** : a court of justice
3 *often capitalized* : the body of congregations, tribunals, and offices through which the pope governs the Roman Catholic Church
— **cu·ri·al** \'kyur-ē-əl, 'kur-\ *adjective*

cu·rie \'kyur-(,)ē, kyu-'rē\ *noun* [Marie & Pierre *Curie*] (1910)
1 : a unit quantity of any radioactive nuclide in which 3.7 × 10¹⁰ disintegrations occur per second
2 : a unit of radioactivity equal to 3.7 × 10¹⁰ disintegrations per second ◆

Curie point *noun* (1911)
1 : the temperature at which there is a transition between the ferromagnetic and paramagnetic phases
2 : a temperature at which the anomalies that characterize a ferroelectric substance disappear — called also *Curie temperature*

cu·rio \'kyur-ē-,ō\ *noun, plural* **cu·ri·os** [short for *curiosity*] (1851)
: something (as a decorative object) considered novel, rare, or bizarre : CURIOSITY; *also* : an unusual or bizarre person

cu·ri·o·sa \,kyur-ē-'ō-sə, -'ō-zə\ *noun plural* [New Latin, from Latin, neuter plural of *curiosus*] (1883)
: CURIOSITIES, RARITIES; *especially* : unusual or erotic books

cu·ri·os·i·ty \,kyur-ē-'ä-s(ə-)tē\ *noun, plural* **-ties** (14th century)
1 : desire to know: **a** : inquisitive interest in others' concerns : NOSINESS **b** : interest leading to inquiry ⟨intellectual *curiosity*⟩
2 *archaic* : undue nicety or fastidiousness
3 a : one that arouses interest especially for uncommon or exotic characteristics **b** : an unusual knickknack : CURIO **c** : a curious trait or aspect

cu·ri·ous \'kyur-ē-əs\ *adjective* [Middle English, from Middle French *curios*, from Latin *curiosus* careful, inquisitive, from *cura* cure] (14th century)
1 a *archaic* : made carefully **b** *obsolete* : ABSTRUSE **c** *archaic* : precisely accurate
2 a : marked by desire to investigate and learn **b** : marked by inquisitive interest in others' concerns : NOSY
3 : exciting attention as strange, novel, or unexpected : ODD ☆
— **cu·ri·ous·ness** *noun*

cu·ri·ous·ly \-lē\ *adverb* (1665)
1 : in a curious manner ⟨seemed *curiously* calm⟩
2 : as is curious ⟨*curiously*, he continues to win reelection⟩

cu·ri·um \'kyur-ē-əm\ *noun* [New Latin, from Marie & Pierre *Curie*] (1946)
: a metallic radioactive element produced artificially — see ELEMENT table

¹curl \'kər(-ə)l\ *verb* [Middle English, from *crul* curly, probably from Middle Dutch; akin to Old High German *krol* curly] (14th century)
transitive verb
1 : to form (as the hair) into coils or ringlets
2 : to form into a curved shape : TWIST ⟨*curled* his lip in a sneer⟩
3 : to furnish with curls
intransitive verb
1 a : to grow in coils or spirals **b** : to form ripples or crinkles ⟨bacon *curling* in a pan⟩
2 : to move or progress in curves or spirals : WIND ⟨the path *curled* along the mountainside⟩
3 : TWIST, CONTORT
4 : to play the game of curling

²curl *noun* (1602)
1 : a lock of hair that coils : RINGLET

2 : something having a spiral or winding form : COIL
3 : the action of curling : the state of being curled
4 : a curved or spiral marking in the grain of wood
5 : a hollow arch of water formed when the crest of a breaking wave spills forward

curl·er \'kər-lər\ *noun* (1638)
1 : a player of curling
2 : one that curls; *especially* : a device on which hair is wound for curling

cur·lew \'kər-(,)lü, 'kər-(,)yü\ *noun, plural* **curlews** *or* **curlew** [Middle English, from Middle French *corlieu*, of imitative origin] (14th century)
: any of various largely brownish chiefly migratory birds (especially genus *Numenius*) having long legs and a long slender downcurved bill and related to the sandpipers and snipes

¹cur·li·cue *also* **cur·ly·cue** \'kər-lē-,kyü, -li-\ *noun* [*curly* + *cue* a braid of hair] (1843)
: a fancifully curved or spiral figure : FLOURISH

²curlicue *verb* **-cued; -cu·ing** (1844)
intransitive verb
: to form curlicues

☆ SYNONYMS

Curious, inquisitive, prying mean interested in what is not one's personal or proper concern. CURIOUS, a neutral term, basically connotes an active desire to learn or to know ⟨children are *curious* about everything⟩. INQUISITIVE suggests impertinent and habitual curiosity and persistent quizzing ⟨dreaded the visits of their *inquisitive* relatives⟩. PRYING implies busy meddling and officiousness ⟨*prying* neighbors who refuse to mind their own business⟩.

◇ WORD HISTORY

curfew In Europe in the Middle Ages people were required to put out or cover their hearth fires by a certain time in the evening. Given the fact that houses were usually of wood and closely adjoining, a hearth fire left unattended overnight might spread and destroy neighboring houses or even the entire town. A bell was rung to let people know that the time had come for covering their fires. In Middle French this signal was called *covrefeu*, a compound of *covrir* "to cover," and *feu* "fire." The meaning of *covrefeu* was extended to any public signal calling on people to retire in the evening, and also to the time of evening when the signal was given. It was in these senses that English borrowed the word as *corfu* or *curfew* in the 14th century. Another English word based on French *covre* and a following noun object is *coverlet*.

curie The unit of measurement called the *curie* is named after Pierre (1859–1906) and Marie (1867–1934) Curie, the French chemists and physicists. The Curies were two of the most important and influential figures in modern physics. Their major joint contributions include the discovery (with Henri Becquerel) of radioactivity and the discovery and isolation of radium and polonium in 1898. In 1910 the first International Congress of Radiology honored the husband and wife team by establishing *curie* as a standard unit of measurement for radioactive material. Later it was used as a unit of radioactivity itself. The Curies were awarded the Nobel Prize for Physics in 1903, and Marie Curie was awarded the Nobel Prize for Chemistry in 1911.

transitive verb
: to embellish with curlicues

curl·ing \'kər-liŋ\ *noun* (1620)
: a game in which two teams of four players each slide curling stones over a stretch of ice toward a target circle

curling iron *noun* (1616)
: a rod-shaped usually metal instrument which is heated and around which a lock of hair to be curled or waved is wound

curling stone *noun* (1620)
: an ellipsoid stone or occasionally piece of iron with a gooseneck handle used in the game of curling

curl·pa·per \'kər-(ə)l-ˌpā-pər\ *noun* (circa 1817)
: a strip or piece of paper around which a lock of hair is wound for curling

curl up *intransitive verb* (1861)
: to arrange oneself in or as if in a ball or curl ⟨*curl up* by the fire⟩ ⟨*curl up* with a good book⟩

curly \'kər-lē\ *adjective* **curl·i·er; -est** (circa 1784)
1 : tending to curl; *also* **:** having curls
2 : having the grain composed of fibers that undulate without crossing and that often form alternating light and dark lines ⟨*curly* maple⟩
— **curl·i·ness** *noun*

curly–coat·ed retriever \'kər-lē-'kō-təd-\ *noun* (1885)
: any of a breed of sporting dogs with a short curly black or liver-colored coat

curly top *noun* (1901)
: a destructive virus disease especially of beets that kills young plants and causes curling and puckering of the leaves in older plants

cur·mud·geon \(ˌ)kər-'mə-jən\ *noun* [origin unknown] (1577)
1 *archaic* **:** MISER
2 : a crusty, ill-tempered, and usually old man
— **cur·mud·geon·li·ness** \-lē-nəs\ *noun*
— **cur·mud·geon·ly** \-lē\ *adjective*

curn \'kərn\ *or* **cur·ran** \'kə-rən\ *noun* [Middle English *curn*; akin to Middle English *corn*] (14th century)
1 *Scottish* **:** GRAIN
2 *Scottish* **:** a small number **:** FEW

curr \'kər\ *intransitive verb* [imitative] (1677)
: to make a murmuring sound (as of doves)

cur·ragh *or* **cur·rach** \'kə-rə, -ˌrak\ *noun* [Middle English *currok*, from Irish *currach, curach*] (15th century)
: a usually large coracle used especially on the west coast of Ireland

cur·rant \'kər-ənt, 'kə-rənt\ *noun* [Middle English *raison of Coraunte*, literally, raisin of Corinth] (14th century)
1 : a small seedless raisin grown chiefly in the Levant
2 : the acid edible fruit of several shrubs (genus *Ribes*) of the saxifrage family; *also* **:** a plant bearing currants

cur·ren·cy \'kər-ən(t)-sē, 'kə-rən(t)-\ *noun, plural* **-cies** (1699)
1 a : circulation as a medium of exchange **b :** general use, acceptance, or prevalence **c :** the quality or state of being current **:** CURRENTNESS
2 a : something (as coins, treasury notes, and banknotes) that is in circulation as a medium of exchange **b :** paper money in circulation **c :** a common article for bartering **d :** a medium of verbal or intellectual expression

¹cur·rent \'kər-ənt, 'kə-rənt\ *adjective* [Middle English *curraunt*, from Old French *curant*, present participle of *courre* to run, from Latin *currere* — more at CAR] (14th century)
1 a *archaic* **:** RUNNING, FLOWING **b** (1) **:** presently elapsing (2) **:** occurring in or existing at the present time (3) **:** most recent ⟨the *current* issue⟩
2 : used as a medium of exchange
3 : generally accepted, used, practiced, or prevalent at the moment
— **cur·rent·ly** *adverb*
— **cur·rent·ness** *noun*

²current *noun* (14th century)
1 a : the part of a fluid body (as air or water) moving continuously in a certain direction **b :** the swiftest part of a stream **c :** a tidal or nontidal movement of lake or ocean water **d :** flow marked by force or strength
2 a : a tendency or course of events that is usually the result of an interplay of forces ⟨*currents* of public opinion⟩ **b :** a prevailing mood **:** STRAIN
3 : a flow of electric charge; *also* **:** the rate of such flow
synonym *see* TENDENCY

current assets *noun plural* (circa 1909)
: assets of a short-term nature that are readily convertible to cash

cur·ri·cle \'kər-i-kəl, 'kə-ri-\ *noun* [Latin *curriculum* running, chariot, from *currere*] (1752)
: a 2-wheeled chaise usually drawn by two horses

cur·ric·u·lar \kə-'ri-kyə-lər\ *adjective* (circa 1909)
: of or relating to a curriculum

cur·ric·u·lum \-ləm\ *noun, plural* **-la** \-lə\ *also* **-lums** [New Latin, from Latin, running, course] (1633)
1 : the courses offered by an educational institution
2 : a set of courses constituting an area of specialization

cur·ric·u·lum vi·tae \kə-'ri-kyə-ləm-'vē-ˌtī, -kə-ləm-, -'wē-ˌtī, -'vī-ˌtē\ *noun, plural* **cur·ric·u·la vitae** \-lə-\ [Latin, course of (one's) life] (1902)
: a short account of one's career and qualifications prepared typically by an applicant for a position

cur·ri·ery \'kər-ē-ə-rē, 'kə-rē-\ *noun, plural* **-er·ies** (circa 1889)
1 : the trade of a currier of leather
2 : a place where currying is done

cur·rish \'kər-ish\ *adjective* (15th century)
1 : IGNOBLE
2 : resembling a cur **:** MONGREL
— **cur·rish·ly** *adverb*

¹cur·ry \'kər-ē, 'kə-rē\ *transitive verb* **cur·ried; cur·ry·ing** [Middle English *currayen*, from Old French *correer* to prepare, curry, from (assumed) Vulgar Latin *conredare*, from Latin *com-* + a base of Germanic origin; akin to Gothic *garaiths* arrayed — more at READY] (13th century)
1 : to clean the coat of (as a horse) with a currycomb
2 : to treat (tanned leather) especially by incorporating oil or grease
3 : BEAT, THRASH
— **cur·ri·er** *noun*
— **curry favor** [Middle English *currayen favel* to curry a chestnut horse] **:** to seek to gain favor by flattery or attention

²cur·ry *also* **cur·rie** \'kər-ē, 'kə-rē\ *noun, plural* **curries** [Tamil *kaṟi*] (1681)
1 : a food, dish, or sauce in Indian cuisine seasoned with a mixture of pungent spices; *also* **:** a food or dish seasoned with curry powder
2 : CURRY POWDER

³curry *transitive verb* **cur·ried; cur·ry·ing** (1839)
: to flavor or cook with curry powder or a curry sauce

cur·ry·comb \-ˌkōm\ *noun* (1573)
: a comb made of rows of metallic teeth or serrated ridges and used especially to curry horses
— **currycomb** *transitive verb*

curry powder *noun* (1810)
: a condiment consisting of several pungent ground spices (as cayenne pepper, fenugreek, and turmeric)

¹curse \'kərs\ *noun* [Middle English *curs*, from Old English] (before 12th century)
1 : a prayer or invocation for harm or injury to come upon one **:** IMPRECATION
2 : something that is cursed or accursed

3 : evil or misfortune that comes as if in response to imprecation or as retribution
4 : a cause of great harm or misfortune **:** TORMENT
5 : MENSTRUATION — used with *the*

²curse *verb* **cursed; curs·ing** (before 12th century)
transitive verb
1 : to use profanely insolent language against **:** BLASPHEME
2 a : to call upon divine or supernatural power to send injury upon **b :** to execrate in fervent and often profane terms
3 : to bring great evil upon **:** AFFLICT
intransitive verb
: to utter imprecations **:** SWEAR
synonym *see* EXECRATE

cursed \'kər-səd, 'kərst\ *also* **curst** \'kərst\ *adjective* (13th century)
: being under or deserving a curse
— **curs·ed·ly** *adverb*
— **curs·ed·ness** *noun*

¹cur·sive \'kər-siv\ *adjective* [French or Medieval Latin; French *cursif*, from Medieval Latin *cursivus*, literally, running, from Latin *cursus*, past participle of *currere* to run] (1784)
: RUNNING, COURSING: as **a** *of writing* **:** flowing often with the strokes of successive characters joined and the angles rounded **b :** having a flowing, easy, impromptu character
— **cur·sive·ly** *adverb*
— **cur·sive·ness** *noun*

²cursive *noun* (1861)
1 : a manuscript written in cursive writing; *also* **:** cursive writing
2 : a style of printed letter resembling handwriting

cur·sor \'kər-sər\ *noun* [Latin, runner, from *currere*] (1594)
: a movable item used to mark a position: as **a** **:** a transparent slide with a line attached to a slide rule **b :** a visual cue (as a flashing rectangle) on a video display that indicates position (as for data entry)

cur·so·ri·al \ˌkər-'sōr-ē-əl, -'sor-\ *adjective* (1836)
: adapted to or involving running

cur·so·ry \'kərs-rē, 'kər-sə-\ *adjective* [Late Latin *cursorius* of running, from Latin *currere*] (1601)
: rapidly and often superficially performed or produced **:** HASTY ⟨a *cursory* glance⟩
synonym *see* SUPERFICIAL
— **cur·so·ri·ly** \-rə-lē\ *adverb*
— **cur·so·ri·ness** \-rē-nəs\ *noun*

curt \'kərt\ *adjective* [Latin *curtus* shortened — more at SHEAR] (1630)
1 a : sparing of words **:** TERSE **b :** marked by rude or peremptory shortness **:** BRUSQUE
2 : shortened in linear dimension
synonym *see* BLUFF
— **curt·ly** *adverb*
— **curt·ness** *noun*

cur·tail \(ˌ)kər-'tā(ə)l\ *transitive verb* [by folk etymology from earlier *curtal* to dock an animal's tail, from *curtal*, noun, animal with a docked tail, from Middle French *courtault* — more at CURTAL] (1580)
: to make less by or as if by cutting off or away some part ⟨*curtail* the power of the executive branch⟩ ⟨*curtail* inflation⟩
synonym *see* SHORTEN
— **cur·tail·er** \-'tā-lər\ *noun*

cur·tail·ment \-'tā(ə)l-mənt\ *noun* (1794)
: the act of curtailing **:** the state of being curtailed

¹cur·tain \'kər-tᵊn\ *noun* [Middle English *curtine*, from Old French, from Late Latin *cortina* (translation of Greek *aulaia*, from *aulē* court),

\ə\ abut \ᵊ\ kitten \ər\ further \a\ ash \ā\ ace
\ä\ mop, mar \aù\ out \ch\ chin \e\ bet \ē\ easy
\g\ go \i\ hit \ī\ ice \j\ job \ŋ\ sing \ō\ go
\ò\ law \òi\ boy \th\ thin \th̲\ the \ü\ loot \ù\ foot
\y\ yet \zh\ vision *see also* Guide to Pronunciation

from Latin *cohort-, cohors* enclosure, court — more at COURT] (14th century)
1 : a hanging screen usually capable of being drawn back or up; *especially* : window drapery
2 : a device or agency that conceals or acts as a barrier — compare IRON CURTAIN
3 a : the part of a bastioned front that connects two neighboring bastions **b** (1) : a similar stretch of plain wall (2) : a nonbearing exterior wall
4 a : the movable screen separating the stage from the auditorium of a theater **b** : the ascent or opening (as at the beginning of a play) of a stage curtain; *also* : its descent or closing (as at the end of an act) **c** : the final situation, line, or scene of an act or play **d** : the time at which a theatrical performance begins **e** *plural* : END; *especially* : DEATH ⟨it will be *curtains* for us if we're caught⟩
— **cur·tain·less** \-ləs\ *adjective*
²curtain *transitive verb* **cur·tained; cur·tain·ing** \'kərt-niŋ, -'kər-tⁿn-iŋ\ (14th century)
1 : to furnish with or as if with curtains
2 : to veil or shut off with or as if with a curtain

curtain call *noun* (1884)
: an appearance by a performer (as after the final curtain of a play) in response to the applause of the audience

curtain lecture *noun* [from its originally being given behind the curtains of a bed] (1633)
: a private lecture by a wife to her husband

cur·tain-rais·er \'kər-tⁿn-ˌrā-zər\ *noun* (1886)
1 : a short play usually of one scene that is presented before the main full-length drama
2 : a usually short preliminary to a main event

curtain wall *noun* (1853)
: a nonbearing exterior wall between columns or piers

cur·tal \'kərt-ᵊl\ *adjective* [Middle French *courtault*, from *court* short, from Latin *curtus*] (1576)
1 *obsolete* : having a docked tail
2 *obsolete* : BRIEF, CURTAILED
3 *archaic* : wearing a short frock

cur·tal ax *or* **cur·tle ax** \'kər-tⁿl-\ *noun* [modification of Middle French *coutelas*] (circa 1580)
archaic : CUTLASS

cur·te·sy \'kər-tə-sē\ *noun, plural* **-sies** [Middle English *corteisie* courtesy] (1523)
: a husband's interest upon the death of his wife in the real property of an estate that she either solely owned or inherited provided they bore a child capable of inheriting the estate
— compare DOWER

cur·ti·lage \'kər-tⁿl-ij\ *noun* [Middle English, from Middle French *cortillage*, from *cortil* courtyard, from *cort* court] (14th century)
: a piece of ground (as a yard or courtyard) within the fence surrounding a house

¹curt·sy *also* **curt·sey** \'kərt-sē\ *intransitive verb* **curt·sied** *also* **curt·seyed; curt·sy·ing** *also* **curt·sey·ing** [alteration of *courtesy*] (circa 1553)
: to make a curtsy

²curtsy *also* **curtsey** *noun, plural* **curtsies** *also* **curtseys** (1575)
: an act of civility, respect, or reverence made mainly by women and consisting of a slight lowering of the body with bending of the knees

cu·rule \'kyùr-ˌül\ *adjective* [Latin *curulis*, perhaps alteration of *currulis* of a chariot, from *currus* chariot, from *currere* to run] (1600)
: privileged to sit in a seat reserved in ancient Rome for the use of the highest dignitaries; *also* : of or relating to a curule chair

cur·va·ceous *also* **cur·va·cious** \ˌkər-'vā-shəs\ *adjective* (circa 1935)
: having curves suggestive of a well-proportioned feminine figure

cur·va·ture \'kər-və-ˌchür, -chər, -ˌtyür, -ˌtür\ *noun* (1603)
1 : the act of curving : the state of being curved
2 : a measure or amount of curving; *specifically* : the rate of change of the angle through which the tangent to a curve turns in moving along the curve and which for a circle is equal to the reciprocal of the radius
3 a : an abnormal curving (as of the spine) **b** : a curved surface of an organ

¹curve \'kərv\ *adjective* [Middle English, from Latin *curvus*; akin to Greek *kyrtos* convex, Middle Irish *cruinn* round] (15th century)
archaic : bent or formed into a curve

²curve *verb* **curved; curv·ing** [Latin *curvare*, from *curvus*] (1594)
intransitive verb
: to have or take a turn, change, or deviation from a straight line or plane surface without sharp breaks or angularity
transitive verb
1 : to cause to curve
2 : to throw a curveball to (a batter)
3 : to grade (as an examination) on a curve

³curve *noun* (1696)
1 a : a line especially when curved: as (1) : the path of a moving point (2) : a line defined by an equation so that the coordinates of its points are functions of a single independent variable or parameter **b** : the graph of a variable
2 : something curved: as **a** : a curving line of the human body **b** *plural* : PARENTHESIS
3 a : CURVEBALL **b** : TRICK, DECEPTION
4 : a distribution indicating the relative performance of individuals measured against each other that is used especially in assigning good, medium, or poor grades to usually predetermined proportions of students rather than in assigning grades based on predetermined standards of achievement
— **curvy** \'kər-vē\ *adjective*

curve·ball \'kərv-ˌbȯl\ *noun* (1936)
: a slow or moderately fast baseball pitch thrown with spin to make it swerve downward and usually to the left when thrown from the right hand or to the right when thrown from the left hand
— **curveball** *verb*

curve fitting *noun* (circa 1924)
: the empirical determination of a curve or function that approximates a set of data

¹cur·vet \(ˌ)kər-'vet\ *noun* [Italian *corvetta*, from Middle French *courbette*, from *courber* to curve, from Latin *curvare*] (1575)
: a prancing leap of a horse in which the hind legs are raised just before the forelegs touch the ground

²curvet *intransitive verb* **-vet·ted** *or* **-vet·ed; -vet·ting** *or* **-vet·ing** (1592)
: to make a curvet; *also* : PRANCE, CAPER

cur·vi·lin·ear \ˌkər-və-'li-nē-ər\ *adjective* [Latin *curvus* + *linea* line] (1710)
1 : consisting of or bounded by curved lines : represented by a curved line
2 : marked by flowing tracery ⟨*curvilinear* Gothic⟩
— **cur·vi·lin·ear·i·ty** \-ˌli-nē-'ar-ə-tē\ *noun*

cu·sec \'kyü-ˌsek\ *noun* [*cu*bic foot per *sec*ond] (circa 1903)
: a volumetric unit of flow equal to a cubic foot per second

cush·at \'kə-shət\ *noun* [Middle English *cowschote*, from Old English *cūscote*] (before 12th century)
chiefly Scottish : RINGDOVE 1

cu·shaw \kù-'shȯ, 'kü-ˌ\ *noun* [origin unknown] (1698)
: a squash of any of several cultivars of a winter squash (*Cucurbita mixta*)

Cush·ing's disease \'kù-shiŋz-\ *noun* [Harvey *Cushing*] (circa 1935)

: Cushing's syndrome especially when caused by excessive production of ACTH by the pituitary gland

Cushing's syndrome *noun* (1937)
: an abnormal bodily condition characterized by obesity and muscular weakness due to excess corticosteroids and especially hydrocortisone from adrenal or pituitary hyperfunction

¹cush·ion \'kù-shən\ *noun* [Middle English *cusshin*, from Middle French *coissin*, from (assumed) Vulgar Latin *coxinus*, from Latin *coxa* hip — more at COXA] (14th century)
1 : a soft pillow or pad usually used for sitting, reclining, or kneeling
2 : a bodily part resembling a pad
3 : something resembling a cushion: as **a** : PILLOW 2 **b** : RAT 3 **c** : a pad of springy rubber along the inside of the rim of a billiard table **d** : a padded insert in a shoe **e** : an elastic body for reducing shock **f** : a mat laid under a large rug to ease the effect of wear
4 a : something (as an economic factor or a medical procedure) serving to mitigate the effects of disturbances or disorders **b** : a reserve supply (of money) **c** : a comfortable lead ⟨a 4–0 *cushion* in the ninth inning⟩
— **cush·ion·less** \-ləs\ *adjective*
— **cush·iony** \-shə-nē\ *adjective*

²cushion *transitive verb* **cush·ioned; cush·ion·ing** \'kù-sh(ə-)niŋ\ (circa 1738)
1 : to seat or place on a cushion
2 : to suppress by ignoring
3 : to furnish with a cushion
4 a : to mitigate the effects of **b** : to protect against force or shock
5 : to check gradually so as to minimize shock of moving parts

Cush·it·ic \kə-'shi-tik, kù-\ *noun* [*Cush* (Kush), Africa] (circa 1903)
: a subfamily of the Afro-Asiatic language family comprising various languages spoken in eastern Africa and especially in Ethiopia, Djibouti, and Somalia
— **Cushitic** *adjective*

cushy \'kù-shē\ *adjective* **cush·i·er; cush·i·est** [Hindi *khush* pleasant, from Persian *khūsh*] (1915)
: entailing little hardship or difficulty ⟨a *cushy* job with a high salary⟩
— **cush·i·ly** \'kù-shə-lē\ *adverb*

cusk \'kəsk\ *noun, plural* **cusk** *or* **cusks** [probably alteration of *tusk*, a kind of codfish] (1616)
1 : a large edible North Atlantic fish (*Brosme brosme*) of the cod family
2 : BURBOT

cusp \'kəsp\ *noun* [Latin *cuspis* point] (1585)
: POINT, APEX: as **a** : either horn of a crescent moon **b** : a fixed point on a mathematical curve at which a point tracing the curve would exactly reverse its direction of motion **c** : an ornamental pointed projection formed by or arising from the intersection of two arcs or foils **d** (1) : a point on the grinding surface of a tooth (2) : a fold or flap of a cardiac valve **e** : a point of transition (as from one astrological sign to another or one historical period to the next) : TURNING POINT; *also* : EDGE, VERGE ⟨on the *cusp* of stardom⟩
— **cus·pate** \'kəs-ˌpāt, -pət\ *adjective*
— **cusped** \'kəspt\ *adjective*

1 cusp c

cus·pid \'kəs-pəd\ *noun* [*bicuspid*] (1878)
: CANINE 1

cus·pi·date \'kəs-pə-ˌdāt\ *adjective* [Latin *cuspidatus*, past participle of *cuspidare* to make pointed, from *cuspid-, cuspis* point] (1692)
: having a cusp : terminating in a point ⟨a *cuspidate* leaf⟩ ⟨*cuspidate* molars⟩

cus·pi·da·tion \ˌkəs-pə-'dā-shən\ *noun* (1848)
: decoration with cusps

cus·pi·dor \'kəs-pə-,dòr, -,dōr\ *noun* [Portuguese *cuspidouro* place for spitting, from *cuspir* to spit, from Latin *conspuere,* from *com-* + *spuere* to spit — more at SPEW] (1735)
: SPITTOON

¹cuss \'kəs\ *noun* [alteration of *curse*] (1775)
1 : FELLOW 4c
2 : CURSE 1, 2

²cuss *verb* (1815)
: CURSE
— **cuss·er** *noun*

cuss·ed \'kə-səd\ *adjective* (1840)
1 : CURSED
2 : OBSTINATE, CANTANKEROUS
— **cuss·ed·ly** *adverb*
— **cuss·ed·ness** \-nəs\ *noun*

cuss·word \'kəs-,wərd\ *noun* (1872)
1 : SWEARWORD
2 : a term of abuse : a derogatory term

cus·tard \'kəs-tərd\ *noun* [Middle English, a kind of pie, alteration of *crustarde, crustade,* probably from (assumed) Anglo-French *crustade,* from Old French *crouste* crust, from Latin *crusta* — more at CRUST] (1740)
: a pudding-like usually sweetened mixture made with eggs and milk
— **cus·tardy** \-tər-dē\ *adjective*

custard apple *noun* (1657)
1 a : any of several chiefly tropical American soft-fleshed edible fruits **b** : any of a genus (*Annona* of the family Annonaceae, the custard-apple family) of trees or shrubs bearing this fruit; *especially* : a small West Indian tree (*A. reticulata*)
2 : PAPAW 2

cus·to·di·al \,kəs-'tō-dē-əl\ *adjective* (1772)
: relating to guardianship; *specifically* : marked by or given to watching and protecting rather than seeking to cure ⟨*custodial* care⟩

cus·to·di·an \,kəs-'tō-dē-ən\ *noun* (1781)
: one that guards and protects or maintains; *especially* : one entrusted with guarding and keeping property or records or with custody or guardianship of prisoners or inmates
— **cus·to·di·an·ship** \-,ship\ *noun*

cus·to·dy \'kəs-tə-dē\ *noun, plural* **-dies** [Middle English *custodie,* from Latin *custodia* guarding, from *custod-, custos* guardian] (15th century)
: immediate charge and control (as over a ward or a suspect) exercised by a person or an authority; *also* : SAFEKEEPING

¹cus·tom \'kəs-təm\ *noun* [Middle English *custume,* from Old French, from Latin *consuetudin-, consuetudo,* from *consuescere* to accustom, from *com-* + *suescere* to accustom; akin to *suus* one's own — more at SUICIDE] (13th century)
1 a : a usage or practice common to many or to a particular place or class or habitual with an individual **b** : long-established practice considered as unwritten law **c** : repeated practice **d** : the whole body of usages, practices, or conventions that regulate social life
2 *plural* **a** : duties, tolls, or imposts imposed by the sovereign law of a country on imports or exports **b** *usually singular in construction* : the agency, establishment, or procedure for collecting such customs
3 a : business patronage **b** : usually habitual patrons : CUSTOMERS
synonym see HABIT

²custom *adjective* (1830)
1 : made or performed according to personal order
2 : specializing in custom work or operation ⟨*custom* tailor⟩

cus·tom·ary \'kəs-tə-,mer-ē\ *adjective* (1535)
1 : based on or established by custom
2 : commonly practiced, used, or observed
synonym see USUAL
— **cus·tom·ar·i·ly** \,kəs-tə-'mer-ə-lē\ *adverb*
— **cus·tom·ar·i·ness** \'kəs-tə-,mer-ē-nəs\ *noun*

cus·tom–built \'kəs-təm-'bilt\ *adjective* (1925)
: built to individual specifications

cus·tom·er \'kəs-tə-mər\ *noun* [Middle English *customer,* from *custume*] (15th century)
1 : one that purchases a commodity or service
2 : an individual usually having some specified distinctive trait ⟨a real tough *customer*⟩

cus·tom·house \'kəs-təm-,haùs\ *also* **cus·toms·house** \-təmz-\ *noun* (15th century)
: a building where customs and duties are paid or collected and where vessels are entered and cleared

cus·tom·ise *British variant of* CUSTOMIZE

cus·tom·ize \'kəs-tə-,mīz\ *transitive verb* **-ized; -iz·ing** (1926)
: to build, fit, or alter according to individual specifications
— **cus·tom·iz·er** *noun*

cus·tom–made \'kəs-tə(m)-'mād\ *adjective* (1855)
: made to individual specifications

cus·tom–tai·lor \-'tā-lər\ *transitive verb* (1895)
: to alter, plan, or build according to individual specifications or needs

¹cut \'kət\ *verb* **cut; cut·ting** [Middle English *cutten*] (13th century)
transitive verb
1 a : to penetrate with or as if with an edged instrument **b** : to hurt the feelings of **c** : to strike sharply with a cutting effect **d** : to strike (a ball) with a glancing blow that imparts a reverse spin **e** : to experience the growth of (a tooth) through the gum
2 a : TRIM, PARE ⟨*cut* one's nails⟩ **b** : to shorten by omissions **c** : DISSOLVE, DILUTE, ADULTERATE **d** : to reduce in amount ⟨*cut* costs⟩
3 a : MOW, REAP **b** : to divide into parts with an edged tool ⟨*cut* bread⟩ (2) : FELL, HEW **c** (1) : to separate or discharge from an organization : DETACH (2) : to single out and isolate ⟨*cut* a calf out from the herd⟩ **d** : to change the direction of sharply **e** : to go or pass around or about
4 a : to divide into segments **b** : INTERSECT, CROSS **c** : BREAK, INTERRUPT ⟨*cut* our supply lines⟩ **d** (1) : to divide (a deck of cards) into two portions (2) : to draw (a card) from the deck **e** : to divide into shares : SPLIT
5 a : to make by or as if by cutting: as (1) : CARVE ⟨*cut* stone⟩ (2) : to shape by grinding ⟨*cut* a diamond⟩ (3) : ENGRAVE (4) : to shear or hollow out **b** : to record sounds (as speech or music) on ⟨*cut* a record⟩ **c** : to type on a stencil
6 a : STOP, CEASE ⟨*cut* the nonsense⟩ **b** : to refuse to recognize (an acquaintance) : OSTRACIZE **c** : to absent oneself from (as a class) **d** : to stop (a motor) by opening a switch **e** : to stop the filming of (a motion-picture scene)
7 a : to engage in (a frolicsome or mischievous action) ⟨on summer nights strange capers are *cut* under the thin guise of a Christian festival —D. C. Peattie⟩ **b** : to give the appearance or impression of ⟨*cut* a fine figure⟩
8 : to be able to manage or handle — usually used in negative constructions ⟨can't *cut* that kind of work anymore⟩
intransitive verb
1 a : to function as or as if as an edged tool **b** : to undergo incision or severance ⟨cheese *cuts* easily⟩ **c** : to perform the operation of dividing, severing, incising, or intersecting **d** : to make a stroke with a whip, sword, or other weapon **e** : to wound feelings or sensibilities **f** : to cause constriction or chafing **g** : to be of effect, influence, or significance ⟨an analysis that *cuts* deep⟩
2 a (1) : to divide a pack of cards especially in order to decide the deal or settle a bet (2) : to draw a card from the pack **b** : to divide spoils : SPLIT

3 a : to proceed obliquely from a straight course ⟨*cut* across the yard⟩ **b** : to move swiftly ⟨a yacht *cutting* through the water⟩ **c** : to describe an oblique or diagonal line **d** : to change sharply in direction : SWERVE **e** : to make an abrupt transition from one sound or image to another in motion pictures, radio, or television
4 : to stop photographing motion pictures
— **cut a deal** : to negotiate an agreement
— **cut both ways** : to have both favorable and unfavorable results or implications
— **cut corners** : to perform some action in the quickest, easiest, or cheapest way
— **cut ice** : to be of importance — usually used in negative constructions
— **cut it** : to cut the mustard
— **cut the mustard** : to achieve the standard of performance necessary for success

²cut *noun* (1548)
1 : a product of cutting: as **a** : a creek, channel, or inlet made by excavation or worn by natural action **b** (1) : an opening made with an edged instrument (2) : a wound made by something sharp : GASH **c** : a surface or outline left by cutting **d** : a passage cut as a roadway **e** : a grade or step especially in a social scale ⟨a *cut* above the ordinary⟩ **f** : a subset of a set such that when it is subtracted from the set the remainder is not connected **g** : a pictorial illustration **h** : TRACK 1e(2)
2 : the act or an instance of cutting: as **a** : a gesture or expression that hurts the feelings ⟨made an unkind *cut*⟩ **b** : a straight passage or course **c** : a stroke or blow with the edge of a knife or other edged tool **d** : a lash with or as if with a whip **e** : the act of reducing or removing a part ⟨a *cut* in pay⟩ **f** : an act or turn of cutting cards; *also* : the result of cutting **g** : the elimination of part of a large field from further competition (as in a golf tournament) — often used with *miss* or *make* to denote respectively being or not being among those eliminated ⟨played poorly and missed the *cut*⟩
3 : something that is cut or cut off: as **a** : a length of cloth varying from 40 to 100 yards (36.6 to 91.4 meters) **b** : the yield of products cut especially during one harvest **c** : a segment or section of a meat carcass or a part of one **d** : a group of animals selected from a herd **e** : SHARE ⟨took his *cut* of the profits⟩
4 : a voluntary absence from a class
5 a : a stroke that cuts a ball: as **a** : the spin imparted by such a stroke **b** : a swing by a batter at a pitched baseball **c** : an exchange of captures in checkers
6 : an abrupt transition from one sound or image to another in motion pictures, radio, or television
7 a : the shape and style in which a thing is cut, formed, or made ⟨clothes of the latest *cut*⟩ **b** : PATTERN, TYPE **c** : HAIRCUT
— **cut of one's jib** : APPEARANCE, STYLE

cut·abil·i·ty \,kə-tə-'bi-lə-tē\ *noun* (1965)
: the proportion of lean salable meat yielded by a carcass

cut–and–dried \,kət-ᵊn-'drīd\ *also* **cut–and–dry** \-'drī\ *adjective* (1710)
: being or done according to a plan, set procedure, or formula : ROUTINE

cut–and–paste \-'pāst\ *adjective* (1953)
: pieced together by excerpting and combining passages from many sources ⟨the book was a *cut-and-paste* job⟩

cut–and–try \-'trī\ *adjective* (1903)
: marked by experimental procedure : EMPIRICAL

cu·ta·ne·ous \kyù-'tā-nē-əs\ *adjective* [New Latin *cutaneus,* from Latin *cutis* skin — more at HIDE] (1578)

\ə\ abut \ᵊ\ kitten \ər\ further \a\ ash \ā\ ace
\ä\ mop, mar \aù\ out \ch\ chin \e\ bet \ē\ easy
\g\ go \i\ hit \ī\ ice \j\ job \ŋ\ sing \ō\ go
\ò\ law \ói\ boy \th\ thin \t̲h̲\ the \ü\ loot \ù\ foot
\y\ yet \zh\ vision *see also* Guide to Pronunciation

: of, relating to, or affecting the skin
— **cu·ta·ne·ous·ly** *adverb*
¹**cut·away** \'kə-tə-,wā\ *adjective* (1841)
: having or showing parts cut away
²**cutaway** *noun* (1849)
1 : a coat with skirts tapering from the front waistline to form tails at the back
2 a : a cutaway picture or representation **b** : a shot that interrupts the main action of a film or television program to take up a related subject or to depict action supposed to be going on at the same time as the main action
3 : a back dive in which the head is lowered toward the board after the takeoff
cut·back \'kət-,bak\ *noun* (1897)
1 : something cut back
2 : REDUCTION
cut back (1871)
transitive verb
: to shorten by cutting : PRUNE
intransitive verb
1 : to interrupt the sequence of a plot (as of a movie) by introducing events prior to those last presented
2 : CUT DOWN ⟨*cut back* on sugar⟩
cutch \'kəch\ *noun* [modification of Malay *kachu*] (1759)
: CATECHU a
cut down (1821)
transitive verb
1 a : to strike down and kill or incapacitate **b** : KNOCK DOWN
2 a : to remodel by removing extras or unwanted furnishings and fittings **b** : to remake in a smaller size
intransitive verb
: to reduce or curtail volume or activity ⟨*cut down* on smoking⟩
— **cut down to size** : to reduce from an inflated or exaggerated importance to true or suitable stature
cute \'kyüt\ *adjective* **cut·er; cut·est** [short for *acute*] (circa 1731)
1 a : clever or shrewd often in an underhanded manner **b** : IMPERTINENT, SMART-ALECKY ⟨don't get *cute* with me⟩
2 : attractive or pretty especially in a dainty or delicate way
3 : obviously straining for effect
— **cute·ly** *adverb*
— **cute·ness** *noun*
cute·sy \'kyüt-sē\ *adjective* **cute·si·er; -est** [*cute* + -*sy* (as in *folksy*)] (1914)
: self-consciously or excessively cute
cut glass *noun* (1800)
: glass ornamented with patterns cut into its surface by an abrasive wheel and polished
cut-grass \'kət-,gras\ *noun* (circa 1818)
: a grass (especially genus *Leersia*) with minute hooked bristles along the edges of the leaf blade
cu·ti·cle \'kyü-ti-kəl\ *noun* [Latin *cuticula*, diminutive of *cutis* skin — more at HIDE] (1615)
1 : SKIN, PELLICLE: as **a** : an external investment (as of an insect) secreted usually by epidermal cells **b** : the outermost layer of animal integument (as in humans) when composed of epidermis **c** : a thin continuous fatty or waxy film on the external surface of many higher plants that consists chiefly of cutin
2 : dead or horny epidermis
— **cu·tic·u·lar** \kyü-'ti-kyə-lər\ *adjective*
cut·ie *or* **cut·ey** \'kyü-tē\ *noun, plural* **cuties** *or* **cuteys** [*cute* + -*ie*] (1908)
: an attractive person; *especially* : a pretty girl
cu·tin \'kyü-tᵊn\ *noun* [International Scientific Vocabulary, from Latin *cutis*] (circa 1872)
: an insoluble mixture containing waxes, fatty acids, soaps, and resinous material that forms a continuous layer on the outer epidermal wall of a plant
cut-in \'kət-,in\ *noun* (1883)
: something cut in
— **cut-in** *adjective*
cut in (1612)
intransitive verb

1 : to thrust oneself into a position between others or belonging to another
2 : to join in something suddenly ⟨*cut in* on the conversation⟩
3 : to interrupt a dancing couple and take one as one's partner
4 : to become automatically connected or started in operation
transitive verb
1 : to mix with cutting motions ⟨after sifting the flour into a mixing bowl, *cut* the lard *in*⟩
2 : to introduce into a number, group, or sequence
3 : to connect into an electrical circuit to a mechanical apparatus so as to permit operation
4 : to include especially among those benefiting or favored ⟨*cut* them *in* on the profits⟩
cu·tin·ized \'kyü-tᵊn-,īzd\ *adjective* (1901)
: infiltrated with cutin ⟨*cutinized* epidermal cells⟩
cu·tis \'kyü-təs\ *noun, plural* **cu·tes** \'kyü-,tēz\ *or* **cu·tis·es** [Latin] (1603)
: DERMIS
cut·lass \'kət-ləs\ *noun* [Middle French *coutelas*, augmentative of *coutel* knife, from Latin *cultellus*, diminutive of *culter* knife, plowshare] (1594)
1 : a short curving sword formerly used by sailors on warships
2 : MACHETE
cut·ler \'kət-lər\ *noun* [Middle English, from Middle French *coutelier*, from Late Latin *cultellarius*, from Latin *cultellus*] (14th century)
: one who makes, deals in, or repairs cutlery
cut·lery \'kət-lə-rē\ *noun* (15th century)
1 : the business of a cutler
2 : edged or cutting tools; *specifically* : implements for cutting and eating food
cut·let \'kət-lət\ *noun* [French *côtelette*, from Old French *costelette*, diminutive of *coste* rib, side, from Latin *costa* — more at COAST] (circa 1706)
1 : a small slice of meat ⟨a veal *cutlet*⟩
2 : a flat croquette of chopped meat or fish
cut·line \'kət-,līn\ *noun* (1943)
: CAPTION, LEGEND
cut·off \'kət-,óf\ *noun* (1741)
1 : the act or action of cutting off
2 a : the new and relatively short channel formed when a stream cuts through the neck of an oxbow **b** : SHORTCUT 1 **c** : a channel made to straighten a stream
3 : a device for cutting off
4 a : something cut off **b** *plural* : shorts originally made from jeans with the legs cut off at the knees or higher
5 : the point, date, or period for a cutoff
— **cutoff** *adjective*
cut off (14th century)
transitive verb
1 : to bring to an untimely end
2 : to stop the passage of
3 : SHUT OFF, BAR
4 : DISCONTINUE, TERMINATE
5 : SEPARATE, ISOLATE
6 : DISINHERIT
7 a : to stop the operation of : TURN OFF **b** : to stop or interrupt while in communication ⟨the operator *cut* me *off*⟩
intransitive verb
: to cease operating
cutoff man *noun* (1967)
: a player in baseball who relays a ball from an outfielder to the infield
cut-out \'kət-,aút\ *noun* (1851)
1 : something cut out or off from something else; *also* : the space or hole left after cutting
2 : one that cuts out
3 : one serving as an intermediary for clandestine operations
— **cutout** *adjective*
¹**cut out** (15th century)
transitive verb
1 : to form by erosion
2 : to determine or assign through necessity ⟨you've got your work *cut out* for you⟩

3 : to take the place of : SUPPLANT
4 : to put an end to : desist from
5 : DEPRIVE, DEFRAUD
6 a : to remove from a series or circuit : DISCONNECT **b** : to make inoperative
intransitive verb
1 : to depart in haste
2 : to cease operating
3 : to swerve out of a traffic line
²**cut out** *adjective* (1645)
: naturally fitted or suited ⟨not *cut out* to be a vet⟩
cut·over \'kət-'ō-vər\ *adjective* (1899)
: having most of the salable timber cut down
cut-price \-'prīs\ *adjective* (1897)
chiefly British : CUT-RATE
cut-purse \'kət-,pərs\ *noun* (14th century)
: PICKPOCKET
cut-rate \'kət-'rāt\ *adjective* (1881)
1 : marked by, offering, or making use of a reduced rate or price ⟨*cut-rate* stores⟩
2 : SECOND-RATE, CHEAP
cut·ta·ble \'kə-tə-bəl\ *adjective* (15th century)
: capable of being cut : ready for cutting
cut·ter \'kə-tər\ *noun* (15th century)
1 : one that cuts: **a** : one whose work is cutting or involves cutting **b** (1) : an instrument, machine, machine part, or tool that cuts (2) : a device for vibrating a cutting stylus in disc recording; *also* : the stylus or its point
2 a : a ship's boat for carrying stores or passengers **b** : a single-masted fore-and-aft rigged sailing vessel **c** : a small armed vessel in government service
3 : a light sleigh
¹**cut-throat** \'kət-,thrōt\ *noun* (1535)
1 : KILLER, MURDERER
2 : a cruel unprincipled person
²**cutthroat** *adjective* (1567)
1 : MURDEROUS, CRUEL
2 : marked by unprincipled practices : RUTHLESS ⟨*cutthroat* competition⟩
3 : characterized by each player playing independently rather than having a permanent partner — used especially of partnership games adapted for three players ⟨*cutthroat* bridge⟩
cutthroat contract *noun* (circa 1944)
: contract bridge in which partnerships are determined by the bidding
cutthroat trout *noun* (circa 1891)
: a large spotted trout (*Oncorhynchus clarki* synonym *Salmo clarki*) chiefly of northwestern North America that has reddish streaks on the integument of the lower jaw — called also *cutthroat*

cutthroat trout

cut time *noun* (1951)
: duple or quadruple time with the beat represented by a half note
¹**cut·ting** \'kə-tin\ *noun* (14th century)
1 : something cut or cut off or out: as **a** : a plant section originating from stem, leaf, or root and capable of developing into a new plant **b** : HARVEST
2 : something made by cutting; *especially* : RECORD 4
²**cutting** *adjective* (15th century)
1 : given to or designed for cutting; *especially* : SHARP, EDGED
2 : marked by sharp piercing cold
3 : inclined or likely to wound the feelings of others especially because of a ruthless incisiveness ⟨a *cutting* remark⟩
4 : INTENSE, PIERCING ⟨a *cutting* pain⟩
— **cut·ting·ly** \-tin-lē\ *adverb*
cutting board *noun* (1825)
: a board on which something (as food or cloth) is placed for cutting
cutting edge *noun* (1951)
1 : the foremost part or place : VANGUARD

2 : a sharp effect or quality

cutting horse *noun* (1881)
: an agile saddle horse trained to separate individual animals from a cattle herd

cut·tle·bone \'kə-t^əl-ˌbōn\ *noun* [Middle English *cotul* cuttlefish (from Old English *cudele*) + English *bone*] (1547)
: the shell of cuttlefishes that is sometimes used for polishing powder or for supplying cage birds with lime and salts

cut·tle·fish \-ˌfish\ *noun* [Middle English *cotul* + English *fish*] (circa 1828)
: any of various 10-armed marine cephalopod mollusks (order Sepioidea, especially genus *Sepia*) differing from the related squid in having a calcified internal shell

cut·ty sark \'kə-tē-ˈsärk\ *noun* [English dialect *cutty* short + *sark*] (1779)
chiefly Scottish : a short garment; *especially* : a woman's short undergarment

cutty stool *noun* (1820)
1 *chiefly Scottish* : a low stool
2 : a seat in a Scottish church where offenders formerly sat for public rebuke

cut·up \'kət-ˌəp\ *noun* (1843)
: a person who clowns or acts boisterously

cut up (1580)
transitive verb
1 a : to cut into parts or pieces **b :** to injure or damage by or as if by cutting : GASH, SLASH
2 : to subject to hostile criticism : CENSURE
intransitive verb
1 : to undergo being cut up
2 : to behave in a comic, boisterous, or unruly manner : CLOWN

cut·wa·ter \'kət-ˌwȯ-tər, -ˌwä-\ *noun* (1644)
: the forepart of a ship's stem

cut·work \-ˌwərk\ *noun* (15th century)
: embroidery usually on linen in which a design is outlined in buttonhole stitch and the enclosed material cut away

cut·worm \-ˌwərm\ *noun* (1816)
: any of various smooth-bodied chiefly nocturnal noctuid moth caterpillars which often feed on young plant stems near ground level

cu·vette \kyü-ˈvet\ *noun* [French, diminutive of *cuve* tub, from Latin *cupa* — more at HIVE] (circa 1909)
: a small often transparent laboratory vessel (as a tube)

cwm \'küm\ *noun* [Welsh, valley] (1853)
chiefly British : CIRQUE 3

-cy *noun suffix* [Middle English *-cie*, from Old French, from Latin *-tia*, partly from *-t-* (final stem consonant) + *-ia* -y, partly from Greek *-tia*, *-teia*, from *-t-* (final stem consonant) + *-ia*, *-eia* -y]
1 : action : practice ⟨mendican*cy*⟩
2 : rank : office ⟨baronet*cy*⟩ ⟨chaplain*cy*⟩
3 : body : class ⟨magistra*cy*⟩
4 : state : quality ⟨accura*cy*⟩ — often replacing a final *-t* or *-te* of the base word

cy·an \'sī-ˌan, -ən\ *noun* [Greek *kyanos*] (circa 1889)
: a greenish blue color — used in photography and color printing of one of the primary colors

cyan- *or* **cyano-** *combining form* [German, from Greek *kyan-*, *kyano-*, from *kyanos* dark blue enamel]
1 : dark blue : blue ⟨*cyano*bacterium⟩
2 : cyanogen ⟨*cyan*ide⟩
3 : cyanide ⟨*cyano*genetic⟩

cy·an·a·mide \sī-ˈa-nə-məd\ *noun* [International Scientific Vocabulary] (1838)
1 : a caustic acidic compound CH_2N_2
2 : CALCIUM CYANAMIDE

cy·a·nate \'sī-ə-ˌnāt, -nət\ *noun* [International Scientific Vocabulary] (circa 1846)
: a salt (as ammonium cyanate) or ester of cyanic acid

cy·an·ic acid \sī-ˌa-nik-\ *noun* (1832)
: a strong acid HOCN used to prepare cyanates

cy·a·nide \'sī-ə-ˌnīd, -nəd\ *noun* [International Scientific Vocabulary] (1826)
1 : a compound of cyanogen with a more electropositive element or group: as **a :** POTASSIUM CYANIDE **b :** SODIUM CYANIDE
2 : CYANOGEN 1

cy·a·nine \'sī-ə-ˌnēn, -nən\ *noun* [International Scientific Vocabulary] (circa 1872)
: any of various dyes that sensitize photographic film to light from the green, yellow, red, and infrared regions of the spectrum

cy·a·no \sī-ˈa-(ˌ)nō, sī-'a-(ˌ)nō\ *adjective* [*cyan-*] (1929)
: relating to or containing the cyanogen group — often used in combination

cy·a·no·ac·ry·late \ˌsī-ə-nō-ˈa-krə-ˌlāt, sī-ˌa-nō-\ *noun* (1963)
: any of several liquid acrylate monomers that readily polymerize as anions and are used as adhesives in industry and in closing wounds in surgery

cy·a·no·bac·te·ri·um \-bak-ˈtir-ē-əm\ *noun* [New Latin] (1974)
: BLUE-GREEN ALGA

cy·a·no·co·bal·a·min \-kō-ˈba-lə-mən\ *also* **cy·a·no·co·bal·a·mine** \-ˌmēn\ *noun* [*cyan-* + *cobal*t + *vitamin*] (1950)
: VITAMIN B_{12} 1

cy·a·no·eth·yl·ate \-ˈe-thə-ˌlāt\ *transitive verb* (1942)
: to introduce a cyano-ethyl group CNC_2H_4 into (a compound) usually by means of acrylonitrile ⟨*cyanoethylate* cotton⟩
— **cy·a·no·eth·yl·a·tion** \-ˌe-thə-ˈlā-shən\ *noun*

cy·a·no·gen \sī-ˈa-nə-jən\ *noun* [French *cyanogène*, from *cyan-* + *gène* -gen] (1826)
1 : a univalent group −CN present in cyanides
2 : a colorless flammable poisonous gas $(CN)_2$

cy·a·no·ge·net·ic \ˌsī-ə-nō-jə-ˈne-tik, sī-ˌa-nō-\ *or* **cy·a·no·gen·ic** \-ˈje-nik\ *adjective* (1902)
: capable of producing cyanide (as hydrogen cyanide) ⟨a *cyanogenetic* plant⟩ ⟨a *cyanogenetic* glucoside⟩
— **cy·a·no·gen·e·sis** \-ˈje-nə-səs\ *noun*

cy·a·no·hy·drin \-ˈhī-drən\ *noun* [International Scientific Vocabulary, from *cyan-* + *hydr-* + [1]*-in*] (1925)
: any of various compounds containing both cyano and hydroxyl groups

cy·a·no·sis \ˌsī-ə-ˈnō-səs\ *noun* [New Latin, from Greek *kyanōsis* dark blue color, from *kyanos*] (1834)
: a bluish or purplish discoloration (as of skin) due to deficient oxygenation of the blood
— **cy·a·not·ic** \-ˈnä-tik\ *adjective*

cy·an·uric acid \ˌsī-ə-ˈnùr-ik-, -ˈnyùr-\ *noun* [*cyan-* + *urea*] (1838)
: a crystalline weak acid $C_3N_3(OH)_3$ that yields cyanic acid when heated

Cyb·e·le \'si-bə-(ˌ)lē\ *noun* [Latin, from Greek *Kybelē*]
: a nature goddess of the ancient peoples of Asia Minor

cy·ber·na·tion \ˌsī-bər-ˈnā-shən\ *noun* [*cybernetics + -ation*] (1962)
: the automatic control of a process or operation (as in manufacturing) by means of computers
— **cy·ber·nat·ed** \'sī-bər-ˌnā-təd\ *adjective*

cy·ber·ne·ti·cian \ˌsī-(ˌ)bər-nə-ˈti-shən\ *noun* (1951)
: a specialist in cybernetics

cy·ber·net·i·cist \ˌsī-bər-ˈne-tə-sist\ *noun* (1948)
: CYBERNETICIAN

cy·ber·net·ics \ˌsī-bər-ˈne-tiks\ *noun plural but singular in construction* [Greek *kybernētēs* pilot, governor (from *kybernan* to steer, govern) + English *-ics*] (1948)
: the science of communication and control theory that is concerned especially with the comparative study of automatic control systems (as the nervous system and brain and mechanical-electrical communication systems)
— **cy·ber·net·ic** \-tik\ *also* **cy·ber·net·i·cal** \-ti-kəl\ *adjective*
— **cy·ber·net·i·cal·ly** \-ti-k(ə-)lē\ *adverb*

cy·ber·punk \'sī-bər-ˌpəŋk\ *noun* [*cyber*netic + [1]*punk*] (1984)
1 : science fiction dealing with future urban societies dominated by computer technology
2 : an opportunistic computer hacker

cy·ber·space \-ˌspās\ *noun* [*cyber*netic + *space*] (1986)
: the on-line world of computer networks

cy·borg \'sī-ˌbȯrg\ *noun* [*cyber*netic + *organ*ism] (1960)
: a bionic human

cy·cad \'sī-kəd\ *noun* [New Latin *Cycad-*, *Cycas*, genus name, from Greek *kykas*, manuscript variant of *koikas*, accusative plural of *koïx*, a kind of palm] (1845)
: any of an order (Cycadales) of dioecious cycadophytes that are represented by a single surviving family (Cycadaceae) of palmlike tropical plants that reproduce by means of spermatozoids

cy·cad·e·oid \sī-ˈka-dē-ˌȯid\ *noun* [New Latin *Cycadeoidales*, group name, ultimately from *Cycad-*, *Cycas*] (1928)
: any of an extinct order (Cycadeoidales or Bennettitales) of Mesozoic cycadophytes that differ from the cycads chiefly in having the reproductive organs on the trunk embedded in a thick external covering of persistent leaf bases

cy·cad·o·phyte \sī-ˈka-də-ˌfīt\ *noun* [ultimately from New Latin *Cycad-*, *Cycas* + Greek *phyton* plant — more at -PHYTE] (1911)
: any of a subclass (Cycadophytae) of usually unbranched gymnosperms with pinnate leaves, large pith, little xylem, and a thick cortex that includes the cycads, cycadeoids, and seed ferns

cy·ca·sin \'sī-kə-sən\ *noun* [New Latin *Cycas* cycad + International Scientific Vocabulary [1]*-in*] (circa 1965)
: a glucoside $C_8H_{16}N_2O_7$ that occurs in cycads and results in toxic and carcinogenic effects when introduced into mammals

cycl- *or* **cyclo-** *combining form* [New Latin, from Greek *kykl-*, *kyklo-*, from *kyklos*]
1 : circle ⟨*cyclo*meter⟩
2 : cyclic ⟨*cyclo*hexane⟩

cy·cla·mate \'sī-klə-ˌmāt, -mət\ *noun* [*cyclo*hexyl-*sulfamate*] (1954)
: an artificially prepared salt of sodium or calcium used especially formerly as a sweetener

cy·cla·men \'sī-klə-mən, 'si-\ *noun* [New Latin, genus name, from Greek *kyklaminos*] (circa 1550)
: any of a genus (*Cyclamen*) of plants of the primrose family having showy nodding flowers

cy·clase \'sī-ˌklās, -ˌklāz\ *noun* [*cycl-* + *-ase*] (1946)
: an enzyme (as adenylate cyclase) that catalyzes cyclization of a compound

cy·claz·o·cine \sī-ˈkla-zə-ˌsēn, -sən\ *noun* [*cycl-* + *azocine* (C_7H_7N), probably from *az-* + *octa-* + [2]*-ine*] (1966)
: an analgesic drug $C_{18}H_{25}NO$ that inhibits the effect of morphine and related addictive drugs and is used in the treatment of drug addiction

[1]cy·cle \'sī-kəl\ *noun* [Middle English *cicle*, from Late Latin *cyclus*, from Greek *kyklos* circle, wheel, cycle — more at WHEEL] (14th century)
1 : an interval of time during which a sequence of a recurring succession of events or phenomena is completed
2 a : a course or series of events or operations that recur regularly and usually lead back to

the starting point **b** : one complete performance of a vibration, electric oscillation, current alternation, or other periodic process **c** : a permutation of a set of ordered elements in which each element takes the place of the next and the last becomes first **3** : a circular or spiral arrangement: as **a** : an imaginary circle or orbit in the heavens **b** : WHORL **c** : RING 10 **4** : a long period of time : AGE **5 a** : a group of poems, plays, novels, or songs treating the same theme **b** : a series of narratives dealing typically with the exploits of a legendary hero **6 a** : BICYCLE **b** : TRICYCLE **c** : MOTORCYCLE **7** : the series of a single, double, triple, and home run hit in any order by one player during one baseball game

²**cycle** verb **cy·cled; cy·cling** \'sī-k(ə-)liŋ\ (1842)
intransitive verb
1 a : to pass through a cycle **b** : to recur in cycles
2 : to ride a cycle; *specifically* : BICYCLE
transitive verb
: to cause to go through a cycle
— **cy·cler** \'sī-k(ə-)lər\ noun

cy·clic \'sī-klik *also* 'si-\ *or* **cy·cli·cal** \'sī-kli-kəl, 'si-\ adjective (1794)
1 a : of, relating to, or being a cycle **b** : moving in cycles ⟨cyclic time⟩ **c** : of, relating to, or being a chemical compound containing a ring of atoms
2 *cyclic* : being a mathematical group that has an element such that every element of the group can be expressed as one of its powers
— **cy·cli·cal·ly** \-k(ə-)lē\ *also* **cy·clic·ly** \'sī-kli-klē, 'si-\ adverb

cyclic AMP noun (1966)
: a cyclic mononucleotide of adenosine that is formed from ATP and is responsible for the intracellular mediation of hormonal effects on various cellular processes — called also *adenosine 3',5'-monophosphate*

cyclic GMP \-ˌjē-(ˌ)em-'pē\ noun [guanosine + *mon-* + *phosphate*] (1969)
: a cyclic mononucleotide of guanosine that acts similarly to cyclic AMP as a secondary messenger in response to hormones

cy·clic·i·ty \sī-'kli-sə-tē, si-\ noun (1944)
: the quality or state of being cyclic ⟨estrous *cyclicity*⟩ — called also *cy·cli·cal·i·ty* \ˌsī-klə-kə-lə-tē, ˌsi-\

cy·clist \'sī-k(ə-)ləst\ noun (1882)
: one who rides a cycle

cy·cli·tol \'sī-klə-ˌtȯl, 'si-, -ˌtōl\ noun [*cycl-* + *-itol* (as in *inositol*)] (1943)
: an alicyclic polyhydroxy compound (as inositol)

cy·cli·za·tion \ˌsī-k(ə-)lə-'zā-shən, ˌsi-\ noun (1909)
: formation of one or more rings in a chemical compound
— **cy·clize** \'sī-kə-ˌlīz, 'si-, -ˌklīz\ verb

cy·clo \'sē-(ˌ)klō, 'si-\ noun, plural **cyclos** [French, bicycle, moped, from *cyclo-* (as in *cyclomoteur* moped), from *cycle* two- or three-wheeled vehicle] (1964)
: a 3-wheeled often motor-driven taxi

cy·clo·ad·di·tion \ˌsī-(ˌ)klō-ə-'di-shən\ noun (1963)
: a chemical reaction leading to ring formation in a compound

cy·clo·al·i·phat·ic \ˌsī-klō-ˌa-lə-'fa-tik\ adjective (1936)
: ALICYCLIC

cy·clo·dex·trin \-'dek-strən\ noun (1960)
: any of a class of complex cyclic sugars that are products of the enzymatic decomposition of starch and that can catalyze reactions between simpler molecules which come together within the cylindrical body of the sugar

cy·clo·di·ene \-'dī-ˌēn, -dī-'\ noun (1942)

: an organic insecticide (as dieldrin or chlordane) with a chlorinated methylene group forming a bridge across a 6-membered carbon ring

cy·clo·gen·e·sis \-'je-nə-səs\ noun [*cyclone* + *genesis*] (circa 1938)
: the development or intensification of a cyclone

cy·clo·hex·ane \ˌsī-klō-'hek-ˌsān\ noun [International Scientific Vocabulary] (circa 1909)
: a pungent saturated cyclic hydrocarbon C_6H_{12} found in petroleum or made synthetically and used chiefly as a solvent and in organic synthesis

cy·clo·hex·a·none \-'hek-sə-ˌnōn\ noun (circa 1909)
: a liquid ketone $C_6H_{10}O$ used especially as a solvent and in organic synthesis

cy·clo·hex·i·mide \-'hek-sə-ˌmīd, -məd\ noun [*cyclohex*ane + *imide*] (1950)
: an agricultural fungicide $C_{15}H_{23}NO_4$ that inhibits protein synthesis and is obtained from a soil bacterium (*Streptomyces griseus*)

cy·clo·hex·yl·amine \-hek-'si-lə-ˌmēn\ noun [*cyclohex*ane + *-yl* + *amine*] (1943)
: a colorless liquid amine $C_6H_{11}NH_2$ that is used in organic synthesis and to prevent corrosion in boilers and that is believed to be harmful as a metabolic breakdown product of cyclamate

¹**cy·cloid** \'sī-ˌklȯid\ noun [French *cycloïde*, from Greek *kykloeidēs* circular, from *kyklos*] (1661)
: a curve that is generated by a point on the circumference of a circle as it rolls along a straight line

cycloid

— **cy·cloi·dal** \sī-'klȯi-dᵊl\ adjective

²**cycloid** adjective (1847)
1 : smooth with concentric lines of growth ⟨*cycloid* scales⟩; *also* : having or consisting of cycloid scales
2 : relating to or being a personality characterized by alternating high and low moods — compare CYCLOTHYMIC

cy·clom·e·ter \sī-'klä-mə-tər\ noun (1880)
: a device made for recording the revolutions of a wheel and often used for registering distance traversed by a wheeled vehicle

cy·clone \'sī-ˌklōn\ noun [modification of Greek *kyklōma* wheel, coil, from *kykloun* to go around, from *kyklos* circle] (1848)
1 a : a storm or system of winds that rotates about a center of low atmospheric pressure, advances at a speed of 20 to 30 miles (about 30 to 50 kilometers) an hour, and often brings heavy rain **b** : TORNADO **c** : LOW 1b
2 : any of various centrifugal devices for separating materials (as solid particles from gases)
— **cy·clon·ic** \sī-'klä-nik\ adjective
— **cy·clon·i·cal·ly** \-ni-k(ə-)lē\ adverb

Cy·clone \'sī-ˌklōn\ trademark
— used for a chain-link fence

cyclone cellar noun (1887)
: STORM CELLAR

cy·clo·ole·fin \ˌsī-klō-'ō-lə-fən\ noun [International Scientific Vocabulary] (circa 1929)
: a hydrocarbon containing a ring having one or more double bonds
— **cy·clo·ole·fin·ic** \-ˌō-lə-'fi-nik\ adjective

cy·clo·par·af·fin \-'par-ə-fən\ noun (1900)
: a saturated cyclic hydrocarbon of the formula C_nH_{2n}

cy·clo·pe·an \ˌsī-klə-'pē-ən, sī-'klō-pē-\ adjective (1626)
1 *often capitalized* : of, relating to, or characteristic of a Cyclops
2 : HUGE, MASSIVE
3 : of or relating to a style of stone construction marked typically by the use of large irregular blocks without mortar

cy·clo·pe·dia *also* **cy·clo·pae·dia** \ˌsī-klə-'pē-dē-ə\ noun (1728)
: ENCYCLOPEDIA
— **cy·clo·pe·dic** \-'pē-dik\ adjective

cy·clo·phos·pha·mide \ˌsī-klō-'fäs-fə-ˌmīd\ noun (1960)
: an immunosuppressive and antineoplastic agent $C_7H_{15}Cl_2N_2O_2P$ used especially in the treatment of lymphomas and some leukemias

cy·clo·pro·pane \ˌsī-klə-'prō-ˌpān\ noun [International Scientific Vocabulary] (1894)
: a flammable gaseous saturated cyclic hydrocarbon C_3H_6 sometimes used as a general anesthetic

cy·clops \'sī-ˌkläps\ noun [Latin, from Greek *Kyklōps*, from *kykl-* cycl- + *ōps* eye] (1513)
1 *plural* **cy·clo·pes** \sī-'klō-(ˌ)pēz\ *capitalized* : any of a race of giants in Greek mythology with a single eye in the middle of the forehead
2 *plural* **cyclops** [New Latin, genus name, from Latin] : any of a genus (*Cyclops*) of freshwater predatory copepods having a median eye

cy·clo·ra·ma \ˌsī-klə-'ra-mə, -'rä-\ noun [*cycl-* + *-orama* (as in *panorama*)] (1840)
1 : a large pictorial representation encircling the spectator and often having real objects as a foreground
2 : a curved curtain or wall used as a background of a stage set to suggest unlimited space
— **cy·clo·ram·ic** \-'ra-mik\ adjective

cy·clo·ser·ine \ˌsī-klō-'ser-ˌēn\ noun (1952)
: an amino antibiotic $C_3H_6N_2O_2$ produced by an actinomycete (*Streptomyces orchidaceus*) and used especially in the treatment of tuberculosis

cy·clo·sis \sī-'klō-səs\ noun [New Latin, from Greek *kyklōsis* encirclement, from *kykloun* to go around] (1835)
: the streaming of protoplasm within a cell

cy·clo·spor·ine \ˌsī-klə-'spȯr-ᵊn, -ˌēn\ noun [International Scientific Vocabulary *cycl-* + *spor-* + ²*-ine*] (1976)
: an immunosuppressive polypeptide drug $C_{62}H_{111}N_{11}O_{12}$ obtained from various imperfect fungi and used especially to prevent rejection of organ transplants

cy·clo·stome \'sī-klə-ˌstōm\ noun [ultimately from Greek *kykl-* + *stoma* mouth — more at STOMACH] (1835)
: any of a class (Cyclostomata) of jawless fishes having a large sucking mouth and comprising the hagfishes and lampreys

cy·clo·style \-ˌstīl\ noun [from *Cyclostyle*, a trademark] (1883)
: a machine for making multiple copies that utilizes a stencil cut by a graver whose tip is a small rowel
— **cyclostyle** transitive verb

cy·clo·thy·mic \ˌsī-klə-'thī-mik\ adjective [New Latin *cyclothymia* (from German *Zyklothymie*, from *zykl-* cycl- + *-thymie* -thymia) + English *-ic*] (1923)
: relating to or being an affective disorder characterized by the alternation of depressed moods with elevated, expansive, or irritable moods without psychotic features — compare CYCLOID 2
— **cy·clo·thy·mia** \-'thī-mē-ə\ noun

cy·clo·tom·ic \-'tä-mik\ adjective [*cyclotomy* mathematical theory of the division of the circle into equal parts, from *cycl-* + *-tomy*] (1879)
: relating to, being, or containing a polynomial of the form $x^{p-1} + x^{p-2} + \ldots + x + 1$ where p is a prime number

cy·clo·tron \'sī-klə-ˌträn\ noun [*cycl-* + *-tron*; from the circular movement of the particles] (1935)
: an accelerator in which charged particles (as protons, deuterons, or ions) are propelled by an alternating electric field in a constant magnetic field

cy·der *British variant of* CIDER

cyg·net \'sig-nət\ *noun* [Middle English *syg-nett,* from Middle French *cygne* swan, from Latin *cycnus, cygnus,* from Greek *kyknos*] (15th century)
: a young swan

Cyg·nus \'sig-nəs\ *noun* [Latin (genitive *Cygni*), literally, swan]
: a northern constellation between Lyra and Pegasus in the Milky Way

cyl·in·der \'si-lən-dər\ *noun* [Middle French or Latin; Middle French *cylindre,* from Latin *cylindrus,* from Greek *kylindros,* from *kylindein* to roll; perhaps akin to Greek *kyklos* wheel — more at WHEEL] (1570)
1 a : the surface traced by a straight line moving parallel to a fixed straight line and intersecting a fixed planar closed curve **b :** the space bounded by a cylinder and two parallel planes cutting all its elements — see VOLUME table
2 : a cylindrical body or space: as **a :** the turning chambered breech of a revolver **b** (1) **:** the piston chamber in an engine (2) **:** a chamber in a pump from which the piston expels the fluid **c :** any of various rotating members in a press (as a printing press); *especially* **:** one that impresses paper on an inked form **d :** a cylindrical clay object inscribed with cuneiform inscriptions
— **cyl·in·dered** \-dərd\ *adjective*

cylinder head *noun* (1884)
: the closed end of an engine or pump cylinder

cylinder seal *noun* (1887)
: a cylinder (as of stone) engraved in intaglio and used especially in ancient Mesopotamia to roll an impression on wet clay

cy·lin·dri·cal \sə-'lin-dri-kəl\ *also* **cy·lin·dric** \-drik\ *adjective* (1646)
: relating to or having the form or properties of a cylinder
— **cy·lin·dri·cal·ly** \-dri-k(ə-)lē\ *adverb*

cylindrical coordinate *noun* (circa 1934)
: any of the coordinates in space obtained by constructing in a plane a polar coordinate system and on a line perpendicular to the plane a linear coordinate system

cy·ma \'sī-mə\ *noun* [Greek *kyma,* literally, wave] (1563)
1 : a projecting molding whose profile is an S-shaped curve
2 : an S-shaped curve formed by the union of a concave line and a convex line

cy·ma·tium \sī-'mā-sh(ē-)əm\ *noun, plural* **-tia** \-sh(ē-)ə\ [Latin, from Greek *kymation,* diminutive of *kymat-, kyma*] (1563)
: a crowning molding in classic architecture; *especially* **:** CYMA

cym·bal \'sim-bəl\ *noun* [Middle English, from Old English *cymbal* & Middle French *cymbale,* from Latin *cymbalum,* from Greek *kymbalon,* from *kymbē* bowl, boat] (before 12th century)
: a concave brass plate that produces a brilliant clashing tone and that is struck with a drumstick or is used in pairs struck glancingly together
— **cym·bal·ist** \-bə-list\ *noun*

cym·bid·i·um \sim-'bi-dē-əm\ *noun* [New Latin, genus name, from Latin *cymba* boat, from Greek *kymbē*] (1815)
: any of a genus (*Cymbidium*) of tropical Old World epiphytic orchids with showy flowers

cyme \'sīm\ *noun* [New Latin *cyma,* from Latin, cabbage sprout, from Greek *kyma* swell, wave, cabbage sprout, from *kyein* to be pregnant; akin to Sanskrit *śvayati* it swells, grows] (1794)
: an inflorescence in which each floral axis terminates in a single flower; *especially* **:** a determinate inflorescence of this type containing several flowers with the first-opening central flower terminating the main axis and subsequent flowers developing from lateral buds — see INFLORESCENCE illustration

cym·ling \'sim-lən, -liŋ\ *noun* [probably alteration of *simnel*] (1779)

: PATTYPAN

cy·mo·phane \'sī-mə-,fān\ *noun* [French, from Greek *kyma* wave + French *-phane* -phane] (circa 1804)
: CHRYSOBERYL; *especially* **:** an opalescent chrysoberyl

cy·mose \'sī-,mōs\ *adjective* (1807)
: of, relating to, being, or bearing a cyme

¹Cym·ric \'kəm-rik, 'kim-\ *adjective* (1839)
: of, relating to, or characteristic of the non-Gaelic Celtic people of Britain or their language; *specifically* **:** WELSH

²Cymric *noun* (circa 1889)
: BRYTHONIC; *specifically* **:** the Welsh language

Cym·ry \'kəm-rē\ *noun* [Welsh] (1833)
: WELSH 2

cyn·ic \'si-nik\ *noun* [Middle French or Latin, Middle French *cynique,* from Latin *cynicus,* from Greek *kynikos,* literally, like a dog, from *kyn-, kyōn* dog — more at HOUND] (circa 1564)
1 *capitalized* **:** an adherent of an ancient Greek school of philosophers who held the view that virtue is the only good and that its essence lies in self-control and independence
2 : a faultfinding captious critic; *especially* **:** one who believes that human conduct is motivated wholly by self-interest ◇
— **cynic** *adjective*

cyn·i·cal \'si-ni-kəl\ *adjective* (1584)
1 : CAPTIOUS, PEEVISH
2 : having or showing the attitude or temper of a cynic; *especially* **:** contemptuously distrustful of human nature and motives ⟨those *cynical* men who say that democracy cannot be honest and efficient —F. D. Roosevelt⟩ ☆
— **cyn·i·cal·ly** \-k(ə-)lē\ *adverb*

cyn·i·cism \'si-nə-,si-zəm\ *noun* (1672)
1 *capitalized* **:** the doctrine of the Cynics
2 : cynical character, attitude, or quality; *also* **:** an expression of such quality

cy·no·mol·gus monkey \,sī-nə-'mäl-gəs-\ *noun* [New Latin, alteration of *cynamolgus,* from Latin, member of an ancient tribe in Africa, from Greek *Kynamolgoi,* literally, dog milkers] (1936)
: a macaque (*Macaca fascicularis* synonym *M. cynomolgus*) of southeastern Asia, Borneo, and the Philippines that sometimes feeds on marine crustaceans and shellfish and is often used in medical research

cy·no·sure \'sī-nə-,shur, 'si-\ *noun* [Middle French & Latin; Middle French, Ursa Minor, guide, from Latin *cynosura* Ursa Minor, from Greek *kynosoura,* from *kynos oura,* literally, dog's tail]
1 *capitalized* **:** the northern constellation Ursa Minor; *also* **:** NORTH STAR
2 : one that serves to direct or guide
3 : a center of attraction or attention

Cyn·thia \'sin(t)-thē-ə\ *noun* [Latin, from feminine of *Cynthius* of Cynthus, from *Cynthus,* mountain on Delos where she was born, from Greek *Kynthos*]
1 : ARTEMIS
2 : MOON 1a

cy·pher *chiefly British variant of* CIPHER

¹cy pres \,sī-'prā, ,sē-\ *noun* [Anglo-French, so near, as near (as may be)] (1802)
: a rule providing for the interpretation of instruments in equity as nearly as possible in conformity to the intention of the testator when literal construction is illegal, impracticable, or impossible — called also *cy pres doctrine*

²cy pres *adverb* (1885)
: in accordance with the rule of cy pres

¹cy·press \'sī-prəs\ *noun* [Middle English, from Middle French *ciprès,* from Latin *cyparissus,* from Greek *kyparissos*] (14th century)
1 a (1) **:** any of a genus (*Cupressus* of the family Cupressaceae, the cypress family) of evergreen trees and shrubs with small overlapping leaves resembling scales (2) **:** any of several coniferous trees of the cypress family or the

bald cypress family; *especially* **:** BALD CYPRESS
1 b : the wood of a cypress tree
2 : branches of cypress used as a symbol of mourning

²cypress *noun* [Middle English *ciprus, cipres,* from *Cyprus,* Mediterranean island] (15th century)
: a silk or cotton usually black gauze formerly used for mourning

cypress vine *noun* (1819)
: a tropical American vine (*Ipomoea quamoclit* synonym *Quamoclit pennata*) of the morning-glory family with usually red or white tubular flowers and finely dissected leaves

cyp·ri·an \'si-prē-ən\ *noun, often capitalized* [Latin *cyprius* of Cyprus, from Greek *kyprios,* from *Kypros* Cyprus, birthplace of Aphrodite] (1819)
: PROSTITUTE

cyp·ri·nid \'si-prə-nəd\ *noun* [ultimately from Latin *cyprinus* carp, from Greek *kyprinos*] (circa 1889)
: any of a family (Cyprinidae) of soft-finned freshwater fishes including the carps and minnows
— **cyprinid** *adjective*

cyp·ri·pe·di·um \,si-prə-'pē-dē-əm\ *noun* [New Latin, genus name, from Late Latin *Cypris,* a name for Venus + Greek *pedilon* sandal] (1813)
1 : any of a genus (*Cypripedium*) of Eurasian and North American terrestrial orchids having large usually showy drooping flowers with the lip inflated or pouched — compare LADY'S SLIPPER
2 : any of a genus (*Paphiopedalum*) of widely cultivated Asian orchids

cy·pro·hep·ta·dine \,sī-prō-'hep-tə-,dēn\ *noun* [cyclic + propyl + hepta- + piperidine] (1971)

☆ SYNONYMS

Cynical, misanthropic, pessimistic mean deeply distrustful. CYNICAL implies having a sneering disbelief in sincerity or integrity ⟨*cynical* about politicians' motives⟩. MISANTHROPIC suggests a rooted distrust and dislike of human beings and their society ⟨a solitary and *misanthropic* artist⟩. PESSIMISTIC implies having a gloomy, distrustful view of life ⟨*pessimistic* about the future⟩.

◇ WORD HISTORY

cynic The ancient school of philosophers known collectively as the Cynics was founded by Antisthenes (c. 445–c. 360 B.C.), a contemporary of Plato. Antisthenes is said to have taught at a gymnasium outside Athens called the Kynosarges, from which the Greek name of the school *kynikoi,* literally, "doglike ones," may be derived. On the other hand, Antisthenes' most famous follower, Diogenes of Sinope (c. 400–c. 325 B.C.), is most closely associated with the appellation. Diogenes rejected social conventions as impeding the most convenient satisfaction of one's needs; whatever was natural and easy could not be indecent, and therefore can and should be done in public. This shamelessness earned him the label *ho kyōn* "the dog," *kyōn* being an epithet applied to shameless or audacious people as far back as Homer. What English *cynic* and *cynical* now reflect, however, is not the Cynics' shamelessness, but their biting criticism of conventional mores.

\ə\ abut \ᵊ\ kitten \ər\ further \a\ ash \ā\ ace
\ä\ mop, mar \au̇\ out \ch\ chin \e\ bet \ē\ easy
\g\ go \i\ hit \ī\ ice \j\ job \ŋ\ sing \ō\ go
\o̊\ law \o̊i\ boy \th\ thin \th\ the \ü\ loot \u̇\ foot
\y\ yet \zh\ vision *see also* Guide to Pronunciation

: a drug C₂₁H₂₁N that acts antagonistically to histamine and serotonin and is used especially in the treatment of asthma

cy·prot·er·one \ˌsī-ˈprä-tə-ˌrōn\ *noun* [probably from *cycl-* + *progesterone*] (1966)
: a synthetic steroid C₂₂H₂₇ClO₃ that inhibits androgenic secretions (as testosterone)

Cy·re·na·ic \ˌsir-ə-ˈnā-ik, ˌsī-rə-\ *noun* [Latin *cyrenaicus*, from Greek *kyrēnaikos*, from *Kyrēnē* Cyrene, Africa, home of Aristippus, author of the doctrine] (1586)
: an adherent of the doctrine that pleasure is the chief end of life
— **Cyrenaic** *adjective*
— **Cy·re·na·icism** \-ˈnā-ə-ˌsi-zəm\ *noun*

Cy·ril·lic \sə-ˈri-lik\ *adjective* [Saint *Cyril*, reputed inventor of the Cyrillic alphabet] (1842)
: of, relating to, or constituting an alphabet used for writing Old Church Slavonic and for Russian and a number of other languages of eastern Europe and Asia

cyst \ˈsist\ *noun* [New Latin *cystis*, from Greek *kystis* bladder, pouch; akin to Sanskrit *śvasiti* he blows, snorts — more at WHEEZE] (circa 1720)
1 : a closed sac having a distinct membrane and developing abnormally in a cavity or structure of the body
2 : a body resembling a cyst: as **a :** a resting spore of many algae **b :** a gas-filled vesicle (as of a rockweed or bladderwort) **c :** a capsule formed about a minute organism going into a resting or spore stage; *also* **:** this capsule with its contents **d :** a resistant cover about a parasite produced by the parasite or the host

cyst- *or* **cysti-** *or* **cysto-** *combining form* [French, from Greek *kyst-*, *kysto-*, from *kystis*]
: bladder ⟨*cyst*itis⟩ **:** sac ⟨*cysto*carp⟩

-cyst *noun combining form* [New Latin *-cystis*, from Greek *kystis*]
: bladder **:** sac ⟨blasto*cyst*⟩

cys·te·amine \sis-ˈtē-ə-mən\ *noun* [*cyste*ine + *amine*] (1943)
: a cysteine derivative C₂H₇NS that has been used experimentally in the prevention of radiation sickness (as of cancer patients)

cys·te·ine \ˈsis-tə-ˌēn\ *noun* [International Scientific Vocabulary, from *cystine* + *-ein*] (1884)
: a crystalline sulfur-containing amino acid C₃H₇NO₂S readily oxidizable to cystine

cys·tic \ˈsis-tik\ *adjective* (1713)
1 : relating to, composed of, or containing cysts
2 : of or relating to the urinary bladder or the gallbladder
3 : enclosed in a cyst

cys·ti·cer·coid \ˌsis-tə-ˈsər-ˌkȯid\ *noun* (1858)
: a tapeworm larva having an invaginated scolex and solid tailpiece

cys·ti·cer·co·sis \ˌsis-tə-(ˌ)sər-ˈkō-səs\ *noun, plural* **-co·ses** \-ˈkō-ˌsēz\ [New Latin] (1905)
: infestation with or disease caused by cysticerci

cys·ti·cer·cus \-ˈsər-kəs\ *noun, plural* **-cer·ci** \-ˈsər-ˌsī, -ˌkī\ [New Latin, from *cyst-* + Greek *kerkos* tail] (circa 1871)
: a tapeworm larva that consists of a fluid-filled sac containing an invaginated scolex and is situated in the tissues of an intermediate host

cystic fibrosis *noun* (1938)
: a common hereditary disease especially among whites that appears usually in early childhood, involves functional disorder of the exocrine glands, and is marked especially by faulty digestion due to a deficiency of pancreatic enzymes, by difficulty in breathing due to mucus accumulation in airways, and by excessive loss of salt in the sweat

cys·tine \ˈsis-ˌtēn\ *noun* [from its discovery in bladder stones] (1843)
: a crystalline amino acid C₆H₁₂N₂O₄S₂ that is widespread in proteins (as keratins) and is a major metabolic sulfur source

cys·tin·uria \ˌsis-tə-ˈnu̇r-ē-ə, -ˈnyu̇r-\ *noun* [New Latin] (1853)
: a metabolic defect characterized by excretion of excessive amounts of cystine in the urine and inherited as an autosomal recessive trait

cys·ti·tis \sis-ˈtī-təs\ *noun* [New Latin] (circa 1783)
: inflammation of the urinary bladder

cys·to·carp \ˈsis-tə-ˌkärp\ *noun* [International Scientific Vocabulary] (1875)
: the fruiting structure produced in the red algae after fertilization

cys·to·lith \ˈsis-tə-ˌlith\ *noun* [German *Zystolith*, from *zyst-* cyst- + *-lith*] (1857)
: a calcium carbonate concretion arising from the cellulose wall of cells of higher plants

cys·to·scope \ˈsis-tə-ˌskōp\ *noun* [International Scientific Vocabulary] (1889)
: a medical instrument for the visual examination of the bladder and for the passage of instruments under visual control
— **cys·to·scop·ic** \ˌsis-tə-ˈskä-pik\ *adjective*
— **cys·tos·co·py** \si-ˈstäs-kə-pē\ *noun*

cyt- *or* **cyto-** *combining form* [German *zyt-*, *zyto-*, from Greek *kytos* hollow vessel — more at HIDE]
1 : cell ⟨*cyto*logy⟩
2 : cytoplasm ⟨*cyto*kinesis⟩

-cyte *noun combining form* [New Latin *-cyta*, from Greek *kytos* hollow vessel]
: cell ⟨leuko*cyte*⟩

Cyth·er·ea \ˌsi-thə-ˈrē-ə\ *noun* [Latin, from Greek *Kythereia*, from *Kythēra* Cythera, island associated with Aphrodite]
: APHRODITE

Cyth·er·e·an \-ˈrē-ən\ *adjective* (1885)
: of or relating to the planet Venus

cy·ti·dine \ˈsi-tə-ˌdēn, ˈsī-\ *noun* [*cytosine* + *-idine*] (1911)
: a nucleoside containing cytosine

cy·ti·dyl·ic acid \ˌsi-tə-ˈdi-lik-, ˌsī-\ *noun* [*cytidine* + *-yl* + ¹*-ic*] (1936)
: a nucleotide containing cytosine

cy·to·cha·la·sin \ˌsī-tō-kə-ˈlā-sən\ *noun* [*cyt-* + Greek *chalasis* slackening + English ¹*-in*] (1967)
: any of a group of metabolites isolated from fungi (especially *Helminthosporium dematioideum*) that inhibit various cell processes

cy·to·chem·is·try \-ˈke-mə-strē\ *noun* (circa 1905)
1 : microscopical biochemistry
2 : the chemistry of cells
— **cy·to·chem·i·cal** \-ˈke-mi-kəl\ *adjective*

cy·to·chrome \ˈsī-tə-ˌkrōm\ *noun* (1925)
: any of several intracellular hemoprotein respiratory pigments that are enzymes functioning in electron transport as carriers of electrons

cytochrome c *noun, often 2d c italic* (1940)
: the most abundant and stable of the cytochromes

cytochrome oxidase *noun* (1942)
: an iron-porphyrin enzyme important in cell respiration because of its ability to catalyze the oxidation of reduced cytochrome c in the presence of oxygen

cy·to·dif·fer·en·ti·a·tion \ˈsī-tō-ˌdi-fə-ˌren(t)-shē-ˈā-shən\ *noun* (1959)
: the development of specialized cells (as muscle, blood, or nerve cells) from undifferentiated precursors

cy·to·ge·net·ics \ˌsī-tō-jə-ˈne-tiks\ *noun plural but singular or plural in construction* [International Scientific Vocabulary] (1942)
: a branch of biology that deals with the study of heredity and variation by the methods of both cytology and genetics
— **cy·to·ge·net·ic** \-jə-ˈne-tik\ *or* **cy·to·ge·net·i·cal** \-ti-kəl\ *adjective*
— **cy·to·ge·net·i·cal·ly** \-ti-k(ə-)lē\ *adverb*
— **cy·to·ge·net·i·cist** \-ˈne-tə-sist\ *noun*

cy·to·kine \ˈsī-tə-ˌkīn\ *noun* [*cyt-* + *-kine* (as in *lymphokine*)] (1979)
: any of a class of immunoregulatory substances (as lymphokines) that are secreted by cells of the immune system

cy·to·ki·ne·sis \ˌsī-tō-kə-ˈnē-səs, -kī-\ *noun* [New Latin] (1919)
1 : the cytoplasmic changes accompanying mitosis
2 : cleavage of the cytoplasm into daughter cells following nuclear division
— **cy·to·ki·net·ic** \-ˈne-tik\ *adjective*

cy·to·ki·nin \ˌsī-tə-ˈkī-nən\ *noun* [*cyt-* + *kinin*] (1965)
: any of various plant growth substances (as kinetin) that are usually derivatives of adenine

cy·tol·o·gy \sī-ˈtä-lə-jē\ *noun* [International Scientific Vocabulary] (1889)
1 : a branch of biology dealing with the structure, function, multiplication, pathology, and life history of cells
2 : the cytological aspects of a process or structure
— **cy·to·log·i·cal** \ˌsī-tᵊl-ˈä-ji-kəl\ *or* **cy·to·log·ic** \-ˈä-jik\ *adjective*
— **cy·to·log·i·cal·ly** \-ji-k(ə-)lē\ *adverb*
— **cy·tol·o·gist** \sī-ˈtä-lə-jist\ *noun*

cy·to·ly·sin \ˌsī-tᵊl-ˈī-sᵊn\ *noun* [International Scientific Vocabulary] (circa 1903)
: a substance (as an antibody that lyses bacteria) producing cytolysis

cy·tol·y·sis \sī-ˈtä-lə-səs\ *noun* [New Latin] (1907)
: the usually pathologic dissolution or disintegration of cells
— **cy·to·lyt·ic** \ˌsī-tᵊl-ˈi-tik\ *adjective*

cy·to·me·gal·ic \ˌsī-tō-mi-ˈga-lik\ *adjective* [New Latin *cytomegalia* condition of having enlarged cells, from *cyt-* + *megal-* + *-ia*] (1952)
: characterized by or causing the formation of enlarged cells

cy·to·meg·a·lo·vi·rus \ˌsī-tə-ˌme-gə-lō-ˈvī-rəs\ *noun* [New Latin, from *cytomegalia* + *-o-* + *virus*] (1963)
: any of several viruses that cause cellular enlargement and formation of eosinophilic inclusion bodies especially in the nucleus and include some acting as opportunistic infectious agents in immunosuppressed conditions (as AIDS)

cy·to·mem·brane \ˌsī-tō-ˈmem-ˌbrān\ *noun* (1962)
: one of the cellular membranes including those of the plasmalemma, endoplasmic reticulum, nuclear envelope, and Golgi apparatus; *specifically* **:** UNIT MEMBRANE

cy·to·path·ic \ˌsī-tə-ˈpa-thik\ *adjective* (1952)
: of, relating to, characterized by, or producing pathological changes in cells

cy·to·path·o·gen·ic \-ˌpa-thə-ˈje-nik\ *adjective* (1952)
: pathologic for or destructive to cells
— **cy·to·path·o·ge·nic·i·ty** \-jə-ˈni-sə-tē\ *noun*

cy·to·phil·ic \ˌsī-tə-ˈfi-lik\ *adjective* (circa 1909)
: having an affinity for cells ⟨*cytophilic* antibodies⟩

cy·to·pho·tom·e·try \-fō-ˈtä-mə-trē\ *noun* (1955)
: photometry applied to the study of the cell or its constituents
— **cy·to·pho·to·met·ric** \-ˌfō-tə-ˈme-trik\ *adjective*

cy·to·plasm \ˈsī-tə-ˌpla-zəm\ *noun* [International Scientific Vocabulary] (1874)
: the organized complex of inorganic and organic substances external to the nuclear membrane of a cell and including the cytosol and membrane-bound organelles (as mitochondria or chloroplasts) — see CELL illustration
— **cy·to·plas·mic** \ˌsī-tə-ˈplaz-mik\ *adjective*
— **cy·to·plas·mi·cal·ly** \-mi-k(ə-)lē\ *adverb*

cy·to·sine \'sī-tə-ˌsēn\ *noun* [International Scientific Vocabulary *cyt-* + *-ose* + ²*-ine*] (1894)
: a pyrimidine base $C_4H_5N_3O$ that codes genetic information in the polynucleotide chain of DNA or RNA — compare ADENINE, GUANINE, THYMINE, URACIL

cy·to·skel·e·ton \ˌsī-tə-'ske-lə-t°n\ *noun* (1940)
: the network of protein filaments and microtubules in the cytoplasm that controls cell shape, maintains intracellular organization, and is involved in cell movement
— **cy·to·skel·e·tal** \-t°l\ *adjective*

cy·to·sol \'sī-tə-ˌsäl, -ˌsȯl\ *noun* (1970)
: the fluid portion of the cytoplasm exclusive of organelles and membranes — called also *hyaloplasm, ground substance*
— **cy·to·sol·ic** \ˌsī-tə-'sä-lik, -'sȯ-\ *adjective*

cy·to·stat·ic \ˌsī-tə-'sta-tik\ *adjective* (1949)
: tending to retard cellular activity and multiplication ⟨*cytostatic* treatment of tumor cells⟩
— **cytostatic** *noun*
— **cy·to·stat·i·cal·ly** \-ti-k(ə-)lē\ *adverb*

cy·to·tax·on·o·my \ˌsī-tō-(ˌ)tak-'sä-nə-mē\ *noun* (1930)
1 : study of the relationships and classification of organisms using both classical systematic techniques and comparative studies of chromosomes
2 : the nuclear cytologic makeup of a kind of organism
— **cy·to·tax·o·nom·ic** \-ˌtak-sə-'nä-mik\ *adjective*
— **cy·to·tax·o·nom·i·cal·ly** \-mi-k(ə-)lē\ *adverb*

cy·to·tech·nol·o·gist \ˌsī-tə-tek-'nä-lə-jist\ *noun* (1961)
: a medical technician trained in the identification of cells and cellular abnormalities (as in cancer)
— **cy·to·tech·nol·o·gy** \-lə-jē\ *noun*

cy·to·tox·ic \ˌsī-tə-'täk-sik\ *adjective* (1904)
1 : of or relating to a cytotoxin
2 : toxic to cells ⟨*cytotoxic* properties of platinum⟩
— **cy·to·tox·ic·i·ty** \-(ˌ)täk-'si-sə-tē\ *noun*

cy·to·tox·in \-'täk-sən\ *noun* (1902)
: a substance (as a toxin or antibody) having a toxic effect on cells

czar \'zär, '(t)sär\ *noun* [New Latin *czar,* from Russian *tsar',* from Old Russian *tsĭsarĭ,* from Gothic *kaisar,* from Greek or Latin; Greek, from Latin *Caesar* — more at CAESAR] (1555)
1 : EMPEROR; *specifically* : the ruler of Russia until the 1917 revolution
2 : one having great power or authority ⟨a banking *czar*⟩ ◇
— **czar·dom** \'zär-dəm, '(t)sär-\ *noun*

czar·das \'chär-ˌdash, -ˌdäsh\ *noun, plural* **czardas** [Hungarian *csárdás*] (1860)
: a Hungarian dance to music in duple time in which the dancers start slowly and finish with a rapid whirl

czar·e·vitch \'zär-ə-ˌvich, '(t)sär-\ *noun* [Russian *tsarevich,* from *tsar'* + *-evich,* patronymic suffix] (1710)
: an heir apparent of a Russian czar

cza·ri·na \zä-'rē-nə, (t)sä-\ *noun* [probably modification of German *Zarin,* from *Zar* czar, from Russian *tsar'*] (1717)
: the wife of a czar

czar·ism \'zär-ˌi-zəm, '(t)sär-\ *noun* (1855)
1 : the government of Russia under the czars
2 : autocratic rule
— **czar·ist** \'zär-ist, '(t)sär-\ *noun or adjective*

Czech \'chek\ *noun* [Czech *Čech*] (1841)
1 : a native or inhabitant of western Czechoslovakia including Bohemia and Moravia
2 : the Slavic language of the Czechs
3 : a native or inhabitant of Czechoslovakia or the Czech Republic
— **Czech** *adjective*
— **Czech·ish** \'che-kish\ *adjective*

◇ WORD HISTORY

czar *Czar* or *tsar* is the English word for a pre-Soviet Russian emperor. *Tsar* is a straightforward transliteration of the Russian word and is now the usual form in Slavic studies; but *czar,* now usually used figuratively (as in "drug czar") has an older and more involved origin. We owe this spelling to the Austrian diplomat Seigmund, Freiherr (Baron) von Herberstein (1486–1566), who was an ambassador to the court at Moscow during the reigns of the Holy Roman Emperors Maximilian I and Charles V. In 1549 he published *Rerum moscovitarum commentarii* ("Commentaries on Muscovite Matters"), one of the first Western books concerning things Russian and long a major source of information about Russia in Western Europe. Herberstein wrote in Latin, but his use of *cz* to represent the sound \ts\ reflected a largely obsolete spelling convention in Hungarian. In English words such as *czardas* and *Czech,* *cz* represents, in contrast, \ch\ which is a convention continued in modern Polish.

D *is the fourth letter of the English alphabet and of most alphabets that are closely related to that of English. It came to Latin through Etruscan from a western Greek alphabet. The Greeks took it from the Phoenician alphabet, naming the letter* delta *after Phoenician* dāleth. *In modern English* d *usually represents the voiced alveolar stop, a consonant sound made with the tip of the tongue touching the inner surface of the gums above the upper front teeth (as the* d *sound in English* dog). *Small* d *evolved from a Roman variant of captial D in which the top of the curved line swept beyond the straight upright line of the letter (* Ɒ *). The straight line was later rounded on the left to form a lobe, and the original curved line ascended above the lobe from its right side (∂). Eventually, this ascender was straightened to produce the modern form of the letter.*

d \'dē\ *noun, plural* **d's** *or* **ds** \'dēz\ *often capitalized, often attributive* (before 12th century)
1 a : the 4th letter of the English alphabet **b :** a graphic representation of this letter **c :** a speech counterpart of orthographic *d*
2 : 500 — see NUMBER table
3 : the 2d tone of a C-major scale
4 : a graphic device for reproducing the letter *d*
5 : one designated *d* especially as the 4th in order or class
6 a : a grade rating a student's work as poor in quality **b :** one graded or rated with a D
7 : something shaped like the letter D; *specifically* **:** a semicircle on a pool table about 23 inches in diameter for use especially in snooker
8 : DEFENSE 2b, 4b ⟨play tough *D*⟩
d- \,dē, 'dē\ *prefix* [International Scientific Vocabulary, from *dextr-*]
1 : dextrorotatory ⟨*d*-tartaric acid⟩
2 : having a similar configuration at a selected carbon atom to the configuration of dextrorotatory glyceraldehyde — usually printed as a small capital ⟨D-fructose⟩
-d *symbol*
— used after the figure 2 or 3 to indicate the ordinal number second or third ⟨2*d*⟩ ⟨53*d*⟩
'd \d, əd, id\ *verb*
1 : HAD
2 : WOULD
3 : DID
DA \,dē-'ā\ *noun* [duck's *a*ss; from its resemblance to the tail of a duck] (1951)
: DUCKTAIL
¹dab \'dab\ *noun* [Middle English *dabbe*] (14th century)
1 : a sudden blow or thrust **:** POKE
2 : a small amount
3 : a gentle touch or stroke **:** PAT
4 : DAUB
²dab *verb* **dabbed; dab·bing** (1562)
transitive verb
1 : to strike or touch lightly **:** PAT
2 : to apply lightly or irregularly **:** DAUB
intransitive verb
: to make a dab
— **dab·ber** *noun*
³dab *noun* [Anglo-French *dabbe*] (15th century)
: FLATFISH; *especially* **:** any of several flounders (genus *Limanda*)
⁴dab *noun* [origin unknown] (1691)
chiefly British **:** a skillful person
dab·ble \'da-bəl\ *verb* **dab·bled; dab·bling**
\-b(ə-)liŋ\ [perhaps frequentative of ²*dab*] (1557)
transitive verb
: to wet by splashing or by little dips or strokes **:** SPATTER
intransitive verb

1 a : to paddle, splash, or play in or as if in water **b :** to reach with the bill to the bottom of shallow water in order to obtain food
2 : to work or involve oneself superficially or intermittently especially in a secondary activity or interest ⟨*dabbles* in art⟩
dab·bler \-b(ə-)lər\ *noun* (1611)
: one that dabbles: as **a :** one not deeply engaged in or concerned with something **b :** a duck (as a mallard or shoveler) that feeds by dabbling — called also *dabbling duck, puddle duck*
synonym see AMATEUR
dab·bling \-b(ə-)liŋ\ *noun* (circa 1847)
: a superficial or intermittent interest, investigation, or experiment ⟨his *dabblings* in philosophy and art⟩
dab·chick \'dab-,chik\ *noun* [probably irregular from obsolete English *dop* (to dive) + English *chick*] (circa 1550)
: any of several small grebes
dab hand *noun* [⁴*dab*] (circa 1828)
chiefly British **:** EXPERT
da ca·po \dä-'kä-(,)pō, də-\ *adverb or adjective* [Italian] (circa 1724)
: from the beginning — used as a direction in music to repeat
dace \'dās\ *noun, plural* **dace** [Middle English *dace, darce,* from Middle French *dars,* from Medieval Latin *darsus*] (15th century)
1 : a small freshwater European cyprinid fish (*Leuciscus leuciscus*)
2 : any of various small North American freshwater cyprinid fishes
da·cha \'dä-chə *also* 'da-\ *noun* [Russian, from Old Russian, land allotted by a prince; akin to Latin *dos* dowry — more at DATE] (1896)
: a Russian country cottage used especially in the summer
dachs·hund \'däks-,hunt, -,hund; 'däk-sənt; *especially British* 'dak-sənd\ *noun* [German, from *Dachs* badger + *Hund* dog] (1882)
: any of a breed of long-bodied, short-legged dogs of German origin that occur in short-haired, long-haired, and wirehaired varieties

dachshund

Da·cron \'dā-,krän, 'da-\ *trademark*
— used for a synthetic polyester textile fiber
dac·tyl \'dak-t°l, -,til\ *noun* [Middle English *dactile,* from Latin *dactylus,* from Greek *daktylos,* literally, finger; from the fact that the first of three syllables is the longest, like the joints of the finger] (14th century)
: a metrical foot consisting of one long and two short syllables or of one stressed and two unstressed syllables (as in *tenderly*)
— **dac·tyl·ic** \dak-'ti-lik\ *adjective or noun*
dactyl- *or* **dactylo-** *combining form* [Greek *daktyl-, daktylo-,* from *daktylos*]

: finger **:** toe **:** digit ⟨*dactylology*⟩
dac·ty·lol·o·gy \,dak-tə-'lä-lə-jē\ *noun* (circa 1656)
: FINGER SPELLING
dad \'dad\ *noun* [probably baby talk] (15th century)
: FATHER 1a
Da·da \'dä-(,)dä\ *noun* [French] (1919)
: a movement in art and literature based on deliberate irrationality and negation of traditional artistic values; *also* **:** the art and literature produced by this movement ◇
da·da·ism \-,i-zəm\ *noun, often capitalized* [French *dadaïsme*] (1919)
: DADA
— **da·da·ist** \-ist\ *noun or adjective, often capitalized*
— **da·da·is·tic** \,dä-dä-'is-tik\ *adjective, often capitalized*
dad·dy \'da-dē\ *noun, plural* **daddies** (15th century)
1 : FATHER 1a
2 : GRANDDADDY 2
dad·dy long·legs \,da-dē-'loŋ-,legz, -,lägz\ *noun, plural* **daddy longlegs** (circa 1814)
1 : CRANE FLY
2 : HARVESTMAN
¹da·do \'dā-(,)dō\ *noun, plural* **da·does** [Italian, die, plinth] (1664)
1 a : the part of a pedestal of a column between the base and the surbase **b :** the lower part of an interior wall when specially decorated or faced; *also* **:** the decoration adorning this part of a wall
2 : a rectangular groove cut to make a joint in woodworking; *specifically* **:** one cut across the grain

dado 1a: *1* surbase, *2* dado, *3* base

²dado *transitive verb* **da·doed; da·do·ing** (1881)
1 : to provide with a dado
2 a : to set into a groove **b :** to cut a dado in (as a plank)
dae·dal \'dē-d°l\ *adjective* [Latin *daedalus,* from Greek *daidalos*] (1590)
1 a : SKILLFUL, ARTISTIC **b :** INTRICATE ⟨the computer's *daedal* circuitry⟩
2 : adorned with many things ⟨visions of cloud and light and *daedal* earth are the airman's daily scene —Laurence Binyon⟩
Dae·da·lus \'de-d°l-əs, 'dē-\ *noun* [Latin, from Greek *Daidalos*]
: the legendary builder of the Cretan labyrinth who makes wings to enable himself and his son Icarus to escape imprisonment

◇ WORD HISTORY
Dada In February 1916, while Europe was engulfed in World War I, a group of aesthetes and war resisters, including the artists Marcel Duchamp and Jean Arp and the poet Tristan Tzara, sought refuge in tranquil, neutral Switzerland. They decided to respond to the madness about them by creating an artistic movement based on irrationality, one that would repudiate traditional values and conventions and would shock bourgeois sensibilities. At a café in Zurich one evening, they hit upon a name for the new movement. Recollections of the movement's founding members differ regarding the arbitrariness of the naming process, but in any case the word chosen was *dada,* in French a child's word for a hobbyhorse; its very childishness was a way the group could mock the world around them. Though the Zurich group soon broke up and Dadaism as a movement lost its steam in the 1920s, it had far-reaching effects on the art of the 20th century, for trends as diverse as surrealism and conceptual art have their roots in Dada.

— **Dae·da·lian** or **Dae·da·lean** \di-'dāl-yən\ adjective

dae·mon variant of DEMON

daff \'daf\ transitive verb [alteration of doff] (1596)
1 archaic **:** to thrust aside
2 obsolete **:** to put off (as with an excuse)

daf·fo·dil \'da-fə-,dil\ noun [perhaps from Dutch de affodil asphodel, from de the (from Middle Dutch) + affodil asphodel, from Middle French afrodille, from Latin asphodelus; akin to Old High German thaz the — more at THAT, ASPHODEL] (1548)
: any of various bulbous herbs (genus Narcissus); especially **:** a plant whose flowers have a large corona elongated into a trumpet — compare JONQUIL

daf·fy \'da-fē\ adjective **daf·fi·er; -est** [obsolete English daff, noun (fool)] (circa 1884)
: CRAZY, FOOLISH
— **daf·fi·ly** \'da-fə-lē\ adverb

daft \'daft also 'däft\ adjective [Middle English dafte gentle, stupid; akin to Old English gedæfte mild, gentle, Middle English defte deft, Old Church Slavonic podobati to be fitting] (14th century)
1 a : SILLY, FOOLISH **b :** MAD, INSANE
2 Scottish **:** frivolously gay
— **daft·ly** adverb
— **daft·ness** \'daf(t)-nəs\ noun

dag \'dag\ noun [Middle English dagge] (14th century)
1 : a hanging end or shred
2 : matted or manure-coated wool

dag·ger \'da-gər\ noun [Middle English] (14th century)
1 : a sharp pointed knife for stabbing
2 a : something that resembles a dagger **b :** a character † used as a reference mark or to indicate a death date
— **dag·ger·like** \-,līk\ adjective
— **at daggers drawn :** in a state of open hostility or conflict

da·go \'dā-(,)gō\ noun, plural **dagos** or **dagoes** [alteration of earlier diego, from Diego, a common Spanish given name] (1832)
: a person of Italian or Spanish birth or descent — usually used disparagingly

da·guerre·o·type \də-'ge-rō-,tīp, -rə- also də-'ge-rē-ō-,tīp\ noun [French daguerréotype, from L. J. M. Daguerre + French -o- + type] (1839)
: an early photograph produced on a silver or a silver-covered copper plate; also **:** the process of producing such photographs
— **daguerreotype** transitive verb
— **da·guerre·o·typ·ist** \-,tī-pist\ noun
— **da·guerre·o·typy** \-,tī-pē\ noun

dah \'dä\ noun [imitative] (1940)
: DASH 7

dahl·ia \'dal-yə, 'däl-, U.S. also & British usually 'dāl-\ noun [New Latin, genus name, from Anders Dahl (died 1789) Swedish botanist] (1840)
: any of a genus (Dahlia) of American tuberous-rooted composite herbs having opposite pinnate leaves and rayed flower heads and including many that are cultivated as ornamentals

dai·kon \'dī-kən\ noun [Japanese, from dai big + kon root] (1876)
: a large long hard white radish used especially in Oriental cuisine; also **:** a plant (Raphanus sativus longipinnatus) whose root is a daikon

dai·li·ness \'dā-lē-nəs, -li-\ noun (1596)
: daily or routine quality **:** ORDINARINESS (the dailiness of family life)

¹dai·ly \'dā-lē\ adjective (15th century)
1 a : occurring, made, or acted upon every day **b :** issued every day or every weekday **c :** of or providing for every day
2 a : reckoned by the day (average daily wage) **b :** covering the period of or based on a day (daily statistics)

²daily adverb (15th century)
1 : every day
2 : every weekday

³daily noun, plural **dai·lies** (1832)
1 : a newspaper published every weekday
2 British **:** a servant who works on a daily basis
3 plural **:** RUSH 6

daily double noun (1942)
: a system of betting (as on horse races) in which the bettor must pick the winners of two stipulated races in order to win

daily dozen noun (1919)
1 : a series of physical exercises to be performed daily **:** WORKOUT
2 : a set of routine duties or tasks

dai·mon \'dī-,mōn\ noun, plural **dai·mo·nes** \'dī-mə-,nēz\ or **daimons** [Greek daimōn] (1852)
: DEMON 2, 3
— **dai·mon·ic** \dī-'mä-nik\ adjective

dai·myo also **dai·mio** \'dī-mē-,ō, -(,)myō\ noun, plural **-myo** or **-myos** also **-mio** or **-mios** [Japanese daimyō] (1727)
: a Japanese feudal baron

¹dain·ty \'dān-tē\ noun, plural **dain·ties** [Middle English deinte, from Old French deintié, from Latin dignitat-, dignitas dignity, worth] (14th century)
1 a : something delicious to the taste **b :** something choice or pleasing
2 obsolete **:** FASTIDIOUSNESS

²dainty adjective **dain·ti·er; -est** (14th century)
1 a : tasting good **:** TASTY **b :** attractively prepared and served
2 : marked by delicate or diminutive beauty, form, or grace
3 obsolete **:** CHARY, RELUCTANT
4 a : marked by fastidious discrimination or finical taste **b :** showing avoidance of anything rough
synonym see CHOICE
— **dain·ti·ly** \'dān-tə-lē\ adverb
— **dain·ti·ness** \'dān-tē-nəs\ noun

dai·qui·ri \'da-kə-rē, 'dī-\ noun [Daiquirí, Cuba] (1920)
: a cocktail made of rum, lime juice, and sugar

dairy \'der-ē, 'dar-\ noun, plural **dair·ies** often attributive [Middle English deyerie, from deye dairymaid, from Old English dæge kneader of bread; akin to Old English dāg dough — more at DOUGH] (14th century)
1 : a room, building, or establishment where milk is kept and butter or cheese is made
2 a : the department of farming or of a farm that is concerned with the production of milk, butter, and cheese **b :** a farm devoted to such production
3 : an establishment for the sale or distribution chiefly of milk and milk products

dairy cattle noun plural (1895)
: cattle kept for milk production

dairy·ing \'der-ē-iŋ\ noun (1649)
: the business of operating a dairy

dairy·maid \-,mād\ noun (1599)
: a woman employed in a dairy

dairy·man \-mən, -,man\ noun (circa 1617)
: one who operates a dairy farm or works in a dairy

da·is \'dā-əs, ÷'dī-\ noun [Middle English deis, from Old French, from Late Latin discus high table, from Latin, dish, quoit — more at DISH] (13th century)
: a raised platform (as in a hall or large room)

dai·shi·ki \dī-'shē-kē\ variant of DASHIKI

dai·sy \'dā-zē\ noun, plural **daisies** [Middle English dayeseye, from Old English dægesēage, from dæg day + ēage eye] (before 12th century)
1 : a composite plant (as of the genera Bellis or Chrysanthemum) having a flower head with well-developed ray flowers usually arranged in one or a few whorls: as **a :** a low European herb (Bellis perennis) with white or pink ray flowers — called also English daisy **b :** a leafy-stemmed perennial herb (Chrysanthemum leucanthemum) with long white ray flowers and a yellow disk that was introduced into the U.S. from Europe — called also ox-eye daisy
2 : the flower head of a daisy
3 : a first-rate person or thing
4 capitalized **:** a member of a program of the Girl Scouts for girls in kindergarten and first grade in school

daisy chain noun (1841)
1 : a string of daisies with stems linked to form a chain
2 : an interlinked series

daisy ham noun (circa 1938)
: a boned and smoked piece of pork from the shoulder

daisy wheel noun [from its resemblance to the flower] (circa 1977)
: a disk with spokes bearing type that serves as the printing element of an electric typewriter or printer; also **:** a printer that uses such a disk

Da·ko·ta \də-'kō-tə\ noun, plural **Dakotas** also **Dakota** (1804)
1 : a member of an American Indian people of the northern Mississippi valley
2 : the language of the Dakota people

dal also **dahl** \'däl\ noun [Hindi dāl] (1673)
: a dried legume (as lentils, beans, or peas); also **:** an Indian dish made of simmered and usually pureed and spiced legumes

Da·lai La·ma \,dä-lī-'lä-mə, ,dä-lä-, ,da-\ noun [Mongolian dalai ocean] (1698)
: the spiritual head of Lamaism

da·la·si \dä-'lä-sē\ noun, plural **dalasi** or **dalasis** [Wolof] (1966)
— see MONEY table

dale \'dā(ə)l\ noun [Middle English, from Old English dæl; akin to Old High German tal valley, Welsh dôl] (before 12th century)
: VALLEY, VALE (went riding over hill and dale)

dales·man \'dā(ə)lz-mən\ noun (1769)
British **:** one living or born in a dale

da·leth \'dä-,leth, -,let also -ləd\ noun [Hebrew dāleth, from deleth door] (1823)
: the 4th letter of the Hebrew alphabet — see ALPHABET table

dal·li·ance \'da-lē-ən(t)s\ noun (14th century)
: an act of dallying: as **a :** PLAY; especially **:** amorous play **b :** frivolous action **:** TRIFLING

Dal·lis grass \'da-ləs-\ noun [A. T. Dallis, 19th century American farmer] (1907)
: a tall tufted tropical perennial grass (Paspalum dilatatum) introduced as a pasture and forage grass in the southern U.S.

Dall por·poise \'dol-\ noun [William H. Dall (died 1927) American naturalist] (1951)
: a black-and-white porpoise (Phocoenoides dalli) of temperate and arctic waters of the rim of the North Pacific Ocean — called also Dall's porpoise \'dolz-\

Dall sheep noun [W. H. Dall] (1887)
: a large white wild sheep (Ovis dalli) of Alaska and northern British Columbia — called also Dall's sheep

dal·ly \'da-lē\ intransitive verb **dal·lied; dal·ly·ing** [Middle English dalyen, from Anglo-French dalier] (15th century)
1 a : to act playfully; especially **:** to play amorously **b :** to deal lightly **:** TOY (accused him of dallying with a serious problem)
2 a : to waste time **b :** LINGER, DAWDLE
synonym see TRIFLE, DELAY
— **dal·li·er** noun

dal·ma·tian \dal-'mā-shən\ noun, often capitalized [from the supposed origin of the breed in Dalmatia] (1824)
: any of a breed of medium-sized dogs having a

\ə\ abut \ᵊ\ kitten \ər\ further \a\ ash \ā\ ace
\ä\ mop, mar \au̇\ out \ch\ chin \e\ bet \ē\ easy
\g\ go \i\ hit \ī\ ice \j\ job \ŋ\ sing \ō\ go
\ȯ\ law \ȯi\ boy \th\ thin \th\ the \ü\ loot \u̇\ foot
\y\ yet \zh\ vision see also Guide to Pronunciation

white short-haired coat with black or brown spots

dal·mat·ic \dal-'ma-tik\ *noun* [Middle English *dalmatyk,* from Old English *dalmatice,* from Late Latin *dalmatica,* from Latin, feminine of *dalmaticus* Dalmatian, from *Dalmatia*] (before 12th century)
1 : a wide-sleeved overgarment with slit sides worn by a deacon or prelate
2 : a robe worn by a British sovereign at his or her coronation

dal se·gno \däl-'sā-(,)nyō\ *adverb* [Italian, from the sign] (circa 1854)
— used as a direction in music to return to the sign that marks the beginning of a repeat

dal·ton \'dȯl-t°n\ *noun* [*John Dalton* (died 1844) English chemist] (circa 1928)
: ATOMIC MASS UNIT — used chiefly in biochemistry

¹dam \'dam\ *noun* [Middle English *dam, dame* lady, dam — more at DAME] (13th century)
: a female parent — used especially of a domestic animal

²dam *noun* [Middle English, probably from Middle Dutch; akin to Old English for*demman* to stop up] (14th century)
1 : a body of water confined by a barrier
2 a : a barrier preventing the flow of water or of loose solid materials (as soil or snow); *especially* : a barrier built across a watercourse for impounding water **b** : a barrier to check the flow of liquid, gas, or air

³dam *transitive verb* **dammed; dam·ming** (15th century)
1 : to provide or restrain with a dam
2 : to stop up : BLOCK

¹dam·age \'da-mij\ *noun* [Middle English, from Middle French, from *dam* damage, from Latin *damnum*] (14th century)
1 : loss or harm resulting from injury to person, property, or reputation
2 *plural* : compensation in money imposed by law for loss or injury
3 : EXPENSE, COST ⟨"What's the *damage*?" he asked the waiter⟩

²damage *transitive verb* **dam·aged; dam·ag·ing** (14th century)
: to cause damage to
synonym see INJURE
— **dam·age·abil·i·ty** \,da-mi-jə-'bi-lə-tē\ *noun*
— **dam·ag·er** *noun*

dam·ag·ing *adjective* (circa 1828)
: causing or able to cause damage : INJURIOUS ⟨has a *damaging* effect on wildlife⟩
— **dam·ag·ing·ly** \'da-mi-jiŋ-lē\ *adverb*

dam·ar *or* **dam·mar** \'da-mər\ *noun* [Malay] (1698)
: any of various resins used in varnishes and inks and obtained chiefly in Malaya and Indonesia from several timber trees (families Dipterocarpaceae and Burseraceae)

¹dam·a·scene \'da-mə-,sēn, ,da-mə-'-\ *noun* (14th century)
1 *capitalized* : a native or inhabitant of Damascus
2 : the characteristic markings of Damascus steel

²damascene *adjective* (14th century)
1 *capitalized* : of, relating to, or characteristic of Damascus or the Damascenes
2 : of or relating to damask or the art of damascening

³damascene *transitive verb* **-scened; -scen·ing** [Middle French *damasquiner,* from *damasquin* of Damascus] (1585)
: to ornament (as iron or steel) with wavy patterns like those of watered silk or with inlaid work of precious metals

dalmatian

Da·mas·cus steel \də-'mas-kəs-\ *noun* (circa 1727)
: hard elastic steel ornamented with wavy patterns and used especially for sword blades

¹dam·ask \'da-məsk\ *noun* [Middle English *damaske,* from Medieval Latin *damascus,* from *Damascus*] (14th century)
1 : a firm lustrous fabric (as of linen, cotton, silk, or rayon) made with flat patterns in a satin weave on a plain-woven ground on jacquard looms
2 : DAMASCUS STEEL; *also* : the characteristic markings of this steel
3 : a grayish red

²damask *adjective* (15th century)
1 : made of or resembling damask
2 : of the color damask

damask rose *noun* [obsolete *Damask* of Damascus, from obsolete *Damask* Damascus] (1540)
: a large hardy fragrant pink rose (*Rosa damascena*) widely introduced from Asia Minor and the major source of attar of roses

dame \'dām\ *noun* [Middle English, from Old French, from Latin *domina,* feminine of *dominus* master; akin to Latin *domus* house — more at DOME] (13th century)
1 : a woman of rank, station, or authority: as **a** *archaic* : the mistress of a household **b** : the wife or daughter of a lord **c** : a female member of an order of knighthood — used as a title prefixed to the given name
2 a : an elderly woman **b** : WOMAN

dame school *noun* (1817)
: a school in which the rudiments of reading and writing were taught by a woman in her own home

dame's rocket *noun* (circa 1900)
: a Eurasian perennial plant (*Hesperis matronalis*) of the mustard family cultivated for its spikes of showy fragrant white or purple flowers — called also *dame's violet, rocket*

damn \'dam\ *verb* **damned; damn·ing** \'da-miŋ\ [Middle English *dampnen,* from Old French *dampner,* from Latin *damnare,* from *damnum* damage, loss, fine] (13th century)
transitive verb
1 : to condemn to a punishment or fate; *especially* : to condemn to hell
2 a : to condemn vigorously and often irascibly for some real or fancied fault or defect ⟨*damned* the storm for their delay⟩ **b** : to condemn as a failure by public criticism
3 : to bring ruin on
4 : to swear at : CURSE — often used to express annoyance, disgust, or surprise
intransitive verb
: CURSE, SWEAR
synonym see EXECRATE

²damn *noun* (1619)
1 : the utterance of the word *damn* as a curse
2 : a minimum amount or degree (as of care or consideration) : the least bit ⟨don't give a *damn*⟩

³damn *adjective or adverb* (1775)
: DAMNED ⟨a *damn* nuisance⟩ ⟨ran *damn* fast⟩
— **damn well** : beyond doubt or question : CERTAINLY ⟨knew *damn well* what would happen⟩

dam·na·ble \'dam-nə-bəl\ *adjective* (14th century)
1 : liable to or deserving condemnation
2 : very bad : DETESTABLE ⟨*damnable* weather⟩
— **dam·na·ble·ness** *noun*
— **dam·na·bly** \-blē\ *adverb*

dam·na·tion \dam-'nā-shən\ *noun* (14th century)
: the act of damning : the state of being damned

dam·na·to·ry \'dam-nə-,tōr-ē, -,tȯr-\ *adjective* (1682)
: expressing, imposing, or causing condemnation : CONDEMNATORY

¹damned \'dam(d)\ *adjective* **damned·er** \'dam-dər\; **damned·est** *or* **damnd·est** \-dəst\ (1563)

1 : DAMNABLE ⟨this *damned* smog⟩
2 : COMPLETE, UTTER — often used as an intensive
3 : EXTRAORDINARY — used in the superlative ⟨the *damnedest* contraption you ever saw⟩

²damned \'dam(d)\ *adverb* (1757)
: EXTREMELY, VERY ⟨a *damned* good job⟩

damned·est *or* **damnd·est** \'dam-dəst\ *noun* (1830)
: UTMOST, BEST — used chiefly in the phrase *do one's damnedest* ⟨doing my *damnedest* to win⟩

dam·ni·fy \'dam-nə-,fī\ *transitive verb* **-fied; -fy·ing** [Middle French *damnifier,* from Old French, from Late Latin *damnificare,* from Latin *damnificus* injurious, from *damnum* damage] (1512)
: to cause loss or damage to

damn·ing \'da-miŋ\ *adjective* (1599)
1 : bringing damnation ⟨a *damning* sin⟩
2 : causing or leading to condemnation or ruin ⟨presented some *damning* testimony⟩
— **damn·ing·ly** \-miŋ-lē\ *adverb*

Dam·o·cles \'da-mə-,klēz\ *noun* [Latin, from Greek *Damoklēs*]
: a courtier of ancient Syracuse held to have been seated at a banquet beneath a sword hung by a single hair
— **Dam·o·cle·an** \,da-mə-'klē-ən\ *adjective*

Da·mon \'dā-mən\ *noun* [Latin, from Greek *Damōn*]
: a legendary Sicilian who pledges his life for his condemned friend Pythias

¹damp \'damp\ *noun* [Middle Dutch or Middle Low German, vapor; akin to Old High German *damph* vapor] (14th century)
1 : a noxious gas — compare BLACK DAMP, FIREDAMP
2 : MOISTURE: **a** : HUMIDITY, DAMPNESS **b** *archaic* : FOG, MIST
3 a : DISCOURAGEMENT, CHECK **b** *archaic* : DEPRESSION, DEJECTION

²damp (14th century)
transitive verb
1 a : to affect with or as if with a noxious gas : CHOKE **b** : to diminish the activity or intensity of ⟨*damping* down the causes of inflation⟩ ⟨liquid *damps* out compass oscillations⟩ **c** : to check the vibration or oscillation of (as a string or voltage)
2 : DAMPEN
intransitive verb
: to diminish progressively in vibration or oscillation

³damp *adjective* (1590)
1 a *archaic* : being confused, bewildered, or shocked : STUPEFIED **b** : DEPRESSED, DULL
2 : slightly or moderately wet : MOIST; *also* : HUMID
synonym see WET
— **damp·ish** \'dam-pish\ *adjective*
— **damp·ly** *adverb*
— **damp·ness** *noun*

damp·en \'dam-pən\ *verb* **damp·ened; damp·en·ing** \'damp-niŋ, 'dam-pə-\ (1547)
transitive verb
1 : to check or diminish the activity or vigor of : DEADEN ⟨the heat *dampened* our spirits⟩
2 : to make damp ⟨the shower barely *dampened* the ground⟩
3 : DAMP 1c
intransitive verb
1 : to become damp
2 : to become deadened or depressed
— **damp·en·er** \-nər\ *noun*

damp·er \'dam-pər\ *noun* (1748)
1 : a dulling or deadening influence ⟨put a *damper* on the celebration⟩
2 : a device that damps: as **a** : a valve or plate (as in the flue of a furnace) for regulating the draft **b** : a small felted block to stop the vibration of a piano string **c** *chiefly British* : SHOCK ABSORBER

damp·ing–off \,dam-piŋ-'ȯf\ *noun* (1890)

: a diseased condition of seedlings or cuttings caused by fungi and marked by wilting or rotting

dam·sel \'dam-zəl\ *also* **dam·o·sel** *or* **dam·o·zel** \'da-mə-,zel\ *noun* [Middle English *damesel*, from Old French *dameisele*, from (assumed) Vulgar Latin *domnicella* young noblewoman, diminutive of Latin *domina* lady] (13th century)

: a young woman: **a** *archaic* : a young unmarried woman of noble birth **b** : GIRL

dam·sel·fish \'dam-zəl-,fish\ *noun* (1904)

: any of numerous often brilliantly colored marine fishes (family Pomacentridae) living especially along coral reefs — called also *demoiselle*

dam·sel·fly \-,flī\ *noun* (1815)

: any of numerous odonate insects (suborder Zygoptera) distinguished from dragonflies by laterally projecting eyes and petiolate wings folded above the body when at rest

dam·son \'dam-zən\ *noun* [Middle English, from Latin (*prunum*) *damascenum*, literally, plum of Damascus] (14th century)

: the small tart fruit of a widely cultivated Asian plum tree (*Prunus insititia*); *also* : this tree

¹**Dan** \'dan\ *noun* [Hebrew *Dān*]

: a son of Jacob and the traditional eponymous ancestor of one of the tribes of Israel

²**Dan** \'dan\ *noun* [Middle English, title of members of religious orders, from Middle French, from Latin *dominus* master] (13th century)

archaic : MASTER, SIR

Dan·aë \'da-nə-,ē\ *noun* [Latin, from Greek *Danaē*]

: a princess of Argos visited by Zeus in the form of a shower of gold and by him the mother of Perseus

¹**dance** \'dan(t)s, 'dȧn(t)s\ *verb* **danced; danc·ing** [Middle English *dauncen*, from Old French *dancier*] (14th century)

intransitive verb

1 : to engage in or perform a dance

2 : to move or seem to move up and down or about in a quick or lively manner

transitive verb

1 : to perform or take part in as a dancer

2 : to cause to dance

3 : to bring into a specified condition by dancing

— **dance·able** \'dan(t)-sə-bəl\ *adjective*

— **danc·er** *noun*

²**dance** *noun, often attributive* (14th century)

1 : an act or instance of dancing

2 : a series of rhythmic and patterned bodily movements usually performed to music

3 : a social gathering for dancing

4 : a piece of music by which dancing may be guided

5 : the art of dancing

dan·de·li·on \'dan-də-,lī-ən, -dē-\ *noun* [Middle French *dent de lion*, literally, lion's tooth] (14th century)

: any of a genus (*Taraxacum*) of yellow-flowered composite plants; *especially* : an herb (*T. officinale*) sometimes grown as a potherb and nearly cosmopolitan as a weed

dan·der \'dan-dər\ *noun* [alteration of *dandruff*] (1786)

1 : DANDRUFF; *specifically* : minute scales from hair, feathers, or skin that may be allergenic

2 : ANGER, TEMPER 〈don't get your *dander* up〉

dan·di·a·cal \dan-'dī-ə-kəl\ *adjective* [¹*dandy* + *-acal* (as in *demoniacal*)] (1831)

: of, relating to, or suggestive of a dandy

Dan·die Din·mont terrier \'dan-dē-'din-,mänt-\ *noun* [*Dandie Dinmont,* character owning six such dogs in the novel *Guy Mannering* by Sir Walter Scott] (1875)

: any of a breed of terriers characterized by short legs, a long body, pendulous ears, a rough coat, and a full silky topknot

dan·di·fy \'dan-di-,fī\ *transitive verb* **-fied; -fy·ing** (1823)

: to cause to resemble a dandy

— **dan·di·fi·ca·tion** \,dan-di-fə-'kā-shən\ *noun*

dan·dle \'dan-dᵊl\ *transitive verb* **dan·dled; dan·dling** \-(d)liŋ, -dᵊl-iŋ\ [origin unknown] (1530)

1 : to move (as a baby) up and down in one's arms or on one's knee in affectionate play

2 : PAMPER, PET

dan·druff \'dan-drəf\ *noun* [probably from *dand-* (origin unknown) + *-ruff*, from Middle English *rove* scabby condition, from Old Norse *hrūfa* scab; akin to Old High German *hruf* scurf, Lithuanian *kraupus* rough] (1545)

: a scurf that forms on skin especially of the scalp and comes off in small white or grayish scales

— **dan·druffy** \-drə-fē\ *adjective*

¹**dan·dy** \'dan-dē\ *noun, plural* **dandies** [probably short for *jack-a-dandy,* from ¹*jack* + *a* (of) + *dandy* (origin unknown)] (circa 1780)

1 : a man who gives exaggerated attention to personal appearance

2 : something excellent in its class

— **dan·dy·ish** \-dē-ish\ *adjective*

— **dan·dy·ish·ly** *adverb*

²**dandy** *adjective* **dan·di·er; -est** (1792)

1 : of, relating to, or suggestive of a dandy : FOPPISH

2 : very good : FIRST-RATE 〈a *dandy* place to stay〉

dan·dy·ism \'dan-dē-,i-zəm\ *noun* (1819)

1 : the style or conduct of a dandy

2 : a literary and artistic style of the latter part of the 19th century marked by artificiality and excessive refinement

Dane \'dān\ *noun* [Middle English *Dan,* from Old Norse *Danr*] (14th century)

1 : a native or inhabitant of Denmark

2 : a person of Danish descent

3 : GREAT DANE

dane·geld \'dān-,geld\ *noun, often capitalized* (before 12th century)

: an annual tax believed to have been imposed originally to buy off Danish invaders in England or to maintain forces to oppose them but continued as a land tax

Dane·law \'dān-,lȯ\ *noun* (before 12th century)

1 : the law in force in the part of England held by the Danes before the Norman Conquest

2 : the part of England under the Danelaw

¹**dang** \'daŋ\ *transitive verb* [euphemism] (1797)

: DAMN 4

²**dang** *adjective or adverb* (1914)

: DAMNED

¹**dan·ger** \'dān-jər\ *noun* [Middle English *daunger,* from Old French *dangier,* alteration of *dongier,* from (assumed) Vulgar Latin *dominiarium,* from Latin *dominium* ownership] (13th century)

1 a *archaic* : JURISDICTION **b** *obsolete* : REACH, RANGE

2 *obsolete* : HARM, DAMAGE

3 : exposure or liability to injury, pain, harm, or loss 〈could play there without *danger*〉

4 : a case or cause of danger 〈the *dangers* of mining〉

²**danger** *transitive verb* (14th century)

archaic : ENDANGER

dan·ger·ous \'dān-jə-rəs; 'dān-jərs, -zhrəs\ *adjective* (15th century)

1 : exposing to or involving danger

2 : able or likely to inflict injury or harm ☆

— **dan·ger·ous·ly** *adverb*

— **dan·ger·ous·ness** *noun*

¹**dan·gle** \'daŋ-gəl\ *verb* **dan·gled; dan·gling** \-g(ə-)liŋ\ [probably of Scandinavian origin; akin to Danish *dangle* to dangle] (circa 1590)

Dandie Dinmont terrier

intransitive verb

1 : to hang loosely and usually so as to be able to swing freely

2 : to be a hanger-on or a dependent

3 : to occur in a sentence without having a normally expected syntactic relation to the rest of the sentence 〈the word *climbing* in "Climbing the mountain the cabin came into view" is *dangling*〉

transitive verb

1 : to cause to dangle : SWING

2 a : to keep hanging uncertainly **b** : to hold out as an inducement

— **dan·gler** \-g(ə-)lər\ *noun*

²**dangle** *noun* (1756)

1 : the action of dangling

2 : something that dangles

Dan·iel \'da-nyəl *also* 'dan°l\ *noun* [Hebrew *Dānī'ēl*]

1 : the Jewish hero of the Book of Daniel who as an exile in Babylon interprets dreams, gives accounts of apocalyptic visions, and is divinely delivered from a den of lions

2 : a book of narratives, visions, and prophecies in canonical Jewish and Christian Scripture — see BIBLE table

da·nio \'dā-nē-,ō\ *noun, plural* **da·ni·os** [New Latin, genus name] (circa 1889)

: any of several small brightly colored Asian cyprinid fishes

¹**Dan·ish** \'dā-nish\ *adjective* (14th century)

: of, relating to, or characteristic of Denmark, the Danes, or the Danish language

²**Danish** *noun* (15th century)

1 : the Germanic language of the Danes

2 *plural* **Danish** : a piece of Danish pastry

Danish pastry *noun* (circa 1928)

: a pastry made of a rich raised dough

dank \'daŋk\ *adjective* [Middle English *danke*] (1573)

: unpleasantly moist or wet

synonym see WET

— **dank·ly** *adverb*

— **dank·ness** *noun*

dan·seur \dȧⁿ-'sər, dän-\ *noun* [French, from *danser* to dance] (1828)

: a male ballet dancer

dan·seuse \dȧⁿ-sœz; däⁿ-'sə(r)z, dän-'süz\ *noun* [French, feminine of *danseur*] (1828)

: a female ballet dancer

Dan·te·an \'dan-tē-ən, 'dän-\ *noun* (circa 1850)

: a student or admirer of Dante

Dao·ism, Dao·ist, Dao·is·tic *variant of* TAOISM, TAOIST, TAOISTIC

daph·ne \'daf-nē\ *noun* [New Latin, genus name, from Latin, laurel, from Greek *daphnē*] (1862)

: any of a genus (*Daphne*) of Eurasian shrubs of the mezereon family with apetalous flowers whose colored calyx resembles a corolla

☆ **SYNONYMS**

Dangerous, hazardous, precarious, perilous, risky mean bringing or involving the chance of loss or injury. DANGEROUS applies to something that may cause harm or loss unless dealt with carefully 〈soldiers on a *dangerous* mission〉. HAZARDOUS implies great and continuous risk of harm or failure 〈claims that smoking is *hazardous* to your health〉. PRECARIOUS suggests both insecurity and uncertainty 〈earned a *precarious* living by gambling〉. PERILOUS strongly implies the immediacy of danger 〈*perilous* mountain roads〉. RISKY often applies to a known and accepted danger 〈made *risky* decisions〉.

\ə\ abut \ᵊ\ kitten \ər\ further \a\ ash \ā\ ace \ä\ mop, mar \au̇\ out \ch\ chin \e\ bet \ē\ easy \g\ go \i\ hit \ī\ ice \j\ job \ŋ\ sing \ō\ go \ȯ\ law \ȯi\ boy \th\ thin \t͟h\ the \ü\ loot \u̇\ foot \y\ yet \zh\ vision *see also* Guide to Pronunciation

Daph·ne \'daf-nē\ *noun* [Latin, from Greek *Daphnē*]
: a nymph who is transformed into a laurel tree to escape the pursuing Apollo

daph·nia \'daf-nē-ə\ *noun* [New Latin, genus name] (1847)
: any of a genus (*Daphnia*) of minute freshwater branchiopod crustaceans with biramous antennae used as locomotor organs — compare WATER FLEA

Daph·nis \'daf-nəs\ *noun* [Latin, from Greek]
: a Sicilian shepherd renowned in Greek mythology as the inventor of pastoral poetry

dap·per \'da-pər\ *adjective* [Middle English *dapyr*, from Middle Dutch *dapper* quick, strong; akin to Old High German *tapfar* heavy, Old Church Slavonic *debelŭ* thick] (15th century)
1 a : neat and trim in appearance **b** : excessively spruce and stylish
2 : alert and lively in movement and manners
— **dap·per·ly** *adverb*
— **dap·per·ness** *noun*

1dap·ple \'da-pəl\ *noun* [Middle English *dappel-gray*, adjective, gray marked with spots of another color] (1580)
1 : any of numerous usually cloudy and rounded spots or patches of a color or shade different from their background
2 : the quality or state of being dappled
3 : a dappled animal

2dapple *verb* **dap·pled**; **dap·pling** \-p(ə-)liŋ\ (1599)
transitive verb
: to mark with dapples
intransitive verb
: to produce a dappled pattern ⟨sun *dappling* through trees⟩

dap·pled *also* **dap·ple** *adjective* (15th century)
: marked with small spots or patches contrasting with the background ⟨a *dappled* fawn⟩

dap·sone \'dap-ˌsōn\ *noun* [*diamine* + *phenyl* + *sulfone*] (1952)
: an antimicrobial agent $C_{12}H_{12}N_2O_2S$ used especially against leprosy

Dar·by and Joan \ˌdär-bē-ən-'jōn\ *noun* [probably from *Darby & Joan*, couple in an 18th century song] (1857)
: a happily married usually elderly couple

Dard \'därd\ *noun* (circa 1885)
: DARDIC

Dar·dan \'där-dᵊn\ *adjective or noun* [Latin *Dardanus*, from Greek *Dardanos*] (1606)
archaic : TROJAN

Dar·da·ni·an \där-'dā-nē-ən\ *adjective* (1596)
: TROJAN

Dar·dic \'där-dik\ *noun* (1910)
: a complex of Indic languages spoken in the upper valley of the Indus

1dare \'dar, 'der\ *verb* **dared**; **dar·ing**; **dares** *or (auxiliary)* **dare** [Middle English *dar* (1st & 3d singular present indicative), from Old English *dear*; akin to Old High German *gitar* (1st & 3d singular present indicative) dare, Greek *tharsos* courage] (before 12th century)
verbal auxiliary
: to be sufficiently courageous to ⟨no one *dared* say a word⟩ ⟨she *dare* not let herself love —G. B. Shaw⟩
intransitive verb
: to have sufficient courage ⟨try it if you *dare*⟩
transitive verb
1 a : to challenge to perform an action especially as a proof of courage ⟨*dared* him to jump⟩ **b** : to confront boldly ⟨*dared* the mob⟩
2 : to have the courage to contend against, venture, or try ⟨the actress *dared* a new interpretation of this classic role⟩
— **dar·er** \'dar-ər, 'der-\ *noun*

2dare *noun* (1594)
1 : an act or instance of daring : CHALLENGE ⟨foolishly took a *dare*⟩
2 : imaginative or vivacious boldness : DARING

1dare·dev·il \'dar-ˌde-vᵊl, 'der-\ *noun* (1794)

: a recklessly bold person
— **dare·dev·il·ry** \-vᵊl-rē\ *noun*
— **dare·dev·il·try** \-vᵊl-trē\ *noun*

2daredevil *adjective* (1832)
: recklessly and often ostentatiously daring
synonym see ADVENTUROUS

dareful *adjective* (1605)
obsolete : DARING

daren't \'dar-ənt, 'der-\
: dare not : dared not

dare·say \ˌdar-'sā, ˌder-\ (13th century)
transitive verb
: venture to say : think probable — used in present 1st singular
intransitive verb
: AGREE, SUPPOSE — used in present 1st singular

1dar·ing *adjective* (1582)
: venturesomely bold in action or thought
synonym see ADVENTUROUS
— **dar·ing·ly** \-iŋ-lē\ *adverb*
— **dar·ing·ness** *noun*

2daring *noun* (1651)
: venturesome boldness

Dar·jee·ling \där-'jē-liŋ\ *noun* [*Darjeeling*, India] (1907)
: a tea of high quality grown especially in the mountainous districts of northern India

1dark \'därk\ *adjective* [Middle English *derk*, from Old English *deorc*; akin to Old High German *tarchannen* to hide] (before 12th century)
1 a : devoid or partially devoid of light : not receiving, reflecting, transmitting, or radiating light **b** : transmitting only a portion of light
2 a : wholly or partially black **b** *of a color* : of low or very low lightness
3 a : arising from or showing evil traits or desires : EVIL ⟨the *dark* powers that lead to war⟩ **b** : DISMAL, GLOOMY ⟨h ̄ a *dark* view of the future⟩ **c** : lacking knowledge or culture
4 : not clear to the understanding
5 : not fair in complexion : SWARTHY
6 : SECRET ⟨kept his plans *dark*⟩
7 : possessing depth and richness ⟨a *dark* voice⟩
8 : closed to the public ⟨the theater is *dark* in the summer⟩
synonym see OBSCURE
— **dark·ish** \'där-kish\ *adjective*
— **dark·ly** *adverb*
— **dark·ness** *noun*

2dark *noun* (13th century)
1 a : a place or time of little or no light : NIGHT, NIGHTFALL **b** : absence of light : DARKNESS
2 : a dark or deep color
— **in the dark 1** : in secrecy ⟨most of his dealings were done *in the dark*⟩ **2** : in ignorance ⟨kept the public *in the dark* about the agreement⟩

3dark (14th century)
intransitive verb
obsolete : to grow dark
transitive verb
: to make dark

dark adaptation *noun* (1909)
: the phenomena including dilation of the pupil, increase in retinal sensitivity, shift of the region of maximum luminosity toward the blue, and regeneration of visual purple by which the eye adapts to conditions of reduced illumination
— **dark–adapt·ed** \ˌdärk-ə-'dap-təd\ *adjective*

dark age *noun* (1730)
1 : a time during which a civilization undergoes a decline: as **a** *plural, D&A capitalized* : the European historical period from about A.D. 476 to about 1000; *broadly* : MIDDLE AGES **b** *often plural, often D&A capitalized* : the Greek historical period of three to four centuries from about 1100 B.C.
2 a *often plural, often D&A capitalized* : the primitive period in the development of something ⟨in the 1890s, way back in baseball's

Dark Ages —R. W. Creamer⟩ **b** *often plural, often D&A capitalized* : a state of stagnation or decline

dark·en \'där-kən\ *verb* **dark·ened**; **dark·en·ing** \'där-kə-niŋ\ (14th century)
intransitive verb
1 : to grow dark : become obscured
2 : to become gloomy
transitive verb
1 : to make dark
2 : to make less clear : OBSCURE ⟨the financial crisis *darkened* the future of the company⟩
3 : TAINT, TARNISH
4 : to cast a gloom over
5 : to make of darker color
— **dark·en·er** \-kə-nər\ *noun*

dark field *noun* (1865)
: the dark area that serves as the background for objects viewed in an ultramicroscope

dark–field microscope *noun* (1926)
: ULTRAMICROSCOPE

dark horse *noun* (1831)
1 a : a usually little known contender (as a racehorse) that makes an unexpectedly good showing **b** : an entrant in a contest that is judged unlikely to succeed
2 : a political candidate unexpectedly nominated usually as a compromise between factions ◇

dark lantern *noun* (1650)
: a lantern that can be closed to conceal the light

dark·le \'där-kəl\ *intransitive verb* **dark·led**; **dark·ling** \-k(ə-)liŋ\ [back-formation from *darkling*] (1800)
1 a : to become clouded or gloomy **b** : to grow dark
2 : to become concealed in the dark

1dark·ling \'där-kliŋ\ *adverb* [Middle English *derkelyng*, from *derk* dark + *-lyng* -ling] (15th century)
: in the dark

2darkling *adjective* (1739)
1 : DARK
2 : done or taking place in the dark

darkling beetle *noun* (1816)
: TENEBRIONID

dark matter *noun* (1982)
: nonluminous matter not yet directly detected by astronomers that is hypothesized to exist because the visible matter in the universe is insufficient to account for various observed gravitational effects

dark reaction *noun* (1927)
: any of a series of chemical reactions in photosynthesis not requiring the presence of light and involving the reduction of carbon dioxide to form carbohydrate; *also* : CALVIN CYCLE

dark·room \'därk-ˌrüm, -ˌrum\ *noun* (1841)
: a room with no light or with a safelight for handling and processing light-sensitive photographic materials

dark·some \'därk-səm\ *adjective* (circa 1530)
: gloomily somber : DARK

darky *or* **dark·ie** \'där-kē\ *noun, plural* **dark·ies** (1775)
: a black person — usually taken to be offensive

1dar·ling \'där-liŋ\ *noun* [Middle English *der-*

◇ WORD HISTORY

dark horse Sometimes in a race a horse whose name and ability are not widely known puts on a surprisingly good show and defeats its more famous rivals. Such a horse is called *dark,* not because of its color (which might be anything), but because of its obscurity. Since the 19th century, the phrase *dark horse* has been extended from racehorses to obscure competitors who do unexpectedly well in contests of other kinds. Now it is perhaps most often applied to candidates for elected office whose chances appear poor.

ling, from Old English *dēorling,* from *dēore* dear] (before 12th century)
1 : a dearly loved person
2 : FAVORITE
²darling *adjective* (1509)
1 : dearly loved **:** FAVORITE
2 : very pleasing **:** CHARMING
— **dar·ling·ly** \-liŋ-lē\ *adverb*
— **dar·ling·ness** *noun*
¹darn \'därn\ *verb* [perhaps from French dialect *darner*] (circa 1600)
transitive verb
1 : to mend with interlacing stitches
2 : to embroider by filling in with long running or interlacing stitches
intransitive verb
: to do darning
— **darn·er** *noun*
²darn *noun* (1720)
: a place that has been darned ⟨a sweater full of *darns*⟩
³darn *adjective or adverb* [euphemism] (1781)
: DAMNED
⁴darn *verb* (1781)
: DAMN
— **darned** \'därn(d)\ *adjective or adverb*
⁵darn *noun* (1840)
: DAMN
dar·nel \'där-n°l\ *noun* [Middle English] (14th century)
: any of several usually weedy grasses (genus *Lolium*)
darning needle *noun* (1761)
1 : a long needle with a large eye for use in darning
2 : DRAGONFLY, DAMSELFLY
¹dart \'därt\ *noun* [Middle English, from Middle French, of Germanic origin; akin to Old High German *tart* dart, Old English *daroth*] (14th century)
1 a *archaic* **:** a light spear **b** (1) **:** a small missile usually with a pointed shaft at one end and feathers at the other (2) *plural but singular in construction* **:** a game in which darts are thrown at a target
2 a : something projected with sudden speed; *especially* **:** a sharp glance **b :** something causing sudden pain or distress ⟨*darts* of sarcasm⟩
3 : something with a slender pointed shaft or outline; *specifically* **:** a stitched tapering fold in a garment
4 : a quick movement ⟨made a *dart* for the door⟩
²dart (1580)
transitive verb
1 : to throw with a sudden movement
2 : to thrust or move with sudden speed
3 : to shoot with a dart containing a usually tranquilizing drug
intransitive verb
: to move suddenly or rapidly ⟨*darted* across the street⟩
dart·board \'därt-,bōrd, -,bȯrd\ *noun* (1901)
: a usually circular board (as of compressed bristles) used as a target in the game of darts
dart·er \'där-tər\ *noun* (1813)
1 : ANHINGA
2 : any of numerous small American freshwater bony fishes (especially genera *Ammocrypta, Etheostoma,* and *Percina* of the family Percidae)
Dar·win·i·an \där-'wi-nē-ən\ *adjective* (1860)
: of or relating to Charles Darwin, his theories especially of evolution, or his followers
— **Darwinian** *noun*
Dar·win·ism \'där-wə-,ni-zəm\ *noun* (1864)
: a theory of the origin and perpetuation of new species of animals and plants that offspring of a given organism vary, that natural selection favors the survival of some of these variations over others, that new species have arisen and may continue to arise by these processes, and that widely divergent groups of plants and animals have arisen from the same ancestors; *broadly* **:** biological evolutionism ◆

— **Dar·win·ist** \-wə-nist\ *noun or adjective*
Dar·win's finches \,där-wənz-\ *noun plural* [Charles *Darwin*] (1947)
: finches of a subfamily (Geospizinae) having great variation in bill shape and confined mostly to the Galapagos islands
Dar·win tulip \,där-wən-\ *noun* (1889)
: a tall late-flowering tulip with the flowers single and of one color
¹dash \'dash\ *verb* [Middle English *dasshen*] (13th century)
transitive verb
1 : to break by striking or knocking
2 : to knock, hurl, or thrust violently
3 : SPLASH, SPATTER
4 a : RUIN, DESTROY ⟨the news *dashed* his hopes⟩ **b :** DEPRESS, SADDEN **c :** to make ashamed
5 : to affect by mixing in something different ⟨his delight was *dashed* with bitterness over the delay⟩
6 : to complete, execute, or finish off hastily — used with *down* or *off* ⟨*dashed* down a drink⟩ ⟨*dash* off a letter⟩
7 [euphemism] **:** ¹DAMN 4
intransitive verb
1 : to move with sudden speed ⟨*dashed* through the rain⟩
2 : SMASH
²dash *noun* (14th century)
1 a *archaic* **:** BLOW **b** (1) **:** a sudden burst or splash (2) **:** the sound produced by such a burst
2 a : a stroke of a pen **b :** a punctuation mark — that is used especially to indicate a break in the thought or structure of a sentence
3 : a small usually distinctive addition ⟨a *dash* of salt⟩ ⟨a *dash* of humor⟩
4 : flashy display
5 : animation in style and action
6 a : a sudden onset, rush, or attempt **b :** a short fast race
7 : a long click or buzz forming a letter or part of a letter (as in Morse code)
8 : DASHBOARD 2
dash·board \'dash-,bōrd, -,bȯrd\ *noun* (1846)
1 : a screen on the front of a usually horse-drawn vehicle to intercept water, mud, or snow
2 : a panel extending across the interior of a vehicle (as an automobile) below the windshield and usually containing dials and controls
dashed \'dasht\ *adjective* (circa 1889)
: made up of a series of dashes
da·sheen \da-'shēn, də-\ *noun* [origin unknown] (circa 1899)
: TARO
dash·er \'da-shər\ *noun* (1790)
1 : a dashing person
2 : one that dashes; *specifically* **:** a device having blades for agitating a liquid or semisolid
dashi \'dä-(,)shē\ *noun* [Japanese, broth] (circa 1961)
: a fish broth made from dried bonito
da·shi·ki \də-'shē-kē, dä-, da-\ *noun* [modification of Yoruba *dànṣíkí*] (circa 1968)
: a usually brightly colored loose-fitting pullover garment
dash·ing *adjective* (1796)
1 : marked by vigorous action **:** SPIRITED ⟨a *dashing* young horse⟩
2 : marked by smartness especially in dress and manners
— **dash·ing·ly** \-iŋ-lē\ *adverb*
dash·pot \'dash-,pät\ *noun* (1861)
: a device for cushioning or damping a movement (as of a mechanical part) to avoid shock
das·sie \'da-sē\ *noun* [Afrikaans] (1786)
: HYRAX
das·tard \'das-tərd\ *noun* [Middle English] (15th century)
1 : COWARD
2 : a person who acts treacherously or underhandedly
das·tard·ly \-lē\ *adjective* (1576)

1 : COWARDLY
2 : characterized by underhandedness or treachery ⟨a *dastardly* attack⟩ ⟨a *dastardly* villain⟩
synonym see COWARDLY
— **das·tard·li·ness** *noun*
da·ta \'dā-tə, 'da- *also* 'dä-\ *noun plural but singular or plural in construction, often attributive* [Latin, plural of *datum*] (1646)
1 : factual information (as measurements or statistics) used as a basis for reasoning, discussion, or calculation ⟨the *data* is plentiful and easily available —H. A. Gleason, Jr.⟩ ⟨comprehensive *data* on economic growth have been published —N. H. Jacoby⟩
2 : information output by a sensing device or organ that includes both useful and irrelevant or redundant information and must be processed to be meaningful
3 : information in numerical form that can be digitally transmitted or processed □
data bank *noun* (1966)
: DATABASE
da·ta·base \'dā-tə-,bās, 'da- *also* 'dä-\ *noun* (circa 1962)
: a usually large collection of data organized especially for rapid search and retrieval (as by a computer)
data processing *noun* (1954)
: the converting of raw data to machine-readable form and its subsequent processing (as storing, updating, combining, rearranging, or printing out) by a computer
— **data processor** *noun*
data structure *noun* (1963)
: any of various methods of organizing data items (as records) in a computer

□ **USAGE**
data *Data* leads a life of its own quite independent of *datum,* of which it was originally the plural. It occurs in two constructions: as a plural noun (like *earnings*), taking a plural verb and plural modifiers (as *these, many, a few*) but not cardinal numbers, and serving as a referent for plural pronouns (as *they, them*); and as an abstract mass noun (like *information*), taking a singular verb and singular modifiers (as *this, much, little*), and being referred to by a singular pronoun (*it*). Both constructions are standard. The plural construction is more common in print, evidently because the house style of several publishers mandates it.

◇ **WORD HISTORY**
Darwinism *Darwinism* is the theory initiated by the British naturalist Charles Robert Darwin (1809–1882). Although he was not the first to question the immutability of species in nature or to conceive the notion of evolution, Darwin is credited with providing voluminous evidence for evolution and with developing the principle of natural selection. In 1831 he embarked on a five-year voyage around the world, making stopovers in South America and the Galápagos Islands, where he gained critical insight into the variation between populations of animals. His landmark *On the Origin of Species by Means of Natural Selection* (1859) brought about a revolution in biological thinking and firmly established the study of evolution as part of the science of biology. *The Descent of Man* (1871) was a follow-up work that presented his related theory of sexual selection.

\ə\ **abut** \ᵊ\ **kitten** \ər\ **further** \a\ **ash** \ā\ **ace**
\ä\ **mop, mar** \aù\ **out** \ch\ **chin** \e\ **bet** \ē\ **easy**
\g\ **go** \i\ **hit** \ī\ **ice** \j\ **job** \ŋ\ **sing** \ō\ **go**
\ȯ\ **law** \ȯi\ **boy** \th\ **thin** \t̲h̲\ **the** \ü\ **loot** \ù\ **foot**
\y\ **yet** \zh\ **vision** *see also* Guide to Pronunciation

¹date \'dāt\ *noun* [Middle English, from Old French, ultimately from Latin *dactylus* — more at DACTYL] (14th century)
1 : the oblong edible fruit of a palm (*Phoenix dactylifera*)
2 : the tall palm with pinnate leaves that yields the date ◇

²date *noun* [Middle English, from Middle French, from Late Latin *data*, from *data* (as in *data Romae* given at Rome), feminine of Latin *datus*, past participle of *dare* to give; akin to Latin *dos* gift, dowry, Greek *didonai* to give] (14th century)
1 a : the time at which an event occurs ⟨the *date* of his birth⟩ **b** : a statement of the time of execution or making ⟨the *date* on the letter⟩
2 : DURATION
3 : the period of time to which something belongs
4 a : an appointment to meet at a specified time; *especially* : a social engagement between two persons that often has a romantic character **b** : a person with whom one has a usually romantic date
5 : an engagement for a professional performance (as of a dance band)
— **to date** : up to the present moment

³date *verb* **dat·ed; dat·ing** (15th century)
transitive verb
1 : to determine the date of ⟨*date* an antique⟩
2 : to record the date of : mark with the date
3 a : to mark with characteristics typical of a particular period **b** : to show up plainly the age of
4 : to make or have a date with
intransitive verb
1 : to reckon chronologically
2 : ORIGINATE ⟨a friendship *dating* from college days⟩
3 : to become dated
— **dat·able** *also* **date·able** \'dā-tə-bəl\ *adjective*
— **dat·er** \'dā-tər\ *noun*

dat·ed *adjective* (1731)
1 : provided with a date ⟨a *dated* document⟩
2 : OUTMODED, OLD-FASHIONED ⟨*dated* formalities⟩
— **dat·ed·ly** *adverb*
— **dat·ed·ness** *noun*

date·less \'dāt-ləs\ *adjective* (1593)
1 : ENDLESS
2 : having no date
3 : too ancient to be dated
4 : TIMELESS ⟨the play's *dateless* theme⟩

date·line \'dāt-,līn\ *noun* (1888)
1 : a line in a written document or a printed publication giving the date and place of composition or issue
2 *usually* **date line** : INTERNATIONAL DATE LINE
— **dateline** *transitive verb*

date rape *noun* (circa 1983)
: rape committed by someone known to the victim

¹da·tive \'dā-tiv\ *adjective* [Middle English *datif*, from Latin *dativus*, from *datus*] (15th century)
: of, relating to, or being the grammatical case that marks typically the indirect object of a verb, the object of some prepositions, or a possessor

²dative *noun* (15th century)
: a dative case or form

dative bond *noun* [from the donation of electrons by one of the atoms] (circa 1929)
: COORDINATE BOND

da·tum \'dā-təm, 'da-, 'dä-\ *noun* [Latin, from neuter of *datus*] (1646)
1 *plural* **da·ta** \-ə\ : something given or admitted especially as a basis for reasoning or inference
2 *plural* **datums** : something used as a basis for calculating or measuring
usage see DATA

da·tu·ra \də-'t(y)ùr-ə\ *noun* [New Latin, genus name, from Hindi *dhatūrā* jimsonweed] (1598)
: any of a genus (*Datura*) of widely distributed strong-scented herbs, shrubs, or trees of the nightshade family including some used as sources of medicinal alkaloids (as stramonium) or in folk rites or illicitly for their poisonous, narcotic, or hallucinogenic properties — compare JIMSONWEED

¹daub \'dòb, 'däb\ *verb* [Middle English, from Middle French *dauber*] (14th century)
transitive verb
1 : to cover or coat with soft adhesive matter : PLASTER
2 : to coat with a dirty substance
3 a : to apply coloring material crudely to **b** : to apply (as paint) crudely
intransitive verb
1 *archaic* : to put on a false exterior
2 : to apply colors crudely
— **daub·er** *noun*

²daub *noun* (15th century)
1 : material used to daub walls
2 : an act or instance of daubing
3 : something daubed on : SMEAR
4 : a crude picture

daube \'dōb\ *noun* [French] (1723)
: a stew of braised meat, vegetables, herbs, and spices

¹daugh·ter \'dò-tər, 'dä-\ *noun* [Middle English, *doughter*, from Old English *dohtor*; akin to Old High German *tohter* daughter, Greek *thygatēr*] (before 12th century)
1 a (1) : a human female having the relation of child to parent (2) : a female offspring of a lower animal **b** : a human female having a specified ancestor or belonging to a group of common ancestry
2 : something considered as a daughter ⟨the United States is a *daughter* of Great Britain⟩
3 : an atomic species that is the product of the radioactive decay of a given element
— **daugh·ter·less** \-ləs\ *adjective*

²daughter *adjective* (1614)
1 : having the characteristics or relationship of a daughter
2 : belonging to the first generation of offspring, organelles, or molecules produced by reproduction, division, or replication ⟨*daughter* cell⟩ ⟨*daughter* DNA molecules⟩

daugh·ter-in-law \'dò-tər-in-,lò, 'dò-tərn-\ *noun, plural* **daugh·ters-in-law** \-tər-zin-\ (14th century)
: the wife of one's son

dau·no·my·cin \,dò-nə-'mī-sən, ,daù-\ *noun* [International Scientific Vocabulary *dauno-* (from Latin *Daunus* Apulian) + *-mycin*] (1964)
: DAUNORUBICIN

dau·no·ru·bi·cin \-'rü-bə-sən\ *noun* [*dauno-* (as in *daunomycin*) + *rubi*domycin, a substance found to be identical with daunomycin (from International Scientific Vocabulary *rubido-* — from Latin *rubidus* red — + *-mycin*)]
: an antibiotic $C_{27}H_{29}NO_{10}$ that is a nitrogenous glycoside and is used especially in the treatment of leukemia

daunt \'dònt, 'dänt\ *transitive verb* [Middle English, from Middle French *danter*, alteration of *donter*, from Latin *domitare* to tame, frequentative of *domare* — more at TAME] (14th century)
: to lessen the courage of : COW, SUBDUE
synonym see DISMAY
— **daunt·ing·ly** \-iŋ-lē\ *adverb*

daunt·less \-ləs\ *adjective* (1593)
: FEARLESS, UNDAUNTED ⟨a *dauntless* hero⟩
— **daunt·less·ly** *adverb*
— **daunt·less·ness** *noun*

dau·phin \'dò-fən, 'dō-; 'dō-'faⁿ\ *noun, often capitalized* [Middle English *dolphin*, from Middle French *dalfin*, from Old French, title of lords of the Dauphiné, from *Dalfin*, a surname] (15th century)
: the eldest son of a king of France

dau·phine \dò-'fēn, dō-\ *noun, often capitalized* [French] (circa 1864)
: the wife of the dauphin

da·ven \'dä-vən\ *intransitive verb* [Yiddish *davnen*] (circa 1930)
: to recite the prescribed prayers in a Jewish liturgy

dav·en·port \'da-vən-,pōrt, 'da-vəm-, -,pòrt\ *noun* [probably from the name *Davenport*] (1853)
1 : a small compact writing desk
2 : a large upholstered sofa often convertible into a bed

Da·vid \'dā-vəd\ *noun* [Hebrew *Dāwïdh*]
1 : a Hebrew shepherd who became the second king of Israel in succession to Saul according to biblical accounts
2 : UNDERDOG 1
— **Da·vid·ic** \də-'vi-dik, dā-\ *adjective*

da·vit \'dā-vət, 'da-\ *noun* [probably from the name *David*] (15th century)
: a crane that projects over the side of a ship or a hatchway and is used especially for boats, anchors, or cargo

Da·vy Jones \,dā-vē-'jōnz\ *noun* (1751)
: the bottom of the sea personified

Da·vy Jones's lock·er \,dā-vē-,jōnz(-əz)-\ *noun* (circa 1777)
: the bottom of the ocean

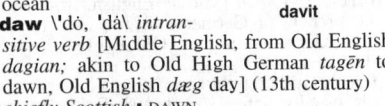
davit

¹daw \'dò, 'dà\ *intransitive verb* [Middle English, from Old English *dagian*; akin to Old High German *tagēn* to dawn, Old English *dæg* day] (13th century)
chiefly Scottish : DAWN

²daw \'dò\ *noun* [Middle English *dawe*; akin to Old High German *taha* jackdaw] (15th century)
: JACKDAW

daw·dle \'dò-d°l\ *verb* **daw·dled; daw·dling** \'dò-dliŋ, -d°l-iŋ\ [origin unknown] (circa 1656)
intransitive verb
1 : to spend time idly
2 : to move lackadaisically ⟨*dawdled* up the hill⟩
transitive verb
: to spend fruitlessly or lackadaisically ⟨*dawdled* the day away⟩
synonym see DELAY
— **daw·dler** \'dò-dlər, -d°l-ər\ *noun*

◇ WORD HISTORY
date The English word *date* in its temporal sense has nothing to do etymologically with *day*, but rather is descended from the Latin verb *dare* "to give." In ancient Rome, the date of a letter was written in the following manner: *Dabam Romae Kal. Aprilis* ("I gave [this letter] at Rome on the calends of April [April 1].") A later formula used *data Romae* "given at Rome," instead of *dabam Romae*. *Data*, past participle of *dare* "to give," had the feminine case ending because it was understood to refer to the unexpressed feminine noun *epistula* "letter." By the 6th century of the modern era, *data* itself had become a noun, used for the formula indicating the date on a letter. Borrowed into French as *date*, it was used not only for the formula on a letter, but also for the time that such a formula indicated, or indeed for any point in time. The English word *date*, borrowed from French in the late Middle Ages, did not come to mean an appointment or engagement until the late 19th century.

¹dawn \'dȯn, 'dän\ *intransitive verb* [Middle English, probably back-formation from *dawning* daybreak, alteration of *dawing*, from Old English *dagung*, from *dagian*] (15th century)
1 : to begin to grow light as the sun rises
2 : to begin to appear or develop
3 : to begin to be perceived or understood ⟨the truth finally *dawned* on us⟩
²dawn *noun* (1599)
1 : the first appearance of light in the morning followed by sunrise
2 : BEGINNING ⟨the *dawn* of the space age⟩
dawn horse *noun* (1930)
: EOHIPPUS
dawn redwood *noun* (1948)
: a metasequoia (*Metasequoia glyptostroboides*) of China resembling the coast redwood but having deciduous foliage
daw·son·ite \'dȯ-sə-ˌnīt\ *noun* [Sir John W. *Dawson*] (1874)
: a mineral consisting of a basic sodium aluminum carbonate
day \'dā\ *noun* [Middle English, from Old English *dæg*; akin to Old High German *tag* day] (before 12th century)
1 a : the time of light between one night and the next **b :** DAYLIGHT 1, 2
2 : the period of rotation of a planet (as earth) or a moon on its axis
3 : the mean solar day of 24 hours beginning at mean midnight
4 : a specified day or date
5 : a specified time or period : AGE ⟨in grandfather's *day*⟩
6 : the conflict or contention of the day ⟨played hard and won the *day*⟩
7 : the time established by usage or law for work, school, or business
8 : a period of existence or prominence of a person or thing
— day after day : for an indefinite or seemingly endless number of days
— day in, day out : for an indefinite number of successive days
Day·ak \'dī-ˌak\ *noun* [Malay, literally, up-country] (1836)
: a member of any of several Indonesian peoples of the interior of Borneo
day·bed \'dā-ˌbed\ *noun* (1818)
1 : a chaise longue of a type made 1680–1780
2 : a couch that can be converted into a bed
day·book \-ˌbuk\ *noun* (1580)
: DIARY, JOURNAL
day·break \-ˌbrāk\ *noun* (1530)
: DAWN
day care *noun* (1947)
1 : supervision of and care for children or disabled adults that is provided during the day by a person or organization
2 : a program, facility, or organization offering day care
¹day·dream \'dā-ˌdrēm\ *noun* (1685)
: a pleasant visionary usually wishful creation of the imagination
— day·dream·like \-ˌlīk\ *adjective*
²daydream *intransitive verb* (1820)
: to have a daydream
— day·dream·er *noun*
day·flow·er \'dā-ˌflau̇(-ə)r\ *noun* (circa 1688)
: any of a genus (*Commelina*) of herbs of the spiderwort family having one petal smaller than the other two; *especially* **:** a blue-flowered weed (*C. communis*) with the smaller petal white
Day-Glo \'dā-ˌglō\ *trademark*
— used for fluorescent materials or colors
day·glow \'dā-ˌglō\ *noun* (circa 1960)
: airglow seen during the day
day laborer *noun* (1548)
: one who works for daily wages especially as an unskilled laborer
day letter *noun* (circa 1913)
: a telegram sent during the day that has a lower priority than a regular telegram
day·light \'dā-ˌlīt\ *noun* (13th century)
1 : the light of day

2 : DAYTIME
3 : DAWN
4 a : knowledge or understanding of something that has been obscure ⟨began to see *daylight* on the problem⟩ **b :** the quality or state of being open : OPENNESS
5 *plural* **a :** CONSCIOUSNESS **b :** mental soundness or stability : WITS ⟨scared the *daylights* out of him⟩
6 : an opening or opportunity especially for action
day·light·ing \'dā-ˌlī-tiŋ\ *noun* (1929)
: illumination of indoor spaces by natural light
daylight saving time *noun* (1919)
: time usually one hour ahead of standard time — called also *daylight saving, daylight time*
day·lily \'dā-ˌli-lē\ *noun* (1597)
: any of various Eurasian plants (genus *Hemerocallis*) of the lily family that have short-lived flowers resembling lilies and are widespread in cultivation and as escapes
day·long \'dā-ˌlȯŋ\ *adjective* (1855)
: lasting all day ⟨a *daylong* tour⟩
day·mare \'dā-ˌmar, -ˌmer\ *noun* [*day* + -*mare* (as in *nightmare*)] (1737)
: a nightmarish fantasy experienced while awake
day–neutral *adjective* (1941)
: developing and maturing regardless of relative length of alternating exposures to light and dark periods — used especially of a plant; compare LONG-DAY, SHORT-DAY
day nursery *noun* (1844)
: a public center for the care and training of young children; *specifically* **:** NURSERY SCHOOL
Day of Atonement (1611)
: YOM KIPPUR
day one *noun, often D&O capitalized* (1971)
: the first day or very beginning of something
day·room \'dā-ˌrüm, -ˌrum\ *noun* (1823)
: a room (as in a hospital) equipped for reading, writing, and recreation
days \'dāz\ *adverb* (before 12th century)
: in the daytime repeatedly : on any day
day school *noun* (1838)
: an elementary or secondary school held on weekdays; *specifically* **:** a private school without boarding facilities
day·side \'dā-ˌsīd\ *noun* (1963)
: the side of a planet in sunlight
days of grace (1726)
: the days allowed for payment of a note or an insurance premium after it becomes due
day·star \'dā-ˌstär\ *noun* (before 12th century)
1 : MORNING STAR
2 : SUN 1a
day student *noun* (1883)
: a student who attends regular classes at a college or preparatory school but does not live at the institution
day·time \'dā-ˌtīm\ *noun, often attributive* (1535)
: the time during which there is daylight
day·times \'dā-ˌtīmz\ *adverb* (1854)
: during the day or during the workday repeatedly : DAYS ⟨has a housekeeper *daytimes*⟩
day–to–day \'dā-tə-ˈdā\ *adjective* (1883)
1 : taking place, made, or done in the course of successive days ⟨*day-to-day* problems⟩
2 : providing for a day at a time with little thought for the future ⟨lived an aimless *day-to-day* existence⟩
day–trip·per \'dā-ˌtri-pər\ *noun* (1897)
: one who takes a trip that does not last overnight
daze \'dāz\ *transitive verb* **dazed; daz·ing** [Middle English *dasen*, from (assumed) Old Norse *dasa*; akin to Old Norse *dasask* to become exhausted] (14th century)
1 : to stupefy especially by a blow : STUN
2 : to dazzle with light
— daze *noun*
— dazed·ly \'dā-zəd-lē\ *adverb*
— dazed·ness \'dā-zəd-nəs, 'dāzd-\ *noun*

daz·zle \'da-zəl\ *verb* **daz·zled; daz·zling** \-z(ə-)liŋ\ [frequentative of *daze*] (15th century)
intransitive verb
1 : to lose clear vision especially from looking at bright light
2 a : to shine brilliantly **b :** to arouse admiration by an impressive display
transitive verb
1 : to overpower with light
2 : to impress deeply, overpower, or confound with brilliance ⟨*dazzled* us with her wit⟩
— dazzle *noun*
— daz·zler \-z(ə-)lər\ *noun*
— daz·zling·ly \-z(ə-)liŋ-lē\ *adverb*
DBCP \ˌdē-(ˌ)bē-(ˌ)sē-ˈpē\ *noun* [*di-* + *brom-* + *chlor-* + *propane*] (1967)
: a halocarbon compound $C_3H_5Br_2Cl$ used as an agricultural pesticide that is a suspected carcinogen and cause of sterility in human males
D day *noun* [*D*, abbreviation for *day*] (1918)
: a day set for launching an operation; *specifically* **:** June 6, 1944, on which Allied forces began the invasion of France in World War II
DDC \ˌdē-(ˌ)dē-ˈsē\ *noun* [*di-* + *deoxy* + *cytidine*] (1987)
: an antiviral drug $C_{10}H_{13}N_3O_3$ used to reduce virus growth and reproduction in AIDS and HIV infection
DDD \ˌdē-(ˌ)dē-ˈdē\ *noun* [*dichlor-* + *diphenyl* + *dichlor-*] (1946)
: an insecticide $(ClC_6H_4)_2CHCHCl_2$ closely related chemically and similar in properties to DDT
DDE \ˌdē-(ˌ)dē-ˈē\ *noun* [*dichlor-* + *diphenyl* + *ethylene*] (1949)
: a persistent organochlorine $C_{15}H_8Cl_4$ that is produced by the metabolic breakdown of DDT
DDI \ˌdē-(ˌ)dē-ˈī\ *noun* [*di-* + *deoxy* + *inosine*, a nucleoside] (1988)
: an antiviral drug $C_{10}H_{12}N_4O_3$ used to reduce virus growth and reproduction in AIDS and HIV infection
DDT \ˌdē-(ˌ)dē-ˈtē\ *noun* [*dichlor-* + *diphenyl* + *trichlor-* (from *tri-* +*chlor-*)] (1943)
: a colorless odorless water-insoluble crystalline insecticide $C_{14}H_9Cl_5$ that tends to accumulate in ecosystems and has toxic effects on many vertebrates
DDVP \ˌdē-(ˌ)dē-(ˌ)vē-ˈpē\ *noun* [*dimethyl* + *dichlor-* + *vinyl* + *phosphate*] (1954)
: DICHLORVOS
de- *prefix* [Middle English, from Old French *de-, des-*, partly from Latin *de-* from, down, away (from *de*, preposition) and partly from Latin *dis-*; Latin *de* akin to Old Irish *di* from, Old English *tō* to — more at TO, DIS-]
1 a : do the opposite of ⟨*de*activate⟩ **b :** reverse of ⟨*de*-emphasis⟩
2 a : remove (a specified thing) from ⟨*de*louse⟩ **b :** remove from (a specified thing) ⟨*de*throne⟩
3 : reduce ⟨*de*value⟩
4 : something derived from (a specified thing) ⟨*de*compound⟩ **:** derived from something (of a specified nature) ⟨*de*nominative⟩
5 : get off of (a specified thing) ⟨*de*train⟩
6 : having a molecule characterized by the removal of one or more atoms (of a specified element) ⟨*de*oxy-⟩
de·acid·i·fy \ˌdē-ə-ˈsi-də-ˌfī\ *transitive verb* (1786)
: to remove acid from **:** reduce the acidity of (as by neutralization)
— de·acid·i·fi·ca·tion \-ˌsi-də-fə-ˈkā-shən\ *noun*
dea·con \'dē-kən\ *noun* [Middle English *dekene*, from Old English *dēacon*, from Late Latin *diaconus*, from Greek *diakonos*, literally,

servant, from *dia-* + *-konos* (akin to en*konein* to be active); perhaps akin to Latin *conari* to attempt] (before 12th century)
: a subordinate officer in a Christian church: as **a** : a Roman Catholic, Anglican, or Eastern Orthodox cleric ranking next below a priest **b** : one of the laymen elected by a church with congregational polity to serve in worship, in pastoral care, and on administrative committees **c** : a Mormon in the lowest grade of the Aaronic priesthood

dea·con·ess \'dē-kə-nəs\ *noun* (15th century)
: a woman chosen to assist in the church ministry; *specifically* : one in a Protestant order

deacon's bench *noun* (1922)
: a bench with usually spindled arms and back

de·ac·ti·vate \(,)dē-'ak-tə-,vāt\ *transitive verb* (1926)
: to make inactive or ineffective
— **de·ac·ti·va·tion** \(,)dē-,ak-tə-'vā-shən\ *noun*
— **de·ac·ti·va·tor** \(,)dē-'ak-tə-,vā-tər\ *noun*

deacon's bench

¹**dead** \'ded\ *adjective* [Middle English *deed*, from Old English *dēad;* akin to Old Norse *dauthr* dead, *deyja* to die, Old High German *tōt* dead — more at DIE] (before 12th century)
1 : deprived of life : having died
2 a (1) : having the appearance of death : DEATHLY ⟨in a *dead* faint⟩ (2) : lacking power to move, feel, or respond : NUMB **b** : very tired **c** (1) : incapable of being stirred emotionally or intellectually : UNRESPONSIVE ⟨*dead* to pity⟩ **2** : grown cold : EXTINGUISHED ⟨*dead* coals⟩
3 a : INANIMATE, INERT ⟨*dead* matter⟩ **b** : BARREN, INFERTILE ⟨*dead* soil⟩ **c** : no longer producing or functioning : EXHAUSTED ⟨a *dead* battery⟩
4 a (1) : lacking power or effect ⟨a *dead* law⟩ (2) : no longer having interest, relevance, or significance ⟨a *dead* issue⟩ **b** : no longer in use : OBSOLETE ⟨a *dead* language⟩ **c** : no longer active : EXTINCT ⟨a *dead* volcano⟩ **d** : lacking in gaiety or animation ⟨a *dead* party⟩ **e** (1) : lacking in commercial activity : QUIET (2) : commercially idle or unproductive ⟨*dead* capital⟩ **f** : lacking elasticity ⟨a *dead* tennis ball⟩ **g** : being out of action or out of use; *specifically* : free from any connection to a source of voltage and free from electric charges **h** (1) : being out of play ⟨a *dead* ball⟩ (2) : temporarily forbidden to play or to make a certain play in croquet
5 a : not running or circulating : STAGNANT ⟨*dead* water⟩ **b** : not turning ⟨a *dead* lathe center⟩ **c** : not imparting motion or power although otherwise functioning ⟨a *dead* rear axle⟩ **d** : lacking warmth, vigor, or taste
6 a : absolutely uniform ⟨a *dead* level⟩ **b** (1) : UNERRING (2) : EXACT ⟨*dead* center of the target⟩ (3) : certain to be doomed ⟨he's *dead* if he's late for curfew⟩ (4) : IRREVOCABLE ⟨a *dead* loss⟩ **c** : ABRUPT ⟨brought to a *dead* stop⟩ **d** (1) : COMPLETE, ABSOLUTE ⟨a *dead* silence⟩ (2) : ALL-OUT ⟨caught it on the *dead* run⟩
7 : devoid of former occupants ⟨*dead* villages⟩ ☆
— **dead·ness** *noun*
— **dead in the water 1** : incapable of being effective : STALLED **2** : ¹DEAD 6b(3)

²**dead** *noun, plural* **dead** (before 12th century)
1 : one that is dead — usually used collectively
2 : the state of being dead ⟨raised him from the *dead* —Colossians 2:12(Revised Standard Version)⟩
3 : the time of greatest quiet ⟨the *dead* of night⟩

³**dead** *adverb* (14th century)

1 : ABSOLUTELY, UTTERLY ⟨*dead* certain⟩
2 : suddenly and completely ⟨stopped *dead*⟩
3 : DIRECTLY ⟨*dead* ahead⟩

dead air *noun* (circa 1943)
: a period of silence especially during a broadcast

dead–air space \'ded-'ar-, -'er-\ *noun* (1902)
: an unventilated air space

¹**dead·beat** \'ded-,bēt\ *noun* (1863)
1 : LOAFER
2 : one who persistently fails to pay personal debts or expenses

²**deadbeat** *adjective* (circa 1864)
: having a pointer that gives a reading with little or no oscillation

dead bolt *noun* (circa 1902)
: a lock bolt that is moved by turning the knob or key without action of a spring

dead duck *noun* (1943)
: one that is doomed

dead·en \'de-dᵊn\ *verb* **dead·ened; dead·en·ing** \'ded-niŋ, 'de-dᵊn-iŋ\ (1665)
transitive verb
1 : to impair in vigor or sensation : BLUNT ⟨*deadened* his enthusiasm⟩
2 a : to deprive of brilliance **b** : to make vapid or spiritless **c** : to make (as a wall) impervious to sound
3 : to deprive of life : KILL
intransitive verb
: to become dead : lose life or vigor
— **dead·en·er** \'ded-nər, -dᵊn-ər\ *noun*
— **dead·en·ing·ly** \-niŋ-lē, -dᵊn-iŋ-\ *adverb*

¹**dead–end** \'ded-,end\ *adjective* (1919)
1 a : lacking opportunities especially for advancement ⟨a *dead-end* job⟩ **b** : lacking an exit ⟨a *dead-end* street⟩
2 : UNRULY ⟨*dead-end* kids⟩
— **dead–end·ed·ness** \,ded-'en-dəd-nəs\ *noun*

²**dead–end** \'ded-'end\ *intransitive verb* (1944)
: to come to a dead end : TERMINATE

dead end \'ded-'end\ *noun* (1886)
1 : an end (as of a street) without an exit
2 : a position, situation, or course of action that leads to nothing further

dead·en·ing *noun* (circa 1874)
: material used to soundproof walls or floors

dead·eye \'ded-,ī\ *noun* (1748)
1 : a rounded wood block encircled by a rope or an iron band and having holes to receive the lanyard that is used especially to set up shrouds and stays
2 : an unerring marksman

dead·fall \-,fol\ *noun* (1611)
1 : a trap so constructed that a weight (as a heavy log) falls on an animal and kills or disables it
2 : a tangled mass of fallen trees and branches

dead hand *noun* (14th century)
1 : MORTMAIN 1
2 : the oppressive influence of the past

¹**dead·head** \'ded-,hed\ *noun* (1841)
1 : one who has not paid for a ticket
2 : a dull or stupid person

²**deadhead** (1911)
intransitive verb
: to make a return trip without a load
transitive verb
: to remove the faded flowers of (a plant) especially to keep a neat appearance and to promote reblooming by preventing seed production

dead heat *noun* (1796)
: a tie with no single winner of a race

dead horse *noun* (1830)
: an exhausted or profitless topic or issue — usually used in the phrases *beat a dead horse* and *flog a dead horse*

dead letter *noun* (1663)
1 : something that has lost its force or authority without being formally abolished
2 : a letter that is undeliverable and unreturnable by the post office

dead lift *noun* (1963)

: a lift in weight lifting in which the weight is lifted from the floor to hip level
— **dead·lift** \'ded-,lift\ *transitive verb*

dead·light \'ded-,līt\ *noun* (1726)
: a metal cover or shutter fitted to a port to keep out light and water

dead·line \-,līn\ *noun* (1864)
1 : a line drawn within or around a prison that a prisoner passes at the risk of being shot
2 a : a date or time before which something must be done **b** : the time after which copy is not accepted for a particular issue of a publication

dead load *noun* (circa 1888)
: a constant load in a structure (as a bridge, building, or machine) that is due to the weight of the members, the supported structure, and permanent attachments or accessories

dead·lock \'ded-,läk\ *noun* (1779)
1 : a state of inaction or neutralization resulting from the opposition of equally powerful uncompromising persons or factions : STANDSTILL
2 : a tie score
— **deadlock** *verb*

¹**dead·ly** \'ded-lē\ *adjective* **dead·li·er; -est** (before 12th century)
1 : likely to cause or capable of producing death
2 a : aiming to kill or destroy : IMPLACABLE ⟨a *deadly* enemy⟩ **b** : highly effective ⟨a *deadly* exposé⟩ **c** : UNERRING ⟨a *deadly* marksman⟩ **d** : marked by determination or extreme seriousness
3 a : tending to deprive of force or vitality ⟨a *deadly* habit⟩ **b** : suggestive of death especially in dullness or lack of animation ⟨*deadly* bores⟩ ⟨a *deadly* conversation⟩
4 : very great : EXTREME ☆
— **dead·li·ness** *noun*

²**deadly** *adverb* (before 12th century)
1 *archaic* : in a manner to cause death : MORTALLY
2 : suggesting death
3 : EXTREMELY ⟨*deadly* serious⟩

deadly nightshade *noun* (1578)
: BELLADONNA 1

deadly sin *noun* (13th century)
: one of seven sins of pride, covetousness, lust, anger, gluttony, envy, and sloth held to be fatal to spiritual progress

dead man's float *noun* (circa 1946)

☆ SYNONYMS
Dead, defunct, deceased, departed, late mean devoid of life. DEAD applies literally to what is deprived of vital force but is used figuratively of anything that has lost any attribute (as energy, activity, radiance) suggesting life ⟨a *dead*, listless performance⟩. DEFUNCT stresses cessation of active existence or operation ⟨a *defunct* television series⟩. DECEASED, DEPARTED, and LATE apply to persons who have died recently. DECEASED is the preferred term in legal use ⟨the estate of the *deceased*⟩. DEPARTED is used usually as a euphemism ⟨our *departed* sister⟩. LATE is used especially with reference to a person in a specific relation or status ⟨the company's *late* president⟩.

Deadly, mortal, fatal, lethal mean causing or capable of causing death. DEADLY applies to an established or very likely cause of death ⟨a *deadly* disease⟩. MORTAL implies that death has occurred or is inevitable ⟨a *mortal* wound⟩. FATAL stresses the inevitability of what has in fact resulted in death or destruction ⟨*fatal* consequences⟩. LETHAL applies to something that is bound to cause death or exists for the destruction of life ⟨*lethal* gas⟩.

: a prone floating position with the arms extended forward

dead march *noun* (1603)
: a solemn march for a funeral

dead metaphor *noun* (1922)
: a word or phrase (as *time is running out*) that has lost its metaphoric force through common usage

dead–on \'ded-ˌon, -ˌän\ *adjective* (circa 1889)
: exactly correct or accurate

¹**dead·pan** \'ded-ˌpan\ *adjective* (circa 1928)
: marked by an impassive matter-of-fact manner, style, or expression ⟨a *deadpan* comedy⟩
— **deadpan** *adverb*

²**deadpan** *noun* (circa 1930)
1 : a completely expressionless face
2 : a deadpan manner of behavior or presentation

³**deadpan** *transitive verb* (circa 1942)
: to express in a deadpan manner
— **dead·pan·ner** *noun*

dead reckoning *noun* (1613)
1 : the determination without the aid of celestial observations of the position of a ship or aircraft from the record of the courses sailed or flown, the distance made, and the known or estimated drift
2 : GUESSWORK
— **dead reckon** *verb*

dead space *noun* (circa 1923)
: the portion of the respiratory system which is external to the bronchioles and through which air must pass to reach the bronchioles and alveoli

dead–stick landing \'ded-ˌstik-\ *noun* (circa 1917)
: a landing of an airplane or spacecraft made without power

dead·weight \'ded-'wāt\ *noun* (1660)
1 : the unrelieved weight of an inert mass
2 : DEAD LOAD
3 : a ship's load including the total weight of cargo, fuel, stores, crew, and passengers

deadweight ton *noun* (circa 1917)
: a long ton used in indicating a ship's gross capacity — abbreviation dwt

dead·wood \-ˌwůd\ *noun* (15th century)
1 : wood dead on the tree
2 : useless personnel or material
3 : solid timbers built in at the extreme bow and stern of a ship when too narrow to permit framing
4 : bowling pins that have been knocked down but remain on the alley

de·aer·ate \ˌdē-'ar-ˌāt, -'er-\ *transitive verb* (1791)
: to remove air or gas from
— **de·aer·a·tion** \ˌdē-ˌar-'ā-shən, -ˌer-\ *noun*
— **de·aer·a·tor** \-'ar-ˌā-tər, -'er-\ *noun*

deaf \'def, *dialect* 'dēf\ *adjective* [Middle English *deef*, from Old English *dēaf*; akin to Greek *typhlos* blind, *typhein* to smoke, Latin *fumus* smoke — more at FUME] (before 12th century)
1 : lacking or deficient in the sense of hearing
2 : unwilling to hear or listen : not to be persuaded ⟨was overwrought and *deaf* to reason⟩
— **deaf·ish** \'de-fish\ *adjective*
— **deaf·ly** *adverb*
— **deaf·ness** *noun*

deaf·en \'de-fən\ *transitive verb* **deaf·ened;** **deaf·en·ing** \-fə-niŋ, 'def-niŋ\ (1597)
: to make deaf

deaf·en·ing *adjective* (1597)
1 : that deafens
2 : very loud : EARSPLITTING ⟨fell with a *deafening* clap⟩
— **deaf·en·ing·ly** *adverb*

deaf–mute \'def-'myüt\ *noun* (circa 1837)
: a deaf person who cannot speak
— **deaf–mute** *adjective*

¹**deal** \'dē(ə)l\ *noun* [Middle English *deel*, from Old English *dæl*; akin to Old English *dāl* division, portion, Old High German *teil* part] (before 12th century)

1 *obsolete* : PART, PORTION
2 : a usually large or indefinite quantity or degree ⟨a great *deal* of support⟩ ⟨a good *deal* faster⟩
3 a : the act or right of distributing cards to players in a card game **b** : HAND 9b

²**deal** *verb* **dealt** \'delt\; **deal·ing** \'dē-liŋ\ (before 12th century)
transitive verb
1 a : to give as one's portion : APPORTION ⟨tried to *deal* justice to all⟩ ⟨*dealt* out three sandwiches apiece⟩ **b** : to distribute (playing cards) to players in a game
2 : ADMINISTER, DELIVER ⟨*dealt* him a blow⟩
3 : SELL ⟨*deals* marijuana⟩
intransitive verb
1 : to distribute the cards in a card game
2 : to concern oneself or itself ⟨the book *deals* with education⟩
3 a : to engage in bargaining : TRADE **b** : to sell or distribute something as a business ⟨*deal* in insurance⟩
4 a : to take action with regard to someone or something ⟨*deal* with an offender⟩ **b** : to reach or try to reach a state of acceptance or reconcilement ⟨trying to *deal* with her son's death⟩
synonym see DISTRIBUTE
— **deal·er** \'dē-lər\ *noun*

³**deal** *noun* (15th century)
1 a : an act of dealing : TRANSACTION **b** : BARGAIN
2 : PACKAGE DEAL
3 : treatment received ⟨a dirty *deal*⟩
4 : an arrangement for mutual advantage
5 : AFFAIR 2 ⟨dinner was an informal *deal*⟩

⁴**deal** *noun* [Middle English *dele*, from Middle Dutch or Middle Low German, plank; akin to Old High German *dili* plank — more at THILL] (14th century)
1 a *British* : a board of fir or pine **b** : sawed yellow-pine lumber nine inches (22.5 centimeters) or wider and three, four, or five inches (7.6 to 12.4 centimeters) thick
2 : pine or fir wood
— **deal** *adjective*

de·alat·ed \ˌdē-'ā-ˌlā-təd\ *adjective* (1904)
: divested of the wings — used of postnuptial adults of insects (as ants) that drop their wings after a nuptial flight
— **de·ala·tion** \ˌdē-ˌ(ˌ)ā-'lā-shən\ *noun*

deal·er·ship \'dē-lər-ˌship\ *noun* (1916)
: an authorized sales agency ⟨an automobile *dealership*⟩

deal·fish \'dē(ə)l-ˌfish\ *noun* [⁴*deal*] (1845)
: any of several long thin fishes (genus *Trachipterus* especially *T. arcticus* of the family Trachipteridae) inhabiting the deep sea

deal·ing *noun* (15th century)
1 : method of business : manner of conduct
2 *plural* : friendly or business interactions

dealing box *noun* (1897)
: a case that holds a deck of playing cards so that they may be dealt one by one

de·am·i·nase \ˌ(ˌ)dē-'a-mi-ˌnās, -ˌnāz\ *noun* [*de-* + *amino* + *-ase*] (1920)
: an enzyme that hydrolyzes amino compounds (as amino acids) with removal of the amino group

de·am·i·nate \-ˌnāt\ *transitive verb* **-nat·ed; -nat·ing** (1926)
: to remove the amino group from (a compound)
— **de·am·i·na·tion** \ˌ(ˌ)dē-ˌa-mi-'nā-shən\ *noun*

dean \'dēn\ *noun* [Middle English *deen*, from Old French *deien*, from Late Latin *decanus* chief of ten, from Greek *dekanos*, from *deka* ten — more at TEN] (13th century)
1 a : the head of the chapter of a collegiate or cathedral church **b** : a Roman Catholic priest who supervises one district of a diocese
2 a : the head of a division, faculty, college, or school of a university **b** : a college or secondary school administrator in charge of counseling and disciplining students
3 : DOYEN 1

— **dean** *intransitive verb*
— **dean·ship** \-ˌship\ *noun*

dean·ery \'dēn-rē, 'dē-nə-rē\ *noun, plural* **-er·ies** (15th century)
: the office, jurisdiction, or official residence of a clerical dean

dean's list *noun* (circa 1926)
: a list of students receiving special recognition from the dean of a college because of superior scholarship

¹**dear** \'dir\ *adjective* [Middle English *dere*, from Old English *dēor*] (before 12th century)
: SEVERE, SORE ⟨in our *dear* peril —Shakespeare⟩

²**dear** *adjective* [Middle English *dere*, from Old English *dēore*; akin to Old High German *tiuri* distinguished, costly] (before 12th century)
1 *obsolete* : NOBLE
2 : highly valued : PRECIOUS ⟨a *dear* friend⟩ — often used in a salutation ⟨*dear* Sir⟩
3 : AFFECTIONATE, FOND
4 : high or exorbitant in price : EXPENSIVE ⟨eggs are very *dear* just now⟩
5 : HEARTFELT
— **dear** *adverb*
— **dear·ly** *adverb*
— **dear·ness** *noun*

³**dear** *noun* (13th century)
1 : a loved one : SWEETHEART
2 : a lovable person

⁴**dear** *interjection* (1694)
— used especially to express annoyance or dismay

Dear John \-'jän\ *noun* (1945)
: a letter (as to a soldier) in which a wife asks for a divorce or a girlfriend breaks off an engagement or a friendship

dearth \'dərth\ *noun* [Middle English *derthe*, from (assumed) Old English *dierth*, from *dēore* dear] (13th century)
1 : scarcity that makes dear; *specifically* : FAMINE
2 : an inadequate supply : LACK

dea·sil \'dē-zəl\ *adverb* [Scottish Gaelic *deiseil*; akin to Latin *dexter* right hand] (1771)
: CLOCKWISE — compare WIDDERSHINS

death \'deth\ *noun* [Middle English *deeth*, from Old English *dēath*; akin to Old Norse *dauthi* death, *deyja* to die — more at DIE] (before 12th century)
1 : a permanent cessation of all vital functions : the end of life — compare BRAIN DEATH
2 : the cause or occasion of loss of life ⟨drinking was the *death* of him⟩
3 *capitalized* : the destroyer of life represented usually as a skeleton with a scythe
4 : the state of being dead
5 a : the passing or destruction of something inanimate ⟨the *death* of vaudeville⟩ **b** : EXTINCTION
6 : CIVIL DEATH
7 : SLAUGHTER
8 *Christian Science* : the lie of life in matter : that which is unreal and untrue : ILLUSION
— **at death's door** : close to death : critically ill
— **to death** : beyond endurance : EXCESSIVELY ⟨bored *to death*⟩

death·bed \'deth-ˌbed\ *noun* (before 12th century)
1 : the bed in which a person dies
2 : the last hours of life
— **on one's deathbed** : near the point of death

death benefit *noun* (1921)
: money payable to the beneficiary of a deceased

death·blow \'deth-ˌblō\ *noun* (1795)
: a destructive or killing stroke or event

\ə\ abut \ᵊ\ kitten \ər\ further \a\ ash \ā\ ace \ä\ mop, mar \aů\ out \ch\ chin \e\ bet \ē\ easy \g\ go \i\ hit \ī\ ice \j\ job \ŋ\ sing \ō\ go \ȯ\ law \ȯi\ boy \th\ thin \th\ the \ü\ loot \ů\ foot \y\ yet \zh\ vision *see also* Guide to Pronunciation

death camas *noun* (circa 1889)
: any of several plants (genus *Zigadenus*) of the lily family that cause poisoning of livestock in the western U.S.

death camp *noun* (1944)
: a concentration camp in which large numbers of prisoners are systematically killed

death cap *noun* (1925)
: a very poisonous mushroom (*Amanita phalloides*) of deciduous woods of North America and Europe that varies in color from pure white to olive or yellow and has a prominent volva at the base — called also *death cup*

death duty *noun* (1881)
chiefly British : DEATH TAX

death instinct *noun* (1922)
: an innate and unconscious tendency toward self-destruction postulated in psychoanalytic theory to explain aggressive and destructive behavior not satisfactorily explained by the pleasure principle — called also *Thanatos*; compare EROS 2

death·less \'deth-ləs\ *adjective* (1589)
: IMMORTAL, IMPERISHABLE ⟨*deathless* fame⟩
— **death·less·ly** *adverb*
— **death·less·ness** *noun*

death·ly \'deth-lē\ *adjective* (before 12th century)
1 : FATAL
2 : of, relating to, or suggestive of death ⟨a *deathly* pallor⟩
— **deathly** *adverb*

death mask *noun* (1877)
: a cast taken from the face of a dead person

death rattle *noun* (1822)
: a rattling or gurgling sound produced by air passing through mucus in the lungs and air passages of a dying person

death ray *noun* (1919)
: a weapon that generates an intense beam of particles or radiation by which it destroys its target

death row *noun* (1950)
: a prison area housing inmates sentenced to death

death's—head \'deths-,hed\ *noun* (1596)
: a human skull or a depiction of a human skull symbolizing death

death's—head hawkmoth *noun* (1879)
: a large dark hawkmoth (*Acherontia atropos*) with markings resembling a human skull on the back of the thorax — called also *death's-head moth*

deaths·man \'deths-mən\ *noun* (1589)
archaic : EXECUTIONER

death squad *noun* (1969)
: any of various right-wing vigilante groups in Latin America whose members kill suspected political adversaries and criminals

death tax *noun* (1937)
: a tax arising on the transmission of property after the owner's death; *especially* : ESTATE TAX

death trap *noun* (1835)
: a structure or situation that is potentially very dangerous to life

death warrant *noun* (1692)
1 : a warrant for the execution of a death sentence
2 : DEATHBLOW

¹death·watch \'deth-,wäch\ *noun* [*death* + *watch* (timepiece); from the superstition that its ticking presages death] (1646)
: a small insect that makes a ticking sound; *especially* : DEATHWATCH BEETLE

²deathwatch *noun* [*death* + *watch* (vigil)] (circa 1890)
1 : a vigil kept over the dead or dying
2 : the guard set over a criminal to be executed

deathwatch beetle *noun* (1877)
: any of various small beetles (family Anobiidae) that are common in old houses where they bore in woodwork and furniture and make a tapping noise as a mating call

death wish *noun* (1913)

: the conscious or unconscious desire for the death of oneself or of another

deb \'deb\ *noun* (1920)
: DEBUTANTE

de·ba·cle \dē-'bä-kəl, -'ba-; ÷'de-bə-kəl\ *also* **dé·bâ·cle** *also* dā-'bäk(l°)\ *noun* [French *débâcle*, from *débâcler* to clear, from Middle French *desbacler*, from *des-* de- + *bacler* to block, perhaps from (assumed) Vulgar Latin *baccular*, from Latin *baculum* staff] (1802)
1 : a tumultuous breakup of ice in a river
2 : a violent disruption (as of an army) : ROUT
3 a : a great disaster **b** : a complete failure : FIASCO

de·bar \di-'bär, dē-\ *transitive verb* [Middle English *debarren*, from Middle French *desbarrer* to unbar, from *des-* de- + *barrer* to bar] (15th century)
: to bar from having or doing something : PRECLUDE
— **de·bar·ment** \-mənt\ *noun*

¹de·bark \di-'bärk, dē-\ *verb* [French *debarquer*, from *de-* + *barque* bark (ship)] (1654)
: DISEMBARK
— **de·bar·ka·tion** \,dē-,bär-'kā-shən\ *noun*

²de·bark \(,)dē-'bärk\ *transitive verb* (1742)
: to remove bark from

de·base \di-'bās, dē-\ *transitive verb* (1565)
1 : to lower in status, esteem, quality, or character
2 a : to reduce the intrinsic value of (a coin) by increasing the base-metal content **b** : to reduce the exchange value of (a monetary unit) ☆
— **de·base·ment** \-'bās-mənt\ *noun*
— **de·bas·er** \-'bā-sər\ *noun*

de·bat·able \di-'bā-tə-bəl, dē-\ *adjective* (1536)
1 : claimed by more than one country ⟨*debatable* border territory⟩
2 a : open to dispute : QUESTIONABLE **b** : open to debate
3 : capable of being debated

de·bate \di-'bāt, dē-\ *noun* (13th century)
: a contention by words or arguments: as **a** : the formal discussion of a motion before a deliberative body according to the rules of parliamentary procedure **b** : a regulated discussion of a proposition between two matched sides

²debate *verb* **de·bat·ed; de·bat·ing** [Middle English, from Middle French *debatre*, from Old French, from *de-* + *batre* to beat, from Latin *battuere*] (14th century)
intransitive verb
1 *obsolete* : FIGHT, CONTEND
2 a : to contend in words **b** : to discuss a question by considering opposed arguments
3 : to participate in a debate
transitive verb
1 a : to argue about **b** : to engage (an opponent) in debate
2 : to turn over in one's mind
synonym see DISCUSS
— **de·bate·ment** \-'bāt-mənt\ *noun*
— **de·bat·er** *noun*

¹de·bauch \di-'bóch, -'bäch, dē-\ *transitive verb* [Middle French *debaucher*, from Old French *desbauchier* to scatter, disperse, from *des-* de- + *bauch* beam, of Germanic origin; akin to Old High German *balko* beam — more at BALK] (1595)
1 a *archaic* : to make disloyal **b** : to seduce from chastity
2 a : to lead away from virtue or excellence **b** : to corrupt by intemperance or sensuality
synonym see DEBASE
— **de·bauch·er** *noun*

²debauch *noun* (1603)
1 : an act or occasion of debauchery
2 : ORGY

de·bauch·ee \di-,bó-'chē, -,bä-; ,de-bə-'shē, -'shä\ *noun* [French *débauché*, from past participle of *débaucher*] (1661)
: one given to debauchery

de·bauch·ery \di-'bó-chə-rē, -chrē, -'bä-\ *noun, plural* **-er·ies** (1642)

1 a : extreme indulgence in sensuality **b** *plural* : ORGIES
2 *archaic* : seduction from virtue or duty

de·beak \(,)dē-'bēk\ *transitive verb* (1937)
: to remove the tip of the upper mandible of (as a chicken) to prevent cannibalism and fighting

de·ben·ture \di-'ben-chər\ *noun* [Middle English *debentur*, from Latin, they are due, 3d plural present passive of *debēre* to owe — more at DEBT] (15th century)
1 *British* : a corporate security other than an equity security : BOND
2 : a bond backed by the general credit of the issuer rather than a specific lien on particular assets

de·bil·i·tate \di-'bi-lə-,tāt, dē-\ *transitive verb* **-tat·ed; -tat·ing** [Latin *debilitatus*, past participle of *debilitare* to weaken, from *debilis* weak] (1533)
: to impair the strength of : ENFEEBLE
synonym see WEAKEN
— **de·bil·i·ta·tion** \-,bi-lə-'tā-shən\ *noun*

de·bil·i·ty \di-'bi-lə-tē, dē-\ *noun, plural* **-ties** [Middle French *debilité*, from Latin *debilitat-, debilitas*, from *debilis*, from *de-* de- + *-bilis*; akin to Sanskrit *bala* strength] (15th century)
: WEAKNESS, INFIRMITY

¹deb·it \'de-bət\ *transitive verb* (1682)
: to enter upon the debit side of an account
: charge with a debit

²debit *noun* [Latin *debitum* debt] (1776)
1 a : a record of an indebtedness; *specifically* : an entry on the left-hand side of an account constituting an addition to an expense or asset account or a deduction from a revenue, net worth, or liability account **b** : the sum of the items entered as debits
2 : a charge against a bank deposit account
3 : DRAWBACK, SHORTCOMING

debit card *noun* (1977)
: a card like a credit card by which money may be withdrawn or the cost of purchases paid directly from the holder's bank account without the payment of interest

deb·o·nair \,de-bə-'nar, -'ner\ *adjective* [Middle English *debonere*, from Old French *debonaire*, from *de bon aire* of good family or nature] (13th century)
1 *archaic* : GENTLE, COURTEOUS
2 a : SUAVE, URBANE **b** : LIGHTHEARTED, NONCHALANT
— **deb·o·nair·ly** *adverb*
— **deb·o·nair·ness** *noun*

de·bone \(,)dē-'bōn\ *transitive verb* (1944)
: BONE ⟨*debone* a roast⟩
— **de·bon·er** *noun*

Deb·o·rah \'de-b(ə-)rə\ *noun* [Hebrew *Dĕbhōrāh*]
: a Hebrew prophetess who rallied the Israelites in their struggles against the Canaanites

☆ **SYNONYMS**

Debase, vitiate, deprave, corrupt, debauch, pervert mean to cause deterioration or lowering in quality or character. DEBASE implies a loss of position, worth, value, or dignity ⟨commercialism has *debased* the holiday⟩. VITIATE implies a destruction of purity, validity, or effectiveness by allowing entrance of a fault or defect ⟨a foreign policy *vitiated* by partisanship⟩. DEPRAVE implies moral deterioration by evil thoughts or influences ⟨the claim that society is *depraved* by pornography⟩. CORRUPT implies loss of soundness, purity, or integrity ⟨the belief that bureaucratese *corrupts* the language⟩. DEBAUCH implies a debasing through sensual indulgence ⟨the long stay on a tropical isle had *debauched* the ship's crew⟩. PERVERT implies a twisting or distorting from what is natural or normal ⟨*perverted* the original goals of the institute⟩.

de·bouch \di-ˈbau̇ch, -ˈbüsh, dē-\ *verb* [French *déboucher,* from *dé-* de- + *bouche* mouth, from Latin *bucca* cheek] (1745)
transitive verb
: to cause to emerge **:** DISCHARGE
intransitive verb
1 : to march out into open ground
2 : EMERGE, ISSUE
— **de·bouch·ment** \-mənt\ *noun*
de·bride·ment \di-ˈbrēd-mənt, dā-, -ˌmänt, dā-brēd-ˈmäⁿ\ *noun* [French *débridement,* from *débrider* to remove adhesions, literally, to unbridle, from Middle French *desbrider,* from *des-* de- + *bride* bridle, from Middle High German *brīdel* — more at BRIDLE] (circa 1842)
: the surgical removal of lacerated, devitalized, or contaminated tissue
— **de·bride** \di-ˈbrēd, dā-\ *transitive verb*
de·brief \(ˌ)dē-ˈbrēf\ *transitive verb* (1945)
: to interrogate (as a pilot) usually upon return (as from a mission) in order to obtain useful information
de·bris \də-ˈbrē, dā-, ˈdā-ˌ, *British usually* ˈde-(ˌ)brē\ *noun, plural* **de·bris** \-ˈbrēz, -ˌbrēz\ [French *débris,* from Middle French, from *debriser* to break to pieces, from Old French *debrisier,* from *de-* + *brisier* to break — more at BRISANCE] (1708)
1 : the remains of something broken down or destroyed
2 : an accumulation of fragments of rock
3 : something discarded **:** RUBBISH
debt \ˈdet\ *noun* [Middle English *dette, debte,* from Old French *dette* something owed, from (assumed) Vulgar Latin *debita,* from Latin, plural of *debitum* debt, from neuter of *debitus,* past participle of *debēre* to owe, from *de-* + *habēre* to have — more at GIVE] (13th century)
1 : SIN, TRESPASS
2 : something owed **:** OBLIGATION
3 : a state of owing
4 : the common-law action for the recovery of money held to be due
— **debt·less** \-ləs\ *adjective*
debt·or \ˈde-tər\ *noun* (13th century)
1 : one guilty of neglect or violation of duty
2 : one who owes a debt
debt service *noun* (1929)
: the amount of interest and sinking fund payments due annually on long-term debt
de·bug \(ˌ)dē-ˈbəg\ *transitive verb* (1944)
1 : to remove insects from
2 : to eliminate errors in or malfunctions of
3 : to remove a concealed microphone or wiretapping device from
— **de·bug·ger** *noun*
de·bunk \(ˌ)dē-ˈbəŋk\ *transitive verb* (1923)
: to expose the sham or falseness of ⟨*debunk* a legend⟩
— **de·bunk·er** *noun*
¹de·but *also* **dé·but** \ˈdā-ˌbyü, dā-ˈ\ *noun* [French *début,* from *débuter* to begin, from Middle French *desbuter* to play first, from *des-* de- + *but* starting point, goal — more at BUTT] (1751)
1 : a first appearance ⟨made her singing *debut*⟩
2 : a formal entrance into society
²debut (1830)
intransitive verb
: to make a debut
transitive verb
: to present to the public for the first time **:** INTRODUCE
deb·u·tant \ˈde-byu̇-ˌtänt\ *noun* [French *débutant,* from present participle of *débuter*] (1821)
: one making a debut
deb·u·tante \ˈde-byu̇-ˌtänt\ *noun* [French *débutante,* feminine of *débutant*] (1801)
: DEBUTANT; *especially* **:** a young woman making her formal entrance into society
deca- *or* **dec-** *or* **deka-** *or* **dek-** *combining form* [Middle English, from Latin, from Greek *deka-, dek-,* from *deka* — more at TEN]
: ten ⟨*deca*syllabic⟩ ⟨*deka*meter⟩

de·cade \ˈde-ˌkād, de-ˈkād; *especially sense* 1b ˈde-kəd\ *noun* [Middle English, from Middle French *décade,* from Late Latin *decad-, decas,* from Greek *dekad-, dekas,* from *deka*] (15th century)
1 : a group or set of 10: as **a :** a period of 10 years **b :** a division of the rosary that consists primarily of 10 Hail Marys
2 : a ratio of 10 to 1 **:** ORDER OF MAGNITUDE
— **dec·a·dal** \ˈde-kə-dᵊl\ *adjective*
dec·a·dence \ˈde-kə-dən(t)s *also* di-ˈkā-\ *noun* [Middle French, from Medieval Latin *decadentia,* from Late Latin *decadent-, decadens,* present participle of *decadere* to fall, sink — more at DECAY] (1549)
1 : the process of becoming decadent **:** the quality or state of being decadent
2 : a period of decline
synonym see DETERIORATION
dec·a·den·cy \-dᵊn-sē\ *noun* (1632)
: DECADENCE 1
¹dec·a·dent \ˈde-kə-dənt *also* di-ˈkā-\ *adjective* [back-formation from *decadence*] (1837)
1 : marked by decay or decline
2 : of, relating to, or having the characteristics of the decadents
3 : characterized by or appealing to self-indulgence
— **dec·a·dent·ly** *adverb*
²decadent *noun* (1886)
1 : one of a group of late 19th century French and English writers tending toward artificial and unconventional subjects and subtilized style
2 : one that is decadent
de·caf \ˈdē-ˌkaf\ *noun* [short for *decaffeinated*] (1984)
: decaffeinated coffee
de·caf·fein·at·ed \(ˌ)dē-ˈka-fə-nā-təd, -fē-ə-\ *adjective* (1921)
: having the caffeine removed ⟨*decaffeinated* coffee⟩ ⟨*decaffeinated* tea⟩
deca·gon \ˈde-kə-ˌgän\ *noun* [New Latin *decagonum,* from Greek *dekagōnon,* from *deka-* deca- + *-gōnon* -gon] (1571)
: a plane polygon of 10 angles and 10 sides
deca·gram \-ˌgram\ *noun* [French *décagramme,* from *déca-* deca- + *gramme* gram] (1810)
: DEKAGRAM
deca·he·dron \ˌde-kə-ˈhē-drən\ *noun* [International Scientific Vocabulary] (circa 1828)
: a polyhedron of 10 faces

decagon

de·cal \ˈdē-ˌkal, di-ˈkal; *Canadian usually* ˈde-kəl\ *noun* [short for *decalcomania*] (1937)
: a picture, design, or label made to be transferred (as to glass) from specially prepared paper
de·cal·ci·fi·ca·tion \(ˌ)dē-ˌkal-sə-fə-ˈkā-shən\ *noun* (1859)
: the removal or loss of calcium or calcium compounds (as from bones or soil)
— **de·cal·ci·fy** \(ˌ)dē-ˈkal-sə-fī\ *transitive verb*
de·cal·co·ma·nia \di-ˌkal-kə-ˈmā-nē-ə\ *noun* [French *décalcomanie,* from *décalquer* to copy by tracing (from *dé-* de- + *calquer* to trace, from Italian *calcare,* literally, to tread, from Latin) + *manie* mania, from Late Latin *mania* — more at CAULK] (1864)
1 : the art or process of transferring pictures and designs from specially prepared paper (as to glass)
2 : DECAL
deca·li·ter \ˈde-kə-ˌlē-tər\ *noun* [French *décalitre,* from *déca-* + *litre* liter] (1810)
: DEKALITER
deca·logue \ˈde-kə-ˌlȯg, -ˌläg\ *noun* [Middle English *decaloge,* from Late Latin *decalogus,* from Greek *dekalogos,* from *deka-* + *logos* word — more at LEGEND] (14th century)
1 *capitalized* **:** TEN COMMANDMENTS

2 : a basic set of rules carrying binding authority
¹deca·me·ter \ˈde-kə-ˌmē-tər\ *noun* [French *décamètre,* from *déca-* + *mètre* meter] (1810)
: DEKAMETER
²de·cam·e·ter \de-ˈka-mə-tər, də-\ *noun* [Greek *dekametron,* from *deka-* + *metron* measure, meter] (1821)
: a line of verse consisting of 10 metrical feet
deca·me·tho·ni·um \ˌde-kə-mə-ˈthō-nē-əm\ *noun* [*deca-* + *methylene* + *-onium*] (circa 1949)
: a synthetic ion used in the form of either its bromide or iodide salts ($C_{16}H_{38}Br_2N_2$ or $C_{16}H_{38}I_2N_2$) as a skeletal muscle relaxant; *also* **:** either of these salts
deca·met·ric \ˌde-kə-ˈme-trik\ *adjective* [*decameter* + *-ic;* from the wavelength range being between 1 and 10 dekameters] (1950)
: of, relating to, or being a radio wave of high frequency
de·camp \di-ˈkamp, dē-\ *intransitive verb* [French *décamper,* from Middle French *descamper,* from *des-* de- + *camper* to camp] (1676)
1 : to break up a camp
2 : to depart suddenly **:** ABSCOND
— **de·camp·ment** \-mənt\ *noun*
dec·ane \ˈde-ˌkān\ *noun* [International Scientific Vocabulary *deca-*] (circa 1875)
: any of several isomeric liquid alkanes $C_{10}H_{22}$
de·cant \di-ˈkant, dē-\ *transitive verb* [New Latin *decantare,* from Latin *de-* + Medieval Latin *cantus* edge, from Latin, iron ring round a wheel — more at CANT] (1633)
1 : to draw off (a liquid) without disturbing the sediment or the lower liquid layers
2 : to pour from one vessel into another
3 : to pour out, transfer, or unload as if by pouring
— **de·can·ta·tion** \ˌdē-ˌkan-ˈtā-shən\ *noun*
de·cant·er \di-ˈkan-tər, dē-\ *noun* (1712)
: a vessel used to decant or to receive decanted liquids; *especially* **:** an ornamental glass bottle used for serving wine
de·cap·i·tate \di-ˈka-pə-ˌtāt, dē-\ *transitive verb* **-tat·ed; -tat·ing** [Late Latin *decapitatus,* past participle of *decapitare,* from Latin *de-* + *capit-, caput* head — more at HEAD] (circa 1611)
1 : to cut off the head of **:** BEHEAD
2 : to make ineffective **:** DESTROY
— **de·cap·i·ta·tion** \-ˌka-pə-ˈtā-shən\ *noun*
— **de·cap·i·ta·tor** \-ˈka-pə-ˌtā-tər\ *noun*

decanter

deca·pod \ˈde-kə-ˌpäd\ *noun* [New Latin *Decapoda,* order name] (1836)
1 : any of an order (Decapoda) of crustaceans (as shrimps, lobsters, and crabs) with five pairs of thoracic appendages one or more of which are modified into pincers, with stalked eyes, and with the head and thorax fused into a cephalothorax and covered by a carapace
2 : any of the cephalopod mollusks (orders Sepioidea and Teuthoidea) with 10 arms including cuttlefishes, squids, and related forms
— **decapod** *adjective*
— **de·cap·o·dan** \di-ˈka-pə-dən\ *adjective or noun*
— **de·cap·o·dous** \-ə-dəs\ *adjective*
de·car·bon·ate \(ˌ)dē-ˈkär-bə-ˌnāt\ *transitive verb* (1831)
: to remove carbon dioxide or carbonic acid from
— **de·car·bon·ation** \-ˌkär-bə-ˈnā-shən\ *noun*

de·car·bon·ize \(ˌ)dē-ˈkär-bə-ˌnīz\ *transitive verb* [International Scientific Vocabulary] (1825)
: to remove carbon from
— **de·car·bon·iz·er** *noun*

de·car·box·yl·ase \dē-kär-ˈbäk-sə-ˌlās, -ˌlāz\ *noun* (1940)
: any of a group of enzymes that accelerate decarboxylation especially of amino acids

de·car·box·yl·ation \-ˌbäk-sə-ˈlā-shən\ *noun* (1922)
: the removal or elimination of carboxyl from a molecule
— **de·car·box·yl·ate** \-ˈbäk-sə-ˌlāt\ *transitive verb*

de·car·bu·rize \(ˌ)dē-ˈkär-b(y)ə-ˌrīz\ *transitive verb* (1856)
: DECARBONIZE
— **de·car·bu·ri·za·tion** \-ˌkär-b(y)ə-rə-ˈzā-shən\ *noun*

dec·are \ˈde-ˌkar, -ˌker, -ˌkär\ *noun* [French *décare*, from *déca-* deca- + *are*] (1810)
: a metric unit of area equal to 10 ares or 0.2471 acre

de·ca·su·al·iza·tion \(ˌ)dē-ˌka-zh(ə-)wə-lə-ˈzā-shən, -ˌka-zhə-lə-\ *noun* (1892)
: the process of eliminating the employment of casual workers to stabilize the work force

deca·syl·lab·ic \ˌde-kə-sə-ˈla-bik\ *adjective* [probably from French *décasyllabique*, from Greek *dekasyllabos*, from *deka-* deca- + *syllabē* syllable] (1771)
: consisting of 10 syllables or composed of verses of 10 syllables
— **decasyllabic** *noun*
— **deca·syl·la·ble** \ˈde-kə-ˌsi-lə-bəl, ˌde-kə-ˈ\ *noun*

de·cath·lete \di-ˈkath-ˌlēt\ *noun* [blend of *decathlon* and *athlete*] (1968)
: an athlete who competes in the decathlon

de·cath·lon \di-ˈkath-lən, -ˌlän\ *noun* [French *décathlon*, from *déca-* deca- + *-athlon* (as in *pentathlon*)] (1912)
: a 10-event athletic contest; *specifically* : a composite contest that consists of the 100-meter, 400-meter, and 1500-meter runs, the 110-meter high hurdles, the javelin and discus throws, shot put, pole vault, high jump, and long jump

¹de·cay \di-ˈkā\ *verb* [Middle English, from Old North French *decair*, from Late Latin *decadere* to fall, sink, from Latin *de-* + *cadere* to fall — more at CHANCE] (15th century) *intransitive verb*
1 : to decline from a sound or prosperous condition
2 : to decrease gradually in quantity, activity, or force
3 : to fall into ruin
4 : to decline in health, strength, or vigor
5 : to undergo decomposition
transitive verb
1 *obsolete* : to cause to decay : IMPAIR ⟨infirmity that *decays* the wise —Shakespeare⟩
2 : to destroy by decomposition ☆
— **de·cay·er** *noun*

²decay *noun* (15th century)
1 : gradual decline in strength, soundness, or prosperity or in degree of excellence or perfection
2 : a wasting or wearing away : RUIN
3 *obsolete* : DESTRUCTION, DEATH
4 a : ROT; *specifically* : aerobic decomposition of proteins chiefly by bacteria **b** : the product of decay
5 : a decline in health or vigor
6 : decrease in quantity, activity, or force: as **a** : spontaneous decrease in the number of radioactive atoms in radioactive material **b** : spontaneous disintegration (as of an atom or a particle)

Dec·ca \ˈde-kə\ *noun* [Decca Co., British firm which developed it] (1946)
: a system of long-range navigation used chiefly in Europe that utilizes the phase differences of continuous-wave signals from synchronized ground transmitters to establish position

de·cease \di-ˈsēs\ *noun* [Middle English *deces*, from Middle French, from Latin *decessus* departure, death, from *decedere* to depart, die, from *de-* + *cedere* to go] (14th century)
: departure from life : DEATH
— **decease** *intransitive verb*

¹de·ceased \-ˈsēst\ *adjective* (15th century)
: no longer living; *especially* : recently dead — used of persons
synonym see DEAD

²deceased *noun, plural* **deceased** (1625)
: a dead person ⟨the will of the *deceased*⟩

de·ce·dent \di-ˈsē-dᵊnt\ *noun* [Latin *decedent-, decedens*, present participle of *decedere*] (1599)
: a deceased person — used chiefly in law

de·ceit \di-ˈsēt\ *noun* [Middle English *deceite*, from Middle French, from Latin *decepta*, feminine of *deceptus*, past participle of *decipere*] (14th century)
1 : the act or practice of deceiving : DECEPTION
2 : an attempt or device to deceive : TRICK
3 : the quality of being deceitful : DECEITFULNESS

de·ceit·ful \-fəl\ *adjective* (15th century)
: having a tendency or disposition to deceive: **a** : not honest ⟨a *deceitful* child⟩ **b** : DECEPTIVE, MISLEADING
synonym see DISHONEST
— **de·ceit·ful·ly** \-fə-lē\ *adverb*
— **de·ceit·ful·ness** *noun*

de·ceiv·able \di-ˈsē-və-bəl\ *adjective* (14th century)
1 *archaic* : DECEITFUL, DECEPTIVE
2 *archaic* : capable of being deceived

de·ceive \di-ˈsēv\ *verb* **de·ceived; de·ceiv·ing** [Middle English, from Middle French *deceivre*, from Latin *decipere*, from *de-* + *capere* to take — more at HEAVE] (13th century)
transitive verb
1 *archaic* : ENSNARE
2 a *obsolete* : to be false to **b** *archaic* : to fail to fulfill
3 *obsolete* : CHEAT
4 : to cause to accept as true or valid what is false or invalid
5 *archaic* : to while away
intransitive verb
: to practice deceit; *also* : to give a false impression ⟨appearances can *deceive*⟩ ☆
— **de·ceiv·er** *noun*
— **de·ceiv·ing·ly** \-ˈsē-viŋ-lē\ *adverb*

de·cel·er·ate \(ˌ)dē-ˈse-lə-ˌrāt\ *verb* **-at·ed; -at·ing** [*de-* + *accelerate*] (1899)
transitive verb
1 : to reduce the speed of : slow down
2 : to decrease the rate of progress of
intransitive verb
: to move at decreasing speed
— **de·cel·er·a·tion** \(ˌ)dē-ˌse-lə-ˈrā-shən\ *noun*
— **de·cel·er·a·tor** \(ˌ)dē-ˈse-lə-ˌrā-tər\ *noun*

De·cem·ber \di-ˈsem-bər, dē-\ *noun* [Middle English *Decembre*, from Old English or Old French, both from Latin *December* (tenth month), from *decem* ten — more at TEN] (before 12th century)
: the 12th month of the Gregorian calendar
word history see SEPTEMBER

De·cem·brist \-ˈbrist\ *noun* (1877)
: one taking part in the unsuccessful uprising against the Russian emperor Nicholas I in December 1825

de·cem·vir \di-ˈsem-vər\ *noun* [Middle English, from Latin, back-formation from *decemviri*, plural, from *decem* + *viri*, plural of *vir* man — more at VIRILE] (1579)
: one of a ruling body of 10; *specifically* : one of a body of 10 magistrates in ancient Rome
— **de·cem·vi·ral** \-vər-əl\ *adjective*
— **de·cem·vi·rate** \-vər-ət\ *noun*

de·cen·cy \ˈdē-sᵊn-sē\ *noun, plural* **-cies** (1567)
1 *archaic* **a** : FITNESS **b** : ORDERLINESS
2 a : the quality or state of being decent : PROPRIETY **b** : conformity to standards of taste, propriety, or quality
3 : standard of propriety — usually used in plural
4 *plural* : conditions or services considered essential for a proper standard of living
5 : literary decorum

de·cen·ni·al \di-ˈse-nē-əl\ *adjective* (circa 1656)
1 : consisting of or lasting for 10 years
2 : occurring or being done every 10 years ⟨the *decennial* census⟩
— **decennial** *noun*
— **de·cen·ni·al·ly** \-nē-ə-lē\ *adverb*

de·cen·ni·um \-nē-əm\ *noun, plural* **-ni·ums** *or* **-nia** \-nē-ə\ [Latin, from *decem* + *annus* year — more at ANNUAL] (1685)
: a period of 10 years : DECADE

de·cent \ˈdē-sᵊnt\ *adjective* [Middle French or Latin; Middle French, from Latin *decent-, decens*, present participle of *decēre* to be fitting; akin to Latin *decus* honor, *dignus* worthy, Greek *dokein* to seem, seem good] (1539)
1 *archaic* **a** : APPROPRIATE **b** : well-formed : HANDSOME
2 a : conforming to standards of propriety, good taste, or morality **b** : modestly clothed
3 : free from immodesty or obscenity
4 : fairly good but not excellent : ADEQUATE, SATISFACTORY ⟨*decent* wages⟩
5 : marked by moral integrity, kindness, and goodwill ⟨hard-working and *decent* folks⟩
synonym see CHASTE
— **de·cent·ly** *adverb*

de·cen·tral·iza·tion \(ˌ)dē-ˌsen-trə-lə-ˈzā-shən\ *noun* (1846)
1 : the dispersion or distribution of functions and powers; *specifically* : the delegation of power from a central authority to regional and local authorities
2 : the redistribution of population and industry from urban centers to outlying areas
— **de·cen·tral·ize** \(ˌ)dē-ˈsen-trə-ˌlīz\ *verb*

de·cep·tion \di-ˈsep-shən\ *noun* [Middle English *decepcioun*, from Middle French *deception*, from Late Latin *deception-, deceptio*, from Latin *decipere* to deceive] (15th century)
1 a : the act of deceiving **b** : the fact or condition of being deceived

2 : something that deceives : TRICK ☆
— **de·cep·tion·al** \-shə-nəl\ *adjective*
de·cep·tive \di-'sep-tiv\ *adjective* (circa 1611)
: tending or having power to deceive : MISLEADING
— **de·cep·tive·ly** *adverb*
— **de·cep·tive·ness** *noun*

¹**de·cer·e·brate** \(,)dē-'ser-ə-brət, -,brāt\ *adjective* (1897)
1 : characteristic of decerebration ⟨*decerebrate* rigidity⟩
2 : having the cerebrum removed or made inactive

²**de·cer·e·brate** \(,)dē-'ser-ə-,brāt\ *transitive verb* (circa 1900)
: to remove the cerebrum from; *also* : to make incapable of cerebral activity
— **de·cer·e·bra·tion** \(,)dē-,ser-ə-'brā-shən\ *noun*

de·cer·ti·fy \(,)dē-'sər-tə-,fī\ *transitive verb* (1918)
: to withdraw or revoke the certification of
— **de·cer·ti·fi·ca·tion** \(,)dē-,sər-tə-fə-'kā-shən\ *noun*

de·chlo·ri·nate \(,)dē-'klōr-ə-,nāt, -'klȯr-\ *transitive verb* (1941)
: to remove chlorine from ⟨*dechlorinate* water⟩
— **de·chlo·ri·na·tion** \(,)dē-,klōr-ə-'nā-shən, -,klȯr-\ *noun*

deci- *combining form* [French *déci-*, from Latin *decimus* tenth, from *decem* ten — more at TEN]
: tenth part ⟨*decimeter*⟩

deci·bel \'de-sə-,bel, -bəl\ *noun* [International Scientific Vocabulary *deci-* + *bel*] (1928)
1 a : a unit for expressing the ratio of two amounts of electric or acoustic signal power equal to 10 times the common logarithm of this ratio **b** : a unit for expressing the ratio of the magnitudes of two electric voltages or currents or analogous acoustic quantities equal to 20 times the common logarithm of the voltage or current ratio
2 : a unit for expressing the relative intensity of sounds on a scale from zero for the average least perceptible sound to about 130 for the average pain level
3 : degree of loudness; *also* : extremely loud sound — usually used in plural

de·cide \di-'sīd, dē-\ *verb* **de·cid·ed; de·cid·ing** [Middle English, from Middle French *decider*, from Latin *decidere*, literally, to cut off, from *de-* + *caedere* to cut] (14th century)
transitive verb
1 a : to arrive at a solution that ends uncertainty or dispute about ⟨*decide* what to do⟩ **b** : to select as a course of action — used with an infinitive ⟨*decided* to go⟩
2 : to bring to a definitive end ⟨one blow *decided* the fight⟩
3 : to induce to come to a choice ⟨her pleas *decided* him to help⟩
intransitive verb
: to make a choice or judgment ☆
— **de·cid·abil·i·ty** \di-,sī-də-'bi-lə-tē\ *noun*
— **de·cid·able** \di-'sī-də-bəl\ *adjective*
— **de·cid·er** *noun*

de·cid·ed *adjective* (1790)
1 : UNQUESTIONABLE ⟨a *decided* advantage⟩
2 : free from doubt or wavering
— **de·cid·ed·ly** *adverb*
— **de·cid·ed·ness** *noun*

de·cid·ing *adjective* (1658)
: that decides : DECISIVE ⟨drove in the *deciding* run⟩

de·cid·ua \di-'si-jə-wə\ *noun, plural* **-u·ae** \-jə-,wē\ [New Latin, from Latin, feminine of *deciduus*] (1785)
1 : the part of the mucous membrane lining the uterus that in higher placental mammals undergoes special modifications in preparation for and during pregnancy and is cast off at parturition

2 : the part of the mucous membrane of the uterus cast off in the process of menstruation
— **de·cid·u·al** \-wəl\ *adjective*

de·cid·u·ate \-wət\ *adjective* (1868)
: having the fetal and maternal tissues firmly interlocked so that a layer of maternal tissue is torn away at parturition and forms part of the afterbirth

de·cid·u·ous \di-'si-jə-wəs\ *adjective* [Latin *deciduus*, from *decidere* to fall off, from *de-* + *cadere* to fall — more at CHANCE] (1688)
1 : falling off or shed seasonally or at a certain stage of development in the life cycle ⟨*deciduous* leaves⟩ ⟨*deciduous* teeth⟩
2 a : having deciduous parts ⟨*deciduous* trees⟩ **b** : having the dominant plants deciduous ⟨a *deciduous* forest⟩
3 : EPHEMERAL
— **de·cid·u·ous·ness** *noun*

deci·gram \'de-sə-,gram\ *noun* [French *décigramme*, from *déci-* + *gramme* gram] (1810)
— see METRIC SYSTEM table

dec·ile \'de-,sīl, -səl\ *noun* [Latin *decem* ten — more at TEN] (1882)
: any one of nine numbers that divide a frequency distribution into 10 classes such that each contains the same number of individuals; *also* : any one of these 10 classes
— **decile** *adjective*

deci·li·ter \'de-sə-,lē-tər\ *noun* [French *décilitre*, from *déci-* + *litre* liter] (1801)
— see METRIC SYSTEM table

de·cil·lion \di-'sil-yən\ *noun, often attributive* [Latin *decem* + English *-illion* (as in *million*)] (1847)
— see NUMBER table

¹**dec·i·mal** \'de-sə-məl, 'des-məl\ *adjective* [French *décimal*, from Medieval Latin *decimalis* of a tithe, from Latin *decima* tithe — more at DIME] (1608)
: numbered or proceeding by tens: **a** : based on the number 10; *especially* : expressed in or utilizing a decimal system especially with a decimal point **b** : subdivided into 10th or 100th units ⟨*decimal* coinage⟩
— **dec·i·mal·ly** \-mə-lē\ *adverb*

²**decimal** *noun* (1651)
: any real number expressed in base 10; *especially* : DECIMAL FRACTION

decimal fraction *noun* (1660)
: a fraction (as $.5 = {}^{25}\!/_{100}$ or $.025 = {}^{25}\!/_{1000}$) or mixed number (as $3.025 = 3{}^{25}\!/_{1000}$) in which the denominator is a power of 10 usually expressed by use of the decimal point

dec·i·mal·i·za·tion \,de-sə-mə-lə-'zā-shən\ *noun* (1855)
: conversion (as of a currency) to a decimal system
— **dec·i·mal·ize** \'de-sə-mə-,līz\ *transitive verb*

decimal point *noun* (circa 1864)
: a period, centered dot, or in some countries a comma at the left of a proper decimal fraction (as .678) or between the parts of a mixed number (as 3.678) expressed by a whole number and a decimal fraction

decimal system *noun* (1864)
1 : a number system that uses a notation in which each number is expressed in base 10 by using one of the first nine integers or 0 in each place and letting each place value be a power of 10
2 : a system of measurement or currency in which the basic units increase by powers of 10

dec·i·mate \'de-sə-,māt\ *transitive verb* **-mat·ed; -mat·ing** [Latin *decimatus*, past participle of *decimare*, from *decimus* tenth, from *decem* ten] (1660)
1 : to select by lot and kill every tenth man of
2 : to exact a tax of 10 percent from ⟨poor as a *decimated* Cavalier —John Dryden⟩
3 a : to reduce drastically especially in number ⟨cholera *decimated* the population⟩ **b** : to destroy a large part of ⟨firebombs *decimated* large sections of the city⟩ ◻

— **dec·i·ma·tion** \,de-sə-'mā-shən\ *noun*

deci·me·ter \'de-sə-,mē-tər\ *noun* [French *décimètre*, from *déci-* deci- + *mètre* meter] (1809)
: see METRIC SYSTEM table

de·ci·pher \dē-'sī-fər\ *transitive verb* (1545)
1 : DECODE 1a
2 *obsolete* : DEPICT
3 a : to make out the meaning of despite indistinctness or obscurity **b** : to interpret the meaning of
— **de·ci·pher·able** \-f(ə-)rə-bəl\ *adjective*
— **de·ci·pher·er** \-fər-ər\ *noun*
— **de·ci·pher·ment** \-fər-mənt\ *noun*

¹de·ci·sion \di-'si-zhən\ *noun* [Middle French, from Latin *decision-, decisio,* from *decidere* to decide] (15th century)
1 a : the act or process of deciding **b** : a determination arrived at after consideration : CONCLUSION
2 : a report of a conclusion
3 : promptness and firmness in deciding : DETERMINATION
4 a : WIN; *specifically* : a victory in boxing decided on points **b** : a win or loss officially credited to a pitcher in baseball
— **de·ci·sion·al** \-'si-zhnəl, -'si-zhə-nºl\ *adjective*

²decision *transitive verb* (1943)
: to win a decision over (a boxing opponent)

decision theory *noun* (1961)
: a branch of statistical theory concerned with quantifying the process of making choices between alternatives

decision tree *noun* (1964)
: a tree diagram which is used for making decisions in business or computer programming and in which the branches represent choices with associated risks, costs, results, or probabilities

de·ci·sive \di-'sī-siv\ *adjective* (1611)
1 : having the power or quality of deciding
2 : RESOLUTE, DETERMINED
3 : UNMISTAKABLE, UNQUESTIONABLE ⟨a *decisive* superiority⟩
synonym see CONCLUSIVE
— **de·ci·sive·ly** *adverb*
— **de·ci·sive·ness** *noun*

¹deck \'dek\ *noun* [Middle English *dekke* covering of a ship, from (assumed) Middle Dutch *dec* covering, probably from Middle Low German *vordeck,* from *vordecken* to cover, from *vor-* for- + *decken* to cover; akin to Old High German *decchen* to cover — more at THATCH] (1509)
1 : a platform in a ship serving usually as a structural element and forming the floor for its compartments
2 : something resembling the deck of a ship: as **a** : a story or tier of a building **b** : the roadway of a bridge **c** : a flat floored roofless area adjoining a house **d** : the lid of the compartment at the rear of the body of an automobile; *also* : the compartment **e** : a layer of clouds
3 a : a pack of playing cards **b** : a packet of narcotics
4 : TAPE DECK
— **on deck 1** : ready for duty **2** : next in line : next in turn

²deck *transitive verb* [Dutch *dekken* to cover; akin to Old High German *decchen*] (1513)
1 *obsolete* : COVER
2 a : to clothe elegantly : ARRAY ⟨*decked* out in furs⟩ **b** : DECORATE ⟨*deck* the halls with boughs of holly —*English carol*⟩ **c** : to portray or present with embellishments
3 [¹*deck*] : to furnish with or as if with a deck
4 [¹*deck*] : to knock down forcibly : FLOOR ⟨*decked* him with one punch⟩
synonym see ADORN

deck chair *noun* (1884)
: a folding chair often having an adjustable leg rest

deck·er \'de-kər\ *noun* (1790)
: something having a specified number of decks, levels, floors, or layers — used in

combination ⟨many of the city's buses are double-*deckers*⟩

deck·hand \'dek-,hand\ *noun* (1844)
: a seaman who performs manual duties

deck·house \-,haus\ *noun* (1856)
: a superstructure on a ship's upper deck

deck·ing \'de-kiŋ\ *noun* (1580)
: DECK; *also* : material for a deck

deck chair

deck·le \'de-kəl\ *noun* [German *Deckel,* literally, cover, from *decken* to cover, from Old High German *decchen*] (1816)
: a frame around the edges of a mold used in making paper by hand; *also* : either of the bands around the edge of the wire of a papermaking machine that determine the width of the web

deckle edge *noun* (circa 1874)
: the rough untrimmed edge of paper left by a deckle or produced artificially
— **deck·le-edged** \-'ejd\ *adjective*

deck tennis *noun* [from its being played on the decks of ocean liners] (1927)
: a game in which players toss a ring or quoit back and forth over a net stretched across a small court

de·claim \di-'klām, dē-\ *verb* [Middle English *declamen,* from Latin *declamare,* from *de-* + *clamare* to cry out; akin to Latin *calare* to call — more at LOW] (14th century)
intransitive verb
1 : to speak rhetorically; *specifically* : to recite something as an exercise in elocution
2 : to speak pompously or bombastically : HARANGUE
transitive verb
: to deliver rhetorically; *specifically* : to recite in elocution
— **de·claim·er** *noun*
— **dec·la·ma·tion** \,de-klə-'mā-shən\ *noun*

de·clam·a·to·ry \di-'kla-mə-,tōr-ē, -,tòr-\ *adjective* (1581)
: of, relating to, or marked by declamation or rhetorical display

de·clar·ant \di-'klar-ənt, -'kler-\ *noun* (1681)
: a person who makes a statement or declaration especially in connection with a legal proceeding

dec·la·ra·tion \,de-klə-'rā-shən\ *noun* (15th century)
1 : the act of declaring : ANNOUNCEMENT
2 a : the first pleading in a common-law action **b** : a statement made by a party to a legal transaction usually not under oath
3 a : something that is declared **b** : the document containing such a declaration

de·clar·a·tive \di-'klar-ə-tiv, -'kler-\ *adjective* (1628)
: making a declaration : DECLARATORY ⟨a *declarative* sentence⟩
— **de·clar·a·tive·ly** *adverb*

de·clar·a·to·ry \-ə-,tōr-ē, -,tòr-\ *adjective* (15th century)
1 : serving to declare, set forth, or explain
2 a : declaring what is the existing law ⟨*declaratory* statute⟩ **b** : declaring a legal right or interpretation ⟨a *declaratory* judgment⟩

de·clare \di-'klar, -'kler\ *verb* **de·clared; de·clar·ing** [Middle English, from Middle French & Latin; Middle French *declarer,* from Latin *declarare,* from *de-* + *clarare* to make visible, from *clarus* clear — more at CLEAR] (14th century)
transitive verb
1 : to make known formally, officially, or explicitly
2 *obsolete* : to make clear
3 : to make evident : SHOW
4 : to state emphatically : AFFIRM ⟨*declares* his innocence⟩

5 : to make a full statement of (one's taxable or dutiable property)
6 a : to announce (as a trump suit) in a card game **b** : MELD
7 : to make payable ⟨*declare* a dividend⟩
intransitive verb
1 : to make a declaration
2 : to avow one's opinion or support ☆
— **de·clar·able** \-'klar-ə-bəl, -'kler-\ *adjective*

de·clar·er \di-'klar-ər, -'kler-\ *noun* (14th century)
: one that declares; *specifically* : the bridge player who names the trump and plays both his own hand and that of the dummy

de·class \(,)dē-'klas\ *transitive verb* (1888)
: to remove from a class; *especially* : to assign to a lower social status

dé·clas·sé \,dā-,kla-'sā, -,klä-\ *adjective* [French, from past participle of *déclasser* to declass] (1887)
1 : fallen or lowered in class, rank, or social position
2 : of inferior status

de·clas·si·fy \(,)dē-'kla-sə-,fī\ *transitive verb* (1945)
: to remove or reduce the security classification of ⟨*declassify* a secret document⟩
— **de·clas·si·fi·ca·tion** \(,)dē-,kla-sə-fə-'kā-shən\ *noun*

de·claw \-'klò\ *transitive verb* (1953)
: to remove the claws of (as a cat) surgically

de·clen·sion \di-'klen(t)-shən\ *noun* [Middle English *declenson,* modification of Middle French *declinaison,* from Latin *declination-, declinatio* grammatical inflection, turning aside, from *declinare* to inflect, turn aside] (15th century)
1 a : noun, adjective, or pronoun inflection especially in some prescribed order of the forms **b** : a class of nouns or adjectives having the same type of inflectional forms
2 : a falling off or away : DETERIORATION
3 : DESCENT, SLOPE
— **de·clen·sion·al** \-'klen(t)-shə-nºl\ *adjective*

dec·li·na·tion \,de-klə-'nā-shən\ *noun* [Middle English *declinacioun,* from Middle French *declination,* from Latin *declination-, declinatio* angle of the heavens, turning aside] (14th century)
1 : angular distance north or south from the celestial equator measured along a great circle passing through the celestial poles
2 : a turning aside or swerving
3 : DETERIORATION ⟨moral *declination*⟩
4 : a bending downward : INCLINATION
5 : a formal refusal
6 : the angle formed between a magnetic needle and the geographical meridian
— **dec·li·na·tion·al** \-shnəl, -shə-nºl\ *adjective*

¹de·cline \di-'klīn, dē-\ *verb* **de·clined; de·clin·ing** [Middle English, from Middle French *decliner,* from Latin *declinare* to turn aside, inflect, from *de-* + *clinare* to incline — more at LEAN] (14th century)
intransitive verb

☆ **SYNONYMS**
Declare, announce, proclaim, promulgate mean to make known publicly. DECLARE implies explicitness and usually formality in making known ⟨the referee *declared* the contest a draw⟩. ANNOUNCE implies the declaration of something for the first time ⟨*announced* their engagement at a party⟩. PROCLAIM implies declaring clearly, forcefully, and authoritatively ⟨the president *proclaimed* a national day of mourning⟩. PROMULGATE implies the proclaiming of a dogma, doctrine, or law ⟨*promulgated* an edict of religious toleration⟩. See in addition ASSERT.

1 *archaic* **:** to turn from a straight course **:** STRAY
2 a : to slope downward **:** DESCEND **b :** to bend down **:** DROOP **c :** to stoop to what is unworthy
3 a *of a celestial body* **:** to sink toward setting **b :** to draw toward a close **:** WANE ⟨the day *declined*⟩
4 : to tend toward an inferior state or weaker condition ⟨his health *declined*⟩
5 : to withhold consent
6 : to become less in amount ⟨prices *declined*⟩ *transitive verb*
1 : to give in prescribed order the grammatical forms of (a noun, pronoun, or adjective)
2 *obsolete* **a :** AVERT **b :** AVOID
3 : to cause to bend or bow downward
4 a : to refuse to undertake, undergo, engage in, or comply with **b :** to refuse especially courteously ⟨*decline* an invitation⟩ ☆
— **de·clin·able** \-'klī-nə-bəl\ *adjective*
— **de·clin·er** \-'klī-nər\ *noun*
²decline *also* 'dē-,klīn\ *noun* (14th century)
1 : the process of declining: **a :** a gradual physical or mental sinking and wasting away **b :** a change to a lower state or level
2 : the period during which something is deteriorating or approaching its end
3 : a downward slope
4 : a wasting disease; *especially* **:** pulmonary tuberculosis
synonym see DETERIORATION
de·clin·ing \-niŋ\ *adjective* (1593)
: of or relating to the period during which something is deteriorating or nearing its end ⟨her *declining* years⟩
de·cliv·i·tous \di-'kliv-ət-əs\ *adjective* (1799)
: moderately steep
de·cliv·i·ty \-ət-ē\ *noun, plural* **-ties** [Latin *declivitat-, declivitas,* from *declivis* sloping down, from *de-* + *clivus* slope, hill; akin to Latin *clinare*] (1612)
1 : downward inclination
2 : a descending slope
de·co \'de-(,)kō, dā-'kō, 'dā-,\ *noun, often capitalized* (1969)
: ART DECO
de·coct \di-'käkt\ *transitive verb* [Latin *decoctus,* past participle of *decoquere,* from *de-* + *coquere* to cook — more at COOK] (15th century)
1 : to extract the flavor of by boiling
2 : BOIL DOWN, CONCENTRATE
de·coc·tion \di-'käk-shən\ *noun* (15th century)
1 : an extract obtained by decocting
2 : the act or process of decocting
de·code \(,)dē-'kōd\ *transitive verb* (1896)
1 a : to convert (as a coded message) into intelligible form **b :** to recognize and interpret (an electronic signal)
2 a : DECIPHER 3a **b :** to discover the underlying meaning of ⟨*decode* the play's imagery⟩
de·cod·er \-'kō-dər\ *noun* (1920)
: one that decodes; *especially* **:** an electronic device for unscrambling a television transmission
de·col·late \dē-'kä-,lāt\ *transitive verb* **-lat·ed; -lat·ing** [Latin *decollatus,* past participle of *decollare,* from *de-* + *collum* neck — more at COLLAR] (1599)
: BEHEAD
— **de·col·la·tion** \,dē-kä-'lā-shən\ *noun*
dé·col·le·tage \(,)dā-,kä-lə-'täzh, (,)dā-,kȯl-'täzh, ,de-klə-\ *noun* [French, action of cutting or wearing a low neckline, from *décolleter*] (1894)
1 : the low-cut neckline of a dress
2 : a décolleté dress
3 : ¹BUST 2
¹dé·col·le·té \(,)dā-,käl-'tā, -,kȯl-, -lə-'tā; *also* dā-'kȯl-tā\ *adjective* [French, from past participle of *décolleter* to give a low neckline to, from *dé-* de- + *collet* collar, from Old French *colet,* from *col* collar, neck, from Latin *collum* neck] (1831)
1 : wearing a strapless or low-necked dress

2 : having a low-cut neckline
²dé·col·le·té *also* **de·col·le·te** *noun* (1900)
: DÉCOLLETAGE
de·col·o·nize \(,)dē-'kä-lə-,nīz\ *transitive verb* (1963)
: to free from colonial status
— **de·col·o·ni·za·tion** \(,)dē-,kä-lə-nə-'zā-shən\ *noun*
de·col·or·ize \(,)dē-'kə-lə-,rīz\ *transitive verb* **-ized; -iz·ing** (1839)
: to remove color from ⟨*decolorize* vinegar by adsorption of impurities on activated charcoal⟩
— **de·col·or·iza·tion** \(,)dē-,kə-lə-rə-'zā-shən\ *noun*
— **de·col·or·iz·er** \(')dē-'kə-lə-,rī-zər\ *noun*
de·com·mis·sion \,dē-kə-'mi-shən\ *transitive verb* (1922)
: to remove (as a ship or nuclear power plant) from service
de·com·pen·sa·tion \(,)dē-,käm-pən-'sā-shən, -,pen-\ *noun* [International Scientific Vocabulary] (circa 1903)
: loss of physiological compensation or psychological balance; *especially* **:** inability of the heart to maintain adequate circulation
— **de·com·pen·sate** \(,)dē-'käm-pən-,sāt, -,pen-\ *verb*
de·com·pose \,dē-kəm-'pōz\ *verb* [French *décomposer,* from *dé-* de- + *composer* to compose] (circa 1751)
transitive verb
1 : to separate into constituent parts or elements or into simpler compounds ⟨*decompose* water by electrolysis⟩ ⟨*decompose* a word into its base and affixes⟩
2 : ROT
intransitive verb
: to break up into constituent parts by or as if by a chemical process **:** DECAY, ROT ⟨fruit *decomposes*⟩
synonym see DECAY
— **de·com·pos·abil·i·ty** \-,pō-zə-'bi-lə-tē\ *noun*
— **de·com·pos·able** \-'pō-zə-bəl\ *adjective*
— **de·com·po·si·tion** \(,)dē-,käm-pə-'zi-shən\ *noun*
de·com·pos·er \,dē-kəm-'pō-zər\ *noun* (1959)
: any of various organisms (as many bacteria and fungi) that return constituents of organic substances to ecological cycles by feeding on and breaking down dead protoplasm
de·com·pound \,dē-'käm-,paund, ,dē-kəm-'\ *adjective* (circa 1793)
of a leaf **:** having divisions that are themselves compound
de·com·press \,dē-kəm-'pres\ (1905)
transitive verb
: to release from pressure or compression
intransitive verb
: to undergo release from pressure; *especially* **:** RELAX ⟨need a week off to *decompress*⟩
— **de·com·pres·sion** \-'pre-shən\ *noun*
decompression sickness *noun* (circa 1941)
: ²BEND 3, AEROEMBOLISM
de·con·cen·trate \(,)dē-'kän(t)-sən-,trāt\ *transitive verb* (circa 1889)
: to reduce or abolish the concentration of **:** DECENTRALIZE
— **de·con·cen·tra·tion** \(,)dē-,kän(t)-sən-'trā-shən\ *noun*
de·con·di·tion \,dē-kən-'di-shən\ *transitive verb* (1941)
1 : to cause extinction of (a conditioned response)
2 : to cause to lose physical fitness
de·con·ges·tant \,dē-kən-'jes-tənt\ *noun* (1947)
: an agent that relieves congestion (as of mucous membranes)
— **decongestant** *adjective*
de·con·ges·tion \,dē-kən-'jes(h)-chən\ *noun* (1908)
: the process of relieving congestion

— **de·con·gest** \-'jest\ *transitive verb*
— **de·con·ges·tive** \-'jes-tiv\ *adjective*
de·con·se·crate \(,)dē-'kän(t)s-ə-,krāt\ *transitive verb* (1876)
: to remove the sacred character of ⟨*deconsecrate* a church⟩
— **de·con·se·cra·tion** \(,)dē-,kän(t)-sə-'krā-shən\ *noun*
de·con·struct \,dē-kən-'strəkt\ *transitive verb* (1973)
: to discuss (as a work of literature) using the methods of deconstruction
— **de·con·struc·tive** \-tiv\ *adjective*
— **de·con·struc·tor** \-tər\ *noun*
de·con·struc·tion \,dē-kən-'strək-shən\ *noun* [French *déconstruction,* from *dé-* de- + *construction*] (1973)
: a method of literary criticism that assumes language refers only to itself rather than to an extratextual reality, that asserts multiple conflicting interpretations of a text, and that bases such interpretations on the philosophical, political, or social implications of the use of language in the text rather than on the author's intention
— **de·con·struc·tion·ist** \-shə-nist\ *noun*
de·con·tam·i·nate \,dē-kən-'ta-mə-,nāt\ *transitive verb* (1936)
: to rid of contamination (as radioactive material)
— **de·con·tam·i·na·tion** \-,ta-mə-'nā-shən\ *noun*
— **de·con·tam·i·na·tor** \-'ta-mə-,nā-tər\ *noun*
de·con·trol \,dē-kən-'trōl\ *transitive verb* (1919)
: to end control of
— **decontrol** *noun*
de·cor *or* **dé·cor** \dā-'kȯr, di-'; 'de-,kȯr, 'dā-,\ *noun* [French *décor,* from *décorer* to decorate, from Latin *decorare*] (1897)
1 : a stage setting
2 a : DECORATION 2 **b :** the style and layout of interior furnishings
dec·o·rate \'de-kə-,rāt\ *transitive verb* **-rat·ed; -rat·ing** [Latin *decoratus,* past participle of *decorare,* from *decor-, decus* ornament, honor — more at DECENT] (1530)
1 : to add honor to
2 : to furnish with something ornamental ⟨*decorate* a room⟩
3 : to award a mark of honor to
synonym see ADORN
dec·o·ra·tion \,de-kə-'rā-shən\ *noun* (1530)
1 : the act or process of decorating
2 : something that adorns, enriches, or beautifies **:** ORNAMENT
3 : a badge of honor (as a U.S. military award)

☆ **SYNONYMS**
Decline, refuse, reject, repudiate, spurn mean to turn away by not accepting, receiving, or considering. DECLINE often implies courteous refusal especially of offers or invitations ⟨*declined* his party's nomination⟩. REFUSE suggests more positiveness or ungraciousness and often implies the denial of something asked for ⟨*refused* to lend them the money⟩. REJECT implies a peremptory refusal by sending away or discarding ⟨*rejected* the manuscript as unpublishable⟩. REPUDIATE implies a casting off or disowning as untrue, unauthorized, or unworthy of acceptance ⟨teenagers who *repudiate* the values of their parents⟩. SPURN stresses contempt or disdain in rejection or repudiation ⟨*spurned* his overtures of friendship⟩.

\ə\ **abut** \ᵊ\ **kitten** \ər\ **further** \a\ **ash** \ā\ **ace**
\ä\ **mop, mar** \au̇\ **out** \ch\ **chin** \e\ **bet** \ē\ **easy**
\g\ **go** \i\ **hit** \ī\ **ice** \j\ **job** \ŋ\ **sing** \ō\ **go**
\ȯ\ **law** \ȯi\ **boy** \th\ **thin** \t̲h̲\ **the** \ü\ **loot** \u̇\ **foot**
\y\ **yet** \zh\ **vision** *see also* Guide to Pronunciation

Decoration Day *noun* [from the custom of decorating graves on this day] (1871)
: MEMORIAL DAY

dec·o·ra·tive \'de-k(ə-)rə-tiv, 'de-kə-,rā-\ *adjective* (1791)
: serving to decorate; *especially* : purely ornamental
— **dec·o·ra·tive·ly** *adverb*
— **dec·o·ra·tive·ness** *noun*

decorative art *noun* (1967)
1 : an art concerned primarily with the creation of useful items (as furniture, ceramics, and textiles) — usually used in plural
2 : objects of decorative art

¹**dec·o·ra·tor** \'de-kə-,rā-tər\ *noun* (circa 1755)
: one that decorates; *especially* : one that designs or executes interiors and their furnishings

²**decorator** *adjective* (1950)
: suitable for interior decoration ⟨*decorator* fabrics⟩

dec·o·rous \'de-kər-əs *also* di-'kōr-əs *or* -'kor-\ *adjective* [Latin *decorus*, from *decor* beauty, grace; akin to Latin *decēre* to be fitting — more at DECENT] (1673)
: marked by propriety and good taste : CORRECT ⟨*decorous* conduct⟩
— **dec·o·rous·ly** *adverb*
— **dec·o·rous·ness** *noun*

de·cor·ti·ca·tion \(,)dē-,kor-tə-'kā-shən\ *noun* [Latin *decortication-, decorticatio,* from *decorticare* to remove the bark from, from *de-* + *cortic-, cortex* bark — more at CUIRASS] (circa 1623)
1 : the act or process of removing the outer coverings (as bark or husks) from something (as fiber or seed)
2 : the surgical removal of the cortex of an organ (as the brain), an enveloping membrane, or a constrictive fibrinous covering
— **de·cor·ti·cate** \(,)dē-'kor-tə-,kāt\ *transitive verb*
— **de·cor·ti·cat·or** \-,kā-tər\ *noun*

de·co·rum \di-'kor-əm, -'kor-\ *noun* [Latin, from neuter of *decorus*] (1576)
1 : literary and dramatic propriety : FITNESS
2 : propriety and good taste in conduct or appearance
3 : ORDERLINESS
4 *plural* : the conventions of polite behavior

de·cou·page *or* **dé·cou·page** \,dā-(,)kü-'päzh\ *noun* [French *découpage,* literally, act of cutting out, from Middle French, from *decouper* to cut out, from *de-* + *couper* to cut — more at COPE] (1946)
1 : the art of decorating surfaces by applying cutouts (as of paper) and then coating with usually several layers of finish (as lacquer or varnish)
2 : work produced by decoupage
— **decoupage** *or* **découpage** *transitive verb*

de·cou·ple \(,)dē-'kə-pəl\ *transitive verb* (1953)
: to eliminate the interrelationship of : SEPARATE

¹**de·coy** \'dē-,koi, di-'\ *noun* [probably from Dutch *de kooi,* literally, the cage, from *de,* masculine definite article (akin to Old English *thæt,* neuter definite article) + *kooi* cage, from Latin *cavea* — more at THAT, CAGE] (1641)
1 : a pond into which wildfowl are lured for capture
2 : someone or something used to lure or lead another into a trap; *especially* : an artificial bird used to attract live birds within shot
3 : someone or something used to draw attention away from another

²**de·coy** \di-'koi, 'dē-\ *transitive verb* (circa 1674)
: to lure by or as if by a decoy : ENTICE
synonym see LURE

¹**de·crease** \di-'krēs, 'dē-\ *verb* **de·creased; de·creas·ing** [Middle English *decreessen,* from (assumed) Anglo-French *de-*

creistre, from Latin *decrescere,* from *de-* + *crescere* to grow — more at CRESCENT] (14th century)
intransitive verb
: to grow progressively less (as in size, amount, number, or intensity)
transitive verb
: to cause to decrease ☆
— **de·creas·ing·ly** \di-'krē-siŋ-lē, dē-\ *adverb*

²**de·crease** \'dē-,krēs, di-'\ *noun* (14th century)
1 : the process of decreasing
2 : an amount of diminution : REDUCTION

¹**de·cree** \di-'krē\ *noun* [Middle English, from Middle French *decré,* from Latin *decretum,* from neuter of *decretus,* past participle of *decernere* to decide, from *de-* + *cernere* to sift, decide — more at CERTAIN] (14th century)
1 : an order usually having the force of law
2 a : a religious ordinance enacted by council or titular head **b** : a foreordaining will
3 a : a judicial decision of the Roman emperor **b** : a judicial decision especially in an equity or probate court

²**decree** *verb* **de·creed; de·cree·ing** (14th century)
transitive verb
1 : to command or enjoin by or as if by decree ⟨*decree* an amnesty⟩
2 : to determine or order judicially ⟨*decree* a punishment⟩
intransitive verb
: ORDAIN
— **de·cre·er** \-'krē-ər\ *noun*

de·cree–law \di-'krē-,lo\ *noun* (1926)
: a decree of a ruler or ministry having the force of a law enacted by the legislature

dec·re·ment \'de-krə-mənt\ *noun* [Latin *decrementum,* from *decrescere*] (1610)
1 : a gradual decrease in quality or quantity
2 a : the quantity lost by diminution or waste **b** : the amount of decrease (as of a variable)
— **dec·re·men·tal** \,de-krə-'men-t²l\ *adjective*

de·crep·it \di-'kre-pət\ *adjective* [Middle English, from Middle French, from Latin *decrepitus*] (15th century)
1 : wasted and weakened by or as if by the infirmities of old age
2 a : impaired by use or wear : WORN-OUT **b** : fallen into ruin or disrepair
3 : DILAPIDATED, RUN-DOWN
synonym see WEAK
— **de·crep·it·ly** *adverb*

de·crep·i·tate \di-'kre-pə-,tāt\ *verb* [probably from (assumed) New Latin *decrepitatus,* past participle of *decrepitare,* from Latin *de-* + *crepitare* to crackle — more at CREPITATE] (1646)
transitive verb
: to roast or calcine (as salt) so as to cause crackling or until crackling stops
intransitive verb
: to become decrepitated
— **de·crep·i·ta·tion** \-,kre-pə-'tā-shən\ *noun*

de·crep·i·tude \di-'kre-pə-,tüd, -,tyüd\ *noun* (1603)
: the quality or state of being decrepit

¹**de·cre·scen·do** \,dā-krə-'shen-(,)dō\ *noun,* *plural* **-dos** [Italian, literally, decreasing, from Latin *decrescendum,* gerund of *decrescere*] (circa 1880)
1 : a gradual decrease in volume of a musical passage
2 : a decrescendo musical passage

²**decrescendo** *adverb or adjective* (circa 1890)
: with a decrease in volume — used as a direction in music

mark indicating decrescendo 2

de·cres·cent \di-'kre-s²nt\ *adjective* [alteration of earlier *decressant,* probably from Anglo-French, present participle of (assumed) Anglo-French *decreistre* to decrease] (1610)
: becoming less by gradual diminution : DECREASING, WANING

de·cre·tal \di-'krē-t²l, 'de-kri-t²l\ *noun* [Middle English, from Middle French, from Late Latin *decretalis* of a decree, from Latin *decretum* decree] (14th century)
: DECREE; *especially* : a papal letter giving an authoritative decision on a point of canon law

de·cre·tive \-'krē-tiv\ *adjective* (1609)
: having the force of a decree : DECRETORY

de·cre·to·ry \'de-krə-,tōr-ē, -,tor-; di-'krē-tər-ē\ *adjective* (circa 1631)
: relating to or fixed by a decree or decision

de·crim·i·nal·ize \(,)dē-'kri-mə-nə-,līz, -'krim-nəl-\ *transitive verb* (1969)
: to remove or reduce the criminal classification or status of; *especially* : to repeal a strict ban on while keeping under some form of regulation ⟨*decriminalize* the possession of marijuana⟩
— **de·crim·i·nal·iza·tion** \(,)dē-,kri-mə-nə-lə-'zā-shən, -,krim-nəl-\ *noun*

de·cry \di-'krī, dē-\ *transitive verb* [French *décrier,* from Old French *descrier,* from *des-* de- + *crier* to cry] (1614)
1 : to depreciate (as a coin) officially or publicly
2 : to express strong disapproval of ⟨*decry* the emphasis on sex⟩ ☆
— **de·cri·er** \-'krī(-ə)r\ *noun*

de·crypt \(,)dē-'kript\ *transitive verb* [International Scientific Vocabulary de- + crypt(ogram, crypt)ograph] (1935)
: DECODE 1a
— **de·cryp·tion** \-'krip-shən\ *noun*

de·cum·bent \di-'kəm-bənt, dē-\ *adjective* [Latin *decumbent-, decumbens,* present participle of *decumbere* to lie down, from *de-* + *-cumbere* to lie down; akin to Latin *cubare* to lie] (1656)
1 : lying down
2 *of a plant* : reclining on the ground but with ascending apex or extremity

dec·u·ple \'de-kyə-pəl\ *adjective* [French *décuple,* from Middle French, from Late Latin *decuplus,* from Latin *decem* ten + *-uplus* (as in *quadruplus* quadruple)] (1613)
1 : TENFOLD
2 : taken in groups of 10

de·cu·ri·on \di-'kyur-ē-ən\ *noun* [Middle English *decurioun,* from Latin *decurion-, decurio,* from *decuria* division of ten, from *decem*] (14th century)
1 : a Roman cavalry officer in command of 10 men
2 : a member of a Roman senate

de·cur·rent \di-'kər-ənt, -'kə-rənt\ *adjective* [Latin *decurrent-, decurrens,* present participle of *decurrere* to run down, from *de-* + *currere* to run — more at CAR] (circa 1753)

☆ **SYNONYMS**
Decrease, lessen, diminish, reduce, abate, dwindle mean to grow or make less. DECREASE suggests a progressive decline in size, amount, numbers, or intensity ⟨slowly *decreased* the amount of pressure⟩. LESSEN suggests a decline in amount rather than in number ⟨has been unable to *lessen* her debt⟩. DIMINISH emphasizes a perceptible loss and implies its subtraction from a total ⟨his visual acuity has *diminished*⟩. REDUCE implies a bringing down or lowering ⟨you must *reduce* your caloric intake⟩. ABATE implies a reducing of something excessive or oppressive in force or amount ⟨the storm *abated*⟩. DWINDLE implies progressive lessening and is applied to things growing visibly smaller ⟨their provisions *dwindled* slowly⟩.

: running or extending downward along the stem ⟨*decurrent* leaves⟩

de·curved \(ˌ)dē-ˈkərvd\ *adjective* [part translation of Late Latin *decurvatus,* from Latin *de-* + *curvatus* curved] (1835)
: curved downward : bent down

¹**de·cus·sate** \ˈde-kə-ˌsāt, di-ˈkə-ˌsāt\ *verb* **-sat·ed; -sat·ing** [Latin *decussatus,* past participle of *decussare* to arrange crosswise, from *decussis* the number ten, numeral X, intersection, from *decem* + *ass-,* as unit — more at ACE] (1658)
: INTERSECT, CROSS

²**de·cus·sate** \ˈde-kə-ˌsāt, di-ˈkə-sət\ *adjective* (circa 1823)
: arranged in pairs each at right angles to the next pair above or below ⟨*decussate* leaves⟩

de·cus·sa·tion \ˌde-kə-ˈsā-shən, ˌdē-kə-\ *noun* (circa 1656)
1 : the action of crossing (as of nerve fibers) especially in the form of an X
2 : a crossed tract of nerve fibers passing between centers on opposite sides of the nervous system

¹**ded·i·cate** \ˈde-di-kət\ *adjective* [Middle English, from Latin *dedicatus,* past participle of *dedicare* to dedicate, from *de-* + *dicare* to proclaim, dedicate — more at DICTION] (14th century)
: DEDICATED

²**ded·i·cate** \ˈde-di-ˌkāt *also* ˈde-ˌdē-\ *transitive verb* **-cat·ed; -cat·ing** (15th century)
1 : to devote to the worship of a divine being; *specifically* : to set apart (a church) to sacred uses with solemn rites
2 a : to set apart to a definite use ⟨money *dedicated* to their vacation fund⟩ **b** : to commit to a goal or way of life ⟨ready to *dedicate* his life to public service⟩
3 : to inscribe or address by way of compliment ⟨*dedicate* a book to a friend⟩
4 : to open to public use
synonym see DEVOTE
— **ded·i·ca·tor** \-ˌkā-tər\ *noun*

ded·i·cat·ed *adjective* (circa 1600)
1 : devoted to a cause, ideal, or purpose : ZEALOUS ⟨a *dedicated* scholar⟩
2 : given over to a particular purpose ⟨a *dedicated* process control computer⟩
— **ded·i·cat·ed·ly** *adverb*

ded·i·ca·tee \ˌde-di-kə-ˈtē\ *noun* (1760)
: one to whom a thing is dedicated

ded·i·ca·tion \ˌde-di-ˈkā-shən\ *noun* (14th century)
1 : an act or rite of dedicating to a divine being or to a sacred use
2 : a devoting or setting aside for a particular purpose
3 : a name and often a message prefixed to a literary, musical, or artistic production in tribute to a person or cause
4 : self-sacrificing devotion
— **ded·i·ca·to·ry** \ˈde-di-kə-ˌtōr-ē, -ˌtȯr-\ *adjective*

de·dif·fer·en·ti·a·tion \(ˌ)dē-ˌdi-fə-ˌren-chē-ˈā-shən\ *noun* (1915)
: reversion of specialized structures (as cells) to a more generalized or primitive condition often as a preliminary to major physiological or structural change
— **de·dif·fer·en·ti·ate** \-ˈren-chē-ˌāt\ *intransitive verb*

de·duce \di-ˈdüs, dē-; *chiefly British* -ˈdyüs\ *transitive verb* **de·duced; de·duc·ing** [Middle English, from Latin *deducere,* literally, to lead away, from *de-* + *ducere* to lead — more at TOW] (15th century)
1 : to determine by deduction; *specifically* : to infer from a general principle
2 : to trace the course of
synonym see INFER
— **de·duc·ible** \-ˈd(y)ü-sə-bəl\ *adjective*

de·duct \di-ˈdəkt, dē-\ *transitive verb* [Latin *deductus,* past participle of *deducere*] (15th century)

1 : to take away (an amount) from a total
: SUBTRACT
2 : DEDUCE, INFER

¹**de·duct·ible** \di-ˈdək-tə-bəl, dē-\ *adjective* (1856)
: allowable as a deduction
— **de·duct·ibil·i·ty** \-ˌdək-tə-ˈbi-lə-tē\ *noun*

²**deductible** *noun* (1929)
: a clause in an insurance policy that relieves the insurer of responsibility for an initial specified loss of the kind insured against; *also* : the amount of the loss specified in such a clause

de·duc·tion \di-ˈdək-shən, dē-\ *noun* (15th century)
1 a : an act of taking away ⟨*deduction* of legitimate business expenses⟩ **b** : something that is or may be subtracted ⟨*deductions* from his taxable income⟩
2 a : the deriving of a conclusion by reasoning; *specifically* : inference in which the conclusion about particulars follows necessarily from general or universal premises — compare INDUCTION **b** : a conclusion reached by logical deduction

de·duc·tive \di-ˈdək-tiv, dē-\ *adjective* (1665)
1 : of, relating to, or provable by deduction
2 : employing deduction in reasoning
— **de·duc·tive·ly** *adverb*

dee \ˈdē\ *noun* (13th century)
1 : the letter *d*
2 : something shaped like the letter D

¹**deed** \ˈdēd\ *noun* [Middle English *dede,* from Old English *dǣd;* akin to Old English *dōn* to do] (before 12th century)
1 : something that is done ⟨evil *deeds*⟩
2 : a usually illustrious act or action : FEAT, EXPLOIT
3 : the act of performing : ACTION ⟨righteous in word and in *deed*⟩
4 : a signed and usually sealed instrument containing some legal transfer, bargain, or contract
— **deed·less** \-ləs\ *adjective*

²**deed** *transitive verb* (1806)
: to convey or transfer by deed

deed poll \-ˈpōl\ *noun, plural* **deeds poll** [¹*deed* + *poll,* adjective (having the edges cut even rather than indented), from ²*poll*] (1588)
British : a deed (as to change one's name) made and executed by only one party

deedy \ˈdē-dē\ *adjective* **deed·i·er; -est** (1615)
dialect chiefly English : INDUSTRIOUS

dee·jay \ˈdē-ˌjā\ *noun* [disc jockey] (circa 1949)
: DISC JOCKEY

deem \ˈdēm\ *verb* [Middle English *demen,* from Old English *dēman;* akin to Old High German *tuomen* to judge, Old English *dōm* doom] (before 12th century)
transitive verb
: to come to think or judge : CONSIDER ⟨*deemed* it wise to go slow⟩
intransitive verb
: to have an opinion : BELIEVE

de–em·pha·size \(ˌ)dē-ˈem(p)-fə-ˌsīz\ *transitive verb* (1938)
: to reduce in relative importance; *also* : PLAY DOWN
— **de–em·pha·sis** \-fə-səs\ *noun*

de–en·er·gize \ˌdē-ˈe-nər-ˌjīz\ *transitive verb* (1925)
: to disconnect from a source of electricity
: shut off the power to

¹**deep** \ˈdēp\ *adjective* [Middle English *dep,* from Old English *dēop;* akin to Old High German *tiof* deep, Old English *dyppan* to dip — more at DIP] (before 12th century)
1 : extending far from some surface or area: as
a : extending far downward ⟨a *deep* well⟩ **b** (1) : extending well inward from an outer surface ⟨a *deep* gash⟩ ⟨a *deep*-chested animal⟩ (2) : not located superficially within the body ⟨*deep* pressure receptors in muscles⟩ **c** : extending well back from a surface accepted as

front ⟨a *deep* closet⟩ **d** : extending far laterally from the center ⟨*deep* borders of lace⟩ **e** : occurring or located near the outer limits of the playing area ⟨hit to *deep* right field⟩ **f** : thrown deep ⟨a *deep* pass⟩
2 : having a specified extension in an implied direction usually downward or backward ⟨a shelf 20 inches *deep*⟩ ⟨cars parked three-*deep*⟩
3 a : difficult to penetrate or comprehend : RECONDITE ⟨*deep* mathematical problems⟩ **b** : MYSTERIOUS, OBSCURE ⟨a *deep* dark secret⟩ **c** : grave in nature or effect ⟨in *deepest* disgrace⟩ **d** : of penetrating intellect : WISE ⟨a *deep* thinker⟩ **e** : INVOLVED, ENGROSSED ⟨*deep* in debt⟩ **f** : characterized by profundity of feeling or quality ⟨a *deep* sleep⟩; *also* : DEEP-SEATED ⟨*deep* religious beliefs⟩
4 a *of color* : high in saturation and low in lightness **b** : having a low musical pitch or pitch range ⟨a *deep* voice⟩
5 a : situated well within the boundaries ⟨a house *deep* in the woods⟩ **b** : remote in time or space **c** : being below the level of the conscious ⟨*deep* neuroses⟩ **d** : covered, enclosed, or filled to a specified degree — usually used in combination ⟨ankle-*deep* in mud⟩
6 : LARGE ⟨*deep* discounts⟩
7 : having many good players ⟨a *deep* bull pen⟩
synonym see BROAD
— **deep·ly** *adverb*
— **deep·ness** *noun*
— **in deep water** : in difficulty or distress

²**deep** *adverb* (before 12th century)
1 : to a great depth : DEEPLY ⟨still waters run *deep*⟩
2 : far on : LATE ⟨danced *deep* into the night⟩
3 a : near the outer limits of the playing area ⟨the shortstop was playing *deep*⟩ **b** : LONG 6

³**deep** *noun* (before 12th century)
1 a : a vast or immeasurable extent : ABYSS **b** (1) : the extent of surrounding space or time (2) : OCEAN
2 : any of the deep portions of a body of water; *specifically* : a generally long and narrow area in the ocean where the depth exceeds 3000 fathoms (5500 meters)
3 : the middle or most intense part ⟨the *deep* of winter⟩
4 : any of the fathom points on a sounding line other than the marks

deep–dish pie *noun* (1918)
: a pie usually with a fruit filling and no bottom crust that is baked in a deep dish

deep·en \ˈdē-pən\ *verb* **deep·ened; deep·en·ing** \ˈdē-pə-niŋ, ˈdēp-niŋ\ (1598)
transitive verb
: to make deep or deeper
intransitive verb
: to become deeper or more profound

deep fat *noun* (1921)
: hot fat or oil deep enough in a cooking utensil to cover the food to be fried

☆ SYNONYMS
Decry, depreciate, disparage, belittle mean to express a low opinion of. DECRY implies open condemnation with intent to discredit ⟨*decried* their defeatist attitude⟩. DEPRECIATE implies a representing as being of less value than commonly believed ⟨critics *depreciate* his plays for being unabashedly sentimental⟩. DISPARAGE implies depreciation by indirect means such as slighting or invidious comparison ⟨*disparaged* polo as a game for the rich⟩. BELITTLE usually suggests a contemptuous or envious attitude ⟨*belittled* the achievements of others⟩.

\ə\ abut \ᵊ\ kitten \ər\ further \a\ ash \ā\ ace
\ä\ mop, mar \au̇\ out \ch\ chin \e\ bet \ē\ easy
\g\ go \i\ hit \ī\ ice \j\ job \ŋ\ sing \ō\ go
\ȯ\ law \ȯi\ boy \th\ thin \t̶h̶\ the \ü\ loot \u̇\ foot
\y\ yet \zh\ vision *see also* Guide to Pronunciation

Deep·freeze \'dēp-ˌfrēz\ *trademark*
— used for a freezer for food storage

deep–freeze \'dēp-'frēz\ *transitive verb* **-froze** \-'frōz\; **-fro·zen** \-'frō-zᵊn\ (1943)
1 : QUICK-FREEZE
2 : to store in a frozen state

deep freeze \'dēp-ˌfrēz\ *noun* (1948)
1 : COLD STORAGE 2 ⟨a bill presently in *deep freeze* awaiting a new congress —*Newsweek*⟩
2 : intense cold

deep–fry \'dēp-'frī\ *transitive verb* (1922)
: to cook in deep fat

deep fryer *noun* (1950)
: a utensil suitable for deep-fat frying

deep pocket *noun* (1976)
1 : a person or an organization having substantial financial resources
2 *plural* **:** substantial financial resources

deep–root·ed \'dēp-'rü-təd, -'rū-\ *adjective* (15th century)
: deeply implanted or established ⟨a *deep-rooted* loyalty⟩
synonym see INVETERATE

deep–sea \'dēp-'sē\ *adjective* (1626)
: of, relating to, or occurring in the deeper parts of the sea ⟨*deep-sea* fishing⟩

deep–seat·ed \'dēp-'sē-təd\ *adjective* (1741)
1 : situated far below the surface ⟨a *deep-seated* inflammation⟩
2 : firmly established ⟨a *deep-seated* tradition⟩
synonym see INVETERATE

deep–six \'dēp-'siks\ *transitive verb* (1952)
1 *slang* **:** to throw away **:** DISCARD
2 *slang* **:** to throw overboard

deep six *noun* [from the leadsman's call *by the deep six* for a depth corresponding to the sixth deep on a sounding line] (1944)
slang **:** a place of disposal or abandonment — used especially in the phrase *give it the deep six*

deep–sky \'dēp-ˌskī\ *adjective* (1968)
: relating to or existing in space outside the solar system ⟨*deep-sky* objects⟩

deep space *noun* (circa 1952)
: space well outside the earth's atmosphere and especially that part lying beyond the earth-moon system

deep structure *noun* (1964)
: a formal representation of the underlying semantic content of a sentence; *also* **:** the structure which such a representation specifies

deep throat *noun, often D&T capitalized* [from the nickname given to such an informant in the Watergate scandal by Bob Woodward (born 1943) U.S. journalist, from the title of a pornographic film (1972)] (1973)
: an informant who divulges damaging information under cover of anonymity

deep·wa·ter \'dēp-ˌwȯ-tər, -,wä-\ *adjective* (1795)
: of, relating to, or characterized by water of considerable depth; *especially* **:** able to accommodate oceangoing vessels ⟨*deepwater* ports⟩

deer \'dir\ *noun, plural* **deer** *also* **deers** [Middle English, deer, animal, from Old English *dēor* beast; akin to Old High German *tior* wild animal, Lithuanian *dvasia* breath, spirit] (before 12th century)
1 *archaic* **:** ANIMAL; *especially* **:** a small mammal
2 : any of numerous ruminant mammals (family Cervidae, the deer family) having two large and two small hooves on each foot and antlers borne by the males of nearly all and by the females of a few forms ◆
— **deer·like** \-,līk\ *adjective*

deer·ber·ry \-,ber-ē\ *noun* (1814)
1 : either of two shrubs (*Vaccinium stamineum* or *V. caesium*) of dry woods and scrub of the eastern U.S.
2 : the edible fruit of a deerberry

deer·fly \'dir-,flī\ *noun* (1853)
: any of numerous small horseflies (as of the genus *Chrysops*) that include important vectors of tularemia

deer·hound \-,hau̇nd\ *noun* (1818)

: SCOTTISH DEERHOUND

deer mouse *noun* [from its agility] (1833)
: WHITE-FOOTED MOUSE; *especially* **:** a mouse (*Peromyscus maniculatus*) widely distributed in forests and grasslands of North America and Mexico

deer·skin \'dir-,skin\ *noun* (14th century)
: leather made from the skin of a deer; *also* **:** a garment of this leather

deer·stalk·er \-,stȯ-kər\ *noun* (1870)
: a close-fitting hat with a visor at the front and the back and with earflaps that may be worn up or down — called also *deerstalker cap, deerstalker hat*

deer tick *noun* (1982)
: an ixodid tick (*Ixodes dammini*) that transmits the bacterium causing Lyme disease

deer·yard \'dir-,yärd\ *noun* (1849)
: a place where deer herd in winter

deerstalker

de–es·ca·late \(ˌ)dē-'es-kə-ˌlāt, ÷-kyə-\ (1964)
transitive verb
: LIMIT 2b
intransitive verb
: to decrease in extent, volume, or scope
— **de–es·ca·la·tion** \(ˌ)dē-,es-kə-'lā-shən, ÷-kyə-\ *noun*
— **de–es·ca·la·to·ry** \(ˌ)dē-'es-kə-lə-,tōr-ē, -,tȯr-, ÷-kyə-\ *adjective*

deet \'dēt\ *noun, often all capitalized* [probably from *d. e. t.*, from *di-* + *ethyl* + *toluamide* (C_8H_9NO)] (1962)
: a colorless oily liquid insect repellent $C_{12}H_{17}NO$

de·face \di-'fās, dē-\ *transitive verb* [Middle English, from Middle French *desfacier*, from Old French, from *des-* de- + *face* front, face] (14th century)
1 : to mar the external appearance of **:** injure by effacing significant details ⟨*deface* an inscription⟩
2 : IMPAIR
3 *obsolete* **:** DESTROY
— **de·face·ment** \-'fās-mənt\ *noun*
— **de·fac·er** *noun*

¹de fac·to \di-'fak-(,)tō, dā-, dē-\ *adverb* [Medieval Latin, literally, from the fact] (1601)
: in reality **:** ACTUALLY

²de facto *adjective* (1696)
1 : ACTUAL; *especially* **:** being such in effect though not formally recognized ⟨a *de facto* state of war⟩
2 : exercising power as if legally constituted ⟨a *de facto* government⟩

de·fal·cate \di-'fal-,kāt, -'fȯl-, dē-; 'de-fəl-\ *verb* **-cat·ed; -cat·ing** [Medieval Latin *defalcatus*, past participle of *defalcare*, from Latin *de-* + *falc-, falx* sickle] (1540)
transitive verb
archaic **:** DEDUCT, CURTAIL
intransitive verb
: to engage in embezzlement
— **de·fal·ca·tor** \-,kā-tər\ *noun*

de·fal·ca·tion \,dē-,fal-'kā-shən, ,dē-,fȯl-, di-; ,de-fəl-\ *noun* (15th century)
1 *archaic* **:** DEDUCTION
2 : the act or an instance of embezzling
3 : a failure to meet a promise or an expectation

def·a·ma·tion \,de-fə-'mā-shən\ *noun* (14th century)
: the act of defaming another **:** CALUMNY
— **de·fam·a·to·ry** \di-'fa-mə-,tōr-ē, dē-, -,tȯr-\ *adjective*

de·fame \di-'fām, dē-\ *transitive verb* **de·famed; de·fam·ing** [Middle English, from Middle French & Medieval Latin; Middle French *defamer*, from Medieval Latin *defamare*, alteration of Latin *diffamare*, from *dis-* + *fama* reputation, fame] (14th century)
1 *archaic* **:** DISGRACE

2 : to harm the reputation of by libel or slander
3 *archaic* **:** ACCUSE
synonym see MALIGN
— **de·fam·er** *noun*

de·fang \(ˌ)dē-'faŋ\ *transitive verb* (1953)
: to make harmless or less powerful

de·fat \(ˌ)dē-'fat\ *transitive verb* (1919)
: to remove fat from

¹de·fault \di-'fȯlt, dē-; 'dē-ˌfȯlt\ *noun* [Middle English *defaute, defaulte*, from Old French *defaute*, from *defaillir* to be lacking, fail, from *de-* + *faillir* to fail] (13th century)
1 : failure to do something required by duty or law **:** NEGLECT
2 *archaic* **:** FAULT
3 : a failure to pay financial debts
4 a : failure to appear at the required time in a legal proceeding **b :** failure to compete in or to finish an appointed contest
5 : a selection automatically used by a computer program in the absence of a choice made by the user
— **in default of :** in the absence of

²default (15th century)
intransitive verb
: to fail to fulfill a contract, agreement, or duty: as **a :** to fail to meet a financial obligation **b :** to fail to appear in court **c :** to fail to compete in or to finish an appointed contest; *also* **:** to forfeit a contest by such failure
transitive verb
1 : to fail to perform, pay, or make good
2 a : FORFEIT **b :** to exclude (a player or a team) from a contest by default
— **de·fault·er** *noun*

de·fea·sance \di-'fē-zən(t)s\ *noun* [Middle English *defesance*, from Anglo-French, from Old French *deffesant*, present participle of *deffaire*] (15th century)
1 a (1) **:** the termination of a property interest in accordance with stipulated conditions (as in a deed) (2) **:** an instrument stating such conditions of limitation **b :** a rendering null or void
2 : DEFEAT, OVERTHROW

de·fea·si·ble \di-'fē-zə-bəl\ *adjective* (15th century)
: capable of being annulled or made void ⟨a *defeasible* claim⟩
— **de·fea·si·bil·i·ty** \-,fē-zə-'bi-lə-tē\ *noun*

¹de·feat \di-'fēt, dē-\ *transitive verb* [Middle English *deffeten*, from Middle French *deffait*, past participle of *deffaire* to destroy, from Old French *desfaire*, from Medieval Latin *disfacere*, from Latin *dis-* + *facere* to do — more at DO] (14th century)
1 *obsolete* **:** DESTROY
2 a : NULLIFY ⟨*defeat* an estate⟩ **b :** FRUSTRATE 2a(1) ⟨*defeat* a hope⟩
3 : to win victory over **:** BEAT ⟨*defeat* the opposing team⟩
synonym see CONQUER

◇ WORD HISTORY
deer In English the development of a word's meaning is sometimes from the general to the specific. For instance, *deer* is used in modern English to refer to several animals, including the white-tailed deer, reindeer, elk, and moose, that belong to the same zoological family. In Old English, however, *dēor* could refer to any animal, tame or wild, or to wild animals collectively. In time, *deer* came to be used only for wild animals that were hunted and then quite specifically for the red deer, which was once the primary object of the hunt in England. From that rather narrow usage, *deer* has expanded to the other members of its family mentioned above, thereby becoming somewhat more general again, though not as general as it once was.

²**defeat** *noun* (1590)
1 : frustration by nullification or by prevention of success ⟨the bill suffered *defeat* in the Senate⟩
2 *obsolete* : DESTRUCTION
3 a : an overthrow especially of an army in battle **b** : the loss of a contest
de·feat·ism \di-'fē-ˌti-zəm, dē-\ *noun* (1918) : acceptance or expectation of or resignation to defeat
— **de·feat·ist** \-tist\ *noun or adjective*
de·fea·ture \di-'fē-chər, dē-\ *noun* [probably from *de-* + *feature*] (1590)
1 *archaic* : DISFIGUREMENT
2 *archaic* : DEFEAT
def·e·cate \'de-fi-ˌkāt\ *verb* **-cat·ed; -cat·ing** [Latin *defaecatus*, past participle of *defaecare*, from *de-* + *faec-, faex* dregs, lees] (1575)
transitive verb
1 : to free from impurity or corruption
2 : to discharge from the anus
intransitive verb
: to discharge feces from the bowels
— **def·e·ca·tion** \ˌde-fi-'kā-shən\ *noun*
¹**de·fect** \'dē-ˌfekt, di-'\ *noun* [Middle English, from Middle French, from Latin *defectus* lack, from *deficere* to desert, fail, from *de-* + *facere* to do — more at DO] (15th century)
1 a : an imperfection that impairs worth or utility : SHORTCOMING ⟨the grave *defects* in our foreign policy⟩ **b** : an imperfection (as a vacancy or a foreign atom) in a crystal lattice
2 [Latin *defectus*] : a lack of something necessary for completeness, adequacy, or perfection : DEFICIENCY ⟨a hearing *defect*⟩
²**de·fect** \di-'fekt\ *intransitive verb* [Latin *defectus*, past participle of *deficere*] (1596)
1 : to forsake one cause, party, or nation for another often because of a change in ideology
2 : to leave one situation (as a job) often to go over to a rival ⟨the reporter *defected* to another network⟩
— **de·fec·tor** \-'fek-tər\ *noun*
de·fec·tion \di-'fek-shən\ *noun* (1552) : conscious abandonment of allegiance or duty (as to a person, cause, or doctrine) : DESERTION
¹**de·fec·tive** \di-'fek-tiv\ *adjective* (14th century)
1 a : imperfect in form or function : FAULTY ⟨a *defective* pane of glass⟩ **b** : falling below the norm in structure or in mental or physical function ⟨*defective* eyesight⟩
2 : lacking one or more of the usual forms of grammatical inflection ⟨*must* is a *defective* verb⟩
— **de·fec·tive·ly** *adverb*
— **de·fec·tive·ness** *noun*
²**defective** *noun* (1881) : a person who is subnormal physically or mentally
de·fem·i·nize \(ˌ)dē-'fe-mə-ˌnīz\ *transitive verb* (1907) : to divest of feminine qualities or characteristics : MASCULINIZE
— **de·fem·i·ni·za·tion** \(ˌ)dē-ˌfe-mə-nə-'zā-shən\ *noun*
de·fence, de·fence·man *chiefly British variant of* DEFENSE, DEFENSEMAN
de·fend \di-'fend\ *verb* [Middle English, from Old French *defendre*, from Latin *defendere*, from *de-* + *-fendere* to strike; akin to Old English *gūth* battle, war, Greek *theinein* to strike] (14th century)
transitive verb
1 a : to drive danger or attack away from **b** (1) : to maintain or support in the face of argument or hostile criticism (2) : to prove (as a doctoral thesis) valid by answering questions in an oral exam **c** : to attempt to prevent an opponent from scoring at ⟨elects to *defend* the south goal⟩
2 *archaic* : PREVENT, FORBID
3 : to act as attorney for

4 : to deny or oppose the right of a plaintiff in regard to (a suit or a wrong charged) : CONTEST
5 : to seek to retain (as a title or position) against a challenge in a contest
intransitive verb
1 : to take action against attack or challenge ⟨couldn't fight back, could only *defend*⟩
2 : to play or be on defense ⟨playing deep to *defend* against a pass⟩
3 : to play against the high bidder in a card game ☆
— **de·fend·able** \'fen-də-bəl\ *adjective*
¹**de·fen·dant** \di-'fen-dənt, *in legal circles often* -ˌdant\ *noun* (14th century) : a person required to make answer in a legal action or suit — compare PLAINTIFF
²**defendant** *adjective* (15th century) : being on the defensive : DEFENDING
de·fend·er \di-'fen-dər\ *noun* (14th century)
1 : one that defends
2 : a player in a sport (as football) assigned to a defensive position
de·fen·es·tra·tion \(ˌ)dē-ˌfe-nə-'strā-shən\ *noun* [*de-* + Latin *fenestra* window] (1620) : a throwing of a person or thing out of a window
— **de·fen·es·trate** \(ˌ)dē-'fe-nə-ˌstrāt\ *transitive verb*
¹**de·fense** \di-'fen(t)s; *as antonym of "offense," often* 'dē-ˌ\ *noun* [Middle English, from Middle French, from Late Latin *defensa* vengeance, from Latin, feminine of *defensus*, past participle of *defendere*] (14th century)
1 a : the act or action of defending ⟨the *defense* of our country⟩ ⟨speak out in *defense* of justice⟩ **b** : a defendant's denial, answer, or plea
2 a : capability of resisting attack **b** : defensive play or ability ⟨a player known for good *defense*⟩
3 a : means or method of defending or protecting oneself, one's team, or another; *also* : a defensive structure **b** : an argument in support or justification **c** : the collected facts and method adopted by a defendant to protect himself against a plaintiff's action **d** : a sequence of moves available in chess to the second player in the opening
4 a : a defending party or group (as in a court of law) ⟨the *defense* rests⟩ **b** : a defensive team
5 : the military and industrial aggregate that authorizes and supervises arms production ⟨appropriations for *defense*⟩ ⟨*defense* contract⟩
— **de·fense·less** \-ləs\ *adjective*
— **de·fense·less·ly** *adverb*
— **de·fense·less·ness** *noun*
²**defense** *transitive verb* **de·fensed; de·fens·ing** (1950) : to take specific defensive action against (an opposing team or player or an offensive play)
de·fense·man \-mən, -ˌman\ *noun* (1895) : a player in a sport (as hockey) who is assigned to a defensive zone or position
defense mechanism *noun* (1913)
1 : an often unconscious mental process (as repression) that makes possible compromise solutions to personal problems
2 : a defensive reaction by an organism
de·fen·si·ble \di-'fen(t)-sə-bəl\ *adjective* (14th century) : capable of being defended
— **de·fen·si·bil·i·ty** \di-ˌfen(t)-sə-'bi-lə-tē, ˌdē-\ *noun*
— **de·fen·si·bly** \-blē\ *adverb*
¹**de·fen·sive** \di-'fen(t)-siv, 'dē-ˌ\ *adjective* (14th century)
1 : serving to defend or protect
2 a : devoted to resisting or preventing aggression or attack **b** : of or relating to the attempt to keep an opponent from scoring in a game or contest
3 a : valuable in defensive play ⟨a *defensive* card in bridge⟩ **b** : designed to keep an opponent from being the highest bidder ⟨a *defensive* bid⟩

— **de·fen·sive·ly** *adverb*
— **de·fen·sive·ness** *noun*
²**defensive** *noun* (1601) : a defensive position
— **on the defensive** : in the state or condition of being prepared for an expected aggression or attack
¹**de·fer** \di-'fər\ *transitive verb* **de·ferred; de·fer·ring** [Middle English *deferren, differren*, from Middle French *differer*, from Latin *differre* to postpone, be different — more at DIFFER] (14th century)
1 : PUT OFF, DELAY
2 : to postpone induction of (a person) into military service ☆
— **de·fer·rer** *noun*
²**defer** *verb* **deferred; deferring** [Middle English *deferren, differren*, from Middle French *deferer, defferer*, from Late Latin *deferre*, from Latin, to bring down, bring, from *de-* + *ferre* to carry — more at BEAR] (15th century)
transitive verb
: to delegate to another ⟨he could *defer* his job to no one —J. A. Michener⟩
intransitive verb
: to submit to another's wishes, opinion, or governance usually through deference or respect ⟨*deferred* to her father's wishes⟩
synonym see YIELD
def·er·ence \'de-fə-rən(t)s, 'def-rən(t)s\ *noun* (1660) : respect and esteem due a superior or an elder; *also* : affected or ingratiating regard for another's wishes
synonym see HONOR
— **in deference to** : in consideration of
def·er·ent \'de-fə-rənt, 'def-rənt\ *adjective* [back-formation from *deference*] (1822) : DEFERENTIAL
def·er·en·tial \ˌde-fə-'ren-chəl\ *adjective* (1822) : showing or expressing deference ⟨*deferential* attention⟩

\ə\ **abut** \ᵊ\ **kitten** \ər\ **further** \a\ **ash** \ā\ **ace**
\ä\ **mop, mar** \au̇\ **out** \ch\ **chin** \e\ **bet** \ē\ **easy**
\g\ **go** \i\ **hit** \ī\ **ice** \j\ **job** \ŋ\ **sing** \ō\ **go**
\ȯ\ **law** \ȯi\ **boy** \th\ **thin** \t͟h\ **the** \ü\ **loot** \u̇\ **foot**
\y\ **yet** \zh\ **vision** *see also* Guide to Pronunciation

— **def·er·en·tial·ly** \-'ren-chə-lē\ *adverb*

de·fer·ment \di-'fər-mənt\ *noun* (1612)
: the act of delaying or postponing; *specifical·ly* : official postponement of military service

de·fer·ra·ble \di-'fər-ə-bəl\ *adjective* (1943)
: capable of or suitable or eligible for being deferred

— **deferrable** *noun*

de·fer·ral \di-'fər-əl\ *noun* (1895)
: the act of delaying : POSTPONEMENT

de·ferred *adjective* (1651)
1 : withheld for or until a stated time ⟨a *deferred* payment⟩
2 : charged in cases of delayed handling ⟨a *deferred* rate⟩

de·fer·ves·cence \,dē-(,)fər-'ve-s°n(t)s, ,defər-\ *noun* [German *Deferveszenz*, from Latin *defervescent-, defervescens*, present participle of *defervescere* to stop boiling, from *de-* + *fervescere* to begin to boil — more at EFFERVESCE] (1866)
: the subsidence of a fever

de·fi·ance \di-'fī-ən(t)s, dē-\ *noun* (15th century)
1 : the act or an instance of defying : CHALLENGE
2 : disposition to resist : willingness to contend or fight
— **in defiance of** : contrary to : DESPITE

de·fi·ant \-ənt\ *adjective* [French *défiant*, from Old French, present participle of *defier* to defy] (circa 1837)
: full of defiance : BOLD
— **de·fi·ant·ly** *adverb*

de·fi·bril·la·tor \(,)dē-'fi-brə-,lā-tər\ *noun* (1952)
: an electronic device that applies an electric shock to restore the rhythm of a fibrillating heart
— **de·fi·bril·late** \-,lāt\ *transitive verb*
— **de·fi·bril·la·tion** \-,fi-brə-'lā-shən\ *noun*

de·fi·brin·ate \(,)dē-'fi-brə-,nāt, -'fī-\ *transitive verb* **-at·ed; -at·ing** (1845)
: to remove fibrin from (blood)
— **de·fi·brin·ation** \(,)dē-,fi-brə-'nā-shən, -,fī-\ *noun*

de·fi·cien·cy \di-'fi-shən-sē\ *noun, plural* **-cies** (1634)
1 : the quality or state of being deficient : INADEQUACY
2 : an amount that is lacking or inadequate : SHORTAGE: as **a** : a shortage of substances necessary to health **b** : DELETION 2b(1)

deficiency disease *noun* (1912)
: a disease (as scurvy) caused by a lack of essential dietary elements and especially a vitamin or mineral

¹**de·fi·cient** \di-'fi-shənt\ *adjective* [Latin *deficient-, deficiens*, present participle of *deficere* to be wanting — more at DEFECT] (1581)
1 : lacking in some necessary quality or element ⟨*deficient* in judgment⟩
2 : not up to a normal standard or complement : DEFECTIVE ⟨*deficient* strength⟩
— **de·fi·cient·ly** *adverb*

²**deficient** *noun* (1906)
: one that is deficient ⟨a mental *deficient*⟩

def·i·cit \'de-fə-sət, *British also* di-'fis-ət *or* 'dē-fə-sət\ *noun* [French *déficit*, from Latin *deficit* it is wanting, 3d singular present indicative of *deficere*] (1782)
1 a (1) : deficiency in amount or quality ⟨a *deficit* in rainfall⟩ (2) : a lack or impairment in a functional capacity ⟨cognitive *deficits*⟩ ⟨a hearing *deficit*⟩ **b** : DISADVANTAGE ⟨scored two runs to overcome a 2–1 *deficit*⟩
2 a : an excess of expenditure over revenue **b** : a loss in business operations

deficit spending *noun* (1938)
: the spending of public funds raised by borrowing rather than by taxation

de·fi·er \di-'fī(-ə)r\ *noun* (1585)
: one that defies

def·i·lade \'de-fə-,lād, -,läd\ *transitive verb* **-lad·ed; -lad·ing** [probably from *de-* + *-filade* (as in *enfilade*)] (1828)
: to arrange (fortifications) so as to protect the lines from frontal or enfilading fire and the interior from fire from above or behind
— **defilade** *noun*

¹**de·file** \di-'fī(ə)l, dē-\ *transitive verb* **de·filed; de·fil·ing** [Middle English, alteration (influenced by Old English *fȳlan* to defile) of *defoulen* to trample, defile, from Old French *defouler* to trample, from *de-* + *fouler* to trample, literally, to full — more at FULL] (14th century)
: to make unclean or impure: as **a** : to corrupt the purity or perfection of : DEBASE ⟨the countryside *defiled* by billboards⟩ **b** : to violate the chastity of : DEFLOWER **c** : to make physically unclean especially with something unpleasant or contaminating ⟨boots *defiled* with blood⟩ **d** : to violate the sanctity of : DESECRATE ⟨*defile* a sanctuary⟩ **e** : SULLY, DISHONOR
synonym see CONTAMINATE
— **de·file·ment** \-'fī(ə)l-mənt\ *noun*
— **de·fil·er** \-'fī-lər\ *noun*

²**de·file** \di-'fī(ə)l, 'dē-,fīl\ *noun* [French *défilé*, from past participle of *défiler*] (1685)
: a narrow passage or gorge

³**de·file** \di-'fī(ə)l, 'dē-,fīl\ *intransitive verb* **de·filed; de·fil·ing** [French *défiler*, from *dé-* + *filer* to move in a column — more at FILE] (1705)
: to march off in a line

de·fin·able \di-'fī-nə-bəl\ *adjective* (circa 1660)
1 : able to be defined
2 : able to be specified to have a particular function or operation ⟨*definable* keys⟩
— **de·fin·ably** \-'fī-nə-blē\ *adverb*

de·fine \di-'fīn\ *verb* **de·fined; de·fin·ing** [Middle English, from Middle French & Latin; Middle French *definer*, from Latin *definire*, from *de-* + *finire* to limit, end, from *finis* boundary, end] (14th century)
transitive verb
1 a : to determine or identify the essential qualities or meaning of ⟨whatever *defines* us as human⟩ **b** : to discover and set forth the meaning of (as a word) **c** : to create on a computer ⟨*define* a window⟩ ⟨*define* a procedure⟩
2 a : to fix or mark the limits of : DEMARCATE ⟨rigidly *defined* property lines⟩ **b** : to make distinct, clear, or detailed especially in outline ⟨the issues aren't too well *defined*⟩
3 : CHARACTERIZE, DISTINGUISH ⟨you *define* yourself by the choices you make —*Denison University Bulletin*⟩
intransitive verb
: to make a definition
— **de·fine·ment** \-'fīn-mənt\ *noun*
— **de·fin·er** \-'fī-nər\ *noun*

de·fin·i·en·dum \di-,fi-nē-'en-dəm\ *noun, plural* **-da** \-də\ [Latin, something to be defined, neuter of *definiendus*, gerundive of *definire*] (1871)
: an expression that is being defined

de·fin·i·ens \di-'fi-nē-,enz\ *noun, plural* **de·fin·i·en·tia** \di-,fi-nē-'en(t)-shē-ə\ [Latin, present participle of *definire*] (1871)
: an expression that defines : DEFINITION

def·i·nite \'de-fə-nit, 'def-nət\ *adjective* [Latin *definitus*, past participle of *definire*] (1553)
1 : having distinct or certain limits ⟨set *definite* standards for pupils to meet⟩
2 a : free of all ambiguity, uncertainty, or obscurity ⟨demanded a *definite* answer⟩ **b** : UNQUESTIONABLE, DECIDED ⟨the quarterback was a *definite* hero today⟩
3 : typically designating an identified or immediately identifiable person or thing ⟨the *definite* article *the*⟩
4 a : being constant in number, usually less than 20, and occurring in multiples of the petal number ⟨stamens *definite*⟩ **b** : CYMOSE ⟨a *definite* inflorescence⟩
synonym see EXPLICIT
— **def·i·nite·ly** *adverb*
— **def·i·nite·ness** *noun*

definite integral *noun* (1860)
: the difference between the values of the integral of a given function *f*(*x*) for an upper value *b* and a lower value *a* of the independent variable *x*

def·i·ni·tion \,de-fə-'ni-shən\ *noun* [Middle English *diffinicioun*, from Middle French *definition*, from Latin *definition-, definitio*, from *definire*] (14th century)
1 : an act of determining; *specifically* : the formal proclamation of a Roman Catholic dogma
2 a : a statement expressing the essential nature of something **b** : a statement of the meaning of a word or word group or a sign or symbol ⟨dictionary *definitions*⟩ **c** : a product of defining
3 : the action or process of defining
4 a : the action or the power of describing, explaining, or making definite and clear ⟨the *definition* of a telescope⟩ ⟨her comic genius is beyond *definition*⟩ **b** (1) : clarity of visual presentation : distinctness of outline or detail ⟨high-*definition* television⟩ (2) : clarity especially of musical sound in reproduction **c** : sharp demarcation of outlines or limits ⟨a jacket with distinct waist *definition*⟩
— **def·i·ni·tion·al** \-'ni-shə-n°l\ *adjective*

¹**de·fin·i·tive** \di-'fi-nə-tiv\ *adjective* [Middle English *diffinityf*, from Middle French *definitif*, from Latin *definitivus*, from *definitus*] (14th century)
1 : serving to provide a final solution or to end a situation ⟨a *definitive* victory⟩
2 : authoritative and apparently exhaustive ⟨a *definitive* edition⟩
3 a : serving to define or specify precisely ⟨*definitive* laws⟩ **b** : serving as a perfect example : QUINTESSENTIAL ⟨a *definitive* bourgeois⟩
4 : fully differentiated or developed ⟨a *definitive* organ⟩
5 *of a postage stamp* : issued as a regular stamp for the country or territory in which it is to be used
synonym see CONCLUSIVE
— **de·fin·i·tive·ly** *adverb*
— **de·fin·i·tive·ness** *noun*

²**definitive** *noun* (1951)
: a definitive postage stamp — compare PROVISIONAL

definitive host *noun* (1901)
: the host in which the sexual reproduction of a parasite takes place — compare INTERMEDIATE HOST 1

de·fi·ni·tize \'de-fə-nə-,tīz, di-'fi-\ *transitive verb* **-tized; -tiz·ing** (1876)
: to make definite

de·fi·ni·tude \di-'fi-nə-,tüd, -,tyüd\ *noun* [irregular from *definite*] (1836)
: PRECISION, DEFINITENESS

def·la·grate \'def-lə-,grāt\ *verb* **-grat·ed; -grat·ing** [Latin *deflagratus*, past participle of *deflagrare* to burn down, from *de-* + *flagrare* to burn — more at BLACK] (circa 1727)
transitive verb
: to cause to deflagrate — compare DETONATE 1
intransitive verb
: to burn rapidly with intense heat and sparks being given off
— **def·la·gra·tion** \,def-lə-'grā-shən\ *noun*

de·flate \di-'flāt, dē-\ *verb* **de·flat·ed; de·flat·ing** [*de-* + *-flate* (as in *inflate*)] (1891)
transitive verb
1 : to release air or gas from
2 : to reduce in size, importance, or effectiveness ⟨*deflate* his ego with cutting remarks⟩
3 : to reduce (a price level) or cause (a volume of credit) to contract
intransitive verb
: to lose firmness through or as if through the escape of contained gas
synonym see CONTRACT
— **de·fla·tor** *also* **de·fla·ter** \-'flā-tər\ *noun*

de·fla·tion \di-'flā-shən, ,dē-\ *noun* (1891)
1 : an act or instance of deflating : the state of being deflated
2 : a contraction in the volume of available money or credit that results in a general decline in prices
3 : the erosion of soil by the wind
— **de·fla·tion·ary** \-shə-,ner-ē\ *adjective*

de·flect \di-'flekt, dē-\ *verb* [Latin *deflectere* to bend down, turn aside, from *de-* + *flectere* to bend] (circa 1555)
transitive verb
: to turn aside especially from a straight course or fixed direction
intransitive verb
: to turn aside : DEVIATE
— **de·flect·able** \-'flek-tə-bəl\ *adjective*
— **de·flec·tive** \-tiv\ *adjective*
— **de·flec·tor** \-tər\ *noun*

de·flec·tion \di-'flek-shən, dē-\ *noun* (1605)
1 : a turning aside or off course : DEVIATION
2 : the departure of an indicator or pointer from the zero reading on the scale of an instrument

de·flexed \'dē-,flekst, di-'\ *adjective* [Latin *deflexus,* past participle of *deflectere*] (1826)
: turned abruptly downward ⟨a *deflexed* leaf⟩

de·flo·ra·tion \,def-lə-'rā-shən, ,dē-flō-\ *noun* [Middle English *defloracioun,* from Middle French & Late Latin; Middle French *defloracion,* from Late Latin *defloration-, defloratio,* from *deflorare*] (15th century)
: rupture of the hymen

de·flow·er \(,)dē-'flaů(-ə)r\ *transitive verb* [Middle English *deflouren,* from Middle French or Late Latin; Old French *desflorer,* from Late Latin *deflorare,* from Latin *de-* + *flor-, flos* flower — more at BLOW] (14th century)
1 : to deprive of virginity
2 : to take away the prime beauty of
— **de·flow·er·er** *noun*

de·fog \(,)dē-'fòg, -'fäg\ *transitive verb* (1904)
: to remove fog or condensed moisture from
— **de·fog·ger** *noun*

de·fo·li·ant \(,)dē-'fō-lē-ənt\ *noun* (1943)
: a chemical spray or dust applied to plants in order to cause the leaves to drop off prematurely

de·fo·li·ate \-lē-,āt\ *transitive verb* [Late Latin *defoliatus,* past participle of *defoliare,* from Latin *de-* + *folium* leaf — more at BLADE] (1791)
: to deprive of leaves especially prematurely
— **de·fo·li·a·tion** \(,)dē-,fō-lē-'ā-shən\ *noun*
— **de·fo·li·a·tor** \(,)dē-'fō-lē-,ā-tər\ *noun*

de·force \(,)dē-'fōrs, -'fòrs\ *transitive verb* [Middle English, from Middle French *deforcier,* from *de-* + *forcier* to force] (15th century)
1 : to keep (as lands) by force from the rightful owner
2 : to eject (a person) from possession by force
— **de·force·ment** \-'fōr-smənt, -'fòr-\ *noun*

de·for·es·ta·tion \(,)dē-,fòr-ə-'stā-shən, -,fär-\ *noun* (1874)
: the action or process of clearing of forests; *also* : the state of having been cleared of forests
— **de·for·est** \(')dē-'fòr-əst, -'fär-\ *transitive verb*

de·form \di-'fòrm, dē-\ *verb* [Middle English, from Old French or Latin; Old French *deformer,* from Latin *deformare,* from *de-* + *formare* to form, from *forma* form] (15th century)
transitive verb
1 : to spoil the form of
2 a : to spoil the looks of : DISFIGURE ⟨a face *deformed* by bitterness⟩ **b** : to mar the character of ⟨a marriage *deformed* by jealousy⟩
3 : to alter the shape of by stress
intransitive verb
: to become misshapen or changed in shape ☆

— **de·form·able** \-mə-bəl\ *adjective*

de·for·mal·ize \(,)dē-'fòr-mə-,līz\ *transitive verb* (1880)
: to make less formal

de·for·ma·tion \,dē-,fòr-'mā-shən, ,de-fər-\ *noun* (15th century)
1 : alteration of form or shape; *also* : the product of such alteration
2 : the action of deforming : the state of being deformed
3 : change for the worse
— **de·for·ma·tion·al** \-shə-nºl\ *adjective*

de·for·ma·tive \di-'fòr-mə-tiv, dē-\ *adjective* (1641)
: tending to deform

de·formed *adjective* (15th century)
: distorted or unshapely in form : MISSHAPEN

de·for·mi·ty \di-'fòr-mə-tē, dē-\ *noun, plural* **-ties** [Middle English *deformite,* from Middle French *defformeteit,* from Latin *deformitat-, deformitas,* from *deformis* deformed, from *de-* + *forma*] (15th century)
1 : the state of being deformed
2 : IMPERFECTION, BLEMISH: as **a** : a physical blemish or distortion : DISFIGUREMENT **b** : a moral or aesthetic flaw or defect

de·fraud \di-'fròd, dē-\ *transitive verb* [Middle English, from Middle French *defrauder,* from Latin *defraudare,* from *de-* + *fraudare* to cheat, from *fraud-, fraus* fraud] (14th century)
: to deprive of something by deception or fraud
synonym see CHEAT
— **de·fraud·er** \di-'frò-dər\ *noun*

de·fray \di-'frā, dē-\ *transitive verb* [Middle French *deffrayer,* from *des-* de- + *frayer* to expend, from Old French, from (assumed) Old French *frai* expenditure, literally, damage by breaking, from Latin *fractum,* neuter of *fractus,* past participle of *frangere* to break — more at BREAK] (1536)
1 : to provide for the payment of : PAY
2 *archaic* : to bear the expenses of
— **de·fray·able** \-ə-bəl\ *adjective*
— **de·fray·al** \-'frā(-ə)l\ *noun*

de·frock \(,)dē-'fräk\ *transitive verb* (1581)
1 : to deprive (as a priest) of the right to exercise the functions of office
2 : to remove from a position of honor or privilege

de·frost \di-'fròst, 'dē-,\ (1895)
transitive verb
1 : to release from a frozen state ⟨*defrost* meat⟩
2 : to free from ice ⟨*defrost* the refrigerator⟩
intransitive verb
: to thaw out especially from a deep-frozen state
— **de·frost·er** *noun*

deft \'deft\ *adjective* [Middle English *defte* gentle — more at DAFT] (15th century)
: characterized by facility and skill
synonym see DEXTEROUS
— **deft·ly** *adverb*
— **deft·ness** \'def(t)-nəs\ *noun*

de·funct \di-'fəŋkt, dē-\ *adjective* [Latin *defunctus,* from past participle of *defungi* to finish, die, from *de-* + *fungi* to perform — more at FUNCTION] (1599)
: no longer living, existing, or functioning ⟨the committee is now *defunct*⟩
synonym see DEAD

de·fund \(,)dē-'fənd\ *transitive verb* (1948)
: to withdraw funding from

de·fuse \(,)dē-'fyüz\ *transitive verb* (1943)
1 : to remove the fuse from (as a mine or bomb)
2 : to make less harmful, potent, or tense ⟨*defuse* the crisis⟩

¹de·fy \di-'fī, dē-\ *transitive verb* **de·fied; de·fy·ing** [Middle English, to renounce faith in, challenge, from Middle French *defier,* from *de-* + *fier* to entrust, from (assumed) Vulgar Latin *fidare,* alteration of Latin *fidere* to trust — more at BIDE] (14th century)
1 *archaic* : to challenge to combat

2 : to challenge to do something considered impossible : DARE
3 : to confront with assured power of resistance : DISREGARD ⟨*defy* public opinion⟩
4 : to resist attempts at : WITHSTAND ⟨the paintings *defy* classification⟩

²de·fy \di-'fī, 'dē-,\ *noun, plural* **defies** (1580)
: CHALLENGE, DEFIANCE

dé·ga·gé \,dā-gä-'zhā\ *adjective* [French, from past participle of *dégager* to put at ease, from Old French *desgagier* to redeem a pledge, free, from *des-* de- + *gage* pledge — more at GAGE] (1696)
1 : free of constraint : NONCHALANT
2 : being free and easy ⟨clothes with a *dégagé* look⟩
3 : extended with toe pointed in preparation for a ballet step

de·gas \(,)dē-'gas\ *transitive verb* (1928)
: to remove gas from ⟨*degas* an electron tube⟩

de Gaull·ism \di-'gō-,li-zəm, -'gò-\ *noun* (1943)
: GAULLISM
— **de Gaull·ist** \-ləst\ *noun*

de·gauss \(,)dē-'gaůs\ *transitive verb* [de- + *gauss,* after Karl F. *Gauss*] (circa 1940)
: to remove or neutralize the magnetic field of ⟨*degauss* a ship⟩ ⟨*degauss* a magnetic tape⟩
— **de·gauss·er** *noun*

de·gen·er·a·cy \di-'jen-rə-sē, -'je-nə-, dē-\ *noun, plural* **-cies** (1664)
1 : the state of being degenerate
2 : the process of becoming degenerate
3 : sexual perversion
4 : the coding of an amino acid by more than one codon

¹de·gen·er·ate \di-'jen-rət, -'je-nə-, dē-\ *adjective* [Middle English *degenerat,* from Latin *degeneratus,* past participle of *degenerare* to degenerate, from *de-* + *gener-, genus* race, kind — more at KIN] (15th century)
1 a : having declined (as in nature, character, structure, or function) from an ancestral or former state **b** : having sunk to a condition below that which is normal to a type; *especially* : having sunk to a lower and usually corrupt and vicious state **c** : DEGRADED 2
2 : being mathematically simpler (as by having a factor or constant equal to zero) than the typical case ⟨a *degenerate* hyperbola⟩
3 : characterized by atoms stripped of their electrons and by very great density ⟨*degenerate* matter⟩; *also* : consisting of degenerate matter ⟨a *degenerate* star⟩
4 : having two or more states or subdivisions ⟨*degenerate* energy level⟩
5 : having more than one codon representing an amino acid; *also* : being such a codon
synonym see VICIOUS
— **de·gen·er·ate·ly** *adverb*
— **de·gen·er·ate·ness** *noun*

☆ **SYNONYMS**

Deform, distort, contort, warp means to mar or spoil by or as if by twisting. DEFORM may imply a change of shape through stress, injury, or some accident of growth ⟨his face was *deformed* by hatred⟩. DISTORT and CONTORT both imply a wrenching from the natural, normal, or justly proportioned, but CONTORT suggests a more involved twisting and a more grotesque and painful result ⟨the odd camera angle *distorts* the figure in the photograph⟩ ⟨disease had painfully *contorted* his body⟩. WARP indicates physically an uneven shrinking that bends or twists out of a flat plane ⟨*warped* floorboards⟩.

\ə\ abut \ə\ kitten \ər\ further \a\ ash \ā\ ace
\ä\ mop, mar \aů\ out \ch\ chin \e\ bet \ē\ easy
\g\ go \i\ hit \ī\ ice \j\ job \ŋ\ sing \ō\ go
\ò\ law \òi\ boy \th\ thin \t͟h\ the \ü\ loot \ů\ foot
\y\ yet \zh\ vision *see also* Guide to Pronunciation

²**de·gen·er·ate** \di-'je-nə-ˌrāt, dē-\ (1545)
intransitive verb
1 : to pass from a higher to a lower type or condition **:** DETERIORATE
2 : to sink into a low intellectual or moral state
3 : to decline in quality ⟨the poetry gradually *degenerates* into jingles⟩
4 : to decline from a condition or from the standards of a species, race, or breed
5 : to evolve or develop into a less autonomous or less functionally active form ⟨*degenerated* into dependent parasites⟩
transitive verb
: to cause to degenerate

³**de·gen·er·ate** \di-'jen-rət, -'je-nə-, dē-\ *noun* (1555)
: one that is degenerate: as **a :** one degraded from the normal moral standard **b :** a sexual pervert **c :** one showing signs of reversion to an earlier culture stage

de·gen·er·a·tion \di-ˌje-nə-'rā-shən, ˌdē-\ *noun* (15th century)
1 : degenerate condition
2 : a lowering of effective power, vitality, or essential quality to an enfeebled and worsened kind or state
3 : intellectual, moral, or artistic decline
4 a : progressive deterioration of physical characters from a level representing the norm of earlier generations or forms **b :** deterioration of a tissue or an organ in which its function is diminished or its structure is impaired
synonym see DETERIORATION

de·gen·er·a·tive \di-'je-nə-rə-tiv, -'jen-rə-; -'je-nə-ˌrā-; dē-\ *adjective* (circa 1846)
: of, relating to, involving, or causing degeneration ⟨a *degenerative* disease⟩

de·gla·ci·a·tion \(ˌ)dē-ˌglā-s(h)ē-'ā-shən\ *noun* (1895)
: the melting of ice; *specifically* **:** the retreat of a glacier or ice sheet
— **de·gla·ci·at·ed** \-'glā-s(h)ē-ˌā-təd\ *adjective*

de·glam·or·ize \(ˌ)dē-'gla-mə-ˌrīz\ *transitive verb* (1938)
: to remove the glamor from
— **de·glam·or·iza·tion** \(ˌ)dē-ˌgla-mə-rə-'zā-shən\ *noun*

¹**de·glaze** \(ˌ)dē-'glāz\ *transitive verb* (circa 1889)
: to remove the glaze from

²**deglaze** *transitive verb* [modification of French *déglacer*, literally, to melt the ice from, from *dé-* + *glacer* to freeze — more at GLACÉ] (1968)
: to dissolve the small particles of sautéed meat remaining in (a pan) by adding a liquid and heating

de·glu·ti·tion \ˌdē-glü-'ti-shən, ˌde-glü-\ *noun* [French *déglutition*, from Latin *deglutire* to swallow down, from *de-* + *glutire, gluttire* to swallow — more at GLUTTON] (1650)
: the act or process of swallowing

de·grad·able \di-'grā-də-bəl, dē-\ *adjective* (circa 1962)
: capable of being chemically degraded ⟨*degradable* detergents⟩ — compare BIODEGRADABLE

deg·ra·da·tion \ˌde-grə-'dā-shən\ *noun* (circa 1535)
1 : the act or process of degrading
2 a : decline to a low, destitute, or demoralized state **b :** moral or intellectual decadence **:** DEGENERATION
— **deg·ra·da·tive** \'de-grə-ˌdā-tiv\ *adjective*

de·grade \di-'grād, dē-\ *verb* [Middle English, from Old French *degrader*, from Late Latin *degradare*, from Latin *de-* + *gradus* step, grade — more at GRADE] (14th century)
transitive verb
1 a : to lower in grade, rank, or status **:** DEMOTE **b :** to strip of rank or honors **c :** to lower to an inferior or less effective level **d :** to scale down in desirability or salability

2 a : to bring to low esteem or into disrepute
b : to drag down in moral or intellectual character **:** CORRUPT
3 : to impair in respect to some physical property
4 : to wear down by erosion
5 : to reduce the complexity of (a chemical compound) **:** DECOMPOSE
intransitive verb
1 : to pass from a higher grade or class to a lower
2 *of a chemical compound* **:** to become reduced in complexity
— **de·grad·er** *noun*
— **de·grad·ing·ly** \-'grā-diŋ-lē\ *adverb*

de·grad·ed *adjective* (1643)
1 : reduced far below ordinary standards of civilized life and conduct
2 : characterized by degeneration of structure or function
— **de·grad·ed·ly** *adverb*

de·gran·u·la·tion \(ˌ)dē-ˌgra-nyə-'lā-shən\ *noun* (circa 1941)
: the process of losing granules ⟨*degranulation* of leukocytes⟩

de·grease \(ˌ)dē-'grēs, -'grēz\ *transitive verb* (circa 1889)
: to remove grease from
— **de·greas·er** \-'grē-sər, -zər\ *noun*

de·gree \di-'grē\ *noun* [Middle English, from Old French *degré*, from (assumed) Vulgar Latin *degradus*, from Latin *de-* + *gradus*] (13th century)
1 : a step or stage in a process, course, or order of classification ⟨advanced by *degrees*⟩
2 a : a rank or grade of official, ecclesiastical, or social position ⟨people of low *degree*⟩ **b** *archaic* **:** a particular standing especially as to dignity or worth **c :** the civil condition or status of a person
3 : a step in a direct line of descent or in the line of ascent to a common ancestor
4 a *obsolete* **:** STEP, STAIR **b** *archaic* **:** a member of a series arranged in steps
5 : a measure of damage to tissue caused by injury or disease — compare FIRST-DEGREE BURN, SECOND-DEGREE BURN, THIRD-DEGREE BURN
6 a : the extent, measure, or scope of an action, condition, or relation ⟨different in *degree* but not in kind⟩ **b :** relative intensity ⟨a high *degree* of stress⟩ **c :** one of the forms or sets of forms used in the comparison of an adjective or adverb **d :** a legal measure of guilt or negligence ⟨found guilty of robbery in the first *degree*⟩
7 a : a title conferred on students by a college, university, or professional school on completion of a program of study **b :** a grade of membership attained in a ritualistic order or society **c :** an academic title conferred to honor distinguished achievement or service **d :** the formal ceremonies observed in the conferral of such a distinction
8 : a unit of measure for angles equal to an angle with its vertex at the center of a circle and its sides cutting off $\frac{1}{360}$ of the circumference; *also* **:** a unit of measure for arcs of a circle equal to the amount of arc that subtends a central angle of one degree
9 *archaic* **:** a position or space on the earth or in the heavens as measured by degrees of latitude
10 a : a step, note, or tone of a musical scale
b : a line or space of the musical staff
11 : one of the divisions or intervals marked on a scale of a measuring instrument; *specifically* **:** any of various units for measuring temperature
12 a : the sum of the exponents of the variables in the term of highest degree in a polynomial, polynomial function, or polynomial equation **b :** the sum of the exponents of the variable factors of a monomial **c :** the greatest power of the derivative of highest order in a differential equation after the equation has

been rationalized and cleared of fractions with respect to the derivative
— **de·greed** \-'grēd\ *adjective*
— **to a degree 1 :** to a remarkable extent **2** **:** in a small way

de·gree–day \di-'grē-ˌdā\ *noun* (1832)
: a unit that represents one degree of difference from a given point (as 65°) in the mean daily outdoor temperature and that is used especially to measure heat requirements

degree of freedom (1867)
1 : any of a limited number of ways in which a body may move or in which a dynamic system may change
2 : one of the capabilities of a statistic for variation of which there are as many as the number of unrestricted and independent variables determining its value

de·gres·sive \di-'gre-siv, 'dē-\ *adjective* [*de-* + *-gressive* (as in *progressive*)] (1886)
: tending to descend or decrease
— **de·gres·sive·ly** *adverb*

dé·grin·go·lade \dā-ˌgraⁿ(ŋ)-gə-'läd\ *noun* [French, from *dégringoler* to tumble down, from Middle French *desgringueler*, from *des-de-* + *gringueler* to tumble, from Middle Dutch *crinkelen* to make curl, from *crinc, cring* ring, circle] (1883)
: a rapid decline or deterioration (as in strength, position, or condition) **:** DOWNFALL

de·gum \(ˌ)dē-'gəm\ *transitive verb* (1887)
: to free from gum, a gummy substance, or sericin

de·gus·ta·tion \ˌdē-gəs-'tā-shən, de-\ *noun* [French *dégustation*, from Latin *degustation-, degustatio*, from *degustare* to taste, from *de-* + *gustare* to taste — more at CHOOSE] (circa 1656)
: the action or an instance of tasting especially in a series of small portions
— **de·gust** \di-'gəst, dē-\ *transitive verb*

de haut en bas \də-ō-täⁿ-bä\ *adjective or adverb* [French, literally, from top to bottom] (1696)
: of superiority **:** of or with condescension

de·hisce \di-'his\ *intransitive verb* **de·hisced; de·hisc·ing** [Latin *dehiscere* to split open, from *de-* + *hiscere* to gape; akin to Latin *hiare* to yawn — more at YAWN] (1657)
: to split along a natural line; *also* **:** to discharge contents by so splitting ⟨seedpods *dehiscing* at maturity⟩

de·his·cence \di-'hi-sᵊn(t)s\ *noun* [New Latin *dehiscentia*, from Latin *dehiscent-, dehiscens*, present participle of *dehiscere*] (circa 1828)
: an act or instance of dehiscing ⟨pollen freed by *dehiscence* of the anther⟩
— **de·his·cent** \-sᵊnt\ *adjective*

de·horn \(ˌ)dē-'hȯrn\ *transitive verb* (1888)
1 : to deprive of horns
2 : to prevent the growth of the horns of
— **de·horn·er** *noun*

de·hu·man·ize \(ˌ)dē-'hyü-mə-ˌnīz, (ˌ)dē-'yü-\ *transitive verb* (1818)
: to deprive of human qualities, personality, or spirit
— **de·hu·man·iza·tion** \(ˌ)dē-ˌhyü-mə-nə-'zā-shən, (ˌ)dē-ˌyü-\ *noun*

de·hu·mid·i·fy \ˌdē-hyü-'mi-də-ˌfī, ˌdē-yü-\ *transitive verb* (1927)
: to remove moisture from (as air)
— **de·hu·mid·i·fi·ca·tion** \-ˌmi-də-fə-'kā-shən\ *noun*
— **de·hu·mid·i·fi·er** \-'mi-də-ˌfī(-ə)r\ *noun*

de·hy·drate \(ˌ)dē-'hī-ˌdrāt\ (1876)
transitive verb
1 a : to remove bound water or hydrogen and oxygen from (a chemical compound) in the proportion in which they form water **b :** to remove water from (as foods)
2 : to deprive of vitality or savor
intransitive verb
: to lose water or body fluids
— **de·hy·dra·tor** \-ˌdrā-tər\ *noun*

de·hy·dra·tion \ˌdē-ˌhī-'drā-shən\ *noun* (1854)
: the process of dehydrating; *especially* **:** an abnormal depletion of body fluids

de·hy·dro·chlo·ri·nase \(ˌ)dē-ˌhī-drə-'klōr-ə-ˌnās, -'klȯr-, -ˌnāz\ *noun* (1956)
: an enzyme that dehydrochlorinates a chlorinated hydrocarbon (as DDT) and is found especially in some DDT resistant insects

de·hy·dro·chlo·ri·na·tion \-ˌklōr-ə-'nā-shən, -ˌklȯr-\ *noun* (1936)
: the process of removing hydrogen and chlorine or hydrogen chloride from a compound
— **de·hy·dro·chlo·ri·nate** \-'klōr-ə-ˌnāt, -'klȯr-\ *transitive verb*

de·hy·dro·ge·nase \ˌdē-(ˌ)hī-'drä-jə-ˌnās, (ˌ)dē-'hī-drə-jə-, -ˌnāz\ *noun* [International Scientific Vocabulary]
: an enzyme that accelerates the removal of hydrogen from metabolites and its transfer to other substances ⟨succinic *dehydrogenase*⟩

de·hy·dro·ge·na·tion \ˌdē-(ˌ)hī-ˌdrä-jə-'nā-shən, (ˌ)dē-ˌhī-drə-jə-\ *noun* (1866)
: the removal of hydrogen from a chemical compound
— **de·hy·dro·ge·nate** \ˌdē-(ˌ)hī-'drä-jə-ˌnāt, (ˌ)dē-'hī-drə-jə-\ *transitive verb*

de·ice \(ˌ)dē-'īs\ *transitive verb* (1934)
: to rid or keep free of ice
— **de·ic·er** *noun*

de·i·cide \'dē-ə-ˌsīd, 'dā-ə-\ *noun* [ultimately from Latin *deus* god + *-cidium, -cida* -cide — more at DEITY] (1611)
1 : the act of killing a divine being or a symbolic substitute of such a being
2 : the killer or destroyer of a god

deic·tic \'dīk-tik *also* 'dāk-\ *adjective* [Greek *deiktikos* able to show, from *deiktos,* verbal of *deiknynai* to show — more at DICTION] (1876)
: showing or pointing out directly ⟨the words *this, that,* and *those* have a *deictic* function⟩

de·i·fi·ca·tion \ˌdē-ə-fə-'kā-shən, ˌdā-\ *noun* (14th century)
: the act or an instance of deifying

de·i·fy \'dē-ə-ˌfī, 'dā-\ *transitive verb* **-fied; -fy·ing** [Middle English, from Middle French *deifier,* from Late Latin *deificare,* from Latin *deus* god + *-ficare* -fy] (14th century)
1 a : to make a god of **b :** to take as an object of worship
2 : to glorify as of supreme worth

deign \'dān\ *verb* [Middle English, from Old French *deignier,* from Latin *dignare, dignari,* from *dignus* worthy — more at DECENT] (14th century)
intransitive verb
: to condescend reluctantly and with a strong sense of the affront to one's superiority that is involved
transitive verb
: to condescend to give or offer

deil \'dē(ə)l\ *noun* [Middle English *devel, del*] (15th century)
Scottish **:** DEVIL

de·in·dus·tri·al·iza·tion \(ˌ)dē-in-ˌdəs-trē-ə-lə-'zā-shən\ *noun* (1940)
: the reduction or destruction of a nation's industrial capacity
— **de·in·dus·tri·al·ize** \(ˌ)dē-in-'dəs-trē-ə-ˌlīz\ *verb*

dei·non·y·chus \(ˌ)dī-'nä-ni-kəs\ *noun* [New Latin, from Greek *deinos* terrifying + *-onychos* -clawed (from *onych-, onyx* claw, nail) — more at DIRE, NAIL] (1969)
: any of a genus (*Deinonychus*) of small bipedal carnivorous dinosaurs from the Cretaceous

de·in·sti·tu·tion·al·iza·tion \(ˌ)dē-ˌin(t)-stə-ˌtü-shə-nə-lə-'zā-shən, -ˌtyü-\ *noun* (1955)
1 : the release of institutionalized individuals (as mental patients) from institutional care to care in the community
2 : the reform or modification of an institution to remove or disguise its institutional character
— **de·in·sti·tu·tion·al·ize** \-'tü-shə-nə-ˌlīz, -'tyü-\ *transitive verb*

de·ion·ize \(ˌ)dē-'ī-ə-ˌnīz\ *transitive verb* (1906)
: to remove ions from ⟨*deionize* water by ion exchange⟩
— **de·ion·iza·tion** \(ˌ)dē-ˌī-ə-nə-'zā-shən\ *noun*
— **de·ion·iz·er** \-ˌnī-zər\ *noun*

de·ism \'dē-ˌi-zəm, 'dā-\ *noun, often capitalized* (1682)
: a movement or system of thought advocating natural religion, emphasizing morality, and in the 18th century denying the interference of the Creator with the laws of the universe
— **de·ist** \'dē-ist, 'dā-\ *noun, often capitalized*
— **de·is·tic** \dē-'is-tik, dā-\ *adjective*
— **de·is·ti·cal** \-ti-kəl\ *adjective*
— **de·is·ti·cal·ly** \-ti-k(ə)lē\ *adverb*

de·i·ty \'dē-ə-tē, 'dā-\ *noun, plural* **-ties** [Middle English *deitee,* from Old French *deité,* from Late Latin *deitat-, deitas,* from Latin *deus* god; akin to Old English *Tīw,* god of war, Latin *divus* god, *dies* day, Greek *dios* heavenly, Sanskrit *deva* heavenly, god] (14th century)
1 a : the rank or essential nature of a god **:** DIVINITY **b** *capitalized* **:** GOD 1, SUPREME BEING
2 : a god or goddess ⟨the *deities* of ancient Greece⟩
3 : one exalted or revered as supremely good or powerful

deix·is \'dīk-sis *also* 'dāk-\ *noun* [Greek, literally, display, from *deiknynai* to show — more at DICTION] (1949)
: the pointing or specifying function of some words (as definite articles and demonstrative pronouns) whose denotation changes from one discourse to another

dé·jà vu \ˌdā-ˌzhä-'vü, dā-zhà-vᴇ̄\ *noun* [French, adjective, literally, already seen] (1903)
1 a : the illusion of remembering scenes and events when experienced for the first time **b :** a feeling that one has seen or heard something before
2 : something overly or unpleasantly familiar

¹de·ject \di-'jekt, dē-\ *adjective* (15th century)
archaic **:** DEJECTED

²deject *transitive verb* [Middle English, to throw down, from Latin *dejectus,* past participle of *deicere,* from *de-* + *jacere* to throw — more at JET] (1581)
: to make gloomy

de·jec·ta \di-'jek-tə, dē-\ *noun plural* [New Latin, from Latin, neuter plural of *dejectus*] (1887)
: FECES, EXCREMENT

de·ject·ed \di-'jek-təd, dē-\ *adjective* (1581)
1 : cast down in spirits **:** DEPRESSED
2 a *obsolete, of the eyes* **:** DOWNCAST **b** *archaic* **:** thrown down
3 *obsolete* **:** lowered in rank or condition
— **de·ject·ed·ly** *adverb*
— **de·ject·ed·ness** *noun*

de·jec·tion \di-'jek-shən, dē-\ *noun* (15th century)
: lowness of spirits

de ju·re \(ˌ)dē-'jùr-ē, (ˌ)dā-'yùr-\ *adverb or adjective* [Medieval Latin] (1611)
: by right **:** of right

deka- or **dek-** — see DECA-

deka·gram \'de-kə-ˌgram\ *noun* (circa 1879)
— see METRIC SYSTEM table

deka·li·ter \-ˌlē-tər\ *noun* (circa 1879)
— see METRIC SYSTEM table

deka·me·ter \-ˌmē-tər\ *noun* (circa 1879)
— see METRIC SYSTEM table

deka·met·ric \ˌde-kə-'me-trik\ *adjective* (1968)
: DECAMETRIC

de·lam·i·na·tion \(ˌ)dē-ˌla-mə-'nā-shən\ *noun* (1877)
1 : gastrula formation in which the endoderm is split off as a layer from the inner surface of the blastoderm and the archenteron is represented by the space between this endoderm and the yolk mass

2 : separation into constituent layers
— **de·lam·i·nate** \(ˌ)dē-'la-mə-ˌnāt\ *intransitive verb*

de·late \di-'lāt, dē-\ *transitive verb* **de·lat·ed; de·lat·ing** [Latin *delatus* (past participle of *deferre* to bring down, report, accuse), from *de-* + *latus,* past participle of *ferre* to bear — more at TOLERATE] (15th century)
1 : ACCUSE, DENOUNCE
2 : REPORT, RELATE
— **de·la·tion** \-'lā-shən\ *noun*
— **de·la·tor** \-'lā-tər\ *noun*

Del·a·ware \'de-lə-ˌwar, -ˌwer, -wər\ *noun, plural* **Delaware** *or* **Delawares** [*Delaware* River] (1721)
1 : a member of an American Indian people originally of the Delaware valley
2 : the Algonquian language of the Delaware

¹de·lay \di-'lā, dē-\ *noun* (13th century)
1 a : the act of delaying **:** the state of being delayed **b :** an instance of being delayed
2 : the time during which something is delayed

²delay *verb* [Middle English, from Old French *delaier,* from *de-* + *laier* to leave, perhaps alteration of *laissier,* from Latin *laxare* to slacken, from *laxus* loose — more at SLACK] (14th century)
transitive verb
1 : PUT OFF, POSTPONE
2 : to stop, detain, or hinder for a time
intransitive verb
: to move or act slowly; *also* **:** to cause delay
☆ ☆
— **de·lay·er** *noun*

¹de·le \'dē-(ˌ)lē\ *transitive verb* **de·led; de·le·ing** [Latin, imperative singular of *delēre*] (1705)
: to delete especially from typeset matter

\ə\ abut \ᵊ\ kitten \ər\ further \a\ ash \ā\ ace
\ä\ mop, mar \aù\ out \ch\ chin \e\ bet \ē\ easy
\g\ go \i\ hit \ī\ ice \j\ job \ŋ\ sing \ō\ go
\ȯ\ law \ȯi\ boy \th\ thin \t͟h\ the \ü\ loot \ù\ foot
\y\ yet \zh\ vision *see also* Guide to Pronunciation

²dele *noun* (circa 1751)
: a mark indicating that something is to be deled

¹de·lec·ta·ble \di-'lek-tə-bəl\ *adjective* [Middle English, from Old French, from Latin *delectabilis,* from *delectare* to delight — more at DELIGHT] (15th century)
1 : highly pleasing **:** DELIGHTFUL
2 : DELICIOUS
— **de·lec·ta·bil·i·ty** \-,lek-tə-'bi-lə-tē\ *noun*
— **de·lec·ta·bly** \-blē\ *adverb*

²delectable *noun* (1921)
: something that is delectable

de·lec·ta·tion \,dē-,lek-'tā-shən, di-; ,de-lək-\ *noun* (14th century)
: DELIGHT, ENJOYMENT

del·e·ga·ble \'de-li-gə-bəl\ *adjective* (1660)
: capable of being delegated

del·e·ga·cy \-gə-sē\ *noun, plural* **-cies** (15th century)
1 : a body of delegates **:** BOARD
2 a : the act of delegating **b :** appointment as delegate

¹del·e·gate \'de-li-gət, -,gāt\ *noun* [Middle English *delegat,* from Medieval Latin *delegatus,* from Latin, past participle of *delegare* to delegate, from *de-* + *legare* to send — more at LEGATE] (15th century)
: a person acting for another: as **a :** a representative to a convention or conference **b :** a representative of a U.S. territory in the House of Representatives **c :** a member of the lower house of the legislature of Maryland, Virginia, or West Virginia

²del·e·gate \-,gāt\ *verb* **-gat·ed; -gat·ing** (1530)
transitive verb
1 : to entrust to another ⟨*delegate* authority⟩
2 : to appoint as one's representative
intransitive verb
: to assign responsibility or authority
— **del·e·ga·tee** \,de-li-gə-'tē\ *noun*
— **del·e·ga·tor** \'de-li-gā-tər\ *noun*

del·e·ga·tion \,de-li-'gā-shən\ *noun* (1612)
1 : the act of empowering to act for another
2 : a group of persons chosen to represent others

de·le·git·i·ma·tion \,dē-lə-,ji-tə-'mā-shən\ *noun* (1968)
: a decline in or loss of prestige or authority

de·lete \di-'lēt, dē-\ *transitive verb* **de·let·ed; de·let·ing** [Latin *deletus,* past participle of *delēre* to wipe out, destroy] (circa 1605)
: to eliminate especially by blotting out, cutting out, or erasing

del·e·te·ri·ous \,de-lə-'ti-rē-əs\ *adjective* [Greek *dēlētērios,* from *dēleisthai* to hurt] (1643)
: harmful often in a subtle or unexpected way ⟨*deleterious* effects⟩ ⟨*deleterious* to health⟩
synonym *see* PERNICIOUS
— **del·e·te·ri·ous·ly** *adverb*
— **del·e·te·ri·ous·ness** *noun*

de·le·tion \di-'lē-shən, dē-\ *noun* [Latin *deletion-, deletio* destruction, from *delēre*] (1590)
1 : the act of deleting
2 a : something deleted **b** (1) **:** the absence of a section of genetic material from a chromosome (2) **:** the mutational process that results in a deletion

delft \'delft\ *noun* [*Delft,* Netherlands] (1723)
1 : tin-glazed Dutch earthenware with blue and white or polychrome decoration
2 : a ceramic ware resembling or imitative of Dutch delft

delft·ware \'delft-,war, -,wer\ *noun* (1714)
: DELFT

deli \'de-lē\ *noun, plural* **del·is** (circa 1954)
: DELICATESSEN

¹de·lib·er·ate \di-'li-bə-,rāt\ *verb* **-at·ed; -at·ing** (14th century)
intransitive verb
: to think about or discuss issues and decisions carefully
transitive verb
: to think about deliberately and often with formal discussion before reaching a decision
synonym *see* THINK

²de·lib·er·ate \di-'li-bə-rət, -'lib-rət\ *adjective* [Latin *deliberatus,* past participle of *deliberare* to consider carefully, perhaps alteration of (assumed) *delibrare,* from *de-* + *libra* scale, pound] (15th century)
1 : characterized by or resulting from careful and thorough consideration ⟨a *deliberate* decision⟩
2 : characterized by awareness of the consequences ⟨*deliberate* falsehood⟩
3 : slow, unhurried, and steady as though allowing time for decision on each individual action involved ⟨a *deliberate* pace⟩
synonym *see* VOLUNTARY
— **de·lib·er·ate·ly** *adverb*
— **de·lib·er·ate·ness** *noun*

de·lib·er·a·tion \di-,li-bə-'rā-shən\ *noun* (14th century)
1 a : the act of deliberating **b :** a discussion and consideration by a group of persons of the reasons for and against a measure
2 : the quality or state of being deliberate
— **de·lib·er·a·tive** \-'li-bə-,rāt-iv, -'lib(ə-)rət-\ *adjective*
— **de·lib·er·a·tive·ly** *adverb*
— **de·lib·er·a·tive·ness** *noun*

del·i·ca·cy \'de-li-kə-sē\ *noun, plural* **-cies** (14th century)
1 *obsolete* **a :** the quality or state of being luxurious **b :** INDULGENCE
2 : something pleasing to eat that is considered rare or luxurious ⟨considered caviar a *delicacy*⟩
3 a : the quality or state of being dainty **:** FINENESS ⟨lace of great *delicacy*⟩ **b :** FRAILTY 1
4 : fineness or subtle expressiveness of touch (as in painting or music)
5 a : precise and refined perception and discrimination **b :** extreme sensitivity **:** PRECISION ⟨an electronic instrument of great *delicacy*⟩
6 a : refined sensibility in feeling or conduct **b :** the quality or state of being squeamish
7 : the quality or state of requiring delicate handling

¹del·i·cate \'de-li-kət\ *adjective* [Middle English *delicat,* from Latin *delicatus* delicate, addicted to pleasure; akin to Latin *delicere* to allure] (14th century)
1 : pleasing to the senses: **a :** generally pleasant ⟨the climate's *delicate,* the air most sweet —Shakespeare⟩ **b :** pleasing to the sense of taste or smell especially in a mild or subtle way ⟨a *delicate* aroma⟩ ⟨a robust wine will dominate *delicate* dishes⟩ **c :** marked by daintiness or charm of color, lines, or proportions ⟨a *delicate* floral print⟩ ⟨an ample tear trilled down her *delicate* cheek —Shakespeare⟩ **d :** marked by fineness of structure, workmanship, or texture ⟨a *delicate* tracery⟩ ⟨a *delicate* lace⟩
2 a : marked by keen sensitivity or fine discrimination ⟨*delicate* insights⟩ ⟨a more *delicate* syntactic analysis —R. H. Robins⟩ **b :** FASTIDIOUS, SQUEAMISH ⟨a person of *delicate* tastes⟩
3 a : not robust in health or constitution **:** WEAK, SICKLY ⟨had been considered a *delicate* child⟩ **b :** easily torn or damaged **:** FRAGILE ⟨the *delicate* chain of life⟩
4 a : requiring careful handling: (1) **:** easily unsettled or upset ⟨a *delicate* balance⟩ ⟨the *delicate* relationships defined by the Constitution —*New Yorker*⟩ (2) **:** requiring skill or tact ⟨in a *delicate* position⟩ ⟨*delicate* negotiations⟩ ⟨a *delicate* operation⟩ (3) **:** involving matters of a deeply personal nature **:** SENSITIVE ⟨this is a

delicate matter. Could I possibly speak to you alone —Daphne Du Maurier⟩ **b :** marked by care, skill, or tact ⟨*delicate* handling of a difficult situation⟩
5 : marked by great precision or sensitivity ⟨a *delicate* instrument⟩
synonym *see* CHOICE
— **del·i·cate·ly** *adverb*

²delicate *noun* (15th century)
: something delicate

del·i·ca·tes·sen \,de-li-kə-'te-sᵊn\ *noun plural* [obsolete German (now *Delikatessen*), plural of *Delicatesse* delicacy, from French *délicatesse,* probably from Old Italian *delicatezza,* from *delicato* delicate, from Latin *delicatus*] (1889)
1 : ready-to-eat food products (as cooked meats and prepared salads)
2 *singular, plural* **delicatessens** [*delicatessen (store)*] **:** a store where delicatessen are sold ◇

de·li·cious \di-'li-shəs\ *adjective* [Middle English, from Middle French, from Late Latin *deliciosus,* from Latin *deliciae* delights, from *delicere* to allure] (14th century)
1 : affording great pleasure **:** DELIGHTFUL ⟨*delicious* anecdotes⟩
2 : appealing to one of the bodily senses especially of taste or smell
— **de·li·cious·ly** *adverb*
— **de·li·cious·ness** *noun*

Delicious *noun, plural* **De·li·cious·es** *or* **Delicious** (circa 1903)
: an important red or yellow market apple of American origin that has a crown of five rounded prominences on the end opposite the stem

de·lict \di-'likt, dē-\ *noun* [Latin *delictum* fault, from neuter of *delictus,* past participle of *delinquere*] (1523)
: an offense against the law

¹de·light \di-'līt, dē-\ *noun* (13th century)
1 : a high degree of gratification **:** JOY; *also* **:** extreme satisfaction
2 : something that gives great pleasure
3 *archaic* **:** the power of affording pleasure

²delight *verb* [Middle English *deliten,* from Old French *delitier,* from Latin *delectare,* frequentative of *delicere* to allure, from *de-* + *lacere* to allure] (13th century)
intransitive verb
1 : to take great pleasure ⟨*delighted* in playing the guitar⟩
2 : to give keen enjoyment ⟨a book certain to *delight*⟩
transitive verb
: to give joy or satisfaction to

◇ **WORD HISTORY**
delicatessen The word *delicatessen,* borrowed from a German plural noun meaning "delicacies," began to appear in U.S. publications toward the end of the 19th century, usually in combination with *store* or *shop.* These collocations are partial translations of German compound words such as *Delikatessenhandlung* or *Delikatessengeschäft.* By the 1920s the noun *store* or *shop* was dropped and the word *delicatessen* was used alone for the store. The delicatessen has become an American institution, especially in large urban centers such as New York City, where the *deli* (a clipping that first appeared in the 1950s) is typically a sparely furnished restaurant that serves traditional American Jewish fare such as pastrami and corned beef sandwiches, knishes, and matzo ball soup. More generally in the U.S., *deli* evokes a store or now more commonly a supermarket department that sells cold cuts and prepared foods. It is worth noting that, contrary to some popular notions, *delicatessen* has no etymological connection with the German verb *essen* "to eat."

— **de·light·er** *noun*
de·light·ed *adjective* (1603)
1 *obsolete* : DELIGHTFUL
2 : highly pleased
— **de·light·ed·ly** *adverb*
— **de·light·ed·ness** *noun*
de·light·ful \di-'līt-fəl, dē-\ *adjective* (circa 1530)
: highly pleasing
— **de·light·ful·ly** \-fə-lē\ *adverb*
— **de·light·ful·ness** *noun*
de·light·some \-'līt-səm\ *adjective* (1520)
: very pleasing : DELIGHTFUL
De·li·lah \di-'lī-lə\ *noun* [Hebrew *Dĕlīlāh*]
: the mistress and betrayer of Samson in the book of Judges
de·lim·it \di-'li-mət\ *transitive verb* [French *délimiter,* from Latin *delimitare,* from *de-* + *limitare* to limit, from *limit-, limes* boundary, limit] (1852)
: to fix or define the limits of
— **de·lim·i·ta·tion** \di-,li-mə-'tā-shən, ,dē-\ *noun*
de·lim·it·er \di-'li-mə-tər\ *noun* (1960)
: a character that marks the beginning or end of a unit of data
de·lin·eate \di-'li-nē-,āt\ *transitive verb* **-eat·ed; -eat·ing** [Latin *delineatus,* past participle of *delineare,* from *de-* + *linea* line] (1559)
1 a : to indicate or represent by drawn or painted lines **b** : to mark the outline of ⟨lights *delineating* the narrow streets⟩
2 : to describe, portray, or set forth with accuracy or in detail ⟨*delineate* a character in the story⟩ ⟨*delineate* the steps to be taken by the government⟩
— **de·lin·ea·tor** \-ē-,ā-tər\ *noun*
de·lin·ea·tion \di-,li-nē-'ā-shən\ *noun* (1570)
1 : the act of delineating
2 : something made by delineating
— **de·lin·ea·tive** \-'li-nē-,ā-tiv\ *adjective*
de·lin·quen·cy \di-'liŋ-kwən-sē, -'lin-\ *noun, plural* **-cies** (1636)
1 a : a delinquent act **b** : conduct that is out of accord with accepted behavior or the law; *especially* : JUVENILE DELINQUENCY
2 : a debt on which payment is overdue
¹**de·lin·quent** \-kwənt\ *noun* (15th century)
: a delinquent person
²**delinquent** *adjective* [Latin *delinquent-, delinquens,* present participle of *delinquere* to fail, offend, from *de-* + *linquere* to leave — more at LOAN] (1603)
1 : offending by neglect or violation of duty or of law
2 : being overdue in payment ⟨a *delinquent* charge account⟩
3 : of, relating to, or characteristic of delinquents : marked by delinquency
— **de·lin·quent·ly** *adverb*
del·i·quesce \,de-li-'kwes\ *intransitive verb* **-quesced; -quesc·ing** [Latin *deliquescere,* from *de-* + *liquescere,* inchoative of *liquēre* to be fluid — more at LIQUID] (1756)
1 : to dissolve or melt away
2 : to become soft or liquid with age — used of plant structures (as mushrooms)
del·i·ques·cent \-'kwe-sᵊnt\ *adjective* [Latin *deliquescent-, deliquescens,* present participle of *deliquescere*] (1791)
1 : tending to melt or dissolve; *especially* : tending to undergo gradual dissolution and liquefaction by the attraction and absorption of moisture from the air
2 : having repeated division into branches ⟨elms are *deliquescent* trees⟩ — compare EXCURRENT 2a
— **del·i·ques·cence** \-sᵊn(t)s\ *noun*
de·lir·i·ous \di-'lir-ē-əs\ *adjective* (1599)
1 : of, relating to, or characteristic of delirium
2 : affected with or marked by delirium
— **de·lir·i·ous·ly** *adverb*
— **de·lir·i·ous·ness** *noun*

de·lir·i·um \di-'lir-ē-əm\ *noun* [Latin, from *delirare* to be crazy, literally, to leave the furrow (in plowing), from *de-* + *lira* furrow — more at LEARN] (circa 1563)
1 : a mental disturbance characterized by confusion, disordered speech, and hallucinations
2 : frenzied excitement ⟨he would stride about his room in a *delirium* of joy —Thomas Wolfe⟩
delirium tre·mens \-'trē-mənz, -'tre-\ *noun* [New Latin, literally, trembling delirium] (1865)
: a violent delirium with tremors that is induced by excessive and prolonged use of alcoholic liquors — called also *d.t.'s*
de·list \(,)dē-'list\ *transitive verb* (1933)
: to remove from a list; *especially* : to remove (a security) from the list of securities that may be dealt in on a particular exchange
de·liv·er \di-'li-vər, dē-\ *verb* **de·liv·ered; de·liv·er·ing** \-v(ə-)riŋ\ [Middle English, from Old French *delivrer,* from Late Latin *deliberare,* from Latin *de-* + *liberare* to liberate] (13th century)
transitive verb
1 : to set free ⟨and lead us not into temptation, but *deliver* us from evil —Matthew 6:13 (Authorized Version)⟩
2 a : to take and hand over to or leave for another : CONVEY ⟨*deliver* a package⟩ **b** : HAND OVER, SURRENDER ⟨*delivered* the prisoners to the sheriff⟩ ⟨*delivered* themselves over to God⟩
3 a (1) : to assist in giving birth (2) : to aid in the birth of **b** : to give birth to **c** : to cause (oneself) to produce as if by giving birth ⟨has *delivered* himself of half an autobiography —H. C. Schonberg⟩
4 : SPEAK, SING, UTTER ⟨*delivered* their lines with style⟩ ⟨*deliver* a song⟩ ⟨*deliver* a speech⟩
5 : to send (something aimed or guided) to an intended target or destination ⟨ability to *deliver* nuclear warheads⟩ ⟨*delivered* a fastball⟩
6 a : to bring (as votes) to the support of a candidate or cause **b** : to come through with : PRODUCE ⟨can *deliver* the goods⟩ ⟨new car *delivers* high gas mileage⟩
intransitive verb
: to produce the promised, desired, or expected results : COME THROUGH ⟨can't *deliver* on all these promises⟩
synonym see RESCUE
— **de·liv·er·abil·i·ty** \-,li-v(ə-)rə-'bi-lə-tē\ *noun*
— **de·liv·er·able** \-'li-v(ə-)rə-bəl\ *adjective*
— **de·liv·er·er** \-'li-vər-ər\ *noun*
— **deliver the goods** : to give results that are promised, expected, or desired
de·liv·er·ance \di-'li-v(ə-)rən(t)s, dē-\ *noun* (14th century)
1 : the act of delivering someone or something : the state of being delivered; *especially* : LIBERATION, RESCUE
2 : something delivered; *especially* : an opinion or decision (as the verdict of a jury) expressed publicly
de·liv·ery \di-'li-v(ə-)rē, dē-\ *noun, plural* **-ies** (15th century)
: the act of delivering something; *also* : something delivered
delivery boy *noun* (1920)
: a person employed by a retail store to deliver small orders to customers on call
de·liv·ery·man \-v(ə-)rē-mən, -,man\ *noun* (1920)
: a person who delivers wholesale or retail goods to customers usually over a regular local route
dell \'del\ *noun* [Middle English *delle;* akin to Middle High German *telle* ravine, Old English *dæl* valley — more at DALE] (13th century)
: a secluded hollow or small valley usually covered with trees or turf
delly *variant of* DELI

Del·mon·i·co steak \del-'mä-ni-(,)kō-\ *noun* [from the *Delmonico* restaurants, New York City, after Lorenzo Delmonico (died 1881) American restaurateur] (1925)
: CLUB STEAK — called also *Delmonico*
de·lo·cal·ize \(,)dē-'lō-kə-,līz\ *transitive verb* (1855)
: to free from the limitations of locality; *specifically* : to remove (a charge or charge carrier) from a particular position
— **de·lo·cal·iza·tion** \(,)dē-,lō-kə-lə-'zā-shən\ *noun*
de·louse \(,)dē-'laús, -'laúz\ *transitive verb* (circa 1919)
: to remove lice from
Del·phi·an \'del-fē-ən\ *adjective* (1625)
: DELPHIC
Del·phic \'del-fik\ *adjective* (circa 1599)
1 : of or relating to ancient Delphi or its oracle
2 *often not capitalized* : AMBIGUOUS, OBSCURE ⟨*Delphic* utterances⟩ ◇
— **del·phi·cal·ly** \-fi-k(ə-)lē\ *adverb*
del·phin·i·um \del-'fi-nē-əm\ *noun* [New Latin, genus name, from Greek *delphinion* larkspur, diminutive of *delphin-, delphis* dolphin; probably from the shape of the nectary] (1664)
: any of a large genus (*Delphinium*) of the buttercup family that comprises chiefly perennial erect branching herbs with palmately divided leaves and irregular flowers in showy spikes and includes several that are poisonous — compare LARKSPUR

delphinium

Del·phi·nus \del-'fī-nəs, -'fē-\ *noun* [Latin (genitive *Delphini*), literally, dolphin, from Greek *delphin-, delphis*]
: a northern constellation nearly west of Pegasus
¹**del·ta** \'del-tə\ *noun* [Middle English *deltha,* from Greek *delta,* of Semitic origin; akin to Hebrew *dāleth* daleth] (13th century)
1 : the 4th letter of the Greek alphabet — see ALPHABET table
2 : something shaped like a capital Greek delta; *especially* : the alluvial deposit at the mouth of a river
3 : an increment of a variable — symbol Δ
— **del·ta·ic** \del-'tā-ik\ *adjective*

\ə\ abut \ᵊ\ kitten \ər\ further \a\ ash \ā\ ace
\ä\ mop, mar \aú\ out \ch\ chin \e\ bet \ē\ easy
\g\ go \i\ hit \ī\ ice \j\ job \ŋ\ sing \ō\ go
\ò\ law \òi\ boy \th\ thin \t͟h\ the \ü\ loot \ú\ foot
\y\ yet \zh\ vision *see also* Guide to Pronunciation

²delta *adjective* (circa 1929)
: fourth in position in the structure of an organic molecule from a particular group or atom — symbol δ
Delta (1952)
— a communications code word for the letter *d*
delta ray *noun* (1908)
: an electron ejected by an ionizing particle in its passage through matter
delta wave *noun* (1936)
: a high amplitude electrical rhythm of the brain with a frequency of less than 6 cycles per second that occurs especially in deep sleep, in infancy, and in many diseased conditions of the brain — called also *delta, delta rhythm*
delta wing *noun* [¹*delta;* from its shape] (1946)
: a triangular swept-back airplane wing with a usually straight trailing edge
¹del·toid \'del-ˌtȯid\ *noun* [New Latin *deltoides,* from Greek *deltoeidēs* shaped like a delta, from *delta*] (circa 1681)
: a large triangular muscle that covers the shoulder joint and serves to raise the arm laterally
²deltoid *adjective* (circa 1753)
1 : having a triangular shape ⟨a *deltoid* leaf⟩ — see LEAF illustration
2 : relating to, associated with, or supplying the deltoid
del·toi·de·us \del-'tȯi-dē-əs\ *noun, plural* **del·toi·dei** \-ē-ˌī\ [New Latin, alteration of *deltoides*] (circa 1860)
: DELTOID
de·lude \di-'lüd, dē-\ *transitive verb* **de·lud·ed; de·lud·ing** [Middle English, from Latin *deludere,* from *de-* + *ludere* to play — more at LUDICROUS] (15th century)
1 : to mislead the mind or judgment of : DECEIVE, TRICK
2 *obsolete* **a** : FRUSTRATE, DISAPPOINT **b** : EVADE, ELUDE
synonym see DECEIVE
— **de·lud·er** *noun*
¹del·uge \'del-ˌyüj, -ˌyüzh; ÷də-'lüj, 'dä-ˌlüj\ *noun* [Middle English, from Old French, from Latin *diluvium,* from *diluere* to wash away, from *dis-* + *lavere* to wash — more at LYE] (14th century)
1 a : an overflowing of the land by water **b** : a drenching rain
2 : an overwhelming amount or number
²deluge *transitive verb* **del·uged; del·ug·ing** (1593)
1 : to overflow with water : INUNDATE
2 : OVERWHELM, SWAMP
de·lu·sion \di-'lü-zhən, dē-\ *noun* [Middle English, from Late Latin *delusion-, delusio,* from *deludere*] (15th century)
1 a : the act of deluding : the state of being deluded **b** : an abnormal mental state characterized by the occurrence of psychotic delusions
2 a : something that is falsely or delusively believed or propagated **b** : a persistent false psychotic belief regarding the self or persons or objects outside the self
— **de·lu·sion·al** \-'lüzh-nəl, -'lü-zhə-n³l\ *adjective*
— **de·lu·sion·ary** \-zhə-ˌner-ē\ *adjective*
de·lu·sive \-'lü-siv, -'lü-ziv\ *adjective* (1605)
1 : likely to delude
2 : constituting a delusion
— **de·lu·sive·ly** *adverb*
— **de·lu·sive·ness** *noun*
de·lu·so·ry \-sə-rē, -zə-\ *adjective* (15th century)
: DECEPTIVE, DELUSIVE
de·lus·ter \(ˌ)dē-'ləs-tər\ *transitive verb* (1926)
: to reduce the sheen of (as yarn or fabric)

de·luxe \di-'ləks, dē- *also* -'lùks, -'lüks\ *adjective* [French *de luxe,* literally, of luxury] (1819)
: notably luxurious, elegant, or expensive ⟨a *deluxe* edition⟩ ⟨*deluxe* hotels⟩
¹delve \'delv\ *verb* **delved; delv·ing** [Middle English, from Old English *delfan;* akin to Old High German *telban* to dig] (before 12th century)
transitive verb
archaic : EXCAVATE
intransitive verb
1 : to dig or labor with or as if with a spade
2 : to make a careful or detailed search for information ⟨*delved* into the past⟩
— **delv·er** *noun*
²delve *noun* (14th century)
archaic : CAVE, HOLLOW
de·mag·ne·tize \(ˌ)dē-'mag-nə-ˌtīz\ *transitive verb* (1839)
: to deprive of magnetic properties
— **de·mag·ne·ti·za·tion** \(ˌ)dē-ˌmag-nə-tə-'zā-shən\ *noun*
— **de·mag·ne·tiz·er** \(ˌ)dē-'mag-nə-ˌtī-zər\ *noun*
dem·a·gog·ic \ˌde-mə-'gä-gik *also* -'gä-jik *or* -'gō-jik\ *adjective* (1831)
: of, relating to, or characteristic of a demagogue : employing demagoguery
— **dem·a·gog·i·cal·ly** \-gi-k(ə-)lē, -ji-\ *adverb*
¹dem·a·gogue *or* **dem·a·gog** \'de-mə-ˌgäg\ *noun* [Greek *dēmagōgos,* from *dēmos* people (perhaps akin to Greek *daiesthai* to divide) + *agōgos* leading, from *agein* to lead — more at TIDE, AGENT] (1648)
1 : a leader who makes use of popular prejudices and false claims and promises in order to gain power
2 : a leader championing the cause of the common people in ancient times
— **dem·a·gogu·ery** \-ˌgä-g(ə-)rē\ *noun*
— **dem·a·gogy** \-ˌgä-gē, -ˌgä-jē, -ˌgō-jē\ *noun*
²demagogue *or* **demagog** *verb* **-gogued** *or* **-goged; -gogu·ing** *or* **-gog·ing** (1656)
intransitive verb
: to behave like a demagogue
transitive verb
: to treat (as an issue) in a demogogic manner
¹de·mand \di-'mand, -'mánd, dē-\ *noun* (13th century)
1 a : an act of demanding or asking especially with authority **b** : something claimed as due
2 *archaic* : QUESTION
3 a : willingness and ability to purchase a commodity or service **b** : the quantity of a commodity or service wanted at a specified price and time
4 a : a seeking or state of being sought after ⟨in great *demand* as an entertainer⟩ **b** : urgent need
5 : the requirement of work or of the expenditure of a resource ⟨equal to the *demands* of the office⟩ ⟨oxygen *demand* for waste oxidation⟩
— **on demand** : upon presentation and request for payment; *also* : when requested or needed
²demand *verb* [Middle English *demaunden,* from Old French *demander,* from Medieval Latin *demandare,* from Latin, to entrust, charge, from *de-* + *mandare* to enjoin — more at MANDATE] (14th century)
intransitive verb
: to make a demand : ASK
transitive verb
1 : to ask or call for with authority : claim as due or just ⟨*demanded* to see a lawyer⟩
2 : to call for urgently, peremptorily, or insistently ⟨*demanded* that the rioters disperse⟩
3 a : to ask authoritatively or earnestly to be informed of **b** : to require to come : SUMMON
4 : to call for as useful or necessary ☆

— **de·mand·able** \-'man-də-bəl\ *adjective*
— **de·mand·er** *noun*
de·man·dant \di-'man-dənt\ *noun* (15th century)
1 *archaic* : the plaintiff in a real action
2 *archaic* : one who makes a demand or claim
demand deposit *noun* (1923)
: a bank deposit that can be withdrawn without advance notice
de·mand·ing *adjective* (1926)
: requiring much time, effort, or attention : EXACTING
— **de·mand·ing·ly** \-'man-diŋ-lē\ *adverb*
— **de·mand·ing·ness** *noun*
demand loan *noun* (1913)
: CALL LOAN
demand note *noun* (1862)
: a note payable on demand
de·mand–pull \di-'man(d)-ˌpúl\ *noun* (1952)
: an increase or upward trend in spendable money that tends to result in increased competition for available goods and services and a corresponding increase in consumer prices — compare COST-PUSH
— **demand–pull** *adjective*
de·mand–side \di-'mand-ˌsīd\ *adjective* (1980)
: of, relating to, or being an economic theory that advocates use of government spending and growth in the money supply to stimulate the demand for goods and services and therefore expand economic activity — compare SUPPLY–SIDE
dem·an·toid \'de-mən-ˌtȯid\ *noun* [German, from obsolete German *Demant* diamond, from Middle High German *diemant,* from Old French *diamant* — more at DIAMOND] (circa 1890)
: a green garnet used as a gem
de·mar·cate \di-'mär-ˌkāt, 'dē-ˌ\ *transitive verb* **-cat·ed; -cat·ing** [back-formation from *demarcation,* from Spanish *demarcación,* from *demarcar* to delimit, from *de-* + *marcar* to mark, probably from Italian *marcare,* of Germanic origin; akin to Old High German *marha* boundary — more at MARK] (1816)
1 : DELIMIT
2 : to set apart : SEPARATE
— **de·mar·ca·tion** \ˌdē-ˌmär-'kā-shən\ *noun*
dé·marche *or* **de·marche** \dā-'märsh, di-', 'dā-ˌ\ *noun* [French *démarche,* literally, gait, from Middle French, from *demarcher* to march, from Old French *demarchier,* from *de-* + *marchier* to march] (1658)
1 a : a course of action : MANEUVER **b** : a diplomatic or political initiative or maneuver
2 : a petition or protest presented through diplomatic channels
de·mark \di-'märk\ *transitive verb* (1834)
: DEMARCATE
de·ma·te·ri·al·ize \ˌdē-mə-'tir-ē-ə-ˌlīz\ (circa 1864)
transitive verb

: to cause to become or appear immaterial
intransitive verb
: to lose or appear to lose materiality
— **de·ma·te·ri·al·iza·tion** \-,tir-ē-ə-lə-'zā-shən\ *noun*

deme \'dēm\ *noun* [Greek *dēmos* people, deme] (1833)
1 : a unit of local government in ancient Attica
2 : a local population of closely related interbreeding organisms
¹de·mean \di-'mēn\ *transitive verb* **de·meaned; de·mean·ing** [Middle English *demenen*, from Middle French *demener* to conduct, from *de-* + *mener* to lead, from Latin *minare* to drive, from *minari* to threaten — more at MOUNT] (14th century)
: to conduct or behave (oneself) usually in a proper manner
²demean *transitive verb* **de·meaned; de·mean·ing** [*de-* + ¹*mean*] (1601)
: to lower in character, status, or reputation
de·mean·or \di-'mē-nər\ *noun* [¹*demean*] (circa 1485)
: behavior toward others : outward manner
synonym see BEARING
demeanour *British variant of* DEMEANOR
de·ment·ed \di-'men-təd\ *adjective* (1644)
: MAD, INSANE
— **de·ment·ed·ly** *adverb*
— **de·ment·ed·ness** *noun*
de·men·tia \di-'men(t)-shə, -shē-ə\ *noun* [Latin, from *dement-*, *demens* mad, from *de-* + *ment-*, *mens* mind — more at MIND] (1806)
1 : a condition of deteriorated mentality often with emotional apathy
2 : MADNESS, INSANITY ⟨a fanaticism bordering on *dementia*⟩
— **de·men·tial** \-shəl\ *adjective*
dementia prae·cox \-'prē-,käks\ *noun* [New Latin, literally, premature dementia] (1899)
: SCHIZOPHRENIA
de·mer·it \di-'mer-ət, dē-\ *noun* [Middle English, from Middle French & Medieval Latin; Middle French *demerite*, from Medieval Latin *demeritum*, from neuter of *demeritus*, past participle of *demerēre* to be undeserving of, from Latin, to earn, from *de-* + *merēre* to merit] (15th century)
1 *obsolete* : OFFENSE
2 a : a quality that deserves blame or lacks merit : FAULT, DEFECT **b** : lack of merit
3 : a mark usually entailing a loss of privilege given to an offender
De·mer·ol \'de-mə-,ról, -,rōl\ *trademark*
— used for meperidine
de·mer·sal \di-'mər-səl\ *adjective* [Latin *demersus* (past participle of *demergere* to sink, from *de-* + *mergere* to dip, sink) + English ¹*-al* — more at MERGE] (1889)
: living near, deposited on, or sinking to the bottom of the sea ⟨*demersal* fish eggs⟩
de·mesne \di-'mān, -'mēn\ *noun* [Middle English, from Anglo-French, modification of Old French *demaine* — more at DOMAIN] (14th century)
1 : legal possession of land as one's own
2 : REALM 4b, DOMAIN
3 : manorial land actually possessed by the lord and not held by tenants
4 a : the land attached to a mansion **b** : landed property : ESTATE **c** : REGION 2, TERRITORY
De·me·ter \di-'mē-tər\ *noun* [Latin, from Greek *Dēmētēr*]
: the Greek goddess of agriculture — compare CERES
demi- *prefix* [Middle English, from *demi*, from Middle French, from (assumed) Vulgar Latin *dimedius*, modification of Latin *dimidius*, from *dis-* + *medius* mid — more at MID]
1 : half ⟨*demi*semiquaver⟩
2 : one that partly belongs to (a specified type or class) ⟨*demi*god⟩
demi·god \'de-mē-,gäd\ *noun* (1530)

1 : a mythological being with more power than a mortal but less than a god
2 : a person so outstanding as to seem to approach the divine
demi·god·dess \'de-mē-,gä-dəs\ *noun* (1603)
: a female demigod
demi·john \'de-mē-,jän\ *noun* [by folk etymology from French *dame-jeanne*, literally, Lady Jane] (1806)
: a large narrow-necked bottle usually enclosed in wickerwork
de·mil·i·ta·rize \(,)dē-'mi-lə-tə-,rīz, di-\ *transitive verb* (1883)
1 a : to do away with the military organization or potential of **b** : to prohibit (as a zone or frontier area) from being used for military purposes
2 : to rid of military characteristics or uses
— **de·mil·i·tar·iza·tion** \(,)dē-,mi-lə-t(ə-)rə-'zā-shən, di-\ *noun*
demi·mon·daine \,de-mi-,män-'dān, -'män-,-mē-\ *noun* [French *demi-mondaine*, from feminine of *demi-mondain*, from *demi-monde*] (1894)
: a woman of the demimonde
demi·monde \'de-mi-,mänd, -mē-\ *noun* [French *demi-monde*, from *demi-* + *monde* world, from Latin *mundus*] (1855)
1 a : a class of women on the fringes of respectable society supported by wealthy lovers **b** : PROSTITUTES
2 : DEMIMONDAINE
3 : a distinctive class, group, or activity that is often an isolated part of a larger class, group, or activity ⟨the pop music *demimonde*⟩ ⟨the literary *demimonde*⟩; *especially* : one having little reputation or prestige
de·min·er·al·iza·tion \(,)dē-,mi-nə-rə-lə-'zā-shən, di-\ *noun* (1903)
1 : loss of bodily minerals (as calcium salts) especially in disease
2 : the process of removing mineral matter or salts (as from water)
— **de·min·er·al·ize** \(,)dē-'mi-nə-rə-,līz\ *transitive verb*
— **de·min·er·al·iz·er** \-,lī-zər\ *noun*
demi·rep \'de-mi-,rep, -mē-\ *noun* [*demi-* + *rep* (reprobate)] (1749)
: DEMIMONDAINE
¹de·mise \di-'mīz\ *verb* **de·mised; de·mis·ing** (15th century)
transitive verb
1 : to convey (as an estate) by will or lease
2 *obsolete* : CONVEY, GIVE
3 : to transmit by succession or inheritance
intransitive verb
1 : DIE, DECEASE
2 : to pass by descent or bequest ⟨the property has *demised* to the king⟩
²demise *noun* [Middle French, feminine of *demis*, past participle of *demettre* to dismiss, from Latin *demittere* to send down, from *de-* + *mittere* to send] (15th century)
1 : the conveyance of an estate
2 : transfer of the sovereignty to a successor
3 a : DEATH **b** : a cessation of existence or activity **c** : a loss of position or status
demi–sec \,de-mi-'sek, -mē-\ *adjective* [French] (1926)
of champagne : moderately sweet
demi·semi·qua·ver \,de-mē-'se-mē-,kwā-vər\ *noun* (circa 1706)
: THIRTY-SECOND NOTE
de·mis·sion \di-'mi-shən\ *noun* [Middle French, from Latin *demission-, demissio* lowering, from *demittere*] (15th century)
: RESIGNATION, ABDICATION
de·mit \di-'mit\ *verb* **de·mit·ted; de·mit·ting** [Middle French *demettre*] (15th century)

transitive verb
1 *archaic* : DISMISS
2 : RESIGN
intransitive verb
: to withdraw from office or membership
demi·tasse \'de-mi-,tas, -,täs, -mē-\ *noun* [French *demi-tasse*, from *demi-* + *tasse* cup, from Middle French, from Arabic *ṭass*, from Persian *tast*] (1842)
: a small cup of black coffee; *also* : the cup used to serve it
demi·urge \'de-mē-,ərj\ *noun* [Late Latin *demiurgus*, from Greek *dēmiourgos*, literally, artisan, one with special skill, from *dēmios* of the people (from *dēmos* people) + *-ourgos* worker (from *ergon* work) — more at DEMAGOGUE, WORK] (1678)
1 *capitalized* **a** : a Platonic subordinate deity who fashions the sensible world in the light of eternal ideas **b** : a Gnostic subordinate deity who is the creator of the material world
2 : one that is an autonomous creative force or decisive power
— **demi·ur·gic** \-jik\ *also* **demi·ur·gi·cal** \-ji-kəl\ *adjective*
demi·world \'de-mē-,wərld\ *noun* (1862)
: DEMIMONDE 3
demo \'de-(,)mō\ *noun, plural* **dem·os** (1793)
1 *capitalized* : DEMOCRAT 2
2 a : DEMONSTRATION 1b **b** *British* : DEMONSTRATION 4
3 a : DEMONSTRATOR a **b** : a recording intended to show off a song or performer to a record producer
¹de·mob \(,)dē-'mäb, di-\ *transitive verb* (1919)
chiefly British : DEMOBILIZE
²demob *noun* (1945)
chiefly British : the act or process of demobilizing
de·mo·bi·lize \di-'mō-bə-,līz, ,dē-\ *transitive verb* (1882)
1 : DISBAND
2 : to discharge from military service
— **de·mo·bi·li·za·tion** \di-,mō-bə-lə-'zā-shən, ,dē-\ *noun*
de·moc·ra·cy \di-'mä-krə-sē\ *noun, plural* **-cies** [Middle French *democratie*, from Late Latin *democratia*, from Greek *dēmokratia*, from *dēmos* + *-kratia* -cracy] (1576)
1 a : government by the people; *especially* : rule of the majority **b** : a government in which the supreme power is vested in the people and exercised by them directly or indirectly through a system of representation usually involving periodically held free elections
2 : a political unit that has a democratic government
3 *capitalized* : the principles and policies of the Democratic party in the U.S.
4 : the common people especially when constituting the source of political authority
5 : the absence of hereditary or arbitrary class distinctions or privileges
dem·o·crat \'de-mə-,krat\ *noun* (1740)
1 a : an adherent of democracy **b** : one who practices social equality
2 *capitalized* : a member of the Democratic party of the U.S.
dem·o·crat·ic \,de-mə-'kra-tik\ *adjective* (1602)
1 : of, relating to, or favoring democracy
2 *often capitalized* : of or relating to one of the two major political parties in the U.S. evolving in the early 19th century from the antifederalists and the Democratic-Republican party and associated in modern times with policies of broad social reform and internationalism

\ə\ abut \ᵊ\ kitten \ər\ further \a\ ash \ā\ ace
\ä\ mop, mar \aú\ out \ch\ chin \e\ bet \ē\ easy
\g\ go \i\ hit \ī\ ice \j\ job \ŋ\ sing \ō\ go
\ó\ law \ói\ boy \th\ thin \th\ the \ü\ loot \ú\ foot
\y\ yet \zh\ vision *see also* Guide to Pronunciation

3 : relating to, appealing to, or available to the broad masses of the people ⟨*democratic* art⟩
4 : favoring social equality **:** not snobbish
— **dem·o·crat·i·cal·ly** \-ti-k(ə-)lē\ *adverb*
democratic centralism *noun* (1926)
: a principle of Communist party organization by which members take part in policy discussions and elections at all levels but must follow decisions made at higher levels
Democratic–Republican *adjective* (1818)
: of or relating to a major American political party of the early 19th century favoring a strict interpretation of the constitution to restrict the powers of the federal government and emphasizing states' rights
de·moc·ra·tize \di-'mä-krə-ˌtīz\ *transitive verb* **-tized; -tiz·ing** (1798)
: to make democratic
— **de·moc·ra·ti·za·tion** \-ˌmä-krə-tə-'zā-shən\ *noun*
— **de·moc·ra·tiz·er** \-'mä-krə-ˌtī-zər\ *noun*
dé·mo·dé \ˌdā-mō-'dā\ *adjective* [French, from *dé-* de- + *mode*] (1873)
: no longer fashionable **:** OUT-OF-DATE
de·mod·ed \(ˌ)dē-'mō-dəd\ *adjective* (1887)
: DÉMODÉ
de·mod·u·late \(ˌ)dē-'mä-jə-ˌlāt\ *transitive verb* (1927)
: to extract the intelligence from (a modulated signal)
— **de·mod·u·la·tion** \(ˌ)dē-ˌmä-jə-'lā-shən\ *noun*
— **de·mod·u·la·tor** \(')dē-'mä-jə-ˌlā-tər\ *noun*
De·mo·gor·gon \ˌdē-mə-'gòr-gən, 'dē-mə-ˌ\ *noun* [Late Latin]
: a mysterious spirit or deity often explained as a primeval creator god who antedates the gods of Greek mythology
de·mo·graph·ic \ˌdē-mə-'gra-fik, ˌdē-mə-\ *also* **de·mo·graph·i·cal** \-fi-kəl\ *adjective* (1882)
1 : of or relating to demography or demographics
2 : relating to the dynamic balance of a population especially with regard to density and capacity for expansion or decline
— **de·mo·graph·i·cal·ly** \-fi-k(ə-)lē\ *adverb*
de·mo·graph·ics \-fiks\ *noun plural* (circa 1966)
1 : the statistical characteristics of human populations (as age or income) used especially to identify markets
2 : the demographic profile of a market (as the viewers of a TV show)
de·mog·ra·phy \di-'mä-grə-fē\ *noun* [French *démographie*, from Greek *dēmos* people + French *-graphie* -graphy] (1880)
: the statistical study of human populations especially with reference to size and density, distribution, and vital statistics
— **de·mog·ra·pher** \-fər\ *noun*
dem·oi·selle \ˌdem-wə-'zel\ *noun* [French, from Old French *dameisele* — more at DAMSEL] (1520)
1 : a young lady
2 : DAMSELFLY
3 : DAMSELFISH
De·Moi·vre's theorem \di-'mói-vərz-, -'mwäv-(rə)z-\ *noun* [Abraham *De Moivre* (died 1754) French mathematician] (circa 1891)
: a theorem of complex numbers: the *n*th power of a complex number has for its absolute value and its argument respectively the *n*th power of the absolute value and *n* times the argument of the complex number
de·mol·ish \di-'mä-lish\ *transitive verb* [Middle French *demoliss-*, stem of *demolir*, from Latin *demoliri*, from *de-* + *moliri* to construct, from *moles* mass — more at MOLE] (1570)
1 a : TEAR DOWN, RAZE **b :** to break to pieces **:** SMASH
2 a : to do away with **:** DESTROY **b :** to strip of any pretense of merit or credence

— **de·mol·ish·er** *noun*
— **de·mol·ish·ment** \-lish-mənt\ *noun*
de·mo·li·tion \ˌde-mə-'li-shən, ˌdē-mə-\ *noun* (1549)
1 : the act of demolishing; *especially* **:** destruction in war by means of explosives
2 *plural* **:** explosives for destruction in war
— **de·mo·li·tion·ist** \-'li-sh(ə-)nəst\ *noun*
demolition derby *noun* (circa 1953)
: a contest in which skilled drivers ram old cars into one another until only one car remains running
de·mon *or* **dae·mon** \'dē-mən\ *noun* [Middle English *demon*, from Late Latin & Latin; Late Latin *daemon* evil spirit, from Latin, divinity, spirit, from Greek *daimōn*, probably from *daiesthai* to distribute — more at TIDE] (13th century)
1 a : an evil spirit **b :** a source or agent of evil, harm, distress, or ruin
2 *usually* **daemon :** an attendant power or spirit **:** GENIUS
3 *usually* **daemon :** a supernatural being of Greek mythology intermediate between gods and men
4 : one that has exceptional enthusiasm, drive, or effectiveness ⟨a *demon* for work⟩
— **de·mo·ni·an** \di-'mō-nē-ən\ *adjective*
— **de·mon·iza·tion** \ˌdē-mə-nə-'zā-shən\ *noun*
— **de·mon·ize** \'dē-mə-ˌnīz\ *transitive verb*
de·mon·e·tize \(ˌ)dē-'mä-nə-ˌtīz, -'mə-\ *transitive verb* [French *démonétiser*, from *dé-* de- + Latin *moneta* coin — more at MINT] (1852)
1 : to stop using (a metal) as a monetary standard
2 : to deprive of value for official payment
— **de·mon·e·ti·za·tion** \(ˌ)dē-ˌmä-nə-tə-'zā-shən, -mä-nə-\ *noun*
¹de·mo·ni·ac \di-'mō-nē-ˌak\ *also* **de·mo·ni·a·cal** \ˌdē-mə-'nī-ə-kəl\ *adjective* [Middle English *demoniac*, from Late Latin *daemoniacus*, from Greek *daimoniakos*, from *daimon-, daimōn*] (14th century)
1 : possessed or influenced by a demon
2 : of, relating to, or suggestive of a demon **:** FIENDISH ⟨*demoniac* cruelty⟩
— **de·mo·ni·a·cal·ly** \ˌdē-mə-'nī-ə-k(ə-)lē\ *adverb*
²demoniac *noun* (14th century)
: one possessed by a demon
de·mon·ic \di-'mä-nik, dē-\ *also* **de·mon·i·cal** \-ni-kəl\ *adjective* (1662)
: DEMONIAC 2
— **de·mon·i·cal·ly** \-ni-k(ə-)lē\ *adverb*
de·mon·ol·o·gy \ˌdē-mə-'nä-lə-jē\ *noun* (1597)
1 : the study of demons or evil spirits
2 : belief in demons **:** a doctrine of evil spirits
3 : a catalog of enemies ⟨the liberal creed at that time put Big Business in a central place in its *demonology* —Carl Kaysen⟩
— **de·mon·olog·i·cal** \ˌdē-mə-nə-'lä-ji-kəl\ *adjective*
— **de·mon·ol·o·gist** \-'nä-lə-jist\ *noun*
de·mon·stra·ble \di-'män(t)-strə-bəl\ *adjective* (15th century)
1 : capable of being demonstrated
2 : APPARENT, EVIDENT
— **de·mon·stra·bil·i·ty** \-ˌmän(t)-strə-'bi-lə-tē\ *noun*
— **de·mon·stra·bly** \-blē\ *adverb*
dem·on·strate \'de-mən-ˌstrāt\ *verb* **-strat·ed; -strat·ing** [Latin *demonstratus*, past participle of *demonstrare*, from *de-* + *monstrare* to show — more at MUSTER] (1552)
transitive verb
1 : to show clearly
2 a : to prove or make clear by reasoning or evidence **b :** to illustrate and explain especially with many examples
3 : to show or prove the value or efficiency of to a prospective buyer

intransitive verb
: to make a demonstration
synonym see SHOW
dem·on·stra·tion \ˌde-mən-'strā-shən\ *noun* (14th century)
1 : an act, process, or means of demonstrating to the intelligence: as **a** (1) **:** conclusive evidence **:** PROOF (2) **:** DERIVATION 5 **b :** a showing of the merits of a product or service to a prospective consumer
2 : an outward expression or display
3 : a show of armed force
4 : a public display of group feelings toward a person or cause
— **dem·on·stra·tion·al** \-shnəl, -shə-nᵊl\ *adjective*
¹de·mon·stra·tive \di-'män(t)-strə-tiv\ *adjective* (14th century)
1 a : demonstrating as real or true **b :** characterized or established by demonstration
2 : pointing out the one referred to and distinguishing it from others of the same class ⟨*demonstrative* pronouns⟩
3 a : marked by display of feeling **b :** inclined to display feelings openly
— **de·mon·stra·tive·ly** *adverb*
— **de·mon·stra·tive·ness** *noun*
²demonstrative *noun* (15th century)
: a demonstrative word or morpheme
dem·on·stra·tor \'de-mən-ˌstrā-tər\ *noun* (1611)
: one that demonstrates: **a :** a product (as an automobile) used to demonstrate performance or merits to prospective buyers **b :** someone who engages in a public demonstration
de·mor·al·ize \di-'mòr-ə-ˌlīz, ˌdē-, -'mär-\ *transitive verb* (circa 1793)
1 : to corrupt the morals of
2 a : to weaken the morale of **:** DISCOURAGE, DISPIRIT **b :** to upset or destroy the normal functioning of **c :** to throw into disorder
— **de·mor·al·iza·tion** \di-ˌmòr-ə-lə-'zā-shən, ˌdē-, -ˌmär-\ *noun*
— **de·mor·al·iz·er** \di-'mòr-ə-ˌlī-zər, ˌdē-, -'mär-\ *noun*
— **de·mor·al·iz·ing·ly** \-ziŋ-lē\ *adverb*
de·mos \'dē-ˌmäs\ *noun* [Greek *dēmos* — more at DEMAGOGUE] (1831)
1 : POPULACE
2 : the common people of an ancient Greek state
de·mote \di-'mōt, ˌdē-\ *transitive verb* **de·mot·ed; de·mot·ing** [*de-* + *-mote* (as in *promote*)] (circa 1891)
1 : to reduce to a lower grade or rank
2 : to relegate to a less important position
— **de·mo·tion** \-'mō-shən\ *noun*
de·mot·ic \di-'mä-tik\ *adjective* [Greek *dēmotikos*, from *dēmotēs* commoner, from *dēmos*] (1822)
1 : of, relating to, or written in a simplified form of the ancient Egyptian hieratic writing
2 : POPULAR, COMMON ⟨*demotic* idiom⟩
3 : of or relating to the form of Modern Greek that is based on everyday speech
de·mount \(ˌ)dē-'maùnt\ *transitive verb* (circa 1930)
1 : to remove from a mounted position
2 : DISASSEMBLE
— **de·mount·able** \-tə-bəl\ *adjective*
¹de·mul·cent \di-'məl-sənt\ *adjective* [Latin *demulcent-, demulcens*, present participle of *demulcēre* to soothe, from *de-* + *mulcēre* to soothe] (1732)
: SOOTHING
²demulcent *noun* (1732)
: a usually mucilaginous or oily substance (as tragacanth) that can soothe or protect an abraded mucous membrane
de·mul·ti·plex·er \(ˌ)dē-'məl-tə-ˌplek-sər\ *noun* (1963)
: an electronic device that separates a multiplex signal into its component parts

¹de·mur \di-'mər\ *intransitive verb* **de·murred; de·mur·ring** [Middle English *demeoren* to linger, from Old French *demorer*, from Latin *demorari*, from *de-* + *morari* to linger, from *mora* delay — more at MORA] (13th century)
1 *archaic* **:** DELAY, HESITATE
2 : to file a demurrer
3 : to take exception **:** OBJECT — often used with *to* or *at*

²demur *noun* (13th century)
1 : hesitation (as in doing or accepting) usually based on doubt of the acceptability of something offered or proposed
2 : the act or an instance of objecting **:** PROTEST
synonym see QUALM

de·mure \di-'myùr\ *adjective* [Middle English] (14th century)
1 : RESERVED, MODEST
2 : affectedly modest, reserved, or serious **:** COY
— **de·mure·ly** *adverb*
— **de·mure·ness** *noun*

de·mur·rage \di-'mər-ij, -'mə-rij\ *noun* (1641)
1 : the detention of a ship by the freighter beyond the time allowed for loading, unloading, or sailing
2 : a charge for detaining a ship, freight car, or truck

de·mur·ral \di-'mər-əl, -'mə-rəl\ *noun* (1810)
: the act or an instance of demurring

¹de·mur·rer \di-'mər-ər, -'mə-rər\ *noun* [Middle French *demorer*, verb] (circa 1521)
1 : a response in a court proceeding in which the defendant does not dispute the truth of the allegation but claims it is not sufficient grounds to justify legal action
2 : OBJECTION

²de·mur·rer \-'mər-ər\ *noun* [¹*demur*] (1711)
: one that demurs

de·my·e·lin·at·ing \(,)dē-'mī-ə-lə-,nā-tiŋ\ *adjective* (1939)
: causing or characterized by the loss or destruction of myelin ⟨*demyelinating* diseases⟩ ⟨a *demyelinating* agent⟩
— **de·my·e·lin·ation** \(,)dē-,mī-ə-lə-'nā-shən\ *noun*

de·mys·ti·fy \(,)dē-'mis-tə-,fī\ *transitive verb* (1963)
: to eliminate the mystifying features of
— **de·mys·ti·fi·ca·tion** \(,)dē-,mis-tə-fə-'kā-shən\ *noun*

de·my·thol·o·gize \,dē-mi-'thä-lə-,jīz\ *transitive verb* (1950)
1 : to divest of mythological forms in order to uncover the meaning underlying them ⟨*demythologize* the Gospels⟩
2 : to divest of mythical elements or associations
— **de·my·thol·o·gi·za·tion** \-,thä-lə-jə-'zā-shən\ *noun*
— **de·my·thol·o·giz·er** \-'thä-lə-,jī-zər\ *noun*

¹den \'den\ *noun* [Middle English, from Old English *denn;* akin to Old English *denu* valley, Old High German *tenni* threshing floor] (before 12th century)
1 : the lair of a wild usually predatory animal
2 a (1) **:** a hollow or cavern used especially as a hideout (2) **:** a center of secret activity **b :** a small usually squalid dwelling
3 : a comfortable usually secluded room
4 : a subdivision of a Cub Scout pack made up of two or more boys

²den *verb* **denned; den·ning** (13th century)
intransitive verb
: to live in or retire to a den
transitive verb
: to drive into a den

de·nar·i·us \di-'nar-ē-əs, -'ner-\ *noun, plural* **de·nar·ii** \-ē-,ī, -ē-,ē\ [Middle English, from Latin — more at DENIER] (14th century)
1 : a small silver coin of ancient Rome
2 : a gold coin of the Roman Empire equivalent to 25 denarii

de·na·tion·al·ize \(')dē-'nash-nə-,līz, -'na-shə-n°l-,īz\ *transitive verb* (1807)
1 : to divest of national character or rights
2 : to remove from ownership or control by the national government
— **de·na·tion·al·iza·tion** \(,)dē-,nash-nə-lə-'zā-shən, -,na-shə-n°l-ə-'zā-\ *noun*

de·nat·u·ral·ize \(,)dē-'na-ch(ə-)rə-,līz\ *transitive verb* (1800)
1 : to make unnatural
2 : to deprive of the rights and duties of a citizen
— **de·nat·u·ral·iza·tion** \(,)dē-,na-ch(ə-)rə-lə-'zā-shən\ *noun*

de·na·ture \(,)dē-'nā-chər\ *verb* **de·na·tured; de·na·tur·ing** \-'nā-ch(ə-)riŋ\ (1685)
transitive verb
1 : DEHUMANIZE
2 : to deprive of natural qualities **:** change the nature of: as **a :** to make (alcohol) unfit for drinking (as by adding an obnoxious substance) without impairing usefulness for other purposes **b :** to modify the molecular structure of (as a protein or DNA) especially by heat, acid, alkali, or ultraviolet radiation so as to destroy or diminish some of the original properties and especially the specific biological activity
intransitive verb
: to become denatured
— **de·na·tur·ant** \(,)dē-'nā-chər-ənt\ *noun*
— **de·na·tur·ation** \(,)dē-,nā-chə-'rā-shən\ *noun*

de·na·zi·fy \(,)dē-'nät-si-,fī, -'nat-\ *transitive verb* **-fied; -fying** (1940)
: to rid of Nazism and its influence
— **de·na·zi·fi·ca·tion** \(,)dē-,nät-si-fə-'kā-shən, -,nat-\ *noun*

dendr- *or* **dendro-** *combining form* [Greek, from *dendron;* akin to Greek *drys* tree — more at TREE]
: tree ⟨*dendro*logy⟩ **:** resembling a tree ⟨*dendrite*⟩

den·dri·form \'den-drə-,fòrm\ *adjective* (circa 1847)
: resembling a tree in structure

den·drite \'den-,drīt\ *noun* (1751)
1 : a branching treelike figure produced on or in a mineral by a foreign mineral; *also* **:** the mineral so marked
2 : a crystallized arborescent form
3 : any of the usually branching protoplasmic processes that conduct impulses toward the body of a nerve cell

den·drit·ic \(,)den-'dri-tik\ *adjective* (1816)
: resembling or having dendrites **:** branching like a tree ⟨a *dendritic* drainage system⟩ ⟨*dendritic* cells⟩

den·dro·chro·nol·o·gy \,den-(,)drō-krə-'nä-lə-jē\ *noun* (circa 1928)
: the science of dating events and variations in environment in former periods by comparative study of growth rings in trees and aged wood
— **den·dro·chro·no·log·i·cal** \-,krä-nə-'lä-ji-kəl, -,krō-\ *adjective*
— **den·dro·chro·no·log·i·cal·ly** \-ji-k(ə-)lē\ *adverb*
— **den·dro·chro·nol·o·gist** \-krə-'nä-lə-jist\ *noun*

den·dro·gram \'den-drə-,gram\ *noun* (circa 1953)
: a branching diagram representing a hierarchy of categories based on degree of similarity or number of shared characteristics especially in biological taxonomy — compare CLADOGRAM

den·droid \'den-,dròid\ *adjective* [Greek *dendroeidēs,* from *dendron*] (circa 1828)
: resembling a tree in form **:** ARBORESCENT

denarius of Julius Caesar, 44 B.C.

den·drol·o·gy \den-'drä-lə-jē\ *noun* (circa 1708)
: the study of trees
— **den·dro·log·ic** \,den-drə-'lä-jik\ *or* **den·dro·log·i·cal** \-ji-kəl\ *adjective*
— **den·drol·o·gist** \den-'drä-lə-jist\ *noun*

dene \'dēn\ *noun* [Middle English, from Old English *denu*] (before 12th century)
British **:** VALLEY

Dé·né \de-'nā, dā-\ *noun, plural* **Déné** *or* **Dé·nés** \-āz\ [Canadian French, from Athabascan; akin to Chipewyan *dene* person] (1891)
: a member of any of the Athabascan-speaking peoples of the interior of Alaska and northwestern Canada; *also* **:** the languages of these peoples

Den·eb \'de-,neb, -nəb\ *noun* [Arabic *dhanab al-dajāja,* literally, the tail of the hen]
: a star of the first magnitude in Cygnus

den·e·ga·tion \,de-ni-'gā-shən\ *noun* [Middle English *denegacioun,* from Middle French or Latin; Middle French *denegation,* from Latin *denegation-, denegatio,* from *denegare* to deny — more at DENY] (15th century)
: DENIAL

de·ner·vate \'dē-(,)nər-,vāt\ *transitive verb* **-vat·ed; -vat·ing** (1905)
: to deprive of a nerve supply (as by cutting a nerve)
— **de·ner·va·tion** \,dē-(,)nər-'vā-shən\ *noun*

den·gue \'deŋ-gē, -,gā\ *noun* [American Spanish] (1828)
: an acute infectious disease caused by an arbovirus, transmitted by aedes mosquitoes, and characterized by headache, severe joint pain, and a rash — called also *breakbone fever, dengue fever*

de·ni·a·bil·i·ty \dē-,nī-ə-'bi-lə-tē\ *noun* (1973)
: the ability to deny something especially on the basis of being officially uninformed

de·ni·able \di-'nī-ə-bəl, dē-\ *adjective* (1548)
: capable of being denied

de·ni·al \di-'nī(-ə)l, dē-\ *noun* (1528)
1 : refusal to satisfy a request or desire
2 a (1) **:** refusal to admit the truth or reality (as of a statement or charge) (2) **:** assertion that an allegation is false **b :** refusal to acknowledge a person or a thing **:** DISAVOWAL
3 : the opposing by the defendant of an allegation of the opposite party in a lawsuit
4 : SELF-DENIAL
5 : negation in logic
6 : a psychological defense mechanism in which confrontation with a personal problem or with reality is avoided by denying the existence of the problem or reality

¹de·ni·er \di-'nī(-ə)r, dē-\ *noun* (15th century)
: one that denies

²de·nier *noun* [Middle English *denere,* from Middle French *denier,* from Latin *denarius,* coin worth ten asses, from *denarius* containing ten, from *deni* ten each, from *decem* ten — more at TEN] (15th century)
1 \də-'ni(ə)r, də-'nyā\ **:** a small originally silver coin formerly used in western Europe
2 \'de-nyər\ **:** a unit of fineness for yarn equal to the fineness of a yarn weighing one gram for each 9000 meters ⟨100-*denier* yarn is finer than 150-*denier* yarn⟩

den·i·grate \'de-ni-,grāt\ *transitive verb* **-grat·ed; -grat·ing** [Latin *denigratus,* past participle of *denigrare,* from *de-* + *nigrare* to blacken, from *nigr-, niger* black] (1526)
1 : to cast aspersions on **:** DEFAME
2 : to deny the importance or validity of **:** BELITTLE
— **den·i·gra·tion** \,de-ni-'grā-shən\ *noun*
— **den·i·gra·tive** \'de-ni-,grā-tiv\ *adjective*
— **den·i·gra·tor** \-,grā-tər\ *noun*

\ə\ abut \ᵊ\ kitten \ər\ further \a\ ash \ā\ ace \ä\ mop, mar \aù\ out \ch\ chin \e\ bet \ē\ easy \g\ go \i\ hit \ī\ ice \j\ job \ŋ\ sing \ō\ go \ò\ law \òi\ boy \th\ thin \t͟h\ the \ü\ loot \ù\ foot \y\ yet \zh\ vision *see also* Guide to Pronunciation

— den·i·gra·to·ry \'de-ni-grə-ˌtōr-ē, -ˌtȯr-\ *adjective*

den·im \'de-nəm\ *noun* [French (*serge*) *de Nîmes* serge of Nîmes, France] (1695)
1 a : a firm durable twilled usually cotton fabric woven with colored warp and white filling threads **b :** a similar fabric woven in colored stripes
2 *plural* **:** overalls or trousers usually of blue denim ◇

den·i·tri·fi·ca·tion \(ˌ)dē-ˌnī-trə-fə-'kā-shən\ *noun* (1883)
: the loss or removal of nitrogen or nitrogen compounds; *specifically* **:** reduction of nitrates or nitrites commonly by bacteria (as in soil) that usually results in the escape of nitrogen into the air
— de·ni·tri·fi·er \-'nī-trə-ˌfī-ər\ *noun*
— de·ni·tri·fy \-'nī-trə-ˌfī\ *transitive verb*

den·i·zen \'de-nə-zən\ *noun* [Middle English *denizeine*, from Anglo-French *denzein* inhabitant, inner part, inner, from Old French *denz* within, from Late Latin *deintus*, from Latin *de-* + *intus* within — more at ENT-] (15th century)
1 : INHABITANT
2 : one admitted to residence in a foreign country; *especially* **:** an alien admitted to rights of citizenship
3 : one that frequents a place

den mother *noun* (1946)
: a female adult leader of a Cub Scout den; *also* **:** a person seen in the role of leader or protector of a group

de·nom·i·nal \dē-'nä-mə-nᵊl\ *adjective* (1951)
: derived from a noun

de·nom·i·nate \di-'nä-mə-ˌnāt, dē-\ *transitive verb* [Latin *denominatus*, past participle of *denominare*, from *de-* + *nominare* to name — more at NOMINATE] (circa 1552)
1 : to give a name to **:** DESIGNATE
2 : to express or designate in some denomination ⟨will *denominate* prices in U.S. dollars⟩

de·nom·i·nate number \di-'nä-mə-nət-\ *noun* [Latin *denominatus*] (1579)
: a number (as *7* in *7 feet*) that specifies a quantity in terms of a unit of measurement

de·nom·i·na·tion \di-ˌnä-mə-'nā-shən\ *noun* (15th century)
1 : an act of denominating
2 : a value or size of a series of values or sizes (as of money)
3 : NAME, DESIGNATION; *especially* **:** a general name for a category
4 : a religious organization uniting local congregations in a single legal and administrative body
— de·nom·i·na·tion·al \-shnəl, -shə-nᵊl\ *adjective*

de·nom·i·na·tion·al·ism \-shə-nə-ˌli-zəm\ *noun* (circa 1855)
1 : devotion to denominational principles or interests
2 : the emphasizing of denominational differences to the point of being narrowly exclusive **:** SECTARIANISM

de·nom·i·na·tive \di-'nä-mə-nə-tiv\ *adjective* [Latin *de* from + *nomin-, nomen* name] (circa 1783)
: derived from a noun or adjective
— denominative *noun*

de·nom·i·na·tor \di-'nä-mə-ˌnā-tər\ *noun* (circa 1542)
1 : the part of a fraction below the line signifying division that functions as the divisor of the numerator and in fractions with 1 as the numerator indicates into how many parts the unit is divided
2 a : a common trait **b :** the average level (as of taste or opinion) **:** STANDARD

de·no·ta·tion \ˌdē-nō-'tā-shən\ *noun* (circa 1532)
1 : an act or process of denoting
2 : MEANING; *especially* **:** a direct specific meaning as distinct from an implied or associated idea

3 a : a denoting term **:** NAME **b :** SIGN, INDICATION ⟨visible *denotations* of divine wrath⟩
4 : the totality of things to which a term is applicable especially in logic — compare CONNOTATION

de·no·ta·tive \'dē-nō-ˌtā-tiv, di-'nō-tə-tiv\ *adjective* (circa 1611)
1 : denoting or tending to denote
2 : relating to denotation

de·note \di-'nōt, dē-\ *transitive verb* [Middle French *denoter*, from Latin *denotare*, from *de-* + *notare* to note] (1592)
1 : to serve as an indication of **:** BETOKEN ⟨the swollen bellies that *denote* starvation⟩
2 : to serve as an arbitrary mark for ⟨red flares *denoting* danger⟩
3 : to make known **:** ANNOUNCE ⟨his crestfallen look *denoted* his distress⟩
4 a : to serve as a linguistic expression of the notion of **:** MEAN **b :** to stand for **:** DESIGNATE
— de·note·ment \-'nōt-mənt\ *noun*

de·noue·ment *also* **dé·noue·ment** \ˌdā-ˌnü-'mäⁿ, dā-'nü-ˌ\ *noun* [French *dénouement*, literally, untying, from Middle French *desnouement*, from *desnouer* to untie, from Old French *des-* de- + *noer* to tie, from Latin *nodare*, from *nodus* knot — more at NODE] (1752)
1 : the final outcome of the main dramatic complication in a literary work
2 : the outcome of a complex sequence of events

de·nounce \di-'naȯn(t)s, dē-\ *transitive verb* **de·nounced; de·nounc·ing** [Middle English, from Old French *denoncier* to proclaim, from Latin *denuntiare*, from *de-* + *nuntiare* to report — more at ANNOUNCE] (13th century)
1 : to pronounce especially publicly to be blameworthy or evil
2 *archaic* **a :** PROCLAIM **b :** to announce threateningly
3 : to inform against **:** ACCUSE
4 *obsolete* **:** PORTEND
5 : to announce formally the termination of (as a treaty)
synonym see CRITICIZE
— de·nounce·ment \-'naȯn(t)-smənt\ *noun*
— de·nounc·er *noun*

de no·vo \di-'nō-(ˌ)vō, dā-, dē-\ *adverb or adjective* [Latin] (1536)
: over again **:** ANEW

dense \'den(t)s\ *adjective* **dens·er; dens·est** [Latin *densus*; akin to Greek *dasys* thick with hair or leaves] (15th century)
1 a : marked by compactness or crowding together of parts **b :** having a high mass per unit volume ⟨carbon dioxide is a *dense* gas⟩
2 a : marked by a stupid imperviousness to ideas or impressions **:** THICKHEADED **b :** EXTREME ⟨*dense* ignorance⟩
3 : having between any two elements at least one element ⟨the set of rational numbers is *dense*⟩
4 : demanding concentration to follow or comprehend ⟨*dense* prose⟩
5 : having high or relatively high opacity ⟨a *dense* fog⟩ ⟨a *dense* photographic negative⟩
synonym see STUPID
— dense·ly *adverb*
— dense·ness \'den(t)-snəs\ *noun*

den·si·fy \'den(t)-sə-ˌfī\ *transitive verb* **-fied; -fy·ing** (1820)
: to make denser **:** COMPRESS
— den·si·fi·ca·tion \ˌden(t)-sə-fə-'kā-shən\ *noun*

den·si·tom·e·ter \ˌden(t)-sə-'tä-mə-tər\ *noun* (1901)
: an instrument for determining optical or photographic density
— den·si·to·met·ric \ˌden(t)-sə-tə-'me-trik\ *adjective*
— den·si·tom·e·try \ˌden(t)-sə-'tä-mə-trē\ *noun*

den·si·ty \'den(t)-sə-tē\ *noun, plural* **-ties** (1603)

1 : the quality or state of being dense
2 : the quantity per unit volume, unit area, or unit length: as **a :** the mass of a substance per unit volume **b :** the distribution of a quantity (as mass, electricity, or energy) per unit usually of space (as length, area, or volume) **c :** the average number of individuals or units per space unit ⟨a population *density* of 500 per square mile⟩ ⟨a housing *density* of 10 houses per acre⟩
3 a : the degree of opacity of a translucent medium **b :** the common logarithm of the opacity

density function *noun* (circa 1962)
: PROBABILITY DENSITY FUNCTION

¹dent \'dent\ *verb* [Middle English, short for *indenten* to make dents in, indent] (14th century)
transitive verb
1 : to make a dent in
2 : to have a weakening effect on
intransitive verb
: to form a dent by sinking inward **:** become dented

²dent *noun* (1565)
1 : a depression or hollow made by a blow or by pressure
2 a : an impression or effect often made against resistance and usually having a weakening effect **b :** initial progress **:** HEADWAY

³dent *noun* [French, literally, tooth, from Latin *dent-, dens*] (1703)
: TOOTH 3a

dent- *or* **denti-** *or* **dento-** *combining form* [Middle English *denti-*, from Latin, from *dent-, dens* tooth — more at TOOTH]
: tooth **:** teeth ⟨*dentiform*⟩

¹den·tal \'den-tᵊl\ *adjective* [Latin *dentalis*, from *dent-, dens*] (1594)
1 : articulated with the tip or blade of the tongue against or near the upper front teeth
2 : of or relating to the teeth or dentistry
— den·tal·ly \-ē\ *adverb*

²dental *noun* (circa 1727)
: a dental consonant

dental floss *noun* (1910)
: a thread used to clean between the teeth

dental hygienist *noun* (circa 1922)
: a licensed dental professional who cleans and examines teeth

den·ta·li·um \den-'tā-lē-əm\ *noun, plural* **-lia** \-lē-ə\ [New Latin, genus name, from Latin *dentalis*] (1864)
: any of a genus (*Dentalium*) of widely distributed tooth shells; *broadly* **:** TOOTH SHELL

dental technician *noun* (1946)
: one who makes dental appliances

den·tate \'den-ˌtāt\ *adjective* [Latin *dentatus*, from *dent-, dens*] (1810)
: having teeth or pointed conical projections ⟨a *dentate* margin of a leaf⟩

dent corn *noun* (1873)
: an Indian corn having kernels that contain both hard and soft starch and that become indented at maturity

den·ti·cle \'den-ti-kəl\ *noun* [Middle English, from Latin *denticulus*, diminutive of *dent-, dens*] (14th century)
: a conical pointed projection (as a small tooth)

◇ WORD HISTORY
denim It is not unusual for fabrics to be named after the places where they were originally made. Nîmes is a city in France known traditionally for its textiles. A heavy serge produced there became known as *serge de Nîmes*, meaning literally, "serge from Nîmes." The "s" in *Nîmes* is not pronounced in French, so when the name of the fabric came into English in the late 17th century, it was often written *serge de Nim* and later *serge denim*. In time the latter was shortened to *denim*.

den·tic·u·late \den-'ti-kyə-lət\ *or* **den·tic·u·lat·ed** \-,lā-təd\ *adjective* (1661)
1 : finely dentate or serrate ⟨a *denticulate* shell⟩ ⟨a *denticulate* margin of a leaf⟩
2 : cut into dentils
— **den·tic·u·la·tion** \(,)den-,ti-kyə-'lā-shən\ *noun*

den·ti·form \'den-tə-,fòrm\ *adjective* (1708)
: shaped like a tooth

den·ti·frice \'den-tə-frəs\ *noun* [Middle French, from Latin *dentifricium*, from *denti-* + *fricare* to rub — more at FRICTION] (15th century)
: a powder, paste, or liquid for cleaning the teeth

den·til \'den-t⁰l, -,til\ *noun* [obsolete French *dentille*, from Middle French, diminutive of *dent*] (1663)
: one of a series of small projecting rectangular blocks forming a molding especially under a cornice
— **den·tiled** \-t⁰ld, -,tild\ *adjective*

den·tin \'den-t⁰n\ *or* **den·tine** \'den-,tēn, den-'\ *noun* (1845)
: a calcareous material similar to but harder and denser than bone that composes the principal mass of a tooth — see TOOTH illustration
— **den·tin·al** \den-'tē-n⁰l, 'den-t⁰n-əl\ *adjective*

den·tist \'den-təst\ *noun* [French *dentiste*, from *dent*] (1752)
: one who is skilled in and licensed to practice the prevention, diagnosis, and treatment of diseases, injuries, and malformations of the teeth, jaws, and mouth and who makes and inserts false teeth

den·tist·ry \'den-tə-strē\ *noun* (1838)
: the art or profession of a dentist

den·ti·tion \den-'ti-shən\ *noun* [Latin *dentition-, dentitio*, from *dentire* to cut teeth, from *dent-, dens*] (1615)
1 : the development and cutting of teeth
2 : the character of a set of teeth especially with regard to their number, kind, and arrangement — see TOOTH illustration
3 : TEETH

den·tu·lous \'den-chə-ləs\ *adjective* [back-formation from *edentulous*] (1926)
: having teeth

den·ture \'den-chər\ *noun* [French, from Middle French, from *dent*] (1874)
1 : a set of teeth
2 : an artificial replacement for one or more teeth; *especially* : a set of false teeth

den·tur·ist \'den-chə-rist\ *noun* (1965)
: a dental technician who makes, fits, and repairs dentures directly for the public

de·nu·cle·ar·ize \(')dē-'n(y)ü-klē-ə-,rīz, ÷-kyə-lə-,rīz\ *transitive verb* **-ized; -iz·ing** (1958)
: to remove nuclear arms from : prohibit the use of nuclear arms in
— **de·nu·cle·ar·iza·tion** \(,)dē-,n(y)ü-klē-ə-rə-'zā-shən, ÷-kyə-lə-rə-\ *noun*

de·nude \di-'n(y)üd, dē-\ *transitive verb* **de·nud·ed; de·nud·ing** [Latin *denudare*, from *de-* + *nudus* bare — more at NAKED] (15th century)
1 : to deprive of something important
2 a : to strip of all covering or surface layers **b** : to lay bare by erosion **c** : to strip (land) of forests
— **de·nu·da·tion** \,dē-(,)n(y)ü-'dā-shən, ,den-yü-\ *noun*
— **de·nude·ment** \di-'n(y)üd-mənt\ *noun*

de·nu·mer·a·ble \di-'n(y)ü-mə-rə-bəl\ *adjective* (1902)
: capable of being put into one-to-one correspondence with the positive integers
— **de·nu·mer·a·bil·i·ty** \-,n(y)ü-mə-rə-'bi-lə-tē\ *noun*
— **de·nu·mer·a·bly** \-'n(y)ü-mə-rə-blē\ *adverb*

de·nun·ci·a·tion \di-,nən(t)-sē-'ā-shən\ *noun* (1842)

: an act of denouncing; *especially* : a public condemnation
— **de·nun·ci·a·tive** \-'nən(t)-sē-,ā-tiv\ *adjective*
— **de·nun·ci·a·to·ry** \-sē-ə-,tòr-ē, -,tòr-\ *adjective*

Den·ver boot \'den-vər-\ *noun* [*Denver*, Colo.] (1968)
: a metal clamp that is locked onto one of the wheels of an automobile to immobilize it especially until its owner pays accumulated parking fines

Denver omelet *noun* (1954)
: WESTERN OMELET

Denver sandwich *noun* (1950)
: WESTERN SANDWICH

de·ny \di-'nī, dē-\ *transitive verb* **de·nied; de·ny·ing** [Middle English, from Middle French *denier*, from Latin *denegare*, from *de-* + *negare* to deny — more at NEGATE] (14th century)
1 : to declare untrue
2 : to disclaim connection with or responsibility for : DISAVOW
3 a : to give a negative answer to **b** : to refuse to grant **c** : to restrain (oneself) from gratification of desires
4 *archaic* : DECLINE
5 : to refuse to accept the existence, truth, or validity of ☆
— **de·ny·ing·ly** \-'nī-iŋ-lē\ *adverb*

deoch an dor·is \,d(y)ók-⁰n-'dòr-əs\ *Scottish & Irish variant of* DOCH-AN-DORRIS

de·o·dar \'dē-ə-,där\ *also* **de·o·da·ra** \,dē-ə-'där-ə\ *noun* [Hindi *deodār*, from Sanskrit *devadāru*, literally, timber of the gods, from *deva* god + *dāru* wood — more at DEITY, TREE] (1842)
: an East Indian cedar (*Cedrus deodara*)

de·odor·ant \dē-'ō-də-rənt\ *noun* (1869)
: a preparation that destroys or masks unpleasant odors
— **deodorant** *adjective*

de·odor·ize \dē-'ō-də-,rīz\ *transitive verb* (1856)
1 : to eliminate or prevent the offensive odor of
2 : to make (something unpleasant or reprehensible) more acceptable ⟨the movie *deodorizes* his scandalous career⟩
— **de·odor·iza·tion** \-,ō-də-rə-'zā-shən\ *noun*
— **de·odor·iz·er** *noun*

de·on·tic \(,)dē-'än-tik\ *adjective* [Greek *deont-, deon* that which is obligatory, from neuter of present participle of *dein* to lack, be needful — more at DEUTER-] (circa 1866)
: of or relating to moral obligation : DEONTOLOGICAL

de·on·tol·o·gy \,dē-,än-'tä-lə-jē\ *noun* (1826)
: the theory or study of moral obligation
— **de·on·to·log·i·cal** \,dē-,än-tə-'lä-ji-kəl\ *adjective*
— **de·on·tol·o·gist** \,dē-,än-'tä-lə-jist\ *noun*

Deo vo·len·te \,dā-(,)ō-vō-'len-tē, ,dē-\ [Latin] (1767)
: God being willing

de·ox·i·dize \(,)dē-'äk-sə-,dīz\ *transitive verb* (1794)
: to remove oxygen from
— **de·ox·i·da·tion** \(,)dē-,äk-sə-'dā-shən\ *noun*
— **de·ox·i·diz·er** \(,)dē-'äk-sə-,dī-zər\ *noun*

de·oxy \(,)dē-'äk-sē\ *also* **des·oxy** \(,)de-'zäk-sē, -'säk-\ *adjective* [International Scientific Vocabulary]
: containing less oxygen in the molecule than the compound from which it is derived ⟨*deoxy* sugars⟩ — usually used in combination ⟨*de·oxy*ribonucleic acid⟩

de·ox·y·gen·ate \(,)dē-'äk-si-jə-,nāt, ,dē-äk-'si-jə-\ *transitive verb* (1799)
: to remove oxygen from
— **de·ox·y·gen·ation** \(,)dē-,äk-si-jə-'nā-shən, ,dē-äk-,si-jə-\ *noun*

de·ox·y·gen·at·ed *adjective* (1799)
: having the hemoglobin in the reduced state

de·oxy·ri·bo·nu·cle·ase \(,)dē-'äk-si-,rī-bō-'n(y)ü-klē-,ās, -,āz\ *noun* (1946)
: an enzyme that hydrolyzes DNA to nucleotides — called also *DNase*

de·oxy·ri·bo·nu·cle·ic acid \(,)dē-'äk-si-,rī-bō-n(y)ü-,klē-ik-, -,klā-\ *noun* [*deoxyribose* + *nucleic acid*] (1938)
: DNA

de·oxy·ri·bo·nu·cle·o·tide \-'n(y)ü-klē-ə-,tīd\ *noun* (1972)
: a nucleotide that contains deoxyribose and is a constituent of DNA

de·oxy·ri·bose \(,)dē-,äk-si-'rī-,bōs, -,bōz\ *noun* [International Scientific Vocabulary] (1957)
: a pentose sugar $C_5H_{10}O_4$ that is a structural element of DNA

de·part \di-'pärt\ *verb* [Middle English, to divide, part company, from Old French *departir*, from *de-* + *partir* to divide, from Latin *partire*, from *part-, pars* part] (13th century) *intransitive verb*
1 a : to go away : LEAVE **b** : DIE
2 : to turn aside : DEVIATE
transitive verb
: to go away from : LEAVE
synonym see SWERVE

de·part·ed *adjective* (14th century)
1 : BYGONE
2 : having died especially recently ⟨mourning our *departed* friend⟩
synonym see DEAD

de·part·ment \di-'pärt-mənt\ *noun* [French *département*, from Old French, act of dividing, from *departir*] (1735)
1 a : a distinct sphere : PROVINCE ⟨that's not my *department*⟩ **b** : a category consisting especially of a measurable activity or attribute ⟨lacking in the trustworthiness *department* —Garrison Keillor⟩
2 : a functional or territorial division: as **a** : a major administrative division of a government **b** : a major territorial administrative subdivision **c** : a division of a college or school giving instruction in a particular subject **d** : a major division of a business **e** : a section of a department store handling a particular kind of merchandise **f** : a territorial subdivision made for the administration and training of military units
— **de·part·men·tal** \di-,pärt-'men-t⁰l, ,dē-\ *adjective*
— **de·part·men·tal·ly** \-t⁰l-ē\ *adverb*

de·part·men·tal·ize \di-,pärt-'men-t⁰l-,īz, ,dē-\ *transitive verb* **-ized; -iz·ing** (circa 1895)
: to divide into departments
— **de·part·men·tal·iza·tion** \-,men-t⁰l-ə-'zā-shən\ *noun*

department store *noun* (1887)
: a store selling a wide variety of goods and arranged in several departments

☆ **SYNONYMS**
Deny, gainsay, contradict, contravene mean to refuse to accept as true or valid. DENY implies a firm refusal to accept as true, to grant or concede, or to acknowledge the existence or claims of ⟨*denied* the charges⟩. GAINSAY implies disputing the truth of what another has said ⟨no one can *gainsay* her claims⟩. CONTRADICT implies an open or flat denial ⟨her account *contradicts* his⟩. CONTRAVENE implies not so much an intentional opposition as some inherent incompatibility ⟨laws that *contravene* tradition⟩.

\ə\ abut \⁰\ kitten \ər\ further \a\ ash \ā\ ace
\ä\ mop, mar \au̇\ out \ch\ chin \e\ bet \ē\ easy
\g\ go \i\ hit \ī\ ice \j\ job \ŋ\ sing \ō\ go
\ȯ\ law \ȯi\ boy \th\ thin \t̲h̲\ the \ü\ loot \u̇\ foot
\y\ yet \zh\ vision *see also* Guide to Pronunciation

de·par·ture \di-'pär-chər\ *noun* (15th century)
1 a (1) : the act or an instance of departing (2) *archaic* : DEATH **b** : a setting out (as on a new course)
2 : DIVERGENCE 2

de·pau·per·ate \di-'pò-pə-rət\ *adjective* [Middle English *depauperat,* from Medieval Latin *depauperatus,* past participle of *depauperare* to impoverish, from Latin *de-* + *pauperare* to impoverish, from *pauper* poor — more at POOR] (1670)
1 : falling short of natural development or size
2 : IMPOVERISHED ⟨a *depauperate* fauna⟩

de·pend \di-'pend\ *intransitive verb* [Middle English, from Middle French *dependre,* modification of Latin *dependēre,* from *de-* + *pendēre* to hang — more at PENDANT] (15th century)
1 : to be determined, based, or contingent ⟨life *depends* on food⟩ ⟨the value of *Y depends* on *X*⟩
2 : to be pending or undecided
3 a : to place reliance or trust ⟨you can *depend* on me⟩ **b** : to be dependent especially for financial support
4 : to hang down

de·pend·able \di-'pen-də-bəl\ *adjective* (1735)
: capable of being depended on : RELIABLE
— **de·pend·abil·i·ty** \-,pen-də-'bi-lə-tē\ *noun*
— **de·pend·able·ness** *noun*
— **de·pend·ably** \-blē\ *adverb*

de·pen·dence *also* **de·pen·dance** \di-'pen-dən(t)s\ *noun* (15th century)
1 : the quality or state of being dependent; *especially* : the quality or state of being influenced or determined by or subject to another
2 : RELIANCE, TRUST
3 : one that is relied on
4 a : drug addiction **b** : HABITUATION 2b

de·pen·den·cy \-dən(t)-sē\ *noun, plural* **-cies** (1594)
1 : DEPENDENCE 1
2 : something that is dependent on something else; *especially* : a territorial unit under the jurisdiction of a nation but not formally annexed by it
3 : a building (as a stable) that is an adjunct to a main dwelling

¹de·pen·dent \di-'pen-dənt\ *adjective* [Middle English *dependant,* from Middle French, present participle of *dependre*] (14th century)
1 : hanging down
2 a : determined or conditioned by another : CONTINGENT **b** (1) : relying on another for support (2) : affected with a drug dependence **c** : subject to another's jurisdiction **d** : SUBORDINATE 3a
3 a : not mathematically or statistically independent ⟨a *dependent* set of vectors⟩ ⟨*dependent* events⟩ **b** : EQUIVALENT 6a ⟨*dependent* equations⟩
— **de·pen·dent·ly** *adverb*

²dependent *also* **de·pen·dant** \-dənt\ *noun* (1523)
1 *archaic* : DEPENDENCY
2 : one that is dependent; *especially* : a person who relies on another for support

dependent variable *noun* (circa 1852)
: a mathematical variable whose value is determined by that of one or more other variables in a function

de·per·son·al·iza·tion \(,)dē-,pər-snə-lə-'zā-shən, -,pər-s°n-ə-lə-\ *noun* (1906)
1 a : an act or process of depersonalizing **b** : the quality or state of being depersonalized
2 : a psychopathological syndrome characterized by loss of identity and feelings of unreality and strangeness about one's own behavior

de·per·son·al·ize \(')dē-'pər-snə-,līz, -'pər-s°n-ə-\ *transitive verb* (1866)
1 : to deprive of the sense of personal identity ⟨schools that *depersonalize* students⟩
2 : to make impersonal

de·phos·phor·y·la·tion \(,)dē-,fäs-fòr-ə-'lā-shən\ *noun* (1931)
: the process of removing phosphate groups from an organic compound (as ATP) by hydrolysis; *also* : the resulting state
— **de·phos·phor·y·late** \(,)dē-fäs-'fòr-ə-,lāt\ *transitive verb*

de·pict \di-'pikt\ *transitive verb* [Latin *depictus,* past participle of *depingere,* from *de-* + *pingere* to paint — more at PAINT] (15th century)
1 : to represent by or as if by a picture
2 : DESCRIBE 1
— **de·pic·ter** \-'pik-tər\ *noun*
— **de·pic·tion** \-'pik-shən\ *noun*

de·pig·men·ta·tion \(,)dē-,pig-mən-'tā-shən, -,men-\ *noun* (1889)
: loss of normal pigmentation

dep·i·la·tion \,de-pə-'lā-shən\ *noun* [Middle French or Medieval Latin; Middle French, from Medieval Latin *depilation-, depilatio,* from Latin *depilare,* from *de-* + *pilus* hair — more at PILE] (1547)
: the removal of hair, wool, or bristles by chemical or mechanical methods
— **dep·i·late** \'de-pə-,lāt\ *transitive verb*

de·pil·a·to·ry \di-'pi-lə-,tōr-ē, -,tòr-\ *noun, plural* **-ries** (1606)
: an agent for removing hair, wool, or bristles
— **depilatory** *adjective*

de·plane \(,)dē-'plān\ *intransitive verb* (1923)
: to disembark from an airplane

de·plete \di-'plēt\ *transitive verb* **de·plet·ed; de·plet·ing** [Latin *depletus,* past participle of *deplēre,* from *de-* + *plēre* to fill — more at FULL] (1807)
1 : to empty of a principal substance
2 : to lessen markedly in quantity, content, power, or value ☆
— **de·plet·able** \-'plē-tə-bəl\ *adjective*
— **de·ple·tion** \-'plē-shən\ *noun*
— **de·ple·tive** \-'plē-tiv\ *adjective*

de·plor·able \di-'plōr-ə-bəl, -'plòr-\ *adjective* (1612)
1 : LAMENTABLE
2 : deserving censure or contempt : WRETCHED
— **de·plor·able·ness** *noun*
— **de·plor·ably** \-blē\ *adverb*

de·plore \di-'plōr, -'plòr\ *transitive verb* **de·plored; de·plor·ing** [Middle French or Latin; Middle French *deplorer,* from Latin *deplorare,* from *de-* + *plorare* to wail] (1567)
1 a : to feel or express grief for **b** : to regret strongly
2 : to consider unfortunate or deserving of deprecation
— **de·plor·er** \-'plōr-ər\ *noun*
— **de·plor·ing·ly** \-iŋ-lē\ *adverb*

de·ploy \di-'plòi\ *verb* [French *déployer,* literally, to unfold, from Old French *desploier,* from *des-* dis- + *ploier, plier* to fold — more at PLY] (1786)
transitive verb
1 a : to extend (a military unit) especially in width **b** : to place in battle formation or appropriate positions
2 : to spread out, utilize, or arrange especially strategically
intransitive verb
: to move in being deployed
— **de·ploy·able** \-ə-bəl\ *adjective*
— **de·ploy·ment** \-mənt\ *noun*

de·po·lar·ize \(,)dē-'pō-lə-,rīz\ *transitive verb* (1818)
1 : to cause to become partially or wholly unpolarized
2 : to prevent or remove polarization of (as a dry cell or cell membrane)
— **de·po·lar·iza·tion** \(,)dē-,pō-lə-rə-'zā-shən\ *noun*
— **de·po·lar·iz·er** \(,)dē-'pō-lə-,rī-zər\ *noun*

de·po·lit·i·cize \,dē-pə-'li-tə-,sīz\ *transitive verb* (1937)

: to remove the political character of : take out of the realm of politics ⟨*depoliticize* foreign aid⟩
— **de·po·lit·i·ci·za·tion** \,dē-pə-,li-tə-sə-'zā-shən\ *noun*

de·po·ly·mer·ize \(,)dē-pə-'li-mə-,rīz, -'pä-lə-mə-\ (circa 1909)
transitive verb
: to decompose (macromolecules) into simpler compounds (as monomers)
intransitive verb
: to undergo decomposition into simpler compounds
— **de·po·ly·mer·iza·tion** \,dē-pə-,li-mə-rə-'zā-shən, (,)dē-,pä-lə-mə-rə-\ *noun*

de·pone \di-'pōn\ *verb* **de·poned; de·pon·ing** [Medieval Latin *deponere,* from Latin, to put down, from *de-* + *ponere* to put — more at POSITION] (15th century)
: TESTIFY

¹de·po·nent \di-'pō-nənt\ *adjective* [Late Latin *deponent-, deponens,* present participle of *deponere*] (15th century)
: occurring with passive or middle voice forms but with active voice meaning ⟨the *deponent* verbs in Latin and Greek⟩

²deponent *noun* (1530)
1 : a deponent verb
2 : one who gives evidence

de·pop·u·late \(,)dē-'pä-pyə-,lāt\ *transitive verb* [Latin *depopulatus,* past participle of *depopulari,* from *de-* + *populari* to ravage] (1548)
1 *obsolete* : RAVAGE
2 : to reduce greatly the population of
— **de·pop·u·la·tion** \(,)dē-,pä-pyə-'lā-shən\ *noun*

de·port \di-'pōrt, -'pòrt, dē-\ *transitive verb* [Middle French *deporter,* from Latin *deportare* to carry away, from *de-* + *portare* to carry — more at FARE] (1598)
1 : to behave or comport (oneself) especially in accord with a code
2 [Latin *deportare*] **a** : to carry away **b** : to send out of the country by legal deportation
synonym see BANISH, BEHAVE

de·port·able \di-'pōr-tə-bəl, -'pòr-, dē-\ *adjective* (1891)
1 : punishable by deportation ⟨*deportable* offenses⟩

☆ **SYNONYMS**

Deplete, drain, exhaust, impoverish, bankrupt mean to deprive of something essential to existence or potency. DEPLETE implies a reduction in number or quantity so as to endanger the ability to function ⟨*depleting* our natural resources⟩. DRAIN implies a gradual withdrawal and ultimate deprivation of what is necessary to an existence ⟨personal tragedy had *drained* him of all spirit⟩. EXHAUST stresses a complete emptying ⟨her lecture *exhausted* the subject⟩. IMPOVERISH suggests a deprivation of something essential to richness or productiveness ⟨*impoverished* soil⟩. BANKRUPT suggests impoverishment to the point of imminent collapse ⟨war had *bankrupted* the nation of resources⟩.

Deplore, lament, bewail, bemoan mean to express grief or sorrow for something. DEPLORE implies regret for the loss or impairment of something of value ⟨*deplores* the breakdown in family values⟩. LAMENT implies a profound or demonstrative expression of sorrow ⟨*lamenting* the loss of their only child⟩. BEWAIL and BEMOAN imply sorrow, disappointment, or protest finding outlet in words or cries, BEWAIL commonly suggesting loudness, and BEMOAN lugubriousness ⟨fans *bewailed* the defeat⟩ ⟨purists *bemoaning* the corruption of the language⟩.

2 : subject to deportation ⟨*deportable* aliens⟩
de·por·ta·tion \,dē-,pōr-'tā-shən, -,pȯr-, -pər-\ *noun* (1595)
1 : an act or instance of deporting
2 : the removal from a country of an alien whose presence is unlawful or prejudicial
de·por·tee \,dē-,pȯr-'tē, di-, -,pȯr-\ *noun* (1865)
: one who has been deported or is under sentence of deportation
de·port·ment \di-'pōrt-mənt, -'pȯrt-, dē-\ *noun* (1601)
: the manner in which one conducts oneself **:** BEHAVIOR
synonym see BEARING
de·pos·al \di-'pō-zəl, dē-\ *noun* (14th century)
: an act of deposing from office
de·pose \di-'pōz, dē-\ *verb* **de·posed; de·pos·ing** [Middle English, from Middle French *deposer,* from Late Latin *deponere* (perfect indicative *deposui*), from Latin, to put down] (14th century)
transitive verb
1 : to remove from a throne or other high position
2 : to put down **:** DEPOSIT
3 a [Middle English, from Medieval Latin *deponere,* from Late Latin] **:** to testify to under oath or by affidavit **b :** AFFIRM, ASSERT
intransitive verb
: to bear witness
¹**de·pos·it** \di-'pä-zət\ *verb* **de·pos·it·ed** \-'pä-zə-təd, -'päz-təd\; **de·pos·it·ing** \-'pä-zə-tiŋ, -'päz-tiŋ\ [Latin *depositus,* past participle of *deponere*] (1624)
transitive verb
1 : to place especially for safekeeping or as a pledge; *especially* **:** to put in a bank
2 a : to lay down **:** PLACE **b :** to let fall (as sediment)
intransitive verb
: to become deposited
— **de·pos·i·tor** \-'pä-zə-tər, -'päz-tər\ *noun*
²**deposit** *noun* (1624)
1 : the state of being deposited
2 : something placed for safekeeping: as **a :** money deposited in a bank **b :** money given as a pledge or down payment
3 : a place of deposit **:** DEPOSITORY
4 : an act of depositing
5 a : something laid down; *especially* **:** matter deposited by a natural process **b :** a natural accumulation (as of iron ore, coal, or gas)
de·pos·i·tary \di-'pä-zə-,ter-ē\ *noun, plural* **-tar·ies** (1605)
1 : a person to whom something is entrusted
2 : DEPOSITORY 2
de·po·si·tion \,de-pə-'zi-shən, ,dē-pə-\ *noun* (14th century)
1 : an act of removing from a position of authority
2 a : a testifying especially before a court **b :** DECLARATION; *specifically* **:** testimony taken down in writing under oath
3 : an act or process of depositing
4 : something deposited **:** DEPOSIT
— **de·po·si·tion·al** \-'zish-nəl, -shə-nᵊl\ *adjective*
de·pos·i·to·ry \di-'pä-zə-,tōr-ē, -,tȯr-\ *noun, plural* **-ries** (1656)
1 : DEPOSITARY 1
2 : a place where something is deposited especially for safekeeping
depository library *noun* (circa 1930)
: a library designated to receive U.S. government publications
de·pot *I & 2 are* 'de-(,)pō *also* 'dē-, *3 is* 'dē- *sometimes* 'de-\ *noun* [French *dépôt,* from Middle French *depost,* Medieval Latin *depositum,* from Latin, neuter of *depositus*] (1795)
1 a : a place for storing goods or motor vehicles **b :** STORE, CACHE
2 a : a place for the storage of military supplies **b :** a place for the reception and forwarding of military replacements

3 : a building for railroad or bus passengers or freight
de·prave \di-'prāv\ *transitive verb* **de·praved; de·prav·ing** [Middle English, from Middle French *depraver,* from Latin *depravare* to pervert, from *de-* + *pravus* crooked, bad] (14th century)
1 *archaic* **:** to speak ill of **:** MALIGN
2 : to make bad **:** CORRUPT; *especially* **:** to corrupt morally
synonym see DEBASE
— **de·pra·va·tion** \,de-prə-'vā-shən, ,dē-,prā-\ *noun*
— **de·prave·ment** \di-'prāv-mənt\ *noun*
— **de·prav·er** \di-'prā-vər\ *noun*
de·praved \di-'prāvd\ *adjective* (14th century)
: marked by corruption or evil; *especially* **:** PERVERTED
— **de·praved·ly** \-'prā-vəd-lē, -'prāvd-lē\ *adverb*
— **de·praved·ness** \-'prā-vəd-nəs, -'prāvd-nəs\ *noun*
de·prav·i·ty \di-'pra-və-tē *also* -'prā-\ *noun, plural* **-ties** (1641)
1 : the quality or state of being depraved
2 : a corrupt act or practice
dep·re·cate \'de-pri-,kāt\ *transitive verb* **-cat·ed; -cat·ing** [Latin *deprecatus,* past participle of *deprecari* to avert by prayer, from *de-* + *precari* to pray — more at PRAY] (1628)
1 a *archaic* **:** to pray against (as an evil) **b :** to seek to avert ⟨*deprecate* the wrath . . . of the Roman people —Tobias Smollett⟩
2 : to express disapproval of
3 a : PLAY DOWN **:** make little of ⟨speaks five languages . . . but *deprecates* this facility —*Time*⟩ **b :** BELITTLE, DISPARAGE ⟨the most reluctantly admired and least easily *deprecated* of . . . novelists —*New Yorker*⟩
— **dep·re·cat·ing·ly** \-,kā-tiŋ-lē\ *adverb*
— **dep·re·ca·tion** \,de-pri-'kā-shən\ *noun*
dep·re·ca·to·ry \'de-pri-kə-,tōr-ē, -,tȯr-, 'de-prə-,kā-tə-rē\ *adjective* (1586)
1 : seeking to avert disapproval **:** APOLOGETIC
2 : serving to deprecate **:** DISAPPROVING
— **dep·re·ca·to·ri·ly** \,de-pri-kə-'tōr-ə-lē, -'tȯr-\ *adverb*
de·pre·ci·ate \di-'prē-shē-,āt\ *verb* **-at·ed; -at·ing** [Late Latin *depretiatus,* past participle of *depretiare,* from Latin *de-* + *pretium* price — more at PRICE] (15th century)
transitive verb
1 : to lower in estimation or esteem
2 : to lower the price or estimated value of
intransitive verb
: to fall in value
synonym see DECRY
— **de·pre·cia·ble** \-shə-bəl\ *adjective*
— **de·pre·ci·at·ing·ly** \-shē-,ā-tiŋ-lē\ *adverb*
— **de·pre·ci·a·tion** \-,prē-shē-'ā-shən\ *noun*
— **de·pre·ci·a·tive** \-'prē-shə-tiv, -shē-,ā-tiv\ *adjective*
— **de·pre·ci·a·tor** \-shē-,ā-tər\ *noun*
— **de·pre·cia·to·ry** \-shə-,tōr-ē, -,tȯr-\ *adjective*
dep·re·date \'de-prə-,dāt\ *verb* **-dat·ed; -dat·ing** [Late Latin *depraedatus,* past participle of *depraedari,* from Latin *de-* + *praedari* to plunder — more at PREY] (1626)
transitive verb
: to lay waste **:** PLUNDER, RAVAGE
intransitive verb
: to engage in plunder
— **dep·re·da·tion** \,de-prə-'dā-shən\ *noun*
— **dep·re·da·tor** \'de-prə-,dā-tər, di-'pre-də-\ *noun*
— **dep·re·da·to·ry** \di-'pre-də-,tōr-ē, 'de-pri-də-, -,tȯr-\ *adjective*
de·press \di-'pres, dē-\ *transitive verb* [Middle English, from Middle French *depresser,* from Latin *depressus,* past participle of *deprimere* to press down, from *de-* + *premere* to press — more at PRESS] (14th century)
1 *obsolete* **:** REPRESS, SUBJUGATE

2 a : to press down ⟨*depress* a typewriter key⟩
b : to cause to sink to a lower position
3 : to lessen the activity or strength of
4 : SADDEN, DISCOURAGE
5 : to decrease the market value or marketability of
— **de·press·ible** \-'pre-sə-bəl\ *adjective*
de·pres·sant \-'pre-sᵊnt, dē-\ *noun* (1876)
: one that depresses; *specifically* **:** an agent that reduces a bodily functional activity or an instinctive desire (as appetite)
— **depressant** *adjective*
de·pressed *adjective* (1621)
1 : low in spirits **:** SAD; *especially* **:** affected by psychological depression
2 a : vertically flattened ⟨a *depressed* cactus⟩ **b :** having the central part lower than the margin **c :** lying flat or prostrate **d :** dorsoventrally flattened
3 : suffering from economic depression; *especially* **:** UNDERPRIVILEGED
4 : being below the standard
de·press·ing *adjective* (1789)
: that depresses; *especially* **:** causing emotional depression ⟨a *depressing* story⟩
— **de·press·ing·ly** \-siŋ-lē\ *adverb*
de·pres·sion \di-'pre-shən, dē-\ *noun* (14th century)
1 a : the angular distance of a celestial object below the horizon **b :** the size of an angle of depression
2 : an act of depressing or a state of being depressed: as **a :** a pressing down **:** LOWERING **b** (1) **:** a state of feeling sad **:** DEJECTION (2) **:** a psychoneurotic or psychotic disorder marked especially by sadness, inactivity, difficulty in thinking and concentration, a significant increase or decrease in appetite and time spent sleeping, feelings of dejection and hopelessness, and sometimes suicidal tendencies **c** (1) **:** a reduction in activity, amount, quality, or force (2) **:** a lowering of vitality or functional activity
3 : a depressed place or part **:** HOLLOW
4 : LOW 1b
5 : a period of low general economic activity marked especially by rising levels of unemployment
Depression glass *noun* [Great *Depression* of 1929 to circa 1939] (1971)
: tinted glassware machine-produced during the 1930s
¹**de·pres·sive** \di-'pre-siv, dē-\ *adjective* (1620)
1 : tending to depress
2 : of, relating to, marked by, or affected by psychological depression
— **de·pres·sive·ly** *adverb*
²**depressive** *noun* (1937)
: one who is affected with or prone to psychological depression
de·pres·sor \di-'pre-sər, dē-\ *noun* [Late Latin, from Latin *deprimere*] (1611)
: one that depresses: as **a :** a muscle that draws down a part — compare LEVATOR **b :** a device for pressing down or aside **c :** a nerve or nerve fiber that decreases the activity or the tone of the organ or part it innervates
de·pres·sur·ize \(,)dē-'pre-shə-,rīz\ *transitive verb* (1944)
: to release pressure from
— **de·pres·sur·iza·tion** \(,)dē-,pre-shə-rə-'zā-shən\ *noun*
dep·ri·va·tion \,de-prə-'vā-shən *also* ,dē-,prī-\ *noun* (15th century)
1 : the state of being deprived **:** PRIVATION; *especially* **:** removal from an office, dignity, or benefice
2 : an act or instance of depriving **:** LOSS

de·prive \di-'prīv\ *transitive verb* **de·prived; de·priv·ing** [Middle English *depriven*, from Medieval Latin *deprivare*, from Latin *de-* + *privare* to deprive — more at PRIVATE] (14th century)
1 *obsolete* **:** REMOVE
2 : to take something away from ⟨*deprived* him of his professorship —J. M. Phalen⟩
3 : to remove from office
4 : to withhold something from ⟨*deprived* a citizen of her rights⟩
de·prived *adjective* (circa 1522)
: marked by deprivation especially of the necessities of life or of healthful environmental influences ⟨culturally *deprived* children⟩
de·pro·gram \(ˌ)dē-'prō-ˌgram, -grəm\ *transitive verb* (1973)
: to dissuade from convictions usually of a religious nature often by coercive means
— **de·pro·gram·mer** \-mər\ *noun*
depth \'depth\ *noun, plural* **depths** \'depths, 'dep(t)s\ [Middle English, probably from *dep* deep] (14th century)
1 a (1) **:** a deep place in a body of water (2) **:** a part that is far from the outside or surface ⟨the *depths* of the woods⟩ (3) **:** ABYSS **2 b** (1) **:** a profound or intense state (as of thought or feeling) ⟨the *depths* of misery⟩; *also* **:** a reprehensibly low condition ⟨hadn't realized that standards had fallen to such *depths*⟩ (2) **:** the middle of a time (as winter) (3) **:** the worst part
2 a : the perpendicular measurement downward from a surface **b :** the direct linear measurement from front to back
3 : the quality of being deep
4 : the degree of intensity ⟨*depth* of a color⟩; *also* **:** the quality of being profound (as in insight) or full (as of knowledge)
5 : the quality or state of being complete or thorough ⟨a study will be made in *depth*⟩
— **depth·less** \'depth-ləs\ *adjective*
depth charge *noun* (1917)
: an antisubmarine weapon that consists essentially of a drum filled with explosives which is dropped near a target and descends to a predetermined depth where it explodes — called also *depth bomb*
depth of field (1911)
: the range of distances of the object in front of an image-forming device (as a camera lens) measured along the axis of the device throughout which the image has acceptable sharpness
depth perception *noun* (circa 1911)
: the ability to judge the distance of objects and the spatial relationship of objects at different distances
depth psychology *noun* (1924)
: PSYCHOANALYSIS; *also* **:** psychology concerned especially with the unconscious mind
dep·u·ta·tion \ˌde-pyə-'tā-shən\ *noun* (14th century)
1 : the act of appointing a deputy
2 : a group of people appointed to represent others
de·pute \di-'pyüt\ *transitive verb* **de·put·ed; de·put·ing** [Middle English, to appoint, from Middle French *deputer*, from Late Latin *deputare* to assign, from Latin, to consider (as), from *de-* + *putare* to consider — more at PAVE] (14th century)
: DELEGATE
dep·u·tize \'de-pyə-ˌtīz\ *verb* **-tized; -tiz·ing** (circa 1736)
transitive verb
: to appoint as deputy
intransitive verb
: to act as deputy
— **dep·u·ti·za·tion** \ˌde-pyə-tə-'zā-shən\ *noun*
dep·u·ty \'de-pyə-tē\ *noun, plural* **-ties** [Middle English, from Middle French *député*, past participle of *deputer*] (15th century)

1 a : a person appointed as a substitute with power to act **b :** a second in command or assistant who usually takes charge when his or her superior is absent
2 : a member of the lower house of some legislative assemblies
de·rac·i·nate \(ˌ)dē-'ra-sᵊn-ˌāt\ *transitive verb* **-nat·ed; -nat·ing** [Middle French *desraciner*, from *des-* de- + *racine* root, from Late Latin *radicina*, from Latin *radic-, radix* — more at ROOT] (1599)
: UPROOT
— **de·rac·i·na·tion** \(ˌ)dē-ˌra-sᵊn-'ā-shən\ *noun*
de·rail \di-'rā(ə)l, dē-\ *verb* [French *dérailler* to throw off the track, from *dé-* de- + *rail*, from English] (1850)
transitive verb
1 : to cause to run off the rails
2 : to obstruct the progress of **:** FRUSTRATE
intransitive verb
: to leave the rails
— **de·rail·ment** \-mənt\ *noun*
de·rail·leur \di-'rā-lər\ *noun* [French *dérailleur*, from *dérailler*] (1930)
: a mechanism for shifting gears on a bicycle that operates by moving the chain from one set of exposed gears to another
de·range \di-'rānj\ *transitive verb* **de·ranged; de·rang·ing** [French *déranger*, from Old French *desrengier*, from *des-* de- + *reng* line, row — more at RANK] (1776)
1 : to disturb the operation or functions of
2 : DISARRANGE ⟨hatless, with tie *deranged* —G. W. Stonier⟩
3 : to make insane
— **de·range·ment** \-mənt\ *noun*
de·rate \(ˌ)dē-'rāt\ *transitive verb* (1947)
: to lower the rated capability of (as electrical or mechanical apparatus) because of deterioration or inadequacy
der·by \'dər-bē, *especially British* 'där-\ *noun, plural* **derbies** [Edward Stanley (died 1834), 12th earl of *Derby*] (1844)
1 : any of several horse races held annually and usually restricted to three-year-olds
2 : a race or contest open to all comers or to a specified category of contestants ⟨bicycle *derby*⟩
3 : a man's stiff felt hat with dome-shaped crown and narrow brim ◇

derby 3

de·re·al·iza·tion \(ˌ)dē-ˌrē-ə-lə-'zā-shən, -ˌri-ə-\ *noun* (1942)
: a feeling of altered reality that occurs often in schizophrenia and in some drug reactions
de·reg·u·la·tion \(ˌ)dē-ˌre-gyə-'lā-shən\ *noun* (1963)
: the act or process of removing restrictions and regulations
— **de·reg·u·late** \(ˈ)dē-'re-gyə-ˌlāt\ *transitive verb*
¹der·e·lict \'der-ə-ˌlikt\ *adjective* [Latin *derelictus*, past participle of *derelinquere* to abandon, from *de-* + *relinquere* to leave — more at RELINQUISH] (1649)
1 : abandoned especially by the owner or occupant **:** RUN-DOWN
2 : lacking a sense of duty **:** NEGLIGENT
²derelict *noun* (1670)
1 a : something voluntarily abandoned; *specifically* **:** a ship abandoned on the high seas **b :** a tract of land left dry by receding water
2 : a destitute homeless social misfit **:** VAGRANT, BUM
der·e·lic·tion \ˌder-ə-'lik-shən\ *noun* (1597)
1 a : an intentional abandonment **b :** the state of being abandoned
2 : a recession of water leaving permanently dry land

3 a : intentional or conscious neglect **:** DELINQUENCY ⟨*dereliction* of duty⟩ **b :** FAULT, SHORTCOMING
de·re·press \ˌdē-ri-'pres\ *transitive verb* (1962)
: to activate (a gene or enzyme) by releasing from a blocked state
— **de·re·pres·sion** \-'pre-shən\ *noun*
de·ride \di-'rīd, dē-\ *transitive verb* **de·rid·ed; de·rid·ing** [Latin *deridēre*, from *de-* + *ridēre* to laugh] (1530)
1 : to laugh at contemptuously
2 : to subject to usually bitter or contemptuous ridicule
synonym see RIDICULE
— **de·rid·er** *noun*
— **de·rid·ing·ly** \-'rī-diŋ-lē\ *adverb*
de ri·gueur \də-(ˌ)rē-'gər\ *adjective* [French] (1833)
: prescribed or required by fashion, etiquette, or custom **:** PROPER
de·ri·sion \di-'ri-zhən\ *noun* [Middle English, from Middle French, from Late Latin *derision-, derisio*, from Latin *deridēre*] (14th century)
1 a : the use of ridicule or scorn to show contempt **b :** a state of being derided
2 : an object of ridicule or scorn
de·ri·sive \di-'rī-siv, -ziv; -'ri-ziv, -'ri-siv\ *adjective* (circa 1662)
: expressing or causing derision
— **de·ri·sive·ly** *adverb*
— **de·ri·sive·ness** *noun*
de·ri·so·ry \di-'rī-sə-rē, -zə-\ *adjective* (1618)
1 : expressing derision **:** DERISIVE
2 : worthy of derision; *especially* **:** laughably small ⟨a *derisory* sum⟩
de·riv·able \di-'rī-və-bəl\ *adjective* (1653)
: capable of being derived
der·i·vate \'der-ə-ˌvāt\ *noun* (1660)
: DERIVATIVE
der·i·va·tion \ˌder-ə-'vā-shən\ *noun* (15th century)
1 a (1) **:** the formation of a word from another word or base (as by the addition of a usually noninflectional affix) (2) **:** an act of ascertaining or stating the derivation of a word (3) **:** ETYMOLOGY 1 **b :** the relation of a word to its base
2 a : SOURCE, ORIGIN **b :** DESCENT, ORIGINATION
3 : something derived **:** DERIVATIVE
4 : an act or process of deriving
5 : a sequence of statements (as in logic or mathematics) showing that a result is a necessary consequence of previously accepted statements
— **der·i·va·tion·al** \-shnəl, -shə-nᵊl\ *adjective*
¹de·riv·a·tive \di-'ri-və-tiv\ *noun* (15th century)
1 : a word formed by derivation
2 : something derived
3 : the limit of the ratio of the change in a function to the corresponding change in its independent variable as the latter change approaches zero

◇ WORD HISTORY
derby The first horse race referred to as a Derby was named after Edward Stanley, the twelfth Earl of Derby (1752–1834). Stanley's inherited title originally derived from the borough and county of Derby in north central England. In 1780 the earl initiated an annual race at Epsom Downs in the southeastern county of Surrey. That race continues to be run up to the present on the first Wednesday of June. The word *derby* has become attached to other horse races usually restricted to three-year-olds, such as the Kentucky Derby, first run in 1875. It is used as well of races that have nothing to do with horses, such as the Soap Box Derby, for small homemade motorless racing cars.

4 a : a chemical substance related structurally to another substance and theoretically derivable from it **b :** a substance that can be made from another substance

²derivative *adjective* (circa 1530)
1 : formed by derivation
2 : made up of or marked by derived elements
3 : lacking originality : BANAL
— **de·riv·a·tive·ly** *adverb*
— **de·riv·a·tive·ness** *noun*

de·riv·a·ti·za·tion \də-,ri-və-tə-'zā-shən\ *noun* (1967)
: the conversion of a chemical compound into a derivative (as for identification)
— **de·riv·a·tize** \də-'ri-və-,tīz\ *transitive verb*

de·rive \di-'rīv, dē-\ *verb* **de·rived; de·riv·ing** [Middle English, from Middle French *deriver*, from Latin *derivare*, literally, to draw off (water), from *de-* + *rivus* stream — more at RUN] (14th century)
transitive verb
1 a : to take, receive, or obtain especially from a specified source **b :** to obtain (a chemical substance) actually or theoretically from a parent substance
2 : INFER, DEDUCE
3 *archaic* **:** BRING
4 : to trace the derivation of
intransitive verb
: to have or take origin : come as a derivative
synonym see SPRING
— **de·riv·er** *noun*

derm- *or* **derma-** *or* **dermo-** *combining form* [New Latin, from Greek *derm-*, *dermo-*, from *derma*, from *derein* to skin — more at TEAR]
: skin ⟨*derma*l⟩

-derm \,dərm\ *noun combining form* [probably from French *-derme*, from Greek *derma*]
: skin : covering ⟨ecto*derm*⟩

-der·ma \'dər-mə\ *noun combining form, plural* **-dermas** *or* **-der·ma·ta** \-mə-tə\ [New Latin, from Greek *dermat-*, *derma* skin]
: skin or skin ailment of a (specified) type ⟨sclero*derma*⟩

derm·abra·sion \,dər-mə-'brā-zhən\ *noun* (circa 1954)
: surgical removal of skin blemishes or imperfections (as scars or tattoos) by abrasion (as with sandpaper or wire brushes)

der·mal \'dər-məl\ *adjective* (circa 1803)
1 : of or relating to skin and especially to the dermis : CUTANEOUS
2 : EPIDERMAL

dermat- *or* **dermato-** *combining form* [Greek, from *dermat-*, *derma*]
: skin ⟨*dermat*itis⟩ ⟨*dermato*logy⟩

der·ma·ti·tis \,dər-mə-'tī-təs\ *noun* (1876)
: inflammation of the skin

der·mat·o·gen \(,)dər-'ma-tə-jən\ *noun* [International Scientific Vocabulary] (1882)
: PROTODERM

der·ma·to·glyph·ics \,dər-mə-tə-'gli-fiks\ *noun plural but singular or plural in construction* [*dermat-* + Greek *glyphein* to carve + English *-ics* — more at CLEAVE] (1926)
1 : skin patterns; *especially* **:** patterns of the specialized skin of the inferior surfaces of the hands and feet
2 : the science of the study of skin patterns
— **der·ma·to·glyph·ic** \-fik\ *adjective*

der·ma·tol·o·gy \,dər-mə-'tä-lə-jē\ *noun* (1819)
: a branch of science dealing with the skin, its structure, functions, and diseases
— **der·ma·to·log·ic** \-mə-t°l-'ä-jik\ *or* **der·ma·to·log·i·cal** \-ji-kəl\ *adjective*
— **der·ma·tol·o·gist** \-mə-'tä-lə-jist\ *noun*

der·ma·tome \'dər-mə-,tōm\ *noun* [International Scientific Vocabulary *dermat-* + *-ome*] (1910)
: the lateral wall of a somite from which the dermis is produced
— **der·ma·to·mal** \,dər-mə-'tō-məl\ *adjective*

der·ma·to·phyte \(,)dər-'ma-tə-,fīt, 'dər-mə-\ *noun* [International Scientific Vocabulary] (1882)
: a fungus parasitic on the skin or skin derivatives (as hair or nails)

der·ma·to·sis \,dər-mə-'tō-səs\ *noun, plural* **-to·ses** \-,sēz\ (1866)
: a disease of the skin

-der·ma·tous \'dər-mə-təs\ *adjective combining form* [Greek *dermat-*, *derma* skin]
: having a (specified) type of skin ⟨pachy*der*matous⟩

der·mes·tid \(,)dər-'mes-təd\ *noun* [ultimately from Greek *dermēstēs*, a leather-eating worm, literally, skin eater, from *derm-* + *edmenai* to eat — more at EAT] (circa 1888)
: any of a family (Dermestidae) of beetles with clubbed antennae that are very destructive to organic material of animal origin (as dried meat, wool, or museum specimens)
— **dermestid** *adjective*

der·mis \'dər-məs\ *noun* [New Latin, from Late Latin *-dermis*] (circa 1830)
: the sensitive vascular inner mesodermic layer of the skin — called also *corium, cutis*

-der·mis \'dər-məs\ *noun combining form* [Late Latin, from Greek, from *derma*]
: layer of skin or tissue ⟨endo*dermis*⟩

der·moid cyst \'dər-,móid-\ *noun* (1872)
: a cystic tumor often of the ovary that contains skin and skin derivatives (as hair or teeth) — called also *dermoid*

der·nier cri \,dern-yā-'krē\ *noun* [French, literally, last cry] (1896)
: the newest fashion

der·o·gate \'der-ə-,gāt\ *verb* **-gat·ed; -gat·ing** [Middle English, from Late Latin *derogatus*, past participle of *derogare*, from Latin, to annul (a law), detract, from *de-* + *rogare* to ask, propose (a law) — more at RIGHT] (15th century)
transitive verb
: to cause to seem inferior : DISPARAGE
intransitive verb
1 : to take away a part so as to impair : DETRACT
2 : to act beneath one's position or character
— **der·o·ga·tion** \,der-ə-'gā-shən\ *noun*
— **de·ro·ga·tive** \di-'rä-gə-tiv\ *adjective*

de·rog·a·to·ry \di-'rä-gə-,tōr-ē, -,tòr-\ *adjective* (1503)
1 : detracting from the character or standing of something — often used with *to, of,* or *from*
2 : expressive of a low opinion : DISPARAGING ⟨*derogatory* remarks⟩
— **de·rog·a·to·ri·ly** \-,rä-gə-'tōr-ə-lē, -'tòr-\ *adverb*

der·rick \'der-ik\ *noun* [obsolete *derrick* hangman, gallows, from *Derick,* name of 17th century English hangman] (circa 1752)
1 : a hoisting apparatus employing a tackle rigged at the end of a beam
2 : a framework or tower over a deep drill hole (as of an oil well) for supporting boring tackle or for hoisting and lowering ◇

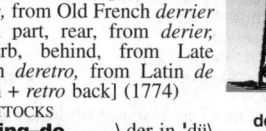
derrick 2

der·ri·ere *or* **der·ri·ère** \,der-ē-'er\ *noun* [French *derrière*, from Old French *derrier* back part, rear, from *derier,* adverb, behind, from Late Latin *deretro,* from Latin *de* from + *retro* back] (1774)
: BUTTOCKS

der·ring–do \,der-iŋ-'dü\ *noun* [Middle English *dorring don* daring to do, from *dorring* (gerund of *dorren* to dare) + *don* to do] (1579)
: daring action ⟨deeds of *derring-do*⟩

der·rin·ger \'der-ən-jər\ *noun* [Henry *Deringer* (died 1869) American inventor] (1853)
: a short-barreled pocket pistol

der·ris \'der-əs\ *noun* [New Latin, genus name, from Greek, skin, from *derein* to skin — more at TEAR] (1919)
1 : a preparation of derris roots and stems used as an insecticide
2 : any of a large genus (*Derris*) of leguminous tropical Old World shrubs and woody vines including sources of poisons and especially commercial sources of rotenone

der·vish \'dər-vish\ *noun* [Turkish *derviş,* literally, beggar, from Persian *darvīsh*] (1585)
1 : a member of a Muslim religious order noted for devotional exercises (as bodily movements leading to a trance)
2 : one that whirls or dances with or as if with the abandonment of a dervish

des- *prefix* [French *dés-*, from Old French *des-* — more at DE-]
: DE- 6 — especially before vowels ⟨*des*oxy⟩

DES \,dē-(,)ē-'es\ *noun* (1971)
: DIETHYLSTILBESTROL

de·sa·cral·ize \(,)dē-'sā-krə-,līz, -'sa-\ *transitive verb* **-ized; -iz·ing** (1911)
: to divest of sacred qualities
— **de·sa·cral·iza·tion** \(,)dē-,sā-krə-lī-'zā-shən, -,sa-\ *noun*

de·sa·li·nate \(')dē-'sa-lə-,nāt *also* -'sā-\ *transitive verb* **-nat·ed; -nat·ing** (1949)
: DESALT
— **de·sa·li·na·tion** \(,)dē-,sa-lə-'nā-shən *also* -,sā-\ *noun*
— **de·sa·li·na·tor** \(,)dē-'sa-lə-,nā-tər *also* -'sā-\ *noun*

de·sa·li·nize \(')dē-'sa-lə-,nīz *also* -'sā-\ *transitive verb* **-nized; -niz·ing** (1963)
: DESALT
— **de·sa·li·ni·za·tion** \(,)dē-,sa-lə-nə-'zā-shən *also* -,sā-\ *noun*

de·salt \(,)dē-'sòlt\ *transitive verb* (circa 1904)
: to remove salt from
— **de·salt·er** *noun*

¹des·cant \'des-,kant\ *noun* [Middle English *dyscant*, from Old North French & Medieval Latin; Old North French *descant*, from Medieval Latin *discantus*, from Latin *dis-* + *cantus* song — more at CHANT] (14th century)
1 a : a melody or counterpoint sung above the plainsong of the tenor **b :** the art of composing or improvising contrapuntal part music; *also* **:** the music so composed or improvised **c :** SOPRANO, TREBLE **d :** a superimposed counterpoint to a simple melody sung typically by some or all of the sopranos
2 : discourse or comment on a theme

◇ **WORD HISTORY**

derrick *Derick* or *Derrick* was apparently the surname of a well-known public executioner active about 1600 at Tyburn, an execution site in what is now central London. Our sole evidence for his existence, however, consists of a few references in plays and popular ballads that circulated in the first decade of the 17th century. According to Thomas Blount's *Glossographia,* an English dictionary published in 1656, *Deric* had become an abusive byword for a hangman. Nothing more is heard of this word for a time, but then *derrick* turns up in the 18th century applied to a kind of block and tackle used aboard ships, and the habitual, if tenuous, assumption is that the famous hangman's name was transferred to a gallows, and the name for a gallows applied to other hoisting apparatuses. In the United States, *derrick* is probably most frequently used for the tower-like structure suspended over an oil well.

\ə\ abut \ᵊ\ kitten \ər\ further \a\ ash \ā\ ace
\ä\ mop, mar \aú\ out \ch\ chin \e\ bet \ē\ easy
\g\ go \i\ hit \ī\ ice \j\ job \ŋ\ sing \ō\ go
\ò\ law \òi\ boy \th\ thin \th\ the \ü\ loot \ú\ foot
\y\ yet \zh\ vision *see also* Guide to Pronunciation

²des·cant \'des-ˌkant, des-', dis-'\ *intransitive verb* (15th century)
1 : to sing or play a descant; *broadly* : SING
2 : COMMENT, DISCOURSE

de·scend \di-'send, dē-\ *verb* [Middle English, from Old French *descendre*, from Latin *descendere*, from *de-* + *scandere* to climb — more at SCAN] (13th century)
intransitive verb
1 : to pass from a higher place or level to a lower one ⟨*descended* from the platform⟩
2 : to pass in discussion from what is logically prior or more comprehensive
3 a : to come down from a stock or source : DERIVE ⟨*descends* from an old merchant family⟩ **b** : to pass by inheritance ⟨a desk that has *descended* in the family⟩ **c** : to pass by transmission ⟨songs *descended* from old ballads⟩
4 : to incline, lead, or extend downward ⟨the road *descends* to the river⟩
5 a : to swoop or pounce down (as in a sudden attack) **b** : to appear suddenly and often disconcertingly as if from above ⟨reporters *descended* on the candidate⟩
6 : to proceed in a sequence or gradation from higher to lower or from more remote to nearer or more recent
7 a : to lower oneself in status or dignity : STOOP **b** : to worsen and sink in condition or estimation
transitive verb
1 : to pass, move, or climb down or down along
2 : to extend down along
— **de·scend·ible** \-'sen-də-bəl\ *adjective*

¹de·scen·dant *or* **de·scen·dent** \di-'sen-dənt\ *adjective* [Middle French & Latin; Middle French *descendant*, from Latin *descendent-*, *descendens*, present participle of *descendere*] (1572)
1 : moving or directed downward
2 : proceeding from an ancestor or source

²descendant *or* **descendent** *noun* [French & Latin; French *descendant*, from Late Latin *descendent-*, *descendens*, from Latin] (1600)
1 : one descended from another or from a common stock
2 : one deriving directly from a precursor or prototype

de·scend·er \di-'sen-dər, 'dē-ˌ\ *noun* (1802)
: the part of a lowercase letter (as p) that descends below the main body of the letter; *also* : a letter that has such a part

de·scen·sion \di-'sen-chən\ *noun* (15th century)
archaic : DESCENT 2

de·scent \di-'sent\ *noun* [Middle English, from Middle French *descente*, from Old French *descendre*] (14th century)
1 a : derivation from an ancestor : BIRTH, LINEAGE ⟨of French *descent*⟩ **b** : transmission or devolution of an estate by inheritance usually in the descending line **c** : the fact or process of originating from an ancestral stock **d** : the shaping or development in nature and character by transmission from a source : DERIVATION
2 : the act or process of descending
3 : a step downward in a scale of gradation; *specifically* : one generation in an ancestral line or genealogical scale
4 a : an inclination downward : SLOPE **b** : a descending way (as a downgrade or stairway) **c** *obsolete* : the lowest part
5 a : ATTACK, INVASION **b** : a sudden disconcerting appearance (as for a visit)
6 : a downward step (as in station or value) : DECLINE ⟨*descent* of the family to actual poverty⟩

de·scribe \di-'skrīb\ *transitive verb* **de·scribed; de·scrib·ing** [Middle English, from Latin *describere*, from *de-* + *scribere* to write — more at SCRIBE] (15th century)
1 : to represent or give an account of in words ⟨*describe* a picture⟩
2 : to represent by a figure, model, or picture : DELINEATE

3 *obsolete* : DISTRIBUTE
4 : to trace or traverse the outline of ⟨*describe* a circle⟩
5 *archaic* : OBSERVE, PERCEIVE
— **de·scrib·able** \-'skrī-bə-bəl\ *adjective*
— **de·scrib·er** *noun*

de·scrip·tion \di-'skrip-shən\ *noun* [Middle English *descripcioun*, from Middle French & Latin; Middle French *description*, from Latin *description-*, *descriptio*, from *describere*] (14th century)
1 a : an act of describing; *specifically* : discourse intended to give a mental image of something experienced **b** : a descriptive statement or account
2 : kind or character especially as determined by salient features ⟨opposed to any tax of so radical a *description*⟩
synonym see TYPE

de·scrip·tive \di-'skrip-tiv\ *adjective* (1751)
1 : serving to describe ⟨a *descriptive* account⟩
2 a : referring to, constituting, or grounded in matters of observation or experience ⟨the *descriptive* basis of science⟩ **b** : factually grounded or informative rather than normative, prescriptive, or emotive ⟨*descriptive* cultural studies⟩
3 *of a modifier* **a** : expressing the quality, kind, or condition of what is denoted by the modified term ⟨*hot* in "hot water" is a *descriptive* adjective⟩ **b** : NONRESTRICTIVE
4 : of, relating to, or dealing with the structure of a language at a particular time usually with exclusion of historical and comparative data ⟨*descriptive* linguistics⟩
— **de·scrip·tive·ly** *adverb*
— **de·scrip·tive·ness** *noun*

de·scrip·tor \di-'skrip-tər\ *noun* (1933)
: something (as a word or characteristic feature) that serves to describe or identify; *especially* : a word or phrase (as an index term) used to identify an item (as a subject or document) in an information retrieval system

¹de·scry \di-'skrī\ *transitive verb* **de·scried; de·scry·ing** [Middle English *descrien*, from Middle French *descrier* to proclaim, decry] (14th century)
1 a : to catch sight of **b** : FIND OUT, DISCOVER
2 *obsolete* : to make known : REVEAL

²descry *noun* (1605)
obsolete : discovery or view from afar

Des·de·mo·na \ˌdez-də-'mō-nə\ *noun*
: the wife of Othello in Shakespeare's *Othello*

des·e·crate \'de-si-ˌkrāt\ *transitive verb* **-crat·ed; -crat·ing** [*de-* + *-secrate* (as in *consecrate*)] (1677)
1 : to violate the sanctity of : PROFANE
2 : to treat disrespectfully, irreverently, or outrageously ⟨the kind of shore development . . . that has *desecrated* so many waterfronts —John Fischer⟩
— **des·e·crat·er** *or* **des·e·cra·tor** \-ˌkrā-tər\ *noun*

des·e·cra·tion \ˌde-si-'krā-shən\ *noun* (circa 1717)
: an act or instance of desecrating : the state of being desecrated

de·seg·re·gate \(ˌ)dē-'se-gri-ˌgāt\ (1944)
transitive verb
: to eliminate segregation in; *specifically* : to free of any law, provision, or practice requiring isolation of the members of a particular race in separate units
intransitive verb
: to become desegregated

de·seg·re·ga·tion \(ˌ)dē-ˌse-gri-'gā-shən\ *noun* (1951)
1 : the action or an instance of desegregating
2 : the state of being desegregated

de·se·lect \ˌdē-sə-'lekt\ *transitive verb* (1965)
: DISMISS, REJECT

de·sen·si·tize \(ˌ)dē-'sen(t)-sə-ˌtīz\ *transitive verb* (1898)
1 : to make (a sensitized or hypersensitive individual) insensitive or nonreactive to a sensitizing agent

2 : to make emotionally insensitive or callous; *specifically* : to extinguish an emotional response (as of fear, anxiety, or guilt) to stimuli that formerly induced it
— **de·sen·si·ti·za·tion** \(ˌ)dē-ˌsen(t)-sə-tə-'zā-shən\ *noun*
— **de·sen·si·tiz·er** \(ˌ)dē-'sen-sə-ˌtī-zər\ *noun*

¹des·ert \'de-zərt\ *noun* [Middle English, from Old French, from Late Latin *desertum*, from Latin, neuter of *desertus*, past participle of *deserere* to desert, from *de-* + *serere* to join together — more at SERIES] (13th century)
1 a : arid barren land; *especially* : a tract incapable of supporting any considerable population without an artificial water supply **b** : an area of water apparently devoid of life
2 *archaic* : a wild uninhabited and uncultivated tract
3 : a desolate or forbidding area ⟨lost in a *desert* of doubt⟩
— **de·ser·tic** \de-'zər-tik\ *adjective*

²des·ert \'de-zərt\ *adjective* (13th century)
1 : desolate and sparsely occupied or unoccupied ⟨a *desert* island⟩
2 : of or relating to a desert
3 *archaic* : FORSAKEN

³de·sert \di-'zərt\ *noun* [Middle English *deserte*, from Old French, from feminine of *desert*, past participle of *deservir* to deserve] (13th century)
1 : the quality or fact of deserving reward or punishment
2 : deserved reward or punishment — usually used in plural ⟨got their just *deserts*⟩
3 : EXCELLENCE, WORTH

⁴de·sert \di-'zərt\ *verb* [French *déserter*, from Late Latin *desertare*, frequentative of Latin *deserere*] (1603)
transitive verb
1 : to withdraw from or leave usually without intent to return
2 a : to leave in the lurch ⟨*desert* a friend in trouble⟩ **b** : to abandon (military service) without leave
intransitive verb
: to quit one's post, allegiance, or service without leave or justification; *especially* : to abandon military duty without leave and without intent to return
synonym see ABANDON
— **de·sert·er** *noun*

de·ser·ti·fi·ca·tion \di-ˌzər-tə-fə-'kā-shən\ *noun* (1974)
: the process of becoming desert (as from land mismanagement or climate change)

de·ser·tion \di-'zər-shən\ *noun* (1591)
1 : an act of deserting; *especially* : the abandonment without consent or legal justification of a person, post, or relationship and the associated duties and obligations ⟨sued for divorce on grounds of *desertion*⟩
2 : a state of being deserted or forsaken

desert locust *noun* (1944)
: a destructive migratory locust (*Schistocerca gregaria*) of southwestern Asia and parts of northern Africa

desert soil *noun* (circa 1938)
: a soil that develops under sparse shrub vegetation in warm to cool arid climates with a light-colored surface soil usually underlain by calcareous material and a hardpan layer

desert varnish *noun* (circa 1898)
: a dark coating which is found on rocks after long exposure in desert regions and whose color is due to iron and manganese oxides

de·serve \di-'zərv\ *verb* **de·served; de·serv·ing** [Middle English, from Old French *deservir*, from Latin *deservire* to devote oneself to, from *de-* + *servire* to serve] (13th century)
transitive verb
: to be worthy of : MERIT ⟨*deserves* another chance⟩
intransitive verb
: to be worthy, fit, or suitable for some reward

or requital ⟨have become recognized as they *deserve* —T. S. Eliot⟩
— **de·serv·er** *noun*

de·served \-'zərvd\ *adjective* (circa 1552)
: of, relating to, or being that which one deserves ⟨a *deserved* reputation⟩
— **de·served·ly** \-'zər-vəd-lē, -'zərvd-lē\ *adverb*
— **de·served·ness** \-'zər-vəd-nəs, -'zərvd-nəs\ *noun*

¹**de·serv·ing** \-'zər-viŋ\ *noun* (14th century)
: DESERT, MERIT ⟨reward the proud according to their *deservings* —Charles Kingsley⟩

²**deserving** *adjective* (1576)
: MERITORIOUS, WORTHY; *especially* : meriting financial aid ⟨scholarships for *deserving* students⟩

de·sex \(ˌ)dē-'seks\ *transitive verb* (1911)
1 : CASTRATE, SPAY
2 : to eliminate perceived sexism from ⟨*desex* the language of church Bible study programs —R. M. Harley⟩

de·sex·u·al·ize \(ˌ)dē-'sek-sh(ə-)wə-ˌlīz, -'sek-shə-ˌlīz\ *transitive verb* (1894)
1 : to deprive of sexual characters or power
2 : to divest of sexual quality
— **de·sex·u·al·iza·tion** \(ˌ)dē-ˌsek-sh(ə-)wə-lə-'zā-shən, -'sek-shə-lə-\ *noun*

des·ha·bille \ˌde-sə-'bē(ə)l, -'bil, -'bē\ *variant of* DISHABILLE

des·ic·cant \'de-si-kənt\ *noun* (1676)
: a drying agent (as calcium chloride)

des·ic·cate \'de-si-ˌkāt\ *verb* **-cat·ed; -cat·ing** [Latin *desiccatus*, past participle of *desiccare* to dry up, from *de-* + *siccare* to dry, from *siccus* dry — more at SACK] (1575)
transitive verb
1 : to dry up
2 : to preserve (a food) by drying : DEHYDRATE
3 : to drain of emotional or intellectual vitality
intransitive verb
: to become dried up
— **des·ic·ca·tion** \ˌde-si-'kā-shən\ *noun*
— **des·ic·ca·tive** \'de-si-ˌkā-tiv\ *adjective*
— **des·ic·ca·tor** \'de-si-ˌkā-tər\ *noun*

de·sid·er·ate \di-'si-də-ˌrāt, -'zi-\ *transitive verb* **-at·ed; -at·ing** [Latin *desideratus*, past participle of *desiderare* to desire] (1645)
: to entertain or express a wish to have or attain
— **de·sid·er·a·tion** \-ˌsi-də-'rā-shən, -ˌzi-\ *noun*
— **de·sid·er·a·tive** \-'si-də-ˌrā-tiv, -'si-d(ə-)rət-, -'zi-\ *adjective*

de·sid·er·a·tum \di-ˌsi-də-'rä-təm, -ˌzi-, -'rā-\ *noun, plural* **-ta** \-tə\ [Latin, neuter of *desideratus*] (1652)
: something desired as essential

¹**de·sign** \di-'zīn\ *verb* [Middle English, to outline, indicate, mean, from Middle French & Medieval Latin; Middle French *designer* to designate, from Medieval Latin *designare*, from Latin, to mark out, from *de-* + *signare* to mark — more at SIGN] (14th century)
transitive verb
1 : to create, fashion, execute, or construct according to plan : DEVISE, CONTRIVE
2 a : to conceive and plan out in the mind ⟨he *designed* the perfect crime⟩ **b** : to have as a purpose : INTEND ⟨she *designed* to excel in her studies⟩ **c** : to devise for a specific function or end ⟨a book *designed* primarily as a college textbook⟩
3 *archaic* : to indicate with a distinctive mark, sign, or name
4 a : to make a drawing, pattern, or sketch of
b : to draw the plans for
intransitive verb
1 : to conceive or execute a plan
2 : to draw, lay out, or prepare a design
— **de·sign·ed·ly** \-'zī-nəd-lē\ *adverb*

²**design** *noun* (1588)
1 a : a particular purpose held in view by an individual or group ⟨he has ambitious *designs* for his son⟩ **b** : deliberate purposive planning ⟨more by accident than *design*⟩

2 : a mental project or scheme in which means to an end are laid down
3 a : a deliberate undercover project or scheme : PLOT **b** *plural* : aggressive or evil intent — used with *on* or *against* ⟨he has *designs* on the money⟩
4 : a preliminary sketch or outline showing the main features of something to be executed : DELINEATION
5 a : an underlying scheme that governs functioning, developing, or unfolding : PATTERN, MOTIF ⟨the general *design* of the epic⟩ **b** : a plan or protocol for carrying out or accomplishing something (as a scientific experiment); *also* : the process of preparing this
6 : the arrangement of elements or details in a product or work of art
7 : a decorative pattern
8 : the creative art of executing aesthetic or functional designs
synonym see INTENTION, PLAN

¹**des·ig·nate** \'de-zig-ˌnāt, -nət\ *adjective* [Latin *designatus*, past participle of *designare*] (1646)
: chosen but not yet installed ⟨ambassador *designate*⟩

²**des·ig·nate** \-ˌnāt\ *transitive verb* **-nat·ed; -nat·ing** (1791)
1 : to indicate and set apart for a specific purpose, office, or duty ⟨*designate* a group to prepare a plan⟩
2 a : to point out the location of ⟨a marker *designating* the battle⟩ **b** : to distinguish as to class ⟨the area we *designate* as that of spiritual values —J. B. Conant⟩ **c** : SPECIFY, STIPULATE ⟨to be sent by a *designated* shipper⟩
3 : DENOTE ⟨associate names with the people they *designate*⟩
4 : to call by a distinctive title, term, or expression ⟨a particle *designated* the neutron⟩
— **des·ig·na·tive** \-ˌnā-tiv\ *adjective*
— **des·ig·na·tor** \-ˌnā-tər\ *noun*
— **des·ig·na·to·ry** \-nə-ˌtōr-ē, -ˌtȯr-\ *adjective*

designated hitter *noun* (1973)
: a baseball player designated at the start of the game to bat in place of the pitcher without causing the pitcher to be removed from the game

des·ig·na·tion \ˌde-zig-'nā-shən\ *noun* (14th century)
1 : the act of indicating or identifying
2 : appointment to or selection for an office, post, or service
3 : a distinguishing name, sign, or title
4 : the relation between a sign and the thing signified

des·ig·nee \ˌde-zig-'nē\ *noun* (1925)
: one who is designated

¹**de·sign·er** \di-'zī-nər\ *noun* (1662)
: one that designs: as **a** : one who creates and often executes plans for a project or structure ⟨urban *designers*⟩ ⟨a theater set *designer*⟩ **b** : one that creates and manufactures a new product style or design; *especially* : one who designs and manufactures high-fashion clothing ⟨the *designer's* new fall line⟩

²**designer** *adjective* (1966)
1 : of, relating to, or produced by a designer ⟨*designer* wallpaper⟩ ⟨wearing a *designer* original⟩; *also* : displaying the name, signature, or logo of a designer or manufacturer ⟨*designer* jeans⟩
2 : intended to reflect the latest in sophisticated taste or fashion ⟨*designer* ice cream⟩ ⟨a *designer* haircut⟩

designer drug *noun* (1983)
: a synthetic version of a controlled substance (as heroin) that is produced with a slightly altered molecular structure to avoid having it classified as an illicit drug

de·sign·ing \di-'zī-niŋ\ *adjective* (1653)
1 : practicing forethought
2 : CRAFTY, SCHEMING

de·sign·ment \di-'zīn-mənt\ *noun* (1583)
obsolete : PLAN, PURPOSE

de·si·pra·mine \də-'zi-prə-ˌmēn\ *noun* [*des*-methyl (from *des-* + *methyl*) + imi*pramine*] (1965)
: a tricyclic antidepressant $C_{18}H_{22}N_2$

de·sir·abil·i·ty \di-ˌzī-rə-'bi-lə-tē\ *noun, plural* **-ties** (1824)
1 *plural* : desirable conditions ⟨had understood and studied certain *desirabilities* —D. D. Eisenhower⟩
2 : the quality, fact, or degree of being desirable

¹**de·sir·able** \di-'zī-rə-bəl\ *adjective* (14th century)
1 : having pleasing qualities or properties : ATTRACTIVE ⟨a *desirable* woman⟩
2 : worth seeking or doing as advantageous, beneficial, or wise : ADVISABLE ⟨*desirable* legislation⟩
— **de·sir·able·ness** *noun*
— **de·sir·ably** \-blē\ *adverb*

²**desirable** *noun* (1645)
: one that is desirable

¹**de·sire** \di-'zīr, dē-\ *verb* **de·sired; de·sir·ing** [Middle English, from Old French *desirer*, from Latin *desiderare*, from *de-* + *sider-*, *sidus* heavenly body] (13th century)
transitive verb
1 : to long or hope for : exhibit or feel desire for
2 a : to express a wish for : REQUEST **b** *archaic* : to express a wish to : ASK
3 *obsolete* : INVITE
4 *archaic* : to feel the loss of
intransitive verb
: to have or feel desire ☆

²**desire** *noun* (14th century)
1 : conscious impulse toward something that promises enjoyment or satisfaction in its attainment
2 a : LONGING, CRAVING **b** : sexual urge or appetite
3 : a usually formal request or petition for some action
4 : something desired

de·sir·ous \di-'zīr-əs\ *adjective* (14th century)
: impelled or governed by desire ⟨*desirous* of fame⟩
— **de·sir·ous·ly** *adverb*
— **de·sir·ous·ness** *noun*

de·sist \di-'zist, -'sist, dē-\ *intransitive verb* [Middle English, from Middle French *desister*, from Latin *desistere*, from *de-* + *sistere* to stand, stop; akin to Latin *stare* to stand — more at STAND] (15th century)
: to cease to proceed or act
synonym see STOP
— **de·sis·tance** \-'zis-tən(t)s, -'sis-\ *noun*

desk \'desk\ *noun* [Middle English *deske*, from Medieval Latin *desca*, modification of Old Italian *desco* table, from Latin *discus* dish, disc — more at DISH] (14th century)
1 a : a table, frame, or case with a sloping or horizontal surface especially for writing and

☆ **SYNONYMS**
Desire, wish, want, crave, covet mean to have a longing for. DESIRE stresses the strength of feeling and often implies strong intention or aim ⟨*desires* to start a new life⟩. WISH sometimes implies a general or transient longing especially for the unattainable ⟨*wishes* for permanent world peace⟩. WANT specifically suggests a felt need or lack ⟨*wants* to have a family⟩. CRAVE stresses the force of physical appetite or emotional need ⟨*craves* sweets⟩. COVET implies strong envious desire ⟨*covets* his rise to fame⟩.

\ə\ abut \ᵊ\ kitten \ər\ further \a\ ash \ā\ ace
\ä\ mop, mar \aȯ\ out \ch\ chin \e\ bet \ē\ easy
\g\ go \i\ hit \ī\ ice \j\ job \ŋ\ go
\ȯ\ law \ȯi\ boy \th\ thin \t͟h\ the \ü\ loot \u̇\ foot
\y\ yet \zh\ vision *see also* Guide to Pronunciation

reading and often with drawers, compartments, and pigeonholes **b :** a reading table or lectern from which a liturgical service is read **c :** a table, counter, stand, or booth at which a person works **2 a :** a division of an organization specializing in a particular phase of activity ⟨the Russian *desk* in the Department of State⟩ **b :** a seating position according to rank in an orchestra ⟨a first-*desk* violinist⟩

desk·bound \'desk-,baùnd\ *adjective* (1944)
: restricted to work at a desk

de–skill \dē-'skil\ *transitive verb* (1941)
1 : to reduce the level of skill needed for (a job)
2 : to reduce the level of skill needed for a job by (a worker)

desk·man \'desk-,man, -mən\ *noun* (1913)
: one that works at a desk; *specifically* **:** a newspaperman who processes news and prepares copy

¹desk·top \'desk-,täp\ *noun* (1929)
1 : the top of a desk; *also* **:** an office desktop simulated by a computer program
2 : a desktop computer

²desktop *adjective* (1958)
: of a size that can be conveniently used on a desk or table ⟨*desktop* computers⟩ — compare LAPTOP

desktop publishing *noun* (1984)
: the production of printed matter by means of a desktop computer having a layout program that integrates text and graphics

desm- *or* **desmo-** *combining form* [New Latin, from Greek, from *desmos*, from *dein* to bind — more at DIADEM]
: bond **:** ligament ⟨*desmo*some⟩

des·mid \'dez-məd\ *noun* [ultimately from Greek *desmos*] (1862)
: any of numerous unicellular or colonial green algae (order Zygnematales)

des·mo·some
\'dez-mə-,sōm\
noun (circa 1932)
: a specialized local thickening of the cell membrane of an epithelial cell that serves to anchor contiguous cells together

desmid

— des·mo·som·al \-,sō-məl\ *adjective*

¹des·o·late \'de-sə-lət, 'de-zə-\ *adjective* [Middle English *desolat*, from Latin *desolatus*, past participle of *desolare* to abandon, from *de-* + *solus* alone] (14th century)
1 : devoid of inhabitants and visitors **:** DESERTED
2 : joyless, disconsolate, and sorrowful through or as if through separation from a loved one
3 a : showing the effects of abandonment and neglect **:** DILAPIDATED **b :** BARREN, LIFELESS ⟨a *desolate* landscape⟩ **c :** devoid of warmth, comfort, or hope **:** GLOOMY ⟨*desolate* memories⟩
synonym see ALONE
— des·o·late·ly *adverb*
— des·o·late·ness *noun*

²des·o·late \-,lāt\ *transitive verb* **-lat·ed; -lat·ing** (14th century)
: to make desolate: **a :** to deprive of inhabitants **b :** to lay waste **c :** FORSAKE **d :** to make wretched
— des·o·lat·er *or* **des·o·la·tor** \-,lā-tər\ *noun*
— des·o·lat·ing·ly \-,lā-tiŋ-lē\ *adverb*

des·o·la·tion \,de-sə-'lā-shən, ,de-zə-\ *noun* (14th century)
1 : the action of desolating
2 a : GRIEF, SADNESS **b :** LONELINESS
3 : DEVASTATION, RUIN
4 : barren wasteland

de·sorb \(,)dē-'sòrb, -'zòrb\ *transitive verb* (1924)
: to remove (a sorbed substance) by the reverse of adsorption or absorption

de·sorp·tion \-'sòrp-shən, -'zòrp-\ *noun* (1924)
: the process of desorbing

desoxy- — see DEOXY-

des·oxy·ri·bo·nu·cle·ic acid \de-,zäk-sē-'rī-bō-n(y)ù-,klē-ik-, -,klä-\ *noun* (1931)
: DNA

¹de·spair \di-'spar, -'sper\ *verb* [Middle English *despeiren*, from Middle French *desperer*, from Latin *desperare*, from *de-* + *sperare* to hope; akin to Latin *spes* hope — more at SPEED] (14th century)
intransitive verb
: to lose all hope or confidence ⟨*despair* of winning⟩
transitive verb
obsolete **:** to lose hope for
— de·spair·er *noun*

²despair *noun* (14th century)
1 : utter loss of hope
2 : a cause of hopelessness ⟨an incorrigible child is the *despair* of his parents⟩

de·spair·ing *adjective* (1589)
: given to, arising from, or marked by despair **:** devoid of hope
synonym see DESPONDENT
— de·spair·ing·ly \-iŋ-lē\ *adverb*

des·patch \dis-'pach\ *variant of* DISPATCH

des·per·a·do \,des-pə-'rä-(,)dō, -'rä-\ *noun*, *plural* **-does** *or* **-dos** [probably alteration of obsolete *desperate* desperado, from *desperate*, adjective] (1647)
: a bold or violent criminal; *especially* **:** a bandit of the western U.S. in the 19th century

des·per·ate \'des-p(ə-)rət, -pərt\ *adjective* [Latin *desperatus*, past participle of *desperare*] (15th century)
1 a : having lost hope ⟨a *desperate* spirit crying for relief⟩ **b :** giving no ground for hope ⟨the outlook was *desperate*⟩
2 a : moved by despair ⟨victims made *desperate* by abuse⟩ **b :** involving or employing extreme measures in an attempt to escape defeat or frustration ⟨made a *desperate* leap for the rope⟩
3 : suffering extreme need or anxiety ⟨*desperate* for money⟩
4 : involving extreme danger or possible disaster ⟨a *desperate* situation⟩
5 : of extreme intensity
6 : SHOCKING, OUTRAGEOUS
synonym see DESPONDENT
— des·per·ate·ly *adverb*
— des·per·ate·ness *noun*

des·per·a·tion \,des-pə-'rā-shən\ *noun* (14th century)
1 : loss of hope and surrender to despair
2 : a state of hopelessness leading to rashness

de·spi·ca·ble \di-'spi-kə-bəl, 'des-(,)pi-\ *adjective* [Late Latin *despicabilis*, from Latin *despicari* to despise] (1553)
: deserving to be despised **:** so worthless or obnoxious as to rouse moral indignation ⟨*despicable* behavior⟩
synonym see CONTEMPTIBLE
— de·spi·ca·ble·ness *noun*
— de·spi·ca·bly \-blē\ *adverb*

de·spir·i·tu·al·ize \(,)dē-'spi-ri-ch(ə-)wə-,līz, -chə-,līz\ *transitive verb* (1868)
: to deprive of spiritual character or influence

de·spise \di-'spīz\ *transitive verb* **de·spised; de·spis·ing** [Middle English, from Old French *despis-*, stem of *despire*, from Latin *despicere*, from *de-* + *specere* to look — more at SPY] (14th century)
1 : to look down on with contempt or aversion ⟨*despised* the weak⟩
2 : to regard as negligible, worthless, or distasteful ☆
— de·spise·ment \-'spīz-mənt\ *noun*
— de·spis·er \-'spī-zər\ *noun*

¹de·spite \di-'spīt\ *noun* [Middle English, from Old French *despit*, from Latin *despectus*, from *despicere*] (13th century)
1 : the feeling or attitude of despising **:** CONTEMPT
2 : MALICE, SPITE
3 a : an act showing contempt or defiance **b :** DETRIMENT, DISADVANTAGE ⟨I know of no government which stands to its obligations, even in its own *despite*, more solidly —Sir Winston Churchill⟩
— in despite of : in spite of

²despite *transitive verb* **de·spit·ed; de·spit·ing** (14th century)
1 *archaic* **:** to treat with contempt
2 *obsolete* **:** to provoke to anger **:** VEX

³despite *preposition* (15th century)
: in spite of ⟨played *despite* an injury⟩

de·spite·ful \di-'spīt-fəl\ *adjective* (15th century)
: expressing malice or hate
— de·spite·ful·ly \-fə-lē\ *adverb*
— de·spite·ful·ness *noun*

de·spit·eous \dis-'pi-tē-əs\ *adjective* (14th century)
archaic **:** feeling or showing despite **:** MALICIOUS
— de·spit·eous·ly *adverb*, *archaic*

de·spoil \di-'spòi(ə)l\ *transitive verb* [Middle English *despoylen*, from Middle French *despoillier*, from Latin *despoliare*, from *de-* + *spoliare* to strip, rob — more at SPOIL] (14th century)
: to strip of belongings, possessions, or value **:** PILLAGE
synonym see RAVAGE
— de·spoil·er *noun*
— de·spoil·ment \-mənt\ *noun*

de·spo·li·a·tion \di-,spō-lē-'ā-shən\ *noun* [Late Latin *despoliation-*, *despoliatio*, from *despoliare*] (circa 1657)
: the condition of being despoiled **:** SPOLIATION

¹de·spond \di-'spänd\ *intransitive verb* [Latin *despondēre*, from *de-* + *spondēre* to promise solemnly — more at SPOUSE] (1655)
: to become despondent

²despond *noun* (1678)
: DESPONDENCY

de·spon·dence \di-'spän-dən(t)s\ *noun* (1676)
: DESPONDENCY

de·spon·den·cy \-dən-sē\ *noun* (1653)
: the state of being despondent **:** DEJECTION, HOPELESSNESS

de·spon·dent \-dənt\ *adjective* [Latin *despondent-*, *despondens*, present participle of *despondēre*] (circa 1699)
: feeling or showing extreme discouragement, dejection, or depression ⟨*despondent* about his health⟩ ☆
— de·spon·dent·ly *adverb*

des·pot \'des-pət, -,pät\ *noun* [Middle French *despote*, from Greek *despotēs* master, lord, autocrat, from *des-* (akin to *domos* house) + *-potēs* (akin to *posis* husband); akin to Sanskrit *dampati* lord of the house — more at DOME, POTENT] (1585)

1 a : a Byzantine emperor or prince **b :** a bishop or patriarch of the Eastern Orthodox Church **c :** an Italian hereditary prince or military leader during the Renaissance
2 a : a ruler with absolute power and authority **b :** a person exercising power tyrannically
des·pot·ic \des-'pä-tik, dis-\ *adjective* (1650) **:** of, relating to, or characteristic of a despot — **des·pot·i·cal·ly** \-ti-k(ə-)lē\ *adverb*
des·po·tism \'des-pə-ˌti-zəm\ *noun* (circa 1727)
1 a : rule by a despot **b :** despotic exercise of power
2 a : a system of government in which the ruler has unlimited power **:** ABSOLUTISM **b :** a despotic state
des·qua·mate \'des-kwə-ˌmāt\ *intransitive verb* **-mat·ed; -mat·ing** [Latin *desquamatus*, past participle of *desquamare* to scale, from *de-* + *squama* scale] (1828) **:** to peel off in scales
— **des·qua·ma·tion** \ˌdes-kwə-'mā-shən\ *noun*
des·sert \di-'zərt\ *noun* [Middle French, from *desservir* to clear the table, from *des-* de- + *servir* to serve, from Latin *servire*] (1600)
1 : a usually sweet course or dish (as of pastry or ice cream) served at the end of a meal
2 *British* **:** a fresh fruit served after a sweet course
des·sert·spoon \-ˌspün\ *noun* (1754)
1 : a spoon intermediate in size between a teaspoon and a tablespoon for use in eating dessert
2 : DESSERTSPOONFUL
des·sert·spoon·ful \di-'zərt-ˌspün-ˌfül\ *noun* (1875)
1 : as much as a dessertspoon will hold
2 *chiefly British* **:** a unit of measure equal to about 2½ fluidrams
dessert wine *noun* (1773) **:** a usually sweet wine typically served with dessert or afterward
de·sta·bi·lize \(ˌ)dē-'stā-bə-ˌlīz\ *transitive verb* (1924)
1 : to make unstable
2 : to cause (as a government) to be incapable of functioning or surviving
— **de·sta·bi·li·za·tion** \(ˌ)dē-ˌstā-bə-lə-'zā-shən\ *noun*
de·stain \(ˌ)dē-'stān\ *transitive verb* (1927) **:** to selectively remove stain from (a specimen for microscopic study)
de–Sta·lin·iza·tion \(ˌ)dē-ˌstä-lə-nə-'zā-shən, -ˌsta-\ *noun* (1951) **:** the discrediting of Stalin and his policies
de Stijl \də-'stī(ə)l, -'stä(ə)l\ *noun* [Dutch *De Stijl*, literally, the style, magazine published by members of the school] (1934) **:** a school of art founded in Holland in 1917 typically using rectangular forms and the primary colors plus black and white and asymmetric balance
des·ti·na·tion \ˌdes-tə-'nā-shən\ *noun* (14th century)
1 : the purpose for which something is destined
2 : an act of appointing, setting aside for a purpose, or predetermining
3 : a place to which one is journeying or to which something is sent ⟨kept their *destination* secret⟩
des·tine \'des-tən\ *transitive verb* **des·tined; des·tin·ing** [Middle English, from Middle French *destiner*, from Latin *destinare*, from *de-* + *-stinare* (akin to Latin *stare* to stand) — more at STAND] (14th century)
1 : to decree beforehand **:** PREDETERMINE
2 a : to designate, assign, or dedicate in advance ⟨the younger son was *destined* for the priesthood⟩ **b :** to direct, devise, or set apart for a specific purpose or place ⟨freight *destined* for European ports⟩
des·ti·ny \'des-tə-nē\ *noun, plural* **-nies** [Middle English *destinee*, from Middle

French, from feminine of *destiné*, past participle of *destiner*] (14th century)
1 : something to which a person or thing is destined **:** FORTUNE
2 : a predetermined course of events often held to be an irresistible power or agency
synonym see FATE
des·ti·tute \'des-tə-ˌtüt, -ˌt(y)üt\ *adjective* [Middle English, from Latin *destitutus*, past participle of *destituere* to abandon, deprive, from *de-* + *statuere* to set up — more at STATUTE] (14th century)
1 : lacking something needed or desirable ⟨a lake *destitute* of fish⟩
2 : lacking possessions and resources; *especially* **:** suffering extreme poverty ⟨a *destitute* old man⟩
— **des·ti·tute·ness** *noun*
des·ti·tu·tion \ˌdes-tə-'tü-shən, -'tyü-\ *noun* (15th century) **:** the state of being destitute; *especially* **:** such extreme want as threatens life unless relieved
synonym see POVERTY
des·tri·er \'des-trē-ər, də-'stri(ə)r\ *noun* [Middle English, from Middle French, from *destre* right hand, from Latin *dextra*, from feminine of *dexter*] (14th century)
archaic **:** WAR-HORSE; *also* **:** a charger used especially in medieval tournaments
de·stroy \di-'stròi, dē-\ *verb* [Middle English, from Old French *destruire*, from (assumed) Vulgar Latin *destrugere*, alteration of Latin *destruere*, from *de-* + *struere* to build — more at STRUCTURE] (13th century)
transitive verb
1 : to ruin the structure, organic existence, or condition of ⟨*destroyed* the files⟩; *also* **:** to ruin as if by tearing to shreds ⟨their reputation was *destroyed*⟩
2 a : to put out of existence **:** KILL **b :** NEUTRALIZE ⟨the moon *destroys* the light of the stars⟩ **c :** ANNIHILATE, VANQUISH ⟨armies had been crippled but not *destroyed* —W. L. Shirer⟩
intransitive verb **:** to cause destruction
de·stroy·er \di-'stròi(-ə)r, dē-\ *noun* (14th century)
1 : one that destroys
2 : a small fast warship used especially to support larger vessels and usually armed with 5-inch guns, depth charges, torpedoes, and often guided missiles
destroyer escort *noun* (1924) **:** a warship similar to but smaller than a destroyer
destroying angel *noun* (circa 1900) **:** DEATH CAP; *also* **:** a related poisonous mushroom (*Amanita verna*)
de·struc·ti·ble \di-'strək-tə-bəl\ *adjective* (circa 1755) **:** capable of being destroyed
— **de·struc·ti·bil·i·ty** \di-ˌstrək-tə-'bi-lə-tē\ *noun*
de·struc·tion \di-'strək-shən\ *noun* [Middle English *destruccion*, from Middle French *destruction*, from Latin *destruction-, destructio*, from *destruere*] (14th century)
1 : the state or fact of being destroyed **:** RUIN
2 : the action or process of destroying something
3 : a destroying agency
de·struc·tion·ist \-sh(ə-)nəst\ *noun* (1833) **:** one who delights in or advocates destruction
de·struc·tive \di-'strək-tiv\ *adjective* (15th century)
1 : causing destruction **:** RUINOUS ⟨*destructive* storm⟩
2 : designed or tending to destroy ⟨*destructive* criticism⟩
— **de·struc·tive·ly** *adverb*
— **de·struc·tive·ness** *noun*
destructive distillation *noun* (circa 1831)

: decomposition of a substance (as wood, coal, or oil) by heat in a closed container and collection of the volatile products produced
de·struc·tiv·i·ty \di-ˌstrək-'ti-və-tē, ˌdē-\ *noun* (1902) **:** capacity for destruction
de·sue·tude \'de-swi-ˌtüd, -ˌtyüd, di-'sü-ə-, -'syü-\ *noun* [Middle English *dissuetude*, from Latin *desuetudo*, from *desuescere* to become unaccustomed, from *de-* + *suescere* to become accustomed; akin to Latin *sodalis* comrade — more at SIB] (15th century) **:** discontinuance from use or exercise **:** DISUSE
de·sul·fur·iza·tion \(ˌ)dē-ˌsəl-fər-ə-'zā-shən\ *noun* (1854) **:** the removal of sulfur or sulfur compounds (as from coal or flue gas)
— **de·sul·fur·ize** \(ˌ)dē-'səl-fər-ˌīz\ *transitive verb*
de·sul·to·ry \'de-səl-ˌtōr-ē, -ˌtòr- *also* -zəl-\ *adjective* [Latin *desultorius*, literally, of a circus rider who leaps from horse to horse, from *desilire* to leap down, from *de-* + *salire* to leap — more at SALLY] (1581)
1 : marked by lack of definite plan, regularity, or purpose ⟨a dragged-out ordeal of . . . *desultory* shopping —Herman Wouk⟩
2 : not connected with the main subject
3 : disappointing in progress or performance **:** SLUGGISH
— **des·ul·to·ri·ly** \ˌde-səl-'tōr-ə-lē, -'tòr-\ *adverb*
— **des·ul·to·ri·ness** \'de-səl-ˌtōr-ē-nəs, -ˌtòr-\ *noun*
de·tach \di-'tach, dē-\ *transitive verb* [French *détacher*, from Old French *destachier*, from *des-* de- + *-tachier* (as in *atachier* to attach)] (1686)
1 : to separate especially from a larger mass and usually without violence or damage
2 : DISENGAGE, WITHDRAW
— **de·tach·abil·i·ty** \-ˌta-chə-'bi-lə-tē\ *noun*
— **de·tach·able** \-'ta-chə-bəl\ *adjective*
— **de·tach·ably** \-blē\ *adverb*
de·tached \di-'tacht, dē-\ *adjective* (circa 1706)
1 : standing by itself **:** SEPARATE, UNCONNECTED; *especially* **:** not sharing any wall with another building ⟨a *detached* house⟩
2 : exhibiting an aloof objectivity usually free from prejudice or self-interest ⟨a *detached* observer⟩
synonym see INDIFFERENT
— **de·tached·ly** \-'ta-chəd-lē, -'tacht-lē\ *adverb*
— **de·tached·ness** \-'ta-chəd-nəs, -'tacht-nəs\ *noun*
detached service *noun* (circa 1889)

☆ SYNONYMS
Despondent, despairing, desperate, hopeless mean having lost all or nearly all hope. DESPONDENT implies a deep dejection arising from a conviction of the uselessness of further effort ⟨*despondent* about yet another rejection⟩. DESPAIRING suggests the slipping away of all hope and often despondency ⟨*despairing* appeals for the return of the kidnapped child⟩. DESPERATE implies despair that prompts reckless action or violence in the face of defeat or frustration ⟨one last *desperate* attempt to turn the tide of battle⟩. HOPELESS suggests despair and the cessation of effort or resistance and often implies acceptance or resignation ⟨the situation of the trapped miners is *hopeless*⟩.

\ə\ abut \ᵊ\ kitten \ər\ further \a\ ash \ā\ ace
\ä\ mop, mar \aù\ out \ch\ chin \e\ bet \ē\ easy
\g\ go \i\ hit \ī\ ice \j\ job \ŋ\ sing \ō\ go
\ò\ law \òi\ boy \th\ thin \th\ the \ü\ loot \ù\ foot
\y\ yet \zh\ vision *see also* Guide to Pronunciation

: military service away from one's assigned organization

de·tach·ment \di-'tach-mənt, dē-\ *noun* (1669)
1 : the action or process of detaching : SEPARATION
2 a : the dispatch of a body of troops or part of a fleet from the main body for a special mission or service **b** : the part so dispatched **c** : a permanently organized separate unit usually smaller than a platoon and of special composition
3 a : indifference to worldly concerns : ALOOFNESS **b** : freedom from bias or prejudice

¹**de·tail** \di-'tāl)l, 'dē-,tāl\ *noun* [French *détail*, from Old French *detail* slice, piece, from *detaillier* to cut in pieces, from *de-* + *taillier* to cut — more at TAILOR] (1603)
1 : extended treatment of or attention to particular items
2 : a part of a whole: as **a** : a small and subordinate part : PARTICULAR; *also* : a reproduction of such a part of a work of art **b** : a part considered or requiring to be considered separately from the whole **c** : the small elements that collectively constitute a work of art **d** : the small elements of a photographic image corresponding to those of the subject
3 a : selection of a person or group for a particular task (as in military service) **b** (1) : the person or group selected (2) : the task to be performed
synonym see ITEM
— **in detail** : with all the particulars

²**detail** (1650)
transitive verb
1 : to report minutely and distinctly : SPECIFY ⟨*detailed* their grievances⟩
2 : to assign to a particular task
3 : to furnish with the smaller elements of design and finish ⟨trimmings that *detail* slips and petticoats⟩
intransitive verb
: to make detail drawings
— **de·tail·er** *noun*

de·tailed \di-'tā(ə)ld, 'dē-,tāld\ *adjective* (1740)
: marked by abundant detail or by thoroughness in treating small items or parts ⟨the *detailed* study of history⟩
synonym see CIRCUMSTANTIAL
— **de·tailed·ly** \di-'tāld-lē, -'tā-ləd-, 'dē-,\ *adverb*
— **de·tailed·ness** \di-'tā-ləd-nəs, -'tāld-, 'dē-,\ *noun*

detail man *noun* (1928)
: a representative of a drug manufacturer who introduces new drugs especially to physicians and pharmacists

de·tain \di-'tān, dē-\ *transitive verb* [Middle English *deteynen*, from Middle French *detenir*, modification of Latin *detinēre*, from *de-* + *tenēre* to hold — more at THIN] (15th century)
1 : to hold or keep in or as if in custody
2 *obsolete* : to keep back (as something due) : WITHHOLD
3 : to restrain especially from proceeding : STOP
synonym see KEEP, DELAY
— **de·tain·ment** \-mənt\ *noun*

de·tain·ee \di-,tā-'nē, ,dē-\ *noun* (circa 1928)
: a person held in custody especially for political reasons

de·tain·er \di-'tā-nər\ *noun* [Anglo-French *detener*, from *detener* to detain, from Latin *detinēre*] (1619)
1 : the act of keeping something in one's possession; *specifically* : the withholding from the rightful owner of something that has lawfully come into the possession of the holder
2 : detention in custody
3 : a writ authorizing the keeper of a prison to continue to hold a person in custody

de·tect \di-'tekt, dē-\ *verb* [Middle English, from Latin *detectus*, past participle of *detegere*

to uncover, detect, from *de-* + *tegere* to cover — more at THATCH] (1581)
transitive verb
1 : to discover the true character of
2 : to discover or determine the existence, presence, or fact of ⟨*detect* alcohol in the blood⟩
3 : DEMODULATE
intransitive verb
: to work as a detective
— **de·tect·abil·i·ty** \-,tek-tə-'bi-lə-tē\ *noun*
— **de·tect·able** \-'tek-tə-bəl\ *adjective*

de·tec·tion \di-'tek-shən\ *noun* (15th century)
1 : the act of detecting : the state or fact of being detected
2 : the process of demodulating

¹**de·tec·tive** \di-'tek-tiv\ *adjective* (1843)
1 : fitted for or used in detecting something ⟨had perfected his *detective* sensibilities⟩
2 : of or relating to detectives or their work ⟨a *detective* novel⟩
— **de·tec·tive·like** \-,līk\ *adjective*

²**detective** *noun* (1850)
: one employed or engaged in detecting lawbreakers or in getting information that is not readily or publicly accessible

de·tec·tor \di-'tek-tər\ *noun* (1541)
: one that detects: as **a** : a device for detecting the presence of electromagnetic waves or of radioactivity **b** : a rectifier of high-frequency current used especially for extracting the intelligence from a radio signal

de·tent \'dē-,tent, di-'\ *noun* [French *détente*, from Middle French *destente*, from *destendre* to slacken, from Old French, from *des-* de- + *tendre* to stretch, from Latin *tendere* — more at THIN] (1688)
: a device (as a catch, dog, or spring-operated ball) for positioning and holding one mechanical part in relation to another so that the device can be released by force applied to one of the parts

dé·tente *or* **detente** \dā-'tänt\ *noun* [French] (1908)
1 : the relaxation of strained relations or tensions (as between nations); *also* : a policy promoting this
2 : a period of détente

de·ten·tion \di-'ten-chən\ *noun* [Middle English *detencion*, from Middle French or Latin; Middle French, from Latin *detention-, detentio*, from *detinēre* to detain] (15th century)
1 : the act or fact of detaining or holding back; *especially* : a holding in custody
2 : the state of being detained; *especially* : a period of temporary custody prior to disposition by a court

detention home *noun* (circa 1930)
: a house of detention for juvenile delinquents usually under the supervision of a juvenile court

de·ter \di-'tər, dē-\ *transitive verb* **de·terred**; **de·ter·ring** [Latin *deterrēre*, from *de-* + *terrēre* to frighten — more at TERROR] (1579)
1 : to turn aside, discourage, or prevent from acting
2 : INHIBIT
— **de·ter·ment** \-'tər-mənt\ *noun*
— **de·ter·ra·bil·i·ty** \-,tər-ə-'bi-lə-tē\ *noun*
— **de·ter·ra·ble** \-'tər-ə-bəl\ *adjective*

de·terge \di-'tərj\ *transitive verb* **de·terged**; **de·terg·ing** [French or Latin; French *déterger*, from Latin *detergēre*, from *de-* + *tergēre* to wipe] (circa 1623)
: to wash off : CLEANSE
— **de·terg·er** *noun*

de·ter·gen·cy \di-'tər-jən(t)-sē\ *noun* (1710)
: cleansing quality or power

¹**de·ter·gent** \-jənt\ *adjective* (1616)
: that cleanses : CLEANSING

²**detergent** *noun* (1676)
: a cleansing agent: as **a** : SOAP **b** : any of numerous synthetic water-soluble or liquid organic preparations that are chemically different from soaps but are able to emulsify oils, hold dirt in suspension, and act as wetting

agents **c** : an oil-soluble substance that holds insoluble foreign matter in suspension and is used in lubricating oils and dry-cleaning solvents

de·te·ri·o·rate \di-'tir-ē-ə-,rāt, dē-\ *verb* **-rat·ed**; **-rat·ing** [Late Latin *deterioratus*, past participle of *deteriorare*, from Latin *deterior* worse, from *de-* + *-ter* (suffix as in Latin *uter* which of two) + *-ior* (comparative suffix) — more at WHETHER, -ER] (1572)
transitive verb
1 : to make inferior in quality or value : IMPAIR
2 : DISINTEGRATE
intransitive verb
: to become impaired in quality, functioning, or condition : DEGENERATE ⟨allowed a tradition of academic excellence to *deteriorate*⟩ ⟨his health *deteriorated*⟩
— **de·te·ri·o·ra·tive** \-,rā-tiv\ *adjective*

de·te·ri·o·ra·tion \di-,tir-ē-ə-'rā-shən, dē-\ *noun* (circa 1658)
: the action or process of deteriorating : the state of having deteriorated ☆

de·ter·min·able \-'tər-mə-nə-bəl\ *adjective* (15th century)
1 : capable of being determined, definitely ascertained, or decided upon
2 : liable to be terminated : TERMINABLE
— **de·ter·min·able·ness** *noun*
— **de·ter·min·ably** \-blē\ *adverb*

de·ter·mi·na·cy \di-'tər-mə-nə-sē\ *noun, plural* **-cies** (1873)
1 : the quality or state of being determinate
2 a : the state of being definitely and unequivocally characterized : EXACTNESS **b** : the state of being determined or necessitated

de·ter·mi·nant \di-'tər-mə-nənt\ *noun* (1686)
1 : an element that identifies or determines the nature of something or that fixes or conditions an outcome
2 : a square array of numbers bordered on the left and right by a vertical line and having a value equal to the algebraic sum of all possible products where the number of factors in each product is the same as the number of rows or columns, each factor in a given product is taken from a different row and column, and the sign of a product is positive or negative depending upon whether the number of permutations necessary to place the indices representing each factor's position in its row or column in the order of the natural numbers is odd or even
3 : GENE
4 : EPITOPE
— **de·ter·mi·nan·tal** \-,tər-mə-'nan-t³l\ *adjective*

de·ter·mi·nate \di-'tər-mə-nət\ *adjective* [Middle English, from Latin *determinatus*, past participle of *determinare*] (14th century)
1 : having defined limits
2 : definitely settled

☆ **SYNONYMS**
Deterioration, degeneration, decadence, decline mean the falling from a higher to a lower level in quality, character, or vitality. DETERIORATION implies generally the impairment of value or usefulness ⟨the *deterioration* of the house through neglect⟩. DEGENERATION stresses physical, intellectual, or especially moral retrogression ⟨the *degeneration* of their youthful idealism into cynicism⟩. DECADENCE presupposes a reaching and passing the peak of development and implies a turn downward with a consequent loss in vitality or energy ⟨cited love of luxury as a sign of cultural *decadence*⟩. DECLINE differs from DECADENCE in suggesting a more markedly downward direction and greater momentum as well as more obvious evidence of deterioration ⟨the meteoric *decline* of his career after the scandal⟩.

3 : conclusively determined : DEFINITIVE
4 : characterized by sequential flowering from the central or uppermost bud to the lateral or basal buds; *also* : characterized by growth in which the main stem ends in an inflorescence and stops growing with only branches from the main stem having further and similarly restricted growth ⟨*determinate* tomato plants⟩ — compare INDETERMINATE 4
5 : relating to, being, or undergoing egg cleavage in which each division irreversibly separates portions of the zygote with specific potencies for further development
— **de·ter·mi·nate·ly** *adverb*
— **de·ter·mi·nate·ness** *noun*

de·ter·mi·na·tion \di-ˌtər-mə-'nā-shən\ *noun* (14th century)
1 a : a judicial decision settling and ending a controversy **b** : the resolving of a question by argument or reasoning
2 *archaic* : TERMINATION
3 a : the act of deciding definitely and firmly; *also* : the result of such an act of decision **b** : the power or habit of deciding definitely and firmly
4 : a fixing or finding of the position, magnitude, value, or character of something: as **a** : the act, process, or result of an accurate measurement **b** : an identification of the taxonomic position of a plant or animal
5 a : the definition of a concept in logic by its essential constituents **b** : the addition of a differentia to a concept to limit its denotation
6 : direction or tendency to a certain end : IMPULSION
7 : the fixation of the destiny of undifferentiated embryonic tissue

de·ter·mi·na·tive \-'tər-mə-ˌnā-tiv, -'tər-mə-nə-\ *adjective* (1655)
: having power or tendency to determine : tending to fix, settle, or define something ⟨regard experiments as *determinative* of the principles from which deductions could be made —S. F. Mason⟩
synonym see CONCLUSIVE
— **determinative** *noun*

de·ter·mi·na·tor \di-'tər-mə-ˌnā-tər\ *noun* (1556)
: DETERMINER

de·ter·mine \di-'tər-mən, dē-\ *verb* **de·ter·mined; de·ter·min·ing** [Middle English, from Middle French *determiner*, from Latin *determinare*, from *de-* + *terminare* to limit, from *terminus* boundary, limit — more at TERM] (14th century)
transitive verb
1 a : to fix conclusively or authoritatively **b** : to decide by judicial sentence **c** : to settle or decide by choice of alternatives or possibilities **d** : RESOLVE
2 a : to fix the form, position, or character of beforehand : ORDAIN ⟨two points *determine* a straight line⟩ **b** : to bring about as a result : REGULATE ⟨demand *determines* the price⟩
3 a : to fix the boundaries of **b** : to limit in extent or scope **c** : to put or set an end to : TERMINATE ⟨*determine* an estate⟩
4 : to find out or come to a decision about by investigation, reasoning, or calculation ⟨*determine* the answer to the problem⟩ ⟨*determine* a position at sea⟩
5 : to bring about the determination of ⟨*determine* the fate of a cell⟩
intransitive verb
1 : to come to a decision
2 : to come to an end or become void
synonym see DECIDE, DISCOVER

de·ter·mined \-'tər-mənd\ *adjective* (1513)
1 : having reached a decision : firmly resolved ⟨*determined* to be a pilot⟩
2 a : showing determination ⟨a *determined* effort⟩ **b** : characterized by determination ⟨will deter all but the most *determined* thief —Security World⟩
— **de·ter·mined·ly** \-mənd-lē, -mə-nəd-lē\ *adverb*

— **de·ter·mined·ness** \-mənd-nəs\ *noun*
de·ter·min·er \-'tər-mə-nər\ *noun* (circa 1530)
: one that determines: as **a** : GENE **b** : a word (as an article, possessive, demonstrative, or quantifier) that makes specific the denotation of a noun phrase

de·ter·min·ism \di-'tər-mə-ˌni-zəm, dē-\ *noun* (1846)
1 a : a theory or doctrine that acts of the will, occurrences in nature, or social or psychological phenomena are causally determined by preceding events or natural laws **b** : a belief in predestination
2 : the quality or state of being determined
— **de·ter·min·ist** \-nəst\ *noun or adjective*
— **de·ter·min·is·tic** \-ˌtər-mə-'nis-tik\ *adjective*
— **de·ter·min·is·ti·cal·ly** \-ti-k(ə-)lē\ *adverb*

de·ter·rence \di-'tər-ən(t)s, -'ter-; -'tə-rən(t)s, dē-\ *noun* (1861)
: the inhibition of criminal behavior by fear especially of punishment; *also* : the maintenance of military power for the purpose of discouraging attack

de·ter·rent \-ənt, -rənt\ *adjective* [Latin *deterrent-, deterrens,* present participle of *deterrēre* to deter] (1829)
1 : serving to deter
2 : relating to deterrence
— **deterrent** *noun*
— **de·ter·rent·ly** *adverb*

de·ter·sive \di-'tər-siv, -ziv\ *adjective* [Middle French *detersif,* from Latin *detersus,* past participle of *detergēre* to deterge] (1586)
: DETERGENT
— **detersive** *noun*

de·test \di-'test, dē-\ *transitive verb* [Middle French *detester* or Latin *detestari;* Middle French *detester,* from Latin *detestari,* literally, to curse while calling a deity to witness, from *de-* + *testari* to call to witness — more at TESTAMENT] (circa 1535)
1 : to feel intense and often violent antipathy toward : LOATHE
2 *obsolete* : CURSE, DENOUNCE
synonym see HATE
— **de·test·er** *noun*

de·test·able \di-'tes-tə-bəl, dē-\ *adjective* (15th century)
: arousing or meriting intense dislike : ABOMINABLE
— **de·test·able·ness** *noun*
— **de·test·ably** \-blē\ *adverb*

de·tes·ta·tion \ˌdē-ˌtes-'tā-shən, di-\ *noun* (15th century)
1 : extreme hatred or dislike : ABHORRENCE, LOATHING
2 : an object of hatred or contempt

de·throne \di-'thrōn, dē-\ *transitive verb* (1609)
: to remove from a throne or place of power or prominence : DEPOSE
— **de·throne·ment** \-mənt\ *noun*
— **de·thron·er** *noun*

de·tick \(ˌ)dē-'tik\ *transitive verb* (1925)
: to remove ticks from
— **de·tick·er** *noun*

det·i·nue \'de-tᵊn-ˌ(y)ü\ *noun* [Middle English *detenewe,* from Middle French *detenue* detention, from feminine of *detenu,* past participle of *detenir* to detain] (15th century)
1 : a common-law action for the recovery of a personal chattel wrongfully detained or of its value
2 : detention of something due; *especially* : the unlawful detention of a personal chattel from another

det·o·na·ble \'de-tᵊn-ə-bəl, -tə-nə-\ *adjective* (1884)
: capable of being detonated
— **det·o·na·bil·i·ty** \ˌdet-ᵊn-ə-'bil-ət-ē, ˌdet-ə-nə-\ *noun*

det·o·nate \'de-tᵊn-ˌāt, 'de-tə-ˌnāt\ *verb* **-nat·ed; -nat·ing** [French *détoner* to explode,

from Latin *detonare* to expend thunder, from *de-* + *tonare* to thunder — more at THUNDER] (1729)
intransitive verb
: to explode with sudden violence
transitive verb
1 : to cause to detonate ⟨*detonate* a bomb⟩ — compare DEFLAGRATE
2 : to set off in a burst of activity : SPARK ⟨programs that *detonated* controversies⟩
— **det·o·nat·able** \-ˌā-tə-bəl, -ˌnā-\ *adjective*
— **det·o·na·tive** \'de-tᵊn-ˌā-tiv, 'de-tə-ˌnā-\ *adjective*

det·o·na·tion \ˌde-tᵊn-'ā-shən, ˌde-tə-'nā-\ *noun* (1686)
1 : the action or process of detonating
2 : rapid combustion in an internal combustion engine that results in knocking

det·o·na·tor \'de-tᵊn-ˌā-tər, -tə-ˌnā-\ *noun* (1822)
: a device or small quantity of explosive used for detonating a high explosive

¹de·tour \'dē-ˌtür *also* di-'tür\ *noun* [French *détour,* from Old French *destor,* from *destorner* to divert, from *des-* de- + *torner* to turn — more at TURN] (1738)
: a deviation from a direct course or the usual procedure; *especially* : a roundabout way temporarily replacing part of a route

²detour (1836)
intransitive verb
: to proceed by a detour ⟨*detour* around road construction⟩
transitive verb
1 : to send by a circuitous route
2 : to avoid by going around : BYPASS

de·tox \'dē-ˌtäks, di-'täks\ *noun, often attributive* (1973)
: detoxification from an intoxicating or an addictive substance
— **detox** *verb*

de·tox·i·cate \(ˌ)dē-'täk-sə-ˌkāt\ *transitive verb* **-cat·ed; -cat·ing** [*de-* + ²*intoxicate*] (1867)
: DETOXIFY 1, 2
— **de·tox·i·cant** \-si-kənt\ *noun*
— **de·tox·i·ca·tion** \(ˌ)dē-ˌtäk-sə-'kā-shən\ *noun*

de·tox·i·fy \(ˌ)dē-'täk-sə-ˌfī\ *transitive verb* **-fied; -fy·ing** (circa 1905)
1 a : to remove a poison or toxin or the effect of such from **b** : to render (a harmful substance) harmless
2 : to free (as a drug user or an alcoholic) from an intoxicating or an addictive substance in the body or from dependence on or addiction to such a substance
3 : NEUTRALIZE 2
— **de·tox·i·fi·ca·tion** \(ˌ)dē-ˌtäk-sə-fə-'kā-shən\ *noun*

de·tract \di-'trakt, dē-\ *verb* [Middle English, from Latin *detractus,* past participle of *detrahere* to pull down, disparage, from *de-* + *trahere* to draw] (15th century)
transitive verb
1 *archaic* : to speak ill of
2 *archaic* : to take away
3 : DIVERT ⟨*detract* attention⟩
intransitive verb
: to diminish the importance, value, or effectiveness of something — often used with *from*
— **de·trac·tor** \-'trak-tər\ *noun*

de·trac·tion \di-'trak-shən, dē-\ *noun* (14th century)
1 : a lessening of reputation or esteem especially by envious, malicious, or petty criticism : BELITTLING, DISPARAGEMENT
2 : a taking away ⟨it is no *detraction* from its dignity or prestige —J. F. Golay⟩

— **de·trac·tive** \-'trak-tiv\ *adjective*
— **de·trac·tive·ly** *adverb*
de·train \(,)dē-'trān\ (1881)
intransitive verb
: to get off a railroad train
transitive verb
: to remove from a railroad train
— **de·train·ment** \-mənt\ *noun*
de·trib·al·ize \(,)dē-'trī-bə-,līz\ *transitive verb* **-ized; -iz·ing** (1920)
: to cause to lose tribal identity : ACCULTURATE
— **de·trib·al·iza·tion** \(,)dē-,trī-bə-lə-'zā-shən\ *noun*
det·ri·ment \'de-trə-mənt\ *noun* [Middle English, from Middle French or Latin; Middle French, from Latin *detrimentum*, from *deterere* to wear away, impair, from *de-* + *terere* to rub — more at THROW] (15th century)
1 : INJURY, DAMAGE ⟨did hard work without *detriment* to his health⟩
2 : a cause of injury or damage ⟨a *detriment* to progress⟩
¹**det·ri·men·tal** \,de-trə-'men-t°l\ *adjective* (1590)
: obviously harmful : DAMAGING ⟨the *detrimental* effects of pollution⟩
synonym see PERNICIOUS
— **det·ri·men·tal·ly** \-t°l-ē\ *adverb*
²**detrimental** *noun* (1831)
: an undesirable or harmful person or thing
de·tri·tion \di-'tri-shən\ *noun* (1674)
: a wearing off or away
de·tri·tus \di-'trī-təs\ *noun, plural* **de·tri·tus** \-'trī-təs, -'trī-,tüs\ [French *détritus*, from Latin *detritus*, past participle of *deterere*] (1802)
1 : loose material (as rock fragments or organic particles) that results directly from disintegration
2 : a product of disintegration, destruction, or wearing away : DEBRIS
— **de·tri·tal** \-'trī-t°l\ *adjective*
de trop \də-'trō\ *adjective* [French] (1752)
: too much or too many : SUPERFLUOUS
de·tu·mes·cence \,dē-t(y)ü-'me-s°n(t)s\ *noun* [Latin *detumescere* to become less swollen, from *de-* + *tumescere* to swell — more at TUMESCENT] (1678)
: subsidence or diminution of swelling or erection
— **de·tu·mes·cent** \-s°nt\ *adjective*
Deu·ca·lion \d(y)ü-'kāl-yən\ *noun* [Latin, from Greek *Deukaliōn*]
: a survivor with his wife Pyrrha of a great flood by which Zeus destroys the rest of the human race
¹**deuce** \'düs *also* 'dyüs\ *noun* [Middle French *deus* two, from Latin *duos*, accusative masculine of *duo* two — more at TWO] (15th century)
1 a (1) : the face of a die that bears two spots (2) : a playing card bearing an index number two **b** : a throw of the dice yielding two points
2 : a tie in tennis after each side has scored 40 requiring two consecutive points by one side to win
3 [obsolete English *deuce* bad luck] **a** : DEVIL, DICKENS — used chiefly as a mild oath ⟨what the *deuce* is he up to now⟩ **b** : something notable of its kind ⟨a *deuce* of a mess⟩
²**deuce** *transitive verb* **deuced; deuc·ing** (1919)
: to bring the score of (a tennis game or set) to deuce
deuc·ed \'dü-səd *also* 'dyü-\ *adjective* (1782)
: DAMNED, CONFOUNDED ⟨in a *deuced* fix⟩
— **deuc·ed** *or* **deuc·ed·ly** *adverb*
deuces wild *noun* (1927)
: a card game (as poker) in which each deuce may represent any card designated by its holder
de·us ex ma·chi·na \'dā-əs-,eks-'mä-ki-nə, -'ma-, -,nä; -,mə-'shē-nə\ *noun* [New Latin, a god from a machine, translation of Greek *theos ek mēchanēs*] (1697)

1 : a god introduced by means of a crane in ancient Greek and Roman drama to decide the final outcome
2 : a person or thing (as in fiction or drama) that appears or is introduced suddenly and unexpectedly and provides a contrived solution to an apparently insoluble difficulty ◇
deuter- *or* **deutero-** *combining form* [alteration of Middle English *deutro-*, modification of Late Latin *deutero-*, from Greek *deuter-, deutero-*, from *deuteros*; probably akin to Greek *dein* to lack, Sanskrit *doṣa* fault, lack]
: second : secondary ⟨*deuter*anopia⟩
deu·ter·ag·o·nist \,dü-tə-'ra-gə-nist *also* ,dyü-\ *noun* [Greek *deuteragōnistēs*, from *deuter-* + *agōnistēs* combatant, actor — more at PROTAGONIST] (1855)
1 : the actor taking the part of second importance in a classical Greek drama
2 : a person who serves as a foil to another
deu·ter·anom·a·lous \,dü-tə-rə-'nä-mə-ləs *also* ,dyü-\ *adjective* [New Latin *deuteranomali*a (from *deuter-* + Latin *anomalia* anomaly) abnormal trichromatism + English *-ous*] (circa 1931)
: exhibiting partial loss of green color vision so that an increased intensity of this color is required in a mixture of red and green to match a given yellow
— **deu·ter·anom·a·ly** \-'nä-mə-lē\ *noun*
deu·ter·an·ope \'dü-tə-rə-,nōp *also* 'dyü-\ *noun* (1902)
: an individual affected with deuteranopia
deu·ter·an·opia \,dü-tə-rə-'nō-pē-ə *also* ,dyü-\ *noun* [New Latin, from *deuter-* + ²*a-* + *-opia*; from the blindness to green, regarded as the second primary color] (circa 1901)
: color blindness marked by confusion of purplish red and green
— **deu·ter·an·opic** \-'nō-pik, -'nä-pik\ *adjective*
deu·ter·ate \'dü-tə-,rāt *also* 'dyü-\ *transitive verb* **-at·ed; -at·ing** (1947)
: to introduce deuterium into (a compound)
— **deu·ter·a·tion** \,dyü-tə-'rā-shən\ *noun*
deu·te·ri·um \dü-'tir-ē-əm *also* dyü-\ *noun* [New Latin, from Greek *deuteros* second] (1933)
: an isotope of hydrogen that has one proton and one neutron in its nucleus and that has twice the mass of ordinary hydrogen — symbol *D*; called also *heavy hydrogen*
deuterium oxide *noun* (1934)
: HEAVY WATER 1
deu·tero·ca·non·i·cal \,dü-tə-rō-kə-'nä-ni-kəl *also* ,dyü-\ *adjective* [New Latin *deuterocanonicus*, from *deuter-* + Late Latin *canonicus* canonical] (1684)
: of, relating to, or constituting the books of Scripture contained in the Septuagint but not in the Hebrew canon
deu·ter·on \'dü-tə-,rän *also* 'dyü-\ *noun* (1933)
: a deuterium nucleus
Deu·ter·o·nom·ic \,dü-tə-rə-'nä-mik *also* ,dyü-\ *adjective* (1857)
: of or relating to the book of Deuteronomy, its style, or its contents
Deu·ter·on·o·mist \,dü-tə-rə-'rä-nə-mist *also* ,dyü-\ *noun* (1862)
: any of the writers or editors of a Deuteronomic body of source material often distinguished in the earlier books of the Old Testament
— **Deu·ter·on·o·mis·tic** \-,rä-nə-'mis-tik\ *adjective*
Deu·ter·on·o·my \,dü-tə-'rä-nə-mē *also* ,dyü-\ *noun* [Middle English *Deutronomie*, from Late Latin *Deuteronomium*, from Greek *Deuteronomion*, from *deuter-* + *nomos* law — more at NIMBLE]
: the fifth book of canonical Jewish and Christian Scripture containing narrative and Mosaic laws — see BIBLE table
deu·tero·stome \'dü-tə-rō-,stōm *also* 'dyü-\ *noun* [New Latin *Deuterostomia*, group name,

from *deuter-* + Greek *stoma* mouth — more at STOMACH] (1950)
: any of a major division (Deuterostomia) of the animal kingdom that includes the bilaterally symmetrical animals (as the chordates) with indeterminate cleavage and a mouth that does not arise from the blastopore
deu·to·plasm \'dü-tō-,pla-zəm *also* 'dyü-\ *noun* [International Scientific Vocabulary *deuter-* + *-plasm*] (1884)
: the nutritive inclusions of protoplasm; *especially* : the yolk reserves of an egg
deut·sche mark \'dòich-,märk, 'doi-chə-\ *noun* [German, German mark] (1948)
— see MONEY table
deut·zia \'düt-sē-ə *also* 'dyüt-\ *noun* [New Latin, from Jean *Deutz* (died 1784?) Dutch patron of botanical research] (1837)
: any of a genus (*Deutzia*) of the saxifrage family of ornamental shrubs with white or pink flowers
de·val·u·ate \(,)dē-'val-yə-,wāt\ *verb* (1898)
: DEVALUE
de·val·u·a·tion \(,)dē-,val-yə-'wā-shən\ *noun* (1914)
1 : an official reduction in the exchange value of a currency by a lowering of its gold equivalency or its value relative to another currency
2 : a lessening especially of status or stature : DECLINE
de·val·ue \(,)dē-'val-(,)yü, -yə(-w)\ (1918)
transitive verb
1 : to institute the devaluation of (money)
2 : to lessen the value of
intransitive verb
: to institute devaluation
De·va·na·ga·ri \,dā-və-'nä-gə-rē\ *noun* [Sanskrit *devanāgarī*, from *deva* divine + *nāgarī* script of the city — more at DEITY] (1781)
: an alphabet usually employed for Sanskrit and also used as a literary hand for various modern languages of India — see ALPHABET table
dev·as·tate \'de-və-,stāt\ *transitive verb* **-tat·ed; -tat·ing** [Latin *devastatus*, past participle of *devastare*, from *de-* + *vastare* to lay waste — more at WASTE] (1638)
1 : to bring to ruin or desolation by violent action
2 : to reduce to chaos, disorder, or helplessness : OVERWHELM ⟨*devastated* by grief⟩ ⟨her wisecrack *devastated* the class⟩
synonym see RAVAGE
— **dev·as·tat·ing·ly** \-,stā-tiŋ-lē\ *adverb*
— **dev·as·ta·tion** \,de-və-'stā-shən\ *noun*
— **dev·as·ta·tive** \'de-və-,stā-tiv\ *adjective*
— **dev·as·ta·tor** \-,stā-tər\ *noun*

de·vein \(,)dē-'vān\ *transitive verb* (1953)
: to remove the dark dorsal vein from (shrimp)

de·vel·op \di-'vel-əp, dē-\ *verb* [French *développer*, from Old French *desveloper, desvoluper* to unwrap, expose, from *des-* de- + *enveloper* to enclose — more at ENVELOP] (1750)
transitive verb
1 a : to set forth or make clear by degrees or in detail : EXPOUND **b** : to make visible or manifest **c** : to treat (as in dyeing) with an agent to cause the appearance of color **d** : to subject (exposed photograph material) especially to chemicals in order to produce a visible image; *also* : to make visible by such a method **e** : to elaborate (a musical idea) by the working out of rhythmic and harmonic changes in the theme
2 : to work out the possibilities of
3 a : to make active or promote the growth of ⟨*developed* his muscles⟩ **b** (1) : to make available or usable ⟨*develop* natural resources⟩ (2) : to make suitable for commercial or residential purposes **c** : to move (as a chess piece) from the original position to one providing more opportunity for effective use
4 a : to cause to unfold gradually ⟨*developed* his argument⟩ **b** : to expand by a process of growth ⟨*developed* a strong organization⟩ **c** : to cause to grow and differentiate along lines natural to its kind ⟨rain and sun *develop* the grain⟩ **d** : to have unfold or differentiate within one ⟨*developed* pneumonia⟩
5 : to acquire gradually ⟨*develop* an appreciation for ballet⟩
intransitive verb
1 a : to go through a process of natural growth, differentiation, or evolution by successive changes ⟨a blossom *develops* from a bud⟩ **b** : to acquire secondary sex characters
2 : to become gradually manifest
3 : to come into being gradually ⟨the situation *developing* in eastern Europe⟩; *also* : TURN OUT ⟨*intransitive verb* 2a ⟨it *developed* that no one had paid the bill⟩
— **de·vel·op·able** \-'ve-lə-pə-bəl\ *adjective*

de·vel·oped \di-'ve-ləpt\ *adjective* (1945)
: having a relatively high level of industrialization and standard of living ⟨a *developed* country⟩

de·vel·op·er \-lə-pər\ *noun* (1883)
: one that develops: as **a** : a chemical used to develop exposed photographic materials **b** : a person who develops real estate

de·vel·op·ing \-lə-piŋ\ *adjective* (1964)
: UNDERDEVELOPED 2 ⟨*developing* nations⟩

de·vel·op·ment \di-'ve-ləp-mənt, dē-\ *noun* (1756)
1 : the act, process, or result of developing
2 : the state of being developed
3 : a developed tract of land; *especially* : one with houses built on it

de·vel·op·men·tal \dē-,ve-ləp-'men-t⁰l\ *adjective* (1849)
1 a : of, relating to, or being development ⟨*developmental* processes⟩; *broadly* : EXPERIMENTAL 2 ⟨*developmental* aircraft⟩ **b** : serving economic development ⟨*developmental* highways⟩
2 : designed to assist growth or bring about improvement (as of a skill) ⟨*developmental* toys⟩
— **de·vel·op·men·tal·ly** \-t⁰l-ē\ *adverb*

developmentally disabled *adjective* (1975)
: having a physical or mental handicap that impedes or prevents normal development

de·verb·al \(,)dē-'vər-bəl\ *adjective* (1943)
: DEVERBATIVE

de·verb·a·tive \(,)dē-'vər-bə-tiv\ *adjective* (1930)
1 : derived from a verb ⟨the *deverbative* noun *developer* is derived from *develop*⟩
2 : used in derivation from a verb ⟨the *deverbative* suffix *-er* in *developer*⟩
— **deverbative** *noun*

de·vest \di-'vest\ *transitive verb* [Middle French *desvestir*, from Medieval Latin *disvestire*, from Latin *dis-* + *vestire* to clothe — more at VEST] (1563)
: DIVEST

de·vi·ance \'dē-vē-ən(t)s\ *noun* (1944)
: deviant quality, state, or behavior

de·vi·an·cy \-ən-sē\ *noun, plural* **-cies** (1947)
: DEVIANCE

de·vi·ant \-ənt\ *adjective* (15th century)
: deviating especially from an accepted norm ⟨*deviant* behavior⟩
— **deviant** *noun*

¹**de·vi·ate** \'dē-vē-,āt\ *verb* **-at·ed; -at·ing** [Late Latin *deviatus*, past participle of *deviare*, from Latin *de-* + *via* way — more at WAY] (circa 1633)
intransitive verb
1 : to stray especially from a standard, principle, or topic
2 : to depart from an established course or norm
transitive verb
: to cause to turn out of a previous course
synonym see SWERVE
— **de·vi·a·tor** \-,ā-tər\ *noun*
— **de·vi·a·to·ry** \-ə-,tōr-ē, -,tòr-\ *adjective*

²**de·vi·ate** \-vē-ət, -vē-,āt\ *noun* (1912)
1 : one that deviates from a norm; *especially* : a person who differs markedly from a group norm
2 : a statistical variable that gives the deviation of another variable from a fixed value (as the mean)

³**de·vi·ate** \-vē-ət, -vē-,āt\ *adjective* (1929)
: departing significantly from the behavioral norms of a particular society

de·vi·a·tion \,dē-vē-'ā-shən\ *noun* (15th century)
: an act or instance of deviating: as **a** : deflection of the needle of a compass caused by local magnetic influences (as in a ship) **b** : the difference between a value in a frequency distribution and a fixed number (as the mean) **c** : departure from an established ideology or party line **d** : noticeable or marked departure from accepted norms of behavior
— **de·vi·a·tion·ism** \-shə-,ni-zəm\ *noun*
— **de·vi·a·tion·ist** \-sh(ə-)nist\ *noun or adjective*

de·vice \di-'vīs\ *noun* [Middle English *devis, devise*, from Middle French, division, intention, from Old French *deviser* to divide, regulate, tell — more at DEVISE] (14th century)
1 : something devised or contrived: as **a** (1) : PLAN, PROCEDURE, TECHNIQUE (2) : a scheme to deceive : STRATAGEM, TRICK **b** : something fanciful, elaborate, or intricate in design **c** : something (as a figure of speech) in a literary work designed to achieve a particular artistic effect **d** *archaic* : MASQUE, SPECTACLE **e** : a conventional stage practice or means (as a stage whisper) used to achieve a particular dramatic effect **f** : a piece of equipment or a mechanism designed to serve a special purpose or perform a special function
2 : DESIRE, INCLINATION ⟨left to my own *devices*⟩
3 : an emblematic design used especially as a heraldic bearing

¹**dev·il** \'de-v⁰l\, *dialect* 'di-v⁰l\ *noun* [Middle English *devel*, from Old English *dēofol*, from Late Latin *diabolus*, from Greek *diabolos*, literally, slanderer, from *diaballein* to throw across, slander, from *dia-* + *ballein* to throw; probably akin to Sanskrit *gurate* he lifts up] (before 12th century)
1 *often capitalized* : the personal supreme spirit of evil often represented in Jewish and Christian belief as the tempter of mankind, the leader of all apostate angels, and the ruler of hell — usually used with *the*; often used as an interjection, an intensive, or a generalized term of abuse ⟨what the *devil* is this?⟩ ⟨the *devil* you say!⟩

2 : an evil spirit : DEMON
3 a : an extremely wicked person : FIEND **b** *archaic* : a great evil
4 : a person of notable energy, recklessness, and dashing spirit; *also* : one who is mischievous ⟨those kids are little *devils* today⟩
5 : FELLOW — usually used in the phrases *poor devil, lucky devil*
6 a : something very trying or provoking ⟨having a *devil* of a time with this problem⟩ **b** : severe criticism or rebuke : HELL — used with *the* ⟨I'll probably catch the *devil* for this⟩
7 : DUST DEVIL
8 *Christian Science* : the opposite of Truth : a belief in sin, sickness, and death : EVIL, ERROR
— **between the devil and the deep blue sea** : faced with two equally objectionable alternatives
— **devil to pay** : severe consequences — used with *the*

²**devil** *transitive verb* **-iled** *or* **-illed; -il·ing** *or* **-il·ling** \'de-v⁰l-in, 'dev-lin\ (1800)
1 : to season highly ⟨*deviled* eggs⟩
2 : TEASE, ANNOY

dev·il·fish \'de-v⁰l-,fish\ *noun* (1709)
1 : any of several extremely large rays (genera *Manta* and *Mobula*) widely distributed in warm seas
2 : OCTOPUS; *broadly* : any large cephalopod

devilfish 1

dev·il·ish \'de-v⁰l-ish, 'dev-lish\ *adjective* (15th century)
1 : resembling or befitting a devil: as **a** : EVIL, SINISTER **b** : MISCHIEVOUS, ROGUISH
2 : EXTREME ⟨in a *devilish* hurry⟩
— **devilish** *adverb*
— **dev·il·ish·ly** *adverb*
— **dev·il·ish·ness** *noun*

dev·il–may–care \,de-v⁰l-(,)mā-'ker, -'kar\ *adjective* (1837)
: EASYGOING, CAREFREE

dev·il·ment \'de-v⁰l-mənt, -,ment\ *noun* (1771)
: MISCHIEF

dev·il·ry \'de-v⁰l-rē\ *or* **dev·il·try** \-v⁰l-trē\ *noun, plural* **-ries** *or* **-tries** (14th century)
1 a : action performed with the help of the devil : WITCHCRAFT **b** : WICKEDNESS **c** : MISCHIEF
2 : an act of devilry

devil's advocate *noun* [translation of New Latin *advocatus diaboli*] (1760)
1 : a Roman Catholic official whose duty is to examine critically the evidence on which a demand for beatification or canonization rests
2 : a person who champions the less accepted cause for the sake of argument

devil's claw *noun* (circa 1900)
: any of several herbs (genus *Proboscidea* synonym *Martynia* of the family Martyniaceae) of the southwestern U.S. and Mexico that have edible pods yielding a black sewing material used in basket making

devil's darning needle *noun* (1809)
1 : DRAGONFLY
2 : DAMSELFLY

devil's food cake *noun* (1905)
: a rich chocolate cake

devil's paintbrush *noun* (1900)
: ORANGE HAWKWEED; *broadly* : any of various hawkweeds that are naturalized weeds in the eastern U.S.

devil theory *noun* (1937)

\ə\ abut \⁰\ kitten \ər\ further \a\ ash \ā\ ace
\ä\ mop, mar \aủ\ out \ch\ chin \e\ bet \ē\ easy
\g\ go \i\ hit \ī\ ice \j\ job \ŋ\ sing \ō\ go
\ò\ law \òi\ boy \th\ thin \th\ the \ü\ loot \ủ\ foot
\y\ yet \zh\ vision *see also* Guide to Pronunciation

: a theory of history: political and social crises arise from the deliberate actions of evil or misguided leaders rather than as a natural result of conditions

dev·il·wood \'de-vᵊl-ˌwu̇d\ *noun* (1818)
: a small tree (*Osmanthus americanus*) of the southern U.S. that is related to the olive

de·vi·ous \'dē-vē-əs, -vyəs\ *adjective* [Latin *devius*, from *de* from + *via* way — more at DE-, WAY] (1599)
1 : OUT-OF-THE-WAY, REMOTE
2 a : WANDERING, ROUNDABOUT ⟨a *devious* path⟩ **b** : moving without a fixed course : ERRANT ⟨*devious* breezes⟩
3 a : deviating from a right, accepted, or common course **b** : not straightforward : CUNNING; *also* : DECEPTIVE
— **de·vi·ous·ly** *adverb*
— **de·vi·ous·ness** *noun*

¹de·vise \di-'vīz\ *transitive verb* **de·vised; de·vis·ing** [Middle English, from Old French *deviser* to divide, regulate, tell, modification of (assumed) Vulgar Latin *divisare*, frequentative of Latin *dividere* to divide] (13th century)
1 a : to form in the mind by new combinations or applications of ideas or principles : INVENT **b** *archaic* : CONCEIVE, IMAGINE **c** : to plan to obtain or bring about : PLOT
2 : to give (real estate) by will — compare BEQUEATH
— **de·vis·able** \-'vī-zə-bəl\ *adjective*
— **de·vis·er** *noun*

²devise *noun* (15th century)
1 : the act of giving or disposing of real property by will
2 : a will or clause of a will disposing of real property
3 : property devised by will

de·vi·see \ˌde-və-'zē, di-ˌvī-'zē\ *noun* (1543)
: one to whom a devise of property is made

de·vi·sor \ˌde-və-'zȯr; di-'vī-zər, -ˌvī-'zȯr\ *noun* (1543)
: one who devises property in a will

de·vi·tal·ize \(ˌ)dē-'vī-tᵊl-ˌīz\ *transitive verb* (1849)
: to deprive of life, vigor, or effectiveness

de·vit·ri·fy \(ˌ)dē-'vi-trə-ˌfī\ *transitive verb* [French *dévitrifier*, from *dé-* de- + *vitrifier* to vitrify] (1832)
: to deprive of glassy luster and transparency; *especially* : to change (as a glass) from a vitreous to a crystalline condition
— **de·vit·ri·fi·ca·tion** \(ˌ)dē-ˌvi-trə-fə-'kā-shən\ *noun*

de·vo·cal·ize \(ˌ)dē-'vō-kə-ˌlīz\ *transitive verb* (1877)
: DEVOICE

de·voice \(ˌ)dē-'vȯis\ *transitive verb* (1932)
: to pronounce (as a sometimes or formerly voiced sound) without vibration of the vocal cords

de·void \di-'vȯid\ *adjective* [Middle English, past participle of *devoiden* to dispel, from Middle French *desvuidier* to empty, from Old French, from *des-* dis- + *vuidier* to empty — more at VOID] (15th century)
: being without a usual, typical, or expected attribute or accompaniment ⟨an argument *devoid* of sense⟩

de·voir \də-'vwär, 'de-ˌ\ *noun* [Middle English, alteration of *dever*, from Anglo-French *deveir*, from Old French *devoir*, *deveir* to owe, be obliged, from Latin *debēre* — more at DEBT] (14th century)
1 : DUTY, RESPONSIBILITY
2 : a usually formal act of civility or respect

de·vo·lu·tion \ˌde-və-'lü-shən *also* ˌdē-və-\ *noun* [Medieval Latin *devolution-*, *devolutio*, from Latin *devolvere*] (1545)
1 : transference (as of rights, power, property, or responsibility) to another; *especially* : the surrender of powers to local authorities by a central government
2 : retrograde evolution : DEGENERATION
— **de·vo·lu·tion·ary** \-shə-ˌner-ē\ *adjective*

— **de·vo·lu·tion·ist** \-sh(ə-)nist\ *noun*

de·volve \di-'välv, -'vȯlv, dē-\ *verb* **devolved; de·volv·ing** [Middle English, from Latin *devolvere*, from *de-* + *volvere* to roll — more at VOLUBLE] (15th century)
transitive verb
: to pass on (as responsibility, rights, or powers) from one person or entity to another ⟨*devolving* to western Europe full responsibility for its own defense —Christopher Lane⟩
intransitive verb
1 a : to pass by transmission or succession ⟨the estate *devolved* on a distant cousin⟩ **b** : to fall or be passed usually as a responsibility or obligation ⟨the responsibility for breadwinning has *devolved* increasingly upon women —Barbara Ehrenreich⟩
2 : to come by or as if by flowing down ⟨his allegedly subversive campaigns . . . *devolve* from his belief in basic American rights —Frank Deford⟩
3 : to degenerate through a gradual change or evolution ⟨where order *devolves* into chaos —Johns Hopkins Magazine⟩

dev·on \'de-vən\ *noun, often capitalized* [*Devon*, England] (1834)
: any of a breed of vigorous red dual-purpose cattle of English origin

De·vo·ni·an \di-'vō-nē-ən\ *adjective* [*Devon*, England] (1612)
1 : of or relating to Devonshire, England
2 : of, relating to, or being the period of the Paleozoic era between the Silurian and the Mississippian or the corresponding system of rocks — see GEOLOGIC TIME table
— **Devonian** *noun*

Dev·on·shire cream \ˌde-vən-ˌshir-, -shər-\ *noun* (1825)
: CLOTTED CREAM

de·vote \di-'vōt, dē-\ *transitive verb* **de·vot·ed; de·vot·ing** [Latin *devotus*, past participle of *devovēre*, from *de-* + *vovēre* to vow] (1586)
1 : to commit by a solemn act ⟨*devoted* herself to serving God⟩
2 : to give over or direct (as time, money, or effort) to a cause, enterprise, or activity ☆
— **de·vote·ment** \-'vōt-mənt\ *noun*

de·vot·ed *adjective* (1593)
: characterized by loyalty and devotion
— **de·vot·ed·ly** *adverb*
— **de·vot·ed·ness** *noun*

dev·o·tee \ˌde-və-'tē, -'tā; dē-ˌvō-'tē\ *noun* (1645)
: an ardent follower, supporter, or enthusiast (as of a religion, art form, or sport)

de·vo·tion \di-'vō-shən, dē-\ *noun* (13th century)
1 a : religious fervor : PIETY **b** : an act of prayer or private worship — usually used in plural **c** : a religious exercise or practice other than the regular corporate worship of a congregation
2 a : the act of devoting **b** : the fact or state of being ardently dedicated and loyal (as to an idea or person)
3 *obsolete* : the object of one's devotion
synonym see FIDELITY

¹de·vo·tion·al \-shnəl, -shə-nᵊl\ *adjective* (1648)
: of, relating to, or characterized by devotion
— **de·vo·tion·al·ly** \-ē\ *adverb*

²devotional *noun* (1659)
: a short worship service

de·vour \di-'vau̇(ə)r, dē-\ *transitive verb* [Middle English, from Middle French *devourer*, from Latin *devorare*, from *de-* + *vorare* to devour — more at VORACIOUS] (14th century)
1 : to eat up greedily or ravenously
2 : to use up or destroy as if by eating ⟨we are *devouring* the world's resources⟩
3 : to prey upon ⟨*devoured* by guilt⟩
4 : to enjoy avidly ⟨*devours* books⟩
— **de·vour·er** *noun*

de·vout \di-'vau̇t\ *adjective* [Middle English *devot*, from Old French, from Late Latin *devo-*

tus, from Latin, past participle of *devovēre*] (13th century)
1 : devoted to religion or to religious duties or exercises
2 : expressing devotion or piety ⟨a *devout* attitude⟩
3 : devoted to a pursuit, belief, or mode of behavior : SERIOUS, EARNEST ⟨a *devout* baseball fan⟩ ⟨born a *devout* coward —G. B. Shaw⟩
— **de·vout·ly** *adverb*
— **de·vout·ness** *noun*

dew \'dü *also* 'dyü\ *noun* [Middle English, from Old English *dēaw*; akin to Old High German *tou* dew, Greek *thein* to run] (before 12th century)
1 : moisture condensed upon the surfaces of cool bodies especially at night
2 : something resembling dew in purity, freshness, or power to refresh
3 : moisture especially when appearing in minute droplets: as **a** : TEARS **b** : SWEAT **c** : droplets of water produced by a plant in transpiration
— **dew** *transitive verb*
— **dew·less** \-ləs\ *adjective*

dew·ar \'dü-ər *also* 'dyü-\ *noun, often capitalized* [Sir James *Dewar*] (circa 1909)
: a glass or metal container made like a vacuum bottle that is used especially for storing liquefied gases — called also *Dewar flask*

de·wa·ter \(ˌ)dē-'wȯt-ər, -'wät-\ *transitive verb* (circa 1909)
: to remove water from
— **de·wa·ter·er** *noun*

dew·ber·ry \'dü-ˌber-ē *also* 'dyü-\ *noun* (circa 1578)
1 : any of several sweet edible berries related to and resembling blackberries
2 : a trailing or decumbent bramble (genus *Rubus*) that bears dewberries

dew·claw \'dü-ˌklȯ *also* 'dyü-\ *noun* (1576)
: a vestigial digit not reaching to the ground on the foot of a mammal; *also* : a claw or hoof terminating such a digit — see COW illustration

dew·drop \'dü-ˌdräp *also* 'dyü-\ *noun* (13th century)
: a drop of dew

Dew·ey decimal classification \'dü-ē *also* 'dyü-\ *noun* [Melvil *Dewey*] (1924)
: a system of classifying books and other publications whereby main classes are designated by a three-digit number and subdivisions are shown by numbers after a decimal point — called also *Dewey decimal system*

dew·fall \'dü-ˌfȯl *also* 'dyü-\ *noun* (1622)
: formation of dew; *also* : the time when dew begins to deposit

dew·lap \'dü-ˌlap *also* 'dyü-\ *noun* (14th century)
1 : loose skin hanging under the neck of an animal — see COW illustration
2 : loose flesh on the human throat
— **dew·lapped** \-ˌlapt\ *adjective*

de·worm \(ˌ)dē-'wərm\ *transitive verb* (1926)
: to rid (as a dog) of worms : WORM 4
— **de·worm·er** \(ˌ)dē-'wər-mər\ *noun*

☆ **SYNONYMS**
Devote, dedicate, consecrate, hallow mean to set apart for a special and often higher end. DEVOTE is likely to imply compelling motives and often attachment to an objective ⟨*devoted* his evenings to study⟩. DEDICATE implies solemn and exclusive devotion to a sacred or serious use or purpose ⟨*dedicated* her life to medical research⟩. CONSECRATE stresses investment with a solemn or sacred quality ⟨*consecrate* a church to the worship of God⟩. HALLOW, often differing little from *dedicate* or *consecrate*, may distinctively imply an attribution of intrinsic sanctity ⟨battlegrounds *hallowed* by the blood of patriots⟩.

dew point *noun* (circa 1833)
 : the temperature at which a vapor begins to condense
dew worm *noun* (1599)
 : NIGHT CRAWLER
dewy \'dü-ē *also* 'dyü-\ *adjective* **dew·i·er; -est** (before 12th century)
 1 : moist with, affected by, or suggestive of dew
 2 : INNOCENT, UNSOPHISTICATED ⟨from a *dewy* bride to an ill-mannered, murderous courtesan —Melvin Gussow⟩
 — dew·i·ly \'dü-ə-lē, 'dyü-\ *adverb*
 — dew·i·ness \'dü-ē-nəs, 'dyü-\ *noun*
dewy–eyed \'dü-ē-ˌīd *also* 'dyü-\ *adjective* (1938)
 : naively credulous
dex \'deks\ *noun* (circa 1961)
 : the sulfate of dextroamphetamine
dexa·meth·a·sone \ˌdek-sə-'me-thə-ˌsōn, -ˌzōn\ *noun* [*dexa-* blend of *deca-* and *hexa-* + *methyl* + *-a-* (perhaps from *pregnane,* a parent compound of corticoid hormones) + *-sone* (as in *cortisone*)] (1958)
 : a synthetic glucocorticoid $C_{22}H_{29}FO_5$ used especially as an anti-inflammatory agent
Dex·e·drine \'dek-sə-ˌdrēn, -drən\ *trademark*
 — used for a preparation of the sulfate of dextroamphetamine
dex·ies \'dek-sēz\ *noun plural* [*Dex*edrine + *-ie* + [1]*-s*] (1956)
 : tablets or capsules of the sulfate of dextroamphetamine
dex·ter \'dek-stər\ *adjective* [Latin; akin to Old High German *zeso* situated on the right, Greek *dexios*] (1562)
 1 : relating to or situated on the right
 2 : being or relating to the side of a heraldic shield at the right of the person bearing it
 — dexter *adverb*
dex·ter·i·ty \dek-'ster-ə-tē\ *noun, plural* **-ties** [Middle French or Latin; Middle French *dexterité,* from Latin *dexteritat-, dexteritas,* from *dexter*] (1527)
 1 : mental skill or quickness **:** ADROITNESS
 2 : readiness and grace in physical activity; *especially* **:** skill and ease in using the hands
dex·ter·ous *also* **dex·trous** \'dek-st(ə-)rəs\ *adjective* [Latin *dextr-, dexter* on the right side, skillful] (1622)
 1 : mentally adroit and skillful **:** CLEVER
 2 : done with dexterity **:** ARTFUL
 3 : skillful and competent with the hands ☆
 — dex·ter·ous·ly *adverb*
 — dex·ter·ous·ness *noun*
dextr- *or* **dextro-** *combining form* [Latin *dextr-, dexter*]
 1 : right **:** on or toward the right ⟨*dextro*rotatory⟩
 2 : *usually* **dextro-** **:** dextrorotatory ⟨*dextro*amphetamine⟩
dex·tral \'dek-strəl\ *adjective* (1646)
 : of or relating to the right: as **a :** RIGHT-HANDED **3 b :** *of a gastropod shell* **:** having the whorls coiling clockwise down the spire when viewed with the apex toward the observer and having the aperture situated on the right of the axis when held with the spire uppermost and with the aperture opening toward the observer — compare SINISTRAL
dex·tran \'dek-stran, -strən\ *noun* [International Scientific Vocabulary] (1879)
 : any of numerous glucose biopolymers of variable molecular weight produced especially by bacteria (as genus *Leuconostoc*), occurring in dental plaque, and used after chemical modification as blood plasma substitutes, as packing materials in chromatography, and as pharmaceutical agents
dex·tran·ase \-strə-ˌnās, -ˌnāz\ *noun* (circa 1949)
 : a hydrolase that prevents tooth decay by breaking down dextran and eliminating dental plaque

dex·trin \'dek-strən\ *also* **dex·trine** \-ˌstrēn, -strən\ *noun* [French *dextrine,* from *dextr-*] (1838)
 : any of various water-soluble gummy polysaccharides $(C_6H_{10}O_5)n$ obtained from starch by the action of heat, acids, or enzymes and used as adhesives, as sizes for paper and textiles, as thickening agents (as in syrups), and in beer
dex·tro \'dek-(ˌ)strō\ *adjective* [*dextr-*] (circa 1929)
 : DEXTROROTATORY
dex·tro·am·phet·amine \ˌdek-(ˌ)strō-am-'fe-tə-ˌmēn, -mən\ *noun* (1943)
 : dextrorotatory amphetamine sulfate
dex·tro·ro·ta·to·ry \-'rō-tə-ˌtōr-ē, -ˌtor-\ *also* **dex·tro·ro·ta·ry** \-'rō-tə-rē\ *adjective* (1878)
 : turning clockwise or toward the right; *especially* **:** rotating the plane of polarization of light toward the right ⟨*dextrorotatory* crystals⟩
 — compare LEVOROTATORY
dex·trose \'dek-ˌstrōs, -ˌstrōz\ *noun* (circa 1869)
 : dextrorotatory glucose
dey \'dā\ *noun* [French, from Turkish *dayı,* literally, maternal uncle] (1659)
 : a ruling official of the Ottoman Empire in northern Africa
[1]**DH** \ˌdē-'āch\ *noun* (1973)
 : DESIGNATED HITTER
[2]**DH** \ˌdē-'āch, 'dē-ˌāch\ *intransitive verb* **DH–d; DH–ing** (1975)
 : to play the position of designated hitter
dhar·ma \'där-mə, 'där-\ *noun* [Sanskrit; akin to Latin *firmus* firm] (1796)
 1 *Hinduism* **:** an individual's duty fulfilled by observance of custom or law
 2 *Hinduism & Buddhism* **a :** the basic principles of cosmic or individual existence **:** divine law **b :** conformity to one's duty and nature
 — dhar·mic \-mik\ *adjective*
dhar·na \'dər-nə, 'där-\ *noun* [Hindi *dharnā,* from Sanskrit *dharaṇa* support, prop; akin to Latin *firmus* firm] (1747)
 : a fast held at the door of an offender in India as an appeal for justice
dhole \'dōl\ *noun* [perhaps from Kannada *tōḷa* wolf] (circa 1827)
 : a wild dog (*Cuon alpinus*) occurring from India to southern Siberia
dho·ti \'dō-tē\ *noun, plural* **dhotis** [Hindi *dhotī*] (1614)
 : a loincloth worn by men in some parts of India
dhow \'dau\ *noun* [Arabic *dāwa*] (1785)
 : an Arab lateen-rigged boat usually having a long overhang forward, a high poop, and a low waist

dhow

Dhu'l–Hij·ja \ˌdül-'hi-(ˌ)jä, ˌthül-\ *noun* [Arabic *Dhū-l-ḥijjah,* literally, the one of the pilgrimage] (circa 1771)
 : the 12th month of the Islamic year — see MONTH table
Dhu'l–Qa'·dah \-'kä-(ˌ)dä\ *noun* [Arabic *Dhū-l-qa'dah,* literally, the one of the sitting] (circa 1771)
 : the 11th month of the Islamic year — see MONTH table
dhur·rie \'də-rē, 'dər-ē\ *noun* [Hindi *darī*] (1880)
 : a thick flat-woven cotton or wool cloth or rug made in India
di- *combining form* [Middle English, from Middle French, from Latin, from Greek; akin to Old English *twi-*]
 1 : twice **:** twofold **:** double ⟨*di*chromatic⟩
 2 : containing two atoms, radicals, or groups ⟨*di*oxide⟩

dia- *also* **di-** *prefix* [Middle English, from Old French, from Latin, from Greek, through, apart, from *dia;* akin to Latin *dis-*]
 : through ⟨*dia*positive⟩ **:** across ⟨*dia*dromous⟩
di·a·base \'dī-ə-ˌbās\ *noun* [French, probably from Greek *diabasis* act of crossing over, from *diabainein* to cross over, from *dia-* + *bainein* to go — more at COME] (circa 1816)
 1 *archaic* **:** DIORITE
 2 *chiefly British* **:** an altered basalt
 3 : a fine-grained rock of the composition of gabbro but with an ophitic texture
 — di·a·ba·sic \ˌdī-ə-'bā-sik\ *adjective*
di·a·be·tes \ˌdī-ə-'bē-tēz, -'bē-təs\ *noun* [Latin, from Greek *diabētēs* diabetes insipidus, from *diabainein* to walk with the legs apart, cross over] (15th century)
 : any of various abnormal conditions characterized by the secretion and excretion of excessive amounts of urine; *especially* **:** DIABETES MELLITUS
diabetes in·sip·i·dus \-in-'si-pə-dəs\ *noun* [New Latin, literally, bland diabetes] (circa 1860)
 : a disorder of the pituitary gland characterized by intense thirst and by the excretion of large amounts of urine
diabetes mel·li·tus \-'me-lə-təs\ *noun* [New Latin, literally, honey-sweet diabetes] (circa 1860)
 : a variable disorder of carbohydrate metabolism caused by a combination of hereditary and environmental factors and usually characterized by inadequate secretion or utilization of insulin, by excessive urine production, by excessive amounts of sugar in the blood and urine, and by thirst, hunger, and loss of weight
[1]**di·a·bet·ic** \ˌdī-ə-'be-tik\ *adjective* (1799)
 1 : of or relating to diabetes or diabetics
 2 : affected with diabetes
 3 : occurring in or caused by diabetes ⟨*diabetic* coma⟩
 4 : suitable for diabetics ⟨*diabetic* food⟩
[2]**diabetic** *noun* (1840)

☆ **SYNONYMS**

Dexterous, adroit, deft mean ready and skilled in physical movement. DEXTEROUS implies expertness with consequent facility and quickness in manipulation ⟨unrolled the sleeping bag with a *dexterous* toss⟩. ADROIT implies dexterity but usually also stresses resourcefulness or artfulness or inventiveness ⟨the magician's *adroit* response to the failure of her prop won applause⟩. DEFT emphasizes lightness, neatness, and sureness of touch or handling ⟨a surgeon's *deft* manipulation of the scalpel⟩.

☐ **USAGE**

diabetes One of the forces in linguistic change is *analogy,* the alteration of one word to make it similar to other words which are perceived to be related. Analogy has probably been the source of the variant pronunciation of *diabetes* in which the last syllable has a reduced form \-təs\, and not the older, fuller \-tēz\. The \-təs\ ending is more like the final syllable of the names of other diseases and conditions: *phlebitis, arthritis, conjunctivitis.* Although *diabetes* shares no word elements with these names, the last syllable has come to be pronounced as if it were parallel in form to these words. The newer pronunciation has been labelled "colloquial" by some, but it is common in all circles today.

\ə\ **abut** \ʿ\ **kitten** \ər\ **further** \a\ **ash** \ā\ **ace**
\ä\ **mop, mar** \au̇\ **out** \ch\ **chin** \e\ **bet** \ē\ **easy**
\g\ **go** \i\ **hit** \ī\ **ice** \j\ **job** \ŋ\ **sing** \ō\ **go**
\ȯ\ **law** \ȯi\ **boy** \th\ **thin** \t͟h\ **the** \ü\ **loot** \u̇\ **foot**
\y\ **yet** \zh\ **vision** *see also* Guide to Pronunciation

: a person affected with diabetes

di·a·be·to·gen·ic \ˌdī-ə-ˌbe-tə-'je-nik, -,bē-\ *adjective* (circa 1903)
: producing diabetes

di·a·be·tol·og·ist \ˌdī-ə-(ˌ)be-'tä-lə-jist, -,bē-\ *noun* (1970)
: a specialist in diabetes

di·a·ble·rie \də̄-'ä-blə-(ˌ)rē, -'a-blə-\ *noun* [French, from Old French, from *diable* devil, from Late Latin *diabolus* — more at DEVIL] (1751)
1 : black magic : SORCERY
2 a : a representation in words or pictures of black magic or of dealings with the devil **b** : demon lore
3 : mischievous conduct or manner

di·a·bol·i·cal \ˌdī-ə-'bä-li-kəl\ *or* **di·a·bol·ic** \-'bä-lik\ *adjective* [Middle English *deabolik*, from Middle French *diabolique*, from Late Latin *diabolicus*, from *diabolus*] (14th century)
: of, relating to, or characteristic of the devil : DEVILISH
— **di·a·bol·i·cal·ly** \-li-k(ə-)lē\ *adverb*
— **di·a·bol·i·cal·ness** \-li-kəl-nəs\ *noun*

di·a·bo·lism \dī-'a-bə-ˌli-zəm\ *noun* (1614)
1 : dealings with or possession by the devil
2 : belief in or worship of devils
3 : evil character or conduct
— **di·ab·o·list** \-list\ *noun*

di·ab·o·lize \-ˌlīz\ *transitive verb* **-lized; -liz·ing** (1702)
: to represent as or make diabolic

dia·chron·ic \ˌdī-ə-'krä-nik\ *adjective* (1927)
: of, relating to, or dealing with phenomena (as of language or culture) as they occur or change over a period of time
— **dia·chron·i·cal·ly** \-'krä-ni-k(ə-)lē\ *adverb*

di·ach·ro·ny \dī-'a-krə-nē\ *noun* [International Scientific Vocabulary *dia-* + *-chrony* (as in *synchrony*)] (circa 1939)
1 : diachronic analysis
2 : change extending through time

¹di·ac·id \(ˌ)dī-'a-səd\ *or* **di·acid·ic** \ˌdī-ə-'si-dik\ *adjective* (1866)
: able to react with two molecules of a monobasic acid or one of a dibasic acid to form a salt or ester — used especially of bases

²diacid *noun* [International Scientific Vocabulary] (circa 1929)
: an acid with two acid hydrogen atoms

di·ac·o·nal \dī-'a-kə-nᵊl, dē-\ *adjective* [Late Latin *diaconalis*, from *diaconus* deacon — more at DEACON] (circa 1611)
: of or relating to a deacon or deaconess

di·ac·o·nate \-'a-kə-nət, -,nāt\ *noun* (circa 1751)
1 : the office or period of office of a deacon or deaconess
2 : an official body of deacons

di·a·crit·ic \ˌdī-ə-'kri-tik\ *noun* (1866)
: an accent near or through an orthographic or phonetic character or combination of characters indicating a phonetic value different from that given the unmarked or otherwise marked element

di·a·crit·i·cal \ˌdī-ə-'kri-ti-kəl\ *also* **di·a·crit·ic** \-'kri-tik\ *adjective* [Greek *diakritikos* separative, from *diakrinein* to distinguish, from *dia-* + *krinein* to separate — more at CERTAIN] (1749)
1 : serving as a diacritic
2 a : DISTINCTIVE ⟨the *diacritical* elements in culture —S. F. Nadel⟩ **b** : capable of distinguishing ⟨students of superior *diacritical* powers⟩

di·adel·phous \ˌdī-ə-'del-fəs\ *adjective* [*di-* + *-adelphous*] (1807)
: united by filaments into two fascicles — used of stamens

di·a·dem \'dī-ə-ˌdem, -dəm\ *noun* [Middle English *diademe*, from Old French, from Latin *diadema*, from Greek *diadēma*, from *diadein* to bind around, from *dia-* + *dein* to bind; akin to Sanskrit *dāman* rope] (13th century)

DIACRITICS

´	(é)	acute accent
`	(è)	grave accent
^ *or* ˆ *or* ~	(ô)	circumflex
~	(ñ)	tilde
ˉ	(ō)	macron
˘	(ŭ)	breve
ˇ	(č)	haček
¨	(oö)	diaeresis
ˏ	(ç)	cedilla

1 a : CROWN 1; *specifically* : a royal headband **b** : CROWN 6a(1)
2 : something that adorns like a crown

di·ad·ro·mous \dī-'a-drə-məs\ *adjective* (circa 1949)
of a fish : migratory between salt and fresh waters

di·aer·e·sis \dī-'er-ə-səs, *British also* -'ir-\ *noun, plural* **-e·ses** \-ˌsēz\ [Late Latin *diaeresis*, from Greek *diairesis*, literally, division, from *diairein* to divide, from *dia-* + *hairein* to take] (circa 1611)
1 : a mark ¨ placed over a vowel to indicate that the vowel is pronounced in a separate syllable (as in *naïve* or *Brontë*)
2 : the break in a verse caused by the coincidence of the end of a foot with the end of a word
— **di·ae·ret·ic** \ˌdī-ə-'re-tik\ *adjective*

di·a·gen·e·sis \ˌdī-ə-'je-nə-səs\ *noun* [New Latin] (circa 1886)
1 : recombination or rearrangement of constituents (as of a chemical or mineral) resulting in a new product
2 : the conversion (as by compaction or chemical reaction) of sediment into rock
— **dia·ge·net·ic** \ˌdī-ə-jə-'ne-tik\ *adjective*
— **dia·ge·net·i·cal·ly** \-'ne-ti-k(ə-)lē\ *adverb*

dia·geo·tro·pic \ˌdī-ə-ˌjē-ə-'trō-pik, -'trä-pik\ *adjective* (1880)
: tending to grow at right angles to the line of gravity ⟨*diageotropic* branches and roots⟩

di·ag·nose \'dī-ig-ˌnōs, -,nōz, ˌdī-ig-', -əg-\ *verb* **-nosed; -nos·ing** [back-formation from *diagnosis*] (circa 1859)
transitive verb
1 a : to recognize (as a disease) by signs and symptoms **b** : to diagnose a disease or condition in ⟨*diagnosed* the patient⟩
2 : to analyze the cause or nature of ⟨*diagnose* the problem⟩
intransitive verb
: to make a diagnosis
— **di·ag·nos·able** *or* **di·ag·nose·able** \ˌdī-ig-'nō-sə-bəl, -əg-, -zə-\ *adjective*

di·ag·no·sis \ˌdī-ig-'nō-səs, -əg-\ *noun, plural* **-no·ses** \-ˌsēz\ [New Latin, from Greek *diagnōsis*, from *diagignōskein* to distinguish, from *dia-* + *gignōskein* to know — more at KNOW] (circa 1681)
1 a : the art or act of identifying a disease from its signs and symptoms **b** : the decision reached by diagnosis
2 : a concise technical description of a taxon
3 a : investigation or analysis of the cause or nature of a condition, situation, or problem ⟨*diagnosis* of engine trouble⟩ **b** : a statement or conclusion from such an analysis

¹di·ag·nos·tic \-'näs-tik\ *also* **di·ag·nos·ti·cal** \-ti-kəl\ *adjective* (1625)
1 a : of, relating to, or used in diagnosis **b** : using the methods of or yielding a diagnosis
2 : serving to distinguish or identify
— **di·ag·nos·ti·cal·ly** \-ti-k(ə-)lē\ *adverb*

²diagnostic *noun* (1625)
1 : the art or practice of diagnosis — often used in plural
2 : a distinguishing mark
— **di·ag·nos·ti·cian** \-(ˌ)näs-'ti-shən\ *noun*

¹di·ag·o·nal \dī-'a-gə-nᵊl, -'a-nəl\ *adjective* [Latin *diagonalis*, from Greek *diagōnios* from angle to angle, from *dia-* + *gōnia* angle; akin to Greek *gony* knee — more at KNEE] (1563)
1 a : joining two vertices of a rectilinear figure that are nonadjacent or two vertices of a polyhedral figure that are not in the same face **b** : passing through two nonadjacent edges of a polyhedron ⟨a *diagonal* plane⟩
2 a : inclined obliquely from a reference line (as the vertical) ⟨wood with a *diagonal* grain⟩ **b** : having diagonal markings or parts ⟨a *diagonal* weave⟩

²diagonal *noun* (1571)
1 : a diagonal straight line or plane
2 a (1) : a diagonal direction (2) : a diagonal row, arrangement, or pattern **b** : something oriented in diagonal position
3 : a mark / used typically to denote "or" (as in *and/or*), "and or" (as in *straggler/deserter*), or "per" (as in *feet/second*) — called also *solidus, virgule*
— **on the diagonal** : in an oblique direction : DIAGONALLY

di·ag·o·nal·ize \-nə-ˌlīz\ *transitive verb* **-ized; -iz·ing** (1942)
: to put (a matrix) in a form with all the nonzero elements along the diagonal from upper left to lower right
— **di·ag·o·nal·iz·able** \-ˌlī-zə-bəl\ *adjective*
— **di·ag·o·nal·iza·tion** \-ˌa-gə-nᵊl-ə-'zā-shən, -ˌag-nə-lə-'zā-\ *noun*

di·ag·o·nal·ly \dī-'a-gə-nᵊl-ē, -'ag-nə-lē\ *adverb* (1541)
: in a diagonal manner

diagonal matrix *noun* (circa 1928)
: a diagonalized matrix

¹di·a·gram \'dī-ə-ˌgram\ *noun* [Greek *diagramma*, from *diagraphein* to mark out by lines, from *dia-* + *graphein* to write — more at CARVE] (1619)
1 : a graphic design that explains rather than represents; *especially* : a drawing that shows arrangement and relations (as of parts)
2 : a line drawing made for mathematical or scientific purposes
— **di·a·gram·ma·ble** \-ˌgra-mə-bəl\ *adjective*
— **di·a·gram·mat·ic** \ˌdī-ə-grə-'ma-tik\ *also* **di·a·gram·mat·i·cal** \-'ma-ti-kəl\ *adjective*
— **di·a·gram·mat·i·cal·ly** \-ti-k(ə-)lē\ *adverb*

²diagram *transitive verb* **-grammed** *or* **-gramed** \-ˌgramd\; **-gram·ming** *or* **-gram·ing** \-ˌgra-miŋ\ (1840)
: to represent by or put into the form of a diagram

dia·ki·ne·sis \ˌdī-ə-kə-'nē-səs, -ˌkī-\ *noun, plural* **-ne·ses** \-ˌsēz\ [New Latin] (circa 1902)
: the final stage of the meiotic prophase marked by contraction of the bivalents

¹di·al \'dī(-ə)l\ *noun* [Middle English *dyal*, from Medieval Latin *dialis* clock wheel revolving daily, from Latin *dies* day — more at DEITY] (15th century)
1 : the face of a sundial
2 *obsolete* : TIMEPIECE
3 : the graduated face of a timepiece
4 a : a face upon which some measurement is registered usually by means of graduations and a pointer ⟨the thermometer *dial* reads 70°F⟩ **b** : a device that may be operated to make electrical connections or to regulate the operation of a machine ⟨a radio *dial*⟩ ⟨a telephone *dial*⟩

²dial *verb* **di·aled** *or* **di·alled; di·al·ing** *or* **di·al·ling** (1821)
transitive verb

1 : to measure with a dial
2 a : to manipulate a device (as a dial) so as to operate, regulate, or select ⟨*dial* your favorite program⟩ **b :** CALL 1m(1) ⟨*dialed* the wrong number⟩ **b :** CALL 1m(1) ⟨*dialed* the office⟩
intransitive verb
1 : to manipulate a dial
2 : to make a telephone call or connection
— **di·al·er** *noun*

di·a·lect \'dī-ə-ˌlekt\ *noun, often attributive* [Middle French *dialecte*, from Latin *dialectus*, from Greek *dialektos* conversation, dialect, from *dialegesthai* to converse — more at DIALOGUE] (1577)
1 a : a regional variety of language distinguished by features of vocabulary, grammar, and pronunciation from other regional varieties and constituting together with them a single language ⟨the Doric *dialect* of ancient Greek⟩ **b :** one of two or more cognate languages ⟨French and Italian are Romance *dialects*⟩ **c :** a variety of a language used by the members of a group ⟨such *dialects* as politics and advertising —Philip Howard⟩ **d :** a variety of language whose identity is fixed by a factor other than geography (as social class) ⟨spoke a rough peasant *dialect*⟩ **e :** REGISTER 4c **f :** a version of a computer programming language
2 : manner or means of expressing oneself **:** PHRASEOLOGY
— **di·a·lec·tal** \ˌdī-ə-'lek-t³l\ *adjective*
— **di·a·lec·tal·ly** \-t³l-ē\ *adverb*
dialect atlas *noun* (1932)
: LINGUISTIC ATLAS
dialect geography *noun* (1929)
: LINGUISTIC GEOGRAPHY
di·a·lec·tic \ˌdī-ə-'lek-tik\ *noun* [Middle English *dialetik*, from Middle French *dialetique*, from Latin *dialectica*, from Greek *dialektikē*, from feminine of *dialektikos* of conversation, from *dialektos*] (14th century)
1 : LOGIC 1a(1)
2 a : discussion and reasoning by dialogue as a method of intellectual investigation; *specifically* **:** the Socratic techniques of exposing false beliefs and eliciting truth **b :** the Platonic investigation of the eternal ideas
3 : the logic of fallacy
4 a : the Hegelian process of change in which a concept or its realization passes over into and is preserved and fulfilled by its opposite; *also* **:** the critical investigation of this process **b** (1) *usually plural but singular or plural in construction* **:** development through the stages of thesis, antithesis, and synthesis in accordance with the laws of dialectical materialism (2) **:** the investigation of this process (3) **:** the theoretical application of this process especially in the social sciences
5 *usually plural but singular or plural in construction* **a :** any systematic reasoning, exposition, or argument that juxtaposes opposed or contradictory ideas and usually seeks to resolve their conflict **b :** an intellectual exchange of ideas
6 : the dialectical tension or opposition between two interacting forces or elements
di·a·lec·ti·cal \ˌdī-ə-'lek-ti-kəl\ *also* **di·a·lec·tic** \-tik\ *adjective* (1548)
1 a : of, relating to, or in accordance with dialectic ⟨*dialectical* method⟩ **b :** practicing, devoted to, or employing dialectic ⟨a *dialectical* philosopher⟩
2 : of, relating to, or characteristic of a dialect
— **di·a·lec·ti·cal·ly** \-ti-k(ə-)lē\ *adverb*
dialectical materialism *noun* (1927)
: the Marxist theory that maintains the material basis of a reality constantly changing in a dialectical process and the priority of matter over mind — compare HISTORICAL MATERIALISM
di·a·lec·ti·cian \ˌdī-ə-ˌlek-'ti-shən\ *noun* (circa 1693)
1 : one who is skilled in or practices dialectic
2 : a student of dialects
di·a·lec·tol·o·gist \-'tä-lə-jist\ *noun* (1883)

: a specialist in dialectology
di·a·lec·tol·o·gy \-jē\ *noun* [International Scientific Vocabulary] (circa 1864)
1 : the systematic study of dialect
2 : the body of data available for study of a dialect
— **di·a·lec·to·log·i·cal** \-ˌlek-tə-'lä-ji-kəl\ *adjective*
— **di·a·lec·to·log·i·cal·ly** \-k(ə-)lē\ *adverb*
di·al·lel \'dī-ə-ˌlel\ *adjective* [Greek *diallēlos* reciprocating, from *dia* through + *allēlōn* one another — more at ALLELO-] (1920)
: relating to or being the crossing of each of several individuals with two or more others in order to determine the relative genetic contribution of each parent to specific characters in the offspring
di·a·log·ic \ˌdī-ə-'lä-jik\ *or* **di·a·log·i·cal** \-ji-kəl\ *adjective* (1833)
: of, relating to, or characterized by dialogue ⟨*dialogic* writing⟩
— **di·a·log·i·cal·ly** \-ji-k(ə-)lē\ *adverb*
di·a·lo·gist \'dī-ə-lə-jist; 'dī-ə-ˌlô-gist, -ˌlä-\ *noun* (circa 1660)
1 : a writer of dialogues
2 : one who participates in a dialogue
— **di·a·lo·gis·tic** \(ˌ)dī-ˌa-lə-'jis-tik; ˌdī-ə-ˌlô-'gis-, -ˌlä-'gis-\ *adjective*
¹**di·a·logue** *also* **di·a·log** \'dī-ə-ˌlôg, -ˌläg\ *noun* [Middle English *dialoge*, from Old French *dialogue*, from Latin *dialogus*, from Greek *dialogos*, from *dialegesthai* to converse, from *dia-* + *legein* to speak — more at LEGEND] (13th century)
1 : a written composition in which two or more characters are represented as conversing
2 a : a conversation between two or more persons; *also* **:** a similar exchange between a person and something else (as a computer) **b :** an exchange of ideas and opinions **c :** a discussion between representatives of parties to a conflict that is aimed at resolution
3 : the conversational element of literary or dramatic composition
4 : a musical composition for two or more parts suggestive of a conversation
²**dialogue** *verb* **-logued; -logu·ing** (1597)
transitive verb
: to express in dialogue
intransitive verb
: to take part in a dialogue
dial tone *noun* (1923)
: a tone emitted by a telephone as a signal that the system is ready for dialing
dial-up \'dī-(ə)l-ˌəp\ *adjective* (1972)
: relating to or being a standard telephone line used for computer communications; *also* **:** accessible via a standard telephone line ⟨a *dial-up* information service⟩
di·al·y·sate \dī-'a-lə-ˌzāt, -ˌsāt\ *also* **di·al·y·zate** \-ˌzāt\ *noun* (circa 1867)
: the material that passes through the membrane in dialysis; *also* **:** the liquid into which this material passes
di·al·y·sis \dī-'a-lə-səs\ *noun, plural* **-y·ses** \-ˌsēz\ [New Latin, from Greek, separation, from *dialyein* to dissolve, from *dia-* + *lyein* to loosen — more at LOSE] (1861)
1 : the separation of substances in solution by means of their unequal diffusion through semipermeable membranes; *especially* **:** such a separation of colloids from soluble substances
2 : HEMODIALYSIS
— **di·a·lyt·ic** \ˌdī-ə-'li-tik\ *adjective*
di·a·lyze \'dī-ə-ˌlīz\ *verb* **-lyzed; -lyz·ing** (1861)
transitive verb
: to subject to dialysis
intransitive verb
: to undergo dialysis
— **di·a·lyz·able** \-ˌlī-zə-bəl\ *adjective*
— **di·a·lyz·er** \-ˌlī-zər\ *noun*
dia·mag·net·ic \ˌdī-ə-mag-'ne-tik\ *adjective* (1846)

: having a magnetic permeability less than that of a vacuum **:** slightly repelled by a magnet
— **dia·mag·ne·tism** \-'mag-nə-ˌti-zəm\ *noun*
di·a·man·té \ˌdē-ə-ˌmän-'tā\ *noun* [French, adjective, like a diamond, from *diamant* diamond, from Middle French] (1904)
: a sparkling decoration (as of sequins) or material decorated with this ⟨a gown trimmed with *diamanté*⟩
di·am·e·ter \dī-'a-mə-tər\ *noun* [Middle English *diametre*, from Middle French, from Latin *diametros*, from Greek, from *dia-* + *metron* measure — more at MEASURE] (14th century)
1 : a chord passing through the center of a figure or body
2 : the length of a straight line through the center of an object
3 : a unit of magnification for an optical instrument equal to the number of times the linear dimensions of an object are apparently increased ⟨a microscope magnifying 60 *diameters*⟩
— **di·am·e·tral** \-'a-mə-trəl\ *adjective*
di·a·met·ric \ˌdī-ə-'me-trik\ *or* **di·a·met·ri·cal** \-tri-kəl\ *adjective* (1553)
1 : of, relating to, or constituting a diameter **:** located at the diameter
2 : completely opposed **:** being at opposite extremes ⟨in *diametric* contradiction to his claims⟩
— **di·a·met·ri·cal·ly** \-tri-k(ə-)lē\ *adverb*
di·am·ide \'dī-ə-ˌmīd, dī-'a-məd\ *noun* (1866)
: a compound containing two amido groups
di·a·mine \'dī-ə-ˌmēn, dī-'a-mən\ *noun* [International Scientific Vocabulary] (1866)
: a compound containing two amino groups
di·am·mo·ni·um phosphate \ˌdī-ə-'mō-nē-əm-\ *noun* (circa 1929)
: a white crystalline compound $(NH_4)_2HPO_4$ used especially as a fertilizer and as a fire retardant
¹**di·a·mond** \'dī-(ə-)mənd\ *noun, often attributive* [Middle English *diamaunde*, from Middle French *diamant*, from Old French, from Late Latin *diamant-, diamas*, alteration of Latin *adamant-, adamas* hardest metal, diamond, from Greek] (14th century)
1 a : native crystalline carbon that is usually nearly colorless, that when transparent and free from flaws is highly valued as a precious stone, and that is used industrially as an abrasive powder and in rock drills because of its great hardness; *also* **:** a piece of this substance **b :** crystallized carbon produced artificially
2 : something that resembles a diamond (as in brilliance, value, or fine quality)
3 : a square or rhombus-shaped figure usually oriented with the long diagonal vertical
4 a : a playing card marked with a stylized figure of a red diamond **b** *plural but singular or plural in construction* **:** the suit comprising cards marked with diamonds
5 : a baseball infield; *also* **:** the entire playing field
²**diamond** *transitive verb* (1751)
: to adorn with or as if with diamonds
³**diamond** *adjective* (1872)
: of, relating to, or being a 60th or 75th anniversary or its celebration ⟨*diamond* jubilee⟩
di·a·mond·back \'dī-(ə-)mən(d)-ˌbak\ *adjective* (1887)
: having marks like diamonds or lozenges on the back
diamondback moth *noun* (1891)
: a nearly cosmopolitan moth (*Plutella xylostella* of the family Plutellidae) whose larva is a pest on cruciferous plants
diamondback rattlesnake *noun* (1894)

\ə\ abut \ə\ kitten \ər\ further \a\ ash \ā\ ace
\ä\ mop, mar \aů\ out \ch\ chin \e\ bet \ē\ easy
\g\ go \i\ hit \ī\ ice \j\ job \ŋ\ sing \ō\ go
\ȯ\ law \ȯi\ boy \th\ thin \th\ the \ü\ loot \ů\ foot
\y\ yet \zh\ vision *see also* Guide to Pronunciation

: either of two large and deadly rattlesnakes (*Crotalus adamanteus* of the southeastern U.S. and *C. atrox* of the south central and southwestern U.S. and Mexico) — called also *diamondback, diamondback rattler*

diamondback terrapin *noun* (1887)
: any of several terrapins (genus *Malaclemys*) formerly widely distributed in salt marshes along the Atlantic and Gulf coasts but now much restricted

di·a·mond·if·er·ous \ˌdī-(ə-)mən-'di-fə-rəs\ *adjective* (1870)
: containing diamonds ⟨*diamondiferous* earth⟩

diamond in the rough (circa 1947)
: a person of exceptional qualities or potential but lacking refinement or polish

Di·ana \dī-'a-nə\ *noun* [Latin]
: an ancient Italian goddess of the forest and of childbirth who was identified with Artemis by the Romans

di·an·thus \dī-'an(t)-thəs\ *noun* [New Latin, genus name, from Greek *dios* heavenly + *anthos* flower — more at DEITY, ANTHOLOGY] (1849)
: ²PINK 1

di·a·pa·son \ˌdī-ə-'pā-z°n, -s°n\ *noun* [Middle English, from Latin, from Greek (*hē*) *dia pasōn* (*chordōn symphōnia*), literally, the concord through all the notes, from *dia* through + *pasōn*, genitive feminine plural of *pas* all — more at DIA-, PAN-] (circa 1501)
1 a : a burst of sound ⟨*diapasons* of laughter⟩
b : the principal foundation stop in the organ extending through the complete range of the instrument **c** (1) : the entire compass of musical tones **2** : RANGE, SCOPE
2 a : TUNING FORK **b** : a standard of pitch

dia·pause \'dī-ə-ˌpȯz\ *noun* [Greek *diapausis* pause, from *diapauein* to pause, from *dia-* + *pauein* to stop] (1893)
: a period of physiologically enforced dormancy between periods of activity

dia·paus·ing \-ˌpȯ-ziŋ\ *adjective* (1944)
: undergoing diapause

di·a·pe·de·sis \ˌdī-ə-pə-'dē-səs\ *noun, plural* **-de·ses** \-ˌsēz\ [New Latin, from Greek *diapēdēsis*, literally, act of leaping through, from *diapēdan* to leap through, from *dia-* + *pēdan* to leap] (1625)
: the passage of blood cells through capillary walls into the tissues

¹di·a·per \'dī-pər *also* 'dī-ə-\ *noun* [Middle English *diapre*, from Medieval Latin *diasprum*] (14th century)
1 : a fabric with a distinctive pattern: **a** : a rich silk fabric **b** : a soft usually white linen or cotton fabric used for tablecloths or towels
2 : an allover pattern consisting of one or more small repeated units of design (as geometric figures) connecting with one another or growing out of one another with continuously flowing or straight lines
3 : a basic garment for infants consisting of a folded cloth or other absorbent material drawn up between the legs and fastened about the waist

diaper 2

²diaper *transitive verb* **di·a·pered; di·a·per·ing** \-p(ə-)riŋ\ (14th century)
1 : to ornament with diaper designs
2 : to put on or change the diaper of (an infant)

diaper rash *noun*
: skin irritation of the diaper-covered area of an infant especially from excessive urinary ammonia

di·a·pha·ne·ity \ˌ(ˌ)dī-ˌa-fə-'nē-ə-tē, ˌdī-ə-fə-, -'nā-\ *noun* (15th century)
: the quality or state of being diaphanous

di·aph·a·nous \dī-'a-fə-nəs\ *adjective* [Medieval Latin *diaphanus*, from Greek *diaphanēs*,

from *diaphainein* to show through, from *dia-* + *phainein* to show — more at FANCY] (1614)
1 : characterized by such fineness of texture as to permit seeing through
2 : characterized by extreme delicacy of form : ETHEREAL ⟨painted *diaphanous* landscapes⟩
3 : INSUBSTANTIAL, VAGUE ⟨had only a *diaphanous* hope of success⟩
— **di·aph·a·nous·ly** *adverb*
— **di·aph·a·nous·ness** *noun*

dia·phone \'dī-ə-ˌfōn\ *noun* (1906)
: a fog signal similar to a siren but producing a blast of two tones

di·aph·o·rase \dī-'a-fə-ˌrās, -ˌrāz\ *noun* [International Scientific Vocabulary *diaphor-* (from Greek *diaphoros* different, from *diapherein* to differ, from *dia-* + *pherein* to carry) + *-ase* — more at BEAR] (1938)
: a flavoprotein enzyme capable of oxidizing the reduced form of NAD

di·a·pho·re·sis \ˌdī-ə-fə-'rē-səs, ˌ(ˌ)dī-ˌa-fə-\ *noun, plural* **-re·ses** \-ˌsēz\ [Late Latin, from Greek *diaphorēsis*, from *diaphorein* to dissipate by perspiration, from *dia-* + *phorein*, frequentative of *pherein* to carry] (circa 1681)
: PERSPIRATION; *especially* : profuse perspiration artificially induced

di·a·pho·ret·ic \-'re-tik\ *adjective* (15th century)
: having the power to increase perspiration
— **diaphoretic** *noun*

di·a·phragm \'dī-ə-ˌfram\ *noun* [Middle English *diafragma*, from Late Latin *diaphragma*, from Greek, from *diaphrassein* to barricade, from *dia-* + *phrassein* to enclose] (14th century)
1 : a body partition of muscle and connective tissue; *specifically* : the partition separating the chest and abdominal cavities in mammals
2 : a dividing membrane or thin partition especially in a tube
3 a : a more or less rigid partition in the body or shell of an invertebrate **b** : a transverse septum in a plant stem
4 : a device that limits the aperture of a lens or optical system — compare IRIS DIAPHRAGM
5 : a thin flexible disk (as in a microphone or loudspeaker) that vibrates when struck by sound waves or that vibrates to generate sound waves
6 : a molded cap usually of thin rubber fitted over the uterine cervix to act as a mechanical contraceptive barrier
— **di·a·phrag·mat·ic** \ˌdī-ə-frə(g)-'ma-tik, -ˌfrag-\ *adjective*
— **di·a·phrag·mat·i·cal·ly** \-'ma-ti-k(ə-)lē\ *adverb*

di·aph·y·sis \dī-'a-fə-səs\ *noun, plural* **-y·ses** \-ˌsēz\ [New Latin, from Greek, spinous process of the tibia, from *diaphyesthai* to grow between, from *dia-* + *phyein* to bring forth — more at BE] (1831)
: the shaft of a long bone
— **di·aph·y·se·al** \ˌ(ˌ)dī-ˌa-fə-'sē-əl\ *or* **di·a·phys·i·al** \ˌdī-ə-fi-'zē-əl\ *adjective*

di·a·pir \'dī-ə-ˌpir\ *noun* [French, probably from Greek *diapeirein* to drive through, from *dia-* + *peirein* to pierce; akin to Greek *poros* passage — more at FARE] (1918)
: an anticlinal fold in which a mobile core has broken through brittle overlying rocks
— **di·a·pir·ic** \ˌdī-ə-'pir-ik\ *adjective*

di·a·pos·i·tive \ˌdī-ə-'pä-zə-tiv, -'päz-tiv\ *noun* (1893)
: a positive photographic image on transparent material (as glass or film)

di·ap·sid \dī-'ap-səd\ *adjective* [ultimately from Greek *di-* + *hapsid-, hapsis* loop, arch — more at APSIS] (circa 1909)
: of, relating to, or including reptiles (as the crocodiles) with two pairs of temporal openings in the skull

di·ar·chy *variant of* DYARCHY

di·a·rist \'dī-ə-rəst\ *noun* (circa 1818)
: one who keeps a diary

di·ar·rhea \ˌdī-ə-'rē-ə\ *noun* [Middle English *diaria*, from Late Latin *diarrhoea*, from Greek *diarrhoia*, from *diarrhein* to flow through, from *dia-* + *rhein* to flow — more at STREAM] (14th century)
1 : abnormally frequent intestinal evacuations with more or less fluid stools
2 : excessive flow ⟨verbal *diarrhea*⟩
— **di·ar·rhe·ic** \-'rē-ik\ *adjective*
— **di·ar·rhe·al** \-'rē-əl\ *adjective*
— **di·ar·rhet·ic** \-'re-tik\ *adjective*

di·ar·rhoea *chiefly British variant of* DIARRHEA

di·ar·thro·sis \ˌdī-är-'thrō-səs\ *noun, plural* **-thro·ses** \-ˌsēz\ [New Latin, from Greek *diarthrōsis*, from *diarthroun* to joint, from *dia-* + *arthroun* to fasten by a joint, from *arthron* joint — more at ARTHR-] (1578)
1 : articulation that permits free movement
2 : a freely movable joint

di·a·ry \'dī-(ə-)rē\ *noun, plural* **-ries** [Latin *diarium*, from *dies* day — more at DEITY] (1581)
1 : a record of events, transactions, or observations kept daily or at frequent intervals : JOURNAL; *especially* : a daily record of personal activities, reflections, or feelings
2 : a book intended or used for a diary

di·as·po·ra \dī-'as-p(ə-)rə, dē-\ *noun* [Greek, dispersion, from *diaspeirein* to scatter, from *dia-* + *speirein* to sow] (1881)
1 *capitalized* **a** : the settling of scattered colonies of Jews outside Palestine after the Babylonian exile **b** : the area outside Palestine settled by Jews **c** : the Jews living outside Palestine or modern Israel
2 a : the breaking up and scattering of a people : MIGRATION ⟨the black *diaspora* to northern cities⟩ **b** : people settled far from their ancestral homelands ⟨African *diaspora*⟩ **c** : the place where these people live

di·a·spore \'dī-ə-ˌspȯr, -ˌspȯr\ *noun* [French, from Greek *diaspora*] (1805)
: a mineral consisting of aluminum hydrogen oxide

di·a·stase \'dī-ə-ˌstās, -ˌstāz\ *noun* [French, from Greek *diastasis* separation, interval, from *diistanai* to separate, from *dia-* + *histanai* to cause to stand — more at STAND] (1838)
1 : AMYLASE; *especially* : a mixture of amylases from malt
2 : ENZYME

di·a·stat·ic \ˌdī-ə-'sta-tik\ *adjective* (1881)
: relating to or having the properties of diastase; *especially* : converting starch into sugar

di·a·ste·ma \ˌdī-ə-'stē-mə\ *noun, plural* **-ma·ta** \-mə-tə\ [New Latin, from Late Latin, interval, from Greek *diastēma*, from *diistanai*] (1854)
: a space between teeth in a jaw

di·a·ste·reo·mer \ˌdī-ə-'ster-ē-ō-(ˌ)mər, -'stir-\ *or* **di·a·ste·reo·iso·mer** \-ˌster-ē-ō-'ī-sə-mər, -ˌstir-\ *noun* (1936)
: a stereoisomer of a compound having two or more chiral centers that is not a mirror image of another stereoisomer of the same compound — compare ENANTIOMORPH
— **di·a·ste·reo·mer·ic** \-ˌster-ē-ō-'mer-ik, -ˌstir-\ *or* **di·a·ste·reo·iso·mer·ic** \-ˌī-sə-'mer-ik\ *adjective*
— **di·a·ste·reo·isom·er·ism** \-ˌī-'sä-mə-ˌri-zəm\ *noun*

di·as·to·le \dī-'as-tə-(ˌ)lē\ *noun* [Greek *diastolē* dilatation, from *diastellein* to expand, from *dia-* + *stellein* to prepare, send] (circa 1578)
: a rhythmically recurrent expansion; *especially* : the dilatation of the cavities of the heart during which they fill with blood
— **di·a·stol·ic** \ˌdī-ə-'stä-lik\ *adjective*

di·as·tro·phism \dī-'as-trə-ˌfi-zəm\ *noun* [Greek *diastrophē* twisting, from *diastrephein* to distort, from *dia-* + *strephein* to twist] (1890)

: the process of deformation that produces in the earth's crust its continents and ocean basins, plateaus and mountains, folds of strata, and faults

— **di·a·stroph·ic** \ˌdī-ə-ˈsträ-fik\ *adjective*
— **di·a·stroph·i·cal·ly** \-fi-k(ə-)lē\ *adverb*

di·a·tes·sa·ron \ˌdī-ə-ˈte-sə-rən\ *noun* [Greek (*Euangelion*) *dia tessarōn*, literally, Gospel out of four, from *dia* through, out of + *tessarōn*, genitive of *tessares* four — more at DIA-, FOUR] (1803)
: a harmony of the four Gospels edited and arranged into a single connected narrative

dia·ther·ma·nous \ˌdī-ə-ˈthər-mə-nəs\ *adjective* [French *diathermane*, modification of Greek *diathermainein* to heat through, from *dia-* + *thermainein* to heat, from *thermos* hot — more at THERM] (1834)
: DIATHERMIC 1

dia·ther·mic \ˌdī-ə-ˈthər-mik\ *adjective* (1840)
1 : transmitting infrared radiation
2 : of or relating to diathermy ⟨*diathermic* treatment⟩

dia·ther·my \ˈdī-ə-ˌthər-mē\ *noun* [International Scientific Vocabulary] (1909)
: the generation of heat in tissue by electric currents for medical or surgical purposes

di·ath·e·sis \dī-ˈa-thə-səs\ *noun, plural* **-e·ses** \-ˌsēz\ [New Latin, from Greek, literally, arrangement, from *diatithenai* to arrange, from *dia-* + *tithenai* to set — more at DO] (1651)
: a constitutional predisposition toward a particular state or condition and especially one that is abnormal or diseased
— **di·a·thet·ic** \ˌdī-ə-ˈthe-tik\ *adjective*

di·a·tom \ˈdī-ə-ˌtäm\ *noun* [ultimately from Greek *diatomos* cut in half, from *diatemnein* to cut through, from *dia-* + *temnein* to cut — more at TOME] (1845)
: any of a class (Bacillariophyceae) of minute planktonic unicellular or colonial algae with silicified skeletons that form diatomite

di·a·to·ma·ceous \ˌdī-ə-tə-ˈmā-shəs, ˌ(ˌ)dī-ˌa-tə-\ *adjective* (1847)
: consisting of or abounding in diatoms or their siliceous remains ⟨*diatomaceous* silica⟩

diatomaceous earth *noun* (1883)
: DIATOMITE

di·atom·ic \ˌdī-ə-ˈtä-mik\ *adjective* [International Scientific Vocabulary] (circa 1859)
: consisting of two atoms : having two atoms in the molecule

di·at·o·mite \dī-ˈa-tə-ˌmīt\ *noun* (1887)
: a light friable siliceous material derived chiefly from diatom remains and used especially as a filter

dia·ton·ic \ˌdī-ə-ˈtä-nik\ *adjective* [Late Latin *diatonicus*, from Greek *diatonikos*, from *diatonos* stretching, from *diateinein* to stretch out, from *dia-* + *teinein* to stretch — more at THIN] (1694)
: of or relating to a major or minor musical scale comprising intervals of five whole steps and two half steps
— **dia·ton·i·cal·ly** \-ˈtä-ni-k(ə-)lē\ *adverb*

di·a·tribe \ˈdī-ə-ˌtrīb\ *noun* [Latin *diatriba*, from Greek *diatribē* pastime, discourse, from *diatribein* to spend (time), wear away, from *dia-* + *tribein* to rub — more at THROW] (1581)
1 *archaic* : a prolonged discourse
2 : a bitter and abusive speech or writing
3 : ironical or satirical criticism

di·az·e·pam \dī-ˈa-zə-ˌpam\ *noun* [benzo*diaz*epine + *-am* (of unknown origin)] (circa 1961)
: a tranquilizer $C_{16}H_{13}ClN_2O$ used especially to relieve anxiety and tension and as a muscle relaxant — compare VALIUM

Di·az·i·non \dī-ˈa-zi-ˌnän\ *trademark*
— used for a cholinesterase-inhibiting organophosphate insecticide

di·azo \dī-ˈa-(ˌ)zō, -ˈā-\ *adjective* [International Scientific Vocabulary *diaz-, diazo-*, from *di-* + *az-*] (1878)

1 a : relating to or containing the group N_2 composed of two nitrogen atoms united to a single carbon atom of an organic radical — often used in combination b : relating to or containing diazonium — often used in combination
2 : of or relating to a photograph or photocopy whose production involves the use of a coating of a diazo compound that is decomposed by exposure to light

di·a·zo·ni·um \ˌdī-ə-ˈzō-nē-əm\ *noun* [International Scientific Vocabulary *di-* + *az-* + *-onium*] (1895)
: the univalent cation N_2^+ that is composed of two nitrogen atoms united to carbon in an organic radical and that usually exists in salts used in the manufacture of azo dyes

di·az·o·tize \dī-ˈa-zə-ˌtīz\ *transitive verb* **-tized; -tiz·ing** [International Scientific Vocabulary *di-* + *azote* nitrogen + *-ize* — more at AZ-] (circa 1889)
: to convert (a compound) into a diazo compound (as a diazonium salt)
— **di·az·o·ti·za·tion** \-ˌa-zə-tə-ˈzā-shən\ *noun*

di·ba·sic \(ˌ)dī-ˈbā-sik\ *adjective* (1868)
: having two replaceable hydrogen atoms — used of acids

dib·ber \ˈdi-bər\ *noun* (circa 1736)
: DIBBLE

¹dib·ble \ˈdi-bəl\ *noun* [Middle English *debylle*] (15th century)
: a small hand implement used to make holes in the ground for plants, seeds, or bulbs

²dibble *transitive verb* **dib·bled; dib·bling** \ˈdi-b(ə-)liŋ\ (1583)
1 : to plant with a dibble
2 : to make holes in (soil) with or as if with a dibble

di·ben·zo·fu·ran \ˌdī-ˌben-zō-ˈfyù-ˌran, -fyə-ˈran\ *noun* (1940)
: a highly toxic chemical compound $C_{12}H_8O$ that is used in chemical synthesis and as an insecticide and is a hazardous pollutant in its chlorinated form

dibs \ˈdibz\ *noun plural* [short for *dibstones* (jacks), from obsolete *dib* (to dab)] (1812)
1 *slang* : money especially in small amounts
2 : CLAIM, RIGHTS ⟨I have *dibs* on that piece of cake⟩

di·bu·tyl phthal·ate \ˌdī-ˌbyü-t⁴l-ˈtha-ˌlāt\ *noun* [*phthal*ic acid + *-ate*] (1925)
: a colorless oily ester $C_{16}H_{22}O_4$ used chiefly as a solvent, plasticizer, pesticide, and repellent (as for chiggers and mites)

di·cal·ci·um silicate \(ˌ)dī-ˈkal-sē-əm-\ *noun* (1925)
: a calcium silicate $2CaO \cdot SiO_2$ that is an essential ingredient of portland cement

di·car·box·yl·ic \ˌdī-ˌkär-ˌbäk-ˈsi-lik\ *adjective* (circa 1890)
: containing two carboxyl groups in the molecule ⟨*dicarboxylic* acids⟩

di·cast \ˈdī-ˌkast, ˈdi-\ *noun* [Greek *dikastēs*, from *dikazein* to judge, from *dikē* judgment — more at DICTION] (1822)
: an ancient Athenian performing the functions of both judge and juror at a trial

¹dice \ˈdīs\ *noun, plural* **dice** [Middle English *dyce*, from *dees, dyce*, plural of *dee* die — more at DIE] (14th century)
1 a : DIE 1 b : a gambling game played with dice
2 *plural also* **dic·es** : a small cubical piece (as of food)
3 : a close contest between two racing-car drivers for position during a race
— **no dice 1** : of no avail : no use : FUTILE 2 : ¹NO 3 ⟨said *no dice* to my request⟩

²dice *verb* **diced; dic·ing** [Middle English *dycen*, from *dyce*] (14th century)
transitive verb
1 a : to cut into small cubes b : to ornament with square markings ⟨*diced* leather⟩

2 a : to bring by playing dice ⟨*dice* himself into debt⟩ b : to lose by dicing ⟨*dice* her money away⟩
intransitive verb
1 : to play games with dice ⟨*dice* for drinks in the bar —Malcolm Lowry⟩
2 : to take a chance ⟨the temptation to *dice* with death —*Newsweek*⟩
— **dic·er** *noun*

di·cen·tric \(ˌ)dī-ˈsen-trik\ *adjective* (1937)
: having two centromeres ⟨a *dicentric* chromosome⟩
— **dicentric** *noun*

dic·ey \ˈdī-sē\ *adjective* **dic·i·er; -est** [¹*dice* + *-y*] (1950)
: RISKY, UNPREDICTABLE ⟨a *dicey* proposition⟩ ⟨*dicey* weather⟩

dich- *or* **dicho-** *combining form* [Late Latin, from Greek, from *dicha;* akin to Greek *di-*]
: in two : apart ⟨*dichogamous*⟩

di·cha·sium \dī-ˈkā-z(h)ē-əm, -zhəm\ *noun, plural* **-sia** \-z(h)ē-ə, -zhə\ [New Latin, from Greek *dichasis* halving, from *dichazein* to halve, from *dicha*] (1875)
: a cymose inflorescence that produces two main axes

dichlor- *or* **dichloro-** *combining form*
: containing two atoms of chlorine ⟨*dichloro*ethane⟩

di·chlo·ro·ben·zene \(ˌ)dī-ˌklōr-ə-ˈben-ˌzēn, -ˌklōr-, -(ˌ)ben-ˈ\ *noun* (1873)
: any of three isomeric compounds $C_6H_4Cl_2$; *especially* : PARADICHLOROBENZENE

di·chlo·ro·di·flu·o·ro·meth·ane \ˌdī-ˌflùr-ə-ˈme-ˌthān\ *noun* (1936)
: a chlorofluoromethane CCl_2F_2

di·chlo·ro·eth·ane \(ˌ)dī-ˌklō-rō-ˈe-ˌthān\ *noun* (1936)
: a colorless toxic liquid compound $C_2H_4Cl_2$ that is used chiefly as a solvent

di·chlor·vos \(ˈ)dī-ˈklōr-ˌväs, -ˈklór-, -vəs\ *noun* [*dichlor-* + *vinyl* + *phos*phate] (1957)
: an organophosphorus insecticide and anthelmintic $C_4H_7Cl_2O_4P$ used especially in veterinary medicine — called also *DDVP*

di·chog·a·my \dī-ˈkä-gə-mē\ *noun, plural* **-mies** [German *Dichogamie*, from *dich-* + *-gamie* -gamy] (1862)
: the production of male and female reproductive elements at different times by a hermaphroditic organism in order to ensure cross-fertilization
— **di·chog·a·mous** \-gə-məs\ *adjective*

di·chon·dra \dī-ˈkän-drə\ *noun* [New Latin, genus name, from *di-* + Greek *chondros* grain — more at GRIND] (1947)
: any of a genus (Dichondra) of chiefly tropical perennial herbs of the morning glory family that includes some (especially *D. repens* or its varieties) used as a ground cover and a substitute for lawn grasses in warmer parts of the U.S.

dich·ot·ic \(ˌ)dī-ˈkō-tik\ *adjective* [*dich-* + ²*-otic*] (circa 1911)
: affecting or relating to the two ears differently in regard to a conscious aspect (as pitch or loudness) or a physical aspect (as frequency or energy) of sound
— **dich·ot·i·cal·ly** \-ti-k(ə-)lē\ *adverb*

di·chot·o·mist \dī-ˈkä-tə-məst *also* də-\ *noun* (circa 1592)
: one that dichotomizes

di·chot·o·mize \-ˌmīz\ *verb* **-mized; -miz·ing** [Late Latin *dichotomos*] (1606)
transitive verb
: to divide into two parts, classes, or groups
intransitive verb
: to exhibit dichotomy
— **di·chot·o·mi·za·tion** \-ˌkä-tə-mə-ˈzā-shən\ *noun*

di·chot·o·mous \dī-'kä-tə-məs *also* də-\ *adjective* [Late Latin *dichotomos,* from Greek, from *dich-* + *temnein* to cut — more at TOME] (1752)
1 : dividing into two parts
2 : relating to, involving, or proceeding from dichotomy
— **di·chot·o·mous·ly** *adverb*
— **di·chot·o·mous·ness** *noun*
dichotomous key *noun* (circa 1889)
: a key for the identification of organisms based on a series of choices between alternative characters
di·chot·o·my \dī-'kä-tə-mē *also* də-\ *noun, plural* **-mies** [Greek *dichotomia,* from *dichotomos*] (1610)
1 : a division or the process of dividing into two especially mutually exclusive or contradictory groups or entities
2 : the phase of the moon or an inferior planet in which half its disk appears illuminated
3 a : BIFURCATION; *especially* : repeated bifurcation (as of a plant's stem) **b** : a system of branching in which the main axis forks repeatedly into two branches **c** : branching of an ancestral line into two equal diverging branches
4 : something with seemingly contradictory qualities
di·chro·ic \dī-'krō-ik\ *adjective* [Greek *dichroos* two-colored, from *di-* + *chrōs* color, literally, skin] (circa 1859)
1 : having the property of dichroism ⟨a *dichroic* crystal⟩ ⟨a *dichroic* mirror⟩
2 : DICHROMATIC
di·chro·ism \dī-(,)krō-,i-zəm\ *noun* (1819)
: the property of some crystals and solutions of absorbing one of two plane-polarized components of transmitted light more strongly than the other; *also* : the property of exhibiting different colors by reflected or transmitted light — compare CIRCULAR DICHROISM
di·chro·mat \dī-krō-,mat, (,)dī-\ *noun* [back-formation from *dichromatic*] (circa 1909)
: one affected with dichromatism
di·chro·mate \(,)dī-'krō-,māt, 'dī-krō-\ *noun* [International Scientific Vocabulary] (circa 1864)
: a usually orange to red chromium salt containing the anion $Cr_2O_7^{2-}$ ⟨*dichromate* of potassium⟩ — called also *bichromate*
di·chro·mat·ic \,dī-krō-'ma-tik\ *adjective* (circa 1847)
1 : having or exhibiting two colors
2 : of, relating to, or exhibiting dichromatism
di·chro·ma·tism \dī-'krō-mə-,ti-zəm\ *noun* (circa 1901)
: partial color blindness in which only two colors are perceptible
di·chro·scope \dī-krə-,skōp\ *noun* (1857)
: an instrument for examining crystals for dichroism
dick \dik\ *noun* [*Dick,* nickname for *Richard*] (1553)
1 *chiefly British* : FELLOW, CHAP
2 : PENIS — usually considered vulgar
3 [by shortening & alteration] : DETECTIVE
dick·cis·sel \dik-'si-səl, 'dik-,\ *noun* [imitative] (1886)
: a common migratory black-throated finch (*Spiza americana*) of the central U.S.
dick·ens \'di-kənz\ *noun* [euphemism] (1598)
: DEVIL, DEUCE
¹dick·er \'di-kər\ *noun* [Middle English *dyker,* from Latin *decuria* quantity of ten, from *decem* ten — more at TEN] (14th century)
: the number or quantity of 10 especially of hides or skins

dickcissel

²dicker *intransitive verb* **dick·ered; dick·er·ing** \'di-k(ə-)riŋ\ [origin unknown] (circa 1802)
: BARGAIN ⟨*dickered* over the price⟩
³dicker *noun* (1823)
1 : BARTER
2 : an act or session of bargaining
dick·ey *or* **dicky** *also* **dick·ie** \'di-kē\ *noun, plural* **dickeys** *or* **dick·ies** [*Dicky,* nickname for *Richard*] (1753)
1 : any of various articles of clothing: as **a** : a man's separate or detachable shirtfront **b** : a small fabric insert worn to fill in the neckline
2 *chiefly British* **a** : the driver's seat in a carriage **b** : a seat at the back of a carriage or automobile
3 : a small bird
Dick test \'dik-\ *noun* [George French *Dick* and Gladys H. *Dick*] (1925)
: a test to determine susceptibility or immunity to scarlet fever by an injection of scarlet fever toxin
di·cli·nous \(,)dī-'klī-nəs\ *adjective* (1830)
: having the stamens and pistils in separate flowers
di·cot \'dī-,kät\ *noun* (1877)
: DICOTYLEDON
di·cot·y·le·don \,dī-,kä-tᵊl-'ē-dᵊn\ *noun* [New Latin] (circa 1727)
: any of a class or subclass (Magnoliopsida or Dicotyledoneae) of angiospermous plants that produce an embryo with two cotyledons and usually have floral organs arranged in cycles of four or five and leaves with reticulate venation — compare MONOCOTYLEDON
— **di·cot·y·le·don·ous** \-dᵊn-əs\ *adjective*
di·cou·ma·rin \(,)dī-'kü-mə-rən\ *noun* (1886)
: DICUMAROL
di·crot·ic \dī-'krä-tik\ *adjective* [Greek *dikrotos,* from *di-* + *krotos* rattling noise, beat] (circa 1811)
1 *of the pulse* : having a double beat
2 : being or relating to the second part of the arterial pulse occurring during diastole of the heart or of an arterial pressure recording made during the same period
— **di·cro·tism** \dī-krə-,ti-zəm\ *noun*
Dic·ta·phone \'dik-tə-,fōn\ *trademark*
— used for a dictating machine
¹dic·tate \'dik-,tāt, dik-'\ *verb* **dic·tat·ed; dic·tat·ing** [Latin *dictatus,* past participle of *dictare* to assert, dictate, frequentative of *dicere* to say — more at DICTION] (1592)
intransitive verb
1 : to give dictation
2 : to speak or act domineeringly : PRESCRIBE
transitive verb
1 : to speak or read for a person to transcribe or for a machine to record
2 a : to issue as an order **b** : to impose, pronounce, or specify authoritatively **c** : to require or determine necessarily ⟨injuries *dictated* the choice of players⟩
²dic·tate \'dik-,tāt\ *noun* (1594)
1 a : an authoritative rule, prescription, or injunction **b** : a ruling principle ⟨according to the *dictates* of your conscience⟩
2 : a command by one in authority
dictating machine *noun* (1907)
: a machine used especially for the recording of human speech for transcription
dic·ta·tion \dik-'tā-shən\ *noun* (circa 1656)
1 a : PRESCRIPTION **b** : arbitrary command
2 a (1) : the act or manner of uttering words to be transcribed (2) : material that is dictated or transcribed **b** (1) : the performing of music to be reproduced by a student (2) : music so reproduced
dic·ta·tor \'dik-,tā-tər, dik-'\ *noun* [Latin, from *dictare*] (14th century)
1 a : a person granted absolute emergency power; *especially* : one appointed by the senate of ancient Rome **b** : one holding complete autocratic control **c** : one ruling absolutely and often oppressively
2 : one that dictates

dic·ta·to·ri·al \,dik-tə-'tōr-ē-əl, -'tòr-\ *adjective* (1701)
1 a : of, relating to, or befitting a dictator ⟨*dictatorial* power⟩ **b** : ruled by a dictator
2 : oppressive to or arrogantly overbearing toward others ☆
— **dic·ta·to·ri·al·ly** \-ē-ə-lē\ *adverb*
— **dic·ta·to·ri·al·ness** *noun*
dic·ta·tor·ship \dik-'tā-tər-,ship, 'dik-,\ *noun* (1542)
1 : the office of dictator
2 : autocratic rule, control, or leadership
3 a : a form of government in which absolute power is concentrated in a dictator or a small clique **b** : a government organization or group in which absolute power is so concentrated **c** : a despotic state
dic·tion \'dik-shən\ *noun* [Latin *diction-, dictio* speaking, style, from *dicere* to say; akin to Old English *tēon* to accuse, Latin *dicare* to proclaim, dedicate, Greek *deiknynai* to show, *dikē* judgment, right] (1581)
1 *obsolete* : verbal description
2 : choice of words especially with regard to correctness, clearness, or effectiveness
3 a : vocal expression : ENUNCIATION **b** : pronunciation and enunciation of words in singing
— **dic·tion·al** \-shnəl, -shə-nᵊl\ *adjective*
— **dic·tion·al·ly** \-ē\ *adverb*
dic·tio·nary \'dik-shə-,ner-ē\ *noun, plural* **-nar·ies** [Medieval Latin *dictionarium,* from Late Latin *diction-, dictio* word, from Latin, speaking] (1526)
1 : a reference book containing words usually alphabetically arranged along with information about their forms, pronunciations, functions, etymologies, meanings, and syntactical and idiomatic uses
2 : a reference book listing alphabetically terms or names important to a particular subject or activity along with discussion of their meanings and applications
3 : a reference book giving for words of one language equivalents in another
4 : a list (as of items of data or words) stored in a computer for reference (as for information retrieval or word processing)
dic·tum \'dik-təm\ *noun, plural* **dic·ta** \-tə\ *also* **dictums** [Latin, from neuter of *dictus,* past participle of *dicere*] (1599)
1 : a noteworthy statement: as **a** : a formal pronouncement of a principle, proposition, or opinion **b** : an observation intended or regarded as authoritative
2 : a judicial opinion on a point other than the precise issue involved in determining a case
dicty- *or* **dictyo-** *combining form* [New Latin, from Greek *dikty-, diktyo-,* from *diktyon,* from *dikein* to throw]
: net ⟨*dicty*ostele⟩ ⟨*dictyo*some⟩

dic·tyo·some \'dik-tē-ə-ˌsōm\ *noun* (circa 1930)
: any of the membranous or vesicular structures making up the Golgi apparatus

dic·tyo·stele \'dik-tē-ə-ˌstēl, ˌdik-tē-ə-'stē-lē\ *noun* (circa 1902)
: a stele in which the vascular cylinder is broken up into a longitudinal series or network of vascular strands around a central pith (as in many ferns)

di·cu·ma·rol *also* **di·cou·ma·rol** \dī-'k(y)ü-mə-ˌról, -ˌról\ *noun* [*di-* + *coumar*in + *¹-ol*] (1943)
: a crystalline compound $C_{19}H_{12}O_6$ originally obtained from spoiled sweet clover hay and used to delay clotting of blood especially in preventing and treating thromboembolic disease

di·cyn·o·dont \(ˌ)dī-'si-nō-ˌdänt, -'sī-\ *noun* [ultimately from Greek *di-* + *kyn-, kyōn* dog + *odont-, odous* tooth — more at HOUND, TOOTH] (1854)
: any of a suborder (Dicynodontia) of small herbivorous therapsid reptiles with reduced dentition
— **dicynodont** *adjective*

did *past of* DO

di·dact \'dī-ˌdakt\ *noun* [back-formation from *didactic*] (1954)
: a didactic person

di·dac·tic \dī-'dak-tik, də-\ *adjective* [Greek *didaktikos,* from *didaskein* to teach] (1658)
1 a : designed or intended to teach **b :** intended to convey instruction and information as well as pleasure and entertainment
2 : making moral observations
— **di·dac·ti·cal** \-ti-kəl\ *adjective*
— **di·dac·ti·cal·ly** \-ti-k(ə-)lē\ *adverb*
— **di·dac·ti·cism** \-tə-ˌsi-zəm\ *noun*

di·dac·tics \-tiks\ *noun plural but singular or plural in construction* (1644)
: systematic instruction : PEDAGOGY

did·dle \'di-d°l\ *verb* **did·dled; did·dling** \'did-liŋ, -d°l-iŋ\ [origin unknown] (1786)
transitive verb
1 *chiefly dialect* : to move with short rapid motions
2 : to waste (as time) in trifling
3 : HOAX, SWINDLE
4 : to copulate with — often considered vulgar
intransitive verb
1 : DAWDLE, FOOL
2 : FIDDLE, TOY — usually used with *with* 〈*diddled* with the machine until it broke〉
— **did·dler** \'did-lər, -d°l-ər\ *noun*

did·dly \'di-d°l-ē, 'did-lē\ *noun* (1964)
: DIDDLY-SQUAT

did·dly–squat \-ˌskwät\ *noun* [probably alteration of *doodly-squat*] (1974)
slang : the least amount : anything at all 〈didn't know *diddly-squat* about sports —Sam Toperoff〉

did·ger·i·doo *also* **did·jer·i·doo** \'di-jə-rē-ˌdü, ˌdi-jə-rē-'\ *noun* [Yolngu (Australian aboriginal language group of Arnhem Land) *didjeridu*] (1919)
: a large bamboo or wooden trumpet of the Australian Aborigines

didn't \'di-d°nt, -d°n, *dialect also* 'dit-°n(t) *or* 'dint\ (1705)
: did not

di·do \'dī-(ˌ)dō\ *noun, plural* **didoes** *or* **didos** [origin unknown] (1807)
1 : a mischievous or capricious act : PRANK, ANTIC — often used in the phrase *cut didoes*
2 : something that is frivolous or showy

Di·do \'dī-(ˌ)dō\ *noun* [Latin, from Greek *Didō*]
: a legendary queen of Carthage in Virgil's *Aeneid* who kills herself when Aeneas leaves her

didst \'didst, 'ditst\ *archaic past 2d singular of* DO

di·dym·i·um \dī-'di-mē-əm\ *noun* [New Latin, from Greek *didymos* twin, from *dyo* two — more at TWO] (1842)
: a mixture of rare-earth elements made up chiefly of neodymium and praseodymium and used especially for coloring glass for optical filters

¹die \'dī\ *intransitive verb* **died; dy·ing** \'dī-iŋ\ [Middle English *dien,* from or akin to Old Norse *deyja;* akin to Old High German *touwen* to die] (12th century)
1 : to pass from physical life : EXPIRE
2 a : to pass out of existence : CEASE 〈their anger *died* at these words〉 **b :** to disappear or subside gradually — often used with *away, down,* or *out* 〈the storm *died* down〉
3 a : SINK, LANGUISH 〈*dying* from fatigue〉 **b :** to long keenly or desperately 〈*dying* to go〉 **c :** to be overwhelmed by emotion 〈*die* of embarrassment〉
4 a : to cease functioning : STOP 〈the motor *died*〉 **b :** to end in failure 〈the bill *died* in committee〉
5 : to become indifferent 〈*die* to worldly things〉
— **die hard 1 :** to be long in dying 〈such rumors *die* hard〉 **2 :** to continue resistance against hopeless odds 〈hard-shell conservatism *dies* hard〉
— **die on the vine :** to fail especially at an early stage through lack of support or enthusiasm 〈let the proposal *die on the vine*〉

²die \'dī\ *noun, plural* **dice** \'dīs\ *or* **dies** \'dīz\ [Middle English *dee,* from Middle French *dé*] (14th century)
1 *plural* **dice :** a small cube marked on each face with from one to six spots and used usually in pairs in various games and in gambling by being shaken and thrown to come to rest at random on a flat surface — often used figuratively in expressions concerning chance or the irrevocability of a course of action 〈the *die* was cast〉
2 *plural* **dies :** DADO 1a
3 *plural* **dies :** any of various tools or devices for imparting a desired shape, form, or finish to a material or for impressing an object or material: as **a** (1) : the larger of a pair of cutting or shaping tools that when moved toward each other produce a desired form in or impress a desired device on an object by pressure or by a blow (2) : a device composed of a pair of such tools **b :** a hollow internally threaded screw-cutting tool used for forming screw threads **c :** a mold into which molten metal or other material is forced **d :** a perforated block through which metal or plastic is drawn or extruded for shaping

die·back \'dī-ˌbak\ *noun* (circa 1886)
: a condition in woody plants in which peripheral parts are killed especially by parasites

di·ecious *variant of* DIOECIOUS

dief·fen·bach·ia \ˌdē-fən-'ba-kē-ə, ˌdi-, -'bä-\ *noun* [New Latin, from Ernst *Dieffenbach* (died 1855) German naturalist] (circa 1900)
: any of a genus (*Dieffenbachia*) of the family Araceae) of erect poisonous tropical American plants that have oblong usually variegated leaves and are often used as houseplants

die–hard \'dī-ˌhärd\ *adjective* (1922)
: strongly or fanatically determined or devoted 〈*die-hard* fans〉; *especially* : strongly resisting change 〈a *die-hard* conservative〉
— **die–hard** *noun*
— **die–hard·ism** \-ˌiz-əm\ *noun*

di·el \'dī-əl, -ˌel\ *adjective* [irregular from Latin *dies* day + English *-al*] (circa 1935)
: involving a 24-hour period that usually includes a day and the adjoining night 〈*diel* fluctuations in temperature〉

diel·drin \'dē(ə)l-drən\ *noun* [*Diels*-Alder reaction (an addition reaction forming a 6-membered ring), after Otto *Diels* & Kurt *Alder*] (circa 1949)
: a white crystalline persistent chlorinated hydrocarbon insecticide $C_{12}H_8Cl_6O$ that accumulates in and becomes toxic to vertebrates

di·elec·tric \ˌdī-ə-'lek-trik\ *noun* [*dia-* + *electric*] (1837)
: a nonconductor of direct electric current
— **dielectric** *adjective*

dielectric constant *noun* (1875)
: PERMITTIVITY

dielectric heating *noun* (1944)
: the rapid and uniform heating throughout a nonconducting material by means of a high-frequency electromagnetic field

di·en·ceph·a·lon \ˌdī-ən-'se-fə-ˌlän, ˌdī-(ˌ)en-, -lən\ *noun* [New Latin, from *dia-* + *encephalon*] (circa 1883)
: the posterior subdivision of the forebrain — called also *betweenbrain*
— **di·en·ce·phal·ic** \-sə-'fa-lik\ *adjective*

di·ene \'dī-ˌēn\ *noun* [*di-* + *-ene*] (1917)
: a compound containing two double bonds between carbon atoms

die–off \'dī-ˌóf\ *noun* (1936)
: a sudden sharp decline of a population (as of rabbits) that is not caused directly by human activity (as hunting)

die off \'dī-ˌóf\ *intransitive verb* (1697)
: to die sequentially either singly or in numbers so that the total number is greatly diminished

die out *intransitive verb* (1853)
: to become extinct

di·er·e·sis *variant of* DIAERESIS

die·sel \'dē-zəl, -səl\ *noun* [Rudolf *Diesel*] (1894)
1 : DIESEL ENGINE
2 : a vehicle driven by a diesel engine

diesel–electric *adjective* (1914)
: of, relating to, or employing the combination of a diesel engine driving an electric generator 〈a *diesel-electric* locomotive〉

diesel engine *noun* (1894)
: an internal combustion engine in which air is compressed to a temperature sufficiently high to ignite fuel injected into the cylinder where the combustion and expansion actuate a piston

die·sel·ing \'dē-zə-liŋ, -sə-\ *noun* (circa 1955)
: the continued operation of an internal combustion engine after the ignition is turned off

die·sel·ize \'dē-zə-ˌlīz, -sə-\ *transitive verb* **-ized; -iz·ing** (1925)
: to equip with a diesel engine or with electric locomotives having generators powered by diesel engines
— **die·sel·iza·tion** \ˌdē-zə-lə-'zā-shən, -sə-\ *noun*

Di·es Irae \ˌdē-(ˌ)ās-'ē-ˌrā\ *noun* [Medieval Latin, day of wrath; from the first words of the hymn] (1860)
: a medieval Latin hymn on the Day of Judgment sung in requiem masses

di·esis \'dī-ə-səs\ *noun, plural* **di·eses** \-ˌsēz\ [probably from Italian, sharp (in music), symbol for a sharp, from Medieval Latin, quarter tone, from Latin, from Greek, from *diienai* to send through, from *dia-* + *hienai* to send — more at JET] (circa 1706)
: DOUBLE DAGGER

di·es·ter \'dī-ˌes-tər\ *noun* (1935)
: a compound containing two ester groups

die·stock \'dī-ˌstäk\ *noun* (circa 1859)
: a stock to hold dies used for cutting threads

di·es·trus \(ˌ)dī-'es-trəs\ *noun* [New Latin, from *dia-* + *estrus*] (1942)
: a period of sexual quiescence that intervenes between two periods of estrus
— **di·es·trous** \-trəs\ *adjective*

¹di·et \'dī-ət\ *noun* [Middle English *diete,* from Old French, from Latin *diaeta,* from Greek *diaita,* literally, manner of living, from *diaitasthai* to lead one's life] (13th century)
1 a : food and drink regularly provided or consumed **b :** habitual nourishment **c :** the kind and amount of food prescribed for a person or animal for a special reason

2 : something provided especially habitually ⟨a *diet* of Broadway shows and nightclubs —Frederick Wyatt⟩

²diet (14th century)
transitive verb
1 : to cause to take food **:** FEED
2 : to cause to eat and drink sparingly or according to prescribed rules
intransitive verb
: to eat sparingly or according to prescribed rules
— **di·et·er** *noun*

³diet *adjective* (1969)
: reduced in calories ⟨a *diet* soft drink⟩

⁴diet *noun* [Middle English *diete* day's journey, day set for a meeting, from Medieval Latin *dieta*, literally, daily regimen, diet (taken as a derivative of Latin *dies* day), from Latin *diaeta*] (1565)
1 : a formal deliberative assembly of princes or estates
2 : any of various national or provincial legislatures

¹di·e·tary \'dī-ə-ˌter-ē\ *noun, plural* **di·e·tar·ies** (1838)
: the kinds and amounts of food available to or eaten by an individual, group, or population

²dietary *adjective* (1614)
: of or relating to a diet or to the rules of a diet
— **di·e·tar·i·ly** \ˌdī-ə-ˈter-ə-lē\ *adverb*

dietary law *noun* (circa 1930)
: any of the laws observed by Orthodox Jews that permit or prohibit certain foods

di·e·tet·ic \ˌdī-ə-ˈte-tik\ *adjective* (1579)
1 : of or relating to diet
2 : adapted for use in special diets
— **di·e·tet·i·cal·ly** \-ti-k(ə-)lē\ *adverb*

di·e·tet·ics \-ˈte-tiks\ *noun plural but singular or plural in construction* (1799)
: the science or art of applying the principles of nutrition to the diet

di·ether \(ˌ)dī-ˈē-thər\ *noun* (1950)
: a compound containing two atoms of oxygen with ether linkages

di·eth·yl·car·bam·a·zine \ˌdī-ˌe-thəl-kär-ˈba-mə-ˌzēn, -zən\ *noun* [*di-* + *ethyl* + *carboxy-* + *amide* + *azine*] (1948)
: an anthelmintic administered in the form of its crystalline citrate $C_{10}H_{21}N_3O \cdot C_6H_8O_7$ especially to control human filariasis and large roundworms in dogs and cats

di·eth·yl ether \(ˌ)dī-ˌe-thəl-\ *noun* (circa 1930)
: ETHER 3a

di·eth·yl·stil·bes·trol \-stil-ˈbes-ˌtrȯl, -ˌtrōl\ *noun* [International Scientific Vocabulary] (1938)
: a colorless crystalline synthetic compound $C_{18}H_{20}O_2$ used as a potent estrogen but contraindicated in pregnancy for its tendency to cause cancer or birth defects in offspring — called also *stilbestrol*

di·eth·yl zinc *noun* (1952)
: a volatile pyrophoric liquid organometallic compound $C_4H_{10}Zn$ used especially to catalyze polymerization reactions and to deacidify paper

di·e·ti·tian *or* **di·e·ti·cian** \ˌdī-ə-ˈti-shən\ *noun* [*dietitian* irregular from ¹*diet* + *-ician*] (circa 1846)
: a specialist in dietetics

dif·fer \'di-fər\ *intransitive verb* **dif·fered; dif·fer·ing** \-f(ə-)riŋ\ [Middle English, from Middle French or Latin; Middle French *differer* to postpone, be different, from Latin *differre*, from *dis-* + *ferre* to carry — more at BEAR] (14th century)
1 a : to be unlike or distinct in nature, form, or characteristics ⟨the law of one state *differs* from that of another⟩ **b :** to change from time to time or from one instance to another **:** VARY ⟨the number of cookies in a box may *differ*⟩
2 : to be of unlike or opposite opinion **:** DISAGREE ⟨they *differ* on religious matters⟩

¹dif·fer·ence \'di-fərn(t)s, 'di-f(ə-)rən(t)s\ *noun* (14th century)

1 a : the quality or state of being different **b :** an instance of differing in nature, form, or quality **c** *archaic* **:** a characteristic that distinguishes one from another or from the average **d :** the element or factor that separates or distinguishes contrasting situations
2 : distinction or discrimination in preference
3 a : disagreement in opinion **:** DISSENSION **b :** an instance or cause of disagreement
4 : the degree or amount by which things differ in quantity or measure; *specifically* **:** REMAINDER 2b(1)
5 : a significant change in or effect on a situation

²difference *transitive verb* **-enced; -enc·ing** (1576)
: DIFFERENTIATE, DISTINGUISH

¹dif·fer·ent \'di-fərnt, 'di-f(ə-)rənt\ *adjective* [Middle French, from Latin *different-, differens*, present participle of *differre*] (14th century)
1 : partly or totally unlike in nature, form, or quality **:** DISSIMILAR ⟨could hardly be more *different*⟩ — often followed by *from, than,* or chiefly British *to* ⟨small, neat hand, very *different* from the captain's tottery characters —R. L. Stevenson⟩ ⟨vastly *different* in size than it was twenty-five years ago —N. M. Pusey⟩ ⟨a very *different* situation to the . . . one under which we live —Sir Winston Churchill⟩
2 : not the same: as **a :** DISTINCT ⟨*different* age groups⟩ **b :** VARIOUS ⟨*different* members of the class⟩ **c :** ANOTHER ⟨switched to a *different* TV program⟩
3 : UNUSUAL, SPECIAL ⟨she was *different* and superior⟩ ☆ □
— **dif·fer·ent·ness** *noun*

²different *adverb* (1744)
: DIFFERENTLY

dif·fer·en·tia \ˌdi-fə-ˈren(t)-sh(ē-)ə\ *noun, plural* **-ti·ae** \-shē-ˌē, -shē-ˌī\ [Latin, difference, from *different-, differens*] (1690)
: an element, feature, or factor that distinguishes one entity, state, or class from another; *especially* **:** a characteristic trait distinguishing a species from other species of the same genus

¹dif·fer·en·tial \ˌdi-fə-ˈren(t)-shəl\ *adjective* (1647)
1 a : of, relating to, or constituting a difference **:** DISTINGUISHING **b :** making a distinction between individuals or classes **c :** based on or resulting from a differential **d :** functioning or proceeding differently or at a different rate
2 : being, relating to, or involving a differential or differentiation
3 a : relating to quantitative differences **b :** producing effects by reason of quantitative differences
— **dif·fer·en·tial·ly** \-ˈren(t)-shə-lē\ *adverb*

²differential *noun* (1704)
1 a : the product of the derivative of a function of one variable by the increment of the independent variable **b :** a sum of products in which each product consists of a partial derivative of a given function of several variables multiplied by the corresponding increment and which contains as many products as there are independent variables in the function
2 : a difference between comparable individuals or classes ⟨a price *differential*⟩; *also* **:** the amount of such a difference
3 a : DIFFERENTIAL GEAR **b :** a case covering a differential gear

differential calculus *noun* (1702)
: a branch of mathematics concerned chiefly with the study of the rate of change of functions with respect to their variables especially through the use of derivatives and differentials

differential equation *noun* (1763)
: an equation containing differentials or derivatives of functions — compare PARTIAL DIFFERENTIAL EQUATION

differential gear *noun* (circa 1859)
: an arrangement of gears forming an epicyclic train for connecting two shafts or axles in the same line, dividing the driving force equally

between them, and permitting one shaft to revolve faster than the other — called also *differential gearing*

differential geometry *noun* (circa 1909)
: a branch of mathematics using calculus to study the geometric properties of curves and surfaces

dif·fer·en·ti·ate \ˌdif-ə-ˈren(t)-shē-ˌāt\ *verb* **-at·ed; -at·ing** (1816)
transitive verb
1 : to obtain the mathematical derivative of
2 : to mark or show a difference in **:** constitute a difference that distinguishes
3 : to develop differential characteristics in
4 : to cause differentiation of in the course of development
5 : to express the specific distinguishing quality of **:** DISCRIMINATE
intransitive verb
1 : to recognize or give expression to a difference
2 : to become distinct or different in character
3 : to undergo differentiation
— **dif·fer·en·tia·bil·i·ty** \-ˌren(t)-sh(ē-)ə-ˈbi-lə-tē\ *noun*
— **dif·fer·en·tia·ble** \-ˈren(t)-sh(ē-)ə-bəl\ *adjective*

dif·fer·en·ti·a·tion \-ˌren(t)-shē-ˈā-shən\ *noun* (1802)
1 : the act or process of differentiating
2 : development from the one to the many, the simple to the complex, or the homogeneous to the heterogeneous
3 a : modification of body parts for performance of particular functions **b :** the sum of the processes whereby apparently indifferent cells, tissues, and structures attain their adult form and function
4 : the processes by which various rock types are produced from a common magma

dif·fer·ent·ly \'di-fərnt-lē, 'di-f(ə-)rənt-\ *adverb* (14th century)
1 : in a different manner
2 : OTHERWISE

dif·fi·cile \ˌdē-fi-ˈsē(ə)l\ *adjective* [French, literally, difficult] (1536)
: STUBBORN, UNREASONABLE

dif·fi·cult \'di-fi-(ˌ)kəlt\ *adjective* [Middle English, back-formation from *difficulty*] (14th century)
1 : hard to do, make, or carry out **:** ARDUOUS ⟨a *difficult* climb⟩

2 a : hard to deal with, manage, or overcome ⟨a *difficult* child⟩ **b :** hard to understand : PUZZLING ⟨*difficult* reading⟩
synonym see HARD
— **dif·fi·cult·ly** *adverb*
dif·fi·cul·ty \-(ˌ)kəl-tē\ *noun, plural* **-ties** [Middle English *difficulte*, from Latin *difficultas*, from *difficilis* not easy, from *dis-* + *facilis* easy — more at FACILE] (14th century)
1 : the quality or state of being difficult
2 : CONTROVERSY, DISAGREEMENT
3 : OBJECTION
4 : something difficult : IMPEDIMENT
5 : EMBARRASSMENT, TROUBLE — usually used in plural
dif·fi·dence \'di-fə-dən(t)s, -fə-ˌden(t)s\ *noun* (14th century)
: the quality or state of being diffident
dif·fi·dent \-dənt, -ˌdent\ *adjective* [Middle English, from Latin *diffident-, diffidens,* present participle of *diffidere* to distrust, from *dis-* + *fidere* to trust — more at BIDE] (15th century)
1 : hesitant in acting or speaking through lack of self-confidence
2 *archaic* **:** DISTRUSTFUL
3 : RESERVED, UNASSERTIVE
synonym see SHY
— **dif·fi·dent·ly** *adverb*
dif·fract \di-'frakt\ *transitive verb* [back-formation from *diffraction*] (1803)
: to cause to undergo diffraction
dif·frac·tion \di-'frak-shən\ *noun* [New Latin *diffraction-, diffractio,* from Latin *diffringere* to break apart, from *dis-* + *frangere* to break — more at BREAK] (1671)
: a modification which light undergoes in passing by the edges of opaque bodies or through narrow slits or in being reflected from ruled surfaces and in which the rays appear to be deflected and to produce fringes of parallel light and dark or colored bands; *also* **:** a similar modification of other waves (as sound waves)
diffraction grating *noun* (1867)
: GRATING 3
dif·frac·tom·e·ter \di-ˌfrak-'tä-mə-tər\ *noun* (circa 1909)
: an instrument for analyzing the structure of a usually crystalline substance from the scattering pattern produced when a beam of radiation or particles (as X rays or neutrons) strikes it
— **dif·frac·to·met·ric** \di-ˌfrak-tə-'me-trik\ *adjective*
— **dif·frac·tom·e·try** \di-ˌfrak-'tä-mə-trē\ *noun*
¹dif·fuse \di-'fyüs\ *adjective* [Middle English, from Latin *diffusus,* past participle of *diffundere* to spread out, from *dis-* + *fundere* to pour — more at FOUND] (15th century)
1 : being at once verbose and ill-organized
2 : not concentrated or localized ⟨*diffuse* sclerosis⟩
synonym see WORDY
— **dif·fuse·ly** *adverb*
— **dif·fuse·ness** *noun*
²dif·fuse \di-'fyüz\ *verb* **dif·fused; dif·fus·ing** [Middle English *diffused,* past participle, from Latin *diffusus,* past participle] (14th century)
transitive verb
1 a : to pour out and permit or cause to spread freely **b :** EXTEND, SCATTER **c :** to spread thinly or wastefully
2 : to subject to diffusion; *especially* **:** to break up and distribute (incident light) by reflection
intransitive verb
1 : to spread out or become transmitted especially by contact
2 : to undergo diffusion
— **dif·fus·ible** \di-'fyü-zə-bəl\ *adjective*
dif·fuse–po·rous \di-ˌfyüs-'pōr-əs, -'pȯr-\ *adjective* [¹*diffuse*] (circa 1902)
: having vessels more or less evenly distributed throughout an annual ring and not varying greatly in size — compare RING-POROUS

dif·fus·er \di-'fyü-zər\ *noun* (circa 1679)
1 : one that diffuses: as **a :** a device (as a reflector) for distributing the light of a lamp evenly **b :** a screen (as of cloth or frosted glass) for softening lighting (as in photography) **c :** a device (as slats at different angles) for deflecting air from an outlet in various directions
2 : a device for reducing the velocity and increasing the static pressure of a fluid passing through a system
dif·fu·sion \di-'fyü-zhən\ *noun* (14th century)
1 : the action of diffusing : the state of being diffused
2 : PROLIXITY, DIFFUSENESS
3 a : the process whereby particles of liquids, gases, or solids intermingle as the result of their spontaneous movement caused by thermal agitation and in dissolved substances move from a region of higher to one of lower concentration **b** (1) **:** reflection of light by a rough reflecting surface (2) **:** transmission of light through a translucent material : SCATTERING
4 : the spread of cultural elements from one area or group of people to others by contact
5 : the softening of sharp outlines in a photographic image
— **dif·fu·sion·al** \-'fyü-zhə-nᵊl\ *adjective*
dif·fu·sion·ist \-'fyü-zhə-nəst\ *noun* (1938)
: an anthropologist who emphasizes the role of diffusion in the history of culture rather than independent invention or discovery
— **dif·fu·sion·ism** \-'fyü-zhə-ˌni-zəm\ *noun*
— **diffusionist** *adjective*
dif·fu·sive \di-'fyü-siv, -ziv\ *adjective* (1614)
: tending to diffuse : characterized by diffusion ⟨*diffusive* motion of atoms⟩
— **dif·fu·sive·ly** *adverb*
— **dif·fu·sive·ness** *noun*
— **dif·fu·siv·i·ty** \di-ˌfyü-'si-və-tē, -'zi-\ *noun*
di·func·tion·al \(ˌ)dī-'fəŋ(k)-shnəl, -shə-nᵊl\ *adjective* (1943)
: of, relating to, or being a compound with two highly reactive sites in each molecule
¹dig \'dig\ *verb* **dug** \'dəg\; **dig·ging** [Middle English *diggen*] (13th century)
transitive verb
1 a : to break up, turn, or loosen (earth) with an implement **b :** to prepare the soil of ⟨*dig* a garden⟩
2 a : to bring to the surface by digging : UNEARTH **b :** to bring to light or out of hiding ⟨*dig* up facts⟩
3 : to hollow out or form by removing earth : EXCAVATE
4 : to drive down so as to penetrate : THRUST
5 : POKE, PROD
6 a : to pay attention to : NOTICE ⟨*dig* that fancy hat⟩ **b :** UNDERSTAND, APPRECIATE ⟨if you . . . do something subtle . . . only one tenth of the audience will *dig* it —Nat Hentoff⟩ **c :** LIKE, ADMIRE ⟨high school students *dig* short poetry —David Burmester⟩
intransitive verb
1 : to turn up, loosen, or remove earth : DELVE
2 : to work hard or laboriously
3 : to advance by or as if by removing or pushing aside material
²dig *noun* (1819)
1 a : THRUST, POKE **b :** a cutting remark
2 *plural* **a :** living accommodations **b** *chiefly British* **:** LODGING, HOTEL
3 : an archaeological excavation site; *also* **:** the excavation itself
dig·a·my \'di-gə-mē\ *noun, plural* **-mies** [Late Latin *digamia,* from Late Greek, from Greek *digamos* married to two people, from *di-* + *-gamos* -gamous] (1635)
: a second marriage after the termination of the first
di·gas·tric \(ˌ)dī-'gas-trik\ *adjective* [New Latin *digastricus,* from *di-* + *gastricus* gastric] (circa 1721)

: of, relating to, or being a muscle with two bellies separated by a median tendon
di·ge·net·ic \ˌdī-jə-'ne-tik\ *adjective* [New Latin *Digenetica,* subclass name (synonym of *Digenea*), from *di-* + *genetica,* neuter plural of *geneticus* genetic] (circa 1883)
: of or relating to a subclass (Digenea) of trematode worms in which sexual reproduction as an internal parasite of a vertebrate alternates with asexual reproduction in a mollusk
¹di·gest \'dī-ˌjest\ *noun* [Middle English, systematic arrangement of laws, from Latin *digesta,* from neuter plural of *digestus,* past participle of *digerere* to arrange, distribute, digest, from *dis-* + *gerere* to carry] (14th century)
1 : a summation or condensation of a body of information: as **a :** a systematic compilation of legal rules, statutes, or decisions **b :** a periodical devoted to condensed versions of previously published articles
2 : a product of digestion
²di·gest \dī-'jest, də-\ *verb* [Middle English, from Latin *digestus*] (14th century)
transitive verb
1 : to distribute or arrange systematically : CLASSIFY
2 : to convert (food) into absorbable form
3 : to take into the mind or memory; *especially* **:** to assimilate mentally
4 a : to soften, decompose, or break down by heat and moisture or chemicals **b :** to extract soluble ingredients from by warming with a liquid
5 : to compress into a short summary
6 : ABSORB 1 ⟨the capacity of the U.S. to *digest* immigrants⟩
intransitive verb
1 : to digest food
2 : to become digested
di·gest·er \-'jes-tər\ *noun* (1614)
1 : one that digests or makes a digest
2 : a vessel for digesting especially plant or animal materials
di·gest·ibil·i·ty \-ˌjes-tə-'bi-lə-tē\ *noun, plural* **-ties** (1740)
1 : the fitness of something for digestion
2 : the percentage of a foodstuff taken into the digestive tract that is absorbed into the body
di·gest·ible \-'jes-tə-bəl\ *adjective* (14th century)
: capable of being digested
di·ges·tion \dī-'jes-chən, də-, -'jesh-\ *noun* (14th century)
: the action, process, or power of digesting: as **a :** the process of making food absorbable by dissolving it and breaking it down into simpler chemical compounds that occurs in the living body chiefly through the action of enzymes secreted into the alimentary canal **b :** the process in sewage treatment by which organic matter in sludge is decomposed by anaerobic bacteria with the release of a burnable mixture of gases
¹di·ges·tive \-'jes-tiv\ *noun* (14th century)
: an aid to digestion especially of food
²digestive *adjective* (15th century)
1 : relating to or functioning in digestion ⟨the *digestive* system⟩
2 : having the power to cause or promote digestion ⟨*digestive* enzymes⟩
— **di·ges·tive·ly** *adverb*
digestive gland *noun* (1940)
: a gland secreting digestive enzymes
dig·ger \'di-gər\ *noun* (15th century)
1 a : one that digs **b :** a tool or machine for digging

\ə\ abut \ᵊ\ kitten \ər\ further \a\ ash \ā\ ace \ä\ mop, mar \au̇\ out \ch\ chin \e\ bet \ē\ easy \g\ go \i\ hit \ī\ ice \j\ job \ŋ\ sing \ō\ go \ȯ\ law \ȯi\ boy \th\ thin \th\ the \ü\ loot \u̇\ foot \y\ yet \zh\ vision *see also* Guide to Pronunciation

2 *capitalized* **:** a North American Indian (as a Paiute) who dug roots for food — usually used disparagingly especially formerly
3 *often capitalized, chiefly Australian & New Zealand* **:** an Australian or New Zealand soldier

dig·ger wasp *noun* (1880)
: a burrowing wasp; *especially* **:** a usually solitary wasp (superfamily Sphecoidea) that digs nest burrows in the soil and provisions them with insects or spiders paralyzed by stinging

dig·gings *noun plural* (1538)
1 : a place of excavating especially for ore, metals, or precious stones
2 : material dug out
3 a : QUARTERS, PREMISES **b** *chiefly British* **:** lodgings for a student

dight \'dīt\ *transitive verb* **dight·ed** *or* **dight; dight·ing** [Middle English, from Old English *dihtan* to arrange, compose, from Latin *dictare* to dictate, compose] (13th century) *archaic* **:** DRESS, ADORN

dig in (1839)
transitive verb
1 : to cover or incorporate by burying ⟨*dig in* compost⟩
2 : to establish in a dug defensive position ⟨the platoon was well *dug in*⟩
intransitive verb
1 : to establish a defensive position especially by digging trenches
2 a : to go resolutely to work **b :** to begin eating
3 : to hold stubbornly to a position
4 : to scuff the ground for better footing while batting (as in baseball)
— dig in one's heels : to take or persist in an uncompromising position or attitude despite opposition

dig·it \'di-jət\ *noun* [Middle English, from Latin *digitus* finger, toe; perhaps akin to Greek *deiknynai* to show — more at DICTION] (14th century)
1 a : any of the Arabic numerals 1 to 9 and usually the symbol 0 **b :** one of the elements that combine to form numbers in a system other than the decimal system
2 : a unit of length based on the breadth of a finger and equal in English measure to ¾ inch
3 : any of the divisions in which the limbs of amphibians and all higher vertebrates terminate, which are typically five in number but may be reduced (as in the horse), and which typically have a series of phalanges bearing a nail, claw, or hoof at the tip — compare FINGER 1, TOE 1a

dig·i·tal \'di-jə-t⁼l\ *adjective* [Latin *digitalis*] (circa 1656)
1 : of or relating to the fingers or toes **:** DIGITATE
2 : done with a finger
3 : of, relating to, or using calculation by numerical methods or by discrete units
4 : of or relating to data in the form of numerical digits
5 : providing a readout in numerical digits ⟨a *digital* voltmeter⟩
6 : relating to an audio recording method in which sound waves are represented digitally (as on magnetic tape) so that in the recording wow and flutter are eliminated and background noise is reduced
— dig·i·tal·ly \-t⁼l-ē\ *adverb*

digital computer *noun* (1947)
: a computer that operates with numbers expressed directly as digits — compare ANALOG COMPUTER, HYBRID COMPUTER

dig·i·tal·in \ˌdi-jə-'ta-lən *also* -'tā-\ *noun* [New Latin *Digitalis*] (1837)
1 : a white crystalline steroid glycoside $C_{36}H_{56}O_{14}$ obtained from seeds especially of the common foxglove
2 : a mixture of the glycosides of digitalis leaves or seeds

dig·i·tal·is \-'ta-ləs *also* -'tā-\ *noun* [New Latin, genus name, from Latin, of a finger, from *digitus*; from its finger-shaped corolla] (1664)
1 : FOXGLOVE
2 : the dried powdered leaf of the common foxglove containing important glycosides and serving as a powerful cardiac stimulant and a diuretic

dig·i·ta·li·za·tion \ˌdi-jə-t⁼l-ə-'zā-shən\ *noun* [*digitalis*] (1882)
: the administration of digitalis until the desired physiological adjustment is attained; *also* **:** the bodily state so produced

¹dig·i·ta·lize \'di-jə-t⁼l-ˌīz\ *transitive verb* **-lized; -liz·ing** [*digitalis*] (1927)
: to subject to digitalization

²dig·i·tal·ize \'di-jə-t⁼l-ˌīz\ *transitive verb* **-ized; -iz·ing** [*digital*] (1962)
: DIGITIZE

dig·i·tate \'di-jə-ˌtāt\ *adjective* (1661)
: having divisions arranged like those of a bird's foot ⟨*digitate* leaves⟩
— dig·i·tate·ly *adverb*

digiti- *combining form* [French, from Latin *digitus*]
: digit **:** finger ⟨*digiti*grade⟩

dig·i·ti·grade \'di-jə-tə-ˌgrād\ *adjective* [French, from *digiti-* + *-grade*] (circa 1833)
: walking on the digits with the posterior of the foot more or less raised

dig·i·tize \'di-jə-ˌtīz\ *transitive verb* **-tized; -tiz·ing** (1953)
: to convert (as data or an image) to digital form
— dig·i·ti·za·tion \ˌdi-jə-tə-'zā-shən\ *noun*
— dig·i·tiz·er \'di-jə-ˌtī-zər\ *noun*

dig·i·to·nin \ˌdi-jə-'tō-nən\ *noun* [International Scientific Vocabulary *digit-* (from New Latin *Digitalis*) + *saponin*] (1875)
: a steroid saponin $C_{56}H_{92}O_{29}$ occurring in the leaves and seeds of foxglove

digi·toxi·gen·in \ˌdi-jə-ˌtäk-sə-'je-nən\ *noun* [International Scientific Vocabulary, blend of *digitoxin* and *-gen*] (circa 1909)
: a steroid lactone $C_{23}H_{34}O_4$ obtained especially by hydrolysis of digitoxin

dig·i·tox·in \ˌdi-jə-'täk-sən\ *noun* [International Scientific Vocabulary, blend of New Latin *Digitalis* and International Scientific Vocabulary *toxin*] (circa 1883)
: a poisonous glycoside $C_{41}H_{64}O_{13}$ that is the most active constituent of digitalis; *also* **:** a mixture of digitalis glycosides consisting chiefly of digitoxin

di·glyc·er·ide \ˌdī-'gli-sə-ˌrīd\ *noun* (1918)
: an ester formed from glycerol by reacting two of its alcohol hydroxy groups with fatty acids

dig·ni·fied \'dig-nə-ˌfīd\ *adjective* (1763)
: showing or expressing dignity

dig·ni·fy \'dig-nə-ˌfī\ *transitive verb* **-fied; -fy·ing** [Middle French *dignifier*, from Late Latin *dignificare*, from Latin *dignus* worthy — more at DECENT] (15th century)
1 : to give distinction to **:** ENNOBLE
2 : to confer dignity upon; *also* **:** to give undue attention or status to ⟨won't *dignify* that remark with a reply⟩

dig·ni·tary \'dig-nə-ˌter-ē\ *noun, plural* **-tar·ies** (1673)
: one who possesses exalted rank or holds a position of dignity or honor
— dignitary *adjective*

dig·ni·ty \'dig-nə-tē\ *noun, plural* **-ties** [Middle English *dignete*, from Old French *digneté*, from Latin *dignitat-, dignitas*, from *dignus*] (13th century)
1 : the quality or state of being worthy, honored, or esteemed
2 a : high rank, office, or position **b :** a legal title of nobility or honor
3 *archaic* **:** DIGNITARY
4 : formal reserve or seriousness of manner, appearance, or language

dig out (14th century)
transitive verb

1 : FIND, UNEARTH
2 : to make hollow by digging
intransitive verb
: TAKE OFF 2a

di·gox·in \di-'jäk-sən, -'gäk-\ *noun* [International Scientific Vocabulary *dig-* (from New Latin *Digitalis*) + *toxin*] (circa 1930)
: a poisonous cardiotonic steroid $C_{41}H_{64}O_{14}$ obtained from a foxglove (*Digitalis lanata*) and used similarly to digitalis

di·graph \'dī-ˌgraf\ *noun* (1780)
1 : a group of two successive letters whose phonetic value is a single sound (as *ea* in *bread* or *ng* in *sing*) or whose value is not the sum of a value borne by each in other occurrences (as *ch* in *chin* where the value is \t\ + \sh\)
2 : a group of two successive letters
3 : LIGATURE 4
— di·graph·ic \dī-'gra-fik\ *adjective*
— di·graph·i·cal·ly \-fi-k(ə-)lē\ *adverb*

di·gress \dī-'gres, də-\ *intransitive verb* [Latin *digressus*, past participle of *digredi*, from *dis-* + *gradi* to step — more at GRADE] (1530)
: to turn aside especially from the main subject of attention or course of argument
synonym see SWERVE

di·gres·sion \-'gre-shən\ *noun* (14th century)
1 : the act or an instance of digressing in a discourse or other usually organized literary work
2 *archaic* **:** a going aside
— di·gres·sion·al \-'gresh-nəl, -ən-⁼l\ *adjective*
— di·gres·sion·ary \-'gre-shə-ˌner-ē\ *adjective*

di·gres·sive \-'gre-siv\ *adjective* (circa 1611)
: characterized by digressions ⟨a *digressive* talk⟩
— di·gres·sive·ly *adverb*
— di·gres·sive·ness *noun*

dig up *transitive verb* (14th century)
: FIND, UNEARTH

di·he·dral \(ˌ)dī-'hē-drəl\ *noun* (circa 1911)
1 : DIHEDRAL ANGLE
2 : the angle between an aircraft supporting surface (as a wing) and a horizontal transverse line

dihedral angle *noun* [*di-* + *-hedral*] (1826)
: a figure formed by two intersecting planes

di·hy·brid \(ˌ)dī-'hī-brəd\ *adjective* [International Scientific Vocabulary] (1907)
: of, relating to, involving, or being an individual or strain that is heterozygous at two genetic loci
— dihybrid *noun*

dihydr- *or* **dihydro-** *combining form*
: combined with two atoms of hydrogen ⟨*dihy-dro*ergotamine⟩

di·hy·dro·er·got·a·mine \(ˌ)dī-ˌhī-drō-ˌər-'gä-tə-ˌmēn\ *noun* (1945)
: a hydrogenated derivative $C_{33}H_{37}N_5O_5$ of ergotamine that is used in the treatment of migraine

dihydroxy- *combining form*
: containing two hydroxyl groups ⟨*dihydroxy*acetone⟩

di·hy·droxy·ac·e·tone \ˌdī-hī-ˌdräk-sē-'a-sə-ˌtōn\ *noun* (1895)
: a glyceraldehyde isomer $C_3H_6O_3$ used especially to stain the skin to resemble a tan

dik–dik \'dik-ˌdik\ *noun, plural* **dik–diks** *or* **dik–dik** [origin unknown] (1883)
: any of a genus (*Madoqua*) of small eastern African antelopes

¹dike \'dīk\ *noun* [Middle English, probably from Old Norse *dīk* ditch and Middle Low German *dīk* dam; akin to Old

dik-dik

English *dīc* ditch — more at DITCH] (13th century)
1 : an artificial watercourse **:** DITCH
2 a : a bank usually of earth constructed to control or confine water **:** LEVEE **b :** a barrier preventing passage especially of something undesirable
3 a : a raised causeway **b :** a tabular body of igneous rock that has been injected while molten into a fissure
²**dike** *transitive verb* **diked; dik·ing** (14th century)
1 : to surround or protect with a dike
2 : to drain by a dike
— **dik·er** *noun*
³**dike** *variant of* ²DYKE
dik·tat \dik-'tät\ *noun* [German, literally, something dictated, from New Latin *dictatum*, from Latin, neuter of *dictatus*, past participle of *dictare* to dictate] (1933)
1 : a harsh settlement unilaterally imposed (as on a defeated nation)
2 : DECREE, ORDER
Di·lan·tin \dī-'lan-tⁿn, də-\ *trademark*
— used for phenytoin
di·lap·i·date \də-'la-pə-ˌdāt\ *verb* **-dat·ed; -dat·ing** [Latin *dilapidatus*, past participle of *dilapidare* to squander, destroy, from *dis-* + *lapidare* to pelt with stones, from *lapid-, lapis* stone] (circa 1570)
transitive verb
1 : to bring into a condition of decay or partial ruin ⟨furniture is *dilapidated* by use —Janet Flanner⟩
2 *archaic* **:** SQUANDER
intransitive verb
: to become dilapidated
— **di·lap·i·da·tion** \-ˌla-pə-'dā-shən\ *noun*
di·lap·i·dat·ed *adjective* (circa 1806)
: decayed, deteriorated, or fallen into partial ruin especially through neglect or misuse ⟨a *dilapidated* old house⟩
di·lat·an·cy \dī-'lā-tⁿn(t)-sē\ *noun* (1885)
: the property of being dilatant
di·lat·ant \-tⁿnt\ *adjective* (1885)
: increasing in viscosity and setting to a solid as a result of deformation by expansion, pressure, or agitation
di·la·ta·tion \ˌdi-lə-'tā-shən, ˌdī-\ *noun* (14th century)
1 : amplification in writing or speech
2 a : the condition of being stretched beyond normal dimensions especially as a result of overwork, disease, or abnormal relaxation ⟨*dilatation* of the heart⟩ ⟨*dilatation* of the stomach⟩ **b :** DILATION 2
3 : the action of expanding **:** the state of being expanded
4 : a dilated part or formation
— **di·la·ta·tion·al** \-shnəl, -shə-nⁿl\ *adjective*
di·late \'dī-ˌlāt, dī-'\ *verb* **di·lat·ed; di·lat·ing** [Middle English, from Middle French *dilater*, from Latin *dilatare*, literally, to spread wide, from *dis-* + *latus* wide — more at LATITUDE] (14th century)
transitive verb
1 *archaic* **:** to describe or set forth at length or in detail
2 : to enlarge or expand in bulk or extent **:** DISTEND, WIDEN
intransitive verb
1 : to comment at length **:** DISCOURSE — usually used with *on* or *upon*
2 : to become wide **:** SWELL
synonym see EXPAND
— **di·lat·abil·i·ty** \(ˌ)dī-ˌlā-tə-'bi-lə-tē\ *noun*
— **di·lat·able** \dī-'lā-tə-bəl, 'dī-ˌ\ *adjective*
— **di·la·tor** \dī-'lā-tər, 'dī-ˌ\ *noun*
di·lat·ed *adjective* (15th century)
1 : expanded laterally; *especially* **:** being flat and widened ⟨*dilated* leaves⟩
2 : expanded normally or abnormally in all dimensions
di·la·tion \dī-'lā-shən\ *noun* (15th century)

1 : the act or action of dilating **:** the state of being dilated **:** EXPANSION, DILATATION
2 : the action of stretching or enlarging an organ or part of the body
di·la·tive \dī-'lā-tiv, 'dī-ˌ\ *adjective* (1634)
: causing dilation **:** tending to dilate
di·la·tom·e·ter \ˌdi-lə-'tä-mə-tər, ˌdī-\ *noun* [International Scientific Vocabulary] (circa 1883)
: an instrument for measuring expansion
— **di·la·to·met·ric** \-tō-'me-trik\ *adjective*
— **di·la·tom·e·try** \-'tä-mə-trē\ *noun*
dil·a·to·ry \'di-lə-ˌtōr-ē, -ˌtȯr-\ *adjective* [Middle English, from Late Latin *dilatorius*, from Latin *differre* (past participle *dilatus*) to postpone, differ — more at DIFFER, TOLERATE] (15th century)
1 : tending or intended to cause delay ⟨*dilatory* tactics⟩
2 : characterized by procrastination **:** TARDY ⟨*dilatory* in answering letters⟩
— **dil·a·to·ri·ly** \ˌdi-lə-'tōr-ə-lē, -'tȯr-\ *adverb*
— **dil·a·to·ri·ness** \'di-lə-ˌtōr-ē-nəs, -ˌtȯr-\ *noun*
dil·do \'dil-(ˌ)dō\ *noun, plural* **dildos** *also* **dil·does** [origin unknown] (circa 1593)
: an object serving as a penis substitute for vaginal insertion
di·lem·ma \də-'le-mə *also* dī-\ *noun* [Late Latin, from Late Greek *dilēmmat-, dilēmma*, probably back-formation from Greek *dilēmmatos* involving two assumptions, from *di-* + *lēmmat-, lēmma* assumption — more at LEMMA] (1523)
1 : an argument presenting two or more equally conclusive alternatives against an opponent
2 a : a usually undesirable or unpleasant choice ⟨faces this *dilemma*: raise interest rates and slow the economy or lower them and risk serious inflation⟩ **b :** a situation involving such a choice ⟨here am I brought to a very pretty *dilemma*; I must commit murder or commit matrimony —George Farquhar⟩; *broadly* **:** PREDICAMENT ⟨lords and bailiffs were in a terrible *dilemma* —G. M. Trevelyan⟩
3 a : a problem involving a difficult choice ⟨the *dilemma* of "liberty versus order" —J. M. Burns⟩ **b :** a difficult or persistent problem ⟨unemployment . . . the great central *dilemma* of our advancing technology —August Heckscher⟩ ▢
— **dil·em·mat·ic** \ˌdi-lə-'ma-tik *also* ˌdī-\ *adjective*
dil·et·tante \'di-lə-ˌtänt, -ˌtant; ˌdi-lə-'\ *noun, plural* **-tantes** *or* **-tan·ti** \-'tän-tē, -'tan-tē\ [Italian, from present participle of *dilettare* to delight, from Latin *dilectare* — more at DELIGHT] (1748)
1 : an admirer or lover of the arts
2 : a person having a superficial interest in an art or a branch of knowledge **:** DABBLER
synonym see AMATEUR
— **dilettante** *adjective*
— **dil·et·tant·ish** \-ˌtän-tish, -ˌtan-, ˌdi-lə-'\ *adjective*
— **dil·et·tan·tism** \-ˌtän-ˌti-zəm, -ˌtan-, ˌdi-lə-'\ *noun*
¹**dil·i·gence** \'di-lə-jən(t)s\ *noun* [Middle English, from Middle French, from Latin *diligentia*, from *diligent-, diligens*] (14th century)
1 a : persevering application **:** ASSIDUITY **b** *obsolete* **:** SPEED, HASTE
2 : the attention and care legally expected or required of a person (as a party to a contract)
²**di·li·gence** \'di-lə-ˌzhäⁿs, 'di-lə-jən(t)s\ *noun* [French, literally, haste, from Middle French, persevering application] (1742)
: STAGECOACH
dil·i·gent \'di-lə-jənt\ *adjective* [Middle English, from Middle French, from Latin *diligent-, diligens*, from present participle of *diligere* to esteem, love, from *di-* (from *dis-* apart) + *legere* to select — more at LEGEND] (14th century)

: characterized by steady, earnest, and energetic effort **:** PAINSTAKING
synonym see BUSY
— **dil·i·gent·ly** *adverb*
dill \'dil\ *noun* [Middle English *dile*, from Old English; akin to Old High German *tilli* dill] (before 12th century)
1 : any of several plants of the carrot family; *especially* **:** a European herb (*Anethum graveolens*) with aromatic foliage and seeds both of which are used in flavoring foods and especially pickles
2 : DILL PICKLE
— **dilled** *adjective*
dill pickle *noun* (1904)
: a pickle seasoned with fresh dill or dill juice
dil·ly \'di-lē\ *noun, plural* **dillies** [obsolete *dilly*, adjective (delightful), perhaps by shortening & alteration from *delightful*] (1935)
: one that is remarkable or outstanding ⟨had a *dilly* of a storm⟩ ⟨for a practical joke, that was a *dilly*⟩
dil·ly bag \'di-lē-\ *noun* [Jagara (Australian aboriginal language of Queensland) *dili* coarse grass, fiber bag] (1867)
: an Australian mesh bag made of native fibers
dil·ly·dal·ly \'di-lē-ˌda-lē\ *intransitive verb* [reduplication of *dally*] (1741)
: to waste time by loitering or delaying **:** DAWDLE
dil·u·ent \'dil-yə-wənt\ *noun* [Latin *diluent-, diluens*, present participle of *diluere*] (circa 1721)
: a diluting agent (as the vehicle in a medicinal preparation)
¹**di·lute** \dī-'lüt, də-\ *transitive verb* **di·lut·ed; di·lut·ing** [Latin *dilutus*, past participle of *diluere* to wash away, dilute, from *di-* + *lavere* to wash — more at LYE] (circa 1555)
1 : ATTENUATE
2 : to make thinner or more liquid by admixture
3 : to diminish the strength, flavor, or brilliance of by admixture
4 : to decrease the per share value of (common stock) by increasing the total number of shares
— **di·lut·er** *or* **di·lu·tor** \-'lü-tər\ *noun*
— **di·lu·tive** \-'lü-tiv\ *adjective*
²**dilute** *adjective* (1605)
: WEAK, DILUTED
— **di·lute·ness** *noun*
di·lu·tion \dī-'lü-shən, də-\ *noun* (1646)
1 : the action of diluting **:** the state of being diluted
2 : something (as a solution) that is diluted
3 : a lessening of real value (as of equity) by a decrease in relative worth; *specifically* **:** a decrease of per share value of common stock by an increase in the total number of shares

▢ **USAGE**
dilemma Although some commentators insist that *dilemma* be restricted to instances in which the alternatives to be chosen are equally unsatisfactory, their concern is misplaced; the unsatisfactoriness of the options is usually a matter of how the author presents them. What is distressing or painful about a dilemma is having to make a choice one does not want to make. The use of such adjectives as *terrible*, *painful*, and *irreconcilable* suggests that *dilemma* is losing some of its unpleasant force. There also seems to be a tendency especially in sense 3b toward applying the word to less weighty problems (solved their goaltending *dilemma* —Pat Calabria).

\ə\ abut \ᵊ\ kitten \ər\ further \a\ ash \ā\ ace
\ä\ mop, mar \aú\ out \ch\ chin \e\ bet \ē\ easy
\g\ go \i\ hit \ī\ ice \j\ job \ŋ\ sing \ō\ go
\ȯ\ law \ȯi\ boy \th\ thin \th\ the \ü\ loot \ú\ foot
\y\ yet \zh\ vision *see also* Guide to Pronunciation

di·lu·vi·al \də-'lü-vē-əl, dī-\ *or* **di·lu·vi·an** \-vē-ən\ *adjective* [Late Latin *diluvialis*, from Latin *diluvium* deluge — more at DELUGE] (circa 1656)
: of, relating to, or brought about by a flood

¹**dim** \'dim\ *adjective* **dim·mer; dim·mest** [Middle English, from Old English *dimm;* akin to Old High German *timber* dark] (before 12th century)
1 a : emitting a limited or insufficient amount of light **b** : DULL, LUSTERLESS **c** : lacking pronounced, clear-cut, or vigorous quality or character
2 a : seen indistinctly or without clear outlines or details **b** : perceived by the senses or mind indistinctly or weakly ⟨had only a *dim* notion of what was going on⟩ **c** : having little prospect of favorable result or outcome ⟨a *dim* future⟩ **d** : characterized by an unfavorable, skeptical, or pessimistic attitude — usually used in the phrase *take a dim view of*
3 : not perceiving clearly and distinctly ⟨*dim* eyes⟩
4 : DIM-WITTED
— **dim·ly** *adverb*
— **dim·ma·ble** \'di-mə-bəl\ *adjective*
— **dim·ness** *noun*

²**dim** *verb* **dimmed; dim·ming** (before 12th century)
transitive verb
1 : to make dim or lusterless
2 : to reduce the light from
intransitive verb
: to become dim

³**dim** *noun* (14th century)
1 *archaic* : DUSK, DIMNESS
2 : LOW BEAM

dim bulb *noun* (1927)
slang : DIMWIT

dime \'dīm\ *noun* [Middle English, tenth part, tithe, from Middle French, from Latin *decima*, from feminine of *decimus* tenth, from *decem* ten — more at TEN] (1786)
1 a : a coin of the U.S. worth ¹⁄₁₀ dollar **b** : a petty sum of money
2 : a Canadian 10-cent piece
— **a dime a dozen** : so plentiful or commonplace as to be of little esteem or slight value
— **on a dime** **1** : in a very small area ⟨these cars can turn *on a dime*⟩ **2** : INSTANTLY

di·men·hy·dri·nate \,dī-,men-'hī-drə-,nāt\ *noun* [*dimethyl* + *amine* + *hydr-* + *amine* + *¹-ate*] (circa 1950)
: a crystalline antihistaminic compound $C_{24}H_{28}ClN_5O_3$ used especially to prevent nausea

dime novel *noun* (1864)
: a usually paperback melodramatic novel; *especially* : one popular in the U.S. from about the mid-19th century to the early 20th often featuring a Western theme

¹**di·men·sion** \də-'men(t)-shən *also* dī-\ *noun* [Middle English, from Middle French, from Latin *dimension-, dimensio*, from *dimetiri* to measure out, from *dis-* + *metiri* to measure — more at MEASURE] (14th century)
1 a (1) : measure in one direction; *specifically* : one of three coordinates determining a position in space or four coordinates determining a position in space and time (2) : one of a group of properties whose number is necessary and sufficient to determine uniquely each element of a system of usually mathematical entities (as an aggregate of points in real or abstract space) ⟨the surface of a sphere has two *dimensions*⟩; *also* : a parameter or coordinate variable assigned to such a property ⟨the three *dimensions* of momentum⟩ (3) : the number of elements in a basis of a vector space **b** : the quality of spatial extension : MAGNITUDE, SIZE **c** : a lifelike or realistic quality **d** : the range over which or the degree to which something extends : SCOPE — usually used in plural **e** : one of the elements or factors making up a complete personality or entity : ASPECT

2 *obsolete* : bodily form or proportions
3 : any of the fundamental units (as of mass, length, or time) on which a derived unit is based; *also* : the power of such a unit
4 : wood or stone cut to pieces of specified size
5 : a level of existence or consciousness
— **di·men·sion·al** \-'mench-nəl, -'men(t)-shə-nºl\ *adjective*
— **di·men·sion·al·i·ty** \-,men(t)-shə-'na-lə-tē\ *noun*
— **di·men·sion·al·ly** \-'mench-nə-lē, -'men(t)-shə-nºl-ē\ *adverb*
— **di·men·sion·less** \-'men(t)-shən-ləs\ *adjective*

²**dimension** *transitive verb* **di·men·sioned; di·men·sion·ing** \-'men(t)-shə-niŋ\ (1754)
1 : to form to the required dimensions
2 : to indicate the dimensions of (as on a drawing)

di·mer \'dī-mər\ *noun* [International Scientific Vocabulary] (circa 1926)
: a compound formed by the union of two radicals or two molecules of a simpler compound; *specifically* : a polymer formed from two molecules of a monomer
— **di·mer·ic** \(,)dī-'mer-ik\ *adjective*
— **di·mer·iza·tion** \,dī-mə-rə-'zā-shən\ *noun*
— **di·mer·ize** \'dī-mə-,rīz\ *transitive verb*

di·mer·cap·rol \,dī-mər-'ka-,pról, -,pról\ *noun* [*di-* + *mercap*tan + *propane* + *¹-ol*] (1947)
: a compound $C_3H_8OS_2$ developed as an antidote against lewisite and used against arsenic, mercury, and gold poisoning — called also *BAL*

dime–store \'dīm-,stór, -,stòr\ *adjective* (1938)
1 : INEXPENSIVE ⟨*dime-store* perfume⟩
2 : TAWDRY, SECOND-RATE ⟨*dime-store* philosophy⟩

dime store *noun* (circa 1928)
: FIVE-AND-TEN

dim·e·ter \'di-mə-tər\ *noun* [Late Latin, from Greek *dimetros*, adjective, being a dimeter, from *di-* + *metron* measure — more at MEASURE] (1589)
: a line of verse consisting of two metrical feet or of two dipodies

di·meth·o·ate \dī-'me-thə-,wāt\ *noun* [*di*methyl + *thio* acid + *¹-ate*] (1960)
: an insecticide $C_5H_{12}NO_3PS_2$ used in agriculture and animal husbandry

di·meth·yl \dī-'me-thəl\ *adjective*
: containing two methyl groups in the molecule — often used in combination

di·meth·yl·hy·dra·zine \,dī-,me-thəl-'hī-drə-,zēn\ *noun* (1961)
: either of two flammable corrosive isomeric liquids $C_2H_8N_2$ which are methylated derivatives of hydrazine and of which one is used as a rocket fuel

di·meth·yl·ni·tro·sa·mine \-nī-'trō-sə-,mēn\ *noun* (1965)
: a carcinogenic nitrosamine $C_2H_6N_2O$ that occurs especially in tobacco smoke

dimethyl sulfoxide *noun* (1964)
: a compound $(CH_3)_2SO$ obtained as a by-product in wood-pulp manufacture and used as a solvent and in veterinary medicine as an anti-inflammatory — called also *DMSO*

di·meth·yl·tryp·ta·mine \-'trip-tə-,mēn\ *noun* (1966)
: a naturally occurring or easily synthesized hallucinogenic drug $C_{12}H_{16}N_2$ that is chemically similar to but shorter acting than psilocybin — called also *DMT*

di·min·ish \də-'mi-nish\ *verb* [Middle English *deminishen*, alteration of *diminuen*, from Middle French *diminuer*, from Late Latin *diminuere*, alteration of Latin *deminuere*, from *de-* + *minuere* to lessen — more at MINOR] (15th century)
transitive verb
1 : to make less or cause to appear less

2 : to lessen the authority, dignity, or reputation of : BELITTLE
3 : to cause to taper
intransitive verb
1 : to become gradually less (as in size or importance) : DWINDLE
2 : TAPER
synonym see DECREASE
— **di·min·ish·able** \-ni-shə-bəl\ *adjective*
— **di·min·ish·ment** \-mənt\ *noun*

di·min·ished *adjective* (circa 1751)
of a musical interval : made one half step less than perfect or minor ⟨a *diminished* fifth⟩

diminishing returns *noun plural* (1815)
: a rate of yield that beyond a certain point fails to increase in proportion to additional investments of labor or capital

di·min·u·en·do \də-,min-yə-'wen-(,)dō *also* -,mi-nə-'\ *adverb or adjective* [Italian, literally, diminishing, from Late Latin *diminuendum*, gerund of *diminuere*] (1775)
: DECRESCENDO
— **diminuendo** *noun*

dim·i·nu·tion \,di-mə-'nü-shən *also* -'nyü-\ *noun* [Middle English *diminucioun*, from Middle French *diminution*, from Medieval Latin *diminution-, diminutio*, alteration of Latin *deminution-, deminutio*, from *deminuere*] (14th century)
: the act, process, or an instance of diminishing : DECREASE

¹**di·min·u·tive** \də-'mi-nyə-tiv\ *noun* [Middle English *diminutif*, from Medieval Latin *diminutivum*, alteration of Late Latin *deminutivum*, from neuter of *deminutivus*, adjective, from *deminutus*, past participle of *deminuere*] (14th century)
1 : a diminutive word, affix, or name
2 : a diminutive individual

²**diminutive** *adjective* (14th century)
1 : indicating small size and sometimes the state or quality of being familiarly known, lovable, pitiable, or contemptible — used of affixes (as *-ette, -kin, -ling*) and of words formed with them (as *kitchenette, manikin, duckling*), of clipped forms (as *Jim*), and of altered forms (as *Peggy*); compare AUGMENTATIVE
2 : exceptionally or notably small : TINY
synonym see SMALL
— **di·min·u·tive·ly** *adverb*
— **di·min·u·tive·ness** *noun*

dim·i·ty \'di-mə-tē\ *noun, plural* **-ties** [alteration of Middle English *demyt*, from Medieval Latin *dimitum*, from Middle Greek *dimitos* of double thread, from Greek *di-* + *mitos* warp thread] (1570)
: a sheer usually corded cotton fabric of plain weave in checks or stripes

dim·mer \'di-mər\ *noun* (circa 1896)
1 : a device for regulating the intensity of an electric lighting unit
2 : LOW BEAM

di·mor·phic \(,)dī-'mòr-fik\ *adjective* (1859)
1 a : DIMORPHOUS 1 **b** : occurring in two distinct forms ⟨*dimorphic* leaves of emergent plants⟩ ⟨sexually *dimorphic* coloration in birds⟩
2 : combining qualities of two kinds of individuals in one

di·mor·phism \-,fi-zəm\ *noun* (1832)
: the condition or property of being dimorphic or dimorphous: as **a** : the existence of two different forms (as of color or size) of a species especially in the same population ⟨sexual *dimorphism*⟩ **b** : the existence of an organ (as the leaves of a plant) in two different forms

di·mor·phous \(,)dī-'mòr-fəs\ *adjective* [Greek *dimorphos* having two forms, from *di-* + *-morphos* -morphous] (1832)
1 : crystallizing in two different forms
2 : DIMORPHIC 1b

dim·out \'dim-,aùt\ *noun* (1942)
: a restriction limiting the use or showing of lights at night especially during the threat of

an air raid; *also* **:** a condition of partial darkness produced by this restriction

¹dim·ple \'dim-pəl\ *noun* [Middle English *dympull;* akin to Old High German *tumphilo* whirlpool, Old English *dyppan* to dip — more at DIP] (15th century)
1 : a slight natural indentation in the surface of some part of the human body
2 : a depression or indentation on a surface (as of a golf ball)
— **dim·ply** \-p(ə-)lē\ *adjective*

²dimple *verb* **dim·pled; dim·pling** \-p(ə-)liŋ\ (1602)
transitive verb
: to mark with dimples
intransitive verb
: to exhibit or form dimples

dim sum \'dim-'səm\ *noun* [Chinese (Guangdong) *dímsām,* from *dím* dot, speck + *sām* heart] (1948)
: traditional Chinese food consisting of a variety of items (as steamed or fried dumplings, pieces of cooked chicken, and rice balls) served in small portions

dim·wit \'dim-,wit\ *noun* (circa 1922)
: a stupid or mentally slow person

dim·wit·ted \-'wi-təd\ *adjective* (1934)
: not mentally bright **:** STUPID
— **dim·wit·ted·ly** *adverb*
— **dim·wit·ted·ness** *noun*

¹din \'din\ *noun* [Middle English, from Old English *dyne;* akin to Old Norse *dynr* din, Sanskrit *dhvanati* it roars] (before 12th century)
1 : a loud continued noise; *especially* **:** a welter of discordant sounds
2 : a situation or condition resembling a din

²din *verb* **dinned; din·ning** (before 12th century)
intransitive verb
: to make a loud noise
transitive verb
1 : to assail with loud continued noise
2 : to impress by insistent repetition — often used with *into*

di·nar \di-'när, 'dē-,\ *noun* [Arabic *dīnār,* from Late Greek *dēnarion* denarius, from Latin *denarius* — more at DENIER] (1634)
1 : a gold coin formerly used in countries of southwest Asia and north Africa
2 a — see MONEY table **b** — see *rial* at MONEY table

¹dine \'dīn\ *verb* **dined; din·ing** [Middle English, from Old French *diner,* from (assumed) Vulgar Latin *disjejunare* to break one's fast, from Latin *dis-* + Late Latin *jejunare* to fast, from Latin *jejunus* fasting] (13th century)
intransitive verb
: to take dinner
transitive verb
: to give a dinner to

²dine *noun* (15th century)
Scottish **:** DINNER

dine out *intransitive verb* (1816)
: to eat a meal away from home
— **dine out on** **:** to use as a subject for dining table conversation

din·er \'dī-nər\ *noun* (1815)
1 : one that dines
2 a : DINING CAR **b :** a restaurant usually resembling a dining car in shape

din·er-out \,dī-nə-'raùt\ *noun, plural* **di·ners-out** \-nər-'zaùt\ (1808)
: one who dines out

di·nette \dī-'net\ *noun* (1925)
: a small space usually off a kitchen used for informal dining; *also* **:** furniture for such a space

¹ding \'diŋ\ *verb* [probably imitative] (1582)
transitive verb
: to dwell on with tiresome repetition ⟨keeps *dinging* it into him that the less he smokes the better —Samuel Butler (died 1902)⟩
intransitive verb
1 : to make a ringing sound **:** CLANG
2 : to speak with tiresome reiteration

²ding *noun* [*ding* (to strike), from Middle English *dingen*] (circa 1945)
: an instance of minor surface damage (as a dent)

ding-a-ling \'diŋ-ə-,liŋ\ *noun* [reduplication of ¹*ding*] (circa 1935)
: NITWIT, KOOK

ding·bat \'diŋ-,bat\ *noun* [origin unknown] (1904)
1 : a typographical symbol or ornament (as *, ¶, or ✠)
2 : NITWIT, KOOK

¹ding·dong \'diŋ-,dòŋ, -,däŋ\ *noun* [imitative] (1611)
: the ringing sound produced by repeated strokes especially on a bell

²dingdong *intransitive verb* (1659)
1 : to make a dingdong sound
2 : to repeat a sound or action tediously or insistently

³dingdong *adjective* (1792)
1 : of, relating to, or resembling the ringing sound made by a bell
2 : marked by a rapid exchange or alternation

dinge \'dinj\ *noun* [back-formation from *dingy*] (1846)
: the condition of being dingy

ding·er \'diŋ-ər\ *noun* [perhaps from *ding* (to strike) + ²*-er*] (1974)
: HOME RUN

din·ghy \'diŋ-ē, -gē\ *noun, plural* **dinghies** [Bengali *ḍiṅgi* & Hindi *ḍiṅgī*] (1810)
1 : an East Indian rowboat or sailboat
2 a : a small boat carried on or towed behind a larger boat as a tender or a lifeboat **b :** a small sailboat
3 : a rubber life raft

din·gle \'diŋ-gəl\ *noun* [Middle English, deep hollow] (13th century)
: a small wooded valley **:** DELL

din·gle·ber·ry \'diŋ-gəl-,ber-ē\ *noun* [origin unknown] (1955)
: a piece of dried fecal matter clinging to the hair around the anus

din·go \'diŋ-(,)gō\ *noun, plural* **dingoes** [Dharuk (Australian aboriginal language of the Port Jackson area) *ḍiṅgu*] (1789)
: a reddish brown wild dog (*Canis dingo*) of Australia

din·gus \'diŋ-(g)əs\ *noun* [Dutch or German; Dutch *dinges,* probably from German *Dings,* from genitive of *Ding* thing, from Old High German — more at THING] (1876)
: DOODAD 2

dingo

din·gy \'din-jē\ *adjective* **din·gi·er; -est** [origin unknown] (circa 1736)
1 : DIRTY, DISCOLORED
2 : SHABBY, SQUALID
— **din·gi·ly** \-jə-lē\ *adverb*
— **din·gi·ness** \-jē-nəs\ *noun*

dining car *noun* (1838)
: a railroad car in which meals are served

dining room *noun* (1601)
: a room used for eating meals

di·ni·tro \(,)dī-'nī-trō\ *adjective*
: containing two nitro groups — often used in combination

di·ni·tro·ben·zene \(,)dī-,nī-trō-'ben-,zēn, -(,)ben-'\ *noun* [International Scientific Vocabulary] (1873)
: any of three isomeric toxic compounds $C_6H_4(NO_2)_2$

di·ni·tro·phe·nol \-'fē-,nòl, -fi-'\ *noun* (circa 1897)
: any of six isomeric crystalline compounds $C_6H_4N_2O_5$ some of whose derivatives are pesticides

¹dink \'diŋk\ *noun* [by shortening & alteration] (1903)
: DINGHY

²dink *noun* [*dink* (to hit with a drop shot), probably of imitative origin] (1939)
: DROP SHOT

³dink *noun* [perhaps from *dink,* disparaging name for a Vietnamese] (1974)
slang **:** NITWIT, JERK, NERD

Din·ka \'diŋ-kə\ *noun, plural* **Dinkas** *also* **Dinka** (1861)
1 : a member of a pastoral people of the Nile Valley in south central Sudan
2 : the Nilotic language of the Dinkas

din·key *or* **din·ky** \'diŋ-kē\ *noun, plural* **dinkeys** *or* **dinkies** [probably from *dinky*] (1874)
: a small locomotive

¹din·kum \'diŋ-kəm\ *adjective* [English dialect *dinkum,* noun, work, share of work] (1905)
Australian & New Zealand **:** AUTHENTIC, GENUINE — often used with *fair*

²dinkum *adverb* (1915)
Australian & New Zealand **:** TRULY, HONESTLY — often used with *fair;* often used interjectionally

din·ky \'diŋ-kē\ *adjective* **din·ki·er; -est** [Scots *dink* neat] (1880)
: SMALL 1a; *also* **:** INSIGNIFICANT

din·ner \'di-nər\ *noun, often attributive* [Middle English *diner,* from Old French, from *diner* to dine] (13th century)
1 a : the principal meal of the day **b :** a formal feast or banquet
2 : TABLE D'HÔTE 2
3 : the food prepared for a dinner ⟨eat your *dinner*⟩
4 : a packaged meal usually for quick preparation ⟨warmed up a frozen *dinner*⟩
— **din·ner·less** \-ləs\ *adjective*

dinner jacket *noun* (1891)
: a jacket for formal evening wear

dinner theater *noun* (1960)
: a restaurant in which a play is presented after the meal is over

din·ner·time \'di-nər-,tīm\ *noun* (14th century)
: the customary time for dinner

din·ner·ware \-,war, -,wer\ *noun* (1895)
: tableware other than flatware

di·no·fla·gel·late \,dī-nō-'fla-jə-lət, -,lāt; -flə-'je-lət\ *noun* [ultimately from Greek *dinos* rotation, eddy + New Latin *flagellum*] (1889)
: any of an order (Dinoflagellata) of chiefly marine planktonic usually solitary unicellular phytoflagellates that include luminescent forms, forms important in marine food chains, and forms causing red tide

di·no·saur \'dī-nə-,sòr\ *noun* [New Latin *Dinosaurus,* genus name, from Greek *deinos* terrifying + *sauros* lizard — more at DIRE] (1841)
1 : any of a group (Dinosauria) of extinct chiefly terrestrial carnivorous or herbivorous reptiles of the Mesozoic era
2 : any of various large extinct reptiles other than the true dinosaurs
3 : one that is impractically large, out-of-date, or obsolete
— **di·no·sau·ri·an** \,dī-nə-'sòr-ē-ən\ *adjective*

¹dint \'dint\ *noun* [Middle English, from Old English *dynt;* akin to Old Norse *dyntr* noise] (before 12th century)
1 *archaic* **:** BLOW, STROKE
2 : FORCE, POWER
3 : ²DENT
— **by dint of** **:** by force of **:** BECAUSE OF

²dint *transitive verb* (1597)
1 : to make a dent in
2 : to impress or drive in with force

\ə\ abut \ᵊ\ kitten \ər\ further \a\ ash \ā\ ace
\ä\ mop, mar \aù\ out \ch\ chin \e\ bet \ē\ easy
\g\ go \i\ hit \ī\ ice \j\ job \ŋ\ sing \ō\ go
\ò\ law \òi\ boy \th\ thin \th\ the \ü\ loot \ù\ foot
\y\ yet \zh\ vision　　*see also* Guide to Pronunciation

di·nu·cle·o·tide \(ˌ)dī-'n(y)ü-klē-ə-ˌtīd\ *noun* (circa 1927)
: a nucleotide consisting of two units each composed of a phosphate, a pentose, and a nitrogen base

di·oc·e·san \dī-'ä-sə-sən *also* 'dī-ə-ˌsē-sᵊn\ *noun* (15th century)
: a bishop having jurisdiction over a diocese

di·o·cese \'dī-ə-səs, -ˌsēs, -ˌsēz\ *noun, plural* **-ces·es** \'dī-ə-sə-səz, -ˌsē-zəz, ÷'dī-ə-ˌsēz\ [Middle English *diocise*, from Middle French, from Late Latin *diocesis*, alteration of *dioecesis*, from Latin, administrative division, from Greek *dioikēsis* administration, administrative division, from *dioikein* to keep house, govern, from *dia-* + *oikein* to dwell, manage, from *oikos* house — more at VICINITY] (14th century)
: the territorial jurisdiction of a bishop
— **di·oc·e·san** \dī-'ä-sə-sən *also* 'dī-ə-ˌsē-sᵊn\ *adjective*

di·ode \'dī-ˌōd\ *noun* [International Scientific Vocabulary] (1919)
: an electronic device that has two electrodes or terminals and is used especially as a rectifier

di·oe·cious \(ˌ)dī-'ē-shəs\ *adjective* [ultimately from Greek *di-* + *oikos*] (1752)
1 : having male reproductive organs in one individual and female in another
2 : having staminate and pistillate flowers borne on different individuals
— **di·oe·cism** \-'ē-ˌsi-zəm\ *noun*
— **di·oe·cy** \'dī-ˌē-sē\ *noun*

di·ol \'dī-ˌōl, -ˌól\ *noun* [International Scientific Vocabulary] (1923)
: a compound containing two hydroxyl groups

di·ole·fin \dī-'ō-lə-fən\ *noun* [International Scientific Vocabulary] (circa 1909)
: DIENE

Di·o·me·des \ˌdī-ə-'mē-dēz\ *noun* [Latin, from Greek *Diomēdēs*]
: one of the Greek heroes of the Trojan War

Di·o·ny·sia \ˌdī-ə-'ni-zhē-ə, -'nē-, -shē-, -zē-, -sē-\ *noun plural* [Latin, from Greek, from neuter plural of *dionysios* of Dionysus, from *Dionysos*] (circa 1895)
: ancient Greek festival observances held in seasonal cycles in honor of Dionysus; *especially* : such observances marked by dramatic performances

Di·o·ny·si·ac \-'ni-zhē-ˌak, -'nē-, -shē-, -zē-, -sē-\ *adjective* [Latin *dionysiacus*, from Greek *dionysiakos*, from *Dionysos*] (1844)
: DIONYSIAN 2
— **Dionysiac** *noun*

Di·o·ny·sian \ˌdī-ə-'ni-zhē-ən, -'nē-, -shē-, -zē-, -sē-; -zhən, -shən\ *adjective* (1607)
1 a : of or relating to Dionysius **b** : of or related to the theological writings once mistakenly attributed to Dionysius the Areopagite
2 a : devoted to the worship of Dionysus **b** : characteristic of Dionysus or the cult of worship of Dionysus; *especially* : being of a frenzied or orgiastic character — compare APOLLONIAN

Di·o·ny·sus \ˌdī-ə-'nī-səs, -'nē-\ *noun* [Latin, from Greek *Dionysos*]
: BACCHUS

Di·o·phan·tine equation \ˌdī-ə-'fan-ˌtīn, -'fan-tᵊn\ *noun* [*Diophantus*, 3d century A.D. Greek mathematician] (circa 1928)
: an indeterminate polynomial equation with integral coefficients for which it is required to find all integral solutions

di·op·side \dī-'äp-ˌsīd\ *noun* [French, from *di-* + Greek *opsis* appearance — more at OPTIC] (circa 1808)
: a green to white mineral that consists of pyroxene containing little or no aluminum
— **di·op·sid·ic** \dī-ˌäp-'si-dik\ *adjective*

di·op·ter \dī-'äp-tər, 'dī-ˌäp-\ *noun* [*diopter* (an optical instrument), from Middle French *dioptre*, from Latin *dioptra*, from Greek, from *dia-* + *opsesthai* to be going to see — more at OPTIC] (circa 1864)
: a unit of measurement of the refractive power of lenses equal to the reciprocal of the focal length in meters

di·op·tric \dī-'äp-trik\ *adjective* [Greek *dioptrikos* of a diopter (instrument), from *dioptra*] (1653)
: REFRACTIVE; *specifically* : assisting vision by refracting and focusing light

di·o·ra·ma \ˌdī-ə-'ra-mə, -'rä-\ *noun* [French, from *dia-* + *-orama* (as in *panorama*, from English)] (1823)
1 : a scenic representation in which a partly translucent painting is seen from a distance through an opening
2 a : a scenic representation in which sculptured figures and lifelike details are displayed usually in miniature so as to blend indistinguishably with a realistic painted background **b** : a life-size exhibit (as of a wildlife specimen or scene) with realistic natural surroundings and a painted background
— **di·o·ram·ic** \-'ra-mik\ *adjective*

di·o·rite \'dī-ə-ˌrīt\ *noun* [French, irregular from Greek *diorizein* to distinguish, from *dia-* + *horizein* to define — more at HORIZON] (1826)
: a granular crystalline igneous rock commonly of acid plagioclase and hornblende, pyroxene, or biotite
— **di·o·rit·ic** \ˌdī-ə-'ri-tik\ *adjective*

Di·os·cu·ri \ˌdī-əs-'kyü(ə)r-ˌī, dī-ˌäs-kyə-ˌrī\ *noun plural* [New Latin, from Greek *Dioskouroi*, literally, sons of Zeus, from *Dios* (genitive of *Zeus*; akin to Latin *divus* divine) + *kouroi*, plural of *kouros, koros* boy — more at DEITY, CRESCENT]
: the twins Castor and Pollux reunited as stars in the sky by Zeus after Castor's death and regarded as patrons of athletes and sailors

di·ox·ane \dī-'äk-ˌsān\ *also* **di·ox·an** \-ˌsan, -sən\ *noun* [International Scientific Vocabulary] (1912)
: a flammable toxic liquid diether $C_4H_8O_2$ used especially as a solvent

di·ox·ide \(ˌ)dī-'äk-ˌsīd\ *noun* [International Scientific Vocabulary] (circa 1847)
: an oxide (as carbon dioxide) containing two atoms of oxygen in the molecule

di·ox·in \(ˌ)dī-'äk-sən\ *noun* (circa 1919)
: any of several heterocyclic hydrocarbons that occur especially as persistent toxic impurities in herbicides; *especially* : TCDD

¹dip \'dip\ *verb* **dipped; dip·ping** [Middle English *dippen*, from Old English *dyppan*; akin to Old High German *tupfen* to wash, Lithuanian *dubus* deep] (before 12th century)
transitive verb
1 a : to plunge or immerse momentarily or partially under the surface (as of a liquid) so as to moisten, cool, or coat ⟨*dip* candles⟩ **b** : to thrust in a way to suggest immersion **c** : to immerse (as a sheep or dog) in an antiseptic or parasiticidal solution
2 a : to lift a portion of by reaching below the surface with something shaped to hold liquid : LADLE **b** : to take a portion of (snuff)
3 a *archaic* : INVOLVE **b** : MORTGAGE
4 a : to lower and then raise again ⟨*dip* a flag in salute⟩ **b** *chiefly British* : DIM 2
intransitive verb
1 a : to plunge into a liquid and quickly emerge **b** : to immerse something into a processing liquid or finishing material
2 a : to suddenly drop down or out of sight **b** *of an airplane* : to drop suddenly before climbing **c** : to decline or decrease moderately and usually temporarily ⟨prices *dipped*⟩ **d** : to lower the body momentarily especially as part of an athletic or dancing motion
3 a : to reach down inside or below or as if inside or below a surface especially to withdraw a part of the contents — used with *into* ⟨*dipped* into the family's savings⟩
4 : to examine or read something casually or superficially — used with *into*

5 : to incline downward from the plane of the horizon
— **dip·pa·ble** \'di-pə-bəl\ *adjective*

²dip *noun* (1599)
1 : an act of dipping; *especially* : a brief plunge into the water for sport or exercise
2 : inclination downward: **a** : PITCH **b** : a sharp downward course : DROP **c** : the angle that a stratum or similar geological feature makes with a horizontal plane
3 : the angle formed with the horizon by a magnetic needle free to rotate in the vertical plane
4 : HOLLOW, DEPRESSION
5 : something obtained by or used in dipping
6 a : a sauce or soft mixture into which food may be dipped **b** : a liquid preparation for the dipping of something; *especially* : an insecticide or parasiticide for the dipping of animals — compare SHEEP-DIP
7 *slang* : PICKPOCKET
8 : a stupid or unsophisticated person

di·pep·ti·dase \dī-'pep-tə-ˌdās, -ˌdāz\ *noun* (1927)
: any of various enzymes that hydrolyze dipeptides but not polypeptides

di·pep·tide \(ˌ)dī-'pep-ˌtīd\ *noun* (1903)
: a peptide that yields two molecules of amino acid on hydrolysis

di·pha·sic \(ˌ)dī-'fā-zik\ *adjective* (1881)
: having two phases

di·phen·hy·dra·mine \ˌdī-ˌfen-'hī-drə-ˌmēn\ *noun* (1948)
: an antihistamine $C_{17}H_{21}NO$ used especially in the form of its hydrochloride to treat allergy symptoms and motion sickness

di·phe·nyl·amine \(ˌ)dī-ˌfe-nᵊl-ə-ˌmēn, -ˌfē-, -nᵊl-'a-mən\ *noun* [International Scientific Vocabulary] (1872)
: a crystalline pleasant-smelling compound $(C_6H_5)_2NH$ used chiefly in the manufacture of dyes and as an indicator

di·phe·nyl·hy·dan·to·in \-hī-'dan-tə-wən\ *noun* [*di-* + *phenyl* + *hyd*rogen + all*antoin*] (1937)
: PHENYTOIN

di·phos·gene \(ˌ)dī-'fäz-ˌjēn\ *noun* [International Scientific Vocabulary] (circa 1922)
: a liquid compound $C_2Cl_4O_2$ used as a poison gas in World War I

di·phos·phate \(ˌ)dī-'fäs-ˌfāt\ *noun* (1826)
: a phosphate containing two phosphate groups

di·phos·pho·gly·cer·ic acid \(ˌ)dī-'fäs-fō-gli-ˌser-ik-\ *noun* (1959)
: a diphosphate of glyceric acid that is an important intermediate in photosynthesis and in glycolysis and fermentation

di·phos·pho·pyr·i·dine nucleotide \-ˌpir-ə-ˌdēn-\ *noun* (1938)
: NAD

diph·the·ria \dif-'thir-ē-ə, ÷dip-\ *noun* [New Latin, from French *diphthérie*, from Greek *diphthera* leather; from the toughness of the false membrane] (circa 1851)
: an acute febrile contagious disease marked by the formation of a false membrane especially in the throat and caused by a bacterium (*Corynebacterium diphtheriae*) that produces a toxin causing inflammation of the heart and nervous system
— **diph·the·ri·al** \-ē-əl\ *adjective*
— **diph·the·rit·ic** \ˌdif-thə-'ri-tik, ÷ˌdip-\ *adjective*

¹diph·the·roid \'dif-thə-ˌroid\ *adjective* (1861)
: resembling diphtheria

²diphtheroid *noun* (1908)
: a bacterium (especially genus *Corynebacterium*) that resembles the bacterium of diphtheria but does not produce diphtheria toxin

diph·thong \'dif-ˌthöŋ, 'dip-\ *noun* [Middle English *diptonge*, from Middle French *diptongue*, from Late Latin *dipthongus*, from Greek *diphthongos*, from *di-* + *phthongos* voice, sound] (15th century)

1 : a gliding monosyllabic speech sound (as the vowel combination at the end of *toy*) that starts at or near the articulatory position for one vowel and moves to or toward the position of another
2 : DIGRAPH
3 : the ligature æ or œ
— **diph·thon·gal** \dif-'thȯṅ-(g)əl, dip-\ *adjective*

diph·thong·i·za·tion \(ˌ)dif-ˌthȯṅ-ə-'zā-shən, (ˌ)dip-\ *noun* (1874)
: the act of diphthongizing **:** the state of being diphthongized

diph·thong·ize \'dif-ˌthȯṅ-ˌīz, 'dip-\ *verb* **-ized; -iz·ing** (1867)
intransitive verb
of a simple vowel **:** to change into a diphthong
transitive verb
: to pronounce as a diphthong

diphy- *or* **diphyo-** *combining form* [New Latin, from Greek *diphy-*, from *diphyēs*, from *di-* + *phyein* to bring forth — more at BE]
: double **:** bipartite 〈*diphy*odont〉

di·phy·let·ic \ˌdī-fī-'le-tik\ *adjective* (1902)
: derived from two lines of evolutionary descent 〈*diphyletic* dinosaurs〉

di·phy·odont \(ˌ)dī-'fī-ə-ˌdänt\ *adjective* [International Scientific Vocabulary] (1854)
: marked by the successive development of deciduous and permanent sets of teeth

dipl- *or* **diplo-** *combining form* [Greek, from *diploos* — more at DOUBLE]
1 : double **:** twofold 〈*diplo*pia〉
2 : diploid 〈*diplo*phase〉

di·ple·gia \dī-'plē-j(ē-)ə\ *noun* [New Latin] (circa 1881)
: paralysis of corresponding parts on both sides of the body

dip·lo·blas·tic \ˌdip-lō-'blas-tik\ *adjective* (circa 1885)
: having two germ layers — used of an embryo or lower invertebrate that lacks a true mesoderm

dip·lo·coc·cus \-'kä-kəs\ *noun* [New Latin, genus name] (circa 1881)
: any of various encapsulated bacteria (as *Streptococcus pneumoniae*, a common cause of pneumonia) that usually occur in pairs and that were formerly grouped in a single taxon (genus *Diplococcus*) but are now all assigned to other genera

di·plod·o·cus \də-'plä-də-kəs, dī-\ *noun* [New Latin, genus name, from *dipl-* + Greek *dokos* beam, from *dekesthai, dechesthai* to receive; akin to Latin *decēre* to be fitting — more at DECENT] (1928)
: any of a genus (*Diplodocus*) of large herbivorous sauropod dinosaurs of the late Jurassic period in Colorado and Wyoming

dip·loe \'di-plə-ˌwē\ *noun* [New Latin, from Greek *diploē*, from *diploos* double] (circa 1696)
: cancellous bony tissue between the external and internal layers of the skull
— **di·plo·ic** \də-'plō-ik, dī-\ *adjective*

¹dip·loid \'di-ˌplȯid\ *adjective* [International Scientific Vocabulary] (1908)
: having the basic chromosome number doubled
— **dip·loi·dy** \-ˌplȯi-dē\ *noun*

²diploid *noun* (1908)
: a single cell, individual, or generation characterized by the diploid chromosome number

di·plo·ma \də-'plō-mə\ *noun, plural* **diplomas** [Latin, passport, diploma, from Greek *diplōma* folded paper, passport, from *diploun* to double, from *diploos*] (1622)
1 *plural also* **di·plo·ma·ta** \-mə-tə\ **:** an official or state document **:** CHARTER
2 : a writing usually under seal conferring some honor or privilege
3 : a document bearing record of graduation from or of a degree conferred by an educational institution

di·plo·ma·cy \də-'plō-mə-sē\ *noun* (1796)

1 : the art and practice of conducting negotiations between nations
2 : skill in handling affairs without arousing hostility **:** TACT

diploma mill *noun* (1914)
: a usually unregulated institution of higher education granting degrees with few or no academic requirements

dip·lo·mat \'di-plə-ˌmat\ *noun* [French *diplomate*, back-formation from *diplomatique*] (1813)
: one employed or skilled in diplomacy

dip·lo·mate \'di-plə-ˌmāt\ *noun* (1879)
: one who holds a diploma; *especially* **:** a physician qualified to practice in a medical specialty by advanced training and experience in the specialty followed by passing an intensive examination by a national board of senior specialists

dip·lo·mat·ic \ˌdi-plə-'ma-tik\ *adjective* [in sense 1, from New Latin *diplomaticus*, from Latin *diplomat-*; in other senses, from French *diplomatique* connected with documents regulating international relations, from New Latin *diplomaticus*] (1711)
1 a : PALEOGRAPHIC **b :** exactly reproducing the original 〈a *diplomatic* edition〉
2 : of, relating to, or concerned with diplomacy or diplomats 〈*diplomatic* relations〉
3 : employing tact and conciliation especially in situations of stress
synonym see SUAVE
— **dip·lo·mat·i·cal·ly** \-ti-k(ə-)lē\ *adverb*

di·plo·ma·tist \də-'plō-mə-tist\ *noun* (1815)
: DIPLOMAT

dip·lont \'di-ˌplänt\ *noun* [International Scientific Vocabulary] (1925)
: an organism with somatic cells having the diploid chromosome number — compare HAPLONT
— **dip·lon·tic** \di-'plän-tik\ *adjective*

dip·lo·phase \'di-plə-ˌfāz\ *noun* (circa 1925)
: a diploid phase in a life cycle

dip·lo·pia \di-'plō-pē-ə\ *noun* [New Latin] (circa 1811)
: a disorder of vision in which two images of a single object are seen because of unequal action of the eye muscles — called also *double vision*
— **di·plo·pic** \-'plō-pik, -'plä-pik\ *adjective*

dip·lo·pod \'di-plə-ˌpäd\ *noun* [ultimately from Greek *dipl-* + *pod-, pous* foot — more at FOOT] (circa 1864)
: MILLIPEDE

dip·lo·tene \'di-plə-ˌtēn\ *noun* [International Scientific Vocabulary] (1925)
: a stage of meiotic prophase which follows the pachytene and during which the paired homologous chromosomes begin to separate and chiasmata become visible
— **diplotene** *adjective*

dip net *noun* (1820)
: a bag net with a handle that is used especially to scoop fish from the water
— **dip·net** \'dip-\ *transitive verb*

dip·no·an \'dip-nə-wən\ *adjective* [ultimately from Greek *dipnoos* having two breathing apertures, from *di-* + *pnoē* breath, from *pnein* to breathe — more at SNEEZE] (1883)
: of or relating to a group (Dipnoi) of fishes with pulmonary circulation, gills, and lungs
— **dipnoan** *noun*

dip·o·dy \'di-pə-dē\ *noun, plural* **-dies** [Late Latin *dipodia*, from Greek, from *dipod-, dipous* having two feet, from *di-* + *pod-, pous*] (circa 1844)
: a prosodic unit or measure of two feet
— **di·pod·ic** \dī-'pä-dik\ *adjective*

di·pole \'dī-ˌpōl\ *noun* [International Scientific Vocabulary] (1912)
1 a : a pair of equal and opposite electric charges or magnetic poles of opposite sign separated especially by a small distance **b :** a body or system (as a molecule) having such charges

2 : a radio antenna consisting of two horizontal rods in line with each other with their ends slightly separated
— **di·po·lar** \'dī-ˌpō-lər, ˌdī-'pō-\ *adjective*

dipole moment *noun* (1926)
: the product of the distance between the two poles (as magnetic or electric) of a dipole and the magnitude of either pole

dip·per \'di-pər\ *noun* (1611)
1 : one that dips: as **a :** a worker who dips articles **b :** something (as a long-handled cup) used for dipping **c** *slang* **:** PICKPOCKET
2 : any of a genus (*Cinclus* and especially *C. cinclus* of the Old World and *C. mexicanus* of North America) of birds that comprise an oscine family (Cinclidae) related to the thrushes and including individuals that are not web-footed but dive into swift mountain streams and walk on the bottom in search of food — called also *water ouzel*
3 *capitalized* **:** a group of stars that resembles a dipper: as **a :** BIG DIPPER **b :** LITTLE DIPPER
— **dip·per·ful** \-ˌfu̇l\ *noun*

dip·py \'di-pē\ *adjective* **dip·pi·er; -est** [origin unknown] (1911)
: FOOLISH

dip·so \'dip-(ˌ)sō\ *noun, plural* **dipsos** [by shortening] (1880)
: one affected with dipsomania

dip·so·ma·nia \ˌdip-sə-'mā-nē-ə, -nyə\ *noun* [New Latin, from Greek *dipsa* thirst + Late Latin *mania*] (circa 1844)
: an uncontrollable craving for alcoholic liquors
— **dip·so·ma·ni·ac** \-nē-ˌak\ *noun*
— **dip·so·ma·ni·a·cal** \ˌdip-sō-mə-'nī-ə-kəl\ *adjective*

dip·stick \'dip-ˌstik\ *noun* (1927)
: a graduated rod for indicating depth (as of oil in a crankcase)

dip·ter·an \'dip-tə-rən\ *adjective* [ultimately from Greek *dipteros* two-winged, from *di-* + *pteron* wing — more at FEATHER] (circa 1842)
: of, relating to, or being a fly (sense 2a)
— **dipteran** *noun*
— **dip·ter·ous** \-dip-t(ə-)rəs\ *adjective*

dip·tero·carp \'dip-tə-rō-ˌkärp\ *noun* [ultimately from Greek *dipteros* + *-karpos* -carpous] (circa 1876)
: any of a family (Dipterocarpaceae) of tall hardwood trees of tropical Asia, Indonesia, and the Philippines that have a 2-winged fruit and are the source of valuable timber, aromatic oils, and resins; *especially* **:** a member of the type genus (*Dipterocarpus*)

dip·ter·on \'dip-tə-ˌrän\ *noun, plural* **-tera** \-rə\ [Greek, neuter of *dipteros*] (circa 1891)
: ⁴FLY 2a

dip·tych \'dip-(ˌ)tik\ *noun* [Late Latin *diptycha*, plural, from Greek, from neuter plural of *diptychos* folded in two, from *di-* + *ptychē* fold] (1622)

1 : a 2-leaved hinged tablet folding together to protect writing on its waxed surfaces
2 : a picture or series of pictures (as an altarpiece) painted or carved on two hinged tablets
3 : a work made up of two matching parts

di·quat \'dī-ˌkwät\ *noun* [*di-* + *quaternary*] (1960)
: a powerful nonpersistent herbicide $C_{12}H_{12}$-Br_2N_2 that has been used to control water weeds (as the water hyacinth)

diptych 2

dir·dum \'dir-dəm, 'dər-\ *noun* [Middle English (northern dialect) *durdan, durdum* uproar, from Celtic; akin to Welsh *dwrdd* noise, clamor, Middle Irish *dordán* humming, droning] (circa 1693)
Scottish : BLAME

dire \'dīr\ *adjective* **dir·er; dir·est** [Latin *dirus;* akin to Greek *deinos* terrifying, Sanskrit *dveṣṭi* he hates] (1567)
1 a : exciting horror ⟨*dire* suffering⟩ **b** : DISMAL, OPPRESSIVE ⟨*dire* days⟩
2 : warning of disaster ⟨a *dire* forecast⟩
3 a : desperately urgent ⟨*dire* need⟩ **b** : EXTREME ⟨*dire* poverty⟩
— dire·ly *adverb*
— dire·ness *noun*

¹di·rect \də-'rekt, dī-\ *verb* [Middle English, from Latin *directus* straight, from past participle of *dirigere* to direct — more at DRESS] (14th century)
transitive verb
1 a *obsolete* : to write (a letter) to a person **b** : to mark with the name and address of the intended recipient **c** : to impart orally **d** : to adapt in expression so as to have particular applicability ⟨a lawyer who *directs* his appeals to intelligence⟩
2 a : to regulate the activities or course of **b** : to carry out the organizing, energizing, and supervising of **c** : to dominate and determine the course of **d** : to train and lead performances of
3 : to cause to turn, move, or point undeviatingly or to follow a straight course ⟨X rays are *directed* through the body⟩
4 : to point, extend, or project in a specified line or course
5 : to request or enjoin with authority
6 : to show or point out the way for
intransitive verb
1 : to point out, prescribe, or determine a course or procedure
2 : to act as director
synonym see COMMAND, CONDUCT

²direct *adjective* [Middle English, from Latin *directus*] (15th century)
1 *of a celestial body* : moving in the general planetary direction from west to east : not retrograde
2 a : stemming immediately from a source ⟨*direct* result⟩ **b** : being or passing in a straight line of descent from parent to offspring : LINEAL ⟨*direct* ancestor⟩ **c** : having no compromising or impairing element ⟨*direct* insult⟩
3 a : proceeding from one point to another in time or space without deviation or interruption : STRAIGHT **b** : proceeding by the shortest way ⟨the *direct* route⟩
4 : NATURAL, STRAIGHTFORWARD ⟨*direct* manner⟩
5 a : marked by absence of an intervening agency, instrumentality, or influence **b** : effected by the action of the people or the electorate and not by representatives ⟨*direct* democracy⟩ **c** : consisting of or reproducing the exact words of a speaker or writer
6 : characterized by close logical, causal, or consequential relationship ⟨*direct* evidence⟩
7 : capable of dyeing without the aid of a mordant

³direct *adverb* (14th century)
: in a direct way: as **a** : from point to point without deviation : by the shortest way ⟨flew *direct* to Miami⟩ **b** : from the source without interruption or diversion ⟨the writer must take his material *direct* from life —Douglas Stewart⟩ **c** : without an intervening agency or step ⟨buy *direct* from the manufacturer⟩

direct action *noun* (1912)
: action that seeks to achieve an end directly and by the most immediately effective means (as boycott or strike)

direct current *noun* (circa 1889)
: an electric current flowing in one direction only and substantially constant in value — abbreviation *DC*

di·rect·ed *adjective* (1891)
1 : subject to supervision or regulation ⟨a *directed* reading program for students⟩
2 : having a positive or negative sense ⟨*directed* line segment⟩
— di·rect·ed·ness *noun*

direct examination *noun* (circa 1859)
: the first examination of a witness by the party calling the witness — compare CROSS-EXAMINATION

di·rec·tion \də-'rek-shən, dī-\ *noun* (15th century)
1 : guidance or supervision of action or conduct : MANAGEMENT
2 *archaic* : SUPERSCRIPTION
3 a : an explicit instruction : ORDER **b** : assistance in pointing out the proper route — usually used in plural ⟨asked for *directions* to the beach⟩
4 : the line or course on which something is moving or is aimed to move or along which something is pointing or facing
5 *archaic* : DIRECTORATE 1
6 a : a channel or direct course of thought or action **b** : TENDENCY, TREND **c** : a guiding, governing, or motivating purpose
7 a : the art and technique of directing an orchestra, band, or a show (as for stage or screen) **b** : a word, phrase, or sign indicating the appropriate tempo, mood, or intensity of a passage or movement in music
— di·rec·tion·less \-ləs\ *adjective*
— di·rec·tion·less·ness \-nəs\ *noun*

di·rec·tion·al \-shnəl, -shə-n°l\ *adjective* (1881)
1 : of, relating to, or indicating direction in space: **a** : suitable for detecting the direction from which radio signals come or for sending out radio signals in one direction only **b** : operating most effectively in a particular direction
2 : relating to direction or guidance especially of thought or effort
— di·rec·tion·al·i·ty \-,rek-shə-'na-lə-tē\ *noun*

direction angle *noun* (circa 1909)
: an angle made by a given line with an axis of reference; *specifically* : such an angle made by a straight line with the three axes of a rectangular Cartesian coordinate system — usually used in plural

direction cosine *noun* (circa 1889)
: any of the cosines of the three angles between a directed line in space and the positive direction of the axes of a rectangular Cartesian coordinate system — usually used in plural

direction finder *noun* (1913)
: a radio receiving device for determining the direction of incoming radio waves that typically consists of a coil antenna rotating freely on a vertical axis

¹di·rec·tive \də-'rek-tiv, dī-\ *adjective* (15th century)
1 : serving or intended to guide, govern, or influence
2 : serving to point direction; *specifically* : DIRECTIONAL 1b
3 : of or relating to psychotherapy or counseling in which the counselor introduces information, content, or attitudes not previously expressed by the client

²directive *noun* (1902)
: something that serves to direct, guide, and usually impel toward an action or goal; *especially* : an authoritative instrument issued by a high-level body or official

di·rec·tiv·i·ty \də-,rek-'ti-və-tē, (,)dī-\ *noun* (1928)
: the property of being directional

direct lighting *noun* (1928)
: lighting in which the greater part of the light goes directly from the source to the area lit

¹di·rect·ly \də-'rek(t)-lē, dī-, *in sense 2 especially* də-'rek-lē *or* 'drek-lē\ *adverb* (15th century)

1 a : in a direct manner ⟨*directly* relevant⟩ ⟨the road runs *directly* east and west⟩ **b** : in immediate physical contact **c** : in the manner of direct variation
2 a : without delay : IMMEDIATELY **b** : in a little while : SHORTLY

²di·rect·ly \də-'rek(t)-lē, dī-; 'drek-lē\ *conjunction* (1795)
chiefly British : immediately after : AS SOON AS ⟨*directly* I received it I rang up the shipping company —F. W. Crofts⟩

directly proportional *noun* (1796)
: related by direct variation — compare INVERSELY PROPORTIONAL

direct mail *noun* (circa 1923)
: printed matter (as circulars) prepared for soliciting business or contributions and mailed directly to individuals

di·rect·ness \də-'rek(t)-nəs, dī-\ *noun* (1598)
1 : the character of being accurate in course or aim
2 : strict pertinence : STRAIGHTFORWARDNESS ⟨her *directness* was disarming —Robin Cook⟩

direct object *noun* (1879)
: a word or phrase denoting the goal or the result of the action of a verb

Di·rec·toire \dē-(,)rek-'twä(r), -'rek-\ *adjective* [French, from *Directoire*, the group of five officials who governed France from 1795–99, from *directeur* director] (1878)
: of, relating to, or imitative of the style of clothing, furniture, or decoration prevalent in France during the period of the Directory

di·rec·tor \də-'rek-tər, dī-\ *noun* (15th century)
: one that directs: as **a** : the head of an organized group or administrative unit (as a bureau or school) **b** : one of a group of persons entrusted with the overall direction of a corporate enterprise **c** : one that supervises the production of a show (as for stage or screen) usually with responsibility for action, lighting, music, and rehearsals **d** : CONDUCTOR c
— di·rec·tor·ship \-,ship\ *noun*

di·rec·tor·ate \də-'rek-t(ə-)rət, dī-\ *noun* (1837)
1 : the office of director
2 a : a board of directors (as of a corporation) **b** : membership on a board of directors
3 : an executive staff (as of a department)

di·rec·to·ri·al \də-,rek-'tōr-ē-əl, (,)dī-, -'tòr-\ *adjective* (1770)
1 : serving to direct
2 : of or relating to a director or to theatrical or motion-picture direction
3 : of, relating to, or administered by a directory

director's chair *noun* [from its use by motion-picture directors on the set] (1953)
: a lightweight folding armchair with a back and seat usually of cotton duck

director's chair

¹di·rec·to·ry \də-'rek-t(ə-)rē, dī-\ *adjective* (15th century)
: serving to direct; *specifically* : providing advisory but not compulsory guidance

²directory *noun, plural* **-ries** [Middle English *directorie* guide, from Medieval Latin *directorium*, from neuter of Late Latin *directorius* directorial, from Latin *dirigere*] (1543)
1 a : a book or collection of directions, rules, or ordinances **b** : an alphabetical or classified list (as of names and addresses)
2 : a body of directors

direct primary *noun* (1900)
: a primary in which nominations of candidates for office are made by direct vote

direct product *noun* (circa 1925)
: CARTESIAN PRODUCT; *especially* : a group that is the Cartesian product of two other groups

di·rec·tress \də-'rek-trəs, dī-\ *noun* (1580)
: a woman who is a director

di·rec·trice \də-ˌrek-'trēs\ *noun* [French, from Medieval Latin *directric-, directrix*] (1631)
: DIRECTRESS

di·rec·trix \-'rek-triks\ *noun, plural* **-trix·es** \-trik-səz\ *also* **-tri·ces** \-trə-ˌsēz\ [Medieval Latin, feminine of Late Latin *director*, from Latin *dirigere*] (1622)
1 *archaic* : DIRECTRESS
2 : a fixed curve with which a generatrix maintains a given relationship in generating a geometric figure; *specifically* : a straight line the distance to which from any point of a conic section is in fixed ratio to the distance from the same point to a focus

direct sum *noun* (circa 1928)
: CARTESIAN PRODUCT — compare DIRECT PRODUCT

direct tax *noun* (1801)
: a tax exacted directly from the taxpayer

direct variation *noun* (1949)
1 : mathematical relationship between two variables that can be expressed by an equation in which one variable is equal to a constant times the other
2 : an equation or function expressing direct variation — compare INVERSE VARIATION

dire·ful \'dīr-fəl\ *adjective* (1583)
1 : DREADFUL
2 : OMINOUS
— **dire·ful·ly** \-fə-lē\ *adverb*

dire wolf *noun* (1925)
: a large extinct lupine mammal (*Canis dirus*) known from Pleistocene deposits of North America

dirge \'dərj\ *noun* [Middle English *dirige*, the Office of the Dead, from the first word of a Late Latin antiphon, from Latin, imperative of *dirigere* to direct — more at DRESS] (13th century)
1 : a song or hymn of grief or lamentation; *especially* : one intended to accompany funeral or memorial rites
2 : a slow, solemn, and mournful piece of music
3 : something (as a poem) that has the qualities of a dirge ◇
— **dirge·like** \-ˌlīk\ *adjective*

dir·ham \'dir-həm\ *noun* [Arabic, from Latin *drachma* drachma] (1788)
1 — see MONEY table
2 — see *dinar, riyal* at MONEY table

¹di·ri·gi·ble \'dir-ə-jə-bəl, də-'ri-jə-\ *adjective* [Latin *dirigere*] (1581)
: capable of being steered

²dirigible *noun* [*dirigible (balloon)*] (1885)
: AIRSHIP

di·ri·gisme \di-ri-'zhi-zᵊm, dē-rē-zhēs-mᵊ\ *noun* [French, from *diriger* to direct (from Latin *dirigere*) + *-isme* -ism] (1947)
: economic planning and control by the state
— **di·ri·giste** \di-ri-'zhēst, dē-rē-\ *adjective*

¹dirk \'dərk\ *noun* [Scots *durk*] (1557)
: a long straight-bladed dagger

²dirk *transitive verb* (1599)
: to stab with a dirk

dirl \'dir(-ə)l, 'dərl\ *intransitive verb* [perhaps alteration of *thirl*] (1715)
Scottish : TREMBLE, QUIVER

dirndl \'dərn-dᵊl\ *noun* [short for German *Dirndlkleid*, from German dialect *Dirndl* girl + German *Kleid* dress] (1937)
1 : a dress style with tight bodice, short sleeves, low neck, and gathered skirt
2 : a full skirt with a tight waistband

dirt \'dərt\ *noun* [Middle English *drit*, from Old Norse; akin to Old English *drītan* to defecate] (13th century)
1 a : EXCREMENT **b** : a filthy or soiling substance (as mud, dust, or grime) **c** *archaic* : something worthless **d** : a contemptible person
2 : loose or packed soil or sand : EARTH

3 a : an abject or filthy state : SQUALOR **b** : CORRUPTION, CHICANERY **c** : licentiousness of language or theme **d** : scandalous or malicious gossip **e** : embarrassing or incriminating information

dirt·bag \'dərt-ˌbag\ *noun* (circa 1967)
slang : a dirty, unkempt, or contemptible person

dirt bike *noun* (1970)
: a usually lightweight motorcycle designed for operation on unpaved surfaces

dirt cheap *adjective or adverb* (1821)
: exceedingly cheap

dirt farmer *noun* (1920)
: a farmer who earns his living by farming his own land especially without the help of hired hands or tenants

dirt–poor \'dərt-'pu̇r\ *adjective* (1937)
: suffering extreme poverty

¹dirty \'dər-tē\ *adjective* **dirt·i·er; -est** (14th century)
1 a : not clean or pure (*dirty* clothes) **b** : likely to befoul or defile with dirt (*dirty* jobs) **c** : tedious, disagreeable, and unrecognized or thankless (had to do the *dirty* work) **d** : contaminated with infecting organisms (*dirty* wounds) **e** : containing impurities (*dirty* coal)
2 a : morally unclean or corrupt: as (1) : INDECENT, VULGAR (*dirty* jokes) (a *dirty* movie) (2) : DISHONORABLE, BASE (*dirty* tricks) (3) : UNSPORTSMANLIKE (*dirty* players) **b** : acquired by disreputable or illegal means : ILL-GOTTEN (*dirty* money)
3 a : ABOMINABLE, HATEFUL (war is a *dirty* business) **b** : highly regrettable (a *dirty* shame)
4 : FOGGY, STORMY (*dirty* weather)
5 a *of color* : not clear and bright : DULLISH (*dirty* blond) **b** : characterized by a husky, rasping, or raw tonal quality (*dirty* trumpet tones)
6 : conveying ill-natured resentment (gave him a *dirty* look)
7 : having considerable fallout (*dirty* bombs) ☆
— **dirt·i·ly** \'dər-tᵊl-ē\ *adverb*
— **dirt·i·ness** \'dər-tē-nəs\ *noun*

²dirty *adverb* **dirt·i·er; -est** (circa 1934)
: in a dirty manner: as **a** : DECEPTIVELY, UNDERHANDEDLY (fight *dirty*) **b** : INDECENTLY (talk *dirty*)

³dirty *verb* **dirt·ied; dirty·ing** (1591)
transitive verb
1 : to make dirty
2 a : to stain with dishonor : SULLY **b** : to debase by distorting the real nature of
intransitive verb
: to become soiled

dirty linen *noun* (1946)
: private matters whose public exposure brings distress and embarrassment — called also **dirty laundry**

dirty old man *noun* (1932)
: a lecherous older man

dirty pool *noun* (1940)
: underhanded or unsportsmanlike conduct

dirty rice *noun* (circa 1967)
: a Cajun dish of white rice cooked with chopped or ground giblets

dirty word *noun* (1842)
: a word, expression, or idea that is disagreeable or unpopular in a particular frame of reference

dis \'dis\ *transitive verb* **dissed; dis·sing** [perhaps short for *disrespect*] (1986)
1 *slang* : to treat with disrespect or contempt : INSULT
2 *slang* : to find fault with : CRITICIZE

Dis \'dis\ *noun* [Latin]
: the Roman god of the underworld — compare PLUTO

dis- *prefix* [Middle English *dis-, des-*, from Old French & Latin; Old French *des-, dis-*, from Latin *dis-*, literally, apart; akin to Old English *te-* apart, Latin *duo* two — more at TWO]
1 a : do the opposite of (*dis*establish) **b** : deprive of (a specified quality, rank, or object)

(*dis*franchise) **c** : exclude or expel from (*dis*bar)
2 : opposite or absence of (*dis*union) (*dis*affection)
3 : not (*dis*agreeable)
4 : completely (*dis*annul)
5 [by folk etymology] : DYS- (*dis*function)

dis·abil·i·ty \ˌdi-sə-'bi-lə-tē\ *noun* (1580)
1 a : the condition of being disabled **b** : inability to pursue an occupation because of physical or mental impairment
2 : lack of legal qualification to do something
3 : a disqualification, restriction, or disadvantage

dis·able \di-'sā-bəl, di-'zā-\ *transitive verb* **dis·abled; dis·abling** \-b(ə-)liŋ\ (15th century)
1 : to deprive of legal right, qualification, or capacity
2 : to make incapable or ineffective; *especially* : to deprive of physical, moral, or intellectual strength
synonym see WEAKEN
— **dis·able·ment** \-bəl-mənt\ *noun*

dis·abled *adjective* (1633)

☆ **SYNONYMS**

Dirty, filthy, foul, nasty, squalid mean conspicuously unclean or impure. DIRTY emphasizes the presence of dirt more than an emotional reaction to it (a *dirty* littered street). FILTHY carries a strong suggestion of offensiveness and typically of gradually accumulated dirt that begrimes and besmears (a stained greasy floor, utterly *filthy*). FOUL implies extreme offensiveness and an accumulation of what is rotten or stinking (a *foul*-smelling open sewer). NASTY applies to what is actually foul or is repugnant to one expecting freshness, cleanliness, or sweetness (it's a *nasty* job to clean up after a sick cat). In practice, *nasty* is often weakened to the point of being no more than a synonym of *unpleasant* or *disagreeable* (had a *nasty* fall) (his answer gave her a *nasty* shock). SQUALID adds to the idea of dirtiness and filth that of slovenly neglect (*squalid* slums). All these terms are also applicable to moral uncleanness or baseness or obscenity. DIRTY then stresses meanness or despicableness (don't ask me to do your *dirty* work), while FILTHY and FOUL describe disgusting obscenity or loathsome behavior (*filthy* street language) (a *foul* story of lust and greed), and NASTY implies a peculiarly offensive unpleasantness (a stand-up comedian known for *nasty* humor). Distinctively, SQUALID implies sordidness as well as baseness and dirtiness (engaged in a series of *squalid* affairs).

◇ **WORD HISTORY**

dirge *Dirge* is a borrowed word whose English meaning is derived from its use, as distinct from its meaning, in its original language. *Dirge* and its earlier form *dirige*, meaning "a song or hymn of mourning," come from the first word of a Latin chant used in the church service for the dead: "*Dirige, Domine deus meus, in conspectu tuo viam meam.*" ("Direct, O Lord my God, my way in thy sight.") Because hymns and chants were often referred to by their first words, *dirge* became the common word for this chant. Later it was used for any slow, solemn piece of music.

: incapacitated by illness, injury, or wounds; *broadly* : physically or mentally impaired

dis·abuse \,di-sə-'byüz\ *transitive verb* [French *désabuser*, from *dés-* dis- + *abuser* to abuse] (1611)
: to free from error, fallacy, or misconception

di·sac·cha·ri·dase \(,)dī-'sa-kə-rə-,dās, -,dāz\ *noun* (1961)
: an enzyme (as maltase or lactase) that hydrolyzes disaccharides

di·sac·cha·ride \(,)dī-'sa-kə-,rīd\ *noun* (1892)
: any of a class of sugars (as sucrose) that yields on hydrolysis two monosaccharide molecules

dis·ac·cord \,di-sə-'kȯrd\ *intransitive verb* [Middle English *disacorden*, from Middle French *desacorder*, from *desacort* disagreement, from *des-* dis- + *acort* accord] (15th century)
: CLASH, DISAGREE
— **disaccord** *noun*

dis·ac·cus·tom \,di-sə-'kəs-təm\ *transitive verb* [Middle French *desaccoustumer*, from Old French *desacostumer*, from *des-* dis- + *acostumer* to accustom] (1530)
: to free from a habit

¹dis·ad·van·tage \,di-səd-'van-tij\ *noun* [Middle English *disavauntage*, from Middle French *desavantage*, from Old French, from *des-* dis- + *avantage* advantage] (14th century)
1 : loss or damage especially to reputation, credit, or finances : DETRIMENT
2 a : an unfavorable, inferior, or prejudicial condition ⟨we were at a *disadvantage*⟩ **b** : HANDICAP ⟨it put us under a serious *disadvantage*⟩

²disadvantage *transitive verb* (circa 1534)
: to place at a disadvantage : HARM

dis·ad·van·taged \-tijd\ *adjective* (1648)
: lacking in the basic resources or conditions (as standard housing, medical and educational facilities, and civil rights) believed to be necessary for an equal position in society
— **dis·ad·van·taged·ness** \-tijd-nəs\ *noun*

dis·ad·van·ta·geous \(,)dis-,ad-,van-'tā-jəs, -vən-\ *adjective* (1603)
1 : constituting a disadvantage
2 : DEROGATORY, DISPARAGING
— **dis·ad·van·ta·geous·ly** *adverb*
— **dis·ad·van·ta·geous·ness** *noun*

dis·af·fect \,di-sə-'fekt\ *transitive verb* (1641)
: to alienate the affection or loyalty of
synonym see ESTRANGE
— **dis·af·fec·tion** \-'fek-shən\ *noun*

dis·af·fect·ed *adjective* (1632)
: discontented and resentful especially against authority : REBELLIOUS

dis·af·fil·i·ate \,di-sə-'fi-lē-,āt\ (1870)
transitive verb
: DISASSOCIATE
intransitive verb
: to terminate an affiliation
— **dis·af·fil·i·a·tion** \-,fil-ē-'ā-shən\ *noun*

dis·af·firm \,di-sə-'fərm\ *transitive verb* (1531)
1 : to refuse to confirm : ANNUL, REPUDIATE
2 : CONTRADICT
— **dis·af·fir·mance** \-'fər-mən(t)s\ *noun*

dis·ag·gre·gate \(,)dis-'a-gri-,gāt\ (circa 1828)
transitive verb
: to separate into component parts ⟨*disaggregate* sandstone⟩ ⟨*disaggregate* demographic data⟩
intransitive verb
: to break up or apart ⟨the molecules of a gel *disaggregate* to form a sol⟩
— **dis·ag·gre·ga·tion** \(,)dis-,a-gri-'gā-shən\ *noun*
— **dis·ag·gre·ga·tive** \(,)dis-'a-gri-,gā-tiv\ *adjective*

dis·agree \,di-sə-'grē\ *intransitive verb* [Middle English, from Middle French *desagreer*, from *des-* dis- + *agreer* to agree] (15th century)
1 : to fail to agree ⟨the two accounts *disagree*⟩
2 : to differ in opinion ⟨he *disagreed* with me on every topic⟩
3 : to cause discomfort or distress ⟨fried foods *disagree* with me⟩

dis·agree·able \-ə-bəl\ *adjective* (15th century)
1 : causing discomfort : UNPLEASANT, OFFENSIVE
2 : marked by ill temper : PEEVISH
— **dis·agree·able·ness** *noun*
— **dis·agree·ably** \-blē\ *adverb*

dis·agree·ment \,di-sə-'grē-mənt\ *noun* (15th century)
1 : the act of disagreeing
2 a : the state of being at variance : DISPARITY **b** : QUARREL

dis·al·low \,di-sə-'laů\ *transitive verb* (14th century)
1 : to deny the force, truth, or validity of
2 : to refuse to allow
— **dis·al·low·ance** \-ən(t)s\ *noun*

dis·am·big·u·ate \,di-sam-'bi-gyə-,wāt\ *transitive verb* **-at·ed; -at·ing** (1963)
: to establish a single semantic or grammatical interpretation for
— **dis·am·big·u·a·tion** \-,bi-gyə-'wā-shən\ *noun*

dis·an·nul \,di-sə-'nəl\ *transitive verb* (15th century)
: ANNUL, CANCEL

dis·ap·pear \,di-sə-'pir\ (15th century)
intransitive verb
1 : to pass from view
2 : to cease to be : pass out of existence or notice
transitive verb
: to cause the disappearance of
— **dis·ap·pear·ance** \-'pir-ən(t)s\ *noun*

dis·ap·point \,di-sə-'pȯint\ *verb* [Middle English *disapoynten*, from Middle French *desapointier*, from *des-* dis- + *apointier* to arrange — more at APPOINT] (15th century)
transitive verb
: to fail to meet the expectation or hope of : FRUSTRATE
intransitive verb
: to cause disappointment ⟨where the show *disappoints* most is in the work of the younger generation —John Ashbery⟩

dis·ap·point·ed *adjective* (1537)
1 : defeated in expectation or hope
2 *obsolete* : not adequately equipped
— **dis·ap·point·ed·ly** *adverb*

dis·ap·point·ing *adjective* (1530)
: failing to meet expectations
— **dis·ap·point·ing·ly** \-'pȯin-tiŋ-lē\ *adverb*

dis·ap·point·ment \,di-sə-'pȯint-mənt\ *noun* (1614)
1 : the act or an instance of disappointing : the state or emotion of being disappointed
2 : one that disappoints

dis·ap·pro·ba·tion \(,)di-,sa-prə-'bā-shən\ *noun* (1647)
: the act or state of disapproving : the state of being disapproved : CONDEMNATION

dis·ap·prov·al \,di-sə-'prü-vəl\ *noun* (1662)
: DISAPPROBATION, CENSURE

dis·ap·prove \-'prüv\ (1647)
transitive verb
1 : to pass unfavorable judgment on
2 : to refuse approval to : REJECT
intransitive verb
: to feel or express disapproval
— **dis·ap·prov·er** *noun*
— **dis·ap·prov·ing·ly** \-'prü-viŋ-lē\ *adverb*

dis·arm \di-'särm, -'zärm, 'di-,särm\ *verb* [Middle English *desarmen*, literally, to divest of arms, from Middle French *desarmer*, from Old French, from *des-* dis- + *armer* to arm] (14th century)
transitive verb
1 a : to deprive of means, reason, or disposition to be hostile **b** : to win over
2 a : to divest of arms **b** : to deprive of a means of attack or defense **c** : to make harmless
intransitive verb
1 : to lay aside arms
2 : to give up or reduce armed forces
— **dis·ar·ma·ment** \-'sär-mə-mənt, -'zär-\ *noun*
— **dis·arm·er** *noun*

dis·arm·ing *adjective* (1839)
: allaying criticism or hostility : INGRATIATING
— **dis·arm·ing·ly** \-'sär-miŋ-lē, -'zär-\ *adverb*

dis·ar·range \,di-sə-'rānj\ *transitive verb* (1744)
: to disturb the arrangement or order of
— **dis·ar·range·ment** \-mənt\ *noun*

¹dis·ar·ray \,di-sə-'rā\ *noun* (15th century)
1 : a lack of order or sequence : CONFUSION, DISORDER
2 : disorderly dress : DISHABILLE

²disarray *transitive verb* [Middle English *disarayen*, from Middle French *desarroyer*, from Old French *desareer*, from *des-* dis- + *areer* to array] (14th century)
1 : to throw into disorder
2 : UNDRESS

dis·ar·tic·u·late \,di-sär-'ti-kyə-,lāt\ (1830)
intransitive verb
: to become disjointed
transitive verb
: DISJOINT
— **dis·ar·tic·u·la·tion** \-,ti-kyə-'lā-shən\ *noun*

dis·as·sem·ble \,di-sə-'sem-bəl\ (1903)
transitive verb
: to take apart ⟨*disassemble* a watch⟩
intransitive verb
1 : to come apart ⟨the frame *disassembles* into sections⟩
2 : DISPERSE, SCATTER ⟨the crowd began to *disassemble*⟩
— **dis·as·sem·bly** \-blē\ *noun*

dis·as·so·ci·ate \,di-sə-'sō-sē-,āt, -shē-\ *transitive verb* (1603)
: to detach from association : DISSOCIATE
— **dis·as·so·ci·a·tion** \-,sō-sē-'ā-shən, -shē-\ *noun*

di·sas·ter \di-'zas-tər, -'sas-\ *noun* [Middle French & Old Italian; Middle French *desastre*, from Old Italian *disastro*, from *dis-* (from Latin) + *astro* star, from Latin *astrum* — more at ASTRAL] (1591)
1 : a sudden calamitous event bringing great damage, loss, or destruction; *broadly* : a sudden or great misfortune or failure
2 *obsolete* : an unfavorable aspect of a planet or star ◇

disaster area *noun* (1953)

: an area officially declared to be the scene of an emergency created by a disaster and therefore qualified to receive certain types of governmental aid (as emergency loans and relief supplies)

di·sas·trous \di-'zas-trəs *also* -'sas-\ *adjective* (1603)
1 : attended by or causing suffering or disaster : CALAMITOUS
2 : TERRIBLE, HORRENDOUS ⟨a *disastrous* score⟩
— **di·sas·trous·ly** *adverb*

dis·avow \ˌdi-sə-'vaü\ *transitive verb* [Middle English *desavowen*, from Middle French *desavouer*, from Old French, from *des-* dis- + *avouer* to avow] (14th century)
1 : to deny responsibility for : REPUDIATE
2 : to refuse to acknowledge : DISCLAIM
— **dis·avow·able** \-ə-bəl\ *adjective*
— **dis·avow·al** \-'vaü-(ə)l\ *noun*

dis·band \dis-'band\ *verb* [Middle French *desbander*, from *des-* dis- + *bande* band] (1591)
transitive verb
: to break up the organization of : DISSOLVE
intransitive verb
: to break up as an organization : DISPERSE
— **dis·band·ment** \-'ban(d)-mənt\ *noun*

dis·bar \dis-'bär\ *transitive verb* (1633)
: to expel from the bar or the legal profession : deprive (an attorney) of legal status and privileges
— **dis·bar·ment** \-mənt\ *noun*

dis·be·lief \ˌdis-bə-'lēf\ *noun* (1672)
: the act of disbelieving : mental rejection of something as untrue

dis·be·lieve \-'lēv\ (circa 1644)
transitive verb
: to hold not worthy of belief : not believe
intransitive verb
: to withhold or reject belief
— **dis·be·liev·er** *noun*

dis·ben·e·fit \(ˌ)dis-'be-nə-fit\ *noun* (1968)
: something disadvantageous or objectionable : DRAWBACK

dis·bud \(ˌ)dis-'bəd\ *transitive verb* (1727)
1 : to thin out flower buds in order to improve the quality of bloom of
2 : to dehorn (cattle) by destroying the undeveloped horn bud

dis·bur·den \(ˌ)dis-'bər-d²n\ (1532)
transitive verb
1 a : to rid of a burden ⟨*disburden* a pack animal⟩ **b** : UNBURDEN ⟨*disburden* your conscience⟩
2 : UNLOAD ⟨*disburdened* their merchandise in the town square⟩
intransitive verb
: DISCHARGE ⟨the vessels *disburdened* at the dock⟩
— **dis·bur·den·ment** \-mənt\ *noun*

dis·burse \dis-'bərs\ *transitive verb* **dis·bursed; dis·burs·ing** [Middle French *desbourser*, from Old French *desborser*, from *des-* dis- + *borser* to get money, from *borse* burse] (1530)
1 a : to pay out : expend especially from a fund **b** : to make a payment in settlement of
2 : DISTRIBUTE
— **dis·burs·er** *noun*

dis·burse·ment \-'bər-smənt\ *noun* (1596)
: the act of disbursing; *also* : funds paid out

disc *variant of* DISK

disc- *or* **disci-** *or* **disco-** *combining form* [Latin, from Greek *disk-*, *disko-*, from *diskos*]
1 : disk ⟨*discoid*⟩
2 : phonograph record ⟨*discophile*⟩

dis·calced \(ˌ)dis-'kalst\ *adjective* [part translation of Latin *discalceatus*, from *dis-* + *calceatus*, past participle of *calceare* to put on shoes, from *calceus* shoe, from *calc-, calx* heel] (1631)
: UNSHOD, BAREFOOT ⟨*discalced* friars⟩

dis·cant \'dis-ˌkant\ *variant of* DESCANT

¹dis·card \dis-'kärd, 'dis-ˌ\ (circa 1586)
transitive verb
1 : to get rid of especially as useless or unpleasant

2 a : to remove (a playing card) from one's hand **b** : to play (any card except a trump) from a suit different from the one led
intransitive verb
: to discard a playing card ☆
— **dis·card·able** \-də-bəl\ *adjective*
— **dis·card·er** *noun*

²dis·card \'dis-ˌkärd\ *noun* (1744)
1 a : the act of discarding in a card game **b** : a card discarded
2 : one that is cast off or rejected

dis·car·nate \dis-'kär-nət, -ˌnāt\ *adjective* [*dis-* + *-carnate* (as in *incarnate*)] (1895)
: having no physical body : INCORPOREAL

disc brake *noun* (1904)
: a brake that operates by the friction of a caliper pressing against the sides of a rotating disc

dis·cern \di-'sərn, -'zərn\ *verb* [Middle English, from Middle French *discerner*, from Latin *discernere* to separate, distinguish between, from *dis-* apart + *cernere* to sift — more at DIS-, CERTAIN] (14th century)
transitive verb
1 a : to detect with the eyes **b** : to detect with senses other than vision
2 : to recognize or identify as separate and distinct : DISCRIMINATE
3 : to come to know or recognize mentally
intransitive verb
: to see or understand the difference
— **dis·cern·er** *noun*
— **dis·cern·ible** *also* **dis·cern·able** \-'sər-nə-bəl, -'zər-\ *adjective*
— **dis·cern·ibly** \-blē\ *adverb*

dis·cern·ing *adjective* (1589)
: showing insight and understanding : DISCRIMINATING ⟨a *discerning* critic⟩
— **dis·cern·ing·ly** \-'sər-niŋ-lē, -'zər-\ *adverb*

dis·cern·ment \di-'sərn-mənt, -'zərn-\ *noun* (1586)
1 : the quality of being able to grasp and comprehend what is obscure : skill in discerning
2 : an act of discerning ☆

¹dis·charge \dis-'chärj, 'dis-ˌ\ *verb* [Middle English, from Middle French *descharger*, from Late Latin *discarricare*, from Latin *dis-* + Late Latin *carricare* to load — more at CHARGE] (14th century)
transitive verb
1 : to relieve of a charge, load, or burden: **a** : UNLOAD **b** : to release from an obligation **c** : to release electrical energy from (as a battery or capacitor) by a discharge
2 a : to let or put off ⟨*discharge* passengers⟩ ⟨*discharge* cargo⟩ **b** : SHOOT ⟨*discharge* an arrow⟩ **c** : to release from confinement, custody, or care ⟨*discharge* a prisoner⟩ **d** : to give outlet or vent to : EMIT
3 a (1) : to dismiss from employment (2) : to release from service or duty ⟨*discharge* a soldier⟩ **b** : to get rid of (as a debt or obligation) by performing an appropriate action (as payment) **c** : to set aside : ANNUL **d** : to order (a legislative committee) to end consideration of a bill in order to bring it before the house for action
4 : to bear and distribute (as the weight of a wall above an opening)
5 : to bleach out or remove (color or dye) in dyeing and printing textiles
6 : to cancel the record of the loan of (a library book) upon return
intransitive verb
1 a : to throw off or deliver a load, charge, or burden **b** : to release electrical energy by a discharge

2 a : GO OFF, FIRE — used of a gun **b** : SPREAD, RUN ⟨some dyes *discharge*⟩ **c** : to pour forth fluid or other contents
synonym SEE PERFORM
— **dis·charge·able** \-jə-bəl\ *adjective*
— **dis·charg·ee** \(ˌ)dis-ˌchär-'jē\ *noun*
— **dis·charg·er** \-'dis-'chär-jər, 'dis-ˌ\ *noun*

²dis·charge \'dis-ˌchärj, dis-'\ *noun* (14th century)
1 a : the act of relieving of something that oppresses : RELEASE **b** : something that discharges or releases; *especially* : a certification of release or payment
2 : the state of being discharged or relieved
3 : the act of discharging or unloading
4 : legal release from confinement
5 : a firing off
6 a : a flowing or issuing out ⟨a *discharge* of spores⟩; *also* : a rate of flow **b** : something that is emitted ⟨a purulent *discharge*⟩
7 : the act of removing an obligation or liability
8 a : release or dismissal especially from an office or employment **b** : complete separation from military service
9 a : the equalization of a difference of electric potential between two points **b** : the conversion of the chemical energy of a battery into electrical energy

discharge lamp *noun* (1936)
: an electric lamp in which an enclosed gas or vapor glows or causes a phosphor coating on the lamp's inner surface to glow

discharge tube *noun* (1898)

disc brake: *1* caliper, *2* disc

: an electron tube which contains gas or vapor at low pressure and through which conduction takes place when a high voltage is applied

disci- — see DISC-

dis·ci·form \'di-sə-ˌfȯrm\ *adjective* (1830)
: round or oval in shape

dis·ci·ple \di-'sī-pəl\ *noun* [Middle English, from Old English *discipul* & Old French *desciple*, from Late Latin and Latin; Late Latin *discipulus* follower of Jesus Christ in his lifetime, from Latin, pupil] (before 12th century)
1 : one who accepts and assists in spreading the doctrines of another: as **a** : one of the twelve in the inner circle of Christ's followers according to the Gospel accounts **b** : a convinced adherent of a school or individual
2 *capitalized* : a member of the Disciples of Christ founded in the U.S. in 1809 that holds the Bible alone to be the rule of faith and practice, usually baptizes by immersion, and has a congregational polity
synonym see FOLLOWER
— **dis·ci·ple·ship** \-ˌship\ *noun*

dis·ci·plin·able \ˌdi-sə-'pli-nə-bəl; 'di-sə-pli-\ *adjective* (15th century)
1 : DOCILE, TEACHABLE
2 : subject to or deserving discipline ⟨a *disciplinable* offense⟩

dis·ci·pli·nar·i·an \ˌdi-sə-plə-'ner-ē-ən\ *noun* (1639)
: one who disciplines or enforces order
— **disciplinarian** *adjective*

dis·ci·plin·ary \'di-sə-plə-ˌner-ē, *especially British* ˌdi-sə-'pli-nə-rē\ *adjective* (1598)
1 a : of or relating to discipline **b** : designed to correct or punish breaches of discipline ⟨took *disciplinary* action⟩
2 : of or relating to a particular field of study
— **dis·ci·plin·ar·i·ly** \ˌdi-sə-plə-'ner-ə-lē\ *adverb*
— **dis·ci·plin·ar·i·ty** \-'nar-ə-tē\ *noun*

¹dis·ci·pline \'di-sə-plən\ *noun* [Middle English, from Old French & Latin; Old French, from Latin *disciplina* teaching, learning, from *discipulus* pupil] (13th century)
1 : PUNISHMENT
2 *obsolete* : INSTRUCTION
3 : a field of study
4 : training that corrects, molds, or perfects the mental faculties or moral character
5 a : control gained by enforcing obedience or order **b** : orderly or prescribed conduct or pattern of behavior **c** : SELF-CONTROL
6 : a rule or system of rules governing conduct or activity
— **dis·ci·plin·al** \-plə-nᵊl\ *adjective*

²discipline *transitive verb* **-plined; -plin·ing** (14th century)
1 : to punish or penalize for the sake of discipline
2 : to train or develop by instruction and exercise especially in self-control
3 a : to bring (a group) under control ⟨*discipline* troops⟩ **b** : to impose order upon ⟨serious writers *discipline* and refine their writing styles⟩
synonym see PUNISH, TEACH
— **dis·ci·plin·er** *noun*

dis·ci·plined *adjective* (14th century)
: marked by or possessing discipline ⟨a *disciplined* mind⟩

disc jockey *noun* (1941)
: an announcer of a radio show of popular recorded music; *also* : one who plays recorded music for dancing at a nightclub or party

dis·claim \dis-'klām\ *verb* [Middle English, from Anglo-French *disclaimer*, from *dis-* + *claimer* to claim, from Old French *clamer*] (15th century)
intransitive verb
1 : to make a disclaimer
2 a *obsolete* : to disavow all part or share **b** : to utter denial
transitive verb
1 : to renounce a legal claim to

2 : DENY, DISAVOW ⟨*disclaimed* any knowledge of the contents of the letter⟩

dis·claim·er \-'klā-mər\ *noun* (15th century)
1 a : a denial or disavowal of legal claim : relinquishment of or formal refusal to accept an interest or estate **b** : a writing that embodies a legal disclaimer
2 a : DENIAL, DISAVOWAL **b** : REPUDIATION

dis·cla·ma·tion \ˌdis-klə-'mā-shən\ *noun* (1592)
: RENUNCIATION, DISAVOWAL

dis·cli·max \(ˌ)dis-'klī-ˌmaks\ *noun* (1935)
: a relatively stable ecological community often including kinds of organisms foreign to the region and displacing the climax because of disturbance especially by man

¹dis·close \dis-'klōz\ *transitive verb* [Middle English, from Middle French *desclos-*, stem of *desclore* to disclose, from Medieval Latin *disclaudere* to open, from Latin *dis-* + *claudere* to close — more at CLOSE] (14th century)
1 *obsolete* : to open up
2 a : to expose to view **b** *archaic* : HATCH **c** : to make known or public ⟨demands that politicians *disclose* the sources of their income⟩
synonym see REVEAL
— **dis·clos·er** *noun*

²disclose *noun* (1548)
obsolete : DISCLOSURE

dis·clos·ing \-'klō-ziŋ\ *adjective* (1965)
: being or using an agent (as a tablet or liquid) that contains a usually red dye that stains dental plaque

dis·clo·sure \dis-'klō-zhər\ *noun* (circa 1598)
1 : the act or an instance of disclosing : EXPOSURE
2 : something disclosed : REVELATION

¹dis·co \'dis-(ˌ)kō\ *noun, plural* **discos** [short for *discotheque*] (1964)
1 : a nightclub for dancing to live and recorded music
2 : popular dance music characterized by hypnotic rhythm, repetitive lyrics, and electronically produced sounds

²disco *intransitive verb* (1979)
: to dance to disco music

disco- — see DISC-

dis·cog·ra·pher \dis-'kä-grə-fər\ *noun* (1941)
: a person who compiles discographies

dis·cog·ra·phy \-fē\ *noun, plural* **-phies** [French *discographie*, from *disc-* + *-graphie* -graphy] (1933)
1 : a descriptive list of phonograph records by category, composer, performer, or date of release
2 : the history of recorded music
— **dis·co·graph·i·cal** \ˌdis-kə-'gra-fi-kəl\ *also* **dis·co·graph·ic** \-fik\ *adjective*

dis·coid \'dis-ˌkȯid\ *adjective* [Late Latin *discoides* quoit-shaped, from Greek *diskoeidēs*, from *diskos* disk] (1794)
1 : relating to or having a disk: as **a** *of a composite floret* : situated in the floral disk **b** *of a composite flower head* : having only tubular florets
2 : flat and circular like a disc

dis·coi·dal \dis-'kȯi-dᵊl\ *adjective* (circa 1706)
: of, resembling, or producing a disk

discoidal cleavage *noun* (circa 1909)
: meroblastic cleavage in which a disk of cells is produced at the animal pole of the zygote (as in bird eggs)

dis·col·or \(ˌ)dis-'kə-lər\ *verb* [Middle English *discolouren*, from Middle French *descolourer*, from Late Latin *discolorari*, from Latin *discolor* of another color, from *dis-* + *color* color] (14th century)
transitive verb
: to alter or change the hue or color of
intransitive verb
: to change color especially for the worse

dis·col·or·ation \(ˌ)dis-ˌkə-lə-'rā-shən\ *noun* (1642)
1 : the act of discoloring : the state of being discolored

2 : a discolored spot or formation : STAIN

dis·com·bob·u·late \ˌdis-kəm-'bä-b(y)ə-ˌlāt\ *transitive verb* **-lat·ed; -lat·ing** [probably alteration of *discompose*] (circa 1916)
: UPSET, CONFUSE ⟨the offensive had *discombobulated* all the German defensive arrangements —A. J. Liebling⟩
— **dis·com·bob·u·la·tion** \-ˌbä-b(y)ə-'lā-shən\ *noun*

¹dis·com·fit \dis-'kəm(p)-fət, *especially Southern* ˌdis-kəm-'fit\ *transitive verb* [Middle English, from Old French *desconfit*, past participle of *desconfire*, from *des-* dis- + *confire* to prepare — more at COMFIT] (13th century)
1 a *archaic* : to defeat in battle **b** : to frustrate the plans of : THWART
2 : to put into a state of perplexity and embarrassment : DISCONCERT
synonym see EMBARRASS

²discomfit *noun* (15th century)
: DISCOMFITURE

dis·com·fi·ture \dis-'kəm(p)-fə-ˌchür, -chər, *especially Southern* -ˌt(y)ùr\ *noun* (14th century)
: the act of discomfiting : the state of being discomfited

¹dis·com·fort \dis-'kəm(p)-fərt\ *transitive verb* [Middle English, from Middle French *desconforter*, from Old French, from *des-* dis- + *conforter* to comfort] (14th century)
1 *archaic* : DISMAY
2 : to make uncomfortable or uneasy
— **dis·com·fort·able** \-'kəm(p)-fər-tə-bəl, -'kəm(p)f-tər-bəl\ *adjective*

²discomfort *noun* (14th century)
1 *archaic* : DISTRESS, GRIEF
2 : mental or physical uneasiness : ANNOYANCE

dis·com·mend \ˌdis-kə-'mend\ *transitive verb* [Middle English *dyscommenden*] (15th century)
1 : DISAPPROVE, DISPARAGE
2 : to cause to be viewed unfavorably

dis·com·mode \ˌdis-kə-'mōd\ *transitive verb* **-mod·ed; -mod·ing** [Middle French *discommoder*, from *dis-* + *commode* convenient — more at COMMODE] (circa 1721)
: to cause inconvenience to : TROUBLE

dis·com·pose \ˌdis-kəm-'pōz\ *transitive verb* [Middle English] (15th century)
1 : to destroy the composure of
2 : to disturb the order of ☆
— **dis·com·po·sure** \-'pō-zhər\ *noun*

dis·con·cert \ˌdis-kən-'sərt\ *transitive verb* [obsolete French *disconcerter*, alteration of Middle French *desconcerter*, from *des-* dis- + *concerter* to concert] (1687)
1 : to throw into confusion

☆ **SYNONYMS**
Discompose, disquiet, disturb, perturb, agitate, upset, fluster mean to destroy capacity for collected thought or decisive action. DISCOMPOSE implies some degree of loss of self-control or self-confidence especially through emotional stress ⟨*discomposed* by the loss of his beloved wife⟩. DISQUIET suggests loss of sense of security or peace of mind ⟨the *disquieting* news of factories closing⟩. DISTURB implies interference with one's mental processes caused by worry, perplexity, or interruption ⟨the discrepancy in accounts *disturbed* me⟩. PERTURB implies deep disturbance of mind and emotions ⟨*perturbed* by her husband's strange behavior⟩. AGITATE suggests obvious external signs of nervous or emotional excitement ⟨in his *agitated* state we could see he was unable to work⟩. UPSET implies the disturbance of normal or habitual functioning by disappointment, distress, or grief ⟨the family's constant bickering *upsets* the youngest child⟩. FLUSTER suggests bewildered agitation ⟨his declaration of love completely *flustered* her⟩.

2 : to disturb the composure of
synonym see EMBARRASS
— **dis·con·cert·ing** *adjective*
— **dis·con·cert·ing·ly** \-tiŋ-lē\ *adverb*
— **dis·con·cert·ment** \-mənt\ *noun*

dis·con·firm \,dis-kən-'fərm\ *transitive verb* (1936)
: to deny the validity of

dis·con·for·mi·ty \,dis-kən-'fòr-mə-tē\ *noun* (1587)
1 : NONCONFORMITY
2 : a break in a sequence of sedimentary rocks all of which have approximately the same dip

dis·con·nect \,dis-kə-'nekt\ (1770) *transitive verb*
1 : to terminate a connection
2 : to sever the connection of or between
~ *intransitive verb*
1 : to terminate a connection
2 : to become detached or withdrawn (*discon*-nects into dark moods)

dis·con·nect·ed *adjective* (1783)
1 : not connected : SEPARATE; *also* : INCOHERENT
— **dis·con·nect·ed·ly** *adverb*
— **dis·con·nect·ed·ness** *noun*

dis·con·so·late \dis-'kän(t)-sə-lət\ *adjective* [Middle English, from Medieval Latin *disconsolatus*, from Latin *dis-* + *consolatus*, past participle of *consolari* to console] (14th century)
1 : CHEERLESS (a clutch of *disconsolate* houses —D. H. Lawrence)
2 : DEJECTED, DOWNCAST (the team returned *disconsolate* from three losses)
— **dis·con·so·late·ly** *adverb*
— **dis·con·so·late·ness** *noun*

dis·con·so·la·tion \(,)dis-,kän(t)-sə-'lā-shən\ *noun*

¹**dis·con·tent** \,dis-kən-'tent\ *adjective* (15th century)
: DISCONTENTED

²**discontent** *transitive verb* (1549)
: to make discontented

³**discontent** *noun* (1591)
1 : lack of contentment : *also* : a sense of grievance : DISSATISFACTION (the winter of our *discontent* —Shakespeare) b : restless aspiration for improvement

⁴**discontent** *noun* (14th century)
: one who is discontented : MALCONTENT

dis·con·tent·ed *adjective* (1525)
: DISSATISFIED, MALCONTENT
— **dis·con·tent·ed·ly** *adverb*
— **dis·con·tent·ed·ness** *noun*

dis·con·tent·ment \-mənt\ *noun*

dis·con·tin·u·ance \,dis-kən-'tin-yə-wən(t)s\ *noun* (14th century)
1 : the act or an instance of discontinuing
2 : the interruption or termination of a legal action by the plaintiff's not continuing it

dis·con·tin·u·a·tion \(,)dis-,kän-tə-'nü-ā-shən\ *noun* (1570)
synonym see STOP

dis·con·tin·ue \,dis-kən-'tin-(,)yü, -yə(-w)\ *verb* [Middle English, from Middle French *discontinuer*, from Medieval Latin *discontinuare*, from Latin *dis-* + *continuare* to continue] (14th century)
transitive verb
1 : to break the continuity of : cease to operate, administer, use, produce, or take
2 : to abandon or terminate by a legal action
~ *intransitive verb*
1 : to come to an end
2 : to cease to be subscribed for
synonym see STOP

dis·con·ti·nu·i·ty \,dis-,kän-tə-'nü-ə-tē, -'nyü-\ *noun* (1570)
1 : lack of continuity or cohesion
2 : GAP 5
3 a : the property of being not mathematically continuous (a point of *discontinuity*) b : an instance of being not mathematically continuous

dis·con·tin·u·ous \,dis-kən-'tin-yə-wəs\ *adjective* (1718)
1 a (1) : not continuous (a *discontinuous* series of events) (2) : not continued : DISCRETE b : lacking sequence or coherence
2 : having one or more mathematical discontinuities — used of a variable or a function
— **dis·con·tin·u·ous·ly** *adverb*

¹**dis·cord** \'dis-,kord\ *noun* (13th century)
1 a : lack of agreement or harmony (as between persons, things, or ideas) b : active quarreling or conflict resulting from discord
2 a (1) : a combination of musical sounds that strikes the ear harshly (2) : DISSONANCE b : a harsh or unpleasant sound

²**dis·cord** \dis-'kord, dis-'\ *intransitive verb* (14th century)
: DISAGREE, CLASH

dis·cor·dance \dis-'kor-d°n(t)s\ *noun* (1607)
1 : DISCORDANCE
2 : DISSONANCE

dis·cor·dan·cy \-d°n-sē\ *noun, plural* **-cies** (14th century)
: DISCORDANCE

dis·cor·dant \dis-'kord°nt\ *adjective* (14th century)
1 a : being at variance : DISAGREEING b : QUARRELSOME
2 : relating to a discord
— **dis·cor·dant·ly** *adverb*

dis·co·theque *or* **discothèque** \'dis-kə-,tek, ,dis-kə-'\ *noun* [French *discothèque*, from *disque* disk, record + *-o-* + *-theque* (as in *bibliothèque* library)] (1954)
: DISCO 1

¹**dis·count** \'dis-,kaunt\ *noun* (1622)
1 a : a reduction made from the gross amount or value of something : as a (1) : a reduction made from a regular or list price (2) : a proportionate deduction from a debt account usually made for cash or prompt payment b : a deduction from interest in advancing money upon or purchasing a bill or note not due
2 : the act or practice of discounting
3 a : a deduction taken or allowance made

²**dis·count** \'dis-,kaunt, dis-'\ *verb* [modification of French *décompter*, from Medieval Latin *discomputare*, from Latin *dis-* + *computare* to count] (1629)
transitive verb
1 a : to make a deduction from usually for cash or prompt payment b : to sell or offer for sale at a discount
2 : to lend money on after deducting the discount
3 a : to leave out of account : DISREGARD b : to minimize the importance of c (1) : to make allowance for bias or exaggeration in (2) : to view with doubt d : to take into account (as a future event) in present calculations
~ *intransitive verb*
: to give or make discounts
— **dis·count·er** \-,kaun-tər, -'kaun-\ *noun*

³**dis·count** \'dis-,kaunt\ *adjective* (1889)
1 a : selling goods or services at a discount (*discount* stores) (a *discount* broker) (*discount* airlines) b : offered or sold at a discount
2 : reflecting a discount (*discount* prices) (*discount* period)

dis·count·able \,dis-'kaun-tə-bəl, 'dis-,\ *adjective* (1800)
1 : set apart for discounting (within the *discountable* period)
2 : subject to being discounted (a *discountable* note)

¹**dis·coun·te·nance** \dis-'kaunt-nən(t)s, -'kaun-tə-\ *transitive verb* (1580)
1 : ABASH, DISCONCERT
2 : to look with disfavor on : discourage by evidence of disapproval

²**discountenance** *noun* (1580)
: DISAPPROBATION, DISFAVOR

discount rate *noun* (circa 1927)
1 : the interest on an annual basis deducted in advance on a loan
2 : the charge levied by a central bank for advances and rediscounts

dis·cour·age \dis-'kər-ij, -'kə-rij\ *transitive verb* **-aged; -ag·ing** [Middle English *discoragen*, from Middle French *descouragier*, from Old French *descoragier*, from *des-* dis- + *corage* courage] (15th century)
1 : to deprive of courage or confidence : DISHEARTEN
2 a : to hinder by disfavoring b : to attempt to dissuade
— **dis·cour·age·able** \-jə-bəl\ *adjective*
— **dis·cour·age·ment** \-mənt\ *noun*
— **dis·cour·ag·er** *noun*
— **dis·cour·ag·ing·ly** \-jiŋ-lē\ *adverb*

¹**dis·course** \'dis-,kors, -,kórs, dis-'\ *noun* [Middle English *discours*, from Medieval Latin & Late Latin *discursus*; Medieval Latin, argument, act of running about, from Late Latin, conversation, from Latin, act of running about, from *discurrere* to run on — more at CAR] (14th century)
1 *archaic* : the capacity of orderly thought or procedure : RATIONALITY
2 : verbal interchange of ideas; *especially* : CONVERSATION
3 a : formal and orderly and usually extended expression of thought on a subject b : connected speech or writing c : a linguistic unit (as a conversation or a story) larger than a sentence
4 *obsolete* : social familiarity

²**dis·course** \'dis-,kors, -,kórs, dis-'\ *verb* **dis·coursed; dis·cours·ing** (1559)
intransitive verb
1 : to express oneself especially in oral discourse

☆ **SYNONYMS**
Discord, strife, conflict, contention, dissension, variance mean a state or condition marked by a lack of agreement or harmony. DISCORD implies an intrinsic or essential lack of harmony producing quarreling, factiousness, or antagonism (a political party long racked by *discord*). STRIFE emphasizes a struggle for superiority rather than the incongruity or incompatibility of the persons or things involved (during his brief reign the empire was never free of civil *strife*). CONFLICT applies to a sharp disagreement or collision in interests or ideas and stresses the clash of forces in opposition but in static applications implies an irreconcilability as of duties or desires (the new zoning law). CONTENTION applies to strife or competition that shows itself in quarreling, disputing, or controversy (several points of *contention* about the new zoning law). DISSENSION implies strife or discord and stresses a division into factions (religious *dissension* threatened to split the colony). VARIANCE implies a clash between persons or things owing to a difference in nature, opinion, or interest (cultural *variances* that work against a national identity).

2 : TALK, CONVERSE
transitive verb
archaic : to give forth : UTTER
— **dis·cours·er** *noun*

discourse analysis *noun* (1952)
: the study of linguistic relations and structures in discourse

dis·cour·te·ous \(ˌ)dis-ˈkər-tē-əs\ *adjective* (1578)
: lacking courtesy : RUDE
— **dis·cour·te·ous·ly** *adverb*
— **dis·cour·te·ous·ness** *noun*

dis·cour·te·sy \ˈ-ˌkər-tə-sē\ *noun* (1555)
1 : RUDENESS
2 : a rude act

dis·cov·er \dis-ˈkə-vər\ *verb* **dis·cov·ered; dis·cov·er·ing** \-ˈkə-v(ə-)riŋ\ [Middle English, from Middle French *descovrir*, from Late Latin *discooperire*, from Latin *dis-* + *cooperire* to cover — more at COVER] (14th century)
transitive verb
1 a : to make known or visible : EXPOSE **b** *archaic* : DISPLAY
2 a : to obtain sight or knowledge of for the first time ⟨*discover* the solution⟩ **b** : FIND OUT ⟨*discovered* he was out of gas⟩
intransitive verb
: to make a discovery
— **dis·cov·er·able** \-ˈkə-v(ə-)rə-bəl\ *adjective*

dis·cov·er·er \-ər-ər\ *noun*

dis·cov·ery \dis-ˈkə-v(ə-)rē\ *noun, plural* **-er·ies** (1539)
1 a : the act or process of discovering **b** (1) *archaic* : DISCLOSURE (2) *obsolete* : DISPLAY **c** *obsolete* : EXPLORATION
2 : something discovered
3 : the usually pretrial disclosure of pertinent facts or documents by one or both parties to a legal action or proceeding

Discovery Day *noun* (circa 1913)
: COLUMBUS DAY

¹**dis·cred·it** \(ˌ)dis-ˈkre-dət\ *transitive verb* (1559)
1 : to refuse to accept as true or accurate : DISBELIEVE
2 : to cause disbelief in the accuracy or authority of
3 : to deprive of good repute : DISGRACE

²**discredit** *noun* (1565)
1 : loss of credit or reputation ⟨I knew stories to the *discredit* of England —W. B. Yeats⟩
2 : lack or loss of belief or confidence : DOUBT ⟨contradictions cast *discredit* on his testimony⟩

dis·cred·it·able \-ˈta-bəl\ *adjective* (1640)
: injurious to reputation : DISGRACEFUL
— **dis·cred·it·ably** \-blē\ *adverb*

dis·creet \di-ˈskrēt\ *adjective* [Middle English, from Middle French *discret*, from Medieval Latin *discretus*, from Latin, past participle of *discernere* to separate, distinguish between — more at DISCERN] (14th century)
1 : having or showing discernment or good judgment in conduct and especially in speech : PRUDENT; *especially* : capable of preserving prudent silence
2 : UNPRETENTIOUS, MODEST ⟨the warmth and *discreet* elegance of a civilized home —Joseph Wechsberg⟩
3 : UNOBTRUSIVE, UNNOTICEABLE ⟨followed at a *discreet* distance⟩
— **dis·creet·ly** *adverb*
— **dis·creet·ness** *noun*

dis·crep·an·cy \dis-ˈkre-pən-sē\ *noun, plural* **-cies** (circa 1623)
1 : the quality or state of being discrepant
2 : an instance of being discrepant

dis·crep·ant \-pənt\ *adjective* [Middle English *discrepaunt*, from Latin *discrepant-, discrepans*, present participle of *discrepare* to sound discordantly, from *dis-* + *crepare* to rattle, creak — more at RAVEN] (15th century)
: being at variance : DISAGREEING ⟨widely *discrepant* conclusions⟩
— **dis·crep·ant·ly** *adverb*

dis·crete \dis-ˈkrēt, ˈdis-ˌ\ *adjective* [Middle English, from Latin *discretus*] (14th century)
1 : constituting a separate entity : individually distinct
2 a : consisting of distinct or unconnected elements : NONCONTINUOUS **b** : taking on or having a finite or countably infinite number of values ⟨*discrete* probabilities⟩ ⟨a *discrete* random variable⟩
synonym see DISTINCT
— **dis·crete·ly** *adverb*
— **dis·crete·ness** *noun*

dis·cre·tion \dis-ˈkre-shən\ *noun* (14th century)
1 : the quality of being discreet : CIRCUMSPECTION; *especially* : cautious reserve in speech
2 : ability to make responsible decisions
3 a : individual choice or judgment ⟨left the decision to his *discretion*⟩ **b** : power of free decision or latitude of choice within certain legal bounds ⟨reached the age of *discretion*⟩
4 : the result of separating or distinguishing

dis·cre·tion·ary \-ˈkre-shə-ˌner-ē\ *adjective* (1698)
1 : left to discretion : exercised at one's own discretion
2 : available for discretionary use ⟨*discretionary* purchasing power⟩

discretionary account *noun* (circa 1920)
: a security or commodity market account in which an agent (as a broker) is given power of attorney so as to be able to make independent decisions and buy and sell for the principal's account

dis·crim·i·na·bil·i·ty \-ˌkri-mə-nə-ˈbi-lə-tē\ *noun, plural* **-ties** (circa 1901)
1 : the quality of being discriminable
2 : the ability to discriminate

dis·crim·i·na·ble \dis-ˈkri-mə-nə-bəl\ *adjective* (1736)
: capable of being discriminated
— **dis·crim·i·na·bly** \-blē\ *adverb*

dis·crim·i·nant \-ˈkri-mə-nənt\ *noun* (circa 1948)
: a mathematical expression providing a criterion for the behavior of another more complicated expression, relation, or set of relations

discriminant function *noun* (circa 1936)
: a function of a set of variables (as measurements of taxonomic specimens) that is evaluated for samples of events or objects and used as an aid in discriminating between or classifying them

dis·crim·i·nate \dis-ˈkri-mə-ˌnāt\ *verb* **-nat·ed; -nat·ing** [Latin *discriminatus*, past participle of *discriminare*, from *discrimin-, discrimen* distinction, from *discernere* to distinguish between — more at DISCERN] (1628)
transitive verb
1 a : to mark or perceive the distinguishing or peculiar features of **b** : DISTINGUISH, DIFFERENTIATE ⟨*discriminate* hundreds of colors⟩
2 : to distinguish by discerning or exposing differences; *especially* : to distinguish from another like object
intransitive verb
1 a : to make a distinction ⟨*discriminate* among historical sources⟩ **b** : to use good judgment
2 : to make a difference in treatment or favor on a basis other than individual merit ⟨*discriminate* in favor of your friends⟩ ⟨*discriminate* against a certain nationality⟩

dis·crim·i·nat·ing *adjective* (1647)
1 : making a distinction : DISTINGUISHING
2 : marked by discrimination: **a** : DISCERNING, JUDICIOUS **b** : DISCRIMINATORY
— **dis·crim·i·nat·ing·ly** \-ˌnā-tiŋ-lē\ *adverb*

dis·crim·i·na·tion \dis-ˌkri-mə-ˈnā-shən\ *noun* (1648)

1 a : the act of discriminating **b** : the process by which two stimuli differing in some aspect are responded to differently
2 : the quality or power of finely distinguishing
3 a : the act, practice, or an instance of discriminating categorically rather than individually **b** : prejudiced or prejudicial outlook, action, or treatment ⟨racial *discrimination*⟩
synonym see DISCERNMENT
— **dis·crim·i·na·tion·al** \-shnəl, -shə-nᵊl\ *adjective*

dis·crim·i·na·tive \dis-ˈkri-mə-ˌnā-tiv, -ˈkri-mə-nə-ˌtiv, -ˈkri-mə-nə-tiv\ *adjective* (1677)
1 : making distinctions
2 : DISCRIMINATORY 2

dis·crim·i·na·tor \dis-ˈkri-mə-ˌnā-tər\ *noun* (1828)
: one that discriminates; *especially* : a circuit that can be adjusted to accept or reject signals of different characteristics (as amplitude or frequency)

dis·crim·i·na·to·ry \dis-ˈkri-mə-nə-ˌtōr-ē, -ˈtȯr-, -ˈkri-mə-nə-ˌtōr-ē\ *adjective* (1828)
1 : DISCRIMINATIVE 1
2 : applying or favoring discrimination in treatment

dis·crim·i·na·to·ri·ly \-ˌkri-mə-nə-ˈtōr-ə-lē, -ˈtȯr-, -ˌkri-mə-ˈtōr-\ *adverb*

dis·cur·sive \dis-ˈkər-siv\ *adjective* [Medieval Latin *discursivus*, from Latin *discursus*, past participle of *discurrere* to run about — more at DISCOURSE] (1598)
1 a : moving from topic to topic without order or coherence **b** : proceeding coherently from topic to topic
2 : marked by analytical reasoning
— **dis·cur·sive·ly** *adverb*
— **dis·cur·sive·ness** *noun*

dis·cus \ˈdis-kəs\ *noun, plural* **dis·cus·es** [Latin — more at DISH] (1656)
: a disk (as of wood or plastic) that is thicker in the center than at the perimeter and that is hurled for distance as a track-and-field event; *also* : the event

discus

dis·cuss \di-ˈskəs\ *transitive verb* [Middle English, from Latin *discussus*, past participle of *discutere* to disperse, from *dis-* apart + *quatere* to shake — more at DIS-, QUASH] (14th century)
1 *obsolete* : DISPEL
2 a : to investigate by reasoning or argument **b** : to present in detail for examination or consideration ⟨*discussed* plans for the party⟩ **c** : to talk about

☆ SYNONYMS

Discover, ascertain, determine, unearth, learn mean to find out what one did not previously know. DISCOVER may apply to something requiring exploration or investigation or to a chance encounter ⟨*discovered* the source of the river⟩. ASCERTAIN implies effort to find the facts or the truth proceeding from awareness of ignorance or uncertainty ⟨attempts to *ascertain* the population of the region⟩. DETERMINE emphasizes the intent to establish the facts definitely or precisely ⟨unable to *determine* the origin of the word⟩. UNEARTH implies bringing to light something forgotten or hidden ⟨*unearth* old records⟩. LEARN may imply acquiring knowledge with little effort or conscious intention (as by simply being told) or it may imply study and practice ⟨I *learned* her name only today⟩ ⟨*learning* Greek⟩.

3 *obsolete* : DECLARE ☆
— **dis·cuss·able** *or* **dis·cuss·ible** \-'skə-sə-bəl\ *adjective*
— **dis·cuss·er** *noun*
dis·cus·sant \di-'skə-sᵊnt\ *noun* (1926)
: one who takes part in a formal discussion or symposium
dis·cus·sion \di-'skə-shən\ *noun* (14th century)
1 : consideration of a question in open and usually informal debate
2 : a formal treatment of a topic in speech or writing
¹dis·dain \dis-'dān\ *noun* [Middle English *desdeyne*, from Old French *desdeign*, from *desdeignier*] (14th century)
: a feeling of contempt for what is beneath one : SCORN
²disdain *transitive verb* [Middle English *desdeynen*, from Middle French *desdeignier*, from Old French, from (assumed) Vulgar Latin *disdignare*, from Latin *dis-* + *dignare* to deign — more at DEIGN] (14th century)
1 : to look on with scorn
2 : to refuse or abstain from because of disdain
3 : to treat as beneath one's notice or dignity
synonym see DESPISE
dis·dain·ful \-fəl\ *adjective* (circa 1542)
: full of or expressing disdain
synonym see PROUD
— **dis·dain·ful·ly** \-fə-lē\ *adverb*
— **dis·dain·ful·ness** *noun*
dis·ease \di-'zēz\ *noun* [Middle English *disese*, from Middle French *desaise*, from *des-* + *aise* ease] (14th century)
1 *obsolete* : TROUBLE
2 : a condition of the living animal or plant body or of one of its parts that impairs normal functioning : SICKNESS, MALADY
3 : a harmful development (as in a social institution)
— **dis·eased** \-'zēzd\ *adjective*
dis·econ·o·my \di-si-'kä-nə-mē\ *noun* (1937)
1 : a lack of economy
2 : a factor responsible for an increase in cost
dis·em·bark \di-səm-'bärk\ *verb* [Middle French *desembarquer*, from *des-* dis- + *embarquer* to embark] (1582)
transitive verb
: to remove to shore from a ship
intransitive verb
1 : to go ashore out of a ship
2 : to get out of a vehicle or craft
— **dis·em·bar·ka·tion** \(ˌ)di-ˌsem-ˌbär-'kā-shən, -bər-\ *noun*
dis·em·bar·rass \di-səm-'bar-əs\ *transitive verb* (1726)
: to free (as oneself) from something troublesome or superfluous
synonym see EXTRICATE
dis·em·body \di-səm-'bä-dē\ *transitive verb* (1714)
: to divest of a body, of corporeal existence, or of reality
dis·em·bogue \di-sim-'bōg\ *verb* -**bogued**; -**bogu·ing** [modification of Spanish *desembocar*, from *des-* (from Latin *dis-*) + *embocar* to put into the mouth, from *en* in (from Latin *in*) + *boca* mouth, from Latin *bucca*] (1595)
intransitive verb
: to flow or come forth from or as if from a channel
transitive verb
archaic : to pour out from or as if from a container
dis·em·bow·el \di-səm-'bau̇(-ə)l\ *transitive verb* (1618)
1 : to take out the bowels of : EVISCERATE
2 : to remove the substance of
— **dis·em·bow·el·ment** \-mənt\ *noun*
dis·en·chant \di-sᵊn-'chant\ *transitive verb* [Middle French *desenchanter*, from *des-* dis- + *enchanter* to enchant] (circa 1586)

: to free from illusion
— **dis·en·chant·er** *noun*
— **dis·en·chant·ing** *adjective*
— **dis·en·chant·ing·ly** \-'chan-tiŋ-lē\ *adverb*
— **dis·en·chant·ment** \-mənt\ *noun*
dis·en·chant·ed \-'chan-təd\ *adjective* (1838)
: DISAPPOINTED, DISSATISFIED
dis·en·cum·ber \di-sᵊn-'kəm-bər\ *transitive verb* [Middle French *desencombrer*, from *des-* dis- + *encombrer* to encumber] (1598)
: to free from encumbrance : DISBURDEN
synonym see EXTRICATE
dis·en·dow \di-sᵊn-'dau̇\ *transitive verb* (1861)
: to strip of endowment
— **dis·en·dow·er** \-'dau̇(-ə)r\ *noun*
— **dis·en·dow·ment** \-'dau̇-mənt\ *noun*
dis·en·fran·chise \di-sᵊn-'fran-ˌchīz\ *transitive verb* (1664)
: DISFRANCHISE
— **dis·en·fran·chise·ment** \-ˌchīz-mənt, -chəz-\ *noun*
dis·en·gage \di-sᵊn-'gāj\ *verb* [French *désengager*, from Middle French, from *des-* dis- + *engager* to engage] (1611)
transitive verb
: to release from something that engages or involves
intransitive verb
: to release or detach oneself : WITHDRAW
— **dis·en·gage·ment** \-mənt\ *noun*
dis·en·tail \di-sᵊn-'tā(ə)l\ *transitive verb* (1641)
: to free from entail
dis·en·tan·gle \di-sᵊn-'taŋ-gəl\ (1598)
transitive verb
: to free from entanglement : UNRAVEL
intransitive verb
: to become disentangled
synonym see EXTRICATE
— **dis·en·tan·gle·ment** \-mənt\ *noun*
dis·en·thrall *also* **dis·en·thral** \di-sᵊn-'thrȯl\ *transitive verb* (1643)
: to free from bondage : LIBERATE
dis·en·ti·tle \di-sᵊn-'tī-tᵊl\ *transitive verb* (1654)
: to deprive of title, claim, or right
dis·equi·li·brate \di-si-'kwi-lə-ˌbrāt\ *transitive verb* (1891)
: to put out of balance
— **dis·equi·li·bra·tion** \-ˌkwi-lə-'brā-shən\ *noun*
dis·equi·lib·ri·um \(ˌ)di-ˌsē-kwə-'li-brē-əm, -ˌse-kwə-\ *noun* (1840)
: loss or lack of equilibrium
dis·es·tab·lish \di-sə-'stab-lish\ *transitive verb* (1598)
: to deprive of an established status; *especially* : to deprive of the status and privileges of an established church
— **dis·es·tab·lish·ment** \-mənt\ *noun*
dis·es·tab·lish·men·tar·i·an \-ˌstab-lish-ˌmen-'ter-ē-ən, -mən-\ *noun, often capitalized* [*disestablishment*] (1885)
: one who opposes an established order
— **dis·es·tab·lish·men·tar·i·an** *adjective, often capitalized*
¹dis·es·teem \di-sə-'stēm\ *transitive verb* (1594)
: to regard with disfavor
²disesteem *noun* (1603)
: DISFAVOR, DISREPUTE
di·seuse \dē-'züz, -'zᵊz\ *noun, plural* **di·seuses** *same*\ [French, feminine of *diseur*, from Old French, from *dire* to say, from Latin *dicere* — more at DICTION] (1896)
: a skilled and usually professional woman reciter
¹dis·fa·vor \(ˌ)dis-'fā-vər\ *noun* [probably from Middle French *desfaveur*, from *des-* + *faveur* favor, from Old French *favor*] (circa 1533)

1 : DISAPPROVAL, DISLIKE ⟨practices looked upon with *disfavor*⟩
2 : the state or fact of being no longer favored ⟨fell into *disfavor*⟩
3 : DISADVANTAGE
²disfavor *transitive verb* (1570)
: to withhold or withdraw favor from
dis·fig·ure \dis-'fi-gyər, *especially British* -'fi-gər\ *transitive verb* [Middle English, from Middle French *desfigurer*, from *des-* dis- + *figure* figure] (14th century)
1 : to impair (as in beauty) by deep and persistent injuries ⟨a face *disfigured* by smallpox⟩
2 *obsolete* : DISGUISE
— **dis·fig·ure·ment** \-mənt\ *noun*
dis·fran·chise \(ˌ)dis-'fran-ˌchīz\ *transitive verb* (15th century)
: to deprive of a franchise, of a legal right, or of some privilege or immunity; *especially* : to deprive of the right to vote
— **dis·fran·chise·ment** \-ˌchīz-mənt, -chəz-\ *noun*
dis·frock \(ˌ)dis-'fräk\ *transitive verb* (1837)
: DEFROCK
dis·func·tion *variant of* DYSFUNCTION
dis·fur·nish \(ˌ)dis-'fər-nish\ *transitive verb* [Middle French *desfourniss-*, stem of *desfournir*, from *des-* dis- + *fournir* to furnish] (1531)
: to make destitute of possessions : DIVEST
— **dis·fur·nish·ment** \-mənt\ *noun*
dis·gorge \(ˌ)dis-'gȯrj\ *verb* [Middle English, from Middle French *desgorger*, from *des-* dis- + *gorge* gorge] (15th century)
transitive verb
1 a : to discharge by the throat and mouth : VOMIT **b** : to discharge or let go of in a manner suggesting vomiting ⟨the train *disgorged* its passengers⟩ **c** : to give up on request or under pressure ⟨refused to *disgorge* his ill-gotten gains⟩
2 : to discharge the contents of (as the stomach)
intransitive verb
: to discharge contents ⟨where the river *disgorges* into the sea⟩
¹dis·grace \di-'skrās, dis-'grās\ *transitive verb* (1580)
1 *archaic* : to humiliate by a superior showing
2 : to be a source of shame to ⟨your actions *disgraced* the family⟩
3 : to cause to lose favor or standing ⟨was *disgraced* by the hint of scandal⟩
— **dis·grac·er** *noun*
²disgrace *noun* [Middle French, from Old Italian *disgrazia*, from *dis-* (from Latin) + *grazia* grace, from Latin *gratia* — more at GRACE] (1586)
1 a : the condition of one fallen from grace or honor **b** : loss of grace, favor, or honor

☆ **SYNONYMS**
Discuss, argue, debate mean to discourse about in order to reach conclusions or to convince. DISCUSS implies a sifting of possibilities especially by presenting considerations pro and con ⟨*discussed* the need for a new highway⟩. ARGUE implies the offering of reasons or evidence in support of convictions already held ⟨*argued* that the project would be too costly⟩. DEBATE suggests formal or public argument between opposing parties ⟨*debated* the merits of the amendment⟩; it may also apply to deliberation with oneself ⟨I'm *debating* whether I should go⟩.

\ə\ **abut** \ᵊ\ **kitten** \ər\ **further** \a\ **ash** \ā\ **ace**
\ä\ **mop, mar** \au̇\ **out** \ch\ **chin** \e\ **bet** \ē\ **easy**
\g\ **go** \i\ **hit** \ī\ **ice** \j\ **job** \ŋ\ **sing** \ō\ **go**
\ȯ\ **law** \ȯi\ **boy** \th\ **thin** \t̲h̲\ **the** \ü\ **loot** \u̇\ **foot**
\y\ **yet** \zh\ **vision** *see also* Guide to Pronunciation

2 : something that disgraces ⟨your manners are a *disgrace*⟩ ☆
dis·grace·ful \-fəl\ *adjective* (1597)
: bringing or involving disgrace
— **dis·grace·ful·ly** \-fə-lē\ *adverb*
— **dis·grace·ful·ness** *noun*
dis·grun·tle \dis-'grən-t²l\ *transitive verb*
dis·grun·tled; dis·grun·tling \-'grənt-liŋ, -'grən-t²l-iŋ\ [*dis-* + *gruntle* (to grumble), from Middle English *gruntlen*, frequentative of *grunten* to grunt] (1682)
: to make ill-humored or discontented — usually used as a participial adjective ⟨they were a very *disgruntled* crew —Flannery O'Connor⟩
— **dis·grun·tle·ment** \-t²l-mənt\ *noun*
¹**dis·guise** \də-'skīz, dis-'gīz *also* diz-\ *transitive verb* **dis·guised; dis·guis·ing** [Middle English *disgisen*, from Middle French *desguiser*, from Old French, from *des-* dis- + *guise* guise] (14th century)
1 a : to change the customary dress or appearance of **b :** to furnish with a false appearance or an assumed identity
2 *obsolete* **:** DISFIGURE
3 : to obscure the existence or true state or character of **:** CONCEAL ☆
— **dis·guis·ed·ly** \-'gīz(-ə)d-lē, -'kīz(-ə)d-\ *adverb*
— **dis·guise·ment** \-'gīz-mənt, -'kīz-\ *noun*
— **dis·guis·er** *noun*
²**disguise** *noun* (14th century)
1 : apparel assumed to conceal one's identity or counterfeit another's
2 : the act of disguising
3 a : form misrepresenting the true nature of something ⟨blessings in *disguise*⟩ **b :** an artificial manner **:** PRETENSE ⟨threw off all *disguise*⟩
¹**dis·gust** \di-'skəst, dis-'gəst *also* diz-\ *noun* (1598)
: marked aversion aroused by something highly distasteful **:** REPUGNANCE
²**disgust** *verb* [Middle French *desgouster*, from *des-* dis- + *goust* taste, from Latin *gustus*; akin to Latin *gustare* to taste — more at CHOOSE] (1616)
transitive verb
1 : to provoke to loathing, repugnance, or aversion **:** be offensive to
2 : to cause (one) to lose an interest or intention
intransitive verb
: to cause disgust
— **dis·gust·ed** *adjective*
— **dis·gust·ed·ly** *adverb*
dis·gust·ful \-fəl\ *adjective* (circa 1616)
1 : provoking disgust
2 : full of or accompanied by disgust
— **dis·gust·ful·ly** \-fə-lē\ *adverb*
dis·gust·ing *adjective* (1754)
: causing disgust
— **dis·gust·ing·ly** \di-'skəs-tiŋ-lē, dis-'gəs- *also* diz-\ *adverb*
¹**dish** \'dish\ *noun* [Middle English, from Old English *disc* plate, from Latin *discus* quoit, disk, dish, from Greek *diskos*, from *dikein* to throw] (before 12th century)
1 a : a more or less concave vessel from which food is served **b :** the contents of a dish ⟨a *dish* of strawberries⟩
2 a : food prepared in a particular way **b :** something one particularly enjoys **:** CUP OF TEA
3 a (1) **:** any of various shallow concave vessels **:** *broadly* **:** anything shallowly concave (2) **:** a directional receiver having a concave usually parabolic reflector; *especially* **:** one used as a microwave antenna **b :** the state of being concave or the degree of concavity
4 a : something that is favored ⟨entertainment that is just his *dish*⟩ **b :** an attractive or sexy person
²**dish** (14th century)
transitive verb

1 : to put (as food for serving) into a dish — often used with *up*
2 : PRESENT — usually used with *up*
3 : to make concave like a dish
intransitive verb
: to pass to a teammate (as in basketball) — usually used with *off*
dis·ha·bille \ˌdis-ə-'bē(ə)l, -'bil\ *noun* [French *déshabillé*, from past participle of *déshabiller* to undress, from *dés-* dis- + *habiller* to dress — more at HABILIMENT] (1673)
1 a *archaic* **:** NEGLIGEE **b :** the state of being dressed in a casual or careless style
2 : a deliberately careless or casual manner
dis·har·mo·ni·ous \ˌdis-(ˌ)här-'mō-nē-əs\ *adjective* (1659)
: lacking in harmony
dis·har·mo·nize \(ˌ)dis-'här-mə-ˌnīz\ *transitive verb* (1801)
: to make disharmonious
dis·har·mo·ny \-nē\ *noun* (circa 1602)
: lack of harmony **:** DISCORD
dish·cloth \'dish-ˌklȯth\ *noun* (circa 1828)
: a cloth for washing dishes
dish·clout \'dish-ˌklau̇t\ *noun* (circa 1530)
British **:** DISHCLOTH
dis·heart·en \(ˌ)dis-'här-t²n\ *transitive verb* (1590)
: to cause to lose spirit or morale
— **dis·heart·en·ing·ly** \-'härt-niŋ-lē, -'här-t²n-iŋ-\ *adverb*
— **dis·heart·en·ment** \-'här-t²n-mənt\ *noun*
dished \'disht\ *adjective* (1737)
: CONCAVE
di·shev·el \di-'shev-əl\ *transitive verb* **di·shev·eled** *or* **di·shev·elled; di·shev·el·ing** *or* **di·shev·el·ling** \-'she-v(ə-)liŋ\ [back-formation from *disheveled*] (1598)
: to throw into disorder or disarray
di·shev·eled *or* **di·shev·elled** *adjective* [Middle English *discheveled* with disordered hair, part translation of Middle French *deschevelé*, from past participle of *descheveler* to disarrange the hair, from *des-* dis- + *chevel* hair, from Latin *capillus*] (1583)
: marked by disorder or disarray
dis·hon·est \(ˌ)di-'sä-nəst *also* -'zä-\ *adjective* [Middle English, from Middle French *deshoneste*, from *des-* dis- + *honeste* honest] (14th century)
1 *obsolete* **:** SHAMEFUL, UNCHASTE
2 : characterized by lack of truth, honesty, or trustworthiness **:** UNFAIR, DECEPTIVE ☆
— **dis·hon·est·ly** *adverb*
dis·hon·es·ty \-nə-stē\ *noun* (1599)
1 : lack of honesty or integrity **:** disposition to defraud or deceive
2 : a dishonest act **:** FRAUD
¹**dis·hon·or** \(ˌ)di-'sä-nər *also* -'zä-\ *noun* [Middle English *dishonour*, from Middle French *deshonor*, from *des-* dis- + *honor* honor] (13th century)
1 : lack or loss of honor or reputation
2 : the state of one who has lost honor or prestige **:** SHAME
3 : a cause of disgrace
4 : the nonpayment or nonacceptance of commercial paper by the party on whom it is drawn
synonym see DISGRACE
— **dis·hon·or·er** \-'sän-ər-ər *also* -'zä-\ *noun*
²**dishonor** *transitive verb* (13th century)
1 a : to treat in a degrading manner **b :** to bring shame on
2 : to refuse to accept or pay (as a bill or check)
dis·hon·or·able \(ˌ)di-'sä-nə-rə-bəl, -'sä-nər-bəl\ *adjective* (1534)
1 : lacking honor **:** SHAMEFUL ⟨*dishonorable* conduct⟩
2 *archaic* **:** not honored
— **dis·hon·or·able·ness** *noun*
— **dis·hon·or·ably** \-blē\ *adverb*

dish out *transitive verb* (1641)
: to give or dispense freely ⟨*dish out* gifts⟩ ⟨*dish out* advice⟩ ⟨*dish out* punishment⟩
dish·pan \'dish-ˌpan\ *noun* (1872)
: a large flat-bottomed pan used for washing dishes
dishpan hands *noun plural but singular or plural in construction* (1944)
: a condition of dryness, redness, and scaling of the hands that results typically from repeated exposure to, sensitivity to, or overuse of cleaning materials (as detergents) used in housework
dish·rag \'dish-ˌrag\ *noun* (1839)
: DISHCLOTH
dish·ware \'dish-ˌwar, -ˌwer\ *noun* (1946)
: tableware (as of china) used in serving food
dish·wash·er \-ˌwȯ-shər, -ˌwä-\ *noun* (15th century)
1 : a worker employed to wash dishes
2 : a machine for washing dishes
dish·wa·ter \-ˌwȯ-tər, -ˌwä-\ *noun* (15th century)
: water in which dishes have been or are to be washed
dishy \'di-shē\ *adjective* **dish·i·er; -est** (1961)
: ATTRACTIVE 2
¹**dis·il·lu·sion** \ˌdi-sə-'lü-zhən\ *noun* (1851)
: the condition of being disenchanted
²**disillusion** *transitive verb* **dis·il·lu·sioned; dis·il·lu·sion·ing** \-'lü-zhə-niŋ\ (1855)
: to leave without illusion or naive faith and trust
— **dis·il·lu·sion·ment** \-'lü-zhən-mənt\ *noun*

dis·il·lu·sioned *adjective* (1871)
: DISAPPOINTED, DISSATISFIED

dis·in·cen·tive \,di-s°n-'sen-tiv\ *noun* (1946)
: DETERRENT

dis·in·cli·na·tion \(,)di-,sin-klə-'nā-shən, -,siŋ-\ *noun* (1647)
: a preference for avoiding something : slight aversion

dis·in·cline \,di-s°n-'klīn\ *transitive verb* (1647)
: to make unwilling

dis·in·clined *adjective* (1647)
: unwilling because of mild dislike or disapproval ☆

dis·in·fect \,di-s°n-'fekt\ *transitive verb* [Middle French *desinfecter,* from *des-* dis- + *infecter* to infect] (1598)
: to free from infection especially by destroying harmful microorganisms; *broadly* : CLEANSE
— **dis·in·fec·tion** \-'fek-shən\ *noun*

dis·in·fec·tant \-'fek-tənt\ *noun* (1837)
: an agent that frees from infection; *especially* : a chemical that destroys vegetative forms of harmful microorganisms especially on inanimate objects but that may be less effective in destroying bacterial spores

dis·in·fest \,di-s°n-'fest\ *transitive verb* (circa 1920)
: to rid of small animal pests (as insects or rodents)
— **dis·in·fes·ta·tion** \(,)di-,sin-,fes-'tā-shən\ *noun*

dis·in·fes·tant \,di-s°n-'fes-tənt\ *noun* (1943)
: a disinfesting agent

dis·in·fla·tion \,di-s°n-'flā-shən\ *noun* (1880)
: a reversal of inflationary pressures
— **dis·in·fla·tion·ary** \-shə-,ner-ē\ *adjective*

dis·in·for·ma·tion \(,)di-,sin-fər-'mā-shən\ *noun* (1939)
: false information deliberately and often covertly spread (as by the planting of rumors) in order to influence public opinion or obscure the truth ◇

dis·in·gen·u·ous \,di-s°n-'jen-yə-wəs\ *adjective* (1655)
: lacking in candor; *also* : giving a false appearance of simple frankness : CALCULATING
— **dis·in·gen·u·ous·ly** *adverb*
— **dis·in·gen·u·ous·ness** *noun*

dis·in·her·it \,di-s°n-'her-ət\ *transitive verb* [Middle English] (15th century)
1 : to prevent deliberately from inheriting something (as by making a will)
2 : to deprive of natural or human rights or of previously held special privileges
— **dis·in·her·i·tance** \-'her-ə-tən(t)s\ *noun*

dis·in·hi·bi·tion \(,)di-,sin-(h)ə-'bi-shən\ *noun* (circa 1927)
: loss or reduction of an inhibition (as by the action of interfering stimuli or events) ⟨*disinhibition* of a reflex⟩ ⟨*disinhibition* of violent tendencies⟩
— **dis·in·hib·it** \(,)di-s°n-'hi-bət\ *transitive verb*

dis·in·te·grate \(,)di-'sin-tə-,grāt\ (1796)
transitive verb
1 : to break or decompose into constituent elements, parts, or small particles
2 : to destroy the unity or integrity of
intransitive verb
1 : to break or separate into constituent elements or parts
2 : to lose unity or integrity by or as if by breaking into parts
3 : to undergo a change in composition ⟨an atomic nucleus that *disintegrates* because of radioactivity⟩
— **dis·in·te·gra·tion** \(,)di-,sin-tə-'grā-shən\ *noun*
— **dis·in·te·gra·tive** \(,)di-'sin-tə-,grā-tiv\ *adjective*
— **dis·in·te·gra·tor** \-,grā-tər\ *noun*

dis·in·ter \,di-s°n-'tər\ *transitive verb* (1611)
1 : to take out of the grave or tomb

2 : to bring back into awareness or prominence; *also* : to bring to light : UNEARTH
— **dis·in·ter·ment** \-mənt\ *noun*

¹dis·in·ter·est \(,)dis-'in-trəst; -'in-tə-,rest, -tə-rəst, -tərst; -'in,trest\ *transitive verb* (1612)
: to cause to regard something with no interest or concern

²disinterest *noun* (1658)
1 : DISINTERESTEDNESS
2 : lack of interest : INDIFFERENCE

dis·in·ter·est·ed \-təd\ *adjective* (circa 1612)
1 a : not having the mind or feelings engaged : not interested ⟨telling them in a *disinterested* voice —Tom Wicker⟩ ⟨Introverted. Unsocial . . . *Disinterested* in women —J. A. Brussel⟩ **b** : no longer interested ⟨husband and wife become *disinterested* in each other —T. I. Rubin⟩
2 : free from selfish motive or interest : UNBIASED ⟨a *disinterested* decision⟩ ⟨*disinterested* intellectual curiosity is the lifeblood of real civilization —G. M. Trevelyan⟩ □
synonym see INDIFFERENT
— **dis·in·ter·est·ed·ly** *adverb*
— **dis·in·ter·est·ed·ness** \-təd-nəs\ *noun* (circa 1682)
: the quality of being objective or impartial

dis·in·ter·me·di·a·tion \,di-,sin-tər-,mē-dē-'ā-shən\ *noun* (1967)
: the diversion of savings from accounts with low fixed interest rates to direct investment in high-yielding instruments

dis·in·tox·i·cate \,di-s°n-'täk-sə-,kāt\ *transitive verb* (1685)
: DETOXIFY 2
— **dis·in·tox·i·ca·tion** \-,täk-sə-'kā-shən\ *noun*

dis·in·vest \(,)di-s°n-'vest\ *intransitive verb* (1945)
: to reduce or eliminate capital investment (as in an industry or area)

dis·in·vest·ment \,di-s°n-'ves(t)-mənt\ *noun* (1936)
: consumption of capital; *also* : the withdrawing of investment

dis·in·vite \(,)di-s°n-'vīt\ *transitive verb* (1580)
: to withdraw an invitation to

dis·join \(,)dis-'jȯin\ *verb* [Middle English *disjoynen,* from Middle French *desjoindre,* from Latin *disjungere,* from *dis-* + *jungere* to join — more at YOKE] (15th century)
transitive verb
: to end the joining of
intransitive verb
: to become detached

¹dis·joint \-'jȯint\ *adjective* [Middle English *disjoynt,* from Middle French *desjoint,* past participle of *desjoindre*] (15th century)
1 *obsolete* : DISJOINTED 1a
2 : having no elements in common ⟨*disjoint* mathematical sets⟩

²disjoint (15th century)
transitive verb
1 : to disturb the orderly structure or arrangement of
2 : to take apart at the joints
intransitive verb
: to come apart at the joints

dis·joint·ed *adjective* (circa 1586)
1 a : being thrown out of orderly function ⟨a *disjointed* society⟩ **b** : lacking coherence or orderly sequence ⟨an incomplete and *disjointed* history⟩
2 : separated at or as if at the joint
— **dis·joint·ed·ly** *adverb*
— **dis·joint·ed·ness** *noun*

¹dis·junct \dis-'jəŋ(k)t\ *adjective* [Middle English, from Latin *disjunctus,* past participle of *disjungere* to disjoin] (15th century)
: marked by separation of or from usually contiguous parts or individuals: as **a** : DISCONTINUOUS **b** : relating to melodic progression by intervals larger than a major second — compare CONJUNCT

Disinclined, hesitant, reluctant, loath, averse mean lacking the will or desire to do something indicated. DISINCLINED implies lack of taste for or inclination ⟨*disinclined* to move again⟩ ⟨*disinclined* for reading⟩. HESITANT implies a holding back especially through fear or uncertainty ⟨*hesitant* about asking for a date⟩. RELUCTANT implies a holding back through unwillingness ⟨a *reluctant* witness⟩. LOATH implies hesitancy because of conflict with one's opinions, predilections, or liking ⟨seems *loath* to trust anyone⟩. AVERSE implies a holding back from or avoiding because of distaste or repugnance ⟨*averse* to hard work⟩.

disinterested *Disinterested* and *uninterested* have a tangled history. *Uninterested* originally meant impartial, but this sense fell into disuse during the 18th century. About the same time the original sense of *disinterested* also disappeared, with *uninterested* developing a new sense—the present meaning—to take its place. The original sense of *uninterested* is still out of use, but the original sense of *disinterested* revived in the early 20th century. The revival has since been under frequent attack as an illiteracy and a blurring or loss of a useful distinction. Actual usage shows otherwise. Sense 2 of *disinterested* is still its most frequent sense, especially in edited prose; it shows no sign of vanishing. A careful writer may choose sense 1a of *disinterested* in preference to *uninterested* for emphasis ⟨teaching the letters of the alphabet to her wiggling and supremely *disinterested* little daughter —C. L. Sulzberger⟩ Further, *disinterested* has developed a sense (1b), perhaps influenced by sense 1 of the prefix *dis-,* that contrasts with *uninterested* ⟨when I grow tired or *disinterested* in anything, I experience a disgust —Jack London (letter, 1914)⟩ Still, use of senses 1a and 1b will incur the disapproval of some who may not fully appreciate the history of this word or the subtleties of its present use.

disinformation Though its roots are several decades older, *disinformation* became a common word in the 1970s and '80s. Many uses of the word during this period associate *disinformation* with the KGB, the Soviet secret police; and claims have been made that the KGB established a branch in the 1950s called, presumably unofficially, the "Department of Disinformation." It has been said that the word first appeared in English in the *Times* of London in 1955, but actually the U.S. magazine *Time* used it a year earlier to refer to Communist propaganda. The earliest known attestation of *disinformation,* however, is in the 1939 book *In Stalin's Secret Police,* a pioneering exposé of Stalin's purges, written by Walter Krivitsky, a Soviet intelligence officer who defected in the fall of 1937 and—meeting a fate common among Stalin's enemies in those days—was found shot in his hotel room in February 1941. In all likelihood, *disinformation* in Krivitsky's book as well as later uses are translations of Russian *dezinformatsiya,* which began to appear in Russian dictionaries in 1949.

²**dis·junct** \'dis-ˌjəŋ(k)t, dis-'\ *noun* (1921)
1 : any of the alternatives that make up a logical disjunction
2 : an adverb or adverbial (as *luckily* in "Luckily we had an extra set" or *in short* in "In short, there is nothing we can do") that is loosely connected to a sentence and conveys the speaker's or writer's comment on its content, truth, or manner — compare ADJUNCT 2b

dis·junc·tion \dis-'jəŋ(k)-shən\ *noun* (14th century)
1 : a sharp cleavage **:** DISUNION, SEPARATION ⟨the *disjunction* between theory and practice⟩
2 : a compound sentence in logic formed by joining two simple statements by *or*: **a :** INCLUSIVE DISJUNCTION **b :** EXCLUSIVE DISJUNCTION

¹**dis·junc·tive** \-'jəŋ(k)-tiv\ *adjective* (15th century)
1 a : relating to, being, or forming a logical disjunction **b :** expressing an alternative or opposition between the meanings of the words connected ⟨the *disjunctive* conjunction *or*⟩ **c :** expressed by mutually exclusive alternatives joined by *or* ⟨*disjunctive* pleading⟩
2 : marked by breaks or disunity ⟨a *disjunctive* narrative sequence⟩
3 *of a pronoun form* **:** stressed and not attached to the verb as an enclitic or proclitic
— **dis·junc·tive·ly** *adverb*

²**disjunctive** *noun* (1530)
: a disjunctive conjunction

dis·junc·ture \-'jəŋ(k)-chər\ *noun* [Middle English, modification (influenced by Latin *disjunctus*) of Middle French *desjointure*, from *desjoint* disjoint] (14th century)
: DISJUNCTION 1

¹**disk** *or* **disc** \'disk\ *noun, often attributive* [Latin *discus* — more at DISH] (1664)
1 a : the seemingly flat figure of a celestial body ⟨the solar *disk*⟩ **b** *archaic* **:** DISCUS
2 : any of various rounded and flattened animal anatomical structures (as an intervertebral disk) — compare SLIPPED DISK
3 : the central part of the flower head of a typical composite made up of closely packed tubular flowers
4 a : a thin circular object **b** *usually disc* **:** a phonograph record **c :** a round flat plate coated with a magnetic substance on which data for a computer is stored **d** *usually disc* **:** OPTICAL DISK: as (1) **:** VIDEODISC (2) **:** COMPACT DISC
5 *usually disc* **:** one of the concave circular steel tools with sharpened edge making up the working part of a disc harrow or plow; *also* **:** an implement employing such tools
— **disk·like** \-ˌlīk\ *adjective*

²**disk** *or* **disc** *transitive verb* (circa 1884)
: to cultivate with an implement (as a harrow or plow) that turns and loosens the soil with a series of disks

dis·kette \ˌdis-'ket\ *noun* (1973)
: FLOPPY DISK

disk flower *noun* (1870)
: one of the tubular flowers in the disk of a composite plant — called also *disk floret*

dis·lik·able *also* **dis·like·able** \(ˌ)dis-'lī-kə-bəl\ *adjective* (1843)
: easy to dislike

¹**dis·like** \(ˌ)dis-'līk, 'dis-ˌ\ *noun* (1577)
1 : a feeling of aversion or disapproval
2 *obsolete* **:** DISCORD

²**dislike** *transitive verb* (1579)
1 *archaic* **:** DISPLEASE
2 : to regard with dislike **:** DISAPPROVE
3 *obsolete* **:** to show aversion to
— **dis·lik·er** *noun*

dis·limn \(ˌ)dis-'lim\ *verb* (1606)
: DIM

dis·lo·cate \'dis-lō-ˌkāt, -lə-; (ˌ)dis-'lō-\ *transitive verb* [Medieval Latin *dislocatus*, past participle of *dislocare*, from Latin *dis-* + *locare* to locate] (1605)
1 : to put out of place; *specifically* **:** to displace (a bone) from normal connections with another bone

2 : to force a change in the usual status, relationship, or order of **:** DISRUPT

dis·lo·ca·tion \ˌdis-(ˌ)lō-'kā-shən, -lə-\ *noun* (14th century)
: the act of dislocating **:** the state of being dislocated: as **a :** displacement of one or more bones at a joint **:** LUXATION **b :** a discontinuity in the otherwise normal lattice structure of a crystal **c :** disruption of an established order

dis·lodge \(ˌ)dis-'läj\ *verb* [Middle English *disloggen*, from Middle French *desloger*, from *des-* dis- + *loger* to lodge, from Old French *loge* lodge] (15th century)
transitive verb
1 : to drive from a position of hiding, defense, or advantage
2 : to force out of a secure or settled position ⟨*dislodged* the rock with a shovel⟩
intransitive verb
: to leave a lodging place
— **dis·lodg·ment** *or* **dis·lodge·ment** *noun*

dis·loy·al \(ˌ)dis-'lȯi(-ə)l\ *adjective* [Middle English, from Middle French *desloial*, from Old French, from *des-* dis- + *loial* loyal] (15th century)
: lacking in loyalty; *also* **:** showing an absence of allegiance, devotion, obligation, faith, or support ⟨his *disloyal* refusal to help his friend⟩
synonym see FAITHLESS
— **dis·loy·al·ly** \-'lȯi-ə-lē\ *adverb*

dis·loy·al·ty \-'lȯi(-ə)l-tē\ *noun* (15th century)
: lack of loyalty

dis·mal \'diz-məl\ *adjective* [Middle English, from *dismal*, noun, days marked as unlucky in medieval calendars, from Anglo-French, from Medieval Latin *dies mali*, literally, evil days] (15th century)
1 *obsolete* **:** DISASTROUS, DREADFUL
2 : showing or causing gloom or depression
3 : lacking merit **:** particularly bad ◆
— **dis·mal·ly** \-mə-lē\ *adverb*
— **dis·mal·ness** *noun*

dis·man·tle \(ˌ)dis-'man-t³l\ *transitive verb*
dis·man·tled; dis·man·tling \-'mant-liŋ, -'man-t³l-\ [Middle French *desmanteler*, from *des-* dis- + *mantel* mantle] (1602)
1 : to take to pieces; *also* **:** to destroy the integrity or functioning of
2 : to strip of dress or covering **:** DIVEST
3 : to strip of furniture and equipment
— **dis·man·tle·ment** \-'man-t³l-mənt\ *noun*

dis·mast \(ˌ)dis-'mast\ *transitive verb* (1747)
: to remove or break off the mast of

¹**dis·may** \dis-'mā, diz-\ *transitive verb* **dis·mayed; dis·may·ing** [Middle English, from (assumed) Old French *desmaiier*, from Old French *des-* dis- + *-maiier* (as in *esmaiier* to dismay), from (assumed) Vulgar Latin *-magare*, of Germanic origin; akin to Old High German *magan* to be able — more at MAY] (13th century)
: to deprive of courage, resolution, and initiative through the pressure of sudden fear or anxiety or great perplexity ☆
— **dis·may·ing·ly** \-iŋ-lē\ *adverb*

²**dismay** *noun* (14th century)
1 : sudden loss of courage or resolution from alarm or fear
2 a : sudden disappointment **b :** PERTURBATION 1

disme \'dīm\ *noun* [obsolete English, tenth, from obsolete French, from Middle French *disme, dime* — more at DIME] (1792)
: a U.S. 10-cent coin struck in 1792

dis·mem·ber \(ˌ)dis-'mem-bər\ *transitive verb* **-bered; -ber·ing** \-b(ə-)riŋ\ [Middle English *dismembren*, from Old French *desmembrer*, from *des-* dis- + *membre* member] (14th century)
1 : to cut off or disjoin the limbs, members, or parts of
2 : to break up or tear into pieces
— **dis·mem·ber·ment** \-bər-mənt\ *noun*

dis·miss \dis-'mis\ *transitive verb* [Middle English, modification of Latin *dimissus*, past participle of *dimittere*, from *dis-* apart + *mittere* to send — more at DIS-, SMITE] (15th century)
1 : to permit or cause to leave ⟨*dismissed* the visitors⟩
2 : to remove from position or service **:** DISCHARGE
3 a : to reject serious consideration of ⟨*dismissed* the thought⟩ **b :** to put out of judicial consideration ⟨*dismissed* all charges⟩
— **dis·mis·sion** \-'mi-shən\ *noun*
— **dis·mis·sive** \-'mi-siv\ *adjective*
— **dis·mis·sive·ly** *adverb*

dis·miss·al \-'mi-səl\ *noun* (1816)
: the act of dismissing **:** the fact or state of being dismissed

¹**dis·mount** \(ˌ)dis-'maunt\ *verb* [probably modification of Middle French *desmonter*, from *des-* dis- + *monter* to mount] (1579)
intransitive verb
1 *obsolete* **:** DESCEND
2 : to alight from an elevated position (as on a horse); *also* **:** to get out of an enclosed craft or vehicle
transitive verb
1 : to throw down or remove from a mount or an elevated position; *especially* **:** UNHORSE
2 : DISASSEMBLE

²**dismount** *noun* (1654)
: the act of dismounting

dis·obe·di·ence \ˌdi-sə-'bē-dē-ən(t)s\ *noun* (15th century)
: refusal or neglect to obey

dis·obe·di·ent \-ənt\ *adjective* [Middle English, from Middle French *desobedient*, from Old French, from *des-* dis- + *obedient* obedient] (15th century)
: refusing or neglecting to obey
— **dis·obe·di·ent·ly** *adverb*

☆ **SYNONYMS**

Dismay, appall, horrify, daunt mean to unnerve or deter by arousing fear, apprehension, or aversion. DISMAY implies that one is disconcerted and at a loss as to how to deal with something ⟨*dismayed* at the size of the job⟩. APPALL implies that one is faced with that which perturbs, confounds, or shocks ⟨I am *appalled* by your behavior⟩. HORRIFY stresses a reaction of horror or revulsion ⟨was *horrified* by such wanton cruelty⟩. DAUNT suggests a cowing, disheartening, or frightening in a venture requiring courage ⟨a cliff that would *daunt* the most intrepid climber⟩.

◇ **WORD HISTORY**

dismal In late antiquity, certain days of each month, called in Latin *dies Aegyptiaci* "Egyptian days," were regarded as unlucky times, when new enterprises of any sort were not to be undertaken. These days of ill omen were probably a relic of ancient Egyptian astrological practices, but their source had been forgotten by the Middle Ages. People then took them to be anniversaries of the plagues visited on Egypt in Moses' time— despite the fact that there were 24 Egyptian days in the year and only ten Biblical plagues. In a 13th century Anglo-French calendar, the Egyptian days were called collectively *dismal* (from Latin *dies mali* "evil days"), and this word was borrowed into Middle English. Any day of the 24 was a *dismal day*, but the original sense "evil days" was forgotten, and *dismal* in the phrase was simply taken as an adjective meaning "disastrous." In Modern English this sense has been weakened to "causing gloom," perhaps by association with *dismay*.

dis·obey \ˌdi-sə-'bā\ verb [Middle English, from Middle French desobeir, from Old French, from des- dis- + obeir to obey] (14th century)
intransitive verb
: to be disobedient
transitive verb
: to fail to obey
— **dis·obey·er** noun

dis·oblige \ˌdi-sə-'blīj\ transitive verb [French désobliger, from Middle French, from des- dis- + obliger to oblige] (1632)
1 : to go counter to the wishes of
2 : INCONVENIENCE

dis·so·di·um phosphate \ˌ(ˌ)dī-'sō-dē-əm-\ noun (circa 1928)
: a sodium phosphate Na_2HPO_4

dis·so·mic \ˌ(ˌ)dī-'sō-mik\ adjective [di- + -somic] (1924)
: having one or more chromosomes present in twice the normal number but not having the entire genome doubled

¹dis·or·der \ˌ(ˌ)di-'sȯr-dər, -'zȯr-\ transitive verb (15th century)
1 : to disturb the order of
2 : to disturb the regular or normal functions of

²disorder noun (1530)
1 : lack of order ⟨clothes in disorder⟩
2 : breach of the peace or public order ⟨troubled times marked by social disorders⟩
3 : an abnormal physical or mental condition : AILMENT ⟨a nervous disorder⟩

dis·or·dered adjective (1548)
1 obsolete **a** : morally reprehensible **b** : UNRULY
2 a : marked by disorder **b** : not functioning in a normal orderly healthy way
— **dis·or·dered·ly** adverb
— **dis·or·dered·ness** noun

¹dis·or·der·ly \-'sȯrd-ər-lē\ adverb (1564)
archaic : in a disorderly manner

²disorderly adjective (1585)
1 : engaged in conduct offensive to public order ⟨charged with being drunk and disorderly⟩
2 : characterized by disorder ⟨a disorderly pile of clothes⟩
— **dis·or·der·li·ness** noun

disorderly conduct noun (circa 1845)
: a petty offense chiefly against public order and decency that falls short of an indictable misdemeanor

disorderly house noun [euphemism] (circa 1809)
: BORDELLO

dis·or·ga·nize \ˌ(ˌ)di-'sȯr-gə-ˌnīz\ transitive verb [French désorganiser, from dés- dis- + organiser to organize] (1793)
: to destroy or interrupt the orderly structure or function of
— **dis·or·ga·ni·za·tion** \ˌ(ˌ)di-ˌsȯr-gə-nə-'zā-shən\ noun

dis·or·ga·nized adjective (1812)
: lacking coherence, system, or central guiding agency ⟨disorganized work habits⟩

dis·ori·ent \ˌ(ˌ)di-'sȯr-ē-ˌent, -'sȯr-\ transitive verb [French désorienter, from dés- dis- + orienter to orient] (1655)
1 a : to cause to lose bearings : displace from normal position or relationship **b** : to cause to lose the sense of time, place, or identity
2 : CONFUSE

dis·ori·en·tate \-ē-ən-ˌtāt, -ē-ˌen-\ transitive verb (circa 1704)
: DISORIENT
— **dis·ori·en·ta·tion** \ˌ(ˌ)di-ˌsȯr-ē-ən-'tā-shən, -ˌsȯr-, -ē-ˌen-\ noun

dis·own \ˌ(ˌ)di-'sōn\ transitive verb (1649)
1 : to refuse to acknowledge as one's own
2 a : to repudiate any connection or identification with **b** : to deny the validity or authority of
— **dis·own·ment** \-mənt\ noun

dis·par·age \di-'spar-ij\ transitive verb -aged; -ag·ing [Middle English, to degrade by marriage below one's class, disparage, from Middle French desparagier to marry below one's class, from Old French, from des- dis- + parage extraction, lineage, from per peer] (14th century)
1 : to lower in rank or reputation : DEGRADE
2 : to depreciate by indirect means (as invidious comparison) : speak slightingly about
synonym see DECRY
— **dis·par·age·ment** \-ij-mənt\ noun
— **dis·par·ag·er** noun
— **dis·par·ag·ing** adjective
— **dis·par·ag·ing·ly** \-ij-in-lē\ adverb

dis·pa·rate \'dis-p(ə-)rət, di-'spar-ət\ adjective [Latin disparatus, past participle of disparare to separate, from dis- + parare to prepare — more at PARE] (15th century)
1 : containing or made up of fundamentally different and often incongruous elements
2 : markedly distinct in quality or character
synonym see DIFFERENT
— **dis·pa·rate·ly** adverb
— **dis·pa·rate·ness** noun
— **dis·par·i·ty** \di-'spar-ə-tē\ noun

dis·part \ˌ(ˌ)dis-'pärt\ verb [Italian & Latin; Italian dispartire, from Latin, from dis- + partire to divide — more at PART] (1590)
archaic : SEPARATE, DIVIDE

dis·pas·sion \ˌ(ˌ)dis-'pa-shən\ noun (1692)
: absence of passion : COOLNESS

dis·pas·sion·ate \-sh(ə-)nət\ adjective (1594)
: not influenced by strong feeling; especially : not affected by personal or emotional involvement ⟨a dispassionate critic⟩ ⟨a dispassionate approach to an issue⟩
synonym see FAIR
— **dis·pas·sion·ate·ly** adverb
— **dis·pas·sion·ate·ness** noun

¹dis·patch \di-'spach\ verb [Spanish despachar or Italian dispacciare, from Provençal despachar to get rid of, from Middle French despeechier to set free, from Old French, from des- dis- + -peechier (as in empeechier to hinder) — more at IMPEACH] (1517)
transitive verb
1 : to send off or away with promptness or speed; especially : to send off on official business
2 a : to kill with quick efficiency **b** obsolete : DEPRIVE
3 : to dispose of (as a task) rapidly or efficiently
4 : DEFEAT 3
intransitive verb
archaic : to make haste : HURRY
synonym see KILL
— **dis·patch·er** noun

²dis·patch \di-'spach, 'dis-ˌpach\ noun (1537)
1 a : a message sent with speed; especially : an important official message sent by a diplomatic, military, or naval officer **b** : a news item filed by a correspondent
2 : the act of dispatching: as **a** obsolete : DISMISSAL **b** : the act of killing **c** (1) : prompt settlement (as of an item of business) (2) : quick riddance **d** : a sending off : SHIPMENT
3 : promptness and efficiency in performance or transmission ⟨done with dispatch⟩
synonym see HASTE

dispatch case noun (circa 1918)
: a case for carrying papers

dis·pel \di-'spel\ transitive verb dis·pelled; dis·pel·ling [Middle English, from Latin dispellere, from dis- + pellere to drive, beat — more at FELT] (15th century)
: to drive away by or as if by scattering : DISSIPATE ⟨dispel a rumor⟩
synonym see SCATTER

dis·pens·able \di-'spen(t)-sə-bəl\ adjective (1649)
: capable of being dispensed with
— **dis·pens·abil·i·ty** \-ˌspen(t)-sə-'bi-lə-tē\ noun

dis·pen·sa·ry \di-'spen(t)s-(ə-)rē\ noun, plural -ries (1699)
: a place where medicine or medical or dental treatment is dispensed

dis·pen·sa·tion \ˌdis-pən-'sā-shən, -ˌpen-\ noun (14th century)
1 a : a general state or ordering of things; specifically : a system of revealed commands and promises regulating human affairs **b** : a particular arrangement or provision especially of providence or nature
2 a : an exemption from a law or from an impediment, vow, or oath **b** : a formal authorization
3 a : the act of dispensing **b** : something dispensed or distributed
— **dis·pen·sa·tion·al** \-shnəl, -shə-nᵊl\ adjective

dis·pen·sa·to·ry \di-'spen(t)-sə-ˌtōr-ē, -ˌtȯr-\ noun, plural -ries (1566)
: a medicinal formulary

dis·pense \di-'spen(t)s\ verb dis·pensed; dis·pens·ing [Middle English, from Medieval Latin & Latin; Medieval Latin dispensare to exempt, from Latin, to distribute, from dis- + pensare to weigh, frequentative of pendere to weigh, pay out — more at SPIN] (14th century)
transitive verb
1 a : to deal out in portions **b** : ADMINISTER ⟨dispense justice⟩
2 : to give dispensation to : EXEMPT
3 : to prepare and distribute (medication)
intransitive verb
archaic : to grant dispensation
synonym see DISTRIBUTE
— **dispense with 1** : to set aside : DISCARD ⟨dispensing with the usual introduction⟩
2 : to do without ⟨could dispense with such a large staff⟩

dis·pens·er \-'spen(t)-sər\ noun (14th century)
: one that dispenses: as **a** : a container that extrudes, sprays, or feeds out in convenient units **b** : a usually mechanical device for vending merchandise

dis·peo·ple \ˌ(ˌ)dis-'pē-pəl\ transitive verb (15th century)
: DEPOPULATE

dis·pers·al \di-'spər-səl\ noun (1821)
: the act or result of dispersing; especially : the process or result of the spreading of organisms from one place to another

dis·per·sant \di-'spər-sənt\ noun (1941)
: a dispersing agent; especially : a substance for promoting the formation and stabilization of a dispersion of one substance in another
— **dispersant** adjective

dis·perse \di-'spərs\ verb dis·persed; dis·pers·ing [Middle English dysparsen, from Middle French disperser, from Latin dispersus, past participle of dispergere to scatter, from dis- + spargere to scatter — more at SPARK] (14th century)
transitive verb
1 a : to cause to break up ⟨police dispersed the crowd⟩ **b** : to cause to become spread widely **c** : to cause to evaporate or vanish ⟨sunlight dispersing the mist⟩
2 : to spread or distribute from a fixed or constant source: as **a** archaic : DISSEMINATE **b** : to subject (as light) to dispersion **c** : to distribute (as fine particles) more or less evenly throughout a medium
intransitive verb
1 : to break up in random fashion ⟨the crowd dispersed on request⟩
2 a : to become dispersed **b** : DISSIPATE, VANISH ⟨the fog dispersed toward morning⟩
synonym see SCATTER
— **dis·persed·ly** \-'spər-səd-lē, -'spərst-lē\ adverb

\ə\ abut \ᵊ\ kitten \ər\ further \a\ ash \ā\ ace \ä\ mop, mar \au̇\ out \ch\ chin \e\ bet \ē\ easy \g\ go \i\ hit \ī\ ice \j\ job \ŋ\ sing \ō\ go \ȯ\ law \ȯi\ boy \th\ thin \th\ the \ü\ loot \u̇\ foot \y\ yet \zh\ vision see also Guide to Pronunciation

— **dis·pers·er** *noun*
— **dis·pers·ible** \-'spər-sə-bəl\ *adjective*
dis·per·sion \di-'spər-zhən, -shən\ *noun* (14th century)
1 *capitalized* : DIASPORA 1a
2 : the act or process of dispersing : the state of being dispersed
3 : the scattering of the values of a frequency distribution from an average
4 : the separation of light into colors by refraction or diffraction with formation of a spectrum; *also* : the separation of radiation into components in accordance with some varying characteristic (as energy)
5 a : a dispersed substance **b** : a system consisting of a dispersed substance and the medium in which it is dispersed : COLLOID 2b
dis·per·sive \-'spər-siv, -ziv\ *adjective* (1677)
1 : of or relating to dispersion ⟨a *dispersive* medium⟩ ⟨the *dispersive* power of a lens⟩
2 : tending to disperse
— **dis·per·sive·ly** *adverb*
— **dis·per·sive·ness** *noun*
dis·per·soid \-'spər-ˌsȯid\ *noun* (1911)
: finely divided particles of one substance dispersed in another
dis·pir·it \(ˌ)dis-'pir-ət\ *transitive verb* [*dis-* + *spirit*] (1647)
: to deprive of morale or enthusiasm
— **dis·pir·it·ed** *adjective*
— **dis·pir·it·ed·ly** *adverb*
— **dis·pir·it·ed·ness** *noun*
dis·pit·eous \di-'spi-tē-əs\ *adjective* [alteration of *despiteous*] (1803)
archaic : CRUEL
dis·place \(ˌ)dis-'plās\ *transitive verb* [probably from Middle French *desplacer*, from *des-* dis- + *place* place] (1553)
1 a : to remove from the usual or proper place; *specifically* : to expel or force to flee from home or homeland **b** : to remove from an office, status, or job **c** *obsolete* : to drive out : BANISH
2 a : to move physically out of position ⟨a floating object *displaces* water⟩ **b** : to take the place of (as in a chemical reaction) : SUPPLANT
synonym see REPLACE
— **dis·place·able** \-'plā-sə-bəl\ *adjective*
dis·place·ment \di-'splā-smənt\ *noun* (1611)
1 : the act or process of displacing : the state of being displaced
2 a : the volume or weight of a fluid (as water) displaced by a floating body (as a ship) of equal weight **b** : the difference between the initial position of something (as a body or geometric figure) and any later position **c** : the volume displaced by a piston (as in a pump or an engine) in a single stroke; *also* : the total volume so displaced by all the pistons in an internal combustion engine (as in an automobile)
3 a : the redirection of an emotion or impulse from its original object (as an idea or person) to another **b** : the substitution of another form of behavior for what is usual or expected especially when the usual response is nonadaptive
dis·plant \(ˌ)dis-'splant\ *transitive verb* [Middle French *desplanter*, from *des-* dis- + *planter* to plant, from Late Latin *plantare*] (15th century)
1 : DISPLACE, REMOVE
2 : SUPPLANT
¹dis·play \di-'splā\ *verb* [Middle English, from Anglo-French *despleer, desploier*, literally, to unfold — more at DEPLOY] (14th century)
transitive verb
1 a : to put or spread before the view ⟨*display* the flag⟩ **b** : to make evident ⟨*displayed* great skill⟩ **c** : to exhibit ostentatiously ⟨liked to *display* his erudition⟩
2 *obsolete* : DESCRY
intransitive verb
1 *obsolete* : SHOW OFF
2 : to make a breeding display ⟨penguins *displayed* and copulated⟩
synonym see SHOW

— **dis·play·able** \-'splā-ə-bəl\ *adjective*
²display *noun, often attributive* (1665)
1 a (1) : a setting or presentation of something in open view ⟨a fireworks *display*⟩ (2) : a clear sign or evidence : EXHIBITION ⟨a *display* of courage⟩ **b** : ostentatious show **c** : type, composition, or printing designed to catch the eye **d** : an eye-catching arrangement by which something is exhibited **e** : an electronic device (as a cathode-ray tube) that temporarily presents information in visual form; *also* : the visual information
2 : a pattern of behavior exhibited especially by male birds in the breeding season
dis·please \(ˌ)dis-'plēz\ *verb* [Middle English *displesen*, from Middle French *desplaisir*, modification of (assumed) Vulgar Latin *displacēre*, from Latin *dis-* + *placēre* to please — more at PLEASE] (14th century)
transitive verb
1 : to incur the disapproval or dislike of especially by annoying ⟨their gossip *displeases* her⟩
2 : to be offensive to ⟨abstract art *displeases* him⟩
intransitive verb
: to give displeasure ⟨behavior calculated to *displease*⟩
dis·plea·sure \(ˌ)dis-'ple-zhər, -'plā-\ *noun* (15th century)
1 : the feeling of one that is displeased : DISFAVOR
2 : DISCOMFORT, UNHAPPINESS
3 *archaic* : OFFENSE, INJURY
dis·plode \di-'splōd\ *verb* **dis·plod·ed; dis·plod·ing** [Latin *displodere*, from *dis-* + *plaudere* to clap, applaud] (1667)
archaic : EXPLODE
— **dis·plo·sion** \-'splō-zhən\ *noun*
¹dis·port \di-'spȯrt, -'spȯrt\ *noun* (14th century)
archaic : SPORT, PASTIME
²disport *verb* [Middle English, from Middle French *desporter*, from *des-* dis- + *porter* to carry, from Latin *portare* — more at FARE] (14th century)
transitive verb
1 : DIVERT, AMUSE
2 : DISPLAY
intransitive verb
: to amuse oneself in light or lively fashion : FROLIC
— **dis·port·ment** \-mənt\ *noun*
¹dis·pos·able \di-'spō-zə-bəl\ *adjective* (1643)
1 : subject to or available for disposal; *specifically* : remaining to an individual after deduction of taxes ⟨*disposable* income⟩
2 : designed to be used once and then thrown away ⟨*disposable* diapers⟩
— **dis·pos·abil·i·ty** \-ˌspō-zə-'bi-lə-tē\ *noun*
²disposable *noun* (1963)
: something that is disposable
dis·pos·al \di-'spō-zəl\ *noun* (1630)
1 : the power or authority to dispose or make use of as one chooses ⟨the car was at my *disposal*⟩
2 : the act or process of disposing: as **a** : orderly placement or distribution **b** : REGULATION, ADMINISTRATION **c** : the act or action of presenting or bestowing something ⟨*disposal* of favors⟩ **d** : systematic destruction; *especially* : destruction or transformation of garbage
3 [*garbage disposal unit*] : a device used to reduce waste matter (as by grinding)
¹dis·pose \di-'spōz\ *verb* **dis·posed; dis·pos·ing** [Middle English, from Middle French *disposer*, from Latin *disponere* to arrange (perfect indicative *disposui*), from *dis-* + *ponere* to put — more at POSITION] (14th century)
transitive verb
1 : to give a tendency to : INCLINE ⟨faulty diet *disposes* one to sickness⟩

2 a : to put in place : set in readiness : ARRANGE ⟨*disposing* troops for withdrawal⟩ **b** *obsolete* : REGULATE **c** : BESTOW
intransitive verb
1 : to settle a matter finally
2 *obsolete* : to come to terms
synonym see INCLINE
— **dis·pos·er** *noun*
— **dispose of 1** : to place, distribute, or arrange especially in an orderly way **2 a** : to transfer to the control of another ⟨*disposing of* personal property to a total stranger⟩ **b** (1) : to get rid of ⟨how to *dispose of* toxic waste⟩ (2) : to deal with conclusively ⟨*disposed of* the matter efficiently⟩
²dispose *noun* (1590)
1 *obsolete* : DISPOSAL
2 *obsolete* **a** : DISPOSITION **b** : DEMEANOR
dis·po·si·tion \ˌdis-pə-'zi-shən\ *noun* [Middle English, from Middle French, from Latin *disposition-, dispositio*, from *disponere*] (14th century)
1 : the act or the power of disposing or the state of being disposed: as **a** : ADMINISTRATION, CONTROL **b** : final arrangement : SETTLEMENT ⟨the *disposition* of the case⟩ **c** (1) : transfer to the care or possession of another (2) : the power of such transferal **d** : orderly arrangement
2 a : prevailing tendency, mood, or inclination **b** : temperamental makeup : the tendency of something to act in a certain manner under given circumstances ☆
— **dis·po·si·tion·al** \-'zish-nəl, -'zi-shə-nᵊl\ *adjective*
dis·pos·i·tive \di-'spä-zə-tiv\ *adjective* (1613)
: directed toward or effecting disposition (as of a case) ⟨*dispositive* evidence⟩
dis·pos·sess \ˌdis-pə-'zes *also* -'ses\ *transitive verb* [Middle French *despossesser*, from *des-* dis- + *possesser* to possess] (1555)
: to put out of possession or occupancy ⟨*dispossessed* the nobles of their land⟩
— **dis·pos·ses·sion** \-'ze-shən *also* -'se-\ *noun*
— **dis·pos·ses·sor** \-'ze-sər *also* -'se-\ *noun*
dis·pos·sessed *adjective* (15th century)
: deprived of homes, possessions, and security
dis·po·sure \di-'spō-zhər\ *noun* (1569)
archaic : DISPOSAL, DISPOSITION
dis·praise \(ˌ)dis-'prāz\ *transitive verb* [Middle English *dispraisen*, from Middle French *despreisier*, from Old French, from *des-* dis- + *preisier* to praise] (13th century)
: to comment on with disapproval or censure
— **dispraise** *noun*
— **dis·prais·er** *noun*
— **dis·prais·ing·ly** \-'prā-ziŋ-lē\ *adverb*
dispread \di-'spred\ *transitive verb* (1590)
: to spread abroad or out

☆ SYNONYMS
Disposition, temperament, temper, character, personality mean the dominant quality or qualities distinguishing a person or group. DISPOSITION implies customary moods and attitude toward the life around one ⟨a cheerful *disposition*⟩. TEMPERAMENT implies a pattern of innate characteristics associated with one's specific physical and nervous organization ⟨an artistic *temperament*⟩. TEMPER implies the qualities acquired through experience that determine how a person or group meets difficulties or handles situations ⟨a resilient *temper*⟩. CHARACTER applies to the aggregate of moral qualities by which a person is judged apart from intelligence, competence, or special talents ⟨strength of *character*⟩. PERSONALITY applies to an aggregate of qualities that distinguish one as a person ⟨a somber *personality*⟩.

dis·prize \(ˌ)dis-ˈprīz\ *transitive verb* [Middle French *despriser,* from Old French *despreisier*] (15th century)
archaic : UNDERVALUE, SCORN
dis·proof \(ˌ)dis-ˈprüf\ *noun* (15th century)
1 : the action of disproving
2 : evidence that disproves
¹dis·pro·por·tion \ˌdis-prə-ˈpōr-shən, -ˈpȯr-\ *noun* (1555)
: lack of proportion, symmetry, or proper relation : DISPARITY; *also* : an instance of such disparity
— **dis·pro·por·tion·al** \-shnəl, -shə-nᵊl\ *adjective*
²disproportion *transitive verb* (1593)
: to make out of proportion : MISMATCH
dis·pro·por·tion·ate \-sh(ə-)nət\ *adjective* (1555)
: being out of proportion ⟨a *disproportionate* share⟩
— **dis·pro·por·tion·ate·ly** *adverb*
dis·pro·por·tion·ation \-ˌpōr-shə-ˈnā-shən, -ˌpȯr-\ *noun* (circa 1929)
: the transformation of a substance into two or more dissimilar substances usually by simultaneous oxidation and reduction
— **dis·pro·por·tion·ate** \-ˈpōr-shə-ˌnāt, -ˈpȯr-\ *intransitive verb*
dis·prove \(ˌ)dis-ˈprüv\ *transitive verb* [Middle English, from Middle French *desprover,* from *des-* dis- + *prover* to prove] (14th century)
: to prove to be false or wrong : REFUTE
— **dis·prov·able** \-ˈprü-və-bəl\ *adjective*
dis·pu·tant \di-ˈspyü-tᵊnt, ˈdis-pyə-tənt\ *noun* (1593)
: one that is engaged in a dispute
dis·pu·ta·tion \ˌdis-pyə-ˈtā-shən\ *noun* (14th century)
1 : the action of disputing : verbal controversy ⟨continuous *disputation* between them⟩ ⟨ideological *disputations*⟩
2 : an academic exercise in oral defense of a thesis by formal logic
dis·pu·ta·tious \-shəs\ *adjective* (1660)
1 a : inclined to dispute **b** : marked by disputation
2 : provoking debate : CONTROVERSIAL
— **dis·pu·ta·tious·ly** *adverb*
— **dis·pu·ta·tious·ness** *noun*
¹dis·pute \di-ˈspyüt\ *verb* **dis·put·ed; dis·put·ing** [Middle English, from Old French *desputer,* from Latin *disputare* to discuss, from *dis-* + *putare* to think] (13th century)
intransitive verb
: to engage in argument : DEBATE; *especially*
: to argue irritably or with irritating persistence
transitive verb
1 a : to make the subject of disputation **b** : to call into question ⟨her honesty was never *disputed*⟩
2 a : to struggle against : OPPOSE ⟨*disputed* the advance of the invaders⟩ **b** : to contend over ⟨both sides *disputed* the bridgehead⟩
— **dis·put·able** \di-ˈspyü-tə-bəl, ˈdis-pyə-\ *adjective*
— **dis·put·ably** \-blē\ *adverb*
— **dis·put·er** *noun*
²dis·pute \di-ˈspyüt, ˈdis-ˌpyüt\ *noun* (1608)
1 a : verbal controversy : DEBATE **b** : QUARREL
2 *obsolete* : physical combat
dis·qual·i·fi·ca·tion \(ˌ)dis-ˌkwä-lə-fə-ˈkā-shən\ *noun* (1714)
1 : something that disqualifies or incapacitates
2 : the act of disqualifying : the state of being disqualified ⟨*disqualification* from office⟩
dis·qual·i·fy \(ˌ)dis-ˈkwä-lə-ˌfī\ *transitive verb* (1723)
1 : to deprive of the required qualities, properties, or conditions : make unfit
2 : to deprive of a power, right, or privilege
3 : to make ineligible for a prize or for further competition because of violations of the rules
dis·quan·ti·ty \(ˌ)dis-ˈkwän-(t)ə-tē\ *transitive verb* (1605)

obsolete : DIMINISH, LESSEN
¹dis·qui·et \(ˌ)dis-ˈkwī-ət\ *transitive verb* (circa 1530)
: to take away the peace or tranquillity of : DISTURB, ALARM
synonym see DISCOMPOSE
— **dis·qui·et·ing** *adjective*
— **dis·qui·et·ing·ly** \-ˈkwī-ə-tiŋ-lē\ *adverb*
²disquiet *noun* (1581)
: lack of peace or tranquillity : ANXIETY
³disquiet *adjective* (1587)
archaic : UNEASY, DISQUIETED
— **dis·qui·et·ly** *adverb*
dis·qui·etude \(ˌ)dis-ˈkwī-ə-ˌt(y)üd\ *noun* (1709)
: ANXIETY, AGITATION
dis·qui·si·tion \ˌdis-kwə-ˈzi-shən\ *noun* [Latin *disquisition-, disquisitio,* from *disquirere* to investigate, from *dis-* + *quaerere* to seek] (1647)
: a formal inquiry into or discussion of a subject : DISCOURSE
dis·rate \(ˌ)dis-ˈrāt\ *transitive verb* (1811)
: to reduce in rank : DEMOTE
¹dis·re·gard \ˌdis-ri-ˈgärd\ *transitive verb* (1641)
: to pay no attention to : treat as unworthy of regard or notice
synonym see NEGLECT
²disregard *noun* (1665)
: the act of disregarding : the state of being disregarded : NEGLECT
— **dis·re·gard·ful** \-fəl\ *adjective*
dis·re·lat·ed \ˌdis-ri-ˈlā-təd\ *adjective* (1894)
: not related
dis·re·la·tion \-ˈlā-shən\ *noun* (1893)
: lack of a fitting or proportionate connection or relationship
¹dis·rel·ish \(ˌ)dis-ˈre-lish\ *transitive verb* (1604)
: to find unpalatable or distasteful
²disrelish *noun* (circa 1625)
: lack of relish : DISTASTE, DISLIKE
dis·re·mem·ber \ˌdis-ri-ˈmem-bər\ *transitive verb* (1815)
: FORGET
dis·re·pair \ˌdis-ri-ˈpar, -ˈper\ *noun* (1798)
: the state of being in need of repair ⟨a building fallen into *disrepair*⟩
dis·rep·u·ta·ble \(ˌ)dis-ˈre-pyə-tə-bəl\ *adjective* (1772)
: not reputable
— **dis·rep·u·ta·bil·i·ty** \(ˌ)dis-ˌre-pyə-tə-ˈbi-lə-tē\ *noun*
— **dis·rep·u·ta·ble·ness** \(ˌ)dis-ˈre-pyə-tə-bəl-nəs\ *noun*
— **dis·rep·u·ta·bly** \-blē\ *adverb*
dis·re·pute \ˌdis-ri-ˈpyüt\ *noun* (1653)
: lack or decline of good reputation : a state of being held in low esteem
synonym see DISGRACE
¹dis·re·spect \ˌdis-ri-ˈspekt\ *transitive verb* (1614)
: to have disrespect for
²disrespect *noun* (1631)
: lack of respect
— **dis·re·spect·ful** \-fəl\ *adjective*
— **dis·re·spect·ful·ly** \-fə-lē\ *adverb*
— **dis·re·spect·ful·ness** *noun*
dis·re·spect·able \ˌdis-ri-ˈspek-tə-bəl\ *adjective* (1813)
: not respectable
— **dis·re·spect·abil·i·ty** \-ˌspek-tə-ˈbi-lə-tē\ *noun*
dis·robe \(ˌ)dis-ˈrōb\ *verb* [Middle French *desrober,* from *des-* dis- + *robe* garment, from Old French] (1581)
intransitive verb
: to take off one's clothing
transitive verb
: to strip of clothing or covering
dis·rupt \dis-ˈrəpt\ *transitive verb* [Latin *disruptus,* past participle of *disrumpere* to break — more at REAVE] (1817)
1 a : to break apart : RUPTURE **b** : to throw into disorder ⟨agitators trying to *disrupt* the meeting⟩

2 : to interrupt the normal course or unity of
— **dis·rupt·er** *noun*
— **dis·rup·tion** \-ˈrəp-shən\ *noun*
— **dis·rup·tive** \-ˈrəp-tiv\ *adjective*
— **dis·rup·tive·ly** *adverb*
— **dis·rup·tive·ness** *noun*
diss *variant of* DIS
dis·sat·is·fac·tion \(ˌ)di(s)-ˌsat-əs-ˈfak-shən\ *noun* (1640)
: the quality or state of being dissatisfied : DISCONTENT
dis·sat·is·fac·to·ry \-ˈfak-t(ə-)rē\ *adjective* (circa 1610)
: causing dissatisfaction
dis·sat·is·fied \(ˌ)di(s)-ˈsa-təs-ˌfīd\ *adjective* (1675)
: expressing or showing lack of satisfaction
: not pleased or satisfied
dis·sat·is·fy \-ˌfī\ *transitive verb* (1666)
: to fail to satisfy : DISPLEASE
dis·save \(ˌ)di(s)-ˈsāv\ *intransitive verb* (1936)
: to use savings for current expenses
dis·seat \(ˌ)di(s)-ˈsēt\ *transitive verb* (1612)
archaic : UNSEAT
dis·sect \di-ˈsekt; ÷dī-ˈsekt, ÷ˈdī-\ *verb* [Latin *dissectus,* past participle of *dissecare* to cut apart, from *dis-* + *secare* to cut — more at SAW] (1607)
transitive verb
1 : to separate into pieces : expose the several parts of (as an animal) for scientific examination
2 : to analyze and interpret minutely
intransitive verb
: to make a dissection
synonym see ANALYZE
— **dis·sec·tor** \-ˈsek-tər\ *noun*
dis·sect·ed *adjective* (1652)
1 : cut deeply into fine lobes ⟨a *dissected* leaf⟩
2 : divided into hills and ridges (as by gorges) ⟨a *dissected* plateau⟩
dis·sect·ing microscope *noun* (circa 1897)
: a microscope with low magnification
dis·sec·tion \di-ˈsek-shən; ÷dī-ˈsek-, ÷ˈdī-\ *noun* (1605)
1 : the act or process of dissecting : the state of being dissected
2 : an anatomical specimen prepared by dissecting
dis·seise *or* **dis·seize** \(ˌ)di(s)-ˈsēz\ *transitive verb* **dis·seised** *or* **dis·seized; dis·seis·ing** *or* **dis·seiz·ing** [Middle English *disseisen,* from Medieval Latin *disseisiare* & Anglo-French *disseisir,* from Old French *dessaisir,* from *des-* dis- + *saisir* to put in possession of — more at SEIZE] (14th century)
: to deprive especially wrongfully of seisin : DISPOSSESS
— **dis·sei·sor** \-ˈsē-zər\ *noun*
dis·sei·sin *or* **dis·sei·zin** \-ˈsē-zᵊn\ *noun* [Middle English *dysseysyne,* from Anglo-French *disseisine,* from Old French *dessaisine,* from *des-* dis- + *saisine* seisin] (14th century)
: the act of disseising : the state of being disseised
dis·sem·ble \di-ˈsem-bəl\ *verb* **dis·sem·bled; dis·sem·bling** \-b(ə-)liŋ\ [Middle English *dissymblen,* alteration of *dissimulen,* from Middle French *dissimuler,* from Latin *dissimulare* — more at DISSIMULATE] (15th century)
transitive verb
1 : to hide under a false appearance
2 : to put on the appearance of : SIMULATE
intransitive verb
: to put on a false appearance : conceal facts, intentions, or feelings under some pretense
— **dis·sem·bler** \-b(ə-)lər\ *noun*

\ə\ abut \ᵊ\ kitten \ər\ further \a\ ash \ā\ ace
\ä\ mop, mar \au̇\ out \ch\ chin \e\ bet \ē\ easy
\g\ go \i\ hit \ī\ ice \j\ job \ŋ\ sing \ō\ go
\ȯ\ law \ȯi\ boy \th\ thin \th̲\ the \ü\ loot \u̇\ foot
\y\ yet \zh\ vision *see also* Guide to Pronunciation

dis·sem·i·nate \di-'se-mə-,nāt\ *transitive verb* **-nat·ed; -nat·ing** [Latin *disseminatus*, past participle of *disseminare*, from *dis-* + *seminare* to sow, from *semin-, semen* seed — more at SEMEN] (1603)
1 : to spread abroad as though sowing seed ⟨*disseminate* ideas⟩
2 : to disperse throughout
— **dis·sem·i·na·tion** \-,se-mə-'nā-shən\ *noun*
— **dis·sem·i·na·tor** \-'se-mə-,nā-tər\ *noun*
dis·sem·i·nat·ed *adjective* (1876)
: widely dispersed in a tissue, organ, or the entire body ⟨*disseminated* gonococcal disease⟩
dis·sem·i·nule \di-'sem-ə-,nyül\ *noun* (1904)
: a part or organ (as a seed or spore) of a plant that ensures propagation
dis·sen·sion *also* **dis·sen·tion** \di-'sen(t)-shən\ *noun* [Middle English, from Middle French, from Latin *dissension-, dissensio,* from *dissentire*] (14th century)
: DISAGREEMENT; *especially* : partisan and contentious quarreling
synonym see DISCORD
dis·sen·sus \(,)di(s)-'sen(t)-səs\ *noun* [*dis-* + *consensus*] (1966)
: difference of opinion
¹dis·sent \di-'sent\ *intransitive verb* [Middle English, from Latin *dissentire,* from *dis-* + *sentire* to feel — more at SENSE] (15th century)
1 : to withhold assent
2 : to differ in opinion
²dissent *noun* (1585)
: difference of opinion: as **a** : religious nonconformity **b** : a justice's nonconcurrence with a decision of the majority — called also *dissenting opinion*
dis·sent·er \di-'sen-tər\ *noun* (1639)
1 : one that dissents
2 *capitalized* : an English Nonconformist
dis·sen·tient \di-'sen(t)-sh(ē-)ənt\ *adjective* [Latin *dissentient-, dissentiens,* present participle of *dissentire*] (1651)
: expressing dissent
— **dissentient** *noun*
dis·sent·ing \di-'sen-tiŋ\ *adjective, often capitalized* (1644)
: of or relating to the English Nonconformists ⟨a *dissenting* church⟩ ⟨*dissenting* merchants⟩
dis·sen·tious \di-'sen(t)-shəs\ *adjective* (1560)
: characterized by dissension or dissent
dis·sep·i·ment \di-'se-pə-mənt\ *noun* [Latin *dissaepimentum* partition, from *dissaepire* to divide, from *dis-* + *saepire* to fence in — more at SEPTUM] (circa 1727)
: a dividing tissue : SEPTUM
dis·sert \di-'sərt\ *intransitive verb* [Latin *dissertus,* past participle of *disserere,* from *dis-* + *serere* to join, arrange — more at SERIES] (1657)
: to speak or write at length
dis·ser·tate \'di-sər-,tāt\ *intransitive verb* **-tat·ed; -tat·ing** [Latin *dissertatus,* past participle of *dissertare,* from *dissertus*] (1766)
: DISSERT; *also* : to write a dissertation
— **dis·ser·ta·tor** \-,tā-tər\ *noun*
dis·ser·ta·tion \,di-sər-'tā-shən\ *noun* (1651)
: an extended usually written treatment of a subject; *specifically* : one submitted for a doctorate
— **dis·ser·ta·tion·al** \-'tāsh-nəl, -'tā-shə-n°l\ *adjective*
dis·serve \(,)di(s)-'sərv\ *transitive verb* (1629)
: to serve badly or falsely : HARM
dis·ser·vice \di-'sər-vəs\ *noun* (1599)
: ill service : HARM; *also* : an unhelpful, unkind, or harmful act
dis·ser·vice·able \di(s)-'sər-və-sə-bəl\ *adjective* (1644)
: COUNTERPRODUCTIVE
dis·sev·er \di-'se-vər\ *verb* [Middle English, from Old French *dessevrer,* from Late Latin *disseparare,* from Latin *dis-* + *separare* to separate] (13th century)

transitive verb
: SEVER, SEPARATE
intransitive verb
: to come apart : DISUNITE
— **dis·sev·er·ance** \-'se-v(ə-)rən(t)s\ *noun*
— **dis·sev·er·ment** \-'se-vər-mənt\ *noun*
dis·si·dence \'di-sə-dən(t)s\ *noun* (circa 1656)
: DISSENT, DISAGREEMENT
dis·si·dent \-dənt\ *adjective* [Latin *dissident-, dissidens,* present participle of *dissidēre* to sit apart, disagree, from *dis-* + *sedēre* to sit — more at SIT] (1837)
: disagreeing especially with an established religious or political system, organization, or belief
— **dissident** *noun*
dis·sim·i·lar \(,)di(s)-'si-mə-lər, -'sim-lər\ *adjective* (1599)
: UNLIKE
— **dis·sim·i·lar·i·ty** \(,)di(s)-,si-mə-'lar-ə-tē\ *noun*
— **dis·sim·i·lar·ly** \(')di(s)-'si-mə-lər-lē, -'sim-lər\ *adverb*
— **dis·sim·i·lars** \-lərz\ *noun plural*
dis·sim·i·late \(,)di-'si-mə-,lāt\ *intransitive verb* **-lat·ed; -lat·ing** [*dis-* + *-similate* (as in *assimilate*)] (1841)
: to undergo dissimilation
— **dis·sim·i·la·to·ry** \-mə-lə-,tōr-ē, -,tȯr-\ *adjective*
dis·sim·i·la·tion \(,)di-,si-mə-'lā-shən\ *noun* (circa 1874)
: the change or omission of one of two identical or closely related sounds in a word
dis·si·mil·i·tude \,di(s)-sə-'mi-lə-,tüd, -,tyüd\ *noun* [Latin *dissimilitudo,* from *dissimilis* unlike, from *dis-* + *similis* like — more at SAME] (15th century)
: lack of resemblance
dis·sim·u·late \(,)di-'sim-yə-,lāt\ *verb* **-lat·ed; -lat·ing** [Latin *dissimulatus,* past participle of *dissimulare,* from *dis-* + *simulare* to simulate] (15th century)
transitive verb
: to hide under a false appearance ⟨smiled to *dissimulate* her urgency —Alice Glenday⟩
intransitive verb
: DISSEMBLE
— **dis·sim·u·la·tion** \(,)di-,sim-yə-'lā-shən\ *noun*
— **dis·sim·u·la·tor** \(')di-'sim-yə-,lā-tər\ *noun*
dis·si·pate \'di-sə-,pāt\ *verb* **-pat·ed; -pat·ing** [Latin *dissipatus,* past participle of *dissipare, dissupare,* from *dis-* + *supare* to throw] (15th century)
transitive verb
1 a : to break up and drive off (as a crowd) **b** : to cause to spread thin or scatter and gradually vanish ⟨one's sympathy is eventually *dissipated* —Andrew Feinberg⟩ **c** : to lose (as heat or electricity) irrecoverably
2 : to spend or use up wastefully or foolishly ⟨lifelong tendency to *dissipate* his gifts in travel and pleasure —Edmund Morris⟩ ⟨his fortune is *dissipated* in imprudent political adventures —John Butt⟩
intransitive verb
1 : to break up and scatter or vanish
2 : to be extravagant or dissolute in the pursuit of pleasure; *especially* : to drink to excess
synonym see SCATTER
— **dis·si·pat·er** *noun*
dis·si·pat·ed *adjective* (1744)
: given to or marked by dissipation : DISSOLUTE
— **dis·si·pat·ed·ly** *adverb*
— **dis·si·pat·ed·ness** *noun*
dis·si·pa·tion \,di-sə-'pā-shən\ *noun* (15th century)
1 : the action or process of dissipating : the state of being dissipated: **a** : DISPERSION, DIFFUSION **b** *archaic* : DISSOLUTION, DISINTEGRATION **c** : wasteful expenditure **d** : intemperate living; *especially* : excessive drinking

2 : an act of self-indulgence; *especially* : one that is not harmful : AMUSEMENT
dis·si·pa·tive \'di-sə-,pā-tiv\ *adjective* (1684)
: relating to dissipation especially of heat
dis·so·cia·ble \(,)di-'sō-sh(ē-)ə-bəl, -sē-ə-\ *adjective* (1833)
: SEPARABLE
— **dis·so·cia·bil·i·ty** \(,)di-,sō-sh(ē-)ə-'bi-lə-tē, -sē-ə-\ *noun*
dis·so·cial \(,)di(s)-'sō-shəl\ *adjective* (1762)
: UNSOCIAL, SELFISH
dis·so·ci·ate \(,)di-'sō-shē-,āt, -sē-\ *verb* **-at·ed; -at·ing** [Latin *dissociatus,* past participle of *dissociare,* from *dis-* + *sociare* to join, from *socius* companion — more at SOCIAL] (1590)
transitive verb
1 : to separate from association or union with another
2 : DISUNITE; *specifically* : to subject to chemical dissociation
intransitive verb
1 : to undergo dissociation
2 : to mutate especially reversibly
dis·so·ci·a·tion \(,)di-,sō-sē-'ā-shən, -shē-\ *noun* (1611)
1 : the act or process of dissociating : the state of being dissociated: as **a** : the process by which a chemical combination breaks up into simpler constituents; *especially* : one that results from the action of energy (as heat) on a gas or of a solvent on a dissolved substance **b** : the separation of whole segments of the personality (as in multiple personality) or of discrete mental processes (as in the schizophrenias) from the mainstream of consciousness or of behavior
2 : the property inherent in some biological stocks (as of certain bacteria) of differentiating into two or more distinct and relatively permanent strains; *also* : such a strain
— **dis·so·ci·a·tive** \(,)di-'sō-shē-,ā-tiv, -sē-, -shə-tiv\ *adjective*
dis·sol·u·ble \di-'säl-yə-bəl\ *adjective* [Latin *dissolubilis,* from *dissolvere* to dissolve] (1534)
: capable of being dissolved or disintegrated
dis·so·lute \'di-sə-,lüt, -lət\ *adjective* [Latin *dissolutus,* from past participle of *dissolvere* to loosen, dissolve] (14th century)
: lacking restraint; *especially* : marked by indulgence in things (as drink or promiscuous sex) deemed vices ⟨*dissolute* and degrading aspects of human nature —Wallace Fowlie⟩
— **dis·so·lute·ly** *adverb*
— **dis·so·lute·ness** *noun*
dis·so·lu·tion \,di-sə-'lü-shən\ *noun* (14th century)
1 : the act or process of dissolving: as **a** : separation into component parts **b** (1) : DECAY, DISINTEGRATION (2) : DEATH **c** : termination or destruction by breaking down, disrupting, or dispersing ⟨the *dissolution* of the republic⟩ **d** : the dissolving of an assembly or organization **e** : LIQUEFACTION
2 : a dissolute act or practice
¹dis·solve \di-'zälv, -'zȯlv *also* -'zäv *or* -'zȯv\ *verb* [Middle English, from Latin *dissolvere,* from *dis-* + *solvere* to loosen — more at SOLVE] (14th century)
transitive verb
1 a : to cause to disperse or disappear : DESTROY **b** : to separate into component parts : DISINTEGRATE **c** : to bring to an end : TERMINATE ⟨*dissolve* parliament⟩ **d** : ANNUL ⟨*dissolve* an injunction⟩
2 a : to cause to pass into solution ⟨*dissolve* sugar in water⟩ **b** : MELT, LIQUEFY **c** : to cause to be emotionally moved **d** : to cause to fade out in a dissolve
3 *archaic* : DETACH, LOOSEN
4 : to clear up ⟨*dissolve* a problem⟩
intransitive verb
1 a : to become dissipated or decomposed **b** : BREAK UP, DISPERSE **c** : to fade away

2 a : to become fluid **:** MELT **b :** to pass into solution **c :** to be overcome emotionally ⟨*dissolved* into tears⟩ **d :** to resolve itself as if by dissolution ⟨hate *dissolved* into fear⟩ **e :** to change by a dissolve ⟨the scene *dissolves* to a Victorian parlor⟩
— **dis·solv·able** \-'zäl-və-bəl, -'zȯl-\ *adjective*
— **dis·sol·vent** \-'zäl-vənt, -'zȯl-\ *noun or adjective*
— **dis·solv·er** *noun*
²**dissolve** *noun* (1916)
: a gradual superimposing of one motion-picture or television shot upon another on a screen
dis·so·nance \'di-sə-nən(t)s\ *noun* (15th century)
1 a : lack of agreement; *especially* **:** inconsistency between the beliefs one holds or between one's actions and one's beliefs — compare COGNITIVE DISSONANCE **b :** an instance of such inconsistency or disagreement
2 : a mingling of discordant sounds; *especially* **:** a clashing or unresolved musical interval or chord
dis·so·nant \-nənt\ *adjective* [Middle French or Latin; Middle French, from Latin *dissonant-, dissonans,* present participle of *dissonare* to be discordant, from *dis-* + *sonare* to sound — more at SOUND] (15th century)
1 : marked by dissonance **:** DISCORDANT
2 : INCONGRUOUS
3 : harmonically unresolved
— **dis·so·nant·ly** *adverb*
dis·suade \di-'swād\ *transitive verb* **dis·suad·ed; dis·suad·ing** [Middle French or Latin; Middle French *dissuader,* from Latin *dissuadēre,* from *dis-* + *suadēre* to urge — more at SWEET] (15th century)
1 a : to advise (a person) against something **b** *archaic* **:** to advise against (an action)
2 : to turn from something by persuasion
— **dis·suad·er** *noun*
dis·sua·sion \di-'swā-zhən\ *noun* [Middle French or Latin; Middle French, from Latin *dissuasion-, dissuasio,* from *dissuadēre*] (15th century)
: the action of dissuading
dis·sua·sive \di-'swā-siv, -ziv\ *adjective* (1609)
: tending to dissuade
— **dis·sua·sive·ly** *adverb*
— **dis·sua·sive·ness** *noun*
dis·syl·la·ble \'di-,si-lə-bəl, (,)di(s)-'si-; 'dī-,si-, (,)dī-'si-\ *variant of* DISYLLABLE
dis·sym·me·try \(,)di(s)-'si-mə-trē\ *noun* (1845)
: the absence of or the lack of symmetry
— **dis·sym·met·ric** \(,)di(s)-sə-'me-trik\ *adjective*
¹**dis·taff** \'dis-,taf\ *noun, plural* **distaffs** \-,tafs, -,tavz\ [Middle English *distaf,* from Old English *distæf,* from *dis-* (akin to Middle Low German *dise* bunch of flax) + *stæf* staff] (before 12th century)
1 a : a staff for holding the flax, tow, or wool in spinning **b :** woman's work or domain
2 : the female branch or side of a family ◇
²**distaff** *adjective* (circa 1633)
: MATERNAL ⟨the *distaff* side of the family⟩ — compare SPEAR; *also* **:** FEMALE ⟨*distaff* executives⟩

distaff 1a

dis·tain \dis-'tān\ *transitive verb* [Middle English *disteynen,* from Middle French *desteindre* to take away the color of, from Old French, from *des-* dis- + *teindre* to dye, from Latin *tingere* to wet, dye — more at TINGE] (14th century)
1 *archaic* **:** STAIN
2 *archaic* **:** DISHONOR

dis·tal \'dis-t°l\ *adjective* [*distant* + *-al*] (1808)
1 : situated away from the point of attachment or origin or a central point especially of the body — compare PROXIMAL
2 : of, relating to, or being the surface of a tooth that is next to the tooth behind it or that is farthest from the middle of the front of the jaw — compare MESIAL 2
— **dis·tal·ly** \-t°l-ē\ *adverb*
distal convoluted tubule *noun* (circa 1901)
: the convoluted portion of the vertebrate nephron that lies between the loop of Henle and the nonsecretory part of the nephron and that is concerned especially with the concentration of urine
¹**dis·tance** \'dis-tən(t)s\ *noun* (14th century)
1 *obsolete* **:** DISCORD
2 a : separation in time **b :** the degree or amount of separation between two points, lines, surfaces, or objects **c** (1) **:** an extent of area or an advance along a route measured linearly (2) **:** an extent of space measured other than linearly ⟨within walking *distance*⟩ **d :** an extent of advance from a beginning **e :** EXPANSE **f** (1) **:** length of a race or contest ⟨won at all *distances*⟩ (2) **:** the full length (as of a prizefight or ball game) (3) **:** a long race ⟨*distance* training⟩
3 : the quality or state of being distant: as **a :** spatial remoteness **b :** personal and especially emotional separation; *also* **:** RESERVE, COLDNESS **c :** DIFFERENCE, DISPARITY
4 : a distant point or region
5 a : AESTHETIC DISTANCE **b :** capacity to observe dispassionately
— **go the distance** *also* **last the distance :** to complete a course of action
²**distance** *transitive verb* **dis·tanced; dis·tanc·ing** (1578)
1 : to place or keep at a distance
2 : to leave far behind **:** OUTSTRIP
dis·tant \'dis-tənt\ *adjective* [Middle English, from Middle French, from Latin *distant-, distans,* present participle of *distare* to stand apart, be distant, from *dis-* + *stare* to stand — more at STAND] (14th century)
1 a : separated in space **:** AWAY **b :** situated at a great distance **:** FAR-OFF **c :** separated by a great distance from each other **:** far apart **d :** far behind ⟨finished a *distant* third⟩
2 : separated in a relationship other than spatial ⟨a *distant* cousin⟩ ⟨the *distant* past⟩
3 : different in kind
4 : reserved or aloof in personal relationship **:** COLD ⟨was *distant* and distracted⟩
5 a : going a long distance ⟨*distant* voyages⟩ **b :** concerned with remote things ⟨*distant* thoughts⟩
— **dis·tant·ly** *adverb*
— **dis·tant·ness** *noun*
¹**dis·taste** \(,)dis-'tāst\ (1592) *transitive verb*
1 *archaic* **:** to feel aversion to
2 *archaic* **:** OFFEND, DISPLEASE
intransitive verb
obsolete **:** to have an offensive taste
²**dis·taste** *noun* (1598)
1 a *archaic* **:** dislike of food or drink **b :** AVERSION, DISINCLINATION ⟨a *distaste* for opera⟩
2 *obsolete* **:** ANNOYANCE, DISCOMFORT
dis·taste·ful \(,)dis-'tāst-fəl\ *adjective* (1607)
1 : objectionable because offensive to one's personal taste **:** DISAGREEABLE
2 : unpleasant to the taste **:** LOATHSOME
— **dis·taste·ful·ly** \-fə-lē\ *adverb*
— **dis·taste·ful·ness** *noun*
dis·tel·fink \'dish-t°l-,fiŋk, 'dis-\ *noun* [Pennsylvania German *dischdelfink,* literally, gold-finch, from *dischdel* thistle + *fink* finch] (1939)
: a traditional Pennsylvania Dutch design motif in the form of a stylized bird
¹**dis·tem·per** \dis-'tem-pər\ *transitive verb* [Middle English *distempren,* from Late Latin

distemperare to temper badly, from Latin *dis-* + *temperare* to temper] (14th century)
1 : to throw out of order
2 *archaic* **:** DERANGE, UNSETTLE
²**distemper** *noun* (circa 1555)
1 : bad humor or temper
2 : a disordered or abnormal bodily state especially of quadruped mammals: as **a :** a highly contagious virus disease especially of dogs marked by fever, leukopenia, and respiratory, gastrointestinal, and neurological symptoms **b :** STRANGLES **c :** PANLEUKOPENIA
3 : AILMENT, DISORDER ⟨political *distemper*⟩ ⟨intellectual *distempers*⟩
— **dis·tem·per·ate** \-p(ə-)rət\ *adjective*
³**distemper** *noun* [obsolete *distemper,* verb, to dilute, mix to produce distemper, from Middle English, from Middle French *destemprer,* from Latin *dis-* + *temperare*] (1632)
1 : a process of painting in which the pigments are mixed with an emulsion of egg yolk, with size, or with white of egg as a vehicle and which is used for painting scenery and murals
2 a : the paint or the prepared ground used in the distemper process **b :** a painting done in distemper
3 : any of various water-based paints
⁴**distemper** *transitive verb* (circa 1873)
: to paint in or with distemper
dis·tem·per·a·ture \di-'stem-p(ə-)rə-,chu̇r, -pə(r)-, -chər, *chiefly Southern* -,t(y)u̇(ə)r\ *noun* (1531)
: a disordered condition
dis·tend \di-'stend\ *verb* [Middle English, from Latin *distendere,* from *dis-* + *tendere* to stretch — more at THIN] (15th century)
transitive verb
1 : EXTEND
2 : to enlarge from internal pressure **:** SWELL
intransitive verb
: to become expanded
synonym see EXPAND
dis·ten·si·ble \-'sten(t)-sə-bəl\ *adjective* [*distens-* (from Latin *distensus,* past participle of *distendere*) + *-ible*] (circa 1828)
: capable of being distended
— **dis·ten·si·bil·i·ty** \-,sten(t)-sə-'bi-lə-tē\ *noun*
dis·ten·sion *or* **dis·ten·tion** \di-'sten(t)-shən\ *noun* [Latin *distention-, distentio,* from *distendere*] (15th century)
: the act of distending or the state of being distended especially unduly or abnormally
dis·tich \'dis-(,)tik\ *noun* [Latin *distichon,* from Greek, from neuter of *distichos* having two rows, from *di-* + *stichos* row, verse; akin to Greek *steichein* to go — more at STAIR] (1553)
: a strophic unit of two lines
dis·ti·chous \'dis-ti-kəs\ *adjective* [Late Latin *distichus,* from Greek *distichos*] (circa 1753)

◇ WORD HISTORY
distaff A distaff was originally a short staff that held a bundle of fibers, such as flax or wool, that were drawn and twisted into yarn or thread either by hand or with the aid of a spinning wheel. The job of spinning customarily fell to women, and since it was such a basic daily task, the distaff naturally came to be a symbol for women's work. This symbolic use of the word *distaff* dates back at least to the time of Chaucer. Eventually *distaff* came to be used figuratively for everything relating to the female domain and for women collectively. The women of a family became known as the *distaff* or the *distaff side.*

\ə\ abut \ᵊ\ kitten \ər\ further \a\ ash \ā\ ace
\ä\ mop, mar \au̇\ out \ch\ chin \e\ bet \ē\ easy
\g\ go \i\ hit \ī\ ice \j\ job \ŋ\ sing \ō\ go
\ȯ\ law \ȯi\ boy \th\ thin \t̲h̲\ the \ü\ loot \u̇\ foot
\y\ yet \zh\ vision *see also* Guide to Pronunciation

: disposed in two vertical rows ⟨*distichous* leaves⟩

dis·till *also* **dis·til** \di-'stil\ *verb* **dis·tilled; dis·till·ing** [Middle English *distillen*, from Middle French *distiller*, from Late Latin *distillare*, alteration of Latin *destillare*, from *de-* + *stillare* to drip, from *stilla* drop] (14th century) *transitive verb*
1 : to let fall, exude, or precipitate in drops or in a wet mist
2 a : to subject to or transform by distillation **b :** to obtain by or as if by distillation **c :** to extract the essence of **:** CONCENTRATE
intransitive verb
1 a : to fall or materialize in drops or in a fine moisture **b :** to appear slowly or in small quantities at a time
2 a : to undergo distillation **b :** to perform distillation

dis·til·late \'dis-tə-ˌlāt, -lət; di-'sti-lət\ *noun* (circa 1859)
1 : a liquid product condensed from vapor during distillation
2 : something concentrated or extracted as if by distilling

dis·til·la·tion \ˌdis-tə-'lā-shən\ *noun* (14th century)
1 a : the process of purifying a liquid by successive evaporation and condensation **b :** a process like distillation; *also* **:** an instance of distilling
2 : something distilled **:** DISTILLATE 2

dis·till·er \di-'sti-lər\ *noun* (1577)
: one that distills especially alcoholic liquors

dis·till·ery \di-'sti-lə-rē, -'stil-rē\ *noun, plural* **-er·ies** (1759)
: the works where distilling (as of alcoholic liquors) is done

dis·tinct \di-'stiŋ(k)t\ *adjective* [Middle English, from Middle French, from Latin *distinctus,* from past participle of *distinguere*] (14th century)
1 : distinguishable to the eye or mind as discrete **:** SEPARATE ⟨a *distinct* cultural group⟩ ⟨teaching as *distinct* from research⟩
2 : presenting a clear unmistakable impression ⟨a neat *distinct* handwriting⟩
3 *archaic* **:** notably decorated
4 a : NOTABLE ⟨a *distinct* contribution to scholarship⟩ **b :** readily and unmistakably apprehended ⟨a *distinct* possibility of snow⟩ ⟨a *distinct* British accent⟩ ☆
— **dis·tinct·ly** \-'stiŋ(k)t-lē, -'stiŋ-klē\ *adverb*
— **dis·tinct·ness** \-'stiŋ(k)t-nəs, -'stiŋk-nəs\ *noun*

dis·tinc·tion \di-'stiŋ(k)-shən\ *noun* (13th century)
1 a *archaic* **:** DIVISION **b :** CLASS 4
2 : the distinguishing of a difference ⟨without *distinction* as to race, sex, or religion⟩; *also* **:** the difference distinguished ⟨the *distinction* between *imply* and *infer*⟩
3 : something that distinguishes ⟨regional *distinctions*⟩
4 : the quality or state of being distinguishable
5 a : the quality or state of being distinguished or worthy ⟨a politician of *distinction*⟩ **b :** special honor or recognition ⟨took a law degree with *distinction*⟩ **c :** achievement that sets one apart ⟨the *distinction* of winning the title⟩

dis·tinc·tive \di-'stiŋ(k)-tiv\ *adjective* (15th century)
1 a : serving to distinguish **b :** having or giving style or distinction
2 : capable of making a segment of utterance different in meaning as well as in sound from an otherwise identical utterance
synonym see CHARACTERISTIC
— **dis·tinc·tive·ly** *adverb*
— **dis·tinc·tive·ness** *noun*

dis·tin·gué \ˌdēs-ˌtaŋ-'gā, (ˌ)dis-; di-'staŋ-ˌ\ *adjective* [French, from past participle of *distinguer*] (1813)
: distinguished especially in manner or bearing

dis·tin·guish \di-'stiŋ-(g)wish\ *verb* [Middle French *distinguer*, from Latin *distinguere*, literally, to separate by pricking, from *dis-* + *-stinguere* (akin to Latin in*stigare* to urge on) — more at STICK] (1561)
transitive verb
1 : to perceive a difference in **:** mentally separate ⟨so alike they could not be *distinguished*⟩
2 a : to mark as separate or different **b :** to separate into kinds, classes, or categories **c :** to give prominence or distinction to ⟨*distinguished* herself in music⟩ **d :** CHARACTERIZE
3 a : DISCERN ⟨*distinguished* a light in the distance⟩ **b :** to single out **:** take special notice of
intransitive verb
: to perceive a difference
— **dis·tin·guish·abil·i·ty** \-ˌstiŋ-(g)wi-shə-'bi-lə-tē\ *noun*
— **dis·tin·guish·able** \-'stiŋ-(g)wi-shə-bəl\ *adjective*
— **dis·tin·guish·ably** \-blē\ *adverb*

dis·tin·guished *adjective* (1714)
1 : marked by eminence, distinction, or excellence
2 : befitting an eminent person
synonym see FAMOUS

Distinguished Conduct Medal *noun* (1862)
: a British military decoration awarded for distinguished conduct in the field

Distinguished Flying Cross *noun* (1918)
1 : a British military decoration awarded for acts of gallantry when flying in operations against an enemy
2 : a U.S. military decoration awarded for heroism or extraordinary achievement while participating in an aerial flight

Distinguished Service Cross *noun* (1914)
1 : a British military decoration awarded for distinguished service against the enemy
2 : a U.S. Army decoration awarded for extraordinary heroism during operations against an armed enemy

Distinguished Service Medal *noun* (1914)
1 : a British military decoration awarded for distinguished conduct in war
2 : a U.S. military decoration awarded for exceptionally meritorious service to the government in a wartime duty of great responsibility

Distinguished Service Order *noun* (1886)
: a British military decoration awarded for special services in action

dis·tort \di-'stȯrt\ *verb* [Latin *distortus,* past participle of *distorquēre,* from *dis-* + *torquēre* to twist — more at TORTURE] (circa 1586)
transitive verb
1 : to twist out of the true meaning or proportion ⟨*distorted* the facts⟩
2 : to twist out of a natural, normal, or original shape or condition ⟨a face *distorted* by pain⟩; *also* **:** to cause to be perceived unnaturally ⟨the new lights *distorted* colors⟩
3 : PERVERT
intransitive verb
: to become distorted; *also* **:** to cause a twisting from the true, natural, or normal
synonym see DEFORM
— **dis·tort·er** *noun*

dis·tor·tion \di-'stȯr-shən\ *noun* (1581)
1 : the act of distorting
2 : the quality or state of being distorted **:** a product of distorting: as **a :** a lack of proportionality in an image resulting from defects in the optical system **b :** falsified reproduction of an audio or video signal caused by change in the wave form of the original signal
— **dis·tor·tion·al** \-shnəl, -shə-nºl\ *adjective*

¹dis·tract \di-'strakt, 'dis-ˌtrakt\ *adjective* (14th century)
archaic **:** INSANE, MAD

²dis·tract \di-'strakt\ *transitive verb* [Middle English, from Latin *distractus,* past participle

of *distrahere,* literally, to draw apart, from *dis-* + *trahere* to draw] (14th century)
1 a : to turn aside **:** DIVERT **b :** to draw or direct (as one's attention) to a different object or in different directions at the same time
2 : to stir up or confuse with conflicting emotions or motives
synonym see PUZZLE
— **dis·tract·i·bil·i·ty** \-ˌstrak-tə-'bi-lə-tē\ *noun*
— **dis·tract·ible** *or* **dis·tract·able** \-'strak-tə-bəl\ *adjective*
— **dis·tract·ing·ly** \-tiŋ-lē\ *adverb*

dis·tract·ed *adjective* (1590)
1 : maddened or deranged especially by grief or anxiety
2 : mentally confused, troubled, or remote
— **dis·tract·ed·ly** *adverb*

dis·trac·tion \di-'strak-shən\ *noun* (15th century)
1 : the act of distracting or the state of being distracted; *especially* **:** mental confusion
2 : something that distracts; *especially* **:** AMUSEMENT
— **dis·trac·tive** \-'strak-tiv\ *adjective*

dis·train \di-'strān\ *verb* [Middle English *distreynen,* from Old French *destreindre,* from Medieval Latin *distringere,* from Latin, to draw apart, detain, from *dis-* + *stringere* to bind tight — more at STRAIN] (14th century)
transitive verb
1 : to force or compel to satisfy an obligation by means of a distress
2 : to seize by distress
intransitive verb
: to levy a distress
— **dis·train·able** \-'strā-nə-bəl\ *adjective*
— **dis·train·er** \-'strā-nər\ *or* **dis·train·or** \-'strā-nər, -ˌstrā-'nȯr\ *noun*

dis·traint \di-'strānt\ *noun* [*distrain* + *-t* (as in *constraint*)] (circa 1736)
: the act or action of distraining

dis·trait \di-'strā\ *adjective* [Middle English, from Old French *destrait,* from Latin *distractus*] (15th century)
: apprehensively divided or withdrawn in attention **:** DISTRACTED 2

dis·traite \di-'strāt\ *adjective* (15th century)
: DISTRAIT — used especially of women

dis·traught \dis-'trȯt\ *adjective* [Middle English, modification of Latin *distractus*] (14th century)
1 : agitated with doubt or mental conflict
2 : INSANE
— **dis·traught·ly** *adverb*

¹dis·tress \di-'stres\ *noun* [Middle English *destresse,* from Old French, from (assumed) Vulgar Latin *districtia,* from Latin *districtus,* past participle of *distringere*] (13th century)
1 a : seizure and detention of the goods of another as pledge or to obtain satisfaction of a claim by the sale of the goods seized **b :** something that is distrained
2 a : pain or suffering affecting the body, a bodily part, or the mind **:** TROUBLE ⟨gastric *distress*⟩ **b :** a painful situation **:** MISFORTUNE
3 : a state of danger or desperate need ⟨a ship in *distress*⟩ ☆

²distress *transitive verb* (14th century)
1 : to subject to great strain or difficulties

2 *archaic* : to force or overcome by inflicting pain
3 : to cause to worry or be troubled : UPSET
4 : to mar (as clothing or wood) deliberately to give an effect of age
— **dis·tress·ing·ly** \-'stre-siŋ-lē\ *adverb*
³**distress** *adjective* (1926)
1 : offered for sale at a loss ⟨*distress* merchandise⟩
2 : involving distress goods ⟨a *distress* sale⟩
dis·tress·ful \di-'stres-fəl\ *adjective* (1591)
: causing distress : full of distress
— **dis·tress·ful·ly** \-fə-lē\ *adverb*
— **dis·tress·ful·ness** *noun*
dis·trib·u·tary \di-'stri-byə-,ter-ē\ *noun, plural* **-tar·ies** (1863)
: a river branch flowing away from the main stream
dis·trib·ute \di-'stri-byət, *British also* 'dis-tri-,byüt\ *verb* **-ut·ed; -ut·ing** [Middle English, from Latin *distributus,* past participle of *distribuere,* from *dis-* + *tribuere* to allot — more at TRIBUTE] (15th century)
transitive verb
1 : to divide among several or many : APPORTION ⟨*distribute* expenses⟩
2 a : to spread out so as to cover something : SCATTER **b** : to give out or deliver especially to members of a group ⟨*distribute* newspapers⟩ ⟨*distribute* leaflets⟩ **c** : to place or position so as to be properly apportioned over or throughout an area ⟨200 pounds *distributed* on a 6-foot frame⟩ **d** : to use (a term) so as to convey information about every member of the class named ⟨the proposition "all men are mortal" *distributes* "man" but not "mortal"⟩
3 a : to divide or separate especially into kinds **b** : to return the units of (as typeset matter) to storage
4 : to use in or as an operation so as to be mathematically distributive
intransitive verb
: to be mathematically distributive ⟨multiplication *distributes* over addition⟩ ☆
— **dis·trib·u·tee** \dis-,tri-byə-'tē\ *noun*
dis·trib·ut·ed *adjective* (1968)
1 : characterized by a statistical distribution of a particular kind ⟨a normally *distributed* random variable⟩
2 : of, relating to, or being a computer network in which at least some of the processing is done by the individual workstations and information is shared by and often stored at the workstations
dis·tri·bu·tion \,dis-trə-'byü-shən\ *noun* (14th century)
1 a : the act or process of distributing **b** : the apportionment by a court of the personal property of an intestate
2 a : the position, arrangement, or frequency of occurrence (as of the members of a group) over an area or throughout a space or unit of time **b** : the natural geographic range of an organism
3 a : something distributed **b** (1) : FREQUENCY DISTRIBUTION (2) : PROBABILITY FUNCTION (3) : PROBABILITY DENSITY FUNCTION 2
4 : the pattern of branching and termination of a ramifying structure (as a nerve)
5 : the marketing or merchandising of commodities
— **dis·tri·bu·tion·al** \-shnəl, -shə-nᵊl\ *adjective*
distribution function *noun* (circa 1909)
: a function that gives the probability that a random variable is less than or equal to the independent variable of the function
dis·trib·u·tive \di-'stri-byə-tiv\ *adjective* (15th century)
1 : of or relating to distribution: as **a** : dealing a proper share to each of a group **b** : diffusing more or less evenly
2 *of a word* : referring singly and without exception to the members of a group ⟨*each, either,* and *none* are *distributive*

3 a : being an operation (as multiplication in $a(b + c) = ab + ac$) that produces the same result when operating on the whole mathematical expression as when operating on each part and collecting the results **b** : being or relating to a rule or property concerning a distributive operation ⟨the *distributive* property of multiplication with respect to addition⟩
— **dis·trib·u·tive·ly** *adverb*
— **dis·trib·u·tiv·i·ty** \-,stri-byə-'ti-və-tē\ *noun*
dis·trib·u·tor \di-'stri-byə-tər\ *noun* (1526)
1 : one that distributes
2 : one that markets a commodity; *especially* : WHOLESALER
3 : an apparatus for directing the secondary current from the induction coil to the various spark plugs of an engine in their proper firing order
¹**dis·trict** \'dis-(,)trikt\ *noun, often attributive* [French, from Medieval Latin *districtus* jurisdiction, district, from *distringere* to distrain — more at DISTRAIN] (1611)
1 a : a territorial division (as for administrative or electoral purposes) **b** : the basic administrative unit for local government in Northern Ireland
2 : an area, region, or section with a distinguishing character
²**district** *transitive verb* (1792)
: to divide or organize into districts
district attorney *noun* (1789)
: the prosecuting officer of a judicial district
district court *noun* (1789)
: a trial court that has jurisdiction over certain cases within a specific judicial district
¹**dis·trust** \(,)dis-'trəst\ *noun* (1513)
: the lack or absence of trust
²**distrust** *transitive verb* (1548)
: to have no trust or confidence in
dis·trust·ful \-'trəs(t)-fəl\ *adjective* (1589)
: having or showing distrust
— **dis·trust·ful·ly** \-fə-lē\ *adverb*
— **dis·trust·ful·ness** *noun*
dis·turb \di-'stərb\ *verb* [Middle English *disturben, destourben,* from Old French & Latin; Old French *destourber,* from Latin *disturbare,* from *dis-* + *turbare* to throw into disorder, from *turba* disorder — more at TURBID] (14th century)
transitive verb
1 a : to interfere with : INTERRUPT **b** : to alter the position or arrangement of **c** : to upset the natural and especially the ecological balance or relations of ⟨land *disturbed* by dumping⟩
2 a : to destroy the tranquillity or composure of **b** : to throw into disorder **c** : ALARM **d** : to put to inconvenience
intransitive verb
: to cause disturbance
synonym see DISCOMPOSE
— **dis·turb·er** *noun*
— **dis·turb·ing·ly** \-'stər-biŋ-lē\ *adverb*
dis·tur·bance \di-'stər-bən(t)s\ *noun* (13th century)
1 : the act of disturbing : the state of being disturbed
2 : a local variation from the average or normal wind conditions
dis·turbed *adjective* (1904)
: showing symptoms of emotional illness ⟨*disturbed* children⟩ ⟨*disturbed* behavior⟩
di·sub·sti·tut·ed \(,)dī-'səb-stə-,tü-təd, -,tyü-\ *adjective* (circa 1909)
: having two substituent atoms or groups in a molecule
di·sul·fide \(,)dī-'səl-,fīd\ *noun* (1872)
1 : a compound containing two atoms of sulfur combined with an element or radical
2 : an organic compound containing the bivalent group SS composed of two sulfur atoms
di·sul·fi·ram \dī-'səl-fə-,ram\ *noun* [*disulf*ide + *thiourea* + *amyl*] (1952)
: a compound $C_{10}H_{20}N_2S_4$ that causes a severe physiological reaction to alcohol and is used especially in the treatment of alcoholism

di·sul·fo·ton \dī-'səl-fə-,tän\ *noun* [*di-* + *sulfo-* + *-ton* (probably from *thion-*)] (1965)
: an organophosphorus systemic insecticide $C_8H_{19}O_2PS_3$
dis·union \(,)dis-'yü-nyən, dish-\ *noun* (15th century)
1 : the termination of union : SEPARATION
2 : DISUNITY
— **dis·union·ist** \-nyə-nist\ *noun*
dis·unite \(,)dis-yü-'nīt, -yə-, dish-\ *transitive verb* (1598)
: DIVIDE, SEPARATE
dis·uni·ty \(,)dis-'yü-nə-tē, dish-\ *noun* (1632)
: lack of unity; *especially* : DISSENSION
¹**dis·use** \(,)dis-'yüz, dish-\ *transitive verb* (15th century)
: to discontinue the use or practice of
²**dis·use** \-'yüs\ *noun* (15th century)
: cessation of use or practice
dis·util·i·ty \(,)dis-yü-'ti-lə-tē, -yə-, dish-\ *noun* (1879)
: the state or fact of being counterproductive
¹**dis·val·ue** \(,)dis-'val-(,)yü, -yə(-w)\ *transitive verb* (1603)
1 *archaic* : UNDERVALUE, DEPRECIATE
2 : to consider of little value
²**disvalue** *noun* (1603)
1 *obsolete* : DISREGARD, DISESTEEM
2 : a negative value
di·syl·la·ble \'dī-,si-lə-bəl, (,)dī-'sil-; 'di-,sil-, (,)di(s)-'sil-\ *noun* [part translation of Middle French *dissilabe,* from Latin *disyllabus* having two syllables, from Greek *disyllabos,* from *di-* + *syllabē* syllable] (1589)
: a linguistic form consisting of two syllables
— **di·syl·lab·ic** \,dī-sə-'la-bik, ,di(s)-sə-\ *adjective*
dit \'dit\ *noun* [imitative] (1940)
: a dot in radio or telegraphic code
¹**ditch** \'dich\ *noun* [Middle English *dich,* from Old English *dīc* dike, ditch; akin to Middle High German *tīch* pond, dike] (before 12th century)

☆ **SYNONYMS**
Distress, suffering, misery, agony mean the state of being in great trouble. DISTRESS implies an external and usually temporary cause of great physical or mental strain and stress ⟨the hurricane put everyone in great *distress*⟩. SUFFERING implies conscious endurance of pain or distress ⟨the *suffering* of famine victims⟩. MISERY stresses the unhappiness attending especially sickness, poverty, or loss ⟨the homeless live with *misery* every day⟩. AGONY suggests pain too intense to be borne ⟨in *agony* over the death of their child⟩.

Distribute, dispense, divide, deal, dole out mean to give out, usually in shares, to each member of a group. DISTRIBUTE implies an apportioning by separation of something into parts, units, or amounts ⟨*distributed* food to the needy⟩. DISPENSE suggests the giving of a carefully weighed or measured portion to each of a group according to due or need ⟨*dispensed* wisdom to the students⟩. DIVIDE stresses the separation of a whole into parts and implies that the parts are equal ⟨three charitable groups *divided* the proceeds⟩. DEAL emphasizes the allotment of something piece by piece ⟨*deal* out equipment and supplies⟩. DOLE OUT implies a carefully measured portion that is often scant or niggardly ⟨*doled out* what little food there was⟩.

\ə\ abut \ᵊ\ kitten \ər\ further \a\ ash \ā\ ace
\ä\ mop, mar \aù\ out \ch\ chin \e\ bet \ē\ easy
\g\ go \i\ hit \ī\ ice \j\ job \ŋ\ sing \ō\ go
\ò\ law \òi\ boy \th\ thin \th̄\ the \ü\ loot \ù\ foot
\y\ yet \zh\ vision *see also* Guide to Pronunciation

: a long narrow excavation dug in the earth (as for drainage)

²**ditch** (14th century)
transitive verb
1 a : to enclose with a ditch **b :** to dig a ditch in
2 : to make a forced landing of (an airplane) on water
3 : to get rid of : DISCARD
intransitive verb
1 : to dig a ditch
2 : to crash-land at sea

ditch·dig·ger \-ˌdi-gər\ *noun* (circa 1897)
1 : one that digs ditches
2 : one employed at menial and usually hard physical labor

dite \'dīt\ *noun* [variant of *doit*] (circa 1877)
dialect : MITE, BIT

¹**dith·er** \'di-ᴛ͟hər\ *intransitive verb* **dith·ered; dith·er·ing** \-ᴛ͟h(ə-)riŋ\ [Middle English *didderen*] (15th century)
1 : SHIVER, TREMBLE
2 : to act nervously or indecisively : VACILLATE
— **dith·er·er** \-ᴛ͟hər-ər\ *noun*

²**dither** *noun* (1819)
: a highly nervous, excited, or agitated state : EXCITEMENT, CONFUSION
— **dith·ery** \'di-ᴛ͟hə-rē\ *adjective*

dithi- *or* **dithio-** *combining form* [International Scientific Vocabulary *di-* + *thi-*]
: containing two atoms of sulfur usually in place of two oxygen atoms ⟨*dithio*carbamate⟩

di·thio·car·ba·mate \ˌdī-ˌthī-ō-'kär-bə-ˌmāt\ *noun* (1929)
: any of several sulfur analogues of the carbamates including some used as fungicides

dith·y·ramb \'di-thi-ˌram(b)\ *noun, plural* **-rambs** \-ˌramz\ [Greek *dithyrambos*] (1656)
1 : a usually short poem in an inspired wild irregular strain
2 : a statement or writing in an exalted or enthusiastic vein
— **dith·y·ram·bic** \ˌdi-thi-'ram-bik\ *adjective*
— **dith·y·ram·bi·cal·ly** \-bi-k(ə-)lē\ *adverb*

di·tran·si·tive \ˌdī-'tran(t)-sə-tiv, -'tran-zə-\ *adjective* (1972)
: able to take both a direct and an indirect object ⟨a *ditransitive* verb⟩
— **ditransitive** *noun*

dit·sy *or* **dit·zy** \'dit-sē\ *adjective* **dits·i·er** *or* **ditz·i·er; -est** [origin unknown] (1973)
: eccentrically silly, giddy, or inane : DIZZY

dit·ta·ny \'di-t°n-ē\ *noun, plural* **-nies** [Middle English *ditoyne*, from Old French *ditayne*, from Latin *dictamnum*, from Greek *diktamnon*] (12th century)
1 : a pink-flowered herb (*Origanum dictamnus*) that is native to Crete
2 : an American herb (*Conila origanoides*) of the mint family that has much-branched stems

¹**dit·to** \'di-(ˌ)tō\ *noun, plural* **dittos** [Italian *ditto, detto,* past participle of *dire* to say, from Latin *dicere* — more at DICTION] (circa 1678)
1 : a thing mentioned previously or above — used to avoid repeating a word; often symbolized by inverted commas or apostrophes
2 : a ditto mark

²**ditto** *adjective* (1776)
: having the same characteristics : SIMILAR

³**ditto** *transitive verb* (1837)
1 : to repeat the action or statement of
2 [from *Ditto,* a trademark] : to copy (as printed matter) on a duplicator

⁴**ditto** *adverb* (circa 1864)
: as before or aforesaid : in the same manner

dit·ty \'di-tē\ *noun, plural* **ditties** [Middle English *ditee,* from Middle French *ditié* poem, from past participle of *ditier* to compose, from Latin *dictare* to dictate, compose] (14th century)
: an especially simple and unaffected song

dit·ty bag \'di-tē-\ *noun* [origin unknown] (circa 1860)

: a bag used especially by sailors to hold small articles (as needles and thread)

ditty box *noun* (circa 1880)
: a box used for the same purpose as a ditty bag

ditz \'dits\ *noun* (1982)
: a ditsy person

di·ure·sis \ˌdī-yə-'rē-səs\ *noun, plural* **-ure·ses** \-ˌsēz\ [New Latin] (circa 1681)
: an increased excretion of urine

di·uret·ic \ˌdī-yə-'re-tik\ *adjective* [Middle English, from Middle French or Late Latin; Middle French *diuretique,* from Late Latin *diureticus,* from Greek *diourētikos,* from *diourein* to urinate, from *dia-* + *ourein* to urinate — more at URINE] (14th century)
: tending to increase the flow of urine
— **diuretic** *noun*
— **di·uret·i·cal·ly** \-ti-k(ə-)lē\ *adverb*

¹**di·ur·nal** \dī-'ər-n°l\ *adjective* [Middle English, from Latin *diurnalis* — more at JOURNAL] (14th century)
1 a : recurring every day ⟨*diurnal* tasks⟩ **b :** having a daily cycle ⟨*diurnal* tides⟩
2 a : of, relating to, or occurring in the daytime ⟨the city's *diurnal* noises⟩ **b :** active chiefly in the daytime ⟨*diurnal* animals⟩ **c :** opening during the day and closing at night ⟨*diurnal* flowers⟩
— **di·ur·nal·ly** \-n°l-ē\ *adverb*

²**diurnal** *noun* (1600)
1 *archaic* : DIARY, DAYBOOK
2 : JOURNAL 2a

di·u·ron \'dī-yə-ˌrän\ *noun* [*dichlor-* + *urea* + ¹*-on*] (1957)
: a persistent herbicide $C_9H_{10}Cl_2N_2O$ used especially to control annual weeds

di·va \'dē-və\ *noun, plural* **divas** *or* **di·ve** \-(ˌ)vā\ [Italian, literally, goddess, from Latin, feminine of *divus* divine, god — more at DEITY] (1883)
: PRIMA DONNA 1

di·va·gate \'dī-və-ˌgāt, 'di-\ *intransitive verb* **-gat·ed; -gat·ing** [Late Latin *divagatus,* past participle of *divagari,* from Latin *dis-* + *vagari* to wander — more at VAGARY] (1599)
: to wander or stray from a course or subject : DIVERGE, DIGRESS
— **di·va·ga·tion** \ˌdī-və-'gā-shən, ˌdi-\ *noun*

di·va·lent \(ˌ)dī-'vā-lənt\ *adjective* (1869)
: having a chemical valence of two; *also* : bonded to two other atoms or groups

di·van \di-'van, 'dī-ˌvan, *especially in senses 1, 2, & 4 also* di-'vän, dī-'van\ *noun* [Turkish, from Persian *dīwān* account book] (1586)
1 a : the privy council of the Ottoman Empire **b :** COUNCIL
2 : a council chamber
3 : a large couch usually without back or arms often designed for use as a bed
4 : a collection of poems in Persian or Arabic usually by one author

di·var·i·cate \dī-'var-ə-ˌkāt, də-\ *transitive verb* **-cat·ed; -cat·ing** [Latin *divaricatus,* past participle of *divaricare,* from *dis-* + *varicare* to straddle — more at PREVARICATE] (1673)
: to spread apart : branch off : DIVERGE

di·var·i·ca·tion \(ˌ)dī-ˌvar-ə-'kā-shən, də-\ *noun* (1578)
1 : the action, process, or fact of divaricating
2 : a divergence of opinion

¹**dive** \'dīv\ *verb* **dived** \'dīvd\ *or* **dove** \'dōv\; **dived** *also* **dove; div·ing** [Middle English *diven, duven,* from Old English *dȳfan* to dip & *dūfan* to dip; akin to Old English *dyppan* to dip — more at DIP] (before 12th century)
intransitive verb
1 a : to plunge into water intentionally and especially headfirst; *also* : to execute a dive **b :** SUBMERGE
2 a : to come or drop down precipitously : PLUNGE 3 **b :** to plunge one's hand into something **c** *of an airplane* : to descend in a dive

3 a : to plunge into some matter or activity **b :** to plunge or dash for some place ⟨*diving* for cover⟩; *also* : to lunge especially in order to seize something ⟨*dove* for the ball⟩
transitive verb
1 : to thrust into something
2 : to cause to dive □

²**dive** *noun* (1700)
1 : the act or an instance of diving: as **a** (1) : a plunge into water executed in a prescribed manner (2) : a submerging of a submarine (3) : a steep descent of an airplane at greater than the maximum horizontal speed **b :** a sharp decline
2 : a disreputable entertainment establishment
3 : a faked knockout — usually used in the phrase *take a dive*
4 : an offensive play in football in which the ballcarrier plunges into the line for short yardage

dive–bomb \'dīv-ˌbäm\ *transitive verb* (1935)
: to bomb from an airplane by making a steep dive toward the target before releasing the bomb
— **dive–bomb·er** *noun*

div·er \'dī-vər\ *noun* (1506)
1 : one that dives
2 a : a person who stays underwater for long periods by having air supplied from the surface or by carrying a supply of compressed air **b :** any of various birds that obtain food by diving in water; *especially* : LOON

di·verge \də-'vərj, dī-\ *verb* **di·verged; di·verg·ing** [Medieval Latin *divergere,* from Latin *dis-* + *vergere* to incline — more at WRENCH] (1665)
intransitive verb
1 a : to move or extend in different directions from a common point : draw apart ⟨*diverging* roads⟩ **b :** to become or be different in character or form : differ in opinion
2 : to turn aside from a path or course : DEVIATE
3 : to be mathematically divergent
transitive verb
: DEFLECT
synonym see SWERVE

di·ver·gence \-'vər-jən(t)s\ *noun* (1656)
1 a : a drawing apart (as of lines extending from a common center) **b :** DIFFERENCE, DISAGREEMENT **c :** the acquisition of dissimilar characters by related organisms in unlike environments
2 : a deviation from a course or standard
3 : the condition of being mathematically divergent

di·ver·gen·cy \-jən(t)-sē\ *noun, plural* **-cies** (1709)
: DIVERGENCE

di·ver·gent \-jənt\ *adjective* [Latin *divergent-, divergens,* present participle of *divergere*] (1696)
1 a : diverging from each other **b :** differing from each other or from a standard : DEVIANT ⟨the *divergent* interests of capital and labor⟩

□ USAGE
dive *Dive,* which was originally a weak verb, developed a past tense *dove,* probably by analogy with verbs like *drive, drove. Dove* exists in some British dialects and has become the standard past tense especially in speech in some parts of Canada. In the U.S. *dived* and *dove* are both widespread in speech as past tense and past participle, with *dove* less common than *dived* in the south Midland area, and *dived* less common than *dove* in the Northern and north Midland areas. In writing, the past tense *dived* is usual in British English and somewhat more common in American English. *Dove* seems relatively rare as a past participle in writing.

2 : relating to or being an infinite sequence that does not have a limit or an infinite series whose partial sums do not have a limit
3 : causing divergence of rays ⟨a *divergent* lens⟩
synonym see DIFFERENT
— di·ver·gent·ly *adverb*
di·vers \'dī-vərz\ *adjective* [Middle English *divers, diverse*] (14th century)
: VARIOUS
di·verse \dī-'vərs, də-\, 'dī-,\ *adjective* [Middle English *divers, diverse,* from Old French & Latin; Old French *divers,* from Latin *diversus,* from past participle of *divertere*] (14th century)
1 : differing from one another **:** UNLIKE
2 : composed of distinct or unlike elements or qualities
synonym see DIFFERENT
— di·verse·ly *adverb*
— di·verse·ness *noun*
di·ver·si·fy \də-'vər-sə-,fī, dī-\ *verb* **-fied; -fy·ing** (15th century)
transitive verb
1 : to make diverse **:** give variety to ⟨*diversify* a course of study⟩
2 : to balance (as an investment portfolio) defensively by dividing funds among securities of different industries or of different classes
3 : to increase the variety of the products of
intransitive verb
1 : to produce variety
2 : to engage in varied operations
— di·ver·si·fi·ca·tion \-,vər-sə-fə-'kā-shən\ *noun*
— di·ver·si·fi·er \-'vər-sə-,fī(-ə)r\ *noun*
di·ver·sion \də-'vər-zhən, dī-, -shən\ *noun* (1600)
1 : the act or an instance of diverting from a course, activity, or use **:** DEVIATION
2 : something that diverts or amuses **:** PASTIME
3 : an attack or feint that draws the attention and force of an enemy from the point of the principal operation
di·ver·sion·ary \də-'vər-zhə-,ner-ē, dī-, -shə-\ *adjective* (1846)
: tending to draw attention away from the principal concern **:** being a diversion
di·ver·sion·ist \-zhə-nəst, -shə-\ *noun* (1937)
1 : one engaged in diversionary activities
2 : one characterized by political deviation
di·ver·si·ty \də-'vər-sə-tē, dī-\ *noun, plural* **-ties** (14th century)
1 : the condition of being diverse **:** VARIETY
2 : an instance of being diverse
di·vert \də-'vərt, dī-\ *verb* [Middle English, from Middle French & Latin; Middle French *divertir,* from Latin *divertere* to turn in opposite directions, from *dis- + vertere* to turn — more at WORTH] (15th century)
intransitive verb
: to turn aside **:** DEVIATE ⟨studied law but *diverted* to diplomacy⟩
transitive verb
1 a : to turn from one course or use to another **:** DEFLECT **b :** DISTRACT
2 : to give pleasure to especially by distracting the attention from what burdens or distresses
synonym see AMUSE
di·ver·tic·u·li·tis \,dī-vər-,ti-kyə-'lī-təs\ *noun* [New Latin] (circa 1900)
: inflammation of a diverticulum
di·ver·tic·u·lo·sis \,dī-vər-,ti-kyə-'lō-səs\ *noun* [New Latin] (1917)
: an intestinal disorder characterized by the presence of many diverticula
di·ver·tic·u·lum \,dī-vər-'ti-kyə-ləm\ *noun, plural* **-la** \-lə\ [New Latin, from Latin, bypath, probably alteration of *deverticulum,* from *devertere* to turn aside, from *de- + vertere*] (circa 1819)
1 : an abnormal pouch or sac opening from a hollow organ (as the intestine or bladder)
2 : a pocket or closed branch opening off a main passage
— di·ver·tic·u·lar \-kyə-lər\ *adjective*

di·ver·ti·men·to \di-,vər-tə-'men-(,)tō, -,ver-\ *noun, plural* **-men·ti** \-'men-(,)tē\ *or* **-mentos** [Italian, literally, diversion, from *divertire* to divert, amuse, from Latin *divertere*] (1823)
1 : an instrumental chamber work in several movements usually light in character
2 : DIVERTISSEMENT 1
di·ver·tisse·ment \di-'vər-təs-mənt, -təz-, French dē-ver-tē-smä[n]\ *noun, plural* **divertissements** \-mən(t)s, -smä[n](z)\ [French, literally, diversion, from *divertiss-* (stem of *divertir*)] (1728)
1 : a dance sequence or short ballet usually used as an interlude
2 : DIVERTIMENTO 1
3 : DIVERSION, ENTERTAINMENT
Di·ves \'dī-(,)vēz\ *noun* [Middle English, from Latin, rich, rich man; misunderstood as a proper name in Luke 16:19] (14th century)
: a rich man
di·vest \dī-'vest, də-\ *transitive verb* [alteration of *devest*] (1563)
1 a : to deprive or dispossess especially of property, authority, or title **b :** to undress or strip especially of clothing, ornament, or equipment **c :** RID, FREE
2 : to take away from a person
— di·vest·ment \-'ves(t)-mənt\ *noun*
di·ves·ti·ture \dī-'ves-tə-,chür, -chər, də-, *chiefly Southern* -t(y)ů(ə)r\ *noun* [*divest + -iture* (as in *investiture*)] (1601)
1 : the act of divesting
2 : the compulsory transfer of title or disposal of interests (as stock in a corporation) upon government order
¹di·vide \də-'vīd\ *verb* **di·vid·ed; di·vid·ing** [Middle English, from Latin *dividere,* from *dis- + -videre* to separate — more at WIDOW] (14th century)
transitive verb
1 a : to separate into two or more parts, areas, or groups **b :** to separate into classes, categories, or divisions **c :** CLEAVE, PART
2 a : to separate into portions and give out in shares **:** DISTRIBUTE **b :** to possess, enjoy, or make use of in common **c :** APPORTION
3 a : to cause to be separate, distinct, or apart from one another **b :** to separate into opposing sides or parties **c :** to cause (a parliamentary body) to vote by division
4 a : to subject (a number or quantity) to the operation of finding how many times it contains another number or quantity ⟨*divide* 42 by 14⟩ **b :** to be used as a divisor with respect to (a dividend) ⟨4 *divides* 16 evenly⟩ **c :** to use as a divisor — used with *into* ⟨*divide* 14 into 42⟩
intransitive verb
1 : to perform mathematical division
2 a (1) **:** to undergo replication, multiplication, fission, or separation into parts (2) **:** to branch out **b :** to become separated or disunited especially in opinion or interest
synonym see SEPARATE, DISTRIBUTE
— di·vid·able \-'vī-də-bəl\ *adjective*
²divide *noun* (1642)
1 : an act of dividing
2 a : a dividing ridge between drainage areas **:** WATERSHED **b :** a point or line of division
di·vid·ed *adjective* (14th century)
1 a : separated into parts or pieces **b** *of a leaf* **:** cut into distinct parts by incisions extending to the base or to the midrib **c :** having a barrier (as a guardrail) to separate lanes of traffic going in opposite directions ⟨a *divided* highway⟩
2 a : disagreeing with each other **:** DISUNITED **b :** directed or moved toward conflicting interests, states, or objects ⟨*divided* loyalties⟩
3 : separated by distance ⟨familiar objects from which she had never dreamed of being *divided* —James Joyce⟩
— di·vid·ed·ly \də-'vī-dəd-lē\ *adverb*
— di·vid·ed·ness \-nəs\ *noun*

div·i·dend \'di-və-,dend, -dənd\ *noun* [Middle English *divident,* from Latin *dividendus,* gerundive of *dividere*] (15th century)
1 : an individual share of something distributed: as **a :** a share in a pro rata distribution (as of profits) to stockholders **b :** a share of surplus allocated to a policyholder in a participating insurance policy
2 a : a resultant return or reward **b :** BONUS
3 a : a number to be divided **b :** a sum or fund to be divided and distributed
— div·i·dend·less \-ləs\ *adjective*
di·vid·er \də-'vī-dər\ *noun* (1534)
1 : one that divides
2 *plural* **:** an instrument for measuring or marking (as in dividing lines)
3 : something serving as a partition between separate spaces within a larger area
di·vi-di·vi \dē-vē-'dē-vē, ,di-vē-'dē-vē\ *noun* [American Spanish *dividivi,* probably from Cumanagoto (extinct Cariban language of northern Venezuela)] (circa 1837)
: a small leguminous tree (*Caesalpinia coriaria*) of tropical America with twisted astringent pods that contain a large proportion of tannin

dividers

div·i·na·tion \,di-və-'nā-shən\ *noun* [Middle English *divinacioun,* from Latin *divination-, divinatio,* from *divinare*] (14th century)
1 : the art or practice that seeks to foresee or foretell future events or discover hidden knowledge usually by the interpretation of omens or by the aid of supernatural powers
2 : unusual insight **:** intuitive perception
— di·vi·na·to·ry \də-'vi-nə-,tōr-ē, də-'vī-nə-, 'di-və-nə-, -,tōr-\ *adjective*
¹di·vine \də-'vīn\ *adjective* **di·vin·er; -est** [Middle English *divin,* from Middle French, from Latin *divinus,* from *divus* god — more at DEITY] (14th century)
1 a : of, relating to, or proceeding directly from God or a god ⟨*divine* love⟩ **b :** being a deity ⟨the *divine* Savior⟩ **c :** directed to a deity ⟨*divine* worship⟩
2 a : supremely good **:** SUPERB ⟨the pie was *divine*⟩ **b :** HEAVENLY, GODLIKE
— di·vine·ly *adverb*
²divine *noun* [Middle English, from Medieval Latin *divinus,* from Latin, soothsayer, from *divinus,* adjective] (14th century)
1 : CLERGYMAN
2 : THEOLOGIAN
³divine *verb* **di·vined; di·vin·ing** [Middle English, from Middle French & Latin; Middle French *diviner,* from Latin *divinare,* from *divinus,* noun] (14th century)
transitive verb
1 : to discover intuitively **:** INFER
2 : to discover or locate (as water or minerals underground) usually by means of a divining rod
intransitive verb
1 : to practice divination **:** PROPHESY
2 : to perceive intuitively
synonym see FORESEE
Divine Liturgy *noun* (1870)
: the eucharistic rite of Eastern churches
Divine Office *noun* (15th century)
: the office for the canonical hours of prayer that priests and religious say daily
di·vin·er \də-'vī-nər\ *noun* (14th century)
1 : one who practices divination **:** SOOTHSAYER
2 : a person who divines the location of water or minerals
divine right *noun* (circa 1600)

\ə\ abut \ᵊ\ kitten \ər\ further \a\ ash \ā\ ace
\ä\ mop, mar \aů\ out \ch\ chin \e\ bet \ē\ easy
\g\ go \i\ hit \ī\ ice \j\ job \ŋ\ sing \ō\ go
\ȯ\ law \ȯi\ boy \th\ thin \t͟h\ the \ü\ loot \ů\ foot
\y\ yet \zh\ vision *see also* Guide to Pronunciation

: the right of a sovereign to rule as set forth by the theory of government that holds that a monarch receives the right to rule directly from God and not from the people

divine service *noun* (14th century)
: a service of Christian worship; *specifically* : such a service that is not sacramental in character

diving beetle *noun* (circa 1889)
: any of various predatory aquatic beetles (family Dytiscidae) that breathe while submerged using air trapped under their elytra

diving bell *noun* (1661)
: a diving apparatus consisting of a container open only at the bottom and supplied with compressed air by a hose

diving board *noun* (1893)
: SPRINGBOARD 1

diving duck *noun* (1813)
: any of various ducks (as a bufflehead) that frequent deep waters and obtain their food by diving

diving suit *noun* (1908)
: a waterproof suit with a removable helmet that is worn by a diver who is supplied with air pumped through a tube

divining rod *noun* (1751)
: a forked rod believed to indicate the presence of water or minerals especially by dipping downward when held over a vein

di·vin·i·ty \də-'vi-nə-tē\ *noun, plural* **-ties** (14th century)
1 : THEOLOGY
2 : the quality or state of being divine
3 *often capitalized* : a divine being: as **a** : GOD 1 **b** (1) : GOD 2 (2) : GODDESS
4 : fudge made of whipped egg whites, sugar, and nuts

divinity school *noun* (circa 1555)
: a professional school having a religious curriculum especially for ministerial candidates

di·vis·i·ble \də-'vi-zə-bəl\ *adjective* (15th century)
: capable of being divided
— **di·vis·i·bil·i·ty** \-,vi-zə-'bi-lə-tē\ *noun*

di·vi·sion \də-'vi-zhən\ *noun* [Middle English, from Middle French, from Latin *division-, divisio,* from *dividere* to divide] (14th century)
1 a : the act or process of dividing : the state of being divided **b** : the act, process, or an instance of distributing among a number : DISTRIBUTION **c** *obsolete* : a method of arranging or disposing (as troops)
2 : one of the parts or groupings into which a whole is divided or is divisible
3 : the condition or an instance of being divided in opinion or interest : DISAGREEMENT, DISUNITY ⟨exploited the *divisions* between the two countries⟩
4 a : something that divides, separates, or marks off **b** : the act, process, or an instance of separating or keeping apart : SEPARATION
5 : the mathematical operation of dividing something
6 a : a self-contained major military unit capable of independent action **b** : a tactical military unit composed of headquarters and usually three to five brigades **c** (1) : the basic naval administrative unit (2) : a tactical subdivision of a squadron of ships **d** : a unit of the U.S. Air Force higher than a wing and lower than an air force
7 a : a portion of a territorial unit marked off for a particular purpose (as administrative or judicial functions) **b** : an administrative or operating unit of a governmental, business, or educational organization
8 : the physical separation into different lobbies of the members of a parliamentary body voting for and against a question
9 : plant propagation by dividing parts and planting segments capable of producing roots and shoots
10 : a group of organisms forming part of a larger group; *specifically* : a primary category of the plant kingdom

11 : a competitive class or category (as in boxing or wrestling)
synonym see PART
— **di·vi·sion·al** \-'vizh-nəl, -'vi-zhə-n°l\ *adjective*

di·vi·sion·ism \-'vi-zhə-,ni-zəm\ *noun, often capitalized* (1901)
: POINTILLISM
— **di·vi·sion·ist** \-'vi-zhə-nəst\ *noun or adjective*

division of labor (1776)
: the breakdown of labor into its components and their distribution among different persons, groups, or machines to increase productive efficiency

division sign *noun* (circa 1934)
1 : the symbol ÷ used to indicate division
2 : the diagonal / used to indicate a fraction

di·vi·sive \də-'vī-siv *also* -'vi- *or* -ziv\ *adjective* (1642)
: creating disunity or dissension
— **di·vi·sive·ly** *adverb*
— **di·vi·sive·ness** *noun*

di·vi·sor \də-'vī-zər\ *noun* (15th century)
: the number by which a dividend is divided

¹di·vorce \də-'vōrs, -'vȯrs *also* dī-\ *noun* [Middle English *divorse,* from Middle French, from Latin *divortium,* from *divertere, divortere* to divert, to leave one's husband] (14th century)
1 : the action or an instance of legally dissolving a marriage
2 : SEPARATION, SEVERANCE

²divorce *verb* **di·vorced; di·vorc·ing** (15th century)
transitive verb
1 a : to end marriage with (one's spouse) by divorce **b** : to dissolve the marriage contract between
2 : to terminate an existing relationship or union : SEPARATE ⟨*divorce* church from state⟩
intransitive verb
: to obtain a divorce
synonym see SEPARATE
— **di·vorce·ment** \-'vōr-smənt, -'vȯr-\ *noun*

di·vor·cé \də-,vȯr-'sā, -,vȯr-, -'sē, -'vȯr-, -'vȯr-,\ *noun* (1877)
: a divorced man

di·vor·cée \də-,vȯr-'sā, -,vȯr-, -'sē, -'vȯr-, -'vȯr-,\ *noun* [French, from feminine of *divorcé,* past participle of *divorcer* to divorce, from Middle French *divorse*] (1813)
: a divorced woman

div·ot \'di-vət\ *noun* [alteration of earlier Scots *devat,* from Middle English (Scots dialect) *duvat*] (1586)
1 *Scottish* : a square of turf or sod
2 : a loose piece of turf (as one dug from a golf fairway in making a shot)

di·vulge \də-'vəlj, dī-\ *transitive verb* **di·vulged; di·vulg·ing** [Middle English, from Latin *divulgare,* from *dis-* + *vulgare* to make known, from *vulgus* mob] (15th century)
1 *archaic* : to make public : PROCLAIM
2 : to make known (as a confidence or secret)
synonym see REVEAL
— **di·vul·gence** \-'vəl-jən(t)s\ *noun*

div·vy \'di-vē\ *transitive verb* **div·vied; div·vy·ing** [by shortening & alteration from *divide*] (1877)
: DIVIDE, SHARE — usually used with *up*

Dix·ie \'dik-sē\ *noun* [name for the Southern states in the song *Dixie* (1859) by Daniel D. Emmett] (1859)
: the Southern states of the U.S.

Dix·ie·crat \-,krat\ *noun* (1948)
: a dissident Southern Democrat; *specifically* : a supporter of a 1948 presidential ticket opposing the civil rights stand of the Democrats
— **Dix·ie·crat·ic** \,dik-sē-'kra-tik\ *adjective*

Dix·ie·land \-,land\ *noun* [probably from the *Original Dixieland Jazz Band*] (1927)
: jazz music in duple time usually played by a small band and characterized by ensemble and solo improvisation

DIY \,dē-(,)ī-'wī\ *noun, often attributive* (1955) *chiefly British* : DO-IT-YOURSELF

di·zen \'dī-z°n, 'di-\ *transitive verb* [earlier *disen* to dress a distaff with flax, from Middle Dutch] (1619)
archaic : BEDIZEN

di·zy·got·ic \,dī-(,)zī-'gä-tik\ *also* **di·zy·gous** \(,)dī-'zī-gəs\ *adjective* (1916)
of twins : FRATERNAL 2

¹diz·zy \'di-zē\ *adjective* **diz·zi·er; -est** [Middle English *disy,* from Old English *dysig* stupid; akin to Old High German *tusig* stupid] (before 12th century)
1 : FOOLISH, SILLY
2 a : having a whirling sensation in the head with a tendency to fall **b** : mentally confused
3 a : causing giddiness or mental confusion **b** : caused by or marked by giddiness **c** : extremely rapid
— **diz·zi·ly** \'di-zə-lē\ *adverb*
— **diz·zi·ness** \-zē-nəs\ *noun*

²dizzy *transitive verb* **diz·zied; diz·zy·ing** (1501)
1 : to make dizzy or giddy
2 : BEWILDER ⟨disasters that *dizzy* the mind⟩
— **diz·zy·ing·ly** \-zē-iŋ-lē\ *adverb*

DJ \'dē-,jā\ *noun, often not capitalized* (1950)
: DISC JOCKEY

djel·la·ba *also* **djel·la·bah** \jə-'lä-bə\ *noun* [French *djellaba,* from Arabic *jallābīya*] (1919)
: a long loose garment with full sleeves and a hood

djin·ni \'jē-nē\ *or* **djinn** *or* **djin** \'jin\ *variant of* JINNI

dl- \(,)dē-el, 'dē-,\ *prefix*
1 *also* **d,l-** : consisting of equal amounts of the dextro and levo forms of a specified compound ⟨*dl*-tartaric acid⟩
2 : consisting of equal amounts of the D- and L- forms of a specified compound ⟨DL-fructose⟩

D layer *noun* (circa 1934)
: a layer that may exist within the D region of the ionosphere; *also* : D REGION

D-mark \'dȯich-,märk, 'doi-chə-,\ *noun* (1948)
: DEUTSCHE MARK

DME \,dē-(,)em-'ē\ *noun* [*d*istance *m*easuring *e*quipment] (1947)
: an electronic device that informs the pilot of an airplane of its distance from a particular ground station

DMSO \,dē-,em-,es-'ō\ *noun* (1964)
: DIMETHYL SULFOXIDE

DMT \,dē-(,)em-'tē\ *noun* (circa 1966)
: DIMETHYLTRYPTAMINE

DNA \,dē-,en-'ā\ *noun* [*d*eoxyribo*n*ucleic *a*cid] (1944)
: any of various nucleic acids that are usually the molecular basis of heredity, are localized especially in cell nuclei, and are constructed of a double helix held together by hydrogen bonds between purine and pyrimidine bases

DNA: *A* molecular model: *1* hydrogen, *2* oxygen, *3* carbon in the helical phosphate ester chains, *4* carbon and nitrogen in the cross-linked purine and pyrimidine bases, *5* phosphorus; *B* double helix

which project inward from two chains containing alternate links of deoxyribose and phosphate — compare RECOMBINANT DNA

DNA fingerprinting *noun* (1984)
: a method of identification (as for forensic purposes) by determining the sequence of base pairs in the DNA especially of a person
— **DNA fingerprint** *noun*

DNA polymerase *noun* (circa 1962)
: any of several polymerases that promote replication or repair of DNA usually using single-stranded DNA as a template

DN·ase \(,)dē-'en-,ās, -,āz\ *also* **DNA·ase** \(,)dē-,en-'ā-,ās, -,āz\ *noun* (circa 1956)
: DEOXYRIBONUCLEASE

¹**do** \'dü, də(-w)\ *verb* **did** \'did, dəd\; **done** \'dən\; **do·ing** \'dü-iŋ\; **does** \'dəz\ [Middle English *don*, from Old English *dōn*; akin to Old High German *tuon* to do, Latin *-dere* to put, *facere* to make, do, Greek *tithenai* to place, set] (before 12th century)
transitive verb
1 : to bring to pass : CARRY OUT
2 : PUT — used chiefly in *do to death*
3 a : PERFORM, EXECUTE ⟨*did* some work⟩ ⟨*did* his duty⟩ **b** : COMMIT ⟨crimes *done* deliberately⟩
4 a : BRING ABOUT, EFFECT ⟨trying to *do* good⟩ ⟨*do* violence⟩ **b** : to give freely : PAY ⟨*do* honor to her memory⟩
5 : to bring to an end : FINISH — used in the past participle ⟨the job is finally *done*⟩
6 : to put forth : EXERT ⟨*did* her best to win the race⟩
7 a : to wear out especially by physical exertion : EXHAUST ⟨at the end of the race they were pretty well *done*⟩ **b** *British* : to attack physically : BEAT; *also* : KILL
8 : to bring into existence : PRODUCE ⟨*do* a biography on the general⟩
9 — used as a substitute verb especially to avoid repetition ⟨if you must make such a racket, *do* it somewhere else⟩
10 a : to play the role or character of **b** : MIMIC; *also* : to behave like ⟨*do* a Houdini and disappear⟩ **c** : to perform in or serve as producer of ⟨*do* a play⟩
11 : to treat unfairly; *especially* : CHEAT ⟨*did* him out of his inheritance⟩
12 : to treat or deal with in any way typically with the sense of preparation or with that of care or attention: **a** (1) : to put in order : CLEAN ⟨was *doing* the kitchen⟩ (2) : WASH ⟨*did* the dishes after supper⟩ **b** : to prepare for use or consumption; *especially* : COOK ⟨like my steak *done* rare⟩ **c** : SET, ARRANGE ⟨had her hair *done*⟩ **d** : to apply cosmetics to ⟨wanted to *do* her face before the party⟩ **e** : DECORATE, FURNISH ⟨*did* the living room in Early American⟩
13 : to be engaged in the study or practice of ⟨*do* science⟩; *especially* : to work at as a vocation ⟨what to *do* after college⟩
14 a : to pass over (as distance) : TRAVERSE **b** : to travel at a speed of ⟨*doing* 55 on the turnpike⟩
15 : TOUR ⟨*doing* 12 countries in 30 days⟩
16 : to spend or serve out (a period of time) ⟨*did* ten years in prison⟩
17 : to serve the needs of : SUIT, SUFFICE ⟨worms will *do* us for bait⟩
18 : to approve especially by custom, opinion, or propriety ⟨you oughtn't to say a thing like that . . . it's not *done* —Dorothy Sayers⟩
19 : to treat with respect to physical comforts ⟨*did* themselves well⟩
20 : USE *transitive verb* 3 ⟨doesn't *do* drugs⟩
intransitive verb
1 : ACT, BEHAVE ⟨*do* as I say⟩
2 a : GET ALONG, FARE ⟨*do* well in school⟩ **b** : to carry on business or affairs : MANAGE ⟨we can *do* without your help⟩
3 : to take place : HAPPEN ⟨what's *doing* across the street⟩
4 : to come to or make an end : FINISH — used in the past participle

5 : to be active or busy ⟨let us then be up and *doing* —H. W. Longfellow⟩
6 : to be adequate or sufficient : SERVE ⟨half of that will *do*⟩
7 : to be fitting : conform to custom or propriety ⟨won't *do* to be late⟩
8 — used as a substitute verb to avoid repetition ⟨wanted to run and play as children *do*⟩; used especially in British English following a modal auxiliary or perfective *have* ⟨a great many people had died, or would *do* —Bruce Chatwin⟩
9 — used in the imperative after an imperative to add emphasis ⟨be quiet *do*⟩
verbal auxiliary
1 a — used with the infinitive without *to* to form present and past tenses in legal and parliamentary language ⟨*do* hereby bequeath⟩ and in poetry ⟨give what she *did* crave —Shakespeare⟩ **b** — used with the infinitive without *to* to form present and past tenses in declarative sentences with inverted word order ⟨fervently *do* we pray —Abraham Lincoln⟩, in interrogative sentences ⟨*did* you hear that⟩, and in negative sentences ⟨we *don't* know⟩ ⟨*don't* go⟩
2 — used with the infinitive without *to* to form present and past tenses expressing emphasis ⟨I *do* say⟩ ⟨*do* be careful⟩
— **do·able** \'dü-ə-bəl\ *adjective*
— **do a number on** : to defeat or confound thoroughly especially by indirect or deceptive means
— **do away with 1** : to put an end to : ABOLISH **2** : to put to death : KILL
— **do by** : to deal with : TREAT
— **do for** *chiefly British* **1** : to attend to the wants and needs of : take care of **2** : to bring about the death or ruin of
— **do it** : to have sexual intercourse
— **do justice 1 a** : to act justly **b** : to treat fairly or adequately **c** : to show due appreciation for **2** : to acquit in a way worthy of one's abilities
— **do proud** : to give cause for pride or gratification
— **do the trick** : to produce a desired result
— **do with** : to make good use of : benefit by ⟨could *do with* a cup of coffee⟩
— **to do** : necessary to be done ⟨I've done my best and all's *to do* again —A. E. Housman⟩

²**do** \'dü\ *noun, plural* **dos** *or* **do's** \'düz\ (1599)
1 *chiefly dialect* : FUSS, ADO
2 *archaic* : DEED, DUTY
3 a : a festive get-together : AFFAIR, PARTY **b** *chiefly British* : BATTLE
4 : a command or entreaty to do something ⟨a list of *dos* and don'ts⟩
5 *British* : CHEAT, SWINDLE
6 : HAIRDO

³**do** \'dō\ *noun* [Italian] (circa 1754)
: the 1st tone of the diatonic scale in solmization

dob·bin \'dä-bən\ *noun* [*Dobbin*, nickname for *Robert*] (1596)
1 : a farm horse
2 : a quiet plodding horse

dob·by \'dä-bē\ *noun, plural* **dobbies** [perhaps from *Dobby*, nickname for *Robert*] (1878)
1 : a loom attachment for weaving small figures
2 : a fabric or figured weave made with a dobby

Dobe \'dōb\ *noun* (1946)
: DOBERMAN PINSCHER

Do·ber·man pin·scher \,dō-bər-mən-'pin-chər\ *noun* [German *Dobermann-pinscher*, from Ludwig *Dobermann*, 19th century German dog breeder + German *Pinscher*, a breed of hunting dog] (1917)

: any of a breed of short-haired medium-sized dogs of German origin — called also *Doberman*

do·bra \'dō-brə, 'dȯ-\ *noun* [Portuguese, from feminine of obsolete *dobro* double, from Latin *duplus* — more at DOUBLE] (1978)
— see MONEY table

Do·bro \'dō-(,)brō\ *trademark*
— used for an acoustic guitar having a metal resonator

dob·son·fly \'däb-sən-,flī\ *noun* [origin unknown] (circa 1904)
: a winged insect (family Corydalidae) that has very long slender mandibles in the male and a large carnivorous aquatic larva and that is now usually considered a neuropteran — compare HELLGRAMMITE

doc \'däk\ *noun* (circa 1850)
: DOCTOR

do·cent \'dō-sᵊnt, dō(t)-'sent\ *noun* [obsolete German (now *Dozent*), from Latin *docent-, docens*, present participle of *docēre*] (1880)
1 : a college or university teacher or lecturer
2 : a person who leads guided tours especially through a museum or art gallery

do·ce·tic \dō-'sē-tik, -'se-\ *adjective, often capitalized* [Late Greek *Dokētai* Docetists, from Greek *dokein* to seem — more at DECENT] (1846)
: of or relating to Docetism or the Docetists

Do·ce·tism \dō-'sē-,ti-zəm, 'dō-sə-\ *noun* (1846)
: a belief opposed as heresy in early Christianity that Christ only seemed to have a human body and to suffer and die on the cross
— **Do·ce·tist** \-'sē-tist, -sə-\ *noun*

doch–an–dor·ris *or* **doch–an–dor·is** \,däk-ən-'dȯr-əs\ *noun* [Scottish Gaelic *deoch an doruis* & Irish *deoch an dorais*, literally, drink of the door] (1691)
Scottish & Irish : a parting drink : STIRRUP CUP

doc·ile \'dä-səl *also* -,sīl, *especially British* 'dō-,sīl\ *adjective* [Latin *docilis*, from *docēre* to teach; akin to Latin *decēre* to be fitting — more at DECENT] (15th century)
1 : easily taught
2 : easily led or managed : TRACTABLE
synonym see OBEDIENT
— **doc·ile·ly** \'dä-s(ə)l-lē\ *adverb*
— **do·cil·i·ty** \dä-'si-lə-tē, dō-\ *noun*

¹**dock** \'däk\ *noun* [Middle English, from Old English *docce*; akin to Middle Dutch *docke* dock] (before 12th century)
1 : any of a genus (*Rumex*) of the buckwheat family of coarse weedy plants that have long taproots and are sometimes used as potherbs
2 : any of several usually broad-leaved weedy plants

²**dock** *noun* [Middle English *dok*, perhaps from Old English *-docca* (as in *fingirdocca* finger muscle); akin to Old High German *tocka* doll, Old Norse *dokka* bundle] (14th century)
1 : the solid part of an animal's tail as distinguished from the hair
2 : the part of an animal's tail left after it has been shortened

³**dock** *transitive verb* (14th century)
1 a : to cut off the end of a body part of; *specifically* : to remove part of the tail of **b** : to cut (as ears or a tail) short
2 a : to take away a part of : ABRIDGE **b** : to subject (as wages) to a deduction **c** : to penalize by depriving of a benefit ordinarily due; *especially* : to fine by a deduction of wages ⟨*docked* him for tardiness⟩

⁴**dock** *noun* [Middle English *dokke*, probably from Middle Dutch *docke*] (15th century)

\ə\ abut \ᵊ\ kitten \ər\ **further** \a\ ash \ā\ ace \ä\ mop, mar \aù\ out \ch\ chin \e\ bet \ē\ easy \g\ go \i\ hit \ī\ ice \j\ job \ŋ\ sing \ō\ go \ȯ\ law \ȯi\ boy \th\ thin \t͟h\ the \ü\ loot \ù\ foot \y\ yet \zh\ vision *see also* Guide to Pronunciation

1 : a usually artificial basin or enclosure for the reception of ships that is equipped with means for controlling the water height
2 : the waterway extending between two piers for the reception of ships
3 : a place (as a wharf or platform) for the loading or unloading of materials □
⁵**dock** (1600)
transitive verb
1 : to haul or guide into a dock
2 : to join (as two spacecraft) mechanically while in space
intransitive verb
1 : to come into dock
2 : to become docked
⁶**dock** *noun* [Flemish *docke* cage] (1586)
: the place in a criminal court where a prisoner stands or sits during trial
— in the dock : on trial
dock·age \'dä-kij\ *noun* (1648)
1 : a charge for the use of a dock
2 : the docking of ships
3 : docking facilities
¹**dock·er** \'dä-kər\ *noun* (1810)
: one that docks the tails of animals
²**docker** *noun* (1887)
: one connected with docks; *especially* **:** LONGSHOREMAN
¹**dock·et** \'dä-kət\ *noun* [Middle English *doggette*] (15th century)
1 : a brief written summary of a document **:** ABSTRACT
2 a (1) **:** a formal abridged record of the proceedings in a legal action (2) **:** a register of such records **b** (1) **:** a list of legal causes to be tried (2) **:** a calendar of business matters to be acted on **:** AGENDA
3 : an identifying statement about a document placed on its outer surface or cover
²**docket** *transitive verb* (1615)
1 : to place on the docket for legal action
2 : to make a brief abstract of (as a legal matter) and inscribe it in a list
3 : to inscribe (as a document) with an identifying statement
dock·hand \'däk-ˌhand\ *noun* (1920)
: LONGSHOREMAN
dock·land \-ˌland\ *noun* (1904)
British **:** the part of a port occupied by docks; *also* **:** a residential section adjacent to docks
dock·mas·ter \'däk-ˌmas-tər\ *noun* (1736)
: a person in charge of a dock or marina or of the docking of ships
dock·side \-ˌsīd\ *noun, often attributive* (1887)
: the shore or area adjacent to a dock
dock·work·er \-ˌwər-kər\ *noun* (1921)
: LONGSHOREMAN
dock·yard \-ˌyärd\ *noun* (1704)
1 : SHIPYARD
2 *British* **:** NAVY YARD
¹**doc·tor** \'däk-tər\ *noun* [Middle English *doctour* teacher, doctor, from Middle French & Medieval Latin; Middle French, from Medieval Latin *doctor*, from Latin, teacher, from *docēre* to teach — more at DOCILE] (14th century)
1 a : an eminent theologian declared a sound expounder of doctrine by the Roman Catholic Church — called also *doctor of the church* **b :** a learned or authoritative teacher **c :** a person who has earned one of the highest academic degrees (as a PhD) conferred by a university **d :** a person awarded an honorary doctorate (as an LLD or Litt D) by a college or university
2 a : one skilled or specializing in healing arts; *especially* **:** a physician, surgeon, dentist, or veterinarian who is licensed to practice **b :** MEDICINE MAN
3 a : material added (as to food) to produce a desired effect **b :** a blade (as of metal) for spreading a coating or scraping a surface
4 : a person who restores or repairs things
— doc·tor·al \-t(ə-)rəl\ *adjective*

— doc·tor·less \-tər-ləs\ *adjective*
— doc·tor·ship \-ˌship\ *noun*
²**doctor** *verb* **doc·tored; doc·tor·ing** \-t(ə-)riŋ\ (1712)
transitive verb
1 a : to give medical treatment to **b :** to restore to good condition **:** REPAIR ⟨*doctor* an old clock⟩
2 a : to adapt or modify for a desired end by alteration or special treatment ⟨*doctored* the play to suit the audience⟩ ⟨the drink was *doctored*⟩ **b :** to alter deceptively ⟨accused of *doctoring* the election returns⟩
intransitive verb
1 : to practice medicine
2 *dialect* **:** to take medicine
doc·tor·ate \'däk-t(ə-)rət\ *noun* (1676)
: the degree, title, or rank of a doctor
¹**doc·tri·naire** \ˌdäk-trə-'nar, -'ner\ *noun* [French, from *doctrine*] (1831)
: one who attempts to put into effect an abstract doctrine or theory with little or no regard for practical difficulties
²**doctrinaire** *adjective* (1834)
: of, relating to, or characteristic of a doctrinaire **:** DOGMATIC
synonym see DICTATORIAL
— doc·tri·nair·ism \-'nar-ˌi-zəm, -'ner-\ *noun*
doc·trin·al \'däk-trə-nᵊl, *especially British* däk-'trī-\ *adjective* (15th century)
: of, relating to, or preoccupied with doctrine
— doc·trin·al·ly \-nᵊl-ē\ *adverb*
doc·trine \'däk-trən\ *noun* [Middle English, from Middle French & Latin; Middle French, from Latin *doctrina*, from *doctor*] (14th century)
1 *archaic* **:** TEACHING, INSTRUCTION
2 a : something that is taught **b :** a principle or position or the body of principles in a branch of knowledge or system of belief **:** DOGMA **c :** a principle of law established through past decisions **d :** a statement of fundamental government policy especially in international relations
docu·dra·ma \'dä-kyə-ˌdrä-mə, -ˌdra-\ *noun* [*documentary* + *drama*] (circa 1961)
: a drama for television, motion pictures, or theater dealing freely with historical events especially of a recent and controversial nature
¹**doc·u·ment** \'dä-kyə-mənt\ *noun* [Middle English, from Middle French, from Late Latin & Latin; Late Latin *documentum* official paper, from Latin, lesson, proof, from *docēre* to teach — more at DOCILE] (15th century)
1 a *archaic* **:** PROOF, EVIDENCE **b :** an original or official paper relied on as the basis, proof, or support of something **c :** something (as a photograph or a recording) that serves as evidence or proof
2 a : a writing conveying information **b :** a material substance (as a coin or stone) having on it a representation of thoughts by means of some conventional mark or symbol **c :** DOCUMENTARY
— doc·u·men·tal \ˌdä-kyə-'men-tᵊl\ *adjective*
²**doc·u·ment** \'dä-kyə-ˌment\ *transitive verb* (1711)
1 : to furnish documentary evidence of
2 : to furnish with documents
3 a : to provide with factual or substantial support for statements made or a hypothesis proposed; *especially* **:** to equip with exact references to authoritative supporting information **b** (1) **:** to construct or produce (as a movie or novel) with authentic situations or events (2) **:** to portray realistically
4 : to furnish (a ship) with ship's papers
— doc·u·ment·able \-ˌmen-tə-bəl, ˌdäk-yə-'\ *adjective*
— doc·u·ment·er \'dä-kyə-ˌmen-tər\ *noun*
doc·u·men·tal·ist \ˌdä-kyə-'men-tᵊl-ist\ *noun* (1939)
: a specialist in documentation

doc·u·men·tar·i·an \ˌdä-kyə-mən-'ter-ē-ən, -ˌmen-\ *noun* [²*documentary*] (1943)
: one who makes a documentary
doc·u·men·ta·rist \-'men-tə-rist\ *noun* [²*documentary*] (1949)
: DOCUMENTARIAN
¹**doc·u·men·ta·ry** \ˌdä-kyə-'men-tə-rē, -'men-trē\ *adjective* (1802)
1 : being or consisting of documents **:** contained or certified in writing ⟨*documentary* evidence⟩
2 : of, relating to, or employing documentation in literature or art; *broadly* **:** FACTUAL, OBJECTIVE ⟨a *documentary* film of the war⟩
— doc·u·men·tar·i·ly \-mən-'ter-ə-lē, -ˌmen-\ *adverb*
²**documentary** *noun, plural* **-ries** (1935)
: a documentary presentation (as a film or novel)
doc·u·men·ta·tion \ˌdä-kyə-mən-'tā-shən, -ˌmen-\ *noun* (1884)
1 : the act or an instance of furnishing or authenticating with documents
2 a : the provision of documents in substantiation; *also* **:** documentary evidence **b** (1) **:** the use of historical documents (2) **:** conformity to historical or objective facts (3) **:** the provision of footnotes, appendices, or addenda referring to or containing documentary evidence
3 : INFORMATION SCIENCE
4 : the usually printed instructions, comments, and information for using a particular piece or system of computer software or hardware
— doc·u·men·ta·tion·al \-shnəl, -shə-nᵊl\ *adjective*
¹**dod·der** \'dä-dər\ *noun* [Middle English *doder;* akin to Middle High German *toter* dodder, egg yolk] (13th century)
: any of a genus (*Cuscuta*) of parasitic wiry twining vines of the morning-glory family that are deficient in chlorophyll and have tiny scales instead of leaves
²**dodder** *intransitive verb* **dod·dered; dod·der·ing** \'dä-d(ə-)riŋ\ [Middle English *da-diren*] (14th century)
1 : to tremble or shake from weakness or age
2 : to progress feebly and unsteadily ⟨was *doddering* down the walk⟩
— dod·der·er \-dər-ər\ *noun*
dod·dered \'dä-dərd\ *adjective* [probably alteration of *dodded*, from past participle of English dialect *dod* to lop, from Middle English *dodden*] (1697)
1 : deprived of branches through age or decay ⟨a *doddered* oak⟩
2 : INFIRM, ENFEEBLED
dod·der·ing \'dä-d(ə-)riŋ\ *adjective* (1898)
: FEEBLE, SENILE
dod·dery \-d(ə-)rē\ *adjective* (1866)
1 : DODDERED 2
2 : DODDERING
dodeca- *or* **dodec-** *combining form* [Latin, from Greek *dōdeka-, dōdek-,* from *dōdeka, dyōdeka,* from *dyō, dyo* two + *deka* ten]
: twelve ⟨*dodeca*phonic⟩

do·deca·gon \dō-'de-kə-ˌgän\ *noun* [Greek *dōdekagōnon*, from *dōdeka-* + *-gōnon* -gon] (circa 1658)
: a polygon of 12 angles and 12 sides
do·deca·he·dron \(ˌ)dō-ˌde-kə-'hē-drən\ *noun, plural* **-drons** *or* **-dra** \-drə\ [Greek *dōdekaedron*, from *dōdeka-* + *-edron* -hedron] (circa 1570)
: a solid having 12 plane faces
— **do·deca·he·dral** \-drəl\ *adjective*
do·deca·phon·ic \(ˌ)dō-ˌde-kə-'fä-nik\ *adjective* [*dodeca-* + *phon-* + *-ic*] (1949)
: TWELVE-TONE
— **do·deca·phon·i·cal·ly** \-ni-k(ə-)lē\ *adverb*
— **do·deca·pho·nist** \dō-'de-kə-fə-nist, -ˌfō-; ˌdō-di-'ka-fə-nist\ *noun*
— **do·deca·pho·ny** \-nē\ *noun*
¹dodge \'däj\ *noun* [origin unknown] (1575)
1 a : an artful device to evade, deceive, or trick **b :** EXPEDIENT
2 : an act of evading by sudden bodily movement
²dodge *verb* **dodged; dodg·ing** (1680) *transitive verb*
1 : to evade (as a duty) usually indirectly or by trickery ⟨*dodged* the draft by leaving the country⟩ ⟨*dodged* questions⟩
2 a : to evade by a sudden or repeated shift of position **b :** to avoid an encounter with *intransitive verb*
1 a : to make a sudden movement in a new direction (as to evade a blow) ⟨*dodged* behind the door⟩ **b :** to move to and fro or from place to place usually in an irregular course ⟨*dodged* through the crowd⟩
2 : to evade a responsibility or duty especially by trickery or deceit
dodge·ball \'däj-ˌbȯl\ *noun* (circa 1922)
: a game in which players stand in a circle and try to hit opponents within the circle with a large inflated ball
dodg·em \'dä-jəm\ *noun, often capitalized* (1921)
: an amusement ride featuring bumper cars
dodgem car *noun* (1945)
: BUMPER CAR
dodg·er \'dä-jər\ *noun* (1568)
1 : one that dodges; *especially* : one who uses tricky devices
2 : a small leaflet : CIRCULAR
3 : CORN DODGER
4 : a usually canvas screen on a boat or ship that provides protection from spray
dodg·ery \'dä-jə-rē\ *noun, plural* **-er·ies** (1670)
: EVASION, TRICKERY
dodgy \'dä-jē\ *adjective* (1861)
1 *chiefly British* : EVASIVE, TRICKY
2 *chiefly British* : not sound, stable, or reliable : SHAKY
3 *British* : requiring skill or care in handling; *also* : CHANCY, RISKY
— **dodg·i·ness** \-nəs\ *noun*
do·do \'dō-(ˌ)dō\ *noun, plural* **dodoes** *or* **do·dos** [Portuguese *doudo*, from *doudo* silly, stupid] (1628)
1 a : an extinct heavy flightless bird (*Raphus cucullatus*, synonym *Didus ineptus*) of the island of Mauritius that is related to the pigeon and larger than a turkey **b :** an extinct bird of the island of Réunion similar to and apparently closely related to the dodo
2 a : one hopelessly behind the times **b :** a stupid person

dodo 1a

do down *transitive verb* (14th century)
British : to get the better of (as by trickery)
doe \'dō\ *noun, plural* **does** *or* **doe** [Middle English *do*, from Old English *dā*; akin to German dialect *tē* doe] (before 12th century)

: the adult female of various mammals (as a deer, rabbit, or kangaroo) of which the male is called buck
doe–eyed \'dō-ˌīd\ *adjective* (1933)
: having large innocent-looking eyes
do·er \'dü-ər\ *noun* (14th century)
: one that takes an active part ⟨a thinker or a *doer*⟩
does *present 3d singular of* DO, *plural of* DOE
doe·skin \'dō-ˌskin\ *noun* (15th century)
1 : the skin of does or leather made of it; *also* : soft leather from sheep- or lambskins
2 : a compact coating and sportswear fabric napped and felted for a smooth surface
doesn't \'də-z⁰nt\ (1860)
: does not
do·est \'dü-əst\ *archaic present 2d singular of* DO
do·eth \'dü-əth\ *archaic present 3d singular of* DO
doff \'däf, 'dȯf\ *transitive verb* [Middle English, from *don* to do + *of* off] (14th century)
1 a : to remove (an article of wear) from the body **b :** to take off (the hat) in greeting or as a sign of respect
2 : to rid oneself of : put aside
— **doff one's hat to** *or* **doff one's cap to :** to show respect to : SALUTE
¹dog \'dȯg, 'däg\ *noun, often attributive* [Middle English, from Old English *docga*] (before 12th century)
1 a : CANID; *especially* : a highly variable domestic mammal (*Canis familiaris*) closely related to the common wolf (*Canis lupus*) **b :** a male dog; *also* : a male usually carnivorous mammal
2 a : a worthless person **b :** FELLOW, CHAP ⟨a lazy *dog*⟩ ⟨you lucky *dog*⟩
3 a : any of various usually simple mechanical devices for holding, gripping, or fastening that consist of a spike, bar, or hook **b :** ANDIRON
4 : uncharacteristic or affected stylishness or dignity ⟨put on the *dog*⟩
5 *capitalized* : either of the constellations Canis Major or Canis Minor
6 *plural* : FEET
7 *plural* : RUIN ⟨going to the *dogs*⟩
8 : one inferior of its kind: as **a :** an investment not worth its price **b :** an undesirable piece of merchandise
9 : an unattractive person and especially a girl or woman
10 : HOT DOG 1
— **dog·like** \'dȯg-ˌlīk\ *adjective*

dog 1a: *1* pastern, *2* chest, *3* flews, *4* muzzle, *5* stop, *6* occiput, *7* leather, *8* crest, *9* withers, *10* loin, *11* point of rump, *12* hock *or* tarsus, *13* knee *or* stifle, *14* brisket, *15* elbow, *16* feathering

²dog *adjective* (14th century)
1 : CANINE
2 : SPURIOUS; *especially* : unlike that used by native speakers or writers ⟨*dog* Latin⟩ ⟨*dog* French⟩
³dog *transitive verb* **dogged** \'dȯgd, 'dägd\; **dog·ging** (1519)
1 a : to hunt or track like a hound **b :** to worry as if by pursuit with dogs : PLAGUE
2 : to fasten with a dog

— **dog it :** to fail to do one's best : GOLDBRICK
⁴dog *adverb* (circa 1552)
: EXTREMELY, UTTERLY ⟨*dog*-tired⟩
dog and pony show *noun* (1965)
: an often elaborate public relations or sales presentation
dog·bane \'dȯg-ˌbān\ *noun* (1597)
: any of a genus (*Apocynum* of the family Apocynaceae, the dogbane family) comprising chiefly tropical and often poisonous plants with milky juice and usually showy flowers
dog biscuit *noun* (circa 1858)
: a hard dry cracker for dogs
dog·cart \'dȯg-ˌkärt\ *noun* (1668)
1 : a cart drawn by a dog
2 : a light two-wheeled carriage with two transverse seats set back to back
dog·catch·er \-ˌka-chər, -ˌke-\ *noun* (1835)
: a community official assigned to catch and dispose of stray dogs
dog collar *noun* (1524)
1 : a collar for a dog
2 *slang* : CLERICAL COLLAR
3 : a wide flexible snug-fitting necklace
dog days *noun plural* [from their being reckoned from the heliacal rising of the Dog Star (Sirius)] (1538)
1 : the period between early July and early September when the hot sultry weather of summer usually occurs in the northern hemisphere
2 : a period of stagnation or inactivity ◇
dog·dom \'dȯg-dəm\ *noun* (1854)
: the world of dogs or of dog fanciers
doge \'dōj\ *noun* [Italian dialect, from Latin *duc-, dux* leader — more at DUKE] (1549)
: the chief magistrate in the republics of Venice and Genoa
dog-ear \'dȯ-ˌgir\ *noun* (circa 1725)
: the turned-down corner of a page especially of a book
— **dog-ear** *transitive verb*
dog-eared \'dȯ-ˌgird\ *adjective* (1784)
1 : having dog-ears ⟨a *dog-eared* book⟩
2 : SHABBY, TIMEWORN ⟨a *dog-eared* resort⟩ ⟨*dog-eared* myths⟩
dog-eat-dog \ˌdȯ-ˌgēt-'dȯg\ *adjective* (1834)
: marked by ruthless self-interest ⟨*dog-eat-dog* competition⟩
dog·face \'dȯg-ˌfās\ *noun* (1941)
: SOLDIER; *especially* : INFANTRYMAN
dog fennel *noun* (14th century)
: a strong-scented chamomile (*Anthemis cotula*) of Europe and Asia naturalized along roadsides in the U.S.
dog·fight \'dȯg-ˌfīt\ *noun* (1656)

◇ WORD HISTORY
dog days The Greek name for the brightest star in the sky was *Seirios*, a word of uncertain origin; the Latin version of this word is *Sirius*, which gives us our name for the star. Our alternative name, the Dog Star, is ultimately a translation of Greek *Kyōn*, literally, "hound." This epithet was given to Sirius because it was considered the hound of the hunter Orion, whose constellation was nearby. Sirius was regarded by the Greeks as the bringer of scorching heat, because its early-morning rising coincided with the hottest summer days of July and August. The Greek writer Plutarch referred to these days as *hēmerai kynades*, literally, "dog days"—the days of the Dog Star—and a later Latin translation of this expression as *dies caniculares* is the source of the English phrase *dog days*.

\ə\ abut \ᵊ\ kitten \ər\ further \a\ ash \ā\ ace
\ä\ mop, mar \au̇\ out \ch\ chin \e\ bet \ē\ easy
\g\ go \i\ hit \ī\ ice \j\ job \ŋ\ sing \ō\ go
\ȯ\ law \ȯi\ boy \th\ thin \t͟h\ the \ü\ loot \u̇\ foot
\y\ yet \zh\ vision *see also* Guide to Pronunciation

1 : a fight between dogs; *broadly* : a fiercely disputed contest
2 : a fight between two or more fighter planes usually at close quarters
— **dogfight** *intransitive verb*
dog·fish \-,fish\ *noun* (15th century)
: any of various usually small bottom-dwelling sharks (as of the families Squalidae, Carcharhinidae, and Scyliorhinidae) that often appear in schools near shore, prey chiefly on fish and invertebrates, and are a valuable food source
dog·ged \'dȯ-gəd\ *adjective* (1653)
: marked by stubborn determination
synonym see OBSTINATE
— **dog·ged·ly** *adverb*
— **dog·ged·ness** *noun*
¹dog·ger·el \'dȯ-g(ə-)rəl, 'dä-\ *adjective* [Middle English *dogerel*, probably diminutive of *dogge* dog] (14th century)
: loosely styled and irregular in measure especially for burlesque or comic effect; *also*
: marked by triviality or inferiority
²doggerel *noun* (1630)
: doggerel verse
dog·gery \'dȯ-gə-rē\ *noun, plural* **-ger·ies** (1830)
: a cheap saloon : DIVE
dog·gie bag *or* **doggy bag** \'dȯ-gē-\ *noun* [¹*doggy*; from the presumption that such leftovers are intended for a pet dog] (1963)
: a container for carrying home leftover food and especially meat from a restaurant meal
dog·gish \'dȯ-gish\ *adjective* (15th century)
1 : CANINE
2 : stylish in a showy way
— **dog·gish·ly** *adverb*
— **dog·gish·ness** *noun*
dog·go \'dȯ-(,)gō\ *adverb* [probably from ¹*dog*] (1893)
: in hiding — used chiefly in the phrase *to lie doggo*
¹dog·gone \'däg-,gän, 'dȯg-'gȯn\ *verb* **dog·goned; dog·gon·ing** [euphemism for *God damn*] (1828)
: DAMN
²dog·gone *or* **dog·goned** \,däg-'gän(d), ,dȯg-,gȯn(d)\ *adjective or adverb* (1851)
: DAMNED
³doggone *noun* (1928)
: DAMN
¹dog·gy *or* **dog·gie** \'dȯ-gē\ *noun, plural* **doggies** (1825)
: a small dog
²dog·gy \'dȯ-gē\ *adjective* **dog·gi·er; -est** (1859)
1 : concerned with or fond of dogs
2 : resembling or suggestive of a dog ⟨*doggy* odor⟩
3 : STYLISH, SHOWY
4 : not worthy or profitable : INFERIOR
dog·house \'dȯg-,haus\ *noun* (1594)
: a shelter for a dog
— **in the doghouse** : in a state of disfavor
do·gie \'dō-gē\ *noun* [origin unknown] (1888) *chiefly West* : a motherless calf in a range herd
dog in the manger [from the fable of the dog who prevented an ox from eating hay which he did not want himself] (1573)
: a person who selfishly withholds from others something useless to himself
¹dog·leg \'dȯg-,leg, -,lāg\ *adjective* (1889)
: crooked or bent like a dog's hind leg
²dogleg *noun* (circa 1909)
1 a : something having an abrupt angle **b** : a sharp bend (as in a road)
2 : a golf hole having an angled fairway
³dogleg *intransitive verb* (1947)
: to proceed along a dogleg course ⟨the single narrow street that *doglegs* through town —Russ Leadabrand⟩
dog·ma \'dȯg-mə, 'däg-\ *noun, plural* **dog·mas** *also* **dog·ma·ta** \-mə-tə\ [Latin *dogmat-, dogma*, from Greek, from *dokein* to seem — more at DECENT] (1638)

1 a : something held as an established opinion; *especially* : a definite authoritative tenet **b** : a code of such tenets ⟨pedagogical *dogma*⟩ **c** : a point of view or tenet put forth as authoritative without adequate grounds
2 : a doctrine or body of doctrines concerning faith or morals formally stated and authoritatively proclaimed by a church
dog·mat·ic \dȯg-'ma-tik, däg-\ *also* **dog·mat·i·cal** \-ti-kəl\ *adjective* (circa 1681)
1 : characterized by or given to the use of dogmatism ⟨a *dogmatic* critic⟩
2 : of or relating to dogma
synonym see DICTATORIAL
— **dog·mat·i·cal·ly** \-ti-k(ə-)lē\ *adverb*
— **dog·mat·i·cal·ness** \-ti-kəl-nəs\ *noun*
dog·mat·ics \-tiks\ *noun plural but singular or plural in construction* (1845)
: a branch of theology that seeks to interpret the dogmas of a religious faith
dogmatic theology *noun* (1846)
: DOGMATICS
dog·ma·tism \'dȯg-mə-,ti-zəm, 'däg-\ *noun* (1603)
1 : positiveness in assertion of opinion especially when unwarranted or arrogant
2 : a viewpoint or system of ideas based on insufficiently examined premises
dog·ma·tist \-mə-tist\ *noun* (1541)
: one who dogmatizes
dog·ma·tize \'dȯg-mə-,tīz, 'däg-\ *verb* **-tized; -tiz·ing** [French *dogmatiser*, from Late Latin *dogmatizare*, from Greek *dogmatizein*, from *dogmat-, dogma*] (1611)
intransitive verb
: to speak or write dogmatically
transitive verb
: to state as a dogma or in a dogmatic manner
— **dog·ma·ti·za·tion** \,dȯg-mə-tə-'zā-shən, ,däg-\ *noun*
— **dog·ma·tiz·er** *noun*
dog·nap \'dȯg-,nap\ *transitive verb* **-napped** *or* **-naped** \-,napt\; **-nap·ping** *or* **-nap·ing** \-,na-piŋ\ [¹*dog* + -*nap* (as in *kidnap*)] (1947)
: to steal (a dog) especially to obtain a reward for its return or to sell to a scientific laboratory
— **dog·nap·per** *or* **dog·nap·er** *noun*
Do·gon \'dō-,gän\ *noun, plural* **Dogon** *or* **Dogons** (circa 1931)
1 : a member of a people of Mali noted for their sculpture
2 : the language of the Dogon
do–good \'dü-,gud\ *adjective* (1952)
: designed or designated sometimes impractically and too zealously toward bettering the conditions under which others live
— **do–good·ism** \-,i-zəm\ *noun*
do–good·er \-,gu-dər\ *noun* (1926)
: an earnest often naive humanitarian or reformer
— **do–good·ing** \-diŋ\ *noun or adjective*
dog paddle *noun* (1904)
: an elementary swimming stroke in which the arms paddle in the water and the legs maintain a kicking motion
— **dog–pad·dle** *intransitive verb*
dog rose *noun* (circa 1597)
: a common European wild rose (*Rosa canina*)
dogs·body \'dȯgz-,bä-dē\ *noun* [British naval slang *dogsbody* pudding made of peas, junior officer] (1922)
chiefly British : DRUDGE
dog's chance *noun* (1902)
: a bare chance in one's favor
dog·sled \'dȯg-,sled\ *noun* (1810)
: a sled drawn by dogs
— **dogsled** *intransitive verb*
— **dog·sled·der** \-,sle-dər\ *noun*
Dog Star *noun*
: SIRIUS
dog tag *noun* (1918)
: an identification tag (as for military personnel or pets)
dog tick *noun* (circa 1552)
: AMERICAN DOG TICK

dog·tooth \'dȯg-,tüth\ *noun* (1552)
1 : CANINE 1, EYETOOTH
2 : an architectural ornament common in early English Gothic consisting usually of four leaves radiating from a raised point at the center
3 *chiefly British* : HOUNDSTOOTH CHECK

dogtooth 2

dogtooth violet *noun* (1629)
: any of a genus (*Erythronium*) of small spring-flowering bulbous herbs of the lily family
¹dog·trot \'dȯg-,trät\ *noun* (15th century)
1 : a quick easy gait suggesting that of a dog
2 *chiefly Southern & Midland* : a roofed passage similar to a breezeway; *especially* : one connecting two parts of a cabin
²dogtrot *intransitive verb* (circa 1900)
: to move or progress at a dogtrot
dog·watch \'dȯg-,wäch\ *noun* (1700)
1 : either of two watches of two hours on shipboard that extend from 4 to 6 and 6 to 8 p.m.
2 : any of various night shifts; *especially* : the last shift
dog·wood \'dȯg-,wud\ *noun* (1617)
: any of various trees and shrubs (genus *Cornus* of the family Cornaceae, the dogwood family) with clusters of small flowers and often large white, pink, or red involucral bracts
doi·ly \'dȯi-lē\ *noun, plural* **doilies** [*Doily* or *Doyley* (flourished 1711) London draper] (1711)
1 : a small napkin
2 : a small often decorative mat
do in *transitive verb* (1905)
1 a : to bring about the defeat or destruction of; *also* : KILL **b** : EXHAUST, WEAR OUT
2 : CHEAT
do·ing \'dü-iŋ\ *noun* (14th century)
1 : the act of performing or executing : ACTION ⟨that will take a great deal of *doing*⟩
2 *plural* **a** : things that are done or that occur : GOINGS-ON ⟨everyday *doings*⟩ **b** : social activities
doit \'dȯit\ *noun* [Dutch *duit*; akin to Old Norse *thveiti* small coin, *thveita* to hew] (1592)
1 : an old Dutch coin equal to about ⅛ stiver
2 : TRIFLE 1
do–it–your·self \,dü-ə-chər-'self, -tyər-\ *noun, often attributive* (1952)
: the activity of doing or making something (as in woodworking or home repair) without professional training or assistance; *broadly*
: an activity in which one does something oneself or on one's own initiative
— **do–it–your·self·er** \-'sel-fər\ *noun*
do·jo \'dō-(,)jō\ *noun, plural* **dojos** [Japanese *dōjō*, from *dō* way, art + -*jō* ground] (1942)
: a school for training in various arts of self-defense (as judo or karate)
Dol·by \'dȯl-bē, 'dōl-\ *trademark*
— used for an electronic device that eliminates noise from recorded sound or sound broadcast on FM radio
dol·ce \'dōl-(,)chä\ *adjective or adverb* [Italian, literally, sweet, from Latin *dulcis* — more at DULCET] (circa 1847)
: SOFT, SMOOTH — used as a direction in music
dol·ce far nien·te \'dōl-chē-,fär-nē-'en-tē\ *noun* [Italian, literally, sweet doing nothing] (1814)
: pleasant relaxation in carefree idleness
dol·ce vi·ta \,dōl-chā-'vē-(,)tä\ *noun* [Italian, literally, sweet life] (1961)
: a life of indolence and self-indulgence
dol·drums \'dōl-drəmz, 'däl-, 'dȯl-\ *noun plural* [probably akin to Old English *dol* foolish] (1811)
1 : a spell of listlessness or despondency
2 *often capitalized* : a part of the ocean near the equator abounding in calms, squalls, and light shifting winds

3 : a state or period of inactivity, stagnation, or slump

¹dole \'dōl\ *noun* [Middle English, from Old English *dāl* portion — more at DEAL] (before 12th century)
1 *archaic* **:** one's allotted share, portion, or destiny
2 a (1) **:** a giving or distribution of food, money, or clothing to the needy (2) **:** a grant of government funds to the unemployed **b :** something distributed at intervals in the needy; *also* **:** HANDOUT 1 **c :** something portioned out bit by bit

²dole *transitive verb* **doled; dol·ing** (15th century)
: to give or distribute as a charity — usually used with *out*

³dole *noun* [Middle English *dol*, from Old French, from Late Latin *dolus*, alteration of Latin *dolor*] (13th century)
archaic **:** GRIEF, SORROW

dole·ful \'dōl-fəl\ *adjective* (13th century)
1 : causing grief or affliction ⟨a *doleful* loss⟩
2 : full of grief **:** CHEERLESS ⟨a *doleful* face⟩
3 : expressing grief **:** SAD ⟨a *doleful* melody⟩
— **dole·ful·ly** \-fə-lē\ *adverb*
— **dole·ful·ness** *noun*

dole out *transitive verb* (1749)
1 : to give or deliver in small portions
2 : DISH OUT
synonym see DISTRIBUTE

dol·er·ite \'dä-lə-ˌrīt\ *noun* [French *dolérite*, from Greek *doleros* deceitful, from *dolos* deceit; from its being easily mistaken for diorite] (1838)
1 : any of various coarse basalts
2 *chiefly British* **:** DIABASE 3
— **dol·er·it·ic** \ˌdä-lə-'ri-tik\ *adjective*

dole·some \'dōl-səm\ *adjective* (1533)
: DOLEFUL

dol·i·cho·ce·phal·ic \ˌdä-li-kō-sə-'fa-lik\ *adjective* [New Latin *dolichocephalus* long-headed, from Greek *dolichos* long + -*kephalos*, from *kephalē* head — more at CEPHALIC] (1852)
: having a relatively long head with cephalic index of less than 75
— **dol·i·cho·ceph·a·ly** \-'se-fə-lē\ *noun*

doll \'däl, 'dȯl\ *noun* [probably from *Doll*, nickname for *Dorothy*] (circa 1700)
1 : a small-scale figure of a human being used especially as a child's plaything
2 a (1) **:** a pretty but often empty-headed young woman (2) **:** WOMAN **b :** DARLING, SWEETHEART **c :** an attractive person
— **doll·ish** \'dä-lish, 'dȯ-\ *adjective*
— **doll·ish·ly** *adverb*
— **doll·ish·ness** *noun*

dol·lar \'dä-lər\ *noun, often attributive* [Dutch or Low German *daler*, from German *Taler*, short for *Joachimstaler*, from Sankt *Joachimsthal*, Bohemia, where talers were first made] (1553)
1 : TALER
2 : any of numerous coins patterned after the taler (as a Spanish peso)
3 a : any of various basic monetary units (as in the U.S. and Canada) — see MONEY table **b :** a coin, note, or token representing one dollar
4 : RINGGIT ◇

dollar cost averaging *noun* (circa 1957)
: investment in a security at regular intervals of a uniform sum regardless of the price level in order to obtain an overall reduction in cost per unit — called also *dollar averaging*

dollar–a–year *adjective* (1918)
: compensated by a token salary usually for government service ⟨a *dollar-a-year* man⟩

dollar day *noun* (1949)
: a day on which special low prices are offered — often used in plural

dollar diplomacy *noun* (1910)
1 : diplomacy used by a country to promote its financial or commercial interests abroad

2 : diplomacy that seeks to strengthen the power of a country or effect its purposes in foreign relations by the use of its financial resources

dollars–and–cents \'dä-lər-z²n-'sen(t)s\ *adjective* (1899)
: dealing with or expressed in terms of money, sales, or profits

dollar sign *noun* (1881)
: a mark $ placed before a number to indicate that it stands for dollars — called also *dollar mark*

doll·house \'däl-ˌhau̇s, 'dȯl-\ *also* **doll's house** *or* **dolls' house** *noun* (1783)
1 : a child's small-scale toy house
2 : a dwelling so small as to suggest a house for dolls

¹dol·lop \'dä-ləp\ *noun* [origin unknown] (circa 1812)
1 *chiefly British* **:** an indefinite often large quantity especially of something liquid ⟨out of heaven, as if a plug had been pulled, fell a jolly *dollop* of rain —E. M. Forster⟩
2 : a lump or glob of something soft or mushy ⟨top it with a *dollop* of jam⟩
3 : an amount given, spooned, or ladled out **:** PORTION ⟨hold out their mess tins for a *dollop* of gruel —Robert Craft⟩
4 : a small lump, portion, or amount ⟨want just a *dollop* of catsup⟩ ⟨a *dollop* of brandy after dinner⟩
5 : something added or served as if in dollops ⟨fantasy with a *dollop* of satire —Lee Rogow⟩ ⟨a delicious *dollop* of gossip —Leon Harris⟩

²dollop *transitive verb* (circa 1860)
: to serve or dispense in dollops

doll up (1906)
transitive verb
1 : to dress elegantly or extravagantly
2 : to make more attractive (as by addition of decorative details)
intransitive verb
: to get dolled up

¹dol·ly \'dä-lē, 'dȯ-lē\ *noun, plural* **dollies** (1790)
1 : DOLL
2 : a wooden-pronged instrument for beating and stirring clothes in the process of washing them in a tub
3 : a compact narrow-gauge railroad locomotive for moving construction trains and for switching
4 a : a platform on a roller or on wheels or casters for moving heavy objects **b :** a wheeled platform for a television or motion-picture camera

²dolly *verb* **dol·lied; dol·ly·ing** (1878)
transitive verb
1 : to treat with a dolly
2 : to move or convey on a dolly
intransitive verb
: to move a motion-picture or television camera about on a dolly while shooting a scene; *also of a camera* **:** to be moved on a dolly

dol·ly bird \'dä-lē-ˌbərd\ *noun* (1964)
British **:** a pretty young woman

dolly shot *noun* (1933)
: TRACKING SHOT

Dol·ly Var·den trout \ˌdä-lē-'vär-d²n-\ *noun* [*Dolly Varden*, gaily dressed coquette in *Barnaby Rudge* (1841), novel by Charles Dickens] (circa 1876)
: a large char (*Salvelinus malma*) widespread in streams of western North America and Japan as well as in coastal salt waters — called also *Dolly Varden*

dol·ma \ˌdōl-'mä, 'dȯl-mə, 'däl-\ *noun, plural* **dolmas** *or* **dol·ma·des** \dȯl-'mä-(ˌ)thēz, dȯl-, däl-\ [Turkish, literally, something stuffed] (circa 1889)
: a stuffed grape leaf or vegetable shell

dolman sleeve *noun* [French *dolman* coat with dolman sleeves, from German *Dolman* or Hungarian *dolmány*, from Turkish *dolama*, a Turkish robe] (1934)

: a sleeve very wide at the armhole and tight at the wrist often cut in one piece with the bodice

dol·men \'dōl-mən, 'dȯl-, 'däl-\ *noun* [French, from Breton *tolmen*, from *tol* table + *men* stone] (1859)
: a prehistoric monument of two or more upright stones supporting a horizontal stone slab found especially in Britain and France and thought to be a tomb

dolmen

dol·o·mite \'dō-lə-ˌmīt, 'dä-\ *noun* [French, from Déodat de *Dolomieu* (died 1801) French geologist] (1794)
1 : a mineral $CaMg(CO_3)_2$ consisting of a calcium magnesium carbonate found in crystals and in extensive beds as a compact limestone
2 : a limestone or marble rich in magnesium carbonate
— **do·lo·mit·ic** \ˌdō-lə-'mi-tik, ˌdä-\ *adjective*

do·lo·mi·ti·za·tion \ˌdȯ-lə-mə-tə-'zā-shən, ˌdä-, -ˌmī-\ *noun* (1862)
: the process of converting into dolomite
— **do·lo·mi·tize** \'dō-lə-mə-ˌtīz, 'dä-\ *transitive verb*

do·lor \'dō-lər *also* 'dä-\ *noun* [Middle English *dolour*, from Middle French, from Latin *dolor* pain, grief, from *dolēre* to feel pain, grieve] (14th century)
: mental suffering or anguish **:** SORROW

do·lor·ous \'dō-lə-rəs *also* 'dä-\ *adjective* (15th century)
: causing, marked by, or expressing misery or grief
— **do·lor·ous·ly** *adverb*
— **do·lor·ous·ness** *noun*

do·lour *chiefly British variant of* DOLOR
dol·phin \'däl-fən, 'dȯl-\ *noun* [Middle English, from Middle French *dophin, daufin*, from Old French *dalfin*, from Old Provençal, from Medieval Latin *dalfinus*, alteration of Latin *delphinus*, from Greek *delphin-, delphis*; akin to Greek *delphys* womb, Sanskrit *garbha*] (14th century)

dolphin 1a

1 a : any of various small toothed whales (family Delphinidae) with the snout more or less elongated into a beak and the neck vertebrae partially fused **b :** PORPOISE 1
2 : either of two active pelagic bony fishes (genus *Coryphaena* of the family Coryphaenidae) of tropical and temperate seas that are used for food — called also *dolphinfish*
3 *capitalized* : DELPHINUS
4 : a spar or buoy for mooring boats; *also* : a cluster of closely driven piles used as a fender for a dock or as a mooring or guide for boats
dolphin striker *noun* (1833)
: a vertical spar under the end of the bowsprit of a sailboat to extend and support the martingale
dolt \'dōlt\ *noun* [probably akin to Old English *dol* foolish] (1553)
: a stupid person
— **dolt·ish** \'dōl-tish\ *adjective*
— **dolt·ish·ly** *adverb*
— **dolt·ish·ness** *noun*
Dom [Latin *dominus* master] (1716)
1 \'däm\ — used as a title for some monks and canons regular
2 \'dōⁿ\ — used as a title prefixed to the Christian name of a Portuguese or Brazilian man of rank
-dom \dəm\ *noun suffix* [Middle English, from Old English *-dōm;* akin to Old High German *-tuom* -dom, Old English *dōm* judgment — more at DOOM]
1 a : dignity : office ⟨duke*dom*⟩ **b :** realm : jurisdiction ⟨king*dom*⟩
2 : state or fact of being ⟨free*dom*⟩
3 : those having a (specified) office, occupation, interest, or character ⟨official*dom*⟩
do·main \dō-'mān, də-\ *noun* [Middle English *domayne,* from Middle French *domaine, demaine,* from Latin *dominium,* from *dominus*] (15th century)
1 a : complete and absolute ownership of land — compare EMINENT DOMAIN **b :** land so owned
2 : a territory over which dominion is exercised
3 : a region distinctively marked by some physical feature ⟨the *domain* of rushing streams, tall trees, and lakes⟩
4 : a sphere of knowledge, influence, or activity ⟨the *domain* of art⟩
5 : the set of elements to which a mathematical or logical variable is limited; *specifically* : the set on which a function is defined
6 : any of the small randomly oriented regions of uniform magnetization in a ferromagnetic substance
7 : INTEGRAL DOMAIN
¹dome \'dōm\ *noun* [French, Italian, & Latin; French *dôme* dome, cathedral, from Italian *duomo* cathedral, from Medieval Latin *domus* church, from Latin, house; akin to Greek *domos* house, Sanskrit *dam*] (1513)
1 *archaic* : a stately building : MANSION
2 : a large hemispherical roof or ceiling
3 : a natural formation or structure that resembles the dome or cupola of a building
4 : a form of crystal composed of planes parallel to a lateral axis that meet above in a horizontal edge like a roof
5 : an upward fold in rock whose sides dip uniformly in all directions
6 : a roofed sports stadium
— **dom·al** \'dō-məl\ *adjective*
²dome *verb* **domed; dom·ing** (1876)
transitive verb
1 : to cover with a dome
2 : to form into a dome
intransitive verb
: to swell upward or outward like a dome
Domes·day Book \'dümz-ˌdā-, 'dōmz-\ *noun* [Middle English, from *domesday* doomsday] (1591)
: a record of a survey of English lands and landholdings made by order of William the Conqueror about 1086

¹do·mes·tic \də-'mes-tik\ *adjective* [Middle English, from Middle French *domestique,* from Latin *domesticus,* from *domus*] (15th century)
1 a : living near or about human habitations **b** : TAME, DOMESTICATED
2 : of, relating to, or originating within a country and especially within one's own country ⟨*domestic* politics⟩ ⟨*domestic* wines⟩
3 : of or relating to the household or the family
4 : devoted to home duties and pleasures
5 : INDIGENOUS
— **do·mes·ti·cal·ly** \-ti-k(ə-)lē\ *adverb*
²domestic *noun* (1613)
1 : a household servant
2 : an article of domestic manufacture — usually used in plural
domestic animal *noun* (circa 1855)
: any of various animals (as the horse or sheep) domesticated so as to live and breed in a tame condition
¹do·mes·ti·cate \də-'mes-ti-ˌkāt\ *transitive verb* **-cat·ed; -cat·ing** (circa 1639)
1 : to bring into domestic use : ADOPT
2 : to adapt (an animal or plant) to life in intimate association with and to the advantage of humans
3 : to make domestic : fit for domestic life
4 : to bring to the level of ordinary people : FAMILIARIZE
— **do·mes·ti·ca·tion** \-ˌmes-ti-'kā-shən\ *noun*
²do·mes·ti·cate \-kət, -ˌkāt\ *noun* (1951)
: a domesticated animal or plant
do·mes·tic·i·ty \ˌdō-ˌmes-'ti-sə-tē, -məs-; ˌdä-\ *noun, plural* **-ties** (1721)
1 : the quality or state of being domestic or domesticated
2 : domestic activities or life
3 *plural* : domestic affairs
domestic prelate *noun* (1929)
: a priest having permanent honorary membership in the papal household
domestic relations court *noun* (circa 1939)
: COURT OF DOMESTIC RELATIONS
domestic science *noun* (1869)
: HOME ECONOMICS
dom·i·cal \'dō-mi-kəl, 'dä-\ *adjective* (1846)
: relating to, shaped like, or having a dome
¹do·mi·cile \'dä-mə-ˌsīl, 'dō-; 'dä-mə-sil\ *also* **dom·i·cil** \'däm-ə-səl\ *noun* [Middle English, from Middle French, from Latin *domicilium,* from *domus*] (15th century)
1 : a dwelling place : place of residence : HOME
2 a : a person's fixed, permanent, and principal home for legal purposes **b :** RESIDENCE 2b
²domicile *transitive verb* **-ciled; -cil·ing** (1809)
: to establish in or provide with a domicile
do·mi·cil·i·ary \ˌdä-mə-'si-lē-ˌer-ē, ˌdō-\ *adjective* (1790)
: of, relating to, or constituting a domicile: as **a :** provided or taking place in the home ⟨*domiciliary* midwifery⟩ **b :** providing care and living space (as for disabled veterans)
do·mi·cil·i·ate \ˌdä-mə-'si-lē-ˌāt, ˌdō-\ *verb* **-at·ed; -at·ing** [Latin *domicilium*] (1778)
transitive verb
: DOMICILE
intransitive verb
: RESIDE
— **do·mi·cil·i·a·tion** \-ˌsi-lē-'ā-shən\ *noun*
dom·i·nance \'dä-mə-nən(t)s, 'däm-nən(t)s\ *noun* (1819)
1 : the fact or state of being dominant: as **a :** dominant position especially in a social hierarchy **b :** the property of one of a pair of alleles or traits that suppresses expression of the other in the heterozygous condition **c :** the influence or control over ecological communities exerted by a dominant

2 : functional asymmetry between a pair of bodily structures (as the right and left hands)
¹dom·i·nant \-nənt\ *adjective* [Middle French or Latin; Middle French, from Latin *dominant-, dominans,* present participle of *dominari*] (circa 1532)
1 : commanding, controlling, or prevailing over all others
2 : overlooking and commanding from a superior position
3 : of, relating to, or exerting ecological or genetic dominance
4 : being the one of a pair of bodily structures that is the more effective or predominant in action ⟨*dominant* eye⟩ ☆
— **dom·i·nant·ly** *adverb*
²dominant *noun* (1819)
1 : the fifth tone of a diatonic scale
2 a : a dominant genetic character or factor **b :** any of one or more kinds of organism (as a species) in an ecological community that exerts a controlling influence on the environment and thereby largely determines what other kinds of organisms are present **c :** a dominant individual in a social hierarchy
dom·i·nate \'dä-mə-ˌnāt\ *verb* **-nat·ed; -nat·ing** [Latin *dominatus,* past participle of *dominari,* from *dominus* master; akin to Latin *domus* house — more at DOME] (1611)
transitive verb
1 : RULE, CONTROL
2 : to exert the supreme determining or guiding influence on
3 : to overlook from a superior elevation or command because of superior height or position
4 : to have a commanding or preeminent place or position in ⟨name brands *dominate* the market⟩
intransitive verb
1 : to have or exert mastery, control, or preeminence
2 : to occupy a more elevated or superior position
— **dom·i·na·tive** \-ˌnā-tiv\ *adjective*
— **dom·i·na·tor** \-ˌnā-tər\ *noun*
dom·i·na·tion \ˌdä-mə-'nā-shən\ *noun* (14th century)
1 : supremacy or preeminence over another
2 : exercise of mastery or ruling power
3 : exercise of preponderant, governing, or controlling influence
4 *plural* : DOMINION 3
do·mi·na·trix \ˌdä-mi-'nā-triks\ *noun, plural* **-trices** \-'nā-trə-ˌsēz, -nə-'trī-ˌsēz\ [Latin, feminine of *dominator*] (1971)
: a woman who physically and psychologically dominates and abuses her partner in sadomasochistic sex; *broadly* : a dominating woman
dom·i·neer \ˌdä-mə-'nir\ *verb* [Dutch *domineren,* from French *dominer,* from Latin *dominari*] (1591)
intransitive verb
: to exercise arbitrary or overbearing control

☆ **SYNONYMS**
Dominant, predominant, paramount, preponderant mean superior to all others in influence or importance. DOMINANT applies to something that is uppermost because ruling or controlling ⟨a *dominant* social class⟩. PREDOMINANT applies to something that exerts, often temporarily, the most marked influence ⟨a *predominant* emotion⟩. PARAMOUNT implies supremacy in importance, rank, or jurisdiction ⟨unemployment was the *paramount* issue in the campaign⟩. PREPONDERANT applies to an element or factor that outweighs all others in influence or effect ⟨*preponderant* evidence in her favor⟩.

transitive verb
: to tyrannize over
dom·i·neer·ing *adjective* (1588)
: inclined to domineer
synonym see MASTERFUL
— **dom·i·neer·ing·ly** \-iŋ-lē\ *adverb*
— **dom·i·neer·ing·ness** *noun*
do·min·i·cal \də-'mi-ni-kəl\ *adjective* [Late Latin *dominicalis*, from *dominicus* (*dies*) the Lord's day, from Latin *dominicus* of a lord, from *dominus* lord, master] (15th century)
1 : of or relating to Jesus Christ as Lord
2 : of or relating to the Lord's day
Do·min·i·can \də-'mi-ni-kən\ *noun* [Saint *Dominic*] (circa 1632)
: a member of a mendicant order of friars founded by Saint Dominic in 1215 and dedicated especially to preaching
— **Dominican** *adjective*
dom·i·nick·er \'dä-mə-,ne-kər, -,ni-\ *also* **dom·i·nick** \-(,)nik, -nek\ *noun, often capitalized* (1806)
: DOMINIQUE
do·mi·nie *I usually* 'dä-mə-nē, *2 usually* 'dō-\ *noun* [Latin *domine*, vocative of *dominus*] (1612)
1 *chiefly Scottish* **:** SCHOOLMASTER
2 : CLERGYMAN
do·min·ion \də-'mi-nyən\ *noun* [Middle English *dominioun*, from Middle French *dominion*, modification of Latin *dominium*, from *dominus*] (14th century)
1 : DOMAIN
2 : supreme authority **:** SOVEREIGNTY
3 *plural* **:** an order of angels — see CELESTIAL HIERARCHY
4 *often capitalized* **:** a self-governing nation of the Commonwealth other than the United Kingdom that acknowledges the British monarch as chief of state
5 : absolute ownership
synonym see POWER
Dominion Day *noun* (1867)
: CANADA DAY
dom·i·nique \'dä-mə-,nēk\ *noun* [*Dominique* (Dominica), one of the Windward islands, West Indies] (1849)
: any of an American breed of domestic fowl with a rose comb, yellow legs, and barred plumage; *broadly* **:** a barred fowl
¹dom·i·no \'dä-mə-,nō\ *noun, plural* **-noes** *or* **-nos** [French, probably from Latin (in the ritual formula *benedicamus Domino* let us bless the Lord)] (circa 1694)
1 a (1) **:** a long loose hooded cloak usually worn with a half mask as a masquerade costume (2) **:** a half mask worn over the eyes with a masquerade costume **b :** a person wearing a domino
2 a : a flat rectangular block (as of wood or plastic) whose face is divided into two equal parts that are blank or bear usually from one to six dots arranged as on dice faces **b** *plural but usually singular in construction* **:** any of several games played with a set of usually 28 dominoes
3 : a member of a group (as of nations) expected to behave in accordance with the domino theory ◇
domino effect *noun* (1966)
: a cumulative effect produced when one event initiates a succession of similar events — compare RIPPLE EFFECT
domino theory *noun* [from the fact that if dominoes are stood on end one slightly behind the other, a slight push on the first will topple the others] (1965)
1 : a theory that if one nation becomes Communist-controlled the neighboring nations will also become Communist-controlled
2 : the theory that if one act or event is allowed to take place a series of similar acts or events will follow
¹don \'dän\ *transitive verb* **donned; don·ning** [Middle English, contraction of *do on*] (14th century)

1 : to put on (an article of clothing)
2 : to wrap oneself in **:** TAKE ON 3a
²don \'dän\ *noun* [Spanish, from Latin *dominus* master — more at DAME] (1523)
1 : a Spanish nobleman or gentleman — used as a title prefixed to the Christian name
2 *archaic* **:** a person of consequence **:** GRANDEE
3 : a head, tutor, or fellow in a college of Oxford or Cambridge University; *broadly* **:** a college or university professor
4 [Italian, title of respect, from *donno*, literally, lord, from Latin *dominus*] **:** a powerful Mafia leader
do·na \,dō-nə\ *noun* [Portuguese, from Latin *domina* lady — more at DAME] (circa 1897)
: a Portuguese or Brazilian woman of rank — used as a title prefixed to the Christian name
do·ña \'dō-nyə\ *noun* [Spanish, from Latin *domina*] (1622)
: a Spanish woman of rank — used as a title prefixed to the Christian name
do·nate \'dō-,nāt, dō-'\ *verb* **do·nat·ed; do·nat·ing** [back-formation from *donation*] (1785)
transitive verb
1 : to make a gift of; *especially* **:** to contribute to a public or charitable cause
2 : to transfer (as electrons) to another atom or molecule
intransitive verb
: to make a donation
synonym see GIVE
do·na·tion \dō-'nā-shən\ *noun* [Middle English *donatyowne*, from Latin *donation-, donatio* from *donare* to present, from *donum* gift; akin to Latin *dare* to give — more at DATE] (15th century)
: the act or an instance of donating: as **a :** the making of a gift especially to a charity or public institution **b :** a free contribution **:** GIFT
Do·na·tism \'dō-nə-,ti-zəm, 'dä-\ *noun* [*Donatus*, 4th century bishop of Carthage] (1588)
: the doctrines of a Christian sect arising in North Africa in 311 and holding that sanctity is essential for the administration of sacraments and church membership
— **Do·na·tist** \-tist\ *noun*
¹do·na·tive \'dō-nə-tiv, 'dä-\ *noun* (15th century)
: a special gift or donation
²do·na·tive *same or* 'dō-,nā-, dō-'\ *adjective* [Latin *donativus*, from *donatus*] (1559)
: of or relating to donation
do·na·tor \'dō-,nā-tər, dō-'\ *noun* (15th century)
: DONOR
¹done \'dən\ *past participle of* DO
²done *adjective* (14th century)
1 : arrived at or brought to an end
2 : doomed to failure, defeat, or death
3 : gone by **:** OVER
4 : physically exhausted
5 : cooked sufficiently
6 : conformable to social convention
do·nee \,dō-'nē\ *noun* [*donor*] (1523)
: a recipient of a gift
done for \'dən-,fòr\ *adjective* (1803)
1 : sunk in defeat **:** BEATEN
2 : mortally stricken **:** DOOMED
done·ness \'dən-nəs\ *noun* (1927)
: the condition of being cooked to the desired degree
¹dong \'dòŋ, 'däŋ\ *noun* [origin unknown] (circa 1930)
: PENIS — usually considered vulgar
²dong *noun, plural* **dong** [Vietnamese *đồng*] (1948)
: — see MONEY table
don·jon \'dän-jən, 'dən-\ *noun* [Middle English — more at DUNGEON] (14th century)
: a massive inner tower in a medieval castle
word history see DUNGEON
Don Juan \'dän-'(h)wän, *chiefly British & in poetry* dän-'jü-ən\ *noun* [Spanish]

1 : a legendary Spaniard proverbial for his seduction of women
2 : a captivating man known as a great lover or seducer of women
— **Don Juan·ism** \-'(h)wän-,i-zəm, -'jü-ə-,ni-\ *noun*

1 donjon

don·key \'däŋ-kē, 'dəŋ-, 'dòŋ-\ *noun, plural* **donkeys** [origin unknown] (circa 1785)
1 : the domestic ass (*Equus asinus*)
2 : a stupid or obstinate person
donkey engine *noun* (1858)
1 : a small usually portable auxiliary engine
2 : a small locomotive used in switching
donkey jacket *noun* (1929)
British **:** a jacket of heavy material worn especially by laborers
donkey's years *noun plural* (1927)
chiefly British **:** a very long time
don·key·work \'däŋ-kē-,wərk, 'dəŋ-, 'dòŋ-\ *noun* (1920)
: monotonous and routine work **:** DRUDGERY
don·na \,dä-nə, ,dò-\ *noun, plural* **don·ne** \-(,)nā\ [Italian, from Latin *domina*] (1740)
: an Italian woman especially of rank — used as a title prefixed to the Christian name
don·née \dò-'nā, (,)də-\ *noun, plural* **don·nées** \-'nā(z)\ [French, from feminine of *donné*, past participle of *donner* to give, from Latin *donare* to donate — more at DONATION] (1876)
: the set of assumptions on which a work of fiction or drama proceeds
don·nick·er *or* **don·ni·ker** \'dä-ni-kər\ *noun* [alteration of English dialect *dunnekin* toilet, cesspool] (circa 1931)
: TOILET 3a
don·nish \'dä-nish\ *adjective* (1848)
: of, relating to, or characteristic of a university don
— **don·nish·ly** *adverb*

◇ WORD HISTORY

domino The origin of dominoes is rather obscure, and that is as true of the word as it is of the game. Both appeared in France shortly after the middle of the 18th century, but details of their history are unrecorded. The word *domino* in both French and English earlier denoted a long hooded cloak worn together with a silk or velvet mask as a costume during carnival season or at a masquerade ball. Dominoes were particularly associated with the carnival in Venice, and masqueraders garbed in domino and mask, together with a three-cornered hat, were often depicted by 18th century Venetian painters. It seems that it is an even earlier sense, however, that links the garment with the playing piece. In French, *domino* originally referred to a cape worn by a priest in winter over his surplice. (Presumably at the source of this sense is some connection with Latin *dominus* "lord," but this is another circumstance that remains conjectural.) Domino pieces were once made with ebony backs and ivory faces, and it has been suggested that the playing piece brought to mind the priest's black domino contrasting with the white surplice.

\ə\ abut \ᵊ\ kitten \ər\ further \a\ ash \ā\ ace
\ä\ mop, mar \aù\ out \ch\ chin \e\ bet \ē\ easy
\g\ go \i\ hit \ī\ ice \j\ job \ŋ\ sing \ō\ go
\ò\ law \òi\ boy \th\ thin \t͟h\ the \ü\ loot \ù\ foot
\y\ yet \zh\ vision *see also* Guide to Pronunciation

— **don·nish·ness** *noun*

don·ny·brook \'dä-nē-ˌbrük\ *noun, often capitalized* [*Donnybrook* Fair, annual Irish event known for its brawls] (1852)
1 : FREE-FOR-ALL, BRAWL
2 a : a usually public quarrel or dispute ◊

do·nor \'dō-nər, -ˌnòr\ *noun* [Middle French *doneur*, from Latin *donator*, from *donare*] (15th century)
1 : one that gives, donates, or presents something
2 : one used as a source of biological material (as blood or an organ)
3 a : a compound capable of giving up a part (as an atom, chemical group, or subatomic particle) for combination with an acceptor **b** : an impurity added to a semiconductor to increase the number of mobile electrons

¹**do–noth·ing** \'dü-ˌnə-thiŋ\ *noun* (1579)
: a shiftless or lazy person

²**do–nothing** *adjective* (1832)
: marked by inactivity or failure to make positive progress
— **do–noth·ing·ism** \-ˌi-zəm\ *noun*

Don Qui·xote \ˌdän-kē-'(h)ō-tē, ˌdän-; *chiefly British* dän-'kwik-sət\ *noun* [Spanish, hero of Cervantes' *Don Quixote*]
: an impractical idealist

don·sie *or* **don·sy** \'dän(t)-sē\ *adjective* [Scottish Gaelic *donas* evil, harm + English *-ie*] (1720)
1 *dialect British* : UNLUCKY
2 *Scottish* **a** : RESTIVE **b** : SAUCY
3 *chiefly northern Midland* : slightly ill

¹**don't** \'dōnt\ (1639)
1 : do not
2 : does not □

²**don't** \'dōnt\ *noun* (1894)
: a command or entreaty not to do something

do·nut \'dō-(ˌ)nət\ *variant of* DOUGHNUT

doo·dad \'dü-ˌdad\ *noun* [origin unknown] (1888)
1 : an ornamental attachment or decoration
2 : an often small article whose common name is unknown or forgotten : GADGET

¹**doo·dle** \'dü-dᵊl\ *verb* **doo·dled; doo·dling** \'düd-liŋ, 'dü-dᵊl-iŋ\ [perhaps from *doodle* (to ridicule)] (1936)
intransitive verb
1 : to make a doodle
2 : DAWDLE, TRIFLE
transitive verb
: to produce by doodling
— **doo·dler** \'düd-lər, 'dü-dᵊl-ər\ *noun*

²**doodle** *noun* (1937)
: an aimless or casual scribble, design, or sketch; *also* : a minor work

doo·dle·bug \'dü-dᵊl-ˌbəg\ *noun* [probably from *doodle* (fool) + *bug*] (circa 1866)
1 : the larva of an ant lion; *also* : any of several other insects
2 : a device (as a divining rod) used in attempting to locate underground gas, water, oil, or ores
3 : BUZZ BOMB

doodley–squat *or* **doodly–squat** \'dü-dᵊl-ē-ˌskwät\ *noun* [perhaps from *doodle* + ⁴*-y* + *squat*, euphemism for *shit*] (1934)
: DIDDLY-SQUAT

doo–doo \'dü-(ˌ)dü\ *noun* [baby talk] (1948)
: EXCREMENT
— **in deep doo–doo** : in trouble

doo·fus \'dü-fəs, -fis\ *noun, plural* **doo·fus·es** \-fə-siz\ [perhaps alteration of ¹*goof*] (1970)
slang : a stupid, incompetent, or foolish person

doo·hick·ey \'dü-ˌhi-kē\ *noun, plural* **-hickeys** *also* **-hickies** [probably from *doodad* + *hickey*] (1914)
: DOODAD 2

¹**doom** \'düm\ *noun* [Middle English, from Old English *dōm*; akin to Old High German *tuom* condition, state, Old English *dōn* to do] (before 12th century)
1 : a law or ordinance especially in Anglo-Saxon England
2 a : JUDGMENT, DECISION; *especially* : a judicial condemnation or sentence **b** (1) : JUDGMENT 3a (2) : JUDGMENT DAY 1
3 a : DESTINY; *especially* : unhappy destiny **b** : DEATH, RUIN
synonym see FATE

²**doom** *transitive verb* (15th century)
1 : to give judgment against : CONDEMN
2 a : to fix the fate of : DESTINE **b** : to make certain the failure or destruction of

doom·ful \'düm-fəl\ *adjective* (1586)
: presaging doom : OMINOUS
— **doom·ful·ly** \-fə-lē\ *adverb*

doom·say·er \'düm-ˌsā-ər\ *noun* (1953)
: one given to forebodings and predictions of impending calamity
— **doom·say·ing** \-ˌsā-iŋ\ *noun*

dooms·day \'dümz-ˌdā\ *noun, often attributive* (before 12th century)
: a day of final judgment

dooms·day·er \-ˌdā-ər, -ˌde(ə)r\ *noun* (1972)
: DOOMSAYER

doom·ster \'düm(p)-stər\ *noun* (15th century)
1 : JUDGE
2 : DOOMSAYER

doomy \'dü-mē\ *adjective* (1971)
: suggestive of doom : DOOMFUL
— **doom·i·ly** \'dü-mi-lē\ *adverb*

door \'dōr, 'dòr\ *noun, often attributive* [Middle English *dure, dor,* from Old English *duru* door & *dor* gate; akin to Old High German *turi* door, Latin *fores,* Greek *thyra*] (before 12th century)
1 : a usually swinging or sliding barrier by which an entry is closed and opened; *also* : a similar part of a piece of furniture
2 : DOORWAY
3 : a means of access or participation : OPPORTUNITY ⟨opens new *doors*⟩ ⟨*door* to success⟩
— **door·less** \-ləs\ *adjective*
— **at one's door** : as a charge against one as being responsible ⟨laid the blame *at our door*⟩

door·bell \'dōr-ˌbel, 'dòr-\ *noun* (circa 1815)
: a bell or set of chimes to be rung usually by a push button at an outer door

do–or–die \'dü-ər-ˌdī, -òr-\ *adjective* (1879)
1 : doggedly determined to reach one's objective : INDOMITABLE
2 : presenting as the only alternatives complete success or complete ruin ⟨a *do-or-die* situation⟩

door·jamb \'dōr-ˌjam, 'dòr-\ *noun* (1837)
: an upright piece forming the side of a door opening

door·keep·er \-ˌkē-pər\ *noun* (1535)
: a person who tends a door

door·knob \-ˌnäb\ *noun* (1846)
: a knob that releases a door latch

door·man \-ˌman, -mən\ *noun* (circa 1897)
: a usually uniformed attendant at the door of a building (as a hotel or apartment house)

door·mat \-ˌmat\ *noun* (1665)
1 : a mat placed before or inside a door for wiping dirt from the shoes
2 : one that submits without protest to abuse or indignities
3 : a team that regularly finishes last

door·nail \-ˌnāl, -'nā(ə)l\ *noun* (14th century)
: a large-headed nail — used chiefly in the phrase *dead as a doornail*

door·plate \-ˌplāt\ *noun* (1823)
: a nameplate on a door

door·post \-ˌpōst\ *noun* (1535)
: DOORJAMB

door prize *noun* (1951)
: a prize awarded to the holder of a winning ticket passed out at the entrance to an entertainment or function

door·sill \'dōr-ˌsil, 'dòr-\ *noun* (1587)
: SILL 1b

door·step \-ˌstep\ *noun* (1767)
: a step before an outer door

— **on one's doorstep** : close at hand; *especially* : too close to be overlooked

door·stop \-ˌstäp\ *noun* (circa 1895)
1 : a device (as a wedge or weight) for holding a door open
2 : a usually rubber-tipped device attached to a wall or floor to prevent damaging contact between an opened door and the wall

door–to–door \ˌdōr-tə-'dōr, ˌdòr-tə-'dòr\ *adjective* (1902)
: going or made by going to each house in a neighborhood ⟨*door-to-door* salesmen⟩ ⟨a *door-to-door* canvass⟩
— **door–to–door** *adverb*

door·way \'dōr-ˌwā, 'dòr-\ *noun* (1799)
1 : the opening that a door closes; *especially* : an entrance into a building or room
2 : DOOR 3

door·yard \-ˌyärd\ *noun* (circa 1764)
: a yard next to the door of a house

doo–wop \'dü-ˌwäp\ *noun* [from nonsense syllables typical of the style] (1969)
: a vocal style of rock and roll characterized by the a cappella singing of nonsense syllables in rhythmical support of the melody

doo·zy *or* **doo·zie** \'dü-zē\ *also* **doo·zer** \-zər\ *noun, plural* **doozies** *or* **doozers** [perhaps alteration of *daisy*] (1916)
: an extraordinary one of its kind

do·pa \'dō-pə, -(ˌ)pä\ *noun* [International Scientific Vocabulary *di*hydroxy- + *p*henylalanine] (1917)
: an amino acid $C_9H_{11}NO_4$ that in the levorotatory form is found in the broad bean and is used in the treatment of Parkinson's disease

do·pa·mine \'dō-pə-ˌmēn\ *noun* [*dopa* + *amine*] (1959)

: a monoamine $C_8H_{11}NO_2$ that is a decarboxylated form of dopa and that occurs especially as a neurotransmitter in the brain

do·pa·mi·ner·gic \ˌdō-pə-ˌmē-'nər-jik\ *adjective* (1970)
: relating to, participating in, or activated by dopamine or related substances

dop·ant \'dō-pənt\ *noun* [²*dope*] (1962)
: an impurity added usually in minute amounts to a pure substance to alter its properties

¹dope \'dōp\ *noun* [Dutch *doop* sauce, from *dopen* to dip; akin to Old English *dyppan* to dip] (1807)
1 a : a thick liquid or pasty preparation **b :** a preparation for giving a desired quality to a substance or surface
2 : absorbent or adsorbent material used in various manufacturing processes (as the making of dynamite)
3 a (1) **:** an illicit, habit-forming, or narcotic drug (2) **:** a preparation given to a racehorse to help or hinder its performance **b** *chiefly Southern* **:** a cola drink **c :** a stupid person
4 : information especially from a reliable source ⟨the inside dope⟩

²dope *verb* **doped; dop·ing** (1889)
transitive verb
1 : to treat or affect with dope; *especially* **:** to give a narcotic to
2 : FIGURE OUT — usually used with *out*
3 : to treat with a dopant
intransitive verb
: to take dope
— **dop·er** *noun*

dope·head \'dōp-ˌhed\ *noun* (1903)
: a drug addict

dope·ster \'dōp-stər\ *noun* (1907)
: a forecaster of the outcome of future events (as sports contests or elections)

dop·ey *also* **dopy** \'dō-pē\ *adjective* **dop·i·er; -est** (1896)
1 a : dulled by alcohol or a narcotic **b :** SLUGGISH, STUPEFIED
2 : STUPID, FATUOUS
— **dop·i·ness** *noun*

dop·pel·gäng·er *or* **dop·pel·gang·er** \'dä-pəl-ˌgaŋ-ər, -ˌgeŋ-, ˌdä-pəl-'-\ *n* [German *Doppelgänger*, from *doppel-* double + *-gänger* goer] (1851)
1 : a ghostly counterpart of a living person
2 a : DOUBLE 2a **b :** ALTER EGO **b c :** a person who has the same name as another

Dopp·ler \'dä-plər\ *adjective* (1905)
: of, relating to, being, or utilizing a shift in frequency in accordance with the Doppler effect; *also* **:** of or relating to Doppler radar

Doppler effect *noun* [Christian J. *Doppler*] (1905)
: a change in the frequency with which waves (as sound or light) from a given source reach an observer when the source and the observer are in motion with respect to each other so that the frequency increases or decreases according to the speed at which the distance is decreasing or increasing

Doppler radar *noun* (1954)
: a radar system that utilizes the Doppler effect for measuring velocity

Dor·cas \'dȯr-kəs\ *noun* [Greek *Dorkas*]
: a Christian woman of New Testament times who made clothing for the poor

Do·ri·an \'dȯr-ē-ən, 'dȯr-\ *noun* [Latin *Dorius* of Doris, from Greek *dōrios*, from *Dōris*, region of ancient Greece] (1662)
: a member of an ancient Hellenic race that completed the overthrow of Mycenaean civilization and settled especially in the Peloponnisos and Crete
— **Dorian** *adjective*

¹Dor·ic \'dȯr-ik, 'där-\ *adjective* (1569)
1 : of, relating to, or characteristic of the Dorians
2 : belonging to the oldest and simplest Greek architectural order — see ORDER illustration
3 : of, relating to, or constituting Doric

²Doric *noun* (1837)

: a dialect of ancient Greek spoken especially in the Peloponnisos, Crete, Sicily, and southern Italy

dork \'dȯrk\ *noun* [perhaps alteration of *dick*] (1972)
slang **:** NERD; *also* **:** JERK 4

dorky \'dȯr-kē\ *adjective* **dork·i·er; -est** (1983)
slang **:** foolishly stupid **:** INEPT

dorm \'dȯrm\ *noun* (1900)
: DORMITORY

dor·man·cy \'dȯr-mən(t)-sē\ *noun* (1789)
: the quality or state of being dormant

dor·mant \'dȯr-mənt\ *adjective* [Middle English, fixed, stationary, from Middle French, from present participle of *dormir* to sleep, from Latin *dormire*; akin to Sanskrit *drāti* he sleeps] (1500)
1 : represented on a coat of arms in a lying position with the head on the forepaws
2 : marked by a suspension of activity: as **a :** temporarily devoid of external activity ⟨a *dormant* volcano⟩ **b :** temporarily in abeyance yet capable of being activated
3 a : ASLEEP, INACTIVE **b :** having the faculties suspended **:** SLUGGISH **c :** having biological activity suspended: as (1) **:** being in a state of suspended animation (2) **:** not actively growing but protected (as by bud scales) from the environment — used of plant parts
4 : associated with, carried out, or applied during a period of dormancy ⟨*dormant* grafting⟩
synonym see LATENT

dor·mer \'dȯr-mər\ *noun* [Middle French *dormeor* dormitory, from Latin *dormitorium*] (1592)
: a window set vertically in a structure projecting through a sloping roof; *also* **:** the roofed structure containing such a window

dor·mie *or* **dor·my** \'dȯr-mē\ *adjective* [origin unknown] (1847)
: being ahead by as many holes in golf as remain to be played

dor·mi·to·ry \'dȯr-mə-ˌtōr-ē, -ˌtȯr-\ *noun, plural* **-ries** [Middle English, from Latin *dormitorium*, from *dormitus*, past participle of *dormire*] (15th century)
1 : a room for sleeping; *especially* **:** a large room containing numerous beds
2 : a residence hall providing rooms for individuals or for groups usually without private baths
3 *chiefly British* **:** a residential community inhabited chiefly by commuters

dor·mouse \'dȯr-ˌmaùs\ *noun, plural* **dor·mice** \-ˌmīs\ [Middle English *dormowse*, perhaps from Middle French *dormir* + Middle English *mous* mouse] (15th century)
: any of numerous small Old World rodents (families Gliridae and Seleviniidae) that are intermediate in form and behavior between mice and squirrels

dor·nick \'dȯr-nik, 'dä-nik\ *noun* [probably from Irish *dornóg*] (1840)
: a stone small enough to throw; *also* **:** a large piece of rock

do·ron·i·cum \də-'rä-ni-kəm\ *noun* [New Latin, genus name, from Arabic *darūnaj*, a plant of this genus] (1892)
: any of a genus (*Doronicum*) of Eurasian perennial composite herbs including several cultivated for their showy yellow flower heads

dorp \'dȯrp\ *noun* [Dutch, from Middle Dutch; akin to Old High German *dorf* village — more at THORP] (circa 1576)
: VILLAGE

dors- *or* **dorsi-** *or* **dorso-** *combining form* [Late Latin *dors-*, from Latin *dorsum*]
1 : back ⟨*dors*ad⟩
2 : dorsal and ⟨*dorso*lateral⟩

dor·sad \'dȯr-ˌsad\ *adverb* (circa 1803)
: toward the back **:** DORSALLY

¹dorsal *variant of* DOSSAL

²dor·sal \'dȯr-səl\ *adjective* [Late Latin *dorsalis*, from Latin *dorsum* back] (1727)

1 : relating to or situated near or on the back especially of an animal or of one of its parts
2 : ABAXIAL
— **dor·sal·ly** \-sə-lē\ *adverb*

³dorsal *noun* (1834)
: a dorsally located part; *especially* **:** a thoracic vertebra

dorsal lip *noun* (1940)
: the margin of the fold of blastula wall that delineates the dorsal limit of the blastopore, constitutes the primary organizer, and forms the point of origin of chordamesoderm

dorsal root *noun* (circa 1934)
: the one of the two roots of a spinal nerve that passes dorsally to the spinal cord and consists of sensory fibers

Dor·set \'dȯr-sət\ *noun* (1891)
: any of a breed of domestic white-faced sheep originally developed in Dorset, England

dor·si·ven·tral \ˌdȯr-si-'ven-trəl\ *adjective* (circa 1882)
1 : having distinct dorsal and ventral surfaces
2 : DORSOVENTRAL 1
— **dor·si·ven·tral·i·ty** \-ven-'tra-lə-tē\ *noun*
— **dor·si·ven·tral·ly** \-'ven-trə-lē\ *adverb*

dor·so·lat·er·al \ˌdȯr-sō-'la-tə-rəl, -'la-trəl\ *adjective* (1835)
: of, relating to, or involving both the back and the sides

dor·so·ven·tral \-'ven-trəl\ *adjective* [International Scientific Vocabulary] (1870)
1 : relating to, involving, or extending along the axis joining the dorsal and ventral sides
2 : DORSIVENTRAL 1
— **dor·so·ven·tral·i·ty** \-ven-'tra-lə-tē\ *noun*
— **dor·so·ven·tral·ly** \-trə-lē\ *adverb*

dor·sum \'dȯr-səm\ *noun, plural* **dor·sa** \-sə\ [Latin] (1840)
1 : the upper surface of an appendage or part
2 : BACK; *especially* **:** the entire dorsal surface of an animal

do·ry \'dȯr-ē, 'dȯr-\ *noun, plural* **dories** [Miskito *dóri* dugout] (1709)
: a flat-bottomed boat with high flaring sides, sharp bow, and deep V-shaped transom

dos *or* **do's** *plural of* ²DO

dos·age \'dō-sij\ *noun* (circa 1867)
1 a : the addition of an ingredient or the application of an agent in a measured dose **b :** the presence and relative representation or strength of a factor or agent
2 a : DOSE 2 **b** (1) **:** the giving of a dose (2) **:** regulation or determination of doses
3 : an exposure to some experience in or as if in measured portions

¹dose \'dōs\ *noun* [Middle English, from Middle French, from Late Latin *dosis*, from Greek, literally, act of giving, from *didonai* to give — more at DATE] (15th century)
1 a : the measured quantity of a therapeutic agent to be taken at one time **b :** the quantity of radiation administered or absorbed
2 : a portion of a substance added during a process
3 : something experienced as if in a prescribed or measured amount ⟨a daily *dose* of hard work⟩
4 : a gonorrheal infection

²dose *transitive verb* **dosed; dos·ing** (1654)
1 : to give a dose to; *especially* **:** to give medicine to
2 : to divide (as a medicine) into doses
3 : to treat with an application or agent

do–si–do \ˌdō-(ˌ)sē-'dō\ *noun, plural* **do-si-dos** [French *dos-à-dos* back to back] (1926)
: a square-dance figure: **a :** a figure in which the dancers pass each other right shoulder to right shoulder and circle each other back to

\ə\ abut \ᵊ\ kitten \ər\ **further** \a\ ash \ā\ ace
\ä\ mop, mar \aù\ out \ch\ chin \e\ bet \ē\ easy
\g\ go \i\ hit \ī\ ice \j\ job \ŋ\ sing \ō\ go
\ȯ\ law \ȯi\ boy \th\ thin \t͟h\ the \ü\ loot \ù\ foot
\y\ yet \zh\ vision *see also* Guide to Pronunciation

back **b** : a figure in which the woman moves in a figure circling first her partner and then the man on her right

do·sim·e·ter \dō-'si-mə-tər\ *noun* [Late Latin *dosis* + International Scientific Vocabulary *-meter*] (1938)
: a device for measuring doses of radiations (as X rays)
— **do·si·met·ric** \ˌdō-sə-'me-trik\ *adjective*
— **do·sim·e·try** \dō-'si-mə-trē\ *noun*

¹doss \'dòs, 'däs\ *intransitive verb* [origin unknown] (circa 1785)
chiefly British : to sleep or bed down in a convenient place — usually used with *down*

²doss *noun* (circa 1789)
chiefly British : a crude or makeshift bed

dos·sal \'dä-səl\ *or* **dor·sal** \'dòr-səl\ *or* **dos·sel** \'dä-səl\ *noun* [Medieval Latin *dossale, dorsale*, from neuter of Late Latin *dorsalis* dorsal] (1851)
: an ornamental cloth hung behind and above an altar

doss–house \'dòs-ˌhaüs, 'däs-\ *noun* (1888)
chiefly British : a cheap rooming house or hotel

dos·sier \'dò-ˌyā, 'däs-; 'dò-sē-ˌā, 'dä-\ *noun* [French, bundle of documents labeled on the back, dossier, from *dos* back, from Latin *dorsum*] (1880)
: a file containing detailed records on a particular person or subject

dost \'dəst\ *archaic present 2d singular of* DO

¹dot \'dät\ *noun* [(assumed) Middle English, from Old English *dott* head of a boil; akin to Old High German *tutta* nipple] (1674)
1 : a small spot : SPECK
2 a (1) : a small point made with a pointed instrument ⟨a *dot* on the chart marked the ship's position⟩ (2) : a small round mark used in orthography or punctuation ⟨put a *dot* over the i⟩ **b** : a centered point used as a multiplication sign (as in 6 · 5 = 30) **c** (1) : a point after a note or rest in music indicating augmentation of the time value by one half (2) : a point over or under a note indicating that it is to be played staccato
3 : a precise point especially in time ⟨arrived at six on the *dot*⟩
4 : a short click or buzz forming a letter or part of a letter in the Morse code

²dot *verb* **dot·ted; dot·ting** (circa 1740)
transitive verb
1 : to mark with a dot
2 : to intersperse with dots or objects scattered at random ⟨boats *dotting* the lake⟩
intransitive verb
: to make a dot
— **dot·ter** *noun*

³dot \'dòt\ *noun* [French, from Latin *dot-, dos* dowry] (1855)
: DOWRY 2

dot·age \'dō-tij\ *noun* [*dote*] (14th century)
: a state or period of senile decay marked by decline of mental poise and alertness

do·tal \'dō-t³l\ *adjective* [Latin *dotalis*, from *dot-, dos*] (1513)
: of or relating to a woman's marriage dowry

dot·ard \'dō-tərd\ *noun* (14th century)
: a person in his or her dotage

dote \'dōt\ *intransitive verb* **dot·ed; dot·ing** [Middle English; akin to Middle Low German *dotten* to be foolish] (13th century)
1 : to exhibit mental decline of or like that of old age : be in one's dotage
2 : to be lavish or excessive in one's attention, fondness, or affection — used especially with *on* ⟨*doted* on her only grandchild⟩
— **dot·er** *noun*
— **dot·ing·ly** \'dō-tiŋ-lē\ *adverb*

doth \'dəth\ *archaic present 3d singular of* DO

dot matrix *noun* (1963)
: a pattern of dots in a grid from which alphanumeric characters can be formed ⟨a *dot matrix* printer⟩

dot product *noun* [¹*dot*; from its being commonly written A · B] (1901)
: SCALAR PRODUCT

dotted swiss *noun* (circa 1924)
: a sheer light muslin ornamented with evenly spaced raised dots

dot·ter·el \'dä-tə-rəl, 'dä-trəl\ *noun* [Middle English *dotrelle*, irregular from *doten* to dote] (15th century)
: a Eurasian plover (*Eudromias morinellus*) formerly common in England; *also* : any of various related plovers chiefly of eastern Asia, Australia, and South America

dot·tle \'dä-t³l, 'dò-\ *noun* [Middle English *dottel* plug, from (assumed) Middle English *dot*] (circa 1825)
: unburned and partially burned tobacco in the bowl of a pipe

¹dot·ty \'dä-tē\ *adjective* **dot·ti·er; -est** [alteration of Scots *dottle* fool, from Middle English *dotel*, from *doten*] (15th century)
1 a : mentally unbalanced : CRAZY **b** : amiably eccentric
2 : being obsessed or infatuated
3 : amusingly absurd : RIDICULOUS ⟨some sublimely *dotty* exchanges of letters⟩
— **dot·ti·ly** \'dä-t³l-ē\ *adverb*
— **dot·ti·ness** \'dä-tē-nəs\ *noun*

²dotty *adjective* (1812)
: composed of or marked by dots

Dou·ay Version \dü-'ā-\ *noun* [*Douay*, France] (1837)
: an English translation of the Vulgate used by Roman Catholics

¹dou·ble \'də-bəl\ *adjective* [Middle English, from Old French, from Latin *duplus*, from Greek *diploos*, from *duo* two + *-plus* multiplied by; akin to Old English *-feald* -fold — more at TWO, -FOLD] (13th century)
1 : having a twofold relation or character : DUAL
2 : consisting of two usually combined members or parts ⟨an egg with a *double* yolk⟩
3 a : being twice as great or as many ⟨*double* the number of expected applicants⟩ **b** *of a coin* : worth two of the specified amount ⟨a *double* eagle⟩ ⟨a *double* crown⟩
4 : marked by duplicity : DECEITFUL
5 : folded in two
6 : of extra size, strength, or value ⟨a *double* martini⟩
7 : having more than the normal number of floral leaves often at the expense of the sporophylls
8 *of rhyme* : involving correspondence of two syllables (as in *exciting* and *inviting*)
9 : designed for the use of two persons ⟨a *double* room⟩ ⟨a *double* bed⟩
— **dou·ble·ness** *noun*

²double *verb* **dou·bled; dou·bling** \'də-b(ə-)liŋ\ (13th century)
transitive verb
1 : to make twice as great or as many: as **a** : to increase by adding an equal amount **b** : to amount to twice the number of **c** : to make a call in bridge that increases the value of odd tricks or undertricks at (an opponent's bid)
2 a : to make of two thicknesses : FOLD **b** : CLENCH ⟨*doubled* his fist⟩ **c** : to cause to stoop
3 : to avoid by doubling : ELUDE
4 a : to replace in a dramatic role **b** : to play (dramatic roles) by doubling
5 a (1) : to advance or score (a base runner) by a double (2) : to bring about the scoring of (a run) by a double **b** : to put out (a base runner) in completing a double play
intransitive verb
1 a : to become twice as much or as many **b** : to double a bid (as in bridge)
2 a : to turn sharply and suddenly; *especially* : to turn back on one's course **b** : to follow a circuitous course
3 : to become bent or folded usually in the middle — usually used with *up* ⟨she *doubled* up in pain⟩

4 a : to serve an additional purpose or perform an additional duty **b** : to play a dramatic role as a double
5 : to make a double in baseball
— **dou·bler** \-b(ə-)lər\ *noun*

³double *adverb* (14th century)
1 : to twice the extent or amount
2 : two together

⁴double *noun* (14th century)
1 : something twice the usual size, strength, speed, quantity, or value: as **a** : a double amount **b** : a base hit that enables the batter to reach second base
2 : one that is the counterpart of another : DUPLICATE: as **a** : a living person that closely resembles another living person **b** : WRAITH **c** (1) : UNDERSTUDY (2) : one who resembles an actor and takes his or her place especially in scenes calling for special skills (3) : an actor who plays more than one role in a production
3 a : a sharp turn (as in running) : REVERSAL **b** : an evasive shift
4 : something consisting of two paired members: as **a** : FOLD **b** : a combined bet placed on two different contests **c** : two consecutive strikes in bowling
5 *plural* : a game between two pairs of players
6 : an act of doubling in a card game
7 : a room (as in a hotel) for two guests — compare SINGLE 4

double agent *noun* (1935)
: a spy pretending to serve one government while actually serving another

double bar *noun* (circa 1674)
: two adjacent vertical lines or a heavy single line separating principal sections of a musical composition

dou·ble–bar·rel \ˌdə-bəl-'bar-əl\ *noun* (1811)
: a double-barreled gun

dou·ble–bar·reled \-əld\ *adjective* (1709)
1 *of a firearm* : having two barrels mounted side by side or one beneath the other
2 : TWOFOLD; *especially* : having a double purpose ⟨asked a *double-barreled* question⟩

double bass *noun* (1752)
: the largest and lowest-pitched of the stringed instruments tuned in fourths
— **double bass·ist** \-'bā-sist\ *noun*

double bassoon *noun* (circa 1876)
: CONTRABASSOON

double bill *noun* (1917)
: a bill (as at a theater) offering two principal features

double bind *noun* (1956)
: a psychological predicament in which a person receives from a single source conflicting messages that allow no appropriate response to be made; *broadly* : DILEMMA 2

double bass

dou·ble–blind \ˌdə-bəl-'blīnd\ *adjective* (1950)
: of, relating to, or being an experimental procedure in which neither the subjects nor the experimenters know the makeup of the test and control groups during the actual course of the experiments — compare SINGLE-BLIND

double boiler *noun* (1879)
: a cooking utensil consisting of two saucepans fitting together so that the contents of the upper can be cooked or heated by boiling water in the lower

double bond *noun* (1889)
: a chemical bond in which two pairs of electrons are shared by two atoms in a molecule — compare SINGLE BOND, TRIPLE BOND

dou·ble–breast·ed \ˌdə-bəl-'bres-təd\ *adjective* (1701)
1 : having one half of the front lapped over the other and usually a double row of buttons

and a single row of buttonholes ⟨a *double-breasted* coat⟩
2 : having a double-breasted coat ⟨a *double-breasted* suit⟩
dou·ble–check \ˌdə-bəl-ˈchek, ˈdə-bəl-ˌ\ (1944)
transitive verb
: to subject to a double check ⟨an article *double-checked* for accuracy⟩
intransitive verb
: to make a double check
double check *noun* (1953)
: a careful checking to determine accuracy, condition, or progress especially of something already checked
dou·ble–clutch \ˌdə-bəl-ˈkləch\ *intransitive verb* (1928)
: to shift gears in an automotive vehicle by shifting into neutral and pumping the clutch before shifting to another gear
dou·ble–crop \ˌdə-bəl-ˈkräp\ *intransitive verb* (1918)
: to grow two or more crops on the same land in the same season or at the same time
dou·ble–cross \ˌdə-bəl-ˈkrós\ *transitive verb* (1903)
: to deceive by double-dealing **:** BETRAY
— dou·ble–cross·er *noun*
double cross *noun* (1834)
1 a : an act of winning or trying to win a fight or match after agreeing to lose it **b :** an act of betraying or cheating an associate
2 : a cross between first-generation hybrids of four separate inbred lines (as in the production of hybrid seed corn)
double dagger *noun* (1706)
: the character ‡ used as a reference mark — called also *diesis*
double date *noun* (circa 1931)
: a date participated in by two couples
— dou·ble–date *intransitive verb*
¹dou·ble–deal·ing \ˌdə-bəl-ˈdē-liŋ\ *noun* (1529)
: action contradictory to a professed attitude **:** DUPLICITY
synonym see DECEPTION
— dou·ble–deal·er \-ˈdē-lər\ *noun*
²double–dealing *adjective* (1587)
: given to or marked by duplicity
dou·ble–deck \ˌdə-bəl-ˈdek\ *or* **dou·ble–decked** \-ˈdekt\ *adjective* (1894)
: having two decks, levels, or layers ⟨a *double-deck* bus⟩ ⟨a *double-deck* sandwich⟩
dou·ble–deck·er \-ˈde-kər\ *noun* (1835)
: something that is double-deck
dou·ble–dig·it \ˌdə-bəl-ˈdi-jət\ *adjective* (1959)
: amounting to 10 percent or more ⟨*double-digit* inflation⟩ ⟨*double-digit* price increases⟩
dou·ble–dip·per \-ˈdi-pər\ *noun* (circa 1974)
: a person who collects both a government pension and a government salary
— dou·ble–dip·ping \-piŋ\ *noun*
dou·ble–dome \ˈdə-bəl-ˌdōm\ *noun* (1938)
: INTELLECTUAL
double door *noun* (1840)
: an opening with two vertical doors that meet in the middle of the opening when closed
— compare DUTCH DOOR
double dribble *noun* (circa 1949)
: an illegal action in basketball made when a player dribbles the ball with two hands simultaneously or continues to dribble after allowing the ball to come to rest in one or both hands
double Dutch *noun* (1876)
1 : unintelligible language **:** GIBBERISH
2 : the jumping of two jump ropes rotating in opposite directions simultaneously
dou·ble–edged \ˌdə-bəl-ˈejd\ *adjective* (15th century)
1 : having two cutting edges
2 a : having two components or aspects ⟨a spy with a *double-edged* mission⟩ **b :** capable of being taken in two ways ⟨a *double-edged* remark⟩

double–edged sword *noun* (15th century)
: something that is or can have both favorable and unfavorable consequences ⟨freedom of expression . . . can be a *double-edged sword* —Linda Connors⟩
dou·ble–end·ed \ˌdə-bəl-ˈen-dəd\ *adjective* (circa 1874)
: similar at both ends ⟨a *double-ended* bolt⟩
dou·ble–end·er \-dər\ *noun* (1864)
: a ship or boat with bow and stern of similar shape
dou·ble en·ten·dre \ˈdüb-ᵊl-än-ˈtänd(-rᵊ); ˌdə-bəl-än-ˈtänd(-rə)\ *noun, plural* **double entendres** *same also* -ˈtänz; -ˈtän-drəz\ [obsolete French, literally, double meaning] (1673)
1 : ambiguity of meaning arising from language that lends itself to more than one interpretation
2 : a word or expression capable of two interpretations with one usually risqué
double entry *noun* (1741)
: a method of bookkeeping that recognizes both sides of a business transaction by debiting the amount of the transaction to one account and crediting it to another account so the total debits equal the total credits
dou·ble–faced \ˌdə-bəl-ˈfāst\ *adjective* (1577)
1 : HYPOCRITICAL, TWO-FACED
2 a : having two faces or sides designed for use ⟨a *double-faced* bookshelf⟩ **b** *also* **dou·ble–face** \-ˈfās\ **:** finished on both sides — REVERSIBLE — used of fabric
double fault *noun* (1909)
: two consecutive serving faults in tennis that result in the loss of a point
— dou·ble–fault \ˌdə-bəl-ˈfólt\ *intransitive verb*
double feature *noun* (1928)
: a movie program with two main films
double fertilization *noun* (circa 1909)
: fertilization characteristic of seed plants in which one sperm nucleus fuses with the egg nucleus to form an embryo and another fuses with polar nuclei to form endosperm
double genitive *noun* (1824)
: a syntactic construction in English in which possession is marked both by the preposition *of* and a noun or pronoun in the possessive case (as in "A friend of Bob's is a friend of mine") — called also *double possessive*
double glazing *noun* (1943)
: two layers of glass set in a window to reduce heat flow in either direction
Double Glouces·ter \-ˈgläs-tər, -ˌglòs-\ *noun* [*Gloucester,* England] (1816)
: a firm mild orange-colored English cheese similar to cheddar
dou·ble–head·er \ˌdə-bəl-ˈhe-dər\ *noun* (1878)
1 : a train pulled by two locomotives
2 : two games, contests, or events held consecutively on the same program
double helix *noun* (1954)
: a helix or spiral consisting of two strands in the surface of a cylinder that coil around its axis; *especially* **:** the structural arrangement of DNA in space that consists of paired polynucleotide strands stabilized by cross-links between purine and pyrimidine bases — compare ALPHA-HELIX, WATSON-CRICK MODEL
— dou·ble–he·li·cal \-ˈhe-li-kəl, -ˈhē-\ *adjective*
dou·ble–hung \ˌdə-bəl-ˈhəŋ\ *adjective* (1823)
of a window **:** having an upper and a lower sash that can slide vertically past each other
double hyphen *noun* (1893)
: a punctuation mark ⸗ used in place of a hyphen at the end of a line to indicate that the word so divided is normally hyphenated
double indemnity *noun* (1924)
: a provision in a life-insurance or accident policy whereby the company agrees to pay twice the face of the contract in case of accidental death
double jeopardy *noun* (1910)

: the putting of a person on trial for an offense for which he or she has previously been put on trial under a valid charge **:** two adjudications for one offense
dou·ble–joint·ed \ˌdə-bəl-ˈjóin-təd\ *adjective* (1831)
: having a joint that permits an exceptional degree of freedom of motion of the parts joined
double knit *noun* (1895)
: a knitted fabric (as wool) made with a double set of needles to produce a double thickness of fabric with each thickness joined by interlocking stitches; *also* **:** an article of clothing made of such fabric
double negative *noun* (1827)
: a now substandard syntactic construction containing two negatives and having a negative meaning ⟨"I didn't hear nothing" is a *double negative*⟩ □
dou·ble–park \ˌdə-bəl-ˈpärk\ (1936)
transitive verb
: to park (a vehicle) beside a row of vehicles already parked parallel to the curb
intransitive verb
: to double-park a vehicle
double play *noun* (1867)
: a play in baseball by which two players are put out
dou·ble–quick \ˈdə-bəl-ˌkwik\ *noun* (1834)
: DOUBLE TIME 1; *broadly* **:** a rapid pace
— double–quick *adjective or adverb*
double reed *noun* (circa 1876)
: two reeds bound together with a slight separation between them so that air passing through them causes them to beat against one another and that are used as a sound-

□ USAGE

double negative The grammarian Otto Jespersen once observed that although negation is very important to the meaning of the sentence, it is often marked in an almost inconspicuous way—perhaps only by an unstressed particle like *-n't.* Hence there has long been a tendency to strengthen the negative idea by adding more negative elements to the sentence. This multiple negation is known popularly as the *double negative.* Multiple negation occurs in Chaucer, and it continued in common use at least through Shakespeare's time ⟨no woman has; nor never none shall mistress be of it —*Twelfth Night*⟩ and the ordinary double negative into the early 18th century ⟨lost no time, nor abated no Diligence —Daniel DeFoe (*Robinson Crusoe,* 1719)⟩. During the 18th century it began to drop out of use in writing but continued in familiar use—conversation and letters. Thus grammarians, seeing it in older literature but not in current literature, decided that it was obsolete. Later grammarians were content to call it wrong. More important than the strictures of the grammarians was the perception that it was associated with the lower classes, both rural and urban, and hence was a construction to be avoided by the socially ambitious. The current status of the double negative remains much the same, confined to the most familiar discourse of those who choose to use it ⟨as you know, Ez hasn't changed none —Archibald MacLeish (letter)⟩ and used as an everyday form only in the speech of less educated people and of some educated people who are comfortable with it. It is not a prestige form, even though it may be used on occasion for effect ⟨the sailplane sure ain't no 747! —Susan Ochshorn (*Saturday Rev.*)⟩.

\ə\ **abut** \ᵊ\ **kitten** \ər\ **further** \a\ **ash** \ā\ **ace**
\ä\ **mop, mar** \aủ\ **out** \ch\ **chin** \e\ **bet** \ē\ **easy**
\g\ **go** \i\ **hit** \ī\ **ice** \j\ **job** \ŋ\ **sing** \ō\ **go**
\ò\ **law** \òi\ **boy** \th\ **thin** \th̲\ **the** \ü\ **loot** \ủ\ **foot**
\y\ **yet** \zh\ **vision** *see also* Guide to Pronunciation

producing device in certain woodwind instruments (as members of the oboe family)

double refraction *noun* (1831)
: BIREFRINGENCE

dou·ble–ring \'də-bəl-ˌriŋ\ *adjective* (circa 1959)
: of or relating to a wedding ceremony in which each partner ceremonially gives the other a wedding ring while reciting vows

double salt *noun* (circa 1849)
: a salt (as an alum) yielding on hydrolysis two different cations or anions

dou·ble–space \ˌdə-bəl-'spās\ (circa 1937) *transitive verb*
: to type (text) leaving alternate lines blank
intransitive verb
: to type on every other line

dou·ble·speak \'də-bəl-ˌspēk\ *noun* (1952)
: language used to deceive usually through concealment or misrepresentation of truth; *also* : GOBBLEDYGOOK
— **dou·ble·speak·er** \-ˌspē-kər\ *noun*

double standard *noun* (1894)
1 : BIMETALLISM
2 : a set of principles that applies differently and usually more rigorously to one group of people or circumstances than to another; *especially* : a code of morals that applies more severe standards of sexual behavior to women than to men

double star *noun* (1781)
1 : BINARY STAR
2 : two stars in very nearly the same line of sight but actually physically separate

dou·ble–stop \ˌdə-bəl-'stäp\ *transitive verb* (circa 1889)
: to produce two or more tones simultaneously on (as a violin)
— **double–stop** *noun*

double sugar *noun* (1956)
: DISACCHARIDE

dou·blet \'dəb-lət\ *noun* [Middle English, from Middle French, from *double*] (14th century)
1 : a man's close-fitting jacket worn in Europe especially during the Renaissance
2 : something consisting of two identical or similar parts: as **a** : a lens consisting of two components; *especially* : a handheld magnifier consisting of two lenses in a metal cylinder **b** : a spectrum line having two close components **c** : a domino with the same number of spots on each end

doublet 1

3 : a set of two identical or similar things: as **a** : two thrown dice with the same number of spots on the upper face **b** : one of nine pairs of microtubules found in cilia and flagella
4 : one of a pair; *specifically* : one of two or more words (as *guard* and *ward*) in the same language derived by different routes of transmission from the same source

dou·ble take \'də-bəl-ˌtāk\ *noun* (1930)
: a delayed reaction to a surprising or significant situation after an initial failure to notice anything unusual — usually used in the phrase *do a double take*

dou·ble–talk \-ˌtȯk\ *noun* (1936)
1 : language that appears to be earnest and meaningful but in fact is a mixture of sense and nonsense
2 : inflated, involved, and often deliberately ambiguous language
— **dou·ble–talk** *intransitive verb*
— **dou·ble–talk·er** *noun*

dou·ble–team \-ˌtēm\ *transitive verb* (1860)
: to block or guard (an opponent) with two players at one time

Double Ten *noun* [translation of Chinese (Beijing) *shuāngshí*; from its being the tenth day of the tenth month] (1940)

: October 10 observed by the Republic of China in commemoration of the revolution of 1911

dou·ble·think \'də-bəl-ˌthiŋk\ *noun* (1949)
: a simultaneous belief in two contradictory ideas

dou·ble–time \'də-bəl-ˌtīm\ *intransitive verb* (1943)
: to move at double time

double time *noun* (1853)
1 : a marching cadence of 180 36-inch steps per minute
2 : payment of a worker at twice the regular wage rate

dou·ble·ton \'də-bəl-tən\ *noun* [*double* + *-ton* (as in *singleton*)] (circa 1894)
: two cards that are the only ones of their suit originally dealt to a player — compare SINGLETON 1, VOID 4

dou·ble–tongue \ˌdə-bəl-'təŋ\ *intransitive verb* (circa 1900)
: to cause the tongue to alternate rapidly between the positions for *t* and *k* so as to produce a fast succession of detached notes on a wind instrument

dou·ble–u \as at w\ *noun* (1840)
: the letter *w*

double up *intransitive verb* (1789)
: to share accommodations designed for one

double vision *noun* (circa 1860)
: DIPLOPIA

double whammy *noun* (1951)
: a combination of two usually adverse forces, circumstances, or effects

double–wide \ˌdə-bəl-'wīd\ *noun* (1970)
: a mobile home consisting of two units which have been fastened together along their length

dou·bloon \ˌdə-'blün\ *noun* [Spanish *doblón*, augmentative of *dobla*, an old Spanish coin, from Latin *dupla*, feminine of *duplus* double — more at DOUBLE] (1622)
: an old gold coin of Spain and Spanish America

dou·bly \'də-b(ə-)lē\ *adverb* (15th century)
1 : in a twofold manner
2 : to twice the degree

¹doubt \'daȯt\ *verb* [alteration of Middle English *douten*, from Old French *douter* to doubt, from Latin *dubitare*; akin to Latin *dubius* dubious] (13th century)
transitive verb
1 *archaic* **a** : FEAR **b** : SUSPECT
2 : to be in doubt about ⟨he *doubts* everyone's word⟩
3 a : to lack confidence in : DISTRUST ⟨find myself *doubting* him when I know that he is honest —H. L. Mencken⟩ **b** : to consider unlikely ⟨I *doubt* if I can go⟩
intransitive verb
: to be uncertain
— **doubt·able** \'daȯ-tə-bəl\ *adjective*
— **doubt·er** *noun*
— **doubt·ing·ly** \-tiŋ-lē\ *adverb*

²doubt *noun* (13th century)
1 a : uncertainty of belief or opinion that often interferes with decision-making **b** : a deliberate suspension of judgment
2 : a state of affairs giving rise to uncertainty, hesitation, or suspense
3 a : a lack of confidence : DISTRUST **b** : an inclination not to believe or accept
synonym see UNCERTAINTY
— **no doubt** : DOUBTLESS

doubt·ful \'daȯt-fəl\ *adjective* (14th century)
1 : giving rise to doubt : open to question ⟨it is *doubtful* that they ever knew what happened⟩
2 a : lacking a definite opinion, conviction, or determination ⟨they were *doubtful* about the advantages of the new system⟩ **b** : uncertain in outcome : UNDECIDED ⟨the outcome of the election remains *doubtful*⟩
3 : marked by qualities that raise doubts about worth, honesty, or validity ⟨of *doubtful* repute⟩
☆
— **doubt·ful·ly** \-fə-lē\ *adverb*
— **doubt·ful·ness** *noun*

doubting Thom·as \-'tä-məs\ *noun* [Saint *Thomas*, apostle who doubted Jesus' resurrection until he had proof of it (John 20:24–29)] (1883)
: a habitually doubtful person

¹doubt·less \'daȯt-ləs\ *adverb* (14th century)
1 : without doubt
2 : PROBABLY

²doubtless *adjective* (14th century)
: free from doubt : CERTAIN
— **doubt·less·ly** *adverb*
— **doubt·less·ness** *noun*

douce \'düs\ *adjective* [Middle English, sweet, pleasant, from Middle French, from feminine of *douz*, from Latin *dulcis* sweet — more at DULCET] (1721)
chiefly Scottish : SOBER, SEDATE ⟨the *douce* faces of the mourners —L. J. A. Bell⟩
— **douce·ly** *adverb, chiefly Scottish*

dou·ceur \dü-'sər\ *noun* [French, pleasantness, from Late Latin *dulcor* sweetness, from Latin *dulcis*] (1763)
: a conciliatory gift

douche \'düsh\ *noun* [French, from Italian *doccia*, from *docciare* to douche, from *doccia* water pipe, probably back-formation from *doccione* conduit, from Latin *duction-, ductio* means of conveying water, from *ducere* to lead — more at TOW] (1766)
1 a : a jet or current especially of water directed against a part or into a cavity of the body **b** : an act of cleansing with a douche
2 : a device for giving douches
3 *British* : a rude awakening ⟨the icy *douche* (what he said about my work) —John Fowles⟩
— **douche** *verb*

douche bag *noun* (circa 1963)
slang : an unattractive or offensive person

dough \'dō\ *noun* [Middle English *dogh*, from Old English *dāg*; akin to Old High German *teic* dough, Latin *fingere* to shape, Greek *teichos* wall] (before 12th century)
1 : a mixture that consists essentially of flour or meal and a liquid (as milk or water) and is stiff enough to knead or roll
2 : something resembling dough especially in consistency
3 : MONEY
4 : DOUGHBOY
— **dough·like** \-ˌlīk\ *adjective*

dough box *noun* (circa 1944)
: a rectangular wooden box mounted on legs that is used as a worktable and storage space

dough·boy \-ˌbȯi\ *noun* (1865)
: an American infantryman especially in World War I

dough·face \-ˌfās\ *noun* (1830)
: a Northern congressman not opposed to slavery in the South before or during the Civil War; *also* : a Northerner sympathetic to the South during the same period
— **dough–faced** \-ˈfāst\ *adjective*

dough·nut \-(ˌ)nət\ *noun* (circa 1809)
1 : a small usually ring-shaped cake fried in fat

☆ **SYNONYMS**
Doubtful, dubious, problematic, questionable mean not affording assurance of the worth, soundness, or certainty of something. DOUBTFUL implies little more than a lack of conviction or certainty (*doubtful* about whether I said the right thing). DUBIOUS stresses suspicion, mistrust, or hesitation (*dubious* about the practicality of the scheme). PROBLEMATIC applies especially to things whose existence, meaning, fulfillment, or realization is highly uncertain (whether the project will ever be finished is *problematic*). QUESTIONABLE may imply no more than the existence of doubt but usually suggests that the suspicions are well-grounded (a man of *questionable* honesty).

2 : something (as a mathematical torus) that resembles a doughnut especially in shape — **dough·nut·like** \-ˌlīk\ *adjective*

dough·ty \'daù-tē\ *adjective* **dough·ti·er; -est** [Middle English, from Old English *dohtig;* akin to Old High German *toug* is useful, Greek *teuchein* to make] (before 12th century)
: marked by fearless resolution **:** VALIANT
— **dough·ti·ly** \'daù-t³l-ē\ *adverb*
— **dough·ti·ness** \'daù-tē-nəs\ *noun*

doughy \'dō-ē\ *adjective* **dough·i·er; -est** (1601)
: resembling dough: as **a :** not thoroughly baked **b :** unhealthily pale **:** PASTY

Doug·las fir \ˌdə-gləs-\ *noun* [David *Douglas* (died 1834) Scottish botanist] (1873)
: any of a genus (*Pseudotsuga*) of tall evergreen timber trees having thick bark, pitchy wood, and pendulous cones; *especially* **:** one (*P. menziesii* synonym *P. taxifolia*) of the western U.S.

Dou·kho·bor \'dü-kə-ˌbòr\ *noun* [Russian *dukhobor, dukhoborets,* from *dukh* spirit + *borets* wrestler] (1876)
: a member of a Christian sect of 18th century Russian origin emphasizing the duty of obeying the inner light and rejecting church or civil authority

do up *transitive verb* (1666)
1 : to prepare (as by cleaning or repairing) for wear or use ⟨*do up* a shirt⟩
2 a : to wrap up ⟨*do up* a package⟩ **b :** PUT UP, CAN
3 a : to deck out **:** CLOTHE **b :** to furnish with something ornamental **:** DECORATE
4 : EXHAUST, WEAR OUT

dour \'dù(-ə)r, 'daù(-ə)r\ *adjective* [Middle English, from Latin *durus* hard — more at DURING] (14th century)
1 : STERN, HARSH
2 : OBSTINATE, UNYIELDING
3 : GLOOMY, SULLEN
— **dour·ly** *adverb*
— **dour·ness** *noun*

dou·rou·cou·li \ˌdùr-ə-'kü-lē\ *noun* [French, from an unidentified American Indian language of Venezuela] (1842)
: any of several small nocturnal monkeys (genus *Aotus*) of tropical America that have round heads, large eyes, and densely furred bodies

¹douse \'daùs *also* 'daùz\ *verb* **doused; dous·ing** [perhaps from obsolete English *douse* (to smite)] (1600)
transitive verb
1 : to plunge into water
2 a : to throw a liquid on **:** DRENCH **b :** SLOSH
3 : EXTINGUISH ⟨*douse* the lights⟩
intransitive verb
: to fall or become plunged into water
— **dous·er** *noun*

²douse \'daùs *also* 'daùz\ *noun* (1881)
: a heavy drenching

³douse \'düs, 'daùs\ *noun* [origin unknown] (circa 1625)
British **:** BLOW, STROKE

⁴douse \'daùs\ *transitive verb* **doused; dous·ing** (1627)
1 a : FURL ⟨*douse* a sail⟩ **b :** SLACKEN ⟨*douse* a rope⟩
2 : TAKE OFF, DOFF

doux \'dü\ *adjective* [French, literally, sweet, from Old French *douz* — more at DOUCE] (circa 1943)
of champagne **:** very sweet

¹dove \'dəv\ *noun* [Middle English, from (assumed) Old English *dūfe;* akin to Old High German *tūba* dove] (13th century)
1 : any of numerous pigeons; *especially* **:** a small wild pigeon
2 : a gentle woman or child
3 : one who takes a conciliatory attitude and advocates negotiations and compromise; *especially* **:** an opponent of war — compare HAWK
— **dov·ish** \'də-vish\ *adjective*
— **dov·ish·ness** *noun*

²dove \'dōv\ *past of* DIVE

dove·cote \'dəv-ˌkōt, -ˌkät\ *also* **dove·cot** \-ˌkät\ *noun* (15th century)
1 : a small compartmented raised house or box for domestic pigeons
2 : a settled or harmonious group or organization

dove·kie \'dəv-kē\ *noun* [diminutive of *dove*] (1821)
: a small short-billed auk (*Alle alle*) breeding on arctic coasts and ranging south in winter

doven *variant of* DAVEN

Dover sole *noun* [probably from *Dover,* England] (circa 1911)
1 : a common European sole (*Solea solea*) esteemed as a food fish
2 : a brownish blotched flatfish (*Microstomus pacificus*) of the Pacific coast of North America that is a market fish in California

Do·ver's powder \ˌdō-vərz-\ *noun* [Thomas *Dover* (died 1742) English physician] (1801)
: a powder of ipecac and opium and used as a pain reliever and diaphoretic

¹dove·tail \'dəv-ˌtāl\ *noun* (1573)
: something resembling a dove's tail; *especially* **:** a flaring tenon and a mortise into which it fits tightly making an interlocking joint between two pieces (as of wood)

dovetail: *1* mortises, *2* tenons, *3* joint

²dovetail (circa 1656)
transitive verb
1 a : to join by means of dovetails **b :** to cut to a dovetail
2 a : to fit skillfully to form a whole **b :** to fit together with
intransitive verb
: to fit together into a whole

dow \'daù\ *intransitive verb* **dought** \'daùt\ *or* **dowed** \'daùd\; **dow·ing** [Middle English *dow, deih* have worth, am able, from Old English *dēah, dēag;* akin to Old High German *toug* is worthy, is useful — more at DOUGHTY] (before 12th century)
chiefly Scottish **:** to be able or capable

Dow \'daù\ *noun* (1949)
: DOW-JONES AVERAGE

dow·a·ger \'daù-i-jər\ *noun* [Middle French *douagiere,* from *douage* dower, from *douer* to endow, from Latin *dotare,* from *dot-, dos* gift, dower — more at DATE] (1530)
1 : a widow holding property or a title from her deceased husband
2 : a dignified elderly woman

dowager's hump *noun* (1948)
: an abnormal curvature of the upper back with round shoulders and stooped posture caused especially by bone loss and anterior compression of the vertebrae in osteoporosis

¹dowdy \'daù-dē\ *noun, plural* **dowd·ies** [diminutive of *dowd* (dowdy), from Middle English *doude*] (1581)
archaic **:** a dowdy woman

²dowdy *adjective* **dowd·i·er; -est** (1676)
1 : not neat or becoming in appearance **:** SHABBY
2 a : lacking smartness or taste **b :** OLD-FASHIONED
— **dowd·i·ly** \'daù-d³l-ē\ *adverb*
— **dowd·i·ness** \'daù-dē-nəs\ *noun*
— **dowdy·ish** \-ish\ *adjective*

³dowdy *noun* [origin unknown] (1936)
: PANDOWDY

¹dow·el \'daù(-ə)l\ *noun* [Middle English *dowle;* akin to Old High German *tubili* plug, Late Greek *typhos* wedge] (14th century)
1 : a pin fitting into a hole in an abutting piece to prevent motion or slipping; *also* **:** a round rod or stick used especially for cutting up into dowels
2 : a piece of wood driven into a wall so that other pieces can be nailed to it

²dowel *transitive verb* **-elled** *also* **-eled; -elling** *also* **-eling** (1713)
: to fasten by or furnish with dowels

¹dow·er \'daù(-ə)r\ *noun* [Middle English *dowere,* from Middle French *douaire,* modification of Medieval Latin *dotarium* — more at DOWRY] (14th century)
1 : the part of or interest in the real estate of a deceased husband given by law to his widow during her life — compare CURTESY
2 : DOWRY 2, 3

²dower *transitive verb* (1605)
: to supply with a dower or dowry **:** ENDOW

dow·itch·er \'daù-i-chər\ *noun, plural* **dow·itchers** *also* **dowitcher** [probably of Iroquoian origin; akin to Oneida *tawístawis* dowitcher] (1841)
: any of several long-billed wading birds (especially *Limnodromus griseus* and *L. scolopaceus* of the family Scolopacidae) related to the sandpipers

Dow–Jones average \ˌdaù-'jōnz-\ *noun* [Charles H. *Dow* (died 1902) & Edward D. *Jones* (died 1920) American financial statisticians] (1922)
: an index of the relative price of securities

¹down \'daùn\ *adverb* [Middle English *doun,* from Old English *dūne,* short for *adūne, of dūne,* from *a-* (from *of*), *of* off, from + *dūne,* dative of *dūn* hill] (before 12th century)
1 a (1) : toward or in a lower physical position (2) **:** to a lying or sitting position (3) **:** toward or to the ground, floor, or bottom **b :** as a down payment ⟨paid $10 *down*⟩ **c :** on paper ⟨put *down* what he says⟩
2 : in a direction that is the opposite of up: as **a :** SOUTHWARD **b :** to or toward a point away from the speaker or the speaker's point of reference
3 : to a lesser degree, level, or rate ⟨cool *down* tensions⟩
4 : to or toward a lower position in a series
5 a : to or in a lower or worse condition or status **b** — used to indicate completion ⟨dusted *down* the house⟩
6 : from a past time
7 : to or in a state of less activity or prominence
8 : to a concentrated state ⟨got the report *down* to three pages⟩
9 : into defeat ⟨voted the motion *down*⟩
— **down to the ground :** PERFECTLY, COMPLETELY ⟨that suits me *down to the ground*⟩

²down *preposition* (14th century)
: down along, around, through, toward, in, into, or on ⟨fell *down* the stairs⟩ ⟨*down* the years⟩

³down (1562)
transitive verb
1 : to cause to go or come down
2 : to cause (a football) to be out of play
3 : DEFEAT
intransitive verb
: to go down

⁴down *adjective* (circa 1565)
1 a (1) : occupying a low position; *specifically* **:** lying on the ground ⟨*down* timber⟩ (2) **:** directed or going downward ⟨attendance is *down*⟩ **b :** lower in price **c :** not being in play in football because of wholly stopped progress or because the officials stop the play **d :** defeated or trailing an opponent (as in points scored) ⟨*down* by two runs⟩ **e** *baseball* **:** OUT
2 a : reduced or low in activity or intensity ⟨a *down* economy⟩ **b :** not operating or able to function ⟨the computer is *down*⟩ **c :** DEPRESSED, DEJECTED; *also* **:** DEPRESSING ⟨a *down* movie⟩ **d :** SICK ⟨*down* with flu⟩

3 : DONE, FINISHED ⟨eight *down* and two to go⟩
4 : completely mastered ⟨had her lines *down*⟩ — often used with *pat*
5 *slang* : COOL 7 ⟨a *down* dude⟩
6 : being a quark with an electric charge of −⅓, zero charm, and zero strangeness ⟨a *down* quark⟩ — compare ²UP 5
7 : being on record ⟨you're *down* for two tickets⟩
— **down on** : having a low opinion of or dislike for

⁵**down** *noun* (1710)
1 : DESCENT, DEPRESSION
2 : an instance of putting down
3 a : a complete play to advance the ball in football **b** : one of a series of four attempts in American football or three attempts in Canadian football to advance the ball 10 yards
4 *chiefly British* : DISLIKE, GRUDGE
5 : DOWNER

⁶**down** *noun* [Middle English *doun* hill, from Old English *dūn*] (14th century)
1 : an undulating usually treeless upland with sparse soil — usually used in plural
2 *often capitalized* : a sheep of any breed originating in the downs of southern England

⁷**down** *noun* [Middle English *doun*, from Old Norse *dūnn*] (14th century)
1 : a covering of soft fluffy feathers; *also* : these feathers
2 : something soft and fluffy like down

down and dirty *adjective or adverb* (1967)
1 : UNVARNISHED ⟨the *down and dirty* truth⟩
2 : made or done hastily : not revised or polished
3 : marked by fierce competition
4 : BAWDY
5 : SEEDY 2

down–and–out \ˌdau̇-nən-'(d)au̇t\ *adjective* (1901)
1 : DESTITUTE, IMPOVERISHED
2 : physically weakened or incapacitated
— **down–and–out** *or* **down–and–out·er** \-'(d)au̇t-ər\ *noun*

down–at–the–heels \ˌdau̇-nət-thə-'hē(ə)lz, -nat-\ *or* **down–at–heel** \-nət-'hē(ə)l\ *also* **down–at–the–heel** \-thə-'hē(ə)l\ *or* **down–at–heel** \-nət-'hē(ə)lz\ *adjective* (1732)
: SHABBY

¹**down·beat** \'dau̇n-ˌbēt\ *noun* (1876)
1 : the downward stroke of a conductor indicating the principally accented note of a measure of music; *also* : the first beat of a measure
2 : a decline in activity or prosperity

²**downbeat** *adjective* (1950)
: PESSIMISTIC, GLOOMY

down–bow \'dau̇n-ˌbō\ *noun* (circa 1889)
: a stroke in playing a bowed instrument (as a violin) in which the bow is drawn across the strings from the frog to the tip

down·burst \-ˌbərst\ *noun* (1978)
: a powerful downdraft usually associated with a thunderstorm that strikes the ground and deflects in all directions and that constitutes a hazard especially for low-flying aircraft; *also* : MICROBURST

down·cast \'dau̇n-ˌkast\ *adjective* (14th century)
1 : low in spirit : DEJECTED
2 : directed downward ⟨with *downcast* eyes⟩

down·court \-'kōrt, -'kȯrt\ *adverb or adjective* (1952)
: in or into the opposite end of the court (as in basketball)

down·draft \-ˌdraft\ *noun* (1849)
: a downward current of gas (as air during a thunderstorm)

down east *adverb, often D&E capitalized* (1825)
: in or into the northeast coastal section of the U.S. and parts of the Maritime Provinces of Canada; *specifically* : in or into coastal Maine

— **down east** *adjective, often D&E capitalized*

down–east·er \ˌdau̇-'nē-stər\ *noun, often D&E capitalized* (1827)
: one born or living down east

down·er \'dau̇-nər\ *noun* (1966)
1 : a depressant drug; *especially* : BARBITURATE
2 : someone or something depressing

down·fall \'dau̇n-ˌfȯl\ *noun* (13th century)
1 a : a sudden fall (as from power) **b** : a fall (as of snow or rain) especially when sudden or heavy
2 : something that causes a downfall (as of a person)
— **down·fall·en** \-ˌfȯ-lən\ *adjective*

down·field \-'fē(ə)ld\ *adverb or adjective* (1944)
: in or into the part of the field toward which the offensive team is headed

¹**down·grade** \'dau̇n-ˌgrād\ *noun* (1858)
1 : a downward grade (as of a road)
2 : a descent toward an inferior state ⟨a career on the *downgrade*⟩

²**downgrade** *transitive verb* (1930)
1 : MINIMIZE, DEPRECIATE
2 : to lower in quality, value, status, or extent

down·haul \'dau̇n-ˌhȯl\ *noun* (1669)
: a rope or line for hauling down or holding down a sail or spar

down·heart·ed \-'här-təd\ *adjective* (circa 1774)
: DOWNCAST, DEJECTED
— **down·heart·ed·ly** *adverb*
— **down·heart·ed·ness** *noun*

¹**down·hill** \ˌdau̇n-'hil\ *adverb* (14th century)
1 : toward the bottom of a hill
2 : toward a worsened or inferior state or level — used especially in the phrase *go downhill*

²**down·hill** \-ˌhil\ *noun* (1591)
1 : a descending slope
2 : a skiing race against time down a trail — often used attributively

³**down·hill** \-ˌhil\ *adjective* (1727)
1 : sloping downhill
2 : closer to the bottom of an incline ⟨your *downhill* ski⟩
3 : not difficult : EASY ⟨after that problem the rest was *downhill*⟩
4 : progressively worse

down·hill·er \-hi-lər\ *noun* (1967)
: a downhill skier

down–home \'dau̇n-ˌhōm\ *adjective* (1938)
: of, relating to, or having qualities (as informality and simplicity) associated with rural or small-town people especially of the Southern U.S. ⟨*down-home* country cooking⟩; *broadly* : SIMPLE, UNPRETENTIOUS

down in the mouth *adjective* (1649)
: DEJECTED 1

down·land \'dau̇n-ˌland\ *noun* (before 12th century)
: ⁶DOWN 1

down·link \'dau̇n-ˌliŋk\ *noun* (circa 1969)
: a communications channel for receiving transmissions from a spacecraft; *also* : such transmissions

down·load \'dau̇n-ˌlōd\ *transitive verb* (1980)
: to transfer (data) from a usually large computer to the memory of another device (as a smaller computer)
— **down·load·able** \-ˌlō-də-bəl\ *adjective*

down–market \'dau̇n-ˌmär-kət\ *adjective* (1970)
: relating or appealing to lower-income consumers

down payment *noun* (1926)
: a part of the full price paid at the time of purchase or delivery with the balance to be paid later; *broadly* : the first step in a process

down·pipe \'dau̇n-ˌpīp\ *noun* (1858)
British : DOWNSPOUT

down·play \'dau̇n-ˌplā\ *transitive verb* (1954)
: PLAY DOWN, DE-EMPHASIZE

down·pour \-ˌpōr, -ˌpȯr\ *noun* (1811)
: a pouring or streaming downward; *especially* : a heavy rain

down·range \-'rānj\ *adverb* (1952)
: away from a launching site

¹**down·right** \-ˌrīt\ *adverb* (13th century)
1 *archaic* : straight down
2 : ABSOLUTELY 1 ⟨*downright* handsome⟩ ⟨*downright* mean⟩
3 *obsolete* : FORTHRIGHT

²**downright** *adjective* (1530)
1 *archaic* : directed vertically downward
2 : OUTRIGHT, THOROUGH ⟨a *downright* lie⟩
3 : PLAIN, BLUNT ⟨stories he had heard of her *downright* tongue —Angus Wilson⟩
— **down·right·ly** *adverb*
— **down·right·ness** *noun*

down·riv·er \'dau̇n-'ri-vər\ *adverb or adjective* (1852)
: toward or at a point nearer the mouth of a river

¹**down·scale** \'dau̇n-ˌskāl\ *transitive verb* **down·scaled; down·scal·ing** (1945)
: to cut back in size or scope ⟨the recession forced us to *downscale* vacation plans⟩

²**downscale** *adjective* (circa 1966)
: lower in class, income, or quality

down·shift \-ˌshift\ *intransitive verb* (1955)
: to shift an automotive vehicle into a lower gear
— **downshift** *noun*

down·side \'dau̇n-ˌsīd\ *noun* (1946)
1 : a downward trend (as of prices)
2 : a negative aspect ⟨the *downside* of fame⟩

down·size \'dau̇n-ˌsīz\ (1975)
transitive verb
: to reduce in size; *especially* : to design or produce in smaller size
intransitive verb
: to undergo a reduction in size

down·slide \'dau̇n-ˌslīd\ *noun* (1926)
: a downward movement

down·slope \'dau̇n-ˌslōp\ *adjective or adverb* (1928)
: toward the bottom of a slope

down·spout \'dau̇n-ˌspau̇t\ *noun* (circa 1896)
: a vertical pipe used to drain rainwater from a roof

Down's syndrome \'dau̇n(z)-\ *noun* [J. L. H. Down (died 1896) English physician] (1961)
: a congenital condition characterized by moderate to severe mental retardation, slanting eyes, a broad short skull, broad hands with short fingers, and trisomy of the human chromosome numbered 21 — called also *Down's, Down syndrome*

¹**down·stage** \'dau̇n-'stāj\ *adverb or adjective* (1898)
1 : toward or at the front of a theatrical stage
2 : toward a motion-picture or television camera

²**downstage** \-ˌstāj\ *noun* (circa 1931)
: the part of a stage that is nearest the audience or camera

¹**down·stairs** \'dau̇n-'starz, -'sterz\ *adverb* (1596)
: down the stairs : on or to a lower floor

²**down·stairs** \'dau̇n-ˌstarz, -ˌsterz\ *adjective* (1819)
: situated on the main, lower, or ground floor of a building

³**down·stairs** \'dau̇n-', 'dau̇n-\ *noun plural but singular or plural in construction* (1843)
: the lower floor of a building

down·state \'dau̇n-ˌstāt\ *noun* (1909)
: the chiefly southerly sections of a state; *also* : the chiefly rural part of a state when the major metropolitan area is to the north
— **down·state** \-'stāt\ *adjective or adverb*
— **down·stat·er** \-'stā-tər\ *noun*

down·stream \'dau̇n-'strēm\ *adverb or adjective* (1706)
1 : in the direction of or nearer to the mouth of a stream

2 : in or toward the latter stages of a usually industrial process or the stages (as marketing) after manufacture

down·stroke \-ˌstrōk\ *noun* (1852)
: a downward stroke

down·swing \-ˌswiŋ\ *noun* (1899)
1 : a downward swing
2 : DOWNTREND

down–the–line *adjective* (1940)
: COMPLETE ⟨a *down-the-line* union supporter⟩

down·time \'daún-ˌtīm\ *noun* (1928)
1 : time during which production is stopped especially during setup for an operation or when making repairs
2 : break time between periods of work ⟨napping during our *downtime*⟩

down–to–earth \ˌdaún-tə-'(w)ərth\ *adjective* (1932)
1 : PRACTICAL ⟨*down-to-earth* traveling tips⟩
2 : UNPRETENTIOUS ⟨surprised to find the movie star so *down-to-earth*⟩

down–to–the–wire \'daún-tə-thə-'wīr\ *adjective* (1952)
: full of suspense; *especially* **:** unsettled until the very end

down·town \ˌdaún-'taún, 'daún-ˌ\ *noun* (1851)
: the lower part of a city; *especially* **:** the main business district — often used attributively
— **downtown** \ˌdaún-'taún\ *adverb*
— **down·town·er** \-'taú-nər\ *noun*

down·trend \-ˌtrend\ *noun* (1926)
: a downturn especially in business and economic activity

down·trod·den \'daún-'trä-d³n\ *adjective* (1595)
: suffering oppression

down·turn \-ˌtərn\ *noun* (1926)
: a downward turn especially toward a decline in business activity

down under *adverb or adjective, often D&U capitalized* (1886)
: to or in Australia or New Zealand

¹**down·ward** \'daún-wərd\ *or* **down·wards** \-wərdz\ *adverb* (13th century)
1 a : from a higher to a lower place **b :** toward a direction that is the opposite of up
2 : from a higher to a lower condition
3 a : from an earlier time **b :** from an ancestor or predecessor

²**downward** *adjective* (circa 1552)
1 : moving or extending downward
2 : descending from a head, origin, or source
— **down·ward·ly** *adverb*
— **down·ward·ness** *noun*

down·wash \'daún-ˌwȯsh, -ˌwäsh\ *noun* (1915)
: an airstream directed downward (as by an airfoil)

down·wind \'daún-'wind\ *adverb or adjective* (1855)
: in the direction that the wind is blowing

downy \'daú-nē\ *adjective* **down·i·er; -est** (1578)
1 : resembling a bird's down
2 : covered with down
3 : made of down
4 : SOFT, SOOTHING

downy mildew *noun* (1886)
1 : any of various parasitic lower fungi (family Peronosporaceae) that produce whitish masses of sporangiophores or conidiophores on the undersurface of the leaves of the host
2 : a plant disease caused by a downy mildew

downy woodpecker *noun* (1808)
: a small black-and-white woodpecker (*Dendrocopos pubescens*) of North America that has a white back and is smaller than the hairy woodpecker

dow·ry \'daú(-ə)-rē\ *noun, plural* **dowries** [Middle English *dowarie*, from Anglo-French, irregular from Medieval Latin *dotarium*, from Latin *dot-, dos* gift, marriage portion — more at DATE] (14th century)
1 *archaic* **:** DOWER 1

2 : the money, goods, or estate that a woman brings to her husband in marriage
3 : a gift of money or property by a man to or for his bride
4 : a natural talent

dowsabel *noun* [*Dowsabel,* feminine name] (circa 1652)
obsolete **:** SWEETHEART

¹**dowse** *variant of* DOUSE

²**dowse** \'daúz\ *verb* **dowsed; dows·ing** [origin unknown] (1894)
intransitive verb
: to use a divining rod
transitive verb
: to find (as water) by dowsing
— **dows·er** \'daú-zər\ *noun* (1838)
: DIVINING ROD; *also* **:** a person who uses it

dowsing rod *noun* (1691)
: DIVINING ROD

dox·ol·o·gy \däk-'sä-lə-jē\ *noun, plural* **-gies** [Medieval Latin *doxologia,* from Late Greek, from Greek *doxa* opinion, glory (from *dokein* to seem, seem good) + *-logia* -logy — more at DECENT] (1649)
: a usually liturgical expression of praise to God

doxo·ru·bi·cin \ˌdäk-sə-'rü-bə-sən\ *noun* [*deoxy-* + *-orubicin* (as in *daunorubicin*)] (circa 1977)
: an antibiotic with broad antitumor activity that is obtained from a bacterium (*Streptomyces peucetius*) and is administered as the hydrochloride $C_{27}H_{29}NO_{11} \cdot HCl$

doxy *also* **dox·ie** \'däk-sē\ *noun, plural* **dox·ies** [perhaps modification of obsolete Dutch *docke* doll, from Middle Dutch] (circa 1530)
1 : FLOOZY, PROSTITUTE
2 : MISTRESS 4a

doxy·cy·cline \ˌdäk-sə-'sī-ˌklēn\ *noun* [*deoxy-* + tetra*cycline*] (1966)
: a broad-spectrum tetracycline antibiotic $C_{22}H_{24}N_2O_8$ with potent antibacterial activity that is often taken orally as a prophylactic against diarrhea by travelers

doy·en \'dȯi-ən, -ˌ(y)en; dwä-ˌyaⁿ(n)\ *noun* [French, from Late Latin *decanus* dean — more at DEAN] (1670)
1 a : the senior member of a body or group **b :** a person considered to be knowledgeable or uniquely skilled as a result of long experience in some field of endeavor
2 : the oldest example of a category

doy·enne \dȯi-'(y)en, dwä-'yen\ *noun* [French, feminine of *doyen*] (circa 1897)
: a woman who is a doyen

doy·ley *chiefly British variant of* DOILY

¹**doze** \'dōz\ *verb* **dozed; doz·ing** [probably of Scandinavian origin; akin to Old Norse *dūsa* to doze] (1693)
transitive verb
: to pass (as time) drowsily
intransitive verb
1 a : to sleep lightly **b :** to fall into a light sleep — usually used with *off*
2 : to be in a dull or stupefied condition
— **doze** *noun*
— **doz·er** *noun*

²**doze** *transitive verb* **dozed; doz·ing** [probably back-formation from *dozer* (bulldozer)] (1945)
: BULLDOZE 2
— **doz·er** *noun*

doz·en \'də-z³n\ *noun, plural* **dozens** *or* **dozen** [Middle English *dozeine,* from Middle French *dozaine,* from *doze* twelve, from Latin *duodecim,* from *duo* two + *decem* ten — more at TWO, TEN] (13th century)
1 : a group of 12
2 : an indefinitely large number ⟨*dozens* of times⟩
3 *plural but singular in construction* **:** a ritualized word game that consists of exchanging insults usually about the members of the opponent's family — used with *the*

— **dozen** *adjective*
— **doz·enth** \-z³n(t)th\ *adjective*

dozy \'dō-zē\ *adjective* **doz·i·er; -est** (1693)
: DROWSY, SLEEPY
— **doz·i·ly** \'dō-zə-lē\ *adverb*
— **doz·i·ness** *noun*

DP \ˌdē-'pē\ *noun, plural* **DP's** *or* **DPs** (circa 1944)
: a displaced person

DPN \ˌdē-ˌpē-'en\ *noun* [*d*iphospho*p*yridine *n*ucleotide] (1938)
: NAD

¹**drab** \'drab\ *noun* [origin unknown] (circa 1515)
1 : SLATTERN
2 : PROSTITUTE

²**drab** *intransitive verb* **drabbed; drab·bing** (1602)
: to associate with prostitutes

³**drab** *noun* [Middle French *drap* cloth, from Late Latin *drappus*] (1541)
1 : any of various cloths of a dull brown or gray color
2 a : a light olive brown **b :** a dull, lifeless, or faded appearance or quality

⁴**drab** *adjective* **drab·ber; drab·best** (1686)
1 a : of the dull brown color of drab **b :** of the color drab
2 : characterized by dullness and monotony
: CHEERLESS
— **drab·ly** *adverb*
— **drab·ness** *noun*

⁵**drab** *noun* [probably alteration of *drib*] (1828)
: a small amount — usually used in the phrase *dribs and drabs*

drab·ble \'dra-bəl\ *verb* **drab·bled; drab·bling** \-b(ə-)liŋ\ [Middle English *drabelen;* akin to Low German *drabbelen*] (15th century)
transitive verb
: DRAGGLE
intransitive verb
: to become wet and muddy

dra·cae·na \drə-'sē-nə\ *noun* [New Latin, from Late Latin, she-serpent, from Greek *drakaina,* feminine of *drakōn* serpent — more at DRAGON] (circa 1823)
: any of two genera (*Dracaena* and *Cordyline*) of Old World tropical shrubs or trees of the agave family that have naked branches ending in tufts of sword-shaped leaves and include some used as houseplants

drachm \'dram\ *noun* [alteration of Middle English *dragme* — more at DRAM] (14th century)
1 : DRACHMA
2 *chiefly British* **:** DRAM

drach·ma \'drak-mə\ *noun, plural* **drach·mas** *or* **drach·mai** \-ˌmī\ *or* **drach·mae** \-ˌ)mē, -ˌmī\ [Latin, from Greek *drachmē* — more at DRAM] (1525)
1 a : any of various ancient Greek units of weight **b :** any of various modern units of weight; *especially* **:** DRAM 1
2 a : an ancient Greek silver coin equivalent to 6 obols **b** — see MONEY table

Dra·co \'drā-ˌkō\ *noun* [Latin (genitive *Draconis*), literally, dragon — more at DRAGON]
: a northern circumpolar constellation within which is the north pole of the ecliptic

dra·co·ni·an \drā-'kō-nē-ən, drə-\ *adjective, often capitalized* [Latin *Dracon-, Draco,* from Greek *Drakōn* Draco (Athenian lawgiver)] (1876)
1 : of, relating to, or characteristic of Draco or the severe code of laws held to have been framed by him

\ə\ abut \ᵊ\ kitten \ər\ further \a\ ash \ā\ ace
\ä\ mop, mar \aú\ out \ch\ chin \e\ bet \ē\ easy
\g\ go \i\ hit \ī\ ice \j\ job \ŋ\ go
\ō\ law \ȯi\ boy \th\ thin \th\ the \ü\ loot \ú\ foot
\y\ yet \zh\ vision *see also* Guide to Pronunciation

2 : CRUEL; *also* **:** SEVERE ⟨*draconian* littering fines⟩ ◇

¹dra·con·ic \drə-'kä-nik\ *adjective* [Latin *dracon-, draco*] (1680)
: of or relating to a dragon

²dra·con·ic \drā-'kä-nik, drə-\ *adjective* (1708)
: DRACONIAN

¹draft \'draft, 'dråft\ *noun* [Middle English *draght;* akin to Old English *dragan* to draw — more at DRAW] (13th century)
1 : the act of drawing a net; *also* **:** the quantity of fish taken at one drawing
2 a : the act or an instance of drinking or inhaling; *also* **:** the portion drunk or inhaled in one such act **b :** a portion poured out or mixed for drinking **:** DOSE
3 a : the force required to pull an implement **b :** load or load-pulling capacity
4 a : the act of moving loads by drawing or pulling **:** PULL **b :** a team of animals together with what they draw
5 a : DELINEATION, REPRESENTATION **b :** SCHEME, DESIGN **c :** a preliminary sketch, outline, or version ⟨the author's first *draft*⟩ ⟨a *draft* treaty⟩
6 : the act, result, or plan of drawing out or stretching
7 a : the act of drawing (as from a cask) **b :** a portion of liquid so drawn ⟨a *draft* of ale⟩ **c :** draft beer ⟨a glass of *draft*⟩
8 : the depth of water a ship draws especially when loaded
9 a (1) **:** a system for or act of selecting individuals from a group (as for compulsory military service) (2) **:** an act or process of selecting an individual (as for political candidacy) without his expressed consent **b :** a group of individuals selected especially by military draft **c :** a system whereby exclusive rights to selected new players are apportioned among professional teams
10 a : an order for the payment of money drawn by one person or bank on another **b :** the act or an instance of drawing from or making demands upon something **:** DEMAND
11 a : a current of air in a closed-in space ⟨felt a *draft*⟩ **b :** a device for regulating the flow of air (as in a fireplace)
12 : ANGLE, TAPER; *specifically* **:** the taper given to a pattern or die so that the work can be easily withdrawn
13 : a pocket of reduced air pressure behind a moving object; *also* **:** the use of such a draft to save energy
— **on draft :** ready to be drawn from a receptacle ⟨beer *on draft*⟩

²draft *adjective* (15th century)
1 : used or adapted for drawing loads ⟨*draft* horses⟩
2 : being or having been on draft ⟨drinking *draft* beer⟩

³draft (1714)
transitive verb
1 : to select for some purpose: as **a :** to conscript for military service **b :** to select (a professional athlete) by draft
2 a : to draw the preliminary sketch, version, or plan of **b :** COMPOSE, PREPARE
3 : to draw off or away ⟨water *drafted* by pumps⟩
4 : to stay close behind (another racer) so as to take advantage of the reduced air pressure created by the leading racer
intransitive verb
1 : to practice draftsmanship
2 : to draft another racer (as in car or bike racing)
— **draft·able** \'draf-tə-bəl, 'dråf-\ *adjective*
— **draft·ee** \draf-'tē, ˌdråf-\ *noun*
— **draft·er** \'draf-tər, 'dråf-\ *noun*

draft board *noun* (1953)
: a civilian board that registers, classifies, and selects men for compulsory military service

drafts·man \'draf(t)s-mən, 'dråf(t)s-\ *noun* (1663)

1 : a person who draws plans and sketches (as of machinery or structures)
2 : a person who draws legal documents or other writings
3 : an artist who excels in drawing
— **drafts·man·ship** \-ˌship\ *noun*

drafts·person \'draf(t)s-ˌpər-sᵊn\ *noun* (1975)
: DRAFTSMAN 1

drafty \'draf-tē, 'dråf-\ *adjective* **draft·i·er; -est** (1846)
: exposed to or abounding in drafts of air
— **draft·i·ly** \-tə-lē\ *adverb*
— **draft·i·ness** \-tē-nəs\ *noun*

¹drag \'drag\ *noun* (14th century)
1 : something used to drag with; *especially* **:** a device for dragging under water to detect or obtain objects
2 : something that is dragged, pulled, or drawn along or over a surface: as **a :** HARROW **b :** a sledge for conveying heavy bodies **c :** CONVEYANCE
3 a : the act or an instance of dragging or drawing: as (1) **:** a drawing along or over a surface with effort or pressure (2) **:** motion effected with slowness or difficulty; *also* **:** the condition of having or seeming to have such motion (3) **:** a draw on a pipe, cigarette, or cigar; *also* **:** a draft of liquid **b :** a movement, inclination, or retardation caused by or as if by dragging **c** *slang* **:** influence securing special favor **:** PULL
4 a : something that retards motion or action **b** (1) **:** the retarding force acting on a body (as an airplane) moving through a fluid (as air) parallel and opposite to the direction of motion (2) **:** friction between engine parts; *also* **:** retardation due to friction **c :** BURDEN, ENCUMBRANCE ⟨the *drag* of population growth on living standards⟩ ⟨maturity is a *drag*⟩ **d :** one that is boring or gets in the way of enjoyment ⟨this sickly kid is going to be a social *drag* —Edmund Morris⟩
5 : an object drawn over the ground to leave a scented trail **b :** a clog fastened to a trap to prevent the escape of a trapped animal
6 : STREET, ROAD ⟨the main *drag*⟩
7 a : COSTUME, OUTFIT ⟨in Victorian *drag*⟩ **b :** clothing typical of one sex worn by a person of the opposite sex — often used in the phrase *in drag*
8 : DRAG RACE

²drag *verb* **dragged; drag·ging** [Middle English *draggen,* from Old Norse *draga* — more at DRAW] (15th century)
transitive verb
1 a (1) **:** to draw slowly or heavily **:** HAUL (2) **:** to cause to move with painful or undue slowness or difficulty ⟨*dragging* the national anthem⟩ (3) **:** to cause to trail along a surface ⟨wandered off *dragging* the leash⟩ **b** (1) **:** to bring by or as if by force or compulsion ⟨had to *drag* her husband to the opera⟩ (2) **:** to extract by or as if by pulling **c :** PROTRACT ⟨*drag* a story out⟩
2 a : to explore with a drag **b :** to catch with a dragnet
3 : to hit (a drag bunt) while moving toward first base
intransitive verb
1 : to hang or lag behind
2 : to fish or search with a drag
3 : to trail along on the ground
4 : to move or proceed laboriously or tediously ⟨the lawsuit *dragged* on for years⟩ ⟨was *dragging* after the long trip⟩
5 : DRAW 4a ⟨*drag* on a cigarette⟩
6 : to make a plucking or pulling movement
7 : to participate in a drag race
— **drag·ging·ly** \'dra-giŋ-lē\ *adverb*
— **drag one's feet** *also* **drag one's heels :** to act in a deliberately slow or dilatory manner

³drag *adjective* (1887)
: of, being, involving, or intended for a person in drag ⟨a *drag* ball⟩

drag bunt *noun* (circa 1949)

: a bunt in baseball made by a left-handed batter by trailing the bat while moving toward first base; *broadly* **:** a bunt made with the object of getting on base safely rather than sacrificing

drag coefficient *noun* (circa 1942)
: a factor representing the drag acting on a body (as an automobile or airfoil)

dra·gée \dra-'zhā\ *noun* [French, from Middle French *dragie* — more at DREDGE] (1853)
1 : a sugar-coated nut
2 : a small silver-colored ball for decorating cakes

drag·ger \'dra-gər\ *noun* (circa 1500)
: one that drags; *specifically* **:** a fishing boat operating a trawl or dragnet

drag·gle \'dra-gəl\ *verb* **drag·gled; drag·gling** \-g(ə-)liŋ\ [frequentative of *drag*] (1513)
transitive verb
: to make wet and dirty by dragging
intransitive verb
1 : to trail on the ground
2 : STRAGGLE

drag·gle–tail \'dra-gəl-ˌtāl\ *noun* (1596)
: SLATTERN

drag·gy \'dra-gē\ *adjective* **drag·gi·er; -est** (15th century)
: SLUGGISH, DULL

drag·line \'drag-ˌlīn\ *noun* (circa 1911)
1 : a line used in or for dragging
2 : an excavating machine in which the bucket is attached by cables and operates by being drawn toward the machine

drag·net \'drag-ˌnet\ *noun* (circa 1541)
1 a : a net drawn along the bottom of a body of water **b :** a net used on the ground (as to capture small game)
2 : a network of measures for apprehension (as of criminals)

drag·o·man \'dra-gə-mən\ *noun, plural* **-mans** *or* **-men** \-mən\ [Middle English *drogman,* from Middle French, from Old Italian *dragomanno,* from Middle Greek *dragomanos,* from Arabic *tarjumān,* from Aramaic *tūrgĕmānā*] (14th century)
: an interpreter chiefly of Arabic, Turkish, or Persian employed especially in the Near East

drag·on \'dra-gən\ *noun* [Middle English, from Old French, from Latin *dracon-, draco* serpent, dragon, from Greek *drakōn* serpent; akin to Old English *torht* bright, Greek *derkesthai* to see, look at] (13th century)
1 *archaic* **:** a huge serpent
2 : a mythical animal usually represented as a monstrous winged and scaly serpent or saurian with a crested head and enormous claws
3 : a violent, combative, or very strict person
4 *capitalized* **:** DRACO
5 : something or someone formidable or baneful
— **drag·on·ish** \-gə-nish\ *adjective*

drag·on·et \ˌdra-gə-'net, 'dra-gə-nət\ *noun* (14th century)
1 : a little dragon

◇ **WORD HISTORY**
draconian According to ancient Athenian tradition, Draco was a lawgiver of the 7th century B.C., associated with the first commitment of Greek law to writing. Draco's code was famed for its harshness, as most criminal offenses required the death penalty. According to the 4th century orator Demades, the statutes were literally written in blood. Not many decades after Draco supposedly lived, the 6th century statesman Solon abolished all of Draco's punishments except those dealing with homicide. Modern scholars are unsure if Draco or his code ever actually existed, but in any event *draconian* remains in English as a synonym for "severe" in reference to laws or other measures taken by persons in a position of power.

2 : any of various small often brightly colored scaleless marine fishes constituting a family (Callionymidae); *especially* **:** a European fish (*Callionymus lyra*) sometimes used as food

drag·on·fly \'dra-gən-ˌflī\ *noun* (1626)
: any of a suborder (Anisoptera) of odonate insects that are larger and stouter than damselflies, hold the wings horizontal in repose, and have rectal gills during the naiad stage; *broadly* **:** ODONATE

dragonfly

drag·on·head \-ˌhed\ *noun* (1784)
: any of several mints (genus *Dracocephalum*) often grown for their showy flower heads; *especially* **:** a North American plant (*D. parviflorum*)

dragon lady *noun* [character in the comic strip "Terry and the Pirates" by Milton Caniff] (1973)
: an overbearing or tyrannical woman; *also* **:** a glamorous often mysterious woman

dragon's blood *noun* (1599)
: any of several resinous mostly dark-red plant products; *specifically* **:** a resin from the fruit of a palm (genus *Daemonorops*) used for coloring varnish and in photoengraving

dragon's teeth *noun plural* [from the dragon's teeth sown by Cadmus which sprang up as armed warriors who killed one another off] (1853)
1 : seeds of strife
2 : wedge-shaped concrete antitank barriers laid in multiple rows

¹dra·goon \drə-'gün, dra-\ *noun* [French *dragon* dragon, dragoon, from Middle French] (1622)
: a member of a European military unit formerly composed of heavily armed mounted troops

²dragoon *transitive verb* (1689)
1 : to subjugate or persecute by harsh use of troops
2 : to force or attempt to force into submission by violent measures **:** COERCE

drag queen *noun* (circa 1941)
: a male homosexual who dresses as a woman

drag race *noun* (1949)
: an acceleration contest between vehicles (as automobiles)
— **drag racing** *noun*

drag·ster \'drag-stər\ *noun* (circa 1954)
1 : a vehicle built or modified for use in a drag race
2 : one who participates in a drag race

drag strip *noun* (1952)
: the site of a drag race; *specifically* **:** a strip of pavement with a racing area at least ¼ mile long

¹drain \'drān\ *verb* [Middle English *draynen*, from Old English *drēahnian* — more at DRY] (before 12th century)
transitive verb
1 *obsolete* **:** FILTER
2 a : to draw off (liquid) gradually or completely ⟨*drained* all the water out⟩ **b :** to cause the gradual disappearance of **c :** to exhaust physically or emotionally
3 a : to make gradually dry ⟨*drain* a swamp⟩ **b :** to carry away the surface water of ⟨the river that *drains* the valley⟩ **c :** to deplete or empty by or as if by drawing off by degrees or in increments **d :** to empty by drinking the contents of
4 : DROP 7c, SINK ⟨*drained* the putt⟩
intransitive verb
1 a : to flow off gradually **b :** to disappear gradually **:** DWINDLE
2 : to become emptied or freed of liquid by its flowing or dropping
3 : to discharge surface or surplus water

synonym see DEPLETE
— **drain·er** *noun*

²drain *noun* (1552)
1 : a means (as a pipe) by which usually liquid matter is drained
2 a : the act of draining **b :** a gradual outflow or withdrawal **:** DEPLETION
3 : something that causes depletion **:** BURDEN
4 : an electrode in a field-effect transistor toward which charge carriers move — compare GATE, SOURCE
— **down the drain :** to a state of being wasted or irretrievably lost

drain·age \'drā-nij\ *noun* (1652)
1 : the act, process, or mode of draining; *also* **:** something drained off
2 : a device for draining **:** DRAIN; *also* **:** a system of drains
3 : an area or district drained

drain·pipe \'drān-ˌpīp\ *noun* (1857)
: a pipe for drainage

Draize test \'drāz-\ *noun* [John H. *Draize* (born 1900) American pharmacologist] (1980)
: a test for harmfulness of chemicals to the human eye that involves dropping the test substance into one eye of a rabbit without anesthesia using the other eye as a control — called also *Draize eye test*

drake \'drāk\ *noun* [Middle English; akin to Old High German an*trahho* drake] (14th century)
: a male duck

dram \'dram\ *noun* [Middle English *dragme*, from Middle French & Late Latin; Middle French, dram, drachma, from Late Latin *dragma*, from Latin *drachma*, from Greek *drachmē*, literally, handful, from *drassesthai* to grasp] (14th century)
1 a — see WEIGHT table **b :** FLUID DRAM
2 a : a small portion of something to drink **b :** a small amount

DRAM \'dram *also* 'dē-ˌram\ *noun* [dynamic + RAM (random-access memory)] (1980)
: a computer memory chip that must be continuously supplied with power in order to retain data

dra·ma \'drä-mə, 'dra-\ *noun* [Late Latin *dramat-, drama,* from Greek, deed, drama, from *dran* to do, act] (1515)
1 : a composition in verse or prose intended to portray life or character or to tell a story usually involving conflicts and emotions through action and dialogue and typically designed for theatrical performance **:** PLAY — compare CLOSET DRAMA
2 : dramatic art, literature, or affairs
3 a : a state, situation, or series of events involving interesting or intense conflict of forces **b :** dramatic state, effect, or quality ⟨the *drama* of the courtroom proceedings⟩

Dram·a·mine \'dra-mə-ˌmēn\ *trademark*
— used for dimenhydrinate

dra·mat·ic \drə-'ma-tik\ *adjective* (1589)
1 : of or relating to the drama
2 a : suitable to or characteristic of the drama **b :** striking in appearance or effect
3 *of an opera singer* **:** having a powerful voice and a declamatory style — compare LYRIC ☆
— **dra·mat·i·cal·ly** \-ti-k(ə-)lē\ *adverb*

dramatic irony *noun* (circa 1907)
: IRONY 3b

dramatic monologue *noun* (circa 1935)
: a literary work in which a character reveals himself in a monologue usually addressed to a second person

dra·mat·ics \drə-'ma-tiks\ *noun plural but singular or plural in construction* (1796)
1 : the study or practice of theatrical arts (as acting and stagecraft)
2 : dramatic behavior or expression

dramatic unities *noun plural* (circa 1922)
: the unities of time, place, and action that are observed in classical drama

dramatisation, dramatise *British variant of* DRAMATIZATION, DRAMATIZE

dra·ma·tis per·so·nae \ˌdra-mə-təs-pər-'sō-(ˌ)nē, ˌdrä-, -ˌnī\ *noun plural* [New Latin] (1730)
1 : the characters or actors in a drama
2 *singular in construction* **:** a list of the characters or actors in a drama
3 : the participants in an event

dra·ma·tist \'dra-mə-tist, 'drä-\ *noun* (1678)
: PLAYWRIGHT

dra·ma·ti·za·tion \ˌdra-mə-tə-'zā-shən, ˌdrä-\ *noun* (1796)
1 : the action of dramatizing
2 : a dramatized version (as of a novel)

dra·ma·tize \'dra-mə-ˌtīz, 'drä-\ *verb* -**tized**; -**tiz·ing** (1783)
transitive verb
1 : to adapt (as a novel) for theatrical presentation
2 : to present or represent in a dramatic manner
intransitive verb
1 : to be suitable for dramatization
2 : to behave dramatically
— **dra·ma·tiz·able** \-ˌtī-zə-bəl\ *adjective*

dra·ma·turge *or* **dra·ma·turg** \'dra-mə-ˌtərj, 'drä-\ *noun* (1870)
: a specialist in dramaturgy

dra·ma·tur·gy \'dra-mə-ˌtər-jē, 'drä-\ *noun* [German *Dramaturgie*, from Greek *dramatourgia* dramatic composition, from *dramat-, drama* + *-ourgia* -urgy] (1801)
: the art or technique of dramatic composition and theatrical representation
— **dra·ma·tur·gic** \ˌdra-mə-'tər-jik, ˌdrä-\ *or* **dra·ma·tur·gi·cal** \-ji-kəl\ *adjective*
— **dra·ma·tur·gi·cal·ly** \-ji-k(ə-)lē\ *adverb*

dra·me·dy \'drä-mə-dē, 'dra-\ *noun* [blend of *drama* and *comedy*] (1978)
: a situation comedy having dramatic scenes

dram·mock \'dra-mək\ *noun* [Scottish Gaelic *dramag*] (1562)
chiefly Scottish **:** raw oatmeal mixed with cold water

dram·shop \'dram-ˌshäp\ *noun* (1725)
: BARROOM

drank *past and past participle of* DRINK

¹drape \'drāp\ *verb* **draped; drap·ing** [probably back-formation from *drapery*] (1847)
transitive verb
1 : to cover or adorn with or as if with folds of cloth
2 : to cause to hang or stretch out loosely or carelessly
3 : to arrange in flowing lines or folds
intransitive verb
: to become arranged in folds ⟨this silk *drapes* beautifully⟩

☆ **SYNONYMS**
Dramatic, theatrical, histrionic, melodramatic mean having a character or an effect like that of acted plays. DRAMATIC applies to situations in life and literature that stir the imagination and emotions deeply ⟨a *dramatic* meeting of world leaders⟩. THEATRICAL implies a crude appeal through artificiality or exaggeration in gesture or vocal expression ⟨a *theatrical* oration⟩. HISTRIONIC applies to tones, gestures, and motions and suggests a deliberate affectation or staginess ⟨a *histrionic* show of grief⟩. MELODRAMATIC suggests an exaggerated emotionalism or an inappropriate theatricalism ⟨made a *melodramatic* plea⟩.

— **drap·abil·i·ty** also **drape·abil·i·ty** \ˌdrā-pə-'bi-lə-tē\ noun
— **drap·able** also **drape·able** \'drā-pə-bəl\ adjective
²**drape** noun (1889)
1 : arrangement in or of folds
2 a : a drapery especially for a window : CURTAIN **b :** a sterile covering used in an operating room — usually used in plural
3 : the cut or hang of clothing
— **drap·ey** \'drā-pē\ adjective
drap·er \'drā-pər\ noun [Middle English, weaver, clothier, from Middle French drapier, from Old French, from drap cloth — more at DRAB] (14th century)
chiefly British **:** a dealer in cloth and sometimes also in clothing and dry goods
drap·ery \'drā-p(ə-)rē\ noun, plural **-er·ies** (14th century)
1 British **:** DRY GOODS
2 a : a decorative piece of material usually hung in loose folds and arranged in a graceful design **b :** hangings of heavy fabric for use as a curtain
3 : the draping or arranging of materials
dras·tic \'dras-tik\ adjective [Greek drastikos, from dran to do] (circa 1691)
1 : acting rapidly or violently ⟨a drastic purgative⟩
2 : extreme in effect or action : SEVERE ⟨drastic measures⟩
— **dras·ti·cal·ly** \-ti-k(ə-)lē\ adverb
drat \'drat\ verb **drat·ted; drat·ting** [probably euphemistic alteration of God rot] (1815)
: DAMN — used as a mild oath
draught \'draft\, **draughty** \'draf-tē\ chiefly British variant of DRAFT, DRAFTY
draughts \'draf(t)s\ noun plural but singular or plural in construction [Middle English draghtes, from plural of draght draft, move in chess] (15th century)
British **:** CHECKERS
draughts·man chiefly British variant of DRAFTSMAN
Dra·vid·i·an \drə-'vi-dē-ən\ noun [Sanskrit Drāviḍa] (1856)
1 : a member of an ancient dark-skinned people of southern India
2 : DRAVIDIAN LANGUAGES
— **Dravidian** adjective
Dravidian languages noun plural (1871)
: a language family of India, Sri Lanka, and Pakistan that includes Tamil, Telugu, Kannada, and Malayalam
¹**draw** \'drȯ\ verb **drew** \'drü\; **drawn** \'drȯn, 'drän\; **draw·ing** [Middle English drawen, dragen, from Old English dragan; akin to Old Norse draga to draw, drag] (before 12th century)
transitive verb
1 : to cause to move continuously toward or after a force applied in advance : PULL ⟨draw your chair up by the fire⟩: as **a :** to move (as a covering) over or to one side ⟨draw the drapes⟩ **b :** to pull up or out of a receptacle or place where seated or carried ⟨draw water from the well⟩ ⟨drew a gun⟩; also : to cause to come out of a container ⟨draw water for a bath⟩
2 : to cause to go in a certain direction (as by leading) ⟨drew him aside⟩
3 a : to bring by inducement or allure : ATTRACT ⟨honey draws flies⟩ **b :** to bring in or gather from a specified group or area ⟨a college that draws its students from many states⟩ **c :** BRING ON, PROVOKE ⟨drew enemy fire⟩ **d :** to bring out by way of response : ELICIT ⟨drew cheers from the audience⟩ **e :** to receive in the course of play ⟨the batter drew a walk⟩ ⟨draw a foul⟩
4 : INHALE ⟨drew a deep breath⟩
5 a : to extract the essence from ⟨draw tea⟩ **b :** EVISCERATE ⟨plucking and drawing a goose before cooking⟩ **c :** to derive to one's benefit ⟨drew inspiration from the old masters⟩

6 : to require (a specified depth) to float in ⟨a ship that draws 12 feet of water⟩
7 a : ACCUMULATE, GAIN ⟨drawing interest⟩ **b :** to take (money) from a place of deposit **c :** to use in making a cash demand ⟨drawing a check against his account⟩ **d :** to receive regularly or in due course ⟨draw a salary⟩
8 a : to take (cards) from a stack or from the dealer **b :** to receive or take at random ⟨drew a winning number⟩
9 : to bend (a bow) by pulling back the string
10 : to cause to shrink, contract, or tighten
11 : to strike (a ball) so as to impart a backward spin
12 : to leave (a contest) undecided : TIE
13 a (1) **:** to produce a likeness or representation of by making lines on a surface ⟨draw a picture⟩ ⟨draw a graph with chalk⟩ (2) **:** to give a portrayal of : DELINEATE ⟨a writer who draws characters well⟩ **b :** to write out in due form ⟨draw a will⟩ **c :** to design or describe in detail : FORMULATE ⟨draw comparisons⟩
14 : to infer from evidence or premises ⟨draw a conclusion⟩
15 : to spread or elongate (metal) by hammering or by pulling through dies; also : to shape (as plastic) by stretching or by pulling through dies
intransitive verb
1 : to come or go steadily or gradually ⟨night draws near⟩
2 a : to move something by pulling ⟨drawing at the well⟩ **b :** to exert an attractive force ⟨the play is drawing well⟩
3 a : to pull back a bowstring **b :** to bring out a weapon ⟨drew, aimed, and fired⟩
4 a : to produce a draft ⟨the chimney draws well⟩ ⟨draw on a cigar⟩ **b :** to swell out in a wind ⟨all sails drawing⟩
5 a : to wrinkle or tighten up : SHRINK **b :** to change shape by pulling or stretching
6 : to cause blood or pus to localize at one point
7 : to create a likeness or a picture in outlines : SKETCH
8 : to come out even in a contest
9 a : to make a written demand for payment of money on deposit **b :** to obtain resources (as of information) ⟨drawing from a common fund of knowledge⟩
— **draw·able** \-ə-bəl\ adjective
— **draw a bead on :** to take aim at
— **draw a blank :** to fail to gain a desired object (as information sought); also : to be unable to think of something
— **draw on** or **draw upon :** to use as a source of supply ⟨drawing on the whole community for support⟩
— **draw straws :** to decide or assign something by lottery in which straws of unequal length are used
— **draw the line** or **draw a line 1 :** to fix an arbitrary boundary between things that tend to intermingle **2 :** to fix a boundary excluding what one will not tolerate or engage in
²**draw** noun (1663)
1 : the act or process of drawing: as **a :** a sucking pull on something held with the lips **b :** a removal of a handgun from its holster ⟨quick on the draw⟩ **c :** backward spin given to a ball by striking it below center — compare FOLLOW
2 : something that is drawn: as **a :** a card drawn to replace a discard in poker **b :** a lot or chance drawn at random **c :** the movable part of a drawbridge
3 : a contest left undecided or deadlocked : TIE
4 : one that draws attention or patronage
5 a : the distance from the string to the back of a drawn bow **b :** the force required to draw a bow fully
6 : a gully shallower than a ravine
7 : the deal in draw poker to improve the players' hands after discarding

8 : a football play that simulates a pass play so a runner can go straight up the middle past the pass rushers
draw away intransitive verb (1670)
: to move ahead (as of an opponent in a race)
draw·back \'drȯ-ˌbak\ noun (1697)
1 : a refund of duties especially on an imported product subsequently exported or used to produce a product for export
2 : an objectionable feature : DISADVANTAGE
draw back \drȯ-'bak\ intransitive verb (14th century)
: to avoid an issue or commitment
draw·bar \'drȯ-ˌbär\ noun (1839)
1 : a railroad coupler
2 : a beam across the rear of a vehicle (as a tractor) to which implements are hitched
draw·bridge \-ˌbrij\ noun (14th century)
: a bridge made to be raised up, let down, or drawn aside so as to permit or hinder passage

drawbridge

draw·down \-ˌdau̇n\ noun (1918)
1 : a lowering of a water level (as in a reservoir)
2 a : the process of depleting **b :** REDUCTION
draw down \ˌdrȯ-'dau̇n\ transitive verb (1949)
: to deplete by using or spending
draw·ee \drȯ-'ē\ noun (1766)
: the party on which an order or bill of exchange is drawn
draw·er \'drȯ(-ə)r\ noun (14th century)
1 : one that draws: as **a :** a person who draws liquor **b :** DRAFTSMAN **c :** one that draws a bill of exchange or order for payment or makes a promissory note
2 : a sliding box or receptacle opened by pulling out and closed by pushing in
3 plural **:** an article of clothing (as underwear) for the lower body
— **drawer·ful** \-ˌfu̇l\ noun
draw in (1558)
transitive verb
1 : to cause or entice to enter or participate
2 : to sketch roughly
intransitive verb
1 a : to draw to an end ⟨the day drew in⟩ **b :** to shorten seasonally ⟨the evenings are already drawing in⟩
2 : to become more cautious or economical
draw·ing \'drȯ(-)iŋ\ noun (14th century)
1 : an act or instance of drawing; especially **:** the process of deciding something by drawing lots
2 : the art or technique of representing an object or outlining a figure, plan, or sketch by means of lines
3 : something drawn or subject to drawing: as **a :** an amount drawn from a fund **b :** a representation formed by drawing : SKETCH
drawing account noun (1920)
: an account showing payments made to an employee in advance of actual earnings or for traveling expenses
drawing board noun (1725)
1 : a board used as a base for drafting on paper
2 : a planning stage ⟨a project still on the drawing board⟩
drawing card noun (1887)
: one that attracts attention or patronage
drawing pin noun (1859)
British **:** THUMBTACK
drawing room noun [short for withdrawing room] (1642)
1 a : a formal reception room **b :** a private room on a railroad passenger car with three berths and an enclosed toilet
2 : a formal reception

drawing table *noun* (1706)
: a table with a surface adjustable for elevation and angle of incline

draw·knife \'drȯ-ˌnīf\ *noun* (1703)
: a woodworker's tool consisting of a blade with a handle at each end for use in shaving off surfaces

¹drawl \'drȯl\ *verb* [probably frequentative of *draw*] (1598)
intransitive verb
: to speak slowly with vowels greatly prolonged
transitive verb
: to utter in a slow lengthened tone
— **drawl·er** *noun*
— **drawl·ing·ly** \'drȯ-liŋ-lē\ *adverb*

²drawl *noun* (1760)
: a drawling manner of speaking
— **drawly** \'drȯ-lē\ *adjective*

¹drawn *past participle of* DRAW

²drawn \'drȯn, 'drän\ *adjective* (1613)
: showing the effects of tension, pain, or illness : HAGGARD

drawn butter *noun* (1826)
: melted clarified butter

drawn·work \'drȯn-ˌwȯrk\ *noun* (1595)
: decoration on cloth made by drawing out threads according to a pattern

draw off (13th century)
transitive verb
: REMOVE, WITHDRAW
intransitive verb
: to move apart or ahead

draw on (15th century)
intransitive verb
: APPROACH ⟨night *draws on*⟩
transitive verb
: BRING ON, CAUSE

draw out *transitive verb* (14th century)
1 : REMOVE, EXTRACT
2 : to extend beyond a minimum in time : PROTRACT 2
3 : to cause to speak freely ⟨a reporter's ability to *draw* a person *out*⟩

draw·plate \'drȯ-ˌplāt\ *noun* (1832)
: a die with holes through which wires are drawn

draw play *noun* (1952)
: DRAW 8

draw poker *noun* (1849)
: poker in which each player is dealt five cards face down and after betting may get replacements for discards

draw·shave \'drȯ-ˌshāv\ *noun* (1828)
: DRAWKNIFE

draw shot *noun* (1897)
: a shot in billiards or pool made by hitting the cue ball with draw so it moves back after striking the object ball

draw·string \'drȯ-ˌstriŋ\ *noun* (1845)
: a string, cord, or tape inserted into hems or casings or laced through eyelets for use in closing a bag or controlling fullness in garments or curtains

draw·tube \-ˌtüb, -ˌtyüb\ *noun* (circa 1891)
: a telescoping tube (as for the eyepiece of a microscope)

draw up (1605)
transitive verb
1 : to bring (as troops) into array
2 : to prepare a draft or version of ⟨*draw up* plans⟩
3 : to bring to a halt
4 : to straighten (oneself) to an erect posture especially as an assertion of dignity or resentment
intransitive verb
: to come to a halt

¹dray \'drā\ *noun* [Middle English *draye*, a wheelless vehicle; akin to Old English *dræge* dragnet, *dragan* to pull — more at DRAW] (14th century)
: a vehicle used to haul goods; *especially* : a strong cart or wagon without sides

²dray *transitive verb* (1857)
: to haul on a dray : CART

dray·age \'drā-ij\ *noun* (1791)
: the work or cost of hauling by dray

dray horse *noun* (1709)
: a horse adapted for drawing heavy loads

dray·man \'drā-mən\ *noun* (1581)
: one whose work is hauling by dray

¹dread \'dred\ *verb* [Middle English *dreden*, from Old English *drædan*] (before 12th century)
transitive verb
1 a : to fear greatly **b** *archaic* : to regard with awe
2 : to feel extreme reluctance to meet or face
intransitive verb
: to be apprehensive or fearful

²dread *noun* (13th century)
1 a : great fear especially in the face of impending evil **b** : extreme uneasiness in the face of a disagreeable prospect ⟨*dread* of a social blunder⟩ **c** *archaic* : AWE
2 : one causing fear or awe
synonym see FEAR

³dread *adjective* (15th century)
1 : causing great fear or anxiety
2 : inspiring awe

¹dread·ful \'dred-fəl\ *adjective* (13th century)
1 a : inspiring dread : causing great and oppressive fear **b** : inspiring awe or reverence
2 : extremely bad, distasteful, unpleasant, or shocking
3 : EXTREME ⟨*dreadful* disorder⟩
— **dread·ful·ly** \-f(ə-)lē\ *adverb*
— **dread·ful·ness** \-fəl-nəs\ *noun*

²dreadful *noun* (1873)
: a cheap and sensational story or periodical

dread·lock \'dred-ˌläk\ *noun* (1960)
1 : a narrow ropelike strand of hair formed by matting or braiding
2 *plural* : a hairstyle consisting of dreadlocks

dread·nought \'dred-ˌnȯt, -ˌnät\ *noun* (1806)
1 : a warm garment of thick cloth; *also* : the cloth
2 [*Dreadnought*, British battleship] : BATTLESHIP
3 : one that is among the largest or most powerful of its kind

¹dream \'drēm\ *noun, often attributive* [Middle English *dreem*, from Old English *drēam* noise, joy, and Old Norse *draumr* dream; akin to Old High German *troum* dream] (13th century)
1 : a series of thoughts, images, or emotions occurring during sleep — compare REM SLEEP
2 : an experience of waking life having the characteristics of a dream: as **a** : a visionary creation of the imagination : DAYDREAM **b** : a state of mind marked by abstraction or release from reality : REVERIE **c** : an object seen in a dreamlike state : VISION
3 : something notable for its beauty, excellence, or enjoyable quality ⟨the new car is a *dream* to operate⟩
4 a : a strongly desired goal or purpose ⟨a *dream* of becoming president⟩ **b** : something that fully satisfies a wish : IDEAL ⟨a meal that was a gourmet's *dream*⟩ ◇
— **dream·ful** \-fəl\ *adjective*
— **dream·ful·ly** \-fə-lē\ *adverb*
— **dream·ful·ness** *noun*
— **dream·less** *adjective*
— **dream·less·ly** *adverb*
— **dream·less·ness** *noun*
— **dream·like** \'drēm-ˌlīk\ *adjective*

²dream *verb* **dreamed** \'drem(p)t, 'drēmd\ *or* **dreamt** \'drem(p)t\; **dream·ing** \'drē-miŋ\ (13th century)
intransitive verb
1 : to have a dream
2 : to indulge in daydreams or fantasies ⟨*dreaming* of a better future⟩
3 : to appear tranquil or dreamy ⟨houses *dream* in leafy shadows —Gladys Taber⟩
transitive verb
1 : to have a dream of
2 : to consider as a possibility : IMAGINE

3 : to pass (time) in reverie or inaction ⟨*dreaming* the hours away⟩
— **dream of** : to consider possible or fitting ⟨wouldn't *dream of* disturbing you⟩

dream·er \'drē-mər\ *noun* (14th century)
1 : one that dreams
2 a : one who lives in a world of fancy and imagination **b** : one who has ideas or conceives projects regarded as impractical : VISIONARY

dream·land \'drēm-ˌland\ *noun* (circa 1834)
: an unreal delightful country existing only in imagination or in dreams : NEVER-NEVER LAND

dream·time \-ˌtīm\ *noun, often capitalized* (1896)
: the time of creation in the mythology of the Australian aborigines

dream up *transitive verb* (1941)
: to form in the mind : DEVISE, CONCOCT

dream vision *noun* (1906)
: a usually medieval poem having a framework in which the poet pictures himself as falling asleep and envisioning in his dream a series of allegorical people and events

dream·world \'drēm-ˌwərld\ *noun* (1817)
: a world of illusion or fantasy

dreamy \'drē-mē\ *adjective* **dream·i·er; -est** (1567)
1 a : full of dreams ⟨a *dreamy* night's sleep⟩ **b** : pleasantly abstracted from immediate reality
2 : given to dreaming or fantasy ⟨a *dreamy* child⟩
3 a : suggestive of a dream in vague or visionary quality **b** : quiet and soothing **c** : DELIGHTFUL, IDEAL ⟨he's so handsome . . . real *dreamy* —Greg Foley⟩
— **dream·i·ly** \-mə-lē\ *adverb*
— **dream·i·ness** \-mē-nəs\ *noun*

drear \'drir\ *adjective* (1629)
: DREARY
— **drear** *noun*

drea·ry \'drir-ē\ *adjective* **drea·ri·er; -est** [Middle English *drery*, from Old English *drēorig* sad, bloody, from *drēor* gore; akin to Old High German *trūrēn* to be sad, Gothic *driusan* to fall] (before 12th century)
1 : feeling, displaying, or reflecting listlessness or discouragement
2 : having nothing likely to provide cheer, comfort, or interest : GLOOMY, DISMAL
— **drea·ri·ly** \'drir-ə-lē\ *adverb*
— **drea·ri·ness** \'drir-ē-nəs\ *noun*

dreck *also* **drek** \'drek\ *noun* [Yiddish *drek* & German *Dreck*, from Middle High German *drec*; akin to Old English *threax* rubbish] (1922)
: TRASH, RUBBISH

◇ WORD HISTORY
dream Not until the 13th century did *dream*, in the Middle English forms *drem* and *dreem*, appear in reference to images seen during sleep; however, the word itself is considerably older. In Old English *drēam* meant "joy, ecstasy" or "melody, music." Yet the shift in sense between Old and Middle English was not simply the result of an adaptation and specialization of the earlier senses. Rather it would appear that after the Scandinavian conquests and settlements in Britain of the 9th and 10th centuries, which had a major impact on the history of English, the Old Norse word *draumr*, referring to a dream during sleep, influenced the meaning of the similar and almost certainly related English word. By the end of the 14th century, the Old English meanings of the word had been entirely replaced.

¹dredge \'drej\ *verb* **dredged; dredg·ing** (1508)
transitive verb
1 a : to dig, gather, or pull out with or as if with a dredge — often used with *up* **b :** to deepen (as a waterway) with a dredging machine
2 : to bring to light by deep searching — often used with *up* ⟨*dredging* up memories⟩
intransitive verb
1 : to use a dredge
2 : to search deeply
— dredg·er *noun*
²dredge *noun* [perhaps from (assumed) Old English *drecge;* akin to Old English *dræge* dragnet, *dragan* to draw] (1602)
1 : an apparatus usually in the form of an oblong iron frame with an attached bag net used especially for gathering fish and shellfish
2 : a machine for removing earth usually by buckets on an endless chain or a suction tube
3 : a barge used in dredging
³dredge *transitive verb* **dredged; dredg·ing** [obsolete *dredge,* noun, sweetmeat, from Middle English *drage, drege,* from Middle French *dragie,* modification of Latin *tragemata* sweetmeats, from Greek *tragēmata,* plural of *tragēma* sweetmeat, from *trōgein* to gnaw] (1596)
: to coat (food) by sprinkling (as with flour)
— dredg·er *noun*
dree \'drē\ *transitive verb* **dreed; dree·ing** [Middle English, from Old English *drēogan;* akin to Gothic *driugan* to perform military service] (before 12th century)
chiefly Scottish **:** ENDURE, SUFFER
dreg \'dreg\ *noun* [Middle English, from Old Norse *dregg;* perhaps akin to Latin *fraces* dregs of oil] (14th century)
1 : sediment contained in a liquid or precipitated from it **:** LEES — usually used in plural
2 : the most undesirable part — usually used in plural
3 : the last remaining part **:** VESTIGE
— dreg·gy \'dre-gē\ *adjective*
D region *noun* (1930)
: the lowest part of the ionosphere occurring approximately between 30 and 55 miles (50 and 90 kilometers) above the surface of the earth
dreich \'drēk\ *adjective* [Middle English, of Scandinavian origin; akin to Old Norse *drjūgr* lasting] (1813)
chiefly Scottish **:** DREARY
drei·del *also* **dreidl** \'drā-dᵊl\ *noun* [Yiddish *dreydl,* from *dreyen* to turn, from Middle High German *dræjen,* from Old High German *drāen* — more at THROW] (1926)
1 : a 4-sided toy marked with Hebrew letters and spun like a top in a game of chance
2 : a children's game of chance played especially at Hanukkah with a dreidel
¹drench \'drench\ *noun* (before 12th century)
1 : a poisonous or medicinal drink; *specifically* **:** a large dose of medicine mixed with liquid and put down the throat of an animal

dreidel 1

2 a : something that drenches **b :** a quantity sufficient to drench or saturate
²drench *transitive verb* [Middle English, from Old English *drencan;* akin to Old English *drincan* to drink] (before 12th century)
1 a *archaic* **:** to force to drink **b :** to administer a drench to (an animal)
2 : to wet thoroughly (as by soaking or immersing in liquid)
3 : to soak or cover thoroughly with liquid that falls or is precipitated
4 : to fill or cover completely as if by soaking or precipitation ⟨was *drenched* in furs and diamonds —Richard Brautigan⟩
synonym see SOAK
— drench·er *noun*

¹dress \'dres\ *verb* [Middle English, from Middle French *dresser,* from Old French *drecier,* from (assumed) Vulgar Latin *directiare,* from Latin *directus* direct, past participle of *dirigere* to direct, from *dis-* + *regere* to lead straight — more at RIGHT] (14th century)
transitive verb
1 a : to make or set straight **b :** to arrange (as troops) in a straight line and at proper intervals
2 : to prepare for use or service; *specifically* **:** to prepare for cooking or for the table
3 : to add decorative details or accessories to **:** EMBELLISH
4 a : to put clothes on **b :** to provide with clothing
5 *archaic* **:** DRESS DOWN
6 a : to apply dressings or medicaments to **b** (1) **:** to arrange (the hair) by combing, brushing, or curling (2) **:** to groom and curry (an animal) **c :** to kill and prepare for market or for consumption — often used with *out* **d :** CULTIVATE, TEND; *especially* **:** to apply manure or fertilizer to **e :** to put through a finishing process; *especially* **:** to trim and smooth the surface of (as lumber or stone)
intransitive verb
1 a : to put on clothing **b :** to put on or wear formal, elaborate, or fancy clothes ⟨*dress* for dinner⟩
2 *of a food animal* **:** to weigh after being dressed — often used with *out*
3 : to align oneself with the next soldier in a line to make the line straight
— dress ship : to ornament a ship for a celebration by hoisting national ensigns at the mastheads and running a line of signal flags and pennants from bow to stern
²dress *noun* (1606)
1 : APPAREL, CLOTHING
2 : an outer garment (as for a woman or girl) usually consisting of a one-piece bodice and skirt
3 : covering, adornment, or appearance appropriate or peculiar to a particular time
4 : a particular form of presentation **:** GUISE
³dress *adjective* (1767)
1 : suitable for a formal occasion
2 : requiring or permitting formal dress ⟨a *dress* affair⟩
3 : relating to or used for a dress
dres·sage \drǝ-'säzh, dre-\ *noun, often attributive* [French, from *dresser* to train, drill, from Middle French] (1936)
: the execution by a trained horse of precision movements in response to barely perceptible signals from its rider
dress circle *noun* (1825)
: the first or lowest curved tier of seats above the main floor in a theater or opera house
dress code *noun* (1968)
: formally or socially imposed standards of dress
dress down (circa 1897)
transitive verb
: to reprove severely
intransitive verb
: to dress casually especially for reasons of fashion
¹dress·er \'dre-sǝr\ *noun* (15th century)
1 *obsolete* **:** a table or sideboard for preparing and serving food
2 : a cupboard to hold dishes and cooking utensils
3 : a chest of drawers or bureau with a mirror
²dresser *noun* (1520)
: one that dresses ⟨a fashionable *dresser*⟩
dresser set *noun* (circa 1934)
: a set of toilet articles including hairbrush, comb, and mirror for use at a dresser or dressing table
dress·ing *noun* (15th century)
1 a : the act or process of one who dresses **b :** an instance of such act or process

2 a : a sauce for adding to a dish (as a salad)
b : a seasoned mixture usually used as a stuffing (as for poultry)
3 a : material (as ointment or gauze) applied to cover a lesion **b :** fertilizing material (as manure or compost)
dres·sing–down \.dre-siŋ-'daùn\ *noun* (circa 1890)
: a severe reprimand
dressing glass *noun* (1714)
: a small mirror set to swing in a standing frame and used at a dresser or dressing table
dressing gown *noun* (1777)
: a robe worn especially while dressing or resting
dressing room *noun* (1675)
: a room used chiefly for dressing; *especially* **:** a room in a theater for changing costumes and makeup
dressing table *noun* (1692)
: a table often fitted with drawers and a mirror in front of which one sits while dressing and grooming oneself
¹dress·mak·er \'dres-.mā-kǝr\ *noun* (1803)
: one that makes dresses
— dress·mak·ing \-.mā-kiŋ\ *noun*
²dressmaker *adjective* (1904)
of women's clothes **:** having softness, rounded lines, and intricate detailing ⟨a *dressmaker* suit⟩
dress rehearsal *noun* (1828)
1 : a full rehearsal (as of a play) in costume and with stage properties shortly before the first performance
2 : a practice exercise for something to come **:** DRY RUN
dress shield *noun* (1884)
: a pad worn inside a part of the clothing liable to be soiled by perspiration (as at the underarm)
dress shirt *noun* (1892)
: a man's shirt especially for wear with evening dress; *broadly* **:** a shirt suitable for wear with a necktie
dress uniform *noun* (circa 1897)
: a uniform for formal wear
dress up (1674)
transitive verb
1 a : to attire in best or formal clothes **b :** to attire in clothes suited to a particular role
2 a : to present in the most attractive or impressive light ⟨a fiasco *dressed up* as a triumph⟩ **b :** to make more attractive, glamorous, or fancy ⟨*dress up* a plain dessert with a rich chocolate sauce⟩
intransitive verb
: to get dressed up
dressy \'dre-sē\ *adjective* **dress·i·er; -est** (1768)
1 : showy in dress
2 : STYLISH, SMART
— dress·i·ness *noun*
drew *past of* DRAW
Drey·fu·sard \.drī-f(y)ǝ-'sär(d), .drā-, -'zär(d)\ *noun* [French] (1898)
: a defender or partisan of Alfred Dreyfus
drib \'drib\ *noun* [probably back-formation from *dribble & driblet*] (circa 1730)
: a small amount — usually used in the phrase *dribs and drabs*
¹drib·ble \'dri-bǝl\ *verb* **drib·bled; drib·bling** \-(ǝ-)liŋ\ [frequentative of *drib* (to dribble)] (circa 1589)
transitive verb
1 : to issue sporadically and in small bits
2 : to let or cause to fall in drops little by little
3 a : to propel by successive slight taps or bounces with hand, foot, or stick **b :** to hit (as a baseball) so as to cause a slow bouncing
intransitive verb
1 : to fall or flow in drops or in a thin intermittent stream **:** TRICKLE
2 : to let saliva trickle from the corner of the mouth **:** DROOL
3 : to come or issue in piecemeal or desultory fashion

4 a : to dribble a ball or puck **b :** to proceed by dribbling **c** *of a ball* **:** to move with short bounces
— **drib·bler** \-b(ə-)lər\ *noun*
²**dribble** *noun* (circa 1680)
1 : a tiny or insignificant bit or quantity
2 : a small trickling stream or flow
3 : an act, instance, or manner of dribbling a ball or puck
— **drib·bly** \'dri-b(ə-)lē\ *adjective*
drib·let \'drib-lət\ *noun* (1678)
1 : a trifling or small sum or part
2 : a drop of liquid
dried–up \'drī-,dəp, ,drī-'\ *adjective* (1885)
: being wizened and shriveled
¹**drier** *comparative of* DRY
²**dri·er** *or* **dry·er** \'drī(-ə)r\ *noun* (1528)
1 : something that extracts or absorbs moisture
2 : a substance that accelerates drying (as of oils, paints, and printing inks)
3 *usually* **dryer :** a device for drying
driest *superlative of* DRY
¹**drift** \'drift\ *noun* [Middle English; akin to Old English *drīfan* to drive — more at DRIVE] (14th century)
1 a : the act of driving something along **b :** the flow or the velocity of the current of a river or ocean stream
2 : something driven, propelled, or urged along or drawn together in a clump by or as if by a natural agency: as **a :** wind-driven snow, rain, cloud, dust, or smoke usually at or near the ground surface **b** (1) **:** a mass of matter (as sand) deposited together by or as if by wind or water (2) **:** a helter-skelter accumulation **c :** DROVE, FLOCK **d :** something (as driftwood) washed ashore **e :** rock debris deposited by natural agents; *specifically* **:** a deposit of clay, sand, gravel, and boulders transported by a glacier or by running water from a glacier
3 a : a general underlying design or tendency **b :** the underlying meaning, import, or purport of what is spoken or written
4 : something (as a tool) driven down upon or forced into a body
5 : the motion or action of drifting especially spatially and usually under external influence: as **a :** the lateral motion of an aircraft due to air currents **b :** an easy moderate more or less steady flow or sweep along a spatial course **c :** a gradual shift in attitude, opinion, or position **d :** an aimless course; *especially* **:** a foregoing of any attempt at direction or control **e :** a deviation from a true reproduction, representation, or reading
6 a : a nearly horizontal mine passageway driven on or parallel to the course of a vein or rock stratum **b :** a small crosscut in a mine connecting two larger tunnels
7 a : an assumed trend toward a general change in the structure of a language over a period of time **b :** GENETIC DRIFT **c :** a gradual change in the zero reading of an instrument or in any quantitative characteristic that is supposed to remain constant
synonym see TENDENCY
— **drifty** \'drif-tē\ *adjective*
²**drift** (circa 1600)
intransitive verb
1 a : to become driven or carried along (as by a current of water, wind, or air) **b :** to move or float smoothly and effortlessly
2 a : to move along a line of least resistance **b :** to move in a random or casual way **c :** to become carried along subject to no guidance or control ⟨the talk *drifted* from topic to topic⟩
3 a : to accumulate in a mass or become piled up in heaps by wind or water **b :** to become covered with a drift
4 : to vary or deviate from a set course or adjustment
transitive verb
1 a : to cause to be driven in a current **b** *West* **:** to drive (livestock) slowly especially to allow grazing

2 a : to pile in heaps **b :** to cover with drifts
— **drift·ing·ly** \'drif-tiŋ-lē\ *adverb*
drift·age \'drif-tij\ *noun* (1768)
: drifted material
drift·er \'drif-tər\ *noun* (1897)
: one that drifts; *especially* **:** one that travels or moves about aimlessly
drift fence *noun* (1907)
: a stretch of fence on rangeland especially in the western U.S. for preventing cattle from drifting from their home range
drift net *noun* (1848)
: a fishing net often miles in extent arranged to drift with the tide or current and buoyed up by floats or attached to a boat
drift·wood \'drift-,wùd\ *noun* (1633)
1 : wood drifted or floated by water
2 : FLOTSAM 2
¹**drill** \'dril\ *verb* [Dutch *drillen*] (1622)
transitive verb
1 a : to fix something in the mind or habit pattern of by repetitive instruction ⟨*drill* pupils in spelling⟩ **b :** to impart or communicate by repetition ⟨impossible to *drill* the simplest idea into some people⟩ **c :** to train or exercise in military drill
2 a (1) **:** to bore or drive a hole in (2) **:** to make by piercing action **b :** to shoot with or as if with a gun **c** (1) **:** to propel (as a ball) with force or accuracy ⟨*drilled* a single to right field⟩ (2) **:** to hit with force ⟨*drilled* the batter with the first pitch⟩
intransitive verb
1 : to make a hole with a drill
2 : to engage in an exercise
— **drill·abil·i·ty** \,dri-lə-'bi-lə-tē\ *noun*
— **drill·able** \-lə-bəl\ *adjective*
— **drill·er** \'dri-lər\ *noun*
²**drill** *noun* (1611)
1 : an instrument with an edged or pointed end for making holes in hard substances by revolving or by a succession of blows; *also* **:** a machine for operating such an instrument
2 : the act or exercise of training soldiers in marching and in executing prescribed movements with a weapon
3 a : a physical or mental exercise aimed at perfecting facility and skill especially by regular practice **b :** a formal exercise by a team of marchers **c** *chiefly British* **:** the approved or correct procedure for accomplishing something efficiently
4 a : a marine snail (*Urosalpinx cinerea*) destructive to oysters by boring through their shells and feeding on the soft parts **b :** any of several mollusks related to the drill
5 : a drilling sound
³**drill** *noun* [origin unknown] (1644)
: a western African baboon (*Papio leucophaeus* synonym *Mandrillus leucophaeus*) having a black face and brown coat and closely related to the typical mandrills
⁴**drill** *noun* [perhaps from *drill* (rill)] (1727)
1 a : a shallow furrow or trench into which seed is sown **b :** a row of seed sown in such a furrow
2 : a planting implement that makes holes or furrows, drops in the seed and sometimes fertilizer, and covers them with earth
⁵**drill** *transitive verb* (circa 1740)
1 : to sow (seeds) by dropping along a shallow furrow
2 a : to sow with seed or set with seedlings inserted in drills **b :** to distribute seed or fertilizer in by means of a drill
⁶**drill** *noun* [short for *drilling*] (1743)
: a durable cotton twilled fabric
dril·ling \'dri-liŋ\ *noun* [modification of German *Drillich*, from Middle High German *drilich* fabric woven with a threefold thread, from Old High German *drilīh* made up of three threads, from Latin *trilic-, trilix*, from *tri- + licium* thread] (1640)
: ⁶DRILL
drill·mas·ter \'dril-,mas-tər\ *noun* (1869)
1 : an instructor in military drill

2 : an instructor or director who maintains severe discipline and often stresses method and detail
drill press *noun* (circa 1864)
: an upright drilling machine in which the drill is pressed to the work by a hand lever or by power
drill team *noun* (1928)
: an exhibition marching team that engages in precision drill
drily *variant of* DRYLY
D ring \'dē-,riŋ\ *noun* (circa 1899)
: a usually metal ring having the shape of a capital D
¹**drink** \'driŋk\ *verb* **drank** \'draŋk\; **drunk** \'drəŋk\ *or* **drank**; **drink·ing** [Middle English, from Old English *drincan*; akin to Old High German *trinkan* to drink] (before 12th century)
transitive verb
1 a : SWALLOW, IMBIBE **b :** to take in or suck up **:** ABSORB ⟨*drinking* air into his lungs⟩ **c :** to take in or receive avidly — usually used with *in* ⟨*drank* in every word of the lecture⟩
2 : to join in a toast to ⟨I'll *drink* your good health⟩
3 : to bring to a specified state by drinking alcoholic beverages ⟨*drank* himself into oblivion⟩
intransitive verb
1 a : to take liquid into the mouth for swallowing **b :** to receive into one's consciousness
2 : to partake of alcoholic beverages
3 : to make or join in a toast ⟨I'll *drink* to that!⟩
²**drink** *noun* (before 12th century)
1 a : a liquid suitable for swallowing **b :** alcoholic beverages
2 : a draft or portion of liquid
3 : excessive consumption of alcoholic beverages
4 : a sizable body of water — used with *the*
¹**drink·able** \'driŋ-kə-bəl\ *adjective* (1611)
: suitable or safe for drinking
— **drink·abil·i·ty** \,driŋ-kə-'bi-lə-tē\ *noun*
²**drinkable** *noun* (1708)
: a liquid suitable for drinking **:** BEVERAGE
drink·er \'driŋ-kər\ *noun* (before 12th century)
1 a : one that drinks **:** a person who drinks alcoholic beverages especially to a notable degree ⟨a heavy *drinker*⟩
2 : WATERER b
drinking fountain *noun* (1860)
: a fixture with nozzle that delivers a stream of water for drinking
drinking song *noun* (1597)
: a song on a convivial theme appropriate for a group engaged in social drinking
¹**drip** \'drip\ *verb* **dripped; drip·ping** [Middle English *drippen*, from Old English *dryppan*; akin to Old English *dropa* drop] (before 12th century)
transitive verb
1 : to let fall in drops
2 : to let out or seem to spill copiously ⟨her voice *dripping* sarcasm⟩
intransitive verb
1 a : to let fall drops of moisture or liquid **b :** to overflow with or as if with moisture ⟨a uniform *dripping* with gold braid⟩
2 : to fall in or as if in drops
3 : to waft or pass gently
— **drip·per** *noun*
²**drip** *noun* (1664)
1 : a part of a cornice or other member that projects to throw off rainwater; *also* **:** an overlapping metal strip or an underneath groove for the same purpose
2 a : a falling in drops **b :** liquid that falls, overflows, or is extruded in drops

\ə\ **abut** \ᵊ\ **kitten** \ər\ **further** \a\ **ash** \ā\ **ace**
\ä\ **mop, mar** \aù\ **out** \ch\ **chin** \e\ **bet** \ē\ **easy**
\g\ **go** \i\ **hit** \ī\ **ice** \j\ **job** \ŋ\ **sing** \ō\ **go**
\ò\ **law** \òi\ **boy** \th\ **thin** \th̲\ **the** \ü\ **loot** \ù\ **foot**
\y\ **yet** \zh\ **vision** *see also* Guide to Pronunciation

3 : the sound made by or as if by falling drops
4 : a device for the administration of a fluid at a slow rate especially into a vein; *also* **:** a material so administered
5 : a dull or unattractive person

³drip *adjective* (1895)
: of, relating to, or being coffee made by letting boiling water drip slowly through finely ground coffee ⟨*drip* coffee⟩ ⟨a *drip* pot⟩

¹drip–dry \'drip-,drī\ (1953)
intransitive verb
: to dry with few or no wrinkles when hung wet
transitive verb
: to hang (as wet clothing) to drip-dry

²drip–dry *adjective* (1957)
: made of a washable fabric that drip-dries

³drip–dry *noun* (1959)
: a drip-dry garment

drip·less \'dri-pləs\ *adjective* (1887)
: designed not to drip ⟨*dripless* candles⟩

drip·ping \'dri-piŋ\ *noun* (15th century)
: fat and juices drawn from meat during cooking — often used in plural

drip·py \'dri-pē\ *adjective* **drip·pi·er; -est** (circa 1718)
1 : characterized by dripping; *especially* **:** RAINY, DRIZZLY
2 : MAWKISH 2

drip·stone \'drip-,stōn\ *noun* (circa 1818)
1 : a stone drip (as over a window)
2 : calcium carbonate in the form of stalactites or stalagmites

¹drive \'drīv\ *verb* **drove** \'drōv\; **driv·en** \'dri-vən\; **driv·ing** \'drī-viŋ\ [Middle English, from Old English *drīfan*; akin to Old High German *trīban* to drive] (before 12th century)
transitive verb
1 a : to frighten or prod (as game or cattle) into moving in a desired direction **b :** to go through (a district) driving game animals
2 : to carry on or through energetically ⟨*drives* a hard bargain⟩
3 a : to impart a forward motion to by physical force ⟨waves *drove* the boat ashore⟩ **b :** to repulse, remove, or cause to go by force, authority, or influence ⟨*drive* the enemy back⟩ **c :** to set or keep in motion or operation ⟨*drive* machinery by electricity⟩
4 a : to direct the motions and course of (a draft animal) **b :** to operate the mechanism and controls and direct the course of (as a vehicle) **c :** to convey in a vehicle **d :** to float (logs) down a stream
5 a : to exert inescapable or coercive pressure on **:** FORCE **b :** to compel to undergo or suffer a change (as in situation or emotional state) ⟨*drove* him crazy⟩ ⟨*drove* her out of business⟩ **c :** to urge relentlessly to continuous exertion ⟨the sergeant *drove* his recruits⟩ **d :** to press or force into an activity, course, or direction ⟨the drug habit *drives* addicts to steal⟩ **e :** to project, inject, or impress incisively ⟨*drove* her point home⟩
6 : to force (a passage) by pressing or digging
7 a : to propel (an object of play) swiftly **b :** to hit (a golf ball) from the tee especially with a driver; *also* **:** to drive a golf ball onto a green **c :** to cause (a run or runner) to be scored in baseball — usually used with *in*
8 : to give shape or impulse to ⟨factors that *drive* the business cycle⟩
intransitive verb
1 a : to dash, plunge, or surge ahead rapidly or violently **b :** to progress with strong momentum ⟨the rain was *driving* hard⟩
2 a : to operate a vehicle **b :** to have oneself carried in a vehicle
3 : to drive a golf ball
synonym see MOVE
— **driv·abil·i·ty** *also* **drive·abil·i·ty** \,drī-və-'bi-lə-tē\ *noun*
— **driv·able** *also* **drive·able** \'drī-və-bəl\ *adjective*
— **drive at :** to intend to express, convey, or accomplish ⟨did not understand what she was *driving* at —Eric Goldman⟩

²drive *noun, often attributive* (1785)
1 : an act of driving: **a :** a trip in a carriage or automobile **b :** a collection and driving together of animals; *also* **:** the animals gathered **c :** a driving of cattle or sheep overland **d :** a hunt or shoot in which the game is driven within the hunter's range **e :** the guiding of logs downstream to a mill; *also* **:** the floating logs amassed in a drive **f** (1) **:** the act or an instance of driving an object of play (as a golf ball) (2) **:** the flight of a ball
2 a : a private road **:** DRIVEWAY **b :** a public road for driving (as in a park)
3 : the state of being hurried and under pressure
4 a : a strong systematic group effort ⟨a fundraising *drive*⟩ **b :** a sustained offensive effort ⟨the *drive* ended in a touchdown⟩
5 a : the means for giving motion to a machine or machine part **b :** the means by which the propulsive power of an automobile is applied to the road ⟨front wheel *drive*⟩ **c :** the means by which the propulsion of an automotive vehicle is controlled and directed ⟨a left-hand *drive*⟩
6 : an offensive, aggressive, or expansionist move; *especially* **:** a strong military attack against enemy-held terrain
7 a : an urgent, basic, or instinctual need **:** a motivating physiological condition of an organism ⟨a sexual *drive*⟩ **b :** an impelling culturally acquired concern, interest, or longing **:** dynamic quality
8 : a device for reading and writing on magnetic media (as tapes or disks)

drive-by \'drīv-'bī\ *adjective* (1986)
: carried out from a moving vehicle ⟨a *drive-by* shooting⟩

drive-in \'drī-,vin\ *noun* (1937)
: an establishment (as a theater or restaurant) so laid out that patrons can be accommodated while remaining in their automobiles
— **drive-in** *adjective*

¹driv·el \'dri-vəl\ *verb* **-eled** *or* **-elled; -eling** *or* **-el·ling** \-v(ə-)liŋ\ [Middle English, from Old English *dreflian*; perhaps akin to Old Norse *draf* malt dregs] (before 12th century)
intransitive verb
1 : to let saliva dribble from the mouth **:** SLAVER
2 : to talk stupidly and carelessly
transitive verb
1 : to utter in an infantile or imbecilic way
2 : to waste or fritter in a childish fashion
— **driv·el·er** \-v(ə-)lər\ *noun*

²drivel *noun* (14th century)
1 *archaic* **:** DROOL 1
2 : NONSENSE

drive·line \'drīv-,līn\ *noun* (1949)
: DRIVETRAIN

driv·en *adjective* (1925)
: having a compulsive or urgent quality ⟨a *driven* sense of obligation⟩
— **driv·en·ness** \'dri-vən-nəs\ *noun*

driv·er \'drī-vər\ *noun* (14th century)
: one that drives: as **a :** COACHMAN **b :** the operator of a motor vehicle **c :** an implement (as a hammer) for driving **d :** a mechanical piece for imparting motion to another piece **e :** a golf wood with a nearly straight face used in driving **f :** an electronic circuit that supplies input to another electronic circuit; *also* **:** LOUDSPEAKER **g :** a piece of computer software that controls input and output operations
— **driv·er·less** \-ləs\ *adjective*

driver ant *noun* (1859)
: ARMY ANT; *specifically* **:** any of various African and Asian ants (*Dorylus* or related genera) that move in vast armies

driver's license *noun* (1926)
: a license issued under governmental authority that permits the holder to operate a motor vehicle

driver's seat *noun* (1923)
: the position of top authority or dominance

drive-shaft \'drīv-,shaft\ *noun* (1895)
: a shaft that transmits mechanical power

drive time *noun* (1966)
: a time during rush hour when radio audiences are swelled by commuters listening to car radios

drive-train \'drīv-,trān\ *noun* (1954)
: the parts (as the universal joint and the driveshaft) that connect the transmission with the driving axles of an automobile

drive-way \-,wā\ *noun* (1871)
: a private road giving access from a public way to a building or abutting grounds

driv·ing *adjective* (14th century)
1 a : communicating force ⟨a *driving* wheel⟩ **b :** exerting pressure ⟨a *driving* influence⟩
2 a : having great force ⟨a *driving* rain⟩ **b :** acting with vigor **:** ENERGETIC ⟨a hard-*driving* worker⟩

driving range *noun* (circa 1949)
: an area equipped with distance markers, clubs, balls, and tees for practicing golf drives

¹driz·zle \'dri-zəl\ *noun* (1554)
: a fine misty rain
— **driz·zly** \'driz-(ə-)lē\ *adjective*

²drizzle *verb* **driz·zled; driz·zling** \-z(ə-)liŋ\ [perhaps alteration of Middle English *drysnen* to fall, from Old English *-drysnian* to disappear; akin to Gothic *driusan* to fall] (1584)
transitive verb
1 : to shed or let fall in minute drops or particles
2 : to make wet with minute drops
intransitive verb
: to rain in very small drops or very lightly **:** SPRINKLE
— **driz·zling·ly** \-z(ə-)liŋ-lē\ *adverb*

drogue \'drōg\ *noun* [probably alteration of ¹*drag*] (1875)
1 : SEA ANCHOR
2 a : a cylindrical or funnel-shaped device towed as a target by an airplane **b :** a small parachute for stabilizing or decelerating something (as an astronaut's capsule) or for pulling a larger parachute out of stowage
3 : a funnel-shaped device which is attached to the end of a long flexible hose suspended from a tanker airplane in flight and into which the probe of another airplane is fitted so as to receive fuel from the tanker

droit \'dròit, 'drwä\ *noun* [Middle English, from Middle French, from Medieval Latin *directum*, from Late Latin, neuter of *directus* just, from Latin, direct — more at DRESS] (15th century)
: a legal right

droit du sei·gneur \drwä-dē-se-n^yœr\ *noun* [French, right of the lord] (1825)
: a supposed legal or customary right of a feudal lord to have sexual relations with a vassal's bride on her wedding night

¹droll \'drōl\ *adjective* [French *drôle*, from *drôle* scamp, from Middle French *drolle*, from Middle Dutch, imp] (1623)
: having a humorous, whimsical, or odd quality
— **droll·ness** *noun*
— **drol·ly** \'drō(l)-lē\ *adverb*

²droll *noun* (circa 1645)
: an amusing person **:** JESTER, COMEDIAN

³droll *intransitive verb* (1654)
archaic **:** to make fun **:** JEST, SPORT

droll·ery \'drōl-rē, 'drō-lə-\ *noun, plural* **-eries** (1597)
1 : something that is droll; *especially* **:** a comic picture or drawing
2 : the act or an instance of jesting or burlesquing
3 : whimsical humor

-drome \,drōm\ *noun combining form* [hippo-*drome*]
1 : racecourse ⟨motor*drome*⟩
2 : large specially prepared place ⟨aero*drome*⟩

drom·e·dary \'drä-mə-,der-ē *also* 'drə-\ *noun, plural* **-dar·ies** [Middle English *dromedarie*,

from Old French *dromedaire,* from Late Latin *dromedarius,* from Latin *dromad-, dromas,* from Greek, running; akin to Greek *dramein* to run, *dromos* racecourse, Sanskrit *dramati* he runs about] (13th century)
: CAMEL 1a

-d·ro·mous \drə-məs\ *adjective combining form* [New Latin *-dromus,* from Greek *-dromos* (akin to Greek *dramein*)]
: running ⟨cata*dromous*⟩

¹drone \'drōn\ *noun* [Middle English, from Old English *drān;* akin to Old High German *treno* drone, Greek *thrēnos* dirge] (before 12th century)
1 : the male of a bee (as the honeybee) that has no sting and gathers no honey
2 : one that lives on the labors of others : PARASITE
3 : an unmanned airplane, helicopter, or ship guided by remote control
4 : DRUDGE

²drone *verb* **droned; dron·ing** (circa 1520)
intransitive verb
1 a : to make a sustained deep murmuring, humming, or buzzing sound **b** : to talk in a persistently dull or monotonous tone
2 : to pass, proceed, or act in a dull, drowsy, or indifferent manner
transitive verb
1 : to utter or pronounce with a drone
2 : to pass or spend in dull or monotonous activity or in idleness
— **dron·er** *noun*
— **dron·ing·ly** \'drō-niŋ-lē\ *adverb*

³drone *noun* (circa 1520)
1 : a deep sustained or monotonous sound : HUM
2 : an instrument or part of an instrument (as one of the fixed-pitch pipes of a bagpipe) that sounds a continuous unvarying tone
3 : PEDAL POINT

¹drool \'drü(-ə)l\ *verb* [perhaps alteration of *drivel*] (1802)
intransitive verb
1 a : to secrete saliva in anticipation of food **b** : DRIVEL 1
2 : to make an effusive show of pleasure or often envious or covetous appreciation
3 : to talk nonsense
transitive verb
: to express sentimentally or effusively

²drool *noun* (1869)
1 : saliva trickling from the mouth
2 : NONSENSE

¹droop \'drüp\ *verb* [Middle English *drupen,* from Old Norse *drūpa;* akin to Old English *dropa* drop] (13th century)
intransitive verb
1 : to hang or incline downward
2 : to sink gradually
3 : to become depressed or weakened : LANGUISH
transitive verb
: to let droop
— **droop·ing·ly** \'drü-piŋ-lē\ *adverb*

²droop *noun* (1647)
: the condition or appearance of drooping

droopy \'drü-pē\ *adjective* **droop·i·er; -est** (13th century)
1 : GLOOMY
2 : drooping or tending to droop

¹drop \'dräp\ *noun, often attributive* [Middle English, from Old English *dropa;* akin to Old High German *tropfo* drop] (before 12th century)
1 a (1) : the quantity of fluid that falls in one spherical mass (2) *plural* : a dose of medicine measured by drops; *especially* : a solution for dilating the pupil of the eye **b** : a minute quantity or degree of something nonmaterial or intangible **c** : a small quantity of drink **d** : the smallest practical unit of liquid measure
2 : something that resembles a liquid drop: as
a : a pendent ornament attached to a piece of jewelry; *also* : an earring with such a pendant
b : a small globular cookie or candy

3 [²*drop*] **a** : the act or an instance of dropping : FALL **b** : a decline in quantity or quality **c** : a descent by parachute; *also* : the people or equipment dropped by parachute **d** : a place or central depository to which something (as mail, money, or stolen property) is brought for distribution or transmission; *also* : the act of depositing something at such a place ⟨made the *drop*⟩
4 a : the distance from a higher to a lower level or through which something drops **b** : a fall of electric potential
5 : a slot into which something is to be dropped
6 [²*drop*] : something that drops, hangs, or falls: as **a** : a movable plate that covers the keyhole of a lock **b** : an unframed piece of cloth stage scenery; *also* : DROP CURTAIN **c** : a hinged platform on a gallows **d** : a fallen fruit
7 : the advantage of having an opponent covered with a firearm; *broadly* : ADVANTAGE, SUPERIORITY — usually used in the phrase *get the drop on*
— **at the drop of a hat** : as soon as the slightest provocation is given : IMMEDIATELY
— **drop in the bucket** : a part so small as to be negligible

²drop *verb* **dropped; drop·ping** (before 12th century)
intransitive verb
1 : to fall in drops
2 a (1) : to fall unexpectedly or suddenly (2) : to descend from one line or level to another **b** : to fall in a state of collapse or death **c** *of a card* : to become played by reason of the obligation to follow suit **d** *of a ball* : to fall or roll into a hole or basket
3 : to enter or pass as if without conscious effort of will into some state, condition, or activity ⟨*dropped* into sleep⟩
4 a : to cease to be of concern : LAPSE ⟨let the matter *drop*⟩ **b** : to pass from view or notice : DISAPPEAR — often used with *out* ⟨*drop* out of sight⟩ **c** : to become less ⟨production *dropped*⟩ — often used with *off*
5 : to move with a favoring wind or current — usually used with *down*
transitive verb
1 : to let fall : cause to fall
2 a : GIVE UP 2, ABANDON ⟨*drop* an idea⟩ ⟨*drop* the charges⟩ **b** : DISCONTINUE ⟨*dropped* what she was doing⟩ **c** : to break off an association or connection with : DISMISS ⟨*drop* a failing student⟩
3 a : to utter or mention in a casual way ⟨*drop* a suggestion⟩ ⟨*drop* names⟩ **b** : WRITE ⟨*drop* us a line soon⟩
4 a : to lower or cause to descend from one level or position to another **b** : to cause to lessen or decrease : REDUCE ⟨*dropped* his speed⟩
5 *of an animal* : to give birth to
6 a : LOSE ⟨*dropped* three games⟩ ⟨*dropped* $50 in a poker game⟩ **b** : SPEND ⟨*drop* $20 for lunch⟩
7 a : to bring down with a shot or a blow **b** : to cause (a high card) to fall **c** : to toss or roll into a hole or basket ⟨*drop* a putt⟩
8 a : to deposit or deliver during a usually brief stop — usually used with *off* ⟨*drop* the kids off at school⟩ **b** : AIR-DROP
9 : to cause (the voice) to be less loud
10 a : to leave (a letter representing a speech sound) unsounded ⟨*drop* the *g* in *running*⟩ **b** : to leave out in writing : OMIT
11 : to draw from an external point ⟨*drop* a perpendicular to the line⟩
12 : to take (a drug) orally : SWALLOW ⟨*drop* acid⟩
— **drop·pa·ble** \'drä-pə-bəl\ *adjective*
— **drop behind** : to fail to keep up

drop back *intransitive verb* (1927)
1 : RETREAT
2 : to move straight back from the line of scrimmage ⟨the quarterback *drops back* to pass⟩

drop by (circa 1905)
intransitive verb
: to pay a brief casual visit
transitive verb
: to visit casually or unexpectedly ⟨*drop by* a friend's house⟩

drop cloth *noun* (circa 1928)
: a protective sheet (as of cloth or plastic) used especially by painters to cover floors and furniture

drop curtain *noun* (1832)
: a stage curtain that can be lowered and raised

drop–dead *adjective* (1970)
: sensationally striking, attractive, or impressive ⟨a *drop-dead* evening gown⟩
— **drop–dead** *adverb*

drop–forge \'dräp-ˌfȯrj, -ˌfȯrj\ *transitive verb* (1886)
: to forge between dies by means of a drop hammer or punch press
— **drop forger** *noun*

drop front *noun* (1925)
: a hinged cover on the front of a desk that may be lowered to provide a surface for writing

drop hammer *noun* (circa 1864)
: a power hammer raised and then released to drop (as on metal resting on an anvil or die)

drop–head \'dräp-ˌhed\ *noun, often attributive* (1932)
British : a convertible automobile

drop–in \'dräp-ˌin\ *noun* (1819)
1 : a casual visit or brief stop
2 : one who drops in : a casual visitor

drop in *intransitive verb* (circa 1600)
: to pay an unexpected or casual visit — often used with *on*

drop·kick \-ˌkik\ *noun* (1857)
: a kick made by dropping a ball to the ground and kicking it at the moment it starts to rebound

drop–kick \-ˌkik\ (circa 1909)
intransitive verb
: to make a dropkick
transitive verb
: to kick by means of a dropkick ⟨*drop-kick* a ball⟩ ⟨*drop-kick* a field goal⟩
— **drop·kick·er** *noun*

drop leaf *noun* (1882)
: a hinged leaf on the side or end of a table that can be folded down

drop·let \'dräp-lət\ *noun* (1607)
: a tiny drop (as of a liquid)

drop·light \'dräp-ˌlīt\ *noun* (1890)
: an electric light suspended by a cord or on a portable extension

drop–off \'dräp-ˌȯf\ *noun* (1923)
1 : a very steep or perpendicular descent
2 : a marked dwindling or decline ⟨a *drop-off* in attendance⟩

drop off \ˌdräp-'ȯf\ *intransitive verb* (1820)
: to fall asleep

drop·out \'dräp-ˌaut\ *noun* (1930)
1 a : one who drops out of school **b** : one who drops out of conventional society **c** : one who abandons an attempt, activity, or chosen path ⟨a corporate *dropout*⟩
2 : a spot on a magnetic tape or disk from which data has disappeared

drop out \ˌdräp-'aut\ *intransitive verb* (1883)
: to withdraw from participation or membership : QUIT; *especially* : to withdraw from conventional society

drop pass *noun* (1949)
: a pass in ice hockey in which the passer skates past the puck leaving it for a teammate following close behind

dropped *adjective* (1953)

: designed to extend or begin lower than normal ⟨a dress with a *dropped* waist⟩ ⟨*dropped* shoulders⟩

dropped egg *noun* (1824)
: a poached egg

drop·per \'drä-pər\ *noun* (circa 1700)
1 : one that drops
2 : a short glass tube fitted with a rubber bulb and used to measure liquids by drops — called also *eyedropper, medicine dropper*
— **drop·per·ful** \-ˌful\ *noun*

drop·ping *noun* (14th century)
1 : something dropped
2 *plural* : DUNG

drop seat *noun* (1926)
1 : a hinged seat (as in a taxi) that may be dropped down
2 : a seat (as in an undergarment) that can be unbuttoned

drop shot *noun* (1908)
: a delicately hit shot (as in tennis or squash) that drops quickly after crossing the net or dies after hitting a wall

drop·si·cal \'dräp-si-kəl\ *adjective* (1678)
1 : relating to or affected with dropsy
2 : TURGID, SWOLLEN

drop·sy \'dräp-sē\ *noun* [Middle English *dropesie*, short for *ydropesie*, from Old French, from Latin *hydropisis*, modification of Greek *hydrōps*, from *hydōr* water — more at WATER] (13th century)
: EDEMA

drop tank *noun* (1943)
: an auxiliary fuel tank for airplanes that can be jettisoned when empty

drop volley *noun* (1907)
: a drop shot made on a volley in tennis

drop zone *noun* (circa 1943)
: the area in which troops, supplies, or equipment are to be air-dropped; *also* : the target on which a skydiver lands

drosh·ky \'dräsh-kē\ *also* **dros·ky** \'dräs-kē\ *noun, plural* **droshkies** *also* **droskies** [Russian *drozhki*, from *droga* pole of a wagon] (1808)
: any of various 2- or 4-wheeled carriages used especially in Russia

dro·soph·i·la \drō-'sä-fə-lə\ *noun* [New Latin, genus name, from Greek *drosos* dew + New Latin *-phila*, feminine of *-philus* -phil] (1910)
: any of a genus (*Drosophila*) of small two-winged flies used in genetic research

dross \'dräs, 'dròs\ *noun* [Middle English *dros*, from Old English *drōs* dregs] (before 12th century)
1 : the scum that forms on the surface of molten metal
2 : waste or foreign matter : IMPURITY
3 : something that is base, trivial, or inferior
— **drossy** \'drä-sē, 'dró-\ *adjective*

drought \'draut\ *also* **drouth** \'drauth\ *noun* [Middle English, from Old English *drūgath*, from *drūgian* to dry up; akin to Old English *drȳge* dry — more at DRY] (before 12th century)
1 : a period of dryness especially when prolonged that causes extensive damage to crops or prevents their successful growth
2 : a prolonged or chronic shortage or lack of something expected or desired
— **drought·i·ness** *noun*
— **droughty** \'drau-tē\ *adjective*

¹drove \'drōv\ *noun* [Middle English, from Old English *drāf*, from *drīfan* to drive — more at DRIVE] (before 12th century)
1 : a group of animals driven or moving in a body
2 : a large number : CROWD — usually used in plural especially with *in* ⟨tourists arriving in *droves*⟩ ⟨stayed away in *droves*⟩

²drove *past of* DRIVE

drov·er \'drō-vər\ *noun* (15th century)
: one that drives cattle or sheep

drown \'draun\ *verb* **drowned** \'draund\; **drown·ing** \'drau-nin\ [Middle English *drounen*] (14th century)

intransitive verb
: to become drowned
transitive verb
1 a : to suffocate by submersion especially in water **b** : to submerge especially by a rise in the water level **c** : to soak, drench, or cover with a liquid
2 : to engage (oneself) deeply and strenuously
3 : to cause (a sound) not to be heard by making a loud noise — usually used with *out*
4 a : to drive out (as a sensation or an idea) ⟨*drowned* his sorrows in liquor⟩ **b** : OVERWHELM

drownd \'draund\ *nonstandard variant of* DROWN

¹drowse \'drauz\ *verb* **drowsed; drows·ing** [probably akin to Gothic *driusan* to fall — more at DREARY] (1573)
intransitive verb
1 : to be inactive
2 : to fall into a light slumber
transitive verb
1 : to make drowsy or inactive
2 : to pass (time) drowsily or in drowsing

²drowse *noun* (1814)
: the act or an instance of drowsing : DOZE

drowsy \'drau-zē\ *adjective* **drows·i·er; -est** (1530)
1 a : ready to fall asleep **b** : inducing or tending to induce sleep **c** : INDOLENT, LETHARGIC
2 : giving the appearance of peaceful inactivity
— **drows·i·ly** \-zə-lē\ *adverb*
— **drows·i·ness** \-zē-nəs\ *noun*

drub \'drəb\ *verb* **drubbed; drub·bing** [perhaps from Arabic *ḍaraba*] (1634)
transitive verb
1 : to beat severely
2 : to abuse with words : BERATE
3 : to defeat decisively
intransitive verb
: DRUM, STAMP
— **drub·ber** *noun*
— **drub·bing** *noun*

¹drudge \'drəj\ *verb* **drudged; drudg·ing** [Middle English *druggen*] (14th century)
intransitive verb
: to do hard, menial, or monotonous work
transitive verb
: to force to do hard, menial, or monotonous work
— **drudg·er** *noun*

²drudge *noun* (15th century)
1 : one who is obliged to do menial work
2 : one whose work is routine and boring

drudg·ery \'drəj-rē, 'drə-jə-rē\ *noun, plural* **-er·ies** (1550)
: dull, irksome, and fatiguing work : uninspiring or menial labor
synonym see WORK

drudg·ing \'drə-jin\ *adjective* (1548)
: MONOTONOUS, TIRING
— **drudg·ing·ly** \-jin-lē\ *adverb*

¹drug \'drəg\ *noun* [Middle English *drogge*] (14th century)
1 a *obsolete* : a substance used in dyeing or chemical operations **b** : a substance used as a medication or in the preparation of medication **c** *according to the Food, Drug, and Cosmetic Act* (1) : a substance recognized in an official pharmacopoeia or formulary (2) : a substance intended for use in the diagnosis, cure, mitigation, treatment, or prevention of disease (3) : a substance other than food intended to affect the structure or function of the body (4) : a substance intended for use as a component of a medicine but not a device or a component, part, or accessory of a device
2 : a commodity that is not salable or for which there is no demand — used in the phrase *drug on the market*
3 : something and often an illegal substance that causes addiction, habituation, or a marked change in consciousness
— **drug·gy** *also* **drug·gie** \'drə-gē\ *adjective*

²drug *verb* **drugged; drug·ging** (1605)
transitive verb
1 : to affect with a drug; *especially* : to stupefy by a narcotic drug
2 : to administer a drug to
3 : to lull or stupefy as if with a drug
intransitive verb
: to take drugs for narcotic effect

³drug *dialect past of* DRAG

drug·get \'drə-gət\ *noun* [Middle French *droguet*, diminutive of *drogue* trash, drug] (1580)
1 : a wool or partly wool fabric formerly used for clothing
2 : a coarse durable cloth used chiefly as a floor covering
3 : a rug having a cotton warp and a wool filling

drug·gie *also* **drug·gy** \'drə-gē\ *noun, plural* **druggies** (1967)
: one who habitually uses drugs

drug·gist \'drə-gist\ *noun* (1611)
: one who sells or dispenses drugs and medicines: as **a** : PHARMACIST **b** : one who owns or manages a drugstore

drug·mak·er \'drəg-ˌmā-kər\ *noun* (1964)
: one that manufactures pharmaceuticals

drug·store \-ˌstōr, -ˌstòr\ *noun* (1810)
: a retail store where medicines and miscellaneous articles are sold : PHARMACY

drugstore cowboy *noun* (1925)
1 : one who wears cowboy clothes but has had no experience as a cowboy
2 : one who loafs on street corners and in drugstores

dru·id \'drü-id\ *noun, often capitalized* [Latin *druides, druidae*, plural, from Gaulish *druides*; akin to Old Irish *druí* druid, and perhaps to Old English *trēow* tree] (1563)
: one of an ancient Celtic priesthood appearing in Irish and Welsh sagas and Christian legends as magicians and wizards
— **dru·id·ic** \drü-'i-dik\ *or* **dru·id·i·cal** \-di-kəl\ *adjective, often capitalized*

dru·id·ism \'drü-ə-ˌdi-zəm\ *noun, often capitalized* (1715)
: the system of religion, philosophy, and instruction of the druids

¹drum \'drəm\ *noun* [probably from Dutch *trom*; akin to Middle High German *trumme* drum] (1539)
1 : a percussion instrument consisting of a hollow shell or cylinder with a drumhead stretched over one or both ends that is beaten with the hands or with some implement (as a stick or wire brush)
2 : TYMPANIC MEMBRANE

drum 1: *1* bass, *2* snare (orchestra), *3* snare (parade)

3 : the sound of a drum; *also* : a sound similar to that of a drum
4 : any of various bony fishes (family Sciaenidae) that make a drumming noise
5 : something resembling a drum in shape: as **a** : a cylindrical machine or mechanical device or part **b** : a cylindrical container; *specifically* : a large usually metal container for liquids ⟨a 55-gallon *drum*⟩ **c** : a disk-shaped magazine for an automatic weapon
— **drum·like** \-ˌlīk\ *adjective*

²drum *verb* **drummed; drum·ming** (1583)
intransitive verb
1 : to make a succession of strokes or vibrations that produce sounds like drumbeats
2 : to beat a drum
3 : to throb or sound rhythmically
4 : to stir up interest : SOLICIT
transitive verb
1 : to summon or enlist by or as if by beating a drum ⟨were *drummed* into service⟩

2 : to dismiss ignominiously **:** EXPEL — usually used with *out*
3 : to drive or force by steady effort or reiteration ⟨*drummed* the speech into her head⟩
4 a : to strike or tap repeatedly **b :** to produce (rhythmic sounds) by such action
³drum *noun* [Scottish Gaelic *druim* back, ridge, from Old Irish *druimm*] (1725)
1 *chiefly Scottish* **:** a long narrow hill or ridge
2 : DRUMLIN
drum·beat \'drəm-ˌbēt\ *noun* (1855)
1 : a stroke on a drum or its sound; *also* **:** a series of such strokes
2 : vociferous advocacy of a cause
3 : DRUMFIRE 2
— **drum·beat·er** \-ˌbē-tər\ *noun*
— **drum·beat·ing** \-tiŋ\ *noun*
drum brake *noun* (1950)
: a brake that operates by the friction of usually a pair of shoes pressing against the inner surface of the cylinder of a rotating drum — compare DISC BRAKE
drum·fire \'drəm-ˌfīr\ *noun* (1916)
1 : artillery firing so continuous as to sound like a drumroll
2 : something suggestive of drumfire in intensity **:** BARRAGE ⟨a *drumfire* of publicity⟩
drum·head \-ˌhed\ *noun* (1622)
1 : the material (as skin or plastic) stretched over one or both ends of a drum
2 : the top of a capstan that is pierced with sockets for the levers used in turning it
drumhead court-martial *noun* [from the use of a drumhead as a table] (1835)
: a summary court-martial that tries offenses on the battlefield
drum·lin \'drəm-lən\ *noun* [Irish *druim* back, ridge (from Old Irish *druimm*) + English *-lin* (alteration of *-ling*)] (circa 1833)
: an elongate or oval hill of glacial drift
drum major *noun* (1844)
: the leader of a marching band
drum ma·jor·ette \ˌdrəm-ˌmā-jə-'ret\ *noun* (1938)
1 : a girl or woman who leads a marching band
2 : a baton twirler who accompanies a marching band
drum·mer \'drə-mər\ *noun* (1580)
1 a : one that plays a drum **b** — used figuratively in expressions denoting an unconventional way of behaving or thinking ⟨march to a different *drummer*⟩
2 : TRAVELING SALESMAN
drum·roll \'drəm-ˌrōl\ *noun* (1887)
: a roll on a drum or its sound
drum·stick \-ˌstik\ *noun* (1589)
1 : a stick for beating a drum
2 : the segment of a fowl's leg between the thigh and tarsus
drum up *transitive verb* (1830)
1 : to bring about by persistent effort ⟨*drum up* some business⟩
2 : INVENT, ORIGINATE ⟨*drum up* a new method⟩
¹drunk *past participle of* DRINK
²drunk \'drəŋk\ *adjective* [Middle English *drunke*, alteration of *drunken*] (14th century)
1 a : having the faculties impaired by alcohol **b :** having a level of alcohol in the blood that exceeds a maximum prescribed by law ⟨legally *drunk*⟩
2 : dominated by an intense feeling ⟨*drunk* with rage⟩
3 : of, relating to, or caused by intoxication **:** DRUNKEN
³drunk *noun* (1779)
1 : a period of drinking to intoxication or of being intoxicated ⟨a 2-day *drunk*⟩
2 : one who is drunk; *especially* **:** DRUNKARD
drunk·ard \'drəŋ-kərd\ *noun* (15th century)
: one who is habitually drunk
drunk·en \'drəŋ-kən\ *adjective* [Middle English, from Old English *druncen*, from past participle of *drincan* to drink] (before 12th century)
1 : DRUNK 1 ⟨a *drunken* driver⟩

2 *obsolete* **:** saturated with liquid
3 a : given to habitual excessive use of alcohol **b :** of, relating to, or characterized by intoxication ⟨they come from . . . broken homes, *drunken* homes —P. B. Gilliam⟩ **c :** resulting from or as if from intoxication ⟨a *drunken* brawl⟩
4 : unsteady or lurching as if from alcoholic intoxication
— **drunk·en·ly** *adverb*
— **drunk·en·ness** \-kən-nəs\ *noun*
drunk tank *noun* (1947)
: a large detention cell for arrested drunks
dru·pa·ceous \drü-'pā-shəs\ *adjective* (1822)
1 : of or relating to a drupe
2 : bearing drupes
drupe \'drüp\ *noun* [New Latin *drupa*, from Latin, overripe olive, from Greek *dryppa* olive] (circa 1753)
: a one-seeded indehiscent fruit having a hard bony endocarp, a fleshy mesocarp, and a thin exocarp that is flexible (as in the cherry) or dry and almost leathery (as in the almond)
drupe·let \'drü-plət\ *noun* (1880)
: a small drupe; *specifically* **:** one of the individual parts of an aggregate fruit (as the raspberry)
druth·ers \'drə-thərz\ *noun plural* [*druther*, alteration of *would rather*] (1875)
dialect **:** free choice **:** PREFERENCE — used especially in the phrase *if one had one's druthers*
Druze or **Druse** \'drüz\ *noun, plural* **Druze** or **Druzes** or **Druse** or **Druses** *often attributive* [Arabic *Durūz*, plural, from Muḥammed ibn-Isma'īl al-*Darazīy* (died 1019) Muslim religious leader] (1786)
: a member of a religious sect originating among Muslims and centered in the mountains of Lebanon and Syria
¹dry \'drī\ *adjective* **dri·er** *also* **dry·er** \'drī(-ə)r\; **dri·est** *also* **dry·est** \'drī-əst\ [Middle English, from Old English *drȳge*; akin to Old High German *truckan* dry, Old English *drēahnian* to drain] (before 12th century)
1 a : free or relatively free from a liquid and especially water **b :** not being in or under water ⟨*dry* land⟩ **c :** lacking precipitation or humidity ⟨*dry* climate⟩
2 a : characterized by exhaustion of a supply of liquid ⟨a *dry* well⟩ **b :** devoid of running water ⟨a *dry* ravine⟩ **c :** devoid of natural moisture ⟨my throat was *dry*⟩ **d :** no longer sticky or damp ⟨the paint is *dry*⟩ **e :** not giving milk ⟨a *dry* cow⟩ **f :** lacking freshness **:** STALE **g :** ANHYDROUS
3 a : marked by the absence or scantiness of secretions ⟨a *dry* cough⟩ **b :** not shedding or accompanied by tears ⟨a *dry* sob⟩
4 *obsolete* **:** involving no bloodshed or drowning ⟨I would fain die a *dry* death —Shakespeare⟩
5 a : marked by the absence of alcoholic beverages ⟨a *dry* party⟩ **b :** prohibiting the manufacture or distribution of alcoholic beverages
6 : served or eaten without butter or margarine ⟨*dry* toast⟩
7 a : lacking sweetness **:** SEC ⟨*dry* champagne⟩ **b :** having all or most sugar fermented to alcohol ⟨a *dry* wine⟩ ⟨*dry* beer⟩
8 a : solid as opposed to liquid ⟨*dry* groceries⟩ **b :** reduced to powder or flakes **:** DEHYDRATED ⟨*dry* milk⟩
9 : functioning without lubrication ⟨a *dry* clutch⟩
10 *of natural gas* **:** containing no recoverable hydrocarbon (as gasoline)
11 : requiring no liquid in preparation or operation ⟨a *dry* photocopying process⟩
12 a : not showing or communicating warmth, enthusiasm, or tender feeling **:** SEVERE ⟨a *dry* style of painting⟩ **b :** WEARISOME, UNINTERESTING ⟨*dry* passages of description⟩ **c :** lacking embellishment **:** PLAIN ⟨the *dry* facts⟩
13 a : not yielding what is expected or desired **:** UNPRODUCTIVE **b :** having no personal bias or emotional concern ⟨the *dry* light of reason⟩ **c :** RESERVED, ALOOF

14 : marked by matter-of-fact, ironic, or terse manner of expression ⟨*dry* wit⟩
15 : lacking smooth sound qualities ⟨a *dry* rasping voice⟩
16 : being a dry run ⟨a *dry* rehearsal⟩
— **dry·ish** \'drī-ish\ *adjective*
— **dry·ly** *adverb*
— **dry·ness** *noun*
²dry *verb* **dried; dry·ing** (before 12th century)
transitive verb
: to make dry
intransitive verb
: to become dry
— **dry·able** \'drī-ə-bəl\ *adjective*
³dry *noun, plural* **drys** (13th century)
1 : the condition of being dry **:** DRYNESS
2 : something dry; *especially* **:** a dry place
3 : PROHIBITIONIST
dry·ad \'drī-əd, -ˌad\ *noun* [Latin *dryad-, dryas*, from Greek, from *drys* tree — more at TREE] (14th century)
: WOOD NYMPH
dry-as-dust \'drī-əz-ˌdəst\ *adjective* (circa 1872)
: BORING
— **dryasdust** *noun*
dry cell *noun* (1893)
: a voltaic cell whose contents are not spillable — called also *dry battery*
dry-clean \'drī-ˌklēn\ *transitive verb* (1817)
transitive verb
: to subject to dry cleaning
intransitive verb
: to undergo dry cleaning
— **dry-clean·able** \-ˌklē-nə-bəl\ *adjective*
dry cleaner *noun* (1897)
: one whose business is dry cleaning
dry cleaning *noun* (1897)
1 : the cleansing of fabrics with substantially nonaqueous organic solvents
2 : something that is dry-cleaned
dry-dock \'drī-ˌdäk\ *transitive verb* (1884)
: to place in a dry dock
dry dock *noun* (circa 1627)
: a dock that can be kept dry for use during the construction or repairing of ships
dry·er *variant of* DRIER
dry-eyed \'drī-ˌīd\ *adjective* (1667)
1 : not moved to tears or to empathy
2 : marked by the absence of sentimentalism or romanticism
dry farming *noun* (1878)
: farming on nonirrigated land with little rainfall that relies on moisture-conserving tillage and drought-resistant crops
— **dry-farm** *transitive verb*
— **dry farm** *noun*
— **dry farmer** *noun*
dry fly *noun* (1846)
: an artificial angling fly designed to float
Dry-gas \'drī-ˌgas\ *trademark*
— used for fuel-line antifreeze for motor vehicles
dry goods \'drī-ˌgu̇dz\ *noun plural* (1657)
: textiles, ready-to-wear clothing, and notions as distinguished especially from hardware and groceries
dry hole *noun* (1883)
: a well (as for gas or oil) that proves unproductive
dry ice *noun* (1925)
: solidified carbon dioxide
drying oil *noun* (circa 1865)
: an oil (as linseed oil) that changes readily to a hard tough elastic substance when exposed in a thin film to air
dry·land \'drī-ˌland\ *adjective* (1893)
: of, relating to, or being a relatively arid region ⟨a *dryland* wheat state⟩; *also* **:** of, adapted

to, practicing, or being agricultural methods (as dry farming) suited to such a region

dry·lot \'drī-,lät\ *noun* (1924)
: an enclosure of limited size usually bare of vegetation and used for fattening livestock

dry measure *noun* (1688)
: a series of units of capacity for dry commodities — see METRIC SYSTEM table, WEIGHT table

dry mop *noun* (1933)
: a long-handled mop for dusting floors

dry–nurse *transitive verb* (1581)
1 : to act as dry nurse to
2 : to give unnecessary supervision to

dry nurse *noun* (1598)
: a nurse who takes care of but does not breast-feed another woman's baby

dryo·pith·e·cine \,drī-ō-'pi-thə-,sīn\ *noun* [ultimately from Greek *drys* tree + *pithēkos* ape] (1948)
: any of a subfamily (Dryopithecinae) of Miocene and Pliocene Old World anthropoid apes sometimes regarded as ancestors of both man and modern anthropoids
— **dryopithecine** *adjective*

dry out *intransitive verb* (1892)
: to undergo an extended period of withdrawal from alcohol or drug use especially at a special clinic

dry·point \'drī-,point\ *noun* (1883)
: an engraving made with a steel or jeweled point directly into the metal plate without the use of acid as in etching; *also* : a print made from such an engraving

dry–rot (1870)
transitive verb
: to affect with dry rot
intransitive verb
: to become affected with dry rot

dry rot *noun* (1795)
1 a : a decay of seasoned timber caused by fungi that consume the cellulose of wood leaving a soft skeleton which is readily reduced to powder **b** : a fungal rot of plant tissue in which the affected areas are dry and often firmer than normal or more or less mummified
2 : a fungus causing dry rot
3 : decay from within caused especially by resistance to new forces

dry run *noun* (circa 1941)
1 : a practice exercise : REHEARSAL, TRIAL
2 : a practice firing without ammunition

dry·salt·er \'drī-,sȯl-tər\ *noun* (1707)
British : a dealer in crude dry chemicals and dyes
— **dry·salt·ery** \-tə-rē\ *noun, British*

dry–shod \'drī-,shäd\ *adjective* (15th century)
: having dry shoes or feet

dry sink *noun* (1951)
: a wooden cabinet with a tray top for holding a wash basin

dry·stone \'drī-,stōn\ *adjective* (circa 1702)
chiefly British : constructed of stone without the use of mortar as an adhesive ⟨a *drystone* wall⟩

dry suit *noun* (1955)
: a close-fitting air-insulated waterproof suit for divers

dry up (14th century)
transitive verb
: to cut off the supply of
intransitive verb
1 : to disappear as if by evaporation, draining, or cutting off of a source of supply
2 : to wither or die through gradual loss of vitality
3 : to stop talking

dry·wall \'drī-,wȯl\ *noun* (1952)
: PLASTERBOARD

dry wash *noun* (1872)
West : WASH 1d

dry well *noun* (circa 1942)
: a hole in the ground filled with gravel or rubble to receive drainage water and allow it to percolate away

d.t.'s \,dē-'tēz\ *noun plural, often D&T capitalized* (1858)
: DELIRIUM TREMENS

¹du·al \'dü-(ə)l *also* 'dyü-əl\ *adjective* [Latin *dualis*, from *duo* two — more at TWO] (1607)
1 *of grammatical number* : denoting reference to two
2 a : consisting of two parts or elements or having two like parts : DOUBLE **b** : having a double character or nature
— **du·al·ly** \-ə(l)-lē\ *adverb*

²dual *noun* (1650)
1 : the dual number of a language
2 : a linguistic form in the dual

dual carriageway *noun* (1933)
chiefly British : a divided highway

dual citizenship *noun* (circa 1924)
: the status of an individual who is a citizen of two or more nations

du·al·ism \'dü-ə-,li-zəm *also* 'dyü-\ *noun* (1794)
1 : a theory that considers reality to consist of two irreducible elements or modes
2 : the quality or state of being dual or of having a dual nature
3 a : a doctrine that the universe is under the dominion of two opposing principles one of which is good and the other evil **b** : a view of human beings as constituted of two irreducible elements (as matter and spirit)
— **du·al·ist** \-list\ *noun*
— **du·al·is·tic** \,dü-ə-'lis-tik, ,dyü-\ *adjective*
— **du·al·is·ti·cal·ly** \-ti-k(ə-)lē\ *adverb*

du·al·i·ty \dü-'a-lə-tē *also* dyü-\ *noun, plural* **-ties** (15th century)
: DUALISM 2; *also* : DICHOTOMY

du·al·ize \'dü-ə-,līz *also* 'dyü-\ *transitive verb* **-ized; -iz·ing** (1838)
: to make dual

dual–purpose *adjective* (1904)
: having breed characteristics that serve two purposes ⟨*dual-purpose* cattle that supply milk and meat⟩

¹dub \'dəb\ *transitive verb* **dubbed; dub·bing** [Middle English *dubben*, from Old English *dubbian*; akin to Old Norse *dubba* to dub, Old High German *tubili* plug] (before 12th century)
1 a : to confer knighthood on **b** : to call by a distinctive title, epithet, or nickname
2 : to trim or remove the comb and wattles of
3 a : to hit (a golf ball) poorly **b** : to execute poorly
— **dub·ber** *noun*

²dub *noun* (1887)
: one who is inept or clumsy

³dub *noun* [Middle English (Scots dialect) *dubbe*] (15th century)
chiefly Scottish : POOL, PUDDLE

⁴dub *transitive verb* **dubbed; dub·bing** [by shortening & alteration from *double*] (1930)
1 : to add (sound effects or new dialogue) to a film or to a radio or television production — usually used with *in*
2 : to provide (a motion-picture film) with a new sound track and especially dialogue in a different language
3 : to make a new recording of (sound or videotape already recorded); *also* : to mix (recorded sound or videotape from different sources) into a single recording
— **dubber** *noun*

⁵dub *noun* (1974)
: Jamaican pop music in which audio effects and spoken or chanted words are imposed on an instrumental reggae background

dub·bin \'də-bən\ *also* **dub·bing** \-bən, -biŋ\ *noun* [*dubbing*, gerund of *dub* (to dress leather)] (1781)
: a dressing of oil and tallow for leather

du·bi·ety \dü-'bī-ət-ē *also* dyü-\ *noun, plural* **-eties** [Late Latin *dubietas*, from Latin *dubius*] (1750)
1 : a usually hesitant uncertainty or doubt that tends to cause vacillation
2 : a matter of doubt
synonym see UNCERTAINTY

du·bi·ous \'dü-bē-əs *also* dyü-\ *adjective* [Latin *dubius*, from *dubare* to vacillate; akin to Latin *duo* two — more at TWO] (1548)
1 : giving rise to uncertainty: as **a** : of doubtful promise or outcome ⟨felt that our plan was a little *dubious*⟩ **b** : questionable or suspect as to true nature or quality ⟨the practice is of *dubious* legality⟩ ⟨the *dubious* honor of being the world's biggest polluter⟩
2 : unsettled in opinion : DOUBTFUL ⟨I was *dubious* about the plan⟩
synonym see DOUBTFUL
— **du·bi·ous·ly** *adverb*
— **du·bi·ous·ness** *noun*

du·bi·ta·ble \'dü-bə-tə-bəl *also* 'dyü-\ *adjective* [Latin *dubitabilis*, from *dubitare* to doubt — more at DOUBT] (circa 1616)
: open to doubt or question

du·bi·ta·tion \,d(y)ü-bə-'tā-shən\ *noun* (15th century)
archaic : DOUBT

du·cal \'dü-kəl *also* 'dyü-\ *adjective* [Middle English, from Middle French, from Late Latin *ducalis* of a leader, from Latin *duc-, dux* leader — more at DUKE] (15th century)
: of or relating to a duke or dukedom
— **du·cal·ly** \-kə-lē\ *adverb*

duc·at \'də-kət\ *noun* [Middle English, from Middle French, from Old Italian *ducato* coin with the doge's portrait on it, from *duca* doge, from Late Greek *douk-, doux* leader, from Latin *duc-, dux*] (14th century)
1 : a usually gold coin formerly used in various European countries
2 : TICKET 2

du·ce \'dü-(,)chā\ *noun* [Italian (*Il*) *Duce*, literally, the leader, title of Benito Mussolini, from Latin *duc-, dux*] (1923)
: LEADER — used especially for the leader of the Italian Fascist party

Du·chenne \dü-'shen, də-\ *also* **Du·chenne's** \-'shenz\ *adjective* [Guillaume Armand *Duchenne* (died 1875) French neurologist] (circa 1882)
: relating to or being a severe form of muscular dystrophy of males that affects the muscles of the pelvic and shoulder girdles and the pectoral muscles first and is inherited as a sex-linked recessive trait

duch·ess \'də-chəs\ *noun* [Middle English *duchesse*, from Middle French, from *duc* duke] (14th century)
1 : the wife or widow of a duke
2 : a woman who holds the rank of duke in her own right
usage see -ESS

duchy \'də-chē\ *noun, plural* **duch·ies** [Middle English *duche*, from Middle French *duché*, from *duc*] (14th century)
1 : the territory of a duke or duchess : DUKEDOM
2 : special domain

¹duck \'dək\ *noun, plural* **ducks** *often attributive* [Middle English *duk, doke*, from Old English *dūce*] (before 12th century)
1 *or plural* **duck a** : any of various swimming birds (family Anatidae, the duck family) in which the neck and legs are short, the body more or less depressed, the bill often broad and flat, and the sexes almost always different from each other in plumage **b** : the flesh of any of these birds used as food
2 : a female duck — compare DRAKE
3 *chiefly British* : DARLING — often used in plural but sing. in construction
4 : PERSON, CREATURE

²duck *verb* [Middle English *douken*; akin to Old High German *tūhhan* to dive, Old English *dūce* duck] (14th century)
transitive verb
1 : to thrust under water
2 : to lower (as the head) quickly : BOW
3 : AVOID, EVADE ⟨*duck* the issue⟩
intransitive verb
1 a : to plunge under the surface of water **b** : to descend suddenly : DIP

2 a : to lower the head or body suddenly **:** DODGE **b :** BOW, BOB **3 a :** to move quickly **b :** to evade a duty, question, or responsibility — **duck·er** noun

³duck noun (1554) **:** an instance of ducking

⁴duck noun [Dutch *doek* cloth; akin to Old High German *tuoh* cloth] (1640) **1 :** a durable closely woven usually cotton fabric **2** *plural* **:** light clothes and especially trousers made of duck

duck·bill \'dək-ˌbil\ noun (1840) **1 :** PLATYPUS **2 :** HADROSAUR

duck–billed dinosaur noun (circa 1928) **:** HADROSAUR

duck–billed platypus *also* **duckbill platypus** noun (1799) **:** PLATYPUS

duck·board \-ˌbōrd, -ˌbȯrd\ noun (1917) **:** a boardwalk or slatted flooring laid on a wet, muddy, or cold surface — usually used in plural

duck call noun (1872) **:** a device for imitating the calls of ducks

duck hook noun (1973) **:** a pronounced and unintended hook in golf

ducking stool noun (1597) **:** a seat attached to a plank and formerly used to plunge culprits tied to it into water

duck·ling \'dək-liŋ, 'də-kliŋ\ noun (15th century) **:** a young duck

duck·pin \-ˌpin\ noun (circa 1911) **1 :** a small bowling pin shorter than a tenpin but proportionally wider at mid-diameter **2** *plural but singular in construction* **:** a bowling game using duckpins

ducks and drakes *or* **duck and drake** noun (1583) **:** the pastime of skimming flat stones or shells along the surface of calm water — **play ducks and drakes with** *or* **make ducks and drakes of :** to use recklessly **:** SQUANDER ⟨played ducks and drakes with his money⟩

duck soup noun (1912) **:** something easy to do

duck·tail \'dək-ˌtāl\ noun [from its resemblance to the tail of a duck] (1948) **:** a hairstyle in which the hair on each side is slicked back to meet in a ridge at the back of the head

duck·walk \'dək-ˌwȯk\ *intransitive verb* (1950) **:** to walk while in a crouch or full squatting position

duck·weed \'dək-ˌwēd\ noun (15th century) **:** a small floating aquatic monocotyledonous plant (family Lemnaceae, the duckweed family)

ducky \'də-kē\ adjective **duck·i·er; -est** (1897) **1 :** DARLING, CUTE ⟨a *ducky* little tearoom⟩ **2 :** SATISFACTORY, FINE ⟨everything is just *ducky*⟩

duck 1a (male): *1* bean, *2* bill, *3* nostril, *4* head, *5* eye, *6* auricular region, *7* neck, *8* cape, *9* shoulder, *10, 11* wing coverts, *12* saddle, *13* secondaries, *14* primaries, *15* rump, *16* drake feathers, *17* tail, *18* tail coverts, *19* down, *20* shank, *21* web, *22* breast, *23* wing front, *24* wing bow

ducktail

¹duct \'dəkt\ noun [New Latin *ductus,* from Medieval Latin, aqueduct, from Latin, act of leading, from *ducere* to lead — more at TOW] (1667) **1 :** a bodily tube or vessel especially when carrying the secretion of a gland **2 a :** a pipe, tube, or channel that conveys a substance **b :** a pipe or tubular runway for carrying an electric power line, telephone cables, or other conductors **3 a :** a continuous tube formed in plant tissue by a row of elongated cells that have lost their intervening end walls **b :** an elongated cavity (as a resin canal of a conifer) formed by disintegration or separation of cells **4 :** a layer (as in the atmosphere or the ocean) which occurs under usually abnormal conditions and in which radio or sound waves are confined to a restricted path — **duct·al** \'dək-tᵊl\ adjective — **duct·less** \'dək(t)-ləs\ adjective

²duct transitive verb (1936) **1 :** to enclose in a duct **2 :** to convey (as a gas) through a duct; *also* **:** to propagate (as radio waves) through a duct

duc·tile \'dək-tᵊl, -ˌtīl\ adjective [Middle French & Latin; Middle French, from Latin *ductilis,* from *ducere*] (14th century) **1 :** capable of being drawn out or hammered thin ⟨*ductile* iron⟩ **2 :** easily led or influenced **3 :** capable of being fashioned into a new form **synonym** see PLASTIC — **duc·til·i·ty** \ˌdək-'ti-lə-tē\ noun

duct·ing \'dək-tiŋ\ noun (1945) **:** a system of ducts; *also* **:** the material composing a duct

ductless gland noun (circa 1852) **:** ENDOCRINE GLAND

duct tape \'dək(t)-\ noun (1970) **:** a wide silvery cloth adhesive tape designed for sealing joints in heating or air-conditioning ducts

duct·ule \'dək-(ˌ)chül\ noun (1883) **:** a small duct

duc·tus ar·te·ri·o·sus \'dək-təs-är-ˌtir-ē-'ō-səs\ noun [New Latin, literally, arterial duct] (1811) **:** a short broad vessel in the fetus that connects the pulmonary artery with the aorta and conducts most of the blood directly from the right ventricle to the aorta bypassing the lungs

duct·work \'dək-ˌwərk\ noun (1934) **:** DUCTING

¹dud \'dəd\ noun [Middle English *dudde*] (1567) **1** *plural* **a :** CLOTHING **b :** personal belongings **2 a :** one that is ineffectual; *also* **:** FAILURE ⟨a box-office *dud*⟩ **b :** MISFIT **3 :** a bomb or missile that fails to explode

²dud adjective (1903) **:** of little or no worth **:** VALUELESS ⟨*dud* checks⟩

dud·die *or* **dud·dy** \'də-dē\ adjective (1718) *Scottish* **:** RAGGED, TATTERED

¹dude \'düd *also* 'dyüd\ noun [origin unknown] (1883) **1 :** a man extremely fastidious in dress and manner **:** DANDY **2 :** a city dweller unfamiliar with life on the range; *especially* **:** an Easterner in the West **3 :** FELLOW, GUY — **dud·ish** \'d(y)üd-ish\ adjective — **dud·ish·ly** adverb

²dude transitive verb **dud·ed; dud·ing** (1899) **:** DRESS UP — usually used with *up*

du·deen \dü-'dēn\ noun [Irish *dúidín,* diminutive of *dúd* pipe] (1841) **:** a short tobacco pipe made of clay

dude ranch noun (1921) **:** a vacation resort offering activities (as horseback riding) typical of western ranches

¹dud·geon \'də-jən\ noun [Middle English *dogeon,* from Anglo-French *digeon*] (15th century) **1** *obsolete* **:** a wood used especially for dagger hilts **2 a** *archaic* **:** a dagger with a handle of dudgeon **b** *obsolete* **:** a haft made of dudgeon

²dudgeon noun [origin unknown] (1573) **:** a fit or state of indignation — often used in the phrase *in high dudgeon* **synonym** see OFFENSE

¹due \'dü, 'dyü\ adjective [Middle English, from Middle French *deu,* past participle of *devoir* to owe, from Latin *debēre* — more at DEBT] (14th century) **1 :** owed or owing as a debt **2 a :** owed or owing as a natural or moral right ⟨everyone's right to dissent . . . is *due* the full protection of the Constitution —Nat Hentoff⟩ **b :** according to accepted notions or procedures **:** APPROPRIATE **3 a :** satisfying or capable of satisfying a need, obligation, or duty **:** ADEQUATE **b :** REGULAR, LAWFUL ⟨*due* proof of loss⟩ **4 :** capable of being attributed **:** ASCRIBABLE — used with *to* ⟨this advance is partly *due* to a few men of genius —A. N. Whitehead⟩ **5 :** having reached the date at which payment is required **:** PAYABLE **6 :** required or expected in the prescribed, normal, or logical course of events **:** SCHEDULED; *also* **:** expected to give birth — **due·ness** noun

²due noun (15th century) **:** something due or owed: as **a :** something that rightfully belongs to one **b :** a payment or obligation required by law or custom **:** DEBT **c** *plural* **:** FEES, CHARGES

³due adverb (1582) **1 :** DIRECTLY, EXACTLY ⟨*due* north⟩ **2** *obsolete* **:** DULY

due diligence noun (1903) **:** the care that a reasonable person exercises under the circumstances to avoid harm to other persons or their property

¹du·el \'dü-əl *also* 'dyü-\ noun [Middle English, from Medieval Latin *duellum,* from Old Latin, war] (15th century) **1 :** a combat between two persons; *specifically* **:** a formal combat with weapons fought between two persons in the presence of witnesses **2 :** a conflict between antagonistic persons, ideas, or forces; *also* **:** a hard-fought contest between two opponents

²duel verb **du·eled** *or* **du·elled; du·el·ing** *or* **du·el·ling** (circa 1645) *intransitive verb* **:** to fight a duel *transitive verb* **:** to encounter (an opponent) in a duel — **du·el·er** *or* **du·el·ler** noun — **du·el·ist** *or* **du·el·list** \'dü-ə-list\ noun

du·el·lo \d(y)ü-'e-(ˌ)lō\ noun, plural **-los** [Italian, from Medieval Latin *duellum*] (1588) **1 :** the rules or practice of dueling **2 :** DUEL

du·en·de \dü-'en-(ˌ)dā\ noun [Spanish dialect, charm, from Spanish, ghost, goblin, probably from *duen de casa,* from *dueño de casa* owner of a house] (1964) **:** the power to attract through personal magnetism and charm

du·en·na \dü-'e-nə, 'dyü-\ noun [Spanish *dueña,* from Latin *domina* mistress — more at DAME] (1623) **1 :** an elderly woman serving as governess and companion to the younger ladies in a Spanish or a Portuguese family **2 :** CHAPERON — **du·en·na·ship** \-ˌship\ noun

due process noun (1791)

1 : a course of formal proceedings (as legal proceedings) carried out regularly and in accordance with established rules and principles — called also *procedural due process*

2 : a judicial requirement that enacted laws may not contain provisions that result in the unfair, arbitrary, or unreasonable treatment of an individual — called also *substantive due process*

¹**du·et** \dü-'et *also* dyü-\ *noun* [Italian *duetto*, diminutive of *duo*] (circa 1740)
: a composition for two performers

²**duet** *intransitive verb* **du·et·ted; du·et·ting** (1822)
: to perform a duet

due to *preposition* (1897)
: as a result of : BECAUSE OF ⟨*due to* the complaints of uptight parents . . . he lost his job —Herbert Gold⟩ □

¹**duff** \'dəf\ *noun* [English dialect, alteration of *dough*] (1816)
1 : a boiled or steamed pudding often containing dried fruit
2 : the partly decayed organic matter on the forest floor
3 : fine coal : SLACK

²**duff** *noun* [origin unknown] (circa 1888)
: BUTTOCKS ⟨get off your *duff*⟩

³**duff** *adjective* [*duff*, noun, something worthless, from ¹*duff*] (circa 1889)
British : INFERIOR, WORTHLESS

duf·fel *or* **duf·fle** \'də-fəl\ *noun* [Dutch *duffel*, from *Duffel*, Belgium] (1677)
1 : a coarse heavy woolen material with a thick nap
2 : transportable personal belongings, equipment, and supplies
3 : DUFFEL BAG
4 : DUFFLE COAT

duffel bag *noun* (1917)
: a large cylindrical fabric bag for personal belongings

duf·fer \'də-fər\ *noun* [perhaps from *duff*, noun, something worthless] (1756)
1 a : a peddler especially of cheap flashy articles **b** : something counterfeit or worthless
2 : an incompetent, ineffectual, or clumsy person; *especially* : a mediocre golfer
3 *Australian* : a cattle rustler

duffle coat \'də-fəl-\ *or* **duffel coat** *noun* (1684)
: a heavy usually woolen medium-length coat with toggle fasteners and a hood

¹**dug** *past and past participle of* DIG

²**dug** \'dəg\ *noun* [perhaps of Scandinavian origin; akin to Old Swedish *dæggia* to suckle; akin to Old English *delu* nipple — more at FEMININE] (1530)
: UDDER; *also* : TEAT — usually used of a suckling animal; usually considered vulgar when used of a woman

du·gong \'dü-,gäŋ, -,gòŋ\ *noun* [New Latin, genus name, modification of Malay *duyong* dugong] (1800)
: an aquatic herbivorous mammal of a monotypic genus (*Dugong*) that has a bilobed tail and in the male upper incisors altered into short tusks, is related to the manatee, and inhabits warm coastal regions — called also *sea cow*

dugong

dug·out \'dəg-,aut\ *noun* (1819)
1 : a boat made by hollowing out a large log
2 a : a shelter dug in a hillside; *also* : a shelter dug in the ground and roofed with sod **b** : an area in the side of a trench for quarters, storage, or protection

3 : either of two low shelters on either side of and facing a baseball diamond that contain the players' benches

dui·ker \'dī-kər\ *noun* [Afrikaans, literally, diver, from *duik* to dive, from Middle Dutch *dūken;* akin to Old High German *tūhhan* to dive — more at DUCK] (1777)
: any of several small African antelopes comprising two genera (*Cephalophus* and *Sylvicapra*)

duit *variant of* DOIT

du jour \dü-'zhər, də-, -'zhùr, -'zhür\ *adjective* [French, literally, of the day] (1969)
1 : made for a particular day — used of an item not specified on the regular menu ⟨soup *du jour*⟩
2 : popular, fashionable, or prominent at a particular time ⟨the buzzword *du jour*⟩

¹**duke** \'dük *also* 'dyük\ *noun* [Middle English, from Old French *duc*, from Latin *duc-*, *dux*, from *ducere* to lead — more at TOW] (12th century)
1 : a sovereign male ruler of a continental European duchy
2 : a nobleman of the highest hereditary rank; *especially* : a member of the highest grade of the British peerage
3 [probably from *dukes of York*, rhyming slang for *fork* (hand, fist)] *slang* : FIST, HAND — usually used in plural
— **duke·dom** \-dəm\ *noun*

²**duke** *intransitive verb* **duked; duk·ing** (circa 1947)
: FIGHT
— **duke it out** : to engage in a fight and especially a fistfight

Du·kho·bor *variant of* DOUKHOBOR

dul·cet \'dəl-sət\ *adjective* [Middle English *doucet*, from Middle French, from *douz* sweet, from Latin *dulcis;* perhaps akin to Greek *glykys* sweet] (14th century)
1 : sweet to the taste
2 : pleasing to the ear
3 : generally pleasing or agreeable
— **dul·cet·ly** *adverb*

dul·ci·fy \'dəl-sə-,fī\ *transitive verb* **-fied; -fy·ing** [Late Latin *dulcificare*, from Latin *dulcis*] (1599)
1 : to make sweet
2 : to make agreeable : MOLLIFY

dul·ci·mer \'dəl-sə-mər\ *noun* [Middle English *dowcemere*, from Middle French *doulcemer*, from Old Italian *dolcimelo*, from *dolce* sweet, from Latin *dulcis*] (15th century)
1 : a stringed instrument of trapezoidal shape played with light hammers held in the hands
2 *or* **dul·ci·more** \-,mōr, -,mór\ : an American folk instrument with three or four strings stretched over an elongate fretted sound box that is held on the lap and played by plucking or strumming

dul·ci·nea \,dəl-sə-'nē-ə, -'si-nē-ə\ *noun* [Spanish, from *Dulcinea* del Toboso, beloved of Don Quixote] (1748)
: MISTRESS, SWEETHEART

¹**dull** \'dəl\ *adjective* [Middle English *dul;* akin to Old English *dol* foolish, Old Irish *dall* blind] (13th century)
1 : mentally slow : STUPID
2 a : slow in perception or sensibility : INSENSIBLE **b** : lacking zest or vivacity : LISTLESS
3 : slow in action : SLUGGISH
4 a : lacking in force, intensity, or sharpness **b** : not resonant or ringing ⟨a *dull* booming sound⟩
5 : lacking sharpness of edge or point
6 : lacking brilliance or luster
7 *of a color* : low in saturation and low in lightness
8 : CLOUDY
9 : TEDIOUS, UNINTERESTING ☆
— **dull·ness** *or* **dul·ness** \'dəl-nəs\ *noun*
— **dul·ly** \'də(l)-lē\ *adverb*

²**dull** (13th century)
transitive verb
: to make dull

intransitive verb
: to become dull

dull·ard \'də-lərd\ *noun* (15th century)
: a stupid or unimaginative person

dull·ish \'də-lish\ *adjective* (14th century)
: somewhat dull
— **dull·ish·ly** *adverb*

dulls·ville \'dəlz-,vil\ *noun* (circa 1960)
: something or some place that is dull or boring; *also* : BOREDOM

dulse \'dəls\ *noun* [modification of Scottish Gaelic *duileasg;* akin to Welsh *delysg* dulse] (circa 1698)
: any of several coarse red seaweeds (especially *Palmaria palmata* synonym *Rhodymenia palmata*) found especially in northern latitudes and used as a food condiment

du·ly \'dü-lē *also* 'dyü-\ *adverb* (14th century)
: in a due manner or time : PROPERLY

du·ma \'dü-mə, -(,)mä\ *noun* [Russian, from Old Russian, council, thought, probably of Germanic origin; akin to Old English *dōm* judgment — more at DOOM] (circa 1870)
: a representative council in Russia; *especially, often capitalized* : the principal legislative assembly in czarist Russia

¹**dumb** \'dəm\ *adjective* [Middle English, from Old English; akin to Old High German *tumb* mute] (before 12th century)
1 : lacking the power of speech ⟨deaf and *dumb* from birth⟩ ⟨*dumb* animals⟩
2 : temporarily unable to speak ⟨as from shock or astonishment⟩ ⟨struck *dumb* with fear⟩
3 : not expressed in uttered words ⟨*dumb* grief⟩
4 : SILENT; *also* : TACITURN
5 : lacking some usual attribute or accompaniment; *especially* : having no means of self-propulsion ⟨*dumb* barge⟩
6 a : markedly lacking in intelligence : STUPID **b** : showing a lack of intelligence **c** : having little or no meaning — sometimes used in the phrase *dumb luck*
7 : not having the capability to process data ⟨a *dumb* terminal⟩ — compare INTELLIGENT 3a □
synonym see STUPID
— **dumb·ly** \'dəm-lē\ *adverb*
— **dumb·ness** *noun*

²**dumb** *transitive verb* (1608)
: to make silent : DEADEN ⟨would lie around, *dumbed* by the drugs —Norman Mailer⟩

dumb·bell \'dəm-,bel\ *noun* (1785)

1 : a short bar with weights at each end that is used usually in pairs for exercise
2 : one that is dull and stupid

dumb·cane \'dəm-ˌkān\ *noun* [from the fact that chewing it causes the tongue and throat to swell] (1696)
: DIEFFENBACHIA

dumb down *transitive verb* (1980)
: to lower the level of difficulty and the intellectual content of (as a textbook)

dumb·found *or* **dum·found** \ˌdəm-'faùnd, 'dəm-ˌ\ *transitive verb* [dumb + -found (as in confound)] (1653)
: to confound briefly and usually with astonishment
synonym see PUZZLE

dumb·foun·der \-'faùn-dər\ *transitive verb* (1710)
British **:** DUMBFOUND

dumb·head \'dəm-ˌhed\ *noun* [probably translation of German *dummkopf*] (1887)
slang **:** a stupid person **:** BLOCKHEAD

dumb show *noun* (1561)
1 : a part of a play presented in pantomime
2 : signs and gestures without words **:** PANTOMIME

dumb·struck \'dəm-ˌstrək\ *adjective* (1887)
: made silent by astonishment

dumb·wait·er \'dəm-ˌwā-tər, ˌdəm-'-\ *noun* (1749)
1 : a portable serving table or stand
2 : a small elevator used for conveying food and dishes from one story of a building to another

dum·dum \'dəm-ˌdəm\ *noun* [*Dum Dum*, arsenal near Calcutta, India] (circa 1889)
: a bullet (as one with a hollow point) that expands more than usual upon hitting an object

dum–dum *noun* [reduplication of ¹*dumb*] (1928)
: a stupid person **:** DUMMY

dum·ka \'dùm-kə\ *noun, plural* **dum·ky** \-kē\ [Czech, elegy, from Ukrainian, diminutive of *duma* narrative folk poem, from Old Russian] (1895)
: a musical composition containing alternating sad and gay passages

dumm·kopf \'dùm-ˌkòpf\ *noun* [German, from *dumm* stupid + *Kopf* head] (1809)
: BLOCKHEAD

¹**dum·my** \'də-mē\ *noun, plural* **dummies** [¹*dumb* + ⁴-*y*] (1598)
1 a : one who is incapable of speaking **b :** one who is habitually silent **c :** one who is stupid
2 a : the exposed hand in bridge played by the declarer in addition to his own hand **b :** a bridge player whose hand is a dummy
3 : an imitation, copy, or likeness of something used as a substitute: as **a :** MANNEQUIN **b :** a stuffed figure or cylindrical bag used by football players for tackling and blocking practice **c :** a large puppet usually having movable features (as mouth and arms) manipulated by a ventriloquist **d** *chiefly British* **:** PACIFIER 2
4 : one seeming to act independently but in reality controlled by another
5 a : a mock-up of a proposed publication (as a book or magazine) **b :** a set of pages (as for a newspaper or magazine) with the position of text and artwork indicated for the printer

²**dummy** *adjective* (1846)
1 a : having the appearance of being real **:** ARTIFICIAL ⟨*dummy* foods in the display case⟩ **b :** existing in name only **:** FICTITIOUS ⟨*dummy* corporations⟩
2 : apparently acting for oneself while really acting for or at the direction of another ⟨a *dummy* director⟩

³**dummy** *transitive verb* **dum·mied; dum·my·ing** (1928)
: to make a dummy of (as a publication) — often used with *up* ⟨*dummied* up the front page⟩

dummy up *intransitive verb* (1926)
: to say nothing **:** CLAM UP

dummy variable *noun* (1957)
: an arbitrary mathematical symbol or variable that can be replaced by another without affecting the value of the expression in which it occurs

du·mor·ti·er·ite \dù-'mòr-tē-ə-ˌrīt *also* dyù-\ *noun* [French *dumortiérite*, from Eugène *Dumortier* (died 1876) French paleontologist] (1881)
: a bright blue or greenish blue mineral consisting of a silicate of aluminum and used especially for jewelry

¹**dump** \'dəmp\ *verb* [perhaps from Middle Dutch *dompen* to immerse, topple; akin to Old Norse *dumpa* to thump, fall suddenly] (14th century)
transitive verb
1 a : to let fall in or as if in a heap or mass **b :** to get rid of unceremoniously or irresponsibly **c :** JETTISON ⟨an airplane *dumping* gasoline⟩
2 *slang* **:** to knock down **:** BEAT ⟨the man rushed out and *dumped* him —John Corry⟩
3 : to sell in quantity at a very low price; *specifically* **:** to sell abroad at less than the market price at home
4 : to copy (data in a computer's internal storage) to an external storage or output device
5 : to throw (as a pass) short and softly — often used with *off*
intransitive verb
1 : to fall abruptly **:** PLUNGE
2 : to dump refuse
— **dump·er** *noun*
— **dump on :** to treat disrespectfully; *especially* **:** BELITTLE, BAD-MOUTH

²**dump** *noun* (1784)
1 a : an accumulation of refuse and discarded materials **b :** a place where such materials are dumped
2 a : a quantity of reserve materials accumulated at one place **b :** a place where such materials are stored ⟨ammunition *dump*⟩
3 : a disorderly, slovenly, or objectionable place
4 : an instance of dumping data stored in a computer
5 : an act of defecation — usually used with *take*; often considered vulgar

dump·ing *noun* (1857)
: the act of one that dumps; *especially* **:** the selling of goods in quantity at below market price

dumping ground *noun* (1857)
: a place to which unwanted people or things are sent

dump·ish \'dəm-pish\ *adjective* [*dumps*] (1519)
: SAD, MELANCHOLY

dump·ling \'dəm-pliŋ\ *noun* [perhaps alteration of *lump*] (circa 1600)
1 a : a small mass of leavened dough cooked by boiling or steaming **b :** a usually baked dessert of fruit wrapped in dough
2 : something soft and rounded like a dumpling; *especially* **:** a short fat person or animal

dumps \'dəm(p)s\ *noun plural* [probably from Dutch *domp* haze, from Middle Dutch *damp* — more at DAMP] (1529)
: a gloomy state of mind **:** DESPONDENCY ⟨in the *dumps*⟩

Dump·ster \'dəm(p)-stər\ *trademark*
— used for a large trash receptacle

dump truck *noun* (1930)
: an automotive truck for the transportation of bulk material that has a body which tilts to dump its contents

dumpy \'dəm-pē\ *adjective* **dump·i·er; -est** [English dialect *dump* (lump)] (1750)
1 : being short and thick in build **:** SQUAT
2 : SHABBY, DINGY
— **dump·i·ly** \-pə-lē\ *adverb*
— **dump·i·ness** \-pē-nəs\ *noun*

dumpy level *noun* (1838)
: a surveyor's level with a short telescope rigidly fixed and rotating only in a horizontal plane

¹**dun** \'dən\ *adjective* [Middle English, from Old English *dunn* — more at DUSK] (before 12th century)
1 a : having the color dun **b** *of a horse* **:** having a grayish yellow coat with black mane and tail
2 : marked by dullness and drabness
— **dun·ness** \'dən-nəs\ *noun*

²**dun** *noun* (14th century)
1 : a dun horse
2 : a variable color averaging a nearly neutral slightly brownish dark gray
3 : a subadult mayfly; *also* **:** an artificial fly tied to imitate such an insect

³**dun** *transitive verb* **dunned; dun·ning** [origin unknown] (circa 1626)
1 : to make persistent demands upon for payment
2 : PLAGUE, PESTER

⁴**dun** *noun* (1628)
1 : one who duns
2 : an urgent request; *especially* **:** a demand for payment

Dun·can Phyfe \ˌdəŋ-kən-'fīf\ *adjective* (1926)
: of, relating to, or constituting furniture designed and built by or in the style of Duncan Phyfe

dunce \'dən(t)s\ *noun* [John *Duns* Scotus, whose once accepted writings were ridiculed in the 16th century] (1587)
: one who is slow-witted or stupid ◇

dunce cap *noun* (1840)
: a conical cap formerly used as a punishment for slow learners at school — called also *dunce's cap*

dun·der·head \'dən-dər-ˌhed\ *noun* [perhaps from Dutch *donder* thunder + English *head*; akin to Old High German *thonar* thunder — more at THUNDER] (circa 1625)
: DUNCE, BLOCKHEAD
— **dun·der·head·ed** \ˌdən-dər-'he-dəd\ *adjective*

dun·drear·ies \ˌdən-'drir-ēz\ *noun plural, often capitalized* [Lord *Dundreary*, character in the play *Our American Cousin* (1858), by Tom Taylor] (circa 1922)
: long flowing sideburns

dune \'dün *also* 'dyün\ *noun* [French, from Old French, from Middle Dutch; akin to Old English *dūn* down — more at DOWN] (1790)
: a hill or ridge of sand piled up by the wind

◇ WORD HISTORY

dunce The irony of *dunce* lies in the fact that this synonym for *dullard* is derived from the name of one of the most brilliant thinkers of the later Middle Ages. *Duns* was the name of a Scottish market town and the birthplace in the mid 13th century of John Duns Scotus, one of the luminaries of Scholasticism. So ingenious were the theological and metaphysical speculations of this thinker that he was given the epithet of *Doctor Subtilis* ("the Subtle Doctor"). His followers, who were known as *Scotists* or *dunsmen*, were a powerful conservative element in English universities through the 16th century. They tended to resist both the new learning of humanism and the complaints of church reformers. As a result, *dunsman* and the shorter form *duns* (later respelled as we have it today) became terms of opprobrium and scorn meaning first "sophist" or "pedant" and gradually taking on the modern sense "slow-witted person."

— **dune·like** \-ˌlīk\ *adjective*
dune buggy *noun* (1956)
: an off-road motor vehicle with oversize tires for use especially on sand
dune·land \'dün-ˌland\ *noun* (1922)
: an area having many dunes
¹**dung** \'dəŋ\ *noun* [Middle English, from Old English; akin to Old Norse *dyngja* manure pile] (before 12th century)
1 : the excrement of an animal : MANURE
2 : something repulsive
— **dungy** \'dəŋ-ē\ *adjective*
²**dung** (before 12th century)
transitive verb
: to fertilize or dress with manure
intransitive verb
: DEFECATE
dun·ga·ree \ˌdəŋ-gə-'rē, 'dəŋ-gə-ˌ\ *noun* [Hindi *dūgrī*] (1673)
1 : a heavy coarse durable cotton twill woven from colored yarns; *specifically* : blue denim
2 *plural* : clothes made usually of blue denim
dung beetle *noun* (circa 1634)
: a beetle (as a tumblebug) that rolls balls of dung in which to lay eggs and on which the larvae feed
Dunge·ness crab \ˌdən-jə-ˌnes-\ *noun* [*Dungeness*, village on the Strait of Juan de Fuca, Washington] (1925)
: a large edible crab (*Cancer magister*) of the Pacific coast of North America from Alaska to California
dun·geon \'dən-jən\ *noun* [Middle English *donjon*, from Middle French, from (assumed) Vulgar Latin *domnion-, domnio* keep, mastery, from Latin *dominus* lord — more at DOMINATE] (14th century)
1 : DONJON
2 : a dark usually underground prison or vault
◇
dung·hill \'dəŋ-ˌhil\ *noun* (14th century)
1 : a heap of dung
2 : something (as a situation or condition) that is repulsive or degraded
du·nite \'dü-ˌnīt, 'də-\ *noun* [Mount *Dun*, New Zealand] (circa 1868)
: a granitoid igneous rock consisting chiefly of olivine
— **du·nit·ic** \dü-'ni-tik, ˌdə-\ *adjective*
¹**dunk** \'dəŋk\ *verb* [Pennsylvania German *dunke*, from Middle High German *dunken*, from Old High German *dunkōn* — more at TINGE] (1919)
transitive verb
1 : to dip (as a piece of bread) into a beverage while eating
2 : to dip or submerge temporarily in liquid
3 : to throw (a basketball) into the basket from above the rim
intransitive verb
1 : to submerge oneself in water
2 : to make a dunk shot in basketball
²**dunk** *noun* (circa 1944)
: the act or action of dunking; *especially*
: DUNK SHOT
Dun·ker \'dəŋ-kər\ *or* **Dun·kard** \-kərd\ *noun* [Pennsylvania German *Dunker*, from *dunke*] (1744)
: a member of the Church of the Brethren or any of several other originally German Baptist denominations practicing trine immersion and love feasts and refusing to take oaths or to perform military service
Dun·kirk \'dən-ˌkərk, ˌdən-'\ *noun* [*Dunkirk* or *Dunkerque*, France, scene of the evacuation of Allied forces in 1940] (1941)
1 : a retreat to avoid total defeat
2 : a crisis situation that requires a desperate last effort to forestall certain failure ⟨a *Dunkirk* for U.S. foreign policy —*Time*⟩
dunk shot *noun* (circa 1961)
: a shot in basketball made by jumping high into the air and throwing the ball down through the basket

dun·lin \'dən-lən\ *noun, plural* **dunlins** *or* **dunlin** [¹*dun* + *-lin* (alteration of *-ling*)] (circa 1532)
: a small widely distributed sandpiper (*Calidris alpina*) largely cinnamon to rusty brown above and white below
Dun·lop \'dən-ˌläp, ˌdən-'\ *noun* [*Dunlop*, Ayrshire, Scotland] (circa 1780)
: a Scottish cheese similar to cheddar
dun·nage \'də-nij\ *noun* [origin unknown] (15th century)
1 : loose materials used to support and protect cargo in a ship's hold; *also* : padding in a shipping container
2 : BAGGAGE
duo \'dü-(ˌ)ō *also* 'dyü-\ *noun, plural* **du·os** [Italian, from Latin, two — more at TWO] (1590)
1 : DUET
2 : PAIR 2
duo- *combining form* [Latin *duo*]
: two ⟨*duo*logue⟩
duo·de·cil·lion \ˌdü-ō-di-'sil-yən, ˌdyü-\ *noun, often attributive* [Latin *duodecim* twelve + English *-illion* (as in *million*)] (1875)
— see NUMBER table
duo·dec·i·mal \ˌdü-ə-'de-sə-məl, ˌdyü-\ *adjective* [Latin *duodecim* — more at DOZEN] (1727)
: of, relating to, or proceeding by twelve or the scale of twelves
— **duodecimal** *noun*
duo·dec·i·mo \-ˌmō\ *noun, plural* **-mos** [Latin, ablative of *duodecimus* twelfth, from *duodecim*] (1658)
: TWELVEMO
du·o·de·num \ˌdü-ə-'dē-nəm, dü-'ä-dᵊn-əm *also* (ˌ)dyü-\ *noun, plural* **-de·na** \-'dē-nə, -dᵊn-ə\ *or* **-denums** [Middle English, from Medieval Latin, from Latin *duodeni* twelve each, from *duodecim* twelve; from its length, about 12 fingers' breadth] (14th century)
: the first part of the small intestine extending from the pylorus to the jejunum
— **du·o·de·nal** \-'dē-nᵊl, -dᵊn-əl\ *adjective*
duo·logue \'dü-ə-ˌlȯg, -ˌläg *also* 'dyü-\ *noun* (1864)
: a dialogue between two persons
duo·mo \'dwȯ-ˌmō\ *noun, plural* **duomos** [Italian, from Latin *domus* house — more at DOME] (1549)
: CATHEDRAL
du·op·o·ly \dü-'ä-pə-lē *also* dyù-\ *noun, plural* **-lies** [*duo-* + *-poly* (as in *monopoly*)] (1920)
1 : an oligopoly limited to two sellers
2 : preponderant influence or control by two political powers
— **du·op·o·lis·tic** \-ˌä-pə-'lis-tik\ *adjective*
dup \'dəp\ *transitive verb* [contraction of *do up*] (1547)
archaic : OPEN
¹**dupe** \'düp *also* 'dyüp\ *noun* [French, from Middle French *duppe*, probably alteration of *huppe* hoopoe] (1681)
: one that is easily deceived or cheated : FOOL
²**dupe** *transitive verb* **duped; dup·ing** (1704)
: to make a dupe of ☆
— **dup·er** *noun*
³**dupe** *noun or verb* (circa 1900)
: DUPLICATE
dup·ery \'dü-pə-rē *also* 'dyü-\ *noun, plural* **-er·ies** (1759)
1 : the condition of being duped
2 : the act or practice of duping
du·ple \'dü-pəl *also* 'dyü-\ *adjective* [Latin *duplus* double — more at DOUBLE] (15th century)
1 : having two elements
2 a : marked by two or a multiple of two beats per measure of music ⟨*duple* time⟩ **b** : of rhythm : consisting of a meter based on disyllabic feet
¹**du·plex** \'dü-ˌpleks *also* 'dyü-\ *adjective* [Latin, from *duo* two + *-plex* -fold — more at TWO, -FOLD] (1567)

1 a : having two principal elements or parts : DOUBLE, TWOFOLD **b** : having complementary polynucleotide strands ⟨*duplex* DNA⟩
2 : allowing telecommunication in opposite directions simultaneously
²**duplex** *transitive verb* (1833)
: to make duplex
³**duplex** *noun* (1922)
: something duplex: as **a** : a 2-family house **b** : DUPLEX APARTMENT **c** : a duplex molecule of DNA or of RNA and DNA
duplex apartment *noun* (circa 1925)
: an apartment having rooms on two floors
du·plex·er \'dü-ˌplek-sər *also* 'dyü-\ *noun* (circa 1932)
: a switching device that permits alternate transmission and reception with the same radio antenna
¹**du·pli·cate** \'dü-pli-kət *also* 'dyü-\ *adjective* [Middle English, from Latin *duplicatus*, past participle of *duplicare* to double, from *duplic-, duplex*] (15th century)
1 : consisting of or existing in two corresponding or identical parts or examples ⟨*duplicate* invoices⟩
2 : being the same as another ⟨*duplicate* copies⟩
²**du·pli·cate** \'dü-pli-ˌkāt *also* 'dyü-\ *verb* **-cat·ed; -cat·ing** (15th century)
transitive verb
1 : to make double or twofold
2 a : to make a copy of ⟨a cell *duplicates* itself when it divides⟩ **b** : to produce something equal to ⟨trying to *duplicate* last year's success⟩ **c** : to do over or again often needlessly ⟨*duplicated* effort⟩
intransitive verb
: to become duplicated; *also* : REPEAT
— **du·pli·ca·tive** \-ˌkā-tiv\ *adjective*
³**du·pli·cate** \-kət\ *noun* (1532)
1 a : either of two things exactly alike and usually produced at the same time or by the

◇ **WORD HISTORY**
dungeon The word *dungeon*, in use in English since the 14th century, originally referred to the keep of a castle—the massive inner tower detached from the rest of the structure that was its most securely located and protected part. During its early history this word had about a dozen different spellings, but nowadays, in the sense of a castle's keep, the usual form is *donjon*. The donjon was the stronghold to which the garrison and residents of the castle retreated if the outer walls had been scaled or breached in a siege. The subterranean part of a donjon was called by the same word in the form *dungeon*, the usual spelling for this sense. This dark, damp chamber was used as a cell for the confinement of prisoners. Both *donjon* and *dungeon* are borrowed from Old French *donjon*, most likely the descendant of an unrecorded vernacular Latin form *domnio*, reflected in Medieval Latin renderings such as *dominionus* and *domnionus*, and ultimately a derivative of Latin *dominus* "lord." The underlying sense of *domnio* would have been "dominating tower," reflecting the relation between the keep and the rest of the castle.

same process **b :** an additional copy of something (as a book or stamp) already in a collection

2 : one that resembles or corresponds to another **:** COUNTERPART

3 : two identical copies — used in the phrase *in duplicate*

synonym see REPRODUCTION

duplicate bridge *noun* (1926)

: a tournament form of contract bridge in which identical deals are played in order to compare individual scores

du·pli·ca·tion \ˌdü-pli-'kā-shən *also* ˌdyü-\ *noun* (15th century)

1 a : the act or process of duplicating **b :** the quality or state of being duplicated

2 : DUPLICATE, COUNTERPART

3 : a part of a chromosome in which the genetic material is repeated; *also* **:** the process of forming a duplication

du·pli·ca·tor \'dü-pli-ˌkā-tər *also* 'dyü-\ *noun* (1893)

: one that duplicates; *specifically* **:** a machine for making copies of graphic matter

du·plic·i·tous \dü-'pli-sə-təs *also* dyü-\ *adjective* (1928)

: marked by duplicity

— **du·plic·i·tous·ly** *adverb*

du·plic·i·ty \dü-'pli-sə-tē *also* dyü-\ *noun, plural* **-ties** [Middle English *duplicite*, from Middle French, from Late Latin *duplicitat-, duplicitas*, from Latin *duplex*] (15th century)

1 : contradictory doubleness of thought, speech, or action; *especially* **:** the belying of one's true intentions by deceptive words or action

2 : the quality or state of being double or twofold

3 : the technically incorrect use of two or more distinct items (as claims, charges, or defenses) in a single legal action

du·ra·ble \'dùr-ə-bəl *also* 'dyùr-\ *adjective* [Middle English, from Middle French, from Latin *durabilis*, from *durare* to last — more at DURING] (14th century)

: able to exist for a long time without significant deterioration; *also* **:** designed to be durable ⟨*durable* goods⟩

synonym see LASTING

— **du·ra·bil·i·ty** \ˌdùr-ə-'bi-lə-tē, ˌdyùr-\ *noun*

— **du·ra·ble·ness** \'dùr-ə-bəl-nəs, 'dyùr-\ *noun*

— **du·ra·bly** \-blē\ *adverb*

durable press *noun* (1966)

: PERMANENT PRESS

du·ra·bles \'dùr-ə-bəlz *also* 'dyùr-\ *noun plural* (1941)

: consumer goods (as vehicles and household appliances) that are typically used repeatedly over a period of years — called also *durable goods*

du·ral·u·min \dù-'ral-yə-mən *also* dyù-\ *noun* [from *Duralumin*, a trademark] (1910)

: a light strong alloy of aluminum, copper, manganese, and magnesium

du·ra ma·ter \'dùr-ə-ˌmā-tər, 'dyùr-, -ˌmä-\ *noun* [Middle English, from Medieval Latin, literally, hard mother] (14th century)

: the tough fibrous membrane that envelops the brain and spinal cord external to the arachnoid and pia mater

du·rance \'dùr-ən(t)s *also* 'dyùr-\ *noun* [Middle English, from Middle French, from *durer* to endure, from Latin *durare*] (15th century)

1 *archaic* **:** ENDURANCE

2 : restraint by or as if by physical force — usually used in the phrase *durance vile*

du·ra·tion \dù-'rā-shən *also* dyù-\ *noun* (14th century)

1 : continuance in time

2 : the time during which something exists or lasts

du·ra·tive \'dùr-ə-tiv, 'dyùr-\ *adjective* (1889)

: CONTINUATIVE

— **durative** *noun*

dur·bar \'dər-ˌbär, ˌdər-'\ *noun* [Hindi *darbār*, from Persian, from *dar* door + *bār* admission, audience] (1609)

1 : court held by an Indian prince

2 : a formal reception held by an Indian prince or an African ruler

du·ress \dù-'res *also* dyù-\ *noun* [Middle English *duresse*, from Middle French *duresce* hardness, severity, from Latin *duritia*, from *durus*] (15th century)

1 : forcible restraint or restriction

2 : compulsion by threat; *specifically* **:** unlawful constraint

Dur·ham \'dər-əm, 'də-rəm, 'dùr-əm\ *noun* [County *Durham*, England] (1810)

: SHORTHORN

Durham Rule *noun* [Monte *Durham*, 20th century American litigant] (1955)

: a legal hypothesis under which a person is not judged responsible for a criminal act that is attributed to a mental disease or defect

du·ri·an \'dùr-ē-ən, -ē-ˌän *also* 'dyùr-\ *noun* [Malay] (1588)

1 : a large oval tasty but foul-smelling fruit with a prickly rind

2 : an East Indian tree (*Durio zibethinus*) of the silk-cotton family that bears durians

dur·ing \'dùr-iŋ *also* 'dyùr-\ *preposition* [Middle English, from present participle of *duren* to last, from Old French *durer*, from Latin *durare* to harden, endure, from *durus* hard; perhaps akin to Sanskrit *dāru* wood — more at TREE] (14th century)

1 : throughout the duration of ⟨swims every day *during* the summer⟩

2 : at a point in the course of ⟨was offered a job *during* a visit to the capital⟩

dur·mast oak \'dər-ˌmast-\ *noun* [perhaps alteration of *dun mast*, from [1]*dun + mast*] (1791)

: a European oak (*Quercus petraea*) valued especially for its dark heavy tough elastic wood and for its tannin-rich bark

durn \'dərn\, **durned** \'dərn(d)\ *variant of* DARN, DARNED

du·ro \'dùr-(ˌ)ō\ *noun, plural* **duros** [Spanish, short for *peso duro* hard peso] (1832)

: a Spanish or Spanish American peso or silver dollar

du·roc \'dùr-ˌäk *also* 'dyùr-\ *noun, often capitalized* [*Duroc*, 19th century American stallion] (1883)

: any of a breed of large vigorous red American hogs

du·rom·e·ter \dù-'rä-mə-tər *also* dyù-\ *noun* [Latin *durus* hard] (circa 1879)

: an instrument for measuring hardness

dur·ra *also* **du·ra** \'dùr-ə\ *noun* [Arabic *dhurah*] (1798)

: any of several grain sorghums widely grown in warm dry regions

durst \'dərst\ *archaic & dialect past of* DARE

du·rum wheat \'dùr-əm-, 'dyùr-, 'dər-əm-, 'də-rəm-\ *noun* [New Latin *durum*, from Latin, neuter of *durus* hard] (circa 1903)

: a wheat (*Triticum durum*) that yields a glutenous flour used especially in pasta — called also *durum*

[1]**dusk** \'dəsk\ *adjective* [Middle English *dosk*, alteration of Old English *dox*; akin to Latin *fuscus* dark brown, Old English *dunn* dun, *dūst* dust] (13th century)

: DUSKY

[2]**dusk** (13th century)

intransitive verb

: to become dark

transitive verb

: to make dark or gloomy

[3]**dusk** *noun* (1622)

1 : the darker part of twilight especially at night

2 : darkness or semidarkness caused by the shutting out of light

dusky \'dəs-kē\ *adjective* **dusk·i·er; -est** (1558)

1 : somewhat dark in color; *specifically* **:** having dark skin

2 : marked by slight or deficient light **:** SHADOWY

— **dusk·i·ly** \-kə-lē\ *adverb*

— **dusk·i·ness** \-kē-nəs\ *noun*

[1]**dust** \'dəst\ *noun* [Middle English, from Old English *dūst*; akin to Old High German *tunst* storm, and probably to Latin *fumus* smoke — more at FUME] (before 12th century)

1 : fine particles of matter (as of earth)

2 : the particles into which something disintegrates

3 a : something worthless **b :** a state of humiliation

4 a : the earth especially as a place of burial **b :** the surface of the ground

5 a : a cloud of dust **b :** CONFUSION, DISTURBANCE

6 *archaic* **:** a single particle (as of earth)

7 *British* **:** refuse ready for collection

— **dust·less** \-ləs\ *adjective*

— **dust·like** \-ˌlīk\ *adjective*

[2]**dust** (1530)

transitive verb

1 *archaic* **:** to make dusty

2 : to make free of dust

3 a : to sprinkle with fine particles **b :** to sprinkle in the form of dust

intransitive verb

1 *of a bird* **:** to work dust into the feathers

2 : to remove dust

3 : to give off dust

dust·bin \'dəs(t)-ˌbin\ *noun* (1848)

1 *British* **:** a can for trash or garbage

2 : DUSTHEAP 2

dust bowl *noun* (1936)

: a region that suffers from prolonged droughts and dust storms

dust·cov·er \-ˌkə-vər\ *noun* (1899)

1 : a cover (as of cloth or plastic) used to protect furniture or equipment from dust

2 : DUST JACKET

dust devil *noun* (1888)

: a small whirlwind containing sand or dust

dust·er \'dəs-tər\ *noun* (1576)

1 : one that removes dust

2 a (1) **:** a long lightweight overgarment to protect clothing from dust (2) **:** a long coat cut like a duster — called also *duster coat* **b :** a dress-length housecoat

3 : one that scatters fine particles; *specifically* **:** a device for applying insecticidal or fungicidal dusts to crops

4 : DUST STORM

dust·heap \'dəst-ˌ(h)ēp\ *noun* (1599)

1 : a pile of refuse

2 : a category of forgotten items ⟨the *dustheap* of history —*New Republic*⟩

dust jacket *noun* (1926)

: a paper cover for a book

dust·man \'dəs(t)-mən\ *noun* (1707)

British **:** a collector of trash or garbage

dust mop *noun* (1953)

: DRY MOP

dust off *transitive verb* (1940)

: to bring out or back to use again

dust·pan \'dəs(t)-ˌpan\ *noun* (1783)

: a shovel-shaped pan for sweepings

dust storm *noun* (1879)

1 : a dust-laden whirlwind that moves across an arid region and is usually associated with hot dry air and marked by high electrical tension

2 : strong winds bearing clouds of dust

dust-up \'dəs-ˌtəp\ *noun* (1897)

: ROW, FIGHT

dust wrapper *noun* (1932)

: DUST JACKET

\ə\ **abut** \ᵊ\ **kitten** \ər\ **further** \a\ **ash** \ā\ **ace** \ä\ **mop, mar** \aù\ **out** \ch\ **chin** \e\ **bet** \ē\ **easy** \g\ **go** \i\ **hit** \ī\ **ice** \j\ **job** \ŋ\ **sing** \ō\ **go** \ò\ **law** \òi\ **boy** \th\ **thin** \t̶h̶\ **the** \ü\ **loot** \ù\ **foot** \y\ **yet** \zh\ **vision** *see also* Guide to Pronunciation

dusty \'dəs-tē\ *adjective* **dust·i·er; -est** (13th century)
1 : covered or abounding with dust
2 : consisting of dust : POWDERY
3 : resembling dust
4 : lacking vitality : DRY ⟨*dusty* scholarship⟩
5 *British* : UNSATISFACTORY — used especially in the phrases *dusty answer* and *not so dusty*
— **dust·i·ly** \'dəs-tə-lē\ *adverb*
— **dust·i·ness** \-tē-nəs\ *noun*

dusty miller *noun* (circa 1825)
: any of several plants having ashy-gray or white tomentose leaves; *especially* : an herbaceous artemisia (*Artemisia stelleriana*) with greyish foliage found along the eastern coast of the U.S.

dutch \'dəch\ *adverb, often capitalized* (1914)
: with each person paying his or her own way

¹Dutch \'dəch\ *adjective* [Middle English *Duch,* from Middle Dutch *duutsch;* akin to Old High German *diutisc* German, Old English *thēod* nation, Gothic *thiudisko* as a gentile, *thiuda* people, Oscan *touto* city] (14th century)
1 a *archaic* : of, relating to, or in any of the Germanic languages of Germany, Austria, Switzerland, and the Low Countries **b** : of, relating to, or in the Dutch of the Netherlands
2 a *archaic* : of or relating to the Germanic peoples of Germany, Austria, Switzerland, and the Low Countries **b** : of or relating to the Netherlands or its inhabitants **c** : ²GERMAN
3 : of or relating to the Pennsylvania Dutch or their language
— **Dutch·ly** *adverb*

²Dutch *noun* (14th century)
1 a *archaic* (1) : any of the Germanic languages of Germany, Austria, Switzerland, and the Low Countries (2) : GERMAN 3 **b** : the Germanic language of the Netherlands
2 Dutch *plural* **a** *archaic* : the Germanic peoples of Germany, Austria, Switzerland, and the Low Countries **b** : GERMANS 2a, b **c** : the people of the Netherlands
3 : PENNSYLVANIA DUTCH
4 : DANDER ⟨her *Dutch* is up⟩
5 : DISFAVOR, TROUBLE ⟨in *Dutch* with the boss⟩

Dutch cheese *noun* (1829)
chiefly Northern : COTTAGE CHEESE

Dutch clover *noun* (1800)
: WHITE CLOVER

Dutch Colonial *adjective* (1922)
: characterized by a gambrel roof with overhanging eaves

Dutch courage *noun* (1809)
: courage artificially stimulated especially by drink; *also* : drink taken for courage

Dutch door *noun* (circa 1890)
: a door divided horizontally so that the lower or upper part can be shut separately

Dutch elm disease *noun* (1927)
: a disease of elms caused by an ascomycetous fungus (*Ceratocystis ulmi*) and characterized by yellowing of the foliage, defoliation, and death

Dutch hoe *noun* (1744)
: SCUFFLE HOE

Dutch door

dutch·man \'dəch-mən\ *noun* (14th century)
1 *capitalized* **a** *archaic* : a member of any of the Germanic peoples of Germany, Austria, Switzerland, and the Low Countries **b** : a native or inhabitant of the Netherlands **c** : a person of Dutch descent **d** : GERMAN 1a, b
2 : a device for hiding or counteracting structural defects

Dutch·man's–breech·es \,dəch-mənz-'brichəz\ *noun plural but singular or plural in construction* (1837)
: a spring-flowering herb (*Dicentra cucullaria*) of the fumitory family occurring in the eastern U.S. and having finely divided leaves and

cream-white double-spurred flowers

Dutchman's–pipe \-'pīp\ *noun, plural* **Dutchman's–pipes** \-'pīps\ (1845)
: a vine (*Aristolochia durior*) with large leaves and early summer flowers having the tube of the calyx curved like the bowl of a pipe

Dutch oven *noun* (1769)
1 : a metal shield for roasting before an open fire
2 : a brick oven in which cooking is done by the preheated walls
3 a : a cast-iron kettle with a tight cover that is used for baking in an open fire **b** : a heavy pot with a tight-fitting domed cover

Dutchman's-breeches

Dutch roll *noun* (1913)
: a combination of directional and lateral oscillation of an airplane

¹dutch treat *noun, often D capitalized* (1887)
: a meal or other entertainment for which each person pays his or her own way

²dutch treat *adverb, often D capitalized* (1942)
: DUTCH ⟨go *dutch treat*⟩

Dutch uncle *noun* (1837)
: one who admonishes sternly and bluntly

du·te·ous \'dü-tē-əs *also* 'dyü-\ *adjective* [irregular from *duty*] (1593)
: DUTIFUL, OBEDIENT

du·ti·able \'dü-tē-ə-bəl *also* 'dyü-\ *adjective* (1774)
: subject to a duty

du·ti·ful \'dü-ti-fəl *also* 'dyü-\ *adjective* (1552)
1 : filled with or motivated by a sense of duty
2 : proceeding from or expressive of a sense of duty
— **du·ti·ful·ly** \-f(ə-)lē\ *adverb*
— **du·ti·ful·ness** \-fəl-nəs\ *noun*

¹du·ty \'dü-tē *also* 'dyü-\ *noun, plural* **duties** [Middle English *duete,* from Anglo-French *dueté,* from Old French *deu* due] (13th century)
1 : conduct due to parents and superiors : RESPECT
2 a : obligatory tasks, conduct, service, or functions that arise from one's position (as in life or in a group) **b** (1) : assigned service or business (2) : active military service (3) : a period of being on duty
3 a : a moral or legal obligation **b** : the force of moral obligation
4 : TAX; *especially* : a tax on imports
5 a : WORK 1a **b** (1) : the service required (as of an electric machine) under specified conditions (2) : functional application : USE ⟨got double *duty* out of the trip⟩ (3) : use as a substitute ⟨making the word do *duty* for the thing —Edward Sapir⟩
synonym see FUNCTION, TASK
— **off duty** : free from assignment or responsibility
— **on duty** : engaged in or responsible for an assigned task or duty

²duty *adjective* (1806)
1 : done as a duty
2 : being on duty : assigned to specified tasks or functions ⟨the *duty* officer⟩

duty–free \,dü-tē-'frē, ,dyü-, ,dü-tē-,\ *adjective or adverb* (1689)
1 : without payment of customs duties : free from duties ⟨imported *duty-free*⟩ ⟨*duty-free* goods⟩
2 : relating to or selling duty-free goods ⟨a *duty-free* shop⟩

du·um·vir \dü-'əm-vər *also* dyù-\ *noun* [Latin, from *duum* (genitive of *duo* two) + *vir* man] (1600)
1 : one of two Roman officers or magistrates constituting a board or court

2 : one of two people jointly holding power
— **du·um·vi·rate** \-və-rət\ *noun*

du·vet \d(y)ù-'vā, 'd(y)ü-,\ *noun* [French] (1758)
: COMFORTER 2b

duve·tyn \'dü-və-,tēn, 'dyü-, 'dəv-,tēn\ *noun* [French *duvetine,* from *duvet* down, from Middle French, alteration of (assumed) Middle French *dumet,* diminutive of Old French *dun, dum* down, from Old Norse *dūnn* — more at DOWN] (1913)
: a smooth lustrous velvety fabric

dux·elles \,dük-'sel, (,)dü-'sel\ *noun* [Marquis Louis Chalon du Blé *d'Uxelles* (died 1658) French nobleman] (1877)
: a garnish or stuffing made especially of finely chopped sautéed mushrooms

¹dwarf \'dwȯrf\ *noun, plural* **dwarfs** \'dwȯrfs\ *also* **dwarves** \'dwȯrvz\ *often attributive* [Middle English *dwerg, dwerf,* from Old English *dweorg, dweorh;* akin to Old High German *twerg* dwarf] (before 12th century)
1 a : a person of unusually small stature; *especially* : one whose bodily proportions are abnormal **b** : an insignificant person
2 : an animal or plant much below normal size
3 : a small legendary manlike being who is usually misshapen and ugly and skilled as an artificer
4 : a star (as the sun) of ordinary or low luminosity and relatively small mass and size
— **dwarf·ish** \'dwȯr-fish\ *adjective*
— **dwarf·ish·ly** *adverb*
— **dwarf·ish·ness** *noun*
— **dwarf·like** \'dwȯr-,flīk\ *adjective*
— **dwarf·ness** \'dwȯrf-nəs\ *noun*

²dwarf (circa 1626)
transitive verb
1 : to restrict the growth of : STUNT
2 : to cause to appear smaller or to seem inferior
intransitive verb
: to become smaller

³dwarf *adjective* (1664)
of a plant : low-growing in habit ⟨*dwarfer* forms of citrus⟩

dwarf·ism \'dwȯr-,fi-zəm\ *noun* (1865)
: the condition of stunted growth ·

dweeb \'dwēb\ *noun* [origin unknown] (1983)
slang : an unattractive, insignificant, or inept person

dwell \'dwel\ *intransitive verb* **dwelled** \'dweld, 'dwelt\ *or* **dwelt** \'dwelt\; **dwelling** [Middle English, from Old English *dwellan* to go astray, hinder; akin to Old High German *twellen* to tarry] (13th century)
1 : to remain for a time
2 a : to live as a resident **b** : EXIST, LIE
3 a : to keep the attention directed — used with *on* or *upon* ⟨tried not to *dwell* on my fears⟩ **b** : to speak or write insistently — used with *on* or *upon* ⟨leering reviewers *dwelled* on a publicity photograph —James Atlas⟩
— **dwell·er** *noun*

dwell·ing *noun* (14th century)
: a shelter (as a house) in which people live

dwin·dle \'dwin-dᵊl\ *verb* **dwin·dled; dwin·dling** \-(d)liŋ, -dᵊl-iŋ\ [probably frequentative of *dwine* to waste away, from Middle English, from Old English *dwīnan;* akin to Old Norse *dvīna* to pine away, *deyja* to die — more at DIE] (1596)
intransitive verb
: to become steadily less : SHRINK
transitive verb
: to make steadily less
synonym see DECREASE

DX \(,)dē-'eks\ *noun* (circa 1924)
: DISTANCE — used of long-distance radio transmission

dy- *or* **dyo-** *combining form* [Late Latin, from Greek, from *dyo* — more at TWO]
: two ⟨*dyarchy*⟩

dy·ad \'dī-,ad, -əd\ *noun* [Late Latin *dyad-, dyas,* from Greek, from *dyo*] (1675)

1 : PAIR; *specifically* : two individuals (as husband and wife) maintaining a sociologically significant relationship
2 : a meiotic chromosome after separation of the two homologous members of a tetrad
3 : a mathematical operator indicated by writing the symbols of two vectors without a dot or cross between (as AB)
— **dy·ad·ic** \dī-'a-dik\ *adjective*
— **dy·ad·i·cal·ly** \-di-k(ə-)lē\ *adverb*
dy·ad·ic \dī-'a-dik\ *noun* (1884)
: a mathematical expression formed by addition or subtraction of dyads
Dy·ak *variant of* DAYAK
dy·ar·chy \'dī-,är-kē\ *noun, plural* **-chies** (1640)
: a government in which power is vested in two rulers or authorities
dyb·buk \'di-bək\ *noun, plural* **dyb·bu·kim** \,di-bù-'kēm\ *also* **dybbuks** [Late Hebrew *dibbūq*] (circa 1903)
: a wandering soul believed in Jewish folklore to enter and control a living body until exorcised by a religious rite
dye \'dī\ *noun* [Middle English *dehe*, from Old English *dēah*, *dēag*] (before 12th century)
1 : color from dyeing
2 : a soluble or insoluble coloring matter
dye *verb* **dyed; dye·ing** (before 12th century)
transitive verb
1 : to impart a new and often permanent color to especially by impregnating with a dye
2 : to impart (a color) by dyeing ⟨*dyeing* blue on yellow⟩
intransitive verb
: to take up or impart color in dyeing
— **dye·abil·i·ty** \,dī-ə-'bi-lə-tē\ *noun*
— **dye·able** \'dī-ə-bəl\ *adjective*
— **dy·er** \'dī-(ə)r\ *noun*
dyed–in–the–wool \,dīd-ᵊn-thə-'wùl\ *adjective* (1580)
: THOROUGHGOING, UNCOMPROMISING ⟨a *dyed-in-the-wool* conservative⟩
dye·stuff \'dī-,stəf\ *noun* (1837)
: DYE 2
dye·wood \-,wùd\ *noun* (1699)
: a wood (as logwood or fustic) from which coloring matter is extracted for dyeing
dying *present participle of* DIE
dyke *chiefly British variant of* DIKE
dyke \'dīk\ *noun* [origin unknown] (circa 1942)
: LESBIAN — often used disparagingly
— **dykey** \'dī-kē\ *adjective*
dy·nam·ic \dī-'na-mik\ *adjective* [French *dynamique*, from Greek *dynamikos* powerful, from *dynamis* power, from *dynasthai* to be able] (1827)
1 *also* **dy·nam·i·cal** \-mi-kəl\ **a** : of or relating to physical force or energy **b** : of or relating to dynamics
2 a : marked by usually continuous and productive activity or change ⟨a *dynamic* city⟩ **b** : ENERGETIC, FORCEFUL ⟨a *dynamic* personality⟩
3 *of random-access memory* : requiring periodic refreshment of charge in order to retain data
— **dy·nam·i·cal·ly** \-mi-k(ə-)lē\ *adverb*
dynamic *noun* (1879)
1 : a dynamic force
2 : DYNAMICS 2; *also* : an underlying cause of change or growth
dynamic range *noun* (1949)
: the ratio of the strongest to the weakest sound intensity that can be transmitted or reproduced by an audio or broadcasting system
dy·nam·ics \dī-'na-miks\ *noun plural but singular or plural in construction* (circa 1789)
1 : a branch of mechanics that deals with forces and their relation primarily to the motion but sometimes also to the equilibrium of bodies
2 : a pattern or process of change, growth, or activity ⟨population *dynamics*⟩

3 : variation and contrast in force or intensity (as in music)
dy·na·mism \'dī-nə-,mi-zəm\ *noun* (circa 1857)
1 a : a theory that all phenomena (as matter or motion) can be explained as manifestations of force — compare MECHANISM **b** : DYNAMICS 2
2 : a dynamic or expansionist quality
— **dy·na·mist** \-mist\ *noun*
— **dy·na·mis·tic** \,dī-nə-'mis-tik\ *adjective*
dy·na·mite \'dī-nə-,mīt\ *noun* (1867)
1 : an explosive that is made of nitroglycerin absorbed in a porous material and that often contains ammonium nitrate or cellulose nitrate; *also* : an explosive (as a mixture of ammonium nitrate and nitrocellulose) that contains no nitroglycerin
2 : one that has a powerful effect; *also* : something that has great potential to cause trouble or conflict
— **dy·na·mit·ic** \,dī-nə-'mi-tik\ *adjective*
dynamite *transitive verb* **-mit·ed; -mit·ing** (1881)
1 : to blow up with dynamite
2 : to cause the failure or destruction of
— **dy·na·mit·er** *noun*
dynamite *adjective* (1940)
: TERRIFIC, WONDERFUL
dy·na·mo \'dī-nə-,mō\ *noun, plural* **-mos** [short for *dynamoelectric machine*] (circa 1882)
1 : GENERATOR 3
2 : a forceful energetic individual
dy·na·mom·e·ter \,dī-nə-'mä-mə-tər\ *noun* [French *dynamomètre*, from Greek *dynamis* power + French *-mètre* -meter] (1810)
1 : an instrument for measuring mechanical force
2 : an apparatus for measuring mechanical power (as of an engine)
— **dy·na·mo·met·ric** \-mō-'me-trik\ *adjective*
— **dy·na·mom·e·try** \-'mä-mə-trē\ *noun*
dy·na·mo·tor \'dī-nə-,mō-tər\ *noun* [*dynamo* + *motor*] (1899)
: a motor generator combining the electric motor and generator
dy·nast \'dī-,nast, -nəst\ *noun* [Latin *dynastes*, from Greek *dynastēs*, from *dynasthai* to be able, have power] (1631)
: RULER 1
dy·nas·ty \'dī-nə-stē *also* -,nas-tē, *especially British* 'di-nə-stē\ *noun, plural* **-ties** (14th century)
1 : a succession of rulers of the same line of descent
2 : a powerful group or family that maintains its position for a considerable time
— **dy·nas·tic** \dī-'nas-tik\ *adjective*
— **dy·nas·ti·cal·ly** \-ti-k(ə-)lē\ *adverb*
dy·na·tron \'dī-nə-,trän\ *noun* [Greek *dynamis* power] (1918)
: a vacuum tube in which the secondary emission of electrons from the plate results in a decrease in the plate current as the plate voltage increases
dyne \'dīn\ *noun* [French, from Greek *dynamis*] (circa 1873)
: the unit of force in the centimeter-gram-second system equal to the force that would give a free mass of one gram an acceleration of one centimeter per second per second
dy·ne·in \'dī-nē-in\ *noun* [*dyne* (force) + *-in*] (1965)
: an ATPase that is associated especially with microtubules involved in the ciliary and flagellar movement of cells
dy·node \'dī-,nōd\ *noun* [Greek *dynamis*] (1939)
: an electrode in an electron tube that functions to produce secondary emission of electrons
dys- *prefix* [Middle English *dis-* bad, difficult, from Middle French & Latin; Middle French

dis-, from Latin *dys-*, from Greek; akin to Old English *tō-*, *te-* apart, Sanskrit *dus-* bad, difficult]
1 : abnormal ⟨*dys*plasia⟩
2 : difficult ⟨*dys*phagia⟩ — compare EU-
3 : impaired ⟨*dys*function⟩
4 : bad ⟨*dys*logistic⟩ — compare EU-
dys·ar·thria \di-'sär-thrē-ə\ *noun* [New Latin, from *dys-* + *arthr-* + *-ia*] (1878)
: difficulty in articulating words due to disease of the central nervous system
dys·cra·sia \dis-'krā-zh(ē-)ə\ *noun* [New Latin, from Medieval Latin, bad mixture of humors, from Greek *dyskrasia*, from *dys-* + *krasis* mixture, from *kerannynai* to mix — more at CRATER] (14th century)
: an abnormal condition of the body and especially the blood
dys·en·ter·ic \,di-sᵊn-'ter-ik\ *adjective* (1727)
: of or relating to dysentery
dys·en·tery \'di-sᵊn-,ter-ē\ *noun, plural* **-ter·ies** [Middle English *dissenterie*, from Latin *dysenteria*, from Greek, from *dys-* + *enteron* intestine — more at INTER-] (14th century)
1 : a disease characterized by severe diarrhea with passage of mucus and blood and usually caused by infection
2 : DIARRHEA
dys·func·tion \(,)dis-'fəŋ(k)-shən\ *noun* (circa 1916)
: impaired or abnormal functioning
— **dys·func·tion·al** \-shnəl, -shə-nᵊl\ *adjective*
dys·gen·e·sis \(,)dis-'je-nə-səs\ *noun* [New Latin] (circa 1883)
: defective development especially of the gonads (as in Klinefelter's syndrome)
dys·gen·ic \(,)dis-'je-nik\ *adjective* (1912)
1 : tending to promote survival of or reproduction by less well-adapted individuals (as the weak or diseased) especially at the expense of well-adapted individuals (as the strong or healthy) ⟨the *dysgenic* effect of war⟩
2 : biologically defective or deficient
dys·ki·ne·sia \,dis-kə-'nē-zh(ē-)ə, -kī-\ *noun* [New Latin, from Greek *dyskinēsia* difficulty in moving, from *dys-* + *-kinesia*, from *kinēsis* motion, from *kinein* to move — more at HIGHT] (circa 1706)
: impairment of voluntary movements resulting in fragmented or jerky motions (as in Parkinson's disease) — compare TARDIVE DYSKINESIA
— **dys·ki·net·ic** \-'net-ik\ *adjective*
dys·lex·ia \dis-'lek-sē-ə\ *noun* [New Latin, from *dys-* + Greek *lexis* word, speech, from *legein* to say — more at LEGEND] (circa 1888)
: a disturbance of the ability to read; *broadly* : disturbance of the ability to use language
— **dys·lex·ic** \-sik\ *adjective or noun*
dys·lo·gis·tic \dis-lə-'jis-tik\ *adjective* [*dys-* + *-logistic* (as in *eulogistic*)] (1812)
: UNCOMPLIMENTARY
— **dys·lo·gis·ti·cal·ly** \-ti-k(ə-)lē\ *adverb*
dys·men·or·rhea \(,)dis-,me-nə-'rē-ə\ *noun* [New Latin] (circa 1810)
: painful menstruation
— **dys·men·or·rhe·ic** \-'rē-ik\ *adjective*
dys·pep·sia \dis-'pep-shə, -sē-ə\ *noun* [Latin, from Greek, from *dys-* + *pepsis* digestion, from *peptein, pessein* to cook, digest — more at COOK] (1706)
1 : INDIGESTION
2 : ill humor : DISGRUNTLEMENT
— **dys·pep·tic** \-'pep-tik\ *adjective or noun*
— **dys·pep·ti·cal·ly** \-ti-k(ə-)lē\ *adverb*
dys·pha·gia \dis-'fā-j(ē-)ə\ *noun* [New Latin] (1783)

\ə\ abut \ᵊ\ kitten \ər\ further \a\ ash \ā\ ace
\ä\ mop, mar \au\ out \ch\ chin \e\ bet \ē\ easy
\g\ go \i\ hit \ī\ ice \j\ job \ŋ\ sing \ō\ go
\o\ law \oi\ boy \th\ thin \th\ the \ü\ loot \ù\ foot
\y\ yet \zh\ vision *see also* Guide to Pronunciation

: difficulty in swallowing

dys·pha·sia \dis-'fā-zh(ē-)ə\ *noun* [New Latin] (circa 1883)
: loss of or deficiency in the power to use or understand language as a result of injury to or disease of the brain
— **dys·pha·sic** \-'fā-zik\ *noun or adjective*

dys·phe·mism \'dis-fə-ˌmi-zəm\ *noun* [*dys-* + *-phemism* (as in *euphemism*)] (1884)
: the substitution of a disagreeable, offensive, or disparaging expression for an agreeable or inoffensive one; *also* : an expression so substituted
— **dys·phe·mis·tic** \ˌdis-fə-'mis-tik\ *adjective*

dys·pho·nia \dis-'fō-nē-ə\ *noun* [New Latin] (circa 1706)
: defective use of the voice

dys·pho·ria \dis-'fōr-ē-ə, -'fȯr-\ *noun* [New Latin, from Greek, from *dysphoros* hard to bear, from *dys-* + *pherein* to bear — more at BEAR] (circa 1842)
: a state of feeling unwell or unhappy
— **dys·phor·ic** \-'fȯr-ik, -'fär-\ *adjective*

dys·pla·sia \dis-'plā-zh(ē-)ə\ *noun* [New Latin] (circa 1923)
: abnormal growth or development (as of organs or cells); *broadly* : abnormal anatomic structure due to such growth
— **dys·plas·tic** \-'plas-tik\ *adjective*

dys·pnea \'dis(p)-nē-ə\ *noun* [Latin *dyspnoea*, from Greek *dyspnoia*, from *dyspnoos* short of breath, from *dys-* + *pnein* to breathe — more at SNEEZE] (circa 1681)
: difficult or labored respiration
— **dys·pne·ic** \-nē-ik\ *adjective*

dyspnoea *chiefly British variant of* DYSPNEA

dys·pro·si·um \dis-'prō-zē-əm, -zh(ē-)əm\ *noun* [New Latin, from Greek *dysprositos* hard to get at, from *dys-* + *prositos* approachable, from *prosienai* to approach, from *pros-* + *ienai* to go — more at ISSUE] (1886)
: an element of the rare-earth group that forms highly magnetic compounds — see ELEMENT table

dys·rhyth·mia \dis-'rith-mē-ə\ *noun* [New Latin, from *dys-* + Latin *rhythmus* rhythm] (circa 1909)
: an abnormal rhythm; *especially* : a disordered rhythm exhibited in a record of electrical activity of the brain or heart
— **dys·rhyth·mic** \-mik\ *adjective*

dys·to·cia \di-'stō-sh(ē-)ə\ *noun* [New Latin, from Greek *dystokia*, from *dys-* + *tokos* child-birth; akin to Greek *tiktein* to give birth to — more at THANE] (circa 1706)
: slow or difficult labor or delivery

dys·to·pia \(ˌ)dis-'tō-pē-ə\ *noun* [New Latin, from *dys-* + *-topia* (as in *utopia*)] (circa 1950)
1 : an imaginary place where people lead dehumanized and often fearful lives
2 : ANTI-UTOPIA 2
— **dys·to·pi·an** \-pē-ən\ *adjective*

dys·tro·phic \dis-'trō-fik\ *adjective* (1893)
1 a : relating to or caused by faulty nutrition **b** : relating to or affected with a dystrophy ⟨a *dystrophic* patient⟩
2 *of a lake* : brownish with much dissolved humic matter, a sparse bottom fauna, and a high oxygen consumption

dys·tro·phy \'dis-trə-fē\ *noun, plural* **-phies** [New Latin *dystrophia*, from *dys-* + *-trophia* -trophy] (1901)
1 : a condition produced by faulty nutrition
2 : any myogenic atrophy; *especially* : MUSCULAR DYSTROPHY

dys·uria \dis-'yu̇r-ē-ə, dish-\ *noun* [New Latin, from Greek *dysouria*, from *dys-* + *-ouria* -uria] (14th century)
: difficult or painful discharge of urine — compare STRANGURY

E *is the fifth letter of the English alphabet and of most alphabets that are closely related to it. It came through Latin from Etruscan and there from Greek, which took it from a Phoenician letter called* he, *representing a sound like English* h. *In Greek the letter, renamed* epsilon *("simple e"), designated a short vowel equivalent to the* e *in English* end. *Although the corresponding long vowel (pronounced like the* a *in English* ale*) was indicated in Greek by the letter* eta *(see* H*), in Latin* E *was used for both the short and the long vowel. English* E *inherited these Latin phonetic values, but in Modern English "long"* e *has come to represent the sound of the letter* e *in* eve. *The small letterform of* e *developed in two main stages: first by a curving of the upright line of capital* E *so as to form a semicircle with the top and bottom bars (ϵ); next by the joining of the top curve and middle bar to form a crescent.*

e \'ē\ *noun, plural* **e's** *or* **es** \'ēz\ *often capitalized, often attributive* (before 12th century)
1 a : the 5th letter of the English alphabet **b :** a graphic representation of this letter **c :** a speech counterpart of orthographic *e*
2 : the 3d tone of a C-major scale
3 : a graphic device for reproducing the letter *e*
4 : one designated *e* especially as the 5th in order or class
5 a : a grade rating a student's work as poor and usually constituting a conditional pass **b :** a grade rating a student's work as failing **c :** one graded or rated with an E
6 : a transcendental number having a value to eight decimal places of 2.71828183 that is the base of natural logarithms
7 : something shaped like the letter E
e- \(')ē, i\ *prefix* [Middle English, from Old French & Latin; Old French, out, forth, away, from Latin, from *ex-*]
1 : missing **:** absent ⟨edentulous⟩
2 : away ⟨eluviation⟩
¹each \'ēch\ *adjective* [Middle English *ech,* from Old English *ǣlc;* akin to Old High German *iogilīh* each; both from a prehistoric West Germanic compound whose first and second constituents respectively are represented by Old English *ā* always and by Old English *gelīc* alike] (before 12th century)
: being one of two or more distinct individuals having a similar relation and often constituting an aggregate
²each *pronoun* (before 12th century)
: each one
³each *adverb* (before 12th century)
: to or for each **:** APIECE
each other *pronoun* (before 12th century)
: each of two or more in reciprocal action or relation ⟨looked at *each other* in surprise⟩ □
ea·ger \'ē-gər\ *adjective* [Middle English *egre,* from Middle French *aigre,* from Latin *acer* — more at EDGE] (14th century)
1 a *archaic* **:** SHARP **b** *obsolete* **:** SOUR
2 : marked by enthusiastic or impatient desire or interest ☆
— ea·ger·ly *adverb*
— ea·ger·ness *noun*
eager beaver *noun* (1943)
: a person who is extremely zealous about performing duties and volunteering for more
ea·gle \'ē-gəl\ *noun* [Middle English *egle,* from Old French *aigle,* from Latin *aquila*] (13th century)
1 : any of various large diurnal birds of prey of the accipiter family noted for their strength, size, keenness of vision, and powers of flight
2 a : the eagle-bearing standard of the ancient Romans **b :** one of a pair of eagle-bearing silver insignia of rank worn by a military colonel or a navy captain

3 : a gold coin of the U.S. bearing an eagle on the reverse and usually having a value of ten dollars
4 : a golf score of two strokes less than par on a hole — compare BIRDIE
5 *capitalized* [Fraternal Order of *Eagles*] **:** a member of a major fraternal order
eagle eye *noun* (1802)
1 : the ability to see or observe with exceptional keenness
2 : one that sees or observes keenly
— eagle–eyed \'ē-gəl-,īd\ *adjective*
eagle ray *noun* (circa 1856)
: any of several widely distributed large active stingrays (family Myliobatidae) with broad pectoral fins like wings
Eagle Scout *noun* (1913)
1 : a Boy Scout who has reached the highest level of achievement in scouting
2 : a straight-arrow and self-reliant man
ea·glet \'ē-glət\ *noun* (1572)
: a young eagle
eal·dor·man \'al-dər-mən\ *noun* [Old English — more at ALDERMAN] (before 12th century)
: the chief officer in a district (as a shire) in Anglo-Saxon England
Eames chair \'ēmz-, 'āmz-\ *noun* [Charles Eames (died 1978) American designer] (1946)
: any of several chairs designed by Charles Eames to fit the contours of the body and to be made from modern materials
-ean — see -AN
¹ear \'ir, ēr\ *noun* [Middle English *ere,* from Old English *ēare;* akin to Old High German *ōra* ear, Latin *auris,* Greek *ous*] (before 12th century)
1 a : the characteristic vertebrate organ of hearing and equilibrium consisting in the typical mammal of a sound-collecting outer ear separated by the tympanic membrane from a sound-transmitting middle ear that in turn is separated from a sensory inner ear by membranous fenestrae **b :** any of various organs capable of detecting vibratory motion
2 : the external ear of humans and most mammals
3 a : the sense or act of hearing **b :** acuity of hearing **c :** sensitivity to musical tone and pitch; *also* **:** the ability to retain and reproduce music that has been heard **d :** sensitivity to nuances of language especially as revealed in the command of verbal melody and rhythm or in the ability to render a spoken idiom accurately
4 : something resembling a mammalian ear in shape, position, or function: as **a :** a projecting part (as a lug or handle) **b :** either of a pair of tufts of lengthened feathers on the head of some birds
5 a : sympathetic attention **b :** ATTENTION, AWARENESS
6 : a space in the upper corner of the front

page of a periodical (as a newspaper) usually containing advertising for the periodical itself or a weather forecast
— by ear : without reference to or memorization of written music ⟨plays *by ear*⟩
— in one ear and out the other : through one's mind without making an impression ⟨everything you say to him goes *in one ear and out the other*⟩
— on one's ear : in or into a state of irritation, shock, or discord ⟨set the racing world *on its ear* by breaking the record⟩
— up to one's ears : deeply involved **:** heavily implicated ⟨*up to his ears* in shady deals⟩

ear 1a: *1* pinna, *2* lobe, *3* auditory meatus, *4* tympanic membrane, *5* eustachian tube, *6* auditory nerve, *7* cochlea, *8* semicircular canals, *9* stapes, *10* incus, *11* malleus, *12* bones of skull

²ear *noun* [Middle English *er,* from Old English *ēar;* akin to Old High German *ahir* ear, Old English *ecg* edge — more at EDGE] (before 12th century)
: the fruiting spike of a cereal (as wheat or Indian corn) including both the seeds and protective structures
³ear *intransitive verb* (14th century)
: to form ears in growing ⟨the rye should be *earing* up⟩
ear·ache \'ir-,āk\ *noun* (1789)
: an ache or pain in the ear
ear candy *noun* (1977)
: music that is pleasing to listen to but lacks depth

ear clip *noun* (1945)
: an earring with a clip fastener
ear·drop \-,dräp\ *noun* (1720)
: EARRING; *especially* : one with a pendant
ear·drum \-,drəm\ *noun* (1645)
: TYMPANIC MEMBRANE
eared \'ird\ *adjective* (14th century)
: having ears especially of a specified kind or number ⟨a big-*eared* man⟩ ⟨golden-*eared* corn⟩
eared seal *noun* (1883)
: any of a family (Otariidae) of seals including the sea lions and fur seals and having independent mobile hind limbs and small well-developed external ears — compare HAIR SEAL
ear·flap \'ir-,flap\ *noun* (1907)
: a warm covering for the ears; *especially* : an extension on the lower edge of a cap that may be folded up or down
ear·ful \'ir-,fúl\ *noun* (1911)
1 : an outpouring of news or gossip
2 : an outpouring of anger, abuse, or complaint
ear·ing \'ir-iŋ\ *noun* [perhaps from ¹*ear*] (1626)
: a line used to fasten a corner of a sail to the yard or gaff or to haul a reef cringle to the yard
earl \'ər(-ə)l\ *noun* [Middle English *erl,* from Old English *eorl* warrior, nobleman; akin to Old Norse *jarl* warrior, nobleman] (12th century)
: a member of the British peerage ranking below a marquess and above a viscount
— **earl·dom** \-dəm\ *noun*
earl marshal *noun* (13th century)
: an officer of state in England serving chiefly as a royal attendant on ceremonial occasions, as marshal of state processions, and as head of the College of Arms
ear·lobe \'ir-,lōb\ *noun* (1859)
: the pendent part of the ear of humans or some fowls
ear·lock \-,läk\ *noun* (circa 1775)
: a curl of hair hanging in front of the ear
¹ear·ly \'ər-lē\ *adverb* **ear·li·er; -est** [Middle English *erly,* from Old English *ǣrlīce,* from *ǣr* early, soon — more at ERE] (before 12th century)
1 a : near the beginning of a period of time ⟨awoke *early* in the morning⟩ **b** : near the beginning of a course, process, or series ⟨*early* in his senatorial career⟩
2 a : before the usual or expected time **b** *archaic* : SOON **c** : sooner than related forms ⟨these apples bear *early*⟩
²early *adjective* **ear·li·er; -est** (13th century)
1 a : of, relating to, or occurring near the beginning of a period of time, a development, or a series **b** (1) : distant in past time (2) : PRIMITIVE
2 a : occurring before the usual or expected time **b** : occurring in the near future ⟨at your *earliest* convenience⟩ **c** : maturing or producing sooner than related forms ⟨an *early* peach⟩
— **ear·li·ness** *noun*
Early American *noun* (1895)
: a style (as of furniture, architecture, or fabric) originating in or characteristic of colonial America
early bird *noun* [from the proverb, "the early bird catches the worm"] (circa 1922)
1 : an early riser
2 : one that arrives early and especially before possible competitors
early on *adverb* (1928)
: at or during an early point or stage ⟨the reasons were obvious *early on* in the experiment⟩
□
ear·ly·wood \'ər-lē-,wúd\ *noun* (circa 1914)
: SPRINGWOOD
¹ear·mark \'ir-,märk\ *noun* (15th century)
1 : a mark of identification on the ear of an animal

2 : a distinguishing mark ⟨all the *earmarks* of poverty⟩
²earmark *transitive verb* (1591)
1 a : to mark (livestock) with an earmark **b** : to mark in a distinguishing manner
2 : to designate (as funds) for a specific use or owner
ear·muff \'ir-,məf\ *noun* (1889)
: one of a pair of ear coverings connected by a flexible band and worn as protection against cold or noises
¹earn \'ərn\ *transitive verb* [Middle English *ernen,* from Old English *earnian;* akin to Old High German *arnōn* to reap, Czech *jeseň* autumn] (before 12th century)
1 a : to receive as return for effort and especially for work done or services rendered **b** : to bring in by way of return ⟨bonds *earning* 10% interest⟩
2 a : to come to be duly worthy of or entitled or suited to ⟨she *earned* a promotion⟩ **b** : to make worthy of or obtain for ⟨the suggestion *earned* him a promotion⟩
— **earn·er** *noun*
²earn *intransitive verb* [probably alteration of *yearn*] (1599)
obsolete : GRIEVE
earned run *noun* (1886)
: a run in baseball that scores without benefit of an error before the fielding team has had a chance to make the third putout of the inning
earned run average *noun* (1947)
: the average number of earned runs per game scored against a pitcher in baseball determined by dividing the total of earned runs scored against him by the total number of innings pitched and multiplying by nine
¹ear·nest \'ər-nəst\ *noun* [Middle English *ernest,* from Old English *eornost;* akin to Old High German *ernust* earnest] (before 12th century)
: a serious and intent mental state ⟨in *earnest*⟩
²earnest *adjective* (before 12th century)
1 : characterized by or proceeding from an intense and serious state of mind
2 : GRAVE, IMPORTANT
synonym see SERIOUS
— **ear·nest·ly** *adverb*
— **ear·nest·ness** \-nəs(t)-nəs\ *noun*
³earnest *noun* [Middle English *ernes, ernest,* from Old French *erres,* plural of *erre* earnest, from Latin *arra,* short for *arrabo,* from Greek *arrhabōn,* of Semitic origin; akin to Hebrew *'ērābhōn* pledge] (13th century)
1 : something of value given by a buyer to a seller to bind a bargain
2 : a token of what is to come : PLEDGE ◇
earn·ings \'ər-niŋz\ *noun plural* (1732)
1 : something (as wages) earned
2 : the balance of revenue after deduction of costs and expenses
ear·phone \'ir-,fōn\ *noun* (1924)
: a device that converts electrical energy into sound waves and is worn over or inserted into the ear
ear pick *noun* (14th century)
: a device often of precious metal for removing wax or foreign bodies from the ear
ear·piece \'ir-,pēs\ *noun* (1853)
1 : a part of an instrument (as a stethoscope or hearing aid) which is applied to the ear; *especially* : EARPHONE
2 : one of the two sidepieces that support eyeglasses by passing over or behind the ears
ear·plug \-,pləg\ *noun* (1904)
1 : an ornament inserted in the lobe of the ear especially to distend it
2 : a device of pliable material for insertion into the outer opening of the ear (as to keep out water or deaden sound)
ear·ring \'ir-(,)iŋ, -,riŋ\ *noun* (before 12th century)
: an ornament for the earlobe
ear rot *noun* (1926)

: a condition of Indian corn that is characterized by molding and decay of the ears and that is caused by fungi (genera *Diplodia, Fusarium,* or *Gibberella*)
ear shell *noun* (circa 1753)
: ABALONE
ear·shot \'ir-,shät\ *noun* (1607)
: the range within which the unaided voice may be heard
ear·split·ting \-,spli-tiŋ\ *adjective* (1884)
: distressingly loud or shrill
synonym see LOUD
¹earth \'ərth\ *noun* [Middle English *erthe,* from Old English *eorthe;* akin to Old High German *erda* earth, Greek *era*] (before 12th century)
1 : the fragmental material composing part of the surface of the globe; *especially* : cultivable soil
2 : the sphere of mortal life as distinguished from spheres of spirit life — compare HEAVEN, HELL
3 a : areas of land as distinguished from sea and air **b** : the solid footing formed of soil : GROUND
4 *often capitalized* : the planet on which we live that is third in order from the sun — see PLANET table
5 a : the people of the planet Earth **b** : the mortal human body **c** : the pursuits, interests, and pleasures of earthly life as distinguished from spiritual concerns
6 : the lair of a burrowing animal
7 : an excessive amount of money — used with *the* ⟨real suede, which costs the *earth* to clean —Joanne Winship⟩
— **earth·like** \-,līk\ *adjective*
— **on earth** — used as an intensive ⟨to find out what *on earth* he was up to —Michael Holroyd⟩
²earth (1575)

transitive verb
1 : to drive to hiding in the earth
2 : to draw soil about (plants) — often used with *up*
3 *chiefly British* **:** GROUND 3
intransitive verb
of a hunted animal **:** to hide in the ground
earth·born \'ərth-ˌbȯrn\ *adjective* (1667)
1 : born on this earth **:** MORTAL
2 : associated with earthly life ⟨*earthborn* cares⟩
earth·bound \-ˌbaůnd\ *adjective* (1605)
1 a : fast in or to the soil ⟨*earthbound* roots⟩ **b :** located on or restricted to land or to the surface of the earth
2 a : bound by earthly interests **b :** PEDESTRIAN, UNIMAGINATIVE
earth color *noun* (1931)
: EARTH TONE
earth·en \'ər-thən, -thən\ *adjective* (13th century)
1 : made of earth
2 : EARTHLY
earth·en·ware \-ˌwar, -ˌwer\ *noun* (1648)
: ceramic ware made of slightly porous opaque clay fired at low heat
earth·i·ly \'ər-thə-lē, -thə-\ *adverb* (1953)
: in an earthy manner
earth·light \'ərth-ˌlīt\ *noun* (1833)
: EARTHSHINE
earth·ling \'ərth-liŋ\ *noun* (1593)
1 : an inhabitant of the earth
2 : WORLDLING
earth·ly \'ərth-lē\ *adjective* (before 12th century)
1 a : characteristic of or belonging to this earth **b :** relating to man's actual life on this earth
2 : POSSIBLE ⟨there is no *earthly* reason for such behavior⟩ ☆
— **earth·li·ness** *noun*
earth mother *noun, often E&M capitalized* (1902)
1 : the earth viewed (as in primitive theology) as the divine source of terrestrial life
2 : the embodiment of the female principle of fertility **:** a nurturing maternal woman
earth·mov·er \'ərth-ˌmü-vər\ *noun* (1941)
: a machine (as a bulldozer) for excavating, pushing, or transporting large quantities of earth (as in road building)
— **earth·mov·ing** \-ˌmü-viŋ\ *noun*
earth·quake \'ərth-ˌkwāk\ *noun* (14th century)
1 : a shaking or trembling of the earth that is volcanic or tectonic in origin
2 : UPHEAVAL 2
earth·rise \'ərth-ˌrīz\ *noun* (1968)
: the rising of the earth above the horizon of the moon as seen from lunar orbit
earth science *noun* (1939)
: any of the sciences (as geology, meteorology, or oceanography) that deal with the earth or with one or more of its parts — compare GEOSCIENCE
— **earth scientist** *noun*
earth·shak·er \'ərth-ˌshā-kər\ *noun* (1953)
: one that is earthshaking
earth·shak·ing \-ˌkiŋ\ *adjective* (1948)
: of great importance **:** MOMENTOUS
— **earth·shak·ing·ly** \-ˌkiŋ-lē\ *adverb*
earth–shat·ter·ing \'ərth-'sha-tə-riŋ\ *adjective* (1970)
: EARTHSHAKING
earth–shel·tered \'ərth-ˌshel-tərd\ *adjective* (1979)
: built partly or mostly underground ⟨an *earth-sheltered* house⟩
earth·shine \'ərth-ˌshīn\ *noun* (1876)
: sunlight reflected by the earth that illuminates the dark part of the moon — called also *earthlight*
earth·star \-ˌstär\ *noun* (1885)
: any of various fungi (*Geastrum*) of globose basidiomycetous fungi with an outer peridium that splits into the shape of a star

earth station *noun* (1970)
: DISH 3a(2); *especially* **:** one used primarily for receiving and transmitting television signals
earth tone *noun* (1973)
: any of various rich colors containing some brown
earth·ward \-wərd\ *also* **earth·wards** \-wərdz\ *adverb* (14th century)
: toward the earth
earth·work \'ərth-ˌwərk\ *noun* (1633)
1 : an embankment or other construction made of earth; *especially* **:** one used as a field fortification
2 : the operations connected with excavations and embankments of earth
3 : a work of art consisting of a portion of land modified by an artist
earth·worm \-ˌwərm\ *noun* (14th century)
: a terrestrial annelid worm (class Oligochaeta); *especially* **:** any of a family (Lumbricidae) of numerous widely distributed hermaphroditic worms that move through the soil by means of setae
earthy \'ər-thē, -thē\ *adjective* **earth·i·er; -est** (14th century)
1 a : of, relating to, or consisting of earth ⟨*earthy* creatures like worms⟩ **b :** suggestive of earth (as in texture, odor, or color) ⟨an *earthy* yellow⟩ **c :** rough, coarse, or plain in taste ⟨*earthy* flavors⟩
2 a *archaic* **:** EARTHLY, WORLDLY **b :** characteristic of or associated with mortal life on the earth ⟨prefers *earthy* to ethereal themes⟩
3 : suggestive of plain or poor people or their ways: as **a :** PRACTICAL, DOWN-TO-EARTH ⟨*earthy* problems of daily life⟩ **b :** CRUDE, GROSS ⟨*earthy* humor⟩ **c :** plain and simple in style **:** UNSOPHISTICATED ⟨*earthy* peasant cookery⟩ ⟨*earthy* decor⟩ ⟨*earthy* clothes⟩
— **earth·i·ness** *noun*
ear·wax \'ir-ˌwaks\ *noun* (14th century)
: CERUMEN
¹ear·wig \-ˌwig\ *noun* [Middle English *erwigge*, from Old English *ēarwicga*, from *ēare* ear + *wicga* insect] (before 12th century)
: any of numerous insects (order Dermaptera) having slender many-jointed antennae and a pair of cerci resembling forceps at the end of the body
²earwig *transitive verb* **ear·wigged; ear·wig·ging** (1837)
: to annoy or attempt to influence by private talk
ear·wit·ness \'ir-'wit-nəs\ *noun* (1594)
: one who overhears something; *especially* **:** one who gives a report on what has been heard
¹ease \'ēz\ *noun* [Middle English *ese*, from Old French *aise* convenience, comfort, from Latin *adjacent-, adjacens* neighboring — more at ADJACENT] (13th century)
1 : the state of being comfortable: as **a :** freedom from pain or discomfort **b :** freedom from care **c :** freedom from labor or difficulty **d :** freedom from embarrassment or constraint **:** NATURALNESS **e :** an easy fit
2 : relief from discomfort or obligation
3 : FACILITY, EFFORTLESSNESS
4 : an act of easing or a state of being eased
— **ease·ful** \-fəl\ *adjective*
— **ease·ful·ly** \-fə-lē\ *adverb*
— **at ease 1 :** free from pain or discomfort
2 a : free from restraint or formality **b :** standing silently (as in a military formation) with the feet apart, the right foot in place, and one or both hands behind the body — often used as a command
²ease *verb* **eased; eas·ing** (14th century)
transitive verb
1 : to free from something that pains, disquiets, or burdens
2 : to make less painful **:** ALLEVIATE ⟨*ease* his suffering⟩

3 a : to lessen the pressure or tension of especially by slackening, lifting, or shifting **b :** to maneuver gently or carefully **c :** to moderate or reduce especially in amount or intensity
4 : to make less difficult ⟨*ease* credit⟩
5 a : to put the helm of (a ship) alee **b :** to let (a helm or rudder) come back a little after having been put hard over
intransitive verb
1 : to give freedom or relief
2 : to move or pass with freedom or with little resistance
3 : MODERATE, SLACKEN
ea·sel \'ē-zəl\ *noun* [Dutch *ezel*, literally, ass, from Middle Dutch *esel*; akin to Old English *esol* ass; both from a prehistoric East Germanic-West Germanic word borrowed from Latin *asinus* ass] (1596)
: a frame for supporting something (as an artist's canvas) ◇
ease·ment \'ēz-mənt\ *noun* (14th century)
1 : an act or means of easing or relieving (as from discomfort)
2 : an interest in land owned by another that entitles its holder to a specific limited use or enjoyment
eas·i·ly \'ēz-lē, 'ē-zə-\ *adverb* (13th century)
1 : in an easy manner **:** without difficulty
2 : without question **:** by far
3 : WELL 10b ⟨it could *easily* have been me⟩
¹east \'ēst\ *adverb* [Middle English *est*, from Old English *ēast*; akin to Old High German *ōstar* to the east, Latin *aurora* dawn, Greek *ēōs, heōs*] (before 12th century)
: to, toward, or in the east
²east *adjective* (before 12th century)
1 : situated toward or at the east ⟨an *east* window⟩
2 : coming from the east ⟨an *east* wind⟩
³east *noun* (before 12th century)
1 a : the general direction of sunrise **:** the direction toward the right of one facing north **b :** the compass point directly opposite to west
2 *capitalized* **a :** regions lying to the east of a specified or implied point of orientation **b :** regions having a culture derived from ancient non-European especially Asian areas
3 : the altar end of a church

☆ SYNONYMS
Earthly, worldly, mundane mean belonging to or characteristic of the earth. EARTHLY often implies a contrast with what is heavenly or spiritual ⟨abandoned *earthly* concerns and entered a convent⟩. WORLDLY and MUNDANE both imply a relation to the immediate concerns and activities of human beings, WORLDLY suggesting tangible personal gain or gratification ⟨*worldly* goods⟩ and MUNDANE suggesting reference to the immediate and practical ⟨a *mundane* discussion of finances⟩.

◇ WORD HISTORY
easel The word *easel* was borrowed into English from Middle Dutch *esel* or Dutch *ezel*, alluding to the frame that supports an artist's canvas. This sense was a metaphorical extension of the literal meaning "ass, donkey," probably from the fact that, like a beast of burden, an easel is used to hold things. If this metaphor seems at all odd, we need only recall that since at least the 18th century English has used *horse* in a very similar way in the compound *sawhorse*, a framework used to support wood for cutting.

\ə\ abut \'ə\ kitten \ər\ further \a\ ash \ā\ ace
\ä\ mop, mar \au̇\ out \ch\ chin \e\ bet \ē\ easy
\g\ go \i\ hit \ī\ ice \j\ job \ŋ\ sing \ō\ go
\ȯ\ law \ȯi\ boy \th\ thin \t͟h\ the \ü\ loot \u̇\ foot
\y\ yet \zh\ vision *see also* Guide to Pronunciation

4 *often capitalized* **a :** the one of four positions at 90-degree intervals that lies to the east or at the right of a diagram **b :** a person (as a bridge player) occupying this position in the course of a specified activity

east·bound \'ēs(t)-ˌbau̇nd\ *adjective* (1880)
: traveling or heading east

east by north (1594)
: a compass point that is one point north of due east **:** N78°45′E

east by south (14th century)
: a compass point that is one point south of due east **:** S78°45′E

East Caribbean dollar *noun* (circa 1974)
: the basic monetary unit shared by a number of islands of the British West Indies

Eas·ter \'ē-stər\ *noun* [Middle English *estre*, from Old English *ēastre*; akin to Old High German *ōstarun* (plural) Easter, Old English *ēast* east] (before 12th century)
: a feast that commemorates Christ's resurrection and is observed with variations of date due to different calendars on the first Sunday after the paschal full moon

EASTER DATES

YEAR	ASH WEDNESDAY	EASTER
1993	February 24	April 11
1994	February 16	April 3
1995	March 1	April 16
1996	February 21	April 7
1997	February 12	March 30
1998	February 25	April 12
1999	February 17	April 4
2000	March 8	April 23
2001	February 28	April 15
2002	February 13	March 31
2003	March 5	April 20
2004	February 25	April 11
2005	February 9	March 27
2006	March 1	April 16
2007	February 21	April 8
2008	February 6	March 23
2009	February 25	April 12
2010	February 17	April 4
2011	March 9	April 24
2012	February 22	April 8

Easter egg *noun* (1804)
: an egg that is dyed and sometimes decorated and that is associated with the celebration of Easter

Easter lily *noun* (1877)
: any of several white cultivated lilies (especially *Lilium longiflorum*) that bloom in early spring

¹east·er·ly \'ē-stər-lē\ *adjective or adverb* [obsolete *easter* (eastern)] (1548)
1 : situated toward or belonging to the east ⟨the *easterly* shore of the lake⟩
2 : coming from the east ⟨an *easterly* storm⟩

²easterly *noun, plural* **-lies** (1901)
: a wind from the east

Easter Monday *noun* (14th century)
: the Monday after Easter observed as a legal holiday in some nations of the Commonwealth and in North Carolina

east·ern \'ē-stərn\ *adjective* [Middle English *estern*, from Old English *ēasterne*; akin to Old High German *ōstrōni* eastern, Old English *ēast* east] (before 12th century)
1 *capitalized* **:** of, relating to, or characteristic of a region conventionally designated East
2 *capitalized* **a :** of, relating to, or being the Christian churches originating in the church of the Eastern Roman Empire **b :** EASTERN ORTHODOX
3 a : lying toward the east **b :** coming from the east ⟨an *eastern* wind⟩
— east·ern·most \-ˌmōst\ *adjective*
East·ern·er \'ē-stə(r)-nər\ *noun* (1840)

: a native or inhabitant of the East; *especially*
: a native or resident of the eastern part of the U.S.

eastern hemisphere *noun, often E&H capitalized* (1624)
: the half of the earth east of the Atlantic Ocean including Europe, Asia, Australia, and Africa

Eastern Orthodox *adjective* (1909)
: of or consisting of the Eastern churches that form a loose federation according primacy of honor to the patriarch of Constantinople and adhering to the decisions of the first seven ecumenical councils and to the Byzantine rite

eastern time *noun, often E capitalized* (1883)
: the time of the 5th time zone west of Greenwich that includes the eastern U.S. — see TIME ZONE illustration

eastern white pine *noun* (1925)
: WHITE PINE 1a

Eas·ter·tide \'ē-stər-ˌtīd\ *noun* [Middle English *estertide*, from Old English *ēastortīd*, from *ēastor* + *tīd* time — more at TIDE] (before 12th century)
: the period from Easter to Ascension Day, to Whitsunday, or to Trinity Sunday

East Germanic *noun* (circa 1901)
: a subdivision of the Germanic languages that includes Gothic — see INDO-EUROPEAN LANGUAGES table

east·ing \'ē-stiŋ\ *noun* (1628)
1 : easterly progress
2 : difference in longitude to the east from the last preceding point of reckoning

east–northeast *noun* (1725)
: a compass point that is two points north of due east **:** N67°30′E

east–southeast *noun* (1555)
: a compass point that is two points south of due east **:** S67°30′E

¹east·ward \'ēs-twərd\ *adverb or adjective* (before 12th century)
: toward the east
— east·wards \-twərdz\ *adverb*

²eastward *noun* (1582)
: eastward direction or part ⟨sail to the *eastward*⟩

¹easy \'ē-zē\ *adjective* **eas·i·er; -est** [Middle English *esy*, from Old French *aaisié*, past participle of *aaisier* to ease, from *a-* ad- (from Latin *ad-*) + *aise* ease] (13th century)
1 a : causing or involving little difficulty or discomfort ⟨within *easy* reach⟩ **b :** requiring or indicating little effort, thought, or reflection ⟨*easy* clichés⟩
2 a : not severe **:** LENIENT **b :** not steep or abrupt ⟨*easy* slopes⟩ **c :** not difficult to endure or undergo ⟨an *easy* penalty⟩ **d :** readily taken advantage of ⟨an *easy* target for takeovers⟩ **e** (1) **:** readily available **:** easily come by ⟨*easy* pickings⟩ (2) **:** plentiful in supply at low or declining interest rates ⟨*easy* money⟩ (3) **:** less in demand and usually lower in price ⟨bonds were *easier*⟩ **f :** PLEASANT ⟨*easy* listening⟩
3 a : marked by peace and comfort ⟨the *easy* life of a courtier⟩ **b :** not hurried or strenuous ⟨an *easy* pace⟩
4 a : free from pain, annoyance, or anxiety ⟨did all she could to make him *easier*⟩ **b :** marked by social ease ⟨an air of *easy* assurance⟩ **c :** EASYGOING ⟨an *easy* disposition⟩
5 a : giving ease, comfort, or relaxation ⟨*easy* chairs⟩ **b :** not burdensome or straitened ⟨bought on *easy* terms⟩ **c :** fitting comfortably **:** allowing freedom of movement ⟨*easy* jackets⟩ **d :** marked by ready facility ⟨an *easy* flowing style⟩ **e :** felt or attained to readily, naturally, and spontaneously ⟨an *easy* smile⟩
☆
— eas·i·ness *noun*

²easy *adverb* **eas·i·er; -est** (14th century)
1 : EASILY 1 ⟨promises come *easy*⟩
2 a : without undue speed or excitement ⟨take it *easy*⟩ **b :** in or with moderation ⟨go *easy* on the mustard⟩

3 a : without worry or care ⟨rest *easy*⟩ **b :** without a severe penalty ⟨got off *easy*⟩ **c :** without violent movement ⟨the boat rode *easy*⟩
4 : EASILY 2 ⟨cost $500 *easy*⟩

easy·go·ing \ˌē-zē-'gō-iŋ, -'gȯ(-)iŋ\ *adjective* (1674)
1 a : relaxed and casual in style or manner ⟨an *easygoing* boss⟩ **b :** morally lax
2 : UNHURRIED, COMFORTABLE ⟨an *easygoing* pace⟩
— easy·go·ing·ness *noun*

easy mark *noun* (circa 1896)
: one easily taken advantage of

easy street *noun* (1900)
: a situation with no worries

easy virtue *noun* (1809)
: sexually promiscuous behavior or habits ⟨ladies of *easy virtue*⟩

¹eat \'ēt\ *verb* **ate** \'āt, *dialect or British* 'et\; **eat·en** \'ē-tᵊn\; **eat·ing** [Middle English *eten*, from Old English *etan*; akin to Old High German *ezzan* to eat, Latin *edere*, Greek *edmenai*] (before 12th century)
transitive verb
1 : to take in through the mouth as food **:** ingest, chew, and swallow in turn
2 a : to destroy, consume, or waste by or as if by eating ⟨expenses *ate* up the profits⟩ **b :** to bear the expense of **:** take a loss on
3 a : to consume gradually **:** CORRODE **b :** to consume with vexation **:** BOTHER ⟨what's *eating* you now⟩
intransitive verb
1 : to take food or a meal
2 : to affect something by gradual destruction or consumption — usually used with *into*, *away*, or *at*
— eat·er *noun*
— eat another's lunch : to deprive of profit, dominance, or success
— eat crow : to accept what one has fought against
— eat humble pie : to apologize or retract under pressure
— eat one's heart out 1 : to grieve bitterly **2 :** to be jealous
— eat one's words : to retract what one has said
— eat out of one's hand : to accept the domination of another

²eat *noun* [Middle English *et*, from Old English *ǣt*; akin to Old High German *āz* food; derivative from the root of ¹*eat*] (before 12th century)
: something to eat **:** FOOD — usually used in plural

¹eat·able \'ē-tə-bəl\ *adjective* (14th century)
: fit or able to be eaten

²eatable *noun* (1672)
1 : something to eat
2 *plural* **:** FOOD

eat·ery \'ē-tə-rē\ *noun, plural* **-er·ies** (1901)

☆ **SYNONYMS**
Easy, facile, simple, light, effortless, smooth mean not demanding effort or involving difficulty. EASY is applicable either to persons or things imposing tasks or to activity required by such tasks ⟨an *easy* college course⟩. FACILE often adds to EASY the connotation of undue haste or shallowness ⟨*facile* answers to complex questions⟩. SIMPLE stresses ease in understanding or dealing with because complication is absent ⟨a *simple* problem in arithmetic⟩. LIGHT stresses freedom from what is burdensome ⟨a *light* teaching load⟩. EFFORTLESS stresses the appearance of ease and usually implies the prior attainment of artistry or expertness ⟨moving with *effortless* grace⟩. SMOOTH stresses the absence or removal of all difficulties, hardships, or obstacles ⟨a *smooth* ride⟩. See in addition COMFORTABLE.

: LUNCHEONETTE, RESTAURANT

eath \ˈēth\ *adverb or adjective* [Middle English *ethe,* from Old English *ēathe;* akin to Old High German *ōdi* easy] (before 12th century) *Scottish* : EASY

eat·ing \ˈē-tiŋ\ *adjective* (15th century)
1 : used for eating ⟨*eating* utensils⟩
2 : suitable to eat ⟨the finest *eating* fish⟩; *also* : suitable to eat raw ⟨an *eating* apple⟩

eau de co·logne \ˌō-də-kə-ˈlōn\ *noun, plural* **eaux de cologne** \ˌō(z)-də-\ [French, literally, Cologne water, from *Cologne,* Germany] (1802)
: COLOGNE

eau–de–vie \ˌō-də-ˈvē\ *noun, plural* **eaux–de–vie** \ˌō(z)-də-\ [French, literally, water of life, translation of Medieval Latin *aqua vitae*] (1748)
: a clear brandy distilled from the fermented juice of fruit (as pears or raspberries)

eaves \ˈēvz\ *noun plural* [Middle English *eves* (singular), from Old English *efes;* akin to Old High German *obasa* portico, Old English *ūp* up — more at UP] (before 12th century)
1 : the lower border of a roof that overhangs the wall
2 : a projecting edge (as of a hill)

eaves·drop \ˈēvz-ˌdräp\ *intransitive verb* [probably back-formation from *eavesdropper,* literally, one standing under the drip from the eaves] (1606)
: to listen secretly to what is said in private ◆
— **eaves·drop·per** *noun*

eaves trough *noun* (1878)
: GUTTER 1a

¹ebb \ˈeb\ *noun* [Middle English *ebbe,* from Old English *ebba;* akin to Middle Dutch *ebbe* ebb, Old English *of* from — more at OF] (before 12th century)
1 : the reflux of the tide toward the sea
2 : a point or condition of decline ⟨our spirits were at a low *ebb*⟩

²ebb *intransitive verb* (before 12th century)
1 : to recede from the flood
2 : to fall from a higher to a lower level or from a better to a worse state
synonym see ABATE

ebb tide *noun* (1823)
1 : the tide while ebbing or at ebb
2 : a period or state of decline

EBCDIC \ˈep-sə-ˌdik, ˈeb-\ *noun* [extended binary coded decimal interchange code] (circa 1966)
: a code for representing alphanumeric information (as on magnetic tape)

Ebo·la virus \ē-ˈbō-lə, i-, e-\ *noun* [Ebola River, Zaire, site of an outbreak of the virus in 1976] (1977)
: an RNA-containing virus of African origin that causes an often fatal hemorrhagic fever — called also *Ebola*

eb·on \ˈe-bən\ *adjective* (15th century)
: EBONY

eb·o·nite \ˈe-bə-ˌnīt\ *noun* (1861)
: hard rubber especially when black

eb·o·nize \-ˌnīz\ *transitive verb* **-nized; -nizing** (circa 1828)
: to stain black in imitation of ebony

¹eb·o·ny \ˈe-bə-nē\ *noun, plural* **-nies** [probably from Late Latin *hebeninus* of ebony, from Greek *ebeninos,* from *ebenos* ebony, from Egyptian *hbnj*] (14th century)
1 : a hard heavy wood yielded by various Old World tropical dicotyledonous trees (genus *Diospyros* of the family Ebonaceae, the ebony family)
2 a : a tree yielding ebony **b** : any of several trees yielding wood like ebony

²ebony *adjective* (1598)
1 : made of or resembling ebony
2 : BLACK, DARK

ebul·lience \i-ˈbu̇l-yən(t)s, -ˈbəl-\ *noun* (1749)
: the quality of lively or enthusiastic expression of thoughts or feelings : EXUBERANCE

ebul·lien·cy \-yən(t)-sē\ *noun* (1676)

: EBULLIENCE

ebul·lient \-yənt\ *adjective* [Latin *ebullient-, ebulliens,* present participle of *ebullire* to bubble out, from *e-* + *bullire* to bubble, boil — more at BOIL] (1599)
1 : BOILING, AGITATED
2 : characterized by ebullience
— **ebul·lient·ly** *adverb*

eb·ul·li·tion \ˌe-bə-ˈli-shən\ *noun* (1534)
1 : a sudden violent outburst or display
2 : the act, process, or state of boiling or bubbling up

EB virus \ˌē-ˈbē-\ *noun* (1968)
: EPSTEIN-BARR VIRUS

¹ec·cen·tric \ik-ˈsen-trik, ek-\ *adjective* [Middle English, from Medieval Latin *eccentricus,* from Greek *ekkentros,* from *ex* out of + *kentron* center] (circa 1630)
1 a : deviating from an established or usual pattern or style **b** : deviating from conventional or accepted usage or conduct especially in odd or whimsical ways
2 a : deviating from a circular path; *especially* : ELLIPTICAL 1 ⟨an *eccentric* orbit⟩ **b** : located elsewhere than at the geometrical center; *also* : having the axis or support so located ⟨an *eccentric* wheel⟩
synonym see STRANGE
— **ec·cen·tri·cal·ly** \-tri-k(ə-)lē\ *adverb*

²eccentric *noun* (1827)
1 : a mechanical device consisting of a disk through which a shaft is keyed eccentrically and a circular strap which works freely round the rim of the disk for communicating its motion to one end of a rod whose other end is constrained to move in a straight line so as to produce reciprocating motion
2 : an eccentric person

ec·cen·tric·i·ty \ˌek-(ˌ)sen-ˈtri-sə-tē\ *noun, plural* **-ties** (1545)
1 a : the quality or state of being eccentric **b** : deviation from an established pattern or norm; *especially* : odd or whimsical behavior
2 a : a mathematical constant that for a given conic section is the ratio of the distances from any point of the conic section to a focus and the corresponding directrix **b** : the eccentricity of an astronomical orbit used as a measure of its deviation from circularity

ec·chy·mo·sis \ˌe-ki-ˈmō-səs\ *noun, plural* **-mo·ses** \-ˌsēz\ [New Latin, from Greek *ekchymōsis,* from *ekchymousthai* to extravasate blood, from *ex-* + *chymos* juice — more at CHYME] (1541)
: the escape of blood into the tissues from ruptured blood vessels
— **ec·chy·mot·ic** \-ˈmä-tik\ *adjective*

ecclesi- *or* **ecclesio-** *combining form* [Middle English *ecclesi-,* from Late Latin *ecclesia,* from Greek *ekklēsia* assembly of citizens, church, from *ekkalein* to call forth, summon, from *ex-* + *kalein* to call — more at LOW]
: church ⟨*ecclesiology*⟩

ec·cle·si·al \i-ˈklē-zē-əl, e-ˈklē-\ *adjective* (1641)
: of or relating to a church

Ec·cle·si·as·tes \i-ˌklē-zē-ˈas-(ˌ)tēz, e-ˌklē-\ *noun* [Greek *Ekklēsiastēs,* literally, preacher (translation of Hebrew *qōheleth*), from *ekklēsiastēs* member of an assembly, from *ekklēsia*] : a book of wisdom literature in canonical Jewish and Christian Scripture — see BIBLE table

¹ec·cle·si·as·tic \-ˈas-tik\ *adjective* (15th century)
: ECCLESIASTICAL

²ecclesiastic *noun* (1651)
: CLERGYMAN

ec·cle·si·as·ti·cal \-ti-kəl\ *adjective* [Middle English, from Late Latin *ecclesiasticus,* from Late Greek *ekklēsiastikos,* from Greek, of an assembly of citizens, from *ekklēsiastēs*] (15th century)
1 : of or relating to a church especially as an established institution
2 : suitable for use in a church

— **ec·cle·si·as·ti·cal·ly** \-ti-k(ə-)lē\ *adverb*

ec·cle·si·as·ti·cism \-tə-ˌsi-zəm\ *noun* (circa 1859)
: excessive attachment to ecclesiastical forms and practices

Ec·cle·si·as·ti·cus \-ti-kəs\ *noun* [Late Latin, from *ecclesiasticus*]
: a didactic book included in the Protestant Apocrypha and as Sirach in the Roman Catholic canon of the Old Testament

ec·cle·si·ol·o·gy \i-ˌklē-zē-ˈä-lə-jē, e-ˌklē-\ *noun, plural* **-gies** (circa 1837)
1 : the study of church architecture and adornment
2 : theological doctrine relating to the church
— **ec·cle·si·o·log·i·cal** \-zē-ə-ˈlä-ji-kəl\ *adjective*
— **ec·cle·si·ol·o·gist** \-zē-ˈä-lə-jist\ *noun*

ec·crine gland \ˈe-krən-, -ˌkrīn-, -ˌkren-\ *noun* [Greek *ekkrinein* to secrete, from *ek-, ex-* out + *krinein* to separate — more at CERTAIN] (circa 1927)
: any of the rather small sweat glands in the human skin that produce a fluid secretion without removing cytoplasm from the secretory cells — called also *eccrine sweat gland*

ec·dys·i·ast \ek-ˈdi-zē-ˌast, -ē-əst\ *noun* [Greek *ekdysīs*] (1940)
: STRIPTEASER

ec·dy·sis \ˈek-də-səs\ *noun, plural* **ec·dy·ses** \-də-ˌsēz\ [New Latin, from Greek *ekdysis* act of getting out, from *ekdyein* to strip, from *ex-* + *dyein* to enter, don] (circa 1854)
: the act of molting or shedding an outer cuticular layer (as in insects and crustaceans)

ec·dy·sone \ˈek-də-ˌsōn\ *also* **ec·dy·son** \-ˌsän\ *noun* [International Scientific Vocabulary *ecdysis* + hormone] (1956)
: any of several arthropod hormones that in insects are produced by the prothoracic gland and that trigger molting and metamorphosis

ece·sis \i-ˈsē-səs, -ˈkē-\ *noun* [New Latin, from Greek *oikēsis* inhabitation, from *oikein* to inhabit — more at ECUMENICAL] (circa 1904)
: the establishment of a plant or animal in a new habitat

echelle \ā-ˈshel\ *noun* [French, literally, ladder, from Old French *eschele*] (1949)

◇ WORD HISTORY

eavesdrop The verb *eavesdrop* first appeared in the 17th century and is probably a back-formation from *eavesdropper,* which is attested in Middle English as *evesdropper* and is apparently a derivative of an earlier noun *evesdrop. Evesdrop,* and a related Old English word *yfesdrype,* occur very rarely and then only in law texts that refer to the ground below the eaves of a house on which rainwater drips. This use comes from an old sanction against building so close to the edge of one's property that water from the eaves falls on a neighbor's land. For a while the word *eavesdropper* too occurred mainly in legal contexts—persons snooping on others' conversations seem to have been considered a sort of public nuisance, like Peeping Toms—but less literal uses of *eavesdropper* and the verb *eavesdrop* appear in the 17th and 18th centuries. Today applications of the words to secret observation by satellite or electronic device are far removed from eaves, rainwater, or stealthy listening outside the walls of someone's house.

\ə\ abut \ᵊ\ kitten \ər\ further \a\ ash \ā\ ace \ä\ mop, mar \au̇\ out \ch\ chin \e\ bet \ē\ easy \g\ go \i\ hit \ī\ ice \j\ job \ŋ\ sing \ō\ go \ȯ\ law \ȯi\ boy \th\ thin \t͟h\ the \ü\ loot \u̇\ foot \y\ yet \zh\ vision *see also* Guide to Pronunciation

: a diffraction grating made by ruling a plane metallic mirror with lines having a relatively wide spacing

¹ech·e·lon \'e-shə-ˌlän\ *noun* [French *échelon,* literally, rung of a ladder, from Old French *eschelon,* from *eschele* ladder, from Late Latin *scala*] (1796)
1 a (1) : an arrangement of a body of troops with its units each somewhat to the left or right of the one in the rear like a series of steps (2) : a formation of units or individuals resembling such an echelon (3) : a flight formation in which each airplane flies at a certain elevation above or below and at a certain distance behind and to the right or left of the airplane ahead **b** : any of several military units in echelon formation
2 a : one of a series of levels or grades (as of leadership or responsibility) in an organization or field of activity **b** : a group of individuals at a particular level or grade in an organization ◊

²echelon (circa 1860)
transitive verb
: to form or arrange in an echelon
intransitive verb
: to take position in an echelon

ech·e·ve·ria \ˌe-chə-və-'rē-ə\ *noun* [New Latin, genus name, after Atanasio *Echeverría* (flourished 1771) Mexican botanical illustrator] (1883)
: any of a large genus (*Echeveria*) of tropical American succulent plants of the orpine family that have showy rosettes of often plushy basal leaves and axillary clusters of flowers with erect petals and that are often grown as ornamentals

echid·na \i-'kid-nə\ *noun* [New Latin, from Latin, viper, from Greek — more at OPHITIC] (1832)
: an oviparous spiny-coated toothless burrowing nocturnal monotreme mammal (*Tachyglossus aculeatus*) of Australia, Tasmania, and New Guinea that has a long extensile tongue and

echidna

long heavy claws and that feeds chiefly on ants; *also* : a related mammal (*Zaglossus bruijni*) of New Guinea having a longer snout and shorter spines

echin- *or* **echino-** *combining form* [Latin, from Greek, from *echinos* sea urchin]
1 : prickle ⟨*echino*derm⟩
2 : sea urchin ⟨*echin*oid⟩

echi·no·coc·co·sis \i-ˌkī-nə-kä-'kō-səs\ *noun, plural* **-co·ses** \-ˌsēz\ [New Latin] (1900)
: infestation with or disease caused by an echinococcus (as *Echinococcus granulosus*)

echi·no·coc·cus \i-ˌkī-nə-'kä-kəs\ *noun, plural* **-coc·ci** \-'käk-ˌ(s)ī, -'käk-ˌ(s)ē\ [New Latin, genus name] (1839)
: any of a genus (*Echinococcus*) of tapeworms that alternate a minute adult living as a commensal in the intestine of carnivores with a hydatid larva invading tissues especially of the liver of cattle, sheep, swine, and humans and acting as a dangerous pathogen

echi·no·derm \i-'kī-nə-ˌdərm\ *noun* [New Latin *Echinodermata,* phylum name, from *echin-* + *-dermata* (from Greek *derma* skin)] (1835)
: any of a phylum (Echinodermata) of radially symmetrical coelomate marine animals including the starfishes, sea urchins, and related forms
— **echi·no·der·ma·tous** \-ˌkī-nə-'dər-mə-təs\ *adjective*

echi·noid \i-'kī-ˌnȯid, 'e-kə-ˌnȯid\ *noun* (1864)
: SEA URCHIN

echi·nus \i-'kī-nəs\ *noun, plural* **-ni** \-ˌnī\ [Middle English, from Latin, from Greek *echinos* hedgehog, sea urchin — more at OPHITE] (14th century)
1 : SEA URCHIN
2 a : the rounded molding forming the bell of the capital in the Greek Doric order **b** : a similar member in other orders

¹echo \'e-(ˌ)kō\ *noun, plural* **ech·oes** *also* **echos** [Middle English *ecco,* from Middle French & Latin; Middle French *echo,* from Latin, from Greek *ēchō;* akin to Latin *vagire* to wail, Greek *ēchē* sound] (14th century)
1 a : the repetition of a sound caused by reflection of sound waves **b** : the sound due to such reflection
2 a : a repetition or imitation of another : REFLECTION **b** : REPERCUSSION, RESULT **c** : TRACE, VESTIGE **d** : RESPONSE
3 : one who closely imitates or repeats another's words, ideas, or acts
4 : a soft repetition of a musical phrase
5 a : the repetition of a received radio signal due especially to reflection of part of the wave from an ionized layer of the atmosphere **b** (1) : the reflection of transmitted radar signals by an object (2) : the visual indication of this reflection on a radarscope
— **echo·ey** \'e-ˌkō-ē\ *adjective*

²echo *verb* **ech·oed; echo·ing** \'e-(ˌ)kō-iŋ, 'e-kə-wiŋ\ (1596)
intransitive verb
1 : to resound with echoes
2 : to produce an echo
transitive verb
1 : REPEAT, IMITATE
2 : to send back (a sound) by the reflection of sound waves

¹Echo *noun* [Greek *Ēchō*]
: a nymph in Greek mythology who pines away for love of Narcissus until nothing is left of her but her voice

²Echo (circa 1952)
— a communications code word for the letter *e*

echo·car·dio·gram \ˌe-kō-'kär-dē-ə-ˌgram\ *noun* (1967)
: a visual record made by echocardiography

echo·car·di·og·ra·phy \-ˌkär-dē-'ä-grə-fē\ *noun, plural* **-phies** (1965)
: the use of ultrasound to examine the structure and functioning of the heart for abnormalities and disease
— **echo·car·di·og·raph·er** \-grə-fər\ *noun*
— **echo·car·dio·graph·ic** \-dē-ə-'gra-fik\ *adjective*

echo chamber *noun* (circa 1937)
: a room with sound-reflecting walls used for producing hollow or echoing sound effects

echo·ic \e-'kō-ik, e-\ *adjective* (circa 1880)
1 : formed in imitation of some natural sound
: ONOMATOPOEIC
2 : of or relating to an echo

echo·la·lia \ˌe-kō-'lā-lē-ə\ *noun* [New Latin] (circa 1885)
: the often pathological repetition of what is said by other people as if echoing them
— **echo·lal·ic** \-'la-lik\ *adjective*

echo·lo·ca·tion \ˌe-kō-lō-'kā-shən\ *noun* (circa 1944)
: a physiological process for locating distant or invisible objects (as prey) by means of sound waves reflected back to the emitter (as a bat) by the objects

echo sounder *noun* (1927)
: an instrument for determining the depth of a body of water or of an object below the surface by sound waves

echo·vi·rus \'e-kō-ˌvī-rəs\ *noun* [enteric cytopathogenic human orphan + virus] (1955)
: any of a group of picornaviruses that are found in the gastrointestinal tract, that cause cytopathic changes in cells in tissue culture, and that are sometimes associated with respiratory ailments and meningitis

éclair \ā-'klar, i-, -'kler, 'ā-ˌ, 'ē-ˌ\ *noun* [French, literally, lightning] (1861)
: a usually chocolate-frosted oblong light pastry with whipped cream or custard filling

éclair·cis·se·ment \ā-kler-sēs-(ə-)mäⁿ\ *noun, plural* **-ments** \-mäⁿ(z)\ [French] (1667)
: a clearing up of something obscure : ENLIGHTENMENT

eclamp·sia \i-'klam(p)-sē-ə\ *noun* [New Latin, from Greek *eklampsis* sudden flashing, from *eklampein* to shine forth, from *ex-* out + *lampein* to shine] (circa 1860)
: a convulsive state; *especially* : an attack of convulsions during pregnancy or parturition
— **eclamp·tic** \-'klam(p)-tik\ *adjective*

éclat \ā-'klä, 'ā-ˌ\ *noun* [French, splinter, burst, *éclat*] (1672)
1 : ostentatious display : PUBLICITY
2 : dazzling effect : BRILLIANCE
3 a : brilliant or conspicuous success **b** : PRAISE, APPLAUSE

¹eclec·tic \e-'klek-tik, i-\ *adjective* [Greek *eklektikos,* from *eklegein* to select, from *ex-* out + *legein* to gather — more at LEGEND] (1683)
1 : selecting what appears to be best in various doctrines, methods, or styles
2 : composed of elements drawn from various sources; *also* : HETEROGENEOUS
— **eclec·ti·cal·ly** \-ti-k(ə-)lē\ *adverb*

²eclectic *noun* (1817)
: one who uses an eclectic method or approach

eclec·ti·cism \-'klek-tə-ˌsi-zəm\ *noun* (1798)
1 : the theory or practice of an eclectic method
2 : a mid-19th-century movement in architecture and design that revived the styles of various historical periods

¹eclipse \i-'klips\ *noun* [Middle English, from Old French, from Latin *eclipsis,* from Greek *ekleipsis,* from *ekleipein* to omit, fail, suffer eclipse, from *ex-* + *leipein* to leave — more at LOAN] (13th century)
1 a : the total or partial obscuring of one celestial body by another **b** : the passing into the shadow of a celestial body — compare OCCULTATION, TRANSIT
2 : a falling into obscurity or decline; *also* : the state of being eclipsed
3 : the state of being in eclipse plumage

²eclipse *transitive verb* **eclipsed; eclipsing** (13th century)
: to cause an eclipse of: as **a** : OBSCURE, DARKEN **b** : to reduce in importance or repute **c** : SURPASS

◇ **WORD HISTORY**
echelon In Old French *eschele* meant "ladder," and its diminutive form *eschelon* meant "a rung of a ladder." From *eschelon* a number of figurative meanings developed, including the sense referring to a formation of troops in which individual units are arranged like a staggered series of steps. It was this extended sense that English borrowed in the 18th century. After the borrowing, the meaning of *echelon* was expanded to cover similar formations of ships and aircraft. The pyramidal formation and the step-like arrangement of an echelon made it easy to apply the word figuratively to the hierarchical structure of a military organization. Subdivisions of a military organization became known as *echelons.* Then in extended and transferred use *echelon* came to refer to a single level of any hierarchical organization or to the individuals occupying such a level.

eclipse 1a: *S* sun, *E* earth, *M* moon in solar eclipse, *M'* moon in lunar eclipse

eclipse plumage *noun* (1906)
: comparatively dull plumage that is usually of seasonal occurrence in birds exhibiting a distinct breeding plumage

¹eclip·tic \i-'klip-tik\ *adjective* [Middle English *ecliptik*, from Late Latin *ecliptica linea*, literally, line of eclipses] (14th century)
: of or relating to the ecliptic or an eclipse

²ecliptic *noun* (15th century)
: the great circle of the celestial sphere that is the apparent path of the sun among the stars or of the earth as seen from the sun **:** the plane of the earth's orbit extended to meet the celestial sphere

ec·logue \'ek-,lȯg, -,läg\ *noun* [Middle English *eclog*, from Latin *Eclogae*, title of Virgil's pastorals, literally, selections, plural of *ecloga*, from Greek *eklogē*, from *eklegein* to select] (15th century)
: a poem in which shepherds converse

eclo·sion \i-'klō-zhən\ *noun* [French *éclosion*, from *éclore* to hatch, from (assumed) Vulgar Latin *exclaudere*, alteration of Latin *excludere* to hatch out, exclude] (circa 1889)
of an insect **:** the act of emerging from the pupal case or hatching from the egg

eco- *combining form* [Late Latin *oeco-* household, from Greek *oik-, oiko-*, from *oikos* house — more at VICINITY]
1 : habitat or environment ⟨*eco*species⟩
2 : ecological or environmental ⟨*eco*catastrophe⟩

eco·ca·tas·tro·phe \ē-(,)kō-kə-'tas-trə-fē, ,e-(,)kō-\ *noun* (1969)
: a major destructive upset in the balance of nature especially when caused by the intervention of humans

ecol·o·gy \i-'kä-lə-jē, e-\ *noun, plural* **-gies** [German *Ökologie*, from *öko-* eco- + *-logie* -logy] (1873)
1 : a branch of science concerned with the interrelationship of organisms and their environments
2 : the totality or pattern of relations between organisms and their environment
3 : HUMAN ECOLOGY
— **eco·log·i·cal** \,ē-kə-'lä-ji-kəl, ,e-kə-\ *also* **eco·log·ic** \-jik\ *adjective*
— **eco·log·i·cal·ly** \-ji-k(ə-)lē\ *adverb*
— **ecol·o·gist** \i-'kä-lə-jist, e-\ *noun*

econo·box \i-'kä-nō-,bäks, ē-\ *noun* [*economical* + ²*box*] (1980)
: a small economical car

econo·met·rics \i-,kä-nə-'me-triks, ē-,kä-\ *noun plural but singular in construction* [blend of *economics* and *metric*] (1933)
: the application of statistical methods to the study of economic data and problems
— **econo·met·ric** \-trik\ *adjective*
— **econo·met·ri·cal·ly** \-tri-k(ə-)lē\ *adverb*
— **econo·me·tri·cian** \-mə-'tri-shən\ *noun*
— **econo·met·rist** \-'me-trist\ *noun*

eco·nom·ic \,e-kə-'nä-mik, ,ē-kə-\ *adjective* (1592)
1 *archaic* **:** of or relating to a household or its management
2 : ECONOMICAL 2
3 a : of or relating to economics **b :** of, relating to, or based on the production, distribution, and consumption of goods and services **c :** of or relating to an economy
4 : having practical or industrial significance or uses **:** affecting material resources

5 : PROFITABLE ☐

eco·nom·i·cal \-'nä-mi-kəl\ *adjective* (15th century)
1 *archaic* **:** ECONOMIC 1
2 : marked by careful, efficient, and prudent use of resources **:** THRIFTY
3 : operating with little waste or at a saving
synonym see SPARING
— **eco·nom·i·cal·ly** \-mi-k(ə-)lē\ *adverb*

economic rent *noun* (1889)
: the return for the use of a factor in excess of the minimum required to bring forth its service

eco·nom·ics \,e-kə-'nä-miks, ,ē-kə-\ *noun plural but singular or plural in construction* (1792)
1 : a social science concerned chiefly with description and analysis of the production, distribution, and consumption of goods and services
2 : economic aspect or significance

economise *British variant of* ECONOMIZE

econ·o·mist \i-'kä-nə-mist\ *noun* (1586)
1 *archaic* **:** one who practices economy
2 : a specialist in economics

econ·o·mize \-,mīz\ *verb* **-mized; -miz·ing** (1820)
intransitive verb
: to practice economy **:** be frugal
transitive verb
: to use more economically **:** SAVE
— **econ·o·miz·er** *noun*

¹econ·o·my \i-'kä-nə-mē, ə-, ē-\ *noun, plural* **-mies** [Middle French *yconomie*, from Medieval Latin *oeconomia*, from Greek *oikonomia*, from *oikonomos* household manager, from *oikos* house + *nemein* to manage — more at VICINITY, NIMBLE] (15th century)
1 *archaic* **:** the management of household or private affairs and especially expenses
2 a : thrifty and efficient use of material resources **:** frugality in expenditures; *also* **:** an instance or a means of economizing **:** SAVING **b** **:** efficient and concise use of nonmaterial resources (as effort, language, or motion)
3 : the arrangement or mode of operation of something **:** ORGANIZATION
4 : the structure of economic life in a country, area, or period; *specifically* **:** an economic system

²economy *adjective* (circa 1906)
: designed to save money ⟨*economy* cars⟩

economy of scale *noun* (1957)
: a reduction in unit costs brought about especially by increased size of production facilities — usually used in plural

eco·phys·i·ol·o·gy \,ē-kō-,fi-zē-'ä-lə-jē, ,e-kō-\ *noun* (1962)
: the science of the interrelationships between the physiology of organisms and their environment
— **eco·phys·i·o·log·i·cal** \-ē-ə-'lä-ji-kəl\ *adjective*

eco·spe·cies \'ē-kō-,spē-(,)shēz, 'e-kō-, -(,)sēz\ *noun, plural* **ecospecies** (1922)
: a subdivision of a cenospecies comparable with a taxonomic species and composed of interbreeding individuals that are less capable of fertile crosses with individuals of other subdivisions

eco·sphere \'ē-kō-,sfir, 'e-kō-\ *noun* (1953)
: the parts of the universe habitable by living organisms; *especially* **:** BIOSPHERE 1

eco·sys·tem \'ē-kō-,sis-təm\ *noun* (1935)
: the complex of a community of organisms and its environment functioning as an ecological unit in nature

eco·tone \'ē-kə-,tōn, 'e-kə-\ *noun* [*ec-* + Greek *tonos* tension — more at TONE] (1904)
: a transition area between two adjacent ecological communities

eco·tour·ism \,ē-kō-'tu̇r-,i-zəm, ,e-kō-\ *noun* (1989)
: the practice of touring natural habitats in a manner meant to minimize ecological impact
— **eco·tour·ist** \-'tu̇r-ist\ *noun*

eco·type \'ē-kə-,tīp, 'e-\ *noun* (1922)
: a subdivision of an ecospecies that survives as a distinct group through environmental selection and isolation and that is comparable with a taxonomic subspecies
— **eco·typ·ic** \,ē-kə-'ti-pik, ,e-kə-\ *adjective*

ecru \'e-(,)krü, 'ā-(,)krü\ *noun* [French *écru*, literally, unbleached, raw, from Old French *escru*, from *es-* completely (from Latin *ex-*) + *cru* raw, from Latin *crudus* — more at RAW] (1850)
: BEIGE 2
— **ecru** *adjective*

ec·sta·sy \'ek-stə-sē\ *noun, plural* **-sies** [Middle English *extasie*, from Middle French, from Late Latin *ecstasis*, from Greek *ekstasis*, from *existanai* to derange, from *ex-* out + *histanai* to cause to stand — more at EX-, STAND] (14th century)
1 a : a state of being beyond reason and self-control **b** *archaic* **:** SWOON
2 : a state of overwhelming emotion; *especially* **:** rapturous delight
3 : TRANCE; *especially* **:** a mystic or prophetic trance
4 : a synthetic amphetamine analogue $C_{11}H_{15}NO_2$ used illicitly for its mood-enhancing and hallucinogenic properties ☆

¹ec·stat·ic \ek-'sta-tik, ik-'sta-\ *adjective* [Medieval Latin *ecstaticus*, from Greek *ekstatikos*, from *existanai*] (1590)
: of, relating to, or marked by ecstasy
— **ec·stat·i·cal·ly** \-'sta-ti-k(ə-)lē\ *adverb*

²ecstatic *noun* (1659)
: one that is subject to ecstasies

ect- *or* **ecto-** *combining form* [New Latin, from Greek *ekto-*, from *ektos*, from *ex* out — more at EX-]
: outside **:** external ⟨*ecto*derm⟩ — compare END-, EXO-

ec·to·derm \'ek-tə-,dərm\ *noun* [International Scientific Vocabulary] (1861)
1 : the outer cellular membrane of a diploblastic animal (as a jellyfish)

\ə\ abut \ᵊ\ kitten \ər\ further \a\ ash \ā\ ace
\ä\ mop, mar \au̇\ out \ch\ chin \e\ bet \ē\ easy
\g\ go \i\ hit \ī\ ice \j\ job \ŋ\ sing \ō\ go
\ȯ\ law \ȯi\ boy \th\ thin \th̲\ the \ü\ loot \u̇\ foot
\y\ yet \zh\ vision *see also* Guide to Pronunciation

2 a : the outermost of the three primary germ layers of an embryo **b :** a tissue (as neural tissue) derived from this germ layer
— **ec·to·der·mal** \ˌek-tə-'dȯr-məl\ adjective

ec·to·morph \'ek-tə-ˌmȯrf\ noun [ectoderm + -morph] (1940)
: an ectomorphic individual

ec·to·mor·phic \ˌek-tə-'mȯr-fik\ adjective [ectoderm + -morphic; from the predominance in such types of structures developed from the ectoderm] (1940)
1 : of or relating to the component in W. H. Sheldon's classification of body types that measures the body's degree of slenderness, angularity, and fragility
2 : characterized by a light body build with slight muscular development

-ec·to·my \'ek-tə-mē\ noun combining form [New Latin -ectomia, from Greek ektemnein to cut out, from ec-, ex- out + temnein to cut — more at TOME]
: surgical removal ⟨gastrectomy⟩

ec·to·par·a·site \ˌek-tō-'par-ə-ˌsīt\ noun [International Scientific Vocabulary] (1861)
: a parasite that lives on the exterior of its host
— **ec·to·par·a·sit·ic** \-ˌpar-ə-'si-tik\ adjective

ec·top·ic \ek-'tä-pik\ adjective [Greek ektopos out of place, from ex- out + topos place] (1873)
: occurring in an abnormal position or in an unusual manner or form ⟨ectopic lesions⟩
— **ec·top·i·cal·ly** \-pi-k(ə-)lē\ adverb

ectopic pregnancy noun (1929)
: gestation elsewhere than in the uterus (as in a fallopian tube or in the peritoneal cavity)

ec·to·plasm \'ek-tə-ˌpla-zəm\ noun (1883)
1 : the outer relatively rigid granule-free layer of the cytoplasm usually held to be a gel reversibly convertible to a sol
2 : a substance held to produce spirit materialization and telekinesis
— **ec·to·plas·mic** \ˌek-tə-'plaz-mik\ adjective

ec·to·therm \'ek-tə-ˌthərm\ noun (1945)
: a cold-blooded animal : POIKILOTHERM
— **ec·to·ther·mic** \ˌek-tə-'thər-mik\ adjective

ec·to·tro·phic \ˌek-tə-'trō-fik\ adjective (circa 1889)
of a mycorrhiza : growing in a close web on the surface of the associated root — compare ENDOTROPHIC

1ecu \'ā-ˌkyü, ā-kē̄\ noun, plural **ecus** \-ˌkyüz, -kē̄z\ [Middle French, literally, shield, from Old French escu, from Latin scutum; from the device of a shield on the coin — more at ESQUIRE] (circa 1593)
: any of various old French units of value; also : a coin representing an ecu

2ecu \ē-(ˌ)sē-'yü\ noun, often E&C&U capitalized [European Currency Unit (influenced by French écu ecu)] (1970)
: a money of account based on the currency units of members of the European Community

ec·u·men·i·cal \ˌe-kyə-'me-ni-kəl\ adjective [Late Latin oecumenicus, from Late Greek oikoumenikos, from Greek oikoumenē the inhabited world, from feminine of oikoumenos, present passive participle of oikein to inhabit, from oikos house — more at VICINITY] (circa 1587)
1 : worldwide or general in extent, influence, or application
2 a : of, relating to, or representing the whole of a body of churches **b :** promoting or tending toward worldwide Christian unity or cooperation
— **ec·u·men·i·cal·ly** \-k(ə-)lē\ adverb
usage see ECONOMIC

ec·u·men·i·cal·ism \-'me-ni-kə-ˌli-zəm\ noun (1888)
: ECUMENISM

ecumenical patriarch noun (1862)

: the patriarch of Constantinople as the dignitary given first honor in the Eastern Orthodox Church

ec·u·men·i·cism \ˌe-kyə-'me-nə-ˌsi-zəm\ noun (1961)
: ECUMENISM
— **ec·u·men·i·cist** \-sist\ noun

ec·u·me·nic·i·ty \ˌe-kyə-mə-'ni-sə-tē, -me-\ noun (1840)
: the quality or state of being drawn close to others especially through Christian ecumenism

ec·u·men·ics \-'me-niks\ noun plural but singular in construction (circa 1937)
: the study of the nature, mission, problems, and strategy of the Christian church from the perspective of its ecumenical character

ec·u·me·nism \e-'kyü-mə-ˌni-zəm, i- also 'e-kyə- or ˌe-kyə-'me-\ noun (1948)
: ecumenical principles and practices especially as shown among religious groups (as Christian denominations)
— **ecu·me·nist** \e-'kyü-mə-nist, i- also 'e-kyə-mə-nist or ˌe-kyə-'me-nist\ noun

ec·ze·ma \ig-'zē-mə, 'eg-zə-mə, 'ek-sə-\ noun [New Latin, from Greek ekzema, from ekzein to erupt, from ex- out + zein to boil — more at EX-, YEAST] (circa 1753)
: an inflammatory condition of the skin characterized by redness, itching, and oozing vesicular lesions which become scaly, crusted, or hardened
— **ec·zem·a·tous** \ig-'ze-mə-təs\ adjective

ed \'ed\ noun (1954)
: EDUCATION ⟨driver's ed⟩ ⟨adult ed⟩

1-ed \d after a vowel or b, g, j, l, m, n, ŋ, r, th, v, z, or zh; əd, id after d or t; t after other sounds; exceptions are pronounced at their entries\ verb suffix or adjective suffix [Middle English, from Old English -ed, -od, -ad; akin to Old High German -t, past participle ending, Latin -tus, Greek -tos, suffix forming verbals]
1 — used to form the past participle of regular weak verbs ⟨ended⟩ ⟨faded⟩ ⟨tried⟩ ⟨patted⟩
2 — used to form adjectives of identical meaning from Latin-derived adjectives ending in -ate ⟨crenulated⟩
3 a : having : characterized by ⟨cultured⟩ ⟨two-legged⟩ **b :** having the characteristics of ⟨bigoted⟩

2-ed verb suffix [Middle English -ede, -de, from Old English -de, -ede, -ode, -ade; akin to Old High German -ta, past ending (1st singular) and probably to Old High German -t, past participle ending]
— used to form the past tense of regular weak verbs ⟨judged⟩ ⟨denied⟩ ⟨dropped⟩

eda·cious \i-'dā-shəs\ adjective [Latin edac-, edax, from edere to eat — more at EAT] (circa 1798)
1 archaic : of or relating to eating
2 : VORACIOUS
— **edac·i·ty** \-'da-sə-tē\ noun

Edam \'ē-dəm, 'ē-ˌdam\ noun [Edam, Netherlands] (1836)
: a yellow pressed cheese of Dutch origin usually made in flattened balls and often coated with red wax

edaph·ic \i-'da-fik\ adjective [Greek edaphos bottom, ground] (circa 1900)
1 : of or relating to the soil
2 : resulting from or influenced by the soil rather than the climate — compare CLIMATIC 2
— **edaph·i·cal·ly** \-'da-fi-k(ə-)lē\ adverb

edaphic climax noun (circa 1934)
: an ecological climax resulting from soil factors and commonly persisting through cycles of climatic and physiographic change — compare CLIMATIC CLIMAX

Ed·dic \'e-dik\ adjective [Old Norse Edda, a 13th century collection of mythological, heroic, and aphoristic poetry] (1868)
: of, relating to, or resembling the Old Norse Edda

1ed·dy \'e-dē\ noun, plural **eddies** [Middle English (Scots dialect) ydy, probably from Old Norse itha] (15th century)
1 a : a current of water or air running contrary to the main current; especially : a circular current : WHIRLPOOL **b :** something moving similarly
2 : a contrary or circular current (as of thought or policy)

2eddy verb **ed·died; ed·dy·ing** (1810)
transitive verb
: to cause to move in an eddy
intransitive verb
: to move in an eddy or in the manner of an eddy

eddy current noun (1887)
: an electric current induced by an alternating magnetic field

edel·weiss \'ā-dᵊl-ˌvīs, -, -ˌwīs\ noun [German, from edel noble + weiss white] (1862)
: a small alpine perennial composite herb (Leontopodium alpinum) of central and southeast Europe that has a dense woolly white pubescence

edelweiss

ede·ma \i-'de-mə\ noun [New Latin, from Greek oidēma swelling, from oidein to swell; akin to Old English ātor poison] (15th century)
1 : an abnormal infiltration and excess accumulation of serous fluid in connective tissue or in a serous cavity — called also dropsy
2 a : watery swelling of plant organs or parts **b :** any of various plant diseases characterized by such swellings
— **edem·a·tous** \-'de-mə-təs\ adjective

Eden \'ē-dᵊn\ noun [Late Latin, from Hebrew 'Ēdhen] (13th century)
1 : PARADISE 2
2 : the garden where according to the account in Genesis Adam and Eve first lived
— **Eden·ic** \i-'de-nik, ē-\ adjective

1eden·tate \(ˌ)ē-'den-ˌtāt\ adjective [Latin edentatus, past participle of edentare to make toothless, from e- + dent-, dens tooth — more at TOOTH] (1828)
1 : lacking teeth
2 : being an edentate

2edentate noun (1835)
: any of an order (Edentata) of mammals having few or no teeth and including the sloths, armadillos, and New World anteaters and formerly also the pangolins and the aardvark

eden·tu·lous \(ˌ)ē-'den-chə-ləs\ adjective [Latin edentulus, from e- + dent-, dens] (1782)
: TOOTHLESS

Ed·gar \'ed-gər\ noun [Edgar Allan Poe, regarded as father of the detective story] (1947)
: a statuette awarded annually by a professional organization for notable achievement in mystery-novel writing

1edge \'ej\ noun [Middle English egge, from Old English ecg; akin to Latin acer sharp, Greek akmē point] (before 12th century)
1 a : the cutting side of a blade **b :** the sharpness of a blade **c** (1) : FORCE, EFFECTIVENESS ⟨blunted the edge of the legislation⟩ (2) : vigor or energy especially of body ⟨maintains his hard edge⟩ **d** (1) : incisive or penetrating quality ⟨writing with a satirical edge⟩ (2) : a noticeably harsh or sharp quality ⟨her voice had an edge to it⟩ **e :** keenness of desire or enjoyment ⟨lost my competitive edge⟩ ⟨took the edge off our appetites⟩
2 a : the line where an object or area begins or ends : BORDER ⟨on the edge of a plain⟩ **b :** the narrow part adjacent to a border ⟨the edge of the deck⟩ **c :** a point near the beginning or the end; especially : BRINK, VERGE ⟨on the edge of disaster⟩ **d :** a favorable margin : ADVANTAGE ⟨has an edge on the competition⟩

3 : a line or line segment that is the intersection of two plane faces (as of a pyramid) or of two planes
— **edge·less** *adjective*
— **on edge :** ANXIOUS, NERVOUS
²**edge** *verb* **edged; edg·ing** (14th century)
transitive verb
1 a : to give an edge to **b :** to be on an edge of ⟨trees *edging* the lake⟩
2 : to move or force gradually ⟨*edged* him off the road⟩
3 : to incline (a ski) sideways so that one edge cuts into the snow
4 : to defeat by a small margin — often used with *out* ⟨*edged* out her opponent⟩
intransitive verb
: to advance by short moves
edged \'ejd, 'e-jid\ *adjective* (before 12th century)
1 : having a specified kind of edge, boundary, or border or a specified number of edges ⟨rough-*edged*⟩ ⟨two-*edged*⟩
2 : SHARP, CUTTING ⟨an *edged* knife⟩ ⟨an *edged* remark⟩
edge effect *noun* (1933)
: the effect of an abrupt transition between two quite different adjoining ecological communities on the numbers and kinds of organisms in the marginal habitat
edge–grain \'ej-,grān\ *or* **edge–grained** \'ej-,gränd\ *adjective* (1906)
: QUARTERSAWN
edge in *transitive verb* (1683)
: to work in : INTERPOLATE ⟨*edged in* a few remarks⟩
edg·er \'e-jər\ *noun* (1591)
: one that edges; *especially* **:** a tool used to trim the edge of a lawn along a sidewalk or curb
edge tool *noun* (14th century)
: a tool with a sharp cutting edge
edge·ways \'ej-,wāz\ *adverb* (1566)
chiefly British **:** SIDEWAYS
edge·wise \-,wīz\ *adverb* (1677)
: SIDEWAYS
edg·ing *noun* (1558)
: something that forms an edge or border
edgy \'e-jē\ *adjective* **edg·i·er; -est** (1775)
1 : having an edge : SHARP
2 a : being on edge : TENSE, IRRITABLE **b :** characterized by tension ⟨*edgy* negotiations⟩
— **edg·i·ly** \'e-jə-lē\ *adverb*
— **edg·i·ness** \'e-jē-nəs\ *noun*
edh \'eth\ *noun* [Icelandic *eth*] (1875)
: the letter ð used in Old English and in Icelandic to represent either of the fricatives \th\ or \th\ and in some phonetic alphabets to represent the fricative \th\
ed·i·ble \'e-də-bəl\ *adjective* [Late Latin *edibilis*, from Latin *edere* to eat — more at EAT] (1594)
: fit to be eaten : EATABLE
— **ed·i·bil·i·ty** \,e-də-'bi-lə-tē\ *noun*
— **edible** *noun*
— **ed·i·ble·ness** \'e-də-bəl-nəs\ *noun*
edict \'ē-,dikt\ *noun* [Middle English, from Latin *edictum*, from neuter of *edictus*, past participle of *edicere* to decree, from *e-* + *dicere* to say — more at DICTION] (14th century)
1 : a proclamation having the force of law
2 : ORDER, COMMAND ⟨we held firm to Grandmother's *edict* —M. F. K. Fisher⟩
— **edic·tal** \i-'dik-t⁰l\ *adjective*
ed·i·fi·ca·tion \,e-də-fə-'kā-shən\ *noun* (14th century)
: an act or process of edifying
ed·i·fice \'e-də-fəs\ *noun* [Middle English, from Middle French, from Latin *aedificium*, from *aedificare*] (14th century)
1 : BUILDING; *especially* **:** a large or massive structure
2 : a large abstract structure ⟨holds together the social *edifice* —R. H. Tawney⟩
ed·i·fy \'e-də-,fī\ *transitive verb* **-fied; -fy·ing** [Middle English, from Middle French *edifier*,

from Late Latin & Latin; Late Latin *aedificare* to instruct or improve spiritually, from Latin, to erect a house, from *aedes* temple, house; akin to Old English *ād* funeral pyre, Latin *aestas* summer] (14th century)
1 *archaic* **a :** BUILD **b :** ESTABLISH
2 : to instruct and improve especially in moral and religious knowledge **:** UPLIFT; *also* **:** ENLIGHTEN 2, INFORM
¹**ed·it** \'e-dət\ *transitive verb* [back-formation from *editor*] (1791)
1 a : to prepare (as literary material) for publication or public presentation **b :** to assemble (as a moving picture or tape recording) by cutting and rearranging **c :** to alter, adapt, or refine especially to bring about conformity to a standard or to suit a particular purpose ⟨carefully *edited* the speech⟩
2 : to direct the publication of ⟨*edits* the daily newspaper⟩
3 : DELETE — usually used with *out*
— **ed·it·able** \'e-di-tə-bəl\ *adjective*
²**edit** *noun* (1955)
: an instance of editing
edi·tion \i-'di-shən\ *noun* [Middle French, from Latin *edition-, editio* publication, edition, from *edere* to bring forth, publish, from *e-* + *-dere* to put or *-dere* (from *dare* to give) — more at DO, DATE] (1555)
1 a : the form or version in which a text is published ⟨a paperback *edition*⟩ ⟨the German *edition*⟩ **b** (1) **:** the whole number of copies published at one time (2) **:** a usually special issue of a newspaper (as for a particular day or purpose) ⟨Sunday *edition*⟩ ⟨international *edition*⟩ (3) **:** one of the usually several issues of a newspaper in a single day ⟨city *edition*⟩ ⟨late *edition*⟩
2 a : one of the forms in which something is presented ⟨this year's *edition* of the annual charity ball⟩ **b :** the whole number of articles of one style put out at one time ⟨a limited *edition* of collectors' pieces⟩
3 : COPY, VERSION
edi·tio prin·ceps \ā-,di-tē-(,)ō-'prin-,keps, i-,di-shē-(,)ō-'prin-,seps\ *noun, plural* **edi·ti·o·nes prin·ci·pes** \ā-,di-tē-'ō-,nās-'prin-kə-,pās, i-,di-shē-'ō-(,)nēz-'prin(t)-sə-,pēz\ [New Latin, literally, first edition] (1802)
: the first printed edition especially of a work that circulated in manuscript before printing became common
ed·i·tor \'e-də-tər\ *noun* (1649)
1 : someone who edits especially as an occupation
2 : a device used in editing motion-picture film or magnetic tape
3 : a computer program that permits the user to create or modify data (as text or graphics) especially on a display screen
— **ed·i·tor·ship** \-,ship\ *noun*
¹**ed·i·to·ri·al** \,e-də-'tōr-ē-əl, -'tór-\ *adjective* (1744)
1 : of or relating to an editor or editing ⟨an *editorial* office⟩
2 : being or resembling an editorial ⟨an *editorial* statement⟩
— **ed·i·to·ri·al·ly** \-ē-ə-lē\ *adverb*
²**editorial** *noun* (1830)
: a newspaper or magazine article that gives the opinions of the editors or publishers; *also* **:** an expression of opinion that resembles such an article ⟨a television *editorial*⟩
ed·i·to·ri·al·ist \-ē-ə-list\ *noun* (1901)
: a writer of editorials
ed·i·to·ri·al·ize \,e-də-'tōr-ē-ə-,līz, -'tór-\ *intransitive verb* **-ized; -iz·ing** (1856)
1 : to express an opinion in the form of an editorial
2 : to introduce opinion into the reporting of facts
3 : to express an opinion (as on a controversial issue)
— **ed·i·to·ri·al·iza·tion** \-,tōr-ē-ə-lə-'zā-shən, -,tór-\ *noun*
— **ed·i·to·ri·al·iz·er** *noun*

editor in chief *noun* (1873)
: an editor who heads an editorial staff
ed·i·tress \'e-də-trəs\ *noun* (1799)
: a woman who is an editor
Edom·ite \'ē-də-,mīt\ *noun* [*Edom* (Esau), ancestor of the Edomites] (1534)
: a member of a Semitic people living south of the Dead Sea in biblical times
EDTA \,ē-(,)dē-(,)tē-'ā\ *noun* [*e*thylene*d*iamine*t*etra*a*cetic *a*cid] (1954)
: a white crystalline acid $C_{10}H_{16}N_2O_8$ used especially as a chelating agent and in medicine as an anticoagulant and in the treatment of lead poisoning
ed·u·ca·ble \'e-jə-kə-bəl\ *adjective* (1845)
: capable of being educated; *specifically* **:** capable of some degree of learning
— **ed·u·ca·bil·i·ty** \,e-jə-kə-'bi-lə-tē\ *noun*
ed·u·cate \'e-jə-,kāt\ *verb* **-cat·ed; -cat·ing** [Middle English, to rear, from Latin *educatus*, past participle of *educare* to rear, educate, from *educere* to lead forth — more at EDUCE] (15th century)
transitive verb
1 a : to provide schooling for **b :** to train by formal instruction and supervised practice especially in a skill, trade, or profession
2 a : to develop mentally, morally, or aesthetically especially by instruction **b :** to provide with information : INFORM
3 : to persuade or condition to feel, believe, or act in a desired way ⟨*educate* the public to support our position⟩
intransitive verb
: to educate a person or thing
synonym see TEACH
ed·u·cat·ed *adjective* (1588)
1 : having an education; *especially* **:** having an education beyond the average
2 a : giving evidence of training or practice **:** SKILLED **b :** befitting one that is educated ⟨*educated* taste⟩ **c :** based on some knowledge of fact ⟨an *educated* guess⟩
— **ed·u·cat·ed·ness** *noun*
ed·u·ca·tion \,e-jə-'kā-shən\ *noun* (1531)
1 a : the action or process of educating or of being educated; *also* **:** a stage of such a process **b :** the knowledge and development resulting from an educational process ⟨a man of little *education*⟩
2 : the field of study that deals mainly with methods of teaching and learning in schools
— **ed·u·ca·tion·al** \-shnəl, -shə-n⁰l\ *adjective*
— **ed·u·ca·tion·al·ly** \-ē\ *adverb*
educational psychology *noun* (1911)
: psychology concerned with human maturation, school learning, teaching methods, guidance, and evaluation of aptitude and progress by standardized tests
— **educational psychologist** *noun*
educational television *noun* (1951)
1 : television that provides instruction especially for students
2 : PUBLIC TELEVISION
ed·u·ca·tion·ese \,e-jə-,kā-shə-'nēz, -'nēs\ *noun* (1954)
: the jargon used especially by educational theorists
ed·u·ca·tion·ist \,e-jə-'kā-sh(ə-)nist\ *also* **ed·u·ca·tion·al·ist** \-shnə-list, -shə-n⁰l-ist\ *noun* (1829)
1 *chiefly British* **:** a professional educator
2 : an educational theorist
ed·u·ca·tive \'e-jə-,kā-tiv\ *adjective* (1856)
1 : tending to educate : INSTRUCTIVE
2 : of or relating to education
ed·u·ca·tor \'e-jə-,kā-tər\ *noun* (1673)
1 : one skilled in teaching : TEACHER

\ə\ **abut** \⁰\ **kitten** \ər\ **further** \a\ **ash** \ā\ **ace**
\ä\ **mop, mar** \au̇\ **out** \ch\ **chin** \e\ **bet** \ē\ **easy**
\g\ **go** \i\ **hit** \ī\ **ice** \j\ **job** \ŋ\ **sing** \ō\ **go**
\ȯ\ **law** \ȯi\ **boy** \th\ **thin** \th\ **the** \ü\ **loot** \u̇\ **foot**
\y\ **yet** \zh\ **vision** *see also* Guide to Pronunciation

2 a : a student of the theory and practice of education : EDUCATIONIST 2 **b :** an administrator in education

educe \i-'düs also -'dyüs\ *transitive verb* **educed; educ·ing** [Latin *educere* to draw out, from *e-* + *ducere* to lead — more at TOW] (1603)
1 : to bring out (as something latent)
2 : DEDUCE ☆
— **educ·ible** \-'dü-sə-bəl also -'dyü-\ *adjective*
— **educ·tion** \-'dək-shən\ *noun*

educ·tor \i-'dək-tər\ *noun* [Late Latin, one that leads out, from Latin *educere*] (1796)
: EJECTOR 2

edul·co·rate \i-'dəl-kə-,rāt\ *transitive verb* **-rat·ed; -rat·ing** [New Latin *edulcoratus*, past participle of *edulcorare*, from Latin *e-* + *dulcor* sweetness, from *dulcis* sweet — more at DULCET] (1641)
: to free from harshness (as of attitude) : SOFTEN

ed·u·tain·ment \,e-jə-'tān-mənt, ,e-dyü-\ *noun* [*education* + enter*tainment*] (1973)
: a form of entertainment (as by games, films, or shows) that is designed to be educational

Ed·war·di·an \e-'dwär-dē-ən, -'dwor-\ *adjective* (1908)
: of, relating to, or characteristic of Edward VII of England or his age; *especially, of clothing* **:** marked by the hourglass silhouette for women and long narrow fitted suits and high collars for men
— **Edwardian** *noun*

¹-ee \'ē, ,ē, ē\ *noun suffix* [Middle English *-e*, from Middle French *-é*, from *-é*, past participle ending, from Latin *-atus*]
1 : recipient or beneficiary of (a specified action) ⟨appoint*ee*⟩ ⟨grant*ee*⟩
2 : person furnished with (a specified thing) ⟨patent*ee*⟩
3 : person that performs (a specified action) ⟨escap*ee*⟩

²-ee *noun suffix* [probably alteration of *-y*]
1 : one associated with ⟨barg*ee*⟩
2 : a particular especially small kind of ⟨boot*ee*⟩
3 : one resembling or suggestive of ⟨goat*ee*⟩

eel \'ē(ə)l\ *noun* [Middle English *ele*, from Old English *ǣl*; akin to Old High German *āl* eel] (before 12th century)
1 a : any of numerous voracious elongate snakelike bony fishes (order Anguilliformes) that have a smooth

eel 1a

slimy skin, lack pelvic fins, and have the median fins confluent around the tail — compare AMERICAN EEL **b :** any of numerous other elongate fishes (as of the order Symbranchii)
2 : any of various nematodes
— **eel·like** \'ē(ə)l-,līk\ *adjective*
— **eely** \'ē-lē\ *adjective*

eel·grass \'ē(ə)l-,gras\ *noun* (1790)
1 : a submerged long-leaved monocotyledonous marine plant (*Zostera marina*) of the eelgrass family that is abundant along the Atlantic coast and has stems used especially in woven products (as mats and hats)
2 : TAPE GRASS

eel·pout \-,paut\ *noun* (before 12th century)
1 : any of various elongate tapered marine fishes (family Zoarcidae) usually living on the bottom of cold seas
2 : BURBOT

eel·worm \-,wərm\ *noun* (1888)
: a nematode worm; *especially* **:** any of various small free-living or plant-parasitic roundworms

-een \'ēn\ *noun suffix* [probably from *ratteen*]
: inferior fabric resembling (a specified fabric) **:** imitation ⟨velvet*een*⟩

e'en \'ēn\ *adverb* (circa 1553)

: EVEN

-eer \'ir\ *noun suffix* [Middle French *-ier*, from Latin *-arius* — more at -ARY]
: one that is concerned with professionally, conducts, or produces ⟨auction*eer*⟩ ⟨pamphlet*eer*⟩ — often in words with derogatory meaning ⟨profit*eer*⟩

e'er \'er, 'ar\ *adverb* (13th century)
: EVER

ee·rie *also* **ee·ry** \'ir-ē, 'ēr-\ *adjective* **ee·ri·er; -est** [Middle English (northern dialect) *eri*] (14th century)
1 *chiefly Scottish* **:** affected with fright **:** SCARED
2 : so mysterious, strange, or unexpected as to send a chill up the spine ⟨a coyote's *eerie* howl⟩ ⟨the similarities were *eerie*⟩; *also* **:** seemingly not of earthly origin ⟨the flames cast an *eerie* glow⟩
synonym see WEIRD
— **ee·ri·ly** \'ir-ə-lē, 'ēr-\ *adverb*
— **ee·ri·ness** \'ir-ē-nəs, 'ēr-\ *noun*

ef \'ef\ *noun* (before 12th century)
: the letter *f*

ef·face \i-'fās, e-\ *transitive verb* **ef·faced; ef·fac·ing** [Middle English, from Middle French *effacer*, from Old French *esfacier*, from *e-* + *face* face] (15th century)
1 : to eliminate or make indistinct by or as if by wearing away a surface ⟨coins with dates *effaced* by wear⟩; *also* **:** to cause to vanish ⟨daylight *effaced* the stars⟩
2 : to make (oneself) modestly or shyly inconspicuous
— **ef·face·able** \-'fā-sə-bəl\ *adjective*
— **ef·face·ment** \-'fā-smənt\ *noun*
— **ef·fac·er** *noun*

¹ef·fect \i-'fekt, e-, ē-\ *noun* [Middle English, from Middle French & Latin; Middle French, from Latin *effectus*, from *efficere* to bring about, from *ex-* + *facere* to make, do — more at DO] (14th century)
1 a : PURPORT, INTENT **b :** basic meaning **:** ESSENCE
2 : something that inevitably follows an antecedent (as a cause or agent)
3 : an outward sign **:** APPEARANCE
4 : ACCOMPLISHMENT, FULFILLMENT
5 : power to bring about a result **:** INFLUENCE ⟨the content itself of television . . . is therefore less important than its *effect* —*Current Biography*⟩
6 *plural* **:** movable property **:** GOODS ⟨personal *effects*⟩
7 a : a distinctive impression ⟨the color gives the *effect* of being warm⟩ **b :** the creation of a desired impression ⟨her tears were purely for *effect*⟩ **c** (1) **:** something designed to produce a distinctive or desired impression — usually used in plural (2) *plural* **:** SPECIAL EFFECTS
8 : the quality or state of being operative **:** OPERATION ⟨the law goes into *effect* next week⟩
— **in effect :** in substance **:** VIRTUALLY ⟨the . . . committee agreed to what was *in effect* a reduction in the hourly wage —*Current Biography*⟩
— **to the effect :** with the meaning ⟨issued a statement *to the effect* that he would resign⟩

²effect *transitive verb* (1533)
1 : to cause to come into being
2 a : to bring about often by surmounting obstacles **:** ACCOMPLISH ⟨*effect* a settlement of a dispute⟩ **b :** to put into operation ⟨the duty of the legislature to *effect* the will of the citizens⟩

synonym see PERFORM

¹ef·fec·tive \i-'fek-tiv, e-, ē-\ *adjective* (14th century)
1 a : producing a decided, decisive, or desired effect **b :** IMPRESSIVE, STRIKING ⟨a gold lamé fabric studded with *effective* . . . precious stones —Stanley Marcus⟩
2 : ready for service or action ⟨*effective* manpower⟩
3 : ACTUAL ⟨the need to increase *effective* demand for goods⟩

4 : being in effect **:** OPERATIVE ⟨the tax becomes *effective* next year⟩
5 *of a rate of interest* **:** equal to the rate of simple interest that yields the same amount when the interest is paid once at the end of the interest period as a quoted rate of interest does when calculated at compound interest over the same period — compare NOMINAL 4 ☆
— **ef·fec·tive·ness** *noun*
— **ef·fec·tiv·i·ty** \,e-,fek-'ti-və-tē, i-, ē-\ *noun*

²effective *noun* (1722)
: one that is effective; *especially* **:** a soldier equipped for duty

ef·fec·tive·ly \-lē\ *adverb* (circa 1536)
1 : in effect **:** VIRTUALLY
2 : in an effective manner

ef·fec·tor \i-'fek-tər, -,tor\ *noun* (1906)
1 : a bodily organ (as a gland or muscle) that becomes active in response to stimulation
2 : a substance (as an inducer or corepressor) that controls protein synthesis by combining allosterically with a genetic repressor

ef·fec·tu·al \i-'fek-chə(-wə)l, -'feksh-wəl\ *adjective* (14th century)
: producing or able to produce a desired effect
synonym see EFFECTIVE
— **ef·fec·tu·al·i·ty** \-,fek-chə-'wa-lə-tē\ *noun*
— **ef·fec·tu·al·ness** \-'fek-chə(-wə)l-nəs, -'feksh-wəl-\ *noun*
— **ef·fec·tu·al·ly** \i-'fek-chə(-wə)-lē, -'fek-shwə-\ *adverb* (14th century)

1 : in an effectual manner
2 : with great effect **:** COMPLETELY
ef·fec·tu·ate \i-'fek-chə-ˌwāt\ *transitive verb* **-at·ed; -at·ing** (1580)
: EFFECT 2
— **ef·fec·tu·a·tion** \-ˌfek-chə-'wā-shən\ *noun*
ef·fem·i·na·cy \ə-'fe-mə-nə-sē\ *noun* (1602)
: the quality of being effeminate
¹ef·fem·i·nate \-nət\ *adjective* [Middle English, from Latin *effeminatus*, from past participle of *effeminare* to make effeminate, from *ex-* + *femina* woman — more at FEMININE] (15th century)
1 : having feminine qualities untypical of a man **:** not manly in appearance or manner
2 : marked by an unbecoming delicacy or overrefinement ⟨*effeminate* art⟩ ⟨an *effeminate* civilization⟩
²effeminate *noun* (1597)
: an effeminate person
ef·fen·di \e-'fen-dē, ə-\ *noun* [Turkish *efendi* master, from New Greek *aphentēs*, alteration of Greek *authentēs* — more at AUTHENTIC] (1614)
: a man of property, authority, or education in an eastern Mediterranean country
ef·fer·ent \'e-fər-ənt, -ˌfer-\ *adjective* [French *efférent*, from Latin *efferent-, efferens*, present participle of *efferre* to carry outward, from *ex-* + *ferre* to carry — more at BEAR] (1856)
: conducting outward from a part or organ; *specifically* **:** conveying nervous impulses to an effector — compare AFFERENT
— **efferent** *noun*
— **ef·fer·ent·ly** *adverb*
ef·fer·vesce \ˌe-fər-'ves\ *intransitive verb* **-vesced; -vesc·ing** [Latin *effervescere*, from *ex-* + *fervescere* to begin to boil, inchoative of *fervēre* to boil — more at BREW] (1784)
1 : to bubble, hiss, and foam as gas escapes
2 : to show liveliness or exhilaration
— **ef·fer·ves·cence** \-'ve-sᵊn(t)s\ *noun*
— **ef·fer·ves·cent** \-sᵊnt\ *adjective*
— **ef·fer·ves·cent·ly** *adverb*
ef·fete \e-'fēt, i-\ *adjective* [Latin *effetus*, from *ex-* + *fetus* fruitful — more at FEMININE] (1660)
1 : no longer fertile
2 a : having lost character, vitality, or strength ⟨the *effete* monarchies . . . of feudal Europe —G. M. Trevelyan⟩ **b :** marked by weakness or decadence ⟨the *effete* East⟩ **c :** soft or delicate from or as if from a pampered existence ⟨peddled . . . trendy tweeds to *effete* Easterners —William Helmer⟩ ⟨*effete* tenderfeet⟩; *also* **:** characteristic of an effete person ⟨a wool scarf . . . a bit *effete* on an outdoorsman —Nelson Bryant⟩
3 : EFFEMINATE 1 ⟨a good-humored, *effete* boy brought up by maiden aunts —Herman Wouk⟩
— **ef·fete·ly** *adverb*
— **ef·fete·ness** *noun*
ef·fi·ca·cious \ˌe-fə-'kā-shəs\ *adjective* [Latin *efficac-, efficax*, from *efficere*] (1528)
: having the power to produce a desired effect
synonym see EFFECTIVE
— **ef·fi·ca·cious·ly** *adverb*
— **ef·fi·ca·cious·ness** *noun*
ef·fi·cac·i·ty \ˌe-fə-'ka-sə-tē\ *noun* (15th century)
: EFFICACY
ef·fi·ca·cy \'e-fi-kə-sē\ *noun, plural* **-cies** (13th century)
: the power to produce an effect
ef·fi·cien·cy \i-'fi-shən-sē\ *noun, plural* **-cies** (1633)
1 : the quality or degree of being efficient
2 a : efficient operation **b** (1) **:** effective operation as measured by a comparison of production with cost (as in energy, time, and money) (2) **:** the ratio of the useful energy delivered by a dynamic system to the energy supplied to it
3 : EFFICIENCY APARTMENT

efficiency apartment *noun* (1930)
: a small usually furnished apartment with minimal kitchen and bath facilities
efficiency expert *noun* (1913)
: one who analyzes methods, procedures, and jobs in order to secure maximum efficiency — called also *efficiency engineer*
ef·fi·cient \i-'fi-shənt\ *adjective* [Middle English, from Middle French or Latin; Middle French, from Latin *efficient-, efficiens*, from present participle of *efficere*] (14th century)
1 : being or involving the immediate agent in producing an effect ⟨the *efficient* action of heat in changing water to steam⟩
2 : productive of desired effects; *especially* **:** productive without waste
synonym see EFFECTIVE
— **ef·fi·cient·ly** *adverb*
ef·fi·gy \'e-fə-jē\ *noun, plural* **-gies** [Middle French *effigie*, from Latin *effigies*, from *effingere* to form, from *ex-* + *fingere* to shape — more at DOUGH] (1539)
: an image or representation especially of a person; *especially* **:** a crude figure representing a hated person
— **in effigy :** publicly in the form of an effigy ⟨the football coach was burned *in effigy*⟩
ef·flo·resce \ˌe-flə-'res\ *intransitive verb* **-resced; -resc·ing** [Latin *efflorescere*, from *ex-* + *florescere* to begin to blossom — more at FLORESCENCE] (1775)
1 : to burst forth **:** BLOOM
2 a : to change to a powder from loss of water of crystallization **b :** to form or become covered with a powdery crust ⟨bricks may *effloresce* owing to the deposition of soluble salts⟩
ef·flo·res·cence \-'re-sᵊn(t)s\ *noun* (1626)
1 a : the action or process of developing and unfolding as if coming into flower **:** BLOSSOMING ⟨periods of . . . intellectual and artistic *efflorescence* —Julian Huxley⟩ **b :** an instance of such development **c :** fullness of manifestation **:** CULMINATION
2 : the period or state of flowering
3 : the process or product of efflorescing chemically
— **ef·flo·res·cent** \-sᵊnt\ *adjective*
ef·flu·ence \'e-ˌflü-ən(t)s; e-'flü-, ə-\ *noun* (1603)
1 : something that flows out
2 : an action or process of flowing out
¹ef·flu·ent \-ənt\ *adjective* [Latin *effluent-, effluens*, present participle of *effluere* to flow out, from *ex-* + *fluere* to flow — more at FLUID] (1726)
: flowing out **:** EMANATING, OUTGOING ⟨an *effluent* river⟩
²effluent *noun* (1859)
: something that flows out: as **a :** an outflowing branch of a main stream or lake **b :** waste material (as smoke, liquid industrial refuse, or sewage) discharged into the environment especially when serving as a pollutant
ef·flu·vi·um \e-'flü-vē-əm\ *also* **ef·flu·via** \-vē-ə\ *noun, plural* **-via** *or* **-vi·ums** [Latin *effluvium* act of flowing out, from *effluere*] (1651)
1 : an invisible emanation; *especially* **:** an offensive exhalation or smell
2 : a by-product especially in the form of waste
ef·flux \'e-ˌfləks\ *noun* [Medieval Latin *effluxus*, from *effluere*] (1647)
1 : something given off in or as if in a stream
2 a : EFFLUENCE 2 **b :** a passing away **:** EXPIRATION
— **ef·flux·ion** \e-'flək-shən\ *noun*
ef·fort \'e-fərt, -ˌfȯrt\ *noun* [Middle English, from Middle French, from Old French *esfort*, from *esforcier* to force, from *ex-* + *forcier* to force] (15th century)
1 : conscious exertion of power **:** hard work
2 : a serious attempt **:** TRY
3 : something produced by exertion or trying ⟨the novel was her most ambitious *effort*⟩

4 : effective force as distinguished from the possible resistance called into action by such a force
5 : the total work done to achieve a particular end ⟨the war *effort*⟩
ef·fort·ful \-fərt-fəl\ *adjective* (circa 1895)
: showing or requiring effort
— **ef·fort·ful·ly** \-fə-lē\ *adverb*
— **ef·fort·ful·ness** \-fəl-nəs\ *noun*
ef·fort·less \-fərt-ləs\ *adjective* (1801)
: showing or requiring little or no effort
synonym see EASY
— **ef·fort·less·ly** *adverb*
— **ef·fort·less·ness** *noun*
ef·fron·tery \i-'frən-tə-rē, e-\ *noun, plural* **-ter·ies** [French *effronterie*, ultimately from Medieval Latin *effront-, effrons* shameless, from Latin *ex-* + *front-, frons* forehead] (1697)
: shameless boldness **:** INSOLENCE
synonym see TEMERITY
ef·ful·gence \i-'fu̇l-jən(t)s, e-, -'fəl-\ *noun* [Late Latin *effulgentia*, from Latin *effulgent-, effulgens*, present participle of *effulgēre* to shine forth, from *ex-* + *fulgēre* to shine — more at FULGENT] (1667)
: radiant splendor **:** BRILLIANCE
— **ef·ful·gent** \-jənt\ *adjective*
¹ef·fuse \i-'fyüz, e-\ *verb* **ef·fused; ef·fus·ing** [Latin *effusus*, past participle of *effundere*, from *ex-* + *fundere* to pour — more at FOUND] (1526)
transitive verb
: to pour out (a liquid)
intransitive verb
: to flow out **:** EMANATE
²ef·fuse \-'fyüs\ *adjective* (circa 1530)
: DIFFUSE; *specifically* **:** spread out flat without definite form ⟨*effuse* lichens⟩
ef·fu·sion \i-'fyü-zhən, e-\ *noun* (15th century)
1 : an act of effusing
2 : unrestrained expression of words or feelings ⟨greeted her with great *effusion* —Olive H. Prouty⟩
3 a (1) **:** the escape of a fluid from anatomical vessels by rupture or exudation (2) **:** the flow of a gas through an aperture whose diameter is small as compared with the distance between the molecules of the gas **b :** the fluid that escapes
ef·fu·sive \i-'fyü-siv, e-, -ziv\ *adjective* (1662)
1 : excessively demonstrative
2 *archaic* **:** pouring freely
3 : characterized or formed by a nonexplosive outpouring of lava ⟨*effusive* rocks⟩
— **ef·fu·sive·ly** *adverb*
— **ef·fu·sive·ness** *noun*
Ef·ik \'e-fik\ *noun* (1849)
1 : a member of a people of southeastern Nigeria
2 : the language of the Efik people
eft \'eft\ *noun* [Middle English *evete, ewte*, from Old English *efete*] (before 12th century)
: NEWT; *especially* **:** the terrestrial phase of a predominantly aquatic newt
eft·soons \eft-'sünz\ *adverb* [Middle English *eftsones*, alteration of Old English *eftsōna*, from Old English *eft* after + *sōna* soon; akin to Old English *æfter* after] (before 12th century)
archaic **:** soon after
egad \i-'gad\ *or* **egads** \-'gadz\ *interjection* [probably euphemism for *oh God*] (1673)
— used as a mild oath
egal \'ē-gəl\ *adjective* [Middle English, from Middle French, from Latin *aequalis*] (14th century)
obsolete **:** EQUAL

\ə\ **abut** \ᵊ\ **kitten** \ər\ **further** \a\ **ash** \ā\ **ace**
\ä\ **mop, mar** \au̇\ **out** \ch\ **chin** \e\ **bet** \ē\ **easy**
\g\ **go** \i\ **hit** \ī\ **ice** \j\ **job** \ŋ\ **sing** \ō\ **go**
\ȯ\ **law** \ȯi\ **boy** \th\ **thin** \th̲\ **the** \ü\ **loot** \u̇\ **foot**
\y\ **yet** \zh\ **vision** *see also* Guide to Pronunciation

egal·i·tar·i·an \i-ˌga-lə-'ter-ē-ən\ *adjective* [French *égalitaire*, from *égalité* equality, from Latin *aequalitat-, aequalitas*, from *aequalis* equal] (1885)
: asserting, promoting, or marked by egalitarianism
— **egalitarian** *noun*
egal·i·tar·i·an·ism \-ē-ə-ˌni-zəm\ *noun* (1905)
1 : a belief in human equality especially with respect to social, political, and economic rights and privileges
2 : a social philosophy advocating the removal of inequalities among people
éga·li·té \ā-gȧ-lē-tā\ *noun* [French] (1794)
: social or political equality
Ege·ria \i-'jir-ē-ə\ *noun* [Latin, a nymph who advised the legendary Roman king Numa Pompilius] (1621)
: a woman adviser or companion
eges·ta \i-'jes-tə\ *noun plural* [New Latin, from Latin, neuter plural of *egestus*] (1727)
: something egested
eges·tion \i-'jes(h)-chən\ *noun* [Middle English *egestioun*, from Middle French or Latin; Middle French *egestion*, from Latin *egestion-, egestio*, from *egerere* to carry outside, discharge, from *e-* + *gerere* to carry] (1547)
: the act or process of discharging undigested or waste material from a cell or organism; *specifically* : DEFECATION
— **egest** \i-'jest\ *transitive verb*
— **eges·tive** \-'jes-tiv\ *adjective*
¹egg \'eg, 'āg\ *transitive verb* [Middle English, from Old Norse *eggja*; akin to Old English *ecg* edge — more at EDGE] (13th century)
: to incite to action — usually used with *on* ⟨*egged* the mob on to riot⟩
²egg *noun, often attributive* [Middle English *egge*, from Old Norse *egg*; akin to Old English *ǣg* egg, Latin *ovum*, Greek *ōion*] (14th century)
1 a : the hard-shelled reproductive body produced by a bird and especially by the common domestic chicken; *also* : its contents used as food **b** : an animal reproductive body consisting of an ovum together with its nutritive and protective envelopes and having the capacity to develop into a new individual capable of independent existence **c** : OVUM
2 : something resembling an egg
3 : PERSON, SORT ⟨a good *egg*⟩
— **egg·less** *adjective*
— **eggy** \-gē\ *adjective*
— **egg on one's face** : a state of embarrassment or humiliation
³egg *transitive verb* (1833)
1 : to cover with egg
2 : to pelt with eggs
egg and dart *noun* (circa 1864)
: a carved ornamental design in relief consisting of an egg-shaped figure alternating with a figure somewhat like an elongated javelin or arrowhead
egg·beat·er \'eg-ˌbē-tər, 'āg-\ *noun* (1828)
1 : a hand-operated kitchen utensil used for beating, stirring, or whipping; *especially* : a rotary device for these purposes
2 : HELICOPTER
egg case *noun* (1847)
: a protective case enclosing eggs : OOTHECA
— called also *egg capsule*
egg cell *noun* (1880)
: OVUM
egg cream *noun* (1954)

: a drink consisting of milk, a flavoring syrup, and soda water
egg·cup \'eg-ˌkəp, 'āg-\ *noun* (1773)
: a cup for holding an egg that is to be eaten from the shell
egg·head \-ˌhed\ *noun, often attributive* (1952)
: INTELLECTUAL, HIGHBROW
egg·head·ed \-'he-dəd\ *adjective* (1938)
: having the characteristics of an egghead
— **egg·head·ed·ness** *noun*
egg·nog \-ˌnäg\ *noun* (circa 1775)
: a drink consisting of eggs beaten with sugar, milk or cream, and often alcoholic liquor
egg·plant \-ˌplant\ *noun* (1767)
1 a : a widely cultivated perennial herb (*Solanum melongena*) of the nightshade family yielding edible fruit **b** : the usually smooth ovoid fruit of the eggplant
2 : a dark grayish or blackish purple
egg roll *noun* (1947)
: a thin egg-dough casing filled with minced vegetables and often bits of meat (as shrimp or chicken) and usually deep-fried
eggs Ben·e·dict \-'be-nə-ˌdikt\ *noun plural but singular or plural in construction* [probably from the name *Benedict*] (1898)
: poached eggs and broiled ham placed on toasted halves of English muffin and covered with hollandaise
¹egg·shell \'eg-ˌshel, 'āg-\ *noun* (14th century)
1 : the hard exterior covering of an egg
2 : something resembling an eggshell especially in fragility
²eggshell *adjective* (1835)
1 : thin and fragile
2 : slightly glossy
3 : yellowish white
egg timer *noun* (1884)
: a small sandglass for timing the boiling of eggs
egg tooth *noun* (1893)
: a hard sharp prominence on the beak of an unhatched bird or the nose of an unhatched reptile that is used to break through the eggshell
egis \'ē-jəs\ *variant of* AEGIS
eg·lan·tine \'e-glən-ˌtīn, -ˌtēn\ *noun* [Middle English *eglentyn*, from Middle French *aiglent*, from (assumed) Vulgar Latin *aculentum*, from Latin *acus* needle; akin to Latin *acer* sharp — more at EDGE] (14th century)
: SWEETBRIER
eglo·mi·se *also* **églo·mi·sé** \ā-glə-(ˌ)mē-'zā, -e-; 'ā-glə-(ˌ)mē-ˌ, -e'\ *adjective* [French, past participle of *églomiser* to decorate a glass panel by painting on its back, from Jean-Baptiste *Glomy* (died 1786) French decorator] (1877)
: made of glass on the back of which is a painted picture that shows through ⟨a clock with *eglomise* panels⟩
ego \'ē-(ˌ)gō *also* 'e-\ *noun, plural* **egos** [New Latin, from Latin, I — more at I] (1789)
1 : the self especially as contrasted with another self or the world
2 a : EGOTISM 2 **b** : SELF-ESTEEM 1
3 : the one of the three divisions of the psyche in psychoanalytic theory that serves as the organized conscious mediator between the person and reality especially by functioning both in the perception of and adaptation to reality — compare ID, SUPEREGO
— **ego·less** *adjective*
ego·cen·tric \ˌē-gō-'sen-trik *also* ˌe-\ *adjective* (1894)
1 : concerned with the individual rather than society
2 : taking the ego as the starting point in philosophy
3 a : limited in outlook or concern to one's own activities or needs **b** : SELF-CENTERED, SELFISH
— **egocentric** *noun*
— **ego·cen·tri·cal·ly** \-tri-k(ə-)lē\ *adverb*

— **ego·cen·tric·i·ty** \-ˌsen-'tri-sə-tē\ *noun*
— **ego·cen·trism** \-'sen-ˌtri-zəm\ *noun*
ego ideal *noun* (1922)
: the standards, ideals, and ambitions that according to psychoanalytic theory are assimilated from the superego
ego·ism \'ē-gə-ˌwi-zəm *also* 'e-\ *noun* (1785)
1 a : a doctrine that individual self-interest is the actual motive of all conscious action **b** : a doctrine that individual self-interest is the valid end of all actions
2 : excessive concern for oneself with or without exaggerated feelings of self-importance — compare EGOTISM 2
ego·ist \-wist\ *noun* (1785)
1 : a believer in egoism
2 : an egocentric or egotistic person
— **ego·is·tic** \ˌē-gə-'wis-tik *also* ˌe-\ *also* **ego·is·ti·cal** \-ti-kəl\ *adjective*
— **ego·is·ti·cal·ly** \-ti-k(ə-)lē\ *adverb*
egoistic hedonism *noun* (1874)
: the ethical theory that achieving one's own happiness is the proper goal of all conduct
ego·ma·nia \ˌē-gō-'mā-nē-ə, -nyə\ *noun* (1825)
: the quality or state of being extremely egocentric
— **ego·ma·ni·ac** \-nē-ˌak\ *noun*
— **ego·ma·ni·a·cal** \-mə-'nī-ə-kəl\ *adjective*
— **ego·ma·ni·a·cal·ly** \-k(ə-)lē\ *adverb*
ego·tism \'ē-gə-ˌti-zəm *also* 'e-\ *noun* [Latin *ego* + English *-tism* (as in *idiotism*)] (1714)
1 a : excessive use of the first person singular personal pronoun **b** : the practice of talking about oneself too much
2 : an exaggerated sense of self-importance : CONCEIT — compare EGOISM 2
— **ego·tist** \-tist\ *noun*
— **ego·tis·tic** \-'tis-tik\ *or* **ego·tis·ti·cal** \-'tis-ti-kəl\ *adjective*
— **ego·tis·ti·cal·ly** \-k(ə-)lē\ *adverb*
ego trip *noun* (1967)
: an act or course of action that enhances and satisfies one's ego
— **ego–trip** *intransitive verb*
— **ego–trip·per** *noun*
egre·gious \i-'grē-jəs\ *adjective* [Latin *egregius*, from *e-* + *greg-, grex* herd — more at GREGARIOUS] (circa 1534)
1 *archaic* : DISTINGUISHED
2 : CONSPICUOUS; *especially* : conspicuously bad : FLAGRANT ⟨an *egregious* mistake⟩ ◇
— **egre·gious·ly** *adverb*
— **egre·gious·ness** *noun*
¹egress \'ē-ˌgres\ *noun* [Latin *egressus*, from *egressus*, past participle of *egredi* to go out, from *e-* + *gradi* to go — more at GRADE] (1538)
1 : the action or right of going or coming out
2 : a place or means of going out : EXIT
²egress \ē-'gres\ *intransitive verb* (1578)
: to go or come out

egg 1a: *1* shell, *2* shell membrane, *3* egg membrane, *4* air space, *5* chalaza, *6* albumen or white layers, *7* yolk layers, *8* blastodisc, *9* vitelline membrane

◇ WORD HISTORY

egregious *Egregious* is one of several English words whose connotations have taken a decided turn for the worse since their appearance in the language. The word is borrowed from *egregius*, a Latin word meaning "outstanding" or "excellent," which was formed from *e* "out of" and *grex* "herd." Thus, a person who was *egregius* stood out from the herd. Originally, English *egregious*, like its Latin source, denoted a positive quality. In the 16th century, however, an opposite sense came into use when *egregious* began to be applied to a person who was conspicuously or outrageously bad. Though it may have been the result of ironic use of the original sense, this pejorative meaning, now applied to things as well as people, is the one that persists in common use today. See in addition GREGARIOUS.

egres·sion \ē-'gre-shən\ *noun* (15th century)
: EGRESS, EMERGENCE

egret \'ē-grət, -,gret *also* i-'gret, 'eg-rət\ *noun* [Middle English *aigrette,* from Middle French *aigrette,* from Old Provençal *aigreta,* of Germanic origin; akin to Old High German *heigaro* heron] (14th century)
: any of various herons that bear long plumes during the breeding season

egret

¹Egyp·tian \i-'jip-shən\ *adjective* (14th century)
: of, relating to, or characteristic of Egypt or the Egyptians

²Egyptian *noun* (14th century)
1 : a native or inhabitant of Egypt
2 : the Afro-Asiatic language of the ancient Egyptians from earliest times to about the 3d century A.D.
3 *often not capitalized* : a typeface having little contrast between thick and thin strokes and squared serifs

Egyptian alfalfa weevil *noun* (1943)
: an Old World weevil (*Hypera brunneipennis*) established in western North America where it feeds on alfalfa and various clovers

Egyptian clover *noun* (circa 1900)
: BERSEEM

Egyptian cotton *noun* (1877)
: a fine long-staple often somewhat brownish cotton grown chiefly in Egypt

Egyp·tol·o·gy \ē-(,)jip-'tä-lə-jē\ *noun* (1862)
: the study of Egyptian antiquities
— **Egyp·to·log·i·cal** \-tə-'lä-jə-kəl\ *adjective*
— **Egyp·tol·o·gist** \-'tä-lə-jist\ *noun*

eh \'ā, 'e, 'a(i)\ *interjection* [Middle English *ey*] (13th century)
— used to ask for confirmation or repetition or to express inquiry; used especially in Canadian English in anticipation of the listener's or reader's agreement

ei·cos·a·noid \ī-'kō-sə-,nóid\ *noun* [*eicosa-* containing 20 atoms (from Greek *eikosa-* twenty, from *eikosi*) + *-noic,* suffix used in names of fatty acids (from *-ane* + *-oic*) + ¹*-oid* — more at VIGESIMAL] (1980)
: any of a class of compounds (as the prostaglandins) derived from polyunsaturated acids (as arachidonic acid) and involved in cellular activity

ei·der \'ī-dər\ *noun* [Dutch, German, or Swedish, from Icelandic *æthur,* from Old Norse *æthr*] (1743)
1 : any of several large northern sea ducks (genera *Somateria* and *Polystica*) having fine soft down that is used by the female for lining the nest — called also *eider duck*
2 : EIDERDOWN 1

ei·der·down \-,daún\ *noun* [probably from German *Eiderdaune,* from Icelandic *æthardūnn,* from *æthur* + *dūnn* ⁷down] (1774)
1 : the down of the eider
2 : a comforter filled with eiderdown
3 : a soft lightweight clothing fabric knitted or woven and napped on one or both sides

ei·det·ic \ī-'de-tik\ *adjective* [Greek *eidētikos* of a form, from *eidos* form — more at WISE] (circa 1924)
: marked by or involving extraordinarily accurate and vivid recall especially of visual images ⟨an *eidetic* memory⟩
— **ei·det·i·cal·ly** \-ti-k(ə-)lē\ *adverb*

ei·do·lon \ī-'dō-lən\ *noun, plural* **-lons** \-lənz\ *or* **-la** \-lə\ [Greek *eidōlon* — more at IDOL] (1828)
1 : an unsubstantial image : PHANTOM
2 : IDEAL

ei·gen·mode \'ī-gən-,mōd\ *noun* [*eigen-* (as in *eigenvector*) + ¹*mode*]
: a normal mode of vibration of an oscillating system

ei·gen·val·ue \'ī-gən-,val-(,)yü, -yə(-w)\ *noun* [part translation of German *Eigenwert,* from *eigen* own, peculiar + *Wert* value] (1927)
: a scalar associated with a given linear transformation of a vector space and having the property that there is some nonzero vector which when multiplied by the scalar is equal to the vector obtained by letting the transformation operate on the vector; *especially* : a root of the characteristic equation of a matrix

ei·gen·vec·tor \-,vek-tər\ *noun* [International Scientific Vocabulary *eigen-* (from German *eigen*) + *vector*] (1941)
: a nonzero vector that is mapped by a given linear transformation of a vector space onto a vector that is the product of a scalar multiplied by the original vector — called also *characteristic vector*

eight \'āt\ *noun* [Middle English *eighte,* from *eighte,* adjective, from Old English *eahta;* akin to Old High German *ahto* eight, Latin *octo,* Greek *oktō*] (before 12th century)
1 — see NUMBER table
2 : the eighth in a set or series ⟨the *eight* of spades⟩
3 : something having eight units or members: as **a** : an 8-oared racing boat or its crew **b** : an 8-cylinder engine or automobile
— **eight** *adjective*
— **eight** *pronoun, plural in construction*

eight ball *noun* (1932)
1 : a black pool ball numbered 8
2 : MISFIT
— **behind the eight ball** : in a highly disadvantageous position

eigh·teen \(')ā(t)-'tēn\ *noun* [Middle English *eightetene,* adjective, from Old English *eahtatīene,* from *eahta* + *-tīene;* akin to Old English *tīen* ten] (before 12th century)
— see NUMBER table
— **eighteen** *adjective*
— **eighteen** *pronoun, plural in construction*
— **eigh·teenth** \-'tēn(t)th\ *adjective or noun*

18–wheel·er *or* **eigh·teen–wheel·er** \,ā(t)-(,)tēn-'wē-lər\ *noun* (1976)
: a trucking rig consisting of a tractor and a trailer and typically having eighteen wheels

eight·fold \'āt-,fōld, -'fōld\ *adjective* (before 12th century)
1 : having eight units or members
2 : being eight times as great or as many
— **eight·fold** \-'fōld\ *adverb*

eightfold way *noun* (1961)
: a unified theoretical scheme for classifying the relationship among strongly interacting elementary particles on the basis of isospin and hypercharge

eighth \'ātth, 'āth\ *noun, plural* **eighths** \'āt(th)s, 'āths\ (1557)
1 — see NUMBER table
2 : OCTAVE
— **eighth** *adjective or adverb*

eighth note *noun* (circa 1864)
: a musical note with the time value of ⅛ of a whole note — see NOTE illustration

eighth rest *noun* (circa 1890)
: a musical rest corresponding in time value to an eighth note — see REST illustration

800 number \,āt-'hən-drəd, -dərd-\ *noun* (1979)
: a toll-free telephone number for long-distance calls (as to a business) that is prefixed by the number 800

eight·pen·ny nail \,āt-,pe-nē-\ *noun* [from its original price per hundred] (15th century)
: a nail typically 2½ inches (6.35 centimeters) long

eighty \'ā-tē\ *noun, plural* **eight·ies** [Middle English *eighty,* adjective, from Old English *eahtatig,* short for *hundeahtatig,* noun, group of eighty, from *hund-,* literally, hundred + *eahta* eight + *-tig* group of ten; akin to Old English *tīen* ten] (before 12th century)
1 — see NUMBER table
2 *plural* : the numbers 80 to 89; *specifically* : the years 80 to 89 in a lifetime or century
— **eight·i·eth** \'ā-tē-əth\ *adjective or noun*
— **eighty** *adjective*
— **eighty** *pronoun, plural in construction*

eighty–six *or* **86** \,ā-tē-'siks\ *transitive verb* [probably rhyming slang for ³*nix*] (1967)
slang : to refuse to serve (a customer); *also* : to get rid of : THROW OUT

ein·korn \'īn-,kórn\ *noun* [German, from Old High German, from *ein* one + *korn* grain — more at ONE, CORN] (circa 1901)
: a one-grained wheat (*Triticum monococcum*) sometimes considered the most primitive wheat and grown especially in poor soils in central Europe — called also *einkorn wheat*

ein·stei·ni·um \īn-'stī-nē-əm\ *noun* [New Latin, from Albert *Einstein*] (1955)
: a radioactive element produced artificially — see ELEMENT table

ei·re·nic *chiefly British variant of* IRENIC

eis·ege·sis \,ī-sə-'jē-səs, 'ī-sə-,\ *noun, plural* **-ege·ses** \-,sēz\ [Greek *eis* into (akin to Greek *en* in) + English *exegesis* — more at IN] (1892)
: the interpretation of a text (as of the Bible) by reading into it one's own ideas — compare EXEGESIS

ei·stedd·fod \ī-'steth-,vòd, ā-\ *noun, plural* **-fods** \-,vòdz\ *or* **-fod·au** \-,steth-'vò-,dī\ [Welsh, literally, session, from *eistedd* to sit + *bod* being] (1822)
: a usually Welsh competitive festival of the arts especially in poetry and singing
— **ei·stedd·fod·ic** \,ī-,steth-'vò-dik, ,ā-\ *adjective*

eis·wein \'īs-,wīn, -,vīn\ *noun, often capitalized* [German, from *Eis* ice + *Wein* wine] (1967)
: a sweet German wine made from grapes that have frozen on the vine

¹ei·ther \'ē-thər *also* 'ī-\ *adjective* [Middle English, from Old English *ǣghwæther* both, each, from *ā* always + *ge-,* collective prefix + *hwæther* which of two, whether — more at AYE, CO-] (before 12th century)
1 : being the one and the other of two : EACH ⟨flowers blooming on *either* side of the walk⟩
2 : being the one or the other of two ⟨take *either* road⟩ □

²either *pronoun* (before 12th century)
: the one or the other

³either *conjunction* (before 12th century)
— used as a function word before two or more coordinate words, phrases, or clauses joined usually by *or* to indicate that what immediately follows is the first of two or more alternatives

☐ **USAGE**
either Americans prefer \ē\ as the first vowel of *either* and *neither,* while the British overwhelmingly prefer \ī\. This *ei* has had still other pronunciations through the centuries, including the vowel sound in *eight.* The variant with \ī\ was not at first accepted by British commentators, but now has become standard in British speech. This entails, by the lights of some, that the British \ī\ should be the standard for the American pronunciation of *either* and *neither* as well. However, the weight of long usage has established the older vowel \ē\ for *either* and *neither* in American speech.

\ə\ abut \ᵊ\ kitten \ər\ further \a\ ash \ā\ ace
\ä\ mop, mar \aú\ out \ch\ chin \e\ bet \ē\ easy
\g\ go \i\ hit \ī\ ice \j\ job \ŋ\ sing \ō\ go
\ó\ law \ói\ boy \th\ thin \th\ the \ü\ loot \ú\ foot
\y\ yet \zh\ vision *see also* Guide to Pronunciation

⁴either *adverb* (15th century)
1 : LIKEWISE, MOREOVER — used for emphasis after a negative ⟨not smart or handsome *either*⟩
2 : for that matter — used for emphasis after an alternative following a question or conditional clause especially where negation is implied ⟨who answers for the Irish parliament? or army *either*? —Robert Browning⟩

¹ei·ther-or \ˌē-thə-ˈrȯr *also* ˌī-\ *noun* (1922)
: an unavoidable choice or exclusive division between only two alternatives

²either-or *adjective* (1926)
: of or marked by either : BLACK-AND-WHITE

¹ejac·u·late \i-ˈja-kyə-ˌlāt\ *verb* **-lat·ed; -lat·ing** [Latin *ejaculatus,* past participle of *ejaculari* to throw out, from *e-* + *jaculari* to throw, from *jaculum* dart, from *jacere* to throw — more at JET] (1578)
transitive verb
1 : to eject from a living body; *specifically* : to eject (semen) in orgasm
2 : to utter suddenly and vehemently
intransitive verb
: to eject a fluid
— **ejac·u·la·tor** \-ˌlā-tər\ *noun*

²ejac·u·late \-lət\ *noun* (1927)
: the semen released by one ejaculation

ejac·u·la·tion \i-ˌja-kyə-ˈlā-shən\ *noun* (1603)
1 : an act of ejaculating; *specifically* : a sudden discharging of a fluid from a duct
2 : something ejaculated; *especially* : a short sudden emotional utterance

ejac·u·la·to·ry \i-ˈja-kyə-lə-ˌtȯr-ē, -ˌtȯr-\ *adjective* (1644)
1 : marked by or given to vocal ejaculation
2 : casting or throwing out; *specifically* : associated with or concerned in physiological ejaculation ⟨*ejaculatory* vessels⟩

ejaculatory duct *noun* (1751)
: a duct through which semen is ejaculated; *specifically* : either of the paired ducts in the human male that are formed by the junction of the duct from the seminal vesicle with the vas deferens and that pass through the prostate to empty into the urethra by means of a small opening

eject \i-ˈjekt\ *transitive verb* [Middle English, from Latin *ejectus,* past participle of *eicere,* from *e-* + *jacere*] (15th century)
1 a : to drive out especially by physical force **b** : to evict from property
2 : to throw out or off from within ⟨*ejects* the empty cartridges⟩ ☆
— **eject·able** \-ˈjek-tə-bəl\ *adjective*
— **ejec·tion** \-ˈjek-shən\ *noun*
— **ejec·tive** \-ˈjek-tiv\ *adjective*

ejec·ta \i-ˈjek-tə\ *noun plural but singular or plural in construction* [New Latin, from Latin, neuter plural of *ejectus*] (1886)
: material thrown out (as from a volcano)

ejection seat *noun* (1945)
: an emergency escape seat for propelling an occupant out and away from an airplane

eject·ment \i-ˈjek(t)-mənt\ *noun* (1523)
1 : the act or an instance of ejecting : DISPOSSESSION
2 : an action for the recovery of possession of real property and damages and costs

ejec·tor \i-ˈjek-tər\ *noun* (1640)
1 : one that ejects; *especially* : a mechanism of a firearm that ejects an empty cartridge
2 : a jet pump for withdrawing a gas, fluid, or powdery substance from a space

eka- \ˈe-kə, ˌā-kə\ *combining form* [International Scientific Vocabulary, from Sanskrit *eka* one — more at ONE]
: standing or assumed to stand next in order beyond (a specified element) in the same family of the periodic table — in names of chemical elements especially when not yet discovered ⟨*eka*-lead is the hypothetical element 114⟩

¹eke \ˈēk\ *adverb* [Middle English, from Old English *ēac;* akin to Old High German *ouh* also, Latin *aut* or, Greek *au* again] (before 12th century)
archaic : ALSO

²eke *transitive verb* **eked; ek·ing** [Middle English, from Old English *īecan, ēcan;* akin to Old High German *ouhhōn* to add, Latin *augēre* to increase, Greek *auxein*] (before 12th century)
1 *archaic* : INCREASE, LENGTHEN
2 : to get with great difficulty — usually used with *out* ⟨*eke* out a living⟩

eke out *transitive verb* (1596)
1 : to make up for the deficiencies of : SUPPLEMENT ⟨*eked out* his income by getting a second job⟩
2 : to make (a supply) last by economy

ekis·tics \i-ˈkis-tiks\ *noun plural but singular in construction* [New Greek *oikistikē,* from feminine of *oikistikos* of settlement, from Greek, from *oikizein* to settle, colonize, from *oikos* house — more at VICINITY] (1958)
: a science dealing with human settlements and drawing on the research and experience of professionals in various fields (as architecture, engineering, city planning, and sociology)
— **ekis·tic** \-tik\ *adjective*

Ek·man dredge \ˌek-mən-\ *noun* [probably from V. W. *Ekman* (died 1954) Swedish oceanographer] (1948)
: a dredge that has opposable jaws operated by a messenger traveling down a cable to release a spring catch and that is used in ecology for sampling the bottom of a body of water

ekue·le \ā-ˈkwā-(ˌ)lā\ *also* **ek·pwe·le** \ek-ˈpwā-\ *noun, plural* **ekuele** *also* **ekpweles** [Fang (Bantu language of western equatorial Africa)] (circa 1973)
: the basic monetary unit of Equatorial Guinea 1975–85

¹el \ˈel\ *noun* (14th century)
: the letter *l*

²el *noun, often capitalized* (circa 1906)
: an urban railway that operates chiefly on an elevated structure; *also* : a train belonging to such a railway

¹elab·o·rate \i-ˈla-b(ə-)rət\ *adjective* [Latin *elaboratus,* from past participle of *elaborare* to work out, acquire by labor, from *e-* + *laborare* to work — more at LABORATORY] (1592)
1 : planned or carried out with great care ⟨took *elaborate* precautions⟩
2 : marked by complexity, fullness of detail, or ornateness ⟨*elaborate* prose⟩
— **elab·o·rate·ly** *adverb*
— **elab·o·rate·ness** *noun*

²elab·o·rate \i-ˈla-bə-ˌrāt\ *verb* **-rat·ed; -rat·ing** (1611)
transitive verb
1 : to produce by labor
2 : to build up (as complex organic compounds) from simple ingredients
3 : to work out in detail : DEVELOP
intransitive verb
1 : to become elaborate
2 : to expand something in detail ⟨would you care to *elaborate* on that statement⟩
— **elab·o·ra·tion** \-ˌla-bə-ˈrā-shən\ *noun*
— **elab·o·ra·tive** \-ˈla-bə-ˌrā-tiv\ *adjective*

Elaine \i-ˈlān\ *noun*
: any of several women in Arthurian legend; *especially* : one who dies for unrequited love of Lancelot

Elam·ite \ˈē-lə-ˌmīt\ *noun* (1874)
: a language of unknown affinities used in Elam approximately from the 25th to the 4th centuries B.C.

élan \ā-ˈläⁿ\ *noun* [French, from Middle French *eslan* rush, from (*s'*)*eslancer* to rush, from *ex-* + *lancer* to hurl — more at LANCE] (1864)
: vigorous spirit or enthusiasm

eland \ˈē-lənd, -ˌland\ *noun, plural* **eland** *also* **elands** [Afrikaans, elk, from Dutch, from obsolete German *Elend,* probably from obsolete

Lithuanian *ellenis;* akin to Old High German *elaho* elk — more at ELK] (1600)
: either of two large African antelopes (*Tragelaphus oryx* and *T. derbianus*) bovine in form with short spirally twisted horns in both sexes

eland

élan vi·tal \ā-ˌläⁿ-vē-ˈtál\ *noun* [French] (1907)
: the vital force or impulse of life; *especially* : a creative principle held by Bergson to be immanent in all organisms and responsible for evolution

el·a·pid \ˈe-lə-pəd\ *noun* [New Latin *Elap-, Elaps,* genus of snakes, from Middle Greek, a fish, alteration of Greek *elops*] (1885)
: any of a family (Elapidae) of venomous snakes with grooved fangs

¹elapse \i-ˈlaps\ *intransitive verb* **elapsed; elaps·ing** [Latin *elapsus,* past participle of *elabi,* from *e-* + *labi* to slip — more at SLEEP] (1644)
: to slip or glide away : PASS ⟨four years *elapsed* before he returned⟩

²elapse *noun* (circa 1677)
: PASSAGE ⟨returned after an *elapse* of 15 years⟩

elapsed time *noun* (circa 1909)
: the actual time taken (as by a boat or automobile in traveling over a racecourse)

elas·mo·branch \i-ˈlaz-mə-ˌbraŋk\ *noun, plural* **-branchs** [ultimately from Greek *elasmos* metal plate (from *elaunein*) + *branchia* gills] (1872)
: any of a subclass (Elasmobranchii) of cartilaginous fishes that have five to seven lateral to ventral gill openings on each side and that comprise the sharks, rays, skates, and extinct related fishes
— **elasmobranch** *adjective*

elas·tase \i-ˈlas-ˌtās, -ˌtāz\ *noun* [*elastin* + *-ase*] (1949)
: an enzyme especially of pancreatic juice that digests elastin

¹elas·tic \i-ˈlas-tik\ *adjective* [New Latin *elasticus,* from Late Greek *elastos* ductile, beaten, from Greek *elaunein* to drive, beat out; probably akin to Greek *ēlythe* he went, Old Irish *luid*] (1674)
1 a *of a solid* : capable of recovering size and shape after deformation **b** : being a collision between particles in which the total kinetic energy of the particles remains unchanged
2 : capable of recovering quickly especially from depression or disappointment
3 : capable of being easily stretched or expanded and resuming former shape : FLEXIBLE
4 a : capable of ready change or easy expansion or contraction : not rigid or constricted **b** : receptive to new ideas : ADAPTABLE ☆
— **elas·ti·cal·ly** \-ti-k(ə-)lē\ *adverb*

²**elastic** *noun* (1847)
1 a : easily stretched rubber usually prepared in cords, strings, or bands **b :** RUBBER BAND
2 a : an elastic fabric usually made of yarns containing rubber **b :** something made from this fabric

elastic fiber *noun* (1849)
: a thick very elastic smooth yellowish anastomosing fiber of connective tissue that contains elastin

elas·tic·i·ty \i-,las-'ti-sə-tē, ,ē-,las-, -'tis-tē\ *noun, plural* **-ties** (1664)
: the quality or state of being elastic: as **a :** the capability of a strained body to recover its size and shape after deformation **:** SPRINGINESS **b :** RESILIENCE 2 **c :** the quality of being adaptable

elas·ti·cized \i-'las-tə-,sīzd\ *adjective* (circa 1909)
: made with elastic thread or inserts

elastic limit *noun* (1898)
: the greatest stress that an elastic solid can sustain without undergoing permanent deformation

elastic modulus *noun* (1904)
: the ratio of the stress in a body to the corresponding strain

elastic scattering *noun* (1933)
: a scattering of particles as the result of an elastic collision

elas·tin \i-'las-tən\ *noun* [International Scientific Vocabulary, from New Latin *elasticus*] (1875)
: a protein that is similar to collagen and is the chief constituent of elastic fibers

elas·to·mer \-tə-mər\ *noun* [*elastic* + *-o-* + *-mer*] (circa 1939)
: any of various elastic substances resembling rubber ⟨polyvinyl *elastomers*⟩
— **elas·to·mer·ic** \i-,las-tə-'mer-ik\ *adjective*

¹**elate** \i-'lāt\ *transitive verb* **elat·ed; elat·ing** [Latin *elatus* (past participle of *efferre* to carry out, elevate), from *e-* + *latus*, past participle of *ferre* to carry — more at TOLERATE, BEAR] (circa 1619)
: to fill with joy or pride

²**elate** *adjective* (1647)
: ELATED

elat·ed *adjective* (circa 1619)
: marked by high spirits : EXULTANT
— **elat·ed·ly** *adverb*
— **elat·ed·ness** *noun*

el·a·ter \'e-lə-tər\ *noun* [New Latin, from Greek *elatēr* driver, from *elaunein* to drive] (1830)
: a plant structure functioning in the distribution of spores: as **a :** one of the elongated filaments among the spores in the capsule of a liverwort **b :** one of the filamentous appendages of the spores in the scouring rushes

elat·er·ite \i-'la-tə-,rīt\ *noun* [German *Elaterit*, from Greek *elatēr*] (1826)
: a dark brown elastic mineral resin occurring in soft flexible masses

ela·tion \i-'lā-shən\ *noun* (14th century)
1 : the quality or state of being elated
2 : pathological euphoria

E layer *noun* (1933)
: a layer of the ionosphere occurring about 65 miles (110 kilometers) above the earth's surface during daylight hours that is capable of reflecting shortwave frequencies

El·ba \'el-bə\ *noun* [*Elba* (Mediterranean island), residence of Napoléon Bonaparte after his first abdication May 14, 1814 to Feb. 26, 1815] (1924)
: a place or state of exile

¹**el·bow** \'el-,bō\ *noun* [Middle English *elbowe*, from Old English *elboga*, from *el-* (akin to *eln* ell) + Old English *boga* bow — more at ELL, BOW] (before 12th century)
1 a : the joint of the human arm **b :** a corresponding joint in the anterior limb of a lower vertebrate

2 : something (as macaroni or an angular pipe fitting) resembling an elbow
— **at one's elbow :** at one's side
— **out at elbows** *or* **out at the elbows**
1 : shabbily dressed **2 :** short of funds

²**elbow** (1605)
transitive verb
1 a : to push with the elbow **:** JOSTLE **b :** to shove aside by pushing with or as if with the elbow
2 : to force (as one's way) by pushing with or as if with the elbow ⟨*elbowing* our way through the crowd⟩ ⟨*elbows* her way into the best social circles⟩
intransitive verb
1 : to advance by pushing with the elbow
2 : to make an angle **:** TURN

elbow grease *noun* (1672)
: vigorously applied physical labor **:** hard work

el·bow·room \'el-,bō-,rüm, -,rum\ *noun* (circa 1540)
1 a : room for moving the elbows freely **b :** adequate space for work or operation ⟨the large house gives plenty of *elbowroom*⟩
2 : free scope ⟨*elbowroom* to try new ideas⟩

el cheapo \(,)el-'chē-(,)pō, 'el-\ *adjective* [Spanish *el* the + English *cheap* + Spanish *-o* (masculine noun ending)] (1969)
: CHEAP 3a, b

eld \'eld\ *noun* [Middle English, from Old English *ieldo*; akin to Old English *eald* old — more at OLD] (before 12th century)
1 : old age
2 *archaic* **:** old times **:** ANTIQUITY

¹**el·der** \'el-dər\ *noun* [Middle English *eldre*, from Old English *ellærn*; perhaps akin to Old English *alor* alder — more at ALDER] (before 12th century)
: ELDERBERRY 2

²**elder** *adjective* [Middle English, from Old English *ieldra*, comparative of *eald* old] (before 12th century)
1 : of earlier birth or greater age ⟨his *elder* brother⟩
2 : of or relating to earlier times **:** FORMER
3 *obsolete* **:** of or relating to a more advanced time of life
4 : prior or superior in rank, office, or validity

³**elder** *noun* (before 12th century)
1 : one living in an earlier period
2 a : one who is older ⟨a child trying to please her *elders*⟩ **b :** an aged person
3 : one having authority by virtue of age and experience ⟨the village *elders*⟩
4 : any of various officers of religious groups: as **a :** PRESBYTER 1 **b :** a permanent officer elected by a Presbyterian congregation and ordained to serve on the session and assist the pastor at communion **c :** MINISTER 2 **d :** a leader of the Shakers **e :** a Mormon ordained to the Melchizedek priesthood
— **el·der·ship** \-,ship\ *noun*

el·der·ber·ry \'el-də(r)-,ber-ē\ *noun* (1589)
1 : the edible black or red berrylike drupe of any of a genus (*Sambucus*) of shrubs or trees of the honeysuckle family bearing flat clusters of small white or pink flowers
2 : a tree or shrub bearing elderberries

¹**el·der·ly** \'el-dər-lē\ *adjective* (1611)
1 a : rather old; *especially* **:** being past middle age **b :** OLD-FASHIONED
2 : of, relating to, or characteristic of later life or elderly persons
— **el·der·li·ness** *noun*

²**elderly** *noun, plural* **-ly** *or* **-lies** (1865)
: an elderly person

elder statesman *noun* (1904)
: an eminent senior member of a group or organization; *especially* **:** a retired statesman who unofficially advises current leaders

el·dest \'el-dəst\ *adjective* (before 12th century)
: of the greatest age or seniority **:** OLDEST

eldest hand *noun* (1599)

: the card player who first receives cards in the deal

El Do·ra·do \,el-də-'rä-(,)dō, -'rā-\ *noun* [Spanish, literally, the gilded one]
1 : a city or country of fabulous riches held by 16th century explorers to exist in South America
2 : a place of fabulous wealth or opportunity

el·dress \'el-drəs\ *noun* (1640)
: a woman elder especially of the Shakers

el·dritch \'el-drich\ *adjective* [perhaps from (assumed) Middle English *elfriche* fairyland, from Middle English *elf* + *riche* kingdom, from Old English *rīce* — more at RICH] (1508)
: WEIRD, EERIE

El·e·at·ic \,el-ē-'a-tik\ *adjective* [Latin *Eleaticus*, from Greek *Eleatikos*, from *Elea* (Velia), ancient town in southern Italy] (1695)
: of or relating to a school of Greek philosophers founded by Parmenides and developed by Zeno and marked by belief in the unity of being and the unreality of motion or change
— **Eleatic** *noun*
— **El·e·at·i·cism** \-'a-tə-,si-zəm\ *noun*

ele·cam·pane \,e-li-,kam-'pān\ *noun* [Middle English *elena campana*, from Medieval Latin *enula campana*, literally, field elecampane, from *inula, enula* elecampane + *campana* of the field] (14th century)
: a large coarse European composite herb (*Inula helenium*) that has yellow ray flowers and is naturalized in the U.S.

¹**elect** \i-'lekt\ *adjective* [Middle English, from Latin *electus*, past participle of *eligere* to select, from *e-* + *legere* to choose — more at LEGEND] (15th century)
1 : carefully selected **:** CHOSEN
2 : chosen for salvation through divine mercy
3 a : chosen for office or position but not yet installed ⟨the president-*elect*⟩ **b :** chosen for marriage at some future time ⟨the bride-*elect*⟩

²**elect** *noun, plural* **elect** (15th century)
1 : one chosen or set apart (as by divine favor)
2 *plural* **:** a select or exclusive group of people

³**elect** *verb* [Middle English, from Latin *electus*] (15th century)
transitive verb
1 : to select by vote for an office, position, or membership ⟨*elected* her class president⟩
2 : to make a selection of ⟨will *elect* an academic program⟩
3 : to choose (as a course of action) especially by preference ⟨might *elect* to sell the business⟩
intransitive verb
: to make a selection

elect·able \i-'lek-tə-bəl\ *adjective* (1879)
: capable of being elected (as to public office)

☆ SYNONYMS
Elastic, resilient, springy, flexible, supple mean able to endure strain without being permanently injured. ELASTIC implies the property of resisting deformation by stretching ⟨an *elastic* waistband⟩. RESILIENT implies the ability to recover shape quickly when the deforming force or pressure is removed ⟨a *resilient* innersole⟩. SPRINGY stresses both the ease with which something yields to pressure and the quickness of its return to original shape ⟨the cake is done when the top is *springy*⟩. FLEXIBLE applies to something which may or may not be resilient or elastic but which can be bent or folded without breaking ⟨*flexible* plastic tubing⟩. SUPPLE applies to something that can be readily bent, twisted, or folded without any sign of injury ⟨*supple* leather⟩.

\ə\ abut \ᵊ\ kitten \ər\ further \a\ ash \ā\ ace
\ä\ mop, mar \au̇\ out \ch\ chin \e\ bet \ē\ easy
\g\ go \i\ hit \ī\ ice \j\ job \ŋ\ sing \ō\ go
\ȯ\ law \ȯi\ boy \th\ thin \t͟h\ the \ü\ loot \u̇\ foot
\y\ yet \zh\ vision *see also* Guide to Pronunciation

— **elect·abil·i·ty** \-ˌlek-tə-'bi-lə-tē\ *noun*

elec·tion \i-'lek-shən\ *noun* (13th century)
1 a : an act or process of electing **b :** the fact of being elected
2 : predestination to eternal life
3 : the right, power, or privilege of making a choice

Election Day *noun* (15th century)
: a day legally established for the election of public officials; *especially* **:** the first Tuesday after the first Monday in November in an even year designated for national elections in the U.S. and observed as a legal holiday in many states

elec·tion·eer \i-ˌlek-shə-'nir\ *intransitive verb* [*election* + *-eer* (as in *privateer,* verb)] (1789)
: to take an active part in an election; *specifically* **:** to work for the election of a candidate or party
— **elec·tion·eer·er** *noun*

¹**elec·tive** \i-'lek-tiv\ *adjective* (1531)
1 a : chosen or filled by popular election ⟨an *elective* official⟩ **b :** of or relating to election **c :** based on the right or principle of election ⟨the presidency is an *elective* office⟩
2 a : permitting a choice **:** OPTIONAL ⟨an *elective* course in school⟩ **b :** beneficial to the patient but not essential for survival ⟨*elective* surgery⟩
3 a : tending to operate on one substance rather than another ⟨*elective* absorption⟩ **b :** favorably inclined to one more than to another **:** SYMPATHETIC ⟨an *elective* affinity⟩
— **elec·tive·ly** *adverb*
— **elec·tive·ness** *noun*

²**elective** *noun* (1850)
: an elective course or subject

elec·tor \i-'lek-tər, -ˌtȯr\ *noun* (15th century)
1 : one qualified to vote in an election
2 : one entitled to participate in an election: as **a :** any of the German princes entitled to take part in choosing the Holy Roman Emperor **b :** a member of the electoral college in the U.S.

elec·tor·al \i-'lek-t(ə-)rəl, ˌē-lek-'tȯr-əl\ *adjective* (1675)
1 : of or relating to an elector ⟨the *electoral* vote⟩
2 : of or relating to election ⟨an *electoral* system⟩
— **elec·tor·al·ly** \-t(ə-)rə-lē, -'tȯr-ə-lē\ *adverb*

electoral college *noun* (circa 1691)
: a body of electors; *especially* **:** one that elects the president and vice president of the U.S.

elec·tor·ate \i-'lek-t(ə-)rət\ *noun* (1675)
1 : the territory, jurisdiction, or dignity of a German elector
2 : a body of people entitled to vote

electr- *or* **electro-** *combining form* [New Latin *electricus*]
1 a : electricity ⟨*electro*meter⟩ **b :** electric ⟨*electro*de⟩ **:** electric and ⟨*electro*chemical⟩ **:** electrically ⟨*electro*positive⟩
2 : electrolytic ⟨*electro*analysis⟩
3 : electron ⟨*electro*philic⟩

Elec·tra \i-'lek-trə\ *noun* [Latin, from Greek *Ēlektra*]
: a sister of Orestes who aids him in killing their mother Clytemnestra

Electra complex *noun* (1913)
: the Oedipus complex when it occurs in a female

elec·tress \i-'lek-trəs\ *noun* (1618)
: the wife or widow of a German elector

elec·tret \i-'lek-trət, -ˌtret\ *noun* [*electr*icity + magn*et*] (1885)
: a dielectric body in which a permanent state of electric polarization has been set up

¹**elec·tric** \i-'lek-trik, ē-\ *adjective* [New Latin *electricus* produced from amber by friction, electric, from Medieval Latin, of amber, from Latin *electrum* amber, electrum, from Greek *ēlektron;* akin to Greek *ēlektōr* beaming sun] (1675)

1 *or* **elec·tri·cal** \-tri-kəl\ **:** of, relating to, or operated by electricity
2 : exciting as if by electric shock ⟨an *electric* performance⟩ ⟨an *electric* personality⟩; *also* **:** charged with strong emotion ⟨the room was *electric* with tension⟩
3 a : ELECTRONIC 3a **b :** amplifying sound by electronic means — used of a musical instrument ⟨an *electric* guitar⟩
4 : very bright ⟨*electric* blue⟩ ⟨*electric* orange⟩
— **elec·tri·cal·ly** \-tri-k(ə-)lē\ *adverb*

²**electric** *noun* (1646)
1 *archaic* **:** a nonconductor of electricity used to excite or accumulate electricity
2 : something (as a light, automobile, or train) operated by electricity

electrical storm *noun* (1941)
: THUNDERSTORM — called also *electric storm*

electric chair *noun* (1889)
1 : a chair used in legal electrocution
2 : the penalty of death by electrocution

electric eel *noun* (1794)
: a large eel-shaped fish (*Electrophorus electricus*) of the Orinoco and Amazon basins that is capable of giving a severe shock with its electric organs

electric eye *noun* (1898)
: PHOTOELECTRIC CELL

electric field *noun* (circa 1889)
: a region associated with a distribution of electric charge or a varying magnetic field in which forces due to that charge or field act upon other electric charges

elec·tri·cian \i-ˌlek-'tri-shən, ē-\ *noun* (1869)
: one who installs, maintains, operates, or repairs electrical equipment

elec·tric·i·ty \i-ˌlek-'tri-sə-tē, ē-ˌ, -'tris-tē\ *noun, plural* **-ties** (1646)
1 a : a fundamental entity of nature consisting of negative and positive kinds, observable in the attractions and repulsions of bodies electrified by friction and in natural phenomena (as lightning or the aurora borealis), and usually utilized in the form of electric currents **b :** electric current or power
2 : a science that deals with the phenomena and laws of electricity
3 : keen contagious excitement

electric organ *noun* (1773)
: a specialized tract of tissue (as in the electric eel) in which electricity is generated

electric ray *noun* (1774)
: any of various round-bodied short-tailed rays (family Torpedinidae) of warm seas with a pair of electric organs

elec·tri·fi·ca·tion \i-ˌlek-trə-fə-'kā-shən, ē-ˌ\ *noun* (1748)
1 : an act or process of electrifying
2 : the state of being electrified

elec·tri·fy \i-'lek-trə-ˌfī, ē-'\ *transitive verb* **-fied; -fy·ing** (1745)
1 a : to charge with electricity **b** (1) **:** to equip for use of electric power (2) **:** to supply with electric power (3) **:** to amplify (music) electronically
2 : to excite intensely or suddenly as if by electric shock

elec·tro·acous·tics \i-ˌlek-trō-ə-'küs-tiks\ *noun plural but singular in construction* (1927)
: a science that deals with the transformation of acoustic energy into electric energy or vice versa
— **elec·tro·acous·tic** \-tik\ *adjective*

elec·tro·anal·y·sis \-ə-'na-lə-səs\ *noun* (1903)
: chemical analysis by electrolytic methods
— **elec·tro·an·a·lyt·i·cal** \-'lit-i-kəl\ *adjective*

elec·tro·car·dio·gram \-'kär-dē-ə-ˌgram\ *noun* (circa 1904)
: the tracing made by an electrocardiograph

elec·tro·car·dio·graph \-ˌgraf\ *noun* (1913)
: an instrument for recording the changes of electrical potential occurring during the heart-

beat used especially in diagnosing abnormalities of heart action
— **elec·tro·car·dio·graph·ic** \-ˌkär-dē-ə-'gra-fik\ *adjective*
— **elec·tro·car·dio·graph·i·cal·ly** \-fi-k(ə-)lē\ *adverb*
— **elec·tro·car·dio·g·ra·phy** \-dē-'ä-grə-fē\ *noun*

elec·tro·chem·is·try \-'ke-mə-strē\ *noun* (1814)
: a science that deals with the relation of electricity to chemical changes and with the interconversion of chemical and electrical energy
— **elec·tro·chem·i·cal** \-'ke-mi-kəl\ *adjective*
— **elec·tro·chem·i·cal·ly** \-k(ə-)lē\ *adverb*

elec·tro·con·vul·sive \i-ˌlek-trō-kən-'vəl-siv\ *adjective* (1947)
: of, relating to, or involving convulsive response to electroshock ⟨*electroconvulsive* shocks⟩

electroconvulsive therapy *noun* (1948)
: ELECTROSHOCK THERAPY

elec·tro·cor·ti·co·gram \i-ˌlek-trō-'kȯr-ti-kə-ˌgram\ *noun* (1939)
: an electroencephalogram made with the electrodes in direct contact with the brain

elec·tro·cute \i-'lek-trə-ˌkyüt\ *transitive verb* **-cut·ed; -cut·ing** [*electr-* + *-cute* (as in *execute*)] (1889)
1 : to execute (a criminal) by electricity
2 : to kill by electric shock
— **elec·tro·cu·tion** \-ˌlek-trə-'kyü-shən\ *noun*

elec·trode \i-'lek-ˌtrōd\ *noun* (1834)
1 : a conductor used to establish electrical contact with a nonmetallic part of a circuit
2 : an element in a semiconductor device (as a transistor) that emits or collects electrons or holes or controls their movements

¹**elec·tro·de·pos·it** \i-ˌlek-trō-di-'pä-zət\ *noun* (1864)
: a deposit formed in or at an electrode by electrolysis

²**electrodeposit** *transitive verb* (1882)
: to deposit (as a metal or rubber) by electrolysis
— **elec·tro·de·po·si·tion** \-ˌde-pə-'zi-shən, -ˌdē-pə-\ *noun*

elec·tro·der·mal \i-ˌlek-trō-'dər-məl\ *adjective* (1946)
: of or relating to electrical activity in or electrical properties of the skin

elec·tro·des·ic·ca·tion \i-ˌlek-trō-ˌde-si-'kā-shən\ *noun* (1919)
: the drying up of tissue by a high-frequency electric current applied with a needle-shaped electrode — called also *fulguration*

elec·tro·di·al·y·sis \i-ˌlek-trō-dī-'a-lə-səs\ *noun* (1921)
: dialysis accelerated by an electromotive force applied to electrodes adjacent to the membranes
— **elec·tro·di·a·lyt·ic** \-ˌdī-ə-'li-tik\ *adjective*

elec·tro·dy·nam·ics \-dī-'na-miks\ *noun plural but singular in construction* (1827)
: a branch of physics that deals with the effects arising from the interactions of electric currents with magnets, with other currents, or with themselves
— **elec·tro·dy·nam·ic** \-mik\ *adjective*

elec·tro·dy·na·mom·e·ter \-ˌdī-nə-'mä-mə-tər\ *noun* [International Scientific Vocabulary] (1876)
: an instrument that measures current by indicating the strength of the forces between a current flowing in fixed coils and one flowing in movable coils

elec·tro·en·ceph·a·lo·gram \-in-'se-f(ə-)lə-ˌgram\ *noun* [International Scientific Vocabulary] (1934)
: the tracing of brain waves made by an electroencephalograph

elec·tro·en·ceph·a·lo·graph \-,graf\ *noun* [International Scientific Vocabulary] (1936) **:** an apparatus for detecting and recording brain waves
— **elec·tro·en·ceph·a·log·ra·pher** \-,se-fə-'lä-grə-fər\ *noun*
— **elec·tro·en·ceph·a·lo·graph·ic** \-,se-f(ə-)lə-'gra-fik\ *adjective*
— **elec·tro·en·ceph·a·lo·graph·i·cal·ly** \-fi-k(ə-)lē\ *adverb*
— **elec·tro·en·ceph·a·log·ra·phy** \-'lä-grə-fē\ *noun*

elec·tro·fish·ing \i-'lek-trō-,fi-shiŋ\ *noun* (1950) **:** the taking of fish by a system based on their tendency to respond positively to a source of direct electric current

elec·tro·form \i-'lek-trə-,fȯrm\ *transitive verb* (1931) **:** to form (shaped articles) by electrodeposition on a mold
— **electroform** *noun*

elec·tro·gen·ic \i-,lek-trə-'je-nik\ *adjective* (circa 1891) **:** of or relating to the production of electrical activity in living tissue ⟨an *electrogenic* pump⟩
— **elec·tro·gen·e·sis** \-'je-nə-sis\ *noun*

elec·tro·gram \i-'lek-trə-,gram\ *noun* (circa 1935) **:** a tracing of the electrical potentials of a tissue (as the brain or heart) made by means of electrodes placed directly in the tissue instead of on the surface of the body

elec·tro·hy·drau·lic \i-,lek-trō-hī-'drȯ-lik, -'drä-\ *adjective* (1922) **1 :** of or relating to a combination of electric and hydraulic mechanisms **2 :** involving or produced by the action of very brief but powerful pulse discharges of electricity under a liquid resulting in the generation of shock waves and highly reactive chemical species ⟨an *electrohydraulic* effect⟩

elec·tro·jet \i-'lek-trə-,jet\ *noun* (1955) **:** an overhead concentration of electric current found in the regions of strong auroral displays and along the magnetic equator

elec·tro·ki·net·ic \i-,lek-trō-kə-'ne-tik, -kī-\ *adjective* (1881) **:** of or relating to the motion of particles or liquids that results from or produces a difference of electric potential

elec·tro·ki·net·ics \-tiks\ *noun plural but singular in construction* (circa 1925) **:** a branch of physics dealing with the motion of electric currents or charged particles

elec·tro·less \i-'lek-,trō-ləs, -trə-\ *adjective* (1947) **:** being or involving chemical deposition of metal instead of electrodeposition

elec·trol·o·gist \i-'lek-'trä-lə-jist\ *noun* [blend of *electrolysis* and *-logist* (from *-logy* + *-ist*)] (circa 1902) **:** one that removes hair, warts, moles, and birthmarks by means of an electric current applied to the body with a needle-shaped electrode
— **elec·trol·o·gy** \-lə-jē\ *noun*

elec·tro·lu·mi·nes·cent \i-,lek-trō-,lü-mə-'ne-sᵊnt\ *adjective* (circa 1909) **:** of or relating to luminescence resulting from a high-frequency discharge through a gas or from application of an alternating current to a layer of phosphor
— **elec·tro·lu·mi·nes·cence** \-sᵊn(t)s\ *noun*

elec·trol·y·sis \i-,lek-'trä-lə-səs\ *noun* (1834) **1 a :** the producing of chemical changes by passage of an electric current through an electrolyte **b :** subjection to this action **2 :** the destruction of hair roots with an electric current

elec·tro·lyte \i-'lek-trə-,līt\ *noun* (1834) **1 :** a nonmetallic electric conductor in which current is carried by the movement of ions

2 : a substance that when dissolved in a suitable solvent or when fused becomes an ionic conductor

elec·tro·lyt·ic \i-,lek-trə-'li-tik\ *adjective* (1842) **:** of or relating to electrolysis or an electrolyte; *also* **:** involving, produced by, or used in electrolysis ⟨*electrolytic* cell⟩
— **elec·tro·lyt·i·cal·ly** \-ti-k(ə-)lē\ *adverb*

elec·tro·lyze \i-'lek-trə-,līz\ *transitive verb* **-lyzed; -lyz·ing** (1834) **:** to subject to electrolysis

elec·tro·mag·net \i-,lek-trō-'mag-nət\ *noun* (1831) **:** a core of magnetic material surrounded by a coil of wire through which an electric current is passed to magnetize the core

elec·tro·mag·net·ic \-mag-'ne-tik\ *adjective* (1821) **:** of, relating to, or produced by electromagnetism
— **elec·tro·mag·net·i·cal·ly** \-ti-k(ə-)lē\ *adverb*

electromagnetic pulse *noun* (1981) **:** high-intensity electromagnetic radiation generated by a nuclear blast high above the earth's surface and held to disrupt electronic and electrical systems

electromagnetic radiation *noun* (1939) **:** a series of electromagnetic waves

electromagnetic spectrum *noun* (circa 1934) **:** the entire range of wavelengths or frequencies of electromagnetic radiation extending from gamma rays to the longest radio waves and including visible light

electromagnetic unit *noun* (circa 1889) **:** any of a system of electrical units based primarily on the magnetic properties of electrical currents

electromagnetic wave *noun* (1908) **:** one of the waves that are propagated by simultaneous periodic variations of electric and magnetic field intensity and that include radio waves, infrared, visible light, ultraviolet, X rays, and gamma rays

elec·tro·mag·ne·tism \i-,lek-trō-'mag-nə-,ti-zəm\ *noun* (1828) **1 :** magnetism developed by a current of electricity **2 a :** a fundamental physical force that is responsible for interactions between charged particles which occur because of their charge and for the emission and absorption of photons, that is about 100 times weaker than the strong force, and that extends over infinite distances but is dominant over atomic and molecular distances — called also *electromagnetic force*; compare GRAVITY 3a(2), STRONG FORCE, WEAK FORCE **b :** a branch of physical science that deals with the physical relations between electricity and magnetism

elec·tro·me·chan·i·cal \-mə-'ka-ni-kəl\ *adjective* (1888) **:** of, relating to, or being a mechanical process or device actuated or controlled electrically; *especially* **:** being a transducer for converting electrical energy to mechanical energy
— **elec·tro·me·chan·i·cal·ly** \-k(ə-)lē\ *adverb*

elec·tro·met·al·lur·gy \-'me-tᵊl-,ər-jē, *especially British* -mə-'ta-lər-\ *noun* (1840) **:** a branch of metallurgy that deals with the application of electric current either for electrolytic deposition or as a source of heat

elec·trom·e·ter \i-,lek-'trä-mə-tər\ *noun* (1749) **:** any of various instruments for detecting or measuring electric-potential differences or ionizing radiations by means of the forces of attraction or repulsion between charged bodies

elec·tro·mo·tive force \i-,lek-trō-,mō-tiv-, -trə-\ *noun* (1827) **:** something that moves or tends to move electricity **:** the potential difference derived from

an electrical source per unit quantity of electricity passing through the source (as a cell or generator)

elec·tro·myo·gram \i-,lek-trō-'mī-ə-,gram\ *noun* (1917) **:** a tracing made with an electromyograph

elec·tro·myo·graph \-,graf\ *noun* [*electr-* + *my-* + *-graph*] (1948) **:** an instrument that converts the electrical activity associated with functioning skeletal muscle into a visual record or into sound and used to diagnose neuromuscular disorders and in biofeedback training
— **elec·tro·myo·graph·ic** \-,mī-ə-'gra-fik\ *adjective*
— **elec·tro·myo·graph·i·cal·ly** \-fi-k(ə-)lē\ *adverb*
— **elec·tro·my·og·ra·phy** \-mī-'ä-grə-fē\ *noun*

elec·tron \i-'lek-,trän\ *noun* [*electr-* + ²*-on*] (1891) **:** an elementary particle consisting of a charge of negative electricity equal to about 1.602×10^{-19} coulomb and having a mass when at rest of about 9.109534×10^{-28} gram or about $1/1836$ that of a proton

electron cloud *noun* (1926) **:** the system of electrons surrounding the nucleus of an atom

elec·tro·neg·a·tive \i-,lek-trō-'ne-gə-tiv\ *adjective* (1834) **:** having a tendency to attract electrons
— **elec·tro·neg·a·tiv·i·ty** \-,ne-gə-'ti-və-tē\ *noun*

electron gas *noun* (circa 1929) **:** a population of free electrons in a vacuum or in a metallic conductor

electron gun *noun* (1924) **:** an electron-emitting cathode and its surrounding assembly (as in a cathode-ray tube) for directing, controlling, and focusing a beam of electrons

elec·tron·ic \i-,lek-'trä-nik\ *adjective* (1902) **1 :** of or relating to electrons **2 :** of, relating to, or utilizing devices constructed or working by the methods or principles of electronics; *also* **:** implemented on or by means of a computer ⟨*electronic* food stamps⟩ ⟨*electronic* banking⟩ **3 a :** generating musical tones by electronic means ⟨an *electronic* organ⟩ **b :** of, relating to, or being music that consists of sounds electronically generated or modified **4 :** of, relating to, or being a medium (as television) by which information is transmitted electronically ⟨*electronic* journalism⟩
— **elec·tron·i·cal·ly** \-ni-k(ə-)lē\ *adverb*

electronic countermeasure *noun* (1962) **:** the disruption of the operation of an enemy's equipment (as by jamming radio or radar signals)

electronic mail *noun* (1977) **:** messages sent and received electronically (as between terminals linked by telephone lines or microwave relays)

electronic publishing *noun* (1980) **:** publishing in which information is distributed by means of a computer network or is produced in a format for use with a computer

elec·tron·ics \i-,lek-'trä-niks\ *noun plural* (1910) **1** *singular in construction* **:** a branch of physics that deals with the emission, behavior, and effects of electrons (as in electron tubes and transistors) and with electronic devices **2 :** electronic devices or equipment

electron lens *noun* (1931) **:** a device for focusing a beam of electrons by means of an electric or a magnetic field

electron micrograph *noun* (1934)

: a micrograph made with an electron microscope

— **electron micrography** \-mī-'krä-grə-fē\ *noun*

electron microscope *noun* (1932)
: an electron-optical instrument in which a beam of electrons focused by means of an electron lens is used to produce an enlarged image of a minute object on a fluorescent screen or photographic plate
— **electron microscopist** *noun*
— **electron microscopy** *noun*

electron multiplier *noun* (1936)
: a device utilizing secondary emission of electrons for amplifying a current of electrons

electron optics *noun plural but singular in construction* (1916)
: a branch of physics in which the principles of optics are applied to beams of electrons
— **elec·tron–op·ti·cal** \i-,lek-,trän-'äp-ti-kəl\ *adjective*

electron probe *noun* (1962)
: a microprobe that uses an electron beam to induce X-ray emissions in a sample

electron transport *noun* (1951)
: the sequential transfer of electrons especially by cytochromes in cellular respiration from an oxidizable substrate to molecular oxygen by a series of oxidation-reduction reactions

electron tube *noun* (1922)
: an electronic device in which conduction by electrons takes place through a vacuum or a gaseous medium within a sealed glass or metal container and which has various uses based on the controlled flow of electrons

electron volt *noun* (1930)
: a unit of energy equal to the energy gained by an electron in passing from a point of low potential to a point one volt higher in potential
: 1.60×10^{-19} joule

elec·tro·oc·u·lo·gram \i-,lek-trō-'ä-kyə-lə-,gram\ *noun* [electr- + Latin *oculus* eye + English *-gram* — more at EYE] (1947)
: a record of the standing voltage between the front and back of the eye that is correlated with eyeball movement (as in REM sleep) and obtained by electrodes placed on the skin near the eye

elec·tro·oc·u·log·ra·phy \-,ä-kyə-'lä-grə-fē\ *noun, plural* **-phies** (1951)
: the preparation and study of electrooculograms

elec·tro–op·ti·cal \i-,lek-trō-'äp-ti-kəl\ *or* **elec·tro–op·tic** \-'äp-tik\ *adjective* (1879)
1 : of or relating to electro-optics
2 a : relating to or being a change in the refractive index of a material due to an electric field ⟨*electro-optical* effect⟩ **b** : using or being a material that exhibits electro-optical properties ⟨an *electro-optical* crystal⟩
3 : relating to or being an electronic device for emitting, modulating, transmitting, or sensing light
— **elec·tro–op·ti·cal·ly** \-k(ə-)lē\ *adverb*

elec·tro–op·tics \-trō-'äp-tiks\ *noun plural* (circa 1889)
1 *singular in construction* : a branch of physics that deals with the effects of an electric field on light traversing it
2 : electro-optical devices

elec·tro·os·mo·sis \i-,lek-trō-äz-'mō-səs, -äs-\ *noun* (1906)
: the movement of a liquid out of or through a porous material or a biological membrane under the influence of an electric field
— **elec·tro·os·mot·ic** \-'mä-tik\ *adjective*

elec·tro·phe·ro·gram \-trə-'fir-ə-,gram, -'fer-\ *noun* [*electr-* + *phero-* (from Greek *pherein* to carry) + *-gram*] (1951)
: ELECTROPHORETOGRAM

elec·tro·phile \i-'lek-trə-,fīl\ *noun* (1943)
: an electrophilic substance (as an electron-accepting reagent)

elec·tro·phil·ic \i-,lek-trə-'fi-lik\ *adjective* (1936)

1 *of an atom, ion, or molecule* : having an affinity for electrons : being an electron acceptor
2 : involving an electrophilic species ⟨an *electrophilic* reaction⟩ — compare NUCLEOPHILIC
— **elec·tro·phi·lic·i·ty** \-trō-fi-'li-sə-tē\ *noun*

elec·tro·pho·re·sis \-trə-fə-'rē-səs\ *noun* [New Latin] (1911)
: the movement of suspended particles through a fluid or gel under the action of an electromotive force applied to electrodes in contact with the suspension
— **elec·tro·pho·rese** \-'rēs, -'rēz\ *transitive verb*
— **elec·tro·pho·ret·ic** \-'re-tik\ *adjective*
— **elec·tro·pho·ret·i·cal·ly** \-ti-k(ə-)lē\ *adverb*

elec·tro·pho·re·to·gram \-'re-tə-,gram\ *noun* [*electrophoret*ic + *-o-* + *-gram*] (1954)
: a record that consists of the separated components of a mixture (as of proteins) produced by electrophoresis in a supporting medium (as filter paper)

elec·troph·o·rus \i-,lek-'trä-fə-rəs\ *noun, plural* **-ri** \-,rī, -,rē\ [New Latin, from *electr-* + *-phorus* -phore] (1778)
: a device for producing electric charges consisting of a disk that is negatively electrified by friction and a metal plate that becomes charged by induction when placed on the disk

elec·tro·pho·tog·ra·phy \i-,lek-trō-fə-'tä-grə-fē\ *noun* (1894)
: photography in which images are produced by electrical means (as in xerography)
— **elec·tro·pho·to·graph·ic** \-trə-,fō-tə-'gra-fik\ *adjective*

elec·tro·phys·i·ol·o·gy \i-,lek-trō-,fi-zē-'ä-lə-jē\ *noun* (1838)
1 : physiology that is concerned with the electrical aspects of physiological phenomena
2 : electrical phenomena associated with a physiological process (as the function of a body or bodily part) ⟨*electrophysiology* of the eye⟩
— **elec·tro·phys·i·o·log·i·cal** \-zē-ə-'lä-ji-kəl\ *also* **elec·tro·phys·i·o·log·ic** \-jik\ *adjective*
— **elec·tro·phys·i·o·log·i·cal·ly** \-ji-k(ə-)lē\ *adverb*
— **elec·tro·phys·i·ol·o·gist** \-zē-'äl-ə-jist\ *noun*

elec·tro·plate \i-'lek-trə-,plāt\ *transitive verb* (circa 1859)
: to plate with an adherent continuous coating by electrodeposition

elec·tro·pos·i·tive \i-,lek-trō-'pä-zə-tiv, -'päz-tiv\ *adjective* (1834)
: having a tendency to release electrons

elec·tro·ret·i·no·gram \-'re-tᵊn-ə-,gram\ *noun* (1936)
: a graphic record of electrical activity of the retina used especially in the diagnosis of retinal conditions

elec·tro·ret·i·no·graph \-,graf\ *noun* (1962)
: an instrument for recording electrical activity in the retina
— **elec·tro·ret·i·no·graph·ic** \-,re-tᵊn-ə-'gra-fik\ *adjective*
— **elec·tro·ret·i·nog·ra·phy** \-tᵊn-'ä-grə-fē\ *noun*

elec·tro·scope \i-'lek-trə-,skōp\ *noun* [probably from French *électroscope*] (1810)
: any of various instruments for detecting the presence of an electric charge on a body, for determining whether the charge is positive or negative, or for indicating and measuring intensity of radiation

elec·tro·shock \-trō-,shäk\ *noun* (1941)
1 : ³SHOCK 5
2 : ELECTROSHOCK THERAPY

electroshock therapy *noun* (1942)
: the treatment of mental disorder and especially depression by the induction of unconsciousness and convulsions through the use of

an electric current now usually on an anesthetized patient — called also *electroconvulsive therapy*

elec·tro·stat·ic \i-,lek-trə-'sta-tik\ *adjective* [International Scientific Vocabulary] (1860)
1 : of or relating to static electricity or electrostatics
2 : of or relating to painting with a spray that utilizes electrically charged particles to ensure complete coating
— **elec·tro·stat·i·cal·ly** \-'sta-ti-k(ə-)lē\ *adverb*

electrostatic generator *noun* (circa 1931)
: VAN DE GRAAFF GENERATOR

electrostatic precipitator *noun* (1949)
: an electrostatic device in chimney flues that removes particles from escaping gases

elec·tro·stat·ics \i-,lek-trə-'sta-tiks\ *noun plural but singular in construction* (1827)
: physics that deals with phenomena due to attractions or repulsions of electric charges but not dependent upon their motion

elec·tro·sur·gery \i-,lek-trō-'sər-jə-rē\ *noun* (circa 1903)
: surgery by means of diathermy
— **elec·tro·sur·gi·cal** \-'sər-ji-kəl\ *adjective*

elec·tro·ther·a·py \-'ther-ə-pē\ *noun* (1881)
: treatment of disease by means of electricity (as in diathermy)

elec·tro·ther·mal \-'thər-məl\ *adjective* (1884)
: relating to or combining electricity and heat; *specifically* : relating to the generation of heat by electricity
— **elec·tro·ther·mal·ly** \-mə-lē\ *adverb*

elec·tro·ton·ic \i-,lek-trə-'tä-nik\ *adjective* (1832)
1 : of, induced by, relating to, or constituting electrotonus
2 : of, relating to, or being the spread of electrical activity through living tissue or cells in the absence of repeated action potentials ⟨an *electrotonic* junction between cells⟩
— **elec·tro·ton·i·cal·ly** \-ni-k(ə-)lē\ *adverb*

elec·trot·o·nus \i-,lek-'trä-tᵊn-əs\ *noun* [New Latin] (1878)
: the altered sensitivity of a nerve when a constant current of electricity passes through any part of it

elec·tro·type \i-'lek-trə-,tīp\ *noun* (1840)
1 : a duplicate printing surface made by an electroplating process
2 : a copy (as of a coin) made by an electroplating process
— **electrotype** *transitive verb*
— **elec·tro·typ·er** \-,tī-pər\ *noun*

elec·tro·weak \i-'lek-trō-,wēk\ *adjective* (1978)
: of, relating to, or being the unification of electromagnetism and the weak force

elec·tro·win·ning \i-'lek-trō-,wi-niŋ\ *noun* (1924)
: the recovery especially of metals from solutions by electrolysis

elec·trum \i-'lek-trəm\ *noun* [Middle English, from Latin — more at ELECTRIC] (14th century)
: a natural pale yellow alloy of gold and silver

elec·tu·ary \i-'lek-chə-,wer-ē\ *noun, plural* **-ar·ies** [Middle English *electuarie*, from Late Latin *electuarium*, probably from Greek *ekleikton*, from *ekleichein* to lick up, from *ex-* + *leichein* to lick — more at LICK] (14th century)
: CONFECTION 2b

el·e·doi·sin \,e-lə-'dȯi-sᵊn\ *noun* [irregular from New Latin *Eledone*, from Greek *eledōnē*, a kind of octopus] (1963)
: a small protein $C_{54}H_{85}N_{13}O_{15}S$ from the salivary glands of several octopuses (genus *Eledone*) that is a powerful vasodilator and hypotensive agent

el·ee·mo·sy·nary \ˌe-li-ˈmä-sᵊn-ˌer-ē, -ˈmō-; -ˈmä-zᵊn-\ *adjective* [Medieval Latin *eleemosynarius*, from Late Latin *eleemosyna* alms — more at ALMS] (circa 1616)
: of, relating to, or supported by charity

el·e·gance \ˈe-li-gən(t)s\ *noun* (circa 1510)
1 a : refined grace or dignified propriety **:** URBANITY **b :** tasteful richness of design or ornamentation ⟨the sumptuous *elegance* of the furnishings⟩ **c :** dignified gracefulness or restrained beauty of style ⟨the essay is marked by lucidity, wit, and *elegance*⟩ **d :** scientific precision, neatness, and simplicity ⟨the *elegance* of a mathematical proof⟩
2 : something that is elegant

el·e·gan·cy \-gən(t)-sē\ *noun, plural* **-cies** (15th century)
: ELEGANCE

el·e·gant \ˈe-li-gənt\ *adjective* [Middle French or Latin; Middle French, from Latin *elegant-, elegans;* akin to Latin *eligere* to select — more at ELECT] (15th century)
1 : marked by elegance
2 : of a high grade or quality **:** SPLENDID ⟨*elegant* gems priced at hundreds of thousands of dollars⟩
synonym see CHOICE
— **el·e·gant·ly** *adverb*

ele·gi·ac \ˌe-lə-ˈjī-ǝk, -ˌak *also* i-ˈlē-jē-ˌak\ *also* **el·e·gi·a·cal** \ˌe-lə-ˈjī-ǝ-kǝl\ *adjective* [Late Latin *elegiacus,* from Greek *elegeiakos,* from *elegeion*] (1542)
1 a : of, relating to, or consisting of two dactylic hexameter lines the second of which lacks the arsis in the third and sixth feet **b** (1) **:** written in or consisting of elegiac couplets (2) **:** noted for having written poetry in such couplets **c :** of or relating to the period in Greece about the seventh century B.C. when poetry written in such couplets flourished
2 : of, relating to, or comprising elegy or an elegy; *especially* **:** expressing sorrow often for something now past ⟨an *elegiac* lament for departed youth⟩
— **elegiac** *noun*
— **el·e·gi·a·cal·ly** \ˌe-lə-ˈjī-ǝ-k(ǝ-)lē\ *adverb*

ele·git \i-ˈlē-jǝt\ *noun* [Latin, literally, he has chosen, from *eligere*] (1504)
: a judicial writ of execution by which a defendant's goods and if necessary his or her lands are delivered for debt to the plaintiff until the debt is paid

el·e·gize \ˈe-lə-ˌjīz\ *verb* **-gized; -giz·ing** (1702)
intransitive verb
: to write an elegy
transitive verb
: to write an elegy on

el·e·gy \ˈe-lə-jē\ *noun, plural* **-gies** [Latin *elegia* poem in elegiac couplets, from Greek *elegeia, elegeion,* from *elegos* song of mourning] (1501)
1 : a poem in elegiac couplets
2 a : a song or poem expressing sorrow or lamentation especially for one who is dead **b :** something (as a speech) resembling such a song or poem
3 a : a pensive or reflective poem that is usually nostalgic or melancholy **b :** a short pensive musical composition

el·e·ment \ˈe-lə-mǝnt\ *noun* [Middle English, from Old French & Latin; Old French, from Latin *elementum*] (13th century)
1 a : any of the four substances air, water, fire, and earth formerly believed to compose the physical universe **b** *plural* **:** weather conditions; *especially* **:** violent or severe weather ⟨battling the *elements*⟩ **c :** the state or sphere natural or suited to a person or thing ⟨at school she was in her *element*⟩
2 : a constituent part: as **a** *plural* **:** the simplest principles of a subject of study **:** RUDIMENTS **b** (1) **:** a part of a geometric magnitude ⟨an infinitesimal *element* of volume⟩ (2) **:** a generator of a geometric figure; *also* **:** a line or

line segment contained in the surface of a cone or cylinder (3) **:** a basic member of a mathematical or logical class or set (4) **:** one of the individual entries in a mathematical matrix or determinant **c :** one of a number of distinct groups composing a larger group or community ⟨the criminal *element* in the city⟩ **d** (1) **:** one of the necessary data or values on which calculations or conclusions are based (2) **:** one of the factors determining the outcome of a process **e :** any of more than 100 fundamental substances that consist of atoms of only one kind and that singly or in combination constitute all matter **f :** a distinct part of a composite device **g :** a subdivision of a military unit
3 *plural* **:** the bread and wine used in the Eucharist ☆

CHEMICAL ELEMENTS

ELEMENT AND SYMBOL		ATOMIC NUMBER	ATOMIC WEIGHT (C = 12)
actinium	Ac	89	227.0278
aluminum	Al	13	26.98154
americium	Am	95	
antimony	Sb	51	121.75
argon	Ar	18	39.948
arsenic	As	33	74.9216
astatine	At	85	
barium	Ba	56	137.33
berkelium	Bk	97	
beryllium	Be	4	9.01218
bismuth	Bi	83	208.9804
boron	B	5	10.81
bromine	Br	35	79.904
cadmium	Cd	48	112.41
calcium	Ca	20	40.08
californium	Cf	98	
carbon	C	6	12.011
cerium	Ce	58	140.12
cesium	Cs	55	132.9054
chlorine	Cl	17	35.453
chromium	Cr	24	51.996
cobalt	Co	27	58.9332
copper	Cu	29	63.546
curium	Cm	96	
dysprosium	Dy	66	162.50
einsteinium	Es	99	
erbium	Er	68	167.26
europium	Eu	63	151.96
fermium	Fm	100	
fluorine	F	9	18.998403
francium	Fr	87	
gadolinium	Gd	64	157.25
gallium	Ga	31	69.72
germanium	Ge	32	72.59
gold	Au	79	196.9665
hafnium	Hf	72	178.49
helium	He	2	4.00260
holmium	Ho	67	164.9304
hydrogen	H	1	1.0079
indium	In	49	114.82
iodine	I	53	126.9045
iridium	Ir	77	192.22
iron	Fe	26	55.847
krypton	Kr	36	83.80
lanthanum	La	57	138.9055
lawrencium	Lr	103	
lead	Pb	82	207.2
lithium	Li	3	6.941
lutetium	Lu	71	174.967
magnesium	Mg	12	24.305
manganese	Mn	25	54.9380
mendelevium	Md	101	
mercury	Hg	80	200.59
molybdenum	Mo	42	95.94
neodymium	Nd	60	144.24
neon	Ne	10	20.179
neptunium	Np	93	237.0482
nickel	Ni	28	58.69
niobium	Nb	41	92.9064
nitrogen	N	7	14.0067
nobelium	No	102	

ELEMENT AND SYMBOL		ATOMIC NUMBER	ATOMIC WEIGHT (C = 12)
osmium	Os	76	190.2
oxygen	O	8	15.9994
palladium	Pd	46	106.42
phosphorus	P	15	30.97376
platinum	Pt	78	195.08
plutonium	Pu	94	
polonium	Po	84	
potassium	K	19	39.0983
praseodymium	Pr	59	140.9077
promethium	Pm	61	
protactinium	Pa	91	231.0359
radium	Ra	88	226.0254
radon	Rn	86	
rhenium	Re	75	186.207
rhodium	Rh	45	102.9055
rubidium	Rb	37	85.4678
ruthenium	Ru	44	101.07
samarium	Sm	62	150.36
scandium	Sc	21	44.9559
selenium	Se	34	78.96
silicon	Si	14	28.0855
silver	Ag	47	107.868
sodium	Na	11	22.98977
strontium	Sr	38	87.62
sulfur	S	16	32.06
tantalum	Ta	73	180.9479
technetium	Tc	43	
tellurium	Te	52	127.60
terbium	Tb	65	158.9254
thallium	Tl	81	204.383
thorium	Th	90	232.0381
thulium	Tm	69	168.9342
tin	Sn	50	118.69
titanium	Ti	22	47.88
tungsten	W	74	183.85
unnilhexium	Unh	106	
unnilpentium	Unp	105	
unnilquadium	Unq	104	
uranium	U	92	238.0289
vanadium	V	23	50.9415
xenon	Xe	54	131.29
ytterbium	Yb	70	173.04
yttrium	Y	39	88.9059
zinc	Zn	30	65.38
zirconium	Zr	40	91.22

el·e·men·tal \ˌe-lə-ˈmen-tᵊl\ *adjective* (15th century)
1 a : of, relating to, or being an element; *specifically* **:** existing as an uncombined chemical element **b** (1) **:** of, relating to, or being the basic or essential constituent of something **:** FUNDAMENTAL ⟨*elemental* biological needs⟩ (2) **:** SIMPLE, UNCOMPLICATED ⟨*elemental* food⟩ **c**

☆ SYNONYMS
Element, component, constituent, ingredient mean one of the parts of a compound or complex whole. ELEMENT applies to any such part and often connotes irreducible simplicity ⟨the basic *elements* of geometry⟩. COMPONENT and CONSTITUENT may designate any of the substances (whether elements or compounds) or the qualities that enter into the makeup of a complex product; COMPONENT stresses its separate entity or distinguishable character ⟨the *components* of a stereo system⟩. CONSTITUENT stresses its essential and formative character ⟨the *constituents* of a chemical compound⟩. INGREDIENT applies to any of the substances which when combined form a particular mixture (as a medicine or alloy) ⟨the *ingredients* of a cocktail⟩.

: of, relating to, or dealing with the rudiments of something : ELEMENTARY ⟨taught *elemental* crafts to the children⟩ **d** : forming an integral part : INHERENT ⟨an *elemental* sense of rhythm⟩ **2** : of, relating to, or resembling a great force of nature ⟨the rains come with *elemental* violence⟩ ⟨*elemental* passions⟩
— **elemental** *noun*
— **el·e·men·tal·ly** \-t°l-ē\ *adverb*
el·e·men·ta·ry \ˌe-lə-ˈmen-tə-rē, -ˈmen-trē\ *adjective* (14th century)
1 a : of, relating to, or dealing with the simplest elements or principles of something ⟨avoids the most *elementary* decision-making⟩ **b** : of or relating to an elementary school ⟨an *elementary* curriculum⟩
2 : ELEMENTAL 1a, 1b
3 : ELEMENTAL 2
— **el·e·men·ta·ri·ly** \-ˌmen-ˈter-ə-lē, -ˈmen-trə-lē\ *adverb*
— **el·e·men·ta·ri·ness** \-ˈmen-tə-rē-nəs, -ˈmen-trē-\ *noun*
elementary particle *noun* (1934)
: any of the particles of which matter and energy are composed or which mediate the fundamental forces of nature; *especially* : one whose existence has not been attributed to the combination of other more fundamental entities
elementary school *noun* (1841)
: a school including usually the first four to the first eight grades and often a kindergarten
el·e·mi \ˈe-lə-mē\ *noun* [New Latin *elimi*, probably from Arabic *al lāmi* the elemi] (1543)
: any of various fragrant oleoresins obtained from tropical trees (family Burseraceae) and used chiefly in varnishes, lacquers, and printing inks
elen·chus \i-ˈleŋ-kəs\ *noun, plural* **-chi** \-ˌkī, -(ˌ)kē\ [Latin, from Greek *elenchos*] (1663)
: REFUTATION; *especially* : one in syllogistic form
el·e·phant \ˈe-lə-fənt\ *noun, plural* **elephants** *also* **elephant** *often attributive* [Middle English, from Middle French & Latin; Middle French *olifant*, from Latin *elephantus*, from Greek *elephant-, elephas*] (14th century)
1 : any of a family (Elephantidae, the elephant family) of thickset usually extremely large nearly hairless herbivorous mammals that have a snout elongated into a muscular trunk and two incisors in the upper jaw developed especially in the male into large ivory tusks and that include two living forms and various extinct relatives: as **a** : a tall large-eared mammal (*Loxodonta africana*) of tropical Africa — called also *African elephant* **b** : a relatively small-eared mammal (*Elephas maximus*) of forests of southeastern Asia — called also *Asian elephant, Indian elephant*
2 : an animal or fossil related to the elephants
3 : one that is uncommonly large or hard to manage

elephant: *1* African, *2* Asian

elephant bird *noun* (circa 1889)
: AEPYORNIS
elephant grass *noun* (1832)
1 : an Old World cattail (*Typha elephantina*) used especially in making baskets

2 : NAPIER GRASS
el·e·phan·ti·a·sis \ˌe-lə-fən-ˈtī-ə-səs, -ˌfan-\ *noun, plural* **-a·ses** \-ˌsēz\ [New Latin, from Latin, a kind of leprosy, from Greek, from *elephant-, elephas*] (1581)
1 : enlargement and thickening of tissues; *specifically* : the enormous enlargement of a limb or the scrotum caused by obstruction of lymphatics by filarial worms (especially *Wuchereria bancrofti*)
2 : an undesirable usually enormous growth, enlargement, or overdevelopment ⟨*elephantiasis* of intellect and atrophy of emotion — Michael Lerner⟩
el·e·phan·tine \ˌe-lə-ˈfan-ˌtēn, -ˌtīn, ˈe-lə-fən-\ *adjective* (1610)
1 a : having enormous size or strength : MASSIVE **b** : CLUMSY, PONDEROUS ⟨*elephantine* verse⟩
2 : of or relating to an elephant
elephant seal *noun* (1841)
: either of two very large seals (genus *Mirounga* of the family Phocidae) characterized by a long inflatable proboscis: **a** : one (*M. angustirostris*) found in Pacific coastal waters from southeastern Alaska to Baja California **b** : one (*M. leonina*) found in coastal waters of subantarctic islands and Patagonia
El·eu·sin·i·an \ˌel-yu̇-ˈsi-nē-ən\ *adjective* (1611)
: of or relating to ancient Eleusis or to the religious mysteries celebrated there in worship of Demeter and Persephone
¹el·e·vate \ˈe-lə-ˌvāt, -vət\ *adjective* (14th century)
archaic : ELEVATED
²el·e·vate \-ˌvāt\ *verb* **-vat·ed; -vat·ing** [Middle English, from Latin *elevatus*, past participle of *elevare*, from *e-* + *levare* to raise — more at LEVER] (15th century)
transitive verb
1 : to lift up : RAISE
2 : to raise in rank or status : EXALT
3 : to improve morally, intellectually, or culturally
4 : to raise the spirits of : ELATE
intransitive verb
: to become elevated : RISE ⟨his voice *elevated* to a shout⟩
synonym see LIFT
¹el·e·vat·ed \-ˌvā-təd\ *adjective* (1553)
1 a : raised especially above the ground or other surface ⟨an *elevated* highway⟩ **b** : increased especially abnormally (as in degree or amount) ⟨*elevated* blood pressure⟩
2 a : being morally or intellectually on a high plane ⟨*elevated* conversation⟩ **b** : FORMAL, DIGNIFIED ⟨*elevated* diction⟩
3 : exhilarated in mood or feeling
²elevated *noun* (1881)
: ²EL
el·e·va·tion \ˌe-lə-ˈvā-shən\ *noun* (14th century)
1 : the height to which something is elevated: as **a** : the angular distance of something (as a celestial object) above the horizon **b** : the degree to which a gun is aimed above the horizon **c** : the height above the level of the sea : ALTITUDE
2 : a ballet dancer's or a skater's leap and seeming suspension in the air; *also* : the ability to achieve an elevation
3 : an act or instance of elevating
4 : something that is elevated: as **a** : an elevated place **b** : a swelling especially on the skin
5 : the quality or state of being elevated
6 : a geometrical projection (as of a building) on a vertical plane
synonym see HEIGHT
el·e·va·tor \ˈe-lə-ˌvā-tər\ *noun* (1646)
1 : one that raises or lifts something up: as **a** : an endless belt or chain conveyor with cleats, scoops, or buckets for raising material **b** : a cage or platform and its hoisting machinery for conveying people or things to different levels **c** : GRAIN ELEVATOR

2 : a movable auxiliary airfoil usually attached to the tail plane of an airplane for controlling pitch — see AIRPLANE illustration
elevator music *noun* (1979)
: instrumental arrangements of popular songs often piped in (as in an elevator or retail store)
elev·en \i-ˈle-vən\ *noun* [Middle English *enleven*, from *enleven*, adjective, from Old English *endleofan*, from *end-* (alteration of *ān* one) + *-leofan;* akin to Old English *lēon* to lend — more at ONE, LOAN] (before 12th century)
1 — see NUMBER table
2 : the 11th in a set or series
3 : something having 11 units or members; *especially* : a football team
— **eleven** *adjective*
— **eleven** *pronoun, plural in construction*
— **elev·enth** \-vən(t)th\ *adjective or noun*
eleven–plus \i-ˌle-vən-ˈpləs\ *noun* (1955)
British : an examination taken by schoolchildren between the ages of 11 and 12 that determines the type of secondary education to which they are assigned
elev·ens·es \-vən-zəz\ *noun plural but sometimes singular in construction* [double plural of *eleven* (o'clock)] (circa 1819)
British : light refreshment (as a snack) taken in the middle of the morning
eleventh hour *noun* (1826)
: the latest possible time ⟨still making changes at the *eleventh hour*⟩
el·e·von \ˈe-lə-ˌvän\ *noun* [*elev*ator + ailer*on*] (1944)
: an airplane control surface that combines the functions of elevator and aileron
elf \ˈelf\ *noun, plural* **elves** \ˈelvz\ [Middle English, from Old English *ælf;* akin to Old Norse *alfr* elf & perhaps to Latin *albus* white — more at ALB] (before 12th century)
1 : a small often mischievous fairy
2 : a small lively creature; *also* : a usually lively mischievous or malicious person
— **elf·ish** \ˈel-fish\ *adjective*
— **elf·ish·ly** *adverb*
elf·in \ˈel-fən\ *adjective* [irregular from *elf*] (1596)
1 a : of, relating to, or produced by an elf **b** : resembling an elf especially in its tiny size ⟨*elfin* portions⟩
2 : having an otherworldly or magical quality or charm
elf·lock \ˈelf-ˌläk\ *noun* (1592)
: hair matted as if by elves — usually used in plural
elf owl *noun* (1887)
: a very small insectivorous owl (*Micrathene whitneyi*) of the Southwestern U.S. and Mexico that often roosts and nests in giant cacti
el·hi \(ˌ)el-ˈhī\ *adjective* [*el*ementary (school) + *hi*gh (school)] (circa 1948)
: of, relating to, or designed for use in grades 1 to 12
Eli \ˈē-ˌlī\ *noun* [Hebrew *'Ēlī*]
: a judge and priest of Israel who according to the account in 1 Samuel was entrusted with the care of the boy Samuel
Eli·as \i-ˈlī-əs\ *noun* [Late Latin, from Greek *Ēlias*, from Hebrew *Ēlīyāh*]
: ELIJAH
elic·it \i-ˈli-sət\ *transitive verb* [Latin *elicitus*, past participle of *elicere*, from *e-* + *lacere* to allure] (1605)
1 : to draw forth or bring out (something latent or potential) ⟨hypnotism *elicited* his hidden fears⟩
2 : to call forth or draw out (as information or a response) ⟨her performance *elicited* wild applause⟩
synonym see EDUCE
— **elic·i·ta·tion** \i-ˌli-sə-ˈtā-shən, ˌē-\ *noun*
— **elic·i·tor** \i-ˈli-sə-tər\ *noun*
elide \i-ˈlīd\ *transitive verb* **elid·ed; elid·ing** [Latin *elidere* to strike out, from *e-* + *laedere* to injure by striking] (1796)

1 a : to suppress or alter (as a vowel or syllable) by elision **b :** to strike out (as a written word)

2 a : to leave out of consideration **:** OMIT **b :** CURTAIL, ABRIDGE

el·i·gi·ble \'e-lə-jə-bəl\ *adjective* [Middle English, from Middle French & Late Latin; Middle French, from Late Latin *eligibilis*, from Latin *eligere* to choose — more at ELECT] (15th century)

1 a : qualified to be chosen **:** ENTITLED ⟨*eligible* to retire⟩ **b :** permitted under football rules to catch a forward pass ⟨an *eligible* receiver⟩ **2 :** worthy of being chosen **:** DESIRABLE ⟨an *eligible* young bachelor⟩
— **el·i·gi·bil·i·ty** \ˌe-lə-jə-'bi-lə-tē\ *noun*
— **eligible** *noun*
— **el·i·gi·bly** \'e-lə-jə-blē\ *adverb*

Eli·jah \i-'lī-jə\ *noun* [Hebrew *Ēlīyāh*]
: a Hebrew prophet of the 9th century B.C. who according to the account in I Kings championed the worship of Jehovah as against Baal

elim·i·nate \i-'li-mə-ˌnāt\ *transitive verb* **-nat·ed; -nat·ing** [Latin *eliminatus*, past participle of *eliminare*, from *e-* + *limin-, limen* threshold] (1568)

1 a : to cast out or get rid of **:** REMOVE, ERADICATE ⟨the need to *eliminate* poverty⟩ **b :** to set aside as unimportant **:** IGNORE
2 : to expel (as waste) from the living body
3 : to cause (as an unknown) to disappear by combining two or more mathematical equations
— **elim·i·na·tive** \-'li-mə-ˌnā-tiv\ *adjective*
— **elim·i·na·tor** \-ˌnā-tər\ *noun*

elim·i·na·tion \i-ˌli-mə-'nā-shən\ *noun, often attributive* (1627)
: the act, process, or an instance of eliminating or discharging: as **a :** the act of discharging or excreting waste products from the body **b :** the removal from a molecule of the constituents of a simpler molecule ⟨ethylene is formed by the *elimination* of water from ethanol⟩ — compare ADDITION 4

ELISA \ē-'lī-sə, -zə\ *noun* (1978)
: ENZYME-LINKED IMMUNOSORBENT ASSAY

Eli·sha \i-'lī-shə\ *noun* [Hebrew *Ēlīshāʻ*]
: a Hebrew prophet and disciple and successor of Elijah

eli·sion \i-'li-zhən\ *noun* [Late Latin *elision-, elisio*, from Latin *elidere*] (1581)
1 a : the use of a speech form that lacks a final or initial sound which a variant speech form has (as *'s* instead of *is* in *there's*) **b :** the omission of an unstressed vowel or syllable in a verse to achieve a uniform metrical pattern
2 : the act or an instance of omitting something **:** OMISSION

elite \ā-'lēt, i-, ē-\ *noun* [French *élite*, from Old French *eslite*, from feminine of *eslit*, past participle of *eslire* to choose, from Latin *eligere*] (1823)
1 a *singular or plural in construction* **:** the choice part **:** CREAM ⟨the *elite* of the entertainment world⟩ **b** *singular or plural in construction* **:** the best of a class ⟨superachievers who dominate the computer *elite* —Marilyn Chase⟩ **c** *singular or plural in construction* **:** the socially superior part of society ⟨how the *elite* live —*A P World*⟩ ⟨how the French-speaking *elite* . . . was changing —*Economist*⟩ **d :** a group of persons who by virtue of position or education exercise much power or influence ⟨members of the ruling *elite*⟩ ⟨the intellectual *elites* of the country⟩ **e :** a member of such an elite — usually used in plural ⟨the *elites* . . ., pursuing their studies in Europe —Robert Wernick⟩
2 : a typewriter type providing 12 characters to the linear inch
— **elite** *adjective*

élite, élitism *chiefly British variant of* ELITE, ELITISM

elit·ism \ā-'lē-ˌti-zəm, i-, ē-\ *noun* (1947)
1 : leadership or rule by an elite

2 : the selectivity of the elite; *especially* **:** SNOBBERY 1 ⟨*elitism* in choosing new members⟩
3 : consciousness of being or belonging to an elite
— **elit·ist** \-'lē-tist\ *noun or adjective*

elix·ir \i-'lik-sər\ *noun* [Middle English, from Medieval Latin, from Arabic *al-iksīr* the elixir, from *al* the + *iksīr* elixir, probably from Greek *xērion* desiccative powder, from *xēros* dry] (14th century)
1 a (1) **:** a substance held capable of changing base metals into gold (2) **:** a substance held capable of prolonging life indefinitely **b** (1) **:** CURE-ALL (2) **:** a medicinal concoction
2 : a sweetened liquid usually containing alcohol that is used in medication either for its medicinal ingredients or as a flavoring
3 : the essential principle

Eliz·a·be·than \i-ˌli-zə-'bē-thən\ *adjective* (1807)
: of, relating to, or characteristic of Elizabeth I of England or her reign
— **Elizabethan** *noun*

elk \'elk\ *noun, plural* **elks** [Middle English, probably from Old English *eolh;* akin to Old High German *elaho* elk, Greek *elaphos* deer] (before 12th century)
1 *plural usually* **elk a :** MOOSE 1 — used for one of the Old World **b :** a large gregarious deer (*Cervus elaphus*) of North America, Europe, Asia, and northwestern Africa — called also *red deer, wapiti* **c :** any of various large Asian deer
2 : soft tanned rugged leather
3 *capitalized* [Benevolent and Protective Order of *Elks*] **:** a member of a major benevolent and fraternal order

elk·hound \'elk-ˌhaünd, 'el-ˌkaünd\ *noun* (1889)
: NORWEGIAN ELKHOUND

¹ell \'el\ *noun* [Middle English *eln*, from Old English; akin to Old High German *elina* ell, Latin *ulna* forearm, Greek *ōlenē* elbow, Sanskrit *aratni*] (before 12th century)
: a former English unit of length (as for cloth) equal to 45 inches (about 1.14 meters); *also* **:** any of various units of length used similarly

²ell *noun* [alteration of ¹*el*] (1773)
1 : an extension at right angles to the length of a building
2 : an elbow in a pipe or conduit

el·lag·ic acid \ə-'la-jik-, e-\ *noun* [French *ellagique*, from *ellag*, anagram of *galle* gall] (1810)
: a crystalline phenolic compound $C_{14}H_6O_8$ with two lactone groupings that is obtained especially from oak galls and some tannins and is used medicinally as a hemostatic

el·lipse \i-'lips, e-\ *noun* [Greek *elleipsis*] (circa 1753)
1 a : OVAL **b :** a closed plane curve generated by a point moving in such a way that the sums of its distances from two fixed points is a constant **:** a plane section of a right circular cone that is a closed curve
2 : ELLIPSIS

ellipse 1b: *F, F'* foci; *P, P', P''* any point on the curve; *FP + PF' = FP'' +* *P''F' = FP' + P'F'*

el·lip·sis \i-'lip-səs, e-\ *noun, plural* **el·lip·ses** \-ˌsēz\ [Latin, from Greek *elleipsis* ellipsis, ellipse, from *elleipein* to leave out, fall short, from *en* in + *leipein* to leave — more at IN, LOAN] (1540)
1 a : the omission of one or more words that are obviously understood but that must be supplied to make a construction grammatically complete **b :** a sudden leap from one topic to another
2 : marks or a mark (as . . . or *** or —) indicating an omission (as of words) or a pause

el·lip·soid \i-'lip-ˌsoid, e-\ *noun* (1721)

: a surface all plane sections of which are ellipses or circles
— **el·lip·soi·dal** \i-ˌlip-'soi-dᵊl, (ˌ)e-\ *also* **ellipsoid** *adjective*

el·lip·ti·cal \i-'lip-ti-kəl, e-\ *or* **el·lip·tic** \-tik\ *adjective* [Greek *elleiptikos* defective, marked by ellipsis, from *elleipein*] (1656)
1 : of, relating to, or shaped like an ellipse
2 a : of, relating to, or marked by ellipsis or an ellipsis **b** (1) **:** of, relating to, or marked by extreme economy of speech or writing (2) **:** of or relating to deliberate obscurity (as of literary or conversational style)
— **el·lip·ti·cal·ly** \-ti-k(ə-)lē\ *adverb*

elliptical galaxy *noun* (1948)
: a galaxy that has a generally elliptical shape and that has no apparent internal structure or spiral arms — called also *elliptical*; compare SPIRAL GALAXY

el·lip·tic·i·ty \i-ˌlip-'ti-sə-tē, (ˌ)e-\ *noun* (1753)
: deviation of an ellipse or a spheroid from the form of a circle or a sphere

elm \'elm\ *noun* [Middle English, from Old English; akin to Old High German *elme* elm, Latin *ulmus*] (before 12th century)
1 : any of a genus (*Ulmus* of the family Ulmaceae, the elm family) comprising large trees with alternate stipulate leaves and small apetalous flowers
2 : the wood of an elm

elm bark beetle *noun* (circa 1909)
: either of two beetles (family Scolytidae) that are vectors for the fungus causing Dutch elm disease: **a :** one (*Hylurgopinus rufipes*) native to eastern North America **b :** one (*Scolytus multistriatus*) introduced from Europe into eastern North America

elm leaf beetle *noun* (1881)
: a small orange-yellow black-striped Old World chrysomelid beetle (*Pyrrhalta luteola*) that in the larval and adult stage is a leaf-eating pest of elms in eastern North America

El Ni·ño \el-'nē-nyō\ *noun, plural* **El Niños** [Spanish, literally, the child (i.e., the Christ child); from the appearance of the flow at the Christmas season] (1925)
: an irregularly occurring flow of unusually warm surface water along the western coast of South America that is accompanied by abnormally high rainfall in usually arid areas and that prevents upwelling of nutrient-rich cold deep water causing a decline in the regional fish population

el·o·cu·tion \ˌe-lə-'kyü-shən\ *noun* [Middle English *elocucioun*, from Latin *elocution-, elocutio*, from *eloqui*] (15th century)
1 : a style of speaking especially in public
2 : the art of effective public speaking
— **el·o·cu·tion·ary** \-shə-ˌner-ē\ *adjective*
— **el·o·cu·tion·ist** \-sh(ə-)nist\ *noun*

elo·dea \i-'lō-dē-ə\ *noun* [New Latin, genus name, from Greek *helōdēs* marshy, from *helos* marsh; akin to Sanskrit *saras* pond] (circa 1868)
: any of a small American genus (*Elodea*) of submerged aquatic monocotyledonous herbs

eloign \i-'lóin\ *transitive verb* [Middle English *eloynen*, from Middle French *esloigner*, from Old French *es- ex-* (from Latin *ex-*) + *loing* (adverb) far, from Latin *longe*, from *longus* long] (15th century)
1 *archaic* **:** to take (oneself) far away
2 *archaic* **:** to remove to a distant or unknown place **:** CONCEAL

¹elon·gate \i-'lóŋ-ˌgāt, (ˌ)ē-, 'ē-ˌ\ *verb* **-gat·ed; -gat·ing** [Late Latin *elongatus*, past participle of *elongare*, to withdraw, from Latin *e-* + *longus*] (1578)
transitive verb

\ə\ abut \ᵊ\ kitten \ər\ further \a\ ash \ā\ ace \ä\ mop, mar \aü\ out \ch\ chin \e\ bet \ē\ easy \g\ go \i\ hit \ī\ ice \j\ job \ŋ\ sing \ō\ go \ó\ law \ói\ boy \th\ thin \th\ the \ü\ loot \ü\ foot \y\ yet \zh\ vision *see also* Guide to Pronunciation

: to extend the length of
intransitive verb
: to grow in length
²**elongate** *or* **elon·gat·ed** *adjective* (1751)
1 : stretched out
2 : SLENDER
elon·ga·tion \(,)ē-,lȯṅ-'gā-shən\ *noun* (14th century)
1 : the angular distance of a celestial body from another around which it revolves or from a particular point in the sky
2 a : the state of being elongated or lengthened; *also* **:** the process of growing or increasing in length **b :** something that is elongated
elope \i-'lōp\ *intransitive verb* **eloped; elop·ing** [Anglo-French *aloper*] (1628)
1 : to slip away **:** ESCAPE
2 a : to run away from one's husband with a lover **b :** to run away secretly with the intention of getting married usually without parental consent
— **elope·ment** \-'lōp-mənt\ *noun*
— **elop·er** *noun*
el·o·quence \'e-lə-kwən(t)s\ *noun* (14th century)
1 : discourse marked by force and persuasiveness; *also* **:** the art or power of using such discourse
2 : the quality of forceful or persuasive expressiveness
el·o·quent \-kwənt\ *adjective* [Middle English, from Middle French, from Latin *eloquent-, eloquens*, from present participle of *eloqui* to speak out, from *e-* + *loqui* to speak] (14th century)
1 : marked by forceful and fluent expression ⟨an *eloquent* preacher⟩
2 : vividly or movingly expressive or revealing ⟨an *eloquent* monument⟩
— **el·o·quent·ly** *adverb*
¹**else** \'el(t)s\ *adverb* [Middle English *elles*, from Old English; akin to Latin *alius* other, *alter* other of two, Greek *allos* other] (before 12th century)
1 a : in a different manner or place or at a different time ⟨how *else* could he have acted⟩ ⟨here and nowhere *else*⟩ **b :** in an additional manner or place or at an additional time ⟨where *else* is gold found⟩
2 : if not **:** OTHERWISE ⟨leave or *else* you'll be sorry⟩ — used absolutely to express a threat ⟨do what I tell you or *else*⟩
²**else** *adjective* (before 12th century)
: OTHER: **a :** being different in identity ⟨it must have been somebody *else*⟩ **b :** being in addition ⟨what *else* did he say⟩
else·where \-,(h)wer, -,(h)war\ *adverb* [Middle English *elleswher*, from Old English *elles hwær*] (before 12th century)
: in or to another place ⟨took my business *elsewhere*⟩
el·u·ant *or* **el·u·ent** \'el-yə-wənt\ *noun* [Latin *eluent-, eluens*, present participle of *eluere*] (1941)
: a solvent used in eluting
el·u·ate \'el-yə-wət, -,wāt\ *noun* [Latin *eluere* + English ¹-*ate*] (1932)
: the washings obtained by eluting
elu·ci·date \i-'lü-sə-,dāt\ *verb* **-dat·ed; -dat·ing** [Late Latin *elucidatus*, past participle of *elucidare*, from Latin *e-* + *lucidus* lucid] (circa 1568)
transitive verb
: to make lucid especially by explanation or analysis
intransitive verb
: to give a clarifying explanation
synonym see EXPLAIN
— **elu·ci·da·tion** \-,lü-sə-'dā-shən\ *noun*
— **elu·ci·da·tive** \-'lü-sə-,dā-tiv\ *adjective*
— **elu·ci·da·tor** \-,dā-tər\ *noun*
elu·cu·brate \i-'lü-k(y)ə-,brāt\ *transitive verb* **-brat·ed; -brat·ing** [Latin *elucubratus*, past participle of *elucubrare* to work on far into the night, from *e-* + *lucubrare* to work by lamplight — more at LUCUBRATION] (circa 1623)

: to work out or express by studious effort
— **elu·cu·bra·tion** \-,lü-k(y)ə-'brā-shən\ *noun*
elude \ē-'lüd\ *transitive verb* **elud·ed; elud·ing** [Latin *eludere*, from *e-* + *ludere* to play — more at LUDICROUS] (1667)
1 : to avoid adroitly **:** EVADE ⟨the mice *eluded* the traps⟩ ⟨managed to *elude* capture⟩
2 : to escape the perception, understanding, or grasp of ⟨subtlety simply *eludes* them⟩ ⟨victory continued to *elude* us⟩
3 : DEFY 4 ⟨it *eludes* explanation⟩
synonym see ESCAPE
Elul \e-'lül\ *noun* [Hebrew *Ĕlūl*] (1535)
: the 12th month of the civil year or the 6th month of the ecclesiastical year in the Jewish calendar — see MONTH table
elu·sion \ē-'lü-zhən\ *noun* [Medieval Latin *elusion-, elusio*, from Late Latin, deception, from Latin *eludere*] (1617)
: an act of eluding
elu·sive \ē-'lü-siv, -'lü-ziv\ *adjective* (1719)
: tending to elude: as **a :** tending to evade grasp or pursuit **b :** hard to comprehend or define ⟨an *elusive* concept⟩ **c :** hard to isolate or identify ⟨a haunting *elusive* aroma⟩
— **elu·sive·ly** *adverb*
— **elu·sive·ness** *noun*
elute \ē-'lüt\ *transitive verb* **elut·ed; elut·ing** [Latin *elutus*, past participle of *eluere* to wash out, from *e-* + *lavere* to wash — more at LYE] (1731)
: EXTRACT; *specifically* **:** to remove (adsorbed material) from an adsorbent by means of a solvent
— **elu·tion** \-'lü-shən\ *noun*
elu·tri·ate \ē-'lü-trē-,āt\ *transitive verb* **-at·ed; -at·ing** [Latin *elutriatus*, past participle of *elutriare* to put in a vat, perhaps from (assumed) *elutrum* vat, from Greek *elytron* reservoir, literally, covering] (circa 1727)
: to purify, separate, or remove by washing
— **elu·tri·a·tion** \ē-,lü-trē-'ā-shən\ *noun*
— **elu·tri·a·tor** \ē-'lü-trē-,ā-tər\ *noun*
elu·vi·a·tion \(,)ē-,lü-vē-'ā-shən\ *noun* [*eluvial* of eluviation (from *e-* + *-luvial*—as in *alluvial*) + *-ation*] (1899)
: the transportation of dissolved or suspended material within the soil by the movement of water when rainfall exceeds evaporation
— **elu·vi·al** \ē-'lü-vē-əl\ *adjective*
— **elu·vi·at·ed** \-'lü-vē-ā-təd\ *adjective*
el·ver \'el-vər\ *noun* [alteration of *eelfare* (migration of eels)] (circa 1640)
: a young eel
elves *plural of* ELF
el·vish \'el-vish\ *adjective* (13th century)
1 : of or relating to elves
2 : MISCHIEVOUS
ely·sian \i-'li-zhən\ *adjective, often capitalized* (1579)
1 : of or relating to Elysium
2 : BLISSFUL, DELIGHTFUL
elysian fields *noun plural, often E capitalized* (1579)
: ELYSIUM
Ely·si·um \i-'li-zhē-əm, -zē-\ *noun, plural* **-si·ums** *or* **-sia** \-zhē-ə, -zē-\ [Latin, from Greek *Ēlysion*]
1 : the abode of the blessed after death in classical mythology
2 : PARADISE 2
el·y·tron \'e-lə-,trän\ *noun, plural* **-tra** \-trə\ [New Latin, from Greek, sheath, wing cover, from *eilyein* to roll, wrap — more at VOLUBLE] (1774)
: one of the anterior wings in beetles and some other insects that serve to protect the posterior pair of functional wings
em \'em\ *noun* (13th century)
1 : the letter *m*
2 : the width of a piece of type about as wide as it is tall used as a unit of measure of typeset matter
em- — see EN-

'em \əm; *after* p,b,f, *or* v *often* ᵊm\ *pronoun* [Middle English *hem*, from Old English *heom, him*, dative plural of *hē* he] (before 12th century)
: THEM
ema·ci·ate \i-'mā-shē-,āt\ *verb* **-at·ed; -at·ing** [Latin *emaciatus*, past participle of *emaciare*, from *e-* + *macies* leanness, from *macer* lean — more at MEAGER] (1646)
intransitive verb
: to waste away physically
transitive verb
1 : to cause to lose flesh so as to become very thin
2 : to make feeble
— **ema·ci·a·tion** \-,mā-s(h)ē-'ā-shən\ *noun*
E-mail \'ē-,māl\ *noun* (1982)
: ELECTRONIC MAIL
emalangeni *plural of* LILANGENI
em·a·nate \'e-mə-,nāt\ *verb* **-nat·ed; -nat·ing** [Latin *emanatus*, past participle of *emanare*, from *e-* + *manare* to flow] (1756)
intransitive verb
: to come out from a source
transitive verb
: EMIT
synonym see SPRING
em·a·na·tion \,e-mə-'nā-shən\ *noun* (1570)
1 a : the action of emanating **b :** the origination of the world by a series of hierarchically descending radiations from the Godhead through intermediate stages to matter
2 a : something that emanates or is produced by emanation **:** EFFLUENCE **b :** an isotope of radon produced by radioactive disintegration ⟨radium *emanation*⟩
— **em·a·na·tive** \'e-mə-,nā-tiv\ *adjective*
eman·ci·pate \i-'man(t)-sə-,pāt\ *transitive verb* **-pat·ed; -pat·ing** [Latin *emancipatus*, past participle of *emancipare*, from *e-* + *mancipare* to transfer ownership of, from *mancip-, manceps* contractor, from *manus* hand + *capere* to take — more at MANUAL, HEAVE] (1613)
1 : to free from restraint, control, or the power of another; *especially* **:** to free from bondage
2 : to release from paternal care and responsibility and make sui juris
3 : to free from any controlling influence (as traditional mores or beliefs)
synonym see FREE
— **eman·ci·pa·tor** \-,pā-tər\ *noun*
eman·ci·pa·tion \i-,man(t)-sə-'pā-shən\ *noun* (1631)
: the act or process of emancipating
— **eman·ci·pa·tion·ist** \-sh(ə-)nist\ *noun*
emar·gin·ate \(,)ē-'mär-jə-nət, -,nāt\ *adjective* [Latin *emarginatus*, past participle of *emarginare* to deprive of a margin, from *e-* + *margin-, margo* margin] (1794)
: having the margin notched
— **emar·gi·na·tion** \(,)ē-,mär-jə-'nā-shən\ *noun*
emas·cu·late \i-'mas-kyə-,lāt\ *transitive verb* **-lat·ed; -lat·ing** [Latin *emasculatus*, past participle of *emasculare*, from *e-* + *masculus* male — more at MALE] (1607)
1 : to deprive of strength, vigor, or spirit **:** WEAKEN
2 : to deprive of virility or procreative power **:** CASTRATE
3 : to remove the androecium of (a flower) in the process of artificial cross-pollination
synonym see UNNERVE
— **emas·cu·late** \-lət\ *adjective*
— **emas·cu·la·tion** \-,mas-kyə-'lā-shən\ *noun*
— **emas·cu·la·tor** \-'mas-kyə-,lā-tər\ *noun*
em·balm \im-'bä(l)m, *New England also* -'bȧm\ *transitive verb* [Middle English *embaumen*, from Middle French *embaumer*, from Old French *embasmer*, from *en-* + *basme* balm — more at BALM] (14th century)
1 : to treat (a dead body) so as to protect from decay
2 : to fill with sweet odors **:** PERFUME

3 : to protect from decay or oblivion **:** PRESERVE
4 : to fix in a static condition
— **em·balm·er** *noun*
— **em·balm·ment** \-'bä(l)m-mənt, -'bám-\ *noun*

em·bank \im-'baŋk\ *transitive verb* (1576)
: to enclose or confine by an embankment
em·bank·ment \-mənt\ *noun* (1786)
1 : a raised structure to hold back water or to carry a roadway
2 : the action of embanking
em·bar·ca·de·ro \(ˌ)em-ˌbär-kə-'der-(ˌ)ō\ *noun, plural* **-ros** [Spanish, from *embarcado*, past participle of *embarcar* to embark, from *em-* (from Latin *in-*) + *barca* bark, from Late Latin] (1846)
West **:** a landing place especially on an inland waterway

¹em·bar·go \im-'bär-(ˌ)gō\ *noun, plural* **-goes** [Spanish, from *embargar* to bar, from (assumed) Vulgar Latin *imbarricare*, from Latin *in-* + (assumed) Vulgar Latin *barra* bar] (1593)
1 : an order of a government prohibiting the departure of commercial ships from its ports
2 : a legal prohibition on commerce ⟨an *embargo* on arms shipments⟩
3 : STOPPAGE, IMPEDIMENT; *especially* **:** PROHIBITION ⟨I lay no *embargo* on anybody's words —Jane Austen⟩
4 : an order by a common carrier or public regulatory agency prohibiting or restricting freight transportation
²embargo *transitive verb* **-goed; -go·ing** (1755)
: to place an embargo on

em·bark \im-'bärk\ *verb* [Middle French *embarquer*, from Old Provençal *embarcar*, from *em-* (from Latin *in-*) + *barca* bark] (1533)
intransitive verb
1 : to go on board a vehicle for transportation
2 : to make a start ⟨*embarked* on a new career⟩
transitive verb
1 : to cause to go on board (as a boat or airplane)
2 : to engage, enlist, or invest in an enterprise
— **em·bar·ka·tion** \ˌem-ˌbär-'kā-shən, -bər-\ *noun*
— **em·bark·ment** \im-'bärk-mənt\ *noun*

em·bar·rass \im-'bar-əs\ *transitive verb* [French *embarrasser*, from Spanish *embarazar*, from Portuguese *embaraçar*, from *em-* (from Latin *in-*) + *baraça* noose] (1672)
1 a : to place in doubt, perplexity, or difficulties **b :** to involve in financial difficulties **c :** to cause to experience a state of self-conscious distress ⟨bawdy stories *embarrassed* him⟩
2 a : to hamper the movement of **b :** HINDER, IMPEDE
3 : to make intricate **:** COMPLICATE
4 : to impair the activity of (a bodily function) or the function of (a bodily part) ⟨digestion *embarrassed* by overeating⟩ ☆
— **em·bar·rass·able** \-sə-bəl\ *adjective*
em·bar·rassed·ly \-əst-lē, -ə-səd-lē\ *adverb* (1883)
: with embarrassment
em·bar·rass·ing·ly \-ə-siŋ-lē\ *adverb* (circa 1864)
: to an embarrassing degree **:** so as to cause embarrassment
em·bar·rass·ment \im-'bar-ə-smənt\ *noun* (1729)
1 a : something that embarrasses **:** IMPEDIMENT **b :** an excessive quantity from which to select — used especially in the phrase *embarrassment of riches*
2 : the state of being embarrassed: as **a :** confusion or disturbance of mind **b :** difficulty arising from the want of money to pay debts **c :** difficulty in functioning as a result of disease ⟨cardiac *embarrassment*⟩
em·bas·sage \'em-bə-sij\ *noun* (1526)

1 : the message or commission entrusted to an ambassador
2 *archaic* **:** EMBASSY
em·bas·sy \'em-bə-sē\ *noun, plural* **-sies** [Middle French *ambassee*, ultimately of Germanic origin; akin to Old High German *ambaht* service] (1534)
1 : a body of diplomatic representatives; *specifically* **:** one headed by an ambassador
2 a : the function or position of an ambassador **b :** a mission abroad undertaken officially especially by an ambassador
3 : EMBASSAGE 1
4 : the official residence and offices of an ambassador
em·bat·tle \im-'ba-t°l\ *transitive verb* **em·bat·tled; em·bat·tling** \-'bat-liŋ, -t°l-iŋ\ [Middle English *embatailen*, from Middle French *embatailler*, from *en-* + *batailler* to battle] (14th century)
1 : to arrange in order of battle **:** prepare for battle
2 : FORTIFY
em·bat·tled *adjective* (15th century)
1 a : ready to fight **:** prepared to give battle ⟨here once the *embattled* farmers stood —R. W. Emerson⟩ **b :** engaged in battle, conflict, or controversy ⟨an *embattled* official accused of extortion⟩
2 a : being a site of battle, conflict, or controversy ⟨the *embattled* capital⟩ **b :** characterized by conflict or controversy ⟨his . . . often *embattled* experience as an educator —Nat Hentoff⟩
em·bat·tle·ment \-'ba-t°l-mənt\ *noun* (15th century)
1 : BATTLEMENT
2 : the state of being embattled
em·bay \im-'bā\ *transitive verb* (1600)
: to trap or catch in or as if in a bay ⟨an *embayed* sailing ship⟩
em·bay·ment \-'bā-mənt\ *noun* (1815)
1 : formation of a bay
2 : a bay or a conformation resembling a bay
Emb·den \'em-dən\ *noun* [*Emden*, Germany] (1903)
: a breed of large white domestic geese with an orange bill and deep orange shanks and toes
em·bed \im-'bed\ *verb* **em·bed·ded; em·bed·ding** (circa 1794)
transitive verb
1 a : to enclose closely in or as if in a matrix ⟨fossils *embedded* in stone⟩ **b :** to make something an integral part of ⟨the prejudices *embedded* in our language⟩ **c :** to prepare (a microscopy specimen) for sectioning by infiltrating with and enclosing in a supporting substance
2 : to surround closely ⟨a sweet pulp *embeds* the plum seed⟩
intransitive verb
: to become embedded
— **em·bed·ment** \-'bed-mənt\ *noun*
em·bed·ded \im-'be-dəd\ *adjective* (1961)
: occurring as a grammatical constituent (as a verb phrase or clause) within a like constituent
— **em·bed·ding** \-diŋ\ *noun*
em·bel·lish \im-'be-lish\ *transitive verb* [Middle English, from Middle French *embeliss-*, stem of *embelir*, from *en-* + *bel* beautiful — more at BEAUTY] (14th century)
1 : to make beautiful with ornamentation **:** DECORATE
2 : to heighten the attractiveness of by adding ornamental details **:** ENHANCE ⟨*embellished* our account of the trip⟩
synonym see ADORN
— **em·bel·lish·er** *noun*
em·bel·lish·ment \-lish-mənt\ *noun* (1591)
1 : the act or process of embellishing
2 : something serving to embellish
3 : ORNAMENT 5
em·ber \'em-bər\ *noun* [Middle English *eymere*, from Old Norse *eimyrja*; akin to Old

English *ǣmerge* ashes, Latin *urere* to burn] (14th century)
1 : a glowing fragment (as of coal) from a fire; *especially* **:** one smoldering in ashes
2 *plural* **:** the smoldering remains of a fire
3 *plural* **:** slowly dying or fading emotions, memories, ideas, or responses still capable of being revived
ember day \'em-bər-\ *noun* [Middle English, from Old English *ymbrendæg*, from *ymbrene* circuit, anniversary + *dæg* day] (before 12th century)
: a Wednesday, Friday, or Saturday following the first Sunday in Lent, Whitsunday, September 14, or December 13 set apart for fasting and prayer in Western churches
em·bez·zle \im-'be-zəl\ *transitive verb* **em·bez·zled; em·bez·zling** \-(ə-)liŋ\ [Middle English *embesilen*, from Anglo-French *em·beseiller*, from Middle French *en-* + *besillier* to destroy] (15th century)
: to appropriate (as property entrusted to one's care) fraudulently to one's own use
— **em·bez·zle·ment** \-zəl-mənt\ *noun*
— **em·bez·zler** \-z(ə-)lər\ *noun*
em·bit·ter \im-'bi-tər\ *transitive verb* (15th century)
1 : to excite bitter feelings in
2 : to make bitter
— **em·bit·ter·ment** \-mənt\ *noun*
¹em·blaze \im-'blāz\ *transitive verb* **em·blazed; em·blaz·ing** (15th century)
1 : to illuminate especially by a blaze
2 : to set ablaze
²emblaze *transitive verb* **em·blazed; em·blaz·ing** [*en-* + *blaze* (to blazon)] (1593)
1 *archaic* **:** EMBLAZON 1
2 : to adorn sumptuously ⟨with gems and golden luster rich *emblazed* —John Milton⟩
em·bla·zon \im-'blā-z°n\ *transitive verb* **em·bla·zoned; em·bla·zon·ing** \-'blāz-niŋ, -'blā-z°n-iŋ\ (1589)
1 a : to inscribe or adorn with or as if with heraldic bearings or devices **b :** to inscribe (as heraldic bearings) on a surface
2 : CELEBRATE, EXTOL ⟨have his . . . deeds *emblazoned* by a poet —Thomas Nash⟩
— **em·bla·zon·er** \-'blāz-nər, -'blā-z°n-ər\ *noun*
— **em·bla·zon·ment** \-'blā-z°n-mənt\ *noun*
em·bla·zon·ry \-z°n-rē\ *noun* (1667)
1 : emblazoned figures **:** brilliant decoration
2 : the act or art of emblazoning
¹em·blem \'em-bləm\ *noun* [Middle English, from Latin *emblema* inlaid work, from Greek *emblēmat-*, *emblēma*, from *emballein* to insert, from *en-* + *ballein* to throw — more at DEVIL] (15th century)

☆ **SYNONYMS**
Embarrass, discomfit, abash, disconcert, rattle mean to distress by confusing or confounding. EMBARRASS implies some influence that impedes thought, speech, or action ⟨*embarrassed* to admit that she liked the movie⟩. DISCOMFIT implies a hampering or frustrating accompanied by confusion ⟨hecklers *discomfited* the speaker⟩. ABASH presupposes some initial self-confidence that receives a sudden check, producing shyness, shame, or a feeling of inferiority ⟨*abashed* by her swift and cutting retort⟩. DISCONCERT implies an upsetting of equanimity or assurance producing uncertainty or hesitancy ⟨*disconcerted* by finding so many in attendance⟩. RATTLE implies an agitation that impairs thought and judgment ⟨*rattled* by all the television cameras⟩.

\ə\ **abut** \°\ **kitten** \ər\ **further** \a\ **ash** \ā\ **ace**
\ä\ **mop, mar** \au̇\ **out** \ch\ **chin** \e\ **bet** \ē\ **easy**
\g\ **go** \i\ **hit** \ī\ **ice** \j\ **job** \ŋ\ **sing** \ō\ **go**
\o̊\ **law** \o̊i\ **boy** \th\ **thin** \th̲\ **the** \ü\ **loot** \u̇\ **foot**
\y\ **yet** \zh\ **vision** *see also* Guide to Pronunciation

1 : a picture with a motto or set of verses intended as a moral lesson
2 : an object or the figure of an object symbolizing and suggesting another object or an idea
3 a : a symbolic object used as a heraldic device **b :** a device, symbol, or figure adopted and used as an identifying mark
²**emblem** *transitive verb* (1584)
: EMBLEMATIZE

em·blem·at·ic \ˌem-blə-'ma-tik\ *also* **em·blem·at·i·cal** \-ti-kəl\ *adjective* (1645)
: of, relating to, or constituting an emblem
: SYMBOLIC, REPRESENTATIVE
— **em·blem·at·i·cal·ly** \-ti-k(ə-)lē\ *adverb*

em·blem·a·tize \em-'ble-mə-ˌtīz\ *transitive verb* **-tized; -tiz·ing** (1615)
: to represent by or as if by an emblem : SYMBOLIZE

em·ble·ments \'em-blə-mən(t)s\ *noun plural* [Middle English *emblayment*, from Middle French *emblaement*, from *emblaer* to sow with grain, from *en-* + *blee* grain, of Germanic origin; akin to Old English *blæd* fruit, growth, leaf — more at BLADE] (15th century)
: crops from annual cultivation legally belonging to the tenant

em·bodi·ment \im-'bä-di-mənt\ *noun* (1828)
1 : one that embodies something ⟨the *embodiment* of all our hopes⟩
2 : the act of embodying : the state of being embodied

em·body \im-'bä-dē\ *transitive verb* **em·bod·ied; em·body·ing** (circa 1548)
1 : to give a body to (a spirit) : INCARNATE
2 a : to deprive of spirituality **b :** to make concrete and perceptible
3 : to cause to become a body or part of a body : INCORPORATE
4 : to represent in human or animal form : PERSONIFY ⟨men who greatly *embodied* the idealism of American life —A. M. Schlesinger (born 1917)⟩
— **em·bodi·er** *noun*

em·bold·en \im-'bōl-dən\ *transitive verb* (15th century)
: to instill with boldness or courage

em·bo·lec·to·my \ˌem-bə-'lek-tə-mē\ *noun, plural* **-mies** (1923)
: surgical removal of an embolus

em·bol·ic \em-'bä-lik, im-\ *adjective* (1866)
: of or relating to an embolus or embolism

em·bo·lism \'em-bə-ˌli-zəm\ *noun* [Middle English *embolisme*, from Medieval Latin *embolismus*, from Greek *embol-* (from *emballein* to insert, intercalate) — more at EMBLEM] (14th century)
1 : the insertion of one or more days in a calendar : INTERCALATION
2 a : the sudden obstruction of a blood vessel by an embolus **b :** EMBOLUS
— **em·bo·lis·mic** \ˌem-bə-'liz-mik\ *adjective*

em·bo·li·za·tion \ˌem-bə-lə-'zā-shən\ *noun* (1942)
: the process or state in which a blood vessel or organ is obstructed by the lodgment of a material mass (as an embolus)

em·bo·lus \'em-bə-ləs\ *noun, plural* **-li** \-ˌlī\ [New Latin, from Greek *embolos* wedge-shaped object, stopper, from *emballein*] (1859)
: an abnormal particle (as an air bubble) circulating in the blood — compare THROMBUS

em·bon·point \äⁿ-bōⁿ-'pwäⁿ\ *noun* [French, from Middle French, from *en bon point* in good condition] (1670)
: plumpness of person : STOUTNESS

em·bos·om \im-'bu̇-zəm *also* -'bü-\ *transitive verb* (circa 1590)
1 *archaic* **:** to take into or place in the bosom
2 : to shelter closely : ENCLOSE ⟨his house *embosomed* in the grove —Alexander Pope⟩

¹**em·boss** \im-'bäs, -'bȯs\ *transitive verb* [Middle English *embosen* to become exhausted from being hunted, ultimately from Middle French *bois* woods] (14th century)
archaic **:** to drive (as a hunted animal) to bay or to exhaustion

²**emboss** *transitive verb* [Middle English *embosen*, from Middle French *embocer*, from *en-* + *boce* boss] (15th century)
1 : to raise the surface of into bosses; *especially* **:** to ornament with raised work
2 : to raise in relief from a surface
3 : ADORN, EMBELLISH
— **em·boss·able** \-'bä-sə-bəl, -'bȯ-\ *adjective*
— **em·boss·er** \-sər\ *noun*
— **em·boss·ment** \-mənt\ *noun*

em·bou·chure \'äm-bu̇-ˌshu̇r, ˌäm-bu̇-'\ *noun* [French, from *(s)emboucher* to flow into, from *en-* + *bouche* mouth — more at DEBOUCH] (1760)
1 : the position and use of the lips, tongue, and teeth in playing a wind instrument
2 : the mouthpiece of a musical instrument

em·bour·geoise·ment \em-'bu̇rzh-ˌwäz-mənt, äm-; äⁿ-bu̇rzh-wàz-mäⁿ\ *noun* [French, from *embourgeoiser* to make bourgeois, from *em-* + *bourgeois*] (1937)
: a shift to bourgeois values and practices

em·bowed \im-'bōd\ *adjective* (15th century)
: bent like a bow : ARCHED

em·bow·el \im-'bau̇(-ə)l\ *transitive verb* **-eled** *or* **-elled; -el·ing** *or* **-el·ling** (1521)
1 : DISEMBOWEL
2 *obsolete* **:** ENCLOSE

em·bow·er \im-'bau̇(-ə)r\ *transitive verb* (1580)
: to shelter or enclose in or as if in a bower ⟨like a rose *embowered* in its own green leaves —P. B. Shelley⟩

¹**em·brace** \im-'brās\ *verb* **em·braced; em·brac·ing** [Middle English, from Middle French *embracer*, from Old French *embracier*, from *en-* + *brace* two arms — more at BRACE] (14th century)
transitive verb
1 a : to clasp in the arms : HUG **b :** CHERISH, LOVE
2 : ENCIRCLE, ENCLOSE
3 a : to take up especially readily or gladly ⟨*embrace* a cause⟩ **b :** to avail oneself of : WELCOME ⟨*embraced* the opportunity to study further⟩
4 a : to take in or include as a part, item, or element of a more inclusive whole ⟨charity *embraces* all acts that contribute to human welfare⟩ **b :** to be equal or equivalent to ⟨his assets *embraced* $10⟩
intransitive verb
: to participate in an embrace
synonym see ADOPT, INCLUDE
— **em·brace·able** \-'brā-sə-bəl\ *adjective*
— **em·brace·ment** \-'brā-smənt\ *noun*
— **em·brac·er** *noun*
— **em·brac·ing·ly** \-'brā-siŋ-lē\ *adverb*

²**embrace** *noun* (1592)
1 : a close encircling with the arms and pressure to the bosom especially as a sign of affection : HUG
2 : GRIP, ENCIRCLEMENT ⟨in the *embrace* of terror⟩
3 : ACCEPTANCE ⟨her *embrace* of new ideas⟩

em·bra·ceor \im-'brā-sər\ *noun* [Anglo-French, from Middle French *embraseor* instigator, from *embraser* to set on fire, from *en-* + *brase, brese* live coals] (15th century)
: one guilty of embracery

em·brac·ery \im-'brā-sə-rē\ *noun, plural* **-er·ies** [Middle English, from Anglo-French *embraceor*] (15th century)
: an attempt to influence a jury corruptly

em·brac·ive \-'brā-siv\ *adjective* (1855)
1 : disposed to embrace
2 : INCLUSIVE, COMPREHENSIVE

em·bran·gle \im-'braŋ-gəl\ *transitive verb* **-gled; -gling** \-g(ə-)liŋ\ [*en-* + *brangle* (squabble)] (1664)
: EMBROIL
— **em·bran·gle·ment** \-gəl-mənt\ *noun*

em·bra·sure \im-'brā-zhər\ *noun* [French, from obsolete *embraser* to widen an opening] (1702)
1 : an opening with sides flaring outward in a wall or parapet of a fortification usually for allowing the firing of cannon
2 : a recess of a door or window

em·brit·tle \im-'bri-t°l\ *verb* **-brit·tled; -brit·tling** \-'brit-liŋ, -t°l-iŋ\ (1902)
transitive verb
: to make brittle
intransitive verb
: to become brittle
— **em·brit·tle·ment** \-'bri-t°l-mənt\ *noun*

E embrasure 2

em·bro·ca·tion \ˌem-brə-'kā-shən\ *noun* [Middle English *embrocacioun*, from Middle French *embrocacion*, from Medieval Latin *embrocation-, embrocatio*, from Late Latin *embrocare* to rub with lotion, from Greek *embroche* lotion, from *en-* + *brechein* to wet] (15th century)
: LINIMENT

em·broi·der \im-'brȯi-dər\ *verb* **em·broi·dered; em·broi·der·ing** \-d(ə-)riŋ\ [Middle English *embroderen*, from Middle French *embroder*, from *en-* + *broder* to embroider, of Germanic origin; akin to Old English *brord* point, *byrst* bristle] (14th century)
transitive verb
1 a : to ornament with needlework **b :** to form with needlework
2 : to elaborate on : EMBELLISH
intransitive verb
1 : to make embroidery
2 : to provide embellishments : ELABORATE
— **em·broi·der·er** \-'brȯi-dər-ər\ *noun*

em·broi·dery \im-'brȯi-d(ə-)rē\ *noun, plural* **-der·ies** (14th century)
1 a : the art or process of forming decorative designs with hand or machine needlework **b :** a design or decoration formed by or as if by embroidery **c :** an object decorated with embroidery
2 : elaboration by use of decorative and often fictitious detail
3 : something pleasing or desirable but unimportant ⟨considered the humanities mere educational *embroidery*⟩

em·broil \im-'brȯi(ə)l\ *transitive verb* [French *embrouiller*, from Middle French, from *en-* + *brouiller* to broil] (1603)
1 : to throw into disorder or confusion
2 : to involve in conflict or difficulties
— **em·broil·ment** \-mənt\ *noun*

em·brown \im-'brau̇n\ *transitive verb* (1667)
1 : DARKEN
2 : to cause to turn brown

embrue *variant of* IMBRUE

embry- *or* **embryo-** *combining form* [Late Latin, from Greek, from *embryon*]
: embryo ⟨*embryo*geny⟩

em·bryo \'em-brē-ˌō\ *noun, plural* **em·bry·os** [Medieval Latin *embryon-, embryo*, from Greek *embryon*, from *en-* + *bryein* to swell; akin to Greek *bryon* catkin] (1548)
1 a *archaic* **:** a vertebrate at any stage of development prior to birth or hatching **b :** an animal in the early stages of growth and differentiation that are characterized by cleavage, the laying down of fundamental tissues, and the formation of primitive organs and organ systems; *especially* **:** the developing human individual from the time of implantation to the end of the eighth week after conception
2 : the young sporophyte of a seed plant usually comprising a rudimentary plant with plumule, radicle, and cotyledons
3 a : something as yet undeveloped **b :** a beginning or undeveloped state of something

⟨productions seen in *embryo* during their out-of-town tryout period —Henry Hewes⟩

em·bryo·gen·e·sis \,em-brē-ō-'je-nə-səs\ *noun* (1830)
: the formation and development of the embryo

— **em·bryo·ge·net·ic** \-jə-'ne-tik\ *adjective*

em·bry·og·e·ny \,em-brē-'ä-jə-nē\ *noun, plural* **-nies** (1835)
: EMBRYOGENESIS

— **em·bryo·gen·ic** \-brē-ō-'je-nik\ *adjective*

em·bry·oid \'em-brē-,ȯid\ *noun* (circa 1927)
: a mass of plant or animal tissue that resembles an embryo

— **embryoid** *adjective*

em·bry·ol·o·gy \,em-brē-'ä-lə-jē\ *noun* [French *embryologie*] (circa 1847)
1 : a branch of biology dealing with embryos and their development
2 : the features and phenomena exhibited in the formation and development of an embryo

— **em·bry·o·log·i·cal** \-brē-ə-'lä-ji-kəl\ *adjective*

— **em·bry·o·log·i·cal·ly** \-ji-k(ə-)lē\ *adverb*

— **em·bry·ol·o·gist** \-brē-'ä-lə-jist\ *noun*

embryon- *or* **embryoni-** *combining form* [Medieval Latin *embryon-, embryo*]
: embryo ⟨*embryonic*⟩

em·bry·o·nal \em-'brī-ə-nᵊl\ *adjective* (1652)
: EMBRYONIC 1

em·bry·o·nat·ed \'em-brē-ə-,nā-təd\ *adjective* (1687)
: having an embryo

em·bry·on·ic \,em-brē-'ä-nik\ *adjective* (circa 1841)
1 : of or relating to an embryo
2 : being in an early stage of development **:** INCIPIENT, RUDIMENTARY

— **em·bry·on·i·cal·ly** \-ni-k(ə-)lē\ *adverb*

embryonic disk *noun* (circa 1938)
1 a : BLASTODISC **b :** BLASTODERM
2 : the part of the inner cell mass of a blastocyst from which the embryo of a placental mammal develops — called also *embryonic shield*

embryonic membrane *noun* (1947)
: a structure (as the amnion) that derives from the fertilized ovum but does not form a part of the embryo

em·bryo·phyte \'em-brē-ə-,fīt\ *noun* (circa 1909)
: any of a subkingdom (Embryophyta) of plants in which the embryo is retained within maternal tissue and which include the bryophytes and tracheophytes

embryo sac *noun* (1872)
: the female gametophyte of a seed plant consisting of a thin-walled sac within the nucellus that contains the egg nucleus and other nuclei which give rise to endosperm on fertilization

embryo transfer *noun* (1969)
: a procedure used especially in animal breeding in which an embryo from a superovulated female is removed and reimplanted in the uterus of another female — called also *embryo transplant*

¹em·cee \,em-'sē\ *noun* [MC] (circa 1933)
: MASTER OF CEREMONIES

²emcee *verb* **em·ceed; em·cee·ing** (1937)
transitive verb
: to act as master of ceremonies of
intransitive verb
: to act as master of ceremonies

-eme \,ēm\ *noun suffix* [French *-ème* (from *phonème* speech sound, phoneme)]
: significantly distinctive unit of language structure ⟨tax*eme*⟩

emend \ē-'mend\ *transitive verb* [Middle English, from Latin *emendare* — more at AMEND] (15th century)
: to correct usually by textual alterations
synonym *see* CORRECT

— **emend·able** \-'men-də-bəl\ *adjective*

— **emend·er** *noun*

emen·da·tion \,ē-,men-'dā-shən; ,e-mən-, e-,men-\ *noun* (1536)
1 : the act or practice of emending
2 : an alteration designed to correct or improve

¹em·er·ald \'em-rəld, 'e-mə-\ *noun* [Middle English *emerallde*, from Middle French *esmeralde*, from (assumed) Vulgar Latin *smaralda*, from Latin *smaragdus*, from Greek *smaragdos*] (14th century)
1 : a rich green variety of beryl prized as a gemstone
2 : any of various green gemstones (as synthetic corundum or demantoid)

²emerald *adjective* (1508)
: brightly or richly green

emerald cut *noun* (1926)
: a rectangular cut for a gem having a series of parallel facets on each side and at each corner

emerald green *noun* (1646)
1 : a clear bright green resembling that of the emerald
2 : any of various strong greens

emerge \i-'mərj\ *intransitive verb* **emerged; emerg·ing** [Latin *emergere*, from *e-* + *mergere* to plunge — more at MERGE] (1563)
1 : to become manifest
2 : to rise from or as if from an enveloping fluid **:** come out into view
3 : to rise from an obscure or inferior position or condition
4 : to come into being through evolution

emer·gence \i-'mər-jən(t)s\ *noun* (1704)
1 : the act or an instance of emerging
2 : any of various superficial outgrowths of plant tissue usually formed from both epidermis and immediately underlying tissues
3 : penetration of the soil surface by a newly germinated plant

emer·gen·cy \i-'mər-jənt-sē\ *noun, plural* **-cies** *often attributive* (circa 1631)
1 : an unforeseen combination of circumstances or the resulting state that calls for immediate action
2 : an urgent need for assistance or relief ⟨the governor declared a state of *emergency* after the flood⟩
synonym *see* JUNCTURE

emergency brake *noun* (1900)
: a brake (as on an automobile) that can be used for stopping in the event of failure of the main brakes and to keep the vehicle from rolling when parked

emergency medical technician *noun* (1980)
: EMT

emergency room *noun* (1964)
: a hospital room or area staffed and equipped for the reception and treatment of persons requiring immediate medical care

¹emer·gent \i-'mər-jənt\ *adjective* [Middle English, from Latin *emergent-, emergens*, present participle of *emergere*] (1593)
1 a : arising unexpectedly **b :** calling for prompt action **:** URGENT
2 : rising out of or as if out of a fluid
3 : arising as a natural or logical consequence
4 : newly formed or prominent

²emergent *noun* (1620)
1 : something emergent
2 a : a tree that rises above the surrounding forest **b :** a plant rooted in shallow water and having most of the vegetative growth above water

emergent evolution *noun* (1923)
: evolution that according to some theories involves the appearance of new characters and qualities at complex levels of organization (as the cell or organism) which cannot be predicted solely from the study of less complex levels (as the atom or molecule) — compare CREATIVE EVOLUTION

emerg·ing *adjective* (1646)
: EMERGENT 4 ⟨the *emerging* nations of Africa⟩

emer·i·ta \i-'mer-ə-tə\ *adjective* [Latin, feminine of *emeritus*] (1928)
: EMERITUS — used of a woman ⟨Professor *Emerita* Mary Smith⟩

¹emer·i·tus \i-'mer-ə-təs\ *noun, plural* **-i·ti** \-ə-,tī, -,tē\ (1750)
: one retired from professional life but permitted to retain as an honorary title the rank of the last office held

²emeritus *adjective* [Latin, past participle of *emereri* to serve out one's term, from *e-* + *mereri, merēre* to earn, deserve, serve — more at MERIT] (1794)
1 : holding after retirement an honorary title corresponding to that held last during active service
2 : retired from an office or position ⟨professor *emeritus*⟩ — converted to *emeriti* after a plural ⟨professors *emeriti*⟩

emersed \(,)ē-'mərst\ *adjective* (1686)
: standing out of or rising above a surface (as of a fluid) ⟨*emersed* aquatic weeds⟩

emer·sion \(,)ē-'mər-zhən, -shən\ *noun* [Latin *emersus*, past participle of *emergere*] (1633)
: an act of emerging **:** EMERGENCE

em·ery \'em-rē, 'e-mə-\ *noun, plural* **em·er·ies** *often attributive* [Middle English, from Middle French *emeri*, from Old Italian *smiriglio*, from Medieval Latin *smiriglum*, from Greek *smyrid-, smyris*] (15th century)
: a dark granular mineral that consists essentially of corundum and is used for grinding and polishing; *also* **:** a hard abrasive powder

emery board *noun* (1725)
: a cardboard nail file covered with emery

eme·sis \'e-mə-səs, i-'mē-\ *noun, plural* **eme·ses** \-,sēz\ [New Latin, from Greek, from *emein*] (circa 1847)
: an act or instance of vomiting

emet·ic \i-'me-tik\ *noun* [Latin *emetica*, from Greek *emetikē*, from feminine of *emetikos* causing vomiting, from *emein* to vomit — more at VOMIT] (1657)
: an agent that induces vomiting

— **emetic** *adjective*

— **emet·i·cal·ly** \-ti-k(ə-)lē\ *adverb*

em·e·tine \'e-mə-,tēn\ *noun* (1819)
: an amorphous alkaloid $C_{29}H_{40}N_2O_4$ extracted from ipecac root and used as an emetic and expectorant

émeute \ā-'mœt\ *noun, plural* **émeutes** \same\ [French, from Old French *esmeute* act of starting, from feminine of *esmeut*, past participle of *esmovoir* to start — more at EMOTION] (1782)
: UPRISING

emf \,ē-(,)em-'ef\ *noun* [*electromotive force*] (1868)
: POTENTIAL DIFFERENCE

-emia \'ē-mē-ə\ *noun combining form* [New Latin *-emia, -aemia*, from Greek *-aimia*, from *haima* blood]
1 : condition of having (such) blood ⟨leuke*mia*⟩
2 : condition of having (a specified thing) in the blood ⟨ure*mia*⟩

emic \'ē-mik\ *adjective* [phon*emic*] (1954)
: of, relating to, or involving analysis of linguistic or behavioral phenomena in terms of the internal structural or functional elements of a particular system — compare ETIC

¹em·i·grant \'e-mi-grənt\ *noun* (1754)
1 : one who emigrates
2 : a migrant plant or animal

²emigrant *adjective* (1794)
: departing or having departed from a country to settle elsewhere

em·i·grate \'e-mə-,grāt\ *intransitive verb* **-grat·ed; -grat·ing** [Latin *emigratus*, past

\ə\ abut \ᵊ\ kitten \ər\ further \a\ ash \ā\ ace \ä\ mop, mar \aù\ out \ch\ chin \e\ bet \ē\ easy \g\ go \i\ hit \ī\ ice \j\ job \ŋ\ sing \ō\ go \ȯ\ law \ȯi\ boy \th\ thin \t͟h\ the \ü\ loot \ù\ foot \y\ yet \zh\ vision *see also* Guide to Pronunciation

participle of *emigrare*, from *e-* + *migrare* to migrate] (1778)
: to leave one's place of residence or country to live elsewhere
— **em·i·gra·tion** \,e-mə-'grā-shən\ *noun*

émi·gré *also* **emi·gre** \'e-mi-,grā, ,e-mi-'\ *noun, often attributive* [French *émigré*, from past participle of *émigrer* to emigrate, from Latin *emigrare*] (1792)
: EMIGRANT; *especially* : a person forced to emigrate for political reasons

em·i·nence \'e-mə-nən(t)s\ *noun* (15th century)
1 : a position of prominence or superiority
2 : one that is eminent, prominent, or lofty: as **a** : an anatomical protuberance (as on a bone) **b** : a person of high rank or attainments — often used as a title for a cardinal **c** : a natural elevation

émi·nence grise \ā-mē-näⁿs-grēz\ *noun, plural* **éminences grises** *same*\ [French, literally, gray eminence, nickname of Père Joseph (François du Tremblay) (died 1638) French monk and diplomat, confidant of Cardinal Richelieu who was known as *Éminence Rouge* red eminence; from the colors of their respective habits] (1925)
: a confidential agent; *especially* : one exercising unsuspected or unofficial power

em·i·nen·cy \'e-mə-nən(t)-sē\ *noun, plural* **-cies** (1605)
archaic : EMINENCE

em·i·nent \'e-mə-nənt\ *adjective* [Middle English, from Middle French or Latin; Middle French, from Latin *eminent-, eminens*, present participle of *eminēre* to stand out, from *e-* + *-minēre*; akin to Latin *mont-, mons* mountain — more at MOUNT] (15th century)
1 : standing out so as to be readily perceived or noted : CONSPICUOUS
2 : jutting out : PROJECTING
3 : exhibiting eminence especially in standing above others in some quality or position : PROMINENT
synonym see FAMOUS

eminent domain *noun* (1783)
: a right of a government to take private property for public use by virtue of the superior dominion of the sovereign power over all lands within its jurisdiction

em·i·nent·ly \-lē\ *adverb* (1641)
: to a high degree : VERY ⟨*eminently* worthy⟩ ⟨an *eminently* sensible plan⟩

emir \i-'mir, ā-\ *noun* [Arabic *amīr* commander] (1595)
: a ruler, chief, or commander in Islamic countries

emir·ate \'e-mə-rət, -,rāt\ *noun* (1863)
: the state or jurisdiction of an emir

em·is·sary \'e-mə-,ser-ē\ *noun, plural* **-saries** [Latin *emissarius*, from *emissus*, past participle of *emittere*] (1616)
1 : one designated as the agent of another : REPRESENTATIVE
2 : a secret agent

emis·sion \ē-'mi-shən\ *noun* (1607)
1 a : an act or instance of emitting : EMANATION **b** *archaic* : PUBLICATION **c** : a putting into circulation
2 a : something sent forth by emitting: as (1) : electromagnetic waves radiated by an antenna or a celestial body (2) : substances discharged into the air (as by a smokestack or an automobile gasoline engine) **b** : EFFLUVIUM
— **emis·sive** \-'mi-siv\ *adjective*

emis·siv·i·ty \,e-mə-'si-və-tē, ,ē-,mi-'siv-\ *noun, plural* **-ties** (1880)
: the relative power of a surface to emit heat by radiation : the ratio of the radiant energy emitted by a surface to that emitted by a blackbody at the same temperature

emit \ē-'mit\ *transitive verb* **emit·ted; emit·ting** [Latin *emittere* to send out, from *e-* + *mittere* to send] (1626)
1 a : to throw or give off or out (as light) **b** : to send out : EJECT

2 a : to issue with authority; *especially* : to put (as money) into circulation **b** *obsolete* : PUBLISH
3 : to give utterance or voice to ⟨*emitted* a groan⟩
— **emit·ter** *noun*

emit·tance \ē-'mi-tⁿn(t)s\ *noun* (1940)
1 : the energy radiated by the surface of a body per second per unit area
2 : EMISSIVITY

Emmanuel *variant of* IMMANUEL

em·men·a·gogue \ə-'me-nə-,gäg, e-\ *noun* [Greek *emmēna* menses (from neuter plural of *emmēnos* monthly, from *en-* + *mēn* month) + English *-agogue* — more at MOON] (circa 1732)
: an agent that promotes the menstrual discharge

Em·men·ta·ler *or* **Em·men·tha·ler** \'e-mən-,tä-lər\ *or* **Em·men·tal** *or* **Em·men·thal** \-,täl\ *noun* [German, from *Emmental*, Switzerland] (1902)
: SWISS CHEESE

em·mer \'e-mər\ *noun* [German, from Old High German *amari*] (circa 1900)
: a wheat (*Triticum dicoccum*) having spikelets with two hard red kernels that remain in the glumes after threshing; *broadly* : a tetraploid wheat — called also *emmer wheat*

em·met \'e-mət\ *noun* [Middle English *emete*, from Old English *æmette* ant — more at ANT] (before 12th century)
chiefly dialect : ANT

Em·my \'e-mē\ *noun, plural* **Emmys** [from alteration of *Immy*, nickname for *image orthicon* (a camera tube used in television)] (1949)
: a statuette awarded annually by a professional organization for notable achievement in television

em·o·din \'e-mə-dən\ *noun* [International Scientific Vocabulary *emodi-* (from New Latin *Rheum emodi*, species of rhubarb) + *-in*] (1858)
: an orange crystalline phenolic compound $C_{15}H_{10}O_5$ that is obtained from plants (as rhubarb and cascara buckthorn) and is used as a laxative

¹emol·lient \i-'mäl-yənt\ *adjective* [Latin *emollient-, emolliens*, present participle of *emollire* to soften, from *e-* + *mollis* soft — more at MOLLIFY] (circa 1640)
1 : making soft or supple; *also* : soothing especially to the skin or mucous membrane
2 : making less intense or harsh : MOLLIFYING ⟨soothe us in our agonies with *emollient* words —H. L. Mencken⟩

²emollient *noun* (1656)
: something that softens or soothes

emol·u·ment \i-'mäl-yə-mənt\ *noun* [Middle English, from Latin *emolumentum* advantage, from *emolere* to produce by grinding, from *e-* + *molere* to grind — more at MEAL] (15th century)
1 : the returns arising from office or employment usually in the form of compensation or perquisites
2 *archaic* : ADVANTAGE

emote \i-'mōt\ *intransitive verb* **emot·ed; emot·ing** [back-formation from *emotion*] (1917)
: to give expression to emotion especially in or as if in acting

emo·tion \i-'mō-shən\ *noun* [Middle French, from *emouvoir* to stir up, from Old French *esmovoir*, from Latin *emovēre* to remove, displace, from *e-* + *movēre* to move] (1579)
1 a *obsolete* : DISTURBANCE **b** : EXCITEMENT
2 a : the affective aspect of consciousness : FEELING **b** : a state of feeling **c** : a psychic and physical reaction (as anger or fear) subjectively experienced as strong feeling and physiologically involving changes that prepare the body for immediate vigorous action
synonym see FEELING

emo·tion·al \-shnəl, -shə-nⁿl\ *adjective* (1834)

1 : of or relating to emotion ⟨an *emotional* disorder⟩
2 : dominated by or prone to emotion ⟨an *emotional* person⟩
3 : appealing to or arousing emotion ⟨an *emotional* sermon⟩
4 : markedly aroused or agitated in feeling or sensibilities ⟨gets *emotional* at weddings⟩
— **emo·tion·al·i·ty** \-,mō-shə-'na-lə-tē\ *noun*
— **emo·tion·al·ly** \-'mō-shnə-lē, -shə-nⁿl-ē\ *adverb*

emo·tion·al·ism \i-'mō-shnə-,li-zəm, -shə-nⁿl-,iz-\ *noun* (1865)
1 : a tendency to regard things emotionally
2 : undue indulgence in or display of emotion

emo·tion·al·ist \-shnə-list, -shə-nⁿl-ist\ *noun* (circa 1866)
1 : one who bases a theory or policy on an emotional conviction
2 : one prone to emotionalism
— **emo·tion·al·is·tic** \-,mō-shnə-'lis-tik, -shə-nⁿl-'is-\ *adjective*

emo·tion·al·ize \i-'mō-shnə-,līz, -shə-nⁿl-,īz\ *transitive verb* **-ized; -iz·ing** (1879)
: to give an emotional quality to

emo·tion·less \i-'mō-shən-ləs\ *adjective* (1862)
: showing, having, or expressing no emotion
— **emo·tion·less·ness** *noun*
— **emo·tion·less·ly** *adverb*

emo·tive \i-'mō-tiv\ *adjective* (1830)
1 : of or relating to the emotions
2 : appealing to or expressing emotion ⟨the *emotive* use of language⟩
— **emo·tive·ly** *adverb*
— **emo·tiv·i·ty** \i-,mō-'ti-və-tē, ,ē-,mō-\ *noun*

em·pa·na·da \,em-pə-'nä-də\ *noun* [American Spanish, from Spanish, feminine of *empanado*, past participle of *empanar* to bread, from *em-* (from Latin *in-*) + *pan* bread, from Latin *panis* — more at FOOD] (circa 1922)
: a turnover with a sweet or savory filling

empanel *variant of* IMPANEL

em·pa·thet·ic \,em-pə-'the-tik\ *adjective* (1932)
: EMPATHIC
— **em·pa·thet·i·cal·ly** \-ti-k(ə-)lē\ *adverb*

em·path·ic \em-'pa-thik, im-\ *adjective* (1909)
: involving, eliciting, characterized by, or based on empathy
— **em·path·i·cal·ly** \-thi-k(ə-)lē\ *adverb*

em·pa·thise *British variant of* EMPATHIZE

em·pa·thize \'em-pə-,thīz\ *intransitive verb* **-thized; -thiz·ing** (circa 1921)
: to experience empathy ⟨adults unable to *empathize* with a child's frustrations⟩

em·pa·thy \'em-pə-thē\ *noun* [Greek *empatheia*, literally, passion, from *empathēs* emotional, from *em-* + *pathos* feelings, emotion — more at PATHOS] (1904)
1 : the imaginative projection of a subjective state into an object so that the object appears to be infused with it
2 : the action of understanding, being aware of, being sensitive to, and vicariously experiencing the feelings, thoughts, and experience of another of either the past or present without having the feelings, thoughts, and experience fully communicated in an objectively explicit manner; *also* : the capacity for this

em·pen·nage \,äm-pə-'näzh, ,em-\ *noun* [French, feathers of an arrow, empennage, from *empenner* to feather an arrow, from *em-* + ¹*en-* + *penne* feather, from Middle French — more at PEN] (1909)
: the tail assembly of an airplane

em·per·or \'em-pər-ər, -prər\ *noun* [Middle English, from Old French *empereor*, from Latin *imperator*, literally, commander, from *imperare* to command, from *in-* + *parare* to prepare, order — more at PARE] (13th century)
: the sovereign or supreme male monarch of an empire
— **em·per·or·ship** \-,ship\ *noun*

emperor penguin *noun* (1885)
: a penguin (*Aptenodytes forsteri*) that is the largest known and that is noted for its habit of brooding the egg or young between the feet and a fold of abdominal skin resembling a pouch

em·pery \'em-p(ə-)rē\ *noun, plural* **em·per·ies** [Middle English *emperie,* from Old French, from *emperer* to command, from Latin *imperare*] (13th century)
: wide dominion : EMPIRE

em·pha·sise *British variant of* EMPHASIZE

em·pha·sis \'em(p)-fə-səs\ *noun, plural* **-pha·ses** \-ˌsēz\ [Latin, from Greek, exposition, emphasis, from *emphainein* to indicate, from *en-* + *phainein* to show — more at FANCY] (1573)
1 a : force or intensity of expression that gives impressiveness or importance to something **b :** a particular prominence given in reading or speaking to one or more words or syllables
2 : special consideration of or stress or insistence on something

em·pha·size \'em(p)-fə-ˌsīz\ *transitive verb* **-sized; -siz·ing** (circa 1806)
: to place emphasis on : STRESS ⟨*emphasized* the need for reform⟩

em·phat·ic \im-'fa-tik, em-\ *adjective* [Greek *emphatikos,* from *emphainein*] (circa 1708)
1 : uttered with or marked by emphasis
2 : tending to express oneself in forceful speech or to take decisive action
3 : attracting special attention
4 : constituting or belonging to a set of tense forms in English consisting of the auxiliary *do* followed by an infinitive without *to* that are used to facilitate rhetorical inversion or to emphasize something
— **em·phat·i·cal·ly** \-'fa-ti-k(ə-)lē\ *adverb*

em·phy·se·ma \ˌem(p)-fə-'zē-mə, -'sē-\ *noun* [New Latin, from Greek *emphysēma,* from *emphysan* to inflate, from *em-* ²*en-* + *physan* to blow, from *physa* breath — more at PUSTULE] (1661)
: a condition characterized by air-filled expansions of body tissues; *specifically* : a condition of the lung marked by abnormal dilation of its air spaces and distension of its walls and frequently by impairment of heart action
— **em·phy·se·ma·tous** \-'ze-mə-təs, -'se-, -'zē-, -'sē-\ *adjective*
— **em·phy·se·mic** \-'zē-mik, -'sē-\ *adjective*

em·pire \'em-ˌpīr\ *noun* [Middle English, from Old French *empire, empirie,* from Latin *imperium* absolute authority, empire, from *imperare*] (14th century)
1 a (1) : a major political unit having a territory of great extent or a number of territories or peoples under a single sovereign authority; *especially* : one having an emperor as chief of state (2) : the territory of such a political unit **b :** something resembling a political empire; *especially* : an extensive territory or enterprise under single domination or control
2 : imperial sovereignty, rule, or dominion

Em·pire \'äm-ˌpir, 'em-ˌpīr\ *adjective* [French, from (*le premier*) *Empire* the first Empire of France] (1869)
: of, relating to, or characteristic of a style (as of clothing or furniture) popular in early 19th century France

Empire Day \'em-ˌpīr-\ *noun* (1902)
: COMMONWEALTH DAY — used before the official adoption of *Commonwealth Day* in 1958

em·pir·ic \im-'pir-ik, em-\ *noun* [Latin *empiricus,* from Greek *empeirikos,* from *empeiria* experience, from *em-* ²*en-* + *peiran* to attempt — more at FEAR] (1562)
1 : CHARLATAN 2
2 : one who relies on practical experience

em·pir·i·cal \-i-kəl\ *also* **em·pir·ic** \-ik\ *adjective* (1569)
1 : originating in or based on observation or experience ⟨*empirical* data⟩

2 : relying on experience or observation alone often without due regard for system and theory
3 : capable of being verified or disproved by observation or experiment ⟨*empirical* laws⟩
4 : of or relating to empiricism
— **em·pir·i·cal·ly** \-i-k(ə-)lē\ *adverb*

empirical formula *noun* (1885)
: a chemical formula showing the simplest ratio of elements in a compound rather than the total number of atoms in the molecule ⟨CH_2O is the *empirical formula* for glucose⟩

em·pir·i·cism \im-'pir-ə-ˌsi-zəm, em-\ *noun* (1657)
1 a : a former school of medical practice founded on experience without the aid of science or theory **b :** QUACKERY, CHARLATANRY
2 a : the practice of relying on observation and experiment especially in the natural sciences **b :** a tenet arrived at empirically
3 : a theory that all knowledge originates in experience
— **em·pir·i·cist** \-sist\ *noun*

em·place \im-'plās\ *transitive verb* [backformation from *emplacement*] (1865)
: to put into position ⟨missiles *emplaced* around the city⟩

em·place·ment \-'plā-smənt\ *noun* [French, from Middle French *emplacer* to emplace, from *en-* + *place*] (1802)
1 : the situation or location of something
2 : a prepared position for weapons or military equipment ⟨radar *emplacements*⟩
3 : a putting into position : PLACEMENT

em·plane \im-'plān\ *variant of* ENPLANE

¹em·ploy \im-'plói, em-\ *transitive verb* [Middle English *emploien,* from Middle French *emploier,* from Latin *implicare* to enfold, involve, implicate, from *in-* + *plicare* to fold — more at PLY] (15th century)
1 a : to make use of (someone or something inactive) ⟨*employ* a pen for sketching⟩ **b :** to use (as time) advantageously **c** (1) : to use or engage the services of (2) : to provide with a job that pays wages or a salary
2 : to devote to or direct toward a particular activity or person ⟨*employed* all her energies to help the poor⟩
synonym see USE
— **em·ploy·er** *noun*

²em·ploy \im-'plói, 'im-ˌ, 'em-ˌ\ *noun* (1666)
1 a : USE, PURPOSE **b :** OCCUPATION, JOB
2 : the state of being employed ⟨in the government's *employ*⟩

¹em·ploy·able \im-'plói-ə-bəl\ *adjective* (1593)
: capable of being employed
— **em·ploy·abil·i·ty** \-ˌplói-ə-'bi-lə-tē\ *noun*

²employable *noun* (1934)
: one who is employable

em·ploy·ee *or* **em·ploye** \im-ˌplói(i)-'ē, (ˌ)em-; im-'plói(i)-ˌē, -ˌē\ *noun* (1822)
: one employed by another usually for wages or salary and in a position below the executive level

em·ploy·ment \im-'plói-mənt\ *noun* (15th century)
1 : USE, PURPOSE
2 a : activity in which one engages or is employed **b :** an instance of such activity
3 : the act of employing : the state of being employed
synonym see WORK

employment agency *noun* (1888)
: an agency whose business is to find jobs for people seeking them or to find people to fill jobs that are open

em·poi·son \im-'pói-zᵊn\ *transitive verb* [Middle English *empoysonen,* from Middle French *empoisoner,* from *en-* + *poison* poison, from Old French] (14th century)
1 *archaic* : POISON
2 : EMBITTER ⟨a look of *empoisoned* acceptance —Saul Bellow⟩
— **em·poi·son·ment** \-mənt\ *noun*

em·po·ri·um \im-'pōr-ē-əm, em-, -'pór-\ *noun, plural* **-ri·ums** *also* **-ria** \-ē-ə\ [Latin, from Greek *emporion,* from *emporos* traveler, trader, from *em-* ²*en-* + *poros* passage, journey — more at FARE] (1586)
1 a : a place of trade; *especially* : a commercial center **b :** a retail outlet ⟨a hardware *emporium*⟩ ⟨a pizza *emporium*⟩
2 : a store carrying a diversity of merchandise

em·pow·er \im-'paú(-ə)r\ *transitive verb* (1648)
1 : to give official authority or legal power to
2 : ENABLE 1a
3 : to promote the self-actualization or influence of ⟨women's movement has been inspiring and empowering women —Ron Hansen⟩
— **em·pow·er·ment** \-mənt\ *noun*

em·press \'em-prəs\ *noun* [Middle English *emperesse,* from Old French, feminine of *empereor* emperor] (12th century)
1 : the wife or widow of an emperor
2 : a woman who is the sovereign or supreme monarch of an empire

em·presse·ment \äⁿ-pres-mäⁿ\ *noun* [French, from (*s'*)*empresser* to hurry, from *en-* + *presser* to press] (1709)
: demonstrative warmth or cordiality

em·prise \em-'prīz\ *noun* [Middle English, from Middle French, from Old French, from *emprendre* to undertake, from (assumed) Vulgar Latin *imprehendere,* from Latin *in-* + *prehendere* to seize — more at GET] (13th century)
: an adventurous, daring, or chivalric enterprise

¹emp·ty \'em(p)-tē\ *adjective* **emp·ti·er; -est** [Middle English, from Old English *æmettig* unoccupied, from *æmetta* leisure, perhaps from *æ-* without + *-metta* (probably akin to *mōtan* to have to) — more at MUST] (before 12th century)
1 a : containing nothing **b :** not occupied or inhabited **c :** UNFREQUENTED **d :** not pregnant ⟨*empty* heifer⟩ **e :** NULL 4a ⟨the *empty* set⟩
2 a : lacking reality, substance, meaning, or value : HOLLOW ⟨an *empty* pleasure⟩ **b :** destitute of effect or force **c :** devoid of sense : FOOLISH
3 : HUNGRY
4 a : IDLE ⟨*empty* hours⟩ **b :** having no purpose or result : USELESS
5 : marked by the absence of human life, activity, or comfort ☆
— **emp·ti·ly** \-tə-lē\ *adverb*
— **emp·ti·ness** \-tē-nəs\ *noun*

²empty *verb* **emp·tied; emp·ty·ing** (1555) *transitive verb*
1 a : to make empty : remove the contents of **b :** DEPRIVE, DIVEST **c :** to discharge (itself) of contents **d :** to fire (a repeating firearm) until empty

☆ **SYNONYMS**
Empty, vacant, blank, void, vacuous mean lacking contents which could or should be present. EMPTY suggests a complete absence of contents ⟨an *empty* bucket⟩. VACANT suggests an absence of appropriate contents or occupants ⟨a *vacant* apartment⟩. BLANK stresses the absence of any significant, relieving, or intelligible features on a surface ⟨a *blank* wall⟩. VOID suggests absolute emptiness as far as the mind or senses can determine ⟨a statement *void* of meaning⟩. VACUOUS suggests the emptiness of a vacuum and especially the lack of intelligence or significance ⟨a *vacuous* facial expression⟩. See in addition VAIN.

\ə\ abut \ᵊ\ kitten \ər\ further \a\ ash \ā\ ace
\ä\ mop, mar \aú\ out \ch\ chin \e\ bet \ē\ easy
\g\ go \i\ hit \ī\ ice \j\ job \ŋ\ sing \ō\ go
\ó\ law \ói\ boy \th\ thin \t͟h\ the \ü\ loot \ú\ foot
\y\ yet \zh\ vision *see also* Guide to Pronunciation

2 : to remove from what holds or encloses ⟨*empty* the grain from sacks⟩
intransitive verb
1 : to become empty
2 : to discharge contents ⟨the river *empties* into the ocean⟩

³**empty** *noun, plural* **emp·ties** (1535)
: something (as a container) that is empty

emp·ty–hand·ed \,em(p)-tē-'han-dəd\ *adjective* (1589)
1 : having or bringing nothing
2 : having acquired or gained nothing ⟨came back *empty-handed*⟩

emp·ty–head·ed \-'he-dəd\ *adjective* (1650)
: SCATTERBRAINED

empty nest·er \-'nes-tər\ *noun* (1962)
: a parent whose children have grown and moved away from home

emp·ty–nest syndrome \,em(p)-tē-'nest-\ *noun* (1972)
: the emotional letdown experienced by an empty nester

em·pur·ple \im-'pər-pəl\ *verb* **em·pur·pled; em·pur·pling** \-'pər-p(ə-)liŋ\ (1590)
transitive verb
: to tinge or color purple
intransitive verb
: to become purple

em·py·ema \,em-,pī-'ē-mə\ *noun, plural* **-ema·ta** \-mə-tə\ *or* **-emas** [Late Latin, from Greek *empyēma*, from *empyein* to suppurate, from *em-* ²*en-* + *pyon* pus — more at FOUL] (circa 1605)
: the presence of pus in a bodily cavity
— em·py·emic \-mik\ *adjective*

em·py·re·al \,em-,pī-'rē-əl, -pə-; em-'pir-ē-əl, -'pī-rē-\ *adjective* [Late Latin *empyrius, empyreus*, from Late Greek *empyrios*, from Greek *em-* ²*en-* + *pyr* fire] (15th century)
1 : of or relating to the empyrean **:** CELESTIAL
2 : SUBLIME

¹**em·py·re·an** \-ən\ *adjective* (15th century)
: EMPYREAL

²**empyrean** *noun* (circa 1610)
1 a : the highest heaven or heavenly sphere in ancient and medieval cosmology usually consisting of fire or light **b :** the true and ultimate heavenly paradise
2 : FIRMAMENT, HEAVENS
3 : an ideal place or state

EMT \,ē-(,)em-'tē\ *noun* [*emergency medical technician*] (1972)
: a specially trained medical technician licensed to provide basic emergency services before and during transportation to a hospital — compare PARAMEDIC 2

emu \'ē-(,)myü\ *noun* [modification of Portuguese *ema* cassowary] (1656)
1 : any of various tall flightless birds (as the rhea)
2 : a swift-running Australian bird (*Dromaius novae-hollandiae*) with undeveloped wings that is related to and smaller than the ostrich

¹**em·u·late** \'em-yə-,lāt\ *transitive verb* **-lat·ed; -lat·ing** [Latin *aemulatus*, past participle of *aemulari*, from *aemulus* rivaling] (1582)

emu 2

1 a : to strive to equal or excel **b :** IMITATE; *especially* **:** to imitate by means of an emulator
2 : to equal or approach equality with

²**em·u·late** \-lət\ *adjective* (1602)
obsolete **:** EMULOUS 1b ⟨pricked on by a most *emulate* pride —Shakespeare⟩

em·u·la·tion \,em-yə-'lā-shən\ *noun* (1542)
1 *obsolete* **:** ambitious or envious rivalry
2 : ambition or endeavor to equal or excel others (as in achievement)
3 a : IMITATION **b :** the use of or technique of using an emulator

— em·u·la·tive \'em-yə-,lā-tiv\ *adjective*
— em·u·la·tive·ly *adverb*
em·u·la·tor \'em-yə-,lā-tər\ *noun* (1589)
1 : one that emulates
2 : hardware or software that permits programs written for one computer to be run on another usually newer computer

em·u·lous \'em-yə-ləs\ *adjective* (1535)
1 a : inspired by or deriving from a desire to emulate **b :** ambitious or eager to emulate
2 *obsolete* **:** JEALOUS
— em·u·lous·ly *adverb*
— em·u·lous·ness *noun*

emul·si·fi·er \i-'məl-sə-,fī(-ə)r\ *noun* (1888)
: one that emulsifies; *especially* **:** a surface-active agent (as a soap) promoting the formation and stabilization of an emulsion

emul·si·fy \-,fī\ *transitive verb* **-fied; -fy·ing** (1859)
: to disperse (as an oil) in an emulsion; *also* **:** to convert (two or more immiscible liquids) into an emulsion
— emul·si·fi·able \i-'məl-sə-,fī-ə-bəl\ *adjective*
— emul·si·fi·ca·tion \i-,məl-sə-fə-'kā-shən\ *noun*

emul·sion \i-'məl-shən\ *noun* [New Latin *emulsion-, emulsio*, from Latin *emulgēre* to milk out, from *e-* + *mulgēre* to milk; akin to Old English *melcan* to milk, Greek *amelgein*] (1612)
1 a : a system (as fat in milk) consisting of a liquid dispersed with or without an emulsifier in an immiscible liquid usually in droplets of larger than colloidal size **b :** the state of such a system
2 : SUSPENSION 2b(3); *especially* **:** a suspension of a sensitive silver salt or a mixture of silver halides in a viscous medium (as a gelatin solution) forming a coating on photographic plates, film, or paper

emul·soid \i-'məl-,sȯid\ *noun* (circa 1909)
1 : a colloidal system consisting of a liquid dispersed in a liquid
2 : a lyophilic sol (as a gelatin solution)
— emul·soi·dal \-,məl-'sȯi-dᵊl\ *adjective*

en \'en\ *noun* (1792)
1 : the width of a piece of type half the width of an em
2 : the letter *n*

¹**en-** *also* **em-** \in *also* en; *sometimes only in* is *shown when* en *is infrequent*\ *prefix* [Middle English, from Old French, from Latin *in-, im-,* from *in*]
1 : put into or onto ⟨*en*throne⟩ **:** cover with ⟨*en*shroud⟩ **:** go into or onto ⟨*en*plane⟩ — in verbs formed from nouns
2 : cause to be ⟨*en*slave⟩ — in verbs formed from adjectives or nouns
3 : provide with ⟨*em*power⟩ — in verbs formed from nouns
4 : so as to cover ⟨*en*wrap⟩ **:** thoroughly ⟨*en*tangle⟩ — in verbs formed from verbs; in all senses usually *em-* before *b, m,* or *p*

²**en-** *also* **em-** *prefix* [Middle English, from Latin, from Greek, from *en* in — more at IN]
: in **:** within ⟨*en*zootic⟩ — usually *em-* before *b, m,* or *p* ⟨*em*pathy⟩

³**en-** *combining form* [International Scientific Vocabulary, from *-ene*]
: chemically unsaturated; *especially* **:** having one double bond ⟨*en*amine⟩

¹**-en** \ən, ᵊn\ *also* **-n** \n\ *adjective suffix* [Middle English, from Old English; akin to Old High German *-īn* made of, Latin *-īnus* of or belonging to, Greek *-inos* made of, of or belonging to]
: made of **:** consisting of ⟨earth*en*⟩ ⟨leather*n*⟩

²**-en** *verb suffix* [Middle English *-nen*, from Old English *-nian;* akin to Old High German *-inōn* -en]
1 a : cause to be ⟨sharp*en*⟩ **b :** cause to have ⟨length*en*⟩
2 a : come to be ⟨steep*en*⟩ **b :** come to have ⟨length*en*⟩

en·able \i-'nā-bəl\ *transitive verb* **en·abled; en·abling** \-b(ə-)liŋ\ (15th century)
1 a : to provide with the means or opportunity ⟨training that *enables* people to earn a living⟩ **b :** to make possible, practical, or easy **c :** to cause to operate ⟨software that *enables* the keyboard⟩
2 : to give legal power, capacity, or sanction to ⟨a law *enabling* admission of a state⟩

en·act \i-'nakt\ *transitive verb* (15th century)
1 : to establish by legal and authoritative act; *specifically* **:** to make (as a bill) into law
2 : ACT OUT ⟨*enact* a role⟩
— en·ac·tor \-'nak-tər\ *noun*
en·act·ment \-'nak(t)-mənt\ *noun* (1817)
1 : the act of enacting **:** the state of being enacted
2 : something (as a law) that has been enacted

¹**enam·el** \i-'na-məl\ *transitive verb* **-eled** *or* **-elled; -el·ing** *or* **-el·ling** \-'nam-liŋ, -'na-mə-\ [Middle English, from Middle French *enamailler*, from *en-* + *esmail* enamel, of Germanic origin; akin to Old High German *smelzan* to melt — more at SMELT] (14th century)
1 : to cover, inlay, or decorate with enamel
2 : to beautify with a colorful surface
3 : to form a glossy surface on (as paper, leather, or cloth)
— enam·el·er *noun*
— enam·el·ist \-mə-list\ *noun*

²**enamel** *noun* (15th century)
1 : a usually opaque vitreous composition applied by fusion to the surface of metal, glass, or pottery
2 : a surface or outer covering that resembles enamel
3 a : something that is enameled **b :** ENAMELWARE
4 : a cosmetic intended to give a smooth or glossy appearance
5 : a hard calcareous substance that forms a thin layer capping the teeth — see TOOTH illustration
6 : a paint that flows out to a smooth coat when applied and that dries with a glossy appearance

enam·el·ware \i-'na-məl-,war, -,wer\ *noun* (1903)
: metalware (as kitchen utensils) coated with enamel

en·amine \'e-nə-,mēn, 'ē-\ *noun* (1942)
: an amine containing the double bond linkage C=C−N

en·am·or \i-'na-mər\ *transitive verb* **-ored; -or·ing** \-mə-riŋ, -'nam-riŋ\ [Middle English *enamouren*, from Middle French *enamourer*, from *en-* + *amour* love — more at AMOUR] (14th century)
1 : to inflame with love — usually used in the passive with *of*
2 : FASCINATE 2b — usually used in the passive with *of* or *with*

en·am·our *chiefly British variant of* ENAMOR

en·an·tio·mer \i-'nan-tē-ə-mər\ *noun* [Greek *enantios* + English *-mer*] (circa 1929)
: either of a pair of chemical compounds whose molecular structures have a mirror-image relationship to each other
— en·an·tio·mer·ic \-,nan-tē-ə-'mer-ik\ *adjective*

en·an·tio·morph \i-'nan-tē-ə-,mȯrf\ *noun* [Greek *enantios* opposite (from *enanti* facing, from *en* in + *anti* against) + International Scientific Vocabulary *-morph* -morph] (1885)
: ENANTIOMER; *also* **:** either of a pair of crystals (as of quartz) that are structural mirror images
— en·an·tio·mor·phic \-,nan-tē-ə-'mȯr-fik\ *adjective*
— en·an·tio·mor·phism \-'mȯr-,fi-zəm\ *noun*
— en·an·tio·mor·phous \-'mȯr-fəs\ *adjective*

ena·tion \i-'nā-shən\ *noun* [Latin *enatus*, past participle of *enasci* to rise out of, from *e-* + *nasci* to be born — more at NATION] (circa 1842)

: an outgrowth from the surface of an organ ⟨a plant virus forming *enations* on leaves⟩

en banc \äⁿ-'bäⁿ\ *adverb or adjective* [French, on the bench] (1863)
: in full court : with full judiciary authority

en bloc \äⁿ-'bläk\ *adverb or adjective* [French] (1861)
: as a whole : in a mass

en bro·chette \äⁿ-brō-'shet\ *adjective* [French] (circa 1909)
of food : cooked or served on a skewer ⟨shrimp *en brochette*⟩

en·cae·nia \en-'sē-nyə\ *noun plural but singular or plural in construction, often capitalized* [New Latin, from Latin, dedication festival, from Greek *enkainia*, from *en* + *kainos* new — more at RECENT] (1691)
: an annual university ceremony (as at Oxford) of commemoration with recital of poems and essays and conferring of degrees

en·cage \in-'kāj, en-\ *transitive verb* (1593)
: CAGE 1

en·camp \in-'kamp, en-\ (1568)
transitive verb
: to place or establish in a camp
intransitive verb
: to set up or occupy a camp

en·camp·ment \-mənt\ *noun* (1598)
1 a : the place where a group (as a body of troops) is encamped **b** : the individuals that make up an encampment
2 : the act of encamping : the state of being encamped

en·cap·su·late \in-'kap-sə-,lāt, en-\ *verb* **-lat·ed; -lat·ing** (1876)
transitive verb
1 : to enclose in or as if in a capsule ⟨a pilot *encapsulated* in the cockpit⟩
2 : EPITOMIZE, SUMMARIZE ⟨*encapsulate* an era in an aphorism⟩
intransitive verb
: to become encapsulated
— **en·cap·su·la·tion** \-,kap-sə-'lā-shən\ *noun*

en·cap·su·lat·ed *adjective* (1894)
1 : surrounded by a gelatinous or membranous envelope ⟨*encapsulated* water bacteria⟩
2 : CONDENSED

en·cap·sule \in-'kap-səl, en-\ (,)sül, en-\ *transitive verb* **-suled; -sul·ing** (1877)
: ENCAPSULATE

en·case \in-'kās, en-\ *transitive verb* (1633)
: to enclose in or as if in a case

en·case·ment \in-'kā-smənt, en-\ *noun* (1741)
: the act or process of encasing : the state of being encased; *also* : CASE, COVERING

en·cash \in-'kash, en-\ *transitive verb* (1861)
British : CASH
— **en·cash·able** \-'ka-shə-bəl\ *adjective, chiefly British*
— **en·cash·ment** \-mənt\ *noun, chiefly British*

en·caus·tic \in-'kȯ-stik\ *noun* [encaustic, adjective, from Latin *encausticus*, from Greek *enkaustikos*, from *enkaiein* to burn in, from *en-* + *kaiein* to burn] (1601)
1 : a paint made from pigment mixed with melted beeswax and resin and after application fixed by heat
2 : the method involving the use of encaustic; *also* : a work produced by this method
— **encaustic** *adjective*

-ence \ən(t)s, ᵊn(t)s\ *noun suffix* [Middle English, from Old French, from Latin *-entia*, from *-ent-, -ens*, present participle ending + *-ia* ²-y]
1 : action or process ⟨emerg*ence*⟩ : instance of an action or process ⟨refer*ence*⟩
2 : quality or state ⟨despond*ence*⟩

¹en·ceinte \äⁿ(n)-'sant\ *adjective* [Middle French, perhaps from (assumed) Vulgar Latin *incenta*, alteration of Latin *incient-, inciens* being with young, modification of Greek *enkyos* pregnant, from *en-* + *kyein* to be pregnant — more at CYME] (1599)

: PREGNANT 3

²enceinte *noun* [French, from Old French, enclosing wall, from *enceindre* to surround, from Latin *incingere*, from *in-* + *cingere* to gird — more at CINCTURE] (circa 1708)
: a line of fortification enclosing a castle or town; *also* : the area so enclosed

encephal- *or* **encephalo-** *combining form* [French *encéphal-*, from Greek *enkephal-*, from *enkephalos*, from *en-* + *kephalē* head — more at CEPHALIC]
: brain ⟨*encephal*itis⟩ ⟨*encephalo*myocarditis⟩

en·ceph·a·li·tis \in-,se-fə-'lī-təs\ *noun, plural* **-lit·i·des** \-'li-tə-,dēz\ (1843)
: inflammation of the brain
— **en·ceph·a·lit·ic** \-'li-tik\ *adjective*

en·ceph·a·li·to·gen·ic \-,lī-tə-'je-nik\ *adjective* (1923)
: tending to cause encephalitis ⟨an *encephalitogenic* virus⟩
— **en·ceph·a·li·to·gen** \-'lī-tə-jən, -,jen\ *noun*

en·ceph·a·lo·gram \in-'se-fə-lə-,gram\ *noun* (1928)
: an X-ray picture of the brain made by encephalography

en·ceph·a·lo·graph \-,graf\ *noun* (1928)
1 : ENCEPHALOGRAM
2 : ELECTROENCEPHALOGRAPH

en·ceph·a·log·ra·phy \in-,se-fə-'lä-grə-fē\ *noun* (1922)
: roentgenography of the brain after the cerebrospinal fluid has been replaced by a gas (as air)

en·ceph·a·lo·my·eli·tis \in-,se-fə-lō-,mī-ə-'lī-təs\ *noun, plural* **-elit·i·des** \-ə-'li-tə-,dēz\ [New Latin] (1908)
: concurrent inflammation of the brain and spinal cord; *specifically* : any of several virus diseases of horses

en·ceph·a·lo·myo·car·di·tis \-,mī-ə-kär-'dī-təs\ *noun* [New Latin] (1947)
: an acute febrile virus disease characterized by degeneration and inflammation of skeletal and cardiac muscle and lesions of the central nervous system

en·ceph·a·lon \in-'se-fə-,län, -lən\ *noun, plural* **-la** \-lə\ [New Latin, from Greek *enkephalos*] (1741)
: the vertebrate brain

en·ceph·a·lop·a·thy \in-,se-fə-'lä-pə-thē\ *noun* (1866)
: a disease of the brain; *especially* : one involving alterations of brain structure
— **en·ceph·a·lo·path·ic** \-lə-'pa-thik\ *adjective*

en·chain \in-'chān\ *transitive verb* [Middle English *encheynen*, from Middle French *enchainer*, from Old French, from *en-* + *chaeine* chain] (14th century)
: to bind or hold with or as if with chains
— **en·chain·ment** \-mənt\ *noun*

en·chant \in-'chant, en-\ *transitive verb* [Middle English, from Middle French *enchanter*, from Latin *incantare*, from *in-* + *cantare* to sing — more at CHANT] (14th century)
1 : to influence by or as if by charms and incantation : BEWITCH
2 : to attract and move deeply : rouse to ecstatic admiration ⟨the scene *enchanted* her to the point of tears —Elinor Wylie⟩
synonym see ATTRACT

en·chant·er *noun* (13th century)
: one that enchants; *especially* : SORCERER

en·chant·ing *adjective* (1606)
: CHARMING
— **en·chant·ing·ly** \-'chan-tiŋ-lē\ *adverb*

en·chant·ment \in-'chant-mənt, en-\ *noun* (13th century)
1 a : the act or art of enchanting **b** : the quality or state of being enchanted
2 : something that enchants

en·chant·ress \in-'chan-trəs, en-\ *noun* (14th century)
1 : a woman who practices magic : SORCERESS
2 : a fascinating woman

en·chase \in-'chās\ *transitive verb* [Middle English, to emboss, from Middle French *enchasser* to enshrine, set, from *en-* + *chasse* reliquary, set, from Latin *capsa* case — more at CASE] (15th century)
1 : ORNAMENT: as **a** : to cut or carve in relief **b** : INLAY
2 : SET ⟨*enchase* a gem⟩

en·chi·la·da \,en-chə-'lä-də\ *noun* [American Spanish, from feminine of *enchilado*, past participle of *enchilar* to season with chili, from Spanish *en-* ¹en- + *chile* chili] (1887)
1 : a rolled filled tortilla covered with chili sauce and usually baked
2 : SCHMEAR, BALL OF WAX ⟨the whole *enchilada*⟩

en·chi·rid·i·on \,en-,kī-'ri-dē-ən, -,ki-'\ *noun, plural* **-rid·ia** \-dē-ə\ [Late Latin, from Greek *encheiridion*, from *en* + *cheir* hand — more at IN, CHIR-] (15th century)
: HANDBOOK, MANUAL

-en·chy·ma \-'eŋ-kə-mə\ *noun combining form, plural* **-en·chy·ma·ta** \en-'ki-mə-tə, -'kī-mə-\ *or* **-enchymas** [New Latin, from *parenchyma*]
: cellular tissue ⟨coll*enchyma*⟩

en·ci·pher \in-'sī-fər, en-\ *transitive verb* (1577)
: to convert (a message) into cipher
— **en·ci·pher·er** \-fər-ər\ *noun*
— **en·ci·pher·ment** \-fər-mənt\ *noun*

en·cir·cle \in-'sər-kəl, en-\ *transitive verb* [Middle English *enserclen*] (15th century)
1 : to form a circle around : SURROUND
2 : to pass completely around
— **en·cir·cle·ment** \-mənt\ *noun*

en clair \äⁿ-'kler\ *adverb or adjective* [French, in clear] (circa 1897)
: in plain language ⟨a message sent *en clair*⟩

en·clasp \in-'klasp, en-\ *transitive verb* (1596)
: to seize and hold : EMBRACE

en·clave \'en-,klāv, ÷'än-,klāv, ÷'äⁿ-\ *noun* [French, from Middle French, from *enclaver* to enclose, from (assumed) Vulgar Latin *inclavare* to lock up, from Latin *in-* + *clavis* key — more at CLAVICLE] (1868)
: a distinct territorial, cultural, or social unit enclosed within or as if within foreign territory ⟨ethnic *enclaves*⟩

en·clit·ic \en-'kli-tik\ *noun* [Late Latin *encliticus*, from Greek *enklitikos*, from *enklinesthai* to lean on, from *en-* + *klinein* to lean — more at LEAN] (circa 1663)
: a clitic that is associated with a preceding word
— **enclitic** *adjective*

en·close \in-'klōz, en-\ *transitive verb* [Middle English, probably from *enclos* enclosed, from Middle French, past participle of *enclore* to enclose, from (assumed) Vulgar Latin *inclaudere*, alteration of Latin *includere* — more at INCLUDE] (14th century)
1 a (1) : to close in : SURROUND ⟨*enclose* a porch with glass⟩ (2) : to fence off (common land) for individual use **b** : to hold in : CONFINE
2 : to include along with something else in a parcel or envelope ⟨a check is *enclosed* herewith⟩

en·clo·sure \in-'klō-zhər, en-\ *noun* (15th century)
1 : the act or action of enclosing : the quality or state of being enclosed
2 : something that encloses
3 : something enclosed ⟨a letter with two *enclosures*⟩

en·code \in-'kōd, en-\ *transitive verb* (circa 1919)

1 : to convert (as a body of information) from one system of communication into another; *especially* **:** to convert (a message) into code **2 :** to specify the genetic code for
— **en·cod·er** *noun*

en·co·mi·ast \en-'kō-mē-ˌast, -mē-əst\ *noun* [Greek *enkōmiastēs*, from *enkōmiazein* to praise, from *enkōmion*] (1610)
: one that praises **:** EULOGIST
— **en·co·mi·as·tic** \-ˌkō-mē-'as-tik\ *adjective*

en·co·mi·um \en-'kō-mē-əm\ *noun, plural* **-mi·ums** *or* **-mia** \-mē-ə\ [Latin, from Greek *enkōmion*, from *en* in + *kōmos* revel, celebration] (1589)
: glowing and warmly enthusiastic praise; *also* **:** an expression of this ☆

en·com·pass \in-'kəm-pəs, en- *also* -'kam-\ *transitive verb* [Middle English] (14th century)
1 a : to form a circle about **:** ENCLOSE **b** *obsolete* **:** to go completely around **2 a :** ENVELOP **b :** INCLUDE ⟨a plan that *encompasses* a number of aims⟩ **3 :** BRING ABOUT, ACCOMPLISH ⟨*encompass* a task⟩
— **en·com·pass·ment** \-pə-smənt\ *noun*

¹en·core \'än-ˌkōr, -ˌkȯr\ *noun* [French, still, again] (1712)
: a demand for repetition or reappearance made by an audience; *also* **:** a reappearance or additional performance in response to such a demand

²encore *transitive verb* **en·cored; en·cor·ing** (1748)
: to request an encore of or by

¹en·coun·ter \in-'kaun-tər, en-\ *verb* **en·coun·tered; en·coun·ter·ing** \-'kaun-t(ə-)riŋ\ [Middle English *encountren*, from Middle French *encontrer*, from Medieval Latin *incontrare*, from Late Latin *incontra* toward, from Latin *in-* + *contra* against — more at COUNTER] (14th century)
transitive verb
1 a : to meet as an adversary or enemy **b :** to engage in conflict with **2 :** to come upon face-to-face **3 :** to come upon especially unexpectedly
intransitive verb
: to meet especially by chance

²encounter *noun* (14th century)
1 a : a meeting especially between hostile factions or persons **b :** a sudden often violent clash **:** COMBAT **2 a :** a chance meeting **b :** a direct often momentary meeting **3 :** a coming into the vicinity of a celestial body ⟨the Martian *encounter* of a spacecraft⟩

encounter group *noun* (1967)
: a usually unstructured group that seeks to develop the capacity of the individual to express feelings and to form emotional ties by unrestrained confrontation of individuals

en·cour·age \in-'kər-ij, -'kə-rij, en-\ *transitive verb* **-aged; -ag·ing** [Middle English *encoragen*, from Middle French *encoragier*, from Old French, from *en-* + *corage* courage] (15th century)
1 : to inspire with courage, spirit, or hope **:** HEARTEN **2 :** to spur on **:** STIMULATE **3 :** to give help or patronage to **:** FOSTER ☆
synonym see HEARTEN
— **en·cour·ag·er** *noun*

en·cour·age·ment \-ij-mənt, -rij-\ *noun* (1568)
1 : the act of encouraging **:** the state of being encouraged **2 :** something that encourages

en·cour·ag·ing \-i-jiŋ, -ri-jiŋ\ *adjective* (1593)
: giving hope or promise **:** INSPIRITING
— **en·cour·ag·ing·ly** \-jiŋ-lē\ *adverb*

en·crim·son \in-'krim-zən\ *transitive verb* (1597)
: to make or dye crimson

en·croach \in-'krōch, en-\ *intransitive verb* [Middle English *encrochen* to get, seize, from Middle French *encrochier*, from Old French, from *en-* + *croc, croche* hook — more at CROCHET] (circa 1534)
1 : to enter by gradual steps or by stealth into the possessions or rights of another **2 :** to advance beyond the usual or proper limits ⟨the gradually *encroaching* sea⟩
synonym see TRESPASS
— **en·croach·er** *noun*
— **en·croach·ment** \-'krōch-mənt\ *noun*

en·crust \in-'krəst, iŋ-\ *verb* [probably from Latin *incrustare*, from *in-* + *crusta* crust] (1641)
transitive verb
: to cover, line, or overlay with or as if with a crust
intransitive verb
: to form a crust

en·crus·ta·tion \(ˌ)in-ˌkrəs-'tā-shən, ˌen-\ *variant of* INCRUSTATION

en·crypt \in-'kript, en-\ *transitive verb* [*en-* + *crypt-* (as in *cryptogram*)] (1944)
1 : ENCIPHER **2 :** ENCODE 1
— **en·cryp·tion** \-'krip-shən\ *noun*

en·cum·ber \in-'kəm-bər\ *transitive verb* **-cum·bered; -cum·ber·ing** \-b(ə-)riŋ\ [Middle English *encombren*, from Middle French *encombrer*, from Old French, from *en-* + (assumed) Old French *combre* dam, weir] (14th century)
1 : WEIGH DOWN, BURDEN **2 :** to impede or hamper the function or activity of **:** HINDER **3 :** to burden with a legal claim (as a mortgage) ⟨*encumber* an estate⟩

en·cum·brance \in-'kəm-brən(t)s\ *noun* (1535)
1 : something that encumbers **:** IMPEDIMENT **2 :** a claim (as a mortgage) against property

en·cum·branc·er \-brən(t)-sər\ *noun* (1858)
: one that holds an encumbrance

-en·cy \ən(t)-sē, ᵊn(t)-\ *noun suffix* [Middle English *-encie*, from Latin *-entia* — more at -ENCE]
: quality or state ⟨despond*ency*⟩

¹en·cyc·li·cal \in-'si-kli-kəl, en-\ *adjective* [Late Latin *encyclicus*, from Greek *enkyklios* circular, general, from *en* in + *kyklos* circle — more at IN, WHEEL] (1647)
: addressed to all the individuals of a group **:** GENERAL

²encyclical *noun* (1837)
: an encyclical letter; *specifically* **:** a papal letter to the bishops of the church as a whole or to those in one country

en·cy·clo·pe·dia *also* **en·cy·clo·pae·dia** \in-ˌsī-klə-'pē-dē-ə\ *noun* [Medieval Latin *encyclopaedia* course of general education, from Greek *enkyklios* + *paideia* education, child rearing, from *paid-, pais* child — more at FEW] (1644)
: a work that contains information on all branches of knowledge or treats comprehensively a particular branch of knowledge usually in articles arranged alphabetically often by subject

en·cy·clo·pe·dic *also* **en·cy·clo·pae·dic** \-'pē-dik\ *adjective* (1824)
: of, relating to, or suggestive of an encyclopedia or its methods of treating or covering a subject **:** COMPREHENSIVE ⟨an *encyclopedic* mind⟩ ⟨an *encyclopedic* collection of armor⟩
— **en·cy·clo·pe·di·cal·ly** \-di-k(ə-)lē\ *adverb*

en·cy·clo·pe·dism \-'pē-ˌdi-zəm\ *noun* (1833)
: the quality or state of being encyclopedic

en·cy·clo·pe·dist \-'pē-dist\ *noun* (1651)
1 : one who compiles or writes for an encyclopedia **2** *often capitalized* **:** one of the writers of a French encyclopedia (1751–80) who were

identified with the Enlightenment and advocated deism and scientific rationalism

en·cyst \in-'sist, en-\ (1845)
transitive verb
: to enclose in a cyst
intransitive verb
: to form or become enclosed in a cyst
— **en·cyst·ment** \-'sis(t)-mənt\ *noun*

¹end \'end\ *noun* [Middle English *ende*, from Old English; akin to Old High German *enti* end, Latin *ante* before, Greek *anti* against] (before 12th century)
1 a : the part of an area that lies at the boundary **b** (1) **:** a point that marks the extent of something (2) **:** the point where something ceases to exist ⟨world without *end*⟩ **c :** the extreme or last part lengthwise **:** TIP **d :** the terminal unit of something spatial that is marked off by units **e :** a player stationed at the extremity of a line (as in football) **2 a :** cessation of a course of action, pursuit, or activity **b :** DEATH, DESTRUCTION **c** (1) **:** the ultimate state (2) **:** RESULT, ISSUE **3 :** something incomplete, fragmentary, or undersized **:** REMNANT **4 a :** an outcome worked toward **:** PURPOSE ⟨the *end* of poetry is to be poetry —R. P. Warren⟩ **b :** the object by virtue of or for the sake of which an event takes place **5 a :** a share in an undertaking ⟨kept your *end* up⟩ **b :** a particular operation or aspect of an undertaking or organization ⟨the sales *end* of the business⟩ **6 :** something that is extreme **:** ULTIMATE — used with *the* **7 :** a period of action or turn in any of various sports events (as archery or lawn bowling)
synonym see INTENTION
— **end·ed** \'en-dəd\ *adjective*
— **in the end :** AFTER ALL, ULTIMATELY
— **no end :** EXCEEDINGLY
— **on end :** without a stop or letup ⟨it rained for days *on end*⟩

²end (before 12th century)
transitive verb
1 a : to bring to an end **b :** DESTROY **2 :** to make up the end of
intransitive verb

1 a : to come to an end **b :** to reach a specified ultimate rank or situation — usually used with *up* ⟨*ended* up as a colonel⟩
2 : DIE
synonym see CLOSE
³**end** *adjective* (13th century)
: FINAL, ULTIMATE ⟨*end* results⟩ ⟨*end* markets⟩ ⟨*end* product⟩
⁴**end** *transitive verb* [probably alteration of English dialect *in* (to harvest)] (1607)
dialect English **:** to put (grain or hay) into a barn or stack
end- *or* **endo-** *combining form* [French, from Greek, from *endon* within; akin to Greek *en* in, Old Latin *indu*, Hittite *andan* within — more at IN]
1 : within **:** inside ⟨*endo*skeleton⟩ — compare ECT-, EXO-
2 : taking in ⟨*endo*thermic⟩
en·dam·age \in-'da-mij\ *transitive verb* [Middle English] (14th century)
: to cause loss or damage to
end·amoe·ba \,en-də-'mē-bə\ *noun* [New Latin, genus name] (circa 1864)
: any of a genus (*Endamoeba*) comprising amoebas parasitic in the intestines of insects — compare ENTAMOEBA
en·dan·ger \in-'dān-jər\ *verb* **-dan·gered; -dan·ger·ing** \-'dānj-riŋ, -'dān-jə-\ (1509)
transitive verb
: to bring into danger or peril
intransitive verb
: to create a dangerous situation ⟨driving to *endanger*⟩
— **en·dan·ger·ment** \-'dān-jər-mənt\ *noun*
en·dan·gered *adjective* (1964)
: being or relating to an endangered species ⟨an *endangered* bird⟩ ⟨put on the *endangered* list⟩
endangered species *noun* (1964)
: a species threatened with extinction; *broadly* **:** anyone or anything whose continued existence is threatened
en·darch \'en-,därk\ *adjective* (circa 1900)
: formed or taking place from inner cells outward ⟨*endarch* xylem⟩
end around *noun* (1926)
: a football play in which an offensive end comes behind the line of scrimmage to take a handoff and attempts to carry the ball around the opposite flank
end·ar·ter·ec·to·my \,en-,där-tə-'rek-tə-mē\ *noun, plural* **-mies** [New Latin *endarterium* intima of an artery (from *end-* + *arteria* artery) + English *-ectomy*] (1950)
: surgical removal of the inner layer of an artery when thickened and atheromatous or occluded (as by intimal plaques)
end·brain \'en(d)-,brān\ *noun* (1927)
: TELENCEPHALON
end brush *noun* (circa 1891)
: END PLATE
en·dear \in-'dir\ *transitive verb* (1580)
1 *obsolete* **:** to make higher in cost, value, or estimation
2 : to cause to become beloved or admired
— **en·dear·ing·ly** \-iŋ-lē\ *adverb*
en·dear·ment \in-'dir-mənt\ *noun* (1610)
1 : a word or an act (as a caress) expressing affection
2 : the act or process of endearing
¹**en·deav·or** \in-'de-vər\ *verb* **en·deav·ored; en·deav·or·ing** \-v(ə-)riŋ\ [Middle English *endeveren* to exert oneself, from *en-* + *dever* duty — more at DEVOIR] (15th century)
transitive verb
1 *archaic* **:** to strive to achieve or reach
2 : to attempt (as the fulfillment of an obligation) by exertion of effort ⟨*endeavors* to finish the race⟩
intransitive verb
: to work with set purpose
synonym see ATTEMPT
²**endeavor** *noun* (15th century)
1 : serious determined effort

2 : activity directed toward a goal **:** ENTERPRISE ⟨fields of *endeavor*⟩
en·deav·our *chiefly British variant of* ENDEAVOR
¹**en·dem·ic** \en-'de-mik, in-\ *adjective* [French *endémique*, from *endémie* endemic disease, from Greek *endēmia* action of dwelling, from *endēmos* endemic, from *en* in + *dēmos* people, populace — more at DEMAGOGUE] (1759)
1 a : belonging or native to a particular people or country **b :** characteristic of or prevalent in a particular field, area, or environment ⟨problems *endemic* to translation⟩ ⟨the self-indulgence *endemic* in the film industry⟩
2 : restricted or peculiar to a locality or region ⟨*endemic* diseases⟩ ⟨an *endemic* species⟩
synonym see NATIVE
— **en·dem·i·cal·ly** \-'de-mi-k(ə-)lē\ *adverb*
— **en·de·mic·i·ty** \,en-,de-'mi-sə-tē, -də-'mi-\ *noun*
— **en·de·mism** \'en-də-,mi-zəm\ *noun*
²**endemic** *noun* (1926)
: an endemic organism
en·der·gon·ic \,en-,dər-'gä-nik\ *adjective* [*end-* + Greek *ergon* work — more at WORK] (1940)
: ENDOTHERMIC 1 ⟨an *endergonic* biochemical reaction⟩
end·ex·ine \(,)en-'dek-,sēn, -,sīn\ *noun* (1947)
: an inner membranous layer of the exine
end·game \'en(d)-,gām\ *noun* (1884)
: the stage of a chess game after major reduction of forces; *also* **:** the final stages of some action
end·ing \'en-diŋ\ *noun* (before 12th century)
: something that constitutes an end: as **a :** CONCLUSION **b :** one or more letters or syllables added to a word base especially in inflection
endite *variant of* INDITE
en·dive \'en-,dīv, ,än-'dēv\ *noun* [Middle English, from Middle French, from Late Latin *endivia*, from Late Greek *entybion*, from Latin *intubus*] (14th century)
1 : an annual or biennial composite herb (*Cichorium endivia*) widely cultivated as a salad plant — called also *escarole*
2 : the developing crown of chicory when blanched for use as a vegetable or in salads by growing in darkness or semidarkness
end·leaf \'end-,lēf\ *noun* (1888)
: ENDPAPER
end·less \'en(d)-ləs\ *adjective* (before 12th century)
1 : being or seeming to be without end ⟨*endless* speech⟩
2 : extremely numerous ⟨all the multiplied, *endless*, nameless iniquities —Edmund Burke⟩
3 : joined at the ends ⟨an *endless* chain⟩
— **end·less·ly** *adverb*
— **end·less·ness** *noun*
end line *noun* (1893)
: a line marking an end or boundary especially of a playing area: as **a :** a line at either end of a football field 10 yards beyond and parallel to the goal line **b :** a line at either end of a court (as in basketball or tennis) perpendicular to the sidelines
end·long \'end-,lòŋ\ *adverb* [Middle English *endelong*, alteration of *andlong*, from Old English *andlang* along, from *andlang*, preposition — more at ALONG] (13th century)
archaic **:** LENGTHWISE
end man *noun* (1865)
: a man at each end of the line of performers in a minstrel show who engages in comic repartee with the interlocutor
end·most \'en(d)-,mōst\ *adjective* (before 12th century)
: situated at the very end
end·note \'en(d)-,nōt\ *noun* (1926)
: a note placed at the end of the text
en·do·bi·ot·ic \,en-dō-,bī-'ä-tik, -bē-\ *adjective* [International Scientific Vocabulary] (circa 1900)

: dwelling within the cells or tissues of a host ⟨*endobiotic* fungi⟩
en·do·car·di·al \,en-dō-'kär-dē-əl\ *adjective* (circa 1849)
1 : situated within the heart
2 : of or relating to the endocardium
en·do·car·di·tis \-,kär-'dī-təs\ *noun* [New Latin] (circa 1839)
: inflammation of the lining of the heart and its valves
en·do·car·di·um \-'kär-dē-əm\ *noun, plural* **-dia** \-dē-ə\ [New Latin, from *end-* + Greek *kardia* heart] (circa 1864)
: a thin serous membrane lining the cavities of the heart
en·do·carp \'en-də-,kärp\ *noun* [French *endocarpe*] (1830)
: the inner layer of the pericarp of a fruit (as an apple or orange) when it consists of two or more layers of different texture or consistency

en·do·cast \'en-dō-,kast\ *noun* (1949)
: ENDOCRANIAL CAST
en·do·chon·dral \,en-də-'kän-drəl\ *adjective* (1882)
: relating to, formed by, or being ossification that takes place from centers arising in cartilage and involves deposition of lime salts in the cartilage matrix followed by secondary absorption and replacement by true bony tissue

endocarp (cross section of a cherry): *1* exocarp, *2* mesocarp, *3* endocarp, *4* seed; *1, 2,* and *3* together form the pericarp

en·do·cra·ni·al cast \,en-də-,krā-nē-əl-\ *noun* (1923)
: a cast of the cranial cavity showing the approximate shape of the brain
¹**en·do·crine** \'en-də-krən, -,krīn, -,krēn\ *adjective* [International Scientific Vocabulary *end-* + Greek *krinein* to separate — more at CERTAIN] (circa 1911)
1 : secreting internally; *specifically* **:** producing secretions that are distributed in the body by way of the bloodstream ⟨an *endocrine* system⟩
2 : of, relating to, affecting, or resembling an endocrine gland or secretion ⟨*endocrine* tumors⟩
²**endocrine** *noun* (1922)
1 : HORMONE
2 : ENDOCRINE GLAND
endocrine gland *noun* (1914)
: a gland (as the thyroid or the pituitary) that produces an endocrine secretion — called also *ductless gland*
en·do·cri·no·log·ic \,en-də-,kri-nᵊl-'ä-jik, -,krī-, -,krē-\ *or* **en·do·cri·no·log·i·cal** \-ji-kəl\ *adjective* (circa 1934)
: involving or relating to the endocrine glands or secretions or to endocrinology
en·do·cri·nol·o·gy \,en-də-kri-'nä-lə-jē, -,krī-\ *noun* [International Scientific Vocabulary] (circa 1913)
: a science dealing with the endocrine glands
— **en·do·cri·nol·o·gist** \-jist\ *noun*
en·do·cy·to·sis \-sī-'tō-səs\ *noun* [New Latin, from *end-* + *-cytosis* (as in *phagocytosis*)] (1963)
: incorporation of substances into a cell by phagocytosis or pinocytosis
— **en·do·cy·tot·ic** \-'tä-tik\ *adjective*
en·do·derm \'en-də-,dərm\ *noun* [French *endoderme*, from *end-* + Greek *derma* skin — more at DERM-] (1861)
: the innermost of the germ layers of an embryo that is the source of the epithelium of the

digestive tract and its derivatives; *also* **:** a tissue that is derived from this germ layer — compare HYPOBLAST

— **en·do·der·mal** \ˌen-də-ˈder-məl\ *adjective*

en·do·der·mis \ˌen-də-ˈder-məs\ *noun* [New Latin] (1884)
: the innermost tissue of the cortex in many roots and stems

end·odon·tics \-ˈdän-tiks\ *noun plural but singular in construction* [*end-* + *odont-* + *-ics*] (1946)
: a branch of dentistry concerned with diseases of the pulp

— **end·odon·tic** \-ˈdän-tik\ *adjective*
— **end·odon·ti·cal·ly** \-ˈdän-ti-k(ə-)lē\ *adverb*
— **end·odon·tist** \-ˈdän-tist\ *noun*

en·do·en·zyme \ˌen-dō-ˈen-ˌzīm\ *noun* [International Scientific Vocabulary] (circa 1909)
: an enzyme that functions inside the cell

en·do·er·gic \ˌen-dō-ˈər-jik\ *adjective* (1940)
: absorbing energy **:** ENDOTHERMIC ⟨*endoergic* nuclear reactions⟩

en·dog·a·my \en-ˈdä-gə-mē\ *noun* (1865)
: marriage within a specific group as required by custom or law

— **en·dog·a·mous** \-məs\ *adjective*

en·do·gen·ic \ˌen-də-ˈje-nik\ *adjective* (circa 1904)
1 : of or relating to metamorphism taking place within a planet or moon
2 : ENDOGENOUS

en·dog·e·nous \en-ˈdä-jə-nəs\ *adjective* (1830)
1 : growing or produced by growth from deep tissue ⟨*endogenous* plant roots⟩
2 a : caused by factors inside the organism or system ⟨an *endogenous* psychic depression⟩ ⟨*endogenous* business cycles⟩ **b :** produced or synthesized within the organism or system ⟨an *endogenous* hormone⟩

— **en·dog·e·nous·ly** *adverb*

en·do·lith·ic \ˌen-də-ˈli-thik\ *adjective* (1886)
: living within or penetrating deeply into stony substances (as rocks, coral, or mollusk shells) ⟨*endolithic* lichens⟩

en·do·lymph \ˈen-də-ˌlim(p)f\ *noun* [International Scientific Vocabulary] (circa 1839)
: the watery fluid in the membranous labyrinth of the ear

— **en·do·lym·phat·ic** \ˌen-də-lim-ˈfa-tik\ *adjective*

en·do·me·tri·o·sis \ˌen-dō-ˌmē-trē-ˈō-səs\ *noun* [New Latin] (1925)
: the presence and growth of functioning endometrial tissue in places other than the uterus that often results in severe pain and infertility

en·do·me·tri·tis \ˌen-dō-mə-ˈtrī-təs\ *noun* [New Latin] (1872)
: inflammation of the endometrium

en·do·me·tri·um \-ˈmē-trē-əm\ *noun, plural* **-tria** \-trē-ə\ [New Latin, from *end-* + Greek *mētra* uterus, from *mētr-*, *mētēr* mother — more at MOTHER] (circa 1882)
: the mucous membrane lining the uterus

— **en·do·me·tri·al** \-trē-əl\ *adjective*

en·do·mi·to·sis \-mī-ˈtō-səs\ *noun* [New Latin] (1942)
: division of chromosomes not followed by nuclear division that results in an increased number of chromosomes in the cell

— **en·do·mi·tot·ic** \-mī-ˈtä-tik\ *adjective*

en·do·mix·is \-ˈmik-səs\ *noun* [New Latin, from *end-* + Greek *mixis* act of mixing, from *mignynai* to mix — more at MIX] (1914)
: a periodic nuclear reorganization in ciliated protozoans

en·do·morph \ˈen-də-ˌmorf\ *noun* [*endo*derm + *-morph*] (1940)
: an endomorphic individual

en·do·mor·phic \ˌen-də-ˈmor-fik\ *adjective* [*endo*derm + *-morphic*; from the predominance in such types of structures developed from the endoderm] (1940)
1 : of or relating to the component in W. H. Sheldon's classification of body types that measures the massiveness of the digestive viscera and the body's degree of roundedness and softness
2 : having a heavy rounded body build often with a marked tendency to become fat

— **en·do·mor·phy** \ˈen-də-ˌmor-fē\ *noun*

en·do·mor·phism \ˌen-də-ˈmor-fi-zəm\ *noun* (1909)
: a homomorphism that maps a mathematical set into itself — compare ISOMORPHISM

en·do·nu·cle·ase \ˌen-dō-ˈnü-klē-ˌās, -,āz, -ˈnyü-\ *noun* (1962)
: an enzyme that breaks down a nucleotide chain into two or more shorter chains by cleaving it at points not adjacent to the end — compare EXONUCLEASE

en·do·nu·cleo·lyt·ic \-ˌnü-klē-ō-ˈli-tik, -ˌnyü-\ *adjective* [*end-* + *nucleo-* + *-lytic*] (1967)
: cleaving a nucleotide chain at an internal point ⟨*endonucleolytic* nicks⟩

en·do·par·a·site \-ˈpar-ə-ˌsīt\ *noun* [International Scientific Vocabulary] (circa 1882)
: a parasite that lives in the internal organs or tissues of its host

— **en·do·par·a·sit·ic** \-ˌpar-ə-ˈsi-tik\ *adjective*
— **en·do·par·a·sit·ism** \-ˈpar-ə-ˌsī-ˌti-zəm, -sə-ˌti-\ *noun*

en·do·pep·ti·dase \-ˈpep-tə-ˌdās, -ˌdāz\ *noun* (1936)
: any of a group of enzymes that hydrolyze peptide bonds within the long chains of protein molecules **:** PROTEASE — compare EXOPEPTIDASE

en·do·per·ox·ide \-pə-ˈräk-ˌsīd\ *noun* (1962)
: any of various biosynthetic intermediates in the formation of prostaglandins

en·do·phyte \ˈen-də-ˌfīt\ *noun* [International Scientific Vocabulary] (1854)
: a plant living within another plant

— **en·do·phyt·ic** \ˌen-də-ˈfi-tik\ *adjective*

en·do·plasm \ˈen-də-ˌpla-zəm\ *noun* [International Scientific Vocabulary] (1882)
: the inner relatively fluid part of the cytoplasm

— **en·do·plas·mic** \ˌen-də-ˈplaz-mik\ *adjective*

endoplasmic reticulum *noun* (1947)
: a system of interconnected vesicular and lamellar cytoplasmic membranes that functions especially in the transport of materials within the cell and that is studded with ribosomes in some places — see CELL illustration

en·dop·o·dite \en-ˈdä-pə-ˌdīt\ *noun* [International Scientific Vocabulary] (1870)
: the mesial or internal branch of a typical limb of a crustacean

en·do·poly·ploidy \ˌen-dō-ˈpä-li-ˌplói-dē\ *noun* (1945)
: a polyploid state in which the chromosomes have divided repeatedly without subsequent division of the nucleus or cell

— **en·do·poly·ploid** \-ˌplói\ *adjective*

end organ *noun* (1878)
: a structure forming the end of a neural path and consisting of an effector or a receptor with its associated nerve terminations

en·dor·phin \en-ˈdor-fən\ *noun* [International Scientific Vocabulary *endo*genous + *mor*phine] (1976)
: any of a group of proteins with potent analgesic properties that occur naturally in the brain — compare ENKEPHALIN

en·dorse \in-ˈdors, en-\ *transitive verb* **en·dorsed; en·dors·ing** [alteration of obsolete *endoss*, from Middle English *endosen*, from Middle French *endosser*, from Old French, to put on the back, from *en-* + *dos* back, from Latin *dorsum*] (1581)
1 a : to write on the back of; *especially* **:** to sign one's name as payee on the back of (a check) in order to obtain the cash or credit represented on the face **b :** to inscribe (one's signature) on a check, bill, or note **c :** to inscribe (as an official document) with a title or memorandum **d :** to make over to another (the value represented in a check, bill, or note) by inscribing one's name on the document **e :** to acknowledge receipt of (a sum specified) by one's signature on a document
2 : to approve openly ⟨*endorse* an idea⟩; *especially* **:** to express support or approval of publicly and definitely ⟨*endorse* a mayoral candidate⟩

synonym see APPROVE

— **en·dors·able** \-ˈdor-sə-bəl\ *adjective*
— **en·dors·ee** \in-ˌdor-ˈsē, ˌen-\ *noun*
— **en·dors·er** \in-ˈdor-sər\ *noun*

en·dorse·ment \in-ˈdors-mənt, en-\ *noun* (1547)
1 : the act or process of endorsing
2 a : something that is written in the process of endorsing **b :** a provision added to an insurance contract altering its scope or application
3 : SANCTION, APPROVAL

en·do·scope \ˈen-də-ˌskōp\ *noun* [International Scientific Vocabulary] (1861)
: an instrument for visualizing the interior of a hollow organ (as the rectum or urethra)

— **en·dos·co·py** \en-ˈdäs-kə-pē\ *noun*

en·do·scop·ic \ˌen-də-ˈskä-pik\ *adjective* (1861)
: of, relating to, or performed by means of an endoscope or endoscopy

— **en·do·scop·i·cal·ly** \-pi-k(ə-)lē\ *adverb*

en·do·skel·e·ton \ˌen-dō-ˈske-lə-tᵊn\ *noun* (circa 1847)
: an internal skeleton or supporting framework in an animal

— **en·do·skel·e·tal** \-lə-tᵊl\ *adjective*

en·do·sperm \ˈen-dō-ˌspərm\ *noun* [French *endosperme*, from *end-* + Greek *sperma* seed — more at SPERM] (circa 1850)
: a nutritive tissue in seed plants formed within the embryo sac

endosperm nucleus *noun* (circa 1902)
: the triploid nucleus formed in the embryo sac of a seed plant by fusion of a sperm nucleus with two polar nuclei or with a nucleus formed by the prior fusion of the polar nuclei

en·do·spore \ˈen-dō-ˌspōr, -ˌspór\ *noun* [International Scientific Vocabulary] (1875)
: an asexual spore developed within the cell especially in bacteria

end·os·te·al \en-ˈdäs-tē-əl\ *adjective* (circa 1868)
1 : of or relating to the endosteum
2 : located within bone or cartilage

— **end·os·te·al·ly** *adverb*

end·os·te·um \en-ˈdäs-tē-əm\ *noun, plural* **-tea** \-tē-ə\ [New Latin, from *end-* + Greek *osteon* bone — more at OSSEOUS] (circa 1881)
: the layer of vascular connective tissue lining the medullary cavities of bone

en·do·style \ˈen-dō-ˌstīl\ *noun* [International Scientific Vocabulary *end-* + Greek *stylos* pillar — more at STEER] (1854)
: a pair of parallel longitudinal folds projecting into the pharyngeal cavity and bounding a furrow lined with glandular ciliated cells in lower chordates (as the tunicates)

en·do·sul·fan \ˌen-də-ˈsəl-fən, -ˌfan\ *noun* [*endo-* + *sulf-* + ³*-an*] (1962)
: a brownish crystalline insecticide $C_9H_6Cl_6O_3S$ that is used in the control of numerous crop insects and some mites

en·do·sym·bi·o·sis \ˌen-dō-ˌsim-bī-ˈō-səs, -bē-\ *noun* (circa 1940)
: symbiosis in which a symbiont dwells within the body of its symbiotic partner

— **en·do·sym·bi·ont** \-ˈsim-bī-ˌänt, -bē-\ *noun*
— **en·do·sym·bi·ot·ic** \-ˌsim-bī-ˈä-tik, -bē-\ *adjective*

en·do·the·ci·um \ˌen-dō-ˈthē-s(h)ē-əm\ *noun, plural* **-cia** \-s(h)ē-ə\ [New Latin] (1832)

: the inner lining of a mature anther

en·do·the·li·o·ma \-ˌthē-lē-'ō-mə\ *noun, plural* **-o·mas** *or* **-o·ma·ta** \-mə-tə\ [New Latin] (1880)

: a tumor developing from endothelial tissue

en·do·the·li·um \ˌen-də-'thē-lē-əm\ *noun, plural* **-lia** \-lē-ə\ [New Latin, from *end-* + *-thelium* (as in *epithelium*)] (1872)

1 : an epithelium of mesodermal origin composed of a single layer of thin flattened cells that lines internal body cavities

2 : the inner layer of the seed coat of some plants

— **en·do·the·li·al** \-lē-əl\ *adjective*

en·do·therm \'en-dō-ˌthərm\ *noun* (1946)

: a warm-blooded animal

en·do·ther·mic \ˌen-də-'thər-mik\ *adjective* [International Scientific Vocabulary] (1884)

1 : characterized by or formed with absorption of heat

2 : WARM-BLOODED

en·do·ther·my \'en-də-ˌthər-mē\ *noun* (1922)

: physiological regulation of body temperature by metabolic means; *especially* : the property or state of being warm-blooded

en·do·tox·in \ˌen-dō-'täk-sən\ *noun* [International Scientific Vocabulary] (1904)

: a toxin of internal origin; *specifically* : a poisonous substance present in bacteria (as the causative agent of typhoid fever) but separable from the cell body only on its disintegration

— **en·do·tox·ic** \-sik\ *adjective*

en·do·tra·che·al \-'trā-kē-əl\ *adjective* (1910)

1 : placed within the trachea ⟨an *endotracheal* tube⟩

2 : applied or effected through the trachea

en·do·tro·phic \ˌen-də-'trō-fik\ *adjective* (1899)

of a mycorrhiza : penetrating into the associated root and ramifying between the cells — compare ECTOTROPHIC

en·dow \in-'dau̇, en-\ *transitive verb* [Middle English, from Anglo-French *endouer,* from Middle French *en-* + *douer* to endow, from Latin *dotare,* from *dot-, dos* gift, dowry — more at DATE] (15th century)

1 : to furnish with an income; *especially* : to make a grant of money providing for the continuing support or maintenance of ⟨*endow* a hospital⟩

2 : to furnish with a dower

3 : to provide with something freely or naturally ⟨*endowed* with a good sense of humor⟩

en·dow·ment \-mənt\ *noun* (15th century)

1 : the act or process of endowing

2 : something that is endowed; *specifically* : the part of an institution's income derived from donations

3 : natural capacity, power, or ability

end·pa·per \'en(d)-ˌpā-pər\ *noun* (1818)

: a once-folded sheet of paper having one leaf pasted flat against the inside of the front or back cover of a book and the other pasted at the base to the first or last page

end plate *noun* (1878)

: a complex terminal treelike branching of a motor nerve cell

end point *noun* (1899)

1 : a point marking the completion of a process or stage of a process; *especially* : a point in a titration at which a definite effect (as a color change) is observed

2 *usually* **end·point** : either of two points or values that mark the ends of a line segment or interval; *also* : a point that marks the end of a ray

en·drin \'en-drən\ *noun* [*end-* + dield*rin*] (1952)

: a chlorinated hydrocarbon insecticide $C_{12}H_8Cl_6O$ that is a stereoisomer of dieldrin and resembles dieldrin in toxicity

end run *noun* (1902)

1 : a football play in which the ballcarrier attempts to run wide around the end of the line; *specifically* : SWEEP 3e

2 : an evasive trick or maneuver

end–stopped \'en(d)-ˌstäpt\ *adjective* (1877)

: marked by a logical or rhetorical pause at the end ⟨an *end-stopped* line of verse⟩ — compare RUN-ON

end table *noun* (1851)

: a small table usually about the height of the arm of a chair that is used beside a larger piece of furniture (as a sofa)

en·due \in-'dü, -'dyü, en-\ *transitive verb* **en·dued; en·du·ing** [Middle English, from Middle French *enduire* to bring in, introduce, from Latin *inducere* — more at INDUCE] (15th century)

1 : PROVIDE, ENDOW

2 : IMBUE, TRANSFUSE

3 [Middle English *induen;* influenced by Latin *induere* to put on] : PUT ON, DON

en·dur·able \in-'du̇r-ə-bəl, -'dyu̇r-, en-\ *adjective* (1800)

: capable of being endured : BEARABLE

— **en·dur·ably** \-blē\ *adverb*

en·dur·ance \in-'du̇r-ən(t)s, -'dyu̇r-, en-\ *noun* (15th century)

1 : PERMANENCE, DURATION

2 : the ability to withstand hardship or adversity; *especially* : the ability to sustain a prolonged stressful effort or activity ⟨a marathon runner's *endurance*⟩

3 : the act or an instance of enduring or suffering ⟨*endurance* of many hardships⟩

en·dure \in-'du̇r, -'dyu̇r, en-\ *verb* **en·dured; en·dur·ing** [Middle English, from Middle French *endurer,* from (assumed) Vulgar Latin *indurare,* from Latin, to harden, from *in-* + *durare* to harden, endure — more at DURING] (14th century)

transitive verb

1 : to undergo (as a hardship) especially without giving in : SUFFER

2 : to regard with acceptance or tolerance ⟨could not *endure* noisy children⟩

intransitive verb

1 : to continue in the same state : LAST

2 : to remain firm under suffering or misfortune without yielding

synonym see BEAR, CONTINUE

en·dur·ing *adjective* (15th century)

: LASTING, DURABLE

— **en·dur·ing·ly** \-'d(y)u̇r-iŋ-lē\ *adverb*

— **en·dur·ing·ness** *noun*

en·duro \in-'du̇r-(ˌ)ō, -'dyu̇r-\ *noun, plural* **en·dur·os** [*endurance* + *-o* (Italian or Spanish masculine noun ending)] (1935)

: a long race (as for automobiles or motorcycles) stressing endurance rather than speed

end user *noun* (circa 1945)

: the ultimate consumer of a finished product

end·ways \'en-ˌdwāz\ *adverb or adjective* (circa 1608)

1 : in or toward the direction of the ends : LENGTHWISE ⟨*endways* pressure⟩

2 : with the end forward (as toward the observer)

3 : on end : UPRIGHT ⟨boxes set *endways*⟩

end·wise \'en-ˌdwīz\ *adverb or adjective* (1657)

: ENDWAYS

En·dym·i·on \en-'di-mē-ən\ *noun* [Latin, from Greek *Endymiōn*]

: a beautiful youth loved by Selene in Greek mythology

end zone *noun* (circa 1916)

: the area at either end of a football field between the goal line and the end line

-ene \ˌēn\ *noun suffix* [International Scientific Vocabulary, from Greek *-ēnē,* feminine of *-ēnos,* adjective suffix]

: unsaturated carbon compound ⟨benz*ene*⟩; *especially* : carbon compound with one double bond ⟨ethyl*ene*⟩

en·e·ma \'e-nə-mə\ *noun, plural* **enemas** *also* **ene·ma·ta** \ˌe-nə-'mä-tə, 'e-nə-mə-tə\ [Late Latin, from Greek, from *enienai* to inject, from *en-* + *hienai* to send — more at JET] (15th century)

1 : the injection of liquid into the intestine by way of the anus

2 : material for injection as an enema

en·e·my \'e-nə-mē\ *noun, plural* **-mies** [Middle English *enemi,* from Old French, from Latin *inimicus,* from *in-* ¹*in-* + *amicus* friend — more at AMIABLE] (13th century)

1 : one that is antagonistic to another; *especially* : one seeking to injure, overthrow, or confound an opponent

2 : something harmful or deadly

3 a : a military adversary **b** : a hostile unit or force

en·er·get·ic \ˌe-nər-'je-tik\ *adjective* [Greek *energētikos,* from *energein* to be active, from *energos*] (1651)

1 : operating with or marked by vigor or effect

2 : marked by energy : STRENUOUS

3 : of or relating to energy ⟨*energetic* equation⟩

synonym see VIGOROUS

— **en·er·get·i·cal·ly** \-ti-k(ə-)lē\ *adverb*

en·er·get·ics \-tiks\ *noun plural but singular in construction* (1855)

1 : a branch of mechanics that deals primarily with energy and its transformations

2 : the total energy relations and transformations of a physical, chemical, or biological system ⟨the *energetics* of an ecological community⟩

en·er·gise *British variant of* ENERGIZE

en·er·gize \'e-nər-ˌjīz\ *verb* **-gized; -giz·ing** (1752)

intransitive verb

: to put forth energy : ACT

transitive verb

1 : to make energetic, vigorous, or active

2 : to impart energy to

3 : to apply voltage to

— **en·er·gi·za·tion** \ˌe-nər-ˌjī-'zā-shən\ *noun*

— **en·er·giz·er** *noun*

en·er·gy \'e-nər-jē\ *noun, plural* **-gies** [Late Latin *energia,* from Greek *energeia* activity, from *energos* active, from *en* in + *ergon* work — more at WORK] (1599)

1 a : dynamic quality ⟨narrative *energy*⟩ **b** : the capacity of acting or being active ⟨intellectual *energy*⟩

2 : vigorous exertion of power : EFFORT ⟨investing time and *energy*⟩

3 : the capacity for doing work

4 : usable power (as heat or electricity); *also* : the resources for producing such power

synonym see POWER

energy level *noun* (1910)

: one of the stable states of constant energy that may be assumed by a physical system — used especially of the quantum states of electrons in atoms and of nuclei; called also *energy state*

¹ener·vate \i-'nər-vət\ *adjective* (1603)

: lacking physical, mental, or moral vigor : ENERVATED

²en·er·vate \'e-nər-ˌvāt\ *transitive verb* **-vat·ed; -vat·ing** [Latin *enervatus,* past participle of *enervare,* from *e-* + *nervus* sinew — more at NERVE] (1614)

1 : to reduce the mental or moral vigor of

2 : to lessen the vitality or strength of

synonym see UNNERVE

— **en·er·va·tion** \ˌe-nər-'vā-shən\ *noun*

en·fant ter·ri·ble \ä(n)-fä(n)-te-rēbl°\ *noun, plural* **enfants terribles** *same*\ [French, literally, terrifying child] (1851)

1 a : a child whose inopportune remarks cause embarrassment **b** : a person known for shocking remarks or outrageous behavior

\ə\ abut \ᵊ\ kitten \ər\ further \a\ ash \ā\ ace \ä\ mop, mar \au̇\ out \ch\ chin \e\ bet \ē\ easy \g\ go \i\ hit \ī\ ice \j\ job \ŋ\ sing \ō\ go \ȯ\ law \ȯi\ boy \th\ thin \t̲h̲\ the \ü\ loot \u̇\ foot \y\ yet \zh\ vision *see also* Guide to Pronunciation

2 : a usually young and successful person who is strikingly unorthodox, innovative, or avant-garde

en·fee·ble \in-'fē-bəl, en-\ *transitive verb* **en·fee·bled; en·fee·bling** \-b(ə-)liŋ\ [Middle English *enfeblen*, from Middle French *enfeblir*, from Old French, from *en-* + *feble* feeble] (14th century)
: to make feeble : deprive of strength
synonym see WEAKEN
— **en·fee·ble·ment** \-bəl-mənt\ *noun*

en·feoff \in-'fef, -'fēf, en-\ *transitive verb* [Middle English *enfeoffen*, from Anglo-French *enfeoffer*, from Old French *en-* + *fief* fief] (15th century)
: to invest with a fief or fee
— **en·feoff·ment** \-mənt\ *noun*

en·fet·ter \in-'fe-tər, en-\ *transitive verb* (1599)
: to bind in fetters : ENCHAIN

en·fe·ver \in-'fē-vər, en-\ *transitive verb* (1647)
: FEVER

En·field rifle \'en-,fēld-\ *noun* [Enfield, England] (1854)
: a .30 caliber bolt-action repeating rifle used by U.S. and British troops in World War I

1en·fi·lade \'en-fə-,lād, -,läd\ *noun* [French, from *enfiler* to thread, enfilade, from Old French, to thread, from *en-* + *fil* thread — more at FILE] (circa 1730)
1 : an interconnected group of rooms arranged usually in a row with each room opening into the next
2 : gunfire directed from a flanking position along the length of an enemy battle line

2enfilade *transitive verb* **-lad·ed; -lad·ing** (1706)
: to rake or be in a position to rake with gunfire in a lengthwise direction

enflame *variant of* INFLAME

en·fleu·rage \,äⁿ-,flər-'äzh\ *noun* [French, from *enfleurer* to saturate with the perfume of flowers, from *en-* 1en- + *fleur* flower, from Old French *flor* — more at FLOWER] (1855)
: a process of extracting perfumes by exposing absorbents to the exhalations of flowers

en·fold \in-'fōld, en-\ *transitive verb* (circa 1674)
1 a : to cover with or as if with folds : ENVELOP **b** : to surround with a covering : CONTAIN
2 : to clasp within the arms : EMBRACE

en·force \in-'fōrs, -'fòrs, en-\ *transitive verb* [Middle English, from Middle French *enforcier*, from Old French, from *en-* + *force* force] (14th century)
1 : to give force to : STRENGTHEN
2 : to urge with energy
3 : CONSTRAIN, COMPEL
4 *obsolete* : to effect or gain by force
5 : to carry out effectively ⟨*enforce* laws⟩
— **en·force·abil·i·ty** \-,fōr-sə-'bi-lə-tē, -,fòr-\ *noun*
— **en·force·able** \-'fōr-sə-bəl, -'fòr-\ *adjective*
— **en·force·ment** \-'fōr-smənt, -'fòr-\ *noun*

en·forc·er \in-'fōr-sər, -'fòr-\ *noun* (1580)
1 : one that enforces
2 a : a violent criminal employed by a crime syndicate; *especially* : HIT MAN 1 **b** : an aggressive player (as in ice hockey) known for rough play and fighting

en·frame \in-'frām\ *transitive verb* (1848)
: FRAME 6
— **en·frame·ment** \-'frām-mənt\ *noun*

en·fran·chise \in-'fran-,chīz, en-\ *transitive verb* **-chised; -chis·ing** [Middle English, from Middle French *enfranchiss-*, stem of *enfranchir*, from Old French, from *en-* + *franc* free — more at FRANK] (15th century)
1 : to set free (as from slavery)
2 : to endow with a franchise: as **a** : to admit to the privileges of a citizen and especially to the right of suffrage **b** : to admit (a municipality) to political privileges or rights

— **en·fran·chise·ment** \-,chīz-mənt, -chəz-\ *noun*

en·gage \in-'gāj, en-\ *verb* **en·gaged; en·gag·ing** [Middle English, from Middle French *engagier*, from Old French, from *en-* + *gage* token, gage] (15th century)
transitive verb
1 : to offer (as one's word) as security for a debt or cause
2 a *obsolete* : to entangle or entrap in or as if in a snare or bog **b** : to attract and hold by influence or power **c** : to interlock with : MESH; *also* : to cause (mechanical parts) to mesh
3 : to bind (as oneself) to do something; *especially* : to bind by a pledge to marry
4 a : to provide occupation for : INVOLVE ⟨*engage* him in a new project⟩ **b** : to arrange to obtain the use or services of : HIRE
5 a : to hold the attention of : ENGROSS ⟨her work *engages* her completely⟩ **b** : to induce to participate ⟨*engaged* the shy boy in conversation⟩
6 a : to enter into contest with **b** : to bring together or interlock (weapons)
7 : to deal with especially at length
intransitive verb
1 a : to pledge oneself : PROMISE **b** : GUARANTEE ⟨he *engages* for the honesty of his brother⟩
2 a : to begin and carry on an enterprise or activity ⟨*engaged* in trade for a number of years⟩ **b** : to take part : PARTICIPATE ⟨at college she *engaged* in gymnastics⟩
3 : to enter into conflict
4 : to come together and interlock (as of machinery parts) : to be or become in gear

en·ga·gé \,äⁿ-,gä-'zhā\ *adjective* [French, past participle of *engager* to engage, from Middle French *engagier*] (1946)
: committed to or supportive of a cause

en·gaged \in-'gājd, en-\ *adjective* (1665)
1 : involved in activity : OCCUPIED
2 : pledged to be married : BETROTHED
3 : greatly interested : COMMITTED
4 : involved especially in a hostile encounter
5 : partly embedded in a wall ⟨an *engaged* column⟩
6 : being in gear : MESHED

en·gage·ment \in-'gāj-mənt, en-\ *noun* (1601)
1 a : an arrangement to meet or be present at a specified time and place ⟨a dinner *engagement*⟩ **b** : a job or period of employment especially as a performer
2 : something that engages : PLEDGE
3 a : the act of engaging : the state of being engaged **b** : emotional involvement or commitment ⟨seesaws between obsessive *engagement* and ambiguous detachment —Gary Taylor⟩ **c** : BETROTHAL
4 : the state of being in gear
5 : a hostile encounter between military forces

en·gag·ing *adjective* (1673)
: tending to draw favorable attention : ATTRACTIVE
— **en·gag·ing·ly** \-'gā-jiŋ-lē\ *adverb*

en·gar·land \in-'gär-lənd, en-\ *transitive verb* (1581)
: to adorn with or as if with a garland

En·gel·mann spruce \,eŋ-gəl-mən-\ *noun* [George *Engelmann* (died 1884) American botanist] (1908)
: a large spruce (*Picea engelmannii*) of the Rocky mountain region and British Columbia that yields a light-colored wood

en·gen·der \in-'jen-dər, en-\ *verb* **en·gen·dered; en·gen·der·ing** \-d(ə-)riŋ\ [Middle English *engendren*, from Middle French *engendrer*, from Latin *ingenerare*, from *in-* + *generare* to generate] (14th century)
transitive verb
1 : BEGET, PROCREATE
2 : to cause to exist or to develop : PRODUCE ⟨angry words *engender* strife⟩
intransitive verb
: to assume form : ORIGINATE

en·gild \in-'gild, en-\ *transitive verb* (15th century)
: to make bright with or as if with light

1en·gine \'en-jən\ *noun* [Middle English *engin*, from Middle French, from Latin *ingenium* natural disposition, talent, from *in-* + *gignere* to beget — more at KIN] (13th century)
1 *obsolete* **a** : INGENUITY **b** : evil contrivance : WILE
2 : something used to effect a purpose : AGENT, INSTRUMENT ⟨mournful and terrible *engine* of horror and of crime —E. A. Poe⟩
3 a : a mechanical tool: as (1) : an instrument or machine of war (2) *obsolete* : a torture implement **b** : MACHINERY **c** : any of various mechanical appliances — often used in combination ⟨fire *engine*⟩
4 : a machine for converting any of various forms of energy into mechanical force and motion; *also* : a mechanism or object that serves as an energy source ⟨black holes may be the *engines* for quasars⟩
5 : a railroad locomotive

2engine *transitive verb* **en·gined; en·gin·ing** (1868)
: to equip with engines

engine driver *noun* (1828)
British : ENGINEER 4

1en·gi·neer \,en-jə-'nir\ *noun* [alteration of earlier *enginer*, from Middle English, alteration of *enginour*, from Middle French *engigneur*, from Old French *enginier* to contrive, from *engin*] (14th century)
1 : a member of a military group devoted to engineering work
2 *obsolete* : a crafty schemer : PLOTTER
3 a : a designer or builder of engines **b** : a person who is trained in or follows as a profession a branch of engineering **c** : a person who carries through an enterprise by skillful or artful contrivance
4 : a person who runs or supervises an engine or an apparatus

2engineer *transitive verb* (1843)
1 : to lay out, construct, or manage as an engineer
2 a : to contrive or plan out usually with more or less subtle skill and craft **b** : to guide the course of
3 : to modify or produce by genetic engineering ⟨grain crops *engineered* to require fewer nutrients and produce higher yields⟩
synonym see GUIDE

en·gi·neer·ing *noun* (1720)
1 : the activities or function of an engineer
2 a : the application of science and mathematics by which the properties of matter and the sources of energy in nature are made useful to people **b** : the design and manufacture of complex products ⟨software *engineering*⟩
3 : calculated manipulation or direction (as of behavior) ⟨social *engineering*⟩ — compare GENETIC ENGINEERING

en·gine·ry \'en-jən-rē\ *noun* (1641)
: instruments of war

en·gird \in-'gərd, en-\ *transitive verb* (1566)
archaic : GIRD, ENCOMPASS

en·gir·dle \in-'gər-d°l, en-\ *transitive verb* (1602)
: to encircle with or as if with a girdle

1En·glish \'iŋ-glish, 'iŋ-lish\ *adjective* [Middle English, from Old English *englisc*, from *Engle* (plural) Angles] (before 12th century)
: of, relating to, or characteristic of England, the English people, or the English language
— **En·glish·ness** *noun*

2English *noun* (before 12th century)
1 a : the language of the people of England and the U.S. and many areas now or formerly under British control **b** : a particular variety of English distinguished by peculiarities (as of pronunciation) **c** : English language, literature, or composition when a subject of study
2 *plural in construction* : the people of England

3 a : an English translation **b :** idiomatic or intelligible English
4 : spin around the vertical axis deliberately imparted to a ball that is driven or rolled — compare DRAW, FOLLOW; BODY ENGLISH

³**English** *transitive verb* (14th century)
1 : to translate into English
2 : to adopt into English **:** ANGLICIZE

English breakfast *noun* (1807)
1 : a substantial breakfast (as of eggs, ham or bacon, toast, and cereal)
2 : CONGOU; *broadly* **:** any similar black tea

English cocker spaniel *noun* (1948)
: any of a breed of spaniels that have square muzzles, wide well-developed noses, and distinctive heads which are ideally half muzzle and half skull with the forehead and skull arched and slightly flattened

English cocker spaniel

English daisy *noun* (circa 1890)
: DAISY 1a

English foxhound *noun* (1929)
: any of a breed of medium-sized foxhounds developed in England and characterized by a muscular body, bi- or tri-colored short coat, and lightly fringed tail

English horn *noun* [translation of Italian *corno inglese*] (1838)
: a double-reed woodwind instrument resembling the oboe in design but having a longer tube and a range a fifth lower than that of the oboe

English ivy *noun* (1624)
: IVY 1

En·glish·man \'iŋ-glish-mən, 'iṇ-lish-\ *noun* (before 12th century)
: a native or inhabitant of England

English muffin *noun* (1902)
: bread dough rolled and cut into rounds, baked on a griddle, and split and toasted just before eating

English pea *noun* (1634)
Southern **:** PEA 1a, b

En·glish·ry \'iŋ-glish-rē, 'iṇ-lish-\ *noun* (1620)
: the state, fact, or quality of being English **:** ENGLISHNESS

English saddle *noun* (1817)
: a saddle with long side bars, steel cantle and pommel, no horn, and a leather seat supported by webbing stretched between the saddlebow and cantle — see SADDLE illustration

English setter *noun* (1859)
: any of a breed of dogs often trained as bird dogs and characterized by a moderately long flat silky coat of white or white with color and by feathering on the tail and legs

English shepherd *noun* (1950)
: any of a breed of vigorous medium-sized working dogs with a long and glossy black coat usually with tan to brown markings that was developed in England for herding sheep and cattle

English sonnet *noun* (circa 1903)
: a sonnet consisting of three quatrains and a couplet with a rhyme scheme of *abab cdcd efef gg* — called also *Shakespearean sonnet*

English sparrow *noun* (1876)
: HOUSE SPARROW

English springer spaniel *noun* (1929)
: any of a breed of springer spaniels having a muscular build and a moderately long silky coat usually of black and white or liver and white hair — called also *English springer*

English system *noun* (1927)
: the foot-pound-second system of units

English toy spaniel *noun* (circa 1934)
: any of a breed of small blocky spaniels with well-rounded upper skull projecting forward toward the short turned-up nose

English walnut *noun* (1772)
: a Eurasian walnut (*Juglans regia*) valued for its large edible nut and its hard richly figured wood; *also* **:** its nut

En·glish·wom·an \'iŋ-glish-ˌwu̇-mən *also* 'iṇ-lish-\ *noun* (15th century)
: a woman of English birth, nationality, or origin

English toy spaniel

English yew *noun* (circa 1930)
: YEW 1a(1)

en·gorge \in-'gȯrj, en-\ *verb* [Middle French *engorgier*, from Old French, to devour, from *en-* + *gorge* throat — more at GORGE] (1515)
transitive verb
: GORGE, GLUT; *especially* **:** to fill with blood to the point of congestion
intransitive verb
: to suck blood to the limit of body capacity
— **en·gorge·ment** \-mənt\ *noun*

en·graft \in-'graft, en-\ *transitive verb* (1585)
1 : to join or fasten as if by grafting
2 : GRAFT 1, 3 ⟨*engrafted* embryonic gill tissue into the back⟩
— **en·graft·ment** \-'graf(t)-mənt\ *noun*

en·grailed \in-'grāld, en-\ *adjective* [Middle English *engreled*, from Middle French *engreslé*, from *en-* + *gresle* slender, from Latin *gracilis*] (15th century)
1 : indented with small concave curves ⟨an *engrailed* heraldic bordure⟩
2 : made of or bordered by a circle of raised dots ⟨an *engrailed* coin⟩

en·grain \in-'grān\ *transitive verb* (circa 1641)
: INGRAIN

en·gram *also* **en·gramme** \'en-ˌgram\ *noun* [International Scientific Vocabulary] (1908)
: a hypothetical change in neural tissue postulated in order to account for persistence of memory

en·grave \in-'grāv, en-\ *transitive verb* **engraved; en·grav·ing** [Middle French *engraver*, from *en-* + *graver* to grave, of Germanic origin; akin to Old English *grafan* to grave] (1509)
1 a : to form by incision (as on wood or metal) **b :** to impress deeply as if with a graver ⟨the incident was *engraved* in his memory⟩
2 a : to cut figures, letters, or designs on for printing; *also* **:** to print from an engraved plate **b :** PHOTOENGRAVE
— **en·grav·er** *noun*

en·grav·ing *noun* (1601)
1 : the act or process of one that engraves
2 : something that is engraved: as **a :** an engraved printing surface **b :** engraved work
3 : an impression from an engraved printing surface

en·gross \in-'grōs, en-\ *transitive verb* [Middle English, from Anglo-French *engrosser*, probably from Medieval Latin *ingrossare*, from Latin *in* + Medieval Latin *grossa* large handwriting, from Latin, feminine of *grossus* thick] (15th century)
1 a : to copy or write in a large hand **b :** to prepare the usually final handwritten or printed text of (an official document)
2 [Middle English, from Middle French *en gros* in large quantities] **a :** to purchase large quantities of (as for speculation) **b** *archaic* **:** AMASS, COLLECT **c :** to take or engage the whole attention of **:** occupy completely ⟨ideas that have *engrossed* the minds of scholars for generations⟩
— **en·gross·er** *noun*

en·gross·ing \-'grō-siŋ\ *adjective* (1820)
: taking up the attention completely **:** ABSORBING
— **en·gross·ing·ly** \-siŋ-lē\ *adverb*

en·gross·ment \in-'grō-smənt, en-\ *noun* (1526)

1 : the act of engrossing
2 : the state of being absorbed or occupied **:** PREOCCUPATION

en·gulf \in-'gȯlf, en-\ *transitive verb* (1555)
1 : to flow over and enclose **:** OVERWHELM ⟨the mounting seas threatened to *engulf* the island⟩
2 : to take in (food) by or as if by flowing over and enclosing
— **en·gulf·ment** \-mənt\ *noun*

en·ha·lo \in-'hā-(ˌ)lō, en-\ *transitive verb* (1842)
: to surround with or as if with a halo

en·hance \in-'han(t)s, en-\ *transitive verb* **enhanced; en·hanc·ing** [Middle English *enhauncen*, from Anglo-French *enhauncer*, alteration of Old French *enhaucier*, from (assumed) Vulgar Latin *inaltiare*, from Latin *in* + *altus* high — more at OLD] (13th century)
1 *obsolete* **:** RAISE
2 : HEIGHTEN, INCREASE; *especially* **:** to increase or improve in value, quality, desirability, or attractiveness
— **en·hance·ment** \-'han(t)-smənt\ *noun*

enhanced recovery *noun* (1970)
: the extraction of oil from a nearly exhausted well by methods more costly and complex than waterflooding alone

en·hanc·er \in-'han(t)-sər, en-\ *noun* (14th century)
1 : one that enhances
2 : a nucleotide sequence that increases the rate of genetic transcription by preferentially increasing the activity of the nearest promoter on the same DNA molecule

en·har·mon·ic \ˌen-(ˌ)här-'mä-nik\ *adjective* [French *enharmonique*, from Middle French, of a scale employing quarter tones, from Greek *enarmonios*, from *en* in + *harmonia* harmony, scale] (1794)
: of, relating to, or being notes that are written differently (as A flat and G sharp) but sound the same in the tempered scale
— **en·har·mon·i·cal·ly** \-ni-k(ə-)lē\ *adverb*

enig·ma \i-'nig-mə, e-\ *noun* [Latin *aenigma*, from Greek *ainigmat-*, *ainigma*, from *ainissesthai* to speak in riddles, from *ainos* fable] (15th century)
1 : an obscure speech or writing
2 : something hard to understand or explain
3 : an inscrutable or mysterious person
synonym see MYSTERY

enig·mat·ic \ˌe-(ˌ)nig-'ma-tik *also* ˌē-(ˌ)nig-\ *also* **enig·mat·i·cal** \-ti-kəl\ *adjective* (1677)
: of, relating to, or resembling an enigma **:** MYSTERIOUS
synonym see OBSCURE
— **enig·mat·i·cal·ly** \-ti-k(ə-)lē\ *adverb*

en·isle \in-'ī(ə)l, en-\ *transitive verb* (1612)
1 : to place apart **:** ISOLATE
2 : to make an island of

en·jamb·ment \in-'jam-mənt\ *or* **en·jambe·ment** *same or* äⁿ-zhäⁿb-mäⁿ\ *noun* [French *enjambement*, from Middle French, encroachment, from *enjamber* to straddle, encroach on, from *en-* + *jambe* leg — more at JAMB] (1839)
: the running over of a sentence from one verse or couplet into another so that closely related words fall in different lines — compare RUN-ON

en·join \in-'jȯin, en-\ *transitive verb* [Middle English, from Old French *enjoindre*, from Latin *injungere*, from *in-* + *jungere* to join — more at YOKE] (13th century)
1 : to direct or impose by authoritative order or with urgent admonition ⟨*enjoined* us to be careful⟩

2 a : FORBID, PROHIBIT ⟨was *enjoined* by conscience from telling a lie⟩ **b :** to prohibit by a judicial order **:** put an injunction on ⟨a book had been *enjoined* prior to publication —David Margolick⟩
synonym see COMMAND
en·joy \in-'jòi, en-\ *verb* [Middle English *enjoie*, from Middle French *enjoir*, from Old French, from *en-* + *joir* to enjoy, from Latin *gaudēre* to rejoice — more at JOY] (15th century)
intransitive verb
: to have a good time
transitive verb
1 : to have for one's use, benefit, or lot **:** EXPERIENCE ⟨*enjoyed* great success⟩
2 : to take pleasure or satisfaction in
— **en·joy·able** \-ə-bəl\ *adjective*
— **en·joy·able·ness** *noun*
— **en·joy·ably** \-blē\ *adverb*
— **en·joy·er** *noun*
— **enjoy oneself :** to have a good time
en·joy·ment \in-'jòi-mənt\ *noun* (1553)
1 a : the action or state of enjoying **b :** possession and use ⟨the *enjoyment* of civic rights⟩
2 : something that gives keen satisfaction
en·keph·a·lin \in-'ke-fə-lən, -(,)lin, en-\ *noun* [*enkephal-* (alteration of *encephal-*) + *-in*] (1975)
: either of two pentapeptides with opiate and analgesic activity that occur naturally in the brain and have a marked affinity for opiate receptors — compare ENDORPHIN
en·kin·dle \in-'kin-dᵊl, en-\ (1542)
transitive verb
1 : to set (as fuel) on fire
2 : to make bright and glowing
intransitive verb
: to take fire **:** FLAME
en·lace \in-'lās, en-\ *transitive verb* [Middle English, from Middle French *enlacier*, from Old French, from *en-* + *lacier* to lace] (14th century)
1 : ENCIRCLE, ENFOLD
2 : ENTWINE, INTERLACE
en·lace·ment \in-'lā-smənt, en-\ *noun* (1830)
1 : the process or result of interlacing
2 : a pattern of interlacing elements
en·large \in-'lärj, en-\ *verb* **en·larged; en·larg·ing** [Middle English, from Middle French *enlargier*, from Old French, from *en-* + *large* large, abundant] (14th century)
transitive verb
1 : to make larger **:** EXTEND
2 : to give greater scope to **:** EXPAND
3 : to set free (as a captive)
intransitive verb
1 : to grow larger
2 : to speak or write at length **:** ELABORATE ⟨let me *enlarge* upon that point⟩
synonym see INCREASE
— **en·large·able** \-'lär-jə-bəl\ *adjective*
— **en·larg·er** *noun*
en·large·ment \in-'lärj-mənt, en-\ *noun* (1540)
1 : an act or instance of enlarging **:** the state of being enlarged
2 : a photographic print larger than the negative that is made by projecting the negative image through a lens onto a photographic printing surface
en·light·en \in-'lī-tᵊn, en-\ *transitive verb* **en·light·ened; en·light·en·ing** \-'līt-niŋ, -tᵊn-iŋ\ (1587)
1 *archaic* **:** ILLUMINATE
2 a : to furnish knowledge to **:** INSTRUCT **b :** to give spiritual insight to
en·light·ened *adjective* (1652)
1 : freed from ignorance and misinformation ⟨an *enlightened* people⟩
2 : based on full comprehension of the problems involved ⟨issued an *enlightened* ruling⟩
en·light·en·ment \in-'lī-tᵊn-mənt, en-\ *noun* (1669)
1 : the act or means of enlightening **:** the state of being enlightened

2 *capitalized* **:** a philosophical movement of the 18th century marked by a rejection of traditional social, religious, and political ideas and an emphasis on rationalism — used with *the*
3 *Buddhism* **:** a final blessed state marked by the absence of desire or suffering
en·list \in-'list, en-\ (1599)
transitive verb
1 a : to secure the support and aid of **:** employ in advancing an interest ⟨*enlist* all the available resources⟩ ⟨*enlist* the community in an experiment⟩ **b :** to win over **:** ATTRACT ⟨trying to *enlist* my sympathies⟩
2 : to engage (a person) for duty in the armed forces
intransitive verb
1 : to enroll oneself in the armed forces
2 : to participate heartily (as in a cause, drive, or crusade)
— **en·list·ee** \-,lis-'tē, -'lis-tē\ *noun*
— **en·list·ment** \-'lis(t)-mənt\ *noun*
en·list·ed \-'lis-təd\ *adjective* (1724)
: of, relating to, or constituting the part of a military or naval force below commissioned or warrant officers
enlisted man *noun* (1724)
: a man or woman in the armed forces ranking below a commissioned or warrant officer; *specifically* **:** one ranking below a noncommissioned officer or petty officer
en·liv·en \in-'lī-vən, en-\ *transitive verb* (1604)
: to give life, action, or spirit to **:** ANIMATE
synonym see QUICKEN
en masse \äⁿ(n)-'mas, -'mäs, en-\ *adverb* [French] (1795)
: in a body **:** as a whole
en·mesh \in-'mesh, en-\ *transitive verb* (1604)
: to catch or entangle in or as if in meshes
— **en·mesh·ment** \-mənt\ *noun*
en·mi·ty \'en-mə-tē\ *noun, plural* **-ties** [Middle English *enmite*, from Middle French *enemité*, from Old French *enemisté*, from *enemi* enemy] (13th century)
: positive, active, and typically mutual hatred or ill will
en·ne·ad \'e-nē-,ad\ *noun* [Greek *ennead-, enneas*, from *ennea* nine — more at NINE] (1550)
: a group of nine
en·no·ble \i-'nō-bəl, e-'nō-\ *transitive verb* **en·no·bled; en·no·bling** \-b(ə-)liŋ\ [Middle English *ennobelen*, from Middle French *ennoblir*, from Old French, from *en-* + *noble* noble] (15th century)
1 : to make noble **:** ELEVATE ⟨seemed *ennobled* by suffering⟩
2 : to raise to the rank of nobility
— **en·no·ble·ment** \-bəl-mənt\ *noun*
en·nui \,än-'wē\ *noun* [French, from Old French *enui* annoyance, from *enuier* to annoy — more at ANNOY] (1732)
: a feeling of weariness and dissatisfaction **:** BOREDOM
Enoch \'ē-nək, -nik\ *noun* [Greek *Enōch*, from Hebrew *Hănōkh*]
: an Old Testament patriarch and father of Methuselah
eno·ki·da·ke \e-,nō-kē-'dä-kē\ *noun* [Japanese *enokitake*, from *enoki* Chinese hackberry (*Celtis sinensis*) + *take* mushroom] (1983)
: ENOKI MUSHROOM
enoki mushroom \e-'nō-kē-\ *noun* [Japanese *enoki*] (circa 1977)
: a small white edible mushroom (*Flammulina velutipes* synonym *Collybia velutipes* of the family Agaricaceae) — called also *enoki*
enol \'ē-,nòl, -,nōl\ *noun* [International Scientific Vocabulary *ene-* (from *-ene*) + *-ol*] (1904)
: an organic compound that contains a hydroxyl group bonded to a carbon atom having a double bond and that is usually characterized by the grouping C=C(OH)
— **eno·lic** \ē-'nō-lik, -'nä-lik\ *adjective*
eno·lase \'ē-nə-,lās, -,lāz\ *noun* [International Scientific Vocabulary *enol* + *-ase*] (1942)

: a crystalline enzyme that is found especially in muscle and yeast and is important in the metabolism of carbohydrates
enol·o·gy \ē-'nä-lə-jē\ *noun* [Greek *oinos* wine + English *-logy* — more at WINE] (1814)
: a science that deals with wine and wine making
— **eno·log·i·cal** \,ē-nə-'lä-ji-kəl\ *adjective*
— **enol·o·gist** \ē-'nä-lə-jist\ *noun*
enor·mi·ty \i-'nòr-mə-tē\ *noun, plural* **-ties** (15th century)
1 : an outrageous, improper, vicious, or immoral act ⟨the *enormities* of state power —Susan Sontag⟩ ⟨other *enormities* too juvenile to mention —Richard Freedman⟩
2 : the quality or state of being immoderate, monstrous, or outrageous; *especially* **:** great wickedness ⟨the *enormity* of the crimes committed during the Third Reich —G. A. Craig⟩
3 : the quality or state of being huge **:** IMMENSITY
4 : a quality of momentous importance □
enor·mous \i-'nòr-məs, ē-\ *adjective* [Latin *enormis*, from *e, ex* out of + *norma* rule] (1531)
1 a *archaic* **:** ABNORMAL, INORDINATE **b :** exceedingly wicked **:** SHOCKING ⟨an *enormous* sin⟩

2 : marked by extraordinarily great size, number, or degree; *especially* **:** exceeding usual bounds or accepted notions ☆
— **enor·mous·ly** *adverb*
— **enor·mous·ness** *noun*

eno·sis \i-'nō-səs\ *noun* [New Greek *henōsis*, from Greek, union, from *henoun* to unite, from *hen-*, *heis* one — more at SAME] (1928) **:** a movement to secure the political union of Greece and Cyprus

¹enough \i-'nəf; *after* t, d, s, z *often* ⁾n-'əf\ *adjective* [Middle English *ynough*, from Old English *genōg* (akin to Old High German *ginuog* enough), from *ge-* (perfective prefix) + *-nōg*; akin to Latin *nancisci* to get, Greek *enenkein* to carry — more at CO-] (before 12th century) **:** occurring in such quantity, quality, or scope as to fully meet demands, needs, or expectations
synonym see SUFFICIENT

²enough *adverb* (before 12th century)
1 : in or to a degree or quantity that satisfies or that is sufficient or necessary for satisfaction **:** SUFFICIENTLY
2 : FULLY, QUITE
3 : in a tolerable degree

³enough *pronoun* (before 12th century) **:** a sufficient number, quantity, or amount ⟨*enough* were present to constitute a quorum⟩ ⟨had *enough* of their foolishness⟩

enounce \ē-'naun(t)s\ *transitive verb* **enounced; enounc·ing** [French *énoncer*, from Latin *enuntiare* to report — more at ENUNCIATE] (1805)
1 : to set forth or state (as a proposition)
2 : to pronounce distinctly **:** ARTICULATE

enow \i-'naú, i-'nō\ *adverb or adjective* [Middle English *inow*, from Old English *genōg*] (before 12th century)
archaic **:** ENOUGH

en pas·sant \ˌäⁿ-ˌpä-'säⁿ, -pə-\ *adverb* [French] (1665)
1 : in passing
2 — used in chess of the capture of a pawn as it makes a first move of two squares by an enemy pawn that threatens the first of these squares

en·plane \in-'plān, en-\ *intransitive verb* (1941)
: to board an airplane

en prise \äⁿ-'prēz\ *adjective* [French, literally, engaged, within grasp] (1899)
of a chess piece **:** exposed to capture

en·quire \in-'kwīr\, **en·qui·ry** \'in-ˌkwīr-ē, in-'; 'in-kwə-rē, -'in\ *variant of* INQUIRE, INQUIRY

en·rage \in-'rāj, en-\ *transitive verb* [Middle French *enrager* to become mad, from Old French *enragier*, from *en-* + *rage* rage] (1589)
: to fill with rage **:** ANGER

en·rapt \in-'rapt, en-\ *adjective* (1606)
: wholly absorbed with rapture

en·rap·ture \in-'rap-chər, en-\ *transitive verb* **en·rap·tured; en·rap·tur·ing** \-'rap-chə-riŋ, -'rap-shriŋ\ (1740)
: to fill with delight

en·reg·is·ter \in-'re-jə-stər, en-\ *transitive verb* [Middle French *enregistrer*, from Old French, from *en-* + *registre* register] (1523)
: to put on record **:** REGISTER

en·rich \in-'rich, en-\ *transitive verb* [Middle English, from Middle French *enrichir*, from Old French, from *en-* + *riche* rich] (14th century)
: to make rich or richer especially by the addition or increase of some desirable quality, attribute, or ingredient (the experience will *enrich* your life): as **a :** to add beauty to **:** ADORN **b :** to enhance the taste of ⟨butter will *enrich* the sauce⟩ **c :** to make (a soil) more fertile **d :** to improve the nutritive value of (a food) by adding nutrients (as vitamins or amino acids) and especially by restoring part of the nutrients lost in processing ⟨*enriched* flour⟩ **e :** to process so as to add or increase the proportion of a desirable ingredient ⟨*enriched* uranium⟩ ⟨*enriched* natural gas⟩

— **en·rich·er** *noun*
— **en·rich·ment** \-'rich-mənt\ *noun*

en·robe \in-'rōb, en-\ *transitive verb* (1593)
1 : to cover with or as if with a robe
2 : COAT 2

en·roll *or* **en·rol** \in-'rōl, en-\ *verb* **en·rolled; en·roll·ing** [Middle English, from Middle French *enroller*, from *en-* + *rolle* roll, register] (14th century)
transitive verb
1 : to insert, register, or enter in a list, catalog, or roll (the school *enrolls* about 800 pupils)
2 : to prepare a final perfect copy of (a bill passed by a legislature) in written or printed form
3 : to roll or wrap up
intransitive verb
: to enroll oneself or cause oneself to be enrolled ⟨we *enrolled* in the history course⟩
— **en·roll·ee** \-rō-'lē\ *noun*
— **en·roll·ment** \-'rōl-mənt\ *noun*

en·root \in-'rüt, -'rút\ *transitive verb* [Middle English] (15th century)
: ESTABLISH, IMPLANT

en route \äⁿ(n)-'rüt, en-, in-, -'raút\ *adverb or adjective* [French] (1779)
: on or along the way ⟨he reads *en route*⟩ ⟨arrived early despite *en route* delays⟩

en·sam·ple \in-'sam-pəl\ *noun* [Middle English, from Middle French *ensample*, *example*] (13th century)
archaic **:** EXAMPLE, INSTANCE

en·san·guine \in-'saŋ-gwən\ *transitive verb* **-guined; -guin·ing** (1667)
1 : to make bloody
2 : CRIMSON

en·sconce \in-'skän(t)s\ *transitive verb* **en·sconced; en·sconc·ing** [*en-* + ²*sconce*] (1598)
1 : SHELTER, CONCEAL
2 : ESTABLISH, SETTLE ⟨*ensconced* in a new job⟩

¹en·sem·ble \än-'säm-bəl, äⁿ-\ *noun* [French, from *ensemble* together, from Latin *insimul* at the same time, from *in-* + *simul* at the same time — more at SAME] (1750)
: a group producing a single effect: as **a :** concerted music of two or more parts **b :** a complete costume of harmonizing or complementary clothing and accessories **c** (1) **:** the musicians engaged in the performance of a musical ensemble (2) **:** a group of supporting players, singers, or dancers; *especially* **:** CORPS DE BALLET

²ensemble *adjective* (circa 1911)
: emphasizing the roles of all performers as a whole rather than a star performance ⟨*ensemble* acting⟩

en·serf \in-'sərf, en-\ *transitive verb* (1882)
: to make a serf of **:** deprive of liberty and personal rights
— **en·serf·ment** \-mənt\ *noun*

en·sheathe \in-'shēth, en-\ *transitive verb* (1593)
: to cover with or as if with a sheath

en·shrine \in-'shrīn, en-, *especially Southern* -'srīn\ *transitive verb* [Middle English] (14th century)
1 : to enclose in or as if in a shrine
2 : to preserve or cherish as sacred
— **en·shrine·ment** \-mənt\ *noun*

en·shri·nee \in-'shrī-nē, -ˌshrī-'nē, en-\ *noun* (1968)
: a person inducted into a Hall of Fame

en·shroud \in-'shraúd, en-, *especially Southern* -'sraúd\ *transitive verb* (1583)
: to cover or enclose with or as if with a shroud

en·si·form \'en(t)-sə-ˌfòrm\ *adjective* [French *ensiforme*, from Latin *ensis* sword + French *-forme* -form; akin to Sanskrit *asi* sword] (1541)
: having sharp edges and tapering to a slender point ⟨*ensiform* leaves of the gladiolus⟩ — see LEAF illustration

en·sign \'en(t)-sən, *also* 'en-ˌsīn *for* 1, 2, & 3a\ *noun* [Middle English *ensigne*, from Middle French *enseigne*, from Latin *insignia* insignia, flags] (15th century)
1 : a flag that is flown (as by a ship) as the symbol of nationality and that may also be flown with a distinctive badge added to its design
2 a : a badge of office, rank, or power **b :** EMBLEM, SIGN
3 a : an infantry officer of what was formerly the lowest commissioned rank **b :** a commissioned officer in the navy or coast guard ranking above a chief warrant officer and below a lieutenant junior grade

en·si·lage \'en(t)-s(ə-)lij, *for 1 also* in-'sī-lij\ *noun* [French, from *ensiler* to ensile, from *en-* + *silo* silo, from Spanish] (1876)
1 : the process of preserving fodder by ensiling
2 : SILAGE

en·sile \en-'sī(ə)l, in-\ *transitive verb* **en·siled; en·sil·ing** (1883)
: to prepare and store (fodder) for silage

en·sky \in-'skī, en-\ *transitive verb* (1603)
: EXALT

en·slave \in-'slāv, en-\ *transitive verb* (1630)
: to reduce to or as if to slavery **:** SUBJUGATE
— **en·slave·ment** \-mənt\ *noun*
— **en·slav·er** *noun*

en·snare \in-'snar, -'sner, en-\ *transitive verb* (1576)
: to take in or as if in a snare
synonym see CATCH

en·snarl \in-'snär(-ə)l, en-\ *transitive verb* (1593)
: to involve in a snarl

en·sor·cell *or* **en·sor·cel** \in-'sòr-səl\ *transitive verb* **-celled** *or* **-celed; -cell·ing** *or* **-cel·ing** [Middle French *ensorceler*, alteration of Old French *ensorcerer*, from *en-* + *-sorcerer*, from *sorcier* sorcerer — more at SORCERY] (circa 1541)
: BEWITCH, ENCHANT
— **en·sor·cell·ment** \-mənt\ *noun*

en·soul \in-'sōl, en-\ *transitive verb* (1605)
: to endow or imbue with a soul

en·sphere \in-'sfir, en-\ *transitive verb* (1612)
: to enclose in or as if in a sphere

en·sue \in-'sü, en-\ *verb* **en·sued; en·su·ing** [Middle English, from Middle French *ensuivre*, from Old French, from *en-* + *suivre* to follow — more at SUE] (14th century)
transitive verb
: to strive to attain **:** PURSUE ⟨I wander, seeking peace, and *ensuing* it —Rupert Brooke⟩
intransitive verb
: to take place afterward or as a result
synonym see FOLLOW

☆ **SYNONYMS**
Enormous, immense, huge, vast, gigantic, colossal, mammoth mean exceedingly large. ENORMOUS and IMMENSE both suggest an exceeding of all ordinary bounds in size or amount or degree, but ENORMOUS often adds an implication of abnormality or monstrousness (an *enormous* expense) (an *immense* shopping mall). HUGE commonly suggests an immensity of bulk or amount (incurred a *huge* debt). VAST usually suggests immensity of extent (the *vast* Russian steppes). GIGANTIC stresses the contrast with the size of others of the same kind (a *gigantic* sports stadium). COLOSSAL applies especially to a human creation of stupendous or incredible dimensions (a *colossal* statue of Lincoln). MAMMOTH suggests both hugeness and ponderousness of bulk (a *mammoth* boulder).

\ə\ abut \ᵊ\ kitten \ər\ further \a\ ash \ā\ ace
\ä\ mop, mar \aú\ out \ch\ chin \e\ bet \ē\ easy
\g\ go \i\ hit \ī\ ice \j\ job \ŋ\ sing \ō\ go
\ò\ law \òi\ boy \th\ thin \t͟h\ the \ü\ loot \ú\ foot
\y\ yet \zh\ vision *see also* Guide to Pronunciation

en suite \äⁿ-'swēt\ *adverb or adjective* [French] (1818)
: so as to form a suite **:** CONNECTED ⟨bathroom *en suite*⟩; *also* **:** so as to make a matching set
en·sure \in-'shùr\ *transitive verb* **en·sured; en·sur·ing** [Middle English, from Anglo-French *enseurer*, probably alteration of Old French *aseürer* — more at ASSURE] (circa 1704)
: to make sure, certain, or safe **:** GUARANTEE ☆
en·swathe \in-'swäth, -'swòth, -'swãth, en-\ *transitive verb* (1597)
: to enfold or enclose with or as if with a covering **:** SWATHE
ent- *or* **ento-** *combining form* [New Latin, from Greek *entos* within; akin to Latin *intus* within, Greek *en* in — more at IN]
: inner **:** within ⟨*ento*derm⟩
en·tab·la·ture \in-'ta-blə-ˌchür, -chər, -ˌt(y)ùr\ *noun* [obsolete French, modification of Italian *intavolatura*, from *intavolare* to put on a board or table, from *in-* (from Latin) + *tavola* board, table, from Latin *tabula*] (1611)
: a horizontal part in classical architecture that rests on the columns and consists of architrave, frieze, and cornice

1 entablature, 2 cornice, 3 frieze, 4 architrave

¹en·tail \in-'tā(ə)l, en-\ *transitive verb* [Middle English *entailen, entaillen*, from ¹*en-* + *taile, taille* limitation — more at TAIL] (14th century)
1 : to restrict (property) by limiting the inheritance to the owner's lineal descendants or to a particular class thereof
2 a : to confer, assign, or transmit as if by entail **:** FASTEN ⟨*entailed* on them indelible disgrace —Robert Browning⟩ **b :** to fix (a person) permanently in some condition or status ⟨*entail* him and his heirs unto the crown —Shakespeare⟩
3 : to impose, involve, or imply as a necessary accompaniment or result ⟨the project will *entail* considerable expense⟩
— **en·tail·er** \-'tā-lər\ *noun*
— **en·tail·ment** \-'tāl-mənt\ *noun*
²en·tail \'en-ˌtāl, in-'tā(ə)l\ *noun* (14th century)
1 a : an entailing especially of lands **b :** an entailed estate
2 : something transmitted as if by entail
ent·amoe·ba \ˌen-tə-'mē-bə\ *noun* [New Latin] (1914)
: any of a genus (*Entamoeba*) comprising various amoebas parasitic in vertebrates and including one (*E. histolytica*) that causes amebic dysentery in humans — compare ENDAMOEBA
en·tan·gle \in-'taŋ-gəl, en-\ *transitive verb* (15th century)
1 a : to wrap or twist together **:** INTERWEAVE **b :** ENSNARE
2 a : to involve in a perplexing or troublesome situation ⟨became *entangled* in a lawsuit⟩ **b :** to make complicated ⟨the story is *entangled* with legends⟩
— **en·tan·gler** \-g(ə-)lər\ *noun*
en·tan·gle·ment \in-'taŋ-gəl-mənt, en-\ *noun* (1535)
1 a : the action of entangling **:** the state of being entangled **b :** something that entangles, confuses, or ensnares
2 : the condition of being deeply involved
en·ta·sis \'en-tə-sis\ *noun, plural* **-ta·ses** \-tə-ˌsēz\ [Greek, literally, distension, stretching, from *enteinein* to stretch tight (from *en-* ²*en-* + *teinein* to stretch) — more at THIN] (1664)
: a slight convexity especially in the shaft of a column

en·tel·e·chy \en-'te-lə-kē, in-\ *noun, plural* **-chies** [Late Latin *entelechia*, from Greek *entelecheia*, from *enteles* complete (from *en-* ²*en-* + *telos* end) + *echein* to have — more at WHEEL, SCHEME] (1603)
1 : the actualization of form-giving cause as contrasted with potential existence
2 : a hypothetical agency not demonstrable by scientific methods that in some vitalist doctrines is considered an inherent regulating and directing force in the development and functioning of an organism
en·tente \äⁿ-'tänt\ *noun* [French, from Old French, intent, understanding — more at INTENT] (1854)
1 : an international understanding providing for a common course of action
2 [French *entente cordiale*] **:** a coalition of parties to an entente
en·tente cor·diale \(')äⁿ-ˌtänt-ˌkòr-'dyäl\ *noun* [French, literally, cordial understanding] (1844)
1 : ENTENTE 1
2 : a friendly agreement or working relationship
en·ter \'en-tər\ *verb* **en·tered; en·ter·ing** \'en-t(ə-)riŋ\ [Middle English *entren*, from Old French *entrer*, from Latin *intrare*, from *intra* within; akin to Latin *inter* between — more at INTER-] (13th century)
intransitive verb
1 : to go or come in
2 : to come or gain admission into a group **:** JOIN — often used with *into*
3 a : to make a beginning ⟨*entering* upon a career⟩ **b :** to begin to consider a subject — usually used with *into* or *upon*
4 : to go upon land for the purpose of taking possession
5 : to play a part **:** be a factor ⟨other considerations *enter* when money is involved⟩
transitive verb
1 : to come or go into ⟨*enter* a room⟩
2 : INSCRIBE, REGISTER ⟨*enter* the names of qualified voters⟩
3 : to cause to be received or admitted ⟨*enter* a child at a school⟩
4 : to put in **:** INSERT ⟨*enter* the new data into the computer⟩
5 a : to make a beginning in ⟨*enter* politics⟩ **b :** to go into (a particular period of time) ⟨*enter* middle age⟩
6 : to become a member of or an active participant in ⟨*enter* the university⟩ ⟨*enter* a race⟩
7 : to make report of (a ship or its cargo) to customs authorities
8 : to place in proper form before a court of law or upon record ⟨*enter* a writ⟩
9 : to go into or upon and take actual possession of (as land)
10 : to put formally on record ⟨*entering* a complaint⟩ ☆
— **en·ter·able** \'en-t(ə-)rə-bəl\ *adjective*
— **enter into 1 :** to make oneself a party to or in ⟨*enter into* an agreement⟩ **2 :** to form or be part of ⟨your prejudices shouldn't *enter into* it⟩ **3 :** to participate or share in ⟨*enter into* the spirit of the occasion⟩
— **enter the lists :** to engage in a fight or struggle
enter- *or* **entero-** *combining form* [Greek, from *enteron* — more at INTER-]
: intestine ⟨*enter*itis⟩
en·ter·al \'en-tə-rəl\ *adjective* (1903)
: ENTERIC
— **en·ter·al·ly** \-rə-lē\ *adverb*
en·ter·ic \en-'ter-ik, in-\ *adjective* (circa 1859)
1 : of or relating to the intestines; *broadly* **:** ALIMENTARY
2 : of, relating to, or being a medicinal preparation treated to pass through the stomach unaltered and disintegrate in the intestines
en·ter·i·tis \ˌen-tə-'rī-təs\ *noun* (1808)
1 : inflammation of the intestines and especially of the human ileum

2 : a disease of domestic animals (as panleucopenia of cats) marked by enteritis and diarrhea
en·tero·bac·te·ri·um \ˌen-tə-rō-bak-'tir-ē-əm\ *noun* [New Latin] (circa 1951)
: any of a family (Enterobacteriaceae) of gram-negative straight rod bacteria (as a salmonella or a colon bacillus) that ferment glucose and include saprophytes as well as some serious plant and animal pathogens
— **en·tero·bac·te·ri·al** \-ē-əl\ *adjective*
en·tero·bi·a·sis \-'bī-ə-səs\ *noun, plural* **-a·ses** \-ˌsēz\ [New Latin, from *Enterobius*, genus name (from Greek *enter-* + *bios* mode of life) + *-iasis*] (circa 1927)
: infestation with or disease caused by pinworms (genus *Enterobius*) that occurs especially in children
en·tero·chro·maf·fin \-'krō-mə-fən\ *adjective* (circa 1941)
: of or relating to epithelial cells of the intestinal mucosa that stain especially with chromium salts and usually contain serotonin
en·tero·coc·cus \-'kä-kəs\ *noun, plural* **-coc·ci** \-'käk-ˌ(s)ī, -'käk-(ˌ)(s)ē\ [New Latin, genus name] (1908)
: STREPTOCOCCUS; *especially* **:** a streptococcus (as *Streptococcus faecalis*) normally present in the intestine
— **en·tero·coc·cal** \-'kä-kəl\ *adjective*
en·tero·coele *or* **en·tero·coel** \'en-tə-rō-ˌsēl\ *noun* (1877)
: a coelom originating by outgrowth from the archenteron
— **en·tero·coe·lous** \ˌen-tə-rō-'sē-ləs\ *adjective*
— **en·tero·coe·lic** \-lik\ *adjective*
en·tero·co·li·tis \ˌen-tə-rō-kə-'lī-təs\ *noun* [New Latin] (circa 1857)
: enteritis affecting both the large and small intestine
en·tero·gas·trone \-'gas-ˌtrōn\ *noun* [*enter-* + *gastr-* + *-one* (as in *hormone*)] (circa 1930)
: a hormone that is produced by the duodenal mucosa and has an inhibitory action on gastric motility and secretion
en·tero·ki·nase \ˌen-tə-rō-'kī-ˌnās, -ˌnāz\ *noun* [International Scientific Vocabulary] (circa 1902)
: an enzyme especially of the upper intestinal mucosa that activates trypsinogen by converting it to trypsin
en·ter·on \'en-tə-ˌrän, -rən\ *noun* [New Latin, from Greek, intestine — more at INTER-] (circa 1842)

: the alimentary canal or system — used especially of the embryo

en·tero·patho·gen·ic \\,en-tə-rō-,pa-thə-'je-nik\\ *adjective* (1961)
: tending to produce disease in the intestinal tract ⟨*enteropathogenic* bacteria⟩

en·ter·op·a·thy \\,en-tə-'rä-pə-thē\\ *noun* (circa 1889)
: a disease of the intestinal tract

en·ter·os·to·my \\,en-tə-'räs-tə-mē\\ *noun, plural* **-mies** [International Scientific Vocabulary] (1878)
: a surgical formation of an opening into the intestine through the abdominal wall
— **en·ter·os·to·mal** \\-tə-məl\\ *adjective*

en·tero·tox·in \\,en-tə-rō-'täk-sən\\ *noun* (circa 1928)
: a toxin that is produced by microorganisms (as some staphylococci) and causes gastrointestinal symptoms (as in some forms of food poisoning or cholera)

en·tero·vi·rus \\-'vī-rəs\\ *noun* [New Latin] (1957)
: any of a group of picornaviruses (as the poliomyelitis virus) that typically occur in the gastrointestinal tract but may be involved in respiratory ailments, meningitis, and neurological disorders
— **en·tero·vi·ral** \\-rəl\\ *adjective*

en·ter·prise \\'en-tə(r)-,prīz\\ *noun* [Middle English, from Middle French, from Old French *entreprendre* to undertake, from *entre-* inter- + *prendre* to take — more at PRIZE] (15th century)
1 : a project or undertaking that is especially difficult, complicated, or risky
2 : readiness to engage in daring action : INITIATIVE
3 a : a unit of economic organization or activity; *especially* : a business organization **b** : a systematic purposeful activity ⟨agriculture is the main economic *enterprise* among these people⟩

en·ter·pris·er \\-,prī-zər\\ *noun* (1523)
: ENTREPRENEUR

en·ter·pris·ing \\-,prī-ziŋ\\ *adjective* (1611)
: marked by an independent energetic spirit and by readiness to undertake or experiment

en·ter·tain \\,en-tər-'tān\\ *verb* [Middle English *entertinen*, from Middle French *entretenir*, from *entre-* inter- + *tenir* to hold — more at TENABLE] (15th century)
transitive verb
1 a *archaic* : MAINTAIN **b** *obsolete* : RECEIVE
2 : to show hospitality to
3 a : to keep, hold, or maintain in the mind ⟨I *entertain* grave doubts about her sincerity⟩ **b** : to receive and take into consideration ⟨refused to *entertain* our plea⟩
4 : to provide entertainment for
5 : to play against (an opposing team) on one's home field or court
intransitive verb
: to provide entertainment especially for guests
synonym see AMUSE
— **en·ter·tain·er** *noun*

en·ter·tain·ing *adjective* (1568)
: providing entertainment : DIVERTING
— **en·ter·tain·ing·ly** \\-'tā-niŋ-lē\\ *adverb*

en·ter·tain·ment \\,en-tər-'tān-mənt\\ *noun* (15th century)
1 : the act of entertaining
2 a *archaic* : MAINTENANCE, PROVISION **b** *obsolete* : EMPLOYMENT
3 : something diverting or engaging: as **a** : a public performance **b** : a usually light comic or adventure novel

en·thal·py \\'en-,thal-pē, en-'\\ *noun* [*en-* + Greek *thalpein* to heat] (circa 1924)
: the sum of the internal energy of a body and the product of its volume multiplied by the pressure

en·thrall *or* **en·thral** \\in-'thrȯl, en-\\ *transitive verb* **en·thralled; en·thrall·ing** [Middle English] (15th century)

1 : to hold in or reduce to slavery
2 : to hold spellbound : CHARM
— **en·thrall·ment** \\-'thrȯl-mənt\\ *noun*

en·throne \\in-'thrōn, en-\\ *transitive verb* (1606)
1 a : to seat ceremonially on a throne **b** : to seat in a place associated with a position of authority or influence
2 : to assign supreme virtue or value to : EXALT
— **en·throne·ment** \\-mənt\\ *noun*

en·thuse \\in-'thüz, en-, *also* -'thyüz\\ *verb* **en·thused; en·thus·ing** [back-formation from *enthusiasm*] (1827)
transitive verb
1 : to make enthusiastic
2 : to express with enthusiasm
intransitive verb
: to show enthusiasm ⟨a splendid performance, and I was *enthusing* over it —Julian Huxley⟩ ▫

en·thu·si·asm \\in-'thü-zē-,a-zəm, en-, *also* -'thyü-\\ *noun* [Greek *enthousiasmos*, from *enthousiazein* to be inspired, irregular from *entheos* inspired, from *en-* + *theos* god] (1603)
1 a : belief in special revelations of the Holy Spirit **b** : religious fanaticism
2 a : strong excitement of feeling : ARDOR **b** : something inspiring zeal or fervor ◆
synonym see PASSION

en·thu·si·ast \\-,ast, -əst\\ *noun* (1570)
: a person filled with enthusiasm: as **a** : one who is ardently attached to a cause, object, or pursuit ⟨a sports car *enthusiast*⟩ **b** : one who tends to become ardently absorbed in an interest

en·thu·si·as·tic \\in-,thü-zē-'as-tik, en-, *also* -,thyü-\\ *adjective* (1603)
: filled with or marked by enthusiasm
— **en·thu·si·as·ti·cal·ly** \\-ti-k(ə-)lē\\ *adverb*

en·thy·meme \\'en(t)-thi-,mēm\\ *noun* [Latin *enthymema*, from Greek *enthymēma*, from *enthymeisthai* to keep in mind, from *en-* + *thymos* mind, soul] (1552)
: a syllogism in which one of the premises is implicit

en·tice \\in-'tīs, en-\\ *transitive verb* **en·ticed; en·tic·ing** [Middle English, from Middle French *enticier*, from (assumed) Vulgar Latin *intitiare*, from Latin *in-* + *titio* firebrand] (14th century)
: to attract artfully or adroitly or by arousing hope or desire : TEMPT
synonym see LURE
— **en·tice·ment** \\-'tī-smənt\\ *noun*
— **en·tic·ing·ly** \\-'tī-siŋ-lē\\ *adverb*

¹en·tire \\in-'tīr, 'en-,\\ *adjective* [Middle English, from Middle French *entir*, from Latin *integer*, literally, untouched, from *in-* + *tangere* to touch — more at TANGENT] (14th century)
1 : having no element or part left out : WHOLE ⟨was alone the *entire* day⟩
2 : complete in degree : TOTAL ⟨their *entire* devotion to their family⟩
3 a : consisting of one piece **b** : HOMOGENEOUS, UNMIXED **c** : INTACT ⟨strove to keep the collection *entire*⟩
4 : not castrated
5 : having the margin continuous or free from indentations ⟨an *entire* leaf⟩
synonym see WHOLE, PERFECT
— **entire** *adverb*
— **en·tire·ness** *noun*

²entire *noun* (1597)
1 *archaic* : the whole : ENTIRETY
2 : STALLION

en·tire·ly *adverb* (14th century)
1 : to the full or entire extent : COMPLETELY ⟨I agree *entirely*⟩ ⟨you are *entirely* welcome⟩
2 : to the exclusion of others : SOLELY ⟨*entirely* by my own efforts⟩

en·tire·ty \\in-'tī-rə-tē, -'tī(-ə)r-tē\\ *noun, plural* **-ties** (1548)
1 : the state of being entire or complete
2 : SUM TOTAL, WHOLE

en·ti·tle \\in-'tī-t°l, en-\\ *transitive verb* **en·ti·tled; en·ti·tling** \\-'tīt-liŋ, -°l-iŋ\\ [Middle English, from Middle French *entituler*, from Late Latin *intitulare*, from Latin *in-* + *titulus* title] (14th century)
1 : to give a title to : DESIGNATE
2 : to furnish with proper grounds for seeking or claiming something ⟨this ticket *entitles* the bearer to free admission⟩

en·ti·tle·ment \\-'tī-t°l-mənt\\ *noun* (1944)
1 a : the state or condition of being entitled : RIGHT **b** : a right to benefits specified especially by law or contract
2 : a government program providing benefits to members of a specified group; *also* : funds supporting or distributed by such a program

en·ti·ty \\'en-tə-tē, 'e-nə-\\ *noun, plural* **-ties** [Medieval Latin *entitas*, from Latin *ent-, ens* existing thing, from coined present participle of *esse* to be — more at IS] (1596)
1 a : BEING, EXISTENCE; *especially* : independent, separate, or self-contained existence **b** : the existence of a thing as contrasted with its attributes
2 : something that has separate and distinct existence and objective or conceptual reality

ento- — see ENT-

en·to·derm \\'en-tə-,dərm\\ *noun* (1879)
: ENDODERM
— **en·to·der·mal** \\,en-tə-'dər-məl\\ *adjective*
— **en·to·der·mic** \\-mik\\ *adjective*

en·toil \\in-'tȯi(ə)l\\ *transitive verb* (1581)
: ENTRAP, ENMESH

entom- *or* **entomo-** *combining form* [French, from Greek *entomon*]
: insect ⟨*entomo*phagous⟩

en·tomb \\in-'tüm, en-\\ *transitive verb* [Middle English *entoumben*, from Middle French *entomber*, from *en-* + *tombe* tomb] (1576)

1 : to deposit in a tomb **:** BURY
2 : to serve as a tomb for
— **en·tomb·ment** \-'tüm-mənt\ *noun*
en·to·mo·fau·na \ˌen-tə-mō-'fȯ-nə, -'fä-\ *noun* [New Latin] (1951)
: a fauna of insects **:** the insects of an environment or region
en·to·mol·o·gy \ˌen-tə-'mä-lə-jē\ *noun* [French *entomologie*, from Greek *entomon* insect (from neuter of *entomos* cut up, from *en-* + *temnein* to cut) + French *-logie* -logy — more at TOME] (1766)
: a branch of zoology that deals with insects
— **en·to·mo·log·i·cal** \-mə-'lä-ji-kəl\ *adjective*
— **en·to·mo·log·i·cal·ly** \-k(ə-)lē\ *adverb*
— **en·to·mol·o·gist** \ˌen-tə-'mä-lə-jist\ *noun*
en·to·moph·a·gous \ˌen-tə-'mä-fə-gəs\ *adjective* (1847)
: feeding on insects
en·to·moph·i·lous \ˌen-tə-'mä-fə-ləs\ *adjective* (1880)
: normally pollinated by insects — compare ZOOPHILIC
— **en·to·moph·i·ly** \-lē\ *noun*
en·to·proct \'en-tə-ˌpräkt\ *noun* [ultimately from *ent-* + Greek *prōktos* anus] (1940)
: any of a phylum (Entoprocta) of animals that are very similar to bryozoans but lack a true coelom and have the anus located near the mouth inside a crown of tentacles
en·tou·rage \ˌän-tü-'räzh\ *noun* [French, from Middle French, from *entourer* to surround, from *entour* around, from *en* in (from Latin *in*) + *tour* circuit — more at TURN] (1834)
1 : one's attendants or associates
2 : SURROUNDINGS
en·tr'acte \'ä(n)-ˌtrakt, -ˌträkt, ä(n)-'\ *noun* [French, from *entre-* inter- + *acte* act] (circa 1842)
1 : a dance, piece of music, or interlude performed between two acts of a play
2 : the interval between two acts of a play
en·trails \'en-ˌtrālz, -trəlz\ *noun plural* [Middle English *entrailles*, from Middle French, from Medieval Latin *intralia*, alteration of Latin *interanea*, plural of *interaneum* intestine, from neuter of *interaneus* interior] (14th century)
1 : BOWELS, VISCERA; *broadly* **:** internal parts
2 : the inner workings of something ⟨the *entrails* of the movie industry⟩
¹**en·train** \in-'trān\ *transitive verb* [Middle French *entrainer*, from *en-* + *trainer* to draw, drag — more at TRAIN] (1568)
1 : to draw along with or after oneself
2 : to draw in and transport (as solid particles or gas) by the flow of a fluid
3 : to incorporate (air bubbles) into concrete
4 : to determine or modify the phase or period of ⟨circadian rhythms *entrained* by a light cycle⟩
— **en·train·er** *noun*
— **en·train·ment** \-'trān-mənt\ *noun*
²**entrain** (1881)
transitive verb
: to put aboard a train
intransitive verb
: to go aboard a train
¹**en·trance** \'en-trən(t)s\ *noun* (15th century)
1 : power or permission to enter **:** ADMISSION
2 : the act of entering
3 : the means or place of entry
4 : the point at which a voice or instrument part begins in ensemble music
5 : the first appearance of an actor in a scene
²**en·trance** \in-'tran(t)s, en-\ *transitive verb*
en·tranced; en·tranc·ing (1593)
1 : to carry away with delight, wonder, or rapture
2 : to put into a trance
— **en·trance·ment** \-'tran(t)-smənt\ *noun*
en·trance·way \'en-trən(t)s-ˌwā\ *noun* (1865)
: ENTRYWAY
en·trant \'en-trənt\ *noun* (1635)

: one that enters; *especially* **:** one that enters a contest
en·trap \in-'trap, en-\ *transitive verb* [Middle French *entraper*, from *en-* + *trape* trap] (1534)
1 : to catch in or as if in a trap
2 : to lure into a compromising statement or act
synonym see CATCH
en·trap·ment \-mənt\ *noun* (1597)
1 a : the action or process of entrapping **b** **:** the condition of being entrapped
2 : the action of luring an individual into committing a crime in order to prosecute the person for it
en·treat \in-'trēt, en-\ *verb* [Middle English *entreten*, from Middle French *entraitier*, from *en-* + *traitier* to treat] (14th century)
intransitive verb
1 *obsolete* **a :** NEGOTIATE **b :** INTERCEDE
2 : to make an earnest request **:** PLEAD
transitive verb
1 : to plead with especially in order to persuade **:** ask urgently ⟨*entreated* his boss for another chance⟩
2 *archaic* **:** to deal with **:** TREAT
synonym see BEG
— **en·treat·ing·ly** \-trē-tiŋ-lē\ *adverb*
— **en·treat·ment** \-mənt\ *noun*
en·treaty \-'trē-tē\ *noun, plural* **-treat·ies** (15th century)
: an act of entreating **:** PLEA
en·tre·chat \'ä(n)-trə-ˌshä\ *noun* [French, modification of Italian (*capriola*) *intrecciata*, literally, intertwined caper] (1775)
: a leap in which a ballet dancer repeatedly crosses the legs and sometimes beats them together
en·tre·côte *also* **en·tre·cote** \'ä(n)-trə-ˌkōt\ *noun* [French *entrecôte*, from *entre-* inter- + *côte* rib, from Latin *costa* — more at INTER-, COAST] (1841)
: a steak cut from between the ribs
en·trée *or* **en·tree** \'än-ˌtrā *also* än-'\ *noun* [French *entrée*, from Old French — more at ENTRY] (1761)
1 a : the act or manner of entering **:** ENTRANCE **b :** freedom of entry or access
2 : the main course of a meal in the U.S. ◆
en·tre·mets *as singular* ˌä(n)-trə-'mā, *as plural* -'mā(z)\ *noun plural but singular or plural in construction* [Middle English, from Middle French, from Old French *entremes*, from Latin *intermissus*, past participle of *intermittere* to intermit] (15th century)
: dishes served in addition to the main course of a meal; *especially* **:** DESSERT
en·trench \in-'trench, en-\ (1555)
transitive verb
1 a : to place within or surround with a trench especially for defense **b :** to place (oneself) in a strong defensive position **c :** to establish solidly ⟨*entrenched* themselves in the business⟩
2 : to cut into **:** FURROW; *specifically* **:** to erode downward so as to form a trench
intransitive verb
1 : to dig or occupy a trench for defensive purposes
2 : to enter upon or take over something unfairly, improperly, or unlawfully **:** ENCROACH — used with *on* or *upon*
— **en·trench·ment** \-mənt\ *noun*
en·tre·pôt \'ä(n)-trə-ˌpō\ *noun* [French, from Middle French *entrepost*, from *entreposer* to put between, from *entre-* inter- + *poser* to pose, put] (1758)
: an intermediary center of trade and transshipment
en·tre·pre·neur \ˌä(n)-trə-p(r)ə-'nər, -'n(y)ùr\ *noun* [French, from Old French, from *entreprendre* to undertake — more at ENTERPRISE] (1852)
: one who organizes, manages, and assumes the risks of a business or enterprise
— **en·tre·pre·neur·ial** \-'n(y)ùr-ē-əl, -'nər-\ *adjective*

— **en·tre·pre·neur·ial·ism** \-ē-ə-li-zəm\ *noun*
— **en·tre·pre·neur·ial·ly** \-ē-ə-lē\ *adverb*
— **en·tre·pre·neur·ship** \-'nər-ˌship, -'n(y)ùr-\ *noun*
en·tre·sol \'ä(n)-trə-ˌsäl, -ˌsȯl\ *noun* [French, from Spanish *entresuelo*, from *entre* between + *suelo* level, from (assumed) Vulgar Latin *sola*, from Latin *solea* sandal, sole, sill — more at SOLE] (1711)
: MEZZANINE
en·tro·pi·on \en-'trō-pē-ˌän, -pē-ən\ *noun* [New Latin, from *en-* ²en- + *ectropion* turning out of the eyelid, from Greek *ektropion*, from *ektrepein* to turn out, from *ex-* out + *trepein* to turn] (circa 1860)
: the inversion or turning inward of the border of the eyelid against the eyeball
en·tro·py \'en-trə-pē\ *noun, plural* **-pies** [International Scientific Vocabulary ²en- + Greek *tropē* change, literally, turn, from *trepein* to turn] (1875)
1 : a measure of the unavailable energy in a closed thermodynamic system that is also usually considered to be a measure of the system's disorder and that is a property of the system's state and is related to it in such a manner that a reversible change in heat in the system produces a change in the measure which varies directly with the heat change and inversely with the absolute temperature at which the change takes place; *broadly* **:** the degree of disorder or uncertainty in a system
2 a : the degradation of the matter and energy in the universe to an ultimate state of inert uniformity **b :** a process of degradation or running down or a trend to disorder
3 : CHAOS, DISORGANIZATION, RANDOMNESS
— **en·tro·pic** \en-'trō-pik, -'trä-pik\ *adjective*
— **en·tro·pi·cal·ly** \-pi-k(ə-)lē\ *adverb*
en·trust \in-'trəst, en-\ *transitive verb* (1602)
1 : to confer a trust on; *especially* **:** to deliver something in trust to
2 : to commit to another with confidence
synonym see COMMIT
— **en·trust·ment** \-'trəs(t)-mənt\ *noun*
en·try \'en-trē\ *noun, plural* **entries** [Middle English *entre*, from Old French *entree*, from feminine of *entré*, past participle of *entrer* to enter] (13th century)
1 : the right or privilege of entering **:** ENTRÉE
2 : the act of entering **:** ENTRANCE
3 : a place of entrance: as **a :** VESTIBULE, PASSAGE **b :** DOOR, GATE

◇ **WORD HISTORY**
entrée *Entrée*, which signifies the main course of a meal in the U.S., is in fact the French word for "entry." The culinary sense of *entrée* can be traced back to 18th century Britain. In those days a formal dinner could be a gastronomic marathon. In addition to the principal courses of soup, fish, meat, and dessert, there would be an impressive array of side dishes, not to mention the salad and cheese courses. Between the fish and meat courses would come a small dish concocted of several ingredients and often garnished and sauced. Because this secondary dish immediately preceded the centerpiece of the whole meal—typically a roast—it was called the *entrée*, being, in effect, the "entrance" to the really important part of the meal. As Anglo-American dining habits changed, meals gradually diminished in their elaborateness; fewer and simpler courses were served. In the U.S. the course following the appetizer course continued to be known as the *entrée*, even if it did turn out to be a roast. Perhaps the continued preference for *entrée* in menu terminology lay in the fact that it was obviously French, and anything French was considered to have prestige.

4 a : the act of making or entering a record **b : **something entered: as (1) **:** a record or notation of an occurrence, transaction, or proceeding (2) **:** a descriptive record (as in a card catalog or an index) (3) **:** HEADWORD (4) **:** a headword with its definition or identification (5) **:** VOCABULARY ENTRY
5 : a person, thing, or group entered in a contest

en·try–lev·el \'en-trē-ˌle-vəl\ *adjective* (1975) **:** of or being at the lowest level of a hierarchy ⟨*entry-level* jobs⟩

en·try·way \-trē-ˌwā\ *noun* (1746) **:** a passage for entrance

entry word *noun* (circa 1908) **:** HEADWORD

en·twine \in-'twīn, en-\ (1590) *transitive verb* **:** to twine together or around *intransitive verb* **:** to become twisted or twined

en·twist \in-'twist, en-\ *transitive verb* (1590) **:** ENTWINE

enu·cle·ate \(ˌ)ē-'nü-klē-ˌāt, -'nyü-\ *transitive verb* **-at·ed; -at·ing** [Latin *enucleatus*, past participle of *enucleare*, literally, to remove the kernel from, from *e-* + *nucleus* kernel — more at NUCLEUS] (1548)
1 *archaic* **:** EXPLAIN
2 : to deprive of a nucleus
3 : to remove without cutting into ⟨*enucleate* a tumor⟩ ⟨*enucleate* the eyeball⟩
— enu·cle·ation \(ˌ)ē-ˌn(y)ü-klē-'ā-shən\ *noun*

enu·mer·a·ble \i-'n(y)üm-rə-bəl, -'n(y)ü-mə-\ *adjective* (circa 1889) **:** DENUMERABLE
— enu·mer·a·bil·i·ty \-ˌn(y)üm-rə-'bi-lə-tē, -ˌn(y)ü-mə-\ *noun*

enu·mer·ate \i-'n(y)ü-mə-ˌrāt\ *transitive verb* **-at·ed; -at·ing** [Latin *enumeratus*, past participle of *enumerare*, from *e-* + *numerare* to count, from *numerus* number] (1616)
1 : to ascertain the number of **:** COUNT
2 : to specify one after another **:** LIST
— enu·mer·a·tion \-ˌn(y)ü-mə-'rā-shən\ *noun*
— enu·mer·a·tive \-'n(y)ü-mə-ˌrā-tiv, -'n(y)üm-rə-, -'n(y)ü-mə-rə-\ *adjective*
enu·mer·a·tor \-'n(y)ü-mə-ˌrā-tər\ *noun* (1856) **:** one that enumerates; *especially* **:** a census taker

enun·ci·ate \ē-'nən(t)-sē-ˌāt\ *verb* **-at·ed; -at·ing** [Latin *enuntiatus*, past participle of *enuntiare* to report, declare, from *e-* + *nuntiare* to report — more at ANNOUNCE] (1623) *transitive verb*
1 a : to make a definite or systematic statement of **b :** ANNOUNCE, PROCLAIM ⟨*enunciated* the new policy⟩
2 : ARTICULATE, PRONOUNCE ⟨*enunciate* all the syllables⟩
intransitive verb **:** to utter articulate sounds
— enun·ci·a·ble \-'nən(t)-sē-ə-bəl, -'nən-ch(ē-)ə-\ *adjective*
— enun·ci·a·tion \-ˌnən(t)-sē-'ā-shən\ *noun*
— enun·ci·a·tor \-'nən(t)-sē-ˌā-tər\ *noun*

enure *variant of* INURE

en·ure·sis \ˌen-yu̇-'rē-səs\ *noun* [New Latin, from Greek *enourein* to urinate in, wet the bed, from *en-* + *ourein* to urinate — more at URINE] (circa 1800) **:** the involuntary discharge of urine **:** incontinence of urine
— en·uret·ic \-'re-tik\ *adjective or noun*

en·vel·op \in-'ve-ləp, en-\ *transitive verb* [Middle English *envolupen*, from Middle French *envoluper, enveloper*, from Old French *envoloper*, from *en-* + *voloper* to wrap] (14th century)
1 : to enclose or enfold completely with or as if with a covering
2 : to mount an attack on (an enemy's flank)

— en·vel·op·ment \-mənt\ *noun*

en·ve·lope \'en-və-ˌlōp, ÷'än-\ *noun* (circa 1714)
1 : a flat usually paper container (as for a letter)
2 : something that envelops **:** WRAPPER ⟨the *envelope* of air around the earth⟩
3 a : the outer covering of an aerostat **b :** the bag containing the gas in a balloon or airship
4 : a natural enclosing covering (as a membrane, shell, or integument)
5 a : a curve tangent to each of a family of curves **b :** a surface tangent to each of a family of surfaces
6 : a set of performance limits (as of an aircraft) that may not be safely exceeded; *also* **:** the set of operating parameters that exists within these limits □

en·ven·om \in-'ve-nəm, en-\ *transitive verb* [Middle English *envenimen*, from Old French *envenimer*, from *en-* + *venim* venom] (13th century)
1 : to make poisonous
2 : EMBITTER

en·ven·om·iza·tion \in-ˌve-nə-mə-'zā-shən, en-\ *noun* (1960) **:** a poisoning caused by a bite or sting

en·vi·able \'en-vē-ə-bəl\ *adjective* (1602) **:** highly desirable
— en·vi·able·ness *noun*
— en·vi·ably \-blē\ *adverb*

en·vi·er \'en-vē-ər\ *noun* (15th century) **:** one that envies

en·vi·ous \'en-vē-əs\ *adjective* (13th century)
1 : feeling or showing envy ⟨*envious* of their neighbor's new car⟩ ⟨*envious* looks⟩
2 *archaic* **a :** EMULOUS **b :** ENVIABLE
— en·vi·ous·ly *adverb*
— en·vi·ous·ness *noun*

en·vi·ron \in-'vī-rən, -'vī(-ə)rn\ *transitive verb* [Middle English *environen*, from Middle French *environner*, from *environ* around, from *en* in (from Latin *in*) + *viron* circle, from *virer* to turn — more at VEER] (14th century) **:** ENCIRCLE, SURROUND

en·vi·ron·ment \in-'vī-rə(n)-mənt, -'vī(-ə)r(n)-\ *noun* (1827)
1 : the circumstances, objects, or conditions by which one is surrounded
2 a : the complex of physical, chemical, and biotic factors (as climate, soil, and living things) that act upon an organism or an ecological community and ultimately determine its form and survival **b :** the aggregate of social and cultural conditions that influence the life of an individual or community
3 : the position or characteristic position of a linguistic element in a sequence
synonym *see* BACKGROUND
— en·vi·ron·men·tal \-ˌvī-rə(n)-'men-t°l, -ˌvī(-ə)r(n)-\ *adjective*
— en·vi·ron·men·tal·ly \-t°l-ē\ *adverb*

en·vi·ron·men·tal·ism \-ˌvī-rə(n)-'men-t°l-ˌi-zəm, -ˌvī(-ə)r(n)-\ *noun* (circa 1922)
1 : a theory that views environment rather than heredity as the important factor in the development and especially the cultural and intellectual development of an individual or group
2 : advocacy of the preservation or improvement of the natural environment; *especially* **:** the movement to control pollution

en·vi·ron·men·tal·ist \-t°l-əst\ *noun* (1916)
1 : an advocate of environmentalism
2 : one concerned about environmental quality especially of the human environment with respect to the control of pollution

en·vi·rons \in-'vī-rənz, -'vī(-ə)rnz\ *noun plural* (1665)
1 : the districts around a city
2 a : environing things **:** SURROUNDINGS **b :** an adjoining region or space **:** VICINITY

en·vis·age \in-'vi-zij, en-\ *transitive verb* **-aged; -ag·ing** [French *envisager*, from *en-* + *visage* face] (1837)
1 : to view or regard in a certain way ⟨*envisages* the slum as a hotbed of crime⟩

2 : to have a mental picture of especially in advance of realization ⟨*envisages* an entirely new system of education⟩
synonym *see* THINK

en·vi·sion \in-'vi-zhən, en-\ *transitive verb* (1919) **:** to picture to oneself ⟨*envisions* a career dedicated to promoting peace⟩
synonym *see* THINK

en·voi *or* **en·voy** \'en-ˌvȯi, 'än-\ *noun* [Middle English *envoye*, from Middle French *envoi*, literally, message, from Old French *envei*, from *envoier* to send on one's way, from (assumed) Vulgar Latin *inviare*, from Latin *in-* + *via* way — more at WAY] (14th century) **:** the usually explanatory or commendatory concluding remarks to a poem, essay, or book; *especially* **:** a short final stanza of a ballade serving as a summary or dedication

en·voy \'en-ˌvȯi, ÷'än-\ *noun* [French *envoyé*, from past participle of *envoyer* to send, from Old French *envoier*] (1635)
1 a : a minister plenipotentiary accredited to a foreign government who ranks between an ambassador and a minister resident — called also *envoy extraordinary* **b :** a person delegated to represent one government in its dealings with another
2 : MESSENGER, REPRESENTATIVE

¹en·vy \'en-vē\ *noun, plural* **envies** [Middle English *envie*, from Old French, from Latin *invidia*, from *invidus* envious, from *invidēre* to look askance at, envy, from *in-* + *vidēre* to see — more at WIT] (13th century)
1 : painful or resentful awareness of an advantage enjoyed by another joined with a desire to possess the same advantage
2 *obsolete* **:** MALICE
3 : an object of envious notice or feeling ⟨his new car made him the *envy* of his friends⟩

²envy *verb* **en·vied; en·vy·ing** (14th century) *transitive verb*
1 : to feel envy toward or on account of
2 *obsolete* **:** BEGRUDGE
intransitive verb *obsolete* **:** to feel or show envy
— en·vy·ing·ly \-vē-iŋ-lē\ *adverb*

en·wheel \in-'hwē(ə)l, -'wē(ə)l, en-\ *transitive verb* (1604) *obsolete* **:** ENCIRCLE

en·wind \in-'wīnd, en-\ *transitive verb* **en·wound** \-'waund\; **en·wind·ing** (1850) **:** to wind on or around **:** ENFOLD

en·womb \in-'wüm, en-\ *transitive verb* (circa 1591) **:** to shut up as if in a womb

en·wrap \in-'rap, en-\ *transitive verb* (14th century)
1 : to wrap in a covering **:** ENFOLD
2 a : ENVELOP **b :** to preoccupy or absorb mentally **:** ENGROSS

en·wreathe \in-'rēth, en-\ *transitive verb* (15th century)

□ **USAGE**
envelope The \'en-\ and \'än-\ pronunciations are used with about equal frequency, and both are fully acceptable, though the \'än-\ version is sometimes decried as "pseudo-French." Actually \'än-\ is exactly what one would expect to hear when a French word like *entrepreneur* is becoming anglicized. *Envelope*, however, has been in English for nearly 300 years, plenty of time for it to become completely anglicized and for both of its pronunciations to win respectability.

\ə\ abut \ᵊ\ kitten \ər\ further \a\ ash \ā\ ace
\ä\ mop, mar \au̇\ out \ch\ chin \e\ bet \ē\ easy
\g\ go \i\ hit \ī\ ice \j\ job \ŋ\ sing \ō\ go
\ȯ\ law \ȯi\ boy \th\ thin \th\ the \ü\ loot \u̇\ foot
\y\ yet \zh\ vision *see also* Guide to Pronunciation

: to encircle with or as if with a wreath **:** EN-
VELOP

en·zo·ot·ic \,en-zə-'wä-tik\ *adjective* [*en-* +
epi*zootic*] (1882)
: *of animal diseases* **:** peculiar to or constantly
present in a locality
— enzootic *noun*

en·zy·mat·ic \,en-zə-'ma-tik\ *also* **en·zy·
mic** \en-'zī-mik\ *adjective* (1900)
: of, relating to, or produced by an enzyme
— en·zy·mat·i·cal·ly \,en-zə-'ma-ti-
k(ə-)lē\ *also* **en·zy·mi·cal·ly** \en-'zī-mi-
k(ə-)lē\ *adverb*

en·zyme \'en-,zīm\ *noun* [German *Enzym*,
from Middle Greek *enzymos* leavened, from
Greek *en-* + *zymē* leaven — more at JUICE]
(1881)
: any of numerous complex proteins that are
produced by living cells and catalyze specific
biochemical reactions at body temperatures

enzyme–linked immunosorbent assay
noun (1977)
: a quantitative in vitro test for an antibody or
antigen in which the test material is adsorbed
on a surface and exposed to a complex of an
enzyme linked to an antibody specific for the
substance being tested for with a positive re-
sult indicated by a treatment yielding a color
in proportion to the amount of antigen or anti-
body in the test material — called also *ELISA*

en·zy·mol·o·gy \,en-,zī-'mä-lə-jē, -zə-\ *noun*
[International Scientific Vocabulary] (circa
1900)
: a branch of biochemistry that deals with en-
zymes, their nature, activity, and significance
— en·zy·mol·o·gist \-jist\ *noun*

eo- *combining form* [Greek *ēo-* dawn, from *ēōs*
— more at EAST]
: earliest : oldest ⟨*eol*ithic⟩

Eo·cene \'ē-ə-,sēn\ *adjective* (1831)
: of, relating to, or being an epoch of the Ter-
tiary between the Paleocene and the Oligocene
or the corresponding system of rocks — see
GEOLOGIC TIME table
— Eocene *noun*

eo·hip·pus \,ē-ō-'hi-pəs\ *noun* [New Latin,
from *eo-* + Greek *hippos* horse — more at
EQUINE] (circa 1879)
: any of a genus (*Hyracotherium* synonym *Eo-
hippus*) of very small primitive horses from
the Lower Eocene having four-toed forefeet
and three-toed hind feet — called also *dawn
horse*

eo·lian \ē-'ō-lē-ən, -'ōl-yən\ *adjective* [Latin
Aeolus, Aeolus] (1853)
: borne, deposited, produced, or eroded by the
wind

eo·lith \'ē-ə-,lith\ *noun* (1895)
: a very crudely chipped flint

Eo·lith·ic \,ē-ə-'li-thik\ *adjective* (1890)
: of or relating to the early period of the Stone
Age marked by the use of eoliths

eon \'ē-ən, 'ē-,än\ *variant of* AEON

eo no·mi·ne \,ē-ō-'nä-mə-nē\ [Latin] (1627)
: by or under that name

Eos \'ē-,äs\ *noun* [Greek *Ēos*]
: the Greek goddess of dawn — compare AU-
RORA

eo·sin \'ē-ə-sən\ *also* **eo·sine** \-sən, -,sēn\
noun [International Scientific Vocabulary,
from Greek *ēos* dawn] (1866)
1 : a red fluorescent dye $C_{20}H_8Br_4O_5$ obtained
by the action of bromine on fluorescein and
used especially in cosmetics and as a toner;
also **:** its red to brown sodium or potassium
salt used especially as a biological stain for
cytoplasmic structures
2 : any of several dyes related to eosin

¹eo·sin·o·phil \,ē-ə-'si-nə-,fil\ *adjective* (circa
1882)
: EOSINOPHILIC 1

²eosinophil \-,fil\ *noun* (circa 1900)
: a white blood cell or other granulocyte with
cytoplasmic inclusions readily stained by
eosin

eo·sin·o·phil·ia \-,si-nə-'fi-lē-ə\ *noun* [New
Latin] (circa 1903)
: abnormal increase in the number of eosino-
phils in the blood that is characteristic of aller-
gic states and various parasitic infections

eo·sin·o·phil·ic \-,si-nə-'fi-lik\ *adjective* (cir-
ca 1900)
1 : staining readily with eosin
2 : of, relating to, or characterized by eosino-
philia

epact \'ē-,pakt, 'e-,pakt\ *noun* [Middle French
epacte, from Late Latin *epacta*, from Greek
epaktē, from *epagein* to bring in, intercalate,
from *epi-* + *agein* to drive — more at AGENT]
(1588)
: a period added to harmonize the lunar with
the solar calendar

ep·ar·chy \'e-,pär-kē\ *noun, plural* **-chies**
[Greek *eparchia* province, from *eparchos* pre-
fect, from *epi-* + *archos* ruler — more at
ARCH] (1796)
: a diocese of an Eastern church

ep·au·let *also* **ep·au·lette** \'e-pə-'let; 'e-pə-
,let, -,lət\ *noun* [French *épaulette*, diminutive
of *épaule* shoulder, from Late Latin *spatula*
shoulder blade, spoon, diminutive of Latin
spatha spoon, sword — more at SPADE]
(1783)
: something that orna-
ments or protects the
shoulder: as **a :** an orna-
mental fringed shoulder
pad formerly worn as
part of a military uni-
form **b :** an ornamental
strip or loop sewn across
the shoulder of a dress
or coat
— ep·au·let·ted \,e-
pə-'le-təd, 'e-pə-,\ *adjec-
tive*

E epaulet

ep·a·zote \'e-pə-,zōt\ *noun* [Mexican Spanish,
from Nahuatl *epazōtl*] (1946)
: WORMSEED b

épée \'e-,pā, ā-'pā\ *noun* [French, from Latin
spatha] (1889)
1 : a fencing or dueling sword having a bowl-
shaped guard and a rigid blade of triangular
section with no cutting edge that tapers to a
sharp point blunted for fencing — compare
⁴FOIL 1, SABER
2 : the art or sport of fencing with the épée

épée·ist \-ist\ *noun* (1910)
: one who fences with an épée

ep·ei·rog·e·ny \,e-,pī-'rä-jə-nē\ *noun, plural*
-nies [Greek *ēpeiros* mainland, continent +
English *-geny*] (1890)
: the deformation of the earth's crust by which
the broader features of relief are produced
— epei·ro·gen·ic \-,pī-rə-'je-nik\ *adjec-
tive*
— epei·ro·gen·i·cal·ly \-ni-k(ə-)lē\ *ad-
verb*

epen·the·sis \i-'pen(t)-thə-səs, e-\ *noun, plu-
ral* **-the·ses** \-,sēz\ [Late Latin, from Greek,
from *epentithenai* to insert a letter, from *epi-*
+ *entithenai* to put in, from *en-* + *tithenai* to
put — more at DO] (1543)
: the insertion or development of a sound or
letter in the body of a word (as \ə\ in \'a-thə-
,lēt\ *athlete*)
— ep·en·thet·ic \,e-pən-'the-tik\ *adjective*

epergne \i-'pərn, ā-\ *noun* [probably from
French *épargne* saving] (1761)
: an often ornate tiered centerpiece consisting
typically of a frame of wrought metal (as sil-
ver or gold) bearing dishes, vases, or candle
holders or a combination of these

ep·ex·e·ge·sis \,e-,pek-sə-'jē-səs\ *noun, plu-
ral* **-ge·ses** \-,sēz\ [Greek *epexēgēsis*, from
epi- + *exēgēsis* exegesis] (circa 1577)
: additional explanation or explanatory matter
— ep·ex·e·get·i·cal \-'je-ti-kəl\ *or* **ep-
ex·e·get·ic** \-'je-tik\ *adjective*
— ep·ex·e·get·i·cal·ly \-'je-ti-k(ə-)lē\ *ad-
verb*

ephah \'ē-fə, 'e-fə\ *noun* [Middle English *ephi*,
from Late Latin, from Hebrew *ēphāh*, from
Egyptian *'pt*] (1611)
: an ancient Hebrew unit of dry measure equal
to ¹⁄₁₀ homer or a little over a bushel

ephebe \'e-,fēb, i-'fēb\ *noun* [Latin *ephebus*]
(1880)
: EPHEBUS; *also* **:** a young man **:** YOUTH

ephe·bic \i-'fē-bik\ *adjective* (1865)
: of, relating to, or characteristic of an ephebe
or ephebus

ephe·bus \i-'fē-bəs, e-\ *noun, plural* **-bi** \-,bī\
[Latin, from Greek *ephēbos*, from *epi-* + *hēbē*
youth, puberty] (1697)
: a youth of ancient Greece; *especially* **:** an
Athenian 18 or 19 years old in training for full
citizenship

ephe·dra \i-'fe-drə, 'e-fə-drə\ *noun* [New Lat-
in, genus name, from Latin, equisetum, from
Greek, from *ephedros* sitting upon, from *epi-*
+ *hedra* seat — more at SIT] (circa 1889)
: any of a large genus (*Ephedra* of the family
Gnetaceae) of jointed nearly leafless desert
shrubs with the leaves reduced to scales at the
nodes

ephed·rine \i-'fe-drən, *British also* 'e-fə-drən\
noun [New Latin *Ephedra*] (1889)
: a crystalline alkaloid $C_{10}H_{15}NO$ extracted
from Chinese ephedras or synthesized and
used in the form of a salt for relief of hay fe-
ver, asthma, and nasal congestion

ephem·era \i-'fe-mər-ə, -'fem-ər-ə\ *noun, plu-
ral* **ephemera** *also* **ephem·er·ae** \-mər-ē,
-rē\ *or* **ephemeras** [New Latin, from Greek
ephēmera, neuter plural of *ephēmeros*] (1751)
1 : something of no lasting significance —
usually used in plural
2 *ephemera plural* **:** collectibles (as posters,
broadsides, and tickets) not intended to have
lasting value

¹ephem·er·al \i-'fem-rəl, -'fēm-; -'fe-mə-,
-'fē-\ *adjective* [Greek *ephēmeros* lasting a
day, daily, from *epi-* + *hēmera* day] (1576)
1 : lasting one day only ⟨an *ephemeral* fever⟩
2 : lasting a very short time ⟨*ephemeral*
pleasures⟩
synonym see TRANSIENT
— ephem·er·al·ly \-rə-lē\ *adverb*

²ephemeral *noun* (1817)
: something ephemeral; *specifically* **:** a plant
that grows, flowers, and dies in a few days

ephem·er·al·i·ty \i-,fe-mə-'ra-lə-tē, -,fē-\
noun, plural **-ties** (1822)
1 : the quality or state of being ephemeral
2 *plural* **:** ephemeral things

ephem·er·id \i-'fe-mə-rəd\ *noun* [ultimately
from Greek *ephēmeron*] (1872)
: MAYFLY

ephem·er·is \-mə-rəs\ *noun, plural* **eph·e·
mer·i·des** \,e-fə-'mer-ə-,dēz\ [Latin, diary,
ephemeris, from Greek *ephēmeris*, from
ephēmeros] (1508)
: a tabular statement of the assigned places of
a celestial body for regular intervals

ephemeris time *noun* (1950)
: a uniform measure of time defined by the or-
bital motions of the planets

Ephe·sians \i-'fē-zhənz\ *noun plural but sin-
gular in construction* [short for *Epistle to the
Ephesians*]
: a letter addressed to early Christians and in-
cluded as a book in the New Testament —
see BIBLE table

eph·od \'e-,fäd, 'ē-,fäd\ *noun* [Middle English,
from Late Latin, from Hebrew *ēphōdh*] (14th
century)
1 : a linen apron worn in ancient Hebrew rites;
especially **:** a vestment for the high priest
2 : an ancient Hebrew instrument of priestly
divination

eph·or \'e-fər, -,fȯr\ *noun* [Latin *ephorus*, from
Greek *ephoros*, from *ephoran* to oversee, from
epi- + *horan* to see — more at WARY] (1579)
1 : one of five ancient Spartan magistrates
having power over the king

2 : a government official in modern Greece; *especially* **:** one who oversees public works
— **eph·or·ate** \'e-fə-ˌrāt\ *noun*

Ephra·im \'ē-frē-əm\ *noun* [Hebrew *Ephrayim*]
: a son of Joseph and the traditional eponymous ancestor of one of the tribes of Israel

Ephra·im·ite \-frē-ə-ˌmīt\ *noun* (1611)
1 : a member of the Hebrew tribe of Ephraim
2 : a native or inhabitant of the biblical northern kingdom of Israel

epi- *or* **ep-** *prefix* [Middle English, from Middle French & Latin; Middle French, from Latin, from Greek, from *epi* on, at, besides, after; akin to Old English *eofot* crime]
1 : upon ⟨*epi*phyte⟩ **:** besides ⟨*epi*phenomenon⟩ **:** attached to ⟨*epi*didymis⟩ **:** over ⟨*epi*center⟩ **:** outer ⟨*epi*blast⟩ **:** after ⟨*epi*genesis⟩
2 a : chemical entity related to (such) another ⟨*epi*mer⟩ **b :** chemical entity distinguished from (such) another by having a bridge connection ⟨*epi*chlorohydrin⟩

epi·blast \'e-pə-ˌblast\ *noun* (1875)
: the outer layer of the blastoderm **:** ECTODERM
— **epi·blas·tic** \ˌe-pə-'blas-tik\ *adjective*

epib·o·ly \i-'pi-bə-lē\ *noun, plural* **-lies** [Greek *epibolē* addition, from *epiballein* to throw on, from *epi-* + *ballein* to throw — more at DEVIL] (1875)
: the growing of one part about another; *especially* **:** such growth of the dorsal lip area during gastrulation
— **ep·i·bol·ic** \ˌe-pə-'bä-lik\ *adjective*

¹ep·ic \'e-pik\ *adjective* [Latin *epicus*, from Greek *epikos*, from *epos* word, speech, poem — more at VOICE] (1589)
1 : of, relating to, or having the characteristics of an epic
2 a : extending beyond the usual or ordinary especially in size or scope ⟨his genius was *epic* —*Times Literary Supplement*⟩ **b :** HEROIC
— **ep·i·cal** \-pi-kəl\ *adjective*
— **ep·i·cal·ly** \-pi-k(ə-)lē\ *adverb*

²epic *noun* (1706)
1 : a long narrative poem in elevated style recounting the deeds of a legendary or historical hero ⟨the *Iliad* and the *Odyssey* are *epics*⟩
2 : a work of art (as a novel or drama) that resembles or suggests an epic
3 : a series of events or body of legend or tradition thought to form the proper subject of an epic ⟨the winning of the West was a great American *epic*⟩

epi·ca·lyx \ˌe-pi-'kā-liks *also* -'ka-liks\ *noun* (1870)
: an involucre resembling the calyx but consisting of a whorl of bracts that is exterior to the calyx or results from the union of the sepal appendages

epi·can·thic fold \ˌe-pə-'kan(t)-thik-\ *noun* [New Latin *epicanthus* epicanthic fold, from *epi-* + *canthus* canthus] (1913)
: a prolongation of a fold of the skin of the upper eyelid over the inner angle or both angles of the eye

epi·car·di·um \ˌe-pə-'kar-dē-əm\ *noun, plural* **-dia** \-dē-ə\ [New Latin] (circa 1865)
: the visceral part of the pericardium that closely envelops the heart
— **epi·car·di·al** \-dē-əl\ *adjective*

epi·carp \'e-pi-ˌkärp\ *noun* [French *épicarpe*, from *épi-* epi- + *-carpe* -carp] (1835)
: EXOCARP

ep·i·cene \'e-pə-ˌsēn\ *adjective* [Middle English, from Latin *epicoenus*, from Greek *epikoinos*, from *epi-* + *koinos* common — more at CO-] (15th century)
1 *of a noun* **:** having but one form to indicate either sex
2 a : having characteristics typical of the other sex **:** INTERSEXUAL **b :** EFFEMINATE
3 : lacking characteristics of either sex
— **epicene** *noun*
— **ep·i·cen·ism** \-ˌsē-ˌni-zəm, ˌe-pə-'\ *noun*

epi·cen·ter \'e-pi-ˌsen-tər\ *noun* [New Latin *epicentrum*, from *epi-* + Latin *centrum* center] (1887)
1 : the part of the earth's surface directly above the focus of an earthquake — compare HYPOCENTER 1
2 : CENTER 2a, b, c ⟨the *epicenter* of world finance⟩
— **epi·cen·tral** \ˌe-pi-'sen-trəl\ *adjective*

epi·chlo·ro·hy·drin \ˌe-pi-ˌklōr-ə-'hī-drən, -ˌklȯr-\ *noun* (circa 1891)
: a volatile liquid toxic epoxide C_3H_5ClO having a chloroform odor and used especially in making epoxy resins and rubbers

epi·con·ti·nen·tal \ˌe-pi-ˌkän-t°n-'en-t°l\ *adjective* (1900)
: lying upon a continent or a continental shelf ⟨*epicontinental* seas⟩

epi·cot·yl \'e-pi-ˌkä-t°l\ *noun* [*epi-* + *cotyledon*] (1880)
: the portion of the axis of a plant embryo or seedling above the cotyledonary node

ep·i·crit·ic \ˌe-pə-'kri-tik\ *adjective* [Greek *epikritikos* determinative, from *epikrinein* to decide, from *epi-* + *krinein* to judge — more at CERTAIN] (circa 1905)
: of, relating to, being, or mediating cutaneous sensory reception marked by accurate discrimination between small degrees of sensation

epic simile *noun* (1931)
: an extended simile that is used typically in epic poetry to intensify the heroic stature of the subject

ep·i·cure \'e-pi-ˌkyùr\ *noun* [*Epicurus*] (1565)
1 *archaic* **:** one devoted to sensual pleasure **:** SYBARITE
2 : one with sensitive and discriminating tastes especially in food or wine ☆ ◇

ep·i·cu·re·an \ˌe-pi-kyù-'rē-ən, -'kyùr-ē-\ *adjective* (1586)
1 *capitalized* **:** of or relating to Epicurus or Epicureanism
2 : of, relating to, or suited to an epicure

Epicurean *noun* (14th century)
1 : a follower of Epicurus
2 *often not capitalized* **:** EPICURE 2

ep·i·cu·re·an·ism \-ə-ˌni-zəm\ *noun* (circa 1751)
1 *capitalized* **a :** the philosophy of Epicurus who subscribed to a hedonistic ethics that considered an imperturbable emotional calm the highest good and whose followers held intellectual pleasures superior to transient sensualism **b :** a mode of life in consonance with Epicureanism
2 : EPICURISM

ep·i·cur·ism \'e-pi-ˌkyùr-i-zəm, ˌe-pi-'\ *noun* (1586)
: the practices or tastes of an epicure or an epicurean

epi·cu·ti·cle \ˌe-pi-'kyü-ti-kəl\ *noun* (1929)
: an outermost waxy layer of the insect exoskeleton
— **epi·cu·tic·u·lar** \-kyù-'ti-kyə-lər\ *adjective*

epi·cy·cle \'e-pə-ˌsī-kəl\ *noun* [Middle English *epicicle*, from Late Latin *epicyclus*, from Greek *epikyklos*, from *epi-* + *kyklos* circle — more at WHEEL] (14th century)
1 *in Ptolemaic astronomy* **:** a circle in which a planet moves and which has a center that is itself carried around at the same time on the circumference of a larger circle
2 : a process going on within a larger one
— **epi·cy·clic** \ˌe-pə-'sī-klik, -'si-klik\ *adjective*

epicyclic train *noun* (circa 1890)
: a train (as of gear wheels) designed to have one or more parts travel around the circumference of another fixed or revolving part

epi·cy·cloid \ˌe-pə-'sī-ˌklȯid\ *noun* (circa 1755)
: a curve traced by a point on a circle that rolls on the outside of a fixed circle
— **epi·cy·cloi·dal** \-sī-'klȯi-d°l\ *adjective*

¹ep·i·dem·ic \ˌe-pə-'de-mik\ *adjective* [French *épidémique*, from Middle French, from *epidemie*, noun, epidemic, from Late Latin *epidemia*, from Greek *epidēmia* visit, epidemic, from *epidēmos* visiting, epidemic, from *epi-* + *dēmos* people — more at DEMAGOGUE] (1603)
1 : affecting or tending to affect a disproportionately large number of individuals within a population, community, or region at the same time ⟨typhoid was *epidemic*⟩
2 a : excessively prevalent **b :** CONTAGIOUS 4 ⟨*epidemic* laughter⟩
3 : of, relating to, or constituting an epidemic ⟨the practice had reached *epidemic* proportions⟩
— **ep·i·dem·i·cal** \-'de-mi-kəl\ *adjective*
— **ep·i·dem·i·cal·ly** \-'de-mi-k(ə-)lē\ *adverb*
— **ep·i·de·mic·i·ty** \-də-'mi-sə-tē\ *noun*

²epidemic *noun* (1799)
1 : an outbreak of epidemic disease
2 : an outbreak or product of sudden rapid spread, growth, or development; *specifically* **:** a natural population suddenly and greatly enlarged

ep·i·de·mi·ol·o·gy \ˌe-pə-ˌdē-mē-'ä-lə-jē, -ˌde-mē-\ *noun* [Late Latin *epidemia* + International Scientific Vocabulary *-logy*] (circa 1860)

epicycloid *E*, traced by point *P*, on circle *R*, rolling on fixed circle *F*

1 : a branch of medical science that deals with the incidence, distribution, and control of disease in a population
2 : the sum of the factors controlling the presence or absence of a disease or pathogen
— **ep·i·de·mi·o·log·i·cal** \-ˌdē-mē-ə-'lä-ji-kəl, -ˌde-mē-\ *also* **ep·i·de·mi·o·log·ic** \-jik\ *adjective*
— **ep·i·de·mi·o·log·i·cal·ly** \-ji-k(ə-)lē\ *adverb*
— **ep·i·de·mi·ol·o·gist** \-ˌdē-mē-'ä-lə-jist, -ˌde-mē-\ *noun*

ep·i·den·drum \ˌe-pə-'den-drəm\ *noun* [New Latin, from Greek *epi-* + *dendron* tree — more at DENDR-] (1791)
: any of a large genus (*Epidendrum*) of chiefly epiphytic orchids found especially in tropical America

epi·der·mal \ˌe-pə-'dər-məl\ *also* **epi·der·mic** \-mik\ *adjective* (1816)
: of, relating to, or arising from the epidermis

epidermal growth factor *noun* (1966)
: a polypeptide hormone that stimulates cell proliferation

epi·der·mis \ˌe-pə-'dər-məs\ *noun* [Late Latin, from Greek, from *epi-* + *derma* skin — more at DERM-] (1626)
1 a : the outer epithelial layer of the external integument of the animal body that is derived from the embryonic epiblast; *specifically* **:** the outer nonsensitive and nonvascular layer of the skin of a vertebrate that overlies the dermis **b :** any of various animal integuments
2 : a thin surface layer of tissue in higher plants formed by growth of a primary meristem

epi·der·moid \-ˌmȯid\ *adjective* (1836)
: resembling epidermis or epidermal cells **:** made up of elements like those of epidermis ⟨*epidermoid* cancer of the lung⟩

epi·dia·scope \ˌe-pə-'dī-ə-ˌskōp\ *noun* [International Scientific Vocabulary] (1903)
1 : a projector for images of both opaque objects and transparencies
2 : EPISCOPE

ep·i·did·y·mis \ˌe-pə-'di-də-məs\ *noun, plural* **-mi·des** \-mə-ˌdēz\ [New Latin, from Greek, from *epi-* + *didymos* testicle, twin, from *dyo* two — more at TWO] (1610)
: a system of ductules emerging posteriorly from the testis that holds sperm during maturation and that forms a tangled mass before uniting into a single coiled duct which is continuous with the vas deferens
— **ep·i·did·y·mal** \-məl\ *adjective*

epi·did·y·mi·tis \ˌe-pə-ˌdi-də-'mī-təs\ *noun* [New Latin] (1852)
: inflammation of the epididymis

ep·i·dote \'e-pə-ˌdōt\ *noun* [French *épidote*, from Greek *epididonai* to give in addition, from *epi-* + *didonai* to give — more at DATE] (1808)
: a yellowish green mineral $Ca_2(Al,Fe)_3$-$Si_3O_{12}OH$ usually occurring in grains or columnar masses and sometimes used as a gemstone

epi·du·ral \ˌe-pi-'d(y)ùr-əl\ *adjective* (1882)
: situated upon or administered outside the dura mater ⟨*epidural* anesthesia⟩ ⟨*epidural* structures⟩

epi·fau·na \-'fȯ-nə, -'fä-\ *noun* [New Latin] (circa 1914)
: benthic fauna living on the substrate (as a hard sea floor) or on other organisms — compare INFAUNA
— **epi·fau·nal** \-'fȯ-n°l, -'fä-\ *adjective*

epi·gas·tric \ˌe-pi-'gas-trik\ *adjective* (circa 1678)
1 : lying upon or over the stomach
2 a : of, relating to, supplying, or draining the anterior walls of the abdomen **b :** of or relating to the abdominal region

epi·ge·al \ˌe-pi-'jē-əl\ *or* **epi·ge·an** \-'jē-ən\ *also* **epi·ge·ous** \-'jē-əs\ *or* **epi·ge·ic** \-'jē-ik\ *adjective* [Greek *epigaios* upon the earth, from *epi-* + *gaia* earth] (1861)

1 *of a cotyledon* **:** forced above ground by elongation of the hypocotyl
2 : marked by the production of epigeal cotyledons ⟨*epigeal* germination⟩
3 : living on or near the surface of the ground; *also* **:** relating to or being the environment near the surface of the ground

epi·gen·e·sis \ˌe-pə-'je-nə-səs\ *noun* [New Latin] (1798)
1 : development of a plant or animal from an egg or spore through a series of processes in which unorganized cell masses differentiate into organs and organ systems; *also* **:** the theory that plant and animal development proceeds in this way — compare PREFORMATION 2
2 : change in the mineral character of a rock owing to outside influences

epi·ge·net·ic \-jə-'ne-tik\ *adjective* (1883)
1 : of, relating to, or produced by the chain of developmental processes in epigenesis that lead from genotype to phenotype after the initial action of the genes
2 *of a deposit or structure* **:** formed after the laying down of the enclosing rock
— **epi·ge·net·i·cal·ly** \-'ne-ti-k(ə-)lē\ *adverb*

epi·glot·tal \ˌe-pə-'glä-t°l\ *also* **epi·glot·tic** \-'glä-tik\ *adjective* (1926)
: of, relating to, or produced with the aid of the epiglottis

epi·glot·tis \-'glä-təs\ *noun* [New Latin, from Greek *epiglōttis*, from *epi-* + *glōttis* glottis] (1615)
: a thin plate of flexible cartilage in front of the glottis that folds back over and protects the glottis during swallowing

ep·i·gone \'e-pə-ˌgōn\ *noun* [German, from Latin *epigonus* successor, from Greek *epigonos*, from *epigignesthai* to be born after, from *epi-* + *gignesthai* to be born — more at KIN] (1865)
: FOLLOWER, DISCIPLE; *also* **:** an inferior imitator
— **ep·i·gon·ic** \ˌe-pə-'gä-nik\ *or* **epig·o·nous** \i-'pi-gə-nəs, e-\ *adjective*
— **epig·o·nism** \-'pi-gə-ˌni-zəm\ *noun*

epig·o·nus \i-'pi-gə-nəs, e-\ *noun, plural* **-ni** \-ˌnī, -ˌnē\ [Latin] (1922)
: EPIGONE — usually used in plural

ep·i·gram \'e-pə-ˌgram\ *noun* [Middle English *epigrame*, from Latin *epigrammat-*, *epigramma*, from Greek, from *epigraphein* to write on, inscribe, from *epi-* + *graphein* to write — more at CARVE] (15th century)
1 : a concise poem dealing pointedly and often satirically with a single thought or event and often ending with an ingenious turn of thought
2 : a terse, sage, or witty and often paradoxical saying
3 : epigrammatic expression
— **ep·i·gram·ma·tism** \ˌe-pə-'gra-mə-ˌti-zəm\ *noun*
— **ep·i·gram·ma·tist** \-'gra-mə-tist\ *noun*

ep·i·gram·mat·ic \ˌe-pə-grə-'ma-tik\ *adjective* (circa 1704)
1 : of, relating to, or resembling an epigram
2 : marked by or given to the use of epigrams
— **ep·i·gram·mat·i·cal·ly** \-'ma-ti-k(ə-)lē\ *adverb*

ep·i·gram·ma·tize \-'gra-mə-ˌtīz\ *verb* **-tized; -tiz·ing** (1691)
transitive verb
1 : to express in the form of an epigram
2 : to make an epigram about
intransitive verb
: to make an epigram
— **ep·i·gram·ma·tiz·er** *noun*

ep·i·graph \'e-pə-ˌgraf\ *noun* [Greek *epigraphē*, from *epigraphein*] (1624)
1 : an engraved inscription
2 : a quotation set at the beginning of a literary work or one of its divisions to suggest its theme

epig·ra·pher \i-'pi-grə-fər, e-\ *noun* (1887)
: EPIGRAPHIST

ep·i·graph·ic \ˌe-pə-'gra-fik\ *also* **ep·i·graph·i·cal** \-fi-kəl\ *adjective* (1858)
: of or relating to epigraphs or epigraphy
— **ep·i·graph·i·cal·ly** \-fi-k(ə-)lē\ *adverb*

epig·ra·phist \i-'pi-grə-fist, e-\ *noun* (circa 1864)
: a specialist in epigraphy

epig·ra·phy \-fē\ *noun* (1851)
1 : EPIGRAPHS, INSCRIPTIONS
2 : the study of inscriptions; *especially* **:** the deciphering of ancient inscriptions

epig·y·nous \i-'pi-jə-nəs, e-\ *adjective* (1830)
1 *of a floral organ* **:** adnate to the surface of the ovary and appearing to grow from the top of it
2 : having epigynous floral organs
— **epig·y·ny** \-nē\ *noun*

ep·i·la·tion \ˌe-pə-'lā-shən\ *noun* [French *épilation*, from *épiler* to remove hair, from *é-* e- + Latin *pilus* hair — more at PILE] (1878)
: the loss or removal of hair

ep·i·lep·sy \'e-pə-ˌlep-sē\ *noun, plural* **-sies** [Middle French *epilepsie*, from Late Latin *epilepsia*, from Greek *epilēpsia*, from *epilambanein* to seize, from *epi-* + *lambanein* to take, seize — more at LATCH] (1543)
: any of various disorders marked by disturbed electrical rhythms of the central nervous system and typically manifested by convulsive attacks usually with clouding of consciousness

epilept- *or* **epilepti-** *or* **epilepto-** *combining form* [Greek *epilēpt-*, from *epilēptos* seized by epilepsy, from *epilambanein*]
: epilepsy ⟨*epilept*oid⟩

ep·i·lep·tic \ˌe-pə-'lep-tik\ *adjective* (1605)
: relating to, affected with, or having the characteristics of epilepsy
— **epileptic** *noun*
— **ep·i·lep·ti·cal·ly** \-ti-k(ə-)lē\ *adverb*

ep·i·lep·ti·form \-'lep-tə-ˌfȯrm\ *adjective* (circa 1859)
: resembling that of epilepsy ⟨an *epileptiform* convulsion⟩

ep·i·lep·to·gen·ic \-ˌlep-tə-'je-nik\ *adjective* (circa 1882)
: inducing or tending to induce epilepsy ⟨an *epileptogenic* drug⟩

ep·i·lep·toid \-'lep-ˌtȯid\ *adjective* (circa 1860)
1 : EPILEPTIFORM
2 : exhibiting symptoms resembling those of epilepsy ⟨the *epileptoid* person⟩

epi·lim·ni·on \ˌe-pə-'lim-nē-ˌän, -nē-ən\ *noun* [New Latin, from *epi-* + Greek *limnion*, diminutive of *limnē* marshy lake — more at LIMNETIC] (circa 1910)
: the water layer overlying the thermocline of a lake

ep·i·logue *also* **ep·i·log** \'e-pə-ˌlȯg, -ˌläg\ *noun* [Middle English *epiloge*, from Middle French *epilogue*, from Latin *epilogus*, from Greek *epilogos*, from *epilegein* to say in addition, from *epi-* + *legein* to say — more at LEGEND] (15th century)
1 : a concluding section that rounds out the design of a literary work
2 a : a speech often in verse addressed to the audience by an actor at the end of a play; *also* **:** the actor speaking such an epilogue **b :** the final scene of a play that comments on or summarizes the main action
3 : the concluding section of a musical composition **:** CODA

epi·mer \'e-pi-mər\ *noun* [*epi-* + is*omer*] (circa 1911)
: either of the stereoisomers of a sugar or sugar derivative that differ in the arrangement of the hydrogen atom and the hydroxyl group on the first asymmetric carbon atom of a chain
— **epi·mer·ic** \ˌe-pi-'mer-ik\ *adjective*

epim·er·ase \i-'pi-mə-ˌrās, e-, -ˌrāz\ *noun* (1960)
: any of various isomerases that catalyze the inversion of asymmetric groups in a substrate with several centers of asymmetry

epi·my·si·um \,e-pə-'mi-zhē-əm, -zē-\ *noun*, *plural* **-sia** \-zhē-ə, -zē-ə\ [New Latin, irregular from *epi-* + Greek *mys* mouse, muscle — more at MOUSE] (1900)
: the external connective-tissue sheath of a muscle

epi·nas·ty \'e-pə-,nas-tē\ *noun* [International Scientific Vocabulary *epi-* + Greek *nastos* close-pressed (from *nassein* to press) + International Scientific Vocabulary ²-y] (1880)
: a nastic movement in which a plant part (as a flower petal) is bent outward and often downward

epi·neph·rine *also* **epi·neph·rin** \,e-pə-'nef-frən\ *noun* [International Scientific Vocabulary *epi-* + Greek *nephros* kidney — more at NEPHRITIS] (1899)
: a colorless crystalline feebly basic sympathomimetic hormone $C_9H_{13}NO_3$ that is the principal blood-pressure raising hormone secreted by the adrenal medulla and is used medicinally especially as a heart stimulant, a vasoconstrictor in controlling hemorrhages of the skin, and a muscle relaxant in bronchial asthma — called also *adrenaline*

epi·neu·ri·um \,e-pə-'n(y)ur-ē-əm\ *noun* [New Latin] (circa 1882)
: the external connective-tissue sheath of a nerve trunk

epi·pe·lag·ic \,e-pi-pə-'la-jik\ *adjective* (1940)
: of, relating to, or constituting the part of the oceanic zone into which enough light penetrates for photosynthesis

ep·i·phan·ic \,e-pə-'fa-nik\ *adjective* (1951)
: of or having the character of an epiphany

epiph·a·nous \i-'pi-fə-nəs\ *adjective* (1823)
: EPIPHANIC

epiph·a·ny \i-'pi-fə-nē\ *noun*, *plural* **-nies** [Middle English *epiphanie*, from Middle French, from Late Latin *epiphania*, from Late Greek, plural, probably alteration of Greek *epiphaneia* appearance, manifestation, from *epiphainein* to manifest, from *epi-* + *phainein* to show — more at FANCY] (14th century)
1 *capitalized* : January 6 observed as a church festival in commemoration of the coming of the Magi as the first manifestation of Christ to the Gentiles or in the Eastern Church in commemoration of the baptism of Christ
2 : an appearance or manifestation especially of a divine being
3 a (1) : a usually sudden manifestation or perception of the essential nature or meaning of something (2) : an intuitive grasp of reality through something (as an event) usually simple and striking (3) : an illuminating discovery **b** : a revealing scene or moment

epi·phe·nom·e·nal \,e-pi-fi-'nä-mə-n³l\ *adjective* (1899)
: of or relating to an epiphenomenon : DERIVATIVE
— **epi·phe·nom·e·nal·ly** \-n³l-ē\ *adverb*

epi·phe·nom·e·nal·ism \-n³l-,i-zəm\ *noun* (1899)
: a doctrine that mental processes are epiphenomena of brain processes

epi·phe·nom·e·non \-'nä-mə-,nän, -nən\ *noun*, *plural* **-na** \-,nä, -nə\ (circa 1706)
: a secondary phenomenon accompanying another and caused by it

ep·i·phragm \'e-pə-,fram\ *noun* [Greek *epiphragma* covering] (circa 1854)
: a closing membrane or septum (as of a snail shell or a moss capsule)

epiph·y·se·al \i-,pi-fə-'sē-əl\ *also* **ep·i·phys·i·al** \,e-pə-'fi-zē-əl\ *adjective* (1842)
: of or relating to an epiphysis

epiph·y·sis \i-'pi-fə-səs\ *noun*, *plural* **-y·ses** \-,sēz\ [New Latin, from Greek, growth, from *epiphyesthai* to grow on, from *epi-* + *phyesthai* to grow, middle voice of *phyein* to bring forth — more at BE] (1634)

1 : a part or process of a bone that ossifies separately and later becomes ankylosed to the main part of the bone; *especially* : an end of a long bone
2 : PINEAL GLAND

epi·phyte \'e-pə-,fīt\ *noun* (circa 1847)
: a plant that derives its moisture and nutrients from the air and rain and grows usually on another plant

epi·phyt·ic \,e-pə-'fi-tik\ *adjective* (1830)
1 : of, relating to, or being an epiphyte
2 : living on the surface of plants
— **epi·phyt·i·cal·ly** \-'fi-ti-k(ə-)lē\ *adverb*
— **epi·phyt·ism** \'e-pə-,fī-,ti-zəm\ *noun*

ep·i·phy·tol·o·gy \,e-pə-fī-'tä-lə-jē\ *noun* [*epiphyto*tic + *-logy*] (1940)
1 : a science that deals with character, ecology, and causes of outbreak of plant diseases
2 : the sum of the factors controlling the occurrence of a disease or pathogen of plants

ep·i·phy·tot·ic \-'tä-tik\ *adjective* [*epi-* + *-phyte* + *-otic* (as in *epizootic*)] (circa 1899)
: of, relating to, or being a plant disease that tends to recur sporadically and to affect large numbers of susceptible plants
— **epiphytotic** *noun*

epi·scia \i-'pi-sh(ē-)ə\ *noun* [New Latin, from Greek *episkios* shaded, from *epi-* + *skia* shadow — more at SHINE] (circa 1868)
: any of a genus (*Episcia*) of tropical American herbs that have hairy foliage and are related to the African violet

epis·co·pa·cy \i-'pis-kə-pə-sē\ *noun*, *plural* **-cies** (1647)
1 : government of the church by bishops or by a hierarchy
2 : EPISCOPATE

epis·co·pal \i-'pis-kə-pəl, -bəl\ *adjective* [Middle English, from Late Latin *episcopalis*, from *episcopus* bishop — more at BISHOP] (15th century)
1 : of or relating to a bishop
2 : of, having, or constituting government by bishops
3 *capitalized* : of or relating to the Protestant Episcopal Church representing the Anglican communion in the U.S.
— **epis·co·pal·ly** \-p(ə-)lē\ *adverb*

Episcopal *noun* (1752)
: EPISCOPALIAN

Epis·co·pa·lian \i-,pis-kə-'pāl-yən\ *noun* (1690)
1 : an adherent of the episcopal form of church government
2 : a member of an episcopal church (as the Protestant Episcopal Church)
— **Episcopalian** *adjective*
— **Epis·co·pa·lian·ism** \-yə-,ni-zəm\ *noun*

epis·co·pate \i-'pis-kə-pət, -,pāt\ *noun* (1641)
1 : the rank, office, or term of bishop
2 : DIOCESE
3 : the body of bishops (as in a country)

epi·scope \'e-pə-,skōp\ *noun* [International Scientific Vocabulary] (circa 1909)
: a projector for images of opaque objects (as photographs)

epi·si·ot·o·my \i-,pi-zē-'ä-tə-mē, -,pē-\ *noun* [International Scientific Vocabulary *episio*-vulva (from Greek *epision* pubic region) + *-tomy*] (1878)
: surgical enlargement of the vulval orifice for obstetrical purposes during parturition

ep·i·sode \'e-pə-,sōd *also* -,zōd\ *noun* [Greek *epeisodion*, from neuter of *epeisodios* coming in besides, from *epi-* + *eisodios* coming in, from *eis* into (akin to Greek *en* in) + *hodos* road, journey — more at IN] (1678)
1 : a usually brief unit of action in a dramatic or literary work: as **a** : the part of an ancient Greek tragedy between two choric songs **b** : a developed situation that is integral to but separable from a continuous narrative : INCIDENT **c** : one of a series of loosely connected stories

or scenes **d** : the part of a serial presented at one performance
2 : an event that is distinctive and separate although part of a larger series
3 : a digressive subdivision in a musical composition
synonym see OCCURRENCE

ep·i·sod·ic \,e-pə-'sä-dik *also* -'zä-\ *also* **ep·i·sod·i·cal** \-di-kəl\ *adjective* (1711)
1 : made up of separate especially loosely connected episodes
2 : having the form of an episode
3 : of or limited in duration or significance to a particular episode : TEMPORARY ⟨may be able to establish whether the sea-floor spreading is continuous or *episodic* —A. I. Hammond⟩
4 : occurring, appearing, or changing at usually irregular intervals : OCCASIONAL ⟨an *episodic* illness⟩
— **ep·i·sod·i·cal·ly** \-di-k(ə-)lē\ *adverb*

epi·some \'e-pə-,sōm, -,zōm\ *noun* (circa 1931)
: a genetic determinant (as the DNA of some bacteriophages) that can replicate autonomously in bacterial cytoplasm or as an integral part of the chromosomes
— **epi·som·al** \,e-pə-'sō-məl, -'zō-\ *adjective*
— **epi·som·al·ly** \-mə-lē\ *adverb*

epis·ta·sis \i-'pis-tə-səs\ *noun*, *plural* **-ta·ses** \-,sēz\ [New Latin, from Greek, act of stopping, from *ephistanai* to stop, from *epi-* + *histanai* to cause to stand — more at STAND] (circa 1917)
: suppression of the effect of a gene by a nonallelic gene
— **ep·i·stat·ic** \,e-pə-'sta-tik\ *adjective*

ep·i·stax·is \,e-pə-'stak-səs\ *noun*, *plural* **-stax·es** \-,sēz\ [New Latin, from Greek, from *epistazein* to drip on, to bleed at the nose again, from *epi-* + *stazein* to drip] (1793)
: NOSEBLEED

ep·i·ste·mic \,e-pə-'stē-mik, -'ste-mik\ *adjective* (1922)
: of or relating to knowledge or knowing : COGNITIVE
— **ep·i·ste·mi·cal·ly** \-mi-k(ə-)lē\ *adverb*

epis·te·mol·o·gy \i-,pis-tə-'mä-lə-jē\ *noun* [Greek *epistēmē* knowledge, from *epistanai* to understand, know, from *epi-* + *histanai* to cause to stand — more at STAND] (circa 1856)
: the study or a theory of the nature and grounds of knowledge especially with reference to its limits and validity
— **epis·te·mo·log·i·cal** \-mə-'lä-ji-kəl\ *adjective*
— **epis·te·mo·log·i·cal·ly** \-k(ə-)lē\ *adverb*
— **epis·te·mol·o·gist** \-'mä-lə-jist\ *noun*

epis·tle \i-'pi-səl\ *noun* [Middle English, letter, Epistle, from Old French, from Latin *epistula*, *epistola* letter, from Greek *epistolē* message, letter, from *epistellein* to send to, from *epi-* + *stellein* to send] (13th century)
1 *capitalized* **a** : one of the letters adopted as books of the New Testament **b** : a liturgical lection usually from one of the New Testament Epistles
2 a : LETTER; *especially* : a formal or elegant letter **b** : a composition in the form of a letter
— **epis·tler** \-'pi-sə-lər\ *noun*

¹epis·to·lary \i-'pis-tə-,ler-ē, ,e-pi-'stò-lə-rē\ *adjective* (circa 1656)
1 : of, relating to, or suitable to a letter
2 : contained in or carried on by letters ⟨an endless sequence of . . . *epistolary* love affairs —*Times Literary Supplement*⟩
3 : written in the form of a series of letters ⟨*epistolary* novel⟩

\ə\ abut \ᵊ\ kitten \ər\ further \a\ ash \ā\ ace
\ä\ mop, mar \aù\ out \ch\ chin \e\ bet \ē\ easy
\g\ go \i\ hit \ī\ ice \j\ job \ŋ\ sing \ō\ go
\ò\ law \òi\ boy \th\ thin \t͟h\ the \ü\ loot \ù\ foot
\y\ yet \zh\ vision *see also* Guide to Pronunciation

²epistolary *noun, plural* **-lar·ies** (circa 1900)
: a lectionary containing a body of liturgical epistles

epis·to·ler \i-'pis-tə-lər\ *noun* (1530)
: the reader of the liturgical Epistle especially in Anglican churches

ep·i·stome \'e-pə-ˌstōm\ *noun* [New Latin *epistoma*] (1852)
: any of several structures or regions situated above or covering the mouth of various invertebrates

epis·tro·phe \i-'pis-trə-(ˌ)fē\ *noun* [Greek *epistrophē*, literally, turning about, from *epi-* + *strophē* turning — more at STROPHE] (circa 1584)
: repetition of a word or expression at the end of successive phrases, clauses, sentences, or verses especially for rhetorical or poetic effect (as Lincoln's "of the people, by the people, for the people") — compare ANAPHORA

ep·i·taph \'e-pə-ˌtaf\ *noun* [Middle English *epitaphe*, from Middle French & Medieval Latin; Middle French, from Medieval Latin *epi taphium*, from Latin, funeral oration, from Greek *epitaphion*, from *epi-* + *taphos* tomb, funeral] (14th century)
1 : an inscription on or at a tomb or a grave in memory of the one buried there
2 : a brief statement commemorating or epitomizing a deceased person or something past
— **ep·i·taph·ial** \ˌe-pə-'ta-fē-əl\ *adjective*
— **ep·i·taph·ic** \-'ta-fik\ *adjective*

epit·a·sis \i-'pi-tə-səs\ *noun, plural* **-a·ses** \-ˌsēz\ [Greek, increased intensity, from *epiteinein* to stretch tighter, from *epi-* + *teinein* to stretch — more at THIN] (1589)
: the part of a play developing the main action and leading to the catastrophe

ep·i·taxy \'e-pə-ˌtak-sē\ *noun* [International Scientific Vocabulary] (circa 1931)
: the growth on a crystalline substrate of a crystalline substance that mimics the orientation of the substrate
— **ep·i·tax·i·al** \ˌe-pə-'tak-sē-əl\ *adjective*
— **ep·i·tax·i·al·ly** \-sē-ə-lē\ *adverb*

ep·i·tha·la·mi·um \ˌe-pə-thə-'lā-mē-əm\ *or* **ep·i·tha·la·mi·on** \-mē-ən\ *noun, plural* **-mi·ums** *or* **-mia** \-mē-ə\ [Latin & Greek; Latin *epithalamium*, from Greek *epithalamion*, from *epi-* + *thalamos* room, bridal chamber; perhaps akin to Greek *tholos* rotunda] (circa 1589)
: a song or poem in honor of a bride and bridegroom
— **ep·i·tha·lam·ic** \-'la-mik\ *adjective*

ep·i·the·li·al \ˌe-pə-'thē-lē-əl\ *adjective* (1845)
: of or relating to epithelium

ep·i·the·li·oid \-lē-ˌóid\ *adjective* (1878)
: resembling epithelium ⟨*epithelioid* cells⟩

ep·i·the·li·o·ma \-ˌthē-lē-'ō-mə\ *noun* (1872)
: a tumor derived from epithelial tissue
— **ep·i·the·li·o·ma·tous** \-mə-təs\ *adjective*

ep·i·the·li·um \ˌe-pə-'thē-lē-əm\ *noun, plural* **-lia** \-lē-ə\ [New Latin, from *epi-* + Greek *thēlē* nipple — more at FEMININE] (1748)
1 : a membranous cellular tissue that covers a free surface or lines a tube or cavity of an animal body and serves especially to enclose and protect the other parts of the body, to produce secretions and excretions, and to function in assimilation
2 : a usually thin layer of parenchyma that lines a cavity or tube of a plant

ep·i·the·li·za·tion \ˌe-pə-ˌthē-lə-'zā-shən\ *or* **ep·i·the·li·al·iza·tion** \-ˌthē-lē-ə-\ *noun* (circa 1934)
: the process of becoming covered with or converted to epithelium
— **ep·i·the·lize** \ˌe-pə-'thē-ˌlīz\ *or* **ep·i·the·li·al·ize** \-'thē-lē-ə-ˌlīz\ *transitive verb*

ep·i·thet \'e-pə-ˌthet *also* -thət\ *noun* [Latin *epitheton*, from Greek, from neuter of *epithe-tos* added, from *epitithenai* to put on, add, from *epi-* + *tithenai* to put — more at DO] (1579)
1 a : a characterizing word or phrase accompanying or occurring in place of the name of a person or thing **b** : a disparaging or abusive word or phrase **c** : the part of a taxonomic name identifying a subordinate unit within a genus
2 *obsolete* : EXPRESSION
— **ep·i·thet·ic** \ˌe-pə-'the-tik\ *or* **ep·i·thet·i·cal** \-ti-kəl\ *adjective*

epit·o·me \i-'pi-tə-mē\ *noun* [Latin, from Greek *epitomē*, from *epitemnein* to cut short, from *epi-* + *temnein* to cut — more at TOME] (1520)
1 a : a summary of a written work **b** : a brief presentation or statement of something
2 : a typical or ideal example : EMBODIMENT ⟨the British monarchy itself is the *epitome* of tradition —Richard Joseph⟩
3 : brief or miniature form — usually used with *in*
— **ep·i·tom·ic** \ˌe-pə-'tä-mik\ *or* **ep·i·tom·i·cal** \-mi-kəl\ *adjective*

epit·o·mise *British variant of* EPITOMIZE

epit·o·mize \-ˌmīz\ *transitive verb* **-mized; -miz·ing** (1594)
1 : to make or give an epitome of
2 : to serve as the typical or ideal example of

epi·tope \'e-pə-ˌtōp\ *noun* [International Scientific Vocabulary, from *epi-* + Greek *topos* place] (1960)
: a molecular region on the surface of an antigen capable of eliciting an immune response and of combining with the specific antibody produced by such a response — called also *determinant, antigenic determinant*

epi·zo·ic \ˌe-pə-'zō-ik\ *adjective* (circa 1857)
: living upon the body of an animal ⟨an *epizoic* plant⟩
— **epi·zo·ite** \-ˌīt\ *noun*

epi·zo·ot·ic \ˌe-pə-zə-'wä-tik\ *noun* [French *épizootie*, from *épizootie* such an outbreak, from *épi-* (as in *épidemie* epidemic) + Greek *zōiotēs* animal nature, from *zōē* life — more at QUICK] (1748)
: an outbreak of disease affecting many animals of one kind at the same time; *also* : the disease itself
— **epizootic** *adjective*

epi·zo·ot·i·ol·o·gy \ˌe-pə-zə-ˌwä-tē-'ä-lə-jē\ *noun* (1910)
1 : the sum of the factors controlling the occurrence of a disease or pathogen of animals
2 : a science that deals with the character, ecology, and causes of outbreaks of animal diseases
— **epi·zo·oti·o·log·i·cal** \-zə-ˌwä-tē-ə-'lä-ji-kəl\ *also* **epi·zo·oti·o·log·ic** \-jik\ *adjective*

ep·och \'e-pək, 'e-ˌpäk, *US also & British usually* 'ē-ˌpäk\ *noun* [Medieval Latin *epocha*, from Greek *epochē* cessation, fixed point, from *epechein* to pause, hold back, from *epi-* + *echein* to hold — more at SCHEME] (1614)
1 a : an event or a time marked by an event that begins a new period or development **b** : a memorable event or date
2 a : an extended period of time usually characterized by a distinctive development or by a memorable series of events **b** : a division of geologic time less than a period and greater than an age
3 : an instant of time or a date selected as a point of reference (as in astronomy)
synonym see PERIOD

ep·och·al \'e-pə-kəl, 'e-ˌpä-kəl\ *adjective* (1685)
1 : of or relating to an epoch
2 : uniquely or highly significant : MOMENTOUS ⟨during his three *epochal* years in the assembly —C. G. Bowers⟩; *also* : UNPARALLELED ⟨*epochal* stupidity⟩
— **ep·och·al·ly** *adverb*

ep·ode \'e-ˌpōd\ *noun* [Latin *epodos*, from Greek *epōidos*, from *epōidos* sung or said after, from *epi-* + *aidein* to sing — more at ODE] (1598)
1 : a lyric poem in which a long verse is followed by a shorter one
2 : the third part of a triadic Greek ode following the strophe and the antistrophe

ep·onym \'e-pə-ˌnim\ *noun* [Greek *epōnymos*, from *epōnymos* eponymous, from *epi-* + *onyma* name — more at NAME] (1846)
1 : one for whom or which something is or is believed to be named
2 : a name (as of a drug or a disease) based on or derived from an eponym
— **ep·onym·ic** \ˌe-pə-'ni-mik\ *adjective*

epon·y·mous \i-'pä-nə-məs, e-\ *adjective* (1846)
: of, relating to, or being an eponym

epon·y·my \-mē\ *noun, plural* **-mies** (1865)
: the explanation of a proper name (as of a town or tribe) by supposing a fictitious eponym

ep·o·pee \'e-pə-ˌpē\ *noun* [French *épopée*, from Greek *epopoiia*, from *epos* + *poiein* to make — more at POET] (1697)
: EPIC; *especially* : an epic poem

ep·os \'e-ˌpäs\ *noun* [Greek, word, epic poem — more at VOICE] (circa 1828)
1 : EPIC
2 : a number of poems that treat an epic theme but are not formally united

ep·ox·i·da·tion \(ˌ)e-ˌpäk-sə-'dā-shən\ *noun* (1944)
: a conversion of a usually unsaturated compound into an epoxide

ep·ox·ide \(ˌ)e-'päk-ˌsīd\ *noun* (1930)
: an epoxy compound

ep·ox·i·dize \(ˌ)e-'päk-sə-ˌdīz\ *transitive verb* **-dized; -diz·ing** (1945)
: to convert into an epoxide ⟨*epoxidized* esters⟩

¹ep·oxy \i-'päk-sē\ *adjective* [*epi-* + *oxy*] (1916)
1 : containing oxygen attached to two different atoms already united in some other way; *specifically* : containing a 3-membered ring consisting of one oxygen and two carbon atoms
2 : of or relating to an epoxide

²epoxy *transitive verb* **ep·ox·ied** *or* **ep·oxyed; ep·oxy·ing** (1966)
: to glue with epoxy resin

epoxy resin *noun* (1950)
: a flexible usually thermosetting resin made by copolymerization of an epoxide with another compound having two hydroxyl groups and used chiefly in coatings and adhesives — called also *epoxy*

EPROM \'ē-ˌpräm\ *noun* [*erasable programmable read-only memory*] (1977)
: a programmable read-only memory that can be erased usually by exposure to ultraviolet radiation

ep·si·lon \'ep-sə-ˌlän, -lən\ *noun* [Greek *e psilon*, literally, simple e] (15th century)
1 : the 5th letter of the Greek alphabet — see ALPHABET table
2 : an arbitrarily small positive quantity in mathematical analysis
— **ep·si·lon·ic** \ˌep-sə-'lä-nik\ *adjective*

Ep·som salt \'ep-səm-\ *noun* (1770)
: EPSOM SALTS

Epsom salts *noun plural but singular in construction* [*Epsom*, England] (1876)
: a bitter colorless or white crystalline salt $MgSO_4 \cdot 7H_2O$ that is a hydrated magnesium sulfate with cathartic properties

Ep·stein–Barr virus \ˌep-ˌstīn-'bär-\ *noun* [Michael Anthony *Epstein* (born 1921) and Y. M. *Barr* (born 1932) English pathologists] (1968)
: a herpesvirus that causes infectious mononucleosis and is associated with Burkitt's lymphoma and nasopharyngeal carcinoma

equa·ble \'e-kwə-bəl, 'ē-\ *adjective* [Latin *aequabilis,* from *aequare* to make level or equal, from *aequus*] (1677)
1 : marked by lack of variation or change **:** UNIFORM
2 : marked by lack of noticeable, unpleasant, or extreme variation or inequality
synonym see STEADY
— **equa·bil·i·ty** \,e-kwə-'bi-lə-tē, ,ē-\ *noun*
— **equa·ble·ness** \'e-kwə-bəl-nəs, 'ē-\ *noun*
— **equa·bly** \-blē\ *adverb*

¹**equal** \'ē-kwəl\ *adjective* [Middle English, from Latin *aequalis,* from *aequus* level, equal] (14th century)
1 a (1) **:** of the same measure, quantity, amount, or number as another (2) **:** identical in mathematical value or logical denotation **:** EQUIVALENT **b :** like in quality, nature, or status **c :** like for each member of a group, class, or society ⟨provide *equal* employment opportunities⟩
2 : regarding or affecting all objects in the same way **:** IMPARTIAL
3 : free from extremes: as **a :** tranquil in mind or mood **b :** not showing variation in appearance, structure, or proportion
4 a : capable of meeting the requirements of a situation or a task **b :** SUITABLE ⟨bored with work not *equal* to his abilities⟩
synonym see SAME

²**equal** *transitive verb* **equaled** or **equalled; equal·ing** or **equal·ling** (1590)
1 : to be equal to; *especially* **:** to be identical in value to
2 *archaic* **:** EQUALIZE
3 : to make or produce something equal to

³**equal** *noun* (1753)
1 : one that is equal ⟨insists that women can be absolute *equals* with men —Anne Bernays⟩
2 : an equal quantity

equal–area *adjective* (circa 1929)
of a map projection **:** maintaining constant ratio of size between quadrilaterals formed by the meridians and parallels and the quadrilaterals of the globe thereby preserving true areal extent of forms represented

equal·ise, equal·is·er *British variant of* EQUALIZE, EQUALIZER

equal·i·tar·i·an \i-,kwä-lə-'ter-ē-ən\ *adjective or noun* (1799)
: EGALITARIAN
— **equal·i·tar·i·an·ism** \-ē-ə-,ni-zəm\ *noun*

equal·i·ty \i-'kwä-lə-tē\ *noun, plural* **-ties** (15th century)
1 : the quality or state of being equal
2 : EQUATION 2a

equal·ize \'ē-kwə-,līz\ *verb* **-ized; -iz·ing** (1622)
transitive verb
1 : to make equal
2 a : to compensate for **b :** to make uniform; *especially* **:** to distribute evenly or uniformly ⟨*equalize* the tax burden⟩ **c :** to adjust or correct the frequency characteristics of (an electronic signal) by restoring to their original level high frequencies that have been attenuated
intransitive verb
chiefly British **:** to tie the score
— **equal·iza·tion** \,ē-kwə-lə-'zā-shən\ *noun*

equal·iz·er \-,lī-zər\ *noun* (1792)
: one that equalizes: as **a :** a score that ties a game **b :** an electronic device (as in a sound-reproducing system) used to adjust response to different audio frequencies

equal·ly \'ē-kwə-lē\ *adverb* (14th century)
1 : in an equal or uniform manner **:** EVENLY
2 : to an equal degree ⟨respected *equally* by young and old⟩

equal opportunity employer *noun* (1963)
: an employer who agrees not to discriminate against any employee or job applicant because of race, color, religion, national origin, sex, physical or mental handicap, or age

equal sign *noun* (circa 1909)
: a sign = indicating mathematical or logical equivalence — called also *equality sign, equals sign*

equa·nim·i·ty \,ē-kwə-'ni-mə-tē, ,e-kwə-\ *noun, plural* **-ties** [Latin *aequanimitas,* from *aequo animo* with even mind] (circa 1616)
1 : evenness of mind especially under stress
2 : right disposition **:** BALANCE ☆

equate \i-'kwāt, 'ē-,\ *verb* **equat·ed; equat·ing** [Middle English, from Latin *aequatus,* past participle of *aequare*] (15th century)
transitive verb
1 a : to make equal **:** EQUALIZE **b :** to make such an allowance or correction in as will reduce to a common standard or obtain a correct result
2 : to treat, represent, or regard as equal, equivalent, or comparable ⟨*equates* disagreement with disloyalty⟩
intransitive verb
: to correspond as equal

equa·tion \i-'kwā-zhən *also* -shən\ *noun* (14th century)
1 a : the act or process of equating **b** (1) **:** an element affecting a process **:** FACTOR (2) **:** a complex of variable factors **c :** a state of being equated; *specifically* **:** a state of close association or identification ⟨bring governmental enterprises and payment for them into immediate *equation* —R. G. Tugwell⟩
2 a : a usually formal statement of the equality or equivalence of mathematical or logical expressions **b :** an expression representing a chemical reaction quantitatively by means of chemical symbols

equa·tion·al \i-'kwāzh-nəl, -'kwā-zhə-n°l *also* -'kwāsh-\ *adjective* (1864)
1 : of, using, or involving equation or equations
2 : dividing into two equal parts — used especially of the mitotic cell division usually following reduction in meiosis
— **equa·tion·al·ly** *adverb*

equation of time (1726)
: the difference between apparent time and mean time usually expressed as a correction which is to be added to apparent time to give local mean time

equa·tor \i-'kwā-tər, 'ē-,\ *noun* [Middle English, from Medieval Latin *aequator,* literally, equalizer, from Latin *aequare*] (14th century)
1 : the great circle of the celestial sphere whose plane is perpendicular to the axis of the earth
2 : a great circle of the earth or a celestial body that is everywhere equally distant from the two poles and divides the surface into the northern and southern hemispheres
3 a : a circle or circular band dividing the surface of a body into two usually equal and symmetrical parts **b :** EQUATORIAL PLANE ⟨the *equator* of a dividing cell⟩
4 : GREAT CIRCLE

equa·to·ri·al \,ē-kwə-'tōr-ē-əl, ,e-kwə-, -'tȯr-\ *adjective* (1664)
1 a : of, relating to, or located at the equator or an equator; *also* **:** being in the plane of the equator ⟨a satellite in *equatorial* orbit⟩ **b :** of, originating in, or suggesting the region around the geographic equator
2 a : being or having a support that includes two axles at right angles to each other with one parallel to the earth's axis of rotation ⟨an *equatorial* telescope⟩ **b :** extending in a direction essentially in the plane of a cyclic structure (as of cyclohexane) ⟨*equatorial* hydrogens⟩ — compare AXIAL

equatorial plane *noun* (circa 1892)
: the plane perpendicular to the spindle of a dividing cell and midway between the poles

equatorial plate *noun* (1887)
1 : METAPHASE PLATE
2 : EQUATORIAL PLANE

equa·tor·ward \i-'kwā-tər-wərd\ *adverb or adjective* (1875)
: toward or near the equator ⟨currents flowing *equatorward*⟩ ⟨*equatorward* winds⟩

equer·ry \'e-kwə-rē, i-'kwer-ē\ *noun, plural* **-ries** [obsolete *escuirie, equerry* stable, from Middle French *escuirie* office of a squire, stable, from *escuier* squire — more at ESQUIRE] (1591)
1 : an officer of a prince or noble charged with the care of horses
2 : an officer of the British royal household in personal attendance on the sovereign or a member of the royal family

¹**eques·tri·an** \i-'kwes-trē-ən\ *adjective* [Latin *equestr-, equester* of a horseman, from *eques* horseman, from *equus* horse — more at EQUINE] (circa 1681)
1 a : of, relating to, or featuring horseback riding **b** *archaic* **:** riding on horseback **:** MOUNTED **c :** representing a person on horseback ⟨an *equestrian* statue⟩
2 : of, relating to, or composed of knights

²**equestrian** *noun* (1791)
: one who rides on horseback

eques·tri·enne \i-,kwes-trē-'en\ *noun* [²*equestrian* + *-enne* (as in *tragedienne*)] (circa 1864)
: a female rider on horseback

equi- *combining form* [Middle English, from Middle French, from Latin *aequi-,* from *aequus* equal]
: equal ⟨*equi*poise⟩ **:** equally ⟨*equi*probable⟩

equi·an·gu·lar \,ē-kwi-'aŋ-gyə-lər, ,e-kwi-\ *adjective* (1660)
: having all or corresponding angles equal ⟨mutually *equiangular* parallelograms⟩

equi·ca·lor·ic \,ē-kwə-kə-'lȯr-ik, ,e-kwə-, -'lär-\ *adjective* (1940)
: capable of yielding equal amounts of energy in the body ⟨*equicaloric* diets⟩

equid \'e-,kwid, 'ē-\ *noun* [New Latin *Equidae,* family name, from *Equus,* genus name, from Latin, horse] (circa 1889)
: any of a family (Equidae) of perissodactyl mammals consisting of the horses, asses, zebras, and extinct related animals

equi·dis·tant \,ē-kwə-'dis-tənt, ,e-kwə-\ *adjective* [Middle French or Late Latin; Middle French, from Late Latin *aequidistant-, aequidistans,* from Latin *aequi-* + *distant-, distans,* present participle of *distare* to stand apart — more at DISTANT] (1593)
1 : equally distant
2 : representing map distances true to scale in all directions
— **equi·dis·tant·ly** *adverb*

equi·lat·er·al \,ē-kwə-'la-tə-rəl, ,e-kwə-, -'la-trəl\ *adjective* [Late Latin *aequilateralis,* from Latin *aequi-* + *later-, latus* side — more at LATERAL] (1570)
1 : having all sides equal ⟨an *equilateral* triangle⟩ ⟨an *equilateral* polygon⟩ — see TRIANGLE illustration

☆ **SYNONYMS**
Equanimity, composure, sangfroid
mean evenness of mind under stress. EQUANIMITY suggests a habit of mind that is only rarely disturbed under great strain ⟨accepted her troubles with *equanimity*⟩. COMPOSURE implies the controlling of emotional or mental agitation by an effort of will or as a matter of habit ⟨maintaining his *composure* even under hostile questioning⟩. SANGFROID implies great coolness and steadiness under strain ⟨handled the situation with professional *sangfroid*⟩.

\ə\ abut \ᵊ\ kitten \ər\ further \a\ ash \ā\ ace
\ä\ mop, mar \au̇\ out \ch\ chin \e\ bet \ē\ easy
\g\ go \i\ hit \ī\ ice \j\ job \ŋ\ sing \ō\ go
\ȯ\ law \ȯi\ boy \th\ thin \th̲\ the \ü\ loot \u̇\ foot
\y\ yet \zh\ vision *see also* Guide to Pronunciation

2 : having all the faces equal ⟨an *equilateral* polyhedron⟩

equilateral hyperbola *noun* (1880)
: a hyperbola with its asymptotes at right angles

equil·i·brant \i-'kwi-lə-brənt, ē-, *also* ,ē-kwə-'li-brənt\ *noun* (1883)
: a force that will balance one or more unbalanced forces

equil·i·brate \i-'kwi-lə-,brāt\ *verb* **-brat·ed; -brat·ing** (1635)
transitive verb
: to bring into or keep in equilibrium : BALANCE
intransitive verb
: to bring about, come to, or be in equilibrium
— **equil·i·bra·tion** \-,kwi-lə-'brā-shən\ *noun*
— **equil·i·bra·tor** \-'kwi-lə-,brā-tər\ *noun*
— **equil·i·bra·to·ry** \-brə-,tōr-ē, -,tȯr-\ *adjective*

equi·li·brist \,ē-kwə-'li-brist, ,e-kwə-; i-'kwi-lə-brist\ *noun* (1760)
: one (as a rope dancer) who performs difficult feats of balancing
— **equil·i·bris·tic** \i-,kwi-lə-'bris-tik\ *adjective*

equi·lib·ri·um \,ē-kwə-'li-brē-əm, ,e-kwə-\ *noun, plural* **-ri·ums** *or* **-ria** \-brē-ə\ [Latin *aequilibrium*, from *aequilibris* being in equilibrium, from *aequi-* + *libra* weight, balance] (1608)
1 a : a state of intellectual or emotional balance : POISE **b** : a state of adjustment between opposing or divergent influences or elements
2 : a state of balance between opposing forces or actions that is either static (as in a body acted on by forces whose resultant is zero) or dynamic (as in a reversible chemical reaction when the velocities in both directions are equal)
3 : BALANCE 6a

equilibrium constant *noun* (1929)
: a number that expresses the relationship between the amounts of products and reactants present at equilibrium in a reversible chemical reaction at a given temperature

equi·mo·lar \-'mō-lər\ *adjective* (circa 1909)
1 : of or relating to an equal number of moles ⟨an *equimolar* mixture⟩
2 : having equal molar concentration

equine \'ē-,kwīn, 'e-,kwīn\ *adjective* [Latin *equinus*, from *equus* horse; akin to Old English *eoh* horse, Greek *hippos*, Sanskrit *aśva*] (1778)
: of, relating to, or resembling a horse or the horse family
— **equine** *noun*
— **equine·ly** *adverb*

¹equi·noc·tial \,ē-kwə-'näk-shəl, ,e-kwə-\ *adjective* (1545)
1 : relating to an equinox or to a state or the time of equal day and night
2 : relating to the regions or climate on or near the equator
3 : relating to the time when the sun passes an equinoctial point

²equinoctial *noun* (1527)
1 : EQUATOR 1
2 : an equinoctial storm

equi·nox \'ē-kwə-,näks, 'e-kwə-\ *noun* [Middle English, from Middle French or Medieval Latin; Middle French *equinoxe*, from Medieval Latin *equinoxium*, alteration of Latin *aequinoctium*, from *aequi-* equi- + *noct-, nox* night — more at NIGHT] (14th century)
1 : either of the two points on the celestial sphere where the celestial equator intersects the ecliptic
2 : either of the two times each year (as about March 21 and September 23) when the sun crosses the equator and day and night are everywhere of equal length

equip \i-'kwip\ *transitive verb* **equipped; equip·ping** [Middle French *equiper*, from

Old French *esciper*, of Germanic origin; akin to Old English *scip* ship] (1523)
1 : to furnish for service or action by appropriate provisioning
2 : DRESS, ARRAY
3 : to make ready : PREPARE
synonym see FURNISH

equ·i·page \'e-kwə-pij\ *noun* (1579)
1 a : material or articles used in equipment : OUTFIT **b** *archaic* (1) : a set of small articles (as for table service) (2) : ETUI **c** : TRAPPINGS
2 *archaic* : RETINUE
3 : a horse-drawn carriage with its servants; *also* : such a carriage alone

equip·ment \i-'kwip-mənt\ *noun* (1717)
1 a : the set of articles or physical resources serving to equip a person or thing: as (1) : the implements used in an operation or activity : APPARATUS (2) : all the fixed assets other than land and buildings of a business enterprise (3) : the rolling stock of a railway **b** : a piece of such equipment
2 a : the equipping of a person or thing **b** : the state of being equipped
3 : mental or emotional traits or resources : ENDOWMENT

¹equi·poise \'e-kwə-,pȯiz, 'ē-\ *noun* (1658)
1 : a state of equilibrium
2 : COUNTERBALANCE

²equipoise *transitive verb* (1664)
1 : to serve as an equipoise to
2 : to put or hold in equipoise

equi·pol·lence \,ē-kwə-'pä-lən(t)s, ,e-kwə-\ *noun* (15th century)
: the quality of being equipollent

equi·pol·lent \-lənt\ *adjective* [Middle English, from Middle French, from Latin *aequipollent-, aequipollens*, from *aequi-* equi- + *pollent-, pollens*, present participle of *pollēre* to be able] (15th century)
1 : equal in force, power, or validity
2 : the same in effect or signification
— **equipollent** *noun*
— **equi·pol·lent·ly** *adverb*

equi·pon·der·ant \-'pän-d(ə-)rənt\ *adjective* [Medieval Latin *aequiponderant-, aequiponderans*, present participle of *aequiponderare*, from Latin *aequi-* + *ponderare* to weigh — more at PONDER] (1630)
: evenly balanced

equi·po·ten·tial \,ē-kwə-pə-'ten(t)-shəl, ,e-kwə-\ *adjective* (circa 1865)
: having the same potential : of uniform potential throughout ⟨*equipotential* points⟩

equi·prob·a·ble \-'prä-bə-bəl\ *adjective* (1921)
: having the same degree of logical or mathematical probability ⟨*equiprobable* alternatives⟩

equi·se·tum \,e-kwə-'sē-təm\ *noun, plural* **-se·tums** *or* **-se·ta** \-'sē-tə\ [New Latin, from Latin *equisaetum* horsetail plant, from *equus* horse + *saeta* bristle] (1830)
: any of a genus (*Equisetum*) of lower tracheophytes comprising perennial plants that spread by creeping rhizomes and have leaves reduced to nodal sheaths on the hollow jointed ribbed shoots — called also *horsetail, scouring rush*

equisetum: 1 vegetative plant, 2 fertile plant

equi·ta·ble \'e-kwə-tə-bəl\ *adjective* (1646)
1 : having or exhibiting equity : dealing fairly and equally with all concerned
2 : existing or valid in equity as distinguished from law
synonym see FAIR

— **eq·ui·ta·bil·i·ty** \,e-kwə-tə-'bi-lə-tē\ *noun*
— **eq·ui·ta·ble·ness** \'e-kwə-tə-bəl-nəs\ *noun*
— **eq·ui·ta·bly** \-blē\ *adverb*

eq·ui·ta·tion \,e-kwə-'tā-shən\ *noun* [Middle French, from Latin *equitation-, equitatio*, from *equitare* to ride on horseback, from *equit-, eques* horseman, from *equus* horse] (1562)
: the act or art of riding on horseback

eq·ui·ty \'e-kwə-tē\ *noun, plural* **-ties** [Middle English *equite*, from Middle French *equité*, from Latin *aequitat-, aequitas*, from *aequus* equal, fair] (14th century)
1 a : justice according to natural law or right; *specifically* : freedom from bias or favoritism **b** : something that is equitable
2 a : a system of law originating in the English chancery and comprising a settled and formal body of legal and procedural rules and doctrines that supplement, aid, or override common and statute law and are designed to protect rights and enforce duties fixed by substantive law **b** : trial or remedial justice under or by the rules and doctrines of equity **c** : a body of legal doctrines and rules developed to enlarge, supplement, or override a narrow rigid system of law
3 a : a right, claim, or interest existing or valid in equity **b** : the money value of a property or of an interest in a property in excess of claims or liens against it **c** : a risk interest or ownership right in property **d** : the common stock of a corporation

equity capital *noun* (1942)
: VENTURE CAPITAL

equiv·a·lence \i-'kwiv-lən(t)s, -'kwi-və-\ *noun* (circa 1541)
1 a : a state or property of being equivalent **b** : the relation holding between two statements if they are either both true or both false so that to affirm one and to deny the other would result in a contradiction
2 : a presentation of terms as equivalent
3 : equality in metrical value of a regular foot and one in which there are substitutions

equivalence class *noun* (1952)
: a set for which an equivalence relation holds between every pair of elements

equivalence relation *noun* (circa 1949)
: a relation (as equality) between elements of a set (as the real numbers) that is symmetric, reflexive, and transitive and for any two elements either holds or does not hold

equiv·a·len·cy \i-'kwiv-lən(t)-sē, -'kwi-və-\ *noun, plural* **-cies** (1535)
1 : EQUIVALENCE
2 : a level of achievement equivalent to completion of an educational or training program ⟨a high school *equivalency* certificate⟩

equiv·a·lent \-lənt\ *adjective* [Middle English, from Middle French or Late Latin; Middle French, from Late Latin *aequivalent-, aequivalens*, present participle of *aequivalēre* to have equal power, from Latin *aequi-* + *valēre* to be strong — more at WIELD] (15th century)
1 : equal in force, amount, or value; *also* : equal in area or volume but not admitting of superposition ⟨a square *equivalent* to a triangle⟩
2 a : like in signification or import **b** : having logical equivalence ⟨*equivalent* statements⟩
3 : corresponding or virtually identical especially in effect or function
4 *obsolete* : equal in might or authority
5 : having the same chemical combining capacity ⟨*equivalent* quantities of two elements⟩
6 a : having the same solution set ⟨*equivalent* equations⟩ **b** : capable of being placed in one-to-one correspondence ⟨*equivalent* sets⟩ **c** : related by an equivalence relation
synonym see SAME
— **equivalent** *noun*
— **equiv·a·lent·ly** *adverb*

equivalent weight *noun* (1904)
: the mass of a substance especially in grams that combines with or is chemically equivalent to eight grams of oxygen or one gram of hydrogen : the atomic or molecular weight divided by the valence

equiv·o·cal \i-'kwi-və-kəl\ *adjective* [Late Latin *aequivocus*, from *aequi-* equi- + *voc-*, *vox* voice — more at VOICE] (1599)
1 a : subject to two or more interpretations and usually used to mislead or confuse **b :** uncertain as an indication or sign
2 a : of uncertain nature or classification **b :** of uncertain disposition or temper toward a person or thing : UNDECIDED **c :** of doubtful advantage, genuineness, or moral rectitude ⟨*equivocal* behavior⟩
synonym see OBSCURE
— **equiv·o·cal·i·ty** \-,kwi-və-'ka-lə-tē\ *noun*
— **equiv·o·cal·ly** \-'kwi-və-k(ə-)lē\ *adverb*
— **equiv·o·cal·ness** \-kəl-nəs\ *noun*

equiv·o·cate \i-'kwi-və-,kāt\ *intransitive verb* **-cat·ed; -cat·ing** (1590)
1 : to use equivocal language especially with intent to deceive
2 : to avoid committing oneself in what one says
synonym see LIE
— **equiv·o·ca·tion** \-,kwi-və-'kā-shən\ *noun*
— **equiv·o·ca·tor** \-'kwi-və-,kā-tər\ *noun*

equi·voque *also* **equi·voke** \'e-kwə-,vōk, 'ē-\ *noun* [French *équivoque*, from *équivoque* equivocal, from Late Latin *aequivocus*] (1599)
1 : an equivocal word or phrase; *specifically* : PUN
2 a : double meaning **b :** WORDPLAY

¹-er \ər; *after some vowels, often* r; *after* ŋ, *usually* gər\ *adjective suffix or adverb suffix* [Middle English *-er*, *-ere*, *-re*, from Old English *-ra* (in adjectives), *-or* (in adverbs); akin to Old High German *-iro*, adjective comparative suffix, Latin *-ior*, Greek *-iōn*]
— used to form the comparative degree of adjectives and adverbs of one syllable ⟨*hotter*⟩ ⟨*drier*⟩ and of some adjectives and adverbs of two syllables ⟨*completer*⟩ and sometimes of longer ones ⟨*beautifuler*⟩

²-er \ər; *after some vowels, often* r\ *also* **-ier** \ē-ər, yər\ *or* **-yer** \yər\ *noun suffix* [Middle English *-er*, *-ere*, *-ier*, *-iere*; partly from Old English *-ere* (from Latin *-arius*); partly from Old French *-ier*, *-iere*, from Latin *-arius*, *-aria*, *-arium* *-ary*; partly from Middle French *-ere*, from Latin *-ator* -or — more at -ARY, -OR]
1 a : person occupationally connected with ⟨*hatter*⟩ ⟨*furrier*⟩ ⟨*lawyer*⟩ **b :** person or thing belonging to or associated with ⟨*header*⟩ ⟨*oldtimer*⟩ **c :** native of : resident of ⟨*cottager*⟩ ⟨New York*er*⟩ **d :** one that has ⟨three-deck*er*⟩ **e :** one that produces or yields ⟨pork*er*⟩
2 a : one that does or performs (a specified action) ⟨report*er*⟩ — sometimes added to both elements of a compound ⟨build*er*-upp*er*⟩ **b :** one that is a suitable object of (a specified action) ⟨broil*er*⟩
3 : one that is ⟨foreign*er*⟩ — in all senses *-yer* in a few words after *w*, *-ier* in a few other words, otherwise *-er*

era \'ir-ə, 'er-ə, 'ē-rə\ *noun* [Late Latin *aera*, from Latin, counters, plural of *aer-*, *aes* copper, money — more at ORE] (1615)
1 a : a fixed point in time from which a series of years is reckoned **b :** a memorable or important date or event; *especially* : one that begins a new period in the history of a person or thing
2 : a system of chronological notation computed from a given date as basis
3 a : a period identified by some prominent figure or characteristic feature **b :** a stage in development; *especially* : one of the four major divisions of geologic time ⟨Paleozoic *era*⟩
synonym see PERIOD

erad·i·cate \i-'ra-də-,kāt\ *transitive verb* **-cat·ed; -cat·ing** [Latin *eradicatus*, past participle of *eradicare*, from *e-* + *radic-*, *radix* root — more at ROOT] (1578)
1 : to pull up by the roots
2 : to do away with as completely as if by pulling up by the roots ⟨programs to *eradicate* illiteracy⟩
synonym see EXTERMINATE
— **erad·i·ca·ble** \-'ra-di-kə-bəl\ *adjective*
— **erad·i·ca·tion** \-,ra-də-'kā-shən\ *noun*
— **erad·i·ca·tor** \-,kā-tər\ *noun*

erase \i-'rās, *British* -'rāz\ *verb* **erased; eras·ing** [Latin *erasus*, past participle of *eradere*, from *e-* + *radere* to scratch, scrape — more at RODENT] (1605)
transitive verb
1 a : to rub or scrape out (as written, painted, or engraved letters) **b :** to remove (recorded matter) from a magnetic medium; *also* : to remove recorded matter from ⟨*erase* a videotape⟩ **c :** to delete from a computer storage device
2 a : to remove from existence or memory as if by erasing **b :** to nullify the effect or force of
intransitive verb
: to yield to being erased
— **eras·abil·i·ty** \-,rā-sə-'bi-lə-tē\ *noun*
— **eras·able** \-'rā-sə-bəl\ *adjective*

eras·er \i-'rā-sər\ *noun* (1790)
: one that erases; *especially* : a device (as a piece of rubber, or a felt pad) used to erase marks (as of ink or chalk)

Eras·tian \i-'ras-tē-ən, -'ras-chən\ *adjective* [Thomas *Erastus* (died 1583) Swiss physician and Zwinglian theologian] (1839)
: of, characterized by, or advocating the doctrine of state supremacy in ecclesiastical affairs
— **Erastian** *noun*
— **Eras·tian·ism** \-,ni-zəm\ *noun*

era·sure \i-'rā-shər *also* -zhər\ *noun* (1734)
: an act or instance of erasing

Er·a·to \'er-ə-,tō\ *noun* [Greek *Eratō*]
: the Greek Muse of lyric and love poetry

er·bi·um \'ər-bē-əm\ *noun* [New Latin, from *Ytterby*, Sweden] (1843)
: a metallic element of the rare-earth group that occurs with yttrium — see ELEMENT table

¹ere \'er, 'ar\ *preposition* [Middle English *er*, from Old English *ær*, adverb, early, soon; akin to Old High German *ēr* earlier, Greek *ēri* early] (before 12th century)
²BEFORE 2 ⟨contrived *ere* the beginning of the world —Norman Douglas⟩

²ere *conjunction* (before 12th century)
: **³BEFORE**

Er·e·bus \'er-ə-bəs\ *noun* [Latin, from Greek *Erebos*]
1 : a personification of darkness in Greek mythology
2 : a place of darkness in the underworld on the way to Hades

¹erect \i-'rekt\ *adjective* [Middle English, from Latin *erectus*, past participle of *erigere* to erect, from *e-* + *regere* to lead straight, guide — more at RIGHT] (14th century)
1 a : vertical in position; *also* : not spread out or decumbent ⟨an *erect* plant stem⟩ **b :** standing up or out from the body ⟨*erect* hairs⟩ **c :** characterized by firm or rigid straightness in bodily posture ⟨an *erect* bearing⟩
2 *archaic* : directed upward
3 *obsolete* : ALERT, WATCHFUL
4 : being in a state of physiological erection
— **erect·ly** \-'rek-(t)lē\ *adverb*
— **erect·ness** \-'rek(t)-nəs\ *noun*

²erect *transitive verb* (15th century)
1 a (1) : to put up by the fitting together of materials or parts : BUILD (2) : to fix in an upright position (3) : to cause to stand up or stand out **b** *archaic* : to direct upward **c :** to change (an image) from an inverted to a normal position
2 : to elevate in status

3 : SET UP, ESTABLISH
4 *obsolete* : ENCOURAGE, EMBOLDEN
5 : to draw or construct (as a perpendicular or figure) upon a given base
— **erect·able** \-'rek-tə-bəl\ *adjective*

erec·tile \i-'rek-t²l, -,tīl\ *adjective* (1830)
: capable of becoming erect ⟨*erectile* tissue⟩ — compare CAVERNOUS 1b
— **erec·til·i·ty** \-,rek-'ti-lə-tē\ *noun*

erec·tion \i-'rek-shən\ *noun* (15th century)
1 a : the state marked by firm turgid form and erect position of a previously flaccid bodily part containing cavernous tissue when that tissue becomes dilated with blood **b :** an occurrence of such a state in the penis or clitoris
2 : the act or process of erecting something : CONSTRUCTION
3 : something erected

erec·tor \i-'rek-tər\ *noun* (1538)
: one that erects; *especially* : a muscle that raises or keeps a part erect

Erector *trademark*
— used for a metal toy construction set

E region *noun* (1930)
: the part of the ionosphere occurring between 55 and 80 miles (90 and 130 kilometers) above the surface of the earth and containing the daytime E layer and the sporadic E layer

ere·long \er-'lóŋ, ar-\ *adverb* (1577)
archaic : before long : SOON

er·e·mite \'er-ə-,mīt\ *noun* [Middle English — more at HERMIT] (13th century)
: HERMIT; *especially* : a religious recluse
— **er·e·mit·ic** \,er-ə-'mi-tik\ *or* **er·e·mit·i·cal** \-ti-kəl\ *adjective*
— **er·e·mit·ism** \'er-ə-,mī-,ti-zəm\ *noun*

er·em·urus \,er-ə-'myùr-əs\ *noun, plural* **-uri** \-'myùr-,ī\ [New Latin, from Greek *erēmos* solitary + *oura* tail — more at ASS] (1829)
: any of a genus (*Eremurus*) of perennial herbs of the lily family that produce tall racemes of showy blooms — called also *foxtail lily*

ere·now \er-'naù, ar-\ *adverb* (14th century)
: before now : HERETOFORE

erep·sin \i-'rep-sən\ *noun* [International Scientific Vocabulary *er-* (probably from Latin *eripere* to snatch away, from *e-* + *rapere* to seize) + *pepsin* — more at RAPID] (1902)
: a proteolytic fraction obtained especially from the intestinal juice and known to be a mixture of exopeptidases

er·e·thism \'er-ə-,thi-zəm\ *noun* [French *éréthisme*, from Greek *erethismos* irritation, from *erethizein* to irritate; akin to Greek *ornynai* to rouse — more at ORIENT] (1800)
: abnormal irritability or responsiveness to stimulation

ere·while \er-'(h)wī(ə)l, ar-\ *also* **ere·whiles** \-'(h)wī(ə)lz\ *adverb* (13th century)
archaic : HERETOFORE

erg \'ərg\ *noun* [Greek *ergon* work — more at WORK] (circa 1873)
: a centimeter-gram-second unit of work equal to the work done by a force of one dyne acting through a distance of one centimeter and equivalent to 10^{-7} joule

erg- *or* **ergo-** *combining form* [Greek, from *ergon*]
: work ⟨*ergo*meter⟩

er·gas·tic \(,)ər-'gas-tik\ *adjective* [Greek *ergastikos* able to work, from *ergazesthai* to work, from *ergon* work] (circa 1896)
: constituting the nonliving by-products of protoplasmic activity ⟨*ergastic* substances⟩

er·gas·to·plasm \-tə-,pla-zəm\ *noun* [International Scientific Vocabulary] (1902)
: ribosome-studded endoplasmic reticulum
— **er·gas·to·plas·mic** \-,gas-tə-'plaz-mik\ *adjective*

\ə\ abut \ᵊ\ kitten \ər\ further \a\ ash \ā\ ace \ä\ mop, mar \aù\ out \ch\ chin \e\ bet \ē\ easy \g\ go \i\ hit \ī\ ice \j\ job \ŋ\ sing \ō\ go \ò\ law \òi\ boy \th\ thin \th\ the \ü\ loot \ù\ foot \y\ yet \zh\ vision *see also* Guide to Pronunciation

er·ga·tive \'ər-gə-tiv\ *adjective* [Greek *ergatēs* worker, from *ergon* work] (1939)
: of, relating to, or being a language (as Inuit or Georgian) in which the objects of transitive verbs and subjects of intransitive verbs are typically marked by the same linguistic forms; *also* : being an inflectional morpheme that typically marks the subject of a transitive verb in an ergative language

-er·gic \(ˌ)ər-jik\ *adjective combining form* [*-ergy* work (from Late Latin *-ergia*, from Greek, from *ergon* work) + *-ic* — more at WORK]
: exhibiting or stimulating activity of ⟨dopamin*ergic*⟩

er·go \'er-(ˌ)gō, 'ər-\ *adverb* [Middle English, from Latin, from Old Latin, because of, from (assumed) Old Latin *e rogo* from the direction (of)] (14th century)
: THEREFORE, HENCE

ergo- *combining form* [French, from *ergot*]
: ergot ⟨*ergo*sterol⟩

er·go·dic \(ˌ)ər-'gä-dik, -'gō-\ *adjective* [International Scientific Vocabulary *erg-* + *-ode*] (1926)
1 : of or relating to a process in which every sequence or sizable sample is equally representative of the whole (as in regard to a statistical parameter)
2 : involving or relating to the probability that any state will recur; *especially* : having zero probability that any state will never recur
— **er·go·dic·i·ty** \ˌər-gə-'di-sə-tē\ *noun*

er·go·graph \'ər-gə-ˌgraf\ *noun* [International Scientific Vocabulary] (1892)
: an apparatus for measuring the work capacity of a muscle

er·gom·e·ter \(ˌ)ər-'gä-mə-tər\ *noun* (circa 1879)
: an apparatus for measuring the work performed (as by a person exercising); *also* : an exercise machine equipped with an ergometer
— **er·go·met·ric** \ˌər-gə-'me-trik\ *adjective*

er·go·nom·ics \ˌər-gə-'nä-miks\ *noun plural but singular or plural in construction* [*erg-* + *-nomics* (as in *economics*)] (1949)
: an applied science concerned with designing and arranging things people use so that the people and things interact most efficiently and safely — called also *human engineering*
— **er·go·nom·ic** \-mik\ *adjective*
— **er·go·nom·i·cal·ly** \-mi-k(ə)lē\ *adverb*
— **er·gon·o·mist** \(ˌ)ər-'gä-nə-mist\ *noun*

er·go·no·vine \ˌər-gə-'nō-ˌvēn\ *noun* [*ergo-* + Latin *novus* new — more at NEW] (circa 1936)
: an alkaloid $C_{19}H_{23}N_3O_2$ from ergot with similar pharmacological action but reduced toxicity

er·gos·ter·ol \(ˌ)ər-'gäs-tə-ˌról, -ˌról\ *noun* [International Scientific Vocabulary] (1906)
: a crystalline steroid alcohol $C_{28}H_{44}O$ that occurs especially in yeast, molds, and ergot and is converted by ultraviolet irradiation ultimately into vitamin D_2

er·got \'ər-gət, -ˌgät\ *noun* [French, literally, cock's spur] (1683)
1 : the black or dark purple sclerotium of fungi (genus *Claviceps*) that occurs as a club-shaped body replacing the seed of a grass (as rye); *also* : a fungus bearing ergots
2 : a disease of rye and other cereals caused by an ergot fungus
3 a : the dried sclerotia of an ergot fungus grown on rye and containing several alkaloids (as ergonovine and ergotamine) **b** : any of such alkaloids used medicinally for their contractile effect on smooth muscle (as of peripheral arterioles)
— **er·got·ic** \(ˌ)ər-'gä-tik\ *adjective*

er·got·a·mine \(ˌ)ər-'gä-tə-ˌmēn\ *noun* [International Scientific Vocabulary] (1921)
: an alkaloid $C_{33}H_{35}N_5O_5$ from ergot that is used chiefly in the form of its tartrate especially in treating migraine

er·got·ism \'ər-gə-ˌti-zəm\ *noun* (circa 1841)

: a toxic condition produced by eating grain, grain products (as rye bread), or grasses infected with ergot fungus or by chronic excessive use of an ergot drug

er·got·ized \-ˌtīzd\ *adjective* (1860)
: infected with ergot ⟨*ergotized* grain⟩; *also*
: poisoned by ergot ⟨*ergotized* cattle⟩

er·i·ca \'er-i-kə\ *noun* [New Latin, from Latin *erice* heather, from Greek *ereikē* — more at BRIER] (1826)
: any of a large genus (*Erica*) of the heath family of low much-branched evergreen shrubs

er·i·ca·ceous \ˌer-ə-'kā-shəs\ *adjective* (circa 1859)
: of, relating to, or being a heath or the heath family

er·i·coid \'er-ə-ˌkóid\ *adjective* (circa 1900)
: resembling heath ⟨*ericoid* foliage⟩

Erie \'ir-ē, 'ēr-ē\ *noun* (circa 1909)
1 : a member of an American Indian people living south of Lake Erie in the 17th century
2 : the extinct and probably Iroquoian language of the Erie people

erig·er·on \ə-'ri-jə-ˌrän\ *noun* [New Latin, from Latin, groundsel, from Greek *ērigerōn*, from *ēri* early + *gerōn* old man; from the hoary down of some species — more at ERE, GERONT-] (1601)
: any of a widely distributed genus (*Erigeron*) of composite herbs with flower heads that resemble asters but have fewer and narrower involucral bracts

Er·i·nys \i-'ri-nəs, -'rī-\ *noun, plural* **Erin·y·es** \-'ri-nē-ˌēz\ [Greek] (1590)
: FURY 2a

er·i·o·phy·id \ˌer-ē-'ä-fē-əd, -ē-ə-'fī-əd\ *noun* [ultimately from Greek *erion* wool + *phyē* growth; akin to Greek *physis* growth — more at PHYSICS] (1942)
: any of a large family (Eriophyidae) of minute plant-feeding mites that have two pairs of legs placed far anterior and lack a respiratory system
— **eriophyid** *adjective*

¹**eris·tic** \i-'ris-tik, e-\ *also* **eris·ti·cal** \-ti-kəl\ *adjective* [Greek *eristikos* fond of wrangling, from *erizein* to wrangle, from *eris* strife] (1637)
: characterized by disputatious and often subtle and specious reasoning
— **eris·ti·cal·ly** \-ti-k(ə)lē\ *adverb*

²**eristic** *noun* (1659)
1 : a person devoted to logical disputation
2 : the art or practice of disputation and polemics

Er·len·mey·er flask \ˌər-lən-ˌmī-(ə)r-, ˌer-lən-\ *noun* [Emil *Erlenmeyer*] (circa 1890)
: a flat-bottomed conical laboratory flask

er·mine \'ər-mən\ *noun, plural* **ermines** [Middle English, from Old French, of Germanic origin; akin to Old High German *harmo* weasel] (12th century)
1 *or plural* **ermine a** : any of several weasels whose coats become white in winter usually with black on the tip of the tail; *especially* : a short-tailed weasel (*Mustela erminea*) of the forests and tundra of Eurasia and North America **b** : the white fur of the ermine
2 : a rank or office whose ceremonial or official robe is ornamented with ermine

er·mined \-mənd\ *adjective* (15th century)
: clothed or adorned with ermine

erne \'ərn, 'ern\ *noun* [Middle English, from Old English *earn*; akin to Old High German *arn* eagle, Greek *ornis* bird] (before 12th century)

ermine 1a: winter coat

: EAGLE; *especially* : a long-winged sea eagle (*Haliäetus albicilla*) with a short white wedge-shaped tail

erode \i-'rōd\ *verb* **erod·ed; erod·ing** [Latin *erodere* to eat away, from *e-* + *rodere* to gnaw — more at RODENT] (1612)
transitive verb
1 : to diminish or destroy by degrees: **a** : to eat into or away by slow destruction of substance (as by acid, infection, or cancer) **b** : to wear away by the action of water, wind, or glacial ice **c** : to cause to deteriorate or disappear as if by eating or wearing away ⟨inflation *eroding* buying power⟩
2 : to produce or form by eroding ⟨glaciers *erode* U-shaped valleys⟩
intransitive verb
: to undergo erosion
— **erod·ibil·i·ty** \-ˌrō-də-'bi-lə-tē\ *noun*
— **erod·ible** \-'rō-də-bəl\ *adjective*

erog·e·nous \i-'rä-jə-nəs\ *adjective* [Greek *erōs* + English *-genous, -genic*] (circa 1889)
1 : producing sexual excitement or libidinal gratification when stimulated : sexually sensitive
2 : of, relating to, or arousing sexual feelings

Eros \'er-ˌäs, 'ir-\ *noun* [Greek *Erōs*, from *erōs* sexual love; akin to Greek *erasthai* to love, desire]
1 : the Greek god of erotic love — compare CUPID
2 : the sum of life-preserving instincts that are manifested as impulses to gratify basic needs, as sublimated impulses, and as impulses to protect and preserve the body and mind — compare DEATH INSTINCT
3 a : love conceived in the philosophy of Plato as a fundamental creative impulse having a sensual element **b** *often not capitalized* : erotic love or desire

erose \i-'rōs\ *adjective* [Latin *erosus,* past participle of *erodere*] (1793)
: IRREGULAR, UNEVEN; *specifically* : having the margin irregularly notched as if gnawed ⟨an *erose* leaf⟩

ero·sion \i-'rō-zhən\ *noun* (1541)
1 a : the action or process of eroding **b** : the state of being eroded
2 : an instance or product of erosive action
— **ero·sion·al** \-'rōzh-nəl, -'rō-zhə-nᵊl\ *adjective*
— **ero·sion·al·ly** \-ē\ *adverb*

ero·sive \i-'rō-siv, -ziv\ *adjective* (1830)
: tending to erode or to induce or permit erosion
— **ero·sive·ness** *noun*
— **ero·siv·i·ty** \i-ˌrō-'si-və-tē\ *noun*

erot·ic \i-'rä-tik\ *also* **erot·i·cal** \-ti-kəl\ *adjective* [Greek *erōtikos*, from *erōt-, erōs*] (1651)
1 : of, devoted to, or tending to arouse sexual love or desire ⟨*erotic* art⟩
2 : strongly marked or affected by sexual desire ◇

— **erotic** *noun*

— **erot·i·cal·ly** \-ti-k(ə-)lē\ *adverb*

erot·i·ca \i-'rä-ti-kə\ *noun plural but singular or plural in construction* [New Latin, from Greek *erōtika,* neuter plural of *erōtikos*] (1854)
1 : literary or artistic works having an erotic theme or quality
2 : depictions of things erotic

erot·i·cism \i-'rä-tə-,si-zəm\ *noun* (1881)
1 : an erotic theme or quality
2 : a state of sexual arousal
3 : insistent sexual impulse or desire

— **erot·i·cist** \-sist\ *noun*

erot·i·cize \-,sīz\ *transitive verb* **-cized; -ciz·ing** (circa 1914)
: to make erotic

— **erot·i·ci·za·tion** \i-,rä-tə-sə-'zā-shən\ *noun*

er·o·tism \'er-ə-,ti-zəm\ *noun* (1849)
: EROTICISM

er·o·tize \'er-ə-,tīz\ *transitive verb* **-tized; -tiz·ing** (1936)
: to invest with erotic significance or sexual feeling

— **er·o·ti·za·tion** \,er-ə-tə-'zā-shən\ *noun*

eroto- *combining form* [New Latin, from Greek *erōto-,* from *erot-, eros*]
: sexual desire ⟨*erotogenic*⟩

ero·to·gen·ic \i-,rō-tə-'je-nik, -,rä-\ *adjective* (circa 1909)
: EROGENOUS

err \'er, 'ər\ *intransitive verb* [Middle English, from Middle French *errer,* from Latin *errare* to wander, err; akin to Old English *ierre* wandering, angry, Old Norse *rās* race — more at RACE] (14th century)
1 *archaic* : STRAY
2 a : to make a mistake **b** : to violate an accepted standard of conduct □

er·ran·cy \'er-ən(t)-sē\ *noun, plural* **-cies** (1621)
: the state or an instance of erring

er·rand \'er-ənd\ *noun* [Middle English *erend* message, business, from Old English *ǣrend;* akin to Old High German *ārunti* message] (before 12th century)
1 *archaic* **a** : an oral message entrusted to a person **b** : EMBASSY, MISSION
2 a : a short trip taken to attend to some business often for another ⟨was on an *errand* for his mother⟩ **b** : the object or purpose of such a trip

er·rant \'er-ənt\ *adjective* [Middle English *erraunt,* from Middle French *errant,* present participle of *errer* to err & *errer* to travel, from Late Latin *iterare,* from Latin *iter* road, journey — more at ITINERANT] (14th century)
1 : traveling or given to traveling ⟨an *errant* knight⟩
2 a : straying outside the proper path or bounds ⟨an *errant* calf⟩ **b** : moving about aimlessly or irregularly ⟨an *errant* breeze⟩ **c** : deviating from a standard (as of truth or propriety) ⟨an *errant* child⟩ **d** : FALLIBLE

— **errant** *noun*

— **er·rant·ly** *adverb*

er·rant·ry \'er-ən-trē\ *noun, plural* **-ries** (1654)
: the quality, condition, or fact of wandering; *especially* : a roving in search of chivalrous adventure

er·ra·ta \e-'rä-tə, -'rā-, -'ra-\ *noun* [Latin, plural of *erratum*] (1589)
: a list of corrigenda; *also* : a page bearing such a list

¹**er·rat·ic** \ir-'a-tik\ *adjective* [Middle English, from Middle French or Latin; Middle French *erratique,* from Latin *erraticus,* from *erratus,* past participle of *errare*] (14th century)
1 a : having no fixed course : WANDERING ⟨an *erratic* comet⟩ **b** *archaic* : NOMADIC
2 : transported from an original resting place especially by a glacier ⟨an *erratic* boulder⟩
3 a : characterized by lack of consistency, regularity, or uniformity **b** : deviating from what is ordinary or standard ⟨an *erratic* genius⟩

synonym see STRANGE

— **er·rat·i·cal** \-ti-kəl\ *adjective*

— **er·rat·i·cal·ly** \-ti-k(ə-)lē\ *adverb*

— **er·rat·i·cism** \-'a-tə-,si-zəm\ *noun*

²**erratic** *noun* (circa 1623)
: one that is erratic; *especially* : an erratic boulder or block of rock

er·ra·tum \e-'rä-təm, -'rā-, -'ra-\ *noun, plural* **-ta** \-tə\ [Latin, from neuter of *erratus*] (1589)
: ERROR; *especially* : CORRIGENDUM

er·ro·ne·ous \i-'rō-nē-əs, e-'rō-\ *adjective* [Middle English, from Latin *erroneus,* from *erron-, erro* wanderer, from *errare*] (15th century)
1 : containing or characterized by error : MISTAKEN ⟨*erroneous* assumptions⟩
2 *archaic* : WANDERING

— **er·ro·ne·ous·ly** *adverb*

— **er·ro·ne·ous·ness** *noun*

er·ror \'er-ər\ *noun* [Middle English *errour,* from Middle French, from Latin *error,* from *errare*] (13th century)
1 a : an act or condition of ignorant or imprudent deviation from a code of behavior **b** : an act involving an unintentional deviation from truth or accuracy **c** : an act that through ignorance, deficiency, or accident departs from or fails to achieve what should be done: as (1) : a defensive misplay other than a wild pitch or passed ball made by a baseball player when normal play would have resulted in an out or prevented an advance by a base runner (2) : the failure of a player (as in tennis) to make a successful return of a ball during play **d** : a mistake in the proceedings of a court of record in matters of law or of fact
2 a : the quality or state of erring **b** *Christian Science* : illusion about the nature of reality that is the cause of human suffering : the contradiction of truth **c** : an instance of false belief
3 : something produced by mistake; *especially* : a postage stamp exhibiting a consistent flaw (as a wrong color) in its manufacture
4 a : the difference between an observed or calculated value and a true value; *specifically* : variation in measurements, calculations, or observations of a quantity due to mistakes or to uncontrollable factors **b** : the amount of deviation from a standard or specification
5 : a deficiency or imperfection in structure or function ⟨an *error* of metabolism⟩ ☆

— **er·ror·less** \'er-ər-ləs\ *adjective*

er·satz \'er-,säts, -,zäts, er-'; 'ər-,sats\ *adjective* [German *ersatz-,* from *Ersatz,* noun, substitute] (1875)
: being a usually artificial and inferior substitute or imitation ⟨*ersatz* turf⟩ ⟨*ersatz* intellectuals⟩

— **ersatz** *noun*

Erse \'ərs\ *noun* [Middle English (Scots) *Erisch,* adjective, Irish, alteration of *Irish*] (15th century)
1 : SCOTTISH GAELIC
2 : IRISH GAELIC

— **Erse** *adjective*

erst \'ərst\ *adverb* [Middle English *erest* earliest, formerly, from Old English *ǣrest,* superlative of *ǣr* early — more at ERE] (12th century)
archaic : ERSTWHILE

¹**erst·while** \'ərst-,(h)wīl\ *adverb* (1569)
: in the past : FORMERLY ⟨cultures, *erstwhile* unknown to each other —Robert Plank⟩

²**erstwhile** *adjective* (1903)
: FORMER, PREVIOUS ⟨her *erstwhile* students⟩

eru·cic acid \i-'rü-sik-\ *noun* [New Latin *Eruca,* genus of herbs, from Latin, colewort] (1869)
: a crystalline fatty acid $C_{22}H_{42}O_2$ found in the form of glycerides especially in rapeseed oil

eruct \i-'rəkt\ *verb* [Latin *eructare,* frequentative of *erugere* to belch, disgorge; akin to Old English *rocettan* to belch, Greek *ereugesthai*] (1666)
: BELCH

eruc·ta·tion \i-,rək-'tā-shən, ,ē-\ *noun* (15th century)
: an act or instance of belching

er·u·dite \'er-ə-,dīt, 'er-yə-\ *adjective* [Middle English *erudit,* from Latin *eruditus,* from past participle of *erudire* to instruct, from *e-* + *rudis* rude, ignorant] (15th century)
: possessing or displaying erudition : LEARNED ⟨an *erudite* scholar⟩

— **er·u·dite·ly** *adverb*

er·u·di·tion \,er-ə-'di-shən, ,er-yə-\ *noun* (15th century)
: extensive knowledge acquired chiefly from books : profound, recondite, or bookish learning

synonym see KNOWLEDGE

erum·pent \i-'rəm-pənt\ *adjective* [Latin *erumpent-, erumpens,* present participle of *erumpere*] (1650)
: bursting forth ⟨*erumpent* fungi⟩

erupt \i-'rəpt\ *verb* [Latin *eruptus,* past participle of *erumpere* to burst forth, from *e-* + *rumpere* to break — more at REAVE] (1657)
intransitive verb
1 a (1) : to burst from limits or restraint (2) *of a tooth* : to emerge through the gum **b** : to force out or release suddenly and often violently something (as lava or steam) that is pent up **c** : to become active or violent especially suddenly
2 : to break out with or as if with a skin eruption

☆ **SYNONYMS**

Error, mistake, blunder, slip, lapse mean a departure from what is true, right, or proper. ERROR suggests the existence of a standard or guide and a straying from the right course through failure to make effective use of this ⟨procedural *errors*⟩. MISTAKE implies misconception or inadvertence and usually expresses less criticism than *error* ⟨dialed the wrong number by *mistake*⟩. BLUNDER regularly imputes stupidity or ignorance as a cause and connotes some degree of blame ⟨diplomatic *blunders*⟩. SLIP stresses inadvertence or accident and applies especially to trivial but embarrassing mistakes ⟨a *slip* of the tongue⟩. LAPSE stresses forgetfulness, weakness, or inattention as a cause ⟨a *lapse* in judgment⟩.

□ **USAGE**

err The sound of the letter *r* often colors a preceding vowel in English, so that the originally distinct vowels of *curt, word, bird,* and *were* are now pronounced the same. Originally *err* and *error* had the same first vowel, but over time *err* developed the pronunciation \'ər\ as well. Commentators have expressed a visceral dislike for the original pronunciation \'er\; perhaps they believe that once usage has established a new pronunciation for a word that there can be no going back. By this reasoning, though, we should embrace the once established innovative pronunciations of *gold* \'gŭld\ and *Rome* \'rüm\ (as seen in Shakespeare's pun on *Rome* and *room* in *Julius Caesar* I.ii.156). For these two words the English language has returned to the older forms, and no sound reason prevents us from accepting again the \'er\ pronunciation of *err,* which is today also the more common variant in American speech.

\ə\ abut \ᵊ\ kitten \ər\ further \a\ ash \ā\ ace
\ä\ mop, mar \au̇\ out \ch\ chin \e\ bet \ē\ easy
\g\ go \i\ hit \ī\ ice \j\ job \ŋ\ sing \ō\ go
\ȯ\ law \ȯi\ boy \th\ thin \t͟h\ the \ü\ loot \u̇\ foot
\y\ yet \zh\ vision *see also* Guide to Pronunciation

transitive verb
: to force out or release usually suddenly and violently
— **erupt·ible** \-'rəp-tə-bəl\ *adjective*
— **erup·tive** \-tiv\ *adjective*
— **erup·tive·ly** *adverb*
erup·tion \i-'rəp-shən\ *noun* (1555)
 1 a : an act, process, or instance of erupting **b :** the breaking out of a rash on the skin or mucous membrane
 2 : a product of erupting (as a skin rash)
-ery \(ə-)rē\ *noun suffix, plural* **-er·ies** [Middle English *-erie*, from Old French, from *-ier -er + -ie -y*]
 1 : qualities collectively **:** character **:** -NESS ⟨snob*bery*⟩
 2 : art **:** practice ⟨quack*ery*⟩
 3 : place of doing, keeping, producing, or selling (the thing specified) ⟨fish*ery*⟩ ⟨bak*ery*⟩
 4 : collection **:** aggregate ⟨fin*ery*⟩
 5 : state or condition ⟨slav*ery*⟩
eryn·go \i-'riŋ-(,)gō\ *noun, plural* **-goes** *or* **-gos** [modification of Latin *eryngion* sea holly, from Greek *ēryngion*] (1543)
 1 : any of various plants (genus *Eryngium*) of the carrot family that have elongate spinulose-margined leaves and flowers in dense bracted heads
 2 *obsolete* **:** candied root of the sea holly made to be used as an aphrodisiac
ery·sip·e·las \,er-ə-'si-p(ə-)ləs, ,ir-\ *noun* [Middle English *erisipila*, from Latin *erysipelas*, from Greek, from *erysi-* (probably akin to Greek *erythros* red) + *-pelas* (probably akin to Latin *pellis* skin) — more at RED, FELL] (14th century)
 : an acute febrile disease associated with intense edematous local inflammation of the skin and subcutaneous tissues caused by a hemolytic streptococcus
er·y·the·ma \,er-ə-'thē-mə\ *noun* [New Latin, from Greek *erythēma*, from *erythainein* to redden, from *erythros*] (circa 1783)
 : abnormal redness of the skin due to capillary congestion
— **er·y·them·a·tous** \-'the-mə-təs\ *adjective*
er·y·thor·bate \,er-ə-'thòr-,bāt\ *noun* (1963)
 : a salt of erythorbic acid that is used in foods as an antioxidant
er·y·thor·bic acid \-,thòr-bik-\ *noun* [*erythr- + ascorbic acid*] (1963)
 : a diastereoisomer of ascorbic acid with optical activity
erythr- *or* **erythro-** *combining form* [Greek, from *erythros* — more at RED]
 1 : red ⟨*erythro*cyte⟩
 2 : erythrocyte ⟨*erythr*oid⟩
er·y·thre·mia \,er-ə-'thrē-mē-ə\ *noun* [New Latin] (1908)
 : POLYCYTHEMIA VERA
er·y·thrism \'er-ə-,thri-zəm\ *noun* (1864)
 : a condition marked by exceptional prevalence of red pigmentation (as in skin or hair)
— **er·y·thris·tic** \,er-ə-'thris-tik\ *also* **er·y·thris·mal** \-'thriz-məl\ *adjective*
er·y·thrite \'er-ə-,thrīt\ *noun* (1844)
 : a usually rose-colored mineral consisting of a hydrous cobalt arsenate occurring especially in monoclinic crystals
eryth·ro·blast \i-'rith-rə-,blast\ *noun* [International Scientific Vocabulary] (circa 1890)
 : a polychromatic nucleated cell of red marrow that synthesizes hemoglobin and that is an intermediate in the initial stage of red blood cell formation; *broadly* **:** a cell ancestral to red blood cells
— **eryth·ro·blas·tic** \-,rith-rə-'blas-tik\ *adjective*
eryth·ro·blas·to·sis \i-,rith-rə-,blas-'tō-səs\ *noun, plural* **-to·ses** \-,sēz\ [New Latin] (circa 1923)
 : abnormal presence of erythroblasts in the circulating blood; *especially* **:** ERYTHROBLASTOSIS FETALIS

erythroblastosis fe·ta·lis \-fi-'ta-ləs\ *noun* [New Latin, fetal erythroblastosis] (circa 1934)
 : a hemolytic disease of the fetus and newborn that occurs when the system of an Rh-negative mother produces antibodies to an antigen in the blood of an Rh-positive fetus which cross the placenta and destroy fetal erythrocytes and that is characterized by an increase in circulating erythroblasts and by jaundice
eryth·ro·cyte \i-'rith-rə-,sīt\ *noun* [International Scientific Vocabulary] (circa 1894)
 : RED BLOOD CELL
— **eryth·ro·cyt·ic** \-,rith-rə-'si-tik\ *adjective*
ery·throid \i-'rith-,ròid, 'er-ə-,thròid\ *adjective* (1927)
 : relating to erythrocytes or their precursors
eryth·ro·my·cin \i-,rith-rə-'mī-sᵊn\ *noun* (1952)
 : a broad-spectrum antibiotic $C_{37}H_{67}NO_{13}$ produced by an actinomycete (*Streptomyces erythreus*)
eryth·ro·poi·e·sis \i-,rith-rō-pòi-'ē-səs\ *noun* [New Latin, from *erythr-* + Greek *poiēsis* creation — more at POESY] (1918)
 : the production of red blood cells (as from the bone marrow)
— **eryth·ro·poi·et·ic** \-'e-tik\ *adjective*
eryth·ro·poi·e·tin \-'pòi-ə-tᵊn\ *noun* (1948)
 : a hormonal substance that is formed especially in the kidney and stimulates red blood cell formation
eryth·ro·sin \i-'rith-rə-sən\ *also* **eryth·ro·sine** \-sən, -,sēn\ *noun* [International Scientific Vocabulary *erythr-* + e*osin*] (circa 1882)
 : any of several dyes made from fluorescein that yield reddish shades
¹-es \əz, iz *after* s, z, sh, ch; z *after* v *or a vowel*\ *noun plural suffix* [Middle English *-es, -s* — more at ¹-S]
 — used to form the plural of most nouns that end in *s* ⟨glass*es*⟩, *z* ⟨fuzz*es*⟩, *sh* ⟨bush*es*⟩, *ch* ⟨peach*es*⟩, or a final *y* that changes to *i* ⟨lad*ies*⟩ and of some nouns ending in *f* that changes to *v* ⟨loav*es*⟩; compare ¹-S
²-es *verb suffix* [Middle English — more at ³-S]
 — used to form the third person singular present of most verbs that end in *s* ⟨bless*es*⟩, *z* ⟨fizz*es*⟩, *sh* ⟨hush*es*⟩, *ch* ⟨catch*es*⟩, or a final *y* that changes to *i* ⟨defi*es*⟩; compare ³-S
Esau \'ē-(,)sò\ *noun* [Latin, from Greek *Ēsau*, from Hebrew *'Ēsāw*]
 : the elder son of Isaac and Rebekah who sold his birthright to his twin brother Jacob
es·ca·drille \'es-kə-,dril, -,drē\ *noun* [French, flotilla, escadrille, from Spanish *escuadrilla*, diminutive of *escuadra* squadron, squad — more at SQUAD] (1912)
 : a unit of a European air command containing usually six airplanes
es·ca·lade \'es-kə-,lād, -,läd\ *noun* [French, from Italian *scalata*, from *scalare* to scale, from *scala* ladder, from Late Latin — more at SCALE] (1598)
 : an act of scaling especially the walls of a fortification
— **escalade** *transitive verb*
— **es·ca·lad·er** *noun*
es·ca·late \'es-kə-,lāt, ÷-kyə-\ *verb* **-lat·ed; -lat·ing** [back-formation from *escalator*] (1944)
intransitive verb
 : to increase in extent, volume, number, amount, intensity, or scope ⟨a little war threatens to *escalate* into a huge ugly one —Arnold Abrams⟩
transitive verb
 : EXPAND 2
— **es·ca·la·tion** \,es-kə-'lā-shən, ÷-kyə-\ *noun*
— **es·ca·la·to·ry** \'es-kə-lə-,tòr-ē, -,tòr-, ÷-kyə-\ *adjective*
¹es·ca·la·tor \'es-kə-,lā-tər, ÷-kyə-\ *noun* [from *Escalator*, a trademark] (1900)

 1 a : a power-driven set of stairs arranged like an endless belt that ascend or descend continuously **b :** an upward course suggestive of an escalator ⟨a never-stopping *escalator* of economic progress —D. W. Brogan⟩
 2 : an escalator clause or provision
²escalator *adjective* (1930)
 : providing for a periodic proportional upward or downward adjustment (as of prices or wages) ⟨an *escalator* arrangement tying the base pay . . . to living costs —*N. Y. Times*⟩
es·cal·lop \is-'kä-ləp, -'ka-\ *variant of* SCALLOP
es·ca·pade \'es-kə-,pād\ *noun* [French, action of escaping, from Spanish *escapada*, from *escapar* to escape, from (assumed) Vulgar Latin *excappare*] (1672)
 : a usually adventurous action that runs counter to approved or conventional conduct
¹es·cape \is-'kāp, es-, *dialect* iks-'käp\ *verb* **es·caped; es·cap·ing** [Middle English, from Old North French *escaper*, from (assumed) Vulgar Latin *excappare*, from Latin *ex-* + Late Latin *cappa* head covering, cloak] (13th century)
intransitive verb
 1 a : to get away (as by flight) ⟨*escaped* from prison⟩ **b :** to issue from confinement ⟨gas is *escaping*⟩ **c** *of a plant* **:** to run wild from cultivation
 2 : to avoid a threatening evil
transitive verb
 1 : to get free of **:** break away from ⟨*escape* the jungle⟩ ⟨*escape* the solar system⟩
 2 : to get or stay out of the way of **:** AVOID
 3 : to fail to be noticed or recallable by ⟨his name *escapes* me⟩
 4 a : to issue from **b :** to be uttered involuntarily by ☆
— **es·cap·er** *noun*
²escape *noun* (14th century)
 1 : an act or instance of escaping: as **a :** flight from confinement **b :** evasion of something undesirable **c :** leakage or outflow especially of a fluid **d :** distraction or relief from routine or reality
 2 : a means of escape
 3 : a cultivated plant run wild
³escape *adjective* (1817)
 1 : providing a means of escape ⟨*escape* literature⟩
 2 : providing a means of evading a regulation, claim, or commitment ⟨an *escape* clause in a contract⟩
escape artist *noun* (1943)
 : one (as a performer or criminal) unusually adept at escaping from confinement
es·cap·ee \is-,kā-'pē, ,es-(,)kā-, ,es-kə-\ *noun* (circa 1866)
 : one that has escaped; *especially* **:** an escaped prisoner

escape hatch *noun* (1925)
1 : a hatch providing an emergency exit from an enclosed space
2 : a means of evading a difficulty, dilemma, or responsibility

escape mechanism *noun* (1927)
: a mode of behavior or thinking adopted to evade unpleasant facts or responsibilities

es·cape·ment \is-ˈkāp-mənt\ *noun* (1779)
1 a : a device in a timepiece which controls the motion of the train of wheelwork and through which the energy of the power source is delivered to the pendulum or balance by means of impulses that permit a tooth to escape from a pallet at regular intervals **b :** a ratchet device (as the spacing mechanism of a typewriter) that permits motion in one direction only in equal steps

escapement 1a
2 a : the act of escaping **b :** a way of escape **:** VENT

escape velocity *noun* (1934)
: the minimum velocity that a moving body (as a rocket) must have to escape from the gravitational field of a celestial body (as the earth) and move outward into space

es·cap·ism \is-ˈkā-ˌpi-zəm\ *noun* (1933)
: habitual diversion of the mind to purely imaginative activity or entertainment as an escape from reality or routine
— es·cap·ist \-pist\ *adjective or noun*

es·cap·ol·o·gy \is-ˌkā-ˈpä-lə-jē, ˌes-(ˌ)\ *noun* (1939)
: the art or practice of escaping
— es·cap·ol·o·gist \-jist\ *noun*

es·car·got \ˌes-ˌkär-ˈgō\ *noun, plural* **-gots** \-ˈgō(z)\ [French, snail, from Middle French, from Old Provençal *escaragol*]
: a snail prepared for use as food

es·ca·role \ˈes-kə-ˌrōl\ *noun* [French, from Late Latin *escariola*, from Latin *escarius* of food, from *esca* food, from *edere* to eat — more at EAT] (1897)
: ENDIVE 1

es·carp·ment \i-ˈskärp-mənt\ *noun* [French *escarpement*, from *escarper* to scarp, from Middle French *escarpe* scarp, from Old Italian *scarpa* — more at SCARP] (circa 1802)
1 : a steep slope in front of a fortification
2 : a long cliff or steep slope separating two comparatively level or more gently sloping surfaces and resulting from erosion or faulting

-es·cence \ˈe-sᵊn(t)s\ *noun suffix* [Middle French, from Latin *-escentia*, from *-escent-*, *-escens* + *-ia* -y]
: state or process of becoming ⟨obsol*escence*⟩

-es·cent \ˈe-sᵊnt\ *adjective suffix* [Middle French, from Latin *-escent-*, *-escens*, present participle suffix of inchoative verbs in *-escere*]
1 : beginning **:** beginning to be **:** slightly ⟨frut*escent*⟩
2 : reflecting or emitting light (in a specified way) ⟨opal*escent*⟩

es·char \ˈes-ˌkär\ *noun* [Middle English *escare* — more at SCAR] (1543)
: a scab formed especially after a burn

es·cha·rot·ic \ˌes-kə-ˈrä-tik\ *adjective* [French or Late Latin; French *escharotique*, from Late Latin *escharoticus*, from Greek *escharōtikos*, from *escharoun* to form an eschar, from *eschara* eschar] (1612)
: producing an eschar
— escharotic *noun*

es·cha·to·log·i·cal \(ˌ)es-ˌka-tᵊl-ˈä-ji-kəl, ˌes-kə-\ *adjective* (1854)
1 : of or relating to eschatology or an eschatology
2 : of or relating to the end of the world or the events associated with it in eschatology
— es·cha·to·log·i·cal·ly \-ji-k(ə-)lē\ *adverb*

es·cha·tol·o·gy \ˌes-kə-ˈtä-lə-jē\ *noun, plural* **-gies** [Greek *eschatos* last, farthest] (1844)

1 : a branch of theology concerned with the final events in the history of the world or of mankind
2 : a belief concerning death, the end of the world, or the ultimate destiny of mankind; *specifically* **:** any of various Christian doctrines concerning the Second Coming, the resurrection of the dead, or the Last Judgment

¹es·cheat \is-ˈchēt, ish-ˈchēt\ *noun* [Middle English *eschete*, from Old French, reversion of property, from *escheoir* to fall, devolve, from (assumed) Vulgar Latin *excadēre*, from Latin *ex-* + (assumed) Vulgar Latin *cadēre* to fall, from Latin *cadere* — more at CHANCE] (14th century)
1 : escheated property
2 a : the reversion of lands in English feudal law to the lord of the fee when there are no heirs capable of inheriting under the original grant **b :** the reversion of property to the crown in England or to the state in the U.S. when there are no legal heirs

²escheat (14th century)
transitive verb
: to cause to revert by escheat
intransitive verb
: to revert by escheat
— es·cheat·able \-ˈchē-tə-bəl\ *adjective*

es·chew \e-ˈshü, i-; es-ˈchü, is-; *also* e-ˈskyü\ *transitive verb* [Middle English, from Middle French *eschiuer*, of Germanic origin; akin to Old High German *sciuhen* to frighten off — more at SHY] (14th century)
: to avoid habitually especially on moral or practical grounds **:** SHUN
synonym see ESCAPE
— es·chew·al \-əl\ *noun*

es·co·lar \ˌes-kə-ˈlär\ *noun, plural* **escolar** *or* **escolars** [Spanish, literally, scholar, from Medieval Latin *scholaris* — more at SCHOLAR] (circa 1890)
: a large widely distributed rough-scaled fish (*Lepidocybium flavobrunneum*) that resembles a mackerel

¹es·cort \ˈes-ˌkȯrt\ *noun* [French *escorte*, from Italian *scorta*, from *scorgere* to guide, from (assumed) Vulgar Latin *excorrigere*, from Latin *ex-* + *corrigere* to make straight, correct — more at CORRECT] (1745)
1 a (1) **:** a person or group of persons accompanying another to give protection or as a courtesy (2) **:** the man who goes on a date with a woman **b :** a protective screen of warships or fighter planes or a single ship or plane used to fend off enemy attack from one or more vulnerable craft
2 : accompaniment by a person or an armed protector (as a ship)

²es·cort \is-ˈkȯrt, es-, ˈes-ˌ\ *transitive verb* (1708)
: to accompany as an escort

es·cot \is-ˈkät\ *transitive verb* [Middle French *escoter*, from *escot* contribution, of Germanic origin; akin to Old Norse *skot* contribution, shot — more at SHOT] (1602)
obsolete **:** SUPPORT, MAINTAIN

es·cri·toire \ˈes-krə-ˌtwär\ *noun* [obsolete French, writing desk, scriptorium, from Medieval Latin *scriptorium*] (1694)
: a writing table or desk; *specifically* **:** SECRETARY 4b

¹es·crow \ˈes-ˌkrō, es-ˈ\ *noun* [Middle French *escroue* scroll — more at SCROLL] (1594)
1 : a deed, a bond, money, or a piece of property held in trust by a third party to be turned over to the grantee only upon fulfillment of a condition
2 : a fund or deposit designed to serve as an escrow
— in escrow : in trust as an escrow ⟨had $1000 *in escrow* to pay taxes⟩

²es·crow \es-ˈkrō, ˈes-ˌ\ *transitive verb* (1949)
: to place in escrow

es·cu·do \is-ˈkü-(ˌ)dō\ *noun, plural* **-dos** [Spanish & Portuguese, literally, shield, from Latin *scutum*] (circa 1821)

1 : any of various former gold or silver coins of Hispanic countries
2 — see MONEY table
3 : the basic monetary unit of Chile between 1960 and 1975
4 : the peso of Guinea-Bissau

es·cu·lent \ˈes-kyə-lənt\ *adjective* [Latin *esculentus*, from *esca* food, from *edere* to eat — more at EAT] (1626)
: EDIBLE
— esculent *noun*

es·cutch·eon \is-ˈkə-chən\ *noun* [Middle English *escochon*, from Middle French *escuchon*, from (assumed) Vulgar Latin *scution-*, *scutio*, from Latin *scutum* shield — more at ESQUIRE] (15th century)
1 : a defined area on which armorial bearings are displayed and which usually consists of a shield
2 : a protective or ornamental plate or flange (as around a keyhole)
3 : the part of a ship's stern on which the name is displayed

Es·dras \ˈez-drəs\ *noun* [Late Latin, from Greek, from Hebrew *'Ezrā*]
1 : either of two books of the Roman Catholic canon of the Old Testament: **a :** EZRA 1 **b :** NEHEMIAH 2
2 : either of two uncanonical books of Scripture included in the Protestant Apocrypha — see BIBLE table

¹-ese \ˈēz, ˈēs\ *adjective suffix* [Portuguese *-ês* & Italian *-ese*, from Latin *-ensis*]
: of, relating to, or originating in (a certain place or country) ⟨Japan*ese*⟩

²-ese *noun suffix, plural* **-ese**
1 : native or resident of (a specified place or country) ⟨Chin*ese*⟩
2 a : language of (a particular place, country, or nationality) ⟨Siam*ese*⟩ **b :** speech, literary style, or diction peculiar to (a specified place, person, or group) — usually in words applied in depreciation ⟨journal*ese*⟩

es·em·plas·tic \ˌe-sem-ˈplas-tik, -səm-\ *adjective* [Greek *es hen* into one + English *plastic*] (1817)
: shaping or having the power to shape disparate things into a unified whole ⟨the *esemplastic* power of the poetic imagination —W. H. Gardner⟩

es·er·ine \ˈe-sə-ˌrēn\ *noun* [French *ésérine*] (1879)
: PHYSOSTIGMINE

es·ker \ˈes-kər\ *noun* [Irish *eiscir* ridge] (1848)
: a long narrow ridge or mound of sand, gravel, and boulders deposited by a stream flowing on, within, or beneath a stagnant glacier

Es·ki·mo \ˈes-kə-ˌmō\ *noun* [obsolete *Esquimawe*, probably from Spanish *esquimao*, from Montagnais (Algonquian language of eastern Canada) *aiachkime8* Micmac, Eskimo; probably akin to modern Montagnais *assime'w* she laces a snowshoe, Ojibwa *aškime'*] (1584)
1 *plural* **Eskimo** *or* **Eskimos :** a member of a group of peoples of northern Canada, Greenland, Alaska, and eastern Siberia
2 : any of the languages of the Eskimo peoples
— Es·ki·mo·an \ˌes-kə-ˈmō-ən\ *adjective*

Eskimo curlew *noun* (1813)
: an extremely rare New World curlew (*Numenius borealis*) that breeds in northern North America and winters in South America

Eskimo curlew

Eskimo dog *noun* (1774)
: a sled dog of American origin

ESOP \'ē-,es-(,)ō-'pē, 'ē-,säp\ *noun* [*e*mployee *s*tock *o*wnership *p*lan] (1975)
: a program by which a corporation's employees acquire its capital stock

esoph·a·gus \i-'sä-fə-gəs\ *noun, plural* **-gi** \-,gī, -,jī\ [Middle English *ysophagus*, from Greek *oisophagos*, from *oisein* to be going to carry + *phagein* to eat — more at BAKSHEESH] (14th century)
: a muscular tube that in humans is about nine inches long and passes from the pharynx down the neck between the trachea and the spinal column and behind the left bronchus where it pierces the diaphragm slightly to the left of the middle line and joins the cardiac end of the stomach
— **esoph·a·ge·al** \i-,sä-fə-'jē-əl\ *adjective*

es·o·ter·ic \,e-sə-'ter-ik\ *adjective* [Late Latin *esotericus*, from Greek *esōterikos*, from *esōterō*, comparative of *eisō, esō* within, from *eis* into; akin to Greek *en* in — more at IN] (circa 1660)
1 a : designed for or understood by the specially initiated alone ⟨a body of *esoteric* legal doctrine —B. N. Cardozo⟩ **b** : of or relating to knowledge that is restricted to a small group
2 a : limited to a small circle ⟨*esoteric* pursuits⟩ **b** : PRIVATE, CONFIDENTIAL ⟨an *esoteric* purpose⟩
— **es·o·ter·i·cal·ly** \-i-k(ə-)lē\ *adverb*

es·o·ter·i·ca \-i-kə\ *noun plural* [New Latin, from Greek *esōterika*, neuter plural of *esōterikos*] (circa 1929)
: esoteric items

es·o·ter·i·cism \-'ter-ə-,si-zəm\ *noun* (1846)
1 : esoteric doctrines or practices
2 : the quality or state of being esoteric

ESP \,ē-,es-'pē\ *noun* [*e*xtra*s*ensory *p*erception] (1934)
: EXTRASENSORY PERCEPTION

es·pa·drille \'es-pə-,dril\ *noun* [French, alteration of *espardille*, ultimately from Latin *spartum*] (1892)
: a sandal usually having a fabric upper and a flexible sole

¹es·pal·ier \is-'pal-yər, -,yā\ *noun* [French, ultimately from Italian *spalla* shoulder, from Late Latin *spatula* shoulder blade — more at EPAULET] (1662)
1 : a plant (as a fruit tree) trained to grow flat against a support (as a wall)
2 : a railing or trellis on which fruit trees or shrubs are trained to grow flat

²espalier *transitive verb* (1810)
1 : to train as an espalier
2 : to furnish with an espalier

es·par·to \is-'pär-(,)tō\ *noun, plural* **-tos** [Spanish, from Latin *spartum*, from Greek *sparton* — more at SPIRE] (1845)
1 : either of two Spanish and Algerian grasses (*Stipa tenacissima* and *Lygeum spartum*) used especially to make cordage, shoes, and paper — called also *esparto grass*
2 : the fiber of esparto

es·pe·cial \is-'pe-shəl\ *adjective* [Middle English, from Middle French — more at SPECIAL] (14th century)
: being distinctive: as **a** : directed toward a particular individual, group, or end ⟨sent *especial* greetings to his son⟩ ⟨took *especial* care to speak clearly⟩ **b** : of special note or importance : unusually great or significant ⟨a decision of *especial* relevance⟩ **c** : highly distinctive or personal : PECULIAR ⟨had an *especial* dislike for music⟩ **d** : CLOSE, INTIMATE ⟨his *especial* crony⟩ **e** : SPECIFIC, PARTICULAR ⟨had no *especial* destination in mind⟩
synonym see SPECIAL
— **in especial** : in particular

es·pe·cial·ly \is-'pesh-lē, -'pe-shə-\ *adverb* (15th century)
1 : SPECIALLY 1

2 a : in particular : PARTICULARLY ⟨food seems cheaper, *especially* meats⟩ **b** : for a particular purpose ⟨built *especially* for research⟩
3 — used as an intensive ⟨an *especially* good essay⟩ ⟨nothing *especially* radical in the remarks⟩

es·per·ance \'es-p(ə-)rən(t)s\ *noun* [Middle English *esperaunce*, from Middle French *esperance*] (15th century)
obsolete : HOPE, EXPECTATION

Es·pe·ran·to \,es-pə-'rän-(,)tō, -'ran-(,)tō\ *noun* [Dr. *Esperanto*, pseudonym of L. L. Zamenhof (died 1917) Polish oculist, its inventor] (1892)
: an artificial international language based as far as possible on words common to the chief European languages
— **Es·pe·ran·tist** \-'rän-tist, -'ran-\ *noun or adjective*

es·pi·al \is-'pī(-ə)l\ *noun* (14th century)
1 : OBSERVATION
2 : an act of noticing : DISCOVERY

es·piè·gle \es-pyegl°\ *adjective* [French, after *Ulespiegle* (Till Eulenspiegel), peasant prankster] (1816)
: FROLICSOME, ROGUISH

es·piè·gle·rie \es-,pyeg-lə-rē\ *noun* [French, from *espiègle*] (1816)
: the quality or state of being roguish or frolicsome

es·pi·o·nage \'es-pē-ə-,näzh, -,näj, -nij, Canadian also* -,nazh; ,es-pē-ə-'näzh; is-'pē-ə-nij\ *noun* [French *espionnage*, from Middle French, from *espionner* to spy, from *espion* spy, from Old Italian *spione*, from *spia*, of Germanic origin; akin to Old High German *spehōn* to spy — more at SPY] (1793)
: the practice of spying or using spies to obtain information about the plans and activities especially of a foreign government or a competing company ⟨industrial *espionage*⟩

es·pla·nade \'es-plə-,näd, ,es-plə-'\ *also* -'nād *or* -,nād\ *noun* [Middle French, from Italian *spianata*, from *spianare* to level, from Latin *explanare* — more at EXPLAIN] (1591)
: a level open stretch of paved or grassy ground; *especially* : one designed for walking or driving along a shore

es·pous·al \is-'pau̇-zəl *also* -səl\ *noun* (14th century)
1 a : BETROTHAL **b** : WEDDING **c** : MARRIAGE
2 : a taking up or adopting of a cause or belief

es·pouse \is-'pau̇z *also* -'pau̇s\ *transitive verb* **es·poused; es·pous·ing** [Middle English, from Middle French *espouser*, from Latin *sponsare* to betroth, from Latin *sponsus* betrothed — more at SPOUSE] (15th century)
1 : MARRY
2 : to take up and support as a cause : become attached to
synonym see ADOPT
— **es·pous·er** *noun*

espres·so \e-'spre-(,)sō\ *noun, plural* **-sos** [Italian (*caffè*) *espresso*, literally, pressed out coffee] (1945)
1 : coffee brewed by forcing steam through finely ground darkly roasted coffee beans
2 : a cup of espresso

es·prit \is-'prē\ *noun* [French, from Latin *spiritus* spirit] (1591)
1 : vivacious cleverness or wit
2 : ESPRIT DE CORPS

es·prit de corps \is-,prē-də-'kȯr, -'kȯr\ *noun* [French] (1780)
: the common spirit existing in the members of a group and inspiring enthusiasm, devotion, and strong regard for the honor of the group

es·py \is-'pī\ *transitive verb* **es·pied; es·py·ing** [Middle English *espien*, from Old French *espier* — more at SPY] (14th century)
: to catch sight of ⟨among the several horses . . . she *espied* the white mustang —Zane Grey⟩

-esque \'esk\ *adjective suffix* [French, from Italian *-esco*, of Germanic origin; akin to Old High German *-isc* -ish — more at -ISH]

: in the manner or style of : like ⟨statu*esque*⟩

Es·qui·mau \'es-kə-,mō\ *noun, plural* **Es·quimau** *or* **Es·qui·maux** \-,mō(z)\ [French, from Montagnais (Algonquian language)] (1744)
: ESKIMO

es·quire \'es-,kwīr, is-'\ *noun* [Middle English, from Middle French *escuier* squire, from Late Latin *scutarius*, from Latin *scutum* shield; akin to Old Irish *sciath* shield] (15th century)
1 : a member of the English gentry ranking below a knight
2 : a candidate for knighthood serving as shield bearer and attendant to a knight
3 — used as a title of courtesy usually placed in its abbreviated form after the surname ⟨John R. Smith, *Esq.*⟩
4 *archaic* : a landed proprietor ◆

ess \'es\ *noun* (1540)
1 : the letter *s*
2 : something resembling the letter *S* in shape; *especially* : an S-shaped curve in a road

-ess \əs, is *also* ,es\ *noun suffix* [Middle English *-esse*, from Old French, from Late Latin *-issa*, from Greek]
: female ⟨giant*ess*⟩ □

¹es·say \e-'sā, ə-'sā, 'e-,sā\ *transitive verb* (14th century)
1 : to put to a test
2 : to make an often tentative or experimental effort to perform : TRY
synonym see ATTEMPT
— **es·say·er** *noun*

²es·say \'e-,sā; *senses* 1, 2 & 4 *also* e-'sā\ *noun* [Middle English, from Middle French *essai*, ultimately from Late Latin *exagium* act of weighing, from *ex-* + *agere* to drive — more at AGENT] (14th century)
1 : TRIAL, TEST
2 a : EFFORT, ATTEMPT; *especially* : an initial tentative effort **b** : the result or product of an attempt
3 a : an analytic or interpretative literary composition usually dealing with its subject from a limited or personal point of view **b** : something resembling such a composition ⟨a photographic *essay*⟩
4 : a proof of an unaccepted design for a stamp or piece of paper money

es·say·ist \'e-,sā-ist\ *noun* (1601)
: a writer of essays

es·say·is·tic \,e-(,)sā-'is-tik\ *adjective* (1862)
1 : of or relating to an essay or an essayist
2 : resembling an essay in quality or character

essay question *noun* (1947)

◇ WORD HISTORY
esquire The word *esquire* in its oldest senses, "young candidate for knighthood" and "member of the English gentry ranking below a knight in social precedence," has been less common than the shortened form *squire* since Middle English. It is only as an abbreviated title placed after a person's name that *esquire* maintains a curious sort of afterlife in English, even in the United States, where there have never been knights or gentry. This peculiar usage came about because the technical stipulations for members of the gentry who could be styled *esquire*, as established by 17th century lawyers and antiquaries, were so complex and so loosely observed that the title became practically equivalent to "gentleman." (The title *knight* never became similarly nebulous because since the 16th century knighthood has been an honor specifically bestowed on individuals by the British sovereign, and not hereditary.) In America, *esquire* is less common than in Britain, persisting mainly among attorneys, who use it, chiefly in the form of its abbreviation *Esq.*, when referring to or addressing each other in writing.

: an examination question that requires an answer in a sentence, paragraph, or short composition

es·sence \'e-s⁰n(t)s\ *noun* [Middle English, from Middle French & Latin; Middle French, from Latin *essentia,* from *esse* to be — more at IS] (14th century)
1 a : the permanent as contrasted with the accidental element of being **b :** the individual, real, or ultimate nature of a thing especially as opposed to its existence **c :** the properties or attributes by means of which something can be placed in its proper class or identified as being what it is
2 : something that exists **:** ENTITY
3 a (1) **:** a volatile substance or constituent (as of perfume) (2) **:** a constituent or derivative possessing the special qualities (as of a plant or drug) in concentrated form; *also* **:** a preparation of such an essence or a synthetic substitute **b :** ODOR, PERFUME
4 : one that possesses or exhibits a quality in abundance as if in concentrated form ⟨she was the *essence* of punctuality⟩
— **in essence :** in or by its very nature **:** ESSENTIALLY, BASICALLY ⟨was *in essence* an honest person⟩
— **of the essence :** of the utmost importance ⟨time is *of the essence*⟩

Es·sene \i-'sēn, 'e-,sēn\ *noun* [Greek *Essēnos*] (1553)
: a member of a monastic brotherhood of Jews in Palestine from the 2d century B.C. to the 2d century A.D.
— **Es·se·ni·an** \i-'sē-nē-ən, e-'se-\ *or* **Es·se·nic** \-'se-nik, -'sē-nik\ *adjective*
— **Es·se·nism** \-ni-zəm\ *noun*

¹es·sen·tial \i-'sen(t)-shəl\ *adjective* (14th century)
1 : of, relating to, or constituting essence **:** INHERENT
2 : of the utmost importance **:** BASIC, INDISPENSABLE, NECESSARY ⟨*essential* foods⟩ ⟨an *essential* requirement for admission to college⟩
3 : IDIOPATHIC ⟨*essential* disease⟩ ☆
— **es·sen·tial·ly** \-'sench-lē, -'sen-chə-\ *adverb*
— **es·sen·tial·ness** \-'sen-chəl-nəs\ *noun*

²essential *noun* (15th century)
1 : something basic ⟨the *essentials* of astronomy⟩
2 : something necessary, indispensable, or unavoidable

essential amino acid *noun* (1935)
: an amino acid (as lysine) required for normal health and growth, manufactured in the body in insufficient quantities or not at all, and usually supplied by dietary protein

es·sen·tial·ism \-,li-zəm\ *noun* (1927)
1 : an educational theory that ideas and skills basic to a culture should be taught to all alike by time-tested methods — compare PROGRESSIVISM
2 : a philosophical theory ascribing ultimate reality to essence embodied in a thing perceptible to the senses — compare NOMINALISM
— **es·sen·tial·ist** \-list\ *adjective or noun*

es·sen·ti·al·i·ty \i-,sen(t)-shē-'a-lə-tē\ *noun, plural* **-ties** (1616)
1 a : essential nature **:** ESSENCE **b :** an essential quality, property, or aspect
2 : the quality or state of being essential ⟨the *essentiality* of freedom and justice —P. G. Hoffman⟩

es·sen·tial·ize \i-'sen(t)-shə-,līz\ *transitive verb* **-ized; -iz·ing** (1913)
: to express or formulate in essential form **:** reduce to essentials

essential oil *noun* (1674)
: any of a class of volatile oils that give plants their characteristic odors and are used especially in perfumes and flavorings — compare FIXED OIL

es·soin \i-'sòin\ *noun* [Middle English *essoine,* from Middle French, from Old French, from *essoinier* to offer an essoin, from *es-* ex-

+ *soine* legal excuse, of Germanic origin; akin to Old Saxon *sunnea* denial, Old English *sōth* truth — more at SOOTH] (14th century)
1 : an excuse for not appearing in an English law court at the appointed time
2 *obsolete* **:** EXCUSE, DELAY

es·so·nite \'e-sⁿ-,īt\ *noun* [French, from Greek *hēsson* inferior; from its being less hard than true hyacinth] (1820)
: a yellow to brown garnet

¹-est \əst, ist\ *adjective suffix or adverb suffix* [Middle English, from Old English *-st, -est, -ost;* akin to Old High German *-isto* (adjective superlative suffix), Greek *-istos*]
— used to form the superlative degree of adjectives and adverbs of one syllable ⟨fatt*est*⟩ ⟨lat*est*⟩, of some adjectives and adverbs of two syllables ⟨lucki*est*⟩ ⟨often*est*⟩, and less often of longer ones ⟨beggarli*est*⟩

²-est \əst, ist\ *or* **-st** \st\ *verb suffix* [Middle English, from Old English *-est, -ast, -st;* akin to Old High German *-ist, -ōst, -ēst,* 2d singular ending]
— used to form the archaic 2d person singular of English verbs (with *thou*) ⟨did*st*⟩

es·tab·lish \is-'ta-blish\ *transitive verb* [Middle English *establissen,* from Middle French *establiss-,* stem of *establir,* from Latin *stabilire,* from *stabilis* stable] (14th century)
1 : to institute (as a law) permanently by enactment or agreement
2 *obsolete* **:** SETTLE 7
3 a : to make firm or stable **b :** to introduce and cause to grow and multiply ⟨*establish* grass on pasturelands⟩
4 a : to bring into existence **:** FOUND ⟨*established* a republic⟩ **b :** BRING ABOUT, EFFECT ⟨*established* friendly relations⟩
5 a : to put on a firm basis **:** SET UP ⟨*establish* his son in business⟩ **b :** to put into a favorable position **c :** to gain full recognition or acceptance of ⟨the role *established* her as a star⟩
6 : to make (a church) a national or state institution
7 : to put beyond doubt **:** PROVE ⟨*established* my innocence⟩
— **es·tab·lish·able** \-shə-bəl\ *adjective*
— **es·tab·lish·er** \-shər\ *noun*

established church *noun* (1731)
: a church recognized by law as the official church of a nation or state and supported by civil authority

es·tab·lish·ment \is-'ta-blish-mənt\ *noun* (15th century)
1 : something established: as **a :** a settled arrangement; *especially* **:** a code of laws **b :** ESTABLISHED CHURCH **c :** a permanent civil or military organization **d :** a place of business or residence with its furnishings and staff **e :** a public or private institution
2 : an established order of society: as **a** *often capitalized* **:** a group of social, economic, and political leaders who form a ruling class (as of a nation) **b** *often capitalized* **:** a controlling group ⟨the literary *establishment*⟩
3 a : the act of establishing **b :** the state of being established

es·tab·lish·men·tar·i·an \is-,ta-blish-mən-'ter-ē-ən, -,men-\ *adjective* (1847)
: of, relating to, or favoring the social or political establishment
— **establishmentarian** *noun*
— **es·tab·lish·men·tar·i·an·ism** \-ē-ə-,ni-zəm\ *noun*

es·ta·mi·net \e-stá-mē-nā\ *noun, plural* **-nets** \-nā(z)\ [French] (1814)
: a small café

es·tate \is-'tāt\ *noun* [Middle English *estat,* from Old French — more at STATE] (13th century)
1 : STATE, CONDITION
2 : social standing or rank especially of a high order
3 : a social or political class; *specifically* **:** one of the great classes (as the nobility, the clergy,

and the commons) formerly vested with distinct political powers
4 a : the degree, quality, nature, and extent of one's interest in land or other property **b** (1) **:** POSSESSIONS, PROPERTY; *especially* **:** a person's property in land and tenements ⟨a man of small *estate*⟩ (2) **:** the assets and liabilities left by a person at death **c :** a landed property usually with a large house on it **d** *British* **:** PROJECT 4
5 *British* **:** STATION WAGON

estate agent *noun* (1880)
British **:** a real estate broker or manager

estate car *noun* (1950)
British **:** STATION WAGON

estate tax *noun* (1928)
: an excise in the form of a percentage of the net estate that is levied on the privilege of an

☆ **SYNONYMS**

Essential, fundamental, vital, cardinal mean so important as to be indispensable. ESSENTIAL implies belonging to the very nature of a thing and therefore being incapable of removal without destroying the thing itself or its character ⟨conflict is *essential* in drama⟩. FUNDAMENTAL applies to something that is a foundation without which an entire system or complex whole would collapse ⟨*fundamental* principles of algebra⟩. VITAL suggests something that is necessary to a thing's continued existence or operation ⟨cut off from *vital* supplies⟩. CARDINAL suggests something on which an outcome turns or depends ⟨a *cardinal* rule in buying a home⟩.

□ **USAGE**

-ess In 1865 Sara Josepha Hale, self-styled editress of *Godey's Lady's Book,* proposed for use a list of more than 50 terms ending in -ess that she thought would lend dignity to women and their work. We are not sure if her plea for the use of these words had any effect on late 19th century usage, but the male commentators of that time mostly disapproved the forms. In the 20th century, attitudes have become no more nearly unanimous. A few male commentators have looked on the forms with approval, if not with the evangelistic fervor of Mrs. Hale, but more, both men and women, find them objectionable in some way. Of course some words with this ending, like *lioness* or *duchess* or *goddess,* have never been in dispute. But actual users always have the final say. If *stewardess* is falling into disuse, it is probably due as much to the increased number of male flight attendants as to language attitudes. *Poetess,* which has been disapproved as archaic or disused since the 18th century, is still used, but in historical reference; it does not appear to be applied to contemporary writers. *Mayoress* and *manageress,* which look a bit strange to American eyes, are quite common in British English. *Actress* and *waitress* are still in common use. *Priestess* in its first sense generally refers to ancient or pagan religions; its second sense, "a woman regarded as a leader," is still in common use, often in such phrases as *high priestess of fashion.* These are a few of the -ess words that have been commented on. You can assume that any -ess word entered in this dictionary is in current acceptable use unless it bears a warning label or usage note.

\ə\ abut \ⁿ\ kitten \ər\ further \a\ ash \ā\ ace \ä\ mop, mar \au\ out \ch\ chin \e\ bet \ē\ easy \g\ go \i\ hit \ī\ ice \j\ job \ŋ\ sing \ō\ law \oi\ boy \th\ thin \th\ the \ü\ loot \u\ foot \y\ yet \zh\ vision *see also* Guide to Pronunciation

owner of property of transmitting the property to others after his or her death — compare IN-HERITANCE TAX 1

¹es·teem \is-'tēm\ *noun* (14th century)
1 *archaic* : WORTH, VALUE
2 *archaic* : OPINION, JUDGMENT
3 : the regard in which one is held; *especially* : high regard ⟨the *esteem* we all feel for her⟩

²esteem *transitive verb* [Middle English *estemen* to estimate, from Middle French *estimer,* from Latin *aestimare*] (15th century)
1 *archaic* : APPRAISE
2 a : to view as : CONSIDER ⟨*esteem* it a privilege⟩ **b** : THINK, BELIEVE
3 : to set a high value on : regard highly and prize accordingly
synonym see REGARD

es·ter \'es-tər\ *noun* [German, from *Essigäther* ethyl acetate, from *Essig* vinegar + *Äther* ether] (circa 1852)
: any of a class of often fragrant compounds that can be represented by the formula RCOOR' and that are usually formed by the reaction between an acid and an alcohol with elimination of water

es·ter·ase \'es-tə-ˌrās, -ˌrāz\ *noun* (1910)
: an enzyme that accelerates the hydrolysis or synthesis of esters

es·ter·i·fy \e-'ster-ə-ˌfī\ *transitive verb* **-fied; -fy·ing** (circa 1905)
: to convert into an ester
— **es·ter·i·fi·ca·tion** \-ˌster-ə-fə-'kā-shən\ *noun*

Es·ther \'es-tər\ *noun* [Latin, from Hebrew *Estēr*]
1 : the Jewish heroine of the Old Testament book of Esther
2 : a narrative book of canonical Jewish and Christian Scripture — see BIBLE table

es·thete, es·thet·ic, es·the·ti·cian, es·the·ti·cism *variant of* AESTHETE, AESTHETIC, AESTHETICIAN, AESTHETICISM

es·ti·ma·ble \'es-tə-mə-bəl\ *adjective* (15th century)
1 : capable of being estimated
2 *archaic* : VALUABLE
3 : worthy of esteem
— **es·ti·ma·ble·ness** *noun*
— **es·ti·ma·bly** \-blē\ *adverb*

¹es·ti·mate \'es-tə-ˌmāt\ *transitive verb* **-mat·ed; -mat·ing** [Latin *aestimatus,* past participle of *aestimare* to value, estimate] (circa 1532)
1 *archaic* **a** : ESTEEM **b** : APPRAISE
2 a : to judge tentatively or approximately the value, worth, or significance of **b** : to determine roughly the size, extent, or nature of **c** : to produce a statement of the approximate cost of
3 : JUDGE, CONCLUDE ☆
— **es·ti·ma·tive** \-ˌmā-tiv\ *adjective*

²es·ti·mate \'es-tə-mət\ *noun* (1563)
1 : the act of appraising or valuing : CALCULATION
2 : an opinion or judgment of the nature, character, or quality of a person or thing ⟨had a high *estimate* of his abilities⟩
3 a : a rough or approximate calculation **b** : a numerical value obtained from a statistical sample and assigned to a population parameter
4 : a statement of the cost of work to be done

es·ti·ma·tion \ˌes-tə-'mā-shən\ *noun* (14th century)
1 : JUDGMENT, OPINION
2 a : the act of estimating something **b** : the value, amount, or size arrived at in an estimate
3 : ESTEEM, HONOR

es·ti·ma·tor \'es-tə-ˌmā-tər\ *noun* (1611)
1 : one that estimates
2 : ESTIMATE 3b; *also* : a statistical function whose value for a sample furnishes an estimate of a population parameter

es·ti·val \'es-tə-vəl\ *adjective* [Middle English, from Middle French or Latin; Middle French, from Latin *aestivalis,* from *aestivus* of

summer, from *aestas* summer — more at EDIFY] (14th century)
: of or relating to the summer

es·ti·vate \-ˌvāt\ *intransitive verb* **-vat·ed; -vat·ing** (1626)
1 : to spend the summer usually at one place
2 : to pass the summer in a state of torpor — compare HIBERNATE

es·ti·va·tion \ˌes-tə-'vā-shən\ *noun* (1625)
: the state of one that estivates

Es·to·ni·an \e-'stō-nē-ən, -nyən\ *noun* (1795)
1 : a native or inhabitant of Estonia
2 : the Finno-Ugric language of the Estonian people
— **Estonian** *adjective*

es·top \e-'stäp\ *transitive verb* **es·topped; es·top·ping** [Middle English *estoppen,* from Middle French *estouper,* from (assumed) Vulgar Latin *stuppare* to stop with a tow — more at STOP] (15th century)
1 *archaic* : to stop up
2 : BAR; *specifically* : to impede by estoppel

es·top·pel \e-'stä-pəl\ *noun* [probably from Middle French *estoupail* bung, from *estouper*] (1531)
: a legal bar to alleging or denying a fact because of one's own previous actions or words to the contrary

estr- *or* **estro-** *combining form*
: estrus ⟨*estro*gen⟩

es·tra·di·ol \ˌes-trə-'dī-ˌól, -ˌōl\ *noun* [International Scientific Vocabulary *estra-* (from *estrane* parent compound of estradiol, from New Latin *estrus* + English *-ane*) + *di-* + ¹*-ol*] (1934)
: an estrogenic hormone that is a phenolic steroid alcohol $C_{18}H_{24}O_2$ usually made synthetically and that is often used combined as an ester especially in treating menopausal symptoms

es·tral cycle \'es-trəl-\ *noun* (1941)
: ESTROUS CYCLE

es·trange \is-'trānj\ *transitive verb* **es·tranged; es·trang·ing** [Middle English, from Middle French *estranger,* from Medieval Latin *extraneare,* from Latin *extraneus* strange — more at STRANGE] (15th century)
1 : to remove from customary environment or associations
2 : to arouse especially mutual enmity or indifference in where there had formerly been love, affection, or friendliness : ALIENATE ☆
— **es·trange·ment** \-'trānj-mənt\ *noun*
— **es·trang·er** *noun*

¹es·tray \is-'trā\ *noun* (circa 1523)
: STRAY 1

²estray *intransitive verb* [Middle French *estraier*] (1572)
archaic : STRAY

es·tri·ol \'es-ˌtrī-ˌól, e-'strī-, -ˌōl\ *noun* [*estrane* + *tri-* + ¹*-ol*] (1933)
: a crystalline estrogenic hormone that is a glycol $C_{18}H_{24}O_3$ usually obtained from the urine of pregnant women

es·tro·gen \'es-trə-jən\ *noun* [New Latin *estrus* + International Scientific Vocabulary *-o- + -gen*] (1927)
: a substance (as a sex hormone) tending to promote estrus and stimulate the development of female secondary sex characteristics
usage see ECONOMIC

es·tro·gen·ic \ˌes-trə-'je-nik\ *adjective* (1930)
1 : promoting estrus
2 : of, relating to, caused by, or being an estrogen
— **es·tro·gen·i·cal·ly** \-ni-k(ə-)lē\ *adverb*

es·trone \'es-ˌtrōn\ *noun* [*estrane*] (1933)
: an estrogenic hormone that is a ketone $C_{18}H_{22}O_2$ usually obtained from the urine of pregnant females and used similarly to estradiol

es·trous \'es-trəs\ *adjective* (1900)
1 : of, relating to, or characteristic of estrus
2 : being in heat

estrous cycle *noun* (1900)

: the correlated phenomena of the endocrine and generative systems of a female mammal from the beginning of one period of estrus to the beginning of the next — called also *estral cycle, estrus cycle*

es·tru·al \'es-trə-wəl\ *adjective* (circa 1857)
: ESTROUS

es·trus \'es-trəs\ *noun* [New Latin, from Latin *oestrus* gadfly, frenzy, from Greek *oistros* — more at IRE] (circa 1890)
: a regularly recurrent state of sexual excitability during which the female of most mammals will accept the male and is capable of conceiving : HEAT; *also* : a single occurrence of this state

es·tu·ar·i·al \ˌes-chə-'wer-ē-əl, ˌesh-\ *adjective* (1883)
: ESTUARINE

es·tu·a·rine \'es-chə-(wə-)ˌrīn, -ˌrēn, -ˌrin, 'esh-\ *adjective* (1846)
: of, relating to, or formed in an estuary ⟨*estuarine* currents⟩ ⟨*estuarine* animals⟩

es·tu·ary \'es-chə-ˌwer-ē, 'esh-\ *noun, plural* **-ar·ies** [Latin *aestuarium,* from *aestus* boiling, tide; akin to Latin *aestas* summer — more at EDIFY] (1538)
: a water passage where the tide meets a river current; *especially* : an arm of the sea at the lower end of a river

esu·ri·ence \i-'sùr-ē-ən(t)s, -'zùr-\ *noun* (1825)
: the quality or state of being esurient

esu·ri·ent \-ənt\ *adjective* [Latin *esurient-, esuriens,* present participle of *esurire* to be hungry; akin to Latin *edere* to eat — more at EAT] (circa 1672)
: HUNGRY, GREEDY
— **esu·ri·ent·ly** *adverb*

et \'et\ *dialect past and past participle of* EAT

¹-et \'et, ˌet, ət, it\ *noun suffix* [Middle English, from Old French *-et,* masculine, & *-ete,* feminine, from Late Latin *-itus & -ita*]
: small one ⟨baron*et*⟩ ⟨cellar*et*⟩

☆ **SYNONYMS**
Estimate, appraise, evaluate, value, rate, assess mean to judge something with respect to its worth or significance. ESTIMATE implies a judgment, considered or casual, that precedes or takes the place of actual measuring or counting or testing out ⟨*estimated* the crowd at two hundred⟩. APPRAISE commonly implies the fixing by an expert of the monetary worth of a thing, but it may be used of any critical judgment ⟨having their house *appraised*⟩. EVALUATE suggests an attempt to determine relative or intrinsic worth in terms other than monetary ⟨*evaluate* a student's work⟩. VALUE equals APPRAISE but without implying expertness of judgment ⟨a watercolor *valued* by the donor at $500⟩. RATE adds to ESTIMATE the notion of placing a thing according to a scale of values ⟨a highly *rated* restaurant⟩. ASSESS implies a critical appraisal for the purpose of understanding or interpreting, or as a guide in taking action ⟨officials are trying to *assess* the damage⟩.

Estrange, alienate, disaffect mean to cause one to break a bond of affection or loyalty. ESTRANGE implies the development of indifference or hostility with consequent separation or divorcement ⟨his *estranged* wife⟩. ALIENATE may or may not suggest separation but always implies loss of affection or interest ⟨managed to *alienate* all his coworkers⟩. DISAFFECT refers especially to those from whom loyalty is expected and stresses the effects (as rebellion or discontent) of alienation without actual separation ⟨conservatives were *disaffected* by the new tax⟩.

²-et *noun suffix* [*duet*]
: group ⟨*octet*⟩

eta \'ā-tə, *chiefly British* 'ē-tə\ *noun* [Middle English, from Late Latin, from Greek *ēta*, of Semitic origin; akin to Hebrew *ḥēth* heth] (15th century)
: the 7th letter of the Greek alphabet — see ALPHABET table

éta·gère *or* **eta·gere** \,ā-tä-'zher, -tə-\ *noun* [French, from Middle French *estagiere*, from *estage* floor of a building, station, from Old French — more at STAGE] (1851)
: a piece of furniture consisting of a set of open shelves for displaying small objects and sometimes having an enclosed cabinet as a base

étagère

et alia \(,)et-'ä-l(ē-)yə, -'ā-, -'a-\ [Latin] (1953)
: and others

eta·mine \'ā-tə-,mēn\ *noun* [French *étamine*] (1714)
: a light cotton or worsted fabric with an open mesh

etat·ism \ā-'tä-,ti-zəm\ *noun* [French *étatisme*, from *état* state, from Old French *estat* — more at STATE] (1923)
: STATE SOCIALISM
 — **etat·ist** \-'tä-tist\ *adjective*

et·cet·era \et-'se-tə-rə, -'se-trə *also* it-, ÷ek-, ÷ik-\ *noun* (1656)
1 : a number of unspecified additional persons or things
2 *plural* **:** unspecified additional items **:** ODDS AND ENDS

et cet·era *same*\ [Latin] (12th century)
: and others especially of the same kind **:** and so forth

¹etch \'ech\ *verb* [Dutch *etsen*, from German *ätzen* to etch, corrode, from Old High German *azzen* to feed; akin to Old High German *ezzan* to eat — more at EAT] (1634)
transitive verb
1 a : to produce (as a pattern or design) on a hard material by eating into the material's surface (as by acid or laser beam) **b :** to subject to such etching
2 : to delineate or impress clearly ⟨scenes *etched* in our minds⟩ ⟨pain was *etched* on his features⟩
intransitive verb
: to practice etching
 — **etch·er** *noun*

²etch *noun* (1896)
1 : the action or effect of etching a surface
2 : a chemical agent used in etching

etch·ant \'e-chənt\ *noun* (1904)
: ETCH 2

etch·ing *noun* (1634)
1 a : the action or process of etching **b :** the art of producing pictures or designs by printing from an etched metal plate
2 a : an etched design **b :** an impression from an etched plate

¹eter·nal \i-'tər-n°l\ *adjective* [Middle English, from Middle French, from Late Latin *aeternalis*, from Latin *aeternus* eternal, from *aevum* age, eternity — more at AYE] (14th century)
1 a : having infinite duration **:** EVERLASTING **b :** of or relating to eternity **c :** characterized by abiding fellowship with God ⟨good teacher, what must I do to inherit *eternal* life? —Mark 10:17 (Revised Standard Version)⟩
2 a : continued without intermission **:** PERPETUAL **b :** seemingly endless
3 *archaic* **:** INFERNAL ⟨some *eternal* villain . . . devised this slander —Shakespeare⟩
4 : valid or existing at all times **:** TIMELESS ⟨*eternal* verities⟩
 — **eter·nal·ize** \-n°l-,īz\ *transitive verb*

 — **eter·nal·ly** \-n°l-ē\ *adverb*
 — **eter·nal·ness** *noun*

²eternal *noun* (1582)
1 *capitalized* **:** GOD 1 — used with *the*
2 : something eternal

eterne \i-'tərn\ *adjective* [Middle English, from Middle French, from Latin *aeternus*] (14th century)
archaic **:** ETERNAL

eter·ni·ty \i-'tər-nə-tē\ *noun, plural* **-ties** [Middle English *eternite*, from Middle French *eternité*, from Latin *aeternitat-, aeternitas*, from *aeternus*] (14th century)
1 : the quality or state of being eternal
2 : infinite time
3 *plural* **:** AGE 3b
4 : the state after death **:** IMMORTALITY
5 : a seemingly endless or immeasurable time

eter·nize \i-'tər-,nīz\ *transitive verb* **-nized; -niz·ing** (1580)
1 a : to make eternal **b :** to prolong indefinitely
2 : IMMORTALIZE
 — **eter·ni·za·tion** \-,tər-nə-'zā-shən\ *noun*

Ete·sian \i-'tē-zhən\ *adjective* [Latin *etesius*, from Greek *etēsios*, from *etos* year — more at WETHER] (1601)
: recurring annually — used of summer winds that blow over the Mediterranean
 — **Etesian** *noun*

eth \'eth\ *variant of* EDH

eth- *combining form* [International Scientific Vocabulary]
: ethyl ⟨*ethene*⟩

¹-eth \əth, ith\ *or* **-th** \th\ *verb suffix* [Middle English, from Old English *-eth, -ath, -th;* akin to Old High German *-it, -ōt, -ēt,* 3d singular ending, Latin *-t, -it*]
— used to form the archaic third person singular present of verbs ⟨do*th*⟩

²-eth — see -TH

eth·a·cryn·ic acid \,e-thə-,kri-nik-\ *noun* [perhaps from *eth-* + *ac*etic + *buty*ryl + *phe*nol] (1964)
: a potent synthetic diuretic $C_{13}H_{12}Cl_2O_4$ used especially in the treatment of edema

eth·am·bu·tol \e-'tham-byù-,tòl, -,tōl\ *noun* [*eth*ylene + *am*ine + *butanol*] (1965)
: a compound $C_{10}H_{24}N_2O_2$ used especially in the treatment of tuberculosis

eth·ane \'e-,thān, *British usually* 'ē-\ *noun* [International Scientific Vocabulary, from *ethyl*] (1873)
: a colorless odorless gaseous alkane C_2H_6 found in natural gas and used as a fuel

eth·a·nol \'e-thə-,nòl, -,nōl, *British also* 'ē-\ *noun* (1900)
: a colorless volatile flammable liquid C_2H_5OH that is the intoxicating agent in liquors and is also used as a solvent — called also *ethyl alcohol, grain alcohol*

eth·a·nol·amine \,e-thə-'nä-lə-,mēn, -'nō-, *British also* ,ē-\ *noun* (1897)
: a colorless liquid amino alcohol C_2H_7NO used especially as a solvent in the synthesis of detergents and in gas purification

eth·ene \'e-,thēn\ *noun* (1873)
: ETHYLENE

eth·e·phon \'e-thə-,fän\ *noun* [*eth*yl + *phos*phonic acid (a dibasic organic acid)] (1971)
: a synthetic plant growth regulator $C_2H_6ClO_3P$ that induces flowering and abscission by promoting the release of ethylene and has been used to cause early ripening (as of apples on the tree)

ether \'ē-thər\ *noun* [Middle English, from Latin *aether*, from Greek *aithēr*, from *aithein* to ignite, blaze; akin to Old English *ād* pyre — more at EDIFY] (14th century)
1 a : the rarefied element formerly believed to fill the upper regions of space **b :** the upper regions of space **:** HEAVENS
2 a : a medium that in the wave theory of light permeates all space and transmits transverse waves **b :** AIRWAVES

3 a : a light volatile flammable liquid $C_4H_{10}O$ used chiefly as a solvent and anesthetic **b :** any of various organic compounds characterized by an oxygen atom attached to two carbon atoms
 — **ethe·ric** \i-'ther-ik, -'thir-\ *adjective*

ethe·re·al \i-'thir-ē-əl\ *adjective* (1513)
1 a : of or relating to the regions beyond the earth **b :** CELESTIAL, HEAVENLY **c :** UNWORLDLY, SPIRITUAL
2 a : lacking material substance **:** IMMATERIAL, INTANGIBLE **b :** marked by unusual delicacy or refinement ⟨this smallest, most *ethereal*, and daintiest of birds —William Beebe⟩
3 : relating to, containing, or resembling a chemical ether
 — **ethe·re·al·i·ty** \-,thir-ē-'a-lə-tē\ *noun*
 — **ethe·re·al·iza·tion** \-ē-ə-lə-'zā-shən\ *noun*
 — **ethe·re·al·ize** \-'thir-ē-ə-,līz\ *transitive verb*
 — **ethe·re·al·ly** \-ē-ə-lē\ *adverb*
 — **ethe·re·al·ness** *noun*

ether extract *noun* (circa 1900)
: the part of a complex organic material that is soluble in ether and consists chiefly of fats and fatty acids

ether·ize \'ē-thə-,rīz\ *transitive verb* **-ized; -iz·ing** (1853)
1 : to treat or anesthetize with ether
2 : to make numb as if by anesthetizing
 — **ether·iza·tion** \,ē-thə-rə-'zā-shən\ *noun*
 — **ether·iz·er** *noun*

eth·ic \'e-thik\ *noun* [Middle English *ethik*, from Middle French *ethique*, from Latin *ethice*, from Greek *ēthikē*, from *ēthikos*] (14th century)
1 *plural but singular or plural in construction* **:** the discipline dealing with what is good and bad and with moral duty and obligation
2 a : a set of moral principles or values **b :** a theory or system of moral values ⟨the present-day materialistic *ethic*⟩ **c** *plural but singular or plural in construction* **:** the principles of conduct governing an individual or a group ⟨professional *ethics*⟩ **d :** a guiding philosophy

eth·i·cal \'e-thi-kəl\ *also* **eth·ic** \-thik\ *adjective* [Middle English *etik*, from Latin *ethicus*, from Greek *ēthikos*, from *ēthos* character — more at SIB] (1607)
1 : of or relating to ethics
2 : involving or expressing moral approval or disapproval
3 : conforming to accepted professional standards of conduct
4 *of a drug* **:** restricted to sale only on a doctor's prescription
synonym see MORAL
 — **eth·i·cal·i·ty** \,e-thə-'ka-lə-tē\ *noun*
 — **eth·i·cal·ly** \'e-thi-k(ə-)lē\ *adverb*
 — **eth·i·cal·ness** \-kəl-nəs\ *noun*

eth·i·cian \e-'thi-shən\ *noun* (1629)
: ETHICIST

eth·i·cist \'e-thə-sist\ *noun* (circa 1890)
: a specialist in ethics

ethid·i·um bromide \e-'thi-dē-əm-\ *noun* [*ethyl* + *-id* + *-ium*] (1963)
: a biological dye used especially to block nucleic acid synthesis (as in mitochondria) and to destroy trypanosomes

ethinyl *variant of* ETHYNYL
— used especially in pharmacology

ethinyl estradiol *noun* (1939)
: a very potent synthetic estrogen $C_{20}H_{24}O_2$ used orally

eth·i·on \'e-thē-,än\ *noun* [blend of *eth-* and *thion-*] (circa 1960)
: an organophosphate $C_9H_{22}O_4P_2S_4$ used as a pesticide

\ə\ abut \°\ kitten \ər\ further \a\ ash \ā\ ace
\ä\ mop, mar \aù\ out \ch\ chin \e\ bet \ē\ easy
\g\ go \i\ hit \ī\ ice \j\ job \ŋ\ sing \ō\ go
\ò\ law \òi\ boy \th\ thin \t̲h̲\ the \ü\ loot \ù\ foot
\y\ yet \zh\ vision *see also* Guide to Pronunciation

eth·i·on·amide \,e-thē-'ä-nə-,mīd\ *noun* (1960)
: a compound $C_8H_{10}N_2S$ used against mycobacteria (as in tuberculosis and leprosy)

ethi·o·nine \e-'thī-ə-,nēn\ *noun* (1938)
: an amino acid $C_6H_{13}NO_2S$ that is the ethyl homologue of methionine and is biologically antagonistic to methionine

Ethi·op \'ē-thē-,äp\ *or* **Ethi·ope** \-,ōp\ *noun* [Middle English *Ethiope*, from Latin *Aethiops*, from Greek *Aithiops*] (13th century)
archaic : ETHIOPIAN

¹**Ethi·o·pi·an** \,ē-thē-'ō-pē-ən\ *noun* (13th century)
1 : a member of any of the mythical or actual peoples usually described by the ancient Greeks as dark-skinned and living far to the south
2 *archaic* : a black person
3 : a native or inhabitant of Ethiopia

²**Ethiopian** *adjective* (1578)
1 : of, relating to, or characteristic of the inhabitants or the country of Ethiopia
2 : of, relating to, or being the biogeographic region that includes Africa south of the Sahara, southern Arabia, and sometimes Madagascar and the adjacent islands

¹**Ethi·o·pic** \-'ä-pik, -'ō-pik\ *adjective* (1654)
1 : ETHIOPIAN
2 a : of, relating to, or constituting Ethiopic **b** : of, relating to, or constituting a group of related Semitic languages spoken in Ethiopia

²**Ethiopic** *noun* (1677)
1 : a Semitic language formerly spoken in Ethiopia and still used as the liturgical language of the Christian church in Ethiopia
2 : the Ethiopic group of Semitic languages

eth·moid \'eth-,mȯid\ *noun* [French *ethmoïde*, from Greek *ēthmoeidēs*, literally, like a strainer, from *ēthmos* strainer] (1842)
: a light spongy cubical bone forming much of the walls of the nasal cavity and part of those of the orbits
— **ethmoid** \same\ *or* **eth·moi·dal** \(,)eth-'mȯi-dᵊl\ *adjective*

¹**eth·nic** \'eth-nik\ *adjective* [Middle English, from Late Latin *ethnicus*, from Greek *ethnikos* national, gentile, from *ethnos* nation, people; akin to Greek *ēthos* custom — more at SIB] (15th century)
1 : HEATHEN
2 a : of or relating to large groups of people classed according to common racial, national, tribal, religious, linguistic, or cultural origin or background ⟨*ethnic* minorities⟩ ⟨*ethnic* enclaves⟩ **b** : being a member of an ethnic group **c** : of, relating to, or characteristic of ethnics ⟨*ethnic* neighborhoods⟩ ⟨*ethnic* foods⟩

²**ethnic** *noun* (1941)
: a member of an ethnic group; *especially* : a member of a minority group who retains the customs, language, or social views of the group

eth·ni·cal \'eth-ni-kəl\ *adjective* (15th century)
1 : ETHNIC
2 : of or relating to ethnology : ETHNOLOGIC
— **eth·ni·cal·ly** \-k(ə-)lē\ *adverb*

ethnic cleansing *noun* (1992)
: the expulsion, imprisonment, or killing of ethnic minorities by a dominant majority group

eth·nic·i·ty \eth-'ni-sə-tē\ *noun* (1950)
: ethnic quality or affiliation

ethno- *combining form* [French, from Greek *ethno-, ethn-,* from *ethnos*]
: race : people : cultural group ⟨*ethno*centric⟩

eth·no·bot·a·ny \,eth-nō-'bä-tᵊn-ē, -'bät-nē\ *noun* (1890)
: the plant lore of a race or people; *also* : the systematic study of such lore
— **eth·no·bo·tan·i·cal** \-bə-'ta-ni-kəl\ *adjective*
— **eth·no·bot·a·nist** \-'bä-tᵊn-ist, -'bät-nist\ *noun*

eth·no·cen·tric \,eth-nō-'sen-trik\ *adjective* (1900)
: characterized by or based on the attitude that one's own group is superior
— **eth·no·cen·tric·i·ty** \-sen-'tri-sə-tē\ *noun*
— **eth·no·cen·trism** \-'sen-,tri-zəm\ *noun*

eth·nog·ra·phy \eth-'nä-grə-fē\ *noun* [French *ethnographie*, from *ethno-* + *-graphie* -graphy] (1834)
: the study and systematic recording of human cultures; *also* : a descriptive work produced from such research
— **eth·nog·ra·pher** \-fər\ *noun*
— **eth·no·graph·ic** \,eth-nə-'gra-fik\ *or* **eth·no·graph·i·cal** \-fi-kəl\ *adjective*
— **eth·no·graph·i·cal·ly** \-fi-k(ə-)lē\ *adverb*

eth·no·his·to·ry \,eth-nō-'his-t(ə-)rē\ *noun* (1943)
: a study of the development of cultures
— **eth·no·his·to·ri·an** \-(h)is-'tȯr-ē-ən, -'tȯr-, -'tär-\ *noun*
— **eth·no·his·to·ric** \-(h)is-'tȯr-ik, -'tär-\ *or* **eth·no·his·to·ri·cal** \-i-kəl\ *adjective*

eth·nol·o·gy \eth-'nä-lə-jē\ *noun* (circa 1828)
1 : a science that deals with the division of human beings into races and their origin, distribution, relations, and characteristics
2 : anthropology dealing chiefly with the comparative and analytical study of cultures : CULTURAL ANTHROPOLOGY
— **eth·no·log·i·cal** \,eth-nə-'lä-ji-kəl\ *also* **eth·no·log·ic** \-jik\ *adjective*
— **eth·nol·o·gist** \eth-'nä-lə-jist\ *noun*

eth·no·meth·od·ol·o·gy \,eth-nō-,me-thə-'dä-lə-jē\ *noun* (1967)
: a branch of sociology dealing with nonspecialists' commonsense understanding of the structure and organization of society
— **eth·no·meth·od·ol·o·gist** \-'dä-lə-jist\ *noun*

eth·no·mu·si·col·o·gy \,eth-nō-,myü-zi-'kä-lə-jē\ *noun* (1950)
1 : the study of music that is outside the European art tradition
2 : the study of music in a sociocultural context
— **eth·no·mu·si·co·log·i·cal** \-kə-'lä-ji-kəl\ *adjective*
— **eth·no·mu·si·col·o·gist** \-'kä-lə-jist\ *noun*

eth·no·sci·ence \'eth-nō-,sī-ən(t)s\ *noun* (1961)
: the nature lore (as folk taxonomy of plants and animals) of primitive peoples

ethol·o·gy \ē-'thä-lə-jē\ *noun* (circa 1843)
1 : a branch of knowledge dealing with human ethos and with its formation and evolution
2 : the scientific and objective study of animal behavior especially under natural conditions
— **etho·log·i·cal** \,ē-thə-'lä-ji-kəl, ,e-thə-\ *adjective*
— **ethol·o·gist** \ē-'thä-lə-jist\ *noun*

ethos \'ē-,thäs\ *noun* [New Latin, from Greek *ēthos* custom, character — more at SIB] (1851)
: the distinguishing character, sentiment, moral nature, or guiding beliefs of a person, group, or institution

eth·oxy \e-'thäk-sē\ *adjective* (circa 1909)
: relating to or containing the univalent group CH_3CH_2O- composed of ethyl united with oxygen

eth·yl \'e-thəl\ *noun* [German *Ethyl* (now *Äthyl*), from *Äther* ether + *-yl*] (1838)
: a univalent hydrocarbon group CH_3CH_2-
— **eth·yl·ic** \e-'thi-lik\ *adjective*

ethyl acetate *noun* (1874)
: a colorless fragrant volatile flammable liquid ester $C_4H_8O_2$ used especially as a solvent

ethyl alcohol *noun* (1869)
: ETHANOL

eth·yl·ben·zene \,e-thil-'ben-,zēn\ *noun* [International Scientific Vocabulary] (1873)
: a liquid hydrocarbon C_8H_{10} that is made usually from benzene and ethylene and is used chiefly in the manufacture of styrene

ethyl cellulose *noun* (1936)
: any of various thermoplastic substances used especially in plastics and lacquers

ethyl chloride *noun* (circa 1891)
: a colorless pungent flammable gaseous or volatile liquid C_2H_5Cl used especially as a local surface anesthetic

eth·yl·ene \'e-thə-,lēn\ *noun* (circa 1852)
1 : a colorless flammable gaseous unsaturated hydrocarbon C_2H_4 that is found in coal gas, can be produced by pyrolysis of petroleum hydrocarbons, and occurs in plants functioning especially as a natural growth regulator that promotes the ripening of fruit
2 : a divalent hydrocarbon group C_2H_4 derived from ethane
— **eth·yl·en·ic** \,e-thə-'lē-nik, -'le-nik\ *adjective*

eth·yl·ene·di·amine·tet·ra·ac·e·tate \,e-thə-,lēn-,dī-ə-,mēn,te-trə-'a-sə-,tāt, -dī-,a-mən-\ *noun* (1954)
: a salt of EDTA

eth·yl·ene·di·amine·tet·ra·ace·tic acid \-(ə-)'sē-tik-\ *noun* (1942)
: EDTA

ethylene di·bro·mide \-(,)dī-'brō-,mīd\ *noun* (circa 1929)
: a colorless toxic liquid compound $C_2H_4Br_2$ that is used chiefly as a fuel additive in leaded gasolines, that has been found to be strongly carcinogenic in laboratory animals, and that was used formerly in the U.S. as an agricultural pesticide — abbreviation *EDB*

ethylene glycol *noun* (1901)
: a thick liquid diol $C_2H_6O_2$ used especially as an antifreeze and in making polyester fibers

ethylene oxide *noun* (1898)
: a colorless flammable toxic compound C_2H_4O used especially in synthesis (as of ethylene glycol) and in sterilization and fumigation

ethyl ether *noun* (1878)
: ETHER 3a

eth·yne \'e-,thīn, e-'\ *noun* [*ethyl* + ²*-ine*] (circa 1929)
: ACETYLENE

eth·y·nyl \e-'thī-nᵊl, 'e-thə-,nil\ *noun* (1929)
: a univalent unsaturated group $HC\equiv C-$ derived from acetylene by removal of one hydrogen atom

et·ic \'e-tik\ *adjective* [*phonetic*] (1954)
: of, relating to, or having linguistic or behavioral characteristics considered without regard to their structural significance — compare EMIC

-et·ic \'e-tik\ *adjective suffix* [Latin & Greek; Latin *-eticus*, from Greek *-etikos, -ētikos,* from *-etos, -ētos,* ending of certain verbals]
: -IC ⟨limn*etic*⟩ — often in adjectives corresponding to nouns ending in *-esis* ⟨gen*etic*⟩

eti·o·late \'ē-tē-ə-,lāt\ *transitive verb* **-lat·ed; -lat·ing** [French *étioler*] (1791)
1 : to bleach and alter the natural development of (a green plant) by excluding sunlight
2 a : to make pale **b** : to deprive of natural vigor : make feeble
— **eti·o·la·tion** \,ē-tē-ə-'lā-shən\ *noun*

eti·o·log·ic \,ē-tē-ə-'lä-jik\ *or* **eti·o·log·i·cal** \-ji-kəl\ *adjective* (circa 1753)
1 : assigning or seeking to assign a cause
2 : of or relating to etiology
— **eti·o·log·i·cal·ly** \-ji-k(ə-)lē\ *adverb*

eti·ol·o·gy \,ē-tē-'ä-lə-jē\ *noun, plural* **-gies** [Medieval Latin *aetiologia* statement of causes, from Greek *aitiologia,* from *aitia* cause] (circa 1555)
1 : CAUSE, ORIGIN; *specifically* : all of the causes of a disease or abnormal condition
2 : a branch of knowledge concerned with causes; *specifically* : a branch of medical science concerned with the causes and origins of diseases

et·i·quette \'e-ti-kət, -ˌket\ *noun* [French *étiquette,* literally, ticket — more at TICKET] (1750)
: the conduct or procedure required by good breeding or prescribed by authority to be observed in social or official life ◆

Eton collar \ˌē-t°n-\ *noun* [*Eton* College, English public school] (1887)
: a large stiff turnover collar

Eto·ni·an \ē-'tō-nē-ən\ *noun* (circa 1770)
: a student or former student of Eton College
— **Etonian** *adjective*

Eton jacket *noun* (1881)
: a short black jacket with long sleeves, wide lapels, and an open front

étouf·fée *also* **etouf·fee** \ˌā-tü-'fā\ *noun* [Louisiana French, from French *à l'étouffée* braised, from feminine of *étouffer,* past participle of *étouffer* to smother, from Old French *estofer,* alteration of *estoper* to plug up — more at ESTOP] (circa 1933)
: a Cajun stew of shellfish or chicken served over rice

Etru·ri·an \i-'trür-ē-ən\ *noun* (1623)
: ETRUSCAN
— **Etrurian** *adjective*

¹Etrus·can \i-'trəs-kən\ *adjective* [Latin *etruscus;* akin to Latin *Etruria,* ancient country] (1706)
: of, relating to, or characteristic of Etruria, the Etruscans, or the Etruscan language

²Etruscan *noun* (1773)
1 : the language of the Etruscans which is of unknown affiliation
2 : a native or inhabitant of ancient Etruria

-ette \'et, ˌet, ət, it\ *noun suffix* [Middle English, from Middle French, feminine diminutive suffix, from Old French *-ete* — more at -ET]
1 : little one ⟨kitchen*ette*⟩
2 : female ⟨farmer*ette*⟩

étude \'ā-ˌtüd, -ˌtyüd\ *noun* [French, literally, study, from Middle French *estude, estudie,* from Old French — more at STUDY] (circa 1837)
1 : a piece of music for the practice of a point of technique
2 : a composition built on a technical motive but played for its artistic value

etui \ā-'twē, 'ā-,\ *noun, plural* **etuis** [French *étui*] (1611)
: a small ornamental case

et·y·mol·o·gise *British variant of* ETYMOLOGIZE

et·y·mol·o·gist \ˌe-tə-'mä-lə-jist\ *noun* (1635)
: a specialist in etymology

et·y·mol·o·gize \-ˌjīz\ *verb* **-gized; -giz·ing** (1530)
transitive verb
: to discover, formulate, or state an etymology for
intransitive verb
: to study or formulate etymologies

et·y·mol·o·gy \-jē\ *noun, plural* **-gies** [Middle English *ethimologie,* from Latin *etymologia,* from Greek, from *etymon* + *-logia* -logy] (14th century)
1 : the history of a linguistic form (as a word) shown by tracing its development since its earliest recorded occurrence in the language where it is found, by tracing its transmission from one language to another, by analyzing it into its component parts, by identifying its cognates in other languages, or by tracing it and its cognates to a common ancestral form in an ancestral language
2 : a branch of linguistics concerned with etymologies
— **et·y·mo·log·i·cal** \-mə-'lä-ji-kəl\ *adjective*
— **et·y·mo·log·i·cal·ly** \-k(ə-)lē\ *adverb*

et·y·mon \'e-tə-ˌmän\ *noun, plural* **-ma** \-mə\ *also* **-mons** [Latin, from Greek, literal meaning of a word according to its origin, from *ety-*

mos true; akin to Greek *eteos* true — more at SOOTH] (circa 1576)
1 a : an earlier form of a word in the same language or an ancestral language **b** : a word in a foreign language that is the source of a particular loanword
2 a : a word or morpheme from which words are formed by composition or derivation

eu- *combining form* [Middle English, from Latin, from Greek, from *eu* well, from neuter of *eys* good; perhaps akin to Latin *esse* to be]
1 a : well : easily ⟨*eu*clase⟩ — compare DYS-
b : good ⟨*eu*daemonism⟩ — compare DYS-
2 : true ⟨*eu*chromatin⟩

eu·ca·lypt \'yü-kə-ˌlipt\ *noun* (1885)
: EUCALYPTUS

eu·ca·lyp·tol *also* **eu·ca·lyp·tole** \ˌyü-kə-'lip-ˌtȯl, -ˌtōl\ *noun* (1879)
: CINEOLE

eu·ca·lyp·tus \ˌyü-kə-'lip-təs\ *noun, plural* **-ti** \-ˌtī, -ˌtē\ *or* **-tus·es** [New Latin, genus name, from *eu-* + Greek *kalyptos* covered, from *kalyptein* to conceal; from the conical covering of the buds — more at HELL] (1801)
: any of a genus (*Eucalyptus*) of mostly Australian evergreen trees or rarely shrubs of the myrtle family that have rigid entire leaves and umbellate flowers and are widely cultivated for their gums, resins, oils, and woods

eu·cary·ote *variant of* EUKARYOTE

Eu·cha·rist \'yü-k(ə-)rəst\ *noun* [Middle English *eukarist,* from Middle French *eucariste,* from Late Latin *eucharistia,* from Greek, Eucharist, gratitude, from *eucharistos* grateful, from *eu-* + *charizesthai* to show favor, from *charis* favor, grace, gratitude; akin to Greek *chairein* to rejoice — more at YEARN] (14th century)
1 : COMMUNION 2a
2 *Christian Science* : spiritual communion with God
— **eu·cha·ris·tic** \ˌyü-kə-'ris-tik\ *adjective, often capitalized*

¹eu·chre \'yü-kər\ *noun* [origin unknown] (1841)
: a card game in which each player is dealt five cards and the player making trump must take three tricks to win a hand

²euchre *transitive verb* **eu·chred; eu·chring** \-k(ə-)riŋ\ (1847)
1 : to prevent from winning three tricks in euchre
2 : CHEAT, TRICK ⟨*euchred* out of their life savings —Pete Martin⟩

eu·chro·ma·tin \(ˌ)yü-'krō-mə-tən\ *noun* [International Scientific Vocabulary] (1932)
: the genetically active portion of chromatin that is largely composed of genes
— **eu·chro·mat·ic** \ˌyü-krō-'ma-tik\ *adjective*

eu·clase \'yü-ˌklās, -ˌklāz\ *noun* [French, from *eu-* (from Latin) + Greek *klasis* breaking, from *klan* to break] (1804)
: a mineral that consists of a brittle silicate of beryllium and aluminum in pale-yellow, green, or blue prismatic crystals and is used especially as a gemstone

eu·clid·e·an *also* **eu·clid·i·an** \yü-'kli-dē-ən\ *adjective, often capitalized* (1660)
: of, relating to, or based on the geometry of Euclid or a geometry with similar axioms

Euclidean algorithm *noun* (circa 1955)
: a method of finding the greatest common divisor of two numbers by dividing the larger by the smaller, the smaller by the remainder, the first remainder by the second remainder, and so on until exact division is obtained whence the greatest common divisor is the exact divisor — called also *Euclid's algorithm*

euclidean geometry *noun, often E capitalized* (circa 1865)
1 : geometry based on Euclid's axioms
2 : the geometry of a euclidean space

euclidean space *noun, often E capitalized* (1883)

: a space in which Euclid's axioms and definitions (as of straight and parallel lines and angles of plane triangles) apply

eu·crite \'yü-ˌkrīt\ *noun* [German *Eukrit,* from Greek *eukritos* easily discerned, from *eu-* + *kritos* separated, from *krinein* to separate — more at CERTAIN] (circa 1899)
1 : a stony meteorite composed essentially of plagioclase and pigeonite
2 : a rock consisting of a very basic gabbro
— **eu·crit·ic** \yü-'kri-tik\ *adjective*

eu·dae·mo·nism \yü-'dē-mə-ˌni-zəm\ *or* **eu·dai·mo·nism** \-'dī-\ *noun* [Greek *eudaimonia* happiness, from *eudaimōn* having a good attendant spirit, happy, from *eu-* + *daimōn* spirit — more at DEMON]
: a theory that the highest ethical goal is happiness and personal well-being
— **eu·dae·mo·nist** \-nist\ *noun*
— **eu·dae·mo·nis·tic** \-ˌdē-mə-'nis-tik\ *adjective*

eu·di·om·e·ter \ˌyü-dē-'ä-mə-tər\ *noun* [modification of Italian *eudiometro,* from Greek *eudia* fair weather (from *eu-* + *-dia* weather— akin to Latin *dies* day) + Italian *-metro* -meter, from Greek *metron* measure] (1777)
: an instrument for the volumetric measurement and analysis of gases
— **eu·di·o·met·ric** \ˌyü-dē-ə-'me-trik\ *adjective*
— **eu·di·o·met·ri·cal·ly** \-tri-k(ə-)lē\ *adverb*

eu·gen·ic \yü-'je-nik\ *adjective* [Greek *eugenēs* wellborn, from *eu-* + *-genēs* born — more at -GEN] (1883)
1 : relating to or fitted for the production of good offspring
2 : of or relating to eugenics
— **eu·gen·i·cal·ly** \-ni-k(ə-)lē\ *adverb*

eu·gen·i·cist \-'je-nə-sist\ *noun* (circa 1909)
: a student or advocate of eugenics

eu·gen·ics \yü-'je-niks\ *noun plural but singular or plural in construction* (1883)
: a science that deals with the improvement (as by control of human mating) of hereditary qualities of a race or breed

eu·gen·ist \yü-'je-nist\ *noun* (1908)
: EUGENICIST

◇ WORD HISTORY

etiquette The Middle French word *estiquette* or *etiquette* denoted a label attached to something, such as a bundle of documents, for description or identification; it was a derivative of a medieval French verb *estichier* or *estiquier* "to stick or attach" (itself ultimately borrowed from a verb akin to Modern English *stick* and *stitch* in the old Germanic language called Frankish). Middle French *etiquette* is the source of the English word *ticket,* and Modern French *étiquette* still retains the primary meaning "label." In the 16th century, the court of the Spanish king and Holy Roman Emperor Charles V borrowed Middle French *etiquette* as Spanish *etiqueta* to denote the written protocols describing order of precedence and other aspects of correct courtly behavior. The *etiqueta* eventually became the court ceremonies themselves as well as the documents that described them. Under the influence of Spanish, French *étiquette* also acquired the meaning "proper court behavior" and in the 18th century was borrowed into English. It then expanded in sense to cover all sorts of proper behavior required by society.

\ə\ **abut** \ᵊ\ **kitten** \ər\ **further** \a\ **ash** \ā\ **ace**
\ä\ **mop, mar** \aú\ **out** \ch\ **chin** \e\ **bet** \ē\ **easy**
\g\ **go** \i\ **hit** \ī\ **ice** \j\ **job** \ŋ\ **sing** \ō\ **go**
\ȯ\ **law** \ȯi\ **boy** \th\ **thin** \ṯh\ **the** \ü\ **loot** \ú\ **foot**
\y\ **yet** \zh\ **vision** *see also* Guide to Pronunciation

eu·ge·nol \'yü-jə-ˌnȯl, -ˌnōl\ *noun* [International Scientific Vocabulary *eugen-*, from New Latin *Eugenia*, genus of tropical trees] (1886) : a colorless aromatic liquid phenol $C_{10}H_{12}O_2$ found especially in clove oil and used commercially in flavors and perfumes and in dentistry as an analgesic

eu·geo·syn·cline \(ˌ)yü-ˌjē-ō-'sin-ˌklīn\ *noun* (1944) : a narrow rapidly subsiding geosyncline usually with volcanic materials mingled with clastic sediments — **eu·geo·syn·cli·nal** \-ˌ(ˌ)sin-'klī-nᵊl\ *adjective*

eu·gle·na \yü-'glē-nə\ *noun* [New Latin, genus name, from *eu-* + Greek *glēnē* eyeball, socket of a joint] (circa 1889) : any of a genus (*Euglena*) of green freshwater flagellates often classed as algae

eu·gle·noid \-ˌnȯid\ *noun* (1885) : any of a taxon (Euglenoidina or Euglenophyta) of varied flagellates (as a euglena) that are typically green or colorless stigma-bearing solitary organisms with one or two flagella emerging from a well-defined gullet — **euglenoid** *adjective*

euglenoid movement *noun* (1940) : writhing usually nonprogressive protoplasmic movement of plastic-bodied euglenoid flagellates

eu·glob·u·lin \yü-'glä-byə-lən\ *noun* [International Scientific Vocabulary] (1904) : a simple protein that does not dissolve in pure water

eu·he·mer·ism \yü-'hē-mə-ˌri-zəm, -'he-mə-\ *noun* [*Euhemerus*, 4th century B.C. Greek mythographer] (1846) : interpretation of myths as traditional accounts of historical persons and events — **eu·he·mer·ist** \-rist\ *noun* — **eu·he·mer·is·tic** \-ˌhē-mə-'ris-tik, -ˌhe-mə-\ *adjective*

eu·kary·ote \(ˌ)yü-'kar-ē-ˌōt, -ē-ət\ *noun* [New Latin *Eukaryotes*, proposed subdivision of protists, from *eu-* + *kary-* + *-otes*, plural noun suffix, from Greek *-ōtos* — more at -OTIC] (1943) : an organism composed of one or more cells containing visibly evident nuclei and organelles — compare PROKARYOTE — **eu·kary·ot·ic** \-ˌkar-ē-'ä-tik\ *adjective*

eu·la·chon \'yü-lə-ˌkän, -li-kən\ *noun, plural* **eulachon** *or* **eulachons** [Chinook Jargon *ulâkân*] (1807) : an anadromous marine food fish (*Thaleichthys pacificus*) of the north Pacific coast related to the smelt — called also *candlefish*

eulogise *British variant of* EULOGIZE

eu·lo·gist \'yü-lə-jist\ *noun* (1808) : one who eulogizes

eu·lo·gi·um \yü-'lō-jē-əm\ *noun, plural* **-gia** \-jē-ə\ *or* **-gi·ums** [Medieval Latin] (1621) : EULOGY

eu·lo·gize \'yü-lə-ˌjīz\ *transitive verb* **-gized; -giz·ing** (1810) : to speak or write in high praise of : EXTOL — **eu·lo·giz·er** *noun*

eu·lo·gy \'yü-lə-jē\ *noun, plural* **-gies** [Middle English *euloge*, from Medieval Latin *eulogium*, from Greek *eulogia* praise, from *eu-* + *-logia* -logy] (15th century) **1** : a commendatory formal statement or set oration **2** : high praise **synonym** see ENCOMIUM — **eu·lo·gis·tic** \ˌyü-lə-'jis-tik\ *adjective* — **eu·lo·gis·ti·cal·ly** \-ti-k(ə-)lē\ *adverb*

Eu·men·i·des \yü-'me-nə-ˌdēz\ *noun plural* [Latin, from Greek, literally, the gracious ones] : the Furies in Greek mythology

eu·nuch \'yü-nək, -nik\ *noun* [Middle English *eunuk*, from Latin *eunuchus*, from Greek *eunouchos*, from *eunē* bed + *echein* to have,

have charge of — more at SCHEME] (15th century) **1** : a castrated man placed in charge of a harem or employed as a chamberlain in a palace **2** : a man or boy deprived of the testes or external genitals **3** : one that lacks virility or power ⟨political eunuchs⟩ — **eu·nuch·ism** \-nə-ˌki-zəm, -ni-\ *noun*

eu·nuch·oid \-nə-ˌkȯid, -ni-\ *noun* (1906) : a sexually deficient individual; *especially* : one lacking in sexual differentiation and tending toward the intersex state — **eunuchoid** *adjective*

eu·on·y·mus \yü-'ä-nə-məs\ *noun* [New Latin, genus name, from Latin *euonymos* spindle tree, from Greek *euōnymos*, from *euōnymos* having an auspicious name, from *eu-* + *onyma* name — more at NAME] (1767) : SPINDLE TREE

eu·pa·trid \yü-'pa-trəd, 'yü-pə-\ *noun, plural* **eu·pat·ri·dae** \yü-'pa-trə-ˌdē\ *often capitalized* [Greek *eupatridēs*, from *eu-* + *patr-*, *patēr* father — more at FATHER] (1836) : one of the hereditary aristocrats of ancient Athens

eu·pep·tic \yü-'pep-tik\ *adjective* (1831) **1** : of, relating to, or having good digestion **2** : CHEERFUL, OPTIMISTIC

eu·phau·si·id \yü-'fȯ-zē-əd\ *noun* [New Latin *Euphausia*, genus of crustaceans] (circa 1893) : any of an order (Euphausiacea) of small usually luminescent malacostracan crustaceans that resemble shrimps and in some areas form an important element in marine plankton — **euphausiid** *adjective*

euphemise *British variant of* EUPHEMIZE

eu·phe·mism \'yü-fə-ˌmi-zəm\ *noun* [Greek *euphēmismos*, from *euphēmos* auspicious, sounding good, from *eu-* + *phēmē* speech, from *phanai* to speak — more at BAN] (circa 1681) : the substitution of an agreeable or inoffensive expression for one that may offend or suggest something unpleasant; *also* : the expression so substituted — **eu·phe·mist** \-mist\ *noun* — **eu·phe·mis·tic** \ˌyü-fə-'mis-tik\ *adjective* — **eu·phe·mis·ti·cal·ly** \-ti-k(ə-)lē\ *adverb*

eu·phe·mize \'yü-fə-ˌmīz\ *transitive verb* **-mized; -miz·ing** (1857) : to express or describe euphemistically ⟨*euphemize* death⟩ — **eu·phe·miz·er** \-ˌmī-zər\ *noun*

eu·phen·ics \yü-'fe-niks\ *noun plural but singular in construction* [*eu-* + *phen-* (from *phenotype*) + *-ics*; after English *genotype* : *eugenics*] (1963) : a science that deals with the biological improvement of human beings after birth — **eu·phen·ic** \-nik\ *adjective*

eu·pho·ni·ous \yü-'fō-nē-əs\ *adjective* (1774) : pleasing to the ear — **eu·pho·ni·ous·ly** *adverb* — **eu·pho·ni·ous·ness** *noun*

eu·pho·ni·um \yü-'fō-nē-əm\ *noun* [Greek *euphōnos* + English *-ium* (as in *harmonium*)] (1865) : a brass instrument smaller than but resembling a tuba and having a range from B flat below the bass staff upward for three octaves

eu·pho·ny \'yü-fə-nē\ *noun, plural* **-nies** [French *euphonie*, from Late Latin *euphonia*, from Greek *euphōnia*, from *euphōnos* sweet-voiced, musical, from *eu-* + *phōnē* voice — more at BAN] (circa 1616)

euphonium

1 : pleasing or sweet sound; *especially* : the acoustic effect produced by words so formed or combined as to please the ear **2** : a harmonious succession of words having a pleasing sound — **eu·phon·ic** \yü-'fä-nik\ *adjective* — **eu·phon·i·cal·ly** \-ni-k(ə-)lē\ *adverb*

eu·phor·bia \yü-'fȯr-bē-ə\ *noun* [New Latin, alteration of Latin *euphorbea*, from *Euphorbus*, 1st century A.D. Greek physician] (14th century) : any of a large genus (*Euphorbia* of the family Euphorbiaceae) of plants that have a milky juice and flowers lacking a calyx and included in an involucre which surrounds a group of several staminate flowers and a central pistillate flower with 3-lobed pistils; *broadly* : SPURGE

eu·pho·ria \yü-'fȯr-ē-ə, -'fȯr-\ *noun* [New Latin, from Greek, from *euphoros* healthy, from *eu-* + *pherein* to bear — more at BEAR] (circa 1751) : a feeling of well-being or elation — **eu·phor·ic** \-'fȯr-ik, -'fär-\ *adjective* — **eu·phor·i·cal·ly** \-i-k(ə-)lē\ *adverb*

eu·pho·ri·ant \yü-'fȯr-ē-ənt, -'fȯr-\ *noun* (1947) : a drug that tends to induce euphoria — **euphoriant** *adjective*

eu·pho·tic \yü-'fō-tik\ *adjective* [International Scientific Vocabulary] (1909) : of, relating to, or constituting the upper layers of a body of water into which sufficient light penetrates to permit growth of green plants

Eu·phros·y·ne \yü-'frä-sᵊn-(ˌ)ē, -zᵊn-\ *noun* [Latin, from Greek *Euphrosynē*] : one of the three Graces

eu·phu·ism \'yü-fyə-ˌwi-zəm\ *noun* [*Euphues*, character in prose romances by John Lyly] (1592) **1** : an elegant Elizabethan literary style marked by excessive use of balance, antithesis, and alliteration and by frequent use of similes drawn from mythology and nature **2** : artificial elegance of language — **eu·phu·ist** \-wist\ *noun* — **eu·phu·is·tic** \ˌyü-fyə-'wis-tik\ *adjective* — **eu·phu·is·ti·cal·ly** \-ti-k(ə-)lē\ *adverb*

eu·ploid \'yü-ˌplȯid\ *adjective* [International Scientific Vocabulary] (1926) : having a chromosome number that is an exact multiple of the monoploid number — compare ANEUPLOID — **euploid** *noun* — **eu·ploi·dy** \-ˌplȯi-dē\ *noun*

eup·nea *also* **eup·noea** \yüp-'nē-ə\ *noun* [New Latin, from Greek *eupnoia*, from *eupnous* breathing freely, from *eu-* + *pnein* to breathe — more at SNEEZE] (circa 1706) : normal respiration — **eup·ne·ic** \-'nē-ik\ *adjective*

Eur- *or* **Euro-** *combining form* [*Europe*] : European and ⟨*Euramerican*⟩ : European ⟨*Eurocentric*⟩ : western European ⟨*Eurocommunism*⟩ : of the European Communities ⟨*Eurocrat*⟩

Eur·amer·i·can \ˌyur-ə-'mer-ə-kən\ *or* **Eu·ro-Amer·i·can** \ˌyur-ō-ə-'mer-\ *adjective* (1941) : common to Europe and America

Eur·asian \yü-'rā-zhən, -shən\ *adjective* (1844) **1** : of a mixed European and Asian origin **2** : of or relating to Europe and Asia — **Eurasian** *noun*

eu·re·ka \yü-'rē-kə\ *interjection* [Greek *heurēka* I have found, from *heuriskein* to find; from the exclamation attributed to Archimedes on discovering a method for determining the purity of gold — more at HEURISTIC] (1603)

— used to express triumph on a discovery ◊

eu·ro \'yúr-(,)ō\ *noun, plural* **euros** [Adnyamadhanha (Australian aboriginal language of South Australia) *yuru*] (1855)
: WALLAROO

Eu·ro·bond \'yúr-ō-,bänd\ *noun* (1966)
: a bond of a U.S. corporation that is sold outside the U.S. and that is denominated and paid for in dollars and yields interest in dollars

Eu·ro·cen·tric \,yúr-ə-'sen-trik\ *adjective* (1963)
: centered on Europe or the Europeans; *especially* **:** reflecting a tendency to interpret the world in terms of western and especially European values and experiences
— **Eu·ro·cen·trism** \-,tri-zəm\ *noun*

Eu·ro·com·mu·nism \,yúr-ō-'käm-yə-,ni-zəm\ *noun* (1976)
: the communism especially of western European Communist parties that is marked by a willingness to reach power through coalitions and by independence from Soviet leadership
— **Eu·ro·com·mu·nist** *noun or adjective*

Eu·ro·crat \'yúr-ə-,krat\ *noun* (1961)
: a staff member of the administrative commission of the European Communities

Eu·ro·cur·ren·cy \,yúr-ō-'kər-ən-sē, -'kə-rən-\ *noun* (1963)
: moneys (as of the U.S. and Japan) held outside their countries of origin and used in the money markets of Europe

Eu·ro·dol·lar \'yúr-ō-,dä-lər\ *noun* (1960)
: a U.S. dollar held as Eurocurrency

Eu·ro·pa \yú-'rō-pə\ *noun* [Latin, from Greek *Európē*]
: a Phoenician princess carried off by Zeus in the form of a white bull and by him mother of Minos, Rhadamanthus, and Sarpedon

¹Eu·ro·pe·an \,yúr-ə-'pē-ən, -'pēn\ *adjective* (1603)
: of, relating to, or characteristic of the continent of Europe or its people
— **Eu·ro·pe·an·iza·tion** \-,pē-ə-nə-'zā-shən\ *noun*
— **Eu·ro·pe·an·ize** \-'pē-ə-,nīz\ *transitive verb*

²European *noun* (1632)
1 : a native or inhabitant of Europe
2 : a person of European descent

European bison *noun* (1860)
: WISENT

European chafer *noun* (1947)
: an Old World beetle (*Rhizotragus majalis* synonym *Amphimallon majalis*) established in parts of eastern North America where its larva is a destructive pest on the roots of turf grasses

European corn borer *noun* (1920)
: an Old World moth (*Ostrinia nubilalis*) that is widespread in eastern North America where its larva is a major pest especially in the stems and crowns of Indian corn, dahlias, and potatoes

European plan *noun* (1834)
: a hotel plan whereby the daily rates cover only the cost of the room — compare AMERICAN PLAN

European red mite *noun* (1940)
: a small bright or brownish red oval mite (*Panonychus ulmi*) that is a destructive orchard pest

eu·ro·pi·um \yú-'rō-pē-əm\ *noun* [New Latin, from *Europa* Europe] (1901)
: a bivalent and trivalent metallic element of the rare-earth group found in monazite sand — see ELEMENT table

Eu·ro·po·cen·tric \yú-,rō-pə-'sen-trik\ *adjective* (1926)
: EUROCENTRIC
— **Eu·ro·po·cen·trism** \-,tri-zəm\ *noun*

eury- *combining form* [New Latin, from Greek, from *eurys;* akin to Sanskrit *uru* broad, wide] **:** broad **:** wide ⟨*euryhaline*⟩

eu·ry·bath·ic \,yúr-i-'ba-thik\ *adjective* [*eury-* + Greek *bathos* depth] (1902)

: capable of living on the bottom in both deep and shallow water

Eu·ryd·i·ce \yú-'ri-də-(,)sē\ *noun* [Latin, from Greek *Eurydikē*]
: the wife of Orpheus whom he attempts to bring back from Hades

eu·ry·ha·line \,yúr-i-'hā-,līn, -'ha-\ *adjective* [International Scientific Vocabulary *eury-* + Greek *halinos* of salt, from *hals* salt — more at SALT] (1888)
: able to live in waters of a wide range of salinity ⟨*euryhaline* crabs⟩

eu·ryp·ter·id \yú-'rip-tə-rəd\ *noun* [ultimately from Greek *eury-* + *pteron* wing — more at FEATHER] (1871)
: any of an order (Eurypterida) of usually large aquatic Paleozoic arthropods related to the horseshoe crabs
— **eurypterid** *adjective*

eu·ry·ther·mal \,yúr-i-'thər-məl\ *adjective* [International Scientific Vocabulary] (1881)
: tolerating a wide range of temperature ⟨*eurythermal* animals⟩

eu·ry·ther·mic \-mik\ *adjective* [International Scientific Vocabulary] (1903)
: EURYTHERMAL

eu·ry·ther·mous \-məs\ *adjective* [International Scientific Vocabulary] (1940)
: EURYTHERMAL

eu·ryth·mic *or* **eu·rhyth·mic** \yú-'rith-mik\ *adjective* (1921)
1 : HARMONIOUS
2 : of or relating to eurythmy or eurythmics

eu·ryth·mics *or* **eu·rhyth·mics** \-miks\ *noun plural but singular or plural in construction* (1912)
: the art of harmonious bodily movement especially through expressive timed movements in response to improvised music

eu·ryth·my *or* **eu·rhyth·my** \-mē\ *noun* [German *Eurhythmie,* from Latin *eurythmia* rhythmical movement, from Greek, from *eurythmos* rhythmical, from *eu-* + *rhythmos* rhythm] (1949)
: a system of harmonious body movement to the rhythm of spoken words

eu·ry·top·ic \,yúr-i-'tä-pik\ *adjective* [International Scientific Vocabulary *eury-* + Greek *topos* place] (circa 1945)
: tolerant of wide variation in one or more physical factors of the environment

eu·sta·chian tube \yú-'stā-sh(ē-)ən-, -'stā-kē-ən-\ *noun, often E capitalized* [Bartolommeo *Eustachio*] (1741)
: a bony and cartilaginous tube connecting the middle ear with the nasopharynx and equalizing air pressure on both sides of the tympanic membrane — called also *auditory tube;* see EAR illustration

eu·stat·ic \yú-'sta-tik\ *adjective* [International Scientific Vocabulary] (1906)
: relating to or characterized by worldwide change of sea level

eu·stele \'yü-,stēl, yú-'stē-lē\ *noun* (circa 1920)
: a stele typical of dicotyledonous plants that consists of vascular bundles of xylem and phloem strands with parenchymal cells between the bundles

eu·tec·tic \yú-'tek-tik\ *adjective* [Greek *eutēktos* easily melted, from *eu-* + *tēktos* melted, from *tēkein* to melt — more at THAW] (1884)
1 *of an alloy or solution* **:** having the lowest melting point possible
2 : of or relating to a eutectic alloy or solution or its melting or freezing point
— **eutectic** *noun*
— **eu·tec·toid** \-,tóid\ *adjective or noun*

Eu·ter·pe \yú-'tər-pē\ *noun* [Latin, from Greek *Euterpē*]
: the Greek Muse of music

eu·tha·na·sia \,yü-thə-'nā-zh(ē-)ə\ *noun* [Greek, easy death, from *euthanatos,* from *eu-* + *thanatos* death — more at THANATOS] (1869)

: the act or practice of killing or permitting the death of hopelessly sick or injured individuals (as persons or domestic animals) in a relatively painless way for reasons of mercy
— **eu·tha·na·sic** \-zik, -sik\ *adjective*

eu·than·a·tize \yú-'tha-nə-,tīz\ *also* **eu·tha·nize** \'yü-thə-,nīz\ *transitive verb* **-tized** *also* **-nized; -tiz·ing** *also* **-niz·ing** [Greek *euthanatos*] (1873)
: to subject to euthanasia

eu·then·ics \yú-'the-niks\ *noun plural but singular or plural in construction* [Greek *euthenein* to thrive, from *eu-* + *-thenein*] (1905)
: a science that deals with development of human well-being by improvement of living conditions
— **eu·the·nist** \yú-'the-nist, 'yü-thə-\ *noun*

eu·the·ri·an \yú-'thir-ē-ən\ *adjective* [ultimately from New Latin *eu-* + Greek *thērion* beast — more at TREACLE] (1880)
: of or relating to a major division (Eutheria) of mammals comprising the placental mammals
— **eutherian** *noun*

eu·thy·roid \(,)yü-'thī-,róid\ *adjective* (1924)
: characterized by normal thyroid function

eu·tro·phic \yú-'trō-fik\ *adjective* [probably from German *Eutroph* eutrophic, from Greek *eutrophos* well-nourished, nourishing, from *eu-* + *trephein* to nourish] (1928)
of a body of water **:** characterized by the state resulting from eutrophication — compare MESOTROPHIC, OLIGOTROPHIC
— **eu·tro·phy** \'yü-trə-fē\ *noun*

eu·tro·phi·ca·tion \yú-,trō-fə-'kā-shən, ,yü-trə-fə-\ *noun* (1946)
: the process by which a body of water becomes enriched in dissolved nutrients (as phosphates) that stimulate the growth of aquatic plant life usually resulting in the depletion of dissolved oxygen

evac·u·ate \i-'va-kyə-,wāt\ *verb* **-at·ed; -at·ing** [Middle English, to draw off morbid humors, from Latin *evacuatus,* past participle of *evacuare* to empty, from *e-* + *vacuus* empty] (15th century)
transitive verb
1 : to remove the contents of **:** EMPTY
2 : to discharge from the body as waste **:** VOID
3 : to remove something (as gas or water) from especially by pumping

◊ WORD HISTORY
eureka When people make an unexpected discovery or have a sudden flash of inspiration, a traditional response is an exclamation of "Eureka!" Whether they know it or not, the elated discoverers are reenacting a legendary event in the life of the Greek mathematician and mechanical inventor Archimedes (ca. 287–212 B.C.). While wrestling with the problem of how to determine the purity of gold, he made the sudden realization that the buoyancy of an object placed in water is equal in magnitude to the weight of the water displaced by the object. According to the most popular and elaborate version of the legend, he made this discovery while at a public bathhouse, whereupon he leapt out of his bath, exclaimed *"Heurēka! Heurēka!"* ("I have found (it)") and ran naked through the streets of Syracuse all the way home. The absence of a contemporary source for the anecdote has done nothing to diminish its popularity over the centuries.

\ə\ abut \ᵊ\ kitten \ər\ further \a\ ash \ā\ ace
\ä\ mop, mar \aú\ out \ch\ chin \e\ bet \ē\ easy
\g\ go \i\ hit \ī\ ice \j\ job \ŋ\ sing \ō\ go
\ó\ law \ói\ boy \th\ thin \t͟h\ the \ü\ loot \ú\ foot
\y\ yet \zh\ vision *see also* Guide to Pronunciation

4 a : to remove especially from a military zone or dangerous area **b** : to withdraw from military occupation of **c** : VACATE ⟨were ordered to *evacuate* the building⟩
intransitive verb
1 : to withdraw from a place in an organized way especially for protection
2 : to pass urine or feces from the body
— **evac·u·a·tive** \-ˌwā-tiv\ *adjective*
evac·u·a·tion \i-ˌva-kyə-ˈwā-shən\ *noun* (14th century)
1 : the act or process of evacuating
2 : something evacuated or discharged
evac·u·ee \i-ˌva-kyə-ˈwē\ *noun* (1918)
: an evacuated person
evade \i-ˈvād\ *verb* **evad·ed; evad·ing** [Middle French & Latin; Middle French *evader*, from Latin *evadere*, from *e-* + *vadere* to go, walk — more at WADE] (1513)
intransitive verb
1 : to slip away
2 : to take refuge in evasion
transitive verb
1 : to elude by dexterity or stratagem
2 a : to avoid facing up to ⟨*evaded* the real issues⟩ **b** : to avoid the performance of : DODGE, CIRCUMVENT; *especially* : to fail to pay (taxes) **c** : to avoid answering directly : turn aside
3 : to be elusive to : BAFFLE ⟨the simple, personal meaning *evaded* them —C. D. Lewis⟩
synonym see ESCAPE
— **evad·able** \-ˈvā-də-bəl\ *adjective*
— **evad·er** *noun*
evag·i·na·tion \i-ˌva-jə-ˈnā-shən\ *noun* [Late Latin *evaginatio-*, *evaginatio*, act of unsheathing, from Latin *evaginatus*, past participle of *evaginare* to unsheathe, from *e-* + *vagina* sheath] (circa 1676)
1 : an act or instance of everting
2 : a product of eversion : OUTGROWTH
eval·u·ate \i-ˈval-yə-ˌwāt\ *transitive verb* **-at·ed; -at·ing** [back-formation from *evaluation*] (1842)
1 : to determine or fix the value of
2 : to determine the significance, worth, or condition of usually by careful appraisal and study
synonym see ESTIMATE
— **eval·u·a·tion** \-ˌval-yə-ˈwā-shən\ *noun*
— **eval·u·a·tive** \-ˈval-yə-ˌwā-tiv\ *adjective*
— **eval·u·a·tor** \-ˌwā-tər\ *noun*
ev·a·nesce \ˌe-və-ˈnes\ *intransitive verb* **-nesced; -nesc·ing** [Latin *evanescere* — more at VANISH] (1822)
: to dissipate like vapor
ev·a·nes·cence \ˌe-və-ˈne-s⁰n(t)s\ *noun* (1751)
1 : the process or fact of evanescing
2 : evanescent quality
ev·a·nes·cent \-s⁰nt\ *adjective* [Latin *evanescent-*, *evanescens*, present participle of *evanescere*] (1717)
: tending to vanish like vapor
synonym see TRANSIENT
¹evan·gel \i-ˈvan-jəl\ *noun* [Middle English *evangile*, from Middle French, from Late Latin *evangelium*, from Greek *euangelion* good news, gospel, from *euangelos* bringing good news, from *eu-* + *angelos* messenger] (14th century)
: GOSPEL
²evangel *noun* (1614)
: EVANGELIST
evan·gel·i·cal \ˌē-ˌvan-ˈje-li-kəl, ˌe-vən-\ *also* **evan·gel·ic** \-ik\ *adjective* (1531)
1 : of, relating to, or being in agreement with the Christian gospel especially as it is presented in the four Gospels
2 : PROTESTANT
3 : emphasizing salvation by faith in the atoning death of Jesus Christ through personal conversion, the authority of Scripture, and the importance of preaching as contrasted with ritual

4 a *capitalized* : of or relating to the Evangelical Church in Germany **b** *often capitalized* : of, adhering to, or marked by fundamentalism : FUNDAMENTALIST **c** *often capitalized* : LOW CHURCH
5 : marked by militant or crusading zeal : EVANGELISTIC ⟨the *evangelical* ardor of the movement's leaders —Amos Vogel⟩
— **Evan·gel·i·cal·ism** \-li-kə-ˌli-zəm\ *noun*
— **evan·gel·i·cal·ly** \-li-k(ə-)lē\ *adverb*
Evangelical *noun* (1532)
: one holding evangelical principles or belonging to an evangelical party or church
evan·ge·lism \i-ˈvan-jə-ˌli-zəm\ *noun* (circa 1626)
1 : the winning or revival of personal commitments to Christ
2 : militant or crusading zeal
— **evan·ge·lis·tic** \-ˌvan-jə-ˈlis-tik\ *adjective*
— **evan·ge·lis·ti·cal·ly** \-ti-k(ə-)lē\ *adverb*
evan·ge·list \i-ˈvan-jə-list\ *noun* (13th century)
1 *often capitalized* : a writer of any of the four Gospels
2 : a person who evangelizes; *specifically* : a Protestant minister or layman who preaches at special services
evan·ge·lize \i-ˈvan-jə-ˌlīz\ *verb* **-lized; -liz·ing** (14th century)
transitive verb
1 : to preach the gospel to
2 : to convert to Christianity
intransitive verb
: to preach the gospel
— **evan·ge·li·za·tion** \-ˌvan-jə-lə-ˈzā-shən\ *noun*
evap·o·rate \i-ˈva-p(ə-)ˌrāt\ *verb* **-rat·ed; -rat·ing** [Middle English, from Latin *evaporatus*, past participle of *evaporare*, from *e-* + *vapor* steam, vapor] (15th century)
transitive verb
1 a : to convert into vapor; *also* : to dissipate or draw off in vapor or fumes **b** : to deposit (as a metal) in the form of a film by sublimation
2 a : to expel moisture from **b** : EXPEL ⟨*evaporate* electrons from a hot wire⟩
intransitive verb
1 a : to pass off in vapor or in invisible minute particles **b** (1) : to pass off or away : DISAPPEAR ⟨my despair *evaporated* —J. F. Wharton⟩ (2) : to diminish quickly
2 : to give forth vapor
— **evap·o·ra·tion** \-ˌva-pə-ˈrā-shən\ *noun*
— **evap·o·ra·tive** \-ˈva-pə-ˌrā-tiv\ *adjective*
— **evap·o·ra·tor** \-ˈva-pə-ˌrā-tər\ *noun*
evaporated milk *noun* (1870)
: unsweetened milk concentrated by partial evaporation
evap·o·rite \i-ˈva-pə-ˌrīt\ *noun* [*evaporation* + *¹-ite*] (1924)
: a sedimentary rock (as gypsum) that originates by evaporation of seawater in an enclosed basin
— **evap·o·rit·ic** \-ˌva-pə-ˈri-tik\ *adjective*
evapo·trans·pi·ra·tion \i-ˌva-pō-ˌtran(t)-spə-ˈrā-shən\ *noun* [*evaporation* + *transpiration*] (1938)
: loss of water from the soil both by evaporation and by transpiration from the plants growing thereon
eva·sion \i-ˈvā-zhən\ *noun* [Middle English, from Middle French or Late Latin; Middle French, from Late Latin *evasion-*, *evasio*, from Latin *evadere* to evade] (15th century)
1 : a means of evading : DODGE
2 : the act or an instance of evading : ESCAPE ⟨suspected of tax *evasion*⟩
eva·sive \i-ˈvā-siv, -ziv\ *adjective* (1725)
: tending or intended to evade : EQUIVOCAL ⟨*evasive* answers⟩
— **eva·sive·ly** *adverb*
— **eva·sive·ness** *noun*

eve \ˈēv\ *noun* [Middle English *eve, even*] (13th century)
1 : EVENING
2 : the evening or the day before a special day
3 : the period immediately preceding
Eve \ˈēv\ *noun* [Old English *Ēfe*, from Late Latin *Eva*, from Hebrew *Ḥawwāh*]
: the first woman and wife of Adam
¹even \ˈē-vən\ *noun* [Middle English *even, eve*, from Old English *ǣfen*] (before 12th century)
archaic : EVENING
²even \ˈē-vən, -bᵉm\ *adjective* [Middle English, from Old English *efen*; akin to Old High German *eban* even] (before 12th century)
1 a : having a horizontal surface : FLAT ⟨*even* ground⟩ **b** : being without break, indentation, or irregularity : SMOOTH **c** : being in the same plane or line
2 a : free from variation : UNIFORM ⟨his disposition was *even*⟩ **b** : LEVEL 4
3 a : EQUAL, FAIR ⟨an *even* exchange⟩ **b** (1) : leaving nothing due on either side : SQUARE ⟨we will not be *even* until you repay my visit⟩ (2) : fully revenged **c** : being in equilibrium : BALANCED; *specifically* : showing neither profit nor loss **d** *obsolete* : CANDID
4 a : being any of the integers (as −2, 0, and +2) that are exactly divisible by two **b** : marked by an even number **c** : being a mathematical function such that $f(x) = f(-x)$ where the value remains unchanged if the sign of the independent variable is reversed
5 : EXACT, PRECISE ⟨an *even* dollar⟩
6 : as likely as not : FIFTY-FIFTY ⟨an *even* chance of winning⟩
synonym see LEVEL, STEADY
— **even·ly** *adverb*
— **even·ness** \-vən-nəs\ *noun*
— **on an even keel** *also* **on even keel** : in a sound or stable condition
³even *adverb* [Middle English, from Old English *efne*, from *efen*, adjective] (before 12th century)
1 a : EXACTLY, PRECISELY **b** : to a degree that extends : FULLY, QUITE ⟨faithful *even* unto death⟩ **c** : at the very time
2 a — used as an intensive to emphasize the identity or character of something ⟨he looked content, *even* happy⟩ **b** — used as an intensive to stress an extreme or highly unlikely condition or instance ⟨so simple *even* a child can do it⟩ **c** — used as an intensive to stress the comparative degree ⟨he did *even* better⟩ **d** — used as an intensive to indicate a small or minimum amount ⟨didn't *even* try⟩
⁴even *verb* **evened; even·ing** \ˈēv-niŋ, ˈē-və-\ (13th century)
transitive verb
: to make even
intransitive verb
: to become even
— **even·er** \-nər\ *noun*
even·fall \ˈē-vən-ˌfȯl\ *noun* (1814)
: the beginning of evening : DUSK
even·hand·ed \ˌē-vən-ˈhan-dəd\ *adjective* (1605)
: FAIR, IMPARTIAL
— **even·hand·ed·ly** *adverb*
— **even·hand·ed·ness** *noun*
¹eve·ning \ˈēv-niŋ\ *noun, often attributive* [Middle English, from Old English *ǣfnung*, from *ǣfnian* to grow toward evening, from *ǣfen* evening; akin to Old High German *āband* evening and perhaps to Greek *epi* on] (before 12th century)
1 a : the latter part and close of the day and early part of the night **b** *chiefly Southern & Midland* : AFTERNOON **c** : the period from sunset or the evening meal to bedtime
2 : the latter portion
3 : the period of an evening's entertainment
²evening *adjective* (1797)
: suitable for formal or semiformal evening social occasions ⟨*evening* dress⟩ ⟨*evening* clothes⟩

evening prayer *noun, often E&P capitalized* (1598)
: the daily evening office of the Anglican liturgy

evening primrose *noun* (1806)
: any of several dicotyledonous plants of a family (Onagraceae, the evening-primrose family) and especially of the type genus (*Oenothera*); *especially* : a coarse biennial herb (*O. biennis*) with yellow flowers that open in the evening

eve·nings \'ēv-niŋz\ *adverb* (1652)
: in the evening repeatedly : on any evening ⟨goes bowling *evenings*⟩

evening star *noun* (1535)
1 : a bright planet (as Venus) seen especially in the western sky at or after sunset
2 : a planet that rises before midnight

even money *noun* (1891)
: a situation in wagering in which the odds are even

even permutation *noun* (circa 1932)
: a permutation that is produced by the successive application of an even number of interchanges of pairs of elements

even so *adverb* (1948)
: in spite of that : NEVERTHELESS

even·song \'ē-vən-,soŋ\ *noun, often capitalized* [Middle English, from Old English *æfensang*, from *æfen* evening + *sang* song] (before 12th century)
1 : VESPERS 1
2 : EVENING PRAYER

event \i-'vent\ *noun* [Middle French or Latin; Middle French, from Latin *eventus*, from *evenire* to happen, from *e-* + *venire* to come — more at COME] (1573)
1 a *archaic* : OUTCOME b : the final outcome or determination of a legal action c : a postulated outcome, condition, or eventuality ⟨in the *event* that I am not there, call the house⟩
2 a : something that happens : OCCURRENCE b : a noteworthy happening c : a social occasion or activity
3 : any of the contests in a program of sports
4 : the fundamental entity of observed physical reality represented by a point designated by three coordinates of place and one of time in the space-time continuum postulated by the theory of relativity
5 : a subset of the possible outcomes of an experiment
synonym see OCCURRENCE
— **event·less** \-ləs\ *adjective*
— **at all events** : in any case
— **in any event** : in any case
— **in the event** *British* : as it turns out

event·ful \i-'vent-fəl\ *adjective* (1600)
1 : full of or rich in events
2 : MOMENTOUS
— **event·ful·ly** \-fə-lē\ *adverb*
— **event·ful·ness** *noun*

event horizon *noun* (1969)
: the surface of a black hole : the boundary of a black hole at which the escape velocity equals the speed of light and beyond which nothing can escape from within it

even·tide \'ē-vən-,tīd\ *noun* (before 12th century)
: the time of evening : EVENING

even·tu·al \i-'ven(t)-sh(ə-)wəl, -'ven-chəl\ *adjective* (1683)
1 *archaic* : CONTINGENT, CONDITIONAL
2 : taking place at an unspecified later time
3 : ultimately resulting ⟨they counted on our *eventual* success⟩
synonym see LAST

even·tu·al·i·ty \i-,ven-chə-'wa-lə-tē\ *noun, plural* **-ties** (1759)
: a possible event or outcome : POSSIBILITY

even·tu·al·ly \-ē\ *adverb* (1680)
: at an unspecified later time : in the end

even·tu·ate \i-'ven-chə-,wāt\ *intransitive verb* **-at·ed; -at·ing** (1789)
: to come out finally : RESULT, COME ABOUT

ev·er \'e-vər\ *adverb* [Middle English, from Old English *æfre*] (before 12th century)
1 : ALWAYS ⟨*ever* striving to improve⟩ ⟨the *ever*-increasing population⟩
2 a : at any time ⟨more than *ever* before⟩ b : in any way ⟨how can I *ever* thank you⟩
3 — used as an intensive ⟨looks *ever* so angry⟩ ⟨am I *ever* happy to see you⟩

ev·er·bloom·ing \,e-vər-'blü-miŋ\ *adjective* (circa 1891)
: blooming more or less continuously throughout the growing season

ev·er·dur·ing \,e-vər-'dür-iŋ, -'dyür-\ *adjective* (15th century)
archaic : EVERLASTING

Ev·er·glade \'e-vər-,glād\ *noun* [the *Everglades*, Fla.] (1823)
: a swampy grassland especially in southern Florida usually containing saw grass and at least seasonally covered by slowly moving water — usually used in plural

¹ev·er·green \'e-vər-,grēn\ *noun* (1644)
1 : an evergreen plant; *also* : CONIFER
2 *plural* : twigs and branches of evergreen plants used for decoration
3 : something that retains its freshness, interest, or popularity

²evergreen *adjective* (1671)
1 : having foliage that remains green and functional through more than one growing season — compare DECIDUOUS 1
2 : retaining freshness or interest : PERENNIAL

evergreen oak *noun* (circa 1682)
: any of various oaks (as a live oak, a holm oak, or a tan oak) with foliage that persists for two years so that the plant is more or less continuously green

¹ev·er·last·ing \,e-vər-'las-tiŋ\ *adjective* (13th century)
1 : lasting or enduring through all time : ETERNAL
2 a (1) : continuing long or indefinitely (2) : having or being flowers or foliage that retain form or color for a long time when dried b : tediously persistent ⟨the *everlasting* sympathy-seeker who demands attention —H. A. Overstreet⟩
3 : wearing indefinitely
— **ev·er·last·ing·ly** \-tiŋ-lē\ *adverb*
— **ev·er·last·ing·ness** *noun*

²everlasting *noun* (14th century)
1 : ETERNITY ⟨from *everlasting*⟩
2 *capitalized* : GOD 1 — used with *the*
3 a : any of several chiefly composite plants (as cudweed) with flowers that can be dried without loss of form or color — compare PEARLY EVERLASTING b : the flower of an everlasting

ev·er·more \,e-vər-'mōr, -'mȯr\ *adverb* (13th century)
1 : FOREVER, ALWAYS
2 : in the future

ever·sion \i-'vər-zhən, -shən\ *noun* (1751)
1 : the act of turning inside out : the state of being turned inside out ⟨*eversion* of the bladder⟩
2 : the condition (as of the foot) of being turned or rotated outward
— **ever·si·ble** \-'vər-sə-bəl\ *adjective*

evert \i-'vərt\ *transitive verb* [Latin *evertere*, from *e-* + *vertere* to turn — more at WORTH] (1538)
1 : OVERTHROW, UPSET
2 : to subject to eversion

ev·ery \'ev-rē\ *adjective* [Middle English *everich, every*, from Old English *æfre ælc*, from *æfre* ever + *ælc* each] (before 12th century)
1 a : being each individual or part of a group without exception b : being each in a series or succession ⟨*every* few days⟩
2 *obsolete* : being all taken severally
3 : being each within a range of possibilities ⟨was given *every* chance⟩
4 : COMPLETE, ENTIRE ⟨we have *every* confidence in her⟩
— **every now and then** *or* **every now and again** *or* **every so often** : at intervals : OCCASIONALLY

ev·ery·body \'ev-ri-,bə-dē, -,bä-\ *pronoun* (1530)
: every person : EVERYONE □

ev·ery·day \,ev-rē-'dā\ *adjective* (circa 1623)
: encountered or used routinely or typically : ORDINARY ⟨*everyday* clothes⟩
— **ev·ery·day·ness** \-'dā-nəs\ *noun*

ev·ery·man \'ev-rē-,man\ *noun, often capitalized* [*Everyman*, allegorical character in *The Summoning of Everyman*, 15th century English morality play] (1906)
: the typical or ordinary person

ev·ery·one \-(,)wən\ *pronoun* (13th century)
: EVERYBODY
usage see EVERYBODY

ev·ery·place \-,plās\ *adverb* (circa 1917)
: EVERYWHERE

ev·ery·thing \'ev-rē-,thiŋ\ *pronoun* (14th century)
1 a : all that exists b : all that relates to the subject
2 : all that is important ⟨you mean *everything* to me⟩
3 : all sorts of other things — used to indicate related but unspecified events, facts, or conditions ⟨all the pains and colds and *everything* —E. B. White⟩

ev·ery·where \'ev-rē-,(h)wer, -,(h)war\ *adverb* (13th century)
: in every place or part

every which way *adverb* [probably by folk etymology from Middle English *everich way* every way] (1824)
1 : in every direction
2 : in a disorderly manner : IRREGULARLY ⟨toys scattered about *every which way*⟩

ev·ery·wom·an \'ev-rē-,wu̇-mən\ *noun, often capitalized* [after *everyman*] (1945)
: the typical or ordinary woman

evict \i-'vikt\ *transitive verb* [Middle English, from Late Latin *evictus*, past participle of *evincere*, from Latin, to vanquish, win a point — more at EVINCE] (15th century)

□ USAGE

everybody The indefinite pronouns *everybody* and *everyone* share with other indefinite pronouns the characteristic of taking a singular verb, and, more often than not, a plural pronoun in reference. The use of the plural pronoun—*they, their, them*—has traditionally been disapproved of by those who insist that agreement in number is more important than avoidance of gender-specific third-person singular pronouns. But the use of the plural pronoun has long been established ⟨*everybody* should marry as soon as they can do it to advantage —Jane Austen (1814)⟩ ⟨*everybody* endeavouring to excuse themselves —Samuel Pepys (1668)⟩. The context of the Jane Austen quotation shows why there has been less resistance to the plural pronoun with *everybody* than with the other indefinite pronouns—the meaning is so clearly plural that a singular pronoun can seem silly. For instance, an unthinking copy editor changed Margaret Mitchell's *they* in this sentence from *Gone With the Wind*: "Everyone was very polite and kind to her because he felt sorry for her" *He* simply sounds out of place in this context. Various kinds of mixed usage still occur ⟨*everyone* allegedly being entitled to his ignorance —John Simon⟩ ⟨*everybody* seems to be enjoying themselves —Truman Capote⟩.

\ə\ abut \ᵊ\ kitten \ər\ further \a\ ash \ā\ ace \ä\ mop, mar \au̇\ out \ch\ chin \e\ bet \ē\ easy \g\ go \i\ hit \ī\ ice \j\ job \ŋ\ sing \ō\ go \ȯ\ law \ȯi\ boy \th\ thin \t̲h̲\ the \ü\ loot \u̇\ foot \y\ yet \zh\ vision *see also* Guide to Pronunciation

1 a : to recover (property) from a person by legal process **b :** to put (a tenant) out by legal process
2 : to force out : EXPEL
synonym see EJECT
— **evic·tion** \-'vik-shən\ *noun*
— **evic·tor** \-'vik-tər\ *noun*

evict·ee \i-,vik-'tē\ *noun* (1879)
: an evicted person

¹ev·i·dence \'e-və-dən(t)s, -və-,den(t)s\ *noun* (14th century)
1 a : an outward sign : INDICATION **b :** something that furnishes proof : TESTIMONY; *specifically* : something legally submitted to a tribunal to ascertain the truth of a matter
2 : one who bears witness : *especially* : one who voluntarily confesses a crime and testifies for the prosecution against his accomplices
— **in evidence 1 :** to be seen : CONSPICUOUS ⟨trim lawns . . . are everywhere *in evidence* —American Guide Series: North Carolina⟩ **2 :** as evidence

²evidence *transitive verb* **-denced; -dencing** (circa 1610)
: to offer evidence of : PROVE, EVINCE
synonym see SHOW

ev·i·dent \'e-və-dənt, -və-,dent\ *adjective* [Middle English, from Middle French, from Latin *evident-, evidens,* from *e- + vident-, videns,* present participle of *vidēre* to see — more at WIT] (14th century)
: clear to the vision or understanding ☆

ev·i·den·tial \,e-və-'den(t)-shəl\ *adjective* (1641)
: EVIDENTIARY 1
— **ev·i·den·tial·ly** *adverb*

ev·i·den·tia·ry \,e-və-'den-chə-rē, -chē-,er-ē\ *adjective* (1810)
1 : being, relating to, or affording evidence ⟨photographs of *evidentiary* value⟩
2 : conducted so that evidence may be presented ⟨an *evidentiary* hearing⟩

ev·i·dent·ly \'e-və-dənt-lē, -ə-,dent-, *especially for 2 often* ,ev-ə-'dent-\ *adverb* (1690)
1 : in an evident manner : CLEARLY, OBVIOUSLY ⟨any style . . . so *evidently* bad or second-rate —T. S. Eliot⟩
2 : on the basis of available evidence ⟨he was born . . . *evidently* in Texas —Robert Coughlan⟩

¹evil \'ē-vəl, *British often & US also* 'ē-(,)vil\ *adjective* **evil·er** *or* **evil·ler; evil·est** *or* **evil·lest** [Middle English, from Old English *yfel;* akin to Old High German *ubil* evil] (before 12th century)
1 a : morally reprehensible : SINFUL, WICKED ⟨an *evil* impulse⟩ **b :** arising from actual or imputed bad character or conduct ⟨a man of *evil* reputation⟩
2 a *archaic* **:** INFERIOR **b :** causing discomfort or repulsion : OFFENSIVE ⟨an *evil* odor⟩ **c :** DISAGREEABLE ⟨woke late and in an *evil* temper⟩
3 a : causing harm : PERNICIOUS ⟨the *evil* institution of slavery⟩ **b :** marked by misfortune : UNLUCKY
— **evil** *adverb, archaic*
— **evil·ly** \-(l)ē\ *adverb*
— **evil·ness** \-nəs\ *noun*

²evil *noun* (before 12th century)
1 a : the fact of suffering, misfortune, and wrongdoing **b :** a cosmic evil force
2 : something that brings sorrow, distress, or calamity

evil-do·er \,ē-vəl-'dü-ər\ *noun* (14th century)
: one who does evil

evil-do·ing \-'dü-iŋ\ *noun* (14th century)
: the act or action of doing evil

evil eye *noun* (before 12th century)
: an eye or glance held capable of inflicting harm; *also* : a person believed to have such an eye or glance

evil-mind·ed \,ē-vəl-'mīn-dəd, -vil-\ *adjective* (1531)
: having an evil disposition or evil thoughts
— **evil-mind·ed·ly** *adverb*
— **evil-mind·ed·ness** *noun*

evince \i-'vin(t)s\ *transitive verb* **evinced; evinc·ing** [Latin *evincere* to vanquish, win a point, from *e- + vincere* to conquer — more at VICTOR] (1621)
1 : to constitute outward evidence of
2 : to display clearly : REVEAL
synonym see SHOW
— **evinc·ible** \-'vin(t)-sə-bəl\ *adjective*

evis·cer·ate \i-'vi-sə-,rāt\ *verb* **-at·ed; -at·ing** [Latin *evisceratus,* past participle of *eviscerare,* from *e- + viscera* viscera] (1621)
transitive verb
1 a : to take out the entrails of : DISEMBOWEL **b :** to deprive of vital content or force
2 : to remove an organ from (a patient) or the contents of (an organ)
intransitive verb
: to protrude through a surgical incision or suffer protrusion of a part through an incision
— **evis·cer·a·tion** \-,vi-sə-'rā-shən\ *noun*

ev·i·ta·ble \'e-və-tə-bəl\ *adjective* [Latin *evitabilis,* from *evitare* to avoid, from *e- + vitare* to shun] (1502)
: capable of being avoided

evo·ca·ble \'e-və-kə-bəl, i-'vō-kə-\ *adjective* (1886)
: capable of being evoked

evo·ca·tion \,ē-vō-'kā-shən, ,e-və-\ *noun* [Latin *evocation-, evocatio,* from *evocare*] (1633)
1 : the act or fact of evoking : SUMMONING: as **a :** the summoning of a spirit **b :** imaginative recreation ⟨an *evocation* of the past⟩
2 : INDUCTION 4e
— **evo·ca·tor** \'ē-vō-,kā-tər, 'e-və-\ *noun*

evoc·a·tive \i-'vä-kə-tiv\ *adjective* (1657)
: evoking or tending to evoke an especially emotional response ⟨settings . . . so *evocative* that they bring tears to the eyes —Eric Malpass⟩
— **evoc·a·tive·ly** *adverb*
— **evoc·a·tive·ness** *noun*

evoke \i-'vōk\ *transitive verb* **evoked; evok·ing** [French *évoquer,* from Latin *evocare,* from *e- + vocare* to call — more at VOCATION] (circa 1626)
1 : to call forth or up: as **a :** CONJURE 2a ⟨*evoke* evil spirits⟩ **b :** to cite especially with approval or for support : INVOKE **c :** to bring to mind or recollection ⟨this place *evokes* memories⟩
2 : to recreate imaginatively
synonym see EDUCE

evo·lute \'e-və-,lüt *also* 'ē-və-\ *noun* (circa 1736)
: the locus of the center of curvature or the envelope of the normals of a curve

evo·lu·tion \,e-və-'lü-shən, ,ē-və-\ *noun* [Latin *evolution-, evolutio* unrolling, from *evolvere*] (1622)
1 : one of a set of prescribed movements
2 a : a process of change in a certain direction : UNFOLDING **b :** the action or an instance of forming and giving something off : EMISSION **c** (1) : a process of continuous change from a lower, simpler, or worse to a higher, more complex, or better state : GROWTH (2) : a process of gradual and relatively peaceful social, political, and economic advance **d :** something evolved
3 : the process of working out or developing
4 a : the historical development of a biological group (as a race or species) : PHYLOGENY **b :** a theory that the various types of animals and plants have their origin in other preexisting types and that the distinguishable differences are due to modifications in successive generations
5 : the extraction of a mathematical root
6 : a process in which the whole universe is a progression of interrelated phenomena
— **evo·lu·tion·ari·ly** \-shə-,ner-ə-lē\ *adverb*
— **evo·lu·tion·ary** \-shə-,ner-ē\ *adjective*
— **evo·lu·tion·ism** \-shə-,ni-zəm\ *noun*
— **evo·lu·tion·ist** \-sh(ə-)nist\ *noun or adjective*

evolve \i-'välv, -'vȯlv, ē- *also* -'väv *or* -'vȯv\ *verb* **evolved; evolv·ing** [Latin *evolvere* to unroll, from *e- + volvere* to roll — more at VOLUBLE] (1641)
transitive verb
1 : EMIT
2 a : DERIVE, EDUCE **b :** to produce by natural evolutionary processes **c :** DEVELOP, WORK OUT ⟨*evolve* social, political, and literary philosophies —L. W. Doob⟩
intransitive verb
: to undergo evolutionary change
— **evolv·able** \-'väl-və-bəl, -'vȯl- *also* -'vä-və- *or* -'vȯ-və-\ *adj*
— **evolve·ment** \-'välv-mənt, -'vȯlv- *also* -'väv- *or* -'vȯv-\ *noun*

evul·sion \i-'vəl-shən\ *noun* [Latin *evulsion-, evulsio,* from *evellere* to pluck out, from *e- + vellere* to pluck — more at VULNERABLE] (circa 1611)
: EXTRACTION

ev·zone \'ev-,zōn\ *noun* [New Greek *euzōnos,* from Greek, active, literally, well girt, from *eu- + zōnē* girdle — more at ZONE] (1897)
: a member of a select Greek infantry unit often serving as a palace guard

ewe \'yü, *in rural dials also* 'yō\ *noun* [Middle English, from Old English *ēowu;* akin to Old High German *ouwi* ewe, Latin *ovis* sheep, Greek *ois*] (before 12th century)
: the female of the sheep especially when mature; *also* : the female of various related animals

Ewe \'ā-,wā, 'ā-,vā\ *noun, plural* **Ewe** *also* **Ewes** (1861)
: a people of Ghana and Togo speaking a Kwa language; *also* : the language itself

ewe-neck \-'nek\ *noun* (1820)
: a thin neck with a concave arch occurring as a defect in dogs and horses
— **ewe-necked** \-'nekt\ *adjective*

ew·er \'yü-ər, 'yü-(-ə)r\ *noun* [Middle English, from Anglo-French, from Old French *evier,* from Latin *aquarium* water source, neuter of *aquarius* of water, from *aqua* water — more at ISLAND] (14th century)
: a vase-shaped pitcher or jug

Ew·ing's sarcoma \'yü-iŋz-\ *noun* [James *Ewing* (died 1943) American pathologist] (1951)

ewer

: a tumor that invades the shaft of a long bone and that tends to recur but rarely metastasizes

¹ex \(')eks\ *preposition* [Latin] (circa 1755)
1 : out of : FROM: as **a :** from a specified place or source **b :** from a specified dam ⟨a promising calf by Eric XVI *ex* Heatherbell⟩
2 : free from : WITHOUT: as **a :** without an indicated value or right — used especially of securities **b :** free of charges precedent to removal from the specified place with purchaser to provide means of subsequent transportation ⟨*ex* dock⟩ ◇

²ex *noun* [¹*ex*-] (1827)
: one that formerly held a specified position or place; *especially* **:** a former spouse

³ex *noun* (circa 1889)
: the letter *x*

¹ex- \e *also occurs in this prefix where only* i *is shown below (as in "express") and* ks *sometimes occurs where only* gz *is shown (as in "exact")*\ *prefix* [Middle English, from Old French & Latin; Old French, from Latin (also, prefix with perfective and causative value), from *ex* out of, from; akin to Greek *ex*, *ex*- out of, from Old Church Slavonic *iz*]
1 : out of : outside ⟨*ex*clave⟩
2 : not ⟨*ex*stipulate⟩
3 \(,)eks, 'eks\ [Middle English, from Late Latin, from Latin] **:** former ⟨*ex*-president⟩

²ex- — see EXO-

exa- *combining form* [International Scientific Vocabulary, modification of Greek *hexa*-]
: quintillion ⟨*exa*joules⟩

ex·ac·er·bate \ig-'za-sər-,bāt\ *transitive verb* **-bat·ed; -bat·ing** [Latin *exacerbatus*, past participle of *exacerbare*, from *ex*- + *acerbus* harsh, bitter, from *acer* sharp — more at EDGE] (1660)
: to make more violent, bitter, or severe ⟨the proposed shutdown . . . would *exacerbate* unemployment problems —*Science*⟩
— **ex·ac·er·ba·tion** \-,za-sər-'bā-shən\ *noun*

¹ex·act \ig-'zakt\ *transitive verb* [Middle English, to require as payment, from Latin *exactus*, past participle of *exigere* to drive out, demand, measure, from *ex*- + *agere* to drive — more at AGENT] (1564)
1 : to call for forcibly or urgently and obtain ⟨from them has been *exacted* the ultimate sacrifice —D. D. Eisenhower⟩
2 : to call for as necessary or desirable
synonym see DEMAND
— **ex·act·able** \-'zak-tə-bəl\ *adjective*
— **ex·ac·tor** *also* **ex·act·er** \-'zak-tər\ *noun*

²exact *adjective* [Latin *exactus*] (1533)
1 : exhibiting or marked by strict, particular, and complete accordance with fact or a standard
2 : marked by thorough consideration or minute measurement of small factual details
synonym see CORRECT
— **ex·act·ness** \-'zak(t)-nəs\ *noun*

ex·ac·ta \ig-'zak-tə\ *noun* [American Spanish (*quiniela*) *exacta* exact quiniela] (1964)
: PERFECTA

exact differential *noun* (1825)
: a differential expression of the form $X_1dx_1 + \ldots + X_ndx_n$ where the X's are the partial derivatives of a function $f(x_1, \ldots, x_n)$ with respect to $x_1, \ldots, x_n$ respectively

ex·act·ing \ig-'zak-tiŋ\ *adjective* (1634)
1 : tryingly or unremittingly severe in making demands
2 : requiring careful attention and precision
synonym see ONEROUS
— **ex·act·ing·ly** \-tiŋ-lē\ *adverb*
— **ex·act·ing·ness** *noun*

ex·ac·tion \ig-'zak-shən\ *noun* (15th century)
1 a : the act or process of exacting **b :** EXTORTION
2 : something exacted; *especially* **:** a fee, reward, or contribution demanded or levied with severity or injustice

ex·ac·ti·tude \ig-'zak-tə-,tüd, -,tyüd\ *noun* (1734)
: the quality or an instance of being exact : EXACTNESS

ex·act·ly \ig-'zak-(t)lē\ *adverb* (1612)
1 a : in a manner or measure or to a degree or number that strictly conforms to a fact or condition ⟨it's *exactly* 3 o'clock⟩ ⟨these two pieces are *exactly* the same size⟩ **b :** in every respect **:** ALTOGETHER, ENTIRELY ⟨that was *exactly* the wrong thing to do⟩ ⟨not *exactly* what I had in mind⟩
2 : quite so — used to express agreement

exact science *noun* (1843)
: a science (as physics, chemistry, or astronomy) whose laws are capable of accurate quantitative expression

ex·ag·ger·ate \ig-'za-jə-,rāt\ *verb* **-at·ed; -at·ing** [Latin *exaggeratus*, past participle of *exaggerare*, literally, to heap up, from *ex*- + *agger* heap, from *aggerere* to carry toward, from *ad*- + *gerere* to carry] (circa 1587)
transitive verb
1 : to enlarge beyond bounds or the truth **:** OVERSTATE ⟨a friend *exaggerates* a man's virtues —Joseph Addison⟩
2 : to enlarge or increase especially beyond the normal **:** OVEREMPHASIZE
intransitive verb
: to make an overstatement
— **ex·ag·ger·at·ed·ly** *adverb*
— **ex·ag·ger·at·ed·ness** *noun*
— **ex·ag·ger·a·tion** \-,za-jə-'rā-shən\ *noun*
— **ex·ag·ger·a·tive** \-'za-jə-,rā-tiv, -'zaj-rə-, -'za-jə-\ *adjective*
— **ex·ag·ger·a·tor** \-'za-jə-,rā-tər\ *noun*
— **ex·ag·ger·a·to·ry** \-'zaj-rə-,tōr-ē, -,tòr-, -'za-jə-\ *adjective*

ex·alt \ig-'zòlt\ *verb* [Middle English, from Middle French & Latin; Middle French *exalter*, from Latin *exaltare*, from *ex*- + *altus* high — more at OLD] (15th century)
transitive verb
1 : to raise in rank, power, or character
2 : to elevate by praise or in estimation **:** GLORIFY
3 *obsolete* **:** ELATE
4 : to raise high **:** ELEVATE
5 : to enhance the activity of **:** INTENSIFY ⟨rousing and *exalting* the imagination —George Eliot⟩
intransitive verb
: to induce exaltation
— **ex·alt·ed·ly** *adverb*
— **ex·alt·er** *noun*

ex·al·ta·tion \,eg-,zòl-'tā-shən, ,ek-,sòl-\ *noun* (14th century)
1 : an act of exalting **:** the state of being exalted
2 : an excessively intensified sense of well-being, power, or importance
3 : an increase in degree or intensity ⟨*exaltation* of virulence of a virus⟩

ex·am \ig-'zam\ *noun* (1877)
: EXAMINATION

ex·a·men \ig-'zā-mən\ *noun* [Latin, tongue of a balance, examination, from *exigere* — more at EXACT] (1606)
1 : EXAMINATION
2 : a critical study

ex·am·i·nant \-'za-mə-nənt\ *noun* (1588)
1 : EXAMINEE
2 : one who examines **:** EXAMINER

ex·am·i·na·tion \ig-,za-mə-'nā-shən\ *noun* (14th century)
1 : the act or process of examining **:** the state of being examined
2 : an exercise designed to examine progress or test qualification or knowledge
3 : a formal interrogation
— **ex·am·i·na·tion·al** \-shnəl, -shə-nᵊl\ *adjective*

ex·am·ine \ig-'za-mən\ *verb* **ex·am·ined; ex·am·in·ing** \-'zam-niŋ, -'za-mə-\ [Middle English, from Middle French *examiner*, from Latin *examinare*, from *examen*] (14th century)
transitive verb
1 a : to inspect closely **b :** to test the condition of **c :** to inquire into carefully **:** INVESTIGATE
2 a : to interrogate closely ⟨*examine* a prisoner⟩ **b :** to test by questioning in order to determine progress, fitness, or knowledge
intransitive verb
: to make or give an examination
synonym see SCRUTINIZE
— **ex·am·in·able** \-'za-mə-nə-bəl\ *adjective*
— **ex·am·in·er** \-'zam-nər, -'za-mə-\ *noun*

ex·am·in·ee \ig-,za-mə-'nē\ *noun* (1788)
: a person who is examined

¹ex·am·ple \ig-'zam-pəl\ *noun* [Middle English, from Middle French, from Latin *exemplum*, from *eximere* to take out, from *ex*- + *emere* to take — more at REDEEM] (14th century)
1 : one that serves as a pattern to be imitated or not to be imitated ⟨a good *example*⟩ ⟨a bad *example*⟩
2 : a punishment inflicted on someone as a warning to others; *also* **:** an individual so punished
3 : one (as an item or incident) that is representative of all of a group or type
4 : a parallel or closely similar case especially when serving as a precedent or model
5 : an instance (as a problem to be solved) serving to illustrate a rule or precept or to act as an exercise in the application of a rule
synonym see INSTANCE, MODEL
— **for example** \fər-ig-'zam-pəl, frig-\ **:** as an example ⟨there are many sources of air pollution; exhaust fumes, *for example*⟩

²example *transitive verb* **ex·am·pled; ex·am·pling** \-p(ə-)liŋ\ (15th century)
1 : to serve as an example of
2 *archaic* **:** to be or set an example to

ex·an·i·mate \eg-'za-nə-mət\ *adjective* [Latin *exanimatus*, past participle of *exanimare* to deprive of life or spirit, from *ex*- + *anima* breath, soul — more at ANIMATE] (circa 1534)
1 : lacking animation **:** SPIRITLESS
2 : being or appearing lifeless

ex·an·them \eg-'zan(t)-thəm, 'ek-,san-,them\ *also* **ex·an·the·ma** \,eg-,zan-'thē-mə\ *noun, plural* **-thems** *also* **-them·a·ta** \,eg-,zan-'the-mə-tə\ *or* **-themas** [Late Latin *exanthema*, from Greek *exanthēma*, from *exanthein* to bloom, break out, from *ex*- + *anthos* flower — more at ANTHOLOGY] (1656)

◇ WORD HISTORY
ex The word *ex* meaning "former spouse" is clearly a shortening of *ex-wife* or *ex-husband*, but the origin of the prefix *ex-* that forms these words is less straightforward. In Latin, both the prefix *ex-* and the preposition *ex* meant "out of, from." The preposition took on the meaning "from being, having formerly been" in phrases describing a man's office and the office he had previously held. For example, *ex assessore praefectus praetorii* meant "prefect of the Praetorian Guard, having formerly held the office of assessor" (literally, "out of assessor, prefect of the Praetorian Guard"). Because of phrases of this type, *ex* in the sense "having formerly been" came to be used in Late Latin simply as a prefix, in words like *exconsul* "person who was formerly consul." Although *ex-* in this meaning has been used sporadically in English since the late Middle Ages, coinages such as *ex-president* and *ex-wife* did not become common until the 19th century.

\ə\ **abut** \ᵊ\ **kitten** \ər\ **further** \a\ **ash** \ā\ **ace**
\ä\ **mop, mar** \aú\ **out** \ch\ **chin** \e\ **bet** \ē\ **easy**
\g\ **go** \i\ **hit** \ī\ **ice** \j\ **job** \ŋ\ **sing** \ō\ **go**
\ò\ **law** \òi\ **boy** \th\ **thin** \th\ **the** \ü\ **loot** \ú\ **foot**
\y\ **yet** \zh\ **vision** *see also* Guide to Pronunciation

: an eruptive disease (as measles) or its symptomatic eruption

— **ex·an·them·a·tous** \,eg-,zan-'the-mə-təs\ *or* **ex·an·the·mat·ic** \-,zan-thə-'ma-tik\ *adjective*

¹**ex·arch** \'ek-,särk\ *noun* [Late Latin *exarchus*, from Late Greek *exarchos*, from Greek, leader, from *exarchein* to begin, take the lead, from *ex-* + *archein* to rule, begin — more at ARCH-] (1588)
1 : a Byzantine viceroy
2 : an Eastern bishop ranking below a patriarch and above a metropolitan; *specifically* : the head of an independent church
— **ex·ar·chal** \ek-'sär-kəl\ *adjective*
— **ex·arch·ate** \'ek-,sär-kət\ *noun*
— **ex·ar·chy** \'ek-,sär-kē\ *noun*

²**exarch** *adjective* [exo- + -arch] (1891)
: formed or taking place from the periphery toward the center ⟨*exarch* xylem⟩

¹**ex·as·per·ate** \ig-'zas-pə-,rāt\ *transitive verb* **-at·ed; -at·ing** [Latin *exasperatus*, past participle of *exasperare*, from *ex-* + *asper* rough — more at ASPERITY] (1534)
1 a : to excite the anger of : ENRAGE **b** : to cause irritation or annoyance to
2 *obsolete* : to make more grievous : AGGRAVATE
synonym see IRRITATE
— **ex·as·per·at·ed·ly** *adverb*
— **ex·as·per·at·ing·ly** \-,rā-tiŋ-lē\ *adverb*

²**ex·as·per·ate** \-p(ə-)rət\ *adjective* (1541)
1 : irritated or annoyed especially to the point of injudicious action : EXASPERATED
2 : roughened with irregular prickles or elevations ⟨*exasperate* seed coats⟩

ex·as·per·a·tion \ig-,zas-pə-'rā-shən\ *noun* (1547)
1 : the state of being exasperated
2 : the act or an instance of exasperating

Ex·cal·i·bur \ek-'ska-lə-bər\ *noun* [Middle English *Excalaber*, from Old French *Escalibor*, from Medieval Latin *Caliburnus*]
: the sword of King Arthur

ex ca·the·dra \,eks-kə-'thē-drə\ *adverb or adjective* [New Latin, literally, from the chair] (1818)
: by virtue of or in the exercise of one's office or position ⟨*ex cathedra* pronouncements⟩

ex·ca·vate \'ek-skə-,vāt\ *verb* **-vat·ed; -vat·ing** [Latin *excavatus*, past participle of *excavare*, from *ex-* + *cavare* to make hollow — more at CAVATINA] (1599)
transitive verb
1 : to form a cavity or hole in
2 : to form by hollowing out
3 : to dig out and remove
4 : to expose to view by or as if by digging away a covering ⟨*excavate* the remains of a temple⟩ ⟨another writer whose work I *excavated* —William Zinsser⟩
intransitive verb
: to make excavations

ex·ca·va·tion \,ek-skə-'vā-shən\ *noun* (circa 1611)
1 : the action or process of excavating
2 : a cavity formed by cutting, digging, or scooping
— **ex·ca·va·tion·al** \-shnəl, -shə-nᵊl\ *adjective*

ex·ca·va·tor \'ek-skə-,vā-tər\ *noun* (circa 1815)
: one that excavates; *especially* : a power-operated shovel

ex·ceed \ik-'sēd\ *verb* [Middle English *exceden*, from Middle French *exceder*, from Latin *excedere*, from *ex-* + *cedere* to go] (14th century)
transitive verb
1 : to extend outside of ⟨the river will *exceed* its banks⟩
2 : to be greater than or superior to
3 : to go beyond a limit set by ⟨*exceeded* his authority⟩
intransitive verb
1 *obsolete* : OVERDO

2 : PREDOMINATE ☆

ex·ceed·ing *adjective* (15th century)
: exceptional in amount, quality, or degree

ex·ceed·ing·ly \-'sē-diŋ-lē\ *also* **ex·ceed·ing** *adverb* (1535)
: to an extreme degree : EXTREMELY

ex·cel \ik-'sel\ *verb* **ex·celled; ex·cel·ling** [Middle English *excellen*, from Latin *excellere*, from *ex-* + *-cellere* to rise, project; akin to Latin *collis* hill — more at HILL] (15th century)
transitive verb
: to be superior to : surpass in accomplishment or achievement
intransitive verb
: to be distinguishable by superiority : surpass others ⟨*excel* in sports⟩ ⟨*excelled* at lipreading⟩
synonym see EXCEED

ex·cel·lence \'ek-s(ə-)lən(t)s\ *noun* (14th century)
1 : the quality of being excellent
2 : an excellent or valuable quality : VIRTUE
3 : EXCELLENCY 2

ex·cel·len·cy \-s(ə-)lən(t)-sē\ *noun, plural* **-cies** (15th century)
1 : EXCELLENCE; *especially* : outstanding or valuable quality — usually used in plural ⟨so crammed, as he thinks, with *excellencies* —Shakespeare⟩
2 — used as a title for high dignitaries of state (as a governor or an ambassador) or church (as a Roman Catholic archbishop or bishop)

ex·cel·lent \'ek-s(ə-)lənt\ *adjective* [Middle English, from Middle French, from Latin *excellent-, excellens*, from present participle of *excellere*] (14th century)
1 *archaic* : SUPERIOR
2 : very good of its kind : eminently good : FIRST-CLASS
— **ex·cel·lent·ly** *adverb*

ex·cel·si·or \ik-'sel-sē-ər, -ȯr\ *noun* [trade name, from Latin, higher, comparative of *excelsus* high, from past participle of *excellere*] (1868)
: fine curled wood shavings used especially for packing fragile items

¹**ex·cept** \ik-'sept\ *also* **ex·cept·ing** \-'sep-tiŋ\ *preposition* (14th century)
: with the exclusion or exception of ⟨daily *except* Sundays⟩

²**except** *verb* [Middle English, from Middle French *excepter*, from Latin *exceptare*, from *exceptus*, past participle of *excipere* to take out, except, from *ex-* + *capere* to take — more at HEAVE] (14th century)
transitive verb
: to take or leave out from a number or a whole : EXCLUDE
intransitive verb
: to take exception : OBJECT
— **ex·cep·tive** \-'sep-təv\ *adjective*

³**except** *also* **excepting** *conjunction* (15th century)
1 : on any other condition than that : UNLESS ⟨*except* you repent⟩
2 : with this exception, namely ⟨was inaccessible *except* by boat⟩
3 : ONLY — often followed by *that* ⟨I would go *except* that it's too far⟩

except for *preposition* (1842)
1 : with the exception of ⟨everyone was gone *except for* me⟩
2 : were it not for ⟨*except for* you I would be dead⟩

ex·cep·tion \ik-'sep-shən\ *noun* (14th century)
1 : the act of excepting : EXCLUSION
2 : one that is excepted; *especially* : a case to which a rule does not apply
3 : QUESTION, OBJECTION ⟨witnesses whose authority is beyond *exception* —T. B. Macaulay⟩
4 : an oral or written legal objection

ex·cep·tion·able \ik-'sep-sh(ə-)nə-bəl\ *adjective* (1691)

: being likely to cause objection : OBJECTIONABLE ⟨visitors even drink the *exceptionable* beer —W. D. Howells⟩
— **ex·cep·tion·abil·i·ty** \-,sep-sh(ə-)nə-'bi-lə-tē\ *noun*
— **ex·cep·tion·ably** \-'sep-sh(ə-)nə-blē\ *adverb*

ex·cep·tion·al \ik-'sep-shnəl, -shə-nᵊl\ *adjective* (circa 1846)
1 : forming an exception : RARE ⟨an *exceptional* number of rainy days⟩
2 : better than average : SUPERIOR ⟨*exceptional* skill⟩
3 : deviating from the norm: as **a** : having above or below average intelligence **b** : physically handicapped
— **ex·cep·tion·al·i·ty** \-,sep-shə-'na-lə-tē\ *noun*
— **ex·cep·tion·al·ness** *noun*

ex·cep·tion·al·ism \ik-'sep-shnə-,li-zəm, -shə-nᵊl-\ *noun* (1937)
: the condition of being different from the norm; *also* : a theory expounding the exceptionalism especially of a nation or region

ex·cep·tion·al·ly \ik-'sep-shnə-lē, -shə-nᵊl-ē\ *adverb* (1848)
: in an exceptional manner : to an exceptional degree; *especially* : more than average or usual ⟨an *exceptionally* difficult task⟩

¹**ex·cerpt** \ek-'sərpt, eg-'zərpt, 'ek-,, 'eg-,\ *transitive verb* [Latin *excerptus*, past participle of *excerpere*, from *ex-* + *carpere* to gather, pluck — more at HARVEST] (15th century)
1 : to select (a passage) for quoting : EXTRACT
2 : to take or publish extracts from (as a book)
— **ex·cerp·tor** *or* **ex·cerpt·er** *noun*
— **ex·cerp·tion** \ek-'sərp-shən, eg-'zərp-\ *noun*

²**ex·cerpt** \'ek-,sərpt, 'eg-,zərpt\ *noun* (1627)
: a passage (as from a book or musical composition) selected, performed, or copied : EXTRACT

¹**ex·cess** \ik-'ses, 'ek-,\ *noun* [Middle English, from Middle French or Late Latin; Middle French *exces*, from Late Latin *excessus*, from Latin, departure, projection, from *excedere* to exceed] (14th century)
1 a : the state or an instance of surpassing usual, proper, or specified limits : SUPERFLUITY **b** : the amount or degree by which one thing or quantity exceeds another ⟨an *excess* of 10 bushels⟩
2 : undue or immoderate indulgence : INTEMPERANCE; *also* : an act or instance of intemperance ⟨prevent *excesses* and abuses by newly created local powers —Albert Shanker⟩
— **in excess of** : to an amount or degree beyond : OVER

²**excess** *adjective* (15th century)
: more than the usual, proper, or specified amount

³**excess** *transitive verb* (1974)
: to eliminate the position of ⟨*excessed* several teachers because of budget cutbacks⟩

☆ **SYNONYMS**

Exceed, surpass, transcend, excel, outdo, outstrip mean to go or be beyond a stated or implied limit, measure, or degree. EXCEED implies going beyond a limit set by authority or established by custom or by prior achievement ⟨*exceed* the speed limit⟩. SURPASS suggests superiority in quality, merit, or skill ⟨the book *surpassed* our expectations⟩. TRANSCEND implies a rising or extending notably above or beyond ordinary limits ⟨*transcended* the values of their culture⟩. EXCEL implies preeminence in achievement or quality and may suggest superiority to all others ⟨*excels* in mathematics⟩. OUTDO applies to a bettering or exceeding what has been done before ⟨*outdid* herself this time⟩. OUTSTRIP suggests surpassing in a race or competition ⟨*outstripped* other firms in sales⟩.

ex·ces·sive \ik-'se-siv\ *adjective* (14th century)
: exceeding what is usual, proper, necessary, or normal ☆
— **ex·ces·sive·ly** *adverb*
— **ex·ces·sive·ness** *noun*

¹**ex·change** \iks-'chānj, 'eks-\ *noun, often attributive* [Middle English *exchaunge*, from Middle French *eschange*, from *eschangier* to exchange, from (assumed) Vulgar Latin *excambiare*, from Latin *ex-* + *cambiare* to change — more at CHANGE] (14th century)
1 : the act of giving or taking one thing in return for another : TRADE ⟨an *exchange* of prisoners⟩
2 a : the act or process of substituting one thing for another **b** : reciprocal giving and receiving
3 : something offered, given, or received in an exchange
4 a : funds payable currently at a distant point either in a foreign currency or in domestic currency **b** (1) : interchange or conversion of the money of two countries or of current and uncurrent money with allowance for difference in value (2) : EXCHANGE RATE (3) : the amount of the difference in value between two currencies or between values of a particular currency at two places **c** : instruments (as checks or bills of exchange) presented in a clearinghouse for settlement
5 : a place where things or services are exchanged: as **a** : an organized market or center for trading in securities or commodities **b** : a store or shop specializing in merchandise usually of a particular type **c** : a cooperative store or society **d** : a central office in which telephone lines are connected to permit communication
— **in exchange** : as a substitute

²**exchange** *verb* **ex·changed; ex·chang·ing** (15th century)
transitive verb
1 a : to part with, give, or transfer in consideration of something received as an equivalent **b** : to have replaced by other merchandise ⟨*exchanged* the shirt for one in a larger size⟩
2 : to part with for a substitute ⟨*exchanging* future security for immediate pleasure⟩
3 : to give and receive reciprocally ⟨*exchange* gifts⟩
intransitive verb
1 : to pass or become received in exchange
2 : to engage in an exchange
— **ex·change·abil·i·ty** \iks-,chān-jə-'bi-lə-tē\ *noun*
— **ex·change·able** \iks-'chān-jə-bəl\ *adjective*
— **ex·chang·er** \iks-'chān-jər, eks-,\ *noun*

exchange rate *noun* (1896)
: the ratio at which the principal unit of two currencies may be traded

exchange student *noun* (circa 1930)
: a student from one country received into an institution in another country in exchange for one sent to an institution in the home country of the first

Ex·chang·ite \iks-'chān-,jīt\ *noun* [(National) *Exchange* (club)] (circa 1934)
: a member of a major national service club

ex·che·quer \'eks-,che-kər, iks-'\ *noun* [Middle English *escheker*, from Anglo-French, from Old French *eschequier* chessboard, counting table — more at CHECKER] (14th century)
1 *capitalized* : a department or office of state in medieval England charged with the collection and management of the royal revenue and judicial determination of all revenue causes
2 *capitalized* : a former superior court having jurisdiction in England and Wales primarily over revenue matters and now merged with King's Bench
3 *often capitalized* **a** : the department or office of state in Great Britain and Northern Ireland charged with the receipt and care of the na-

tional revenue **b** : the national banking account of this realm
4 : TREASURY; *especially* : a national or royal treasury
5 : pecuniary resources : FUNDS

ex·ci·mer laser \'ek-si-,mər-\ *noun* [*excited* + *dimer*] (1973)
: a laser that uses a noble-gas halide to generate radiation usually in the ultraviolet region of the spectrum

ex·cip·i·ent \ik-'si-pē-ənt\ *noun* [Latin *excipient-, excipiens,* present participle of *excipere* to take out, take up — more at EXCEPT] (1753)
: a usually inert substance (as gum arabic or starch) that forms a vehicle (as for a drug)

ex·ci·ple \'ek-sə-pəl\ *noun* [New Latin *excipulum,* from Latin, receptacle, from *excipere*] (circa 1866)
: a saucer-shaped rim around the hymenium of various lichens

ex·cis·able \'ek-,sī-zə-bəl, -,sī-sə-, ek-'\ *adjective* (1689)
: subject to excise

¹**ex·cise** \'ek-,sīz, -,sīs\ *noun* [obsolete Dutch *excijs* (now *accijus*), from Middle Dutch, probably modification of Old French *assise* session, assessment — more at ASSIZE] (15th century)
1 : an internal tax levied on the manufacture, sale, or consumption of a commodity
2 : any of various taxes on privileges often assessed in the form of a license or fee

²**ex·cise** \'ek-,sīz, -,sīs, ik-'sīz\ *transitive verb* **ex·cised; ex·cis·ing** (1652)
: to impose an excise on

³**ex·cise** \ik-'sīz\ *transitive verb* **ex·cised; ex·cis·ing** [Latin *excisus,* past participle of *excidere,* from *ex-* + *caedere* to cut] (1634)
: to remove by or as if by excision

ex·cise·man \'ek-,sīz-mən, -,sīs-, -,man, ek-'\ *noun* (1647)
: an officer who inspects and rates articles liable to excise under British law

ex·ci·sion \ik-'si-zhən\ *noun* [Middle English *excysion,* from Middle French *excision,* from Latin *excision-, excisio,* from *excidere*] (1541)
: the act or procedure of removing by or as if by cutting out; *especially* : surgical removal or resection
— **ex·ci·sion·al** \-'sizh-nəl, -zhⁿ-əl\ *adjective*

ex·cit·able \ik-'sī-tə-bəl\ *adjective* (1609)
1 : capable of being readily roused into action or a state of excitement or irritability
2 : capable of being activated by and reacting to stimuli
— **ex·cit·abil·i·ty** \-,sī-tə-'bi-lə-tē\ *noun*
— **ex·cit·able·ness** \-'sī-tə-bəl-nəs\ *noun*

ex·ci·tant \ik-'sī-tⁿnt, 'ek-sə-tənt\ *adjective* (1607)
: tending to excite or augment ⟨*excitant* drugs⟩
— **excitant** *noun*

ex·ci·ta·tion \,ek-,sī-'tā-shən, ,ek-sə-\ *noun* (14th century)
: EXCITEMENT; *especially* : the disturbed or altered condition resulting from stimulation of an individual, organ, tissue, or cell

ex·ci·ta·tive \ik-'sī-tə-tiv\ *adjective* (15th century)
: tending to induce excitation (as of a neuron) ⟨*excitative* substances⟩

ex·ci·ta·to·ry \ik-'sī-tə-,tōr-ē, -,tor-\ *adjective* (1803)
: exhibiting, resulting from, related to, or producing excitement or excitation ⟨*excitatory* nerve fibers⟩

ex·cite \ik-'sīt, ek-\ *transitive verb* **ex·cit·ed; ex·cit·ing** [Middle English, from Middle French *exciter,* from Latin *excitare,* from *ex-* + *citare* to rouse — more at CITE] (14th century)
1 a : to call to activity **b** : to rouse to an emotional response ⟨scenes to *excite* the hardest

man to pity⟩ **c** : to arouse (as a strong emotional response) by appropriate stimuli ⟨*excite* enthusiasm for the new regime —Arthur Knight⟩
2 a : ENERGIZE ⟨*excite* an electromagnet⟩ **b** : to produce a magnetic field in ⟨*excite* a dynamo⟩
3 : to increase the activity of (as a living organism) : STIMULATE
4 : to raise (as an atomic nucleus, an atom, or a molecule) to a higher energy level
synonym see PROVOKE
— **ex·cit·ed·ly** \-'sī-təd-lē\ *adverb*

excited state *noun* (1927)
: a state of a physical system (as an atomic nucleus, an atom, or a molecule) that is higher in energy than the ground state

ex·cite·ment \ik-'sīt-mənt\ *noun* (1604)
1 : something that excites or rouses
2 : the action of exciting : the state of being excited

ex·cit·er \ik-'sī-tər\ *noun* (14th century)
1 : one that excites
2 a : a generator or battery that supplies the electric current used to produce the magnetic field in another generator or motor **b** : an electrical oscillator that generates the carrier frequency (as for a radio transmitter)

ex·cit·ing \ik-'sī-tiŋ\ *adjective* (circa 1811)
: producing excitement
— **ex·cit·ing·ly** \-iŋ-lē\ *adverb*

ex·ci·ton \'ek-sə-,tän, -,sī-\ *noun* [International Scientific Vocabulary *excitation* + ²*-on*] (1936)
: a mobile combination of an electron and a hole in an excited crystal (as of a semiconductor)
— **ex·ci·ton·ic** \,ek-sə-'tä-nik, -,sī-\ *adjective*

ex·ci·tor \ik-'sī-tər\ *noun* (1816)
: an afferent nerve arousing increased action of the part that it supplies

ex·claim \iks-'klām\ *verb* [Middle French *exclamer,* from Latin *exclamare,* from *ex-* + *clamare* to cry out — more at CLAIM] (circa 1570)
intransitive verb
1 : to cry out or speak in strong or sudden emotion ⟨*exclaimed* in delight⟩
2 : to speak loudly or vehemently ⟨*exclaimed* against immorality⟩
transitive verb
: to utter sharply, passionately, or vehemently : PROCLAIM
— **ex·claim·er** *noun*

ex·cla·ma·tion \,eks-klə-'mā-shən\ *noun* (14th century)
1 : a sharp or sudden utterance

☆ **SYNONYMS**
Excessive, immoderate, inordinate, extravagant, exorbitant, extreme mean going beyond a normal limit. EXCESSIVE implies an amount or degree too great to be reasonable or acceptable (*excessive* punishment). IMMODERATE implies lack of desirable or necessary restraint (*immoderate* spending). INORDINATE implies an exceeding of the limits dictated by reason or good judgment (*inordinate* pride). EXTRAVAGANT implies an indifference to restraints imposed by truth, prudence, or good taste (*extravagant* claims for the product). EXORBITANT implies a departure from accepted standards regarding amount or degree (*exorbitant* prices). EXTREME may imply an approach to the farthest limit possible or conceivable but commonly means only to a notably high degree (*extreme* shyness).

\ə\ abut \ᵊ\ kitten \ər\ **further** \a\ ash \ā\ ace
\ä\ mop, mar \au̇\ out \ch\ chin \e\ bet \ē\ easy
\g\ go \i\ hit \ī\ ice \j\ job \ŋ\ sing \ō\ go
\ȯ\ law \ȯi\ boy \th\ thin \t̲h\ the \ü\ loot \u̇\ foot
\y\ yet \zh\ vision *see also* Guide to Pronunciation

2 : vehement expression of protest or complaint

ex·cla·ma·tion point *noun* (1824)
: a mark ! used especially after an interjection or exclamation to indicate forceful utterance or strong feeling — called also *exclamation mark*

ex·clam·a·to·ry \iks-'kla-mə-,tōr-ē, -,tor-\ *adjective* (1593)
: containing, expressing, using, or relating to exclamation ⟨an *exclamatory* phrase⟩

ex·clave \'eks-,klāv, -,kläv\ *noun* [*ex-* + *-clave* (as in *enclave*)] (1888)
: a portion of a country separated from the main part and constituting an enclave in respect to the surrounding territory

ex·clud·able *or* **ex·clud·ible** \iks-'klü-də-bəl\ *adjective* (1916)
: subject to exclusion ⟨*excludable* income⟩
— **ex·clud·abil·i·ty** \-,klü-də-'bi-lə-tē\ *noun*

ex·clude \iks-'klüd\ *transitive verb* **ex·clud·ed; ex·clud·ing** [Middle English, from Latin *excludere,* from *ex-* + *claudere* to close — more at CLOSE] (14th century)
1 a : to prevent or restrict the entrance of **b :** to bar from participation, consideration, or inclusion
2 : to expel or bar especially from a place or position previously occupied
— **ex·clud·er** *noun*

ex·clu·sion \iks-'klü-zhən\ *noun* [Latin *exclusion-, exclusio,* from *excludere*] (15th century)
1 : the act or an instance of excluding
2 : the state of being excluded
— **ex·clu·sion·ary** \-zhə-,ner-ē\ *adjective*

exclusionary rule *noun* (1964)
: a legal rule that bars unlawfully obtained evidence from being used in court proceedings

ex·clu·sion·ist \iks-'klüzh-nist, -'klü-zhə-\ *noun* (1822)
: one who would exclude another from some right or privilege
— **exclusionist** *adjective*

exclusion principle *noun* (1926)
: a principle in physics: no two particles (as electrons) in an atom or molecule can have the same set of quantum numbers

¹ex·clu·sive \iks-'klü-siv, -ziv\ *adjective* (1515)
1 a : excluding or having power to exclude **b :** limiting or limited to possession, control, or use by a single individual or group
2 a : excluding others from participation **b :** snobbishly aloof
3 a : accepting or soliciting only a socially restricted patronage (as of the upper class) **b :** STYLISH, FASHIONABLE **c :** restricted in distribution, use, or appeal because of expense
4 a : SINGLE, SOLE ⟨*exclusive* jurisdiction⟩ **b :** WHOLE, UNDIVIDED ⟨his *exclusive* attention⟩
— **ex·clu·sive·ly** *adverb*
— **ex·clu·sive·ness** *noun*

²exclusive *noun* (15th century)
: something exclusive: as **a :** a newspaper story at first released to or printed by only one newspaper **b :** an exclusive right (as to sell a particular product in a certain area)

exclusive disjunction *noun* (1942)
: a compound proposition in logic that is true when one and only one of its constituent statements is true — see TRUTH TABLE table

exclusive of *preposition* (1762)
: not taking into account ⟨there were four of us *exclusive of* the guide⟩

ex·clu·siv·ism \iks-'klü-sə-,vi-zəm, -'klü-zə-\ *noun* (circa 1834)
: the practice of excluding or of being exclusive
— **ex·clu·siv·ist** \-vist\ *noun or adjective*

ex·clu·siv·i·ty \,eks-,klü-'si-və-tē, iks-, -'zi-\ *noun, plural* **-ties** (1926)
1 : the quality or state of being exclusive
2 : exclusive rights or services

ex·cog·i·tate \ek-'skä-jə-,tāt\ *transitive verb* [Latin *excogitatus,* past participle of *excogitare,* from *ex-* + *cogitare* to cogitate] (circa 1530)
: to think out **:** DEVISE
— **ex·cog·i·ta·tion** \(,)ek-,skä-jə-'tā-shən\ *noun*
— **ex·cog·i·ta·tive** \ek-'skä-jə-,tā-tiv\ *adjective*

¹ex·com·mu·ni·cate \,ek-skə-'myü-nə-,kāt\ *transitive verb* [Middle English, from Late Latin *excommunicatus,* past participle of *excommunicare,* from Latin *ex-* + Late Latin *communicare* to communicate] (15th century)
: to subject to excommunication
— **ex·com·mu·ni·ca·tor** \-,kā-tər\ *noun*

²ex·com·mu·ni·cate \-ni-kət\ *adjective* (1551)
: excluded from the rites of the church **:** EXCOMMUNICATED
— **excommunicate** *noun*

ex·com·mu·ni·ca·tion \-,myü-nə-'kā-shən\ *noun* (15th century)
1 : an ecclesiastical censure depriving a person of the rights of church membership
2 : exclusion from fellowship in a group or community
— **ex·com·mu·ni·ca·tive** \-'myü-nə-,kā-tiv, -ni-kət-\ *adjective*

ex·co·ri·ate \ek-'skōr-ē-,āt, -'skòr-\ *transitive verb* **-at·ed; -at·ing** [Middle English, from Late Latin *excoriatus,* past participle of *excoriare,* from Latin *ex-* + *corium* skin, hide — more at CUIRASS] (15th century)
1 : to wear off the skin of **:** ABRADE
2 : to censure scathingly
— **ex·co·ri·a·tion** \(,)ek-,skōr-ē-'ā-shən, -,skòr-\ *noun*

ex·cre·ment \'ek-skrə-mənt\ *noun* [Latin *excrementum,* from *excernere*] (1533)
: waste matter discharged from the body; especially **:** waste (as feces) discharged from the alimentary canal
— **ex·cre·men·tal** \,ek-skrə-'men-t°l\ *adjective*
— **ex·cre·men·ti·tious** \-,men-'ti-shəs, -mən-\ *adjective*

ex·cres·cence \ik-'skre-s°n(t)s, ek-\ *noun* (15th century)
1 : a projection or outgrowth especially when abnormal ⟨warty *excrescences* in the colon⟩
2 : a disfiguring, extraneous, or unwanted mark or part **:** BLOT

ex·cres·cen·cy \-s°n-sē\ *noun, plural* **-cies** (1545)
: EXCRESCENCE

ex·cres·cent \-s°nt\ *adjective* [Latin *excrescent-, excrescens,* present participle of *excrescere* to grow out, from *ex-* + *crescere* to grow — more at CRESCENT] (1633)
1 : forming an abnormal, excessive, or useless outgrowth
2 : of, relating to, or constituting epenthesis
— **ex·cres·cent·ly** *adverb*

ex·cre·ta \ik-'skrē-tə\ *noun plural* [New Latin, from Latin, neuter plural of *excretus*] (1857)
: waste matter eliminated or separated from an organism; especially **:** EXCRETIONS
— **ex·cre·tal** \-'skrē-t°l\ *adjective*

ex·crete \ik-'skrēt\ *transitive verb* **ex·cret·ed; ex·cret·ing** [Latin *excretus,* past participle of *excernere* to sift out, discharge, from *ex-* + *cernere* to sift — more at CERTAIN] (1620)
: to separate and eliminate or discharge (waste) from the blood or tissues or from the active protoplasm
— **ex·cret·er** *noun*

ex·cre·tion \ik-'skrē-shən\ *noun* (1603)
1 : the act or process of excreting
2 : something excreted; *especially* **:** metabolic waste products (as urea and carbon dioxide) that are eliminated from the body and differ from a secretion in not being produced to perform a useful function

ex·cre·to·ry \'ek-skrə-,tōr-ē, -,tòr-\ *adjective* (circa 1681)
: of, relating to, or functioning in excretion ⟨*excretory* ducts⟩

ex·cru·ci·ate \ik-'skrü-shē-,āt\ *transitive verb* **-at·ed; -at·ing** [Latin *excruciatus,* past participle of *excruciare,* from *ex-* + *cruciare* to crucify, from *cruc-, crux* cross] (circa 1570)
1 : to inflict intense pain on **:** TORTURE
2 : to subject to intense mental distress
— **ex·cru·ci·a·tion** \-,skrü-shē-'ā-shən, -sē-\ *noun*

ex·cru·ci·at·ing *adjective* (1599)
1 : causing great pain or anguish **:** AGONIZING ⟨the nation's most *excruciating* dilemma —W. H. Ferry⟩
2 : very intense **:** EXTREME ⟨*excruciating* pain⟩
— **ex·cru·ci·at·ing·ly** \-,ā-tiŋ-lē\ *adverb*

ex·cul·pate \'ek-(,)skəl-,pāt, (,)ek-'\ *transitive verb* **-pat·ed; -pat·ing** [Medieval Latin *exculpatus,* past participle of *exculpare,* from Latin *ex-* + *culpa* blame] (circa 1681)
: to clear from alleged fault or guilt ☆
— **ex·cul·pa·tion** \,ek-(,)skəl-'pā-shən\ *noun*

ex·cul·pa·to·ry \ek-'skəl-pə-,tōr-ē, -,tòr-\ *adjective* (1781)
: tending or serving to exculpate

ex·cur·rent \(,)ek-'skər-ənt, -'skə-rənt\ *adjective* [Latin *excurrent-, excurrens,* present participle of *excurrere* to run out, extend, from *ex-* + *currere* to run — more at CAR] (1826)
1 : characterized by a current that flows outward ⟨*excurrent* canals of a sponge⟩
2 a : having the axis prolonged to form an undivided main stem or trunk (as in conifers) — compare DELIQUESCENT 2 **b :** projecting beyond the apex — used especially of the midrib of a mucronate leaf

ex·cur·sion \ik-'skər-zhən\ *noun* [Latin *excursion-, excursio,* from *excurrere*] (1587)
1 a : a going out or forth **:** EXPEDITION **b** (1) **:** a usually brief pleasure trip (2) **:** a trip at special reduced rates
2 : deviation from a direct, definite, or proper course; *especially* **:** DIGRESSION ⟨needless *excursions* into abstruse theory⟩
3 a : a movement outward and back or from a mean position or axis; *also* **:** the distance traversed **:** AMPLITUDE ⟨the *excursion* of a piston⟩
b : one complete movement of expansion and contraction of the lungs and their membranes (as in breathing)

ex·cur·sion·ist \-'skərzh-nist, -'skər-zhə-\ *noun* (1830)
: a person who goes on an excursion

ex·cur·sive \-'skər-siv\ *adjective* (1749)
: constituting a digression **:** characterized by digression
— **ex·cur·sive·ly** *adverb*

— **ex·cur·sive·ness** *noun*

ex·cur·sus \ik-'skər-səs\ *noun, plural* **ex·cur·sus·es** *also* **ex·cur·sus** \-səs, -ˌsüs\ [Latin, digression, from *excurrere*] (1803)
: an appendix or digression that contains further exposition of some point or topic

ex·cu·sa·to·ry \ik-'skyü-zə-ˌtōr-ē, -ˌtȯr-\ *adjective* (1535)
: making or containing excuse

¹**ex·cuse** \ik-'skyüz, *imperatively often* 'skyüz\ *transitive verb* **ex·cused; ex·cus·ing** [Middle English, from Old French *excuser*, from Latin *excusare*, from *ex-* + *causa* cause, explanation] (13th century)
1 a : to make apology for **b** : to try to remove blame from
2 : to forgive entirely or disregard as of trivial import : regard as excusable ⟨graciously *excused* his tardiness⟩
3 a : to grant exemption or release to ⟨was *excused* from jury duty⟩ **b** : to allow to leave ⟨*excused* the class⟩
4 : to serve as excuse for : JUSTIFY ⟨nothing can *excuse* such neglect⟩ ☆
— **ex·cus·able** \ik-'skyü-zə-bəl\ *adjective*
— **ex·cus·able·ness** *noun*
— **ex·cus·ably** \-blē\ *adverb*
— **ex·cus·er** *noun*

²**ex·cuse** \ik-'skyüs\ *noun* (14th century)
1 : the act of excusing
2 a : something offered as justification or as grounds for being excused **b** *plural* : an expression of regret for failure to do something **c** : a note of explanation of an absence
3 : JUSTIFICATION, REASON
synonym see APOLOGY

ex·di·rec·to·ry \ˌeks-də-'rek-t(ə-)rē, -dī-\ *adjective* [Latin *ex* out of — more at EX-] (1936)
British : not listed in a telephone book : UNLISTED

ex·ec \ig-'zek\ *noun* (1896)
1 : EXECUTIVE OFFICER
2 : EXECUTIVE

ex·e·cra·ble \'ek-si-krə-bəl\ *adjective* (14th century)
1 : deserving to be execrated : DETESTABLE ⟨*execrable* crimes⟩
2 : very bad : WRETCHED ⟨*execrable* hotel food⟩
— **ex·e·cra·ble·ness** *noun*
— **ex·e·cra·bly** \-blē\ *adverb*

ex·e·crate \'ek-sə-ˌkrāt\ *transitive verb* **-crat·ed; -crat·ing** [Latin *exsecratus*, past participle of *exsecrari* to put under a curse, from *ex* + *sacr-, sacer* sacred] (1561)
1 : to declare to be evil or detestable : DENOUNCE
2 : to detest utterly
— **ex·e·cra·tive** \-ˌkrā-tiv\ *adjective*
— **ex·e·cra·tor** \-ˌkrā-tər\ *noun*

ex·e·cra·tion \ˌek-sə-'krā-shən\ *noun* (14th century)
1 : the act of cursing or denouncing; *also* : the curse so uttered
2 : an object of curses : something detested

ex·ec·u·tant \ig-'ze-k(y)ə-tənt\ *noun* (1858)
: one who executes or performs; *especially* : one skilled in the technique of an art : PERFORMER

ex·e·cute \'ek-si-ˌkyüt\ *verb* **-cut·ed; -cut·ing** [Middle English, from Middle French *executer*, back-formation from *execution*] (14th century)
transitive verb
1 : to carry out fully : put completely into effect ⟨*execute* a command⟩
2 : to do what is provided or required by ⟨*execute* a decree⟩
3 : to put to death especially in compliance with a legal sentence
4 : to make or produce (as a work of art) especially by carrying out a design
5 : to perform what is required to give validity to ⟨*execute* a deed⟩
6 : PLAY ⟨*execute* a piece of music⟩

intransitive verb
1 : to perform properly or skillfully the fundamentals of a sport or of a particular play ⟨never had a team *execute* better —Bobby Knight⟩
2 : to perform indicated tasks according to encoded instructions — used of a computer program or routine
synonym see KILL, PERFORM
— **ex·e·cut·able** \-ˌkyü-tə-bəl\ *adjective*

ex·e·cu·tion \ˌek-si-'kyü-shən\ *noun* [Middle English, from Middle French, from Latin *exsecution-, exsecutio*, from *exsequi* to execute, from *ex-* + *sequi* to follow — more at SUE] (14th century)
1 : the act or process of executing : PERFORMANCE
2 : a putting to death especially as a legal penalty
3 : the process of enforcing a legal judgment (as against a debtor); *also* : a judicial writ directing such enforcement
4 : the act or mode or result of performance
5 *archaic* : effective or destructive action ⟨his brandished steel, which smoked with bloody *execution* —Shakespeare⟩ — usually used with *do* ⟨as soon as day came, we went out to see what *execution* we had done —Daniel Defoe⟩

ex·e·cu·tion·er \-sh(ə-)nər\ *noun* (1536)
: one who executes; *especially* : one who puts to death

¹**ex·ec·u·tive** \ig-'ze-k(y)ə-tiv\ *adjective* (1649)
1 a : of or relating to the execution of the laws and the conduct of public and national affairs **b** : belonging to the branch of government that is charged with such powers as diplomatic representation, superintendence of the execution of the laws, and appointment of officials and that usually has some power over legislation (as through veto) — compare JUDICIAL, LEGISLATIVE
2 a : designed for or relating to execution or carrying into effect ⟨*executive* board⟩ **b** : having administrative or managerial responsibility ⟨*executive* director⟩
3 : of or relating to an executive ⟨the *executive* offices⟩

²**executive** *noun* (1774)
1 : the executive branch of a government; *also* : the person or persons who constitute the executive magistracy of a state
2 : a directing or controlling office of an organization
3 : one that exercises administrative or managerial control

executive agreement *noun* (1942)
: an agreement between the U.S. and a foreign government made by the executive branch of the government either alone or with Congressional approval and dealing usually with routine matters

executive council *noun* (1778)
1 : a council constituted to advise or share in the functions of a political executive
2 : a council that exercises supreme executive power

executive officer *noun* (1881)
: the officer second in command of a military or naval organization

executive order *noun* (1883)
: REGULATION 2b

executive privilege *noun* (1940)
: exemption from legally enforced disclosure of communications within the executive branch of government when such disclosure would adversely affect the functions and decision-making processes of the executive branch

executive secretary *noun* (1950)
: a secretary having administrative duties; *especially* : an official responsible for administering the activities and business affairs of an organization

executive session *noun* (1840)

: a usually closed session (as of a legislative body) that functions as an executive council (as of the U.S. Senate when considering appointments or the ratification of treaties)

ex·ec·u·tor \ig-'ze-k(y)ə-tər *or in sense 1* 'ek-sə-ˌkyü-\ *noun* [Middle English, from Old French, from Latin *exsecutor*, from *exsequi*] (13th century)
1 a : one who executes something **b** *obsolete* : EXECUTIONER
2 a : the person appointed by a testator to execute a will **b** : LITERARY EXECUTOR
— **ex·ec·u·to·ri·al** \ig-ˌze-k(y)ə-'tōr-ē-əl, -'tȯr-\ *adjective*

ex·ec·u·to·ry \ig-'ze-k(y)ə-ˌtōr-ē, -ˌtȯr-\ *adjective* (1592)
1 : designed or of such a nature as to be executed in time to come or to take effect on a future contingency
2 : relating to administration

ex·ec·u·trix \ig-'ze-k(y)ə-(ˌ)triks\ *noun, plural* **ex·ec·u·tri·ces** \-ˌze-k(y)ə-'trī-(ˌ)sēz\ *or* **ex·ec·u·trix·es** \-'ze-k(y)ə-ˌtrik-səz\ (15th century)
: a woman who is an executor

ex·e·dra \'ek-sə-drə\ *noun, plural* **-drae** \-ˌdrē, -ˌdrī\ [Latin, from Greek, from *ex-* + *hedra* seat — more at SIT] (1706)
1 : a room (as in a temple or house) in ancient Greece and Rome used for conversation and formed by an open or columned recess often semicircular in shape and furnished with seats
2 : a large outdoor nearly semicircular seat with a solid back

ex·e·ge·sis \ˌek-sə-'jē-səs, 'ek-sə-ˌ\ *noun, plural* **-ge·ses** \-'jē-(ˌ)sēz\ [New Latin, from Greek *exēgēsis*, from *exēgeisthai* to explain, interpret, from *ex-* + *hēgeisthai* to lead — more at SEEK] (1619)
: EXPOSITION, EXPLANATION; *especially* : an explanation or critical interpretation of a text

ex·e·gete \'ek-sə-ˌjēt\ *noun* [Greek *exēgētēs*, from *exēgeisthai*] (circa 1736)
: one who practices exegesis

ex·e·get·i·cal \ˌek-sə-'je-ti-kəl\ *also* **ex·e·get·ic** \-tik\ *adjective* [Greek *exēgētikos*, from *exēgeisthai*] (1623)
: of or relating to exegesis : EXPLANATORY

ex·e·get·ist \-'jē-tist, -'je-\ *noun* (1848)
: EXEGETE

ex·em·plar \ig-'zem-ˌplär, -plər, eg-\ *noun* [Middle English, from Latin, from *exemplum* example] (15th century)

☆ **SYNONYMS**
Excuse, condone, pardon, forgive
mean to exact neither punishment nor redress. EXCUSE may refer to specific acts especially in social or conventional situations or the person responsible for these ⟨*excuse* an interruption⟩ ⟨*excused* them for interrupting⟩. Often the term implies extenuating circumstances ⟨injustice *excuses* strong responses⟩. CONDONE implies that one overlooks without censure behavior (as dishonesty or violence) that involves a serious breach of a moral, ethical, or legal code, and the term may refer to the behavior or to the agent responsible for it ⟨a society that *condones* alcohol but not narcotics⟩. PARDON implies that one remits a penalty due for an admitted or established offense ⟨*pardon* a criminal⟩. FORGIVE implies that one gives up all claim to requital and to resentment or vengeful feelings ⟨could not *forgive* their rudeness⟩.

\ə\ abut \ᵊ\ kitten \ər\ further \a\ ash \ā\ ace \ä\ mop, mar \au̇\ out \ch\ chin \e\ bet \ē\ easy \g\ go \i\ hit \ī\ ice \j\ job \ŋ\ sing \ō\ go \ȯ\ law \ȯi\ boy \th\ thin \t͟h\ the \ü\ loot \u̇\ foot \y\ yet \zh\ vision *see also* Guide to Pronunciation

: one that serves as a model or example: as **a** : an ideal model **b** : a typical or standard specimen **c** : a copy of a book or writing **d** : IDEA 1a

synonym see MODEL

ex·em·pla·ry \ig-'zem-plə-rē\ *adjective* (1589)
1 a : serving as a pattern **b** : deserving imitation : COMMENDABLE ⟨his courage was *exemplary*⟩; *also* : deserving imitation because of excellence ⟨they serve *exemplary* pastries —G. V. Higgins⟩
2 : serving as a warning : MONITORY
3 : serving as an example, instance, or illustration
— **ex·em·plar·i·ly** \eg-,zem-'pler-ə-lē\ *adverb*
— **ex·em·pla·ri·ness** \ig-'zem-plə-rē-nəs\ *noun*
— **ex·em·plar·i·ty** \eg-,zem-'plar-ə-tē\ *noun*

ex·em·pli·fi·ca·tion \ig-,zem-plə-fə-'kā-shən\ *noun* (1510)
1 a : the act or process of exemplifying **b** : EXAMPLE, CASE IN POINT
2 : an exemplified copy of a document

ex·em·pli·fy \ig-'zem-plə-,fī\ *transitive verb* **-fied; -fy·ing** [Middle English *exemplifien*, from Middle French *exemplifier*, from Medieval Latin *exemplificare*, from Latin *exemplum*] (15th century)
1 : to show or illustrate by example
2 : to make an attested copy or transcript of (a document) under seal
3 a : to be an instance of or serve as an example : EMBODY **b** : to be typical of

ex·em·pli gra·tia \ig-,zem-(,)plē-'grä-tē-,ä, -'grā-sh(ē-)ə\ *adverb* [Latin] (1602)
: for example

ex·em·plum \ig-'zem-pləm, eg-\ *noun, plural* **-pla** \-plə\ [Latin] (1890)
1 : EXAMPLE, MODEL
2 : an anecdote or short narrative used to point a moral or sustain an argument

¹ex·empt \ig-'zem(p)t\ *adjective* [Middle English, from Latin *exemptus*, past participle of *eximere* to take out — more at EXAMPLE] (14th century)
1 *obsolete* : set apart
2 : free or released from some liability or requirement to which others are subject ⟨was *exempt* from jury duty⟩ ⟨the estate was *exempt* from taxes⟩

²exempt *transitive verb* (15th century)
1 : to release or deliver from some liability or requirement to which others are subject : EXCUSE ⟨a man *exempted* from military service⟩
2 *obsolete* : to set apart

³exempt *noun* (1670)
: one exempted or freed from duty

ex·emp·tion \ig-'zem(p)-shən\ *noun* (14th century)
1 : the act of exempting or state of being exempt : IMMUNITY
2 : one that exempts or is exempted; *especially* : a source or amount of income exempted from taxation

ex·en·ter·ate \ig-'zen-tə-,rāt\ *transitive verb* **-at·ed; -at·ing** [Latin *exenteratus*, past participle of *exenterare* to disembowel, modification of Greek *exenterizein*, from *ex-* + *enteron* intestine — more at INTER-] (1607)
: to remove the contents of (as the orbit or pelvis)
— **ex·en·ter·a·tion** \-,zen-tə-'rā-shən\ *noun*

¹ex·er·cise \'ek-sər-,sīz\ *noun* [Middle English, from Middle French *exercice*, from Latin *exercitium*, from *exercitare* to train, exercise, frequentative of *exercēre* to train, occupy, from *ex-* + *arcēre* to enclose, hold off — more at ARK] (14th century)

1 a : the act of bringing into play or realizing in action : USE **b** : the discharge of an official function or professional occupation **c** : the act or an instance of carrying out the terms of an agreement (as an option)
2 a : regular or repeated use of a faculty or bodily organ **b** : bodily exertion for the sake of developing and maintaining physical fitness
3 : something performed or practiced in order to develop, improve, or display a specific power or skill ⟨arithmetic *exercises*⟩
4 : a performance having a strongly marked secondary or ulterior aspect ⟨party politics has always been an *exercise* in compromise —H. S. Ashmore⟩
5 a : a maneuver, operation, or drill carried out for training and discipline **b** *plural* : a program including speeches, announcements of awards and honors, and various traditional practices of secular or religious character ⟨commencement *exercises*⟩

²exercise *verb* **-cised; -cis·ing** (14th century)
transitive verb
1 a : to make effective in action : USE ⟨didn't *exercise* good judgment⟩ **b** : to bring to bear : EXERT ⟨*exercise* influence⟩ **c** : to implement the terms of (as an option)
2 a : to use repeatedly in order to strengthen or develop **b** : to train (as troops) by drills and maneuvers **c** : to put through exercises ⟨*exercise* the horses⟩
3 a : to engage the attention and effort of **b** : to cause anxiety, alarm, or indignation in ⟨the issues *exercising* voters this year⟩
intransitive verb
: to take exercise
— **ex·er·cis·able** \-,sī-zə-bəl\ *adjective*

ex·er·cis·er \'ek-sər-,sī-zər\ *noun* (1552)
1 : one that exercises
2 : an apparatus for use in physical exercise

ex·er·ci·ta·tion \ig-,zər-sə-'tā-shən\ *noun* [Middle English *exercitacioun*, from Latin *exercitation-, exercitatio*, from *exercitare*] (14th century)
: EXERCISE

Ex·er·cy·cle \'ek-sər-,sī-kəl\ *trademark*
— used for a stationary bicycle

ex·er·gon·ic \,ek-(,)sər-'gä-nik\ *adjective* [*exo-* + Greek *ergon* work — more at WORK] (1940)
: EXOTHERMIC ⟨an *exergonic* biochemical reaction⟩

ex·ergue \'ek-,sərg, 'eg-,zərg\ *noun* [French, from New Latin *exergum*, from Greek *ex* out of + *ergon* work] (1697)
: a space on a coin, token, or medal usually on the reverse below the central part of the design

ex·ert \ig-'zərt\ *transitive verb* [Latin *exsertus*, past participle of *exserere* to thrust out, from *ex-* + *serere* to join — more at SERIES] (1681)
1 a : to put forth (as strength) **b** : to put (oneself) into action or to tiring effort
2 : to bring to bear especially with sustained effort or lasting effect
3 : EMPLOY, WIELD ⟨*exerted* her leadership abilities intelligently⟩

ex·er·tion \ig-'zər-shən\ *noun* (1677)
: the act or an instance of exerting; *especially* : a laborious or perceptible effort

ex·e·unt \'ek-sē-(,)ənt, -,ùnt\ [Latin, they go out, from *exire* to go out — more at EXIT] (15th century)
— used as a stage direction to specify that all or certain named characters leave the stage

ex·fo·li·ate \(,)eks-'fō-lē-,āt\ *verb* **-at·ed; -at·ing** [Late Latin *exfoliatus*, past participle of *exfoliare* to strip of leaves, from Latin *ex-* + *folium* leaf — more at BLADE] (1612)
transitive verb
1 : to cast off in scales, laminae, or splinters
2 : to remove the surface of in scales or laminae
3 : to spread or extend by or as if by opening out leaves
intransitive verb

1 : to split into or give off scales, laminae, or body cells
2 : to come off in thin layers or scales
3 : to grow by or as if by producing or unfolding leaves
— **ex·fo·li·a·tion** \(,)eks-,fō-lē-'ā-shən\ *noun*
— **ex·fo·li·a·tive** \eks-'fō-lē-,ā-tiv\ *adjective*

ex gra·tia \(,)eks-'grā-sh(ē-)ə\ *adjective or adverb* [New Latin] (1769)
: as a favor : not compelled by legal right ⟨*ex gratia* pension payments⟩

ex·hal·ant *or* **ex·hal·ent** \eks-'hā-lənt, ek-'sā-\ *adjective* (1771)
: bearing out or outward : EMISSIVE ⟨an *exhalant* siphon of a clam⟩

ex·ha·la·tion \,eks-hə-'lā-shən, ,ek-sə-\ *noun* (14th century)
1 : something exhaled or given off : EMANATION
2 : an act of exhaling

ex·hale \eks-'hā(ə)l, ek-'sā(ə)l\ *verb* **ex·haled; ex·hal·ing** [Middle English *exalen*, from Latin *exhalare*, from *ex-* + *halare* to breathe] (14th century)
intransitive verb
1 : to rise or be given off as vapor
2 : to emit breath or vapor
transitive verb
1 a : to breathe out **b** : to give forth (gaseous matter) : EMIT
2 *archaic* : to cause to be emitted in vapor

¹ex·haust \ig-'zòst\ *verb* [Latin *exhaustus*, past participle of *exhaurire*, from *ex-* + *haurire* to draw; akin to Middle High German *œsen* to empty, Greek *auein* to take] (1533)
transitive verb
1 a : to consume entirely : USE UP ⟨*exhausted* our funds in a week⟩ **b** : to tire extremely or completely ⟨*exhausted* by overwork⟩ **c** : to deprive of a valuable quality or constituent ⟨*exhaust* a photographic developer⟩ ⟨*exhaust* a soil of fertility⟩
2 a : to draw off or let out completely **b** : to empty by drawing off the contents; *specifically* : to create a vacuum in
3 a : to develop (a subject) completely **b** : to try out the whole number of ⟨*exhausted* all the possibilities⟩
intransitive verb
: DISCHARGE, EMPTY ⟨the engine *exhausts* through the muffler⟩

synonym see DEPLETE, TIRE
— **ex·haust·er** *noun*
— **ex·haust·ibil·i·ty** \-,zò-stə-'bi-lə-tē\ *noun*
— **ex·haust·ible** \-'zò-stə-bəl\ *adjective*

²exhaust *noun* (1848)
1 a : the escape of used gas or vapor from an engine **b** : the gas or vapor thus escaping
2 a : the conduit through which used gases escape **b** : an arrangement for removing fumes, dusts, or odors from an enclosure
3 : EXHAUSTION

ex·haus·tion \ig-'zòs-chən\ *noun* (1646)
: the act or process of exhausting : the state of being exhausted

ex·haus·tive \ig-'zò-stiv\ *adjective* (1786)
: testing all possibilities or considering all elements : THOROUGH ⟨conducted an *exhaustive* investigation⟩
— **ex·haus·tive·ly** *adverb*
— **ex·haus·tive·ness** *noun*
— **ex·haus·tiv·i·ty** \-,zò-'sti-və-tē\ *noun*

ex·haust·less \ig-'zòst-ləs\ *adjective* (1712)
: not to be exhausted : INEXHAUSTIBLE
— **ex·haust·less·ly** *adverb*
— **ex·haust·less·ness** *noun*

¹ex·hib·it \ig-'zi-bət\ *verb* [Middle English, from Latin *exhibitus*, past participle of *exhibēre*, from *ex-* + *habēre* to have, hold — more at GIVE] (15th century)
transitive verb

exhibit 639 **ex libris**

1 : to submit (as a document) to a court or officer in course of proceedings; *also* **:** to present or offer officially or in legal form **2 :** to present to view: as **a :** to show or display outwardly especially by visible signs or actions ⟨*exhibited* no fear⟩ **b :** to have as a readily discernible quality or feature ⟨in all cultures we know, men *exhibit* an aesthetic sense —H. J. Muller⟩ **c :** to show publicly especially for purposes of competition or demonstration
intransitive verb
: to display something for public inspection
synonym see SHOW
— **ex·hib·i·tive** \-bə-tiv\ *adjective*
— **ex·hib·i·tor** \-bə-tər\ *noun*
— **ex·hib·i·to·ry** \-bə-ˌtōr-ē, -ˌtȯr-\ *adjective*

²**exhibit** *noun* (1626)
1 : a document or material object produced and identified in court or before an examiner for use as evidence
2 : something exhibited
3 : an act or instance of exhibiting
ex·hi·bi·tion \ˌek-sə-ˈbi-shən\ *noun* (14th century)
1 : an act or instance of exhibiting
2 *British* **:** a grant drawn from the funds of a school or university to help maintain a student
3 : a public showing (as of works of art, objects of manufacture, or athletic skill) ⟨a one-man *exhibition*⟩ ⟨an *exhibition* game⟩
ex·hi·bi·tion·er \-ˈbish-nər, -ˈbi-shə-\ *noun* (1679)
British **:** one who holds a grant from a school or university
ex·hi·bi·tion·ism \-ˈbi-shə-ˌni-zəm\ *noun* (1893)
1 a : a perversion marked by a tendency to indecent exposure **b :** an act of such exposure
2 : the act or practice of behaving so as to attract attention to oneself
— **ex·hi·bi·tion·ist** \-ˈbish-nist, -ˈbi-shə-\ *noun or adjective*
— **ex·hi·bi·tion·is·tic** \-ˌbi-shə-ˈnis-tik\ *adjective*
— **ex·hi·bi·tion·is·ti·cal·ly** \-ti-k(ə-)lē\ *adverb*
ex·hil·a·rate \ig-ˈzi-lə-ˌrāt\ *transitive verb* **-rat·ed; -rat·ing** [Latin *exhilaratus*, past participle of *exhilarare*, from *ex-* + *hilarare* to gladden, from *hilarus* cheerful — more at HILARIOUS] (1540)
1 a : to make cheerful **b :** ENLIVEN, EXCITE
2 : REFRESH, STIMULATE
— **ex·hil·a·rat·ing·ly** \ig-ˈzi-lə-ˌrā-tiŋ-lē\ *adverb*
— **ex·hil·a·ra·tive** \-ˌrā-tiv\ *adjective*
ex·hil·a·ra·tion \ig-ˌzi-lə-ˈrā-shən\ *noun* (circa 1626)
1 : the action of exhilarating
2 : the feeling or the state of being exhilarated
ex·hort \ig-ˈzȯrt\ *verb* [Middle English, from Middle French *exhorter*, from Latin *exhortari*, from *ex-* + *hortari* to incite — more at YEARN] (15th century)
transitive verb
: to incite by argument or advice **:** urge strongly
intransitive verb
: to give warnings or advice **:** make urgent appeals
— **ex·hort·er** *noun*
ex·hor·ta·tion \ˌek-ˌsȯr-ˈtā-shən, -sər-; ˌeg-ˌzȯr-, -zər-\ *noun* (14th century)
1 : an act or instance of exhorting
2 : language intended to incite and encourage
ex·hor·ta·tive \ig-ˈzȯr-tə-tiv\ *adjective* (15th century)
: serving to exhort
ex·hor·ta·to·ry \-tə-ˌtōr-ē, -ˌtȯr-\ *adjective* (15th century)
: using exhortation **:** EXHORTATIVE ⟨an *exhortatory* appeal⟩
ex·hume \ig-ˈzüm, igz-ˈyüm, iks-ˈ(h)yüm\ *transitive verb* **ex·humed; ex·hum·ing**

[French or Medieval Latin; French *exhumer*, from Medieval Latin *exhumare*, from Latin *ex* out of + *humus* earth — more at EX-, HUMBLE] (15th century)
1 : DISINTER
2 : to bring back from neglect or obscurity
— **ex·hu·ma·tion** \ˌeks-(h)yü-ˈmā-shən, ˌeg-zü-, ˌegz-yü-\ *noun*
— **ex·hum·er** \ig-ˈzü-mər, igz-ˈyü-, iks-ˈ(h)yü-\ *noun*
ex hy·po·the·si \ˌeks-hī-ˈpä-thə-ˌsī\ *adverb* [New Latin, from a hypothesis] (1603)
: according to assumptions made **:** by hypothesis ⟨regard . . . all elites as *ex hypothesi* incompatible with democracy —P. G. J. Pulzer⟩
ex·i·gence \ˈek-sə-jən(t)s\ *noun* (15th century)
: EXIGENCY
ex·i·gen·cy \ˈek-sə-jən(t)-sē, ig-ˈzi-jən(t)-\ *noun, plural* **-cies** (1581)
1 : that which is required in a particular situation — usually used in plural
2 a : the quality or state of being exigent **b :** a state of affairs that makes urgent demands ⟨a leader must act in any sudden *exigency*⟩
synonym see JUNCTURE
ex·i·gent \ˈek-sə-jənt\ *adjective* [Latin *exigent-, exigens*, present participle of *exigere* to demand — more at EXACT] (1629)
1 : requiring immediate aid or action
2 : requiring or calling for much **:** DEMANDING
— **ex·i·gent·ly** *adverb*
ex·i·gu·i·ty \ˌeg-zi-ˈgyü-ə-tē\ *noun, plural* **-ities** (circa 1626)
: the quality or state of being exiguous **:** SCANTINESS
ex·ig·u·ous \ig-ˈzi-gyə-wəs\ *adjective* [Latin *exiguus*, from *exigere*] (1651)
: excessively scanty **:** INADEQUATE ⟨wrest an *exiguous* existence from the land⟩ ⟨*exiguous* evidence⟩
— **ex·ig·u·ous·ly** *adverb*
— **ex·ig·u·ous·ness** *noun*
¹**ex·ile** \ˈeg-ˌzīl, ˈek-ˌsīl\ *noun* [Middle English *exil*, from Middle French, from Latin *exilium* from *exul, exsul* an exile] (14th century)
1 a : the state or a period of forced absence from one's country or home **b :** the state or a period of voluntary absence from one's country or home
2 : a person who is in exile
— **ex·il·ic** \eg-ˈzi-lik\ *adjective*
²**exile** *transitive verb* **ex·iled; ex·il·ing** (14th century)
: to banish or expel from one's own country or home
synonym see BANISH
ex·im·i·ous \eg-ˈzi-mē-əs\ *adjective* [Latin *eximius*, from *eximere* to take out — more at EXAMPLE] (1547)
archaic **:** CHOICE, EXCELLENT
ex·ine \ˈek-ˌsēn, -ˌsīn\ *noun* [International Scientific Vocabulary *ex-* + *in-* fibrous tissue, from Greek *in-, is* tendon] (circa 1884)
: the outer of the two major layers forming the walls of some spores and especially pollen grains
ex·ist \ig-ˈzist\ *intransitive verb* [Latin *exsistere* to come into being, exist, from *ex-* + *sistere* to stand, stop; akin to Latin *stare* to stand — more at STAND] (1602)
1 a : to have real being whether material or spiritual ⟨did unicorns *exist*⟩ ⟨the largest galaxy known to *exist*⟩ **b :** to have being in a specified place or with respect to understood limitations or conditions ⟨strange ideas *existed* in his mind⟩
2 : to continue to be ⟨racism still *exists* in society⟩
3 a : to have life or the functions of vitality ⟨we cannot *exist* without oxygen⟩ **b :** to live at an inferior level or under adverse circumstances ⟨the hungry *existing* from day to day⟩
ex·is·tence \ig-ˈzis-tən(t)s\ *noun* (14th century)

1 a *obsolete* **:** reality as opposed to appearance **b :** reality as presented in experience **c** (1) **:** the totality of existent things (2) **:** a particular being ⟨all the fair *existences* of heaven —John Keats⟩ **d :** sentient or living being **:** LIFE
2 a : the state or fact of having being especially independently of human consciousness and as contrasted with nonexistence **b :** the manner of being that is common to every mode of being **c :** being with respect to a limiting condition or under a particular aspect
3 : continued or repeated manifestation
ex·is·tent \-tənt\ *adjective* [Latin *existent-, exsistens*, present participle of *exsistere*] (1561)
1 : having being **:** EXISTING
2 : existing now **:** PRESENT
— **existent** *noun*
ex·is·ten·tial \ˌeg-(ˌ)zis-ˈten(t)-shəl, ˌek-(ˌ)sis-\ *adjective* (1693)
1 : of, relating to, or affirming existence ⟨*existential* propositions⟩
2 a : grounded in existence or the experience of existence **:** EMPIRICAL **b :** having being in time and space
3 [translation of Danish *eksistentiel* & German *existential*] **:** EXISTENTIALIST
— **ex·is·ten·tial·ly** *adverb*
ex·is·ten·tial·ism \-ˈten(t)-shə-ˌli-zəm\ *noun* (1941)
: a chiefly 20th century philosophical movement embracing diverse doctrines but centering on analysis of individual existence in an unfathomable universe and the plight of the individual who must assume ultimate responsibility for his acts of free will without any certain knowledge of what is right or wrong or good or bad
¹**ex·is·ten·tial·ist** \-list\ *noun* (1942)
: an adherent of existentialism
²**existentialist** *adjective* (1946)
: of or relating to existentialism or existentialists
— **ex·is·ten·tial·is·tic** \-ˌten(t)-shə-ˈlis-tik\ *adjective*
— **ex·is·ten·tial·is·ti·cal·ly** \-ti-k(ə-)lē\ *adverb*
existential quantifier *noun* (1940)
: a quantifier (as *for some* in "for some x, 2x + 5 = 8") that asserts that there exists at least one value of a variable — called also *existential operator*
¹**ex·it** \ˈeg-zət, ˈek-sət\ [Latin, he goes out, from *exire* to go out, from *ex-* + *ire* to go — more at ISSUE] (1538)
— used as a stage direction to specify who goes off stage
²**exit** *noun* [Latin *exitus*, from *exire*] (1588)
1 [¹*exit*] **:** a departure from a stage
2 a : the act of going out or going away **b :** DEATH
3 : a way out of an enclosed place or space
4 : one of the designated points of departure from an expressway
— **ex·it·less** *adjective*
³**exit** (1607)
intransitive verb
1 : to go out or away **:** DEPART
2 : DIE
transitive verb
: LEAVE 3a
exit poll *noun* (1980)
: a poll taken (as by news media) of voters leaving the voting place that is usually used for predicting the winners
— **exit polling** *noun*
ex li·bris \eks-ˈlē-brəs, -ˈbrēs\ *noun, plural* **ex libris** [New Latin, from the books; used before the owner's name on bookplates] (1880)
: BOOKPLATE

\ə\ abut	\ᵊ\ kitten	\ər\ further	\a\ ash	\ā\ ace	
\ä\ mop, mar	\au̇\ out	\ch\ chin	\e\ bet	\ē\ easy	
\g\ go	\i\ hit	\ī\ ice	\j\ job	\ŋ\ sing	\ō\ go
\ȯ\ law	\ȯi\ boy	\th\ thin	\t̶h\ the	\ü\ loot	\u̇\ foot
\y\ yet	\zh\ vision			*see also* Guide to Pronunciation	

Ex·moor \'ek-ˌsmu̇r, -ˌsmȯr, -ˌsmȯr\ *noun* [*Exmoor*, England] (1808)

1 : any of a breed of horned sheep of Devonshire in England valued especially for mutton
2 : any of a breed of hardy ponies native to the Exmoor district and having a mealy-colored muzzle

Exmoor 1

ex ni·hi·lo \(ˌ)eks-'nē-(h)ə-ˌlō, -'ni-, -'nī-\ *adverb or adjective* [Latin] (1580)
: from or out of nothing ⟨creation *ex nihilo*⟩

exo- or **ex-** *combining form* [Greek *exō* out, outside, from *ex* out of — more at EX-]
1 : outside ⟨*exogamy*⟩ **:** outer ⟨*exoskeleton*⟩ — compare ECT-, END-
2 : turning out ⟨*exo*ergic⟩

exo·bi·ol·o·gy \ˌek-sō-bī-'ä-lə-jē\ *noun* (1960)
: a branch of biology concerned with the search for life outside the earth and with the effects of extraterrestrial environments on living organisms
— **exo·bi·o·log·i·cal** \-ˌbī-ə-'lä-ji-kəl\ *adjective*
— **exo·bi·ol·o·gist** \-bī-'ä-lə-jist\ *noun*

exo·carp \'ek-sō-ˌkärp\ *noun* [International Scientific Vocabulary] (circa 1845)
: the outermost layer of the pericarp of a fruit — see ENDOCARP illustration

exo·crine \'ek-sə-krən, -ˌkrīn, -ˌkrēn\ *adjective* [International Scientific Vocabulary *exo-* + Greek *krinein* to separate — more at CERTAIN] (circa 1911)
: producing, being, or relating to a secretion that is released outside its source ⟨*exocrine* pancreatic cells⟩

exocrine gland *noun* (circa 1927)
: a gland (as a salivary gland or part of the pancreas) that releases a secretion external to or at the surface of an organ by means of a canal or duct

exo·cy·clic \ˌek-sō-'sī-klik, -'si-\ *adjective* (1888)
: situated outside of a ring in a chemical structure

exo·cy·to·sis \ˌek-sō-sī-'tō-səs\ *noun, plural* **-to·ses** \-ˌsēz\ [New Latin, from *exo-* + *cyt-* + *-osis*] (1963)
: the release of cellular substances (as secretory products) contained in cell vesicles by fusion of the vesicular membrane with the plasma membrane and subsequent release of the contents to the exterior of the cell
— **exo·cy·tot·ic** \-'tä-tik\ *adjective*

exo·der·mis \ˌek-sō-'dər-məs\ *noun* [New Latin] (circa 1900)
: a layer of the outer living cortical cells of plants that takes over the functions of the epidermis in roots lacking secondary thickening

ex·odon·tia \ˌek-sə-'dän(t)-sh(ē-)ə\ *noun* [New Latin, from *ex-* + *-odontia*] (1913)
: a branch of dentistry that deals with the extraction of teeth
— **ex·odon·tist** \-'dän-tist\ *noun*

ex·o·dus \'ek-sə-dəs, 'eg-zə-\ *noun* [Latin, from Greek *Exodos*, literally, road out, from *ex-* + *hodos* road]
1 *capitalized* **:** the mainly narrative second book of canonical Jewish and Christian Scripture — see BIBLE table
2 : a mass departure **:** EMIGRATION

exo·en·zyme \ˌek-sō-'en-ˌzīm\ *noun* [International Scientific Vocabulary] (circa 1923)
: an extracellular enzyme

exo·er·gic \ˌek-sō-'ər-jik\ *adjective* (1942)
: releasing energy **:** EXOTHERMIC

exo·eryth·ro·cyt·ic \ˌek-sō-i-ˌri-thrə-'si-tik\ *adjective* (1942)
: occurring outside the red blood cells — used especially of stages of malaria parasites

ex of·fi·cio \ˌek-sə-'fi-shē-ˌō, -sē-\ *adverb or adjective* [Late Latin] (1533)
: by virtue or because of an office ⟨the Vice President serves *ex officio* as president of the Senate⟩

ex·og·a·my \ek-'sä-gə-mē\ *noun, plural* **-mies** (1865)
: marriage outside of a specific group especially as required by custom or law
— **ex·og·a·mous** \ek-'sä-gə-məs\ or **exo·gam·ic** \ˌek-sə-'ga-mik\ *adjective*

ex·og·e·nous \ek-'sä-jə-nəs\ *adjective* [French *exogène* exogenous, from *exo-* + *-gène* (from Greek *-genēs* born) — more at -GEN] (1830)
1 : produced by growth from superficial tissue ⟨*exogenous* roots produced by leaves⟩
2 a : caused by factors (as food or a traumatic factor) or an agent (as a disease-producing organism) from outside the organism or system ⟨*exogenous* obesity⟩ ⟨*exogenous* psychic depression⟩ **b :** introduced from or produced outside the organism or system; *specifically* **:** not synthesized within the organism or system
— **ex·og·e·nous·ly** *adverb*

ex·on \'ek-ˌsän\ *noun* [*expressed sequence* + [2]*-on*] (circa 1978)
: a polynucleotide sequence in a nucleic acid that codes information for protein synthesis and that is copied and spliced together with other such sequences to form messenger RNA — compare INTRON
— **ex·on·ic** \ig-'zä-nə-ˌrāt, eg-\ *adjective*

ex·on·er·ate \ig-'zä-nə-ˌrāt, eg-\ *transitive verb* **-at·ed; -at·ing** [Middle English, from Latin *exoneratus*, past participle of *exonerare* to unburden, from *ex-* + *oner-, onus* load] (1524)
1 : to relieve of a responsibility, obligation, or hardship
2 : to clear from accusation or blame
synonym see EXCULPATE
— **ex·on·er·a·tion** \-ˌzä-nə-'rā-shən\ *noun*
— **ex·on·er·a·tive** \-'zä-nə-ˌrā-tiv\ *adjective*

exo·nu·cle·ase \ˌek-sō-'nü-klē-ˌās, -'nyü-, -ˌāz\ *noun* (1963)
: an enzyme that breaks down a nucleic acid by removing nucleotides one by one from the end of a chain — compare ENDONUCLEASE

exo·nu·mia \ˌek-sō-'nü-mē-ə, -'nyü-\ *noun plural* [New Latin, from *exo-* + English *numismatic* + New Latin *-ia*] (1966)
: numismatic items (as tokens, medals, or scrip) other than coins and paper money

exo·pep·ti·dase \-'pep-tə-ˌdās, -ˌdāz\ *noun* (1936)
: any of a group of enzymes that hydrolyze peptide bonds formed by the terminal amino acids of peptide chains **:** PEPTIDASE — compare ENDOPEPTIDASE

ex·oph·thal·mos also **ex·oph·thal·mus** \ˌek-ˌsäf-'thal-məs, -səf-, -ˌsäp-\ *noun* [New Latin, from Greek *exophthalmos* having prominent eyes, from *ex* out + *ophthalmos* eye; akin to Greek *ōps* eye — more at EYE] (1872)
: abnormal protrusion of the eyeball
— **ex·oph·thal·mic** \-mik\ *adjective*

ex·or·bi·tance \ig-'zȯr-bə-tən(t)s\ *noun* (1611)
1 : an exorbitant action or procedure; *especially* **:** excessive or gross deviation from rule, right, or propriety
2 : the tendency or disposition to be exorbitant

ex·or·bi·tant \-tənt\ *adjective* [Middle English, from Middle French, from Late Latin *exorbitant-, exorbitans*, present participle of *exorbitare* to deviate, from Latin *ex-* + *orbita* track of a wheel, rut, from *orbis* disk, hoop] (15th century)
1 : not coming within the scope of the law
2 : exceeding in intensity, quality, amount, or size the customary or appropriate limits
synonym see EXCESSIVE

ex·or·bi·tant·ly *adverb*

ex·or·cise also **ex·or·cize** \'ek-ˌsȯr-ˌsīz, -sər-\ *transitive verb* **-cised** also **-cized; -cis·ing** also **-ciz·ing** [Middle English, from Middle French *exorciser*, from Late Latin *exorcizare*, from Greek *exorkizein*, from *ex-* + *horkizein* to bind by oath, adjure, from *horkos* oath] (1539)
1 a : to expel (an evil spirit) by adjuration **b :** to get rid of (something troublesome, menacing, or oppressive)
2 : to free of an evil spirit
— **ex·or·cis·er** *noun*

ex·or·cism \-ˌsi-zəm\ *noun* (14th century)
1 : the act or practice of exorcising
2 : a spell or formula used in exorcising
— **ex·or·cist** \-ˌsist, -səst\ *noun*
— **ex·or·cis·tic** \ˌek-ˌsȯr-'sis-tik, -sər-\ or **ex·or·cis·ti·cal** \-ti-kəl\ *adjective*

ex·or·di·um \eg-'zȯr-dē-əm\ *noun, plural* **-diums** or **-dia** \-dē-ə\ [Latin, from *exordiri* to begin, from *ex-* + *ordiri* to begin — more at ORDER] (1577)
: a beginning or introduction especially to a discourse or composition
— **ex·or·di·al** \-dē-əl\ *adjective*

exo·skel·e·ton \ˌek-sō-'ske-lə-t³n\ *noun* (1847)
1 : an external supportive covering of an animal (as an arthropod)
2 : bony or horny parts of a vertebrate produced from epidermal tissues
— **exo·skel·e·tal** \-lə-t³l\ *adjective*

exo·sphere \'ek-sō-ˌsfir\ *noun* [International Scientific Vocabulary] (1949)
: the outer fringe region of the atmosphere of the earth or a planet
— **exo·spher·ic** \ˌek-sō-'sfir-ik, -'sfer-\ *adjective*

exo·spore \'ek-sə-ˌspōr, -ˌspȯr\ *noun* [International Scientific Vocabulary] (1859)
: an asexual spore cut off from a parent sporophore by the formation of septa

ex·os·to·sis \ˌek-(ˌ)säs-'tō-səs\ *noun, plural* **-to·ses** \-ˌsēz\ [New Latin, from Greek *exostōsis*, from *ex* out of + *osteon* bone — more at EX-, OSSEOUS] (1736)
: a spur or bony outgrowth from a bone or the root of a tooth

ex·o·ter·ic \ˌek-sə-'ter-ik\ *adjective* [Latin & Greek; Latin *exotericus*, from Greek *exōterikos*, literally, external, from *exōterō* more outside, comparative of *exō* outside — more at EXO-] (1660)
1 a : suitable to be imparted to the public ⟨the *exoteric* doctrine⟩ — compare ESOTERIC **b :** belonging to the outer or less initiate circle
2 : relating to the outside **:** EXTERNAL
— **ex·o·ter·i·cal·ly** \-i-k(ə-)lē\ *adverb*

exo·ther·mal \ˌek-sō-'thər-məl\ (1906)
: EXOTHERMIC
— **exo·ther·mal·ly** \-mə-lē\ *adverb*

exo·ther·mic \-mik\ *adjective* [International Scientific Vocabulary] (1884)
: characterized by or formed with evolution of heat
— **exo·ther·mi·cal·ly** \-mi-k(ə-)lē\ *adverb*
— **exo·ther·mi·ci·ty** \-ˌthər-'mis-ə-tē\ *noun*

[1]**ex·ot·ic** \ig-'zä-tik\ *adjective* [Latin *exoticus*, from Greek *exōtikos*, from *exō*] (1599)
1 : introduced from another country **:** not native to the place where found
2 *archaic* **:** FOREIGN, ALIEN
3 : strikingly, excitingly, or mysteriously different or unusual
4 : of or relating to striptease ⟨*exotic* dancing⟩
— **ex·ot·i·cal·ly** \-ti-k(ə-)lē\ *adverb*
— **ex·ot·ic·ness** \-tik-nəs\ *noun*

[2]**exotic** *noun* (1645)
1 : one (as a plant or animal) that is exotic
2 : STRIPTEASER

ex·ot·i·ca \ig-'zä-ti-kə\ *noun plural* [New Latin, from Latin, neuter plural of *exoticus*] (1876)

: things excitingly different or unusual; *especially* : literary or artistic items having an exotic theme or nature

ex·ot·i·cism \ig-'zä-tə-ˌsi-zəm\ *also* **ex·o·tism** \'eg-zə-ˌti-zəm, 'ek-sə-\ *noun* (1827)
: the quality or state of being exotic

exo·tox·in \ˌek-sō-'täk-sən\ *noun* [International Scientific Vocabulary] (1920)
: a soluble poisonous substance produced during growth of a microorganism and released into the surrounding medium

ex·pand \ik-'spand\ *verb* [Middle English expaunden, from Latin expandere, from ex- + pandere to spread — more at FATHOM] (15th century)
transitive verb
1 : to open up : UNFOLD
2 : to increase the extent, number, volume, or scope of : ENLARGE
3 a : to express at length or in greater detail **b :** to write out in full ⟨expand all abbreviations⟩ **c :** to subject to mathematical expansion ⟨expand a function in a power series⟩
intransitive verb
1 : to open out : SPREAD
2 : to increase in extent, number, volume, or scope
3 : to speak or write fully or in detail ⟨expanded on the theme⟩
4 : to feel generous or optimistic ☆
— **ex·pand·abil·i·ty** \-ˌspan-də-'bi-lə-tē\ *noun*
— **ex·pand·able** \-'span-də-bəl\ *adjective*

ex·pand·ed *adjective* (1875)
of a typeface : EXTENDED

expanded metal *noun* (1890)
: sheet metal cut and expanded into a lattice and used especially as lath

expanded plastic *noun* (1945)
: lightweight cellular plastic used especially as insulation and protective packing material — called also *foamed plastic, plastic foam*

ex·pand·er \ik-'span-dər\ *noun* (1862)
: one that expands; *specifically* : any of several colloidal substances (as dextran) of high molecular weight used as a blood or plasma substitute for increasing the blood volume

ex·panse \ik-'span(t)s\ *noun* [New Latin expansum, from Latin, neuter of expansus, past participle of expandere] (1667)
1 : FIRMAMENT
2 : great extent of something spread out ⟨an expanse of calm ocean⟩

ex·pan·si·ble \ik-'span(t)-sə-bəl\ *adjective* (circa 1691)
: capable of being expanded
— **ex·pan·si·bil·i·ty** \-ˌspan(t)-sə-'bi-lə-tē\ *noun*

ex·pan·sion \ik-'span(t)-shən\ *noun* (1611)
1 : EXPANSE
2 : the act or process of expanding ⟨territorial expansion⟩
3 : the quality or state of being expanded
4 : the increase in volume of working fluid (as steam) in an engine cylinder after cutoff or in an internal combustion engine after explosion
5 a : an expanded part **b :** something that results from an act of expanding ⟨the book is an expansion of a lecture series⟩
6 : the result of carrying out an indicated mathematical operation : the expression of a function in the form of a series
— **ex·pan·sion·al** \-'panch-nəl, -chə-nᵊl\ *adjective*

ex·pan·sion·ary \ik-'span(t)-shə-ˌner-ē\ *adjective* (1936)
: tending toward expansion ⟨an expansionary economy⟩

ex·pan·sion·ism \ik-'span-(t)-shə-ˌni-zəm\ *noun* (1899)
: a policy or practice of expansion and especially of territorial expansion by a nation
— **ex·pan·sion·ist** \-'span(t)-sh(ə-)nist\ *noun*
— **expansionist** *also* **ex·pan·sion·is·tic** \-ˌspan(t)-shə-'nis-tik\ *adjective*

ex·pan·sive \ik-'span(t)-siv\ *adjective* (1651)
1 : having a capacity or a tendency to expand
2 : causing or tending to cause expansion
3 a : characterized by high spirits, generosity, or readiness to talk : OPEN ⟨grew expansive after dinner⟩ **b :** marked by or indicative of exaggerated euphoria and delusions of self-importance ⟨an expansive patient⟩
4 : marked by expansion; *especially* : having a great expanse or extent : SIZABLE, EXTENSIVE
5 : characterized by richness, abundance, or magnificence ⟨expansive living⟩
— **ex·pan·sive·ly** *adverb*
— **ex·pan·sive·ness** *noun*

ex·pan·siv·i·ty \ˌek-ˌspan-'si-və-tē, ik-\ *noun* (1837)
: the quality or state of being expansive; *especially* : the capacity to expand

ex par·te \(ˌ)eks-'pär-tē\ *adverb or adjective* [Medieval Latin] (1672)
1 : on or from one side or party only — used of legal proceedings
2 : from a one-sided or partisan point of view

ex·pat \'eks-ˌpat\ *noun* (1962)
chiefly British : an expatriate person : EXPATRIATE

ex·pa·ti·ate \ek-'spā-shē-ˌāt\ *intransitive verb* **-at·ed; -at·ing** [Latin exspatiatus, past participle of exspatiari to wander, digress, from ex- + spatium space, course] (1538)
1 : to move about freely or at will : WANDER
2 : to speak or write at length or in detail ⟨expatiating upon the value of the fabric —Thomas Hardy⟩
— **ex·pa·ti·a·tion** \(ˌ)ek-ˌspā-shē-'ā-shən\ *noun*

¹ex·pa·tri·ate \ek-'spā-trē-ˌāt\ *verb* **-at·ed; -at·ing** [Medieval Latin expatriatus, past participle of expatriare to leave one's own country, from Latin ex- + patria native country, from feminine of patrius of a father, from patr-, pater father — more at FATHER] (1784)
transitive verb
1 : to withdraw (oneself) from residence in or allegiance to one's native country
2 : BANISH, EXILE
intransitive verb
: to leave one's native country to live elsewhere; *also* : to renounce allegiance to one's native country
— **ex·pa·tri·ate** \-ˌāt, -ət\ *noun*
— **ex·pa·tri·a·tion** \(ˌ)ek-ˌspā-trē-'ā-shən\ *noun*

²ex·pa·tri·ate \ek-'spā-trē-ət, -trē-ˌāt\ *adjective* (1812)
: living in a foreign land

ex·pa·tri·a·tism \ek-'spā-trē-ə-ˌti-zəm\ *noun* (1937)
: the fact or state of being an expatriate

ex·pect \ik-'spekt\ *verb* [Latin exspectare to look forward to, from ex- + spectare to look at, from spectus, past participle of specere to look — more at SPY] (1560)
intransitive verb
1 *archaic* : WAIT, STAY
2 : to look forward
3 : to be pregnant : await the birth of one's child — used in progressive tenses ⟨she's expecting next month⟩
transitive verb
1 *archaic* : AWAIT
2 : SUPPOSE, THINK
3 : to anticipate or look forward to the coming or occurrence of ⟨we expect them any minute now⟩ ⟨expected a telephone call⟩
4 a : to consider probable or certain ⟨expect to be forgiven⟩ ⟨expect that things will improve⟩ **b :** to consider reasonable, due, or necessary ⟨expected hard work from the students⟩ **c :** to consider bound in duty or obligated ⟨they expect you to pay your bills⟩ ☆
— **ex·pect·able** \-'spek-tə-bəl\ *adjective*
— **ex·pect·ably** \-blē\ *adverb*
— **ex·pect·ed·ly** *adverb*
— **ex·pect·ed·ness** *noun*

ex·pec·tance \ik-'spek-tən(t)s\ *noun* (1603)

: EXPECTANCY

ex·pec·tan·cy \-tən(t)-sē\ *noun, plural* **-cies** (1600)
1 a : the act, action, or state of expecting **b :** the state of being expected
2 a : something expected **b :** the expected amount (as of the number of years of life) based on statistical probability ⟨life expectancy⟩

¹ex·pec·tant \-tənt\ *adjective* (14th century)
1 : characterized by expectation
2 : expecting the birth of a child ⟨expectant mothers⟩
— **ex·pec·tant·ly** *adverb*

²expectant *noun* (1628)
: one who is looking forward to something

ex·pec·ta·tion \ˌek-spek-'tā-shən, ik-\ *noun* (1540)
1 : the act or state of expecting : ANTICIPATION
2 a : something expected ⟨not up to expectations⟩ **b :** basis for expecting : ASSURANCE ⟨they have every expectation of success⟩ **c :** prospects of inheritance — usually used in plural
3 : the state of being expected
4 a : EXPECTANCY 2b **b :** EXPECTED VALUE
— **ex·pec·ta·tion·al** \-'tā-shə-nᵊl, -shnəl\ *adjective*

ex·pec·ta·tive \ik-'spek-tə-tiv\ *adjective* (15th century)
: of, relating to, or constituting an object of expectation

expected value *noun* (1947)
1 : the sum of the values of a random variable with each value multiplied by its probability of occurrence
2 : the integral of the product of a probability density function of a continuous random variable and the random variable itself when taken over all possible values of the variable

ex·pec·to·rant \ik-'spek-t(ə-)rənt\ *noun* (1782)

☆ **SYNONYMS**
Expand, amplify, swell, distend, inflate, dilate mean to increase in size or volume. EXPAND may apply whether the increase comes from within or without and regardless of manner (as growth, unfolding, addition of parts). AMPLIFY implies the extension or enlargement of something inadequate. SWELL implies gradual expansion beyond a thing's original or normal limits. DISTEND implies outward extension caused by pressure from within. INFLATE implies expanding by introduction of air or something insubstantial and suggests a resulting vulnerability and liability to sudden collapse. DILATE applies especially to expansion of circumference.

Expect, hope, look mean to await some occurrence or outcome. EXPECT implies a high degree of certainty and usually involves the idea of preparing or envisioning ⟨expects to be finished by Tuesday⟩. HOPE implies little certainty but suggests confidence or assurance in the possibility that what one desires or longs for will happen ⟨hopes to find a job soon⟩. LOOK, with *to*, implies assurance that expectations will be fulfilled ⟨looks to a tidy profit from the sale⟩; with *for* it implies less assurance and suggests an attitude of expectancy and watchfulness ⟨look for rain when the wind shifts to the northeast⟩.

\ə\ abut \ᵊ\ kitten \ər\ further \a\ ash \ā\ ace
\ä\ mop, mar \aú\ out \ch\ chin \e\ bet \ē\ easy
\g\ go \i\ hit \ī\ ice \j\ job \ŋ\ sing \ō\ go
\ó\ law \ói\ boy \th\ thin \th\ the \ü\ loot \ú\ foot
\y\ yet \zh\ vision *see also* Guide to Pronunciation

: an agent that promotes the discharge or expulsion of mucus from the respiratory tract; *broadly* **:** an antitussive agent
— **expectorant** *adjective*

ex·pec·to·rate \-tə-ˌrāt\ *verb* **-rat·ed; -rat·ing** [Latin *expectoratus,* past participle of *expectorare* to banish from the mind (taken to mean literally "to expel from the chest"), from *ex-* + *pector-, pectus* breast, soul — more at PECTORAL] (1601)
transitive verb
1 : to eject from the throat or lungs by coughing or hawking and spitting
2 : SPIT
intransitive verb
1 : to discharge matter from the throat or lungs by coughing or hawking and spitting
2 : SPIT
— **ex·pec·to·ra·tion** \-ˌspek-tə-ˈrā-shən\ *noun*

ex·pe·di·ence \ik-ˈspē-dē-ən(t)s\ *noun* (1593)
: EXPEDIENCY

ex·pe·di·en·cy \-dən-sē\ *noun, plural* **-cies** (1612)
1 : the quality or state of being suited to the end in view **:** SUITABILITY, FITNESS
2 *obsolete* **a :** HASTE, DISPATCH **b :** an enterprise requiring haste or caution
3 : adherence to expedient means and methods ⟨put more emphasis on *expediency* than on principle —W. H. Jones⟩
4 : a means of achieving a particular end **:** EXPEDIENT
— **ex·pe·di·en·tial** \-ˌspē-dē-ˈen-chəl\ *adjective*

¹ex·pe·di·ent \ik-ˈspē-dē-ənt\ *adjective* [Middle English, from Middle French or Latin; Middle French, from Latin *expedient-, expediens,* present participle of *expedire* to extricate, prepare, be useful, from *ex-* + *ped-, pes* foot — more at FOOT] (14th century)
1 : suitable for achieving a particular end in a given circumstance
2 : characterized by concern with what is opportune; *especially* **:** governed by self-interest
☆
— **ex·pe·di·ent·ly** *adverb*

²expedient *noun* (1653)
: something expedient **:** a temporary means to an end
synonym see RESOURCE

ex·pe·dite \ˈek-spə-ˌdīt\ *transitive verb* **-dit·ed; -dit·ing** [Latin *expeditus,* past participle of *expedire*] (15th century)
1 : to execute promptly
2 : to accelerate the process or progress of **:** speed up
3 : ISSUE, DISPATCH

ex·pe·dit·er *also* **ex·pe·di·tor** \-ˌdī-tər\ *noun* (1891)
: one that expedites; *specifically* **:** one employed to ensure efficient movement of goods or supplies in a business

ex·pe·di·tion \ˌek-spə-ˈdi-shən\ *noun* (15th century)
1 a : a journey or excursion undertaken for a specific purpose **b :** the group of persons making such a journey
2 : efficient promptness **:** SPEED
3 : a sending or setting forth
synonym see HASTE

ex·pe·di·tion·ary \-ˈdi-shə-ˌner-ē\ *adjective* (1817)
: of, relating to, or being an expedition; *also* **:** sent on military service abroad ⟨an *expeditionary* force⟩

ex·pe·di·tious \ˌek-spə-ˈdi-shəs\ *adjective* (1559)
: characterized by or acting promptly and efficiently
synonym see FAST
— **ex·pe·di·tious·ly** *adverb*
— **ex·pe·di·tious·ness** *noun*

ex·pel \ik-ˈspel\ *transitive verb* **ex·pelled; ex·pel·ling** [Middle English *expellen,* from

Latin *expellere,* from *ex-* + *pellere* to drive — more at FELT] (14th century)
1 : to force out **:** EJECT ⟨*expelled* the smoke from her lungs⟩
2 : to force to leave (as a place or organization) by official action **:** take away rights or privileges of membership ⟨*expelled* from college⟩
synonym see EJECT
— **ex·pel·la·ble** \-ˈspe-lə-bəl\ *adjective*

ex·pel·lee \ˌek-spe-ˈlē, ik-\ *noun* (1888)
: a person who is expelled especially from a native or adopted country

ex·pend \ik-ˈspend\ *transitive verb* [Middle English, from Latin *expendere* to weigh out, expend, from *ex-* + *pendere* to weigh — more at SPIN] (15th century)
1 : to pay out **:** SPEND ⟨the social services upon which public revenue is *expended* —J. A. Hobson⟩
2 : to make use of for a specific purpose **:** UTILIZE ⟨projects on which they *expended* great energy⟩; *also* **:** USE UP
— **ex·pend·er** *noun*

¹ex·pend·able \ik-ˈspen-də-bəl\ *adjective* (1805)
: that may be expended: as **a :** normally used up or consumed in service ⟨*expendable* supplies like pencils and paper⟩ **b :** more easily or economically replaced than rescued, salvaged, or protected
— **ex·pend·abil·i·ty** \-ˌspen-də-ˈbi-lə-tē\ *noun*

²expendable *noun* (1942)
: one that is expendable — usually used in plural

ex·pen·di·ture \ik-ˈspen-di-chər, -də-ˌchùr, -də-ˌt(y)ùr\ *noun* [irregular from *expend*] (1769)
1 : the act or process of expending ⟨an *expenditure* of energy⟩
2 : something expended **:** DISBURSEMENT, EXPENSE ⟨income should not exceed *expenditures*⟩

¹ex·pense \ik-ˈspen(t)s\ *noun* [Middle English, from Anglo-French or Late Latin; Anglo-French, from Late Latin *expensa,* from Latin, feminine of *expensus,* past participle of *expendere*] (14th century)
1 *archaic* **:** the act or an instance of expending **:** EXPENDITURE
2 a : something expended to secure a benefit or bring about a result **b :** financial burden or outlay **:** COST ⟨built the monument at their own *expense*⟩ **c :** an item of business outlay chargeable against revenue for a specific period
3 : a cause or occasion of expenditure ⟨an estate is a great *expense*⟩
4 : a loss, detriment, or embarrassment that results from some action or gain **:** SACRIFICE ⟨everyone had a good laugh at my *expense*⟩ — usually used in the phrase *at the expense of* ⟨develop a boy's physique at the *expense* of his intelligence —Bertrand Russell⟩

²expense *transitive verb* **ex·pensed; ex·pens·ing** (circa 1909)
1 : to charge with expenses
2 a : to charge to an expense account **b :** to write off as an expense

expense account *noun* (1872)
: an account of expenses reimbursable to an employee; *also* **:** the right of charging expenses to such an account

ex·pen·sive \ik-ˈspen(t)-siv\ *adjective* (1634)
1 : involving high cost or sacrifice ⟨an *expensive* hobby⟩
2 a : commanding a high price and especially one that is not based on intrinsic worth or is beyond a prospective buyer's means **b :** characterized by high prices ⟨*expensive* shops⟩
— **ex·pen·sive·ly** *adverb*
— **ex·pen·sive·ness** *noun*

¹ex·pe·ri·ence \ik-ˈspir-ē-ən(t)s\ *noun* [Middle English, from Middle French, from Latin *experientia* act of trying, from *experient-, experiens,* present participle of *experiri* to try,

from *ex-* + *-periri* (akin to *periculum* attempt) — more at FEAR] (14th century)
1 a : direct observation of or participation in events as a basis of knowledge **b :** the fact or state of having been affected by or gained knowledge through direct observation or participation
2 a : practical knowledge, skill, or practice derived from direct observation of or participation in events or in a particular activity **b :** the length of such participation ⟨has 10 years *experience* in the job⟩
3 a : the conscious events that make up an individual life **b :** the events that make up the conscious past of a community or nation or mankind generally
4 : something personally encountered, undergone, or lived through
5 : the act or process of directly perceiving events or reality

²experience *transitive verb* **-enced; -enc·ing** (1580)
1 : to learn by experience ⟨I have *experienced* that a landscape and the sky unfold the deepest beauty —Nathaniel Hawthorne⟩
2 : to have experience of **:** UNDERGO ⟨*experienced* severe hardships as a child⟩

ex·pe·ri·enced \-ən(t)st\ *adjective* (1576)
: made skillful or wise through experience **:** PRACTICED ⟨an *experienced* driver⟩

ex·pe·ri·en·tial \ik-ˌspir-ē-ˈen(t)-shəl\ *adjective* (1816)
: relating to, derived from, or providing experience **:** EMPIRICAL ⟨*experiential* knowledge⟩ ⟨*experiential* lessons⟩
— **ex·pe·ri·en·tial·ly** \-ˈen(t)-sh(ə-)lē\ *adverb*

¹ex·per·i·ment \ik-ˈsper-ə-mənt *also* -ˈspir-\ *noun* [Middle English, from Middle French, from Latin *experimentum,* from *experiri*] (14th century)
1 a : TEST, TRIAL ⟨make another *experiment* of his suspicion —Shakespeare⟩ **b :** a tentative procedure or policy **c :** an operation carried out under controlled conditions in order to discover an unknown effect or law, to test or establish a hypothesis, or to illustrate a known law
2 *obsolete* **:** EXPERIENCE
3 : the process of testing **:** EXPERIMENTATION

²ex·per·i·ment \-ˌment\ *intransitive verb* (1787)
: to carry out experiments **:** try out a new procedure, idea, or activity
— **ex·per·i·men·ta·tion** \ik-ˌsper-ə-mən-ˈtā-shən, -ˌmen- *also* -ˌspir-\ *noun*
— **ex·per·i·ment·er** \-ˈsper-ə-ˌmen-tər *also* -ˈspir-\ *noun*

ex·per·i·men·tal \ik-ˌsper-ə-ˈmen-tᵊl *also* -ˌspir-\ *adjective* (15th century)
1 : of, relating to, or based on experience or experiment
2 a : serving the ends of or used as a means of experimentation ⟨an *experimental* school⟩ **b :** relating to or having the characteristics of experiment **:** TENTATIVE ⟨still in the *experimental* stage⟩
— **ex·per·i·men·tal·ly** \-tᵊl-ē\ *adverb*

ex·per·i·men·tal·ism \-tᵊl-ˌi-zəm\ *noun* (circa 1834)

☆ **SYNONYMS**
Expedient, politic, advisable mean dictated by practical or prudent motives. EXPEDIENT usually implies what is immediately advantageous without regard for ethics or consistent principles ⟨a politically *expedient* decision⟩. POLITIC stresses judiciousness and tactical value but usually implies some lack of candor or sincerity ⟨a *politic* show of interest⟩. ADVISABLE applies to what is practical, prudent, or advantageous but lacks the derogatory implication of EXPEDIENT and POLITIC ⟨sometimes it's *advisable* to say nothing⟩.

: reliance on or advocacy of experimental or empirical principles and procedures; *specifically* **:** INSTRUMENTALISM

ex·per·i·men·tal·ist \-t°l-əst\ *noun* (1762)
: one who experiments; *specifically* **:** a person conducting scientific experiments

experiment station *noun* (1874)
: an establishment for scientific research (as in agriculture) where experiments are carried out, studies of practical application are made, and information is disseminated

¹**ex·pert** \'ek-ˌspərt, ik-'\ *adjective* [Middle English, from Middle French & Latin; Middle French, from Latin *expertus,* from past participle of *experiri*] (14th century)
1 *obsolete* **:** EXPERIENCED
2 : having, involving, or displaying special skill or knowledge derived from training or experience
synonym see PROFICIENT
— **ex·pert·ly** *adverb*
— **ex·pert·ness** *noun*
²**ex·pert** \'ek-ˌspərt\ *noun* [French, from *expert,* adjective] (1535)
: one with the special skill or knowledge representing mastery of a particular subject
³**ex·pert** \'ek-ˌspərt\ *intransitive verb* (circa 1889)
: to serve as an expert

ex·per·tise \ˌek-(ˌ)spər-'tēz, -'tēs\ *noun* [French, from Middle French, expertness, from *expert*] (1868)
1 : expert opinion or commentary
2 : the skill of an expert

ex·pert·ism \'ek-ˌspər-ˌti-zəm\ *noun* (1886)
: EXPERTISE 2

ex·pert·ize \'ek-spər-ˌtīz\ *verb* **-ized; -iz·ing** (1889)
intransitive verb
: to give a professional opinion usually after careful study
transitive verb
: to examine and give expert judgment on

expert system *noun* (1977)
: computer software that attempts to mimic the reasoning of a human specialist

ex·pi·ate \'ek-spē-ˌāt\ *verb* **-at·ed; -at·ing** [Latin *expiatus,* past participle of *expiare* to atone for, from *ex- + piare* to atone for, appease, from *pius* faithful, pious] (1594)
transitive verb
1 *obsolete* **:** to put an end to
2 a : to extinguish the guilt incurred by **b :** to make amends for 〈permission to *expiate* their offences by their assiduous labours —Francis Bacon〉
intransitive verb
: to make expiation
— **ex·pi·a·ble** \'ek-spē-ə-bəl\ *adjective*
— **ex·pi·a·tor** \-spē-ˌā-tər\ *noun*

ex·pi·a·tion \ˌek-spē-'ā-shən\ *noun* (15th century)
1 : the act of making atonement
2 : the means by which atonement is made

ex·pi·a·to·ry \'ek-spē-ə-ˌtōr-ē, -ˌtȯr-\ *adjective* (15th century)
: serving to expiate

ex·pi·ra·tion \ˌek-spə-'rā-shən\ *noun* (1526)
1 a : the last emission of breath **:** DEATH **b** (1) **:** the act or process of releasing air from the lungs through the nose or mouth (2) **:** the escape of carbon dioxide from the body protoplasm (as through the blood and lungs or by diffusion)
2 : the fact of coming to an end or the point at which something ends **:** TERMINATION

ex·pi·ra·to·ry \ik-'spī-rə-ˌtōr-ē, ek-', -ˌtȯr-; 'ek-sp(ə-)rə-\ *adjective* (circa 1847)
: of, relating to, or employed in the expiration of air from the lungs

ex·pire \ik-'spīr, *oftenest for intransitive verb 3 and transitive verb 2* ek-\ *verb* **ex·pired; ex·pir·ing** [Middle English, from Middle French or Latin; Middle French *expirer,* from Latin *exspirare,* from *ex- + spirare* to breathe] (14th century)

intransitive verb
1 : to breathe one's last breath **:** DIE
2 : to come to an end
3 : to emit the breath
transitive verb
1 *obsolete* **:** CONCLUDE
2 : to breathe out from or as if from the lungs
3 *archaic* **:** EMIT

ex·pi·ry \ik-'spīr-ē, 'ek-spə-rē\ *noun, plural* **-ries** (1752)
: EXPIRATION: as **a :** exhalation of breath **b :** DEATH **c :** TERMINATION; *especially* **:** the termination of a time or period fixed by law, contract, or agreement

ex·plain \ik-'splān\ *verb* [Middle English *explanen,* from Latin *explanare,* literally, to make level, from *ex- + planus* level, flat — more at FLOOR] (15th century)
transitive verb
1 a : to make known **b :** to make plain or understandable 〈footnotes that *explain* the terms〉
2 : to give the reason for or cause of
3 : to show the logical development or relationships of
intransitive verb
: to make something plain or understandable ☆
— **ex·plain·able** \-'splā-nə-bəl\ *adjective*
— **ex·plain·er** *noun*
— **explain oneself :** to clarify one's statements or the reasons for one's conduct

explain away *transitive verb* (1704)
1 : to get rid of by or as if by explanation
2 : to minimize the significance of by or as if by explanation

ex·pla·na·tion \ˌek-splə-'nā-shən\ *noun* (14th century)
1 : the act or process of explaining
2 : something that explains 〈gave no *explanation*〉

ex·plan·a·tive \ik-'spla-nə-tiv\ *adjective* (circa 1616)
: EXPLANATORY
— **ex·plan·a·tive·ly** *adverb*

ex·plan·a·to·ry \ik-'spla-nə-ˌtōr-ē, -ˌtȯr-\ *adjective* (1618)
: serving to explain 〈*explanatory* notes〉
— **ex·plan·a·to·ri·ly** \-ˌspla-nə-'tōr-ə-lē, -'tȯr-\ *adverb*

¹**ex·plant** \(ˌ)ek-'splant\ *transitive verb* [*ex- + -plant* (as in *implant*)] (1915)
: to remove (living tissue) especially to a medium for tissue culture
— **ex·plan·ta·tion** \ˌek-ˌsplan-'tā-shən\ *noun*

²**ex·plant** \'ek-ˌsplant\ *noun* (1917)
: living tissue removed from an organism and placed in a medium for tissue culture

¹**ex·ple·tive** \'ek-splə-tiv\ *noun* (1612)
1 a : a syllable, word, or phrase inserted to fill a vacancy (as in a sentence or a metrical line) without adding to the sense; *especially* **:** a word (as *it* in "make it clear which you prefer") that occupies the position of the subject or object of a verb in normal English word order and anticipates a subsequent word or phrase that supplies the needed meaningful content **b :** an exclamatory word or phrase; *especially* **:** one that is obscene or profane
2 : one that serves to fill out or as a filling

²**expletive** *adjective* [Late Latin *expletivus,* from Latin *expletus,* past participle of *explēre* to fill out, from *ex- + plēre* to fill — more at FULL] (1666)
1 : serving to fill up 〈*expletive* phrases〉
2 : marked by the use of expletives

ex·ple·to·ry \'ek-splə-ˌtōr-ē, -ˌtȯr-\ *adjective* (1672)
: EXPLETIVE

ex·pli·ca·ble \ek-'spli-kə-bəl, 'ek-(ˌ)splik-\ *adjective* (1556)
: capable of being explained
— **ex·pli·ca·bly** \-blē\ *adverb*

ex·pli·cate \'ek-splə-ˌkāt\ *transitive verb* **-cat·ed; -cat·ing** [Latin *explicatus,* past

participle of *explicare,* literally, to unfold, from *ex- + plicare* to fold — more at PLY] (1531)
1 : to give a detailed explanation of
2 : to develop the implications of **:** analyze logically
synonym see EXPLAIN
— **ex·pli·ca·tion** \ˌek-splə-'kā-shən\ *noun*
— **ex·pli·ca·tor** \'ek-splə-ˌkā-tər\ *noun*

ex·pli·ca·tion de texte \ek-splē-kä-syōⁿ-də-tekst\ *noun, plural* **explications de texte** *same*\ [French, literally, explanation of text] (1935)
: a method of literary criticism involving a detailed analysis of a work

ex·pli·ca·tive \ek-'spli-kə-tiv, 'ek-splə-ˌkāt-\ *adjective* (1649)
: serving to explicate; *specifically* **:** serving to explain logically what is contained in the subject 〈an *explicative* proposition〉
— **ex·pli·ca·tive·ly** *adverb*

ex·pli·ca·to·ry \ek-'spli-kə-ˌtōr-ē, 'ek-(ˌ)spli-, -ˌtȯr-\ *adjective* (1625)
: EXPLICATIVE

ex·plic·it \ik-'spli-sət\ *adjective* [French or Medieval Latin; French *explicite,* from Medieval Latin *explicitus,* from Latin, past participle of *explicare*] (circa 1609)
1 a : fully revealed or expressed without vagueness, implication, or ambiguity **:** leaving no question as to meaning or intent 〈*explicit* instructions〉 **b :** open in the depiction of nudity or sexuality 〈*explicit* books and films〉
2 : fully developed or formulated 〈an *explicit* plan〉 〈an *explicit* notion of our objective〉
3 : unambiguous in expression 〈was very *explicit* on how we are to behave〉
4 *of a mathematical function* **:** defined by an expression containing only independent variables — compare IMPLICIT 1c ☆
— **ex·plic·it·ly** *adverb*
— **ex·plic·it·ness** *noun*

ex·plode \ik-'splōd\ *verb* **ex·plod·ed; ex·plod·ing** [Latin *explodere* to drive off the

stage by clapping, from *ex-* + *plaudere* to clap] (circa 1611)
transitive verb
1 *archaic* **:** to drive from the stage by noisy disapproval
2 : to bring into disrepute or discredit ⟨*explode* a theory⟩
3 : to cause to explode or burst noisily ⟨*explode* a bomb⟩
intransitive verb
1 : to burst forth with sudden violence or noise from internal energy: as **a :** to undergo a rapid chemical or nuclear reaction with the production of noise, heat, and violent expansion of gases ⟨dynamite *explodes*⟩ **b :** to burst violently as a result of pressure from within
2 a : to give forth a sudden strong and noisy outburst of emotion ⟨*exploded* in anger⟩ **b :** to move with sudden speed and force ⟨*exploded* from the starting gate⟩
3 : to increase rapidly ⟨the population of the city *exploded*⟩ ◇
— **ex·plod·er** *noun*

ex·plod·ed *adjective* (1944)
: showing the parts separated but in correct relationship to each other ⟨an *exploded* view of a carburetor⟩

¹**ex·ploit** \'ek-ˌsplȯit, ik-'\ *noun* [Middle English, outcome, success, from Middle French, from Latin *explicitum*, neuter of *explicitus*, past participle] (circa 1538)
: DEED, ACT; *especially* **:** a notable or heroic act
synonym see FEAT
²**ex·ploit** \ik-'splȯit, 'ek-\ *transitive verb* (1838)
1 : to make productive use of **:** UTILIZE ⟨*exploiting* your talents⟩ ⟨*exploit* your opponent's weakness⟩
2 : to make use of meanly or unjustly for one's own advantage ⟨*exploiting* migrant farm workers⟩
— **ex·ploit·able** \-'splȯi-tə-bəl\ *adjective*
— **ex·ploit·er** *noun*
ex·ploi·ta·tion \ˌek-ˌsplȯi-'tā-shən\ *noun* (1803)
: an act or instance of exploiting ⟨*exploitation* of natural resources⟩ ⟨*exploitation* of immigrant laborers⟩ ⟨clever *exploitation* of the system⟩
ex·ploit·ative \ik-'splȯi-tə-tiv, 'ek-ˌsplȯi-\ *adjective* (1885)
: exploiting or tending to exploit; *especially* **:** unfairly or cynically using another person or group for profit or advantage ⟨*exploitative* terms of employment⟩ ⟨an *exploitative* film⟩
— **ex·ploit·ative·ly** *adverb*
ex·ploit·ive \ik-'splȯi-tiv\ *adjective* (1921)
: EXPLOITATIVE
ex·plo·ra·tion \ˌek-splə-'rā-shən, -ˌsplō-\ *noun* (1537)
: the act or an instance of exploring
— **ex·plo·ra·tion·al** \-shnəl, -shə-nᵊl\ *adjective*
ex·plor·ative \ik-'splȯr-ə-tiv, -'splȯr-\ *adjective* (1738)
: EXPLORATORY
— **ex·plor·ative·ly** *adverb*
ex·plor·a·to·ry \-ə-ˌtȯr-ē, -ˌtȯr-\ *adjective* (1620)
: of, relating to, or being exploration ⟨*exploratory* surgery⟩ ⟨*exploratory* drilling for oil⟩
ex·plore \ik-'splȯr, -'splȯr\ *verb* **ex·plored; ex·plor·ing** [Latin *explorare*, from *ex-* + *plorare* to cry out] (1585)
transitive verb
1 a : to investigate, study, or analyze **:** look into ⟨*explore* the relationship between social class and learning ability⟩ — sometimes used with indirect questions ⟨to *explore* where ethical issues arise —R. T. Blackburn⟩ **b :** to become familiar with by testing or experimenting ⟨*explore* new cuisines⟩
2 : to travel over (new territory) for adventure or discovery
3 : to examine minutely especially for diagnostic purposes ⟨*explore* the wound⟩

intransitive verb
: to make or conduct a systematic search ⟨*explore* for oil⟩
ex·plor·er \ik-'splȯr-ər, -'splȯr-\ *noun* (1685)
1 : one that explores; *especially* **:** a person who travels in search of geographical or scientific information
2 *capitalized* **:** a member of a coed scouting program of the Boy Scouts of America for young people ages 14 to 20 focusing on career awareness
ex·plo·sion \ik-'splō-zhən\ *noun* [Latin *explosion-, explosio* act of driving off by clapping, from *explodere*] (circa 1616)
1 : the act or an instance of exploding ⟨injured in a laboratory *explosion*⟩
2 : a large-scale, rapid, or spectacular expansion or bursting out or forth ⟨the *explosion* of suburbia⟩ ⟨an *explosion* of red hair⟩
3 : the release of occluded breath that occurs in one kind of articulation of stop consonants
¹**ex·plo·sive** \ik-'splō-siv, -ziv\ *adjective* (1667)
1 a : relating to, characterized by, or operated by explosion ⟨an *explosive* hatch⟩ **b :** resulting from or as if from an explosion ⟨*explosive* population growth⟩
2 a : tending to explode ⟨an *explosive* person⟩ **b :** likely to erupt in or produce hostile reaction or violence ⟨an *explosive* ghetto situation⟩
— **ex·plo·sive·ly** *adverb*
— **ex·plo·sive·ness** *noun*
²**explosive** *noun* (1874)
1 : an explosive substance
2 : a consonant characterized by explosion in its articulation when it occurs in certain environments **:** STOP
ex·po \'ek-(ˌ)spō\ *noun, plural* **expos** (1913)
: EXPOSITION 3
ex·po·nent \ik-'spō-nənt, 'ek-\ *noun* [Latin *exponent-, exponens*, present participle of *exponere*] (1706)
1 : a symbol written above and to the right of a mathematical expression to indicate the operation of raising to a power
2 a : one that expounds or interprets **b :** one that champions, practices, or exemplifies
ex·po·nen·tial \ˌek-spə-'nen-chəl\ *adjective* (1704)
1 : of or relating to an exponent
2 : involving a variable in an exponent ⟨10^x is an *exponential* expression⟩
3 : expressible or approximately expressible by an exponential function; *especially* **:** characterized by or being an extremely rapid increase (as in size or extent) ⟨an *exponential* growth rate⟩
— **ex·po·nen·tial·ly** \-'nench-(ə-)lē\ *adverb*
exponential function *noun* (circa 1890)
: a mathematical function in which an independent variable appears in one of the exponents — called also *exponential*
ex·po·nen·ti·a·tion \ˌek-spə-ˌnen(t)-shē-'ā-shən\ *noun* (1903)
: the act or process of raising a quantity to a power — called also *involution*
¹**ex·port** \ek-'spȯrt, -'spȯrt, 'ek-\ *verb* [Middle English, from Latin *exportare*, from *ex-* + *portare* to carry — more at FARE] (15th century)
transitive verb
1 : to carry away **:** REMOVE
2 : to carry or send (as a commodity) to some other place (as another country)
intransitive verb
: to export something abroad
— **ex·port·abil·i·ty** \(ˌ)ek-ˌspȯr-tə-'bi-lə-tē, -ˌspȯr-\ *noun*
— **ex·port·able** \ek-'spȯr-tə-bəl, -'spȯr-, 'ek-\ *adjective*
²**ex·port** \'ek-ˌspȯrt, -ˌspȯrt\ *noun* (1690)
1 : something exported; *specifically* **:** a commodity conveyed from one country or region to another for purposes of trade
2 : the act of exporting **:** EXPORTATION ⟨the *export* of wheat⟩

³**ex·port** \'ek-ˌ\ *adjective* (1795)
: of or relating to exportation or exports ⟨*export* duties⟩
ex·por·ta·tion \ˌek-spȯr-'tā-shən, -ˌspȯr-, -spər-\ *noun* (1641)
: the act of exporting; *also* **:** a commodity exported
ex·port·er \ek-'spȯr-tər, -'spȯr-, 'ek-ˌ\ *noun* (1691)
: one that exports; *specifically* **:** a wholesaler who sells to merchants or industrial consumers in foreign countries
ex·pose \ik-'spōz\ *transitive verb* **ex·posed; ex·pos·ing** [Middle English, from Middle French *exposer*, from Latin *exponere* to set forth, explain (perfect indicative *exposui*), from *ex-* + *ponere* to put, place — more at POSITION] (15th century)
1 a : to deprive of shelter, protection, or care **:** subject to risk from a harmful action or condition ⟨*expose* troops needlessly⟩ ⟨has not yet been *exposed* to measles⟩ **b :** to submit or make accessible to a particular action or influence ⟨*expose* children to good books⟩; *especially* **:** to subject (a sensitive photographic film, plate, or paper) to radiant energy **c :** to abandon (an infant) especially by leaving in the open
2 a : to make known **:** bring to light (as something shameful) **b :** to disclose the faults or crimes of ⟨*expose* a murderer⟩
3 : to cause to be visible or open to view **:** DISPLAY: as **a :** to offer publicly for sale **b :** to exhibit for public veneration **c :** to reveal the face of (a playing card) or the cards of (a player's hand) **d :** to engage in indecent exposure of (oneself)
synonym see SHOW
— **ex·pos·er** *noun*
ex·po·sé *also* **ex·po·se** \ˌek-spō-'zā, -spə-\ *noun* [French *exposé*, from past participle of *exposer*] (1803)
1 : a formal statement of facts
2 : an exposure of something discreditable ⟨a newspaper *exposé* of government corruption⟩
ex·posed \ik-'spōzd\ *adjective* (circa 1623)
1 : open to view
2 : not shielded or protected; *also* **:** not insulated ⟨an *exposed* electric wire⟩
synonym see LIABLE
ex·pos·it \ik-'spä-zət\ *transitive verb* [Latin *expositus*, past participle of *exponere*] (1882)
: EXPOUND
ex·po·si·tion \ˌek-spə-'zi-shən\ *noun* (14th century)
1 : a setting forth of the meaning or purpose (as of a writing)
2 a : discourse or an example of it designed to convey information or explain what is difficult to understand **b** (1) **:** the first part of a musical composition in sonata form in which the thematic material of the movement is presented (2) **:** the opening section of a fugue
3 : a public exhibition or show

◇ WORD HISTORY
explode A modern audience often expresses its disapproval of a performer or performance by hissing. But in ancient Rome a customary expression of audience disapproval was loud clapping, sometimes expressly intended to drive the performer from the stage. The Latin verb meaning "to drive off by clapping" was *explodere*, a compound of *ex-*, meaning "out of, from" and *plaudere*, meaning "to clap." *Explodere* was, of course, the source of English *explode*, which initially also meant "to drive from the stage by a noisy expression of dislike." This sense is no longer current, but the senses that have replaced it have kept the notion either of dismissal and rejection or of a loud, violent burst.

— ex·po·si·tion·al \-'zish-nəl, -'zi-shə-nᵊl\ *adjective*

ex·pos·i·tive \ik-'spä-zə-tiv\ *adjective* (15th century)
: DESCRIPTIVE, EXPOSITORY

ex·pos·i·tor \-zə-tər\ *noun* [Middle English *expositour,* from Middle French *expositeur,* from Late Latin *expositor,* from Latin *exponere*] (14th century)
: a person who explains **:** COMMENTATOR

ex·pos·i·to·ry \-zə-,tōr-ē, -,tór-\ *adjective* (1628)
: of, relating to, or containing exposition ⟨*expository* writing⟩

¹ex post fac·to \,eks-,pōs(t)-'fak-(,)tō\ *adverb* [Late Latin, literally, from a thing done afterward] (1621)
: after the fact **:** RETROACTIVELY

²ex post facto *adjective* (1787)
: done, made, or formulated after the fact **:** RETROACTIVE ⟨*ex post facto* approval⟩ ⟨*ex post facto* laws⟩

ex·pos·tu·late \ik-'späs-chə-,lāt\ *verb* [Latin *expostulatus,* past participle of *expostulare* to demand, dispute, from *ex-* + *postulare* to ask for — more at POSTULATE] (1573)
transitive verb
obsolete **:** DISCUSS, EXAMINE
intransitive verb
: to reason earnestly with a person for purposes of dissuasion or remonstrance

ex·pos·tu·la·tion \-,späs-chə-'lā-shən\ *noun* (1540)
: an act or an instance of expostulating
— ex·pos·tu·la·to·ry \-'späs-chə-lə-,tōr-ē, -,tór-\ *adjective*

ex·po·sure \ik-'spō-zhər\ *noun* (1606)
1 : the fact or condition of being exposed: as **a :** the condition of being presented to view or made known ⟨a politician seeks a lot of *exposure*⟩ **b :** the condition of being unprotected especially from severe weather ⟨died of *exposure*⟩ **c :** the condition of being subject to some effect or influence ⟨risk *exposure* to the flu⟩ **d :** the condition of being at risk of financial loss; *also* **:** an amount at risk
2 : the act or an instance of exposing: as **a :** disclosure of something secret ⟨tried to prevent *exposure* of their past⟩ **b :** the treating of sensitized material (as film) to controlled amounts of radiant energy; *also* **:** the amount of such energy or length of such treatment ⟨a 3-second *exposure*⟩
3 a : the manner of being exposed **b :** the position (as of a house) with respect to weather influences or compass points ⟨a room with a southern *exposure*⟩
4 : a piece or section of sensitized material (as film) on which an exposure is or can be made ⟨36 *exposures* per roll⟩

exposure meter *noun* (1891)
: a device for indicating correct photographic exposure under varying conditions of illumination

ex·pound \ik-'spaúnd\ *verb* [Middle English, from Middle French *expondre,* from Latin *exponere* to explain — more at EXPOSE] (14th century)
transitive verb
1 a : to set forth **:** STATE **b :** to defend with argument
2 : to explain by setting forth in careful and often elaborate detail ⟨*expound* a law⟩
intransitive verb
: to make a statement **:** COMMENT
synonym see EXPLAIN
— ex·pound·er *noun*

¹ex·press \ik-'spres\ *adjective* [Middle English, from Middle French *expres,* from Latin *expressus,* past participle of *exprimere* to press out, express, from *ex-* + *premere* to press — more at PRESS] (14th century)
1 a : directly, firmly, and explicitly stated ⟨my *express* orders⟩ **b :** EXACT, PRECISE

2 a : designed for or adapted to its purpose **b :** of a particular sort **:** SPECIFIC ⟨for that *express* purpose⟩
3 a : traveling at high speed; *specifically* **:** traveling with few or no stops along the way ⟨*express* train⟩ **b :** adapted or suitable for travel at high speed ⟨an *express* highway⟩ **c :** British **:** designated to be delivered without delay by special messenger
synonym see EXPLICIT

²express *adverb* (14th century)
1 *obsolete* **:** EXPRESSLY
2 : by express ⟨delivered *express*⟩

³express *noun* (1619)
1 a *British* **:** a messenger sent on a special errand **b** *British* **:** a dispatch conveyed by a special messenger **c** (1) **:** a system for the prompt and safe transportation of parcels, money, or goods at rates higher than standard freight charges (2) **:** a company operating such a merchandise freight service **d** *British* **:** SPECIAL DELIVERY
2 : an express vehicle

⁴express *transitive verb* [Middle English, from Middle French & Latin; Middle French *expresser,* from Old French, from *expres,* adjective, from Latin *expressus,* past participle] (14th century)
1 a : DELINEATE, DEPICT **b :** to represent in words **:** STATE **c :** to give or convey a true impression of **:** SHOW, REFLECT **d :** to make known the opinions or feelings of (oneself) **e :** to give expression to the artistic or creative impulses or abilities of (oneself) **f :** to represent by a sign or symbol **:** SYMBOLIZE
2 a : to force out (as the juice of a fruit) by pressure **b :** to subject to pressure so as to extract something
3 : to send by express
4 : to cause (a gene) to manifest its effects in the phenotype ☆
— ex·press·er *noun*
— ex·press·ible \-ə-bəl\ *adjective*

ex·press·age \ik-'spre-sij\ *noun* (1857)
: a carrying of parcels by express; *also* **:** a charge for such carrying

ex·pres·sion \ik-'spre-shən\ *noun* (15th century)
1 a : an act, process, or instance of representing in a medium (as words) **:** UTTERANCE ⟨freedom of *expression*⟩ **b** (1) **:** something that manifests, embodies, or symbolizes something else ⟨this gift is an *expression* of my admiration for you⟩ (2) **:** a significant word or phrase (3) **:** a mathematical or logical symbol or a meaningful combination of symbols (4) **:** the detectable effect of a gene; *also* **:** EXPRESSIVITY 1
2 a : a mode, means, or use of significant representation or symbolism; *especially* **:** felicitous or vivid indication or depiction of mood or sentiment ⟨read the poem with *expression*⟩ **b** (1) **:** the quality or fact of being expressive (2) **:** facial aspect or vocal intonation as indicative of feeling
3 : an act or product of pressing out
— ex·pres·sion·al \-'spresh-nəl, -'spre-shə-nᵊl\ *adjective*

ex·pres·sion·ism \ik-'spre-shə-,ni-zəm\ *noun, often capitalized* (circa 1901)
: a theory or practice in art of seeking to depict the subjective emotions and responses that objects and events arouse in the artist
— ex·pres·sion·ist \-'spre-shə-nist\ *noun or adjective, often capitalized*
— ex·pres·sion·is·tic \-,spre-shə-'nis-tik\ *adjective*
— ex·pres·sion·is·ti·cal·ly \-ti-k(ə-)lē\ *adverb*

ex·pres·sion·less \ik-'spre-shən-ləs\ *adjective* (1831)
: lacking expression ⟨an *expressionless* face⟩
— ex·pres·sion·less·ly *adverb*
— ex·pres·sion·less·ness *noun*

ex·pres·sive \ik-'spre-siv\ *adjective* (15th century)

1 : of or relating to expression ⟨the *expressive* function of language⟩
2 : serving to express, utter, or represent ⟨foul and novel terms *expressive* of rage —H. G. Wells⟩
3 : effectively conveying meaning or feeling ⟨an *expressive* silence⟩ ⟨*expressive* line drawings⟩
— ex·pres·sive·ly *adverb*
— ex·pres·sive·ness *noun*

ex·pres·siv·i·ty \,ek-,spre-'si-və-tē\ *noun, plural* **-ties** (1934)
1 : the relative capacity of a gene to affect the phenotype of the organism of which it is a part
2 : the quality of being expressive

ex·press·ly \ik-'spres-lē\ *adverb* (14th century)
1 : in an express manner **:** EXPLICITLY ⟨*expressly* rejected the proposal⟩
2 : for the express purpose **:** PARTICULARLY, SPECIFICALLY ⟨made *expressly* for me⟩

Express Mail *service mark*
— used for overnight delivery of mail

ex·press·man \ik-'spres-,man, -mən\ *noun* (1839)
: a person employed in the express business

ex·press·so \ik-'spre-(,)sō\ *variant of* ESPRESSO

ex·press·way \ik-'spres-,wā\ *noun* (1944)
: a high-speed divided highway for through traffic with access partially or fully controlled

ex·pro·pri·ate \ek-'sprō-prē-,āt\ *transitive verb* **-at·ed; -at·ing** [Medieval Latin *expropriatus,* past participle of *expropriare,* from Latin *ex-* + *proprius* own] (1611)
1 : to deprive of possession or proprietary rights
2 : to transfer (the property of another) to one's own possession
— ex·pro·pri·a·tor \-,ā-tər\ *noun*

ex·pro·pri·a·tion \(,)ek-,sprō-prē-'ā-shən\ *noun* (15th century)
: the act of expropriating or the state of being expropriated; *specifically* **:** the action of the state in taking or modifying the property rights of an individual in the exercise of its sovereignty

ex·pulse \ik-'spəls\ *transitive verb* **expulsed; ex·puls·ing** (15th century)
: EXPEL

ex·pul·sion \ik-'spəl-shən\ *noun* [Middle English, from Latin *expulsion-, expulsio,* from *expellere* to expel] (15th century)
: the act of expelling **:** the state of being expelled
— ex·pul·sive \-'spəl-siv\ *adjective*

☆ **SYNONYMS**
Express, vent, utter, voice, broach, air mean to make known what one thinks or feels. EXPRESS suggests an impulse to reveal in words, gestures, actions, or what one creates or produces ⟨*expressed* her feelings in music⟩. VENT stresses a strong inner compulsion to express especially in words ⟨a tirade *venting* his frustration⟩. UTTER implies the use of the voice not necessarily in articulate speech ⟨*utter* a groan⟩. VOICE does not necessarily imply vocal utterance but does imply expression or formulation in words ⟨an editorial *voicing* their concerns⟩. BROACH adds the implication of disclosing for the first time something long thought over or reserved for a suitable occasion ⟨*broached* the subject of a divorce⟩. AIR implies an exposing or parading of one's views often in order to gain relief or sympathy or attention ⟨publicly *airing* their differences⟩.

\ə\ abut \ᵊ\ kitten \ər\ further \a\ ash \ā\ ace
\ä\ mop, mar \aú\ out \ch\ chin \e\ bet \ē\ easy
\g\ go \i\ hit \ī\ ice \j\ job \ŋ\ sing \ō\ go
\ó\ law \ói\ boy \th\ thin \t͟h\ the \ü\ loot \ú\ foot
\y\ yet \zh\ vision *see also* Guide to Pronunciation

ex·punc·tion \ik-'spəŋ(k)-shən\ *noun* [Latin *expungere*] (1606)
: the act of expunging : the state of being expunged : ERASURE

ex·punge \ik-'spənj\ *transitive verb* **expunged; ex·pung·ing** [Latin *expungere* to mark for deletion by dots, from *ex-* + *pungere* to prick — more at PUNGENT] (1602)
1 : to strike out, obliterate, or mark for deletion
2 : to efface completely : DESTROY
— **ex·pung·er** *noun*

ex·pur·gate \'ek-spər-ˌgāt\ *transitive verb* **-gat·ed; -gat·ing** [Latin *expurgatus*, past participle of *expurgare*, from *ex-* + *purgare* to purge] (1678)
: to cleanse of something morally harmful, offensive, or erroneous; *especially* : to expunge objectionable parts from before publication or presentation ⟨an *expurgated* edition of the letters⟩
— **ex·pur·ga·tion** \ˌek-spər-'gā-shən\ *noun*
— **ex·pur·ga·tor** \-ˌgā-tər\ *noun*

ex·pur·ga·to·ri·al \(ˌ)ek-ˌspər-gə-'tōr-ē-əl, -ˌtör-\ *adjective* (1807)
: relating to expurgation or an expurgator : EXPURGATORY

ex·pur·ga·to·ry \ek-'spər-gə-ˌtōr-ē, -ˌtör-\ *adjective* (1625)
: serving to purify from something morally harmful, offensive, or erroneous

¹ex·qui·site \ek-'skwi-zət, 'ek-(ˌ)\ *adjective* [Middle English *exquisit*, from Latin *exquisitus*, past participle of *exquirere* to search out, from *ex-* + *quaerere* to seek] (15th century)
1 : carefully selected : CHOICE
2 *archaic* : ACCURATE
3 a : marked by flawless craftsmanship or by beautiful, ingenious, delicate, or elaborate execution **b** : marked by nice discrimination, deep sensitivity, or subtle understanding ⟨*exquisite* taste⟩ **c** : ACCOMPLISHED, PERFECTED ⟨an *exquisite* gentleman⟩
4 a : pleasing through beauty, fitness, or perfection ⟨an *exquisite* white blossom⟩ **b** : ACUTE, INTENSE ⟨*exquisite* pain⟩ **c** : having uncommon or esoteric appeal ◆
synonym see CHOICE
— **ex·qui·site·ly** *adverb*
— **ex·qui·site·ness** *noun*

²exquisite *noun* (1819)
: one who is overly fastidious in dress or ornament

ex·san·gui·na·tion \(ˌ)ek(s)-ˌsaŋ-gwə-'nā-shən\ *noun* [Latin *exsanguinatus* drained of blood, from *ex-* + *sanguin-, sanguis* blood] (circa 1909)
: the action or process of draining or losing blood
— **ex·san·gui·nate** \ek(s)-'saŋ-gwə-ˌnāt\ *transitive verb*

ex·scind \ek-'sind\ *transitive verb* [Latin *exscindere*, from *ex-* + *scindere* to cut, tear — more at SHED] (1662)
: to cut off or out : EXCISE

ex·sert \ek-'sərt\ *transitive verb* [Latin *exsertus*, past participle of *exserere* — more at EXERT] (1836)
: to thrust out
— **ex·ser·tile** \-'sər-tᵊl, -'sər-ˌtīl\ *adjective*
— **ex·ser·tion** \-'sər-shən\ *noun*

ex·sert·ed *adjective* (1816)
: projecting beyond an enclosing organ or part

ex·sic·cate \'ek-si-ˌkāt\ *transitive verb* **-cat·ed; -cat·ing** [Middle English, from Latin *exsiccatus*, past participle of *exsiccare*, from *ex-* + *siccare* to dry, from *siccus* dry — more at SACK] (15th century)
: to remove moisture from : DRY
— **ex·sic·ca·tion** \ˌek-si-'kā-shən\ *noun*

ex·so·lu·tion \ˌek-sə-'lü-shən\ *noun* (1929)
: the process of separating or precipitating from a solid crystalline phase

ex·tant \'ek-stənt; ek-'stant, 'ek-ˌ\ *adjective* [Latin *exstant-, exstans*, present participle of *exstare* to stand out, be in existence, from *ex-* + *stare* to stand — more at STAND] (1545)
1 *archaic* : standing out or above
2 a : currently or actually existing ⟨the most charming writer *extant* —G. W. Johnson⟩ **b** : not destroyed or lost ⟨*extant* manuscripts⟩

ex·tem·po·ral \ek-'stem-p(ə-)rəl\ *adjective* [Latin *extemporalis*, from *ex tempore*] (1570)
archaic : EXTEMPORANEOUS
— **ex·tem·po·ral·ly** \-ē\ *adverb*

ex·tem·po·ra·ne·i·ty \(ˌ)ek-ˌstem-pə-rə-'nē-ə-tē, -'nā-\ *noun* (1937)
: the quality or state of being extemporaneous

ex·tem·po·ra·ne·ous \(ˌ)ek-ˌstem-pə-'rā-nē-əs\ *adjective* [Late Latin *extemporaneus*, from Latin *ex tempore*] (1673)
1 a (1) : composed, performed, or uttered on the spur of the moment : IMPROMPTU (2) : carefully prepared but delivered without notes or text **b** : skilled at or given to extemporaneous utterance **c** : happening suddenly and often unexpectedly and usually without clearly known causes or relationships ⟨a great deal of criminal and delinquent behavior is . . . *extemporaneous* —W. C. Reckless⟩
2 : provided, made, or put to use as an expedient : MAKESHIFT
— **ex·tem·po·ra·ne·ous·ly** *adverb*
— **ex·tem·po·ra·ne·ous·ness** *noun*

ex·tem·po·rary \ik-'stem-pə-ˌrer-ē\ *adjective* (1596)
: EXTEMPORANEOUS
— **ex·tem·po·rar·i·ly** \-ˌstem-pə-'rer-ə-lē\ *adverb*

ex·tem·po·re \ik-'stem-pə-(ˌ)rē\ *adverb or adjective* [Latin *ex tempore*, from *ex* + *tempore*, ablative of *tempus* time] (1553)
: in an extemporaneous manner ⟨speaking *extempore*⟩

ex·tem·por·i·sa·tion, ex·tem·po·rise *British variant of* EXTEMPORIZATION, EXTEMPORIZE

ex·tem·po·ri·za·tion \ik-ˌstem-pə-rə-'zā-shən\ *noun* (circa 1860)
1 : the act of extemporizing : IMPROVISATION
2 : something extemporized

ex·tem·po·rize \ik-'stem-pə-ˌrīz\ *verb* **-rized; -riz·ing** (1644)
intransitive verb
1 : to do something extemporaneously : IMPROVISE; *especially* : to speak extemporaneously
2 : to get along in a makeshift manner
transitive verb
: to compose, perform, or utter extemporaneously : IMPROVISE
— **ex·tem·po·riz·er** *noun*

ex·tend \ik-'stend\ *verb* [Middle English, from Middle French or Latin; Middle French *estendre*, from Latin *extendere*, from *ex-* + *tendere* to stretch — more at THIN] (14th century)
transitive verb
1 : to spread or stretch forth : UNBEND ⟨*extended* both her arms⟩
2 a : to stretch out to fullest length **b** : to cause (as a horse) to move at full stride **c** : to exert (oneself) to full capacity ⟨could work long and hard without seeming to *extend* himself⟩ **d** (1) : to increase the bulk of (as by adding a cheaper substance or a modifier) (2) : ADULTERATE
3 [Middle English, from Medieval Latin *extendere* (from Latin) or Anglo-French *estendre*, from Old French] **a** *British* : to take possession of (as lands) by a writ of extent **b** *obsolete* : to take by force
4 a : to make the offer of : PROFFER ⟨*extending* aid to the needy⟩ **b** : to make available ⟨*extending* credit to customers⟩
5 a : to cause to reach (as in distance or scope) ⟨national authority was *extended* over new territories⟩ **b** : to cause to be longer : PROLONG ⟨*extend* the side of a triangle⟩ ⟨*extended* their visit another day⟩; *also* : to prolong the time of payment of **c** : ADVANCE, FURTHER ⟨*extending* her potential through job training⟩

6 a : to cause to be of greater area or volume : ENLARGE **b** : to increase the scope, meaning, or application of : BROADEN ⟨beauty, I suppose, opens the heart, *extends* the consciousness —Algernon Blackwood⟩ **c** *archaic* : EXAGGERATE
intransitive verb
1 : to stretch out in distance, space, or time : REACH ⟨their jurisdiction *extended* over the whole area⟩
2 : to reach in scope or application ⟨his concern *extends* beyond mere business to real service to his customers⟩ ☆
— **ex·tend·abil·i·ty** \-ˌsten-də-'bi-lə-tē\ *noun*
— **ex·tend·able** *also* **ex·tend·ible** \-'sten-də-bəl\ *adjective*

ex·tend·ed *adjective* (15th century)
1 : drawn out in length especially of time ⟨an *extended* visit⟩
2 a : fully stretched out ⟨an *extended* battle line⟩ **b** *of a horse's gait* : performed with a greatly lengthened stride but without a break — compare COLLECTED **c** : INTENSIVE ⟨*extended* efforts⟩
3 : having spatial magnitude : being larger than a point ⟨an *extended* source of light⟩
4 : EXTENSIVE 1 ⟨made available *extended* information —Ruth G. Strickland⟩
5 : DERIVATIVE 1, SECONDARY 2a ⟨an *extended* sense of a word⟩
6 *of a typeface* : having a wider face than that of a standard typeface
— **ex·tend·ed·ly** *adverb*
— **ex·tend·ed·ness** *noun*

extended family *noun* (circa 1935)
: a family that includes in one household near relatives in addition to a nuclear family

ex·tend·er \ik-'sten-dər\ *noun* (1611)
: one that extends: as **a** : a substance added to a product especially in the capacity of a diluent, adulterant, or modifier **b** : an added ingredient used to increase the bulk of a food (as soup or meat)

ex·ten·si·ble \ik-'sten(t)-sə-bəl\ *adjective* (1611)
: capable of being extended
— **ex·ten·si·bil·i·ty** \-ˌsten(t)-sə-'bi-lə-tē\ *noun*

ex·ten·sile \ik-'sten(t)-səl, -'sten-ˌsīl\ *adjective* (1744)
: EXTENSIBLE

ex·ten·sion \ik-'sten(t)-shən\ *noun* [Middle English, from Middle French or Late Latin; Middle French, from Late Latin *extension-, extensio*, from Latin *extendere*] (15th century)

☆ **SYNONYMS**
Extend, lengthen, prolong, protract mean to draw out or add to so as to increase in length. EXTEND and LENGTHEN imply a drawing out in space or time but EXTEND may also imply increase in width, scope, area, or range ⟨*extend* a vacation⟩ ⟨*extend* welfare services⟩ ⟨*lengthen* a skirt⟩ ⟨*lengthen* the workweek⟩. PROLONG suggests chiefly increase in duration especially beyond usual limits ⟨*prolonged* illness⟩. PROTRACT adds to PROLONG implications of needlessness, vexation, or indefiniteness ⟨*protracted* litigation⟩.

◇ **WORD HISTORY**
exquisite The source of English *exquisite* is the Latin verb *exquirere*, which meant "to ask about" or "to seek." The past participle of this verb, *exquisitus*, came to be used as an adjective, eventually acquiring not just the meaning of "sought out" but also "sought out with care"—in other words, "choice." This was the sense that was adopted into Middle English as *exquisit* and from which the modern senses of *exquisite* have developed.

1 a : the action of extending **:** state of being extended **b :** an enlargement in scope or operation ⟨tools are *extensions* of human hands⟩ **2 a :** the total range over which something extends **:** COMPASS **b :** DENOTATION 4 **3 a :** the stretching of a fractured or dislocated limb so as to restore it to its natural position **b :** an unbending movement around a joint in a limb (as the knee or elbow) that increases the angle between the bones of the limb at the joint — compare FLEXION 4a **4 :** a property whereby something occupies space **5 :** an increase in length of time; *specifically* **:** an increase in time allowed under agreement or concession ⟨was granted an *extension*⟩ **6 :** a program that geographically extends the educational resources of an institution by special arrangements (as correspondence courses) to persons otherwise unable to take advantage of such resources **7 a :** a part constituting an addition **b :** a section or line segment forming an additional length **c :** an extra telephone connected to the principal line **8 :** a mathematical set (as a field or group) that includes a given and similar set as a subset

extension agent *noun* (1949)
: COUNTY AGENT

ex·ten·sion·al \ik-'stench-nəl, -'sten(t)-shə-n°l\ *adjective* (1647)
1 : of, relating to, or marked by extension; *specifically* **:** DENOTATIVE
2 : concerned with objective reality
— **ex·ten·sion·al·i·ty** \-,sten(t)-shə-'na-lə-tē\ *noun*
— **ex·ten·sion·al·ly** \-'stench-nə-lē, -'sten(t)-shə-n°l-ē\ *adverb*

extension cord *noun* (1946)
: an electric cord fitted with a plug at one end and a receptacle at the other

ex·ten·si·ty \ik-'sten(t)-sə-tē\ *noun, plural* **-ties** (circa 1834)
1 a : the quality of having extension **b :** degree of extension **:** RANGE
2 : an attribute of sensation whereby space or size is perceived

ex·ten·sive \ik-'sten(t)-siv\ *adjective* (1605)
1 : having wide or considerable extent ⟨*extensive* reading⟩
2 : EXTENSIONAL
3 : of, relating to, or constituting farming in which large areas of land are utilized with minimum outlay and labor
— **ex·ten·sive·ly** *adverb*
— **ex·ten·sive·ness** *noun*

ex·ten·som·e·ter \,ek-,sten-'sä-mə-tər\ *noun* [*extension* + -*o*- + -*meter*] (1887)
: an instrument for measuring minute deformations of test specimens caused by tension, compression, bending, or twisting

ex·ten·sor \ik-'sten(t)-sər\ *noun* (1713)
: a muscle serving to extend a bodily part (as a limb)

ex·tent \ik-'stent\ *noun* [Middle English, from Anglo-French & Middle French; Anglo-French *extente* land valuation, from Middle French, area, surveying of land, from *extendre, estendre* to extend] (14th century)
1 *archaic* **:** valuation (as of land) in Great Britain especially for taxation
2 a : seizure (as of land) in execution of a writ of extent in Great Britain **:** the condition of being so seized **b :** a writ giving to a creditor temporary possession of his debtor's property
3 a : the range over which something extends **:** SCOPE ⟨the *extent* of her jurisdiction⟩ **b :** the point, degree, or limit to which something extends ⟨using talents to the greatest *extent*⟩ **c :** the amount of space or surface that something occupies or the distance over which it extends **:** MAGNITUDE ⟨the *extent* of the forest⟩

ex·ten·u·ate \ik-'sten-yə-,wāt\ *transitive verb* **-at·ed; -at·ing** [Latin *extenuatus*, past parti-

ciple of *extenuare*, from *ex-* + *tenuis* thin — more at THIN] (1529)
1 a *archaic* **:** to make light of **b :** to lessen or to try to lessen the seriousness or extent of by making partial excuses **:** MITIGATE **c** *obsolete* **:** DISPARAGE
2 a *archaic* **:** to make thin or emaciated **b :** to lessen the strength or effect of
— **ex·ten·u·a·tor** \-,wā-tər\ *noun*
— **ex·ten·u·a·to·ry** \-wə-,tōr-ē, -,tòr-\ *adjective*

ex·ten·u·a·tion \ik-,sten-yə-'wā-shən\ *noun* (circa 1543)
1 : the act of extenuating or state of being extenuated; *especially* **:** partial justification
2 : something extenuating; *especially* **:** a partial excuse

¹ex·te·ri·or \ek-'stir-ē-ər\ *adjective* [Latin, comparative of *exter, exterus* being on the outside, foreign, from *ex*] (1528)
1 : being on an outside surface **:** situated on the outside
2 : observable by outward signs ⟨his *exterior* quietness is belied by an occasional nervous twitch —*Current Biography*⟩
3 : suitable for use on outside surfaces
— **ex·te·ri·or·ly** *adverb*

²exterior *noun* (1591)
1 a : an exterior part or surface **:** OUTSIDE **b :** outward manner or appearance
2 : a representation (as on stage or film) of an outdoor scene; *also* **:** a scene filmed outdoors

exterior angle *noun* (circa 1864)
1 : the angle between a side of a polygon and an extended adjacent side
2 : an angle formed by a transversal as it cuts one of two lines and situated on the outside of the line

ega, egb, fhc, fhd
exterior angle
2

ex·te·ri·or·ise *British variant of* EXTERIORIZE
ex·te·ri·or·i·ty \(,)ek-,stir-ē-'òr-ə-tē, -'är-\ *noun* (1611)
: the quality or state of being exterior or exteriorized **:** EXTERNALITY

ex·te·ri·or·ize \ek-'stir-ē-ə-,rīz\ *transitive verb* **-ized; -iz·ing** (1879)
1 : EXTERNALIZE
2 : to bring out of the body (as for surgery)
— **ex·te·ri·or·iza·tion** \-,stir-ē-ə-rə-'zā-shən\ *noun*

ex·ter·mi·nate \ik-'stər-mə-,nāt\ *transitive verb* **-nat·ed; -nat·ing** [Latin *exterminatus*, past participle of *exterminare*, from *ex-* + *terminus* boundary — more at TERM] (1591)
: to get rid of completely usually by killing off ⟨*exterminate* crabgrass from a lawn⟩ ☆
— **ex·ter·mi·na·tion** \-,stər-mə-'nā-shən\ *noun*
— **ex·ter·mi·na·tor** \-'stər-mə-,nā-tər\ *noun*

ex·ter·mi·na·to·ry \ik-'stər-mə-nə-,tōr-ē, -,tòr-\ *adjective* (1790)
: of, relating to, or marked by extermination

ex·ter·mine \ik-'stər-mən\ *transitive verb* **-mined; -min·ing** (1539)
obsolete **:** EXTERMINATE

¹ex·tern \ek-'stərn, 'ek-,\ *adjective* [Middle French or Latin; Middle French *externe*, from Latin *externus*] (1530)
archaic **:** EXTERNAL

²ex·tern *also* **ex·terne** \'ek-,stərn\ *noun* (circa 1610)
: a person connected with an institution but not living or boarding in it; *specifically* **:** a nonresident doctor or medical student at a hospital

¹ex·ter·nal \ek-'stər-n°l\ *adjective* [Latin *externus* external, from *exter*] (1556)
1 a : capable of being perceived outwardly ⟨*external* signs of a disease⟩ ⟨*external* reality⟩ **b** (1) **:** having merely the outward appearance of something **:** SUPERFICIAL (2) **:** not intrinsic or essential ⟨*external* circumstances⟩

2 a : of, relating to, or connected with the outside or an outer part **b :** applied or applicable to the outside
3 a (1) **:** situated outside, apart, or beyond; *specifically* **:** situated near or toward the surface of the body (2) **:** arising or acting from outside ⟨*external* force⟩ **b :** of or relating to dealings or relationships with foreign countries **c :** having existence independent of the mind ⟨*external* reality⟩
— **ex·ter·nal·ly** \-n°l-ē\ *adverb*

²external *noun* (circa 1635)
: something that is external: as **a :** an outer part **b :** an external feature or aspect — usually used in plural

external combustion engine *noun* (1915)
: a heat engine (as a steam engine) that derives its heat from fuel consumed outside the engine cylinder

external degree *noun* (1928)
: a degree conferred on a student who has not attended the university but has passed the qualifying examination

ex·ter·nal·isa·tion, ex·ter·nal·ise *British variant of* EXTERNALIZATION, EXTERNALIZE
ex·ter·nal·ism \ek-'stər-n°l-,i-zəm\ *noun* (1856)
1 : attention to externals; *especially* **:** excessive preoccupation with externals
2 : EXTERNALITY 1

ex·ter·nal·i·ty \,ek-,stər-'na-lə-tē\ *noun, plural* **-ties** (1673)
1 : the quality or state of being external or externalized
2 : something that is external
3 : a secondary or unintended consequence ⟨pollution and other *externalities* of manufacturing⟩

ex·ter·nal·iza·tion \ek-,stər-n°l-ə-'zā-shən\ *noun* (1803)
1 a : the action or process of externalizing **b :** the quality or state of being externalized
2 : something externalized **:** EMBODIMENT

ex·ter·nal·ize \ek-'stər-n°l-,īz\ *transitive verb* **-ized; -iz·ing** (1852)
1 : to make external or externally manifest
2 : to attribute to causes outside the self **:** RATIONALIZE

external respiration *noun* (1940)
: exchange of gases between the external environment and a distributing system of the animal body (as the lungs of higher vertebrates or the tracheal tubes of insects) or between the alveoli of the lungs and the blood — compare INTERNAL RESPIRATION

ex·tern·ship \'ek-,stərn-,ship\ *noun* (1945)
: a training program that is part of a course of study of an educational institution and is taken in private business

☆ SYNONYMS
Exterminate, extirpate, eradicate, uproot mean to effect the destruction or abolition of something. EXTERMINATE implies complete and immediate extinction by killing off all individuals ⟨*exterminate* cockroaches⟩. EXTIRPATE implies extinction of a race, family, species, or sometimes an idea or doctrine by destruction or removal of its means of propagation ⟨many species have been *extirpated* from the area⟩. ERADICATE implies the driving out or elimination of something that has established itself ⟨a campaign to *eradicate* illiteracy⟩. UPROOT implies a forcible or violent removal and stresses displacement or dislodgment rather than immediate destruction ⟨the war *uprooted* thousands⟩.

\ə\ abut \ᵊ\ kitten \ər\ further \a\ ash \ā\ ace
\ä\ mop, mar \aù\ out \ch\ chin \e\ bet \ē\ easy
\g\ go \i\ hit \ī\ ice \j\ job \ŋ\ sing \ō\ go
\ò\ law \òi\ boy \th\ thin \th\ the \ü\ loot \ù\ foot
\y\ yet \zh\ vision *see also* Guide to Pronunciation

ex·tero·cep·tive \ˌek-stə-rō-'sep-tiv\ *adjective* [*exterior* + *-o-* + *-ceptive* (as in *receptive*)] (circa 1921)
: activated by, relating to, or being stimuli received by an organism from outside
ex·tero·cep·tor \-tər\ *noun* (1906)
: a sense organ excited by exteroceptive stimuli
ex·ter·ri·to·ri·al \ˌek-ster-ə-'tōr-ē-əl, -'tȯr-\ *adjective* (circa 1880)
: EXTRATERRITORIAL
— **ex·ter·ri·to·ri·al·i·ty** \-ˌtōr-ē-'a-lə-tē, -ˌtȯr-\ *noun*
¹ex·tinct \ik-'stiŋ(k)t, 'ek-ˌ\ *adjective* [Middle English, from Latin *exstinctus*, past participle of *exstinguere*] (15th century)
1 a : no longer burning **b :** no longer active ⟨an *extinct* volcano⟩
2 : no longer existing ⟨an *extinct* animal⟩
3 a : gone out of use : SUPERSEDED **b :** having no qualified claimant ⟨an *extinct* title⟩
²extinct *transitive verb* (15th century)
archaic : EXTINGUISH
ex·tinc·tion \ik-'stiŋ(k)-shən\ *noun* (15th century)
1 : the act of making extinct or causing to be extinguished
2 : the condition or fact of being extinct or extinguished; *also* : the process of becoming extinct ⟨*extinction* of a species⟩
3 : the process of eliminating or reducing a conditioned response by not reinforcing it
extinction coefficient *noun* (1902)
: a measure of the rate of diminution of transmitted light via scattering and absorption for a medium
ex·tinc·tive \ik-'stiŋ(k)-tiv\ *adjective* (1600)
: tending or serving to extinguish or make extinct
ex·tin·guish \ik-'stiŋ-(g)wish\ *transitive verb* [Latin *exstinguere* (from *ex-* + *stinguere* to extinguish) + English *-ish* (as in *abolish*); akin to Latin in*stigare* to incite — more at STICK] (1551)
1 a : to cause to cease burning : QUENCH **b** (1) : to bring to an end : make an end of ⟨hope for their safety was slowly *extinguished*⟩ (2) : to reduce to silence or ineffectiveness **c :** to cause extinction of (a conditioned response) **d :** to dim the brightness of : ECLIPSE
2 a : to cause to be void : NULLIFY ⟨*extinguish* a claim⟩ **b :** to get rid of usually by payment ⟨*extinguish* a debt⟩
— **ex·tin·guish·able** \-(g)wi-shə-bəl\ *adjective*
— **ex·tin·guish·er** \-shər\ *noun*
— **ex·tin·guish·ment** \-mənt\ *noun*
ex·tir·pate \'ek-stər-ˌpāt\ *transitive verb* **-pat·ed; -pat·ing** [Latin *exstirpatus*, past participle of *exstirpare*, from *ex-* + *stirp-, stirps* trunk, root — more at TORPID] (1535)
1 a : to destroy completely : WIPE OUT **b :** to pull up by the root
2 : to cut out by surgery
synonym see EXTERMINATE
— **ex·tir·pa·tion** \ˌek-stər-'pā-shən\ *noun*
— **ex·tir·pa·tor** \'ek-stər-ˌpā-tər\ *noun*
ex·tol *also* **ex·toll** \ik-'stōl\ *transitive verb* **ex·tolled; ex·tol·ling** [Middle English, from Latin *extollere*, from *ex-* + *tollere* to lift up — more at TOLERATE] (15th century)
: to praise highly : GLORIFY
— **ex·tol·ler** *noun*
— **ex·tol·ment** \-'stōl-mənt\ *noun*
ex·tort \ik-'stȯrt\ *transitive verb* [Latin *extortus*, past participle of *extorquēre* to wrench out, extort, from *ex-* + *torquēre* to twist — more at TORTURE] (1529)
: to obtain from a person by force, intimidation, or undue or illegal power : WRING; *also* : to gain especially by ingenuity or compelling argument
synonym see EDUCE
— **ex·tort·er** *noun*
— **ex·tor·tive** \-'stȯr-tiv\ *adjective*

ex·tor·tion \ik-'stȯr-shən\ *noun* (14th century)
1 : the act or practice of extorting especially money or other property; *especially* : the offense committed by an official engaging in such practice
2 : something extorted; *especially* : a gross overcharge
— **ex·tor·tion·er** \-sh(ə-)nər\ *noun*
— **ex·tor·tion·ist** \-sh(ə-)nist\ *noun*
ex·tor·tion·ary \-shə-ˌner-ē\ *adjective* (1805)
archaic : EXTORTIONATE 1
ex·tor·tion·ate \ik-'stȯr-sh(ə-)nət\ *adjective* (1789)
1 : characterized by extortion
2 : EXCESSIVE, EXORBITANT ⟨*extortionate* prices⟩
— **ex·tor·tion·ate·ly** *adverb*
¹ex·tra \'ek-strə\ *adjective* [probably short for *extraordinary*] (1776)
1 a : more than is due, usual, or necessary : ADDITIONAL ⟨*extra* work⟩ **b :** subject to an additional charge ⟨room service is *extra*⟩
2 : SUPERIOR ⟨*extra* quality⟩
²extra *noun* (1793)
1 : one that is extra or additional: as **a :** a special edition of a newspaper **b :** an added charge **c :** an additional worker; *specifically* : one hired to act in a group scene in a motion picture or stage production
2 : something of superior quality or grade
³extra *adverb* (1823)
: beyond the usual size, extent, or degree ⟨*extra* large⟩
extra- *prefix* [Middle English, from Latin, from *extra,* adverb & preposition, outside, except, beyond, from *exter* being on the outside — more at EXTERIOR]
: outside : beyond ⟨*extra*judicial⟩
extra–base hit *noun* (circa 1949)
: a hit in baseball that lets the batter take more than one base
ex·tra·cel·lu·lar \ˌek-strə-'sel-yə-lər\ *adjective* (1867)
: situated or occurring outside a cell or the cells of the body ⟨*extracellular* digestion⟩ ⟨*extracellular* enzymes⟩
— **ex·tra·cel·lu·lar·ly** *adverb*
ex·tra·chro·mo·som·al \-ˌkrō-mə-'sō-məl, -'zō-\ *adjective* (1940)
: situated or controlled by factors outside the chromosome ⟨*extrachromosomal* inheritance⟩
ex·tra·cor·po·re·al \-kȯr-'pōr-ē-əl, -'pȯr-\ *adjective* (1865)
: occurring or based outside the living body ⟨heart surgery employing *extracorporeal* circulation⟩
— **ex·tra·cor·po·re·al·ly** \-ē-ə-lē\ *adverb*
ex·tra·cra·ni·al \-'krā-nē-əl\ *adjective* (circa 1884)
: situated or occurring outside the cranium
¹ex·tract \ik-'strakt, oftenest in sense 5 'ek-ˌ\ *transitive verb* [Middle English, from Latin *extractus*, past participle of *extrahere*, from *ex-* + *trahere* to draw] (15th century)
1 a : to draw forth (as by research) ⟨*extract* data⟩ **b :** to pull or take out forcibly ⟨*extracted* a wisdom tooth⟩ **c :** to obtain by much effort from someone unwilling ⟨*extracted* a confession⟩
2 : to withdraw (as a juice or fraction) by physical or chemical process; *also* : to treat with a solvent so as to remove a soluble substance
3 : to separate (a metal) from an ore
4 : to determine (a mathematical root) by calculation
5 : to select (excerpts) and copy out or cite
synonym see EXTRACT
— **ex·tract·abil·i·ty** \ik-ˌstrak-tə-'bi-lə-tē, (ˌ)ek-\ *noun*
— **ex·tract·able** \ik-'strak-tə-bəl, 'ek-ˌ\ *adjective*
²ex·tract \'ek-ˌstrakt\ *noun* (15th century)
1 : a selection from a writing or discourse : EXCERPT

2 : a product (as an essence or concentrate) prepared by extracting; *especially* : a solution (as in alcohol) of essential constituents of a complex material (as meat or an aromatic plant)
ex·trac·tion \ik-'strak-shən\ *noun* (15th century)
1 : the act or process of extracting something
2 : ANCESTRY, ORIGIN
3 : something extracted
¹ex·trac·tive \ik-'strak-tiv, 'ek-ˌ\ *adjective* (1599)
1 a : of, relating to, or involving extraction **b :** tending toward or resulting in withdrawal of natural resources by extraction with no provision for replenishment ⟨*extractive* agriculture⟩
2 : capable of being extracted
— **ex·trac·tive·ly** *adverb*
²extractive *noun* (1847)
: something extracted or extractable : EXTRACT
ex·trac·tor \ik-'strak-tər\ *noun* (1611)
: one that extracts; *especially* : the mechanism in a firearm that dislodges a spent cartridge from the chamber
ex·tra·cur·ric·u·lar \ˌek-strə-kə-'ri-kyə-lər\ *adjective* (1925)
1 : not falling within the scope of a regular curriculum; *specifically* : of or relating to officially or semiofficially approved and usually organized student activities (as athletics) connected with school and usually carrying no academic credit
2 a : lying outside one's regular duties or routine **b :** EXTRAMARITAL
— **extracurricular** *noun*
ex·tra·dit·able \'ek-strə-ˌdī-tə-bəl\ *adjective* (1881)
1 : subject or liable to extradition
2 : making one liable to extradition ⟨an *extraditable* offense⟩
ex·tra·dite \'ek-strə-ˌdīt\ *transitive verb* **-dit·ed; -dit·ing** [back-formation from *extradition*] (1864)
1 : to deliver up to extradition
2 : to obtain the extradition of
ex·tra·di·tion \ˌek-strə-'di-shən\ *noun* [French, from *ex-* + Latin *tradition-, traditio* act of handing over — more at TREASON] (1839)
: the surrender of an alleged criminal usually under the provisions of a treaty or statute by one authority (as a state) to another having jurisdiction to try the charge
ex·tra·dos \'ek-strə-ˌdäs, -ˌdō; ek-'strā-ˌdäs *noun, plural* **-dos·es** \-ˌdä-səz\ *or* **-dos** \-ˌdōz, -ˌdäs\ [French, from Latin *extra* + French *dos* back — more at DOSSIER] (1772)
: the exterior curve of an arch — see ARCH illustration
ex·tra·em·bry·on·ic \ˌek-strə-ˌem-brē-'ä-nik\ *adjective* (circa 1903)
: situated outside the embryo; *especially* : developed from the zygote but not part of the embryo ⟨*extraembryonic* membranes⟩
ex·tra·ga·lac·tic \ˌek-strə-gə-'lak-tik\ *adjective* [International Scientific Vocabulary] (1851)
: lying or coming from outside the Milky Way; *also* : of or relating to extragalactic space ⟨*extragalactic* astronomy⟩
ex·tra·he·pat·ic \-hi-'pa-tik\ *adjective* (circa 1923)
: situated or originating outside the liver
ex·tra·ju·di·cial \-jù-'di-shəl\ *adjective* (1630)
1 a : not forming a valid part of regular legal proceedings ⟨an *extrajudicial* investigation⟩ **b :** delivered without legal authority : PRIVATE 2a(2) ⟨the judge's *extrajudicial* statements⟩
2 : done in contravention of due process of law ⟨an *extrajudicial* execution⟩
— **ex·tra·ju·di·cial·ly** \-'dish-lē, -'di-shə-\ *adverb*
ex·tra·le·gal \ˌek-strə-'lē-gəl\ *adjective* (1644)
: not regulated or sanctioned by law

— **ex·tra·le·gal·ly** \-gə-lē\ *adverb*

ex·tra·lim·it·al \-'li-mə-t°l\ *adjective* (1874)
: not present in a given area — used of kinds of organisms (as species)

ex·tra·lin·guis·tic \-liŋ-'gwis-tik\ *adjective* (1927)
: lying outside the province of linguistics
— **ex·tra·lin·guis·ti·cal·ly** \-ti-kə-lē\ *adverb*

ex·tra·lit·er·ary \-'li-tə-‚rer-ē\ *adjective* (1945)
: lying outside the field of literature

ex·tral·i·ty \ek-'stra-lə-tē\ *noun* [by contraction] (1925)
: EXTRATERRITORIALITY

ex·tra·log·i·cal \‚ek-strə-'lä-ji-kəl\ *adjective* (1833)
: not guided or determined by considerations of logic

ex·tra·mar·i·tal \‚ek-strə-'mar-ə-t°l\ *adjective* (1925)
: of, relating to, or being sexual intercourse between a married person and someone other than his or her spouse : ADULTEROUS

ex·tra·mun·dane \‚ek-strə-‚mən-'dān, -'mən-‚dān\ *adjective* [Late Latin *extramundanus*, from Latin *extra* + *mundus* the world] (1665)
: situated in or relating to a region beyond the material world

ex·tra·mu·ral \-'myùr-əl\ *adjective* (1854)
1 : existing or functioning outside or beyond the walls, boundaries, or precincts of an organized unit (as a school or hospital)
2 *chiefly British* : of, relating to, or taking part in extension courses or facilities
— **ex·tra·mu·ral·ly** \-ə-lē\ *adverb*

ex·tra·mu·si·cal \-'myü-zi-kəl\ *adjective* (1923)
: lying outside the province of music

ex·tra·ne·ous \ek-'strā-nē-əs\ *adjective* [Latin *extraneus* — more at STRANGE] (1638)
1 : existing on or coming from the outside
2 a : not forming an essential or vital part ⟨*extraneous* ornamentation⟩ **b** : having no relevance ⟨an *extraneous* digression⟩
3 : being a number obtained in solving an equation that is not a solution of the equation ⟨*extraneous* roots⟩
synonym see EXTRINSIC
— **ex·tra·ne·ous·ly** *adverb*
— **ex·tra·ne·ous·ness** *noun*

ex·tra·nu·cle·ar \‚ek-strə-'nü-klē-ər, -'nyü-, ÷-kyə-lər\ *adjective* (1887)
1 : situated in or affecting the parts of a cell external to the nucleus : CYTOPLASMIC
2 : situated outside the nucleus of an atom

ex·tra·oc·u·lar muscle \‚ek-strə-'ä-kyə-lər-\ *noun* (1939)
: any of six small voluntary muscles that pass between the eyeball and the orbit and control the movement of the eyeball in relation to the orbit

ex·traor·di·naire \ik-‚strò(r)-d°n-'er, ek-\ *adjective* [French] (1940)
: EXTRAORDINARY — used postpositively ⟨a chef *extraordinaire*⟩

ex·traor·di·nary \ik-'strór-d°n-‚er-ē, ‚ek-strə-'òr-\ *adjective* [Middle English *extraordinarie*, from Latin *extraordinarius*, from *extra ordinem* out of course, from *extra* + *ordinem*, accusative of *ordin-*, *ordo* order] (15th century)
1 a : going beyond what is usual, regular, or customary ⟨*extraordinary* powers⟩ **b** : exceptional to a very marked extent ⟨*extraordinary* beauty⟩ **c** *of a financial transaction* : NONRECURRING
2 : employed for or sent on a special function or service ⟨an ambassador *extraordinary*⟩
— **ex·traor·di·nari·ly** \ik-‚strór-d°n-'er-ə-lē, ‚ek-strə-‚òr-\ *adverb*
— **ex·traor·di·nari·ness** \ik-'strór-d°n-‚er-ē-nəs, ‚ek-strə-'òr-\ *noun*

extra point *noun* (circa 1949)
: a point gained on a conversion in football

ex·trap·o·late \ik-'stra-pə-‚lāt\ *verb* **-lat·ed; -lat·ing** [Latin *extra* outside + English *-polate* (as in *interpolate*) — more at EXTRA-] (1874)
transitive verb
1 : to infer (values of a variable in an unobserved interval) from values within an already observed interval
2 a : to project, extend, or expand (known data or experience) into an area not known or experienced so as to arrive at a usually conjectural knowledge of the unknown area ⟨*extrapolates* present trends to construct an image of the future⟩ **b** : to predict by projecting past experience or known data ⟨*extrapolate* public sentiment on one issue from known public reaction on others⟩
intransitive verb
: to perform the act or process of extrapolating
— **ex·trap·o·la·tion** \-‚stra-pə-'lā-shən\ *noun*
— **ex·trap·o·la·tive** \-'stra-pə-‚lā-tiv\ *adjective*
— **ex·trap·o·la·tor** \-‚lā-tər\ *noun*

ex·tra·py·ra·mi·dal \‚ek-strə-pə-'ra-mə-d°l, -‚pir-ə-'mi-d°l\ *adjective* (circa 1902)
: situated outside of and especially involving descending nerve tracts other than the pyramidal tracts

ex·tra·sen·so·ry \‚ek-strə-'sen(t)s-rē, -'sen(t)-sə-\ *adjective* (1934)
: residing beyond or outside the ordinary senses

extrasensory perception *noun* (1934)
: perception (as in telepathy, clairvoyance, and precognition) that involves awareness of information about events external to the self not gained through the senses and not deducible from previous experience — called also *ESP*

ex·tra·sys·to·le \-'sis-tə-(‚)lē\ *noun* [New Latin] (circa 1900)
: a premature beat of one of the chambers of the heart that leads to momentary arrhythmia

¹ex·tra·ter·res·tri·al \-tə-'res-trē-əl, -'res(h)-chəl\ *adjective* (1868)
: originating, existing, or occurring outside the earth or its atmosphere ⟨*extraterrestrial* life⟩

²extraterrestrial *noun* (1960)
: an extraterrestrial being

ex·tra·ter·ri·to·ri·al \-‚ter-ə-'tòr-ē-əl, -'tòr-\ *adjective* (1869)
: existing or taking place outside the territorial limits of a jurisdiction

ex·tra·ter·ri·to·ri·al·i·ty \-‚tòr-ē-'a-lə-tē, -‚tòr-\ *noun* (1836)
: exemption from the application or jurisdiction of local law or tribunals

ex·tra·tex·tu·al \‚ek-strə-'teks-chə-wəl, -chəl\ *adjective* (1960)
: of, relating to, or being something outside a literary text

ex·tra·trop·i·cal cyclone \‚ek-strə-‚trä-pi-kəl-\ *noun* (1923)
: a cyclone in the middle latitudes often being 1500 miles (2400 kilometers) in diameter and usually containing a cold front that extends toward the equator for hundreds of miles

ex·tra·uter·ine \‚ek-strə-'yü-tə-rən, -‚rīn\ *adjective* (1709)
: situated or occurring outside the uterus ⟨*extrauterine* pregnancy⟩

ex·trav·a·gance \ik-'stra-vi-gən(t)s\ *noun* (1650)
1 a : an instance of excess or prodigality; *specifically* : an excessive outlay of money **b** : something extravagant
2 : the quality or fact of being extravagant

ex·trav·a·gan·cy \-gən(t)-sē\ *noun, plural* **-cies** (1625)
: EXTRAVAGANCE

ex·trav·a·gant \ik-'stra-vi-gənt\ *adjective* [Middle English, from Middle French, from Medieval Latin *extravagant-, extravagans*, from Latin *extra-* + *vagant-, vagans*, present participle of *vagari* to wander about, from *vagus* wandering] (15th century)

1 a *obsolete* : STRANGE, CURIOUS **b** *archaic* : WANDERING
2 a : exceeding the limits of reason or necessity ⟨*extravagant* claims⟩ **b** : lacking in moderation, balance, and restraint ⟨*extravagant* praise⟩
c : extremely or excessively elaborate
3 a : spending much more than necessary **b** : PROFUSE, LAVISH
4 : unreasonably high in price ◊
synonym see EXCESSIVE
— **ex·trav·a·gant·ly** *adverb*

ex·trav·a·gan·za \ik-‚stra-və-'gan-zə\ *noun* [Italian *estravaganza*, literally, extravagance, from *estravagante* extravagant, from Medieval Latin *extravagant-, extravagans*] (1754)
1 : a literary or musical work marked by extreme freedom of style and structure and usually by elements of burlesque or parody
2 : a lavish or spectacular show or event
3 : something extravagant

ex·trav·a·gate \ik-'stra-və-‚gāt\ *intransitive verb* **-gat·ed; -gat·ing** (circa 1755)
archaic : to go beyond proper limits

ex·trav·a·sate \ik-'stra-və-‚sāt, -‚zāt\ *verb* **-sat·ed; -sat·ing** [Latin *extra* + *vas* vessel] (1668)
transitive verb
: to force out or cause to escape from a proper vessel or channel
intransitive verb
: to pass by infiltration or effusion from a proper vessel or channel (as a blood vessel) into surrounding tissue
— **ex·trav·a·sa·tion** \-‚stra-və-'sā-shən, -'zā-\ *noun*

ex·tra·vas·cu·lar \‚ek-strə-'vas-kyə-lər\ *adjective* (1804)
: not occurring or contained in body vessels ⟨*extravascular* tissue fluids⟩

ex·tra·ve·hic·u·lar \-vē-'hi-kyə-lər\ *adjective* (1965)
: taking place outside a vehicle (as a spacecraft) ⟨*extravehicular* activity⟩

¹ex·treme \ik-'strēm\ *adjective* [Middle English, from Middle French, from Latin *extremus*, superlative of *exter, exterus* being on the outside — more at EXTERIOR] (15th century)
1 a : existing in a very high degree ⟨*extreme* poverty⟩ **b** : going to great or exaggerated lengths : RADICAL ⟨went on an *extreme* diet⟩ **c** : exceeding the ordinary, usual, or expected ⟨*extreme* weather conditions⟩
2 *archaic* : LAST
3 : situated at the farthest possible point from a center ⟨the country's *extreme* north⟩
4 a : most advanced or thoroughgoing ⟨the *extreme* political left⟩ **b** : MAXIMUM
synonym see EXCESSIVE

◊ **WORD HISTORY**
extravagant A person who buys an extravagant gift has in all likelihood strayed quite far from the amount originally budgeted for the purchase. The notion of wandering far afield actually is inherent in the word *extravagant*, which comes from a word in Medieval Latin. *Extravagans* is formed from the Latin prefix *extra-* "outside" or "beyond" and the verb *vagari* "to wander about." Originally *extravagant* was used literally of things that wandered beyond their usual confines. In Shakespeare's *Hamlet* the restless ghost of Hamlet's father is spoken of as an "extravagant and erring spirit." From this literal use of *extravagant*, the extended meanings "exceeding the limits of reason or necessity" and "lacking in moderation, balance, and restraint" developed.

\ə\ abut \ᵊ\ kitten \ər\ further \a\ ash \ā\ ace
\ä\ mop, mar \aù\ out \ch\ chin \e\ bet \ē\ easy
\g\ go \i\ hit \ī\ ice \j\ job \ŋ\ sing \ō\ go
\ò\ law \òi\ boy \th\ thin \th\ the \ü\ loot \ù\ foot
\y\ yet \zh\ vision *see also* Guide to Pronunciation

— **ex·treme·ness** *noun*

²**extreme** *noun* (1555)
1 a : something situated at or marking one end or the other of a range ⟨*extremes* of heat and cold⟩ **b** : the first term or the last term of a mathematical proportion **c** : the major term or minor term of a syllogism
2 a : a very pronounced or excessive degree **b** : highest degree : MAXIMUM
3 : an extreme measure or expedient ⟨going to *extremes*⟩
— **in the extreme** : to the greatest possible extent

ex·treme·ly *adverb* (1531)
1 : in an extreme manner
2 : to an extreme extent

extremely high frequency *noun* (1952)
: a radio frequency in the highest range of the radio spectrum — see RADIO FREQUENCY table

extremely low frequency *noun* (1966)
: a radio frequency in the lowest range of the radio spectrum — see RADIO FREQUENCY table

extreme unction \ik-ˌstrēm-ˈəŋ(k)-shən, ˌek-(ˌ)strēm-\ *noun* (15th century)
: a sacrament in which a priest anoints and prays for the recovery and salvation of a critically ill or injured person

ex·trem·ism \ik-ˈstrē-ˌmi-zəm\ *noun* (1865)
1 : the quality or state of being extreme
2 : advocacy of extreme political measures : RADICALISM
— **ex·trem·ist** \-mist\ *noun or adjective*

ex·trem·i·ty \ik-ˈstre-mə-tē\ *noun, plural* **-ties** (14th century)
1 a : the farthest or most remote part, section, or point **b** : a limb of the body; *especially* : a human hand or foot
2 a : extreme danger or critical need **b** : a moment marked by imminent destruction or death
3 a : an intense degree ⟨the *extremity* of his participation —*Saturday Review*⟩ **b** : the utmost degree (as of emotion or pain)
4 : a drastic or desperate act or measure ⟨driven to *extremities*⟩

ex·tre·mum \ik-ˈstrē-məm\ *noun, plural* **-ma** \-mə\ [New Latin, from Latin, neuter of *extremus*] (1904)
: a maximum or a minimum of a mathematical function — called also *extreme value*

ex·tri·cate \ˈek-strə-ˌkāt\ *transitive verb* **-cat·ed; -cat·ing** [Latin *extricatus*, past participle of *extricare*, from *ex-* + *tricae* trifles, perplexities] (1614)
1 a *archaic* : UNRAVEL **b** : to distinguish from a related thing
2 : to free or remove from an entanglement or difficulty ☆
— **ex·tri·ca·ble** \ik-ˈstri-kə-bəl, ek-ˈ, ˈek-(ˌ)\ *adjective*
— **ex·tri·ca·tion** \ˌek-strə-ˈkā-shən\ *noun*

ex·trin·sic \ek-ˈstrin-zik, -ˈstrin(t)-sik\ *adjective* [French & Late Latin; French *extrinsèque*, from Late Latin *extrinsecus*, from Latin, adverb, from without; akin to Latin *exter* outward and to Latin *sequi* to follow — more at EXTERIOR, SUE] (1613)
1 a : not forming part of or belonging to a thing : EXTRANEOUS **b** : originating from or on the outside; *especially* : originating outside a part and acting upon the part as a whole ⟨*extrinsic* muscles of the tongue⟩
2 : EXTERNAL ☆
— **ex·trin·si·cal·ly** \-zi-k(ə-)lē, -si-\ *adverb*

extrinsic factor *noun* (1938)
: VITAMIN B₁₂

extro- *prefix* [alteration of Latin *extra-*]
: outward ⟨*extrovert*⟩ — compare INTRO-

ex·trorse \ˈek-ˌstrȯrs\ *adjective* [probably from (assumed) New Latin *extrorsus*, from Late Latin, adverb, outward, from Latin *extra-* + *-orsus* (as in *introrsus*) — more at INTRORSE] (1858)
: facing outward ⟨an *extrorse* anther⟩

ex·tro·ver·sion *or* **ex·tra·ver·sion** \ˌek-strə-ˈvər-zhən, -shən\ *noun* [German *Extraver-*

sion, from Latin *extra-* + *versus*, past participle of *vertere* to turn — more at WORTH] (1915)
: the act, state, or habit of being predominantly concerned with and obtaining gratification from what is outside the self

ex·tro·vert *also* **ex·tra·vert** \ˈek-strə-ˌvərt\ *noun* [modification of German *extravertiert*, from Latin *extra-* + *vertere*] (1918)
: one whose personality is characterized by extroversion; *broadly* : a gregarious and unreserved person
— **extrovert** *also* **extravert** *adjective*
— **ex·tro·vert·ed** *also* **ex·tra·vert·ed** \-ˌvər-təd, ˌek-strə-ˈvər-\ *adjective*

ex·trude \ik-ˈstrüd\ *verb* **ex·trud·ed; ex·trud·ing** [Latin *extrudere*, from *ex-* + *trudere* to thrust — more at THREAT] (1566)
transitive verb
1 : to force, press, or push out
2 : to shape (as metal or plastic) by forcing through a die
intransitive verb
: to become extruded
— **ex·trud·abil·i·ty** \-ˌstrü-də-ˈbi-lə-tē\ *noun*
— **ex·trud·able** \-ˈstrü-də-bəl\ *adjective*
— **ex·trud·er** \-ˈstrü-dər\ *noun*

ex·tru·sion \ik-ˈstrü-zhən\ *noun* [Medieval Latin *extrusion-, extrusio*, from Latin *extrudere*] (1540)
: the act or process of extruding; *also* : a form or product produced by this process

ex·tru·sive \ik-ˈstrü-siv, -ziv\ *adjective* (1816)
: relating to or formed by geological extrusion from the earth in a molten state or as volcanic ash

ex·u·ber·ance \ig-ˈzü-b(ə-)rən(t)s\ *noun* (1631)
1 : the quality or state of being exuberant
2 : an exuberant act or expression

ex·u·ber·ant \-b(ə-)rənt\ *adjective* [Middle English, from Middle French, from Latin *exuberant-, exuberans*, present participle of *exuberare* to be abundant, from *ex-* + *uber* fruitful, from *uber* udder — more at UDDER] (15th century)
1 : extreme or excessive in degree, size, or extent
2 a : joyously unrestrained and enthusiastic **b** : unrestrained or elaborate especially in style : FLAMBOYANT ⟨*exuberant* architecture⟩
3 : produced in extreme abundance : PLENTIFUL
synonym see PROFUSE
— **ex·u·ber·ant·ly** *adverb*

ex·u·ber·ate \-bə-ˌrāt\ *intransitive verb* **-at·ed; -at·ing** (15th century)
1 *archaic* : to have something in abundance : OVERFLOW
2 : to become exuberant : show exuberance ⟨*exuberated* over his victory⟩

ex·u·date \ˈek-s(y)ù-ˌdāt, -shü-\ *noun* (1876)
: exuded matter

ex·u·da·tion \ˌek-s(y)ù-ˈdā-shən, -shü-\ *noun* (1612)
1 : the process of exuding
2 : EXUDATE
— **ex·u·da·tive** \ig-ˈzü-də-tiv; ˈek-s(y)ù-ˌdā-tiv, -shü-\ *adjective*

ex·ude \ig-ˈzüd\ *verb* **ex·ud·ed; ex·ud·ing** [Latin *exsudare*, from *ex-* + *sudare* to sweat — more at SWEAT] (1574)
intransitive verb
1 : to ooze out
2 : to undergo diffusion
transitive verb
1 : to cause to ooze or spread out in all directions
2 : to display conspicuously or abundantly ⟨*exudes* charm⟩

ex·ult \ig-ˈzəlt\ *intransitive verb* [Middle French *exulter*, from Latin *exsultare*, literally, to leap up, from *ex-* + *saltare* to leap — more at SALTATION] (1570)
1 *obsolete* : to leap for joy

2 : to be extremely joyful : REJOICE
— **ex·ult·ing·ly** \-ˈzəl-tiŋ-lē\ *adverb*

ex·ul·tance \ig-ˈzəl-t²n(t)s\ *noun* (1650)
: EXULTATION

ex·ul·tan·cy \-ˈzəl-t²n(t)-sē\ *noun* (1621)
: EXULTATION

ex·ul·tant \ig-ˈzəl-t²nt\ *adjective* (1653)
: filled with or expressing great joy or triumph : JUBILANT
— **ex·ul·tant·ly** *adverb*

ex·ul·ta·tion \ˌek-(ˌ)səl-ˈtā-shən, ˌeg-(ˌ)zəl-\ *noun* (15th century)
: the act of exulting : the state of being exultant

ex·urb \ˈek-ˌsərb, ˈeg-ˌzərb\ *noun* [*ex-* + suburb] (1955)
: a region or settlement that lies outside a city and usually beyond its suburbs and that often is inhabited chiefly by well-to-do families
— **ex·ur·ban** \ek-ˈsər-bən; eg-ˈzər-, ig-\ *adjective*

ex·ur·ban·ite \ek-ˈsər-bə-ˌnīt; eg-ˈzər-, ig-\ *noun* (1955)
: one who lives in an exurb

ex·ur·bia \-bē-ə\ *noun* (1955)
: the generalized region of exurbs

ex·u·vi·ae \ig-ˈzü-vē-ˌē, -vē-ˌī\ *noun plural* [Latin, from *exuere* to take off, from *ex-* + *-uere* to put on; akin to Old Church Slavonic *obuti* to put on (footwear)] (1653)
: sloughed off natural animal coverings (as the skins of snakes)
— **ex·u·vi·al** \-vē-əl\ *adjective*

ex·u·vi·a·tion \-ˌzü-vē-ˈā-shən\ *noun* (1839)
: the process of molting

¹**ex-vo·to** \(ˌ)eks-ˈvō-(ˌ)tō\ *noun, plural* **ex-votos** [Latin *ex voto* according to a vow] (1787)
: a votive offering

²**ex-voto** *adjective* (1823)
: VOTIVE

-ey — see -Y

ey·as \ˈī-əs\ *noun* [Middle English, alteration (by incorrect division of *a neias*) of *neias*, from Middle French *niais* fresh from the nest,

☆ **SYNONYMS**
Extricate, disentangle, untangle, disencumber, disembarrass mean to free from what binds or holds back. EXTRICATE implies the use of care or ingenuity in freeing from a difficult position or situation ⟨*extricated* himself from financial difficulties⟩. DISENTANGLE and UNTANGLE suggest painstaking separation of a thing from other things ⟨*disentangling* fact from fiction⟩ ⟨*untangle* a web of deceit⟩. DISENCUMBER implies a release from something that clogs or weighs down ⟨an article *disencumbered* of jargon⟩. DISEMBARRASS suggests a release from something that impedes or hinders ⟨*disembarrassed* herself of her advisers⟩.

Extrinsic, extraneous, foreign, alien mean external to a thing, its essential nature, or its original character. EXTRINSIC applies to what is distinctly outside the thing in question or is not contained in or derived from its essential nature ⟨sentimental value that is *extrinsic* to the house's market value⟩. EXTRANEOUS applies to what is on or comes from the outside and may or may not be capable of becoming an essential part ⟨arguments *extraneous* to the issue⟩. FOREIGN applies to what is so different as to be rejected or repelled or to be incapable of becoming assimilated ⟨techniques *foreign* to French cuisine⟩. ALIEN is stronger than FOREIGN in suggesting opposition, repugnance, or irreconcilability ⟨a practice totally *alien* to her nature⟩.

from (assumed) Vulgar Latin *nidax* nestling, from Latin *nidus* nest — more at NEST] (15th century)

: an unfledged bird; *specifically* : a nestling hawk

¹eye \'ī\ *noun* [Middle English, from Old English *ēage;* akin to Old High German *ouga* eye, Latin *oculus*, Greek *ōps* eye, face, Sanskrit *akṣi* eye] (before 12th century)

1 a : an organ of sight; *especially* : a nearly spherical hollow organ that is lined with a sensitive retina, is lodged in a bony orbit in the skull, is the vertebrate organ of sight, and is normally paired **b** : all the visible structures within and surrounding the orbit and including eyelids, eyelashes, and eyebrows **c** (1) : the faculty of

eye 1a: *1* optic nerve, *2* blind spot, *3* fovea, *4* sclera, *5* choroid, *6* retina, *7* ciliary body, *8* posterior chamber, *9* anterior chamber, *10* cornea, *11* lens, *12* iris, *13* suspensory ligament, *14* conjunctiva, *15* vitreous humor

seeing with eyes (2) : the faculty of intellectual or aesthetic perception or appreciation ⟨an *eye* for beauty⟩ **d** : LOOK, GLANCE ⟨cast an eager *eye*⟩ **e** (1) : an attentive look ⟨kept an *eye* on his valuables⟩ (2) : ATTENTION, NOTICE ⟨caught his *eye*⟩ (3) : close observation : SCRUTINY ⟨works under the *eye* of her boss⟩ ⟨in the public *eye*⟩ **f** : POINT OF VIEW, JUDGMENT ⟨beauty is in the *eye* of the beholder⟩ — often used in plural ⟨an offender in the *eyes* of the law⟩ **g** : VIEW 5 ⟨with an *eye* to the future⟩

2 : something having an appearance suggestive of an eye: as **a** : the hole through the head of a needle **b** : a usually circular marking (as on a peacock's tail) **c** : LOOP; *especially* : a loop or catch to receive a hook **d** : an undeveloped bud (as on a potato) **e** : an area like a hole in the center of a tropical cyclone marked by only light winds or complete calm with no precipitation **f** : the center of a flower especially when differently colored or marked; *specifically* : the disk of a composite **g** (1) : a triangular piece of beef cut from between the top and bottom of a round (2) : the chief muscle of a chop (3) : a compact mass of muscular tissue usually embedded in fat in a rib or loin cut of meat **h** : a device (as a photoelectric cell) that functions in a manner analogous to human vision

3 : something central : CENTER ⟨the *eye* of the problem —Norman Mailer⟩

4 : the direction from which the wind is blowing

— **eye·less** \'ī-ləs\ *adjective*
— **eye·like** \-,līk\ *adjective*
— **an eye for an eye** : retribution in kind
— **my eye** — used to express mild disagreement or sometimes surprise ⟨a diamond, *my eye!* That's glass⟩

²eye *verb* **eyed; eye·ing** *or* **ey·ing** (15th century)
transitive verb
1 a : to fix the eyes on : look at **b** : to watch closely
2 : to furnish with an eye
intransitive verb
obsolete : SEEM, LOOK
— **ey·er** \'ī-(-ə)r\ *noun*

¹eye·ball \'ī-,bȯl\ *noun* (1590)
: the more or less globular capsule of the vertebrate eye formed by the sclera and cornea together with their contained structures

²eyeball *transitive verb* (1901)
: to look at intently

³eyeball *adjective* (1971)
: based on observation ⟨*eyeball* judgment⟩

eyeball–to–eyeball *adverb or adjective* (1962)
: FACE-TO-FACE

eye bank *noun* (1944)
: a storage place for human corneas from the newly dead for transplanting to the eyes of those blind through corneal defects

eye-bar \'ī-,bär\ *noun* (circa 1889)
: a metal bar having a closed loop at one or both ends

eye-bolt \'ī-'bȯlt\ *noun* (1769)
: a bolt with a looped head

eye-bright \'ī-,brīt\ *noun* (1533)
: any of a genus (*Euphrasia*) of herbs of the snapdragon family with opposite toothed or cut leaves

eye·brow \'ī-,braù\ *noun* (15th century)
: the ridge over the eye or the hair growing on it

eyebrow pencil *noun* (1881)
: a cosmetic pencil for the eyebrows

eye-catch·er \'ī-,ka-chər, -,ke-\ *noun* (1923)
: something that arrests the eye
— **eye-catch·ing** \-chiŋ\ *adjective*
— **eye-catch·ing·ly** \-chiŋ-lē\ *adverb*

eye chart *noun* (1943)
: a chart read at a fixed distance for purposes of testing sight; *especially* : one with rows of letters or objects of decreasing size

eye contact *noun* (1955)
: visual contact with another person's eyes

eye-cup \'ī-,kəp\ *noun* (circa 1874)
1 : a small oval cup with a rim curved to fit the orbit of the eye used for applying liquid remedies to the eyes
2 : OPTIC CUP
3 : a usually rubber cup at the eyepiece of an optical instrument (as binoculars) for keeping out extraneous light

eyed \'īd\ *adjective* (14th century)
: having an eye or eyes especially of a specified kind or number — often used in combination ⟨an almond-*eyed* girl⟩

eyed·ness \'īd-nəs\ *noun* [-*eyed* (as in *right-eyed, left-eyed*)] (1924)
: preference for the use of one eye instead of the other (as in using a monocular microscope)

eye-drop·per \'ī-,drä-pər\ *noun* (1937)
: DROPPER 2

eye·drops \-,dräps\ *noun plural* (1926)
: a medicated solution for the eyes applied in drops

eye·ful \'ī-,fùl\ *noun* (circa 1864)
1 : a full or completely satisfying view
2 : one that is visually attractive; *especially* : a strikingly beautiful woman

eye·glass \'ī-,glas\ *noun* (1664)
1 a : EYEPIECE **b** : a lens worn to aid vision; *specifically* : MONOCLE **c** *plural* : GLASSES, SPECTACLES
2 : EYECUP 1

eye·hole \'ī-,hōl\ *noun* (1637)
1 : ¹ORBIT
2 : PEEPHOLE

eye·lash \'ī-,lash\ *noun* (1752)
1 : the fringe of hair edging the eyelid — usually used in plural
2 : a single hair of the eyelashes

eye lens *noun* (1871)
: the lens nearest the eye in an eyepiece

eye·let \'ī-lət\ *noun* [alteration of Middle English *oilet*, from Middle French *oillet*, diminutive of *oil* eye, from Latin *oculus*] (14th century)
1 a : a small hole designed to receive a cord or used for decoration (as in embroidery) **b** : a small typically metal ring to reinforce an eyelet : GROMMET
2 : PEEPHOLE, LOOPHOLE

eye·lid \'ī-,lid\ *noun* (13th century)
: either of the movable folds of skin and muscle that can be closed over the eyeball

eye·lin·er \'ī-,lī-nər\ *noun* (1947)
: makeup used to emphasize the contour of the eyes

ey·en \'ī-(-ə)n\ *archaic plural of* EYE

eye–open·er \'ī-,ōp-nər, -,ō-pə-\ *noun* (1818)
1 : a drink intended to wake one up
2 : something startling, surprising, or enlightening
— **eye–open·ing** \-niŋ\ *adjective*

eye·piece \'ī-,pēs\ *noun* (1790)
: the lens or combination of lenses at the eye end of an optical instrument

eye·pop·per \'ī-,pä-pər\ *noun* (1941)
: something that excites, astonishes, or attracts the eye
— **eye–pop·ping** \-,pä-piŋ\ *adjective*

eye rhyme *noun* (1871)
: an imperfect rhyme that appears to have identical vowel sounds from similarity of spelling (as *move* and *love*)

eye·shade \'ī-,shād\ *noun* (1845)
: a visor that shields the eyes from strong light and is fastened on with a headband

eye shadow *noun* (1930)
: a cosmetic cream or powder in one of various colors that is applied to the eyelids to accent the eyes

eye·shot \'ī-,shät\ *noun* (1599)
: the range of the eye : VIEW

eye·sight \'ī-,sīt\ *noun* (13th century)
1 : SIGHT 4a
2 *archaic* : OBSERVATION 1

eye socket *noun* (circa 1844)
: ¹ORBIT

eyes only *adjective* (1972)
: to be read by only the person addressed

eye·sore \'ī-,sōr, -,sȯr\ *noun* (1530)
: something offensive to view

eye·spot \'ī-,spät\ *noun* (1877)
1 a : a simple visual organ of pigment or pigmented cells covering a sensory termination : OCELLUS **b** : a small pigmented body of various unicellular algae
2 : a spot of color
3 : any of several fungal diseases of plants characterized by yellowish oval lesions on the leaves and stem; *especially* : a disease of various grasses (as sugarcane) caused by a fungus (*Helminthosporium sacchari*)

eye·stalk \'ī-,stȯk\ *noun* (1854)
: one of the movable peduncles bearing an eye at the tip in a decapod crustacean

eye·strain \'ī-,strān\ *noun* (1874)
: weariness or a strained state of the eye

eye·strings \'ī-,striŋz\ *noun plural* (1590)
obsolete : organic eye attachments formerly believed to break at death or blindness

eye·tooth \'ī-,tüth\ *noun* (circa 1545)
: a canine tooth of the upper jaw

eye view *noun* (circa 1771)
: POINT OF VIEW ⟨an alien *eye view*⟩

eye·wash \'ī-,wȯsh, -,wäsh\ *noun* (circa 1859)
1 : an eye lotion
2 : misleading or deceptive statements, actions, or procedures

eye·wear \'ī-,war, -,wer\ *noun* (1926)
: corrective or protective devices (as glasses or contact lenses) for the eyes

eye·wink \'ī-,wiŋk\ *noun* (1598)
: LOOK, GLANCE

eye·wit·ness \'ī-'wit-nəs\ *noun* (1539)
: one who sees an occurrence or an object; *especially* : one who gives a report on what he or she has seen

eyre \'ar, 'er\ *noun* [Middle English *eire*, from Anglo-French *eire*, from Old French *erre* trip, from *errer* to travel — more at ERRANT] (14th century)
: a circuit traveled by an itinerant justice in medieval England or the court he presided over

ey·rie \'ir-ē, *or same as* AERIE\ *variant of* AERIE

\ə\ abut \ᵊ\ kitten \ər\ further \a\ ash \ā\ ace
\ä\ mop, mar \aù\ out \ch\ chin \e\ bet \ē\ easy
\g\ go \i\ hit \ī\ ice \j\ job \ŋ\ sing \ō\ go
\ȯ\ law \ȯi\ boy \th\ thin \th\ the \ü\ loot \ù\ foot
\y\ yet \zh\ vision *see also* Guide to Pronunciation

ey·rir \'ā-,rir\ *noun, plural* **au·rar** \'au̇-,rär, 'o͝ei-\ [Icelandic, from Old Norse, money (in plural), probably from Latin *aureus* a gold coin] (circa 1927)
— see *krona* at MONEY table

Eze·chiel \i-'zē-kyəl, -kē-əl\ *noun* [Late Latin]
: EZEKIEL

Eze·kiel \i-'zē-kyəl, -kē-əl\ *noun* [Late Latin *Ezechiel*, from Hebrew *Yĕḥezqēl*]
1 : a Hebrew priest and prophet of the 6th century B.C.
2 : a prophetic book of canonical Jewish and Christian Scripture written by Ezekiel — see BIBLE table

Ez·ra \'ez-rə\ *noun* [Late Latin, from Hebrew *'Ezrā*]
1 : a Hebrew priest, scribe, and reformer of Judaism of the 5th century B.C. in Babylon and Jerusalem
2 : a narrative book of canonical Jewish and Christian Scripture — see BIBLE table

F is the sixth letter of the English, Latin, and early Greek alphabets. Corresponding to the Phoenician wāw, which represented a bilabial fricative, a consonant with a sound somewhat like that of a breathy English w, it came into Greek as digamma (written "ϝ"). This letter dropped out of Classical Greek but was preserved in western Greek alphabets, from which it passed into Etruscan, taking there the value of a voiceless labiodental fricative with the sound of f in English flag. Latin adopted both the Etruscan letterform and pronunciation of f, which has the same phonetic value in English, except in the word of and its compounds, where it is voiced (pronounced with vibrating vocal cords). Small f evolved from the capital form through lengthening of the upright stem, shortening of the top and middle horizontal bars, and rounding of the top bar.

f \'ef\ *noun, plural* **f's** *or* **fs** \'efs\ *often capitalized, often attributive* (before 12th century)
1 a : the 6th letter of the English alphabet **b :** a graphic representation of this letter **c :** a speech counterpart of orthographic *f*
2 : the 4th tone of a C-major scale
3 : a graphic device for reproducing the letter *f*
4 : one designated *f* especially as the 6th in order or class
5 a : a grade rating a student's work as failing **b :** one graded or rated with an F
6 : something shaped like the letter F
fa \'fä\ *noun* [Middle English, from Medieval Latin, from the syllable sung to this note in a medieval hymn to Saint John the Baptist] (13th century)
: the 4th tone of the diatonic scale in solmization
Fa·bi·an \'fā-bē-ən\ *adjective* (1777)
1 a : of, relating to, or in the manner of the Roman general Quintus Fabius Maximus known for his defeat of Hannibal in the Second Punic War by the avoidance of decisive contests **b :** CAUTIOUS, DILATORY
2 [the *Fabian* Society; from the members' belief in slow rather than revolutionary change in government] **:** of, relating to, or being a society of socialists organized in England in 1884 to spread socialist principles gradually
— Fabian *noun*
— Fa·bi·an·ism \-ə-,ni-zəm\ *noun*
¹fa·ble \'fā-bəl\ *noun* [Middle English, from Middle French, from Latin *fabula* conversation, story, play, from *fari* to speak — more at BAN] (14th century)
: a fictitious narrative or statement: as **a :** a legendary story of supernatural happenings **b :** a narration intended to enforce a useful truth; *especially* **:** one in which animals speak and act like human beings **c :** FALSEHOOD, LIE
²fable *verb* **fa·bled; fa·bling** \-b(ə-)liŋ\ (14th century)
intransitive verb
archaic **:** to tell fables
transitive verb
: to talk or write about as if true
— fa·bler \-b(ə-)lər\ *noun*
fa·bled \'fā-bəld\ *adjective* (1606)
1 : FICTITIOUS
2 : told or celebrated in fables
3 : RENOWNED, FAMOUS
fab·li·au \'fa-blē-,ō\ *noun, plural* **-aux** \-,ō(z)\ [French, from Old French, diminutive of *fable*] (1804)
: a short, usually comic, frankly coarse, and often cynical tale in verse popular especially in the 12th and 13th centuries
fab·ric \'fa-brik\ *noun* [Middle French *fabrique*, from Latin *fabrica* workshop, structure] (15th century)
1 a : STRUCTURE, BUILDING **b :** underlying structure **:** FRAMEWORK ⟨the *fabric* of society⟩

2 : an act of constructing **:** ERECTION; *specifically* **:** the construction and maintenance of a church building
3 a : structural plan or style of construction **b :** TEXTURE, QUALITY — used chiefly of textiles **c :** the arrangement of physical components (as of soil) in relation to each other
4 a : CLOTH 1a **b :** a material that resembles cloth
5 : the appearance or pattern produced by the shapes and arrangement of the crystal grains in a rock
fab·ri·cant \'fa-bri-kənt\ *noun* (1757)
: MANUFACTURER
fab·ri·cate \'fa-bri-,kāt\ *transitive verb* **-cat·ed; -cat·ing** [Middle English, from Latin *fabricatus*, past participle of *fabricari*, from *fabrica*] (15th century)
1 a : INVENT, CREATE **b :** to make up for the purpose of deception
2 : CONSTRUCT, MANUFACTURE; *specifically* **:** to construct from diverse and usually standardized parts
— fab·ri·ca·tor \'fa-bri-,kā-tər\ *noun*
fab·ri·ca·tion \,fa-bri-'kā-shən\ *noun* (15th century)
1 : the act or process of fabricating
2 : a product of fabrication; *especially* **:** LIE, FALSEHOOD
fabric softener *noun* (1965)
: a product used to make laundered fabrics softer and fluffier
fab·u·lar \'fa-byə-lər\ *adjective* (1684)
: of, relating to, or having the form of a fable
fab·u·list \'fa-byə-list\ *noun* (1593)
1 : a creator or writer of fables
2 : LIAR
— fabulist *or* **fab·u·lis·tic** \,fa-byə-'lis-tik\ *adjective*
fab·u·lous \'fa-byə-ləs\ *adjective* [Middle English, from Latin *fabulosus*, from *fabula*] (15th century)
1 a : resembling or suggesting a fable **:** of an incredible, astonishing, or exaggerated nature ⟨*fabulous* wealth⟩ **b :** WONDERFUL, MARVELOUS ⟨had a *fabulous* time⟩
2 : told in or based on fable
synonym see FICTITIOUS
— fab·u·lous·ly *adverb*
— fab·u·lous·ness *noun*
fa·cade *also* **fa·çade** \fə-'säd\ *noun* [French *façade*, from Italian *facciata*, from *faccia* face, from (assumed) Vulgar Latin *facia*] (circa 1681)

facade 1

1 : the front of a building; *also* **:** any face of a building given special architectural treatment ⟨a museum's east *facade*⟩
2 : a false, superficial, or artificial appearance or effect
¹face \'fās\ *noun, often attributive* [Middle English, from Old French, from (assumed) Vulgar Latin *facia*, from Latin *facies* make, form, face, from *facere* to make, do — more at DO] (13th century)
1 a : the front part of the human head including the chin, mouth, nose, cheeks, eyes, and usually the forehead **b :** the face as a means of identification **:** COUNTENANCE ⟨would know that *face* anywhere⟩
2 *archaic* **:** PRESENCE, SIGHT
3 a : facial expression **b :** GRIMACE **c :** MAKEUP 3a(1)
4 a : outward appearance ⟨suspicious on the *face* of it⟩ **b :** DISGUISE, PRETENSE **c** (1) **:** ASSURANCE, CONFIDENCE ⟨maintaining a firm *face* in spite of adversity⟩ (2) **:** EFFRONTERY ⟨how anyone could have the *face* to ask that question⟩ **d :** DIGNITY, PRESTIGE ⟨afraid to lose *face*⟩
5 : SURFACE: **a** (1) **:** a front, upper, or outer surface (2) **:** the front of something having two or four sides (3) **:** FACADE (4) **:** an exposed surface of rock (5) **:** any of the plane surfaces that bound a geometric solid **b :** a surface specially prepared: as (1) **:** the principal dressed surface (as of a disk) (2) **:** the right side (as of cloth or leather) (3) **:** an inscribed, printed, or marked side **c** (1) **:** the surface (as of type) that receives the ink and transfers it to the paper (2) **:** a style of type
6 : the end or wall of a mine tunnel, drift, or excavation at which work is progressing
7 : FACE VALUE
8 : PERSON ⟨lots of new *faces* around here⟩
— in the face of *also* **in face of :** face-to-face with **:** DESPITE ⟨succeed *in the face of* great difficulties⟩
— to one's face : in one's presence or so that one is fully aware of what is going on **:** FRANKLY
²face *verb* **faced; fac·ing** (15th century)
transitive verb
1 : to confront impudently
2 a : to line near the edge especially with a different material **b :** to cover the front or surface of ⟨*faced* the building with marble⟩
3 : to meet face-to-face or in competition
4 a : to stand or sit with the face toward **b :** to have the front oriented toward ⟨a house *facing* the park⟩
5 a : to recognize and deal with straightforwardly ⟨*face* the facts⟩ **b :** to master by confronting with determination — used with *down* ⟨*faced* down his critics⟩
6 a : to have as a prospect **:** be confronted by ⟨*face* a grim future⟩ **b :** to be a prospect or a source of concern for ⟨the problems that *face* us⟩ **c :** to bring face-to-face ⟨he was *faced* with ruin⟩
7 : to make the surface of (as a stone) flat or smooth
8 : to cause (troops) to face in a particular direction on command
intransitive verb
1 : to have the face or front turned in a specified direction
2 : to turn the face in a specified direction
— face the music : to meet an unpleasant situation, a danger, or the consequences of one's actions
face angle *noun* (1913)
: an angle formed by two edges of a polyhedral angle
face card *noun* (1826)
: a king, queen, or jack in a deck of cards

\ə\ abut \ᵊ\ kitten \ər\ further \a\ ash \ā\ ace
\ä\ mop, mar \au̇\ out \ch\ chin \e\ bet \ē\ easy
\g\ go \i\ hit \ī\ ice \j\ job \ŋ\ sing \ō\ go
\ȯ\ law \ȯi\ boy \th\ thin \t͟h\ the \ü\ loot \u̇\ foot
\y\ yet \zh\ vision *see also* Guide to Pronunciation

face–cen·tered \'fās-ˌsen-tərd\ *adjective* (1913)
: relating to or being a crystal space lattice in which each cubic unit cell has an atom at the center and at the corners of each face — compare BODY-CENTERED

face-cloth \'fās-ˌklȯth\ *noun* (1602)
: WASHCLOTH

face cord *noun* (circa 1926)
: a unit of wood cut for fuel equal to a stack 4 × 8 feet with lengths of pieces from about 12 to 16 inches

-faced \ˌfāst\ *adjective combining form*
: having (such) a face or (so many) faces ⟨rosy-*faced*⟩ ⟨two-*faced*⟩

face·down \ˌfās-ˈdaùn\ *adverb* (1949)
: with the face down ⟨sliding *facedown*⟩

face fly *noun* (1961)
: a European fly (*Musca autumnalis*) that is similar to the housefly, is widely established in North America, and causes distress to livestock by clustering about the face

face·less \'fās-ləs\ *adjective* (1596)
1 : lacking a face
2 a : lacking character or individuality : NONDESCRIPT ⟨the *faceless* masses⟩ **b** : not identified : ANONYMOUS ⟨a *faceless* accuser⟩
— face·less·ness *noun*

face–lift \'fās-ˌlift\ *noun* (1934)
1 : a cosmetic operation for removal of facial defects (as wrinkles) typical of aging
2 : an alteration, restoration, or restyling (as of a building) intended especially to modernize
— face–lift *transitive verb*

face mask *noun* (1906)
: a mask covering the face (as in football or scuba diving) : MASK 3

face-off \'fās-ˌȯf\ *noun* (1896)
1 : a method of beginning play (as in hockey or lacrosse) in which two opponents face each other and attempt to gain control of a puck or ball dropped between them
2 : CONFRONTATION

face·plate \'fās-ˌplāt\ *noun* (1841)
1 : a disk fixed with its face at right angles to the live spindle of a lathe for the attachment of the work
2 a : a protective plate for a machine or device **b** : a protective cover for the human face (as of a diver)
3 : the glass front of a cathode-ray tube on which the image is seen

fac·er \'fā-sər\ *noun* (15th century)
1 : one that faces
2 *British* : a sudden often stunning check or obstacle

face–sav·er \'fā(s)-ˌsā-vər\ *noun* (1923)
: something (as a compromise) that saves face
— face–sav·ing \-ˌsā-viŋ\ *adjective or noun*

fac·et \'fa-sət\ *noun* [French *facette*, diminutive of *face*] (1625)
1 : a small plane surface (as on a cut gem)
2 : any of the definable aspects that make up a subject (as of contemplation) or an object (as of consideration)
3 : the external corneal surface of an ommatidium
4 : a smooth flat circumscribed anatomical surface (as of a bone)
— fac·et·ed *or* **fac·et·ted** \'fa-sə-təd\ *adjective*

fa·cete \fə-ˈsēt\ *adjective* [Latin *facetus*] (1603)
archaic : FACETIOUS, WITTY

fa·ce·ti·ae \fə-ˈsē-shē-ˌē, -ˌī\ *noun plural* [Latin, from plural of *facetia* jest, from *facetus* elegant, witty] (1529)
: witty or humorous writings or sayings

fa·ce·tious \fə-ˈsē-shəs\ *adjective* [Middle French *facetieux*, from *facetie* jest, from Latin *facetia*] (1599)
1 : joking or jesting often inappropriately : WAGGISH ⟨just being *facetious*⟩

2 : meant to be humorous or funny : not serious ⟨a *facetious* remark⟩
synonym see WITTY
— fa·ce·tious·ly *adverb*
— fa·ce·tious·ness *noun*

face–to–face *adverb or adjective* (14th century)
1 : within each other's sight or presence ⟨met and talked *face-to-face*⟩ ⟨a *face-to-face* consultation⟩
2 : in or into direct contact or confrontation ⟨came *face-to-face* with the problem⟩

face–up \'fā-ˌsəp\ *adverb* (1897)
: with the face up

face up *intransitive verb* (1920)
: to confront or deal directly with someone or something previously avoided — usually used with *to* ⟨*faced up* to the situation⟩

face value *noun* (1876)
1 : the value indicated on the face (as of a postage stamp or a stock certificate)
2 : the apparent value or significance ⟨if their remarks may be taken at *face value*⟩

facia *variant of* FASCIA

¹fa·cial \'fā-shəl\ *adjective* (circa 1818)
1 : of or relating to the face
2 : concerned with or used in improving the appearance of the face
— fa·cial·ly \-shə-lē\ *adverb*

²facial *noun* (1914)
: a facial treatment

facial index *noun* (circa 1889)
: the ratio of the breadth of the face to its length multiplied by 100

facial nerve *noun* (circa 1818)
: either of the 7th pair of cranial nerves that supply motor fibers especially to the muscles of the face and jaw and sensory and parasympathetic fibers to the tongue, palate, and fauces

-fa·cient \'fā-shənt\ *adjective combining form* [Latin *-facient-, -faciens* (as in *calefacient-, calefaciens* making warm, present participle of *calefacere* to warm)]
: making : causing ⟨somni*facient*⟩

fa·cies \'fā-sh(ē-ˌ)ēz\ *noun, plural* **facies** [New Latin, from Latin, face] (circa 1736)
1 : an appearance and expression of the face characteristic of a particular condition especially when abnormal ⟨adenoid *facies*⟩
2 : general appearance ⟨a plant species with a particularly distinct *facies*⟩
3 : a part of a rock or group of rocks that differs from the whole formation (as in composition, age, or fossil content)

fac·ile \'fa-səl\ *adjective* [Middle French, from Latin *facilis*, from *facere* to do — more at DO] (15th century)
1 a (1) : easily accomplished or attained ⟨a *facile* victory⟩ (2) : SPECIOUS, SUPERFICIAL ⟨I am not concerned . . . with offering any *facile* solution for so complex a problem —T. S. Eliot⟩ **b** : used or comprehended with ease **c** : readily manifested and often lacking sincerity or depth ⟨*facile* tears⟩
2 *archaic* : mild or pleasing in manner or disposition
3 a : READY, FLUENT ⟨*facile* prose⟩ **b** : POISED, ASSURED
synonym see EASY
— fac·ile·ly \-sə(l)-lē\ *adverb*
— fac·ile·ness \-səl-nəs\ *noun*

fa·cil·i·tate \fə-ˈsi-lə-ˌtāt\ *transitive verb* **-tat·ed; -tat·ing** (1611)
: to make easier : help bring about ⟨*facilitate* economic recovery⟩
— fa·cil·i·ta·tive \-ˌtā-tiv\ *adjective*
— fa·cil·i·ta·tor \-ˌtā-tər\ *noun*

fa·cil·i·ta·tion \fə-ˌsi-lə-ˈtā-shən\ *noun* (1619)
1 : the act of facilitating : the state of being facilitated
2 a : the lowering of the threshold for reflex conduction along a particular neural pathway especially from repeated use of that pathway **b** : the increasing of the ease or intensity of a response by repeated stimulation

fa·cil·i·ta·to·ry \fə-ˈsi-lə-tə-ˌtōr-ē, -ˌtȯr-\ *adjective* (1944)
: inducing or involved in facilitation especially of a reflex action

fa·cil·i·ty \fə-ˈsi-lə-tē\ *noun, plural* **-ties** (1531)
1 : the quality of being easily performed
2 : ease in performance : APTITUDE
3 : readiness of compliance
4 a (1) : something that makes an action, operation, or course of conduct easier — usually used in plural ⟨*facilities* for study⟩ (2) : LAVATORY 2 — often used in plural **b** : something (as a hospital) that is built, installed, or established to serve a particular purpose

fac·ing \'fā-siŋ\ *noun* (1566)
1 a : a lining at the edge especially of a garment **b** *plural* : the collar, cuffs, and trimmings of a uniform coat
2 : an ornamental or protective layer
3 : material for facing

fac·sim·i·le \fak-ˈsi-mə-lē\ *noun* [Latin *fac simile* make similar] (1691)
1 : an exact copy
2 : a system of transmitting and reproducing graphic matter (as printing or still pictures) by means of signals sent over telephone lines
synonym see REPRODUCTION

fact \'fakt\ *noun* [Latin *factum*, from neuter of *factus*, past participle of *facere*] (15th century)
1 : a thing done: as **a** *obsolete* : FEAT **b** : CRIME ⟨accessory after the *fact*⟩ **c** *archaic* : ACTION
2 *archaic* : PERFORMANCE, DOING
3 : the quality of being actual : ACTUALITY ⟨a question of *fact* hinges on evidence⟩
4 a : something that has actual existence ⟨space exploration is now a *fact*⟩ **b** : an actual occurrence ⟨prove the *fact* of damage⟩
5 : a piece of information presented as having objective reality
— in fact : in truth

fact finder *noun* (1926)
: one that tries to determine the realities of a case, situation, or relationship; *especially* : an impartial examiner designated by a government agency to appraise the facts underlying a particular matter (as a labor dispute)
— fact–find·ing *noun or adjective*

fac·tic·i·ty \fak-ˈti-sə-tē\ *noun* [French or German; French *facticité*, from German *Faktizität*, from *Factum* fact, from Latin *factum*] (1945)
: the quality or state of being a fact

fac·tion \'fak-shən\ *noun* [Middle French & Latin; Middle French, from Latin *faction-, factio* act of making, faction — more at FASHION] (1509)
1 : a party or group (as within a government) that is often contentious or self-seeking : CLIQUE
2 : party spirit especially when marked by dissension
— fac·tion·al \-shnəl, -shə-nᵊl\ *adjective*
— fac·tion·al·ism \-shnə-ˌli-zəm, -shə-nᵊl-ˌiz-\ *noun*
— fac·tion·al·ly \-ē\ *adverb*

-fac·tion \'fak-shən\ *noun combining form* [Middle English *-faccioun*, from Middle French & Latin; Middle French *-faction*, from Latin *-faction-, -factio* (as in *satisfaction-, satisfactio* satisfaction)]
: making : -FICATION ⟨petri*faction*⟩

fac·tious \'fak-shəs\ *adjective* [Middle French or Latin; Middle French *factieux*, from Latin *factiosus*, from *factio*] (1532)
: of or relating to faction: as **a** : caused by faction ⟨*factious* disputes⟩ **b** : inclined to faction or the formation of factions **c** : SEDITIOUS
— fac·tious·ly *adverb*
— fac·tious·ness *noun*

fac·ti·tious \fak-ˈti-shəs\ *adjective* [Latin *facticius*, from *factus*, past participle of *facere* to make, do — more at DO] (1646)
1 : produced by humans rather than by natural forces

2 a : formed by or adapted to an artificial or conventional standard **b :** produced by special effort **:** SHAM ⟨created a *factitious* demand by spreading rumors of shortage⟩
— **fac·ti·tious·ly** *adverb*
— **fac·ti·tious·ness** *noun*

fac·ti·tive \'fak-tə-tiv\ *adjective* [probably from Latin *factitare* to do habitually, frequentative of *facere*] (1846)
: of, relating to, or being a transitive verb that in some constructions requires an objective complement as well as an object
— **fac·ti·tive·ly** *adverb*

-fac·tive \'fak-tiv\ *adjective combining form* [Middle French *-factif*, from *-faction*]
: making **:** causing ⟨putre*factive*⟩

fact of life (1854)
1 : something that exists and must be taken into consideration
2 *plural* **:** the fundamental physiological processes and behavior involved in sex and reproduction

fac·toid \'fak-ˌtȯid\ *noun* (1973)
1 : an invented fact believed to be true because of its appearance in print
2 : a brief and usually trivial news item

¹**fac·tor** \'fak-tər\ *noun* [Middle English, from Middle French *facteur*, from Latin *factor* doer, from *facere*] (15th century)
1 : one who acts or transacts business for another: as **a :** BROKER 1b **b :** one that lends money to producers and dealers (as on the security of accounts receivable)
2 a (1) **:** one that actively contributes to the production of a result **:** INGREDIENT ⟨price wasn't a *factor* in the decision⟩ (2) **:** a substance that functions in or promotes the function of a particular physiological process or bodily system **b :** a good or service used in the process of production
3 : GENE
4 a : any of the numbers or symbols in mathematics that when multiplied together form a product; *also* **:** a number or symbol that divides another number or symbol **b :** a quantity by which a given quantity is multiplied or divided in order to indicate a difference in measurement ⟨costs increased by a *factor* of 10⟩
— **fac·tor·ship** \-ˌship\ *noun*

²**factor** *verb* **fac·tored; fac·tor·ing** \-t(ə-)riŋ\ (1621)
intransitive verb
: to work as a factor
transitive verb
1 : to resolve into factors
2 a : to include or admit as a factor — used with *in* or *into* ⟨*factor* inflation into our calculations⟩ **b :** to exclude as a factor — used with *out*
— **fac·tor·able** \-t(ə-)rə-bəl\ *adjective*

fac·tor·age \-t(ə-)rij\ *noun* (1613)
1 : the charges made by a factor for services
2 : the business of a factor

factor analysis *noun* (1931)
: the analytical process of transforming statistical data (as measurements) into linear combinations of usually independent variables
— **factor analytic** *adjective*

factor VIII \-'āt\ *noun* (1954)
: a glycoprotein of blood plasma that is essential for blood clotting and is absent or inactive in hemophilia — called also *antihemophilic factor*

factor group *noun* (1897)
: QUOTIENT GROUP

¹**fac·to·ri·al** \fak-'tȯr-ē-əl, -'tȯr-\ *adjective* (1837)
: of, relating to, or being a factor or a factorial

²**factorial** *noun* (1869)
1 : the product of all the positive integers from 1 to *n* — symbol *n*!
2 : the quantity 0! arbitrarily defined as equal to 1

fac·tor·iza·tion \ˌfak-tə-rə-'zā-shən\ *noun* (1886)

: the operation of resolving a quantity into factors; *also* **:** a product obtained by factorization
— **fac·tor·ize** \'fak-tə-ˌrīz\ *transitive verb*

fac·to·ry \'fak-t(ə-)rē\ *noun, plural* **-ries** (1582)
1 : a station where resident factors trade
2 a : a building or set of buildings with facilities for manufacturing **b :** the seat of some kind of production ⟨the vice *factories* of the slums⟩
— **fac·to·ry·like** \-ˌlīk\ *adjective*

factory ship *noun* (1927)
: a ship equipped to process a whale or fish catch at sea

fac·to·tum \fak-'tō-təm\ *noun* [New Latin, literally, do everything, from Latin *fac* (imperative of *facere* do) + *totum* everything] (1566)
1 : a person having many diverse activities or responsibilities
2 : a general servant

fac·tu·al \'fak-chə-wəl, -chəl, 'faksh-wəl\ *adjective* [*fact* + *-ual* (as in *actual*)] (circa 1834)
1 : of or relating to facts
2 : restricted to or based on fact
— **fac·tu·al·i·ty** \ˌfak-chə-'wa-lə-tē\ *noun*
— **fac·tu·al·ly** \'fak-chə-wə-lē, -chə-lē, 'faksh-wə-\ *adverb*
— **fac·tu·al·ness** *noun*

fac·tu·al·ism \'fak-chə-wə-ˌli-zəm, -chə-ˌli-, 'faksh-wə-\ *noun* (1936)
: adherence or dedication to facts
— **fac·tu·al·ist** \-list\ *noun*

fac·ture \'fak-chər\ *noun* [Middle English, from Middle French, from Latin *factura* action of making, from *factus*] (15th century)
: the manner in which something (as an artistic work) is made **:** EXECUTION

fac·u·la \'fa-kyə-lə\ *noun, plural* **-lae** \-ˌlē, -ˌlī\ [New Latin, from Latin, diminutive of *fac-, fax* torch] (1706)
: any of the bright regions of the sun's photosphere seen most easily near the sun's edge

fac·ul·ta·tive \'fa-kəl-ˌtā-tiv, *British* -tə-tiv\ *adjective* (1820)
1 a : of or relating to the grant of permission, authority, or privilege ⟨*facultative* legislation⟩ **b :** OPTIONAL
2 : of or relating to a mental faculty
3 a : taking place under some conditions but not under others ⟨*facultative* diapause⟩ **b :** exhibiting an indicated lifestyle under some environmental conditions but not under others ⟨*facultative* anaerobes⟩
— **fac·ul·ta·tive·ly** *adverb*

fac·ul·ty \'fa-kəl-tē\ *noun, plural* **-ties** [Middle English *faculte*, from Middle French *faculté*, from Medieval Latin & Latin; Medieval Latin *facultat-, facultas* branch of learning or teaching, from Latin, ability, abundance, from *facilis* facile] (14th century)
1 : ABILITY, POWER: as **a :** innate or acquired ability to act or do **b :** an inherent capability, power, or function ⟨the *faculty* of hearing⟩ **c :** any of the powers of the mind formerly held by psychologists to form a basis for the explanation of all mental phenomena **d :** natural aptitude ⟨has a *faculty* for saying the right things⟩
2 a : a branch of teaching or learning in an educational institution **b** *archaic* **:** something in which one is trained or qualified
3 a : the members of a profession **b :** the teaching and administrative staff and those members of the administration having academic rank in an educational institution **c :** *faculty plural* **:** faculty members ⟨many *faculty* were present⟩
4 : power, authority, or prerogative given or conferred
synonym see GIFT

fad \'fad\ *noun* [origin unknown] (1867)
: a practice or interest followed for a time with exaggerated zeal **:** CRAZE
synonym see FASHION
— **fad·dish** \'fa-dish\ *adjective*
— **fad·dish·ness** *noun*

— **fad·dism** \'fa-ˌdi-zəm\ *noun*
— **fad·dist** \'fa-dist\ *noun*
— **fad·dy** \-dē\ *adjective*

FAD \ˌef-ˌā-'dē\ *noun* (1944)
: FLAVIN ADENINE DINUCLEOTIDE

¹**fade** \'fād\ *verb* **fad·ed; fad·ing** [Middle English, from Middle French *fader*, from *fade* feeble, insipid, from (assumed) Vulgar Latin *fatidus*, alteration of Latin *fatuus* fatuous, insipid] (14th century)
intransitive verb
1 : to lose freshness, strength, or vitality **:** WITHER
2 : to lose freshness or brilliance of color
3 : to sink away **:** VANISH
4 : to change gradually in loudness, strength, or visibility — used of a motion-picture image or of an electronics signal and usually with *in* or *out*
5 *of an automobile brake* **:** to lose braking power gradually
6 : to move back from the line of scrimmage — used of a quarterback
transitive verb
: to cause to fade
— **fad·er** *noun*

²**fade** *noun* (1918)
1 a : FADE-OUT **b :** a gradual changing of one picture to another in a motion-picture or television sequence
2 : a fading of an automobile brake
3 : a slight to moderate and usually intentional slice in golf

³**fade** \'fād\ *adjective* [Middle English, from Middle French] (15th century)
: INSIPID, COMMONPLACE

fade·away \'fā-də-ˌwā\ *noun* (1909)
1 a : SCREWBALL 1 **b :** a slide in which a base runner throws his body sideways to avoid the tag
2 : an act or instance of fading away

fade-in \'fā-ˌdin\ *noun* (1917)
: a gradual increase in a motion-picture or television image's visibility at the beginning of a sequence

fade·less \'fād-ləs\ *adjective* (1652)
: not susceptible to fading

fade-out \'fā-ˌdaut\ *noun* (1917)
: an act or instance of fading out; *especially* **:** a gradual decrease in a motion-picture or television image's visibility at the end of a sequence

fa·do \'fä-(ˌ)thü, 'fä-\ *noun, plural* **fados** [Portuguese, literally, fate, from Latin *fatum*] (1902)
: a plaintive Portuguese folk song

fae·cal, fae·ces *variant of* FECAL, FECES

fa·e·na \fä-'ā-(ˌ)nä\ *noun* [Spanish, literally, task, from obsolete Catalan, from Latin *facienda* things to be done, from *facere* to do — more at DO] (1927)
: a series of final passes leading to the kill made by the matador in a bullfight

fa·er·ie *also* **fa·ery** \'fā-(ə-)rē, 'far-ē, 'fer-ē\ *noun, plural* **fa·er·ies** [Middle French *faerie* — more at FAIRY] (1590)
1 : FAIRYLAND
2 : FAIRY
— **faery** *adjective*

Faer·oese \ˌfar-ə-'wēz, ˌfer-, -'wēs\ *noun, plural* **Faeroese** (1855)
1 : a member of the people inhabiting the Faeroes
2 : the North Germanic language of the Faeroese people
— **Faeroese** *adjective*

Faf·nir \'fäv-nər, 'fäf-, -ˌnir\ *noun* [Old Norse *Fáfnir*]
: a dragon in Norse mythology that guards the Nibelungs' gold hoard until slain by Sigurd

\ə\ abut \ᵊ\ kitten \ər\ further \a\ ash \ā\ ace
\ä\ mop, mar \aù\ out \ch\ chin \e\ bet \ē\ easy
\g\ go \i\ hit \ī\ ice \j\ job \ŋ\ sing \ō\ go
\ȯ\ law \ȯi\ boy \th\ thin \th\ the \ü\ loot \ù\ foot
\y\ yet \zh\ vision *see also* Guide to Pronunciation

¹**fag** \'fag\ *verb* **fagged; fag·ging** [obsolete *fag* to droop, perhaps from *fag* (fag end)] (1772)
intransitive verb
1 : to work hard : TOIL
2 : to act as a fag especially in an English public school ⟨*fagging* for older boys during his first year⟩
transitive verb
: to tire by strenuous activity : EXHAUST
synonym see TIRE
²**fag** *noun* (1780)
1 *chiefly British* : TOIL, DRUDGERY
2 a : an English public-school boy who acts as servant to an older schoolmate **b** : DRUDGE
³**fag** *noun* [*fag end*] (circa 1888)
: CIGARETTE
⁴**fag** *noun* [probably by shortening] (circa 1931)
: FAGGOT — usually used disparagingly
— **fag·gy** \'fa-gē\ *adjective*
fag end *noun* [earlier *fag*, from Middle English *fagge* flap] (1613)
1 a : a poor or worn-out end : REMNANT **b** : the extreme end
2 a : the last part or coarser end of a web of cloth **b** : the untwisted end of a rope
fag·got \'fa-gət\ *noun* [origin unknown] (1914)
: a male homosexual — usually used disparagingly
— **fag·got·ry** \-gə-trē\ *noun*
— **fag·goty** \-gə-tē\ *adjective*
fa·gin \'fā-gən\ *noun, often capitalized* [*Fagin*, character in Charles Dickens' *Oliver Twist* (1839)] (1847)
: an adult who instructs others (as children) in crime
¹**fag·ot** *or* **fag·got** \'fa-gət\ *noun* [Middle English *fagot*, from Middle French] (14th century)
: BUNDLE: as **a** : a bundle of sticks **b** : a bundle of pieces of wrought iron to be shaped by rolling or hammering at high temperature
²**fagot** *or* **faggot** *transitive verb* (circa 1598)
: to make a fagot of : bind together into a bundle ⟨*fagoted* sticks⟩
fag·ot·ing *or* **fag·got·ing** *noun* (1885)
1 : an embroidery produced by pulling out horizontal threads from a fabric and tying the remaining cross threads into groups of an hourglass shape

fagoting 1

2 : an openwork stitch joining hemmed edges
Fahr·en·heit \'far-ən-ˌhīt, 'fer-\ *adjective* [Gabriel D. *Fahrenheit*] (1753)
: relating or conforming to a thermometric scale on which under standard atmospheric pressure the boiling point of water is at 212 degrees above the zero of the scale, the freezing point is at 32 degrees above zero, and the zero point approximates the temperature produced by mixing equal quantities by weight of snow and common salt — abbreviation *F* ◇
fa·ience *or* **fa·ïence** \fä-'än(t)s, fī-, -'äⁿs\ *noun* [French, from *Faenza*, Italy] (1714)
: earthenware decorated with opaque colored glazes
¹**fail** \'fā(ə)l\ *verb* [Middle English *failen*, from Old French *faillir*, from (assumed) Vulgar Latin *fallire*, alteration of Latin *fallere* to deceive, disappoint] (13th century)
intransitive verb
1 a : to lose strength : WEAKEN ⟨her health was *failing*⟩ **b** : to fade or die away ⟨until our family line *fails*⟩ **c** : to stop functioning ⟨the patient's heart *failed*⟩
2 a : to fall short ⟨*failed* in his duty⟩ **b** : to be or become absent or inadequate ⟨the water supply *failed*⟩ **c** : to be unsuccessful (as in passing an examination) **d** : to become bankrupt or insolvent

transitive verb
1 a : to disappoint the expectations or trust of ⟨her friends *failed* her⟩ **b** : to miss performing an expected service or function for ⟨his wit *failed* him⟩
2 : to be deficient in : LACK ⟨never *failed* an invincible courage —Douglas MacArthur⟩
3 : to leave undone : NEGLECT ⟨*fail* to lock the door⟩
4 a : to be unsuccessful in passing (as a test) **b** : to grade (as a student) as not passing
— **fail·ing·ly** \'fā-liŋ-lē\ *adverb*
²**fail** *noun* (13th century)
1 : FAILURE — usually used in the phrase *without fail*
2 : a failure (as by a security dealer) to deliver or receive securities within a prescribed period after purchase or sale
¹**fail·ing** \'fā-liŋ\ *noun* (1590)
: a usually slight or insignificant defect in character, conduct, or ability
synonym see FAULT
²**failing** *preposition* (1810)
: in absence or default of ⟨*failing* specific instructions, use your own judgment⟩
faille \'fī(ə)l\ *noun* [French, from Old French] (1869)
: a somewhat shiny closely woven silk, rayon, or cotton fabric characterized by slight ribs in the weft
fail-safe \'fā(ə)l-ˌsāf\ *adjective* (1946)
1 : incorporating some feature for automatically counteracting the effect of an anticipated possible source of failure
2 : being or relating to a safeguard that prevents continuing on a bombing mission according to a preconceived plan
3 : having no chance of failure : infallibly problem-free
fail·ure \'fā(ə)l-yər\ *noun* [alteration of earlier *failer*, from Anglo-French, from Old French *faillir* to fail] (1643)
1 a : omission of occurrence or performance; *specifically* : a failing to perform a duty or expected action **b** : a state of inability to perform a normal function ⟨kidney *failure*⟩ — compare HEART FAILURE **c** : a fracturing or giving way under stress ⟨structural *failure*⟩
2 a : lack of success **b** : a failing in business : BANKRUPTCY
3 a : a falling short : DEFICIENCY ⟨a crop *failure*⟩ **b** : DETERIORATION, DECAY
4 : one that has failed
¹**fain** \'fān\ *adjective* [Middle English *fagen*, *fayn*, from Old English *fægen*; akin to Old Norse *feginn* happy, Old English *fæger* fair] (before 12th century)
1 *archaic* : HAPPY, PLEASED
2 *archaic* : INCLINED, DESIROUS
3 a : WILLING ⟨he was very *fain*, for the young widow was "altogether fair and lovely . . ." —Amy Kelly⟩ **b** : being obliged or constrained : COMPELLED ⟨Great Britain was *fain* to devote its whole energy . . . to the business of slaying and being slain —G. M. Trevelyan⟩
²**fain** *adverb* (12th century)
1 : with pleasure : GLADLY ⟨a speech of fire that *fain* would blaze —Michael Billington⟩
2 a : by preference ⟨knew it, too, though he would *fain* not admit it publicly —John Lukacs⟩ **b** : by desire ⟨I would *fain* consult you —W. S. Gilbert⟩
¹**fai·né·ant** \fā-nā-'äⁿ\ *noun, plural* **fainéants** \-'äⁿ(z)\ [French, from Middle French *fait-nient*, literally, does nothing, by folk etymology from *faignant*, from present participle of *faindre*, *feindre* to feign] (1619)
: an irresponsible idler
²**fai·né·ant** \fā-nā-'äⁿ\ *or* **fai·ne·ant** \'fā-nē-ənt\ *adjective* (1855)
: idle and ineffectual : INDOLENT
¹**faint** \'fānt\ *adjective* [Middle English *faint*, *feint*, from Middle French, from past participle

of *faindre*, *feindre* to feign, shirk — more at FEIGN] (14th century)
1 : lacking courage and spirit : COWARDLY
2 : weak, dizzy, and likely to faint
3 : lacking strength or vigor : performed, offered, or accomplished weakly or languidly
4 : producing a sensation of faintness : OPPRESSIVE ⟨the *faint* atmosphere of a tropical port⟩
5 : lacking distinctness : DIM
— **faint·ish** \'fān-tish\ *adjective*
— **faint·ish·ness** *noun*
— **faint·ly** *adverb*
— **faint·ness** *noun*
²**faint** *intransitive verb* (14th century)
1 *archaic* : to lose courage or spirit
2 *archaic* : to become weak
3 : to lose consciousness because of a temporary decrease in the blood supply to the brain
³**faint** *noun* (1808)
: the physiological action of fainting; *also* : the resulting condition : SYNCOPE 1
faint·heart·ed \'fānt-'här-təd\ *adjective* (15th century)
: lacking courage or resolution : TIMID
— **faint·heart·ed·ly** *adverb*
— **faint·heart·ed·ness** *noun*
¹**fair** \'far, 'fer\ *adjective* [Middle English *fager*, *fair*, from Old English *fæger*; akin to Old High German *fagar* beautiful] (before 12th century)
1 : pleasing to the eye or mind especially because of fresh, charming, or flawless quality
2 : superficially pleasing : SPECIOUS ⟨she trusted his *fair* promises⟩
3 a : CLEAN, PURE ⟨*fair* sparkling water⟩ **b** : CLEAR, LEGIBLE
4 : not stormy or foul : FINE ⟨*fair* weather⟩
5 : AMPLE ⟨a *fair* estate⟩
6 a : marked by impartiality and honesty : free from self-interest, prejudice, or favoritism ⟨a very *fair* person to do business with⟩ **b** (1) : conforming with the established rules : ALLOWED (2) : consonant with merit or importance : DUE ⟨a *fair* share⟩ **c** : open to legitimate pursuit, attack, or ridicule ⟨*fair* game⟩
7 a : PROMISING, LIKELY ⟨in a *fair* way to win⟩ **b** : favorable to a ship's course ⟨a *fair* wind⟩
8 *archaic* : free of obstacles
9 : not dark : BLOND
10 : sufficient but not ample : ADEQUATE ⟨a *fair* understanding of the work⟩
11 : being such to the utmost : UTTER ⟨a *fair* treat to watch him —*New Republic*⟩ ☆
— **fair·ness** *noun*
²**fair** *noun* (before 12th century)
1 *obsolete* : BEAUTY, FAIRNESS
2 : something that is fair or fortunate
3 *archaic* : WOMAN; *especially* : SWEETHEART
— **for fair** : to the greatest extent or degree : FULLY ⟨the rush is on *for fair*⟩
— **no fair** : something that is not according to the rules ⟨that's *no fair*⟩
³**fair** *adverb* (before 12th century)
chiefly British : FAIRLY 5
⁴**fair** (1836)
intransitive verb
of the weather : CLEAR

◇ **WORD HISTORY**
Fahrenheit The Fahrenheit scale memorializes the German physicist Daniel Gabriel Fahrenheit (1686–1736). Fahrenheit devoted his career to the making of precision scientific instruments. In 1709 he developed an alcohol thermometer, superseding it with a mercury thermometer in 1714. His most important achievement was his development, from the work of Olaus Roemer, of the thermometric scale that bears his name.

transitive verb
: to join so that the external surfaces blend smoothly
⁵fair *noun* [Middle English *feire*, from Old French, from Medieval Latin *feria* weekday, fair, from Late Latin, festal day, from Latin *feriae* (plural) holidays — more at FEAST] (13th century)
1 : a gathering of buyers and sellers at a particular place and time for trade
2 a : a competitive exhibition (as of farm products) usually with accompanying entertainment and amusements **b :** an exhibition designed to acquaint prospective buyers or the general public with a product
3 : a sale of assorted articles usually for a charitable purpose
fair ball *noun* (1856)
: a batted baseball that lands within the foul lines or that is within the foul lines when bounding to the outfield past first or third base or when going beyond the outfield for a home run
fair catch *noun* (circa 1876)
: a catch of a kicked football by a player who gives a prescribed signal, may not advance the ball, and may not be tackled
fair copy *noun* (1709)
: a neat and exact copy especially of a corrected draft
fair·ground \'far-,graúnd, 'fer-\ *noun* (1741)
: an area where outdoor fairs, circuses, or exhibitions are held — often used in plural with singular construction ⟨what a spot for a *fairgrounds* —W. L. Gresham⟩
fair–haired \'far-'hard, 'fer-'herd\ *adjective* (1909)
: specially favored **:** WHITE-HEADED — used especially in the phrase *fair-haired boy*
¹fair·ing \'far-iŋ, 'fer-\ *noun* (1574)
1 *British* **a :** a present bought or given at a fair **b :** GIFT
2 *British* **:** ³DESERT 2
²fairing *noun* (1914)
: a member or structure whose primary function is to produce a smooth outline and to reduce drag (as on an airplane)
fair·ish \'far-ish, 'fer-\ *adjective* (1611)
: fairly good ⟨a *fairish* wage for those days⟩
— **fair·ish·ly** *adverb*
Fair Isle *noun* (1851)
: a style of knitting originating in the Shetland Islands that is characterized by bands of multicolored geometric patterns; *also* **:** an article of clothing knitted in this style
fair·lead \'far-,lēd, 'fer-\ *noun* (circa 1841)
1 *also* **fair·lead·er** \-,lē-dər\ **:** a block, ring, or strip of plank with holes that serves as a guide for the running rigging or any ship's rope and keeps it from chafing
2 : a course of running ship's rope that avoids all chafing
fair·ly \'far-lē, 'fer-\ *adverb* (12th century)
1 : in a handsome manner ⟨a table *fairly* set⟩
2 *obsolete* **a :** in a gentle manner **:** QUIETLY **b :** in a courteous manner
3 : in a manner of speaking ⟨*fairly* bursting with pride⟩
4 a : in a proper or legal manner ⟨*fairly* priced stocks⟩ **b :** without bias or distortion **:** IMPARTIALLY ⟨a story told *fairly* and objectively⟩
5 : to a full degree or extent **:** PLAINLY, DISTINCTLY ⟨had *fairly* caught sight of him⟩
6 : RATHER 5, MODERATELY ⟨a *fairly* easy job⟩
fair market value *noun* (1901)
: a price at which both buyers and sellers are willing to do business
fair–mind·ed \'far-,mīn-dəd, 'fer-\ *adjective* (1874)
: marked by impartiality and honesty **:** JUST, UNPREJUDICED
— **fair–mind·ed·ness** *noun*
fairness doctrine *noun* (1967)
: a tenet of licensed broadcasting that ensures a reasonable opportunity for the airing of conflicting viewpoints on controversial issues

fair play *noun* (1595)
: equitable or impartial treatment **:** JUSTICE
fair shake *noun* (1830)
: a fair chance or fair treatment ⟨give the negative side a *fair shake* —S. L. Payne⟩
fair–spo·ken \'far-,spō-kən, 'fer-\ *adjective* (15th century)
: pleasant and courteous in speech ⟨a *fair-spoken* youth⟩
fair–trade \'far-'trād, 'fer-\ *transitive verb* (1947)
: to market (a commodity) in compliance with the provisions of a fair-trade agreement
— **fair trade** *noun*
— **fair trader** *noun*
fair–trade agreement *noun* (1937)
: an agreement between a producer and a seller that commodities bearing a trademark, label, or brand name belonging to the producer be sold at or above a specified price
fair·way \'far-,wā, 'fer-\ *noun* (1584)
1 a : a navigable part of a river, bay, or harbor **b :** an open path or space
2 : the closely mowed part of a golf course between a tee and a green
fair–weather *adjective* (1736)
1 : loyal only during a time of success ⟨a *fair-weather* friend⟩
2 : suitable for or done during fair weather ⟨a *fair-weather* sail⟩
fairy \'far-ē, 'fer-\ *noun, plural* **fair·ies** [Middle English *fairie* fairyland, fairy people, from Old French *faerie*, from *feie, fee* fairy, from Latin *Fata*, goddess of fate, from *fatum* fate] (14th century)
1 : a mythical being of folklore and romance usually having diminutive human form and magic powers
2 : a male homosexual — usually used disparagingly
— **fairy** *adjective*
— **fairy·like** \-,līk\ *adjective*
fairy godmother *noun* (1851)
: a generous friend or benefactor
fairy·ism \-,i-zəm\ *noun* (1715)
archaic **:** the power to enchant
fairy·land \-,land\ *noun* (1590)
1 : the land of fairies
2 : a place of delicate beauty or magical charm
fairy ring *noun* [from the folk belief that such rings were dancing places of the fairies] (1599)
1 : a ring of basidiomycetous mushrooms produced at the periphery of a body of mycelium which has grown outward from an initial growth point; *also* **:** a ring of luxuriant vegetation especially when associated with these mushrooms
2 : a mushroom (especially *Marasmius oreades*) that commonly grows in fairy rings
fairy shrimp *noun* (1857)
: any of several delicate transparent freshwater branchiopod crustaceans (order Anostraca)
fairy–tale *adjective* (1924)
: characteristic of or suitable to a fairy tale; *especially* **:** marked by seemingly unreal beauty, perfection, luck, or happiness
fairy tale *noun* (1749)
1 : a story (as for children) involving fantastic forces and beings (as fairies, wizards, and goblins) — called also *fairy story*
2 : a made-up story usually designed to mislead
fait ac·com·pli \'fā-tə-,käm-'plē, 'fe-, 'fe-,ta-, -,kōⁿ(m)-, *British usually* -'käm-(,)plē\ *noun, plural* **faits accomplis** *same, or* -'plēz\ [French, accomplished fact] (1845)
: a thing accomplished and presumably irreversible
¹faith \'fāth\ *noun, plural* **faiths** \'fāths, *sometimes* 'fāthz\ [Middle English *feith*, from Old

French *feid, foi*, from Latin *fides*; akin to Latin *fidere* to trust — more at BIDE] (13th century)
1 a : allegiance to duty or a person **:** LOYALTY **b** (1) **:** fidelity to one's promises (2) **:** sincerity of intentions
2 a (1) **:** belief and trust in and loyalty to God (2) **:** belief in the traditional doctrines of a religion **b** (1) **:** firm belief in something for which there is no proof (2) **:** complete trust
3 : something that is believed especially with strong conviction; *especially* **:** a system of religious beliefs ◊
synonym see BELIEF
— **in faith :** without doubt or question **:** VERILY
²faith *transitive verb* (15th century)
archaic **:** BELIEVE, TRUST
¹faith·ful \'fāth-fəl\ *adjective* (14th century)
1 *obsolete* **:** full of faith
2 : steadfast in affection or allegiance **:** LOYAL
3 : firm in adherence to promises or in observance of duty **:** CONSCIENTIOUS
4 : given with strong assurance **:** BINDING ⟨*faithful* promise⟩

☆ **SYNONYMS**
Fair, just, equitable, impartial, unbiased, dispassionate, objective mean free from favor toward either or any side. FAIR implies an elimination of one's own feelings, prejudices, and desires so as to achieve a proper balance of conflicting interests ⟨a *fair* decision⟩. JUST implies an exact following of a standard of what is right and proper ⟨a *just* settlement of territorial claims⟩. EQUITABLE implies a less rigorous standard than JUST and usually suggests equal treatment of all concerned ⟨the *equitable* distribution of the property⟩. IMPARTIAL stresses an absence of favor or prejudice ⟨an *impartial* third party⟩. UNBIASED implies even more strongly an absence of all prejudice ⟨your *unbiased* opinion⟩. DISPASSIONATE suggests freedom from the influence of strong feeling and often implies cool or even cold judgment ⟨a *dispassionate* summation of the facts⟩. OBJECTIVE stresses a tendency to view events or persons as apart from oneself and one's own interest or feelings ⟨I can't be *objective* about my own child⟩. See in addition BEAUTIFUL.

◇ **WORD HISTORY**
faith *Faith* exemplifies how a language can retain in a word borrowed from another language a sound which that source language has lost or modified drastically. The final \th\ sound of *faith* existed in the northern variety of French from which English borrowed the word, probably not long after the Norman Conquest of 1066. Subsequently, all dialects of French lost this sound entirely, and the usual form of the Old French word was *fei* (later *foi*, leading to the identically spelled Modern French word, pronounced \fwä\). English, on the other hand, from its remote Germanic past to the present day, has retained the sound \th\, and so has kept it in *faith* (perhaps with encouragement from the *-th* suffix of abstract nouns such as *truth*). Like archaeological relics protected by the earth until they are uncovered, words such as *faith* are valuable instruments for studying the history of language change.

\ə\ abut \ᵊ\ kitten \ər\ further \a\ ash \ā\ ace \ä\ mop, mar \aú\ out \ch\ chin \e\ bet \ē\ easy \g\ go \i\ hit \ī\ ice \j\ job \ŋ\ sing \ō\ go \ò\ law \òi\ boy \th\ thin \t͟h\ the \ü\ loot \ú\ foot \y\ yet \zh\ vision *see also* Guide to Pronunciation

5 : true to the facts, to a standard, or to an original ⟨a *faithful* copy⟩ ☆
— **faith·ful·ly** \-fə-lē\ *adverb*
— **faith·ful·ness** *noun*

²**faithful** *noun* (1558)
1 *plural in construction* **a** : church members in full communion and good standing — used with *the* **b** : the body of believers in Islam — used with *the*
2 *plural* **faithful** *or* **faithfuls** : one who is faithful; *especially* : a loyal follower, member, or fan ⟨party *faithfuls*⟩

faith healing *noun* (1885)
: a method of treating diseases by prayer and exercise of faith in God
— **faith healer** *noun*

faith·less \'fāth-ləs\ *adjective* (14th century)
1 : not true to allegiance or duty : TREACHEROUS, DISLOYAL ⟨a *faithless* servant⟩
2 : not to be relied on : UNTRUSTWORTHY ⟨a *faithless* tool⟩ ☆
— **faith·less·ly** *adverb*
— **faith·less·ness** *noun*

fai·tour \'fā-tər\ *noun* [Middle English, from Anglo-French, from Old French *faitor* perpetrator, from Latin *factor* doer — more at FACTOR] (14th century)
archaic : CHEAT, IMPOSTER

fa·ji·ta \fə-'hē-tə, fä-\ *noun* [American Spanish, diminutive of Spanish *faja* sash, belt, probably from Catalan *faixa*, from Latin *fascia* band — more at FASCIA] (1984)
: a marinated strip usually of beef or chicken grilled or broiled and served usually with a flour tortilla and various savory fillings — usually used in plural

¹**fake** \'fāk\ *transitive verb* **faked; fak·ing** [Middle English] (15th century)
: to coil in fakes

²**fake** *noun* (1627)
: one loop of a coil (as of ship's rope or a fire hose) coiled free for running

³**fake** *adjective* [origin unknown] (1775)
: COUNTERFEIT, SHAM

⁴**fake** *noun* (1827)
: one that is not what it purports to be: as **a** : a worthless imitation passed off as genuine **b** : IMPOSTOR, CHARLATAN **c** : a simulated movement in a sports contest (as a pretended kick, pass, or jump or a quick movement in one direction before going in another) designed to deceive an opponent **d** : a device or apparatus used by a magician to achieve the illusion of magic in a trick
synonym see IMPOSTURE

⁵**fake** *verb* **faked; fak·ing** (1851)
transitive verb
1 : to alter, manipulate, or treat so as to give a spuriously genuine appearance to : DOCTOR ⟨*faked* the lab results⟩
2 : COUNTERFEIT, SIMULATE, CONCOCT
3 : to deceive (an opponent) in a sports contest by means of a fake
4 : IMPROVISE, AD-LIB ⟨whistle a few bars . . . and I'll *fake* the rest —Robert Sylvester⟩
intransitive verb
1 : to engage in faking something : PRETEND
2 : to give a fake to an opponent
— **fak·er** *noun*
— **fak·ery** \'fā-k(ə-)rē\ *noun*

fake out *transitive verb* (1968)
: to deliberately mislead : FOOL, TRICK

fa·kir *noun* [Arabic *faqīr*, literally, poor man] (1609)
1 \fə-'kir, fä-, fa-; 'fā-kər\ **a** : a Muslim mendicant : DERVISH **b** : an itinerant Hindu ascetic or wonder-worker
2 \'fā-kər\ : IMPOSTOR; *especially* : SWINDLER

fa la \fä-'lä\ *noun* [*fa-la*, meaningless syllables often occurring in its refrain] (1597)
: a 16th and 17th century part-song

fa·la·fel \fə-'lä-fəl\ *noun, plural* **falafel** [Arabic *falāfil*] (1950)
: a spicy mixture of ground vegetables (as chick-peas or fava beans) formed into balls or patties and then fried

Fa·lan·gist \fə-'lan-jist, 'fä-\ *noun* [Spanish *falangista*, from *Falange española* Spanish Phalanx, a fascist organization] (1936)
: a member of the fascist political party governing Spain after the civil war of 1936–39

Fa·la·sha \fə-'lä-shə\ *noun, plural* **-sha** *or* **-shas** [Amharic *fälaša*] (1710)
: a member of a people of highland Ethiopia who practice a variety of Judaism

fal·cate \'fal-ˌkāt, 'fȯl-\ *adjective* [Latin *falcatus*, from *falc-, falx* sickle, scythe] (1826)
: hooked or curved like a sickle

fal·chion \'fȯl-chən\ *noun* [Middle English *fauchoun*, from Middle French *fauchon*, from *fauchier* to mow, from (assumed) Vulgar Latin *falcare*, from Latin *falc-, falx*] (14th century)
1 : a broad-bladed slightly curved sword of medieval times
2 *archaic* : SWORD

fal·ci·form \'fal-sə-ˌfȯrm, 'fȯl-\ *adjective* [Latin *falc-, falx* + English *-iform*] (1766)
: having the shape of a scythe or sickle

fal·con \'fal-kən, 'fȯl- *also* 'fȯ-kən\ *noun* [Middle English, from Old French, from Late Latin *falcon-, falco*, probably from Latin *falc-, falx*] (13th century)
1 : any of various hawks trained for use in falconry; *especially* : PEREGRINE — used technically only of a female; compare TIERCEL
2 : any of various hawks (family Falconidae) that have long pointed wings, a long tail, and a notched beak and that usually inhabit open areas

fal·con·er \-kə-nər\ *noun* (14th century)
: a person who breeds, trains, or hunts with hawks

falcon 1: *1* hood, *2* jess, *3* gauntlet

fal·con·et \ˌfal-kə-'net, ˌfȯl- *also* ˌfȯ-\ *noun* (1559)
1 : a very small cannon used in the 16th and 17th centuries
2 : any of several very small falcons (genera *Microhierax, Prolihierax,* and *Spiziapteryx*)

fal·con-gen·tle \-kən-'jen-t°l\ *noun* [Middle English *faucon gentil* peregrine falcon, from Middle French *faucon gentil*, literally, noble falcon] (15th century)
: the female peregrine falcon

fal·co·nine \'fal-kə-ˌnīn, 'fȯl- *also* 'fȯ-\ *adjective* (circa 1889)
: of or resembling a falcon ⟨a *falconine* face⟩

fal·con·ry \'fal-kən-rē, 'fȯl- *also* 'fȯ-kən-\ *noun* (1575)
1 : the art of training hawks to hunt in cooperation with a person
2 : the sport of hunting with hawks

fal·de·ral \'fal-də-ˌral\ *variant of* FOLDEROL

fald·stool \'fȯl(d)-ˌstül\ *noun* [Medieval Latin *faldistolium*, of Germanic origin; akin to Old High German *faltstuol* folding chair, from *falt* (akin to Old High German *faldan* to fold) + *stuol* chair — more at FOLD, STOOL] (1603)
1 : a folding stool or chair; *specifically* : one used by a bishop
2 : a folding stool or small desk at which one kneels during devotions; *especially* : one used by the sovereigns of England at their coronation
3 : the desk from which the litany is read in Anglican churches

faldstool 1

¹**fall** \'fȯl\ *verb* **fell** \'fel\; **fall·en** \'fȯ-lən\; **fall·ing** [Middle English, from Old English *feallan*; akin to Old High German *fallan* to fall and perhaps to Lithuanian *pulti*] (before 12th century)

intransitive verb
1 a : to descend freely by the force of gravity **b** : to hang freely ⟨her hair *falls* over her shoulders⟩ **c** : to drop oneself to a lower position ⟨*fell* to his knees⟩ **d** : to come or go as if by falling ⟨darkness *falls* early in the winter⟩
2 : to become born — usually used of lambs
3 a : to become lower in degree or level ⟨the temperature *fell* 10°⟩ **b** : to drop in pitch or volume ⟨their voices *fell* to a whisper⟩ **c** : ISSUE 1a,b ⟨wisdom that *fell* from his lips⟩ **d** : to become lowered ⟨her eyes *fell*⟩
4 a : to leave an erect position suddenly and involuntarily ⟨slipped and *fell* on the ice⟩ **b** : to enter as if unawares : STUMBLE, STRAY ⟨*fell* into error⟩ **c** : to drop down wounded or dead; *especially* : to die in battle **d** : to suffer military capture ⟨after a long siege the city *fell*⟩ **e** : to lose office ⟨the party *fell* from power⟩ **f** : to suffer ruin, defeat, or failure ⟨the deal *fell* through⟩
5 : to commit an immoral act; *especially* : to lose one's chastity
6 a : to move or extend in a downward direction ⟨the land *falls* away to the east⟩ **b** : SUBSIDE, ABATE ⟨the wind is *falling*⟩ **c** : to decline in quality, activity, or quantity ⟨production *fell* off⟩ **d** : to lose weight — used with *off* or *away* **e** : to assume a look of shame, disappointment, or dejection ⟨his face *fell*⟩ **f** : to decline in financial value or price ⟨stocks *fell* sharply⟩
7 a : to occur at a certain time **b** : to come by chance ⟨*fell* in with a fast crowd⟩ **c** : to come or pass by lot, assignment, or inheritance : DEVOLVE ⟨it *fell* to him to break the news⟩ **d** : to have a certain or proper position, place, or station ⟨the accent *falls* on the second syllable⟩

8 : to come within the limits, scope, or jurisdiction of something ⟨this word *falls* into the class of verbs⟩
9 : to pass suddenly and passively into a state of body or mind or a new state or condition ⟨*fall* asleep⟩ ⟨*fall* in love⟩
10 : to set about heartily or actively ⟨*fell* to work⟩
11 : STRIKE, IMPINGE ⟨music *falling* on the ear⟩ *transitive verb* **: FELL** 1

— **fall apart 1 :** DISINTEGRATE **2 :** to succumb to mental or emotional stress **:** BREAK DOWN
— **fall behind 1 :** to lag behind **2 :** to be in arrears
— **fall between two stools :** to fail because of inability to choose between or reconcile two alternative or conflicting courses of action
— **fall flat :** to produce no response or result ⟨the joke *fell flat*⟩
— **fall for 1 :** to fall in love with **2 :** to become a victim of ⟨*fell for* the trick⟩
— **fall foul :** to have a quarrel **:** CLASH — often used with *of*
— **fall from grace :** BACKSLIDE 1
— **fall home :** to curve inward; used of the timbers or upper parts of a ship's side
— **fall into line :** to comply with a certain course of action
— **fall on** *or* **fall upon :** to meet with ⟨*fell on* hard times⟩
— **fall over oneself** *or* **fall over backward :** to display excessive eagerness
— **fall short 1 :** to be deficient **2 :** to fail to attain something (as a goal or target)

²fall *noun* (13th century)
1 : the act of falling by the force of gravity
2 a : a falling out, off, or away **:** DROPPING ⟨the *fall* of leaves⟩ ⟨a *fall* of snow⟩ **b :** the season when leaves fall from trees **:** AUTUMN **c :** a thing or quantity that falls or has fallen ⟨a *fall* of rock at the base of the cliff⟩; *especially* **:** one or more meteorites or their fragments that have fallen together **d** (1) **:** BIRTH (2) **:** the quantity born — usually used of lambs
3 a : a costume decoration of lace or thin fabric arranged to hang loosely and gracefully **b :** a very wide turned-down collar worn in the 17th century **c :** the part of a turnover collar from the crease to the outer edge **d :** a wide front flap on trousers (as those worn by sailors) **e :** the freely hanging lower edge of the skirt of a coat **f :** one of the three outer and often drooping segments of the flower of an iris **g :** long hair overhanging the face of dogs of some breeds **h :** a usually long straight portion of hair that is attached to a person's own hair
4 : a hoisting-tackle rope or chain; *especially* **:** the part of it to which the power is applied
5 a : loss of greatness **:** COLLAPSE ⟨the *fall* of the Roman Empire⟩ **b :** the surrender or capture of a besieged place ⟨the *fall* of Troy⟩ **c :** lapse or departure from innocence or goodness **d :** loss of a woman's chastity
6 a : the downward slope (as of a hill) **:** DECLIVITY **b :** a precipitous descent of water **:** WATERFALL — usually used in plural but sing. or plural in construction **c :** a musical cadence **d :** a falling-pitch intonation in speech
7 : a decrease in size, quantity, degree, or value
8 a : the distance which something falls **b :** INCLINATION, PITCH
9 a : the act of felling something **b :** the quantity of trees cut down **c** (1) **:** an act of forcing a wrestler's shoulders to the mat for a specified time (as one second) (2) **:** a bout of wrestling
10 *Scottish* **:** DESTINY, LOT

³fall *adjective* (1677)
: of, relating to, or suitable for autumn ⟨a new *fall* coat⟩

fal·la·cious \fə-ˈlā-shəs\ *adjective* (1509)
1 : embodying a fallacy

2 : tending to deceive or mislead **:** DELUSIVE
— **fal·la·cious·ly** *adverb*
— **fal·la·cious·ness** *noun*

fal·la·cy \ˈfa-lə-sē\ *noun, plural* **-cies** [Latin *fallacia*, from *fallac-, fallax* deceitful, from *fallere* to deceive] (14th century)
1 a *obsolete* **:** GUILE, TRICKERY **b :** deceptive appearance **:** DECEPTION
2 a : a false or mistaken idea ⟨popular *fallacies*⟩ **b :** erroneous character **:** ERRONEOUSNESS
3 : an often plausible argument using false or invalid inference

fal–lal \fa-ˈlal, ˈfa(l)-ˌlal\ *noun* [perhaps alteration of *falbala* furbelow, from French, from French dialect *ferbelà, farbélla*] (circa 1706)
: a fancy ornament especially in dress
— **fal·lal·ery** \ˈfa-ˈla-lə-rē\ *noun*

fall armyworm *noun* (1881)
: a migratory American moth (*Spodoptera frugiperda*) that is especially destructive to small grains and grasses as a larva

fall–away \ˈfȯ-lə-ˌwā\ *adjective* (1966)
: made while moving away from the basket in basketball ⟨a *fallaway* jumper⟩
— **fallaway** *noun*

fall away *intransitive verb* (1535)
1 a : to withdraw friendship or support **b :** to renounce one's faith
2 a : to diminish gradually in size **b :** to drift off a course

fall·back \ˈfȯl-ˌbak\ *noun* (1851)
1 : something on which one can fall back **:** RESERVE
2 : a falling back **:** RETREAT
3 : something that falls back ⟨the *fallback* from an explosion⟩

fall back *intransitive verb* (1607)
: RETREAT, RECEDE
— **fall back on** *or* **fall back upon :** to have recourse to ⟨had to *fall back on* their reserves⟩

fall down *intransitive verb* (1873)
: to fail to meet expectations or requirements ⟨*fell down* on the job⟩

fall·er \ˈfȯ-lər\ *noun* (1677)
1 : a machine part that acts by falling
2 : a logger who fells trees

fall·fish \ˈfȯl-ˌfish\ *noun* (circa 1811)
: a common cyprinid fish (*Semotilus corporalis*) of the streams of northeastern North America

fall guy *noun* (1906)
1 : one that is easily duped
2 : SCAPEGOAT

fal·li·bil·i·ty \ˌfa-lə-ˈbi-lə-tē\ *noun* (1634)
: liability to err

fal·li·ble \ˈfa-lə-bəl\ *adjective* [Middle English, from Medieval Latin *fallibilis*, from Latin *fallere*] (15th century)
1 : liable to be erroneous ⟨a *fallible* generalization⟩
2 : capable of making a mistake ⟨all men are *fallible*⟩
— **fal·li·bly** \-blē\ *adverb*

fall in *intransitive verb* (1719)
1 : to sink inward ⟨the roof *fell in*⟩
2 : to take one's proper place in a military formation
— **fall in with 1 :** to concur with ⟨had to *fall in with* her wishes⟩ **2 :** to harmonize with ⟨it *falls in* exactly *with* my views⟩

falling diphthong *noun* (1888)
: a diphthong (as \ȯi\ in \ˈnȯiz\ *noise*) composed of a vowel followed by a less sonorous glide

fall·ing–out \ˌfȯ-liŋ-ˈau̇t\ *noun, plural* **fallings–out** *or* **falling–outs** (1568)
: an instance of falling out **:** QUARREL

falling rhythm *noun* (1918)
: rhythm with stress occurring regularly on the first syllable of each foot — compare RISING RHYTHM

falling star *noun* (1563)
: METEOR 2a

fall line *noun* (1882)

1 : a line joining the waterfalls on numerous rivers that marks the point where each river descends from the upland to the lowland and the limit of the navigability of each river
2 : the natural downhill course (as for skiing) between two points on a slope

fall–off \ˈfȯ-ˌlȯf\ *noun* (1880)
: a decline especially in quantity or quality ⟨a *falloff* in exports⟩ ⟨a *falloff* of light intensity⟩

fall off *intransitive verb* (1613)
1 : TREND 1b
2 *of a ship* **:** to deviate to leeward of the point to which the bow was directed

fal·lo·pi·an tube \fə-ˈlō-pē-ən-\ *noun, often F* capitalized [Gabriel *Fallopius* (died 1562) Italian anatomist] (circa 1706)
: either of the pair of tubes conducting the egg from the ovary to the uterus

fall·out \ˈfȯ-ˌlau̇t\ *noun* (1949)
1 a : the often radioactive particles stirred up by or resulting from a nuclear explosion and descending through the atmosphere; *also* **:** other polluting particles (as volcanic ash) descending likewise **b :** descent (as of fallout) through the atmosphere
2 : a secondary and often lingering effect, result, or set of consequences ⟨have to take a position and accept the political *fallout* —Andy Logan⟩

fall out *intransitive verb* (15th century)
1 : QUARREL; *also* **:** to cut off relations over a quarrel ⟨former friends who have *fallen out*⟩
2 : TURN OUT, HAPPEN ⟨expected to be in the States . . . , but things *fell out* otherwise —Mark Twain⟩
3 a : to leave one's place in the ranks **b :** to leave a building in order to take one's place in a military formation

¹fal·low \ˈfa-(ˌ)lō, -lə-(w)\ *adjective* [Middle English *falow*, from Old English *fealu*; akin to Old High German *falo* pale, fallow, Latin *pallēre* to be pale, Greek *polios* gray] (before 12th century)
: of a light yellowish brown color

²fallow *noun* [Middle English *falwe, falow*, from Old English *fealg* — more at FELLY] (before 12th century)
1 : usually cultivated land that is allowed to lie idle during the growing season
2 *obsolete* **:** plowed land
3 : the state or period of being fallow
4 : the tilling of land without sowing it for a season

³fallow *transitive verb* (15th century)
: to plow, harrow, and break up (land) without seeding to destroy weeds and conserve soil moisture

⁴fallow *adjective* (15th century)
1 : left untilled or unsown after plowing
2 : DORMANT, INACTIVE — used especially in the phrase *to lie fallow* ⟨at this very moment there are probably important inventions lying *fallow* —Harper's⟩
— **fal·low·ness** *noun*

fallow deer *noun* [¹*fallow*] (15th century)
: a deer (*Cervus dama* synonym *Dama dama*) of variable color with broad antlers and typically a yellow-brown coat spotted with white in the summer that was originally found in Europe and Asia Minor but has been introduced elsewhere

fall to *intransitive verb* (1593)

fallow deer

: to begin doing something (as working or eating) especially vigorously — often used in invitation or command

¹false \'fȯls\ *adjective* **fals·er; fals·est** [Middle English *fals,* from Old French & Latin; Old French, from Latin *falsus,* from past participle of *fallere* to deceive] (12th century) **1 :** not genuine ⟨*false* documents⟩ ⟨*false* teeth⟩ **2 a :** intentionally untrue ⟨*false* testimony⟩ **b :** adjusted or made so as to deceive ⟨*false* scales⟩ ⟨a trunk with a *false* bottom⟩ **c :** intended or tending to mislead ⟨a *false* promise⟩ **3 :** not true ⟨*false* concepts⟩ **4 a :** not faithful or loyal **:** TREACHEROUS ⟨a *false* friend⟩ **b :** lacking naturalness or sincerity ⟨*false* sympathy⟩ **5 a :** not essential or permanent — used of parts of a structure that are temporary or supplemental **b :** fitting over a main part to strengthen it, to protect it, or to disguise its appearance ⟨a *false* ceiling⟩ **6 :** inaccurate in pitch ⟨a *false* note⟩ **7 a :** based on mistaken ideas ⟨*false* pride⟩ **b :** inconsistent with the facts ⟨a *false* position⟩ ⟨a *false* sense of security⟩ **8 :** threateningly sudden or deceptive ⟨don't make a *false* move⟩
synonym see FAITHLESS
— **false·ly** *adverb*
— **false·ness** *noun*

²false *adverb* (13th century)
: in a false or faithless manner **:** TREACHEROUSLY ⟨his friends played him *false*⟩

false alarm *noun* (1579)
1 : one causing alarm or excitement that proves to be unfounded
2 : an alarm (as a fire or burglar alarm) that is set off needlessly

false arrest *noun* (1926)
: an arrest not justifiable under law

false color *noun* (1968)
: color in an image (as a photograph) of an object that does not actually appear in the object but is used to enhance, contrast, or distinguish details which are evident solely or chiefly from differences in the absorption and reflection of electromagnetic radiation at wavelengths outside the visual spectrum

false·hood \'fȯls-ˌhu̇d\ *noun* (13th century)
1 : an untrue statement **:** LIE
2 : absence of truth or accuracy
3 : the practice of lying **:** MENDACITY

false imprisonment *noun* (14th century)
: imprisonment of a person contrary to law

false mi·ter·wort \-'mī-tər-ˌwȯrt, -ˌwȯrt\ *noun* [*miterwort* from the resemblance of the plant's capsule to a bishop's miter] (1868)
: FOAMFLOWER

false morel *noun* (1942)
: any of a genus (*Gyromitra*) of fungi that are often poisonous and have a cap with convolutions resembling a brain

false pregnancy *noun* (circa 1860)
: PSEUDOCYESIS, PSEUDOPREGNANCY

false rib *noun* (15th century)
: a rib whose cartilages unite indirectly or not at all with the sternum — compare FLOATING RIB

false Solomon's seal *noun* (circa 1856)
: any of a genus (*Smilacina*) of herbs of the lily family that differ from Solomon's seal in having flowers in a terminal raceme or panicle — called also *false Solomonseal*

false start *noun* (1815)
1 : a premature start (as of a race)
2 : an unsuccessful attempt to begin something (as a career)

¹fal·set·to \fȯl-'se-(ˌ)tō\ *noun, plural* **-tos** [Italian, from diminutive of *falso* false, from Latin *falsus*] (1774)
1 : an artificially high voice; *especially* **:** an artificially produced singing voice that overlaps and extends above the range of the full voice especially of a tenor
2 : a singer who uses falsetto

²falsetto *adverb* (1940)

: in falsetto

false·work \'fȯls-ˌwərk\ *noun* (circa 1874)
: temporary construction work on which a main work is wholly or partly built and supported until the main work is strong enough to support itself

fals·ie \'fȯl-sē\ *noun* (circa 1943)
: an artificial addition to a bodily part worn to enhance appearance; *specifically* **:** a breast-shaped usually fabric or rubber cup used to pad a brassiere — usually used in plural

fal·si·fy \'fȯl-sə-ˌfī\ *verb* **-fied; -fy·ing** [Middle English *falsifien,* from Middle French *falsifier,* from Medieval Latin *falsificare,* from Latin *falsus*] (15th century)
transitive verb
1 : to prove or declare false
2 : to make false: as **a :** to make false by mutilation or addition ⟨the accounts were *falsified* to conceal a theft⟩ **b :** to represent falsely **:** MISREPRESENT
3 : to prove unsound by experience
intransitive verb
: to tell lies **:** LIE
— **fal·si·fi·abil·i·ty** \ˌfȯl-sə-ˌfī-ə-'bi-lə-tē\ *noun*
— **fal·si·fi·able** \-'fī-ə-bəl\ *adjective*
— **fal·si·fi·ca·tion** \ˌfȯl-sə-fə-'kā-shən\ *noun*
— **fal·si·fi·er** \'fȯl-sə-ˌfī(-ə)r\ *noun*

fal·si·ty \'fȯl-sə-tē\ *noun, plural* **-ties** (13th century)
1 : something false **:** LIE
2 : the quality or state of being false

Fal·staff \'fȯl-ˌstaf\ *noun*
: a fat, convivial, roguish character in Shakespeare's *Merry Wives of Windsor* and *Henry IV*
— **Fal·staff·ian** \fȯl-'sta-fē-ən\ *adjective*

¹fal·ter \'fȯl-tər\ *verb* **fal·tered; fal·ter·ing** \-t(ə-)riŋ\ [Middle English] (14th century)
intransitive verb
1 a : to walk unsteadily **:** STUMBLE **b :** to give way **:** TOTTER ⟨could feel my legs *faltering*⟩ **c :** to move waveringly or hesitatingly
2 : to speak brokenly or weakly **:** STAMMER
3 a : to hesitate in purpose or action **:** WAVER **b :** to lose drive or effectiveness ⟨the business was *faltering*⟩
transitive verb
: to utter hesitatingly or brokenly
synonym see HESITATE
— **fal·ter·er** \-tər-ər\ *noun*
— **fal·ter·ing·ly** \-t(ə-)riŋ-lē\ *adverb*

²falter *noun* (1834)
: an act or instance of faltering

¹fame \'fām\ *noun* [Middle English, from Old French, from Latin *fama* report, fame; akin to Latin *fari* to speak — more at BAN] (13th century)
1 a : public estimation **:** REPUTATION **b :** popular acclaim **:** RENOWN
2 *archaic* **:** RUMOR

²fame *transitive verb* **famed; fam·ing** (14th century)
1 *archaic* **:** REPORT, REPUTE
2 : to make famous

famed \'fāmd\ *adjective* (circa 1533)
: known widely and well **:** FAMOUS

fa·mil·ial \fə-'mil-yəl, -'mi-lē-əl\ *adjective* [French, from Latin *familia*] (circa 1900)
1 : tending to occur in more members of a family than expected by chance alone ⟨a *familial* disorder⟩
2 : of, relating to, or suggestive of a family

¹fa·mil·iar \fə-'mil-yər\ *noun* (13th century)
1 : a member of the household of a high official
2 : one that is familiar; *especially* **:** an intimate associate **:** COMPANION
3 : a spirit often embodied in an animal and held to attend and serve or guard a person
4 a : one who is well acquainted with something **b :** one who frequents a place

²familiar *adjective* [Middle English *familier,* from Middle French, from Latin *familiaris,* from *familia*] (14th century)

1 : closely acquainted **:** INTIMATE ⟨a *familiar* family friend⟩
2 *obsolete* **:** AFFABLE, SOCIABLE
3 a : of or relating to a family ⟨remembering past *familiar* celebrations⟩ **b :** frequented by families ⟨a *familiar* resort⟩
4 a : being free and easy ⟨the *familiar* association of old friends⟩ **b :** marked by informality ⟨a *familiar* essay⟩ **c :** overly free and unrestrained ⟨grossly *familiar* behavior⟩ **d :** moderately tame ⟨*familiar* animals⟩
5 a : frequently seen or experienced **:** easily recognized ⟨a *familiar* theme⟩ **b :** of everyday occurrence **c :** possibly known but imperfectly remembered ⟨her face looked *familiar*⟩
6 : having personal or intimate knowledge — used with *with* ⟨*familiar* with the facts of the case⟩
synonym see COMMON
— **fa·mil·iar·ly** *adverb*
— **fa·mil·iar·ness** *noun*

fa·mil·iar·ise *British variant of* FAMILIARIZE

fa·mil·iar·i·ty \fə-ˌmi-lē-'(y)ar-ə-tē, -ˌmil-'yar-\ *noun, plural* **-ties** (13th century)
1 a : the quality or state of being familiar **b :** a state of close relationship **:** INTIMACY
2 a : absence of ceremony **:** INFORMALITY **b :** an unduly informal act or expression **:** IMPROPRIETY **c :** a sexual liberty
3 : close acquaintance with something ⟨my *familiarity* with American history⟩

fa·mil·iar·ize \fə-'mil-yə-ˌrīz\ *transitive verb* **-ized; -iz·ing** (1608)
1 : to make known or familiar ⟨Shakespeare . . . *familiarizes* the wonderful —Samuel Johnson⟩
2 : to make well acquainted ⟨*familiarize* students with good literature⟩
— **fa·mil·iar·iza·tion** \-ˌmil-yə-rə-'zā-shən\ *noun*

familiar spirit *noun* (1565)
1 : a spirit or demon that serves or prompts an individual
2 : the spirit of a dead person invoked by a medium to advise or prophesy

fam·i·lism \'fa-mə-ˌli-zəm\ *noun* (1925)
: a social pattern in which the family assumes a position of ascendance over individual interests
— **fam·i·lis·tic** \ˌfa-mə-'lis-tik\ *adjective*

fa·mille rose \fə-'mē-\ *noun* [French, literally, rose family] (circa 1898)
: Chinese porcelain in the decoration of which a rose color predominates

fa·mille verte \fə-'mē-'vert\ *noun* [French, literally, green family] (1872)
: Chinese porcelain in the decoration of which green predominates

¹fam·i·ly \'fam-lē, 'fa-mə-\ *noun, plural* **-lies** [Middle English *familie,* from Latin *familia* household (including servants as well as kin of the householder), from *famulus* servant] (15th century)
1 : a group of individuals living under one roof and usually under one head **:** HOUSEHOLD
2 a : a group of persons of common ancestry **:** CLAN **b :** a people or group of peoples regarded as deriving from a common stock **:** RACE
3 a : a group of people united by certain convictions or a common affiliation **:** FELLOWSHIP **b :** the staff of a high official (as the President)
4 : a group of things related by common characteristics: as **a :** a closely related series of elements or chemical compounds **b :** a group of soils that have similar profiles and include one or more series **c :** a group of related languages descended from a single ancestral language
5 a : the basic unit in society traditionally consisting of two parents rearing their own or adopted children; *also* **:** any of various social units differing from but regarded as equivalent to the traditional family ⟨a single-parent *family*⟩ **b :** spouse and children ⟨want to spend more time with my *family*⟩

6 a : a group of related plants or animals forming a category ranking above a genus and below an order and usually comprising several to many genera **b** *in livestock breeding* (1) : the descendants or line of a particular individual especially of some outstanding female (2) : an identifiable strain within a breed **7 :** a set of curves or surfaces whose equations differ only in parameters **8 :** a unit of a crime syndicate (as the Mafia) operating within a geographical area

²family *adjective* (1602)
1 : of or relating to a family
2 : designed or suitable for both children and adults ⟨*family* restaurants⟩ ⟨*family* movies⟩

family Bible *noun* (1740)
: a large Bible usually having special pages for recording births, marriages, and deaths

family court *noun* (circa 1931)
: COURT OF DOMESTIC RELATIONS

family doctor *noun* (1846)
1 : a doctor regularly consulted by a family
2 : a doctor specializing in family practice

family jewels *noun plural* (circa 1946)
slang : a man's testicles

family man *noun* (1856)
1 : a man with a wife and children dependent on him
2 : a responsible man of domestic habits

family name *noun* (1699)
: SURNAME 2

family physician *noun* (1807)
: FAMILY DOCTOR

family planning *noun* (1939)
: planning intended to determine the number and spacing of one's children through birth control

family practice *noun* (1969)
: a medical practice or specialty which provides continuing general medical care for the individual and family — called also *family medicine*

family practitioner *noun* (1846)
: FAMILY DOCTOR

family room *noun* (1853)
: a large room designed as a recreation center for members of a family

family style *adverb or adjective* (1932)
: with the food placed on the table in serving dishes from which those eating may help themselves

family tree *noun* (1807)
1 : a genealogical diagram
2 : GENEALOGY

family way *noun* (1796)
: condition of being pregnant — used with *in* and *the* or *a* ⟨she is in a *family way*⟩

fam·ine \'fa-mən\ *noun* [Middle English, from Middle French, from *faim* hunger, from Latin *fames*] (14th century)
1 : an extreme scarcity of food
2 *archaic* : STARVATION
3 *archaic* : a ravenous appetite
4 : a great shortage

fam·ish \'fa-mish\ *verb* [Middle English, probably alteration of *famen*, from Middle French *afamer*, from (assumed) Vulgar Latin *affamare*, from Latin *ad-* + *fames*] (15th century)
transitive verb
1 : to cause to suffer severely from hunger
2 *archaic* : to cause to starve to death
intransitive verb
1 *archaic* : STARVE
2 : to suffer for lack of something necessary ⟨a moment when French poetry in particular was *famishing* for such invention —T. S. Eliot⟩
— **fam·ish·ment** \-mənt\ *noun*

fam·ished \'fa-misht\ *adjective* (15th century)
: intensely hungry; *also* : NEEDY

fa·mous \'fā-məs\ *adjective* [Middle English, from Middle French *fameux*, from Latin *famosus*, from *fama* fame] (14th century)
1 a : widely known **b :** honored for achievement
2 : EXCELLENT, FIRST-RATE ⟨*famous* weather for a walk⟩ ☆

— **fa·mous·ness** *noun*
fa·mous·ly *adverb* (1579)
1 : in a celebrated manner
2 : in a superlative fashion
3 : to an unusual degree : VERY

fam·u·lus \'fam-yə-ləs\ *noun, plural* **-li** \-,lī, -,lē\ [German, assistant to a professor, from Latin, servant] (1837)
: a private secretary or attendant

¹fan \'fan\ *noun* [Middle English, from Old English *fann*, from Latin *vannus* — more at WINNOW] (before 12th century)
1 : any of various devices for winnowing grain
2 : an instrument for producing a current of air: as **a :** a device for cooling the person that is usually shaped like a segment of a circle and is composed of material (as feathers or paper) mounted on thin rods or slats moving about a pivot so that the device may be closed compactly when not in use **b :** a device that consists of a series of vanes radiating from a hub rotated on its axle by a motor **c** *slang* : an airplane propeller
3 a : something resembling an open fan **b :** a gently sloping fan-shaped body of detritus; *especially* : ALLUVIAL FAN
— **fan·like** \-,līk\ *adjective*

²fan *verb* **fanned; fan·ning** (before 12th century)
transitive verb
1 a : to drive away the chaff of (grain) by means of a current of air **b :** to eliminate (as chaff) by winnowing
2 : to move or impel (air) with a fan
3 : to blow or breathe upon ⟨the breeze *fanning* her hair⟩
4 a : to direct a current of air upon with a fan **b :** to stir up to activity as if by fanning : STIMULATE ⟨*fanning* the fires of nationalism⟩
5 *archaic* : WAVE
6 *slang* : SPANK
7 : to spread like a fan ⟨the peacock *fanned* his tail⟩
8 : to strike (a batter) out in baseball
9 : to fire a series of shots from (a single-action revolver) by holding the trigger back and successively striking the hammer to the rear with the free hand
intransitive verb
1 : to move like a fan : FLUTTER
2 : to spread like a fan — often used with *out* ⟨deputies *fanning* out on the hunt⟩
3 : STRIKE OUT 3
— **fan·ner** \'fa-nər\ *noun*

³fan *noun* [probably short for *fanatic*] (1682)
1 : an enthusiastic devotee (as of a sport or a performing art) usually as a spectator
2 : an ardent admirer or enthusiast (as of a celebrity or a pursuit) ⟨science-fiction *fans*⟩
word history see FANATIC

fa·nat·ic \fə-'na-tik\ *or* **fa·nat·i·cal** \-ti-kəl\ *adjective* [Latin *fanaticus* inspired by a deity, frenzied, from *fanum* temple — more at FEAST] (1550)
: marked by excessive enthusiasm and often intense uncritical devotion ⟨they're *fanatic* about politics⟩ ◇
— **fanatic** *noun*
— **fa·nat·i·cal·ly** \fə-'na-ti-k(ə-)lē\ *adverb*
— **fa·nat·i·cal·ness** \-kəl-nəs\ *noun*

fa·nat·i·cism \fə-'na-tə-,si-zəm\ *noun* (1652)
: fanatic outlook or behavior

fa·nat·i·cize \-,sīz\ *transitive verb* **-cized; -ciz·ing** (1812)
: to cause to become fanatic

fan·ci·er \'fan(t)-sē-ər\ *noun* (1765)
1 : one that has a special liking or interest
2 : a person who breeds or grows a particular animal or plant for points of excellence ⟨a pigeon *fancier*⟩

fan·ci·ful \'fan(t)-si-fəl\ *adjective* (circa 1627)
1 : marked by fancy or unrestrained imagination rather than by reason and experience ⟨a *fanciful* person⟩
2 : existing in fancy only ⟨a *fanciful* notion⟩

3 : marked by or as if by fancy or whim ⟨gave their children *fanciful* names⟩
synonym see IMAGINARY
— **fan·ci·ful·ly** \-f(ə-)lē\ *adverb*
— **fan·ci·ful·ness** \-fəl-nəs\ *noun*

fan·ci·fy \'fan(t)-sə-,fī\ *transitive verb* **-fied; -fy·ing** (1890)
: to make ornate, elaborate, or fancy ⟨a *fancified* hamburger⟩

¹fan·cy \'fan(t)-sē\ *transitive verb* **fan·cied; fan·cy·ing** (14th century)
1 : to have a fancy for : LIKE
2 : to form a conception of : IMAGINE ⟨*fancy* our embarrassment⟩
3 a : to believe mistakenly or without evidence **b :** to believe without being certain ⟨she *fancied* she had met him before⟩
4 : to visualize or interpret as ⟨*fancied* myself a child again⟩
synonym see THINK

²fancy *noun, plural* **fancies** [Middle English *fantasie, fantsy* fantasy, fancy, from Middle French *fantasie*, from Latin *phantasia*, from

Greek, appearance, imagination, from *phantazein* to present to the mind (middle voice, to imagine), from *phainein* to show; akin to Old English *gebōned* polished, Greek *phōs* light] (15th century)

1 a : a liking formed by caprice rather than reason **:** INCLINATION ⟨took a *fancy* to the strange little animal⟩ **b :** amorous fondness **:** LOVE

2 a : NOTION, WHIM **b :** an image or representation of something formed in the mind
3 *archaic* **:** fantastic quality or state
4 a : imagination especially of a capricious or delusive sort **b :** the power of conception and representation used in artistic expression (as by a poet)
5 : TASTE, JUDGMENT
6 a : devotees of some particular art, practice, or amusement **b :** the object of interest of such a fancy; *especially* **:** ²BOXING

³**fancy** *adjective* **fan·ci·er; -est** (1646)
1 : dependent or based on fancy **:** WHIMSICAL
2 a (1) **:** not plain **:** ORNAMENTAL ⟨a *fancy* hairdo⟩ (2) **:** SWANKY 2, POSH ⟨a *fancy* restaurant⟩ **b** (1) **:** of particular excellence or highest grade ⟨*fancy* tuna⟩ (2) **:** IMPRESSIVE ⟨posted some *fancy* numbers⟩ **c** *of an animal or plant* **:** bred especially for bizarre or ornamental qualities that lack practical utility
3 : based on conceptions of the fancy ⟨*fancy* sketches⟩
4 a : dealing in fancy goods **b :** EXTRAVAGANT ⟨paying *fancy* prices⟩
5 : executed with technical skill and style ⟨*fancy* footwork⟩ ⟨*fancy* diving⟩
6 : PARTI-COLOR ⟨*fancy* carnations⟩
— **fan·ci·ly** \'fan(t)-sə-lē\ *adverb*
— **fan·ci·ness** \-sē-nəs\ *noun*

fancy-dan \'fan(t)-sē-ˌdan, -ˌdan\ *adjective, often D capitalized* (1938)
: SHOWY 2, FANCY

fancy Dan *noun, often F capitalized* (circa 1943)
: one given to flamboyant display especially of technique or dress

fancy dress *noun* (1770)
: a costume (as for a masquerade) chosen to suit the wearer's fancy

fan·cy-free \ˌfan(t)-sē-'frē\ *adjective* (1590)
1 : free from amorous attachment or engagement
2 : free to imagine or fancy

fancy man *noun* (1811)
: a woman's paramour; *also* **:** PIMP

fancy-pants *adjective* (1945)
: overly elegant or refined **:** LA-DI-DA

fancy up *transitive verb* (1934)
: to add superficial adornment to

fancy woman *noun* (1812)
: a woman of questionable morals; *specifically* **:** PROSTITUTE

fan·cy-work \'fan(t)-sē-ˌwərk\ *noun* (1810)
: decorative needlework

fan·dan·go \fan-'daŋ-(ˌ)gō\ *noun, plural* **-gos** [Spanish] (1774)
1 : a lively Spanish or Spanish-American dance in triple time that is usually performed by a man and a woman to the accompaniment of guitar and castanets; *also* **:** music for this dance
2 : TOMFOOLERY

fan·dom \'fan-dəm\ *noun* (1903)
: all the fans (as of a sport)

fane \'fān\ *noun* [Middle English, from Latin *fanum* — more at FEAST] (15th century)
1 : TEMPLE
2 : CHURCH

fan·fare \'fan-ˌfar, -ˌfer\ *noun* [French] (1676)
1 : a showy outward display
2 : a short and lively sounding of trumpets

fan·far·o·nade \ˌfan-ˌfar-ə-'nād, -'näd\ *noun* [French *fanfaronnade*, from Spanish *fanfarronada*, from *fanfarrón* braggart] (1652)
: empty boasting **:** BLUSTER

fan·fold \'fan-ˌfōld\ *noun* (1925)

: paper (as business forms or tape) made from a web and folded like a fan lengthwise and sometimes crosswise
— **fanfold** *transitive verb*

fang \'faŋ\ *noun* [Middle English, that which is taken, from Old English; akin to Old High German *fang* seizure, Old English *fōn* to seize — more at PACT] (1555)
1 a : a long sharp tooth: as (1) **:** one by which an animal's prey is seized and held or torn (2) **:** one of the long hollow or grooved and often erectile teeth of a venomous snake **b :** one of the chelicerae of a spider at the tip of which a poison gland opens
2 : the root of a tooth or one of the processes or prongs into which a root divides
3 : a projecting tooth or prong
— **fanged** \'faŋd\ *adjective*

Fang \'faŋ, 'fäŋ\ *also* **Fan** \'fan, 'fän\ *noun, plural* **Fang** *or* **Fangs** *also* **Fan** *or* **Fans** (1861)
1 : a member of a Bantu-speaking people of northern Gabon, mainland Equatorial Guinea, and southern Cameroon
2 : the language of the Fang people

fan-jet \'fan-ˌjet\ *noun* (1962)
: a jet engine having a fan that operates in a duct and draws in extra air whose compression and expulsion provide extra thrust; *also* **:** an airplane powered by a fan-jet engine

fan letter *noun* (1932)
: a letter sent to a public figure by an admirer

fan·light \'fan-ˌlīt\ *noun* (1819)
: a semicircular window with radiating bars like the ribs of a fan that is placed over a door or window

fan mail *noun* (1924)
: FAN LETTERS

fan·ny \'fa-nē\ *noun, plural* **fannies** [perhaps from *Fanny*, nickname of *Frances*] (1928)
1 : BUTTOCKS
2 *slang British* **:** VULVA

fanny pack *noun* (1967)
: a pack for carrying personal articles that straps to the waist

fan·tab·u·lous \fan-'ta-byə-ləs\ *adjective* [blend of *fantastic* and *fabulous*] (1959)
slang **:** marvelously good

fan·tail \'fan-ˌtāl\ *noun* (1728)
1 : a fan-shaped tail or end
2 : a domestic pigeon having a broad rounded tail often with 30 or 40 feathers
3 : an architectural part resembling a fan
4 : a counter or after overhang of a ship shaped like a duck's bill

fan-tan \'fan-ˌtan\ *noun* [Chinese (Guangdong) *fāantāan*] (1878)
1 : a Chinese gambling game in which the banker divides a pile of objects (as beans) into fours and players bet on what number will be left at the end of the count
2 : a card game in which players must build in sequence upon sevens and attempt to be the first one out of cards

fan·ta·sia \fan-'tā-zhə, -z(h)ē-ə; ˌfan-tə-'zē-ə\ *noun* [Italian, literally, fancy, from Latin *phantasia* — more at FANCY] (1724)
1 : a free usually instrumental composition not in strict form
2 a : a work (as a poem or play) in which the author's fancy roves unrestricted **b :** something possessing grotesque, bizarre, or unreal qualities

fan·ta·sie \ˌfan-tə-'zē, ˌfän-\ *noun* [German *Phantasie*, from Latin *phantasia*] (circa 1859)
: FANTASIA

fan·ta·sied \'fan-tə-sēd, -zēd\ *adjective* (1561)
1 : existing only in the imagination **:** FANCIED
2 *obsolete* **:** full of fancies or strange whims

fan·ta·sise *British variant of* FANTASIZE

fan·ta·sist \-sist, -zist\ *noun* (1896)
: one who creates fantasias or fantasies

fan·ta·size \-ˌsīz\ *verb* **-sized; -siz·ing** (1926)
intransitive verb

: to indulge in reverie **:** create or develop imaginative and often fantastic views or ideas ⟨doing things I'd *fantasized* about in my sheltered childhood —Diane Arbus⟩
transitive verb
: to portray in the mind **:** FANCY ⟨likes to *fantasize* herself as very wealthy⟩
— **fan·ta·siz·er** \-ˌsī-zər\ *noun*

fan·tasm *variant of* PHANTASM

fan·tast \'fan-ˌtast\ *noun* [German, from Medieval Latin *fantasta*, probably back-formation from Late Latin *phantasticus*] (1588)
1 : VISIONARY
2 : a fantastic or eccentric person
3 : FANTASIST

¹**fan·tas·tic** \fan-'tas-tik, fən-\ *also* **fan·tas·ti·cal** \-ti-kəl\ *adjective* [Middle English *fantastic, fantastical*, from Middle French & Late Latin; Middle French *fantastique*, from Late Latin *phantasticus*, from Greek *phantastikos* producing mental images, from *phantazein* to present to the mind] (14th century)
1 a : based on fantasy **:** not real **b :** conceived or seemingly conceived by unrestrained fancy **c :** so extreme as to challenge belief **:** UNBELIEVABLE; *broadly* **:** exceedingly large or great
2 : marked by extravagant fantasy or extreme individuality **:** ECCENTRIC
3 *fantastic* **:** EXCELLENT, SUPERLATIVE ⟨a *fantastic* dinner⟩
— **fan·tas·ti·cal·i·ty** \(ˌ)fan-ˌtas-tə-'ka-lə-tē, fən-\ *noun*
— **fan·tas·ti·cal·ness** \-'tas-tə-kəl-nəs\ *noun*

²**fantastic** *noun* (1598)
: ECCENTRIC 2

fan·tas·ti·cal·ly \fan-'tas-ti-k(ə-)lē, fən-\ *adverb* (1543)
1 : in a fantastic manner
2 : to a fantastic degree **:** EXTREMELY ⟨*fantastically* expensive clothes⟩

fan·tas·ti·cate \fan-'tas-tə-ˌkāt, fən-\ *transitive verb* **-cat·ed; -cat·ing** (1600)
: to make fantastic
— **fan·tas·ti·ca·tion** \(ˌ)fan-ˌtas-tə-'kā-shən, fən-\ *noun*

fan·tas·ti·co \fan-'tas-ti-ˌkō, fən-\ *noun, plural* **-coes** [Italian, fantastic (adjective), from Late Latin *phantasticus*] (1596)
: a ridiculously fantastic individual

¹**fan·ta·sy** \'fan-tə-sē, -zē\ *noun, plural* **-sies** [Middle English *fantasie* — more at FANCY] (14th century)
1 *obsolete* **:** HALLUCINATION
2 : FANCY; *especially* **:** the free play of creative imagination
3 : a creation of the imaginative faculty whether expressed or merely conceived: as **a :** a fanciful design or invention **b :** a chimerical or fantastic notion **c :** FANTASIA 1 **d :** imaginative fiction featuring especially strange settings and grotesque characters — called also *fantasy fiction*
4 : CAPRICE

5 : the power or process of creating especially unrealistic or improbable mental images in response to psychological need ⟨an object of *fantasy*⟩; *also* **:** a mental image or a series of mental images (as a daydream) so created ⟨sexual *fantasies* of adolescence⟩
6 : a coin usually not intended for circulation as currency and often issued by a dubious authority (as a government-in-exile)

²**fantasy** *verb* **-sied; -sy·ing** (15th century)
: FANTASIZE

fan·ta·sy·land \-ˌland\ *noun* (1967)
: an imaginary or ideal place or situation

fan·toc·ci·ni \ˌfän-tə-'chē-nē, ˌfan-\ *noun plural* [Italian, plural of *fantoccino*, diminutive of *fantoccio* doll, augmentative of *fante* child, from Latin *infant-, infans* infant] (1771)
: a puppet show using puppets operated by strings or mechanical devices; *also* **:** such puppets

fan·tod \'fan-ˌtäd\ *noun* [perhaps alteration of English dialect *fantique, fanteeg*] (1839)
1 *plural* **a :** a state of irritability and tension **b :** FIDGETS
2 : an emotional outburst **:** FIT

fan·tom *variant of* PHANTOM

fan vault *noun* (circa 1901)
: a Gothic vault in which the ribs from each springer spread out like the vanes of a fan
— **fan vaulting** *noun*

fan·wise \'fan-ˌwīz\ *adverb or adjective* (1882)
: in the manner or position of the slats of an open fan ⟨boats anchored *fanwise* at the pier⟩

fan·zine \'fan-ˌzēn\ *noun* [³*fan* + maga*zine*] (1949)
: a magazine written by and for fans especially of science fiction or fantasy writing

¹**far** \'fär\ *adverb* **far·ther** \-thər\ *or* **fur·ther** \'fər-\; **far·thest** *or* **fur·thest** \-thəst\ [Middle English *fer*, from Old English *feorr*; akin to Old High German *ferro* far, Old English *faran* to go — more at FARE] (before 12th century)
1 : at or to a considerable distance in space ⟨wandered *far* from home⟩
2 a : to a great extent **:** MUCH ⟨*far* better methods⟩ **b :** by a broad interval **:** WIDELY ⟨the *far* distant future⟩
3 : to or at a definite distance, point, or degree ⟨as *far* as I know⟩
4 : to an advanced point or extent ⟨a bright student will go *far*⟩ ⟨worked *far* into the night⟩
5 : at a considerable distance in time ⟨not *far* from the year 1870⟩
— **by far :** far and away ⟨is *by far* the best runner⟩
— **far be it from :** it would be inappropriate or impossible for ⟨*far be it from* God, that he should do wickedness —Job 34:10 (Authorized Version)⟩
— **far from :** of a distinctly different and especially opposite quality than ⟨the trip was *far from* a failure⟩
— **how far :** to what extent, degree, or distance ⟨didn't know *how far* to trust them⟩
— **so far 1 :** to a certain extent, degree, or distance ⟨when the water rose *so far*, the villagers sought higher ground⟩ **2 :** up to the present ⟨has written just one novel *so far*⟩
— **thus far :** so far ⟨*thus far* our findings have been negative⟩

²**far** *adjective* **farther** *or* **further; farthest** *or* **furthest** (before 12th century)
1 a : remote in space **b :** distinctly different in quality or relationship **c :** remote in time
2 a : LONG ⟨a *far* journey⟩ **b :** of notable extent **:** COMPREHENSIVE ⟨a man of *far* vision⟩
3 : the more distant of two
4 : EXTREME ⟨the *far* left⟩ ⟨a *far* right political organization⟩

far·ad \'far-ˌad, 'far-əd\ *noun* [Michael Fara*day*] (1873)
: the unit of capacitance equal to the capacitance of a capacitor between whose plates

there appears a potential of one volt when it is charged by one coulomb of electricity

far·a·day \'far-ə-ˌdā, -ə-dē\ *noun* [Michael *Faraday*] (1904)
: the quantity of electricity transferred in electrolysis per equivalent weight of an element or ion equal to about 96,500 coulombs

fa·rad·ic \fə-'ra-dik, fa-'ra-\ *also* **far·a·da·ic** \ˌfar-ə-'dā-ik\ *adjective* (1875)
: of or relating to an asymmetric alternating current of electricity produced by an induction coil ⟨*faradic* stimulation of the muscles⟩

far·a·dism \'far-ə-ˌdi-zəm\ *noun* (1876)
: the application of a faradic current of electricity (as for therapeutic purposes)

far and away *adverb* (1852)
: by a considerable margin ⟨was *far and away* the better team⟩

far·an·dole \'far-ən-ˌdōl\ *noun* [French *farandole*, from Provençal *farandoulo*] (1863)
1 : a lively Provençal dance in which men and women hold hands, form a chain, and follow a leader through a serpentine course
2 : music in sextuple time for a farandole

far and wide *adverb* (before 12th century)
: in every direction **:** EVERYWHERE ⟨searched *far and wide*⟩

far·away \'fär-ə-ˌwā\ *adjective* (1735)
1 : lying at a great distance **:** REMOTE
2 : DREAMY, ABSTRACTED ⟨a *faraway* look in her eyes⟩

¹**farce** \'färs\ *transitive verb* **farced; farc·ing** [Middle English *farsen*, from Middle French *farcir*, from Latin *farcire*] (14th century)
1 : STUFF
2 : to improve as if by stuffing ◆

²**farce** *noun* [Middle English *farse*, from Middle French *farce*, from (assumed) Vulgar Latin *farsa*, from Latin, feminine of *farsus*, past participle of *farcire*] (14th century)
1 : a savory stuffing **:** FORCEMEAT
2 : a light dramatic composition marked by broadly satirical comedy and improbable plot
3 : the broad humor characteristic of farce or pretense
4 a : ridiculous or empty show **b :** MOCKERY ⟨the enforcement of this law became a *farce*⟩

far·ceur \fär-'sər\ *noun* [French, from Middle French, from *farcer* to joke, from Old French, from *farce*] (1781)
1 : JOKER, WAG
2 : a writer or actor of farce

far·ci *or* **far·cie** \fär-'sē\ *adjective* [French, from past participle of *farcir*] (1903)
: stuffed especially with forcemeat ⟨oysters *farci*⟩

far·ci·cal \'fär-si-kəl\ *adjective* (1716)
1 : of, relating to, or resembling farce **:** LUDICROUS
2 : laughably inept **:** ABSURD
— **far·ci·cal·i·ty** \ˌfär-sə-'ka-lə-tē\ *noun*
— **far·ci·cal·ly** \'fär-si-k(ə-)lē\ *adverb*

far·cy \'fär-sē\ *noun* [Middle English *farsin, farsi*, from Middle French *farcin*, from Late Latin *farcimen*, from Latin, sausage, from *farcire*] (15th century)
: GLANDERS; *especially* **:** cutaneous glanders

fard \'färd\ *transitive verb* [Middle English, from Middle French *farder*, of Germanic origin; akin to Old High German *faro* colored — more at PERCH] (15th century)
1 : to paint (the face) with cosmetics
2 *archaic* **:** to gloss over
— **fard** *noun, archaic*

far·del \'fär-d°l\ *noun* [Middle English, from Middle French, probably from Arabic *fardah*] (14th century)
1 : BUNDLE
2 : BURDEN

¹**fare** \'far, 'fer\ *intransitive verb* **fared; far·ing** [Middle English *faren*, from Old English *faran*; akin to Old High German *faran* to go, Latin *portare* to carry, Greek *peran* to pass through, *poros* passage, journey] (before 12th century)

1 : GO, TRAVEL
2 : GET ALONG, SUCCEED ⟨how did you *fare* on your exam?⟩
3 : EAT, DINE

²**fare** *noun* [Middle English, journey, passage, supply of food, from Old English *faru, fær*; akin to Old English *faran* to go] (15th century)
1 a : range of food **:** DIET **b :** material provided for use, consumption, or enjoyment
2 a : the price charged to transport a person **b :** a paying passenger on a public conveyance

fare–thee–well \'far-(ˌ)thē-ˌwel, 'fer-\ *also* **fare–you–well** \-yə-, -yü-, -yē-\ *noun* (1884)
1 : the utmost degree ⟨researched the story to a *fare-thee-well*⟩
2 : a state of perfection ⟨imitated the speaker's pompous manner to a *fare-thee-well*⟩

¹**fare·well** \far-'wel, fer-\ *verb imperative* (14th century)
: get along well — used interjectionally to or by one departing

²**farewell** *noun* (14th century)
1 : a wish of well-being at parting **:** GOOD-BYE
2 a : an act of departure **:** LEAVE-TAKING **b :** a formal occasion honoring a person about to leave or retire

³**fare·well** *transitive verb* (1580)
chiefly Australian & New Zealand **:** to bid farewell to

⁴**fare·well** \'far-ˌwel, 'fer-\ *adjective* (1669)
: of or relating to leave-taking **:** FINAL ⟨a *farewell* appearance⟩

far·fel *or* **far·fal** \'fär-fəl\ *noun* [Yiddish *farfl* (plural), from Middle High German *varveln* noodles, noodle soup] (1892)
: noodles in the form of small pellets or granules

far–fetched \'fär-'fecht\ *adjective* (1583)
1 : brought from a remote time or place
2 : not easily or naturally deduced or introduced **:** IMPROBABLE ⟨a *far-fetched* story⟩
— **far–fetched·ness** \-'fech(t)-nəs, -'fe-chəd-nəs\ *noun*

far–flung \-'fləŋ\ *adjective* (1895)
1 : widely spread or distributed ⟨a *far-flung* empire⟩
2 : REMOTE ⟨a *far-flung* correspondent⟩

fa·ri·na \fə-'rē-nə\ *noun* [Latin, meal, flour, from *far* spelt — more at BARLEY] (14th century)

◇ **WORD HISTORY**
farce When *farce* first appeared in English, its connection was with cooking, not comedy. In the 14th century English adopted *farce* (spelling it *farse* until the 18th century) from French, retaining its original meaning of "stuffing or forcemeat." The comedic sense of *farce* in English dates back to the 16th century, when England imported a kind of knockabout comedy that was already well-established in France and Italy. This dramatic genre had its origins in the 13th century practice of interlarding or "stuffing" Latin liturgical texts with explanatory passages in the vernacular. By the 15th century the practice arose of inserting unscripted buffoonery into performances of religious plays. Such farces, which included clowning, acrobatics, reversal of social roles, and indecency, soon developed into a distinct dramatic genre, a kind of broad comedy with a slapstick element. Since its introduction into England, farce in one guise or another has continued its popularity into the age of television.

\ə\ abut \ᵊ\ kitten \ər\ further \a\ ash \ā\ ace \ä\ mop, mar \au̇\ out \ch\ chin \e\ bet \ē\ easy \g\ go \i\ hit \ī\ ice \j\ job \ŋ\ sing \ō\ go \ȯ\ law \ȯi\ boy \th\ thin \t̶h̶\ the \ü\ loot \u̇\ foot \y\ yet \zh\ vision *see also* Guide to Pronunciation

1 : a fine meal of vegetable matter (as cereal grains) used chiefly for puddings or as a breakfast cereal
2 : any of various powdery or mealy substances
far·i·na·ceous \,far-ə-'nā-shəs\ *adjective* (1646)
1 : having a mealy texture or surface
2 : containing or rich in starch
far·in·fra·red \'fär-,in-frə-'red\ *adjective* (1923)
: of or relating to the longer wavelengths of radiation in the infrared spectrum and especially to those between 10 and 1000 micrometers
fa·ri·nha \fə-'rēn-yə\ *noun* [Portuguese, flour, cassava meal, from Latin *farina*] (1726)
: cassava meal
far·kle·ber·ry \'fär-kəl-,ber-ē\ *noun* [origin unknown] (1765)
: a shrub or small tree (*Vaccinium arboreum*) of the heath family of the southeastern U.S. having a black berry with stony seeds
farl \'fär(-ə)l\ *noun* [contraction of Scots *fardel*, literally, fourth part, from Middle English (Scots), from *ferde del*; from *ferde* fourth + *del* part] (1686)
Scottish : a small thin triangular cake or biscuit made especially with oatmeal or wheat flour
¹farm \'färm\ *noun, often attributive* [Middle English *ferme* rent, lease, from Old French, lease, from *fermer* to fix, make a contract, from Latin *firmare* to make firm, from *firmus* firm] (14th century)
1 *obsolete* : a sum or due fixed in amount and payable at fixed intervals
2 : a letting out of revenues or taxes for a fixed sum to one authorized to collect and retain them
3 : a district or division of a country leased out for the collection of government revenues
4 : a tract of land devoted to agricultural purposes
5 a : a plot of land devoted to the raising of animals and especially domestic livestock **b** : a tract of water reserved for the artificial cultivation of some aquatic life form
6 : a minor-league team (as in baseball) associated with a major-league team as a subsidiary
7 : an area containing a number of similar structures (as radio antennas or storage tanks)
²farm (15th century)
transitive verb
1 *obsolete* : RENT
2 : to collect and take the fees or profits of (an occupation or business) on payment of a fixed sum
3 : to give up (as an estate or a business) to another on condition of receiving in return a fixed sum
4 a : to devote to agriculture **b** : to manage and cultivate as a farm **c** : to grow or cultivate in quantity ⟨*farm* trees for fuel⟩ ⟨*farm* salmon⟩
intransitive verb
: to engage in raising crops, animals, or fish
farm·er \'fär-mər\ *noun* (14th century)
1 : a person who pays a fixed sum for some privilege or source of income
2 : a person who cultivates land or crops or raises animals or fish
3 : YOKEL, BUMPKIN
farmer cheese *noun* (1949)
: a pressed unripened cheese similar to but drier and firmer than cottage cheese
farm·er·ette \,fär-mə-'ret\ *noun* (1902)
: a woman who is a farmer or farmhand
farmer's lung *noun* (1945)
: an acute pulmonary disorder characterized by sudden onset, fever, cough, expectoration, and breathlessness that results from the inhalation of dust from moldy hay or straw
farm·hand \'färm-,hand\ *noun* (1843)
1 : a farm laborer; *especially* : a hired laborer on a farm

2 : a player on a farm team
farm·house \-,haùs\ *noun* (1598)
: a dwelling on a farm
farm·ing *noun* (1733)
: the practice of agriculture or aquaculture
farm·land \'färm-,land\ *noun* (1638)
: land used or suitable for farming
farm out *transitive verb* (1607)
1 : to turn over (as a job) for performance by another usually under contract
2 a : to put (as children) into the hands of another for care **b** : to send (as a baseball player) to a farm team
3 : to exhaust (land) by farming especially by continuously raising one crop
farm·stead \'färm-,sted\ *noun* (1807)
: the buildings and adjacent service areas of a farm; *broadly* : a farm with its buildings
farm·wife \'färm-,wīf\ *noun* (1880)
: a farmer's wife
farm·work·er \'färm-,wər-kər\ *noun* (1946)
: FARMHAND 1
— **farm·work** \-,wərk\ *noun*
farm·yard \-,yärd\ *noun* (1748)
: land around or enclosed by farm buildings; *especially* : BARNYARD
faro \'far-,ō, 'fer-\ *noun* [probably alteration of earlier *pharaoh*, translation of French *pharaon*] (circa 1735)
: a gambling game in which players bet on cards drawn from a dealing box
Faro·ese *variant of* FAEROESE
far–off \'fär-,óf\ *adjective* (15th century)
: remote in time or space
fa·rouche \fə-'rüsh\ *adjective* [French, wild, shy, from Late Latin *forasticus* living outside, from Latin *foras* outdoors; akin to Latin *fores* door — more at DOOR] (1765)
1 : WILD
2 : marked by shyness and lack of social graces
far–out \'fär-,aùt\ *adjective* (1954)
: marked by a considerable departure from the conventional or traditional ⟨*far-out* clothes⟩
— **far–out·ness** *noun*
far·rag·i·nous \fə-'ra-jə-nəs\ *adjective* (1615)
: consisting of a farrago
far·ra·go \fə-'rä-(,)gō, -'rā-\ *noun, plural* **-goes** [Latin *farragin-, farrago* mixed fodder, mixture, from *far* spelt — more at BARLEY] (1632)
: a confused mixture : HODGEPODGE
far–reach·ing \'fär-,rē-chin\ *adjective* (1824)
: having a wide range or effect
far–red \-'red\ *adjective* (1951)
: NEAR-INFRARED
far·ri·er \'far-ē-ər\ *noun* [alteration of Middle English *ferrour*, from Middle French *ferrour* blacksmith, from Old French *ferreor*, from *ferrer* to fit with iron, from (assumed) Vulgar Latin *ferrare*, from Latin *ferrum* iron] (15th century)
: a person who shoes horses
¹far·row \'far-(,)ō, -ə(-w)\ *verb* [Middle English *farwen*, from (assumed) Old English *feargian*, from Old English *fearh* young pig; akin to Old High German *farah* young pig, Latin *porcus* pig] (13th century)
transitive verb
: to give birth to (a farrow)
intransitive verb
of swine : to bring forth young — often used with *down*
²farrow *noun* (1577)
1 : a litter of pigs
2 : an act of farrowing
³farrow *adjective* [Middle English (Scots) *ferow*]
of a cow : not pregnant
far–see·ing \'fär-,sē-iɳ\ *adjective* (1837)
: FARSIGHTED 1
Far·si \'fär-sē\ *noun* [Persian *fārsī*, from *Fārs* Persia] (1878)
: PERSIAN 2b
far·side *noun* (15th century)

: the farther side; *especially* : the side of the moon away from the earth
— **on the far side of** : BEYOND ⟨just *on the far side of* 40⟩
far·sight·ed \'fär-,sī-təd\ *adjective* (1609)
1 a : seeing or able to see to a great distance **b** : having or showing foresight or good judgment : SAGACIOUS
2 : affected with hyperopia
— **far·sight·ed·ly** *adverb*
far·sight·ed·ness *noun* (circa 1829)
1 : the quality or state of being farsighted
2 : HYPEROPIA
¹fart \'färt\ *intransitive verb* [Middle English *ferten, farten;* akin to Old High German *ferzan* to break wind, Old Norse *freta*, Greek *perdesthai*, Sanskrit *pardate* he breaks wind] (13th century)
: to expel intestinal gas from the anus — often considered vulgar
²fart *noun* (14th century)
1 : an expulsion of intestinal gas — often considered vulgar
2 : a foolish or contemptible person ⟨couldn't stand the old *fart*⟩ — seldom in polite use
¹far·ther \'fär-thər\ *adverb* [Middle English *ferther*, alteration of *further*] (14th century)
1 : at or to a greater distance or more advanced point ⟨got no *farther* than the first page⟩ ⟨nothing could be *farther* from the truth⟩
2 : to a greater degree or extent ⟨see to it that I do not have to act any *farther* in the matter —Bernard DeVoto⟩ ▢
²farther *adjective* (14th century)
1 : more distant : REMOTER ⟨the *farther* side of town⟩
2 : FURTHER 2 ⟨clearing his throat preparatory to *farther* revelations —Edith Wharton⟩
far·ther·most \-,mōst\ *adjective* (15th century)
: most distant : FARTHEST
¹far·thest \'fär-thəst\ *adjective* (14th century)
: most distant especially in space or time
²farthest *adverb* (15th century)
1 : to or at the greatest distance in space or time ⟨who can jump the *farthest*⟩
2 : to the most advanced point ⟨goes *farthest* toward answering the question⟩
3 : by the greatest degree or extent : MOST ⟨the painting *farthest* removed from reality⟩
far·thing \'fär-thin\ *noun* [Middle English *ferthing*, from Old English *fēorthung* (akin to Middle High German *vierdunc* fourth part), from Old English *fēortha* fourth] (before 12th century)
1 a : a former British monetary unit equal to ¼ of a penny **b** : a coin representing this unit
2 : something of small value : MITE
far·thin·gale \'fär-thən-,gāl, -thin-\ *noun* [modification of Middle French *verdugale*, from Old Spanish *verdugado*, from *verdugo* young shoot of a tree, from *verde* green, from Latin *viridis* — more at VERDANT] (1552)

▢ USAGE
farther *Farther* and *further* have been used more or less interchangeably throughout most of their history, but currently they are showing signs of diverging. As adverbs they continue to be used interchangeably whenever spatial, temporal, or metaphorical distance is involved. But where there is no notion of distance, *further* is used ⟨our techniques can be *further* refined⟩. *Further* is also used as a sentence modifier ⟨*further*, the workshop participants were scarcely optimistic —L. B. Mayhew⟩, but *farther* is not. A polarizing process appears to be taking place in their adjective use. *Farther* is taking over the meaning of distance ⟨the *farther* shore⟩ and *further* the meaning of addition ⟨needed no *further* invitation⟩.

: a support (as of hoops) worn especially in the 16th century beneath a skirt to expand it at the hipline

far ultraviolet *adjective* (1947)
: of, relating to, or being the shortest wavelengths of radiation in the ultraviolet spectrum and especially those between 100 and 300 nanometers

fas·ces \'fas-,ēz\ *noun plural but singular or plural in construction* [Latin, from plural of *fascis* bundle; akin to Latin *fascia*] (1598)
: a bundle of rods and among them an ax with projecting blade borne before ancient Roman magistrates as a badge of authority

fas·cia *1 & 3 are usually* 'fā-sh(ē-)ə, *2 is usually* 'fa-\ *noun, plural* **-ci·ae** \-shē-,ē\ *or* **-cias** [Italian, from Latin, band, bandage; akin to Middle Irish *basc* necklace] (1563)
1 : a flat usually horizontal member of a building having the form of a flat band or broad fillet: as **a** : a flat piece used as a molding **b** : a horizontal piece (as a board) covering the joint between the top of a wall and the projecting eaves — called also *fascia board* **c** : a nameplate over the front of a shop
2 : a sheet of connective tissue covering or binding together body structures; *also* : tissue of this character
3 *or* **fa·cia** \'fā-sh(ē-)ə\ *British* : the dashboard of an automobile
— **fas·cial** \'fash(ē-)əl\ *adjective*

fas·ci·at·ed \'fa-shē-,ā-təd\ *adjective* (circa 1835)
1 : exhibiting fasciation
2 : arranged in fascicles

fas·ci·a·tion \,fa-s(h)ē-'ā-shən\ *noun* (1677)
: a malformation of plant stems commonly manifested as enlargement and flattening as if several stems were fused

fas·ci·cle \'fa-si-kəl\ *noun* [Latin *fasciculus*, diminutive of *fascis*] (15th century)
1 : a small or slender bundle (as of pine needles or nerve fibers)
2 : one of the divisions of a book published in parts
— **fas·ci·cled** \-kəld\ *adjective*

fas·cic·u·lar \fə-'si-kyə-lər, fa-\ *adjective* (1816)
: of, relating to, or consisting of fascicles or fasciculi
— **fas·cic·u·lar·ly** *adverb*

fas·cic·u·late \-lət\ *also* **fas·cic·u·lat·ed** \-,lā-təd\ *adjective* (1794)
: FASCICULAR

fas·cic·u·la·tion \fə-,si-kyə-'lā-shən, fa-\ *noun* (1938)
: muscular twitching involving the simultaneous contraction of contiguous groups of muscle fibers

fas·ci·cule \'fa-si-,kyü(ə)l\ *noun* [French, from Latin *fasciculus*] (1880)
: FASCICLE 2

fas·cic·u·lus \fə-'si-kyə-ləs, fa-\ *noun, plural* **-li** \-,lī\ [New Latin, from Latin] (1713)
1 : a slender bundle of anatomical fibers
2 : FASCICLE 2

fas·ci·nate \'fa-sᵊn-,āt\ *verb* **fas·ci·nat·ed; fas·ci·nat·ing** \'fa-,nā-tiŋ, 'fa-sᵊn-,ā-\ [Latin *fascinatus*, past participle of *fascinare*, from *fascinum* evil spell] (1598)
transitive verb
1 *obsolete* : BEWITCH
2 a : to transfix and hold spellbound by an irresistible power ⟨believed that the serpent could *fascinate* its prey⟩ **b** : to command the interest of : ALLURE ⟨was *fascinated* by carnivals⟩
intransitive verb
: to be irresistibly attractive ⟨the novel's flamboyant cover *fascinates*⟩ ◇
synonym see ATTRACT
fas·ci·nat·ing *adjective* (1648)

: extremely interesting or charming : CAPTIVATING
— **fas·ci·nat·ing·ly** \-,ā-tiŋ-lē\ *adverb*

fas·ci·na·tion \,fa-sᵊn-'ā-shən\ *noun* (1605)
1 a : the quality or power of fascinating **b** : something fascinating
2 : the state of being fascinated

fas·ci·na·tor \'fa-sᵊn-,ā-tər\ *noun* (1750)
1 : one that fascinates
2 : a woman's lightweight head scarf usually of crochet or lace

fas·cine \fa-'sēn, fə-\ *noun* [French, from Latin *fascina*, from *fascis*] (circa 1688)
: a long bundle of sticks of wood bound together and used for such purposes as filling ditches and making revetments for riverbanks

fas·ci·o·li·a·sis \fə-,sē-ə-'lī-ə-səs, -,sī-\ *noun, plural* **-a·ses** \-,sēz\ [New Latin, from *Fasciola*, genus of flukes + *-iasis*] (1890)
: infestation with or disease caused by liver flukes (genus *Fasciola*)

fas·cism \'fa-,shi-zəm *also* 'fa-,si-\ *noun* [Italian *fascismo*, from *fascio* bundle, fasces, group, from Latin *fascis* bundle & *fasces* fasces] (1921)
1 *often capitalized* : a political philosophy, movement, or regime (as that of the Fascisti) that exalts nation and often race above the individual and that stands for a centralized autocratic government headed by a dictatorial leader, severe economic and social regimentation, and forcible suppression of opposition
2 : a tendency toward or actual exercise of strong autocratic or dictatorial control ⟨early instances of army *fascism* and brutality —J. W. Aldridge⟩ ◇
— **fas·cist** \-shist *also* -sist\ *noun or adjective, often capitalized*
— **fas·cis·tic** \fa-'shis-tik *also* -'sis-\ *adjective, often capitalized*
— **fas·cis·ti·cal·ly** \-ti-k(ə-)lē\ *adverb, often capitalized*

Fa·sci·sta \fä-'shē-(,)stä\ *noun, plural* **-sti** \-(,)stē\ [Italian, from *fascio*] (1921)
: a member of an Italian political organization under Mussolini governing Italy 1922–1943 according to the principles of fascism

fash \'fash\ *verb* [Middle French *fascher*, from (assumed) Vulgar Latin *fastidiare* to disgust, from Latin *fastidium* disgust — more at FASTIDIOUS] (1533)
chiefly Scottish : VEX
— **fash** *noun, chiefly Scottish*

¹fash·ion \'fa-shᵊn\ *noun* [Middle English *facioun, fasoun* shape, manner, from Middle French *façon*, from Latin *faction-, factio* act of making, faction, from *facere* to make — more at DO] (14th century)
1 a : the make or form of something **b** *archaic* : KIND, SORT
2 a : a distinctive or peculiar and often habitual manner or way ⟨he will, after his sour *fashion*, tell you —Shakespeare⟩ **b** : mode of action or operation ⟨assembled in an orderly *fashion*⟩
3 a : a prevailing custom, usage, or style **b** (1) : the prevailing style (as in dress) during a particular time (2) : a garment in such a style ⟨always wears the latest *fashions*⟩ **c** : social standing or prominence especially as signalized by dress or conduct ⟨men and women of *fashion*⟩ ☆
— **after a fashion** : in an approximate or rough way ⟨became an artist *after a fashion*⟩

²fashion *transitive verb* **fash·ioned; fash·ion·ing** \'fash-niŋ, 'fa-shᵊn-iŋ\ (15th century)
1 a : to give shape or form to : MOLD **b** : ALTER, TRANSFORM **c** : to mold into a particular character by influencing or training **d** : to make or construct usually with the use of imagination and ingenuity ⟨*fashion* a lamp from an old churn⟩
2 : FIT, ADAPT
3 *obsolete* : CONTRIVE
— **fash·ion·er** \'fash-nər, 'fa-shᵊn-ər\ *noun*

Fashion, style, mode, vogue, fad, rage, craze mean the usage accepted by those who want to be up-to-date. FASHION is the most general term and applies to any way of dressing, behaving, writing, or performing that is favored at any one time or place ⟨the current *fashion*⟩. STYLE often implies a distinctive fashion adopted by people of taste ⟨a media baron used to traveling in *style*⟩. MODE suggests the fashion of the moment among those anxious to appear elegant and sophisticated ⟨slim bodies are the *mode* at this resort⟩. VOGUE stresses the wide acceptance of a fashion ⟨short skirts are back in *vogue*⟩. FAD suggests caprice in taking up or in dropping a fashion ⟨last year's *fad* is over⟩. RAGE and CRAZE stress intense enthusiasm in adopting a fad ⟨Cajun food was the *rage* nearly everywhere for a time⟩ ⟨crossword puzzles once seemed just a passing *craze* but have lasted⟩. See in addition METHOD.

◇ **WORD HISTORY**

fascinate The word *fascinate* has its roots in a world where witchcraft and enchantment were taken much more seriously than they are in our time. Synonyms such as *bewitch* and *charm* have a magical side that is still apparent enough from the literal meanings of the words themselves, but this aspect of *fascinate* is clear only if we look at its etymology. In Latin the verb *fascinare* meant "to cast a spell on, bewitch" and was a derivative of a noun *fascinum*. The original meaning of *fascinum* seems to have been "bewitchment," though this usage is very sparsely attested. More frequently *fascinum* referred to a sort of counter charm, an amulet worn around the neck to avert the evil eye. *Fascinum* is similar in sound to Greek *baskanos* "malicious" (with derivatives such as *baskanein* "to avert the evil eye" and *baskanion* "charm, amulet"), but the ultimate source of both words is uncertain.

fascism The words *fascism* and *fascist* have long been associated with the Fascisti of Benito Mussolini and the bundle of rods called *fasces*, which the Fascisti adopted as a symbol of authoritarianism. However, Mussolini did not introduce the word *fascista* when his black-shirted organization, the *Fasci di combattimento*, was organized in 1919, nor did the fasces have any direct connection with the origin of *fascista*. In Italian, the word *fascio* (plural *fasci*) means literally "bundle," and figuratively "group." From at least 1872 *fascio* was used in the names of labor and agrarian unions, and in October 1914 a political coalition was formed called the *Fascio rivoluzionario d'azione internazionalista* ("revolutionary group for international action"), which advocated Italian participation in World War I on the side of the Allies. Members of this group were first called *fascisti* in January 1915. Although Mussolini was closely associated with this interventionist movement, it had no direct link with the postwar *Fasci di combattimento*, and in 1919 the word *fascista* was already in political circulation. Of course, it is to the Fascisti in their 1919 incarnation—who seized power in Italy three years later—that we owe the customary meanings of our *fascism* and *fascist*.

\ə\ **abut** \ᵊ\ **kitten** \ər\ **further** \a\ **ash** \ā\ **ace** \ä\ **mop, mar** \aù\ **out** \ch\ **chin** \e\ **bet** \ē\ **easy** \g\ **go** \i\ **hit** \ī\ **ice** \j\ **job** \ŋ\ **sing** \ō\ **go** \ò\ **law** \òi\ **boy** \th\ **thin** \t̲h̲\ **the** \ü\ **loot** \ù\ **foot** \y\ **yet** \zh\ **vision** *see also* Guide to Pronunciation

¹fash·ion·able \'fash-nə-bəl, 'fa-shᵊn-ə-\ *adjective* (1606)
1 : conforming to the custom, fashion, or established mode
2 : of or relating to the world of fashion
— **fash·ion·abil·i·ty** \,fash-nə-'bi-lə-tē, ,fa-shᵊn-ə-\ *noun*
— **fash·ion·able·ness** \'fash-nə-bəl-nəs, 'fa-shə-\ *noun*
— **fash·ion·ably** \-blē\ *adverb*
²fashionable *noun* (circa 1800)
: a fashionable person
fash·ion·mon·ger \'fa-shᵊn-,män-gər, -,mən-\ *noun* (1599)
: one that studies, imitates, or sets the fashion
fashion plate *noun* (1851)
1 : an illustration of a clothing style
2 : a person who dresses in the latest fashions
¹fast \'fast\ *adjective* [Middle English, from Old English *fæst;* akin to Old High German *festi* firm, Old Norse *fastr,* Armenian *hast*] (before 12th century)
1 a : firmly fixed ⟨roots *fast* in the ground⟩ **b :** tightly shut ⟨the drawers were *fast*⟩ **c :** adhering firmly **d :** not easily freed : STUCK ⟨a ball *fast* in the mouth of the cannon⟩ **e :** STABLE ⟨movable items were made *fast* to the deck⟩
2 : firmly loyal ⟨became *fast* friends⟩
3 a : characterized by quick motion, operation, or effect: (1) **:** moving or able to move rapidly **:** SWIFT (2) **:** taking a comparatively short time (3) **:** imparting quickness of motion ⟨a *fast* bowler⟩ (4) **:** accomplished quickly (5) **:** agile of mind; *especially* **:** quick to learn ⟨a class for *fast* students⟩ **b :** conducive to rapidity of play or action **c** (1) *of a timepiece or weighing device* **:** indicating in advance of what is correct (2) **:** according to or being daylight saving time **d :** contributing to a shortening of exposure time ⟨*fast* film⟩ **e :** acquired with unusually little effort and often by shady or dishonest methods ⟨had a keen eye for a *fast* buck —R. A. Keith⟩
4 a : securely attached ⟨a rope *fast* to the wharf⟩ **b :** TENACIOUS ⟨a *fast* hold on her purse⟩
5 a *archaic* **:** sound asleep **b** *of sleep* **:** not easily disturbed
6 : not fading or changing color readily
7 a : WILD ⟨a pretty *fast* crowd⟩ **b :** sexually promiscuous
8 : resistant to change (as from destructive action or fading) ⟨*fast* dyes⟩ — often used in combination ⟨sun*fast*⟩ ⟨acid-*fast* bacteria⟩ ☆
²fast *adverb* (before 12th century)
1 : in a firm or fixed manner ⟨stuck *fast*⟩
2 : in a sound manner : DEEPLY ⟨*fast* asleep⟩
3 a : in a rapid manner : QUICKLY **b :** in quick succession ⟨kaleidoscopic impressions that come so thick and *fast* —M. B. Tucker⟩
4 : in a reckless or dissipated manner
5 : ahead of a correct time or schedule
6 *archaic* **:** CLOSE, NEAR
³fast *intransitive verb* [Middle English, from Old English *fæstan*] (before 12th century)
1 : to abstain from food
2 : to eat sparingly or abstain from some foods
⁴fast *noun* (before 12th century)
1 : the practice of fasting
2 : a time of fasting
⁵fast *noun* [alteration of Middle English *fest,* from Old Norse *festr* rope, mooring cable, from *fastr* firm] (15th century)
: something that fastens (as a mooring line) or holds a fastening
fast and loose *adverb* (1557)
1 : in a reckless or irresponsible manner ⟨played *fast and loose* with the public purse strings —Paul Stuewe⟩
2 : in a craftily deceitful way ⟨manipulated evidence . . . and played *fast and loose* with the truth —C. V. Woodward⟩
fast·back \'fas(t)-,bak\ *noun* (1954)
: an automobile with a roof having a long curving downward slope to the rear; *also* **:** the back of such an automobile
fast·ball \'fas(t)-,bȯl\ *noun* (1912)

: a baseball pitch thrown at full speed and often rising slightly as it nears the plate
— **fast–ball·er** \-,bȯ-lər\ *noun*
fast break *noun* (circa 1949)
: a quick offensive drive toward a goal (as in basketball) in an attempt to score before the opponent's defense is set up
— **fast–break** *intransitive verb*
fas·ten \'fa-sᵊn\ *verb* **fas·tened; fas·ten·ing** \'fas-nin, 'fa-sᵊn-\ [Middle English *fastnen,* from Old English *fæstnian* to make fast; akin to Old High German *festinōn* to make fast, Old English *fæst* fast] (before 12th century)
transitive verb
1 a : to attach especially by pinning, tying, or nailing **b :** to make fast and secure **c :** to fix firmly or securely **d :** to secure against opening
2 : to fix or set steadily ⟨*fastened* her attention on the main problem⟩
3 : to take a firm grip with ⟨the dog *fastened* its teeth in the shoe⟩
4 a : to attach (oneself) persistently and usually objectionably **b :** IMPOSE ⟨*fastened* the blame on the wrong person⟩
intransitive verb
1 : to become fast or fixed
2 a : to take a firm grip or hold **b :** to focus attention ☆
— **fas·ten·er** \'fas-nər, 'fa-sᵊn-ər\ *noun*
fas·ten·ing *noun* (12th century)
: something that fastens : FASTENER
fast–food \'fas(t)-,füd\ *adjective* (1951)
1 : of, relating to, or specializing in food that can be prepared and served quickly ⟨a *fast-food* restaurant⟩
2 : designed for ready availability, use, or consumption and with little consideration given to quality or significance ⟨*fast-food* TV programming⟩
— **fast food** *noun*
¹fast–for·ward \,fas(t)-'fȯr-wərd\ *noun, often attributive* (1948)
1 : a function of a tape player by which the tape is advanced at a higher speed than when it is playing normally
2 : a state or an instance of rapid advancement ⟨put her career in *fast-forward*⟩
²fast–forward (1974)
transitive verb
1 : to advance (a magnetic tape) using the fast-forward of a tape player
2 : to bypass (as a commercial) by fast-forwarding
intransitive verb
1 : to advance a magnetic tape using the fast-forward
2 : to proceed rapidly forward especially in time ⟨*fast-forward* to the future⟩
fas·tid·i·ous \fa-'sti-dē-əs, fə-\ *adjective* [Middle English, from Latin *fastidiosus,* from *fastidium* disgust, probably from *fastus* arrogance (probably akin to Latin *fastigium* top) + *taedium* irksomeness — more at TEDIUM] (15th century)
1 *archaic* **:** SCORNFUL
2 a : having high and often capricious standards **:** difficult to please ⟨critics . . . so *fastidious* that they can talk only to a small circle of initiates —Granville Hicks⟩ **b :** showing or demanding excessive delicacy or care **c :** reflecting a meticulous, sensitive, or demanding attitude ⟨*fastidious* workmanship⟩
3 : having complex nutritional requirements ⟨*fastidious* microorganisms⟩
— **fas·tid·i·ous·ly** *adverb*
— **fas·tid·i·ous·ness** *noun*
fas·ti·gi·ate \fa-'sti-jē-ət\ *adjective* [probably from (assumed) New Latin *fastigiatus,* from Latin *fastigium* — more at BRISTLE] (1662)
: narrowing toward the top; *especially* **:** having upright usually clustered branches ⟨*fastigiate* trees⟩
fast lane *noun* (1966)

1 : a traffic lane intended for vehicles traveling at higher speeds
2 : a way of life marked by a fast pace and usually the pursuit of immediate gratification
3 : FAST TRACK
— **fast–lane** *adjective*
fast·ness \'fas(t)-nəs\ *noun* (before 12th century)
1 : the quality or state of being fast: as **a :** the quality or state of being fixed **b :** the quality or state of being swift **c :** colorfast quality **:** resistance (as of an organism) to the action of a usually toxic substance
2 a : a fortified or secure place **b :** a remote and secluded place ⟨vacationed in their mountain *fastness*⟩
Fast of Esther (1887)
: a Jewish fast day observed the day before Purim in commemoration of a fast proclaimed by Queen Esther
fast–talk \'fas(t)-,tȯk\ *transitive verb* (1946)
: to influence or persuade by fluent, facile, and usually deceptive or tricky talk ⟨*fast-talked* him into buying a lemon⟩
¹fast–track \'fas(t)-,trak\ *adjective* (1967)
1 : of, relating to, or moving along a fast track ⟨*fast-track* executives⟩
2 : of, relating to, or being a construction procedure in which work on a building begins before designs are completed
²fast–track *transitive verb* (1971)
: to speed up the processing, production, or construction of in order to meet a goal
— **fast–track·er** *noun*
fast track *noun* (1980)
: a course leading to rapid advancement or success
fast–twitch \'fas(t)-,twich\ *adjective* (1970)
: of, relating to, or being muscle fiber that contracts quickly especially during brief high-intensity physical activity requiring strength — compare SLOW-TWITCH
fas·tu·ous \'fas-chə-wəs\ *adjective* [Latin *fastuosus,* from *fastus* arrogance] (1638)
1 : HAUGHTY, ARROGANT ⟨a *fastuous* air of finality —Carl Van Vechten⟩

☆ **SYNONYMS**
Fast, rapid, swift, fleet, quick, speedy, hasty, expeditious mean moving, proceeding, or acting with celerity. FAST and RAPID are very close in meaning, but FAST applies particularly to the thing that moves ⟨*fast* horses⟩ and RAPID to the movement itself ⟨*rapid* current⟩. SWIFT suggests great rapidity coupled with ease of movement ⟨returned the ball with one *swift* stroke⟩. FLEET adds the implication of lightness and nimbleness ⟨*fleet* runners⟩. QUICK suggests promptness and the taking of little time ⟨a *quick* wit⟩. SPEEDY implies quickness of successful accomplishment ⟨*speedy* delivery of mail⟩ and may also suggest unusual velocity. HASTY suggests hurry and precipitousness and often connotes carelessness ⟨a *hasty* inspection⟩. EXPEDITIOUS suggests efficiency together with rapidity of accomplishment ⟨the *expeditious* handling of an order⟩.

Fasten, fix, attach, affix mean to make something stay firmly in place. FASTEN implies an action such as tying, buttoning, nailing, locking, or otherwise securing ⟨*fasten* the reins to a post⟩. FIX usually implies a driving in, implanting, or embedding ⟨*fixed* the stake in the ground⟩. ATTACH suggests a connecting or uniting by a bond, link, or tie in order to keep things together ⟨*attach* the W-2 form here⟩. AFFIX implies an imposing of one thing on another by gluing, impressing, or nailing ⟨*affix* your address label here⟩.

2 : OSTENTATIOUS, SHOWY ⟨disdained *fastuous* ceremonies⟩

¹fat \'fat\ *adjective* **fat·ter; fat·test** [Middle English, from Old English *fǣtt*, past participle of *fǣtan* to cram; akin to Old High German *feizit* fat] (before 12th century)
1 : notable for having an unusual amount of fat: **a :** PLUMP **b :** OBESE **c** *of a meat animal* **:** fattened for market **d** *of food* **:** OILY, GREASY
2 a : well filled out **:** THICK, BIG ⟨a *fat* book⟩ **b :** full in tone and quality **:** RICH ⟨a gorgeous *fat* bass voice —*Irish Digest*⟩ **c :** well stocked ⟨a *fat* larder⟩ **d :** PROSPEROUS, WEALTHY ⟨grew *fat* on the war —*Time*⟩ **e :** being substantial and impressive ⟨a *fat* bank account⟩
3 a : richly rewarding or profitable ⟨a *fat* part in a movie⟩ ⟨a *fat* contract⟩ **b :** practically non-existent ⟨a *fat* chance⟩
4 : PRODUCTIVE, FERTILE ⟨a *fat* year for crops⟩
5 : STUPID, FOOLISH
6 : being swollen ⟨got a *fat* lip from the fight⟩
7 *of a baseball pitch* **:** easy to hit
— **fat·ness** *noun*

²fat *transitive verb* **fat·ted; fat·ting** (before 12th century)
: to make fat **:** FATTEN

³fat *noun* (14th century)
1 : animal tissue consisting chiefly of cells distended with greasy or oily matter
2 a : oily or greasy matter making up the bulk of adipose tissue and often abundant in seeds **b :** any of numerous compounds of carbon, hydrogen, and oxygen that are glycerides of fatty acids, are the chief constituents of plant and animal fat, are a major class of energy-rich food, and are soluble in organic solvents but not in water **c :** a solid or semisolid fat as distinguished from an oil
3 : the best or richest part
4 : OBESITY
5 : something in excess **:** SUPERFLUITY ⟨trim the *fat* from the news operation —Ray Olson⟩
— **fat·less** \-ləs\ *adjective*

fa·tal \'fā-t°l\ *adjective* [Middle English, from Middle French & Latin; Middle French, from Latin *fatalis*, from *fatum*] (14th century)
1 *obsolete* **:** FATED
2 : FATEFUL ⟨a *fatal* hour⟩
3 a : of or relating to fate **b :** resembling fate in proceeding according to a fixed sequence **c :** determining one's fate
4 a : causing death **b :** bringing ruin ☐
synonym see DEADLY

fa·tal·ism \-,i-zəm\ *noun* (1678)
: a doctrine that events are fixed in advance so that human beings are powerless to change them; *also* **:** a belief in or attitude determined by this doctrine
— **fa·tal·ist** \-ist\ *noun*
— **fa·tal·is·tic** \,fā-t°l-'is-tik\ *adjective*
— **fa·tal·is·ti·cal·ly** \-ti-k(ə-)lē\ *adverb*

fa·tal·i·ty \fā-'ta-lə-tē, fə-\ *noun, plural* **-ties** [Middle English, from Middle French *fatalité*, from Late Latin *fatalitat-, fatalitas*, from Latin *fatalis*] (15th century)
1 a : the quality or state of causing death or destruction **b :** the quality or condition of being destined for disaster
2 : something established by fate
3 a : FATE 1 **b :** FATALISM
4 : the agent or agency of fate
5 a : death resulting from a disaster **b :** one that experiences a fatal outcome

fa·tal·ly \'fā-t°l-ē\ *adverb* (15th century)
1 : in a way determined by fate
2 : in a manner suggesting fate or an act of fate: as **a :** in a manner resulting in death **:** MORTALLY ⟨*fatally* wounded⟩ **b :** beyond repair **:** IRREVOCABLY **c :** in a manner resulting in ruin or evil ⟨it is *fatally* easy to pass off our prejudices as our opinions —W. F. Hambly⟩ **d :** in a manner that cannot be easily resisted ⟨thinks she is *fatally* attractive —J. W. Krutch⟩

fa·ta mor·ga·na \,fä-tə-mór-'gä-nə, -'ga-\ *noun* [Italian, literally, Morgan le Fay (sorceress of Arthurian legend)] (1818)

: MIRAGE

fat-back \'fat-,bak\ *noun* (1903)
: the strip of fat from the back of a hog carcass usually cured by drying and salting

fat body *noun* (1869)
: a fatty tissue especially of nearly mature insect larvae that serves as a food reserve

fat cat *noun* (1928)
1 a : a wealthy contributor to a political campaign fund **b :** a wealthy and privileged person **c :** BIG SHOT
2 : a lethargic complacent person
— **fat–cat** \'fat-,kat\ *adjective*

fat cell *noun* (1845)
: one of the fat-laden cells making up adipose tissue

fat depot *noun* (1946)
: ADIPOSE TISSUE

¹fate \'fāt\ *noun* [Middle English, from Middle French or Latin; Middle French, from Latin *fatum*, literally, what has been spoken, from neuter of *fatus*, past participle of *fari* to speak — more at BAN] (14th century)
1 : the principle or determining cause or will by which things in general are believed to come to be as they are or events to happen as they do **:** DESTINY
2 a : an inevitable and often adverse outcome, condition, or end **b :** DISASTER; *especially* **:** DEATH
3 a : final outcome **b :** the expected result of normal development ⟨prospective *fate* of embryonic cells⟩
4 *plural, capitalized* **:** the three goddesses who determine the course of human life in classical mythology ☆

²fate *transitive verb* **fat·ed; fat·ing** (1601)
: DESTINE; *also* **:** DOOM

fat·ed *adjective* (circa 1606)
: decreed, controlled, or marked by fate

fate·ful \'fāt-fəl\ *adjective* (circa 1720)
1 : having a quality of ominous prophecy ⟨a *fateful* remark⟩
2 a : involving momentous consequences **:** DECISIVE ⟨made his *fateful* decision to declare war —W. L. Shirer⟩ **b :** DEADLY, CATASTROPHIC
3 : controlled by fate **:** FOREORDAINED
synonym see OMINOUS
usage see FATAL
— **fate·ful·ly** \-fə-lē\ *adverb*
— **fate·ful·ness** *noun*

fat farm *noun* (1969)
: a health spa that specializes in weight reduction

fat-head \'fat-,hed\ *noun* (1842)
: a stupid person
— **fat·head·ed** \-'he-dəd\ *adjective*
— **fat·head·ed·ly** *adverb*
— **fat·head·ed·ness** *noun*

¹fa·ther \'fä-thər, 'fä-\ *noun* [Middle English *fader*, from Old English *fæder*; akin to Old High German *fater* father, Latin *pater*, Greek *patēr*] (before 12th century)
1 a : a man who has begotten a child; *also* **:** SIRE **3 b** *capitalized* (1) **:** GOD 1 (2) **:** the first person of the Trinity
2 : FOREFATHER
3 a : one related to another in a way suggesting that of father to child **b :** an old man — used as a respectful form of address
4 *often capitalized* **:** a pre-Scholastic Christian writer accepted by the church as an authoritative witness to its teaching and practice — called also *church father*
5 a : one that originates or institutes ⟨the *father* of modern science⟩ **b :** SOURCE ⟨the sun, the *father* of warmth and light —Lena M. Whitney⟩ **c :** PROTOTYPE
6 : a priest of the regular clergy; *broadly* **:** PRIEST — used especially as a title
7 : one of the leading men (as of a city) — usually used in plural
— **fa·ther·hood** \-,hùd\ *noun*
— **fa·ther·less** \-ləs\ *adjective*
— **fa·ther·like** \-,līk\ *adjective or adverb*

²father *verb* **fa·thered; fa·ther·ing** \'fäth-riŋ, 'fåth-; 'fä-thə-, 'fä-\ (15th century)
transitive verb
1 a : BEGET **b :** to make oneself the founder, producer, or author of ⟨*fathered* the improvement plan⟩ **c :** to accept responsibility for
2 a : to fix the paternity or origin of **b :** to place responsibility for the origin or cause of ⟨collected gossip and *fathered* it on responsible men —J. A. Williamson⟩
3 : FOIST, IMPOSE
intransitive verb
: to care for or look after someone as a father might

Father Christmas *noun*
British **:** SANTA CLAUS

father figure *noun* (1934)
: one often of particular power or influence who serves as an emotional substitute for a father

father image *noun* (1937)
: an idealization of one's father often projected onto someone to whom one looks for guidance and protection

father–in–law \'fä-thə-rən-,lò, -,thərn-,lò, 'fä-\ *noun, plural* **fa·thers–in–law** \-thər-zən-\ (14th century)

☆ **SYNONYMS**

Fate, destiny, lot, portion, doom mean a predetermined state or end. FATE implies an inevitable and usually an adverse outcome ⟨the *fate* of the submarine is unknown⟩. DESTINY implies something foreordained and often suggests a great or noble course or end ⟨the country's *destiny* to be a model of liberty to the world⟩. LOT and PORTION imply a distribution by fate or destiny, LOT suggesting blind chance ⟨it was her *lot* to die childless⟩, PORTION implying the apportioning of good and evil ⟨remorse was his daily *portion*⟩. DOOM distinctly implies a grim or calamitous fate ⟨if the rebellion fails, his *doom* is certain⟩.

☐ **USAGE**

fatal *Fatal* and *fateful* have long shared a meaning ⟨a *fatal* or *fateful* day⟩ and in the second half of the 20th century a curious opinion has grown up that *fatal* ought to be restricted to its fourth sense and its second sense abandoned to *fateful*. The purpose of this newly imposed distinction is presumably to tidy up the language and to reduce confusion. But these uses seem plain enough at ⟨Pearl Harbor on the *fatal* day —David McCullough⟩ ⟨weeping when she thinks of the *fatal* moment when they first met —Samuel Eliot Morison⟩. Here, as in most similar uses of *fatal*, the direction of the portent is toward evil or the undesirable. *Fateful* may be used in a less ominous way ⟨the day when the *fateful* letter from the college admission office is due —James B. Conant⟩. Sometimes *fatal* is similarly used ⟨when the *fatal* call comes over the public address system—"Jones, city desk"—Jones can feel his colleagues thinking as he walks past them, "I hope he gets a lousy assignment . . . " —Robert Darnton⟩. *Fatal* doesn't share its sense "causing death or destruction" ⟨a *fatal* shooting⟩. This sense is also used frequently with weakened force ⟨tediousness is the most *fatal* of all faults —Samuel Johnson⟩ ⟨to assume that the listeners know all about it already . . . is a *fatal* mistake —George Bernard Shaw⟩.

\ə\ abut \ə\ kitten \ər\ further \a\ ash \ā\ ace
\ä\ mop, mar \aù\ out \ch\ chin \e\ bet \ē\ easy
\g\ go \i\ hit \ī\ ice \j\ job \ŋ\ sing \ō\ go
\ò\ law \òi\ boy \th\ thin \th\ the \ü\ loot \ù\ foot
\y\ yet \zh\ vision *see also* Guide to Pronunciation

1 : the father of one's spouse
2 *archaic* **:** STEPFATHER

fa·ther·land \'fä-thər-,land, 'fä-\ *noun* (12th century)
1 : the native land or country of one's father or ancestors
2 : one's native land or country

fa·ther·ly \'fä-thər-lē, 'fä-\ *adjective* (15th century)
1 : of, relating to, or befitting a father ⟨*fatherly* responsibilities⟩
2 : resembling a father (as in affection or care) ⟨a *fatherly* old man⟩
— **fa·ther·li·ness** \-lē-nəs\ *noun*
— **fatherly** *adverb*

Father's Day *noun* (1927)
: the third Sunday in June appointed for the honoring of fathers

¹**fath·om** \'fa-thəm\ *noun* [Middle English *fadme*, from Old English *fæthm*, length of the outstretched arms; akin to Old Norse *fathmr* fathom, Latin *patēre* to be open, *pandere* to spread out, Greek *petannynai*] (before 12th century)
1 : a unit of length equal to six feet (1.83 meters) used especially for measuring the depth of water
2 : COMPREHENSION

²**fathom** (1607)
intransitive verb
1 : PROBE
2 : to take soundings
transitive verb
1 : to measure by a sounding line
2 : to penetrate and come to understand ⟨couldn't *fathom* the problem⟩
— **fath·om·able** \'fa-thə-mə-bəl\ *adjective*

Fa·thom·e·ter \fa-'thä-mə-tər, 'fa-thə-,mē-\ *trademark*
— used for a sonic depth finder

fath·om·less \'fa-thəm-ləs\ *adjective* (1638)
: incapable of being fathomed
— **fath·om·less·ly** *adverb*
— **fath·om·less·ness** *noun*

fa·tid·ic \fā-'ti-dik, fə-\ or **fa·tid·i·cal** \-di-kəl\ *adjective* [Latin *fatidicus*, from *fatum* fate + *dicere* to say — more at DICTION] (1607)
: of or relating to prophecy

fa·ti·ga·ble \fə-'tē-gə-bəl, 'fa-ti-gə-\ *adjective* (1608)
: susceptible to fatigue
— **fa·ti·ga·bil·i·ty** \fə-,tē-gə-'bi-lə-tē, ,fa-ti-gə-\ *noun*

¹**fa·tigue** \fə-'tēg\ *noun* [French, from Middle French, from *fatiguer* to fatigue, from Latin *fatigare*; akin to Latin af*fatim* sufficiently] (1669)
1 a : LABOR **b :** manual or menial work performed by military personnel **c** *plural* **:** the uniform or work clothing worn on fatigue and in the field
2 a : weariness or exhaustion from labor, exertion, or stress **b :** the temporary loss of power to respond induced in a sensory receptor or motor end organ by continued stimulation
3 : the tendency of a material to break under repeated stress

²**fatigue** *verb* **fa·tigued; fa·tigu·ing** (1693)
transitive verb
1 : to weary with labor or exertion
2 : to induce a condition of fatigue in
intransitive verb
: to suffer fatigue
synonym see TIRE
— **fa·tigu·ing·ly** \-'tē-giŋ-lē\ *adverb*

³**fatigue** *adjective* (1774)
1 : consisting of, done, or used in fatigue ⟨*fatigue* detail⟩
2 : belonging to fatigues ⟨a *fatigue* cap⟩

fat·ling \'fat-liŋ\ *noun* (circa 1534)
: a young animal fattened for slaughter

fat·ly \'fat-lē\ *adverb* (15th century)
1 : RICHLY
2 : in the manner of one that is fat ⟨waddled *fatly*⟩

3 : in a smug manner **:** COMPLACENTLY ⟨snickered *fatly*⟩

fats·hed·era \,fats-'he-d(ə-)rə, ,fat-'se-\ *noun* [New Latin *Fatsia*, genus of shrubs + *Hedera*, genus of vines (from Latin, ivy)] (1948)
: a vigorous upright hybrid ornamental foliage plant (*Hedera helix* × *Aralia elata*) with glossy deeply lobed palmate leaves

fat·so \'fat-(,)sō\ *noun, plural* **fat·soes** [probably from *Fats*, nickname for a fat person + -*o*] (1944)
: a fat person — often used disparagingly

fat·stock \-,stäk\ *noun* (1880)
chiefly British **:** livestock that is fat and ready for market

fat–tailed sheep \'fat-,tāld-\ *noun* (1842)
: a coarse-wooled mutton sheep that has great quantities of fat on each side of the tail bones

fat·ten \'fa-t°n\ *verb* **fat·tened; fat·ten·ing** \'fat-niŋ, 'fa-t°n-iŋ\ (1552)
transitive verb
1 a : to make fat, fleshy, or plump; *especially* **:** to feed (as a stock animal) for slaughter **b :** to make more substantial
2 : to make fertile
intransitive verb
: to become fat
— **fat·ten·er** \'fat-nər, 'fa-t°n-ər\ *noun*

fat·tish \'fa-tish\ *adjective* (14th century)
: somewhat fat

¹**fat·ty** \'fa-tē\ *adjective* **fat·ti·er; -est** (14th century)
1 : containing fat especially in unusual amounts; *also* **:** unduly stout **:** CORPULENT
2 : GREASY
3 : derived from or chemically related to fat
— **fat·ti·ness** *noun*

²**fatty** *noun, plural* **fat·ties** (1797)
: one that is fat; *especially* **:** an overweight person

fatty acid *noun* (circa 1872)
1 : any of numerous saturated aliphatic monocarboxylic acids $C_nH_{2n+1}COOH$ (as acetic acid) including many that occur naturally usually in the form of esters in fats, waxes, and essential oils
2 : any of the saturated or unsaturated monocarboxylic acids (as palmitic acid) usually with an even number of carbon atoms that occur naturally in the form of glycerides in fats and fatty oils

fa·tu·ity \fə-'tü-ət-ē, fa-, -'chü-, -'tyü-\ *noun, plural* **-ities** [Middle French *fatuité* foolishness, from Latin *fatuitat-, fatuitas*, from *fatuus*] (1538)
1 a : something foolish or stupid **b :** STUPIDITY, FOOLISHNESS
2 *archaic* **:** IMBECILITY, DEMENTIA

fat·u·ous \'fa-chü-əs, -tyü-\ *adjective* [Latin *fatuus* foolish] (1633)
: complacently or inanely foolish **:** SILLY
synonym see SIMPLE
— **fat·u·ous·ly** *adverb*
— **fat·u·ous·ness** *noun*

fat·wa \'fət-wə\ *noun* [Arabic *fatwā*] (1947)
: a legal opinion or decree handed down by an Islamic religious leader

fat–wit·ted \'fat-,wi-təd\ *adjective* (1596)
: STUPID, IDIOTIC

fat·wood \'fat-,wúd\ *noun* (1904)
chiefly Southern **:** LIGHTWOOD

fau·bourg \fō-'bùr\ *noun* [Middle English *fabour*, from Middle French *fauxbourg*, alteration of *forsbourg*, from Old French *forsborc*, from *fors* outside + *borc* town — more at BOURG] (15th century)
1 : SUBURB; *especially* **:** a suburb of a French city
2 : a city quarter

fau·ces \'fò-,sēz\ *noun plural but singular or plural in construction* [Latin, plural, throat, fauces] (1541)
: the narrow passage from the mouth to the pharynx situated between the soft palate and the base of the tongue
— **fau·cial** \'fò-shəl\ *adjective*

fau·cet \'fò-sət, 'fäs-\ *noun* [Middle English, bung, faucet, from Middle French *fausset* bung, perhaps from *fausser* to damage, from Late Latin *falsare* to falsify, from Latin *falsus* false] (15th century)
: a fixture for drawing or regulating the flow of liquid especially from a pipe

faugh \a strong p-sound or lip trill; often read as th(k)\ *interjection* (1542)
— used to express contempt, disgust, or abhorrence

¹**fault** \'fòlt, *in poetry also* 'fòt\ *noun* [Middle English *faute*, from Middle French, from (assumed) Vulgar Latin *fallita*, from feminine of *fallitus*, past participle of Latin *fallere* to deceive, disappoint] (14th century)
1 *obsolete* **:** LACK
2 a : WEAKNESS, FAILING; *especially* **:** a moral weakness less serious than a vice **b :** a physical or intellectual imperfection or impairment **:** DEFECT **c :** an error especially in service in a net or racket game

fault 5: *1* fault with displaced strata
a, b, c, d, e; 2 scarp

3 a : MISDEMEANOR **b :** MISTAKE
4 : responsibility for wrongdoing or failure ⟨the accident was the driver's *fault*⟩
5 : a fracture in the crust of a planet (as the earth) or moon accompanied by a displacement of one side of the fracture with respect to the other usually in a direction parallel to the fracture ☆
— **at fault 1 :** unable to find the scent and continue chase **2 :** open to blame **:** RESPONSIBLE ⟨couldn't determine who was really *at fault*⟩
— **to a fault :** to an excessive degree ⟨precise *to a fault*⟩

²**fault** (15th century)
intransitive verb
1 : to commit a fault **:** ERR
2 : to fracture so as to produce a geologic fault
transitive verb
1 : to find a fault in ⟨easy to praise this book and to *fault* it —H. G. Roepke⟩
2 : to produce a geologic fault in
3 : BLAME, CENSURE ⟨can't *fault* them for not coming⟩

fault·find·er \'fòlt-,fīn-dər\ *noun* (1561)
: one given to faultfinding

¹**fault·find·ing** \-diŋ\ *adjective* (1622)
: disposed to find fault **:** captiously critical
synonym see CRITICAL

²**faultfinding** *noun* (1626)
: petty, nagging, or unreasonable criticism

fault·less \'fòlt-ləs\ *adjective* (14th century)
: having no fault **:** IRREPROACHABLE ⟨*faultless* workmanship⟩
— **fault·less·ly** *adverb*
— **fault·less·ness** *noun*

fault line *noun* (1869)
: something resembling a fault : SPLIT, RIFT ⟨a major conceptual *fault line* in foreign policy —Morton Kondracke⟩

faulty \'fȯl-tē\ *adjective* **fault·i·er; -est** (14th century)
: marked by fault or defect : IMPERFECT
— **fault·i·ly** \-tə-lē\ *adverb*
— **fault·i·ness** \-tē-nəs\ *noun*

faun \'fȯn, 'fän\ *noun* [Middle English, from Latin *faunus*, from *Faunus*] (14th century)
: a figure in Roman mythology similar to but gentler than the satyr

fau·na \'fȯ-nə, 'fä-\ *noun, plural* **faunas** *also* **fau·nae** \-,nē, -,nī\ [New Latin, from Latin *Fauna*, sister of Faunus] (1771)
: animal life; *especially* : the animals characteristic of a region, period, or special environment — compare FLORA
— **fau·nal** \-n°l\ *adjective*
— **fau·nal·ly** \-n°l-ē\ *adverb*

fau·nis·tic \fȯ-'nis-tik, fä-\ *adjective* (1881)
: of or relating to zoogeography : FAUNAL
— **fau·nis·ti·cal·ly** \-ti-k(ə-)lē\ *adverb*

Fau·nus \'fȯ-nəs, 'fä-\ *noun* [Latin]
: the Roman god of animals

Faust \'faůst\ *or* **Fau·stus** \'faů-stəs, 'fȯ-\ *noun* [German]
: a magician of German legend who enters into a compact with the devil

Faust·ian \'faů-stē-ən, 'fȯ-\ *adjective* (1876)
: of, relating to, resembling, or suggesting Faust; *especially* : made or done for present gain without regard for future cost or consequences ⟨a *Faustian* bargain⟩

faute de mieux \,fōt-də-'myə(r), -'myœ̄\ *adverb* [French] (1766)
: for lack of something better or more desirable ⟨sherry made him dopey but he drank it *faute de mieux* —F. T. Marsh⟩

fau·teuil \fō-'tœy; 'fō-,til\ *noun, plural* **fauteuils** \fō-'tœy; -,tilz\ [French, from Old French *faudestuel*, of Germanic origin; akin to Old High German *faltistuol* folding chair — more at FALDSTOOL] (1744)
: ARMCHAIR; *especially* : an upholstered chair with open arms

¹**fauve** \'fōv\ *noun, often capitalized* [French, literally, wild animal, from *fauve* tawny, wild, from Old French *falve* tawny, of Germanic origin; akin to Old High German *falo* fallow — more at FALLOW] (1931)
: a painter practicing fauvism : FAUVIST

²**fauve** *adjective* (1945)
1 *often capitalized* : of or relating to the fauves
2 : vivid in color

fau·vism \'fō-,vi-zəm\ *noun, often capitalized* (1922)
: a movement in painting typified by the work of Matisse and characterized by vivid colors, free treatment of form, and a resulting vibrant and decorative effect
— **fau·vist** \-vist\ *noun, often capitalized*

faux \'fō\ *adjective* [French, false] (1975)
: IMITATION, ERSATZ ⟨*faux* marble⟩

faux pas \'fō-,pä, fō-'\ *noun, plural* **faux pas** \-,pä(z), -'pä(z)\ [French, literally, false step] (1676)
: BLUNDER; *especially* : a social blunder

fa·va \'fä-və\ *noun* [Italian, from Latin *faba* bean] (1928)
: BROAD BEAN — called also **fava bean**

fave \'fāv\ *noun* (1938)
: FAVORITE 1
— **fave** *adjective*

fa·ve·la *also* **fa·vel·la** \fə-'ve-lə\ *noun* [Brazilian Portuguese *favela*, perhaps from *Favela*, hill outside Rio de Janeiro] (1946)
: a settlement of jerry-built shacks lying on the outskirts of a Brazilian city

fa·vism \'fä-,vi-zəm\ *noun* (circa 1927)
: a hereditary condition especially of males of Mediterranean descent that involves a severe allergic reaction to the broad bean or its pollen

which is characterized by hemolytic anemia, fever, and jaundice

fa·vo·ni·an \fə-'vō-nē-ən\ *adjective* [Latin *favonianus*, from *Favonius*, the west wind] (circa 1681)
: of or relating to the west wind : MILD

¹**fa·vor** \'fā-vər\ *noun* [Middle English, friendly regard, attractiveness, from Old French *favor* friendly regard, from Latin, from *favēre* to be favorable; perhaps akin to Old High German *gouma* attention, Old Church Slavonic *govĕti* to revere] (14th century)
1 a (1) : friendly regard shown toward another especially by a superior : APPROVING consideration or attention : APPROBATION **b** : PARTIALITY **c** *archaic* : LENIENCY **d** *archaic* : PERMISSION **e** : POPULARITY
2 *archaic* **a** : APPEARANCE **b** (1) : FACE (2) : a facial feature
3 a : gracious kindness; *also* : an act of such kindness **b** *archaic* : AID, ASSISTANCE **c** *plural* : effort in one's behalf or interest : ATTENTION
4 a : a token of love (as a ribbon) usually worn conspicuously **b** : a small gift or decorative item given out at a party **c** : BADGE
5 a : a special privilege or right granted or conceded **b** : sexual privileges — usually used in plural
6 *archaic* : LETTER
7 : BEHALF, INTEREST
— **in favor of 1 a** : in accord or sympathy with **b** : for the acquittal of ⟨a verdict *in favor of* the accused⟩ **c** : in support of **2** : to the order of **3** : in order to choose : out of preference for ⟨turned down the scholarship *in favor of* a pro career⟩
— **in one's favor 1** : in one's good graces **2** : to one's advantage ⟨the odds were *in my favor*⟩
— **out of favor** : UNPOPULAR, DISLIKED ⟨was *out of favor* with his neighbors⟩

²**favor** *transitive verb* **fa·vored; fa·vor·ing** \'fā-v(ə-)riŋ\ (14th century)
1 a : to regard or treat with favor **b** (1) : to do a kindness for : OBLIGE (2) : ENDOW **c** : to treat gently or carefully ⟨*favored* his injured leg⟩
2 : to show partiality toward : PREFER
3 a : to give support or confirmation to : SUSTAIN **b** : to afford advantages for success to : FACILITATE ⟨good weather *favored* the outing⟩
4 : to bear a resemblance to ⟨he *favors* his father⟩
— **fa·vor·er** \'fā-vər-ər\ *noun*

fa·vor·able \'fā-v(ə-)rə-bəl, 'fā-vər-bəl\ *adjective* (14th century)
1 a : disposed to favor : PARTIAL **b** : expressing approval : COMMENDATORY **c** : giving a result that is in one's favor ⟨a *favorable* comparison⟩ **d** : AFFIRMATIVE
2 : winning approval : PLEASING
3 a : tending to promote or facilitate : ADVANTAGEOUS ⟨*favorable* wind⟩ **b** : marked by success ☆
— **fa·vor·able·ness** *noun*
— **fa·vor·ably** \-blē\ *adverb*

fa·vored \'fā-vərd\ *adjective* (15th century)
1 : having an appearance or features of a particular kind ⟨hard-*favored*⟩
2 : endowed with special advantages or gifts
3 : providing preferential treatment

¹**fa·vor·ite** \'fā-v(ə-)rət, 'fā-vərt, *chiefly dialect* 'fā-və-,rīt\ *noun* [Italian *favorito*, past participle of *favorire* to favor, from *favore* favor, from Latin *favor*] (1583)
1 : one that is treated or regarded with special favor or liking; *especially* : one unusually loved, trusted, or provided with favors by a person of high rank or authority
2 : a competitor judged most likely to win

²**favorite** *adjective* (1711)
: constituting a favorite; *especially* : markedly popular

favorite son *noun* (1788)
1 : one favored by the delegates of his state as presidential candidate at a national political convention

2 : a famous person who is popular with hometown people

fa·vor·it·ism \'fā-v(ə-)rə-,ti-zəm, 'fā-vər-\ *noun* (1763)
1 : the showing of special favor : PARTIALITY
2 : the state or fact of being a favorite

fa·vour *chiefly British variant of* FAVOR

fa·vus \'fā-vəs\ *noun* [New Latin, from Latin, honeycomb] (circa 1543)
: a contagious skin disease caused by a fungus (as *Trichophyton schoenleinii*) and occurring in humans and many domestic animals and fowls

¹**fawn** \'fȯn, 'fän\ *intransitive verb* [Middle English *faunen*, from Old English *fagnian* to rejoice, from *fægen, fagan* glad — more at FAIN] (13th century)
1 : to show affection — used especially of a dog
2 : to court favor by a cringing or flattering manner ☆
— **fawn·er** *noun*
— **fawn·ing·ly** \'fȯ-niŋ-lē, 'fä-\ *adverb*

²**fawn** *noun* [Middle English *foun*, from Middle French *feon, faon* young of an animal, from (assumed) Vulgar Latin *feton-, feto*, from Latin *fetus* offspring — more at FETUS] (14th century)
1 : a young deer; *especially* : one still unweaned or retaining a distinctive baby coat
2 : KID 1
3 : a light grayish brown

fawn lily *noun* (circa 1894)
: DOGTOOTH VIOLET

fawny \'fȯ-nē, 'fä-\ *adjective* (1849)
: of a color approximating fawn

fax \'faks\ *noun* [by shortening & alteration] (1948)
1 : FACSIMILE 2
2 : a machine used to send or receive facsimile communications
3 : a facsimile communication
— **fax** *transitive verb*

¹**fay** \'fā\ *verb* [Middle English *feien*, from Old English *fēgan*; akin to Old High German *fuogen* to fit, Latin *pangere* to fasten — more at PACT] (before 12th century)

: to fit or join closely or tightly

²fay *noun* [Middle English *fai, fei,* from Old French *feid, fei* — more at FAITH] (13th century)
obsolete : FAITH

³fay *noun* [Middle English *faie,* from Middle French *feie, fee* — more at FAIRY] (14th century)
: FAIRY, ELF

⁴fay *adjective* (14th century)
: resembling an elf

⁵fay *noun* (1927)
: OFAY

faze \'fāz\ *transitive verb* **fazed; faz·ing** [alteration of *feeze* (to drive away, frighten), from Middle English *fesen,* from Old English *fēsian* to drive away] (1830)
: to disturb the composure of : DISCONCERT, DAUNT ⟨nothing *fazed* her⟩

F clef *noun* (1596)
: BASS CLEF

F distribution *noun* [Sir Ronald *Fisher* (died 1962) English geneticist and statistician] (1947)
: a probability density function that is used especially in analysis of variance and is a function of the ratio of two independent random variables each of which has a chi-square distribution and is divided by its number of degrees of freedom

fe·al·ty \'fē(-ə)l-tē\ *noun, plural* **-ties** [alteration of Middle English *feute,* from Old French *feelté, fealté,* from Latin *fidelitat-, fidelitas* — more at FIDELITY] (14th century)
1 a : the fidelity of a vassal or feudal tenant to his lord **b :** the obligation of such fidelity
2 : intense fidelity
synonym see FIDELITY

¹fear \'fir\ (before 12th century)
transitive verb
1 *archaic* : FRIGHTEN
2 *archaic* : to feel fear in (oneself)
3 : to have a reverential awe of ⟨*fear* God⟩
4 : to be afraid of : expect with alarm
intransitive verb
: to be afraid or apprehensive
— **fear·er** *noun*

²fear *noun* [Middle English *fer,* from Old English *fǣr* sudden danger; akin to Latin *periculum* attempt, peril, Greek *peiran* to attempt] (12th century)
1 a : an unpleasant often strong emotion caused by anticipation or awareness of danger **b** (1) : an instance of this emotion (2) : a state marked by this emotion
2 : anxious concern : SOLICITUDE
3 : profound reverence and awe especially toward God
4 : reason for alarm : DANGER ☆

fear·ful \'fir-fəl\ *adjective* (14th century)
1 : causing or likely to cause fear, fright, or alarm especially because of dangerous quality ⟨a *fearful* storm⟩
2 a : full of fear **b :** indicating or arising from fear ⟨a *fearful* glance⟩ **c :** inclined to fear : TIMOROUS
3 : very great or bad — used as an intensive ⟨a *fearful* waste⟩ ⟨*fearful* slum conditions⟩ ☆
— **fear·ful·ly** \-f(ə-)lē\ *adverb*
— **fear·ful·ness** \-fəl-nəs\ *noun*

fear·less \'fir-ləs\ *adjective* (1591)
: free from fear : BRAVE
— **fear·less·ly** *adverb*
— **fear·less·ness** *noun*

fear·some \'fir-səm\ *adjective* (1768)
1 : causing fear
2 : TIMID, TIMOROUS
— **fear·some·ly** *adverb*
— **fear·some·ness** *noun*

fea·si·ble \'fē-zə-bəl\ *adjective* [Middle English *faisible,* from Middle French, from *fais-,* stem of *faire* to make, do, from Latin *facere* — more at DO] (15th century)
1 : capable of being done or carried out ⟨a *feasible* plan⟩

2 : capable of being used or dealt with successfully : SUITABLE
3 : REASONABLE, LIKELY
synonym see POSSIBLE
— **fea·si·bil·i·ty** \,fē-zə-'bi-lə-tē\ *noun*
— **fea·si·bly** \'fē-zə-blē\ *adverb*

¹feast \'fēst\ *noun* [Middle English *feste* festival, feast, from Middle French, festival, from Latin *festa,* plural of *festum* festival, from neuter of *festus* solemn, festal; akin to Latin *feriae* holidays, *fanum* temple] (13th century)
1 a : an elaborate meal often accompanied by a ceremony or entertainment : BANQUET **b :** something that gives unusual or abundant pleasure
2 : a periodic religious observance commemorating an event or honoring a deity, person, or thing

²feast (14th century)
intransitive verb
1 : to take part in a feast
2 : to enjoy some unusual pleasure or delight
transitive verb
1 : to give a feast for
2 : DELIGHT, GRATIFY
— **feast·er** *noun*

Feast of Tabernacles (14th century)
: SUKKOTH

¹feat \'fēt\ *noun* [Middle English *fait,* from Middle French, from Latin *factum,* from neuter of *factus,* past participle of *facere* to make, do — more at DO] (14th century)
1 : ACT, DEED
2 a : a deed notable especially for courage **b :** an act or product of skill, endurance, or ingenuity ☆

²feat *adjective* [Middle English *fete, fayt,* from Middle French *fait,* past participle of *faire*] (15th century)
1 *archaic* : BECOMING, NEAT
2 *archaic* : SMART, DEXTEROUS

¹feath·er \'fe-thər\ *noun* [Middle English *fether,* from Old English; akin to Old High German *federa* wing, Latin *petere* to go to, seek, Greek *petesthai* to fly, *piptein* to fall, *pteron* wing] (before 12th century)
1 a : any of the light horny epidermal outgrowths that form the external covering of the body of birds and that consist of a shaft bearing on each side a series of barbs which bear barbules which in turn bear barbicels commonly ending in hooked hamuli and interlocking with the barbules of an adjacent barb to link the barbs into a continuous vane **b** : PLUME **c :** the vane of an arrow
2 a : PLUMAGE **b :** KIND, NATURE ⟨birds of a *feather* flock together⟩ **c :** ATTIRE, DRESS **d :** CONDITION, MOOD
3 : FEATHERING 2
4 : a projecting strip, rib, fin, or flange
5 : a feathery flaw in the eye or in a precious stone
6 : the act of feathering an oar
— **feath·ered** \-thərd\ *adjective*
— **feath·er·less** *adjective*
— **a feather in one's cap :** a mark of distinction : HONOR

²feather *verb* **feath·ered; feath·er·ing** \'feth-riŋ, 'fe-tho-\ (13th century)
transitive verb
1 a : to furnish (as an arrow) with a feather **b :** to cover, clothe, or adorn with or as if with feathers

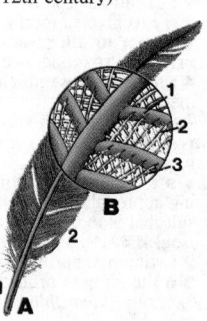

feather 1a: *A: 1* quill, *2* vane; *B: 1* barb, *2* barbule, *3* barbicel with hamulus

2 a : to turn (an oar blade) almost horizontal when lifting from the water at the end of a stroke to reduce air resistance **b** (1) : to change the angle of (airplane propeller blades) so that the chords become approximately parallel to the line of flight; *also* : to change the angle of airplane propeller blades of (an engine) in such a manner (2) : to change the angle of (a rotor blade of a rotorcraft) periodically in forward flight
3 : to reduce the edge of to a featheredge
4 : to cut (as air) with or as if with a wing
5 : to join by a tongue and groove
intransitive verb
1 : to grow or form feathers
2 : to have or take on the appearance of a feather or something feathered
3 : to soak in and spread : BLUR — used of ink or a printed impression
4 : to feather an oar or an airplane propeller blade
— **feather one's nest :** to provide for oneself especially while in a position of trust

¹feath·er·bed \'fe-thər-,bed\ *adjective* (1938)
: calling for, sanctioning, or resulting from featherbedding

²featherbed (1949)
intransitive verb
1 a : to require that more workers be hired than are needed **b :** to limit production under a featherbed rule
2 : to do featherbed work or put in time under a featherbed rule
transitive verb
1 : to bring under a featherbed rule
2 : to assist (as an industry) by government aid

feather bed *noun* (before 12th century)
1 : a feather mattress
2 : a bed having a feather mattress

feath·er·bed·ding *noun* (1921)

: the requiring of an employer usually under a union rule or safety statute to hire more employees than are needed or to limit production

feath·er·brain \-,brān\ *noun* (1839)
: a foolish scatterbrained person
— **feath·er·brained** \-,brānd\ *adjective*

feath·er·edge \'fe-thə-,rej, ,fe-thə-\ *noun* (1616)
: a very thin sharp edge; *especially* : one that is easily broken or bent over
— **featheredge** *transitive verb*

feath·er·head \'fe-thər-,hed\ *noun* (1831)
: FEATHERBRAIN
— **feath·er·head·ed** \,fe-thər-'he-dəd\ *adjective*

feath·er·ing \'feth-riŋ, 'fe-thə-\ *noun* (1721)
1 : a covering of feathers : PLUMAGE
2 : a fringe of hair (as on the legs of a dog)
— see DOG illustration

feath·er·light \'fe-thər-'līt\ *adjective* (circa 1837)
: extremely light

feather star *noun* (1862)
: any of an order (Comatulida) of free-swimming stalkless crinoids

feath·er·stitch \'fe-thər-,stich\ *noun* (1835)
: an embroidery stitch consisting of a line of diagonal blanket stitches worked alternately to the left and right
— **featherstitch** *verb*

feath·er·weight \-,wāt\ *noun, often attributive* (1812)
1 : one that is very light in weight; *especially* : a boxer in a weight division having a maximum limit of 126 pounds for professionals and 125 pounds for amateurs — compare BANTAMWEIGHT, LIGHTWEIGHT
2 : LIGHTWEIGHT 2

featherstitch

feath·ery \'feth-rē, 'fe-thə-\ *adjective* (1580)
: resembling, suggesting, or covered with feathers; *especially* : extremely light

¹feat·ly \'fēt-lē\ *adverb* [Middle English *fetly,* from *fete* feat (adjective)] (14th century)
1 : in a graceful manner : NIMBLY
2 : in a suitable manner : PROPERLY
3 : with skill and ingenuity

²featly *adjective* (1801)
: GRACEFUL, NEAT

¹fea·ture \'fē-chər\ *noun* [Middle English *feture,* from Middle French, from Latin *factura* act of making, from *factus,* past participle of *facere* to make — more at DO] (14th century)
1 a : the structure, form, or appearance especially of a person **b** *obsolete* : physical beauty
2 a : the makeup or appearance of the face or its parts **b** : a part of the face : LINEAMENT
3 a : a prominent part or characteristic **b** : any of the properties (as voice or gender) that are characteristic of a grammatical element (as a phoneme or morpheme); *especially* : one that is distinctive
4 : a special attraction: as **a** : the principal motion picture shown on a program with other pictures **b** : a featured article, story, or department in a newspaper or magazine **c** : something offered to the public or advertised as particularly attractive
— **fea·ture·less** \-ləs\ *adjective*

²feature *verb* **fea·tured; fea·tur·ing** \'fēch-riŋ, 'fē-chə-\ (circa 1755)
transitive verb
1 *chiefly dialect* : to resemble in features
2 : to portray or portray in the mind : IMAGINE
3 a : to give special prominence to **b** : to have as a characteristic or feature
intransitive verb
: to play an important part

fea·tured \'fē-chərd\ *adjective* (15th century)
1 : having facial features of a particular kind — used in combination ⟨a heavy-*featured* lout⟩
2 : displayed, advertised, or presented as a special attraction

fea·tur·ette \'fē-chə-,ret, ,fē-chə-'\ *noun* (1940)
: a short film

feaze \'fēz, 'fāz\ *variant of* FAZE

febri- *combining form* [Late Latin, from Latin *febris*]
: fever ⟨*febrific*⟩

fe·brif·ic \fi-'brif-ik\ *adjective* (1710)
archaic : FEVERISH

feb·ri·fuge \'fe-brə-,fyüj\ *noun* [French *fébrifuge,* probably from (assumed) New Latin *febrifuga,* from Late Latin *febrifuga, febrifugia* centaury, from *febri-* + Late Latin *-fuga* -fuge] (1686)
: ANTIPYRETIC
— **febrifuge** *adjective*

fe·brile \'fe-,brīl also 'fē-\ *adjective* [Medieval Latin *febrilis,* from Latin *febris* fever] (1651)
: FEVERISH

Feb·ru·ary \÷'fe-b(y)ə-,wer-ē, 'fe-brə-\ *noun, plural* **-ar·ies** *or* **-ar·ys** [Middle English *Februarie,* from Old English *Februarius,* from Latin, from *Februa,* plural, feast of purification] (before 12th century)
: the 2d month of the Gregorian calendar ▢

fe·cal \'fē-kəl\ *adjective* (1541)
: of, relating to, or constituting feces

fe·ces \'fē-(,)sēz\ *noun plural* [Middle English, from Latin *faec-, faex* (singular) dregs] (14th century)
: bodily waste discharged through the anus : EXCREMENT

feck·less \'fek-ləs\ *adjective* [Scots, from *feck* effect, majority, from Middle English (Scots) *fek,* alteration of Middle English *effect*] (circa 1585)
1 : WEAK, INEFFECTIVE
2 : WORTHLESS, IRRESPONSIBLE
— **feck·less·ly** *adverb*
— **feck·less·ness** *noun*

feck·ly \'fek-lē\ *adverb* [*feck* + *-ly*] (1768)
chiefly Scottish : ALMOST, NEARLY

fec·u·lent \'fe-kyə-lənt\ *adjective* [Middle English, from Latin *faeculentus,* from *faec-, faex*] (15th century)
: foul with impurities : FECAL
— **fec·u·lence** \-lən(t)s\ *noun*

fe·cund \'fe-kənd, 'fē-\ *adjective* [Middle English, from Middle French *fecond,* from Latin *fecundus* — more at FEMININE] (15th century)
1 : fruitful in offspring or vegetation : PROLIFIC
2 : intellectually productive or inventive to a marked degree
synonym see FERTILE
— **fe·cun·di·ty** \fi-'kən-də-tē, fe-\ *noun*

fe·cun·date \'fe-kən-,dāt, 'fē-\ *transitive verb* **-dat·ed; -dat·ing** [Latin *fecundatus,* past participle of *fecundare,* from *fecundus*] (circa 1631)
1 : to make fecund
2 : IMPREGNATE
— **fe·cun·da·tion** \,fe-kən-'dā-shən, ,fē-\ *noun*

fed \'fed\ *noun, often capitalized* (1916)
: a federal agent, officer, or official — usually used in plural

fe·da·yee \fi-,da-'(y)ē, -,dä-\ *noun, plural* **fe·da·yeen** \-'(y)ēn\ [Arabic *fidā'ī,* literally, one who sacrifices himself] (1955)
: a member of an Arab commando group operating especially against Israel — usually used in plural

fed·er·al \'fe-d(ə-)rəl\ *adjective* [Latin *foeder-, foedus* compact, league; akin to Latin *fidere* to trust — more at BIDE] (1660)
1 *archaic* : of or relating to a compact or treaty
2 a : formed by a compact between political units that surrender their individual sovereignty to a central authority but retain limited residuary powers of government **b** : of or constituting a form of government in which power is distributed between a central authority and a number of constituent territorial units **c** : of or relating to the central government of a federa-

tion as distinguished from the governments of the constituent units
3 *capitalized* : advocating or friendly to the principle of a federal government with strong centralized powers; *especially* : of or relating to the American Federalists
4 *often capitalized* : of, relating to, or loyal to the federal government or the Union armies of the U.S. in the American Civil War
5 *capitalized* : being or belonging to a style of architecture and decoration current in the U.S. following the Revolution
— **fed·er·al·ly** \-d(ə-)rə-lē\ *adverb*

Federal *noun* (1861)
1 : a supporter of the U.S. government in the Civil War; *especially* : a soldier in the federal armies
2 : FED — usually used in plural

federal case *noun* (1955)
: BIG DEAL ⟨don't make a *federal case* out of it⟩

federal court *noun* (1789)
: a court established by a federal government; *especially* : one established under the constitution and laws of the U.S.

federal district *noun* (circa 1934)
: a district set apart as the seat of the central government of a federation

federal district court *noun* (1948)
: a district trial court of law and equity that hears cases under federal jurisdiction

fed·er·al·ese \,fe-d(ə-)rə-'lēz, -'lēs; 'fe-d(ə-)rə-,\ *noun* (1944)
: BUREAUCRATESE

federal funds *noun plural* (1950)
: reserve funds lent overnight by one Federal Reserve bank to another

fed·er·al·ism \'fe-d(ə-)rə-,li-zəm\ *noun* (1789)
1 a *often capitalized* : the distribution of power in an organization (as a government) between a central authority and the constituent units — compare CENTRALISM **b** : support or advocacy of this principle
2 *capitalized* : Federalist principles

fed·er·al·ist \-list\ *noun* (1787)
1 : an advocate of federalism: as **a** *often capitalized* : an advocate of a federal union between the American colonies after the Revolution and of the adoption of the U.S. Constitution **b** *often capitalized* : WORLD FEDERALIST
2 *capitalized* : a member of a major political party in the early years of the U.S. favoring a strong centralized national government
— **federalist** *adjective, often capitalized*

fed·er·al·iza·tion \,fe-d(ə-)rə-lə-'zā-shən\ *noun* (circa 1860)
1 : the act of federalizing
2 : the state of being federalized

fed·er·al·ize \'fe-d(ə-)rə-,līz\ *transitive verb* **-ized; -iz·ing** (1801)
1 : to unite in or under a federal system
2 : to bring under the jurisdiction of a federal government

▢ USAGE
February Dissimilation may occur when a word contains two identical or closely related sounds, resulting in the change or loss of one of them. This happens regularly in *February,* which is more often pronounced \'fe-b(y)ə-,wer-ē\ than \'fe-brə-,wer-ē\, though all of these variants are in frequent use and widely accepted. The \y\ heard from many speakers is not an intrusion but rather a common pronunciation of the vowel *u* after a consonant, as in *January* and *annual.*

Federal Reserve bank *noun* (1914)
: one of 12 reserve banks set up under the Federal Reserve Act to hold reserves and discount commercial paper for affiliated banks in their respective districts

¹**fed·er·ate** \'fe-d(ə-)rət\ *adjective* [Latin *foederatus,* from *foeder-, foedus*] (1710)
: united in an alliance or federation : FEDERATED

²**fed·er·ate** \'fe-də-ˌrāt\ *transitive verb* **-at·ed; -at·ing** (1837)
: to join in a federation

federated church *noun* (circa 1926)
: a local church uniting two or more congregations that maintain different denominational ties — compare UNION CHURCH

fed·er·a·tion \ˌfe-də-'rā-shən\ *noun* (1791)
1 : something formed by federation: as **a** : a federal government **b** : a union of organizations
2 : the act of federating; *especially* : the forming of a federal union

fed·er·a·tive \'fe-də-ˌrā-tiv, 'fe-d(ə-)rə-\ *adjective* (1690)
: FEDERAL
— **fed·er·a·tive·ly** *adverb*

fe·do·ra \fi-'dōr-ə, -'dòr-\ *noun* [*Fédora* (1882), drama by V. Sardou] (1895)
: a low soft felt hat with the crown creased lengthwise ◇

fed up *adjective* (1900)
: tired, sated, or disgusted beyond endurance

¹**fee** \'fē\ *noun* [Middle English, from Middle French *fé, fief,* from Old French, of Germanic origin; akin to Old English *feoh* cattle, property, Old High German *fihu* cattle; akin to Latin *pecus* cattle, *pecunia* money] (14th century)
1 a (1) : an estate in land held in feudal law from a lord on condition of homage and service (2) : a piece of land so held **b** : an inherited or heritable estate in land
2 a : a fixed charge **b** : a sum paid or charged for a service
— **in fee** : in absolute and legal possession

²**fee** *transitive verb* **feed; fee·ing** (15th century)
1 *chiefly Scottish* : HIRE
2 : ⁹TIP 2

fee·ble \'fē-bəl\ *adjective* **fee·bler** \-b(ə-)lər\; **fee·blest** \-b(ə-)ləst\ [Middle English *feble,* from Old French, from Latin *flebilis* lamentable, wretched, from *flēre* to weep — more at BLEAT] (12th century)
1 a : markedly lacking in strength **b** : indicating weakness
2 a : deficient in qualities or resources that indicate vigor, authority, force, or efficiency **b** : INADEQUATE, INFERIOR
synonym see WEAK
— **fee·ble·ness** \-bəl-nəs\ *noun*
— **fee·bly** \-blē\ *adverb*

fee·ble·mind·ed \ˌfē-bəl-'mīn-dəd\ *adjective* (1534)
1 *obsolete* : IRRESOLUTE, VACILLATING
2 : mentally deficient
3 : FOOLISH, STUPID
— **fee·ble·mind·ed·ly** *adverb*
— **fee·ble·mind·ed·ness** *noun*

fee·blish \'fē-b(ə-)lish\ *adjective* (1674)
: somewhat feeble

¹**feed** \'fēd\ *verb* **fed** \'fed\; **feed·ing** [Middle English *feden,* from Old English *fēdan;* akin to Old English *fōda* food — more at FOOD] (before 12th century)
transitive verb
1 a : to give food to **b** : to give as food
2 a : to furnish something essential to the growth, sustenance, maintenance, or operation of **b** : to supply (material to be operated on) to a machine
3 : to produce or provide food for
4 a : SATISFY, GRATIFY **b** : SUPPORT, ENCOURAGE
5 a (1) : to supply for use or consumption (2) : CHANNEL, ROUTE **b** (1) : to supply (a signal) to an electronic circuit (2) : to send (as by wire or satellite) to a transmitting station for broadcast

6 : to supply (a fellow actor) with cues and situations that make a role more effective
7 : to pass a ball or puck to (a teammate) especially for a shot at the goal
intransitive verb
1 a : to consume food : EAT **b** : PREY — used with *on, upon,* or *off*
2 : to become nourished or satisfied or sustained as if by food
3 a : to become channeled or directed **b** : to move into a machine or opening in order to be used or processed

²**feed** *noun* (1576)
1 a : an act of eating **b** : MEAL; *especially* : a large meal
2 a : food for livestock; *specifically* : a mixture or preparation for feeding livestock **b** : the amount given at each feeding
3 a : material supplied (as to a furnace or machine) **b** : a mechanism by which the action of feeding is effected **c** : the motion or process of carrying forward the material to be operated upon (as in a machine) **d** : the process of feeding a television program (as to a local station)
4 : the action of passing a ball or puck to a team member who is in position to score

feed·back \'fēd-ˌbak\ *noun* (1920)
1 : the return to the input of a part of the output of a machine, system, or process (as for producing changes in an electronic circuit that improve performance or in an automatic control device that provide self-corrective action)
2 a : the partial reversion of the effects of a process to its source or to a preceding stage **b** : the transmission of evaluative or corrective information to the original or controlling source about an action, event, or process; *also* : the information so transmitted

feedback inhibition *noun* (1960)
: inhibition of an enzyme controlling an early stage of a series of biochemical reactions by the end product when it reaches a critical concentration

feed dog *noun* (circa 1939)
: a notched piece of metal on a sewing machine that feeds material into position under the needle

feed·er \'fē-dər\ *noun* (14th century)
1 : one that feeds: as **a** : one that fattens livestock for slaughter **b** : a device or apparatus for supplying food
2 : one that eats or takes nourishment; *especially* : an animal being fattened or one suitable for fattening
3 a : one that supplies, replenishes, or connects **b** : TRIBUTARY **c** : a heavy wire conductor supplying electricity at some point of an electric distribution system (as from a substation) **d** : BRANCH; *especially* : a branch transportation line **e** : FEEDER ROAD

feeder road *noun* (1938)
: a road that provides access to a major artery

feeding frenzy *noun* (1973)
: a frenzy of eating; *also* : the excited pursuit of something by a group

feed·lot \'fēd-ˌlät\ *noun* (1889)
: a plot of land on which livestock are fattened for market

feed·stock \-ˌstäk\ *noun* (1932)
: raw material supplied to a machine or processing plant

feed·stuff \-ˌstəf\ *noun* (1856)
: FEED 2a; *also* : any of the constituent nutrients of an animal ration

¹**feel** \'fē(ə)l\ *verb* **felt** \'felt\; **feel·ing** [Middle English *felen,* from Old English *fēlan;* akin to Old High German *fuolen* to feel, Latin *palpare* to caress] (before 12th century)
transitive verb
1 a : to handle or touch in order to examine, test, or explore some quality **b** : to perceive by a physical sensation coming from discrete end organs (as of the skin or muscles)
2 a : to undergo passive experience of **b** : to have one's sensibilities markedly affected by

3 : to ascertain by cautious trial — usually used with *out*
4 a : to be aware of by instinct or inference **b** : BELIEVE, THINK
intransitive verb
1 a : to receive or be able to receive a tactile sensation **b** : to search for something by using the sense of touch
2 a : to be conscious of an inward impression, state of mind, or physical condition **b** : to have a marked sentiment or opinion ⟨*feels* strongly about it⟩
3 : SEEM ⟨it *feels* like spring today⟩
4 : to have sympathy or pity ⟨I *feel* for you⟩
— **feel like** : to have an inclination for ⟨*feel* like a walk?⟩

²**feel** *noun* (13th century)
1 : SENSATION, FEELING
2 : the sense of touch
3 a : the quality of a thing as imparted through or as if through touch **b** : typical or peculiar quality or atmosphere; *also* : an awareness of such a quality or atmosphere
4 : intuitive knowledge or ability

feel·er \'fē-lər\ *noun* (1526)
: one that feels: as **a** : a tactile process (as a tentacle) of an animal **b** : something (as a proposal) ventured to ascertain the views of others

feeler gauge *noun* (1925)
: a thin metal strip or wire of known thickness used as a gauge

feel–good \'fē(ə)l-ˌgùd\ *adjective* (1978)
: relating to or promoting an often specious sense of satisfaction or well-being

¹**feel·ing** \'fē-liŋ\ *noun* (12th century)
1 a : the one of the basic physical senses of which the skin contains the chief end organs and of which the sensations of touch and temperature are characteristic : TOUCH (2) : a sensation experienced through this sense **b** : generalized bodily consciousness or sensation **c** : appreciative or responsive awareness or recognition
2 a : an emotional state or reaction ⟨had a kindly *feeling* toward the child⟩ **b** *plural* : susceptibility to impression : SENSITIVITY ⟨the remark hurt her *feelings*⟩
3 a : the undifferentiated background of one's awareness considered apart from any identifiable sensation, perception, or thought **b** : the overall quality of one's awareness **c** : conscious recognition : SENSE
4 a : often unreasoned opinion or belief : SENTIMENT **b** : PRESENTIMENT

◇ **WORD HISTORY**
fedora The hat known as a *fedora* is generally thought to have some connection with *Fédora,* a melodrama by the French playwright Victorien Sardou (1831–1908), though the exact nature of the connection has yet to be established. Sardou, a popular dramatist in the 19th century, though now nearly forgotten except by literary and theater historians, premiered *Fédora* in 1882, with the celebrated actress Sarah Bernhardt in the title role of Fédora Romanoff, a Russian princess. There is some evidence that the long plume worn by Bernhardt in the play made an impression on Parisian fashion, but the word *fédora,* if it was used for the plume in French, did not survive. Sardou's play ran successfully in New York in 1883 with the American actress Fanny Davenport in the title role. Sometime afterward, *fedora* found its way into American English as a name for a man's soft felt hat, with no obvious link to either Sarah Bernhardt's or Fanny Davenport's headgear. By 1895 the word appeared in a Montgomery Ward catalog—clearly a sign that the hat style had entered mainstream American fashion.

5 : capacity to respond emotionally especially with the higher emotions
6 : the character ascribed to something **:** ATMOSPHERE
7 a : the quality of a work of art that conveys the emotion of the artist **b :** sympathetic aesthetic response
8 FEEL 4 ☆
²**feeling** *adjective* (14th century)
1 a : SENTIENT, SENSITIVE **b :** easily moved emotionally
2 *obsolete* **:** deeply felt
3 : expressing emotion or sensitivity
— **feel·ing·ly** \-liŋ-lē\ *adverb*
— **feel·ing·ness** *noun*
feel up *transitive verb* (1930)
: to touch or fondle (someone) for sexual pleasure
fee simple *noun, plural* **fees simple** (14th century)
: a fee without limitation to any class of heirs or restrictions on transfer of ownership
fee splitting *noun* (1943)
: payment by a specialist (as a doctor or a lawyer) of a part of his fee to the person who made the referral
feet *plural of* FOOT
fee tail *noun, plural* **fees tail** (15th century)
: a fee limited to a particular class of heirs
feet·first \ˌfēt-'fərst\ *adverb* (circa 1901)
: with the feet foremost
feet of clay [from the feet of the idol in Daniel 2:33] (1814)
: a flaw of character that is usually not readily apparent
feeze \'fēz, 'fāz\ *noun* [Middle English *veze,* from *fesen, vesen* to drive away — more at FAZE] (14th century)
1 *chiefly dialect* **:** RUSH
2 *dialect* **:** a state of alarm or excitement
Feh·ling's solution \'fā-liŋ(z)-\ *noun* [Hermann *Fehling* (died 1885) German chemist] (1873)
: a blue solution of Rochelle salt and copper sulfate used as an oxidizing agent in a test for sugars and aldehydes
feign \'fān\ *verb* [Middle English, from Old French *feign-,* stem of *feindre,* from Latin *fingere* to shape, feign — more at DOUGH] (13th century)
intransitive verb
: PRETEND, DISSEMBLE
transitive verb
1 a : to give a false appearance of **:** induce as a false impression ⟨*feign* death⟩ **b :** to assert as if true **:** PRETEND
2 *archaic* **a :** INVENT, IMAGINE **b :** to give fictional representation to
3 *obsolete* **:** DISGUISE, CONCEAL
synonym see ASSUME
— **feign·er** *noun*
feigned *adjective* (14th century)
1 : FICTITIOUS
2 : not genuine or real
fei·joa \fā-'yō-ə, -'hō-ə\ *noun* [New Latin, genus name, from João da Silva *Feijó* (died 1824) Brazilian naturalist] (1898)
: the green edible fruit of a shrub or small tree (*Feijoa sellowiana*) of the myrtle family that is native to South America and is grown commercially especially in New Zealand; *also* **:** the tree or shrub
¹**feint** \'fānt\ *noun* [French *feinte,* from Old French, from *feint,* past participle of *feindre*] (1679)
: something feigned; *specifically* **:** a mock blow or attack on or toward one part in order to distract attention from the point one really intends to attack
synonym see TRICK
²**feint** (1810)
intransitive verb
: to make a feint
transitive verb
1 : to lure or deceive with a feint
2 : to make a pretense of

fei·rie \'fē-rē\ *adjective* [Middle English (Scots) *fery,* from Middle English *fere* strong, from Old English *fēre* able to go; akin to Old English *faran* to travel, fare] (before 12th century)
Scottish **:** NIMBLE, STRONG
feist \'fīst\ *noun* [obsolete *fisting hound,* from obsolete *fist* (to break wind)] (1770)
chiefly dialect **:** a small dog
feisty \'fī-stē\ *adjective* **feist·i·er; -est** (1896)
1 *chiefly Southern & Midland* **a :** full of nervous energy **:** FIDGETY **b :** being touchy and quarrelsome **c :** being frisky and exuberant
2 : having or showing a lively aggressiveness **:** SPUNKY ◇
— **feist·i·ness** *noun*
fe·la·fel \fə-'lä-fəl\ *variant of* FALAFEL
feld·sher \'fel(d)-shər\ *noun* [Russian *fel'dsher,* from German *Feldscher, Feldscherer* field surgeon, from *Feld* field + *Scherer* barber, surgeon] (1877)
: a medical or surgical practitioner without full professional qualifications or status in some east European countries and especially Russia
feld·spar \'fel(d)-ˌspär\ *noun* [modification of obsolete German *Feldspath* (now *Feldspat*), from German *Feld* field + obsolete German *Spath* (now *Spat*) spar] (1772)
: any of a group of crystalline minerals that consist of aluminum silicates with either potassium, sodium, calcium, or barium and that are an essential constituent of nearly all crystalline rocks
feld·spath·ic \fel(d)-'spa-thik\ *adjective* [*feldspath* (variant of *feldspar*), from obsolete German] (circa 1828)
: relating to or containing feldspar — used especially of a porcelain glaze
fe·li·cif·ic \ˌfē-lə-'si-fik\ *adjective* [Latin *felic-, felix*] (1865)
: causing or intended to cause happiness
felicific calculus *noun* (1945)
: a method of determining the rightness of an action by balancing the probable pleasures and pains that it would produce
¹**fe·lic·i·tate** \fi-'li-sə-ˌtāt\ *adjective* [Late Latin *felicitatus,* past participle of *felicitare* to make happy, from Latin *felicitas*] (1605)
obsolete **:** made happy
²**felicitate** *transitive verb* **-tat·ed; -tat·ing** (1628)
1 *archaic* **:** to make happy
2 a : to consider happy or fortunate **b :** to offer congratulations to
— **fe·lic·i·ta·tion** \-ˌli-sə-'tā-shən\ *noun*
— **fe·lic·i·ta·tor** \-'li-sə-ˌtā-tər\ *noun*
fe·lic·i·tous \fi-'li-sə-təs\ *adjective* (1789)
1 : very well suited or expressed **:** APT ⟨a *felicitous* remark⟩
2 : PLEASANT, DELIGHTFUL
synonym see FIT
— **fe·lic·i·tous·ly** *adverb*
— **fe·lic·i·tous·ness** *noun*
fe·lic·i·ty \fi-'li-sə-tē\ *noun, plural* **-ties** [Middle English *felicite,* from Middle French *félicité,* from Latin *felicitat-, felicitas,* from *felic-, felix* fruitful, happy — more at FEMININE] (14th century)
1 a : the quality or state of being happy; *especially* **:** great happiness **b :** an instance of happiness
2 : something that causes happiness
3 : a pleasing manner or quality especially in art or language
4 : an apt expression
fe·lid \'fē-ləd\ *noun* [New Latin *Felidae,* family name, from *Felis,* genus of cats, from Latin, cat] (circa 1889)
: CAT 1b
— **felid** *adjective*
fe·line \'fē-ˌlīn\ *adjective* [Latin *felinus,* from *felis*] (1681)
1 : of, relating to, or affecting cats or the cat family

2 : resembling a cat: as **a :** sleekly graceful **b :** SLY, TREACHEROUS **c :** STEALTHY
— **feline** *noun*
— **fe·line·ly** *adverb*
— **fe·lin·i·ty** \fē-'li-nə-tē\ *noun*
feline distemper *noun* (1942)
: PANLEUKOPENIA
feline panleukopenia *noun* (circa 1943)
: PANLEUKOPENIA
¹**fell** \'fel\ *noun* [Middle English, from Old English; akin to Old High German *fel* skin, Latin *pellis*] (before 12th century)
1 : SKIN, HIDE, PELT
2 : a thin tough membrane covering a carcass directly under the hide
²**fell** *transitive verb* [Middle English, from Old English *fellan;* akin to Old English *feallan* to fall — more at FALL] (before 12th century)
1 a : to cut, knock, or bring down **b :** KILL
2 : to sew (a seam) by folding one raw edge under the other and sewing flat on the wrong side
— **fell·able** \'fe-lə-bəl\ *adjective*
— **fell·er** *noun*
³**fell** *past of* FALL
⁴**fell** *adjective* [Middle English *fel,* from Middle French, from Old French — more at FELON] (14th century)

☆ SYNONYMS

Feeling, emotion, affection, sentiment, passion mean a subjective response to a person, thing, or situation. FEELING denotes any partly mental, partly physical response marked by pleasure, pain, attraction, or repulsion; it may suggest the mere existence of a response but imply nothing about the nature or intensity of it ⟨the *feelings* that once moved me are gone⟩. EMOTION carries a strong implication of excitement or agitation but, like FEELING, encompasses both positive and negative responses ⟨the drama portrays the *emotions* of adolescence⟩. AFFECTION applies to feelings that are also inclinations or likings ⟨a memoir of childhood filled with *affection* for her family⟩. SENTIMENT often implies an emotion inspired by an idea ⟨her feminist *sentiments* are well known⟩. PASSION suggests a very powerful or controlling emotion ⟨revenge became his ruling *passion*⟩.

◇ WORD HISTORY

feisty As *feisty* is a word now generally used with approval, its malodorous origins may come as a surprise to both user and subject. *Feisty* is ultimately derivative of *fist* (not the same word as *fist* denoting a clenched hand), which is attested in late Middle English as both a noun meaning "the act of breaking wind" and a verb meaning "to break wind." By the 16th century the participle *fisting* had become common in contemptuous expressions for a small dog, such as "fisting cur" and "fisting hound." Although *fist* and *fisting* became obsolete in Britain, the word resurfaced in the 19th century U.S., now spelled *feist* and meaning "a small dog of mixed breed," a usage that still survives, mostly in South Midland and Southern states. In the same area an adjective derivative *feisty* was formed, meaning variously "fidgety" and "irritable," supposed qualities of such dogs. Growing out of regional use, *feisty* has entered mainstream American English in the sense "spunky."

\ə\ abut \ᵊ\ kitten \ər\ further \a\ ash \ā\ ace
\ä\ mop, mar \au̇\ out \ch\ chin \e\ bet \ē\ easy
\g\ go \i\ hit \ī\ ice \j\ job \ŋ\ sing \ō\ go
\ȯ\ law \ȯi\ boy \th\ thin \t͟h\ the \ü\ loot \u̇\ foot
\y\ yet \zh\ vision *see also* Guide to Pronunciation

1 a : FIERCE, CRUEL, TERRIBLE **b :** SINISTER, MALEVOLENT ⟨a *fell* purpose⟩ **c :** very destructive **:** DEADLY ⟨a *fell* disease⟩
2 *Scottish* **:** SHARP, PUNGENT
— **fell·ness** *noun*
— **fel·ly** \'fel-lē\ *adverb*
— **at one fell swoop** *or* **in one fell swoop :** all at once; *also* **:** with a single concentrated effort

⁵**fell** *noun* [Middle English, from Old Norse *fell, fjall* mountain; akin to Old High German *felis* rock] (14th century)
dialect British **:** a high barren field or moor

fel·lah \'fe-lə, fə-'lä\ *noun, plural* **fel·la·hin** *or* **fel·la·heen** \,fel-ə-'hēn, fə-,lä-'hēn\ [Arabic *fallāḥ*] (1743)
: a peasant or agricultural laborer in an Arab country (as Egypt)

fel·late \'fe-,lāt, fə-'lāt\ *verb* **fel·lat·ed; fel·lat·ing** [back-formation from *fellatio*] (1948)
transitive verb
: to perform fellatio on
intransitive verb
: to fellate someone
— **fel·la·tor** \-,lā-tər, -'lā-tər\ *noun*

fel·la·tio \fə-'lā-shē-,ō, fe-\ *also* **fel·la·tion** \-'lā-shən\ *noun* [New Latin *fellation-, fellatio,* from Latin *felare, fellare,* literally, to suck — more at FEMININE] (circa 1893)
: oral stimulation of the penis

fell·mon·ger \'fel-,məŋ-gər, -,mäŋ-\ *noun* [¹*fell*] (1530)
British **:** one who removes hair or wool from hides in preparation for leather making
— **fell·mon·gered** \-gərd\ *adjective, British*
— **fell·mon·ger·ing** \-g(ə-)riŋ\ *noun, British*
— **fell·mon·gery** \-g(ə-)rē\ *noun, British*

fel·low \'fe-(,)lō, -lə(-w)\ *noun, often attributive* [Middle English *felawe,* from Old English *fēolaga,* from Old Norse *fēlagi,* from *fēlag* partnership, from *fē* cattle, money + *lag* act of laying] (before 12th century)
1 : COMRADE, ASSOCIATE
2 a : an equal in rank, power, or character **:** PEER **b :** one of a pair **:** MATE
3 : a member of a group having common characteristics; *specifically* **:** a member of an incorporated literary or scientific society
4 a *obsolete* **:** a person of one of the lower social classes **b :** a worthless man or boy **c :** MAN, BOY **d :** BOYFRIEND, BEAU
5 : an incorporated member of a college or collegiate foundation especially in a British university
6 : a person appointed to a position granting a stipend and allowing for advanced study or research ◊

fellow feeling *noun* (1712)
: a feeling of community of interest or of mutual understanding

fel·low·ly \-lō-lē, -lə-lē\ *adjective* (13th century)
: SOCIABLE
— **fellowly** *adverb*

fel·low·man \,fe-lō-'man, -lə-\ *noun* (1667)
: a kindred human being

fellow servant *noun* (1900)
: an employee working with another employee under such circumstances that each one if negligent may expose the other to harm which the employer cannot reasonably be expected to guard against or be held legally liable for

¹**fel·low·ship** \'fe-lə-,ship, -lō-\ *noun* (before 12th century)
1 : COMPANIONSHIP, COMPANY
2 a : community of interest, activity, feeling, or experience **b :** the state of being a fellow or associate
3 : a company of equals or friends **:** ASSOCIATION
4 : the quality or state of being comradely
5 *obsolete* **:** MEMBERSHIP, PARTNERSHIP

6 a : the position of a fellow (as of a university) **b :** the stipend of a fellow **c :** a foundation for the providing of such a stipend

²**fellowship** *verb* **-shipped** *also* **-shiped** \-,shipt\; **-ship·ping** *also* **-ship·ing** \-,shi-piŋ\ (14th century)
intransitive verb
: to join in fellowship especially with a church member
transitive verb
: to admit to fellowship (as in a church)

fellow traveler *noun* [translation of Russian *poputchik*] (1925)
: one that sympathizes with and often furthers the ideals and program of an organized group (as the Communist party) without membership in the group or regular participation in its activities
— **fel·low–trav·el·ing** *adjective*

fel·ly \'fe-lē\ *or* **fel·loe** \-(,)lō\ *noun, plural* **fellies** *or* **felloes** [Middle English *fely, felive,* from Old English *felg;* akin to Old High German *felga* felly, Old English *fealg* piece of plowed land] (before 12th century)
: the exterior rim or a segment of the rim of a wheel supported by the spokes

felo-de-se \,fe-lō-də-'sā, -'sē\ *noun, plural* **fe·lo·nes-de-se** \fə-,lō-(,)nēz-də-\ *or* **felos-de-se** \,fe-lōz-də-\ [Medieval Latin *felo de se, fello de se,* literally, evildoer in respect to oneself] (1607)
1 : one who deliberately kills himself or who dies from the effects of his commission of an unlawful malicious act
2 : an act of deliberate self-destruction **:** SUICIDE

¹**fel·on** \'fe-lən\ *noun* [Middle English, from Middle French *felon, fel* evildoer, probably of Germanic origin; akin to Old High German *fillen* to beat, whip, *fel* skin — more at FELL] (13th century)
1 : one who has committed a felony
2 *archaic* **:** VILLAIN
3 : WHITLOW

²**felon** *adjective* (13th century)
1 *archaic* **a :** CRUEL **b :** EVIL
2 *archaic* **:** WILD

fe·lo·ni·ous \fə-'lō-nē-əs\ *adjective* (1575)
1 *archaic* **:** very evil **:** VILLAINOUS
2 : of, relating to, or having the nature of a felony
— **fe·lo·ni·ous·ly** *adverb*
— **fe·lo·ni·ous·ness** *noun*

fel·on·ry \'fe-lən-rē\ *noun* (1837)
: FELONS; *especially* **:** the convict population of a penal colony

fel·o·ny \'fe-lə-nē\ *noun, plural* **-nies** (14th century)
1 : an act on the part of a feudal vassal involving the forfeiture of his fee
2 a : a grave crime formerly differing from a misdemeanor under English common law by involving forfeiture in addition to any other punishment **b :** a grave crime declared to be a felony by the common law or by statute regardless of the punishment actually imposed **c :** a crime declared a felony by statute because of the punishment imposed **d :** a crime for which the punishment in federal law may be death or imprisonment for more than one year

fel·site \'fel-,sīt\ *noun* [felspar + -ite] (1794)
: a dense igneous rock consisting almost entirely of feldspar and quartz
— **fel·sit·ic** \fel-'si-tik\ *adjective*

fel·spar *chiefly British variant of* FELDSPAR

¹**felt** \'felt\ *noun* [Middle English, from Old English; akin to Old High German *filz* felt, Latin *pellere* to drive, beat] (before 12th century)
1 a : a cloth made of wool and fur often mixed with natural or synthetic fibers through the action of heat, moisture, chemicals, and pressure **b :** a firm woven cloth of wool or cotton heavily napped and shrunk
2 : an article made of felt

3 : a material resembling felt: as **a :** a heavy paper of organic or asbestos fibers impregnated with asphalt and used in building construction **b :** semirigid pressed fiber insulation used in building
— **felt·like** *adjective*

²**felt** *transitive verb* (14th century)
1 : to make out of or cover with felt
2 : to cause to adhere and mat together
3 : to make into felt or a similar substance

³**felt** *past and past participle of* FEEL

felt·ing \'fel-tiŋ\ *noun* (1686)
1 : the process of making felt
2 : FELT

fe·luc·ca \fə-'lü-kə, -'lə-kə\ *noun* [Italian *feluca*] (1615)
: a narrow fast lateen-rigged sailing vessel chiefly of the Mediterranean area

felucca

¹**fe·male** \'fē-,māl\ *adjective* (14th century)
1 a : of, relating to, or being the sex that bears young or produces eggs **b :** PISTILLATE
2 : having some quality (as gentleness) associated with the female sex
3 : designed with a hollow or groove into which a corresponding male part fits ⟨*female* coupling of a hose⟩ ◊
— **fe·male·ness** *noun*

²**female** *noun* [Middle English, alteration of *femel, femelle,* from Middle French & Medieval Latin; Middle French *femelle,* from Medieval Latin *femella,* from Latin, girl, diminutive of *femina*] (14th century)
1 a : a female person **:** WOMAN, GIRL **b :** an individual that bears young or produces large usually immobile gametes (as eggs) that are fertilized by small usually motile gametes of a male
2 : a pistillate plant

◊ WORD HISTORY
fellow *Fellow* is one of a significant number of words—from *law* and *outlaw* in the social sphere to *egg* and *sky* in the everyday world—that English owes to the Scandinavian conquests and settlement of Britain in the 9th and 10th centuries. *Fēolaga,* the late Old English ancestor of *fellow,* was borrowed from Old Norse *fēlagi,* literally, a "fee-layer," that is, someone who put down property, typically in the form of livestock or money in a joint venture with another person, for trade or some other common goal. This sense, which we might render more loosely as "partner" or "business associate," has been lost in Modern English, but *fellow* over the course of centuries has acquired a wide variety of other meanings, one of the most common now being simply "male person."

female In the 14th century *female* first appears in Middle English as one spelling alongside others such as *femel* and *femelle.* All are borrowed, through medieval French, from Latin *femella* "young woman, girl," a diminutive of *femina* "woman." French *femelle* had no etymological connection to English *male,* but the phonetic similarity of the words and the fact that "male" and "female" are naturally paired concepts led English speakers to reshape the French word to make it look more similar to *male.* This process reflects the simple operation of folk etymology, that is, the alteration of less familiar words in the direction of more familiar ones.

¹fem·i·nine \'fe-mə-nən\ *adjective* [Middle English, from Middle French *feminin*, from Latin *femininus*, from *femina* woman; akin to Old English *delu* nipple, Latin *filius* son, *felix*, *fetus*, & *fecundus* fruitful, *felare* to suck, Greek *thēlē* nipple] (14th century)
1 : FEMALE 1a
2 : characteristic of or appropriate or unique to women
3 : of, relating to, or constituting the gender that ordinarily includes most words or grammatical forms referring to females ⟨a *feminine* noun⟩
4 a : being an unstressed and usually hypermetric final syllable ⟨*feminine* ending⟩ **b** *of rhyme* : having an unstressed final syllable **c** : having the final chord occurring on a weak beat ⟨music in *feminine* cadences⟩
— **fem·i·nine·ly** *adverb*
— **fem·i·nine·ness** \-nə(n)-nəs\ *noun*
²feminine *noun* (15th century)
1 a : a noun, pronoun, adjective, or inflectional form or class of the feminine gender **b** : the feminine gender
2 : the female principle ⟨eternal *feminine*⟩
fem·i·nin·i·ty \ˌfe-mə-'ni-nə-tē\ *noun* (14th century)
1 : the quality or nature of the female sex
2 : EFFEMINACY
3 : WOMEN, WOMANKIND
fem·i·nise *British variant of* FEMINIZE
fem·i·nism \'fe-mə-ˌni-zəm\ *noun* (1895)
1 : the theory of the political, economic, and social equality of the sexes
2 : organized activity on behalf of women's rights and interests
— **fem·i·nist** \-nist\ *noun or adjective*
— **fem·i·nis·tic** \ˌfe-mə-'nis-tik\ *adjective*
fe·min·i·ty \fe-'mi-nə-tē, fə-\ *noun* (14th century)
: FEMININITY
fem·i·nize \'fe-mə-ˌnīz\ *transitive verb* **-nized; -niz·ing** (1652)
1 : to give a feminine quality to
2 : to cause (a male or castrate) to take on feminine characters (as by implantation of ovaries or administration of estrogenic substances)
— **fem·i·ni·za·tion** \ˌfe-mə-nə-'zā-shən\ *noun*
femme *also* **fem** \'fem\ *noun* [probably from French *femme* woman, from Latin *femina*] (1958)
: a lesbian who plays the female role in a homosexual relationship
femme fa·tale \ˌfem-fə-'tal, ˌfam-, -'täl\ *noun, plural* **femmes fa·tales** \-'tal(z), -'täl(z)\ [French, literally, disastrous woman] (1912)
1 : a seductive woman who lures men into dangerous or compromising situations
2 : a woman who attracts men by an aura of charm and mystery
fem·o·ral \'fe-mə-rəl, 'fem-rəl\ *adjective* (circa 1771)
: of or relating to the femur or thigh
femoral artery *noun* (circa 1771)
: the chief artery of the thigh lying in its anterior inner part
fem·to- \ˌfem(p)-tō\ *combining form* [International Scientific Vocabulary, from Danish or Norwegian *femten* fifteen, from Old Norse *fimmtān;* akin to Old English *fīftēne* fifteen]
: one quadrillionth (10^{-15}) part of ⟨*femto*second⟩
fem·to·sec·ond \'fem(p)-tə-ˌse-kənd, -kənt, -tō-\ *noun* (1976)
: one quadrillionth of a second
fe·mur \'fē-mər\ *noun, plural* **fe·murs** *or* **fem·o·ra** \'fe-mə-rə, 'fem-rə\ [New Latin *femor-, femur,* from Latin, thigh] (circa 1771)
1 : the proximal bone of the hind or lower limb — called also *thighbone*
2 : the segment of an insect's leg that is third from the body

¹fen \'fen\ *noun* [Middle English, from Old English *fenn;* akin to Old High German *fenna* fen, Sanskrit *paṅka* mud] (before 12th century)
: low land covered wholly or partly with water unless artificially drained
²fen \'fən\ *noun, plural* **fen** [Chinese (Beijing) *fēn*] (1916)
— see *yuan* at MONEY table
¹fence \'fen(t)s\ *noun, often attributive* [Middle English *fens,* short for *defens* defense] (14th century)
1 *archaic* : a means of protection : DEFENSE
2 : a barrier intended to prevent escape or intrusion or to mark a boundary; *especially* : such a barrier made of posts and wire or boards
3 : FENCING 1
4 a : a receiver of stolen goods **b** : a place where stolen goods are bought
— **fence·less** \-ləs\ *adjective*
— **fence·less·ness** *noun*
— **on the fence** : in a position of neutrality or indecision
²fence *verb* **fenced; fenc·ing** (15th century)
transitive verb
1 a : to enclose with a fence **b** (1) : to keep in or out with a fence (2) : to ward off
2 : to provide a defense for
3 : to sell (stolen property) to a fence
intransitive verb
1 a : to practice fencing **b** (1) : to use tactics of attack and defense resembling those of fencing (2) : to parry arguments by shifting ground
2 *archaic* : to provide protection
— **fenc·er** *noun*
fence–mend·ing \'fen(t)s-ˌmen-diŋ\ *noun* (1947)
: the rehabilitating of a deteriorated political relationship
fence·row \'fen(t)s-ˌrō\ *noun* (1842)
: the land occupied by a fence including the uncultivated area on each side
fence–sit·ting \'fen(t)s-ˌsi-tiŋ\ *noun* (1904)
: a state of indecision or neutrality with respect to conflicting positions
— **fence–sit·ter** *noun*
fenc·ing *noun* (1581)
1 : the art or practice of attack and defense with the foil, épée, or saber
2 a (1) : FENCE 2 (2) : the fences of a property or region **b** : material used for building fences
¹fend \'fend\ *verb* [Middle English *fenden,* short for *defenden*] (14th century)
transitive verb
1 : DEFEND
2 : to keep or ward off : REPEL — often used with *off*
3 *dialect British* : to provide for : SUPPORT
intransitive verb
1 *dialect British* : to make an effort : STRUGGLE
2 a : to try to get along without help : SHIFT ⟨had to *fend* for themselves⟩ **b** : to provide a livelihood
²fend *noun* (1721)
chiefly Scottish : an effort or attempt especially for oneself
fend·er \'fen-dər\ *noun* (13th century)
: a device that protects: as **a** (1) : a cushion (as foam rubber or a wood float) between a boat and a dock or between two boats that lessens shock and prevents chafing (2) : a pile or a row or cluster of piles placed to protect a dock or bridge pier from damage by ships or floating objects **b** : RAILING **c** : a device in front of locomotives and streetcars to lessen injury to animals or pedestrians in case of collision **d** : a guard over the wheel of a motor vehicle **e** : a low metal frame or a screen before an open fireplace **f** : an oblong or triangular shield of leather attached to the stirrup leather of a saddle to protect a rider's legs
— **fend·ered** \-dərd\ *adjective*

— **fend·er·less** *adjective*
fender bender *noun* (circa 1962)
: a minor automobile accident
fe·nes·tra \fə-'nes-trə\ *noun, plural* **-trae** \-ˌtrē, -ˌtrī\ [New Latin, from Latin, window] (circa 1737)
1 : a small anatomical opening (as in a bone): as **a** : an oval opening between the middle ear and the vestibule having the base of the stapes or columella attached to its membrane — called also *fenestra ova·lis* \-ō-'vā-ləs\, *fenestra ves·tib·u·li* \-ves-'ti-byə-ˌ()lē\, *oval window* **b** : a round opening between the middle ear and the cochlea — called also *fenestra cochleae, fenestra ro·tun·da* \-rō-'tən-də\, *round window*
2 : an opening cut in bone
— **fe·nes·tral** \-trəl\ *adjective*
fe·nes·trate \fə-'nes-ˌtrāt, 'fe-nə-ˌstrāt\ *adjective* [Latin *fenestratus,* from *fenestra*] (1835)
: FENESTRATED
fen·es·trat·ed \'fe-nə-ˌstrā-təd\ *adjective* (circa 1852)
: having one or more openings or pores ⟨*fenestrated* blood capillaries⟩
fen·es·tra·tion \ˌfe-nə-'strā-shən\ *noun* (1846)
1 : the arrangement, proportioning, and design of windows and doors in a building
2 : an opening in a surface (as a wall or membrane)
3 : the operation of cutting an opening in the bony labyrinth between the inner ear and tympanum to replace natural fenestrae that are not functional
Fe·ni·an \'fē-nē-ən\ *noun* [Irish *féinne,* plural of *fiann,* legendary band of Irish warriors] (1816)
1 : a member of a legendary band of warriors defending Ireland in the 2d and 3d centuries A.D.
2 : a member of a secret 19th century Irish and Irish-American organization dedicated to the overthrow of British rule in Ireland
— **Fenian** *adjective*
— **Fe·ni·an·ism** \-ə-ˌni-zəm\ *noun*
fen·land \'fen-ˌland\ *noun* (before 12th century)
: an area of low often marshy ground
fen·nec \'fe-nik\ *noun* [Arabic *fanak*] (1790)
: a small pale-fawn fox (*Vulpes zerda* synonym *Fennecus zerda*) with large ears that inhabits the deserts of northern Africa and Arabia
fen·nel \'fe-nᵊl\ *noun* [Middle English *fenel,* from Old English *finugl,* from (assumed) Vulgar Latin *fenuculum,* from Latin *feniculum* fennel, irregular diminutive of *fenum* hay] (before 12th century)
: a perennial European herb (*Foeniculum vulgare*) of the carrot family introduced into North America and cultivated for its foliage and aromatic seeds
fen·ny \'fe-nē\ *adjective* (before 12th century)
1 : having the characteristics of a fen : BOGGY
2 *archaic* : peculiar to or found in a fen
fenu·greek \'fen-yə-ˌgrēk\ *noun* [Middle English *fenugrek,* from Middle French *fenugrec,* from Latin *fenum Graecum,* literally, Greek hay] (14th century)
: a leguminous annual Asian herb (*Trigonella foenumgraecum*) with aromatic seeds
feoff·ee \fe-'fē, fē-'fē\ *noun* (15th century)
: one to whom a feoffment is made
feoff·ment \'fef-mənt, 'fēf-\ *noun* [Middle English *feoffement,* from Anglo-French, from *feoffer* to invest with a fee, from Old French *fief* fee] (14th century)
: the granting of a fee

\ə\ abut \ᵊ\ kitten \ər\ further \a\ ash \ā\ ace
\ä\ mop, mar \au̇\ out \ch\ chin \e\ bet \ē\ easy
\g\ go \i\ hit \ī\ ice \j\ job \ŋ\ sing \ō\ go
\ȯ\ law \ȯi\ boy \th\ thin \t͟h\ the \ü\ loot \u̇\ foot
\y\ yet \zh\ vision *see also* Guide to Pronunciation

feof·for \'fe-fər, 'fē-; fe-'fȯr, fē-\ *or* **feoff·er** \'fef-ər, 'fēf-\ *noun* (15th century)
: one who makes a feoffment

-fer \fər\ *noun combining form* [French & Latin; French *-fère,* from Latin *-fer* bearing, one that bears, from *ferre* to carry — more at BEAR]
: one that bears ⟨aqui*fer*⟩

fe·rae na·tu·rae \'fer-ˌī-nə-'tùr-ˌī\ *adjective* [Latin, of a wild nature] (circa 1661)
: wild by nature and not usually tamed

fe·ral \'fir-əl, 'fer-\ *adjective* [Medieval Latin *feralis,* from Latin *fera* wild animal, from feminine of *ferus* wild — more at FIERCE] (1604)
1 : of, relating to, or suggestive of a wild beast : SAVAGE
2 a : not domesticated or cultivated : WILD **b** : having escaped from domestication and become wild
synonym see BRUTAL

fer–de–lance \'fer-dᵊl-'an(t)s, -'än(t)s\ *noun,* *plural* **fer–de–lance** [French, literally, lance iron, spearhead] (1880)
: a large extremely venomous pit viper (*Bothrops atrox*) of Central and South America

fere \'fir\ *noun* [Middle English, from Old English *gefēra;* akin to Old English *faran* to go, travel — more at FARE] (before 12th century)
1 *archaic* : COMPANION, COMRADE
2 *archaic* : SPOUSE

¹fe·ria \'fir-ē-ə\ *noun* [Medieval Latin — more at FAIR] (15th century)
: a weekday of a church calendar on which no feast falls
— **fe·ri·al** \-ē-əl\ *adjective*

²fe·ria \'fer-ē-ə, -ē-ˌä\ *noun* [Spanish, fair, market, from Medieval Latin — more at FAIR] (1844)
: an Hispanic market festival often in observance of a religious holiday

fe·rine \'fir-ˌīn\ *adjective* [Latin *ferinus,* from *fera*] (1640)
: FERAL

fer·i·ty \'fer-ət-ē\ *noun, plural* **-ties** [Latin *feritas,* from *ferus*] (1534)
archaic : the quality or state of being feral; *also* : BARBARITY

fer·lie *also* **fer·ly** \'fer-lē\ *noun, plural* **fer·lies** [Middle English, from *ferly* strange, from Old English *fǣrlīc* unexpected, from *fǣr* sudden danger — more at FEAR] (13th century)
Scottish : WONDER

fer·ma·ta \fer-'mä-tə\ *noun* [Italian, literally, stop, from *fermare* to stop, from Latin *firmare* to make firm] (circa 1859)
: a prolongation at the discretion of the performer of a musical note, chord, or rest beyond its given time value; *also* : the sign ⌢ denoting such a prolongation — called also *hold*

¹fer·ment \(ˌ)fər-'ment\ (14th century)
intransitive verb
1 : to undergo fermentation
2 : to be in a state of agitation or intense activity
transitive verb
1 : to cause to undergo fermentation
2 : to work up (as into a state of agitation) : FOMENT ⟨quick-spreading rumors *fermented* the city and violence soon broke out⟩
— **fer·ment·able** \-'men-tə-bəl\ *adjective*

²fer·ment \'fər-ˌment *also* (ˌ)fər-'\ *noun* [Middle English, from Latin *fermentum* yeast — more at BARM] (15th century)
1 a : a living organism (as a yeast) that causes fermentation by virtue of its enzymes **b** : ENZYME
2 a : a state of unrest : AGITATION **b** : a process of active often disorderly development ⟨the great period of creative *ferment* in literature —William Barrett⟩

fer·men·ta·tion \ˌfər-mən-'tā-shən, -ˌmen-\ *noun* (1601)
1 a : a chemical change with effervescence **b** : an enzymatically controlled anaerobic break-

down of an energy-rich compound (as a carbohydrate to carbon dioxide and alcohol or to an organic acid); *broadly* : an enzymatically controlled transformation of an organic compound
2 : FERMENT 2

fer·men·ta·tive \(ˌ)fər-'men-tə-tiv\ *adjective* (1661)
1 : causing or producing a substance that causes fermentation ⟨*fermentative* organisms⟩
2 : of, relating to, or produced by fermentation

fer·men·ter \(ˌ)fər-'men-tər\ *noun* (1918)
1 : an organism that causes fermentation
2 *or* **fer·men·tor** : an apparatus for carrying out fermentation

fer·mi \'fer-(ˌ)mē, 'fər-\ *noun* [Enrico *Fermi*] (1955)
: a unit of length equal to 10^{-13} centimeter

fer·mi·on \'fer-mē-ˌän, 'fər-\ *noun* [Enrico *Fermi* + English ²*-on*] (1947)
: a particle (as an electron, proton, or neutron) whose spin quantum number is an odd multiple of ½ — compare BOSON

fer·mi·um \'fer-mē-əm, 'fər-\ *noun* [Enrico *Fermi*] (1955)
: a radioactive metallic element artificially produced (as by bombardment of plutonium with neutrons) — see ELEMENT table

fern \'fərn\ *noun* [Middle English, from Old English *fearn;* akin to Old High German *farn* fern, Sanskrit *parṇa* wing, leaf] (before 12th century)
: any of a large class (Filicopsida) of flowerless spore-producing vascular plants; *especially* : any of an order (Filicales) of homosporous plants possessing roots, stems, and leaflike fronds
— **fern·like** \-ˌlīk\ *adjective*
— **ferny** \'fər-nē\ *adjective*

fern bar *noun* (1976)
: a bar or restaurant fashionably decorated with green plants and especially ferns

fern·ery \'fər-nə-rē\ *noun, plural* **-er·ies** (1840)
1 : a place or stand where ferns grow
2 : a collection of growing ferns

fern seed *noun* (1596)
: the dustlike asexual spores of ferns formerly thought to be seeds and believed to make the possessor invisible

fe·ro·cious \fə-'rō-shəs\ *adjective* [Latin *feroc-, ferox,* literally, fierce looking, from *ferus* + *-oc-, -ox* (akin to Greek *ōps* eye) — more at EYE] (1646)
1 : exhibiting or given to extreme fierceness and unrestrained violence and brutality
2 : extremely intense ⟨*ferocious* heat⟩
synonym see FIERCE
— **fe·ro·cious·ly** *adverb*
— **fe·ro·cious·ness** *noun*

fe·roc·i·ty \fə-'rä-sə-tē\ *noun* (1606)
: the quality or state of being ferocious

-ferous *adjective combining form* [Middle English, from Middle French & Latin; Middle French *-fere* -fer, from Latin *-fer*]
: bearing : producing ⟨carboni*ferous*⟩

fer·re·dox·in \ˌfer-ə-'däk-sən\ *noun* [Latin *ferrum* + English *redox* + *-in*] (1962)
: any of a group of iron-containing plant proteins that function as electron carriers in photosynthetic organisms and in some anaerobic bacteria

¹fer·ret \'fer-ət\ *noun* [Middle English *furet, ferret,* from Middle French *furet,* from (assumed) Vulgar Latin *furittus,* literally, little thief, diminutive of Latin *fur* thief — more at FURTIVE] (14th century)
1 : a partially domesticated usually albino European polecat that is sometimes classed as a separate species (*Mustela furo*)
2 : an active and persistent searcher ◇
— **fer·rety** \-ə-tē\ *adjective*

²ferret (15th century)
intransitive verb
1 : to hunt with ferrets
2 : to search about
transitive verb

1 a (1) : to hunt (as rabbits) with ferrets (2) : to force out of hiding : FLUSH **b** : to find and bring to light by searching — usually used with *out* ⟨*ferret* out the answers⟩
2 : HARRY, WORRY
— **fer·ret·er** *noun*

³ferret *noun* [probably modification of Italian *fioretti* floss silk, from plural of *fioretto,* diminutive of *fiore* flower, from Latin *flor-, flos* — more at BLOW] (1649)
: a narrow cotton, silk, or wool tape — called also *ferreting*

ferri- *combining form* [Latin, from *ferrum*]
1 : iron ⟨*ferri*ferous⟩
2 : ferric iron ⟨*ferri*cyanide⟩

fer·ri·age \'fer-ē-ij\ *noun* [Middle English] (14th century)
1 : the fare paid for a ferry passage
2 : the act or business of transporting by ferry

fer·ric \'fer-ik\ *adjective* (1799)
1 : of, relating to, or containing iron
2 : being or containing iron usually with a valence of three

ferric ammonium citrate *noun* (circa 1924)
: a complex salt containing varying amounts of iron and used especially for making blueprints

ferric chloride *noun* (1885)
: a deliquescent dark salt $FeCl_3$ that readily hydrates to the yellow-orange form and that is used in sewage treatment and as an astringent

ferric hydroxide *noun* (1885)
: a hydrate $Fe_2O_3 \cdot nH_2O$ of ferric oxide that is capable of acting both as a base and as a weak acid

ferric oxide *noun* (1882)
: the red or black oxide of iron Fe_2O_3 found in nature as hematite and as rust and also obtained synthetically and used as a pigment and for polishing

fer·ri·cy·a·nide \ˌfer-ˌī-'sī-ə-ˌnīd, ˌfer-i-\ *noun* [International Scientific Vocabulary] (1845)
1 : the trivalent anion $Fe(CN)_6{}^{3-}$
2 : a compound containing the ferricyanide anion; *especially* : the red salt $K_3Fe(CN)_6$ used in making blue pigments

fer·rif·er·ous \fə-'ri-f(ə-)rəs, fe-\ *adjective* (1811)
: containing or yielding iron

fer·ri·mag·net·ic \'fer-ˌī-mag-'ne-tik, ˌfer-i-\ *adjective* (1951)
: of or relating to a substance (as ferrite) characterized by magnetization in which one group of magnetic ions is polarized in a direction opposite to the other
— **fer·ri·mag·net** \'fer-ˌī-ˌmag-nət, 'fer-i-\ *noun*
— **fer·ri·mag·net·i·cal·ly** \'fer-ˌī-mag-'ne-ti-k(ə-)lē, ˌfer-i-\ *adverb*
— **fer·ri·mag·ne·tism** \-'mag-nə-ˌti-zəm\ *noun*

Fer·ris wheel \'fer-əs-\ *noun* [G. W. G. *Ferris* (died 1896) American engineer] (1893)

◇ WORD HISTORY
ferret The *ferret* is a partially domesticated breed of the European polecat. For centuries the ferret has been used in Europe in hunting rats and sometimes rabbits. But both the wild polecat and his domestic relative have rather bad reputations, especially as poultry thieves. The polecat's name (Middle English *polcat*) is of uncertain origin, but one suggestion is that it may be a compound of Middle French *pol* (or *poul*) "cock," and Middle English *cat.* And the ferret is a "little thief": Middle English *ferret* (or *furet*) comes from Middle French *furet,* which ultimately goes back to Latin *fur* "thief." The sport of ferreting out rodents and rabbits gives us the common modern sense of the verb *ferret,* "to find and bring to light by searching."

: an amusement device consisting of a large upright power-driven wheel carrying seats that remain horizontal around its rim

fer·rite \'fer-ˌīt\ *noun* (1851)
1 : any of several magnetic substances that consist essentially of ferric oxide combined with the oxides of one or more metals (as manganese, nickel, or zinc), have high magnetic permeability and high electrical resistivity, and are used especially in electronic devices
2 : a solid solution in which alpha iron is the solvent
— **fer·rit·ic** \fə-'ri-tik, fe-\ *adjective*

fer·ri·tin \'fer-ə-t³n\ *noun* [International Scientific Vocabulary, alteration of *ferratin,* iron-containing protein, from Latin *ferrat*us bound with iron (from *ferrum*) + International Scientific Vocabulary *-in*] (1937)
: a crystalline iron-containing protein that functions in the storage of iron and is found especially in the liver and spleen

ferro- *combining form* [Medieval Latin, from Latin *ferrum*]
1 : iron ⟨*ferro*concrete⟩
2 : ferrous iron ⟨*ferro*cyanide⟩

fer·ro–ce·ment \ˌfer-ō-si-'ment\ *noun* (1956)
: a building material made of thin cement slabs reinforced with steel mesh

fer·ro·cene \'fer-ō-ˌsēn\ *noun* [ferro- + cycl- + -ene] (1952)
: a crystalline stable organometallic coordination compound (C_5H_5)$_2$Fe; *also* : an analogous compound with a heavy metal (as chromium)

fer·ro·con·crete \ˌfer-ō-'kän-ˌkrēt, -kän-'\ *noun* (1900)
: REINFORCED CONCRETE

fer·ro·cy·a·nide \-'sī-ə-ˌnīd\ *noun* (circa 1826)
1 : the tetravalent anion Fe(CN)$_6{}^{4-}$
2 : a compound containing the ferrocyanide anion; *especially* : the salt $K_4Fe(CN)_6$ used in making blue pigments (as Prussian blue)

fer·ro·elec·tric \ˌfer-ō-i-'lek-trik\ *adjective* (1935)
: of or relating to crystalline substances having spontaneous electric polarization reversible by an electric field
— **ferroelectric** *noun*
— **fer·ro·elec·tric·i·ty** \-ˌlek-'tri-sə-tē, -'tris-tē\ *noun*

fer·ro·mag·ne·sian \-mag-'nē-zhən, -shən\ *adjective* (1899)
: containing iron and magnesium ⟨*ferromagnesian* minerals⟩

fer·ro·mag·net·ic \-'ne-tik\ *adjective* (1896)
: of or relating to substances with an abnormally high magnetic permeability, a definite saturation point, and appreciable residual magnetism and hysteresis
— **fer·ro·mag·net** \'fer-ə-ˌmag-nət\ *noun*
— **fer·ro·mag·ne·tism** \ˌfer-ō-'mag-nə-ˌti-zəm\ *noun*

fer·ro·man·ga·nese \-'maŋ-gə-ˌnēz, -ˌnēs\ *noun* (1864)
: an alloy of iron and manganese containing usually about 80 percent manganese and used in the manufacture of steel

fer·ro·sil·i·con \-'si-li-kən, -lə-ˌkän\ *noun* (1882)
: an alloy of iron and silicon containing 15 to 95 percent silicon and used for deoxidizing molten steel and making silicon steel and high-silicon cast iron

fer·ro·type \'fer-ə-ˌtīp\ *noun* (1844)
1 : a positive photograph made by a collodion process on a thin iron plate having a darkened surface
2 : the process by which a ferrotype is made

fer·rous \'fer-əs\ *adjective* [New Latin *ferrosus,* from Latin *ferrum*] (1865)
1 : of, relating to, or containing iron
2 : being or containing divalent iron

ferrous oxide *noun* (1873)
: a black easily oxidizable powder FeO that is the monoxide of iron

ferrous sulfate *noun* (1865)
: a salt $FeSO_4$; *especially* : COPPERAS

fer·ru·gi·nous \fə-'rü-jə-nəs, fe-\ *adjective* [Latin *ferrugineus, ferruginus,* from *ferrugin-, ferrugo* iron rust, from *ferrum*] (circa 1661)
1 : of, relating to, or containing iron ⟨a *ferruginous* soil⟩
2 : resembling iron rust in color

fer·rule \'fer-əl\ *noun* [alteration of Middle English *virole,* from Middle French, from Latin *viriola,* diminutive of *viria* bracelet, of Celtic origin; akin to Old Irish *fiar* oblique] (1611)
1 : a ring or cap usually of metal put around a slender shaft (as a cane or a tool handle) to strengthen it or prevent splitting
2 : a usually metal sleeve used especially for joining or binding one part to another (as pipe sections or the bristles and handle of a brush)
— **fer·ruled** *adjective*

¹**fer·ry** \'fer-ē\ *verb* **fer·ried; fer·ry·ing** [Middle English *ferien,* from Old English *ferian* to carry, convey; akin to Old English *faran* to go — more at FARE] (before 12th century)
transitive verb
1 a : to carry by boat over a body of water **b** : to cross by a ferry
2 a : to convey (as by aircraft or motor vehicle) from one place to another : TRANSPORT **b** : to fly (an airplane) from the factory or other shipping point to a designated delivery point or from one base to another
intransitive verb
: to cross water in a boat

²**ferry** *noun, plural* **fer·ries** (15th century)
1 : a place where persons or things are carried across a body of water (as a river) in a boat
2 : FERRYBOAT
3 : a franchise or right to operate a ferry service across a body of water
4 : an organized service and route for flying airplanes especially across a sea or continent for delivery to the user

fer·ry·boat \'fer-ē-ˌbōt\ *noun* (15th century)
: a boat used to ferry passengers, vehicles, or goods

fer·ry·man \-mən\ *noun* (15th century)
: a person who operates a ferry

fer·tile \'fər-t³l\ *adjective* [Middle English, from Middle French & Latin; Middle French, from Latin *fertilis,* from *ferre* to carry, bear — more at BEAR] (15th century)
1 a : producing or bearing fruit in great quantities : PRODUCTIVE **b** : characterized by great resourcefulness of thought or imagination : INVENTIVE ⟨a *fertile* mind⟩ **c** *obsolete* : PLENTIFUL
2 a (1) : capable of sustaining abundant plant growth ⟨*fertile* soil⟩ (2) : affording abundant possibilities for development ⟨a *fertile* area for research⟩ **b** : capable of growing or developing ⟨*fertile* egg⟩ **c** (1) : capable of producing fruit (2) *of an anther* : containing pollen (3) : developing spores or spore-bearing organs **d** : capable of breeding or reproducing
3 : capable of being converted into fissionable material ⟨*fertile* uranium 238⟩ ☆
— **fer·tile·ly** \-t³l-(l)ē\ *adverb*
— **fer·tile·ness** \-t³l-nəs\ *noun*

fer·til·i·ty \(ˌ)fər-'ti-lə-tē\ *noun* (15th century)
1 : the quality or state of being fertile
2 : the birthrate of a population

fer·til·iza·tion \ˌfər-t³l-ə-'zā-shən\ *noun* (circa 1787)
: an act or process of making fertile: as **a** : the application of fertilizer **b** (1) : an act or process of fecundation, insemination, or pollination — not used technically (2) : the process of union of two gametes whereby the somatic chromosome number is restored and the development of a new individual is initiated

fertilization membrane *noun* (1931)
: a resistant membranous layer in eggs of many animals that forms following fertilization by the thickening and separation of the vitelline membrane from the cell surface and that prevents multiple fertilization

fer·til·ize \'fər-t³l-ˌīz\ *transitive verb* **-ized; -iz·ing** (1648)
: to make fertile: as **a** : to apply a fertilizer to ⟨*fertilize* land⟩ **b** : to cause the fertilization of
— **fer·til·iz·able** \-ˌī-zə-bəl\ *adjective*

fer·til·iz·er \-ˌī-zər\ *noun* (circa 1661)
: one that fertilizes; *specifically* : a substance (as manure or a chemical mixture) used to make soil more fertile

fer·ule \'fer-əl\ *also* **fer·u·la** \'fer-(y)ə-lə\ *noun* [Latin *ferula* giant fennel, ferule] (1580)
1 : an instrument (as a flat piece of wood like a ruler) used to punish children
2 : school discipline

fe·ru·lic acid \fə-'rü-lik-\ *noun* [ferula] (1876)
: a white crystalline acid that is structurally related to vanillin and is obtained especially from plant sources (as aspen bark)

fer·ven·cy \'fər-vən(t)-sē\ *noun, plural* **-cies** (15th century)
: FERVOR

fer·vent \'fər-vənt\ *adjective* [Middle English, from Middle French & Latin; Middle French, from Latin *fervent-, fervens,* present participle of *fervēre* to boil, froth — more at BARM] (14th century)
1 : very hot : GLOWING
2 : exhibiting or marked by great intensity of feeling : ZEALOUS ⟨*fervent* prayers⟩
synonym see IMPASSIONED
— **fer·vent·ly** *adverb*

fer·vid \'fər-vəd\ *adjective* [Latin *fervidus,* from *fervēre*] (1599)
1 : very hot : BURNING
2 : marked by often extreme fervor ⟨a *fervid* crusader⟩
synonym see IMPASSIONED
— **fer·vid·ly** *adverb*
— **fer·vid·ness** *noun*

fer·vor \'fər-vər\ *noun* [Middle English *fervour,* from Middle French & Latin; Middle French *ferveur,* from Latin *fervor,* from *fervēre*] (14th century)
1 : intensity of feeling or expression ⟨booing and cheering with almost equal *fervor* —Alan Rich⟩
2 : intense heat
synonym see PASSION

fer·vour *chiefly British variant of* FERVOR

fes·cen·nine \'fe-s³n-ˌīn, -ˌēn\ *adjective* [Latin *fescennini* (*versus*), ribald songs sung at rustic weddings, probably from *Fescinninus* of Fescennium, from *Fescennium,* town in Etruria] (1601)
: SCURRILOUS, OBSCENE

fes·cue \'fes-(ˌ)kyü\ *noun* [Middle English *festu* stalk, straw, from Middle French, from Late Latin *festucum,* from Latin *festuca*] (1513)
1 : a small pointer (as a stick) used to point out letters to children learning to read

☆ **SYNONYMS**
Fertile, fecund, fruitful, prolific mean producing or capable of producing offspring or fruit. FERTILE implies the power to reproduce in kind or to assist in reproduction and growth ⟨*fertile* soil⟩; applied figuratively, it suggests readiness of invention and development ⟨a *fertile* imagination⟩. FECUND emphasizes abundance or rapidity in bearing fruit or offspring ⟨a *fecund* herd⟩. FRUITFUL adds to FERTILE and FECUND the implication of desirable or useful results ⟨*fruitful* research⟩. PROLIFIC stresses rapidity of spreading or multiplying by or as if by natural reproduction ⟨a *prolific* writer⟩.

\ə\ abut \³\ kitten \ər\ further \a\ ash \ā\ ace
\ä\ mop, mar \au̇\ out \ch\ chin \e\ bet \ē\ easy
\g\ go \i\ hit \ī\ ice \j\ job \ŋ\ sing \ō\ go
\ȯ\ law \ȯi\ boy \th\ thin \t̲h̲\ the \ü\ loot \u̇\ foot
\y\ yet \zh\ vision *see also* Guide to Pronunciation

2 : any of a genus (*Festuca*) of tufted perennial grasses with panicled spikelets
fescue foot *noun* (1949)
: a disease of the feet of cattle resembling ergotism that is associated with feeding on fescue grass and especially tall fescue
¹**fess** *also* **fesse** \'fes\ *noun* [Middle English *fesse*, from Middle French *faisse*, from Latin *fascia* band — more at FASCIA] (15th century)
1 : a broad horizontal bar across the middle of a heraldic field
2 : the center point of an armorial escutcheon
²**fess** \'fes\ *intransitive verb* [short for *confess*] (1840)
: to own up : CONFESS — usually used with *up*
-fest \,fest\ *noun combining form* [German, from *Fest* celebration, from Latin *festum* — more at FEAST]
: meeting or occasion marked by (such) activity ⟨song*fest*⟩
fes·tal \'fes-t°l\ *adjective* [Latin *festum*] (15th century)
: of or relating to a feast or festival : FESTIVE
— **fes·tal·ly** \-t°l-ē\ *adverb*
¹**fes·ter** \'fes-tər\ *noun* [Middle English, from Middle French *festre*, from Latin *fistula* pipe, fistulous ulcer] (14th century)
: a suppurating sore : PUSTULE
²**fester** *verb* **fes·tered; fes·ter·ing** \-t(ə-)riŋ\ (14th century)
intransitive verb
1 : to generate pus
2 : PUTREFY, ROT
3 a : to cause increasing poisoning, irritation, or bitterness : RANKLE ⟨dissent *festered* unchecked⟩ **b :** to undergo or exist in a state of progressive deterioration ⟨allowed slums to *fester*⟩
transitive verb
: to make inflamed or corrupt
¹**fes·ti·nate** \'fes-tə-,nāt\ *verb* **-nat·ed; -nat·ing** (1596)
: HASTEN
²**fes·ti·nate** \-nət, -,nāt\ *adjective* [Latin *festinatus*, past participle of *festinare* to hasten; perhaps akin to Middle Irish *bras* forceful, Welsh *brys* haste] (1605)
: HASTY
— **fes·ti·nate·ly** *adverb*
¹**fes·ti·val** \'fes-tə-vəl\ *adjective* [Middle English, from Middle French, from Latin *festivus* festive] (14th century)
: of, relating to, appropriate to, or set apart as a festival
²**festival** *noun* (1589)
1 a : a time of celebration marked by special observances **b :** FEAST 2
2 : a periodic season or program of cultural events or entertainment
3 : GAIETY, CONVIVIALITY
fes·ti·val·go·er \-,gō-(-ə)r\ *noun* (1959)
: one who attends a festival
fes·tive \'fes-tiv\ *adjective* [Latin *festivus*, from *festum*] (1651)
1 : of, relating to, or suitable for a feast or festival
2 : JOYFUL, GAY
— **fes·tive·ly** *adverb*
— **fes·tive·ness** *noun*
fes·tiv·i·ty \fes-'ti-və-tē, fəs-\ *noun, plural* **-ties** (14th century)
1 : FESTIVAL 1
2 : the quality or state of being festive : GAIETY
3 : festive activity
¹**fes·toon** \fes-'tün\ *noun* [French *feston*, from Italian *festone*, from *festa* festival, from Latin — more at FEAST] (1630)
1 : a decorative chain or strip hanging between two points
2 : a carved, molded, or painted ornament representing a decorative chain
²**festoon** *transitive verb* (1800)
1 : to hang or form festoons on
2 : to shape into festoons

3 : DECORATE, ADORN
fes·toon·ery \fes-'tü-nə-rē\ *noun* (1836)
: an arrangement of festoons
Fest·schrift \'fes(t)-,shrift\ *noun, plural* **Fest·schrif·ten** \-,shrif-tən\ *or* **Fest·schrifts** [German, from *Fest* celebration + *Schrift* writing] (1898)
: a volume of writings by different authors presented as a tribute or memorial especially to a scholar
fe·ta \'fe-tə, 'fe-,tä\ *noun, often capitalized* [New Greek (*tyri*) *pheta*, from *tyri* cheese + *pheta* slice, from Italian *fetta* — more at FETTUCCINE] (1940)
: a white moderately hard and crumbly Greek cheese made from sheep's or goat's milk and cured in brine
fe·tal \'fē-t°l\ *adjective* (1811)
: of, relating to, or being a fetus
fetal alcohol syndrome *noun* (1974)
: a highly variable group of birth defects including mental retardation, deficient growth, and defects of the skull, face, and brain that tend to occur in the infants of women who consume large amounts of alcohol during pregnancy
fetal hemoglobin *noun* (1950)
: a hemoglobin variant that predominates in the blood of a newborn and persists in increased proportions in some forms of anemia (as thalassemia)
fetal position *noun* (1963)
: a position (as of a sleeping person) in which the body lies on one side, curled up with the arms and legs drawn up toward the chest and the head bowed forward
¹**fetch** \'fech\ *verb* [Middle English *fecchen*, from Old English *fetian, feccan*; perhaps akin to Old English *fōt* foot — more at FOOT] (before 12th century)
transitive verb
1 a : to go or come after and bring or take back **b :** DERIVE, DEDUCE
2 a : to cause to come **b :** to bring in (as a price) : REALIZE **c :** INTEREST, ATTRACT
3 a : to give (a blow) by striking : DEAL **b** *chiefly dialect* : BRING ABOUT, ACCOMPLISH **c** (1) : to take in (as a breath) : DRAW (2) : to bring forth (as a sound) : HEAVE ⟨*fetch* a sigh⟩
4 a : to reach by sailing especially against the wind or tide **b :** to arrive at : REACH
intransitive verb
1 : to get and bring something; *specifically* : to retrieve killed game
2 : to take a roundabout way : CIRCLE
3 a : to hold a course on a body of water **b** : VEER
— **fetch·er** *noun*
²**fetch** *noun* (circa 1530)
1 : TRICK, STRATAGEM
2 : an act or instance of fetching
3 a : the distance along open water or land over which the wind blows **b :** the distance traversed by waves without obstruction
³**fetch** *noun* [origin unknown] (circa 1787)
: DOPPELGÄNGER 1
fetch·ing \'fe-chiŋ\ *adjective* (1880)
: ATTRACTIVE, PLEASING
— **fetch·ing·ly** \-chiŋ-lē\ *adverb*
fetch up (1599)
transitive verb
1 : to bring up or out : PRODUCE
2 : to make up (as lost time)
3 : to bring to a stop
intransitive verb
: to reach a standstill, stopping place, or goal : end up ⟨may have *fetched up* running a village store —Geoffrey Household⟩
¹**fete** *or* **fête** \'fāt, 'fet\ *noun* [Middle English *fete*, from Middle French, from Old French *feste* — more at FEAST] (15th century)
1 : FESTIVAL
2 a : a lavish often outdoor entertainment **b** : a large elaborate party
²**fete** *or* **fête** *transitive verb* **fet·ed** *or* **fêt·ed; fet·ing** *or* **fêt·ing** (1819)

1 : to honor or commemorate with a fete
2 : to pay high honor to
fête cham·pê·tre \,fāt-,shä(m)-'petr°, ,fet-\ *noun, plural* **fêtes cham·pê·tres** *same*\ [French, literally, rural festival] (1774)
: an outdoor entertainment
fe·ti·cide \'fē-tə-,sīd\ *noun* (circa 1844)
: the act of causing the death of a fetus
fet·id \'fe-təd, *especially British* 'fē-tid\ *adjective* [Middle English, from Latin *foetidus*, from *foetēre* to stink] (15th century)
: having a heavy offensive smell
synonym see MALODOROUS
— **fet·id·ly** *adverb*
— **fet·id·ness** *noun*
fe·tish *also* **fe·tich** \'fe-tish *also* 'fē-\ *noun* [French & Portuguese; French *fétiche*, from Portuguese *feitiço*, from *feitiço* artificial, false, from Latin *facticius* factitious] (1613)
1 a : an object (as a small stone carving of an animal) believed to have magical power to protect or aid its owner; *broadly* : a material object regarded with superstitious or extravagant trust or reverence **b :** an object of irrational reverence or obsessive devotion : PREPOSSESSION **c :** an object or bodily part whose real or fantasied presence is psychologically necessary for sexual gratification and that is an object of fixation to the extent that it may interfere with complete sexual expression
2 : a rite or cult of fetish worshipers
3 : FIXATION ◇
fe·tish·ism *also* **fe·tich·ism** \-tish-,i-zəm\ *noun* (1801)
1 : belief in magical fetishes
2 : extravagant irrational devotion
3 : the pathological displacement of erotic interest and satisfaction to a fetish
— **fe·tish·ist** \-tish-ist\ *noun*
— **fe·tish·is·tic** \,fe-ti-'shis-tik *also* ,fē-\ *adjective*
— **fe·tish·is·ti·cal·ly** \-ti-k(ə-)lē\ *adverb*
fet·lock \'fet-,läk\ *noun* [Middle English *fitlok, fetlak*; akin to Old English *fōt* foot] (14th century)
1 a : a projection bearing a tuft of hair on the back of the leg above the hoof of a horse or similar animal — see HORSE illustration **b** : the tuft of hair itself
2 : the joint of the limb at the fetlock
feto- *or* **feti-** *combining form* [New Latin *fetus*]
: fetus ⟨*feti*cide⟩
fe·tol·o·gy \fē-'tä-lə-jē\ *noun* (1965)

◇ WORD HISTORY
fetish The Portuguese word *feitiço* "charm, amulet" is descended from Latin *facticius* "made, artificial," a derivative of *facere* "to make, do." These Latin words are also the source of English *factitious*. When in the 15th century the Portuguese began to encounter and soon enslave peoples of West Africa, they applied *feitiço* to African religious objects, whether natural or man-made. English borrowed this word in the 17th century, at first directly from Portuguese (in spellings such as *fetisso*). Later it was borrowed again through French *fétiche*, itself ultimately from Portuguese, which gave rise to the current English form *fetish*. Both in English and other languages that borrowed it, the meaning of the word was extended to any object thought to be irrationally or obsessively worshiped. *Fetish* was given new life when it was used at the end of the 19th century by Havelock Ellis, a pioneering student of human sexuality, to refer to objects of displaced sexual obsession, and the term was adopted by psychoanalytic theorists such as Sigmund Freud, who first used the German equivalent *Fetisch* in 1905.

: a branch of medical science concerned with the study and treatment of the fetus in the uterus
— **fe·tol·o·gist** \-jist\ *noun*

fe·to·pro·tein \ˌfē-tō-'prō-ˌtēn, -'prō-tē-ən\ *noun* (1965)
: any of several fetal antigens present in the adult in some abnormal conditions

fe·tor \'fē-tər, 'fē-ˌtȯr\ *noun* [Middle English *fetoure*, from Latin *foetor*, from *foetēre*] (15th century)
: a strong offensive smell : STENCH

fe·tos·co·py \fē-'täs-kə-pē\ *noun, plural* **-pies** (1971)
: examination of the pregnant uterus by means of a fiber-optic tube
— **fe·to·scope** \'fē-tə-ˌskōp\ *noun*

¹**fet·ter** \'fe-tər\ *noun* [Middle English *feter*, from Old English; akin to Old English *fōt* foot] (before 12th century)
1 : a chain or shackle for the feet
2 : something that confines : RESTRAINT

²**fetter** *transitive verb* (before 12th century)
1 : to put fetters on : SHACKLE
2 : to restrain from motion, action, or progress
synonym see HAMPER

¹**fet·tle** \'fe-tᵊl\ *noun* (1740)
: state or condition of health, fitness, wholeness, spirit, or form — often used in the phrase *in fine fettle*

²**fettle** *transitive verb* **fet·tled; fet·tling** \'fet-liŋ, 'fe-tᵊl-iŋ\ [Middle English *fetlen* to shape, prepare; perhaps akin to Old English *fæt* vessel — more at VAT] (1881)
: to cover or line the hearth of (as a reverberatory furnace) with loose material (as sand or gravel)

fet·tuc·ci·ne *or* **fet·tuc·ci·ni** *or* **fet·tu·ci·ne** *or* **fet·tu·ci·ni** \ˌfe-tə-'chē-nē\ *noun plural but singular or plural in construction* [Italian, plural of *fettuccina*, diminutive of *fettuccia* small slice, ribbon, diminutive of *fetta* slice, probably alteration of (assumed) *offetta*, from *offa* flour cake, from Latin] (1912)
: pasta in the form of narrow ribbons; *also* : a dish of which fettuccine forms the base

fettuccine Al·fre·do \-ˌ(ˌ)al-'frā-(ˌ)dō, -ˌ(ˌ)äl-\ *noun* [from *Alfredo all'Augusteo*, restaurant in Rome where it originated] (1961)
: a dish consisting of fettuccine with butter, Parmesan cheese, cream, and seasonings — called also *fettuccine all'Alfredo* \-ˌal-(ˌ)al-, -ˌäl-(ˌ)äl-\

fe·tus \'fē-təs\ *noun* [Middle English, from Latin, act of bearing young, offspring; akin to Latin *fetus* newly delivered, fruitful — more at FEMININE] (14th century)
: an unborn or unhatched vertebrate especially after attaining the basic structural plan of its kind; *specifically* : a developing human from usually three months after conception to birth

¹**feud** \'fyüd\ *noun* [alteration of Middle English *feide*, from Middle French, of Germanic origin; akin to Old High German *fēhida* hostility, feud, Old English *fāh* hostile — more at FOE] (15th century)
: a mutual enmity or quarrel that is often prolonged or inveterate; *especially* : a lasting state of hostilities between families or clans marked by violent attacks for revenge
— **feud** *intransitive verb*

²**feud** *noun* [Medieval Latin *feodum, feudum*, of Germanic origin; akin to Old English *feoh* cattle, property — more at FEE] (1614)
: FEE 1a

feu·dal \'fyü-dᵊl\ *adjective* (1612)
1 : of, relating to, or having the characteristics of a medieval fee
2 : of, relating to, or suggestive of feudalism ⟨*feudal* law⟩
— **feu·dal·ly** \-dᵊl-ē\ *adverb*

feu·dal·ism \'fyü-dᵊl-ˌi-zəm\ *noun* (circa 1818)
1 : the system of political organization prevailing in Europe from the 9th to about the 15th centuries having as its basis the relation of lord to vassal with all land held in fee and as chief characteristics homage, the service of tenants under arms and in court, wardship, and forfeiture
2 : any of various political or social systems similar to medieval feudalism
— **feu·dal·ist** \-dᵊl-ist\ *noun*
— **feu·dal·is·tic** \ˌfyü-dᵊl-'is-tik\ *adjective*

feu·dal·i·ty \fyü-'da-lə-tē\ *noun, plural* **-ties** (1790)
1 : the quality or state of being feudal
2 : a feudal holding, domain, or concentration of power

feu·dal·ize \'fyü-dᵊl-ˌīz\ *transitive verb* **-ized; -iz·ing** (1828)
: to make feudal
— **feu·dal·iza·tion** \ˌfyü-dᵊl-ə-'zā-shən\ *noun*

¹**feu·da·to·ry** \'fyü-də-ˌtȯr-ē, -ˌtȯr-\ *adjective* [Medieval Latin *feudatorius*, from *feudatus*, past participle of *feudare* to enfeoff, from *feudum*] (1592)
1 : owing feudal allegiance
2 : being under the overlordship of a foreign state

²**feudatory** *noun, plural* **-ries** (1644)
1 : a dependent lordship : FEE
2 : one holding lands by feudal tenure

¹**feud·ist** \'fyü-dist\ *noun* (1607)
: a specialist in feudal law

²**feudist** *noun* (1901)
: one who feuds

feuil·le·ton \ˌfə-yə-'tōⁿ, -fər-, -fœ-\ *noun* [French, from *feuillet* sheet of paper, from Old French *foillet*, diminutive of *foille* leaf — more at FOIL] (1845)
1 : a part of a European newspaper or magazine devoted to material designed to entertain the general reader
2 : something (as an installment of a novel) printed in a feuilleton
3 a : a novel printed in installments **b** : a work of fiction catering to popular taste
4 : a short literary composition often having a familiar tone and reminiscent content
— **feuil·le·ton·ism** \-'tō(ⁿ)-ˌni-zəm\ *noun*
— **feuil·le·ton·ist** \-nist\ *noun*

Feul·gen \'fȯil-gən\ *adjective* (1928)
: of, relating to, utilizing, or staining by the Feulgen reaction ⟨positive *Feulgen* mitochondria⟩

Feulgen reaction *noun* [Robert *Feulgen* (died 1955) German physiologist] (1928)
: the development of a brilliant purple color by DNA in a microscopic preparation stained with a modified Schiff's reagent

¹**fe·ver** \'fē-vər\ *noun* [Middle English, from Old English *fēfer*, from Latin *febris*] (before 12th century)
1 a : a rise of body temperature above the normal **b** : any of various diseases of which fever is a prominent symptom
2 a : a state of heightened or intense emotion or activity **b** : a contagious usually transient enthusiasm : CRAZE

²**fever** *verb* **fe·vered; fe·ver·ing** \'fē-v(ə-)riŋ\ (1606)
transitive verb
: to throw into a fever : AGITATE
intransitive verb
: to contract or be in a fever : become feverish

fever blister *noun* (circa 1860)
: COLD SORE

fe·ver·few \'fē-vər-ˌfyü\ *noun* [Middle English, from Old English *feferfuge*, from Late Latin *febrifugia* centaury — more at FEBRIFUGE] (15th century)
: a perennial European composite herb (*Chrysanthemum parthenium*) widely cultivated as an ornamental

fe·ver·ish \'fē-v(ə-)rish\ *adjective* (14th century)
1 a : tending to cause fever **b** : having the symptoms of a fever **c** : indicating or relating to fever
2 : marked by intense emotion, activity, or instability
— **fe·ver·ish·ly** *adverb*
— **fe·ver·ish·ness** *noun*

fe·ver·ous \'fē-v(ə-)rəs\ *adjective* (14th century)
: FEVERISH

fever pitch *noun* (1915)
: a state of intense excitement and agitation

fever tree *noun* (1868)
: any of several shrubs or trees that are thought to indicate regions free from fever or that yield remedies for fever; *especially* : an African acacia (*Acacia xanthlophloea*)

fe·ver·wort \'fē-vər-ˌwərt, -ˌwȯrt\ *noun* (circa 1814)
: a coarse American herb (*Triosteum perfoliatum*) of the honeysuckle family — called also *horse gentian*

¹**few** \'fyü\ *pronoun, plural in construction* [Middle English *fewe*, pronoun & adjective, from Old English *fēawa;* akin to Old High German *fō* little, Latin *paucus* little, *pauper* poor, Greek *paid-, pais* child, Sanskrit *putra* son] (before 12th century)
: not many persons or things ⟨*few* were present⟩ ⟨*few* of his stories are true⟩

²**few** *adjective* (before 12th century)
1 : consisting of or amounting to only a small number ⟨one of our *few* pleasures⟩
2 : at least some but indeterminately small in number — used with *a* ⟨caught a *few* fish⟩
— **few·ness** *noun*
— **few and far between** : few in number and infrequently met : RARE

³**few** *noun, plural in construction* (before 12th century)
1 : a small number of units or individuals ⟨a *few* of them⟩
2 : a special limited number ⟨the discriminating *few*⟩

¹**few·er** \'fyü-ər, 'fyür\ *pronoun, plural in construction* (before 12th century)
: a smaller number of persons or things

²**fewer** *adjective, comparative of* FEW
usage see LESS

few·trils \'fyü-trəlz\ *noun plural* [origin unknown] (circa 1750)
dialect English : things of little value : TRIFLES

fey \'fā\ *adjective* [Middle English *feye*, from Old English *fǣge;* akin to Old High German *feigi* fey and perhaps to Old English *fāh* hostile, outlawed — more at FOE] (before 12th century)
1 a *chiefly Scottish* : fated to die : DOOMED **b** : marked by a foreboding of death or calamity
2 a : able to see into the future : VISIONARY **b** : marked by an otherworldly air or attitude **c** : CRAZY, TOUCHED
3 b : UNCONVENTIONAL, CAMPY **3 b** : PRECIOUS
— **fey·ly** *adverb*
— **fey·ness** *noun*

fez \'fez\ *noun, plural* **fez·zes** *also* **fez·es** [French, from *Fez*, Morocco] (circa 1803)
: a brimless cone-shaped flat-crowned hat that usually has a tassel, is usually made of red felt, and is worn especially by men in eastern Mediterranean countries
— **fezzed** \'fezd\ *adjective*

fez

fi·acre \fē-'äkrᵊ\ *noun, plural* **fi·acres** *same, or* -'äk-rəz\ [French, from the Hotel Saint *Fiacre*, Paris] (1699)
: a small hackney coach

fi·an·cé \ˌfē-ˌän-'sā, fē-'än-\ *noun* [French, from Middle French, from past participle of *fiancer* to promise, betroth, from

Old French *fiancier,* from *fiance* promise, trust, from *fier* to trust, from (assumed) Vulgar Latin *fidare,* alteration of Latin *fidere —* more at BIDE] (1864)
: a man engaged to be married

fi·an·cée \ˌfē-ˌän-'sā, fē-'än-\ *noun* [French, feminine of *fiancé*] (1853)
: a woman engaged to be married

fi·an·chet·to \ˌfē-ən-'ke-(ˌ)tō, -'che-\ *verb* [*fianchetto* (an opening in chess), from Italian, diminutive of *fianco* side, flank, from Old French *flanc —* more at FLANK] (1927)
transitive verb
: to develop (a bishop) in a chess game to the second square on the adjacent knight's file
intransitive verb
: to fianchetto a bishop in a chess game

¹fi·as·co \fē-'as-(ˌ)kō *also* -'äs-\ *noun, plural* **-coes** [French, from Italian, from *fare fiasco,* literally, to make a bottle] (circa 1854)
: a complete failure ◇

²fi·as·co \fē-'as-(ˌ)kō, -'as-\ *noun, plural* **-coes** *also* **fi·as·chi** \-(ˌ)kē\ [Italian, from Late Latin *flasco* bottle — more at FLASK] (1887)
: BOTTLE, FLASK; *especially* : a bulbous long-necked straw-covered bottle for wine

fi·at \'fē-ət, -ˌat, -ˌät; 'fī-ət, -ˌat\ *noun* [Latin, let it be done, 3d singular present subjunctive of *fieri* to become, be done — more at BE] (circa 1631)
1 : a command or act of will that creates something without or as if without further effort
2 : an authoritative determination : DICTATE ⟨a *fiat* of conscience⟩
3 : an authoritative or arbitrary order : DECREE ⟨government by *fiat*⟩

fiat money *noun* (1876)
: money (as paper currency) not convertible into coin or specie of equivalent value

¹fib \'fib\ *noun* [perhaps by shortening & alteration from *fable*] (1611)
: a trivial or childish lie

²fib *intransitive verb* **fibbed; fib·bing** (1690)
: to tell a fib
synonym see LIE
— **fib·ber** *noun*

³fib *verb* **fibbed; fib·bing** [origin unknown] (circa 1665)
British : BEAT, PUMMEL

fi·ber *or* **fi·bre** \'fī-bər\ *noun* [French *fibre,* from Latin *fibra*] (1540)
1 : a thread or a structure or object resembling a thread: as **a** (1) : a slender root (as of a grass) (2) : an elongated tapering thick-walled plant cell void at maturity that imparts elasticity, flexibility, and tensile strength **b** (1) : a strand of nerve tissue : AXON, DENDRITE (2) : one of the filaments composing most of the intercellular matrix of connective tissue (3) : one of the elongated contractile cells of muscle tissue **c** : a slender and greatly elongated natural or synthetic filament (as of wool, cotton, asbestos, gold, glass, or rayon) typically capable of being spun into yarn **d** : indigestible material in human food that stimulates the intestine to peristalsis — called also *bulk,* *roughage*
2 : material made of fibers; *especially* : VULCANIZED FIBER
3 a : an element that gives texture or substance **b** : basic toughness : STRENGTH, FORTITUDE **c** : essential structure or character ⟨the very *fiber* of a person's being⟩
— **fi·bered** \-bərd\ *adjective*

fi·ber·board *also* **fi·bre·board** \-ˌbōrd, -ˌbòrd\ *noun* (1897)
: a material made by compressing fibers (as of wood) into stiff sheets; *also* : PAPERBOARD

fi·ber·fill *also* **fi·bre·fill** \-ˌfil\ *noun* (1962)
: synthetic fibers used as a filling material (as for cushions)

¹fi·ber·glass *also* **fi·bre·glass** \-ˌglas\ *noun* (1937)

1 : glass in fibrous form used in making various products (as glass wool for insulation)
2 : a composite structural material of plastic and fiberglass

²fiberglass *transitive verb* (1967)
: to protect or repair by the application of fiberglass

fi·ber·ize \'fī-bə-ˌrīz\ *transitive verb* **-ized; -iz·ing** (1925)
: to make or break down into fibers
— **fi·ber·iza·tion** \ˌfī-b(ə-)rə-'zā-shən\ *noun*

fi·ber–op·tic \'fī-bə-ˌräp-tik\ *adjective* (1961)
: of, relating to, or using fiber optics

fiber optics *noun plural* (1956)
1 : thin transparent fibers of glass or plastic that are enclosed by material of a lower index of refraction and that transmit light throughout their length by internal reflections; *also* : a bundle of such fibers used in an instrument (as for viewing body cavities)
2 *singular in construction* : the technique of the use of fiber optics

fi·ber·scope \'fī-bər-ˌskōp\ *noun* (1954)
: a flexible instrument utilizing fiber optics and used for examination of inaccessible areas

Fi·bo·nac·ci number \ˌfē-bə-'nä-chē-, ˌfī-bə-\ *noun* [Leonardo *Fibonacci* (died *about* 1250) Italian mathematician] (1914)
: an integer in the infinite sequence 1, 1, 2, 3, 5, 8, 13, . . . of which the first two terms are 1 and 1 and each succeeding term is the sum of the two immediately preceding

fibr- *or* **fibro-** *combining form* [Latin *fibra*]
: fiber : fibrous tissue ⟨*fibroid*⟩ : fibrous and ⟨*fibro*vascular⟩

fi·branne \'fī-ˌbran, fī-\ *noun* [French, viscose rayon, from *fibre*] (1941)
: a fabric made of spun-rayon yarn

fi·bril \'fī-brəl, 'fi-\ *noun* [New Latin *fibrilla,* diminutive of Latin *fibra*] (1664)
: a small filament or fiber: as **a** : ROOT HAIR **b** (1) : one of the fine threads into which a striated muscle fiber can be longitudinally split (2) : NEUROFIBRIL
— **fi·bril·lar** \'fi-brə-lər, 'fī-\ *adjective*

fi·bril·late \'fi-brə-ˌlāt, 'fī-\ *verb* **-lat·ed; -lat·ing** (circa 1847)
intransitive verb
: to undergo or exhibit fibrillation
transitive verb
: to cause to undergo fibrillation

fi·bril·la·tion \ˌfi-brə-'lā-shən, ˌfī-\ *noun* (1845)
1 : an act or process of forming fibers or fibrils
2 a : a muscular twitching involving individual muscle fibers acting without coordination **b** : very rapid irregular contractions of the muscle fibers of the heart resulting in a lack of synchronism between heartbeat and pulse

fi·brin \'fī-brən\ *noun* (1800)
: a white insoluble fibrous protein formed from fibrinogen by the action of thrombin especially in the clotting of blood

fi·brin·o·gen \fī-'bri-nə-jən\ *noun* [International Scientific Vocabulary] (1872)
: a plasma protein that is produced in the liver and is converted into fibrin during blood clot formation

fi·bri·noid \'fi-brə-ˌnòid, 'fī-\ *noun, often attributive* (1910)
: a homogeneous acidophilic refractile material that somewhat resembles fibrin and is formed in the walls of blood vessels and in connective tissue in some pathological conditions and normally in the placenta

fi·bri·no·ly·sin \ˌfī-brə-nºl-'ī-sºn\ *noun* [International Scientific Vocabulary] (1915)
: any of several proteolytic enzymes that promote the dissolution of blood clots; *especially* : PLASMIN

fi·bri·no·ly·sis \-'ī-səs, -brə-'nä-lə-səs\ *noun* [New Latin] (1907)

: the usually enzymatic breakdown of fibrin
— **fi·bri·no·lyt·ic** \-brə-nºl-'i-tik\ *adjective*

fi·bri·no·pep·tide \ˌfī-brə-nō-'pep-ˌtīd\ *noun* (1960)
: any of the vertebrate polypeptides that are cleaved from fibrinogen by thrombin during blood clot formation

fi·bro·blast \'fī-brə-ˌblast, 'fi-\ *noun* [International Scientific Vocabulary] (1876)
: a connective-tissue cell of mesenchymal origin that secretes proteins and especially molecular collagen from which the extracellular fibrillar matrix of connective tissue forms
— **fi·bro·blas·tic** \ˌfī-brə-'blas-tik, ˌfi-\ *adjective*

fi·bro·cys·tic \ˌfī-brə-'sis-tik, ˌfi-\ *adjective* (1854)
: characterized by the presence or development of fibrous tissue and cysts

¹fi·broid \'fī-ˌbròid, 'fi-\ *adjective* (1852)
: resembling, forming, or consisting of fibrous tissue

²fibroid *noun* (circa 1860)
: a benign tumor that consists of fibrous and muscular tissue and occurs especially in the uterine wall

fi·bro·in \'fī-brə-wən, 'fi-\ *noun* [French *fibroïne,* from *fibr-* + *-ine* -in] (1878)
: an insoluble protein comprising the filaments of the raw silk fiber

fi·bro·ma \fī-'brō-mə\ *noun, plural* **-mas** *also* **-ma·ta** \-mə-tə\ (circa 1849)
: a benign tumor consisting mainly of fibrous tissue
— **fi·bro·ma·tous** \-mə-təs\ *adjective*

fi·bro·nec·tin \ˌfī-brō-'nek-tən\ *noun* [*fibr-* + Latin *nectere* to tie, bind + English *-in*] (1976)
: any of a group of glycoproteins of cell surfaces, blood plasma, and connective tissue that promote cellular adhesion and migration

fi·bro·sar·co·ma \ˌfī-brə-sär-'kō-mə, ˌfi-\ *noun* (1878)
: a sarcoma of relatively low malignancy consisting chiefly of spindle-shaped cells that tend to form collagenous fibrils

fi·bro·sis \fī-'brō-səs\ *noun* [New Latin] (1873)
: a condition marked by increase of interstitial fibrous tissue
— **fi·brot·ic** \-'brä-tik\ *adjective*

fi·bro·si·tis \ˌfī-brə-'sī-təs, -brə-\ *noun* [New Latin, from *fibrosus* fibrous, from International Scientific Vocabulary *fibrous*] (1904)

: a rheumatic disorder of fibrous tissue

fi·brous \'fī-brəs\ *adjective* [modification of French *fibreux,* from *fibre* fiber] (1626)
1 a : containing, consisting of, or resembling fibers **b :** characterized by fibrosis **c :** capable of being separated into fibers ⟨a *fibrous* mineral⟩
2 : TOUGH, SINEWY ⟨*fibrous* texture⟩

fibrous root *noun* (1626)
: a root (as in most grasses) that has no prominent central axis and that branches in all directions

fi·bro·vas·cu·lar \ˌfī-brō-'vas-kyə-lər, ˌfi-\ *adjective* (1845)
: having or consisting of fibers and conducting cells

fibrovascular bundle *noun* (circa 1889)
: VASCULAR BUNDLE

fib·u·la \'fi-byə-lə\ *noun, plural* **-lae** \-lē, -lī\ *or* **-las** [Latin, pin, clasp; akin to Latin *figere* to fasten] (1615)
1 : the outer and usually smaller of the two bones between the knee and ankle in the hind or lower limbs of vertebrates
2 : a clasp resembling a safety pin used especially by the ancient Greeks and Romans
— **fib·u·lar** \-lər\ *adjective*

fibula 2

-fic \fik\ *adjective suffix* [Middle French & Latin; Middle French *-fique,* from Latin *-ficus,* from *facere* to make — more at DO]
: making : causing ⟨felici*fic*⟩

-fi·ca·tion \fə-'kā-shən\ *noun combining form* [Middle English *-ficacioun,* from Middle French & Latin; Middle French *-fication,* from Latin *-fication-, -ficatio,* from *-ficare* to make, from *-ficus*]
: making : production ⟨rei*fication*⟩

fice \'fīs\ *variant of* FEIST

fiche \'fēsh *also* 'fish\ *noun, plural* **fiche** *also* **fiches** (1951)
: MICROFICHE

fi·chu \'fi-ˌshü, 'fē-\ *noun* [French, from past participle of *ficher* to stick in, throw on, from (assumed) Vulgar Latin *figicare,* from Latin *figere* to fasten, pierce] (1803)
: a woman's light triangular scarf that is draped over the shoulders and fastened in front or worn to fill in a low neckline

fi·cin \'fī-sᵊn\ *noun* [Latin *ficus* fig] (1930)
: a protease obtained from the latex of fig trees and used as an anthelmintic and protein digestive

fick·le \'fi-kəl\ *adjective* [Middle English *fikel* deceitful, inconstant, from Old English *ficol* deceitful; akin to Old English be*fician* to deceive, and probably to Old English *fāh* hostile — more at FOE] (13th century)
: marked by lack of steadfastness, constancy, or stability : given to erratic changeableness
synonym see INCONSTANT
— **fick·le·ness** *noun*
— **fick·ly** \'fi-k(ə-)lē\ *adverb*

fi·co \'fē-(ˌ)kō\ *noun, plural* **ficoes** [obsolete *fico,* obscene gesture of contempt, modification of Italian *fica* fig, vulva, gesture of contempt, from (assumed) Vulgar Latin *fica* fig — more at FIG] (1598)
archaic : FIG 2

fic·tile \'fik-tᵊl, -ˌtīl\ *adjective* [Latin *fictilis* molded of clay, from *fingere*] (1626)
1 *archaic* : PLASTIC 2a
2 : of or relating to pottery
3 : MALLEABLE 2a

fic·tion \'fik-shən\ *noun* [Middle English *ficcioun,* from Middle French *fiction,* from Latin *fiction-, fictio* act of fashioning, fiction, from *fingere* to shape, fashion, feign — more at DOUGH] (14th century)
1 a : something invented by the imagination

or feigned; *specifically* : an invented story **b** : fictitious literature (as novels or short stories) **c :** a work of fiction; *especially* : NOVEL
2 a : an assumption of a possibility as a fact irrespective of the question of its truth ⟨a legal *fiction*⟩ **b :** a useful illusion or pretense
3 : the action of feigning or of creating with the imagination
— **fic·tion·al** \-shnəl, -shə-nᵊl\ *adjective*
— **fic·tion·al·i·ty** \ˌfik-shə-'na-lə-tē\ *noun*
— **fic·tion·al·ly** \'fik-shnə-lē, -shə-nᵊl-ē\ *adverb*

fictionalise *British variant of* FICTIONALIZE

fic·tion·al·ize \'fik-shnə-ˌlīz, -shə-nᵊl-ˌīz\ *transitive verb* **-ized; -iz·ing** (1918)
: to make into or treat in the manner of fiction ⟨*fictionalize* a biography⟩
— **fic·tion·al·iza·tion** \ˌfik-shnə-lə-'zā-shən, -shə-nᵊl-ə-\ *noun*

fic·tion·eer \ˌfik-shə-'nir\ *noun* (1923)
: one who writes fiction especially in quantity and without high standards
— **fic·tion·eer·ing** *noun*

fic·tion·ist \'fik-sh(ə-)nist\ *noun* (1829)
: a writer of fiction; *especially* : NOVELIST

fic·tion·ize \'fik-shə-ˌnīz\ *transitive verb* **-ized; -iz·ing** (1831)
: FICTIONALIZE
— **fic·tion·iza·tion** \ˌfik-shə-nə-'zā-shən\ *noun*

fic·ti·tious \fik-'ti-shəs\ *adjective* [Latin *ficticius* artificial, feigned, from *fictus*] (1634)
1 : of, relating to, or characteristic of fiction : IMAGINARY
2 a : conventionally or hypothetically assumed or accepted ⟨a *fictitious* concept⟩ **b** *of a name* : FALSE, ASSUMED
3 : not genuinely felt ☆
— **fic·ti·tious·ly** *adverb*
— **fic·ti·tious·ness** *noun*

fic·tive \'fik-tiv\ *adjective* (1612)
1 : not genuine : FEIGNED
2 : of, relating to, or capable of imaginative creation
3 : of, relating to, or having the characteristics of fiction : FICTIONAL
— **fic·tive·ly** *adverb*
— **fic·tive·ness** *noun*

fi·cus \'fī-kəs\ *noun, plural* **ficus** *or* **fi·cus·es** [New Latin, from Latin, fig] (1864)
: FIG 1b

fid \'fid\ *noun* [origin unknown] (1615)
: a tapered usually wooden pin used in opening the strands of a rope

-fid \fəd, ˌfid\ *adjective combining form* [Latin *-fidus,* from *findere* to split — more at BITE]
: divided into (so many) parts or (such) parts ⟨pinnati*fid*⟩

¹fid·dle \'fi-dᵊl\ *noun* [Middle English *fidel,* from (assumed) Old English *fithele,* probably from Medieval Latin *vitula*] (13th century)
1 : VIOLIN
2 : a device (as a slat, rack, or light railing) to keep dishes from sliding off a table aboard ship
3 : FIDDLESTICKS — used as an interjection
4 [²*fiddle*] *chiefly British* : SWINDLE

²fiddle *verb* **fid·dled; fid·dling** \'fid-liŋ, 'fi-dᵊl-iŋ\ (14th century)
intransitive verb
1 : to play on a fiddle
2 a : to move the hands or fingers restlessly **b** : to spend time in aimless or fruitless activity : PUTTER, TINKER ⟨*fiddled* around with the engine for hours⟩ **c :** MEDDLE, TAMPER
transitive verb
1 : to play (as a tune) on a fiddle
2 : CHEAT, SWINDLE
3 : to alter or manipulate deceptively for fraudulent gain ⟨accountants *fiddling* the books —Stanley Cohen⟩
— **fid·dler** \'fid-lər, 'fi-dᵊl-ər\ *noun*

fiddle away *transitive verb* (1667)
: to fritter away ⟨*fiddling* away the time⟩

fid·dle·back \'fi-dᵊl-ˌbak\ *noun* (1890)
: something resembling a fiddle

fid·dle·fad·dle \'fi-dᵊl-ˌfa-dᵊl\ *noun* [reduplication of *fiddle* (fiddlesticks)] (1577)
: NONSENSE — often used as an interjection

fid·dle·foot·ed \ˌfi-dᵊl-'fù-təd\ *adjective* (1941)
1 : SKITTISH, JUMPY ⟨a *fiddle-footed* horse⟩
2 : prone to wander ⟨the nameless *fiddle-footed* drifters, the shifty riders who traveled the back trails —Luke Short⟩

fid·dle·head \'fi-dᵊl-ˌhed\ *noun* (1882)
: one of the young unfurling fronds of some ferns that are often eaten as greens

fiddler crab *noun* (1843)
: any of a genus (*Uca*) of burrowing crabs in which the male has one claw that is greatly enlarged

fiddler crab

fid·dle·stick \'fi-dᵊl-ˌstik\ *noun* (15th century)
1 : a violin bow
2 a : something of little value : TRIFLE ⟨didn't care a *fiddlestick* for that⟩ **b** *plural* : NONSENSE — used as an interjection

fid·dling \'fid-liŋ, -lən\ *adjective* (1652)
: TRIFLING, PETTY ⟨a *fiddling* excuse⟩

fid·dly \'fi-dᵊl-ē\ *adjective* (1926)
chiefly British : requiring close attention to detail : FUSSY

fi·de·ism \'fē-(ˌ)dā-ˌi-zəm\ *noun* [probably from French *fidéisme,* from Latin *fides*] (1885)
: reliance on faith rather than reason in pursuit of religious truth
— **fi·de·ist** \-ˌdā-ist\ *noun*
— **fi·de·is·tic** \ˌfē-(ˌ)dā-'is-tik\ *adjective*

Fi·del·is·ta \ˌfē-də-'lē-stə\ *noun* [American Spanish, from *Fidel* Castro + *-ista* -ist] (1960)
: an adherent of Castroism

fi·del·i·ty \fə-'de-lə-tē, fī-\ *noun, plural* **-ties** [Middle English *fidelite,* from Middle French *fidelité,* from Latin *fidelitat-, fidelitas,* from *fidelis* faithful, from *fides* faith, from *fidere* to trust — more at BIDE] (15th century)
1 a : the quality or state of being faithful **b :** accuracy in details : EXACTNESS
2 : the degree to which an electronic device (as a record player, radio, or television) accu-

\ə\ abut \ᵊ\ kitten \ər\ further \a\ ash \ā\ ace \ä\ mop, mar \aù\ out \ch\ chin \e\ bet \ē\ easy \g\ go \i\ hit \ī\ ice \j\ job \ŋ\ sing \ō\ go \ò\ law \òi\ boy \th\ thin \t̷h\ the \ü\ loot \ù\ foot \y\ yet \zh\ vision *see also* Guide to Pronunciation

rately reproduces its effect (as sound or picture) ☆

fidge \'fij\ *intransitive verb* **fidged; fidg·ing** [probably alteration of English dialect *fitch*, from Middle English *fichen*] (1575) *chiefly Scottish* **:** FIDGET

¹**fidg·et** \'fi-jət\ *noun* [irregular from *fidge*] (1674)
1 : uneasiness or restlessness as shown by nervous movements — usually used in plural
2 [²*fidget*] **:** one that fidgets

²**fidget** (1754)
intransitive verb
: to move or act restlessly or nervously
transitive verb
: to cause to move or act nervously

fidg·ety \'fi-jə-tē\ *adjective* (circa 1736)
1 : inclined to fidget
2 : making unnecessary fuss **:** FUSSY
— **fidg·et·i·ness** *noun*

fi·do \'fī-(,)dō\ *noun, plural* **fidos** [*freaks + irregulars + defects + oddities*] (1967)
: a coin having a minting error

fi·du·cial \fə-'dü-shəl, -'dyü-, fī-\ *adjective* (1571)
1 : taken as standard of reference ⟨a *fiducial* mark⟩
2 : founded on faith or trust
3 : having the nature of a trust **:** FIDUCIARY
— **fi·du·cial·ly** \-shə-lē\ *adverb*

¹**fi·du·cia·ry** \-'dü-shē-,er-ē, -shə-rē, -'dyü-\ *noun, plural* **-ries** (1631)
: one that holds a fiduciary relation or acts in a fiduciary capacity

²**fiduciary** *adjective* [Latin *fiduciarius*, from *fiducia* confidence, trust, from *fidere*] (circa 1641)
: of, relating to, or involving a confidence or trust: as **a :** held or founded in trust or confidence **b :** holding in trust **c :** depending on public confidence for value or currency ⟨*fiduciary* fiat money⟩

fie \'fī\ *interjection* [Middle English *fi*, from Old French] (14th century)
— used to express disgust or disapproval

fief \'fēf\ *noun* [French, from Old French — more at FEE] (circa 1611)
1 : a feudal estate **:** FEE
2 : something over which one has rights or exercises control ⟨a politician's *fief*⟩
— **fief·dom** \-dəm\ *noun*

¹**field** \'fē(ə)ld\ *noun* [Middle English, from Old English *feld;* akin to Old High German *feld* field, Old English *flōr* floor — more at FLOOR] (before 12th century)
1 (1) **:** an open land area free of woods and buildings (2) **:** an area of land marked by the presence of particular objects or features ⟨dune *field*⟩ **b** (1) **:** an area of cleared enclosed land used for cultivation or pasture ⟨a *field* of wheat⟩ (2) **:** land containing a natural resource (3) **:** AIRFIELD **c :** the place where a battle is fought; *also* **:** BATTLE **d :** a large unbroken expanse (as of ice)
2 a : an area or division of an activity **b :** the sphere of practical operation outside a base (as a laboratory, office, or factory) ⟨geologists working in the *field*⟩ **c :** an area for military exercises or maneuvers **d** (1) **:** an area constructed, equipped, or marked for sports (2) **:** the portion of an indoor or outdoor sports area within the running track on which field events are held (3) **:** any of the three sections of a baseball outfield ⟨hits to all *fields*⟩
3 : a space on which something is drawn or projected: as **a :** the space on the surface of a coin, medal, or seal that does not contain the design **b :** the ground of each division in a flag **c :** the whole surface of an escutcheon
4 : the individuals that make up all or part of the participants in a sports activity; *especially* **:** all participants with the exception of the favorite or the winner in a contest where more than two are entered
5 : the area visible through the lens of an optical instrument

6 a : a region or space in which a given effect (as magnetism) exists **b :** a region of embryonic tissue capable of a particular type of differentiation ⟨a morphogenetic *field*⟩
7 : a set of mathematical elements that is subject to two binary operations the second of which is distributive relative to the first and that constitutes a commutative group under the first operation and also under the second if the zero or unit element under the first is omitted
8 : a complex of forces that serve as causative agents in human behavior
9 : a series of drain tiles and an absorption area for septic-tank overflow
10 : a particular area (as of a record in a database) in which the same type of information is regularly recorded

²**field** *adjective* (12th century)
: of or relating to a field: as **a :** growing in or inhabiting the fields or open country **b :** made, conducted, or used in the field **c :** operating or active in the field

³**field** (1823)
transitive verb
1 a : to catch or pick up (a batted ball) and usually to throw to a teammate **b :** to take care of or respond to (as a telephone call or a request) **c :** to give an impromptu answer or solution to ⟨the senator *fielded* the reporters' questions⟩
2 : to put into the field ⟨*field* an army⟩ ⟨*field* a team⟩; *also* **:** to enter in competition
intransitive verb
: to play as a fielder

field artillery *noun* (1644)
: artillery other than antiaircraft artillery used with armies in the field

field bed *noun* (1926)
: a four-poster with a canopy arched at the center

field corn *noun* (1856)
: an Indian corn (as dent corn or flint corn) with starchy kernels grown for feeding stock or for market grain

field crop *noun* (1860)
: an agricultural crop (as hay, grain, or cotton) grown on large areas

field day *noun* (1747)
1 a : a day for military exercises or maneuvers **b :** an outdoor meeting or social gathering **c :** a day of sports and athletic competition
2 : a time of extraordinary pleasure or opportunity ⟨TV had a *field day* with the scandal⟩

field–ef·fect transistor \'fēl-də-,fekt-\ *noun* (1959)
: a transistor in which the output current is controlled by a variable electric field

field·er \'fēl-dər\ *noun* (1832)
: one that fields; *especially* **:** a defensive player stationed in the field (as in baseball)

fielder's choice *noun* (1902)
: a situation in baseball in which a batter reaches base safely because the fielder attempts to put out another base runner on the play

field event *noun* (1899)
: an event (as weight-throwing or jumping) in a track-and-field meet other than a race

field·fare \'fē(ə)l(d)-,far, -,fer\ *noun* [Middle English *feldefare*, from Old English, from *feld* + *-fare;* probably akin to Old English *fara* companion; akin to Old English *faran* to go — more at FARE] (before 12th century)
: a medium-sized Eurasian thrush (*Turdus pilaris*) with an ash-colored head and chestnut wings

field glass *noun* (1836)
: a binocular without prisms especially for use outdoors — usually used in plural

field goal *noun* (1902)
1 : a score of three points in football made by drop-kicking or place-kicking the ball over the crossbar from ordinary play
2 : a goal in basketball made while the ball is in play

field grade *noun* (1944)
: the rank of a field officer

field guide *noun* (1934)
: a manual for identifying natural objects, flora, or fauna in the field

field hand *noun* (1826)
: an outdoor farm laborer

field hockey *noun* (1903)
: a game played on a turfed field between two teams of 11 players each whose object is to direct a ball into the opponent's goal with a hockey stick

field house *noun* (1895)
1 : a building at an athletic field for housing equipment or providing dressing facilities
2 : a building enclosing a large area suitable for various forms of athletics and usually providing seats for spectators

fielding average *noun* (1947)
: the average (as of a baseball fielder) determined by dividing the number of putouts and assists by the number of chances — compare BATTING AVERAGE

field judge *noun* (circa 1929)
: a football official whose duties include covering action on kicks and forward passes and timing intermission periods and time-outs

field lens *noun* (1837)
: the lens in a compound eyepiece that is nearer the objective

field magnet *noun* (1883)
: a magnet for producing and maintaining a magnetic field especially in a generator or electric motor

field marshal *noun* (1614)
: the highest ranking military officer (as in the British army)

field mouse *noun* (15th century)
: any of various mice and voles that inhabit fields

field officer *noun* (1656)
: a commissioned officer in the army, air force, or marine corps of the rank of colonel, lieutenant colonel, or major — compare COMPANY OFFICER, GENERAL OFFICER

field of force (1850)
: FIELD 6a

field of honor (1824)
1 : BATTLEFIELD
2 : a place where a duel is fought

field of view (circa 1816)
: FIELD 5

field of vision (1862)
: VISUAL FIELD

field pea *noun* (1709)
: a small-seeded pea (*Pisum sativum* variety *arvense*) widely grown for forage and food

field·piece \'fē(ə)l(d)-,pēs\ *noun* (1590)
: a gun or howitzer for use in the field

field spaniel *noun* (1867)
: any of a breed of medium-sized hunting and retrieving spaniels that have a flat dense usually black, liver, red, or roan coat

field·stone \'fē(ə)l(d)-,stōn\ *noun* (1799)
: stone (as in building) in usually unaltered form as taken from the field

☆ **SYNONYMS**
Fidelity, allegiance, fealty, loyalty, devotion, piety mean faithfulness to something to which one is bound by pledge or duty. FIDELITY implies strict and continuing faithfulness to an obligation, trust, or duty ⟨marital *fidelity*⟩. ALLEGIANCE suggests an adherence like that of citizens to their country ⟨pledging *allegiance*⟩. FEALTY implies a fidelity acknowledged by the individual and as compelling as a sworn vow ⟨*fealty* to the truth⟩. LOYALTY implies a faithfulness that is steadfast in the face of any temptation to renounce, desert, or betray ⟨valued the *loyalty* of his friends⟩. DEVOTION stresses zeal and service amounting to self-dedication ⟨a painter's *devotion* to her art⟩. PIETY stresses fidelity to obligations regarded as natural and fundamental ⟨filial *piety*⟩.

field·strip \-ˌstrip\ *transitive verb* (1947)
: to take apart (a weapon) to the extent authorized for routine cleaning, lubrication, and minor repairs

field–test \-ˌtest\ *transitive verb* (1948)
: to test (as a procedure or product) in a natural environment
— **field test** *noun*

field theory *noun* (1901)
: a detailed mathematical description of the assumed physical properties of a region under some influence (as gravitation)

field trial *noun* (1895)
1 : a trial of sporting dogs in actual performance
2 : a trial of a new product in actual situations for which it is intended

field trip *noun* (1926)
: a visit (as to a factory, farm, or museum) made (as by students and a teacher) for purposes of firsthand observation

field winding *noun* (1893)
: the winding of a field magnet

field·work \ˈfē(ə)l-ˌdwərk\ *noun* (1819)
1 : a temporary fortification thrown up by an army in the field
2 : work done in the field (as by students) to gain practical experience and knowledge through firsthand observation
3 : the gathering of anthropological or sociological data through the interviewing and observation of subjects in the field
— **field–work·er** *noun*

fiend \ˈfēnd\ *noun* [Middle English, from Old English *fēond*; akin to Old High German *fīant* enemy, Sanskrit *pīyati* he scorns] (before 12th century)
1 a : DEVIL 1 **b :** DEMON **c :** a person of great wickedness or maliciousness
2 : a person extremely devoted to a pursuit or study **:** FANATIC ⟨a golf *fiend*⟩
3 : ADDICT 1 ⟨a dope *fiend*⟩
4 : WIZARD 3 ⟨a *fiend* at mathematics⟩

fiend·ish \ˈfēn-dish\ *adjective* (1529)
1 : perversely diabolical ⟨took a *fiendish* pleasure in hurting people⟩
2 : extremely cruel or wicked
3 : excessively bad, unpleasant, or difficult ⟨*fiendish* weather⟩
— **fiend·ish·ly** *adverb*
— **fiend·ish·ness** *noun*

fierce \ˈfirs\ *adjective* **fierc·er; fierc·est** [Middle English *fiers*, from Middle French, from Latin *ferus* wild, savage; akin to Greek *thēr* wild animal] (14th century)
1 a : violently hostile or aggressive in temperament **b :** given to fighting or killing **:** PUGNACIOUS
2 a : marked by unrestrained zeal or vehemence ⟨a *fierce* argument⟩ **b :** extremely vexatious, disappointing, or intense ⟨*fierce* pain⟩
3 : furiously active or determined ⟨make a *fierce* effort⟩
4 : wild or menacing in appearance ☆
— **fierce·ly** *adverb*
— **fierce·ness** *noun*

fi·eri fa·cias \ˌfī-(ə-)rē-ˈfā-sh(ē-)əs\ *noun* [Latin, cause (it) to be done] (15th century)
: a writ authorizing the sheriff to obtain satisfaction of a judgment in debt or damages from the goods and chattels of the defendant

fi·ery \ˈfī-(ə)-rē\ *adjective* **fi·er·i·er; -est** [Middle English, from *fire, fier* fire] (13th century)
1 a : consisting of fire **b :** BURNING, BLAZING **c :** using or carried out with fire **d :** liable to catch fire or explode **:** FLAMMABLE ⟨a *fiery* vapor⟩
2 a : hot like a fire **b** (1) **:** being in an inflamed state or condition ⟨a *fiery* boil⟩ (2) **:** feverish and flushed ⟨a *fiery* forehead⟩
3 : of the color of fire **:** RED ⟨a *fiery* sunset⟩
4 : full of or exuding emotion or spirit ⟨a *fiery* sermon⟩ **b :** easily provoked **:** IRRITABLE
— **fi·eri·ly** \ˈfī-rə-lē\ *adverb*
— **fi·eri·ness** \ˈfī-rē-nəs\ *noun*

— **fiery** *adverb*

fi·es·ta \fē-ˈes-tə\ *noun* [Spanish, from Latin *festa* — more at FEAST] (1844)
: FESTIVAL; *specifically* **:** a saint's day celebrated in Spain and Latin America with processions and dances

fife \ˈfīf\ *noun* [German *Pfeife* pipe, fife, from Old High German *pfīfa*, from (assumed) Vulgar Latin *pipa* pipe — more at PIPE] (1539)
: a small transverse flute with six to eight finger holes and usually no keys

fife rail *noun* (circa 1800)
: a rail about the mast near the deck to which rigging is belayed

fif·teen \ˌfif-ˈtēn, ˈfif-\ *noun* [Middle English *fiftene*, adjective, from Old English *fīftēne*, from *fīf* five + *-tēne* (akin to Old English *tīen* ten) — more at FIVE, TEN] (before 12th century)
1 — see NUMBER table
2 : the first point scored by a side in a game of tennis — called also *five*
— **fifteen** *adjective*
— **fifteen** *pronoun, plural in construction*
— **fif·teenth** \-ˈtēn(t)th, -ˌtēn(t)th\ *adjective or noun*

fifth \ˈfith, ˈfif(t)th, ˈfift\ *noun, plural* **fifths** \ˈfiths, ˈfif(t)ths, ˈfif(t)s\ (before 12th century)
1 — see NUMBER table
2 a : the musical interval embracing five diatonic degrees **b :** a tone at this interval; *specifically* **:** DOMINANT 1 **c :** the harmonic combination of two tones at this interval
3 : a unit of measure for liquor equal to one fifth of a U.S. gallon (0.757 liter)
4 *capitalized* **:** the Fifth Amendment of the U.S. Constitution
— **fifth** *adjective or adverb*
— **fifth·ly** *adverb*

fifth column *noun* [name applied to rebel sympathizers in Madrid in 1936 when four rebel columns advanced on the city] (1936)
: a group of secret sympathizers or supporters of an enemy that engage in espionage or sabotage within defense lines or national borders ◇
— **fifth col·um·nism** \-ˈkä-ləm-ˌ(n)i-zəm\ *noun*
— **fifth col·um·nist** \-(n)ist\ *noun*

fifth wheel *noun* (circa 1874)
1 a : a horizontal wheel or segment of a wheel that consists of two parts rotating on each other above the fore axle of a carriage and that forms support to prevent tipping **b :** a similar coupling between tractor and trailer of a semitrailer
2 : one that is superfluous, unnecessary, or burdensome

fif·ty \ˈfif-tē\ *noun, plural* **fifties** [Middle English, from *fifty*, adjective, from Old English *fīftig*, from *fīftig*, noun, group of 50, from *fīf* five + *-tig* group of ten; akin to *tīen* ten] (before 12th century)
1 — see NUMBER table
2 *plural* **:** the numbers 50 to 59; *specifically* **:** the years 50 to 59 in a lifetime or century
3 : a 50-dollar bill
— **fif·ti·eth** \-tē-əth\ *adjective or noun*
— **fifty** *adjective*
— **fifty** *pronoun, plural in construction*
— **fif·ty·ish** \-tē-ish\ *adjective*

fif·ty–fif·ty \ˌfif-tē-ˈfif-tē\ *adjective* (1913)
1 : shared, assumed, or borne equally ⟨a *fifty-fifty* proposition⟩
2 : half favorable and half unfavorable ⟨a *fifty-fifty* chance⟩
— **fifty–fifty** *adverb*

¹fig \ˈfig\ *noun* [Middle English *fige*, from Old French, from Provençal *figa*, from (assumed) Vulgar Latin *fica*, from Latin *ficus* fig tree, fig] (13th century)
1 a : an oblong or pear-

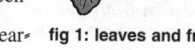

fig 1: leaves and fruit

shaped fruit that is a syconium **b :** any of a genus (*Ficus*) of trees of the mulberry family bearing fruits that are syconia; *especially* **:** a widely cultivated tree (*F. carica*) that produces edible figs
2 : a worthless trifle **:** the least bit ⟨doesn't care a *fig*⟩

²fig *noun* [*fig*, verb (to adorn)] (1835)
: DRESS, ARRAY ⟨a young woman in dazzling royal full *fig* —Mollie Panter-Downes⟩

¹fight \ˈfīt\ *verb* **fought** \ˈfȯt\; **fight·ing** [Middle English, from Old English *feohtan*; akin to Old High German *fehtan* to fight and perhaps to Latin *pectere* to comb — more at PECTINATE] (before 12th century)
intransitive verb
1 a : to contend in battle or physical combat; *especially* **:** to strive to overcome a person by blows or weapons **b :** to engage in boxing
2 : to put forth a determined effort
transitive verb
1 a (1) **:** to contend against in or as if in battle or physical combat (2) **:** to box against in the

☆ **SYNONYMS**
Fierce, ferocious, barbarous, savage, cruel mean showing fury or malignity in looks or actions. FIERCE applies to humans and animals that inspire terror because of their wild and menacing aspect or fury in attack ⟨*fierce* warriors⟩. FEROCIOUS implies extreme fierceness and unrestrained violence and brutality ⟨a *ferocious* dog⟩. BARBAROUS implies a ferocity or mercilessness regarded as unworthy of civilized people ⟨*barbarous* treatment of prisoners⟩. SAVAGE implies the absence of inhibitions restraining civilized people filled with rage, lust, or other violent passion ⟨a *savage* criminal⟩. CRUEL implies indifference to suffering and even positive pleasure in inflicting it ⟨the *cruel* jokes of schoolboys⟩.

◇ **WORD HISTORY**
fifth column *Fifth column* apparently first appeared in English in *New York Times* dispatches by William Carney, a correspondent reporting on the Spanish Civil War. On October 16, 1936, Carney mentioned raids in Republican-held Madrid that "apparently were instigated by a recent broadcast over the Rebel radio station by General Emilio Mola. He stated he was counting on four columns of troops outside Madrid and another column of persons hiding within the city who would join the invaders as soon as they entered the capital." Carney was accurately reflecting the fact that Spanish *quinta columna* "fifth column" was an epithet for subversive Nationalist ("Rebel") elements in the city. But subsequent literature on the war makes no mention of a radio broadcast by Mola, which Carney himself seems not to have heard, and Nationalist biographies of Mola do not attribute the phrase to him. In fact, the first documented use of *quinta columna* was on October 2, in a newspaper article by the Communist leader "La Pasionaria" (Dolores Ibárruri). The phrase may actually have been a propaganda invention of the Republicans attributed to Mola in order to justify reprisals against supposed Nationalist supporters in Madrid. In any event, *fifth column* soon became an international catchphrase for a conspiracy of traitors within one's own camp.

\ə\ abut \ᵊ\ kitten \ər\ further \a\ ash \ā\ ace
\ä\ mop, mar \aú\ out \ch\ chin \e\ bet \ē\ easy
\g\ go \i\ hit \ī\ ice \j\ job \ŋ\ sing \ō\ go
\ȯ\ law \ȯi\ boy \th\ thin \ṯh\ the \ü\ loot \ú\ foot
\y\ yet \zh\ vision *see also* Guide to Pronunciation

ring **b** (1) : to attempt to prevent the success or effectiveness of ⟨the company *fought* the takeover attempt⟩ (2) : to oppose the passage or development of ⟨*fight* a bill in Congress⟩ **2 a** : WAGE, CARRY ON ⟨*fight* a battle⟩ **b** : to take part in (as a boxing match) **3** : to struggle to endure or surmount ⟨*fight* a cold⟩ **4 a** : to gain by struggle ⟨*fights* his way through⟩ **b** : to resolve by struggle ⟨*fought* out their differences in court⟩ **5 a** : to manage (a ship) in a battle or storm **b** : to cause to struggle or contend **c** : to manage in an unnecessarily rough or awkward manner — **fight shy of** : to avoid facing or meeting

²**fight** *noun* (before 12th century) **1 a** : a hostile encounter : BATTLE, COMBAT **b** : a boxing match **c** : a verbal disagreement : ARGUMENT **2** : a struggle for a goal or an objective ⟨a *fight* for justice⟩ **3** : strength or disposition for fighting : PUGNACITY ⟨still full of *fight*⟩

fight·er \'fī-tər\ *noun* (13th century) : one that fights: as **a** (1) : WARRIOR, SOLDIER (2) : a pugnacious or game individual (3) : ¹BOXER 1 **b** : an airplane of high speed and maneuverability with armament designed to destroy enemy aircraft

fight·er–bomb·er \-'bä-mər\ *noun* (1936) : a fighter aircraft fitted to carry bombs and rockets in addition to its normal armament

fighting chair *noun* (1950) : a chair from which a salt-water angler plays a hooked fish

fighting chance *noun* (1889) : a chance that may be realized by a struggle ⟨the patient had a *fighting chance* to live⟩

fighting word *noun* (1917) : a word likely to provoke a fight

fight song *noun* (1954) : a song used to inspire enthusiasm usually during an athletic competition

fig leaf *noun* (14th century) **1** : the leaf of a fig tree **2** [from the use by Adam and Eve of fig leaves to cover their nakedness after eating the forbidden fruit (Genesis 3:7)] : something that conceals or camouflages usually inadequately or dishonestly

fig marigold *noun* (1731) : any of several herbs (genus *Mesembryanthemum*) of the carpetweed family with showy white or pink flowers

fig·ment \'fig-mənt\ *noun* [Middle English, from Latin *figmentum*, from *fingere* to shape — more at DOUGH] (15th century) : something made up or contrived

fig·ur·al \'fi-g(y)ə-rəl\ *adjective* (1813) : of, relating to, or consisting of human or animal figures ⟨a *figural* composition⟩

fig·u·ra·tion \,fi-g(y)ə-'rā-shən\ *noun* (14th century) **1** : FORM, OUTLINE **2** : the act or process of creating or providing a figure **3** : an act or instance of representation in figures and shapes ⟨cubism was explained as a synthesis of colored *figurations* of objects —Janet Flanner⟩ **4** : ornamentation of a musical passage by using decorative and usually repetitive figures

fig·u·ra·tive \'fi-g(y)ə-rə-tiv\ *adjective* (14th century) **1 a** : representing by a figure or resemblance : EMBLEMATIC **b** : of or relating to representation of form or figure in art ⟨*figurative* sculpture⟩ **2 a** : expressing one thing in terms normally denoting another with which it may be regarded as analogous : METAPHORICAL ⟨*figurative* language⟩ **b** : characterized by figures of speech ⟨a *figurative* description⟩ — **fig·u·ra·tive·ly** *adverb* — **fig·u·ra·tive·ness** *noun*

¹**fig·ure** \'fi-gyər, *British & often US* 'fi-gər\ *noun* [Middle English, from Old French, from Latin *figura*, from *fingere*] (13th century) **1 a** : a number symbol : NUMERAL, DIGIT ⟨a salary running into six *figures*⟩ **b** *plural* : arithmetical calculations ⟨good at *figures*⟩ **c** : a written or printed character **d** : value especially as expressed in numbers : SUM, PRICE ⟨sold at a low *figure*⟩ **2 a** : a geometric form (as a line, triangle, or sphere) especially when considered as a set of geometric elements (as points) in space of a given number of dimensions ⟨a square is a plane *figure*⟩ **b** : bodily shape or form especially of a person ⟨a slender *figure*⟩ : an object noticeable only as a shape or form ⟨*figures* moving in the dusk⟩ **3 a** : the graphic representation of a form especially of a person or geometric entity **b** : a diagram or pictorial illustration of textual matter **4** : a person, thing, or action representative of another **5 a** : FIGURE OF SPEECH **b** : an intentional deviation from the ordinary form or syntactical relation of words **6** : the form of a syllogism with respect to the relative position of the middle term **7** : an often repetitive pattern or design in a manufactured article (as cloth) or natural product (as wood) ⟨a polka-dot *figure*⟩ **8** : appearance made : impression produced ⟨the couple cut quite a *figure*⟩ **9 a** : a series of movements in a dance **b** : an outline representation of a form traced by a series of evolutions (as with skates on an ice surface or by an airplane in the air) **10** : a prominent personality : PERSONAGE ⟨great *figures* of history⟩ **11** : a short coherent group of notes or chords that may constitute part of a phrase, theme, or composition

²**figure** *verb* **fig·ured; fig·ur·ing** \'fi-gyə-riŋ, 'fi-g(ə-)riŋ\ (14th century) *transitive verb* **1** : to represent by or as if by a figure or outline **2** : to decorate with a pattern; *also* : to write figures over or under (the bass) in order to indicate the accompanying chords **3** : to indicate or represent by numerals **4 a** : CALCULATE **b** : CONCLUDE, DECIDE ⟨*figured* there was no use in further effort⟩ **c** : REGARD, CONSIDER **d** : to appear likely ⟨*figures* to win⟩ *intransitive verb* **1 a** : to be or appear important or conspicuous **b** : to be involved or implicated ⟨*figured* in a robbery⟩ **2** : to perform a figure in dancing **3** : COMPUTE, CALCULATE **4** : to seem rational, normal, or expected ⟨that *figures*⟩ — **fig·ur·er** \-g(y)ər-ər\ *noun* — **figure on 1** : to take into consideration ⟨*figuring on* the extra income⟩ **2** : to rely on **3** : PLAN ⟨I *figure on* going into town⟩

fig·ured \-g(y)ərd\ *adjective* (15th century) **1** : adorned with, formed into, or marked with a figure ⟨*figured* muslin⟩ ⟨*figured* wood⟩ **2** : being represented : PORTRAYED **3** : indicated by figures

figured bass *noun* (1801) : CONTINUO

figure eight *noun* (1887) : something resembling the Arabic numeral eight in form or shape: as **a** : a small knot — see KNOT illustration **b** : an embroidery stitch **c** : a dance pattern **d** : a skater's figure — called also *figure-of-eight*

fig·ure·head \'fi-g(y)ər-,hed\ *noun* (1765) **1** : the figure on a ship's bow **2** : a head or chief in name only

figure in *transitive verb* (circa 1934) : to include especially in a reckoning

figure of merit (circa 1865) : a numerical quantity based on one or more characteristics of a system or device that represents a measure of efficiency or effectiveness

figure of speech (1824) : a form of expression (as a simile or metaphor) used to convey meaning or heighten effect often by comparing or identifying one thing with another that has a meaning or connotation familiar to the reader or listener

figure out *transitive verb* (1833) **1** : DISCOVER, DETERMINE ⟨try to *figure out* a way to do it⟩ **2** : SOLVE, FATHOM ⟨*figure out* a problem⟩

figure skating *noun* (1852) : skating characterized by the performance of various jumps, spins, and dance movements and formerly by the tracing of prescribed figures — **figure skater** *noun*

fig·u·rine \,fi-g(y)ə-'rēn\ *noun* [French, from Italian *figurina*, diminutive of *figura* figure, from Latin — more at FIGURE] (1854) : a small carved or molded figure : STATUETTE

fig wasp *noun* (1883) : a minute wasp (*Blastophaga psenes* of the family Agaontidae) that breeds in the caprifig and is the agent of caprification; *broadly* : any wasp of the same family

fig·wort \'fig-,wərt, -,wort\ *noun* (1548) : any of a genus (*Scrophularia*) of chiefly herbaceous plants of the snapdragon family with leaves having no stipules, an irregular bilabiate corolla, and a 2-celled ovary

Fi·ji·an \'fē-(,)jē-ən, fi-\ *noun* (1809) **1** : a member of a Melanesian people of Fiji **2** : the Austronesian language of the Fijians — **Fijian** *adjective*

fil·a·ment \'fi-lə-mənt\ *noun* [Middle French, from Medieval Latin *filamentum*, from Late Latin *filare* to spin — more at FILE] (1594) : a single thread or a thin flexible threadlike object, process, or appendage: as **a** : a tenuous conductor (as of carbon or metal) made incandescent by the passage of an electric current; *specifically* : a cathode in the form of a metal wire in an electron tube **b** (1) : a thin and fine elongated constituent part of a gill (2) : an elongated thin series of cells attached one to another or a very long thin cylindrical single cell (as of some algae, fungi, or bacteria) **c** : the anther-bearing stalk of a stamen — see FLOWER illustration — **fil·a·men·ta·ry** \,fil-ə-'men-t(ə-)rē\ *adjective* — **fil·a·men·tous** \-'men-təs\ *adjective*

fi·lar \'fī-lər\ *adjective* [Latin *filum* thread] (circa 1859) : of or relating to a thread or line; *especially* : having threads across the field of view ⟨a *filar* eyepiece⟩

fi·lar·ia \fə-'lar-ē-ə, -'ler-\ *noun, plural* **-i·ae** \-ē-,ē, -ē-,ī\ [New Latin, genus name, from Latin *filum*] (1834) : any of numerous slender filamentous nematodes (*Filaria* and related genera) that as adults are parasites in the blood or tissues of mammals and as larvae usually develop in biting insects — **fi·lar·i·al** \-ē-əl\ *adjective* — **fi·lar·i·id** \-ē-əd\ *adjective or noun*

fil·a·ri·a·sis \,fi-lə-'rī-ə-səs\ *noun, plural* **-a·ses** \-,sēz\ [New Latin] (1879) : infestation with or disease caused by filariae

fil·a·ture \'fil-ə-,chú(ə)r, -chər, -,t(y)ù(ə)r\ *noun* [French, from Late Latin *filatus*, past participle of *filare*] (1759) : a factory where silk is reeled

fil·bert \'fil-bərt\ *noun* [Middle English, from Anglo-French *philber*, from Saint *Philibert* (died 684) Frankish abbot whose feast day falls in the nutting season] (14th century) **1** : either of two European hazels (*Corylus avellana* and *C. maxima*); *also* : the sweet thick-shelled nut of the filbert

2 : HAZELNUT ◆

filch \'filch\ *transitive verb* [Middle English] (1561)
: to appropriate furtively or casually ⟨*filch* a cookie⟩
synonym see STEAL

¹file \'fī(ə)l\ *noun* [Middle English, from Old English *fēol;* akin to Old High German *fīla* file] (before 12th century)
1 : a tool usually of hardened steel with cutting ridges for forming or smoothing surfaces especially of metal
2 : a shrewd or crafty person

²file *transitive verb* **filed; fil·ing** (13th century)
: to rub, smooth, or cut away with or as if with a file

³file *transitive verb* **filed; fil·ing** [Middle English, from Old English *fȳlan,* from *fūl* foul] (before 12th century)
chiefly dialect **:** DEFILE, CORRUPT

⁴file *verb* **filed; fil·ing** [Middle English, from Middle French *filer* to string documents on a string or wire, from *fil* thread, from Old French, from Latin *filum;* akin to Armenian *jil* sinew] (15th century)
transitive verb
1 : to arrange in order for preservation and reference ⟨*file* letters⟩
2 a : to place among official records as prescribed by law ⟨*file* a mortgage⟩ **b :** to send (copy) to a newspaper ⟨*filed* a story⟩ **c :** to return to the office of the clerk of a court without action on the merits
3 : to initiate (as a legal action) through proper formal procedure ⟨threatened to *file* charges⟩
intransitive verb
1 : to register as a candidate especially in a primary election
2 : to place items in a file
— **fil·er** \'fī-lər\ *noun*

⁵file *noun* (1525)
1 : a device (as a folder, case, or cabinet) by means of which papers are kept in order
2 a *archaic* **:** ROLL, LIST **b :** a collection of papers or publications usually arranged or classified **c** (1) **:** a collection of related data records (as for a computer) (2) **:** a complete collection of data (as text or a program) treated by a computer as a unit especially for purposes of input and output
— **on file :** in or as if in a file for ready reference

⁶file *noun* [Middle French, from *filer* to spin, from Late Latin *filare,* from Latin *filum*] (1598)
1 : a row of persons, animals, or things arranged one behind the other
2 : any of the rows of squares that extend across a chessboard from one player's side to the other player's side

⁷file *intransitive verb* **filed; fil·ing** (1616)
: to march or proceed in file

filé *also* **file** \fə-'lā, (,)fē-'lā, 'fē-(,)lā\ *noun* [Louisiana French, from French, past participle of *filer* to twist, spin] (1806)
: powdered young leaves of sassafras used to thicken soups or stews

file clerk *noun* (1919)
: a clerk who works on files

file-fish \'fī(ə)l-,fish\ *noun* (1814)
: any of various bony fishes (order Tetraodontiformes and especially genera *Aluterus, Cantherhines,* and *Monacanthus* of the family Balistidae) with rough granular leathery skins

fi·let \fi-'lā\ *noun* [French, literally, net] (1881)
: a lace with a square mesh and geometric designs

fi·let mi·gnon \,fi-(,)lā-mēn-'yōⁿ, fi-,lā-\ *noun, plural* **filets mignons** \,fi-(,)lā-mēn-'yōⁿz, fi-,lā-\ [French, literally, dainty fillet] (1906)
: a thick slice of beef cut from the narrow end of a beef tenderloin

fili- *or* **filo-** *combining form* [Latin *filum*]
: thread ⟨*filiform*⟩

fil·ial \'fi-lē-əl, 'fil-yəl\ *adjective* [Middle English, from Late Latin *filialis,* from Latin *filius* son — more at FEMININE] (14th century)
1 : of, relating to, or befitting a son or daughter ⟨*filial* obedience⟩
2 : having or assuming the relation of a child or offspring
— **fil·ial·ly** \-lē-ə-lē, -yə-lē\ *adverb*

filial generation *noun* (1909)
: a generation in a breeding experiment that is successive to a mating between parents of two distinctively different but usually relatively pure genotypes

fil·i·a·tion \,fi-lē-'ā-shən\ *noun* (15th century)
1 a : filial relationship especially of a son to his father **b :** the adjudication of paternity
2 a : descent or derivation especially from a culture or language **b :** the act or process of determining such relationship

¹fil·i·bus·ter \'fi-lə-,bəs-tər\ *noun* [Spanish *filibustero,* literally, freebooter] (1851)
1 : an irregular military adventurer; *specifically* **:** an American engaged in fomenting insurrections in Latin America in the mid-19th century
2 [²*filibuster*] **a :** the use of extreme dilatory tactics in an attempt to delay or prevent action especially in a legislative assembly **b :** an instance of this practice ◆

²filibuster *verb* **-tered; -ter·ing** \-t(ə-)riŋ\ (1853)
intransitive verb
1 : to carry out insurrectionist activities in a foreign country
2 : to engage in a filibuster
transitive verb
: to subject to a filibuster
— **fil·i·bus·ter·er** \-tər-ər\ *noun*

fi·li·form \'fi-lə-,fôrm, 'fī-\ *adjective* (1757)
: shaped like a filament

¹fil·i·gree \'fi-lə-,grē\ *noun* [modification of French *filigrane,* from Italian *filigrana,* from Latin *filum* + *granum* grain — more at CORN] (1693)
1 : ornamental work especially of fine wire of gold, silver, or copper applied chiefly to gold and silver surfaces
2 a : ornamental

filigree 2a

openwork of delicate or intricate design **b :** a pattern or design resembling such openwork ⟨a *filigree* of frost⟩ **c :** ORNAMENTATION, EMBELLISHMENT ⟨writings . . . heavy with late Victorian *filigree* —Jack Beatty⟩

²filigree *transitive verb* **fil·i·greed; fil·i·gree·ing** (1831)
: to adorn with or as if with filigree

fil·ing \'fī-liŋ\ *noun* (14th century)
1 : an act or instance of using a file
2 : a fragment rubbed off in filing ⟨iron *filings*⟩

fil·io·pi·etis·tic \'fi-lē-ō-,pī-ə-'tis-tik\ *adjective* [*filial* + *-o-* + *pietistic*] (1893)
: of or relating to an often excessive veneration of ancestors or tradition

Fil·i·pi·na \,fi-lə-'pē-nə\ *noun* [Spanish] (1899)
: a Filipino girl or woman

Fil·i·pi·no \-'pē-(,)nō\ *noun, plural* **Filipinos** [Spanish] (circa 1889)
1 : a native of the Philippine islands
2 : a citizen of the Republic of the Philippines
— **Filipino** *adjective*

¹fill \'fil\ *verb* [Middle English, from Old English *fyllan;* akin to Old English *full* full] (before 12th century)
transitive verb
1 a : to put into as much as can be held or conveniently contained ⟨*fill* a cup with water⟩

b : to supply with a full complement ⟨the class is already *filled*⟩ **c** (1) **:** to cause to swell or billow ⟨wind *filled* the sails⟩ (2) **:** to trim (a sail) to catch the wind **d :** to raise the level of with fill ⟨*filled* land⟩ **e :** to repair the cavities of (teeth) **f :** to stop up **:** OBSTRUCT, PLUG ⟨wreckage *filled* the channel⟩ **g :** to stop up the interstices, crevices, or pores of (as cloth, wood, or leather) with a foreign substance
2 a : FEED, SATIATE **b :** SATISFY, FULFILL ⟨*fills* all requirements⟩ **c :** MAKE OUT, COMPLETE — used with *out* or *in* ⟨*fill* out a form⟩ ⟨*fill* in the blanks⟩ **d :** to draw the playing cards necessary to complete (as a straight or flush in poker)
3 a : to occupy the whole of ⟨smoke *filled* the room⟩ **b :** to spread through **c :** to make full ⟨a mind *filled* with fantasies⟩
4 a : to possess and perform the duties of **:** HOLD ⟨*fill* an office⟩ **b :** to place a person in ⟨*fill* a vacancy⟩
5 : to supply as directed ⟨*fill* a prescription⟩
6 : to cover the surface of with a layer of precious metal
intransitive verb
: to become full
— **fill one's shoes :** to take over one's job, position, or responsibilities

²fill *noun* (before 12th century)
1 : a full supply; *especially* **:** a quantity that satisfies or satiates ⟨eat your *fill*⟩
2 : something that fills: as **a :** material used to fill a receptacle, cavity, passage, or low place

\ə\ abut \ə\ kitten \ər\ further \a\ ash \ā\ ace
\ä\ mop, mar \aù\ out \ch\ chin \e\ bet \ē\ easy
\g\ go \i\ hit \ī\ ice \j\ job \ŋ\ sing \ō\ go
\ò\ law \òi\ boy \th\ thin \ṯh\ the \ü\ loot \ù\ foot
\y\ yet \zh\ vision *see also* Guide to Pronunciation

b : a bit of instrumental music that fills the pauses between phrases (as of a vocalist or soloist)

fill away *intransitive verb* (1840)
1 : to trim a sail to catch the wind
2 : to proceed on the course especially after being brought up in the wind

¹**fill·er** \'fi-lər\ *noun* (15th century)
: one that fills: as **a :** a substance added to a product (as to increase bulk, weight, viscosity, opacity, or strength) **b :** a composition used to fill the pores and grain especially of a wood surface before painting or varnishing **c :** a piece used to cover or fill in a space between two parts of a structure **d :** tobacco used to form the core of a cigar **e :** material used to fill extra space in a column or page of a newspaper or magazine **f :** a pack of paper for a loose-leaf notebook **g :** a sound, word, or phrase (as "you know?") used to fill pauses in speaking

²**fil·ler** \'fi-lər\ *noun, plural* **fillers** *or* **filler** [Hungarian *fillér*] (1904)
— see *forint* at MONEY table

¹**fil·let** \'fi-lət, *in sense 2b also* fi-'lā, 'fi-(,)lā\ *also* **fi·let** \fi-'lā, 'fi-(,)lā\ *noun* [Middle English *filet*, from Middle French, diminutive of *fil* thread — more at FILE] (14th century)
1 : a ribbon or narrow strip of material used especially as a headband
2 a : a thin narrow strip of material **b :** a piece or slice of boneless meat or fish; *especially* **:** the tenderloin of beef
3 a : a concave junction formed where two surfaces meet (as at an angle) **b :** a strip that gives a rounded appearance to such a junction; *also* **:** a strip to reinforce the corner where two surfaces meet
4 : a narrow flat architectural member: **a :** a flat molding separating others — see BASE illustration **b :** the space between two flutings in a shaft

²**fil·let** \'fi-lət, *in sense 2 also* fi-'lā, 'fi-(,)lā\ *transitive verb* (1604)
1 : to bind, furnish, or adorn with or as if with a fillet
2 : to cut into fillets

fillet weld *noun* (1926)
: a weld of approximately triangular cross section used to join two pieces especially perpendicularly

fill-in \'fil-,in\ *noun* (1917)
: someone or something that fills in

fill in (1840)
transitive verb
1 : to give necessary or recently acquired information to (I'll *fill* you *in*)
2 : to enrich (as a design) with detail
intransitive verb
: to fill a vacancy usually temporarily

fill·ing \'fi-liŋ\ *noun* (14th century)
1 : an act or instance of filling
2 : something used to fill a cavity, container, or depression
3 : something that completes: as **a :** the yarn interlacing the warp in a fabric; *also* **:** yarn for the shuttle **b :** a food mixture used to fill pastry or sandwiches

filling station *noun* (1921)
: SERVICE STATION 1

¹**fil·lip** \'fi-ləp\ *transitive verb* [probably of imitative origin] (15th century)
1 a : to make a filliping motion with **b :** to strike or tap with a fillip (*filliped* him on the nose)
2 : to project quickly by or as if by a fillip (*fillip* crumbs off the table)
3 : STIMULATE (with this to *fillip* his spirits —Robert Westerby)

²**fillip** *noun* (1519)
1 a : a blow or gesture made by the sudden forcible straightening of a finger curled up against the thumb **b :** a short sharp blow **:** BUFFET
2 : something tending to arouse or excite: as **a :** STIMULUS (just the *fillip* my confidence need-

ed) (lent a *fillip* of danger to the sport) **b :** trivial addition **:** EMBELLISHMENT (showy *fillips* of language) **c :** a significant and often unexpected development **:** WRINKLE (plot twists and *fillips*)

fill out *intransitive verb* (1888)
: to put on flesh

fill-up \'fil-,əp\ *noun* (1853)
: an action or instance of filling up something

fil·ly \'fi-lē\ *noun, plural* **fillies** [Middle English *fyly*, from Old Norse *fylja;* akin to Old English *fola* foal] (15th century)
1 : a young female horse usually of less than four years
2 : a young woman **:** GIRL

¹**film** \'film, *Southern also* 'fi(ə)m\ *noun, often attributive* [Middle English *filme*, from Old English *filmen;* akin to Greek *pelma* sole of the foot, Old English *fell* skin — more at FELL] (before 12th century)
1 a : a thin skin or membranous covering **:** PELLICLE **b :** an abnormal growth on or in the eye
2 : a thin covering or coating (a *film* of ice)
3 a : an exceedingly thin layer **:** LAMINA **b** (1) **:** a thin flexible transparent sheet (as of plastic) used especially as a wrapping (2) **:** such a sheet of cellulose acetate or nitrocellulose coated with a radiation-sensitive emulsion for taking photographs
4 : MOTION PICTURE

²**film** (1602)
transitive verb
1 : to cover with or as if with a film
2 : to make a motion picture of or from (*film* a scene)
intransitive verb
1 : to become covered or obscured with or as if with a film
2 : to make a motion picture
— **film·able** \'fil-mə-bəl\ *adjective*

film badge *noun* (1945)
: a small pack of sensitive photographic film worn as a badge for indicating exposure to radiation

film·dom \'film-dəm\ *noun* (1914)
: the motion-picture industry

film·go·er \-,gō(-ə)r\ *noun* (1919)
: one who frequently attends films

film·ic \'fil-mik\ *adjective* (circa 1930)
: of, relating to, or resembling motion pictures
— **film·i·cal·ly** \-mi-k(ə-)lē\ *adverb*

film·land \'film-,land\ *noun* (1913)
: FILMDOM

film·mak·er \'film-,mā-kər\ *noun* (1908)
: one who makes motion pictures

film·mak·ing \-,mā-kiŋ\ *noun* (1913)
: the making of motion pictures

film noir \-'nwär\ *noun* [French, literally, black film] (1958)
: a type of crime film featuring cynical malevolent characters in a sleazy setting and an ominous atmosphere that is conveyed by shadowy photography and foreboding background music; *also* **:** a film of this type

film·og·ra·phy \fil-'mä-grə-fē\ *noun, plural* **-phies** [*film* + *-ography* (as in *bibliography*)] (1962)
: a list of motion pictures featuring the work of a prominent film figure or relating to a particular topic

film·set·ting \'film-,se-tiŋ\ *noun* (1954)
: PHOTOCOMPOSITION
— **film·set** *adjective*
— **filmset** *transitive verb*
— **film·set·ter** *noun*

film·strip \'film-,strip\ *noun* (1930)
: a strip of film bearing a sequence of images for projection as still pictures

filmy \'fil-mē\ *adjective* **film·i·er; -est** (1604)
1 : of, resembling, or composed of film **:** GAUZY (*filmy* draperies)
2 : covered with a haze or film
— **film·i·ly** \-mə-lē\ *adverb*
— **film·i·ness** \-mē-nəs\ *noun*

filo *also* **fil·lo** *variant of* PHYLLO

filo- — see FILI-

fils \'fils\ *noun, plural* **fils** [Arabic] (1931)
— see *dinar, dirham, rial* at MONEY table

¹**fil·ter** \'fil-tər\ *noun* [Middle English *filtre*, from Medieval Latin *filtrum* piece of felt used as a filter, of Germanic origin; akin to Old High German *filz* felt — more at FELT] (1563)
1 a : a porous article or mass (as of paper or sand) through which a gas or liquid is passed to separate out matter in suspension **b :** something that has the effect of a filter
2 : an apparatus containing a filter medium
3 a : a device or material for suppressing or minimizing waves or oscillations of certain frequencies (as of electricity, light, or sound) **b :** a transparent material (as colored glass) that absorbs light of certain wavelengths or colors selectively and is used for modifying light that reaches a sensitized photographic material — called also *color filter*

²**filter** *verb* **fil·tered; fil·ter·ing** \-t(ə-)riŋ\ (1576)
transitive verb
1 : to subject to the action of a filter
2 : to remove by means of a filter
intransitive verb
1 : to pass or move through or as if through a filter
2 : to come or go in small units over a period of time (people began *filtering* in)

fil·ter·able *also* **fil·tra·ble** \'fil-t(ə-)rə-bəl\ *adjective* (1908)
: capable of being filtered or of passing through a filter
— **fil·ter·abil·i·ty** \,fil-t(ə-)rə-'bi-lə-tē\ *noun*

filterable virus *noun* (1911)
: any of the infectious agents that pass through a filter of diatomite or unglazed porcelain with the filtrate and remain virulent and that include the viruses as presently understood and various other groups (as the mycoplasmas and rickettsias) which were originally considered viruses before their cellular nature was established

filter bed *noun* (circa 1874)
: a sand or gravel bed for filtering water or sewage

filter feeder *noun* (1928)
: an animal that obtains its food by filtering organic matter or minute organisms from a current of water that passes through some part of its system

filter paper *noun* (circa 1846)
: porous unsized paper used especially for filtering

filter tip *noun* (1932)
: a cigar or cigarette tip designed to filter the smoke before it enters the smoker's mouth; *also* **:** a cigar or cigarette provided with such a tip
— **fil·ter-tipped** \,fil-tər-'tipt\ *adjective*

filth \'filth\ *noun* [Middle English, from Old English *fȳlth*, from *fūl* foul] (before 12th century)
1 : foul or putrid matter; *especially* **:** loathsome dirt or refuse
2 a : moral corruption or defilement **b :** something that tends to corrupt or defile

filthy \'fil-thē\ *adjective* **filth·i·er; -est** (14th century)
1 : covered with or containing filth **:** offensively dirty
2 a : UNDERHAND, VILE **b :** OBSCENE
synonym see DIRTY
— **filth·i·ly** \-thə-lē\ *adverb*
— **filth·i·ness** \-thē-nəs\ *noun*

fil·trate \'fil-,trāt\ *noun* (circa 1846)
: material that has passed through a filter

fil·tra·tion \fil-'trā-shən\ *noun* (1605)
1 : the process of filtering
2 : the process of passing through or as if through a filter; *also* **:** DIFFUSION

fim·bria \'fim-brē-ə\ *noun, plural* **-bri·ae** \-brē-ē, -ˌī\ [New Latin, from Latin, fringe] (1752)
: a bordering fringe especially at the entrance of the fallopian tubes
— **fim·bri·al** \-brē-əl\ *adjective*

fim·bri·at·ed \'fim-brē-ˌā-təd\ *also* **fim·bri·ate** \-ˌāt\ *adjective* (15th century)
: having the edge or extremity bordered by slender processes : FRINGED
— **fim·bri·a·tion** \ˌfim-brē-'ā-shən\ *noun*

¹fin \'fin\ *noun* [Middle English *finn,* from Old English] (before 12th century)
1 : an external membranous process of an aquatic animal (as a fish) used in propelling or guiding the body — see FISH illustration
2 : something resembling a fin: as **a** : HAND, ARM **b** (1) : an appendage of a boat (as a submarine) (2) : an airfoil attached to an airplane for directional stability **c** : FLIPPER 1b **d** : any of the projecting ribs on a radiator or an engine cylinder
— **fin·like** \-ˌlīk\ *adjective*
— **finned** \'find\ *adjective*

²fin *verb* **finned; fin·ning** (1933)
transitive verb
: to equip with fins
intransitive verb
1 : to show the fins above the water
2 : to move through the water propelled by fins

³fin *noun* [Yiddish *finf* five, from Middle High German, from Old High German — more at FIVE] (1925)
slang : a 5-dollar bill

fi·na·gle \fə-'nā-gəl\ *verb* **fi·na·gled; fi·na·gling** \-g(ə-)liŋ\ [perhaps alteration of *fainaigue* (to renege)] (circa 1924)
transitive verb
1 : to obtain by indirect or involved means
2 : to obtain by trickery
intransitive verb
: to use devious or dishonest methods to achieve one's ends
— **fi·na·gler** \-g(ə-)lər\ *noun*

¹fi·nal \'fī-nᵊl\ *adjective* [Middle English, from Middle French, from Latin *finalis,* from *finis* boundary, end] (14th century)
1 a : not to be altered or undone ⟨all sales are *final*⟩ **b** : of or relating to a concluding court action or proceeding ⟨*final* decree⟩
2 : coming at the end : being the last in a series, process, or progress ⟨the *final* chapter⟩
3 : of or relating to the ultimate purpose or result of a process ⟨our *final* goal⟩
synonym see LAST
— **fi·nal·ly** \'fī-nᵊl-ē, 'fīn-lē\ *adverb*

²final *noun* (1609)
: something that is final: as **a** : a deciding match, game, heat, or trial — usually used in plural **b** : the last examination in a course — often used in plural

fi·na·le \fə-'na-lē, fi-'nä-\ *noun* [Italian, from *finale,* adjective, final, from Latin *finalis*] (1783)
: the close or termination of something: as **a** : the last section of an instrumental musical composition **b** : the closing part, scene, or number in a public performance **c** : the last and often climactic event or item in a sequence

fi·nal·ise *British variant of* FINALIZE

fi·nal·ist \'fī-nᵊl-ist\ *noun* (1898)
: a contestant in the finals of a competition

fi·nal·i·ty \fī-'na-lə-tē, fə-\ *noun, plural* **-ties** (1833)
1 a : the character or condition of being final, settled, irrevocable, or complete **b** : the condition of being at an ultimate point especially of development or authority
2 : something final; *especially* : a fundamental fact, action, or belief

fi·nal·ize \'fī-nᵊl-ˌīz\ *transitive verb* **-ized; -iz·ing** (1901)
1 : to put in final or finished form ⟨soon my conclusion will be *finalized* —D. D. Eisenhower⟩
2 : to give final approval to ⟨*finalizing* the papers prepared . . . by his staff —*Newsweek*⟩ □
— **fi·nal·iza·tion** \ˌfī-nᵊl-ə-'zā-shən\ *noun*

final solution *noun, often F&S capitalized* (1947)
: the Nazi program for extermination of all Jews in Europe

¹fi·nance \fə-'nan(t)s, 'fī-ˌ, fī-'\ *noun* [Middle English, payment, ransom, from Middle French, from *finer* to end, pay, from *fin* end — more at FINE] (1739)
1 *plural* : money or other liquid resources of a government, business, group, or individual
2 : the system that includes the circulation of money, the granting of credit, the making of investments, and the provision of banking facilities
3 : the science or study of the management of funds
4 : the obtaining of funds or capital : FINANCING □

²finance *transitive verb* **fi·nanced; fi·nanc·ing** (1866)
1 a : to raise or provide funds or capital for ⟨*finance* a new house⟩ **b** : to furnish with necessary funds ⟨*finance* a son through college⟩
2 : to sell something to on credit

finance company *noun* (circa 1924)
: a company that makes usually small short-term loans usually to individuals

fi·nan·cial \fə-'nan(t)-shəl, fī-\ *adjective* (1769)
: relating to finance or financiers
— **fi·nan·cial·ly** \-'nan(t)-sh(ə-)lē\ *adverb*

fi·nan·cier \ˌfi-nən-'sir; fə-ˌnan-, ˌfī-\ *noun* (1618)
1 : one who specializes in raising and expending public moneys
2 : one who deals with finance and investment on a large scale

fi·nanc·ing *noun* (1827)
: the act or process or an instance of raising or providing funds; *also* : the funds thus raised or provided

fin·back \'fin-ˌbak\ *noun* (1725)
: FIN WHALE

finch \'finch\ *noun* [Middle English, from Old English *finc;* akin to Old High German *fincho* finch and perhaps to Greek *spiza* chaffinch] (before 12th century)
: any of numerous songbirds (especially families Fringillidae, Estrildidae, and Emberizidae) having a short stout usually conical bill adapted for crushing seeds — compare BUNTING, CROSSBILL, GOLDFINCH, GROSBEAK, LINNET, SPARROW

¹find \'fīnd\ *verb* **found** \'faund\; **find·ing** [Middle English, from Old English *findan;* akin to Old High German *findan* to find, Latin *pont-, pons* bridge, Greek *pontos* sea, Sanskrit *patha* way, course] (before 12th century)
transitive verb
1 a : to come upon often accidentally : ENCOUNTER **b** : to meet with (a particular reception) ⟨hoped to *find* favor⟩
2 a : to come upon by searching or effort ⟨must *find* a suitable person for the job⟩ **b** : to discover by study or experiment ⟨*find* an answer⟩ **c** : to obtain by effort or management ⟨*find* the time to study⟩ **d** : ATTAIN, REACH ⟨the bullet *found* its mark⟩
3 a : to discover by the intellect or the feelings ⟨*find* much pleasure in your company⟩ **b** : to perceive (oneself) to be in a certain place or condition **c** : to gain or regain the use or power of ⟨trying to *find* his tongue⟩ **d** : to bring (oneself) to a realization of one's powers or of one's proper sphere of activity ⟨must help the student to *find* himself as an individual —N. M. Pusey⟩

4 a : PROVIDE, SUPPLY **b** : to furnish (room and board) especially as a condition of employment
5 : to determine and make a statement about ⟨*find* a verdict⟩ ⟨*found* her guilty⟩
intransitive verb
: to determine a case judicially by a verdict ⟨*find* for the defendant⟩
— **find·able** \'fīn-də-bəl\ *adjective*
— **find fault** : to criticize unfavorably

²find *noun* (1825)
1 : an act or instance of finding
2 : something found: as **a** : a valuable discovery ⟨an archaeological *find*⟩ **b** : a person whose ability proves to be unexpectedly good

find·er \'fīn-dər\ *noun* (14th century)
1 : one that finds
2 : a small astronomical telescope of low power and wide field attached to a larger telescope for finding an object
3 : VIEWFINDER

fin de siè·cle \ˌfan-də-sē-'e-kᵊl; faⁿ-də-syeklᵊ\ *adjective* [French, end of the century] (1890)
: of, relating to, or characteristic of the close of the 19th century and especially its literary and artistic climate of sophistication, world-weariness, and fashionable despair

find·ing \'fīn-diŋ\ *noun* (14th century)
1 a : the act of one that finds **b** : FIND 2
2 *plural* : small tools and supplies used by an artisan (as a dressmaker, jeweler, or shoemaker)
3 a : the result of a judicial examination or inquiry **b** : the results of an investigation — usually used in plural

find out (13th century)
transitive verb
1 : to learn by study, observation, or search : DISCOVER
2 a : to catch in an offense (as a crime) ⟨the culprits were soon *found out*⟩ **b** : to ascertain the true character or identity of ⟨the informer was *found out*⟩
intransitive verb
: to discover, learn, or verify something ⟨I don't know, but I'll *find out* for you⟩

¹fine \'fīn\ *noun* [Middle English, from Old French *fin,* from Latin *finis* boundary, end] (13th century)
1 *obsolete* : END, CONCLUSION

□ **USAGE**

finalize *Finalize* has been frequently castigated as an unnecessary neologism or as U.S. government gobbledygook. It appears to have first gained currency in Australia (where it has been acceptable all along) in the early 1920s. The U.S. Navy picked it up in the late 20s, and from there it came into widespread use. It is a standard formation (see -IZE). Our current evidence indicates it is most frequently used in government, business dealings, and child adoption; it usually is not found in belles-lettres.

finance Some critics have decreed that the American variant of *finance* with stress on the first syllable is to be avoided, perhaps because it is not the original stress pattern. By this reasoning, however, the original but now obsolete pronunciation of *balcony* and *abdomen,* with stress on the second syllable, should be revived and prescribed, while the British pronunciation of *garage* with stress on the first syllable should be condemned as an innovation. Long usage has proved both stressings of *finance* to be acceptable.

\ə\ abut \ᵊ\ kitten \ər\ further \a\ ash \ā\ ace \ä\ mop, mar \aú\ out \ch\ chin \e\ bet \ē\ easy \g\ go \i\ hit \ī\ ice \j\ job \ŋ\ sing \ō\ go \ó\ law \ói\ boy \th\ thin \th\ the \ü\ loot \ú\ foot \y\ yet \zh\ vision *see also* Guide to Pronunciation

2 : a compromise of a fictitious suit used as a form of conveyance of lands
3 a : a sum imposed as punishment for an offense **b :** a forfeiture or penalty paid to an injured party in a civil action
— **in fine :** in short
²**fine** *transitive verb* **fined; fin·ing** (1559)
: to impose a fine on : punish by a fine
³**fine** *adjective* **fin·er; fin·est** [Middle English *fin,* from Old French, from Latin *finis,* noun, end, limit] (13th century)
1 a : free from impurity **b** *of a metal* **:** having a stated proportion of pure metal in the composition expressed in parts per thousand ⟨a gold coin .9166 *fine*⟩
2 a (1) **:** very thin in gauge or texture ⟨*fine* thread⟩ (2) **:** not coarse ⟨*fine* sand⟩ (3) **:** very small ⟨*fine* print⟩ (4) **:** KEEN ⟨a knife with a *fine* edge⟩ (5) **:** very precise or accurate ⟨a *fine* adjustment⟩ ⟨trying to be too *fine* with his pitches⟩ **b :** physically trained or hardened close to the limit of efficiency — used of an athlete or animal
3 : delicate, subtle, or sensitive in quality, perception, or discrimination ⟨a *fine* distinction⟩
4 : superior in kind, quality, or appearance **:** EXCELLENT ⟨a *fine* job⟩ ⟨a *fine* day⟩ ⟨*fine* wines⟩
5 a : ORNATE 1 ⟨*fine* writing⟩ **b :** marked by or affecting elegance or refinement ⟨*fine* manners⟩
6 a : very well ⟨feel *fine*⟩ **b :** ALL RIGHT ⟨that's *fine* with me⟩
7 — used as an intensive ⟨the leader, in a *fine* frenzy, beheaded one of his wives —Brian Crozier⟩
— **fine·ness** \'fīn-nəs\ *noun*
⁴**fine** *adverb* (14th century)
1 : FINELY: as **a :** very well **b :** ALL RIGHT
2 : with a very narrow margin of time or space ⟨she had not intended to cut her escape so *fine* —Melinda Beck *et al.*⟩
⁵**fine** *verb* **fined; fin·ing** (14th century)
transitive verb
1 : PURIFY, CLARIFY ⟨*fine* and filter wine⟩
2 : to make finer in quality or size
intransitive verb
1 : to become pure or clear ⟨the ale will *fine*⟩
2 : to become smaller in lines or proportions
⁶**fi·ne** \'fē-(ˌ)nā\ *noun* [Italian, from Latin *finis* end] (circa 1798)
: END — used as a direction in music to mark the closing point after a repeat
fine art *noun* (1767)
1 a : art (as painting, sculpture, or music) concerned primarily with the creation of beautiful objects — usually used in plural **b :** objects of fine art
2 : an activity requiring a fine skill
fine·ly \'fīn-lē\ *adverb* (14th century)
: in a fine manner: as **a :** extremely well **:** EXCELLENTLY ⟨plays the hero very *finely* —New Yorker⟩ **b :** with close discrimination **:** PRECISELY **c :** with delicacy or subtlety **:** SENSITIVELY ⟨a leader *finely* attuned to the needs of the people⟩ **d :** MINUTELY ⟨*finely* ground meal⟩
fine print *noun* (1951)
: something thoroughly and often deliberately obscure; *especially* **:** a part of an agreement or document restricting out restrictions and limitations often in small type or obscure language
fin·ery \'fīn-rē, 'fī-nə-\ *noun, plural* **-er·ies** (1680)
: ORNAMENT, DECORATION; *especially* **:** dressy or showy clothing and jewels
fines \'fīnz\ *noun plural* [³*fine*] (circa 1903)
: finely crushed or powdered material (as ore); *also* **:** very small particles in a mixture of various sizes
fines herbes \fēⁿ-'zerb, fē-'nerb\ *noun plural* [French, literally, fine herbs] (1846)
: a mixture of herbs used as a seasoning or garnish
fine-spun \'fīn-'spən\ *adjective* (1647)

: developed with extreme care or delicacy; *also* **:** developed in excessively fine or subtle detail
¹**fi·nesse** \fə-'nes\ *noun* [Middle English, from Middle French, from *fin*] (1528)
1 : refinement or delicacy of workmanship, structure, or texture
2 : skillful handling of a situation **:** adroit maneuvering
3 : the withholding of one's highest card or trump in the hope that a lower card will take the trick because the only opposing higher card is in the hand of an opponent who has already played
²**finesse** *verb* **fi·nessed; fi·ness·ing** (1746)
intransitive verb
: to make a finesse in playing cards
transitive verb
1 : to play (a card) in a finesse
2 a : to bring about or manage by adroit maneuvering ⟨*finesse* his way through tight places —Marquis James⟩ **b :** EVADE, TRICK
fin·est \'fī-nəst\ *noun, plural in construction* [superlative of ³*fine*] (1951)
: POLICE OFFICERS — usually used with the possessive form of a city or area ⟨the city's *finest*⟩
fine structure *noun* (1935)
: microscopic structure of a biological entity or one of its parts especially as studied in preparations for the electron microscope
— **fine structural** *adjective*
fine-tooth comb \'fīn-ˌtüth-\ *noun* (1839)
1 : a comb with close-set teeth used especially for clearing parasites or foreign matter from the hair
2 : an attitude or system of thorough searching or scrutinizing ⟨went over the report with a *fine-tooth comb*⟩
fine-tune \'fīn-'tün\ *transitive verb* (1967)
1 a : to adjust precisely so as to bring to the highest level of performance or effectiveness ⟨*fine-tune* a TV set⟩ ⟨*fine-tune* the format⟩ **b :** to improve through minor alteration or revision ⟨*fine-tune* the temperature of the room⟩
2 : to stabilize (an economy) by small-scale fiscal and monetary manipulations
fin·fish \'fin-ˌfish\ *noun* (circa 1890)
: FISH 1b — compare SHELLFISH
¹**fin·ger** \'fiŋ-gər\ *noun* [Middle English, from Old English; akin to Old High German *fingar* finger] (before 12th century)
1 : any of the five terminating members of the hand **:** a digit of the forelimb; *especially* **:** one other than the thumb
2 a : something that resembles a finger ⟨a narrow *finger* of land⟩ **b :** a part of a glove into which a finger is inserted **c :** a projecting piece (as a pawl for a ratchet) brought into contact with an object to affect its motion
3 : the breadth of a finger
4 : INTEREST, SHARE — often used in the phrase *have a finger in the pie*
5 : BIRD 10 — usually used with *the*
— **fin·ger·like** \-ˌlīk\ *adjective*
²**finger** *verb* **fin·gered; fin·ger·ing** \-g(ə-)riŋ\ (15th century)
transitive verb
1 : to touch or feel with the fingers
2 a : to play (a musical instrument) with the fingers **b :** to play (as notes or chords) with a specific fingering **c :** to mark the notes of (a music score) as a guide in playing
3 : to point out **:** IDENTIFY
4 : to extend into or penetrate in the shape of a finger
intransitive verb
1 : to touch or handle something
2 a : to use the fingers in playing a musical instrument **b :** to have a certain fingering — used of a musical instrument
3 : to extend in the shape or manner of a finger
fin·ger·board \'fiŋ-gər-ˌbȯrd, -ˌbȯrd\ *noun* (circa 1672)

: the part of a stringed instrument against which the fingers press the strings to vary the pitch — see VIOLIN illustration
finger bowl *noun* (circa 1860)
: a small water bowl for rinsing the fingers at the table
fin·gered \'fiŋ-gərd\ *adjective* (circa 1529)
1 : having fingers especially of a specified kind or number — used in combination ⟨stubby-*fingered*⟩ ⟨five-*fingered*⟩
2 : having projections or processes like fingers ⟨the *fingered* roots of giant trees⟩
finger food *noun* (1928)
: a food that is to be held with the fingers for eating
fin·ger·hold \'fiŋ-gər-ˌhōld\ *noun* (1909)
1 : a hold or place of support for the fingers
2 : a tenuous hold or support
finger hole *noun* (1854)
1 : any of several holes in the side of a wind instrument (as a recorder) which may be covered or left open by the fingers to change the pitch of the tone
2 : a hole (as in a telephone dial or a bowling ball) into which the finger is placed to provide a grip
fin·ger·ing \'fiŋ-g(ə-)riŋ\ *noun* (14th century)
1 a : the act or method of using the fingers in playing an instrument **b :** the marking (as by figures on a musical score) of the method of fingering
2 : the act or process of handling or touching with the fingers
fin·ger·ling \'fiŋ-gər-liŋ\ *noun* (1836)
: a small fish especially up to one year of age
fin·ger·nail \'fiŋ-gər-ˌnāl, ˌfiŋ-gər-'nā(ə)l\ *noun* (13th century)
: the nail of a finger
finger painting *noun* (1937)
: a technique of spreading pigment on wet paper chiefly with the fingers; *also* **:** a picture so produced
fin·ger·pick·ing \'fiŋ-gər-ˌpi-kiŋ\ *noun* (1969)
: a method of playing a stringed instrument (as a guitar) with the thumb and tips of the fingers rather than with a pick
— **fin·ger·pick** *verb*
fin·ger–point·ing \-ˌpȯin-tiŋ\ *noun* (1949)
: the act of making explicit and often unfair accusations of blame
fin·ger·post \'fiŋ-gər-ˌpōst\ *noun* (1785)
1 : a post bearing one or more signs often terminating in a pointing finger
2 : something serving as a guide to understanding or knowledge
fin·ger·print \-ˌprint\ *noun* (1859)
1 : the impression of a fingertip on any surface; *also* **:** an ink impression of the lines upon the fingertip taken for the purpose of identification
2 : something that identifies: as **a :** a trait, trace, or characteristic revealing origin or responsibil-

fingerprint 1: *1* arch, *2* loop, *3* whorl, *4* composite

ity **b :** analytical evidence (as a spectrogram) that characterizes an object or substance; *especially* **:** the chromatogram or electropherotogram obtained by cleaving a protein by enzymatic action and subjecting the resulting collection of peptides to two-dimensional chromatography or electrophoresis
— **fingerprint** *transitive verb*
— **fin·ger·print·ing** *noun*

finger spelling *noun* (1918)
: communication by signs made with the fingers — called also *dactylology*

¹**fin·ger·tip** \-,tip\ *noun* (1842)
1 : the tip of a finger
2 : a protective covering for the end of a finger
— **at one's fingertips** : instantly or readily available

²**fingertip** *adjective* (1926)
1 : readily accessible : being within easy reach ⟨*fingertip* information⟩ ⟨*fingertip* controls⟩
2 : extending from head or shoulders to mid-thigh — used of clothing

finger wave *noun* (circa 1934)
: a method of setting hair by dampening with water or wave solution and forming waves or curls with the fingers and a comb

fin·i·al \'fi-nē-əl\ *noun* [Middle English, from *final, finial* final] (15th century)
1 : a usually foliated ornament forming an upper extremity especially in Gothic architecture
2 : a crowning ornament or detail (as a decorative knob)

fin·i·cal \'fi-ni-kəl\ *adjective* [probably from ³*fine*] (1592)
: FINICKY
— **fin·i·cal·ly** \-k(ə-)lē\ *adverb*
— **fin·i·cal·ness** \-kəl-nəs\ *noun*

fin·ick·ing \-kiŋ, -kən\ *adjective* [alteration of *finical*] (1661)
: FINICKY

fin·icky \'fi-ni-kē\ *adjective* [alteration of *finicking*] (circa 1825)
1 : extremely or excessively nice, exacting, or meticulous in taste or standards
2 : requiring much care, precision, or attentive effort ⟨a *finicky* recipe⟩
— **fin·ick·i·ness** *noun*

fi·nis \'fi-nəs, 'fī-nəs; fə-'nē\ *noun* [Middle English, from Latin] (15th century)
: END, CONCLUSION

¹**fin·ish** \'fi-nish\ *verb* [Middle English *finisshen,* from Middle French *finiss-,* stem of *finir,* from Latin *finire,* from *finis*] (14th century)
intransitive verb
1 a : to come to an end : TERMINATE **b** : END 1b
2 a : to come to the end of a course, task, or undertaking **b** : to end relations — used with *with* ⟨decided to *finish* with him for good⟩
3 : to end a competition in a specified manner or position ⟨*finished* third in the race⟩
transitive verb
1 a : to bring to an end : TERMINATE ⟨*finished* the speech and sat down⟩ **b** : to use or dispose of entirely ⟨her sandwich *finished* the loaf⟩
2 a : to bring to completion or issue ⟨hope to *finish* their new home before winter⟩ **b** : to provide with a finish; *especially* : to put a final coat or surface on ⟨*finish* a table with varnish⟩
3 a : to defeat or ruin utterly and finally ⟨the scandal *finished* his career⟩ **b** : to bring about the death of
synonym see CLOSE
— **fin·ish·er** *noun*

²**finish** *noun* (1779)
1 : something that completes or perfects: as **a** : the fine or decorative work required for a building or one of its parts **b** : a finishing material used in painting **c** : the final treatment or coating of a surface **d** : the taste in the mouth after swallowing a beverage (as wine)
2 a : final stage : END **b** : the cause of one's ruin
3 : the result or product of a finishing process
4 : the quality or state of being perfected

fin·ished *adjective* (1709)
: marked by the highest quality : CONSUMMATE

finishing school *noun* (circa 1837)
: a private school for girls that emphasizes cultural studies and prepares students especially for social activities

finish line *noun* (1899)
: a line marking the end of a racecourse

fi·nite \'fī-,nīt\ *adjective* [Middle English *finit,* from Latin *finitus,* past participle of *finire*] (15th century)
1 a : having definite or definable limits ⟨*finite* number of possibilities⟩ **b** : having a limited nature or existence ⟨*finite* beings⟩
2 : completely determinable in theory or in fact by counting, measurement, or thought ⟨the *finite* velocity of light⟩
3 a : less than an arbitrary positive integer and greater than the negative of that integer **b** : having a finite number of elements ⟨a *finite* set⟩
4 : of, relating to, or being a verb or verb form that can function as a predicate or as the initial element of one and that is limited (as in tense, person, and number)
— **finite** *noun*
— **fi·nite·ly** *adverb*
— **fi·nite·ness** *noun*

finite difference *noun* (1807)
: any of a sequence of differences obtained by incrementing successively the dependent variable of a function by a fixed amount; *especially* : any of such differences obtained from a polynomial function using successive integral values of its dependent variable

fi·ni·tude \'fī-nə-,tüd, -,tyüd, 'fin-ə-\ *noun* (1644)
: finite quality or state

¹**fink** \'fiŋk\ *noun* [origin unknown] (1903)
1 : one who is disapproved of or is held in contempt
2 : STRIKEBREAKER
3 : INFORMER 2

²**fink** *intransitive verb* (circa 1925)
: to turn informer : SQUEAL

fink out *intransitive verb* (1956)
: BACK OUT, COP OUT

Fin·land·isa·tion *British variant of* FINLANDIZATION

Fin·land·iza·tion \,fin-lən-də-'zā-shən, (,)fin-,lan-\ *noun* [Finland] (1969)
: a foreign policy of neutrality under the influence of the Soviet Union; *also* : the conversion to such a policy
— **Fin·land·ize** \'fin-lən-,dīz, (,)fin-'lan-\ *transitive verb*

Finn \'fin\ *noun* [Swedish *Finne*] (before 12th century)
1 : a member of a people speaking Finnish or a Finnic language
2 a : a native or inhabitant of Finland **b** : one who is of Finnish descent

fin·nan had·die \,fi-nən-'ha-dē\ *noun* [alteration of *findon haddock,* from *Findon,* village in Scotland] (1811)
: smoked haddock — called also *finnan haddock*

Finn·ic \'fi-nik\ *adjective* (1668)
1 : of or relating to the Finns
2 : of, relating to, or constituting the branch of the Finno-Ugric subfamily that includes Finnish, Estonian, and Lapp

¹**Finn·ish** \'fi-nish\ *adjective* (1699)
: of, relating to, or characteristic of Finland, the Finns, or Finnish

²**Finnish** *noun* (circa 1845)
: a Finno-Ugric language spoken in Finland, Karelia, and small areas of Sweden and Norway

Fin·no–Ugri·an \,fi-(,)nō-'(y)ü-grē-ən\ *adjective* (1880)
: FINNO-UGRIC
— **Finno–Ugrian** *noun*

Fin·no–Ugric \,fi-nō-'(y)ü-grik\ *adjective* (1879)
1 : of, relating to, or constituting a subfamily of the Uralic family of languages comprising various languages spoken in Hungary, Lapland, Finland, Estonia, and parts of western Russia
2 : of or relating to any of the peoples speaking Finno-Ugric languages
— **Finno–Ugric** *noun*

fin·ny \'fi-nē\ *adjective* (1590)
1 : provided with or characterized by fins
2 : relating to or being fish

fino \'fē-(,)nō\ *noun, plural* **finos** [Spanish, from *fino* fine, from *fin* end, from Latin *finis*] (1846)
: a very dry Spanish sherry

fin whale *noun* (1885)
: a baleen whale (*Balaenoptera physalus*) that attains a length of over 60 feet (18.3 meters) and is found in arctic to tropical waters worldwide — called also *finback*

fin whale

fiord *variant of* FJORD

fio·ri·tu·ra \fē-,ȯr-ə-'tur-ə\ *noun, plural* **-tu·re** \-'tur-ē\ [Italian, literally, flowering, from *fiorito,* past participle of *fiorire* to flower, from (assumed) Vulgar Latin *florire* — more at FLOURISH] (1841)
: ORNAMENT 5

fip·ple flute \'fi-pəl-\ *noun* [origin unknown] (1911)
: any of a group of wind instruments (as a flageolet or recorder) having a straight tubular shape, a whistle mouthpiece, and finger holes

fir \'fər\ *noun* [Middle English, from Old English *fyrh;* akin to Old High German *forha* fir, Latin *quercus* oak] (before 12th century)
1 : any of a genus (*Abies*) of north temperate evergreen trees of the pine family that have flattish leaves, circular leaf scars, and erect female cones and are valued for their wood; *also* : any of various conifers (as the Douglas fir) of other genera
2 : the wood of a fir

¹**fire** \'fīr\ *noun, often attributive* [Middle English, from Old English *fyr;* akin to Old High German *fiur* fire, Greek *pyr*] (before 12th century)
1 a (1) : the phenomenon of combustion manifested in light, flame, and heat **(2)** : one of the four elements of the alchemists **b (1)** : burning passion : ARDOR **(2)** : liveliness of imagination : INSPIRATION
2 a : fuel in a state of combustion (as on a hearth) **b** *British* : a small gas or electric space heater
3 a : a destructive burning (as of a building) **b (1)** : death or torture by fire **(2)** : severe trial or ordeal
4 : BRILLIANCY, LUMINOSITY ⟨the *fire* of a gem⟩
5 a : the firing of weapons (as firearms, artillery, or missiles) **b** : intense verbal attack or criticism **c** : a rapidly delivered series (as of remarks)
— **fire·less** \-ləs\ *adjective*
— **on fire 1** : being consumed by fire : AFLAME **2** : EAGER, BURNING
— **under fire 1** : exposed to fire from an enemy's weapons **2** : under attack

²**fire** *verb* **fired; fir·ing** (13th century)
transitive verb
1 a : to set on fire : KINDLE; *also* : IGNITE ⟨*fire* a rocket engine⟩ **b (1)** : to give life or spirit to : INSPIRE **(2)** : to fill with passion or enthusiasm — often used with *up* **c** : to light up as if by fire **d** : to cause to start operating — usually used with *up*
2 a : to drive out or away by or as if by fire **b** : to dismiss from a position

3 a (1) : to cause to explode : DETONATE (2) : to propel from or as if from a gun — DISCHARGE, LAUNCH ⟨*fire* a rocket⟩ (3) : SHOOT 1b ⟨*fire* a gun⟩ (4) : to score (a number) in a game or contest **b** : to throw with speed or force ⟨*fired* the ball to first base⟩ ⟨*fire* a left jab⟩ **c** : to utter with force and rapidity
4 : to apply fire or fuel to: as **a** : to process by applying heat **b** : to feed or serve the fire of ~ *intransitive verb*
1 a : to take fire : KINDLE, IGNITE **b** : to begin operation : START ⟨the engine *fired*⟩ **c** : to operate especially as the result of the application of an electrical impulse ⟨the spark plug *fires*⟩
2 a : to become irritated or angry — often used with *up* **b** : to become filled with excitement or enthusiasm
3 a : to discharge a firearm **b** : to emit or let fly an object
4 : to tend a fire
5 : to transmit a nerve impulse
— **fire·able** \'fīr-ə-bəl, 'fī-rə-\ *adjective*
— **fir·er** *noun*

fire and brimstone *noun* (13th century)
: the torments suffered by sinners in hell
— **fire–and–brimstone** *adjective*

fire ant *noun* (1796)
: any of a genus (*Solenopsis*) of fiercely stinging omnivorous ants; *especially* : IMPORTED FIRE ANT

fire·arm \'fīr-,ärm\ *noun* (1646)
: a weapon from which a shot is discharged by gunpowder — usually used of small arms

fire away *intransitive verb* (1840)
: to speak without hesitation — usually used as an imperative

fire·back \-,bak\ *noun* (1847)
: an often decorated cast-iron plate lining the back wall of a fireplace

fire·ball \'fīr-,bȯl\ *noun* (1555)
1 : a ball of fire; *also* : something resembling such a ball ⟨the primordial *fireball* associated with the beginning of the universe —*Scientific American*⟩
2 : a brilliant meteor that may trail bright sparks
3 : the highly luminous cloud of vapor and dust created by a nuclear explosion
4 : a highly energetic person

fire·ball·er \-,bȯ-lər\ *noun* (1946)
: a baseball pitcher known for throwing fastballs
— **fire·ball·ing** \-liŋ\ *adjective*

fire·base \-,bās\ *noun* (1968)
: a secured site from which field artillery can lay down interdicting fire

fire blight *noun* (1817)
: a destructive infectious disease especially of apples, pears, and related fruits caused by a bacterium (*Erwinia amylovora*)

fire·boat \'fīr-,bōt\ *noun* (1849)
: a ship equipped with fire-fighting apparatus

fire·bomb \-,bäm\ *noun* (1895)
: an incendiary bomb
— **firebomb** *transitive verb*

fire·box \-,bäks\ *noun* (1791)
1 : a chamber (as of a furnace or steam boiler) that contains a fire
2 : a box containing an apparatus for transmitting an alarm to a fire station

fire·brand \-,brand\ *noun* (13th century)
1 : a piece of burning wood
2 : one that creates unrest or strife (as in aggressively promoting a cause) : AGITATOR

fire·brat \-,brat\ *noun* (1895)
: a wingless insect (*Thermobia domestica*) related to the silverfish and found in warm moist places

fire·break \-,brāk\ *noun* (1841)
: a barrier of cleared or plowed land intended to check a forest or grass fire

fire–breath·ing \-,brē-thiŋ\ *adjective* (1933)
: intimidatingly or violently aggressive in speech and manner ⟨a *fire-breathing* orator⟩

fire·brick \-,brik\ *noun* (1793)
: a refractory brick capable of sustaining high temperatures that is used especially for lining furnaces or fireplaces

fire brigade *noun* (1838)
: a body of firefighters: as **a** : a usually private or temporary fire-fighting organization **b** *British* : FIRE DEPARTMENT

fire·bug \'fīr-,bəg\ *noun* (1872)
: INCENDIARY, PYROMANIAC

fire chief *noun* (1889)
: the head of a fire department

fire·clay \'fīr-,klā\ *noun* (1819)
: clay capable of withstanding high temperatures that is used especially for firebrick and crucibles

fire control *noun* (1864)
: the planning, preparation, and delivery of fire on targets

fire·crack·er \'fīr-,kra-kər\ *noun* (1829)
: a usually paper cylinder containing an explosive and a fuse and set off to make a noise

fired \'fīrd\ *adjective* (1889)
: using a specified fuel — usually used in combination ⟨oil-*fired* power plant⟩

fire·damp \-,damp\ *noun* (1677)
: a combustible mine gas that consists chiefly of methane; *also* : the explosive mixture of this gas with air

fire department *noun* (1825)
1 : an organization for preventing or extinguishing fires; *especially* : a government division (as in a municipality) having these duties
2 : the members of a fire department

fire·dog \-,dȯg\ *noun* (1792)
chiefly Southern & Midland : ANDIRON

fire·drake \'fīr-,drāk\ *noun* [Middle English *firdrake*, from Old English *fȳrdraca*, from *fȳr* + *draca* dragon, from Latin *draco* — more at DRAGON] (before 12th century)
: a fire-breathing dragon especially in Germanic mythology

fire drill *noun* (circa 1890)
: a practice drill in extinguishing fires or in the conduct and manner of exit in case of fire

fire–eat·er \'fīr-,ē-tər\ *noun* (1672)
1 : a performer who pretends to eat fire
2 a : a violent or pugnacious person **b** : a person who displays very militant or aggressive partisanship

fire–eat·ing \-,ē-tiŋ\ *adjective* (1819)
: violent or highly militant in disposition, bearing, or policy ⟨a *fire-eating* radical⟩

fire engine *noun* (circa 1680)
: a usually mobile apparatus for directing an extinguishing agent upon fires; *especially* : FIRE TRUCK

fire–en·gine red \'fīr-,en-jən-\ *noun* (1954)
: a bright red

fire escape *noun* (1788)
: a device for escape from a burning building; *especially* : a metal stairway attached to the outside of a building

fire extinguisher *noun* (1849)
: a portable or wheeled apparatus for putting out small fires by ejecting extinguishing chemicals

fire·fight \'fīr-,fīt\ *noun* (1899)
1 a : a usually brief intense exchange of fire between opposing military units **b** : a hostile confrontation that involves gunfire
2 : SKIRMISH 2b

fire·fight·er \-,fī-tər\ *noun* (1903)
: a person who fights fires : FIREMAN 2
— **fire fighting** *noun*

fire·fly \-,flī\ *noun* (1658)
: any of various winged nocturnal beetles (especially family Lampyridae) that produce a bright soft intermittent light by oxidation of luciferin especially for courtship purposes

fire·guard \-,gärd\ *noun* (1833)
1 : a person who watches for the outbreak of fire; *also* : a person whose duty is to extinguish fires
2 : FIRE SCREEN
3 : FIREBREAK

fire hall *noun* (1881)
chiefly Canadian : FIRE STATION

fire·house \'fīr-,haus\ *noun* (1901)
: FIRE STATION

fire irons *noun plural* (1648)
: utensils (as tongs) for tending a fire especially in a fireplace

fire·light \'fīr-,līt\ *noun* (before 12th century)
: the light of a fire (as in a fireplace)
— **fire·lit** \-,lit\ *adjective*

fire·lock \-,läk\ *noun* (1547)
1 : a gun's lock employing a slow match to ignite the powder charge; *also* : a gun having such a lock
2 a : FLINTLOCK **b** : WHEEL LOCK

fire·man \-mən\ *noun* (14th century)
1 : a person who tends or feeds fires : STOKER
2 : a member of a fire department : FIREFIGHTER
3 : an enlisted man in the navy who works with engineering machinery
4 : a relief pitcher in baseball

fire·man·ic \-,ma-nik\ *adjective* [*fireman* + [1]-*ic*] (1902)
: of or relating to firefighters or fire fighting

fire off *transitive verb* (1888)
: to write and send usually in haste or anger ⟨*fired off* a memo⟩

fire opal *noun* (1816)
: GIRASOLE 2

fire·place \'fīr-,plās\ *noun* (1698)
1 : a framed opening made in a chimney to hold an open fire : HEARTH; *also* : a metal container with a smoke pipe used for the same purpose
2 : an outdoor structure of brick, stone, or metal for an open fire
— **fire·placed** \-,plāst\ *adjective*

fire·plug \-,pləg\ *noun* (1713)
: HYDRANT

fire·pot \-,pät\ *noun* (1627)
1 : a clay pot filled with combustibles formerly used as a missile in war
2 : a vessel used in Oriental cuisine for cooking foods in broth at the table; *also* : the food cooked in it

fire·pow·er \-,pau(-ə)r\ *noun* (1913)
1 : the capacity (as of a military unit) to deliver effective fire on a target **b** : effective fire
2 a : effective power or force ⟨intellectual *firepower*⟩ **b** : the scoring action or potential of a team or player

¹fire·proof \-,prüf\ *adjective* (circa 1638)
: proof against or resistant to fire

²fireproof *transitive verb* (1867)
: to make fireproof

fire sale *noun* (1891)
: a sale of merchandise damaged in a fire; *also* : a sale at very low prices

fire screen *noun* (15th century)
: a protective screen before a fireplace

fire ship *noun* (1588)
: a ship carrying combustibles or explosives sent among the enemy's ships or works to set them on fire

¹fire·side \'fīr-,sīd\ *noun* (1563)
1 : a place near the fire or hearth
2 : HOME

²fireside *adjective* (1740)
: having an informal or intimate quality ⟨a *fireside* chat⟩

fire station *noun* (1877)
: a building housing fire apparatus and usually firefighters

fire·stone \'fīr-,stōn\ *noun* (before 12th century)
1 : pyrite formerly used for striking fire; *also* : FLINT
2 : a stone that will endure high heat

fire·stop \-,stäp\ *noun* (1897)
: material used to close open parts especially of a building for preventing the spread of fire
— **fire·stop** *transitive verb*

fire·storm \-,stȯrm\ *noun* (1945)
1 : a large usually stationary fire characterized by very high temperatures in which the central

column of rising heated air induces strong inward winds which supply oxygen to the fire
2 : a sudden or violent outburst ⟨a *firestorm* of public protest⟩

fire·thorn \-,thȯrn\ *noun* (circa 1900)
: any of a genus (*Pyracantha*) of usually thorny ornamental shrubs of the rose family; *especially* : a European semievergreen shrub (*P. coccinea*) with orange-red berries

fire tower *noun* (1827)
: a tower (as in a forest) from which a watch for fires is maintained

fire·trap \'fīr-,trap\ *noun* (1881)
: a place (as a building) apt to catch on fire or difficult to escape from in case of fire

fire truck *noun* (1935)
: an automotive vehicle equipped with firefighting apparatus

fire wall *noun* (1759)
: a wall constructed to prevent the spread of fire

fire·wa·ter \'fīr-,wȯ-tər, -,wä-\ *noun* (1817)
: strong alcoholic liquor

fire·weed \-,wēd\ *noun* (1784)
: any of several plants that grow especially in clearings or burned districts: as **a :** a weedy composite (*Erechtites hieracifolia*) of the eastern U.S. and Canada that has clusters of brush-shaped flower heads with no ray flowers **b :** a tall perennial (*Epilobium angustifolium*) of the evening-primrose family that has long spikes of pinkish purple flowers and is an important honey plant in some areas — called also *willow herb*

fire·wood \-,wu̇d\ *noun* (14th century)
: wood used for fuel

fire·work \-,wərk\ *noun* (1575)
1 : a device for producing a striking display by the combustion of explosive or flammable compositions
2 *plural* : a display of fireworks
3 *plural* : a display of temper or intense conflict **b :** a spectacular display ⟨the *fireworks* of autumn leaves⟩

fir·ing \'fīr-iŋ\ *noun* (14th century)
1 : the act or process of one that fires
2 : the process of maturing ceramic products by the application of heat

firing line *noun* (1881)
1 : a line from which fire is delivered against a target
2 : the forefront of an activity — used especially in the phrase *on the firing line*

firing pin *noun* (1874)
: the pin that strikes the cartridge primer in the breech mechanism of a firearm

firing squad *noun* (1904)
1 : a detachment detailed to fire volleys over the grave of one buried with military honors
2 : a detachment detailed to carry out a sentence of death by shooting

fir·kin \'fər-kən\ *noun* [Middle English, ultimately from Middle Dutch *veerdel* fourth, from *veer* four; akin to Old English *fēower* — more at FOUR] (14th century)
1 : a small wooden vessel or cask
2 : any of various British units of capacity usually equal to ¼ barrel

¹firm \'fərm\ *adjective* [Middle English *ferm,* from Middle French, from Latin *firmus;* akin to Greek *thronos* chair, throne] (14th century)
1 a : securely or solidly fixed in place **b :** not weak or uncertain : VIGOROUS **c :** having a solid or compact structure that resists stress or pressure
2 a (1) **:** not subject to change or revision (2) **:** not subject to price weakness : STEADY **b :** not easily moved or disturbed : STEADFAST **c :** WELL-FOUNDED
3 : indicating firmness or resolution ⟨a *firm* mouth⟩
— **firm·ly** *adverb*
— **firm·ness** *noun*

²firm *adverb* (14th century)
: in a firm manner : STEADFASTLY, FIXEDLY

³firm (14th century)
transitive verb
1 a : to make secure or fast : TIGHTEN ⟨*firming* her grip on the racquet⟩ — often used with *up* **b :** to make solid or compact ⟨*firm* the soil⟩
2 : to put into final form : SETTLE ⟨*firm* a contract⟩ ⟨*firm* up plans⟩
3 : to give additional support to : STRENGTHEN — usually used with *up*
intransitive verb
1 : to become firm : HARDEN — often used with *up*
2 : to recover from a decline : IMPROVE ⟨the market is *firming*⟩

⁴firm *noun* [German *Firma,* from Italian, signature, ultimately from Latin *firmare* to make firm, confirm, from *firmus*] (1744)
1 : the name or title under which a company transacts business
2 : a partnership of two or more persons that is not recognized as a legal person distinct from the members composing it
3 : a business unit or enterprise

fir·ma·ment \'fər-mə-mənt\ *noun* [Middle English, from Late Latin & Latin; Late Latin *firmamentum,* from Latin, support, from *firmare*] (13th century)
1 : the vault or arch of the sky : HEAVENS
2 *obsolete* : BASIS
3 : the field or sphere of an interest or activity ⟨the international fashion *firmament*⟩
— **fir·ma·men·tal** \,fər-mə-'men-t²l\ *adjective*

fir·mer chisel \'fər-mər-\ *noun* [French *fermoir* chisel, alteration of Middle French *formoir,* from *former* to form, from Old French *forme* form] (1823)
: a woodworking chisel with a thin flat blade

firm·ware \'fərm-,war, -,wer\ *noun* (1967)
: computer programs contained permanently in a hardware device (as a read-only memory)

firn \'firn\ *noun* [German, from Old High German *firni* old; akin to Old English *faran*] (1853)
: NÉVÉ

¹first \'fərst\ *adjective* [Middle English, from Old English *fyrst;* akin to Old High German *furist* first, Old English *faran* to go — more at FARE] (before 12th century)
: preceding all others in time, order, or importance: as **a :** EARLIEST **b :** being the lowest forward gear or speed of a motor vehicle **c :** having the highest or most prominent part among a group of similar voices or instruments ⟨*first* violins⟩

²first *adverb* (before 12th century)
1 a : before another in time, space, or importance **b :** in the first place — often used with *of all* **c :** for the first time
2 : in preference to something else : SOONER

³first *noun* (13th century)
1 — see NUMBER table
2 : something that is first: as **a :** the first occurrence or item of a kind **b :** the first forward gear or speed of a motor vehicle **c :** the highest or chief voice or instrument of a group **d :** an article of commerce of the finest grade **e :** the winning or highest place in a competition, examination, or contest
3 : FIRST BASE
— **at first :** at the beginning : INITIALLY

first aid *noun* (1882)
: emergency care or treatment given to an ill or injured person before regular medical aid can be obtained

first base *noun* (1845)
1 : the base that must be touched first by a base runner in baseball
2 : the player position for defending the area around first base
3 : the first step or stage in a course of action ⟨plans never got to *first base*⟩
— **first base·man** \-'bā-smən\ *noun*

first·born \'fərs(t)-'bȯrn\ *adjective* (14th century)
: first brought forth : ELDEST

— **firstborn** *noun*

first cause *noun* (14th century)
: the self-created ultimate source of all being

first-class \'fərs(t)-'klas\ *adjective* (circa 1838)
1 : of or relating to first class
2 : of the highest quality ⟨a *first-class* meal⟩
— **first-class** *adverb*

first class *noun* (1750)
: the first or highest group in a classification: as **a :** the highest of usually three classes of travel accommodations **b :** a class of mail that comprises letters, postcards, or matter sealed against inspection

first cousin *noun* (1661)
: COUSIN 1a

first day cover *noun* (1932)
: a philatelic cover franked with a newly issued postage stamp and postmarked on the first day of issue at a city officially chosen for first day sale

first-degree burn *noun* (circa 1929)
: a mild burn characterized by heat, pain, and reddening of the burned surface but not exhibiting blistering or charring of tissues

first down *noun* (1897)
1 : the first of a series of usually four downs in which a football team must net a 10-yard gain to retain possession of the ball
2 : a gain of a total of 10 or more yards within usually four downs giving the team the right to start a new series of downs

first edition *noun* (circa 1828)
: the copies of a literary work first printed from the same type and issued at the same time; *also* : a single copy from a first edition

first estate *noun, often F&E capitalized* (1935)
: the first of the traditional political estates; *specifically* : CLERGY

first floor *noun* (15th century)
1 : GROUND FLOOR 1
2 *chiefly British* : the floor next above the ground floor

first-fruits \'fərs(t)-'früts\ *noun plural* (14th century)
1 : the earliest gathered fruits offered to the Deity in acknowledgment of the gift of fruitfulness
2 : the earliest products or results of an endeavor

first-hand \'fərst-'hand\ *adjective* (1748)
: obtained by, coming from, or being direct personal observation or experience ⟨a *firsthand* account of the war⟩
— **firsthand** *adverb*

first lady *noun, often F&L capitalized* (1834)
1 : the wife or hostess of the chief executive of a country or jurisdiction
2 : the leading woman of an art or profession

first lieutenant *noun* (1782)
1 : a commissioned officer in the army, air force, or marine corps ranking above a second lieutenant and below a captain
2 : a naval officer responsible for a ship's upkeep

first·ling \'fərst-liŋ\ *noun* (1535)
1 : the first of a class or kind
2 : the first produce or result of something

first·ly \-lē\ *adverb* (circa 1532)
: in the first place : FIRST

first mortgage *noun* (1855)
: a mortgage that has priority as a lien over all mortgages and liens except those imposed by law

first name *noun* (13th century)
: the name that stands first in one's full name

first night *noun* (1711)

: the night on which a theatrical production is first performed at a given place; *also* **:** the performance itself

first–night·er \'fərs(t)-'nī-tər\ *noun* (1882)
: a spectator at a first-night performance

first off *adverb* (1880)
: in the first place **:** before anything else

first offender *noun* (1849)
: one convicted of an offense for the first time

first papers *noun plural* (1912)
: papers declaring intention filed by an applicant for citizenship as the first step in the naturalization process

first person *noun* (1520)
1 a : a set of linguistic forms (as verb forms, pronouns, and inflectional affixes) referring to the speaker or writer of the utterance in which they occur **b :** a linguistic form belonging to such a set **c :** reference of a linguistic form to the speaker or writer of the utterance in which it occurs
2 : a style of discourse marked by general use of verbs and pronouns of the first person

¹first–rate \'fərs(t)-'rāt\ *adjective* (1671)
: of the first order of size, importance, or quality
— **first–rate·ness** *noun*
— **first–rat·er** \-'rā-tər\ *noun*

²first–rate *adverb* (1844)
: very well ⟨is getting along *first-rate*, now —Mark Twain⟩

First Reader *noun* (1895)
: a Christian Scientist chosen to conduct meetings for a specified time and specifically to read aloud from the writings of Mary Baker Eddy

first reading *noun* (circa 1703)
: the first submitting of a bill before a quorum of a legislative assembly usually by title or number only

first–run \'fərs(t)-'rən\ *adjective* (1912)
: available for public viewing for the first time ⟨*first-run* movies⟩; *also* **:** exhibiting first-run movies ⟨*first-run* theaters⟩

first sergeant *noun* (circa 1860)
1 : a noncommissioned officer serving as the chief assistant to the commander of a military unit (as a company or squadron)
2 : the rank of a first sergeant; *specifically* **:** a rank in the army above a platoon sergeant and below a command sergeant major and in the marine corps above a gunnery sergeant and below a sergeant major

first strike *noun* (1960)
: a preemptive nuclear attack
— **first–strike** *adjective*

first–string \'fərs(t)-'striŋ\ *adjective* (1917)
1 : being a regular as distinguished from a substitute (as on a team)
2 : FIRST-RATE

first water *noun* (1753)
1 : the purest luster — used of gems
2 : the highest grade, degree, or quality

first world *noun, often F&W capitalized* [after *third world*] (1967)
: the highly developed industrialized nations often considered the westernized countries of the world

firth \'fərth\ *noun* [Middle English, from Old Norse *fjǫrthr* — more at FORD] (14th century)
: ESTUARY

fisc \'fisk\ *noun* [Latin *fiscus*] (1598)
: a state or royal treasury

¹fis·cal \'fis-kəl\ *adjective* [Latin *fiscalis*, from *fiscus* basket, treasury] (1563)
1 : of or relating to taxation, public revenues, or public debt ⟨*fiscal* policy⟩
2 : of or relating to financial matters
— **fis·cal·ly** \-kə-lē\ *adverb*

²fiscal *noun* (1929)
1 : REVENUE STAMP
2 : FISCAL YEAR

fiscal year *noun* (1843)
: an accounting period of 12 months

¹fish \'fish\ *noun, plural* **fish** *or* **fish·es** *often attributive* [Middle English, from Old English *fisc;* akin to Old High German *fisc* fish, Latin *piscis*] (before 12th century)
1 a : an aquatic animal — usually used in combination ⟨star*fish*⟩ ⟨cuttle*fish*⟩ **b :** any of numerous cold-blooded strictly aquatic craniate vertebrates that include the bony fishes and usually the cartilaginous and jawless fishes and that have typically an elongated somewhat spindle-shaped body terminating in a broad caudal fin, limbs in the form of fins when present at all, and a 2-chambered heart by which blood is sent through thoracic gills to be oxygenated
2 : the flesh of fish used as food
3 a : a person who is caught or is wanted (as in a criminal investigation) **b :** FELLOW, PERSON ⟨an odd *fish*⟩ **c :** SUCKER 5a
4 : something that resembles a fish: as **a** *plural, capitalized* **:** PISCES 1, 2a **b :** TORPEDO 2b
— **fish·less** \'fish-ləs\ *adjective*
— **fish·like** \-ˌlīk\ *adjective*
— **fish out of water :** a person who is in an unnatural or uncomfortable sphere or situation
— **fish to fry :** concerns or interests to pursue — usually used with *other*
— **neither fish nor fowl :** one that does not belong to a particular class or category

fish 1b: **1** mandible, **2** nasal opening, **3** eye,
4 cheek, **5** operculum, **6** dorsal fins, **7** lateral line,
8 caudal fin, **9** scales, **10** anal fin, **11** anus,
12 pectoral fin, **13** pelvic fin, **14** maxilla,
15 premaxilla, **16** upper jaw

²fish (before 12th century)
intransitive verb
1 : to attempt to catch fish
2 : to seek something by roundabout means ⟨*fishing* for a compliment⟩
3 a : to search for something underwater ⟨*fish* for pearls⟩ **b :** to engage in a search by groping or feeling ⟨*fishing* around in her purse for her keys⟩
transitive verb
1 a : to try to catch fish in **b :** to fish with **:** use (as a boat, net, or bait) in fishing
2 a : to go fishing for ⟨*fish* salmon⟩ **b :** to pull or draw as if fishing ⟨*fished* the ball from under the car⟩ ⟨*fish* wires through a conduit⟩
— **fish·abil·i·ty** \ˌfi-shə-'bi-lə-tē\ *noun*
— **fish·able** \'fi-shə-bəl\ *adjective*
— **fish or cut bait :** to make a choice between alternatives

fish–and–chips \ˌfi-shʰn-'chips\ *noun plural* (1876)
: fried fish and french fried potatoes

fish–bowl \'fish-ˌbōl\ *noun* (1906)
1 : a bowl for the keeping of live fish
2 : a place or condition that affords no privacy

fish cake *noun* (1854)
: a round fried cake made of shredded fish and mashed potato

fish duck *noun* (1858)
: MERGANSER

fish·er \'fi-shər\ *noun* (before 12th century)
1 : one that fishes
2 a : a large dark brown North American carnivorous mammal (*Martes pennanti*) related to the weasels **b :** the fur or pelt of this animal

fish·er·folk \'fi-shər-ˌfōk\ *noun plural* (1854)
: people who fish especially for a living

fish·er·man \-mən\ *noun* (15th century)
1 : one who engages in fishing as an occupation or for pleasure
2 : a ship used in commercial fishing

fisherman's bend *noun* (1823)
: a knot made by passing the end twice round a spar or through a ring and then back under both turns — see KNOT illustration

fish·er·wo·man \'fi-shər-ˌwu̇-mən\ *noun* (1816)
: a woman who fishes as an occupation or for pleasure

fish·ery \'fi-shə-rē\ *noun, plural* **-er·ies** (1528)
1 : the occupation, industry, or season of taking fish or other sea animals (as sponges, shrimp, or seals) **:** FISHING
2 : a place for catching fish or taking other sea animals
3 : a fishing establishment; *also* **:** its fishermen
4 : the legal right to take fish at a particular place or in particular waters
5 : the technology of fishery — usually used in plural

fish–eye \'fish-ˌī\ *adjective* (1943)
: being, having, or produced by a wide-angle photographic lens that has a highly curved protruding front, that covers an angle of about 180 degrees, and that gives a circular image

fish farm *noun* (1865)
: a commercial facility for raising aquatic animals for human food
— **fish–farm** \'fish-ˌfärm\ *transitive verb*

fish finger *noun* (1962)
British **:** FISH STICK

fish fry *noun* (1824)
1 : a picnic or supper featuring fried fish
2 : fried fish

fish hawk *noun* (1709)
: OSPREY 1

fish·hook \'fish-ˌhu̇k\ *noun* (14th century)
: a usually barbed hook for catching fish

fish·ing *noun* (13th century)
1 : the sport or business of catching fish
2 : a place for catching fish

fishing expedition *noun* (circa 1925)
1 : a legal interrogation or examination to discover information for a later proceeding
2 : an investigation that does not stick to a stated objective but hopes to uncover incriminating or newsworthy evidence

fish ladder *noun* (1865)
: a series of pools arranged like steps by which fish can pass over a dam in going upstream

fish meal *noun* (1854)
: ground dried fish and fish waste used as fertilizer and animal food

fish·mong·er \'fish-ˌmäŋ-gər, -ˌməŋ-\ *noun* (15th century)
chiefly British **:** a fish dealer

fish·net \-ˌnet\ *noun* (before 12th century)
1 : netting fitted with floats and weights or a supporting frame for catching fish
2 : a coarse open-mesh fabric

fish out *transitive verb* (1892)
: to exhaust the supply of fish in by fishing

fish·plate \-ˌplāt\ *noun* (1855)
: a steel plate used to lap a butt joint

fish·pond \-ˌpänd\ *noun* (14th century)
: a pond stocked with fish

fish protein concentrate *noun* (1961)
: a protein-rich food additive made from ground whole fish

fish stick *noun* (1953)
: a small elongated breaded fillet of fish

fish story *noun* [from the traditional exaggeration by fishermen of the size of fish almost caught] (1819)
: an extravagant or incredible story

fish·tail \'fish-ˌtāl\ *intransitive verb* (1927)
1 : to swing the tail of an airplane from side to side to reduce speed especially when landing
2 : to have the rear end slide from side to side out of control while moving forward ⟨the car *fishtailed* on the icy curve⟩

fish·way \-ˌwā\ noun (1845)
: a contrivance for enabling fish to pass around a fall or dam in a stream; specifically : FISH LADDER

fish·wife \-ˌwīf\ noun [Middle English] (15th century)
1 : a woman who sells fish
2 : a vulgar abusive woman

fishy \'fi-shē\ adjective **fish·i·er; -est** (15th century)
1 : of or resembling fish especially in taste or odor
2 : creating doubt or suspicion : QUESTIONABLE

fis·sile \'fi-səl, 'fi-ˌsīl\ adjective [Latin fissilis, from findere] (1661)
1 : capable of being split or divided in the direction of the grain or along natural planes of cleavage ⟨fissile wood⟩ ⟨fissile crystals⟩
2 : capable of undergoing fission
— **fis·sil·i·ty** \fi-'si-lə-tē\ noun

¹fis·sion \'fi-shən, -zhən\ noun [Latin fission-, fissio, from findere to split — more at BITE] (circa 1617)
1 : a splitting or breaking up into parts
2 : reproduction by spontaneous division of the body into two or more parts each of which grows into a complete organism
3 : the splitting of an atomic nucleus resulting in the release of large amounts of energy
— **fis·sion·al** \-ᵊl\ adjective

²fission (1929)
intransitive verb
: to undergo fission
transitive verb
: to cause to undergo fission

fis·sion·able \'fi-shə-n-ə-bəl, -zhᵊn-; 'fish-nə-, 'fizh-\ adjective (1945)
: FISSILE 2
— **fis·sion·abil·i·ty** \ˌfi-shᵊn-ə-'bi-lə-tē, -zhᵊn-; ˌfish-nə-, ˌfizh-\ noun
— **fissionable** noun

fis·sip·a·rous \fi-'si-p(ə-)rəs\ adjective [Latin fissus, past participle of findere + English -parous] (1874)
: tending to break up into parts : DIVISIVE
— **fis·sip·a·rous·ness** noun

¹fis·sure \'fi-shər\ noun [Middle English, from Middle French, from Latin fissura, from fissus] (14th century)
1 : a narrow opening or crack of considerable length and depth usually occurring from some breaking or parting
2 a : a natural cleft between body parts or in the substance of an organ b : a break or slit in tissue usually at the junction of skin and mucous membrane
3 : a separation or disagreement in thought or viewpoint : SCHISM ⟨fissures in a political party⟩

²fissure verb **fis·sured; fis·sur·ing** (1656)
transitive verb
: to break into fissures : CLEAVE
intransitive verb
: CRACK, DIVIDE

¹fist \'fist\ noun [Middle English, from Old English fȳst; akin to Old High German fūst fist, Polish pięść, and probably to Old English fīf five] (before 12th century)
1 : the hand clenched with the fingers doubled into the palm and the thumb doubled inward across the fingers
2 : the hand closed as in grasping : CLUTCH
3 : INDEX 5

²fist transitive verb (1607)
1 : to grip with the fist : HANDLE
2 : to clench into a fist

-fist·ed \'fis-təd\ combining form
: having (such or so many) fists ⟨two-fisted⟩ ⟨tightfisted⟩

fist·fight \'fist-ˌfīt\ noun (1603)
: a usually spontaneous fight with bare fists

fist·ful \-ˌfúl\ noun (1611)
1 : HANDFUL ⟨a fistful of coins⟩
2 : a considerable number or amount ⟨a whole fistful of musicians —Thomas Lask⟩

fist·ic \'fis-tik\ adjective (1806)
: of or relating to boxing or to fighting with the fists

fist·i·cuffs \'fis-ti-ˌkəfs\ noun plural [alteration of fisty cuff, from fisty (fistic) + cuff] (1605)
: a fight with the fists

fist·note \'fis(t)-ˌnōt\ noun (circa 1934)
: matter in a text to which attention is directed by means of an index mark

fis·tu·la \'fis(h)-chə-lə\ noun, plural **-las** or **-lae** \-ˌlē, -ˌlī\ [Middle English, from Latin, pipe, fistula] (14th century)
: an abnormal passage leading from an abscess or hollow organ to the body surface or from one hollow organ to another and permitting passage of fluids or secretions

fis·tu·lous \-ləs\ adjective (15th century)
1 : of, relating to, or having the form or nature of a fistula
2 : hollow like a pipe or reed

fistulous withers noun plural but singular or plural in construction (circa 1900)
: a deep-seated chronic inflammation of the withers of the horse in which bloody fluid is discharged

¹fit \'fit\ noun [Middle English, from Old English fitt; akin to Old Saxon fittea division of a poem, Old High German fizza skein] (before 12th century)
archaic : a division of a poem or song

²fit adjective **fit·ter; fit·test** [Middle English; akin to Middle English fitten] (14th century)
1 a (1) : adapted to an end or design : suitable by nature or by art (2) : adapted to the environment so as to be capable of surviving **b** : acceptable from a particular viewpoint (as of competence or morality) : PROPER ⟨a movie fit for the whole family⟩
2 a : put into a suitable state : made ready ⟨get the house fit for company⟩ **b** : being in such a state as to be or seem ready to do or suffer something ⟨fair fit to cry I was —Bryan MacMahon⟩ ⟨laughing fit to burst⟩
3 : sound physically and mentally : HEALTHY ☆
— **fit·ly** adverb
— **fit to be tied** : extremely angry or irritated
— **fit to kill** : in a striking manner ⟨dressed fit to kill⟩

³fit noun [Middle English, from Old English fitt strife] (circa 1541)
1 a : a sudden violent attack of a disease (as epilepsy) especially when marked by convulsions or unconsciousness : PAROXYSM **b** : a sudden but transient attack of a physical disturbance
2 : a sudden burst or flurry (as of activity) ⟨cleaned the whole house in a fit of efficiency⟩
3 : an emotional reaction (as in anger or frustration) ⟨has a fit when I show up late⟩
— **by fits** or **by fits and starts** or **in fits and starts** : in an impulsive and irregular manner

⁴fit verb **fit·ted** also **fit; fit·ting** [Middle English fitten to marshal troops, from or akin to Middle Dutch vitten to be suitable; akin to Old High German fizza skein] (15th century)
transitive verb
1 a : to be suitable for or to : harmonize with **b** archaic : to be seemly or proper for ⟨it fits us then to be as provident as fear may teach us —Shakespeare⟩
2 a : to conform correctly to the shape or size of ⟨it doesn't fit me anymore⟩ **b** (1) : to insert or adjust until correctly in place ⟨fit the mechanism into the box⟩ (2) : to make or adjust to the right shape and size ⟨fitting the jacket to the customer⟩ (3) : to measure for determining the specifications of something to be worn by ⟨fitted him for a new suit⟩ **c** : to make a place or room for : ACCOMMODATE
3 : to be in agreement or accord with ⟨the theory fits all the facts⟩
4 a : to put into a condition of readiness **b** : to cause to conform to or suit something

5 : SUPPLY, EQUIP ⟨fitted the ship with new engines⟩ — often used with out
6 : to adjust (a smooth curve of a specified type) to a given set of points
intransitive verb
1 archaic : to be seemly, proper, or suitable
2 : to conform to a particular shape or size; also : to be accommodated ⟨will we all fit into the car?⟩
3 : to be in harmony or accord : BELONG — often used with in
— **fit·ter** noun

⁵fit noun (1823)
: the fact, condition, or manner of fitting or being fitted: as **a** : the way clothing fits the wearer **b** : the degree of closeness between surfaces in an assembly of parts **c** : GOODNESS OF FIT

⁶fit dialect past and past participle of FIGHT

fitch \'fich\ or **fitch·ew** \'fich-(ˌ)ü\ noun [Middle English fiche, ficheux, from Middle French or Middle Dutch; Middle French fichau, from Middle Dutch vitsau] (15th century)
1 : POLECAT 1
2 : the fur or pelt of the polecat

fitch·et \'fi-chət\ noun (1535)
: POLECAT 1

fit·ful \'fit-fəl\ adjective (1592)
1 obsolete : characterized by fits or paroxysms
2 : having an erratic or intermittent character : IRREGULAR ☆
— **fit·ful·ly** \-fə-lē\ adverb
— **fit·ful·ness** noun

fit·ment \'fit-mənt\ noun [⁴fit] (1851)
chiefly British : FURNISHING 2, FIXTURE, CABINETRY — usually used in plural

fit·ness \'fit-nəs\ noun (1580)
1 : the quality or state of being fit
2 : the capacity of an organism to survive and transmit its genotype to reproductive offspring as compared to competing organisms; also : the contribution of an allele or genotype to

☆ **SYNONYMS**
Fit, suitable, meet, proper, appropriate, fitting, apt, happy, felicitous mean right with respect to some end, need, use, or circumstance. FIT stresses adaptability and sometimes special readiness for use or action ⟨fit for battle⟩. SUITABLE implies an answering to requirements or demands ⟨clothes suitable for camping⟩. MEET suggests a just proportioning ⟨meet payment⟩. PROPER suggests a suitability through essential nature or accordance with custom ⟨proper acknowledgement⟩. APPROPRIATE implies eminent or distinctive fitness ⟨an appropriate gift⟩. FITTING implies harmony of mood or tone ⟨a fitting end⟩. APT connotes a fitness marked by nicety and discrimination ⟨apt quotations⟩. HAPPY suggests what is effectively or successfully appropriate ⟨a happy choice of words⟩. FELICITOUS suggests an aptness that is opportune, telling, or graceful ⟨a felicitous phrase⟩.

Fitful, spasmodic, convulsive mean lacking steadiness or regularity in movement. FITFUL implies intermittence, a succession of starts and stops or risings and fallings ⟨fitful sleep⟩. SPASMODIC adds to FITFUL the implication of rapid or violent activity alternating with inactivity ⟨spasmodic growth⟩. CONVULSIVE suggests the breaking of regularity or quiet by uncontrolled movement ⟨convulsive shocks⟩.

\ə\ abut \ᵊ\ kitten \ər\ further \a\ ash \ā\ ace
\ä\ mop, mar \au̇\ out \ch\ chin \e\ bet \ē\ easy
\g\ go \i\ hit \ī\ ice \j\ job \ŋ\ sing \ō\ go
\ȯ\ law \ȯi\ boy \th\ thin \t͟h\ the \ü\ loot \u̇\ foot
\y\ yet \zh\ vision see also Guide to Pronunciation

the gene pool of subsequent generations as compared to that of other alleles or genotypes

fit·ted \'fi-təd\ *adjective* (circa 1666)
1 : FIT, SUITABLE
2 : shaped for a precise fit ⟨a *fitted* sheet⟩; *especially* : shaped to conform to the lines of the body ⟨a *fitted* shirt⟩

¹**fit·ting** \'fi-tiŋ\ *adjective* (15th century)
: of a kind appropriate to the situation : SUITABLE
synonym see FIT
— **fit·ting·ly** \-tiŋ-lē\ *adverb*
— **fit·ting·ness** *noun*

²**fitting** *noun* (1607)
1 : an action or act of one that fits; *specifically* : a trying on of clothes which are in the process of being made or altered
2 : a small often standardized part ⟨an electrical *fitting*⟩

five \'fīv\ *noun* [Middle English, from *five*, adjective, from Old English *fīf*; akin to Old High German *fīnf* five, Latin *quinque*, Greek *pente*] (before 12th century)
1 — see NUMBER table
2 *plural* : a British handball game
3 : the fifth in a set or series ⟨the *five* of clubs⟩
4 : something having five units or members; *especially* : a basketball team
5 : a 5-dollar bill
6 : FIFTEEN 2
— **five** *adjective*
— **five** *pronoun, plural in construction*

five–and–ten \ˌfī-vən-'ten\ *noun* [from the fact that all articles in such stores were formerly priced at either 5 or 10 cents] (1880)
: a retail store that carries chiefly inexpensive merchandise (as notions and household goods) — called also *five-and-dime*

five–fin·ger \'fīv-ˌfiŋ-gər\ *noun* (before 12th century)
: CINQUEFOIL 1

five·fold \'fīv-ˌfōld, -'fōld\ *adjective* (before 12th century)
1 : having five units or members
2 : being five times as great or as many
— **five·fold** \-'fōld\ *adverb*

five of a kind (1897)
: four cards of the same rank plus a wild card in one hand — see POKER illustration

fiv·er \'fī-vər\ *noun* (1843)
1 *slang* : a 5-dollar bill
2 *British* : a 5-pound bill

five–spice powder \'fīv-ˈspīs-\ *noun* (1970)
: a blend of spices typically including anise, pepper, fennel, cloves, and cinnamon that is used in Chinese cooking

five–star \'fīv-ˌstär\ *adjective* (1913)
: of first class or quality

¹**fix** \'fiks\ *verb* [Middle English, from Latin *fixus*, past participle of *figere* to fasten; akin to Lithuanian *dygti* to sprout, break through] (14th century)
transitive verb
1 a : to make firm, stable, or stationary **b** : to give a permanent or final form to: as (1) : to change into a stable compound or available form ⟨bacteria that *fix* nitrogen⟩ (2) : to kill, harden, and preserve for microscopic study (3) : to make the image of (a photographic film) permanent by removing unused salts **c** : AFFIX, ATTACH
2 a : to hold or direct steadily ⟨*fixes* his eyes on the horizon⟩ **b** : to capture the attention of ⟨*fixed* her with a stare⟩
3 a : to set or place definitely : ESTABLISH **b** : to make an accurate determination of : DISCOVER ⟨*fixing* our location on the chart⟩ **c** : ASSIGN ⟨*fix* the blame⟩
4 : to set in order : ADJUST
5 : to get ready : PREPARE ⟨*fix* lunch⟩
6 a : RESTORE, CURE ⟨the doctor *fixed* him up⟩ **b** : RESTORE, MEND ⟨*fix* the clock⟩ **c** : SPAY, CASTRATE
7 a : to get even with **b** : to influence the actions, outcome, or effect of by improper or illegal methods ⟨the race had been *fixed*⟩

intransitive verb
1 : to become firm, stable, or fixed
2 : to get set : be on the verge ⟨we're *fixing* to leave soon⟩
3 : to direct one's attention or efforts : FOCUS; *also* : DECIDE, SETTLE — usually used with *on*
synonym see FASTEN
— **fix·able** \'fik-sə-bəl\ *adjective*

²**fix** *noun* (1809)
1 : a position of difficulty or embarrassment : PREDICAMENT
2 a : the position (as of a ship) determined by bearings, observations, or radio; *also* : a determination of one's position **b** : an accurate determination or understanding especially by observation or analysis
3 : an act or instance of improper or illegal fixing ⟨the *fix* was in⟩
4 : a supply or dose of something strongly desired or craved; *especially* : a shot of a narcotic
5 : FIXATION
6 : something that fixes or restores ⟨a quick *fix*⟩

fix·ate \'fik-ˌsāt\ *verb* **fix·at·ed; fix·at·ing** (1885)
transitive verb
1 : to make fixed, stationary, or unchanging
2 : to focus one's gaze on
3 : to direct (the libido) toward an infantile form of gratification
intransitive verb
1 : to focus or concentrate one's gaze or attention intently or obsessively
2 : to undergo arrestment at a stage of development

fix·at·ed *adjective* (1926)
: arrested in development or adjustment; *especially* : arrested at a pregenital level of psychosexual development

fix·a·tion \fik-'sā-shən\ *noun* (14th century)
: the act, process, or result of fixing, fixating, or becoming fixated: as **a** : a persistent concentration of libidinal energies upon objects characteristic of psychosexual stages of development preceding the genital stage **b** : stereotyped behavior (as in response to frustration) **c** : an obsessive or unhealthy preoccupation or attachment

fix·a·tive \'fik-sə-tiv\ *noun* (circa 1859)
: something that fixes or sets: as **a** : a substance added to a perfume especially to prevent too rapid evaporation **b** : a substance used to fix living tissue **c** : a varnish used especially for the protection of drawings (as in pastel or charcoal)
— **fixative** *adjective*

fixed \'fikst\ *adjective* (14th century)
1 a : securely placed or fastened : STATIONARY **b** (1) : NONVOLATILE (2) : formed into a chemical compound **c** (1) : not subject to change or fluctuation ⟨a *fixed* income⟩ (2) : firmly set in the mind ⟨a *fixed* idea⟩ (3) : having a final or crystallized form or character (4) : recurring on the same date from year to year ⟨*fixed* holidays⟩ **d** : IMMOBILE, CONCENTRATED ⟨a *fixed* stare⟩
2 : supplied with something (as money) needed ⟨comfortably *fixed*⟩
— **fixed·ly** \'fik-səd-lē, 'fiks-tlē\ *adverb*
— **fixed·ness** \'fik-səd-nəs, 'fiks(t)-nəs\ *noun*

fixed charge *noun* (circa 1901)
: a regularly recurring expense (as rent, taxes, or interest) that must be met when due

fixed oil *noun* (circa 1800)
: a nonvolatile oil; *especially* : a fatty oil — compare ESSENTIAL OIL

fixed–point *adjective* (1960)
: involving or being a mathematical notation (as in a decimal system) in which the point separating whole numbers and fractions is fixed — compare FLOATING-POINT

fixed star *noun* (1561)
: a star so distant that its motion can be measured only by very precise observations over long periods

fix·er \'fik-sər\ *noun* (1849)
: one that fixes: as **a** : one who intervenes to enable a person to circumvent the law or obtain a political favor **b** : one who adjusts matters or disputes by negotiation **c** : ²HYPO

fix·ing \-siŋ\ *noun* (1605)
1 : the act or process of one that fixes
2 *plural* ⟨*often* -sənz⟩ : customary accompaniments : TRIMMINGS ⟨a turkey dinner with all the *fixings*⟩

fix·i·ty \'fik-sə-tē\ *noun, plural* **-ties** (1666)
1 : the quality or state of being fixed or stable
2 : something that is fixed

fix·ture \'fiks-chər\ *noun* [modification of Late Latin *fixura*, from Latin *fixus*] (1598)
1 : the act or process of fixing : the state of being fixed
2 a : something that is fixed or attached (as to a building) as a permanent appendage or as a structural part ⟨a plumbing *fixture*⟩ **b** : a device for supporting work during machining **c** : an item of movable property so incorporated into real property that it may be regarded as legally a part of it
3 : a familiar or invariably present element or feature in some particular setting; *especially* : a person long associated with a place or activity
4 : a settled date or time especially for a sporting or festive event; *also* : such an event especially as a regularly scheduled affair

fix up *transitive verb* (1831)
1 : REFURBISH ⟨*fix up* the attic⟩
2 : to set right : SETTLE ⟨*fixed up* their dispute⟩
3 : to provide with something needed or wanted; *especially* : to arrange a date for

¹**fizz** \'fiz\ *intransitive verb* [probably of imitative origin] (1685)
1 : to make a hissing or sputtering sound : EFFERVESCE
2 : to show excitement or exhilaration

²**fizz** *noun* (1842)
1 a : a hissing sound **b** : SPIRIT, LIVELINESS
2 : an effervescent beverage
— **fizzy** \'fi-zē\ *adjective*

¹**fiz·zle** \'fi-zəl\ *intransitive verb* **fiz·zled; fiz·zling** \-z(ə-)liŋ\ [probably alteration of *fist* (to break wind)] (circa 1841)
1 : FIZZ
2 : to fail or end feebly especially after a promising start — often used with *out*

²**fizzle** *noun* (1842)
: an abortive effort : FAILURE

fjord \fē-'ȯrd, 'fē-ˌ; 'fyȯrd\ *noun* [Norwegian *fjord*, from Old Norse *fjǫrthr* — more at FORD] (1674)
: a narrow inlet of the sea between cliffs or steep slopes

flab \'flab\ *noun* [back-formation from *flabby*] (1951)
: soft flabby body tissue

flab·ber·gast \'fla-bər-ˌgast\ *transitive verb* [origin unknown] (1772)
: to overwhelm with shock, surprise, or wonder : DUMBFOUND
synonym see SURPRISE
— **flab·ber·gast·ing·ly** \-ˌgas-tiŋ-lē\ *adverb*

flab·by \'fla-bē\ *adjective* **flab·bi·er; -est** [alteration of *flappy*] (1697)
1 : lacking resilience or firmness : FLACCID
2 : weak and ineffective : FEEBLE
— **flab·bi·ly** \'fla-bə-lē\ *adverb*
— **flab·bi·ness** \'fla-bē-nəs\ *noun*

fjord

fla·bel·late \flə-'be-lət, 'fla-bə-ˌlāt\ *adjective* [Latin *flabellum* fan] (1819)
: shaped like a fan
fla·bel·li·form \flə-'be-lə-ˌfȯrm\ *adjective* (1777)
: FLABELLATE
flac·cid \÷'fla-səd *also* 'flak-səd\ *adjective* [Latin *flaccidus*, from *flaccus* flabby] (1620)
1 a : not firm or stiff; *also* **:** lacking normal or youthful firmness ⟨*flaccid* muscles⟩ **b** *of a plant part* **:** deficient in turgor
2 : lacking vigor or force ⟨*flaccid* leadership⟩
— **flac·cid·i·ty** \fla(k)-'si-də-tē\ *noun*
— **flac·cid·ly** \'fla(k)-səd-lē\ *adverb*
¹**flack** \'flak\ *noun* [origin unknown] (1939)
: one who provides publicity; *especially*
: PRESS AGENT
— **flack·ery** \'fla-k(ə-)rē\ *noun*
²**flack** *variant of* FLAK
³**flack** *intransitive verb* (1965)
: to provide publicity **:** engage in press-agentry
fla·con \'fla-kən, -ˌkän; fla-'kōⁿ\ *noun* [French, from Middle French, bottle — more at FLAGON] (1824)
: a small usually ornamental bottle with a tight cap
¹**flag** \'flag *also* 'flȧg\ *noun* [Middle English *flagge* reed, rush] (14th century)
: any of various monocotyledonous plants with long ensiform leaves: as **a :** IRIS; *especially* **:** a wild iris **b :** SWEET FLAG
²**flag** *noun, often attributive* [perhaps from ¹*flag*] (1530)
1 : a usually rectangular piece of fabric of distinctive design that is used as a symbol (as of a nation), as a signaling device, or as a decoration
2 a : the tail of some dogs (as a setter or hound); *also* **:** the long hair fringing a dog's tail **b :** the tail of a deer
3 a : something used like a flag to signal or attract attention **b :** one of the cross strokes of a musical note less than a quarter note in value
4 : something represented by a flag: as **a :** FLAGSHIP **b :** an admiral functioning in his office of command **c :** NATIONALITY; *especially* **:** the nationality of registration of a ship or aircraft
³**flag** *transitive verb* **flagged; flag·ging** (1856)
1 : to signal with or as if with a flag; *especially* **:** to signal to stop ⟨*flagged* the train⟩ — often used with *down*
2 : to put a flag on (as for identification)
3 : to call a penalty on **:** PENALIZE ⟨a lineman *flagged* for being offside⟩
⁴**flag** *intransitive verb* **flagged; flag·ging** [probably from ²*flag*] (1545)
1 : to hang loose without stiffness
2 a : to become unsteady, feeble, or spiritless **b :** to decline in interest or attraction
⁵**flag** *noun* [Middle English *flagge* turf, from Old Norse *flaga* slab; akin to Old English *flōh* chip] (1604)
: a hard evenly stratified stone that splits into flat pieces suitable for paving; *also* **:** a piece of such stone
⁶**flag** *transitive verb* **flagged; flag·ging** (1615)
: to lay (as a pavement) with flags
flag day *noun* (1894)
1 *F&D capitalized* **:** June 14 observed in various states in commemoration of the adoption in 1777 of the official U.S. flag
2 *British* **:** a day on which charitable contributions are solicited in exchange for small flags
fla·gel·lant \'fla-jə-lənt, flə-'je-lənt\ *noun* (circa 1587)
1 : a person who scourges himself as a public penance
2 : a person who responds sexually to being beaten by or to beating another person
— **flagellant** *adjective*
— **fla·gel·lant·ism** \-lən-ˌti-zəm\ *noun*
fla·gel·lar \flə-'je-lər, 'fla-jə-lər\ *adjective* (circa 1889)

: of or relating to a flagellum
¹**flag·el·late** \'fla-jə-ˌlāt\ *transitive verb* **-lat·ed; -lat·ing** [Latin *flagellatus*, past participle of *flagellare*, from *flagellum*, diminutive of *flagrum* whip; perhaps akin to Old Norse *blaka* to wave] (circa 1623)
1 : WHIP, SCOURGE
2 : to drive or punish as if by whipping
²**fla·gel·late** \'fla-jə-lət, -ˌlāt; flə-'je-lət\ *adjective* [New Latin *flagellatus*, from *flagellum*] (circa 1859)
1 a *or* **flag·el·lat·ed** \'fla-jə-ˌlā-təd\ **:** having flagella **b :** shaped like a flagellum
2 : [³*flagellate*] **:** of, relating to, or caused by flagellates ⟨*flagellate* diarrhea⟩
³**flagellate** *same as* ²\ *noun* [New Latin *Flagellata*, class of unicellular organisms, from neuter plural of *flagellatus*] (1879)
: a flagellate protozoan or alga
flag·el·la·tion \ˌfla-jə-'lā-shən\ *noun* (15th century)
: the act or practice of flagellating; *especially* **:** the practice of a flagellant
fla·gel·lin \flə-'je-lən\ *noun* [*flagellum* + ¹-*in*] (1955)
: a polymeric protein that is the chief constituent of bacterial flagella and is responsible for the specificity of their flagellar antigens
fla·gel·lum \flə-'je-ləm\ *noun, plural* **-la** \-lə\ *also* **-lums** [New Latin, from Latin, whip, shoot of a plant] (1852)
: any of various elongated filiform appendages of plants or animals: as **a :** the slender distal part of an antenna **b :** a long tapering process that projects singly or in groups from a cell and is the primary organ of motion of many microorganisms
¹**fla·geo·let** \ˌfla-jə-'let, -'lā\ *noun* [French, from Old French *flajolet*, from *flajol* flute, from (assumed) Vulgar Latin *flabeolum*, from Latin *flare* to blow — more at BLOW] (1659)
: a small fipple flute resembling the treble recorder
²**flageolet** *noun* [French, diminutive of *flageolle* kidney bean, modification of Italian *fagiolo*, from Latin *phaseolus* — more at FRIJOLE] (1877)
: a green kidney bean used in French cuisine
flag football *noun* (1954)
: a variation of football in which a player must remove a flag attached to the ballcarrier's clothing to stop the play
flag·ging \'fla-giŋ, *also* 'flā-\ *adjective* (1545)
1 : LANGUID, WEAK
2 : becoming progressively less **:** DWINDLING
— **flag·ging·ly** \-giŋ-lē\ *adverb*
fla·gi·tious \flə-'ji-shəs\ *adjective* [Middle English *flagicious*, from Latin *flagitiosus*, from *flagitium* shameful thing] (14th century)
: marked by scandalous crime or vice **:** VILLAINOUS
— **fla·gi·tious·ly** *adverb*
— **fla·gi·tious·ness** *noun*
flag·man \'flag-mən\ *noun* (1832)
: a person who signals with a flag
flag of convenience (1956)
: registry of a merchant ship under a foreign flag in order to profit from less restrictive regulations
flag officer *noun* [from his being entitled to display a flag with one or more stars indicating his rank] (1665)
: any of the officers in the navy or coast guard above captain — compare GENERAL OFFICER
flag of truce (1627)
: a white flag carried or displayed to an enemy as an invitation to conference or parley
flag·on \'fla-gən\ *noun* [Middle English, from Middle French *flascon, flacon* bottle, from Late Latin *flascon-, flasco* — more at FLASK] (15th century)
1 a : a large usually metal or pottery vessel (as for wine) with handle and spout and often a lid **b :** a large bulging short-necked bottle
2 : the contents of a flagon
flag·pole \'flag-ˌpōl\ *noun* (1884)

: a pole on which to raise a flag
fla·grance \'flā-grən(t)s *also* 'fla-\ *noun* (circa 1615)
: FLAGRANCY
fla·gran·cy \'flā-grən(t)-sē *also* 'fla-\ *noun* (1599)
: the quality or state of being flagrant
flag rank *noun* (1894)
: the rank of a flag officer
fla·grant \'flā-grənt *also* 'fla-\ *adjective* [Latin *flagrant-, flagrans*, present participle of *flagrare* to burn — more at BLACK] (1513)
1 *archaic* **:** fiery hot **:** BURNING
2 : conspicuously offensive ⟨*flagrant* errors⟩; *especially* **:** so obviously inconsistent with what is right or proper as to appear to be a flouting of law or morality ⟨*flagrant* violations of human rights⟩ ☆
— **fla·grant·ly** *adverb*

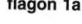
flagon 1a

fla·gran·te de·lic·to \flə-ˌgrän-tē-di-'lik-(ˌ)tō, -ˌgran-\ *adverb or adjective* [Medieval Latin, literally, while the crime is blazing] (1826)
: in the very act of committing a misdeed **:** RED-HANDED; *also* **:** in the midst of sexual activity
flag·ship \'flag-ˌship\ *noun* (1672)
1 : the ship that carries the commander of a fleet or subdivision of a fleet and flies his flag
2 : the finest, largest, or most important one of a series, network, or chain
flag·staff \-ˌstaf\ *noun* (circa 1613)
: a staff on which a flag is hoisted
flag·stick \-ˌstik\ *noun* (1926)
: a staff for a flag marking the location of the cup on a golf putting green
flag·stone \-ˌstōn\ *noun* (1730)
: ⁵FLAG
flag stop *noun* (1941)
: a point at which a vehicle in public transportation stops only on prearrangement or signal
flag-wav·er \'flag-ˌwā-vər\ *noun* (1894)
1 : one who is intensely and conspicuously patriotic
2 : one who waves a flag in signaling
3 : a song intended to rouse patriotic sentiment
flag-wav·ing \-viŋ\ *noun* (1892)
: passionate appeal to patriotic or partisan sentiment **:** CHAUVINISM
¹**flail** \'flā(ə)l\ *noun* [Middle English *fleil, flail*, partly from (assumed) Old English *flegel* (whence Old English *fligel*), from Late Latin *flagellum* flail, from Latin, whip & partly from Middle French *flaiel*, from Late Latin *flagellum* — more at FLAGELLATE] (before 12th century)

\ə\ abut \ᵊ\ kitten \ər\ further \a\ ash \ā\ ace
\ä\ mop, mar \aù\ out \ch\ chin \e\ bet \ē\ easy
\g\ go \i\ hit \ī\ ice \j\ job \ŋ\ sing \ō\ go
\ȯ\ law \ȯi\ boy \th\ thin \t͟h\ the \ü\ loot \ù\ foot
\y\ yet \zh\ vision *see also* Guide to Pronunciation

: a hand threshing implement consisting of a wooden handle at the end of which a stouter and shorter stick is so hung as to swing freely

²**flail** (15th century)
transitive verb
1 a : to strike with or as if with a flail ⟨arms *flailing* the water⟩ **b :** to move, swing, or beat as if wielding a flail ⟨*flailing* a club to drive away the insects⟩
2 : to thresh (grain) with a flail
intransitive verb
: to move, swing, or beat like a flail

flair \'flar, 'fler\ *noun* [French, literally, sense of smell, from Old French, odor, from *flairier* to give off an odor, from Late Latin *flagrare*, alteration of Latin *fragrare*] (1881)
1 : a skill or instinctive ability to appreciate or make good use of something **:** TALENT ⟨a *flair* for color⟩; *also* **:** INCLINATION, TENDENCY ⟨a *flair* for the dramatic⟩
2 : a uniquely attractive quality **:** STYLE ⟨fashionable dresses with a *flair* all their own⟩

flak \'flak\ *noun, plural* **flak** [German, from *Fliegerabwehrkanonen*, from *Flieger* flyer + *Abwehr* defense + *Kanonen* cannons] (1938)
1 : antiaircraft guns
2 : the bursting shells fired from flak
3 : CRITICISM, OPPOSITION

¹**flake** \'flāk\ *noun* [Middle English, of Scandinavian origin; akin to Norwegian *flak* disk] (14th century)
1 : a small loose mass or bit ⟨snow *flakes*⟩
2 : a thin flattened piece or layer **:** CHIP
3 *slang* **:** COCAINE

²**flake** *verb* **flaked; flak·ing** (1627)
intransitive verb
: to separate into flakes; *also* **:** to peel in flakes
transitive verb
1 : to form or break into flakes **:** CHIP
2 : to cover with or as if with flakes
— **flak·er** *noun*

³**flake** *noun* [Middle English, hurdle, from Old Norse *flaki*] (1623)
: a stage, platform, or tray for drying fish or produce

⁴**flake** *noun* [perhaps from *flake out*] (1964)
: a person who is flaky **:** ODDBALL

flake out *intransitive verb* [probably from dialect *flake* to lie, bask] (1939)
1 *slang* **:** to fall asleep
2 *slang* **:** to be overcome especially by exhaustion

flake tool *noun* (circa 1947)
: a Stone-Age tool that is a flake of stone struck off from a larger piece

flak jacket *noun* (1950)
: a jacket containing metal plates for protection against flak; *broadly* **:** a bulletproof vest — called also *flak vest*

¹**flaky** *also* **flak·ey** \'flā-kē\ *adjective* **flak·i·er; -est** (1580)
1 : consisting of flakes ⟨*flaky* snow⟩
2 : tending to flake ⟨a *flaky* crust⟩
— **flak·i·ness** *noun*

²**flaky** *adjective* **flak·i·er; -est** [⁴*flake*] (circa 1963)
: markedly odd or unconventional **:** OFFBEAT, WACKY
— **flak·i·ness** *noun*

flam \'flam\ *noun* [probably imitative] (1819)
: a drumbeat of two strokes of which the first is a very quick grace note

¹**flam·bé** \fläm-'bā, flä-'-\ *adjective* [French *flambé*, from past participle of *flamber* to flame, singe, from Old French, from *flambe* flame] (1914)
: dressed or served covered with flaming liquor — usually used postpositively ⟨crepes suzette *flambé*⟩

²**flambé** *transitive verb* **flam·béed; flam·bé·ing** (circa 1946)
: to douse with a liquor (as brandy, rum, or cognac) and ignite

flam·beau \'flam-,bō\ *noun, plural* **flam·beaux** \-,bōz\ *or* **flambeaus** [French, from Middle French, from *flambe* flame] (1632)

: a flaming torch; *broadly* **:** TORCH

flam·boy·ance \flam-'bȯi-ən(t)s\ *noun* (1891)
: the quality or state of being flamboyant

flam·boy·an·cy \-ən(t)-sē\ *noun* (circa 1889)
: FLAMBOYANCE

¹**flam·boy·ant** \-ənt\ *adjective* [French, from present participle of *flamboyer* to flame, from Old French, from *flambe*] (1832)
1 *often capitalized* **:** characterized by waving curves suggesting flames ⟨*flamboyant* tracery⟩ ⟨*flamboyant* architecture⟩
2 : marked by or given to strikingly elaborate or colorful display or behavior
— **flam·boy·ant·ly** *adverb*

²**flamboyant** *noun* (1879)
: ROYAL POINCIANA

¹**flame** \'flām\ *noun* [Middle English *flaume, flaumbe*, from Middle French *flamme* (from Latin *flamma*) & *flambe*, from Old French, from *flamble*, from Latin *flammula*, diminutive of *flamma* flame; akin to Latin *flagrare* to burn — more at BLACK] (14th century)
1 : the glowing gaseous part of a fire
2 a : a state of blazing combustion ⟨the car burst into *flame*⟩ **b :** a condition or appearance suggesting a flame or burning: as (1) **:** burning zeal or passion (2) **:** a strong reddish orange color
3 : BRILLIANCE, BRIGHTNESS
4 : SWEETHEART
5 : an angry, hostile, or abusive electronic message

²**flame** *verb* **flamed; flam·ing** (14th century)
intransitive verb
1 : to burn with a flame **:** BLAZE
2 a : to burst or break out violently or passionately ⟨*flaming* with indignation⟩ **b :** to send an angry, hostile, or abusive electronic message
3 : to shine brightly **:** GLOW ⟨color *flaming* up in her cheeks⟩
transitive verb
1 : to send or convey by means of flame ⟨*flame* a message by signal fires⟩
2 : to treat or affect with flame: as **a :** to sear, sterilize, or destroy by fire **b :** FLAMBÉ
3 : to send an angry, hostile, or abusive electronic message to or about
— **flam·er** *noun*

flame cell *noun* (1888)
: a hollow cell that has a tuft of vibratile cilia and is part of some lower invertebrate excretory systems (as of a flatworm)

fla·men \'flā-mən\ *noun, plural* **flamens** *or* **flam·i·nes** \'fla-mə-,nēz\ [Middle English *flamin*, from Latin *flamin-, flamen*] (14th century)
: a priest especially in ancient Rome

fla·men·co \flə-'meŋ-(,)kō\ *noun, plural* **-cos** [Spanish, from *flamenco* of the Gypsies, literally, Flemish, from Middle Dutch *Vlaminc* Fleming] (1896)
1 : a vigorous rhythmic dance style of the Andalusian Gypsies; *also* **:** a dance in flamenco style
2 : music or song suitable to accompany a flamenco dance

flame·out \'flā-,maut\ *noun* (1950)
1 : the unintentional cessation of operation of a jet airplane engine
2 : a sudden or spectacular failure
3 : a person whose successful career ends abruptly

flame photometer *noun* (1945)
: a spectrophotometer in which a spray of metallic salts in solution is vaporized in a very hot flame and subjected to quantitative analysis by measuring the intensities of the spectral lines of the metals present
— **flame photometric** *adjective*
— **flame photometry** *noun*

flame·proof \'flām-,prüf\ *adjective* (1886)
: resistant to damage or burning on contact with flame
— **flameproof** *transitive verb*

— **flame·proof·er** *noun*

flame-retardant *adjective* (1947)
: made or treated so as to resist burning

flame stitch *noun* (1936)
: a needlepoint stitch that produces a pattern resembling flames

flame·throw·er \-,thrō(-ə)r\ *noun* (1917)
1 : a device that expels from a nozzle a burning stream of liquid or semiliquid fuel under pressure
2 : a pitcher who throws hard **:** a fastball pitcher

flame tree *noun* (1860)
: any of several trees or shrubs with showy scarlet or yellow flowers: as **a :** a tree (*Brachychiton acerifolium*) of the family Sterculiaceae) of southern Australia with panicles of brilliant scarlet flowers **b :** ROYAL POINCIANA

flam·ing \'flā-miŋ\ *adjective* (14th century)
1 : resembling or suggesting a flame in color, brilliance, or wavy outline ⟨the *flaming* sunset sky⟩ ⟨*flaming* red hair⟩
2 : being on fire **:** BLAZING
3 : INTENSE, PASSIONATE ⟨*flaming* youth⟩
4 — used as an intensive ⟨you *flaming* idiot⟩
— **flam·ing·ly** \-miŋ-lē\ *adverb*

fla·min·go \flə-'miŋ-(,)gō\ *noun, plural* **-gos** *also* **-goes** [obsolete Spanish *flamengo* (now *flamenco*), literally, Fleming, German (conventionally thought of as ruddy-complexioned)] (1565)
: any of several large aquatic birds (family Phoenicopteridae) with long legs and neck, webbed feet, a broad lamellate bill resembling that of a duck but abruptly bent downward, and usually rosy-white plumage with scarlet wing coverts and black wing quills

flamingo

flam·ma·bil·i·ty \,fla-mə-'bi-lə-tē\ *noun* (1646)
: ability to support combustion; *especially* **:** a high capacity for combustion

flam·ma·ble \'fla-mə-bəl\ *adjective* [Latin *flammare* to flame, set on fire, from *flamma*] (1813)

◇ WORD HISTORY
flamenco The Spanish word *flamenco* means literally "Flemish," and its usage in the sense "Gypsy-like," especially in reference to a distinctive song, dance, and guitar-music style of Andalusia, has inspired a number of hypotheses. It has been speculated that Gypsies were called *flamenco* because they reached Spain in the 16th century via Germany or Flanders, or that *flamenco* became a derogatory epithet for any foreigner because certain Flemish courtiers of the Spanish king and Holy Roman Emperor Charles V were much disliked in Spain. These notions of such an early origin for the "Gypsy-like" sense of *flamenco* all look implausible in light of the fact that this meaning is unattested in Spanish before 1870. In the later 19th century *flamenco* also meant "jaunty, cocky" and, in reference to women, "provocatively attractive," and the suggestion has been made that "Gypsy-like" is a secondary development from these senses. In any event, a direct connection between the senses "Flemish" and "Gypsy-like" has not been demonstrated. The ordinary Spanish word for "Gypsy" is *gitano*, which, like English *Gypsy*, is altered from a word meaning "Egyptian."

: capable of being easily ignited and of burning quickly
— **flammable** *noun*

flan \'flan, 'fläⁿ(n)\ *noun* [French, from Old French *flaon*, from Late Latin *fladon-*, *flado* flat cake, of Germanic origin; akin to Old High German *flado* flat cake] (1846)
1 a : an open pie containing any of various sweet or savory fillings **b :** custard baked with a caramel glaze
2 : the metal disk of a coin, token, or medal as distinguished from the design and lettering stamped on it

fla·neur \flä-'nər\ *noun* [French *flâneur*] (1854)
: an idle man-about-town

¹flange \'flanj\ *noun* [perhaps alteration of *flanch* (a curving charge on a heraldic shield)] (circa 1735)
1 : a rib or rim for strength, for guiding, or for attachment to another object ⟨a *flange* on a pipe⟩ ⟨a *flange* on a wheel⟩
2 : a projecting edge of cloth used for decoration on clothing ⟨a jacket with *flange* shoulders⟩

²flange *transitive verb* **flanged; flang·ing** (circa 1859)
: to furnish with a flange

¹flank \'flaŋk\ *noun* [Middle English, from Old French *flanc*, of Germanic origin; akin to Old High German *hlanca* loin, flank — more at LANK] (before 12th century)
1 a : the fleshy part of the side between the ribs and the hip; *broadly* **:** the side of a quadruped **b :** a cut of meat from this part of an animal — see BEEF illustration
2 a : SIDE **b :** the right or left of a formation
3 : the area along either side of a heraldic shield

²flank *transitive verb* (1596)
1 : to protect a flank of
2 : to attack or threaten the flank of (as a body of troops)
3 a : to be situated at the side of; *especially* **:** to be situated on both sides of ⟨a road *flanked* with linden trees⟩ **b :** to place something on each side of

flan·ken \'flän-kən\ *noun* [Yiddish, plural of *flank*, literally, flank, ultimately from Old French *flanc*] (1950)
: beef flank cooked especially by boiling

flank·er \'flaŋ-kər\ *noun* (1940)
: a football player stationed wide of the formation slightly behind the line of scrimmage as a pass receiver — called also *flanker back*

flank steak *noun* (1902)
: a pear-shaped muscle of the beef flank; *also* **:** a steak cut from this muscle — see BEEF illustration

flan·nel \'fla-n°l\ *noun* [Middle English *flaunneol* woolen cloth or garment] (1503)
1 a : a soft twilled wool or worsted fabric with a loose texture and a slightly napped surface **b :** a napped cotton fabric of soft yarns simulating the texture of wool flannel **c :** a stout cotton fabric usually napped on one side
2 *plural* **a :** flannel underwear **b :** outer garments of flannel; *especially* **:** men's trousers
3 *British* **:** WASHCLOTH
4 *British* **:** flattering or evasive talk; *also* **:** NONSENSE, RUBBISH
— **flannel** *adjective*
— **flan·nel·ly** \-n°l-ē\ *adjective*

flan·nel·ette \,fla-n°l-'et\ *noun* (circa 1882)
: a lightweight cotton flannel

flan·nel·mouthed \'fla-n°l-,maůth, -,maůthd\ *adjective* (circa 1893)
1 : speaking indistinctly
2 : speaking in a tricky or ingratiating way

¹flap \'flap\ *noun* [Middle English *flappe*] (14th century)
1 : a stroke with something broad **:** SLAP
2 *obsolete* **:** something broad and flat used for striking
3 : something that is broad, limber, or flat and usually thin and that hangs loose or projects freely: as **a :** a piece on a garment that hangs free **b :** a part of a book jacket that folds under the book's cover **c :** a piece of tissue partly severed from its place of origin for use in surgical grafting **d :** an extended part forming the closure (as of an envelope or carton)
4 : the motion of something broad and limber (as a sail or wing)
5 : a movable auxiliary airfoil usually attached to an airplane wing's trailing edge to increase lift or drag — see AIRPLANE illustration
6 a : a state of excitement or agitation **:** TIZZY, UPROAR **b :** something (as an incident or remark) that generates an uproar
7 : a consonant (as the sound \d\ in *ladder* and \t\ in *latter*) characterized by a single rapid contact of the tongue or lower lip against another point in the mouth — called also *tap*

²flap *verb* **flapped; flap·ping** (14th century)
transitive verb
1 : to beat with or as if with a flap
2 : to toss sharply **:** FLING
3 : to move or cause to move in flaps
intransitive verb
1 : to sway loosely usually with a noise of striking and especially when moved by wind
2 a : to beat or pulsate wings or something suggesting wings **b :** to progress by flapping **c :** to flutter ineffectively
3 : to talk foolishly and persistently

flap·doo·dle \'flap-,dü-d°l\ *noun* [origin unknown] (1878)
: NONSENSE

flap·jack \-,jak\ *noun* (circa 1600)
: PANCAKE

flap·pa·ble \'fla-pə-bəl\ *adjective* (1968)
: easily upset

flap·per \'fla-pər\ *noun* (circa 1570)
1 a : one that flaps **b :** something used in flapping or striking **c :** FLIPPER 1
2 : a young woman; *specifically* **:** a young woman of the period of World War I and the following decade who showed freedom from conventions (as in conduct)

flap·py \'fla-pē\ *adjective* (1905)
: flapping or tending to flap

¹flare \'flar, 'fler\ *verb* **flared; flar·ing** [origin unknown] (circa 1700)
intransitive verb
1 a : to burn with an unsteady flame **b :** to stream in the wind
2 a : to shine with a sudden light ⟨a match *flares* in the darkness⟩ **b** (1) **:** to become suddenly excited or angry — usually used with *up* (2) **:** to break out or intensify usually suddenly or violently — often used with *up* ⟨fighting *flared* up after a two-week lull⟩ **c :** to express strong emotion (as anger) ⟨*flaring* out at such abuses⟩
3 : to open or spread outward ⟨the pants *flare* at the bottom⟩
transitive verb
1 : to display conspicuously ⟨*flaring* her scarf to attract attention⟩
2 : to cause to flare ⟨the breeze *flares* the candle⟩
3 : to signal with a flare or by flaring
4 : to burn (a jet of waste gas) in the open air

²flare *noun* (1814)
1 : an unsteady glaring light
2 a : a fire or blaze of light used especially to signal, illuminate, or attract attention; *also* **:** a device or composition used to produce such a flare **b :** SOLAR FLARE; *also* **:** a sudden increase and decrease in the brightness of a star often amounting to a difference of several magnitudes
3 : a sudden outburst (as of excitement or anger)
4 a : a spreading outward; *also* **:** a place or part that spreads **b :** an area of skin flush
5 : light resulting from reflection (as between lens surfaces) or an effect of this light (as a fogged or dense area in a photographic negative)

flare-up \-,əp\ *noun* (1839)

1 : a sudden outburst or intensification
2 : a sudden bursting (as of a smoldering fire) into flame or light

flar·ing \'flar-iŋ, 'fler-\ *adjective* (1593)
1 : opening or spreading outward ⟨*flaring* nostrils⟩
2 a : flaming or as if flaming brightly or unsteadily **b :** GAUDY ⟨a *flaring* resort hotel⟩
— **flar·ing·ly** \-iŋ-lē\ *adverb*

¹flash \'flash\ *verb* [Middle English *flaschen*, of imitative origin] (13th century)
intransitive verb
1 : RUSH, DASH — used of flowing water
2 : to break forth in or like a sudden flame or flare
3 a : to appear suddenly ⟨an idea *flashes* into her mind⟩ **b :** to move with great speed ⟨the days *flash* by⟩
4 a : to break forth or out so as to make a sudden display ⟨the sun *flashed* from behind a cloud⟩ **b :** to act or speak vehemently and suddenly especially in anger
5 a : to give off light suddenly or in transient bursts **b :** to glow or gleam especially with animation or passion ⟨her eyes *flashed* with anger⟩
6 : to change suddenly or violently into vapor ⟨hot water *flashing* to steam under reduced pressure⟩
7 : to expose one's genitals usually suddenly and briefly in public
8 : to have sudden insight — often used with *on*
transitive verb
1 a *archaic* **:** SPLASH **b :** to fill by a sudden inflow of water
2 a : to cause the sudden appearance of (light) **b :** to cause to burst violently into flame **c** (1) **:** to cause (light) to reflect (2) **:** to cause (as a mirror) to reflect light (3) **:** to cause (a lamp) to flash **d :** to convey by means of flashes of light
3 a : to make known or cause to appear with great speed ⟨*flash* a message on the screen⟩ **b :** to display obtrusively and ostentatiously ⟨always *flashing* a roll of bills⟩ **c :** to expose to view suddenly and briefly ⟨*flashed* a badge⟩
4 : to cover with or form into a thin layer: as **a :** to protect against rain by covering with sheet metal or a substitute **b :** to coat (as glass) with a thin layer (as of metal or a differently colored glass)
5 : to subject (an exposed photographic negative or positive) to a supplementary uniform exposure to light before development in order to modify detail or tone ☆

²flash *noun* (1566)

☆ **SYNONYMS**
Flash, gleam, glint, sparkle, glitter, glisten, glimmer, shimmer mean to send forth light. FLASH implies a sudden and transient outburst of bright light ⟨lightning *flashed*⟩. GLEAM suggests a steady light seen through an obscuring medium or against a dark background ⟨lights *gleamed* in the valley⟩. GLINT implies a cold glancing light ⟨*glinting* steel⟩. SPARKLE suggests innumerable moving points of bright light ⟨the *sparkling* waters of the gulf⟩. GLITTER connotes a brilliant sparkling or gleaming ⟨*glittering* diamonds⟩. GLISTEN applies to the soft sparkle from a wet or oily surface ⟨*glistening* rain-drenched sidewalks⟩. GLIMMER suggests a faint or wavering gleam ⟨a distant *glimmering* light⟩. SHIMMER implies a soft tremulous gleaming or a blurred reflection ⟨a *shimmering* satin dress⟩.

\ə\ abut \°\ kitten \ər\ further \a\ ash \ā\ ace
\ä\ mop, mar \aů\ out \ch\ chin \e\ bet \ē\ easy
\g\ go \i\ hit \ī\ ice \j\ job \ŋ\ sing \ō\ go
\ȯ\ law \ȯi\ boy \th\ thin \th\ the \ü\ loot \ů\ foot
\y\ yet \zh\ vision *see also* Guide to Pronunciation

1 a : a sudden burst of light **b :** a movement of a flag in signaling
2 : a sudden and often brilliant burst ⟨a *flash* of wit⟩
3 : a brief time ⟨I'll be back in a *flash*⟩
4 a : SHOW, DISPLAY; *especially* **:** a vulgar ostentatious display **b** *archaic* **:** a showy ostentatious person **c :** one that attracts notice; *especially* **:** an outstanding athlete **d :** PIZZAZZ
5 *obsolete* **:** thieves' slang
6 : something flashed: as **a :** GLIMPSE, LOOK **b :** SMILE **c :** a first brief news report **d :** FLASHLIGHT 1,2 **e :** a quick-spreading flame or momentary intense outburst of radiant heat **f :** a device for producing a brief and very bright flash of light for taking photographs
7 : RUSH 7a
8 : the rapid conversion of a liquid into vapor
³**flash** *adjective* (circa 1700)
1 a : FLASHY, SHOWY **b :** of, relating to, or characteristic of flashy people or things ⟨*flash* behavior⟩ **c :** of, relating to, or characteristic of persons considered social outcasts ⟨*flash* language⟩
2 a : of sudden origin and short duration ⟨a *flash* fire⟩ **b :** involving very brief exposure to an intense altering agent (as heat or cold) ⟨*flash* drying of milk⟩ ⟨*flash* freezing of food⟩
flash·back \'flash-ˌbak\ *noun* (1903)
1 : a recession of flame to an unwanted position (as into a blowpipe)
2 a : interruption of chronological sequence (as in a film or literary work) by interjection of events of earlier occurrence; *also* **:** an instance of flashback **b :** a past incident recurring vividly in the mind
flash back *intransitive verb* (1944)
1 : to focus one's mind on or vividly remember a past time or incident — usually used with *to*
2 : to employ a flashback (as in a film) — usually used with *to*
flash·board \-ˌbȯrd, -ˌbȯrd\ *noun* (circa 1774)
: one or more boards projecting above the top of a dam to increase the depth of the water
flash·bulb \-ˌbəlb\ *noun* (1935)
: an electric bulb that can be used only once to produce a brief and very bright flash of light for taking photographs
flash card *noun* (1923)
: a card bearing words, numbers, or pictures that is briefly displayed (as by a teacher to a class) usually as a learning aid
flash·cube \'flash-ˌkyüb\ *noun* (1965)
: a cubical device incorporating four flashbulbs
flash·er \'fla-shər\ *noun* (1686)
: one that flashes: as **a :** a light (as a traffic signal or automobile light) that catches the attention by flashing **b :** a device for automatically flashing a light **c :** an exhibitionist who flashes
flash flood *noun* (1940)
: a local flood of great volume and short duration generally resulting from heavy rainfall in the immediate vicinity
— **flash flood** *verb*
flash-for·ward \'flash-ˈfȯr-wərd\ *noun* (1949)
: interruption of chronological sequence (as in a film or literary work) by interjection of events of future occurrence; *also* **:** an instance of flash-forward
flash·gun \-ˌgən\ *noun* (1925)
: a device for producing a bright flash of light for photography
flash·ing \'fla-shiŋ\ *noun* (1742)
: sheet metal used in waterproofing (as at roof valleys or hips or the angle between a chimney and a roof)
flash in the pan [from the firing of the priming in the pan of a flintlock musket without discharging the piece] (1901)
1 : a sudden spasmodic effort that accomplishes nothing
2 : one that appears promising but turns out to be disappointing or worthless

flash·lamp \'flash-ˌlamp\ *noun* (1890)
: a lamp for producing a brief but intense flash of light (as for taking photographs)
flash·light \'flash-ˌlīt\ *noun* (1886)
1 a : a sudden bright artificial light used in taking photographic pictures **b :** a photograph taken by such a light
2 : a small battery-operated portable electric light
flash·over \-ˌō-vər\ *noun* (1892)
1 : an abnormal electrical discharge (as through the air to the ground from a high potential source or between two conducting portions of a structure)
2 : the sudden spread of flame over an area when it becomes heated to the flash point
flash point *noun* (1878)
1 : the lowest temperature at which vapors above a volatile combustible substance ignite in air when exposed to flame
2 : a point at which someone or something bursts suddenly into action or being
3 : TINDERBOX 2
flash·tube \'flash-ˌt(y)üb\ *noun* (1945)
: a gas discharge tube that produces very brief intense flashes of light and is used especially in photography
flashy \'fla-shē\ *adjective* **flash·i·er; -est** (circa 1598)
1 *chiefly dialect* **:** lacking in substance or flavor **:** INSIPID
2 : momentarily dazzling
3 a : superficially attractive or impressive **b :** ostentatious or showy often beyond the bounds of good taste; *especially* **:** marked by gaudy brightness
synonym see GAUDY
— **flash·i·ly** \'fla-shə-lē\ *adverb*
— **flash·i·ness** \'fla-shē-nəs\ *noun*
flask \'flask, flȧsk\ *noun* [Middle French *flasque* powder flask, ultimately from Late Latin *flascon-, flasco* bottle, probably of Germanic origin; akin to Old High German *flaska* bottle] (1549)
: a container often somewhat narrowed toward the outlet and often fitted with a closure: as **a :** a broad flattened necked vessel used especially to carry alcoholic beverages on the person **b** *British* **:** VACUUM BOTTLE
¹**flat** \'flat\ *adjective* **flat·ter; flat·test** [Middle English, from Old Norse *flatr;* akin to Old High German *flaz* flat, and probably Greek *platys* broad — more at PLACE] (14th century)
1 a : lying at full length or spread out upon the ground **:** PROSTRATE **b :** utterly ruined or destroyed **c :** resting with a surface against something
2 a : having a continuous horizontal surface **b :** being or characterized by a horizontal line or tracing without peaks or depressions ⟨a *flat* EEG⟩
3 : having a relatively smooth or even surface
4 : arranged or laid out so as to be level or even
5 a : having the major surfaces essentially parallel and distinctly greater than the minor surfaces ⟨a *flat* piece of wood⟩ **b** *of a heel* **:** very low and broad
6 a : clearly unmistakable **:** DOWNRIGHT ⟨a *flat* denial⟩ **b** (1) **:** not varying **:** FIXED ⟨a *flat* rate⟩ (2) **:** having no fraction either lacking or in excess **:** EXACT ⟨in a *flat* 10 seconds⟩ (3) *of a frequency response* **:** not varying significantly throughout its range
7 a : lacking in animation, zest, or vigor **:** DULL ⟨life seemed *flat* without her⟩ **b :** lacking flavor **:** TASTELESS **c :** lacking effervescence or sparkle ⟨*flat* ginger ale⟩ **d :** commercially inactive; *also* **:** characterized by no significant rise or decline from one period to another ⟨sales were *flat*⟩ **e** *of a tire* **:** lacking air **:** DEFLATED **f** *chiefly British, of a battery* **:** DEAD 3c, DISCHARGED

8 a (1) *of a tone* **:** lowered a half step in pitch (2) **:** lower than the proper pitch **b** *of the vowel a* **:** pronounced as in *bad* or *bat*
9 a : having a low trajectory **b** *of a tennis stroke* **:** made so as to give little or no spin to the ball
10 *of a sail* **:** TAUT
11 a : uniform in hue or shade **b :** having little or no illusion of depth **c** *of a photograph or negative* **:** lacking contrast **d** *of lighting conditions* **:** lacking shadows or contours **e :** free from gloss ⟨*flat* paint⟩ **f :** TWO-DIMENSIONAL 2
12 : of, relating to, or used in competition on the flat ⟨a *flat* horse⟩
synonym see LEVEL, INSIPID
— **flat·ly** *adverb*
— **flat·ness** *noun*
— **flat·tish** \'fla-tish\ *adjective*
²**flat** *noun* (14th century)
1 a : a level surface of land — usually used in plural ⟨sagebrush *flats*⟩ ⟨tidal *flats*⟩ **b :** a stretch of land without obstacles; *especially* **:** a track or course for a flat race — usually used with *the* ⟨has won twice on the *flat*⟩
2 : a flat part or surface ⟨the *flat* of one's hand⟩
3 a : a musical note or tone one half step lower than a specified note or tone **b :** a character ♭ on a line or space of the musical staff indicating a half step drop in pitch
4 : something flat: as **a :** a shallow container for shipping produce **b :** a shallow box in which seedlings are started **c :** a flat piece of theatrical scenery **d :** a shoe or slipper having a flat heel or no heel
5 *chiefly British* **:** an apartment on one floor
6 : a deflated tire
7 : the area to either side of an offensive football formation
³**flat** *adverb* (1531)
1 : in a flat manner **:** DIRECTLY, POSITIVELY
2 : in a complete manner **:** ABSOLUTELY ⟨*flat* broke⟩
3 : below the proper musical pitch
4 : without interest charge; *especially* **:** without allowance or charge for accrued interest ⟨bonds sold *flat*⟩
⁴**flat** *verb* **flat·ted; flat·ting** (circa 1604)
transitive verb
1 : FLATTEN
2 : to lower in pitch especially by a half step
intransitive verb
: to sing or play below the true pitch
¹**flat·bed** \'flat-ˌbed\ *adjective* (1892)
: having a horizontal bed on which the work rests ⟨a *flatbed* printing press⟩ ⟨a *flatbed* plotter⟩
²**flatbed** *noun* (1944)
: a motortruck or trailer with a body in the form of a platform or shallow box
flat·boat \-ˌbōt\ *noun* (1660)
: a boat with a flat bottom and square ends used for transportation of bulky freight especially in shallow waters
flat·car \-ˌkär\ *noun* (1881)
: a railroad freight car without permanent raised sides, ends, or covering
flat–coated retriever \'flat-ˌkō-təd-\ *noun* (1929)
: any of an English breed of medium-sized sporting dogs that have a dense smooth black or liver-colored coat
flat–earth·er \ˌflat-ˈər-thər\ *also* **flat–earth·ist** \-thist\ *noun* (1926)
: a person who believes that the Earth is flat
flat·fish \'flat-ˌfish\ *noun* (1710)
: any of an order (Heterosomata) of marine typically bottom-dwelling bony fishes (as the halibuts, flounders, turbots, and soles) that as adults swim on one side of the laterally compressed body and have both eyes on the upper side
flat·foot \-ˌfût (*always so in sense 3*), ˌflat-ˈ\ *noun, plural* **flat·feet** \-ˌfēt, -ˈfēt\ (1860)

1 : a condition in which the arch of the instep is flattened so that the entire sole rests upon the ground

2 : a foot affected with flatfoot

3 a *or plural* **flatfoots** *slang* : POLICE OFFICER; *especially* : a patrolman walking a regular beat **b** *slang* : SAILOR

¹**flat-foot-ed** \'flat-,fu̇-təd, ,flat-'\ *adjective* (1601)

1 : affected with flatfoot; *broadly* : walking with a dragging or shambling gait

2 a : firm and well balanced on the feet **b** : free from reservation : FORTHRIGHT ⟨had an honest *flat-footed* way of saying a thing⟩

3 : not ready : UNPREPARED — used chiefly in the phrase *catch one flat-footed*

4 : proceeding in a plodding or unimaginative way : PEDESTRIAN ⟨*flat-footed* prose⟩

— **flat-foot-ed-ly** *adverb*

— **flat-foot-ed-ness** *noun*

²**flat-footed** *adverb* (1828)

1 : in an open and determined manner : FLATLY

2 : with the feet flat on a surface (as the ground)

flat-hat \'flat-,hat\ *intransitive verb* [from an alleged incident in which a pedestrian's hat was crushed by a low-flying plane] (1940)

: to fly low in an airplane in a reckless manner : HEDGEHOP

— **flat-hat-ter** *noun*

Flat-head \-,hed\ *noun, plural* **Flatheads** *or* **Flathead** (1709)

1 : a member of any of several North American Indian peoples that practiced head-flattening

2 : an American Indian people of Montana

3 *not capitalized* : any of a family (Platycephalidae) of mostly Australian and East Indian marine food fishes that resemble sculpins

flat-head catfish \'flat-,hed-\ *noun* (1945)

: a large yellowish brown-mottled catfish (*Pylodictis olivaris*) of the central and Gulf states of the U.S.

flat-iron \'flat-,ī(-ə)rn\ *noun* (1744)

: IRON 2c

flat-land \'flat-,land\ *noun* (1735)

1 : a region in which the land is predominantly flat — usually used in plural

2 : land that lacks significant variation in elevation

— **flat-land-er** \-,lan-dər\ *noun*

flat-let \'flat-lət\ *noun* (1925)

British : EFFICIENCY APARTMENT

flat-ling \'flat-liŋ\ *or* **flat-lings** \-liŋz\ *adverb* (15th century)

dialect British : with a flat side or edge

flat-mate \'flat-,māt\ *noun* (1955)

chiefly British : one of two or more persons sharing the same flat

flat-out \'flat-,au̇t\ *adjective* (1906)

1 : being or going at maximum effort or speed

2 : OUT-AND-OUT, DOWNRIGHT ⟨it was a *flat-out* lie⟩

flat out *adverb* (1932)

1 : in a blunt and direct manner : OPENLY ⟨called *flat out* for revolution —*National Review*⟩

2 : at top speed or peak performance ⟨the car does 180 m.p.h. *flat out*⟩

3 *usually* **flat-out** : to the greatest degree : COMPLETELY — usually used as an intensive ⟨is just *flat-out* confusing⟩

flat-picking \'flat-,pi-kiŋ\ *noun* (1970)

: a method of playing a stringed instrument (as a guitar) with a plectrum held between the thumb and forefinger

flat race *noun* (1848)

: a race (as for horses) on a level course without obstacles (as hurdles) — compare STEEPLECHASE

— **flat racing** *noun*

flat-ten \'fla-tᵊn\ *verb* **flat-tened; flat-ten-ing** \'flat-niŋ, 'fla-tə-\ (1630)

transitive verb

: to make flat: as **a** : to make level or smooth **b** : to knock down; *also* : to defeat decisively **c** : to make dull or uninspired — often used with *out* **d** : to make (as paint) lusterless **e** : to stabilize especially at a lower level

intransitive verb

: to become flat or flatter: as **a** : to become dull or spiritless **b** : to extend in or into a flat position or form **c** : to become uniform or stabilized often at a new lower level — usually used with *out*

— **flat-ten-er** \-nər\ *noun*

¹**flat-ter** \'fla-tər\ *verb* [Middle English *flateren*, from Old French *flater* to lick, flatter, of Germanic origin; akin to Old High German *flaz* flat] (13th century)

transitive verb

1 : to praise excessively especially from motives of self-interest

2 a *archaic* : BEGUILE 4 **b** : to encourage or gratify especially with the assurance that something is right ⟨I *flatter* myself that my interpretation is correct⟩

3 a : to portray too favorably ⟨the portrait *flatters* him⟩ **b** : to display to advantage ⟨candlelight often *flatters* the face⟩

intransitive verb

: to use flattery

— **flat-ter-er** \-tər-ər\ *noun*

— **flat-ter-ing-ly** \-tə-riŋ-lē\ *adverb*

²**flatter** *noun* (1714)

: one that flattens; *especially* : a flat-faced swage used in smithing

flat-tery \'fla-tə-rē\ *noun, plural* **-ter-ies** (14th century)

1 a : the act or practice of flattering **b** (1) : something that flatters (2) : insincere or excessive praise

2 *obsolete* : a pleasing self-deception

flat-top \'flat-,täp\ *noun* (1940)

: something with a flat or flattened upper surface: as **a** : AIRCRAFT CARRIER **b** : a modified crew cut

flat-u-lence \'fla-chə-lən(t)s\ *noun* (1711)

: the quality or state of being flatulent

flat-u-len-cy \-lən(t)-sē\ *noun* (1660)

: FLATULENCE

flat-u-lent \-lənt\ *adjective* [Middle French, from Latin *flatus* act of blowing, wind, from *flare* to blow — more at BLOW] (1599)

1 a : marked by or affected with gas generated in the intestine or stomach **b** : likely to cause gas

2 : pompously or portentously overblown : INFLATED

— **flat-u-lent-ly** *adverb*

fla-tus \'flā-təs\ *noun* [Latin, act of blowing, act of breaking wind] (1651)

: gas generated in the stomach or bowels

flat-ware \'flat-,war, -,wer\ *noun* (1851)

: tableware more or less flat and usually formed or cast in a single piece; *especially* : eating and serving utensils (as knives, forks, and spoons) — compare HOLLOWWARE

flat-ways \-,wāz\ *adverb* (1692)

: FLATWISE

flat-wise \-,wīz\ *adverb* (1601)

: with the flat surface presented in some expressed or implied position

flat-work \-,wərk\ *noun* (1925)

: laundry that can be finished mechanically and does not require hand ironing

flat-worm \-,wərm\ *noun* (circa 1889)

: PLATYHELMINTH; *especially* : TURBELLARIAN

flaunt \'flȯnt, 'flänt\ *verb* [perhaps of Scandinavian origin; akin to Old Norse *flana* to rush around — more at PLANET] (1566)

intransitive verb

1 : to display or obtrude oneself to public notice

2 : to wave or flutter showily ⟨the flag *flaunts* in the breeze⟩

transitive verb

1 : to display ostentatiously or impudently : PARADE ⟨*flaunting* his superiority⟩

2 : to treat contemptuously ⟨*flaunted* the rules —Louis Untermeyer⟩ □

synonym see SHOW

— **flaunt** *noun*

— **flaunt-ing-ly** \'flȯn-tiŋ-lē, 'flän-\ *adverb*

— **flaunty** \-tē\ *adjective*

flau-tist \'flȯ-tist, 'flau̇-\ *noun* [Italian *flautista*, from *flauto* flute, from Old Provençal *flaut*] (1860)

: FLUTIST

fla-va-none \'flā-və-,nōn\ *noun* [Latin *flavus* + International Scientific Vocabulary *-ane* + *-one*] (1949)

: a colorless crystalline ketone $C_{15}H_{12}O_2$; *also* : any of the derivatives of this ketone many of which occur in plants often in the form of glycosides

fla-vin \'flā-vən\ *noun* [International Scientific Vocabulary, from Latin *flavus* yellow — more at BLUE] (1933)

: any of a class of yellow water-soluble nitrogenous pigments derived from isoalloxazine and occurring in the form of nucleotides as coenzymes of flavoproteins; *especially* : RIBOFLAVIN

flavin adenine dinucleotide *noun* (1960)

: a coenzyme $C_{27}H_{33}N_9O_{15}P_2$ of some flavoproteins

fla-vine \'flā-,vēn\ *noun* [International Scientific Vocabulary, from Latin *flavus*] (circa 1853)

: any of a series of yellow acridine dyes (as acriflavine) often used medicinally for their antiseptic properties

flavin mononucleotide *noun* (circa 1953)

: FMN

fla-vone \'flā-,vōn\ *noun* [International Scientific Vocabulary, from Latin *flavus*] (1897)

: a colorless crystalline ketone $C_{15}H_{10}O_2$ found in the leaves, stems, and seed capsules of many primroses; *also* : any of the derivatives of this ketone many of which occur as yellow plant pigments in the form of glycosides and are used as dyestuffs

fla-vo-noid \'flā-və-,nȯid\ *noun* [*flavone* + *-oid*] (1947)

: any of a group of aromatic compounds that includes many common pigments (as the anthocyanins and flavones)

fla-vo-nol \'flā-və-,nȯl, -,nōl\ *noun* (1898)

: any of various hydroxy derivatives of flavone

fla-vo-pro-tein \,flā-vō-'prō-,tēn, -'prō-tē-ən\ *noun* [International Scientific Vocabulary *flavin* + *-o-* + *protein*] (1934)

□ **USAGE**

flaunt Although transitive sense 2 of *flaunt* undoubtedly arose from confusion with *flout*, the contexts in which it appears cannot be called substandard ⟨meting out punishment to the occasional mavericks who operate rigged games, tolerate rowdyism, or otherwise *flaunt* the law —Oscar Lewis⟩ ⟨observed with horror the *flaunting* of their authority in the suburbs, where men . . . put up buildings that had no place at all in a Christian commonwealth —Marchette Chute⟩ ⟨in our profession . . . very rarely do we publicly chastise a colleague who has *flaunted* our most basic principles —R. T. Blackburn, *AAUP Bulletin*⟩. If you use it, however, you should be aware that many people will consider it a mistake. Use of *flout* in the sense of *flaunt* 1 is found occasionally ⟨"The proper pronunciation," the blonde said, *flouting* her refined upbringing, "is pree feeks" —Mike Royko⟩.

\ə\ abut \ᵊ\ kitten \ər\ further \a\ ash \ā\ ace
\ä\ mop, mar \au̇\ out \ch\ chin \e\ bet \ē\ easy
\g\ go \i\ hit \ī\ ice \j\ job \ŋ\ sing \ō\ go
\ȯ\ law \ȯi\ boy \th\ thin \th\ the \ü\ loot \u̇\ foot
\y\ yet \zh\ vision *see also* Guide to Pronunciation

: a dehydrogenase that contains a flavin and often a metal and plays a major role in biological oxidations

¹fla·vor \'flā-vər\ *noun* [Middle English, from Middle French *flaor*, *flavor*, from (assumed) Vulgar Latin *flator*, alteration of Latin *flatus* breath, act of blowing — more at FLATULENT] (14th century)
1 a *archaic* : ODOR, FRAGRANCE **b** : the quality of something that affects the sense of taste **c** : the blend of taste and smell sensations evoked by a substance in the mouth ⟨the *flavor* of apples⟩
2 : a substance that flavors ⟨artificial *flavors*⟩
3 : characteristic or predominant quality ⟨the ethnic *flavor* of a neighborhood⟩
4 a : VARIETY 3a **b** : a property that distinguishes different types of elementary particles (as quarks and neutrinos); *also* : any of the different types of particles that are distinguished by flavor
— **fla·vored** \-vərd\ *adjective*
— **fla·vor·ful** \-vər-fəl\ *adjective*
— **fla·vor·ful·ly** \-fə-lē\ *adverb*
— **fla·vor·less** \-vər-ləs\ *adjective*
— **fla·vor·some** \-səm\ *adjective*

²flavor *transitive verb* **fla·vored; fla·vor·ing** \'flā-v(ə-)riŋ\ (1542)
: to give or add flavor to

fla·vor·ing *noun* (1845)
: FLAVOR 2

fla·vor·ist \'flā-vər-ist\ *noun* (1964)
: a specialist in the creation of artificial flavors

fla·vour *chiefly British variant of* FLAVOR

¹flaw \'flȯ\ *noun* [of Scandinavian origin; akin to Norwegian *flaga* gust] (1513)
1 : a sudden brief burst of wind; *also* : a spell of stormy weather
2 *obsolete* : an outburst especially of passion

²flaw *noun* [Middle English, flake, probably of Scandinavian origin; akin to Swedish *flaga* flake, flaw; akin to Old English *flōh* flat stone] (1586)
1 a : a defect in physical structure or form **b** : an imperfection or weakness and especially one that detracts from the whole or hinders effectiveness ⟨vanity was the *flaw* in his character⟩ ⟨a *flaw* in the book's plot⟩
2 *obsolete* : FRAGMENT
— **flawed** \'flȯd\ *adjective*
— **flaw·less** \-ləs\ *adjective*
— **flaw·less·ly** *adverb*
— **flaw·less·ness** *noun*

³flaw (1610)
transitive verb
: to make flaws in : MAR
intransitive verb
: to become defective

flax \'flaks\ *noun, often attributive* [Middle English, from Old English *fleax*; akin to Old High German *flahs* flax, Latin *plectere* to braid — more at PLY] (before 12th century)
1 : any of a genus (*Linum* of the family Linaceae, the flax family) of herbs; *especially* : a slender erect annual (*Linum usitatissimum*) with blue flowers commonly cultivated for its bast fiber and seed
2 : the fiber of the flax plant especially when prepared for spinning
3 : any of several plants resembling flax

flax·en \'flak-sən\ *adjective* (15th century)
1 : made of flax
2 : resembling flax especially in pale soft strawy color ⟨*flaxen* hair⟩

flax·seed \'flak(s)-ˌsēd\ *noun* (1562)
: the seed of flax used as a source of oil and medicinally as a demulcent and emollient

flaxy \'flak-sē\ *adjective* **flax·i·er; -est** (1634)
: resembling flax especially in texture

flay \'flā\ *transitive verb* [Middle English *flen*, from Old English *flēan*; akin to Old Norse *flā* to flay, Lithuanian *plėšti* to tear] (before 12th century)
1 : to strip off the skin or surface of : SKIN
2 : to criticize harshly : EXCORIATE

3 : LASH 1b ⟨the wind whipped up to gale fury, *flaying* his face —Richard Kent⟩

F layer *noun* (1928)
: the highest and most densely ionized regular layer of the ionosphere occurring at night within the F region

flea \'flē\ *noun* [Middle English *fle*, from Old English *flēa*; akin to Old High German *flōh* flea] (before 12th century)
: any of an order (Siphonaptera) of small wingless bloodsucking insects that have a hard laterally compressed body and legs adapted to leaping and that feed on warm-blooded animals
— **flea in one's ear** : REBUKE ⟨sent him away with a *flea in his ear*⟩

flea·bag \'flē-ˌbag\ *noun* (1839)
: an inferior hotel or rooming house

flea·bane \-ˌbān\ *noun* (1548)
: any of various composite plants (as of the genus *Erigeron*) that were once believed to drive away fleas

flea beetle *noun* (1842)
: any of a subfamily (Alticinae, especially genera *Alticia* and *Epitrix*) of small chrysomelid beetles with legs adapted for leaping that feed on foliage and sometimes serve as vectors of virus diseases of plants

flea·bite \'flē-ˌbīt\ *noun* (circa 1570)
1 : the bite of a flea; *also* : the red spot caused by such a bite
2 : a trifling pain or annoyance

flea–bit·ten \-ˌbi-t⁵n\ *adjective* (1570)
1 *of a horse* : having a white or gray coat flecked with a darker color
2 : bitten by or infested with fleas

flea collar *noun* (1953)
: a collar for animals (as dogs and cats) that contains insecticide for killing fleas

flea–flick·er \-ˌfli-kər\ *noun* (1927)
: any of various deceptive football plays in which the ball is quickly transferred between players (as by a lateral) before or after a forward pass

flea·hop·per \-ˌhä-pər\ *noun* (1902)
: any of various small jumping bugs that feed on cultivated plants

flea market *noun* [translation of French *Marché aux Puces*, a market in Paris] (1922)
: a usually open-air market for secondhand articles and antiques

flea·pit \-ˌpit\ *noun* (1937)
British : a dilapidated building usually housing a movie theater

flea·wort \'flē-ˌwərt, -ˌwȯrt\ *noun* (before 12th century)
: any of three Old World plantains (especially *Plantago psyllium*) whose seeds are sometimes used as a mild laxative — compare PSYLLIUM SEED

flèche \'flāsh, 'flesh\ *noun* [French, literally, arrow, from Old French *fleche*, of Germanic origin; akin to Middle Dutch *vlieke* arrow, Old English *flēogan* to fly] (1848)
: SPIRE; *especially* : a slender spire above the intersection of the nave and transepts of a church

flé·chette \flā-'shet, fle-\ *noun* [French, from diminutive of *flèche* arrow] (1915)
: a small dart-shaped projectile that is clustered in an explosive warhead, dropped as a missile from an airplane, or fired from a handheld gun

¹fleck \'flek\ *transitive verb* [back-formation from *flecked* spotted, from Middle English, probably from Old Norse *flekkōttr*, from *flekkr* spot] (14th century)
1 : STREAK, SPOT ⟨whitecaps *flecked* the blue sea⟩
2 : to color as if by sprinkling with flecks ⟨his wit is *flecked* with sarcasm —James Atlas⟩

²fleck *noun* (1598)
1 : SPOT, MARK ⟨a brown tweed with *flecks* of yellow⟩
2 : FLAKE, PARTICLE ⟨*flecks* of snow drifted down⟩

fledge \'flej\ *verb* **fledged; fledg·ing** [*fledge* capable of flying, from Middle English *flegge*, from Old English *-flycge*; akin to Old High German *flucki* capable of flying, Old English *flēogan* to fly — more at FLY] (1566)
intransitive verb
of a bird : to acquire the feathers necessary for flight or independent activity
transitive verb
1 : to rear until ready for flight or independent activity
2 : to cover with or as if with feathers or down
3 : to furnish (as an arrow) with feathers

fledg·ling \'flej-liŋ\ *noun* (1830)
1 : a young bird just fledged
2 : an immature or inexperienced person
3 : one that is new ⟨a *fledgling* company⟩

flee \'flē\ *verb* **fled** \'fled\; **flee·ing** [Middle English *flen*, from Old English *flēon*; akin to Old High German *fliohan* to flee] (before 12th century)
intransitive verb
1 a : to run away often from danger or evil : FLY **b** : to hurry toward a place of security
2 : to pass away swiftly : VANISH
transitive verb
: to run away from : SHUN

¹fleece \'flēs\ *noun* [Middle English *flees*, from Old English *flēos*; akin to Middle High German *vlius* fleece and perhaps to Latin *pluma* feather, down] (before 12th century)
1 a : the coat of wool covering a wool-bearing animal (as a sheep) **b** : the wool obtained from a sheep at one shearing
2 a : any of various soft or woolly coverings **b** : a soft bulky deep-piled knitted or woven fabric used chiefly for clothing

²fleece *transitive verb* **fleeced; fleec·ing** (1537)
1 a : to strip of money or property by fraud or extortion **b** : to charge excessively for goods or services
2 : to remove the fleece from : SHEAR
3 : to dot or cover with fleecy masses

fleeced \'flēst\ *adjective* (1580)
1 : covered with or as if with a fleece
2 *of a textile* : having a soft nap

fleech \'flēch\ *verb* [Middle English (Scots) *flechen*] (14th century)
dialect : COAX, WHEEDLE

fleecy \'flē-sē\ *adjective* **fleec·i·er; -est** (1590)
: covered with, made of, or resembling fleece ⟨a *fleecy* winter coat⟩

¹fleer \'flir\ *intransitive verb* [Middle English *fleryen*, of Scandinavian origin; akin to Norwegian *flire* to giggle] (15th century)
: to laugh or grimace in a coarse derisive manner : SNEER
synonym see SCOFF
— **fleer·ing·ly** \-iŋ-lē\ *adverb*

²fleer *noun* (1604)
: a word or look of derision or mockery

¹fleet \'flēt\ *verb* [Middle English *fleten*, from Old English *flēotan*; akin to Old High German *fliozzan* to float, Old English *flōwan* to flow] (before 12th century)
intransitive verb
1 *obsolete* : DRIFT
2 a *archaic* : FLOW **b** : to fade away : VANISH
3 [³*fleet*] : to fly swiftly
transitive verb
: to cause (time) to pass usually quickly or imperceptibly

²fleet *noun* [Middle English *flete*, from Old English *flēot* ship, from *flēotan*] (13th century)
1 : a number of warships under a single command; *specifically* : an organization of ships and aircraft under the command of a flag officer
2 : GROUP 2a, b; *especially* : a group (as of ships, planes, or trucks) operated under unified control

³fleet *adjective* [probably from ¹*fleet*] (circa 1529)
1 : swift in motion : NIMBLE

2 : EVANESCENT, FLEETING
synonym see FAST
— **fleet·ly** *adverb*
— **fleet·ness** *noun*
fleet admiral *noun* (1946)
: an admiral of the highest rank in the navy whose insignia is five stars
fleet–foot·ed \-,fu̇-təd\ *adjective* (circa 1743)
: able to run fast
fleet·ing *adjective* (1563)
: passing swiftly : TRANSITORY
synonym see TRANSIENT
— **fleet·ing·ly** \'flē-tiŋ-lē\ *adverb*
— **fleet·ing·ness** *noun*
Fleet Street \'flēt-\ *noun* [*Fleet Street*, London, England, center of the London newspaper district] (1882)
: the London press
flei·shig \'flā-shik\ *adjective* [Yiddish *fleyshik*, from Middle High German *vleischic* meaty, from *vleisch* flesh, meat, from Old High German *fleisk*] (1943)
: made of, prepared with, or used for meat or meat products — compare MILCHIG, PAREVE
Flem·ing \'fle-miŋ\ *noun* [Middle English, from Middle Dutch *Vlaminc* (akin to Middle Dutch *Vlander* Flanders)] (12th century)
: a member of the Germanic people inhabiting northern Belgium and a small section of northern France
¹Flem·ish \'fle-mish\ *adjective* (14th century)
: of, relating to, or characteristic of Flanders or the Flemings or their language
²Flemish *noun* (circa 1741)
1 : the Germanic language of the Flemings that is made up of dialects of Dutch
2 *plural in construction* : FLEMINGS
Flemish giant *noun* (1898)
: any of a breed of very large solid-colored rabbits probably of Belgian origin
flense \'flen(t)s\ *transitive verb* **flensed; flens·ing** [Dutch *flensen* or Danish & Norwegian *flense*] (1820)
: to strip (as a whale) of blubber or skin
¹flesh \'flesh\ *noun* [Middle English, from Old English *flǣsc;* akin to Old High German *fleisk* flesh and perhaps to Old Norse *flā* to flay — more at FLAY] (before 12th century)
1 a : the soft parts of the body of an animal and especially of a vertebrate; *especially* : the parts composed chiefly of skeletal muscle as distinguished from visceral structures, bone, and integuments **b** : sleek well-fatted condition of body **c** : SKIN
2 a : edible parts of an animal **b** : flesh of a mammal or fowl eaten as food
3 a : the physical nature of human beings ⟨the spirit indeed is willing, but the *flesh* is weak —Matthew 26:41 (Authorized Version)⟩ **b** : HUMAN NATURE
4 a : human beings : MANKIND **b** : living beings **c** : STOCK, KINDRED
5 : a fleshy plant part used as food; *also* : the fleshy part of a fruit
6 *Christian Science* : an illusion that matter has sensation
7 : SUBSTANCE ⟨insights buried in the *flesh* of the narrative —Jan Carew⟩
— **in the flesh** : in person and alive
²flesh (1530)
transitive verb
1 : to initiate or habituate especially by giving a foretaste
2 *archaic* : GRATIFY
3 : to clothe or cover with or as if with flesh; *broadly* : to give substance to — usually used with *out*
4 : to free from flesh
intransitive verb
: to become fleshy — often used with *up* or *out*
flesh and blood *noun* (before 12th century)
1 : corporeal nature as composed of flesh and of blood
2 : near kindred — used chiefly in the phrase *one's own flesh and blood*

3 : SUBSTANCE, REALITY
fleshed \'flesht\ *adjective* (15th century)
: having flesh especially of a specified kind — often used in combination ⟨pink-*fleshed*⟩ ⟨thick-*fleshed*⟩
flesh fly *noun* (14th century)
: a dipteran fly whose maggots feed on flesh; *especially* : any of a family (Sarcophagidae) of flies some of which cause myiasis
flesh·ings \'fle-shiŋz\ *noun plural* (1860)
: material removed in fleshing a hide
flesh·ly \'flesh-lē\ *adjective* (before 12th century)
1 a : CORPOREAL, BODILY **b** : of, relating to, or characterized by indulgence of bodily appetites; *especially* : LASCIVIOUS ⟨*fleshly* desires⟩ **c** : not spiritual : WORLDLY
2 : FLESHY, PLUMP
3 : having a sensuous quality ⟨*fleshly* art⟩
synonym see CARNAL
flesh·ment \'flesh-mənt\ *noun* [²*flesh*] (1605)
obsolete : excitement associated with a successful beginning
flesh out *transitive verb* (1886)
: to make fuller or more nearly complete ⟨museums *fleshing out* their collections with borrowed works⟩
— **fleshed–out** *adjective*
flesh·pot \'flesh-,pät\ *noun* (1592)
1 *plural* : bodily comfort : LUXURY
2 : a place of lascivious entertainment — usually used in plural
flesh wound *noun* (circa 1674)
: an injury involving penetration of the body musculature without damage to bones or internal organs
fleshy \'fle-shē\ *adjective* **flesh·i·er; -est** (14th century)
1 a : marked by, consisting of, or resembling flesh **b** : marked by abundant flesh; *especially* : CORPULENT
2 a : SUCCULENT, PULPY ⟨the *fleshy* texture of a melon⟩ **b** : not thin, dry, or membranous ⟨*fleshy* fungi⟩
— **flesh·i·ness** *noun*
fleshy fruit *noun* (1929)
: a fruit (as a berry, drupe, or pome) consisting largely of soft succulent tissue
fletch \'flech\ *transitive verb* [back-formation from *fletcher*] (circa 1656)
: FEATHER ⟨*fletch* an arrow⟩
fletch·er \'fle-chər\ *noun* [Middle English *fleccher*, from Old French *flechier*, from *fleche* arrow — more at FLÈCHE] (14th century)
: a maker of arrows
fletch·ing \-chiŋ\ *noun* (circa 1930)
: the feathers on an arrow; *also* : the arrangement of such feathers
fleur de coin \,flər-də-'kwaⁿ\ *adjective* [French *à fleur de coin*, literally, with the bloom of the die] (circa 1889)
: being in the preserved mint condition
fleur–de–lis *or* **fleur–de–lys** \,flər-d²l-'ē, ,flu̇r-\ *noun, plural* **fleurs–de–lis** *or* **fleur–de–lis** *or* **fleurs–de–lys** *or* **fleur–de–lys** \,flər-d²l-'ē(z), ,flu̇r-\ [Middle English *flourdelis*, from Middle French *flor de lis*, literally, lily flower] (14th century)
1 : IRIS 3
2 : a conventionalized iris in artistic design and heraldry
fleu·ry \'flu̇r-ē\ *adjective* [alteration of Middle English *flory*, from Old French *floré*, from *flor* flower — more at FLOWER] (15th century)
of a heraldic cross : having the ends of the arms broadening out into the heads of fleurs-de-lis — see CROSS illustration
flew *past of* FLY
flews \'flüz\ *noun plural* [origin unknown] (1575)

fleur-de-lis 2

: the pendulous lateral parts of a dog's upper lip — see DOG illustration
¹flex \'fleks\ *verb* [Latin *flexus*, past participle of *flectere* to bend] (circa 1521)
transitive verb
1 : to bend especially repeatedly
2 a : to move muscles so as to cause flexion of (a joint) **b** : to move or tense (a muscle) by contraction
intransitive verb
: BEND
— **flex one's muscles** : to demonstrate one's strength ⟨an exaggerated need to *flex* his political *muscles* —J. P. Lash⟩
²flex *noun* [short for *flexible cord*] (1905)
chiefly British : an electric cord
³flex *noun* (circa 1934)
: an act or instance of flexing
flex·i·ble \'flek-sə-bəl\ *adjective* (15th century)
1 : capable of being flexed : PLIANT
2 : yielding to influence : TRACTABLE
3 : characterized by a ready capability to adapt to new, different, or changing requirements ⟨a *flexible* foreign policy⟩ ⟨a *flexible* schedule⟩
synonym see ELASTIC
— **flex·i·bil·i·ty** \,flek-sə-'bi-lə-tē\ *noun*
— **flex·i·bly** \'flek-sə-blē\ *adverb*
flex·ile \'flek-səl, -,sīl\ *adjective* (1633)
: FLEXIBLE
flex·ion \'flek-shən\ *noun* [Latin *flexion-, flexio*, from *flectere*] (1615)
1 : the act of flexing or bending
2 : a part bent : BEND
3 : INFLECTION 3
4 a : a bending movement around a joint in a limb (as the knee or elbow) that decreases the angle between the bones of the limb at the joint — compare EXTENSION 3b **b** : a forward raising of the arm or leg by a movement at the shoulder or hip joint
flex·og·ra·phy \flek-'sä-grə-fē\ *noun* [*flexible* + *-o-* + *-graphy*] (1954)
: a process of rotary letterpress printing using flexible plates and fast-drying inks
— **flexo·graph·ic** \,flek-sə-'gra-fik\ *adjective*
— **flexo·graph·i·cal·ly** \-fi-k(ə-)lē\ *adverb*
flex·or \'flek-sər, -,sȯr\ *noun* (1615)
: a muscle serving to bend a body part (as a limb)
flex·time \'flek-,stīm\ *or* **flexi·time** \'flek-si-,tīm\ *noun* (1972)
: a system that allows employees to choose their own times for starting and finishing work within a broad range of available hours
flex·u·ous \'flek-sh(ə-)wəs\ *adjective* [Latin *flexuosus*, from *flexus* bend, from *flectere*] (1605)
1 : having curves, turns, or windings
2 : lithe or fluid in action or movement
flex·ur·al \'flek-sh(ə-)rəl\ *adjective* (1879)
1 : of, relating to, or resulting from flexure
2 : characterized by flexure
flex·ure \'flek-shər\ *noun* (1592)
1 : the quality or state of being flexed : FLEXION
2 : TURN, BEND, FOLD
fley \'flā\ *transitive verb* [Middle English *flayen*, from Old English *āflēgan*, from *ā-*, perfective prefix + *-flēgan* to put to flight] (13th century)
Scottish : FRIGHTEN
flib·ber·ti·gib·bet \,fli-bər-tē-'ji-bət\ *noun* [Middle English *flepergebet*] (15th century)
: a silly flighty person
— **flib·ber·ti·gib·bety** \-bə-tē\ *adjective*
flic \'flēk\ *noun* [French] (1899)
: a French police officer

¹flick \'flik\ *noun* [imitative] (15th century)
1 : a light sharp jerky stroke or movement
2 : a sound produced by a flick
3 : FLICKER 1
²flick (1816)
transitive verb
1 a : to move or propel with or as if with a flick ⟨*flicked* her hair back over her shoulder⟩ ⟨*flick* a switch⟩ **b :** to activate, deactivate, or change by or as if by flicking a switch ⟨*flick* on a cigarette lighter⟩ ⟨*flick* off the radio⟩
2 a : to strike lightly with a quick sharp motion ⟨*flicked* the horse with a whip⟩ **b :** to remove with light blows ⟨*flicked* an ash off her sleeve⟩
intransitive verb
1 : to go or pass quickly or abruptly ⟨a bird *flicked* by⟩ ⟨*flicking* through some papers⟩
2 : to direct flicks at something
³flick *noun* [short for ²*flicker*] (1926)
: MOVIE
¹flick·er \'fli-kər\ *verb* **flick·ered; flick·er·ing** \-k(ə-)riŋ\ [Middle English *flikeren*, from Old English *flicorian*] (before 12th century)
intransitive verb
1 : to move irregularly or unsteadily **:** FLUTTER
2 : to burn or shine fitfully or with a fluctuating light
3 : to appear briefly
transitive verb
1 : to cause to flicker
2 : to produce by flickering
— **flick·er·ing·ly** \-k(ə-)riŋ-lē\ *adverb*
²flicker *noun* (1849)
1 a : an act of flickering **b :** a sudden brief movement **c :** a momentary quickening ⟨a *flicker* of anger⟩ **d :** a slight indication **:** HINT ⟨a *flicker* of recognition⟩
2 : a wavering light
3 : MOVIE — often used in plural
— **flick·ery** \'fli-k(ə-)rē\ *adjective*
³flicker *noun* [probably imitative of its call] (1809)
: a large barred and spotted North American woodpecker (*Colaptes auratus*) with a brown back that commonly forages on the ground for ants — compare RED-SHAFTED FLICKER, YELLOW-SHAFTED FLICKER
flick–knife \'flik-ˌnīf\ *noun* (1957)
British **:** SWITCHBLADE
flied *past and past participle of* ³FLY
fli·er \'flī-(ə-)r\ *noun* (15th century)
1 : one that flies; *specifically* **:** AIRMAN
2 : a reckless or speculative venture — usually used in the phrase *take a flier*
3 *usually* **fly·er :** an advertising circular
¹flight \'flīt\ *noun, often attributive* [Middle English, from Old English *flyht*; akin to Middle Dutch *vlucht* flight, Old English *flēogan* to fly] (before 12th century)
1 a : an act or instance of passing through the air by the use of wings ⟨the *flight* of a bee⟩ **b :** the ability to fly ⟨*flight* is natural to birds⟩
2 a : a passing through the air or through space outside the earth's atmosphere ⟨*flight* of an arrow⟩ ⟨*flight* of a rocket to the moon⟩ **b :** the distance covered in such a flight **c :** swift movement
3 a : a trip made by or in an airplane or spacecraft **b :** a scheduled airplane trip
4 : a group of similar beings or objects flying through the air together
5 : a brilliant, imaginative, or unrestrained exercise or display ⟨a *flight* of fancy⟩
6 a : a continuous series of stairs from one landing or floor to another **b :** a series (as of terraces or conveyors) resembling a flight of stairs
7 : a unit of the U.S. Air Force below a squadron
— **flight·less** \-ləs\ *adjective*
²flight (1873)
intransitive verb
: to rise, settle, or fly in a flock ⟨geese *flighting* on the marsh⟩

transitive verb
: ¹FLUSH
³flight *noun* [Middle English *fluht, fliht*; akin to Old High German *fluht* flight, Old English *flēon* to flee] (13th century)
: an act or instance of running away
flight attendant *noun* (1947)
: a person who attends passengers on an airplane
flight bag *noun* [¹*flight*] (1943)
1 : a lightweight traveling bag with zippered outside pockets
2 : a small canvas satchel
flight deck *noun* (1924)
1 : the uppermost complete deck of an aircraft carrier
2 : the forward compartment in some airplanes
flight engineer *noun* (1938)
: a flight crewman responsible for mechanical operation
flight feather *noun* (1735)
: one of the quills of a bird's wing or tail that support it in flight — compare CONTOUR FEATHER
flight lieutenant *noun* (1914)
: a commissioned officer in the British air force who ranks with a captain in the army
flight line *noun* (1943)
: a parking and servicing area for airplanes
flight path *noun* (1911)
: the path in the air or space made or followed by something (as a particle, an airplane, or a spacecraft) in flight
flight pay *noun* (1928)
: an additional allowance paid to military personnel who take part in regular authorized aircraft flights
flight plan *noun* (circa 1936)
: a usually written statement (as by a pilot) of the details of an intended flight (as of an airplane or spacecraft) usually filed with an authority
flight recorder *noun* (1939)
: a crashworthy instrument for recording flight data (as airspeed and altitude)
flight suit *noun* (1944)
: a usually one-piece garment especially of fire-resistant fabric worn especially by military aircrews
flight surgeon *noun* (1925)
: a military medical officer trained in aerospace medicine
flight–test \'flīt-ˌtest\ *transitive verb* (1930)
: to test (as an airplane or spacecraft) in flight
flighty \'flī-tē\ *adjective* **flight·i·er; -est** (1552)
1 : SWIFT
2 : lacking stability or steadiness: **a :** easily upset **:** VOLATILE ⟨a *flighty* temper⟩ **b :** easily excited **:** SKITTISH ⟨a *flighty* horse⟩ **c :** CAPRICIOUS, SILLY
— **flight·i·ly** \'flī-tᵊl-ē\ *adverb*
— **flight·i·ness** \'flī-tē-nəs\ *noun*
¹flim·flam \'flim-ˌflam\ *noun* [probably of Scandinavian origin; akin to Old Norse *flim* mockery] (circa 1538)
1 : DECEPTION, FRAUD
2 : deceptive nonsense
²flimflam *transitive verb* **flim·flammed; flim·flam·ming** (1660)
: to subject to a flimflam
— **flim·flam·mer** *noun*
— **flim·flam·mery** \-ˌfla-mə-rē\ *noun*
¹flim·sy \'flim-zē\ *adjective* **flim·si·er; -est** [perhaps alteration of ¹*film* + -*sy* (as in *tricksy*)] (1702)
1 a : lacking in physical strength or substance ⟨*flimsy* silks⟩ **b :** of inferior materials and workmanship
2 : having little worth or plausibility
— **flim·si·ly** \-zə-lē\ *adverb*
— **flim·si·ness** \-zē-nəs\ *noun*
²flimsy *noun, plural* **flim·sies** (1857)

chiefly British **:** a lightweight paper used especially for multiple copies; *also* **:** a document printed on flimsy
flinch \'flinch\ *intransitive verb* [Middle French *flenchir* to bend, of Germanic origin; akin to Middle High German *lenken* to bend, Old High German *hlanca* flank — more at LANK] (1579)
: to withdraw or shrink from or as if from pain **:** WINCE; *also* **:** to tense the muscles involuntarily in anticipation of discomfort
synonym *see* RECOIL
— **flinch** *noun*
— **flinch·er** *noun*
flin·ders \'flin-dərz\ *noun plural* [Middle English *flendris*] (15th century)
: SPLINTERS, FRAGMENTS
¹fling \'fliŋ\ *verb* **flung** \'fləŋ\; **fling·ing** \'fliŋ-iŋ\ [Middle English, perhaps of Scandinavian origin; akin to Old Norse *flengja* to whip] (14th century)
intransitive verb
1 : to move in a brusque or headlong manner ⟨*flung* out of the room in a rage⟩
2 *of an animal* **:** to kick or plunge vigorously
3 *Scottish* **:** CAPER
transitive verb
1 a : to throw forcefully, impetuously, or casually ⟨*flung* herself down on the sofa⟩ ⟨clothes were *flung* on the floor⟩ **b :** to cast as if by throwing ⟨*flung* off all restraint⟩
2 : to place or send suddenly and unceremoniously ⟨was arrested and *flung* into prison⟩
3 : to give unrestrainedly ⟨*flung* himself into music⟩
synonym *see* THROW
— **fling·er** \'fliŋ-ər\ *noun*
²fling *noun* (1589)
1 : an act or instance of flinging
2 a : a casual try or involvement **b :** a casual or brief love affair
3 : a period devoted to self-indulgence
flint \'flint\ *noun* [Middle English, from Old English; akin to Old High German *flins* pebble, hard stone] (before 12th century)
1 : a massive hard quartz that produces a spark when struck by steel
2 : an implement of flint used in prehistoric cultures
3 a : a piece of flint **b :** a material used for producing a spark; *especially* **:** an alloy (as of iron and cerium) used in lighters
4 : something resembling flint in hardness
— **flint·like** \-ˌlīk\ *adjective*
flint corn *noun* (1705)
: an Indian corn (*Zea mays indurata*) having hard horny usually rounded kernels with the soft endosperm enclosed by a hard outer layer
flint glass *noun* (1683)
: heavy brilliant glass that contains lead oxide, has a relatively high index of refraction, and is used in lenses and prisms
flint·lock \'flint-ˌläk\ *noun* (1683)
1 : a lock for a gun or pistol having a flint in the hammer for striking a spark to ignite the charge
2 : a firearm fitted with a flintlock
flinty \'flin-tē\ *adjective* **flint·i·er; -est** (1536)
1 : resembling flint; *especially* **:** STERN, UNYIELDING
2 : composed of or covered with flint
— **flint·i·ly** \'flin-tᵊl-ē\ *adverb*
— **flint·i·ness** \'flin-tē-nəs\ *noun*
¹flip \'flip\ *verb* **flipped; flip·ping** [probably imitative] (1616)
transitive verb
1 : to toss so as to cause to turn over in the air ⟨*flip* a coin⟩; *also* **:** TOSS ⟨*flip* me the ball⟩ ⟨*flip* one end of the scarf over your shoulder⟩
2 a : to cause to turn and especially to turn over ⟨*flipped* the car⟩ ⟨*flipping* the pages of⟩ **b :** to move with a small quick motion ⟨*flip* a switch⟩
intransitive verb

1 : to make a twitching or flicking movement ⟨the fish *flipped* and flopped on the deck⟩; *also* **:** to change from one position to another and especially turn over ⟨the car *flipped*⟩
2 : LEAF 2 ⟨*flipped* through the pages⟩
3 *slang* **a :** to lose one's mind or composure — often used with *out* **b :** to become very enthusiastic
²**flip** *noun* (1695)
1 : a mixed drink usually consisting of a sweetened spiced liquor with beaten eggs
2 : an act or instance of flipping
3 : the motion used in flipping
4 : a somersault especially in the air
³**flip** *adjective* (circa 1847)
: FLIPPANT, IMPERTINENT
flip–flop \'flip-ˌfläp\ *noun* (1600)
1 : the sound or motion of something flapping loosely
2 a : a backward handspring **b :** a sudden reversal (as of direction or point of view)
3 : a usually electronic device or a circuit (as in a computer) capable of assuming either of two stable states
4 : a rubber sandal loosely fastened to the foot by a thong
— **flip–flop** *intransitive verb*
flip·pan·cy \'fli-pən(t)-sē\ *noun, plural* **-cies** (1746)
: unbecoming levity or pertness especially in respect to grave or sacred matters
flip·pant \'fli-pənt\ *adjective* [probably from ¹*flip*] (1605)
1 *archaic* **:** GLIB, TALKATIVE
2 : lacking proper respect or seriousness
— **flip·pant·ly** *adverb*
flip·per \'fli-pər\ *noun* (1822)
1 a : a broad flat limb (as of a seal or cetacean) adapted for swimming **b :** a flat rubber shoe with the front expanded into a paddle used in skin diving
2 : one that flips
flip·py \'fli-pē\ *adjective* (1967)
: loose and flaring at the bottom ⟨a *flippy* skirt⟩
flip side *noun* (1949)
1 : the reverse and usually less popular side of a phonograph record
2 : a reverse or opposite side, aspect, or result ⟨the *flip side* of deficient saving . . . is overconsumption —R. S. Gay⟩
¹**flirt** \'flərt\ *verb* [origin unknown] (1583)
transitive verb
1 : FLICK
2 : to move in a jerky manner
intransitive verb
1 : to move erratically **:** FLIT
2 a : to behave amorously without serious intent **b :** to show superficial or casual interest or liking ⟨*flirted* with the idea⟩; *also* **:** EXPERIMENT ⟨a novelist *flirting* with poetry⟩
3 : to come close to — used with *with* ⟨the temperature *flirted* with 100°⟩
synonym see TRIFLE
— **flir·ta·tion** \ˌflər-'tā-shən\ *noun*
— **flirt·er** *noun*
— **flirty** \'flər-tē\ *adjective*
²**flirt** *noun* (circa 1590)
1 : an act or instance of flirting
2 : a person who flirts
flir·ta·tious \ˌflər-'tā-shəs\ *adjective* (1834)
: inclined to flirt **:** COQUETTISH
— **flir·ta·tious·ly** *adverb*
— **flir·ta·tious·ness** *noun*
flit \'flit\ *intransitive verb* **flit·ted; flit·ting** [Middle English *flitten*, of Scandinavian origin; akin to Old Norse *flytjask* to move, Old English *flēotan* to float] (13th century)
1 : to pass quickly or abruptly from one place or condition to another
2 *archaic* **:** ALTER, SHIFT
3 : to move in an erratic fluttering manner
— **flit** *noun*
flitch \'flich\ *noun* [Middle English *flicche*, from Old English *flicce;* akin to Old High German *fleisk* flesh — more at FLESH] (before 12th century)

1 : a side of cured meat; *especially* **:** a side of bacon
2 a : a longitudinal section of a log **b :** a bundle of sheets of veneer laid together in sequence
¹**flit·ter** \'fli-tər\ *intransitive verb* [frequentative of *flit*] (1534)
: FLUTTER, FLICKER
²**flitter** *noun* (1554)
: one that flits
fliv·ver \'fli-vər\ *noun* [origin unknown] (1910)
: a small cheap usually old automobile
¹**float** \'flōt\ *noun* [Middle English *flote* boat, float, from Old English *flota* ship; akin to Old High German *flōz* raft, stream, Old English *flēotan* to float — more at FLEET] (before 12th century)
1 : an act or instance of floating
2 : something that floats in or on the surface of a fluid: as **a :** a device (as a cork) buoying up the baited end of a fishing line **b :** a floating platform anchored near a shoreline for use by swimmers or boats **c :** a hollow ball that floats at the end of a lever in a cistern, tank, or boiler and regulates the liquid level **d :** a sac containing air or gas and buoying up the body of a plant or animal — compare PNEUMATOPHORE 1 **e :** a watertight structure giving an airplane buoyancy on water
3 : a tool or apparatus for smoothing a surface (as of wet concrete)
4 : a government grant of a fixed amount of land not yet located by survey out of a larger specific tract
5 a : a vehicle with a platform used to carry an exhibit in a parade **b :** the vehicle and exhibit together
6 a : an amount of money represented by checks outstanding and in process of collection **b :** the time between a transaction (as the writing of a check or a purchase on credit) and the actual withdrawal of funds to cover it **c :** the volume of a company's shares available for active trading in the auction market
7 : a soft drink with ice cream floating in it
— **floaty** \'flō-tē\ *adjective*
²**float** (before 12th century)
intransitive verb
1 : to rest on the surface of or be suspended in a fluid
2 a : to drift on or through or as if on or through a fluid ⟨yellow leaves *floated* down⟩ **b :** WANDER
3 *of a currency* **:** to find a level in the international exchange market in response to the law of supply and demand and without any restrictive effect of artificial support or control
transitive verb
1 a : to cause to float in or on the surface of a fluid **b :** to cause to float as if in a fluid
2 : FLOOD ⟨*float* a cranberry bog⟩
3 : to smooth (as plaster or cement) with a float
4 a : to put forth (as a proposal) for acceptance **b :** to place (an issue of securities) on the market **c :** to obtain money for the establishment or development of (an enterprise) by issuing and selling securities **d :** NEGOTIATE ⟨*float* a loan⟩
floa·ta·tion *variant of* FLOTATION
float·er \'flō-tər\ *noun* (1717)
1 a : one that floats **b :** a person who floats something
2 : a person who votes illegally in various polling places
3 a : a person without a permanent residence or regular employment **b :** a worker who moves from job to job; *especially* **:** one without fixed duties
4 : a policy insuring specific items of personal property (as jewelry or art)
float glass *noun* (1959)
: flat glass produced by solidifying molten glass on the surface of a bath of molten tin
float·ing *adjective* (1600)

1 : buoyed on or in a fluid
2 : located out of the normal position ⟨a *floating* kidney⟩
3 a : continually drifting or changing position ⟨the *floating* population⟩ **b :** not presently committed or invested ⟨*floating* capital⟩ **c :** short-term and usually not funded ⟨*floating* debt⟩ **d :** having no fixed value or rate ⟨*floating* currencies⟩ ⟨*floating* interest rates⟩
4 : connected or constructed so as to operate and adjust smoothly ⟨a *floating* axle⟩
floating dock *noun* (1866)
: a dock that floats on the water and can be partly submerged to permit entry of a ship and raised to keep the ship high and dry — called also *floating drydock*
floating island *noun* (1771)
: a dessert consisting of custard with floating masses of beaten egg whites
floating–point *adjective* (1948)
: expressed in, using, or being a mathematical notation in which a number is represented (as in a computer display) by an integer or a decimal fraction multiplied by a power of the number base indicated by an exponent (as in 4.52E2 for 452) — compare FIXED-POINT
floating rib *noun* (1831)
: a rib (as one of either of the last two pairs in humans) that has no attachment to the sternum — compare FALSE RIB
float·plane \'flōt-ˌplān\ *noun* (1922)
: a seaplane supported on the water by one or more floats
floc \'fläk\ *noun* [short for *floccule*] (1921)
: a flocculent mass formed by the aggregation of a number of fine suspended particles
floc·cu·late \'flä-kyə-ˌlāt\ *verb* **-lat·ed; -lat·ing** (1877)
transitive verb
: to cause to aggregate into a flocculent mass ⟨*flocculate* clay⟩
intransitive verb
: to become flocculent
— **floc·cu·lant** \-lənt\ *noun*
— **floc·cu·la·tion** \ˌflä-kyə-'lā-shən\ *noun*
— **floc·cu·la·tor** \'flä-kyə-ˌlā-tər\ *noun*
floc·cule \'flä-(ˌ)kyü(ə)l\ *noun* [Late Latin *flocculus*] (circa 1846)
: FLOC
floc·cu·lent \-lənt\ *adjective* [Latin *floccus* + English *-ulent*] (1800)
1 : resembling wool especially in loose fluffy organization
2 : made up of flocs or floccules ⟨a *flocculent* precipitate⟩
floc·cu·lus \-ləs\ *noun, plural* **-li** \-ˌlī, -ˌlē\ [Late Latin, diminutive of Latin *floccus* tuft of wool] (1799)
1 : a small loosely aggregated mass
2 : a bright or dark patch on the sun
¹**flock** \'fläk\ *noun* [Middle English, from Old English *flocc* crowd, band; akin to Old Norse *flokkr* crowd, band] (13th century)
1 : a group of birds or mammals assembled or herded together
2 : a group under the guidance of a leader; *especially* **:** a church congregation
3 : a large number ⟨a *flock* of tourists⟩
²**flock** *intransitive verb* (14th century)
: to gather or move in a flock ⟨they *flocked* to the beach⟩
³**flock** *noun* [Middle English *flok*, from Old French *floc*, from Latin *floccus*] (13th century)
1 : a tuft of wool or cotton fiber
2 : woolen or cotton refuse used for stuffing furniture and mattresses
3 : very short or pulverized fiber used especially to form a velvety pattern on cloth or paper or a protective covering on metal
4 : FLOC

\ə\ abut \ᵊ\ kitten \ər\ further \a\ ash \ā\ ace
\ä\ mop, mar \au̇\ out \ch\ chin \e\ bet \ē\ easy
\g\ go \i\ hit \ī\ ice \j\ job \ŋ\ sing \ō\ go
\ȯ\ law \ȯi\ boy \th\ thin \t͟h\ the \ü\ loot \u̇\ foot
\y\ yet \zh\ vision *see also* Guide to Pronunciation

⁴flock *transitive verb* (1530)
1 : to fill with flock
2 : to decorate with flock
flock·ing \'flä-kiŋ\ *noun* (circa 1874)
: a design in flock
floe \'flō\ *noun* [probably from Norwegian *flo* flat layer] (1817)
1 : floating ice formed in a large sheet on the surface of a body of water
2 : ICE FLOE
flog \'fläg\ *verb* **flogged; flog·ging** [perhaps modification of Latin *flagellare* to whip — more at FLAGELLATE] (circa 1676)
transitive verb
1 a : to beat with or as if with a rod or whip **b** : to criticize harshly
2 : to force or urge into action : DRIVE
3 a *chiefly British* : to sell (as stolen goods) illegally ⟨*flogged* their employers' petrol to ordinary motorists —*Economist*⟩ **b** : SELL 7 ⟨traveled by horse, *flogging* encyclopedias —Robert Darnton⟩ **c** : to promote aggressively : PLUG ⟨flying around the world *flogging* your movies —Peter Bogdanovich⟩
4 *British* : STEAL 1
intransitive verb
1 : FLAP, FLUTTER ⟨sails *flogging*⟩
2 *British* : to move along with difficulty : SLOG
— **flog·ger** *noun*
flo·ka·ti \flō-'kä-tē\ *noun* [New Greek *phlokatē*] (1967)
: a hand-woven Greek woolen rug with a thick shaggy pile
¹flood \'fləd\ *noun* [Middle English, from Old English *flōd;* akin to Old High German *fluot* flood, Old English *flōwan* to flow] (before 12th century)
1 a : a rising and overflowing of a body of water especially onto normally dry land; *also* : a condition of overflowing ⟨rivers in *flood*⟩ **b** *capitalized* : a flood described in the Bible as covering the earth in the time of Noah
2 : the flowing in of the tide
3 : an overwhelming quantity or volume; *also* : a state of abundant flow or volume ⟨a debate in full *flood*⟩
4 : FLOODLIGHT
²flood (1663)
transitive verb
1 : to cover with a flood : INUNDATE
2 a : to fill abundantly or excessively ⟨*flood* the market⟩ **b** : to supply to (the carburetor of an internal combustion engine) an excess of fuel so that engine operation is hampered
intransitive verb
1 : to pour forth, go, or come in a flood
2 : to become filled with a flood
— **flood·er** *noun*
flood·gate \'fləd-ˌgāt\ *noun* [Middle English *flodgate*] (13th century)
1 : a gate for shutting out, admitting, or releasing a body of water : SLUICE
2 : something serving to restrain an outburst ⟨opened the *floodgates*⟩
¹flood·light \-ˌlīt\ *transitive verb* **-lit** \-ˌlit\ *also* **-light·ed; -light·ing** (1923)
: to illuminate by means of one or more floodlights
²floodlight *noun* (1924)
1 a : artificial illumination in a broad beam **b** : a source of such illumination
2 : a lighting unit for projecting a beam of light
flood·plain \'fləd-ˌplān\ *noun* (1873)
1 : level land that may be submerged by floodwaters
2 : a plain built up by stream deposition
flood tide *noun* (1719)
1 : a rising tide
2 a : an overwhelming quantity **b** : a high point : PEAK
flood·wa·ter \-ˌwȯ-tər, -ˌwä-\ *noun* (1791)
: the water of a flood
flood·way \-ˌwā\ *noun* (1928)
: a channel for diverting floodwaters

floo·ey \'flü-ē\ *adjective* [origin unknown] (1920)
: AWRY, ASKEW ⟨go *flooey*⟩
¹floor \'flōr, 'flȯr\ *noun, often attributive* [Middle English *flor*, from Old English *flōr;* akin to Old High German *fluor* meadow, Latin *planus* level, and perhaps to Greek *planasthai* to wander] (before 12th century)
1 : the level base of a room
2 a : the lower inside surface of a hollow structure (as a cave or bodily part) **b** : a ground surface ⟨the ocean *floor*⟩
3 a : a structure dividing a building into stories; *also* : STORY **b** : the occupants of such a floor
4 : the surface of a structure on which one travels ⟨the *floor* of a bridge⟩
5 a : a main level space (as in a stock exchange or legislative chamber) distinguished from a platform or gallery **b** : the members of an assembly ⟨took questions from the *floor*⟩ **c** : the right to address an assembly ⟨the senator from Utah has the *floor*⟩
6 : a lower limit : BASE
— **floored** *adjective*
²floor *transitive verb* (15th century)
1 : to cover with a floor or flooring
2 a : to knock or bring down **b** : FLABBERGAST, DUMBFOUND
3 : to press (the accelerator of a vehicle) to the floorboard; *also* : to accelerate rapidly ⟨*floored* the van⟩
— **floor·er** *noun*
floor·board \'flȯr-ˌbōrd, 'flȯr-ˌbȯrd\ *noun* (1881)
1 : a board in a floor
2 : the floor of an automobile
floor·cloth \-ˌklȯth\ *noun, plural* **-cloths** \-ˌklȯthz, -ˌklȯths\ (1746)
: a usually decorated heavy cloth (as of canvas) used for a floor covering
floor exercise *noun* (1961)
: an event in gymnastics competition consisting of various ballet and tumbling movements (as jumps, somersaults, and handstands) performed without apparatus
floor·ing \'flōr-iŋ, 'flȯr-\ *noun* (1624)
1 : FLOOR, BASE
2 : material for floors
floor lamp *noun* (1892)
: a tall lamp that stands on the floor
floor leader *noun* (1899)
: a member of a legislative body chosen by a party to have charge of its organization and strategy on the floor
floor–length *adjective* (1939)
: reaching to the floor ⟨a *floor-length* gown⟩
floor manager *noun* (1887)
: a person who directs something from the floor (as of a nominating convention)
floor show *noun* (1927)
: a series of acts presented in a nightclub
floor–through \'flōr-ˌthrü, 'flȯr-\ *noun* (1967)
: an apartment that occupies an entire floor of a building
floor·walk·er \'flōr-ˌwȯ-kər, 'flȯr-\ *noun* (1876)
: a person employed in a retail store to oversee the salespeople and aid customers
floo·zy *or* **floo·zie** \'flü-zē\ *noun, plural* **floozies** [origin unknown] (1911)
: a usually young woman of loose morals
¹flop \'fläp\ *verb* **flopped; flop·ping** [alteration of ²*flap*] (1602)
intransitive verb
1 : to swing or move loosely : FLAP
2 : to throw or move oneself in a heavy, clumsy, or relaxed manner ⟨*flopped* into the chair⟩
3 : to change or turn suddenly
4 : to go to bed ⟨a place to *flop* at night⟩
5 : to fail completely ⟨the play *flopped*⟩
transitive verb
: to move or drop heavily or noisily : cause to flop ⟨*flopped* the bundles down⟩ ⟨*flop* the rag over⟩
— **flop·per** *noun*

²flop *adverb* (1728)
: RIGHT, SQUARELY ⟨fell *flop* on my face⟩
³flop *noun* (1823)
1 : an act or sound of flopping
2 : a complete failure
3 *slang* : a place to sleep; *especially* : FLOPHOUSE
4 : DUNG ⟨cow *flop*⟩; *also* : a piece of dung
flop·house \'fläp-ˌhaús\ *noun* (1916)
: a cheap rooming house or hotel
¹flop·py \'flä-pē\ *adjective* **flop·pi·er; -est** (1858)
: tending to flop; *especially* : being both soft and flexible
— **flop·pi·ly** \'flä-pə-lē\ *adverb*
— **flop·pi·ness** \'flä-pē-nəs\ *noun*
²floppy *noun, plural* **-pies** (1974)
: FLOPPY DISK
floppy disk *noun* (1972)
: a small flexible plastic disk coated with magnetic material on which data for a computer can be stored
flo·ra \'flōr-ə, 'flȯr-\ *noun, plural* **floras** *also* **flo·rae** \'flōr-ˌē, 'flȯr-, -ˌī\ [New Latin, from Latin *Flora*, Roman goddess of flowers, from Latin *flōr-, flos*] (1777)
1 : a treatise on or list of the plants of an area or period
2 : plant or bacterial life; *especially* : such life characteristic of a region, period, or special environment ⟨fossil *flora*⟩ ⟨intestinal *flora*⟩ — compare FAUNA
¹flo·ral \'flōr-əl, 'flȯr-\ *adjective* [Latin *flōr-, flos* flower — more at BLOW] (1753)
: of or relating to flowers or a flora
²floral *noun* (1897)
: a design, pattern, or picture in which flowers predominate
floral envelope *noun* (circa 1829)
: PERIANTH
Flor·ence flask \'flȯr-ən(t)s-, 'flär-\ *noun* [*Florence*, Italy; from the use of flasks of this shape for certain Italian wines] (1744)
: a round usually flat-bottomed laboratory vessel with a long neck
Flor·en·tine \'flȯr-ən-ˌtēn, 'flär-, -ˌtīn\ *adjective* [Medieval Latin *Florentinus*] (1597)
1 a : of or relating to Florence, Italy **b** : MACHIAVELLIAN ⟨*Florentine* politics⟩
2 : served or dressed with spinach ⟨poached eggs *Florentine*⟩
3 : having a matte brushed finish ⟨*Florentine* gold⟩
flo·res·cence \flō-'re-s³n(t)s, flə-\ *noun* [New Latin *florescentia*, from Latin *florescent-, florescens*, present participle of *florescere*, inchoative of *florēre* to blossom, flourish — more at FLOURISH] (1793)
: a state or period of flourishing
— **flo·res·cent** \-s³nt\ *adjective*
flo·ret \'flōr-ət, 'flȯr-\ *noun* [Middle English *flourette*, from Middle French *flouret*, diminutive of *flour* flower] (1671)
1 : a small flower; *especially* : one of the small flowers forming the head of a composite plant
2 : a cluster of flower buds separated from a head especially when used as food ⟨cauliflower *florets*⟩
flori- *combining form* [Latin, from *flōr-, flos*]
: flower or flowers ⟨*floriculture*⟩
flo·ri·at·ed \'flōr-ē-ˌā-təd, 'flȯr-\ *adjective* (1845)
: having floral ornaments or a floral form
— **flo·ri·a·tion** \ˌflōr-ē-'ā-shən, ˌflȯr-\ *noun*
flo·ri·bun·da \ˌflōr-ə-'bən-də, ˌflȯr-\ *noun* [New Latin, feminine of *floribundus* flowering freely] (1898)
: any of various bush roses with large flowers in open clusters that derive from crosses of polyantha and tea roses
flo·ri·cul·ture \'flōr-ə-ˌkəl-chər, 'flȯr-\ *noun* (1822)
: the cultivation and management of ornamental and especially flowering plants

— **flo·ri·cul·tur·al** \ˌflōr-ə-ˈkəlch-rəl, -ˈkəl-chə-, ˌflòr-\ *adjective*
— **flo·ri·cul·tur·ist** \-rist\ *noun*
flor·id \ˈflòr-əd, ˈflär-\ *adjective* [Latin *floridus* blooming, flowery, from *florēre*] (circa 1656) **1 a** *obsolete* : covered with flowers **b** : very flowery in style : ORNATE ⟨*florid* prose⟩ ⟨*florid* declamations⟩; *also* : having a florid style ⟨a *florid* writer⟩ **c** : elaborately decorated ⟨a *florid* interior⟩ **2 a** : tinged with red : RUDDY ⟨a *florid* complexion⟩ **b** : marked by emotional or sexual fervor ⟨a *florid* secret life⟩ ⟨a *florid* sensibility⟩ **3** *archaic* : HEALTHY **4** : fully developed : manifesting a complete and typical clinical syndrome ⟨the *florid* stage of a disease⟩
— **flo·rid·i·ty** \flə-ˈri-də-tē, flò-\ *noun*
— **flor·id·ly** \ˈflòr-əd-lē, ˈflär-\ *adverb*
— **flor·id·ness** \-nəs\ *noun*
flo·rif·er·ous \flò-ˈri-f(ə-)rəs\ *adjective* [Latin *florifer*, from *flori-* + *-fer* fer] (1678) : bearing flowers; *especially* : blooming freely
— **flo·rif·er·ous·ness** *noun*
flo·ri·gen \ˈflōr-ə-jən, ˈflòr-\ *noun* [International Scientific Vocabulary] (1936) : a hormone or hormonal agent that promotes flowering
— **flo·ri·gen·ic** \ˌflōr-ə-ˈje-nik, ˌflòr-\ *adjective*
flo·ri·le·gium \ˌflōr-ə-ˈlē-j(ē-)əm, ˌflòr-\ *noun*, *plural* **-gia** \-j(ē-)ə\ [New Latin, from Latin *florilegus* culling flowers, from *flori-* + *legere* to gather — more at LEGEND] (1647) : a volume of writings : ANTHOLOGY
flo·rin \ˈflòr-ən, ˈflär-, ˈflōr-\ *noun* [Middle English, from Middle French, from Old Italian *fiorino*, from *fiore* flower, from Latin *flor-*, *flos*; from the lily on the coins] (14th century) **1 a** : an old gold coin first struck at Florence in 1252 **b** : any of various European gold coins patterned after the Florentine florin **2 a** : a British silver coin worth two shillings **b** : any of several similar coins issued in Commonwealth countries **3** : GULDEN **4** : FORINT
flo·rist \ˈflōr-ist, ˈflòr-, ˈflär-\ *noun* (1623) : one who sells or grows for sale flowers and ornamental plants
— **flo·rist·ry** \-ə-strē\ *noun*
flo·ris·tic \flò-ˈris-tik\ *adjective* (1898) : of or relating to flowers, a flora, or the phytogeographical study of plants and plant groups
— **flo·ris·ti·cal·ly** \-ti-k(ə-)lē\ *adverb*
flo·ru·it \ˈflòr-(y)ə-wət, ˈflär-\ *noun* [Latin, he flourished, from *florēre* to flourish] (1843) : a period of flourishing (as of a person or movement)
¹floss \ˈfläs, ˈflòs\ *noun* [probably modification of French *floche* soft, weak (of silk fiber), from Gascon, from Latin *fluxus*, literally, loose, flowing, past participle of *fluere* to flow — more at FLUID] (1759) **1 a** : soft thread of silk or mercerized cotton for embroidery **b** : DENTAL FLOSS **2** : fluffy fibrous material
²floss (1974) *transitive verb* : to use dental floss on *intransitive verb* : to use dental floss
flossy \ˈflä-sē, ˈflò-\ *adjective* **floss·i·er; -est** (1839) **1** : of, relating to, or having the characteristics of floss **2** : stylish or glamorous especially at first impression ⟨*flossy* new hotels⟩
— **floss·i·ly** \ˈflä-sə-lē\ *adverb*
flo·ta \ˈflō-tə\ *noun* [Spanish] (1527) : a fleet of Spanish ships
flo·ta·tion \flō-ˈtā-shən\ *noun* [²*float*] (1806) **1** : the act, process, or state of floating **2** : an act or instance of financing (as an issue of stock)

3 : the separation of the particles of a mass of pulverized ore according to their relative capacity for floating on a given liquid; *also* : any of various similar processes involving the relative capacity of materials for floating **4** : the ability (as of a tire or snowshoes) to stay on the surface of soft ground or snow
flo·til·la \flō-ˈti-lə\ *noun* [Spanish, diminutive of *flota* fleet, from Old French *flote*, from Old Norse *floti*; akin to Old English *flota* ship, fleet — more at FLOAT] (1711) **1** : a fleet of ships or boats; *especially* : a navy organizational unit consisting of two or more squadrons of small warships **2** : an indefinite large number ⟨a *flotilla* of changes⟩
flot·sam \ˈflät-səm\ *noun* [Anglo-French *floteson*, from Old French *floter* to float, of Germanic origin; akin to Old English *flotian* to float, *flota* ship] (circa 1607) **1** : floating wreckage of a ship or its cargo; *broadly* : floating debris **2 a** : a floating population (as of emigrants or castaways) **b** : an accumulation of miscellaneous or unimportant stuff
¹flounce \ˈflaun(t)s\ *intransitive verb* **flounced; flounc·ing** [perhaps of Scandinavian origin; akin to Norwegian *flunsa* to hurry] (1542) **1 a** : to move with exaggerated jerky or bouncy motions ⟨*flounced* about the room, jerking her shoulders, gesticulating —Agatha Christie⟩; *also* : to move so as to draw attention to oneself ⟨*flounced* into the lobby⟩ **b** : to go with sudden determination ⟨*flounced* out of the room in a huff⟩ **2** : FLOUNDER, STRUGGLE
²flounce *noun* (1583) : an act or instance of flouncing
— **flouncy** \ˈflaun(t)-sē\ *adjective*
³flounce *transitive verb* **flounced; flounc·ing** [alteration of earlier *frounce*, from Middle English *frouncen* to curl] (1711) : to trim with flounces
⁴flounce *noun* (1713) : a strip of fabric attached by one edge; *also* : a wide ruffle
— **flouncy** \ˈflaun(t)-sē\ *adjective*
flounc·ing \ˈflaun(t)-siŋ\ *noun* (1865) : material used for flounces
¹floun·der \ˈflaun-dər\ *noun*, *plural* **flounder** *or* **flounders** [Middle English, from Anglo-French *floundre*, of Scandinavian origin; akin to Old Norse *flythra* flounder] (15th century) : FLATFISH; *especially* : a fish of either of two families (Pleuronectidae and Bothidae) that include important marine food fishes
²flounder *intransitive verb* **floun·dered; floun·der·ing** \-d(ə-)riŋ\ [probably alteration of *founder*] (1592) **1** : to struggle to move or obtain footing : thrash about wildly **2** : to proceed or act clumsily or ineffectually
¹flour \ˈflaur\ *noun* [Middle English — more at FLOWER] (13th century) **1** : finely ground meal of wheat usually largely freed from bran; *also* : a similar meal of another material (as a cereal grain, an edible seed, or dried processed fish) **2** : a fine soft powder
— **flour·less** *adjective*
— **floury** \-ē\ *adjective*
²flour (circa 1657) *transitive verb* : to coat with or as if with flour *intransitive verb* : to break up into particles
¹flour·ish \ˈflər-ish, ˈflə-rish\ *verb* [Middle English *florisshen*, from Middle French *floriss-*, stem of *florir*, from (assumed) Vulgar Latin *florire*, alteration of Latin *florēre*, from *flor-*, *flos* flower] (14th century) *intransitive verb* **1** : to grow luxuriantly : THRIVE **2 a** : to achieve success : PROSPER **b** : to be in a state of activity or production ⟨*flourished*

around 1850⟩ **c** : to reach a height of development or influence **3** : to make bold and sweeping gestures *transitive verb* : to wield with dramatic gestures : BRANDISH **synonym** see SWING
— **flour·ish·er** *noun*
— **flour·ish·ing·ly** \-i-shiŋ-lē\ *adverb*
²flourish *noun* (1597) **1 a** : a period of thriving **b** : a luxuriant growth or profusion ⟨a *flourish* of white hair⟩ ⟨a springtime *flourish* of color⟩ **2 a** : a florid bit of speech or writing ⟨rhetorical *flourishes*⟩ **b** : an ornamental stroke in writing or printing **c** : a decorative or finishing detail ⟨a house with clever little *flourishes*⟩ **3** : FANFARE **4** : an act or instance of brandishing or waving **5** : showiness in the doing of something ⟨opened the door with a *flourish*⟩ **6** : a sudden burst (as of activity) ⟨the week ends with a *flourish* of tests⟩
¹flout \ˈflaut\ *verb* [probably from Middle English *flouten* to play the flute, from *floute* flute] (1551) *transitive verb* : to treat with contemptuous disregard : SCORN ⟨*flouting* the rules⟩ *intransitive verb* : to indulge in scornful behavior **synonym** see SCOFF **usage** see FLAUNT
— **flout·er** *noun*
²flout *noun* (circa 1570) : JEER
¹flow \ˈflō\ *verb* [Middle English, from Old English *flōwan*; akin to Old High German *flouwen* to rinse, wash, Latin *pluere* to rain, Greek *plein* to sail, float] (before 12th century) *intransitive verb* **1 a** (1) : to issue or move in a stream (2) : CIRCULATE **b** : to move with a continual change of place among the constituent particles ⟨molasses *flows* slowly⟩ **2** : RISE ⟨the tide ebbs and *flows*⟩ **3** : ABOUND **4** : to proceed smoothly and readily ⟨conversation *flowed* easily⟩ **b** : to have a smooth continuity **5** : to hang loose and billowing **6** : to derive from a source : COME ⟨the wealth that *flows* from trade⟩ **7** : to deform under stress without cracking or rupturing — used especially of minerals and rocks **8** : MENSTRUATE *transitive verb* **1** : to cause to flow **2** : to discharge in a flow **synonym** see SPRING
— **flow·ing·ly** \-iŋ-lē\ *adverb*
²flow *noun* (15th century) **1** : an act of flowing **2** : FLOOD 1a, 2 **3 a** : a smooth uninterrupted movement or progress ⟨a *flow* of information⟩ **b** : STREAM; *also* : a mass of material which has flowed when molten ⟨an old lava *flow*⟩ **c** : the direction of movement or development ⟨go with the *flow*⟩ **4** : the quantity that flows in a certain time **5** : MENSTRUATION **6 a** : the motion characteristic of fluids **b** : a continuous transfer of energy
flow·age \ˈflō-ij\ *noun* (1830) **1 a** : an overflowing onto adjacent land **b** : a body of water formed by overflowing or damming **c** : floodwater especially of a stream

\ə\ abut \ᵊ\ kitten \ər\ further \a\ ash \ā\ ace \ä\ mop, mar \aù\ out \ch\ chin \e\ bet \ē\ easy \g\ go \i\ hit \ī\ ice \j\ job \ŋ\ sing \ō\ go \ò\ law \òi\ boy \th\ thin \t͟h\ the \ü\ loot \ù\ foot \y\ yet \zh\ vision *see also* Guide to Pronunciation

2 : gradual deformation of a body of plastic solid (as rock) by intermolecular shear

flow·chart \-ˌchärt\ *noun* (1920)
: a diagram that shows step-by-step progression through a procedure or system especially using connecting lines and a set of conventional symbols
— **flow·chart·ing** \-ˌchär-tiŋ\ *noun*

flow cy·tom·e·try \-sī-ˈtä-mə-trē\ *noun* (1978)
: a technique for identifying and sorting cells and their components (as DNA) by staining with a fluorescent dye and detecting the fluorescence usually by laser beam illumination

flow diagram *noun* (1943)
: FLOWCHART

¹**flow·er** \ˈflaú-(ə)r\ *noun* [Middle English *flour* flower, best of anything, flour, from Old French *flor, flour,* from Latin *flor-, flos* — more at BLOW] (13th century)

1 a : BLOSSOM, INFLORESCENCE **b :** a shoot of the sporophyte of a higher plant that is modified for reproduction and consists of a shortened axis bearing modified leaves; *especially* : one of a seed plant differentiated into a calyx, corolla, stamens, and carpels **c :** a plant cultivated for its blossoms

cross section of flower 1b: *1 filament, 2 anther, 3 stigma, 4 style, 5 petal, 6 ovary, 7 sepal, 8 pedicel, 9 stamen, 10 pistil, 11 perianth*

2 a : the best part or example ⟨the *flower* of our youth⟩ **b :** the finest most vigorous period **c :** a state of blooming or flourishing ⟨in full *flower*⟩
3 *plural* : a finely divided powder produced especially by condensation or sublimation ⟨*flowers* of sulfur⟩
— **flow·ered** \ˈflaú-(ə)rd\ *adjective*
— **flow·er·ful** \ˈflaú-(ə)r-fəl\ *adjective*
— **flow·er·less** \-ləs\ *adjective*
— **flow·er·like** \-ˌlīk\ *adjective*

²**flower** (13th century)
intransitive verb
1 a : DEVELOP ⟨*flowered* into young womanhood⟩ **b :** FLOURISH
2 : to produce flowers : BLOSSOM
transitive verb
1 : to cause to bear flowers
2 : to decorate with flowers or floral designs
— **flow·er·er** \ˈflaú-(ə)r-ər\ *noun*

flow·er·age \ˈflaú-(ə)r-ij\ *noun* (1840)
: a flowering process, state, or condition

flower bud *noun* (1828)
: a plant bud that produces only a flower

flower bug *noun* (circa 1889)
: any of various small mostly black-and-white predaceous bugs (family Anthocoridae) that frequent flowers and feed on pest insects (as aphids and thrips)

flower child *noun* (1967)
: a hippie who advocates love, beauty, and peace

flow·er·et *also* **flow·er·ette** \ˈflaú-(ə)r-ət\ *noun* (15th century)
: FLORET 1

flower girl *noun* (1925)
: a little girl who carries flowers at a wedding

flower head *noun* (1845)
: a capitulum (as of a composite) having sessile flowers so arranged that the whole inflorescence looks like a single flower

flowering dogwood *noun* (1843)
: a common spring-flowering white-bracted dogwood (*Cornus florida*)

flowering plant *noun* (1745)
: ANGIOSPERM

flower people *noun plural* (1967)
: FLOWER CHILDREN

flow·er·pot \ˈflaú-(ə)r-ˌpät\ *noun* (1598)
: a pot in which to grow plants

flow·ery \ˈflaú-(ə)r-ē\ *adjective* (14th century)
1 : of, relating to, or resembling flowers
2 : marked by or given to rhetorical elegance
— **flow·er·i·ly** \ˈflaú-(ə)r-ə-lē\ *adverb*
— **flow·er·i·ness** *noun*

flow·me·ter \ˈflō-ˌmē-tər\ *noun* (1915)
: an instrument for measuring one or more properties (as velocity or pressure) of a flow (as of a liquid in a pipe)

¹**flown** \ˈflōn\ *past participle of* FLY

²**flown** *adjective* [archaic past participle of ¹*flow*] (1626)
: filled to excess

flow sheet *noun* (1912)
: FLOWCHART

flow·stone \ˈflō-ˌstōn\ *noun* (1925)
: calcite deposited by a thin sheet of flowing water usually along the walls or floor of a cave

flu \ˈflü\ *noun* [by shortening] (1839)
1 : INFLUENZA
2 : any of several virus diseases marked especially by respiratory symptoms

¹**flub** \ˈfləb\ *verb* **flubbed; flub·bing** [origin unknown] (1904)
transitive verb
: to make a mess of : BOTCH ⟨*flubbed* my lines⟩
intransitive verb
: BLUNDER

²**flub** *noun* (1948)
: an act or instance of flubbing

flub·dub \ˈfləb-ˌdəb\ *noun* [origin unknown] (1888)
: BUNKUM, BALDERDASH

fluc·tu·ant \ˈflək-chə-wənt\ *adjective* (1560)
1 : moving in waves
2 : VARIABLE, UNSTABLE
3 : being movable and compressible ⟨a *fluctuant* abscess⟩

fluc·tu·ate \ˈflək-chə-ˌwāt\ *verb* **-at·ed; -at·ing** [Latin *fluctuatus,* past participle of *fluctuare,* from *fluctus* flow, wave, from *fluere* — more at FLUID] (1634)
intransitive verb
1 : to shift back and forth uncertainly
2 : to ebb and flow in waves
transitive verb
: to cause to fluctuate
synonym see SWING
— **fluc·tu·a·tion** \ˌflək-chə-ˈwā-shən\ *noun*
— **fluc·tu·a·tion·al** \-ˈwā-shnəl, -shə-nᵊl\ *adjective*

flue \ˈflü\ *noun* [origin unknown] (1582)
: an enclosed passageway for directing a current: as **a :** a channel in a chimney for conveying flame and smoke to the outer air **b :** a pipe for conveying flame and hot gases around or through water in a steam boiler **c :** an air channel leading to the lip of a wind instrument **d :** FLUE PIPE

flue–cured \-ˌkyúrd\ *adjective* (1905)
: cured with heat transmitted through a flue without exposure to smoke or fumes ⟨*flue-cured* tobacco⟩

flu·en·cy \ˈflü-ən(t)-sē\ *noun* (1636)
: the quality or state of being fluent

flu·ent \ˈflü-ənt\ *adjective* [Latin *fluent-, fluens,* present participle of *fluere*] (1599)
1 a : capable of flowing : FLUID **b :** capable of moving with ease and grace ⟨the *fluent* body of a dancer⟩
2 a : ready or facile in speech ⟨*fluent* in Spanish⟩ **b :** effortlessly smooth and rapid : POLISHED ⟨a *fluent* performance⟩
— **flu·ent·ly** *adverb*

flue pipe *noun* (1852)
: an organ pipe whose tone is produced by an air current striking the lip and causing the air within to vibrate — compare REED PIPE

flue stop *noun* (1855)
: an organ stop made up of flue pipes

¹**fluff** \ˈfləf\ *noun* [perhaps blend of *flue* (fluff) and *puff*] (1790)
1 : NAP, DOWN

2 : something fluffy
3 : something inconsequential
4 : BLUNDER; *especially* : an actor's lapse of memory

²**fluff** (1875)
intransitive verb
1 : to become fluffy
2 : to make a mistake; *especially* : to forget or bungle one's lines in a play
transitive verb
1 : to make fluffy
2 a : to spoil by a mistake : BOTCH **b :** to deliver badly or forget (one's lines) in a play

fluffy \ˈflə-fē\ *adjective* **fluff·i·er; -est** (circa 1825)
1 a : covered with or resembling fluff **b :** being light and soft or airy ⟨a *fluffy* omelet⟩
2 : lacking in meaning or substance : SUPERFICIAL 2c
— **fluff·i·ly** \ˈflə-fə-lē\ *adverb*
— **fluff·i·ness** \ˈflə-fē-nəs\ *noun*

flü·gel·horn *or* **flue·gel·horn** \ˈflü-gəl-ˌhórn, ˈflǖ-\ *noun* [German, from *Flügel* wing, flank + *Horn* horn; from its use to signal the flanking drivers in a battue] (1854)
: a valved brass instrument resembling a cornet but having a larger bore
— **flü·gel·horn·ist** \-ˌhór-nist\ *noun*

¹**flu·id** \ˈflü-əd\ *adjective* [French or Latin; French *fluide,* from Latin *fluidus,* from *fluere* to flow; akin to Greek *phlyzein* to boil over] (1603)
1 a : having particles that easily move and change their relative position without a separation of the mass and that easily yield to pressure : capable of flowing **b :** subject to change or movement ⟨boundaries became *fluid*⟩
2 : characterized by or employing a smooth easy style ⟨the ballerina's *fluid* movements⟩
3 a : available for a different use **b :** LIQUID 4 ⟨*fluid* assets⟩
— **flu·id·ly** *adverb*
— **flu·id·ness** *noun*

²**fluid** *noun* (1661)
: a substance (as a liquid or gas) tending to flow or conform to the outline of its container
— **flu·id·al** \ˈflü-ə-dᵊl\ *adjective*
— **flu·id·al·ly** \-dᵊl-ē\ *adverb*

fluid dram *or* **flu·i·dram** \ˌflü-ə(d)-ˈdram\ *noun* (circa 1860)
: a unit of liquid capacity equal to ⅛ fluid ounce — see WEIGHT table

flu·id·ex·tract \ˌflü-ə-ˈdek-ˌstrakt\ *noun* (1851)
: an alcohol preparation of a vegetable drug containing the active constituents of one gram of the dry drug in each milliliter

flu·id·ic \flü-ˈi-dik\ *adjective* (1960)
: of, relating to, or being a device (as an amplifier or control) that depends for operation on the pressures and flows of a fluid in precisely shaped channels
— **fluidic** *noun*
— **flu·id·ics** \-diks\ *noun plural but singular in construction*

flu·id·i·ty \flü-ˈi-də-tē\ *noun* (1603)
1 : the quality or state of being fluid
2 : the physical property of a substance that enables it to flow

flu·id·ize \ˈflü-ə-ˌdīz\ *transitive verb* **-ized; -iz·ing** (circa 1855)
1 : to cause to flow like a fluid
2 : to suspend (as solid particles) in a rapidly moving stream of gas or vapor to induce flowing motion of the whole
— **flu·id·iza·tion** \ˌflü-ə-də-ˈzā-shən\ *noun*
— **flu·id·iz·er** \ˈflü-ə-ˌdī-zər\ *noun*

fluidized bed *noun* (1949)
: a bed of small solid particles (as in a coal burning furnace) suspended and kept in motion by an upward flow of a fluid (as a gas) — called also *fluid bed*

fluid mechanics *noun plural but singular or plural in construction* (1937)
: a branch of mechanics dealing with the properties of liquids and gases

fluid ounce *noun* (circa 1860)
1 : a U.S. unit of liquid capacity equal to ¹⁄₁₆ pint — see WEIGHT table
2 : a British unit of liquid capacity equal to ¹⁄₂₀ pint — see WEIGHT table

¹**fluke** \'flük\ *noun* [Middle English, from Old English *flōc*; akin to Old English *flōh* chip, Old High German *flah* smooth, Greek *plax* flat surface, and probably to Old English *flōr* floor — more at FLOOR] (before 12th century)
1 : FLATFISH
2 : a flattened digenetic trematode worm; *broadly* : TREMATODE — compare LIVER FLUKE

²**fluke** *noun* [perhaps from ¹*fluke*] (1561)
1 : the part of an anchor that fastens in the ground — see ANCHOR illustration
2 : one of the lobes of a whale's tail

³**fluke** *noun* [origin unknown] (1857)
1 : an accidentally successful stroke at billiards or pool
2 : a stroke of luck ⟨the discovery was a *fluke*⟩

fluky *also* **fluk·ey** \'flü-kē\ *adjective* **fluk·i·er; -est** (1867)
1 : happening by or depending on chance
2 : being unsteady or uncertain — used especially of wind

flume \'flüm\ *noun* [probably from Middle English *flum* river, from Old French, from Latin *flumen*, from *fluere* — more at FLUID] (1748)
1 : an inclined channel for conveying water (as for power)
2 : a ravine or gorge with a stream running through it

flum·mery \'fləm-rē, 'flə-mə-\ *noun, plural* **-mer·ies** [Welsh *llymru*] (1623)
1 a : a soft jelly or porridge made with flour or meal **b** : any of several sweet desserts
2 : MUMMERY, MUMBO JUMBO

flum·mox \'flə-məks, -miks\ *transitive verb* [origin unknown] (1837)
: CONFUSE

¹**flump** \'fləmp\ [imitative] (1816)
intransitive verb
: to move or fall suddenly and heavily ⟨*flumped* down into the chair⟩
transitive verb
: to place or drop with a flump

²**flump** *noun* (1832)
: a dull heavy sound (as of a fall)

flung *past and past participle of* FLING

¹**flunk** \'fləŋk\ *verb* [perhaps blend of *flinch* and *funk*] (1823)
intransitive verb
: to fail especially in an examination or course
transitive verb
1 : to give a failing grade to
2 : to get a failing grade in
— **flunk·er** *noun*

²**flunk** *noun* (1846)
: an act or instance of flunking

flunk out (1920)
intransitive verb
: to be dismissed from a school or college for failure
transitive verb
: to dismiss from a school or college for failure

flun·ky *or* **flun·key** \'flən-kē\ *noun, plural* **flunkies** *or* **flunkeys** [Scots, of unknown origin] (circa 1782)
1 a : a liveried servant **b** : one performing menial or miscellaneous duties
2 : YES-MAN

flu·o·cin·o·lone ac·e·to·nide \,flü-ə-'si-nᵊl-,ōn-,a-sə-'tō-,nīd\ *noun* [*fluor-* + *-cinolone*, probably alteration of *-nisolone* (as in *prednisolone*)] (1963)
: a glucocorticoid steroid $C_{24}H_{30}F_2O_6$ used especially as an anti-inflammatory agent in the treatment of skin diseases

flu·or \'flü-,ȯr, 'flü-ər\ *noun* [New Latin, mineral belonging to a group used as fluxes and including fluorite, from Latin, flow, from *fluere* — more at FLUID] (1661)
: FLUORITE

fluor- *or* **fluoro-** *combining form* [French]
1 : fluorine ⟨*fluoride*⟩
2 *also* **fluori-** : fluorescence ⟨*fluoroscope*⟩ ⟨*fluorimeter*⟩

fluo·resce \flù-'res, flȯ-, flō-\ *intransitive verb* **-resced; -resc·ing** [back-formation from *fluorescence*] (1874)
: to produce, undergo, or exhibit fluorescence
— **fluo·resc·er** *noun*

fluo·res·ce·in \-'re-sē-ən\ *noun* (1876)
: a yellow or red crystalline dye $C_{20}H_{12}O_5$ with a bright yellow-green fluorescence in alkaline solution

fluo·res·cence \-'re-sᵊn(t)s\ *noun* [*fluorspar* + *opalescence*] (1852)
: luminescence that is caused by the absorption of radiation at one wavelength followed by nearly immediate reradiation usually at a different wavelength and that ceases almost immediately when the incident radiation stops; *also* : the radiation emitted — compare PHOSPHORESCENCE

fluo·res·cent \-sᵊnt\ *adjective* (1853)
1 : having or relating to fluorescence
2 : bright and glowing as a result of fluorescence ⟨*fluorescent* inks⟩; *broadly* : very bright in color
— **fluorescent** *noun*

fluorescent lamp *noun* (1896)
: a tubular electric lamp having a coating of fluorescent material on its inner surface and containing mercury vapor whose bombardment by electrons from the cathode provides ultraviolet light which causes the material to emit visible light

fluo·ri·date \'flür-ə-,dāt, 'flȯr-, 'flōr-\ *transitive verb* **-dat·ed; -dat·ing** (1949)
: to add a fluoride to (as drinking water) to reduce tooth decay
— **fluo·ri·da·tion** \,flür-ə-'dā-shən, ,flȯr-, ,flōr-\ *noun*

fluo·ride \'flȯr-,īd, 'flür-\ *noun, often attributive* (1826)
1 : a compound of fluorine
2 : the monovalent anion of flourine

fluo·ri·nate \'flȯr-ə-,nāt, 'flȯr-, 'flür-\ *transitive verb* **-nat·ed; -nat·ing** (circa 1929)
: to treat or cause to combine with fluorine or a compound of fluorine
— **fluo·ri·na·tion** \,flȯr-ə-'nā-shən, ,flȯr-, ,flür-\ *noun*

fluo·rine \'flür-,ēn, 'flȯr-, 'flōr-\ *noun* [French, from New Latin *fluor*] (1813)
: a nonmetallic halogen element that is isolated as a pale yellowish flammable irritating toxic diatomic gas — see ELEMENT table

fluo·rite \'flür-,īt, 'flȯr-, 'flōr-\ *noun* [Italian, from New Latin *fluor*] (1868)
: a transparent or translucent mineral of different colors that consists of the fluoride of calcium and is used as a flux and in the making of opalescent and opaque glasses

fluo·ro·car·bon \,flür-ō-'kär-bən, ,flȯr-, ,flōr-\ *noun* (1937)
: any of various chemically inert compounds containing carbon and fluorine used chiefly as lubricants, refrigerants, nonstick coatings, and formerly aerosol propellants and in making resins and plastics; *also* : CHLOROFLUOROCARBON

fluo·ro·chrome \'flür-ə-,krōm, ,flȯr-, ,flōr-\ *noun* (1943)
: any of various fluorescent substances used in biological staining to produce fluorescence in a specimen

fluo·rog·ra·phy \flù-'rä-grə-fē, flȯ-, flō-\ *noun* (1941)
: PHOTOFLUOROGRAPHY
— **fluo·ro·graph·ic** \,flür-ə-'gra-fik, ,flȯr-, ,flōr-\ *adjective*

fluo·rom·e·ter \flü-'rä-mə-tər, flȯ-, flō-\ *or* **fluo·rim·e·ter** \-'ri-\ *noun* (1897)
: an instrument for measuring fluorescence and related phenomena (as intensity of radiation)

— **fluo·ro·met·ric** *or* **fluo·ri·met·ric** \,flür-ə-'me-trik, ,flȯr-, ,flōr-\ *adjective*
— **fluo·rom·e·try** \flù-'rä-mə-trē, flȯ-, flō-\ *or* **fluo·rim·e·try** \-'ri-mə-trē\ *noun*

¹**fluo·ro·scope** \'flür-ə-,skōp, 'flȯr-, 'flōr-\ *noun* [International Scientific Vocabulary] (1896)
: an instrument used for observing the internal structure of an opaque object (as the living body) by means of X rays
— **fluo·ro·scop·ic** \,flür-ə-'skä-pik, ,flȯr-, ,flōr-\ *adjective*
— **fluo·ro·scop·i·cal·ly** \-pi-k(ə-)lē\ *adverb*
— **fluo·ros·co·pist** \flù-'räs-kə-pist, flȯ-, flō-\ *noun*
— **fluo·ros·co·py** \-pē\ *noun*

²**fluoroscope** *transitive verb* **-scoped; -scop·ing** (1898)
: to examine by fluoroscopy

fluo·ro·sis \flù-'rō-səs, flō-\ *noun* [New Latin] (1927)
: an abnormal condition (as mottling of the teeth) caused by fluorine or its compounds
— **fluo·rot·ic** \-'rä-tik\ *adjective*

fluo·ro·ura·cil \,flür-ō-'yùr-ə-,sil, -,səl, ,flȯr-, ,flōr-\ *noun* [*fluor-* + *uracil*] (circa 1958)
: a fluorine-containing pyrimidine base $C_4H_3FN_2O_2$ used to treat some kinds of cancer

fluor·spar \'flür-,spär, 'flȯr-, 'flōr-\ *noun* (1794)
: FLUORITE

flu·phen·azine \flü-'fe-nə-,zēn\ *noun* [*fluor-* + *phenazine*] (circa 1960)
: a tranquilizing compound $C_{22}H_{26}F_3N_3OS$ used especially combined as a salt

¹**flur·ry** \'flər-ē, 'flə-rē\ *noun, plural* **flurries** [probably from *flurr* (to throw scatteringly)] (1686)
1 a : a gust of wind **b** : a brief light snowfall
2 a : a brief period of commotion or excitement **b** : a sudden occurrence of many things at once : BARRAGE 2 ⟨a *flurry* of insults⟩
3 : a brief advance or decline in prices : a short-lived outburst of trading activity

²**flurry** *verb* **flur·ried; flur·ry·ing** (1757)
transitive verb
: to cause to become agitated and confused
intransitive verb
: to move in an agitated or confused manner

¹**flush** \'fləsh\ *verb* [Middle English *flusshen*] (13th century)
intransitive verb
: to take wing suddenly
transitive verb
1 : to cause (a bird) to flush
2 : to expose or chase from a place of concealment ⟨*flushed* the boys from their hiding place⟩

²**flush** *noun* [Middle French *flus, fluz*, from Latin *fluxus* flow, flux] (circa 1529)
1 : a hand of playing cards all of the same suit; *specifically* : a poker hand containing five cards of the same suit but not in sequence — see POKER illustration
2 : a series of three or more slalom gates set vertically on a slope

³**flush** *noun* [perhaps modification of Latin *fluxus*] (1529)
1 : a sudden flow (as of water); *also* : a rinsing or cleansing with or as if with a flush of water
2 a : a sudden increase or expansion; *especially* : sudden and usually abundant new plant growth **b** : a surge of emotion ⟨felt a *flush* of anger at the insult⟩
3 a : a tinge of red : BLUSH **b** : a fresh and vigorous state ⟨in the first *flush* of womanhood⟩
4 : a transitory sensation of extreme heat — compare HOT FLASH

⁴flush (1548)
intransitive verb
1 : to flow and spread suddenly and freely
2 a : to glow brightly **b :** BLUSH
3 : to produce new growth ⟨the plants *flush* twice during the year⟩
transitive verb
1 a : to cause to flow **b :** to pour liquid over or through; *especially* **:** to cleanse or wash out with or as if with a rush of liquid ⟨*flush* the toilet⟩ ⟨*flush* the lungs with air⟩
2 : INFLAME, EXCITE — usually used passively ⟨*flushed* with pride⟩
3 : to cause to blush
⁵flush *adjective* (1594)
1 a : of a ruddy healthy color **b :** full of life and vigor **:** LUSTY
2 a : filled to overflowing **b :** AFFLUENT
3 : readily available **:** ABUNDANT
4 a : having or forming a continuous plane or unbroken surface ⟨*flush* paneling⟩ **b :** directly abutting or immediately adjacent: as (1) **:** set even with an edge of a type page or column **:** having no indention (2) **:** arranged edge to edge so as to fit snugly
— flush·ness *noun*
⁶flush *adverb* (1700)
1 : in a flush manner
2 : SQUARELY ⟨hit him *flush* on the chin⟩
⁷flush *transitive verb* (circa 1842)
: to make flush ⟨*flush* the headings on a page⟩
flush·able \'flə-shə-bəl\ *adjective* (1973)
: suitable for disposal by flushing down a toilet
¹flus·ter \'fləs-tər\ *verb* **flus·tered; flus·ter·ing** \-t(ə-)riŋ\ [probably of Scandinavian origin; akin to Icelandic *flaustur* hurry] (1604)
transitive verb
1 : to make tipsy
2 : to put into a state of agitated confusion **:** UPSET
intransitive verb
: to move or behave in an agitated or confused manner
synonym see DISCOMPOSE
— flus·tered·ly *adverb*
²fluster *noun* (1728)
: a state of agitated confusion
¹flute \'flüt\ *noun* [Middle English *floute*, from Middle French *fleute*, from Old French *flaüte*, probably from Old Provençal *flaut*] (14th century)
1 a : RECORDER 3 **b :** a keyed wood-wind instrument consisting of a cylindrical tube which is stopped at one end and which has a side hole over which air is blown to produce the tone and having a range from middle C upward for three octaves

flute 1b

2 : something long and slender: as **a :** a tall slender wineglass **b :** a grooved pleat (as on a hat brim)
3 : a rounded groove; *specifically* **:** one of the vertical parallel grooves on a classical architectural column
— flute·like \-,līk\ *adjective*
— fluty *or* **flut·ey** \'flü-tē\ *adjective*
²flute *verb* **flut·ed; flut·ing** (14th century)
intransitive verb
1 : to play a flute
2 : to produce a flutelike sound
transitive verb
1 : to utter with a flutelike sound
2 : to form flutes in
— flut·er *noun*
flut·ed *adjective* (1611)
: having or marked by grooves
flut·ing \'flü-tin\ *noun* (1611)
1 : a series of flutes ⟨the *fluting* of a column⟩
2 : fluted material
flut·ist \'flü-tist\ *noun* (1603)

: one who plays a flute
¹flut·ter \'flə-tər\ *verb* [Middle English *floteren* to float, flutter, from Old English *floterian*, frequentative of *flotian* to float; akin to Old English *flēotan* to float — more at FLEET] (before 12th century)
intransitive verb
1 : to flap the wings rapidly
2 a : to move with quick wavering or flapping motions **b :** to vibrate in irregular spasms
3 : to move about or behave in an agitated aimless manner
transitive verb
: to cause to flutter
— flut·ter·er \-tər-ər\ *noun*
— flut·tery \-tə-rē\ *adjective*
²flutter *noun* (1641)
1 : an act of fluttering
2 a : a state of nervous confusion or excitement **b :** FLURRY, COMMOTION **c :** abnormal spasmodic fluttering of a body part ⟨treatment of atrial *flutter*⟩
3 a : a distortion in reproduced sound similar to but of a higher pitch than wow **b :** fluctuation in the brightness of a television image
4 : an unwanted oscillation (as of an aileron or a bridge) set up by natural forces
5 *chiefly British* **:** a small speculative venture or gamble
flut·ter·board \'flə-tər-,bōrd, -,bórd\ *noun* (1950)
: a rectangular board used by swimmers in practicing leg strokes
flutter kick *noun* (circa 1934)
: an alternating whipping motion of the legs used in various swimming styles (as the crawl)
flutter sleeve *noun* (1973)
: a loose-fitting tapered sleeve falling in folds over the upper arm
flu·vi·al \'flü-vē-əl\ *adjective* [Latin *fluvialis*, from *fluvius* river, from *fluere*] (14th century)
1 : of, relating to, or living in a stream or river
2 : produced by the action of a stream
flu·vi·a·tile \'flü-vē-ə-,tīl\ *adjective* [Middle French, from Latin *fluviatilis*, from *fluvius*] (1599)
: FLUVIAL
¹flux \'fləks\ *noun* [Middle English, from Middle French & Medieval Latin; Middle French, from Medieval Latin *fluxus*, from Latin, flow, from *fluere* to flow — more at FLUID] (14th century)
1 : a flowing of fluid from the body; *especially* **:** an excessive abnormal discharge from the bowels
2 : a continuous moving on or passing by (as of a stream)
3 : a continued flow **:** FLOOD
4 a : INFLUX **b :** CHANGE, FLUCTUATION ⟨in a state of *flux*⟩
5 : a substance used to promote fusion (as of metals or minerals); *especially* **:** one (as rosin) applied to surfaces to be joined by soldering, brazing, or welding to clean and free them from oxide and promote their union
6 : the rate of transfer of fluid, particles, or energy across a given surface
²flux (15th century)
transitive verb
1 : to cause to become fluid
2 : to treat with a flux
intransitive verb
: to become fluid **:** FUSE
flux·gate \'fləks-,gāt\ *noun* (1944)
: a device used to indicate the direction and intensity of the magnetic field (as on a planet)
flux·ion \'flək-shən\ *noun* (1599)
1 : the action of flowing or changing; *also* **:** something subjected to such action
2 : DERIVATIVE 3 — compare METHOD OF FLUXIONS
— flux·ion·al \-shnəl, -shə-nᵊl\ *adjective*
¹fly \'flī\ *verb* **flew** \'flü\; **flown** \'flōn\; **fly·ing** [Middle English *flien*, from Old English *flēogan*; akin to Old High German *fliogan* to

fly and probably Old English *flōwan* to flow] (before 12th century)
intransitive verb
1 a : to move in or pass through the air with wings **b :** to move through the air or before the wind or through outer space **c :** to float, wave, or soar in the air ⟨flags *flying* at half-mast⟩
2 a : to take flight **:** FLEE **b :** to fade and disappear **:** VANISH
3 a : to move, pass, or spread quickly ⟨rumors were *flying*⟩ **b :** to be moved with sudden extreme emotion ⟨*flew* into a rage⟩ **c :** to seem to pass quickly ⟨the time simply *flew*⟩
4 : to become expended or dissipated rapidly
5 : to operate or travel in an airplane or spacecraft
6 : to work successfully **:** win popular acceptance ⟨knew . . . a pure human-rights approach would not *fly* —Charles Brydon⟩
transitive verb
1 a : to cause to fly, float, or hang in the air ⟨*flying* a kite⟩ **b :** to operate (as a balloon, aircraft, rocket, or spacecraft) in flight **c :** to journey over or through by flying
2 a : to flee or escape from **b :** AVOID, SHUN
3 : to transport by aircraft or spacecraft
— fly at : to assail suddenly and violently
— fly blind : to fly an airplane solely by instruments
— fly high : to be elated
— fly in the face of *or* **fly in the teeth of :** to stand or act forthrightly or brazenly in defiance or contradiction of
²fly *noun, plural* **flies** (before 12th century)
1 : the action or process of flying **:** FLIGHT
2 a : a device consisting of two or more radial vanes capable of rotating on a spindle to act as a fan or to govern the speed of clockwork or very light machinery **b :** FLYWHEEL
3 *plural* **:** the space over a theater stage where scenery and equipment can be hung
4 : something attached by one edge: as **a :** a garment closing concealed by a fold of cloth extending over the fastener **b** (1) **:** the length of an extended flag from its staff or support (2) **:** the outer or loose end of a flag
5 : a baseball hit high into the air
6 : FLYLEAF
7 : a sheet of material (as canvas) that is attachable to a tent for use as a double top or as a rooflike extension
8 : a football pass pattern in which the receiver runs straight downfield
— on the fly 1 : in motion **:** BUSY **2 :** while still in the air **:** without the ball bouncing ⟨the home run carried 450 feet *on the fly*⟩
³fly *intransitive verb* **flied; fly·ing** (1893)
: to hit a fly in baseball
⁴fly *noun, plural* **flies** [Middle English *flie*, from Old English *flēoge*; akin to Old High German *flioga* fly, Old English *flēogan* to fly] (before 12th century)
1 : a winged insect — used chiefly in combination ⟨mayflies⟩ ⟨butterfly⟩
2 a : any of a large order (Diptera) of winged or rarely wingless insects (as the housefly, mosquito, or gnat) that have segmented often headless, eyeless, and legless larvae, the anterior wings functional, and the posterior wings reduced to halteres **b :** a large stout-bodied fly
3 : a fishhook dressed (as with feathers or tinsel) to suggest an insect
— fly in the ointment : a detracting factor or element
⁵fly *adjective* [probably from ¹fly] (1811)
chiefly British **:** KEEN, ARTFUL
fly·able \'flī-ə-bəl\ *adjective* (circa 1909)
: suitable for flying or for being flown
fly agaric *noun* (1788)
: a poisonous mushroom (*Amanita muscaria*) with a usually bright red cap
fly ash *noun* (1931)
: fine solid particles of ashes, dust, and soot carried out from burning fuel (as coal or oil) by the draft

fly·away \'flī-ə-ˌwā\ *adjective* (1844)
1 : loose and flowing especially because of unconfined fullness at the back ⟨a *flyaway* jacket⟩
2 : of, relating to, or being an aircraft that is ready to fly ⟨a *flyaway* price⟩

fly ball *noun* (1865)
: ²FLY 5

¹**fly·blow** \-ˌblō\ *transitive verb* **-blew; -blown** [⁴*fly* + ¹*blow*] (1603)
1 : TAINT, CONTAMINATE
2 : to deposit eggs or young larvae of a flesh fly or blowfly in

²**flyblow** *noun* (1825)
: FLY-STRIKE

fly·blown \'flī-ˌblōn\ *adjective* (circa 1529)
1 a : not pure : TAINTED ⟨a world *flyblown* with the vices of irresponsible power —V. L. Parrington⟩ **b** : not bright and new : SEEDY, MOTH-EATEN **c** : TRITE, HACKNEYED ⟨a long list of *flyblown* metaphors —*Horizon*⟩
2 a : infested with eggs or young larvae of a flesh fly or blowfly **b** : covered with flyspecks

fly·boat \-ˌbōt\ *noun* [modification of Dutch *vlieboot*, from *Vlie*, channel between North Sea & Wadden Zee + *boot* boat] (1577)
: any of various fast boats

fly·boy \'flī-ˌbȯi\ *noun* (1946)
: a member of the air force; *broadly* : an aircraft pilot

fly·bridge \'flī-ˌbrij\ *noun* (1965)
: an open deck on a cabin cruiser located above the bridge on the cabin roof and usually having a duplicate set of navigating equipment

fly·by \'flī-ˌbī\ *noun, plural* **flybys** (1953)
1 : a prearranged usually low-altitude flight by one or more airplanes over a public gathering (as an air show)
2 a : a flight of a spacecraft past a celestial body (as Mars) close enough to obtain scientific data **b** : a spacecraft that makes a flyby

¹**fly-by-night** \'flī-bī-ˌnīt\ *noun* (1822)
1 : one that seeks to evade responsibilities and especially creditors by flight
2 : one without established reputation or standing; *especially* : a shaky business enterprise

²**fly-by-night** *adjective* (1914)
1 : given to making a quick profit usually by shady or irresponsible acts
2 : TRANSITORY, PASSING ⟨*fly-by-night* fashions⟩

fly-by-night·er \ˌflī-bī-'nī-tər\ *noun* (1946)
: FLY-BY-NIGHT

fly-by-wire \'flī-bī-ˌwīr\ *adjective* (1968)
: of, relating to, being, or utilizing a flight-control system in which controls are operated electrically rather than mechanically

fly casting *noun* (circa 1889)
: the casting of artificial flies in fly-fishing or as a competitive sport

fly·catch·er \'flī-ˌka-chər, -ˌke-\ *noun* (1678)
: any of various passerine birds (families Muscicapidae and Tyrannidae) that feed on insects taken on the wing

fly dope *noun* (1897)
: an insect repellent

fly·er *variant of* FLIER

fly fisherman *noun* (1886)
: an angler who uses the technique of fly-fishing

fly-fish·ing \'flī-ˌfi-shin\ *noun* (1653)
: a method of fishing in which an artificial fly is cast by use of a fly rod, a reel, and a relatively heavy oiled or treated line

fly front *noun* (1893)
: a concealed closing on the front of a coat, skirt, shirt, dress, or pants
— **fly-front** \'flī-ˌfrənt\ *adjective*

fly gallery *noun* (1888)
: a narrow raised platform at the side of a theater stage from which flying scenery lines are operated

¹**fly·ing** \'flī-in\ *adjective* (before 12th century)
1 a : moving or capable of moving in the air **b** : moving or made by moving rapidly ⟨*flying* feet⟩ ⟨a *flying* leap⟩ **c** : very brief

2 : intended for ready movement or action ⟨a *flying* squad car⟩
3 : having stylized wings — used especially of livestock brand marks
4 : of or relating to the operation of aircraft ⟨a *flying* club⟩
5 : traversed or to be traversed (as in speed-record trials) after a running start ⟨a *flying* kilometer⟩
— **with flying colors** : with complete or eminent success

²**flying** *noun* (1548)
1 : travel by air
2 : the operation of an aircraft or spacecraft

flying boat *noun* (1913)
: a seaplane with a hull designed for floating

flying bomb *noun* (1944)
chiefly British : BUZZ BOMB

flying bridge *noun* (circa 1909)
1 : the highest navigational bridge on a ship
2 : FLYBRIDGE

flying buttress *noun* (1669)
: a masonry structure that typically consists of a straight inclined bar carried on an arch and a solid pier or buttress against which it abuts and that receives the thrust of a roof or vault

Flying Dutchman *noun*
1 : a legendary Dutch mariner condemned to sail the seas until Judgment Day
2 : a spectral ship that according to legend haunts the seas near the Cape of Good Hope

flying fish *noun* (circa 1511)
: any of numerous fishes (family Exocoetidae) chiefly of tropical and warm seas that are capable of long gliding flights out of water by spreading their large pectoral fins like wings

1 flying buttress

flying fox *noun* (1759)
: FRUIT BAT

flying gurnard *noun* (1884)
: any of several marine fishes (family Dactylopteridae) that resemble gurnards and have large pectoral fins allowing them to glide above the water for short distances

flying jib *noun* (1711)
: a sail outside the jib on an extension of the jibboom — see SAIL illustration

flying lemur *noun* (1883)
: either of two East Indian or Philippine arboreal nocturnal mammals (*Cynocephalus volans* and *C. variegatus*) that are about the size of a cat, that make long gliding leaps using a broad fold of skin on each side attached to and extending between the limbs, and that are placed in a separate order (Dermoptera)

flying machine *noun* (1736)
: an apparatus for navigating the air

flying mare *noun* (1754)
: a wrestling maneuver in which the aggressor seizes his opponent's wrist, turns about, and jerks him over his back

flying officer *noun* (1913)
: a commissioned officer in the British air force who ranks with a first lieutenant in the army

flying saucer *noun* (1947)
: any of various unidentified flying objects usually described as being saucer-shaped or disk-shaped

flying spot *noun* (1933)
: a spot of light moved over a surface (as one bearing printing or an image) so that light reflected from or transmitted by different parts of the surface is translated into electrical signals for transmission (as in television or computers)

flying squad *noun* (1927)
: a usually small standby group of people ready to move or act swiftly; *especially* : a police unit formed to respond quickly in an emergency

flying squirrel *noun* (1624)
: either of two small nocturnal North American squirrels (*Glaucomys volans* and *G. sabrinus*) with folds of skin connecting the forelegs and hind legs that enable it to make long gliding leaps; *also* : any of various squirrels that possess a patagium

flying start *noun* (1851)
1 : a start in racing in which the participants are already moving when they cross the starting line or receive the starting signal
2 : a favorable start of something

flying wedge *noun* (1909)
: a moving formation (as of guards or police) resembling a wedge

fly·leaf \'flī-ˌlēf\ *noun, plural* **fly·leaves** \-ˌlēvz\ (1832)
: one of the free endpapers of a book

fly·man \-mən, -ˌman\ *noun* (1883)
: a worker in the flies of a theater who manipulates curtains and scenery

fly net *noun* (before 12th century)
: a net to exclude or keep off insects (as from a harness horse)

fly·over \'flī-ˌō-vər\ *noun* (1931)
1 : FLYBY 1
2 *British* : OVERPASS

fly·pa·per \-ˌpā-pər\ *noun* (1847)
: paper coated with a sticky often poisonous substance for killing flies

fly·past \-ˌpast\ *noun* (1914)
chiefly British : FLYBY 1

fly rod *noun* (1684)
: a light springy fishing rod used in fly casting

flysch \'flish\ *noun* [German dialect] (1853)
: a thick and extensive deposit largely of sandstone that is formed in a geosyncline adjacent to a rising mountain belt and is especially common in the Alpine region of Europe

fly sheet *noun* (1833)
1 : a small loose advertising sheet : HANDBILL
2 : a sheet of a folder, booklet, or catalog giving directions for the use of or information about the material that follows

fly·speck \'flī-ˌspek\ *noun* (circa 1847)
1 : a speck made by fly excrement
2 : something small and insignificant
— **flyspeck** *transitive verb*

fly-strike \-ˌstrīk\ *noun* (1940)
: infestation with fly maggots
— **fly-struck** \-ˌstrək\ *adjective*

fly·swat·ter \-ˌswä-tər\ *noun* (1917)
: a device for killing insects that consists of a flat piece of perforated rubber or plastic or fine-mesh wire netting attached to a handle

fly·ti·er \'flī-ˌtī(-ə)r\ *noun* [*fly* + *tier* (one that ties)] (1881)
: a person who makes flies for fishing

flyt·ing \'flī-tin\ *noun* [Scots, literally, contention, gerund of *flyte* to contend, argue, from Middle English *fliten*, from Old English *flītan*; akin to Old High German *flīzan* to argue] (1508)
: a dispute or exchange of personal abuse in verse form

fly·way \'flī-ˌwā\ *noun* (1891)
: an established air route of migratory birds

fly·weight \-ˌwāt\ *noun* (1911)
: a boxer in a weight division having a maximum limit of 112 pounds — compare BANTAMWEIGHT

fly·wheel \-ˌhwēl, -ˌwēl\ *noun* (1784)
: a heavy wheel for opposing and moderating by its inertia any fluctuation of speed in the machinery with which it revolves; *also* : a

\ə\ abut \ᵊ\ kitten \ər\ further \a\ ash \ā\ ace
\ä\ mop, mar \aů\ out \ch\ chin \e\ bet \ē\ easy
\g\ go \i\ hit \ī\ ice \j\ job \ŋ\ sing \ō\ go
\ȯ\ law \ȯi\ boy \th\ thin \th\ the \ü\ loot \ů\ foot
\y\ yet \zh\ vision *see also* Guide to Pronunciation

similar wheel used for storing kinetic energy (as for motive power)

fly whisk *noun* (1841)
: a whisk for brushing away flies

FM \'ef-,em\ *noun, often attributive* [*frequency modulation*] (1940)
: a broadcasting system using frequency modulation; *also* : a radio receiver of such a system

FMN \,ef-,em-'en\ *noun* [*flavin mononucleotide*] (circa 1953)
: a yellow crystalline phosphoric ester $C_{17}H_{21}N_4O_9P$ of riboflavin that is a coenzyme of several flavoprotein enzymes

f-num·ber \'ef-,nəm-bər\ *noun* [*focal length*] (circa 1903)
1 : the ratio of the focal length to the aperture in an optical system
2 : a number following the symbol f/ that expresses the effectiveness of the aperture of a camera lens in relation to brightness of image so that the smaller the number the brighter the image and therefore the shorter the exposure required

¹foal \'fōl\ *noun* [Middle English *fole*, from Old English *fola*; akin to Latin *pullus* young of an animal, Greek *pais* child — more at FEW] (before 12th century)
: a young animal of the horse family; *especially* : one under one year
— **in foal** : PREGNANT 3

²foal *intransitive verb* (14th century)
: to give birth to a foal

¹foam \'fōm\ *noun* [Middle English *fome*, from Old English *fām*; akin to Old High German *feim* foam, Latin *spuma* foam, *pumex* pumice] (before 12th century)
1 : a light frothy mass of fine bubbles formed in or on the surface of a liquid: as **a** : a frothy mass formed in salivating or sweating **b** : a stabilized froth produced chemically or mechanically and used especially in fighting oil fires **c** : a material in a lightweight cellular form resulting from introduction of gas bubbles during manufacture
2 : SEA
3 : something resembling foam
— **foam·less** \-ləs\ *adjective*

²foam (before 12th century)
intransitive verb
1 a : to produce or form foam **b** : to froth at the mouth especially in anger; *broadly* : to be angry
2 : to gush out in foam
3 : to become covered with or as if with foam ⟨streets . . . *foaming* with life —Thomas Wolfe⟩
transitive verb
1 : to cause to foam; *specifically* : to cause air bubbles to form in
2 : to convert (as a plastic) into a foam
— **foam·able** \'fō-mə-bəl\ *adjective*
— **foam·er** \'fō-mər\ *noun*

foamed plastic *noun* (1945)
: EXPANDED PLASTIC

foam·flow·er \'fōm-,flau̇(-ə)r\ *noun* (1895)
: an American woodland spring-flowering herb (*Tiarella cordifolia*) that has white flowers with very long stamens and no stem leaves — called also *false miterwort*

foam rubber *noun* (circa 1939)
: spongy rubber of fine texture made from latex by foaming (as by whipping) before vulcanization

foamy \'fō-mē\ *adjective* **foam·i·er; -est** (before 12th century)
1 : covered with foam : FROTHY
2 : full of, consisting of, or resembling foam
— **foam·i·ly** \-mə-lē\ *adverb*
— **foam·i·ness** \-mē-nəs\ *noun*

¹fob \'fäb\ *transitive verb* **fobbed; fob·bing** [Middle English *fobben*] (14th century)
archaic : DECEIVE, CHEAT

²fob *noun* [perhaps akin to German dialect *Fuppe* pocket] (1653)
1 : WATCH POCKET

2 : a short strap, ribbon, or chain attached especially to a pocket watch
3 : an ornament attached to a fob chain

fob off *transitive verb* (1597)
1 : to put off with a trick, excuse, or inferior substitute
2 : to pass or offer (something spurious) as genuine
3 : to put aside ⟨now *fob off* what once they would have welcomed eagerly —Walter Lippmann⟩

fo·cac·cia \fō-'kä-ch(ē-)ə\ *noun* [Italian, from Late Latin *focacia* (neuter plural), from Latin *focus* hearth] (1969)
: a flat Italian bread typically seasoned with herbs and olive oil

fo·cal \'fō-kəl\ *adjective* (1693)
: of, relating to, being, or having a focus
— **fo·cal·ly** \-kə-lē\ *adverb*

focal infection *noun* (circa 1923)
: a persistent bacterial infection of some organ or region; *especially* : one causing symptoms elsewhere in the body

fo·cal·ize \'fō-kə-,līz\ *verb* **-ized; -iz·ing** (1845)
transitive verb
1 : to bring to a focus
2 : LOCALIZE
intransitive verb
1 : to come to a focus : CONCENTRATE
2 : LOCALIZE
— **fo·cal·iza·tion** \,fō-kə-lə-'zā-shən\ *noun*

focal length *noun* (1753)
: the distance of a focus from the surface of a lens or curved mirror

focal plane *noun* (1889)
: a plane that is perpendicular to the axis of a lens or mirror and passes through the focus

focal point *noun* (1713)
: FOCUS 1a, 5a

focal ratio *noun* (1926)
: F-NUMBER

fo'·c'sle *variant of* FORECASTLE

¹fo·cus \'fō-kəs\ *noun, plural* **fo·ci** \'fō-,sī *also* -,kī\ *also* **fo·cus·es** [New Latin, from Latin, hearth] (1644)
1 a : a point at which rays (as of light, heat, or sound) converge or from which they diverge or appear to diverge; *specifically* : the point where the geometrical lines or their prolongations conforming to the rays diverging from or converging toward another point intersect and give rise to an image after reflection by a mirror or refraction by a lens or optical system **b** : a point of convergence of a beam of particles (as electrons)
2 a : FOCAL LENGTH **b** : adjustment for distinct vision; *also* : the area that may be seen distinctly or resolved into a clear image **c** : a state or condition permitting clear perception or understanding ⟨tried to bring the issues into *focus*⟩ **d** : DIRECTION 6c
3 : one of the fixed points that with the corresponding directrix defines a conic section
4 : a localized area of disease or the chief site of a generalized disease or infection
5 a : a center of activity, attraction, or attention ⟨the *focus* of the meeting was drug abuse⟩ **b** : a point of concentration
6 : the place of origin of an earthquake or moonquake
7 : directed attention : EMPHASIS ◊
— **fo·cus·less** \-ləs\ *adjective*
— **in focus** : having or giving the proper sharpness of outline due to good focusing
— **out of focus** : not in focus

²focus *verb* **fo·cused** *also* **fo·cussed; fo·cus·ing** *also* **fo·cus·sing** (1775)
transitive verb
1 a : to bring into focus **b** : to adjust the focus of (as the eye or a lens)
2 : to cause to be concentrated ⟨*focused* their attention on the most urgent problems⟩
3 : to bring (as light rays) to a focus : CONCENTRATE

intransitive verb
1 : to come to a focus : CONVERGE
2 : to adjust one's eye or a camera to a particular range
3 : to concentrate attention or effort
— **fo·cus·able** \-kə-sə-bəl\ *adjective*
— **fo·cus·er** *noun*

fod·der \'fä-dər\ *noun* [Middle English, from Old English *fōdor*; akin to Old High German *fuotar* food — more at FOOD] (before 12th century)
1 : something fed to domestic animals; *especially* : coarse food for cattle, horses, or sheep
2 : inferior or readily available material used to supply a heavy demand ⟨routine entertainment *fodder*⟩ ⟨*fodder* for gossip columnists⟩
— **fodder** *transitive verb*

fod·gel \'fä-jəl\ *adjective* [origin unknown] (1724)
Scottish : BUXOM

foe \'fō\ *noun* [Middle English *fo*, from Old English *fāh*, from *fāh*, adjective, hostile; akin to Old High German *gifēh* hostile] (before 12th century)
1 : one who has personal enmity for another
2 a : an enemy in war **b** : ADVERSARY, OPPONENT
3 : one who opposes on principle ⟨a *foe* of needless expenditures⟩
4 : something prejudicial or injurious

foehn *or* **föhn** \'fa(r)n, 'fēn, 'fän\ *noun* [German *Föhn*] (1861)
: a warm dry wind blowing down the side of a mountain

foe·man \'fō-mən\ *noun* (before 12th century)
: FOE 2

foe·tal, foe·tus *chiefly British variant of* FETAL, FETUS

foe·tid *variant of* FETID

foeto- *or* **foeti-** *chiefly British variant of* FETO-

¹fog \'fȯg, 'fäg\ *noun* [probably of Scandinavian origin; akin to Danish *fog* spray, shower] (1544)
1 a : vapor condensed to fine particles of water suspended in the lower atmosphere that differs from cloud only in being near the ground **b** : a fine spray or a foam for fire fighting
2 : a murky condition of the atmosphere or a substance causing it
3 a : a state of confusion or bewilderment **b** : something that confuses or obscures ⟨hid behind a *fog* of rhetoric⟩
4 : cloudiness or partial opacity in a developed photographic image caused by chemical action or stray radiation
— **fog·less** \-ləs\ *adjective*

²fog *verb* **fogged; fog·ging** (1599)
transitive verb

◇ **WORD HISTORY**
focus The Latin word *focus* meant "hearth, fireplace." In the spoken Latin of the Roman Empire, the word must have shifted to the more general meaning "fire" and then ousted the literary Latin word *ignis*. It is the sense "fire" that we see reflected in the Romance languages, where the offspring of *focus* include Italian *fuoco*, Spanish *fuego*, French *feu*, and Romanian *foc*. In the scientific Latin of treatises written in the 17th century, the classical Latin word *focus* reappears, used to refer to the point at which rays of light refracted by a lens converge. Because rays of sunlight when directed by a magnifying glass can produce enough heat to burn paper, a word meaning "fireplace" is quite appropriate metaphorically to describe their convergence point. From this optical sense of *focus* have arisen more extended senses in English such as "point of concentration" or "emphasis."

1 : to cover, envelop, or suffuse with or as if with fog ⟨*fog* the barns with pesticide⟩
2 : to make obscure or confusing ⟨accusations which *fogged* the real issues⟩
3 : to make confused
4 : to produce fog on (as a photographic film) during development
intransitive verb
1 : to become covered or thick with fog
2 a : to become blurred by a covering of fog or mist **b :** to become indistinct through exposure to light or radiation

fog·bound \'fȯg-ˌbau̇nd, 'fäg-\ *adjective* (circa 1855)
1 : unable to move because of fog ⟨*fogbound* ship⟩
2 : covered with or surrounded by fog ⟨*fogbound* coast⟩

fog·bow \-ˌbō\ *noun* (1831)
: a nebulous arc or circle of white or yellowish light sometimes seen in fog

fog·gage \'fȯ-gij, 'fä-\ *noun* [Scots, from Middle English (Scots) *fogage*, from Anglo Latin *fogagium*, from Middle English *fogge* second growth of grass + Medieval Latin *-agium* -age] (1786)
Scottish **:** a second growth of grass

fog·gy \'fȯ-gē, 'fä-\ *adjective* **fog·gi·er; -est** (15th century)
1 a : filled or abounding with fog **b :** covered or made opaque by moisture or grime
2 : blurred or obscured as if by fog ⟨hadn't the *foggiest* notion⟩
— **fog·gi·ly** \'fȯ-gə-lē, 'fä-\ *adverb*
— **fog·gi·ness** \'fȯ-gē-nəs, 'fä-\ *noun*

Foggy Bottom *noun* [*Foggy Bottom*, district in Washington, D.C.] (1951)
: the U.S. Department of State

fog·horn \'fȯg-ˌhȯrn, 'fäg-\ *noun* (1858)
1 : a horn (as on a ship) sounded in a fog to give warning
2 : a loud hoarse voice

fo·gy *also* **fo·gey** \'fō-gē\ *noun, plural* **fo·gies** *also* **fogeys** [origin unknown] (1780)
: a person with old-fashioned ideas — usually used with *old*
— **fo·gy·ish** \-gē-ish\ *adjective*
— **fo·gy·ism** \-gē-ˌi-zəm\ *noun*

foi·ble \'fȯi-bəl\ *noun* [obsolete French (now *faible*), from obsolete *foible* weak, from Old French *feble* feeble] (circa 1648)
1 : the part of a sword or foil blade between the middle and point
2 : a minor flaw or shortcoming in character or behavior **:** WEAKNESS
synonym see FAULT

foie gras \'fwä-'grä\ *noun* [French, literally, fat liver] (1818)
: the fatted liver of an animal and especially of a goose usually served as a pâté

¹foil \'fȯi(ə)l\ *transitive verb* [Middle English, to trample, full cloth, from Middle French *fouler* — more at FULL] (14th century)
1 *obsolete* **:** TRAMPLE
2 a : to prevent from attaining an end **:** DEFEAT **b :** to bring to naught **:** THWART
synonym see FRUSTRATE

²foil *noun* [Middle English, leaf, from Middle French *foille* (from Latin *folia*, plural of *folium*) & *foil*, from Latin *folium* — more at BLADE] (14th century)
1 : very thin sheet metal ⟨aluminum *foil*⟩
2 : a thin piece of material (as metal) put under an inferior or paste stone to add color or brilliance
3 : someone or something that serves as a contrast to another ⟨acted as a *foil* for a comedian⟩
4 a : an indentation between cusps in Gothic tracery **b :** one of several arcs that enclose a complex figure
5 : HYDROFOIL 1

³foil *noun* (15th century)
1 *archaic* **:** DEFEAT
2 *archaic* **:** the track or trail of an animal

⁴foil *noun* [origin unknown] (1594)
1 : a light fencing sword having a usually circular guard and a flexible blade of rectangular section tapering to a blunted point — compare ÉPÉE, SABER
2 : the art or sport of fencing with the foil — often used in plural

⁵foil *transitive verb* (1611)
1 : to back or cover with foil
2 : to enhance by contrast

foiled \'fȯi(ə)ld\ *adjective* (1835)
: ornamented with foils ⟨a *foiled* arch⟩

foils·man \'fȯi(ə)lz-mən\ *noun* (1927)
: one who fences with a foil

¹foin \'fȯin\ *intransitive verb* [Middle English, from *foin* fork for spearing fish, from Middle French *foisne*] (14th century)
archaic **:** to thrust with a pointed weapon **:** LUNGE

²foin *noun* (15th century)
archaic **:** a pass in fencing **:** LUNGE

foi·son \'fȯi-z⁾n\ *noun* [Middle English *foisoun*, from Middle French *foison*, from Latin *fusion-, fusio* pouring, effusion — more at FUSION] (14th century)
1 *archaic* **:** rich harvest
2 *chiefly Scottish* **:** physical energy or strength
3 *plural, obsolete* **:** RESOURCES

foist \'fȯist\ *transitive verb* [probably from obsolete Dutch *vuisten* to take into one's hand, from Middle Dutch *vuysten*, from *vuyst* fist; akin to Old English *fȳst* fist] (circa 1587)
1 a : to introduce or insert surreptitiously or without warrant **b :** to force another to accept especially by stealth or deceit
2 : to pass off as genuine or worthy ⟨*foist* costly and valueless products on the public —Jonathan Spivak⟩

fo·la·cin \'fō-lə-sən\ *noun* [*folic acid* + *-in*] (1949)
: FOLIC ACID

fo·late \'fō-ˌlāt\ *noun* (1951)
: FOLIC ACID

¹fold \'fōld\ *noun* [Middle English, from Old English *falod*; akin to Old Saxon *faled* enclosure] (before 12th century)
1 : an enclosure for sheep
2 a : a flock of sheep **b :** a group of people or institutions that share a common faith, belief, activity, or enthusiasm

²fold *transitive verb* (before 12th century)
: to pen up or confine (as sheep) in a fold

³fold *verb* [Middle English, from Old English *fealdan*; akin to Old High German *faldan* to fold, Greek *diplasios* twofold] (before 12th century)
transitive verb
1 : to lay one part over another part of ⟨*fold* a letter⟩
2 : to reduce the length or bulk of by doubling over ⟨*fold* a tent⟩
3 : to clasp together **:** ENTWINE ⟨*fold* the hands⟩
4 : to clasp or enwrap closely **:** EMBRACE
5 : to bend (as a layer of rock) into folds
6 a : to incorporate (a food ingredient) into a mixture by repeated gentle overturnings without stirring or beating **b :** to incorporate closely
7 a : to concede defeat by withdrawing (one's cards) from play (as in poker) **b :** to bring to an end
intransitive verb
1 : to become doubled or pleated
2 : to fail completely **:** COLLAPSE; *especially* **:** to go out of business
3 : to fold one's cards (as in poker)
— **fold·able** \'fōl-də-bəl\ *adjective*

⁴fold *noun* (13th century)
1 : a part doubled or laid over another part **:** PLEAT
2 : something that is folded together or that enfolds
3 a : a bend or flexure produced in rock by forces operative after the depositing or consolidation of the rock **b** *chiefly British* **:** an undulation in the landscape

4 : a margin apparently formed by the doubling upon itself of a flat anatomical structure (as a membrane)
5 : a crease made by folding something (as a newspaper)

-fold \ˌfōld, 'fōld\ *suffix* [Middle English, from Old English *-feald*; akin to Old High German *-falt* -fold, Latin *-plex, -plus*, Old English *fealdan*]
1 : multiplied by (a specified number) **:** times — in adjectives ⟨a six*fold* increase⟩ and adverbs ⟨repay you ten*fold*⟩
2 : having (so many) parts ⟨three*fold* aspect of the problem⟩

fold·away \'fōl-də-ˌwā\ *adjective* (1948)
: designed to be folded for storage or portability ⟨*foldaway* doors⟩ ⟨*foldaway* bed⟩ ⟨a *foldaway* table⟩

fold·boat \'fōl(d)-ˌbōt\ *noun* [translation of German *Faltboot*] (1938)
: a small collapsible canoe made of rubberized sailcloth stretched over a framework

fold·er \'fōl-dər\ *noun* (1552)
1 : one that folds
2 : a folded printed circular
3 : a folded cover or large envelope for holding or filing loose papers

fol·de·rol \'fäl-də-ˌräl\ *noun* [*fol-de-rol*, a nonsense refrain in songs] (1820)
1 : a useless ornament or accessory **:** TRIFLE
2 : NONSENSE

fold·ing \'fōl-diŋ\ *adjective* (15th century)
: capable of being folded into a more compact shape ⟨*folding* chairs⟩ ⟨a *folding* door⟩

folding money *noun* (circa 1930)
: PAPER MONEY

fold·out \'fōl-ˌdau̇t\ *noun, often attributive* (1950)
: a folded leaf in a publication (as a book) that is larger in some dimension than the page ⟨a *foldout* map⟩

fo·li·a·ceous \ˌfō-lē-'ā-shəs\ *adjective* [Latin *foliaceus*, from *folium* leaf + *-aceus* -aceous] (1658)
: of, relating to, or resembling an ordinary green leaf as distinguished from a modified leaf (as a petal, bract, or scale)

fo·liage \'fō-lē-ij *also* -lyij; ÷'fō-lij, ÷'fȯi-lij\ *noun* [Middle French *fuellage*, from *foille* leaf — more at FOIL] (1598)
1 : a representation of leaves, flowers, and branches for architectural ornamentation
2 : the aggregate of leaves of one or more plants
3 : a cluster of leaves, flowers, and branches
☐
— **fo·liaged** \-lē-ijd *also* -lyijd; ÷'fō-lijd, ÷'fȯi-\ *adjective*

foliage plant *noun* (1862)
: a plant grown primarily for its decorative foliage

fo·li·ar \'fō-lē-ər\ *adjective* [French *foliaire*, from Latin *folium* leaf + French *-aire* -ar] (circa 1859)

☐ **USAGE**
foliage The disyllabic pronunciation \'fō-lij\ is very common. Some commentators insist that *foliage* requires a trisyllabic pronunciation because of its spelling, but words of a similar pattern such as *carriage* and *marriage* do not fall under their prescription. The pronunciation \'fȯi-lij\ is disapproved because it suggests the transposition of the *l* and *i* in the spelling. It is not as common as \'fō-lij\ and may be associated with the nonstandard spelling *foilage*.

\ə\ **abut**	\ᵊ\ **kitten**	\ər\ **further**	\a\ **ash**	\ā\ **ace**	
\ä\ **mop, mar**	\au̇\ **out**	\ch\ **chin**	\e\ **bet**	\ē\ **easy**	
\g\ **go**	\i\ **hit**	\ī\ **ice**	\j\ **job**	\ŋ\ **sing**	\ō\ **go**
\ȯ\ **law**	\ȯi\ **boy**	\th\ **thin**	\t̲h̲\ **the**	\ü\ **loot**	\u̇\ **foot**
\y\ **yet**	\zh\ **vision**		*see also* Guide to Pronunciation		

foli·ate : of, relating to, or applied to leaves ⟨*foliar* sprays⟩

fo·li·ate \'fō-lē-ət, -ˌāt\ *adjective* [Latin *foliatus* leafy, from *folium* leaf — more at BLADE] (circa 1658)
1 : shaped like a leaf ⟨a *foliate* sponge⟩
2 : FOLIATED

fo·li·at·ed \-ˌā-təd\ *adjective* (1650)
1 : composed of or separable into layers ⟨a *foliated* rock⟩
2 : ornamented with foils or a leaf design

fo·li·a·tion \ˌfō-lē-'ā-shən\ *noun* (circa 1623)
1 a : the process of forming into a leaf **b** : the state of being in leaf **c** : VERNATION
2 : the numbering of the leaves of a manuscript or early printed book
3 a : ornamentation with foliage **b** : a decoration resembling a leaf
4 : the enrichment of an opening by foils
5 : foliated texture

fo·lic acid \ˌfō-lik-\ *noun* [Latin *folium*] (1941)
: a crystalline vitamin $C_{19}H_{19}N_7O_6$ of the B complex that is used especially in the treatment of nutritional anemias — called also *pteroylglutamic acid*

fo·lie à deux \ˌfō-lē-à-'dœ, ˌfä-lē-ˌä-'də(r)\ *noun* [French, literally, double madness] (circa 1892)
: the presence of the same or similar delusional ideas in two persons closely associated with one another

¹fo·lio \'fō-lē-ˌō\ *noun, plural* **fo·li·os** [Middle English, from Latin, ablative of *folium*] (1447)
1 a : a leaf especially of a manuscript or book **b** : a leaf number **c** : a page number **d** : an identifying reference in accounting used in posting
2 a : a sheet of paper folded once **b** : a case or folder for loose papers
3 a : the size of a piece of paper cut two from a sheet; *also* : paper or a page of this size **b** : a book printed on folio pages **c** : a book of the largest size
4 : a certain number of words taken as a unit or division in a document for purposes of measurement or reference

²folio *transitive verb* (1858)
: to put a serial number on each leaf or page of

fo·li·ose \'fō-lē-ˌōs\ *adjective* [Latin *foliosus* leafy] (1758)
: having a flat, thin, and usually lobed thallus attached to the substratum ⟨*foliose* lichens⟩ — compare CRUSTOSE, FRUTICOSE

¹folk \'fōk\ *noun, plural* **folk** *or* **folks** [Middle English, from Old English *folc;* akin to Old High German *folc* people] (before 12th century)
1 *archaic* : a group of kindred tribes forming a nation : PEOPLE
2 : the great proportion of the members of a people that determines the group character and that tends to preserve its characteristic form of civilization and its customs, arts and crafts, legends, traditions, and superstitions from generation to generation
3 *plural* : a certain kind, class, or group of people ⟨old *folks*⟩ ⟨just plain *folk*⟩ ⟨country *folk*⟩ ⟨media *folk*⟩
4 *folks plural* : people generally
5 *folks plural* : the persons of one's family; *especially* : PARENTS

²folk *adjective* (before 12th century)
1 : originating or traditional with the common people of a country or region and typically reflecting their lifestyle ⟨*folk* hero⟩ ⟨*folk* music⟩
2 : of or relating to the common people or to the study of the common people ⟨*folk* sociology⟩

folk etymology *noun* (1882)
: the transformation of words so as to give them an apparent relationship to other better-known or better-understood words (as in the change of Spanish *cucaracha* to English *cockroach*)

¹folk·ie *also* **folky** \'fō-kē\ *noun, plural* **folk·ies** (1965)
: a folk singer or instrumentalist

²folkie *or* **folky** *adjective* (1965)
: of or relating to folk music

folk·ish \'fō-kish\ *adjective* (1938)
: FOLKLIKE
— **folk·ish·ness** *noun*

folk·life \'fōk-ˌlīf\ *noun* (1864)
: the traditions, activities, skills, and products (as handicrafts) of a particular people or group

folk·like \'fō-ˌklīk\ *adjective* (1939)
: having a folk character

folk·lore \'fō-ˌklōr, -ˌklȯr\ *noun* (1846)
1 : traditional customs, tales, sayings, dances, or art forms preserved among a people
2 : a branch of knowledge that deals with folklore
3 : an often unsupported notion, story, or saying that is widely circulated
— **folk·lor·ic** \-ˌklōr-ik, -ˌklȯr-\ *adjective*
— **folk·lor·ish** \-ish\ *adjective*
— **folk·lor·ist** \-ist\ *noun*
— **folk·lor·is·tic** \ˌfō-ˌklōr-'is-tik, -ˌklȯr-\ *adjective*

folk mass *noun* (1966)
: a mass in which traditional liturgical music is replaced by folk music

folk medicine *noun* (1878)
: traditional medicine as practiced nonprofessionally especially by people isolated from modern medical services and usually involving the use of plant-derived remedies on an empirical basis

folk·moot \'fōk-ˌmüt\ *or* **folk·mote** \-ˌmōt\ *noun* [alteration of Old English *folcmōt, folcgemōt*, from *folc* people + *mōt, gemōt* meeting — more at MOOT] (before 12th century)
: a general assembly of the people (as of a shire) in early England

folk·sing·er \-ˌsiŋ-ər\ *noun* (1884)
: one who sings folk songs or sings in a style associated with folk songs
— **folk·sing·ing** \-ˌsiŋ-iŋ\ *noun*

folk song *noun* (1847)
: a traditional or composed song typically characterized by stanzaic form, refrain, and simplicity of melody

folksy \'fōk-sē\ *adjective* **folks·i·er; -est** (1852)
1 : SOCIABLE, FRIENDLY
2 : informal, casual, or familiar in manner or style ⟨*folksy* humor⟩
— **folks·i·ly** \-sə-lē\ *adverb*
— **folks·i·ness** \-sē-nəs\ *noun*

folk·tale \'fōk-ˌtāl\ *noun* (1852)
: a characteristically anonymous, timeless, and placeless tale circulated orally among a people

folk·way \'fō-ˌkwā\ *noun* (circa 1906)
: a mode of thinking, feeling, or acting common to a given group of people; *especially* : a traditional social custom

fol·li·cle \'fä-li-kəl\ *noun* [New Latin *folliculus*, from Latin, diminutive of *follis* bag — more at FOOL] (1646)
1 a : a small anatomical cavity or deep narrow-mouthed depression **b** : a small lymph node **c** : a vesicle in the mammalian ovary that contains a developing egg surrounded by a covering of cells; *especially* : GRAAFIAN FOLLICLE
2 : a dry dehiscent one-celled many-seeded fruit (as of the milkweed) that has a single carpel and opens along one suture
— **fol·lic·u·lar** \fə-'li-kyə-lər, fä-\ *adjective*

follicle mite *noun* (1925)
: any of several minute mites (genus *Demodex*) parasitic in hair follicles

follicle–stimulating hormone *noun* (circa 1943)
: a hormone produced by the anterior lobe of the pituitary gland that stimulates the growth of the ovum-containing follicles in the ovary and activates sperm-forming cells

fol·lic·u·li·tis \fə-ˌli-kyə-'lī-təs\ *noun* [New Latin, from *folliculus* + *-itis*] (circa 1860)
: inflammation of one or more follicles especially of the hair

¹fol·low \'fä-(ˌ)lō, -lə(-w)\ *verb* [Middle English *folwen*, from Old English *folgian;* akin to Old High German *folgēnoun* to follow] (before 12th century)
transitive verb
1 : to go, proceed, or come after ⟨*followed* the guide⟩
2 a : to engage in as a calling or way of life : PURSUE ⟨wheat-growing is generally *followed* here⟩ **b** : to walk or proceed along ⟨*follow* a path⟩
3 a : to be or act in accordance with ⟨*follow* directions⟩ **b** : to accept as authority : OBEY ⟨*followed* his conscience⟩
4 a : to pursue in an effort to overtake **b** : to seek to attain ⟨*follow* knowledge⟩
5 : to come into existence or take place as a result or consequence of ⟨disaster *followed* the blunder⟩
6 : to come or take place after in time, sequence, or order **b** : to cause to be followed ⟨*followed* dinner with a liqueur⟩
7 : to copy after : IMITATE
8 a : to watch steadily ⟨*followed* the flight of the ball⟩ **b** : to keep the mind on ⟨*follow* a speech⟩ **c** : to attend closely to : keep abreast of ⟨*followed* his career with interest⟩ **d** : to understand the sense or logic of (as a line of thought)
intransitive verb
1 : to go or come after a person or thing in place, time, or sequence
2 : to result or occur as a consequence, effect, or inference ☆
— **as follows** : as comes next — used impersonally
— **follow one's nose 1** : to go in a straight or obvious course **2** : to proceed without plan or reflection : obey one's instincts
— **follow suit 1** : to play a card of the same suit as the card led **2** : to follow an example set

²follow *noun* (1870)
1 : the act or process of following
2 : forward spin given to a ball by striking it above center — compare DRAW, ENGLISH

fol·low·er \'fä-lə-wər\ *noun* (before 12th century)
1 a : one in the service of another : RETAINER **b** : one that follows the opinions or teachings of another **c** : one that imitates another
2 *archaic* : one that chases
3 : a sheet added to the first sheet of an indenture or other deed
4 : a machine part that receives motion from another part
5 : a spring-loaded plate at the bottom of a firearm's magazine that angles cartridges for proper insertion into the chamber

☆ **SYNONYMS**
Follow, succeed, ensue, supervene mean to come after something or someone. FOLLOW may apply to a coming after in time, position, or logical sequence ⟨speeches *followed* the dinner⟩. SUCCEED implies a coming after immediately in a sequence determined by natural order, inheritance, election, or laws of rank ⟨she *succeeded* her father as head of the business⟩. ENSUE commonly suggests a logical consequence or naturally expected development ⟨after the talk a general discussion *ensued*⟩. SUPERVENE suggests the following or beginning of something unforeseen or unpredictable ⟨*supervening* events brought unhappiness to him⟩. See in addition CHASE.

6 : FAN, DEVOTEE ☆
fol·low·er·ship \-ˌship\ *noun* (circa 1928)
1 : FOLLOWING
2 : the capacity or willingness to follow a leader
¹fol·low·ing \ˈfä-lə-wiŋ\ *adjective* (15th century)
1 : being next in order or time ⟨the *following* day⟩
2 : listed or shown next ⟨trains will leave at the *following* times⟩
²following *noun* (15th century)
: a group of followers, adherents, or partisans
³following *preposition* (circa 1926)
: SUBSEQUENT TO ⟨*following* the lecture tea was served⟩
fol·low-on \ˈfä-lə-ˌwòn, -ˌwän\ *adjective* (1960)
: being or relating to something that follows as a natural or logical consequence, development, or progression
— follow-on *noun*
follow out *transitive verb* (1762)
1 : to follow to the end or to a conclusion
2 : CARRY OUT, EXECUTE ⟨*followed out* their orders⟩
follow shot *noun* (circa 1909)
1 : a shot in billiards or pool made by striking the cue ball above its center to cause it to continue forward after striking the object ball
2 : a camera shot in which the camera follows the movement of the subject
fol·low-through \ˈfä-lō-ˌthrü, ˌfä-lō-ˈ, -lə-\ *noun* (circa 1899)
1 : the act or an instance of following through
2 : the part of the stroke following the striking of a ball
follow through *intransitive verb* (1895)
1 : to continue a stroke or motion to the end of its arc
2 : to press on in an activity or process especially to a conclusion
¹fol·low-up \ˈfä-lə-ˌwəp\ *noun* (1916)
1 a : the act or an instance of following up **b :** something that follows up
2 : maintenance of contact with or reexamination of a person (as a patient) especially following treatment
3 : a news story presenting new information on a story published earlier
²follow-up *adjective* (1912)
1 : of, relating to, or being something that follows up ⟨*follow-up* action by the police —Frank Faulkner⟩
2 : done, conducted, or administered in the course of following up persons ⟨*follow-up* care for discharged hospital patients⟩
follow up (1792)
transitive verb
1 : to follow with something similar, related, or supplementary ⟨*following up* his convictions with action —G. P. Merrill⟩
2 : to maintain contact with (a person) so as to monitor the effects of earlier activities or treatments
3 : to pursue in an effort to take further action ⟨the police *follow up* leads⟩
intransitive verb
: to take appropriate action ⟨*follow up* on complaints⟩
fol·ly \ˈfä-lē\ *noun, plural* **follies** [Middle English *folie*, from Old French, from *fol* fool] (13th century)
1 : lack of good sense or normal prudence and foresight
2 a : criminally or tragically foolish actions or conduct **b** *obsolete* **:** EVIL, WICKEDNESS; *especially* **:** lewd behavior
3 : a foolish act or idea
4 : an excessively costly or unprofitable undertaking
5 : an often extravagant picturesque building erected to suit a fanciful taste
Fol·som \ˈfōl-səm\ *adjective* [*Folsom*, town in New Mexico] (1928)

: of, relating to, or characteristic of a prehistoric culture of North America on the east side of the Rocky Mountains that is characterized by flint projectile points having a concave base with side projections and a longitudinal groove on each face
fo·ment \ˈfō-ˌment, fō-ˈ\ *transitive verb* [Middle English *fomenten* to apply a warm substance to, from Late Latin *fomentare*, from Latin *fomentum* compress, from *fovēre* to heat, soothe; akin to Lithuanian *degti* to burn, Sanskrit *dahati* it burns] (circa 1613)
: to promote the growth or development of **:** ROUSE, INCITE ⟨*foment* a rebellion⟩
synonym see INCITE
— fo·ment·er *noun*
fo·men·ta·tion \ˌfō-mən-ˈtā-shən, -ˌmen-\ *noun* (14th century)
1 a : the application of hot moist substances to the body to ease pain **b :** the material so applied
2 : the act of fomenting **:** INSTIGATION
¹fond \ˈfänd\ *adjective* [Middle English, from *fonne* fool] (14th century)
1 : FOOLISH, SILLY ⟨*fond* pride⟩
2 a : prizing highly **:** DESIROUS ⟨*fond* of praise⟩ **b :** having an affection or liking — used with *of* ⟨*fond* of music⟩
3 a : foolishly tender **:** INDULGENT ⟨a *fond* mother⟩ **b :** AFFECTIONATE, LOVING ⟨absence makes the heart grow *fonder*⟩
4 : cherished with great affection **:** doted on ⟨our *fondest* hopes⟩
²fond *intransitive verb* (1530)
obsolete **:** to lavish affection **:** DOTE
³fond \ˈfōⁿ\ *noun, plural* **fonds** \ˈfōⁿ(z)\ [French, from Latin *fundus* bottom, piece of property — more at BOTTOM] (1664)
1 : BACKGROUND, BASIS
2 *obsolete* **:** FUND
fon·dant \ˈfän-dənt\ *noun* [French, from present participle of *fondre* to melt — more at FOUND] (1877)
1 : a soft creamy preparation of sugar, water, and flavorings that is used as a basis for candies or icings
2 : a candy consisting chiefly of fondant
fon·dle \ˈfän-dᵊl\ *verb* **fon·dled; fon·dling** \-(d)liŋ, -dᵊl-iŋ\ [frequentative of obsolete *fond* to fondle] (1694)
transitive verb
1 *obsolete* **:** PAMPER
2 : to handle tenderly, lovingly, or lingeringly **:** CARESS
intransitive verb
: to show affection or desire by caressing
— fon·dler \-(d)lər, -dᵊl-ər\ *noun*
fond·ly \ˈfän-dlē\ *adverb* (14th century)
1 *archaic* **:** in a foolish manner **:** FOOLISHLY
2 : in a fond manner **:** AFFECTIONATELY
3 : in a willingly credulous manner ⟨it would stun, I *fondly* hoped, the reader —Annie Dillard⟩
fond·ness \ˈfän(d)-nəs\ *noun* (14th century)
1 *obsolete* **:** FOOLISHNESS, FOLLY
2 : tender affection
3 : APPETITE, RELISH ⟨had a *fondness* for argument⟩
fon·due *also* **fon·du** \fän-ˈdü, -ˈdyü, ˈfän-\ *noun* [French *fondue*, from feminine of *fondu*, past participle of *fondre* to melt] (1878)
1 a (1) **:** a preparation of melted cheese (as Swiss cheese and Gruyère) usually flavored with white wine and kirsch (2) **:** a dish that consists of small pieces of food (as meat or fruit) cooked in or dipped into a hot liquid ⟨beef *fondue*⟩ ⟨chocolate *fondue*⟩ **b :** a chafing dish in which fondue is made
2 : a dish similar to a soufflé usually made with cheese and bread crumbs
F₁ layer \ˈef-ˈwən-\ *noun* (1933)
: the lower of the two layers into which the F region of the ionosphere splits in the daytime that occurs at varying heights from about 80 to 120 miles (130 to 200 kilometers) above the earth's surface

¹font \ˈfänt\ *noun* [Middle English, from Old English, from Late Latin *font-, fons*, from Latin, fountain] (before 12th century)
1 a : a receptacle for baptismal water **b :** a receptacle for holy water **c :** a receptacle for various liquids
2 : SOURCE, FOUNTAIN ⟨a *font* of information⟩
— font·al \ˈfän-tᵊl\ *adjective*
²font *noun* [Middle French *fonte* act of founding, from (assumed) Vulgar Latin *fundita*, feminine of *funditus*, past participle of Latin *fundere* to found, pour — more at FOUND] (circa 1688)
: an assortment or set of type all of one size and style
fon·ta·nel *or* **fon·ta·nelle** \ˌfän-tᵊn-ˈel, ˈfän-tᵊn-ˌ\ *noun* [Middle English *fontinelle* a bodily hollow or pit, from Middle French *fontenele*, diminutive of *fontaine* fountain] (1741)
: a membrane-covered opening in bone or between bones; *specifically* **:** any of the spaces closed by membranous structures between the uncompleted angles of the parietal bones and the neighboring bones of a fetal or young skull
fon·ti·na \fän-ˈtē-nə\ *noun, often capitalized* [Italian] (1938)
: a cheese that is semisoft to hard in texture and mild to medium sharp in flavor
food \ˈfüd\ *noun, often attributive* [Middle English *fode*, from Old English *fōda;* akin to Old High German *fuotar* food, fodder, Latin *panis* bread, *pascere* to feed] (before 12th century)
1 a : material consisting essentially of protein, carbohydrate, and fat used in the body of an organism to sustain growth, repair, and vital processes and to furnish energy; *also* **:** such food together with supplementary substances (as minerals, vitamins, and condiments) **b :** inorganic substances absorbed by plants in gaseous form or in water solution
2 : nutriment in solid form
3 : something that nourishes, sustains, or supplies ⟨*food* for thought⟩
— food·less \-ləs\ *adjective*
— food·less·ness *noun*
food chain *noun* (1926)
: an arrangement of the organisms of an ecological community according to the order of predation in which each uses the next usually lower member as a food source
food·ie \ˈfü-dē\ *noun* (1982)
: a person having an avid interest in the latest food fads
foo dog \ˈfü-\ *noun, often F capitalized* [Chinese (Beijing) *fó* Buddha; from the use of such figures in ceramic or stone as guardians of Buddhist temples] (1953)
: a mythical lion-dog used as a decorative motif in Far Eastern art
food poisoning *noun* (1887)
: an acute gastrointestinal disorder caused by bacteria or their toxic products or by chemical residues in food
food processor *noun* (1974)

\ə\ abut \ᵊ\ kitten \ər\ further \a\ ash \ā\ ace
\ä\ mop, mar \aù\ out \ch\ chin \e\ bet \ē\ easy
\g\ go \i\ hit \ī\ ice \j\ job \ŋ\ sing \ō\ go
\ò\ law \òi\ boy \th\ thin \th\ the \ü\ loot \ù\ foot
\y\ yet \zh\ vision *see also* Guide to Pronunciation

: an electric kitchen appliance with a set of interchangeable blades revolving inside a container

food pyramid *noun* (1949)
: an ecological hierarchy of food relationships in which a chief predator is at the top, each level preys on the next lower level, and usually green plants are at the bottom

food stamp *noun* (1940)
: a government-issued coupon that is sold or given to low-income persons and is redeemable for food

food·stuff \'füd-,stəf\ *noun* (1872)
: a substance with food value; *specifically* : the raw material of food before or after processing

food vacuole *noun* (circa 1889)
: a membrane-bound vacuole (as in an amoeba) in which ingested food is digested — see AMOEBA illustration

food·ways \'füd-,wāz\ *noun plural* (1946)
: the eating habits and culinary practices of a people, region, or historical period

food web *noun* (1949)
: the totality of interacting food chains in an ecological community

foo·fa·raw \'fü-fə-,rò\ *noun* [origin unknown] (1934)
1 : frills and flashy finery
2 : a disturbance or to-do over a trifle : FUSS

¹fool \'fül\ *noun* [Middle English, from Old French *fol*, from Late Latin *follis*, from Latin, bellows, bag; akin to Old High German *bolla* blister, *balg* bag — more at BELLY] (13th century)
1 : a person lacking in judgment or prudence
2 a : a retainer formerly kept in great households to provide casual entertainment and commonly dressed in motley with cap, bells, and bauble **b** : one who is victimized or made to appear foolish : DUPE
3 a : a harmlessly deranged person or one lacking in common powers of understanding **b** : one with a marked propensity or fondness for something ⟨a dancing *fool*⟩ ⟨a *fool* for candy⟩
4 : a cold dessert of pureed fruit mixed with whipped cream or custard

²fool *adjective* (13th century)
: FOOLISH, SILLY ⟨barking its *fool* head off⟩

³fool (1593)
intransitive verb
1 a : to behave foolishly ⟨why old men *fool* and children calculate —Shakespeare⟩ — often used with *around* **b** : to meddle, tamper, or experiment especially thoughtlessly or ignorantly ⟨don't *fool* with that gun⟩ — often used with *around*
2 a : to play or improvise a comic role **b** : to speak in jest : JOKE ⟨I was only *fooling*⟩
3 : to contend or fight without serious intent or with less than full strength : TOY ⟨a dangerous man to *fool* with⟩
transitive verb
1 : to make a fool of : DECEIVE
2 *obsolete* : INFATUATE
3 : to spend on trifles or without advantage : FRITTER — used with *away*

fool around *intransitive verb* (1837)
1 : to spend time idly, aimlessly, or frivolously
2 : to engage in casual sexual activity

fool·ery \'fül-rē, 'fü-lə-\ *noun, plural* **-er·ies** (1552)
1 : a foolish act, utterance, or belief
2 : foolish behavior

fool·har·dy \'fül-,här-dē\ *adjective* (13th century)
: foolishly adventurous and bold : RASH
synonym see ADVENTUROUS
— **fool·har·di·ly** \-,här-d°l-ē\ *adverb*
— **fool·har·di·ness** \-,här-dē-nəs\ *noun*

fool·ish \'fü-lish\ *adjective* (13th century)
1 : lacking in sense, judgment, or discretion
2 a : ABSURD, RIDICULOUS **b** : marked by a loss of composure : NONPLUSSED, ABASHED
3 : INSIGNIFICANT, TRIFLING, HUMBLE
synonym see SIMPLE

— **fool·ish·ly** *adverb*
fool·ish·ness *noun* (15th century)
1 : foolish behavior : FOLLY
2 : a foolish act or idea

fool·proof \'fül-,prüf\ *adjective* (1902)
: so simple, plain, or reliable as to leave no opportunity for error, misuse, or failure ⟨a *foolproof* plan⟩

fools·cap *also* **fool's cap** \'fül-,skap\ *noun* (1632)
1 : a cap or hood usually with bells worn by jesters
2 : a conical cap for slow or lazy students
3 *usually* foolscap [from the watermark of a foolscap formerly applied to such paper] : a size of paper formerly standard in Great Britain; *broadly* : a piece of writing paper

foolscap 1

fool's gold *noun* (1872)
: PYRITE; *broadly* : any of various pyritic minerals resembling gold

fool's paradise *noun* (15th century)
: a state of delusory happiness

fool's parsley *noun* (1755)
: a poisonous European weed (*Aethusa cynapium*) of the carrot family that resembles parsley and is naturalized in the northern U.S. and southern Canada

¹foot \'fut\ *noun, plural* **feet** \'fēt\ *also* **foot** [Middle English *fot*, from Old English *fōt*; akin to Old High German *fuot* foot, Latin *ped-, pes*, Greek *pod-, pous*] (before 12th century)
1 : the terminal part of the vertebrate leg upon which an individual stands
2 : an invertebrate organ of locomotion or attachment; *especially* : a ventral muscular surface or process of a mollusk — see CLAM illustration
3 : any of various units of length based on the length of the human foot; *especially* : a unit equal to ⅓ yard and comprising 12 inches — plural *foot* used between a number and a noun ⟨a 10-*foot* pole⟩; plural *feet* or *foot* used between a number and an adjective ⟨6 *feet* tall⟩; see WEIGHT table
4 : the basic unit of verse meter consisting of any of various fixed combinations or groups of stressed and unstressed or long and short syllables
5 a : motion or power of walking or running : STEP ⟨fleet of *foot*⟩ **b** : SPEED, SWIFTNESS ⟨showed early *foot*⟩
6 : something resembling a foot in position or use: as **a** : the lower end of the leg of a chair or table **b** (1) : the basal portion of the sporogonium in mosses (2) : a specialized outgrowth by which the embryonic sporophyte of many ferns and related plants and some seed plants absorbs nourishment from the gametophyte **c** : a piece on a sewing machine that presses the cloth against the feed
7 *foot plural, chiefly British* : INFANTRY
8 : the lower edge (as of a sail)
9 : the lowest part : BOTTOM ⟨the *foot* of the hill⟩
10 a : the end that is lower or opposite the head ⟨the *foot* of the bed⟩ **b** : the part (as of a stocking) that covers the foot
11 foots *plural but singular or plural in construction* : material deposited especially in aging or refining : DREGS
12 foots *plural* : FOOTLIGHTS
— **at one's feet** : under one's spell or influence
— **foot in the door** : the initial step toward a goal
— **off one's feet** : in a sitting or lying position
— **on foot** : by walking or running ⟨tour the campus *on foot*⟩
— **on one's feet 1** : in a standing position **2** : in an established position or state **3** : in a

recovered condition (as from illness) ⟨back *on my feet*⟩ **4** : in an extemporaneous manner : while in action ⟨good debaters can think on their *feet*⟩
— **to one's feet** : to a standing position ⟨brought the crowd *to its feet*⟩

²foot (15th century)
intransitive verb
1 : DANCE
2 : to go on foot
3 *of a sailboat* : to make speed : MOVE
transitive verb
1 a : to perform the movements of (a dance) **b** : to walk, run, or dance on, over, or through
2 *archaic* **a** : KICK **b** : REJECT
3 *archaic* : ESTABLISH
4 a : to add up **b** : to pay or stand credit for ⟨*foot* the bill⟩
5 : to make or renew the foot of (as a stocking)

foot·age \'fu-tij\ *noun* (1892)
: length or quantity expressed in feet: as **a** : BOARD FEET **b** : the total number of running feet of motion-picture film used (as for a scene or subject); *also* : the material contained on such footage

foot–and–mouth disease *noun* (1862)
: an acute contagious febrile virus disease especially of cloven-footed animals marked by ulcerating vesicles in the mouth, about the hooves, and on the udder and teats — called also *foot-and-mouth, hoof-and-mouth disease*

foot·ball \'fut-,bòl\ *noun* (15th century)
1 : any of several games played between two teams on a rectangular field having two goalposts at each end and whose object is to get the ball over a goal line or between goalposts by running, passing, or kicking: as **a** *British* : SOCCER **b** *British* : RUGBY **c** : an American game played between two teams of 11 players each in which the ball is in possession of one side at a time and is advanced by running or passing **d** *Australian* : AUSTRALIAN RULES FOOTBALL **e** *Canadian* : CANADIAN FOOTBALL
2 a : an inflated oval ball used in the game of football **b** *British* : a soccer ball
3 : something treated roughly especially as the subject of a prolonged dispute ⟨the issue became a political *football* in Congress⟩
— **foot·ball·er** \-,bò-lər\ *noun*

foot·bath \'fut-,bath, -,bàth\ *noun* (1599)
: a bath (as at the entrance to an indoor swimming pool) for cleansing, warming, or disinfecting the feet

foot·board \'fut-,bōrd, -,bòrd\ *noun* (1766)
1 : a narrow platform on which to stand or brace the feet
2 : a board forming the foot of a bed

foot·boy \-,bòi\ *noun* (1590)
: a serving boy : PAGE, ATTENDANT

foot·bridge \'fut-,brij\ *noun* (14th century)
: a bridge for pedestrians

foot–can·dle \-'kan-d°l\ *noun* (1906)
: a unit of illuminance on a surface that is everywhere one foot from a uniform point source of light of one candle and equal to one lumen per square foot

foot·cloth \-,klòth\ *noun* (14th century)
1 *archaic* : an ornamental cloth draped over the back of a horse to reach the ground on each side
2 : CARPET

foot–drag·ger \-,dra-gər\ *noun* (1957)
: one who engages in foot-dragging

foot–drag·ging \-,dra-gin\ *noun* (1952)
: failure to act with the necessary promptness or vigor

foot·ed \'fu-təd\ *adjective* (14th century)
: having a foot or feet especially of a specified kind or number — often used in combination ⟨a four-*footed* animal⟩

foot·er \'fu-tər\ *noun* (1608)
archaic : PEDESTRIAN

-foot·er \'fu-tər\ *noun combining form*
: one that is a specified number of feet in height, length, or breadth ⟨a six-*footer*⟩

foot·fall \'fŭt-ˌfȯl\ *noun* (1610)
: the sound of a footstep

foot fault *noun* (1886)
: an infraction of the service rules (as in tennis, racquetball, or volleyball) that results from illegal placement of the server's feet
— **foot·fault** \'fŭt-ˌfȯlt\ *intransitive verb*

foot·gear \'fŭt-ˌgir\ *noun* (1837)
: FOOTWEAR

foot·hill \-ˌhil\ *noun* (1850)
1 : a hill at the foot of higher hills
2 *plural* : a hilly region at the base of a mountain range

foot·hold \-ˌhōld\ *noun* (1625)
1 : a hold for the feet : FOOTING
2 : a position usable as a base for further advance

foot·ing \'fŭ-tiŋ\ *noun* (14th century)
1 : a stable position or placing of the feet
2 : a surface or its condition with respect to one walking or running on it; *especially* : the condition of a racetrack
3 : the act of moving on foot : STEP, TREAD
4 a : a place or space for standing : FOOTHOLD
b : established position : STATUS; *especially* : position or rank in relation to others ⟨they all started off on an equal *footing*⟩
5 : BASIS
6 : terms of social intercourse
7 : an enlargement at the lower end of a foundation wall, pier, or column to distribute the load
8 : the sum of a column of figures

foot·lam·bert \'fŭt-ˌlam-bərt\ *noun* (1925)
: a unit of luminance equal to the luminance of a perfectly diffusing surface that emits or reflects one lumen per square foot

foo·tle \'fü-tᵊl\ *intransitive verb* **foo·tled;** **foo·tling** \-tᵊl-iŋ, 'fŭt-liŋ\ [alteration of *footer* (to footle)] (1892)
1 : to talk or act foolishly
2 : to waste time : TRIFLE, FOOL
— **footle** *noun*
— **foo·tler** \-tᵊl-ər, 'fŭt-lər\ *noun*

foot·less \'fŭt-ləs\ *adjective* (14th century)
1 a : having no feet **b** : lacking foundation : UNSUBSTANTIAL
2 : STUPID, INEPT
— **foot·less·ly** *adverb*
— **foot·less·ness** *noun*

foot·lights \-ˌlīts\ *noun plural* (circa 1839)
1 : a row of lights set across the front of a stage floor
2 : the stage as a profession

foo·tling \'fü-tᵊl-iŋ, 'fŭt-liŋ\ *adjective* [*footle*] (circa 1897)
1 : lacking judgment or ability : INEPT ⟨*footling* amateurs who understand nothing —E. R. Bentley⟩
2 : lacking use or value : TRIVIAL

foot·lock·er \'fŭt-ˌlä-kər\ *noun* (circa 1942)
: a small trunk designed to be placed at the foot of a bed (as in a barracks)

foot·loose \-ˌlüs\ *adjective* (1873)
: having no ties : free to move about

foot·man \-mən\ *noun* (14th century)
1 a *archaic* : a traveler on foot : PEDESTRIAN **b** : INFANTRYMAN
2 a : a servant in livery formerly attending a rider or required to run in front of his master's carriage **b** : a servant who serves at table, tends the door, and runs errands

foot·mark \-ˌmärk\ *noun* (1826)
: FOOTPRINT

¹foot·note \-ˌnōt\ *noun* (1822)
1 : a note of reference, explanation, or comment usually placed below the text on a printed page
2 : something that is subordinately related to a larger event or work : COMMENTARY ⟨that biography is an illuminating *footnote* to our times⟩

²footnote *transitive verb* (1864)
: to furnish with a footnote : ANNOTATE

foot·pace \'fŭt-ˌpās\ *noun* (1538)
1 : a walking pace
2 : PLATFORM, DAIS

¹foot·pad \-ˌpad\ *noun* [*foot* + *pad* (highwayman)] (1683)
: one who robs a pedestrian

²footpad *noun* [*foot* + ¹*pad*] (1966)
: a flattish foot on the leg of a spacecraft for distributing weight to minimize sinking into a surface

foot·path \'fŭt-ˌpath, -ˌpàth\ *noun* (1526)
: a narrow path for pedestrians

foot–pound \-ˈpaúnd\ *noun, plural* **foot–pounds** (1850)
: a unit of work equal to the work done by a force of one pound acting through a distance of one foot in the direction of the force

foot–pound–second *adjective* (1892)
: being or relating to a system of units based upon the foot as the unit of length, the pound as the unit of weight and the second as the unit of time — abbreviation *fps*

foot·print \'fŭt-ˌprint\ *noun* (1552)
1 : an impression of the foot on a surface
2 : the area on a surface covered by something ⟨a tire with a wide *footprint*⟩ ⟨the *footprint* of a laser beam on the surface of a planet⟩

foot·race \-ˌrās\ *noun* (1663)
: a race run by humans on foot

foot·rest \-ˌrest\ *noun* (1861)
: a support for the feet

foot·rope \-ˌrōp\ *noun* (1772)
1 : the part of a boltrope sewed to the lower edge of a sail
2 : a rope rigged below a yard for men to stand on

foot rot *noun* (1807)
1 : a progressive inflammation of the feet of sheep or cattle that is associated with bacterial infection
2 : a plant disease marked by rot of the stem near the ground

foot·sie *or* **foot·sy** \'fŭt-sē\ *noun* [diminutive of ¹*foot*] (1944)
1 : a furtive flirtatious caressing with the feet (as under a table)
2 : a usually surreptitious cooperation or negotiation with someone supposed hostile to one's own interests — usually used with *play*

foot·slog \'fŭt-ˌsläg\ *intransitive verb* (1899)
: to march or tramp through mud
— **foot·slog·ger** *noun*

foot soldier *noun* (1622)
: INFANTRYMAN

foot·sore \'fŭt-ˌsōr, -ˌsȯr\ *adjective* (1719)
: having sore or tender feet (as from much walking)
— **foot·sore·ness** *noun*

foot·step \-ˌstep\ *noun* (13th century)
1 : the mark of the foot : TRACK
2 a : TREAD **b** : distance covered by a step : PACE
3 : a step on which to ascend or descend
4 : a way of life, conduct, or action ⟨followed in his father's *footsteps*⟩

foot·stone \-ˌstōn\ *noun* (1724)
: a stone placed at the foot of a grave

foot·stool \-ˌstül\ *noun* (1530)
: a low stool used to support the feet

foot·wall \-ˌwȯl\ *noun* (1860)
1 : the lower underlying wall of a vein, ore deposit, or coal seam in a mine
2 : the lower wall of an inclined fault

foot·way \-ˌwā\ *noun* (15th century)
: a narrow way or path for pedestrians

foot·wear \-ˌwar, -ˌwer\ *noun* (1881)
: wearing apparel (as shoes or boots) for the feet

foot·work \-ˌwərk\ *noun* (1895)
1 : the management of the feet (as in boxing); *also* : the work done with them
2 : the activity of moving from place to place ⟨the investigation entailed a lot of *footwork*⟩
3 : active and adroit maneuvering to achieve an end ⟨fancy political *footwork*⟩

¹foo·zle \'fü-zəl\ *noun* (1890)
: an act of foozling; *especially* : a bungling golf stroke

²foozle *transitive verb* **foo·zled; foo·zling** \'füz-liŋ, 'fü-zə-\ [perhaps from German dialect *fuseln* to work carelessly] (1892)
: to manage or play awkwardly : BUNGLE

¹fop \'fäp\ *noun* [Middle English; akin to Middle English *fobben* to deceive, Middle High German *voppen*] (15th century)
1 *obsolete* : a foolish or silly person
2 : a man who is devoted to or vain about his appearance or dress : COXCOMB, DANDY

²fop *transitive verb* **fopped; fop·ping** (1602) *obsolete* : FOOL, DUPE

fop·pery \'fä-p(ə-)rē\ *noun, plural* **-per·ies** (1546)
1 : foolish character or action : FOLLY
2 : the behavior or dress of a fop

fop·pish \'fä-pish\ *adjective* (1599)
1 *obsolete* : FOOLISH, SILLY
2 a : characteristic of a fop ⟨a *foppish* dressing gown⟩ **b** : behaving or dressing in the manner of a fop
— **fop·pish·ly** *adverb*
— **fop·pish·ness** *noun*

¹for \fər, (ˈ)fȯr, *Southern also* (ˈ)fär\ *preposition* [Middle English, from Old English; akin to Latin *per* through, *prae* before, *pro* before, for, ahead, Greek *pro*, Old English *faran* to go — more at FARE] (before 12th century)
1 a — used as a function word to indicate purpose ⟨a grant *for* studying medicine⟩ **b** — used as a function word to indicate an intended goal ⟨left *for* home⟩ ⟨acted *for* the best⟩ **c** — used as a function word to indicate the object or recipient of a perception, desire, or activity ⟨now *for* a good rest⟩ ⟨run *for* your life⟩ ⟨an eye *for* a bargain⟩
2 a : as being or constituting ⟨taken *for* a fool⟩ ⟨eggs *for* breakfast⟩ **b** — used as a function word to indicate an actual or implied enumeration or selection ⟨*for* one thing, the price is too high⟩
3 : because of ⟨can't sleep *for* the heat⟩
4 — used as a function word to indicate suitability or fitness ⟨it is not *for* you to choose⟩ ⟨ready *for* action⟩
5 a : in place of ⟨go to the store *for* me⟩ **b** (1) : on behalf of : REPRESENTING ⟨speaks *for* the court⟩ (2) : in favor of ⟨all *for* the plan⟩
6 : in spite of — usually used with *all* ⟨*for* all his large size, he moves gracefully⟩
7 : with respect to : CONCERNING ⟨a stickler *for* detail⟩ ⟨heavy *for* its size⟩
8 a — used as a function word to indicate equivalence in exchange ⟨$10 *for* a hat⟩, equality in number or quantity ⟨point *for* point⟩, or correspondence or correlation ⟨*for* every one that works, you'll find five that don't⟩ **b** — used as a function word to indicate number of attempts ⟨0 *for* 4⟩
9 — used as a function word to indicate duration of time or extent of space ⟨gone *for* two days⟩
10 : in honor of : AFTER ⟨named *for* her grandmother⟩

²for *conjunction* (12th century)
: for the reason that : on this ground : BECAUSE

for- *prefix* [Middle English, from Old English; akin to Old High German *far-* for-, Old English ¹*for*]
1 : so as to involve prohibition, exclusion, omission, failure, neglect, or refusal ⟨*for*bid⟩
2 : destructively or detrimentally ⟨*for*do⟩
3 : completely : excessively : to exhaustion : to pieces ⟨*for*spent⟩

fora *plural of* FORUM

¹for·age \'fȯr-ij, 'fär-\ *noun* [Middle English, from Old French, from *forre* fodder, of Germanic origin; akin to Old High German *fuotar* food, fodder — more at FOOD] (14th century)

1 : food for animals especially when taken by browsing or grazing
2 [²*forage*] **:** the act of foraging **:** search for provisions
²**forage** *verb* **for·aged; for·ag·ing** (15th century)
transitive verb
1 : to strip of provisions **:** collect forage from
2 : to secure by foraging ⟨*foraged* a chicken for the feast⟩
intransitive verb
1 : to wander in search of forage or food
2 : to secure forage (as for horses) by stripping the country
3 : RAVAGE, RAID
4 : to make a search **:** RUMMAGE
— **for·ag·er** *noun*
fo·ram \ˈfōr-əm, ˈfȯr-\ *noun* (1927)
: FORAMINIFER
fo·ra·men \fə-ˈrā-mən\ *noun, plural* **fo·ram·i·na** \-ˈra-mə-nə\ *or* **fo·ra·mens** \-ˈrā-mənz\ [Latin *foramin-, foramen,* from *forare* to bore — more at BORE] (1671)
: a small opening, perforation, or orifice **:** FENESTRA
— **fo·ram·i·nal** \fə-ˈra-mə-nᵊl\ *or* **fo·ram·i·nous** \-mə-nəs\ *adjective*
fo·ra·men mag·num \fə-ˌrā-mən-ˈmag-nəm\ *noun* [New Latin, literally, large opening] (1860)
: the opening in the skull through which the spinal cord passes to become the medulla oblongata
foramen ova·le \-ō-ˈva-lē, -ˈvä-, -ˈvā-\ *noun* [New Latin, literally, oval opening] (circa 1860)
: an opening in the septum between the two atria of the heart that is normally present only in the fetus
fo·ra·min·i·fer \ˌfōr-ə-ˈmi-nə-fər, ˌfär-\ *noun* (circa 1842)
: any of an order (Foraminifera) of large chiefly marine rhizopod protozoans usually having calcareous shells that often are perforated with minute holes for protrusion of slender pseudopodia and form the bulk of chalk and nummulitic limestone
— **fo·ra·mi·nif·er·al** \fə-ˌra-mə-ˈni-f(ə-)rəl; ˌfōr-ə-mə-ˈni-, ˌfär-\ *adjective*
fo·ra·mi·nif·era \fə-ˌra-mə-ˈni-f(ə-)rə; ˌfōr-ə-mə-ˈni-, ˌfär-\ *noun plural* [New Latin, from Latin *foramin-, foramen* + *-fera,* neuter plural of *-fer* -fer] (circa 1836)
: organisms that are foraminifers
fo·ra·mi·nif·er·an \-f(ə-)rən\ *noun* (1920)
: FORAMINIFER
for and *conjunction* (circa 1529)
obsolete **:** and also
for·as·much as \ˈfȯr-əz-ˌmə-chəz\ *conjunction* (13th century)
: in view of the fact that
¹**for·ay** \ˈfȯr-ˌā, ˈfȯr-, ˈfär- *also* fȯ-ˈrā *or* fə-ˈ\ *verb* [Middle English *forrayen,* from Middle French *forrer,* from *forre* fodder — more at FORAGE] (14th century)
transitive verb
archaic **:** to ravage in search of spoils **:** PILLAGE
intransitive verb
: to make a raid or brief invasion ⟨*forayed* into enemy territory⟩
— **for·ay·er** *noun*
²**foray** *noun* (14th century)
1 : a sudden or irregular invasion or attack for war or spoils **:** RAID
2 : a brief excursion or attempt especially outside one's accustomed sphere ⟨the novelist's *foray* into nonfiction⟩
forb \ˈfȯrb\ *noun* [Greek *phorbē* fodder, food, from *pherbein* to graze] (1924)
: an herb other than grass
¹**for·bear** \fȯr-ˈbar, fər-, -ˈber\ *verb* **-bore** \-ˈbōr, -ˈbȯr\; **-borne** \-ˈbōrn, -ˈbȯrn\; **-bear·ing** [Middle English *forberen,* from Old English *forberan* to endure, do without, from *for-* + *beran* to bear] (before 12th century)

transitive verb
1 *obsolete* **:** to do without
2 : to hold oneself back from especially with an effort
3 *obsolete* **:** to leave alone **:** SHUN ⟨*forbear* his presence —Shakespeare⟩
intransitive verb
1 : HOLD BACK, ABSTAIN ⟨can write with ease what I *forbear* to read —Flannery O'Connor⟩
2 : to control oneself when provoked **:** be patient
— **for·bear·er** *noun*
²**forbear** *variant of* FOREBEAR
for·bear·ance \fȯr-ˈbar-ən(t)s, fər-, -ˈber-\ *noun* (1576)
1 : a refraining from the enforcement of something (as a debt, right, or obligation) that is due
2 : the act of forbearing **:** PATIENCE
3 : the quality of being forbearing **:** LENIENCY
¹**for·bid** \fər-ˈbid, fȯr-\ *transitive verb* **-bade** \-ˈbad, -ˈbād\ *also* **-bad** \-ˈbad\; **-bid·den** \-ˈbi-dᵊn\; **-bid·ding** [Middle English *forbidden,* from Old English *forbēodan,* from *for-* + *bēodan* to bid — more at BID] (before 12th century)
1 : to proscribe from or as if from the position of one in authority **:** command against ⟨the law *forbids* stores to sell liquor to minors⟩ ⟨her mother *forbids* her to go⟩
2 : to hinder or prevent as if by an effectual command ⟨space *forbids* further treatment here⟩ ☆
— **for·bid·der** *noun*
²**forbid** *adjective* (1606)
archaic **:** ACCURSED ⟨he shall live a man *forbid* —Shakespeare⟩
for·bid·dance \fər-ˈbi-dᵊn(t)s, fȯr-\ *noun* (circa 1611)
: the act of forbidding
for·bid·den \-ˈbi-dᵊn\ *adjective* (13th century)
1 : not permitted or allowed
2 : not conforming to the usual selection principles — used of quantum phenomena ⟨*forbidden* transition⟩ ⟨*forbidden* radiation⟩ ⟨*forbidden* spectral line⟩
forbidden fruit *noun* [from the forbidden fruit of the Garden of Eden in Genesis 3:2–19] (1662)
: an immoral or illegal pleasure
for·bid·ding *adjective* (1712)
1 : such as to make approach or passage difficult or impossible ⟨*forbidding* walls⟩
2 : DISAGREEABLE, REPELLENT ⟨a *forbidding* task⟩
3 : GRIM, MENACING ⟨a dark *forbidding* sky⟩
— **for·bid·ding·ly** \-ˈbi-diŋ-lē\ *adverb*
forbode *variant of* FOREBODE
¹**for·by** *or* **for·bye** \fȯr-ˈbī\ *preposition* [Middle English *forby,* preposition & adverb, from *fore-* + *by*] (14th century)
1 *archaic* **a :** PAST **b :** NEAR
2 *chiefly Scottish* **:** BESIDES
²**forby** *or* **forbye** *adverb* (1590)
chiefly Scottish **:** BESIDES **:** in addition
¹**force** \ˈfōrs, ˈfȯrs\ *noun* [Middle English, from Middle French, from (assumed) Vulgar Latin *fortia,* from Latin *fortis* strong] (14th century)
1 a (1) **:** strength or energy exerted or brought to bear **:** cause of motion or change **:** active power ⟨the *forces* of nature⟩ ⟨the motivating *force* in her life⟩ (2) *usually capitalized* — used with a number to indicate the strength of the wind according to the Beaufort scale ⟨a *Force* 10 hurricane⟩ **b :** moral or mental strength **c :** capacity to persuade or convince ⟨the *force* of the argument⟩
2 a : military strength **b** (1) **:** a body (as of troops or ships) assigned to a military purpose (2) *plural* **:** the whole military strength (as of a nation) **c :** a body of persons or things available for a particular end ⟨a labor *force*⟩ ⟨the missile *force*⟩ **d :** an individual or group having the power of effective action ⟨join *forces*

to prevent violence⟩ ⟨a *force* in politics⟩ **e** *often capitalized* **:** POLICE FORCE — usually used with *the*
3 : violence, compulsion, or constraint exerted upon or against a person or thing
4 a : an agency or influence that if applied to a free body results chiefly in an acceleration of the body and sometimes in elastic deformation and other effects **b :** any of the natural influences (as electromagnetism, gravity, the strong force, and the weak force) that exist especially between particles and determine the structure of the universe
5 : the quality of conveying impressions intensely in writing or speech
synonym *see* POWER
— **force·less** \-ləs\ *adjective*
— **in force 1 :** in great numbers ⟨picnickers were out *in force*⟩ **2 :** VALID, OPERATIVE ⟨the ban remains *in force*⟩
²**force** *transitive verb* **forced; forc·ing** (14th century)
1 : to do violence to; *especially* **:** RAPE
2 : to compel by physical, moral, or intellectual means
3 : to make or cause especially through natural or logical necessity ⟨*forced* to admit my error⟩
4 a : to press, drive, attain to, or effect against resistance or inertia ⟨*force* your way through⟩ **b :** to impose or thrust urgently, importunately, or inexorably ⟨*force* unwanted attentions on a woman⟩
5 : to achieve or win by strength in struggle or violence: as **a :** to win one's way into ⟨*force* a castle⟩ ⟨*forced* the mountain passes⟩ **b :** to break open or through ⟨*force* a lock⟩
6 a : to raise or accelerate to the utmost ⟨*forcing* the pace⟩ **b :** to produce only with unnatural or unwilling effort ⟨*forced* a smile⟩ **c :** to wrench, strain, or use (language) with marked unnaturalness and lack of ease
7 a : to hasten the rate of progress or growth of **b :** to bring (as plants) to maturity out of the normal season ⟨*forcing* lilies for Easter⟩
8 : to induce (as a particular bid or play by another player) in a card game by some conventional act, play, bid, or response
9 a : to cause (a runner in baseball) to be put out on a force-out **b :** to cause (a run) to be scored in baseball by giving a base on balls when the bases are full ☆
— **forc·er** *noun*
— **force one's hand :** to cause one to act precipitously **:** force one to reveal one's purpose or intention
forced \ˈfōrst, ˈfȯrst\ *adjective* (circa 1537)
1 : compelled by force or necessity **:** INVOLUNTARY ⟨a *forced* landing⟩
2 : done or produced with effort, exertion, or pressure ⟨a *forced* laugh⟩
— **forc·ed·ly** \ˈfōr-səd-lē, ˈfȯr-\ *adverb*
force–feed *transitive verb* **-fed; -feed·ing** (1901)
1 : to feed (as an animal) by forcible administration of food

☆ **SYNONYMS**
Forbid, prohibit, interdict, inhibit mean to debar one from doing something or to order that something not be done. FORBID implies that the order is from one in authority and that obedience is expected ⟨smoking is *forbidden* in the building⟩. PROHIBIT suggests the issuing of laws, statutes, or regulations ⟨*prohibited* the sale of liquor⟩. INTERDICT implies prohibition by civil or ecclesiastical authority usually for a given time or a declared purpose ⟨practices *interdicted* by the church⟩. INHIBIT implies the imposition of restraints or restrictions that amount to prohibitions, not only by authority but also by the exigencies of the time or situation ⟨conditions *inhibiting* the growth of free trade⟩.

2 : to force to take in ⟨*force-feed* students the classics⟩ — also used with a single object ⟨*force-feed* the classics to students⟩ ⟨*force-feed* students with the classics⟩

force·ful \'fōrs-fəl, 'fȯrs-\ *adjective* (1571)
: possessing or filled with force **:** EFFECTIVE
— **force·ful·ly** \-fə-lē\ *adverb*
— **force·ful·ness** *noun*

force ma·jeure \ˌfȯr-smä-'zhər, ˌfȯr-, -smə-\ *noun* [French, superior force] (1883)
1 : superior or irresistible force
2 : an event or effect that cannot be reasonably anticipated or controlled — compare ACT OF GOD

force·meat \'fōrs-ˌmēt, 'fȯrs-\ *noun* [*force* (alteration of ²*farce*) + *meat*] (circa 1688)
: finely chopped and highly seasoned meat or fish that is either served alone or used as a stuffing — called also *farce*

force of habit (circa 1925)
: behavior made involuntary or automatic by repeated practice

force of nature (1981)
: FORCE 4b

force·out \'fōrs-ˌaut, 'fȯrs-\ *noun* (1896)
: a play in baseball in which a runner is put out by being forced to advance to the next base but failing to do so safely

force play *noun* (1912)
: FORCE-OUT

for·ceps \'fȯr-səps, -ˌseps\ *noun, plural* **forceps** [Latin, tongs, perhaps from *formus* warm + *capere* to take — more at THERM, HEAVE] (1634)
: an instrument for grasping, holding firmly, or exerting traction upon objects especially for delicate operations (as by jewelers or surgeons)
— **for·ceps·like** \-ˌlīk\ *adjective*

force pump *noun* (1659)
: a pump with a solid piston for drawing and forcing through valves a liquid (as water) to a considerable height above the pump or under a considerable pressure

forc·ible \'fōr-sə-bəl, 'fȯr-\ *adjective* (15th century)
1 : effected by force used against opposition or resistance
2 : characterized by force, efficiency, or energy **:** POWERFUL
— **forc·ible·ness** *noun*
— **forc·ibly** \-blē\ *adverb*

¹**ford** \'fōrd, 'fȯrd\ *noun* [Middle English, from Old English; akin to Old Norse *fjǫrthr* fjord, Latin *portus* port, Old English *faran* to go — more at FARE] (before 12th century)
: a shallow part of a body of water that may be crossed by wading

²**ford** *transitive verb* (1614)
: to cross (a body of water) by wading
— **ford·able** \'fōr-də-bəl, 'fȯr-\ *adjective*

for·do \fȯr-'dü, fōr-\ *transitive verb* **-did** \-'did\; **-done** \-'dən\; **-do·ing** \-'dü-iŋ\ [Middle English *fordon*, from Old English *fordōn*, from *for-* + *dōn* to do] (before 12th century)
1 *archaic* **:** to do away with **:** DESTROY
2 : to overcome with fatigue — used only as past participle ⟨quite *fordone* with the heat⟩

¹**fore** \'fōr, 'fȯr\ *adverb* [Middle English, from Old English; akin to Old English *for*] (before 12th century)
1 *obsolete* **:** at an earlier time or period
2 : in, toward, or adjacent to the front **:** FORWARD

²**fore** *also* ¹**fore** *preposition* (before 12th century)
1 *chiefly dialect* **:** BEFORE
2 : in the presence of

³**fore** *adjective* [*fore-*] (15th century)
1 : situated in front of something else **:** FORWARD
2 : prior in order of occurrence **:** FORMER

⁴**fore** *noun* (1842)
: something that occupies a front position
— **to the fore :** in or into a position of prominence **:** FORWARD

⁵**fore** *interjection* [probably short for *before*] (circa 1878)
— used by a golfer to warn anyone within range of the probable line of flight of the ball

fore- *combining form* [Middle English *for-*, *fore-*, from Old English *fore-*, from *fore*, adverb]
1 a : earlier **:** beforehand ⟨*foresee*⟩ **b :** occurring earlier **:** occurring beforehand ⟨*foreshock*⟩
2 a : situated at the front **:** in front ⟨*foreleg*⟩ **b :** front part of (something specified) ⟨*forearm*⟩
c : foremast ⟨*foretop*⟩

fore–and–aft \ˌfōr-ə-'naft, ˌfȯr-\ *adjective* (1820)
1 : lying, running, or acting in the general line of the length of a construction (as a ship or a house) **:** LONGITUDINAL
2 : having no square sails

fore and aft *adverb* (circa 1618)
1 : lengthwise of a ship **:** from stem to stern
2 : in, at, or toward both the bow and stern
3 : in or at the front and back or the beginning and end

fore–and–aft·er \-'naf-tər\ *noun* (1823)
: a ship with a fore-and-aft rig; *especially* **:** SCHOONER

fore–and–aft rig *noun* (1879)
: a sailing-ship rig in which most or all of the sails are not attached to yards but are bent to gaffs or set on the masts or on stays in a fore-and-aft line

¹**fore·arm** \(ˌ)fōr-'ärm, (ˌ)fȯr-\ *transitive verb* (1592)
: to arm in advance **:** PREPARE

²**fore·arm** \'fōr-ˌärm, 'fȯr-\ *noun* (1741)
: the part of the arm between the elbow and the wrist; *also* **:** the corresponding part in other vertebrates

fore·bay \'fōr-ˌbā, 'fȯr-\ *noun* (1770)
: a reservoir or canal from which water is taken to run equipment (as a waterwheel or turbine)

fore·bear \-ˌbar, -ˌber\ *noun* [Middle English (Scots), from *fore-* + *-bear* (from *been* to be)] (15th century)
: ANCESTOR, FOREFATHER; *also* **:** PRECURSOR — usually used in plural

fore·bode \(ˌ)fōr-'bōd, (ˌ)fȯr-\ (1603)
transitive verb
1 : to have an inward conviction of (as coming ill or misfortune)
2 : FORETELL, PORTEND
intransitive verb
: AUGUR, PREDICT
— **fore·bod·er** *noun*

¹**fore·bod·ing** \-'bō-diŋ\ *noun* (14th century)
: the act of one who forebodes; *also* **:** an omen, prediction, or presentiment especially of coming evil **:** PORTENT

²**foreboding** *adjective* (1679)
: indicative of or marked by foreboding
— **fore·bod·ing·ly** \-diŋ-lē\ *adverb*
— **fore·bod·ing·ness** *noun*

fore·brain \'fōr-ˌbrān, 'fȯr-\ *noun* (1879)
: the anterior of the three primary divisions of the developing vertebrate brain or the corresponding part of the adult brain that includes especially the cerebral hemispheres, the thalamus, and the hypothalamus and that especially in higher vertebrates is the main control center for sensory and associative information processing, visceral functions, and voluntary motor functions — called also *prosencephalon*; compare DIENCEPHALON, TELENCEPHALON

fore·cad·die \-ˌka-dē\ *noun* (1792)
: a golf caddie who is stationed in the fairway and who indicates the position of balls on the course

¹**fore·cast** \-ˌkast; fōr-'kast, fȯr-\ *verb* **forecast** *also* **fore·cast·ed; fore·cast·ing** (15th century)
transitive verb
1 a : to calculate or predict (some future event or condition) usually as a result of study and analysis of available pertinent data; *especially* **:** to predict (weather conditions) on the basis of correlated meteorological observations **b :** to indicate as likely to occur
2 : to serve as a forecast of **:** PRESAGE ⟨such events may *forecast* peace⟩
intransitive verb
: to calculate the future
synonym see FORETELL
— **fore·cast·able** \-ˌkas-tə-bəl\ *adjective*
— **fore·cast·er** *noun*

²**fore·cast** \'fōr-ˌkast, 'fȯr-\ *noun* (circa 1541)
1 *archaic* **:** foresight of consequences and provision against them **:** FORETHOUGHT
2 : a prophecy, estimate, or prediction of a future happening or condition

fore·cas·tle \'fōk-səl; 'fōr-ˌka-səl, 'fȯr-\ *noun* (15th century)
1 : the forward part of the upper deck of a ship
2 : the crew's quarters usually in a ship's bow

fore·check \'fōr-ˌchek, 'fȯr-\ *intransitive verb* (1951)
: to check an opponent in ice hockey in his own defensive zone
— **fore·check·er** \-ˌche-kər\ *noun*

fore·close \(ˌ)fōr-'klōz, (ˌ)fȯr-\ *verb* [Middle English, from Middle French *forclos*, past participle of *forclore*, from *fors* outside (from Latin *foris*) + *clore* to close — more at FORUM] (15th century)
transitive verb
1 : to shut out **:** PRECLUDE
2 : to hold exclusively
3 : to deal with or close in advance
4 : to subject to foreclosure proceedings
intransitive verb
: to foreclose a mortgage

fore·clo·sure \-'klō-zhər\ *noun* (1728)
: an act or instance of foreclosing; *specifically* **:** a legal proceeding that bars or extinguishes a mortgagor's right of redeeming a mortgaged estate

fore·court \'fōr-ˌkōrt, 'fȯr-, -ˌkȯrt\ *noun* (1535)
1 : an open court in front of a building
2 : the area near the net in a court game

fore·deck \'fōr-ˌdek, 'fȯr-\ *noun* (1565)
: the forepart of a ship's main deck

fore·do *variant of* FORDO

fore·doom \(ˌ)fōr-'düm, (ˌ)fȯr-\ *transitive verb* (1603)
: DOOM 2

fore·face \'fōr-ˌfās, 'fȯr-\ *noun* (1545)
: the part of the head of a quadruped that is in front of the eyes

fore·fa·ther \-ˌfä-<u>th</u>ər, -ˌfȧ-\ *noun* (14th century)
1 : ANCESTOR 1a
2 : a person of an earlier period and common heritage

☆ **SYNONYMS**
Force, compel, coerce, constrain, oblige mean to make someone or something yield. FORCE is the general term and implies the overcoming of resistance by the exertion of strength, power, or duress ⟨*forced* to flee for their lives⟩. COMPEL typically suggests overcoming of resistance or unwillingness by an irresistible force ⟨*compelled* to admit my mistake⟩. COERCE suggests overcoming resistance or unwillingness by actual or threatened violence or pressure ⟨*coerced* into signing over the rights⟩. CONSTRAIN suggests the effect of a force or circumstance that limits freedom of action or choice ⟨*constrained* by conscience⟩. OBLIGE implies the constraint of necessity, law, or duty ⟨felt *obliged* to go⟩.

\ə\ abut \ᵊ\ kitten \ər\ further \a\ ash \ā\ ace
\ä\ mop, mar \au̇\ out \ch\ chin \e\ easy
\g\ go \i\ hit \ī\ ice \j\ job \ŋ\ sing \ō\ go
\ȯ\ law \ȯi\ boy \th\ thin \<u>th</u>\ the \ü\ loot \u̇\ foot
\y\ yet \zh\ vision *see also* Guide to Pronunciation

fore·feel \(ˌ)fōr-'fēl, (ˌ)fòr-\ *transitive verb* **-felt** \-'felt\; **-feel·ing** (1580)
: to have a presentiment of

fore·fend *variant of* FORFEND

fore·fin·ger \'fōr-ˌfiŋ-gər, 'fòr-\ *noun* (15th century)
: the finger next to the thumb — called also *index finger*

fore·foot \-ˌfút\ *noun* (14th century)
1 a : one of the anterior feet especially of a quadruped **b** : the front part of the human foot **2** : the forward part of a ship where the stem and keel meet

fore·front \-ˌfrənt\ *noun* (15th century)
: the foremost part or place

fore·gath·er *variant of* FORGATHER

¹fore·go \fōr-'gō, fòr-\ *transitive verb* **-went** \-'went\; **-gone** \-'gòn *also* -'gän\; **-go·ing** \-'gō-iŋ, -'gó(-)iŋ\ (before 12th century)
: to go before : PRECEDE
— **fore·go·er** \-'gō-(-ə)r\ *noun*

²forego *variant of* FORGO

fore·go·ing \-'gō-iŋ, -'gó(-)iŋ\ *adjective* (15th century)
: listed, mentioned, or occurring before ⟨the *foregoing* statement can be proven⟩
synonym *see* PRECEDING

fore·gone \'fōr-ˌgòn, 'fòr- *also* -ˌgän\ *adjective* (circa 1600)
: PREVIOUS, PAST

foregone conclusion *noun* (1604)
1 : a conclusion that has preceded argument or examination
2 : an inevitable result : CERTAINTY ⟨the victory was a *foregone conclusion*⟩

¹fore·ground \'fōr-ˌgraùnd, 'fòr-\ *noun* (1695)
1 : the part of a scene or representation that is nearest to and in front of the spectator
2 : a position of prominence : FOREFRONT

²foreground *transitive verb* (1892)
: to bring to the foreground; *especially* : to give prominence or emphasis to

fore·gut \'fōr-ˌgət, 'fòr-\ *noun* (circa 1889)
: the anterior part of the alimentary canal of a vertebrate embryo that develops into the pharynx, esophagus, stomach, and extreme anterior part of the intestine

¹fore·hand \-ˌhand\ *noun* (1557)
1 *archaic* : superior position : ADVANTAGE
2 : the part of a horse that is before the rider
3 : a forehand stroke (as in tennis or racquets); *also* : the side on which such strokes are made

forehand 3

²forehand *adjective* (1599)
1 *obsolete* : done or given in advance : PRIOR
2 : made with the palm of the hand turned in the direction in which the hand is moving ⟨a *forehand* tennis stroke⟩

³forehand *adverb* (1925)
: with a forehand stroke

fore·hand·ed \(ˌ)fōr-'han-dəd, (ˌ)fòr-\ *adjective* (1650)
1 a : mindful of the future : PRUDENT **b** : WELL-TO-DO
2 : FOREHAND 2
— **fore·hand·ed·ly** *adverb*
— **fore·hand·ed·ness** *noun*

fore·head \'fär-əd, 'fòr-; 'fōr-ˌhed, 'fòr- *also* -ˌed\ *noun* (before 12th century)
1 : the part of the face above the eyes
2 : the front or forepart of something ⟨flames in the *forehead* of the morning sky —John Milton⟩

fore·hoof \'fōr-ˌhúf, 'fòr- -ˌhüf\ *noun* (1770)
: the hoof of a forefoot

for·eign \'fòr-ən, 'fär-\ *adjective* [Middle English *forein*, from Old French, from Late Latin *foranus* on the outside, from Latin *foris* outside — more at FORUM] (13th century)

1 : situated outside a place or country; *especially* : situated outside one's own country
2 : born in, belonging to, or characteristic of some place or country other than the one under consideration
3 : of, relating to, or proceeding from some other person or material thing than the one under consideration
4 : alien in character : not connected or pertinent
5 : related to or dealing with other nations
6 : occurring in an abnormal situation in the living body and often introduced from outside
7 : not being within the jurisdiction of a political unit (as a state)
synonym *see* EXTRINSIC
— **for·eign·ness** \-ən-nəs\ *noun*

foreign affairs *noun plural* (1611)
: matters having to do with international relations and with the interests of the home country in foreign countries

foreign aid *noun* (1949)
: assistance (as economic aid) provided by one nation to another

foreign bill *noun* (1682)
: a bill of exchange that is not both drawn and payable within a particular jurisdiction

for·eign–born \ˌfòr-ən-'bòrn, ˌfär-\ *adjective* (1856)
: foreign by birth

foreign correspondent *noun* (1948)
: a correspondent employed to send news or comment from a foreign country

for·eign·er \'fòr-ə-nər, 'fär-\ *noun* (15th century)
1 : a person belonging to or owing allegiance to a foreign country
2 *chiefly dialect* : one not native to a place or community : STRANGER 1c

foreign exchange *noun* (1691)
1 : a process of settling accounts or debts between persons residing in different countries
2 : foreign currency or current short-term credit instruments payable in such currency

for·eign·ism \'fòr-ə-ˌni-zəm, 'fär-\ *noun* (1855)
: something peculiar to a foreign language or people; *specifically* : a foreign idiom or custom

foreign minister *noun* (1709)
: a governmental minister for foreign affairs

foreign office *noun* (1859)
: a government office (as a ministry) that deals with foreign affairs

foreign policy *noun* (1859)
: the policy of a sovereign state in its interaction with other sovereign states

foreign service *noun* (1927)
: the field force of a foreign office comprising diplomatic and consular personnel

¹fore·judge \fər-'jəj, fōr-, fòr-\ *transitive verb* [Middle English *forjuggen*, from Middle French *forjugier*, from *fors* outside (from Latin *foris*) + *jugier* to judge] (15th century)
: to expel, oust, or put out by judgment of a court

²fore·judge \(ˌ)fōr-'jəj, (ˌ)fòr-\ *transitive verb* (1561)
: PREJUDGE

fore·know \(ˌ)fōr-'nō, (ˌ)fòr-\ *transitive verb* **-knew** \-'nü, -'nyü\; **-known** \-'nōn\; **-know·ing** (14th century)
: to have previous knowledge of : known beforehand especially by paranormal means or by revelation
synonym *see* FORESEE
— **fore·knowl·edge** \-'nä-lij\ *noun*

fore·la·dy \'fōr-ˌlā-dē, 'fòr-\ *noun* (circa 1889)
: FOREWOMAN

fore·land \'fōr-lənd, 'fòr-\ *noun* (14th century)
: PROMONTORY, HEADLAND

fore·leg \'fōr-ˌleg, 'fòr-, -ˌlāg\ *noun* (15th century)
: a front leg

fore·limb \-ˌlim\ *noun* (circa 1796)

: a limb (as an arm, wing, fin, or leg) that is situated anteriorly ⟨the *forelimb* of a bat⟩

fore·lock \-ˌläk\ *noun* (1589)
: a lock of hair growing from the front of the head

fore·man \'fōr-mən, 'fòr-\ *noun* (15th century)
: a first or chief person: as **a** : a member of a jury who acts as chairman and spokesman **b** (1) : a chief and often specially trained worker who works with and commonly leads a gang or crew (2) : a person in charge of a group of workers, a particular operation, or a section of a plant
— **fore·man·ship** \-ˌship\ *noun*

fore·mast \'fōr-ˌmast, 'fòr-, -məst\ *noun* (1582)
: the mast nearest the bow of a ship

¹fore·most \-ˌmōst\ *adjective* [Middle English *formest*, from Old English, superlative of *forma* first; akin to Old High German *fruma* advantage, Old English *fore* fore] (before 12th century)
1 : first in a series or progression
2 : of first rank or position : PREEMINENT

²foremost *adverb* (before 12th century)
1 : in the first place
2 : most importantly ⟨first and *foremost*⟩

fore·moth·er \'fōr-mə-<u>th</u>ər, 'fòr-\ *noun* (1582)
: a female ancestor

fore·name \-ˌnām\ *noun* (1533)
: a name that precedes one's surname

fore·named \-ˌnāmd\ *adjective* (13th century)
: named previously : AFORESAID

fore·noon \'fōr-ˌnün, 'fòr-ˌ, fōr-', 'fòr-\ *noun* (15th century)
: the early part of the day ending with noon : MORNING

¹fo·ren·sic \fə-'ren(t)-sik, -'ren-zik\ *adjective* [Latin *forensis* public, forensic, from *forum* forum] (1659)
1 : belonging to, used in, or suitable to courts of judicature or to public discussion and debate
2 : ARGUMENTATIVE, RHETORICAL
3 : relating to or dealing with the application of scientific knowledge to legal problems ⟨*forensic* medicine⟩ ⟨*forensic* science⟩ ⟨*forensic* pathologist⟩ ⟨*forensic* experts⟩
— **fo·ren·si·cal·ly** \-si-k(ə-)lē, -zi-\ *adverb*

²forensic *noun* (1814)
1 : an argumentative exercise
2 *plural but singular or plural in construction* : the art or study of argumentative discourse

fore·or·dain \ˌfōr-òr-'dān, ˌfòr-\ *transitive verb* (15th century)
: to dispose or appoint in advance : PREDESTINE
— **fore·or·di·na·tion** \-ˌòr-dᵊn-'ā-shən\ *noun*

fore·part \'fōr-ˌpärt, 'fòr-\ *noun* (14th century)
1 : the anterior part of something
2 : the earlier part of a period of time

fore·passed *or* **fore·past** \-ˌpast\ *adjective* (1557)
: BYGONE

fore·paw \-ˌpò\ *noun* (1825)
: the paw of a foreleg

fore·peak \-ˌpēk\ *noun* (1693)
: the extreme forward lower compartment or tank usually used for trimming or storage in a ship

fore·play \-ˌplā\ *noun* (1929)
1 : erotic stimulation preceding sexual intercourse
2 : action or behavior that precedes an event

fore·quar·ter \-ˌkwò(r)-tər, -ˌkòr-\ *noun* (15th century)
: the front half of a lateral half of the body or carcass of a quadruped ⟨a *forequarter* of beef⟩

fore·reach \fòr-'rēch, fòr-\ (1644)
intransitive verb
of a ship : to gain ground in tacking
transitive verb
: to gain on or go ahead of (a ship) when close-hauled

fore·run \-'rən\ *transitive verb* **-ran** \-'ran\; **-run; -run·ning** (before 12th century)
1 : to run before
2 : to come before as a token of something to follow
3 : FORESTALL, ANTICIPATE
fore·run·ner \'fōr-ˌrə-nər, 'fȯr-\ *noun* (13th century)
1 : one that precedes and indicates the approach of another: as **a** : a premonitory sign or symptom **b** : a skier who runs the course before the start of a race
2 : PREDECESSOR, ANCESTOR ☆
fore·said \-ˌsed\ *adjective* (before 12th century)
archaic : AFORESAID
fore·sail \'fōr-ˌsāl, 'fȯr-, -səl\ *noun* (15th century)
1 : the lowest sail set on the foremast of a square-rigged ship or schooner — see SAIL illustration
2 : the sole or principal headsail (as of a sloop, cutter, or schooner)
fore·see \fōr-'sē, fȯr-\ *transitive verb* **-saw** \-'sȯ\; **-seen** \-'sēn\; **-see·ing** (before 12th century)
: to see (as a development) beforehand ☆
— **fore·seer** \-'sē-ər, fȯr-, -'si-(ə)r\ *noun*
fore·see·able \-'sē-ə-bəl\ *adjective* (1804)
1 : being such as may be reasonably anticipated (*foreseeable* problems)
2 : lying within the range for which forecasts are possible (in the *foreseeable* future)
— **fore·see·abil·i·ty** \-ˌsē-ə-'bi-lə-tē\ *noun*
fore·shad·ow \-'sha-(ˌ)dō, -də-(w)\ *transitive verb* (1577)
: to represent, indicate, or typify beforehand : PREFIGURE
— **fore·shad·ow·er** \-də-wər\ *noun*
fore·shank \'fōr-ˌshaŋk, 'fȯr-\ *noun* (1924)
: the upper part of the foreleg of cattle; *also* : meat cut from this part
fore·sheet \-ˌshēt\ *noun* (1667)
1 : one of the sheets of a foresail
2 *plural* : the forward part of an open boat
fore·shock \-ˌshäk\ *noun* (1902)
: any of the usually minor tremors commonly preceding the principal shock of an earthquake
fore·shore \-ˌshōr, -ˌshȯr\ *noun* (1764)
1 : a strip of land margining a body of water
2 : the part of a seashore between high-water and low-water marks
fore·short·en \fōr-'shȯrt-tᵊn, fȯr-\ *transitive verb* (1606)
1 : to shorten by proportionately contracting in the direction of depth so that an illusion of projection or extension in space is obtained
2 : to make more compact : ABRIDGE, SHORTEN
fore·side \'fōr-ˌsīd, 'fȯr-\ *noun* (14th century)
: the front side or part : FRONT
fore·sight \'fōr-ˌsīt, 'fȯr-\ *noun* (14th century)
1 : an act or the power of foreseeing : PRESCIENCE
2 : provident care : PRUDENCE (had the *foresight* to invest his money wisely)
3 : an act of looking forward; *also* : a view forward
— **fore·sight·ed** \-ˌsī-təd\ *adjective*
— **fore·sight·ed·ly** *adverb*
— **fore·sight·ed·ness** *noun*
— **fore·sight·ful** \-ˌsīt-fəl\ *adjective*
fore·skin \-ˌskin\ *noun* (1535)
: a fold of skin that covers the glans of the penis — called also *prepuce*
fore·speak \fōr-'spēk, fȯr-\ *transitive verb* **-spoke** \-'spōk\; **-spo·ken** \-'spō-kən\; **-speak·ing** (14th century)
1 : FORETELL, PREDICT
2 : to arrange for in advance
¹fore·est \'fȯr-əst, 'fär-\ *noun, often attributive* [Middle English, from Old French, from Late Latin *forestis (silva)* unenclosed (woodland), from Latin *foris* outside — more at FORUM] (13th century)
1 : a dense growth of trees and underbrush covering a large tract

2 : a tract of wooded land in England formerly owned by the sovereign and used for game
3 : something resembling a forest especially in profusion (a *forest* of microphones)
— **for·est·al** \-əs-tᵊl\ *or* **fo·res·tial** \fə-'res-tē-əl, fȯ-, -'res(h)-chəl\ *adjective*
— **for·est·ed** \'fȯr-ə-stəd, 'fär-\ *adjective*
²forest *transitive verb* (circa 1828)
: to cover with trees or forest
— **for·es·ta·tion** \ˌfȯr-ə-'stā-shən, ˌfär-\ *noun*
fore·stage \'fȯr-ˌstāj, 'fȯr-\ *noun* (1923)
: APRON 2e
fore·stall \fȯr-'stȯl, fȯr-\ *transitive verb* [Middle English, from *forstall* act of waylaying, from Old English *foresteall*, from *fore-* + *steall* position, stall] (before 12th century)
1 : to prevent the normal trading in by buying or diverting goods or by persuading persons to raise prices
2 *archaic* : INTERCEPT
3 *obsolete* : OBSTRUCT, BESET
4 : to exclude, hinder, or prevent by prior occupation or measures
5 : to get ahead of : ANTICIPATE
synonym see PREVENT
— **fore·stall·er** *noun*
— **fore·stall·ment** \-'stȯl-mənt\ *noun*
fore·stay \'fȯr-ˌstā, 'fȯr-\ *noun* (13th century)
: a stay from the foremast to the foredeck or bow of a ship
fore·stay·sail \-ˌsāl, -səl\ *noun* (1742)
: the triangular aftermost headsail of a schooner, ketch, or yawl set on the forestay — see SAIL illustration
for·est·er \'fȯr-ə-stər, 'fär-\ *noun* [Middle English *forster, forester*, from Old French *forestier*, from *forest*] (14th century)
1 : a person trained in forestry
2 : an inhabitant of a forest
3 : any of various woodland moths (family Agaristidae)
4 *capitalized* : a member of a major benevolent and fraternal order
forest floor *noun* (1849)
: the richly organic layer of soil and debris characteristic of forested land
forest green *noun* (1810)
: a dark yellowish or moderate olive green
for·est·land \'fȯr-əst-ˌland, 'fär-\ *noun* (1649)
: land covered with forest or reserved for the growth of forests
forest ranger *noun* (1830)
: an officer charged with the patrolling and guarding of a forest; *especially* : one in charge of the management and protection of a portion of a public forest
for·est·ry \'fȯr-ə-strē, 'fär-\ *noun* (1823)
1 : FORESTLAND
2 a : the science of developing, caring for, or cultivating forests **b** : the management of growing timber
forest tent caterpillar *noun* (1854)
: a moth (*Malacosoma disstria* of the family Lasiocampidae) whose orange-marked larva is a tent caterpillar and a serious defoliator of deciduous trees
foreswear, foresworn *variant of* FORSWEAR, FORSWORN
¹fore·taste \'fȯr-ˌtāst, 'fȯr-\ *noun* (15th century)
1 : a small anticipatory sample
2 : an advance indication or warning
synonym see PROSPECT
²fore·taste \'fȯr-ˌtāst, fȯr-', 'fȯr-ˌ, 'fȯr-\ *transitive verb* (15th century)
: to taste beforehand : ANTICIPATE
fore·tell \fȯr-'tel, fȯr-\ *transitive verb* **-told** \-'tōld\; **-tell·ing** (14th century)
: to tell beforehand : PREDICT ☆
— **fore·tell·er** *noun*
¹fore·thought \'fȯr-ˌthȯt, 'fȯr-\ *noun* (14th century)
1 : a thinking or planning out in advance : PREMEDITATION
2 : consideration for the future

²forethought *adjective* (15th century)
archaic : AFORETHOUGHT
fore·thought·ful \-fəl\ *adjective* (1809)
: full of or having forethought
— **fore·thought·ful·ly** \-fə-lē\ *adverb*
— **fore·thought·ful·ness** *noun*
fore·time \'fȯr-ˌtīm, 'fȯr-\ *noun* (circa 1540)
: former or past time : the time before the present
¹fore·to·ken \'fȯr-ˌtō-kən, 'fȯr-\ *noun* (before 12th century)
: a premonitory sign
²fore·to·ken \fȯr-'tō-kən, fȯr-\ *transitive verb* **fore·to·kened; fore·to·ken·ing** \-'tōk-niŋ, -'tō-kə-\ (15th century)
: to indicate or warn of in advance
fore·top \'fȯr-ˌtäp, 'fȯr-; -ˌtəp\ *noun* (1509)
: the platform at the head of a ship's foremast
fore·top·man \'fȯr-ˌtäp-mən, 'fȯr-; -ˌtəp-\ *noun* (1816)
: a sailor on duty on the foremast and above
fore–top·mast \'fȯr-ˌtäp-məst, 'fȯr-; -ˌtəp-ˌmast\ *noun* (1626)

☆ **SYNONYMS**
Forerunner, precursor, harbinger, herald mean one that goes before or announces the coming of another. FORERUNNER is applicable to anything that serves as a sign or presage (the blockade was the *forerunner* of war). PRECURSOR applies to a person or thing paving the way for the success or accomplishment of another (18th-century poets like Burns were *precursors* of the Romantics). HARBINGER and HERALD both apply, chiefly figuratively, to one that proclaims or announces the coming or arrival of a notable event (their early victory was the *harbinger* of a winning season) (the *herald* of a new age in medicine).

Foresee, foreknow, divine, anticipate mean to know beforehand. FORESEE implies nothing about how the knowledge is derived and may apply to ordinary reasoning and experience (economists should have *foreseen* the recession). FOREKNOW usually implies supernatural assistance, as through revelation (if only we could *foreknow* our own destinies). DIVINE adds to FORESEE the suggestion of exceptional wisdom or discernment (was able to *divine* Europe's rapid recovery from the war). ANTICIPATE implies taking action about or responding emotionally to something before it happens (the waiter *anticipated* our every need).

Foretell, predict, forecast, prophesy, prognosticate mean to tell beforehand. FORETELL applies to the telling of the coming of a future event by any procedure or any source of information (seers *foretold* the calamity). PREDICT commonly implies inference from facts or accepted laws of nature (astronomers *predicted* an eclipse). FORECAST adds the implication of anticipating eventualities and differs from PREDICT in being usually concerned with probabilities rather than certainties (*forecast* snow). PROPHESY connotes inspired or mystic knowledge of the future especially as the fulfilling of divine threats or promises (*prophesying* a new messiah). PROGNOSTICATE is used less often than the other words; it may suggest learned or skilled interpretation, but more often it is simply a colorful substitute for PREDICT or PROPHESY (*prognosticating* the future).

\ə\ abut \ᵊ\ kitten \ər\ further \a\ ash \ā\ ace
\ä\ mop, mar \au̇\ out \ch\ chin \e\ bet \ē\ easy
\g\ go \i\ hit \ī\ ice \j\ job \ŋ\ sing \ō\ go
\ȯ\ law \ȯi\ boy \th\ thin \th̯\ the \ü\ loot \u̇\ foot
\y\ yet \zh\ vision *see also* Guide to Pronunciation

: a mast next above the foremast

¹for·ev·er \fə-'rev-ər, fȯ-; *Southern often* fə-'e-və\ *adverb* (1629)
1 : for a limitless time ⟨wants to live *forever*⟩
2 : at all times : CONTINUALLY ⟨is *forever* making bad puns⟩

²forever *noun* (1858)
: a seemingly interminable time : excessively long ⟨it took her *forever* to find the answer⟩

for·ev·er·more \-ˌre-və(r)-'mȯr, -'mȯr\ *adverb* (1837)
: FOREVER 1

for·ev·er·ness \-'re-vər-nəs\ *noun* (1945)
: ETERNITY

fore·warn \fȯr-'wȯrn, fȯr-\ *transitive verb* (14th century)
: to warn in advance

fore·wing \'fȯr-ˌwiŋ, 'fȯr-\ *noun* (circa 1889)
: either of the anterior wings of a 4-winged insect

fore·wom·an \'fȯr-ˌwu̇-mən, 'fȯr-\ *noun* (1709)
: a woman who is a foreman

fore·word \'fȯr-(ˌ)wərd, 'fȯr-\ *noun* (1842)
: prefatory comments (as for a book) especially when written by someone other than the author

fore·worn *archaic variant of* FORWORN

¹for·feit \'fȯr-fət\ *noun* [Middle English *forfait*, from Middle French, from past participle of *forfaire* to commit a crime, forfeit, from *fors* outside (from Latin *foris*) + *faire* to do, from Latin *facere* — more at FORUM, DO] (14th century)
1 : something forfeited or subject to being forfeited (as for a crime, offense, or neglect of duty) : PENALTY
2 : forfeiture especially of civil rights
3 a : something deposited (as for making a mistake in a game) and then redeemed on payment of a fine **b** *plural* : a game in which forfeits are exacted

²forfeit *transitive verb* (14th century)
1 : to lose or lose the right to by some error, offense, or crime
2 : to subject to confiscation as a forfeit
— **for·feit·able** \-fə-tə-bəl\ *adjective*
— **for·feit·er** *noun*

³forfeit *adjective* (14th century)
: forfeited or subject to forfeiture

for·fei·ture \'fȯr-fə-ˌchu̇r, -chər, -ˌt(y)u̇r\ *noun* (14th century)
1 : the act of forfeiting : the loss of property or money because of a breach of a legal obligation
2 : something (as money or property) that is forfeited : PENALTY

for·fend \fȯr-'fend, fȯr-\ *transitive verb* (14th century)
1 a *archaic* : FORBID **b** : to ward off : PREVENT
2 : PROTECT, PRESERVE

for·gath·er \fȯr-'ga-thər, fȯr-\ *intransitive verb* (1513)
1 : to come together : ASSEMBLE
2 : to meet someone usually by chance

¹forge \'fȯrj, 'fȯrj\ *noun* [Middle English, from Old French, from Latin *fabrica*, from *fabr-, faber* smith] (13th century)
1 : a furnace or a shop with its furnace where metal is heated and wrought : SMITHY
2 : a workshop where wrought iron is produced or where iron is made malleable

²forge *verb* **forged; forg·ing** (14th century)
transitive verb
1 a : to form (as metal) by heating and hammering **b** : to form (metal) by a mechanical or hydraulic press with or without heat
2 : to make or imitate falsely especially with intent to defraud : COUNTERFEIT
3 : to form or bring into being especially by an expenditure of effort ⟨working to *forge* party unity⟩
intransitive verb
1 : to work at a forge
2 : to commit forgery

forge·abil·i·ty \ˌfȯr-jə-'bi-lə-tē, ˌfȯr-\ *noun*

forge·able \'fȯr-jə-bəl, 'fȯr-\ *adjective*

³forge *intransitive verb* **forged; forg·ing** [origin unknown] (1611)
1 : to move forward slowly and steadily ⟨the ship *forged* ahead through heavy seas⟩
2 : to move with a sudden increase of speed and power ⟨*forged* into the lead⟩ ⟨*forged* ahead in marketing the product⟩

forg·er \'fȯr-jər, 'fȯr-\ *noun* [²*forge*] (14th century)
1 : one that forges metals
2 a : one that falsifies; *especially* : a creator of false tales **b** : a person guilty of forgery

forg·ery \'fȯrj-rē, 'fȯrj-; 'fȯr-jə-, 'fȯr-\ *noun, plural* **-er·ies** (1583)
1 *archaic* : INVENTION
2 : something forged
3 : an act of forging; *especially* : the crime of falsely and fraudulently making or altering a document (as a check)

for·get \fər-'get, fȯr-\ *verb* **-got** \-'gät\; **-got·ten** \-'gä-t°n\ *or* **-got; -get·ting** [Middle English, from Old English *forgietan*, from *for-* + *-gietan* (akin to Old Norse *geta* to get)] (before 12th century)
transitive verb
1 a : to lose the remembrance of : be unable to think of or recall ⟨I *forget* his name⟩ **b** *obsolete* : to cease from doing
2 : to treat with inattention or disregard ⟨*forgot* their old friends⟩
3 : to disregard intentionally : OVERLOOK — usually used in the imperative ⟨*forget* it⟩
intransitive verb
1 : to cease remembering or noticing ⟨forgive and *forget*⟩
2 : to fail to become mindful at the proper time ⟨*forget* about paying the bill⟩
synonym see NEGLECT
— **for·get·ter** *noun*
— **forget oneself** : to lose one's dignity, temper, or self-control

for·get·ful \-'get-fəl\ *adjective* (14th century)
1 : likely to forget
2 : characterized by negligent failure to remember : NEGLECTFUL
3 : inducing oblivion ⟨*forgetful* sleep⟩
— **for·get·ful·ly** \-fə-lē\ *adverb*
— **for·get·ful·ness** *noun*

for·ge·tive \'fȯr-jə-tiv, 'fȯr-\ *adjective* [probably from ²*forge* + *-tive* (as in *inventive*)] (1597)
archaic : INVENTIVE, IMAGINATIVE

for·get–me–not \fər-'get-mē-ˌnät, fȯr-\ *noun* (1532)
: any of a genus (*Myosotis*) of small herbs of the borage family having bright-blue or white flowers usually arranged in a curving spike

for·get·ta·ble \fər-'ge-tə-bəl, 'fȯr-\ *adjective* (1845)
: fit or likely to be forgotten ⟨a *forgettable* movie⟩

forg·ing \'fȯr-jiŋ, 'fȯr-\ *noun* (14th century)
1 : the art or process of forging
2 : a piece of forged work
3 : FORGERY 3

for·give \fər-'giv, fȯr-\ *verb* **-gave** \-'gāv\; **-giv·en** \-'gi-vən\; **-giv·ing** [Middle English, from Old English *forgifan*, from *for-* + *gifan* to give] (before 12th century)
transitive verb
1 a : to give up resentment of or claim to requital for ⟨*forgive* an insult⟩ **b** : to grant relief from payment of ⟨*forgive* a debt⟩
2 : to cease to feel resentment against (an offender) : PARDON ⟨*forgive* one's enemies⟩
intransitive verb
: to grant forgiveness
synonym see EXCUSE
— **for·giv·able** \-'gi-və-bəl\ *adjective*
— **for·giv·ably** \-blē\ *adverb*
— **for·giv·er** *noun*

for·give·ness \-'giv-nəs\ *noun* (before 12th century)
: the act of forgiving

for·giv·ing *adjective* (1690)
1 : willing or able to forgive
2 : allowing room for error or weakness ⟨designed to be a *forgiving* tennis racquet⟩
— **for·giv·ing·ly** \-'gi-viŋ-lē\ *adverb*
— **for·giv·ing·ness** *noun*

for·go \fȯr-'gō, fȯr-\ *transitive verb* **-went** \-'went\; **-gone** \-'gȯn *also* -'gän\; **-go·ing** \-'gō-iŋ, -'gȯ(-)iŋ\ [Middle English, from Old English *forgān* to pass by, forgo, from *for-* + *gān* to go] (before 12th century)
1 : to give up the enjoyment or advantage of : do without
2 *archaic* : FORSAKE
— **for·go·er** \-'gō-(-ə)r\ *noun*

forgotten man *noun* (1925)
: a person or category of persons that receives less attention than is merited

for instance \fə-'rin(t)-stənts, 'frin(t)-\ *noun* (1959)
: EXAMPLE ⟨I'll give you a *for instance*⟩

fo·rint \'fȯr-ˌint\ *noun, plural* **forints** *also* **forint** [Hungarian] (circa 1916)
— see MONEY table

for·judge *variant of* FOREJUDGE

¹fork \'fȯrk\ *noun* [Middle English *forke*, from Old English & Old North French; Old English *forca* & Old North French *forque*, from Latin *furca*] (before 12th century)
1 : an implement with two or more prongs used especially for taking up (as in eating), pitching, or digging
2 : a forked part, tool, or piece of equipment
3 a : a division into branches or the place where something divides into branches **b** : CONFLUENCE
4 : one of the branches into which something forks
5 : an attack by one chess piece (as a knight) on two pieces simultaneously
— **fork·ful** \-ˌfu̇l\ *noun*

²fork (15th century)
intransitive verb
1 : to divide into two or more branches ⟨where the road *forks*⟩
2 a : to use or work with a fork **b** : to turn into a fork
transitive verb
1 : to give the form of a fork to ⟨*forking* her fingers⟩
2 : to attack (two chessmen) simultaneously
3 : to raise, pitch, dig, or work with a fork ⟨*fork* hay⟩
4 : PAY, CONTRIBUTE — used with *over, out,* or *up* ⟨had to *fork* over $5000⟩
— **fork·er** *noun*

fork·ball \'fȯrk-ˌbȯl\ *noun* (1936)
: a baseball pitch in which the ball is gripped between the forked index and middle fingers

forked \'fȯrkt, 'fȯr-kəd\ *adjective* (13th century)
1 : resembling a fork especially in having one end divided into two or more branches or points ⟨*forked* lightning⟩
2 : shaped like a fork or having a forked part ⟨a *forked* road⟩

forked tongue *noun* (1836)
: intent to mislead or deceive — usually used in the phrase *to speak with forked tongue*

fork·lift \'fȯr-ˌklift\ *noun* (1944)
: a self-propelled machine for hoisting and transporting heavy objects by means of steel fingers inserted under the load

fork–ten·der \'fȯrk-'ten-dər\ *adjective* (1973)
: tender enough to be easily pierced or cut with a fork ⟨*fork-tender* filet mignon⟩

forky \'fȯr-kē\ *adjective* **fork·i·er; -est** (1697)
: FORKED ⟨a *forky* beard⟩

for·lorn \fər-'lȯrn, fȯr-\ *adjective* [Middle English *forloren*, from Old English, past participle of *forlēosan* to lose, from *for-* + *lēosan* to lose — more at LOSE] (before 12th century)

1 a : BEREFT, FORSAKEN ⟨left quite *forlorn* of hope⟩ **b :** sad and lonely because of isolation or desertion **:** DESOLATE
2 : being in poor condition **:** MISERABLE, WRETCHED ⟨*forlorn* tumbledown buildings⟩
3 : nearly hopeless ⟨a *forlorn* attempt⟩
synonym see ALONE
— **for·lorn·ly** *adverb*
— **for·lorn·ness** \-'lȯrn-nəs\ *noun*
forlorn hope *noun* [by folk etymology from Dutch *verloren hoop*, literally, lost band] (1579)
1 : a body of men selected to perform a perilous service
2 : a desperate or extremely difficult enterprise
¹**form** \'fȯrm\ *noun* [Middle English *forme*, from Old French, from Latin *forma* form, beauty] (13th century)
1 a : the shape and structure of something as distinguished from its material **b :** a body (as of a person) especially in its external appearance or as distinguished from the face **:** FIGURE **c** *archaic* **:** BEAUTY
2 : the essential nature of a thing as distinguished from its matter: as **a :** IDEA 1a **b :** the component of a thing that determines its kind
3 a : established method of expression or proceeding **:** procedure according to rule or rote **b :** a prescribed and set order of words **:** FORMULA ⟨the *form* of the marriage service⟩
4 : a printed or typed document with blank spaces for insertion of required or requested information ⟨tax *forms*⟩
5 a (1) **:** conduct regulated by extraneous controls (as of custom or etiquette) **:** CEREMONY (2) **:** show without substance **b :** manner or conduct as tested by a prescribed or accepted standard ⟨rudeness is simply bad *form*⟩ **c :** manner or style of performing or accomplishing according to recognized standards of technique ⟨a strong swimmer but weak on *form*⟩
6 a : the resting place or nest of a hare **b :** a long seat **:** BENCH
7 a : a supporting frame model of the human figure or part (as the torso) of the human figure usually used for displaying apparel **b :** a proportioned and often adjustable model for fitting clothes **c :** a mold in which concrete is placed to set
8 : the printing type or other matter arranged and secured in a chase ready for printing
9 a : one of the different modes of existence, action, or manifestation of a particular thing or substance **:** KIND ⟨one *form* of respiratory disorder⟩ ⟨a *form* of art⟩ **b :** a distinguishable group of organisms **c :** LINGUISTIC FORM **d :** one of the different aspects a word may take as a result of inflection or change of spelling or pronunciation ⟨verbal *forms*⟩ **e :** a mathematical expression of a particular type ⟨a bilinear *form*⟩ ⟨a polynomial *form*⟩
10 a (1) **:** orderly method of arrangement (as in the presentation of ideas) **:** manner of coordinating elements (as of an artistic production or course of reasoning) (2) **:** a particular kind or instance of such arrangement ⟨the sonnet is a poetical *form*⟩ **b :** PATTERN, SCHEMA ⟨arguments of the same logical *form*⟩ **c :** the structural element, plan, or design of a work of art — compare CONTENT 2c **d :** a visible and measurable unit defined by a contour **:** a bounded surface or volume
11 : a grade in a British school or in some American private schools
12 a (1) **:** the past performance of a race horse (2) **:** RACING FORM **b :** known ability to perform ⟨a singer at the top of her *form*⟩ **c :** condition suitable for performing (as in athletic competition) ⟨back on *form*⟩
²**form** (13th century)
transitive verb
1 a : to give a particular shape to **:** shape or mold into a certain state or after a particular model ⟨*form* the dough into a ball⟩ ⟨a state

formed along republican lines⟩ **b :** to arrange themselves in ⟨the dancers *formed* a line⟩ **c :** to model by instruction and discipline ⟨a mind *formed* by classical education⟩
2 : to give form or shape to **:** FASHION, CONSTRUCT
3 : to serve to make up or constitute **:** be an essential or basic element of
4 : DEVELOP, ACQUIRE ⟨*form* a habit⟩
5 : to arrange in order **:** DRAW UP
6 a : to assume an inflection so as to produce (as a tense) ⟨*forms* the past in *-ed*⟩ **b :** to combine to make (a compound word)
intransitive verb
1 : to become formed or shaped
2 : to take form **:** come into existence **:** ARISE
3 : to take on a definite form, shape, or arrangement
— **form·abil·i·ty** \ˌfȯr-mə-'bi-lə-tē\ *noun*
— **form·able** \'fȯr-mə-bəl\ *adjective*
— **form on :** to take up a formation next to
form- *or* **formo-** *combining form* [*formic*]
: formic acid ⟨*formate*⟩
-form \ˌfȯrm\ *adjective combining form* [Middle French & Latin; Middle French *-forme*, from Latin *-formis*, from *forma*]
: in the form or shape of **:** resembling ⟨filiform⟩
¹**for·mal** \'fȯr-məl\ *adjective* [Middle English, from Middle French or Latin; Middle French, from Latin *formalis*, from *forma*] (14th century)
1 a : belonging to or constituting the form or essence of a thing ⟨*formal* cause⟩ **b :** relating to or involving the outward form, structure, relationships, or arrangement of elements rather than content ⟨*formal* logic⟩ ⟨*formal* style of painting⟩ ⟨*formal* approach to comparative linguistics⟩
2 a : following or according with established form, custom, or rule ⟨lacked *formal* schooling⟩ ⟨a *formal* dinner party⟩ ⟨*formal* attire⟩ **b :** done in due or lawful form ⟨a *formal* contract⟩ ⟨received *formal* recognition⟩
3 a : characterized by punctilious respect for form **:** METHODICAL ⟨very *formal* in all his dealings⟩ **b :** rigidly ceremonious **:** PRIM
4 : having the appearance without the substance ⟨*formal* Christians who go to church only at Easter⟩
synonym see CEREMONIAL
— **for·mal·ly** \-mə-lē\ *adverb*
— **for·mal·ness** *noun*
²**formal** *noun* (1605)
: something (as a dance or a dress) formal in character
³**formal** *adjective* [*formula + ¹-al*] (circa 1934)
: ³MOLAR
form·al·de·hyde \fȯr-'mal-də-ˌhīd, fər-\ *noun* [International Scientific Vocabulary *form-* + *aldehyde*] (1872)
: a colorless pungent irritating gas CH_2O used chiefly as a disinfectant and preservative and in chemical synthesis
for·ma·lin \'fȯr-mə-lən, -ˌlēn\ *noun* [*Formalin*, a trademark] (1893)
: a clear aqueous solution of formaldehyde containing a small amount of methanol
for·mal·ise *British variant of* FORMALIZE
for·mal·ism \'fȯr-mə-ˌli-zəm\ *noun* (circa 1840)
1 : the practice or the doctrine of strict adherence to prescribed or external forms (as in religion or art); *also* **:** an instance of this
2 : marked attention to arrangement, style, or artistic means (as in art or literature) usually with corresponding de-emphasis of content
— **for·mal·ist** \-list\ *noun or adjective*
— **for·mal·is·tic** \ˌfȯr-mə-'lis-tik\ *adjective*
for·mal·i·ty \fȯr-'ma-lə-tē\ *noun, plural* **-ties** (1597)
1 : compliance with formal or conventional rules **:** CEREMONY
2 : the quality or state of being formal
3 : an established form or procedure that is required or conventional

for·mal·ize \'fȯr-mə-ˌlīz\ *transitive verb* **-ized; -iz·ing** (1646)
1 : to give a certain or definite form to **:** SHAPE
2 a : to make formal **b :** to give formal status or approval to
— **for·mal·iz·able** \-ˌlī-zə-bəl\ *adjective*
— **for·mal·iza·tion** \ˌfȯr-mə-lə-'zā-shən\ *noun*
— **for·mal·iz·er** \'fȯr-mə-ˌlī-zər\ *noun*
form·am·ide \fȯr-'ma-ˌmīd; 'fȯr-ə-ˌmīd, -məd\ *noun* (1852)
: a colorless hygroscopic liquid $CHONH_2$ used chiefly as a solvent
for·mant \'fȯr-mənt, -ˌmant\ *noun* (1901)
: a characteristic component of the quality of a speech sound; *specifically* **:** any of several resonance bands held to determine the phonetic quality of a vowel
¹**for·mat** \'fȯr-ˌmat\ *noun* [French or German; French, from German, from Latin *formatus*, past participle of *formare* to form, from *forma*] (1840)
1 : the shape, size, and general makeup (as of something printed)
2 : general plan of organization, arrangement, or choice of material (as for a television show)
²**format** *transitive verb* **for·mat·ted; for·mat·ting** (1964)
: to arrange (as material to be printed or stored data) in a particular format
— **for·mat·ter** *noun*
for·mate \'fȯr-ˌmāt\ *noun* (1807)
: a salt or ester of formic acid
for·ma·tion \fȯr-'mā-shən\ *noun* (15th century)
1 : an act of giving form or shape to something or of taking form **:** DEVELOPMENT
2 : something that is formed ⟨new word *formations*⟩
3 : the manner in which a thing is formed **:** STRUCTURE ⟨the peculiar *formation* of the heart⟩
4 : the largest unit in an ecological community comprising two or more associations and their precursors ⟨grassland *formation*⟩
5 a : any igneous, sedimentary, or metamorphic rock represented as a unit **b :** any sedimentary bed or consecutive series of beds sufficiently homogeneous or distinctive to be a unit
6 : an arrangement of a body or group of persons or things in some prescribed manner or for a particular purpose
¹**for·ma·tive** \'fȯr-mə-tiv\ *adjective* (15th century)
1 a : giving or capable of giving form **:** CONSTRUCTIVE ⟨a *formative* influence⟩ **b :** used in word formation or inflection
2 : capable of alteration by growth and development; *also* **:** producing new cells and tissues
3 : of, relating to, or characterized by formative effects or formation ⟨*formative* years⟩
— **for·ma·tive·ly** *adverb*
²**formative** *noun* (1816)
: the element (as a suffix) in a word that serves to give the word appropriate form and is not part of the base
form class *noun* (1921)
: a class of linguistic forms that can be used in the same position in a construction and that have one or more morphological or syntactical features in common
form–critical *adjective* (1933)
: based on or applying form criticism
form criticism *noun* (1928)
: a method of criticism for determining the sources and historicity of biblical writings through analysis of the writings in terms of ancient literary forms and oral traditions (as love poems, parables, and proverbs)

\ə\ abut \ᵊ\ kitten \ər\ further \a\ ash \ā\ ace
\ä\ mop, mar \au̇\ out \ch\ chin \e\ bet \ē\ easy
\g\ go \i\ hit \ī\ ice \j\ job \ŋ\ sing \ō\ go
\ȯ\ law \ȯi\ boy \th\ thin \th\ the \ü\ loot \u̇\ foot
\y\ yet \zh\ vision *see also* Guide to Pronunciation

— form critic *noun*

forme \'fōm, 'fȯrm\ *noun* (15th century)
British **:** FORM 8

formed \'fȯrmd\ *adjective* (1605)
: organized in a way characteristic of living matter ⟨mitochondria are *formed* bodies of the cell⟩

for·mée \'fȯr-ˌmā, fȯr-'\ *adjective* [French, feminine past participle of *former* to form, from Latin *formare*] (15th century)
of a heraldic cross **:** having the arms narrow at the center and expanding toward the ends — see CROSS illustration

¹for·mer \'fȯr-mər\ *adjective* [Middle English, from *forme* first, from Old English *forma* — more at FOREMOST] (12th century)
1 a : coming before in time **b :** of, relating to, or occurring in the past ⟨*former* correspondence⟩
2 : preceding in place or arrangement **:** FOREGOING ⟨*former* part of the chapter⟩
3 : first in order of two or more things cited or understood ⟨of the two given, the *former* spelling is more common⟩ ⟨of the two spellings, the *former* is more common⟩
4 : having been previously **:** ONETIME ⟨a *former* athlete⟩
synonym see PRECEDING

²form·er \'fȯr-mər\ *noun* (14th century)
1 : one that forms
2 *chiefly British* **:** a member of a school form — usually used in combination ⟨sixth *former*⟩

for·mer·ly \'fȯr-mə(r)-lē\ *adverb* (1534)
1 : at an earlier time **:** PREVIOUSLY
2 *obsolete* **:** just before

form-fit·ting \'fȯrm-ˌfi-tiŋ\ *adjective* (1897)
: conforming to the outline of the body **:** fitting snugly ⟨a *formfitting* sweater⟩

form·ful \'fȯrm-fəl\ *adjective* (1832)
: exhibiting or notable for form

form genus *noun* (1873)
: an artificial taxonomic category established for organisms (as imperfect fungi) of obscure true relationships

For·mi·ca \fȯr-'mī-kə, fər-\ *trademark*
— used for any of various laminated plastic products used especially for surface finish

for·mic acid \'fȯr-mik-\ *noun* [irregular from Latin *formica* ant — more at PISMIRE] (1791)
: a colorless pungent fuming vesicant liquid acid CH_2O_2 found especially in ants and in many plants and used chiefly in dyeing and finishing textiles

for·mi·cary \'fȯr-mə-ˌker-ē\ *noun, plural* **-car·ies** [Medieval Latin *formicarium,* from Latin *formica*] (1816)
: an ant nest

for·mi·da·ble \'fȯr-mə-də-bəl; fȯr-'mi-, fər-'mi-\ *adjective* [Middle English, from Latin *formidabilis,* from *formidare* to fear, from *formido* terror, bogey; akin to Greek *mormō* bogey] (15th century)
1 : causing fear, dread, or apprehension ⟨a *formidable* prospect⟩
2 : having qualities that discourage approach or attack
3 : tending to inspire awe or wonder
— for·mi·da·bil·i·ty \ˌfȯr-mə-də-'bi-lə-tē; fȯr-ˌmi-, fər-ˌ\ *noun*
— for·mi·da·ble·ness \'fȯr-mə-də-bəl-nəs; fȯr-'mi-, fər-'\ *noun*
— for·mi·da·bly \-blē\ *adverb*

form·less \'fȯrm-ləs\ *adjective* (1591)
1 : having no regular form or shape
2 : lacking order or arrangement
3 : having no physical existence
— form·less·ly *adverb*
— form·less·ness *noun*

form letter *noun* (1909)
1 : a letter on a subject of frequent recurrence that can be sent to different people without essential change except in the address
2 : a letter for mass circulation that is printed in many copies and has a very general salutation (as *Dear Friend*)

formo- — see FORM-

¹for·mu·la \'fȯr-myə-lə\ *noun, plural* **-las** *or* **-lae** \-ˌlē, -ˌlī\ [Latin, diminutive of *forma* form] (1618)
1 a : a set form of words for use in a ceremony or ritual **b :** a conventionalized statement intended to express some fundamental truth or principle especially as a basis for negotiation or action
2 a (1) **:** RECIPE (2) **:** PRESCRIPTION **b :** a milk mixture or substitute for feeding an infant
3 a : a general fact, rule, or principle expressed in usually mathematical symbols **b :** a symbolic expression of the chemical composition or constitution of a substance **c :** a group of symbols (as letters and numbers) associated to express concisely facts or data (as the number and kinds of teeth in the jaw) **d :** a combination of signs in a logical calculus
4 : a customary or set form or method allowing little room for originality
— for·mu·la·ic \ˌfȯr-myə-'lā-ik\ *adjective*
— for·mu·la·ical·ly \-'lā-ə-k(ə-)lē\ *adverb*

²formula *adjective* (1927)
: of, relating to, or being an open-wheel open-cockpit rear-engine racing car conforming to prescribed specifications as to size, weight, and engine displacement

for·mu·la·rize \'fȯr-myə-lə-ˌrīz\ *transitive verb* **-rized; -riz·ing** (1852)
: to state in or reduce to a formula **:** FORMULATE
— for·mu·la·ri·za·tion \ˌfȯr-myə-lə-rə-'zā-shən\ *noun*
— for·mu·la·riz·er \'fȯr-myə-lə-ˌrī-zər\ *noun*

for·mu·lary \'fȯr-myə-ˌler-ē\ *noun, plural* **-lar·ies** (1541)
1 : a collection of prescribed forms (as oaths or prayers)
2 : FORMULA 1
3 : a book listing medicinal substances and formulas
— formulary *adjective*

for·mu·late \'fȯr-myə-ˌlāt\ *transitive verb* **-lat·ed; -lat·ing** (1860)
1 a : to reduce to or express in a formula **b :** to put into a systematized statement or expression **c :** DEVISE ⟨*formulate* a policy⟩
2 a : to develop a formula for the preparation of (as a soap or plastic) **b :** to prepare according to a formula
— for·mu·la·tor \-ˌlā-tər\ *noun*

for·mu·la·tion \ˌfȯr-myə-'lā-shən\ *noun* (1876)
: an act or the product of formulating

formula weight *noun* (circa 1920)
: MOLECULAR WEIGHT — used especially of ionic compounds

for·mu·lize \'fȯr-myə-ˌlīz\ *transitive verb* **-lized; -liz·ing** (1842)
: FORMULATE 1

form word *noun* (1875)
: FUNCTION WORD

form·work \'fȯrm-ˌwərk\ *noun* (1918)
: a set of forms in place to hold wet concrete until it sets

for·myl \'fȯr-ˌmil\ *noun* [International Scientific Vocabulary] (circa 1859)
: the radical HCO of formic acid that is also characteristic of aldehydes

for·ni·cate \'fȯr-nə-ˌkāt\ *verb* **-cat·ed; -cat·ing** [Late Latin *fornicatus,* past participle of *fornicare* to have intercourse with prostitutes, from Latin *fornic-, fornix* arch, vault, brothel] (1552)
intransitive verb
: to commit fornication
transitive verb
: to commit fornication with
— for·ni·ca·tor \-ˌkā-tər\ *noun*

for·ni·ca·tion \ˌfȯr-nə-'kā-shən\ *noun* (14th century)
: consensual sexual intercourse between two persons not married to each other — compare ADULTERY

for·nix \'fȯr-niks\ *noun, plural* **for·ni·ces** \-nə-ˌsēz\ [New Latin, from Latin] (1681)
: an anatomical arch or fold

for·rad·er *also* **for·rard·er** \'fär-ə-dər\ *adverb* [English dialect, comparative of English *forward*] (1888)
chiefly British **:** further ahead

for·sake \fər-'sāk, fȯr-\ *transitive verb* **for·sook** \-'sük\; **for·sak·en** \-'sā-kən\; **for·sak·ing** [Middle English, from Old English *forsacan,* from *for-* + *sacan* to dispute; akin to Old English *sacu* action at law — more at SAKE] (before 12th century)
: to renounce or turn away from entirely ⟨friends have *forsaken* her⟩ ⟨*forsook* the theater for politics⟩
synonym see ABANDON

for·sooth \fər-'süth\ *adverb* [Middle English *for soth,* from Old English *forsōth,* from *for* + *sōth* sooth] (before 12th century)
: in truth **:** INDEED — often used to imply contempt or doubt

for·spent \fər-'spent, fȯr-\ *adjective* (1563)
archaic **:** WORN-OUT, EXHAUSTED

for·swear \fȯr-'swar, fōr-, -'swer\ *verb* **-swore** \-'swōr, -'swȯr\; **-sworn** \-'swōrn, -'swȯrn\; **-swear·ing** [Middle English *forsweren,* from Old English *forswerian,* from *for-* + *swerian* to swear] (before 12th century)
transitive verb
1 : to make a liar of (oneself) under or as if under oath
2 a : to reject or renounce under oath **b :** to renounce earnestly
3 : to deny under oath
intransitive verb
: to swear falsely
synonym see ABJURE

for·sworn \-'swōrn, -'swȯrn\ *adjective* (before 12th century)
1 : guilty of perjury
2 : marked by perjury

for·syth·ia \fər-'si-thē-ə, *chiefly British* -'sī-\ *noun* [New Latin, genus name, from William *Forsyth* (died 1804) British botanist] (circa 1814)
: any of a genus (*Forsythia*) of ornamental shrubs of the olive family with opposite leaves and yellow bell-shaped flowers appearing before the leaves in early spring

forsythia

fort \'fȯrt, 'fōrt\ *noun* [Middle English *forte,* from Middle French *fort,* from *fort,* adjective, strong, from Latin *fortis*] (15th century)
1 : a strong or fortified place; *especially* **:** a fortified place occupied only by troops and surrounded with such works as a ditch, rampart, and parapet **:** FORTIFICATION
2 : a permanent army post — often used in place names

for·ta·lice \'fȯr-tᵊl-əs\ *noun* [Middle English, from Medieval Latin *fortalitia* — more at FORTRESS] (15th century)
1 *archaic* **:** FORTRESS
2 *archaic* **:** a small fort

¹forte \'fȯrt, 'fȯrt; *2 is often* 'fȯr-ˌtā *or* fȯr-'tā *or* 'fȯr-tē\ *noun* [French *fort,* from *fort,* adjective, strong] (circa 1648)
1 : the part of a sword or foil blade that is between the middle and the hilt and that is the strongest part of the blade
2 : one's strong point ☐

²for·te \'fȯr-ˌtā, 'fȯr-tē\ *adverb or adjective* [Italian, from *forte* strong, from Latin *fortis*] (circa 1724)
: LOUD — used as a direction in music

³for·te \'fȯr-ˌtā, 'fȯr-tē\ *noun* (1759)
: a tone or passage played forte

for·te·pia·no \ˌfȯr-ˌtā-pē-'a-(ˌ)nō *also* -'ä-(ˌ)nō\ *noun* [French or Italian; French, from Italian, from *forte* loud + *piano* soft] (1771)

: an early form of the piano originating in the 18th and early 19th centuries and having a smaller range and softer timbre than a modern piano

word history see PIANO

for·te·pi·a·no \,fȯr-,tā-pē-'ä-(,)nō, ,fȯr-tē-\ *adverb or adjective* (circa 1889)
: loud then immediately soft — used as a direction in music

¹forth \'fōrth, 'fȯrth\ *adverb* [Middle English, from Old English; akin to Old English *for*] (before 12th century)
1 : onward in time, place, or order : FORWARD ⟨from that day *forth*⟩
2 : out into notice or view ⟨put *forth* leaves⟩
3 *obsolete* : AWAY, ABROAD

²forth *preposition* (circa 1577)
archaic : forth from : OUT OF

forth·com·ing \fōrth-'kə-miŋ, fȯrth-; 'fōrth-,, 'fȯrth-\ *adjective* [obsolete *forthcome* (to come forth)] (circa 1532)
1 : being about to appear or to be produced or made available ⟨the *forthcoming* holidays⟩ ⟨your *forthcoming* novel⟩ ⟨funds are *forthcoming*⟩
2 a : RESPONSIVE, OUTGOING ⟨a *forthcoming* and courteous man⟩ **b** : characterized by openness, candidness, and forthrightness ⟨not *forthcoming* about his memories of medical school —Mark Kramer⟩

forth of *preposition* (13th century)
archaic : out from : OUT OF

¹forth·right \'fōr-,thrīt, 'fȯr-\ *adverb* [Middle English, from Old English *forthriht*, from *forth* + *riht* right] (before 12th century)
1 *archaic* **a** : directly forward **b** : without hesitation : FRANKLY
2 *archaic* : at once

²forthright *adjective* (before 12th century)
1 *archaic* : proceeding straight on
2 : free from ambiguity or evasiveness : going straight to the point ⟨a *forthright* critic⟩ ⟨was *forthright* in appraising the problem⟩
3 : notably simple in style or quality ⟨*forthright* furniture⟩
— **forth·right·ly** *adverb*
— **forth·right·ness** *noun*

³forthright *noun* (1606)
archaic : a straight path

forth·with \(,)fōrth-'with, (,)fȯrth- *also* -'with\ *adverb* (14th century)
: IMMEDIATELY

for·ti·fi·ca·tion \,fȯr-tə-fə-'kā-shən\ *noun* (15th century)
1 : an act or process of fortifying
2 : something that fortifies, defends, or strengthens; *especially* : works erected to defend a place or position

fortified wine *noun* (1906)
: a wine (as sherry) to which alcohol usually in the form of grape brandy has been added during or after fermentation

for·ti·fi·er \'fȯr-tə-,fī(-ə)r\ *noun* (circa 1552)
: one that fortifies

for·ti·fy \-,fī\ *verb* **-fied; -fy·ing** [Middle English *fortifien*, from Middle French *fortifier*, from Late Latin *fortificare*, from Latin *fortis* strong] (15th century)
transitive verb
: to make strong: as **a** : to strengthen and secure (as a town) by forts or batteries **b** : to give physical strength, courage, or endurance to **c** : to add mental or moral strength to : ENCOURAGE ⟨*fortified* by prayer⟩ **d** : to add material to for strengthening or enriching
intransitive verb
: to erect fortifications

for·tis \'fȯr-təs\ *adjective* [New Latin, from Latin, strong] (1897)
: produced with relatively great articulatory tenseness and strong expiration ⟨\t\ in *toe* is *fortis*, \d\ in *doe* is lenis⟩

¹for·tis·si·mo \fȯr-'ti-sə-,mō\ *adverb or adjective* [Italian, superlative of *forte*] (1724)
: very loud — used especially as a direction in music

²fortissimo *noun, plural* **-mos** *or* **-mi** \-,mē\ (1856)
: a very loud passage, sound, or tone

for·ti·tude \'fȯr-tə-,tüd, -,tyüd\ *noun* [Middle English, from Latin *fortitudin-, fortitudo,* from *fortis*] (12th century)
1 : strength of mind that enables a person to encounter danger or bear pain or adversity with courage
2 *obsolete* : STRENGTH

fort·night \'fōrt-,nīt, 'fȯrt-\ *noun* [Middle English *fourtenight,* alteration of *fourtene night,* from Old English *fēowertȳne niht* fourteen nights] (before 12th century)
: a period of 14 days : two weeks

¹fort·night·ly \-lē\ *adjective* (1800)
: occurring or appearing once in a fortnight

²fortnightly *adverb* (1820)
: once in a fortnight : every fortnight

³fortnightly *noun, plural* **-lies** (1940)
: a publication issued fortnightly

FOR·TRAN *or* **For·tran** \'fȯr-,tran\ *noun* [*formula translation*] (1956)
: a computer programming language that resembles algebra in its notation and is widely used for scientific applications

for·tress \'fȯr-trəs\ *noun* [Middle English *forteresse,* from Middle French *forteresce,* from Medieval Latin *fortalitia,* from Latin *fortis* strong] (14th century)
: a fortified place : STRONGHOLD; *especially* : a large and permanent fortification sometimes including a town
— **for·tress·like** \-,līk\ *adjective*

for·tu·itous \fȯr-'tü-ə-təs, -'tyü-, fər-\ *adjective* [Latin *fortuitus;* akin to Latin *fort-, fors*] (1653)
1 : occurring by chance
2 a : FORTUNATE, LUCKY ⟨from a cost standpoint, the company's timing is *fortuitous* —Business Week⟩ **b** : coming or happening by a lucky chance ⟨belted down the stairs, and there was a *fortuitous* train —Doris Lessing⟩
□
synonym see ACCIDENTAL
— **for·tu·itous·ly** *adverb*
— **for·tu·itous·ness** *noun*

for·tu·ity \-ə-tē\ *noun, plural* **-ities** (circa 1747)
1 : the quality or state of being fortuitous
2 : a chance event or occurrence

for·tu·nate \'fȯrch-nət, 'fȯr-chə-\ *adjective* (14th century)
1 : bringing some good thing not foreseen as certain : AUSPICIOUS
2 : receiving some unexpected good
synonym see LUCKY
— **for·tu·nate·ness** *noun*

for·tu·nate·ly \-lē\ *adverb* (1548)
1 : in a fortunate manner
2 : it is fortunate that

¹for·tune \'fȯr-chən\ *noun* [Middle English, from Middle French, from Latin *fortuna;* akin to Latin *fort-, fors* chance, luck, and perhaps to *ferre* to carry — more at BEAR] (14th century)
1 *often capitalized* : a hypothetical force or personified power that unpredictably determines events and issues favorably or unfavorably
2 *obsolete* : ACCIDENT, INCIDENT
3 a : prosperity attained partly through luck : SUCCESS **b** : LUCK **c** *plural* : the turns and courses of luck accompanying one's progress (as through life) ⟨her *fortunes* varied but she never gave up⟩
4 : DESTINY, FATE ⟨can tell your *fortune*⟩; *also* : a prediction of fortune
5 a : RICHES, WEALTH ⟨a man of *fortune*⟩ **b** : a store of material possessions ⟨the family *fortune*⟩ **c** : a very large sum of money ⟨spent a *fortune* redecorating⟩

²fortune *verb* **for·tuned; for·tun·ing** (14th century)
transitive verb
1 *obsolete* : to give good or bad fortune to

2 *archaic* : to endow with a fortune
intransitive verb
archaic : HAPPEN, CHANCE

fortune cookie *noun* (1962)
: a thin cookie folded to contain a slip of paper on which is printed a fortune, proverb, or humorous statement

fortune hunter *noun* (1689)
: a person who seeks wealth especially by marriage

for·tune–tell·er \-,te-lər\ *noun* (1590)
: one that professes to foretell future events
— **for·tune–tell·ing** \-liŋ\ *noun or adjective*

for·ty \'fȯr-tē\ *noun, plural* **forties** [Middle English *fourty,* from Old English *fēowertig,* from *fēowertig* group of 40, from *fēower* four + *-tig* group of 10; akin to Old English *tīen* ten] (before 12th century)
1 — see NUMBER table
2 *plural* : the numbers 40 to 49; *specifically* : the years 40 to 49 in a lifetime or century
3 : the third point scored by a side in a game of tennis
— **for·ti·eth** \'fȯr-tē-əth\ *adjective or noun*
— **forty** *adjective*
— **forty** *pronoun, plural in construction*
— **for·ty·ish** \-tē-ish\ *adjective*

for·ty–five \,fȯr-tē-'fīv\ *noun* (1904)
1 — see NUMBER table
2 : a .45 caliber handgun — usually written .45
3 : a phonograph record designed to be played at 45 revolutions per minute — usually written 45
— **forty–five** *adjective*
— **forty–five** *pronoun, plural in construction*

Forty Hours *noun plural but singular or plural in construction* (1759)
: a Roman Catholic devotion in which the churches of a diocese on two-day turns have the Blessed Sacrament exposed on the altar for continuous daytime veneration

for·ty–nin·er \,fȯr-tē-'nī-nər\ *noun* (1853)
: one taking part in the rush to California for gold in 1849

forty winks *noun plural but singular or plural in construction* (1872)
: a short sleep : NAP

\ə\ abut \ᵊ\ kitten \ər\ further \a\ ash \ā\ ace
\ä\ mop, mar \au̇\ out \ch\ chin \e\ bet \ē\ easy
\g\ go \i\ hit \ī\ ice \j\ job \ŋ\ sing \ō\ go
\ȯ\ law \ȯi\ boy \th\ thin \t͟h\ the \ü\ loot \u̇\ foot
\y\ yet \zh\ vision *see also* Guide to Pronunciation

fo·rum \'fōr-əm, 'fòr-\ *noun, plural* **forums** *also* **fo·ra** \-ə\ [Latin; akin to Latin *foris* outside, *fores* door — more at DOOR] (15th century)
1 a : the marketplace or public place of an ancient Roman city forming the center of judicial and public business **b :** a public meeting place for open discussion **c :** a medium (as a newspaper) of open discussion or expression of ideas
2 : a judicial body or assembly **:** COURT
3 a : a public meeting or lecture involving audience discussion **b :** a program (as on radio or television) involving discussion of a problem usually by several authorities

¹for·ward \'fòr-wərd, *also* 'fò- *or* 'fò-, *Southern also* 'fär-\ *adjective* [Middle English, from Old English *foreweard*, from *fore-* + *-weard* -ward] (before 12th century)
1 a : near, being at, or belonging to the forepart **b :** situated in advance
2 a : strongly inclined **:** READY **b :** lacking modesty or reserve **:** BRASH
3 : notably advanced or developed **:** PRECOCIOUS
4 : moving, tending, or leading toward a position in front; *also* **:** moving toward an opponent's goal
5 a : advocating an advanced policy in the direction of what is considered progress **b :** EXTREME, RADICAL
6 : of, relating to, or getting ready for the future ⟨*forward* buying of produce⟩
— **for·ward·ly** *adverb*
— **for·ward·ness** *noun*

²forward *adverb* (before 12th century)
: to or toward what is ahead or in front ⟨from that time *forward*⟩ ⟨moved slowly *forward*⟩

³forward *transitive verb* (1596)
1 : to help onward **:** PROMOTE ⟨*forwarded* his friend's career⟩
2 a : to send forward **:** TRANSMIT ⟨will *forward* the goods on receipt of your check⟩ **b :** to send or ship onward from an intermediate post or station in transit ⟨*forward* mail⟩
synonym *see* ADVANCE

⁴forward *noun* (1879)
: a player who plays at the front of his team's formation near the goal at which his team is attempting to score

for·ward·er \-wər-dər\ *noun* (1549)
: one that forwards; *especially* **:** an agent who performs services (as receiving, transshipping, or delivering) designed to move goods to their destination

for·ward–look·ing \'fòr-wərd-ˌlu̇-kiŋ\ *adjective* (1800)
: concerned with or planning for the future

forward pass *noun* (1903)
: a pass (as in football) made in the direction of the opponents' goal

for·wards \'fòr-wərdz\ *adverb* (15th century)
: FORWARD

for·worn \fər-'wòrn, -'wòrn\ *adjective* (1528)
archaic **:** WORN-OUT

for·zan·do \fòrt-'sän-(ˌ)dō\ *adjective or adverb* [Italian] (circa 1828)
: SFORZANDO

¹fos·sa \'fä-sə\ *noun, plural* **fos·sae** \-ˌsē, -ˌsī\ [New Latin, from Latin, ditch] (1771)
: an anatomical pit, groove, or depression

²fossa *noun* [Malagasy] (1838)
: a slender lithe carnivorous mammal (*Cryptoprocta ferox*) of Madagascar that resembles a cat especially in having retractile claws but is usually considered a viverrid

fosse *or* **foss** \'fäs\ *noun* [Middle English *fosse*, from Old French, from Latin *fossa*, from feminine of *fossus*] (15th century)
: DITCH, MOAT

fos·sick \'fä-sik\ *verb* [English dialect *fossick* to ferret out] (1852)
intransitive verb
1 *Australian & New Zealand* **:** to search for gold or gemstones typically by picking over abandoned workings

2 *chiefly Australian & New Zealand* **:** to search about **:** RUMMAGE
transitive verb
chiefly Australian & New Zealand **:** to search for by or as if by rummaging **:** ferret out
— **fos·sick·er** *noun, chiefly Australian & New Zealand*

¹fos·sil \'fä-səl\ *adjective* [Latin *fossilis* obtained by digging, from *fodere* to dig — more at BED] (1665)
1 : preserved from a past geologic age ⟨*fossil* plants⟩ ⟨*fossil* water in an underground reservoir⟩
2 : being or resembling a fossil
3 : of or relating to fossil fuel

²fossil *noun* (1736)
1 : a remnant, impression, or trace of an organism of past geologic ages that has been preserved in the earth's crust — compare LIVING FOSSIL
2 a : one whose views are outmoded **:** FOGY **b :** something (as a theory) that has become rigidly fixed
3 : an old word or word element preserved only by idiom (as *fro* in *to and fro*)

fossil fuel *noun* (1835)
: a fuel (as coal, oil, or natural gas) that is formed in the earth from plant or animal remains
— **fos·sil–fueled** \-ˌfyü(-ə)ld\ *adjective*

fos·sil·if·er·ous \ˌfä-sə-'li-f(ə-)rəs\ *adjective* (circa 1846)
: containing fossils

fos·sil·ise *chiefly British variant of* FOSSILIZE
fos·sil·ize \'fä-sə-ˌlīz\ *verb* **-ized; -iz·ing** (1794)
transitive verb
1 : to convert into a fossil
2 : to make outmoded, rigid, or fixed
intransitive verb
: to become changed into a fossil
— **fos·sil·iza·tion** \ˌfä-sə-lə-'zā-shən\ *noun*

fos·so·ri·al \fä-'sōr-ē-əl, -'sòr-\ *adjective* [Medieval Latin *fossorius* used for digging, from Latin *fossor* digger, from *fodere*] (1837)
: adapted to digging ⟨a *fossorial* foot⟩

¹fos·ter \'fòs-tər, 'fäs-\ *adjective* [Middle English, from Old English *fōstor-*, from *fōstor* food, feeding; akin to Old English *fōda* food] (before 12th century)
: affording, receiving, or sharing nurture or parental care though not related by blood or legal ties

²foster *transitive verb* **fos·tered; fos·ter·ing** \-t(ə-)riŋ\ (12th century)
1 : to give parental care to **:** NURTURE
2 : to promote the growth or development of **:** ENCOURAGE
— **fos·ter·er** \-tər-ər\ *noun*

fos·ter·age \-tə-rij\ *noun* (1614)
1 : the act of fostering
2 : a custom once prevalent in Ireland, Wales, and Scotland of entrusting one's child to foster parents to be brought up

foster home *noun* (1886)
: a household in which an orphaned, neglected, or delinquent child is placed for care

fos·ter·ling \-tər-liŋ\ *noun* (before 12th century)
: a foster child

fou \'fü\ *adjective* [Middle English (Scots) *fow* full, from Middle English *full*] (1535)
Scottish **:** DRUNK 1a

Fou·cault pendulum \ˌfü-'kō-\ *noun* [J.B.L. *Foucault*] (1931)
: a freely swinging pendulum that consists of a heavy weight hung by a long wire and that swings in a constant direction which appears to change showing that the earth rotates

fouet·té \(ˌ)fwe-'tā\ *noun* [French, from past participle of *fouetter* to whip, from Middle French, from *fouet* whip, from Old French, from *fou* beech, from Latin *fagus* — more at BEECH] (1830)
: a quick whipping movement of the raised leg in ballet usually accompanying a pirouette

fought *past and past participle of* FIGHT

¹foul \'fau̇(ə)l\ *adjective* [Middle English, from Old English *fūl*; akin to Old High German *fūl* rotten, Latin *pus* pus, *putēre* to stink, Greek *pyon* pus] (before 12th century)
1 a : offensive to the senses **:** LOATHSOME **b :** filled or covered with offensive matter
2 : full of dirt or mud
3 a : morally or spiritually odious **:** DETESTABLE ⟨a *foul* crime⟩ **b :** notably unpleasant or distressing **:** WRETCHED, HORRID ⟨in a *foul* mood⟩
4 : OBSCENE, ABUSIVE ⟨*foul* language⟩
5 a : being wet and stormy **b :** obstructive to navigation ⟨a *foul* tide⟩
6 *dialect British* **:** HOMELY, UGLY
7 a : TREACHEROUS, DISHONORABLE ⟨fair means or *foul*⟩ **b :** constituting an infringement of rules in a game or sport ⟨a *foul* blow in boxing⟩
8 : containing marked-up corrections ⟨*foul* manuscript⟩ ⟨*foul* proofs⟩
9 : encrusted, clogged, or choked with a foreign substance ⟨the chimney was *foul* and smoked badly⟩
10 : being odorous and impure **:** POLLUTED ⟨*foul* air⟩
11 : placed in a situation that impedes physical movement **:** ENTANGLED
12 : being outside the foul lines in baseball
synonym *see* DIRTY
— **foul·ly** \'fau̇(l)-lē\ *adverb*
— **foul·ness** *noun*

²foul *noun* (before 12th century)
1 *archaic* **:** something foul
2 : an entanglement or collision especially in angling or sailing
3 a : an infringement of the rules in a game or sport **b :** FREE THROW
4 : FOUL BALL

³foul (before 12th century)
intransitive verb
1 : to become or be foul: as **a :** DECOMPOSE, ROT **b :** to become encrusted, clogged, or choked with a foreign substance **c :** to become entangled or come into collision
2 : to commit a violation of the rules in a sport or game
3 : to hit a foul ball
transitive verb
1 : to make foul: as **a :** to make dirty **:** POLLUTE **b :** to tangle or come into collision with **c :** to encrust with a foreign substance ⟨a ship's bottom *fouled* with barnacles⟩ **d :** OBSTRUCT, BLOCK
2 : DISHONOR, DISCREDIT
3 : to commit a foul against
4 : to hit (a baseball) foul

⁴foul *adverb* (13th century)
: in a foul manner **:** so as to be foul

fou·lard \fu̇-'lärd\ *noun* [French] (1830)
1 a : a lightweight plain-woven or twilled silk usually decorated with a printed pattern **b :** an imitation of this fabric
2 : an article of clothing made of foulard

foul ball *noun* (1860)
: a baseball batted into foul territory

foul·brood \'fau̇l-ˌbrüd\ *noun* (1863)
: a destructive disease of honeybee larvae caused by bacteria (as *Bacillus larvae*)

foul·ing *noun* (14th century)
: DEPOSIT, INCRUSTATION ⟨*fouling* on a ship's bottom⟩

foul line *noun* (1878)
1 : either of two straight lines extending from the rear corner of home plate through the outer corners of first and third base respectively and prolonged to the boundary of a baseball field
2 : a line across a bowling alley that a player must not step over when delivering the ball
3 : either of two lines on a basketball court parallel to and 15 feet from the backboards behind which a player must stand while shooting a free throw

foul–mouthed \'fau̇l-ˌmau̇t͟hd, -ˌmau̇tht\ *adjective* (1596)

: given to the use of obscene, profane, or abusive language

foul out *intransitive verb* (1948)
: to be put out of a basketball game for exceeding the number of fouls permitted

foul play *noun* (15th century)
1 : VIOLENCE; *especially* : MURDER
2 : FREE THROW

foul shot *noun* (circa 1949)
: FREE THROW

foul tip *noun* [¹foul + tip (tap)] (1870)
: a pitched ball in baseball that is slightly deflected by the bat; *specifically* : a tipped pitch legally caught by the catcher and counting as a full strike with the ball remaining in play

foul-up \'faul-,əp\ *noun* (1950)
1 : a state of confusion or an error caused by ineptitude, carelessness, or mismanagement ⟨*foul-ups* in transportation⟩
2 : a mechanical difficulty

foul up (1947)
transitive verb
1 : to make dirty : CONTAMINATE
2 : to spoil by making mistakes or using poor judgement : CONFUSE
3 : ENTANGLE, BLOCK ⟨*fouled up* communications⟩
~ *intransitive verb*
: to cause a foul-up : BUNGLE ⟨it was his fault. He had *fouled up*⟩ —Pat Frank

¹**found** \'faund\ *past and past participle of* FIND

²**found** *adjective* (1793)
1 : having all usual, standard, or reasonably expected equipment : such ⟨the boat comes fully *found*, ready to go⟩ —*Holiday*
2 : presented as or incorporated into an artistic work essentially as found ⟨sculpture of fabric, wood, and other *found* materials —Hilton Kramer⟩

³**found** *noun* (1830)
: free food and lodging in addition to wages ⟨they're paid $175 a month and *found* —*New Yorker*⟩

⁴**found** *transitive verb* [Middle English, from Old French *fonder*, from Latin *fundare*, from *fundus* bottom — more at BOTTOM] (13th century)
1 : to take the first steps in building
2 : to set or ground on something solid : BASE
3 : to establish (as an institution) often with provision for future maintenance

⁵**found** *transitive verb* [Middle French *fondre* to pour, melt, from Latin *fundere*; akin to Old English *gēotan* to pour, Greek *chein*] (1562)
: to melt (as metal) and pour into a mold

foun·da·tion \faun-'dā-shən\ *noun* (14th century)
1 : the act of founding
2 : a basis (as a tenet, principle, or axiom) upon which something stands or is supported ⟨the *foundations* of geometry⟩ ⟨the rumor is without *foundation* in fact⟩
3 a : funds given for the permanent support of an institution or institution established **b** : an organization or institution established by endowment with provision for future maintenance
4 : an underlying base or support; *especially* : the whole masonry substructure of a building
5 a : a body or ground upon which something is built up or overlaid **b** : a woman's supporting undergarment : CORSET **c** : a cosmetic usually used as a base for makeup
— **foun·da·tion·al** \-shnal, -sha-nʲl\ *adjective*
— **foun·da·tion·al·ly** *adverb*
— **foun·da·tion·less** \-shan-ləs\ *adjective*

foundation stone *noun* (1651)
1 : BASIS, GROUNDWORK
2 : a stone in the foundation of a building; *especially* : such a stone laid with public ceremony — compare CORNERSTONE

¹**found·er** \'faun-dər\ *noun* [¹found] (14th century)
: one that founds or establishes

²**found·er** \'faun-dər\ *verb* [Middle English *foundren* to send to the bottom, collapse, from Middle French *fondrer*; ultimately from Latin *fundus*] (14th century)
intransitive verb
1 : to become disabled; *especially* : to go lame
2 : to give way : COLLAPSE
3 : to sink below the surface of the water
4 : to come to grief : FAIL
~ *transitive verb*
: to disable (an animal) especially by excessive feeding

³**found·er** *noun* (circa 1547)
: one that founds metal; *especially* : TYPE-FOUNDER

founding father *noun* (1914)
1 : an originator of an institution or movement : FOUNDER
2 *often both F's capitalized* : a leading figure in the founding of the U.S.; *specifically* : a member of the American Constitutional Convention of 1787

found·ling \'faun(d)-lin\ *noun* (14th century)
: an infant found after its unknown parents have abandoned it

found object *noun* (1950)
: OBJET TROUVÉ

found poem *noun* (1966)
: a poem consisting of words found in a nonpoetic context (as a product label) and usually broken into lines that convey a verse rhythm

found·ry \'faun-drē\ *noun, plural* **foundries** (1536)
1 : an establishment where founding is carried on
2 : the act, process, or art of casting metals

¹**fount** \'faunt\ *noun* [Middle English, from Middle French *font*, from Latin *font-, fons*] (15th century)
1 : SOURCE
2 : FOUNTAIN, SOURCE

²**fount** \'faunt, 'faunt\ *noun* [Middle French *fonte*, from Middle French *fondre*, from Late Latin *fontana*, from Latin, feminine of *fontanus* of a spring, from *font-, fons*] (14th century)
1 : the source from which something proceeds or is supplied
2 : a spring of water issuing from the earth
3 : an artificially produced jet of water; *also* : the structure from which it rises
4 : a reservoir containing a liquid that can be drawn off as needed
5 : SODA FOUNTAIN 2

²**fountain** (1903)
intransitive verb
: to flow or spout like a fountain
~ *transitive verb*
: to cause to flow like a fountain

foun·tain·head \-,hed\ *noun* (1585)
1 : a spring that is the source of a stream
2 : principal source : ORIGIN

fountain pen *noun* (1710)
: a pen containing a reservoir that automatically feeds the writing point with ink

¹**four** \'fōr, 'fȯr\ *noun* [Middle English, from Old English *fēower*; akin to Old High German *fior* four, Latin *quattuor*, Greek *tessares, tettares*] (before 12th century)
1 — see NUMBER table
2 : the fourth in a set or series (the *four* of hearts)
3 : something having four units or members: as **a** : a 4-oared racing shell or its crew **b** : a 4-cylinder engine or automobile
— **four** *adjective*
— **four** *pronoun, plural in construction*

²**four** *adjective*

four-bag·ger \-'ba-gər\ *noun* (1926)
: HOME RUN

four-ball \-,bȯl\ *adjective* (1904)
: relating to or being a golf match in which the best individual score of one partnership is matched against the best individual score of another partnership for each hole

four·chée \fur-'shā\ *adjective* [French (feminine of a heraldic cross, forked] (1706)
: having the end of each arm forked — see CROSS illustration

four-dimensional *adjective* (1880)
: relating to or having four dimensions ⟨*four-dimensional* space-time continuum⟩; *especially* : consisting of or relating to elements requiring four coordinates to determine them

four·dri·ni·er \'fȯr-drə-'nir, ,fȯr-\ *noun, often capitalized* [Henry & Sealy *Fourdrinier*] (1839)
: a machine for making paper in an endless web

four-eyed \'fȯr-,īd, 'fȯr-\ *adjective* (1926)
: wearing glasses

4-F \'fȯr-'ef, 'fȯr-\ *noun* (1944)
: classification as unfit for military service; *also* : a person having this classification

four-flush *intransitive verb* (1896)
: to bluff in poker holding a four flush; *broadly* : to make a false claim : BLUFF
— **four-flush·er** \-'flə-shər\ *noun*

four flush *noun* (1887)
: four cards of the same suit in a 5-card poker hand

four·fold \'fȯr-,fōld, 'fȯr-, -'fōld\ *adjective* [Middle English, from Old English *fēower-feald*, from *fēower* + *-feald* -fold] (before 12th century)
1 : being four times as great or as many
2 : having four units or members
— **four·fold** \-'fōld\ *adverb*

four-foot·ed \-'fu-təd\ *adjective* (14th century)
: having four feet : QUADRUPED

four·gon \für-'gō⁽ⁿ⁾\ *noun, plural* **fourgons** \-'gō⁽ⁿ⁾(z)\ [French] (1848)
: a wagon for carrying baggage

4-H \'fȯr-'āch, 'fȯr-\ *adjective* [from the fourfold aim of improving the head, heart, hands, and health] (1926)
: of or relating to a program set up by the U.S. Department of Agriculture originally in rural areas to help young people become productive citizens by instructing them in useful skills (as in agriculture, animal husbandry, and carpentry), community service, and personal development
— **4-H'er** *also* **4-H-er** \-'āch-ər\ *noun*

four-hand \'fȯr-,hand, 'fȯr-\ *adjective* (circa 1909)
: FOUR-HANDED

four-hand·ed \-'han-dəd\ *adjective* (1824)
1 : engaged in by four persons (a *four-handed* card game)
2 : designed for four hands (a *four-handed* musical composition)

Four Horsemen *noun plural* [from the apocalyptic vision in Revelation 6:2–8] (1918)
: war, famine, pestilence, and death personified as the four major plagues of mankind

Four Hundred *or* **400** *noun* (1888)
: the exclusive social set of a community — used with *the*

Fou·ri·er analysis \für-ē-ə-\ *noun* J.B.J. *Fourier* (died 1830) French geometrician & physicist (circa 1928)
: the process of using the terms of a Fourier series to find a function that approximates a periodic function

Fou·ri·er·ism \für-ē-ə-,ri-zəm, -ē-,ā-i-\ *noun* [French *fouriérisme*, from F.M.C. *Fourier*] (1843)
: a system for reorganizing society into cooperative communities of small self-sustaining groups
— **Fou·ri·er·ist** \-ē-ə-rist, -ē-,ā-ist\ *noun*
— **Fou·ri·er series** \für-ē-,ā-\ *noun* [Baron J.B.J. *Fourier*] (1877)

\ə\ abut \ᵊ\ kitten \ər\ further \a\ ash \ā\ ace \ä\ mop, mar \au̇\ out \ch\ chin \e\ bet \ē\ easy \g\ go \i\ hit \ī\ ice \j\ job \ŋ\ sing \ō\ go \ȯ\ law \ȯi\ boy \th\ thin \t̲h\ this \ü\ loot \u̇\ foot \y\ yet \zh\ vision see also Guide to Pronunciation

: an infinite series in which the terms are constants multiplied by sine or cosine functions of integer multiples of the variable and which is used in the analysis of periodic functions

Fourier's theorem noun (1834)
: a theorem in mathematics: under suitable conditions any periodic function can be represented by a Fourier series

Fourier transform noun (1923)
: any of various functions (as $F(u)$) that under suitable conditions can be obtained from given functions (as $f(x)$) by multiplying by e^{iux} and integrating over all values of x and that in scientific instrumentation describe the dependence of the average of a series of measurements (as of a spectrum) on a quantity of interest (as brightness) especially of a very small magnitude — called also *Fourier transformation* (1793)

four-in-hand \fōr-ən-ˌhand, ˈfōr-\ noun (1793)
1 a : a team of four horses driven by one person b : a vehicle drawn by such a team
2 : a necktie tied in a slipknot with long ends overlapping vertically in front

four-letter adjective (1897)
: of, relating to, or being four-letter words

four-letter word noun (1897)
: any of a group of vulgar or obscene words typically made up of four letters

four-line octave noun [from the four accent marks appended to the letters representing its notes] (1931)
: the musical octave that begins on the third C above middle C — see PITCH illustration

four-o'clock \ˈfōr-ə-ˌkläk, ˈfōr-\ noun (1756)
: any of a genus (*Mirabilis*) of chiefly American annual or perennial herbs (family Nyctaginaceae, the four-o'clock family) having apetalous flowers with a showy involucre simulating a calyx; *especially* : a garden plant (*M. jalapa*) with fragrant yellow, red, or white flowers opening late in the afternoon

four of a kind (1934)
: four cards of the same rank in one hand — see POKER illustration

four-plex \ˈfōr-ˌpleks, ˈfōr-\ noun (1952)
: a building that contains four separate apartments

four-post-er \fōr-ˈpō-star, ˌfōr-\ noun (1836)
: a bed with tall or ten carved corner posts originally designed to support curtains or a canopy

four-poster

four-ra-gère \ˌfu̇r-ə-ˈzher\ noun [French, from feminine of *fourrager* of forage, from *fourrage* forage] (1919)
: a braided cord worn usually around the left shoulder; *especially* : such a cord awarded as a decoration to a military unit

four-score \ˈfōr-ˈskōr, ˈfōr-ˈskȯr\ adjective (13th century)
: being four times twenty : EIGHTY

four-some \ˈfōr-səm, ˈfōr-\ noun (14th century)
1 a : a group of four persons or things : QUARTET b : two couples
2 : a golf match in which two players compete against two others with players on each side taking turns playing one ball; *broadly* : any golf match involving four players

four-square \-ˈskwer, -ˈskwar\ adjective (14th century)
1 : SQUARE
2 : marked by boldness and conviction : FORTHRIGHT
— **foursquare** adverb

four-star \-ˈstär\ adjective [from the number of asterisks used to denote relative excellence in guidebooks] (1921)

: of a superior degree of excellence (a *four-star* French restaurant)

four-teen \fōr-ˈtēn, fȯr-; ˈfōr(t)-ˌtēn, ˈfȯr(t)-\ noun [Middle English *fourtene*, from Old English *fēowertīene*, from *fēowertiene*, adjective, from *fēower* + *-tiene*; akin to Old English *tīen*] (before 12th century)
— see NUMBER table
— **fourteen** adjective
— **fourteen** pronoun, plural in construction
— **four-teenth** \-ˈtēn(t)th; -ˌtēn(t)th\ adjective or noun

four-teen-er \-ˈtē-nər\ noun (1884)
: a verse consisting of 14 syllables or especially of 7 iambic feet

fourth \ˈfōrth, ˈfȯrth\ noun, plural **fourths** \ˈfōr(th)s, ˈfȯr(th)s\ (before 12th century)
1 — see NUMBER table
2 a : a musical interval embracing four tones specifically: SUBDOMINANT 1 c : the harmonic combination of two tones a fourth apart b : a tone at this interval; *specifically* : SUBDOMINANT 1 c : the harmonic combination of two tones a fourth apart
3 : the 4th forward gear or speed of a motor vehicle
4 *capitalized* : INDEPENDENCE DAY — used with *the*
— **fourth** adjective or adverb
— **fourth-ly** adverb

fourth class noun (1862)
1 : a class or group ranking fourth in a series
2 : a class of mail in the U.S. that comprises merchandise and non-second-class printed matter and is not sealed against inspection

fourth dimension noun (1875)
1 : a dimension in addition to length, breadth, and depth; *specifically* : a coordinate in addition to three rectangular coordinates especially when interpreted as the time coordinate in a space-time continuum
2 : something outside the range of ordinary experience
— **fourth-dimensional** adjective

fourth estate noun, often F&E capitalized (1752)
: the public press ◇

Fourth of July (1779)
: INDEPENDENCE DAY

fourth world noun, often F&W capitalized (1974)
: a group of nations especially in Africa and Asia characterized by extremely low per capita income and an absence of valuable natural resources

four-way \ˈfōr-ˈwā, ˈfōr-\ adjective (1824)
1 : allowing or affecting passage in any of four directions
2 : including four participants

four-wheel \ˈfōr-ˌhwēl, ˈfȯr-, -ˌwēl\ or **four-wheeled** \-ˌhwē(ə)ld, -ˌwē(ə)ld\ adjective (1740)
1 : having four wheels
2 : acting on or by means of four wheels of an automotive vehicle ⟨*four-wheel* drive⟩

four-wheel-er \-ˌhwē-lər, -ˌwē-\ noun (1846)
: a vehicle with four wheels

fo-vea \ˈfō-vē-ə\ noun, plural **fo-ve-ae** \-vē-ˌī\ [New Latin, from Latin, pit] (1849)
1 : a small fossa
2 : a small rodless area of the retina that affords most acute vision — see EYE illustration
— **fo-ve-al** \-vē-əl\ adjective
— **fo-ve-ate** \-vē-ˌāt, -ət\ adjective

fovea cen-tra-lis \-sen-ˈtra-ləs, -ˈträ-\ noun [New Latin, central fovea] (1858)
: FOVEA 2

fowl \ˈfau̇(ə)l\ noun, plural **fowl** or **fowls** [Middle English *foul*, from Old English *fugel*; akin to Old High German *fogal* bird, and probably to Old English *flēogan* to fly — more at FLY] (before 12th century)
1 : a bird of any kind — compare WATERFOWL, WILDFOWL
2 a : a cock or hen of the domestic chicken (*Gallus gallus*); *especially* : an adult hen b

: any of several domesticated or wild gallinaceous birds — compare GUINEA FOWL, JUNGLE FOWL
3 : the meat of fowls used as food

²fowl intransitive verb (before 12th century)
: to seek, catch, or kill wildfowl
— **fowl-er** noun

fowling piece noun (1596)
: a shotgun for shooting birds or small quadrupeds

¹fox \ˈfäks\ noun, plural **fox-es** also **fox** often attributive [Middle English, from Old English; akin to Old High German *fuhs* fox and perhaps to Sanskrit *puccha* tail] (before 12th century)
1 a : any of various carnivorous mammals (especially genus *Vulpes*) of the dog family related to but smaller than wolves with shorter legs, more pointed muzzle, large erect ears, and long bushy tail b : the fur of a fox
2 : a clever crafty person
3 *archaic* : SWORD
4 *capitalized* : a member of an American Indian people formerly living in what is now Wisconsin
5 : a good-looking young woman or man
word history see VIXEN

²fox transitive verb (1611)
1 *obsolete* : INTOXICATE
2 a : to trick by ingenuity or cunning : OUTWIT b : BAFFLE

foxed \ˈfäkst\ adjective (1847)
: discolored with yellowish brown stains

fox fire noun (15th century)
: an eerie phosphorescent light (as of decaying wood; *also* : a luminous fungus (as *Armillaria mellea*) that causes decaying wood to glow

fox-glove \ˈfäks-ˌgləv\ noun (before 12th century)
: any of a genus (*Digitalis*) of erect herbs of the snapdragon family; *especially* : a common European biennial or perennial (*D. purpurea*) cultivated for its showy racemes of dotted white or purple tubular flowers and as a source of digitalis

fox grape noun (1657)
: any of several native grapes (especially *Vitis labrusca*) of eastern North America with sour or musky fruit

fox-hole \ˈfäks-ˌhōl\ noun (1919)
: a pit dug usually hastily for individual cover from enemy fire

fox-hound \-ˌhau̇nd\ noun (circa 1763)
: any of various large swift powerful hounds of great endurance used in hunting foxes and developed to form several breeds and many distinctive strains — compare AMERICAN FOXHOUND, ENGLISH FOXHOUND

fox-hunt \-ˌhant\ noun (1692)
1 : one who engages in foxhunting

fox-hunt-er \-ˌhən-tər\ noun (1674)
2 : HUNTER 1c

fox-hunt-ing \-ˌhən-tiŋ\ noun (1674)
: a pastime in which participants on horseback ride over the countryside following a pack of hounds on the trail of a fox
— **fox-hunt** \ˈfäks-ˌhənt\ intransitive verb
— **fox-tail** \-ˌtāl\ noun (14th century)

1 a : the tail of a fox **b :** something resembling the tail of a fox
2 : any of several grasses (especially genera *Alopecurus*, *Hordeum*, and *Setaria*) with spikes resembling brushes — called also *foxtail grass*
foxtail lily *noun* (1946)
: EREMURUS
foxtail millet *noun* (circa 1899)
: a coarse drought-resistant but frost-sensitive annual grass (*Setaria italica*) grown for grain, hay, and forage
fox terrier *noun* (1823)
: any of a smooth-haired or a wirehaired breed of small lively terriers formerly used to dig out foxes

fox terrier

Fox·trot \'fäks-ˌträt\ (1952)
— a communications code word for the letter *f*
¹**fox–trot** \'fäks-ˌträt\ *noun* (1872)
1 : a short broken slow trotting gait in which the hind foot of the horse hits the ground a trifle before the diagonally opposite forefoot
2 : a ballroom dance in duple time that includes slow walking steps, quick running steps, and the step of the two-step
²**fox–trot** *intransitive verb* (1916)
: to dance the fox-trot
foxy \'fäk-sē\ *adjective* **fox·i·er; -est** (1528)
1 : resembling or suggestive of a fox ⟨a narrow *foxy* face⟩: as **a :** cunningly shrewd **b :** of a warm reddish brown color ⟨*foxy* eyebrows⟩
2 : having a sharp brisk flavor ⟨*foxy* grapes⟩
3 : physically attractive ⟨a *foxy* lady⟩
synonym see SLY
— **fox·i·ly** \'fäk-sə-lē\ *adverb*
— **fox·i·ness** \-sē-nəs\ *noun*
foy \'fȯi\ *noun* [Dutch dialect *fooi* feast at end of the harvest] (circa 1645)
chiefly Scottish **:** a farewell feast or gift
foy·er \'fȯi-(-ə)r, 'fȯi-ˌ(y)ā *also* 'fwä-ˌyā\ *noun* [French, literally, fireplace, from (assumed) Vulgar Latin *focarium*, from Latin *focus* hearth] (1859)
: an anteroom or lobby especially of a theater; *also* **:** an entrance hallway **:** VESTIBULE
Fra \'frä\ *noun* [Italian, short for *frate*, from Latin *frater* — more at BROTHER] (circa 1890)
— used as a title equivalent to *brother* preceding the name of an Italian monk or friar
fra·cas \'frā-kəs, *British* 'fra-ˌkä\ *noun, plural* **fra·cas·es** \-kə-səz\ *or British* **fracas** \-ˌkäz\ [French, din, row, from Italian *fracasso*, from *fracassare* to shatter] (1727)
: a noisy quarrel **:** BRAWL
frac·tal \'frak-t°l\ *noun* [French *fractale*, from Latin *fractus* broken, uneven (past participle of *frangere* to break) + French *-ale* -al (noun suffix)] (1975)
: any of various extremely irregular curves or shapes for which any suitably chosen part is similar in shape to a given larger or smaller part when magnified or reduced to the same size
— **fractal** *adjective*
fract·ed \'frak-təd\ *adjective* [Latin *fractus*] (1547)
obsolete **:** BROKEN
frac·tion \'frak-shən\ *noun* [Middle English *fraccioun*, from Late Latin *fraction-, fractio*

act of breaking, from Latin *frangere* to break — more at BREAK] (14th century)
1 a : a numerical representation (as ¾, ⅝, 3.234) indicating the quotient of two numbers **b** (1) **:** a piece broken off **:** FRAGMENT (2) **:** a discrete unit **:** PORTION
2 : one of several portions (as of a distillate) separable by fractionation
3 : BIT, LITTLE ⟨a *fraction* closer⟩
frac·tion·al \-shnəl, -shə-n°l\ *adjective* (1675)
1 : of, relating to, or being a fraction
2 : of, relating to, or being fractional currency
3 : relatively small **:** INCONSIDERABLE
4 : of, relating to, or involving a process for separating components of a mixture through differences in physical or chemical properties ⟨*fractional* distillation⟩
— **frac·tion·al·ly** *adverb*
fractional currency *noun* (1862)
1 : paper money in denominations of less than one dollar issued by the U.S. 1863–76
2 : currency in denominations less than the basic monetary unit
frac·tion·al·ize \'frak-shnə-ˌlīz, -shə-n°l-ˌīz\ *transitive verb* **-ized; -iz·ing** (1924)
: to break up into parts or sections
— **frac·tion·al·iza·tion** \ˌfrak-shnə-lə-'zā-shən, -shə-n°l-ə-'zā-\ *noun*
frac·tion·ate \'frak-shə-ˌnāt\ *transitive verb* **-at·ed; -at·ing** (1867)
1 : to separate (as a mixture) into different portions
2 : to divide or break up
— **frac·tion·ation** \ˌfrak-shə-'nā-shən\ *noun*
— **frac·tion·ator** \'frak-shə-ˌnā-tər\ *noun*
frac·tious \'frak-shəs\ *adjective* [*fraction* (discord) + *-ous*] (1725)
1 : tending to be troublesome **:** UNRULY
2 : QUARRELSOME, IRRITABLE
— **frac·tious·ly** *adverb*
— **frac·tious·ness** *noun*
¹**frac·ture** \'frak-chər, -shər\ *noun* [Middle English, from Latin *fractura*, from *fractus*] (15th century)
1 : the result of fracturing **:** BREAK
2 a : the act or process of breaking or the state of being broken; *especially* **:** the breaking of hard tissue (as bone) **b :** the rupture (as by tearing) of soft tissue ⟨kidney *fracture*⟩
3 : the general appearance of a freshly broken surface of a mineral
²**fracture** *verb* **frac·tured; frac·tur·ing** \-chə-riŋ, -shriŋ\ (1612)
transitive verb
1 a : to cause a fracture in **:** BREAK ⟨*fracture* a rib⟩ **b :** RUPTURE, TEAR
2 a : to damage or destroy as if by rupturing **b :** to cause great disorder in **c :** to break up **:** FRACTIONATE **d :** to go beyond the limits of (as rules) **:** VIOLATE ⟨*fractured* the English language with malaprops —Goodman Ace⟩
intransitive verb
: to undergo fracture
fracture zone *noun* (1946)
: an area of suboceanic crust characterized by fractures
frae \'frā\ *preposition* [Middle English (northern) *fra, frae*, from Old Norse *frā;* akin to Old English *fram* from] (1700)
Scottish **:** FROM
frag·ile \'fra-jəl, -ˌjīl\ *adjective* [Middle French, from Latin *fragilis* — more at FRAIL] (1607)
1 a : easily broken or destroyed **b :** constitutionally delicate **:** lacking in physical vigor
2 : TENUOUS, SLIGHT ☆
— **fra·gil·i·ty** \frə-'ji-lə-tē\ *noun*
¹**frag·ment** \'frag-mənt\ *noun* [Middle English, from Latin *fragmentum*, from *frangere* to break — more at BREAK] (15th century)
: a part broken off, detached, or incomplete
synonym see PART
²**frag·ment** \-ˌment\ (1818)
intransitive verb
: to fall to pieces

transitive verb
: to break up or apart into fragments
frag·men·tal \frag-'men-t°l\ *adjective* (1798)
: FRAGMENTARY
— **frag·men·tal·ly** \-t°l-ē\ *adverb*
frag·men·tary \'frag-mən-ˌter-ē\ *adjective* (1611)
: consisting of fragments **:** INCOMPLETE
— **frag·men·tari·ly** \ˌfrag-mən-'ter-ə-lē\ *adverb*
— **frag·men·tari·ness** \-ˌter-ē-nəs\ *noun*
frag·men·ta·tion \ˌfrag-mən-'tā-shən, -ˌmen-\ *noun* (1881)
1 : the act or process of fragmenting or making fragmentary
2 : the state of being fragmented or fragmentary
— **frag·men·tate** \'frag-mən-ˌtāt\ *verb*
fragmentation bomb *noun* (1918)
: a bomb or shell whose relatively thick casing is splintered upon explosion and thrown in fragments in all directions
frag·men·tize \'frag-mən-ˌtīz\ *transitive verb* **-tized; -tiz·ing** (1815)
: FRAGMENT
fra·grance \'frā-grən(t)s\ *noun* (1667)
1 a : a sweet or delicate odor (as of fresh flowers, pine trees, or perfume) **b :** something (as a perfume) compounded to give off a sweet or pleasant odor
2 : the quality or state of having a sweet odor ☆
fra·gran·cy \-grən(t)-sē\ *noun* (1578)
fra·grant \'frā-grənt\ *adjective* [Middle English, from Latin *fragrant-, fragrans*, from present participle of *fragrare* to be fragrant] (15th century)
: marked by fragrance
synonym see ODOROUS
— **fra·grant·ly** *adverb*
frail \'frā(ə)l\ *adjective* [Middle English, from Middle French *fraile*, from Latin *fragilis* fragile, from *frangere*] (14th century)
1 : easily led into evil ⟨*frail* humanity⟩
2 : easily broken or destroyed **:** FRAGILE
3 a : physically weak **b :** SLIGHT, UNSUBSTANTIAL
synonym see WEAK

☆ **SYNONYMS**
Fragile, frangible, brittle, crisp, friable mean breaking easily. FRAGILE implies extreme delicacy of material or construction and need for careful handling ⟨a *fragile* antique chair⟩. FRANGIBLE implies susceptibility to being broken without implying weakness or delicacy ⟨*frangible* stone used for paving⟩. BRITTLE implies hardness together with lack of elasticity or flexibility or toughness ⟨patients with *brittle* bones⟩. CRISP implies a firmness and brittleness desirable especially in some foods ⟨*crisp* lettuce⟩. FRIABLE applies to substances that are easily crumbled or pulverized ⟨*friable* soil⟩. See in addition WEAK.

Fragrance, perfume, scent, redolence mean a sweet or pleasant odor. FRAGRANCE suggests the odors of flowers or other growing things ⟨the *fragrance* of pine⟩. PERFUME may suggest a stronger or heavier odor ⟨the *perfume* of lilacs⟩. SCENT is very close to PERFUME but of wider application because more neutral in connotation ⟨*scent*-free soaps⟩. REDOLENCE implies a mixture of fragrant or pungent odors ⟨the *redolence* of a forest after a rain⟩.

\ə\ **abut** \°\ **kitten** \ər\ **further** \a\ **ash** \ā\ **ace**
\ä\ **mop, mar** \au̇\ **out** \ch\ **chin** \e\ **bet** \ē\ **easy**
\g\ **go** \i\ **hit** \ī\ **ice** \j\ **job** \ŋ\ **sing** \ō\ **go**
\ȯ\ **law** \ȯi\ **boy** \th\ **thin** \th\ **the** \ü\ **loot** \u̇\ **foot**
\y\ **yet** \zh\ **vision** *see also* Guide to Pronunciation

— **frail·ly** \\'frā(ə)(l)-lē\\ *adverb*

— **frail·ness** *noun*

frail·ty \\'frā(-ə)l-tē\\ *noun, plural* **frailties** (14th century)

1 : the quality or state of being frail

2 : a fault due to weakness especially of moral character

synonym *see* FAULT

fraise \\'frāz\\ *noun* [French] (1775)

: an obstacle of pointed stakes driven into the ramparts of a fortification in a horizontal or inclined position

Frak·tur *also* **Frac·tur** \\fräk-'tùr\\ *noun* [German, from Latin *fractura* fracture] (1904)

1 : a German style of black letter

2 *often not capitalized* : a Pennsylvania German document (as a birth or wedding certificate) that is written in calligraphy and illuminated with decorative motifs (as tulips, birds, and scrolls)

fram·be·sia \\fram-'bē-zh(ē-)ə\\ *noun* [New Latin, from French *framboise* raspberry; from the appearance of the lesions] (1803)

: YAWS

fram·boise \\frän-'bwäz\\ *noun* [French, literally, raspberry, from Old French, of Germanic origin; akin to Dutch *braambes* blackberry, literally, bramble berry, Old High German *brāmberi* — more at BROOM, BERRY] (circa 1945)

: a brandy or liqueur made from raspberries

¹frame \\'frām\\ *verb* **framed; fram·ing** [Middle English, to benefit, construct, from Old English *framian* to benefit, make progress; akin to Old Norse *fram* forward, Old English *fram* from] (14th century)

transitive verb

1 : to construct by fitting and uniting the parts of the skeleton of (a structure)

2 a : PLAN, CONTRIVE ⟨*framed* a new method of achieving their purpose⟩ **b** : SHAPE, CONSTRUCT **c** : to give expression to : FORMULATE **d** : to draw up (a document)

3 a : to devise falsely (as a criminal charge) **b** : to contrive the evidence against (an innocent person) so that a verdict of guilty is assured **c** : FIX 7b

4 : to fit or adjust especially to something or for an end : ARRANGE

5 *obsolete* : PRODUCE

6 : to enclose in a frame; *also* : to enclose as if in a frame

intransitive verb

1 *archaic* : PROCEED, GO

2 *obsolete* : MANAGE

— **fram·able** *or* **frame·able** \\'frā-mə-bəl\\ *adjective*

— **fram·er** *noun*

²frame *noun* (14th century)

1 a : something composed of parts fitted together and united **b** : the physical makeup of an animal and especially a human body : PHYSIQUE, FIGURE

2 a : the constructional system that gives shape or strength (as to a building); *also* : a frame dwelling **b** : such a skeleton not filled in or covered

3 *obsolete* : the act or manner of framing

4 a : a machine built upon or within a framework ⟨a spinning *frame*⟩ **b** : an open case or structure made for admitting, enclosing, or supporting something ⟨a window *frame*⟩ **c** (1) : a part of a pair of glasses that holds one of the lenses (2) *plural* : that part of a pair of glasses other than the lenses **d** : a structural unit in an automobile chassis supported on the axles and supporting the rest of the chassis and the body

5 a : an enclosing border **b** : the matter or area enclosed in such a border: as (1) : one of the squares in which scores for each round are recorded (as in bowling); *also* : a round in bowling (2) : an individual drawing in a comic strip usually enclosed by a bordering line (3) : one picture of the series on a length of film (4) : a complete image for display (as on a television

set) **c** : an inning in baseball **d** (1) : FRAMEWORK 1a (2) : FRAMEWORK, FRAME OF REFERENCE **e** : an event that forms the background for the action of a novel or play

6 : FRAME-UP

³frame *adjective* (1775)

: having a wood frame ⟨*frame* houses⟩

frame of mind (1665)

: mental attitude or outlook : MOOD

frame of reference (1897)

1 : an arbitrary set of axes with reference to which the position or motion of something is described or physical laws are formulated

2 : a set of ideas, conditions, or assumptions that determine how something will be approached, perceived, or understood ⟨a Marxian *frame of reference*⟩

frame·shift \\'frām-,shift\\ *adjective* (1967)

: relating to, being, or causing a mutation in which a number of nucleotides not divisible by three is inserted or deleted so as to change the reading frame of some triplet codons during genetic translation

— **frameshift** *noun*

frame-up \\'frā-,məp\\ *noun* (1889)

1 : an act or series of actions in which someone is framed

2 : an action that is framed

frame·work \\'frām-,wərk\\ *noun* (1644)

1 a : a basic conceptional structure (as of ideas) ⟨the *framework* of the constitution⟩ **b** : a skeletal, openwork, or structural frame

2 : FRAME OF REFERENCE

3 : the larger branches of a tree that determine its shape

fram·ing \\'frā-miŋ\\ *noun* (1703)

: FRAME, FRAMEWORK

franc \\'fraŋk\\ *noun* [French] (14th century)

— *see* MONEY table

¹fran·chise \\'fran-,chīz\\ *noun* [Middle English, from Middle French, from *franchir* to free, from Old French *franc* free — more at FRANK] (14th century)

1 : freedom or immunity from some burden or restriction vested in a person or group

2 a : a special privilege granted to an individual or group; *especially* : the right to be and exercise the powers of a corporation **b** : a constitutional or statutory right or privilege; *especially* : the right to vote **c** (1) : the right or license granted to an individual or group to market a company's goods or services in a particular territory; *also* : a business granted such a right or license (2) : the territory involved in such a right

3 a : the right of membership in a professional sports league **b** : a team and its operating organization having such membership

²franchise *transitive verb* **fran·chised; fran·chis·ing** (14th century)

1 *archaic* : FREE

2 : to grant a franchise to

fran·chi·see \\,fran-,chī-'zē, -chə-\\ *noun* (1954)

: one granted a franchise

fran·chis·er \\'fran-,chī-zər\\ *noun* [in sense 1, from ¹*franchise;* in sense 2, from ²*franchise*] (1843)

1 : FRANCHISEE

2 : FRANCHISOR

fran·chi·sor \\,fran-,chī-'zòr, -chə-\\ *noun* [²*franchise* + ¹*-or*] (1967)

: one that grants a franchise

Fran·cis·can \\fran-'sis-kən\\ *noun* [Medieval Latin *Franciscus* Francis] (1599)

: a member of the Order of Friars Minor founded by Saint Francis of Assisi in 1209 and dedicated especially to preaching, missions, and charities

— **Franciscan** *adjective*

fran·ci·um \\'fran(t)-sē-əm\\ *noun* [New Latin, from *France*] (1946)

: a radioactive element of the alkali-metal group discovered as a disintegration product of actinium and obtained artificially by the

bombardment of thorium with protons — see ELEMENT table

Franco- *combining form* [Medieval Latin, from *Francus* Frenchman, from Late Latin, Frank]

1 : French and ⟨*Franco*-American⟩

2 : French ⟨*Franco*phile⟩

Fran·co-Amer·i·can \\,fran-kō-ə-'mer-ə-kən\\ *noun* (1859)

: an American of French or especially French-Canadian descent

— **Franco–American** *adjective*

fran·co·lin \\'fran-k(ə-)lən\\ *noun* [French, from Italian *francolino*] (1653)

: any of a genus (*Francolinus*) of partridges of southern Asia and Africa

Fran·co·phile \\'fran-kə-,fīl, -kō-\\ *or* **Fran·co·phil** \\-,fil\\ *adjective* (1889)

: markedly friendly to France or French culture

— **Francophile** *noun*

— **Fran·co·phil·ia** \\,fran-kə-'fi-lē-ə, -lyə, -kō-\\ *noun*

Fran·co·phobe \\-,fōb\\ *adjective* (1891)

: marked by a fear or strong dislike of France or French culture or customs

— **Francophobe** *noun*

— **Fran·co·pho·bia** \\,fran-kə-'fō-bē-ə, -kō-\\ *noun*

fran·co·phone \\-,fōn\\ *adjective, often capitalized* (1962)

: of, having, or belonging to a population using French as its first or sometimes second language

— **Francophone** *noun*

franc–ti·reur \\,fräⁿ-(,)tē-'rər\\ *noun* [French, from *franc* free + *tireur* shooter] (1808)

: a civilian fighter or sniper

fran·gi·ble \\'fran-jə-bəl\\ *adjective* [Middle English, from Middle French & Medieval Latin; Middle French, from Medieval Latin *frangibilis*, from Latin *frangere* to break — more at BREAK] (15th century)

: readily or easily broken

synonym *see* FRAGILE

— **fran·gi·bil·i·ty** \\,fran-jə-'bi-lə-tē\\ *noun*

fran·gi·pane \\'fran-jə-,pān, fräⁿ-zhē-'pán\\ *noun* [French, frangipani (perfume), fragipane, from Italian] (1858)

: a custard usually flavored with almonds

fran·gi·pa·ni *also* **fran·gi·pan·ni** \\,fran-jə-'pa-nē, -'pä-\\ *noun, plural* **-pani** *also* **-panni** [modification of Italian *frangipane*, from Muzio *Frangipane*, 16th century Italian nobleman] (1676)

1 : a perfume derived from or imitating the odor of the flower of a frangipani (*Plumeria rubra*)

2 : any of a genus (*Plumeria*) of shrubs or small trees of the dogbane family that are native to the American tropics and widely cultivated as ornamentals

fran·glais \\frä-'glä\\ *noun, often capitalized* [French, blend of *français* French and *anglais* English] (1964)

: French marked by a considerable number of borrowings from English

¹frank \\'fraŋk\\ *adjective* [Middle English, free, from Old French *franc*, from Medieval Latin *francus*, from Late Latin *Francus* Frank] (1548)

1 : marked by free, forthright, and sincere expression ⟨a *frank* reply⟩

2 a : unmistakably evident ⟨*frank* materialism⟩ **b** : clinically evident and unmistakable ⟨*frank* pus⟩ ☆ ◇

— **frank·ness** *noun*

²frank *transitive verb* (1708)

1 a : to mark (a piece of mail) with an official signature or sign indicating the right of the sender to free mailing **b** : to mail free **c** : to affix to (mail) a stamp or a marking indicating the payment of postage

2 : to enable to pass or go freely or easily

— **frank·able** \\'fraŋ-kə-bəl\\ *adjective*

— **frank·er** *noun*

³frank *noun* (1713)

1 a : the signature of the sender on a piece of franked mail serving in place of a postage stamp **b :** a mark or stamp on a piece of mail indicating postage paid **c :** a franked envelope **2 :** the privilege of sending mail free of charge

⁴frank *noun* (1904)
: FRANKFURTER

Frank \'frank\ *noun* [Middle English, partly from Old English *Franca*; partly from Old French *Franc*, from Late Latin *Francus*, of Germanic origin; akin to Old High German *Franko* Frank, Old English *Franca*] (before 12th century)
: a member of a West Germanic people that entered the Roman provinces in A.D. 253, occupied the Netherlands and most of Gaul, and established themselves along the Rhine

Fran·ken·stein \'fran-kən-ˌstīn *also* -ˌstēn\ *noun*
1 a : the title character in Mary W. Shelley's novel *Frankenstein* who creates a monster by which he is eventually killed **b :** a monster in the shape of a man especially in popularized versions of the Frankenstein story **2 :** a monstrous creation; *especially* **:** a work or agency that ruins its originator
— **Fran·ken·stein·ian** \ˌfran-kən-'stī-nē-ən, -'sti-\ *adjective*

frank·furt·er \'frank-fə(r)t-ər, -ˌfərt-\ *or* **frank·furt** \-fərt\ *noun* [German *Frankfurter* of Frankfurt, from *Frankfurt am Main*, Germany] (1894)
: a cured cooked sausage (as of beef or beef and pork) that may be skinless or stuffed in a casing

frank·in·cense \'fran-kən-ˌsen(t)s\ *noun* [Middle English *fraunk encense*, from Old French *franc encens*, from *franc* (perhaps in sense "of high quality") + *encens* incense] (14th century)
: a fragrant gum resin from trees of a genus (*Boswellia* of the family Burseraceae) of Somalia and southern coastal Arabia that is an important incense resin and was used in ancient times in religious rites and in embalming

¹Frank·ish \'fran-kish\ *adjective* (14th century)
: of or relating to the Franks

²Frankish *noun* (1863)
: the Germanic language of the Franks

frank·lin \'fran-klən\ *noun* [Middle English *frankeleyn*, from Anglo-French *fraunclein*, from Old French *franc*] (14th century)
: a medieval English landowner of free but not noble birth

frank·lin·ite \-klə-ˌnīt\ *noun* [*Franklin*, N.J.] (1820)
: a black slightly magnetic mineral consisting of an oxide of iron and zinc

Frank·lin stove \'fran-klən-\ *noun* [Benjamin *Franklin*, its inventor] (1787)
: a metal heating stove resembling an open fireplace but designed to be set out in a room

Franklin stove

frank·ly \'fran-klē\ *adverb* (1537)
1 : in a frank manner
2 : in truth **:** INDEED
usage see HOPE-FULLY

frank·pledge \'frank-ˌplej\ *noun* [Middle English *frankeplegge*, from Anglo-French *fraunc plege* (probably translation of Middle English *friborg* peace pledge), from *fraunc* free (from Old French *franc*) + *plege* pledge] (15th century)
: an Anglo-Saxon system under which each adult male member of a tithing was responsible for the good conduct of the others; *also* **:** the member himself or the tithing

fran·tic \'fran-tik\ *adjective* [Middle English *frenetik, frantik* — more at FRENETIC] (14th century)
1 a *archaic* **:** mentally deranged **b :** emotionally out of control 〈*frantic* with anger and frustration〉
2 : marked by fast and nervous, disordered, or anxiety-driven activity 〈made a *frantic* search for the lost child〉
— **fran·ti·cal·ly** \-ti-k(ə-)lē\ *adverb*
— **fran·tic·ness** \-tik-nəs\ *noun*

frap \'frap\ *transitive verb* **frapped; frapping** [Middle English, to strike, beat, from Middle French *fraper*] (1548)
: to draw tight (as with ropes or cables) 〈*frap* a sail〉

¹frap·pé \fra-'pā\ *adjective* [French, from past participle of *frapper* to strike, chill, from Middle French *fraper* to strike] (1848)
: chilled or partly frozen

²frap·pé \fra-'pā\ *or* **frappe** \'frap, fra-'pā\ *noun* (1903)
1 a : a partly frozen drink (as of fruit juice) **b :** a liqueur served over shaved ice
2 : a thick milk shake

Fra·ser fir \'frā-zər-\ *noun* [John *Fraser* (died 1811) British botanist] (1897)
: a southern Appalachian fir (*Abies fraseri*) that resembles the balsam fir

frass \'fras\ *noun* [German, insect damage, literally, eating away, from Old High German *vrāz* food, from *frezzan* to devour — more at FRET] (1854)
: debris or excrement produced by insects

frat \'frat\ *noun* (circa 1895)
: FRATERNITY 1c

fra·ter·nal \frə-'tər-n°l\ *adjective* [Middle English, from Medieval Latin *fraternalis*, from Latin *fraternus*, from *frater* brother — more at BROTHER] (15th century)
1 a : of, relating to, or involving brothers **b :** of, relating to, or being a fraternity or society 〈a *fraternal* order〉
2 : derived from two ova **:** DIZYGOTIC 〈*fraternal* twins〉
3 : FRIENDLY, BROTHERLY
— **fra·ter·nal·ism** \-n°l-ˌiz-əm\ *noun*
— **fra·ter·nal·ly** \-n°l-ē\ *adverb*

fra·ter·ni·ty \frə-'tər-nə-tē\ *noun, plural* **-ties** (14th century)
1 : a group of people associated or formally organized for a common purpose, interest, or pleasure: as **a :** a fraternal order **b :** GUILD **c :** a men's student organization formed chiefly for social purposes having secret rites and a name consisting of Greek letters **d :** a student organization for scholastic, professional, or extracurricular activities 〈a debating *fraternity*〉
2 : the quality or state of being brothers **:** BROTHERLINESS
3 : persons of the same class, profession, character, or tastes 〈the racetrack *fraternity*〉

frat·er·nize \'fra-tər-ˌnīz\ *intransitive verb* **-nized; -niz·ing** (1611)
1 : to associate or mingle as brothers or on fraternal terms
2 a : to associate on close terms with members of a hostile group especially when contrary to military orders **b :** to be friendly or amiable
— **frat·er·ni·za·tion** \ˌfra-tər-nə-'zā-shən\ *noun*
— **frat·er·niz·er** \'fra-tər-ˌnī-zər\ *noun*

frat·ri·cide \'fra-trə-ˌsīd\ *noun* [in sense 1, from Middle English, from Middle French or Latin; Middle French, from Latin *fratricida*, from *fratr-, frater* brother + *-cida* -cide; in sense 2, from Middle French or Latin; Middle French, from Latin *fratricidium*, from *fratr-, frater* brother + *-cidium* -cide] (15th century)
1 : one that murders or kills his or her own brother or sister or an individual (as a countryman) having a relationship like that of a brother or sister
2 : the act of a fratricide
— **frat·ri·cid·al** \ˌfra-trə-'sī-d°l\ *adjective*

Frau \'frau̇\ *noun, plural* **Frau·en** \'frau̇(-ə)n\ [German, woman, wife, from Old High German *frouwa* mistress, lady; akin to Old English *frēa* lord, Old High German *fruma* advantage — more at FOREMOST] (circa 1813)
: a German married woman **:** WIFE — used as a title equivalent to *Mrs.*

fraud \'frȯd\ *noun* [Middle English *fraude*, from Middle French, from Latin *fraud-, fraus*] (14th century)
1 a : DECEIT, TRICKERY; *specifically* **:** intentional perversion of truth in order to induce another to part with something of value or to surrender a legal right **b :** an act of deceiving or misrepresenting **:** TRICK
2 a : a person who is not what he or she pretends to be **:** IMPOSTOR; *also* **:** one who defrauds **:** CHEAT **b :** one that is not what it seems or is represented to be
synonym see DECEPTION, IMPOSTURE

fraud·u·lence \'frȯ-jə-lən(t)s\ *noun* (1601)
: the quality or state of being fraudulent

fraud·u·lent \-lənt\ *adjective* (15th century)
: characterized by, based on, or done by fraud **:** DECEITFUL
— **fraud·u·lent·ly** *adverb*
— **fraud·u·lent·ness** *noun*

¹fraught \'frȯt\ *noun* [Middle English, freight, load, from Middle Dutch or Middle Low German *vracht, vrecht*] (14th century)
chiefly Scottish **:** LOAD, CARGO

²**fraught** *transitive verb* **fraught·ed** *or* **fraught; fraught·ing** [Middle English *fraughten,* from ¹*fraught*] (14th century) *chiefly Scottish* : LOAD, FREIGHT

³**fraught** \'frȯt\ *adjective* [Middle English, from past participle of *fraughten*] (14th century)
1 *archaic* **a** : LADEN **b** : well supplied or provided
2 : full of or accompanied by something specified — used with *with* ⟨a situation *fraught* with danger⟩
3 *chiefly British* : causing or characterized by emotional distress or tension : UNEASY

fräu·lein \'froi-,līn\ *noun* [German, diminutive of *Frau*] (circa 1689)
1 *capitalized* : an unmarried German woman — used as a title equivalent to *Miss*
2 : a German governess

frax·i·nel·la \,frak-sə-'ne-lə\ *noun* [New Latin, diminutive of Latin *fraxinus* ash tree — more at BIRCH] (1664)
: a Eurasian perennial herb (*Dictamnus albus*) of the rue family with flowers that exhale a flammable vapor in hot weather — called also *gas plant*

¹**fray** \'frā\ *transitive verb* [Middle English *fraien,* short for *affraien* to affray] (14th century)
archaic : SCARE; *also* : to frighten away

²**fray** *noun* (14th century)
: a usually disorderly or protracted fight, struggle, or dispute

³**fray** *verb* [Middle English *fraien,* from Middle French *froyer, frayer* to rub, from Latin *fricare* — more at FRICTION] (15th century)
transitive verb
1 a : to wear (as an edge of cloth) by or as if by rubbing : FRET **b** : to separate the threads at the edge of
2 : STRAIN, IRRITATE ⟨tempers became a bit *frayed*⟩
intransitive verb
1 : to wear out or into shreds
2 : to show signs of strain ⟨*fraying* nerves⟩

⁴**fray** *noun* (1630)
: a raveled place or worn spot (as on fabric)

fray·ing *noun* (1637)
: something rubbed or worn off by fraying

¹**fraz·zle** \'fra-zəl\ *verb* **fraz·zled; fraz·zling** \'fraz-liŋ, 'fra-zə-\ [alteration of English dialect *fazle* (to tangle, fray)] (circa 1825)
transitive verb
1 : ³FRAY
2 a : to put in a state of extreme physical or nervous fatigue **b** : UPSET
intransitive verb
: to become frazzled

²**frazzle** *noun* (1865)
1 : the state of being frazzled
2 : a condition of fatigue or nervous exhaustion ⟨worn to a *frazzle*⟩

¹**freak** \'frēk\ *noun* [origin unknown] (1563)
1 a : a sudden and odd or seemingly pointless idea or turn of the mind **b** : a seemingly capricious action or event
2 *archaic* : a whimsical quality or disposition
3 : one that is markedly unusual or abnormal: as **a** : a person or animal with a physical oddity who appears in a circus sideshow **b** *slang* (1) : a sexual deviate (2) : a person who uses an illicit drug **c** : HIPPIE **d** : an atypical postage stamp usually caused by a unique defect in paper (as a crease) or a unique event in the manufacturing process (as a speck of dirt on the plate) that does not produce a constant or systematic effect
4 : an ardent enthusiast ⟨film *freaks*⟩

²**freak** *adjective* (circa 1887)
: having the character of a freak ⟨a *freak* accident⟩

³**freak** (1965)
intransitive verb
1 : to withdraw from reality especially by taking drugs — often used with *out*

2 : to experience nightmarish hallucinations as a result of taking drugs — often used with *out*
3 a : to behave irrationally or unconventionally under the influence of drugs — often used with *out* **b** : to react with extreme or irrational distress or discomposure — often used with *out*
transitive verb
1 : to put under the influence of a psychedelic drug — often used with *out*
2 : to make greatly distressed, astonished, or discomposed — often used with *out* ⟨the news *freaked* them out⟩
— **freaked** *adjective*
— **freaked-out** *adjective*

⁴**freak** *transitive verb* [perhaps from or akin to ¹*freckle*] (1637)
: to streak especially with color ⟨silver and mother-of-pearl *freaking* the intense azure —Robert Bridges (died 1930)⟩

freak·ing \'frē-k°n, -kiŋ\ *adjective or adverb* [euphemism for *frigging* or *fucking*] (1963)
: DAMNED — used as an intensive

freak·ish \'frē-kish\ *adjective* (1653)
1 : WHIMSICAL, CAPRICIOUS
2 : markedly strange or abnormal
— **freak·ish·ly** *adverb*
— **freak·ish·ness** *noun*

freak of nature (1883)
: FREAK 3a

freak-out \'frē-,kaut\ *noun* (1966)
1 : an act or instance of freaking out
2 : a gathering of hippies

freak show *noun* (1887)
: an exhibition (as a sideshow) featuring freaks of nature

freaky \'frē-kē\ *adjective* **freak·i·er; -est** (1824)
: FREAKISH
— **freak·i·ness** *noun*

¹**freck·le** \'fre-kəl\ *noun* [Middle English *freken, frekel,* of Scandinavian origin; akin to Old Norse *freknōttr* freckled] (14th century)
: any of the small brownish spots in the skin usually due to precipitation of pigment that increase in number and intensity on exposure to sunlight
— **freck·ly** \'fre-k(ə-)lē\ *adjective*

²**freckle** *verb* **freck·led; freck·ling** \'fre-k(ə-)liŋ\ (1613)
transitive verb
: to sprinkle or mark with freckles or small spots
intransitive verb
: to become marked with freckles

¹**free** \'frē\ *adjective* **fre·er; fre·est** [Middle English, from Old English *frēo;* akin to Old High German *frī* free, Welsh *rhydd,* Sanskrit *priya* own, dear] (before 12th century)
1 a : having the legal and political rights of a citizen **b** : enjoying civil and political liberty ⟨*free* citizens⟩ **c** : enjoying political independence or freedom from outside domination **d** : enjoying personal freedom : not subject to the control or domination of another
2 a : not determined by anything beyond its own nature or being : choosing or capable of choosing for itself **b** : determined by the choice of the actor or performer ⟨*free* actions⟩ **c** : made, done, or given voluntarily or spontaneously
3 a : relieved from or lacking something unpleasant or burdensome ⟨*free* from pain⟩ ⟨a speech *free* of political rhetoric⟩ **b** : not bound, confined, or detained by force
4 a : having no trade restrictions **b** : not subject to government regulation **c** *of foreign exchange* : not subject to restriction or official control
5 a : having no obligations (as to work) or commitments ⟨I'll be *free* this evening⟩ **b** : not taken up with commitments or obligations ⟨a *free* evening⟩
6 : having a scope not restricted by qualification ⟨a *free* variable⟩

7 a (1) : not obstructed or impeded : CLEAR (2) : not being used or occupied ⟨waved with his *free* hand⟩ **b** : not hampered or restricted in its normal operation
8 a : not fastened ⟨the *free* end of the rope⟩ **b** : not confined to a particular position or place; *also* : not having a specific opponent to cover in football ⟨a *free* safety⟩ **c** : capable of moving or turning in any direction ⟨a *free* particle⟩ **d** : performed without apparatus ⟨*free* tumbling⟩ **e** : done with artificial aids (as pitons) used only for protection against falling and not for support ⟨a *free* climb⟩
9 a : not parsimonious ⟨*free* spending⟩ **b** : OUTSPOKEN **c** : availing oneself of something without stint **d** : FRANK, OPEN **e** : overly familiar or forward in action or attitude **f** : LICENTIOUS
10 : not costing or charging anything
11 a (1) : not united with, attached to, combined with, or mixed with something else : SEPARATE ⟨*free* ores⟩ ⟨a *free* surface of a bodily part⟩ (2) : FREESTANDING ⟨a *free* column⟩ **b** : chemically uncombined ⟨*free* oxygen⟩ ⟨*free* acids⟩ **c** : not permanently attached but able to move about ⟨a *free* electron in a metal⟩ **d** : capable of being used alone as a meaningful linguistic form ⟨the word *hats* is a *free* form⟩ — compare ⁵BOUND 7
12 a : not literal or exact ⟨*free* translation⟩ **b** : not restricted by or conforming to conventional forms ⟨*free* skating⟩
13 : FAVORABLE — used of a wind blowing from a direction more than six points from dead ahead
14 : not allowing slavery
15 : open to all comers ☆ □
— **free·ness** \-nəs\ *noun*
— **for free** : without charge

☆ SYNONYMS
Free, independent, sovereign, autonomous mean not subject to the rule or control of another. FREE stresses the complete absence of external rule and the full right to make all of one's own decisions ⟨you're *free* to do as you like⟩. INDEPENDENT implies a standing alone; applied to a state it implies lack of connection with any other having power to interfere with its citizens, laws, or policies ⟨the colony's struggle to become *independent*⟩. SOVEREIGN stresses the absence of a superior power and implies supremacy within a thing's own domain or sphere ⟨separate and *sovereign* armed services⟩. AUTONOMOUS stresses independence in matters pertaining to self-government ⟨in this denomination each congregation is regarded as *autonomous*⟩.

□ USAGE
free The idiomatic phrase *for free* apparently came into common use only in the early 1940s—our earliest printed evidence is from 1942—and it was no sooner popular than it was censured. The earliest complaint appeared barely six months after the earliest printed citation. Ever since, the critics have been denigrating the phrase, and others have kept on using it. One reason for the phrase's usefulness is that the preposition provides a little space between *free* and the preceding text ⟨it seemed best to find a way to live *for free* then —Jane Harriman⟩. In this example the *for* eliminates the ambiguous *live free.* But in many instances no potential ambiguity is involved; people seem to use the phrase simply because it sounds right to them. This American idiom is well established in speech and in general prose, but it is not used in writing of high solemnity.

²free *transitive verb* **freed; free·ing** (before 12th century)
1 a : to cause to be free **b :** to relieve or rid of what restrains, confines, restricts, or embarrasses ⟨*free* a person from debt⟩ **c :** DISENTANGLE, CLEAR
2 *obsolete* **:** BANISH ☆
— **fre·er** *noun*

³free *adverb* (1559)
1 : in a free manner
2 : without charge
3 : with the wind more than six points from dead ahead ⟨sailing *free*⟩

free agent *noun* (1955)
: a professional athlete (as a baseball player) who is free to negotiate a contract with any team
— **free agency** *noun*

free alongside ship *adverb or adjective* (circa 1903)
: with delivery at the side of the ship free of charges and the buyer's liability then beginning

free and easy *adjective* (1699)
1 : marked by informality and lack of constraint ⟨the *free and easy*, open-air life of the plains —Allan Murray⟩
2 : not observant of strict demands ⟨too *free and easy* in accepting political contributions⟩
— **free–and–eas·i·ness** \ˌfrē-ən-'(d)ē-zē-nəs\ *noun*
— **free and easy** *adverb*

free association *noun* (1899)
1 a : the expression (as by speaking or writing) of the content of consciousness without censorship as an aid in gaining access to unconscious processes especially in psychoanalysis **b :** the reporting of the first thought that comes to mind in response to a given stimulus (as a word)
2 : an idea or image elicited by free association
3 : a method using free association
— **free–as·so·ci·ate** \ˌfrē-ə-'sō-s(h)ē-ˌāt\ *intransitive verb*
— **free–as·so·ci·at·ive** \-s(h)ē-ˌā-tiv, -shə-tiv\ *adjective*

¹free·base \'frē-ˌbās\ (1980)
intransitive verb
: to prepare or use freebase cocaine
transitive verb
: to prepare or use (cocaine) as freebase
— **free·bas·er** *noun*

²freebase *noun* (1980)
: cocaine freed from impurities by treatment (as with ether) and heated to produce vapors for inhalation or smoked as crack

free beach *noun* (1975)
: a beach at which nudity is permitted

free·bie *or* **free·bee** \'frē-bē\ *noun* [by alteration from obsolete *freeby* gratis, irregular from *free*] (1942)
: something (as a theater ticket) given without charge

free·board \'frē-ˌbōrd, -ˌbȯrd\ *noun* (1726)
1 : the distance between the waterline and the main deck or weather deck of a ship or between the level of the water and the upper edge of the side of a small boat
2 : the height above the recorded high-water mark of a structure (as a dam) associated with the water

free·boo·ter \'frē-ˌbü-tər\ *noun* [by folk etymology from Dutch *vrijbuiter*, from *vrijbuit* plunder, from *vrij* free + *buit* booty] (1570)
: PIRATE, PLUNDERER
— **free·boot** \-ˌbüt\ *intransitive verb*

free·born \'frē-'bȯrn\ *adjective* (13th century)
1 : not born in vassalage or slavery
2 : of, relating to, or befitting one that is freeborn

free diver *noun* (1953)
: one who engages in skin diving
— **free diving** *noun*

freed·man \'frēd-mən, -ˌman\ *noun* (1601)
: a man freed from slavery

free·dom \'frē-dəm\ *noun* (before 12th century)
1 : the quality or state of being free: as **a :** the absence of necessity, coercion, or constraint in choice or action **b :** liberation from slavery or restraint or from the power of another **:** INDEPENDENCE **c :** the quality or state of being exempt or released usually from something onerous ⟨*freedom* from care⟩ **d :** EASE, FACILITY ⟨spoke the language with *freedom*⟩ **e :** the quality of being frank, open, or outspoken ⟨answered with *freedom*⟩ **f :** improper familiarity **g :** boldness of conception or execution **h :** unrestricted use ⟨gave him the *freedom* of their home⟩
2 a : a political right **b :** FRANCHISE, PRIVILEGE ☆

freedom of the seas (1917)
: the right of a merchant ship to travel any waters except territorial waters either in peace or war

freedom ride *noun, often F&R capitalized* (1961)
: a ride made by civil rights workers through states of the southern U.S. to ascertain whether public facilities (as bus terminals) are desegregated
— **freedom rider** *noun*

freed·wom·an \'frēd-ˌwu̇-mən\ *noun* (1866)
: a woman freed from slavery

free–elec·tron laser \'frē-i-'lek-ˌträn-\ *noun* (1979)
: a laser that can be tuned over a wide range of frequencies and that produces electromagnetic radiation by the motion of electrons moving at relativistic velocities in a magnetic field

free enterprise *noun* (1890)
: freedom of private business to organize and operate for profit in a competitive system without interference by government beyond regulation necessary to protect public interest and keep the national economy in balance

free enterpriser *noun* (1943)
: a supporter or advocate of free enterprise

free fall *noun* (1919)
1 : the condition of unrestrained motion in a gravitational field; *also* **:** such motion
2 a : the part of a parachute jump before the parachute opens **b :** a rapid and continuing drop or decline ⟨a *free fall* in stock prices⟩
— **free–fall** *intransitive verb*

free–fire zone \'frē-ˌfīr-\ *noun* (1967)
: a combat area in which any moving thing is a legitimate target

free–float·ing \-'flō-tiŋ\ *adjective* (1921)
1 a : floating freely ⟨*free-floating* vegetation⟩ **b :** lacking specific attachment, direction, or purpose ⟨*free-floating* ideas⟩
2 : felt as an emotion without apparent cause ⟨*free-floating* anxiety⟩

free–flow·ing \-ˌflō-iŋ\ *adjective* (1920)
: characterized by easy freedom in movement, progression, or style ⟨a *free-flowing* essay⟩

free–for–all \'frē-fə-ˌrȯl\ *noun* (1881)
: a competition, dispute, or fight open to all comers and usually with no rules **:** BRAWL
— **free–for–all** *adjective*

free–form \'frē-'fȯrm\ *adjective* (1950)
1 : having or being an irregular or asymmetrical shape or design ⟨*free-form* furniture⟩
2 : FREE 12b ⟨*free-form* dancing⟩

free·hand \'frē-ˌhand\ *adjective* (circa 1862)
: done without mechanical aids or devices ⟨*freehand* drawing⟩
— **freehand** *adverb*

free hand \-'hand\ *noun* (1929)
: freedom of action or decision

free·hand·ed \'frē-'han-dəd\ *adjective* (circa 1656)
: GENEROUS, OPENHANDED
— **free·hand·ed·ly** *adverb*
— **free·hand·ed·ness** *noun*

free·heart·ed \-'här-təd\ *adjective* (14th century)
1 : FRANK, UNRESERVED
2 : GENEROUS

— **free·heart·ed·ly** *adverb*

free·hold \'frē-ˌhōld\ *noun* (15th century)
1 : a tenure of real property by which an estate of inheritance in fee simple or fee tail or an estate for life is held; *also* **:** an estate held by such tenure — compare FEE 1
2 *British* **:** an estate held in fee simple
— **freehold** *adjective or adverb*
— **free·hold·er** \-ˌhōl-dər\ *noun*

free kick *noun* (1882)
: a kick (as in football, soccer, or rugby) with which an opponent may not interfere; *especially* **:** such a kick in any direction awarded because of an infraction of the rules by an opponent

¹free–lance \'frē-ˌlan(t)s\ *noun* (1820)
1 a *usually* **free lance :** a mercenary soldier especially of the Middle Ages **:** CONDOTTIERE **b :** a person who acts independently without being affiliated with or authorized by an organization
2 : a person who pursues a profession without a long-term commitment to any one employer

²freelance *adjective* (1901)
1 a : of, relating to, or being a freelance **:** INDEPENDENT ⟨a *freelance* photographer⟩ ⟨*freelance* fees⟩ **b :** done by a freelance ⟨*freelance* reviewing⟩ ⟨*freelance* jobs⟩
2 : not sponsored by an organization ⟨*freelance* terrorists⟩ ⟨a *freelance* demonstration⟩
— **freelance** *adverb*

³freelance (1902)
intransitive verb
: to act or work as a freelance
transitive verb
: to produce as a freelance ⟨*freelancing* magazine articles⟩

free·lanc·er \'frē-ˌlan(t)-sər\ *noun* (1937)
: FREELANCE 1b, 2

free–liv·ing \'frē-'li-viŋ\ *adjective* (1818)
1 : marked by more than usual freedom in the gratification of appetites

☆ **SYNONYMS**

Free, release, liberate, emancipate, manumit mean to set loose from restraint or constraint. FREE implies a usually permanent removal from whatever binds, confines, entangles, or oppresses ⟨*freed* the animals from their cages⟩. RELEASE suggests a setting loose from confinement, restraint, or a state of pressure or tension, often without implication of permanent liberation ⟨*released* his anger on a punching bag⟩. LIBERATE stresses particularly the resulting state of liberty ⟨*liberated* their country from the tyrant⟩. EMANCIPATE implies the liberation of a person from subjection or domination ⟨labor-saving devices *emancipated* us from household drudgery⟩. MANUMIT implies emancipation from slavery ⟨the document *manumitted* the slaves⟩.

Freedom, liberty, license mean the power or condition of acting without compulsion. FREEDOM has a broad range of application from total absence of restraint to merely a sense of not being unduly hampered or frustrated ⟨*freedom* of the press⟩. LIBERTY suggests release from former restraint or compulsion ⟨the released prisoner had difficulty adjusting to his new *liberty*⟩. LICENSE implies freedom specially granted or conceded and may connote an abuse of freedom ⟨freedom without responsibility may degenerate into *license*⟩.

\ə\ abut \ᵊ\ kitten \ər\ further \a\ ash \ā\ ace
\ä\ mop, mar \au̇\ out \ch\ chin \e\ bet \ē\ easy
\g\ go \i\ hit \ī\ ice \j\ job \ŋ\ sing \ō\ go
\ȯ\ law \ȯi\ boy \th\ thin \t͟h\ the \ü\ loot \u̇\ foot
\y\ yet \zh\ vision *see also* Guide to Pronunciation

2 a : not fixed to the substrate but capable of motility ⟨a *free-living* protozoan⟩ **b :** being metabolically independent **:** neither parasitic nor symbiotic

free·load \-ˌlōd\ *intransitive verb* (circa 1934) **:** to impose upon another's generosity or hospitality without sharing in the cost or responsibility involved — SPONGE
— **free·load·er** *noun*

free love *noun* (1822)
1 : the practice of living openly with one of the opposite sex without marriage
2 : sexual relations without any commitments by either partner

free lunch *noun* (1975)
: something one does not have to pay for; *also* **:** FREE RIDE

free·ly \ˈfrē-lē\ *adverb* (before 12th century)
: in a free manner: as **a :** of one's own accord ⟨left home *freely*⟩ **b :** with freedom from external control ⟨a *freely* elected government⟩ **c :** without restraint or reservation ⟨spent *freely* on clothes⟩ **d :** without hindrance ⟨a gate swinging *freely*⟩ ⟨currencies are *freely* convertible⟩ **e :** not strictly following a model, convention, or rule ⟨*freely* translated⟩

free·man \ˈfrē-mən, -ˌman\ *noun* (before 12th century)
1 : one enjoying civil or political liberty
2 : one having the full rights of a citizen

free market *noun* (1907)
: an economic market operating by free competition

free–mar·ke·teer \ˈfrē-ˌmär-kə-ˈtir\ *noun* (1954)
: a proponent of a free-market economy

free–mar·tin \ˈfrē-ˌmär-tᵊn\ *noun* [origin unknown] (1681)
: a sexually imperfect usually sterile female calf twinborn with a male

Free·ma·son \-ˈmā-sᵊn\ *noun* (1646)
: a member of a major fraternal organization called Free and Accepted Masons or Ancient Free and Accepted Masons that has certain secret rituals

free·ma·son·ry \-rē\ *noun* (1741)
1 *capitalized* **:** the principles, institutions, or practices of Freemasons — called also *Masonry*
2 : natural fellowship based on some common experience

free on board *adverb or adjective* (1924)
: without charge for delivery to and placing on board a carrier at a specified point

free port *noun* (1711)
: an enclosed port or section of a port where goods are received and shipped free of customs duty

freer *comparative of* FREE

free radical *noun* (1900)
: an especially reactive atom or group of atoms that has one or more unpaired electrons

free–range \ˈfrē-ˌrānj\ *adjective* (1912)
: allowed to range and forage with relative freedom ⟨*free-range* chickens⟩; *also* **:** of, relating to, or produced by free-range poultry ⟨*free-range* eggs⟩

free reed *noun* (1855)
: a reed in a musical instrument (as a harmonium) that vibrates in an air opening just large enough to allow the reed to move freely — compare BEATING REED

free rein *noun* (1952)
: unrestricted liberty of action or decision

free ride *noun* (1899)
: a benefit obtained at another's expense or without the usual cost or effort
— **free ride** *intransitive verb*
— **free rider** *noun*

free safety *noun* (1973)
: a safety in football who has no particular receiver to cover in a man-to-man defense

free·sia \ˈfrē-zh(ē-)ə, -zē-ə\ *noun* [New Latin, from F. H. T. *Freese* (died 1876) German physician] (circa 1882)
: any of a genus (*Freesia*) of the iris family of sweet-scented African herbs with red, pink, white, or yellow flowers

free–soil *adjective* (1846)
1 : characterized by free soil ⟨*free-soil* states⟩
2 *F&S capitalized* **:** opposing the extension of slavery into U.S. territories and the admission of slave states into the Union prior to the Civil War; *specifically* **:** of, relating to, or constituting a minor U.S. political party having these aims
— **Free–Soil·er** \-ˈsȯi-lər\ *noun*
— **Free–Soil·ism** \-ˈsȯi(ə)-ˌli-zəm\ *noun*

free soil *noun* (1848)
: U.S. territory where prior to the Civil War slavery was prohibited

free–spo·ken \ˈfrē-ˈspō-kən\ *adjective* (1625)
: speaking freely **:** OUTSPOKEN

freest *superlative of* FREE

free·stand·ing \ˈfrē-ˈstan-diŋ\ *adjective* (1876)
1 : standing alone or on its own foundation free of support or attachment ⟨a *freestanding* wall⟩
2 : being independent; *especially* **:** not part of or affiliated with another organization ⟨a *freestanding* clinic⟩ ⟨a *freestanding* city⟩ ⟨a *freestanding* computer store⟩

Free State *noun* (1819)
: a state of the U.S. in which slavery was prohibited before the Civil War

free·stone \ˈfrē-ˌstōn\ *noun* (13th century)
1 : a stone that may be cut freely without splitting
2 a : a fruit stone to which the flesh does not cling **b :** a fruit having such a stone

free·style \ˈfrē-ˌstīl\ *noun, often attributive* (circa 1934)
1 : a competition in which the contestant is given more latitude than in related events; *especially* **:** swimming competition in which the swimmer may use any stroke
2 : CRAWL 2
— **free·styl·er** *noun*

free–swim·ming \-ˈswi-miŋ\ *adjective* (circa 1890)
: able to swim about **:** not attached ⟨the *free-swimming* larva of the barnacle⟩

free–swing·ing \-ˈswiŋ-iŋ\ *adjective* (1949)
: bold, forthright, and heedless of personal consequences ⟨a *free-swinging* soldier of fortune —Will Herberg⟩

free–tailed bat \ˈfrē-ˌtāld-\ *noun* (1895)
: any of a family (Molossidae) of bats characterized by a tail that projects beyond the posterior part of the flight membrane and found in warm regions of the world

free·think·er \-ˈthiŋ-kər\ *noun* (1692)
: one that forms opinions on the basis of reason independently of authority; *especially* **:** one who doubts or denies religious dogma
— **free·think·ing** \-kiŋ\ *noun or adjective*

free thought *noun* (1711)
: unorthodox attitudes or beliefs; *specifically* **:** 18th century deism

free throw *noun* (circa 1929)
: an unhindered shot in basketball made from behind a set line and awarded because of a foul by an opponent

free throw lane *noun* (circa 1929)
: a 12 or 16 foot wide lane on a basketball court that extends from underneath the goal to a line 15 feet in front of the backboard and that players may not enter during a free throw

free trade *noun* (1823)
: trade based on the unrestricted international exchange of goods with tariffs used only as a source of revenue

free trader *noun* (1832)
: one that practices or advocates free trade

free verse *noun* (1908)
: verse whose meter is irregular in some respect or whose rhythm is not metrical

free·way \ˈfrē-ˌwā\ *noun* (1930)
1 : an expressway with fully controlled access
2 : a toll-free highway

¹free·wheel \-ˈ(h)wē(ə)l\ *noun* (1930)
1 : a clutch fitted in the rear hub of a bicycle that permits the rear wheel to run on free from the rear sprocket when the pedals are stopped
2 : a power-transmission system in a motor vehicle with a device that permits the propeller shaft to run freely when its speed is greater than that of the engine shaft

²freewheel *intransitive verb* (1903)
1 : to roll along freely independent of a gear
2 : to move, live, or play freely or irresponsibly

— **free·wheel·er** *noun*

free·wheel·ing \ˌfrē-ˈhwē-liŋ, -ˈwē-\ *adjective* (1931)
: free and loose in form or manner: as **a :** heedless of social norms or niceties ⟨the raider style of his *freewheeling* father —Garry Wills⟩ **b :** not repressed or restrained ⟨*freewheeling* promiscuity⟩ ⟨a *freewheeling* competitive spirit⟩ ⟨*freewheeling* vocabulary⟩ **c :** not bound by formal rules, procedures, or guidelines ⟨a *freewheeling* investigation⟩ ⟨*freewheeling* improvisation⟩ **d :** loose and undisciplined **:** not defensive ⟨a *freewheeling* style of hockey⟩
— **free·wheel·ing·ly** *adverb*

free·will \ˈfrē-ˌwil\ *adjective* (1535)
: VOLUNTARY, SPONTANEOUS

free will *noun* (13th century)
1 : voluntary choice or decision ⟨I do this of my own *free will*⟩
2 : freedom of humans to make choices that are not determined by prior causes or by divine intervention

Freewill Baptist *noun* (1732)
: a member of a Baptist group holding to Arminian doctrine and practicing open communion

free world *noun, often F&W capitalized* (1949)
: the part of the world where democracy and capitalism or moderate socialism rather than totalitarian or Communist political and economic systems prevail

free·writ·ing \ˈfrē-ˌrī-tiŋ\ *noun* (1980)
: automatic writing done especially as a classroom exercise

¹freeze \ˈfrēz\ *verb* **froze** \ˈfrōz\; **fro·zen** \ˈfrō-zᵊn\; **freez·ing** [Middle English *fresen*, from Old English *frēosan*; akin to Old High German *friosan* to freeze, Latin *pruina* hoarfrost, Old English *frost* frost] (before 12th century)
intransitive verb
1 a : to become congealed into ice by cold **b :** to solidify as a result of abstraction of heat **c :** to withstand freezing ⟨the bread *freezes* well⟩
2 : to become chilled with cold ⟨almost *froze* to death⟩
3 : to adhere solidly by or as if by freezing ⟨pressure caused the metals to *freeze*⟩
4 : to become fixed or motionless; *especially* **:** to become incapable of acting or speaking
5 : to become clogged with ice ⟨the water pipes *froze*⟩
transitive verb
1 a : to harden into ice **b :** to convert from a liquid to a solid by cold
2 : to make extremely cold **:** CHILL
3 a : to act on usually destructively by frost **b :** to anesthetize by cold
4 : to cause to grip tightly or remain in immovable contact
5 a : to cause to become fixed, immovable, unavailable, or unalterable ⟨*freeze* interest rates⟩ **b :** to immobilize by governmental regulation the expenditure, withdrawal, or exchange of ⟨*freeze* foreign assets⟩ **c :** to render motionless ⟨a fake *froze* the defender⟩
6 : to attempt to retain continuous possession of (a ball or puck) without an attempt to score usually in order to protect a small lead
— **freez·ing·ly** *adverb*

²freeze *noun* (15th century)
1 a : an act or instance of freezing **b :** the state of being frozen

2 : a state of weather marked by low temperature especially when below the freezing point
3 : a halt in the production, testing, and deployment of military weapons ⟨a nuclear *freeze*⟩

freeze–dried \-'drīd\ *adjective* (1946)
: being in a state produced by or as if by freeze-drying

freeze–dry \-'drī\ *transitive verb* (1949)
: to dry (as food) in a frozen state under high vacuum especially for preservation

freeze–etch·ing \'frē-,ze-chiŋ\ *noun* (1968)
: preparation of a specimen (as of tissue) for electron microscopic examination by freezing, fracturing along natural structural lines, and preparing a replica (as by simultaneous vapor deposition of carbon and platinum)
— **freeze–etch** \-'zech\ *adjective*
— **freeze–etched** \-'zecht\ *adjective*

freeze fracture *noun* (1973)
: FREEZE-ETCHING

freeze–frame \'frēz-'frām\ *noun* (1948)
1 a : a frame of a motion-picture film that is repeated so as to give the illusion of a static picture **b :** a static picture produced from a videodisc or videotape recording
2 : something resembling a freeze-frame especially in unchanging quality

freeze out *transitive verb* (1861)
: EXCLUDE
— **freeze–out** \'frē-,zaût\ *noun*

freez·er \'frē-zər\ *noun* (1847)
: one that freezes or keeps cool; *especially* **:** a compartment, room, or device for freezing food or keeping it frozen

freezer burn *noun* (1926)
: light-colored spots developed in frozen foods as a result of surface evaporation and drying when inadequately wrapped or packaged

freezing point *noun* (1747)
: the temperature at which a liquid solidifies

free zone *noun* (1900)
: an area within which goods may be received and stored without payment of duty

F region *noun* (1923)
: the highest region of the ionosphere occurring from 80 miles (130 kilometers) to more than 300 miles (500 kilometers)

¹freight \'frāt\ *noun, often attributive* [Middle English, from Middle Dutch or Middle Low German *vracht, vrecht*] (15th century)
1 a : the compensation paid for the transportation of goods **b :** COST ⟨help pay the *freight*⟩
2 a : goods to be shipped **:** CARGO **b :** LOAD, BURDEN **c :** MEANING 3, SIGNIFICANCE
3 a : the ordinary transportation of goods by a common carrier and distinguished from express **b :** a train designed or used for such transportation

²freight *transitive verb* (15th century)
1 a : to load with goods for transportation **b :** BURDEN, CHARGE ⟨*freighted* with memories⟩
2 : to transport or ship by freight

freight·age \'frā-tij\ *noun* (1694)
: FREIGHT

freight·er \-tər\ *noun* (1622)
1 : one that loads or charters and loads a ship
2 : SHIPPER
3 : a ship or airplane used chiefly to carry freight

frem·i·tus \'fre-mə-təs\ *noun* [New Latin, from Latin, murmur, from *fremere* to murmur; akin to Old English *bremman* to roar] (1879)
: a sensation felt by a hand placed on a part of the body (as the chest) that vibrates during speech

french \'french\ *transitive verb, often capitalized* (1941)
1 : to trim the meat from the end of the bone of (as a chop)
2 : to cut (green beans) in thin lengthwise strips before cooking

¹French \'french\ *adjective* [Middle English, from Old English *frencisc*, from *Franca* Frank] (before 12th century)
1 : of, relating to, or characteristic of France, its people, or their language

2 : of or relating to the overseas descendents of the French people
— **French·ness** *noun*

²French *noun* (12th century)
1 : a Romance language that developed out of the Vulgar Latin spoken in northern and central Transalpine Gaul and that became the literary and official language of France
2 *plural in construction* **:** the French people
3 : strong language ⟨pardon my *French*⟩

French bean *noun* (1632)
1 *chiefly British* **:** a bean (as a green bean) of which the whole young pod is eaten
2 *chiefly British* **:** KIDNEY BEAN 2

French bread *noun* (15th century)
: a crusty white bread baked usually in long thin loaves

French bulldog *noun* (1875)
: any of a breed of small compact heavy-boned dogs developed in France and having erect ears

French Canadian *noun* (1758)
: one of the descendants of French settlers in Lower Canada
— **French–Canadian** *adjective*

French chalk *noun* (circa 1728)
: a soft white granular variety of steatite used especially for drawing lines on cloth and for removing grease in dry cleaning

French cuff *noun* (1916)
: a soft double cuff that is made by turning back half of a wide cuff band and fastening with cuff links

french curve *noun, often F capitalized* (1885)
: a curved piece of flat often plastic material used as a guide in drawing curves

French door *noun* (1923)
: a door with rectangular glass panes extending the full length; *also* **:** FRENCH WINDOW

French dressing *noun* (1876)
1 : a salad dressing made with oil and vinegar or lemon juice, and spices
2 : a commercial salad dressing that is tomato-flavored and creamy consistency

¹french fry *noun, often 1st F capitalized* (1918)
: a strip of potato fried in deep fat — usually used in plural

²french fry *transitive verb, often 1st F capitalized* (circa 1930)
: to fry (as strips of potato) in deep fat until brown

French horn *noun* (1682)
: a circular valved brass instrument having a conical bore, a funnel-shaped mouthpiece, and a usual range from B below the bass staff upward for more than three octaves

French horn

french·ify \'fren-chə-,fī\ *transitive verb* **-ified; -ify·ing** *often capitalized* (1592)
: to make French in qualities, traits, or typical practices
— **french·i·fi·ca·tion** \,fren-chə-fi-'kā-shən\ *noun, often capitalized*

French kiss *noun* (circa 1923)
: an open-mouth kiss usually involving tongue-to-tongue contact
— **French–kiss** *verb*

French leave *noun* [from an 18th century French custom of leaving a reception without taking leave of the host or hostess] (1771)
: an informal, hasty, or secret departure

French letter *noun* (circa 1856)
chiefly British **:** CONDOM

French·man \'french-mən\ *noun* (before 12th century)
1 : a native or inhabitant of France
2 : one who is of French descent

French pastry *noun* (1922)

: a rich pastry filled especially with custard or fruit

French provincial *noun, often P capitalized* (1945)
: a style of furniture, architecture, or fabric originating in or characteristic of the 17th and 18th century French provinces

French seam *noun* (circa 1890)
: a strong seam stitched on both sides of the fabric to enclose all raw edges

French telephone *noun* (1932)
: HANDSET

French toast *noun* (1871)
: bread dipped in a mixture of egg and milk and sautéed

French window *noun* (1801)
: a pair of casement windows that reaches to the floor, opens in the middle, and is placed in an exterior wall

French·wom·an \'french-,wù-mən\ *noun* (1593)
1 : a woman who is a native or inhabitant of France
2 : a woman of French descent

fre·net·ic \fri-'ne-tik\ *adjective* [Middle English *frenetik* insane, from Middle French *frenetique*, from Latin *phreneticus*, modification of Greek *phrenitikos*, from *phrenitis* inflammation of the brain, from *phren-, phrēn* diaphragm, mind] (14th century)
: FRENZIED, FRANTIC
— **fre·net·i·cal·ly** \-ti-k(ə-)lē\ *adverb*
— **fre·net·i·cism** \'ne-tə-,si-zəm\ *noun*

fren·u·lum \'fren-yə-ləm\ *noun, plural* **-la** \-lə\ [New Latin, diminutive of Latin *frenum*] (circa 1706)
1 : a connecting fold of membrane serving to support or restrain a part (as the tongue)
2 : a bristle or group of bristles on the front edge of the posterior wing of some lepidoptera that unites the wings by interlocking with the retinaculum of the forewings

fre·num \'frē-nəm\ *noun, plural* **frenums** *or* **fre·na** \-nə\ [New Latin, from Latin, bridle, reins, and bit; probably akin to Latin *frendere* to grind — more at GRIND] (1741)
: FRENULUM 1

fren·zied \'fren-zēd\ *adjective* (1796)
: marked by frenzy
— **fren·zied·ly** *adverb*

¹fren·zy \'fren-zē\ *noun, plural* **frenzies** [Middle English *frenesie*, from Middle French, from Medieval Latin *phrenesia*, alteration of Latin *phrenesis*, from *phreneticus*] (14th century)
1 a : a temporary madness **b :** a violent mental or emotional agitation
2 : intense usually wild and often disorderly compulsive or agitated activity

²frenzy *transitive verb* **fren·zied; fren·zy·ing** (1791)
: to affect with frenzy

Fre·on \'frē-,än\ *trademark*
— used for any of various nonflammable fluorocarbons used as refrigerants and as propellants for aerosols

fre·quence \'frē-kwən(t)s\ *noun* (1603)
: FREQUENCY

fre·quen·cy \'frē-kwən(t)-sē\ *noun, plural* **-cies** (1600)
1 : the fact or condition of occurring frequently
2 a : the number of times that a periodic function repeats the same sequence of values during a unit variation of the independent variable **b :** the number of individuals in a single class when objects are classified according to variations in a set of one or more specified attributes

\ə\ **abut** \ᵊ\ **kitten** \ər\ **further** \a\ **ash** \ā\ **ace**
\ä\ **mop, mar** \aû\ **out** \ch\ **chin** \e\ **bet** \ē\ **easy**
\g\ **go** \i\ **hit** \ī\ **ice** \j\ **job** \ŋ\ **sing** \ō\ **go**
\ò\ **law** \òi\ **boy** \th\ **thin** \t͟h\ **the** \ü\ **loot** \ù\ **foot**
\y\ **yet** \zh\ **vision** *see also* Guide to Pronunciation

3 : the number of repetitions of a periodic process in a unit of time: as **a :** the number of complete alternations per second of an alternating current **b :** the number of complete oscillations per second of energy (as sound or electromagnetic radiation) in the form of waves

frequency distribution *noun* (1895)
: an arrangement of statistical data that exhibits the frequency of the occurrence of the values of a variable

frequency modulation *noun* (1922)
: modulation of the frequency of the carrier wave in accordance with speech or a signal; *also* **:** FM

frequency response *noun* (1926)
: the ability of a device (as an audio amplifier) to handle the frequencies applied to it; *also* **:** a graph representing this ability

¹**fre·quent** \frē-'kwent, 'frē-kwənt\ *transitive verb* (15th century)
1 : to associate with, be in, or resort to often or habitually
2 *archaic* **:** to read systematically or habitually
— **fre·quen·ta·tion** \,frē-,kwen-'tā-shən, -kwən-\ *noun*
— **fre·quent·er** *noun*

²**fre·quent** \'frē-kwənt\ *adjective* [Middle English, ample, from Middle French or Latin; Middle French, crowded, from Latin *frequent-, frequens*] (1531)
1 a : COMMON, USUAL **b :** happening at short intervals **:** often repeated or occurring
2 *obsolete* **:** FULL, THRONGED
3 : HABITUAL, PERSISTENT
4 *archaic* **:** INTIMATE, FAMILIAR
— **fre·quent·ness** *noun*

fre·quen·ta·tive \frē-'kwen-tə-tiv\ *adjective* (1533)
: denoting repeated or recurrent action or state — used of a verb aspect, verb form, or meaning
— **frequentative** *noun*

fre·quent·ly \'frē-kwənt-lē\ *adverb* (1531)
: at frequent or short intervals

fres·co \'fres-(,)kō\ *noun, plural* **frescoes** [Italian, from *fresco* fresh, of Germanic origin; akin to Old High German *frisc* fresh] (1598)
1 : the art of painting on freshly spread moist lime plaster with water-based pigments
2 : a painting executed in fresco ◇
— **fresco** *transitive verb*

¹**fresh** \'fresh\ *adjective* [Middle English, from Old French *freis*, of Germanic origin; akin to Old High German *frisc* fresh, Old English *fersc* fresh] (13th century)
1 a : having its original qualities unimpaired: as (1) **:** full of or renewed in vigor **:** REFRESHED ⟨rose *fresh* from a good night's sleep⟩ (2) **:** not stale, sour, or decayed ⟨*fresh* bread⟩ (3) **:** not faded ⟨the lessons remain *fresh* in her memory⟩ (4) **:** not worn or rumpled ⟨a *fresh* white shirt⟩ **b :** not altered by processing ⟨*fresh* vegetables⟩
2 a : not salt **b** (1) **:** free from taint **:** PURE ⟨*fresh* air⟩ (2) *of wind* **:** moderately strong
3 a (1) **:** experienced, made, or received newly or anew ⟨form *fresh* friendships⟩ (2) **:** ADDITIONAL, ANOTHER ⟨a *fresh* start⟩ **b :** ORIGINAL, VIVID ⟨a *fresh* portrayal⟩ **c :** lacking experience **:** RAW **d :** newly or just come or arrived ⟨*fresh* from school⟩ **e :** having the milk flow recently established ⟨a *fresh* cow⟩
4 [probably by folk etymology from German *frech*] **:** disposed to take liberties **:** IMPUDENT
synonym see NEW
— **fresh·ly** *adverb*
— **fresh·ness** *noun*

²**fresh** *adverb* (14th century)
: just recently **:** NEWLY ⟨we're *fresh* out of eggs⟩ ⟨*fresh* caught fish⟩

³**fresh** *noun* (1538)
1 : an increased flow or rush (as of water) **:** FRESHET
2 *archaic* **:** a stream, spring, or pool of freshwater

fresh breeze *noun* (circa 1881)

: wind having a speed of 19 to 24 miles per hour (30 to 38 kilometers per hour) — see BEAUFORT SCALE table

fresh·en \'fre-shən\ *verb* **fresh·ened; fresh·en·ing** \-sh(ə-)niŋ\ (1697)
intransitive verb
1 : to grow or become fresh: as **a** *of wind* **:** to increase in strength **b :** to become fresh in appearance or vitality — usually used with *up* ⟨*freshen* up with a shower⟩
2 *of a milk animal* **:** to begin lactating
transitive verb
: to make fresh; *also* **:** REFRESH, REVIVE
— **fresh·en·er** \-sh(ə-)nər\ *noun*

fresh·et \'fre-shət\ *noun* (1596)
1 *archaic* **:** STREAM 1
2 a : a great rise or overflowing of a stream caused by heavy rains or melted snow **b :** something resembling or suggesting a freshet ⟨a *freshet* of visitors⟩

fresh gale *noun* (1582)
: wind having a speed of 39 to 46 miles per hour (62 to 74 kilometers per hour) — see BEAUFORT SCALE table

fresh·man \'fresh-mən\ *noun, often attributive* (1550)
1 : a first-year student
2 : BEGINNER, NEWCOMER

¹**fresh·wa·ter** \'fresh-'wȯ-tər, -'wä-\ *noun* (14th century)
: water that is not salty especially when considered as a natural resource

²**freshwater** *adjective* (1528)
1 : of, relating to, being, or living in freshwater
2 : accustomed to navigating only in inland waters ⟨a *freshwater* sailor⟩; *also* **:** UNSKILLED
3 : inland and usually provincial ⟨a *freshwater* college⟩

freshwater drum *noun* (1879)
: a croaker (*Aplodinotus grunniens*) of the Great Lakes and Mississippi valley that may attain a weight of 50 pounds (23 kilograms) or more — called also *sheepshead, white perch*

freshwater pearl *noun* (1918)
: a usually very small pearl produced by a freshwater mollusk

Fres·nel lens \'frez-nəl-, frā-'nel-\ *noun* [Augustin J. *Fresnel*] (circa 1884)
: a lens that has a surface consisting of a concentric series of simple lens sections so that a thin lens with a short focal length and large diameter is possible and that is used especially for spotlights

¹**fret** \'fret\ *verb* **fret·ted; fret·ting** [Middle English, to devour, fret, from Old English *fretan* to devour; akin to Old High German *frezzan* to devour, *ezzan* to eat — more at EAT] (12th century)
transitive verb
1 a : to eat or gnaw into **:** CORRODE; *also* **:** FRAY **b :** RUB, CHAFE **c :** to make by wearing away a substance ⟨the stream *fretted* a channel⟩
2 : to cause to suffer emotional strain **:** VEX
3 : to pass (as time) in fretting
4 : AGITATE, RIPPLE
intransitive verb
1 a : to eat into something **b :** to affect something as if by gnawing or biting **:** GRATE
2 a : WEAR, CORRODE **b :** CHAFE **c :** FRAY 1
3 a : to become vexed or worried **b** *of running water* **:** to become agitated

²**fret** *noun* (15th century)
1 a : the action of wearing away **:** EROSION **b :** a worn or eroded spot
2 : an agitation of mind **:** IRRITATION

³**fret** *transitive verb* **fret·ted; fret·ting** [Middle English, back-formation from *fret, fretted* adorned, interwoven, from Middle French *freté*, from Old French, past participle of *freter, ferter* to tie, bind, probably from (assumed) Vulgar Latin *firmitare*, from Latin *firmus* firm] (14th century)
1 a : to decorate with interlaced designs **b :** to form a pattern upon

2 : to enrich with embossed or pierced carved patterns

⁴**fret** *noun* (14th century)
1 : an ornamental network; *especially* **:** a medieval metallic or jeweled net for a woman's headdress
2 : an ornament or ornamental work often in relief consisting of small straight bars intersecting one another in right or oblique angles

⁵**fret** *noun* [perhaps from Middle French *frete* ferrule, from *freter*] (circa 1500)
: one of a series of ridges fixed across the fingerboard of a stringed musical instrument (as a guitar)
— **fret·less** *adjective*
— **fret·ted** *adjective*

fret 2

⁶**fret** *transitive verb* **fret·ted; fret·ting** (1602)
: to press (the strings of a stringed instrument) against the frets

fret·ful \'fret-fəl\ *adjective* (1602)
: disposed to fret **:** IRRITABLE
— **fret·ful·ly** \-fə-lē\ *adverb*
— **fret·ful·ness** *noun*

fret·saw \'fret-,sȯ\ *noun* (1865)
: a narrow-bladed fine-toothed saw held under tension in a frame and used for cutting curved outlines

fret·work \-,wərk\ *noun* (1601)
1 : decoration consisting of work adorned with frets
2 : ornamental openwork or work in relief

Freud·ian \'frȯi-dē-ən\ *adjective* (1910)
: of, relating to, or according with the psychoanalytic theories or practices of Freud ◇
— **Freudian** *noun*
— **Freud·ian·ism** \-ə-,ni-zəm\ *noun*

Freudian slip *noun* (1953)

: a slip of the tongue that is motivated by and reveals some unconscious aspect of the mind

Frey \'frā\ *noun* [Old Norse *Freyr*]
: the Norse god of fertility, crops, peace, and prosperity

Freya \'frā-ə\ *noun* [Old Norse *Freyja*]
: the Norse goddess of love and beauty

fri·a·ble \'frī-ə-bəl\ *adjective* [Middle French or Latin; Middle French, from Latin *friabilis*, from *friare* to crumble — more at FRICTION] (1563)
: easily crumbled or pulverized ⟨*friable* soil⟩
synonym see FRAGILE
— **fri·a·bil·i·ty** \,frī-ə-'bi-lə-tē\ *noun*

fri·ar \'frī-(ə)r\ *noun* [Middle English *frere, fryer*, from Old French *frere*, literally, brother, from Latin *fratr-, frater* — more at BROTHER] (13th century)
: a member of a mendicant order

fri·ar·ly \-lē\ *adjective* (1549)
: resembling a friar : relating to friars

friar's lantern *noun* (1632)
obsolete : IGNIS FATUUS

fri·ary \'frī-(ə)r-ē\ *noun, plural* **-ar·ies** (1538)
: a monastery of friars

¹frib·ble \'fri-bəl\ *verb* **frib·bled; frib·bling** \-b(ə-)liŋ\ [origin unknown] (1633)
intransitive verb
1 : TRIFLE
2 *obsolete* : DODDER
transitive verb
: to trifle or fool away

²fribble *noun* (1664)
: a frivolous person, thing, or idea : TRIFLER
— **frib·ble** *adjective*

fric·an·deau \'fri-kən-,dō\ *noun* [French, from Middle French, probably from *fricasser* + *-ande* (as in *viande* meat) + *-eau*, noun suffix] (1706)
: larded veal roasted and glazed in its own juices

¹fric·as·see *also* **fric·as·sée** \'fri-kə-,sē, ,fri-kə-'\ *noun* [Middle French, from feminine of *fricassé*, past participle of *fricasser* to fricassee] (1568)
: a dish of cut-up pieces of meat (as chicken) stewed in stock and served in a white sauce

²fricassee *transitive verb* **-seed; -see·ing** (1657)
: to cook as a fricassee

fric·a·tive \'fri-kə-tiv\ *noun* [Latin *fricatus*, past participle of *fricare*] (1863)
: a consonant characterized by frictional passage of the expired breath through a narrowing at some point in the vocal tract
— **fricative** *adjective*

fric·tion \'frik-shən\ *noun* [Middle English, from Middle French or Latin; Middle French, from Latin *friction-, frictio*, from *fricare* to rub; akin to Latin *friare* to crumble, and perhaps to Sanskrit *bhriṇanti* they injure] (1704)
1 a : the rubbing of one body against another **b** : the force that resists relative motion between two bodies in contact
2 : the clashing between two persons or parties of opposed views : DISAGREEMENT
— **fric·tion·less** \-ləs\ *adjective*
— **fric·tion·less·ly** *adverb*

fric·tion·al \'frik-shnəl, -shə-nªl\ *adjective* (1850)
1 : of or relating to friction
2 : moved or produced by friction
— **fric·tion·al·ly** *adverb*

friction clutch *noun* (circa 1842)
: a clutch in which connection is made through sliding friction

friction drive *noun* (1907)
: a power-transmission system that transmits motion by surface friction instead of teeth

friction tape *noun* (1920)
: a usually cloth tape impregnated with water-resistant insulating material and an adhesive and used especially to protect, insulate, and support electrical conductors

Fri·day \'frī-dē, -(,)dā\ *noun* [Middle English, from Old English *frīgedæg* (akin to Old High

German *frīatag* Friday), from (assumed) *Frīg* Frigga + *dæg* day, prehistoric translation of Latin *dies Veneris* Venus' day] (before 12th century)
: the sixth day of the week
— **Fri·days** \-dēz, -(,)dāz\ *adverb*

fridge *also* **frig** \'frij\ *noun* [by shortening & alteration] (1926)
: REFRIGERATOR

fried \'frīd\ *adjective* (1926)
: INTOXICATED

fried·cake \'frīd-,kāk\ *noun* (1839)
: DOUGHNUT, CRULLER

¹friend \'frend\ *noun* [Middle English *frend*, from Old English *frēond*; akin to Old High German *friunt* friend, Old English *frēon* to love, *frēo* free] (before 12th century)
1 a : one attached to another by affection or esteem **b** : ACQUAINTANCE
2 a : one that is not hostile **b** : one that is of the same nation, party, or group
3 : one that favors or promotes something (as a charity)
4 : a favored companion
5 *capitalized* : a member of a Christian sect that stresses Inner Light, rejects sacraments and an ordained ministry, and opposes war — called also *Quaker*
— **friend·less** \'fren(d)-ləs\ *adjective*
— **friend·less·ness** *noun*
— **be friends with** : to have a friendship or friendly relationship with
— **make friends with** : to establish a friendship or friendly relations with

²friend *transitive verb* (13th century)
: to act as the friend of : BEFRIEND

¹friend·ly \'fren(d)-lē\ *adjective* **friend·li·er; -est** (before 12th century)
1 : of, relating to, or befitting a friend: as **a** : showing kindly interest and goodwill **b** : not hostile ⟨a *friendly* merger offer⟩; *also* : involving or coming from actions of one's own forces ⟨*friendly* fire⟩ **c** : CHEERFUL, COMFORTING ⟨the *friendly* glow of the fire⟩
2 : serving a beneficial or helpful purpose
3 : easy to use or understand ⟨*friendly* computer software⟩
synonym see AMICABLE
— **friend·li·ly** \'fren(d)-lə-lē\ *adverb*
— **friend·li·ness** *noun*

²friendly *adverb* (before 12th century)
: in a friendly manner : AMICABLY

³friendly *noun, plural* **friendlies** (1861)
1 : one that is friendly; *especially* : a native who is friendly to settlers or invaders
2 *British* : a match between sports teams and especially international teams that has no connection with league or championship play

friendly society *noun* (1703)
British : a mutual association for providing life and health insurance and old-age pension benefits to members

friend of the court (1944)
: AMICUS CURIAE

friend·ship \'fren(d)-,ship\ *noun* (before 12th century)
1 : the state of being friends
2 : the quality or state of being friendly : FRIENDLINESS
3 *obsolete* : AID

fri·er *variant of* FRYER

Frie·sian \'frē-zhən\ *noun* [variant of *Frisian*] (1923)
chiefly British : HOLSTEIN

¹frieze \'frēz *or* frē-'zā\ *noun* [Middle English *frise*, from Middle French, from Middle Dutch *vriese*] (15th century)
1 : a heavy durable coarse wool and shoddy fabric with a rough surface
2 : a pile surface of uncut loops or of patterned cut and uncut loops

²frieze \'frēz\ *noun* [Middle French *frise*, perhaps from Medieval Latin *phrygium, frisium* embroidered cloth, from Latin *phrygium*, from neuter of *Phrygius* Phrygian, from *Phrygia*] (1563)

1 : the part of an entablature between the architrave and the cornice — see ENTABLATURE illustration
2 : a sculptured or richly ornamented band (as on a building or piece of furniture)
3 : a band, line, or series suggesting a frieze ⟨a constant *frieze* of visitors wound its way around the . . . ruins —Mollie Panter-Downes⟩
— **frieze·like** *adjective*

frig \'frig\ *intransitive verb* **frigged; frig·ging** [Middle English *fryggen* to wriggle] (1598)
: COPULATE — usually considered vulgar; sometimes used in present participle as a meaningless intensive

frig·ate \'fri-gət\ *noun* [Middle French, from Old Italian *fregata*] (1585)
1 : a light boat propelled originally by oars but later by sails
2 : a square-rigged war vessel intermediate between a corvette and a ship of the line
3 : a warship that is smaller than a destroyer

frigate bird *noun*
: any of a family (Fregatidae) of tropical seabirds having a forked tail and large wingspans that are noted for aggressively taking food from other birds

Frig·ga \'fri-gə\ *noun* [Old Norse *Frigg*]
: the wife of Odin and Norse goddess of married love and of the hearth

¹fright \'frīt\ *noun* [Middle English, from Old English *fyrhto, fryhto*; akin to Old High German *forhta* fear] (before 12th century)
1 : fear excited by sudden danger : ALARM
2 : something strange, ugly, or shocking
synonym see FEAR

²fright *transitive verb* (before 12th century)
: to alarm suddenly : FRIGHTEN

fright·en \'frī-tªn\ *verb* **fright·ened; fright·en·ing** \'frī-tªn-iŋ, 'frīt-niŋ\ (1666)
transitive verb
1 : to make afraid : TERRIFY
2 : to drive or force by frightening ⟨*frightened* the boy into confessing⟩
intransitive verb
: to become frightened
— **fright·en·ing·ly** \-tªn-iŋ-lē, -niŋ-lē\ *adverb*

fright·ful \'frīt-fəl\ *adjective* (1607)
1 : causing intense fear or alarm : TERRIFYING
2 : startling especially in being bad or objectionable ⟨a *frightful* novel⟩
3 : EXTREME ⟨*frightful* thirst⟩
— **fright·ful·ly** \-fə-lē\ *adverb*
— **fright·ful·ness** *noun*

fright wig *noun* (1886)
: a wig with hair that stands out from the head

frig·id \'fri-jəd\ *adjective* [Latin *frigidus*, from *frigēre* to be cold; akin to Latin *frigus* frost, cold, Greek *rhigos*] (1622)
1 a : intensely cold **b** : lacking warmth or ardor : INDIFFERENT
2 : lacking imaginative qualities : INSIPID
3 a : abnormally averse to sexual intercourse — used especially of women **b** *of a female* : unable to achieve orgasm during sexual intercourse
— **frig·id·ly** *adverb*
— **frig·id·ness** *noun*

Frig·i·daire \,fri-jə-'dar, -'der\ *trademark*
— used for a mechanical refrigerator

fri·gid·i·ty \fri-'ji-də-tē\ *noun* (15th century)
: the quality or state of being frigid; *specifically* : marked or abnormal sexual indifference especially in a woman

frigid zone *noun* (1622)
: the area or region between the arctic circle and the north pole or between the antarctic circle and the south pole

\ə\ abut \ª\ kitten \ər\ further \a\ ash \ā\ ace
\ä\ mop, mar \aů\ out \ch\ chin \e\ bet \ē\ easy
\g\ go \i\ hit \ī\ ice \j\ job \ŋ\ sing \ō\ go
\ȯ\ law \ȯi\ boy \th\ thin \th\ the \ü\ loot \ů\ foot
\y\ yet \zh\ vision *see also* Guide to Pronunciation

frig·o·rif·ic \ˌfri-gə-ˈri-fik\ *adjective* [Latin *frigorificus,* from *frigor-, frigus* frost] (1667)
: causing cold **:** CHILLING

fri·jo·le \frē-ˈhōl, ˈfrē-\ *also* **fri·jol** \frē-ˈhōl, ˈfrē-\ *noun, plural* **fri·jo·les** \frē-ˈhō-lēz, ˈfrē-\ [American Spanish *frijol,* from Spanish, kidney bean, from earlier *fesol, fresol,* probably modification of Galician *feijoo,* from Latin *phaseolus,* diminutive of *phaselus* cowpea, from Greek *phasēlos*] (1577)
: any of various beans used in Mexican style cooking — usually used in plural

¹frill \ˈfril\ *transitive verb* (1574)
: to provide or decorate with a frill

²frill *noun* [perhaps from Flemish *frul*] (1591)
1 a : a gathered, pleated, or bias-cut fabric edging used on clothing **b :** a strip of paper curled at one end and rolled to be slipped over the bone end (as of a chop) in serving
2 : a ruff of hair or feathers or a bony projection about the neck of an animal
3 a : AFFECTATION, AIR — usually used in plural ⟨an honest . . . man who had no *frills,* . . . no nonsense about him —W. A. White⟩ **b :** something decorative or useful and desirable but not essential **:** LUXURY
— **frilly** \ˈfri-lē\ *adjective*

¹fringe \ˈfrinj\ *noun, often attributive* [Middle English *frenge,* from Middle French, from (assumed) Vulgar Latin *frimbia,* from Latin *fimbriae* (plural)] (14th century)
1 : an ornamental border consisting of short straight or twisted threads or strips hanging from cut or raveled edges or from a separate band
2 a : something resembling a fringe **:** EDGE, PERIPHERY — often used in plural ⟨operated on the *fringes* of the law⟩ **b :** one of various light or dark bands produced by the interference or diffraction of light **c :** an area bordering a putting green on a golf course with grass trimmed longer than on the green itself
3 a : something that is marginal, additional, or secondary to some activity, process, or subject **b :** a group with marginal or extremist views **c :** FRINGE BENEFIT
— **fringy** \ˈfrin-jē\ *adjective*

²fringe *transitive verb* **fringed; fring·ing** \ˈfrin-jiŋ\ (15th century)
1 : to furnish or adorn with a fringe
2 : to serve as a fringe for **:** BORDER

fringe area *noun* (1950)
: a region in which reception from a given broadcasting station is weak or subject to serious distortion

fringe benefit *noun* (1948)
1 : an employment benefit (as a pension, a paid holiday, or health insurance) granted by an employer that has a monetary value but does not affect basic wage rates
2 : any additional benefit

fringe tree *noun* (circa 1730)
: a small tree (*Chionanthus virginicus*) of the olive family that has clusters of white flowers and is native to the southern U.S. but is widely cultivated as an ornamental

frip·pery \ˈfri-p(ə-)rē\ *noun, plural* **-per·ies** [Middle French *friperie,* alteration of Old French *freperie,* from *frepe* old garment] (1568)
1 *obsolete* **a :** cast-off clothes **b** *archaic* **:** a place where old clothes are sold
2 a : FINERY; *also* **:** an elegant or showy garment **b :** something showy, frivolous, or nonessential **:** LUXURY, TRIFLE **c :** OSTENTATION; *especially* **:** something foolish or affectedly elegant

Fris·bee \ˈfriz-bē\ *trademark*
— used for a plastic disk several inches in diameter sailed between players by a flip of the wrist

fri·sé \frē-ˈzā\ *noun* [French, from past participle of *friser* to curl] (1884)
: ¹FRIEZE

Frise aileron \ˈfrēz-\ *noun* [Leslie George Frise (born 1897) English engineer] (circa 1934)
: an aileron having a nose portion projecting ahead of the hinge axis and a lower surface in line with the lower surface of the wing

fri·seur \frē-ˈzər\ *noun* [French, from *friser*] (1750)
: HAIRDRESSER

¹Fri·sian \ˈfri-zhən, ˈfrē-\ *adjective* [Latin *Frisius* Frisian; akin to Old English *Frīsa, Frēsa* a Frisian] (1598)
: of, relating to, or characteristic of Friesland, the Frisians, or Frisian

²Frisian *noun* (1601)
1 : a member of a people that inhabit principally the Netherlands province of Friesland and the Frisian islands in the North Sea
2 : the Germanic language of the Frisian people

¹frisk \ˈfrisk\ *verb* [obsolete *frisk* (lively)] (1519)
intransitive verb
: to leap, skip, or dance in a lively or playful way **:** GAMBOL
transitive verb
: to search (a person) for something (as a concealed weapon) by running the hand rapidly over the clothing and through the pockets
— **frisk·er** *noun*

²frisk *noun* (1525)
1 a *archaic* **:** CAPER **b :** GAMBOL, ROMP **c :** DIVERSION
2 : an act of frisking

fris·ket \ˈfris-kət\ *noun* [French *frisquette,* from Middle French] (circa 1898)
: a masking device or material used especially in printing or graphic arts

frisky \ˈfris-kē\ *adjective* **frisk·i·er; -est** (circa 1500)
: inclined to frisk **:** PLAYFUL; *also* **:** LIVELY
— **frisk·i·ly** \ˈfris-kə-lē\ *adverb*
— **frisk·i·ness** \-kē-nəs\ *noun*

fris·son \frē-ˈsōⁿ\ *noun, plural* **frissons** \-ˈsōⁿ(z)\ [French, shiver, from Old French *friçon,* from Late Latin *friction-, frictio,* from Latin, literally, friction (taken in Late Latin as derivative of *frigēre* to be cold)] (1777)
: a brief moment of emotional excitement **:** SHUDDER, THRILL

¹frit \ˈfrit\ *noun* [Italian *fritta,* from feminine of *fritto,* past participle of *friggere* to fry, from Latin *frigere* to roast — more at FRY] (1662)
1 : the calcined or partly fused materials of which glass is made
2 : any of various chemically complex glasses used ground especially to introduce soluble or unstable ingredients into glazes or enamels

²frit *transitive verb* **frit·ted; frit·ting** (1832)
1 : to prepare (materials for glass) by heat **:** FUSE
2 : to convert into a frit

frith \ˈfrith\ *noun* (14th century)
archaic **:** ESTUARY

frit·il·lar·ia \ˌfri-tᵊl-ˈer-ē-ə, -ˈar-\ *noun* [New Latin, from Latin *fritillus* dice cup; from the markings of the petals] (1664)
: any of a widespread genus (*Fritillaria*) of bulbous herbs of the lily family with variably colored and often mottled or checkered flowers

frit·il·lary \ˈfri-tᵊl-ˌer-ē, *plural* **-lar·ies** [New Latin *fritillaria*] (1633)
1 : FRITILLARIA
2 : any of numerous nymphalid butterflies (*Argynnis, Speyeria,* and related genera) that usually are orange with black spots on the upper side of both wings and silver spotted on the underside of the hind wing

fritillaria

frit·ta·ta \frē-ˈtä-tə\ *noun* [Italian, from *fritto*] (1931)
: an unfolded omelet often containing chopped vegetables or meats

frit·ted *adjective* [²*frit*] (1879)
: being porous glass made of sintered powdered glass or fiberglass

¹frit·ter \ˈfri-tər\ *noun* [Middle English *fritour,* from Middle French *friture,* from (assumed) Vulgar Latin *frictura,* from Latin *frictus,* past participle of *frigere* to roast] (14th century)
: a small mass of fried or sautéed batter often containing fruit or meat

²fritter *verb* [*fritter,* noun (fragment, shred)] (1728)
transitive verb
1 : to spend or waste bit by bit, on trifles, or without commensurate return — usually used with *away*
2 : to break into small fragments
intransitive verb
: DISSIPATE, DWINDLE
— **frit·ter·er** \-tər-ər\ *noun*

frit·to mi·sto \ˈfrē-(ˌ)tō-ˈmē-(ˌ)stō\ *noun* [Italian, literally, mixed fried (food)] (1903)
: small morsels of meat, seafood, or vegetables coated with batter and deep fried

fritz \ˈfrits\ *noun* [origin unknown] (1902)
: a state of disorder or disrepair — used in the phrase *on the fritz*

friv·ol \ˈfri-vᵊl\ *intransitive verb* **-oled** *or* **-olled; -ol·ing** *or* **-ol·ling** \-vᵊl-iŋ, -və-liŋ\ [back-formation from *frivolous*] (1866)
: to act frivolously **:** TRIFLE
— **friv·ol·er** *or* **friv·ol·ler** \-vᵊl-ər, -və-lər\ *noun*

fri·vol·i·ty \fri-ˈvä-lə-tē\ *noun, plural* **-ties** (1796)
1 : the quality or state of being frivolous
2 : a frivolous act or thing

friv·o·lous \ˈfri-vᵊl-əs, -və-ləs\ *adjective* [Middle English, from Latin *frivolus*] (15th century)
1 a : of little weight or importance **b :** having no sound basis (as in fact or law) ⟨a *frivolous* lawsuit⟩
2 a : lacking in seriousness **b :** marked by unbecoming levity
— **friv·o·lous·ly** *adverb*
— **friv·o·lous·ness** *noun*

¹frizz \ˈfriz\ *verb* [French *friser*] (1660)
transitive verb
: to form into small tight curls
intransitive verb
of hair **:** to form a mass of tight curls

²frizz *noun* (1668)
1 : a tight curl
2 : hair that is tightly curled

³frizz *verb* [alteration of ¹*fry*] (1835)
transitive verb
: to fry or sear with a sizzling noise
intransitive verb
: SIZZLE

¹friz·zle \ˈfri-zᵊl\ *verb* **friz·zled; friz·zling** \-zᵊl-iŋ, -zə-liŋ\ [probably akin to Old Frisian *frīsle* curl] (1573)
: FRIZZ, CURL

²frizzle *noun* (1613)
: a crisp curl

³frizzle *verb* **friz·zled; friz·zling** [¹*fry* + *sizzle*] (1839)
transitive verb
1 : to fry until crisp and curled
2 : BURN, SCORCH
intransitive verb
: to cook with a sizzling noise

frizzy \ˈfri-zē\ *adjective* **frizz·i·er; -est** (circa 1864)
: tightly curled
— **frizz·i·ness** *noun*

¹fro \frə, ˈfrō\ *preposition* [Middle English, from Old Norse *frā;* akin to Old English *fram* from] (13th century)
dialect British **:** FROM

²fro \ˈfrō\ *adverb* (14th century)
: BACK, AWAY — used in the phrase *to and fro*

¹**frock** \'fräk\ noun [Middle English *frok*, from Middle French *froc*, of Germanic origin; akin to Old High German *hroch* mantle, coat] (14th century)
1 : an outer garment worn by monks and friars **:** HABIT
2 : an outer garment worn chiefly by men: **a :** a long loose mantle **b :** a workman's outer shirt; *especially* **:** SMOCK FROCK **c :** a woolen jersey worn especially by sailors
3 : a woman's dress
²**frock** *transitive verb* (1828)
1 : to clothe in a frock
2 : to make a cleric of
frock coat noun (1823)
: a man's knee-length usually double-breasted coat
froe \'frō\ noun [perhaps alteration of obsolete *froward* turned away, from Middle English; from the position of the handle] (1574)
: a cleaving tool for splitting cask staves and shingles from the block
frog \'frȯg, 'fräg\ noun [Middle English *frogge*, from Old English *frogga*; akin to Old High German *frosk* frog; senses 2, 3, 5, 7, 8 unclearly derived & perhaps of distinct origin] (before 12th century)
1 : any of various smooth-skinned web-footed largely aquatic tailless agile leaping amphibians (as a ranid) — compare TOAD
2 : the triangular elastic horny pad in the middle of the sole of the foot of a horse — see HOOF illustration
3 a : a loop attached to a belt to hold a weapon or tool **b :** an ornamental braiding for fastening the front of a garment that consists of a button and a loop through which it passes
4 *often capitalized* **:** FRENCHMAN — usually taken to be offensive
5 : a device permitting the wheels on one rail of a track to cross an intersecting rail
6 : a condition in the throat that produces hoarseness ⟨had a *frog* in his throat⟩
7 : the nut of a violin bow
8 : a small holder (as of metal, glass, or plastic) with perforations or spikes for holding flowers in place in a bowl or vase
frog·eye \-,ī\ noun (circa 1909)
: any of numerous leaf diseases characterized by concentric rings about the diseased spots
frog·hop·per \-,hä-pər\ noun (1711)
: SPITTLEBUG
frog kick noun (1940)
: a breaststroke kick executed with the knees turned outward and the legs separated and then swung together
frog·man \'frȯg-,man, 'fräg-, -mən\ noun (1945)
: a person equipped (as with face mask, flippers, and air supply) for extended periods of underwater swimming; *especially* **:** a person so equipped for military reconnaissance and demolition
frog–march \-,märch\ *transitive verb* (1923)
: to seize from behind roughly and forcefully propel forward ⟨*frog-marched* him out the door⟩
frog spit noun (circa 1825)
: CUCKOO SPIT 1
¹**frol·ic** \'frä-lik\ adjective [Dutch *vroolijk*, from Middle Dutch *vrolijc*, from *vro* happy; akin to Old High German *frō* happy] (1538)
: full of fun **:** MERRY
²**frolic** *intransitive verb* **frol·icked; frol·ick·ing** (1593)
1 : to amuse oneself **:** make merry
2 : to play and run about happily **:** ROMP
³**frolic** noun (1616)
1 : a playful or mischievous action
2 a : an occasion or scene of fun **:** PARTY **b :** FUN, MERRIMENT
frol·ic·some \'frä-lik-səm\ adjective (1699)
: full of gaiety **:** SPORTIVE, PLAYFUL
from \'frəm, 'främ *also* fəm\ preposition [Middle English, from Old English *from, fram*; akin to Old High German *fram*, adverb, forth,

away, Old English *faran* to go — more at FARE] (before 12th century)
1 — used as a function word to indicate a starting point of a physical movement or a starting point in measuring or reckoning or in a statement of limits ⟨came here *from* the city⟩ ⟨a week *from* today⟩ ⟨cost *from* $5 to $10⟩
2 — used as a function word to indicate physical separation or an act or condition of removal, abstention, exclusion, release, subtraction, or differentiation ⟨protection *from* the sun⟩ ⟨relief *from* anxiety⟩
3 — used as a function word to indicate the source, cause, agent, or basis ⟨we conclude *from* this⟩ ⟨a call *from* my lawyer⟩ ⟨inherited a love of music *from* his father⟩ ⟨worked hard *from* necessity⟩
frond \'fränd\ noun [Latin *frond-, frons* foliage] (1785)
1 : a large leaf (especially of a palm or fern) usually with many divisions
2 : a thallus or thalloid shoot (as of a lichen or seaweed) resembling a leaf
— **frond·ed** \'frän-dəd\ adjective
fron·deur \frōⁿ-'dər\ noun [French, literally, slinger, participant in a 17th century revolt in which the rebels were compared to schoolboys using slings only when the teacher was not looking] (1798)
: REBEL, MALCONTENT
¹**front** \'frənt\ noun [Middle English, from Old French, from Latin *front-, frons*] (13th century)
1 a : FOREHEAD; *also* **:** the whole face **b :** external and often feigned appearance especially in the face of danger or adversity
2 a (1) **:** VANGUARD (2) **:** a line of battle (3) **:** a zone of conflict between armies **b** (1) **:** a stand on an issue **:** POLICY (2) **:** an area of activity (as study or debate) ⟨progress on the educational *front*⟩ (3) **:** a movement linking divergent elements to achieve common objectives; *especially* **:** a political coalition
3 : a side of a building; *especially* **:** the side that contains the principal entrance
4 a : the forward part or surface **b** (1) **:** FRONTAGE (2) **:** a beach promenade at a seaside resort **c :** DICKEY 1a **d :** the boundary between two dissimilar air masses
5 *archaic* **:** BEGINNING
6 a (1) **:** a position ahead of a person or of the foremost part of a thing (2) — used as a call by a hotel desk clerk in summoning a bellhop **b :** a position of leadership or superiority
7 a : a person, group, or thing used to mask the identity or true character or activity of the actual controlling agent **b :** a person who serves as the nominal head or spokesman of an enterprise or group to lend it prestige
— **in front of :** directly before or ahead of
— **out front :** in the audience
²**front** (1523)
intransitive verb
1 : to have the front or principal side adjacent to something; *also* **:** to have frontage on something ⟨a ten-acre plot *fronting* on a lake —*Current Biography*⟩
2 : to serve as a front ⟨*fronting* for special interests⟩
transitive verb
1 a : CONFRONT ⟨went to the woods because I wished . . . to *front* only the essential facts of life —H. D. Thoreau⟩ **b :** to appear before ⟨daily *fronted* him in some fresh splendor —Alfred Tennyson⟩
2 a : to be in front of ⟨lawn *fronting* the house⟩ **b :** to be the leader of (a musical group) ⟨appeared as a soloist and *fronted* bands⟩
3 : to face toward or have frontage on ⟨the house *fronts* the street⟩
4 : to supply a front to ⟨*fronted* the building with bricks⟩
5 a : to articulate (a sound) with the tongue farther forward **b :** to move (a word or phrase) to the beginning of a sentence

6 *basketball* **:** to play in front of (an opposing player) rather than between the player and the basket
³**front** *adjective* (1600)
1 a : of, relating to, or situated at the front **b :** acting as a front ⟨*front* company⟩
2 : articulated at or toward the front of the oral passage ⟨*front* vowels⟩
3 : constituting the first nine holes of an 18-hole golf course
— **front** *adverb*
front·age \'frən-tij\ noun (1622)
1 a : a piece of land that lies adjacent (as to a street or the ocean) **b :** the land between the front of a building and the street **c :** the length of a frontage
2 : the act or fact of facing a given way
3 : the front side of a building
frontage road noun (1949)
: a local street that parallels an expressway or through street and that provides access to property near the expressway — called also *service road*
¹**fron·tal** \'frən-tᵊl\ noun (14th century)
1 [Middle English *frontel*, from Medieval Latin *frontellum*, diminutive of Latin *front-, frons*] **:** a cloth hanging over the front of an altar
2 : FACADE 1
²**frontal** *adjective* [New Latin *frontalis*, from Latin *front-, frons*] (1656)
1 : of, relating to, or adjacent to the forehead or the frontal bone
2 a : of, relating to, or situated at the front **b :** directed against the front or at the main point or issue **:** DIRECT ⟨*frontal* assault⟩
3 : parallel to the main axis of the body and at right angles to the sagittal plane
4 : of or relating to a meteorological front
— **fron·tal·ly** \-tᵊl-ē\ adverb
frontal bone noun (1741)
: a bone that forms the forehead and roofs over most of the orbits and nasal cavity and that at birth consists of two halves separated by a suture
fron·tal·i·ty \,frən-'ta-lə-tē\ noun (1905)
1 *sculpture* **:** a schematic composition of the front view that is complete without lateral movement
2 *painting* **:** the depiction of an object, figure, or scene in a plane parallel to the plane of the picture surface
frontal lobe noun (1879)
: the anterior division of each cerebral hemisphere
front and center adverb (1951)
: in or to the forefront of activity or consideration
front bench noun (circa 1889)
: either of the two benches nearest the chair in a British legislature (as the House of Commons) occupied by government and opposition leaders; *also* **:** the leaders themselves — compare BACKBENCH
— **front–bench·er** \-'ben-chər\ noun
front burner noun (1973)
: the condition of being in active consideration or development — compare BACK BURNER
front·court \'frənt-'kȯrt, -,kȯrt\ noun (circa 1949)
: a basketball team's offensive half of the court; *also* **:** the positions of forward and center on a basketball team
front dive noun (circa 1934)
: a dive from a position facing the water
front–end *adjective* (1962)
: relating to or required at the beginning of an undertaking ⟨no *front-end* charge at the time of investment⟩
front end noun (1973)

: a unit in a computer system devoted to controlling the data communications link between terminals and the main computer and often to the preliminary processing of data

front–end load *noun* (1962)
: the part of the total commission and expenses taken out of early payments under a contract plan for the periodic purchase of investment-company shares

front–end loader *noun* (1954)
: a usually wheeled vehicle with a hydraulically operated scoop in front for excavating and loading loose material — called also *front loader*

fron·tier \‚frən-'tir, 'frən-‚, frän-', 'frän-‚\ *noun* [Middle English *fronter*, from Middle French *frontiere*, from *front*] (15th century)
1 a : a border between two countries **b** *obsolete* : a stronghold on a frontier
2 a : a region that forms the margin of settled or developed territory **b :** the farthermost limits of knowledge or achievement in a particular subject **c :** a line of division between different or opposed things ⟨the *frontiers* separating science and the humanities —R. W. Clark⟩ **d :** a new field for exploitative or developmental activity
— **frontier** *adjective*

fron·tiers·man \‚frən-'tirz-mən, frän-\ *noun* (1782)
: one who lives or works on a frontier

fron·tis·piece \'frən-tə-‚spēs\ *noun* [Middle French *frontispice*, from Late Latin *frontispicium* facade, from Latin *front-, frons* + *-i-* + *specere* to look at — more at SPY] (circa 1598)
1 a : the principal front of a building **b :** a decorated pediment over a portico or window
2 : an illustration preceding and usually facing the title page of a book or magazine ◇

front·less \'frənt-ləs\ *adjective* (1605)
archaic : SHAMELESS

front·let \-lət\ *noun* [Middle English *frontlette*, from Middle French *frontelet*, diminutive of *frontel*, from Latin *frontale*, from *front-, frons*] (15th century)
1 : a band or phylactery worn on the forehead
2 : the forehead especially of an animal

front·line \'frənt-‚līn\ *adjective* (1915)
1 : relating to, being, or involved in a front line ⟨*frontline* ambulances⟩
2 : FIRST-RATE ⟨*frontline* teachers⟩; *also* : FIRST-STRING ⟨*frontline* goalie⟩

front line *noun* (1917)
1 a : a military line formed by the most advanced tactical combat units; *also* : FRONT 2a(2) **b :** an area of potential or actual conflict or struggle
2 : the most advanced, responsible, or visible position in a field or activity

front–load *transitive verb* (1976)
: to assign costs or benefits to the early stages of (as a contract, project, or time period)

front man *noun* (1927)
1 : a person serving as a front or figurehead
2 : the lead performer in a musical group

front matter *noun* (circa 1909)
: matter preceding the main text of a book

front money *noun* (circa 1928)
: money that is paid in advance for a promised service or product

fronto- *combining form* [¹*front*]
: boundary of an air mass ⟨*fronto*genesis⟩

front office *noun, often attributive* (1900)
: the policy-making officials of an organization

front·o·gen·e·sis \‚frən-tō-'je-nə-səs\ *noun* [New Latin] (1931)
: the coming together into a distinct front of two dissimilar air masses that commonly react upon each other to induce cloud and precipitation

front·ol·y·sis \‚frən-'tä-lə-səs\ *noun* [New Latin] (circa 1938)
: a process tending to destroy a meteorological front

fron·ton \'frän-‚tän\ *noun* [Spanish *frontón* gable, wall of a pelota court, fronton, from augmentative of *frente* forehead, from Latin *front-, frons*] (1896)
: a jai alai arena

¹front–page \'frənt-'pāj\ *adjective* (1917)
: printed on the front page of a newspaper; *also* : very newsworthy

²front–page *transitive verb* (1929)
: to print or report on the front page

front room *noun* (1853)
: LIVING ROOM, PARLOR

front–run·ner \'frənt-‚rə-nər\ *noun* (1914)
1 : a contestant who runs best when in the lead
2 : a leading contestant in or as if in a rivalry or competition ⟨a political *front-runner*⟩ ⟨dubbed . . . *front-runner* for the title of "worst Senator" —Edward Roeder⟩

front·ward \'frənt-wərd\ *or* **front·wards** \-wərdz\ *adverb or adjective* (1865)
: toward the front

frore \'frōr, 'frȯr\ *adjective* [Middle English *froren*, from Old English, past participle of *frēosan* to freeze] (13th century)
: FROSTY, FROZEN

frosh \'fräsh\ *noun, plural* **frosh** [by shortening & alteration] (1915)
: FRESHMAN

¹frost \'frȯst\ *noun* [Middle English, from Old English; akin to Old High German *frost* — more at FREEZE] (before 12th century)
1 a : the process of freezing **b :** a covering of minute ice crystals on a cold surface; *also* : ice particles formed from a gas **c :** the temperature that causes freezing
2 a : coldness of deportment or temperament : an indifferent, reserved, or unfriendly manner **b :** FAILURE ⟨the play was . . . a most dreadful *frost* —Arnold Bennett⟩

²frost (1635)
transitive verb
1 a : to cover with or as if with frost; *especially* : to put icing on (cake) **b :** to produce a fine-grained slightly roughened surface on (as metal or glass)
2 : to injure or kill (as plants) by frost
3 : to make angry or irritated ⟨your attitude really *frosts* me⟩
intransitive verb
: to become frosted

¹frost·bite \'frȯs(t)-‚bīt\ *transitive verb* **-bit** \-‚bit\; **-bit·ten** \-‚bi-t°n\; **-bit·ing** \-‚bī-tiŋ\ (1601)
: to affect or injure by frost or frostbite

²frostbite *noun* (1813)
: the freezing or the local effect of a partial freezing of some part of the body

³frostbite *adjective* (1953)
: done in cold weather ⟨*frostbite* sailing⟩; *also* : of or relating to cold-weather sailing ⟨*frostbite* sailors⟩

frost·bit·ing \-‚bī-tiŋ\ *noun* (1965)
: the sport of sailing in cold weather

frost·ed \'frȯ-stəd\ *adjective* (1947)
: having undergone frosting ⟨*frosted* hair⟩

frost heave *noun* (1941)
: an upthrust of ground or pavement caused by freezing of moist soil — called also *frost heaving*

frost·ing \'frȯ-stiŋ\ *noun* (1858)
1 a : ICING **b :** TRIMMING, ORNAMENTATION
2 : lusterless finish of metal or glass : MAT; *also* : a white finish produced on glass (as by etching)
3 : the lightening (as by chemicals) of small strands of hair throughout the entire head to produce a two-tone effect — compare STREAKING

frost·work \'frȯs(t)-‚wərk\ *noun* (1729)
: the figures that moisture sometimes forms in freezing (as on a windowpane)

frosty \'frȯ-stē\ *adjective* **frost·i·er; -est** (before 12th century)
1 a : attended with or producing frost : FREEZING **b :** briskly cold : CHILLY

2 : covered or appearing as if covered with frost : HOARY ⟨a man of 65, with *frosty* eyebrows and hair —Nan Robertson⟩
3 : marked by coolness or extreme reserve in manner ⟨his smile was distinctly *frosty* —Erle Stanley Gardner⟩
— **frost·i·ly** \-stə-lē\ *adverb*
— **frost·i·ness** \-stē-nəs\ *noun*

¹froth \'frȯth\ *noun, plural* **froths** \'frȯths, 'frȯthz\ [Middle English, from Old Norse *frotha*; akin to Old English *āfrēothan* to froth] (14th century)
1 a : bubbles formed in or on a liquid : FOAM **b :** a foamy slaver sometimes accompanying disease or exhaustion
2 : something resembling froth (as in being unsubstantial, worthless, or light and airy)

²froth \'frȯth, 'frȯth\ (14th century)
intransitive verb
1 : to foam at the mouth
2 : to throw froth out or up
3 : to become covered with or as if with froth ⟨whole groves *froth* with nodding blossoms —Amy Lovejoy⟩
transitive verb
1 : to cause to foam
2 : to cover with froth
3 : VENT, VOICE

frothy \'frȯ-thē, -thē\ *adjective* **froth·i·er; -est** (15th century)
1 : full of or consisting of froth
2 a : gaily frivolous or light in content or treatment : INSUBSTANTIAL ⟨a *frothy* comedy⟩ **b :** made of light thin material
— **froth·i·ly** \-thə-lē, -thə-\ *adverb*
— **froth·i·ness** \-thē-nəs, -thē-\ *noun*

frot·tage \frȯ-'täzh\ *noun* [French, from *frotter* to rub] (1935)
: the technique of creating a design by rubbing (as with a pencil) over an object placed underneath the paper; *also* : a composition so made

frou-frou \'frü-‚frü\ *noun* [French, of imitative origin] (1870)
1 : a rustling especially of a woman's skirts
2 : showy or frilly ornamentation

frow \'frō\ *variant of* FROE

fro·ward \'frō-(w)ərd\ *adjective* [Middle English, turned away, froward, from *fro* from + *-ward* -ward] (13th century)
1 : habitually disposed to disobedience and opposition
2 *archaic* : ADVERSE
— **fro·ward·ly** *adverb*
— **fro·ward·ness** *noun*

¹frown \'fraun\ *verb* [Middle English *frounen*, from Middle French *froigner* to snort, frown, of Celtic origin; akin to Welsh *ffroen* nostril, Old Irish *srón* nose] (14th century)
intransitive verb

◇ WORD HISTORY

frontispiece Folk etymology is a process whereby unfamiliar words are altered to give them an apparent relationship to more familiar ones. One word that reflects the workings of folk etymology is *frontispiece*, which has nothing at all to do with the word *piece*. The earliest form of the word in English, *frontispice*, is a loan, via French, from Late Latin *frontispicium*, meaning "façade of a building." Virtually as soon as the word was introduced, English writers began to spell the final syllable as *piece*. *Frontispiece* was applied early on not only to building fronts and decorated pediments, but also to the title page of a book, which in the 17th century often had columns, pediments, and other architectural detail framing the title itself. As the original architectural sense of the word became secondary in users' minds, associations evoked by *front* ("the foremost part") and *piece* ("an artistic composition") made it natural to apply the word to an illustration preceding the title page.

1 : to contract the brow in displeasure or concentration
2 : to give evidence of displeasure or disapproval by or as if by facial expression ⟨critics *frown* on the idea⟩
transitive verb
: to show displeasure with or disapproval of especially by facial expression
— **frown·er** *noun*
— **frown·ing·ly** \'fraù-niŋ-lē\ *adverb*
²frown *noun* (1581)
1 : an expression of displeasure
2 : a wrinkling of the brow in displeasure or concentration
frows·ty \'fraù-stē\ *adjective* **frowst·i·er; -est** [alteration of *frowsy*] (1865)
1 *chiefly British* **:** MUSTY
2 *chiefly British* **:** FROWSY 2
frow·sy *or* **frow·zy** \'fraù-zē\ *adjective* **frow·si·er** *or* **frow·zi·er; -est** [origin unknown] (1681)
1 : MUSTY, STALE ⟨a *frowsy* smell of stale beer and stale smoke —W. S. Maugham⟩
2 : having a slovenly or uncared-for appearance ⟨a couple of *frowsy* stuffed chairs —R. M. Williams⟩
froze *past of* FREEZE
fro·zen \'frō-z°n\ *adjective* (14th century)
1 a : treated, affected, or crusted over by freezing **b :** subject to long and severe cold ⟨*frozen* north⟩
2 a : incapable of being changed, moved, or undone **:** FIXED; *specifically* **:** debarred by official action from movement or from change in status ⟨*frozen* wages⟩ **b :** not available for present use ⟨*frozen* capital⟩ **c** (1) **:** drained or incapable of emotion (2) **:** expressing or characterized by cold unfriendliness
— **fro·zen·ly** *adverb*
— **fro·zen·ness** \-z°n-(n)əs\ *noun*
fruc·ti·fi·ca·tion \ˌfrək-tə-fə-'kā-shən, ˌfrùk-\ *noun* (1764)
: the reproductive organs or fruit of a plant; *especially* **:** SPOROPHORE
fruc·ti·fy \'frək-tə-ˌfī, 'frùk-\ *verb* **-fied; -fy·ing** [Middle English *fructifien*, from Middle French *fructifier*, from Latin *fructificare*, from *fructus* fruit] (14th century)
intransitive verb
: to bear fruit ⟨its seeds shall *fructify* —Amy Lowell⟩ ⟨no partnership can *fructify* without candor on both sides —D. M. Ogilvy⟩
transitive verb
: to make fruitful or productive
fruc·tose \'frək-ˌtōs, 'frùk-, 'frùk-, -ˌtōz\ *noun* (circa 1864)
1 : an optically active sugar $C_6H_{12}O_6$ that differs from glucose in having a ketonic rather than aldehydic carbonyl group
2 : the very sweet soluble levorotatory D-form of fructose that occurs especially in fruit juices and honey — called also *levulose*
fruc·tu·ous \'frək-chə-wəs, 'frùk-\ *adjective* (14th century)
: FRUITFUL ⟨a *fructuous* land⟩
fru·gal \'frü-gəl\ *adjective* [Middle French or Latin; Middle French, from Latin *frugalis* virtuous, frugal, from *frug-, frux* fruit, value; akin to Latin *frui* to enjoy] (1598)
: characterized by or reflecting economy in the use of resources
synonym see SPARING
— **fru·gal·i·ty** \frü-'ga-lə-tē\ *noun*
— **fru·gal·ly** \'frü-gə-lē\ *adverb*
fru·giv·o·rous \frü-'ji-və-rəs\ *adjective* [Latin *frug-, frux* + English *-vorous*] (1713)
: feeding on fruit
— **fru·gi·vore** \'frü-ji-ˌvōr, -ˌvòr\ *noun*
¹fruit \'früt\ *noun, often attributive* [Middle English, from Old French, from Latin *fructus* fruit, use, from *frui* to enjoy, have the use of — more at BROOK] (12th century)
1 a : a product of plant growth (as grain, vegetables, or cotton) ⟨the *fruits* of the field⟩ **b** (1) **:** the usually edible reproductive body of a seed plant; *especially* **:** one having a sweet

pulp associated with the seed ⟨the *fruit* of the tree⟩ (2) **:** a succulent plant part (as the petioles of a rhubarb plant) used chiefly in a dessert or sweet course **c :** a dish, quantity, or diet of fruits ⟨live on *fruit*⟩ **d :** a product of fertilization in a plant with its modified envelopes or appendages; *specifically* **:** the ripened ovary of a seed plant and its contents **e :** the flavor or aroma of fresh fruit in mature wine
2 : OFFSPRING, PROGENY
3 a : the state of bearing fruit ⟨a tree in *fruit*⟩ **b :** the effect or consequence of an action or operation **:** PRODUCT, RESULT ⟨the *fruits* of our labor⟩
4 : a male homosexual — often used disparagingly
— **fruit·ed** \'frü-təd\ *adjective*
²fruit (14th century)
intransitive verb
: to bear fruit
transitive verb
: to cause to bear fruit
fruit·age \'frü-tij\ *noun* (15th century)
1 a : FRUIT **b :** the condition or process of bearing fruit
2 : the product or result of an action
frui·tar·i·an \(ˌ)frü(t)-'ter-ē-ən\ *noun* (1893)
: a person who lives on fruit
fruit bat *noun* (1877)
: any of a family (Pteropodidae of the suborder Megachiroptera) of often large tropical and subtropical Old World bats that feed on ripe fruit, pollen, and nectar and that usually use visual navigation rather than echolocation — called also *flying fox*

fruit bat

fruit·cake \'früt-ˌkāk\ *noun* (1848)
1 : a rich cake containing nuts, dried or candied fruits, and spices
2 : NUT 6a
fruit·er·er \'frü-tər-ər\ *noun* [Middle English, modification of Middle French *fruitier*, from *fruit*] (15th century)
chiefly British **:** a person who deals in fruit
fruit fly *noun* (circa 1753)
: any of various small dipteran flies (as a drosophila) whose larvae feed on fruit or decaying vegetable matter
fruit·ful \'früt-fəl\ *adjective* (14th century)
1 a : yielding or producing fruit **b :** conducive to an abundant yield
2 : abundantly productive
synonym see FERTILE
— **fruit·ful·ly** \-fə-lē\ *adverb*
— **fruit·ful·ness** *noun*
fruiting body *noun* (1918)
: a plant organ specialized for producing spores; *especially* **:** SPOROPHORE
fru·ition \frü-'i-shən\ *noun* [Middle English *fruicioun*, from Middle French or Late Latin; Middle French *fruition*, from Late Latin *fruition-, fruitio*, from Latin *frui*] (15th century)
1 : pleasurable use or possession **:** ENJOYMENT
2 a : the state of bearing fruit **b :** REALIZATION
fruit·less \'früt-ləs\ *adjective* (14th century)
1 : UNSUCCESSFUL
2 : lacking or not bearing fruit
synonym see FUTILE
— **fruit·less·ly** *adverb*
— **fruit·less·ness** *noun*
fruit·let \-lət\ *noun* (1882)
1 : a small fruit
2 : a unit of a collective fruit
fruit machine *noun* (1933)
British **:** SLOT MACHINE 2
fruit sugar *noun* (circa 1889)
: FRUCTOSE 2
fruit·wood \'früt-ˌwùd\ *noun, often attributive* (1927)

: the wood of a fruit tree (as the apple, cherry, or pear) ⟨*fruitwood* furniture⟩
fruity \'frü-tē\ *adjective* **fruit·i·er; -est** (1657)
1 a : relating to, made with, or resembling fruit **b :** having the flavor or aroma of ripe fruit
2 a : extremely effective, interesting, or enjoyable **b :** sweet or sentimental especially to excess **c** *of a voice* **:** rich and deep
3 a *slang* **:** CRAZY, SILLY **b :** HOMOSEXUAL — often used disparagingly
— **fruit·i·ness** *noun*
fru·men·ty \'frü-mən-tē\ *noun, plural* **-ties** [Middle English, from Middle French *frumentee*, from *frument* grain, from Latin *frumentum*, from *frui* to enjoy — more at BROOK] (14th century)
: a dish of wheat boiled in milk and usually sweetened and spiced
frump \'frəmp\ *noun* [probably from *frumple* (to wrinkle)] (1817)
1 : a dowdy unattractive girl or woman
2 : a staid, drab, old-fashioned person
frump·ish \'frəm-pish\ *adjective* (circa 1847)
: DOWDY, DRAB
frumpy \'frəm-pē\ *adjective* **frump·i·er; -est** (circa 1840)
: DOWDY, DRAB
¹frus·trate \'frəs-ˌtrāt\ *transitive verb* **frus·trat·ed; frus·trat·ing** [Middle English, from Latin *frustratus*, past participle of *frustrare* to deceive, frustrate, from *frustra* in error, in vain] (15th century)
1 a : to balk or defeat in an endeavor **b :** to induce feelings of discouragement in
2 a (1) **:** to make ineffectual **:** bring to nothing (2) **:** IMPEDE, OBSTRUCT **b :** to make invalid or of no effect ☆
²frustrate *adjective* (15th century)
: characterized by frustration
frus·trat·ing \-ˌtrā-tiŋ\ *adjective* (1871)
: tending to produce or characterized by frustration
— **frus·trat·ing·ly** \-tiŋ-lē\ *adverb*
frus·tra·tion \(ˌ)frəs-'trā-shən\ *noun* (1555)
1 : the act of frustrating
2 a : the state or an instance of being frustrated **b :** a deep chronic sense or state of insecurity and dissatisfaction arising from unresolved problems or unfulfilled needs
3 : something that frustrates
frus·tule \'frəs-(ˌ)chü(ə)l, -(ˌ)t(y)ü(ə)l\ *noun* [French, from Latin *frustulum*, diminutive of *frustum*] (1857)
: the 2-valved siliceous shell of a diatom
frus·tum \'frəs-təm\ *noun, plural* **frustums** *or* **frus·ta** \-tə\ [New Latin, from Latin, piece, bit — more at BRUISE] (1658)

☆ **SYNONYMS**
Frustrate, thwart, foil, baffle, balk mean to check or defeat another's plan or block achievement of a goal. FRUSTRATE implies making vain or ineffectual all efforts however vigorous or persistent ⟨*frustrated* attempts at government reform⟩. THWART suggests frustration or checking by crossing or opposing ⟨the army *thwarted* his attempt at a coup⟩. FOIL implies checking or defeating so as to discourage further effort ⟨*foiled* by her parents, he stopped trying to see her⟩. BAFFLE implies frustration by confusing or puzzling ⟨*baffled* by the maze of rules and regulations⟩. BALK suggests the interposing of obstacles or hindrances ⟨officials felt that legal restrictions had *balked* their efforts to control crime⟩.

\ə\ abut \°\ kitten \ər\ further \a\ ash \ā\ ace
\ä\ mop, mar \aù\ out \ch\ chin \e\ bet \ē\ easy
\g\ go \i\ hit \ī\ ice \j\ job \ŋ\ sing \ō\ go
\ò\ law \òi\ boy \th\ thin \th\ the \ü\ loot \ù\ foot
\y\ yet \zh\ vision *see also* Guide to Pronunciation

: the basal part of a solid cone or pyramid formed by cutting off the top by a plane parallel to the base; *also* : the part of a solid intersected between two usually parallel planes

fru·tes·cent \frü-'te-s°nt\ *adjective* [Latin *frutex* + English *-escent*] (1709)
: having or approaching the habit or appearance of a shrub : SHRUBBY

fru·ti·cose \'frü-ti-ˌkōs\ *adjective* [Latin *fruticosus*, from *frutic-, frutex* shrub] (1882)
: having a shrubby often branched thallus that grows perpendicular to the substrate 〈*fruticose* lichens〉 — compare CRUSTOSE, FOLIOSE

¹fry \'frī\ *verb* **fried; fry·ing** [Middle English *frien*, from Old French *frire*, from Latin *frigere* to roast; akin to Greek *phrygein* to roast, fry, Sanskrit *bhṛjjati* he roasts] (13th century)
transitive verb
: to cook in a pan or on a griddle over heat especially with the use of fat
intransitive verb
1 : to undergo frying
2 : to get very hot or burn as if being fried 〈bodies *frying* on the beach〉

²fry *noun, plural* **fries** (1833)
1 : a social gathering or picnic where food is fried and eaten 〈a fish *fry*〉
2 a : a dish of something fried **b** : FRENCH FRY — usually used in plural

³fry *noun, plural* **fry** [Middle English, probably from Old North French *fri*, from Old French *frier, froyer* to rub, spawn — more at FRAY] (14th century)
1 a : recently hatched or juvenile fishes **b** : the young of other animals
2 : very small adult fishes
3 : members of a group or class : INDIVIDUALS 〈small *fry*〉 〈a great part of the earth is peopled with these *fry* —Katherine Mansfield〉

fry bread *noun* (1950)
: quick bread cooked (as by American Indians) by deep-frying

fry·er \'frī(-ə)r\ *noun* (1851)
: something intended for or used in frying: as **a** : a young chicken; *especially* : one weighing 2½ to 4 pounds (1.1 to 1.8 kilograms) when dressed **b** : a deep utensil for frying foods

frying pan *noun* (14th century)
: a metal pan with a handle that is used for frying foods — called also *fry pan*
— out of the frying pan into the fire : clear of one difficulty only to fall into a greater one

fry–up \'frī-ˌəp\ *noun* (1967)
British : a dish or meal of fried food

f–stop \'ef-ˌstäp\ *noun* (1946)
: a camera lens aperture setting indicated by an f-number

F₂ layer \'ef-ˌtü-\ *noun* (1933)
: the upper of the two layers into which the F region of the ionosphere splits in the daytime at varying heights from about 120 miles (200 kilometers) to more than 300 miles (500 kilometers) above the earth

fubsy \'fəb-zē\ *adjective* [obsolete English *fubs* (chubby person)] (1780)
: chubby and somewhat squat

fuch·sia \'fyü-shə\ *noun* [New Latin, from Leonhard *Fuchs* (died 1566) German botanist] (1846)
1 : any of a genus (*Fuchsia*) of decorative shrubs of the evening-primrose family having showy nodding flowers usually in deep pinks, reds, and purples
2 : a vivid reddish purple

fuch·sin *or* **fuch·sine** \'fyük-sən, -ˌsēn\ *noun* [French *fuchsine*, probably from New Latin *Fuchsia*; from its color] (1865)
: a dye that is produced by oxidation of a mixture of aniline and toluidines and yields a brilliant bluish red

fuchsia 1

¹fuck \'fək\ *verb* [akin to Dutch *fokken* to breed (cattle), Swedish dialect *fokka* to copulate] (15th century)
intransitive verb
1 : COPULATE — usually considered obscene; sometimes used in the present participle as a meaningless intensive
2 : MESS 3 — used with *with;* usually considered vulgar
transitive verb
1 : to engage in coitus with — usually considered obscene; sometimes used interjectionally with an object (as a personal or reflexive pronoun) to express anger, contempt, or disgust
2 : to deal with unfairly or harshly : CHEAT, SCREW — usually considered vulgar

²fuck *noun* (1680)
1 : an act of copulation — usually considered obscene
2 : a sexual partner — usually considered obscene
3 a : DAMN 2 — usually considered vulgar **b** — used especially with *the* as a meaningless intensive; usually considered vulgar 〈what the *fuck* do they want from me〉

fucked–up \'fək-ˌtəp\ *adjective* (1966)
: thoroughly confused or disordered — usually considered vulgar

fuck·er \'fə-kər\ *noun* (1598)
: one that fucks — often used as a generalized term of abuse; usually considered vulgar

fuck off *intransitive verb* (1929)
: SCRAM — usually used as a command; usually considered vulgar

fuck up (1951)
intransitive verb
: to act foolishly or stupidly : BLUNDER — usually considered vulgar
transitive verb
: to ruin or spoil especially through stupidity or carelessness : BUNGLE — usually considered vulgar
— fuck–up \'fək-ˌəp\ *noun*

¹fu·coid \'fyü-ˌkȯid\ *adjective* [New Latin *Fucus*, from Latin] (1839)
: relating to or resembling the rockweeds

²fucoid *noun* (circa 1841)
: a fucoid seaweed or fossil

fu·cose \'fyü-ˌkōs, -ˌkōz\ *noun* [International Scientific Vocabulary *fuc-* (from Latin *fucus*) + *-ose*] (circa 1909)
: an aldose sugar that occurs in bound form in the dextrorotatory form in various glycosides and in the levorotatory form in some brown algae and in mammalian polysaccharides typical of some blood groups

fu·co·xan·thin \ˌfyü-kō-'zan-thən\ *noun* (1873)
: a brown carotenoid pigment $C_{40}H_{60}O_6$ occurring especially in the chloroplasts of brown algae

fu·cus \'fyü-kəs\ *noun* [Latin, seaweed, archil, dye obtained from archil, from Greek *phykos*] (1599)
1 *obsolete* : a face paint
2 [New Latin, genus name, from Latin] : any of a genus (*Fucus*) of cartilaginous brown algae used in the kelp industry; *broadly* : any of various brown algae

fud \'fəd\ *noun* (1913)
: FUDDY-DUDDY

fud·dle \'fə-d°l\ *verb* **fud·dled; fud·dling** \'fəd-liŋ, 'fə-d°l-iŋ\ [origin unknown] (1588)
intransitive verb
: BOOZE, TIPPLE
transitive verb
1 : to make drunk : INTOXICATE
2 : to make confused : MUDDLE

fud·dy–dud·dy \'fə-dē-ˌdə-dē\ *noun, plural* **-dies** [origin unknown] (circa 1904)
: one that is old-fashioned, unimaginative, or conservative
— fuddy–duddy *adjective*

¹fudge \'fəj\ *verb* **fudged; fudg·ing** [origin unknown] (1674)

transitive verb
1 a : to devise as a substitute : FAKE **b** : FALSIFY 〈*fudged* the figures〉
2 : to fail to come to grips with : DODGE 〈*fudged* the issue〉
intransitive verb
1 : to exceed the proper bounds or limits of something 〈feel that the author has *fudged* a little on the . . . rules for crime fiction —*Newsweek*〉; *also* : CHEAT 〈*fudging* on an exam〉
2 : to fail to perform as expected
3 : to avoid commitment : HEDGE 〈the government's tendency to *fudge* on delicate matters of policy —Claire Sterling〉

²fudge *noun* (1766)
1 : foolish nonsense — often used interjectionally to express annoyance, disappointment, or disbelief
2 : a soft creamy candy made typically of sugar, milk, butter, and flavoring
3 : something that is fudged; *especially* : a bending of rules or a compromise

fudge factor *noun* (1962)
: an arbitrary mathematical term inserted into a calculation in order to arrive at an expected solution or to allow for errors especially of underestimation; *broadly* : any arbitrary unspecified factor

fu dog *often F capitalized, variant of* FOO DOG

¹fu·el \'fyü(-ə)l\ *noun, often attributive* [Middle English *fewel*, from Old French *fouaille*, from (assumed) Vulgar Latin *focalia*, from Latin *focus* hearth] (13th century)
1 a : a material used to produce heat or power by burning **b** : nutritive material **c** : a material from which atomic energy can be liberated especially in a reactor
2 : a source of sustenance or incentive : REINFORCEMENT

²fuel *verb* **-eled** *or* **-elled; -el·ing** *or* **-el·ling** (1592)
transitive verb
1 : to provide with fuel
2 : SUPPORT, STIMULATE 〈movement is *fueled* by massive grants-in-aid —Allen Schick〉
intransitive verb
: to take in fuel — often used with *up*

fuel cell *noun* (1922)
: a device that continuously changes the chemical energy of a fuel (as hydrogen) and an oxidant directly into electrical energy

fuel oil *noun* (1893)
: an oil that is used for fuel and that usually has a higher flash point than kerosene

fuel·wood \'fyü(-ə)l-ˌwu̇d\ *noun* (14th century)
: wood grown or used for fuel

¹fug \'fəg\ *noun* [perhaps alteration of ¹*fog*] (1888)
: the stuffy atmosphere of a poorly ventilated space; *also* : a stuffy or malodorous emanation
— fug·gy \'fə-gē\ *adjective*

²fug *verb* **fugged; fug·ging** (circa 1889)
intransitive verb
: to loll indoors in a stuffy atmosphere
transitive verb
: to make stuffy and odorous

fu·ga·cious \fyü-'gā-shəs\ *adjective* [Latin *fugac-, fugax*, from *fugere*] (1634)
1 : lasting a short time : EVANESCENT
2 : disappearing before the usual time — used chiefly of plant parts (as stipules) other than floral organs

fu·gac·i·ty \fyü-'ga-sə-tē\ *noun* [*fugacious*] (circa 1929)
: the vapor pressure of a vapor assumed to be an ideal gas obtained by correcting the determined vapor pressure and useful as a measure of the escaping tendency of a substance from a heterogeneous system

fu·gal \'fyü-gəl\ *adjective* (1854)
: of, relating to, or being in the style of a musical fugue
— fu·gal·ly \-gə-lē\ *adverb*

-fuge *noun combining form* [French, from Late Latin *-fuga,* from Latin *fugare* to put to flight, from *fuga*]
: one that drives away ⟨febri*fuge*⟩

¹**fu·gi·tive** \'fyü-jə-tiv\ *adjective* [Middle English, from Middle French & Latin; Middle French *fugitif,* from Latin *fugitivus,* from *fugitus,* past participle of *fugere* to flee; akin to Greek *pheugein* to flee] (14th century)
1 : running away or intending flight ⟨*fugitive* slave⟩ ⟨*fugitive* debtor⟩
2 : moving from place to place : WANDERING
3 a : being of short duration **b** : difficult to grasp or retain : ELUSIVE **c** : likely to evaporate, deteriorate, change, fade, or disappear ⟨dyed with *fugitive* colors⟩
4 : being of transient interest ⟨*fugitive* essays⟩
synonym see TRANSIENT
— **fu·gi·tive·ly** *adverb*
— **fu·gi·tive·ness** *noun*
²**fugitive** *noun* (14th century)
1 : a person who flees or tries to escape; *especially* : REFUGEE
2 : something elusive or hard to find

fu·gle·man \'fyü-gəl-mən\ *noun* [modification of German *Flügelmann,* from *Flügel* wing + *Mann* man] (1804)
1 : a trained soldier formerly posted in front of a line of soldiers at drill to serve as a model in their exercises
2 : one at the head or forefront of a group or movement

fu·gu \'f(y)ü-(ˌ)gü\ *noun* [Japanese] (1909)
: any of various very poisonous puffers (sense 2a) that contain tetrodotoxin and that are used as food in Japan after the toxin-containing organs are removed

fugue \'fyüg\ *noun* [probably from Italian *fuga* flight, fugue, from Latin, flight, from *fugere*] (1597)
1 a : a musical composition in which one or two themes are repeated or imitated by successively entering voices and contrapuntally developed in a continuous interweaving of the voice parts **b** : something that resembles a fugue especially in interweaving repetitive elements
2 : a disturbed state of consciousness in which the one affected seems to perform acts in full awareness but upon recovery cannot recollect the deeds
— **fugue** *verb*
— **fugu·ist** \'fyü-gist\ *noun*

füh·rer *or* **fueh·rer** \'fyür-ər, 'fir-\ *noun* [German *(der) Führer,* literally, the leader (title assumed by Adolf Hitler), from Middle High German *vüerer,* from *vüeren* to lead, bear, from Old High German *fuoren* to lead; akin to Old English *faran* to go — more at FARE] (1934)
: LEADER 2; *especially* : TYRANT

fu·ji \'fü-(ˌ)jē\ *noun* [*Fuji,* mountain in Japan] (1925)
: a spun silk clothing fabric in plain weave originally made in Japan

¹**-ful** *adjective suffix, sometimes* **-ful·er** *sometimes* **-ful·lest** [Middle English, from Old English, from *full,* adjective]
1 : full of ⟨pride*ful*⟩
2 : characterized by ⟨peace*ful*⟩
3 : having the qualities of ⟨master*ful*⟩
4 : tending, given, or liable to ⟨help*ful*⟩
²**-ful** *noun suffix*
: number or quantity that fills or would fill ⟨room*ful*⟩ □

Fu·la *or* **Fu·lah** \'fü-lə\ *noun, plural* **Fula** *or* **Fulas** *or* **Fulah** *or* **Fulahs** (1832)
1 : a member of a mainly pastoral African people dispersed over savanna and desert from Senegal to eastern Sudan
2 : the language of the Fula people
Fu·la·ni \'fü-ˌlä-nē, fü-'\ *noun, plural* **-ni** *or* **-nis** (1860)
1 : FULA 1; *especially* : the Fula of northern Nigeria and adjacent areas
2 : FULA 2

ful·crum \'fül-krəm, 'fəl-\ *noun, plural* **ful·crums** *or* **ful·cra** \-krə\ [Late Latin, from Latin, bedpost, from *fulcire* to prop — more at BALK] (1674)
1 a : PROP; *specifically* : the support about which a lever turns **b** : one that supplies capability for action
2 : a part of an animal that serves as a hinge or support

ful·fill *or* **ful·fil** \fu̇(l)-'fil *also* fə(l)-\ *transitive verb* **ful·filled; ful·fill·ing** [Middle English *fulfillen,* from Old English *fullfyllan,* from *full + fyllan* to fill] (before 12th century)
1 *archaic* : to make full : FILL ⟨her subtle, warm, and golden breast . . . *fulfills* him with beatitude —Alfred Tennyson⟩
2 a : to put into effect : EXECUTE **b** : to bring to an end **c** : to measure up to : SATISFY
3 a : to convert into reality **b** : to develop the full potentialities of
synonym see PERFORM
— **ful·fill·er** *noun*
— **ful·fill·ment** \-mənt\ *noun*

ful·gent \'fül-jənt, 'fəl-\ *adjective* [Middle English, from Latin *fulgent-, fulgens,* present participle of *fulgēre* to shine; akin to Latin *flagrare* to burn — more at BLACK] (15th century)
: dazzlingly bright : RADIANT
— **ful·gent·ly** *adverb*

ful·gu·rant \'fül-g(y)ə-rənt, 'fül-jə-, 'fəl-\ *adjective* (1647)
: flashing like lightning; *also* : BRILLIANT

ful·gu·ra·tion \ˌfül-g(y)ə-'rā-shən, ˌfül-jə-, fəl-\ *noun* [Latin *fulguration-, fulguratio* sheet lightning, from *fulgurare* to flash with lightning, from *fulgur* lightning, from *fulgēre*] (1633)
1 : the act or process of flashing like lightning
2 : ELECTRODESICCATION
— **ful·gu·rate** \'fül-g(y)ə-ˌrāt, 'fül-jə-, 'fəl-\ *transitive verb*

ful·gu·rite \'fül-g(y)ə-ˌrīt, 'fül-jə-, 'fəl-\ *noun* [International Scientific Vocabulary, from Latin *fulgur*] (1834)
: an often tubular vitrified crust produced by the fusion of sand or rock by lightning

ful·gu·rous \-rəs\ *adjective* [Latin *fulgur*] (1865)
: flashing with lightning

ful·ham \'fu̇-ləm\ *noun* [alteration of earlier *fullan,* perhaps from ¹*full +* ³*one*] (circa 1592)
archaic : a loaded die

fu·lig·i·nous \fyü-'li-jə-nəs\ *adjective* [Late Latin *fuliginosus,* from Latin *fuligin-, fuligo* soot; akin to Lithuanian *dūlis* cloud, vapor, and probably to Latin *fumus* smoke — more at FUME] (1621)
1 a : SOOTY **b** : OBSCURE, MURKY
2 : having a dark or dusky color
— **fu·lig·i·nous·ly** *adverb*

¹**full** \'fu̇l *also* 'fəl\ *adjective* [Middle English, from Old English; akin to Old High German *fol* full, Latin *plenus* full, *plēre* to fill, Greek *plērēs* full, *plēthein* to be full] (before 12th century)
1 : containing as much or as many as is possible or normal ⟨a bin *full* of corn⟩
2 a : complete especially in detail, number, or duration ⟨a *full* report⟩ ⟨my *full* share⟩ ⟨gone a *full* hour⟩ **b** : lacking restraint, check, or qualification ⟨*full* retreat⟩ ⟨*full* support⟩ **c** : having all distinguishing characteristics : enjoying all authorized rights and privileges ⟨*full* member⟩ ⟨*full* professor⟩ **d** : not lacking in any essential : PERFECT ⟨in *full* control of your senses⟩
3 a : being at the highest or greatest degree : MAXIMUM ⟨*full* speed⟩ ⟨*full* strength⟩ **b** : being at the height of development ⟨*full* bloom⟩
4 : rounded in outline ⟨a *full* figure⟩
5 a : possessing or containing a great number or amount — used with *of* ⟨a room *full* of pictures⟩ ⟨*full* of hope⟩ **b** : having an abundance of material especially in the form of gathered, pleated, or flared parts ⟨a *full* skirt⟩ **c** : rich in experience ⟨a *full* life⟩

6 a : satisfied especially with food or drink **b** : large enough to satisfy ⟨a *full* meal⟩
7 *archaic* : completely weary
8 : having both parents in common ⟨*full* sisters⟩
9 : having volume or depth of sound ⟨*full* tones⟩
10 : completely occupied especially with a thought or plan ⟨*full* of their own concerns⟩
11 : possessing a rich or pronounced quality ⟨a food of *full* flavor⟩ ☆
— **full·ness** *also* **ful·ness** \'fu̇l-nəs\ *noun*
— **full of it** : not to be believed
²**full** *adverb* (before 12th century)
1 a : VERY, EXTREMELY ⟨knew *full* well they had lied to me⟩ **b** : ENTIRELY ⟨swung *full* around —Morley Callaghan⟩
2 : STRAIGHT, SQUARELY ⟨got hit *full* in the face⟩
3 — used as an intensive ⟨wound up winning by a *full* four strokes —William Johnson⟩
³**full** *noun* (14th century)
1 a : the highest or fullest state or degree ⟨the *full* of the moon⟩ **b** : the utmost extent ⟨enjoy to the *full*⟩
2 : the requisite or complete amount ⟨paid in *full*⟩
⁴**full** (1794)
intransitive verb
of the moon : to become full
transitive verb
: to make full in sewing
⁵**full** *transitive verb* [Middle English, from Middle French *fouler* to trample under foot, from Medieval Latin *fullare* to walk, trample, full, from Latin *fullo* fuller] (14th century)
: to shrink and thicken (woolen cloth) by moistening, heating, and pressing

full·back \'fül-ˌbak\ *noun* (1887)
1 : an offensive football back used primarily for line plunges and blocking

☆ **SYNONYMS**
Full, complete, plenary, replete mean containing all that is wanted or needed or possible. FULL implies the presence or inclusion of everything that is wanted or required by something or that can be held, contained, or attained by it ⟨a *full* schedule⟩. COMPLETE applies when all that is needed is present ⟨a *complete* picture of the situation⟩. PLENARY adds to COMPLETE the implication of fullness without qualification ⟨given *plenary* power⟩. REPLETE implies being filled to the brim or to satiety ⟨*replete* with delightful details⟩.

□ **USAGE**
-ful Nouns ending in *-ful,* like *cupful* and *spoonful,* regularly form the plural by adding *-s* at the end: *cupfuls, spoonfuls.* But these words have long been a puzzle to the public. Part of the problem stems from the fact that most words were originally two words with the noun pluralized—many people will recall the nursery rhyme and its "yes sir, yes sir, three bags full." Another factor is that many people remember having been taught that internal pluralization was correct, although we have not yet found a schoolbook giving such a prescription. The result of the continuing uncertainty is the existence of less frequent variants such as *cupsful* and *teaspoonsful.* These variants are not wrong, but most people use *cupfuls* and *teaspoonfuls.*

\ə\ abut \ᵊ\ kitten \ər\ further \a\ ash \ā\ ace
\ä\ mop, mar \au̇\ out \ch\ chin \e\ bet \ē\ easy
\g\ go \i\ hit \ī\ ice \j\ job \ŋ\ sing \ō\ go
\ȯ\ law \ȯi\ boy \th\ thin \th\ the \ü\ loot \u̇\ foot
\y\ yet \zh\ vision *see also* Guide to Pronunciation

2 : a primarily defensive player usually stationed nearest the defended goal (as in soccer or field hockey)

full blast *adverb* (1909)
: at full capacity **:** with great intensity

¹**full–blood** \'fúl-ˌbləd\ *adjective* (1812)
: FULL-BLOODED 1

²**full–blood** *noun* (1846)
: a full-blooded individual

full–blood·ed \'fúl-ˌblə-dəd\ *adjective* (1774)
1 : of unmixed ancestry **:** PUREBRED
2 : FLORID, RUDDY ⟨of *full-blooded* face⟩
3 : FORCEFUL ⟨*full-blooded* prose style⟩
4 a : lacking no particulars **:** GENUINE **b :** containing fullness of substance **:** RICH
— **full–blood·ed·ness** *noun*

full–blown \-'blōn\ *adjective* (1601)
1 a : fully mature **b :** being at the height of bloom **c :** FULL-FLEDGED
2 : possessing all the usual or necessary features ⟨a general philosophy, if not a *full-blown* ideology, is emerging —W. H. Jones⟩

full–bod·ied \-ˌbä-dēd\ *adjective* (1686)
1 : having a large body
2 *of a beverage* **:** imparting to the palate the general impression of substantial weight and rich texture
3 : having importance, significance, or meaningfulness ⟨a *full-bodied* study of literature⟩

full circle *adverb* (1879)
: through a series of developments that lead back to the original source, position, or situation or to a complete reversal of the original position — usually used in the phrase *come full circle*

full–dress *adjective* (1761)
: involving attention to every detail in preparation or execution ⟨a *full-dress* rehearsal⟩ ⟨a *full-dress* investigation⟩

full dress *noun* (1790)
: the style of dress prescribed for ceremonial or formal social occasions

¹**full·er** \'fú-lər\ *noun* [Middle English, from Old English *fullere*, from Latin *fullo*] (before 12th century)
: one that fulls cloth

²**ful·ler** \'fú-lər\ *noun* [*fuller* (to form a groove in)] (circa 1864)
: a blacksmithing hammer for grooving and spreading iron

ful·ler·ene \ˌfú-lə-'rēn\ *noun* [R. Buckminster *Fuller*; from the resemblance of the molecules to the geodesic domes designed by Fuller] (1988)
: any of a class of closed hollow aromatic carbon compounds that are made up of twelve pentagonal and differing numbers of hexagonal faces

fuller's earth *noun* [¹*fuller*; from its earlier use as fulling agent] (15th century)
: an earthy substance that consists chiefly of clay mineral but lacks plasticity and that is used as an adsorbent, a filter medium, and a carrier for catalysts

ful·ler's teasel *noun* (15th century)
: TEASEL 1a

full–fash·ioned \'fúl-'fa-shənd\ *adjective* (1883)
: employing or produced by a knitting process for shaping to conform to body lines ⟨*full-fashioned* hosiery⟩

full–fledged \-'flejd\ *adjective* (1883)
1 : fully developed **:** TOTAL, COMPLETE ⟨a *full-fledged* war⟩
2 : having attained complete status ⟨*full-fledged* lawyer⟩

full house *noun* (1887)
: a poker hand containing three of a kind and a pair — see POKER illustration

full–length \'fúl-ˌleŋ(k)th\ *adjective* (1760)
1 : showing or adapted to the entire length especially of the human figure ⟨a *full-length* mirror⟩ ⟨a *full-length* dress⟩
2 : having a length as great as that which is normal or standard for an object of its kind ⟨a *full-length* play⟩

full marks *noun plural* (1916)
chiefly British **:** due credit or commendation

full moon *noun* (before 12th century)
: the moon with its whole apparent disk illuminated

full–mouthed \'fúl-'maúthd, -'maútht\ *adjective* (1577)
1 : having a full complement of teeth ⟨*full-mouthed* ewes⟩
2 : uttered loudly

full nelson *noun* (circa 1922)
: a wrestling hold gained from behind an opponent by thrusting the arms under the opponent's arms and clasping the hands behind the opponent's head — compare HALF NELSON

full–out \-ˌaút\ *adjective* (14th century)
: COMPLETE, TOTAL

full–scale \-ˌskā(ə)l\ *adjective* (1933)
1 : identical to an original in proportion and size ⟨*full-scale* drawing⟩
2 a : involving full use of available resources ⟨a *full-scale* biography⟩ ⟨*full-scale* war⟩ **b :** TOTAL, COMPLETE ⟨a *full-scale* musical renaissance —*Current Biography*⟩

full–ser·vice \-'sər-vəs\ *adjective* (1957)
: providing comprehensive service of a particular kind ⟨a *full-service* bank⟩

full–size \-ˌsīz\ *adjective* (1832)
1 : having the usual or normal size of its kind
2 : having the dimensions 54 inches by 75 inches (about 1.4 by 1.9 meters) — used of a bed; compare KING-SIZE, QUEEN-SIZE, TWIN-SIZE

full stop *noun* (1596)
: PERIOD 5a

full tilt *adverb* [³*tilt*] (1600)
: at high speed

full–time *adjective* (1898)
1 : employed for or involving full time ⟨*full-time* employees⟩
2 : devoting one's full attention and energies to something ⟨a *full-time* gambler⟩
— **full–time** *adverb*

full time *noun* (1898)
: the amount of time considered the normal or standard amount for working during a given period

full–tim·er \'fúl-'tī-mər\ *noun* (1864)
: a person who works full-time

ful·ly \'fú(l)-lē\ *adverb* (before 12th century)
1 : in a full manner or degree **:** COMPLETELY
2 : at least ⟨*fully* nine tenths of us⟩
usage *see* PLENTY

ful·mar \'fúl-mər, -ˌmär\ *noun* [of Scandinavian origin; akin to Old Norse *fúlmār* fulmar, from *fúll* foul + *mār* gull — more at MEW] (1698)
: a seabird (*Fulmarus glacialis*) of colder northern seas closely related to the petrels; *also* **:** a related bird (*F. glacialoides*) of circumpolar distribution in colder southern seas

ful·mi·nant \'fúl-mə-nənt, 'fəl-\ *adjective* (1602)
: FULMINATING 3

¹**ful·mi·nate** \-ˌnāt\ *verb* **-nat·ed; -nat·ing** [Middle English, from Medieval Latin *fulminatus*, past participle of *fulminare*, from Latin, to strike (of lightning), from *fulmin-*, *fulmen* lightning; akin to Latin *flagrare* to burn — more at BLACK] (15th century)
transitive verb
: to utter or send out with denunciation
intransitive verb
: to send forth censures or invectives
— **ful·mi·na·tion** \ˌfúl-mə-'nā-shən, ˌfəl-\ *noun*

²**fulminate** *noun* [*fulminic acid*, from Latin *fulmin-*, *fulmen*] (1826)
: an often explosive salt (as mercury fulminate) containing the group −CNO

ful·mi·nat·ing *adjective* (1626)
1 : hurling denunciations or menaces
2 : EXPLOSIVE
3 : coming on suddenly with great severity

ful·mine \'fúl-mən, 'fəl-\ *verb* (1590)
archaic **:** FULMINATE

ful·some \'fúl-səm\ *adjective* [Middle English *fulsom* copious, cloying, from *full* + *-som* -some] (13th century)
1 a : characterized by abundance **:** COPIOUS ⟨describes in *fulsome* detail —G. N. Shuster⟩ ⟨*fulsome* bird life. The feeder overcrowded —Maxine Kumin⟩ **b :** generous in amount, extent, or spirit ⟨the passengers were *fulsome* in praise of the plane's crew —Don Oliver⟩ ⟨a *fulsome* victory for the far left —Bruce Rothwell⟩ ⟨the greetings have been *fulsome*, the farewells tender —Simon Gray⟩ **c :** being full and well developed ⟨she was in generally *fulsome*, limpid voice —Thor Eckert, Jr.⟩
2 : aesthetically, morally, or generally offensive ⟨*fulsome* lies and nauseous flattery —William Congreve⟩ ⟨the devil take thee for a . . . *fulsome* rogue —George Villiers⟩
3 : exceeding the bounds of good taste **:** OVERDONE ⟨the *fulsome* chromium glitter of the escalators dominating the central hall —Lewis Mumford⟩
4 : excessively complimentary or flattering **:** EFFUSIVE ⟨an admiration whose extent I did not express, lest I be thought *fulsome* —A. J. Liebling⟩ ▢
— **ful·some·ly** *adverb*
— **ful·some·ness** *noun*

ful·vous \'fúl-vəs, 'fəl-\ *adjective* [Latin *fulvus*; perhaps akin to Latin *flavus* yellow — more at BLUE] (1664)
: of a dull brownish yellow **:** TAWNY

Fu Man·chu mustache \ˌfü-(ˌ)man-'chü-\ *noun* [*Fu Manchu*, Chinese villain in stories by "Sax Rohmer" (A. S. Ward) (died 1955)] (1968)
: a long mustache with ends that turn down to the chin

fu·ma·rase \'fyü-mə-ˌrās, -ˌrāz\ *noun* (1936)
: an enzyme that catalyzes the interconversion (as in the Krebs cycle) of fumaric acid and malic acid or their salts

fu·ma·rate \-ˌrāt\ *noun* (1864)
: a salt or ester of fumaric acid

fu·mar·ic acid \fyü-'mar-ik-\ *noun* [International Scientific Vocabulary, from New Latin *Fumaria*, genus of herbs, from Late Latin, fumitory, from Latin *fumus*] (circa 1864)
: a crystalline acid $C_4H_4O_4$ found in various plants or made synthetically and used especially in making resins

fu·ma·role \'fyü-mə-ˌrōl\ *noun* [Italian *fumarola*, from Italian dialect (Neapolitan), from Late Latin *fumariolum* vent, from Latin *fumarium* smoke chamber for aging wine, from *fumus*] (1811)
: a hole in a volcanic region from which hot gases and vapors issue
— **fu·ma·rol·ic** \ˌfyü-mə-'rō-lik\ *adjective*

¹**fum·ble** \'fəm-bəl\ *verb* **fum·bled; fum·bling** \-b(ə-)liŋ\ [probably of Scandinavian origin; akin to Swedish *fumla* to fumble] (1534)
intransitive verb

▢ **USAGE**
fulsome The senses shown above are the chief living senses of *fulsome*. Sense 2, which was a generalized term of disparagement in the late 17th century, is the least common of these. *Fulsome* became a point of dispute when sense 1, thought to be obsolete in the 19th century, began to be revived in the 20th. The dispute was exacerbated by the fact that the large dictionaries of the first half of the century missed the beginnings of the revival. Sense 1 has not only been revived but has spread in its application and continues to do so. The chief danger for the user of *fulsome* is ambiguity. Unless the context is made very clear, the reader or hearer can't be sure whether such an expression as "fulsome praise" or "a fulsome tribute" is meant in sense 1b or in sense 4.

1 a : to grope for or handle something clumsily or aimlessly **b :** to make awkward attempts to do or find something ⟨*fumbled* in his pocket for a coin⟩ **c :** to search by trial and error **d :** BLUNDER
2 : to feel one's way or move awkwardly
3 a : to drop or juggle or fail to play cleanly a grounder **b :** to lose hold of a football while handling or running with it
transitive verb
1 : to bring about by clumsy manipulation
2 a : to feel or handle clumsily **b :** to deal with in a blundering way : BUNGLE
3 : to make (one's way) in a clumsy manner
4 a : MISPLAY ⟨*fumble* a grounder⟩ **b :** to lose hold of (a football) while handling or running
— **fum·bler** \-b(ə-)lər\ *noun*
— **fum·bling·ly** \-b(ə-)liŋ-lē\ *adverb*

²**fumble** *noun* (1634)
1 : an act or instance of fumbling
2 : a fumbled ball

¹**fume** \'fyüm\ *noun* [Middle English, from Middle French *fum,* from Latin *fumus;* akin to Old High German *toumen* to be fragrant, Sanskrit *dhūma* smoke, Old Church Slavonic *dymŭ*] (14th century)
1 a : a smoke, vapor, or gas especially when irritating or offensive ⟨engine exhaust *fumes*⟩ **b :** an often noxious suspension of particles in a gas (as air)
2 : something (as an emotion) that impairs one's reasoning ⟨sometimes his head gets a little hot with the *fumes* of patriotism —Matthew Arnold⟩
3 : a state of excited irritation or anger — usually used in the phrase *in a fume*
— **fumy** \'fyü-mē\ *adjective*

²**fume** *verb* **fumed; fum·ing** (14th century)
transitive verb
1 : to expose to or treat with fumes
2 : to give off in fumes ⟨*fuming* thick black smoke⟩
3 : to utter while in a state of excited irritation or anger
intransitive verb
1 a : to emit fumes **b :** to be in a state of excited irritation or anger ⟨fretted and *fumed* over the delay⟩
2 : to rise in or as if in fumes

fu·met \fyü-'mā, 'fyü-mət\ *noun* [French, literally, pleasant aroma (of meat cooking), from Middle French, from *fumer* to give off smoke or steam, from Latin *fumare,* from *fumus*] (1906)
: a reduced and seasoned fish, meat, or vegetable stock

fu·mi·gant \'fyü-mi-gənt\ *noun* (1890)
: a substance used in fumigating

fu·mi·gate \'fyü-mə-ˌgāt\ *transitive verb* **-gat·ed; -gat·ing** [Latin *fumigatus,* past participle of *fumigare,* from *fumus* + *-igare* (akin to Latin *agere* to drive) — more at AGENT] (1781)
: to apply smoke, vapor, or gas to especially for the purpose of disinfecting or of destroying pests
— **fu·mi·ga·tion** \ˌfyü-mə-'gā-shən\ *noun*
— **fu·mi·ga·tor** \'fyü-mə-ˌgā-tər\ *noun*

fu·mi·to·ry \'fyü-mə-ˌtōr-ē, -ˌtȯr-\ *noun* [Middle English *fumeterre,* from Medieval Latin *fumus terrae,* literally, smoke of the earth, from Latin *fumus* + *terrae,* genitive of *terra* earth — more at TERRACE] (14th century)
: any of a genus (*Fumaria* of the family Fumariaceae, the fumitory family) of erect or climbing herbs; *especially* : a common European herb (*F. officinalis*)

¹**fun** \'fən\ *noun* [English dialect *fun* to hoax, perhaps alteration of Middle English *fonnen,* from *fonne* dupe] (1727)
1 : what provides amusement or enjoyment; *specifically* : playful often boisterous action or speech ⟨full of *fun*⟩
2 : a mood for finding or making amusement ⟨all in *fun*⟩

3 a : AMUSEMENT, ENJOYMENT ⟨sickness takes all the *fun* out of life⟩ **b :** derisive jest : SPORT, RIDICULE ⟨a figure of *fun*⟩
4 : violent or excited activity or argument ⟨let a snake loose in the classroom; then the *fun* began⟩ ☆

²**fun** *intransitive verb* **funned; fun·ning** (1833)
: to indulge in banter or play : JOKE

³**fun** *adjective, sometimes* **fun·ner;** *sometimes* **fun·nest** (circa 1846)
1 : providing entertainment, amusement, or enjoyment ⟨a *fun* party⟩ ⟨a *fun* person to be with⟩
2 : full of fun : PLEASANT ⟨a *fun* night⟩ ⟨have a *fun* time⟩

fu·nam·bu·lism \fyü-'nam-byə-ˌli-zəm\ *noun* [Latin *funambulus* ropewalker, from *funis* rope + *ambulare* to walk] (1824)
1 : tightrope walking
2 : a show especially of mental agility
— **fu·nam·bu·list** \-list\ *noun*

fun and games *noun plural but singular or plural in construction* (1920)
: light amusement

¹**func·tion** \'fəŋ(k)-shən\ *noun* [Latin *function-, functio* performance, from *fungi* to perform; probably akin to Sanskrit *bhuṅkte* he enjoys] (1533)
1 : professional or official position : OCCUPATION
2 : the action for which a person or thing is specially fitted or used or for which a thing exists : PURPOSE
3 : any of a group of related actions contributing to a larger action; *especially* : the normal and specific contribution of a bodily part to the economy of a living organism
4 : an official or formal ceremony or social gathering
5 a : a mathematical correspondence that assigns exactly one element of one set to each element of the same or another set **b :** a variable (as a quality, trait, or measurement) that depends on and varies with another ⟨height is a *function* of age⟩; *also* : RESULT ⟨illnesses that are a *function* of stress⟩
6 : characteristic behavior of a chemical compound due to a particular reactive unit; *also* : FUNCTIONAL GROUP
7 : a computer subroutine; *specifically* : one that performs a calculation with variables provided by a program and supplies the program with a single result ☆
— **func·tion·less** \-ləs\ *adjective*

²**function** *intransitive verb* **func·tioned; func·tion·ing** \-sh(ə-)niŋ\ (1856)
1 : to have a function : SERVE ⟨an attributive noun *functions* as an adjective⟩
2 : to carry on a function or be in action : OPERATE ⟨a government *functions* through numerous divisions⟩

func·tion·al \'fəŋ(k)-shnəl, -shə-nᵊl\ *adjective* (1631)
1 a : of, connected with, or being a function **b :** affecting physiological or psychological functions but not organic structure ⟨*functional* heart disease⟩
2 : used to contribute to the development or maintenance of a larger whole ⟨*functional* and practical school courses⟩; *also* : designed or developed chiefly from the point of view of use ⟨*functional* clothing⟩
3 : performing or able to perform a regular function
— **func·tion·al·i·ty** \ˌfəŋ(k)-shə-'na-lə-tē\ *noun*
— **func·tion·al·ly** \'fəŋ(k)-shnə-lē, -shə-nᵊl-ē\ *adverb*

functional calculus *noun* (1933)
: PREDICATE CALCULUS

functional group *noun* (1943)
: a characteristic reactive unit of a chemical compound especially in organic chemistry

functional illiterate *noun* (1946)

: a person having had some schooling but not meeting a minimum standard of literacy
— **functionally illiterate** *adjective*

func·tion·al·ism \'fəŋ(k)-shnə-ˌli-zəm, -shə-nᵊl-ˌi-\ *noun* (1914)
1 : a philosophy of design (as in architecture) holding that form should be adapted to use, material, and structure
2 : a theory that stresses the interdependence of the patterns and institutions of a society and their interaction in maintaining cultural and social unity
3 : a doctrine or practice that emphasizes practical utility or functional relations
— **func·tion·al·ist** \-shnə-list, -shə-nᵊl-ist\ *noun*
— **functionalist** *or* **func·tion·al·is·tic** \ˌfəŋ(k)-shnə-'lis-tik, -shə-nᵊl-'is-\ *adjective*

functional shift *noun* (1942)
: the process by which a word or form comes to be used in another grammatical function

func·tion·ary \'fəŋ(k)-shə-ˌner-ē\ *noun, plural* **-ar·ies** (1791)
1 : one who serves in a certain function
2 : one holding office in a government or political party

function word *noun* (1940)
: a word (as a preposition, auxiliary verb, or conjunction) expressing primarily grammatical relationship

func·tor \'fəŋ(k)-tər\ *noun* (1935)
: something that performs a function or an operation

¹**fund** \'fənd\ *noun* [Latin *fundus* bottom, country estate — more at BOTTOM] (1694)

☆ **SYNONYMS**
Fun, jest, sport, game, play mean action or speech that provides amusement or arouses laughter. FUN usually implies laughter or gaiety but may imply merely a lack of serious or ulterior purpose ⟨played cards just for *fun*⟩. JEST implies lack of earnestness in what is said or done and may suggest a hoaxing or teasing ⟨hurt by remarks said only in *jest*⟩. SPORT applies especially to the arousing of laughter against someone ⟨teasing begun in *sport* led to anger⟩. GAME is close to SPORT, and often stresses mischievous or malicious fun ⟨made *game* of their poor relations⟩. PLAY stresses the opposition to *earnest* without implying any element of malice or mischief ⟨pretended to strangle his brother in *play*⟩.

Function, office, duty, province mean the acts or operations expected of a person or thing. FUNCTION implies a definite end or purpose that the one in question serves or a particular kind of work it is intended to perform ⟨the *function* of language is two-fold: to communicate emotion and to give information —Aldous Huxley⟩. OFFICE is typically applied to the function or service expected of a person by reason of his trade or profession or his special relationship to others ⟨they exercise the *offices* of the judge, the priest, the counsellor —W. E. Gladstone⟩. DUTY applies to a task or responsibility imposed by one's occupation, rank, status, or calling ⟨it is the judicial *duty* of the court, to examine the whole case —R. B. Taney⟩. PROVINCE applies to a function, office, or duty that naturally or logically falls to one ⟨nursing does not belong to a man; it is not his *province* —Jane Austen⟩.

\ə\ abut \ᵊ\ kitten \ər\ further \a\ ash \ā\ ace
\ä\ mop, mar \au̇\ out \ch\ chin \e\ bet \ē\ easy
\g\ go \i\ hit \ī\ ice \j\ job \ŋ\ sing \ō\ go
\ȯ\ law \ȯi\ boy \th\ thin \ṯẖ\ the \ü\ loot \u̇\ foot
\y\ yet \zh\ vision *see also* Guide to Pronunciation

1 a : a sum of money or other resources whose principal or interest is set apart for a specific objective **b :** money on deposit on which checks or drafts can be drawn — usually used in plural **c :** CAPITAL **d** *plural* **:** the stock of the British national debt — usually used with *the*
2 : an available quantity of material or intangible resources **:** SUPPLY
3 *plural* **:** available pecuniary resources
4 : an organization administering a special fund

²**fund** *transitive verb* (1789)
1 a : to make provision of resources for discharging the interest or principal of **b :** to provide funds for ⟨a science program federally *funded*⟩
2 : to place in a fund **:** ACCUMULATE
3 : to convert into a debt that is payable either at a distant date or at no definite date and that bears a fixed interest ⟨*fund* a floating debt⟩

fun·da·ment \'fən-də-mənt\ *noun* [Middle English, from Old French *fondement*, from Latin *fundamentum*, from *fundare* to found, from *fundus*] (13th century)
1 : an underlying ground, theory, or principle
2 a : BUTTOCKS **b :** ANUS
3 : the part of a land surface that has not been altered by human activities

¹**fun·da·men·tal** \,fən-də-'men-t°l\ *adjective* (15th century)
1 a : serving as an original or generating source **:** PRIMARY ⟨a discovery *fundamental* to modern computers⟩ **b :** serving as a basis supporting existence or determining essential structure or function **:** BASIC
2 a : of or relating to essential structure, function, or facts **:** RADICAL ⟨*fundamental* change⟩; *also* **:** of or dealing with general principles rather than practical application ⟨*fundamental* science⟩ **b :** adhering to fundamentalism
3 : of, relating to, or produced by the lowest component of a complex vibration
4 : of central importance **:** PRINCIPAL ⟨*fundamental* purpose⟩
5 : belonging to one's innate or ingrained characteristics **:** DEEP-ROOTED ⟨her *fundamental* good humor⟩
synonym see ESSENTIAL
— **fun·da·men·tal·ly** \-t°l-ē\ *adverb*

²**fundamental** *noun* (1637)
1 : something fundamental; *especially* **:** one of the minimum constituents without which a thing or a system would not be what it is
2 a : the principal musical tone produced by vibration (as of a string or column of air) on which a series of higher harmonics is based **b :** the root of a chord
3 : the harmonic component of a complex wave that has the lowest frequency and commonly the greatest amplitude

fundamental group *noun* (1957)
: a set that is a subset of all paths defined on a set of points each pair of which is joined by a path and that is the quotient group of the group of all paths beginning and ending with a given point

fun·da·men·tal·ism \-t°l-,i-zəm\ *noun* (1922)
1 a *often capitalized* **:** a movement in 20th century Protestantism emphasizing the literally interpreted Bible as fundamental to Christian life and teaching **b :** the beliefs of this movement **c :** adherence to such beliefs
2 : a movement or attitude stressing strict and literal adherence to a set of basic principles
— **fun·da·men·tal·ist** \-t°l-ist\ *noun*
— **fundamentalist** *or* **fun·da·men·tal·is·tic** \-,men-t°l-'is-tik\ *adjective*

fundamental law *noun* (circa 1914)
: the organic or basic law of a political unit as distinguished from legislative acts; *specifically* **:** CONSTITUTION

fundamental particle *noun* (1947)
: ELEMENTARY PARTICLE

fun·dic \'fən-dik\ *adjective* (circa 1927)

: of or relating to a fundus

fund–rais·er \'fən-,drā-zər\ *noun* (1957)
1 : a person employed to raise funds
2 : a social event (as a cocktail party) held for the purpose of raising funds

fund–rais·ing \-ziŋ\ *noun, often attributive* (1940)
: the organized activity of raising funds (as for an institution or political cause)

fun·dus \'fən-dəs\ *noun, plural* **fun·di** \-,dī, -,dē\ [New Latin, from Latin, bottom] (1764)
: the bottom of or part opposite the aperture of the internal surface of a hollow organ: as **a :** the greater curvature of the stomach **b :** the lower back part of the bladder **c :** the large upper end of the uterus **d :** the part of the eye opposite the pupil

¹**fu·ner·al** \'fyün-rəl, 'fyü-nə-\ *adjective* [Middle English, from Late Latin *funeralis*, from Latin *funer-*, *funus* funeral (noun)] (14th century)
1 : of, relating to, or constituting a funeral
2 : FUNEREAL 2

²**funeral** *noun* [Middle English *funerelles* (plural), from Middle French *funerailles* (plural), from Medieval Latin *funeralia* (plural), from Late Latin, neuter plural of *funeralis*, adjective] (circa 1512)
1 : the observances held for a dead person usually before burial or cremation
2 *chiefly dialect* **:** a funeral sermon
3 : a funeral procession
4 : an end of something's existence
5 : a matter of concern to one **:** WORRY ⟨if you flunk, that's your *funeral*⟩

funeral director *noun* (1886)
: one whose profession is the management of funerals and who is usually an embalmer

funeral home *noun* (1926)
: an establishment with facilities for the preparation of the dead for burial or cremation, for the viewing of the body, and for funerals — called also *funeral parlor*

fu·ner·ary \'fyü-nə-,rer-ē\ *adjective* (circa 1693)
: of, used for, or associated with burial ⟨a pharaoh's *funerary* chamber⟩

fu·ne·re·al \fyù-'nir-ē-əl\ *adjective* [Latin *funereus*, from *funer-*, *funus*] (1725)
1 : of or relating to a funeral
2 : befitting or suggesting a funeral (as in solemnity)
— **fu·ne·re·al·ly** \-ə-lē\ *adverb*

fun·fair \'fən-,far, -,fer\ *noun* (1925)
chiefly British **:** AMUSEMENT PARK

fun·gal \'fən-gəl\ *adjective* (1835)
1 : of, relating to, or having the characteristics of fungi
2 : caused by a fungus

fungi- *combining form* [Latin *fungus*]
: fungus ⟨*fungi*form⟩

¹**fun·gi·ble** \'fən-jə-bəl\ *noun* (circa 1765)
: something that is fungible — usually used in plural

²**fungible** *adjective* [New Latin *fungibilis*, from Latin *fungi* to perform — more at FUNCTION] (1818)
1 : being of such a nature that one part or quantity may be replaced by another equal part or quantity in the satisfaction of an obligation ⟨oil, wheat, and lumber are *fungible* commodities⟩
2 : INTERCHANGEABLE
— **fun·gi·bil·i·ty** \,fən-jə-'bi-lə-tē\ *noun*

fun·gi·cid·al \,fən-jə-'sī-d°l, ,fən-gə-\ *adjective* (1905)
: ANTIFUNGAL
— **fun·gi·cid·al·ly** \-d°l-ē\ *adverb*

fun·gi·cide \'fən-jə-,sīd, 'fən-gə-\ *noun* [International Scientific Vocabulary] (1889)
: an agent that destroys fungi or inhibits their growth

fun·gi·form \'fən-jə-,förm, 'fən-gə-\ *adjective* (1823)
: shaped like a mushroom

fun·gi·stat·ic \,fən-jə-'sta-tik\ *adjective* (1922)
: inhibiting the growth of fungi without destroying them

fun·go \'fən-(,)gō\ *noun, plural* **fungoes** [origin unknown] (circa 1867)
1 : a fly ball hit especially for practice fielding by a player who tosses a ball in the air and hits it as it comes down
2 : FUNGO BAT

fungo bat *noun* (1926)
: a long thin bat used for hitting fungoes

fun·goid \'fən-,göid\ *adjective* (circa 1836)
: resembling, characteristic of, caused by, or being a fungus ⟨a *fungoid* growth⟩
— **fungoid** *noun*

fun·gous \'fən-gəs\ *adjective* (15th century)
: FUNGAL

fun·gus \'fən-gəs\ *noun, plural* **fun·gi** \'fən-,jī, 'fən-,gī\ *also* **fun·gus·es** \'fən-gə-səz\ *often attributive* [Latin] (1527)
: any of a major group (Fungi) of saprophytic and parasitic spore-producing organisms usually classified as plants that lack chlorophyll and include molds, rusts, mildews, smuts, mushrooms, and yeasts

fun house *noun* (1948)
: a building in an amusement park that contains various devices designed to startle or amuse

¹**fu·nic·u·lar** \fyù-'ni-kyə-lər, fə-\ *adjective* [Latin *funiculus*] (1664)
1 : having the form of or associated with a cord usually under tension
2 [New Latin *funiculus*] **:** of, relating to, or being a funiculus
3 : of, relating to, or being a funicular ⟨a *funicular* system⟩

²**funicular** *noun* (1911)
: a cable railway ascending a mountain; *especially* **:** one in which an ascending car counterbalances a descending car

fu·nic·u·lus \-ləs\ *noun, plural* **-li** \-,lī, -,lē\ [New Latin, from Latin, diminutive of *funis* rope] (1826)
1 : a bodily structure suggesting a cord; *especially* **:** a bundle of nerve fibers
2 : the stalk of a plant ovule

¹**funk** \'fəŋk\ (circa 1739)
intransitive verb
: to become frightened and shrink back
transitive verb
1 : to be afraid of **:** DREAD
2 : to shrink from undertaking or facing

²**funk** *noun* [probably from obsolete Flemish *fonck*] (1743)
1 a : a state of paralyzing fear **b :** a depressed state of mind
2 : one that funks **:** COWARD

³**funk** *noun* [back-formation from ²*funky*] (1959)
1 : music that combines traditional forms of black music (as blues, gospel, or soul) and is characterized by a strong backbeat
2 : the quality or state of being funky ⟨jeans . . . have lost much of their *funk* —Tom Wolfe⟩

funk hole *noun* (1900)
1 : DUGOUT 2
2 : a place of safe retreat

fun·kia \'fən-kē-ə, 'fùŋ-\ *noun* [New Latin, genus name, from C. H. *Funck* (died 1839) German botanist] (1839)
: PLANTAIN LILY

¹**funky** \'fən-kē\ *adjective* (1845)
: being in a funk **:** PANICKY

²**funky** *adjective* **funk·i·er; -est** [*funk* (offensive odor)] (circa 1899)
1 : having an offensive odor **:** FOUL
2 : having an earthy unsophisticated style and feeling; *especially* **:** having the style and feeling of older black American music (as blues or gospel) or of funk ⟨a slick, heavy beat that is unmistakably contemporary and irresistibly *funky* —Jay Cocks⟩

3 a : odd or quaint in appearance or feeling **b :** lacking style or taste **c :** unconventionally stylish : HIP ◇
— **funk·i·ness** noun

¹**fun·nel** \'fə-nᵊl\ noun [Middle English fonel, from Old Provençal fonill, from Medieval Latin fundibulum, short for Latin infundibulum, from infundere to pour in, from in- + fundere to pour — more at FOUND] (15th century)
1 a : a utensil that is usually a hollow cone with a tube extending from the smaller end and that is designed to catch and direct a downward flow **b :** something shaped like a funnel
2 : a stack or flue for the escape of smoke or for ventilation (as on a ship)

²**funnel** verb **-neled** also **-nelled; -nel·ing** also **-nel·ling** (1594)
intransitive verb
1 : to have or take the shape of a funnel
2 : to pass through or as if through a funnel or conduit
transitive verb
1 : to form in the shape of a funnel ⟨funneled his hands and shouted through them⟩
2 : to move to a focal point or into a conduit or central channel ⟨contributions were funneled into one account⟩

funnel cloud noun (circa 1909)
: a funnel-shaped cloud that projects from the base of a thundercloud and that often betokens the formation of a tornado; also : TORNADO 2b

fun·nel·form \'fə-nᵊl-ˌfȯrm\ adjective (circa 1828)
: INFUNDIBULIFORM

¹**fun·ny** \'fə-nē\ adjective **fun·ni·er; -est** (1756)
1 a : affording light mirth and laughter : AMUSING **b :** seeking or intended to amuse : FACETIOUS
2 : differing from the ordinary in a suspicious, perplexing, quaint, or eccentric way : PECULIAR — often used as a sentence modifier ⟨funny, things didn't turn out the way we planned⟩
3 : involving trickery or deception ⟨told his prisoner not to try anything funny⟩
— **fun·ni·ly** \'fə-nᵊl-ē\ adverb
— **fun·ni·ness** \'fə-nē-nəs\ noun
— **funny** adverb

²**funny** noun, plural **funnies** (1852)
1 : one that is funny; especially : JOKE
2 plural : comic strips or the comic section of a periodical — usually used with the

funny bone noun [from the tingling felt when it is struck] (1840)
1 : the place at the back of the elbow where the ulnar nerve rests against a prominence of the humerus
2 : a sense of humor

funny book noun (1947)
: COMIC BOOK

funny car noun (1969)
: a specialized dragster that has a one-piece molded body resembling the body of a mass-produced car

funny farm noun (1963)
slang : a psychiatric hospital

fun·ny·man \'fə-nē-ˌman\ noun (1852)
: COMEDIAN 2, HUMORIST

funny money noun (1943)
1 : artificially inflated currency
2 : counterfeit money

funny paper noun (1924)
: a comic section of a newspaper

¹**fur** \'fər\ verb **furred; fur·ring** [Middle English furren, from Middle French fourrer, from Old French forrer, from fuerre sheath, of Germanic origin; akin to Old High German fuotar sheath; akin to Greek pōma lid, cover, Sanskrit pāti he protects] (14th century)
transitive verb
1 : to cover, line, trim, or clothe with fur
2 : to coat or clog as if with fur
3 : to apply furring to

intransitive verb
: to become coated or clogged as if with fur ◇

²**fur** noun, often attributive (14th century)
1 : a piece of the dressed pelt of an animal used to make, trim, or line wearing apparel
2 : an article of clothing made of or with fur
3 : the hairy coat of a mammal especially when fine, soft, and thick; also : such a coat with the skin
4 : a coating resembling fur: as **a :** a coat of epithelial debris on the tongue **b :** the thick pile of a fabric (as chenille)
— **fur·less** \'fər-ləs\ adjective

fu·ran \'fyu̇r-ˌan, fyu̇-'ran\ also **fu·rane** \'fyu̇r-ˌān, fyu̇-'rān\ noun [International Scientific Vocabulary, from furfural] (1894)
: a flammable liquid C_4H_4O that is obtained from wood oils of pines or made synthetically and is used especially in organic synthesis; also : a derivative of furan

fu·ra·nose \'fyu̇r-ə-ˌnōs, -ˌnōz\ noun (1927)
: a sugar having an oxygen-containing ring of five atoms

fu·ran·o·side \fyu̇-'ra-nə-ˌsīd\ noun (1932)
: a glycoside containing the ring characteristic of furanose

fu·ra·zol·i·done \ˌfyu̇r-ə-'zä-lə-ˌdōn\ noun [furfural + azole + -ide + -one] (1955)
: an antimicrobial drug $C_8H_7N_3O_5$ used against bacteria and some protozoa especially in infections of the gastrointestinal tract

fur·bear·er \'fər-ˌbar-ər, -ˌber-\ noun (1875)
: an animal that bears fur especially of a commercially desired quality

fur·be·low \'fər-bə-ˌlō\ noun [by folk etymology from French dialect farbella] (1706)
1 : a pleated or gathered piece of material; especially : a flounce on women's clothing
2 : something that suggests a furbelow especially in being showy or superfluous
— **furbelow** transitive verb

fur·bish \'fər-bish\ transitive verb [Middle English furbisshen, from Middle French fourbiss-, stem of fourbir, of Germanic origin; akin to Old High German furben to polish] (14th century)
1 : to make lustrous : POLISH
2 : to give a new look to : RENOVATE — often used with up
— **fur·bish·er** noun

fur·ca·tion \ˌfər-'kā-shən\ noun [Medieval Latin furcation-, furcatio, from furcare to branch, from Latin furca fork] (1646)
1 : something that is branched : FORK
2 : the act or process of branching

fur·cu·la \'fər-kyə-lə\ noun, plural **-lae** \-ˌlē, -ˌlī\ [New Latin, from Latin, forked prop, diminutive of furca] (1859)
: a forked process or part: as **a :** WISHBONE **b :** the forked leaping appendage arising from the fourth abdominal segment of a springtail

fur·fu·ral \'fər-f(y)ə-ˌral\ noun [Latin furfur bran + International Scientific Vocabulary ³-al] (1879)
: a liquid aldehyde $C_5H_4O_2$ of penetrating odor that is usually made from plant materials and used especially in making furan or phenolic resins and as a solvent

fu·ri·o·so \ˌfyu̇r-ē-'ō-(ˌ)sō, -(ˌ)zō\ adverb or adjective [Italian, literally, furious] (circa 1823)
: with great force or vigor — used as a direction in music

fu·ri·ous \'fyu̇r-ē-əs\ adjective [Middle English, from Middle French furieus, from Latin furiosus, from furia madness, fury] (14th century)
1 a (1) : exhibiting or goaded by anger (2) : indicative of or proceeding from anger **b :** giving a stormy or turbulent appearance ⟨furious bursts of flame⟩ **c :** marked by noise, excitement, activity, or rapidity
2 : INTENSE 1a ⟨the furious growth of tropical vegetation⟩
— **fu·ri·ous·ly** adverb

¹**furl** \'fər(-ə)l\ verb [Middle French ferler, from Old North French ferlier to tie tightly, from Old French fer, ferm tight (from Latin firmus firm) + lier to tie, from Latin ligare — more at LIGATURE] (1556)
transitive verb
: to wrap or roll (as a sail or a flag) close to or around something
intransitive verb
: to curl or fold as in being furled

²**furl** noun (1643)
1 : a furled coil
2 : the act of furling

fur·long \'fər-ˌlȯŋ\ noun [Middle English, from Old English furlang, from furh furrow + lang long] (14th century)
: a unit of distance equal to 220 yards (about 201 meters)

¹**fur·lough** \'fər-(ˌ)lō\ noun [Dutch verlof, literally, permission, from Middle Dutch, from ver- for- + lof permission; akin to Middle High German loube permission — more at FOR-, LEAVE] (1625)
: a leave of absence from duty granted especially to a soldier; also : a document authorizing such a leave of absence

²**furlough** transitive verb (1781)
1 : to grant a furlough to

\ə\ abut \ᵊ\ kitten \ər\ further \a\ ash \ā\ ace
\ä\ mop, mar \au̇\ out \ch\ chin \e\ bet \ē\ easy
\g\ go \i\ hit \ī\ ice \j\ job \ŋ\ sing \ō\ go
\ȯ\ law \ȯi\ boy \th\ thin \th̲\ the \ü\ loot \u̇\ foot
\y\ yet \zh\ vision see also Guide to Pronunciation

2 : to lay off from work

fur·mi·ty \'fər-mə-tē\ *variant of* FRUMENTY

fur·nace \'fər-nəs\ *noun* [Middle English *furnas*, from Old French *fornaise*, from Latin *fornac-*, *fornax*; akin to Latin *formus* warm — more at THERM] (13th century)
: an enclosed structure in which heat is produced (as for heating a house or for reducing ore)

fur·nish \'fər-nish\ *transitive verb* [Middle English *furnisshen*, from Middle French *fourniss-*, stem of *fournir* to complete, equip, of Germanic origin; akin to Old High German *frummen* to further, *fruma* advantage — more at FOREMOST] (15th century)
1 : to provide with what is needed; *especially* **:** to equip with furniture
2 : SUPPLY, GIVE ⟨*furnished* food and shelter for the refugees⟩ ☆
— **fur·nish·er** *noun*

fur·nish·ing *noun* (1594)
1 : an article or accessory of dress — usually used in plural
2 : an object that tends to increase comfort or utility; *especially* **:** an article of furniture for the interior of a building — usually used in plural

fur·ni·ture \'fər-ni-chər\ *noun* [Middle French *fourniture*, from *fournir*] (1542)
: equipment that is necessary, useful, or desirable: as **a** *archaic* **:** the trappings of a horse **b :** movable articles used in readying an area (as a room or patio) for occupancy or use

furniture beetle *noun* (1925)
: a widespread deathwatch beetle (*Anobium punctatum*) noted for boring in and damaging furniture and seasoned wood

fu·ror \'fyùr-ˌòr, -ˌōr, -ər\ *noun* [Middle French & Latin; Middle French, from Latin, from *furere* to rage] (15th century)
1 : an angry or maniacal fit **:** RAGE
2 : FURY 4
3 : a fashionable craze **:** VOGUE
4 a : furious or hectic activity **b :** an outburst of public excitement or indignation **:** UPROAR

fu·rore \'fyùr-ˌōr, -ˌòr, -ər, *especially British* fyù-'rō-ri\ *noun* [Italian, from Latin *furor*] (1790)
1 : FUROR 4b
2 : FUROR 3

fu·ro·se·mide \fyù-'rō-sə-ˌmīd\ *noun* [*furfural* + *-o-* + *sulf-* + *-emide*, probably alteration of *amide*] (1965)
: a powerful diuretic $C_{12}H_{11}ClN_2O_5S$ used especially to treat edema

furred \'fərd\ *adjective* [Middle English] (14th century)
1 : lined, trimmed, or faced with fur
2 : coated as if with fur; *specifically* **:** having a coating consisting chiefly of mucus and dead epithelial cells ⟨a *furred* tongue⟩
3 : bearing or wearing fur
4 : provided with furring ⟨*furred* wall⟩

fur·ri·er \'fər-ē-ər, 'fə-rē-\ *noun* [alteration of Middle English *furrer*, from Anglo-French *furrere*, from Old French *forrer* to fur — more at FUR] (14th century)
1 : a fur dealer
2 a : one that dresses furs **b :** one that makes, repairs, alters, or cleans fur garments

fur·ri·ery \-ə-rē\ *noun* (circa 1864)
1 : the fur business
2 : fur craftsmanship

fur·rin·er \'fər-ə-nər\ *noun* [alteration of *foreigner*] (1849)
: FOREIGNER 2 — used to represent a dialectal pronunciation

fur·ring \'fər-iŋ\ *noun* (14th century)
1 : a fur trimming or lining
2 a : the application of thin wood, brick, or metal to joists, studs, or walls to form a level surface (as for attaching wallboard) or an air space **b :** the material used in this process

¹fur·row \'fər-ˌō, 'fə-ˌrō\ *noun* [Middle English *furgh, forow*, from Old English *furh*;

akin to Old High German *furuh* furrow, Latin *porca*] (before 12th century)
1 a : a trench in the earth made by a plow **b :** plowed land **:** FIELD
2 : something that resembles the track of a plow: as **a :** a marked narrow depression **:** GROOVE **b :** a deep wrinkle ⟨*furrows* in his brow⟩

²furrow (15th century)
transitive verb
: to make furrows, grooves, wrinkles, or lines in
intransitive verb
: to make or form furrows, grooves, wrinkles, or lines

fur·ry \'fər-ē\ *adjective* **fur·ri·er; -est** (circa 1674)
1 : consisting of or resembling fur ⟨animals with *furry* coats⟩
2 : covered with fur
3 : thick in quality ⟨spoke with a *furry* voice⟩

fur seal *noun* (1775)
: any of two genera (*Callorhinus* and *Arctocephalus*) of eared seals that have a double coat with a dense soft underfur

¹fur·ther \'fər-thər\ *adverb* [Middle English, from Old English *furthor* (akin to Old High German *furthar* further), comparative, from the base of Old English *forth* forth] (before 12th century)
1 : FARTHER 1 ⟨my ponies are tired, and I have *further* to go —Thomas Hardy⟩
2 : in addition **:** MOREOVER
3 : to a greater degree or extent ⟨*further* annoyed by a second intrusion⟩
usage see FARTHER

²further *transitive verb* **fur·thered; fur·ther·ing** \'fərth-riŋ, 'fər-thə-\ (before 12th century)
: to help forward **:** PROMOTE
synonym see ADVANCE
— **fur·ther·er** \'fər-thər-ər\ *noun*

³further *adjective* (13th century)
1 : FARTHER 1 ⟨rode . . . across the valley and up the *further* slopes —T. E. Lawrence⟩
2 : going or extending beyond **:** ADDITIONAL ⟨*further* volumes⟩ ⟨*further* education⟩
usage see FARTHER

fur·ther·ance \'fərth-rən(t)s, 'fər-thə-\ *noun* (15th century)
: the act of furthering **:** ADVANCEMENT

further education *noun* (1937)
British **:** ADULT EDUCATION

fur·ther·more \'fər-thə(r)-ˌmōr, -ˌmòr\ *adverb* (13th century)
: in addition to what precedes **:** BESIDES

fur·ther·most \-thər-ˌmōst\ *adjective* (15th century)
: most distant **:** FARTHEST

fur·thest \'fər-thəst\ *adverb or adjective* (14th century)
: FARTHEST

fur·tive \'fər-tiv\ *adjective* [French or Latin; French *furtif*, from Latin *furtivus*, from *furtum* theft, from *fur* thief, from or akin to Greek *phōr* thief, *pherein* to carry — more at BEAR] (1612)
1 a : done by stealth **:** SURREPTITIOUS **b :** expressive of stealth **:** SLY ⟨had a *furtive* look about him⟩
2 : obtained underhandedly **:** STOLEN
synonym see SECRET
— **fur·tive·ly** *adverb*
— **fur·tive·ness** *noun*

fu·run·cle \'fyùr-ˌəŋ-kəl\ *noun* [Latin *furunculus* petty thief, boil, diminutive of *furon-, furo* ferret, thief, from *fur*] (1676)
: ²BOIL

fu·run·cu·lo·sis \fyù-ˌrəŋ-kyə-'lō-səs\ *noun, plural* **-lo·ses** \-ˌsēz\ [New Latin] (1886)
1 : the condition of having or tending to develop multiple furuncles
2 : a highly infectious disease of various salmonoid fishes (as trout) that is caused by a

bacterium (*Bacterium salmonicida*) and is especially virulent in dense fish populations (as in hatcheries)

fu·ry \'fyùr-ē\ *noun, plural* **furies** [Middle English *furie*, from Middle French & Latin; Middle French, from Latin *furia*, from *furere* to rage] (14th century)
1 : intense, disordered, and often destructive rage
2 a *capitalized* **:** any of the avenging deities in Greek mythology who torment criminals and inflict plagues **b :** an avenging spirit **c :** one who resembles an avenging spirit; *especially* **:** a spiteful woman
3 : extreme fierceness or violence
4 : a state of inspired exaltation **:** FRENZY ◇
synonym see ANGER

furze \'fərz\ *noun* [Middle English *firse*, from Old English *fyrs*; akin to Russian *pyreĭ* quack grass, Greek *pyros* wheat] (before 12th century)
: GORSE
— **furzy** \'fər-zē\ *adjective*

fus·cous \'fəs-kəs\ *adjective* [Latin *fuscus* — more at DUSK] (1662)
: of any of several colors averaging a brownish gray

¹fuse \'fyüz\ *verb* **fused; fus·ing** [Latin *fusus*, past participle of *fundere* to pour, melt — more at FOUND] (1592)
transitive verb
1 : to reduce to a liquid or plastic state by heat
2 : to blend thoroughly by or as if by melting together **:** COMBINE ⟨in her richest work she *fuses* comedy and tragedy —T. A. Gullason⟩
3 : to stitch by applying heat and pressure with or without the use of an adhesive
intransitive verb
1 a : to become fluid with heat **b** *British* **:** to fail because of the blowing of a fuse
2 : to become blended or joined by or as if by melting together
synonym see MIX

²fuse *noun* (1884)
: an electrical safety device consisting of or including a wire or strip of fusible metal that

☆ **SYNONYMS**
Furnish, equip, outfit, appoint, accoutre mean to supply one with what is needed. FURNISH implies the provision of any or all essentials for performing a function ⟨a sparsely *furnished* apartment⟩. EQUIP suggests the provision of something making for efficiency in action or use ⟨a fully *equipped* kitchen⟩. OUTFIT implies provision of a complete list or set of articles as for a journey, an expedition, or a special occupation ⟨*outfitted* the family for a ski trip⟩. APPOINT implies provision of complete and usually elegant or elaborate equipment or furnishings ⟨a lavishly *appointed* apartment⟩. ACCOUTRE suggests the supplying of personal dress or equipment for a special activity ⟨fully *accoutred* members of a polar expedition⟩.

◇ **WORD HISTORY**
fury No more fearsome figures darkened Greek mythology than the Erinyes. Born of the blood drops from the emasculation of Uranus, with snakes coiled in their hair, they roamed the land avenging perjury and murder and carrying out the curses of parent against son. Neither prayer nor tears could sway them, nor sacrifice stave off their wrath. To the Romans they were known as the *Dirae* or the *Furiae*. The latter name is a personified form of the plural noun *furiae* "frenzy," a derivative of *furere* "to rage." English *fury* is borrowed via French from the singular form *furia*.

melts and interrupts the circuit when the current exceeds a particular amperage

³**fuse** noun [Italian fuso spindle, from Latin fusus, of unknown origin] (1644)
1 : a continuous train of a combustible substance enclosed in a cord or cable for setting off an explosive charge by transmitting fire to it
2 usually **fuze :** a mechanical or electrical detonating device for setting off the bursting charge of a projectile, bomb, or torpedo

⁴**fuse** or **fuze** \'fyüz\ transitive verb **fused** or **fuzed; fus·ing** or **fuz·ing** (1802)
: to equip with a fuse

fused quartz noun (1925)
: QUARTZ GLASS — called also **fused silica**

fu·see \fyü-'zē\ noun [French fusée, literally, spindleful of yarn, from Old French, from fus spindle, from Latin fusus] (1622)
1 : a conical spirally grooved pulley in a timepiece from which a cord or chain unwinds onto a barrel containing the spring and which by its increasing diameter compensates for the lessening power of the spring
2 : a red signal flare used especially for protecting stalled trains and trucks

fu·se·lage \'fyü-sə-,läzh, -zə-\ noun [French, from fuselé spindle-shaped, from Middle French, from fusel, diminutive of fus] (1909)
: the central body portion of an aircraft designed to accommodate the crew and the passengers or cargo — see AIRPLANE illustration

fu·sel oil \'fyü-zəl-\ noun [German Fusel bad liquor] (1850)
: an acrid oily liquid occurring in insufficiently distilled alcoholic liquors, consisting chiefly of amyl alcohol, and used especially as a source of alcohols and as a solvent

fus·ible \'fyü-zə-bəl\ adjective (14th century)
: capable of being fused and especially liquefied by heat ⟨fusible alloy⟩
— **fus·ibil·i·ty** \,fyü-zə-'bi-lə-tē\ noun

fu·si·form \'fyü-zə-,förm\ adjective [Latin fusus spindle] (1746)
: tapering toward each end ⟨fusiform bacteria⟩

¹**fu·sil** \'fyü-zəl\ or **fu·sile** \'fyü-zəl, -,zīl\ adjective [Middle English, from Latin fusilis, from fundere] (14th century)
1 archaic **a :** made by melting and pouring into forms **:** CAST **b :** liquefied by heat
2 archaic **:** FUSIBLE

²**fusil** noun [French, literally, steel for striking fire, from Old French foisil, from (assumed) Vulgar Latin focilis, from Late Latin focus fire — more at FUEL] (1680)
: a light flintlock musket

fu·sil·ier or **fu·sil·eer** \,fyü-zə-'lir\ noun [French fusilier, from fusil] (1680)
1 : a soldier armed with a fusil
2 : a member of a British regiment formerly armed with fusils

fu·sil·lade \'fyü-sə-,läd, -,lād, ,fyü-sə-', -zə-\ noun [French, from fusiller to shoot, from fusil] (1801)
1 a : a number of shots fired simultaneously or in rapid succession **b :** something that gives the effect of a fusillade ⟨a fusillade of rocks and bottles⟩
2 : a spirited outburst especially of criticism

fu·sil·li \fyü-'si-lē, -'sē-\ noun [Italian, plural of fusillo, from Italian dialect (southern Italy), diminutive of fuso spindle, from Latin fusus] (1948)
: spiral-shaped pasta

fu·sion \'fyü-zhən\ noun, often attributive [Latin fusion-, fusio, from fundere] (1555)
1 : the act or process of liquefying or rendering plastic by heat
2 : a union by or as if by melting: as **a :** a merging of diverse, distinct, or separate elements into a unified whole **b :** a political partnership **:** COALITION **c :** popular music combining different styles (as jazz and rock)

3 : the union of atomic nuclei to form heavier nuclei resulting in the release of enormous quantities of energy when certain light elements unite

fu·sion·ist \'fyü-zhə-nist\ noun (1851)
: a person involved in a political fusion or in nuclear or musical fusion

¹**fuss** \'fəs\ noun [origin unknown] (1701)
1 a : needless bustle or excitement **:** COMMOTION **b :** a show of flattering attention ⟨made a big fuss over his favorite niece⟩
2 a : a state of agitation especially over a trivial matter **b :** OBJECTION, PROTEST **c :** an often petty controversy or quarrel ⟨ended up having a pretty good fuss with my wife —Mac Hyman⟩

²**fuss** (1792)
intransitive verb
1 a : to create or be in a state of restless activity; especially **:** to shower flattering attentions ⟨fussing over the grandchildren⟩ **b :** to pay close or undue attention to small details ⟨fussed with her hair⟩
2 a : to become upset **:** WORRY **b :** to express annoyance or pique **:** COMPLAIN
transitive verb
: AGITATE, UPSET
— **fuss·er** noun

fuss·bud·get \'fəs-,bə-jət\ noun (circa 1904)
: one who fusses or is fussy especially about trifles
— **fuss·bud·gety** \-jə-tē\ adjective

fuss·pot \'fəs-,pät\ noun (1921)
: FUSSBUDGET

fussy \'fə-sē\ adjective **fuss·i·er; -est** (1831)
1 : easily upset **:** IRRITABLE
2 : overly decorative ⟨a fussy wallpaper pattern⟩
3 a : requiring or giving close attention to details ⟨fussy bookkeeping procedures⟩ **b :** revealing a sometimes extreme concern for niceties **:** FASTIDIOUS, PICKY
— **fuss·i·ly** \'fə-sə-lē\ adverb
— **fuss·i·ness** \'fə-sē-nəs\ noun

fus·tian \'fəs-chən\ noun [Middle English, from Old French fustaine, from Medieval Latin fustaneum, perhaps from fustis tree trunk, from Latin, club] (13th century)
1 a : a strong cotton and linen fabric **b :** a class of cotton fabrics usually having a pile face and twill weave
2 : highflown or affected writing or speech; broadly **:** anything highflown or affected in style
— **fus·tian** adjective

fus·tic \'fəs-tik\ noun [Middle English fustyk smoke tree, from Middle French fustoc, from Arabic fustuq, from Greek pistakē pistachio tree — more at PISTACHIO] (15th century)
: the wood of a tropical American tree (Chlorophora tinctoria) of the mulberry family that yields a yellow dye; also **:** any of several similar dyewoods

fus·ti·gate \'fəs-tə-,gāt\ transitive verb **-gat·ed; -gat·ing** [Late Latin fustigatus, past participle of fustigare, from Latin fustis + -igare (as in fumigare to fumigate)] (circa 1661)
1 : CUDGEL
2 : to criticize severely
— **fus·ti·ga·tion** \,fəs-tə-'gā-shən\ noun

fusty \'fəs-tē\ adjective **fus·ti·er; -est** [Middle English, from fust wine cask, from Middle French, club, cask, from Latin fustis] (14th century)
1 British **:** impaired by age or dampness **:** MOLDY
2 : saturated with dust and stale odors **:** MUSTY
3 : rigidly old-fashioned or reactionary
synonym see MALODOROUS
— **fus·ti·ly** \-tə-lē\ adverb
— **fus·ti·ness** \-tē-nəs\ noun

fu·su·li·nid \,fyü-zə-'lī-nid, -'lē-, -'li-\ noun [New Latin Fusulinidae, from Fusulina, a genus, from Latin fusus spindle + -ulus -ule + New Latin -ina, diminutive suffix] (1941)

: any of a family (Fusulinidae) of extinct marine foraminifers

fu·thark \'fü-,thärk\ also **fu·thorc** or **fu·thork** \-,thörk\ noun [from the first six letters, f, u, þ (th), o (or a), r, c (=k)] (1851)
: the runic alphabet — see RUNE illustration

fu·tile \'fyü-t°l, 'fyü-,tīl\ adjective [Middle French or Latin; Middle French, from Latin futilis brittle, pointless, probably from fu- (akin to fundere to pour) — more at FOUND] (circa 1555)
1 : serving no useful purpose **:** completely ineffective ⟨efforts to convince him were futile⟩
2 : occupied with trifles **:** FRIVOLOUS ☆
— **fu·tile·ly** \-t°l-(l)ē, -,tīl-lē\ adverb
— **fu·tile·ness** \-t°l-nəs, -,tīl-nəs\ noun

fu·til·i·tar·i·an \fyü-,ti-lə-'ter-ē-ən, ,fyü-\ noun [blend of futile and utilitarian] (1827)
: one who believes that human striving is futile
— **futilitarian** adjective
— **fu·til·i·tar·i·an·ism** \-ē-ə-,ni-zəm\ noun

fu·til·i·ty \fyü-'ti-lə-tē\ noun, plural **-ties** (1623)
1 : the quality or state of being futile **:** USELESSNESS
2 : a useless act or gesture ⟨the futilities of debate for its own sake —W. A. White⟩

fu·ton \'fü-,tän\ noun, plural **futons** also **futon** [Japanese] (1876)
: a usually cotton-filled mattress used on the floor or in a frame as a bed

fut·tock \'fə-tək\ noun [Middle English votek, futtek] (13th century)
: one of the curved timbers scarfed together to form the lower part of the compound rib of a ship

futtock shroud noun (1840)
: a short iron rod connecting the topmast rigging with the lower mast

¹**fu·ture** \'fyü-chər\ adjective [Middle English, from Middle French & Latin; Middle French futur, from Latin futurus about to be — more at BE] (14th century)
1 : that is to be; specifically **:** existing after death
2 : of, relating to, or constituting a verb tense expressive of time yet to come
3 : existing or occurring at a later time ⟨met his future wife⟩

²**future** noun (15th century)
1 a : time that is to come **b :** what is going to happen
2 : an expectation of advancement or progressive development
3 : something (as a bulk commodity) bought for future acceptance or sold for future delivery — usually used in plural ⟨grain futures⟩
4 a : the future tense of a language **b :** a verb form in the future tense

fu·ture·less \'fyü-chər-ləs\ adjective (1863)
: having no future
— **fu·ture·less·ness** noun

future perfect adjective (circa 1898)

☆ SYNONYMS
Futile, vain, fruitless mean producing no result. FUTILE may connote completeness of failure or unwisdom of undertaking ⟨resistance had proved so futile that surrender was the only choice left⟩. VAIN usually implies simple failure to achieve a desired result ⟨a vain attempt to get the car started⟩. FRUITLESS comes close to VAIN but often suggests long and arduous effort or severe disappointment ⟨fruitless efforts to obtain a lasting peace⟩.

\ə\ abut \ᵊ\ kitten \ər\ further \a\ ash \ā\ ace
\ä\ mop, mar \aů\ out \ch\ chin \e\ bet \ē\ easy
\g\ go \i\ hit \ī\ ice \j\ job \ŋ\ sing \ō\ go
\ȯ\ law \ȯi\ boy \th\ thin \t͟h\ the \ü\ loot \ů\ foot
\y\ yet \zh\ vision see also Guide to Pronunciation

: of, relating to, or constituting a verb tense that is traditionally formed in English with *will have* and *shall have* and that expresses completion of an action by a specified time that is yet to come
— **future perfect** *noun*
future shock *noun* (1965)
: the physical and psychological distress suffered by one who is unable to cope with the rapidity of social and technological changes
fu·tur·ism \'fyü-chə-‚ri-zəm\ *noun* (1909)
1 : a movement in art, music, and literature begun in Italy about 1909 and marked especially by an effort to give formal expression to the dynamic energy and movement of mechanical processes
2 : a point of view that finds meaning or fulfillment in the future rather than in the past or present
fu·tur·ist \'fyü-chə-rist\ *noun* (1911)
1 : one who advocates or practices futurism
2 : one who studies and predicts the future especially on the basis of current trends
— **futurist** *adjective*
fu·tur·is·tic \‚fyü-chə-'ris-tik\ *adjective* (1915)
: of, relating to, or characteristic of the future, futurism, or futurology; *also* **:** very modern
— **fu·tur·is·ti·cal·ly** \-ti-k(ə-)lē\ *adverb*
fu·tur·is·tics \-tiks\ *noun plural but singular in construction* (1969)

: FUTUROLOGY
fu·tu·ri·ty \fyu̇-'tu̇r-ə-tē, -'tyu̇r-, -'chu̇r-\ *noun, plural* **-ties** (1604)
1 : time to come **:** FUTURE
2 : the quality or state of being future
3 *plural* **:** future events or prospects
4 a : a horse race usually for two-year-olds in which the competitors are nominated at birth or before **b :** a race or competition for which entries are made well in advance of the event
fu·tur·ol·o·gy \‚fyü-chə-'rä-lə-jē\ *noun* (1946)
: a study that deals with future possibilities based on current trends
— **fu·tur·olog·i·cal** \-rə-'lä-ji-kəl\ *adjective*
— **fu·tur·olo·gist** \-'rä-lə-jist\ *noun*
futz \'fəts\ *intransitive verb* [perhaps part modification, part translation of Yiddish *arumfartsn zikh*, literally, to fart around] (1932)
slang **:** FOOL AROUND 1 — often used with *around* ⟨*futz* around without producing any worthwhile music —John Koegel⟩
fuze, fu·zee *variant of* FUSE, FUSEE
¹fuzz \'fəz\ *noun* [probably back-formation from *fuzzy*] (1674)
1 : fine light particles or fibers (as of down or fluff)
2 : a blurred effect
²fuzz (circa 1702)
intransitive verb

1 : to fly off in or become covered with fluffy particles
2 : to become blurred ⟨her frame of reference *fuzzing* at the edges —Jane O'Reilly⟩
transitive verb
1 : to make fuzzy
2 : to envelop in a haze **:** BLUR
³fuzz *noun* [origin unknown] (1927)
: POLICE; *also* **:** a police officer
fuzzy \'fə-zē\ *adjective* **fuzz·i·er; -est** [perhaps from Low German *fussig* loose, spongy] (1713)
1 : marked by or giving a suggestion of fuzz ⟨a *fuzzy* covering of felt⟩
2 : lacking in clarity or definition ⟨moving the camera causes *fuzzy* photos⟩ ⟨*fuzzy* thinking⟩
— **fuzz·i·ly** \'fə-zə-lē\ *adverb*
— **fuzz·i·ness** \'fə-zē-nəs\ *noun*
-fy \‚fī\ *verb suffix* [Middle English *-fien*, from Old French *-fier*, from Latin *-ficare*, from *-ficus* -fic]
1 : make **:** form into ⟨dandi*fy*⟩
2 : invest with the attributes of **:** make similar to ⟨citi*fy*⟩
fyce \'fīs\ *variant of* FEIST
fyke \'fīk\ *noun* [Dutch *fuik*] (1832)
: a long bag net kept open by hoops
fyl·fot \'fil-‚fät\ *noun* [Middle English, device used to fill the lower part of a painted glass window (from a conjectural manuscript reading)] (1842)
: SWASTIKA

G *G is the seventh letter of the English alphabet and of most modern alphabets closely related to that of English. It came from Latin, where it was introduced to distinguish the voiced velar stop (the sound of g in go) from the corresponding voiceless stop (the sound of k in king), both of which had until then been represented by C. In Modern English, g represents two chief sounds, commonly called "hard g" and "soft g." The former, as in go, was the earlier sound, the latter, equivalent to j, as in gem, appears chiefly in words from Latin and Old French. The small g developed from a late Roman form of the capital letter that had a short curved flourish extending below the line (Ꮐ). The upper half of the letter closed to form a full oval, while the tail below the line also closed to form a loop (ꬶ or ꬶ).*

g \'jē\ *noun, plural* **g's** *or* **gs** \'jēz\ *often capitalized, often attributive* (before 12th century)
1 a : the 7th letter of the English alphabet **b :** a graphic representation of this letter **c :** a speech counterpart of orthographic *g*
2 : the 5th tone of a C-major scale
3 : a graphic device for reproducing the letter *g*
4 : one designated *g* especially as the 7th in order or class
5 [gravity] **:** ACCELERATION OF GRAVITY; *also* **:** a unit of force equal to the force exerted by gravity on a body at rest and used to indicate the force to which a body is subjected when accelerated
6 [grand] *slang* **:** a sum of $1000
7 : something shaped like the letter G

G *certification mark*
— used to certify that a motion picture is of such a nature that persons of all ages may be allowed admission; compare NC-17, PG, PG-13, R

¹gab \'gab\ *intransitive verb* **gabbed; gabbing** [probably short for *gabble*] (1786)
: to talk in a rapid or thoughtless manner **:** CHATTER
— **gab·ber** *noun*

²gab *noun* (1790)
: TALK; *especially* **:** idle talk

³gab *noun* (1939)
: GABARDINE 2

gab·ar·dine \'ga-bər-,dēn\ *noun* [Middle French *gaverdine*] (1520)
1 : GABERDINE 1
2 a : a firm hard-finish durable fabric (as of wool or rayon) twilled with diagonal ribs on the right side **b :** a garment of gabardine

gab·ble \'ga-bəl\ *verb* **gab·bled; gab·bling** \-b(ə-)liŋ\ [probably of imitative origin] (1577)
intransitive verb
1 : to talk fast or foolishly **:** JABBER
2 : to utter inarticulate or animal sounds
transitive verb
: to say with incoherent rapidity **:** BABBLE
— **gabble** *noun*
— **gab·bler** \-b(ə-)lər\ *noun*

gab·bro \'ga-(,)brō\ *noun, plural* **gabbros** [Italian, probably modification of Latin *glaber* smooth — more at GLAD] (circa 1828)
: a granular igneous rock composed essentially of calcic plagioclase, a ferromagnesian mineral, and accessory minerals
— **gab·bro·ic** \ga-'brō-ik\ *adjective*

gab·by \'ga-bē\ *adjective* **gab·bi·er; -est** (1719)
: TALKATIVE, GARRULOUS

ga·belle \gə-'bel\ *noun* [Middle English, from Middle French, from Old Italian *gabella* tax, from Arabic *qabālah*] (15th century)
: a tax on salt levied in France prior to 1790

gab·er·dine \'ga-bər-,dēn\ *noun* [Middle French *gaverdine*] (1520)

1 : a long loose outer garment worn in medieval times and associated especially with Jews since the 16th century
2 : GABARDINE 2

gab·fest \'gab-,fest\ *noun* (1897)
1 : an informal gathering for general talk ⟨political *gabfests*⟩
2 : an extended conversation

ga·bi·on \'ga-bē-ən, 'ga-\ *noun* [Middle French, from Old Italian *gabbione*, literally, large cage, augmentative of *gabbia* cage, from Latin *cavea* — more at CAGE] (1579)
: a basket or cage filled with earth or rocks and used especially in building a support or abutment

ga·ble \'gā-bəl\ *noun* [Middle English, from Middle French, of Germanic origin; akin to Old Norse *gafl* gable — more at CEPHALIC] (14th century)
1 a : the vertical triangular end of a building from cornice or eaves to ridge **b :** the similar end of a gambrel roof **c :** the end wall of a building
2 : a triangular part or structure
— **ga·bled** \-bəld\ *adjective*

1 gable 1a

gable roof *noun* (1850)
: a double-sloping roof that forms a gable at each end

gab·oon \gä-'bün, gə-\ *noun* [alteration of ¹*gob* + -*oon* (as in *spittoon*)] (1929)
dialect **:** SPITTOON

Ga·bri·el \'gā-brē-əl\ *noun* [Hebrew *Gabhrī'ēl*]
: one of the four archangels named in Hebrew tradition

ga·by \'gā-bē\ *noun, plural* **gabies** [perhaps of Scandinavian origin; akin to Old Norse *gapa* to gape — more at GAPE] (circa 1796)
dialect chiefly English **:** SIMPLETON

¹gad \'gad\ *noun* [Middle English, spike, from Old Norse *gaddr*; akin to Old English *geard* rod — more at YARD] (1671)
1 : a chisel or pointed iron or steel bar for loosening ore or rock
2 *chiefly dialect* **:** a long stick

²gad *intransitive verb* **gad·ded; gad·ding** [Middle English *gadden*] (15th century)
: to be on the go without a specific aim or purpose — usually used with *about*

³gad *interjection* [euphemism for *God*] (1608)
— used as a mild oath

Gad \'gad\ *noun* [Hebrew *Gādh*]
: a son of Jacob and the traditional eponymous ancestor of one of the tribes of Israel
— **Gad·ite** \'ga-,dīt\ *noun*

gad·about \'ga-də-,baůt\ *noun* (1837)
: a person who flits about in social activity
— **gadabout** *adjective*

gad·a·rene \'ga-də-,rēn\ *adjective, often capitalized* [from the demon-possessed *Gadarene* swine in Matthew 8:28 that rushed into the sea] (1922)
: HEADLONG, PRECIPITATE ⟨a *gadarene* rush to the cities⟩

gad·fly \'gad-,flī\ *noun* [¹*gad*] (1626)
1 : any of various flies (as a horsefly, botfly, or warble fly) that bite or annoy livestock
2 : a person who stimulates or annoys especially by persistent criticism

gad·get \'ga-jət\ *noun* [origin unknown] (1886)
: an often small mechanical or electronic device with a practical use but often thought of as a novelty
— **gad·ge·teer** \,ga-jə-'tir\ *noun*
— **gad·get·ry** \'ga-jə-trē\ *noun*
— **gad·gety** \-jə-tē\ *adjective*

ga·doid \'gā-,doid, 'ga-\ *adjective* [New Latin *Gadus*, genus of fishes, from Greek *gados*, a fish] (circa 1842)
: resembling or related to the cods
— **gadoid** *noun*

gad·o·lin·ite \'ga-d°l-ə-,nīt\ *noun* [German *Gadolinit*, from Johann *Gadolin* (died 1852) Finnish chemist] (1802)
: a black or brown mineral that is a source of rare earths and consists of a silicate of iron, beryllium, yttrium, cerium, and erbium

gad·o·lin·i·um \,ga-də-'li-nē-əm\ *noun* [New Latin, from J. *Gadolin*] (1886)
: a magnetic metallic element of the rare-earth group occurring in combination in gadolinite and several other minerals — see ELEMENT table

ga·droon \gə-'drün\ *noun* [French *godron* round plait, gadroon] (circa 1724)
1 : the ornamental notching or carving of a rounded molding
2 : a short often oval fluting or reeding used in decoration
— **gadroon** *transitive verb*
— **ga·droon·ing** *noun*

gad·wall \'gad-,wȯl\ *noun, plural* **gadwalls** *or* **gadwall** [origin unknown] (1666)
: a grayish brown medium-sized dabbling duck (*Anas strepera*)

gad·zook·ery \gad-'zü-kə-rē, -'zu̇-\ *noun* (1955)
British **:** the use of archaisms (as in a historical novel)

gad·zooks \gad-'züks, -'zu̇ks\ *interjection, often capitalized* [perhaps from *God's hooks*, the nails of the Crucifixion] (1694)
archaic — used as a mild oath

Gaea \'jē-ə\ *noun* [Greek *Gaia*]
: the Greek earth goddess and mother of the Titans

Gael \'gā(ə)l\ *noun* [Scottish Gaelic *Gàidheal* & Irish *Gaedheal*] (1753)
1 : a Scottish Highlander
2 : a Celtic especially Gaelic-speaking inhabitant of Ireland, Scotland, or the Isle of Man
— **Gael·dom** \-dəm\ *noun*

Gael·ic \'gā-lik, 'ga-, 'gä-\ *adjective* [Scottish Gaelic *Gàidhlig* the Scottish Gaelic language, from *Gàidheal* Gaelic] (1741)
1 : of or relating to the Gaels and especially the Celtic Highlanders of Scotland
2 : of, relating to, or constituting the Goidelic speech of the Celts in Ireland, the Isle of Man, and the Scottish Highlands
— **Gaelic** *noun*

Gael·tacht \'gā(ə)l-təkt\ *noun* [Irish, from *Gaelic*, spelling variant of *Gaedheal* Irishman, Gael] (1929)
: any of the Irish-speaking regions remaining in Ireland

\ə\ **abut** \ᵊ\ **kitten** \ər\ **further** \a\ **ash** \ā\ **ace**
\ä\ **mop, mar** \aů\ **out** \ch\ **chin** \e\ **bet** \ē\ **easy**
\g\ **go** \i\ **hit** \ī\ **ice** \j\ **job** \ŋ\ **sing** \ō\ **go**
\ȯ\ **law** \ȯi\ **boy** \th\ **thin** \th̲\ **the** \ü\ **loot** \u̇\ **foot**
\y\ **yet** \zh\ **vision** *see also* Guide to Pronunciation

¹**gaff** \'gaf\ *noun* [French *gaffe,* from Provençal *gaf*] (circa 1656)
1 a : a spear or spearhead for taking fish or turtles **b :** a handled hook for holding or lifting heavy fish **c :** a metal spur for a gamecock **d :** a butcher's hook **e :** a climbing iron or its steel point used by a telephone lineman
2 : the spar on which the head of a fore-and-aft sail is extended
3 : GAFFE

²**gaff** *transitive verb* (1844)
1 : to strike or secure with a gaff
2 : to fit (a gamecock) with a gaff

³**gaff** *noun* [origin unknown] (1812)
British : a cheap theater or music hall

⁴**gaff** *noun* [origin unknown] (1896)
1 a : something painful or difficult to bear **:** ORDEAL — usually used in the phrase *stand the gaff; especially :* persistent raillery or criticism **b :** rough treatment **:** ABUSE
2 a : HOAX, FRAUD **b :** GIMMICK, TRICK

⁵**gaff** *transitive verb* (1933)
1 : DECEIVE, TRICK; *also :* FLEECE
2 : to fix for the purpose of cheating ⟨*gaff* the dice⟩

gaffe \'gaf\ *noun* [French, gaff, gaffe] (1909)
: a social or diplomatic blunder

gaf·fer \'ga-fər\ *noun* [alteration of *godfather*] (1575)
1 : an old man — compare GAMMER
2 *British* **a :** FOREMAN, OVERSEER **b :** EMPLOYER
3 : a head glassblower
4 : a lighting electrician on a motion-picture or television set

gaff–top·sail \'gaf-'täp-ˌsāl, -səl\ *noun* (1794)
: a usually triangular topsail with its foot extended upon the gaff — see SAIL illustration

¹**gag** \'gag\ *verb* **gagged; gag·ging** [Middle English *gaggen* to strangle, of imitative origin] (1509)
transitive verb
1 a : to restrict use of the mouth of by inserting a gag **b :** to prevent from exercising freedom of speech or expression **c :** to pry or hold open with a gag
2 : to provide or write quips or pranks for ⟨*gag* a show⟩
3 : to choke or cause to retch
intransitive verb
1 a : CHOKE; *also :* to suffer a throat spasm that makes swallowing or breathing difficult **b :** RETCH
2 : to be unable to endure something **:** BALK
3 : to make quips
— **gag·ger** *noun*

²**gag** *noun* (1553)
1 : something thrust into the mouth to keep it open or to prevent speech or outcry
2 : an official check or restraint on debate or free speech ⟨a *gag* order⟩ ⟨a *gag* rule⟩
3 : a laugh-provoking remark or act
4 : PRANK, TRICK

ga·ga \'gä-(ˌ)gä\ *adjective* [French, from *gaga* fool, of imitative origin] (1920)
1 : CRAZY, FOOLISH
2 : marked by wild enthusiasm **:** INFATUATED, DOTING

ga·ga·ku \gä-'gä-(ˌ)kü\ *noun* [Japanese, from *ga* elegance + *gaku* music] (1929)
: the ancient court music of Japan

¹**gage** \'gāj\ *noun* [Middle English, from Middle French, of Germanic origin; akin to Old High German *wetti* pledge — more at WED] (14th century)
1 : a token of defiance; *specifically :* a glove or cap cast on the ground to be taken up by an opponent as a pledge of combat
2 : something deposited as a pledge of performance

²**gage** *transitive verb* (15th century)
1 *archaic* **:** PLEDGE
2 *archaic* **:** STAKE, RISK

³**gage** *variant of* GAUGE

⁴**gage** *noun* (1847)
: GREENGAGE

gag·gle \'ga-gəl\ *noun* [Middle English *gagyll,* from *gagelen* to cackle] (15th century)
1 : FLOCK; *especially :* a flock of geese when not in flight — compare SKEIN
2 : AGGREGATION, CLUSTER ⟨a *gaggle* of reporters and photographers⟩

gag·man \'gag-ˌman\ *noun* (1928)
1 : a gag writer
2 : COMEDIAN 2

gag·ster \'gag-stər\ *noun* (1935)
: GAGMAN; *also :* one who plays practical jokes

gahn·ite \'gä-ˌnīt\ *noun* [German *Gahnit,* from J. G. *Gahn* (died 1818) Swedish chemist] (circa 1808)
: a usually dark green mineral consisting of an oxide of zinc and aluminum

gai·ety \'gā-ə-tē\ *noun, plural* **-eties** [French *gaieté*] (1634)
1 : MERRYMAKING; *also :* festive activity — often used in plural
2 : high spirits **:** MERRIMENT
3 : ELEGANCE, FINERY

gai·jin \'gī-(ˌ)jēn, -(ˌ)jin\ *noun, plural* **gaijin** [Japanese, from *gai-* outer, foreign + *-jin* person] (1964)
: a foreigner in Japan

gail·lar·dia \gə-'lär-d(ē-)ə\ *noun* [New Latin, from *Gaillard* de Marentonneau, 18th century French botanist] (1888)
: any of a genus (*Gaillardia*) of chiefly western American composite herbs with showy flower heads

gai·ly \'gā-lē\ *adverb* (14th century)
: in a gay manner **:** marked by gaiety

¹**gain** \'gān\ *noun* [Middle English *gayne,* from Middle French *gaigne, gain,* from Old French *gaaigne, gaaing,* from *gaaignier* to till, earn, gain, of Germanic origin; akin to Old High German *weidanōn* to hunt for food, Old English *wāth* pursuit, hunt] (14th century)
1 : resources or advantage acquired or increased **:** PROFIT ⟨made substantial *gains* last year⟩
2 : the act or process of gaining
3 a : an increase in amount, magnitude, or degree ⟨a *gain* in efficiency⟩ **b :** the increase (as of voltage or signal intensity) caused by an amplifier; *especially :* the ratio of output over input **c :** the signal-gathering ability of an antenna

²**gain** (14th century)
transitive verb
1 a : to acquire or get possession of usually by industry, merit, or craft ⟨*gain* an advantage⟩ ⟨he stood to *gain* a fortune⟩ **b :** to win in competition or conflict ⟨the troops *gained* territory⟩ **c** (1) **:** to arrive at **:** REACH, ATTAIN ⟨*gained* the river that night⟩ (2) **:** TRAVERSE, COVER ⟨*gained* 10 yards on the play⟩ **d :** to get by a natural development or process ⟨*gain* strength⟩ **e :** to establish a specific relationship with ⟨*gain* a friend⟩
2 a : to make an increase of (a specified amount) ⟨*gained* 3% in the past month⟩ **b :** to increase in (a particular quality) ⟨*gain* momentum⟩
3 : to win to one's side **:** PERSUADE ⟨*gain* adherents to a cause⟩
4 : to cause to be obtained or given **:** ATTRACT ⟨*gain* attention⟩
5 *of a timepiece* **:** to run fast by the amount of ⟨the clock *gains* a minute a day⟩
intransitive verb
1 : to get advantage **:** PROFIT ⟨hoped to *gain* by the deal⟩
2 a : INCREASE ⟨the day was *gaining* in warmth⟩ **b :** to increase in weight **c :** to improve in health or ability
3 *of a timepiece* **:** to run fast
4 : to get closer to something pursued — usually used with *on* or *upon*
— **gain·er** *noun*
— **gain ground :** to make progress

gain·ful \'gān-fəl\ *adjective* (1555)
: productive of gain **:** PROFITABLE ⟨*gainful* employment⟩

— **gain·ful·ly** \-fə-lē\ *adverb*
— **gain·ful·ness** *noun*

gain·giv·ing \'gān-ˌgi-viŋ, ˌgān-'\ *noun* [*gain-* (against) + *giving*] (1602)
archaic : MISGIVING

gain·say \ˌgān-'sā\ *transitive verb* **-said** \-'sād, -'sed\; **-say·ing** \-'sā-iŋ\; **-says** \-'sāz, -'sez\ [Middle English *gainsayen,* from *gain-* against (from Old English *gēan-*) + *sayen* to say — more at AGAIN] (14th century)
1 : to declare to be untrue or invalid
2 : CONTRADICT, OPPOSE
synonym see DENY
— **gain·say·er** *noun*

¹**gait** \'gāt\ *noun* [Middle English *gait, gate* gate, way] (1509)
1 : a manner of walking or moving on foot
2 : a sequence of foot movements (as a walk, trot, pace, or canter) by which a horse or a dog moves forward
3 : a manner or rate of movement or progress ⟨the leisurely *gait* of summer⟩

²**gait** (circa 1900)
transitive verb
1 : to train (a horse or a dog) to use a particular gait or set of gaits
2 : to lead (a show dog) before a judge to display carriage and movement
intransitive verb
: to walk with a particular gait

gait·ed \'gā-təd\ *adjective* (1588)
: having a particular gait or so many gaits ⟨slow-*gaited*⟩ ⟨a *gaited* horse⟩

gai·ter \'gā-tər\ *noun* [French *guêtre*] (1775)
1 : a cloth or leather leg covering reaching from the instep to above the ankle or to mid-calf or knee
2 a : an overshoe with fabric upper **b :** an ankle-high shoe with elastic gores in the sides

¹**gal** \'gal\ *noun* [by alteration] (1795)
: GIRL, WOMAN

²**gal** *noun* [*Galileo* Galilei] (1914)
: a unit of acceleration equivalent to one centimeter per second per second — used especially for values of gravity

ga·la \'gā-lə, 'ga-, 'gä-\ *noun* [Italian, from Middle French *gale* festivity, pleasure — more at GALLANT] (1777)
: a festive celebration; *especially :* a public entertainment marking a special occasion
— **gala** *adjective*

ga·la·bia *or* **ga·la·bi·eh** *or* **ga·la·bi·ya** \gə-'lä-b(ē-)ə\ *noun* [Arabic dialect (Egyptian) *gallābīyah*] (1725)
: DJELLABA

galact- *or* **galacto-** *combining form* [Latin *galact-,* from Greek *galakt-, galakto-,* from *galakt-, gala*]
1 : milk ⟨*galacto*rrhea⟩
2 : related to galactose ⟨*galacto*semia⟩

ga·lac·tic \gə-'lak-tik\ *adjective* (1839)
1 : of or relating to a galaxy and especially the Milky Way galaxy
2 : HUGE ⟨a *galactic* sum of money⟩

ga·lac·tor·rhea \gə-ˌlak-tə-'rē-ə\ *noun* (circa 1860)
: a spontaneous flow of milk from the nipple

ga·lac·tos·amine \gə-ˌlak-'tō-sə-ˌmēn, -zə-\ *noun* (1900)
: an amino derivative $C_6H_{13}O_5N$ of galactose that occurs in cartilage

ga·lac·tose \gə-'lak-ˌtōs, -ˌtōz\ *noun* [French, from *galact-*] (1869)
: a sugar $C_6H_{12}O_6$ less soluble and less sweet than glucose

ga·lac·to·semia \gə-ˌlak-tə-'sē-mē-ə\ *noun* (1934)
: an inherited metabolic disorder in which galactose accumulates in the blood due to deficiency of an enzyme catalyzing its conversion to glucose
— **ga·lac·to·semic** \-mik\ *adjective*

ga·lac·to·si·dase \gə-ˌlak-'tō-sə-ˌdās, -zə-ˌdāz\ *noun* (1917)
: an enzyme (as lactase) that hydrolyzes a galactoside

ga·lac·to·side \gə-'lak-tə-ˌsīd\ *noun* (1862)
: a glycoside that yields galactose on hydrolysis

ga·lac·to·syl \gə-'lak-tə-ˌsil\ *noun* (1950)
: a glycosyl radical $C_6H_{11}O_5$ that is derived from galactose

ga·lact·uron·ic acid \gə-ˌlak-tů-'rä-nik-, -tyů-\ *noun* [International Scientific Vocabulary] (1917)
: a crystalline aldehyde-acid $C_6H_{10}O_7$ that occurs especially in polymerized form in pectin

ga·la·go \gə-'lä-(ˌ)gō, -'lä-\ *noun, plural* **-gos** [New Latin, perhaps from Wolof *golokh* monkey] (circa 1848)
: any of several small active nocturnal arboreal African primates (*Galago* and related genera) with large eyes, long ears, a long tail, and elongated hind limbs that enable them to leap with great agility — called also *bush baby*

ga·lah \gə-'lä\ *noun* [Yuwaalaraay (Australian aboriginal language of northern New South Wales) *gilaa*] (1862)
: a showy Australian cockatoo (*Eolophus roseicapillus*) that is a pest in wheat-growing areas and is often kept as a cage bird

galago

Gal·a·had \'ga-lə-ˌhad\ *noun*
1 : the knight of the Round Table who successfully seeks the Holy Grail
2 : one who is pure, noble, and unselfish

gal·an·tine \'ga-lən-ˌtēn\ *noun* [French, from Old French *galentine, galatine* fish sauce, from Medieval Latin *galatina*, probably from Latin *gelatus*, past participle of *gelare* to congeal, freeze — more at COLD] (1725)
: a cold dish consisting of boned meat or fish that has been stuffed, poached, and covered with aspic

Gal·a·tea \ˌga-lə-'tē-ə\ *noun* [Latin, from Greek *Galateia*]
: a female figure sculpted by Pygmalion and given life by Aphrodite in fulfillment of his prayer

Ga·la·tians \gə-'lā-shənz\ *noun plural but singular in construction*
: an argumentative letter of Saint Paul written to the Christians of Galatia and included as a book in the New Testament — see BIBLE table

gal·a·vant *variant of* GALLIVANT

ga·lax \'gā-ˌlaks\ *noun* [New Latin] (circa 1753)
: an evergreen herb (*Galax urceolata* synonym *G. aphylla* of the order Diapensiales) of the southeastern U.S. that has glossy leaves and is related to the heaths (order Ericales)

gal·axy \'ga-lək-sē\ *noun, plural* **-ax·ies** [Middle English *galaxie, galaxias*, from Late Latin *galaxias*, from Greek, from *galakt-, gala* milk; akin to Latin *lac* milk] (14th century)
1 a *often capitalized* **:** MILKY WAY GALAXY — used with *the* **b :** any of the very large groups of stars and associated matter that are found throughout the universe
2 : an assemblage of brilliant or notable persons or things ⟨a *galaxy* of artists⟩ ◇

gal·ba·num \'gal-bə-nəm, 'gȯl-\ *noun* [Middle English, from Latin, from Greek *chalbanē*, of Semitic origin; akin to Hebrew *ḥelbĕnāh* galbanum] (14th century)
: a yellowish to green or brown aromatic bitter gum resin derived from several Asian plants (as *Ferula galbaniflua*) and used in incense

gale \'gā(ə)l\ *noun* [origin unknown] (circa 1547)
1 a : a strong current of air: (1) **:** a wind from 32 to 63 miles per hour (about 51 to 101 kilometers per hour) (2) **:** FRESH GALE — see BEAUFORT SCALE table **b** *archaic* **:** BREEZE
2 : an emotional outburst ⟨*gales* of laughter⟩

ga·lea \'gā-lē-ə\ *noun* [New Latin, from Latin, helmet] (1834)
: an anatomical part suggesting a helmet: as **a :** the upper lip of the corolla of a mint **b :** the outer or lateral lobe of the maxilla in mandibulate insects
— **ga·le·ate** \-lē-ˌāt\ *adjective*

ga·le·na \gə-'lē-nə\ *noun* [Latin, lead ore] (1671)
: a bluish gray mineral with metallic luster consisting of lead sulfide, showing highly perfect cubic cleavage, and constituting the principal ore of lead

ga·len·i·cal \gə-'le-ni-kəl, gā-\ *noun* [*Galen* + ¹*-ic* + ¹*-al*] (1768)
: a medicine prepared by extracting one or more active constituents of a plant

ga·lère \ga-'ler\ *noun* [French, galley, from Middle French, from Catalan *galera*, from Middle Greek *galea*] (1756)
: a group of people having an attribute in common

gal Friday *noun* (1958)
: GIRL FRIDAY

Gal·i·le·an \ˌga-lə-'lē-ən, -'lā-\ *adjective* (circa 1751)
: of, relating to, or discovered by Galileo Galilei

gal·i·lee \'ga-lə-ˌlē\ *noun* [Anglo-French, from Medieval Latin *galilaea*, probably from *Galilaea* Galilee, from Latin] (15th century)
: a chapel or porch at the entrance of an English church

gal·in·gale \'ga-lən-ˌgāl, -liŋ-\ *noun* [Middle English, a kind of ginger, from Middle French *galingal*, from Arabic *khalanjān*] (1578)
: an Old World sedge (*Cyperus longus*) that is used for papermaking and basket-weaving and has an aromatic root; *broadly* **:** any of various other sedges of the same genus

gal·i·ot *variant of* GALLIOT

¹gall \'gȯl\ *noun* [Middle English, from Old English *gealla*; akin to Greek *cholē, cholos* gall, wrath, Old English *geolu* yellow — more at YELLOW] (before 12th century)
1 a : BILE; *especially* **:** bile obtained from an animal and used in the arts or medicine **b :** something bitter to endure **c :** bitterness of spirit **:** RANCOR
2 : brazen boldness coupled with impudent assurance and insolence
synonym see TEMERITY

²gall *noun* [Middle English *galle*, from Old English *gealla*, from Latin *galla* gallnut] (before 12th century)
1 a : a skin sore caused by chronic irritation **b :** a cause or state of exasperation
2 *archaic* **:** FLAW

³gall *verb* (14th century)
transitive verb
1 : to fret and wear away by friction **:** CHAFE ⟨the loose saddle *galled* the horse's back⟩ ⟨the *galling* of a metal bearing⟩
2 : IRRITATE, VEX ⟨sarcasm *galls* her⟩
intransitive verb
1 : to become sore or worn by rubbing
2 : SEIZE 2

⁴gall *noun* [Middle English *galle*, from Middle French, from Latin *galla*] (14th century)
: a swelling of plant tissue usually due to fungi or insect parasites and sometimes forming an important source of tannin

Gal·la \'ga-lə\ *noun, plural* **Galla** *or* **Gallas** (1875)
: OROMO

gal·la·mine tri·eth·io·dide \'ga-lə-ˌmēn-ˌtrī-ˌe-'thī-ə-ˌdīd\ *noun* [*pyrogallol* + *amine* + *triethyl* + *iodide*] (1951)
: a substituted ammonium salt $C_{30}H_{60}I_3N_3O_3$ that is used to produce muscle relaxation especially during anesthesia — called also *gallamine*

¹gal·lant \gə-'lant, gə-'länt, 'ga-lənt\ *noun* (14th century)
1 : a young man of fashion
2 a : LADIES' MAN **b :** SUITOR **c :** PARAMOUR

²gal·lant \'ga-lənt (*usually in sense 2*); gə-'lant, gə-'länt (*usually in sense 3*)\ *adjective* [Middle English *galaunt*, from Middle French *galant*, from present participle of *galer* to have a good time, from *gale* pleasure, of Germanic origin; akin to Old English *wela* weal — more at WEAL] (15th century)
1 : showy in dress or bearing **:** SMART
2 a : SPLENDID, STATELY ⟨a *gallant* ship⟩ **b :** SPIRITED, BRAVE ⟨*gallant* efforts against the enemy⟩ **c :** nobly chivalrous and often self-sacrificing
3 : courteously and elaborately attentive especially to ladies
synonym see CIVIL
— **gal·lant·ly** *adverb*

³gal·lant \gə-'lant, -'länt\ (1672) *transitive verb*
1 : to pay court to (a lady) **:** ATTEND ⟨used to *gallant* her in his youth —Washington Irving⟩
2 *obsolete* **:** to manipulate (a fan) in a modish manner
intransitive verb
: to pay court to ladies

gal·lant·ry \'ga-lən-trē\ *noun, plural* **-ries** (1613)
1 *archaic* **:** gallant appearance
2 a : an act of marked courtesy **b :** courteous attention to a lady **c :** amorous attention or pursuit
3 : spirited and conspicuous bravery

gal·late \'ga-ˌlāt, 'gȯ-\ *noun* (1794)
: a salt or ester of gallic acid

gall·blad·der \'gȯl-ˌbla-dər\ *noun* (1676)
: a membranous muscular sac in which bile from the liver is stored

gal·le·ass \'ga-lē-əs\ *noun* [Middle French *galeasse*, from Old French *galie* galley] (1544)
: a large fast galley used especially as a warship by Mediterranean countries in the 16th and 17th centuries and having both sails and oars but usually propelled chiefly by rowing

gal·le·on \'ga-lē-on\ *noun* [Old Spanish *galeón*, from Middle French *galion*, from Old French *galie*] (1529)
: a heavy square-rigged sailing ship of the 15th to early 18th centuries used for war or commerce especially by the Spanish

galleon

gal·le·ria \,ga-lə-'rē-ə\ *noun* [Italian, gallery, from Medieval Latin *galeria*] (circa 1901)
: a roofed and usually glass-enclosed promenade or court (as at a mall)

gal·lery \'ga-lə-rē, 'gal-rē\ *noun, plural* **-ler·ies** [Middle English *galerie*, from Medieval Latin *galeria*, probably alteration of *galilaea* galilee] (15th century)
1 a : a roofed promenade : COLONNADE **b** : CORRIDOR
2 a : an outdoor balcony **b** *Southern & Midland* : PORCH, VERANDA **c** : a platform at the quarters or stern of a ship
3 a : a long and narrow passage, apartment, or corridor **b** : a subterranean passageway in a cave or military mining system; *also* : a working drift or level in mining **c** : an underground passage made by a mole or ant or a passage made in wood by an insect
4 a : a room or building devoted to the exhibition of works of art **b** : an institution or business exhibiting or dealing in works of art **c** : COLLECTION, AGGREGATION ⟨the rich *gallery* of characters in this novel —H. S. Canby⟩
5 a : a structure projecting from one or more interior walls of an auditorium to accommodate additional people; *especially* : the highest balcony in a theater commonly having the cheapest seats **b** : the part of a theater audience seated in the top gallery **c** : the undiscriminating general public **d** : the spectators at a tennis or golf match
6 : a small ornamental barrier or railing (as along the edge of a table or shelf)
7 : a photographer's studio
— **gal·ler·ied** \-rēd\ *adjective*
— **gal·lery·ite** \-rē-,īt\ *noun*

gallery forest *noun* (1920)
: a forest growing along a watercourse in a region otherwise devoid of trees

gal·lery-go·er \'ga-lə-rē-,gō(-ə)r, 'gal-rē-\ *noun* (1888)
: one who frequently goes to art galleries

ga·lle·ta \gə-'ye-tə, gī-'e-tə\ *noun* [Spanish, hardtack] (1872)
: either of two perennial forage grasses (*Hilaria rigida* and *H. jamesii*) used for hay in the southwestern U.S. and in Mexico

gal·ley \'ga-lē\ *noun, plural* **galleys** [Middle English *galeie*, from Old French *galie, galee*, ultimately from Middle Greek *galea*] (13th century)
1 : a ship or boat propelled solely or chiefly by oars: as **a** : a long low ship used for war and trading especially in the Mediterranean Sea from the Middle Ages to the 19th century; *also* : GALLEASS **b** : a warship of classical antiquity — compare BIREME, TRIREME **c** : a large open boat (as a gig) formerly used in England
2 : the kitchen and cooking apparatus especially of a ship or airplane
3 a : an oblong tray to hold especially a single column of set type **b** : a proof of typeset matter especially in a single column before being made into pages

gal·ley-west \,ga-lē-'west\ *adverb* [probably alteration of English dialect *collywest* (badly askew)] (1875)
: into destruction or confusion ⟨was knocked *galley-west*⟩

gall·fly \'gȯl-,flī\ *noun* (circa 1834)
: an insect (as a gall wasp) that deposits its eggs in plants causing the formation of galls in which the larvae feed

¹gal·liard \'gal-yərd\ *adjective* [Middle English *gaillard*, from Middle French] (14th century)
archaic : GAY, LIVELY

²galliard *noun* (1533)
: a sprightly dance with five steps to a phrase popular in the 16th and 17th centuries

Gal·lic \'ga-lik\ *adjective* [Latin *Gallicus*, from *Gallia* Gaul] (1672)
: of or relating to Gaul or France

gallic acid \'ga-lik-, 'gȯ-lik-\ *noun* [French *gallique*, from *galle* gall] (1791)
: a white crystalline acid $C_7H_6O_5$ found widely in plants or combined in tannins and used especially in dyes and as a photographic developer

Gal·li·can \'ga-li-kən\ *adjective* (14th century)
1 : GALLIC
2 *often not capitalized* : of or relating to Gallicanism
— **Gallican** *noun*

Gal·li·can·ism \-kə-,ni-zəm\ *noun* (1858)
: a movement originating in France and advocating administrative independence from papal control for the Roman Catholic Church in each nation

gal·li·cism \'ga-lə-,si-zəm\ *noun, often capitalized* (circa 1656)
1 : a characteristic French idiom or expression appearing in another language
2 : a French trait

gal·li·cize \-,sīz\ *transitive verb* **-cized; -ciz·ing** *often capitalized* (1773)
: to cause to conform to a French mode or idiom
— **gal·li·ci·za·tion** \,ga-lə-sə-'zā-shən\ *noun, often capitalized*

gal·li·gas·kins \,ga-li-'gas-kənz\ *noun plural* [probably modification of Middle French *garguesques*, from Old Spanish *gregüescos*, from *griego* Greek, from Latin *Graecus*] (1577)
1 a : loose wide hose or breeches worn in the 16th and 17th centuries **b** : very loose trousers
2 *dialect chiefly British* : LEGGINGS

gal·li·mau·fry \,ga-lə-'mȯ-frē\ *noun, plural* **-fries** [Middle French *galimafree* stew] (circa 1556)
: HODGEPODGE ⟨a *gallimaufry* of opinions⟩

gal·li·na·ceous \,ga-lə-'nā-shəs\ *adjective* [Latin *gallinaceus* of domestic fowl, from *gallina* hen, from *gallus* cock] (1783)
: of or relating to an order (Galliformes) of heavy-bodied largely terrestrial birds including the pheasants, turkeys, grouse, and the common domestic fowl

gall·ing \'gȯ-liŋ\ *adjective* [³*gall*] (1583)
: markedly irritating : VEXING ⟨a most *galling* defeat⟩
— **gall·ing·ly** \-liŋ-lē\ *adverb*

gal·li·nip·per \'ga-lə-,ni-pər\ *noun* [origin unknown] (1709)
chiefly Southern & Midland : any of various insects (as a large mosquito or crane fly)

gal·li·nule \'ga-lə-,nü(ə)l, -,nyü(ə)l\ *noun* [New Latin *Gallinula*, genus of birds, from Latin, pullet, diminutive of *gallina*] (1776)
: any of several aquatic birds of the rail family with long thin feet and a platelike frontal area on the head; *especially* : one (*Gallinula chloropus*) widespread in the New World, Eurasia, and Africa that has a largely red bill, red frontal area on the head, and a white band on the flanks

gal·li·ot \'ga-lē-ət\ *noun* [Middle English *galiote*, from Middle French, from Medieval Latin *galeota*, diminutive of *galea* galley, from Middle Greek] (14th century)
1 : a small swift galley formerly used in the Mediterranean
2 [Dutch *galjoot*, from Middle French *galiote*] : a long narrow shallow-draft Dutch merchant sailing ship

gal·li·pot \'ga-li-,pät\ *noun* [Middle English *galy pott*] (15th century)
1 : a small usually ceramic vessel
2 *archaic* : DRUGGIST

gal·li·um \'ga-lē-əm\ *noun* [New Latin, from Latin *gallus* cock (intended as translation of surname of Paul *Lecoq* de Boisbaudran (died 1912) French chemist)] (1875)
: a rare bluish white metallic element that is hard and brittle at low temperatures but melts just above room temperature and expands on freezing — see ELEMENT table

gallium arsenide *noun* (circa 1961)
: a synthetic compound GaAs used especially as a semiconducting material

gal·li·vant \'ga-lə-,vant\ *intransitive verb* [perhaps alteration of ³*gallant*] (1823)
1 : to go about usually ostentatiously or indiscreetly with members of the opposite sex
2 : to travel, roam, or move about for pleasure

gall midge *noun* (circa 1889)
: any of numerous minute dipteran flies (family Cecidomyiidae) most of which cause gall formation in plants

gall mite *noun* (1881)
: any of various minute 4-legged mites (family Eriophyidae) that form galls on plants

gall·nut \'gȯl-,nət\ *noun* [⁴*gall*] (1572)
: a gall resembling a nut

gal·lon \'ga-lən\ *noun* [Middle English *galon*, a liquid measure, from Old North French, from Medieval Latin *galeta* pail, a liquid measure] (13th century)
: a unit of liquid capacity equal to 231 cubic inches or four quarts — see WEIGHT table

gal·lon·age \'ga-lə-nij\ *noun* (circa 1909)
: amount in gallons

gal·loon \gə-'lün\ *noun* [French *galon*] (1604)
: a narrow trimming (as of lace, embroidery, or braid with metallic threads) having both edges scalloped

¹gal·lop \'ga-ləp\ (15th century)
intransitive verb
1 : to progress or ride at a gallop
2 : to run fast
transitive verb
1 : to cause to gallop
2 : to transport at a gallop
— **gal·lop·er** *noun*

²gallop *noun* [Middle French *galop*] (1523)
1 : a bounding gait of a quadruped; *specifically* : a fast natural 3-beat gait of the horse — compare ³CANTER, RUN
2 : a ride or run at a gallop
3 : a stretch of land suitable for galloping horses
4 : a rapid or hasty progression or pace

gal·lo·pade \,ga-lə-'pād, -'päd\ *noun* (1831)
: GALOP

Gal·lo·phile \'ga-lə-,fīl\ *adjective* [Latin *Gallus* Gaul + English *-phile*] (1923)
: FRANCOPHILE
— **Gallophile** *noun*

gal·lop·ing *adjective* (1642)
: progressing, developing, or increasing rapidly ⟨*galloping* inflation⟩ ⟨a *galloping* farce⟩ ⟨*galloping* alcoholism⟩

Gal·lo·way \'ga-lə-,wā\ *noun* [*Galloway*, Scotland] (1805)
: any of a breed of hardy medium-sized hornless chiefly black beef cattle native to southwestern Scotland

gal·low·glass \'ga-lō-,glas\ *noun* [alteration of Irish *gallóglach*, from *gall* foreigner + *óglach* young man, warrior] (circa 1515)
1 : a mercenary or retainer of an Irish chief
2 : an armed Irish foot soldier

¹gal·lows \'ga-(,)lōz, -ləz, *in sense 3 also* -ləs\ *noun, plural* **gallows** *or* **gal·lows·es** [Middle English *galwes*, plural of *galwe*, from Old English *gealga*; akin to Old Norse *gelgja* pole, stake, Armenian *jałk* twig] (before 12th century)
1 a : a frame usually of two upright posts and a transverse beam from which criminals are hanged — called also *gallows tree* **b** : the punishment of hanging
2 : a structure consisting of an upright frame with a crosspiece
3 : SUSPENDER 2a

²gallows *adjective* (15th century)
: deserving the gallows

gallows bird *noun* (circa 1785)
: a person who deserves hanging

gallows humor *noun* (1901)
: humor that makes fun of a life-threatening, disastrous, or terrifying situation

gall·stone \'gȯl-,stōn\ *noun* (1758)

: a calculus formed in the gallbladder or biliary passages

gal·lus \'ga-ləs\ *noun* [alteration of ¹*gallows*] (1836)

: SUSPENDER 2a — usually used in plural

gal·lused \'ga-ləst\ *adjective* (1927)

: wearing galluses

gall wasp *noun* (1879)

: any of a family (Cynipidae) of hymenopterous gallflies

gal·ly \'ga-lē\ *transitive verb* **gal·lied; gal·ly·ing** [origin unknown] (1605)

chiefly dialect **:** FRIGHTEN, TERRIFY

Ga·lois theory \(ˌ)gal-'wä-, 'gal-ˌwä-\ *noun* [Évariste *Galois*] (1893)

: a part of the theory of mathematical groups concerned especially with the conditions under which a solution to a polynomial equation with coefficients in a given mathematical field can be obtained in the field by the repetition of operations and the extraction of nth roots

ga·loot \gə-'lüt\ *noun* [origin unknown] (1866)

slang **:** FELLOW; *especially* **:** one who is strange or foolish

ga·lop \'ga-ləp, ga-'lō\ *noun* [French] (1831)

: a lively dance in duple measure; *also* **:** the music of a galop

ga·lore \gə-'lōr, -'lȯr\ *adjective* [Irish *go leor* enough] (1628)

: ABUNDANT, PLENTIFUL — used postpositively ⟨bargains *galore*⟩

ga·losh \gə-'läsh\ *noun* [Middle English *galoche*, from Middle French] (14th century)

1 *obsolete* **:** a shoe with a heavy sole

2 : a high overshoe worn especially in snow and slush

— **ga·loshed** \-'läsht\ *adjective*

ga·lumph \gə-'ləm(p)f\ *intransitive verb* [probably alteration of ¹*gallop*] (1872)

: to move with a clumsy heavy tread

gal·van·ic \gal-'va-nik\ *adjective* (1797)

1 : of, relating to, or producing a direct current of electricity ⟨a *galvanic* cell⟩

2 a : having an electric effect **:** intensely exciting ⟨a *galvanic* performance⟩ **b :** produced as if by an electric shock ⟨had a *galvanic* effect on the audience⟩

— **gal·van·i·cal·ly** \-ni-k(ə-)lē\ *adverb*

galvanic skin response *noun* (1942)

: a change in the electrical resistance of the skin that is a physiochemical response to an emotional change

gal·va·nise *British variant of* GALVANIZE

gal·va·nism \'gal-və-ˌni-zəm\ *noun* [French or Italian; French *galvanisme*, from Italian *galvanismo*, from Luigi *Galvani*] (1797)

1 : a direct current of electricity especially when produced by chemical action

2 : the therapeutic use of direct electric current

3 : vital or forceful activity

gal·va·nize \'gal-və-ˌnīz\ *verb* **-nized; -niz·ing** (1802)

transitive verb

1 a : to subject to the action of an electric current especially for the purpose of stimulating physiologically ⟨*galvanize* a muscle⟩ **b :** to stimulate or excite as if by an electric shock ⟨an issue that would *galvanize* public opinion⟩

2 : to coat (iron or steel) with zinc; *especially* **:** to immerse in molten zinc to produce a coating of zinc-iron alloy

intransitive verb

: to react as if stimulated by an electric shock ⟨they *galvanized* into action⟩

— **gal·va·ni·za·tion** \ˌgal-və-nə-'zā-shən\ *noun*

— **gal·va·niz·er** \'gal-və-ˌnī-zər\ *noun*

galvano- *combining form* [*galvanic*]

: galvanic current ⟨*galvanometer*⟩

gal·va·nom·e·ter \ˌgal-və-'nä-mə-tər\ *noun* (1802)

: an instrument for detecting or measuring a small electric current by movements of a magnetic needle or of a coil in a magnetic field

— **gal·va·no·met·ric** \-nō-'me-trik\ *adjective*

gal·va·no·scope \gal-'va-nə-ˌskōp, 'gal-və-nə-\ *noun* (1832)

: an instrument for detecting the presence and direction of an electric current by the deflection of a magnetic needle

¹gam \'gam\ *noun* [probably ultimately from Lingua Franca *gamba* leg, from Italian, from Late Latin] (1781)

slang **:** LEG

²gam *noun* [perhaps short for obsolete *gammon* (talk)] (1846)

1 : a visit or friendly conversation at sea or ashore especially between whalers

2 : a school of whales

³gam *verb* **gammed; gam·ming** (1849)

intransitive verb

: to engage in a gam

transitive verb

1 : to have a gam with

2 : to spend or pass (as time) talking

gam- *or* **gamo-** *combining form* [New Latin, from Greek, from *gamos*, from *gamein* to marry]

: united **:** joined ⟨*gamo*petalous⟩

gama grass \'ga-mə-\ *noun* [probably alteration of *grama*] (1833)

: a tall coarse American grass (*Tripsacum dactyloides*) valuable for forage

ga·may \ga-'mā, 'ga-ˌmā\ *noun, often capitalized* [French, from *Gamay*, village in Burgundy] (circa 1941)

: a light dry red table wine made from the same grape used for French Beaujolais ⟨*gamay* rosé⟩

gam·ba \'gäm-bə, 'gam-\ *noun* (1598)

: VIOLA DA GAMBA

¹gam·ba·do \gam-'bā-(ˌ)dō\ *noun, plural* **-does** *also* **-dos** [perhaps modification of Italian *gambale*, from *gamba* leg] (circa 1656)

: a horseman's legging

²gambado *noun, plural* **-does** *also* **-dos** [modification of French *gambade* — more at GAMBOL] (1820)

1 : a spring of a horse

2 : CAPER, GAMBOL

gam·bier *also* **gam·bir** \'gam-ˌbir\ *noun* [Malay *gambir*] (1830)

: a yellowish catechu that is obtained from a Malayan woody vine (*Uncaria gambir*) of the madder family and is used for chewing with the betel nut and for tanning and dyeing

gam·bit \'gam-bət\ *noun* [Italian *gambetto*, literally, act of tripping someone, from *gamba* leg, from Late Latin *gamba, camba*, from Greek *kampē* bend; probably akin to Gothic *hamfs* maimed, Lithuanian *kampas* corner] (1656)

1 : a chess opening in which a player risks one or more minor pieces to gain an advantage in position

2 a (1) : a remark intended to start a conversation or make a telling point **(2) :** TOPIC **b :** a calculated move **:** STRATAGEM

¹gam·ble \'gam-bəl\ *verb* **gam·bled; gam·bling** \-b(ə-)liŋ\ [probably back-formation from *gambler*, probably alteration of obsolete *gamner*, from obsolete *gamen* (to play)] (circa 1775)

intransitive verb

1 a : to play a game for money or property **b :** to bet on an uncertain outcome

2 : to stake something on a contingency **:** take a chance

transitive verb

1 : to risk by gambling **:** WAGER

2 : VENTURE, HAZARD

— **gam·bler** \-blər\ *noun*

²gamble *noun* (1823)

1 a : an act having an element of risk **b :** something chancy

2 : the playing of a game of chance for stakes

gam·boge \gam-'bōj, -'büzh\ *noun* [New Latin *gambogium*, alteration of *cambugium*, from or akin to Portuguese *Camboja* Cambodia] (1712)

1 : an orange to brown gum resin from southeast Asian trees (genus *Garcinia*) of the Saint-John's-wort family that is used as a yellow pigment and cathartic

2 : a strong yellow

¹gam·bol \'gam-bəl\ *intransitive verb* **-boled** *or* **-bolled; -bol·ing** *or* **-bol·ling** \-bə-liŋ *also* -bliŋ\ (1508)

: to skip about in play **:** FRISK, FROLIC

²gambol *noun* [modification of Middle French *gambade* spring of a horse, gambol, probably from Old Provençal *camba* leg, from Late Latin] (circa 1510)

: a skipping or leaping about in play

gam·brel \'gam-brəl\ *noun* [Old North French *gamberel*, from *gambe* leg, from Late Latin *gamba*] (1547)

: a stick or iron for suspending slaughtered animals

gambrel roof *noun* (1765)

: a roof with a lower steeper slope and an upper less steep one on each of its two sides — see ROOF illustration

gam·bu·sia \gam-'bü-zh(ē-)ə, -'byü-\ *noun* [New Latin, modification of American Spanish *gambusino* gambusia] (circa 1889)

: any of a genus (*Gambusia*) of live-bearers (family Poeciliidae) introduced as exterminators of mosquito larvae in warm fresh waters

¹game \'gām\ *noun* [Middle English, from Old English *gamen*; akin to Old High German *gaman* amusement] (before 12th century)

1 a (1) : activity engaged in for diversion or amusement **:** PLAY **(2) :** the equipment for a game **b :** often derisive or mocking jesting **:** FUN, SPORT ⟨make *game* of a nervous player⟩

2 a : a procedure or strategy for gaining an end **:** TACTIC **b :** an illegal or shady scheme or maneuver **:** RACKET

3 a (1) : a physical or mental competition conducted according to rules with the participants in direct opposition to each other **(2) :** a division of a larger contest **(3) :** the number of points necessary to win **(4) :** points scored in certain card games (as in all fours) by a player whose cards count up the highest **(5) :** the manner of playing in a contest **(6) :** the set of rules governing a game **(7) :** a particular aspect or phase of play in a game or sport ⟨a football team's kicking *game*⟩ **b** *plural* **:** organized athletics **c (1) :** a field of gainful activity **:** LINE ⟨the newspaper *game*⟩ **(2) :** any activity undertaken or regarded as a contest involving rivalry, strategy, or struggle ⟨the dating *game*⟩ ⟨the *game* of politics⟩; *also* **:** the course or period of such an activity ⟨got into aviation early in the *game*⟩ **(3) :** area of expertise **:** SPECIALTY 3 ⟨comedy is not my *game*⟩

4 a (1) : animals under pursuit or taken in hunting; *especially* **:** wild animals hunted for sport or food **(2) :** the flesh of game animals **b** *archaic* **:** PLUCK **c :** a target or object especially of ridicule or attack — often used in the phrase *fair game*

synonym see FUN

— **game·like** \-ˌlīk\ *adjective*

²game *verb* **gamed; gam·ing** (1529)

intransitive verb

: to play for a stake

transitive verb

archaic **:** to lose or squander by gambling

³game *adjective* (1610)

1 a : having or showing a resolute unyielding spirit ⟨*game* to the end⟩ **b :** willing or ready to proceed ⟨were *game* for anything⟩

2 : of or relating to game ⟨*game* laws⟩

— **game·ly** *adverb*

— **game·ness** *noun*

\ə\ abut \ᵊ\ kitten \ər\ further \a\ ash \ā\ ace
\ä\ mop, mar \au̇\ out \ch\ chin \e\ bet \ē\ easy
\g\ go \i\ hit \ī\ ice \j\ job \ŋ\ sing \ō\ go
\ȯ\ law \ȯi\ boy \th\ thin \t͟h\ the \ü\ loot \u̇\ foot
\y\ yet \zh\ vision *see also* Guide to Pronunciation

⁴game *adjective* [origin unknown] (circa 1787)
: LAME ⟨a *game* leg⟩

game ball *noun* (1966)
: a ball (as a football) presented to a player or coach in recognition of an outstanding contribution to a team victory

game bird *noun* (1866)
: a bird that may be legally hunted according to the laws especially of a state of the U.S.

game·cock \'gām-ˌkäk\ *noun* (1677)
: a rooster of the domestic chicken trained for fighting

game fish *noun* (1862)
1 : a fish of a family (Salmonidae) including salmons, trouts, chars, and whitefishes
2 : SPORT FISH; *especially* : a fish made a legal catch by law

game·keep·er \'gām-ˌkē-pər\ *noun* (circa 1671)
: a person in charge of the breeding and protection of game animals or birds on a private preserve

gam·elan \'ga-mə-ˌlan\ *noun* [Javanese] (1817)
: an Indonesian orchestra made up especially of percussion instruments (as gongs, xylophones, and drums)

game of chance (circa 1925)
: a game (as a dice game) in which chance rather than skill determines the outcome

game plan *noun* (1941)
: a strategy for achieving an objective

game point *noun* (circa 1949)
: a situation (as in tennis) in which one player will win the game by winning the next point; *also* : the point itself

gam·er \'gā-mər\ *noun* (circa 1630)
: a player who is game; *especially* : an athlete who relishes competition

game show *noun* (1958)
: a television program on which contestants compete for prizes in a game (as a quiz)

games·man \'gāmz-mən, -ˌman\ *noun* (1947)
: one who practices gamesmanship; *also* : one who plays games

games·man·ship \'gāmz-mən-ˌship\ *noun* (1947)
1 : the art or practice of winning games by questionable expedients without actually violating the rules
2 : the use of ethically dubious methods to gain an objective ◇

game·some \'gām-səm\ *adjective* [Middle English] (14th century)
: MERRY, FROLICSOME
— **game·some·ly** *adverb*
— **game·some·ness** *noun*

game·ster \'gām-stər\ *noun* (1553)
: one who plays games; *especially* : GAMBLER

gamet- *or* **gameto-** *combining form* [New Latin, from *gameta*]
: gamete ⟨*gameto*phore⟩

gam·etan·gi·um \ˌga-mə-'tan-jē-əm\ *noun*, *plural* **-gia** \-jē-ə\ [New Latin, from *gamet-* + Greek *angeion* vessel — more at ANGI-] (1886)
: a cell or organ in which gametes are developed

gam·ete \'ga-ˌmēt *also* gə-'mēt\ *noun* [New Latin *gameta*, from Greek *gametēs* husband, from *gamein* to marry] (1886)
: a mature male or female germ cell usually possessing a haploid chromosome set and capable of initiating formation of a new diploid individual by fusion with a gamete of the opposite sex
— **ga·met·ic** \gə-'me-tik, -'mē-\ *adjective*
— **ga·met·i·cal·ly** \-ti-k(ə-)lē\ *adverb*

game theory *noun* (1949)
: the analysis of a situation involving conflicting interests (as in business or military strategy) in terms of gains and losses among opposing players
— **game theorist** *noun*

ga·me·to·cyte \gə-'mē-tə-ˌsīt\ *noun* [International Scientific Vocabulary] (1899)
: a cell (as of a protozoan causing malaria) that divides to produce gametes

ga·me·to·gen·e·sis \gə-ˌmē-tə-'je-nə-səs, ˌga-mə-tə-\ *noun* [New Latin] (circa 1900)
: the production of gametes
— **ga·me·to·gen·ic** \-'je-nik\ *or* **gam·etog·e·nous** \ˌga-mə-'tä-jə-nəs\ *adjective*

ga·me·to·phore \gə-'mē-tə-ˌfōr, -ˌfȯr\ *noun* (1895)
: a modified branch (as of a moss) bearing gametangia

ga·me·to·phyte \gə-'mē-tə-ˌfīt\ *noun* [International Scientific Vocabulary] (circa 1889)
: the individual or generation of a plant exhibiting alternation of generations that bears sex organs — compare SPOROPHYTE
— **ga·me·to·phyt·ic** \-ˌmē-tə-'fi-tik\ *adjective*

-gamic *adjective combining form* [International Scientific Vocabulary, from Greek *-gamos* *-gamous*]
: having (such) reproductive organs ⟨cleisto*gamic*⟩

gam·in \'ga-mən\ *noun* [French] (1840)
1 : a boy who hangs around on the streets : URCHIN
2 : GAMINE 2

¹ga·mine \ga-'mēn, 'ga-ˌmēn\ *noun* [French, feminine of *gamin*] (1889)
1 : a girl who hangs around on the streets
2 : a small playfully mischievous girl

²gamine *adjective* (1925)
: of, relating to, or suggesting a gamine

gam·ing \'gā-miŋ\ *noun* (1501)
1 : the practice of gambling
2 : the playing of games that simulate actual conditions (as of business or war) especially for training or testing purposes

¹gam·ma \'ga-mə\ *noun* [Middle English, from Late Latin, from Greek, of Semitic origin; akin to Hebrew *gīmel* gimel] (15th century)
1 : the 3d letter of the Greek alphabet — see ALPHABET table
2 : the degree of contrast of a developed photographic image or of a television image
3 : a unit of magnetic flux density equal to one nanotesla
4 : GAMMA RAY — usually used as the attributive form of gamma ray ⟨*gamma* counter⟩
5 : MICROGRAM

²gamma *adjective* (1896)
1 : of, relating to, or being one of three or more closely related chemical substances
2 : third in position in the structure of an organic molecule from a particular group or atom — symbol γ

gam·ma-ami·no·bu·tyr·ic acid \ˌga-mə-ə-ˌmē-(ˌ)nō-byü-'tir-ik-, ˌga-mə-ˌa-mə-(ˌ)nō-\ *noun* (1957)
: an amino acid $C_4H_9NO_2$ that is a neurotransmitter in the central nervous system

gamma camera *noun* (1964)
: a camera that detects the radiation from a radioactive tracer injected into the body and is used especially in medical diagnostic scanning

gamma globulin *noun* (1937)
1 a : a protein fraction of blood rich in antibodies **b** : a sterile solution of gamma globulin from pooled human blood administered especially for passive immunity against measles, German measles, infectious hepatitis, or poliomyelitis
2 : any of numerous globulins of blood plasma or serum that have less electrophoretic mobility at alkaline pH than serum albumins, alpha globulins, or beta globulins and that include most antibodies — compare ANTIBODY

gamma radiation *noun* (1904)
: radiation composed of gamma rays

gamma ray *noun* (1903)
: a photon emitted spontaneously by a radioactive substance; *also* : a high-energy photon — usually used in plural

gam·mer \'ga-mər\ *noun* [alteration of *godmother*] (1575)
archaic : an old woman — compare GAFFER

¹gam·mon \'ga-mən\ *noun* [Middle English, from Old North French *gambon* ham, from *gambe* leg — more at GAM] (15th century)
1 *chiefly British* : HAM 2
2 *chiefly British* **a** : a side of bacon **b** : the lower end of a side of bacon

²gammon *noun* [perhaps alteration of Middle English *gamen* game] (circa 1734)
1 *archaic* : BACKGAMMON
2 : the winning of a backgammon game before the loser removes any men from the board

³gammon *transitive verb* (1735)
: to beat by scoring a gammon

⁴gammon (1789)
intransitive verb
1 : to talk gammon
2 : PRETEND, FEIGN
transitive verb
: DECEIVE, FOOL

⁵gammon *noun* [obsolete *gammon* (talk)] (1805)
: talk intended to deceive : HUMBUG

gam·my \'ga-mē\ *adjective* [perhaps from *⁴game*] (1870)
British : LAME, GAME

gamo- — see GAM-

gamo·pet·al·ous \ˌga-mə-'pe-tᵊl-əs\ *adjective* (1830)
: having the corolla composed of united petals ⟨the morning glory is *gamo*petalous⟩

-gamous *adjective combining form* [Greek *-gamos*, from *gamos* marriage, from *gamein* to marry]
1 : characterized by having or practicing (such) a marriage or (such or so many) marriages ⟨exo*gamous*⟩
2 : -GAMIC ⟨hetero*gamous*⟩

gamp \'gamp\ *noun* [Sarah *Gamp*, nurse with a large umbrella in *Martin Chuzzlewit* by Charles Dickens] (1864)
British : a large umbrella

gam·ut \'ga-mət\ *noun* [Medieval Latin *gamma*, lowest note of a medieval scale (from Late Latin, 3d letter of the Greek alphabet) + *ut* ut] (15th century)
1 : the whole series of recognized musical notes

2 : an entire range or series ⟨ran the *gamut* from praise to contempt⟩ ◇
synonym see RANGE

gamy *or* **gam·ey** \'gā-mē\ *adjective* **gam·i·er; -est** (1844)
1 : BRAVE, PLUCKY — used especially of animals
2 a : having the flavor of game; *especially* : having the flavor of game near tainting **b** : SMELLY
3 a : SORDID, SCANDALOUS ⟨gave us all the *gamy* details⟩ **b** : CORRUPT, DISREPUTABLE ⟨a *gamy* character⟩ **c** : sexually suggestive : RACY ⟨*gamy* witticisms⟩
— **gam·i·ly** \-mə-lē\ *adverb*
— **gam·i·ness** \-mē-nəs\ *noun*

-gamy *noun combining form* [Middle English *-gamie*, from Late Latin *-gamia*, from Greek, from *gamein* to marry]
1 : marriage ⟨exo*gamy*⟩
2 : union for propagation or reproduction ⟨allo*gamy*⟩
3 : possession of (such) reproductive organs or (such) a mode of fertilization ⟨cleisto*gamy*⟩

gan *past of* GIN

ga·nache \(ˌ)gä-'näsh, gə-\ *noun* [French, literally, jowl, from Italian *ganascia*, modification of Greek *gnathos* jaw — more at -GNATHOUS] (1977)
: a sweet creamy chocolate mixture used especially as a filling or frosting

Gan·da \'gan-də, 'gän-\ *noun, plural* **Ganda** *or* **Gandas** (1934)
1 : a member of a Bantu-speaking people of Uganda
2 : LUGANDA

¹gan·der \'gan-dər\ *noun* [Middle English, from Old English *gandra*; akin to Old English *gōs* goose] (before 12th century)
1 : the adult male goose
2 : SIMPLETON

²gander *noun* [probably from ¹*gander*; from the outstretched neck of a person craning to look at something] (circa 1914)
: LOOK, GLANCE ⟨take a *gander*⟩

gan·dy dancer \'gan-dē-\ *noun* [origin unknown] (1923)
1 : a laborer in a railroad section gang
2 : an itinerant or seasonal laborer ◇

ga·nef \'gä-nəf\ *noun* [Yiddish, from Hebrew *gannābh* thief] (1923)
slang : THIEF, RASCAL

Ga·ne·lon \ˌga-nᵊl-'ōⁿ\ *noun* [French]
: the traitor in the Charlemagne romances who is responsible for the death of Roland

¹gang \'gaŋ\ *intransitive verb* [Middle English, from Old English; akin to Lithuanian *žengti* to stride] (before 12th century)
Scottish : GO

²gang *noun* [Middle English, walking, journey, from Old English; akin to Old English *gangan*] (15th century)
1 a (1) : a set of articles : OUTFIT ⟨a *gang* of oars⟩ (2) : a combination of similar implements or devices arranged for convenience to act together ⟨a *gang* of saws⟩ **b** : GROUP: as (1) : a group of persons working together (2) : a group of persons working to unlawful or antisocial ends; *especially* : a band of antisocial adolescents
2 : a group of persons having informal and usually close social relations

³gang (1856)
transitive verb
1 a : to assemble or operate simultaneously as a group **b** : to arrange in or produce as a gang
2 : to attack in a gang
intransitive verb
: to move or act as a gang

gang bang *noun* (1950)
1 : copulation by several persons in succession with the same passive partner — often considered vulgar
2 : GANG RAPE — often considered vulgar
— **gang–bang** *verb*

gang·bang·er \'gaŋ-ˌbaŋ-ər\ *noun* (circa 1972)
: a member of a street gang

gang·bust·er \'gaŋ-ˌbəs-tər\ *noun* (1940)
: one engaged in the aggressive breakup of organized criminal gangs
— **like gangbusters** : with great or excessive force or aggressiveness ⟨came on *like gangbusters*⟩; *also* : with great speed or success ⟨making money *like gangbusters* —Martha Hume⟩

gangbusters *also* **gangbuster** *adjective* (1971)
: outstandingly excellent or successful ⟨doesn't make her a *gangbusters* . . . player —Tim Allis⟩
— **gangbusters** *adverb*

gang·er \'gaŋ-ər\ *noun* (1849)
British : the foreman of a gang of workers

gang hook *noun* (circa 1934)
: two or three fishhooks with their shanks joined together

gang·land \'gaŋ-ˌland, -lənd\ *noun, often attributive* (1912)
: the world of organized crime

gan·gling \'gaŋ-gliŋ, -glən\ *adjective* [perhaps alteration of Scots *gangrel* vagrant, lanky person] (circa 1825)
: loosely and awkwardly built : LANKY

gan·gli·on \'gaŋ-glē-ən\ *noun, plural* **-glia** \-glē-ə\ *also* **-gli·ons** [Late Latin, from Greek] (circa 1681)
1 : a small cystic tumor connected either with a joint membrane or tendon sheath
2 a : a mass of nerve tissue containing nerve cells external to the brain or spinal cord; *also* : NUCLEUS 2b **b** : something likened to a nerve ganglion
— **gan·gli·on·at·ed** \'gaŋ-glē-ə-ˌnā-təd\ *adjective*
— **gan·gli·on·ic** \ˌgaŋ-glē-'ä-nik\ *adjective*

gan·gli·o·side \'gaŋ-glē-ə-ˌsīd\ *noun* [International Scientific Vocabulary *ganglion* + ²-*ose* + -*ide*] (1943)
: any of a group of glycolipids that yield a hexose sugar on hydrolysis and are found especially in the plasma membrane of cells of the gray matter

gan·gly \'gaŋ-glē\ *adjective* **gan·gli·er; -est** (1872)
: GANGLING

gang·plank \'gaŋ-ˌplaŋk\ *noun* (1846)
: a movable bridge used in boarding or leaving a ship at a pier

gang·plow \-ˌplau̇\ *noun* (1850)
: a plow designed to turn two or more furrows at one time

gang rape *noun* (1968)
: rape of one person by several attackers in succession
— **gang–rape** *transitive verb*

gang·rel \'gaŋ-(ə-)rəl\ *noun* [Middle English, from *gangen* to go, from Old English *gangan*] (14th century)
Scottish : VAGRANT

¹gan·grene \'gaŋ-ˌgrēn, gaŋ-', 'gan-ˌ, gan-'\ *noun* [Latin *gangraena*, from Greek *gangraina*; akin to Greek *gran* to gnaw] (1543)
1 : local death of soft tissues due to loss of blood supply
2 : pervasive decay or corruption : ROT ⟨moral *gangrene*⟩
— **gan·gre·nous** \'gaŋ-grə-nəs\ *adjective*

²gangrene *verb* **gan·grened; gan·gren·ing** (1607)
transitive verb
: to make gangrenous
intransitive verb
: to become gangrenous

gang·ster \'gaŋ-stər\ *noun* (1896)
: a member of a gang of criminals : RACKETEER
— **gang·ster·dom** \-dəm\ *noun*
— **gang·ster·ish** \-stə-rish\ *adjective*
— **gang·ster·ism** \-stə-ˌri-zəm\ *noun*

gang–tackle \'gaŋ-ˌta-kəl\ *transitive verb* (1951)
: to bring down (a ballcarrier in football) with several tacklers

gangue \'gaŋ\ *noun* [French, from German *Gang* vein of metal, from Old High German, act of going] (1809)
: the worthless rock or vein matter in which valuable metals or minerals occur

gang up *intransitive verb* (1925)
1 : to make a joint assault ⟨*ganged up* on him and beat him up⟩
2 : to combine for a specific purpose ⟨*ganged up* to raise prices⟩
3 : to exert group pressure ⟨the class *ganged up* against the teacher⟩

gang·way \'gaŋ-ˌwā\ *noun* (before 12th century)
1 : PASSAGEWAY; *especially* : a temporary way of planks
2 a : either of the sides of the upper deck of a ship **b** : the opening by which a ship is boarded **c** : GANGPLANK
3 *British* : AISLE
4 a : a cross aisle dividing the front benches from the backbenches in the British House of Commons **b** : an aisle in the British House of Commons that separates government and opposition benches
5 : a clear passage through a crowd — often used as an interjection

◇ **WORD HISTORY**

gamut In the 11th century, Guido d'Arezzo, a musician and former Benedictine monk, devised a system of musical notation that was later adopted throughout Europe. Guido's system consisted of groups of six notes, which he named *ut, re, mi, fa, sol,* and *la,* from the initial syllables of six lines of a Latin hymn to St. John the Baptist. Guido called the first line of the bass staff *gamma,* and we can assume that *gamma ut* was the term his followers used for the note falling on this line, that is, the first note of the lowest group of six. This was later contracted to *gamut* and used for the whole scale as well as the lowest note. The term was further generalized to mean the whole range of a voice or instrument. Eventually *gamut* came to be used for an entire range of any sort.

gandy dancer *Gandy dancer* is a colorful and now perhaps vanishing expression for a laborer who helped lay and maintain railroad tracks. Such work was hard, relatively unskilled, low-paying, and often taken up temporarily by homeless drifters, so that *gandy dancer* was also applied on occasion to itinerant laborers in general, as well as to hoboes. Though *dancer* plausibly alludes to the repetitive motion involved in tamping ballast around ties, the origin of *gandy* remains mysterious. It has been claimed that the word derives from the Gandy Manufacturing Company of Chicago, which supposedly made tools for section gangs, though no such business appears in Chicago city directories of the early part of the century, nor in railroad trade publications of the period. The suggestion that *gandy* is altered from *gander,* alluding to the rocking motion of a worker as he moved along the track, is phonetically implausible. *Gandy dancer,* like other originally slang and argot expressions, arose in a social milieu that left behind few written records to illuminate the context in which the phrase first was used.

\ə\ abut \ᵊ\ kitten \ər\ further \a\ ash \ā\ ace
\ä\ mop, mar \au̇\ out \ch\ chin \e\ bet \ē\ easy
\g\ go \i\ hit \ī\ ice \j\ job \ŋ\ sing \ō\ go
\ȯ\ law \ȯi\ boy \th\ thin \t͟h\ the \ü\ loot \u̇\ foot
\y\ yet \zh\ vision *see also* Guide to Pronunciation

gan·is·ter *also* **gan·nis·ter** \'ga-nə-stər\ *noun* [origin unknown] (1811)
: a fine-grained quartzite used in the manufacture of refractory brick

gan·ja \'gän-jə, 'gan-\ *noun* [Hindi *gā̃jā*, from Sanskrit *gañjā* hemp] (1689)
: a potent and selected preparation of marijuana used especially for smoking; *broadly* : MARIJUANA

gan·net \'ga-nət\ *noun, plural* **gannets** *also* **gannet** [Middle English *ganet*, from Old English *ganot;* akin to Old English *gōs* goose] (before 12th century)
: any of a genus (*Morus* of the family Sulidae) of large fish-eating seabirds that breed in colonies chiefly on offshore islands

¹**gan·oid** \'ga-ˌnȯid\ *adjective* [ultimately from Greek *ganos* brightness; akin to Greek *gēthein* to rejoice — more at JOY] (circa 1847)
: of, having, or being fish scales consisting of bone and an outer shiny layer resembling enamel; *also* : relating to or being fish with ganoid scales

²**ganoid** *noun* (circa 1839)
: a fish (as a sturgeon or gar) with ganoid scales

gante·lope *or* **gant·lope** \'gant-ˌlōp\ *noun* [modification of Swedish *gatlopp*, from Old Swedish *gatulop*, from *gata* road + *lop* course] (1646)
archaic : ²GAUNTLET

gant·let \'gȯnt-lət, 'gänt-\ *variant of* GAUNTLET

gan·try \'gan-trē\ *noun, plural* **gantries** [perhaps modification of Old North French *gantier*, from Latin *cantherius* trellis] (circa 1574)
1 : a frame for supporting barrels
2 : a frame structure raised on side supports so as to span over or around something: as **a** : a platform made to carry a traveling crane and supported by towers or side frames running on parallel tracks; *also* : a movable structure with platforms at different levels used for erecting and servicing rockets before launching **b** : a structure spanning several railroad tracks and displaying signals for each

Gan·y·mede \'ga-ni-ˌmēd\ *noun* [Latin *Ganymedes*, from Greek *Ganymēdēs*]
: a beautiful youth in classical mythology carried off to Olympus to be the cupbearer of the gods

gaol \'jā(ə)l\, **gaol·er** \'jā-lər\ *chiefly British variant of* JAIL, JAILER

¹**gap** \'gap\ *noun* [Middle English, from Old Norse, chasm, hole; akin to Old Norse *gapa* to gape] (14th century)
1 a : a break in a barrier (as a wall, hedge, or line of military defense) **b** : an assailable position
2 a : a mountain pass **b** : RAVINE
3 : SPARK GAP
4 a : a separation in space **b** : an incomplete or deficient area ⟨a *gap* in her knowledge⟩
5 : a break in continuity : HIATUS
6 : a break in the vascular cylinder of a plant where a vascular trace departs from the central cylinder
7 : lack of balance : DISPARITY ⟨the *gap* between imports and exports⟩
8 : a wide difference in character or attitude ⟨the generation *gap*⟩
9 : a problem caused by some disparity ⟨a communication *gap*⟩ ⟨credibility *gap*⟩
— **gap·py** \'ga-pē\ *adjective*

²**gap** *verb* **gapped; gap·ping** (1879)
transitive verb
1 : to make an opening in
2 : to adjust the space between the electrodes of (a spark plug)
intransitive verb
: to fall or stand open

¹**gape** \'gāp *sometimes* 'gap\ *intransitive verb* **gaped; gap·ing** [Middle English, from Old Norse *gapa;* perhaps akin to Latin *hiare* to gape, yawn — more at YAWN] (13th century)
1 a : to open the mouth wide **b** : to open or part widely ⟨holes *gaped* in the pavement⟩

2 : to gaze stupidly or in openmouthed surprise or wonder
3 : YAWN
— **gap·ing·ly** \'gā-piŋ-lē, 'ga-piŋ-\ *adverb*

²**gape** *noun* (1535)
1 : an act of gaping: **a** : YAWN **b** : an openmouthed stare
2 : an unfilled space or extent
3 a : the median margin-to-margin length of the open mouth **b** : the line along which the mandibles of a bird close **c** : the width of an opening
4 *plural but singular in construction* **a** : a disease of birds and especially young birds in which gapeworms invade and irritate the trachea **b** : a fit of yawning

gap·er \'gā-pər *sometimes* 'ga-pər\ *noun* (circa 1637)
1 : one that gapes
2 : any of several large sluggish burrowing clams (families Myacidae and Mactridae) including several used for food

gape·worm \'gāp-ˌwərm *sometimes* 'gap-\ *noun* (1873)
: a nematode worm (*Syngamus trachea*) that causes gapes in birds

gap·ing \'gā-piŋ\ *adjective* (1588)
: wide open ⟨a *gaping* hole⟩

gap junction *noun* (1967)
: an area of contact between adjacent cells characterized by modification of the cell membranes for intercellular communication or transfer of low molecular-weight substances

gapped scale *noun* (1910)
: a musical scale derived from a larger system of tones by omitting certain tones

gap–toothed \'gap-ˌtütht\ *adjective* (1567)
: having gaps between the teeth

¹**gar** \'gär\ *interjection* [euphemism for *God*] (1598)
— used as a mild oath in the phrase *by gar*

²**gar** *noun* [short for *garfish*] (1765)
: any of various fishes that have an elongate body resembling that of a pike and long and narrow jaws: as **a** : NEEDLEFISH 1 **b** : any of several predaceous North American freshwater bony fishes (family Lepisosteidae) with heavy ganoid scales

¹**ga·rage** \gə-'räzh, -'räj; *chiefly New England* -'razh, -'räj; *Canadian also* -'razh, -'raj; *British usually* 'gar-(ˌ)äzh, -(ˌ)äj, -ij\ *noun* [French, act of docking, garage, from *garer* to dock, of Germanic origin; akin to Old High German bi-*warōn* to protect — more at WARE] (1902)
: a shelter or repair shop for automotive vehicles

²**garage** *transitive verb* **ga·raged; ga·rag·ing** (1905)
: to keep or put in a garage

ga·rage·man \-ˌman\ *noun* (1919)
: one who works in a garage

garage sale *noun* (1964)
: a sale of used household or personal articles (as furniture, tools, or clothing) held at the seller's own premises

ga·ram ma·sa·la \gä-'räm-mə-'sä-lə\ *noun* [Hindi *garam masālā*, literally, hot spices] (1970)
: a pungent and aromatic mixture of ground spices used in Indian cooking

Ga·rand rifle \gə-'rand-, 'gar-ənd-\ *noun* [John C. *Garand*] (1931)
: M1 RIFLE

¹**garb** \'gärb\ *noun* [Middle French or Old Italian; Middle French *garbe* graceful contour, grace, from Old Italian *garbo* grace] (1599)
1 *obsolete* : FASHION, MANNER
2 a : a style of apparel **b** : outward form : APPEARANCE

²**garb** *transitive verb* (1846)
: to cover with or as if with clothing ⟨*garbed* in T-shirt and blue jeans⟩

gar·bage \'gär-bij\ *noun* [Middle English, offal] (15th century)
1 a : food waste **b** : discarded or useless material

2 a : TRASH 1b **b** : inaccurate or useless data

gar·bage·man \-ˌman\ *noun* (1888)
: one who collects and hauls away garbage

gar·ban·zo \gär-'bän-(ˌ)zō, *also* -'ban-\ *noun, plural* **-zos** [Spanish] (1759)
: CHICKPEA

garbanzo bean *noun* (1944)
: CHICKPEA

¹**gar·ble** \'gär-bəl\ *transitive verb* **gar·bled; gar·bling** \-b(ə-)liŋ\ [Middle English *garbelen*, from Old Italian *garbellare* to sift, from Arabic *gharbala*, from Late Latin *cribellare*, from *cribellum* sieve; akin to Latin *cernere* to sift — more at CERTAIN] (15th century)
1 *archaic* : CULL
2 : to sift impurities from
3 a : to so alter or distort as to create a wrong impression or change the meaning ⟨*garble* a story⟩ **b** : to introduce textual error into (a message) by inaccurate encipherment, transmission, or decipherment
— **gar·bler** \-b(ə-)lər\ *noun*

²**garble** *noun* (1502)
1 : the impurities removed from spices in sifting
2 : an act or an instance of garbling

gar·board \'gär-ˌbȯrd, -ˌbȯrd\ *noun* [obsolete Dutch *gaarboord*] (1627)
: the strake next to a ship's keel

gar·boil \-ˌbȯil\ *noun* [Middle French *garbouil*, from Old Italian *garbuglio*] (1548)
archaic : a confused disordered state : TURMOIL

gar·çon \gär-'sōⁿ\ *noun, plural* **garçons** \-'sōⁿ(z)\ [French, boy, servant, from Old French, of Germanic origin; akin to Old High German *hrechjo* fugitive — more at WRETCH] (1788)
: WAITER

garde–man·ger \ˌgärd-ˌmäⁿ-'zhā\ *noun, plural* **garde–mangers** \-'zhā(z)\ [French, literally, one who keeps food] (1928)
: a cook who specializes in the preparation of cold foods (as meats, fish, and salads)

¹**gar·den** \'gär-dᵊn\ *noun* [Middle English *gardin*, from Old North French, of Germanic origin; akin to Old High German *gart* enclosure — more at YARD] (13th century)
1 a : a plot of ground where herbs, fruits, flowers, or vegetables are cultivated **b** : a rich well-cultivated region **c** : a container (as a window box) planted with usually a variety of small plants
2 a : a public recreation area or park usually ornamented with plants and trees ⟨a botanical *garden*⟩ **b** : an open-air eating or drinking place **c** : a large hall for public entertainment
— **gar·den·ful** \-ˌfül\ *noun*

²**garden** *verb* **gar·dened; gar·den·ing** \'gär-dᵊn-iŋ, 'gärd-niŋ\ (1577)
intransitive verb
: to lay out or work in a garden
transitive verb
1 : to make into a garden
2 : to ornament with gardens
— **gar·den·er** \'gär-dᵊn-ər, 'gärd-nər\ *noun*

³**garden** *adjective* (1622)
1 : of, relating to, used in, or frequenting a garden
2 a : of a kind grown in the open as distinguished from one more delicate ⟨*garden* plant⟩ **b** : commonly found : GARDEN-VARIETY

garden apartment *noun* (1946)
: a multiple-unit low-rise dwelling having considerable lawn or garden space

garden city *noun* (1898)
: a planned residential community with park and planted areas

garden cress *noun* (1577)
: an annual herb (*Lepidium sativum*) of the mustard family sometimes cultivated for its pungent basal leaves

garden heliotrope *noun* (circa 1902)

: a tall rhizomatous Old World valerian (*Valeriana officinalis*) widely cultivated for its fragrant tiny flowers and for its roots which yield the drug valerian

gar·de·nia \gär-'dē-nyə\ *noun* [New Latin, from Alexander *Garden* (died 1791) Scottish naturalist] (1760)
: any of a large genus (*Gardenia*) of Old World tropical trees and shrubs of the madder family with showy fragrant white or yellow flowers

Garden of Eden (1535)
: EDEN

garden rocket *noun* (1832)
: ARUGULA

garden–variety *adjective* (1928)
: ORDINARY, COMMONPLACE

garde·robe \'gär-ˌdrōb\ *noun* [Middle English, from Middle French; akin to Old North French *warderobe* wardrobe] (15th century)
1 : a wardrobe or its contents
2 : a private room : BEDROOM
3 : PRIVY 1

gar·dy·loo \ˌgär-dē-'lü\ *interjection* [perhaps from French *garde à l'eau!* look out for the water!] (1622)
— used in Edinburgh as a warning cry when it was customary to throw slops from the windows into the streets

Gar·eth \'gar-əth\ *noun*
: a knight of the Round Table and nephew of King Arthur

gar·fish \'gär-ˌfish\ *noun* [Middle English *garfysshe*] (15th century)
: GAR

Gar·gan·tua \gär-'gan(t)-shə-)wə\ *noun* [French]
: a gigantic king in Rabelais' *Gargantua* having a great capacity for food and drink

gar·gan·tuan \-wən\ *adjective, often capitalized* [*Gargantua*] (1596)
: of tremendous size or volume : GIGANTIC, COLOSSAL ⟨*gargantuan* waterfalls⟩

¹gar·gle \'gär-gəl\ *verb* **gar·gled; gar·gling** \-g(ə-)liŋ\ [Middle French *gargouiller*, of imitative origin] (1527)
transitive verb
1 a : to hold (a liquid) in the mouth or throat and agitate with air from the lungs **b** : to cleanse or disinfect (the oral cavity) in this manner
2 : to utter with a gargling sound
intransitive verb
1 : to use a gargle
2 : to speak or sing as if gargling

²gargle *noun* (1657)
1 : a liquid used in gargling
2 : a sound of or like that of gargling

gar·goyle \'gär-ˌgȯil\ *noun* [Middle English *gargoyl*, from Middle French *gargouille;* akin to Middle French *gargouiller*] (13th century)
1 a : a spout in the form of a grotesque human or animal figure projecting from a roof gutter to throw rainwater clear of a building **b** : a grotesquely carved figure
2 : a person with an ugly face
— **gar·goyled** \-ˌgȯild\ *adjective*

gargoyle 1a

gar·i·bal·di \ˌgar-ə-'bȯl-dē\ *noun* (1862)
: a woman's blouse copied from the red shirt worn by the Italian patriot Garibaldi

ga·rigue \gə-'rēg\ *noun* [French] (1896)
: a low open scrubland with many evergreen shrubs, low trees, aromatic herbs, and bunchgrasses found in poor or dry soil in the Mediterranean region

gar·ish \'gar-ish, 'ger-\ *adjective* [origin unknown] (1545)
1 : clothed in vivid colors
2 a : excessively vivid : FLASHY **b** : offensively or distressingly bright : GLARING

3 : tastelessly showy
synonym see GAUDY
— **gar·ish·ly** *adverb*
— **gar·ish·ness** *noun*

¹gar·land \'gär-lənd\ *noun* [Middle English, from Middle French *garlande*] (14th century)
1 : WREATH, CHAPLET
2 : ANTHOLOGY, COLLECTION

²garland *transitive verb* (15th century)
1 : to form into a garland
2 : to adorn with or as if with a garland

gar·lic \'gär-lik\ *noun* [Middle English *garlek*, from Old English *gārlēac*, from *gār* spear + *lēac* leek — more at GORE] (before 12th century)
1 : a European bulbous herb (*Allium sativum*) of the lily family widely cultivated for its pungent compound bulbs much used in cookery; *broadly* : any plant of the same genus
2 : a bulb of garlic
— **gar·licky** \-li-kē\ *adjective*

gar·licked \'gär-likt\ *adjective* (1950)
: containing or prepared with garlic

garlic salt *noun* (1927)
: a seasoning of ground dried garlic and salt

¹gar·ment \'gär-mənt\ *noun* [Middle English, from Middle French *garnement*, from Old French, from *garnir* to equip — more at GARNISH] (14th century)
: an article of clothing

²garment *transitive verb* (1547)
: to clothe with or as if with a garment

garment bag *noun* (1927)
: a bag used by travelers that folds in half and has a center handle for easy carrying

¹gar·ner \'gär-nər\ *noun* [Middle English, from Old French *gernier, grenier*, from Latin *granarium*, from *granum* grain — more at CORN] (12th century)
1 a : GRANARY **b** : a grain bin
2 : something that is collected : ACCUMULATION

²garner *transitive verb* **gar·nered; gar·ner·ing** \'gärn-riŋ, 'gär-nə-\ (14th century)
1 a : to gather into storage **b** : to deposit as if in a granary ⟨volumes in which he has *garnered* the fruits of his lifetime labors —Reinhold Niebuhr⟩
2 a : to acquire by effort : EARN **b** : ACCUMULATE, COLLECT

gar·net \'gär-nət\ *noun* [Middle English *grenat*, from Middle French, from *grenat*, adjective, red like a pomegranate, from (*pomme*) *grenate* pomegranate] (14th century)
1 : a brittle and more or less transparent usually red silicate mineral that has a vitreous luster, occurs mainly in crystals but also in massive form and in grains, is found commonly in gneiss and mica schist, and is used as a semiprecious stone and as an abrasive
2 : a variable color averaging a dark red
— **gar·net·if·er·ous** \ˌgär-nə-'ti-f(ə-)rəs\ *adjective*

garnet paper *noun* (circa 1902)
: an abrasive paper with crushed garnet as the abrasive

gar·ni·er·ite \'gär-nē-ə-ˌrīt\ *noun* [Jules *Garnier* (died 1904) French geologist] (1875)
: a soft mineral consisting of hydrous nickel magnesium silicate and constituting an important ore of nickel

¹gar·nish \'gär-nish\ *transitive verb* [Middle English, from Middle French *garniss-*, stem of *garnir* to warn, equip, garnish, of Germanic origin; akin to Old High German *warnōn* to take heed — more at WARN] (14th century)
1 a : DECORATE, EMBELLISH **b** : to add decorative or savory touches to (food or drink)
2 : to equip with accessories : FURNISH
3 : GARNISHEE
synonym see ADORN

²garnish *noun* (1596)
1 : EMBELLISHMENT, ORNAMENT
2 : something (as lemon wedges or parsley) used to garnish food or drink

3 a : an unauthorized fee formerly extorted from a new inmate of an English jail **b** : a similar payment required of a new worker

¹gar·nish·ee \ˌgär-nə-'shē\ *noun* (1627)
: a person who is served with a legal process of garnishment

²garnishee *transitive verb* **-eed; -ee·ing** (circa 1876)
1 : to serve with a garnishment
2 : to take (as a debtor's wages) by legal authority

gar·nish·ment \'gär-nish-mənt\ *noun* (1550)
1 : GARNISH
2 : a legal summons or warning concerning the attachment of property to satisfy a debt
3 : a stoppage of a specified sum from wages to satisfy a creditor

gar·ni·ture \'gär-ni-chər, -nə-ˌchur\ *noun* [Middle French, equipment, alteration of Old French *garnesture*, from *garnir*] (1667)
1 : EMBELLISHMENT, TRIMMING
2 : a set of decorative objects (as vases, urns, or clocks)

gar·pike \'gär-ˌpīk\ *noun* (1776)
: GAR b

gar·ret \'gar-ət\ *noun* [Middle English *garette* watchtower, from Middle French *garite* watchtower, refuge, from Old French *garir*] (14th century)
: a room or unfinished part of a house just under the roof

¹gar·ri·son \'gar-ə-sən\ *noun* [Middle English *garisoun* protection, from Old French *garison*, from *garir* to protect, of Germanic origin; akin to Old High German *werien* to defend — more at WEIR] (15th century)
1 : a military post; *especially* : a permanent military installation
2 : the troops stationed at a garrison

²garrison *transitive verb* **gar·ri·soned; gar·ri·son·ing** \'gar-ə-s(ə-)niŋ\ (1569)
1 : to station troops in
2 a : to assign as a garrison **b** : to occupy with troops

garrison cap *noun* (1944)
: a visorless folding cap worn as part of a military uniform — compare SERVICE CAP

Gar·ri·son finish \'gar-ə-sən-\ *noun* [probably from Edward "Snapper" *Garrison*, 19th century American jockey] (1935)
: a finish in which the winner comes from behind at the end

garrison house *noun* (1676)
1 : a house fortified against Indian attack
2 : BLOCKHOUSE
3 : a house having the second story overhanging the first in the front

garrison state *noun* (1937)
: a state organized to serve primarily its own need for military security; *also* : a state maintained by military power

gar·ron \'gar-ən, gə-'rȯn\ *noun* [Irish *gearrán* & Scottish Gaelic *gearran*, gelding] (1540)
Scottish & Irish : a small sturdy workhorse

¹gar·rote *or* **ga·rotte** \gə-'rät, -'rōt; 'gar-ət\ *noun* [Spanish *garrote*] (1622)
1 a : a method of execution by strangulation **b** : the apparatus used
2 : an implement (as a wire with a handle at each end) for strangulation

²garrote *or* **garotte** *transitive verb* **gar·rot·ed** *or* **ga·rott·ed; gar·rot·ing** *or* **ga·rott·ing** (1851)
: to strangle with or as if with a garrote
— **gar·rot·er** *noun*

gar·ru·li·ty \gə-'rü-lə-tē, ga-\ *noun* (1581)
: the quality or state of being garrulous

gar·ru·lous \'gar-ə-ləs *also* 'gar-yə-\ *adjective* [Latin *garrulus*, from *garrire* to chatter — more at CARE] (circa 1611)

1 : given to prosy, rambling, or tedious lo-quacity : pointlessly or annoyingly talkative
2 : WORDY 1 ⟨*garrulous* speeches⟩
synonym see TALKATIVE
— **gar·ru·lous·ly** *adverb*
— **gar·ru·lous·ness** *noun*

¹**gar·ter** \'gär-tər\ *noun* [Middle English, from Old North French *gartier*, from *garet* bend of the knee, of Celtic origin; akin to Welsh *gar* shank] (14th century)
1 a : a band worn to hold up a stocking or sock **b** : a band worn to hold up a shirt sleeve **c** : a strap hanging from a girdle or corset to support a stocking
2 *capitalized* **a** : the British Order of the Garter; *also* : the blue velvet garter that is its badge **b** : membership in the order

²**garter** *transitive verb* (15th century)
: to support with or as if with a garter

garter snake *noun* (1769)
: any of a genus (*Thamnophis*) of harmless vi-viparous American snakes with longitudinal stripes on the back

garth \'gärth\ *noun* [Middle English, from Old Norse *garthr* yard; akin to Old High German *gart* enclosure — more at YARD] (14th century)
: a small yard or enclosure : CLOSE

gar·vey \'gär-vē\ *noun, plural* **garveys** [probably from the name *Garvey*] (circa 1896)
: a small scow especially of the New Jersey coast

¹**gas** \'gas\ *noun, plural* **gas·es** *also* **gas·ses** [New Latin, alteration of Latin *chaos* space, chaos] (1779)
1 : a fluid (as air) that has neither independent shape nor volume but tends to expand indefinitely
2 a : a combustible gas or gaseous mixture for fuel or lighting; *especially* : NATURAL GAS **b** : a gaseous product of digestion; *also* : discomfort from this **c** : a gas or gaseous mixture used to produce anesthesia **d** : a substance that can be used to produce a poisonous, asphyxiating, or irritant atmosphere
3 : empty talk : BOMBAST
4 : GASOLINE; *also* : the accelerator pedal of an automotive vehicle
5 : driving force : ENERGY ⟨I was young, and full of *gas* —H. L. Mencken⟩ ⟨ran out of *gas* in the seventh inning⟩
6 *slang* : something that gives pleasure : DE-LIGHT ⟨the party was a *gas*⟩

²**gas** *verb* **gassed; gas·sing** (1852)
intransitive verb
1 : to talk idly or garrulously
2 : to give off gas
3 : to fill the tank (as of an automobile) with gasoline — usually used with *up*
transitive verb
1 : to supply with gas or especially gasoline ⟨*gas* up the car⟩
2 a : to treat chemically with gas **b** : to poison or otherwise affect adversely with gas
3 *slang* : to please greatly

gas·bag \'gas-ˌbag\ *noun* (1827)
1 : a bag for holding gas
2 : an idle or garrulous talker

gas chamber *noun* (1945)
: a chamber in which prisoners are executed by poison gas

gas chromatograph *noun* (1958)
: an instrument used to separate a sample into components in gas chromatography

gas chromatography *noun* (1952)
: chromatography in which the sample mixture is vaporized and injected into a stream of carrier gas (as nitrogen or helium) moving through a column containing a stationary phase composed of a liquid or particulate solid and is separated into its component compounds according to their affinity for the stationary phase
— **gas chromatographic** *adjective*
gas·con \'gas-kən\ *noun* (14th century)

¹*capitalized* **a** : a native of Gascony **b** : the Romance speech of Gascony
2 : a boastful swaggering person
— **Gascon** *adjective*

gas·co·nade \ˌgas-kə-ˈnād\ *noun* [French *gasconnade*, from *gasconner* to boast, from *gascon* gascon, boaster] (1709)
: BRAVADO, BOASTING
— **gasconade** *intransitive verb*
— **gas·con·ad·er** *noun*

gas·eous \'ga-sē-əs, 'ga-shəs\ *adjective* (1799)
1 : having the form of or being gas; *also* : of or relating to gases
2 a : lacking substance or solidity **b** : GASSY 3 ⟨trick phrases and *gaseous* circumlocutions —Edwin Newman⟩
— **gas·eous·ness** *noun*

gas fitter *noun* (circa 1858)
: a worker who installs or repairs gas pipes and appliances

gas gangrene *noun* (1914)
: progressive gangrene marked by impregnation of the dead and dying tissue with gas and caused by one or more toxin-producing clostridia

gas–guz·zler \'gas-ˈgəz-lər, -ˈgə-zə-\ *noun* (1973)
: a usually large automobile that gets relatively poor mileage
— **gas–guz·zling** \-liŋ\ *adjective*

¹**gash** \'gash\ *noun* (1548)
1 : a deep long cut in flesh
2 : a deep narrow depression or cut ⟨cut a *gash* through the forest⟩ ⟨a *gash* in the hull⟩

²**gash** *verb* [alteration of Middle English *garsen*, from Old North French *garser*, from (assumed) Vulgar Latin *charissare*, from Greek *charassein* to scratch, engrave] (1570)
transitive verb
: to make a gash in
intransitive verb
: to make a gash : CUT

³**gash** *adjective* [origin unknown] (1706)
1 *chiefly Scottish* : KNOWING, WITTY
2 *chiefly Scottish* : well-dressed : TRIM

gas·hold·er \'gas-ˌhōl-dər\ *noun* (1802)
: a container for gas; *especially* : a huge cylindrical tank for storing fuel gas under pressure

gas·house \-ˌhaus\ *noun* (1880)
: GASWORKS

gas·i·fi·ca·tion \ˌga-sə-fə-ˈkā-shən\ *noun* (1812)
: conversion into gas; *especially* : conversion of coal into natural gas

gas·i·fy \'ga-sə-ˌfī\ *verb* **-i·fied; -i·fy·ing** (circa 1828)
transitive verb
: to convert into gas ⟨*gasify* coal⟩
intransitive verb
: to become gaseous
— **gas·i·fi·er** \'ga-sə-ˌfī-(-ə)r\ *noun*

gas·ket \'gas-kət\ *noun* [perhaps modification of French *garcette*] (circa 1889)
: a material (as rubber) or a member (as an O-ring) used to make a joint fluid-tight

gas·kin \'gas-kən\ *noun* [probably short for *galligaskins*] (1573)
1 *plural, obsolete* : HOSE, BREECHES
2 : a part of the hind leg of a quadruped between the stifle and the hock — see HORSE illustration

gas·light \'gas-ˌlīt, -ˈlīt\ *noun* (1808)
1 : light made by burning illuminating gas
2 : a gas flame or gas lighting fixture

gas–liquid chromatography *noun* (1952)
: gas chromatography in which the stationary phase is a liquid
— **gas–liquid chromatographic** *adjective*

gas·lit \-ˌlit, -ˈlit\ *adjective* (1837)
: illuminated by gaslight

gas log *noun* (1885)
: a hollow perforated imitation log used as a gas burner in a fireplace

gas mask *noun* (1915)

: a mask connected to a chemical air filter and used to protect the face and lungs from toxic gases; *broadly* : RESPIRATOR 1

gas·o·gene \'ga-sə-ˌjēn\ *noun* [French *gazogène*, from *gaz* gas (from New Latin *gas*) + *-o-* + *-gène* -gen] (circa 1853)
1 : a portable apparatus for carbonating liquids
2 : an apparatus carried by a vehicle to produce gas for fuel by partial burning of charcoal or wood

gas·o·hol \'ga-sə-ˌhol\ *noun* [blend of *gasoline* and *alcohol*] (1977)
: a fuel consisting of a blend usually of 10 percent ethyl alcohol and 90 percent gasoline

gas oil *noun* (1901)
: a hydrocarbon oil used as a fuel oil; *especially* : a petroleum distillate intermediate in boiling range and viscosity between kerosene and lubricating oil

gas·olier \ˌga-sə-ˈlir\ *noun* [alteration of *gaselier*, from *gas* + *-elier* (as in *chandelier*)] (1905)
: a gaslight chandelier

gas·o·line *also* **gas·o·lene** \'ga-sə-ˌlēn, ˌga-sə-ˈ *also* -zə-\ *noun* [¹*gas* + ²*-ol* + ²*-ine* or *-ene*] (1865)
: a volatile flammable liquid hydrocarbon mixture used as a fuel especially for internal combustion engines and usually blended from several products of natural gas and petroleum
— **gas·o·lin·ic** \ˌga-sə-ˈlē-nik, -ˈli-\ *adjective*

gas·om·e·ter \ga-ˈsä-mə-tər\ *noun* [French *gazomètre*, from *gaz* + *-o-* + *-mètre* -meter] (1808)
1 : GASHOLDER
2 : a laboratory apparatus for holding and measuring gases

gas–operated *adjective* (1944)
of a firearm : using part of the force of expanding propellant gases to operate the action

gasp \'gasp\ *verb* [Middle English; akin to Old Norse *geispa* to yawn] (14th century)
intransitive verb
1 : to catch the breath convulsively and audibly (as with shock)
2 : to breathe laboriously
transitive verb
: to utter in a gasping manner
— **gasp** *noun*

gasp·er \'gäs-pə(r)\ *noun* (1914)
slang British : CIGARETTE

gas plant *noun* (circa 1909)
: FRAXINELLA

gas ring *noun* (1901)
: a ring-shaped portable gas burner for cooking

gassed \'gast\ *adjective* (circa 1925)
: DRUNK 1

gas·ser \'ga-sər\ *noun* (circa 1944)
slang : something outstanding

gas station *noun* (1925)
: SERVICE STATION 1

gas·sy \'ga-sē\ *adjective* **gas·si·er; -est** (1757)
1 : full of or containing gas
2 : having the characteristics of gas
3 : characterized by many words but little content : emptily verbose
— **gas·si·ly** \'ga-sə-lē\ *adverb*
— **gas·si·ness** *noun*

gast \'gast\ *transitive verb* [Middle English, from *gast, gost* ghost — more at GHOST] (14th century)
obsolete : SCARE ⟨*gasted* by the noise I made, full suddenly he fled —Shakespeare⟩

Gast·ar·beit·er \'gast-(ˌ)är-ˌbī-tər\ *noun, plural* **Gastarbeiter** *also* **Gastarbeiters** [German, from *Gast* guest + *Arbeiter* worker] (1970)
: a foreign worker especially in Germany

gas·ter \'gas-tər\ *noun* [Greek *gastēr*] (circa 1909)
: the enlarged part of the abdomen behind the pedicel in hymenopterous insects (as ants)

gas·tight \'gas-ˌtīt\ *adjective* (1831)
: impervious to gas
— **gas·tight·ness** *noun*

gast·ness \'gas(t)-nəs\ *noun* (14th century)
obsolete : FRIGHT, TERROR

gastr- *or* **gastro-** *also* **gastri-** *combining form* [Greek, from *gastr-, gastēr*]
1 : stomach ⟨*gastr*ectomy⟩
2 : gastric and ⟨*gastro*intestinal⟩

gas·trea *also* **gas·traea** \ga-'strē-ə\ *noun* [New Latin, from Greek *gastr-, gastēr*] (1879)
: a hypothetical metazoan ancestral form corresponding in organization to a simple invaginated gastrula

gas·trec·to·my \ga-'strek-tə-mē\ *noun, plural* **-mies** [International Scientific Vocabulary] (1886)
: surgical removal of all or part of the stomach

gas·tric \'gas-trik\ *adjective* [Greek *gastr-, gastēr*, alteration of (assumed) Greek *grastēr*, from Greek *gran* to gnaw, eat] (1656)
: of or relating to the stomach

gastric gland *noun* (1900)
: any of various glands in the walls of the stomach that secrete gastric juice

gastric juice *noun* (circa 1736)
: a thin watery acid digestive fluid secreted by glands in the mucous membrane of the stomach

gastric ulcer *noun* (circa 1910)
: a peptic ulcer situated in the stomach

gas·trin \'gas-trən\ *noun* (1905)
: any of various polypeptide hormones that are secreted by the gastric mucosa and induce secretion of gastric juice

gas·tri·tis \ga-'strī-təs\ *noun* (1806)
: inflammation especially of the mucous membrane of the stomach

gas·troc·ne·mi·us \ˌgas-(ˌ)träk-'nē-mē-əs, -trək-\ *noun, plural* **-mii** \-mē-ˌī\ [New Latin, from Greek *gastroknēmē* calf of the leg, from *gastr-* + *knēmē* shank — more at HAM] (1676)
: the largest and most superficial muscle of the calf of the leg arising by two heads from the condyles of the femur and attaching to a tendon that becomes part of the Achilles tendon

gas·tro·du·o·de·nal \ˌgas-trō-ˌd(y)ü-ə-'dē-nᵊl, -d(y)ù-'ä-dᵊn-əl\ *adjective* (1854)
: of, relating to, or involving the stomach and the duodenum

gas·tro·en·ter·i·tis \ˌgas-trō-ˌen-tə-'rī-təs\ *noun* (circa 1829)
: inflammation of the lining membrane of the stomach and the intestines

gas·tro·en·ter·ol·o·gy \-ˌen-tə-'rä-lə-jē\ *noun* [International Scientific Vocabulary] (circa 1904)
: a branch of medicine concerned with the structure, functions, diseases, and pathology of the stomach and intestines
— **gas·tro·en·ter·o·log·i·cal** \-rə-'lä-ji-kəl\ *adjective*
— **gas·tro·en·ter·ol·o·gist** \-ˌen-tə-'rä-lə-jist\ *noun*

gas·tro·esoph·a·ge·al \'gas-trō-i-ˌsä-fə-'jē-əl\ *adjective* (circa 1909)
: of, relating to, or involving the stomach and esophagus

gas·tro·in·tes·ti·nal \ˌgas-trō-in-'tes-tə-nᵊl, -'tes(t)-nəl\ *adjective* (1831)
: of, relating to, affecting, or including both stomach and intestine ⟨*gastrointestinal* tract⟩

gas·tro·lith \'gas-trə-ˌlith\ *noun* (1854)
: a stone or pebble ingested by an animal and functioning to grind food in gastric digestion

gas·tro·nome \'gas-trə-ˌnōm\ *noun* [French, back-formation from *gastronomie*] (1823)
: a lover of good food; *especially* : one with a serious interest in gastronomy
synonym *see* EPICURE

gas·tro·nom·i·cal·ly \ˌgas-trə-'nä-mi-k(ə-)lē\ *adverb* (1875)
1 : from the standpoint of gastronomy ⟨*gastronomically* fashionable⟩

2 : toward gastronomy ⟨*gastronomically* inclined⟩

gas·tron·o·mist \ga-'strä-nə-mist\ *noun* (1825)
: GASTRONOME

gas·tron·o·my \-mē\ *noun* [French *gastronomie*, from Greek *Gastronomia*, title of a 4th century B.C. poem, from *gastro-* gastr- + -nomia -nomy] (1814)
1 : the art or science of good eating
2 : culinary customs or style
— **gas·tro·nom·ic** \ˌgas-trə-'nä-mik\ *also* **gas·tro·nom·i·cal** \-mi-kəl\ *adjective*

gas·tro·pod \'gas-trə-ˌpäd\ *noun* [New Latin *Gastropoda*, class name] (1826)
: any of a large class (Gastropoda) of mollusks (as snails and slugs) usually with a univalve shell or none and a distinct head bearing sensory organs
— **gastropod** *adjective*

gas·tro·scope \'gas-trə-ˌskōp\ *noun* [International Scientific Vocabulary] (1888)
: an instrument for viewing the interior of the stomach
— **gas·tro·scop·ic** \ˌgas-trə-'skä-pik\ *adjective*
— **gas·tros·co·pist** \ga-'sträs-kə-pist\ *noun*
— **gas·tros·co·py** \-pē\ *noun*

gas·tro·trich \'gas-trə-ˌtrik\ *noun* [ultimately from Greek *gastr-* + *trich-, thrix* hair — more at TRICH-] (1940)
: any of a phylum (Gastrotricha) of minute aquatic pseudocoelomate animals that usually have a spiny or scaly cuticle and cilia on the ventral surface

gas·tro·vas·cu·lar \ˌgas-trō-'vas-kyə-lər\ *adjective* [International Scientific Vocabulary] (1876)
: functioning in both digestion and circulation ⟨the *gastrovascular* cavity of a coelenterate⟩

gas·tru·la \'gas-trə-lə\ *noun, plural* **-las** *or* **-lae** \-ˌlē, -ˌlī\ [New Latin, from *gastr-*] (1877)
: an early metazoan embryo in which the ectoderm, mesoderm, and endoderm are established either by invagination of the blastula (as in fish and amphibians) to form a multilayered cellular cup with a blastopore opening into the archenteron or by differentiation of the blastodisc (as in reptiles, birds, and mammals) and inward cellular migration — compare BLASTULA, MORULA
— **gas·tru·lar** \-lər\ *adjective*

gas·tru·la·tion \ˌgas-trə-'lā-shən\ *noun* (1879)
: the process of becoming or of forming a gastrula
— **gas·tru·late** \'gas-trə-ˌlāt\ *intransitive verb*

gas turbine *noun* (1904)
: an internal combustion engine in which expanding gases from the combustion chamber drive the blades of a turbine

gas·works \'gas-ˌwərks\ *noun plural but singular or plural in construction* (1819)
: a plant for manufacturing gas and especially illuminating gas

¹gat \'gat\ *archaic past of* GET

²gat *noun* [probably from Dutch, literally, hole; akin to Old English *geat* gate] (1723)
: a natural or artificial channel or passage

³gat *noun* [short for *Gatling gun*] (1904)
slang : HANDGUN

¹gate \'gāt\ *noun* [Middle English, from Old English *geat*; akin to Old Norse *gat* opening] (before 12th century)
1 : an opening in a wall or fence
2 : a city or castle entrance often with defensive structures (as towers)
3 a : the frame or door that closes a gate **b** : a movable barrier (as at a grade crossing)

4 a : a means of entrance or exit **b** : STARTING GATE **c** : an area (as at a railroad station or an airport) for departure or arrival **d** : a space between two markers through which a competitor must pass in the course of a slalom race
5 a : a door, valve, or other device for controlling the passage especially of a fluid **b** (1) : an electronic switch that allows or prevents the flow of current in a circuit (2) : an electrode in a field-effect transistor that modulates the current flowing through the transistor according to the voltage applied to the electrode — compare DRAIN, SOURCE **c** : a device (as in a computer) that outputs a signal when specified input conditions are met ⟨logic *gate*⟩ **d** : a molecular mechanism controlling the flow of a fluid, ion, or molecule through a channel especially in a cell membrane
6 *slang* : DISMISSAL ⟨gave him the *gate*⟩
7 : the total admission receipts or the number of spectators (as at a sports event)

²gate *transitive verb* **gat·ed; gat·ing** (1835)
1 *British* : to punish by confinement to a campus or dormitory
2 : to supply with a gate
3 : to control by means of a gate

³gate *noun* [Middle English, from Old Norse *gata* road; akin to Old High German *gazza* road] (13th century)
1 *archaic* : WAY, PATH
2 *dialect* : METHOD, STYLE

-gate \ˌgāt\ *noun combining form* [Watergate]
: usually political scandal often involving the concealment of wrongdoing ⟨Iran*gate*⟩

gâ·teau *or* **ga·teau** \(ˌ)gä-'tō\ *noun, plural* **gâ·teaux** *or* **ga·teaux** \-'tō(z)\ *also* **ga·teaus** [French, from Old French *gastel*, probably of Germanic origin; akin to Old English *wist* sustenance, food] (1845)
1 : food baked or served in the form of a cake ⟨eggplant *gâteau*⟩
2 : a rich or fancy cake

gate–crash·er \'gāt-ˌkra-shər\ *noun* (1921)
: a person who enters, attends, or participates without ticket or invitation
— **gate–crash** *verb*

gate·fold \-ˌfōld\ *noun* (1946)
: FOLDOUT; *especially* : one with a single fold that opens out like a gate

gate·house \-ˌhaùs\ *noun* (14th century)
: a building or house connected or associated with a gate

gate·keep·er \-ˌkē-pər\ *noun* (1572)
1 : one that tends or guards a gate
2 : a person who controls access
— **gate·keep·ing** \-piŋ\ *adjective*

gate·leg table \'gāt-ˌleg-, -ˌlāg-\ *noun* (1926)
: a table with drop leaves supported by movable paired legs

gate·post \'gāt-ˌpōst\ *noun* (1522)
: the post to which a gate is hung or the one against which it closes

gateleg table

gate·way \-ˌwā\ *noun* (1707)
1 : an opening for a gate
2 : GATE 4a

¹gath·er \'ga-thər *also* 'ge-\ *verb* **gath·ered; gath·er·ing** \'gath-riŋ, 'ga-thə-\ [Middle English *gaderen*, from Old English *gaderian*; akin to Sanskrit *gadhya* what one clings to — more at GOOD] (before 12th century) *transitive verb*
1 : to bring together : COLLECT ⟨tried to *gather* a crowd⟩ ⟨*gathered* firewood⟩

2 a : PICK, HARVEST ⟨*gather* flowers⟩ **b :** to pick up or accumulate as if by harvesting ⟨*gathering* ideas for the project⟩ **c :** to assemble (the signatures of a book) in sequence for binding
3 : to serve as a center of attraction for
4 : to effect the collection of (as tax)
5 a : to summon up ⟨*gathered* his courage⟩ **b :** to gain by gradual increase : ACCUMULATE ⟨*gather* speed⟩ **c :** to prepare (as oneself) by mustering strength
6 : to reach a conclusion often intuitively from hints or through inferences ⟨I *gather* that you want to leave⟩
7 a : to pull (fabric) along a line of stitching so as to draw into puckers **b :** to draw about or close to something ⟨*gathering* her cloak about her⟩ **c :** to bring together the parts of **d :** to haul in
intransitive verb
1 a : to come together in a body **b :** to cluster around a focus of attraction
2 a : to swell and fill with pus **b :** GROW, INCREASE ☆
— **gath·er·er** \-thər-ər\ *noun*

²gather *noun* (1555)
1 : something gathered: as **a :** a puckering in cloth made by gathering **b :** a mass of molten glass collected for use in glassblowing
2 : an act or instance of gathering
gath·er·ing *noun* (before 12th century)
1 : ASSEMBLY, MEETING
2 : a suppurating swelling : ABCESS
3 : the collecting of food or raw materials from the wild
4 : COLLECTION, COMPILATION
5 : a gather in cloth
Gat·ling gun \'gat-liŋ-\ *noun* [Richard J. *Gatling* (died 1903) American inventor] (1867) **:** a machine gun with a revolving cluster of barrels fired once each per revolution
ga·tor \'gā-tər\ *noun* (1844)
: ALLIGATOR
gauche \'gōsh\ *adjective, sometimes* **gauch·er** *sometimes* **gauch·est** [French, literally, left] (1751)
1 a : lacking social experience or grace; *also* **:** not tactful : CRUDE ⟨it would be *gauche* to mention the subject⟩ **b :** crudely made or done ⟨a *gauche* turn of phrase⟩
2 : not planar ⟨*gauche* conformation of molecules⟩
synonym see AWKWARD
— **gauche·ly** *adverb*
— **gauche·ness** *noun*
gau·che·rie \,gō-sh(ə-)'rē\ *noun* [French] (1826)
: a tactless or awkward act
Gau·cher's disease \(,)gō-'shāz-\ *noun* [Philippe C. E. *Gaucher* (died 1918) French physician] (1902)
: a rare hereditary disorder of lipid metabolism caused by an enzyme deficiency and characterized by enlargement of the spleen and neurological impairment
gau·cho \'gaů-(,)chō\ *noun, plural* **gauchos** [American Spanish] (1824)
: a cowboy of the South American pampas
gaud \'gȯd, 'gäd\ *noun* [Middle English *gaude*] (15th century)
: ORNAMENT, TRINKET
gaud·ery \'gȯ-də-rē, 'gä-\ *noun* (circa 1598)
: showy ornamentation; *especially* **:** personal finery
¹gau·dy \'gȯ-dē, 'gä-\ *adjective* **gaud·i·er; -est** (1582)
1 : ostentatiously or tastelessly ornamented
2 : marked by dazzling brilliance, showiness, or extravagance ⟨*gaudy* praise⟩ ☆
— **gaud·i·ly** \'gȯ-dºl-ē, 'gä-\ *adverb*
— **gaud·i·ness** \'gȯ-dē-nəs, 'gä-\ *noun*
²gaudy *noun, plural* **gaudies** [probably from Latin *gaudium* joy — more at JOY] (1651)
: a feast or entertainment especially in the form of an annual college dinner at a British university

gauf·fer \'gä-fər, 'gȯ-, 'gō-\ *variant of* GOFFER
¹gauge \'gāj\ *noun* [Middle English *gauge*, from Old North French] (15th century)
1 a : a measurement (as of linear dimension) according to some standard or system: as (1) **:** the distance between the rails of a railroad (2) **:** the size of a shotgun barrel's inner diameter nominally expressed as the number of lead balls each just fitting that diameter required to make a pound ⟨a 12-*gauge* shotgun⟩ (3) **:** the thickness of a thin material (as sheet metal or plastic film) (4) **:** the diameter of a slender object (as wire or a hypodermic needle) (5) **:** the fineness of a knitted fabric expressed by the number of loops per unit width **b :** DIMENSIONS, SIZE **c :** MEASURE 1 ⟨surveys are a *gauge* of public sentiment⟩
2 : an instrument or a means of measuring or testing: as **a :** an instrument for measuring a dimension or for testing mechanical accuracy **b :** an instrument with a graduated scale or dial for measuring or indicating quantity
3 : relative position of a ship with reference to another ship and the wind
4 : a function introduced into a field equation to produce a convenient form of the equation but having no observable physical consequences
synonym see STANDARD
²gauge *transitive verb* **gauged; gaug·ing** (15th century)
1 a : to measure precisely the size, dimensions, or other measurable quantity of **b :** to determine the capacity or contents of **c :** ESTIMATE, JUDGE ⟨hard to *gauge* his moods⟩
2 a : to check for conformity to specifications or limits **b :** to measure off or set out
gauged \'gājd\ *adjective* (1823)
of masonry **:** dressed to size
gaug·er \'gā-jər\ *noun* (15th century)
1 : one that gauges
2 *chiefly British* **:** an exciseman who inspects dutiable bulk goods
gauge theory *noun* (1925)
: any of several theories in physics that explain the transmission of a fundamental force between two interacting particles by the exchange of an elementary particle
Gaul \'gȯl\ *noun* (1625)
1 : a Celt of ancient Gaul
2 : FRENCHMAN
¹Gaul·ish \'gȯ-lish\ *adjective* (1659)
: of or relating to the Gauls or their language or land
²Gaulish *noun* (1668)
: the Celtic language of the ancient Gauls — see INDO-EUROPEAN LANGUAGES table
Gaull·ism \'gō-,li-zəm, 'gȯ-\ *noun* [Charles de *Gaulle*] (1943)
1 : a French political movement during World War II led by Charles de Gaulle in opposition to the Vichy government
2 : a postwar French political movement led by Charles de Gaulle
— **Gaull·ist** \-list\ *adjective or noun*
gault \'gȯlt\ *noun* [probably of Scandinavian origin; akin to Old Norse *gald* hard-packed snow] (1575)
chiefly British **:** a heavy thick clay soil
gaum \'gȯm, 'gäm\ *transitive verb* [origin unknown] (1796)
dialect **:** SMUDGE, SMEAR
gaunt \'gȯnt, 'gänt\ *adjective* [Middle English] (15th century)
1 : excessively thin and angular ⟨a long *gaunt* face⟩
2 : BARREN, DESOLATE
synonym see LEAN
— **gaunt·ly** *adverb*
— **gaunt·ness** *noun*
¹gaunt·let \'gȯnt-lət, 'gänt-\ *noun* [Middle English, from Middle French *gantelet*, diminutive of *gant* glove, of Germanic origin; akin to Middle Dutch *want* glove, Old Norse *vǫttr*] (15th century)

1 : a glove worn with medieval armor to protect the hand
2 : any of various protective gloves used especially in industry
3 : an open challenge (as to combat) — used in phrases like *throw down the gauntlet*
4 : a dress glove extending above the wrist
— **gaunt·let·ed** \-lə-təd\ *adjective*
²gauntlet *noun* [by folk etymology from *gantelope*] (1661)
1 : a severe trial : ORDEAL ⟨ran the *gauntlet* of criticism and censure⟩
2 a : a double file of men facing each other and armed with clubs or other weapons with which to strike at an individual who is made to run between them — used with *run* **b :** a long line (as of guards or well-wishers)
gaur \'gaůr\ *noun* [Hindi, from Sanskrit *gaura*; akin to Sanskrit *go* bull, cow — more at COW] (1806)
: a large wild ox (*Bos gaurus*) of India and southeast Asia with a broad forehead and short thick curved horns

gaur

gauss \'gaůs\ *noun, plural* **gauss** *also* **gauss·es** [Karl F. *Gauss*] (1882)
: the centimeter-gram-second unit of magnetic flux density that is equal to 1×10^{-4} tesla
Gauss·ian \'gaů-sē-ən\ *adjective* [Karl F. *Gauss*] (1905)
: being or having the shape of a Gaussian curve or a Gaussian distribution
Gaussian curve *noun* (1905)
: NORMAL CURVE
Gaussian distribution *noun* (1905)
: NORMAL DISTRIBUTION
gauze \'gȯz\ *noun* [Middle French *gaze*] (1561)
1 a : a thin often transparent fabric used chiefly for clothing or draperies **b :** a loosely woven cotton surgical dressing **c :** a firm woven fabric of metal or plastic filaments
2 : HAZE

☆ **SYNONYMS**
Gather, collect, assemble, congregate mean to come or bring together into a group, mass, or unit. GATHER is the most general term for bringing or coming together from a spread-out or scattered state ⟨a crowd quickly *gathered*⟩. COLLECT often implies careful selection or orderly arrangement ⟨*collected* books on gardening⟩. ASSEMBLE implies an ordered union or organization of persons or things often for a definite purpose ⟨experts *assembled* for a conference⟩. CONGREGATE implies a spontaneous flocking together into a crowd or huddle ⟨*congregating* under shelter in a storm⟩. See in addition INFER.

Gaudy, tawdry, garish, flashy, meretricious mean vulgarly or cheaply showy. GAUDY implies a tasteless use of overly bright, often clashing colors or excessive ornamentation ⟨circus performers in *gaudy* costumes⟩. TAWDRY applies to what is at once gaudy and cheap and sleazy ⟨*tawdry* saloons⟩. GARISH describes what is distressingly or offensively bright ⟨*garish* neon signs⟩. FLASHY implies an effect of brilliance quickly and easily seen to be shallow or vulgar ⟨a *flashy* nightclub act⟩. MERETRICIOUS stresses falsity and may describe a tawdry show that beckons with a false allure or promise ⟨a *meretricious* wasteland of casinos and bars⟩.

— **gauze·like** \-₁līk\ *adjective*
— **gauz·i·ly** \'gȯ-zə-lē\ *adverb*
— **gauzy** \-zē\ *adjective*

ga·vage \gə-'väzh, gä-\ *noun* [French, from *gaver* to stuff, force-feed, from Middle French dialect (Picardy) *gave* gullet, crop] (1889)
: introduction of material into the stomach by a tube

gave *past of* GIVE

¹**gav·el** \'ga-vəl\ *noun* [Middle English, from Old English *gafol;* akin to Old English *giefan* to give] (before 12th century)
: rent or tribute in medieval England

²**gavel** *noun* [origin unknown] (circa 1859)
: a mallet used (as by a presiding officer or auctioneer) for commanding attention or confirming an action (as a vote or sale)

³**gavel** *transitive verb* **-eled** *or* **-elled; -el·ing** *or* **-el·ling** \'gav-liŋ, 'ga-və-\ (1925)
: to bring or force by use of a gavel ⟨*gaveled* the audience to silence⟩

gav·el·kind \'ga-vəl-₁kīnd\ *noun* [Middle English *gavelkynde,* from ¹*gavel* + *kinde* kind] (14th century)
: a tenure of land existing chiefly in Kent from Anglo-Saxon times until 1925 and providing for division of an intestate's estate equally among the sons or other heirs

gavel–to–gavel *adjective* (1968)
: extending from the beginning to the end of a meeting or session ⟨*gavel-to-gavel* television coverage⟩

ga·vi·al \'gä-vē-əl\ *noun* [French, modification of Bengali *ghāṛiyal* or Hindi *ghaṛyal,* from Sanskrit *ghaṇṭika* crocodilian] (circa 1825)
: a large long-snouted crocodilian (*Gavialis gangeticus*) of India

ga·votte \gə-'vät\ *noun* [French, from Middle French, from Old Provençal *gavato,* from *gavot* Alpine dweller] (1696)
1 : a dance of French peasant origin marked by the raising rather than sliding of the feet
2 : a tune for the gavotte in moderately quick ¼ time
— **gavotte** *intransitive verb*

Ga·wain \gə-'wän, 'gä-₁wän, 'gaü-ən\ *noun*
: a knight of the Round Table and nephew of King Arthur

¹**gawk** \'gȯk\ *noun* [probably from English dialect *gawk* (left-handed)] (1757)
: a clumsy stupid person : LOUT

²**gawk** *intransitive verb* [perhaps alteration of obsolete *gaw* (to stare)] (1785)
: to gape or stare stupidly
— **gawk·er** *noun*

gawk·ish \'gȯ-kish\ *adjective* (1876)
: GAWKY
— **gawk·ish·ly** *adverb*
— **gawk·ish·ness** *noun*

gawky \'gȯ-kē\ *adjective* **gawk·i·er; -est** (1759)
: AWKWARD, CLUMSY ⟨a *gawky* adolescent⟩
— **gawk·i·ly** \-kə-lē\ *adverb*
— **gawky** *noun*

gawp \'gȯp, 'gäp\ *intransitive verb* [English dialect *gawp* to yawn, gape, from obsolete *galp,* from Middle English] (1855)
chiefly British : GAWK
— **gawp·er** \'gȯ-pər, 'gä-\ *noun*

¹**gay** \'gā\ *adjective* [Middle English, from Middle French *gai*] (14th century)
1 a : happily excited : MERRY **b** : keenly alive and exuberant : having or inducing high spirits ⟨abandoned a sober traditional style for one more timely and *gay*⟩
2 a : BRIGHT, LIVELY ⟨*gay* sunny meadows⟩ **b** : brilliant in color
3 : given to social pleasures; *also* : LICENTIOUS
4 a : HOMOSEXUAL **b** : of, relating to, or used by homosexuals ⟨the *gay* rights movement⟩ ⟨a *gay* bar⟩

synonym *see* LIVELY
— **gay** *adverb*
— **gay·ness** *noun*

²**gay** *noun* (1953)
: HOMOSEXUAL

gay·ety, gay·ly *variant of* GAIETY, GAILY

ga·za·nia \gə-'zä-nē-ə, -nyə\ *noun* [New Latin, from Theodorus *Gaza* (died 1478) Greek scholar] (1813)
: any of a genus (*Gazania*) of South African composite herbs often cultivated for their brightly colored flowers

ga·zar \gə-'zär\ *noun* [origin unknown] (1967)
: a silk organza

¹**gaze** \'gāz\ *intransitive verb* **gazed; gaz·ing** [Middle English] (14th century)
: to fix the eyes in a steady and intent look and often with eagerness or studious attention
— **gaz·er** *noun*

²**gaze** *noun* (1566)
: a fixed intent look

ga·ze·bo \gə-'zē-(₁)bō *also* -'zä-\ *noun, plural* **-bos** [perhaps from ¹*gaze* + Latin *-ebo* (as in *videbo* I shall see)] (1752)
1 : BELVEDERE
2 : a freestanding roofed structure usually open on the sides

gaze·hound \'gāz-₁haund\ *noun* (1610)
: a dog that hunts by sight rather than by scent; *especially* : GREYHOUND

ga·zelle \gə-'zel\ *noun, plural* **gazelles** *also* **gazelle** [French, from Middle French, from Arabic *ghazāl*] (1600)
: any of numerous small to medium graceful and swift African and Asian antelopes (*Gazella* and related genera)

gazelle

¹**ga·zette** \gə-'zet\ *noun* [French, from Italian *gazetta*] (circa 1598)
1 : NEWSPAPER
2 : an official journal
3 *British* : an announcement in an official gazette

²**gazette** *transitive verb* **ga·zett·ed; ga·zett·ing** (1678)
1 *chiefly British* : to announce or publish in a gazette
2 *British* : to announce the appointment or status of in an official gazette

gaz·et·teer \₁ga-zə-'tir\ *noun* (1611)
1 *archaic* : JOURNALIST, PUBLICIST
2 [*The Gazetteer's: or, Newsman's Interpreter,* a geographical index edited by Laurence Echard] : a geographical dictionary; *also* : a book in which a subject is treated especially in regard to geographic distribution and regional specialization

gaz·o·gene \'ga-zə-₁jēn\ *variant of* GASOGENE

gaz·pa·cho \gəz-'pä-(₁)chō, gə-'spä-\ *noun, plural* **-chos** [Spanish] (1845)
: a spicy soup that is usually made from chopped raw vegetables (as tomato, onion, pepper, and cucumber) and that is served cold

GB \₁jē-'bē\ *noun* [code name] (1961)
: SARIN

G clef *noun* (1596)
: TREBLE CLEF

ge- *or* **geo-** *combining form* [Middle English *geo-,* from Middle French & Latin; Middle French, from Latin, from Greek *gē-, geō-,* from *gē*]
1 : earth : ground : soil ⟨*geanticline*⟩ ⟨*geophyte*⟩
2 : geographic : geography and ⟨*geopolitics*⟩

ge·an·ti·cline \jē-'an-ti-₁klīn\ *noun* (1889)
: a great upward flexure of the earth's crust
— *compare* GEOSYNCLINE

¹**gear** \'gir\ *noun* [Middle English *gere,* from Old Norse *gervi, gǫrvi;* akin to Old English *gearwe* equipment, clothing, *gearu* ready — more at YARE] (14th century)
1 a : CLOTHING, GARMENTS **b** : movable property : GOODS
2 : EQUIPMENT, PARAPHERNALIA ⟨fishing *gear*⟩

3 a : the rigging of a ship or boat **b** : the harness especially of horses
4 *dialect chiefly British* : absurd talk : NONSENSE
5 *dialect chiefly British* : DOINGS
6 a (1) : a mechanism that performs a specific function in a complete machine ⟨steering *gear*⟩ (2) : a toothed wheel (3) : working relation, position, order, or adjustment ⟨got her career in *gear*⟩ **b** : one of two or more adjustments of a transmission (as of a bicycle or motor vehicle) that determine mechanical advantage, relative speed, and direction of travel
— **gear·less** \-ləs\ *adjective*

²**gear** (1851)
transitive verb
1 a : to provide (as machinery) with gearing **b** : to connect by gearing
2 a : to make ready for effective operation **b** : to adjust so as to match, blend with, or satisfy something ⟨*gearing* wages to productivity⟩
intransitive verb
1 a *British, of machinery* : to be in gear : MESH **b** : SHIFT 1c ⟨*gear* down⟩
2 : to become adjusted so as to match, blend, or harmonize

gear·box \'gir-₁bäks\ *noun* (1887)
1 : GEARING 2
2 : TRANSMISSION 3

gear·change \-₁chānj\ *noun* (1927)
British : GEARSHIFT

gear·ing \'gir-iŋ\ *noun* (1833)
1 : the act or process of providing or fitting with gears
2 : the parts by which motion is transmitted from one portion of machinery to another; *especially* : a train of gears

gear·shift \'gir-₁shift\ *noun* (1926)
: a mechanism by which the transmission gears in a power-transmission system are engaged and disengaged; *also* : a lever for controlling such a mechanism

gear up *intransitive verb* (1951)
: to get ready ⟨the team is *gearing up* for the big game⟩

gear·wheel \'gir-₁hwēl, -₁wēl\ *noun* (circa 1874)
: GEAR 6a(2)

Geat \'gēt, 'gä-ət, 'yaət\ *noun* [Old English *Gēat*] (before 12th century)
: a member of a Scandinavian people of southern Sweden to which the legendary hero Beowulf belonged
— **Geat·ish** \'gē-tish, 'gä-, 'yaə-\ *adjective*

gecko \'ge-(₁)kō\ *noun, plural* **geck·os** *or* **geck·oes** [perhaps from Malay dialect *ge²kok*] (1774)
: any of numerous small harmless chiefly tropical and nocturnal insectivorous lizards (family Gekkonidae)

gecko

ge·dank·en·ex·per·i·ment \gə-'däŋ-kən-ik-₁sper-ə-mənt *also* -₁spir-\ *noun* [German, from *Gedanke* thought + *Experiment* experiment] (1941)
: an experiment carried out in thought only

¹**gee** \'jē\ *verb* [origin unknown] (1628)
verb imperative
— used as a direction to turn to the right or move ahead; compare ⁵HAW
intransitive verb
geed; gee·ing : to turn to the right side

²**gee** *interjection* [euphemism for *Jesus*] (1895)
— used as an introductory expletive or to express surprise or enthusiasm

\ə\ abut \ᵊ\ kitten \ər\ further \a\ ash \ā\ ace
\ä\ mop, mar \aú\ out \ch\ chin \e\ bet \ē\ easy
\g\ go \i\ hit \ī\ ice \j\ job \ŋ\ sing \ō\ go
\ȯ\ law \ȯi\ boy \th\ thin \th̲\ the \ü\ loot \ú\ foot
\y\ yet \zh\ vision *see also* Guide to Pronunciation

³gee *noun* (1926)
1 : the letter *g*
2 [*grand*] *slang* **:** a thousand dollars

gee·gaw \'jē-(,)gȯ, 'gē-\ *variant of* GEWGAW

geek \'gēk\ *noun* [probably from English dialect *geek, geck* fool, from Low German *geck,* from Middle Low German] (1914)
1 : a person often of an intellectual bent who is disapproved of
2 : a carnival performer often billed as a wild man whose act usually includes biting the head off a live chicken or snake
— **geeky** \'gē-kē\ *adjective*

geese *plural of* GOOSE

gee–whiz \'jē-,hwiz, -,wiz\ *adjective* (1934)
1 : designed to arouse wonder or excitement or to amplify the merits or significance of something especially by the use of clever or sensational language ⟨play-by-play specialists who wallow in *gee-whiz* banality —Jack Gould⟩
2 : marked by spectacular or astonishing qualities or achievement ⟨*gee-whiz* technology⟩
3 : characterized by wide-eyed enthusiasm, excitement, and wonder

gee whiz \(,)jē-\ *interjection* (1885)
: ²GEE

geez *variant of* JEEZ

Ge·ez \'gē-,ez; 'gē-(,)ez, 'gā-\ *noun* (1790)
: a Semitic language formerly spoken in Ethiopia and still used as the liturgical language of the Christian church in Ethiopia

gee·zer \'gē-zər\ *noun* [probably alteration of Scots *guiser* (one in disguise)] (1885)
: a queer, odd, or eccentric person — used especially of elderly men

ge·fil·te fish \gə-'fil-tə-\ *noun* [Yiddish, literally, stuffed fish] (1892)
: balls or cakes of seasoned minced fish usually simmered in a fish stock or baked in a tomato sauce

ge·gen·schein \'gā-gən-,shīn\ *noun, often capitalized* [German, from *gegen* against, counter- + *Schein* shine] (1880)
: a faint light about 20° across on the celestial sphere opposite the sun probably caused by backscatter of sunlight by solar-system dust

Ge·hen·na \gi-'he-nə\ *noun* [Late Latin, from Greek *Geenna,* from Hebrew *Gē' Hinnōm,* literally, valley of Hinnom] (1594)
1 : a place or state of misery
2 : HELL 1a(2)

Gei·ger counter \'gī-gər-\ *noun* [Hans *Geiger* (died 1945) German physicist] (1924)
: an instrument for detecting the presence and intensity of radiations (as cosmic rays or particles from a radioactive substance) by means of the ionizing effect on an enclosed gas which results in a pulse that is amplified and fed to a device giving a visible or audible indication ◆

Gei·ger–Mül·ler counter \-'myü-lər, -'mi-, -'mə-\ *noun* [W. *Müller,* 20th century German physicist] (1932)
: GEIGER COUNTER

gei·sha \'gā-shə, *also* 'gē-\ *noun, plural* **gei·sha** *or* **geishas** [Japanese, from *gei* art + *-sha* person] (1887)
: a Japanese girl or woman who is trained to provide entertaining and lighthearted company especially for a man or a group of men

¹gel \'jel\ *noun* [*gelatin*] (1899)
1 : a colloid in a more solid form than a sol; *broadly* : JELLY 2
2 : a thin colored transparent sheet used over a stage light to color it
3 : a gelatinous preparation used in styling hair

²gel *intransitive verb* **gelled; gel·ling** (1917)
: to change into or take on the form of a gel
: SET
— **gel·able** \'je-lə-bəl\ *adjective*

gel·a·da baboon \'je-lə-də-, 'gē-; jə-'lä-də-\ *noun* [Amharic *čällada*] (1878)
: a large long-haired primate (*Theropithecus gelada*) of Ethiopia related to the baboon — called also *gelada*

ge·län·de·sprung \gə-'len-də-,shprŭn, -,sprŭn\ *noun* [German, from *Gelände* open fields + *Sprung* jump] (1931)
: a jump usually over an obstacle in skiing that is made from a low crouch with the aid of both ski poles

gel·ate \'je-,lāt\ *intransitive verb* **gel·at·ed; gel·at·ing** (1915)
: GEL

gel·a·tin *also* **gel·a·tine** \'je-lə-tᵊn\ *noun* [French *gélatine* edible jelly, gelatin, from Italian *gelatina,* from *gelato,* past participle of *gelare* to freeze, from Latin — more at COLD] (1800)
1 : glutinous material obtained from animal tissues by boiling; *especially* : a colloidal protein used as a food, in photography, and in medicine
2 a : any of various substances (as agar) resembling gelatin **b :** an edible jelly made with gelatin
3 : GEL 2

ge·la·ti·ni·za·tion \jə-,la-tᵊn-ə-'zā-shən, ,je-lə-tᵊn-\ *noun* (1843)
: the process of converting into a gelatinous form or into a jelly
— **ge·la·ti·nize** \jə-'la-tᵊn-,īz, 'je-lə-tᵊn-\ *verb*

ge·lat·i·nous \jə-'lat-nəs, -'la-tᵊn-əs\ *adjective* (1766)
1 : resembling gelatin or jelly : VISCOUS ⟨a *gelatinous* precipitate⟩
2 : of, relating to, or containing gelatin
— **ge·lat·i·nous·ly** *adverb*
— **ge·lat·i·nous·ness** *noun*

¹ge·la·tion \ji-'lā-shən\ *noun* [Latin *gelation-, gelatio,* from *gelare*] (1854)
: the action or process of freezing

²gel·ation \je-'lā-shən\ *noun* [¹*gel* + *-ation*] (1915)
: the formation of a gel from a sol

ge·la·to \je-'lä-(,)tō\ *noun, plural* **-ti** \-tē\ *also* **-tos** [Italian, literally, frozen] (1929)
: a soft rich ice cream containing little or no air

¹geld \'geld\ *transitive verb* [Middle English, from Old Norse *gelda;* akin to Old English *gelde* sterile] (14th century)
1 : CASTRATE
2 : to deprive of a natural or essential part ⟨sick of workingmen being *gelded* of their natural expression —*Atlantic*⟩

²geld *noun* [Old English *gield, geld* service, tribute; akin to Old English *gieldan* to pay, yield — more at YIELD] (1610)
: the crown tax paid under Anglo-Saxon and Norman kings

geld·ing \'gel-diŋ\ *noun* [Middle English, from Old Norse *geldingr,* from *gelda*] (14th century)
1 : a castrated animal; *specifically* : a castrated male horse
2 *archaic* **:** EUNUCH

ge·lée \zhə-'lā\ *noun* [French, jelly, from Middle French — more at JELLY] (1966)
: a cosmetic gel

gel electrophoresis *noun* (1960)
: electrophoresis in which molecules (as proteins and nucleic acids) migrate through a gel and especially a polyacrylamide gel and separate into bands according to size

gel·id \'je-ləd\ *adjective* [Latin *gelidus,* from *gelu* frost, cold — more at COLD] (1599)
: extremely cold : ICY ⟨*gelid* water⟩ ⟨a man of *gelid* reserve —*New Yorker*⟩
— **ge·lid·i·ty** \jə-'li-də-tē, je-\ *noun*
— **gel·id·ly** \'je-ləd-lē\ *adverb*

gel·ig·nite \'je-lig-,nīt\ *noun* [*gel*atin + Latin *ignis* fire + English *-ite* — more at IGNEOUS] (1889)
: a dynamite in which the adsorbent base is largely potassium nitrate or a similar nitrate usually with some wood pulp

gel·lant \'je-lənt\ *noun* (1956)
: a substance used to produce gelling

gel permeation chromatography *noun* (1966)
: chromatography in which macromolecules (as polymers) in a solution are separated by size on a column packed with a gel (as of polystyrene)

gelt \'gelt\ *noun* [Dutch & German *geld* & Yiddish *gelt;* all akin to Old English *geld* ²*geld*] (circa 1529)
: MONEY

¹gem \'jem\ *noun* [Middle English *gemme,* from Middle French, from Latin *gemma* bud, gem] (14th century)
1 a : JEWEL **b :** a precious or sometimes semiprecious stone cut and polished for ornament
2 a : something prized especially for great beauty or perfection **b :** a highly prized or well-beloved person
3 : MUFFIN

²gem *transitive verb* **gemmed; gem·ming** (1610)
: to adorn with or as if with gems

Ge·ma·ra \gə-'mär-ə, -'mȯr-\ *noun* [Aramaic *gĕmārā* completion] (1613)
: a commentary on the Mishnah forming the second part of the Talmud
— **Ge·ma·ric** \-ik\ *adjective*
— **Ge·ma·rist** \-ist\ *noun*

ge·mein·schaft \gə-'mīn-,shäft\ *noun* [German, community, from *gemein* common, general (from Old High German *gimeini*) + *-schaft* -ship — more at MEAN] (1937)
: a spontaneously arising organic social relationship characterized by strong reciprocal bonds of sentiment and kinship within a common tradition; *also* : a community or society characterized by this relationship — compare GESELLSCHAFT

gem·i·nal \'je-mə-nᵊl\ *adjective* [Latin *geminus* twin] (1967)
: relating to or characterized by two usually similar substituents on the same atom
— **gem·i·nal·ly** \-nᵊl-ē\ *adverb*

¹gem·i·nate \'je-mə-nət, -,nāt\ *adjective* [Latin *geminatus,* past participle of *geminare* to double, from *geminus* twin] (15th century)
1 : arranged in pairs : DUPLICATE
2 : being a sequence of identical speech sounds (as in *meanness* or Italian *notte* \'nȯt-te\ "night")

²gem·i·nate \-,nāt\ *verb* **-nat·ed; -nat·ing** (1637)
transitive verb
: to make geminate
intransitive verb
: to be or become geminate
— **gem·i·na·tion** \,je-mə-'nā-shən\ *noun*

Gem·i·ni \'je-mə-(,)nē, -,nī; 'ge-mə-,nē\ *noun plural but singular in construction* [Latin (genitive *Geminorum*), literally, the twins (Castor and Pollux)]
1 : the 3d zodiacal constellation pictorially represented as the twins Castor and Pollux sitting together and located on the opposite side of the Milky Way from Taurus and Orion

◇ **WORD HISTORY**
Geiger counter The Geiger counter is named after the German physicist Hans Wilhelm Geiger (1882–1945). Geiger is credited with significant research on atomic theory, radioactivity, and cosmic rays. He developed a number of techniques and instruments for the detection of individual charged particles. With the British physicist Ernest Rutherford he developed in 1908 the first radiation counter, an instrument that counted alpha particles. Aided by fellow German physicist Walther Müller, he introduced an improved version of the Geiger counter in 1928. The Geiger-Müller counter marked the introduction of modern electrical devices into radiation research.

2 a : the 3d sign of the zodiac in astrology — see ZODIAC table **b** : one born under the sign of Gemini

gem·ma \'je-mə\ *noun, plural* **gem·mae** \-ˌmē\ [Latin] (1830)
: BUD; *broadly* : an asexual reproductive body that becomes detached from a parent plant

gem·ma·tion \je-'mā-shən\ *noun* (circa 1839)
: reproduction by gemmae

gem·mule \'jem-(ˌ)yü(ə)l\ *noun* [French, from Latin *gemmula*, diminutive of *gemma*] (circa 1841)
: a small bud: **a** : a theoretical particle proposed in the theory of pangenesis that is shed by a somatic cell and contains all the information necessary to reproduce that cell type (as in an offspring) **b** : a reproductive bud produced by freshwater and some marine sponges that consists of a usually hardened aggregate of cells

gem·my \'je-mē\ *adjective* (15th century)
1 : having the characteristics desired in a gemstone
2 : BRIGHT, GLITTERING

gem·ol·o·gist *also* **gem·mol·o·gist** \je-'mä-lə-jist, jə-\ *noun* (1931)
: a specialist in gems; *specifically* : one who appraises gems

gem·ol·o·gy *or* **gem·mol·o·gy** \-jē\ *noun* [Latin *gemma* gem] (1811)
: the science of gems
— **gem·olog·i·cal** \ˌje-mə-'lä-ji-kəl\ *adjective*

ge·mot *or* **ge·mote** \gə-'mōt, yə-\ *noun* [Old English *gemōt*, from *ge-* (perfective prefix) + *mōt* assembly — more at CO-, MOOT] (before 12th century)
: a judicial or legislative assembly in Anglo-Saxon England

gems·bok \'gemz-ˌbäk\ *noun* [Afrikaans, from German *Gemsbock* male chamois, from *Gems* chamois + *Bock* male goat] (1777)
: a large and strikingly marked oryx (*Oryx gazella*) formerly abundant in southern Africa

gem·stone \'jem-ˌstōn\ *noun* (before 12th century)
: a mineral or petrified material that when cut and polished can be used in jewelry

ge·müt·lich \gə-'müt-lik, -'müt-lik\ *adjective* [German, from Middle High German *gemüetlich* pleasant, from *gemüete* mentality, mind] (1852)
: agreeably pleasant : COMFORTABLE

gemsbok

ge·müt·lich·keit \gə-'müt-lik-ˌkīt, -'müt-lik-\ *noun* [German, from *gemütlich* + *-keit*, alteration of *-heit* -hood] (1892)
: CORDIALITY, FRIENDLINESS

gen \'jen\ *noun* [perhaps from *general information*] (1940)
chiefly British : INFORMATION 2a

¹gen- *or* **geno-** *combining form* [Greek *genos* birth, race, kind — more at KIN]
1 : race ⟨*geno*cide⟩
2 : genus : kind ⟨*geno*type⟩

²gen- *or* **geno-** *combining form*
: gene ⟨*geno*me⟩

-gen *also* **-gene** *noun combining form* [French *-gène*, from Greek *-genēs* born; akin to Greek *genos* birth]
1 : producer ⟨andro*gen*⟩
2 : one that is (so) produced ⟨culti*gen*⟩

gen·darme \'zhän-ˌdärm *also* -ˌjän-\ *noun* [French, from Middle French, back-formation from *gensdarmes*, plural of *gent d'armes*, literally, armed people] (1796)
1 : a member of a body of soldiers especially in France serving as an armed police force for the maintenance of public order
2 : POLICE OFFICER

gen·dar·mer·ie *or* **gen·dar·mery** \zhän-'där-mə-ˌrē, jän-\ *noun, plural* **-mer·ies** [French *gendarmerie*, from *gendarme*] (circa 1796)
: a body of gendarmes

¹gen·der \'jen-dər\ *noun* [Middle English *gendre*, from Middle French *genre*, *gendre*, from Latin *gener-*, *genus* birth, race, kind, gender — more at KIN] (14th century)
1 a : a subclass within a grammatical class (as noun, pronoun, adjective, or verb) of a language that is partly arbitrary but also partly based on distinguishable characteristics (as shape, social rank, manner of existence, or sex) and that determines agreement with and selection of other words or grammatical forms **b** : membership of a word or a grammatical form in such a subclass **c** : an inflectional form showing membership in such a subclass
2 a : SEX ⟨the feminine *gender*⟩ **b** : the behavioral, cultural, or psychological traits typically associated with one sex ▯

²gender *verb* **gen·dered; gen·der·ing** \-d(ə-)riŋ\ [Middle English *gendren*, from Middle French *gendrer*, from Latin *generare* — more at GENERATE] (14th century)
: ENGENDER

gender bender *noun* (1980)
: a person who dresses and behaves like a member of the opposite sex
— **gender–bending** *adjective or noun*

gen·dered \'jen-dərd\ *adjective* (1972)
: reflecting the experience, prejudices, or orientations of one sex more than the other ⟨*gendered* language⟩

gene \'jēn\ *noun* [German *Gen*, short for *Pangen*, from *pan-* + *-gen*] (1911)
: a specific sequence of nucleotides in DNA or RNA that is located in the germ plasm usually on a chromosome and that is the functional unit of inheritance controlling the transmission and expression of one or more traits by specifying the structure of a particular polypeptide and especially a protein or controlling the function of other genetic material

ge·ne·al·o·gist \ˌjē-nē-'ä-lə-jist *also* -'a-lə-*also* ˌje-nē-\ *noun* (1605)
: a person who traces or studies the descent of persons or families

ge·ne·al·o·gy \-jē\ *noun, plural* **-gies** [Middle English *genealogie*, from Middle French, from Late Latin *genealogia*, from Greek, from *genea* race, family + *-logia* -logy; akin to Greek *genos* race] (14th century)
1 : an account of the descent of a person, family, or group from an ancestor or from older forms
2 : regular descent of a person, family, or group of organisms from a progenitor or older form : PEDIGREE
3 : the study of family pedigrees
— **ge·ne·a·log·i·cal** \ˌjē-nē-ə-'lä-ji-kəl, ˌje-nē-\ *adjective*
— **ge·ne·a·log·i·cal·ly** \-k(ə-)lē\ *adverb*

gene amplification *noun* (1968)
: replication and especially massive replication (as in the polymerase chain reaction) of the genetic material in part of a genome

gene conversion *noun* (1955)
: a genetic process in which a heterozygote with one damaged strand of DNA produces gametes in an aberrant allelic ratio (as 3:1) instead of the normal 1:1 Mendelian ratio due to repair of the damaged strand with genetic material complementary to the other strand

gene flow *noun* (1947)
: the passage and establishment of genes typical of one breeding population into the gene pool of another by hybridization and backcrossing

gene frequency *noun* (1930)
: the ratio of the number of a specified allele in a population to the total of all alleles at its genetic locus

gene mutation *noun* (1927)
: POINT MUTATION

gene pool *noun* (1946)
: the collection of genes of all the individuals in an interbreeding population

genera *plural of* GENUS

gen·er·a·ble \'jen-rə-bəl, 'je-nə-\ *adjective* (15th century)
: capable of being generated

¹gen·er·al \'jen-rəl, 'je-nə-\ *adjective* [Middle English, from Middle French, from Latin *generalis*, from *gener-*, *genus* kind, class — more at KIN] (14th century)
1 : involving, applicable to, or affecting the whole
2 : involving, relating to, or applicable to every member of a class, kind, or group ⟨the *general* equation of a straight line⟩
3 : not confined by specialization or careful limitation
4 : belonging to the common nature of a group of like individuals : GENERIC
5 a : applicable to or characteristic of the majority of individuals involved : PREVALENT **b** : concerned or dealing with universal rather than particular aspects
6 : relating to, determined by, or concerned with main elements rather than limited details ⟨bearing a *general* resemblance to the original⟩
7 : holding superior rank or taking precedence over others similarly titled ⟨the *general* manager⟩

²general *noun* (14th century)
1 : something (as a concept, principle, or statement) that involves or is applicable to the whole
2 : SUPERIOR GENERAL
3 *archaic* : the general public : PEOPLE
4 a : GENERAL OFFICER **b** : a commissioned officer in the army, air force, or marine corps who ranks above a lieutenant general and whose insignia is four stars — compare ADMIRAL
— **in general** : for the most part : GENERALLY

\ə\ **abut** \ᵊ\ **kitten** \ər\ **further** \a\ **ash** \ā\ **ace**
\ä\ **mop, mar** \au̇\ **out** \ch\ **chin** \e\ **bet** \ē\ **easy**
\g\ **go** \i\ **hit** \ī\ **ice** \j\ **job** \ŋ\ **sing** \ō\ **go**
\ȯ\ **law** \ȯi\ **boy** \th\ **thin** \t͟h\ **the** \ü\ **loot** \u̇\ **foot**
\y\ **yet** \zh\ **vision** *see also* Guide to Pronunciation

general admission *noun* (circa 1949)
: a fee paid for admission to a usually unreserved seating area (as in an auditorium or stadium)

general agent *noun* (1835)
1 : one employed to transact generally all legal business entrusted to him by his principal
2 : an insurance company agent working within a specified area

general assembly *noun* (1619)
1 : the highest governing body in a religious denomination (as the United Presbyterian Church)
2 : a legislative assembly; *especially* : a U.S. state legislature
3 *G&A capitalized* : the supreme deliberative body of the United Nations

general aviation *noun* (1966)
: the operation of civilian aircraft not under the control of a common carrier; *also* : such aircraft collectively

General Court *noun* (1629)
: a legislative assembly; *specifically* : the state legislature in Massachusetts and New Hampshire

general delivery *noun* (1846)
: a department of a post office that handles the delivery of mail at a post office window to persons who call for it

general election *noun* (1716)
: an election usually held at regular intervals in which candidates are elected in all or most constituencies of a nation or state

gen·er·al·isa·tion, gen·er·al·ise, gen·er·al·ised *British variant of* GENERALIZATION, GENERALIZE, GENERALIZED

gen·er·a·lis·si·mo \,jen-rə-'li-sə-,mō, ,je-nə-\ *noun, plural* **-mos** [Italian, from *generale* general] (1621)
: the chief commander of an army

gen·er·al·ist \'jen-rə-list, 'je-nə-\ *noun* (1611)
: one whose skills, interests, or habits are varied or unspecialized

gen·er·al·i·ty \,je-nə-'ra-lə-tē\ *noun, plural* **-ties** (15th century)
1 : the quality or state of being general
2 a : GENERALIZATION 2 **b** : a vague or inadequate statement
3 : the greatest part : BULK ⟨the *generality* of the population⟩

gen·er·al·iza·tion \,jen-rə-lə-'zā-shən, ,je-nə-\ *noun* (1761)
1 : the act or process of generalizing
2 : a general statement, law, principle, or proposition
3 : the act or process whereby a response is made to a stimulus similar to but not identical with a reference stimulus

gen·er·al·ize \'jen-rə-,līz, 'je-nə-\ *verb* **-ized; -iz·ing** (circa 1751)
transitive verb
1 : to give a general form to
2 a : to derive or induce (a general conception or principle) from particulars **b** : to draw a general conclusion from
3 : to give general applicability to ⟨*generalize* a law⟩; *also* : to make indefinite
intransitive verb
1 : to form generalizations; *also* : to make vague or indefinite statements
2 : to spread or extend throughout the body
— **gen·er·al·iz·abil·i·ty** \,jen-rə-,lī-zə-'bi-lə-tē, ,je-nə-\ *noun*
— **gen·er·al·iz·able** \-,lī-zə-bəl\ *adjective*
— **gen·er·al·iz·er** *noun*

gen·er·al·ized *adjective* (circa 1843)
: made general; *especially* : not highly differentiated biologically nor strictly adapted to a particular environment

gen·er·al·ly \'jen-rə-lē, 'je-nə-, 'je-nər-lē\ *adverb* (14th century)
: in a general manner: as **a** : in disregard of specific instances and with regard to an overall picture ⟨*generally* speaking⟩ **b** : as a rule : USUALLY

general officer *noun* (1681)

: any of the officers in the army, air force, or marine corps above colonel — compare COMPANY OFFICER, FIELD OFFICER, FLAG OFFICER

general of the air force (1949)
: a general of the highest rank in the air force whose insignia is five stars

general of the army (1945)
: a general of the highest rank in the army whose insignia is five stars

general paresis *noun* (1874)
: insanity caused by syphilitic alteration of the brain that leads to dementia and paralysis — called also *general paralysis of the insane*

general partner *noun* (1887)
: a partner whose liability for partnership debts and obligations is unlimited

general practitioner *noun* (circa 1885)
: a physician or veterinarian whose practice is not limited to a specialty; *broadly* : GENERALIST

general–purpose *adjective* (1894)
: suitable to be used for two or more basic purposes

general quarters *noun plural* (1902)
: a condition of maximum readiness of a warship for action

general relativity *noun* (1916)
: RELATIVITY 3b

general semantics *noun plural but singular or plural in construction* (1933)
: a doctrine and educational discipline intended to improve habits of response of human beings to their environment and one another especially by training in the more critical use of words and other symbols

gen·er·al·ship \'jen-rəl-,ship, 'je-nə-\ *noun* (1610)
1 : office or tenure of office of a general
2 : LEADERSHIP
3 : military skill in a high commander

general store *noun* (1835)
: a retail store located usually in a small or rural community that carries a wide variety of goods including groceries but is not divided into departments

general theory of relativity (1921)
: RELATIVITY 3b

general will *noun* (circa 1902)
: the collective will of a community that is the embodiment or expression of its common interest

gen·er·ate \'je-nə-,rāt\ *transitive verb* **-at·ed; -at·ing** [Latin *generatus*, past participle of *generare*, from *gener-, genus* descent, birth — more at KIN] (1509)
1 : to bring into existence: as **a** : PROCREATE, BEGET **b** : to originate by a vital, chemical, or physical process : PRODUCE ⟨*generate* electricity⟩
2 : to be the cause of (a situation, action, or state of mind) ⟨these stories . . . *generate* a good deal of psychological suspense —*Atlantic*⟩
3 : to define or originate (as a mathematical or linguistic set or structure) by the application of one or more rules or operations; *especially* : to trace out (as a curve) by a moving point or trace out (as a surface) by a moving curve

gen·er·a·tion \,je-nə-'rā-shən\ *noun* (14th century)
1 a : a body of living beings constituting a single step in the line of descent from an ancestor **b** : a group of individuals born and living contemporaneously **c** : a group of individuals having contemporaneously a status (as that of students in a school) which each one holds only for a limited period **d** : a type or class of objects usually developed from an earlier type ⟨first of the . . . new *generation* of powerful supersonic fighters —Kenneth Koyen⟩
2 a : the action or process of producing offspring : PROCREATION **b** : the process of coming or bringing into being ⟨*generation* of income⟩ **c** : origination by a generating process : PRODUCTION; *especially* : formation of a geometric figure by motion of another

3 : the average span of time between the birth of parents and that of their offspring
— **gen·er·a·tion·al** \-shnəl, -shə-nᵊl\ *adjective*
— **gen·er·a·tion·al·ly** \-shnə-lē, shə-nᵊl-ē\ *adverb*

gen·er·a·tive \'jen-rə-tiv, 'je-nə-, -,rā-tiv\ *adjective* (14th century)
: having the power or function of generating, originating, producing, or reproducing

generative cell *noun* (circa 1892)
: a sexual reproductive cell : GAMETE

generative grammar *usually* 'je-nə-rə-tiv-\ *noun* (1959)
1 : a description in the form of an ordered set of rules for producing the grammatical sentences of a language
2 : TRANSFORMATIONAL GRAMMAR

generative nucleus *noun* (circa 1892)
: the one of the two nuclei resulting from the first division in the pollen grain of a seed plant that gives rise to sperm nuclei — compare TUBE NUCLEUS

generative semantics *usually* 'je-nə-rə-tiv-\ *noun plural but usually singular in construction* (1970)
: a description of a language emphasizing a semantic deep structure that is logical in form, that provides syntactic structure, and that is related to surface structure by transformations

gen·er·a·tor \'je-nə-,rā-tər\ *noun* (1646)
1 : one that generates
2 : an apparatus in which vapor or gas is formed
3 : a machine by which mechanical energy is changed into electrical energy
4 : a mathematical entity that when subjected to one or more operations yields another mathematical entity or its elements; *specifically* : GENERATRIX

gen·er·a·trix \,je-nə-'rā-triks\ *noun, plural* **-er·a·tri·ces** \-trə-,sēz, -ə-rə-'trī-(,)sēz\ (1840)
: a point, line, or surface whose motion generates a line, surface, or solid

¹ge·ner·ic \jə-'ner-ik\ *adjective* [French *générique*, from Latin *gener-, genus* birth, kind, class] (1676)
1 a : relating to or characteristic of a whole group or class : GENERAL **b** : being or having a nonproprietary name **c** : having no particularly distinctive quality or application
2 : relating to or having the rank of a biological genus
— **ge·ner·i·cal·ly** \-i-k(ə-)lē\ *adverb*
— **ge·ner·ic·ness** *noun*

²generic *noun* (1967)
: a generic product (as a drug)

gen·er·os·i·ty \,je-nə-'rä-sə-tē, -'räs-tē\ *noun, plural* **-ties** (circa 1616)
1 a : the quality or fact of being generous **b** : a generous act
2 : ABUNDANCE

gen·er·ous \'jen-rəs, 'je-nə-\ *adjective* [Middle French or Latin; Middle French *genereus*, from Latin *generosus*, from *gener-, genus*] (1588)
1 *archaic* : HIGHBORN
2 a : characterized by a noble or forbearing spirit : MAGNANIMOUS, KINDLY **b** : liberal in giving : OPENHANDED **c** : marked by abundance or ample proportions : COPIOUS
synonym see LIBERAL
— **gen·er·ous·ly** *adverb*
— **gen·er·ous·ness** *noun*

gen·e·sis \'je-nə-səs\ *noun, plural* **-e·ses** \-,sēz\ [Latin, from Greek, from *gignesthai* to be born — more at KIN] (circa 1604)
: the origin or coming into being of something

Genesis *noun* [Greek]
: the mainly narrative first book of canonical Jewish and Christian Scriptures — see BIBLE table

gene–splic·ing \'jēn-ˌsplī-siŋ\ *noun* (circa 1978)
: any of various techniques by which recombinant DNA is produced and made to function in an organism

gen·et \'je-nət\ *noun* [Middle English *genete*, from Middle French, from Arabic *jarnayṭ*] (15th century)
: any of a genus (*Genetta*) of small Old World usually carnivorous mammals related to the civets and having retractile claws, spotted or striped fur, and a ringed tail

gene therapy *noun* (1974)
: the insertion of normal or genetically altered genes into cells usually to replace defective genes especially in the treatment of genetic disorders

ge·net·ic \jə-'ne-tik\ *also* **ge·net·i·cal** \-ti-kəl\ *adjective* [*genesis*] (1831)
1 : relating to or determined by the origin, development, or causal antecedents of something
2 a : of, relating to, or involving genetics b : GENIC
— **ge·net·i·cal·ly** \-ti-k(ə-)lē\ *adverb*

-ge·net·ic *adjective combining form*
: -GENIC 1, 2 ⟨psycho*genetic*⟩

genetic code *noun* (1961)
: the biochemical basis of heredity consisting of codons in DNA and RNA that determine the specific amino acid sequence in proteins and appear to be uniform for all known forms of life

genetic counseling *noun* (1968)
: medical education of affected individuals and the general public concerning inherited disorders

genetic drift *noun* (1945)
: random changes in gene frequency especially in small populations when leading to preservation or extinction of particular genes

genetic engineering *noun* (1966)
: the directed alteration of genetic material by intervention in genetic processes; *especially* : GENE-SPLICING
— **genetically engineered** *adjective*
— **genetic engineer** *noun*

genetic map *noun* (circa 1960)
: MAP 3

genetic marker *noun* (1950)
: a usually dominant gene or trait that serves especially to identify genes or traits linked with it

ge·net·ics \jə-'ne-tiks\ *noun plural but singular in construction* (1905)
1 : a branch of biology that deals with the heredity and variation of organisms
2 : the genetic makeup and phenomena of an organism, type, group, or condition
— **ge·net·i·cist** \-'ne-tə-sist\ *noun*

ge·ne·va \jə-'nē-və\ *noun* [modification of obsolete Dutch *genever* (now *jenever*), literally, juniper, from Middle Dutch, from Old French *geneivre*, ultimately from Latin *juniperus*] (1706)
: a highly aromatic bitter gin originally made in the Netherlands

Ge·ne·va bands \jə-'nē-və-\ *noun plural* [*Geneva*, Switzerland; from their use by the Calvinist clergy of Geneva] (1882)
: two strips of white cloth suspended from the front of a clerical collar and sometimes used by Protestant clergymen — called also *Geneva tabs*

Geneva convention *noun* (1880)
: one of a series of agreements concerning the treatment of prisoners of war and of the sick, wounded, and dead in battle first made at Geneva, Switzerland in 1864 and subsequently accepted in later revisions by most nations

Geneva bands

Geneva cross *noun* [from its adoption by the Geneva convention] (circa 1889)
: RED CROSS

Geneva gown *noun* [from its use by the Calvinist clergy of Geneva] (1820)
: a loose large-sleeved black academic gown widely used as a vestment by members of the Protestant clergy

Ge·ne·van \jə-'nē-vən\ *adjective* (1573)
1 : of or relating to Geneva, Switzerland
2 : of or relating to Calvinism
— **Genevan** *noun*

¹**ge·nial** \'jēn-yəl, 'jē-nē-əl\ *adjective* [Latin *genialis*, from *genius*] (1566)
1 *obsolete* : of or relating to marriage or generation ⟨the *genial* bed —John Milton⟩
2 *obsolete* : INBORN, NATIVE
3 a : favorable to growth or comfort : MILD ⟨*genial* sunshine⟩ b : marked by or diffusing sympathy or friendliness ⟨your *genial* host⟩
4 : displaying or marked by genius
synonym see GRACIOUS
— **ge·nial·i·ty** \ˌjē-nē-'a-lə-tē, jēn-'yal-\ *noun*
— **ge·nial·ly** \'jēn-yə-lē\ *adverb*

²**ge·ni·al** \ji-'nī(-ə)l\ *adjective* [Greek *geneion* chin, from *genys* jaw — more at CHIN] (1831)
: of or relating to the chin

gen·ic \'jē-nik, 'je-\ *adjective* (1918)
: of, relating to, or being a gene
— **gen·i·cal·ly** \-ni-k(ə-)lē\ *adverb*

-gen·ic *adjective combining form* [International Scientific Vocabulary *-gen* & *-geny* + *-ic*]
1 : producing : forming ⟨carcino*genic*⟩
2 : produced by : formed from ⟨bio*genic*⟩
3 [*photogenic*] : suitable for production or reproduction by (such) a medium ⟨tele*genic*⟩

ge·nic·u·late \jə-'ni-kyə-lət\ *or* **ge·nic·u·lat·ed** \-ˌlā-təd\ *adjective* [Latin *geniculatus*, from *geniculum*, diminutive of *genu* knee — more at KNEE] (1657)
: bent abruptly at an angle like a bent knee

ge·nie \'jē-nē\ *noun, plural* **ge·nies** *also* **ge·nii** \'jē-nē(-ˌī)\ [French *génie*, from Arabic *jinnīy*] (1748)
1 : JINNI 1
2 : a magic spirit believed to take human form and serve the person who calls it

gen·i·tal \'je-nə-tᵊl\ *adjective* [Middle English, from Latin *genitalis*, from *genitus*, past participle of *gignere* to beget — more at KIN] (14th century)
1 : GENERATIVE
2 : of, relating to, or being a sexual organ
3 : of, relating to, or characterized by the stage of psychosexual development in psychoanalytic theory during which oral and anal impulses are subordinated to adaptive interpersonal mechanisms
— **gen·i·tal·ly** \-tə-lē\ *adverb*

genital herpes *noun* (1968)
: herpes simplex of the type typically affecting the genitalia

gen·i·ta·lia \ˌje-nə-'tāl-yə\ *noun plural* [Latin, from neuter plural of *genitalis*] (1876)
: the organs of the reproductive system; *especially* : the external genital organs
— **gen·i·ta·lic** \-'ta-lik, -'tā-\ *adjective*

gen·i·tals \'je-nə-tᵊlz\ *noun plural* (14th century)
: GENITALIA

gen·i·ti·val \ˌje-nə-'tī-vəl\ *adjective* (1818)
: of, relating to, or formed with or from the genitive case
— **gen·i·ti·val·ly** \-və-lē\ *adverb*

gen·i·tive \'je-nə-tiv\ *adjective* [Middle English, from Latin *genetivus*, *genitivus*, literally, of generation (erroneous translation of Greek *genikos* genitive), from *genitus*] (14th century)
1 : of, relating to, or constituting a grammatical case marking typically a relationship of possessor or source — compare POSSESSIVE
2 : expressing a relationship that in some inflected languages is often marked by a genitive case — used especially of English prepositional phrases introduced by *of*
— **genitive** *noun*

genito- *combining form* [*genital*]
: genital and ⟨*genito*urinary⟩

gen·i·to·uri·nary \ˌje-nə-tō-'yur-ə-ˌner-ē\ *adjective* (circa 1836)
: of or relating to the genital and urinary organs or functions

gen·i·ture \'je-nə-ˌchur, -chər, -ˌt(y)ur\ *noun* (15th century)
: NATIVITY, BIRTH

ge·nius \'jēn-yəs, 'jē-nē-əs\ *noun, plural* **ge·nius·es** *or* **ge·nii** \-nē-ˌī\ [Latin, tutelary spirit, natural inclinations, from *gignere* to beget] (1513)
1 a *plural genii* : an attendant spirit of a person or place b *plural usually genii* : a person who influences another for good or bad
2 : a strong leaning or inclination : PENCHANT
3 a : a peculiar, distinctive, or identifying character or spirit b : the associations and traditions of a place c : a personification or embodiment especially of a quality or condition
4 *plural usually genii* : SPIRIT, JINNI
5 *plural usually geniuses* a : a single strongly marked capacity or aptitude ⟨had a *genius* for getting along with boys —Mary Ross⟩ b : extraordinary intellectual power especially as manifested in creative activity c : a person endowed with transcendent mental superiority; *especially* : a person with a very high intelligence quotient ◇
synonym see GIFT

genius lo·ci \-'lō-ˌsī, -ˌkē\ *noun* [Latin] (1605)
1 : the pervading spirit of a place
2 : a tutelary deity of a place

geno- — see GEN-

gen·oa \'je-nə-wə\ *noun* [*Genoa*, Italy] (1932)
: a large jib that overlaps the mainsail and is used especially in racing

geno·cide \'je-nə-ˌsīd\ *noun* (1944)
: the deliberate and systematic destruction of a racial, political, or cultural group
— **geno·cid·al** \ˌje-nə-'sī-dᵊl\ *adjective*

gé·noise *or* **gé·noise** \zhā-'nwäz\ *noun* [French *génoise*, from feminine of *génois* of Genoa, Italy] (1931)

◇ **WORD HISTORY**
genius For the Romans, *genius* was something between "soul" and "life," a spirit resident in every male human during his lifetime, with a counterpart in women called the *juno*. Originally, the *genius* seems to have resided only in the *paterfamilias*, the head of an extended family, for whom it was the expression of his procreative potency, in line with the etymological link between *genius* and the verbal base *gen-* (as in *gignere* "to beget" and *genitor* "parent"). The *genius* was thought of as the personification of a person's natural desires and so was used in phrases such as *indulgere genio* "to indulge oneself" (literally, "to indulge one's genius"). Corporate entities, such as military units, as well as places, were thought of as having their own *genius*. In late Roman religious belief, *genius* was detached from the individual and regarded as a tutelary spirit who presided over a person's well-being. The English word *genius*, borrowed from Latin in the 16th century, has drawn to some degree on several nuances of the Latin word and added complexities of its own. The sense "extraordinary intellectual power" arose in the 18th century, influenced in part by the meanings of French *génie*, itself descended from Latin *genius*.

\ə\ abut \ᵊ\ kitten \ər\ further \a\ ash \ā\ ace
\ä\ mop, mar \aù\ out \ch\ chin \e\ bet \ē\ easy
\g\ go \i\ hit \ī\ ice \j\ job \ŋ\ sing \ō\ go
\ò\ law \òi\ boy \th\ thin \t͟h\ the \ü\ loot \ù\ foot
\y\ yet \zh\ vision *see also* Guide to Pronunciation

: a sponge cake containing butter and leavened by stiffly beaten eggs

ge·nome \ˈjē-ˌnōm\ *noun* [German *Genom*, from *Gen* gene + *-om* (as in *Chromosom* chromosome)] (1930)
: one haploid set of chromosomes with the genes they contain; *broadly* : the genetic material of an organism
— **ge·no·mic** \ji-ˈnō-mik, -ˈnä-\ *adjective*

ge·no·type \ˈjē-nə-ˌtīp, ˈje-\ *noun* (1897)
1 [International Scientific Vocabulary ¹*gen-*] : TYPE SPECIES
2 [International Scientific Vocabulary ²*gen-*] : all or part of the genetic constitution of an individual or group — compare PHENOTYPE
— **ge·no·typ·ic** \ˌjē-nə-ˈti-pik, ˌje-\ *also* **ge·no·typ·i·cal** \-pi-kəl\ *adjective*
— **ge·no·typ·i·cal·ly** \-pi-k(ə-)lē\ *adverb*

-genous *adjective combining form* [-*gen* + -*ous*]
1 : producing : yielding ⟨erogenous⟩
2 : having (such) an origin ⟨terrigenous⟩

genre \ˈzhän-rə, ˈzhä̃-; ˈzhäⁿr; ˈjän-rə\ *noun* [French, from Middle French, kind, gender — more at GENDER] (1770)
1 : a category of artistic, musical, or literary composition characterized by a particular style, form, or content
2 : KIND, SORT
3 : painting that depicts scenes or events from everyday life usually realistically

gen·ro \ˈgen-ˈrō\ *noun plural, often capitalized* [Japanese *genrō*] (1876)
: the elder statesmen of Japan who formerly advised the emperor

gens \ˈjenz, ˈgen(t)s\ *noun, plural* **gen·tes** \ˈjen-ˌtēz, ˈgen-ˌtās\ [Latin *gent-, gens* — more at GENTLE] (1847)
1 : a Roman clan embracing the families of the same stock in the male line with the members having a common name and worshiping a common ancestor
2 : CLAN; *especially* : a patrilineal clan
3 : a distinguishable group of related organisms

¹gent \ˈjent\ *adjective* [Middle English, noble, graceful, from Old French, from Latin *genitus*, past participle of *gignere* to beget — more at KIN] (13th century)
archaic : PRETTY, GRACEFUL

²gent *noun* (1564)
: GENTLEMAN

gen·ta·mi·cin \ˌjen-tə-ˈmī-sⁿn\ *noun* [alteration of earlier *gentamycin*, from *gent*ian violet + kan*amycin*; from the color of the actinomycete] (1963)
: a broad-spectrum antibiotic that is derived from an actinomycete (*Micromonospora purpurea* or *M. echinospora*) and is extensively used as the sulfate in treating infections especially of the urinary tract

gen·teel \jen-ˈtēl\ *adjective* [Middle French *gentil* gentle] (1599)
1 a : having an aristocratic quality or flavor : STYLISH **b** : of or relating to the gentry or upper class **c** : elegant or graceful in manner, appearance, or shape **d** : free from vulgarity or rudeness : POLITE
2 a : maintaining or striving to maintain the appearance of superior or middle-class social status or respectability **b** (1) : marked by false delicacy, prudery, or affectation (2) : conventionally or insipidly pretty ⟨timid and *genteel* artistic style⟩
— **gen·teel·ly** \-ˈtē(ə)(l)-lē\ *adverb*
— **gen·teel·ness** *noun*

gen·teel·ism \-ˈtē(ə)(l)-ˌli-zəm\ *noun* (1926)
: a word believed by its user to be more polite or less vulgar than a common synonym; *also* : the use of genteelisms

gen·tian \ˈjen(t)-shən\ *noun* [Middle English *gencian*, from Middle French *gentiane*, from Latin *gentiana*] (14th century)
1 : any of numerous herbs (family Gentianaceae, the gentian family, and especially genus

Gentiana) with opposite smooth leaves and showy usually blue flowers
2 : the rhizome and roots of a yellow-flowered gentian (*Gentiana lutea*) of southern Europe that is used as a tonic, stomachic, and flavoring in vermouth

gentian violet *noun, often G&V capitalized* (1897)
: any of several dyes or dye mixtures consisting of one or more methyl derivatives of pararosaniline; *especially* : a dark green or greenish mixture used especially as a bactericide, fungicide, and anthelmintic

¹gen·tile \ˈjen-ˌtīl\ *noun* [Middle English, from Late Latin *gentilis*, from Latin *gent-, gens* nation] (14th century)
1 *often capitalized* : a person of a non-Jewish nation or of non-Jewish faith; *especially* : a Christian as distinguished from a Jew
2 : HEATHEN, PAGAN
3 *often capitalized* : a non-Mormon ◇

²gentile *adjective* (15th century)
1 *often capitalized* **a** : of or relating to the nations at large as distinguished from the Jews; *also* : of or relating to Christians as distinguished from the Jews **b** : of or relating to non-Mormons
2 : HEATHEN, PAGAN
3 [Latin *gentilis*] : relating to a tribe or clan

gen·ti·lesse \ˌjen-tⁿl-ˈes\ *noun* [Middle English, from Middle French, from *gentil*] (14th century)
: decorum of conduct befitting a member of the gentry

gen·til·i·ty \jen-ˈti-lə-tē\ *noun, plural* **-ties** (14th century)
1 a : the condition of belonging to the gentry **b** : GENTLEFOLK, GENTRY
2 a (1) : decorum of conduct : COURTESY (2) : attitudes or activity marked by false delicacy, prudery, or affectation **b** : superior social status or prestige evidenced by manners, possessions, or mode of life

¹gen·tle \ˈjen-tⁿl\ *adjective* **gen·tler** \ˈjent-lər, -tⁿl-ər\; **gen·tlest** \ˈjent-ləst, -tⁿl-əst\ [Middle English *gentil*, from Old French, from Latin *gentilis* of a gens, of one's family, from *gent-, gens* gens, nation; akin to Latin *gignere* to beget — more at KIN] (13th century)
1 a : belonging to a family of high social station **b** *archaic* : CHIVALROUS **c** : HONORABLE, DISTINGUISHED; *specifically* : of or relating to a gentleman **d** : KIND, AMIABLE — used especially in address as a complimentary epithet ⟨*gentle* reader⟩ **e** : suited to a person of high social station
2 a : TRACTABLE, DOCILE **b** : free from harshness, sternness, or violence
3 : SOFT, DELICATE
4 : MODERATE
— **gent·ly** \ˈjent-lē\ *adverb*

²gentle *noun* (14th century)
: a person of gentle birth or status

³gentle *verb* **gen·tled; gen·tling** \ˈjent-liŋ, ˈjen-tⁿl-iŋ\ (14th century)
transitive verb
1 : to raise from the commonalty : ENNOBLE
2 a : to make gentler **b** : to make (an animal) tame and docile **c** : MOLLIFY, PLACATE **d** : to stroke soothingly : PET
intransitive verb
: to become gentle ⟨the wind *gentled*⟩

gentle breeze *noun* (circa 1881)
: wind having a speed of 8 to 12 miles per hour (about 13 to 19 kilometers per hour) — see BEAUFORT SCALE table

gen·tle·folk \ˈjen-tⁿl-ˌfōk\ *also* **gen·tle·folks** \-ˌfōks\ *noun plural* (1594)
: persons of gentle or good family and breeding

gen·tle·man \ˈjen-tⁿl-mən, ˈje-nⁿl-, *in rapid speech also* ˈjen-tə-mən, ˈje-nə-\ *noun, often attributive* [Middle English *gentilman*] (12th century)

1 a : a man of noble or gentle birth **b** : a man belonging to the landed gentry **c** (1) : a man who combines gentle birth or rank with chivalrous qualities (2) : a man whose conduct conforms to a high standard of propriety or correct behavior **d** (1) : a man of independent means who does not engage in any occupation or profession for gain (2) : a man who does not engage in a menial occupation or in manual labor for gain
2 : VALET — often used in the phrase *gentleman's gentleman*
3 : a man of any social class or condition — often used in a courteous reference ⟨show this *gentleman* to a seat⟩ or usually in the plural in address ⟨ladies and *gentlemen*⟩
— **gen·tle·man·like** \-mən-ˌlīk\ *adjective*
— **gen·tle·man·li·ness** *noun*

gentleman–at–arms *noun, plural* **gentlemen–at–arms** (1859)
: one of a military corps of 40 gentlemen who attend the British sovereign on state occasions

gentleman–commoner *noun, plural* **gentlemen–commoners** (1687)
: any of a privileged class of commoners formerly required to pay higher fees than ordinary commoners at the universities of Oxford and Cambridge

gentleman farmer *noun, plural* **gentlemen farmers** (1749)
: a man who farms mainly for pleasure rather than for profit

gen·tle·man·ly \-lē\ *adjective* (15th century)
: characteristic of or having the character of a gentleman
— **gen·tle·man·li·ness** *noun*

gentleman of fortune (1883)
: ADVENTURER

gentleman's agreement *or* **gentlemen's agreement** *noun* (1886)
: an agreement secured only by the honor of the participants

gen·tle·ness \ˈjen-tⁿl-nəs\ *noun* (14th century)
: the quality or state of being gentle; *especially* : mildness of manners or disposition

gen·tle·per·son \ˈjen-tⁿl-ˌpər-sⁿn\ *noun* (1943)
: a gentleman or lady

gentle sex *noun* (1583)
: the female sex : women in general

gen·tle·wom·an \ˈjen-tⁿl-ˌwu̇-mən\ *noun* (13th century)
1 a : a woman of noble or gentle birth **b** : a woman attendant upon a lady of rank
2 : a woman of refined manners or good breeding : LADY

◇ **WORD HISTORY**

gentile The Latin word *gens*, from the same Indo-European root as English *kin*, originally denoted a Roman clan, that is, a group of people sharing—either as a matter of legend or in reality—a common male ancestor. Early on, however, *gens*, especially in the plural *gentes*, was extended to any non-Roman people who, like the members of the clan, were ultimately all related to each other. Thus, it also meant simply "people, nation." The derived adjective *gentilis* meant accordingly both "of a clan" and "of a people, native." In the later Latin of the Christian church, *gentes* was used to translate Greek *ta ethnē* "the pagan peoples, those who were not the people of God." *Ta ethnē* in turn was a translation of Hebrew *goyim* in the Septuagint, the Greek translation of Jewish scripture. Correspondingly, the adjective *gentilis* was used in church Latin to mean "pagan" or "non-Jewish," the latter being the usual sense of English *gentile*, borrowed from Latin in the 14th century.

Gen·too \'jen-(,)tü\ *noun, plural* **Gentoos** [Portuguese *gentio*, literally, gentile, from Late Latin *gentilis*] (1638) *archaic* : HINDU

gen·too penguin \'jen-(,)tü-\ *noun* [perhaps from *Gentoo*] (1860) : a penguin (*Pygoscelis papua*) of Antarctica and nearby islands with a gray back and throat, white underparts, and white spots above the eyes — called also *gentoo*

gen·trice \'jen-trəs\ *noun* [Middle English *gentrise*, from Old French *genterise*, alteration of *gentelise*, from *gentil* gentle] (14th century) *archaic* : gentility of birth : RANK

gen·tri·fi·ca·tion \,jen-trə-fə-'kā-shən\ *noun* (1964) : the process of renewal and rebuilding accompanying the influx of middle-class or affluent people into deteriorating areas that often displaces earlier usually poorer residents

gen·tri·fy \'jen-trə-,fī\ *verb* **-fied; -fying** (1972) *transitive verb* : to attempt or accomplish the gentrification of *intransitive verb* : to become gentrified — **gen·tri·fi·er** \-,fī(-ə)r\ *noun*

gen·try \'jen-trē\ *noun, plural* **gentries** [Middle English *gentrie*, alteration of *gentrise*] (14th century) **1 a** *obsolete* : the qualities appropriate to a person of gentle birth; *especially* : COURTESY **b** : the condition or rank of a gentleman **2 a** : upper or ruling class : ARISTOCRACY **b** : a class whose members are entitled to bear a coat of arms though not of noble rank; *especially* : the landed proprietors having such status **3** : people of a specified class or kind : FOLKS ⟨no real heroes or heroines among the academic *gentry* —R. G. Hanvey⟩

gents \'jen(t)s\ *noun, often capitalized* (1938) *chiefly British* : MEN'S ROOM

gen·u·flect \'jen-yə-,flekt\ *intransitive verb* [Late Latin *genuflectere*, from Latin *genu* knee + *flectere* to bend — more at KNEE] (1630) **1 a** : to bend the knee **b** : to touch the knee to the floor or ground especially in worship **2** : to be servilely obedient or respectful — **gen·u·flec·tion** \,jen-yə-'flek-shən\ *noun*

gen·u·ine \'jen-yə-wən, -(,)wīn, ÷-,wīn\ *adjective* [Latin *genuinus* innate, genuine; akin to Latin *gignere* to beget — more at KIN] (circa 1639) **1 a** : actually having the reputed or apparent qualities or character ⟨*genuine* vintage wines⟩ **b** : actually produced by or proceeding from the alleged source or author ⟨the signature is *genuine*⟩ **c** : sincerely and honestly felt or experienced ⟨a deep and *genuine* love⟩ **d** : ACTUAL, TRUE ⟨a *genuine* improvement⟩ **2** : free from hypocrisy or pretense : SINCERE □ *synonym see* AUTHENTIC — **gen·u·ine·ly** *adverb* — **gen·u·ine·ness** \-wə(n)-nəs\ *noun*

ge·nus \'jē-nəs, 'je-\ *noun, plural* **gen·era** \'je-nə-rə\ [Latin *gener-, genus* birth, race, kind — more at KIN] (1551) **1** : a class, kind, or group marked by common characteristics or by one common characteristic; *specifically* : a category of biological classification ranking between the family and the species, comprising structurally or phylogenetically related species or an isolated species exhibiting unusual differentiation, and being designated by a Latin or latinized capitalized singular noun **2** : a class of objects divided into several subordinate species *word history see* SPICE

-geny *noun combining form* [Greek *-geneia* act of being born, from *-genēs* born — more at -GEN] : generation : production ⟨phylo*geny*⟩

geo- — *see* GE-

geo·bot·a·ny \,jē-ō-'bä-t°n-ē, -'bät-nē\ *noun* (1904) : PHYTOGEOGRAPHY — **geo·bo·tan·i·cal** \-bə-'ta-ni-kəl\ *also* **geo·bo·tan·ic** \-nik\ *adjective* — **geo·bot·a·nist** \-'bä-t°n-ist, -'bät-nist\ *noun*

geo·cen·tric \,jē-ō-'sen-trik\ *adjective* (1686) **1 a** : relating to, measured from, or as if observed from the earth's center — compare TOPOCENTRIC **b** : having or relating to the earth as center — compare HELIOCENTRIC **2** : taking or based on the earth as the center of perspective and valuation — **geo·cen·tri·cal·ly** \-tri-k(ə-)lē\ *adverb*

geo·chem·is·try \,jē-ō-'ke-mə-strē\ *noun* (1902) **1** : a science that deals with the chemical composition of and chemical changes in the solid matter of the earth or a celestial body (as the moon) **2** : the related chemical and geological properties of a substance — **geo·chem·i·cal** \-'ke-mi-kəl\ *adjective* — **geo·chem·i·cal·ly** \-k(ə-)lē\ *adverb* — **geo·chem·ist** \-'ke-mist\ *noun*

geo·chro·nol·o·gy \-krə-'nä-lə-jē\ *noun* (1893) **1** : the chronology of the past as indicated by geologic data **2** : the study of geochronology — **geo·chro·no·log·i·cal** \-,krä-n°l-'ä-ji-kəl, -,krō-\ *also* **geo·chro·no·log·ic** \-'ä-jik\ *adjective* — **geo·chro·no·log·i·cal·ly** \-ji-k(ə-)lē\ *adverb* — **geo·chro·nol·o·gist** \-krə-'nä-lə-jist\ *noun*

ge·ode \'jē-,ōd\ *noun* [Latin *geodes*, a gem, from Greek *geōdēs* earthlike, from *gē* earth] (circa 1732) **1** : a nodule of stone having a cavity lined with crystals or mineral matter **2** : the cavity in a geode

¹geo·de·sic \,jē-ə-'de-sik, -'dē-, -zik\ *adjective* (1821) **1** : GEODETIC **2** : made of light straight structural elements mostly in tension ⟨a *geodesic* dome⟩

²geodesic *noun* (1883) : the shortest line between two points that lies in a given surface

ge·od·e·sy \jē-'ä-də-sē\ *noun* [Greek *geōdaisia*, from *geō-* ge- + *daiesthai* to divide — more at TIDE] (1570) : a branch of applied mathematics concerned with the determination of the size and shape of the earth and the exact positions of points on its surface and with the description of variations of its gravity field — **ge·od·e·sist** \-də-sist\ *noun*

geo·det·ic \,jē-ə-'de-tik\ *also* **geo·det·i·cal** \-ti-kəl\ *adjective* [*geodesy*; after such pairs as *heresy : heretic*] (circa 1828) : of, relating to, or determined by geodesy

geodetic survey *noun* (1880) : a survey of a large land area in which corrections are made for the curvature of the earth's surface

Geo·dim·e·ter \,jē-ə-'di-mə-tər\ *trademark* — used for an electronic-optical device that measures distance using the velocity of light

geo·duck \'gü-ē-,dək\ *noun* [Lushootseed (Salishan language of the Puget Sound region) *gʷídəq*] (1883) : a large edible clam (*Panopea abrupta* synonym *P. generosa*) of the Pacific coast that sometimes weighs over five pounds

ge·og·ra·pher \jē-'ä-grə-fər\ *noun* (1542) : a specialist in geography

geo·graph·ic \,jē-ə-'gra-fik\ *or* **geo·graph·i·cal** \-fi-kəl\ *adjective* (1559) **1** : of or relating to geography **2** : belonging to or characteristic of a particular region — **geo·graph·i·cal·ly** \-fi-k(ə-)lē\ *adverb*

geographical mile *noun* (1823) : NAUTICAL MILE a

ge·og·ra·phy \jē-'ä-grə-fē\ *noun, plural* **-phies** [Latin *geographia*, from Greek *geōgraphia*, from *geōgraphein* to describe the earth's surface, from *geo-* + *graphein* to write — more at CARVE] (15th century) **1** : a science that deals with the description, distribution, and interaction of the diverse physical, biological, and cultural features of the earth's surface **2** : the geographic features of an area **3** : a treatise on geography **4** : a delineation or systematic arrangement of constituent elements : CONFIGURATION ⟨the philosophers . . . have tried to construct *geographies* of human reason —*Times Literary Supplement*⟩

geo·hy·drol·o·gy \,jē-ō-hī-'drä-lə-jē\ *noun* (circa 1909) : a science that deals with the character, source, and mode of occurrence of underground water — **geo·hy·dro·log·ic** \-,hī-drə-'lä-jik\ *adjective* — **geo·hy·drol·o·gist** \-hī-'drä-lə-jist\ *noun*

ge·oid \'jē-,óid\ *noun* [German, from Greek *geoeidēs* earthlike, from *gē*] (1881) : the surface within or around the earth that is everywhere normal to the direction of gravity and coincides with mean sea level in the oceans — **ge·oi·dal** \jē-'ói-d°l\ *adjective*

geo·log·ic \,jē-ə-'lä-jik\ *or* **geo·log·i·cal** \-ji-kəl\ *adjective* (1791) : of, relating to, or based on geology — **geo·log·i·cal·ly** \-ji-k(ə-)lē\ *adverb*

geologic time *noun* (1861) : the long period of time occupied by the earth's geologic history

▶ The Geologic Time table is on page 768.

ge·ol·o·gize \jē-'ä-lə-,jīz\ *intransitive verb* **-gized; -giz·ing** (1831) : to study geology or make geologic investigations

ge·ol·o·gy \jē-'ä-lə-jē\ *noun, plural* **-gies** [New Latin *geologia*, from *ge-* + *-logia* -logy] (1735) **1 a** : a science that deals with the history of the earth and its life especially as recorded in rocks **b** : a study of the solid matter of a celestial body (as the moon) **2** : geologic features **3** : a treatise on geology — **ge·ol·o·gist** \-jist\ *noun*

geo·mag·net·ic \,jē-ō-mag-'ne-tik\ *adjective* (1904) : of or relating to terrestrial magnetism — **geo·mag·net·i·cal·ly** \-ti-k(ə-)lē\ *adverb* — **geo·mag·ne·tism** \-'mag-nə-,ti-zəm\ *noun*

geomagnetic storm *noun* (1941) : MAGNETIC STORM

□ **USAGE**

genuine The objection which some commentators make to the pronunciation \'jen-yə-,wīn\ is perhaps occasioned by the fact that it is more frequent among those with less schooling. However, this variant is heard in the speech of cultured or highly educated speakers sufficiently frequently for it to be recognized as a widespread pronunciation at all social levels. This variant was recorded as early as 1890 and appears to be simply a long-standing spelling pronunciation.

\ə\ abut \°\ kitten \ər\ further \a\ ash \ā\ ace
\ä\ mop, mar \aú\ out \ch\ chin \e\ bet \ē\ easy
\g\ go \i\ hit \ī\ ice \j\ job \ŋ\ sing \ō\ go
\ó\ law \ói\ boy \th\ thin \th\ the \ü\ loot \ù\ foot
\y\ yet \zh\ vision *see also* Guide to Pronunciation

GEOLOGIC TIME

EON	ERA	PERIODS AND SYSTEMS	EPOCHS AND SERIES	BEGINNING OF INTERVAL*	BIOLOGICAL FORMS
Phanerozoic	Cenozoic	Quaternary	Holocene	0.01	
			Pleistocene	1.6	Earliest humans
		Tertiary	Pliocene	5	
			Miocene	24	Earliest hominids
			Oligocene	37	
			Eocene	58	Earliest grasses
			Paleocene	65	Earliest large mammals
	Cretaceous-Tertiary boundary (65 million years ago): extinction of dinosaurs				
	Mesozoic	Cretaceous	Upper	98	
			Lower	144	Earliest flowering plants; dinosaurs in ascendance
		Jurassic		208	Earliest birds & mammals
		Triassic		245	Age of Dinosaurs begins
	Paleozoic	Permian		286	
		Carboniferous			
		Pennsylvanian		320	Earliest reptiles
		Mississippian		360	Earliest winged insects
		Devonian		408	Earliest vascular plants (as ferns & mosses) & amphibians
		Silurian		438	Earliest land plants & insects
		Ordovician		505	Earliest corals
		Cambrian		570	Earliest fish
Proterozoic	Precambrian			2500	Earliest colonial algae & soft-bodied invertebrates
Archean				4000	Life appears: earliest algae & primitive bacteria

*In millions of years before the present

geo·man·cy \'jē-ə-,man(t)-sē\ *noun* [Middle English *geomancie*, from Middle French, from Medieval Latin *geomantia*, from Late Greek *geōmanteia*, from Greek *geō-* + *-manteia* -mancy] (14th century) : divination by means of figures or lines or geographic features
— **geo·man·cer** \-sər\ *noun*
— **geo·man·tic** \,jē-ə-'man-tik\ *adjective*
ge·om·e·ter \jē-'ä-mə-tər\ *noun* (15th century)
1 : a specialist in geometry
2 : GEOMETRID
geo·met·ric \,jē-ə-'me-trik\ *or* **geo·met·ri·cal** \-'me-tri-kəl\ *adjective* (14th century)
1 a : of, relating to, or according to the methods or principles of geometry **b** : increasing in a geometric progression ⟨*geometric* population growth⟩

2 *capitalized* : of or relating to a style of ancient Greek pottery characterized by geometric decorative motifs
3 a : utilizing rectilinear or simple curvilinear motifs or outlines in design **b** : of or relating to art based on simple geometric shapes (as straight lines, circles, or squares) ⟨*geometric* abstractions⟩
— **geo·met·ri·cal·ly** \-tri-k(ə-)lē\ *adverb*
geo·me·tri·cian \(,)jē-,ä-mə-'tri-shən, ,jē-ə-mə-\ *noun* (15th century)
: GEOMETER 1
geometric mean *noun* (circa 1901)
: the nth root of the product of *n* numbers; *specifically* : a number that is the second term of three consecutive terms of a geometric progression ⟨the *geometric mean* of 9 and 4 is 6⟩
geometric progression *noun* (circa 1856)
: a sequence (as 1, ½ , ¼) in which the ratio of a term to its predecessor is always the same

— called also *geometrical progression, geometric sequence*
geo·met·rics \,jē-ə-'me-triks\ *noun plural* (1977)
: decorative patterns or designs based on geometric shapes
geometric series *noun* (circa 1909)
: a series (as $1 + x + x^2 + x^3 + \ldots$) whose terms form a geometric progression
geo·me·trid \jē-'ä-mə-trəd, ,jē-ə-'me-trəd\ *noun* [ultimately from Greek *geōmetrēs* geometer, from *geōmetrein*] (1876)
: any of a family (Geometridae) of usually medium-sized moths with large wings and larvae that are loopers
— **geometrid** *adjective*
ge·om·e·trise *British variant of* GEOMETRIZE
ge·om·e·trize \jē-'ä-mə-,trīz\ *verb* **-trized; -triz·ing** (1603)
intransitive verb
: to work by or as if by geometric methods or laws
transitive verb
1 : to represent geometrically
2 : to make conform to geometric principles and laws
— **ge·om·e·tri·za·tion** \-,ä-mə-trə-'zā-shən\ *noun*
ge·om·e·try \jē-'ä-mə-trē\ *noun, plural* **-tries** [Middle English *geometrie*, from Middle French, from Latin *geometria*, from Greek *geōmetria*, from *geōmetrein* to measure the earth, from *geō-* ge- + *metron* measure — more at MEASURE] (14th century)
1 a : a branch of mathematics that deals with the measurement, properties, and relationships of points, lines, angles, surfaces, and solids; *broadly* : the study of properties of given elements that remain invariant under specified transformations **b** : a particular type or system of geometry
2 a : CONFIGURATION **b** : surface shape
3 : an arrangement of objects or parts that suggests geometric figures
geo·mor·phic \,jē-ə-'mȯr-fik\ *adjective* (1893)
: GEOMORPHOLOGICAL
geo·mor·pho·log·i·cal \-mȯr-fə-'lä-ji-kəl\ *adjective* (1896)
: of or relating to the form or surface features of the earth or other celestial body (as the moon)
geo·mor·phol·o·gy \-mȯr-'fä-lə-jē\ *noun, plural* **-gies** [International Scientific Vocabulary] (1893)
1 : a science that deals with the relief features of the earth or of another celestial body (as the moon) and seeks a genetic interpretation of them
2 : the features dealt with in geomorphology
— **geo·mor·phol·o·gist** \-mȯr-'fä-lə-jist\ *noun*
ge·oph·a·gy \jē-'ä-fə-jē\ *noun* [International Scientific Vocabulary] (1850)
: a practice in rural or preindustrial societies of eating earthy substances (as clay) to augment a scanty or mineral-deficient diet — compare ¹PICA
geo·phone \'jē-ə-,fōn\ *noun* (1919)
: an instrument for detecting vibrations passing through rocks, soil, or ice
geo·phys·ics \,jē-ə-'fi-ziks\ *noun plural but singular or plural in construction* [International Scientific Vocabulary] (circa 1889)
: a branch of earth science dealing with the physical processes and phenomena occurring especially in the earth and in its vicinity
— **geo·phys·i·cal** \-zi-kəl\ *adjective*
— **geo·phys·i·cal·ly** \-zi-k(ə-)lē\ *adverb*
— **geo·phys·i·cist** \-'fi-zə-sist\ *noun*
geo·phyte \'jē-ə-,fīt\ *noun* (circa 1900)
: a perennial plant that bears its perennating buds below the surface of the soil
geo·pol·i·ti·cian \,jē-ō-,pä-lə-'ti-shən\ *noun* (1941)
: a specialist in geopolitics

geo·pol·i·tics \-'pä-lə-,tiks\ *noun plural but singular in construction* (1904)
1 : a study of the influence of such factors as geography, economics, and demography on the politics and especially the foreign policy of a state
2 : a governmental policy guided by geopolitics
3 : a combination of political and geographic factors relating to something (as a state or particular resources)
— **geo·po·lit·i·cal** \-pə-'li-ti-kəl\ *adjective*
— **geo·po·lit·i·cal·ly** \-ti-k(ə-)lē\ *adverb*

geo·pres·sured \,jē-ō-'pre-shərd\ *adjective* (1968)
: subjected to great pressure from geologic forces ⟨*geopressured* methane⟩

Geor·die \'jȯr-dē\ *noun* [from *Geordie,* diminutive of the name *George*] (1866)
chiefly British : an inhabitant of Newcastle upon Tyne or its environs; *also* : the dialect of English spoken by Geordies

George \'jȯrj\ *noun* [Saint *George*] (1506)
1 : either of two of the insignia of the British Order of the Garter
2 : a British coin bearing the image of Saint George

geor·gette \jȯr-'jet\ *noun* [from *Georgette,* a trademark] (1915)
: a sheer crepe woven from hard-twisted yarns to produce a dull pebbly surface

¹Geor·gian \'jȯr-jən\ *noun* (15th century)
1 : a native or inhabitant of Georgia in the Caucasus
2 : the language of the Georgian people

²Georgian *adjective* (1607)
: of, relating to, or constituting Georgia in the Caucasus, the Georgians, or Georgian

³Georgian *noun* (1741)
: a native or resident of the state of Georgia

⁴Georgian *adjective* (1762)
: of, relating to, or characteristic of the state of Georgia or its people

⁵Georgian *adjective* (circa 1855)
1 : of, relating to, or characteristic of the reigns of the first four Georges of Great Britain
2 : of, relating to, or characteristic of the reign of George V of Great Britain

⁶Georgian *noun* (1901)
1 : one belonging to either of the Georgian periods; *especially* : a poet of the second decade of the 20th century
2 : Georgian taste or style especially in architecture

¹geor·gic \'jȯr-jik\ *noun* [the *Georgics,* poem by Virgil, from Latin *georgicus*] (1513)
: a poem dealing with agriculture

²georgic *adjective* [Latin *georgicus,* from Greek *geōrgikos,* from *geōrgos* farmer, from *geō-* ge- + *ergon* work — more at WORK] (circa 1720)
: of or relating to agriculture

geo·sci·ence \,jē-ō-'sī-ən(t)s\ *noun* (1942)
1 : the sciences (as geology, geophysics, and geochemistry) dealing with the earth
2 : any of the geosciences — compare EARTH SCIENCE
— **geo·sci·en·tist** \-ən-tist\ *noun*

geo·sta·tion·ary \-'stā-shə-,ner-ē\ *adjective* (1961)
: being or having an equatorial orbit requiring an angular velocity the same as that of the earth so that the position of a satellite in such an orbit is fixed with respect to the earth

geo·strat·e·gy \-'stra-tə-jē\ *noun* (1942)
1 : a branch of geopolitics that deals with strategy
2 : the combination of geopolitical and strategic factors characterizing a particular geographic region
3 : the use by a government of strategy based on geopolitics
— **geo·stra·te·gic** \-strə-'tē-jik\ *adjective*
— **geo·strat·e·gist** \-'stra-tə-jist\ *noun*

geo·stroph·ic \,jē-ə-'strä-fik\ *adjective* [ge- + Greek *strophikos* turned, from *strophē* turning — more at STROPHE] (1916)
: of, relating to, or arising from the Coriolis force
— **geo·stroph·i·cal·ly** \-fi-k(ə-)lē\ *adverb*

geo·syn·chro·nous \,jē-ō-'siŋ-krə-nəs, -'sin-\ *adjective* (1968)
: GEOSTATIONARY

geo·syn·cline \-'sin-,klīn\ *noun* (1895)
: a great downward flexure of the earth's crust — compare GEANTICLINE
— **geo·syn·cli·nal** \-,sin-'klī-nəl\ *adjective*

geo·tac·tic \,jē-ō-'tak-tik\ *adjective* (1899)
: of or relating to geotaxis

geo·tax·is \-'tak-səs\ *noun* [New Latin] (1899)
: a taxis in which the force of gravity is the directive factor

geo·tech·ni·cal \-'tek-ni-kəl\ *adjective* (1967)
: of or relating to geotechnical engineering

geotechnical engineering *noun* (1974)
: a science that deals with the application of geology to engineering

geo·tec·ton·ic \-tek-'tä-nik\ *adjective* (1882)
: of or relating to the form, arrangement, and structure of rock masses of the earth's crust resulting from folding or faulting
— **geo·tec·ton·i·cal·ly** \-ni-k(ə-)lē\ *adverb*

geo·ther·mal \-'thər-məl\ *adjective* [International Scientific Vocabulary] (1875)
: of, relating to, or utilizing the heat of the earth's interior; *also* : produced or permeated by such heat ⟨*geothermal* steam⟩ ⟨*geothermal* region⟩
— **geo·ther·mal·ly** \-mə-lē\ *adverb*

geo·tro·pic \,jē-ə-'trō-pik, -'trä-\ *adjective* (1875)
: of or relating to geotropism
— **geo·tro·pi·cal·ly** \-'trō-pi-k(ə-)lē, -'trä-\ *adverb*

ge·ot·ro·pism \jē-'ä-trə-,pi-zəm\ *noun* [International Scientific Vocabulary] (1875)
: a tropism (as of plant roots) in which gravity is the orienting factor

ge·rah \'gir-ə\ *noun* [Hebrew *gērāh*] (1530)
: an ancient Hebrew unit of weight equal to ¹⁄₂₀ shekel

ge·ra·ni·ol \jə-'rā-nē-,ȯl, -,ōl\ *noun* [International Scientific Vocabulary, from New Latin *Geranium*] (1871)
: a fragrant liquid unsaturated alcohol $C_{10}H_{18}O$ used chiefly in perfumes and soap

ge·ra·ni·um \jə-'rā-nē-əm, -nyəm\ *noun* [New Latin, from Latin, geranium, from Greek *geranion,* from diminutive of *geranos* crane — more at CRANE] (1548)
1 : any of a widely distributed genus (*Geranium* of the family Geraniaceae, the geranium family) of plants having regular usually white, pink, or purple flowers with elongated styles and glands that alternate with the petals
2 : PELARGONIUM
3 : a vivid or strong red

ge·rar·dia \jə-'rär-dē-ə\ *noun* [New Latin, from John *Gerard* (died 1612) English botanist] (1851)
: any of a genus (*Agalinis* synonym *Gerardia*) of often root-parasitic herbs of the snapdragon family having pink, purple, or yellow flowers

ger·bera \'gər-bə-rə, 'jər-\ *noun* [New Latin, from Traugott *Gerber* (died 1743) German naturalist] (1889)
: any of a genus (*Gerbera*) of Old World composite herbs having basal tufted leaves and showy heads of yellow, pink, or orange flowers with prominent rays

ger·bil *also* **ger·bille** \'jər-bəl\ *noun* [French *gerbille,* from New Latin *Gerbillus,* diminutive of *gerboa, jerboa* jerboa] (1849)
: any of numerous Old World burrowing desert rodents (*Gerbillus* and related genera) with long hind legs adapted for leaping

ge·rent \'jir-ənt\ *noun* [Latin *gerent-, gerens,* present participle of *gerere* to bear, carry on] (1576)
: one that rules or manages

ge·re·nuk \'ger-ə-,nůk, gə-'re-nək\ *noun, plural* **gerenuk** *or* **gerenuks** [Somali *gáránúug*] (1895)
: a large-eyed antelope (*Litocranius walleri*) of eastern Africa with a long neck and limbs

ger·fal·con *variant of* GYRFALCON

¹ge·ri·at·ric \,jer-ē-'a-trik, ,jir-\ *noun* (1909)
1 *plural but singular in construction* : a branch of medicine that deals with the problems and diseases of old age and aging people — compare GERONTOLOGY
2 : an aged person

gerenuk

²geriatric *adjective* [Greek *gēras* old age + English *-iatric*] (1926)
1 a : of or relating to geriatrics or the process of aging **b** : of, relating to, or appropriate for elderly people ⟨the *geriatric* set⟩
2 a : OLD, ELDERLY ⟨a *geriatric* dachshund⟩ **b** : being old and outmoded ⟨*geriatric* airplanes⟩

ger·i·a·tri·cian \,jer-ē-ə-'tri-shən, ,jir-\ *noun* (1926)
: a specialist in geriatrics

germ \'jərm\ *noun* [French *germe,* from Latin *germin-, germen,* from *gignere* to beget — more at KIN] (1644)
1 a : a small mass of living substance capable of developing into an organism or one of its parts **b** : the embryo with the scutellum of a cereal grain that is usually separated from the starchy endosperm during milling
2 : something that initiates development or serves as an origin : RUDIMENTS, BEGINNING
3 : MICROORGANISM; *especially* : a microorganism causing disease

¹ger·man \'jər-mən\ *adjective* [Middle English *germain,* from Middle French, from Latin *germanus* having the same parents, from *germen*] (14th century)
: having the same parents or the same grandparents on either the maternal or paternal side — usually used after the noun which it modifies and joined to it by a hyphen ⟨brother-*german*⟩ ⟨cousin-*german*⟩

²german *noun* (15th century)
obsolete : a near relative

¹Ger·man \'jər-mən\ *noun* [Middle English, from Medieval Latin *Germanus,* from Latin] (14th century)
1 : a member of any of the Germanic peoples inhabiting western Europe in Roman times
2 a : a native or inhabitant of Germany **b** : a person of German descent **c** : one whose native language is German and who is a native of a country other than Germany
3 a : the Germanic language spoken mainly in Germany, Austria, and parts of Switzerland **b** : the literary and official language of Germany
4 *often not capitalized* **a** : a dance consisting of intricate figures that are intermingled with waltzes **b** *chiefly Midland* : a dancing party; *specifically* : one at which the german is danced

²German *adjective* (1552)
: of, relating to, or characteristic of Germany, the Germans, or German

German cockroach *noun* (1896)
: a small active winged cockroach (*Blattella germanica*) probably of African origin that is a

common household pest in the U.S. — called also *Croton bug*

ger·man·der \(ˌ)jər-'man-dər\ *noun* [ultimately from Greek *chamaidrys,* from *chamai* on the ground + *drys* tree — more at HUMBLE, TREE] (15th century)
: any of a genus (*Teucrium*) of plants of the mint family with flowers having four exserted stamens, a short corolla tube, and a prominent lower lip

ger·mane \(ˌ)jər-'mān\ *adjective* [Middle English *germain,* literally, having the same parents, from Middle French] (14th century)
1 *obsolete* : closely akin
2 : being at once relevant and appropriate : FITTING ⟨omit details that are not *germane* to the discussion⟩
synonym see RELEVANT
— **ger·mane·ly** *adverb*

¹Ger·man·ic \(ˌ)jər-'ma-nik\ *adjective* (1633)
1 : GERMAN
2 : of, relating to, or characteristic of the Germanic-speaking peoples
3 : of, relating to, or constituting Germanic

²Germanic *noun* (1892)
: a branch of the Indo-European language family containing English, German, Dutch, Afrikaans, Flemish, Frisian, the Scandinavian languages, and Gothic — see INDO-EUROPEAN LANGUAGES table

Ger·man·ism \'jər-mə-ˌni-zəm\ *noun* (1611)
1 : a characteristic feature of German occurring in another language
2 : partiality for Germany or German customs
3 : the practices or objectives characteristic of the Germans

Ger·man·ist \-nist\ *noun* (1831)
: a specialist in German or Germanic language, literature, or culture

ger·ma·ni·um \(ˌ)jər-'mā-nē-əm\ *noun* [New Latin, from Medieval Latin *Germania* Germany] (1886)
: a grayish white hard brittle metalloid element that resembles silicon and is used as a semiconductor — see ELEMENT table

ger·man·ize \'jər-mə-ˌnīz\ *verb* **-ized; -iz·ing** *often capitalized* (1598)
transitive verb
1 *archaic* : to translate into German
2 : to cause to acquire German characteristics
intransitive verb
: to have or acquire German customs or leanings
— **ger·man·iza·tion** \ˌjər-mə-nə-'zā-shən\ *noun, often capitalized*

German measles *noun plural but singular or plural in construction* (circa 1875)
: an acute contagious virus disease that is milder than typical measles but is damaging to the fetus when occurring early in pregnancy

Ger·mano- *combining form*
: German ⟨*Germano*phile⟩

¹Ger·mano·phile \(ˌ)jər-'ma-nə-ˌfīl\ *adjective* (1898)
: approving or favoring the German people and their institutions and customs

²Germanophile *noun* (1911)
: one that is Germanophile

German shepherd *noun* (1926)
: any of a breed of working dogs of German origin that are intelligent and responsive and are often used in police work and as guide dogs for the blind — called also *Alsatian*

German shorthaired pointer *noun* (1931)
: any of a breed of gundogs of German origin that have a liver or liver and white coat

German silver *noun* (1830)
: a silver-white alloy of copper, zinc, and nickel

German wirehaired pointer *noun* (circa 1964)
: any of a breed of gundogs of German origin that have a liver or liver and white flat-lying wiry coat

germ cell *noun* (circa 1855)

: a gamete (as an egg or sperm cell) or one of its antecedent cells

ger·men \'jər-mən\ *noun* [Latin] (1605)
archaic : GERM 1a, 2

germ-free \'jərm-ˌfrē\ *adjective* (1926)
: free of microorganisms : AXENIC

ger·mi·cid·al \ˌjər-mə-'sī-dᵊl\ *adjective* (circa 1888)
: of or relating to a germicide; *also* : destroying germs

ger·mi·cide \'jər-mə-ˌsīd\ *noun* (1881)
: an agent that destroys germs

ger·mi·na·bil·i·ty \ˌjər-mə-nə-'bi-lə-tē\ *noun* (1896)
: the capacity to germinate

ger·mi·nal \'jərm-nəl, 'jer-mə-nᵊl\ *adjective* [French, from Latin *germin-, germen* — more at GERM] (1808)
1 a : being in the earliest stage of development **b** : CREATIVE, PRODUCTIVE
2 : of, relating to, or having the characteristics of a germ cell or early embryo
— **ger·mi·nal·ly** *adverb*

germinal vesicle *noun* (circa 1856)
: the enlarged nucleus of the egg before completion of meiosis

ger·mi·nate \'jər-mə-ˌnāt\ *verb* **-nat·ed; -nat·ing** [Latin *germinatus,* past participle of *germinare* to sprout, from *germin-, germen* bud, germ] (1610)
transitive verb
: to cause to sprout or develop
intransitive verb
1 : to come into being : EVOLVE ⟨before Western civilization began to *germinate* —A. L. Kroeber⟩
2 : to begin to grow : SPROUT
— **ger·mi·na·tion** \ˌjər-mə-'nā-shən\ *noun*
— **ger·mi·na·tive** \'jər-mə-ˌnā-tiv, -mə-nə-\ *adjective*

germ layer *noun* (1879)
: any of the three primary layers of cells differentiated in most embryos during and immediately following gastrulation

germ plasm *noun* (1889)
1 : germ cells and their precursors serving as the bearers of heredity and being fundamentally independent of other cells
2 : the hereditary material of the germ cells : GENES

germ-proof \'jərm-ˌprüf\ *adjective* (1902)
: impervious to the penetration or action of germs

germ theory *noun* (1871)
: a theory in medicine: infections, contagious diseases, and various other conditions result from the action of microorganisms

germ warfare *noun* (1938)
: the use of harmful microorganisms (as bacteria) as weapons in war

germy \'jər-mē\ *adjective* **germ·i·er; -est** (1912)
: full of germs

geront- *or* **geronto-** *combining form* [French *géront-, géronto-,* from Greek *geront-, geronto-,* from *geront-, gerōn* old man; akin to Greek *gēras* old age, Sanskrit *jarati* he grows old]
: aged one : old age ⟨*geronto*logy⟩

ge·ron·tic \jə-'rän-tik\ *adjective* (1885)
: of or relating to decadence or old age

ger·on·toc·ra·cy \ˌjer-ən-'tä-krə-sē\ *noun, plural* **-cies** [French *gérontocratie,* from *géronto-* geront- + *-cratie* -cracy] (1830)
: rule by elders; *specifically* : a form of social organization in which a group of old men or a council of elders dominates or exercises control
— **ge·ron·to·crat** \jə-'rän-tə-ˌkrat\ *noun*
— **ge·ron·to·crat·ic** \-ˌrän-tə-'kra-tik\ *adjective*

ger·on·tol·o·gy \ˌjer-ən-'tä-lə-jē\ *noun* [International Scientific Vocabulary] (1903)
: the comprehensive study of aging and the problems of the aged — compare GERIATRIC 1

— **ge·ron·to·log·i·cal** \jə-ˌränt-ᵊl-'ä-ji-kəl\ *also* **ge·ron·to·log·ic** \-jik\ *adjective*
— **ger·on·tol·o·gist** \ˌjer-ən-'tä-lə-jist\ *noun*

ge·ron·to·mor·phic \jə-ˌrän-tə-'mȯr-fik\ *adjective* (1939)
: characterized by physical specialization most fully developed in the aged male of a species ⟨*gerontomorphic* traits⟩

¹ger·ry·man·der \'jer-ē-ˌman-dər, *also* 'ger-; *originally* 'ger-\ *noun* [Elbridge *Gerry* + sala*mander;* from the shape of an election district formed during Gerry's governorship of Mass.] (1812)
1 : the act or method of gerrymandering
2 : a district or pattern of districts varying greatly in size or population as a result of gerrymandering ◇

²gerrymander *transitive verb* **-dered; -der·ing** \-d(ə-)riŋ\ (1812)
1 : to divide (a territorial unit) into election districts to give one political party an electoral majority in a large number of districts while concentrating the voting strength of the opposition in as few districts as possible
2 : to divide (an area) into political units to give special advantages to one group ⟨*gerrymander* a school district⟩

ger·und \'jer-ənd\ *noun* [Late Latin *gerundium,* from Latin *gerundus,* gerundive of *gerere* to bear, carry on] (1513)
1 : a verbal noun in Latin that expresses generalized or uncompleted action
2 : any of several linguistic forms analogous to the Latin gerund in languages other than Latin; *especially* : the English verbal noun in *-ing* that has the function of a substantive and at the same time shows the verbal features of tense, voice, and capacity to take adverbial qualifiers and to govern objects □

ge·run·dive \jə-'rən-div\ *noun* (15th century)
1 : the Latin future passive participle that functions as the verbal adjective, that expresses the fitness or necessity of the action to be performed, and that has the same suffix as the gerund
2 : a verbal adjective in a language other than Latin analogous to the gerundive

ge·sell·schaft \gə-'zel-ˌshäft\ *noun* [German, companionship, society] (1887)
: a rationally developed mechanistic type of social relationship characterized by impersonally contracted associations between persons;

◇ WORD HISTORY

gerrymander Elbridge Gerry (1744–1814), a Massachusetts politician who signed the Declaration of Independence and was a U.S. vice president, is now chiefly remembered for a bit of political flimflam. As a Democratic-Republican, Gerry was twice elected to the governorship of Massachusetts. His second administration achieved notoriety because of a measure of February 11, 1812, that has since become known as the "Gerrymander Bill." Its purpose was to redistrict the state in such a way as to give the Democratic-Republicans a majority in the state senate. During the ensuing election campaign a member of the opposition Federalists sketched an animal's head, wings, and claws onto an outline of one irregularly shaped senatorial district in Essex County. The fancied resemblance of the resulting image to the mythical salamander inspired the coinage *gerrymander.* This caricature of the district as a winged monster—with Gerry's profile superimposed upon its back—was widely reproduced, and *gerrymander* immediately caught on, at first applied to the caricature itself and then to the actual act of redistricting in such a way as to favor the party in power. Before long it was being used as a verb, too.

ges·ne·ri·ad \ges-'nir-ē-,ad\ *noun* [New Latin *Gesneria*, genus name, from Konrad *Gesner* (died 1565) Swiss naturalist] (circa 1925)
: any of a family (Gesneriaceae) of tropical herbs (as an African violet or gloxinia) with chiefly opposite leaves and highly zygomorphic flowers

ges·so \'je-(,)sō\ *noun, plural* **gessoes** [Italian, literally, gypsum, from Latin *gypsum*] (1596)
1 : plaster of paris or gypsum prepared with glue for use in painting or making bas-reliefs
2 : a paste prepared by mixing whiting with size or glue and spread upon a surface to fit it for painting or gilding
— **ges·soed** \-(,)sōd\ *adjective*

gest *or* **geste** \'jest\ *noun* [Middle English *geste* — more at JEST] (13th century)
1 : a tale of adventures; *especially* : a romance in verse
2 : ADVENTURE, EXPLOIT

ge·stalt \gə-'stält, -'shtält, -'stólt, -'shtólt\ *noun, plural* **ge·stalt·en** \-'stäl-t³n, -'shtäl-, -'stól-, -'shtól-\ *or* **gestalts** [German, literally, shape, form] (1922)
: a structure, configuration, or pattern of physical, biological, or psychological phenomena so integrated as to constitute a functional unit with properties not derivable by summation of its parts

ge·stalt·ist \-'stäl-tist, -'shtäl-, -'stól-, -'shtól-\ *noun, often capitalized* (1931)
: a specialist in Gestalt psychology

Gestalt psychology *noun* (1927)
: the study of perception and behavior from the standpoint of an individual's response to configurational wholes with stress on the uniformity of psychological and physiological events and rejection of analysis into discrete events of stimulus, percept, and response

ge·sta·po \gə-'stä-(,)pō\ *noun, plural* **-pos** [German, from *Geheime Staatspolizei*, literally, secret state police] (1934)
: a secret-police organization employing underhanded and terrorist methods against persons suspected of disloyalty

ges·tate \'jes-,tāt\ *verb* **ges·tat·ed; ges·tat·ing** [back-formation from *gestation*] (1866)
transitive verb
1 : to carry in the uterus during pregnancy
2 : to conceive and gradually develop in the mind
intransitive verb
: to be in the process of gestation

ges·ta·tion \je-'stä-shən\ *noun* [Latin *gestation-, gestatio*, from *gestare* to bear, frequentative of *gerere* to bear] (1615)
1 : the carrying of young in the uterus : PREGNANCY
2 : conception and development especially in the mind
— **ges·ta·tion·al** \-shnəl, -shə-n³l\ *adjective*

geste *also* **gest** \'jest\ *noun* [Middle French *geste*, from Latin *gestus*, from *gerere*] (14th century)
1 *archaic* : DEPORTMENT
2 *archaic* : GESTURE

ges·tic \'jes-tik\ *adjective* (1764)
: relating to or consisting of bodily movements or gestures

ges·tic·u·lant \je-'sti-kyə-lənt\ *adjective* (1877)
: making gesticulations ⟨the little wiry man *gesticulant* and wild —William Faulkner⟩

ges·tic·u·late \je-'sti-kyə-,lāt\ *intransitive verb* **-lat·ed; -lat·ing** [Latin *gesticulatus*, past participle of *gesticulari*, from (assumed) Latin *gesticulus*, diminutive of Latin *gestus*] (circa 1609)
: to make gestures especially when speaking
— **ges·tic·u·la·tive** \je-'sti-kyə-,lā-tiv\ *adjective*

— **ges·tic·u·la·tor** \-,lā-tər\ *noun*
— **ges·tic·u·la·to·ry** \-lə-,tōr-ē, -,tór-\ *adjective*

ges·tic·u·la·tion \je-,sti-kyə-'lā-shən\ *noun* (15th century)
1 : the act of making gestures
2 : GESTURE; *especially* : an expressive gesture made in showing strong feeling or in enforcing an argument

¹ges·ture \'jes-chər, 'jesh-\ *noun* [Middle English, from Medieval Latin *gestura* mode of action, from Latin *gestus*, past participle of *gerere*] (15th century)
1 *archaic* : CARRIAGE, BEARING
2 : a movement usually of the body or limbs that expresses or emphasizes an idea, sentiment, or attitude
3 : the use of motions of the limbs or body as a means of expression
4 : something said or done by way of formality or courtesy, as a symbol or token, or for its effect on the attitudes of others ⟨a political *gesture* to draw popular support —V. L. Parrington⟩
— **ges·tur·al** \-chə-rəl\ *adjective*
— **ges·tur·al·ly** \-chə-rə-lē\ *adverb*

²gesture *verb* **ges·tured; ges·tur·ing** (1542)
intransitive verb
: to make a gesture
transitive verb
: to express or direct by a gesture

gesture language *noun* (1865)
: communication by gestures; *especially* : SIGN LANGUAGE — called also *gestural language*

ge·sund·heit \gə-'zunt-,hīt\ *interjection* [German, literally, health, from *gesund* healthy (from Old High German *gisunt*) + *-heit* -hood — more at SOUND] (1914)
— used to wish good health especially to one who has just sneezed

¹get \'get, ÷'git\ *verb* **got** \'gät\; **got** *or* **got·ten** \'gä-t³n\; **get·ting** [Middle English, from Old Norse *geta* to get, beget; akin to Old English bi*getan* to beget, Latin pre*hendere* to seize, grasp, Greek *chandanein* to hold, contain] (13th century)
transitive verb
1 a : to gain possession of **b** : to receive as a return : EARN ⟨he *got* a bad reputation for carelessness⟩
2 a : to obtain by concession or entreaty ⟨*get* your mother's permission to go⟩ **b** : to become affected by (a disease or bodily condition) : CATCH ⟨*got* measles from his sister⟩
3 a : to seek out and obtain ⟨hoped to *get* dinner at the inn⟩ **b** : to obtain and bring where wanted or needed ⟨*get* a pencil from the desk⟩
4 : BEGET
5 a : to cause to come or go ⟨quickly *got* his luggage through customs⟩ **b** : to cause to move ⟨*get* it out of the house⟩ **c** : to cause to be in a certain position or condition ⟨*got* his feet wet⟩ **d** : to make ready : PREPARE ⟨*get* breakfast⟩
6 a : to be subjected to ⟨*got* a bad fall⟩ **b** : to receive by way of punishment **c** : to suffer a specified injury to ⟨*got* my nose broken⟩
7 a : to achieve as a result of military activity **b** : to obtain or receive by way of benefit or advantage ⟨he *got* little for his trouble⟩ ⟨*get* the better of an enemy⟩
8 a : SEIZE **b** : OVERCOME **c** : to have an emotional effect on ⟨the final scene always *gets* me⟩ **d** : IRRITATE ⟨the delays were starting to *get* her⟩ **e** : PUZZLE **f** : to take vengeance on; *specifically* : KILL **g** : HIT
9 : to prevail on : CAUSE ⟨finally *got* them to tidy up their room⟩
10 a : HAVE — used in the present perfect tense form with present meaning ⟨I've *got* no money⟩ **b** : to have as an obligation or necessity — used in the present perfect tense form with present meaning ⟨you have *got* to come⟩
11 a : to find out by calculation ⟨*get* the answer to a problem⟩ **b** : MEMORIZE ⟨*got* the verse by heart⟩ **c** : HEAR **d** : UNDERSTAND
12 : to establish communication with
13 : to put out in baseball
14 : DELIVER 6b ⟨the car *gets* 20 miles to the gallon⟩
intransitive verb

☐ **USAGE**

gerund A question discussed in many grammars and handbooks is whether the possessive case of a noun or pronoun must be used before a gerund: must it be "I approve of Pat's going" only or is "I approve of Pat going" also acceptable? Actually both forms have been used side by side for many centuries. When grammarians first discovered this fact in the 18th century, they were perplexed; it never occurred to them that there could be two right ways of doing anything—one of them must be wrong. The 18th century grammarians disagreed as to which was right, and 20th century handbooks opt for the possessive and disapprove the objective pronoun and the common-case noun. Historical grammarians have in the meantime been studying the evidence, and they have discovered that certain circumstances influence the choice of the common (or objective) case or the possessive case. If the gerund is certainly a noun, as in Samuel Pepys' "and thence to Jacob Hall's dancing on the ropes"—where *dancing* could be replaced by the noun *performance*—the possessive is always used. Unfortunately, clearcut noun gerunds are relatively uncommon; most gerunds seem to be more verblike. Verblike gerunds can take either the possessive case or the common (or objective) case, but again subtle influences are at work. Pronouns, for instance, are more often possessive ⟨if you don't mind *my* saying so⟩ ⟨no chance of *its* being ignored⟩, but if the pronoun is linked to a noun in the common case, the objective is usual ⟨they joked about my brother and *me* liking rice pudding⟩. Words intervening between the pronoun and the gerund can also trigger the objective case ⟨I don't understand *you*, of all people, *complaining*⟩. The objective case may also be felt to be more emphatic ⟨I can't imagine *me* letting that happen⟩. These same considerations can bring on the common case of nouns ⟨imagine *John*, of all people, *being* frightened⟩. Nouns appear to be somewhat more evenly divided between possessive and common case ⟨afraid of the *money's* being wasted⟩ ⟨seemed pleased at the *book* being out of print⟩. But the possessive is usually not used after nouns ending in an \s\ sound ⟨afraid of the *house* being robbed⟩. Some plurals without final *-s* are used in the common case because the possessive simply sounds wrong ⟨whatever is responsible for my *feet* swelling⟩. Using the common case permits the addition of a parallel construction with the gerund omitted ⟨was sorry to see *Tom* getting all the credit and Paul none⟩. Some words lack a possessive form ⟨never dreamed of *there* being a different way to do it⟩. And the more informal, the more conversational the context, the less likely is the possessive. All of these constructions are standard English, and when there is no reason prompting one form or the other, the choice is open.

1 a : to succeed in coming or going : to bring or move oneself ⟨*get away* to the country⟩ ⟨*got* into the car⟩ **b :** to reach or enter into a certain condition ⟨*got* to sleep after midnight⟩ **c :** to make progress ⟨hasn't *gotten* far with the essay⟩
2 : to acquire wealth
3 a : to be able ⟨never *got* to go to college⟩ **b :** to come to be — often used with following present participle ⟨*got* talking about old times⟩
4 a : to succeed in becoming : BECOME ⟨how to *get* clear of all the debts I owe —Shakespeare⟩ **b :** to become involved ⟨people who *get* into trouble with the law⟩
5 : to leave immediately ⟨told them to *get*⟩
verbal auxiliary
— used with the past participle of transitive verbs as a passive voice auxiliary ⟨they *got* caught in the act⟩ □
— get a bead on : to gain a precise and telling knowledge or understanding of ⟨*got a bead on* his motives⟩
— get after : to pursue with exhortation, reprimand, or attack
— get ahead : to achieve success ⟨determined to *get ahead* in life⟩
— get a move on : HURRY
— get at 1 : to reach effectively **2 :** to influence corruptly : BRIBE **3 :** to turn one's attention to **4 :** to try to prove or make clear ⟨what is he *getting at*⟩
— get away with : to avoid criticism or punishment for or the consequences of (as a reprehensible act)
— get cracking : to make a start : get going ⟨ought to *get cracking* on that assignment⟩
— get even : to get revenge
— get even with : to repay in kind
— get going : to make a start
— get into : to become strongly involved with or deeply interested in
— get it : to receive a scolding or punishment
— get it on 1 : to become enthusiastic, energetic, or excited **2 :** to engage in sexual intercourse
— get on : to produce an unfortunate effect on : UPSET ⟨the noise *got on* my nerves⟩
— get one's act together 1 : to put one's life, thoughts, or emotions in order : cease to be confused or misdirected **2 :** to begin to function in a skillful or efficient manner ⟨the company finally *got its act together*⟩
— get one's goat : to make one angry or annoyed
— get over 1 a : OVERCOME, SURMOUNT **b :** to recover from **c :** to reconcile oneself to : become accustomed to **2 :** to move or travel across
— get somewhere : to be successful
— get there : to be successful
— get through : to reach the end of : COMPLETE
— get to 1 a : BEGIN ⟨*gets to* worrying over nothing at all⟩ **b :** to be ready to begin or deal with ⟨I'll *get to* the accounts as soon as I can⟩ **2 :** to have an effect on: as **a :** INFLUENCE **b :** BOTHER
— get together 1 : to bring together : ACCUMULATE **2 :** to come together : ASSEMBLE, MEET **3 :** to reach agreement
— get wind of : to become aware of
— get with it : to become alert or aware : show sophisticated consciousness
²**get** \'get\ *noun* (14th century)
1 a : something begotten: (1) : OFFSPRING (2) : the entire progeny of a male animal **b :** LINEAGE
2 : a return of a difficult shot in a game (as tennis)
³**get** \'get\ *noun, plural* **git·tin** \gē-'tēn, 'gi-tin\ [Late Hebrew *gēṭ*] (1892)
1 : a document of release from obligation in Jewish law; *specifically* : a bill of divorce
2 : a religious divorce by Jewish law

ge·ta \'ge-(,)tä, -tə\ *noun, plural* **geta** *or* **ge·tas** [Japanese] (1884)
: a Japanese wooden clog for outdoor wear

geta

get about *intransitive verb* (1816)
1 : to become current : CIRCULATE
2 : to be up and about : begin to walk ⟨able to *get about* again⟩
get across (1913)
intransitive verb
: to become clear or convincing
transitive verb
: to make clear or convincing ⟨we couldn't *get* our point *across*⟩
get along *intransitive verb* (1768)
1 a : to proceed toward a destination : PROGRESS **b :** to approach an advanced stage; *especially* : to approach old age
2 : to meet one's needs : MANAGE ⟨we *got along* on a minimum of clothing⟩
3 : to be or remain on congenial terms
get around (1875)
transitive verb
1 : CIRCUMVENT, EVADE
2 : to get the better of
intransitive verb
1 a : to find or take the necessary time or effort — used with *to* **b :** to give attention or consideration — used with *to*
2 : to go from place to place
3 : to become known or current ⟨word *got around* that he was resigning⟩
get·at·able \get-'a-tə-bəl\ *adjective* (1799)
: ACCESSIBLE, APPROACHABLE
get·away \'ge-tə-,wā\ *noun* (1890)
1 : an act or instance of getting away: as **a :** ESCAPE **b :** START
2 : a place suitable for a vacation
3 : a vacation especially of brief duration
get back (1605)
intransitive verb
1 : to come or go again to a person, place, or condition : RETURN, REVERT ⟨*getting back* to the main topic of the lecture⟩
2 : to gain revenge : RETALIATE — used with *at*
transitive verb
: to regain possession of : RECOVER
get by *intransitive verb* (1908)
1 : to succeed with the least possible effort or accomplishment
2 : to make ends meet : SURVIVE
3 : to proceed without being discovered, criticized, or punished
get down (1757)
intransitive verb
1 : to alight especially from a vehicle : DESCEND
2 : to give one's attention or consideration — used with *to* ⟨*get down* to business⟩
transitive verb
1 : to cause to be physically, mentally, or emotionally exhausted : DEPRESS ⟨the weather was *getting* her *down*⟩
2 : to manage to swallow
3 : to commit to writing : DESCRIBE
get-go \'git-,gō, 'get-\ *noun* (1980)
: the very beginning — used in the phrase *from the get-go* ⟨didn't like me from the *get-go*⟩
Geth·sem·a·ne \geth-'se-mə-nē\ *noun* [Greek *Gethsēmanē*]
1 : the garden outside Jerusalem mentioned in Mark 14 as the scene of the agony and arrest of Jesus
2 : a place or occasion of great mental or spiritual suffering
get in (circa 1533)
intransitive verb
1 a : ENTER **b :** ARRIVE
2 a : to become friendly **b :** to become involved
3 : to become accepted for membership or chosen for office

transitive verb
1 : to succeed in doing, making, or delivering
2 : to include in one's schedule
3 : INVOLVE 2a, b
get off (1640)
intransitive verb
1 : to avoid the most serious consequences of a dangerous situation or punishment ⟨*got off* with a light sentence⟩
2 : START, LEAVE ⟨*got off* on the trip early⟩
3 : to leave work with permission or as scheduled
4 : to get high on a drug
5 : to experience orgasm
6 : to experience great pleasure — often used with *on*
transitive verb
1 : to secure the release of or procure a modified penalty for ⟨his lawyers *got* him *off*⟩
2 a : UTTER ⟨*get off* a joke⟩ **b :** to write and send
3 : to succeed in doing, making, or delivering
4 : to cause to get off
get on *intransitive verb* (1816)
1 : GET ALONG ⟨was *getting on* in years⟩ ⟨*got on* well with the boss⟩ ⟨*get on* with the game⟩
2 : to gain knowledge or understanding ⟨*got on* to the racket⟩
get out (14th century)
intransitive verb
1 : LEAVE, ESCAPE ⟨doubted that he would *get out* alive⟩
2 : to become known : leak out ⟨their secret *got out*⟩
transitive verb
1 : to cause to leave or escape
2 : to bring before the public; *especially* : PUBLISH
get round *intransitive verb* (1748)
: GET AROUND
get·ter \'ge-tər\ *noun* (15th century)
1 : one that gets
2 : a substance introduced into a vacuum tube or electric lamp to remove traces of gas
get through *intransitive verb* (1694)
1 : to reach a destination
2 : to gain approval or a desired outcome
3 a : to make something clear **b :** to complete a communications connection
get-to-geth-er \'get-tə-,ge-thər\ *noun* (1911)
: MEETING; *especially* : an informal social gathering
get-up \'get-,əp\ *noun* (1847)
1 : OUTFIT, COSTUME
2 : general composition or structure
get up (14th century)
intransitive verb
1 a : to arise from bed **b :** to rise to one's feet **c :** CLIMB, ASCEND
2 : to go ahead or faster — used in the imperative as a command especially to driven animals
transitive verb
1 : to make preparations for : ORGANIZE ⟨*got up* a party for the newcomers⟩
2 : to arrange as to external appearance : DRESS
3 : to acquire a knowledge of
4 : to create in oneself ⟨cannot *get up* the courage to tell them⟩

□ **USAGE**
get The pronunciation \'git\ has been noted as a feature of some British and American dialects since the 16th century. In the phonetic spelling of his own speech Benjamin Franklin records *git*. However, since at least 1687 some grammarians and teachers have disapproved this pronunciation. It nonetheless remains in widespread and unpredictable use in many dialects, often, but not exclusively, when *get* is a passive auxiliary (as in *get married*) or an imperative (as in *get up!*).

get–up–and–go \get-,əp-ᵊn-'gō, ,git-, -ᵊm-, -ᵊn̩-\ *noun* (1906)
: ENERGY, DRIVE

ge·um \'jē-əm\ *noun* [Latin] (circa 1548)
: AVENS

gew·gaw \'g(y)ü-(,)gȯ\ *noun* [origin unknown] (circa 1529)
: a showy trifle : BAUBLE, TRINKET

ge·würz·tra·mi·ner \gə-'vùrt-,stra-mə-nər, -'vərt-, -,strä; -strə-'mē-nər, *often capitalized* [German, variety of grape, from *Gewürz* spice + *Traminer,* variety of grape, from *Tramin* (Termeno, Italy)] (circa 1950)
: a light dry Alsatian white wine with a spicy bouquet; *also* : a similar wine made elsewhere

gey \'gā\ *adverb* [alteration of *gay,* adverb] (1796)
chiefly Scottish : VERY, QUITE

gey·ser \'gī-zər, *British sometimes* 'gā- *or* 'gē- *for* 1 & *usually* 'gē- *for* 2\ *noun* [Icelandic *Geysir,* hot spring in Iceland, from *geysa* to rush forth, from Old Norse; akin to Old English *gēotan* to pour — more at FOUND] (1780)
1 : a spring that throws forth intermittent jets of heated water and steam
2 *British* : an apparatus for heating water rapidly with a gas flame (as for a bath)

gey·ser·ite \-zə-,rīt\ *noun* [French *geysérite,* from *geyser,* from Icelandic *Geysir*] (circa 1814)
: a hydrous silica that constitutes one variety of opal and is deposited around some hot springs and geysers in white or grayish concretions

g–fac·tor \'jē-,fak-tər\ *noun* (1942)
: GYROMAGNETIC RATIO

gha·ri·al \'ger-ē-əl\ *noun* [Hindi *ghaṛyāl*] (circa 1809)
: GAVIAL

ghar·ry \'gar-ē, 'gär-\ *noun, plural* **gharries** [Hindi *gāṛī*] (1810)
: a horse-drawn cab used especially in India and Egypt

ghast \'gast\ *adjective* (1622)
archaic : GHASTLY

ghast·ful \-fəl\ *adjective* (14th century)
archaic : FRIGHTFUL
— **ghast·ful·ly** *adverb, archaic*

ghast·ly \'gast-lē\ *adjective* **ghast·li·er; -est** [Middle English *gastly,* from *gasten* to terrify — more at GAST] (14th century)
1 a : terrifyingly horrible to the senses : FRIGHTENING ⟨a *ghastly* crime⟩ **b** : intensely unpleasant, disagreeable, or objectionable ⟨such a life seems *ghastly* in its emptiness and sterility —Aldous Huxley⟩
2 : resembling a ghost
3 *obsolete* : filled with fear
4 : very great ⟨*ghastly* mistake⟩ ☆
— **ghast·li·ness** *noun*
— **ghastly** *adverb*

ghat \'gȯt, 'gät\ *noun* [Hindi *ghāṭ,* from Sanskrit *ghaṭṭa*] (1783)
: a broad flight of steps that is situated on an Indian riverbank and that provides access to the water especially for bathing

ghee *or* **ghi** \'gē\ *noun* [Hindi *ghī,* from Sanskrit *ghṛta*] (1665)
: a semifluid clarified butter made especially in India

gher·kin \'gər-kən\ *noun* [Dutch *gurken,* plural of *gurk* cucumber, ultimately from Middle Greek *agouros*] (1661)
1 : a small prickly fruit used for pickling; *also* : the slender annual vine (*Cucumis anguria*) of the gourd family that bears it
2 : the immature fruit of the cucumber

¹ghet·to \'ge-(,)tō\ *noun, plural* **ghettos** *also* **ghettoes** [Italian, from Venetian dialect *ghèto* island where Jews were forced to live, literally, foundry (located on the island), from *ghetàr* to cast, from Latin *jactare* to throw — more at JET] (1611)
1 : a quarter of a city in which Jews were formerly required to live

2 : a quarter of a city in which members of a minority group live especially because of social, legal, or economic pressure
3 a : an isolated group ⟨a geriatric *ghetto*⟩ **b** : a situation that resembles a ghetto especially in conferring inferior status or limiting opportunity ⟨stuck in daytime TV's *ghetto*⟩ ◇

²ghetto *transitive verb* (1936)
: GHETTOIZE

ghetto blaster *noun* (1983)
: BOOM BOX

ghet·to·ize \'ge-tō-,īz\ *transitive verb* **-ized; -iz·ing** (1939)
: to isolate in or as if in a ghetto
— **ghet·to·iza·tion** \,ge-tō-ə-'zā-shən\ *noun*

Ghib·el·line \'gi-bə-,lēn, -,līn, -lən\ *noun* [Italian *Ghibellino*] (1573)
: a member of an aristocratic political party in medieval Italy supporting the authority of the German emperors — compare GUELF

ghib·li \'gib-lē\ *noun* [Arabic dialect *giblīy* south wind, from Arabic *qiblī* southern] (1942)
: a hot desert wind of northern Africa

ghil·lie *variant of* GILLIE

¹ghost \'gōst\ *noun* [Middle English *gost, gast,* from Old English *gāst;* akin to Old High German *geist* spirit, Sanskrit *heḍa* anger] (before 12th century)
1 : the seat of life or intelligence : SOUL ⟨give up the *ghost*⟩
2 : a disembodied soul; *especially* : the soul of a dead person believed to be an inhabitant of the unseen world or to appear to the living in bodily likeness
3 : SPIRIT, DEMON
4 a : a faint shadowy trace ⟨a *ghost* of a smile⟩ **b** : the least bit ⟨not a *ghost* of a chance⟩
5 : a false image in a photographic negative or on a television screen caused especially by reflection
6 : one who ghostwrites
7 : a red blood cell that has lost its hemoglobin ◇
— **ghost·like** \-,līk\ *adjective*
— **ghosty** \'gō-stē\ *adjective*

²ghost (1606)
transitive verb
1 : to haunt like a ghost
2 : GHOSTWRITE
intransitive verb
1 a : to move silently like a ghost **b** : to sail quietly in light winds
2 : GHOSTWRITE

Ghost Dance *noun* (1890)
: a group dance of a late 19th century American Indian messianic cult believed to promote the return of the dead and the restoration of traditional ways of life

ghost·ing *noun* (circa 1957)
: a false image on a television screen; *also* : the formation of such images

ghost·ly \'gōst-lē\ *adjective* **ghost·li·er; -est** (before 12th century)
1 : of or relating to the soul : SPIRITUAL
2 : of, relating to, or having the characteristics of a ghost : SPECTRAL
— **ghost·li·ness** *noun*
— **ghostly** *adverb*

ghost story *noun* (1819)
1 : a story about ghosts
2 : a tale based on imagination rather than fact

ghost town *noun* (1931)
: a once-flourishing town wholly or nearly deserted usually as a result of the exhaustion of some natural resource

ghost word *noun* (1886)
: a word form never in established usage

ghost·write \'gōs(t)-,rīt\ *verb* **-wrote** \-,rōt\; **-writ·ten** \-,ri-tᵊn\ [back-formation from *ghostwriter*] (1927)
intransitive verb
: to write for and in the name of another

◇ WORD HISTORY
ghetto The etymology of Italian *ghetto* was formerly the subject of much speculation; among many hypotheses were suggestions that it had been shortened from Italian *borghetto,* a diminutive of *borgo* "small town, suburb," or that it had developed from Talmudic Hebrew *gēṭ* "document of release." Today there is little doubt on historical and linguistic grounds that the word comes from an Italian dialect form *ghèto* "foundry." A foundry for cannons was once located on an island forming part of Venice, where in 1516 the Venetians restricted Jewish residence. The word *ghèto* became the name for the quarter and was borrowed into standard Tuscan-based Italian as *ghetto,* with the generic meaning "quarter of a city where Jews are forced to live." From there it passed into most of the languages of Europe. The word took on its darkest connotations during World War II, when Nazi imprisonment of Jews in sectors of Warsaw, Lódź, and other Polish cities led to thousands of deaths through malnutrition and disease. Since the late 19th century, the reference of *ghetto* has been extended to crowded urban districts where other ethnic or racial groups have been confined by poverty and prejudice, and this is probably its most frequent current use.

ghost English *ghost* is descended directly from Old English *gāst,* which meant "soul" or "spirit." These senses now survive mainly in the idiom *to give up the ghost,* and in the Christian epithet *Holy Ghost* for the third person of the Trinity. Not untypically for English, a loanword, *spirit* (from Latin *spiritus*), fills in for the primary sense of an old native word that later developed a very restricted sense. *Ghost* now usually alludes to the spirit of a dead person that supposedly appears to the living in its bodily likeness—a meaning not attested in English before the 14th century. This situation contrasts with the history of German *Geist,* an exact cognate of *ghost,* which from Old High German to the present has retained its primary sense, "spirit." The peculiar spelling of English *ghost* with an initial *gh,* which did not become general until the end of the 16th century, was apparently introduced by the 15th century English printer and translator William Caxton. Having lived in the Low Countries for many years, Caxton most likely adopted the *gh* from Middle Dutch *gheest,* another Germanic cognate of *ghost.*

transitive verb
: to write (as a speech) for another who is the presumed author
— **ghost·writ·er** *noun*

ghoul \'gül\ *noun* [Arabic *ghūl*] (1786)
1 : a legendary evil being that robs graves and feeds on corpses
2 : one suggestive of a ghoul
— **ghoul·ish** \'gü-lish\ *adjective*
— **ghoul·ish·ly** *adverb*
— **ghoul·ish·ness** *noun*

ghou·lie \'gü-lē\ *noun* (1928)
: GHOUL 1

¹GI \,jē-'ī\ *adjective* [galvanized iron; from abbreviation used in listing such articles as garbage cans, but taken as abbreviation for *government issue*] (circa 1935)
1 : provided by an official U.S. military supply department ⟨*GI* shoes⟩
2 : of, relating to, or characteristic of U.S. military personnel
3 : conforming to military regulations or customs ⟨a *GI* haircut⟩

²GI *noun, plural* **GIs** or **GI's** \-'īz\ (1943)
: a member or former member of the U.S. armed forces; *especially* : a man enlisted in the army

³GI *adverb* (1949)
: in a strictly regulation manner

⁴GI *transitive verb* **GI'd** \-'īd\; **GI'·ing** \-'ī-iŋ\ (1951)
: to clean thoroughly (as floors) in preparation for or as if for a military inspection

¹gi·ant \'jī-ənt\ *noun* [Middle English *giaunt*, from Old French *geant*, from Latin *gigant-, gigas*, from Greek] (14th century)
1 : a legendary humanlike being of great stature and strength
2 a : a living being of great size **b** : a person of extraordinary powers
3 : something unusually large or powerful
— **gi·ant·like** \-,līk\ *adjective*

²giant *adjective* (15th century)
: having extremely large size, proportion, or power

giant anteater *noun* (1940)
: a large bushy-tailed anteater (*Myrmecophaga tridactyla*) of Central and South America

giant cactus *noun* (circa 1884)
: SAGUARO

giant clam *noun* (circa 1889)
: a very large clam (*Tridacna gigas*) found on the coral reefs of the Indian and Pacific oceans that sometimes weighs more than 500 pounds (227 kilograms)

gi·ant·ess \'jī-ən-təs\ *noun* (14th century)
: a female giant

gi·ant·ism \'jī-ən-,ti-zəm\ *noun* (1639)
1 : the quality or state of being a giant ⟨*giantism* in industry⟩
2 : GIGANTISM 2

giant panda *noun* (1920)
: a large black-and-white mammal (*Ailuropoda melanoleuca*) of chiefly central China now usually classified with the bears (family Ursidae) — see PANDA illustration

giant reed *noun* (1851)
: a tall European grass (*Arundo donax*) with woody stems used especially in making organ reeds, baskets, and shelters

giant schnauzer *noun* (circa 1934)
: any of a breed of powerful heavyset schnauzers that attain a height of 23½ to 27½ inches (60 to 70 centimeters)

giant sequoia *noun* (circa 1931)
: BIG TREE

giant slalom *noun* (1952)
: a slalom race for skiers on a longer and steeper course than that used for the regular slalom

giant squid *noun* (circa 1890)
: any of a genus (*Architeuthis*) of extremely large squids that include the largest mollusks known

giant star *noun* (1912)
: a star of great luminosity and of large mass

giant tortoise *noun* (circa 1909)
: any of various large long-lived herbivorous land tortoises (genus *Geochelone*) formerly common on the islands of the western Indian Ocean and on the Galapagos Islands

giant water bug *noun* (1901)
: any of a family (Belostomatidae and especially genus *Lethocerus*) of very large predatory bugs capable of inflicting a painful bite

giaour \'jaù-(-ə)r\ *noun* [French, from Italian dialect (Venetian) *giaur*, from Turkish *gâvur*, from Persian *gawr*] (1564)
: one outside the Islamic faith : INFIDEL 2a

giar·di·a·sis \(,)jē-,är-'dī-ə-səs, jē-ər-, jär-\ *noun, plural* **-a·ses** \-,sēz\ [New Latin, from *Giardia*, from Alfred M. *Giard* (died 1908) French biologist] (1919)
: infestation with or disease caused by a flagellate protozoan (genus *Giardia* and especially *G. lamblia* in humans) that is often characterized by diarrhea

¹gib \'gib\ *noun* [Middle English, from *Gib*, nickname for *Gilbert*] (1561)
: a male cat; *specifically* : a castrated male cat

²gib *noun* [origin unknown] (1795)
: a plate of metal or other material machined to hold other parts in place, to afford a bearing surface, or to provide means for overcoming looseness

gib·ber \'ji-bər\ *intransitive verb* **gib·bered; gib·ber·ing** \-b(ə-)riŋ\ [imitative] (1604)
: to speak rapidly, inarticulately, and often foolishly
— **gibber** *noun*

gib·ber·el·lic acid \,ji-bə-'re-lik-\ *noun* (1954)
: a crystalline acid $C_{19}H_{22}O_6$ that is a gibberellin used especially in the malting of barley

gib·ber·el·lin \-'re-lən\ *noun* [New Latin *Gibberella fujikoroi*, fungus from which it was first isolated] (1939)
: any of several growth-regulating plant hormones that promote cell elongation and activity of the cambium, induce parthenocarpy, and stimulate synthesis of nucleic acids and proteins

gib·ber·ish \'ji-b(ə-)rish, 'gi-\ *noun* [probably from *gibber*] (circa 1554)
: unintelligible or meaningless language: **a** : a technical or esoteric language **b** : pretentious or needlessly obscure language

¹gib·bet \'ji-bət\ *noun* [Middle English *gibet*, from Old French] (13th century)
1 : GALLOWS
2 : an upright post with a projecting arm for hanging the bodies of executed criminals as a warning

²gibbet *transitive verb* (1646)
1 a : to expose to infamy or public scorn **b** : to hang on a gibbet
2 : to execute by hanging on a gibbet

gib·bon \'gi-bən\ *noun* [French] (1774)
: any of a genus (*Hylobates*) of brachiating tailless apes of southeastern Asia that are the smallest and most arboreal anthropoid apes

gib·bos·i·ty \ji-'bä-sə-tē, gi-\ *noun, plural* **-ties** (14th century)
: PROTUBERANCE, SWELLING

gib·bous \'ji-bəs, 'gi-\ *adjective* [Middle English, from Middle French *gibbeux*, from Late Latin *gibbosus* humpbacked, from Latin *gibbus* hump] (14th century)
1 a : marked by convexity or swelling **b** *of the moon or a planet* : seen with more than half but not all of the apparent disk illuminated
2 : having a hump : HUMPBACKED

gibe \'jīb\ *verb* **gibed; gib·ing** [perhaps from Middle French *giber* to shake, handle roughly] (1567)

gibbon

intransitive verb
: to utter taunting words
transitive verb
: to deride or tease with taunting words
synonym see SCOFF
— **gibe** *noun*
— **gib·er** *noun*

gib·lets \'jib-ləts *also* 'gib-\ *noun plural* [Middle English *gibelet* entrails, garbage, from Middle French, stew of wildfowl] (15th century)
: the edible viscera of a fowl

Gi·bral·tar \jə-'bròl-tər\ *noun* [*Gibraltar*, fortress in the British colony of Gibraltar] (1856)
: an impregnable stronghold

Gib·son \'gib-sən\ *noun* [from the name *Gibson*] (1948)
: a martini garnished with a cocktail onion

Gibson girl *adjective* [Charles D. *Gibson*] (1936)
: of or relating to a style especially in women's clothing characterized by high necks, full sleeves, and wasp waists

gid \'gid\ *noun* [back-formation from *giddy*] (1601)
: a disease especially of sheep caused by the larva of a tapeworm (*Multiceps multiceps*) in the brain

gid·dap \gi-'dap, -'dəp\ *also* **gid·dy·ap** \,gi-dē-'ap, -'əp\ *verb imperative* [alteration of *get up*] (circa 1897)
— a command to a horse to go ahead or go faster

¹gid·dy \'gi-dē\ *adjective* **gid·di·er; -est** [Middle English *gidy* mad, foolish, from Old English *gydig* possessed, mad; akin to Old English *god* god] (14th century)
1 a : DIZZY ⟨*giddy* from the unaccustomed exercise⟩ **b** : causing dizziness ⟨a *giddy* height⟩ **c** : whirling rapidly
2 a : lightheartedly silly : FRIVOLOUS **b** : joyfully elated : EUPHORIC ◆
— **gid·di·ly** \'gi-dᵊl-ē\ *adverb*
— **gid·di·ness** \'gi-dē-nəs\ *noun*

²giddy *verb* **gid·died; gid·dy·ing** (1602)
transitive verb
: to make giddy
intransitive verb
: to become giddy

Gid·e·on \'gi-dē-ən\ *noun* [Hebrew *Gidh'ōn*]
1 : an early Hebrew hero noted for his defeat of the Midianites
2 : a member of an interdenominational organization whose activities include the placing of Bibles in hotel rooms

gie \'gē\ *chiefly Scottish variant of* GIVE

Gi·em·sa stain \gē-'em-zə-\ *noun* [Gustav *Giemsa* (died 1948) German chemotherapist] (circa 1909)
: a stain consisting of eosin and a blue dye and used chiefly in the differential staining of blood films — called also *Giemsa, Giemsa's stain*

¹**gift** \'gift\ *noun* [Middle English, from Old Norse, something given, talent; akin to Old English *giefan* to give] (12th century)
1 : a notable capacity, talent, or endowment
2 : something voluntarily transferred by one person to another without compensation
3 : the act, right, or power of giving ☆

²**gift** *transitive verb* (circa 1550)
1 : to endow with some power, quality, or attribute
2 : PRESENT ⟨generously *gifted* us with a copy —*Saturday Review*⟩

gift certificate *noun* (1942)
: a certificate entitling the recipient to purchase goods or services in the establishment of the issuer to the amount specified

gift·ed \'gif-təd\ *adjective* (1644)
1 : having great natural ability : TALENTED ⟨*gifted* children⟩
2 : revealing a special gift ⟨*gifted* voices⟩
— **gift·ed·ly** *adverb*
— **gift·ed·ness** *noun*

gift of gab (circa 1890)
: the ability to talk glibly and persuasively

gift of tongues [from the gifts of the Spirit in 1 Corinthians 12:1–13] (1560)
: the charismatic gift of ecstatic speech

gift·ware \'gift-,war, -,wer\ *noun* (1904)
: wares or goods suitable for gifts

gift wrap *transitive verb* (1936)
: to wrap (merchandise intended as a gift) decoratively

¹**gig** \'gig\ *noun* [Middle English *-gyge* (in *whyrlegyge* whirligig), of unknown origin] (1570)
1 : something that whirls or is whirled: as **a** *obsolete* : TOP, WHIRLIGIG **b** : a 3-digit selection in a numbers game
2 : a person of odd or grotesque appearance
3 a : a long light ship's boat **b** : a rowboat designed for speed rather than for work
4 : a light two-wheeled one-horse carriage

²**gig** *intransitive verb* **gigged; gig·ging** (1807)
: to travel in a gig

³**gig** *noun* [short for earlier *fizgig, fishgig*, of unknown origin] (1722)
1 : a pronged spear for catching fish
2 : an arrangement of hooks to be drawn through a school of fish in order to hook their bodies

⁴**gig** *verb* **gigged; gig·ging** (1803)
transitive verb
1 : to spear with a gig
2 a *chiefly West* : SPUR, JAB **b** : GOAD, PROVOKE
intransitive verb
: to fish with a gig

⁵**gig** *noun* [origin unknown] (1926)
: a job usually for a specified time; *especially* : an entertainer's engagement

⁶**gig** *intransitive verb* **gigged; gig·ging** (1939)
: to work as a musician ⟨*gigged* with various bands —*Downbeat*⟩

⁷**gig** *noun* [origin unknown] (circa 1941)
: a military demerit

⁸**gig** *transitive verb* **gigged; gig·ging** (circa 1941)
: to give a military gig to

giga- \'ji-gə, 'gi-\ *combining form* [International Scientific Vocabulary, from Greek *gigas* giant]
: billion ⟨*giga*hertz⟩ ⟨*giga*watt⟩

giga·bit \-,bit\ *noun* (1970)
: a unit of information equal to one billion bits

giga·byte \-,bīt\ *noun* (1975)
: 1,073,741,824 bytes

giga·hertz \-,hərts, -,herts\ *noun* (1964)
: a unit of frequency equal to one billion hertz

gi·gan·tesque \,jī-,gan-'tesk, -gən-\ *adjective* (1821)
: of enormous or grotesquely large proportions

¹**gi·gan·tic** \jī-'gan-tik, jə-\ *adjective* [Greek *gigantikos*, from *gigant-, gigas* giant] (1651)
: exceeding the usual or expected (as in size, force, or prominence) ⟨a man of *gigantic* stature⟩ ⟨made a last *gigantic* effort⟩ ⟨*gigantic* industrial combines⟩
synonym see ENORMOUS
— **gi·gan·ti·cal·ly** \-ti-k(ə-)lē\ *adverb*

gi·gan·tism \jī-'gan-,ti-zəm, jə-; 'jī-gən-\ *noun* (circa 1885)
1 : GIANTISM 1
2 : development to abnormally large size
3 : excessive vegetative growth often accompanied by the inhibiting of reproduction

gi·gas \'jī-gəs\ *adjective* [New Latin, from Latin, giant, from Greek] (1915)
of a polyploid plant : having thicker stem, taller growth, darker thicker leaves, and larger flowers and seeds than a corresponding diploid

giga·watt \'ji-gə-,wät, 'gi-\ *noun* (circa 1962)
: a unit of power equal to one billion watts

¹**gig·gle** \'gi-gəl\ *verb* **gig·gled; gig·gling** \-g(ə-)liŋ\ [imitative] (1509)
intransitive verb
: to laugh with repeated short catches of the breath
transitive verb
: to utter with a giggle
— **gig·gler** \-g(ə-)lər\ *noun*
— **gig·gling·ly** \-g(ə-)liŋ-lē\ *adverb*
— **gig·gly** \-g(ə-)lē\ *adjective*

²**giggle** *noun* (circa 1677)
1 : the act of giggling
2 *chiefly British* : a source of amusement

gig·o·lo \'ji-gə-,lō, 'zhi-\ *noun, plural* **-los** [French] (1922)
1 : a man supported by a woman usually in return for his attentions
2 : a professional dancing partner or male escort

gi·got \'ji-gət, zhē-'gō\ *noun, plural* **gi·gots** \-gəts, -'gō(z)\ [Middle French, diminutive of *gigue* fiddle; from its shape — more at JIG] (1526)
1 : a leg of meat (as lamb) especially when cooked
2 : a leg-of-mutton sleeve

gigue \'zhēg\ *noun* [French, from English *jig*] (1685)
: a lively dance movement (as of a suite) having compound triple rhythm and composed in fugal style

Gi·la monster \'hē-lə-\ *noun* [*Gila* River, Ariz.] (1877)
: a large orange and black venomous lizard (*Heloderma suspectum*) of the southwestern U.S.; *also* : a related lizard (*H. horridum*) of Mexico

Gila monster

gil·bert \'gil-bərt\ *noun* [William *Gilbert*] (1893)
: the centimeter-gram-second unit of magnetomotive force equivalent to 10÷4π ampere-turn

¹**gild** \'gild\ *transitive verb* **gild·ed** \'gil-dəd\ *or* **gilt** \'gilt\; **gild·ing** [Middle English, from Old English *gyldan;* akin to Old English *gold* gold] (14th century)
1 : to overlay with or as if with a thin covering of gold
2 a : to give money to **b** : to give an attractive but often deceptive appearance to **c** *archaic* : to make bloody
— **gild·er** *noun*
— **gild the lily** : to add unnecessary ornamentation to something beautiful in its own right

²**gild** *variant of* GUILD

Gil·ga·mesh \'gil-gə-,mesh\

: a legendary Sumerian king and hero of the *Gilgamesh Epic*

¹**gill** \'jil\ *noun* [Middle English *gille*, from Medieval Latin *gillus*, from Late Latin *gillo, gello* water pot] (14th century)
— see WEIGHT table

²**gill** \'gil\ *noun* [Middle English *gile*, of Scandinavian origin; akin to Swedish *gäl* gill, Old Norse *gjǫlnar* lips; akin to Greek *chelynē* lip, jawbone] (14th century)
1 : an organ (as of a fish) for obtaining oxygen from water
2 a : WATTLE 2 **b** : the flesh under or about the chin or jaws — usually used in plural **c** : one of the radiating plates forming the undersurface of the cap of a mushroom fungus
— **gilled** \'gild\ *adjective*
— **to the gills** : as full as possible

³**gill** \'gil\ (1884)
transitive verb
: GILLNET
intransitive verb
of fish : to become entangled in a gill net
— **gill·er** *noun*

⁴**gill** \'gil\ *noun* [Middle English *gille*, from Old Norse *gil;* akin to Old High German *gil* hernia] (14th century)
1 *British* : RAVINE
2 *British* : a narrow stream or rivulet

⁵**gill** \'jil\ *noun, often capitalized* [Middle English, from *Gill*, nickname for *Gillian*] (15th century)
: GIRL, SWEETHEART

gill arch *noun* (1879)
1 : any of the bony or cartilaginous arches or curved bars extending dorsoventrally and placed one behind the other on each side of the pharynx and supporting the gills of fishes and amphibians
2 : any of the rudimentary ridges in the embryos of all higher vertebrates that correspond to the gill arches

gill cleft *noun* (circa 1889)
: GILL SLIT 1, 2

gill cover *noun* (1776)
: OPERCULUM 1b

¹**gil·lie** \'gi-lē\ *noun* [Scottish Gaelic *gille* & Irish *giolla* youth, gillie] (1705)
1 : a male attendant on a Scottish Highland chief; *broadly* : ATTENDANT
2 *chiefly Scottish & Irish* : a fishing and hunting guide
3 : a shoe with a low top and decorative lacing

²**gillie** *intransitive verb* **gil·lied; gil·ly·ing** (1900)

☆ **SYNONYMS**
Gift, faculty, aptitude, bent, talent, genius, knack mean a special ability for doing something. GIFT often implies special favor by God or nature ⟨the *gift* of singing beautifully⟩. FACULTY applies to an innate or less often acquired ability for a particular accomplishment or function ⟨a *faculty* for remembering names⟩. APTITUDE implies a natural liking for some activity and the likelihood of success in it ⟨a mechanical *aptitude*⟩. BENT is nearly equal to APTITUDE but it stresses inclination perhaps more than specific ability ⟨a family with an artistic *bent*⟩. TALENT suggests a marked natural ability that needs to be developed ⟨has enough *talent* to succeed⟩. GENIUS suggests impressive inborn creative ability ⟨has no great *genius* for poetry⟩. KNACK implies a comparatively minor but special ability making for ease and dexterity in performance ⟨the *knack* of getting along⟩.

\ə\ **abut** \ᵊ\ **kitten** \ər\ **further** \a\ **ash** \ā\ **ace**
\ä\ **mop, mar** \aů\ **out** \ch\ **chin** \e\ **bet** \ē\ **easy**
\g\ **go** \i\ **hit** \ī\ **ice** \j\ **job** \ŋ\ **sing** \ō\ **go**
\ȯ\ **law** \ȯi\ **boy** \th\ **thin** \ṯh\ **the** \ü\ **loot** \ů\ **foot**
\y\ **yet** \zh\ **vision** *see also* Guide to Pronunciation

: to serve as a gillie

gill-net \'gil-ˌnet\ *transitive verb* (1949)
: to catch (fish) with a gill net

gill net *noun* (1796)
: a flat net suspended vertically in the water with meshes that allow the head of a fish to pass but entangle it as it seeks to withdraw

gill-net-ter \-ˌne-tər\ *noun* (circa 1889)
: a boat equipped for or engaged in fishing with gill nets; *also* : a person who fishes with a gill net

gill raker *noun* (1880)
: any of the bony processes on a gill arch that divert solid substances away from the gills

gill slit *noun* (1854)
1 : any of the openings or clefts between the gill arches in vertebrates that breathe by gills through which water taken in at the mouth passes to the exterior and so bathes the gills
2 : any of the rudimentary grooves in the neck region of the embryos of air-breathing vertebrates that correspond to the gill slits
3 : the external opening to the cavity containing the gills when a protective covering of the gills is present

gil-ly-flow-er \'ji-lē-ˌflaü-(ə-)r\ *noun* [by folk etymology from Middle English *gilofre* clove, from Middle French *girofle, gilofre*, from Latin *caryophyllum*, from Greek *karyophyllon*, from *karyon* nut + *phyllon* leaf — more at CAREEN, BLADE] (1551)
: CARNATION 2

Gil-son-ite \'gil-sə-ˌnīt\ *trademark*
— used for uintaite

¹gilt \'gilt\ *adjective* [Middle English, from past participle of *gilden* to gild] (14th century)
: covered with gold or gilt : of the color of gold

²gilt *noun* (15th century)
1 : gold or something that resembles gold laid on a surface
2 *slang* : MONEY
3 : superficial brilliance
4 : a bond issued by the government of the United Kingdom

³gilt *noun* [Middle English *gylte*, from Old Norse *gyltr*; akin to Old English *gelde* sterile — more at GELD] (14th century)
: a young female swine

gilt–edged \'gilt-ˌejd\ *or* **gilt–edge** \-ˈej\ *adjective* (1818)
1 : having a gilt edge
2 : of the best quality or rating ⟨*gilt-edged* securities⟩

¹gim-bal \'gim-bəl, 'jim-\ *noun* [alteration of obsolete *gemel* (double ring)] (1780)
: a device that permits a body to incline freely in any direction or suspends it so that it will remain level when its support is tipped — usually used in plural; called also *gimbal ring*

²gimbal *transitive verb* **-balled** *or* **-baled**; **-bal-ling** *or* **-bal-ing** (1875)
: to provide with or support on gimbals

gim-crack \'jim-ˌkrak\ *noun* [origin unknown] (1676)
: a showy object of little use or value : GEWGAW
— **gimcrack** *adjective*
— **gim-crack-ery** \-ˌkra-k(ə-)rē\ *noun*

gim-el \'gi-məl\ *noun* [Hebrew *gīmel*] (1828)
: the 3d letter of the Hebrew alphabet — see ALPHABET table

¹gim-let \'gim-lət\ *noun* [Middle English, from Middle French *guimbelet*, probably modification of Middle Dutch *wimmelkijn*, from *wimmel* wimble] (14th century)
: a small tool with a screw point, grooved shank, and cross handle for boring holes

²gimlet *adjective* (1752)
: having a piercing or penetrating quality

³gimlet *transitive verb* (1840)
: to pierce as if with a gimlet

⁴gimlet *noun* [probably from ¹*gimlet*] (1928)
: a drink consisting of sweetened lime juice and gin or vodka and sometimes carbonated or plain water

gim-let–eyed \-ˈīd\ *adjective* (1752)
: SHARP-SIGHTED

gim-mal \'gi-məl, 'ji-\ *noun* [alteration of obsolete *gemel* (double ring)] (1598)
1 *plural* : joined work (as in a clock) whose parts move within each other
2 : a pair or series of interlocked rings

gim-me \'gi-mē\ *noun, plural* **gimmes** [from *gimme*, contraction of *give me*] (1982)
: something easily achieved or won especially in a contest

¹gim-mick \'gi-mik\ *noun* [origin unknown] (circa 1926)
1 a : a mechanical device for secretly and dishonestly controlling gambling apparatus **b** : an ingenious or novel mechanical device : GADGET
2 a : an important feature that is not immediately apparent : CATCH ⟨what's the *gimmick* . . . what's in it for you —Maxwell Griffith⟩ **b** : an ingenious and usually new scheme or angle
— **gim-micky** \-mi-kē\ *adjective*

²gimmick *transitive verb* (1928)
1 : to alter or influence by means of a gimmick
2 : to provide with a gimmick — often used with *up*

gim-mick-ry \'gi-mi-krē\ *noun, plural* **-ries** (1948)
: an array or profusion of gimmicks; *also* : use of gimmicks

¹gimp \'gimp\ *noun* [perhaps from Dutch] (1664)
: an ornamental flat braid or round cord used as a trimming

²gimp *noun* [perhaps from *gimp* (fish line strengthened with wire)] (1901)
: SPIRIT, VIM

³gimp *noun* [origin unknown] (1929)
1 : CRIPPLE
2 : LIMP ⟨walks with a *gimp* —Damon Runyon⟩
— **gimpy** \'gim-pē\ *adjective*

⁴gimp *intransitive verb* (1948)
: LIMP, HOBBLE ⟨*gimping* up the stairs⟩

¹gin \'gin\ *verb* **gan** \'gan\; **gin-ning** [Middle English *ginnen*, short for *beginnen*] (13th century)
archaic : BEGIN

²gin \'jin\ *noun* [Middle English *gin*, modification of Old French *engin* — more at ENGINE] (13th century)
: any of various tools or mechanical devices: as **a** : a snare or trap for game **b** : COTTON GIN

³gin \'jin\ *transitive verb* **ginned**; **gin-ning** (circa 1625)
1 : SNARE
2 : to separate (cotton fiber) from seeds and waste material
— **gin-ner** *noun*

⁴gin \'gin\ *conjunction* [perhaps by contraction from dialect *gif* if + *an* if] (1580)
dialect : IF

⁵gin \'jin\ *noun* [by shortening & alteration from *geneva*] (1714)
1 : a colorless alcoholic beverage made from distilled or redistilled neutral grain spirits flavored with juniper berries and aromatics (as anise and caraway seeds)
2 a : GIN RUMMY **b** : the act of laying down a full hand of matched cards in gin rummy ◇
— **gin-ny** \'jin-ē\ *adjective*

¹gin-ger \'jin-jər\ *noun* [Middle English, from Old English *gingifer*, from Medieval Latin *gingiber*, alteration of Latin *zingiber*, from Greek *zingiberi*, ultimately from Pali *siṅgivēra*] (before 12th century)
1 a (1) : a thickened pungent aromatic rhizome that is used as a spice and sometimes medicinally (2) : the spice usually prepared by drying and grinding ginger **b** : any of a genus (*Zingiber* of the family Zingiberaceae, the ginger family) of herbs with pungent aromatic rhizomes; *especially* : a widely cultivated tropical herb (*Z. officinale*) that supplies most of the ginger of commerce
2 : high spirit : PEP ⟨the *ginger* to care hard and work hard —Willa Cather⟩
3 : a strong brown
— **gin-gery** \'jinj-rē, 'jin-jə-\ *adjective*

²ginger *transitive verb* **gin-gered; gin-ger-ing** \'jinj-riŋ, 'jin-jə-\ (1849)
: to make lively : pep up ⟨*ginger* up the tourist trade —*N.Y. Times*⟩

ginger ale *noun* (1886)
: a sweetened carbonated nonalcoholic beverage flavored mainly with ginger extract

ginger beer *noun* (1809)
: a sweetened carbonated nonalcoholic beverage heavily flavored with ginger or capsicum or both

gin-ger-bread \'jin-jər-ˌbred\ *noun* (15th century)
1 : a cake whose ingredients include molasses and ginger
2 [from the fancy shapes and gilding formerly often applied to gingerbread] : lavish or superfluous ornament especially in architecture
— **gingerbread** *adjective*
— **gin-ger-bread-ed** \-ˌbre-dəd\ *adjective*
— **gin-ger-bready** \-dē\ *adjective*

ginger group *noun* (1925)
chiefly British : a group that serves as an energizing force within a larger body (as a political party)

gin-ger-ly \'jin-jər-lē\ *adjective* [perhaps from ¹*ginger*] (1594)
: very cautious or careful
— **gin-ger-li-ness** *noun*
— **gingerly** *adverb*

ginger nut *noun* (1842)
British : GINGERSNAP

gin-ger-root \'jin-jər-ˌüt, -ˌ(r)üt\ *noun* (1831)
: GINGER 1a(1)

gin-ger-snap \-ˌsnap\ *noun* (1805)
: a thin brittle cookie sweetened with molasses and flavored with ginger

ging-ham \'giŋ-əm\ *noun* [modification of Malay *genggang* striped cloth] (1615)
: a clothing fabric usually of yarn-dyed cotton in plain weave

gin-gi-va \'jin-jə-və, jin-ˈjī-\ *noun, plural* **-vae** \-ˌvē\ [Latin] (circa 1889)
: ¹GUM

gin-gi-val \'jin-jə-vəl\ *adjective*

gimlet

◇ WORD HISTORY

gin *Genever* (now spelled with an initial *j*) was the Dutch word for a drink made of distilled spirits and flavored with juniper berries. Ultimately it came from Latin *juniperus* by way of Middle Dutch and Old French. Both the word and the beverage were introduced into Britain around the end of the 17th century, probably by soldiers returning from wars in the Low Countries. In its new land, however, the word was influenced by the similar-sounding name of a city in Switzerland, and thus the earliest name for the drink is *geneva*, which appeared in print in 1706. The creation of new words by clipping longer words to a monosyllable was as popular in 18th century English as it is today, and so a shortened form *gin* arose, to designate not only the Dutch drink but also a similar liquor made in Britain, not necessarily flavored with juniper but remarkably popular. So popular did it become, in fact, that gin drinking among the poorer classes became a major social problem. The epidemic proportions of this menace are long past, but the liquor and its clipped name are still with us.

gin·gi·vec·to·my \ˌjin-jə-'vek-tə-mē\ *noun, plural* **-mies** (circa 1927)
: the excision of a portion of the gingiva
gin·gi·vi·tis \ˌjin-jə-'vī-təs\ *noun* (1874)
: inflammation of the gums
gink \'giŋk\ *noun* [origin unknown] (1908)
slang : PERSON, GUY
gink·go *also* **ging·ko** \'giŋ-(ˌ)kō *also* 'giŋk-(ˌ)gō\ *noun, plural* **ginkgoes** *or* **ginkgos** [New Latin *Ginkgo*, from Japanese *ginkyō*] (1773)
: a gymnospermous tree (*Ginkgo biloba*) of eastern China that is widely grown as an ornamental or shade tree and has fan-shaped leaves and yellow fruit
gin mill *noun* (1865)
: BAR, SALOON
gin rummy *noun* [⁵*gin*] (1941)
: a rummy game for two players in which each player is dealt 10 cards and in which a player may win a hand by matching all the cards in it or may end play when the unmatched cards count up to 10 points or less
gin·seng \'jin-ˌseŋ, -ˌsiŋ\ *noun* [Chinese (Beijing) *rénshēn*] (1654)
1 : a Chinese perennial herb (*Panax schinseng* of the family Araliaceae, the ginseng family) having 5-foliolate leaves, scarlet berries, and an aromatic root valued especially locally as a medicine **b** : any of several plants related to ginseng; *especially* : a North American herb (*P. quinquefolius*)
2 : the root of a ginseng
Gip·sy *chiefly British variant of* GYPSY
gi·raffe \jə-'raf\ *noun, plural* **giraffes** [Italian *giraffa*, from Arabic *zirāfah*] (circa 1600)
1 *or plural* **giraffe** : a large fleet African ruminant mammal (*Giraffa camelopardalis*) that is the tallest of living quadrupeds and has a very long neck and a short coat with dark blotches separated by pale lines
2 *capitalized* : CAMELOPARDALIS
— **gi·raff·ish** \-'ra-fish\ *adjective*

giraffe 1

gir·an·dole \'jir-ən-ˌdōl\ *noun* [French & Italian; French, from Italian *girandola*, from *girare* to turn, from Late Latin *gyrare*, from Latin *gyrus* gyre] (1749)
1 : a radiating and showy composition (as a cluster of skyrockets fired together)
2 : an ornamental branched candlestick
3 : a pendant earring usually with three ornaments hanging from a central piece
gir·a·sole *also* **gir·a·sol** \'jir-ə-ˌsòl, -ˌsōl, -ˌsäl\ *noun* [Italian *girasole* sunflower, from *girare* + *sole* sun, from Latin *sol* — more at SOLAR] (circa 1586)
1 : JERUSALEM ARTICHOKE
2 *usually* **girasol** : an opal of varying color that gives out fiery reflections in bright light

girandole 2

¹gird \'gərd\ *verb* **gird·ed** \'gər-dəd\ *or* **girt** \'gərt\; **gird·ing** [Middle English, from Old English *gyrdan;* akin to Old English *geard* yard — more at YARD] (before 12th century)
transitive verb
1 a : to encircle or bind with a flexible band (as a belt) **b** : to make fast (as a sword by a belt or clothing with a cord) **c** : SURROUND

2 : PROVIDE, EQUIP; *especially* : to invest with the sword of knighthood
3 : to prepare (oneself) for action
intransitive verb
: to prepare for action
— **gird one's loins** : to prepare for action : muster up one's resources
²gird *verb* [Middle English, to strike, thrust] (1546)
intransitive verb
: GIBE, RAIL
transitive verb
: to sneer at : MOCK
³gird *noun* (1566)
: a sarcastic remark
gird·er \'gər-dər\ *noun* [¹*gird*] (1611)
: a horizontal main structural member (as in a building or bridge) that supports vertical loads and that consists of a single piece or of more than one piece bound together
¹gir·dle \'gər-dᵊl\ *noun* [Middle English *girdel*, from Old English *gyrdel;* akin to Old High German *gurtil* girdle, Old English *gyrdan* to gird] (before 12th century)
1 : something that encircles or confines: as **a** : an article of dress encircling the body usually at the waist **b** : a woman's close-fitting undergarment often boned and usually elasticized that extends from the waist to below the hips **c** (1) : PECTORAL GIRDLE (2) : PELVIC GIRDLE
2 : the edge of a brilliant that is grasped by the setting
²girdle *transitive verb* **gir·dled; gir·dling** \'gər-dᵊl-iŋ\ (1582)
1 : to encircle with or as if with a girdle
2 : to cut away the bark and cambium in a ring around (a plant) usually to kill by interrupting the circulation of water and nutrients
3 : to move around : CIRCLE ⟨*girdled* the world⟩
girl \'gər(-ə)l\ *noun* [Middle English *gurle, girle* young person of either sex] (14th century)
1 a : a female child **b** : a young unmarried woman **c** : a single or married woman of any age — sometimes taken to be offensive
2 a : SWEETHEART **b** : a female servant or employee — sometimes taken to be offensive **c** : DAUGHTER ◇
— **girl·hood** \-ˌhùd\ *noun*
girl Friday *noun* [*girl* + *Friday* (as in *man Friday*)] (1940)
: a female assistant (as in an office) entrusted with a wide variety of tasks
girl·friend \'gər(-ə)l-ˌfrend\ *noun* (1859)
1 : a female friend
2 : a frequent or regular female companion of a boy or man
3 : MISTRESS 4a
Girl Guide *noun* (1909)
: a member of a worldwide scouting movement for girls 7 to 18 years of age that is equivalent to the Girl Scouts in the U.S.
girl·ie *also* **girly** \'gər-lē\ *adjective* (1942)
: featuring scantily clothed women ⟨*girlie* magazines⟩ ⟨*girlie* show⟩
girl·ish \'gər-lish\ *adjective* (1565)
: of, relating to, or having the characteristics of a girl or girlhood
— **girl·ish·ly** *adverb*
— **girl·ish·ness** *noun*
Girl Scout *noun* (1909)
: a member of any of the scouting programs of the Girl Scouts of the United States of America for girls ages 5 through 17
girn \'girn\ *intransitive verb* [Middle English, alteration of *grinnen* to grin, snarl] (12th century)
chiefly Scottish : SNARL
— **girn** *noun, chiefly Scottish*
gi·ro \'jir-(ˌ)ō, 'zhir-ō, 'jē-(ˌ)rō, 'zhē-, *especially British* 'jī-\ *noun* [German, circulation (of currency), from Italian, from Latin *gyrus* gyre] (1890)

: a service of many European banks that permits authorized direct transfer of funds among account holders as well as conventional transfers by check
gi·ron *variant of* GYRON
Gi·ron·din \jə-'rän-din, zhə-\ *noun* [French, from *girondin* of Gironde] (1837)
: GIRONDIST
Gi·rond·ist \-dist\ *noun* [French *girondiste*, from *Gironde*, a political party, from *Gironde*, department of France represented by its leaders] (1795)
: a member of the moderate republican party in the French legislative assembly in 1791
girt \'gərt\ *verb* [Middle English *girten*, alteration of *girden*] (15th century)
transitive verb
1 : GIRD
2 : to fasten by means of a girth
intransitive verb
: to measure in girth
¹girth \'gərth\ *noun* [Middle English, from Old Norse *gjorth;* akin to Old English *gyrdan* to gird] (13th century)
1 : a band or strap that encircles the body of an animal to fasten something (as a saddle) on its back
2 a : a measure around a body ⟨a man of more than average *girth*⟩ **b** : SIZE, DIMENSIONS
²girth *transitive verb* (15th century)
1 : ENCIRCLE
2 : to bind or fasten with a girth
3 : to measure the girth of
gi·sarme \gi-'zärm\ *noun* [Middle English, from Old French] (13th century)
: a medieval weapon consisting of a blade mounted on a long staff and carried by foot soldiers
gist \'jist\ *noun* [Anglo-French, it lies, from Middle English *gesir* to lie, ultimately from Latin *jacēre* — more at ADJACENT] (circa 1711)
1 : the ground of a legal action
2 : the main point or part : ESSENCE ⟨the *gist* of an argument⟩
git \'git\ *noun* [variant of *get*, term of abuse, from ²*get*] (1943)
British : a foolish or worthless person

◇ WORD HISTORY
girl Words in European languages that correspond to "boy" or "girl" are often of relatively recent origin and of obscure etymology, having floated upwards into standard use from the most colloquial and innovative varieties of speech. The English word *girl* is no exception. It first appeared in Middle English, about the end of the 13th century, in the forms *gurle, gerle,* and *girle,* denoting a child of either sex. Toward the end of the 14th century it was applied specifically to a female, a sense that became dominant by Shakespeare's time. Attempts have been made to relate the Middle English word to Old English *gierela, gerela* "apparel, banner." The connection may be possible on semantic grounds—witness the now fading English use of *flapper* to mean "young woman"—but it offers phonetic difficulties, as the expected Old English ancestor of *girl* would more plausibly be an unattested *gyrela.* The word *girl* shows a variety of dialect pronunciations in Modern English, often with a dropped \r\ even in accents that do not normally lose \r\ before a consonant. One such form, *gal,* is well-established in American English, though now somewhat old-fashioned and restricted in context.

\ə\ abut \ᵊ\ kitten \ər\ further \a\ ash \ā\ ace
\ä\ mop, mar \aù\ out \ch\ chin \e\ bet \ē\ easy
\g\ go \i\ hit \ī\ ice \j\ job \ŋ\ sing \ō\ go
\ò\ law \òi\ boy \th\ thin \t͟h\ the \ü\ loot \ù\ foot
\y\ yet \zh\ vision *see also* Guide to Pronunciation

git–go \\'git-ˌgō\ *variant of* GET-GO

git·tern \\'gi-tərn\ *noun* [Middle English *giterne*, from Middle French *guiterne*, modification of Old Spanish *guitarra* guitar] (14th century)
: a medieval guitar

¹**give** \\'giv\ *verb* **gave** \\'gāv\; **giv·en** \\'gi-vən\; **giv·ing** [Middle English, of Scandinavian origin; akin to Old Swedish *giva* to give; akin to Old English *giefan, gifan* to give, and perhaps to Latin *habēre* to have, hold] (13th century)
transitive verb
1 : to make a present of ⟨*give* a doll to a child⟩
2 a : to grant or bestow by formal action ⟨the law *gives* citizens the right to vote⟩ **b** : to accord or yield to another ⟨*gave* him her confidence⟩
3 a : to put into the possession of another for his use **b** (1) : to administer as a sacrament (2) : to administer as a medicine **c** : to commit to another as a trust or responsibility and usually for an expressed reason **d** : to transfer from one's authority or custody ⟨the sheriff *gave* the prisoner to the warden⟩ **e** : to execute and deliver ⟨all employees must *give* bond⟩ **f** : to convey to another ⟨*give* them my regards⟩
4 a : to offer to the action of another : PROFFER ⟨*gave* her his hand⟩ **b** : to yield (oneself) to a man in sexual intercourse
5 a : to present in public performance ⟨*give* a concert⟩ **b** : to present to view or observation ⟨*give* the signal to start⟩
6 : to provide by way of entertainment ⟨*give* a party⟩
7 : to propose as a toast
8 a : to designate as a share or portion : ALLOT ⟨all the earth to thee and to thy race I *give* —John Milton⟩ **b** : to make assignment of (a name) **c** : to set forth as an actual or hypothetical datum ⟨*give* the dimensions of the room⟩ **d** : to attribute in thought or utterance : ASCRIBE ⟨*gave* the credit to you⟩
9 a : to yield as a product, consequence, or effect : PRODUCE ⟨cows *give* milk⟩ ⟨84 divided by 12 *gives* 7⟩ **b** : to bring forth : BEAR
10 a : to yield possession of by way of exchange : PAY **b** : to dispose of for a price : SELL
11 a : to deliver by some bodily action ⟨*gave* him a push⟩ **b** : to carry out (as a bodily movement) ⟨*gave* a cynical smile⟩ **c** : to inflict as punishment **d** : to award by formal verdict ⟨judgment was *given* against the plaintiff⟩
12 : to offer for consideration, acceptance, or use ⟨*gives* no reason for his absence⟩
13 a : to suffer the loss of : SACRIFICE **b** : to offer as appropriate or due especially to something higher or more worthy ⟨*gave* his spirit to God⟩ **c** : to apply freely or fully : DEVOTE ⟨*gave* themselves to their work⟩ **d** : to offer as a pledge ⟨I *give* you my word⟩
14 a : to cause one to have or receive ⟨mountains always *gave* him pleasure⟩ **b** : to cause a person to catch by contagion, infection, or exposure
15 a : to allow one to have or take ⟨*give* me time⟩ **b** : to lead or attempt to lead — used with an infinitive ⟨you *gave* me to understand you'd be late⟩
16 : to care to the extent of ⟨didn't *give* a hang⟩
intransitive verb
1 : to make gifts or presents
2 a : to yield to physical force or strain **b** : to collapse from the application of force or pressure **c** : to undergo or submit to change ⟨for the strike to be settled, something has to *give*⟩
3 : to afford a view or passage : OPEN
4 : to enter wholeheartedly into an activity
5 *slang* : GO ON, HAPPEN ⟨wants to know what *gives*⟩ ☆
— **give a good account of** : to acquit (oneself) well
— **give birth** : to have a baby ⟨*gave* birth last Thursday⟩

— **give birth to 1** : to produce as offspring ⟨*gave* birth to a son⟩ **2** : to be the source of
— **give chase** : to set off in pursuit
— **give ground** : to withdraw before superior force : RETREAT
— **give of** : to make available : provide generously ⟨freely *gave* of their time⟩
— **give or take** : as an estimate accurate within (an amount to be added or subtracted)
— **give place to** : to be replaced or succeeded by ⟨optimism *gave place to* worry⟩
— **give rise to** : to be the cause or source of : PRODUCE
— **give the gun** : to open the throttle of : speed up
— **give the lie to 1** : to accuse of falsehood **2** : to show to be false, inaccurate, or invalid
— **give tongue** *of hounds* : to begin barking on the scent
— **give way 1 a** : RETREAT **b** : to yield the right of way **2** : to yield oneself without restraint or control **3 a** : to yield to or as if to physical stress **b** : to yield to entreaty or insistence **4** : to yield place **5** : to begin to row

²**give** *noun* (1868)
1 : capacity or tendency to yield to force or strain : FLEXIBILITY
2 : the quality or state of being springy

give–and–go \ˌgiv-ən-'gō\ *noun* (1965)
: a play (as in basketball or hockey) in which a player passes to a teammate and immediately cuts toward the net or goal to receive a return pass

give–and–take \ˌgiv-ən-'tāk\ *noun* (1778)
1 : the practice of making mutual concessions : COMPROMISE
2 : a usually good-natured exchange (as of ideas or comments)

give·away \\'gi-və-ˌwā\ *noun* (1882)
1 : an unintentional revelation or betrayal
2 a : something given away free; *specifically* : PREMIUM 1d **b** : the act of giving something away free ⟨staging a promotional *giveaway*⟩
3 : a radio or television program on which prizes are given away

give away *transitive verb* (14th century)
1 : to make a present of
2 : to deliver (a bride) ceremonially to the bridegroom at a wedding
3 a : BETRAY **b** : DISCLOSE, REVEAL
4 : to give (as weight) by way of a handicap

give·back \\'giv-ˌbak\ *noun* (1978)
: a previous gain (as an increase in wages or benefits) given back to management by workers (as in a labor contract)

give back (1548)
intransitive verb
: RETIRE, RETREAT
transitive verb
: to send in return or reply : RESTORE, RETURN

give in (1602)
transitive verb
: DELIVER, SUBMIT ⟨*gave in* his resignation⟩
intransitive verb
: to yield under insistence or entreaty : SURRENDER

¹**giv·en** \\'gi-vən\ *adjective* (14th century)
1 : PRONE, DISPOSED ⟨*given* to swearing⟩
2 : presented as a gift : bestowed without compensation
3 : PARTICULAR, SPECIFIED ⟨at a *given* time⟩
4 *of an official document* : having been executed : DATED
5 : immediately present in experience

²**given** *noun* (1879)
: something given; *especially* : something taken for granted : a basic condition or assumption

³**given** *preposition* (1904)
: in view of : CONSIDERING ⟨*given* what she knew about others' lives, how could she complain about her own? —Marilyn French⟩

given name *noun* (1827)
: a name that precedes one's surname; *especially* : FIRST NAME

give off (1831)
transitive verb
1 : to send out as a branch
2 : EMIT ⟨*gave off* an unpleasant smell⟩
intransitive verb
: to branch off

give out (14th century)
transitive verb
1 a : DECLARE, PUBLISH ⟨*giving out* that the doctor . . . required a few days of complete rest —Charles Dickens⟩ **b** : to read aloud the words of (a hymn or psalm) for congregational singing
2 : EMIT ⟨*gave out* a constant hum⟩
3 : ISSUE ⟨*gave out* new uniforms⟩
intransitive verb
1 : BREAK DOWN, FAIL
2 : to become exhausted : COLLAPSE

give over (14th century)
transitive verb
1 : CEASE
2 : ENTRUST
3 a : to yield without restraint or control : ABANDON ⟨*gave* themselves *over* to laughter⟩ **b** : to set apart for a particular purpose or use
4 *archaic* : to pronounce incurable
intransitive verb
British : to cease an activity : STOP ⟨told him to *give over* and let me alone —Brendan Behan⟩

giv·er \\'gi-vər\ *noun* (14th century)
: one that gives : DONOR

give up (13th century)
transitive verb
1 : to yield control or possession of : SURRENDER ⟨forced to *give up* his job⟩
2 : to desist from : ABANDON ⟨refused to *give up* her efforts⟩
3 : to declare incurable or insoluble
4 a : to abandon (oneself) to a particular feeling, influence, or activity ⟨*gave* himself *up* to despair⟩ **b** : to devote to a particular purpose or use
5 : to despair of seeing ⟨we'd *given* you *up*⟩
6 : to allow (a hit or run in baseball) while pitching
intransitive verb
: to cease doing or attempting something especially as an admission of defeat : QUIT — often used with *on* ⟨don't *give up* on the project⟩
— **give up the ghost** : to cease to live or function : DIE

giz·mo *also* **gis·mo** \\'giz-(ˌ)mō\ *noun, plural* **gizmos** *also* **gismos** [origin unknown] (1943)
: GADGET

giz·zard \\'gi-zərd\ *noun* [alteration of Middle English *giser*, from Old French *guisier, giser*, from Latin *gigeria* (plural) giblets] (1565)
1 a : the muscular enlargement of the alimentary canal of birds that has usually thick muscular walls and a tough horny lining for grinding the food and when the crop is present

☆ SYNONYMS
Give, present, donate, bestow, confer, afford mean to convey to another as a possession. GIVE, the general term, is applicable to any passing over of anything by any means ⟨*give* alms⟩ ⟨*gave* her a ride on a pony⟩ ⟨*give* my love to your mother⟩. PRESENT carries a note of formality and ceremony ⟨*present* an award⟩. DONATE is likely to imply a publicized giving (as to charity) ⟨*donate* a piano to the orphanage⟩. BESTOW implies the conveying of something as a gift and may suggest condescension on the part of the giver ⟨*bestow* unwanted advice⟩. CONFER implies a gracious giving (as of a favor or honor) ⟨*confer* an honorary degree⟩. AFFORD implies a giving or bestowing usually as a natural or legitimate consequence of the character of the giver ⟨the trees *afford* shade⟩ ⟨a development that *affords* us some hope⟩.

follows it and the proventriculus **b** : a thickened part of the alimentary canal in some animals (as an insect or an earthworm) that is similar in function to the crop of a bird
2 : INNARDS

gla·bel·la \glə-'be-lə\ *noun, plural* **-bel·lae** \-'be-(,)lē, -,lī\ [New Latin, from Latin, feminine of *glabellus* hairless, diminutive of *glaber*] (circa 1823)
: the smooth prominence between the eyebrows
— **gla·bel·lar** \-'be-lər\ *adjective*

gla·bres·cent \glā-'bre-s⁰nt\ *adjective* (1857)
1 : somewhat glabrous
2 : tending to become glabrous

gla·brous \'glā-brəs\ *adjective* [Latin *glabr-, glaber* smooth, bald — more at GLAD] (1640)
: SMOOTH; *especially* : having a surface without hairs or projections ⟨*glabrous* skin⟩ ⟨*glabrous* leaves⟩

gla·cé \gla-'sā\ *adjective* [French, from past participle of *glacer* to freeze, ice, glaze, from Latin *glaciare*, from *glacies*] (1847)
1 : made or finished so as to have a smooth glossy surface ⟨*glacé* silk⟩
2 *also* **gla·céed** \-'sād\ : coated with a glaze : CANDIED ⟨*glacé* cherries⟩

gla·cial \'glā-shəl\ *adjective* [Latin *glacialis*, from *glacies*] (1656)
1 a : extremely cold : FRIGID ⟨a *glacial* wind⟩ **b** : devoid of warmth and cordiality ⟨a *glacial* handshake⟩ **c** : coldly imperturbable ⟨maintained a *glacial* calm⟩
2 : resembling ice in appearance ⟨*glacial* acetic acid⟩
3 a (1) : of, relating to, or being any of those parts of geologic time from Precambrian onward when a much larger portion of the earth was covered by glaciers than at present (2) *capitalized* : PLEISTOCENE **b** : of, relating to, or produced by glaciers **c** : suggestive of the very slow movement of glaciers ⟨progress on the bill has been *glacial*⟩
— **gla·cial·ly** \-shə-lē\ *adverb*

gla·ci·ate \'glā-shē-,āt, -sē-\ *transitive verb* **-at·ed; -at·ing** (circa 1623)
1 : FREEZE
2 a : to subject to glacial action; *also* : to produce glacial effects in or on **b** : to cover with a glacier
— **gla·ci·a·tion** \,glā-shē-'ā-shən, -sē-\ *noun*

gla·cier \'glā-shər *also* -zhər, *especially British* 'gla-sē-ər *or* 'glā-sē-\ *noun* [French dialect, from Middle French dialect, from Middle French *glace* ice, from Latin *glacies*; akin to Latin *gelu* frost — more at COLD] (1744)
: a large mass of ice moving slowly down a slope or valley or spreading outward on a land surface

gla·ci·ol·o·gy \,glā-shē-'ä-lə-jē, -sē-\ *noun* [Latin *glacies* + International Scientific Vocabulary *-logy*] (1889)
: any of the branches of science dealing with snow or ice accumulation, glaciation, or glacial epochs
— **gla·ci·o·log·i·cal** \-ə-'lä-ji-kəl\ *adjective*
— **gla·ci·ol·o·gist** \-'ä-lə-jist\ *noun*

gla·cis \gla-'sē, 'gla-sē\ *noun, plural* **glacis** \-'sēz, -sēz\ [French, from *glacer* to freeze, slide] (1672)
1 a : a gentle slope : INCLINE **b** : a slope that runs downward from a fortification
2 : BUFFER STATE; *also* : BUFFER ZONE

¹glad \'glad\ *adjective* **glad·der; glad·dest** [Middle English, shining, glad, from Old English *glæd*; akin to Old High German *glat* shining, smooth, Latin *glaber* smooth, bald] (before 12th century)
1 *archaic* : having a cheerful or happy disposition by nature
2 a : experiencing pleasure, joy, or delight : made happy **b** : made pleased, satisfied, or grateful — often used with *of* ⟨was *glad* of their help⟩ **c** : very willing ⟨*glad* to do it⟩

3 a : marked by, expressive of, or caused by happiness and joy ⟨a *glad* shout⟩ **b** : causing happiness and joy : PLEASANT ⟨*glad* tidings⟩
4 : full of brightness and cheerfulness ⟨a *glad* spring morning⟩
— **glad·ly** *adverb*
— **glad·ness** *noun*

²glad *verb* **glad·ded; glad·ding** (before 12th century)
archaic : GLADDEN

³glad *noun* (1923)
: GLADIOLUS 1

glad·den \'gla-d⁰n\ *verb* **glad·dened; glad·den·ing** \'gla-d⁰n-iŋ\ (13th century)
intransitive verb
archaic : to be glad
transitive verb
: to make glad

glade \'glād\ *noun* [perhaps from ¹*glad*] (1529)
: an open space surrounded by woods
— **glady** \'glā-dē\ *adjective*

glad–hand \'glad-,hand\ (1903)
transitive verb
: to extend a glad hand to ⟨candidates *glad-handing* everyone they meet⟩
intransitive verb
: to extend a glad hand ⟨*glad-handing* as if he were running for mayor⟩
— **glad–hand·er** \'glad-,han-dər\ *noun*

glad hand *noun* (circa 1895)
: a warm welcome or greeting often prompted by ulterior reasons

glad·i·a·tor \'gla-dē-,ā-tər\ *noun* [Latin, from *gladius* sword, of Celtic origin; akin to Welsh *cleddyf* sword] (15th century)
1 : a person engaged in a fight to the death as public entertainment for ancient Romans
2 : a person engaging in a public fight or controversy
3 : a trained fighter; *especially* : a professional boxer
— **glad·i·a·to·ri·al** \,gla-dē-ə-'tōr-ē-əl, -'tòr-\ *adjective*

glad·i·o·la \,gla-dē-'ō-lə\ *noun* [back-formation from *gladiolus*, taken as a plural] (1926)
: GLADIOLUS 1

glad·i·o·lus \,gla-dē-'ō-ləs\ *noun, plural* **-li** \-(,)lē, -,lī\ [New Latin, from Latin, gladiolus, from diminutive of *gladius*] (15th century)
1 *or plural* **gladiolus** *also* **glad·i·o·lus·es** : any of a genus (*Gladiolus*) of chiefly African plants of the iris family with erect sword-shaped leaves and spikes of brilliantly colored irregular flowers arising from corms
2 : the large middle portion of the sternum

glad rags *noun plural* (1896)
: dressy clothes

glad·some \'glad-səm\ *adjective* (14th century)
: giving or showing joy : CHEERFUL
— **glad·some·ly** *adverb*
— **glad·some·ness** *noun*

glad·stone \'glad-,stōn, chiefly British -stən\ *noun, often capitalized* [W. E. *Gladstone*] (1889)
: a suitcase with flexible sides on a rigid frame that opens flat into two equal compartments — called also *gladstone bag*

gladiolus 1

glai·kit *or* **glai·ket** \'glā-kət\ *adjective* [Middle English (Scots) *glaikit*] (15th century)
chiefly Scottish : FOOLISH, GIDDY

glair *or* **glaire** \'glar, 'gler\ *noun* [Middle English *gleyre* egg white, from Middle French *glaire*, modification of (assumed) Vulgar Latin *claria*, from Latin *clarus* clear — more at CLEAR] (13th century)
1 : a sizing liquid made from egg white

2 : a viscid substance suggestive of an egg white
— **glairy** \-ē\ *adjective* **glair·i·er; -est** (1662)
: having the characteristics of or overlaid with glair

glaive \'glāv\ *noun* [Middle English, from Middle French, javelin, sword, modification of Latin *gladius* sword] (15th century)
archaic : SWORD; *especially* : BROADSWORD

glam·or·ise *British variant of* GLAMORIZE

glam·or·ize *also* **glam·our·ize** \'gla-mə-,rīz\ *transitive verb* **-ized; -iz·ing** (1936)
1 : to look upon or depict as glamorous : ROMANTICIZE ⟨the novel *glamorizes* war⟩
2 : to make glamorous ⟨*glamorize* the living room⟩
— **glam·or·iza·tion** \,gla-mə-rə-'zā-shən\ *noun*
— **glam·or·iz·er** \'gla-mə-,rī-zər\ *noun*

glam·or·ous *also* **glam·our·ous** \'glam-rəs, 'gla-mə-\ *adjective* (1882)
: full of glamour
— **glam·or·ous·ly** *adverb*
— **glam·or·ous·ness** *noun*

glam·our *or* **glam·or** \'gla-mər\ *noun* [Scots *glamour*, alteration of English *grammar*; from the popular association of erudition with occult practices] (1715)
1 : a magic spell ⟨the girls appeared to be under a *glamour* —Llewelyn Powys⟩
2 : an exciting and often illusory and romantic attractiveness; *especially* : alluring or fascinating personal attraction — often used attributively ⟨*glamour* stock⟩ ⟨*glamour* boy⟩ ⟨*glamour* girl⟩ ◇
— **glamour** *transitive verb*
— **glam·our·less** \-ləs\ *adjective*

glam·our–puss \-,pùs\ *noun* (1941)
: a glamorously attractive person

¹glance \'glan(t)s\ *verb* **glanced; glanc·ing** [Middle English *glencen, glenchen*] (15th century)
intransitive verb
1 : to strike a surface obliquely so as to go off at an angle ⟨the bullet *glanced* off the wall⟩
2 a : to make sudden quick movements ⟨dragonflies *glancing* over the pond⟩ **b** : to flash or gleam with quick intermittent rays of light ⟨brooks *glancing* in the sun⟩

◇ **WORD HISTORY**
glamour In classical antiquity the Greek and Latin ancestors of the English word *grammar* were used in reference not only to the study of language but also to the study of literature. In the medieval period, Latin *grammatica* and its outcomes in other languages were extended to include learning in general. Since almost all learning was couched in a language not spoken or understood by the unschooled populace, it was commonly believed that subjects such as magic and astrology were included in *grammatica*. Scholars were sometimes regarded with awe and more than a little suspicion, and the Faust legend illustrates the popular intertwining of learning and alchemical studies with necromancy and the devil. This connection between grammar and the black arts was evident in a number of languages, and in Scotland by the 18th century a form of *grammar*, altered by dissimilation to *glamer* or *glamour*, meant "a magic spell." As *glamour* passed into more general English usage, it came to have its current meanings "an exciting and often deceptive attractiveness" and particularly "alluring personal attractiveness."

3 : to touch on a subject or refer to it briefly or indirectly ⟨the work *glances* at the customs of ancient cultures⟩
4 a *of the eyes* **:** to move swiftly from one thing to another **b :** to take a quick look at something ⟨*glanced* at his watch⟩
transitive verb
1 *archaic* **a :** to take a quick look at **b :** to catch a glimpse of
2 : to give an oblique path of direction to: **a :** to throw or shoot so that the object glances from a surface **b** *archaic* **:** to aim (as an innuendo) indirectly **:** INSINUATE
— **glanc·er** *noun*
²**glance** *noun* (1503)
1 a : a quick intermittent flash or gleam **b** *archaic* **:** a sudden quick movement
2 a *archaic* **:** a rapid oblique movement **b :** a deflected impact or blow
3 a : a swift movement of the eyes **b :** a quick or cursory look
4 *archaic* **a :** a brief satirical reference to something **:** GIBE **b :** ALLUSION
— **at first glance :** on first consideration ⟨*at first glance* the subject seems harmless enough⟩
glanc·ing \'glan(t)-siŋ\ *adjective* (circa 1541)
1 : hitting so as to glance off ⟨a *glancing* blow⟩
2 : INCIDENTAL, INDIRECT ⟨made *glancing* allusions to her past⟩
— **glanc·ing·ly** \-siŋ-lē\ *adverb*
¹**gland** \'gland\ *noun* [French *glande*, from Old French, glandular swelling on the neck, gland, ultimately from Latin *gland-*, *glans* acorn; akin to Greek *balanos* acorn] (1692)
1 a : a cell, group of cells, or organ of endothelial origin that selectively removes materials from the blood, concentrates or alters them, and secretes them for further use in the body or for elimination from the body **b :** any of various animal structures suggestive of glands though not secretory in function
2 : any of various secreting organs (as a nectary) of plants
— **gland·less** \'gland-ləs\ *adjective*
²**gland** *noun* [origin unknown] (1839)
1 : a device for preventing leakage of fluid past a joint in machinery
2 : the movable part of a stuffing box by which the packing is compressed
glan·dered \'glan-dərd\ *adjective* (1667)
: affected with glanders
glan·ders \-dərz\ *noun plural but singular or plural in construction* [Middle French *glandre* glandular swelling on the neck, from Latin *glandula*, from plural of *glandula*, diminutive of *gland-*, *glans*] (1523)
: a contagious and destructive disease especially of horses caused by a bacterium (*Pseudomonas mallei* synonym *Actinobacillus mallei*) and characterized by caseating nodular lesions especially on the respiratory mucosae and lungs that tend to break down and form ulcers
glan·du·lar \'glan-jə-lər\ *adjective* (circa 1740)
1 a : of, relating to, or involving glands, gland cells, or their products **b :** having the characteristics or function of a gland
2 a : INNATE, INHERENT ⟨the almost *glandular* . . . instinct for adventure and romance —*Newsweek*⟩ **b :** PHYSICAL, SEXUAL
— **glan·du·lar·ly** *adverb*
glandular fever *noun* (1902)
: INFECTIOUS MONONUCLEOSIS
glans \'glanz\ *noun, plural* **glan·des** \'glan-,dēz\ [Latin *gland-*, *glans*, literally, acorn] (1650)
1 : a conical vascular body forming the extremity of the penis — called also *glans penis*
2 : a structure of the clitoris similar to the glans penis — called also *glans cli·to·ri·dis* \-klə-'tòr-ə-dəs\

¹**glare** \'glar, 'gler\ *verb* **glared; glar·ing** [Middle English *glaren;* akin to Old English *glǣs* glass] (13th century)
intransitive verb
1 a : to shine with a harsh uncomfortably brilliant light **b :** STAND OUT, OBTRUDE
2 : to stare angrily or fiercely
transitive verb
1 : to express (as hostility) by staring angrily
2 *archaic* **:** to cause to be sharply reflected
²**glare** *noun* (15th century)
1 a : a harsh uncomfortably bright light ⟨the *glare* of a neon sign⟩ ⟨the *glare* of publicity⟩; *especially* **:** painfully bright sunlight **b :** cheap showy brilliance **:** GARISHNESS
2 : an angry or fierce stare
3 : a surface or sheet of smooth and slippery ice
glar·ing \'glar-iŋ, 'gler-\ *adjective* (14th century)
1 : having a fixed look of hostility, fierceness, or anger
2 : shining with or reflecting an uncomfortably bright light **b** (1) **:** GARISH (2) **:** vulgarly ostentatious
3 : obtrusively and often painfully obvious ⟨a *glaring* error⟩
synonym see FLAGRANT
— **glar·ing·ly** \-iŋ-lē\ *adverb*
— **glar·ing·ness** *noun*
glary \'glar-ē, 'gler-\ *adjective* **glar·i·er; -est** (1632)
: having a dazzling brightness **:** GLARING
glas·nost \'glaz-(,)nóst, 'glas-, 'gläz-, 'gläs-\ *noun* [Russian *glasnost'*, literally, publicity, from *glasnyĭ* public, from *glas* voice, from Old Church Slavonic *glasŭ* — more at CALL] (1986)
: a Soviet policy permitting open discussion of political and social issues and freer dissemination of news and information
¹**glass** \'glas, 'glás\ *noun, often attributive* [Middle English *glas*, from Old English *glæs;* akin to Old English *geolu* yellow — more at YELLOW] (before 12th century)
1 : any of various amorphous materials formed from a melt by cooling to rigidity without crystallization: as **a :** a usually transparent or translucent material consisting especially of a mixture of silicates **b :** a material (as obsidian) produced by fast cooling of magma
2 a : something made of glass: as (1) **:** TUMBLER; *also* **:** GLASSWARE (2) **:** MIRROR (3) **:** BAROMETER (4) **:** HOURGLASS (5) **:** BACKBOARD **b** (1) **:** an optical instrument or device that has one or more lenses and is designed to aid in the viewing of objects not readily seen (2) **:** FIELD GLASSES, BINOCULARS — usually used in plural **c** *plural* **:** a device used to correct defects of vision or to protect the eyes that consists typically of a pair of glass or plastic lenses and the frame by which they are held in place — called also *eyeglasses*, *spectacles*
3 : the quantity held by a glass container
4 : FIBERGLASS
— **glass·ful** \'glas-,fùl\ *noun*
— **glass·less** \-ləs\ *adjective*
²**glass** (14th century)
transitive verb
1 a : to provide with glass **:** GLAZE 1 **b :** to enclose, case, or wall with glass ⟨the sunroom was *glassed* in⟩
2 : to make glassy
3 a : REFLECT **b :** to see mirrored
4 : to look at through an optical instrument (as binoculars)
intransitive verb
: ¹GLAZE 1
glass·blow·ing \-,blō-iŋ\ *noun* (circa 1829)
: the art of shaping a mass of glass that has been softened by heat by blowing air into it through a tube
— **glass·blow·er** \-,blō(-ə)r\ *noun*
glass ceiling *noun* (1986)

: an intangible barrier within the hierarchy of a company that prevents women or minorities from obtaining upper-level positions
glass eye *noun* (1687)
1 : an artificial eye made of glass
2 : an eye having a pale, whitish, or colorless iris
— **glass–eyed** \-,īd\ *adjective*
glass fiber *noun* (1882)
: FIBERGLASS
glass harmonica *noun* (circa 1909)
: a musical instrument consisting of a series of rotating glass bowls of differing sizes played by touching the dampened edges with a finger
glass·house \'glas-,haús\ *noun* (14th century)
1 : a place where glass is made
2 *chiefly British* **:** GREENHOUSE
3 *British* **:** a military prison
glass·ie \'gla-sē\ *or* **glassy** *noun, plural* **glass·ies** (1887)
: a playing marble made of glass
glass·ine \gla-'sēn\ *noun* (1916)
: a thin dense transparent or semitransparent paper highly resistant to the passage of air and grease
glass jaw *noun* (1940)
: vulnerability (as of a boxer) to knockout punches
glass·mak·er \'glas-,mā-kər\ *noun* (1576)
: one that makes glass
— **glass·mak·ing** \-kiŋ\ *noun*
glass·pa·per \'gläs-,pā-pər\ *noun* (1815)
British **:** abrasive paper coated with pulverized glass and used like sandpaper
— **glasspaper** *verb*
glass snake *noun* (1709)
: any of a genus (*Ophisaurus*) of limbless snakelike lizards of the southern U.S., Eurasia, and Africa with a fragile tail that readily breaks into pieces
glass sponge *noun* (1875)
: any of a class (Hexactinellida synonym Hyalospongiae) of chiefly deep-water siliceous sponges with 6-rayed spicules and a skeleton often resembling glass when dried
glass·ware \'glas-,war, -,wer\ *noun* (1745)
: articles made of glass
glass wool *noun* (1879)
: glass fibers in a mass resembling wool and being used especially for thermal insulation and air filters
glass·work \'glas-,wərk\ *noun* (1611)
1 a : the manufacture of glass or glassware; *also* **:** glaziers' work **b** *plural* **:** GLASSHOUSE 1
2 : GLASSWARE
— **glass·work·er** \-,wər-kər\ *noun*
glass·wort \-,wört, -,wòrt\ *noun* [from its former use in the manufacture of glass] (1597)
: any of a genus (*Salicornia*) of woody jointed succulent herbs of the goosefoot family with leaves reduced to fleshy sheaths
glassy \'gla-sē\ *adjective* **glass·i·er; -est** (14th century)
1 : resembling or made of glass
2 : having little animation **:** DULL, LIFELESS ⟨*glassy* eyes⟩
— **glass·i·ly** \'gla-sə-lē\ *adverb*
— **glass·i·ness** \'gla-sē-nəs\ *noun*
glassy–eyed \-,īd\ *adjective* (1895)
: marked by or having glassy eyes
Glau·ber's salt \'glaú-bər(z)-\ *noun* [Johann R. *Glauber* (died 1668) German chemist] (1736)
: a colorless crystalline sulfate of sodium $Na_2SO_4 \cdot 10H_2O$ used especially in dyeing, as a cathartic, and in solar energy systems — called also *Glauber salt*; sometimes used in plural
glau·co·ma \glaú-'kō-mə, glò-\ *noun* [Latin, cataract, from Greek *glaukōma*, from *glaukoun* to have a cataract, from *glaukos*] (1885)
: a disease of the eye marked by increased pressure within the eyeball that can result in damage to the optic disk and gradual loss of vision

glau·co·nite \'glȯ-kə-ˌnīt\ *noun* [German *Glaukonit,* irregular from Greek *glaukos*] (1836)
: a mineral consisting of a dull green earthy iron potassium silicate occurring in greensand — **glau·co·nit·ic** \ˌglȯ-kə-'ni-tik\ *adjective*

glau·cous \'glȯ-kəs\ *adjective* [Latin *glaucus,* from Greek *glaukos* gleaming, gray] (1671)
1 a : of a pale yellow-green color **b :** of a light bluish gray or bluish white color
2 : having a powdery or waxy coating that gives a frosted appearance and tends to rub off — **glau·cous·ness** *noun*

¹glaze \'glāz\ *verb* **glazed; glaz·ing** [Middle English *glasen,* from *glas* glass] (14th century)
transitive verb
1 : to furnish or fit with glass
2 a : to coat with or as if with a glaze ⟨the storm *glazed* trees with ice⟩ **b :** to apply a glaze to ⟨*glaze* doughnuts⟩
3 : to give a smooth glossy surface to
intransitive verb
1 : to become glazed or glassy ⟨my eyes *glazed* over⟩
2 : to form a glaze
— **glaz·er** *noun*

²glaze *noun* (1752)
1 : a smooth slippery coating of thin ice
2 a (1) **:** a liquid preparation applied to food on which it forms a firm glossy coating (2) **:** a mixture mostly of oxides (as silica and alumina) applied to the surface of ceramic wares to form a moisture-impervious and often lustrous or ornamental coating **b :** a transparent or translucent color applied to modify the effect of a painted surface **c :** a smooth glossy or lustrous surface or finish
3 : a glassy film

³glaze *intransitive verb* **glazed; glaz·ing** [probably blend of *glare* and *gaze*] (1601)
archaic **:** STARE

glazed \'glāzd\ *adjective* (15th century)
1 : covered with or as if with a glassy film ⟨*glazed* eyes⟩
2 : marked by lack of expression

gla·zier \'glā-zhər, -zē-ər\ *noun* (14th century)
: one who sets glass
— **gla·ziery** \'glā-zh(ə-)rē, 'glā-zē-ə-rē\ *noun*

glaz·ing \'glā-ziŋ\ *noun* (1677)
1 : the action, process, or trade of fitting windows with glass
2 a : GLASSWORK **b :** GLAZE
3 : transparent material (as glass) used for windows

¹gleam \'glēm\ *noun* [Middle English *gleem,* from Old English *glǣm;* akin to Old English *geolu* yellow — more at YELLOW] (15th century)
1 a : a transient appearance of subdued or partly obscured light ⟨the *gleam* of dawn in the east⟩ **b** (1) **:** a small bright light ⟨the *gleam* of a match⟩ (2) **:** GLINT ⟨a *gleam* in his eyes⟩
2 : a brief or faint appearance ⟨a *gleam* of hope⟩
— **gleamy** \'glē-mē\ *adjective*

²gleam (1508)
intransitive verb
1 : to shine with or as if with subdued steady light or moderate brightness
2 : to appear briefly or faintly ⟨a light *gleamed* in the distance⟩
transitive verb
: to cause to gleam
synonym see FLASH

glean \'glēn\ *verb* [Middle English *glenen,* from Middle French *glener,* from Late Latin *glennare,* of Celtic origin; akin to Old Irish *do·glenn* he selects] (14th century)
intransitive verb
1 : to gather grain or other produce left by reapers
2 : to gather information or material bit by bit
transitive verb

1 a : to pick up after a reaper **b :** to strip (as a field) of the leavings of reapers
2 a : to gather (as information) bit by bit **b :** to pick over in search of relevant material ⟨*gleaning* old files for information⟩
3 : FIND OUT
— **glean·able** \'glē-nə-bəl\ *adjective*
— **glean·er** *noun*

glean·ings \'glē-niŋz\ *noun plural* (15th century)
: things acquired by gleaning

glebe \'glēb\ *noun* [Latin *gleba* clod, land] (14th century)
1 *archaic* **:** LAND; *specifically* **:** a plot of cultivated land
2 : land belonging or yielding revenue to a parish church or ecclesiastical benefice

glede \'glēd\ *noun* [Middle English, from Old English *glida;* akin to Old English *glīdan* to glide] (before 12th century)
: any of several birds of prey (as a kite of Europe)

glee \'glē\ *noun* [Middle English, from Old English *glēo* entertainment, music; akin to Old Norse *glȳ* joy, and perhaps to Greek *chleuē* joke] (before 12th century)
1 : exultant high-spirited joy **:** MERRIMENT
2 : a part-song for usually male voices

glee club *noun* (1844)
: a chorus organized for singing usually short pieces

gleed \'glēd\ *noun* [Middle English, from Old English *glēd;* akin to Old English *glōwan* to glow] (before 12th century)
archaic **:** a glowing coal

glee·ful \'glē-fəl\ *adjective* (1586)
: full of glee **:** MERRY
— **glee·ful·ly** \-fə-lē\ *adverb*
— **glee·ful·ness** *noun*

gleek \'glēk\ *intransitive verb* [origin unknown] (1590)
archaic **:** GIBE, JOKE

glee·man \'glē-mən\ *noun* [Middle English *gleman,* from Old English *glēoman,* from *glēo* + *man* man] (before 12th century)
: JONGLEUR

glee·some \'glē-səm\ *adjective* (1603)
archaic **:** GLEEFUL

gleet \'glēt\ *noun* [Middle English *glet* slimy or mucous matter, from Middle French *glete,* from Latin *glittus* viscous; akin to Latin *gluten* glue — more at CLAY] (14th century)
: a chronic inflammation (as gonorrhea) of a bodily orifice usually accompanied by an abnormal discharge; *also* **:** the discharge itself

gleg \'gleg\ *adjective* [Middle English, from Old Norse *glǫggr* clear-sighted] (14th century)
Scottish **:** marked by quickness of perception or movement

glei·za·tion \glā-'zā-shən\ *noun* (1938)
: development of or conversion into gley

glen \'glen\ *noun* [Middle English (Scots), valley, from (assumed) Scottish Gaelic *glenn;* akin to Middle Irish *glend* valley] (15th century)
: a secluded narrow valley

glen·gar·ry \glen-'gar-ē\ *noun, plural* **-ries** *often capitalized* [Glengarry, valley in Scotland] (1845)
: a woolen cap of Scottish origin — called also *glengarry bonnet*

glen plaid \'glen-\ *noun* [short for *glenurquhart plaid,* from *Glen Urquhart,* valley in Inverness-shire, Scotland] (1926)
: a twill pattern of broken checks; *also* **:** a fabric woven in this pattern — called also *glen check*

gley \'glā\ *noun, often attributive* [Ukrainian *gleĭ* clayey earth; akin to Old English *clǣg* clay — more at CLAY] (1927)
: a sticky clay soil or soil layer formed under the surface of some waterlogged soils
— **gleyed** *adjective*

gley·ing \'glā-iŋ\ *noun* (1949)
: GLEIZATION

glia \'glē-ə, 'glī-ə\ *noun* [New Latin, from Middle Greek, glue — more at CLAY] (1891)
: NEUROGLIA
— **gli·al** \-əl\ *adjective*

gli·a·din \'glī-ə-dən\ *noun* [Italian *gliadina,* from Middle Greek *glia*] (circa 1828)
: PROLAMIN; *especially* **:** one obtained by alcoholic extraction of gluten from wheat and rye

glib \'glib\ *adjective* **glib·ber; glib·best** [probably modification of Low German *glibberig* slippery] (1593)
1 a : marked by ease and informality **:** NONCHALANT **b :** showing little forethought or preparation **:** OFFHAND ⟨*glib* answers⟩ **c :** lacking depth and substance **:** SUPERFICIAL ⟨*glib* solutions to knotty problems⟩
2 *archaic* **:** SMOOTH, SLIPPERY
3 : marked by ease and fluency in speaking or writing often to the point of being insincere or deceitful ⟨a *glib* politician⟩
— **glib·ly** *adverb*
— **glib·ness** *noun*

¹glide \'glīd\ *verb* **glid·ed; glid·ing** [Middle English, from Old English *glīdan;* akin to Old High German *glītan* to glide] (before 12th century)
intransitive verb
1 : to move smoothly, continuously, and effortlessly ⟨swans *gliding* over the lake⟩
2 : to go or pass imperceptibly ⟨hours *glided* by⟩
3 a *of an airplane* **:** to descend gradually in controlled flight **b :** to fly in a glider
4 : to produce a glide (as in music or speech)
transitive verb
: to cause to glide

²glide *noun* (1596)
1 : the act or action of gliding
2 : a calm stretch of shallow water flowing smoothly
3 : PORTAMENTO
4 a : a less prominent vowel sound produced by the passing of the vocal organs to or from the articulatory position of a speech sound — compare DIPHTHONG **b :** SEMIVOWEL
5 : a device for facilitating movement of something; *especially* **:** a circular usually metal button attached to the bottom of furniture legs to provide a smooth surface

glide path *noun* (1936)
: GLIDE SLOPE

glid·er \'glī-dər\ *noun* (15th century)
1 : one that glides: as **a :** an aircraft similar to an airplane but without an engine **b :** a porch seat suspended from an upright framework
2 : something that aids gliding

glide slope *noun* (circa 1949)
1 : the proper path of descent for an aircraft preparing to land; *especially* **:** such a path indicated by a radio beam
2 : the radio beam that marks a glide slope

glim \'glim\ *noun* [perhaps short for ²*glimmer*] (circa 1700)
: something that furnishes light (as a lantern or candle); *also* **:** illumination given off by such a source

¹glim·mer \'gli-mər\ *intransitive verb* **glim·mered; glim·mer·ing** \'glim-riŋ, 'gli-mə-\ [Middle English *glimeren;* akin to Old English *glǣm* gleam] (15th century)
1 a : to shine faintly or unsteadily **b :** to give off a subdued unsteady reflection
2 : to appear indistinctly with a faintly luminous quality
synonym see FLASH

²glimmer *noun* (1590)
1 a : a feeble or intermittent light **b :** a subdued unsteady shining or sparkle

\ə\ abut \ᵊ\ kitten \ər\ **further** \a\ ash \ā\ ace
\ä\ mop, mar \au̇\ out \ch\ chin \e\ bet \ē\ easy
\g\ go \i\ hit \ī\ ice \j\ job \ŋ\ sing \ō\ go
\ȯ\ law \ȯi\ boy \th\ thin \th\ the \ü\ loot \u̇\ foot
\y\ yet \zh\ vision *see also* Guide to Pronunciation

2 a : a dim perception or faint idea **:** INKLING **b
:** HINT, SPARK ⟨a *glimmer* of intelligence⟩
glim·mer·ing *noun* (15th century)
: GLIMMER

¹glimpse \'glim(p)s\ *verb* **glimpsed;
glimps·ing** [Middle English *glimsen;* akin to
Middle High German *glimsen* to glimmer, Old
English *glǣm* gleam] (14th century)
intransitive verb
1 *archaic* **:** GLIMMER
2 : to look briefly
transitive verb
: to get a brief look at
— glimps·er *noun*
²glimpse *noun* (circa 1540)
1 *archaic* **:** GLIMMER
2 : a fleeting view or look

¹glint \'glint\ *verb* [Middle English, to dart ob-
liquely, glint, alteration of *glenten,* of Scandi-
navian origin; akin to Swedish dialect *glänta*
to clear up; akin to Old High German *glanz*
bright, Old English *geolu* yellow — more at
YELLOW] (14th century)
intransitive verb
1 a *archaic* **:** to glance off an object **b** *of rays
of light* **:** to be reflected at an angle from a sur-
face
2 : to give off reflection in brilliant flashes;
also **:** GLEAM
3 : to look quickly or briefly **:** GLANCE
4 : to appear briefly or faintly
transitive verb
: to cause to glint
synonym see FLASH
²glint *noun* (14th century)
1 : a tiny bright flash of light
2 : a brief or faint manifestation **:** GLIMMER ⟨a
glint of recognition⟩; *also* **:** a trace of emotion
expressed through the eyes ⟨a steely *glint* in
his eye⟩

glio·blas·to·ma \ˌglī-ō-ˌbla-'stō-mə\ *noun,
plural* **-mas** *or* **-ma·ta** \-mə-tə\ [New Latin,
from *glia* neuroglia + *blast-* + *-oma*] (circa
1923)
: a malignant tumor of the central nervous sys-
tem and usually of a cerebral hemisphere
gli·o·ma \glē-'ō-mə, glī-\ *noun, plural* **-mas**
or **-ma·ta** \-mə-tə\ [New Latin, from *glia*]
(1870)
: a tumor arising from neuroglia

¹glis·sade \gli-'säd, -'sād\ *intransitive verb*
glis·sad·ed; glis·sad·ing [French, noun,
slide, glissade, from *glisser* to slide, from Old
French *glicier,* alteration of *glier,* of Germanic
origin; akin to Old High German *glītan* to
glide] (1837)
1 : to perform a ballet glissade
2 : to slide in a standing or squatting position
down a snow-covered slope without the aid of
skis
— glis·sad·er *noun*
²glissade *noun* (1843)
1 : a gliding step in ballet
2 : the action of glissading
glis·san·do \gli-'sän-(ˌ)dō\ *noun, plural* **-di**
\-(ˌ)dē\ *or* **-dos** [probably modification of
French *glissade*] (circa 1854)
: a rapid sliding up or down the musical scale
¹glis·ten \'gli-sᵊn\ *intransitive verb* **glis·
tened; glis·ten·ing** \'gli-sᵊn-iŋ\ [Middle
English *glistnen,* from Old English *glisnian;*
akin to Old English *glisian* to glitter, *geolu*
yellow — more at YELLOW] (before 12th cen-
tury)
: to give off a sparkling or lustrous reflection
of or as if of a moist or polished surface
synonym see FLASH
²glisten *noun* (1840)
: GLITTER, SPARKLE
glis·ter \'gli-tər\ *intransitive verb* **glis·
tered; glis·ter·ing** \-t(ə-)riŋ\ [Middle En-
glish *glistren;* akin to Old English *glisian*]
(14th century)
: GLITTER
— glister *noun*

glitch \'glich\ *noun* [perhaps from Yiddish
glitsh slippery place, from *glitshn* (*zikh*) to
slide, glide; akin to Old High German *glītan*
to glide — more at GLIDE] (1962)
1 a : a usually minor malfunction ⟨a *glitch* in
a spacecraft's fuel cell⟩; *also* **:** ²BUG 2 **b :** a mi-
nor problem that causes a temporary setback
: SNAG
2 : a false or spurious electronic signal
¹glit·ter \'gli-tər\ *intransitive verb* [Middle En-
glish *gliteren,* from Old Norse *glitra;* akin to
Old English *geolu* yellow] (14th century)
1 a : to shine by reflection with many small
flashes of brilliant light **:** SPARKLE ⟨sequins
glittered in the spotlight⟩ **b :** to shine with
strong emotion **:** FLASH ⟨eyes *glittering* in an-
ger⟩
2 : to be brilliantly attractive, lavish, or spec-
tacular; *also* **:** to be superficially attractive or
exciting
synonym see FLASH
— glit·ter·ing·ly \-tə-riŋ-lē\ *adverb*
²glitter *noun* (1602)
1 a : sparkling brilliance of something that
glitters **b :** a bright usually superficial attrac-
tiveness **c :** the quality of being spectacular
2 : small glittering objects used for ornamen-
tation
— glit·tery \'gli-tə-rē\ *adjective*
glit·te·ra·ti \ˌgli-tə-'rä-tē\ *noun plural* [blend
of ²*glitter* and *literati*] (1940)
: CELEBRITIES, BEAUTIFUL PEOPLE
glitter rock *noun* (1973)
: rock music characterized by performers
wearing glittering costumes and bizarre often
grotesque makeup
glitz \'glits\ *noun* [perhaps modification of
German *glitzern* to glitter, from Middle High
German *glitzen;* akin to Old Norse *glitra* to
glitter] (1971)
: extravagant showiness **:** GLITTER, OSTENTA-
TION
— glitzy \'glit-sē\ *adjective*
gloam \'glōm\ *noun* [Scots *gloam* to become
twilight, back-formation from *gloaming*] (cir-
ca 1821)
archaic **:** TWILIGHT
gloam·ing \'glō-miŋ\ *noun* [Middle English
(Scots) *gloming,* from Old English *glōming,*
from *glōm* twilight; akin to Old English
glōwan to glow] (before 12th century)
: TWILIGHT, DUSK
¹gloat \'glōt\ *intransitive verb* [probably of
Scandinavian origin; akin to Old Norse *glotta*
to grin scornfully] (1676)
1 *obsolete* **:** to look or glance admiringly or
amorously
2 : to observe or think about something with
triumphant and often malicious satisfaction,
gratification, or delight ⟨*gloat* over an enemy's
misfortune⟩
— gloat·er *noun*
— gloat·ing·ly *adverb*
²gloat *noun* (1899)
: the act or feeling of one who gloats
glob \'gläb\ *noun* [perhaps blend of *globe* and
blob] (1900)
1 : a small drop **:** BLOB
2 : a usually large and rounded mass
— glob·by \'glä-bē\ *adjective*
glob·al \'glō-bəl\ *adjective* (1676)
1 : SPHERICAL
2 : of, relating to, or involving the entire
world **:** WORLDWIDE ⟨*global* warfare⟩ ⟨a *global*
system of communication⟩; *also* **:** of or relat-
ing to a celestial body (as the moon)
3 : of, relating to, or applying to a whole (as a
mathematical function or a computer program)
⟨a *global* search of a file⟩
— glob·al·ly \'glō-bə-lē\ *adverb*
glob·al·ise *British variant of* GLOBALIZE
glob·al·ism \'glō-bə-ˌli-zəm\ *noun* (1943)
: a national policy of treating the whole world
as a proper sphere for political influence —
compare IMPERIALISM, INTERNATIONALISM
— glob·al·ist \-list\ *noun*

glob·al·ize \'glō-bə-ˌlīz\ *transitive verb* **-ized;
-iz·ing** (1944)
: to make global; *especially* **:** to make world-
wide in scope or application
— glob·al·iza·tion \ˌglō-bə-lə-'zā-shən\
noun
global village *noun* (1960)
: the world viewed as a community in which
distance and isolation have been dramatically
reduced by electronic media (as television)
¹globe \'glōb\ *noun* [Middle French, from Lat-
in *globus*] (15th century)
: something spherical or rounded: as **a :** a
spherical representation of the earth, a celes-
tial body, or the heavens **b :** EARTH 4 **c :** ORB 5
²globe *transitive verb* **globed; glob·ing**
(1641)
archaic **:** to form into a globe
globe artichoke *noun* (circa 1858)
: ARTICHOKE 1
globe·fish \'glōb-ˌfish\ *noun* (1668)
: PUFFER 2a
globe·flow·er \-ˌflau(-ə)r\ *noun* (1597)
: any of a genus (*Trollius*) of plants of the but-
tercup family with globose yellow flowers
globe thistle *noun* (1597)
: any of a genus (*Echinops*) of widely-
cultivated Asian and Mediterranean composite
herbs with spiky globose blue or white flowers
globe–trot·ter \-ˌträ-tər\ *noun* (1875)
: a person who travels widely
— globe–trot·ting \-ˌträ-tiŋ\ *noun or ad-
jective*
glo·bin \'glō-bən\ *noun* [International Scientif-
ic Vocabulary, from *hemoglobin*] (1877)
: a colorless protein obtained by removal of
heme from a conjugated protein and especially
hemoglobin
glo·boid \'glō-ˌbȯid\ *adjective* (1887)
: shaped like a sphere
glo·bose \'glō-ˌbōs\ *adjective* (15th century)
: GLOBULAR 1a(1) ⟨*globose* pollen⟩
glob·u·lar \'glä-byə-lər, 1b *is also* 'glō-\ *adjec-
tive* [partly from Latin *globus* + English *-ular;*
partly from Latin *globulus* + English *-ar*]
(1654)
1 a (1) **:** having the shape of a globe or glob-
ule (2) **:** having a compact folded molecular
structure ⟨*globular* proteins⟩ **b :** GLOBAL
2 : having or consisting of globules
globular cluster *noun* (1859)
: any of various approximately spherical clus-
ters of gravitationally associated stars that typ-
ically populate galactic halos
glob·ule \'glä-(ˌ)byü(ə)l\ *noun* [French, from
Latin *globulus,* diminutive of *globus*] (1661)
: a tiny globe or ball especially of a liquid
⟨*globules* of mercury⟩
glob·u·lin \'glä-byə-lən\ *noun* (1845)
: any of a class of simple proteins (as myosin)
that are insoluble in pure water but are soluble
in dilute salt solutions and that occur widely in
plant and animal tissues — compare ALPHA
GLOBULIN, BETA GLOBULIN, GAMMA GLOBULIN
glo·chid·i·um \glō-'ki-dē-əm\ *noun, plural*
-ia \-dē-ə\ [New Latin, from Greek *glōchis*
projecting point + New Latin *-idium*] (1882)
: the larva of a freshwater mussel (family
Unionidae) that develops as an external para-
site on fish
glock·en·spiel \'glä-kən-ˌspēl, -ˌshpēl\ *noun*
[German, from *Glocke* bell + *Spiel* play] (circa
1834)
: a percussion instrument con-
sisting of a series of graduated
metal bars tuned to the chro-
matic scale and played with
two hammers
glogg *or* **glögg** \'glüg, 'glüg\
noun [Swedish *glögg,* from
glödga to burn, mull, from
glöd glowing coal, from Old
Norse *glōth;* akin to Old En-
glish *glēd* glowing coal —
more at GLEED] (1927)

glockenspiel

: a hot spiced wine and liquor punch served in Scandinavian countries as a Christmas drink

glom \\'gläm\\ *transitive verb* **glommed; glom·ming** [alteration of English dialect *glaum* to grab] (1907)
1 : TAKE, STEAL
2 : SEIZE, CATCH
— **glom on to :** to grab hold of **:** appropriate to oneself

glo·mer·u·lar \\glə-'mer-(y)ə-lər, glō-\\ *adjective* (1885)
: of, relating to, or produced by a glomerulus ⟨*glomerular* nephritis⟩ ⟨*glomerular* capillaries⟩

glom·er·ule \\'glä-mə-,rül, -mər-,yü(ə)l\\ *noun* [New Latin *glomerulus*] (1793)
: a compacted cyme of almost sessile and usually small flowers

glo·mer·u·lo·ne·phri·tis \\glä-,mer-(y)ə-lō-ni-'frī-təs\\ *noun, plural* **-phrit·i·des** \\-'fri-tə-,dēz\\ (circa 1886)
: nephritis marked by inflammation of the capillaries of the renal glomeruli

glo·mer·u·lus \\glə-'mer-(y)ə-ləs, glō-\\ *noun, plural* **-li** \\-,lī, -,lē\\ [New Latin, glomerulus, glomerule, diminutive of Latin *glomer-, glomus* ball; akin to Latin *globus* globe] (1856)
: a small convoluted or intertwined mass; *especially* **:** a tuft of capillaries at the point of origin of each vertebrate nephron that passes a protein-free filtrate to the surrounding Bowman's capsule

glo·mus \\'glō-məs\\ *noun, plural* **glo·mera** \\'glä-mə-rə, 'glō-\\ [New Latin, from Latin *glomer-, glomus*] (1903)
: a small arteriovenous anastomosis together with its supporting structures

¹**gloom** \\'glüm\\ *verb* [Middle English *gloumen*] (14th century)
intransitive verb
1 : to look, feel, or act sullen or despondent
2 : to be or become overcast
3 : to loom up dimly
transitive verb
: to make dark, murky, or somber **:** make gloomy

²**gloom** *noun* (1629)
1 a : partial or total darkness **b :** a dark or shadowy place
2 a : lowness of spirits **:** DEJECTION **b :** an atmosphere of despondency ⟨a *gloom* fell over the household⟩

gloomy \\'glü-mē\\ *adjective* **gloom·i·er; -est** (1588)
1 a : partially or totally dark; *especially* **:** dismally and depressingly dark ⟨*gloomy* weather⟩ **b :** having a frowning or scowling appearance **:** FORBIDDING ⟨a *gloomy* countenance⟩ **c :** low in spirits **:** MELANCHOLY
2 a : causing gloom **:** DEPRESSING ⟨a *gloomy* story⟩ ⟨a *gloomy* landscape⟩ **b :** lacking in promise or hopefulness **:** PESSIMISTIC ⟨*gloomy* prophecies⟩ ⟨a *gloomy* future⟩
synonym see SULLEN
— **gloom·i·ly** \\-mə-lē\\ *adverb*
— **gloom·i·ness** \\-mē-nəs\\ *noun*

glop \\'gläp\\ *noun* [origin unknown] (circa 1944)
1 : a thick semiliquid substance (as food) that is usually unattractive in appearance
2 : tasteless or worthless material
— **glop·py** \\'glä-pē\\ *adjective*

Glo·ria \\'glōr-ē-ə, 'glȯr-\\ *noun* [Latin, glory] (13th century)
1 : GLORIA IN EXCELSIS
2 : GLORIA PATRI

Gloria in Ex·cel·sis \\-,in-eks-'chel-səs, -ek-'shel-\\ [Late Latin, glory (be to God) on high] (14th century)
: a Christian liturgical hymn having the verse form of the Psalms

Gloria Pa·tri \\-'pä-(,)trē\\ *noun* [Late Latin, glory (be) to the Father] (13th century)
: a 2-verse doxology to the Trinity

glo·ri·fy \\'glōr-ə-,fī, 'glȯr-\\ *transitive verb* **-fied; -fy·ing** [Middle English *glorifien*, from

Middle French *glorifier*, from Late Latin *glorificare*, from *gloria*] (14th century)
1 a : to make glorious by bestowing honor, praise, or admiration **b :** to elevate to celestial glory
2 : to light up brilliantly ⟨a large chandelier *glorifies* the whole room⟩
3 a : to represent as glorious **:** EXTOL ⟨a song *glorifying* romantic love⟩ **b :** to cause to be or seem to be better than the actual condition ⟨the new position is just a *glorified* version of the old stockroom job⟩
4 : to give glory to (as in worship)
— **glo·ri·fi·ca·tion** \\,glōr-ə-fə-'kā-shən, ,glȯr-\\ *noun*
— **glo·ri·fi·er** \\'glōr-ə-,fī(-ə)r, 'glȯr-\\ *noun*

glo·ri·ous \\'glōr-ē-əs, 'glȯr-\\ *adjective* [Middle English, from Old French & Latin; Old French *glorieus, glorios*, from Latin *gloriosus* glorious, vainglorious, from *gloria*] (13th century)
1 a : possessing or deserving glory **:** ILLUSTRIOUS **b :** entitling one to glory ⟨a *glorious* victory⟩
2 : marked by great beauty or splendor **:** MAGNIFICENT
3 : DELIGHTFUL, WONDERFUL ⟨had a *glorious* weekend⟩
synonym see SPLENDID
— **glo·ri·ous·ly** *adverb*
— **glo·ri·ous·ness** *noun*

¹**glo·ry** \\'glōr-ē, 'glȯr-\\ *noun, plural* **glories** [Middle English *glorie*, from Middle French & Latin; Middle French, from Latin *gloria*] (14th century)
1 a : praise, honor, or distinction extended by common consent **:** RENOWN **b :** worshipful praise, honor, and thanksgiving ⟨giving *glory* to God⟩
2 a : something that secures praise or renown ⟨the *glory* of a brilliant career⟩ **b :** a distinguished quality or asset
3 a (1) **:** great beauty and splendor **:** MAGNIFICENCE ⟨the *glory* that was Greece and the grandeur that was Rome —E. A. Poe⟩ (2) **:** something marked by beauty or resplendence ⟨a perfect *glory* of a day⟩ **b :** the splendor and beatific happiness of heaven; *broadly* **:** ETERNITY
4 a : a state of great gratification or exaltation ⟨when she's acting she's in her *glory*⟩ **b :** a height of prosperity or achievement
5 : a ring or spot of light: as **a :** AUREOLE **b :** CORONA 2a, b

²**glory** *intransitive verb* **glo·ried; glo·ry·ing** (14th century)
: to rejoice proudly — used with *in*

³**glory** *or* **glory be** *interjection* (1816)
— used to express surprise or delight

glory–of–the–snow *noun* (circa 1890)
: any of a genus (*Chionodoxa*) of hardy spring-flowering bulbous herbs of the lily family with narrow basal leaves and terminal racemes of blue, white, or pink flowers

¹**gloss** \\'gläs, 'glȯs\\ *noun* [probably of Scandinavian origin; akin to Icelandic *glossa* to glow; akin to Old English *geolu* yellow] (1538)
1 : a surface luster or brightness **:** SHINE
2 a : a deceptively attractive appearance ⟨selfishness that had a *gloss* of humanitarianism about it⟩ **b :** bright often superficial attractiveness ⟨show-biz *gloss*⟩
3 : a transparent cosmetic preparation for adding shine and usually color to the lips

²**gloss** *transitive verb* (1656)
1 a : to mask the true nature of **:** give a deceptively attractive appearance to — used with *over* ⟨the misery was general, where not *glossed* over by liberal application of alcohol —Marston Bates⟩ **b :** to deal with (a subject or problem) too lightly or not at all — used with *over* ⟨*glosses* over scholarly controversies rather than confronting them head-on —John Israel⟩
2 : to give a gloss to

³**gloss** *noun* [alteration of *gloze*, from Middle English *glose*, from Middle French, from Me-

dieval Latin *glosa, glossa*, from Greek *glōssa, glōtta* tongue, language, obscure word; akin to Greek *glōchis* projecting point] (1548)
1 a : a brief explanation (as in the margin or between the lines of a text) of a difficult or obscure word or expression **b :** a false and often willfully misleading interpretation (as of a text)
2 a : GLOSSARY **b :** an interlinear translation **c :** a continuous commentary accompanying a text
3 : COMMENTARY, INTERPRETATION

⁴**gloss** *transitive verb* (1603)
1 a : to provide a gloss for **:** EXPLAIN, DEFINE **b :** INTERPRET
2 : to dispose of by false or perverse interpretation ⟨trying to *gloss* away the irrationalities of the universe —Irwin Edman⟩

gloss- *or* **glosso-** *combining form* [Latin, from Greek *gloss-, glosso-*, from *glōssa*]
1 : tongue ⟨*gloss*itis⟩
2 : language ⟨*glosso*lalia⟩

glos·sa \\'glä-sə, 'glȯ-\\ *noun, plural* **glos·sae** \\-,sē, -,sī\\ *also* **glossas** [New Latin, from Greek *glōssa*] (circa 1852)
: a tongue or lingual structure especially in an insect; *especially* **:** the median distal lobe of the labium of an insect

glos·sa·rist \\'glä-sə-rist, 'glȯ-\\ *noun* (1774)
: GLOSSATOR

glos·sa·ry \\-sə-rē\\ *noun, plural* **-ries** (14th century)
: a collection of textual glosses or of specialized terms with their meanings
— **glos·sar·i·al** \\glä-'sar-ē-əl, glȯ-, -'ser-\\ *adjective*

glos·sa·tor \\'glä-,sā-tər, 'glȯ-\\ *noun* (14th century)
1 : one that makes textual glosses
2 : a compiler of a glossary

glos·si·tis \\glä-'sī-təs, 'glȯ-\\ *noun* (circa 1834)
: inflammation of the tongue

glos·sog·ra·pher \\glä-'sä-grə-fər, glȯ-\\ *noun* [Greek *glōssographos*, from *glōssa* + *graphein* to write — more at CARVE] (1607)
: GLOSSATOR

glos·so·la·lia \\,glä-sə-'lā-lē-ə, ,glȯ-\\ *noun* [New Latin] (1879)
: TONGUE 4c
— **glos·so·la·list** \\-'lā-list\\ *noun*

glos·so·pha·ryn·geal nerve \\,glä-sō-,far-ən-'jē-əl-, ,glȯ-, -fə-'rin-j(ē-)əl-\\ *noun* (circa 1823)
: either of the 9th pair of cranial nerves that are mixed nerves and supply chiefly the pharynx, posterior tongue, and parotid gland — called also *glossopharyngeal*

¹**glossy** \\'glä-sē, 'glȯ-\\ *adjective* **gloss·i·er; -est** (1556)
1 : having a surface luster or brightness ⟨rich *glossy* leather⟩ ⟨*glossy* paper⟩
2 : attractive in an artificially opulent, sophisticated, or smoothly captivating manner **:** SLICK ⟨lots of *glossy* and phony chatter⟩
synonym see SLEEK
— **gloss·i·ly** \\-sə-lē\\ *adverb*
— **gloss·i·ness** \\-sē-nəs\\ *noun*

²**glossy** *noun, plural* **gloss·ies** (1928)
1 : a photograph printed on smooth shiny paper
2 *chiefly British* **:** SLICK 3

glott- *or* **glotto-** *combining form* [Greek *glōtt-, glōtto-* tongue, from *glōssa, glōtta*]
: language ⟨*glotto*chronology⟩

glot·tal \\'glä-t°l\\ *adjective* (circa 1846)
: of, relating to, or produced in or by the glottis ⟨*glottal* constriction⟩

glottal stop *noun* (1888)
: the interruption of the breath stream during speech by closure of the glottis

\\ə\\ abut \\ᵊ\\ kitten \\ər\\ further \\a\\ ash \\ā\\ ace
\\ä\\ mop, mar \\aù\\ out \\ch\\ chin \\e\\ bet \\ē\\ easy
\\g\\ go \\i\\ hit \\ī\\ ice \\j\\ job \\ŋ\\ sing \\ō\\ go
\\ȯ\\ law \\ȯi\\ boy \\th\\ thin \\t̲h̲\\ the \\ü\\ loot \\ù\\ foot
\\y\\ yet \\zh\\ vision *see also* Guide to Pronunciation

glot·tis \'glä-təs\ *noun, plural* **glot·tis·es** or **glot·ti·des** \-tə-ˌdēz\ [Greek *glōttid-, glōttis,* from *glōtta* tongue — more at GLOSS] (1578) : the elongated space between the vocal cords; *also* : the structures that surround this space — compare EPIGLOTTIS

glot·to·chro·nol·o·gy \ˌglä-tō-krə-'nä-lə-jē\ *noun* (1953) : a linguistic method that uses the rate of vocabulary replacement to estimate the date of divergence for distinct but genetically related languages — **glot·to·chro·no·log·i·cal** \-ˌkrä-nᵊl-'ä-ji-kəl, -ˌkrō-\ *adjective*

glout \'glüt, 'glaut\ *intransitive verb* [Middle English, probably of Scandinavian origin; akin to Old Norse *glotta* to grin scornfully] (14th century) *archaic* : FROWN, SCOWL

¹glove \'gləv\ *noun* [Middle English, from Old English *glōf;* akin to Old Norse *glōfi* glove] (before 12th century)
1 a : a covering for the hand having separate sections for each of the fingers and the thumb and often extending part way up the arm **b :** ¹GAUNTLET 1, 3
2 a (1) **:** a padded leather covering for the hand used in baseball to catch a thrown or batted ball; *specifically* **:** one having individual thumb and finger sections usually connected with a lacing or webbing — compare MITT (2) **:** fielding ability ⟨he's got a good *glove* at three positions and can pinch-hit —Casey Stengel⟩ **b :** BOXING GLOVE

²glove *transitive verb* **gloved; glov·ing** (15th century)
1 a : to cover with or as if with a glove **b :** to furnish with gloves
2 : to catch (a baseball) in one's gloved hand

glove box *noun* (1946)
1 : GLOVE COMPARTMENT
2 : a sealed protectively lined compartment having holes to which are attached gloves for use in handling dangerous materials inside the compartment

glove compartment *noun* (1939) **:** a small storage cabinet in the dashboard of an automobile

glove leather *noun* (1721) **:** a soft lightweight leather

glov·er \'glə-vər\ *noun* (14th century) **:** one that makes or sells gloves

¹glow \'glō\ *intransitive verb* [Middle English, from Old English *glōwan;* akin to Old English *geolu* yellow — more at YELLOW] (before 12th century)
1 a : to shine with or as if with an intense heat ⟨embers *glowing* in the darkness⟩ **b** (1) **:** to have a rich warm typically ruddy color ⟨cheeks *glowing* with health⟩ (2) **:** FLUSH, BLUSH ⟨the children *glowed* with excitement⟩
2 a : to experience a sensation of or as if of heat ⟨*glowing* with rage⟩ **b :** to show exuberance or elation ⟨*glow* with pride⟩
— **glow·ing·ly** \-iŋ-lē\ *adverb*

²glow *noun* (1600)
1 : brightness or warmth of color; *especially* **:** REDNESS
2 a : warmth of feeling or emotion **b :** a sensation of warmth ⟨the drug produces a sustained *glow*⟩
3 a : the state of glowing with heat and light **b :** light such as is emitted by a solid body heated to luminosity **:** INCANDESCENCE

glow discharge *noun* (1844) **:** a luminous electrical discharge without sparks through a gas

¹glow·er \'glaù-(-ə)r, ÷'glō-(-ə)r\ *intransitive verb* [Middle English (Scots) *glowren;* perhaps of Scandinavian origin; akin to Norwegian dialect *glȳra* to look askance, Icelandic *glossa* to glow — more at GLOSS] (15th century) **:** to look or stare with sullen annoyance or anger

²glower *noun* (1715)

: a sullen brooding look of annoyance or anger

glow lamp *noun* (1884) **:** a gas-discharge electric lamp in which most of the light proceeds from the glow of the gas near the cathode

glow plug *noun* (circa 1941) **:** a heating element in a diesel-engine cylinder to preheat the air and facilitate starting; *also* **:** a similar element for ignition in other internal-combustion engines

glow·worm \'glō-ˌwərm\ *noun* [Middle English] (14th century) **:** any of various luminous insect larvae or adults with wings rudimentary or lacking; *especially* **:** a larva or wingless female of a firefly (family Lampyridae) that emits light from the abdomen

glox·in·ia \gläk-'si-nē-ə\ *noun* [New Latin, from B. P. *Gloxin* 18th century German botanist] (circa 1820) **:** any of a genus (*Sinningia*) of Brazilian tuberous herbaceous gesneriads; *especially* **:** a plant (*S. speciosa*) widely cultivated for its showy bell-shaped or slipper-shaped flowers

gloxinia

¹gloze \'glōz\ *transitive verb* **glozed; gloz·ing** [Middle English *glosen* to gloss, flatter, from *glose* gloss] (14th century) *archaic* **:** ⁴GLOSS 1

²gloze *transitive verb* **glozed; gloz·ing** (14th century) **:** ²GLOSS 1 — often used with *over*

gluc- or gluco- *combining form* [International Scientific Vocabulary]
1 : glucose ⟨*gluco*kinase⟩
2 : related to or containing glucose ⟨*gluco*samine⟩

glu·ca·gon \'glü-kə-ˌgän\ *noun* [*gluc-* + *-agon* (perhaps from Greek *agōn,* present participle of *agein* to lead, drive) — more at AGENT] (1923) **:** a protein hormone that is produced especially by the islets of Langerhans and that promotes an increase in the sugar content of the blood by increasing the rate of glycogen breakdown in the liver

glu·can \'glü-ˌkan, -kən\ *noun* (1941) **:** a polysaccharide (as glycogen or cellulose) that is a polymer of glucose

glu·co·cor·ti·coid \ˌglü-kō-'kȯr-ti-ˌkȯid\ *noun* (1950) **:** any of a group of corticoids (as hydrocortisone) that are involved especially in carbohydrate, protein, and fat metabolism, that are anti-inflammatory and immunosuppressive, and that are used widely in medicine (as in the alleviation of the symptoms of rheumatoid arthritis) — compare MINERALOCORTICOID

glu·co·ki·nase \-'kī-ˌnās, -ˌnāz\ *noun* (1950) **:** a hexokinase found especially in the liver that catalyzes the phosphorylation of glucose

glu·co·nate \'glü-kə-ˌnāt\ *noun* (1884) **:** a salt or ester of gluconic acid

glu·co·neo·gen·e·sis \ˌglü-kə-ˌnē-ə-'je-nə-səs\ *noun* [New Latin] (1912) **:** formation of glucose within the animal body especially by the liver from substances (as fats and proteins) other than carbohydrates

glu·con·ic acid \(ˌ)glü-'kä-nik-\ *noun* [International Scientific Vocabulary, irregular from *glucose* + *-ic*] (1871) **:** a crystalline acid $C_6H_{12}O_7$ obtained by oxidation of glucose and used chiefly in cleaning metals

glu·cos·amine \glü-'kō-sə-ˌmēn, -zə-\ *noun* (1884) **:** an amino derivative $C_6H_{13}NO_5$ of glucose that occurs especially as a constituent of polysaccharides in animal supporting structures and some plant cell walls

glu·cose \'glü-ˌkōs, -ˌkōz\ *noun* [French, modification of Greek *gleukos* must, sweet wine; akin to Greek *glykys* sweet — more at DULCET] (1840)
1 : an optically active sugar $C_6H_{12}O_6$ that has an aldehydic carbonyl group; *especially* **:** the sweet colorless soluble dextrorotatory form that occurs widely in nature and is the usual form in which carbohydrate is assimilated by animals
2 : a light-colored syrup made from cornstarch

glucose–1–phosphate *noun* [from the position at which the phosphate group is attached] (1938) **:** an ester $C_6H_{13}O_9P$ that reacts in the presence of a phosphorylase with aldoses and ketoses to yield disaccharides or with itself in liver and muscle to yield glycogen and phosphoric acid

glucose phosphate *noun* (1912) **:** a phosphate ester of glucose: as **a :** GLUCOSE-1-PHOSPHATE **b :** GLUCOSE-6-PHOSPHATE

glucose–6–phosphate *noun* [from the position at which the phosphate group is attached] (1954) **:** an ester $C_6H_{13}O_9P$ that is formed from glucose and ATP in the presence of a glucokinase and that is an essential early stage in glucose metabolism

glucose–6–phosphate dehydrogenase *noun* (1954) **:** an enzyme found especially in red blood cells that dehydrogenates glucose-6-phosphate in a glucose degradation pathway alternative to the Krebs cycle

glu·co·si·dase \glü-'kō-sə-ˌdās, -zə-ˌdāz\ *noun* (circa 1926) **:** an enzyme (as maltase) that hydrolyzes a glucoside

glu·co·side \'glü-kə-ˌsīd\ *noun* (1855) **:** GLYCOSIDE; *especially* **:** a glycoside that yields glucose on hydrolysis — **glu·co·sid·ic** \ˌglü-kə-'si-dik\ *adjective*

glu·cu·ron·ic acid \ˌglü-kyə-'rä-nik-\ *noun* (1911) **:** a compound $C_6H_{10}O_7$ that occurs especially as a constituent of mucopolysaccharides (as hyaluronic acid) and combined as a glucuronide

glu·cu·ron·i·dase \-'rä-nə-ˌdās, -ˌdāz\ *noun* (1945) **:** an enzyme that hydrolyzes a glucuronide; *especially* **:** one that occurs widely (as in liver and spleen) and hydrolyzes the beta form of a glucuronide

glu·cu·ro·nide \glü-'kyùr-ə-ˌnīd\ *noun* (1934) **:** any of various derivatives of glucuronic acid that are formed especially as combinations with often toxic aromatic hydroxyl compounds and are excreted in the urine

¹glue \'glü\ *noun* [Middle English *glu,* from Middle French, from Late Latin *glut-, glus;* akin to Latin *gluten* glue — more at CLAY] (14th century)
1 a : any of various strong adhesive substances; *especially* **:** a hard protein chiefly gelatinous substance that absorbs water to form a viscous solution with strong adhesive properties and that is obtained by cooking down collagenous materials (as hides or bones) **b :** a solution of glue used for sticking things together
2 : something that binds together ⟨enough social *glue* . . . to satisfy the human desire for community —E. D. Hirsch, Jr.⟩
— **glu·ey** \'glü-ē\ *adjective*
— **glu·i·ly** \'glü-ə-lē\ *adverb*

²glue *transitive verb* **glued; glu·ing** *also* **glue·ing** (14th century)
1 : to cause to stick tightly with or as if with glue ⟨*gluing* the wings onto the model airplane⟩ ⟨used that war to *glue* together a frail story —Gloria Emerson⟩
2 : to fix (as the eyes) on an object steadily or with deep concentration ⟨kept his eyes *glued* to the TV screen⟩

glum \'gləm\ *adjective* **glum·mer; glum·mest** [akin to Middle English *gloumen* to gloom] (1547)
1 : broodingly morose 〈became *glum* when they heard the news〉
2 : DREARY, GLOOMY 〈a *glum* countenance〉
synonym see SULLEN
— **glum·ly** *adverb*
— **glum·ness** *noun*

glume \'glüm\ *noun* [New Latin *gluma*, from Latin, hull, husk; akin to Latin *glubere* to peel — more at CLEAVE] (1789)
: a chaffy bract; *specifically* **:** either of two empty bracts at the base of the spikelet in grasses

glu·on \'glü-,än\ *noun* [¹*glue* + ²*-on*] (1971)
: a hypothetical neutral massless particle held to bind together quarks to form hadrons

¹glut \'glət\ *verb* **glut·ted; glut·ting** [Middle English *glouten*, probably from Middle French *gloutir* to swallow, from Latin *gluttire* — more at GLUTTON] (14th century)
transitive verb
1 : to fill especially with food to satiety
2 : to flood (the market) with goods so that supply exceeds demand
intransitive verb
: to eat gluttonously
synonym see SATIATE

²glut *noun* (circa 1546)
1 : an excessive quantity **:** OVERSUPPLY
2 *archaic* **:** the act or process of glutting

³glut *transitive verb* **glut·ted; glut·ting** [probably from obsolete *glut,* noun, swallow] (1600)
archaic **:** to swallow greedily

glu·ta·mate \'glü-tə-,māt\ *noun* (1876)
: a salt or ester of glutamic acid — compare MONOSODIUM GLUTAMATE

glu·tam·ic acid \(,)glü-'ta-mik-\ *noun* [International Scientific Vocabulary *gluten* + *amino* + *-ic*] (1871)
: a crystalline amino acid $C_5H_9NO_4$ widely distributed in plant and animal proteins

glu·ta·min·ase \'glü-tə-mə-,nās, glü-'ta-mə-, -,nāz\ *noun* (1938)
: an enzyme that hydrolyzes glutamine to glutamic acid and ammonia

glu·ta·mine \'glü-tə-,mēn\ *noun* [International Scientific Vocabulary *gluten* + *amine*] (circa 1885)
: a crystalline amino acid $C_5H_{10}N_2O_3$ that is found both free and in proteins in plants and animals and that yields glutamic acid and ammonia on hydrolysis

glu·tar·al·de·hyde \,glü-tə-'ral-də-,hīd\ *noun* [*glutaric* acid + *aldehyde*] (1951)
: a compound $C_5H_8O_2$ that contains two aldehyde groups and is used especially in tanning leather and in the fixation of biological tissues

glu·tar·ic acid \glü-'tar-ik-\ *noun* [probably from *gluten* + *-aric* (as in *tartaric acid*)] (circa 1885)
: a crystalline acid $C_5H_8O_4$ used especially in organic synthesis

glu·ta·thi·one \,glü-tə-'thī-,ōn\ *noun* [International Scientific Vocabulary *gluta-* (from *glutamic acid*) + *thi-* + *-one*] (1921)
: a peptide $C_{10}H_{17}N_3O_6S$ that contains one amino-acid residue each of glutamic acid, cysteine, and glycine, that occurs widely in plant and animal tissues, and that plays an important role in biological oxidation-reduction processes and as a coenzyme

glu·te·al \'glü-tē-əl, glü-'tē-\ *adjective* (1804)
: of or relating to the gluteus muscles

glu·ten \'glü-tᵊn\ *noun* [Latin *glutin-, gluten* glue — more at CLAY] (1803)
: a tenacious elastic protein substance especially of wheat flour that gives cohesiveness to dough
— **glu·ten·ous** \'glüt-nəs, 'glü-tᵊn-əs\ *adjective*

glu·teth·i·mide \glü-'te-thə-,mīd, -məd\ *noun* [*gluten* + *eth-* + *imide*] (1955)

: a sedative-hypnotic drug $C_{13}H_{15}NO_2$ that induces sleep with less depression of respiration than occurs with comparable doses of barbiturates

glu·te·us \'glü-tē-əs, glü-'tē-\ *noun, plural* **glu·tei** \'glü-tē-,ī, -tē-,ē; glü-'tē-,ī\ [New Latin *glutaeus, gluteus,* from Greek *gloutos* buttock — more at CLOUD] (circa 1681)
: any of the large muscles of the buttocks; *especially* **:** GLUTEUS MAXIMUS

gluteus max·i·mus \-'mak-sə-məs\ *noun, plural* **glutei max·i·mi** \-'mak-sə-,mī\ [New Latin, literally, largest gluteus] (1886)
: the outermost muscle of the three glutei found in each of the human buttocks

glu·ti·nous \'glüt-nəs, 'glü-tᵊn-əs\ *adjective* [Middle French or Latin; Middle French *glutineux,* from Latin *glutinosus,* from *glutin-, gluten*] (15th century)
: having the quality of glue **:** GUMMY
— **glu·ti·nous·ly** *adverb*

glut·ton \'glə-tᵊn\ *noun* [Middle English *glotoun,* from Old French *gloton,* from Latin *glutton-, glutto;* akin to Latin *gluttire* to swallow, *gula* throat, Old English *ceole*] (13th century)
1 a : one given habitually to greedy and voracious eating and drinking **b :** one that has a great capacity for accepting or enduring something 〈a *glutton* for punishment〉
2 : WOLVERINE 1a

glut·ton·ous \'glət-nəs, 'glə-tᵊn-əs\ *adjective* (14th century)
: marked by or given to gluttony
synonym see VORACIOUS
— **glut·ton·ous·ly** *adverb*
— **glut·ton·ous·ness** *noun*

glut·tony \'glət-nē, 'glə-tᵊn-ē\ *noun, plural* **-ton·ies** (13th century)
1 : excess in eating or drinking
2 : greedy or excessive indulgence

glyc- *or* **glyco-** *combining form* [International Scientific Vocabulary, from Greek *glyk-* sweet, from *glykys*]
1 : carbohydrate and especially sugar 〈*glyco*protein〉
2 : glycine 〈*glycyl*〉

gly·can \'glī-,kan\ *noun* (1953)
: POLYSACCHARIDE

glyc·er·al·de·hyde \,gli-sə-'ral-də-,hīd\ *noun* [*glyceric* acid + *aldehyde*] (1882)
: a sweet crystalline compound $C_3H_6O_3$ that is formed as an intermediate in carbohydrate metabolism by the breakdown of sugars and that yields glycerol on reduction

gly·cer·ic acid \gli-'ser-ik-\ *noun* [International Scientific Vocabulary, from *glycerin*] (circa 1864)
: a syrupy acid $C_3H_6O_4$ obtainable by oxidation of glycerol or glyceraldehyde

glyc·er·ide \'gli-sə-,rīd\ *noun* (circa 1864)
: an ester of glycerol especially with fatty acids
— **glyc·er·id·ic** \,gli-sə-'ri-dik\ *adjective*

glyc·er·in *or* **glyc·er·ine** \'glis-rən, 'gli-sə-\ *noun* [French *glycérine,* from Greek *glykeros* sweet; akin to Greek *glykys*] (1838)
: GLYCEROL

glyc·er·in·ate \'glis-rə-,nāt, 'gli-sə-\ *transitive verb* **-at·ed; -at·ing** (1897)
: to treat with or preserve in glycerin

glyc·er·ol \'gli-sə-,ról, -,rōl\ *noun* [*glycerin* + *-ol*] (1884)
: a sweet syrupy hygroscopic trihydroxy alcohol $C_3H_8O_3$ usually obtained by the saponification of fats and used especially as a solvent and plasticizer

glyc·er·yl \'glis-rəl, 'gli-sə-\ *noun* (1845)
: a radical derived from glycerol by removal of hydroxide; *especially* **:** a trivalent radical CH_2CHCH_2

gly·cine \'glī-,sēn, 'glī-sᵊn\ *noun* (1851)
: a sweet crystalline amino acid $C_2H_5NO_2$ obtained especially by hydrolysis of proteins

gly·co·gen \'glī-kə-jən\ *noun* (circa 1864)

: a white amorphous tasteless polysaccharide $(C_6H_{10}O_5)_x$ that is the principal form in which carbohydrate is stored in animal tissues and especially muscle and liver tissue

gly·co·gen·e·sis \,glī-kə-'je-nə-səs\ *noun* [New Latin] (circa 1886)
: the formation and storage of glycogen

gly·co·gen·ol·y·sis \,glī-kə-jə-'nä-lə-səs\ *noun, plural* **-y·ses** \-,sēz\ [New Latin] (1909)
: the breakdown of glycogen especially to glucose in the animal body
— **gly·co·gen·o·lyt·ic** \-jə-nᵊl-'i-tik, -,je-\ *adjective*

gly·col \'glī-,kól, -,kōl\ *noun* [International Scientific Vocabulary *glyc-* + *-ol*] (1858)
: DIOL; *especially* **:** ETHYLENE GLYCOL

gly·col·ic acid *or* **gly·col·lic acid** \(,)glī-'kä-lik-\ *noun* [International Scientific Vocabulary *glycol* + ¹*-ic*] (1852)
: a translucent crystalline compound $C_2H_4O_3$ found especially in unripe grapes and sugar beets and used especially in textile and leather processing

gly·co·lip·id \,glī-kō-'li-pəd\ *noun* (1936)
: a lipid (as a ganglioside or a cerebroside) that contains a carbohydrate radical

gly·col·y·sis \glī-'kä-lə-səs\ *noun* [New Latin] (1892)
: the enzymatic breakdown of a carbohydrate (as glucose) by way of phosphate derivatives with the production of pyruvic or lactic acid and energy stored in high-energy phosphate bonds of ATP
— **gly·co·lyt·ic** \,glī-kə-'li-tik\ *adjective*

gly·co·pep·tide \,glī-kō-'pep-,tīd\ *noun* (1959)
: GLYCOPROTEIN

gly·co·pro·tein \-'prō-,tēn, -'prō-tē-ən\ *noun* (circa 1908)
: a conjugated protein in which the nonprotein group is a carbohydrate

gly·cos·ami·no·gly·can \,glī-kō-sə-,mē-nō-'glī-,kan, -kō-,sa-mə-nō-\ *noun* [*glyc-* + *hexosamine* (amine derived from a hexose) + *-o-* + *glycan*] (1962)
: any of various polysaccharides derived from an amino hexose that are constituents of mucoproteins, glycoproteins, and blood-group substances — called also *mucopolysaccharide*

gly·co·si·dase \glī-'kō-sə-,dās, -zə-,dāz\ *noun* (1944)
: an enzyme that catalyzes the hydrolysis of a bond joining a sugar of a glycoside to an alcohol or another sugar unit

gly·co·side \'glī-kə-,sīd\ *noun* [alteration of *glucoside*] (circa 1889)
: any of numerous sugar derivatives that contain a nonsugar group bonded to an oxygen or nitrogen atom and that on hydrolysis yield a sugar (as glucose)
— **gly·co·sid·ic** \,glī-kə-'si-dik\ *adjective*
— **gly·co·sid·i·cal·ly** \-di-k(ə-)lē\ *adverb*

gly·cos·uria \,glī-kō-'shùr-ē-ə, ,glī-kəs-'yùr-\ *noun* [New Latin, from International Scientific Vocabulary *glycose* glucose + New Latin *-uria*] (1860)
: the presence in the urine of abnormal amounts of sugar

gly·co·syl \'glī-kə-,sil\ *noun* [International Scientific Vocabulary *glycose* glucose] (1945)
: a univalent radical derived from a cyclic form of glucose by removal of the hemiacetal hydroxyl group

gly·co·syl·a·tion \,glī-kō-sə-'lā-shən\ *noun* (1946)
: the process of adding glycosyl groups to a protein to form a glycoprotein
— **gly·co·sy·late** \,glī-kō-'sī-,lāt\ *transitive verb*

gly·cyl \'glī-səl\ *noun* (1901)
: the univalent acyl radical NH₂CH₂CO– of glycine

glyph \'glif\ *noun* [Greek *glyphē* carved work, from *glyphein* to carve — more at CLEAVE] (1775)
1 : an ornamental vertical groove especially in a Doric frieze
2 : a symbolic figure or a character (as in the Mayan system of writing) usually incised or carved in relief
3 : a symbol (as a curved arrow on a road sign) that conveys information nonverbally
— **glyph·ic** \'gli-fik\ *adjective*

Glyp·tal \'glip-t⁰l\ *trademark*
— used for an alkyd

glyp·tic \'glip-tik\ *noun* [probably from French *glyptique*, from Greek *glyptikē*, from *glyphein*] (circa 1818)
: the art or process of carving or engraving especially on gems

G–man \'jē-,man\ *noun* [probably from *government-man*] (1928)
: a special agent of the Federal Bureau of Investigation

gnar *or* **gnarr** \'när\ *intransitive verb* **gnarred; gnar·ring** [imitative] (15th century)
: SNARL, GROWL

¹gnarl \'när(-ə)l\ *intransitive verb* [probably frequentative of *gnar*] (1593)
: SNARL, GROWL

²gnarl *transitive verb* [back-formation from *gnarled*] (1814)
: to twist into a state of deformity

³gnarl *noun* (1824)
: a hard protuberance with twisted grain on a tree

gnarled \'när(-ə)ld\ *adjective* [probably alteration of *knurled*] (1603)
1 : full of knots or gnarls : KNOTTY ⟨*gnarled* hands⟩
2 : crabbed in disposition, aspect, or character

gnarly \'när-lē\ *adjective* (1829)
1 : GNARLED
2 *slang* — used as a generalized term of approval or disparagement

gnash \'nash\ *transitive verb* [alteration of Middle English *gnasten*] (15th century)
: to strike or grind (as the teeth) together
— **gnash** *noun*

gnat \'nat\ *noun* [Middle English, from Old English *gnætt*; akin to Old English *gnagan* to gnaw] (before 12th century)
: any of various small usually biting dipteran flies
— **gnat·ty** \-ē\ *adjective*

gnat·catch·er \'nat-,ka-chər, -,ke-\ *noun* (1839)
: any of a genus (*Polioptila*) of several small North and South American insectivorous oscine birds

gnath·ic \'na-thik\ *or* **gna·thal** \'nā-thəl, 'na-\ *adjective* [Greek *gnathos* jaw] (1882)
: of or relating to the jaw

-gnathous *adjective combining form* [New Latin *-gnathus*, from Greek *gnathos*; akin to Greek *genys* jaw — more at CHIN]
: having (such) a jaw ⟨*prognathous*⟩

gnaw \'nȯ\ *verb* [Middle English *gnawen*, from Old English *gnagan*; akin to Old High German *gnagan* to gnaw] (before 12th century)
transitive verb
1 a : to bite or chew on with the teeth; *especially* : to wear away by persistent biting or nibbling ⟨a dog *gnawing* a bone⟩ **b** : to make by gnawing ⟨rats *gnawed* a hole⟩
2 a : to be a source of vexation to : PLAGUE ⟨anxiety always *gnawing* him⟩ **b** : to affect like gnawing ⟨hunger *gnawing* her vitals⟩
3 : ERODE, CORRODE
intransitive verb
1 : to bite or nibble persistently ⟨*gnawing* at his underlip⟩

2 : to produce an effect of or as if of gnawing ⟨waves *gnawing* away at the cliffs⟩
— **gnaw·er** \'nȯ(-ə)r\ *noun*

gneiss \'nīs\ *noun* [German *Gneis*, alteration of Middle High German *gneiste* spark, from Old High German *gneisto*; akin to Old English *fȳrgnāst* spark] (1757)
: a foliated metamorphic rock corresponding in composition to a feldspathic plutonic rock (as granite)
— **gneiss·ic** \'nī-sik\ *adjective*
— **gneiss·oid** \-,sȯid\ *adjective*
— **gneiss·ose** \-,sōs\ *adjective*

gnoc·chi \'nȯ-kē, 'nyȯ-, 'nä-\ *noun plural* [Italian, plural of *gnocco*, from Italian dialect (Veneto), probably of Germanic origin; akin to Middle High German *knöchel* knuckle, *knoche* bone — more at KNUCKLE] (1891)
: dumplings usually made with potato or semolina and served with sauce

¹gnome \'nōm\ *noun* [Greek *gnōmē*, from *gignōskein* to know — more at KNOW] (1577)
: MAXIM, APHORISM

²gnome *noun* [French, from New Latin *gnomus*] (1712)
1 : an ageless and often deformed dwarf of folklore who lives in the earth and usually guards treasure
2 : an elemental being in the theory of Paracelsus that inhabits earth
— **gnome·like** \-,līk\ *adjective*
— **gnom·ish** \'nō-mish\ *adjective*

gno·mic \'nō-mik\ *adjective* (1815)
1 : characterized by aphorism ⟨*gnomic* utterances⟩
2 : given to the composition of gnomic writing ⟨a *gnomic* poet⟩

gno·mon \'nō-,män, -,mən\ *noun* [Latin, from Greek *gnōmōn* interpreter, pointer on a sundial, from *gignōskein*] (1546)
1 : an object that by the position or length of its shadow serves as an indicator especially of the hour of the day: as **a** : the pin of a sundial **b** : a column or shaft erected perpendicular to the horizon

bcdefg gnomon 2

2 : the remainder of a parallelogram after the removal of a similar parallelogram containing one of its corners

gno·sis \'nō-səs\ *noun* [Greek *gnōsis*, literally, knowledge, from *gignōskein*] (1703)
: esoteric knowledge of spiritual truth held by the ancient Gnostics to be essential to salvation

gnos·tic \'näs-tik\ *noun, often capitalized* [Late Latin *gnosticus*, from Greek *gnōstikos* of knowledge, from *gignōskein*] (circa 1587)
: an adherent of gnosticism
— **gnostic** *adjective, often capitalized*

gnos·ti·cism \'näs-tə-,si-zəm\ *noun, often capitalized* (1664)
: the thought and practice especially of various cults of late pre-Christian and early Christian centuries distinguished by the conviction that matter is evil and that emancipation comes through gnosis

gno·to·bi·ot·ic \,nō-tō-bī-'ä-tik, -bē-\ *adjective* [Greek *gnōtos* known (from *gignōskein* to know) + *biotē* way of life — more at KNOW, BIOTA] (1949)
: of, relating to, living in, or being a controlled environment containing one or a few kinds of organisms; *also* : AXENIC
— **gno·to·bi·ot·i·cal·ly** \-ti-k(ə-)lē\ *adverb*

gnu \'nü *also* 'nyü\ *noun, plural* **gnu** *or* **gnus** [Khoikhoi *t'gnu*] (1777)
: either of two large African antelopes (*Connochaetes gnou* and *C. taurinus*) with a head like that of an ox, short mane, long tail, and horns in both sexes that curve downward and outward

gnu

¹go \'gō\ *verb* **went** \'went\; **gone** \'gȯn *also* 'gän\; **go·ing** \'gō-iŋ, 'gȯ(-)iŋ; "*going to*" in sense 13 is *often* 'gȯə-nə *or* 'gȯ-nə *or* 'gə-nə\; **goes** \'gōz\ [Middle English *gon*, from Old English *gān*; akin to Old High German *gān* to go, Greek *kichanein* to reach, attain] (before 12th century)
intransitive verb
1 : to move on a course : PROCEED ⟨*go* slow⟩ ⟨*went* by train⟩ — compare STOP
2 : to move out of or away from a place expressed or implied : LEAVE, DEPART ⟨*went* from school to the party⟩ ⟨*going* away for vacation⟩
3 a : to take a certain course or follow a certain procedure ⟨reports *go* through channels to the president⟩ **b** : to pass by means of a process like journeying ⟨the message *went* by wire⟩ **c** : to proceed without delay and often in a thoughtless or reckless manner — used especially to intensify a complementary verb ⟨why did you *go* and spoil it⟩ ⟨*go* jump in a lake⟩ **d** (1) : to extend from point to point or in a certain direction ⟨the road *goes* to the lake⟩ (2) : to give access : LEAD ⟨that door *goes* to the cellar⟩
4 *obsolete* : WALK
5 : to be habitually in a certain state or condition ⟨*go* bareheaded⟩
6 a : to become lost, consumed, or spent ⟨our time has *gone*⟩ **b** : DIE **c** : to slip away : ELAPSE ⟨the evening *went* quickly⟩ **d** : to come to be given up or discarded ⟨these slums have to *go*⟩ **e** : to pass by sale ⟨*went* for a good price⟩ **f** : to become impaired or weakened ⟨his hearing started to *go*⟩ **g** : to give way especially under great force or pressure : BREAK ⟨the roof *went*⟩
7 a : to move along in a specified manner : FARE ⟨everything was *going* well⟩ **b** : to be in general or on an average ⟨cheap, as yachts *go*⟩ **c** : to be or become especially as the result of a contest ⟨the election *went* in her favor⟩ **d** : to turn out well : SUCCEED ⟨worked hard to make the party *go*⟩
8 a : to apply oneself ⟨*went* to work⟩ **b** : to put or subject oneself ⟨*went* to unnecessary expense⟩ **c** *chiefly Southern & Midland* : INTEND ⟨I didn't *go* to do it⟩
9 : to have recourse to another for corroboration, vindication, or decision : RESORT ⟨*go* to court to recover damages⟩
10 a : to begin an action or motion ⟨here *goes*⟩ **b** : to maintain or perform a certain action or motion ⟨still *going* strong⟩ **c** : to function in the proper or expected manner : RUN ⟨the motor won't *go*⟩
11 : to be known ⟨*goes* by an alias⟩
12 a : to act in accordance or harmony ⟨a good rule to *go* by⟩ **b** : to come to be determined ⟨dreams *go* by contraries⟩ **c** : to come to be applied or appropriated ⟨all proceeds *go* to charity⟩ **d** : to pass by award, assignment, or lot ⟨the prize *went* to a sophomore⟩ **e** (1) : to contribute to an end or result ⟨qualities that *go* to make a hero⟩ (2) : to be of advantage ⟨has a lot *going* for her⟩
13 : to be about, intending, or expecting something — used in a progressive tense before an infinitive ⟨is *going* to leave town⟩
14 a : EXTEND ⟨his knowledge fails to *go* very deep⟩ **b** : to come or arrive at a certain state or condition ⟨*go* to sleep⟩ **c** : to come to be : BECOME ⟨the tire *went* flat⟩ — often used to express conversion to specified values or a specified state ⟨*gone* Hollywood⟩ ⟨*go* condo⟩ **d** : to undergo a change ⟨leaves *go* from green to red⟩
15 a : to be in phrasing or expression : READ ⟨as the story *goes*⟩ **b** : to be capable of being sung or played ⟨the tune *goes* like this⟩

16 : to be compatible, suitable, or becoming **:** HARMONIZE ⟨the tie *goes* with his suit⟩
17 a : to be capable of passing, extending, or being contained or inserted ⟨will these clothes *go* in your suitcase⟩ **b :** to have a usual or proper place or position **:** BELONG ⟨these books *go* on the top shelf⟩
18 : to have a tendency **:** CONDUCE ⟨it *goes* to show⟩
19 a (1) **:** to carry authority ⟨what she said *went*⟩ (2) **:** to be acceptable, satisfactory, or adequate ⟨anything *goes* here⟩ **b :** to hold true **:** be valid ⟨the rule *goes* for you, too⟩
20 : to empty the bladder or bowels
transitive verb
1 : to proceed along or according to **:** FOLLOW ⟨if I were *going* his way⟩ ⟨*went* the conventional route⟩
2 : to travel through or along **:** TRAVERSE ⟨*went* the length of the street⟩
3 a : to make a wager of **:** BET ⟨*go* a dollar on the outcome⟩ **b :** to make an offer of **:** BID ⟨willing to *go* $50 for the clock⟩
4 a : to assume the function or obligation of ⟨promised to *go* bail for his friend⟩ **b :** to participate to the extent of ⟨decided to *go* halves on the winnings⟩
5 : YIELD, WEIGH ⟨this fish *goes* ten pounds⟩
6 a : to put up with **:** TOLERATE ⟨couldn't *go* the noise⟩ **b :** AFFORD ⟨can't *go* the price⟩ **c :** ENJOY ⟨I could *go* a soda⟩
7 a : to cause (a characteristic sound) to occur ⟨the gun *went* bang⟩ **b :** SAY — used chiefly in oral narration of speech
8 : to engage in ⟨don't *go* telling everyone⟩
9 *of a sports team or player* **:** to have a record of ⟨*went* 11-0 last season⟩
— **go·er** \'gō-(ə)r\ *noun*
— **go about :** to set about
— **go after :** to try to get **:** SEEK
— **go all the way 1 :** to enter into complete agreement **2 :** to engage in sexual intercourse
— **go at 1 a :** to make an attack on **b :** to make an approach to **2 :** UNDERTAKE
— **go back on 1 :** ABANDON **2 :** BETRAY **3 :** FAIL
— **go begging :** to be in little demand
— **go by the board 1 :** to be carried over a ship's side **2 :** to be discarded
— **go down the line :** to give wholeheartedly support
— **go easy :** to be sparing ⟨*go easy* with the sugar⟩ ⟨*go easy* on the kid⟩
— **go fly a kite :** to stop being an annoyance or disturbance ⟨told him to *go fly a kite*⟩
— **go for 1 :** to pass for or serve as **2 :** to try to secure or attain (as a goal) ⟨*go for* the prize⟩ **3 a :** FAVOR, ACCEPT ⟨cannot *go for* your idea⟩ **b :** to have an interest in or liking for ⟨she *went for* him in a big way —Chandler Brossard⟩ **4 :** ATTACK, ASSAIL ⟨my dog *went for* the intruder⟩
— **go for broke :** to put forth all one's strength or resources
— **go great guns :** to achieve great success
— **go hang :** to cease to be of interest or concern
— **go into :** to be contained in ⟨5 *goes into* 60 12 times⟩
— **go it 1 :** to behave in a reckless, excited, or impromptu manner **2 :** to proceed in a rapid or furious manner **3 :** to conduct one's affairs **:** ACT ⟨insists on *going it* alone⟩
— **go missing** *chiefly British* **:** to become lost **:** DISAPPEAR
— **go one better :** OUTDO, SURPASS
— **go over 1 :** EXAMINE **2 a :** REPEAT **b :** STUDY, REVIEW
— **go places :** to be on the way to success
— **go public 1** *of a close corporation* **:** to offer shares for sale to the general public **2 :** to make a public disclosure
— **go steady :** to date one person exclusively and frequently

— **go the vole :** to risk all for great gains
— **go through 1 :** to subject to thorough examination, consideration, or study **2 :** EXPERIENCE, UNDERGO **3 :** CARRY OUT, PERFORM ⟨*went through* his work in a daze⟩
— **go to bat for :** to give active support or assistance to **:** DEFEND, CHAMPION
— **go to bed with :** to have sexual intercourse with
— **go to one's head 1 :** to cause one to become confused, excited, or dizzy **2 :** to cause one to become conceited or overconfident
— **go to pieces :** to become shattered (as in nerves or health)
— **go to the mat :** to make an all-out combative effort (as in support of a position)
— **go to town 1 :** to work or act rapidly or efficiently **2 :** to be markedly successful **3 :** to indulge oneself excessively
— **go with 1 :** DATE **2 :** CHOOSE **2** ⟨*went with* an iron off the tee⟩
— **go without saying :** to be self-evident
— **go with the flow :** CONFORM **2b**
— **to go 1 :** still remaining ⟨ten minutes *to go*⟩ **2** *of prepared food* **:** sold for consumption off the premises

²go \'gō\ *noun, plural* **goes** (1727)
1 : the act or manner of going
2 : the height of fashion **:** RAGE ⟨elegant shawls labeled . . . "quite the *go*" —R. S. Surtees⟩
3 : an often unexpected turn of affairs **:** OCCURRENCE
4 : the quantity used or furnished at one time ⟨you can obtain a *go* of brandy for sixpence —C. B. Fairbanks⟩
5 : ENERGY, VIGOR
6 a : a turn in an activity (as a game) ⟨it's your *go*⟩ **b :** ATTEMPT, TRY ⟨have a *go* at painting⟩
7 : a spell of activity ⟨finished the job at one *go*⟩
8 : SUCCESS ⟨made a *go* of the business⟩
9 : permission to proceed **:** GO-AHEAD ⟨gave the astronauts a *go* for another orbit⟩
— **no go :** to no avail **:** USELESS
— **on the go :** constantly or restlessly active

³go *adjective* (1961)
: functioning properly **:** being in good and ready condition ⟨declared all systems *go*⟩
⁴go *noun, often capitalized* [Japanese] (1890)
: a Japanese game played between two players who alternately place black and white stones on a board checkered by 19 vertical lines and 19 horizontal lines in an attempt to enclose the larger area on the board

¹goad \'gōd\ *noun* [Middle English *gode*, from Old English *gād* spear, goad; akin to Langobardic *gaida* spear, and perhaps to Sanskrit *hinoti* he urges on] (before 12th century)
1 a : something that pricks like a goad **:** THORN **b :** something that urges or stimulates into action **:** SPUR
2 : a pointed rod used to urge on an animal
synonym see MOTIVE
²goad *transitive verb* (1579)
1 : to incite or rouse as if with a goad
2 : to drive (as cattle) with a goad
¹go-ahead \'gō-ə-ˌhed\ *adjective* (1834)
1 : marked by energy and enterprise **:** PROGRESSIVE ⟨a vigorous *go-ahead* company⟩
2 : indicating that one may proceed ⟨*go-ahead* signal⟩
3 : being a score that gives a team the lead in a game ⟨drove in the *go-ahead* run⟩
²go-ahead *noun* (1840)
1 a : ENERGY, SPIRIT ⟨had a great deal of courage and *go-ahead*⟩ **b :** one possessing go-ahead
2 : a sign, signal, or authority to proceed **:** GREEN LIGHT
goal \'gōl, *chiefly Northern especially in 1b &* *3a also* 'gül\ *noun* [Middle English *gol* boundary, limit] (1531)

1 a : the terminal point of a race **b :** an area to be reached safely in children's games
2 : the end toward which effort is directed **:** AIM
3 a : an area or object toward which players in various games attempt to advance a ball or puck and usually through or into which it must go to score points **b :** the act or action of causing a ball or puck to go through or into such a goal **c :** the score resulting from such an act
synonym see INTENTION
— **goal** *intransitive verb*
— **goal·less** \'gō(l)-ləs\ *adjective*
goal·ie \'gō-lē\ *noun* (1921)
: GOALKEEPER
goal·keep·er \'gōl-ˌkē-pər\ *noun* (1658)
: a player who defends the goal in any of various games (as hockey, lacrosse, or soccer)
goal kick *noun* (1891)
: a free kick in soccer awarded to a defensive player when the ball is driven out of bounds over the end line by an opposing player
goal line *noun* (1867)
: a line at either end and usually running the width of a playing area on which a goal or goalpost is situated
goal·mouth \'gōl-ˌmau̇th\ *noun* (1882)
: the area directly in front of the goal (as in soccer or hockey)
go along *intransitive verb* (1602)
1 : to move along **:** PROCEED
2 : to go or travel as a companion
3 : to act in cooperation or express agreement ⟨*go along* with the crowd⟩
goal·post \'gōl-ˌpōst\ *noun* (1857)
: one of usually two vertical posts that with or without a crossbar constitute the goal in various games
goal·tend·er \'gōl-ˌten-dər\ *noun* (circa 1909)
: GOALKEEPER
goal·tend·ing \-diŋ\ *noun* (1968)
1 : the act of guarding a goal (as in hockey)
2 : a violation in basketball that involves touching or deflecting a ball that is on its downward path toward the basket or on or within the rim of the basket
goal·ward \'gōl-wərd\ *adverb or adjective* (1949)
: toward a goal
go·an·na \gō-'a-nə\ *noun* [alteration of *iguana*] (1831)
: any of several large Australian monitor lizards (genus *Varanus* of the family Varanidae)
go-around \'gō-ə-ˌrau̇nd\ *noun* (circa 1929)
1 : RUNAROUND ⟨gave me the *go-around*⟩
2 a : ROUND ⟨reached an agreement during the first *go-around*⟩ **b :** a heated argument or struggle ⟨had a real *go-around* with her about it⟩
3 : an act or instance of going around (as in an air traffic pattern)
go around *intransitive verb* (circa 1520)
1 a : to pass from place to place **:** go here and there **b :** to have currency **:** CIRCULATE ⟨an amusing story is *going around*⟩
2 : to satisfy demand **:** fill the need ⟨not enough jobs to *go around*⟩
goat \'gōt\ *noun, plural* **goats** [Middle English *gote*, from Old English *gāt*; akin to Old High German *geiz* goat, Old Norse *geit*, Latin *haedus* kid] (before 12th century)
1 a *or plural* **goat :** any of various hollow-horned ruminant mammals (especially of the genus *Capra*) related to the sheep but of lighter build and with backwardly arching horns, a short tail, and usually straight hair **b** *capitalized* **:** CAPRICORN
2 : a licentious man **:** LECHER
3 : SCAPEGOAT **2**
— **goat·ish** \'gō-tish\ *adjective*

\ə\ **abut** \ᵊ\ **kitten** \ər\ **further** \a\ **ash** \ā\ **ace**
\ä\ **mop, mar** \au̇\ **out** \ch\ **chin** \e\ **bet** \ē\ **easy**
\g\ **go** \i\ **hit** \ī\ **ice** \j\ **job** \ŋ\ **sing**
\ō\ **law** \ȯi\ **boy** \th\ **thin** \t͟h\ **the** \ü\ **loot** \u̇\ **foot**
\y\ **yet** \zh\ **vision** *see also* Guide to Pronunciation

— **goat·like** \-,līk\ *adjective*
goat cheese *noun* (1893)
: any of various cheeses made from goat's milk
goa·tee \gō-'tē\ *noun* [from its resemblance to the beard of a he-goat] (1844)
: a small pointed or tufted beard on a man's chin
— **goa·teed** \-'tēd\ *adjective*
goat·fish \'gōt-,fish\ *noun* (circa 1639)
: any of a family (Mullidae) of moderate-sized usually red or golden fishes with two barbels on the chin — called also *red mullet*
goat·herd \-,hərd\ *noun* [Middle English *goteherd*, from Old English *gāthyrd*] (before 12th century)
: a person who tends goats
goat·skin \-,skin\ *noun* (14th century)
1 : the skin of a goat
2 : leather made from goatskin
goat·suck·er \-,sə-kər\ *noun* (1611)
: NIGHTJAR
¹**gob** \'gäb\ *noun* [Middle English *gobbe*, from Middle French *gobe* large piece of food, back-formation from *gobet*] (14th century)
1 : LUMP
2 : a large amount — usually used in plural ⟨*gobs* of money⟩
²**gob** \'gòb, 'gäb\ *noun* [probably from Scottish Gaelic, mouth & Irish, beak, pursed mouth] (circa 1550)
chiefly British : MOUTH
³**gob** \'gäb, 'gòb\ *noun* [origin unknown] (1915)
: SAILOR
gob·bet \'gä-bət\ *noun* [Middle English *gobet*, from Middle French, mouthful, piece] (14th century)
1 : a piece or portion (as of meat)
2 : LUMP, MASS
3 : a small fragment or extract ⟨a *gobbet* of information⟩
4 : a small quantity of liquid : DROP
¹**gob·ble** \'gä-bəl\ *transitive verb* **gob·bled; gob·bling** \-b(ə-)liŋ\ [probably irregular from ¹*gob*] (1601)
1 : to swallow or eat greedily
2 : to take eagerly — usually used with *up*
3 : to read rapidly or greedily — usually used with *up*
²**gobble** *intransitive verb* **gob·bled; gob·bling** \-b(ə-)liŋ\ [imitative] (1680)
1 : to make the natural guttural noise of a male turkey
2 : to make a sound resembling a gobble
— **gobble** *noun*
gob·ble·dy·gook *also* **gob·ble·de·gook** \'gä-bəl-dē-,gúk, -,gük\ *noun* [irregular from *gobble*, noun] (1944)
: wordy and generally unintelligible jargon
¹**gob·bler** \'gä-blər\ *noun* (circa 1737)
: a male turkey
²**gobbler** *noun* (circa 1755)
: one that gobbles
Go·be·lin \'gō-bə-lən, ,gō-bə-'laⁿ\ *adjective* [*Gobelin* dye and tapestry works, Paris, France] (1788)
: of, relating to, or characteristic of tapestry produced at the Gobelin works in Paris
— **Gobelin** *noun*
go–be·tween \'gō-bə-,twēn\ *noun* (1598)
: an intermediate agent : BROKER
gob·let \'gäb-lət\ *noun* [Middle English *gobelet*, from Middle French] (14th century)
1 *archaic* : a bowl-shaped drinking vessel without handles
2 : a drinking vessel (as of glass) with a foot and stem — compare TUMBLER
goblet cell *noun* [from its shape] (1878)
: a mucus-secreting epithelial cell (as of intestinal columnar epithelium) that is distended at the free end
gob·lin \'gäb-lən\ *noun* [Middle English *gobelin*, from Middle French, from Medieval Latin *gobelinus*, ultimately from Greek *kobalos* rogue] (14th century)

: an ugly or grotesque sprite that is mischievous and sometimes evil and malicious
go·bo \'gō-(,)bō\ *noun, plural* **gobos** *also* **goboes** [origin unknown] (circa 1930)
1 : a dark strip (as of wallboard) to shield a motion-picture or television camera from light
2 : a device to shield a microphone from sound
go·by \'gō-bē\ *noun, plural* **gobies** *also* **goby** [Latin *gobius* gudgeon, from Greek *kōbios*] (1769)
: any of numerous spiny-finned fishes (family Gobiidae) that usually have the pelvic fins united to form a ventral sucking disk

goby

go by *intransitive verb* (1508)
: PASS 3b ⟨as time *goes by*⟩
go–cart \'gō-,kärt\ *noun* (1689)
1 a : WALKER **b** : STROLLER
2 : HANDCART
3 : a light open carriage
¹**god** \'gäd *also* 'gòd\ *noun* [Middle English, from Old English; akin to Old High German *got* god] (before 12th century)
1 *capitalized* : the supreme or ultimate reality: as **a** : the Being perfect in power, wisdom, and goodness who is worshipped as creator and ruler of the universe **b** *Christian Science* : the incorporeal divine Principle ruling over all as eternal Spirit : infinite Mind
2 : a being or object believed to have more than natural attributes and powers and to require human worship; *specifically* : one controlling a particular aspect or part of reality
3 : a person or thing of supreme value
4 : a powerful ruler
²**god** *transitive verb* **god·ded; god·ding** (1595)
: to treat as a god : IDOLIZE, DEIFY
god–aw·ful \gä-'dò-fəl\ *adjective* [*god*damned + *awful*] (1878)
: extremely unpleasant or disagreeable : ABOMINABLE ⟨*god-awful* weather⟩
god·child \'gäd-,chīld *also* 'gòd-\ *noun* (13th century)
: a person for whom another person becomes sponsor at baptism
¹**god·damn** *or* **god·dam** \'gä(d)-'dam\ *noun, often capitalized* (1640)
: DAMN ⟨they were in no mood to give a good *goddamn* about anything —Robert Lowry⟩
²**goddamn** *or* **goddam** *verb, often capitalized* (1928)
: DAMN
god·damned \,gä(d)-'damd\ *or* **god·damn** *or* **god·dam** \-,dam\ *adjective or adverb* (1918)
: DAMNED
god·daugh·ter \'gäd-,dò-tər *also* 'gòd-\ *noun* (before 12th century)
: a female godchild
god·dess \'gä-dəs *also* 'gò-\ *noun* (14th century)
1 : a female god
2 : a woman whose great charm or beauty arouses adoration
usage see -ESS
Go·del's theorem \'gō-dəlz, 'gər-, 'gœ-\ *noun* [Kurt Gödel (died 1978) American mathematician] (1933)
: a theorem in advanced logic: in any logical system as complex as or more complex than the arithmetic of the integers there can always be found either a statement which can be shown to be both true and false or a statement whose truth or falsity cannot be deduced from other statements in the system — called also *Godel's incompleteness theorem*
go·det \gō-'det, -'dā\ *noun, often attributive* [French, from *goder* to form creases, probably from *goderon* rounded pleat on a ruffle, gadroon] (1872)

: an inset of cloth placed in a seam to give fullness (as at the bottom of a skirt)
go–dev·il \'gō-,de-vəl\ *noun* (1852)
: any of various devices: as **a** : a cultivator with wooden runners **b** : a weight dropped in a bored hole (as of an oil well) to set off an explosive **c** : a cleaning scraper propelled through a pipeline **d** : a handcar or small gasoline car used on a railroad **e** : a child's sled
¹**god·fa·ther** \'gäd-,fä-thər, -,fà-, *also* 'gòd-\ *noun* (before 12th century)
1 : a man who sponsors a person at baptism
2 : one having a relation to someone or something analogous to that of a male sponsor to his godchild: as **a** : one that founds, supports, or inspires ⟨made him the *godfather* of a whole generation of rebels —*Times Literary Supplement*⟩ **b** : the leader of an organized crime syndicate
²**godfather** *transitive verb* (1780)
: to act as godfather to
God–fear·ing \-,fir-iŋ\ *adjective* (1835)
: having a reverent feeling toward God : DEVOUT
god·for·sak·en \-fər-,sā-kən\ *adjective* (1860)
1 : REMOTE, DESOLATE
2 : neglected and miserable in appearance or circumstances
god·head \-,hed\ *noun* [Middle English *godhed*, from *god* + *-hed* -hood; akin to Middle English *-hod* -hood] (13th century)
1 : divine nature or essence : DIVINITY
2 *capitalized* **a** : GOD 1 **b** : the nature of God especially as existing in three persons — used with *the*
god·hood \-,húd\ *noun* [Middle English *godhod*, from Old English *godhād*, from *god* + *-hād* -hood] (1563)
: DIVINITY
Go·di·va \gə-'dī-və\ *noun*
: an English earl's wife who in legend rode naked through Coventry to save its citizens from a tax
god·less \'gäd-ləs *also* 'gòd-\ *adjective* (1528)
: not acknowledging a deity or divine law
— **god·less·ness** *noun*
god·like \-,līk\ *adjective* (before 12th century)
: resembling or having the qualities of God or a god : DIVINE
— **god·like·ness** *noun*
god·ling \-liŋ\ *noun* (circa 1500)
: an inferior or local god
god·ly \-lē\ *adjective* **god·li·er; -est** (14th century)
1 : DIVINE
2 : PIOUS, DEVOUT
— **god·li·ness** *noun*
— **godly** *adverb, archaic*
god·moth·er \-,mə-thər\ *noun* (before 12th century)
: a woman who sponsors a person at baptism
go·down \'gō-,daùn\ *noun* [by folk etymology from Malay *gudang*] (1552)
: a warehouse in an oriental country
go down *intransitive verb* (14th century)
1 a : to go below the horizon : SET ⟨the sun *went down*⟩ **b** : to fall to or as if to the ground ⟨the plane *went down* in flames⟩ **c** : to become submerged ⟨the ship *went down* with all hands⟩
2 : to admit of being swallowed ⟨the medicine *went down* easily⟩
3 a : to find acceptance ⟨will the plan *go down* with the farmers⟩ **b** : to come to be remembered especially in posterity ⟨will he *go down* in history as a great president⟩
4 *British* : to leave a university
5 a : to undergo defeat or failure **b** *chiefly British* : to become incapacitated ⟨*went down* with . . . acute tonsillitis —Helen Cathcart⟩
6 *slang* : to take place : HAPPEN
— **go down on** : to perform fellatio or cunnilingus on
god·par·ent \'gäd-,par-ənt, -,per- *also* 'gòd-\ *noun* (1865)

: a sponsor at baptism

God's acre *noun* (1617)
: CHURCHYARD

god·send \'gäd-ˌsend *also* 'gód-\ *noun* [back-formation from *god-sent*] (1820)
: a desirable or needed thing or event that comes unexpectedly

god·son \-ˌsən\ *noun* (before 12th century)
: a male godchild

God-speed \-'spēd\ *noun* [Middle English *god speid,* from the phrase *God spede you* God prosper you] (15th century)
: a prosperous journey : SUCCESS ⟨bade him *Godspeed*⟩

god·wit \'gäd-ˌwit\ *noun* [origin unknown] (1552)
: any of a genus (*Limosa*) of wading birds that are related to the curlews and sandpipers and have a long slender slightly upturned or straight bill

goes *present 3d singular of* GO, *plural of* GO

goe·thite \'gə(r)-ˌtīt\ *noun* [German *Göthit,* from J. W. von *Goethe*] (circa 1823)
: a mineral that consists of an iron hydrogen oxide and is the commonest constituent of many forms of natural rust

go·fer \'gō-fər\ *noun* [alteration of *go for*] (1967)
: an employee whose duties include running errands

gof·fer \'gä-fər, 'gó-\ *transitive verb* [French *gaufrer,* from *gaufre* honeycomb, waffle, from Old French, of Germanic origin; akin to Middle Dutch *wafel* waffle] (1706)
: to crimp, plait, or flute (as linen or lace) especially with a heated iron
— **goffer** *noun*

go–get·ter \'gō-ˈge-tər, -ˌge-\ *noun* (1921)
: an aggressively enterprising person
— **go–get·ting** \-ˌge-tiŋ\ *adjective or noun*

¹**gog·gle** \'gä-gəl\ *intransitive verb* **gog·gled; gog·gling** [Middle English *gogelen* to squint] (1616)
: to stare with wide or protuberant eyes
— **gog·gler** \'gä-gəl-ər\ *noun*

²**goggle** *adjective* (1540)
: PROTUBERANT, STARING ⟨*goggle* eyes⟩
— **gog·gly** \'gä-gəl-ē\ *adjective*

gog·gle–eye \'gä-gəl-ˌī\ *noun* (1840)
1 : ROCK BASS
2 : WARMOUTH

gog·gle–eyed \-ˌīd\ *adjective* (1711)
: having bulging or rolling eyes

gog·gles \'gä-gəlz\ *noun plural* (1715)
: protective glasses set in a flexible frame (as of rubber or plastic) that fits snugly against the face
— **gog·gled** \-gəld\ *adjective*

go–go \'gō-(ˌ)gō\ *adjective* [partly from *a-go-go,* partly from reduplication of ¹*go*] (1965)
1 a : employed to entertain in a disco ⟨*go-go* dancers⟩ **b** : of, relating to, or being a disco or the music or dances performed there
2 : marked by spirited or aggressive action ⟨*go-go* baseball⟩
3 a : relating to or dealing in popular often speculative investment expected to yield high returns ⟨*go-go* mutual funds⟩ **b** : relating to, involved in, or marked by business growth and prosperity and aggressive efforts to turn a quick profit ⟨*go-go* bankers and entrepreneurs . . . who put together the megabuck deals —Ken Auletta⟩

¹**Goi·del·ic** \gói-'de-lik\ *adjective* [Middle Irish *Goídel* Gael, Irishman] (1896)
1 : of, relating to, or characteristic of the Gaels
2 : of, relating to, or constituting Goidelic

²**Goidelic** *noun* (1882)
: the branch of the Celtic languages that includes Irish, Scottish Gaelic, and Manx — see INDO-EUROPEAN LANGUAGES table

go in *intransitive verb* (1812)
1 : to make an approach (as in attacking)

2 a : to take part in a game or contest **b** : to call the opening bet in poker : STAY
3 *of a celestial body* : to become obscured by a cloud
4 : to form a union or alliance : JOIN — often used with *with* ⟨asked the rest of us to *go in* with them⟩
— **go in for 1** : to give support to : ADVOCATE **2** : to have or show an interest in or a liking for **3** : to engage in : take part in

¹**go·ing** \'gō-iŋ, 'gó(-)iŋ\ *noun* (14th century)
1 : an act or instance of going
2 *plural* : BEHAVIOR, ACTIONS ⟨for his eyes are upon the ways of man, and he seeth all his *goings* —Job 34:21 (Authorized Version)⟩
3 : the condition of the ground (as for walking)
4 : advance toward an objective ⟨when the *going* gets tough⟩

²**going** *adjective* (14th century)
1 a : that goes — often used in combination ⟨easy*going*⟩ ⟨out*going*⟩ **b** : WORKING, MOVING ⟨everything was in *going* order⟩
2 : LIVING, EXISTING ⟨the best novelist *going*⟩
3 : CURRENT, PREVAILING ⟨*going* price⟩
4 : conducting business with the expectation of indefinite continuance ⟨*going* concern⟩
— **going on** : drawing near to : APPROACHING ⟨is six years old *going on* seven⟩

go·ing–over \ˌgō-iŋ-'ō-vər, ˌgó(-)iŋ-\ *noun, plural* **go·ings–over** (1872)
1 a : a severe scolding **b** : BEATING
2 : a thorough examination or investigation

go·ings–on \ˌgō-iŋ-'zón, ˌgó(-)iŋ-, -'zän\ *noun plural* (1775)
1 : ACTIONS, EVENTS
2 : irregular or reprehensible happenings or conduct ⟨titillating stories about the *goings-on* of the carefree millionaires —Eleanor Early⟩

goi·ter \'gói-tər\ *noun* [French *goitre,* from Middle French, back-formation from *goitron* throat, from (assumed) Vulgar Latin *guttrion-, guttrio,* from Latin *guttur*] (1625)
: an enlargement of the thyroid gland visible as a swelling of the front of the neck — compare HYPERTHYROIDISM, HYPOTHYROIDISM
— **goi·trous** \'gói-trəs, 'gói-tə-rəs\ *adjective*

goi·tre chiefly British variant of GOITER

goi·tro·gen \'gói-trə-jən\ *noun* [*goiter* + -*o*- + -*gen*] (1946)
: a substance (as thiourea or thiouracil) that induces goiter formation

goi·tro·gen·ic \ˌgói-trə-'je-nik\ *adjective* (1929)
: producing or tending to produce goiter
— **goi·tro·ge·nic·i·ty** \ˌgói-trə-jə-'ni-sə-tē\ *noun*

Gol·con·da \gäl-'kän-də\ *noun* [*Golconda,* India, famous for its diamonds] (1884)
: a rich mine; *broadly* : a source of great wealth

gold \'gōld\ *noun, often attributive* [Middle English, from Old English; akin to Old High German *gold* gold, Old English *geolu* yellow — more at YELLOW] (before 12th century)
1 : a malleable ductile yellow metallic element that occurs chiefly free or in a few minerals and is used especially in coins, jewelry, and dentures — see ELEMENT table
2 a (1) : gold coins (2) : a gold piece **b** : MONEY **c** : GOLD STANDARD
3 : a variable color averaging deep yellow
4 : something resembling gold; *especially* : something valued as the finest of its kind ⟨a heart of *gold*⟩
5 : a medal awarded as the top prize in a competition : a gold medal

¹**gold-brick** \'gōld-ˌbrik\ *noun* (1881)
1 a : a worthless brick that appears to be of gold **b** : something that appears to be valuable but is actually worthless
2 : a person who shirks assigned work

²**goldbrick** (1902)
transitive verb

: SWINDLE
intransitive verb
: to shirk duty or responsibility

gold-bug \-ˌbəg\ *noun* (1878)
1 : a supporter of the gold standard
2 : a person who invests in or hoards gold

gold coast *noun, often G&C capitalized* (1877)
: an exclusive residential district

gold digger *noun* (1830)
1 : one who digs for gold
2 : a woman who uses charm to extract money or gifts from others

gold·en \'gōl-dən\ *adjective* [Middle English] (13th century)
1 : consisting of, relating to, or containing gold
2 a : being or having the color gold or the color of gold **b** : BLOND 1a
3 : LUSTROUS, SHINING
4 : of a high degree of excellence : SUPERB
5 : PROSPEROUS, FLOURISHING ⟨*golden* days⟩
6 a : radiantly youthful and vigorous **b** : possessing talents that promise worldly success — often used with *boy* **c** : highly favored : POPULAR
7 : FAVORABLE, ADVANTAGEOUS ⟨a *golden* opportunity⟩
8 : of, relating to, or being a 50th anniversary or its celebration
9 : MELLOW, RESONANT ⟨a smooth *golden* tenor⟩
— **gold·en·ly** *adverb*
— **gold·en·ness** \-də(n)-nəs\ *noun*

golden age *noun* (1555)
: a period of great happiness, prosperity, and achievement

gold·en·ag·er \'gōl-dən-ˈā-jər\ *noun* (1961)
: an elderly and often retired person usually engaging in club activities

golden al·ex·an·ders \-ˌa-lig-'zan-dərz, -ˌe-lig-\ *noun plural but singular or plural in construction, often A capitalized* [Medieval Latin *alexandrum*] (circa 1923)
: a North American yellow-flowered perennial herb (*Zizia aurea*) of the carrot family occurring in moist woods and meadows; *also* : any of several related herbs

golden–brown alga *noun* (circa 1957)
: any of a division (Chrysophyta) of marine and freshwater algae (as diatoms) containing yellowish green to golden brown pigments that obscure the chlorophyll — called also *chrysophyte, golden alga*

golden club *noun* (1837)
: an American aquatic plant (*Orontium aquaticum*) of the arum family with a spadix of tiny yellow flowers

golden eagle *noun* (1839)
: a brown eagle (*Aquila chrysaetos*) of the northern hemisphere with gold-colored feathers on the back of the head and neck

gold·en·eye \'gōl-dən-ˌī\ *noun* (circa 1678)
1 : either of two diving ducks (genus *Bucephala*); *especially* : a large-headed swift-flying Holarctic diving duck (*B. clangula*) with the male having a green head and striking black and white markings
2 : a lacewing (family Chrysopidae) with yellow eyes

Golden Fleece *noun* (14th century)

golden eagle

: a fleece of gold placed by the king of Colchis in a dragon-guarded grove and recovered by the Argonauts

golden glow *noun* (1902)
: a tall branching composite herb (*Rudbeckia laciniata hortensia*) with showy yellow flower heads

golden hamster *noun* (1939)
: a small tawny hamster (*Mesocricetus auratus*) native to Asia Minor — called also *Syrian hamster*

golden hamster

golden handshake *noun* (1960)
: a generous severance agreement given especially as an inducement to early retirement

Golden Horde *noun* (1863)
: a body of Mongols that overran eastern Europe in the 13th century and dominated Russia until 1486

golden lion tamarin *noun* (1975)
: a marmoset (*Leontopithecus rosalia rosalia*) with a reddish gold coat and long mane that occurs in remnants of tropical forest in southeastern Brazil

golden mean *noun* (1587)
: the medium between extremes : MODERATION

golden nematode *noun* (1946)
: a small yellowish Old World nematode worm (*Globodera rostochiensis* synonym *Heterodera rostochiensis*) established locally as a pest of potatoes in eastern North America

golden oldie *noun* (1970)
: one that was a hit or favorite in the past

golden parachute *noun* (1981)
: a generous severance agreement for an executive in the event of a sudden dismissal (as because of a merger)

golden plover *noun* (1785)
: either of two gregarious plovers (genus *Pluvialis*); *especially* : one (*P. dominica*) that breeds in arctic America and Siberia and winters in Hawaii and the southern hemisphere

gold·en·rain tree \'gōl-dən-ˌrān-\ *noun* (1923)
: an Asian tree (*Koelreuteria paniculata* of the family Sapindaceae) that has a rounded crown with very long showy clusters of yellow flowers

golden retriever *noun* (1919)
: any of a breed of medium-sized retrievers having a flat moderately long golden coat

gold·en·rod \'gōl-dən-ˌräd\ *noun* (1568)
: any of numerous chiefly North American composite biennial or perennial plants (especially of the genus *Solidago*) with alternate leaves and heads of small yellow or sometimes white flowers often clustered in panicles

golden rule *noun* (1861)
1 : a guiding principle
2 *G&R capitalized* : a rule of ethical conduct referring to Matthew 7:12 and Luke 6:31: do to others as you would have them do to you

gold·en·seal \'gōl-dən-ˌsēl\ *noun* (1839)
: a perennial American herb (*Hydrastis canadensis*) of the buttercup family with large rounded leaves and a thick knotted yellow rootstock sometimes used in pharmacy

golden section *noun* (1875)
: a proportion (as one involving a line divided into two segments or the length and width of a rectangle and their sum) in which the ratio of the whole to the larger part is the same as the ratio of the larger part to the smaller

golden shiner *noun* (circa 1889)
: a common cyprinid fish (*Notemigonus crysoleucas*) of eastern North America having silvery sides with bright golden reflections

golden syrup *noun* (1860)
chiefly British : TREACLE 2b

gold·field \'gōl(d)-ˌfēld\ *noun* (1851)
: a gold-mining district

gold–filled \-'fild\ *adjective* (circa 1903)
: consisting of a base metal covered with a layer of gold ⟨a *gold-filled* bracelet⟩

gold·finch \-ˌfinch\ *noun* (before 12th century)
1 : a small Palearctic finch (*Carduelis carduelis*) with a red, white, and black head and yellow and black wings
2 : any of three small American finches (genus *Carduelis* and especially *C. tristis*) having the breeding plumage of the male variably yellow with black markings on the wings, tail, and crown

gold·fish \-ˌfish\ *noun* (1791)
: a small usually golden yellow or orange cyprinid fish (*Carassius auratus*) often kept as an aquarium and pond fish

goldfish bowl *noun* (1935)
: a place or situation offering no privacy

gold leaf *noun* (circa 1741)
: an extremely thin sheet of gold that is used especially for gilding

gold mine *noun* (1833)
: a rich source of something desired

gold of pleasure (1597)
: a European herb (*Camelina sativa*) of the mustard family that is cultivated for its oil-rich seeds

gold rush *noun* (1876)
1 : a rush to newly discovered goldfields in pursuit of riches
2 : the headlong pursuit of sudden wealth in a new or lucrative field
— **gold rush·er** \-ˌrə-shər\ *noun*

gold·smith \'gōl(d)-ˌsmith\ *noun* (before 12th century)
: one who makes or deals in articles of gold

gold standard *noun* (1831)
: a monetary standard under which the basic unit of currency is defined by a stated quantity of gold and which is usually characterized by the coinage and circulation of gold, unrestricted convertibility of other money into gold, and the free export and import of gold for the settlement of international obligations

gold·stone \'gōl(d)-ˌstōn\ *noun* (circa 1889)
: aventurine glass spangled close and fine with particles of gold-colored material

go·lem \'gō-ləm, 'gȯi-, 'gä-\ *noun* [Yiddish *goylem*, from Hebrew *gōlem* shapeless mass] (1897)
1 : an artificial human being in Hebrew folklore endowed with life
2 : something or someone resembling a golem: as **a** : AUTOMATON **b** : BLOCKHEAD

golf \'gälf, 'gȯlf, 'gäf, 'gȯf *sometimes* 'gəlf\ *noun, often attributive* [Middle English (Scots)] (15th century)
: a game in which a player using special clubs attempts to sink a ball with as few strokes as possible into each of the 9 or 18 successive holes on a course □
— **golf** *intransitive verb*
— **golf·er** *noun*

Golf (1952)
— a communications code word for the letter *g*

golf ball *noun* (1545)
1 : a small hard dimpled ball used in golf
2 : the spherical printing element of an electric typewriter or printer

golf cart *noun* (1899)
1 : a small cart for wheeling a golf bag around a golf course
2 : a motorized cart for carrying golfers and their equipment over a golf course — called also *golf car*

golf course *noun* (1890)
: an area of land laid out for golf with a series of 9 or 18 holes each including tee, fairway,

and putting green and often one or more natural or artificial hazards — called also *golf links*

Gol·gi \'gȯl-(ˌ)jē\ *adjective* (1891)
: of or relating to the Golgi apparatus, Golgi bodies, or a method of staining nerve tissue ⟨*Golgi* vesicles⟩

Golgi apparatus *noun* [Camillo *Golgi*] (1916)
: a cytoplasmic organelle that consists of a stack of smooth membranous saccules and associated vesicles and that is active in the modification and transport of proteins — called also *Golgi complex;* see CELL illustration

Golgi body *noun* (1925)
: GOLGI APPARATUS; *also* : DICTYOSOME

go·liard \'gōl-yərd, -ˌyärd\ *noun* [Middle English, from Middle French, goliard, glutton, from *gole* throat, from Latin *gula* — more at GLUTTON] (15th century)
: a wandering student of the 12th or 13th century given to the writing of satiric Latin verse and to convivial living and minstrelsy
— **go·liar·dic** \gōl-'yär-dik\ *adjective*

Go·li·ath \gə-'lī-əth\ *noun* [Hebrew *Golyath*]
1 : a Philistine champion who in I Samuel 17 is killed by David
2 : GIANT

gol·li·wog *also* **gol·ly·wog** *or* **gol·li·wogg** \'gä-lē-ˌwäg\ *noun* [*Golliwogg*, an animated doll in children's fiction by Bertha Upton (died 1912) American writer] (1895)
1 : a grotesque black doll
2 : a person resembling a golliwog

gol·ly \'gä-lē\ *interjection* [euphemism for *God*] (1775)
— used as a mild oath or to express surprise

Go·mor·rah \gə-'mȯr-ə\ *noun* [from *Gomorrah*, ancient city destroyed by God for its wickedness in Genesis 19] (1907)
: a place notorious for vice and corruption

gon- *or* **gono-** *combining form* [Greek, from *gonos* procreation, seed, from *gignesthai* to be born — more at KIN]
: sexual : generative : semen : seed ⟨*gono*cyte⟩

-gon *noun combining form* [New Latin *-gonum*, from Greek *-gōnon*, from *gōnia* angle; akin to Greek *gony* knee — more at KNEE]
: figure having (so many) angles ⟨deca*gon*⟩

go·nad \'gō-ˌnad\ *noun* [New Latin *gonad-, gonas*, from Greek *gonos*] (1916)
: a reproductive gland (as an ovary or testis) that produces gametes
— **go·nad·al** \gō-'na-dᵊl\ *adjective*

go·nad·ec·to·my \ˌgō-nə-'dek-tə-mē\ *noun, plural* **-mies** (1915)
: surgical removal of an ovary or testis
— **go·nad·ec·to·mized** \-ˌmīzd\ *adjective*

go·nad·o·trop·ic \gō-ˌna-də-'trä-pik\ *also* **go·nad·o·tro·phic** \-'trō-fik, -'trä-\ *adjective* (circa 1923)
: acting on or stimulating the gonads

go·nad·o·tro·pin \-'trō-pən\ *also* **go·nad·o·tro·phin** \-fən\ *noun* (1931)
: a gonadotropic hormone (as follicle-stimulating hormone)

Gond \'gänd\ *noun* (1801)
: a member of a Dravidian or pre-Dravidian people of central India

Gondi \'gän-dē\ *noun* (1855)

□ USAGE

golf Like *assault* and *fault, golf* went through the earliest phase of its life as a word with no *l* either in spelling or in pronunciation. Though one no longer hears *assault* and *fault* sounded without an \l\, *golf* is still pronounced without it by some. The pronunciation without \l\ has been proscribed by some critics as "old-fashioned." The forms with an audible \l\ are more common, but no one should be penalized for using the older form without \l\.

: the Dravidian language of the Gonds

gon·do·la \'gän-də-lə (*usual for sense 1*), gän-'dō-\ *noun* [Italian dialect (Venetian), probably from Middle Greek *kontoura* small vessel] (1549)
1 : a long narrow flat-bottomed boat with a high prow and stern used on the canals of Venice

gondola 1

2 : a heavy flat-bottomed boat used on New England rivers and on the Ohio and Mississippi rivers
3 : a railroad car with no top, a flat bottom, and fixed sides that is used chiefly for hauling heavy bulk commodities
4 a : an elongated car attached to the underside of an airship **b** : an often spherical airtight enclosure suspended from a balloon for carrying passengers or instruments **c** : an enclosed car suspended from a cable and used for transporting passengers; *especially* : one used as a ski lift

gon·do·lier \ˌgän-də-'lir\ *noun* (1603)
: one who propels a gondola

gone \'gȯn *also* 'gän\ *adjective* [from past participle of *go*] (1598)
1 a : DEAD **b** : LOST, RUINED ⟨lost looks and *gone* faculties —Penelope Gilliatt⟩ **c** : characterized by sinking or dropping ⟨the empty or *gone* feeling in the abdomen so common in elevators —H. G. Armstrong⟩
2 a : INVOLVED, ABSORBED ⟨far *gone* in hysteria⟩ **b** : possessed with a strong attachment or a foolish or unreasoning love or desire : INFATUATED — often used with *on* ⟨was real *gone* on that man —Pete Martin⟩ **c** : PREGNANT ⟨she's six months *gone*⟩
3 : PAST ⟨memories of *gone* summers —John Cheever⟩
4 *slang* : GREAT ⟨a real *gone* fashion reporter —Inez Robb⟩

G₁ phase \ˌjē-'wən-\ *noun* [growth] (1966)
: the period in the cell cycle from the end of cell division to the beginning of DNA replication — compare G₂ PHASE, M PHASE, S PHASE

gon·er \'gȯ-nər *also* 'gä-nər\ *noun* (1854)
: one whose case is hopeless

gon·fa·lon \'gän-fə-ˌlän, -lən\ *noun* [Italian *gonfalone*] (1595)
1 : the ensign of certain princes or states (as the medieval republics of Italy)
2 : a flag that hangs from a crosspiece or frame

gong \'gäŋ, 'gȯŋ\ *noun* [Malay & Javanese, of imitative origin] (circa 1590)
1 : a disk-shaped percussion instrument that produces a resounding tone when struck with a usually padded hammer
2 a : a saucer-shaped bell (as in a fire alarm) that is struck by a mechanical hammer **b** : a wire rod wound in a flat spiral for sounding the time or chime or alarm (as in a clock)
3 *British* : MEDAL
— **gong** *intransitive verb*

Gon·go·rism \'gäŋ-gə-ˌri-zəm\ *noun* [Spanish *gongorismo*, from Luis de *Góngora* y Argote (died 1627) Spanish poet] (1813)
: a literary style characterized by studied obscurity and by the use of various ornate devices
— **gon·go·ris·tic** \ˌgäŋ-gə-'ris-tik\ *adjective*

go·nid·i·um \gō-'ni-dē-əm\ *noun, plural* **-ia** \-dē-ə\ [New Latin, from *gon-* + *-idium*] (1882)
: an asexual reproductive cell or group of cells especially in algae (as volvox)

gon·if, gon·iff \'gä-nəf\ *variant of* GANEF

go·ni·om·e·ter \ˌgō-nē-'ä-mə-tər\ *noun* [Greek *gōnia* angle] (1766)
1 : an instrument for measuring angles
2 : DIRECTION FINDER
— **go·ni·o·met·ric** \-nē-ə-'me-trik\ *adjective*
— **go·ni·om·e·try** \-nē-'ä-mə-trē\ *noun*

-gonium *combining form* [New Latin, from Greek *gonos*]
1 : germ cell ⟨spermato*gonium*⟩
2 : reproductive structure of a plant or fungus ⟨oo*gonium*⟩

gon·o·coc·cus \ˌgä-nə-'kä-kəs\ *noun, plural* **-coc·ci** \-'käk-ˌsī, -(ˌ)sē; -'kä-ˌkī, -(ˌ)kē\ [New Latin] (1889)
: a pus-producing bacterium (*Neisseria gonorrhoeae*) that causes gonorrhea
— **gon·o·coc·cal** \-'kä-kəl\ *adjective*

gon·o·cyte \'gä-nə-ˌsīt\ *noun* [International Scientific Vocabulary] (1900)
: a cell that produces gametes; *especially* : GAMETOCYTE

go–no–go \ˌgō-'nō-ˌgō\ *adjective* (circa 1945)
1 : being or relating to a required decision to continue or stop a course of action
2 : being or relating to a point at which a go-no-go decision must be made

gon·o·phore \'gä-nə-ˌfōr, -ˌfȯr\ *noun* [International Scientific Vocabulary] (1859)
: an attached reproductive zooid of a hydroid colony

gon·o·pore \'gä-nə-ˌpōr, -ˌpȯr\ *noun* (1897)
: a genital pore in some invertebrates and especially some insects

gon·or·rhea \ˌgä-nə-'rē-ə\ *noun* [New Latin, from Late Latin, morbid loss of semen, from Greek *gonorrhoia*, from *gon-* + *-rrhoia* -rrhea] (circa 1526)
: a contagious inflammation of the genital mucous membrane caused by the gonococcus — called also *clap*
— **gon·or·rhe·al** \-'rē-əl\ *adjective*

-gony *noun combining form* [Latin *-gonia*, from Greek, from *gonos*]
: generation : reproduction : manner of coming into being ⟨iso*gony*⟩

gon·zo \'gän-(ˌ)zō\ *adjective* [origin unknown] (1971)
: idiosyncratically subjective but engagé ⟨*gonzo* journalism⟩; *also* : BIZARRE

goo \'gü\ *noun* [perhaps short for *burgoo*] (1900)
1 : a viscid or sticky substance
2 : sentimental tripe
— **goo·ey** \-ē\ *adjective*
— **goo·ey·ness** \-nəs\ *noun*

goo·ber \'gü-bər, 'gù-\ *noun* [of Bantu origin; akin to Kimbundu *ŋguba* peanut] (1833) *Southern & Midland* : PEANUT

¹good \'gùd\ *adjective* **bet·ter** \'be-tər\; **best** \'best\ [Middle English, from Old English *gōd*; akin to Old High German *guot* good, Sanskrit *gadhya* what one clings to] (before 12th century)
1 a (1) : of a favorable character or tendency ⟨*good* news⟩ (2) : BOUNTIFUL, FERTILE ⟨*good* land⟩ (3) : HANDSOME, ATTRACTIVE ⟨*good* looks⟩ **b** (1) : SUITABLE, FIT ⟨*good* to eat⟩ (2) : free from injury or disease ⟨one *good* arm⟩ (3) : not depreciated ⟨bad money drives out *good*⟩ (4) : commercially sound ⟨a *good* risk⟩ (5) : that can be relied on ⟨*good* for another year⟩ ⟨*good* for a hundred dollars⟩ ⟨always *good* for a laugh⟩ (6) : PROFITABLE, ADVANTAGEOUS ⟨made a very *good* deal⟩ **c** (1) : AGREEABLE, PLEASANT ⟨had a *good* time⟩ (2) : SALUTARY, WHOLESOME ⟨*good* for a cold⟩ (3) : AMUSING, CLEVER ⟨a *good* joke⟩ **d** (1) : of a noticeably large size or quantity : CONSIDERABLE ⟨won by a *good* margin⟩ ⟨a *good* bit of the time⟩ (2) : FULL ⟨waited a *good* hour⟩ (3) — used as an intensive ⟨a

good many of us⟩ **e** (1) : WELL-FOUNDED, COGENT ⟨*good* reasons⟩ (2) : TRUE ⟨holds *good* for society at large⟩ (3) : deserving of respect : HONORABLE ⟨in *good* standing⟩ (4) : legally valid or effectual ⟨*good* title⟩ **f** (1) : ADEQUATE, SATISFACTORY ⟨*good* care⟩ — often used in faint praise ⟨his serve is only *good* —Frank Deford⟩ (2) : conforming to a standard ⟨*good* English⟩ (3) : CHOICE, DISCRIMINATING ⟨*good* taste⟩ (4) : containing less fat and being less tender than higher grades — used of meat and especially of beef
2 a (1) : VIRTUOUS, RIGHT, COMMENDABLE ⟨a *good* person⟩ ⟨*good* conduct⟩ (2) : KIND, BENEVOLENT ⟨*good* intentions⟩ **b** : UPPER-CLASS ⟨a *good* family⟩ **c** : COMPETENT, SKILLFUL ⟨a *good* doctor⟩ **d** (1) : LOYAL ⟨a *good* party man⟩ ⟨a *good* Catholic⟩ (2) : CLOSE ⟨a *good* friend⟩ **e** : free from infirmity or sorrow ⟨I feel *good*⟩ □
— **good·ish** \'gù-dish\ *adjective*
— **as good as** : in effect : VIRTUALLY ⟨*as good as* dead⟩
— **as good as gold 1** : of the highest worth or reliability ⟨his promise is *as good as gold*⟩ **2** : well-behaved ⟨the child was *as good as gold*⟩
— **good and** \ˌgùd-ᵊn\ : VERY, ENTIRELY ⟨was *good and* mad⟩

²good *noun* (before 12th century)
1 a : something that is good **b** (1) : something conforming to the moral order of the universe (2) : praiseworthy character : GOODNESS **c** : a good element or portion
2 a : advancement of prosperity or well-being ⟨the *good* of the community⟩ ⟨it's for your own *good*⟩ **b** : something useful or beneficial ⟨it's no *good* trying⟩
3 a : something that has economic utility or satisfies an economic want **b** *plural* : personal property having intrinsic value but usually excluding money, securities, and negotiable instruments **c** *plural* : CLOTH **d** *plural* : something manufactured or produced for sale : WARES, MERCHANDISE ⟨canned *goods*⟩ **e** *plural, British* : FREIGHT
4 : good persons — used with *the*
5 *plural* **a** : the qualities required to achieve an end **b** : proof of wrongdoing ⟨didn't have the *goods* on him —T. G. Cooke⟩
— **for good** *also* **for good and all** : FOREVER, PERMANENTLY
— **in good with** : in a favored position with
— **to the good 1** : for the best : BENEFICIAL ⟨efforts to restrict credit were all *to the good* —Time⟩ **2** : in a position of net gain or profit ⟨wound up $10 *to the good*⟩

³good *adverb* (13th century)
1 : WELL ⟨he showed me how *good* I was doing —Herbert Gold⟩

□ **USAGE**
good An old notion that it is wrong to say "I feel good" in reference to health still occasionally appears in print. The origins of this notion, which goes back to the turn of the century, are obscure, but they seem to combine someone's idea that *good* should be reserved to describe virtue and uncertainty about whether an adverb or an adjective should follow *feel*. Today nearly everyone agrees that both *good* and *well* can be predicate adjectives after *feel*. Both are used to express good health, but *good* may connote good spirits in addition to good health.

\ə\ **abut** \ᵊ\ **kitten** \ər\ **further** \a\ **ash** \ā\ **ace**
\ä\ **mop, mar** \au̇\ **out** \ch\ **chin** \e\ **bet** \ē\ **easy**
\g\ **go** \i\ **hit** \ī\ **ice** \j\ **job** \ŋ\ **sing** \ō\ **go**
\ȯ\ **law** \ȯi\ **boy** \th\ **thin** \t͟h\ **the** \ü\ **loot** \ù\ **foot**
\y\ **yet** \zh\ **vision** *see also* Guide to Pronunciation

2 — used as an intensive ⟨a *good* 200 pounds⟩ ⟨a *good* long time⟩ □

good book *noun, often G&B capitalized* (1860)
: BIBLE

good–bye *or* **good–by** \gu̇d-'bī, gə(d)-\ *noun* [alteration of *God be with you*] (circa 1580)
1 : a concluding remark or gesture at parting — often used interjectionally
2 : a taking of leave ⟨a tearful *good-bye*⟩ ◊

good deal *noun* (1881)
: a considerable quantity or extent : LOT ⟨knows a *good deal* about disease⟩ ⟨a *good deal* faster⟩

good faith *noun* (1893)
: honesty or lawfulness of purpose

good fellow *noun* (13th century)
: an affable companionable person
— **good–fel·low·ship** \'gu̇d-'fe-lō-,ship, -'fe-lə-\ *noun*

good–for–noth·ing \'gu̇d-fər-,nə-thiŋ\ *adjective* (1533)
: of no use or value
— **good–for–nothing** *noun*

Good Friday *noun* [from its special sanctity] (13th century)
: the Friday before Easter observed in churches as the anniversary of the crucifixion of Christ and in some states of the U.S. as a legal holiday

good–heart·ed \'gu̇d-'här-təd\ *adjective* (1552)
: having a kindly generous disposition
— **good–heart·ed·ly** *adverb*
— **good–heart·ed·ness** *noun*

good–hu·mored \-'(h)yü-mərd\ *adjective* (1662)
: GOOD-NATURED, CHEERFUL
— **good–hu·mored·ly** *adverb*
— **good–hu·mored·ness** *noun*

good life *noun* (1946)
: a life marked by a high standard of living

good–look·ing \'gu̇d-'lu̇-kiŋ\ *adjective* (1780)
: having a pleasing or attractive appearance
— **good–look·er** \-'lu̇-kər\ *noun*

good·ly \'gu̇d-lē\ *adjective* **good·li·er; -est** (before 12th century)
1 : pleasantly attractive
2 : significantly large : CONSIDERABLE ⟨a *goodly* number⟩

good·man \'gu̇d-mən\ *noun* (13th century)
1 *archaic* : the master of a household
2 *archaic* : MR.

good–na·tured \-'nā-chərd\ *adjective* (1577)
: of a pleasant cheerful cooperative disposition
synonym see AMIABLE
— **good–na·tured·ly** *adverb*
— **good–na·tured·ness** *noun*

good–neighbor *adjective* (1936)
: marked by principles of friendship, cooperation, and noninterference in the internal affairs of another country ⟨a *good-neighbor* policy⟩

good·ness \'gu̇d-nəs\ *noun* (before 12th century)
1 : the quality or state of being good
2 — used interjectionally or in phrases especially to express mild surprise or shock ⟨oh, my *goodness*!⟩ ⟨*goodness* knows⟩
3 : the nutritious, flavorful, or beneficial part of something

goodness of fit (circa 1939)
: the conformity between an experimental result and theoretical expectation or between data and an approximating curve

good offices *noun plural* (1904)
: services as a mediator

good old boy *or* **good ol' boy** *or* **good ole boy** \'gu̇d-dōl(d)-,bȯi\ *noun* (circa 1967)
: a usually white Southerner who conforms to the social behavior of his peers

Good Samaritan *noun* (1846)
: SAMARITAN 2

good–tem·pered \'gu̇d-'tem-pərd\ *adjective* (1768)
: not easily vexed
— **good–tem·pered·ly** *adverb*

good–tem·pered·ness *noun*

good·wife \'gu̇d-,wīf\ *noun* (13th century)
1 *archaic* : the mistress of a household
2 *archaic* : MRS.

good·will \,gu̇d-'wil\ *noun* (before 12th century)
1 a : a kindly feeling of approval and support : benevolent interest or concern **b** (1) : the favor or prestige that a business has acquired beyond the mere value of what it sells (2) : the value of projected earnings increases of a business especially as part of its purchase price (3) : the value of other intangible assets (as tax credits) of a business especially as part of its purchase price
2 a : cheerful consent **b** : willing effort
— **good·willed** \-'wild\ *adjective*

¹good·y \'gu̇-dē\ *noun* [alteration of *goodwife*] (1559)
archaic : a usually married woman of lowly station — used as a title preceding a surname

²goody *or* **good·ie** *noun, plural* **good·ies** (1756)
1 : something that is particularly attractive, pleasurable, good, or desirable
2 *chiefly British* : one that is good; *especially* : an opponent of the villain (as in a motion picture)

goody–goody \,gu̇-dē-'gu̇-dē\ *adjective* (1871)
: affectedly or ingratiatingly good or proper
— **goody–goody** *noun*

Goody Two–shoes \'gu̇-dē-'tü-,shüz\ *noun, often S capitalized* [from *Goody Two-Shoes*, heroine of a children's story perhaps by Oliver Goldsmith] (1934)
: a person who is goody-goody; *also* : a person who is uncommonly good
— **goody–two–shoes** *adjective*

¹goof \'güf\ *noun* [probably alteration of English dialect *goff* (simpleton)] (1915)
1 : a silly or stupid person
2 : BLUNDER

²goof (1932)
intransitive verb
1 a : to spend time idly or foolishly — usually used with *off* **b** : to engage in playful activity — usually used with *around*
2 : to make a usually foolish or careless mistake : BLUNDER — often used with *up*
transitive verb
: to make a mess of : BUNGLE — usually used with *up*
— **goof on** *slang* : to make fun of : KID, PUT ON ⟨you're *goofing on* me, right?⟩

goof·ball \'güf-,bȯl\ *noun* (1950)
1 *slang* : a barbiturate sleeping pill
2 : a goofy person

go off *intransitive verb* (1579)
1 : EXPLODE
2 : to burst forth or break out suddenly or noisily
3 : to go forth, out, or away : LEAVE
4 : to undergo decline or deterioration
5 : to follow the expected or desired course : PROCEED ⟨the party *went off* well⟩
6 : to make a characteristic noise : SOUND
— **go off the deep end 1** : to enter recklessly on a course **2** : to become very much excited

goof–off \'gü-,fȯf\ *noun* (1953)
: one who evades work or responsibility

goofy \'gü-fē\ *adjective* **goof·i·er; -est** (1921)
: being crazy, ridiculous, or mildly ludicrous : SILLY
— **goof·i·ly** \-fə-lē\ *adverb*
— **goof·i·ness** \-fē-nəs\ *noun*

goo·gly–eyed \'gü-glē-,īd\ *adjective* [by alteration] (1901)
: GOGGLE-EYED

goo·gol \'gü-,gȯl\ *noun* [coined by Milton Sirotta (born about 1929) nephew of Edward Kasner (died 1955) American mathematician] (1938)
: the figure 1 followed by 100 zeroes equal to 10^{100} ◊

goo·gol·plex \-,pleks\ *noun* (1938)
: the figure 1 followed by a googol of zeroes equal to

$$10^{googol} \text{ or } 10^{10^{100}}$$

¹goo–goo \'gü-(,)gü\ *adjective* [perhaps alteration of ²*goggle*] (1900)
: LOVING, ENTICING — used chiefly in the phrase *goo-goo eyes*

²goo–goo *noun, plural* **goo–goos** [from *good government*] (1912)
: a member or advocate of a political reform movement

¹gook \'gük\ *noun* [origin unknown] (1935)
: a nonwhite or non-American person; *specifically* : ASIAN — usually used disparagingly

²gook \'gu̇k, 'gük\ *variant of* GUCK

goon \'gün\ *noun* [probably short for English dialect *gooney* (simpleton)] (1921)
1 : a stupid person
2 : a man hired to terrorize or eliminate opponents

go on *intransitive verb* (15th century)

□ USAGE
good Adverbial *good* has been under attack from the schoolroom since the 19th century. Insistence on *well* rather than *good* has resulted in a split in connotation: *well* is standard, neutral, and colorless, while *good* is emotionally charged and emphatic. This makes *good* the adverb of choice in sports ⟨"I'm seeing the ball real *good*" is what you hear —Roger Angell⟩. In such contexts as ⟨listen up. And listen *good* —Alex Karras⟩ ⟨lets fly with his tomatoes before they can flee. He gets Clarence *good* —Charles Dickinson⟩ *good* cannot be adequately replaced by *well*. Adverbial *good* is primarily a spoken form; in writing it occurs in reported and fictional speech and in generally familiar or informal contexts.

◊ WORD HISTORY
good-bye In Spanish *adios* and French *adieu* "farewell, good-bye," we see an explicit wish that the person addressed should be in the care of God (*dios, dieu*). The same sentiment lies at the origin of *good-bye*, which comes from the phrase *God be with you*. Gradually eroded over time, it appears in such versions as *God be wy you* (in the 16th century), *God b'y you* (a century later), and numerous other versions before settling into *good-bye* in the 19th century, the final form buttressed by the example of *good night* and *good day*. Good-bye was further shortened simply to *bye*, at which point reduction could scarcely proceed further. To some speakers, indeed, this meager monosyllable seemed in need of fattening, so they produced the reduplication *bye-bye*.

googol A *googol* is a very big number whose name was coined by a small boy. In the late 1930s American mathematician Edward Kasner (1878–1955) found himself working with numbers as large as 1 followed by a hundred zeroes. While it is possible to write this number, using scientific notation, simply as 10^{100}, Kasner felt that having a name for it would facilitate discussing it. According to his own account, he asked his nine-year-old nephew Milton Sirotta to supply a name, promising that he would indeed use the word. Milton produced *googol*, Kasner kept his promise, and the word was accepted in the mathematical community.

1 a : to continue on or as if on a journey ⟨life *goes on*⟩ ⟨*went on* to greater things⟩ **b :** to keep on : CONTINUE ⟨*went on* smoking⟩ **c :** PROCEED ⟨*went on* to win the election⟩
2 : to take place : HAPPEN ⟨what's *going on*⟩
3 : to talk especially in an effusive manner ⟨the way people *go on* about their ancestors —Hamilton Basso⟩

goo·ney *or* **goo·ny** \ˈgü-nē\ *noun, plural* **gooneys** *or* **goonies** [probably from English dialect *gooney* (simpleton)] (1895)
: BLACK-FOOTED ALBATROSS; *broadly* **:** ALBATROSS

goop \ˈgüp\ *noun* [probably alteration of *goo*] (circa 1958)
: GOO, GUNK

goo·san·der \gü-ˈsan-dər\ *noun* [origin unknown] (1766)
: the common merganser (*Mergus merganser*) of the northern hemisphere

¹goose \ˈgüs\ *noun, plural* **geese** \ˈgēs\ [Middle English *gos*, from Old English *gōs;* akin to Old High German *gans* goose, Latin *anser*, Greek *chēn*] (before 12th century)
1 a : any of numerous large waterfowl (family Anatidae) that are intermediate between the swans and ducks and have long necks, feathered lores, and reticulate tarsi **b :** a female goose as distinguished from a gander
2 : SIMPLETON, DOLT
3 *plural* **goos·es :** a tailor's smoothing iron with a gooseneck handle
4 *plural* **goos·es :** a poke between the buttocks

²goose *transitive verb* **goosed; goos·ing** (circa 1880)
1 : to poke between the buttocks with an upward thrust
2 : to increase the activity, speed, power, intensity, or amount of : SPUR ⟨an effort to *goose* newsstand sales⟩

goose·ber·ry \ˈgüs-ˌber-ē, ˈgüz-, -b(ə-)rē, *chiefly British* ˈgüz-\ *noun* (1573)
1 a : the acid usually prickly fruit of any of several shrubs (genus *Ribes*) of the saxifrage family **b :** a shrub bearing gooseberries
2 : CURRANT 2

gooseberry: leaves and fruit

goose bumps *noun plural* (1933)
: a roughness of the skin produced by erection of its papillae especially from cold, fear, or a sudden feeling of excitement

goose egg *noun* (1866)
: ZERO, NOTHING; *especially* **:** a score of zero in a game or contest

goose·fish \ˈgüs-ˌfish\ *noun* (1807)
: any of a family (Lophiidae) of pediculate fishes with a large flattened head, a fringe of flaps along each side of the lower jaw, head, and body, and a long stalk on the head with a flap of flesh at the tip for attracting prey; *especially* **:** MONKFISH

goose·flesh \ˈgüs-ˌflesh\ *noun* (circa 1810)
: GOOSE BUMPS

goose·foot \-ˌfu̇t\ *noun, plural* **goose·foots** (1548)
: any of a genus (*Chenopodium*) or family (Chenopodiaceae, the goosefoot family) of glabrous herbs with utricular fruit

goose·grass \-ˌgras\ *noun* (1530)
1 : CLEAVERS
2 : YARD GRASS

goose·neck \ˈgüs-ˌnek\ *noun, often attributive* (1688)
1 : something (as a flexible jointed metal pipe) curved like the neck of a goose or U-shaped
2 : a truck trailer (as for transporting livestock) with a projecting front end designed to attach to the bed of a pickup truck
— **goose·necked** \-ˌnekt\ *adjective*

goose pimples *noun plural* (circa 1889)
: GOOSE BUMPS

goose–step \ˈgüs-ˌstep\ *intransitive verb* (1879)
1 : to march in a goose step
2 : to practice an unthinking conformity

goose step *noun* (1806)
: a straight-legged stiff-kneed step used by troops of some armies when passing in review

goos·ey \ˈgü-sē\ *adjective* **goos·i·er; -est** (1811)
1 : resembling a goose
2 a : affected with goose bumps : SCARED **b :** very nervous **c :** reacting strongly when goosed or startled

go out *intransitive verb* (before 12th century)
1 a : to go forth, abroad, or outdoors; *specifically* **:** to leave one's house **b** (1) **:** to take the field as a soldier (2) **:** to participate as a principal in a duel **c :** to travel as or as if a colonist or immigrant **d :** to work away from home
2 a : to come to an end **b :** to give up office **:** RESIGN **c :** to become obsolete or unfashionable **d** (1) **:** to play the last card of one's hand (2) **:** to reach or exceed the total number of points required for game in cards
3 : to take part in social activities
4 : to go on strike
5 : BREAK, COLLAPSE
6 : to become a candidate ⟨*went out* for the football team⟩

go over *intransitive verb* (1645)
1 : to go on a journey
2 : to become converted
3 : to receive approval : SUCCEED ⟨his plan *went over* well⟩

¹go·pher \ˈgō-fər\ *noun* [origin unknown] (1791)
1 : a burrowing land tortoise (*Gopherus polyphemus*) of the southern U.S.; *broadly* **:** any of several related land tortoises — called also *gopher tortoise*
2 a : any of a family (Geomyidae) of burrowing rodents of western North America, Central America, and the southern U.S. that are the size of a large rat and have large cheek pouches opening beside the mouth — called also *pocket gopher* **b :** any of several small ground squirrels (genus *Citellus*) of the prairie region of North America closely related to the chipmunks
3 : GOPHER BALL

²gopher *variant of* GOFER

gopher ball *noun* (circa 1949)
: a pitched baseball hit for a home run

gopher snake *noun* (1837)
1 : INDIGO SNAKE
2 : BULL SNAKE

Gor·di·an knot \ˈgȯr-dē-ən-\ *noun*
1 : an intricate problem; *especially* **:** a problem insoluble in its own terms — usually used in the phrase *cut the Gordian knot*
2 : a knot tied by Gordius, king of Phrygia, held to be capable of being untied only by the future ruler of Asia, and cut by Alexander the Great with his sword

Gor·don setter \ˈgȯr-dᵊn-\ *noun* [Alexander, 4th Duke of *Gordon* (died 1827) Scottish sportsman] (1865)
: any of a breed of large bird dogs that have a long flat black-and-tan coat

¹gore \ˈgōr, ˈgȯr\ *noun* [Middle English, from Old English *gāra;* akin to Old English *gār* spear, and perhaps to Greek *chaion* shepherd's staff] (before 12th century)
1 : a small usually triangular piece of land
2 a : a tapering or triangular piece (as of cloth in a skirt) **b :** an elastic gusset for providing a snug fit in a shoe

²gore *transitive verb* **gored; gor·ing** (1548)

Gordon setter

1 : to cut into a tapering triangular form
2 : to provide with a gore

³gore *transitive verb* **gored; gor·ing** [Middle English] (15th century)
: to pierce or wound with something pointed (as a horn or knife) ⟨*gored* by a bull⟩

⁴gore *noun* [Middle English, filth, from Old English *gor*] (1563)
: BLOOD; *especially* **:** clotted blood

¹gorge \ˈgȯrj\ *noun* [Middle English, from Middle French, from Late Latin *gurga*, alteration of *gurges*, from Latin, whirlpool — more at VORACIOUS] (14th century)
1 : THROAT — often used with *rise* to indicate revulsion accompanied by a sensation of constriction ⟨my *gorge* rises at the sight of blood⟩
2 a : a hawk's crop **b :** STOMACH, BELLY
3 : the entrance into an outwork (as a bastion) of a fort
4 : a narrow passage through land; *especially* **:** a narrow steep-walled canyon or part of a canyon
5 : a primitive device used instead of a fishhook that consists of an object (as a piece of bone attached in the middle of a line) easy to swallow but difficult to eject
6 : a mass choking a passage ⟨a river dammed by an ice *gorge*⟩
7 : the line on the front of a coat or jacket formed by the crease of the lapel and collar

²gorge *verb* **gorged; gorg·ing** (14th century)
intransitive verb
: to eat greedily or to repletion
transitive verb
1 a : to stuff to capacity : GLUT **b :** to fill completely or to the point of distension ⟨veins *gorged* with blood⟩
2 : to consume greedily
synonym see SATIATE
— **gorg·er** *noun*

³gorge *noun* (1854)
: the act or an instance of gorging

gor·geous \ˈgȯr-jəs\ *adjective* [Middle English *gorgayse*, from Middle French *gorgias* elegant, from *gorgias* wimple, from *gorge* gorget] (15th century)
: splendidly or showily brilliant or magnificent
synonym see SPLENDID
— **gor·geous·ly** *adverb*
— **gor·geous·ness** *noun*

gor·get \ˈgȯr-jət\ *noun* [Middle English, from Middle French, from *gorge*] (15th century)
1 : a piece of armor protecting the throat — see ARMOR illustration
2 a : an ornamental collar **b :** a part of a wimple covering the throat and shoulders

gor·gon \ˈgȯr-gən\ *noun* [Latin *Gorgon-, Gorgo,* from Greek *Gorgōn*]
1 *capitalized* **:** any of three snake-haired sisters in Greek mythology whose appearance turns the beholder to stone
2 : an ugly or repulsive woman
— **Gor·go·ni·an** \gȯr-ˈgō-nē-ən\ *adjective*

gor·go·ni·an \gȯr-ˈgō-nē-ən\ *noun* [New Latin *Gorgonia*, a coral genus, from Latin, coral, from *Gorgon-, Gorgo*] (1835)
: any of an order (Gorgonacea) of colonial anthozoans with a usually horny and branching axial skeleton
— **gorgonian** *adjective*

gor·gon·ize \ˈgȯr-gə-ˌnīz\ *transitive verb* **-ized; -iz·ing** (1609)
: to have a paralyzing or mesmerizing effect on : STUPEFY, PETRIFY

Gor·gon·zo·la \ˌgȯr-gən-ˈzō-lə\ *noun* [Italian, from *Gorgonzola*, Italy] (1878)
: a pungent blue cheese of Italian origin

go·ril·la \gə-ˈri-lə\ *noun* [New Latin, from Greek *Gorillai*, plural, a tribe of hairy women

mentioned in an account of a voyage around Africa] (1847)
1 : an anthropoid ape (*Gorilla gorilla*) of western equatorial Africa related to the chimpanzee but less erect and much larger
2 a : an ugly or brutal man **b :** THUG, GOON ◆
gor·man·dise *chiefly British variant of* GORMANDIZE
gor·man·dize \'gȯr-mən-ˌdīz\ *verb* **-dized; -diz·ing** [*gormand*, alteration of *gourmand*] (1548)
intransitive verb
: to eat gluttonously or ravenously
transitive verb
: to eat greedily **:** DEVOUR
— **gor·man·diz·er** *noun*
gorm·less \'gȯrm-ləs\ *adjective* [alteration of English dialect *gaumless*, from *gaum* attention, understanding (from Middle English *gome*, from Old Norse *gaum, gaumr*) + *-less*] (1883)
chiefly British **:** lacking intelligence **:** STUPID
go–round \'gō-ˌraůnd\ *noun* (1891)
: GO-AROUND
gorp \'gȯrp\ *noun* [origin unknown] (1968)
: a snack consisting of high-energy food (as raisins and nuts)
gorse \'gȯrs\ *noun* [Middle English *gorst*, from Old English; akin to Old High German *gersta* barley, Latin *hordeum*] (before 12th century)
: a spiny yellow-flowered European shrub (*Ulex europaeus*) of the legume family; *broadly* **:** any of several related plants (genera *Ulex* and *Genista*)
— **gorsy** \'gȯr-sē\ *adjective*
gory \'gōr-ē, 'gȯr-\ *adjective* **gor·i·er; -est** (15th century)
1 : covered with gore **:** BLOODSTAINED
2 : BLOODCURDLING, SENSATIONAL ⟨wanted to hear the *gory* details⟩
synonym see BLOODY
gosh \'gäsh, 'gȯsh\ *interjection* [euphemism for *God*] (1757)
— used as a mild oath or to express surprise
gos·hawk \'gäs-ˌhȯk\ *noun* [Middle English *goshawke*, from Old English *gōshafoc*, from *gōs* goose + *hafoc* hawk] (before 12th century)
: any of several long-tailed accipitrine hawks with short rounded wings; *especially* **:** a hawk (*Accipiter gentilis*) of the northern parts of both the Old and the New World that is larger than a crow and has a white stripe above and behind the eye
gos·ling \'gäz-liŋ, 'gȯz-, -lən\ *noun* [Middle English, from *gos* goose] (14th century)
1 : a young goose
2 : a foolish or callow person
go–slow \ˌgō-'slō\ *noun* (1926)
British **:** SLOWDOWN
¹gos·pel \'gäs-pəl\ *noun* [Middle English, from Old English *gōdspel* (translation of Late Latin *evangelium*), from *gōd* good + *spell* tale — more at SPELL] (before 12th century)
1 a *often capitalized* **:** the message concerning Christ, the kingdom of God, and salvation **b** *capitalized* **:** one of the first four New Testament books telling of the life, death, and resurrection of Jesus Christ; *also* **:** a similar apocryphal book **c :** an interpretation of the Christian message ⟨the social *gospel*⟩
2 *capitalized* **:** a lection from one of the New Testament Gospels
3 : the message or teachings of a religious teacher
4 : something accepted as infallible truth or as a guiding principle ⟨the *gospel* of conservation —R. M. Hodesh⟩
5 : gospel music
²gospel *adjective* (before 12th century)
1 a : having a basis in or being in accordance with the gospel **:** EVANGELICAL ⟨ordained to the *gospel* ministry —*Christian Century*⟩ **b** **:** marked by special or fervid emphasis on the gospel ⟨a *gospel* meeting⟩

2 : of, relating to, or being religious songs of American origin associated with evangelism and popular devotion and marked by simple melody and harmony and elements of folk songs and blues
gos·pel·er *or* **gos·pel·ler** \'gäs-p(ə-)lər\ *noun* (1506)
1 : one who reads or sings the liturgical Gospel
2 : one who preaches or propounds a gospel
gospel side *noun, often G capitalized* [from the custom of reading the Gospel from this side] (1891)
: the left side of an altar or chancel as one faces it
¹gos·sa·mer \'gä-sə-mər *also* 'gäz-mər, 'gä-zə-\ *noun* [Middle English *gossomer*, from *gos* goose + *somer* summer] (14th century)
1 : a film of cobwebs floating in air in calm clear weather
2 : something light, delicate, or insubstantial ⟨the *gossamer* of youth's dreams —Andrea Parke⟩
— **gos·sa·mery** \-mə-rē\ *adjective*
²gossamer *adjective* (circa 1807)
: extremely light, delicate, or tenuous
gos·san \'gä-sᵊn\ *noun* [Cornish *gossen*, from *gōs* blood] (1776)
: decomposed rock or vein material of reddish or rusty color that results from oxidized pyrites
¹gos·sip \'gä-səp\ *noun* [Middle English *gossib*, from Old English *godsibb*, from *god* god + *sibb* kinsman, from *sibb* related — more at SIB] (before 12th century)
1 a *dialect British* **:** GODPARENT **b** **:** COMPANION, CRONY **c :** a person who habitually reveals personal or sensational facts about others
2 a : rumor or report of an intimate nature **b** **:** a chatty talk **c :** the subject matter of gossip ◆
— **gos·sip·ry** \-sə-prē\ *noun*
²gossip *intransitive verb* (1627)
: to relate gossip
— **gos·sip·er** *noun*
gos·sip·mon·ger \'gä-səp-ˌməŋ-gər, -ˌmäŋ-\ *noun* (1836)
: a person who starts or spreads gossip
gos·sipy \'gä-sə-pē\ *adjective* (1818)
: characterized by, full of, or given to gossip ⟨a *gossipy* letter⟩ ⟨*gossipy* neighbors⟩
gos·sy·pol \'gä-si-ˌpȯl, -ˌpōl\ *noun* [International Scientific Vocabulary, ultimately from Latin *gossypion* cotton] (1899)
: a toxic phenolic pigment $C_{30}H_{30}O_8$ in cottonseed
got *past and past participle of* GET
Goth \'gäth\ *noun* [Middle English *Gothes, Gotes* (plural), partly from Old English *Gotan* (plural); partly from Late Latin *Gothi* (plural)] (14th century)
: a member of a Germanic people that overran the Roman Empire in the early centuries of the Christian era
¹Goth·ic \'gä-thik\ *adjective* (1591)
1 a : of, relating to, or resembling the Goths, their civilization, or their language **b :** TEUTONIC, GERMANIC **c :** MEDIEVAL **d :** UNCOUTH, BARBAROUS
2 a : of, relating to, or having the characteristics of a style of architecture developed in northern France and spreading through western Europe from the middle of the 12th century to the early 16th century that is characterized by the converging of weights and strains at isolated points upon slender vertical piers and counterbalancing buttresses and by pointed arches and vaulting **b :** of or relating to an architectural style reflecting the influence of the medieval Gothic
3 *often not capitalized* **:** of or relating to a style of fiction characterized by the use of desolate or remote settings and macabre, mysterious, or violent incidents
— **goth·i·cal·ly** \-thi-k(ə-)lē\ *adverb*
— **Goth·ic·ness** \-thik-nəs\ *noun*

²Gothic *noun* (1691)
1 a : BLACK LETTER **b :** SANS SERIF
2 : Gothic art style or decoration; *specifically* **:** the Gothic architectural style
3 : the East Germanic language of the Goths — see INDO-EUROPEAN LANGUAGES table
4 *often not capitalized* **:** a work of fiction in the gothic style
Gothic arch *noun* (1739)
: a pointed arch; *especially* **:** one with a joint instead of a keystone at its apex
Goth·i·cism \'gä-thə-ˌsi-zəm\ *noun* (1710)
1 : barbarous lack of taste or elegance
2 : conformity to or practice of Gothic style
— **Goth·i·cist** \-sist\ *noun*
goth·i·cize \-ˌsīz\ *transitive verb* **-cized; -ciz·ing** *often capitalized* (1712)
: to make Gothic
Goth·ick *chiefly British variant of* GOTHIC
Gothic Revival *noun* (1869)
: an artistic style or movement of the 18th and 19th centuries inspired by and imitative of the Gothic style especially in architecture
go through *intransitive verb* (1513)
1 : to continue firmly or obstinately to the end ⟨I was *going through* with it if it killed me —A. W. Long⟩
2 a : to receive approval or sanction **:** PASS **b** **:** to come to a desired or satisfactory conclusion

◇ **WORD HISTORY**

gorilla In the sixth or early fifth century B.C., the Carthaginian navigator Hanno made a voyage around the west coast of Africa, perhaps sailing as far as Sherbro Island in modern Sierra Leone. An account of his journey was inscribed on tablets that have since disappeared, though a Greek translation survives. Near the furthest point on their voyage Hanno and his men came upon an island "full of wild people, the greater part of whom were females, hairy on their bodies, whom our interpreters called Gorillas. We pursued them, but could not capture the males . . . but we captured three females, who, biting and scratching their captors, refused to go along with them. We killed and skinned them and brought the skins to Carthage." Whether Hanno actually saw a species of anthropoid ape or something else we will never know, but when the gorilla of western equatorial Africa was first described scientifically in 1847, it was given the Latin name *Troglodytes gorilla*. This binomial was superseded by *Gorilla gorilla*, and the vernacular name of the animal in English and other European languages has become simply *gorilla*.

gossip In Old English *sibb* occurs as a noun meaning "kinship" and as an adjective meaning "related by blood or kinship." By the 11th century a compound had been formed from the noun *sibb* prefixed by *god*, the predecessor of Modern English *god*. A *godsibb*, therefore, was a person spiritually related to another, specifically by being a sponsor at baptism. Today we would call such a person a *godmother* or *godfather*, using *god* in the same way. By the 14th century the *d* had begun to disappear, and *godsibb* developed into *gossib* and then, through devoicing of the final consonant, to *gossip*, the form that is still current. The meaning, too, had begun to change, and the sense of *gossip* as a close friend or comrade developed alongside the sense of a godparent. Since close friends naturally talk about family and other friends, it was only a short step to the *gossip* of today, a person no longer necessarily friend, relative, or sponsor, but someone filled with irresistible tidbits of rumor.

go to *intransitive verb* (15th century)
1 *archaic* — used interjectionally as an exhortation ⟨and they said one to another, *go to*, let us make brick —Genesis 11:3 (Authorized Version)⟩
2 *archaic* — used interjectionally to express disapproval or disbelief ⟨*go to, go to;* you have known what you should not —Shakespeare⟩
gotten *past participle of* GET
Göt·ter·däm·mer·ung \ˌgə(r)-tər-'de-mə-ˌrüṅ, -'dä-\ *noun* [German, literally, twilight of the gods, from *Götter* (plural of *Gott* god) + *Dämmerung* twilight] (1909)
: a collapse (as of a society or regime) marked by catastrophic violence and disorder
gouache \'gwäsh\ *noun* [French, from Italian *guazzo,* literally, puddle, probably from Latin *aquatio* watering place, from *aquari* to fetch water, from *aqua* water — more at ISLAND] (1882)
1 : a method of painting with opaque watercolors
2 a : a picture painted by gouache **b :** the pigment used in gouache
Gou·da \'gü-də\ *noun* [*Gouda,* Netherlands] (1885)
: a mild cheese of Dutch origin that is similar to Edam but contains more fat
¹gouge \'gaüj\ *noun* [Middle English *gowge,* from Middle French *gouge,* from Late Latin *gulbia,* of Celtic origin; akin to Old Irish *gulban* beak, sting] (14th century)
1 : a chisel with a concavo-convex cross section
2 a : the act of gouging **b :** a groove or cavity scooped out
3 : an excessive or improper exaction **:** EXTORTION
²gouge *transitive verb* **gouged; goug·ing** (1570)
1 : to scoop out with or as if with a gouge
2 a : to force out (an eye) with the thumb **b :** to thrust the thumb into the eye of
3 : to subject to extortion or undue exaction **:** OVERCHARGE
— **goug·er** *noun*
gou·lash \'gü-ˌläsh, -ˌlash\ *noun* [Hungarian *gulyás,* short for *gulyáshús,* literally, herdsman's meat] (1866)
1 : a stew made with meat (as beef), assorted vegetables, and paprika
2 : a round in bridge played with hands produced by a redistribution of previously dealt cards
3 : a mixture of heterogeneous elements **:** JUMBLE
go under *intransitive verb* (1848)
: to be overwhelmed, destroyed, or defeated **:** FAIL
go up *intransitive verb* (15th century)
1 *chiefly British* **:** to attend a university
2 *of an actor* **:** to become confused
— **go up in flames :** BURN
— **go up in smoke :** to be destroyed by or as if by burning
gou·ra·mi \gü-'rä-mē\ *noun, plural* **-mi** *or* **-mis** *also* **-mies** [Malay dialect (Java), from Javanese *gramĕh*] (1878)
: any of numerous African and Asian tropical freshwater fishes (order Perciformes): as **a :** a large Asian food fish (*Osphronemus goramy,* family Osphronemidae) **b :** any of various small fishes (families Belontiidae and Helostomatidae) often kept in aquariums
gourd \'gōrd, 'górd, 'gürd\ *noun* [Middle English *gourde,* from Middle French, from Latin *cucurbita*] (14th century)
1 : any of a family (Cucurbitaceae, the gourd family) of chiefly herbaceous tendril-bearing vines including the cucumber, melon, squash, and pumpkin
2 : the fruit of a gourd **:** PEPO; *especially* **:** any of various hard-rinded inedible fruits of plants

of two genera (*Lagenaria* and *Cucurbita*) often used for ornament or for vessels and utensils
— **out of one's gourd** *also* **off one's gourd :** CRAZY
gourde \'gürd\ *noun* [American French] (circa 1858)
— see MONEY table
gour·mand \'gür-ˌmänd, -mənd\ *noun* [Middle English, from Middle French *gourmant*] (15th century)
1 : one who is excessively fond of eating and drinking
2 : one who is heartily interested in good food and drink
synonym see EPICURE
— **gour·mand·ism** \'gür-ˌmän-ˌdi-zəm, -mən-\ *noun*
— **gour·man·dize** \-ˌdīz\ *intransitive verb*
gour·man·dise \ˌgür-män-'dēz\ *noun* [French, from Middle French, from *gourmand*] (15th century)
: appreciation of or interest in good food and drink **:** GOURMANDISM
gour·met \'gür-ˌmā, gür-'\ *noun* [French, from Middle French, alteration of *gromet* boy servant, vintner's assistant, probably ultimately from Middle English *grom* groom] (1820)
: a connoisseur of food and drink; *broadly* **:** CONNOISSEUR 2 ⟨a film *gourmet*⟩
synonym see EPICURE
— **gourmet** *adjective*
gout \'gaüt\ *noun* [Middle English *goute,* from Old French, gout, drop, from Latin *gutta* drop] (13th century)
1 : a metabolic disease marked by a painful inflammation of the joints, deposits of urates in and around the joints, and usually an excessive amount of uric acid in the blood
2 : a mass or aggregate especially of something fluid often gushing or bursting forth
— **gouty** \-ē\ *adjective*
gov·ern \'gə-vərn\ *verb* [Middle English, from Old French *governer,* from Latin *gubernare* to steer, govern, from Greek *kybernan*] (14th century)
transitive verb
1 a : to exercise continuous sovereign authority over; *especially* **:** to control and direct the making and administration of policy in **b :** to rule without sovereign power and usually without having the authority to determine basic policy
2 a *archaic* **:** MANIPULATE **b :** to control the speed of (as a machine) especially by automatic means
3 a : to control, direct, or strongly influence the actions and conduct of **b :** to exert a determining or guiding influence in or over ⟨income must *govern* expenditure⟩ **c :** to hold in check **:** RESTRAIN
4 : to require (a word) to be in a certain case
5 : to serve as a precedent or deciding principle for ⟨customs that *govern* human decisions⟩
intransitive verb
1 : to prevail or have decisive influence **:** CONTROL
2 : to exercise authority
— **gov·ern·able** \-vər-nə-bəl\ *adjective*
gov·er·nance \'gə-vər-nən(t)s\ *noun* (14th century)
: GOVERNMENT
gov·ern·ess \'gə-vər-nəs\ *noun* (15th century)
1 : a woman who governs
2 : a woman entrusted with the care and supervision of a child especially in a private household
gov·ern·essy \'gə-vər-ni-sē\ *adjective* (1872)
: characteristic of or resembling a governess (as in primness)
gov·ern·ment \'gə-vər(n)-mənt, -və-mənt; 'gə-bᵊm-ənt, -vᵊm-\ *noun, often attributive* (14th century)
1 : the act or process of governing; *specifically* **:** authoritative direction or control

2 *obsolete* **:** moral conduct or behavior **:** DISCRETION
3 a : the office, authority, or function of governing **b** *obsolete* **:** the term during which a governing official holds office
4 : the continuous exercise of authority over and the performance of functions for a political unit **:** RULE
5 a : the organization, machinery, or agency through which a political unit exercises authority and performs functions and which is usually classified according to the distribution of power within it **b :** the complex of political institutions, laws, and customs through which the function of governing is carried out
6 : the body of persons that constitutes the governing authority of a political unit or organization: as **a :** the officials comprising the governing body of a political unit and constituting the organization as an active agency **b** *capitalized* **:** the executive branch of the U.S. federal government **c** *capitalized* **:** a small group of persons holding simultaneously the principal political executive offices of a nation or other political unit and being responsible for the direction and supervision of public affairs: (1) **:** such a group in a parliamentary system constituted by the cabinet or by the ministry (2) **:** ADMINISTRATION 4b
7 : POLITICAL SCIENCE
— **gov·ern·men·tal** \ˌgə-vər(n)-'men-tᵊl\ *adjective*
— **gov·ern·men·tal·ize** \-tᵊl-ˌīz\ *transitive verb*
— **gov·ern·men·tal·ly** \-tᵊl-ē\ *adverb*
gov·ern·men·tal·ism \ˌgə-vər(n)-'men-tᵊl-ˌi-zəm\ *noun* (1848)
1 : a theory advocating extension of the sphere and degree of government activity
2 : the tendency toward extension of the role of government
— **gov·ern·men·tal·ist** \-tᵊl-ist\ *noun*
gov·ern·men·tese \ˌgə-vər-mən-'tēz\ *noun* (1944)
: jargon held to be characteristic of government officials
gov·er·nor \'gə-vᵊn-ər *also* 'gə-vər-nər\ *noun* (14th century)
1 : one that governs: as **a :** one that exercises authority especially over an area or group **b :** an official elected or appointed to act as ruler, chief executive, or nominal head of a political unit **c :** COMMANDING OFFICER **d :** the managing director and usually the principal officer of an institution or organization **e :** a member of a group that directs or controls an institution or society
2 : TUTOR
3 a *slang* **:** one looked upon as governing **b :** MISTER, SIR — usually used as a term of address
4 a : an attachment to a machine (as a gasoline engine) for automatic control or limitation of speed **b :** a device giving automatic control (as of pressure or temperature)
— **gov·er·nor·ate** \-ət, -ˌāt\ *noun*
governor–general *noun, plural* **governors–general** *or* **governor–generals** (1586)
: a governor of high rank; *especially* **:** one who governs a large territory or has deputy governors under him
gov·er·nor·ship \'gə-vᵊn-ər-ˌship *also* 'gə-vər-nər-\ *noun* (1658)
1 : the office of governor
2 : the period of incumbency of a governor
gow·an \'gaü-ən\ *noun* [probably alteration of Middle English *gollan*] (1570)
chiefly Scottish **:** DAISY 1; *broadly* **:** a white or yellow field flower

— gow·any \-ə-nē\ *adjective, chiefly Scottish*

gown \ˈgaun\ *noun* [Middle English, from Middle French *goune*, from Late Latin *gunna*, a fur or leather garment] (14th century) **1 a :** a loose flowing outer garment formerly worn by men **b :** a distinctive robe worn by a professional or academic person **c :** a woman's dress **d** (1) : DRESSING GOWN (2) : NIGHTGOWN **e :** a coverall worn in an operating room **2 :** the body of students and faculty of a college or university ⟨rivalry between town and *gown*⟩
— gown *transitive verb*

gowns·man \ˈgaunz-mən\ *noun* (1627) : a professional or academic person

goy \ˈgȯi\ *noun, plural* **goy·im** \ˈgȯi-əm\ *also* **goys** [Yiddish, from Hebrew *gōy* people, nation] (1841) : GENTILE 1 — sometimes used disparagingly
— goy·ish \ˈgȯi-ish\ *adjective*

graaf·ian follicle \ˈgrä-fē-ən-, ˌgra-\ *noun, often G capitalized* [Regnier de *Graaf* (died 1673) Dutch anatomist] (1883) : a liquid-filled cavity in a mammalian ovary containing a mature egg before ovulation

¹grab \ˈgrab\ *verb* **grabbed; grab·bing** [obsolete Dutch or Low German *grabben*] (circa 1581) *transitive verb* **1 :** to take or seize by or as if by a sudden motion or grasp ⟨*grab* up an ax⟩ ⟨*grabbed* the opportunity⟩ ⟨*grab* attention⟩ **2 :** to obtain unscrupulously ⟨*grab* public lands⟩ **3 :** to take hastily ⟨*grab* a bite to eat⟩ ⟨*grab* a cab⟩ **4 a :** to seize the attention of ⟨the technique of *grabbing* an audience —Pauline Kael⟩ **b :** to impress favorably and deeply *intransitive verb* : to make a grab **synonym** see TAKE
— grab·ber *noun*

²grab *adjective* (1608) **1 :** intended to be grabbed ⟨a *grab* rail⟩ **2 :** taken at random ⟨*grab* samples of rocks⟩

³grab *noun* (1777) **1 a :** something grabbed **b :** a sudden snatch **c :** an unlawful or unscrupulous seizure **2** *chiefly British* **a :** a device for clutching an object **b :** CLAMSHELL
— up for grabs : available for anyone to take, win, or settle

grab bag *noun* (1855) **1 :** a receptacle (as a bag) containing small articles which are to be drawn (as at a party or fair) without being seen **2 :** a miscellaneous collection : POTPOURRI

grab·ble \ˈgra-bəl\ *intransitive verb* **grab·bled; grab·bling** \-b(ə-)liŋ\ [Dutch *grabbelen*, from Middle Dutch, frequentative of *grabben*] (circa 1580) **1 :** to search with the hand : GROPE **2 :** to lie or fall prone : SPRAWL
— grab·bler \-b(ə-)lər\ *noun*

grab·by \ˈgra-bē\ *adjective* **grab·bi·er; -est** (1910) **1 :** tending to grab : GRASPING, GREEDY **2 :** having the power to grab the attention ⟨*grabby* previews⟩

gra·ben \ˈgrä-bən\ *noun* [German, ditch, from Old High German *grabo*, from *graban* to dig — more at GRAVE] (1896) : a depressed segment of the crust of the earth or a celestial body (as the moon) bounded on at least two sides by faults

¹grace \ˈgrās\ *noun* [Middle English, from Old French, from Latin *gratia* favor, charm, thanks, from *gratus* pleasing, grateful; akin to Sanskrit *gṛṇāti* he praises] (12th century) **1 a :** unmerited divine assistance given humans for their regeneration or sanctification **b :** a virtue coming from God **c :** a state of sanctification enjoyed through divine grace

2 a : APPROVAL, FAVOR ⟨stayed in his good *graces*⟩ **b** *archaic* : MERCY, PARDON **c :** a special favor : PRIVILEGE ⟨each in his place, by right, not *grace*, shall rule his heritage —Rudyard Kipling⟩ **d :** disposition to or an act or instance of kindness, courtesy, or clemency **e :** a temporary exemption : REPRIEVE **3 a :** a charming or attractive trait or characteristic **b :** a pleasingly graceful appearance or effect : CHARM **c :** ease and suppleness of movement or bearing **4** — used as a title of address or reference for a duke, a duchess, or an archbishop **5 :** a short prayer at a meal asking a blessing or giving thanks **6** *plural, capitalized* : three sister goddesses in Greek mythology who are the givers of charm and beauty **7 :** a musical trill, turn, or appoggiatura **8 a :** sense of propriety or right ⟨had the *grace* not to run for elective office —Calvin Trillin⟩ **b :** the quality or state of being considerate or thoughtful
synonym see MERCY

²grace *transitive verb* **graced; grac·ing** (1585) **1 :** to confer dignity or honor on **2 :** ADORN, EMBELLISH ⟨graveled walks *graced* with statues —J. A. Michener⟩

grace·ful \ˈgrās-fəl\ *adjective* (circa 1586) : displaying grace in form or action : pleasing or attractive in line, proportion, or movement
— grace·ful·ly \-fə-lē\ *adverb*
— grace·ful·ness *noun*

grace·less \ˈgrās-sləs\ *adjective* (14th century) **1 :** lacking in divine grace : IMMORAL, UNREGENERATE **2 a :** lacking a sense of propriety **b :** devoid of attractive qualities **3 :** artistically inept or unbeautiful
— grace·less·ly *adverb*
— grace·less·ness *noun*

grace note *noun* (circa 1823) **1 :** a musical note added as an ornament; *especially* : APPOGGIATURA **2 :** a small addition or embellishment

grace period *noun* (1945) : a period of time beyond a due date during which a financial obligation may be met without penalty or cancellation

grac·ile \ˈgra-səl, -ˌsīl\ *adjective* [Latin *gracilis*] (1623) **1 :** SLENDER, SLIGHT **2 :** GRACEFUL **3 :** relating to, resembling, or being any of the primitive relatively small slender hominids (genus *Australopithecus*) characterized especially by molars and incisors of similar size that are adapted to an omnivorous diet — compare ROBUST
— grac·ile·ness *noun*
— gra·cil·i·ty \gra-ˈsi-lə-tē\ *noun*

gra·ci·o·so \ˌgrä-sē-ˈō-(ˌ)sō, -(ˌ)zō\ *noun, plural* **-sos** [Spanish, from *gracioso*, adjective, agreeable, amusing, from Latin *gratiosus*] (1749) : a buffoon in Spanish comedy

gra·cious \ˈgrā-shəs\ *adjective* [Middle English, from Middle French *gracieus*, from Latin *gratiosus* enjoying favor, agreeable, from *gratia*] (14th century) **1 a** *obsolete* : GODLY **b** *archaic* : PLEASING, ACCEPTABLE **2 a :** marked by kindness and courtesy **b :** GRACEFUL **c :** marked by tact and delicacy : URBANE **d :** characterized by charm, good taste, generosity of spirit, and the tasteful leisure of wealth and good breeding ⟨*gracious* living⟩ **3 :** MERCIFUL, COMPASSIONATE — used conventionally of royalty and high nobility ☆
— gra·cious·ly *adverb*
— gra·cious·ness *noun*

grack·le \ˈgra-kəl\ *noun* [New Latin *Gracula*, genus name, alteration of Latin *graculus* jackdaw] (1772)

1 : any of a genus (*Quiscalus* of the family Icteridae) of large American blackbirds having iridescent black plumage **2 :** any of various Asian starlings (as the hill mynahs)

¹grad \ˈgrad\ *noun or adjective* [by shortening] (circa 1871) : GRADUATE

²grad *noun* [French *grade* degree, from Latin *gradus*] (1898) : one hundredth of a right angle

gra·da·tion \grā-ˈdā-shən, grə-\ *noun* (1549) **1 a :** a series forming successive stages **b :** a step or place in an ordered scale **2 :** an advance by regular degrees **3 :** a gradual passing from one tint or shade to another **4 :** the act or process of grading **5 :** ABLAUT
— gra·da·tion·al \-shnəl, -shə-nᵊl\ *adjective*
— gra·da·tion·al·ly *adverb*

¹grade \ˈgrād\ *noun* [French, from Latin *gradus* step, degree, from Latin *gradi* to step, go; akin to Lithuanian *gridyti* to go, wander] (1796) **1 a** (1) : a stage in a process (2) : a position in a scale of ranks or qualities (3) : a degree of severity in illness ⟨*grade* III carcinoma⟩ **c :** a class organized for the work of a particular year of a school course **d :** a military or naval rank **2 a :** a class of things of the same stage or degree **b :** a mark indicating a degree of accomplishment in school **c :** a standard of food quality **3 a :** the degree of inclination of a road or slope; *also* : a sloping road **b :** a datum or reference level; *especially* : ground level **4 :** a domestic animal with one parent purebred and the other of inferior breeding **5** *plural* : the elementary school system
— grade·less \-ləs\ *adjective*

²grade *verb* **grad·ed; grad·ing** (1659) *transitive verb* **1 a :** to arrange in grades : SORT **b :** to arrange in a scale or series **c :** to assign to a grade or assign a grade to **2 :** to level off to a smooth horizontal or sloping surface *intransitive verb* **1 a :** to form a series **b :** BLEND **2 :** to be of a particular grade
— grad·able \ˈgrā-də-bəl\ *adjective*

³grade *adjective* (1852) : being, involving, or yielding domestic animals of improved but not pure stock ⟨*grade* ewes⟩ ⟨*grade* breeding⟩

-grade \ˌgrād\ *adjective combining form* [French, from Latin *-gradus*, from *gradi*] : walking ⟨plantigrade⟩

grade crossing *noun* (circa 1890) : a crossing of highways, railroad tracks, or pedestrian walks or combinations of these on the same level

grade point *noun* (1951)

☆ **SYNONYMS**
Gracious, cordial, affable, genial, sociable mean markedly pleasant and easy in social intercourse. GRACIOUS implies courtesy and kindly consideration ⟨the *gracious* award winner thanked her colleagues⟩. CORDIAL stresses warmth and heartiness ⟨our host was *cordial* as he greeted us⟩. AFFABLE implies easy approachability and readiness to respond pleasantly to conversation or requests or proposals ⟨though wealthy, she was *affable* to all⟩. GENIAL stresses cheerfulness and even joviality ⟨a *genial* companion with a ready quip⟩. SOCIABLE suggests a genuine liking for the companionship of others ⟨*sociable* people who enjoy entertaining⟩.

: one of the points assigned to each course credit (as in a college) in accordance with the letter grade earned in the course — called also *quality point*

grade point average *noun* (1966)
: the average obtained by dividing the total number of grade points earned by the total number of credits attempted — called also *quality point average*

grad·er \'grā-dər\ *noun* (1832)
1 : one that grades
2 : a machine for leveling earth
3 : a pupil in a school grade ⟨a fifth *grader*⟩

grade school *noun* (1869)
: ELEMENTARY SCHOOL
— **grade–school·er** \'grād-ˌskü-lər\ *noun*

grade separation *noun* (circa 1949)
: a highway or railroad crossing using an underpass or overpass

grade up *transitive verb* (1903)
: to improve by breeding females to purebred males

gra·di·ent \'grā-dē-ənt\ *noun* [Latin *gradient-, gradiens,* present participle of *gradi*] (1835)
1 a : the rate of regular or graded ascent or descent : INCLINATION **b** : a part sloping upward or downward
2 : change in the value of a quantity (as temperature, pressure, or concentration) with change in a given variable and especially per unit distance in a specified direction
3 : the vector sum of the partial derivatives with respect to the three coordinate variables *x, y,* and *z* of a scalar quantity whose value varies from point to point
4 : a graded difference in physiological activity along an axis (as of the body or an embryonic field)
5 : change in response with distance from the stimulus

gra·di·om·e·ter \ˌgrā-dē-ˈä-mə-tər\ *noun* [*gradient* + *-o-* + *-meter*] (1899)
: an instrument for measuring the gradient of a physical quantity (as the earth's magnetic field)

¹grad·u·al \'gra-jə-wəl, -jəl, 'graj-wəl\ *noun, often capitalized* [Middle English, from Medieval Latin *graduale,* from Latin *gradus* step, from its being sung on the steps of the altar] (15th century)
1 : a book containing the choral parts of the Mass
2 : a pair of verses (as from the Psalms) proper after the Epistle in the Mass

²gradual *adjective* [Medieval Latin *gradualis,* from Latin *gradus*] (1692)
1 : proceeding by steps or degrees
2 : moving, changing, or developing by fine or often imperceptible degrees
— **grad·u·al·ly** *adverb*
— **grad·u·al·ness** *noun*

grad·u·al·ism \-jə-wə-ˌli-zəm, -jə-ˌli-\ *noun* (1835)
1 : the policy of approaching a desired end by gradual stages
2 : the evolution of new species by gradual accumulation of small genetic changes over long periods of time; *also* : a theory or model of evolution emphasizing this — compare PUNCTUATED EQUILIBRIUM
— **grad·u·al·ist** \-list\ *noun or adjective*

grad·u·and \ˌgra-jə-ˈwand\ *noun* [Medieval Latin *graduandus,* gerundive of *graduare*] (1882)
British : one about to graduate : a candidate for a degree

¹grad·u·ate \'gra-jə-wət, -ˌwāt, 'graj-wət\ *noun* (15th century)
1 : a holder of an academic degree or diploma
2 : a graduated cup, cylinder, or flask

²graduate *adjective* (15th century)
1 : holding an academic degree or diploma
2 : of, relating to, or engaged in studies beyond the first or bachelor's degree ⟨*graduate* school⟩ ⟨a *graduate* student⟩

³grad·u·ate \'gra-jə-ˌwāt\ *verb* **-at·ed; -at·ing** [Medieval Latin *graduare,* from Latin *gradus* step, degree] (15th century)
transitive verb
1 a : to grant an academic degree or diploma to **b** : to be graduated from
2 a : to mark with degrees of measurement **b** : to divide into grades or intervals
3 : to admit to a particular standing or grade
intransitive verb
1 : to receive an academic degree or diploma
2 : to pass from one stage of experience, proficiency, or prestige to a usually higher one
3 : to change gradually □
— **grad·u·a·tor** \-ˌwā-tər\ *noun*

grad·u·at·ed *adjective* (1861)
of a tax : increasing in rate with increase in taxable base : PROGRESSIVE ⟨*graduated* income tax⟩

graduated cylinder *noun* (1948)
: a tall narrow container with a volume scale used especially for measuring liquids

grad·u·a·tion \ˌgra-jə-ˈwā-shən\ *noun* (1594)
1 : a mark on an instrument or vessel indicating degrees or quantity; *also* : these marks
2 a : the award or acceptance of an academic degree or diploma **b** : COMMENCEMENT
3 : arrangement in degrees or ranks

Graeco- — see GRECO-

graf·fi·to \grə-ˈfē-(ˌ)tō, gra-, grä-\ *noun, plural* **-ti** \-(ˌ)tē\ [Italian, incised inscription, from *graffiare* to scratch, probably from *grafio* stylus, from Latin *graphium*] (1851)
: an inscription or drawing made on some public surface (as a rock or wall); *also* : a message or slogan written as or as if as a graffito □
— **graf·fi·tist** \-ˈfē-tist\ *noun*

¹graft \'graft\ *noun* [Middle English *graffe, grafte,* from Middle French *grafe,* from Medieval Latin *graphium,* from Latin, stylus, from Greek *grapheion,* from *graphein* to write — more at CARVE] (14th century)
1 a : a grafted plant **b** : SCION 1 **c** : the point of insertion of a scion upon a stock
2 a : the act of grafting **b** : something grafted; *specifically* : living tissue used in grafting

²graft (14th century)
transitive verb
1 a : to cause (a scion) to unite with a stock; *also* : to unite (plants or scion and stock) to form a graft **b** : to propagate (a plant) by grafting
2 a : to join or unite as if by grafting **b** : to attach (a chemical unit) to a main molecular chain
3 : to implant (living tissue) surgically
intransitive verb
1 : to become grafted
2 : to perform grafting
— **graft·er** *noun*

³graft *noun* [English dialect *graft,* verb, to work, perhaps alteration of ¹*grave* (to dig)] (1853)
chiefly British : WORK, LABOR

⁴graft [origin unknown] (1859)
transitive verb
: to get (illicit gain) by graft
intransitive verb
: to practice graft

⁵graft *noun* (1865)
: the acquisition of gain (as money) in dishonest or questionable ways; *also* : illegal or unfair gain

graft·age \'graf-tij\ *noun* (circa 1895)
: the principles and practice of grafting

graft–versus–host *adjective* (1972)
: relating to or being the bodily condition that results when cells from a tissue or organ transplant mount an immunological attack against the cells or tissues of the host

gra·ham cracker \'gram-, 'grā-əm-\ *noun* [*graham flour*] (1882)
: a slightly sweet cracker made of whole wheat flour

graham flour *noun* [Sylvester *Graham* (died 1851) American dietary reformer] (1834)
: whole wheat flour

grail \'grā(ə)l\ *noun* [Middle English *graal,* from Middle French, bowl, grail, from Medieval Latin *gradalis*]
1 *capitalized* : the cup or platter used according to medieval legend by Christ at the Last Supper and thereafter the object of knightly quests
2 : the object of an extended or difficult quest

¹grain \'grān\ *noun* [Middle English, partly from Middle French *grain* cereal grain, from Latin *granum;* partly from Middle French *graine* seed, kermes, from Latin *grana,* plural of *granum* — more at CORN] (14th century)
1 a (1) *obsolete* : a single small hard seed (2) : a seed or fruit of a cereal grass : CARYOPSIS **b** : the seeds or fruits of various food plants including the cereal grasses and in commercial and statutory usage other plants (as the soybean) **c** : plants producing grain
2 a (1) : a small hard particle or crystal (2) : any of the particles produced in a photographic material by its development; *also* : the size of such grains in the aggregate (3) : an individual crystal in a metal **b** : a minute portion or particle **c** : the least amount possible ⟨a *grain* of truth⟩
3 a : kermes or a scarlet dye made from it **b** : cochineal or a brilliant scarlet dye made from it **c** : a fast dye **d** *archaic* : COLOR, TINT
4 a : a granulated surface or appearance **b** : the outer or hair side of a skin or hide
5 : a unit of weight based on the weight of a grain of wheat taken as an average of the weight of grains from the middle of the ear — see WEIGHT table
6 a : the stratification of the wood fibers in a piece of wood **b** : a texture due to constituent particles or fibers ⟨the *grain* of a rock⟩ **c** : the direction of threads in cloth
7 : tactile quality
8 a : natural disposition : TEMPER ⟨against my *grain*⟩ **b** : a basic or characteristic quality ⟨doctrines . . . very much in the American *grain* —R. W. Noland⟩
— **grained** \'grānd\ *adjective*

²grain (1530)
transitive verb
1 : INGRAIN

graft 1c:
a scion, *b* stock

□ **USAGE**

graduate In the 19th century the transitive sense (1a) was prescribed; the intransitive (I *graduated* from college) was condemned. The intransitive prevailed nonetheless, and today it is the sense likely to be prescribed and the newer transitive (sense 1b) the one condemned. All three are standard. The intransitive is currently the most common, the new transitive the least common.

graffito The plural *graffiti* is sometimes used with a singular verb as a mass noun ⟨the *graffiti* is being covered with fresh paint —*Springfield (Mass.) Union*⟩ ⟨*graffiti* comes in various styles —S. K. Oberbeck⟩ but this use is not yet as well established as the mass-noun use of *data.* Use of *graffiti* as a singular count noun is still quite rare and is not standard.

\ə\ abut \ᵊ\ kitten \ər\ further \a\ ash \ā\ ace
\ä\ mop, mar \au̇\ out \ch\ chin \e\ bet \ē\ easy
\g\ go \i\ hit \ī\ ice \j\ job \ŋ\ sing \ō\ go
\ȯ\ law \ȯi\ boy \th\ thin \t͟h\ the \ü\ loot \u̇\ foot
\y\ yet \zh\ vision *see also* Guide to Pronunciation

2 : to form into grains **:** GRANULATE
3 : to paint in imitation of the grain of wood or stone
4 : to feed with grain
intransitive verb
: to become granular **:** GRANULATE
— **grain·er** *noun*

grain alcohol *noun* (1889)
: ETHANOL

grain elevator *noun* (1852)
: a building for elevating, storing, discharging, and sometimes processing grain

grain·field \'grān-ˌfēld\ *noun* (circa 1818)
: a field where grain is grown

grain of salt (1647)
: a skeptical attitude

grains of paradise (15th century)
: the pungent seeds of a West African plant (*Aframomum melegueta*) of the ginger family that are used as a spice

grain sorghum *noun* (1920)
: any of several sorghums cultivated primarily for grain — compare SORGO

grainy \'grā-nē\ *adjective* **grain·i·er; -est** (15th century)
1 : resembling or having some characteristic of grain **:** not smooth or fine
2 *of a photograph* **:** appearing to be composed of grain-like particles
— **grain·i·ness** *noun*

¹gram \'gram\ *noun* [obsolete Portuguese (now spelled *grão*), grain, from Latin *granum*] (1702)
: any of several leguminous plants (as a chickpea) grown especially for their seed; *also* **:** their seeds

²gram \'gram\ *noun* [French *gramme*, from Late Latin *gramma*, a small weight, from Greek *grammat-*, *gramma* letter, writing, a small weight, from *graphein* to write — more at CARVE] (1810)
1 : a metric unit of mass equal to ¹⁄₁₀₀₀ kilogram and nearly equal to the mass of one cubic centimeter of water at its maximum density — see METRIC SYSTEM table
2 : the weight of a gram under standard gravity

³gram *noun* [by shortening & alteration] (circa 1934)
: GRANDMOTHER

-gram \ˌgram\ *noun combining form* [Latin *-gramma*, from Greek, from *gramma*]
: drawing **:** writing **:** record ⟨chrono*gram*⟩ ⟨tele*gram*⟩

grama \'gra-mə\ *noun* [Spanish, from Latin *gramina*, plural of *gramen* grass] (1828)
: any of several pasture grasses (genus *Bouteloua*) of the western U.S.

gram-atomic weight *noun* (1927)
: the mass of one mole of an element equal in grams to the atomic weight — called also *gram-atom*

gram calorie *noun* (1902)
: CALORIE 1a

gram equivalent *noun* (circa 1897)
: the quantity of an element, group, or compound that has a mass in grams equal to the equivalent weight

gra·mer·cy \grə-ˈmər-sē\ *interjection* [Middle English *grand mercy*, from Middle French *grand merci* great thanks] (14th century)
archaic — used to express gratitude or surprise

gram·i·ci·din \ˌgra-mə-ˈsī-d⁵n\ *noun* [*gram* positive + *-i-* + *-cide* + *-in*] (1940)
: any of several toxic crystalline polypeptide antibiotics produced by a soil bacterium (*Bacillus brevis*) and used against gram-positive bacteria in local infections

gra·min·e·ous \grə-ˈmi-nē-əs\ *adjective* [Latin *gramineus*, from *gramin-, gramen* grass] (circa 1658)
: of or relating to a grass

gram·i·niv·o·rous \ˌgra-mə-ˈniv-(ə-)rəs\ *adjective* [Latin *gramin-, gramen*] (1739)
: feeding on grass or the seeds of grass ⟨*graminivorous* locusts⟩ ⟨*graminivorous* birds⟩

gram·mar \'gra-mər\ *noun* [Middle English *gramere*, from Middle French *gramaire*, modification of Latin *grammatica*, from Greek *grammatikē*, from feminine of *grammatikos* of letters, from *grammat-, gramma* — more at GRAM] (14th century)
1 a : the study of the classes of words, their inflections, and their functions and relations in the sentence **b :** a study of what is to be preferred and what avoided in inflection and syntax
2 a : the characteristic system of inflections and syntax of a language **b :** a system of rules that defines the grammatical structure of a language
3 a : a grammar textbook **b :** speech or writing evaluated according to its conformity to grammatical rules
4 : the principles or rules of an art, science, or technique ⟨a *grammar* of the theater⟩
word history see GLAMOUR
— **gram·mar·i·an** \grə-ˈmer-ē-ən, -ˈmar-\ *noun*

grammar school *noun* (14th century)
1 a : a secondary school emphasizing Latin and Greek in preparation for college **b :** a British college preparatory school
2 : a school intermediate between primary school and high school
3 : ELEMENTARY SCHOOL

gram·mat·i·cal \grə-ˈma-ti-kəl\ *adjective* (1530)
1 : of or relating to grammar
2 : conforming to the rules of grammar
— **gram·mat·i·cal·i·ty** \-ˌma-tə-ˈka-lə-tē\ *noun*
— **gram·mat·i·cal·ly** \-ˈma-ti-k(ə-)lē\ *adverb*
— **gram·mat·i·cal·ness** \-kəl-nəs\ *noun*

grammatical meaning *noun* (1769)
: the part of meaning that varies from one inflectional form to another (as from *plays* to *played* to *playing*) — compare LEXICAL MEANING

gramme *chiefly British variant of* ²GRAM

gram molecular weight *noun* (circa 1902)
: the mass of one mole of a compound equal in grams to the molecular weight — called also *gram-molecule*

Gram·my \'gra-mē\ *service mark*
— used for the annual presentation of a statuette for notable achievement in the recording industry

gram–neg·a·tive \'gram-'ne-gə-tiv\ *adjective* (1907)
: not holding the purple dye when stained by Gram's stain — used chiefly of bacteria

gram·o·phone \'gra-mə-ˌfōn\ *noun* [from *Gramophone*, a trademark] (1887)
: PHONOGRAPH

gramp \'gramp\ *or* **gramps** \'gram(p)s\ *noun, plural* **gramps** [by shortening & alteration] (circa 1900)
: GRANDFATHER

gram–pos·i·tive \'gram-'pä-zə-tiv, -'päz-tiv\ *adjective* (1907)
: holding the purple dye when stained by Gram's stain — used chiefly of bacteria

gram·pus \'gram-pəs\ *noun* [alteration of Middle English *graspey, grapay*, from Middle French *graspeis* + *peis* fish, from Latin *crassus*) + *peis* fish, from Latin *piscis* — more at CRASS, FISH] (circa 1529)
1 : a dolphin (*Grampus griseus*) of temperate and tropical seas; *also* **:** any of various small cetaceans
2 : the giant whip scorpion (*Mastigoproctus giganteus*) of the southern U.S.

Gram's stain \'gramz-\ *or* **Gram stain** \'gram-\ *noun* [Hans C. J. *Gram* (died 1938) Danish physician] (1903)
1 : a method for the differential staining of bacteria by treatment with a watery solution of iodine and the iodide of potassium after staining with a triphenylmethane dye (as crystal violet) — called also *Gram's method*
2 : the chemicals used in Gram's stain

gram–vari·able \'gram-'ver-ē-ə-bəl, -'var-\ *adjective* (1956)
: staining irregularly or inconsistently by Gram's stain

grana *plural of* GRANUM

gran·a·dil·la \ˌgran-ə-'di-lə, -'dē-(y)ə\ *noun* [Spanish, diminutive of *granada* pomegranate, from Late Latin *granata* — more at GRENADE] (1613)
: the oblong fruit of various passionflowers (especially *Passiflora quadrangularis* of tropical America) used as a dessert; *also* **:** a plant that produces granadillas

gra·na·ry \'grā-nə-rē, 'gra-\ *noun, plural* **-ries** [Latin *granarium*, from *granum* grain] (1530)
1 a : a storehouse for threshed grain **b :** a region producing grain in abundance
2 : a chief source or storehouse

¹grand \'grand\ *adjective* [Middle French, large, great, grand, from Latin *grandis*] (1584)
1 a : having more importance than others **:** FOREMOST **b :** having higher rank than others bearing the same general designation ⟨the *grand* champion⟩
2 a : INCLUSIVE, COMPREHENSIVE ⟨the *grand* total of all money paid out⟩ **b :** DEFINITIVE, INCONTROVERTIBLE ⟨*grand* example⟩
3 : CHIEF, PRINCIPAL
4 : large and striking in size, scope, extent, or conception ⟨*grand* design⟩
5 a : LAVISH, SUMPTUOUS ⟨a *grand* celebration⟩ **b :** marked by a regal form and dignity **c :** fine or imposing in appearance or impression **d :** LOFTY, SUBLIME ⟨writing in the *grand* style⟩
6 a : pretending to social superiority **:** SUPERCILIOUS **b :** intended to impress ⟨a person of *grand* gestures⟩
7 : very good **:** WONDERFUL ⟨a *grand* time⟩ ☆
— **grand·ly** \'gran-(d)lē\ *adverb*
— **grand·ness** \'gran(d)-nəs\ *noun*

²grand *noun* (1840)
1 : GRAND PIANO
2 *slang* **:** a thousand dollars

gran·dam \'gran-ˌdam, -dəm\ *noun* [Middle English *graundam*, from Anglo-French *graund dame*, literally, great lady] (13th century)
1 *or* **gran·dame** \-ˌdām\ **a :** GRANDMOTHER **b :** an old woman
2 *or* **grand·dam** \-ˌdam, -dəm\ **:** a dam's or sire's dam — used of an animal

grand·aunt \'gran-ˌdant, -ˌdänt\ *noun* (1826)
: the aunt of one's father or mother — called also *great-aunt*

grand·ba·by \'gran(d)-ˌbā-bē\ *noun* (1916)
: an infant grandchild

grand·child \-ˌchīld\ *noun* (1587)
: the child of one's son or daughter

grand·dad *or* **gran·dad** \'gran-ˌdad\ *noun* (1782)
: GRANDFATHER

grand·dad·dy \-ˌda-dē\ *also* **gran·dad·dy** *noun* (1769)
1 : GRANDFATHER
2 : one that is the first, earliest, or most venerable of its kind

grand·daugh·ter \-ˌdȯ-tər\ *noun* (1611)
: the daughter of one's son or daughter

grand duchess *noun* (circa 1757)
1 : a woman who rules a grand duchy in her own right
2 : the wife or widow of a grand duke

grand duchy *noun* (1835)
: the territory or dominion of a grand duke or grand duchess

grand duke *noun* (circa 1693)
1 : the sovereign duke of any of various European states
2 : a male descendant of a Russian czar in the male line

grande dame \'grän-'däm, 'gräⁿd-dàm\ *noun, plural* **grandes dames** \-'däm(z), -dàm(z)\ *also* **grande dames** \same\ [French, literally, great lady] (1775)
: a usually elderly woman of great prestige or ability

gran·dee \gran-'dē\ *noun* [Spanish *grande*, from *grande*, adjective, large, great, from Latin *grandis*] (1598)
: a man of elevated rank or station; *especially* : a Spanish or Portuguese nobleman of the first rank

gran·deur \'gran-jər, -ˌjùr, -ˌd(y)ùr, -d(y)ər\ *noun* [Middle English, from Middle French, from *grand*] (1600)
1 : the quality or state of being grand : MAGNIFICENCE ⟨the glory that was Greece and the *grandeur* that was Rome —E. A. Poe⟩
2 : an instance or example of grandeur

¹**grand·fa·ther** \'gran(d)-ˌfä-thər, -ˌfà-\ *noun* (15th century)
: the father of one's father or mother; *also*
: ANCESTOR 1a
— **grand·fa·ther·ly** \-lē\ *adjective*

²**grandfather** *transitive verb* (1972)
: to permit to continue under a grandfather clause

grandfather clause *noun* (1900)
: a clause creating an exemption based on circumstances previously existing; *especially* : a provision in several southern state constitutions designed to enfranchise poor whites and disfranchise Negroes by waiving high voting requirements for descendants of men voting before 1867

grandfather clock *noun* [from the song *My Grandfather's Clock* (1876) by Henry C. Work (died 1884) American songwriter] (1909)
: a tall pendulum clock that stands on the floor — called also *grandfather, grandfather's clock*

grand finale *noun* (1800)
: a climactic finale (as of an opera)

grand fir *noun* (1897)
: a lofty fir tree (*Abies grandis*) of the northwestern Pacific coastal region of North America with cylindrical greenish cones and soft wood

Grand Gui·gnol \ˌgräⁿ-gēn-'yȯl, -'yōl\ *noun* [*Le Grand Guignol*, small theater in Montmartre, Paris, specializing in such performances] (1908)
: dramatic entertainment featuring the gruesome or horrible ◇
— **Grand Guignol** *adjective*

gran·di·flo·ra \ˌgran-də-'flȯr-ə, -'flȯr-\ *noun* [New Latin, from Latin *grandis* great + *flor-, flos* flower — more at BLOW] (1944)
: a bush rose derived from crosses of floribunda and hybrid tea roses and characterized by production of blooms both singly and in clusters on the same plant

gran·dil·o·quence \gran-'di-lə-kwən(t)s\ *noun* [probably from Middle French, from Latin *grandiloquus* using lofty language, from *grandis* + *loqui* to speak] (1589)
: a lofty, extravagantly colorful, pompous, or bombastic style, manner, or quality especially in language
— **gran·dil·o·quent** \-kwənt\ *adjective*
— **gran·dil·o·quent·ly** *adverb*

gran·di·ose \'gran-dē-ˌōs, ˌgran-dē-'\ *adjective* [French, from Italian *grandioso*, from *grande* great, from Latin *grandis*] (1840)
1 : characterized by affectation of grandeur or splendor or by absurd exaggeration
2 : impressive because of uncommon largeness, scope, effect, or grandeur
synonym see GRAND
— **gran·di·ose·ly** *adverb*
— **gran·di·ose·ness** *noun*
— **gran·di·os·i·ty** \ˌgran-dē-'ä-sə-tē\ *noun*

gran·di·o·so \ˌgran-dē-'ō-(ˌ)sō, ˌgran-, -(ˌ)zō\ *adverb or adjective* [Italian] (circa 1859)
: in a broad and noble style — used as a direction in music

grand jury *noun* (15th century)
: a jury that examines accusations against persons charged with crime and if the evidence warrants makes formal charges on which the accused persons are later tried
— **grand juror** *noun*

grand·kid \'gran(d)-ˌkid\ *noun* (1927)
: GRANDCHILD

Grand Lama *noun* (1807)
: DALAI LAMA

grand larceny *noun* (1828)
: larceny of property of a value greater than that fixed as constituting petit larceny

grand·ma \'gran(d)-ˌmä, -ˌmȯ; 'gra-ˌmä, -ˌmȯ\ *noun* (1867)
: GRANDMOTHER

grand mal \'gran(d)-ˌmäl, 'grän-ˌmäl, -ˌmal; 'gran(d)-ˌmal\ *noun* [French, literally, great illness] (1897)
: severe epilepsy

grand manner *noun* (1775)
: an elevated or grand style (as in music or literature)

grand march *noun* (1898)
: an opening ceremony at a ball that consists of a march participated in by all the guests

grand marshal *noun* (1951)
: a person honored as the ceremonial marshal of a parade

grand master *noun* (1724)
1 : the chief officer of a principal lodge in various fraternal orders (as Freemasonry)
2 : an expert player (as of chess) who has consistently scored high in international competition

grand·moth·er \'gran(d)-ˌmə-thər\ *noun* (15th century)
: the mother of one's father or mother; *also* : a female ancestor
— **grand·moth·er·ly** \-lē\ *adjective*

grand·neph·ew \'gran(d)-'nef-(ˌ)yü, *chiefly British* -'nev-\ *noun* (circa 1639)
: a grandson of one's brother or sister

grand·niece \-'nēs\ *noun* (circa 1830)
: a granddaughter of one's brother or sister

grand old man *noun* (1860)
: a venerated practitioner or former practitioner of an art, profession, or sport ⟨the *grand old man* of jazz⟩

grand opera *noun* (1803)
: opera in which the plot is serious or tragic and the entire text is set to music

grand·pa \'gran(d)-ˌpä, -ˌpȯ; 'gram-ˌpä, -ˌpȯ\ *noun* (circa 1889)
: GRANDFATHER

grand·par·ent \'gran(d)-ˌpar-ənt, -ˌper-\ *noun* (1830)
: a parent of one's father or mother

— **grand·pa·ren·tal** \ˌgran(d)-pə-'ren-t²l\ *adjective*
— **grand·par·ent·hood** \'gran(d)-'par-ent-ˌhùd, -'per-\ *noun*

grand piano *noun* (1834)
: a piano with horizontal frame and strings — compare UPRIGHT PIANO

grand prix \'grän-'prē\ *noun, plural* **grand prix** *also* **grands prix** \-'prē(z)\ *often G&P capitalized* [French *Grand Prix de Paris*, an international horse race established 1863, literally, grand prize of Paris] (1863)
1 : the highest level of international equestrian competition; *also* : a contest at this level
2 : one of a series of international formula car races

grand·sire \'gran(d)-ˌsīr\ *noun* [Middle English] (14th century)
1 *or* **grand·sir** \'gran(t)-sər\ *dialect* : GRANDFATHER
2 *archaic* : FOREFATHER
3 *archaic* : an aged man
4 : a dam's or sire's sire — used of an animal

grand slam *noun* (1814)
1 : the winning of all the tricks in one hand of a card game (as bridge)
2 : a clean sweep or total success; *specifically* : the winning of all the major or specified tournaments on a tour ⟨twice won the tennis *grand slam*⟩
3 : a home run made with the bases loaded
— **grand–slam** *adjective*

grand·son \'gran(d)-ˌsən\ *noun* (1586)
: the son of one's son or daughter

¹**grand·stand** \-ˌstand\ *noun* (1834)
1 : a usually roofed stand for spectators at a racecourse or stadium
2 : AUDIENCE

²**grandstand** *adjective* (1893)
: done for show or to impress onlookers ⟨a *grandstand* play⟩

³**grandstand** *intransitive verb* (circa 1917)
: to play or act so as to impress onlookers
— **grand·stand·er** *noun*

grand theft *noun* (circa 1930)
: GRAND LARCENY

grand tour *noun* (1670)
1 : an extended tour of the Continent that was formerly a usual part of the education of young British gentlemen
2 : an extensive and usually educational tour

◇ WORD HISTORY
Grand Guignol Long before cinematic violence became explicit, the Grand-Guignol theater in the Montmartre district of Paris presented to audiences graphic depictions of stabbings, assaults with sulphuric acid, and assorted other mayhem. Founded in 1895 as the Théâtre Salon, it adopted its better-known name and characteristic formula in 1897. On a single night's bill, one-act light comedies alternated with dramas of horror, the latter featuring cleverly arranged (for the time) special effects and plenty of gore. *Guignol* in French denotes both "hand puppet" and, as a proper noun, the leading character in a tradition of children's puppet theater, but aside from the uniformity of repertoire there was nothing puppetlike about the Grand-Guignol. The theater remained a Parisian attraction until 1962, when it finally closed, having outlived an era when stage violence could provide a real shock.

grand touring car *noun* (1970)
: a usually 2-passenger coupe

grand·un·cle \'gran-'dən-kəl\ *noun* (15th century)
: an uncle of one's father or mother

grand touring car

grand unified theory *noun* (1978)
: any of several theories that seek to unite in a single mathematical framework the electromagnetic and weak forces with the strong force or with the strong force and gravity — called also *grand unification theory*

grange \'grānj\ *noun* [Middle English, from Middle French, from Medieval Latin *granica*, from Latin *granum* grain] (14th century)
1 *archaic* : GRANARY, BARN
2 : FARM; *especially* : a farmhouse with outbuildings
3 *capitalized* : one of the lodges of a national fraternal association originally made up of farmers; *also* : the association itself

grang·er \'grān-jər\ *noun* (1873)
1 *capitalized* : a member of a Grange
2 *chiefly West* : FARMER, HOMESTEADER

grang·er·ism \'grān-jə-ˌri-zəm\ *noun* (1875)
: the policy or methods of the grangers

gra·ni·ta \grä-'nē-tə\ *noun* [Italian, from feminine of *granito*, past participle of *granire*] (1869)
: a coarse-textured ice confection typically made from fruit

gran·ite \'gra-nət\ *noun* [Italian *granito*, from past participle of *granire* to granulate, from *grano* grain, from Latin *granum*] (1646)
1 : a very hard natural igneous rock formation of visibly crystalline texture formed essentially of quartz and orthoclase or microcline and used especially for building and for monuments
2 : unyielding firmness or endurance ⟨the cold *granite* of Puritan formalism —V. L. Parrington⟩
— **gran·ite·like** \-ˌlīk\ *adjective*
— **gra·nit·ic** \gra-'ni-tik\ *adjective*
— **gran·it·oid** \'gra-nə-ˌtȯid\ *adjective*

gran·ite·ware \'gra-nət-ˌwar, -ˌwer\ *noun* (1878)
: ironware with grayish or bluish mottled enamel

gra·niv·o·rous \grə-'niv-rəs, grä-, -'ni-və-\ *adjective* [Latin *granum* grain] (1646)
: feeding on seeds or grain ⟨*granivorous* rodents⟩

gran·ny *or* **gran·nie** \'gra-nē\ *noun*, *plural* **grannies** [by shortening & alteration] (1663)
1 a : GRANDMOTHER **b** : a fussy person
2 *chiefly Southern & south Midland* : MIDWIFE

granny dress *noun* (1909)
: a long loose-fitting dress usually with high neck and long sleeves

granny glasses *noun plural* (1966)
: spectacles with usually small oval, round, or square lenses and metal frames

granny knot *noun* (1853)
: an insecure knot often made instead of a square knot — see KNOT illustration

Granny Smith \-'smith\ *noun* [Maria Ann Smith (died 1870) who cultivated it near Sydney, Australia] (1895)
: a tart green apple of Australian origin

grano- *combining form* [German, from *granit*, from Italian *granito*]
: granite : granitic ⟨*grano*diorite⟩

grano·di·o·rite \ˌgra-nō-'dī-ə-ˌrīt\ *noun* (1893)
: a granular intrusive quartzose igneous rock intermediate between granite and quartz-containing diorite with plagioclase predominant over orthoclase
— **grano·di·o·rit·ic** \-ˌdī-ə-'ri-tik\ *adjective*

gra·no·la \grə-'nō-lə\ *noun* [from *Granola*, a trademark] (1970)
: a mixture typically of rolled oats and various added ingredients (as brown sugar, raisins, coconut, and nuts) that is eaten especially for breakfast or as a snack

grano·lith·ic \ˌgra-nə-'li-thik\ *adjective* (1881)
: relating to or composed of a mixture of crushed granite and cement

grano·phyre \'gran-ə-ˌfī(-ə)r\ *noun* [International Scientific Vocabulary, from *grano-* + French *-phyre* (as in *porphyre* porphyry)] (1882)
: a porphyritic igneous rock chiefly of feldspar and quartz with granular groundmass
— **grano·phyr·ic** \ˌgran-ə-'fir-ik\ *adjective*

¹grant \'grant\ *transitive verb* [Middle English, from Old French *creanter, graanter*, from (assumed) Vulgar Latin *credentare*, from Latin *credent-, credens*, present participle of *credere* to believe — more at CREED] (13th century)
1 a : to consent to carry out for a person : allow fulfillment of ⟨*grant* a request⟩ **b** : to permit as a right, privilege, or favor ⟨luggage allowances *granted* to passengers⟩
2 : to bestow or transfer formally ⟨*grant* a scholarship to a student⟩; *specifically* : to give the possession or title of by a deed
3 a : to be willing to concede **b** : to assume to be true ⟨*granting* that you are correct, you may find it hard to prove your point⟩ ☆
— **grant·able** \'gran-tə-bəl\ *adjective*
— **grant·er** \-tər\ *noun*
— **grant·or** \'gran-tər, -ˌtȯr; gran-'tȯr\ *noun*

²grant *noun* (13th century)
1 : the act of granting
2 : something granted; *especially* : a gift (as of land or money) for a particular purpose
3 a : a transfer of property by deed or writing **b** : the instrument by which such a transfer is made; *also* : the property so transferred
4 : a minor territorial division of Maine, New Hampshire, or Vermont originally granted by the state to an individual or institution

grant·ee \gran-'tē\ *noun* (15th century)
: one to whom a grant is made

grant–in–aid \ˌgran-tᵊn-'ād\ *noun*, *plural* **grants–in–aid** \ˌgran(t)-sᵊn-'ād\ (1851)
1 : a grant or subsidy for public funds paid by a central to a local government in aid of a public undertaking
2 : a grant or subsidy to a school or individual for an educational or artistic project

grants·man \'gran(t)-smən\ *noun* (1966)
: a specialist in grantsmanship

grants·man·ship \-ˌship\ *noun* [*grants* + *-manship*] (1961)
: the art of obtaining grants (as for research)
word history see GAMESMANSHIP

granul- *or* **granuli-** *or* **granulo-** *combining form* [Late Latin *granulum*]
: granule ⟨*granulo*cyte⟩

gran·u·lar \'gran-yə-lər\ *adjective* (1794)
: consisting of or appearing to consist of granules : GRAINY
— **gran·u·lar·i·ty** \ˌgran-yə-'lar-ə-tē\ *noun*

gran·u·late \'gran-yə-ˌlāt\ *verb* **-lat·ed; -lat·ing** (1666)
transitive verb
: to form or crystallize into grains or granules
intransitive verb
: to form granulations ⟨an open *granulating* wound⟩
— **gran·u·la·tor** \-ˌlā-tər\ *noun*

gran·u·la·tion \ˌgran-yə-'lā-shən\ *noun* (1612)
1 : the act or process of granulating : the condition of being granulated
2 : one of the minute red granules of new capillaries formed on the surface of a wound in healing
3 : GRANULE 2

granulation tissue *noun* (1873)
: tissue made up of granulations that temporarily replaces lost tissue in a wound

gran·ule \'gran-(ˌ)yü(ə)l\ *noun* [Late Latin *granulum*, diminutive of Latin *granum* grain] (1652)
1 : a small particle; *especially* : one of numerous particles forming a larger unit
2 : any of the small short-lived brilliant spots on the sun's photosphere

gran·u·lite \'gran-yə-ˌlīt\ *noun* (1849)
: a granular metamorphic rock consisting mainly of feldspar and quartz
— **gran·u·lit·ic** \ˌgran-yə-'li-tik\ *adjective*

gran·u·lo·cyte \'gran-yə-lō-ˌsīt\ *noun* [International Scientific Vocabulary] (1906)
: a polymorphonuclear white blood cell with granule-containing cytoplasm
— **gran·u·lo·cyt·ic** \ˌgran-yə-lō-'si-tik\ *adjective*

gran·u·lo·cy·to·poi·e·sis \ˌgran-yə-lō-ˌsī-tə-ˌpȯi-'ē-səs\ *noun* [New Latin] (1944)
: the formation of blood granulocytes typically in the bone marrow

gran·u·lo·ma \ˌgran-yə-'lō-mə\ *noun*, *plural* **-mas** *or* **-ma·ta** \-mə-tə\ (1861)
: a mass or nodule of chronically inflamed tissue with granulations that is usually associated with an infective process
— **gran·u·lo·ma·tous** \-mə-təs\ *adjective*

granuloma in·gui·na·le \-ˌiŋ-gwə-'na-lē, -'nä-, -'nā-\ *noun* [New Latin, literally, inguinal granuloma] (1918)
: a sexually transmitted disease characterized by ulceration and formation of granulations on the genitalia and in the groin area and caused by a bacterium (*Calymmatobacterium granulomatis*, synonym *Donovania granulomatis*)

gran·u·lo·sa cell \ˌgran-yə-'lō-sə-\ *noun* [New Latin *granulosa*, from feminine of *granulosus* granulose] (1936)
: one of the estrogen-secreting cells of the epithelial lining of a graafian follicle or its follicular precursor

gran·u·lose \'gran-yə-ˌlōs\ *adjective* (1852)
: GRANULAR; *especially* : having the surface roughened with granules

gran·u·lo·sis \ˌgran-yə-'lō-səs\ *noun*, *plural* **-lo·ses** \-ˌsēz\ [New Latin] (1949)
: a virus disease of insect larvae distinguished by the presence of minute granular inclusions in infected cells

gra·num \'grā-nəm\ *noun*, *plural* **gra·na** \-nə\ [New Latin, from Latin, grain — more at CORN] (1894)
: one of the lamellar stacks of chlorophyll-containing thylakoids found in plant chloroplasts

grape \'grāp\ *noun*, *often attributive* [Middle English, from Old French *crape, grape* hook, grape stalk, bunch of grapes, grape, of Germanic origin; akin to Old High German *krapfo* hook] (14th century)
1 : a smooth-skinned juicy greenish white to deep red or purple berry eaten dried or fresh as a fruit or fermented to produce wine

2 : any of numerous woody vines (genus *Vitis* of the family Vitaceae, the grape family) that usually climb by tendrils, produce clustered fruits that are grapes, and are nearly cosmopolitan in cultivation
3 : GRAPESHOT
— **grape·like** \-,līk\ *adjective*
grape·fruit \'grāp-,früt\ *noun* (1814)
1 *plural* **grapefruit** *or* **grapefruits :** a large citrus fruit with a bitter yellow rind and inner skin and a highly flavored somewhat acid juicy pulp
2 : a small roundheaded tree (*Citrus paradisi*) that produces grapefruit
grape hyacinth *noun* (1733)
: any of several small bulbous spring-flowering herbs (genus *Muscari*) of the lily family with racemes of usually blue flowers
grape·shot \'grāp-,shät\ *noun* (1747)
: an antipersonnel weapon consisting of a cluster of small iron balls shot from a cannon
grape sugar *noun* (1831)
: DEXTROSE
grape·vine \'grāp-,vīn\ *noun* (circa 1736)
1 : GRAPE 2
2 a : an informal person-to-person means of circulating information or gossip ⟨heard about the meeting through the *grapevine*⟩ **b :** a secret source of information
¹graph \'graf\ *noun* [short for *graphic formula*] (1886)
1 : the collection of all points whose coordinates satisfy a given relation (as a function)
2 : a diagram (as a series of one or more points, lines, line segments, curves, or areas) that represents the variation of a variable in comparison with that of one or more other variables
²graph *transitive verb* (1898)
1 : to represent by a graph
2 : to plot on a graph
³graph *noun* [probably from *-graph*] (1933)
1 : a written or printed representation of a basic unit of speech (as a phoneme or syllable); *especially* **:** GRAPHEME 2
2 : a single occurrence of a letter of an alphabet in any of its various shapes
-graph \,graf\ *noun combining form* [Middle French *-graphe*, from Latin *-graphum*, from Greek *-graphon*, from neuter of *-graphos* written, from *graphein* to write — more at CARVE]
1 : something written or drawn ⟨mono*graph*⟩
2 [French *-graphe*, from Late Latin *-graphus*] **:** instrument for making or transmitting records or images ⟨chrono*graph*⟩
graph·eme \'gra-,fēm\ *noun* (1935)
1 : the set of units of a writing system (as letters and letter combinations) that represent a phoneme
2 : a unit (as a letter) of a writing system
— **gra·phe·mic** \gra-'fē-mik\ *adjective*
— **gra·phe·mi·cal·ly** \-mi-k(ə-)lē\ *adverb*
gra·phe·mics \gra-'fē-miks\ *noun plural but singular or plural in construction* (1951)
: the study and analysis of a writing system in terms of graphemes
¹graph·ic \'gra-fik\ *also* **graph·i·cal** \-fi-kəl\ *adjective* [Latin *graphicus*, from Greek *graphikos*, from *graphein*] (1637)
1 : formed by writing, drawing, or engraving
2 *usually* **graphic a :** marked by clear lifelike or vividly realistic description **b :** vividly or plainly shown or described
3 a : of or relating to the pictorial arts; *also* **:** PICTORIAL **b :** of, relating to, or involving such reproductive methods as those of engraving, etching, lithography, photography, serigraphy, and woodcut **c :** of or relating to the art of printing **d :** relating to or according to graphics
4 *usually* **graphical :** of, relating to, or represented by a graph

5 : of or relating to the written or printed word or the symbols or devices used in writing or printing to represent sound or convey meaning ☆
— **graph·i·cal·ly** \-fi-k(ə-)lē\ *adverb*
— **graph·ic·ness** \-fik-nəs\ *noun*
²graphic *noun* (1944)
1 a : a product of graphic art **b** *plural* **:** the graphic media
2 a : a graphic representation (as a picture, map, or graph) used especially for illustration **b** *plural but singular or plural in construction* **:** the art or science of drawing a representation of an object on a two-dimensional surface according to mathematical rules of projection
3 *plural but singular or plural in construction* **:** the process whereby a computer displays graphics on a CRT and an operator can manipulate them (as with a light pen)
4 : a printed message superimposed on a television picture
-graphic *or* **-graphical** *adjective combining form* [Late Latin *-graphicus*, from Greek *-graphikos*, from *graphikos*]
: written or transmitted in a (specified) way ⟨stylo*graphic*⟩
graphic arts *noun plural* (1882)
: the fine and applied arts of representation, decoration, and writing or printing on flat surfaces together with the techniques and crafts associated with them
graphic design *noun* (1956)
: the art or profession of using design elements (as typography and images) to convey information or create an effect; *also* **:** a product of this art
— **graphic designer** *noun*
graphic equalizer *noun* (1969)
: an electronic device for adjusting the frequency response of an audio system by means of a number of slides each of which controls the response for a band centered on a particular frequency
graphic novel *noun* (1978)
: a fictional story for adults that is presented in comic-strip format and published as a book
graphics tablet *noun* (1980)
: a device by which pictorial information is entered into a computer in a manner similar to drawing
graph·ite \'gra-,fīt\ *noun* [German *Graphit*, from Greek *graphein* to write] (1796)
1 : a soft black lustrous form of carbon that conducts electricity and is used in lead pencils and electrolytic anodes, as a lubricant, and as a moderator in nuclear reactors
2 : a composite material in which carbon fibers are the reinforcing material
— **gra·phit·ic** \gra-'fi-tik\ *adjective*
graph·i·tize \'gra-fə-,tīz, -,fīt-,īz\ *transitive verb* **-tized; -tiz·ing** (1899)
: to convert into graphite
— **graph·i·tiz·able** \-,tī-zə-bəl, -,fīt-,īz-\ *adjective*
— **graph·i·ti·za·tion** \,gra-fə-tə-'zā-shən, -,fī-\ *noun*
grapho- *combining form* [French, from Middle French, from Greek, from *graphē*, from *graphein* to write]
: writing ⟨*grapho*lect⟩
graph·o·lect \'gra-fə-,lekt\ *noun* [*grapho-* + *-lect* (as in *dialect*)] (1977)
: a standard written language
gra·phol·o·gist \gra-'fä-lə-jist\ *noun* (1885)
: a specialist in graphology
gra·phol·o·gy \-jē\ *noun* [French *graphologie*, from *grapho-* + *-logie* -logy] (1886)
: the study of handwriting especially for the purpose of character analysis
— **graph·o·log·i·cal** \,gra-fə-'lä-ji-kəl\ *adjective*
graph paper *noun* (1927)
: paper ruled for drawing graphs
-graphy *noun combining form* [Latin *-graphia*, from Greek, from *graphein*]

1 : writing or representation in a (specified) manner or by a (specified) means or of a (specified) object ⟨steno*graphy*⟩ ⟨photo*graphy*⟩
2 : writing on a (specified) subject or in a (specified) field ⟨hagio*graphy*⟩
grap·nel \'grap-nᵊl\ *noun* [Middle English *grapenel*, from (assumed) Middle French *grapinel*, diminutive of *grapin*, diminutive of *grape* hook — more at GRAPE] (14th century)
: a small anchor with usually four or five flukes used in dragging or grappling operations and for anchoring a dory or skiff — see ANCHOR illustration
grap·pa \'grä-pə\ *noun* [Italian, from Italian dialect, grape stalk, of Germanic origin; akin to Old High German *krāpfo* hook] (circa 1893)
: a dry colorless brandy distilled from fermented grape pomace
¹grap·ple \'gra-pəl\ *noun* [Old French *grappelle*, diminutive of *grape* hook — more at GRAPE] (1601)
1 a : the act or an instance of grappling **b :** a hand-to-hand struggle **c :** a contest for superiority or mastery
2 : a bucket similar to a clamshell but usually having more jaws
²grapple *verb* **grap·pled; grap·pling** \'gra-p(ə-)liŋ\ (1530)
transitive verb
1 : to seize with or as if with a grapple
2 : to come to grips with **:** WRESTLE
3 : to bind closely
intransitive verb
1 : to make a ship fast with a grappling iron
2 : to come to grips
3 : to use a grapple
— **grap·pler** \-p(ə-)lər\ *noun*
grap·pling *noun* (1582)
1 : GRAPNEL
2 : GRAPPLING IRON
grappling iron *noun* (1538)
: a hooked iron for anchoring a boat, grappling ships to each other, or recovering sunken objects — called also *grappling hook*
grap·to·lite \'grap-tə-,līt\ *noun* [Greek *graptos* painted (from *graphein* to write, paint) + English *-lite* — more at CARVE] (1841)
: any of numerous extinct fossil colonial Paleozoic animals (group Graptolitoidea) with zooids in cups along a chitinous support
grapy *or* **grap·ey** \'grā-pē\ *adjective* **grap·i·er; -est** (1594)
: of or relating to grapes; *especially, of wine* **:** having the taste or aroma of fresh grapes
— **grap·i·ness** \-nəs\ *noun*
¹grasp \'grasp\ *verb* [Middle English *graspen*] (14th century)
intransitive verb
: to make the motion of seizing **:** CLUTCH
transitive verb
1 : to take or seize eagerly
2 : to clasp or embrace especially with the fingers or arms

☆ SYNONYMS
Graphic, vivid, picturesque mean giving a clear visual impression in words. GRAPHIC stresses the evoking of a clear lifelike picture ⟨a *graphic* account of combat⟩. VIVID suggests an impressing on the mind of the vigorous aliveness of something ⟨a *vivid* re-creation of an exciting event⟩. PICTURESQUE suggests the presentation of a striking or effective picture composed of features notable for their distinctness and charm ⟨a *picturesque* account of his travels⟩.

\ə\ abut \ᵊ\ kitten \ər\ further \a\ ash \ā\ ace \ä\ mop, mar \au̇\ out \ch\ chin \e\ bet \ē\ easy \g\ go \i\ hit \ī\ ice \j\ job \ŋ\ sing \ō\ go \ȯ\ law \ȯi\ boy \th\ thin \t̷h\ the \ü\ loot \u̇\ foot \y\ yet \zh\ vision *see also* Guide to Pronunciation

3 : to lay hold of with the mind **:** COMPREHEND
synonym see TAKE
— **grasp·able** \'gras-pə-bəl\ *adjective*
— **grasp·er** *noun*
— **grasp at straws :** to reach for or try anything in desperation
— **grasp the nettle :** to act boldly
²grasp *noun* (1561)
1 a : HANDLE **b :** EMBRACE
2 : HOLD, CONTROL
3 a : the reach of the arms **b :** the power of seizing and holding or attaining
4 : mental hold or comprehension especially when broad
grasp·ing *adjective* (1748)
: desiring material possessions urgently and excessively and often to the point of ruthlessness
synonym see COVETOUS
— **grasp·ing·ly** \'gras-piŋ-lē\ *adverb*
— **grasp·ing·ness** *noun*
¹grass \'gras\ *noun, often attributive* [Middle English *gras*, from Old English *græs*; akin to Old High German *gras* grass, Old English *grōwan* to grow] (before 12th century)
1 : herbage suitable or used for grazing animals
2 : any of a large family (Gramineae) of monocotyledonous mostly herbaceous plants with jointed stems, slender sheathing leaves, and flowers borne in spikelets of bracts
3 : land (as a lawn or a turf racetrack) covered with growing grass ⟨keep off the *grass*⟩ ⟨the horse had never won on *grass*⟩
4 *plural* **:** leaves or plants of grass
5 : a state or place of retirement ⟨put out to *grass*⟩
6 [short for *grasshopper*, rhyming slang for *copper*] *slang British* **:** a police informer
7 : electronic noise on a radarscope that takes the form of vertical lines resembling lawn grass
8 : MARIJUANA
— **grass·less** \-ləs\ *adjective*
— **grass·like** \-ˌlīk\ *adjective*
²grass (circa 1500)
transitive verb
1 : to feed (livestock) on grass sometimes without grain or other concentrates
2 : to cover with grass; *especially* **:** to seed to grass
intransitive verb
1 : to produce grass
2 *slang British* **:** INFORM **2** — often used with *on*
grass carp *noun* (1885)
: an herbivorous cyprinid fish (*Ctenopharyngodon idella*) of Russia and mainland China that has been introduced elsewhere to control aquatic weeds — called also *white amur*
grass cloth *noun* (1857)
: a lustrous plain textile of usually loosely woven fibers
grass court *noun* (1883)
: a tennis court with a grass surface
grass·hop·per \'gras-ˌhä-pər\ *noun* (14th century)
1 : any of numerous plant-eating orthopterous insects (Acrididae, Tettigoniidae, and some related families) having the hind legs adapted for leaping and sometimes engaging in migratory flights in which whole regions may be stripped of vegetation
2 : a cocktail made with crème de menthe, crème de cacao, and light cream
grass·land \-ˌland\ *noun* (1682)
1 : farmland occupied chiefly by forage plants and especially grasses
2 a : land on which the natural dominant plant forms are grasses and forbs **b :** an ecological community in which the characteristic plants are grasses
grass·roots \'gras-ˌrüts, -ˌruts\ *also* **grass·root** \-ˌrüt, -ˌrut\ *adjective* (1907)
1 : BASIC, FUNDAMENTAL ⟨the *grassroots* factor in deciding to buy a house⟩

2 : being, originating, or operating in or at the grass roots ⟨a *grassroots* organization⟩ ⟨*grassroots* political support⟩
3 : not adapted from or added to an existing facility or operation **:** totally new ⟨a *grassroots* refinery⟩
grass roots *noun plural but singular or plural in construction, often attributive* (1901)
1 : the very foundation or source
2 : the basic level of society or of an organization especially as viewed from higher or more centralized positions of power
grass tree *noun* (1802)
: any of a genus (*Xanthorrhoea*) of Australian plants of the lily family with a thick woody trunk bearing a cluster of stiff linear leaves and a terminal spike of small flowers
grass widow *noun* (1528)
1 *chiefly dialect* **a :** a discarded mistress **b :** a woman who has had an illegitimate child
2 a : a woman whose husband is temporarily away from her **b :** a woman divorced or separated from her husband
grass widower *noun* (1862)
1 : a man divorced or separated from his wife
2 : a man whose wife is temporarily away from him
grassy \'gra-sē\ *adjective* **grass·i·er; -est** (15th century)
1 a : covered or abounding with grass ⟨*grassy* lawns⟩ **b :** having a flavor or odor of grass ⟨*grassy* tea⟩ ⟨wine with a *grassy* bouquet⟩
2 : resembling grass especially in color
grat *past of* GREET
¹grate \'grāt\ *verb* **grat·ed; grat·ing** [Middle English, from Middle French *grater* to scratch, of Germanic origin; akin to Old High German *krazzōn* to scratch] (14th century)
transitive verb
1 *archaic* **:** ABRADE
2 : to reduce to small particles by rubbing on something rough ⟨*grate* cheese⟩
3 : FRET, IRRITATE
4 a : to gnash or grind noisily **b :** to cause to make a rasping sound **c :** to utter in a harsh voice
intransitive verb
1 : to rub or rasp noisily
2 : to cause irritation **:** JAR ⟨dry, cerebral talk that tends to *grate* on the nerves —Hollis Alpert⟩
— **grat·er** *noun*
— **grat·ing·ly** \'grā-tiŋ-lē\ *adverb*
²grate *noun* [Middle English, from Medieval Latin *crata, grata* hurdle, alteration of Latin *cratis* — more at HURDLE] (14th century)
1 a : a barred frame for cooking over a fire **b :** a frame or bed of iron bars to hold a stove or furnace fire **c :** FIREPLACE
2 : GRATING 2
3 *obsolete* **:** CAGE, PRISON
³grate *transitive verb* **grat·ed; grat·ing** (1547)
: to furnish with a grate
grate·ful \'grāt-fəl\ *adjective* [obsolete *grate* pleasing, thankful, from Latin *gratus* — more at GRACE] (1552)
1 a : appreciative of benefits received **b :** expressing gratitude
2 a : affording pleasure or contentment **:** PLEASING **b :** pleasing by reason of comfort supplied or discomfort alleviated
— **grate·ful·ly** \-fə-lē\ *adverb*
— **grate·ful·ness** *noun*
grat·i·cule \'gra-tə-ˌkyü(ə)l\ *noun* [French, from Latin *craticula* fine latticework, diminutive of *cratis* wickerwork, hurdle] (1914)
1 : RETICLE
2 : the network of lines of latitude and longitude upon which a map is drawn
grat·i·fi·ca·tion \ˌgra-tə-fə-'kā-shən\ *noun* (1576)
1 : REWARD, RECOMPENSE; *especially* **:** GRATUITY
2 : the act of gratifying **:** the state of being gratified

3 : a source of satisfaction or pleasure
grat·i·fy \'gra-tə-ˌfī\ *transitive verb* **-fied; -fy·ing** [Middle French *gratifier*, from Latin *gratificari* to show kindness to, from *gratus* + *-ificari*, passive of *-ificare* -ify] (1539)
1 *archaic* **:** REMUNERATE, REWARD
2 : to be a source of or give pleasure or satisfaction to ⟨it *gratified* him to have his wife wear jewels —Willa Cather⟩
3 : to give in to **:** INDULGE, SATISFY ⟨*gratify* a whim⟩
grat·i·fy·ing *adjective* (circa 1611)
: giving pleasure or satisfaction **:** PLEASING
— **grat·i·fy·ing·ly** \-iŋ-lē\ *adverb*
gra·tin \'gra-t⁼n, 'grä-\ *noun* [French, from Middle French *grater* to scratch] (1806)
: a brown crust formed on food that has been cooked au gratin; *also* **:** a dish so cooked
2 : UPPER CRUST ⟨the *gratin* of London society⟩
gra·ti·né *or* **gra·ti·née** \ˌgra-t⁼n-'ā, ˌgrä-\ *adjective* [French, from past participle of *gratiner* to cook au gratin, from *gratin*] (1931)
: AU GRATIN
gra·ti·née *or* **gra·ti·nee** \ˌgra-t⁼n-'ā, ˌgrä-\ *transitive verb, past & past part* **gra·ti·néed** *or* **gra·ti·need** (1974)
: to cook au gratin
grat·ing \'grā-tiŋ\ *noun* (1626)
1 : a wooden or metal lattice used to close or floor any of various openings
2 : a partition, covering, or frame of parallel bars or crossbars
3 : a system of close equidistant and parallel lines or bars ruled on a polished surface to produce spectra by diffraction
gra·tis \'gra-təs, 'grä-\ *adverb or adjective* [Middle English, from Latin *gratiis, gratis*, from ablative plural of *gratia* favor — more at GRACE] (15th century)
: without charge or recompense **:** FREE
grat·i·tude \'gra-tə-ˌtüd, -ˌtyüd\ *noun* [Middle English, from Middle French or Medieval Latin; Middle French, from Medieval Latin *gratitudo*, from Latin *gratus* grateful] (1565)
: the state of being grateful **:** THANKFULNESS
gra·tu·itous \grə-'tü-ə-təs, -'tyü-\ *adjective* [Latin *gratuitus*, from *gratus*] (1656)
1 a : given unearned or without recompense **b :** not involving a return benefit, compensation, or consideration **c :** costing nothing **:** FREE
2 : not called for by the circumstances **:** UNWARRANTED ⟨*gratuitous* insolence⟩ ⟨a *gratuitous* assumption⟩
— **gra·tu·itous·ly** *adverb*
— **gra·tu·itous·ness** *noun*
gra·tu·ity \grə-'tü-ə-tē, -'tyü-\ *noun, plural* **-ities** (1540)
: something given voluntarily or beyond obligation usually for some service; *especially* **:** TIP
grat·u·late \'gra-chə-ˌlāt\ *transitive verb* [Latin *gratulatus*, past participle of *gratulari* — more at CONGRATULATE] (1584)
archaic **:** CONGRATULATE
— **grat·u·la·tion** \ˌgra-chə-'lā-shən\ *noun*
— **grat·u·la·to·ry** \'gra-chə-lə-ˌtōr-ē, -ˌtòr-\ *adjective*
grau·pel \'graú-pəl\ *noun* [German] (1889)
: granular snow pellets — called also *soft hail*
Grau·stark \'graú-ˌstärk, 'grò-\ *noun* [*Graustark*, imaginary country in the novel *Graustark* (1901) by George B. McCutcheon (died 1928) American novelist] (1941)
: an imaginary land of high romance; *also* **:** a highly romantic piece of writing
— **Grau·stark·ian** \graú-'stär-kē-ən, grò-\ *adjective*
gra·va·men \grə-'vā-mən\ *noun, plural* **-va·mens** *or* **-vam·i·na** \-'va-mə-nə\ [Late Latin, burden, from Latin *gravare* to burden, from *gravis*] (1647)
: the material or significant part of a grievance or complaint
¹grave \'grāv\ *transitive verb* **graved; grav·en** \'grā-vən\ *or* **graved; grav·ing** [Middle

English, from Old English *grafan;* akin to Old High German *graban* to dig, Old Church Slavonic po*greti* to bury] (before 12th century)
1 *archaic* **:** DIG, EXCAVATE
2 a : to carve or shape with a chisel **:** SCULPTURE **b :** to carve or cut (as letters or figures) into a hard surface **:** ENGRAVE
3 : to impress or fix (as a thought) deeply
²**grave** *noun* [Middle English, from Old English *græf;* akin to Old High German *grab* grave, Old English *grafan* to dig] (before 12th century)
1 : an excavation for burial of a body; *broadly* **:** a burial place
2 : DEATH 1, 4
³**grave** *transitive verb* **graved; grav·ing** [Middle English *graven*] (15th century)
: to clean and pay with pitch ⟨*grave* a ship's bottom⟩
⁴**grave** \'grāv, *in sense 5 often* 'gräv\ *adjective* **grav·er; grav·est** [Middle French, from Latin *gravis* heavy, grave — more at GRIEVE] (1539)
1 a *obsolete* **:** AUTHORITATIVE, WEIGHTY **b** **:** meriting serious consideration **:** IMPORTANT ⟨*grave* problems⟩ **c :** likely to produce great harm or danger ⟨a *grave* mistake⟩ **d :** significantly serious **:** CONSIDERABLE, GREAT ⟨*grave* importance⟩
2 : having a serious and dignified quality or demeanor ⟨a *grave* and thoughtful look⟩
3 : drab in color **:** SOMBER
4 : low-pitched in sound
5 a *of an accent mark* **:** having the form ` **b** **:** marked with a grave accent **c :** of the variety indicated by a grave accent
synonym *see* SERIOUS
— **grave·ly** *adverb*
— **grave·ness** *noun*
⁵**grave** \'grāv, 'gräv\ *noun* (1609)
: a grave accent ` used to show that a vowel is pronounced with a fall of pitch (as in ancient Greek), that a vowel has a certain quality (as *è* in French), that a final *e* is stressed and close and that a final *o* is stressed and low (as in Italian), that a syllable has a degree of stress between maximum and minimum (as in phonetic transcription), or that the *e* of the English ending -*ed* is to be pronounced (as in "this cursèd day")
⁶**gra·ve** \'grä-(,)vā\ *adverb or adjective* [Italian, literally, grave, from Latin *gravis*] (1683)
: slowly and solemnly — used as a direction in music
¹**grav·el** \'gra-vəl\ *noun* [Middle English, from Old French *gravele,* diminutive of *grave, greve* pebbly ground, beach] (13th century)
1 *obsolete* **:** SAND
2 a : loose rounded fragments of rock **b :** a stratum or deposit of gravel; *also* **:** a surface covered with gravel ⟨a *gravel* road⟩
3 : a deposit of small calculous concretions in the kidneys and urinary bladder
²**gravel** *transitive verb* **-eled** *or* **-elled; -el·ing** *or* **-el·ling** \'grav-liŋ, 'gra-və-\ (1543)
1 : to cover or spread with gravel
2 a : PERPLEX, CONFOUND **b :** IRRITATE, NETTLE
³**gravel** *adjective* (1939)
: GRAVELLY 2 — used of the human voice
grav·el–blind \'gra-vəl-,blīnd\ *adjective* [suggested by *sand-blind*] (1596)
: having very weak vision
grave·less \'grāv-ləs\ *adjective* (1606)
1 : not buried ⟨these *graveless* bones⟩
2 : not requiring graves **:** DEATHLESS ⟨the *graveless* home of the blessed⟩
grav·el·ly \'grav-lē, 'gra-və-\ *adjective* (14th century)
1 : of, containing, or covered with gravel
2 : having a rough or grating sound ⟨a *gravelly* voice⟩
graven image *noun* [*graven,* past participle of ¹*grave*] (14th century)
: an object of worship carved usually from wood or stone **:** IDOL

grav·er \'grā-vər\ *noun* [Middle English] (13th century)
1 : SCULPTOR, ENGRAVER
2 : any of various cutting or shaving tools used in graving or in hand metal-turning
Graves' disease \'grāvz-\ *noun* [Robert J. Graves (died 1853) Irish physician] (1868)
: a common form of hyperthyroidism characterized by goiter and often a slight protrusion of the eyeballs
grave·side \'grāv-,sīd\ *noun* (1838)
: the area beside a grave ⟨mourners at *graveside*⟩
grave·stone \'grāv-,stōn\ *noun* (14th century)
: a burial monument
grave·yard \-,yärd\ *noun* (1773)
1 : CEMETERY
2 : something resembling a graveyard ⟨an automobile *graveyard*⟩
graveyard shift *noun* (1908)
: a work shift beginning late at night (as 11 o'clock); *also* **:** the workers on such a shift
gravi- *combining form* [Middle French, from Latin, from *gravis*]
: weight ⟨*gravimetric*⟩
grav·id \'gra-vəd\ *adjective* [Latin *gravidus,* from *gravis* heavy] (1597)
1 : PREGNANT
2 : distended with or full of eggs
— **gra·vid·i·ty** \gra-'vi-də-tē\ *noun*
grav·i·da \'gra-və-də\ *noun, plural* **-i·das** *or* **-i·dae** \-və-,dē\ [Latin, from feminine of *gravidus*] (1926)
: a pregnant woman — often used with a number to indicate the number of pregnancies a woman has had ⟨a 4-*gravida*⟩
gra·vim·e·ter \gra-'vi-mə-tər, 'gra-və-,mē-\ *noun* [French *gravimètre,* from *gravi-* + *-mètre* -meter] (1932)
: a sensitive weighing instrument for measuring variations in the gravitational field of the earth or moon
gravi·met·ric \,gra-və-'me-trik\ *adjective* (1873)
1 : of or relating to measurement by weight
2 : of or relating to variations in the gravitational field determined by means of a gravimeter
— **gravi·met·ri·cal·ly** \-tri-k(ə-)lē\ *adverb*
gra·vim·e·try \gra-'vi-mə-trē\ *noun* (1858)
: the measurement of weight, a gravitational field, or density
graving dock *noun* (1840)
: DRY DOCK
grav·i·tas \'gra-və-,täs, -,tas\ *noun* [Latin] (1924)
: high seriousness (as in a person's bearing or in the treatment of a subject)
grav·i·tate \'gra-və-,tāt\ *intransitive verb* **-tat·ed; -tat·ing** (1692)
1 : to move under the influence of gravitation
2 a : to move toward something **b :** to be drawn or attracted especially by natural inclination ⟨youngsters . . . *gravitate* toward a strong leader —Rose Friedman⟩
grav·i·ta·tion \,gra-və-'tā-shən\ *noun* (circa 1645)
1 : a force manifested by acceleration toward each other of two free material particles or bodies or of radiant-energy quanta **:** GRAVITY 3a(2)
2 : the action or process of gravitating
— **grav·i·ta·tion·al** \-shnəl, -shə-nºl\ *adjective*
— **grav·i·ta·tion·al·ly** *adverb*
— **grav·i·ta·tive** \'gra-və-,tā-tiv\ *adjective*
gravitational lens *noun* (1950)
: a massive celestial object (as a galaxy) that bends and focuses the light of another more distant object (as a quasar) by gravity and that is usually detected by the multiple images it forms of the second object
gravitational wave *noun* (1906)
: a hypothetical wave held to travel at the speed of light and to propagate the gravitational field — called also *gravity wave*

grav·i·ton \'gra-və-,tän\ *noun* [International Scientific Vocabulary *gravity* + ²-*on*] (1942)
: a hypothetical particle with zero charge and rest mass that is held to be the quantum of the gravitational field
grav·i·ty \'gra-və-tē\ *noun, plural* **-ties** *often attributive* [Middle French or Latin; Middle French *gravité,* from Latin *gravitat-, gravitas,* from *gravis*] (1509)
1 a : dignity or sobriety of bearing **b :** IMPORTANCE, SIGNIFICANCE; *especially* **:** SERIOUSNESS **c :** a serious situation or problem
2 : WEIGHT
3 a (1) **:** the gravitational attraction of the mass of the earth, the moon, or a planet for bodies at or near its surface (2) **:** a fundamental physical force that is responsible for interactions which occur because of mass between particles, between aggregations of matter (as stars and planets), and between particles (as photons) and aggregations of matter, that is 10^{39} times weaker than the strong force, and that extends over infinite distances but is dominant over macroscopic distances especially between aggregations of matter — called also *gravitation, gravitational force;* compare ELECTROMAGNETISM 2a, STRONG FORCE, WEAK FORCE **b :** ACCELERATION OF GRAVITY **c :** SPECIFIC GRAVITY
grav·lax *or* **grav·laks** \'gräv-,läks\ *noun* [Swedish *gravlax* or Norwegian *gravlaks,* from *grav* buried + Swedish *lax,* Norwegian *laks* salmon — more at LOX] (1977)
: salmon usually cured with salt, pepper, dill, and aquavit
gra·vure \grə-'vyu̇r, grä-\ *noun* [French, from *graver* to grave, of Germanic origin; akin to Old High German *graban* to dig, engrave — more at GRAVE] (1893)
: PHOTOGRAVURE
gra·vy \'grā-vē\ *noun, plural* **gravies** [Middle English *gravey,* from Middle French *gravé*] (14th century)
1 : a sauce made from the thickened and seasoned juices of cooked meat
2 a : something additional or unexpected that is pleasing or valuable ⟨with expenses now paid, future money is pure *gravy* —K. Crossen⟩ **b :** unearned or illicit gain **:** ⁵GRAFT
gravy train *noun* (circa 1927)
: a much exploited source of easy money; *also* **:** GRAVY 2a
¹**gray** \'grā\ *adjective* [Middle English, from Old English *græg;* akin to Old High German *grīs, grāo* gray] (before 12th century)
1 a : of the color gray **b :** tending toward gray ⟨blue-*gray* eyes⟩ **c :** dull in color
2 : having the hair gray **:** HOARY
3 : clothed in gray
4 a : lacking cheer or brightness in mood, outlook, style, or flavor; *also* **:** DISMAL, GLOOMY ⟨a *gray* day⟩ **b :** prosaically ordinary **:** DULL, UNINTERESTING
5 : having an intermediate and often vaguely defined position, condition, or character ⟨an ethically *gray* area⟩
— **gray·ly** *adverb*
— **gray·ness** *noun*
²**gray** *noun* (13th century)
1 : something (as an animal, garment, cloth, or spot) of a gray color
2 : any of a series of neutral colors ranging between black and white
3 : one who wears a gray uniform: as **a :** a soldier in the Confederate army during the American Civil War **b :** the Confederate army
³**gray** (14th century)
transitive verb
: to make gray
intransitive verb

\ə\ **abut** \ᵊ\ **kitten** \ər\ **further** \a\ **ash** \ā\ **ace**
\ä\ **mop, mar** \au̇\ **out** \ch\ **chin** \e\ **bet** \ē\ **easy**
\g\ **go** \i\ **hit** \ī\ **ice** \j\ **job** \ŋ\ **sing** \ō\ **go**
\ȯ\ **law** \ȯi\ **boy** \th\ **thin** \t̲h̲\ **the** \ü\ **loot** \u̇\ **foot**
\y\ **yet** \zh\ **vision** *see also* Guide to Pronunciation

1 : to become gray ⟨*graying* hair⟩
2 : AGE; *also* : to contain an increasing percentage of older people
gray·beard \'grā-ˌbird\ *noun* (circa 1580)
: an old man
gray birch *noun* (1851)
1 : a small birch (*Betula populifolia*) of northeastern North America that has many lateral branches, grayish white bark, triangular leaves, and soft weak wood and that occurs especially in old fields reverting to woodland
2 : YELLOW BIRCH
gray eminence *noun* [translation of French *Éminence grise*, nickname of Père Joseph (François Joseph du Tremblay) (died 1638) French monk and diplomat who was confidant of Cardinal Richelieu, styled *Éminence rouge* (red eminence); from the colors of their respective habits] (1941)
: a person who exercises power behind the scenes
gray·fish \'grā-ˌfish\ *noun* (1917)
: DOGFISH
gray fox *noun* (circa 1679)
: a fox (*Urocyon cinereoargenteus*) with coarse gray hair and white underparts that occurs from southern Canada to northern South America
gray·ish \'grā-ish\ *adjective* (1562)
1 : somewhat gray
2 *of a color* : low in saturation
gray·ling \'grā-liŋ\ *noun, plural* **grayling** *also* **graylings** (15th century)
: any of several freshwater salmonoid fishes (genus *Thymallus*) valued as food and sport fishes
gray market *noun* (1946)
: a market employing irregular but not illegal methods; *especially* : a market that legally circumvents authorized channels of distribution to sell goods at prices lower than those intended by the manufacturer
gray matter *noun* (1840)
1 : neural tissue especially of the brain and spinal cord that contains nerve-cell bodies as well as nerve fibers and has a brownish gray color
2 : BRAINS, INTELLECT
gray squirrel *noun* (1674)
: a common light gray to black squirrel (*Sciurus carolinensis*) that is native to eastern North America and has been introduced into England
gray·wacke \'grā-ˌwak, -ˌwa-kə\ *noun* [partial translation of German *Grauwacke*] (1811)
: a coarse usually dark gray sandstone or fine-grained conglomerate composed of firmly cemented fragments (as of quartz or feldspar)
gray whale *noun* (1860)
: a large baleen whale (*Eschrichtius robustus*) of the northern Pacific having short jaws and no dorsal fin
gray wolf *noun* (1814)
: a large usually gray Holarctic wolf (*Canis lupus*) now restricted to northern North America and Asia — called also *timber wolf*
¹graze \'grāz\ *verb* **grazed; graz·ing** [Middle English *grasen*, from Old English *grasian*, from *græs* grass] (before 12th century)
intransitive verb
1 : to feed on growing herbage, attached algae, or phytoplankton
2 : to eat small amounts of various foods several times a day
transitive verb
1 a : to crop and eat in the field **b** : to feed on the herbage of
2 a : to put to graze ⟨*grazed* the cows on the meadow⟩ **b** : to put cattle to graze on
3 : to supply herbage for the grazing of
— **graze·able** *or* **graz·able** \'grā-zə-bəl\ *adjective*
— **graz·er** *noun*
²graze *noun* (1692)
1 : an act of grazing
2 : herbage for grazing

³graze *verb* **grazed; graz·ing** [perhaps from ¹*graze*] (1604)
transitive verb
1 : to touch lightly in passing
2 : ABRADE, SCRATCH ⟨*grazed* her knee when she fell⟩
intransitive verb
: to touch or rub against something in passing
⁴graze *noun* (1847)
: a scraping along a surface or an abrasion made by it; *especially* : a superficial abrasion of the skin
gra·zier \'grā-zhər\ *noun* (15th century)
1 : a person who grazes cattle; *broadly* : RANCHER
2 *Australian* : a sheep raiser
grazing *noun* (1517)
: herbage or land for grazing
¹grease \'grēs\ *noun* [Middle English *grese*, from Old French *craisse, graisse*, from (assumed) Vulgar Latin *crassia*, from Latin *crassus* fat] (13th century)
1 a : rendered animal fat **b** : oily matter **c** : a thick lubricant
2 : wool as it comes from the sheep retaining the natural oils or fats
— **grease·less** \'grēs-ləs\ *adjective*
— **grease·proof** \'grēs-ˈprüf\ *adjective*
— **in the grease** *of wool or fur* : in the natural uncleaned condition
²grease \'grēs, 'grēz\ *transitive verb* **greased; greas·ing** (14th century)
1 : to smear or daub with grease
2 : to lubricate with grease
3 : to soil with grease
4 : to hasten the process or progress of; *also* : FACILITATE
— **grease the hand of** *or* **grease the palm of** : BRIBE
grease·ball \'grēs-ˌbȯl\ *noun* (circa 1922)
: a person of Hispanic or Mediterranean descent — usually used disparagingly
grease monkey *noun* (1928)
: MECHANIC
grease·paint \'grēs-ˌpānt\ *noun* (1886)
1 : a melted tallow or grease used in theater makeup
2 : theater makeup
grease pencil *noun* (1944)
: a pencil in which the marking substance is pigment and grease
greaseproof paper *noun* (1900)
British : a heavy stiff waxed paper — called also *greaseproof*
greas·er \'grē-zər, -sər\ *noun* [¹*grease*] (1641)
1 : one that greases
2 : a native or inhabitant of Latin America or a Mediterranean land; *especially* : MEXICAN — usually used disparagingly
3 : an aggressive swaggering young white male usually of working-class background
grease·wood \'grēs-ˌwu̇d\ *noun* (1838)
: a low stiff shrub (*Sarcobatus vermiculatus*) of the goosefoot family common in alkaline soils in the western U.S.; *also* : any of various related or similar shrubs
greasy \'grē-sē, -zē\ *adjective* **greas·i·er; -est** (1514)
1 a : smeared or soiled with grease ⟨*greasy* clothes⟩ **b** : oily in appearance, texture, or manner ⟨his *greasy* smile —Jack London⟩ **c** : SLIPPERY
2 : containing an unusual amount of grease ⟨*greasy* food⟩
— **greas·i·ly** \-sə-lē, -zə-\ *adverb*
— **greas·i·ness** \-sē-nəs, -zē-\ *noun*
greasy spoon *noun* (circa 1925)
: a dingy small cheap restaurant
¹great \'grāt, *Southern also* 'gre(ə)t\ *adjective* [Middle English *grete*, from Old English *grēat*; akin to Old High German *grōz* large] (before 12th century)
1 a : notably large in size : HUGE **b** : of a kind characterized by relative largeness — used in plant and animal names **c** : ELABORATE, AMPLE ⟨*great* detail⟩

2 a : large in number or measure : NUMEROUS ⟨*great* multitudes⟩ **b** : PREDOMINANT ⟨the *great* majority⟩
3 : remarkable in magnitude, degree, or effectiveness ⟨*great* bloodshed⟩
4 : full of emotion ⟨*great* with anger⟩
5 a : EMINENT, DISTINGUISHED ⟨a *great* poet⟩ **b** : chief or preeminent over others — often used in titles ⟨Lord *Great* Chamberlain⟩ **c** : ARISTOCRATIC, GRAND ⟨*great* ladies⟩
6 : long continued ⟨a *great* while⟩
7 : PRINCIPAL, MAIN ⟨a reception in the *great* hall⟩
8 : more remote in a family relationship by a single generation than a specified relative ⟨*great*-grandfather⟩
9 : markedly superior in character or quality; *especially* : NOBLE ⟨*great* of soul⟩
10 a : remarkably skilled ⟨*great* at tennis⟩ **b** : marked by enthusiasm : KEEN ⟨*great* on science fiction⟩
11 — used as a generalized term of approval ⟨had a *great* time⟩ ⟨it was just *great*⟩
— **great·ness** *noun*
²great *adverb* (13th century)
: in a great manner : SUCCESSFULLY, WELL ⟨things are going *great*⟩
³great *noun, plural* **great** *or* **greats** (13th century)
: an outstandingly superior or skillful person
great ape *noun* (1949)
: any of a family (Pongidae) of primates including the gorilla, orangutan, and chimpanzees — called also *pongid*
great auk *noun* (circa 1828)
: an extinct large flightless auk (*Pinguinus impennis*) formerly abundant along North Atlantic coasts
great–aunt *noun* (1656)
: GRANDAUNT
Great Bear *noun*
: URSA MAJOR
great blue heron *noun* (1835)
: a large slaty-blue American heron (*Ardea herodias*) with a crested head
great circle *noun* (1594)
: a circle formed on the surface of a sphere by the intersection of a plane that passes through the center of the sphere; *specifically* : such a circle on the surface of the earth an arc of which connecting two terrestrial points constitutes the shortest distance on the earth's surface between them
great·coat \'grāt-ˌkōt\ *noun* (circa 1685)
: a heavy overcoat
Great Dane *noun* (1774)
: any of a breed of tall massive powerful smooth-coated dogs
great divide *noun* [the *Great Divide*, North American watershed] (1868)
: a significant point of division; *especially* : DEATH
great·en \'grā-tᵊn\ *verb* **great·ened; great·en·ing** \'grā-tᵊn-iŋ\ (1614)
transitive verb
: to make greater
intransitive verb
: to become greater
great·er *adjective, often capitalized* [comparative of *great*] (1882)
: consisting of a central city together with adjacent areas that are naturally or administratively connected with it ⟨*Greater* London⟩
greater yellowlegs *noun plural but singular or plural in construction* (circa 1909)
: a common North American marsh and shorebird (*Tringa melanoleuca*) that is largely gray above and white below with black or dark gray flecks and yellow legs — compare LESSER YELLOWLEGS
greatest common divisor *noun* (circa 1924)
: the largest integer or the polynomial of highest degree that is an exact divisor of each of two or more integers or polynomials — called also *greatest common factor*

great group *noun* (1960)
: a group of soils that is characterized by common characteristics usually developed under the influence of environmental factors (as vegetation and climate) active over a considerable geographic range and that comprises one or more families of soil — called also *great soil group*

great·heart·ed \'grāt-,här-təd\ *adjective* (14th century)
1 : characterized by bravery : COURAGEOUS
2 : GENEROUS, MAGNANIMOUS
— **great·heart·ed·ly** *adverb*
— **great·heart·ed·ness** *noun*

great horned owl *noun* (1812)
: a large American owl (*Bubo virginianus*) with conspicuous ear tufts

great laurel *noun* (1784)
: a large-leaved evergreen rhododendron (*Rhododendron maximum*) of eastern North America with rosy bell-shaped flowers more or less speckled with green — called also *rosebay rhododendron*

great·ly \'grāt-lē\ *adverb* (13th century)
1 : to a great extent or degree : very much ⟨contributed *greatly* to improved relations⟩ ⟨not *greatly* bothered⟩
2 : in a great manner : NOBLY, MAGNANIMOUSLY ⟨a man may live *greatly* in the law —O. W. Holmes (died 1935)⟩

Great Mogul *noun* (1588)
: the sovereign of the empire founded in India by the Moguls in the 16th century

great–nephew *noun* (1581)
: GRANDNEPHEW

great–niece *noun* (1884)
: GRANDNIECE

great octave *noun* (circa 1854)
: the musical octave that begins on the second C below middle C — see PITCH illustration

great power *noun, often G&P capitalized* (circa 1890)
: one of the nations that figure most decisively in international affairs : SUPERPOWER

Great Pyr·e·nees \-'pir-ə-,nēz\ *noun, plural*
Great Pyrenees (1938)
: any of a breed of large heavy-coated white dogs often used to guard livestock

great room *noun* (1700)
: a large room usually combining several functions (as of a dining room, living room, and family room)

Great Russian *noun* (1854)
: RUSSIAN 1b
— **Great Russian** *adjective*

Great Pyrenees

great seal *noun* (15th century)
: a large seal that constitutes an emblem of sovereignty and is used especially for the authentication of important documents

great skua *noun* (circa 1954)
: a large seabird (*Catharacta skua*) that is related to the jaeger, has dusky plumage and broad rounded wings, breeds chiefly along arctic and antarctic shores, and forages over most cold and temperate seas

great–uncle *noun* (1656)
: GRANDUNCLE

great vowel shift *noun, often G&V&S capitalized* (1909)
: a change in pronunciation of the long vowels of Middle English that began in the 15th century and continued into the 16th century in which the high vowels were diphthongized and the other vowels were raised

great white shark *noun* (circa 1931)
: a large mackerel shark (*Carcharodon carcharias*) of warm seas that is bluish when young but becomes whitish with age and is a man-eater — called also *white shark*; see SHARK illustration

great year *noun* (circa 1741)
: the period of about 25,800 years required for one complete cycle of the equinoxes around the ecliptic

greave \'grēv\ *noun* [Middle English *greve*, from Middle French] (14th century)
: armor for the leg below the knee

grebe \'grēb\ *noun* [French *grèbe*] (1766)
: any of a family (Podicipedidae) of swimming and diving birds closely related to the loons but having lobate toes — compare DABCHICK

Gre·cian \'grē-shən\ *adjective* [Middle English *greciane*, from Latin *Graecia* Greece] (15th century)
: GREEK
— **Grecian** *noun*
— **gre·cian·ize** \-shə-,nīz\ *transitive verb, often capitalized*

Gre·cism \'grē-,si-zəm\ *noun* (1570)
1 : a Greek idiom
2 : a quality or style imitative of Greek art or culture

gre·cize \-,sīz\ *transitive verb* **gre·cized; gre·ciz·ing** *often capitalized* (1692)
: to make Greek or Hellenistic in character

Gre·co- \'gre-kō, 'grē-\ *or* **Grae·co-** \'gre-kō\ *combining form* [Latin *Graeco-*, from *Graecus*]
1 : Greece : Greeks ⟨*Greco*phile⟩
2 : Greek and ⟨*Graeco*-Roman⟩

¹**gree** \'grē\ *noun* [Middle English, from Middle French *gré* step, degree, from Latin *gradus* — more at GRADE] (14th century)
Scottish : MASTERY, SUPERIORITY

²**gree** *verb* **greed; gree·ing** [Middle English *green*, short for *agreen*] (14th century)
dialect : AGREE

greed \'grēd\ *noun* [back-formation from *greedy*] (1609)
: excessive or reprehensible acquisitiveness : AVARICE

greedy \'grē-dē\ *adjective* **greed·i·er; -est** [Middle English *gredy*, from Old English *grǣdig*; akin to Old High German *grātac* greedy] (before 12th century)
1 : having a strong desire for food or drink
2 : marked by greed
3 : EAGER, KEEN ⟨elated and *greedy* for the future —Frances G. Patton⟩
synonym see COVETOUS
— **greed·i·ly** \'grē-dᵊl-ē\ *adverb*
— **greed·i·ness** \'grē-dē-nəs\ *noun*

¹**Greek** \'grēk\ *noun* [Middle English *Greke*, from Old English *Grēca*, from Latin *Graecus*, from Greek *Graikos*] (before 12th century)
1 a : a native or inhabitant of ancient or modern Greece **b** : a person of Greek descent
2 a : the language used by the Greeks from prehistoric times to the present constituting a branch of Indo-European — see INDO-EUROPEAN LANGUAGES table **b** : ancient Greek as used from the time of the earliest records to the end of the 2d century A.D. — see INDO-EUROPEAN LANGUAGES table **c** *often not capitalized* [translation of Latin *Graecum* (in the medieval phrase *Graecum est; non potest legi* It is Greek; it cannot be read)] : something unintelligible ⟨it's *Greek* to me⟩
3 : a member of a Greek-letter fraternity or sorority

²**Greek** *adjective* (14th century)
1 : of, relating to, or characteristic of Greece, the Greeks, or Greek ⟨*Greek* architecture⟩
2 a : EASTERN ORTHODOX **b** : of or relating to an Eastern church using the Byzantine rite in Greek **c** : of or relating to the established Orthodox church of Greece

Greek Catholic *noun* (1909)
1 : a member of an Eastern church
2 : a member of an Eastern rite of the Roman Catholic Church

Greek cross *noun* (1725)
: a cross having an upright and a transverse shaft equal in length and intersecting at their middles — see CROSS illustration

Greek fire *noun* (circa 1823)
: an incendiary composition used in warfare by the Byzantine Greeks that is said to have burst into flame on wetting

Greek·less \'grēk-ləs\ *adjective* (1891)
: not proficient in Greek

Greek Orthodox *adjective* (circa 1900)
: EASTERN ORTHODOX; *specifically* : GREEK 2c

Greek Revival *noun* (1918)
1 : a style of architecture in the first half of the 19th century marked by the use or imitation of Greek orders
2 : a style of decoration (as of furniture) using or imitating the decorative motifs of ancient Greece

¹**green** \'grēn\ *adjective* [Middle English *grene*, from Old English *grēne*; akin to Old English *grōwan* to grow] (before 12th century)
1 : of the color green
2 a : covered by green growth or foliage ⟨*green* fields⟩ **b** *of winter* : MILD, CLEMENT **c** : consisting of green plants and usually edible herbage ⟨a *green* salad⟩
3 : pleasantly alluring
4 : YOUTHFUL, VIGOROUS
5 : not ripened or matured : IMMATURE ⟨*green* apples⟩ ⟨tender *green* grasses⟩
6 : FRESH, NEW
7 a : marked by a pale, sickly, or nauseated appearance **b** : ENVIOUS 1 — used especially in the phrase *green with envy*
8 a : not fully processed or treated: as (1) : not aged ⟨*green* liquor⟩ (2) : not dressed or tanned ⟨*green* hides⟩ (3) : freshly sawed : UNSEASONED **b** : not in condition for a particular use
9 a : deficient in training, knowledge, or experience **b** : deficient in sophistication and savoir faire : NAIVE **c** : not fully qualified for or experienced in a particular function ⟨*green* horse⟩
10 a *often capitalized* : relating to or being an environmentalist political movement **b** : concerned with or supporting environmentalism
— **green·ish** \'grē-nish\ *adjective*
— **green·ish·ness** *noun*
— **green·ly** *adverb*
— **green·ness** \'grē(n)-nəs\ *noun*
— **green around the gills** : pale or sickly in appearance

²**green** (before 12th century)
intransitive verb
: to become green
transitive verb
1 : to make green
2 : REJUVENATE, REVITALIZE

³**green** *noun* (13th century)
1 : a color whose hue is somewhat less yellow than that of growing fresh grass or of the emerald or is that of the part of the spectrum lying between blue and yellow
2 : something of a green color
3 : green vegetation: as **a** *plural* : leafy parts of plants for use as decoration **b** *plural* (1) : leafy herbs (as spinach, dandelions, Swiss chard) that are cooked as a vegetable : POTHERBS (2) : GREEN VEGETABLES
4 : a grassy plain or plot: as **a** : a common or park in the center of a town or village **b** : PUTTING GREEN
5 : MONEY; *especially* : GREENBACKS
6 *often capitalized* : ENVIRONMENTALIST; *especially* : a member of an environmentalist political party
— **greeny** \'grē-nē\ *adjective*

green alga *noun* (1903)

: any of a division (Chlorophyta) of green-colored algae that have chloroplasts and occur especially in freshwater

green·back \'grēn-,bak\ *noun* (1862)
: a legal-tender note issued by the U.S. government

green·back·er \-,ba-kər\ *noun* (1876)
1 *capitalized* : a member of a post-Civil War American political party opposing reduction in the amount of paper money in circulation **2** : one who advocates a paper currency backed only by the U.S. government
— **green·back·ism** \-,ki-zəm\ *noun*

green bean *noun* (1847)
: a kidney bean that is used as a snap bean when the pods are colored green

green·belt \'grēn-,belt\ *noun* (1932)
: a belt of parkways, parks, or farmlands that encircles a community

Green Beret *noun* [from the beret worn by Special Forces soldiers] (1962)
: a member of the U.S. Army Special Forces

green·bri·er \-,brī-(-ə)r\ *noun* (circa 1785)
: any of a genus (*Smilax*) of woody or herbaceous vines of the lily family; *especially* : a prickly vine (*S. rotundifolia*) of the eastern U.S. with umbels of small greenish flowers

green·bug \-,bəg\ *noun* (1712)
: a green aphid (*Schizaphis graminum*) very destructive to small grains

green card *noun* [from the fact that it was formerly colored green] (1969)
: an identity card attesting the permanent resident status of an alien in the U.S.
— **green–carder** *noun*

green corn *noun* (1645)
: the young tender ears of Indian corn

green dragon *noun* (circa 1818)
: an American arum (*Arisaema dracontium*) with digitate leaves, slender green spathe, and elongated spadix

green·ery \'grēn-rē, 'grē-nər-ē\ *noun, plural* **-er·ies** (1797)
1 : green foliage or plants
2 : GREEN 3a

green–eyed \'grē-,nīd\ *adjective* (1596)
: JEALOUS

green–eyed monster *noun* (1604)
: JEALOUSY

green·finch \'grēn-,finch\ *noun* (15th century)
: a very common European finch (*Carduelis chloris*) having olive-green and yellow plumage

green fingers *noun plural* (1934)
: GREEN THUMB

green flash *noun* (1912)
: a momentary green appearance of the uppermost part of the sun's disk at sunrise or sunset that results from atmospheric refraction

green·fly \'grēn-,flī\ *noun* (circa 1750)
British : APHID; *especially* : GREEN PEACH APHID

green·gage \-,gāj\ *noun* [*green* + Sir William *Gage* (died 1820) English botanist] (1724)
: any of several rather small rounded greenish or greenish yellow cultivated plums

green gland *noun* (circa 1890)
: one of a pair of large green glands in some crustaceans (as crayfishes) that have an excretory function and open at the bases of the larger antennae

green·gro·cer \'grēn-,grō-sər, -shər\ *noun* (1723)
chiefly British : a retailer of fresh vegetables and fruit
— **green·gro·cery** \-,grō-sə-rē, -,grōsh-rē\ *noun*

green·head \'grēn-,hed\ *noun* (1837)
: any of several green-eyed horseflies (as *Tabanus nigrovittatus*)

green·heart \-,härt\ *noun* (1756)
: a tropical South American evergreen tree (*Ocotea rodiaei* synonym *Nectandra rodiaei*) of the laurel family with a hard greenish wood; *also* : its wood

green·horn \-,hòrn\ *noun* [obsolete *greenhorn* (animal with young horns)] (1682)

1 : an inexperienced or unsophisticated person
2 : a newcomer (as to a country) unacquainted with local manners and customs

¹green·house \-,haús\ *noun* (1664)
1 : a structure enclosed (as by glass) and used for the cultivation or protection of tender plants
2 : a clear plastic shell (as a canopy) covering a section of an airplane; *also* : a compartment (as for a bombardier) enclosed by such a shell

²greenhouse *adjective* (1969)
: of, relating to, or caused by the greenhouse effect ⟨*greenhouse* warming⟩ ⟨*greenhouse* gas⟩

greenhouse effect *noun* (1937)
: warming of the surface and lower atmosphere of a planet (as the earth or Venus) that is caused by conversion of solar radiation into heat in a process involving selective transmission of short wave solar radiation by the atmosphere, its absorption by the planet's surface, and reradiation as infrared which is absorbed and partly reradiated back to the surface by atmospheric gases

green·ing \'grē-niŋ\ *noun* (1664)
: any of several green-skinned apples

green·keep·er \'grēn-,kē-pər\ *or* **greens·keep·er** \'grēnz-\ *noun* (circa 1730)
: a person responsible for the care and upkeep of a golf course

green·let \'grēn-lət\ *noun* (1831)
: VIREO

green light *noun* [from the green traffic light which signals permission to proceed] (1937)
: authority or permission to proceed

green·ling \'grēn-liŋ\ *noun* (circa 1898)
: any of several food fishes (family Hexagrammidae) of the rocky coasts of the northern Pacific; *especially* : a common food and sport fish (*Hexagrammos decagrammus*)

green·mail \'grēn-,mā(ə)l\ *noun* (1983)
: the practice of buying enough of a company's stock to threaten a hostile takeover and reselling it to the company at a price above market value; *also* : the money paid for such stock
— **greenmail** *transitive verb*
— **green·mail·er** \-,mā-lər\ *noun*

green manure *noun* (1842)
: an herbaceous crop (as clover) plowed under while green to enrich the soil
— **green–manure** *transitive verb*

green mold *noun* (1919)
: a green or green-spored mold (as of the genera *Penicillium* or *Aspergillus*)

green monkey *noun* (1840)
: a long-tailed monkey of any of several African races of a guenon (*Cercopithecus aethiops*) having greenish-appearing hair and often used in medical research

gree·nock·ite \'grē-nə-,kīt\ *noun* [Charles M. Cathcart, Lord *Greenock* (died 1859) English soldier] (1844)
: a mineral consisting of native cadmium sulfide occurring in yellow translucent hexagonal crystals or as an earthy incrustation

green onion *noun* (1847)
: a young onion pulled before the bulb has enlarged and used especially in salads

green paper *noun, often G&P capitalized* (1967)
British : a government document that proposes and invites discussion on approaches to a problem

green peach aphid *noun* (1922)
: a nearly cosmopolitan yellowish green aphid (*Myzus persicae*) that is frequently a vector of plant virus diseases

green pepper *noun* (1700)
: a sweet pepper before it turns red at maturity

green revolution *noun* (1968)
: the great increase in production of food grains (as rice and wheat) due to the introduction of high-yielding varieties, to the use of pesticides, and to better management techniques

green·room \'grēn-,rüm, -,rùm\ *noun* (1701)

: a room in a theater or concert hall where performers can relax before or after appearances

green·sand \-,sand\ *noun* (1796)
: a sedimentary deposit that consists largely of dark greenish grains of glauconite often mingled with clay or sand

greens fee \'grēnz-\ *noun* (1909)
: a fee paid for the privilege of playing on a golf course — called also *green fee*

green·shank \'grēn-,shaŋk\ *noun* (1766)
: an Old World sandpiper (*Tringa nebularia*) with greenish legs and a slightly upturned bill

green·sick·ness \-,sik-nəs\ *noun* (1583)
: CHLOROSIS
— **green·sick** *adjective*

green snake *noun* (1709)
: either of two bright green harmless largely insectivorous North American colubrid snakes (*Opheodrys vernalis* and *O. aestivus*)

green soap *noun* (circa 1840)
: a soft soap made from vegetable oils and used especially in the treatment of skin diseases

green·stick fracture \'grēn-,stik-\ *noun* (circa 1885)
: a bone fracture in a young individual in which the bone is partly broken and partly bent

green·stone \'grēn-,stōn\ *noun* (circa 1784)
1 : NEPHRITE
2 : any of numerous usually altered dark green compact rocks (as diorite)

green·stuff \-,stəf\ *noun* (1851)
: green vegetation used as foodstuff

green sunfish *noun* (circa 1896)
: a sunfish (*Lepomis cyanellus*) of the Great Lakes region and southwestward to the Rio Grande that is largely greenish above with a blue spot on each scale

green·sward \-,swòrd\ *noun* (1600)
: turf green with growing grass

green tea *noun* (1704)
: tea that is light in color from incomplete fermentation of the leaf before firing

green thumb *noun* (1943)
: an unusual ability to make plants grow
— **green–thumbed** \'grēn-'thəmd\ *adjective*

green turtle *noun* (1657)
: a large usually herbivorous sea turtle (*Chelonia mydas*) of warm waters with a smooth greenish or olive-colored shell

green vegetable *noun* (1826)
: a vegetable whose foliage or foliage-bearing stalks are the chief edible part

green·way \'grēn-,wā\ *noun* (1966)
: a corridor of undeveloped land in or near a city that is designed for recreational use

Green·wich mean time \'gri-nij, 'gre-, -nich\ *noun, often M&T capitalized* [*Greenwich*, England] (1938)
: the mean solar time of the meridian of Greenwich used as the prime basis of standard time throughout the world — called also *Greenwich time*

green·wing \'grēn-,wiŋ\ *noun* (circa 1889)
: GREEN-WINGED TEAL

green–winged teal \'grēn-,wiŋ(d)-\ *noun* (1792)
: a small dabbling duck (*Anas crecca*) the male of which has a chestnut head with a green eye patch and a metallic green area on the wing speculum

green·wood \'grēn-,wùd\ *noun* (14th century)
: a forest green with foliage

¹greet \'grēt\ *transitive verb* [Middle English *greten*, from Old English *grētan*; akin to Old English *grǣtan* to weep] (before 12th century)
1 : to address with expression of kind wishes : HAIL
2 a : to meet or react to in a specified manner ⟨*greeted* him with boos⟩ **b** : to occur as a response to ⟨apathy *greeted* the plan⟩
3 : to appear to the perception of ⟨a surprising sight *greeted* her eyes⟩
— **greet·er** *noun*

²greet *intransitive verb* **grat** \'grat\; **grut-ten** \'grə-t°n\ [Middle English *greten*, from Old English *grǣtan*; akin to Old Norse *grāta* to weep] (before 12th century)
Scottish : WEEP, LAMENT

greet·ing *noun* (before 12th century)
1 : a salutation at meeting
2 : an expression of good wishes : REGARDS — usually used in plural ⟨holiday *greetings*⟩

greeting card *noun* (1898)
: a piece of paper or thin paperboard having any of a variety of shapes and formats and bearing a greeting or message of sentiment

greg·a·rine \'gre-gə-ˌrīn\ *noun* [ultimately from Latin *gregarius*] (1867)
: any of a subclass (Gregarinia) of parasitic vermiform sporozoan protozoans that occur especially in insects and other invertebrates
— **gregarine** *adjective*

gre·gar·i·ous \gri-'gar-ē-əs, -'ger-\ *adjective* [Latin *gregarius* of a flock or herd, from *greg-, grex* flock, herd] (1668)
1 a : tending to associate with others of one's kind : SOCIAL **b** : marked by or indicating a liking for companionship : SOCIABLE **c** : of or relating to a social group
2 a *of a plant* : growing in a cluster or a colony **b** : living in contiguous nests but not forming a true colony — used especially of wasps and bees ◇
— **gre·gar·i·ous·ly** *adverb*
— **gre·gar·i·ous·ness** *noun*

¹Gre·go·ri·an \gri-'gōr-ē-ən, -'gȯr-\ *adjective* (1642)
: of or relating to Pope Gregory XIII or the Gregorian calendar

²Gregorian *adjective* (1653)
1 : of or relating to Pope Gregory I
2 : of, relating to, or having the characteristics of Gregorian chant

³Gregorian *adjective* [Saint *Gregory* the Illuminator (died 332), apostle of Armenia] (1955)
: of or relating to the Armenian national church

Gregorian calendar *noun* (circa 1771)
: a calendar in general use introduced in 1582 by Pope Gregory XIII as a revision of the Julian calendar, adopted in Great Britain and the American colonies in 1752, marked by the suppression of 10 days or after 1700 11 days, and having leap years in every year divisible by four with the restriction that centesimal years are leap years only when divisible by 400 — see MONTH table

Gregorian chant *noun* (1751)
: a monodic and rhythmically free liturgical chant of the Roman Catholic Church

greige \'grā(zh)\ *adjective* [French *grège* raw (of silk), from Italian *greggio*] (1926)
: being in an unbleached undyed state as taken from a loom — used of textiles

grei·sen \'grī-z°n\ *noun* [German] (1878)
: a crystalline rock consisting of quartz and mica that is common in Cornwall and Saxony

grem·lin \'grem-lən\ *noun* [origin unknown] (1941)
: a cause of error or equipment malfunction (as in aircraft) conceived of as a small mischievous gnome

gre·nade \grə-'nād\ *noun* [Middle French, pomegranate, from Late Latin *granata*, from Latin, feminine of *granatus* seedy, from *granum* grain — more at CORN] (1591)
: a small missile that contains an explosive or a chemical agent (as tear gas, a flame producer, or a smoke producer) and that is thrown by hand or projected (as by a rifle or special launcher)

gren·a·dier \ˌgren-ə-'dir\ *noun* [French, from *grenade* grenade] (1676)
1 a : a soldier who carries and throws grenades **b** : a member of a special regiment or corps formerly armed with grenades
2 : any of various deep-sea fishes (family Macruridae) that are related to the cods and

have an elongate tapering body and compressed pointed tail

gren·a·dine \ˌgren-ə-'dēn, 'gre-nə-ˌ\ *noun* [French, from *grenade* coarse silk fabric, pomegranate] (1852)
1 : an open-weave fabric of various fibers
2 : a moderate reddish orange
3 : a syrup flavored with pomegranates and used in mixed drinks

Gren·del \'gren-d°l\ *noun* [Old English]
: a monstrous man-eating descendant of Cain slain by Beowulf in the Old English poem *Beowulf*

Gresh·am's law \'gre-shəmz-\ *noun* [Sir Thomas *Gresham*] (1858)
: an observation in economics: when two coins are equal in debt-paying value but unequal in intrinsic value, the one having the lesser intrinsic value tends to remain in circulation and the other to be hoarded or exported as bullion; *broadly* : any process by which inferior products or practices drive out superior ones

Gret·na Green \ˌgret-nə-'grēn\ *noun* [*Gretna Green*, village in Scotland] (1813)
: a place where many eloping couples are married

Gre·vy's zebra \(ˌ)grā-'vēz-\ *noun* [Jules *Grévy*] (1891)
: a zebra (*Equus grevyi*) of eastern Africa with narrow stripes and a white belly

grew *past of* GROW

grew·some *variant of* GRUESOME

grey *variant of* GRAY

grey friar *noun, often G&F capitalized* (14th century)
: a Franciscan friar

grey·hound \'grā-ˌhau̇nd\ *noun* [Middle English *grehound*, from Old English *grīghund*, from *grīg-* (akin to Old Norse *grey* bitch) + *hund* hound] (before 12th century)
: any of a breed of tall slender graceful smooth-coated dogs characterized by swiftness and keen sight and used for coursing game and racing; *also* : any of several related dogs

greyhound

grey·lag \-ˌlag\ *noun* [perhaps from *gray* + *lag* (last)] (circa 1713)
: the common gray wild goose (*Anser anser*) of Europe — called also *greylag goose*

grib·ble \'gri-bəl\ *noun* [perhaps alteration of ²*grub*] (1838)
: either of two small marine isopods (*Limnoria lignorum* and *L. tripunctata*) that destroy submerged timber

grid \'grid\ *noun* [back-formation from *gridiron*] (1839)
1 : GRATING
2 a (1) : a perforated or ridged metal plate used as a conductor in a storage battery (2) : an electrode consisting of a mesh or a spiral of fine wire in an electron tube (3) : a network of conductors for distribution of electric power; *also* : a network of radio or television stations **b** : a network of uniformly spaced horizontal and perpendicular lines (as for locating points on a map); *also* : something resembling such a network ⟨a road *grid*⟩ **c** : GRIDIRON 3; *broadly* : FOOTBALL
3 : the starting positions of cars on a racecourse
4 : a device in a photocomposer on which are located the characters to be exposed as the text is composed

grid·der \'gri-dər\ *noun* (1928)
: a football player

grid·dle \'gri-d°l\ *noun* [Middle English *gredil* gridiron, from Old North French, from Latin *craticulum*, diminutive of *cratis* wickerwork — more at HURDLE] (14th century)

: a flat metal surface or pan on which food is cooked by dry heat

griddle cake *noun* (1783)
: PANCAKE

grid·iron \'grid-ˌī(-ə)rn\ *noun* [Middle English *gredire*] (14th century)
1 : a grate for broiling food
2 : something consisting of or covered with a network
3 : a football field

grid·lock \-ˌläk\ *noun* (1980)
1 : a traffic jam in which a grid of intersecting streets is so completely congested that no vehicular movement is possible
2 : a situation resembling a gridlock
— **gridlock** *transitive verb*

grief \'grēf\ *noun* [Middle English *gref*, from Middle French, heavy, grave, from (assumed) Vulgar Latin *grevis*, alteration of Latin *gravis*] (15th century)
1 *obsolete* : GRIEVANCE 3
2 a : deep and poignant distress caused by or as if by bereavement **b** : a cause of such suffering
3 a : an unfortunate outcome : DISASTER — used chiefly in the phrase *come to grief* **b** : MISHAP, MISADVENTURE **c** : TROUBLE, ANNOYANCE ⟨enough *grief* for one day⟩
synonym see SORROW

griev·ance \'grē-vən(t)s\ *noun* (14th century)
1 *obsolete* : SUFFERING, DISTRESS
2 : a cause of distress (as an unsatisfactory working condition) felt to afford reason for complaint or resistance
3 : the formal expression of a grievance : COMPLAINT
synonym see INJUSTICE

grievance committee *noun* (1927)
: a committee formed by a labor union or by employer and employees jointly to discuss and where possible to eliminate grievances

griev·ant \-vənt\ *noun* (1958)
: one who submits a grievance for arbitration

grieve \'grēv\ *verb* **grieved; griev·ing** [Middle English *greven*, from Old French *grever*, from Latin *gravare* to burden, from *gravis* heavy, grave; akin to Greek *barys* heavy, Sanskrit *guru*] (13th century)
transitive verb
: to cause to suffer : DISTRESS
intransitive verb
: to feel grief : SORROW
— **griev·er** *noun*

griev·ous \'grē-vəs\ *adjective* (13th century)
1 : causing or characterized by severe pain, suffering, or sorrow ⟨a *grievous* wound⟩ ⟨a *grievous* loss⟩
2 : OPPRESSIVE, ONEROUS ⟨*grievous* costs of war⟩
3 : SERIOUS, GRAVE ⟨*grievous* fault⟩

◇ **WORD HISTORY**

gregarious *Gregarious*, which is not usually an unfavorable word, is the improbable linguistic cousin of *egregious*, which is now usually used of something conspicuously bad. Both have as their base *grex,* the Latin word for "herd" or "flock." Whereas *egregious* is etymologically "apart from the herd or flock," *gregarious* literally means "of or relating to a herd or flock." When *gregarious* first appeared in English in the 17th century, with the meaning "inclined to associate with others of one's kind," it was used of animals naturally living and breeding in groups. Not till the next century was the word applied to people with a marked fondness for companionship. See in addition EGREGIOUS.

\ə\ abut \ᵊ\ kitten \ər\ further \a\ ash \ā\ ace
\ä\ mop, mar \au̇\ out \ch\ chin \e\ bet \ē\ easy
\g\ go \i\ hit \ī\ ice \j\ job \ŋ\ sing \ō\ go
\ȯ\ law \ȯi\ boy \th\ thin \t͟h\ the \ü\ loot \u̇\ foot
\y\ yet \zh\ vision *see also* Guide to Pronunciation

— **griev·ous·ly** *adverb*

— **griev·ous·ness** *noun*

grif·fin *or* **grif·fon** \'gri-fən\ *noun* [Middle English *griffon*, from Middle French *grifon*, from *grif*, from Latin *gryphus*, from Greek *gryp-*, *gryps*] (14th century)
: a mythical animal typically having the head, forepart, and wings of an eagle and the body, hind legs, and tail of a lion

grif·fon \'gri-fən\ *noun* [French, literally, griffin] (1882)
1 : BRUSSELS GRIFFON
2 : WIREHAIRED POINTING GRIFFON

griffin

grift \'grift\ *transitive verb* [*grift*, noun, perhaps alteration of *graft*] (1915)
slang : to obtain (money) illicitly (as in a confidence game)

— **grift** *noun, slang*

— **grift·er** *noun, slang*

grig \'grig\ *noun* [Middle English *grege*] (1566)
: a lively lighthearted usually small or young person

gri·gri *variant of* GRIS-GRIS

¹grill \'gril\ *transitive verb* (1668)
1 : to broil on a grill; *also* : to fry or toast on a griddle
2 a : to torment as if by broiling **b** : to question intensely ⟨the police *grilled* the suspect⟩

— **grill·er** *noun*

²grill *noun* [French *gril*, from Latin *craticulum* — more at GRIDDLE] (1685)
1 : a cooking utensil of parallel bars on which food is exposed to heat (as from charcoal or electricity)
2 : food that is broiled usually on a grill — compare MIXED GRILL
3 : a usually informal restaurant or dining room

gril·lage \'gri-lij\ *noun* [French, from *griller* to supply with grillwork, from *gril*] (1776)
1 : a framework of timber or steel for support in marshy or treacherous soil
2 : a framework for supporting a load (as a column)

grille *or* **grill** \'gril\ *noun* [French *grille*, alteration of Old French *greille*, from Latin *craticula*, diminutive of *cratis* wickerwork — more at HURDLE] (1686)
1 : a grating forming a barrier or screen; *especially* : an ornamental one at the front end of an automobile
2 : an opening covered with a grille

grill·room \'gril-,rüm, -,rum\ *noun* (1883)
: GRILL 3

grill·work \'gril-,wərk\ *noun* (1896)
: work constituting or resembling a grille

grilse \'grils\ *noun, plural* **grilse** [Middle English *grills*] (15th century)
: a young Atlantic salmon returning to its native river to spawn for the first time after one winter at sea; *broadly* : any of various salmon at such a stage of development

grim \'grim\ *adjective* **grim·mer; grim·mest** [Middle English, from Old English *grimm;* akin to Old High German *grimm* fierce, Greek *chremetizein* to neigh] (before 12th century)
1 : fierce in disposition or action : SAVAGE
2 a : stern or forbidding in action or appearance ⟨a *grim* taskmaster⟩ **b** : SOMBER, GLOOMY
3 : ghastly, repellent, or sinister in character ⟨a *grim* tale⟩
4 : UNFLINCHING, UNYIELDING ⟨*grim* determination⟩

— **grim·ly** *adverb*

— **grim·ness** *noun*

gri·mace \'gri-məs, gri-'mās\ *noun* [French, from Middle French, alteration of *grimache*, of Germanic origin; akin to Old English *grīma* mask] (1651)
: a facial expression usually of disgust or disapproval

— **grimace** *intransitive verb*

— **gri·mac·er** *noun*

gri·mal·kin \gri-'mo̅(l)-kən, -'mal-\ *noun* [*gray* + *malkin*] (1630)
: a domestic cat; *especially* : an old female cat

grime \'grīm\ *noun* [Middle Dutch *grime* soot, mask; akin to Old English *grīma* mask] (14th century)
: soot, smut, or dirt adhering to or embedded in a surface; *broadly* : accumulated dirtiness and disorder

— **grime** *transitive verb*

Grimm's law \'grimz-\ *noun* [Jacob *Grimm*] (1838)
: a statement in historical linguistics: Proto-Indo-European voiceless stops became Proto-Germanic voiceless fricatives (as in Greek *pyr*, *treis*, *kardia* compared with English *fire*, *three*, *heart*), Proto-Indo-European voiced stops became Proto-Germanic voiceless stops (as in Latin *duo*, *genus* compared with English *two*, *kin*), and Proto-Indo-European voiced aspirated stops became Proto-Germanic voiced fricatives (as in Sanskrit *nābhi*, *madhya* "mid" compared with English *navel*, Old Norse *mithr* "mid")

grim reaper *noun, often G&R capitalized* (circa 1927)
: death especially when personified as a man or skeleton with a scythe

grimy \'grī-mē\ *adjective* **grim·i·er; -est** (1612)
: full of or covered with grime : DIRTY

— **grim·i·ness** *noun*

grin \'grin\ *intransitive verb* **grinned; grin·ning** [Middle English *grennen*, from Old English *grennian;* akin to Old High German *grennen* to snarl] (before 12th century)
: to draw back the lips so as to show the teeth especially in amusement or laughter; *broadly* : SMILE

— **grin** *noun*

— **grin·ner** *noun*

— **grin·ning·ly** \'gri-niŋ-lē\ *adverb*

grinch \'grinch\ *noun* [from the *Grinch*, character in the children's story *How the Grinch Stole Christmas* (1957) by Dr. Seuss] (1979)
: KILLJOY, SPOILSPORT

¹grind \'grīnd\ *verb* **ground** \'grȧund\; **grind·ing** [Middle English, from Old English *grindan;* akin to Latin *frendere* to crush, grind] (before 12th century)
transitive verb
1 : to reduce to powder or small fragments by friction (as in a mill or with the teeth)
2 : to wear down, polish, or sharpen by friction ⟨*grind* an ax⟩
3 a : OPPRESS, HARASS **b** : to weaken or destroy gradually — usually used with *down* ⟨poverty *ground* her spirit down⟩
4 a : to press together with a rotating motion ⟨*grind* the teeth⟩ **b** : to rub or press harshly ⟨*ground* the cigarette out⟩
5 : to operate or produce by turning a crank ⟨*grind* a hand organ⟩
intransitive verb
1 : to perform the operation of grinding
2 : to become pulverized, polished, or sharpened by friction
3 : to move with difficulty or friction especially so as to make a grating noise ⟨gears *grinding*⟩
4 : DRUDGE; *especially* : to study hard ⟨*grind* for an exam⟩
5 : to rotate the hips in an erotic manner (as in a burlesque striptease)

— **grind·ing·ly** \'grīn-diŋ-lē\ *adverb*

²grind *noun* (13th century)
1 a : an act of grinding **b** : the sound of grinding
2 a : dreary, monotonous, or difficult labor, study, or routine **b** : one who works or studies excessively

3 : the result of grinding; *also* : material ground to a particular degree of fineness ⟨a drip *grind* of coffee⟩
4 : the act of rotating the hips in an erotic manner

synonym see WORK

grind·er \'grīn-dər\ *noun* (14th century)
1 a : MOLAR **b** *plural* : TEETH
2 : one that grinds
3 : a machine or device for grinding
4 : SUBMARINE 2

grind house *noun* (1927)
: an often shabby movie theater having continuous showings especially of pornographic or violent films

grind out *transitive verb* (1868)
: to produce in a mechanical way

grind·stone \'grīn-,stōn\ *noun* (13th century)
1 : MILLSTONE 1
2 : a flat circular stone of natural sandstone that revolves on an axle and is used for grinding, shaping, or smoothing

grin·go \'griŋ-(,)gō\ *noun, plural* **gringos** [Spanish, alteration of *griego* Greek, stranger, from Latin *Graecus* Greek] (1849)
: a foreigner in Spain or Latin America especially when of English or American origin; *broadly* : a non-Hispanic person — often used disparagingly ◇

gri·ot \'grē-,ō\ *noun* [French] (1906)
: any of a class of musician-entertainers of western Africa whose performances include tribal histories and genealogies

¹grip \'grip\ *transitive verb* **gripped; grip·ping** [Middle English *grippen*, from Old English *grippan;* akin to Old English *grīpan*] (before 12th century)
1 : to seize or hold firmly
2 : to hold the interest of strongly ⟨a story that *grips* the reader⟩

— **grip·per** *noun*

— **grip·ping·ly** \'gri-piŋ-lē\ *adverb*

²grip *noun* (before 12th century)
1 a : a strong or tenacious grasp **b** : strength in gripping **c** : manner or style of gripping
2 a : a firm tenacious hold typically giving control, mastery, or understanding **b** : mental grasp
3 : a part or device for gripping
4 : a part by which something is grasped; *especially* : HANDLE
5 : SUITCASE
6 : STAGEHAND

¹gripe \'grīp\ *verb* **griped; grip·ing** [Middle English, from Old English *grīpan;* akin to Old High German *grīfan* to grasp, Lithuanian *griebti*] (before 12th century)
transitive verb
1 *archaic* : SEIZE, GRASP
2 a : AFFLICT, DISTRESS **b** : IRRITATE, VEX
3 : to cause pinching and spasmodic pain in the bowels of
intransitive verb
1 : to experience gripes

◇ **WORD HISTORY**

gringo In English the expression "it's all Greek to me" is nearly equivalent to "I haven't a clue as to what it means." Similarly, Spanish *hablar en griego* means literally "to speak Greek" and figuratively "to speak unintelligibly." In the 18th century, *gringo*, usually explained as an alteration of *griego*, appeared in Spanish with the same sense "unintelligible speech," and became common in Latin America in the meaning "foreigner." *Gringo* made its way into English because Mexicans used it freely to refer derogatorily to Anglo-Americans. There is no basis to the story that American soldiers during the Mexican War (1846–48) often sang Robert Burns's "Green Grow the Rashes, O!" and that "green grow" was misinterpreted as *gringo* by the Mexicans.

2 : to complain with grumbling
— **grip·er** *noun*

²gripe *noun* (13th century)
1 *archaic* **:** CLUTCH, GRASP; *broadly* **:** CONTROL, MASTERY
2 : a pinching spasmodic intestinal pain — usually used in plural
3 : GRIEVANCE, COMPLAINT

grip·man \'grip-mən, -ˌman\ *noun* (1886)
: a cable car operator

grippe \'grip\ *noun* [French, literally, seizure] (1776)
: an acute febrile contagious virus disease; *especially* **:** INFLUENZA 1
— **grippy** \'gri-pē\ *adjective*

grip·sack \'grip-ˌsak\ *noun* (1877)
: SUITCASE

gri·saille \gri-'zī, -'zā(ə)l\ *noun* [French, from *gris* gray, from Middle French — more at GRIZZLE] (1848)
: decoration in tones of a single color and especially gray designed to produce a three-dimensional effect

Gri·sel·da \gri-'zel-də\ *noun* [Middle English, from Italian]
: a woman of humble origins in medieval legend who endures tests of wifely patience laid on her by her wellborn husband

gris·eo·ful·vin \ˌgri-zē-ō-'ful-vən, ˌgri-sē-, -'fəl-\ *noun* [New Latin *griseofulvum*, specific epithet of *Penicillium griseofulvum*, mold from which it is obtained] (1939)
: an antibiotic $C_{17}H_{17}ClO_6$ used systematically in treating superficial fungal infections

gri·sette \gri-'zet\ *noun* [French, grisette, cheap unbleached cloth, from *gris*] (1723)
1 : a young French working-class woman
2 : a young woman combining part-time prostitution with some other occupation

gris–gris \'grē-(ˌ)grē\ *noun, plural* **gris–gris** \-(ˌ)grēz\ [French] (1698)
: an amulet or incantation used chiefly by people of black African ancestry

gris·ly \'griz-lē\ *adjective* **gris·li·er; -est** [Middle English, from Old English *grislic*, from *gris-* (akin to Old English *āgrīsan* to fear); akin to Old High German *grīsenlīh* terrible] (12th century)
1 : inspiring horror or intense fear ⟨houses that were dark and *grisly* under the blank, cold sky —D. H. Lawrence⟩
2 : inspiring disgust or distaste ⟨a *grisly* account of the fire⟩
synonym see GHASTLY
— **gris·li·ness** *noun*

grist \'grist\ *noun* [Middle English, from Old English *grīst*; akin to Old English *grindan* to grind] (before 12th century)
1 a : grain or a batch of grain for grinding **b :** the product obtained from a grist of grain including the flour or meal and the grain offals
2 : a required or usual amount
3 : matter of interest or value forming the basis of a story or analysis
4 : something turned to advantage or use — used especially in the phrase *grist for one's mill*

gris·tle \'gri-səl, -zəl\ *noun* [Middle English *gristil*, from Old English *gristle*; akin to Middle Low German *gristel* gristle] (before 12th century)
: CARTILAGE; *broadly* **:** tough cartilaginous, tendinous, or fibrous matter especially in table meats

gris·tly \'gri-sə-lē, 'gris-lē, 'griz-\ *adjective* **gris·tli·er; -est** (14th century)
: consisting of or containing gristle ⟨*gristly* steak⟩
— **gris·tli·ness** *noun*

grist·mill \'grist-ˌmil\ *noun* (1602)
: a mill for grinding grain

¹grit \'grit\ *noun* [Middle English *grete*, from Old English *grēot*; akin to Old High German *grioz* sand] (before 12th century)

1 a : SAND, GRAVEL **b :** a hard sharp granule (as of sand); *also* **:** material (as many abrasives) composed of such granules
2 : any of several sandstones
3 a : the structure of a stone that adapts it to grinding **b :** the size of abrasive particles usually expressed as their mesh
4 : firmness of mind or spirit **:** unyielding courage in the face of hardship or danger
5 *capitalized* **:** a Liberal in Canadian politics

²grit *verb* **grit·ted; grit·ting** (1762)
intransitive verb
: to give forth a grating sound
transitive verb
1 : to cause (as one's teeth) to grind or grate
2 : to cover or spread with grit; *especially* **:** to smooth (as marble) with a coarse abrasive

grith \'grith\ *noun* [Middle English, from Old English, from Old Norse, security] (before 12th century)
: peace, security, or sanctuary imposed or guaranteed in early medieval England under various special conditions

grits \'grits\ *noun plural but singular or plural in construction* [perhaps partly from ¹grit, partly from dialect *grit* coarse meal, from Old English *grytt*; akin to Old English *grēot*] (1579)
: coarsely ground hulled grain; *especially* **:** ground hominy with the germ removed

grit·ty \'gri-tē\ *adjective* **grit·ti·er; -est** (1598)
1 : containing or resembling grit
2 : courageously persistent **:** PLUCKY
3 : having strong qualities of tough uncompromising realism ⟨a *gritty* novel⟩
— **grit·ti·ly** \'gri-tᵊl-ē\ *adverb*
— **grit·ti·ness** \'gri-tē-nəs\ *noun*

¹griz·zle \'gri-zəl\ *noun* [Middle English *grisel*, adjective, gray, from Middle French, from *gris*, of Germanic origin; akin to Old High German *grīs* gray] (1601)
1 *archaic* **:** gray hair
2 a : a roan coat pattern or color **b :** a gray or roan animal

²griz·zle *verb* **griz·zled; griz·zling** \'griz-liŋ, 'gri-zə-\ (1740)
transitive verb
: to make grayish
intransitive verb
1 : GRIPE, GRUMBLE
2 : to become grayish

griz·zled \'gri-zəld\ *adjective* (15th century)
: sprinkled or streaked with gray **:** GRAYING ⟨a *grizzled* beard⟩

¹griz·zly \'griz-lē\ *adjective* **griz·zli·er; -est** (1594)
: GRIZZLED

²grizzly *variant of* GRISLY

grizzly bear *noun* (1791)
: a very large brown bear (*Ursus arctos horribilis*) of the uplands of western North America — called also *grizzly*

groan \'grōn\ *verb* [Middle English *gronen*, from Old English *grānian*; akin to Old High German *grīnan* to growl] (before 12th century)
intransitive verb
1 : to utter a deep moan indicative of pain, grief, or annoyance
2 : to make a harsh sound (as of creaking) under sudden or prolonged strain
transitive verb
: to utter or express with groaning
— **groan** *noun*

groan·er \'grō-nər\ *noun* (1795)
1 : one that groans
2 : a stale or corny joke, observation, or story

¹groat \'grōt\ *noun* [Middle English *grotes*, plural, from Old English *grotan*, plural of *grot*; akin to Old English *grēot* grit] (12th century)
1 *usually plural but singular or plural in construction* **:** hulled grain broken into fragments larger than grits
2 : a grain (as of oats) exclusive of the hull

²groat *noun* [Middle English *groot*, from Middle Dutch] (14th century)
: an old British coin worth four pennies

gro·cer \'grō-sər, -shər\ *noun* [Middle English, from Middle French *grossier* wholesaler, from *gros* coarse, wholesale — more at GROSS] (15th century)
: a dealer in staple foodstuffs, meats, produce, and dairy products and usually household supplies

gro·cery \'grōs-rē, 'grō-sə-; 'grōsh-rē\ *noun, plural* **-cer·ies** (15th century)
1 *plural* **:** commodities sold by a grocer — usually singular in British usage
2 : a grocer's store

grog \'gräg\ *noun* [*Old Grog*, nickname of Edward Vernon (died 1757) English admiral responsible for diluting the sailors' rum] (1770)
1 : alcoholic liquor; *especially* **:** liquor (as rum) cut with water and now often served hot with lemon juice and sugar sometimes added
2 : refractory materials (as crushed pottery and firebricks) used in the manufacture of refractory products (as crucibles) to reduce shrinkage in drying and firing ◇

grog·gy \'grä-gē\ *adjective* **grog·gi·er; -est** [*grog*] (1832)
: weak and unsteady on the feet or in action
— **grog·gi·ly** \'grä-gə-lē\ *adverb*
— **grog·gi·ness** \'grä-gē-nəs\ *noun*

gro·gram \'grä-grəm, 'grō-\ *noun* [Middle French *gros grain* coarse texture] (1562)
: a coarse loosely woven fabric of silk, silk and mohair, or silk and wool — compare GROSGRAIN

grog·shop \'gräg-ˌshäp\ *noun* (1790)
chiefly British **:** a usually low-class barroom

¹groin \'grȯin\ *noun* [alteration of Middle English *grynde*, from Old English, abyss; akin to Old English *grund* ground] (circa 1532)
1 : the fold or depression marking the juncture of the lower abdomen and the inner part of the thigh; *also* **:** the region of this line
2 a : the projecting curved line along which two intersecting vaults meet **b :** a rib that covers this edge
3 : a rigid structure built out from a shore to protect the shore

groin 2a

◇ **WORD HISTORY**
grog The English admiral Edward Vernon (1684–1757) is reputed to have been in the habit of wearing a grogram cloak and to have thereby won the nickname "Old Grog" among the sailors under his command. Seamen of the Royal Navy in the West Indies had been given by custom a half-pint of rum as a daily ration, but in 1740 Vernon, alarmed at damage to the physical and moral health of his crews, ordered that the rum should be diluted with water. This mixture, not immediately approved, was christened *grog*, after its godfather. *Grog* eventually gained in popularity, however, and the word was sometimes used as a general term for any liquor, even undiluted. A drunkard could be called *groggy*, and now anyone whose mental state seems impaired, whether it be from drugs or from a blow or from fatigue, can be labeled with that word.

\ə\ abut \ᵊ\ kitten \ər\ further \a\ ash \ā\ ace
\ä\ mop, mar \au̇\ out \ch\ chin \e\ bet \ē\ easy
\g\ go \i\ hit \ī\ ice \j\ job \ŋ\ sing \ō\ go
\ȯ\ law \ȯi\ boy \th\ thin \t͟h\ the \ü\ loot \u̇\ foot
\y\ yet \zh\ vision *see also* Guide to Pronunciation

from erosion, to trap sand, or to direct a current for scouring a channel

²**groin** *transitive verb* (circa 1816)
: to build or equip with groins

grom·met \'grä-mət, 'grə-\ *noun* [obsolete French *gormette* curb of a bridle] (1626)
1 : a flexible loop that serves as a fastening, support, or reinforcement
2 : an eyelet of firm material to strengthen or protect an opening or to insulate or protect something passed through it

grom·well \'gräm-,wel, -wəl\ *noun* [Middle English *gromil,* from Middle French] (14th century)
: any of a genus (*Lithospermum*) of plants of the borage family having polished white stony nutlets

¹**groom** \'grüm, 'grům\ *noun* [Middle English *grom*] (14th century)
1 *archaic* : MAN, FELLOW
2 a (1) *archaic* : MANSERVANT (2) : one of several officers of the English royal household **b** : a person responsible for the feeding, exercising, and stabling of horses
3 : BRIDEGROOM

²**groom** (1809)
transitive verb
1 : to clean and condition (as a horse or dog)
2 : to make neat or attractive ⟨an impeccably *groomed* woman⟩
3 : to get into readiness for a specific objective : PREPARE ⟨was being *groomed* as a presidential candidate⟩
intransitive verb
: to groom oneself

groom·er \'grü-mər\ *noun* (circa 1890)
: one who grooms (as dogs)

grooms·man \'grümz-mən, 'grůmz-\ *noun* (1698)
: a male friend who attends a bridegroom at his wedding

¹**groove** \'grüv\ *noun* [Middle English *groof;* akin to Old English *grafan* to dig — more at GRAVE] (1659)
1 : a long narrow channel or depression
2 a : a fixed routine : RUT **b** : a situation suited to one's abilities or interests : NICHE
3 : top form ⟨a great talker when he is in the *groove*⟩
4 : the middle of the strike zone in baseball where a pitch is most easily hit ⟨a fastball right in the *groove*⟩
5 : an enjoyable or exciting experience
6 : a pronounced enjoyable rhythm

²**groove** *verb* **grooved; groov·ing** (1686)
transitive verb
1 a : to make a groove in **b** : to join by a groove
2 : to perfect by repeated practice ⟨*grooved* her golf swing⟩
3 : to throw (a pitch) in the groove
intransitive verb
1 : to become joined or fitted by a groove
2 : to form a groove
3 : to enjoy oneself intensely
4 : to interact harmoniously ⟨contemporary minds and rock *groove* together —Benjamin DeMott⟩
— **groov·er** *noun*

groovy \'grü-vē\ *adjective* **groov·i·er; -est** (circa 1937)
1 : MARVELOUS, WONDERFUL, EXCELLENT ⟨felt that this poetry was . . . enjoyable, not to mention *groovy* —R. M. Muccigrosso⟩
2 : HIP ⟨a younger and *groovier* audience —Robert MacKenzie⟩

grope \'grōp\ *verb* **groped; grop·ing** [Middle English, from Old English *grāpian;* akin to Old English *grīpan* to seize] (before 12th century)
intransitive verb
1 : to feel about blindly or uncertainly in search ⟨*grope* for the light switch⟩
2 : to look for something blindly or uncertainly ⟨*grope* for the right words⟩
3 : to feel one's way

transitive verb
1 : FEEL UP
2 : to find (as one's way) by groping
— **grope** *noun*
— **grop·er** *noun*

gros·beak \'grōs-,bēk\ *noun* [part translation of French *grosbec,* from *gros* thick + *bec* beak] (circa 1678)
: any of several finches of Europe or America having large stout conical bills

gro·schen \'grō-shən, 'grò-\ *noun, plural* **groschen** [German] (1946)
— see *schilling* at MONEY table

gros·grain \'grō-,grān\ *noun* [French *gros grain* coarse texture] (1869)
: a strong close-woven corded fabric usually of silk or rayon and often with cotton filler — compare GROGRAM

¹**gross** \'grōs\ *adjective* [Middle English, from Middle French *gros* thick, coarse, from Latin *grossus*] (14th century)
1 a *archaic* : immediately obvious **b** (1) : glaringly noticeable usually because of inexcusable badness or objectionableness ⟨*gross* error⟩ (2) : OUT-AND-OUT, UTTER ⟨*gross* injustice⟩ **c** : visible without the aid of a microscope
2 a : BIG, BULKY; *especially* : excessively fat **b** : growing or spreading with excessive luxuriance
3 a : of, relating to, or dealing with general aspects or broad distinctions **b** : consisting of an overall total exclusive of deductions ⟨*gross* income⟩ — compare NET
4 : made up of material or perceptible elements
5 *archaic* : not fastidious in taste : UNDISCRIMINATING
6 a : coarse in nature or behavior : UNREFINED **b** : gravely deficient in civility or decency : crudely vulgar ⟨merely *gross,* a scatological rather than a pornographic impropriety —Aldous Huxley⟩ **c** *slang* : inspiring disgust or distaste ⟨that sandwich looks *gross*⟩
7 : deficient in knowledge : IGNORANT, UNTUTORED
synonym see COARSE, FLAGRANT
— **gross·ly** *adverb*
— **gross·ness** *noun*

²**gross** *noun* (1579)
1 *obsolete* : AMOUNT, SUM
2 : overall total exclusive of deductions

³**gross** *transitive verb* (1884)
: to earn or bring in (an overall total) exclusive of deductions (as for taxes or expenses)
— **gross·er** *noun*

⁴**gross** *noun, plural* **gross** [Middle English *groce,* from Middle French *grosse,* from feminine of *gros*] (14th century)
: an aggregate of 12 dozen things ⟨a *gross* of pencils⟩

gross anatomy *noun* (1888)
: a branch of anatomy that deals with the macroscopic structure of tissues and organs

gross national product *noun* (1947)
: the total value of the goods and services produced by the residents of a nation during a specified period (as a year)

gross–out \'grō-,saůt\ *noun, often attributive* (1973)
: something inspiring disgust or distaste

gross out *transitive verb* (1968)
: to offend, insult, or disgust by something gross

gros·su·lar \'gräs-yə-lər\ *noun* [New Latin *Grossularia,* genus name of the gooseberry] (1819)
: a variety of garnet that is most commonly green and consists of calcium aluminum silicate

gros·su·la·rite \-lə-,rīt\ *noun* [German *Grossularit,* from New Latin *Grossularia*] (circa 1847)
: GROSSULAR

gro·szy \'grò-shē\ *also* **grosz** *or* **grosze** \'grösh\ *noun, plural* **groszy** [Polish] (1916)
— see *zloty* at MONEY table

grot \'grät\ *noun* [Middle French *grotte,* from Italian *grotta*] (1506)
: GROTTO

¹**gro·tesque** \grō-'tesk\ *noun* [Middle French & Old Italian; Middle French, from Old Italian (*pittura*) *grottesca,* literally, cave painting, feminine of *grottesco* of a cave, from *grotta*] (1561)
1 a : a style of decorative art characterized by fanciful or fantastic human and animal forms often interwoven with foliage or similar figures that may distort the natural into absurdity, ugliness, or caricature **b** : a piece of work in this style
2 : one that is grotesque
: SANS SERIF ◇

²**grotesque** *adjective* (1603)
: of, relating to, or having the characteristics of the grotesque: as **a** : FANCIFUL, BIZARRE **b** : absurdly incongruous **c** : departing markedly from the natural, the expected, or the typical
synonym see FANTASTIC
— **gro·tesque·ly** *adverb*
— **gro·tesque·ness** *noun*

gro·tes·que·rie *also* **gro·tes·que·ry** \grō-'tes-kə-rē\ *noun, plural* **-ries** [*grotesque* + French *-erie* -ery] (circa 1666)
1 : something that is grotesque
2 : the quality or state of being grotesque : GROTESQUENESS

grot·to \'grä-,tō\ *noun, plural* **grottoes** *also* **grottos** [Italian *grotta, grotto,* from Latin *crypta* cavern, crypt] (1617)
1 : CAVE
2 : an artificial recess or structure made to resemble a natural cave

grot·ty \'grä-tē\ *adjective* **grot·ti·er; -est** [origin unknown] (1964)
chiefly British : wretchedly shabby : of poor quality

grouch \'graůch\ *noun* [probably alteration of *grutch* (grudge)] (circa 1895)
1 a : a fit of bad temper **b** : GRUDGE, COMPLAINT
2 : a habitually irritable or complaining person : GRUMBLER
— **grouch** *intransitive verb*

grouchy \'graů-chē\ *adjective* **grouch·i·er; -est** (circa 1895)
: given to grumbling : PEEVISH
— **grouch·i·ly** \-chə-lē\ *adverb*
— **grouch·i·ness** \-chē-nəs\ *noun*

¹**ground** \'graůnd\ *noun, often attributive* [Middle English, from Old English *grund;* akin to Old High German *grunt* ground] (before 12th century)

◇ **WORD HISTORY**
grotesque In the middle of the 15th century at Rome, when antiquarian interest in the city's cultural legacy was high, remnants of ancient Roman decorative painting were found in underground chambers of the Domus Aurea, the vast palace of the emperor Nero that had been largely demolished and covered over by newer structures. Inspired by these finds, Renaissance painters and sculptors created a style of decorative art with fantastic combinations of human and animal forms interwoven with strange fruits and flowers. Examples of the style were dubbed after their ancient inspiration *grottesche,* short for *pitture grottesche,* literally, "cave paintings." The adjective *grottesco,* which acquired the sense " having the characteristics of *grottesche*" was borrowed into French and English, with the English word eventually copying the French form. By about the middle of the 17th century *grotesque* in both languages had developed the more extended senses "bizarre" or "absurdly incongruous" that the word still has today.

1 a : the bottom of a body of water **b** *plural* (1) **:** SEDIMENT 1 (2) **:** ground coffee beans after brewing
2 a : a basis for belief, action, or argument ⟨*ground* for complaint⟩ — often used in plural **b** (1) **:** a fundamental logical condition (2) **:** a basic metaphysical cause
3 a : a surrounding area **:** BACKGROUND **b :** material that serves as a substratum
4 a : the surface of the earth **b :** an area used for a particular purpose ⟨parade *ground*⟩ ⟨fishing *grounds*⟩ **c** *plural* **:** the area around and belonging to a house or other building **d :** an area to be won or defended in or as if in battle **e :** an area of knowledge or special interest ⟨covered a lot of *ground* in his lecture⟩
5 a : SOIL, EARTH **b :** a special soil
6 a : an object that makes an electrical connection with the earth **b :** a large conducting body (as the earth) used as a common return for an electric circuit and as an arbitrary zero of potential **c :** electric connection with a ground
7 : a football offense utilizing primarily running plays
— from the ground up 1 : entirely new or afresh **2 :** from top to bottom **:** THOROUGHLY
— into the ground : beyond what is necessary or tolerable **:** to exhaustion ⟨labored an issue *into the ground* —*Newsweek*⟩
— off the ground : in or as if in flight **:** off to a good start ⟨the program never got *off the ground*⟩
— on the ground : at the scene of action
— to ground 1 : into a burrow ⟨the fox went *to ground*⟩ **2 :** into hiding ⟨might need to make a run for it and go *to ground* someplace —Edward Hoagland⟩
²ground (13th century)
transitive verb
1 a : to bring to or place on the ground **b :** to cause to run aground
2 a : to provide a reason or justification for ⟨our fears about technological change may be well *grounded* —L. K. Williams⟩ **b :** to furnish with a foundation of knowledge **:** BASE ⟨an understanding . . . that is *grounded* in fact —Michael Kimmelman⟩
3 : to connect electrically with a ground
4 a : to restrict to the ground ⟨*ground* a pilot⟩ **b :** to prohibit from taking part in some usual activities ⟨*grounded* her for a week⟩
5 : to throw (a football) intentionally to the ground to avoid being tackled for a loss
intransitive verb
1 : to have a ground or basis **:** RELY
2 : to run aground
3 : to hit a grounder
³ground *past and past participle of* GRIND
ground ball *noun* (1857)
: a batted baseball that bounds or rolls along the ground
ground bass *noun* (1699)
: a short bass passage continually repeated below constantly changing melody and harmony
ground beetle *noun* (1848)
: any of a large cosmopolitan family (Carabidae) of soil-inhabiting usually carnivorous often shiny black or metallic beetles commonly having fused elytra
ground·break·er \'graún(d)-ˌbrā-kər\ *noun* (1940)
: one that innovates **:** PIONEER
ground·break·ing \-ˌbrā-kiŋ\ *adjective* (1907)
: markedly innovative ⟨has written a *groundbreaking* work⟩
ground·burst \-ˌbərst\ *noun* (circa 1951)
: the detonation of a nuclear warhead at ground level
ground–cher·ry \'graún(d)-ˈcher-ē\ *noun* (1807)
: any of numerous chiefly New World plants (genus *Physalis*) of the nightshade family with pulpy fruits in papery husks; *also* **:** the fruit of the ground-cherry

ground cloth *noun* (1931)
: a waterproof sheet placed on the ground for protection (as of a sleeping bag) against soil moisture
ground cover *noun* (1900)
1 : the small plants on a forest floor except young trees
2 a : a planting of low plants (as ivy) that covers the ground in place of turf **b :** a plant adapted for use as ground cover
ground crew *noun* (1934)
: the mechanics and technicians who maintain and service an airplane
ground–effect machine *noun* [from the lift provided by compression of air between the vehicle and the ground] (1962)
: HOVERCRAFT
ground·er \'graún-dər\ *noun* (circa 1867)
: GROUND BALL
ground·fish \'graún(d)-ˌfish\ *noun* (1856)
: a bottom fish; *especially* **:** a marine fish (as a cod, haddock, pollack, or flounder) of commercial importance
ground floor *noun* (1601)
1 : the floor of a house most nearly on a level with the ground — compare FIRST FLOOR
2 : a favorable position or privileged opportunity usually obtained by early participants — used especially in the phrase *in on the ground floor*
ground glass *noun* (1848)
: glass with a light-diffusing surface produced by etching or abrading
ground·hog \'graún(d)-ˌhóg, -ˌhäg\ *noun* (1742)
: WOODCHUCK
Groundhog Day *noun* [from the legend that a groundhog emerging from its burrow returns to hibernate if it sees its shadow on this day] (1871)
: February 2 that traditionally indicates six more weeks of winter if sunny or an early spring if cloudy
ground·ing \'graún-diŋ\ *noun* (1644)
: training or instruction in the fundamentals of a field of knowledge
ground ivy *noun* (14th century)
: a trailing mint (*Glechoma hederacea*) with rounded leaves and blue-purple flowers
ground·less \'graún(d)-ləs\ *adjective* (1620)
: having no ground or foundation ⟨*groundless* fears⟩
— ground·less·ly *adverb*
— ground·less·ness *noun*
ground·ling \'graún(d)-liŋ\ *noun* (1602)
1 a : a spectator who stood in the pit of an Elizabethan theater **b :** a person of unsophisticated taste
2 : one that lives or works on or near the ground
ground loop *noun* (1928)
: a sharp uncontrollable turn made by an aircraft on the ground and usually caused by an unbalanced drag (as from a wingtip touching the ground)
ground·mass \'graún(d)-ˌmas\ *noun* (1879)
: the fine-grained or glassy base of a porphyry in which the larger distinct crystals are embedded
ground meristem *noun* (1938)
: the part of a primary apical meristem remaining after differentiation of protoderm and procambium
ground·nut \'graún(d)-ˌnət\ *noun* (1602)
1 a : any of several plants having edible tuberous roots; *especially* **:** a North American leguminous vine (*Apios americana*) with pinnate leaves and clusters of brownish purple fragrant flowers **b :** the root of a groundnut
2 *chiefly British* **:** PEANUT
ground·out \'graún-ˌdaút\ *noun* (1965)
: a play in baseball in which a batter is put out after hitting a grounder to an infielder
ground pine *noun* (1551)
1 : a European bugle (*Ajuga chamaepitys*) with a resinous odor

2 : any of several club mosses (especially *Lycopodium clavatum* and *L. complanatum*) with long creeping stems and erect branches
ground plan *noun* (1731)
1 : a plan of a floor of a building as distinguished from an elevation
2 : a first or basic plan
ground rent *noun* (1667)
: the rent paid by a lessee for the use of land especially for building
ground rule *noun* (1890)
1 : a sports rule adopted to modify play on a particular field, court, or course
2 : a rule of procedure ⟨*ground rules* for selecting a superintendent —*American School Board Journal*⟩
¹ground·sel \'graún(d)-səl\ *noun* [Middle English *groundeswele*, from Old English *grundeswelge*, from *grund* ground + *swelgan* to swallow — more at SWALLOW] (before 12th century)
: any of various senecios (as the nearly cosmopolitan weed *Senecio vulgaris*)
²groundsel *noun* [Middle English *ground sille*, from *ground* + *sille* sill] (15th century)
: a foundation timber
ground·sheet \'graún(d)-ˌshēt\ *noun* (1907)
: GROUND CLOTH
grounds·keep·er \'graún(d)z-ˌkē-pər\ *noun* (1903)
: a person who cares for the grounds of a usually large property (as a sports field)
ground sloth *noun* (1860)
: any of various often huge extinct American edentates related to the recent sloths
grounds·man \'graún(d)z-mən\ *noun* (1886) *chiefly British* **:** GROUNDSKEEPER
ground speed *noun* (1917)
: the speed (as of an airplane) with relation to the ground — compare AIRSPEED
ground squirrel *noun* (1688)
: any of various burrowing rodents (especially genus *Spermophilus*) of North America and Eurasia that are related to the squirrels and often live in colonies especially in open areas — called also *spermophile*
ground state *noun* (1926)
: the state of a physical system (as of an atomic nucleus or an atom) having the least energy of all the possible states — called also *ground level*
ground stroke *noun* (1895)
: a stroke made (as in tennis) by hitting a ball that has rebounded from the ground — compare VOLLEY
ground substance *noun* (1882)
: a more or less homogeneous matrix in which the specific differentiated elements of a system are suspended: **a :** the intercellular substance of tissues **b :** CYTOSOL
ground·swell \'graún-ˌswel\ *noun* (1818)
1 *usually* **ground swell :** a broad deep undulation of the ocean caused by an often distant gale or seismic disturbance
2 : a rapid spontaneous growth (as of political opinion) ⟨a *groundswell* of support⟩
ground·wa·ter \-ˌwó-tər, -ˌwä-\ *noun* (circa 1889)
: water within the earth that supplies wells and springs
ground wave *noun* (1925)
: a radio wave that is propagated along the surface of the earth
ground·wood \'graún(d)-ˌwúd\ *noun* [³*ground*] (1885)
: wood ground up and used to make pulp for paper
ground·work \'graún(d)-ˌwərk\ *noun* (15th century)

\ə\ abut \ᵊ\ kitten \ər\ further \a\ ash \ā\ ace
\ä\ mop, mar \aú\ out \ch\ chin \e\ bet \ē\ easy
\g\ go \i\ hit \ī\ ice \j\ job \ŋ\ sing \ō\ go
\ó\ law \ói\ boy \th\ thin \t͟h\ the \ü\ loot \ú\ foot
\y\ yet \zh\ vision *see also* Guide to Pronunciation

: FOUNDATION, BASIS ⟨laid the *groundwork* for a new program⟩; *also* : preparation made beforehand ⟨the *groundwork* was done before the winter tour —Susan Reiter⟩

ground zero *noun* (1946)
1 : the point directly above, below, or at which a nuclear explosion occurs
2 : the center or origin of rapid, intense, or violent activity or change
3 : the very beginning : SQUARE ONE

¹group \'grüp\ *noun, often attributive* [French *groupe*, from Italian *gruppo*, of Germanic origin; akin to Old High German *kropf* craw — more at CROP] (1686)
1 : two or more figures forming a complete unit in a composition
2 a : a number of individuals assembled together or having some unifying relationship **b** : an assemblage of objects regarded as a unit **c** (1) : a military unit consisting of a headquarters and attached battalions (2) : a unit of the U.S. Air Force higher than a squadron and lower than a wing
3 a : an assemblage of related organisms — often used to avoid taxonomic connotations when the kind or degree of relationship is not clearly defined **b** (1) : two or more atoms joined together or sometimes a single atom forming part of a molecule; *especially* : FUNCTIONAL GROUP ⟨a methyl *group*⟩ (2) : an assemblage of elements forming one of the vertical columns of the periodic table **c** : a stratigraphic division comprising rocks deposited during an era
4 : a mathematical set that is closed under a binary associative operation, contains an identity element, and has an inverse for every element

²group (1718)
transitive verb
1 : to combine in a group
2 : to assign to a group : CLASSIFY
intransitive verb
1 : to form a group
2 : to belong to a group
3 : to make groups of closely spaced hits on a target ⟨the gun *grouped* beautifully —R. C. Ruark⟩
— **group·able** \'grü-pə-bəl\ *adjective*

group captain *noun* (1919)
: a commissioned officer in the British air force who ranks with a colonel in the army

group dynamics *noun plural but singular or plural in construction* (1939)
: the interacting forces within a small human group; *also* : the sociological study of these forces

grou·per \'grü-pər\ *noun, plural* **groupers** *also* **grouper** [Portuguese *garoupa*] (1671)
: any of numerous fishes (family Serranidae and especially genera *Epinephelus* and *Mycteroperca*) that are typically large solitary bottom-dwelling fishes of warm seas

group·ie \'grü-pē\ *noun* (1967)
1 : a fan of a rock group who usually follows the group around on concert tours
2 : an admirer of a celebrity who attends as many of his or her public appearances as possible
3 : ENTHUSIAST, AFICIONADO ⟨a political *groupie*⟩ ⟨golf *groupies*⟩

group·ing \'grü-piŋ\ *noun* (1748)
1 : the act or process of combining in groups
2 : a set of objects combined in a group ⟨a furniture *grouping*⟩

group practice *noun* (1942)
: medicine practiced by a group of associated physicians or dentists (as specialists in different fields) working as partners or as partners and employees

group theory *noun* (1898)
: a branch of mathematics concerned with finding all mathematical groups and determining their properties

group therapy *noun* (1943)

: therapy in the presence of a therapist in which several patients discuss and share their personal problems — called also *group psychotherapy*
— **group therapist** *noun*

group·think \'grüp-,thiŋk\ *noun* [¹group + -think (as in *doublethink*)] (1952)
: a pattern of thought characterized by self-deception, forced manufacture of consent, and conformity to group values and ethics

grou·pus·cule \grü-'pəs-,kyül\ *noun* [French, from *groupe* group + *-uscule* (as in *corpuscule* corpuscle)] (1969)
: a small group of political activists

¹grouse \'graùs\ *noun, plural* **grouse** *or* **grouses** [origin unknown] (1531)
: any of numerous chiefly ground-dwelling birds (family Tetraonidae) that are usually of reddish brown or other protective color and have feathered legs and that include many important game birds

²grouse *intransitive verb* **groused; grous·ing** [origin unknown] (1887)
: COMPLAIN, GRUMBLE
— **grous·er** *noun*

³grouse *noun* (1918)
: COMPLAINT

¹grout \'graùt\ *noun* [Middle English, coarse meal, from Old English *grūt;* akin to Old English *grēot* grit] (1638)
1 a : thin mortar used for filling spaces (as the joints in masonry); *also* : any of various other materials (as a mixture of cement and water or chemicals that solidify) used for a similar purpose **b** : PLASTER
2 : LEES

²grout *transitive verb* (1838)
1 : to fill up or finish with grout
2 : to fix in place by means of grout ⟨*grout* a bolt into a wall⟩
— **grout·er** *noun*

grove \'grōv\ *noun* [Middle English, from Old English *grāf*] (before 12th century)
1 : a small wood without underbrush ⟨a picnic *grove*⟩
2 : a planting of fruit or nut trees

grov·el \'grä-vəl, 'grə-\ *intransitive verb* **-eled** *or* **-elled; -el·ing** *or* **-el·ling** [back-formation from *groveling* prone, from *groveling,* adverb, from Middle English, from *gruf,* adverb, on the face (from Old Norse *ā grūfu*) + -*ling*] (1593)
1 : to creep with the face to the ground : CRAWL
2 a : to lie or creep with the body prostrate in token of subservience or abasement **b** : to abase oneself
3 : to give oneself over to what is base or unworthy : WALLOW ⟨*groveling* in self-pity⟩
— **grov·el·er** \-v°l-ər\ *noun*
— **grov·el·ing·ly** \-v°l-iŋ-lē\ *adverb*

groves of academe *often A capitalized* (1849)
: the academic world

grow \'grō\ *verb* **grew** \'grü\; **grown** \'grōn\; **grow·ing** [Middle English, from Old English *grōwan;* akin to Old High German *gruowan* to grow] (before 12th century)
intransitive verb
1 a : to spring up and develop to maturity **b** : to be able to grow in some place or situation ⟨trees that *grow* in the tropics⟩ **c** : to assume some relation through or as if through a process of natural growth ⟨ferns *growing* from the rocks⟩
2 a : to increase in size by assimilation of material into the living organism or by accretion of material in a nonbiological process (as crystallization) **b** : INCREASE, EXPAND ⟨*grows* in wisdom⟩
3 : to develop from a parent source ⟨the book *grew* out of a series of lectures⟩

4 a : to pass into a condition : BECOME ⟨*grew* pale⟩ **b** : to have an increasing influence ⟨habit *grows* on a person⟩ **c** : to become increasingly acceptable or attractive ⟨didn't like it at first, but it *grew* on him⟩
transitive verb
1 : to cause to grow ⟨*grow* wheat⟩
2 : DEVELOP 5
— **grow·er** \'grō(-ə)r\ *noun*
— **grow·ing·ly** \'grō-iŋ-lē\ *adverb*

growing pains *noun plural* (1810)
1 : pains in the legs of growing children having no demonstrable relation to growth
2 : the stresses and strains attending a new project or development

growing point *noun* (1835)
: the undifferentiated end of a plant shoot from which additional shoot tissues differentiate

¹growl \'graù(ə)l\ *verb* [Middle English *groulen, grollen*] (14th century)
intransitive verb
1 a : RUMBLE ⟨his stomach *growled*⟩ **b** : to utter a growl ⟨the dog *growled* at the stranger⟩
2 : to complain angrily
transitive verb
: to utter with a growl : utter angrily

²growl *noun* (1727)
: a deep guttural inarticulate sound

growl·er \'graù-lər\ *noun* (1753)
1 : one that growls
2 : a container (as a can or pitcher) for beer bought by the measure
3 : a small iceberg

growl·ing \'graù-liŋ\ *adjective* (1752)
: marked by a growl ⟨a low *growling* voice⟩ ⟨listened to the *growling* thunder⟩
— **growl·ing·ly** \-liŋ-lē\ *adverb*

growly \'graù-lē\ *adjective* **growl·i·er; -est** (1920)
: resembling a growl ⟨a *growly* voice⟩
— **growl·i·ness** *noun*

grown \'grōn\ *adjective* (1645)
1 : fully grown : MATURE ⟨*grown* men and women⟩
2 : covered or surrounded with vegetation ⟨land well *grown* with trees⟩
3 a : cultivated or produced in a specified way or locality — used in combination ⟨shade-*grown* tobacco⟩ **b** : overgrown with — used in combination ⟨a weed-*grown* patio⟩

¹grown–up \'grō-,nəp\ *adjective* (1633)
: not childish or immature : ADULT

²grown–up *noun* (1813)
: ADULT

growth \'grōth\ *noun* (1557)
1 a (1) : a stage in the process of growing : SIZE (2) : full growth **b** : the process of growing **c** : progressive development : EVOLUTION **d** : INCREASE, EXPANSION ⟨the *growth* of the oil industry⟩
2 a : something that grows or has grown **b** : an abnormal proliferation of tissue (as a tumor) **c** : OUTGROWTH **d** : the result of growth : PRODUCT
3 : a producing especially by growing ⟨fruits of his own *growth*⟩

growth company *noun* (1959)
: a company that grows at a greater rate than the economy as a whole and that usually directs a relatively high proportion of income back into the business

growth factor *noun* (1926)
: a substance (as a vitamin B_{12} or an interleukin) that promotes growth and especially cellular growth

growth hormone *noun* (1924)
1 : a vertebrate polypeptide hormone that is secreted by the anterior lobe of the pituitary gland and regulates growth — called also *somatotropin*
2 : GROWTH REGULATOR

growth regulator *noun* (1936)
: any of various synthetic or naturally occurring plant substances (as an auxin or gibberellin) that regulate growth

growth ring *noun* (1907)

: a layer of wood (as an annual ring) produced during a single period of growth

growthy \'grō-thē\ *adjective* **growth·i·er; -est** (1884)
of livestock : exceptionally fast in growing and gaining weight
— **growth·i·ness** \-nəs\ *noun*

grow up *intransitive verb* (1535)
: to grow toward or arrive at full stature or physical or mental maturity ⟨*growing up* intellectually, socially, and physically⟩

groyne \'gróin\ *noun* [by alteration] (1582)
: GROIN 3

¹**grub** \'grəb\ *verb* **grubbed; grub·bing** [Middle English *grubben;* akin to Old English *grafan* to dig — more at GRAVE] (14th century)
transitive verb
1 : to clear by digging up roots and stumps
2 : to dig up by or as if by the roots
intransitive verb
1 a : to dig in the ground especially for something that is difficult to find or extract **b** : to search about ⟨*grubbed* in the countryside for food —*Lamp*⟩
2 : TOIL, DRUDGE ⟨folks who *grub* for money —James Street⟩
— **grub·ber** *noun*

²**grub** *noun* [Middle English *grubbe,* from *grubben*] (15th century)
1 : a soft thick wormlike larva of an insect
2 a : one who does menial work : DRUDGE **b** : a slovenly person
3 : FOOD

grub·by \'grə-bē\ *adjective* **grub·bi·er; -est** (1725)
1 : infested with fly maggots
2 a : DIRTY, GRIMY ⟨*grubby* hands⟩ **b** : SLOVENLY, SLOPPY
3 : worthy of contempt : BASE ⟨*grubby* political motives⟩
— **grub·bi·ly** \'grə-bə-lē\ *adverb*
— **grub·bi·ness** \'grə-bē-nəs\ *noun*

¹**grub·stake** \'grəb-ˌstāk\ *noun* (1863)
1 : supplies or funds furnished a mining prospector on promise of a share in his discoveries
2 : material assistance (as a loan) provided for launching an enterprise or for a person in difficult circumstances

²**grubstake** *transitive verb* (1879)
: to provide with a grubstake
— **grub·stak·er** *noun*

Grub Street \'grəb-\ *noun* [Grub Street, London, formerly inhabited by literary hacks] (1630)
: the world or category of needy literary hacks

¹**grudge** \'grəj\ *transitive verb* **grudged; grudg·ing** [Middle English *grucchen, grudgen* to grumble, complain, from Middle French *groucier,* of Germanic origin; akin to Middle High German *grogezen* to howl] (14th century)
: to be unwilling to give or admit : give or allow reluctantly or resentfully ⟨didn't *grudge* the time⟩
— **grudg·er** *noun*

²**grudge** *noun* (15th century)
: a feeling of deep-seated resentment or ill will
synonym SEE MALICE

grudg·ing \'grə-jiŋ\ *adjective* (circa 1533)
1 : UNWILLING, RELUCTANT
2 : done, given, or allowed unwillingly, reluctantly, or sparingly ⟨*grudging* compliance⟩
— **grudg·ing·ly** \-jiŋ-lē\ *adverb*

gru·el \'grü-əl\ *noun* [Middle English *grewel,* from Middle French *gruel,* of Germanic origin; akin to Old English *grūt* grout] (14th century)
1 : a thin porridge
2 *chiefly British* : PUNISHMENT

gru·el·ing *or* **gru·el·ling** \'grü-ə-liŋ\ *adjective* [from present participle of obsolete *gruel* (to exhaust)] (1852)
: trying or taxing to the point of exhaustion : PUNISHING ⟨a *grueling* race⟩
— **gru·el·ing·ly** \-liŋ-lē\ *adverb*

grue·some \'grü-səm\ *adjective* [alteration of earlier *growsome,* from English dialect *grow, grue* to shiver, from Middle English *gruen,* probably from Middle Dutch *grūwen;* akin to Old High German in*grūēn* to shiver] (1816)
: inspiring horror or repulsion : GRISLY
synonym SEE GHASTLY
— **grue·some·ly** *adverb*
— **grue·some·ness** *noun*

¹**gruff** \'grəf\ *adjective* [Dutch *grof;* akin to Old High German *grob* coarse, *hruf* scurf — more at DANDRUFF] (1706)
1 : rough, brusque, or stern in manner, speech, or aspect ⟨a *gruff* reply⟩
2 : being deep and harsh : HOARSE ⟨a *gruff* voice⟩
synonym SEE BLUFF
— **gruff·ly** *adverb*
— **gruff·ness** *noun*

²**gruff** *transitive verb* (1706)
: to utter in a gruff voice or manner

grum·ble \'grəm-bəl\ *verb* **grum·bled; grum·bling** \-b(ə-)liŋ\ [probably from Middle French *grommeler,* ultimately from Middle Dutch *grommen;* akin to Old High German *grimm* grim] (circa 1586)
intransitive verb
1 : to mutter in discontent
2 : GROWL, RUMBLE
transitive verb
: to express with grumbling
— **grumble** *noun*
— **grum·bler** \-b(ə-)lər\ *noun*
— **grum·bling·ly** \-b(ə-)liŋ-lē\ *adverb*
— **grum·bly** \-b(ə-)lē\ *adjective*

grum·met \'grə-mət\ *variant of* GROMMET

¹**grump** \'grəmp\ *noun* [obsolete English *grumps* (snubs, slights)] (1844)
1 : a fit of ill humor or sulkiness — usually used in plural
2 : a person given to complaining

²**grump** (1875)
intransitive verb
1 : SULK
2 : GRUMBLE, COMPLAIN
transitive verb
: to utter in a grumpy manner

grumpy \'grəm-pē\ *adjective* **grump·i·er; -est** (1778)
: moodily cross : SURLY
— **grump·i·ly** \-pə-lē\ *adverb*
— **grump·i·ness** \-pē-nəs\ *noun*

grunge \'grənj\ *noun* [back-formation from *grungy*] (1965)
1 : one that is grungy
2 : rock music incorporating elements of punk rock and heavy metal; *also* : the untidy working-class fashions typical of fans of grunge

grun·gy \'grən-jē\ *adjective* **grun·gi·er; -est** [origin unknown] (1965)
: shabby or dirty in character or condition

grun·ion \'grən-yən\ *noun* [probably from Spanish *gruñón* grunter] (1917)
: a silversides (*Leuresthes tenuis*) of the California coast notable for the regularity with which it comes inshore to spawn at nearly full moon

¹**grunt** \'grənt\ *verb* [Middle English *grunten,* from Old English *grunnettan,* frequentative of *grunian,* of imitative origin] (before 12th century)
intransitive verb
: to utter a grunt
transitive verb
: to utter with a grunt
— **grunt·er** *noun*

²**grunt** *noun* (1553)
1 a : the deep short sound characteristic of a hog **b** : a similar sound
2 [from the noise it makes when taken from the water] : any of a family (Haemulidae synonym Pomadasyidae) of chiefly tropical marine bony fishes

3 : a dessert made by dropping biscuit dough on top of boiling berries and steaming ⟨blueberry *grunt*⟩
4 : a U.S. army or marine foot soldier especially in the Vietnam war
5 : one who does routine unglamorous work — often used attributively ⟨*grunt* work⟩

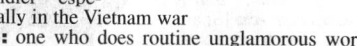

grunt 2

grun·tle \'grən-t[ə]l\ *transitive verb* **grun·tled; grun·tling** \'grənt-liŋ, 'grən-t[ə]l-iŋ\ [back-formation from *disgruntle*] (1926)
: to put in a good humor ⟨were *gruntled* with a good meal and good conversation —W. P. Webb⟩

grutch \'grəch\ *transitive verb* [Middle English *grucchen*] (14th century)
obsolete : BEGRUDGE

grutten *past participle of* GREET

Gru·yère \grü-'yer, grē-\ *noun* [*Gruyère,* district in Switzerland] (1802)
1 : a firm cheese with small holes and a nutty flavor that is of Swiss origin
2 : a process cheese made from natural Gruyère

gryph·on *variant of* GRIFFIN

G–string \'jē-ˌstriŋ\ *noun* [origin unknown] (1878)
: a strip of cloth passed between the legs and supported by a waist cord that is worn especially by striptease dancers

G suit *noun* [gravity *suit*] (1944)
: a suit designed to counteract the physiological effects of acceleration on an aviator or astronaut

GT \ˌjē-'tē\ *noun* [Italian *Gran Turismo*] (1966)
: GRAND TOURING CAR

GTP \ˌjē-(ˌ)tē-'pē\ *noun* [guanosine *t*riphosphate] (1961)
: an energy-rich nucleotide analogous to ATP that is composed of guanine, ribose, and three phosphate groups and is necessary for peptide-bond formation during protein synthesis — called also *guanosine triphosphate*

G_2 phase \ˌjē-'tü-\ *noun* [*growth*] (1968)
: the period in the cell cycle from the completion of DNA replication to the beginning of cell division — compare G_1 PHASE, M PHASE, S PHASE

gua·ca·mo·le \ˌgwä-kə-'mō-lē\ *noun* [Mexican Spanish, from Nahuatl *āhuacamōlli,* from *āhuacatl* avocado + *mōlli* sauce] (1920)
: pureed or mashed avocado seasoned with condiments
word history SEE AVOCADO

gua·cha·ro \'gwä-chə-ˌrō\ *noun, plural* **-ros** *or* **-roes** [American Spanish *guácharo*] (1830)
: OILBIRD

guai·ac \'gwī-ˌak, 'gī-\ *noun* [New Latin *Guaiacum*] (circa 1751)
: GUAIACUM 2

guai·a·cum \'gwī-ə-kəm, 'gī-\ *noun* [New Latin, from Spanish *guayaco,* from Taino *guayacan*] (1553)
1 : any of a genus (*Guaiacum*) of the caltrop family of tropical American evergreen trees and shrubs having pinnate leaves, usually blue flowers, and capsular fruit
2 a : the hard greenish brown wood of a guaiacum (especially *Guaiacum officinale*) **b** : a resin with a faint balsamic odor that is obtained from the trunk of two guaiacums (*G. officinale* and *G. sanctum*) and often used as a clinical reagent

\ə\ abut \ə\ kitten \ər\ further \a\ ash \ā\ ace
\ä\ mop, mar \aù\ out \ch\ chin \e\ bet \ē\ easy
\g\ go \i\ hit \ī\ ice \j\ job \ŋ\ sing \ō\ go
\ò\ law \òi\ boy \th\ thin \t̸h\ the \ü\ loot \ù\ foot
\y\ yet \zh\ vision *see also* Guide to Pronunciation

guan \\'gwän\\ *noun* [alteration of earlier *quam*, probably from Cuna (Chibchan language of Panama) *kwama*] (1743)
: any of various large tropical American lowland-forest birds (family Cracidae) that somewhat resemble turkeys

guan

gua·na·co \\gwə-'nä-(,)kō\\ *noun, plural* **-cos** *also* **-co** [Spanish, from Quechua *wanaku*] (1604)
: a South American mammal (*Lama guanicoe*) of dry open country that has a soft thick fawn-colored coat and is related to the camel but lacks a dorsal hump

gua·neth·i·dine \\gwä-'ne-thə-,dēn\\ *noun* [*guanidine* + *eth-*] (1959)
: a drug $C_{10}H_{22}N_4$ used especially as the sulfate in treating severe high blood pressure

gua·ni·dine \\'gwä-nə-,dēn\\ *noun* [International Scientific Vocabulary, from *guanine*] (circa 1864)
: a base CH_5N_3 derived from guanine, found especially in young tissues, and used in organic synthesis and as a parasympathetic stimulant in medicine especially as the hydrochloride salt

gua·nine \\'gwä-,nēn\\ *noun* [*guano* + *-ine*; from its being found especially in guano] (1850)
: a purine base $C_5H_5N_5O$ that codes genetic information in the polynucleotide chain of DNA or RNA — compare ADENINE, CYTOSINE, THYMINE, URACIL

gua·no \\'gwä-(,)nō\\ *noun* [Spanish, from Quechua *wanu* fertilizer, dung] (1604)
: a substance composed chiefly of the excrement of seafowl and used as a fertilizer; *also*
: a similar substance (as bat excrement or cannery waste) especially when used for fertilizer

gua·no·sine \\'gwä-nə-,sēn\\ *noun* [*guan-* (as in *guanine*) + *ribose* + *-ine*] (1909)
: a nucleoside $C_{10}H_{13}N_5O_5$ composed of guanine and ribose

guanosine triphosphate *noun* (circa 1962)
: GTP

guar \\'gwär\\ *noun* [Hindi *guār*] (1882)
: a drought-tolerant legume (*Cyamopsis tetragonoloba*) cultivated in warm regions as a vegetable, for forage, and for its seeds which produce guar gums

gua·ra·ni \\,gwär-ə-'nē\\ *noun* [Spanish *guaraní*] (1797)
1 *capitalized* **a** *plural* **guarani** *or* **guaranis** : a member of a Tupi-Guaranian people of Bolivia, Paraguay, and southern Brazil **b** : the language of the Guarani
2 *plural* **guaranies** *also* **guaranis** — see MONEY table

¹guar·an·tee \\,gar-ən-'tē, ,gär- *also* 'gar-ən-, *or* 'gär-ən-,\\ *noun* [probably alteration of ¹*guaranty*] (1710)
1 : GUARANTOR
2 : GUARANTY 1
3 : an assurance for the fulfillment of a condition: as **a** : an agreement by which one person undertakes to secure another in the possession or enjoyment of something **b** : an assurance of the quality of or of the length of use to be expected from a product offered for sale often with a promise of reimbursement
4 : GUARANTY 4

²guarantee *transitive verb* **-teed; -tee·ing** (1791)
1 : to undertake to answer for the debt, default, or miscarriage of
2 : to engage for the existence, permanence, or nature of : undertake to do or secure ⟨*guarantee* the winning of three tricks⟩
3 : to give security to
4 : to assert confidently

guar·an·tor \\,gar-ən-'tòr, 'gar-ən-tər, ,gär-, 'gär-\\ *noun* (circa 1828)
1 : one that makes or gives a guaranty
2 : one that guarantees

¹guar·an·ty \\'gar-ən-tē, 'gär-\\ *noun, plural* **-ties** [Middle French *garantie*, from Old French, from *garantir* to guarantee, from *garant* warrant, of Germanic origin; akin to Old High German *werēnto* guarantor — more at WARRANT] (1592)
1 : an undertaking to answer for the payment of a debt or the performance of a duty of another in case of the other's default or miscarriage
2 : GUARANTEE 3
3 : GUARANTOR
4 : something given as security : PLEDGE
5 : the protection of a right afforded by legal provision (as in a constitution)

²guaranty *transitive verb* **-tied; -ty·ing** (1753)
: GUARANTEE

¹guard \\'gärd\\ *noun* [Middle English *garde*, from Middle French, from Old French, from *garder* to guard, defend, of Germanic origin; akin to Old High German *wartēn* to watch, take care — more at WARD] (15th century)
1 : one assigned to protect or oversee another: as **a** : a person or a body of persons on sentinel duty **b** *plural* : troops attached to the person of the sovereign **c** *British* : CONDUCTOR
2 **a** : a defensive state or attitude ⟨asked him out when his *guard* was down⟩ **b** : a defensive position (as in boxing)
3 **a** : the act or duty of protecting or defending **b** : the state of being protected : PROTECTION
4 : a protective or safety device; *specifically* : a device for protecting a machine part or the operator of a machine
5 *archaic* : PRECAUTION
6 **a** : a position or player next to the center in a football line **b** : a player stationed in the backcourt in basketball
— **off guard** : in an unprepared or unsuspecting state
— **on guard** : defensively watchful : ALERT

²guard (1500)
transitive verb
1 : to protect an edge of with an ornamental border
2 **a** : to protect from danger especially by watchful attention : make secure ⟨police *guarding* our cities⟩ **b** : to stand at the entrance of as if on guard or as a barrier **c** : to tend to carefully : PRESERVE, PROTECT ⟨*guarded* their privacy⟩
3 *archaic* : ESCORT
4 **a** : to watch over so as to prevent escape, disclosure, or indiscretion **b** : to attempt to prevent (an opponent) from playing effectively or scoring
intransitive verb
: to watch by way of caution or defense
: stand guard
synonym see DEFEND
— **guard·er** *noun*

¹guar·dant \\'gär-d°nt\\ *adjective* [Middle French *gardant*, present participle of *garder* to guard, look at] (1572)
: having the head turned toward the spectator — used of a heraldic animal whose body is seen from the side ⟨a lion passant *guardant*⟩

²guardant *noun* (1591)
obsolete : GUARDIAN

guard cell *noun* (1875)
: one of the two crescent-shaped epidermal cells that border and open and close a plant stoma

guard·ed \\'gär-dəd\\ *adjective* (1709)
: CAUTIOUS, CIRCUMSPECT
— **guard·ed·ly** *adverb*
— **guard·ed·ness** *noun*

guard hair *noun* (1913)
: one of the long coarse hairs forming a protective coating over the undercoat of a mammal

guard·house \\'gärd-,haùs\\ *noun* (1592)
1 : a building occupied by a guard or used as a headquarters for soldiers on guard duty
2 : a military jail

guard·ian \\'gär-dē-ən\\ *noun* (15th century)
1 : one that guards : CUSTODIAN
2 : a superior of a Franciscan monastery
3 : one who has the care of the person or property of another
— **guard·ian·ship** \\-,ship\\ *noun*

guardian angel *noun* (circa 1631)
: an angel believed to have special care of a particular individual; *broadly* : SAVIOR 1, PROTECTOR

guard of honor (1887)
: HONOR GUARD

guard·rail \\'gär-,drāl\\ *noun* (1860)
: a railing for guarding against danger or trespass; *especially* : a barrier (as of steel cables) placed along the edge of a highway at dangerous points

guard·room \\'gär-,drüm, -,drùm\\ *noun* (1762)
1 : a room occupied by a military guard during its term of duty
2 : a room where military prisoners are confined

guards·man \\'gärdz-mən\\ *noun* (1817)
: a member of a military body called *guard* or *guards*

guar gum *noun* (1950)
: a gum that consists of the ground endosperm of guar seeds and is used especially as a thickening agent and as a sizing material for paper and textiles

Guar·ne·ri·us \\gwär-'nir-ē-əs, -'ner-\\ *noun* [New Latin, from Italian *Guarneri*] (1866)
: a violin made by one of the Italian Guarneri family in the 17th and 18th centuries

gua·va \\'gwä-və\\ *noun* [Spanish *guaba, guayaba*, perhaps from Taino] (1604)
1 : any of several tropical American shrubs or small trees (genus *Psidium*) of the myrtle family; *especially* : a shrubby tree (*P. guajava*) widely cultivated for its sweet acid yellow or pink fruit
2 : the globose or pear-shaped fruit of a guava

gua·ya·be·ra \\,gwī-ə-'ber-ə\\ *noun* [American Spanish] (1947)
: a usually short-sleeved lightweight sport shirt designed to be worn untucked

gua·yu·le \\gwī-'ü-lē, wī-\\ *noun* [American Spanish, from Nahuatl *cuauholli* or *huauholli*] (1906)
: a much-branched composite shrub (*Parthenium argentatum*) of Mexico and the southwestern U.S. cultivated as a source of rubber

gu·ber·na·to·ri·al \\,gü-bə(r)-nə-'tōr-ē-əl, ,gyü-, ,gù-, -'tòr-\\ *adjective* [Latin *gubernator* governor, steersman, from *gubernare* to govern — more at GOVERN] (1734)
: of or relating to a governor

guck \\'gək\\ *noun* [perhaps alteration of *goo*] (1949)
: oozy sloppy dirt or debris; *broadly* : GOO, GUNK

¹gud·geon \\'gə-jən\\ *noun* [Middle English *gudyon*, from Middle French *goujon*] (15th century)
1 : PIVOT 1, JOURNAL
2 : a socket for a rudder pintle

²gudgeon *noun* [Middle English *gojune*, from Middle French *gouvion, gougon*, from Latin *gobion-, gobio*, alteration of *gobius* — more at GOBY] (15th century)
: a small European freshwater fish (*Gobio gobio*) related to the carps and often used for food or bait

gudgeon pin *noun* (1891)
: WRIST PIN

Gud·run \\'gùd-,rün\\ *noun* [Old Norse *Guthrūn*]
: the wife of Sigurd and later of Atli in Norse mythology

guel·der rose \\'gel-də(r)-\\ *noun* [*Guelderland, Gelderland*, Netherlands] (1597)

: a bush of a cultivated variety of the cranberry bush with large globose heads of sterile flowers

Guelf *or* **Guelph** \'gwelf\ *noun* [Italian *Guelfo*] (1579)
: a member of a papal and popular political party in medieval Italy that opposed the authority of the German emperors in Italy — compare GHIBELLINE

gue·non \'gwe-nən; gə-nōⁿ\ *noun* [French] (1838)
: any of various long-tailed chiefly arboreal African monkeys (genera *Cercopithecus* and *Erythrocebus*)

guer·don \'gər-dⁿn\ *noun* [Middle English, from Middle French, from Old French, of Germanic origin; akin to Old High German *widarlōn* reward] (14th century)
: REWARD, RECOMPENSE
— **guerdon** *transitive verb*

gue·ri·don \gä-rē-dōⁿ\ *noun* [French *guéridon*, from *Gueridon*, character in 17th century farces and popular songs] (1853)
: a small usually ornately carved and embellished stand or table

guern·sey \'gərn-zē\ *noun, plural* **guernseys** *often capitalized* [*Guernsey*, Channel islands] (1834)
: any of a breed of fawn and white dairy cattle that are larger than the jersey and produce rich yellowish milk

guernsey

¹guer·ril·la *or* **gue·ril·la** \gə-'ri-lə, ge-, g(y)i-\ *noun* [Spanish *guerrilla*, from diminutive of *guerra* war, of Germanic origin; akin to Old High German *werra* strife — more at WAR] (1809)
: a person who engages in irregular warfare especially as a member of an independent unit carrying out harassment and sabotage ◊
²guerrilla *adjective* (1811)
: of, relating to, or characteristic of guerrillas especially in being aggressive, radical, or unconventional

guerrilla theater *noun* (1968)
: STREET THEATER

¹guess \'ges\ *verb* [Middle English *gessen*, probably of Scandinavian origin; akin to Old Norse *geta* to get, guess — more at GET] (14th century)
transitive verb
1 : to form an opinion of from little or no evidence
2 : BELIEVE, SUPPOSE ⟨I *guess* you're right⟩
3 : to arrive at a correct conclusion about by conjecture, chance, or intuition ⟨*guess* the answer⟩
intransitive verb
: to make a guess
— **guess·able** \'ge-sə-bəl\ *adjective*
— **guess·er** *noun*
²guess *noun* (14th century)
: CONJECTURE, SURMISE

guess·ti·mate \'ges-tə-mət\ *noun* [blend of *guess* and *estimate*] (1923)
: an estimate usually made without adequate information
— **guess·ti·mate** \-ˌmāt\ *transitive verb*

guess·work \'ges-ˌwərk\ *noun* (1725)
: work performed or results obtained by guess
: CONJECTURE

¹guest \'gest\ *noun* [Middle English *gest,* from Old Norse *gestr;* akin to Old English *giest* guest, stranger, Latin *hostis* stranger, enemy] (13th century)
1 a : a person entertained in one's house **b** : a person to whom hospitality is extended **c** : a person who pays for the services of an establishment (as a hotel or restaurant)

2 : an organism (as an insect) sharing the dwelling of another; *especially* : INQUILINE
3 : a substance that is incorporated in a host substance
4 : a usually prominent person not a regular member of a cast or organization who appears in a program or performance
²guest (14th century)
transitive verb
: to receive as a guest
intransitive verb
: to appear as a guest

guest worker *noun* (1967)
: a foreign laborer working temporarily in an industrialized usually European country

guff \'gəf\ *noun* [probably imitative] (1888)
: NONSENSE, HUMBUG

guf·faw \(ˌ)gə-'fȯ, 'gə-ˌfȯ\ *noun* [imitative] (1720)
: a loud or boisterous burst of laughter
— **guf·faw** \(ˌ)gə-'fȯ\ *intransitive verb*

gug·gle \'gə-gəl\ *intransitive verb* **gug·gled; gug·gling** \-g(ə-)liŋ\ [imitative] (1611)
: GURGLE
— **guggle** *noun*

guid·able \'gī-də-bəl\ *adjective* (1676)
: capable of being guided

guid·ance \'gī-dⁿn(t)s\ *noun* (1590)
1 : the act or process of guiding
2 a : the direction provided by a guide **b** : advice on vocational or educational problems given to students
3 : the process of controlling the course of a projectile by a built-in mechanism

¹guide \'gīd\ *noun* [Middle English, from Middle French, from Old Provençal *guida*, of Germanic origin; akin to Old English *wītan* to look after, *witan* to know — more at WIT] (14th century)
1 a : one that leads or directs another's way **b** : a person who exhibits and explains points of interest **c** : something that provides a person with guiding information **d** : SIGNPOST 1 **e** : a person who directs another's conduct or course of life
2 a : a device for steadying or directing the motion of something **b** : a ring or loop for holding the line of a fishing rod in position **c** : a sheet or a card with projecting tab for labeling inserted in a card index to facilitate reference
3 : a member of a unit on whom the movements or alignments of a military command are regulated — used especially in commands ⟨*guide* right⟩
²guide *verb* **guid·ed; guid·ing** (14th century)
transitive verb
1 : to act as a guide to : direct in a way or course
2 a : to direct, supervise, or influence usually to a particular end **b** : to superintend the training or instruction of
intransitive verb
: to act or work as a guide ☆
— **guid·er** *noun*

guide·book \'gīd-ˌbu̇k\ *noun* (1814)
: HANDBOOK 1; *especially* : a book of information for travelers

guided missile *noun* (1945)
: a missile whose course may be altered during flight (as by a target-seeking radar device)

guide dog *noun* (1932)
: a dog trained to lead the blind

guide·line \'gīd-ˌlīn\ *noun* (1785)
: a line by which one is guided: as **a** : a cord or rope to aid a passer over a difficult point or to permit retracing a course **b** : an indication or outline of policy or conduct

guide·post \-ˌpōst\ *noun* (1761)
1 : INDICATION, SIGN
2 : GUIDELINE 2

guide·way \-ˌwā\ *noun* (1876)
: a channel or track for controlling the line of motion of something

guide word *noun* (circa 1928)

: either of the terms at the head of a page of an alphabetical reference work (as a dictionary) indicating the alphabetically first and last words on the page

gui·don \'gī-ˌdän, -dⁿn\ *noun* [Middle French, from *guide*] (1548)
1 : a small flag; *especially* : one borne by a military unit as a unit marker
2 : one who carries a guidon

guid·will·ie \ˌgēd-'wi-lē, gid-\ *adjective* [Scots *guidwill* goodwill] (1788)
Scottish : CORDIAL, CHEERING

guild \'gild\ *noun* [Middle English *gilde*, from Old Norse *gildi* payment, guild; akin to Old English *gield* tribute, guild — more at GELD] (14th century)
: an association of people with similar interests or pursuits; *especially* : a medieval association of merchants or craftsmen
— **guild·ship** \'gild)-ˌship\ *noun*

guil·der \'gil-dər\ *noun* [Middle English *gylder, gyldren,* modification of Middle Dutch *gulden*] (15th century)
: GULDEN

guild·hall \'gild-ˌhȯl\ *noun* (14th century)
: a hall where a guild or corporation usually assembles

guilds·man \'gil(d)z-mən\ *noun* (1873)
1 : a guild member
2 : an advocate of guild socialism

guild socialism *noun* (1912)

\ə\ **abut** \ᵊ\ **kitten** \ər\ **further** \a\ **ash** \ā\ **ace**
\ä\ **mop, mar** \au̇\ **out** \ch\ **chin** \e\ **bet** \ē\ **easy**
\g\ **go** \i\ **hit** \ī\ **ice** \j\ **job** \ŋ\ **sing** \ō\ **go**
\ȯ\ **law** \ȯi\ **boy** \th\ **thin** \t͟h\ **the** \ü\ **loot** \u̇\ **foot**
\y\ **yet** \zh\ **vision** *see also* Guide to Pronunciation

: an early 20th century English socialistic theory advocating state ownership of industry with control and management by guilds of workers

guile \'gī(ə)l\ *noun* [Middle English, from Old French, probably of Germanic origin; akin to Old English *wigle* divination — more at WITCH] (13th century)
1 : deceitful cunning : DUPLICITY
2 *obsolete* : STRATAGEM, TRICK
— **guile·ful** \-fəl\ *adjective*
— **guile·ful·ly** \-fə-lē\ *adverb*
— **guile·ful·ness** *noun*
guile·less \'gī(ə)l-ləs\ *adjective* (1728)
: INNOCENT, NAIVE
— **guile·less·ly** *adverb*
— **guile·less·ness** *noun*
Guil·lain–Bar·ré syndrome \,gē-,lan-,bä-'rā-, ,gē-yaⁿ-\ *noun* [Georges *Guillain* (died 1961) French physician and Jean A. *Barré* (born 1880) French neurologist] (1940)
: a polyneuritis of unknown cause characterized especially by muscle weakness and paralysis
guil·le·met \,gē-(y)ə-'mā, ,gi-lə-'met\ *noun* [French, from diminutive of *Guillaume* William (perhaps a printer's name)] (circa 1905)
: either of the marks « or » used as quotation marks in French writing
guil·le·mot \'gi-lə-,mät\ *noun* [French, from Middle French, diminutive of *Guillaume* William] (1678)
1 *British* : a common murre (*Uria aalge*)
2 : any of a genus (*Cepphus*) of narrow-billed auks of northern seas
guil·loche \gi-'lōsh, gē-'(y)ōsh\ *noun* [French *guillochis*] (circa 1842)
1 : an architectural ornament formed of two or more interlaced bands with openings containing round devices
2 : a pattern (as on metalwork) made by interlacing curved lines
guil·lo·tine \'gi-lə-,tēn, ,gē-(y)ə-', 'gē-(y)ə-,\ *noun* [French, from Joseph *Guillotin* (died 1814) French physician] (1793)
1 : a machine for beheading by means of a heavy blade that slides down in vertical guides
2 : a shearing machine or instrument (as a paper cutter) that in action resembles a guillotine
3 *chiefly British* : closure by the imposition of a predetermined time limit on the consideration of specific sections of a bill or portions of other legislative business ◆
— **guillotine** *transitive verb*
guilt \'gilt\ *noun* [Middle English, delinquency, guilt, from Old English *gylt* delinquency] (before 12th century)
1 : the fact of having committed a breach of conduct especially violating law and involving a penalty; *broadly* : guilty conduct
2 a : the state of one who has committed an offense especially consciously **b** : feelings of culpability especially for imagined offenses or from a sense of inadequacy : SELF-REPROACH
3 : a feeling of culpability for offenses
guilt·less \'gilt-ləs\ *adjective* (13th century)
: INNOCENT
— **guilt·less·ly** *adverb*
— **guilt·less·ness** *noun*
guilty \'gil-tē\ *adjective* **guilt·i·er; -est** (before 12th century)
1 : justly chargeable with or responsible for a usually grave breach of conduct or a crime
2 *obsolete* : justly liable to or deserving of a penalty
3 a : suggesting or involving guilt ⟨*guilty* looks⟩ **b** : aware of or suffering from guilt ⟨*guilty* conscience⟩
synonym see BLAMEWORTHY
— **guilt·i·ly** \-tə-lē\ *adverb*
— **guilt·i·ness** \-tē-nəs\ *noun*
guimpe \'gamp, 'gimp\ *noun* [French, from Old French *guimple*, of Germanic origin; akin to Old English *wimpel* wimple] (1850)
1 : a blouse worn under a jumper or pinafore

2 : a wide cloth used by some nuns to cover the neck and shoulders
3 [by alteration] : ¹GIMP
guin·ea \'gi-nē\ *noun* [*Guinea*, Africa, supposed source of the gold from which it was made] (1664)
1 : an English gold coin issued from 1663 to 1813 and fixed in 1717 at 21 shillings
2 : a unit of value equal to one pound and one shilling
guinea fowl *noun* (1788)
: an African bird (*Numida meleagris*) related to the pheasants, raised for food in many parts of the world, and marked by a bare neck and head and slaty plumage speckled with white; *broadly* : any of several related birds

guinea fowl

guinea grass *noun* (1785)
: a tall African forage grass (*Panicum maximum*) introduced into tropical America and the southern U.S.
guinea hen *noun* (1599)
: a female guinea fowl; *broadly* : GUINEA FOWL
guinea pepper *noun* (1597)
: GRAINS OF PARADISE
guinea pig *noun* (1664)
1 : a small stout-bodied short-eared tailless domesticated rodent (*Cavia porcellus*) often kept as a pet and widely used in biological research — called also *cavy*
2 : a subject of research, experimentation, or testing
guinea worm *noun* (1699)
: a slender nematode worm (*Dracunculus medinensis*) of tropical regions parasitic in mammals including humans and having an adult female that infests subcutaneous tissues and may attain a length of several feet
Guin·e·vere \'gwi-nə-,vir, *British also* 'gi-\ *noun*
: the wife of King Arthur and mistress of Lancelot
gui·pure \gi-'pyur, -'pur\ *noun* [French] (1843)
: a heavy large-patterned decorative lace
gui·ro \'wē-(,)rō, 'gwir-(,)ō\ *noun* [American Spanish *güiro*, literally, calabash] (1898)
: a percussion instrument of Latin-American origin made of a serrated gourd and played by scraping a stick along its surface
gui·sard \'gī-zərd\ *noun* [obsolete Scots *gyze* to disguise, from Middle English *gyzen* to dress, from *guise, gyze* guise] (1626)
chiefly Scottish : MASKER, MUMMER
guise \'gīz\ *noun* [Middle English, from Old French, of Germanic origin; akin to Old High German *wīsa* manner — more at WISE] (13th century)
1 : a form or style of dress : COSTUME
2 a *obsolete* : MANNER, FASHION **b** *archaic* : a customary way of speaking or behaving
3 a : external appearance : SEMBLANCE **b** : PRETEXT
gui·tar \gə-'tär, gi-, *especially Southern & Midland also* 'gi-,tär\ *noun* [French *guitare*, from Spanish *guitarra*, from Arabic *qītār*, from Greek *kithara* cithara] (1621)
: a flat-bodied stringed instrument with a long fretted neck and usually six strings plucked with a pick or with the fingers

guitar: *1* electric,
2 acoustic

— **gui·tar·ist** \-ist\ *noun*
gui·tar·fish \-,fish\ *noun* (circa 1900)
: any of several viviparous rays (family Rhinobatidae) somewhat like a guitar in shape viewed from above
Gu·ja·ra·ti \,gü-jə-'rä-tē, ,gù-\ *noun* [Hindi *gujarātī*, from *Gujarāt* Gujarat] (1808)
1 *or* **Gu·je·ra·ti** *same*\ : the Indo-Aryan language of Gujarat and neighboring regions in northwestern India
2 *or* **Guj·ra·ti** \güj-'rä-, gùj-'rä-\ : a member of a people chiefly of Gujarat speaking the Gujarati language
gul \'gül\ *noun* [Persian] (1813)
archaic : ROSE 1
gu·lag \'gü-,läg\ *noun, often capitalized* [Russian, from *Glavnoe upravlenie ispravitel'no-trudovykh lagereĭ* chief administration of corrective labor camps] (1974)
: the penal system of the U.S.S.R. consisting of a network of labor camps; *also* : LABOR CAMP 1
gu·lar \'g(y)ü-lər\ *adjective* [Latin *gula* throat — more at GLUTTON] (1828)
: of, relating to, or situated on the throat
gulch \'gəlch\ *noun* [perhaps from English dialect *gulch* to gulp, from Middle English *gulchen*] (1832)
: a deep or precipitous cleft : RAVINE; *especially* : one occupied by a torrent
gul·den \'gül-dən, 'gùl-\ *noun, plural* **guldens** *or* **gulden** [Middle English (Scots), from Middle Dutch *gulden florijn* golden florin] (15th century)
— see MONEY table
gules \'gyü(ə)lz\ *noun, plural* **gules** [Middle English *goules*, from Middle French] (14th century)
: the heraldic color red
¹gulf \'gəlf\ *noun* [Middle English *goulf*, from Middle French *golfe*, from Italian *golfo*, from Late Latin *colpus*, from Greek *kolpos* bosom, gulf; akin to Old English *hwealf* vault, Old High German *walbo*] (15th century)
1 : a part of an ocean or sea extending into the land
2 : a deep chasm : ABYSS
3 : WHIRLPOOL
4 : a wide gap ⟨the *gulf* between generations⟩
²gulf *transitive verb* (1807)
: ENGULF
gulf·weed \'gəlf-,wēd\ *noun* [*Gulf* of Mexico] (1674)
: any of several sargassums; *especially* : a branching olive-brown seaweed (*Sargassum bacciferum*) of tropical American seas with numerous berrylike air vesicles

¹gull \'gəl\ *noun* [Middle English, of Celtic origin; akin to Welsh *gwylan* gull] (15th century) : any of numerous long-winged web-footed aquatic birds (subfamily Larinae of the family Laridae); *especially* : a usually gray and white bird (as of the genus *Larus*) differing from a tern in usually larger size, stouter build, thicker and somewhat hooked bill, less pointed wings, and short unforked tail

²gull *transitive verb* [probably from *²gull*] (1550) : to take advantage of (one who is foolish or unwary) **: DECEIVE**
synonym see DUPE

³gull *noun* (1594) : a person who is easily deceived or cheated **: DUPE**

Gul·lah \'gə-lə\ *noun* (1822) **1 a :** a member of a group of blacks inhabiting the sea islands and coastal districts of South Carolina, Georgia, and northeastern Florida **2 :** an English-based creole spoken by the Gullahs that is marked by vocabulary and grammatical elements from various African languages

gul·let \'gə-lət\ *noun* [Middle English *golet*, from Middle French *goulet*, diminutive of *goule* throat, from Latin *gula*] (14th century) **1 : ESOPHAGUS;** *broadly* **: THROAT 2 :** an invagination of the protoplasm in various protozoans (as a paramecium) that sometimes functions in the intake of food **3 :** the space between the tips of adjacent saw teeth

gull·ible *also* **gull·able** \'gə-lə-bəl\ *adjective* (1818) : easily duped or cheated
— **gull·ibil·i·ty** \ˌgə-lə-'bi-lə-tē\ *noun*
— **gul·libly** \'gə-lə-blē\ *adverb*

¹gul·ly \'gə-lē\ *noun, plural* **gullies** [short for English dialect *gully knife*] (1582) *British* : a large knife

²gul·ly *also* **gul·ley** \'gə-lē\ *noun, plural* **gullies** [obsolete English *gully* (gullet)] (1637) **1 :** a trench which was originally worn in the earth by running water and through which water often runs after rains **2 :** a small valley or gulch

³gul·ly \'gə-lē\ *verb* **gullied; gul·ly·ing** (1754) : to make gullies in — *transitive verb*

gully erosion *noun* (1928) : soil erosion produced by running water

gu·los·i·ty \g(y)ü-'lä-sə-tē\ *noun* [Late Latin *gulositas*, from Latin *gulosus* gluttonous, from *gula* gullet] (15th century) : excessive appetite **: GREEDINESS**

gulp \'gəlp\ *verb* [Middle English, from a Middle Dutch or Middle Low German word akin to Dutch & Frisian *gulpen* to bubble forth, boast — more at YELP] (14th century) *transitive verb* **1 :** to swallow hurriedly or greedily or in one swallow **2 :** to keep back as if by swallowing ⟨*gulp* down a sob⟩ **:** to take in readily as if by swallowing ⟨*gulp* down knowledge⟩ ~ *intransitive verb* : to catch the breath as if in taking a long drink
— **gulp** *noun*
— **gulp·er** *noun*

¹gum \'gəm\ *noun* [Middle English *gome* from Old English *gōma* palate; akin to Old High German *guomo* palate, and perhaps to Greek *chaos* abyss] (before 12th century) : the tissue that surrounds the necks of teeth and covers the alveolar parts of the jaws; *broadly* : the alveolar portion of a jaw with its enveloping soft tissues

²gum *transitive verb* **gummed; gum·ming** (1777) **1 :** to enlarge gullets of (a saw) **2 :** to chew with the gums

³gum *noun* [Middle English *gomme*, from Middle French, from Latin *cummi, gummi*, from Greek *kommi*, from Egyptian *qmyt*] (14th century) **1 a :** any of numerous colloidal polysaccharide substances of plant origin that are gelatinous when moist but harden on drying and are salts of complex organic acids — compare MUCILAGE 1 **b :** any of various plant exudates (as an oleoresin or gum resin) **2 a :** a substance or deposit resembling a plant gum (as in sticky or adhesive quality) **b :** a tree (as a black gum) that yields gum **3 a :** a tree (as a black gum) that yields gum **4 :** the wood or lumber of a gum; *especially* : the sweet gum **5 : CHEWING GUM**

⁴gum *verb* **gummed; gum·ming** (1597) *transitive verb* **1 :** to clog, impede, or damage with or as if with gum ⟨*gum* up the works⟩ ~ *intransitive verb* **1 :** to exude or form gum **2 :** to become gummy
— **gum·mer** *noun*

gum arabic *noun* (14th century) : a water-soluble gum obtained from several acacias (especially *Acacia senegal*) and used especially in the manufacture of inks, adhesives, pharmaceuticals, and confections

¹gum·bo \'gəm-(ˌ)bō\ *noun, plural* **gumbos** [American French *gombo*, of Bantu origin; akin to Umbundu *ochinggômbo* okra] (1805) **1 :** a soup thickened with okra pods or filé and containing meat or seafoods and usually vegetables **2 : OKRA 1 3 a :** any of various fine-grained silty soils especially of the central U.S. that when wet become impervious and soapy or waxy and very sticky **b :** a heavy sticky mud **4 : MIXTURE, MÉLANGE**

²gumbo *adjective*

gumbo *noun, often capitalized* [American French *gombo*, perhaps from Kongo *nkômbó* runaway slave] (1838) **: CREOLE 4a**

gum·boil \'gəm-ˌbȯil\ *noun* (1753) : an abscess in the gum

gum·bo-lim·bo \ˌgəm-bō-'lim-(ˌ)bō\ *noun* [origin unknown] (1837) : a tree (*Bursera simaruba* of the family Burseraceae) of southern Florida and the American tropics that has a smooth coppery bark and supplies a reddish resin used locally in cements and varnishes

gum boot *noun* (1850) : a rubber boot

gum·drop \'gəm-ˌdräp\ *noun* (1860) : a sugar-coated candy made usually from corn syrup with gelatin or gum arabic

gum·ma \'gə-mə\ *noun, plural* **gummas** *also* **gum·ma·ta** \'gə-mə-tə\ [New Latin *gummat-, gumma*, from Late Latin *gummi*, gum, alteration of Latin *gummi* gum] (circa 1722) : a tumor of gummy or rubbery consistency that is characteristic of the tertiary stage of syphilis
— **gum·ma·tous** \-mə-təs\ *adjective*

gum·mite \'gə-ˌmīt\ *noun* (1868) : a yellow to reddish brown mixture of hydrous oxides of uranium, thorium, and lead

gum·mo·sis \ˌgə-'mō-səs\ *noun* [New Latin] (1882) : a pathological production of gummy exudate in a plant; *also* : a plant disease marked by gummosis

gum·mous \'gə-məs\ *adjective* (1669) : resembling or composed of gum

gum·my \'gə-mē\ *adjective* **gum·mi·er; -est** (14th century) **1 : VISCOUS, STICKY 2 a :** consisting of or containing gum **b :** covered with gum
— **gum·mi·ness** *noun*

gump·tion \'gəm(p)-shən\ *noun* [origin unknown] (1719) **1** *chiefly dialect* **: COMMON SENSE, HORSE SENSE 2 : ENTERPRISE, INITIATIVE** ⟨lacked the *gumption* to try⟩

gum resin *noun* (1712) : a product consisting essentially of a mixture of gum and resin usually obtained by making an incision in a plant and allowing the juice which exudes to solidify

¹gum·shoe \'gəm-ˌshü\ *noun* (1906) **1 : DETECTIVE**

²gumshoe *intransitive verb* **gum·shoed; gum·shoe·ing** (1930) : to engage in detective work

gum tragacanth *noun* (1573) **: TRAGACANTH**

gum tree *noun* (1676)

gum turpentine *noun* (1926) **: TURPENTINE 2a**

gum·wood \'gəm-ˌwu̇d\ *noun* (1709) **: ³GUM 4**

¹gun \'gən\ *noun* [Middle English *gonne, gunne*] (14th century) **1 a :** a piece of ordnance usually with high muzzle velocity and comparatively flat trajectory **b :** a portable firearm (as a rifle or handgun) **c :** a device that throws a projectile **2 a :** a discharge of a gun especially as a salute or signal **b :** a signal marking a beginning or ending **3 a : HUNTER b : GUNMAN 4 :** something suggesting a gun in shape or function **5 : THROTTLE**
— **gunned** *adjective*
— **under the gun :** under pressure or attack

²gun *verb* **gunned; gun·ning** (1622) *transitive verb* : to hunt with a gun **1 a :** to fire on ⟨*gunned* down by a hit man⟩ **2 a :** to open up the throttle of so as to increase speed ⟨*gun* the engine⟩ **b : FIRE 3b** ⟨*gunned* the ball to first base⟩
— **gun for :** to aim at or go after with determination or effort

gun·boat \'gən-ˌbōt\ *noun* (1777) : an armed ship of shallow draft

gunboat diplomacy *noun* (1927) : diplomacy backed by the use or threat of military force

gun control *noun* (1969) : regulation of the selling, owning, and use of guns

gun·cot·ton \-ˌkä-tʰn\ *noun* (1846) **: NITROCELLULOSE;** *especially* : highly nitrated product used chiefly in smokeless powder

gun·dog \-ˌdȯg\ *noun* (1744) : a dog trained to work with hunters by locating and retrieving game

gun·fight \-ˌfīt\ *noun* (1659) : a hostile encounter in which antagonists fire upon each other
— **gun·fight·er** \-ˌfī-tər\ *noun*

gun·fire \-ˌfīr\ *noun* (1801)
: the firing of guns

gun·flint \-ˌflint\ *noun* (1731)
: a small sharp flint fashioned to ignite the priming in a flintlock

gung ho \ˈgən-ˈhō\ *adjective* [*Gung ho!*, motto (interpreted as meaning "work together") adopted by certain U.S. marines, from Chinese (Beijing) *gōnghé*, short for *Zhōngguó Gōngyè Hézuò Shè* Chinese Industrial Cooperative Society] (1942)
: extremely or overly zealous or enthusiastic

◊ **gun·ite** \ˈgən-ˌnīt\ *noun* (1914)
: a building material consisting of a mixture of cement, sand, and water that is sprayed onto a mold

gunk \ˈgəŋk\ *noun* [from *Gunk*, trademark for a cleaning solvent] (1943)
: filthy, sticky, or greasy matter
— **gunky** \ˈgəŋ-kē\ *adjective*

gun lap *noun* (circa 1949)
: the final lap of a race signaled by the firing of a gun as the leader begins the lap

gun·man \-mən\ *noun* (1624)
1 : a man armed with a gun; *especially* : a professional killer
2 : a man noted for speed or skill in handling a gun

gun·met·al \ˈgən-ˌme-t'l\ *noun* (1541)
1 : a metal used for guns; *specifically* : a bronze formerly much used as a material for cannon
2 : an alloy or metal treated to imitate nearly black tarnished copper-alloy gunmetal
3 : a bluish gray color

gun moll \-ˌmäl, -ˌmōl\ *noun* [slang *gun* thief, alteration from *gonoph*, *ganef* thief — more at GANEF] (circa 1908)
slang : MOLL 2b

Gun·nar \ˈgu̇-ˌnär, ˈgu̇-, -nər\ *noun* [Old Norse *Gunnarr*]
: the king of the Nibelungs and husband of Brynhild in Norse mythology

[1]**gun·nel** \ˈgən-n'l\ *variant of* GUNWALE

[2]**gunnel** *noun* [origin unknown] (1740)
: a small slimy elongate north Atlantic blenny (*Pholis gunnellus*); *broadly* : any fish of the family (Pholidae) to which the gunnel belongs

gun·ner \ˈgə-nər\ *noun* (14th century)
1 : a soldier or airman who operates or aims a gun
2 : one who hunts with a gun
3 : a warrant officer who supervises ordnance and ordnance stores

gun·nery \ˈgən-rē, ˈgə-nə-\ *noun* (1605)
: the use of guns; *especially* : the science of the flight of projectiles and of the effective use of guns

gunnery sergeant *noun* (circa 1961)
: a noncommissioned officer in the marine corps ranking above a staff sergeant and below a master sergeant or first sergeant

gun·ny·sack \ˈgə-nē-ˌsak\ *noun* [*gunny* coarse fabric, of Indo-Aryan origin; akin to Hindi *gon* sack, Punjabi *gūṇ*] (1862)
: a sack made of a coarse heavy fabric (as burlap)

gun·play \ˈgən-ˌplā\ *noun* (1881)
: the shooting of small arms with intent to scare or kill

gun·point \-ˌpȯint\ *noun* (1951)
: the muzzle of a gun
— **at gunpoint** : under a threat of death by being shot

gun·pow·der \-ˌpau̇-dər\ *noun* (15th century)
: an explosive mixture of potassium nitrate, charcoal, and sulfur used in gunnery and blasting; *broadly* : any of various powders used in guns as propelling charges

gun room *noun* (1626)
: quarters on a British warship originally used by the gunner and his mates but now by midshipmen and junior officers

gun·run·ner \ˈgən-ˌrə-nər\ *noun* (1899)
: one that traffics in contraband arms and ammunition
— **gun·run·ning** \-ˌrə-niŋ\ *noun*

gun·sel \ˈgən(t)-səl\ *noun* [slang *gunsel* catamite, perhaps modification of Yiddish *gendzl* gosling] (1944)
slang : GUNMAN

gun·ship \ˈgən-ˌship\ *noun* (1966)
: a helicopter or cargo aircraft armed with rockets and machine guns

gun·shot \ˈgən-ˌshät\ *noun* (15th century)
1 : shot or a projectile fired from a gun
2 : the range of a gun
3 : the firing of a gun

gun·shy \-ˌshī\ *adjective* (1884)
1 : afraid of loud noise (as that of a gun)
2 : markedly distrustful, afraid, or cautious

gun·sling·er \-ˌsliŋ-ər\ *noun* (1928)
: a person noted for speed and skill in handling and shooting a gun especially in the American West

gun·sling·ing \-ˌsliŋ-iŋ\ *noun* (circa 1944)
: the shooting of a gun especially in a gunfight

gun·smith \-ˌsmith\ *noun* (1588)
: one who designs, makes, or repairs small firearms
— **gun·smith·ing** \-ˌsmi-thiŋ\ *noun*

Gun·ter's chain \ˈgən-tərz-\ *noun* [Edmund *Gunter* (died 1626)] (1679)
: a chain 66 feet (20.1 meters) long that is the unit of length for surveys of U.S. public lands

Gun·ther \ˈgu̇n-tər\ *noun* [German]
: a Burgundian king and husband of Brunhild in Germanic legend

gun·wale *also* **gun·nel** \ˈgə-n'l\ *noun* [Middle English *gonne-wale*, from *gonne* gun + *wale*; from its former use as a support for guns] (15th century)
— **to the gunwales** : as full as possible
: the upper edge of a ship's or boat's side

gup·py \ˈgə-pē\ *noun*, *plural* **guppies** [R.J.L. *Giúppy* (died 1916) Trinidadian naturalist] (1925)
: a small live-bearer (*Poecilia reticulata* of the family Poeciliidae) of Barbados, Trinidad, and Venezuela often kept as an aquarium fish

gur·gle \ˈgər-gəl\ *intransitive verb* **gur·gled; gur·gling** \-g(ə-)liŋ\ [probably imitative] (1713)
1 : to flow in a broken irregular current ⟨the brook *gurgling* over the rocks⟩
2 : to make a sound like that of a gurgling liquid ⟨the baby *gurgling* in his crib⟩
— **gurgle** *noun*

Gur·kha \ˈgu̇r-kə, ˈgər-\ *noun* [*Gurkha*, member of a Rajput clan who dominated Nepal in the 18th century] (1811)
: a soldier from Nepal in the British or Indian army

gur·nard \ˈgər-nərd\ *noun*, *plural* **gurnard** *or* **gurnards** [Middle English, from Middle French *gornart*, irregular from *grognier* to grunt, from Latin *grunnire*, of imitative origin] (14th century)
: SEA ROBIN — compare FLYING GURNARD

gur·ney \ˈgər-nē\ *noun*, *plural* **gurneys** [probably from the name *Gurney*] (1939)
: a wheeled cot or stretcher

gur·ry \ˈgər-ē, ˈgə-rē\ *noun* [origin unknown] (1850)
: fishing offal

gu·ru \ˈgu̇r-(ˌ)ü *also* gə-ˈrü\ *noun*, *plural* **gu·rus** [Hindi *gurū*, from Sanskrit *guru*, from *guru*, adjective, heavy, venerable — more at GRIEVE] (1613)
1 : a personal religious teacher and spiritual guide in Hinduism
2 a : a teacher and especially intellectual guide in matters of fundamental concern b : one who is an acknowledged leader or chief

proponent c : a person with knowledge or expertise : EXPERT

[1]**gush** \ˈgəsh\ *verb* [Middle English *guschen*] (15th century)
intransitive verb
1 : to issue copiously or violently
2 : to emit a sudden copious flow
3 : to make an effusive display of affection or enthusiasm ⟨an aunt *gushing* over the baby⟩
transitive verb
1 : to emit in a copious free flow
2 : to say or write effusively
— **gush·ing·ly** \ˈgə-shiŋ-lē\ *adverb*

[2]**gush** *noun* (circa 1682)
1 a : a sudden outpouring b : something emitted in a gushing forth
2 : an effusive display or outpouring

gush·er \ˈgə-shər\ *noun* (1864)
: one that gushes; *specifically* : an oil well with a copious natural flow

gushy \ˈgə-shē\ *adjective* **gush·i·er; -est** (1845)
: marked by effusive sentimentality
— **gush·i·ly** \ˈgə-shə-lē\ *adverb*
— **gush·i·ness** \-gə-shē-nəs\ *noun*

gus·set \ˈgə-sət\ *noun* [Middle English, piece of armor covering the joints in a suit of armor, from Middle French *goussel*] (circa 1570)
1 : a usually diamond-shaped or triangular insert in a seam (as of a sleeve, pocketbook, or shoe upper) to provide expansion or reinforcement
2 : a plate or bracket for strengthening an angle in a framework (as in a building or bridge)
— **gusset** *transitive verb*

gus·sy up \ˈgə-sē-ˈəp\ *transitive verb* **gus·sied up; gus·sy·ing up** [origin unknown] (1952)
: DRESS UP, EMBELLISH

[1]**gust** \ˈgəst\ *noun* [Middle English *guste*, from Latin *gustus*; akin to CHOOSE] (15th century)
1 *obsolete* a : the sensation of taste b : INCLINATION, LIKING
2 : keen delight

[2]**gust** *noun* [probably from Old Norse *gustr*; akin to Old High German *gussa* flood, and perhaps to Old English *gēotan* to pour — more at FOUND] (1588)
1 : a sudden brief rush of wind
2 : a sudden outburst : SURGE ⟨a *gust* of emotion⟩
— **gust·i·ly** \ˈgəs-tə-lē\ *adverb*

guppy: 1 female, 2 male

— **gust·i·ness** \-tē-nəs\ *noun*
— **gusty** \-tē\ *adjective*
³**gust** *intransitive verb* (1813)
: to blow in gusts ⟨winds *gusting* up to 40 mph⟩
gus·ta·tion \ˌgəs-'tā-shən\ *noun* [Latin *gustation-, gustatio,* from *gustare*] (1599)
: the act or sensation of tasting
gus·ta·to·ry \'gəs-tə-ˌtōr-ē, -ˌtȯr-\ *adjective* (1684)
: relating to or associated with eating or the sense of taste
— **gus·ta·to·ri·ly** \ˌgəs-tə-'tōr-ə-lē, -'tȯr-\ *adverb*
gus·to \'gəs-(ˌ)tō\ *noun, plural* **gustoes** [Italian, from Latin *gustus,* past participle] (1620)
1 a : an individual or special taste ⟨different *gustoes*⟩ **b :** enthusiastic and vigorous enjoyment or appreciation **c :** vitality marked by an abundance of vigor and enthusiasm
2 *archaic* **:** artistic style
¹**gut** \'gət\ *noun* [Middle English, from Old English *guttas,* plural; probably akin to Old English *gēotan* to pour] (before 12th century)
1 a (1) **:** BOWELS, ENTRAILS — usually used in plural (2) **:** the basic visceral or emotional part of a person **b :** the alimentary canal or part of it (as the intestine or stomach) **c :** BELLY, ABDOMEN **d :** CATGUT
2 *plural* **:** the inner essential parts ⟨the *guts* of a car⟩
3 : a narrow passage; *also* **:** a narrow waterway or small creek
4 : the sac of silk taken from a silkworm ready to spin its cocoon and drawn out into a thread for use as a snell
5 *plural* **:** fortitude and stamina in coping with what alarms, repels, or discourages **:** COURAGE, PLUCK
6 : GUT COURSE
²**gut** *transitive verb* **gut·ted; gut·ting** (14th century)
1 a : EVISCERATE **b :** to extract all the essential passages or portions from
2 a : to destroy the inside of ⟨fire *gutted* the building⟩ **b :** to destroy the essential power or effectiveness of ⟨inflation *gutting* the economy⟩
— **gut it out :** PERSEVERE
³**gut** *adjective* (1964)
1 : arising from one's inmost self **:** VISCERAL ⟨a *gut* reaction⟩
2 : having strong impact or immediate relevance ⟨*gut* issues⟩
gut·buck·et \'gət-ˌbə-kət\ *noun* (1929)
1 : BARRELHOUSE 2
2 : a homemade bass fiddle consisting of a stick attached to an inverted washtub and having a single string
gut course *noun* (1948)
: a course (as in college) that is easily passed
gut·less \'gət-ləs\ *adjective* (1900)
1 : lacking courage **:** COWARDLY
2 : lacking significance or vitality
— **gut·less·ness** *noun*
gutsy \'gət-sē\ *adjective* **guts·i·er; -est** (circa 1893)
1 : marked by courage, pluck, or determination ⟨a *gutsy* little fighter⟩ ⟨a *gutsy* decision⟩
2 a : expressing or characterized by basic physical senses or passions ⟨*gutsy* macho talk⟩ ⟨*gutsy* country blues⟩ **b :** rough or plain in style **:** not bland or sophisticated ⟨a *gutsy* soup⟩
— **gut·si·ly** \-sə-lē\ *adverb*
— **guts·i·ness** *noun*
gut·ta \'gə-tə, 'gu̇-tə\ *noun, plural* **gut·tae** \'gə-ˌtē, 'gu̇-, -ˌtī\ [Latin, literally, drop] (1563)
: one of a series of ornaments in the Doric entablature that is usually in the form of a frustum of a cone
gut·ta-per·cha \ˌgə-tə-'pər-chə\ *noun* [Malay *gětah-pěrcha,* from *gětah* sap, latex + *pěrcha* scrap, rag] (1845)
: a tough plastic substance from the latex of several Malaysian trees (genera *Payena* and

Palaquium) of the sapodilla family that resembles rubber but contains more resin and is used especially as insulation and in dentistry
gut·ta·tion \ˌgə-'tā-shən\ *noun* [Latin *gutta* drop] (circa 1889)
: the exudation of liquid water from the uninjured surface of a plant leaf
¹**gut·ter** \'gə-tər\ *noun* [Middle English *goter,* from Middle French *goutiere,* from *goute* drop, from Latin *gutta*] (14th century)
1 a : a trough along the eaves to catch and carry off rainwater **b :** a low area (as at the edge of a street) to carry off surface water (as to a sewer) **c :** a trough or groove to catch and direct something ⟨the *gutters* of a bowling alley⟩
2 : a white space formed by the adjoining inside margins of two facing pages (as of a book)
3 : the lowest or most vulgar level or condition of human life
²**gutter** (14th century)
transitive verb
1 : to cut or wear gutters in
2 : to provide with a gutter
intransitive verb
1 a : to flow in rivulets **b** *of a candle* **:** to melt away through a channel out of the side of the cup hollowed out by the burning wick
2 : to incline downward in a draft ⟨the candle flame *guttering*⟩
³**gutter** *adjective* (15th century)
: of, relating to, or characteristic of the gutter; *especially* **:** marked by extreme vulgarity, cheapness, and indecency ⟨*gutter* politics⟩
gut·ter·ing \-iŋ\ *noun* (1703)
1 : material for gutters
2 : GUTTER 1a
gutter out *intransitive verb* (1875)
1 : to become gradually weaker and then go out ⟨the candle *guttered out*⟩
2 : to end feebly or undramatically ⟨his screen career had slowly *guttered out*⟩
gut·ter·snipe \'gə-tər-ˌsnīp\ *noun* (circa 1869)
1 : STREET ARAB
2 : a person of the lowest moral or economic station
— **gut·ter·snip·ish** \-ˌsnī-pish\ *adjective*
gut·tur·al \'gə-tə-rəl, 'gə-trəl\ *adjective* [Middle French, probably from Medieval Latin *gutturalis,* from Latin *guttur* throat] (1594)
1 : articulated in the throat ⟨*guttural* sounds⟩
2 : VELAR
3 : being or marked by utterance that is strange, unpleasant, or disagreeable
— **guttural** *noun*
— **gut·tur·al·ism** \'gə-tə-rə-ˌli-zəm, 'gə-trə-\ *noun*
gut·ty \'gə-tē\ *adjective* **gut·ti·er; -est** (1947)
1 : GUTSY 1 ⟨a *gutty* quarterback⟩
2 : having a vigorous challenging quality ⟨*gutty* realism⟩
gut–wrench·ing \'gət-ˌren-chiŋ\ *adjective* (1974)
: causing mental or emotional anguish
¹**guy** \'gī\ *noun* [probably from Dutch *gei* brail] (1623)
: a rope, chain, rod, or wire attached to something as a brace or guide — called also **guyline**
²**guy** *transitive verb* (1712)
: to steady or reinforce with a guy
³**guy** *noun* [*Guy* Fawkes] (1806)
1 *often capitalized* **:** a grotesque effigy of Guy Fawkes traditionally displayed and burned in England on Guy Fawkes Day
2 *chiefly British* **:** a person of grotesque appearance
3 a : MAN, FELLOW **b :** PERSON — used in plural to refer to the members of a group regardless of sex ⟨saw her and the rest of the *guys*⟩ ◆
⁴**guy** *transitive verb* (1854)
: to make fun of **:** RIDICULE

Guy Fawkes Day \'gī-'fȯks-\ *noun* (1825)
: November 5 observed in England in commemoration of the seizure of Guy Fawkes in 1605 for an attempt to blow up the houses of Parliament
guy·ot \'gē-(ˌ)ō\ *noun* [Arnold H. *Guyot* (died 1884) American geographer & geologist] (1946)
: a flat-topped seamount
guz·zle \'gə-zəl\ *verb* **guz·zled; guz·zling** \'gəz-liŋ, 'gə-zə-\ [origin unknown] (1583)
intransitive verb
: to drink especially liquor greedily, continually, or habitually
transitive verb
: to drink greedily or habitually ⟨*guzzle* beer⟩
— **guz·zler** \'gəz-lər, 'gə-zə-\ *noun*
gwe·duc \'gü-ē-ˌdək\ *variant of* GEODUCK
gybe \'jīb\ *variant of* JIBE
gym \'jim\ *noun* (circa 1871)
1 : GYMNASIUM
2 : PHYSICAL EDUCATION
3 : a usually metal frame supporting an assortment of outdoor play equipment (as a swing, seesaw, and rings)
gym·kha·na \jim-'kä-nə, -'ka-\ *noun* [probably modification of Hindi *gēdkhāna,* literally, ball court] (1877)
: a meet featuring sports contests or athletic skills: as **a :** competitive games on horseback **b :** a timed contest for automobiles featuring a series of events designed to test driving skill
gym·na·si·um *sense 1* jim-'nā-zē-əm, -zhəm; *sense 2 usually* gim-'nä-zē-əm\ *noun, plural* **-na·si·ums** *or* **-na·sia** \-'nā-zē-ə, -'nä-zhə; -'nä-zē-ə\ [Latin, exercise ground, school, from Greek *gymnasion,* from *gymnazein* to exercise naked, from *gymnos* naked — more at NAKED] (1598)
1 a : a large room used for various indoor sports (as basketball or boxing) and usually equipped with gymnastic apparatus **b :** a building (as on a college campus) containing space and equipment for various indoor sports activities and usually including spectator accommodations, locker and shower rooms, offices, classrooms, and a swimming pool

◇ WORD HISTORY
guy On November 4, 1605, Guy Fawkes was arrested in London and later executed for having planted barrels of gunpowder in the cellars of the houses of Parliament as part of a conspiracy to blow up the buildings. The failure of this conspiracy, now known as the Gunpowder Plot, is still celebrated in England on the evening of November 5, Guy Fawkes Day, when bonfires are traditionally lit and fireworks set off. On the bonfires are burned effigies of Guy Fawkes made from old clothes stuffed with straw and rags. By the early part of the 19th century these effigies had come to be called *guys.* The use of this word was extended to other similar effigies and then to a person of grotesque appearance or dress. In the U.S., where Guy Fawkes' demise has apparently never been celebrated, the word *guy* has had an extraordinary career, passing in the course of the last two centuries from the meaning "person who is an object of derision or pity" to "man, fellow" to a gender-neutral "person." The last sense is heard particularly in the phrase *you guys,* first attested in 1896, which sometimes amounts to little more than a familiar plural form of the second-person pronoun.

\ə\ abut \ᵊ\ kitten \ər\ further \a\ ash \ā\ ace
\ä\ mop, mar \au̇\ out \ch\ chin \e\ bet \ē\ easy
\g\ go \i\ hit \ī\ ice \j\ job \ŋ\ sing \ō\ go
\ȯ\ law \ȯi\ boy \th\ thin \t̲h̲\ the \ü\ loot \u̇\ foot
\y\ yet \zh\ vision *see also* Guide to Pronunciation

2 [German, from Latin, school] : a European secondary school that prepares students for the university ◇

gym·nast \'jim-ˌnast, -nəst\ noun [Middle French gymnaste, from Greek gymnastēs trainer, from gymnazein] (1594)
: one trained in gymnastics

¹gym·nas·tic \jim-'nas-tik\ adjective (1574)
: of or relating to gymnastics : ATHLETIC
— **gym·nas·ti·cal·ly** \-ti-k(ə-)lē\ adverb

²gymnastic noun (1652)
1 plural but singular in construction **a** : physical exercises designed to develop strength and coordination **b** : a competitive sport in which individuals perform optional and prescribed acrobatic feats mostly on special apparatus in order to demonstrate strength, balance, and body control
2 : an exercise in intellectual or artistic dexterity ⟨my earlier philosophic study had been an intellectual gymnastic —John Dewey⟩ ⟨mental gymnastics⟩
3 : a physical feat or contortion ⟨the gymnastics necessary for the killer to have swung from the fire escape —E. D. Radin⟩

gym·nos·o·phist \jim-'nä-sə-fist\ noun [Latin gymnosophista, from Greek gymnosophistēs, from gymnos + sophistēs wise man, sophist] (15th century)
: any of a sect of ascetics in ancient India who went naked and practiced meditation

gym·no·sperm \'jim-nə-ˌspərm\ noun [ultimately from Greek gymnos + sperma seed — more at SPERM] (circa 1838)
: any of a class (Gymnospermae) of woody vascular seed plants (as conifers) that produce naked seeds not enclosed in an ovary and that in some instances have motile spermatozoids
— **gym·no·sper·mous** \ˌjim-nə-'spər-məs\ adjective
— **gym·no·sper·my** \'jim-nə-ˌspər-mē\ noun

gyn- or **gyno-** combining form [Greek gyn-, from gynē woman — more at QUEEN]
: female reproductive organ : ovary ⟨gynophore⟩

gy·nae·col·o·gy chiefly British variant of GYNECOLOGY

gyn·an·dro·morph \ˌgīn-'an-drə-ˌmȯrf, ˌjin-\ noun [International Scientific Vocabulary, from Greek gynandros + -morph] (circa 1890)
: an abnormal individual exhibiting characters of both sexes in various parts of the body : a sexual mosaic
— **gyn·an·dro·mor·phic** \(ˌ)gīn-ˌan-drə-'mȯr-fik, (ˌ)jin-\ adjective
— **gyn·an·dro·mor·phism** \-ˌfi-zəm\ noun
— **gyn·an·dro·mor·phy** \ˌgīn-'an-drə-ˌmȯr-fē, ˌjin-\ noun

gyn·an·drous \gīn-'an-drəs, ˌjin-\ adjective [Greek gynandros of doubtful sex, from gynē woman + andr-, anēr man — more at ANDR-] (1807)
: having the androecium and gynoecium united in a column

-gyne noun combining form [Greek gynē]
: female reproductive organ ⟨trichogyne⟩

gynec- or **gyneco-** also **gynaec-** or **gynaeco-** combining form [Greek gynaik-, gynaiko-, from gynaik-, gynē woman — more at QUEEN]
: woman ⟨gynecology⟩

gy·ne·coc·ra·cy \ˌgī-ni-'kä-krə-sē, ˌji-\ noun, plural **-cies** [Greek gynaikokratia, from gynaik- + -kratia -cracy] (1612)
: political supremacy of women
— **gy·ne·co·crat·ic** \ˌgī-ni-kō-'kra-tik, ˌji-\ adjective

gy·ne·coid \'gī-ni-ˌkȯid, 'ji-\ adjective (1907)
: typical or characteristic of the human female ⟨gynecoid pelvis⟩

gy·ne·col·o·gy \ˌgī-nə-'kä-lə-jē, ˌji-\ noun [International Scientific Vocabulary] (circa 1847)

: a branch of medicine that deals with the diseases and routine physical care of the reproductive system of women
— **gy·ne·co·log·ic** \ˌgī-ni-kə-'lä-jik, ˌji-\ or **gy·ne·co·log·i·cal** \-ji-kəl\ adjective
— **gy·ne·col·o·gist** \ˌgī-nə-'kä-lə-jist, ˌji-\ noun

gy·neco·mas·tia \ˌgī-nə-kō-'mas-tē-ə\ noun [New Latin, from gyneco- + Greek mastos breast + New Latin -ia] (1881)
: excessive development of the breast in the male

gy·noe·ci·um \ji-'nē-shē-əm, gī-, -sē-\ noun, plural **-cia** \-shē-ə, -sē-\ [New Latin, alteration of Latin gynaeceum women's apartments, from Greek gynaikeion, from gynaik-, gynē] (1832)
: the aggregate of carpels or pistils in a flower

gy·no·gen·e·sis \ˌgī-nə-'je-nə-səs\ noun [New Latin] (1925)
: development in which the embryo contains only maternal chromosomes due to activation of an egg by a sperm that degenerates without fusing with the egg nucleus
— **gy·no·ge·net·ic** \-jə-'ne-tik\ adjective

gy·no·phore \'gī-nə-ˌfōr, 'ji-, -ˌfȯr\ noun (1821)
: a prolongation of the receptacle (as in a caper flower) with the gynoecium at its apex

-gynous adjective combining form [New Latin -gynus, from Greek -gynos, from gynē woman — more at QUEEN]
1 : of, relating to, or having (such or so many) wives ⟨monogynous⟩
2 : situated (in a specified place) in relation to a female organ of a plant ⟨hypogynous⟩

-gyny noun combining form
1 : existence of or condition of having (such or so many) wives ⟨polygyny⟩
2 : condition of being situated (in a specified place) in relation to a female organ of a plant ⟨epigyny⟩

¹gyp \'jip\ noun [probably short for gypsy] (1750)
1 British : a college servant
2 a : CHEAT, SWINDLER **b** : FRAUD, SWINDLE

²gyp verb **gypped; gyp·ping** (1880)
: CHEAT

gyp·se·ous \'jip-sē-əs\ adjective (1661)
: resembling, containing, or consisting of gypsum ⟨gypseous clay loam⟩

gyp·sif·er·ous \jip-'si-f(ə-)rəs\ adjective (circa 1847)
: containing gypsum

gyp·soph·i·la \jip-'sä-fə-lə\ noun [New Latin, from Latin gypsum + New Latin -phila -phil] (1771)
: any of a large genus (Gypsophila) of Old World herbs of the pink family having small delicate usually paniculate flowers

gyp·sum \'jip-səm\ noun [Latin, from Greek gypsos] (14th century)
1 : a widely distributed mineral consisting of hydrous calcium sulfate that is used especially as a soil amendment and in making plaster of paris
2 : PLASTERBOARD

gyp·sy \'jip-sē\ intransitive verb **gyp·sied; gyp·sy·ing** (circa 1627)
: to live or roam like a Gypsy

Gyp·sy \'jip-sē\ noun, plural **Gypsies** [by shortening & alteration from Egyptian] (1537)
1 : a member of a traditionally itinerant people who originated in northern India and now live chiefly in south and southwest Asia, Europe, and North America
2 : ROMANY 2
3 not capitalized : one that resembles a Gypsy; especially : WANDERER

gypsy cab noun (1964)
: a taxicab licensed only to answer calls; especially : such a cab that cruises in search of passengers

gypsy moth noun (1819)
: an Old World tussock moth (Lymantria dispar) that was introduced about 1869 into the

U.S. and has a grayish brown mottled hairy caterpillar which is a destructive defoliator of many trees

gyr- or **gyro-** combining form [probably from Middle French, from Latin, from Greek, from gyros rounded]
1 : ring : circle : spiral ⟨gyromagnetic⟩
2 : gyroscope ⟨gyrocompass⟩

gyr·ase \'jī-ˌrās\ noun [gyr- + -ase] (1976)
: an enzyme that catalyzes the breaking and rejoining of bonds linking adjacent nucleotides in DNA to generate supercoiled DNA helices

¹gy·rate \'jī-ˌrāt\ adjective (1830)
: winding or coiled around : CONVOLUTED ⟨gyrate branches of a tree⟩

²gyrate intransitive verb **gy·rat·ed; gy·rat·ing** (1830)
1 : to revolve around a point or axis
2 : to oscillate with or as if with a circular or spiral motion
— **gy·ra·tor** \-ˌrā-tər\ noun
— **gy·ra·to·ry** \'jī-rə-ˌtōr-ē, -ˌtȯr-\ adjective

gy·ra·tion \jī-'rā-shən\ noun (1615)
1 : an act or instance of gyrating
2 : something (as a coil of a shell) that is gyrate
— **gy·ra·tion·al** \-shnəl, -shə-n°l\ adjective

¹gyre \'jī(-ə)r\ noun [Latin gyrus, from Greek gyros] (1566)
: a circular or spiral motion or form; especially : a giant circular oceanic surface current
— **gy·ral** \'jī-rəl\ adjective

²gyre intransitive verb **gyred; gyr·ing** [Late Latin gyrare, from Latin gyrus] (1593)
: to move in a circle or spiral

gy·rene \jī-'rēn\ noun [probably alteration of marine] (1944)
slang : a U.S. marine

gyr·fal·con \'jər-ˌfal-kən, -ˌfȯl- also -ˌfȯ-kən\ noun [Middle English gerfaucun, from Old French girfaucon, probably from gir vulture (from Old High German gīr) + faucon falcon] (14th century)
: an arctic falcon (Falco rusticolus) that occurs in several color forms and is the largest of all falcons

gyrfalcon

¹**gy·ro** \'jī-(,)rō\ *noun, plural* **gyros** (1910)
 1 : GYROCOMPASS
 2 : GYROSCOPE
²**gy·ro** \'yē-,rō, 'zhir-ō\ *noun, plural* **gyros**
[New Greek *gyros* turn, from Greek; from the
rotation of the meat on a spit] (1971)
 : a sandwich especially of lamb and beef, to-
mato, and onion on pita bread
Gy·ro \'jī-(,)rō\ *noun, plural* **Gyros** [*Gyro* In-
ternational (association)] (1971)
 : a member of a major international service
club
gy·ro·com·pass \'jī-rō-,kəm-pəs *also* -,käm-\
noun (1910)
 : a compass consisting of a continuously driv-
en gyroscope whose spinning axis is confined
to a horizontal plane so that the earth's rota-
tion causes it to assume a position parallel to
the earth's axis and thus point to the true north
gy·ro·fre·quen·cy \-,frē-kwən(t)-sē\ *noun*
(1938)
 : the frequency with which a charged particle
(as an electron) executes spiral gyrations in
moving obliquely across a magnetic field
gyro horizon *noun* (1938)
 : ARTIFICIAL HORIZON

gy·ro·mag·net·ic \,jī-rō-mag-'ne-tik\ *adjec-
tive* (1922)
 : of or relating to the magnetic properties of a
rotating electrical particle
gyromagnetic ratio *noun* (1922)
 : the ratio of the magnetic moment of a spin-
ning charged particle to its angular momentum
gy·ron \'jī-rən\ *noun* [Middle French *giron*
gore, of Germanic origin; akin to Old High
German *gēra* wedge-shaped object, Old En-
glish *gār* spear — more at GORE] (1572)
 : a heraldic charge of triangular form having
one side at the edge of the field and the oppo-
site angle usually at the fess point
gy·ro·plane \'jī-rə-,plān\ *noun* [International
Scientific Vocabulary] (1907)
 : an airplane balanced and supported by the
aerodynamic forces acting on rapidly rotating
horizontal or slightly inclined airfoils
gy·ro·scope \'jī-rə-,skōp, *British also* 'gī-\
noun [French] (1856)
 : a wheel or disk mounted to spin rapidly
about an axis and also free to rotate about one
or both of two axes perpendicular to each oth-
er and to the axis of spin so that a rotation of
one of the two mutually perpendicular axes re-
sults from application of torque to the other

when the wheel is spinning and so that the en-
tire apparatus offers considerable opposition
depending on the angular momentum to any
torque that would change the direction of the
axis of spin
— **gy·ro·scop·ic** \,jī-rə-'skä-pik\ *adjective*
— **gy·ro·scop·i·cal·ly** \-pi-k(ə-)lē\ *adverb*
gy·ro·sta·bi·liz·er \,jī-rō-'stā-bə-,lī-zər\ *noun*
(1921)
 : a stabilizing device (as for a ship or airplane)
that consists of a continuously driven gyro
spinning about a vertical axis and pivoted so
that its axis of spin may be tipped fore-and-aft
in the vertical plane and that serves to oppose
sideways motion — called also *gy·ro·stat*
\'jī-rə-,stat\
gy·rus \'jī-rəs\ *noun, plural* **gy·ri** \'jī-,rī\ [New
Latin, from Latin, circle — more at GYRE]
(circa 1842)
 : a convoluted ridge (as a convolution of the
brain) between anatomical grooves
gyve \'jīv, 'gīv\ *noun* [Middle English] (13th
century)
 : FETTER, SHACKLE
— **gyve** *transitive verb*

H

H *is the eighth letter of the English alphabet and of most alphabets closely related to that of English. It came through Latin via Etruscan from Greek, which took it from a Phoenician letter* hēth, *standing for a laryngeal aspirate (a consonant with the sound of a very forceful English* h). *In Greek it was called* eta *and was assigned to the long open* e *sound (as in English* café; *see* E) *except in the western alphabet, where it designated the rough breathing (that is, the sound of* h *in* helium). *This aspirated pronunciation passed through Etruscan and Latin to English. Small* h *evolved from a late Roman form of the capital in which the second upright line had been shortened to nearly the height of the horizontal cross-stroke. In a later Roman cursive script, the cross-stroke and shortened right vertical stroke were merged into a single downward-curving line.*

h \'āch\ *noun, plural* **h's** *or* **hs** \'ā-chəz\ *often capitalized, often attributive* (before 12th century)
1 a : the 8th letter of the English alphabet **b :** a graphic representation of this letter **c :** a speech counterpart of orthographic *h*
2 : a graphic device for reproducing the letter *h*
3 : one designated *h* especially as the 8th in order or class
4 : something shaped like the letter H

ha \'hä\ *interjection* [Middle English, from Old English] (before 12th century)
— used especially to express surprise or joy

Ha·ba·cuc \'ha-bə-,kək, hə-'ba-kək\ *noun* [Late Latin, from Hebrew *Ḥăbhaqqūq*]
: HABAKKUK

Ha·bak·kuk \'ha-bə-,kək, hə-'ba-kək\ *noun* [Hebrew *Ḥăbhaqqūq*]
1 : a Hebrew prophet of 7th century B.C. Judah who prophesied an imminent Chaldean invasion
2 : a prophetic book of canonical Jewish and Christian Scripture — see BIBLE table

ha·ba·ne·ra \,(h)ä-bə-'ner-ə\ *noun* [Spanish *(danza) habanera,* literally, Havanan dance] (1878)
1 : a Cuban dance in slow duple time
2 : the music for the habanera

hab·da·lah \,häv-də-'lä, häv-'dò-lə\ *noun, often capitalized* [Hebrew *habhdālāh* separation] (1733)
: a Jewish ceremony marking the close of a Sabbath or holy day

ha·be·as cor·pus \'hā-bē-əs-'kòr-pəs\ *noun* [Middle English, from Medieval Latin, literally, you should have the body (the opening words of the writ)] (15th century)
1 : any of several common-law writs issued to bring a party before a court or judge; *especially* **:** HABEAS CORPUS AD SUBJICIENDUM
2 : the right of a citizen to obtain a writ of habeas corpus as a protection against illegal imprisonment

habeas corpus ad sub·ji·ci·en·dum \-,ad-səb-,yi-kē-'en-dəm\ *noun* [New Latin, literally, you should have the body for submitting] (1768)
: a writ for inquiring into the lawfulness of the restraint of a person who is imprisoned or detained in another's custody

hab·er·dash·er \'ha-bə(r)-,da-shər\ *noun* [Middle English *haberdassher,* from modification of Anglo-French *hapertas* petty merchandise] (14th century)
1 *British* **:** a dealer in notions
2 : a dealer in men's clothing and accessories

hab·er·dash·ery \-,da-sh(ə-)rē\ *noun, plural* **-er·ies** (1593)
1 : goods sold by a haberdasher
2 : a haberdasher's shop

ha·ber·geon \'ha-bər-jən, hə-'bər-jē-ən, -jən\ *noun* [Middle English *haubergeoun,* from Middle French *haubergeon,* diminutive of *hauberc* hauberk] (14th century)
1 : a medieval jacket of mail shorter than a hauberk
2 : HAUBERK

Ha·ber process \'hä-bər-\ *noun* [Fritz *Haber* (died 1934) German chemist] (1916)
: a catalytic process for synthesizing ammonia from nitrogen and hydrogen

hab·ile \'ha-bəl, -,bīl\ *adjective* [French, from Latin *habilis* — more at ABLE] (15th century)
: having general skill **:** ABLE, SKILLFUL

hab·il·i·ment \hə-'bi-lə-mənt\ *noun* [Middle French *habillement,* from *habiller* to dress, prepare, from Old French *abiller,* from *bille* log — more at BILLET] (15th century)
1 *plural* **:** characteristic apparatus **:** FITTINGS ⟨the *habiliments* of civilization —W. P. Webb⟩
2 a : the dress characteristic of an occupation or occasion — usually used in plural **b :** CLOTHES — usually used in plural

ha·bil·i·tate \hə-'bi-lə-,tāt\ *verb* **-tat·ed; -tat·ing** [Late Latin *habilitatus,* past participle of *habilitare,* from Latin *habilitas* ability — more at ABILITY] (1604)
transitive verb
1 : to make fit or capable (as for functioning in society)
2 : CLOTHE, DRESS
intransitive verb
: to qualify oneself
— **ha·bil·i·ta·tion** \-,bi-lə-'tā-shən\ *noun*

¹hab·it \'ha-bət\ *noun* [Middle English, from Old French, from Latin *habitus* condition, character, from *habēre* to have, hold — more at GIVE] (13th century)
1 *archaic* **:** CLOTHING
2 a : a costume characteristic of a calling, rank, or function ⟨a nun's *habit*⟩ **b :** a costume worn for horseback riding
3 : manner of conducting oneself **:** BEARING
4 : bodily appearance or makeup ⟨a man of fleshy *habit*⟩
5 : the prevailing disposition or character of a person's thoughts and feelings **:** mental makeup
6 : a settled tendency or usual manner of behavior
7 a : a behavior pattern acquired by frequent repetition or physiologic exposure that shows itself in regularity or increased facility of performance **b :** an acquired mode of behavior that has become nearly or completely involuntary **c :** ADDICTION
8 : characteristic mode of growth or occurrence ⟨a grass similar to Indian corn in *habit*⟩
9 *of a crystal* **:** characteristic assemblage of forms at crystallization leading to a usual appearance ☆

²habit *transitive verb* (1594)
: CLOTHE, DRESS

hab·it·able \'ha-bə-tə-bəl *also* hə-'bi-tə-\ *adjective* (14th century)
: capable of being lived in **:** suitable for habitation
— **hab·it·abil·i·ty** \,ha-bə-tə-'bi-lə-tē\ *noun*
— **hab·it·able·ness** \'ha-bə-tə-bəl-nes\ *noun*
— **hab·it·ably** \-blē\ *adverb*

ha·bi·tant *noun* (15th century)
1 \'ha-bə-tənt\ **:** INHABITANT, RESIDENT
2 \,(h)a-bi-'täⁿ\ *also* **ha·bi·tan** \-'täⁿ\ **:** a settler or descendant of a settler of French origin working as a farmer in Canada

hab·i·tat \'ha-bə-,tat\ *noun* [Latin, it inhabits, from *habitare*] (1796)
1 a : the place or environment where a plant or animal naturally or normally lives and grows **b :** the typical place of residence of a person or a group **c :** a housing for a controlled physical environment in which people can live under surrounding inhospitable conditions (as under the sea)
2 : the place where something is commonly found

hab·i·ta·tion \,ha-bə-'tā-shən\ *noun* [Middle English *habitacioun,* from Middle French *habitation,* from Latin *habitation-, habitatio,* from *habitare* to inhabit, frequentative of *habēre*] (14th century)
1 : the act of inhabiting **:** OCCUPANCY
2 : a dwelling place **:** RESIDENCE
3 : SETTLEMENT, COLONY

hab·it–form·ing \'ha-bət-,fòr-miŋ\ *adjective* (1913)
: inducing the formation of an addiction

ha·bit·u·al \hə-'bi-ch(ə-)wəl, ha-, -'bi-chəl\ *adjective* (1611)
1 : having the nature of a habit **:** being in accordance with habit **:** CUSTOMARY ⟨*habitual* smoking⟩
2 : doing, practicing, or acting in some manner by force of habit ⟨*habitual* drunkard⟩
3 : resorted to on a regular basis ⟨our *habitual* diet⟩
4 : inherent in an individual ⟨*habitual* grace⟩
synonym see USUAL
— **ha·bit·u·al·ly** *adverb*
— **ha·bit·u·al·ness** *noun*

ha·bit·u·ate \hə-'bi-chə-,wāt, ha-\ *verb* **-at·ed; -at·ing** (15th century)
transitive verb
1 : to make used to something **:** ACCUSTOM
2 : FREQUENT 1
intransitive verb
1 : to cause habituation
2 : to undergo habituation ⟨*habituate* to a stimulus⟩

ha·bit·u·a·tion \-,bi-chə-'wā-shən\ *noun* (15th century)
1 : the process of habituating **:** the state of being habituated

☆ **SYNONYMS**
Habit, practice, usage, custom, wont mean a way of acting fixed through repetition. HABIT implies a doing unconsciously and often compulsively ⟨had a *habit* of tapping his fingers⟩. PRACTICE suggests an act or method followed with regularity and usually through choice ⟨our *practice* is to honor all major credit cards⟩. USAGE suggests a customary action so generally followed that it has become a social norm ⟨western-style dress is now common *usage* in international business⟩. CUSTOM applies to a practice or usage so steadily associated with an individual or group as to have almost the force of unwritten law ⟨the *custom* of wearing black at funerals⟩. WONT usually applies to an habitual manner, method, or practice of an individual or group ⟨as was her *wont,* she slept until noon⟩.

2 a : tolerance to the effects of a drug acquired through continued use **b :** psychological dependence on a drug after a period of use — compare ADDICTION

3 : decrease in responsiveness upon repeated exposure to a stimulus

hab·i·tude \'ha-bə-ˌtüd, ˌtyüd\ *noun* (14th century)
1 *archaic* **:** native or essential character
2 *obsolete* **:** habitual association
3 a : habitual disposition or mode of behavior or procedure **b :** CUSTOM

ha·bi·tué *also* **ha·bi·tue** \hə-'bi-chə-ˌwā, ha-ˌbi-chə-\ *noun* [French, from past participle of *habituer* to frequent, from Late Latin *habituare* to habituate, from Latin *habitus*] (1818)
1 : one who may be regularly found in or at a particular place or kind of place 〈café *habitués*〉
2 : DEVOTEE 〈an *habitué* of science-fiction movies〉

hab·i·tus \'ha-bə-təs\ *noun, plural* **habitus** \-təs, -ˌtüs\ [New Latin, from Latin] (1886)
: HABIT; *specifically* **:** body build and constitution especially as related to predisposition to disease

ha·boob \hə-'büb\ *noun* [Arabic *habūb* violent storm] (1897)
: a violent dust storm or sandstorm especially of Sudan

Habs·burg \'haps-, 'häps-\ *variant of* HAPSBURG

ha·ček \'hä-ˌchek\ *noun* [Czech *háček*, literally, little hook] (1953)
: a diacritic ˇ placed over a letter (as in č) to modify it **:** an inverted circumflex

ha·cen·da·do \ˌ(h)ä-sⁿn-'dä-(ˌ)dō\ *also* **ha·ci·en·da·do** \ˌhä-sē-en-\ *noun, plural* **-dos** [Spanish, from *hacienda*] (1840)
: the owner or proprietor of a hacienda

¹ha·chure \ha-'shür\ *noun* [French, from *hacher* to chop up, hash] (1858)
: a short line used for shading and denoting surfaces in relief (as in map drawing) and drawn in the direction of slope

²hachure *transitive verb* **ha·chured; ha·chur·ing** (circa 1859)
: to shade in or show by hachures

ha·ci·en·da \ˌ(h)ä-sē-'en-də\ *noun* [Spanish, from Old Spanish *facienda*, from Latin, literally, things to be done, neuter plural of *faciendus*, gerundive of *facere* to do — more at DO] (circa 1772)
1 : a large estate especially in a Spanish-speaking country **:** PLANTATION
2 : the main dwelling of a hacienda

¹hack \'hak\ *verb* [Middle English *hakken*, from Old English *-haccian*; akin to Old High German *hacchōn* to hack, Old English *hōc* hook] (13th century)
transitive verb
1 a : to cut or sever with repeated irregular or unskillful blows **b :** to cut or shape by or as if by crude or ruthless strokes 〈*hacking* out new election districts〉 **c :** ANNOY, VEX — often used with *off*
2 : to clear or make by or as if by cutting away vegetation 〈*hacked* his way through the brush〉
3 a : to manage successfully 〈just couldn't *hack* the new job〉 **b :** TOLERATE 〈I can't *hack* all this noise〉
intransitive verb
1 a : to make chopping strokes or blows 〈*hacked* at the weeds〉; *also* **:** to make cuts as if by chopping 〈*hacking* away at the work force〉 **b :** to play inexpert golf
2 : to cough in a short dry manner
3 : LOAF — usually used with *around*
4 a : to write computer programs for enjoyment **b :** to gain access to a computer illegally

²hack *noun* (14th century)
1 : an implement for hacking
2 : NICK, NOTCH
3 : a short dry cough
4 : a hacking stroke or blow

5 : restriction to quarters as punishment for naval officers — usually used in the phrase *under hack*

³hack *noun* [short for *hackney*] (circa 1721)
1 a (1) **:** a horse let out for common hire (2) **:** a horse used in all kinds of work **b :** a horse worn out in service **:** JADE **c :** a light easy saddle horse; *especially* **:** a three-gaited saddle horse **d :** a ride on a horse
2 a : HACKNEY **b** (1) **:** TAXICAB (2) **:** CABDRIVER
3 a : a person who works solely for mercenary reasons **:** HIRELING 〈party *hacks*〉 **b :** a writer who works on order; *also* **:** a writer who aims solely for commercial success

⁴hack *adjective* (circa 1734)
1 : working for hire especially with mediocre professional standards
2 : performed by, suited to, or characteristic of a hack 〈*hack* writing〉
3 : HACKNEYED, TRITE

⁵hack (circa 1888)
intransitive verb
1 : to ride or drive at an ordinary pace or over the roads especially as distinguished from racing or hunting
2 : to operate a taxicab
transitive verb
: to ride (a horse) at an ordinary pace

⁶hack *noun* [origin unknown] (circa 1914)
slang **:** a guard especially at a prison

hack·a·more \'ha-kə-ˌmōr, -ˌmȯr\ *noun* [by folk etymology from Spanish *jáquima* bridle] (1850)
: a bridle with a loop capable of being tightened about the nose in place of a bit or with a slip noose passed over the lower jaw

hack·ber·ry \'hak-ˌber-ē\ *noun* [alteration of *hagberry* (a cherry resembling the chokecherry)] (1779)
: any of a genus (*Celtis*) of trees and shrubs of the elm family with small often edible berries; *also* **:** its wood

hack·er \'ha-kər\ *noun* (14th century)
1 : one that hacks
2 : a person who is inexperienced or unskilled at a particular activity 〈a tennis *hacker*〉
3 : an expert at programming and solving problems with a computer
4 : a person who illegally gains access to and sometimes tampers with information in a computer system

hack·ie \'ha-kē\ *noun* (circa 1926)
: CABDRIVER

¹hack·le \'ha-kəl\ *noun* [Middle English *hakell*; akin to Old High German *hāko* hook — more at HOOK] (15th century)
1 a : one of the long narrow feathers on the neck or saddle of a bird **b :** the neck plumage of the domestic fowl
2 : a comb or board with long metal teeth for dressing flax, hemp, or jute
3 *plural* **a :** erectile hairs along the neck and back especially of a dog **b :** TEMPER, DANDER
4 a : an artificial fishing fly made chiefly of the filaments of a cock's neck feathers **b :** filaments of cock feather projecting from the head of an artificial fly

²hackle *transitive verb* **hack·led; hack·ling** \'ha-k(ə-)liŋ\ (1616)
: to comb out with a hackle
— **hack·ler** \-k(ə-)lər\ *noun*

hack·ly \'ha-k(ə-)lē\ *adjective* (1796)
: having the appearance of something hacked **:** JAGGED

hack·man \'hak-mən\ *noun* (1796)
: CABDRIVER

hack·ma·tack \'hak-mə-ˌtak\ *noun* [earlier *hakmantak*, probably from Western Abenaki (Algonquian language of New Hampshire and Vermont)] (1792)
: TAMARACK

¹hack·ney \'hak-nē\ *noun, plural* **hack·neys** [Middle English *hakeney*] (14th century)

1 a : a horse suitable for ordinary riding or driving **b :** a trotting horse used chiefly for driving **c** *often capitalized* **:** any of an English breed of rather compact usually chestnut, bay, or brown high-stepping horses

hackney 1c

2 *obsolete* **:** one that works for hire
3 : a carriage or automobile kept for hire

²hackney *adjective* (1589)
1 : kept for public hire
2 : HACKNEYED
3 *archaic* **:** done or suitable for doing by a drudge

³hackney *transitive verb* **hack·neyed; hack·ney·ing** (1596)
1 a : to make common or frequent use of **b :** to make trite, vulgar, or commonplace
2 *archaic* **:** to make sophisticated or jaded

hackney coach *noun* (1635)
: a coach kept for hire; *especially* **:** a four-wheeled carriage drawn by two horses and having seats for six persons

hack·neyed \'hak-nēd\ *adjective* (1749)
: lacking in freshness or originality
synonym see TRITE

hack·saw \'hak-ˌsȯ\ *noun* (1654)
: a fine-tooth saw with a blade under tension in a frame that is used for cutting hard materials (as metal)

hack·work \-ˌwərk\ *noun* (1851)
: literary, artistic, or professional work done on order usually according to formula and in conformity with commercial standards

had *past and past participle of* HAVE

ha·dal \'ha-dᵊl\ *adjective* [French, from *Hadès* Hades] (1959)
: of, relating to, or being the parts of the ocean below 6000 meters

had·dock \'ha-dək\ *noun, plural* **haddock** *also* **haddocks** [Middle English *haddok*] (14th century)
: an important food fish (*Melanogrammus aeglefinus*) that is usually smaller than the related cod and that occurs on both sides of the North Atlantic

Ha·des \'hā-(ˌ)dēz\ *noun* [Greek *Haidēs*]
1 : PLUTO
2 : the underground abode of the dead in Greek mythology
3 : SHEOL
4 *often not capitalized* **:** HELL

ha·dith \hə-'dēth\ *noun, plural* **hadith** *or* **ha·diths** *often capitalized* [Arabic *hadīth*, literally, speech, report] (circa 1817)
1 : a narrative record of the sayings or customs of Muhammad and his companions
2 : the collective body of traditions relating to Muhammad and his companions

hadj, hadji *variant of* HAJJ, HAJJI

Had·ley cell \'had-lē-\ *noun* [George *Hadley* (died 1768) English scientific writer] (1969)
: a pattern of atmospheric circulation in which warm air rises near the equator, cools as it travels poleward at high altitude, sinks as cold air, and warms as it travels equatorward; *also* **:** a similar atmospheric circulation pattern on another planet (as Mars)

hadn't \'ha-dᵊnt, -dᵊn, *dialect also* 'ha-tᵊn(t) *or* 'hant\ (1695)
: had not

had·ron \'ha-ˌdrän\ *noun* [International Scientific Vocabulary *hadr-* thick, heavy (from Greek *hadros* thick) + ²-*on*] (1962)

\ə\ abut \ᵊ\ kitten \ər\ further \a\ ash \ā\ ace
\ä\ mop, mar \aú\ out \ch\ chin \e\ bet \ē\ easy
\g\ go \i\ hit \ī\ ice \j\ job \ŋ\ sing \ō\ go
\ȯ\ law \ȯi\ boy \th\ thin \th\ the \ü\ loot \ù\ foot
\y\ yet \zh\ vision *see also* Guide to Pronunciation

: any of the subatomic particles that are made up of quarks and are subject to the strong force
— **ha·dron·ic** \ha-'drä-nik\ *adjective*

had·ro·saur \'ha-drə-,sȯr\ *noun* [New Latin *Hadrosaurus*, genus name, from Greek *hadros* thick, bulky + *sauros* lizard] (1877)
: any of a family (Hadrosauridae) of medium-sized bipedal herbivorous dinosaurs of the Upper Cretaceous with long flat snouts and an often crested skull

hadst \'hadst, hədst, or t for d\ *archaic past 2d singular of* HAVE

hae \'hā\ *chiefly Scottish variant of* HAVE

haem *chiefly British variant of* HEME

haem- *or* **haemo-** *chiefly British variant of* HEM-

haema- *chiefly British variant of* HEMA-

haemat- *or* **haemato-** *chiefly British variant of* HEMAT-

hae·ma·tite *British variant of* HEMATITE

-haemia *chiefly British variant of* -EMIA

haet \'hāt\ *noun* [contraction of Scots *hae it* (as in *Deil hae it!* Devil take it!)] (1603)
chiefly Scottish : a small quantity : WHIT, BIT

haf·fet \'haf-fət\ *noun* [Middle English (Scots) *halfheid*, from Middle English *half* half + *hed* head] (1513)
Scottish : CHEEK, TEMPLE

haf·ni·um \'haf-nē-əm\ *noun* [New Latin, from *Hafnia* (Copenhagen), Denmark] (1923)
: a metallic element that resembles zirconium in its chemical properties and occurs in zirconium minerals and that readily absorbs neutrons — see ELEMENT table

¹haft \'haft\ *noun* [Middle English, from Old English *hæft*; akin to Old English *hebban* to lift — more at HEAVE] (before 12th century)
: the handle of a weapon or tool

²haft *transitive verb* (15th century)
: to set in or furnish with a haft

haf·ta·rah *or* **haf·to·rah** \häf-'tȯr-ə, ,häf-tə-'rä\ *noun* [Hebrew *haphṭārāh* conclusion] (1723)
: one of the biblical selections from the Books of the Prophets read after the parashah in the Jewish synagogue service

¹hag \'hag\ *noun* [Middle English *hagge* demon, old woman] (14th century)
1 : an ugly, slatternly, or evil-looking old woman
2 *archaic* **a** : a female demon **b** : an evil or frightening spirit : HOBGOBLIN
3 : WITCH
— **hag·gish** \'ha-gish\ *adjective*

²hag *noun* [Scots, break in a moor, from Old Norse *hǫgg* cut, cleft; akin to Old English *hēawan* to hew] (1662)
1 *British* : QUAGMIRE, BOG
2 *British* : a firm spot in a bog

Ha·gar \'hā-,gär, -gər\ *noun* [Hebrew *Hāghār*]
: a concubine of Abraham driven into the desert with her son Ishmael because of Sarah's jealousy according to the account in Genesis

hag·fish \'hag-,fish\ *noun* (1611)
: any of a family (Myxinidae) of marine cyclostomes that are related to the lampreys and in general resemble eels but have a round mouth surrounded by barbels and that feed upon other fishes and invertebrates by boring into their bodies

Hag·ga·dah \hə-'gä-də, hä-, -'gȯ-\ *noun, plural* **Hag·ga·doth** \-'gä-,dōt, -'gȯ-, -,dōth\ [Hebrew *haggādhāh*] (1856)
1 : ancient Jewish lore forming especially the nonlegal part of the Talmud
2 : the prayer book containing the seder ritual
— **hag·ga·dic** \-'gä-dik, -'gȯ-\ *adjective*, *often capitalized*

hag·ga·dist \-'gä-dist, -'gȯ-\ *noun, often capitalized* (1886)
1 : a haggadic writer
2 : a student of the Haggadah
— **hag·ga·dis·tic** \,ha-gə-'dis-tik, hä-\ *adjective, often capitalized*

Hag·gai \'ha-gē-,ī, 'ha-,gī\ *noun* [Hebrew *Ḥaggai*]

1 : a Hebrew prophet who flourished about 500 B.C. and who advocated that the Temple in Jerusalem be rebuilt
2 : a prophetic book of canonical Jewish and Christian Scriptures — see BIBLE table

¹hag·gard \'ha-gərd\ *adjective* [Middle French *hagard*] (1567)
1 *of a hawk* : not tamed
2 a : wild in appearance **b** : having a worn or emaciated appearance : GAUNT ⟨*haggard* faces looked up sadly from out of the straw —W. M. Thackeray⟩
— **hag·gard·ly** *adverb*
— **hag·gard·ness** *noun*

²haggard *noun* (1567)
1 : an adult hawk caught wild
2 *obsolete* : an intractable person

hag·gis \'ha-gəs\ *noun* [Middle English *hagese*] (15th century)
: a traditionally Scottish dish that consists of the heart, liver, and lungs of a sheep or a calf minced with suet, onions, oatmeal, and seasonings boiled in the stomach of the animal

¹hag·gle \'ha-gəl\ *verb* **hag·gled; hag·gling** \-g(ə-)liŋ\ [frequentative of *hag* (to hew)] (1599)
transitive verb
1 : to cut roughly or clumsily : HACK
2 *archaic* : to annoy or exhaust with wrangling
intransitive verb
: BARGAIN, WRANGLE
— **hag·gler** \-g(ə-)lər\ *noun*

²haggle *noun* (1858)
: an act or instance of haggling

hagi- *or* **hagio-** *combining form* [Late Latin, from Greek, from *hagios*]
1 : holy ⟨*hagioscope*⟩
2 : saints ⟨*hagiography*⟩

Ha·gi·og·ra·pha \,ha-gē-'ä-grə-fə, ,hā-, -jē-\ *noun plural but singular or plural in construction* [Late Latin, from Late Greek, from *hagio-* + *graphein* to write — more at CARVE] (1583)
: the third part of the Jewish scriptures — see BIBLE table

ha·gi·og·ra·pher \-fər\ *noun* (1849)
: a writer of hagiography

ha·gi·o·graph·ic \,ha-gē-ə-'gra-fik, ,hā-, -jē-\ *also* **ha·gi·o·graph·i·cal** \-fi-kəl\ *adjective* (1819)
1 : of or relating to hagiography
2 : of or relating to the Hagiographa

ha·gi·og·ra·phy \-gē-'ä-grə-fē, -jē-\ *noun* (1821)
1 : biography of saints or venerated persons
2 : idealizing or idolizing biography

ha·gi·ol·o·gy \-gē-'ä-lə-jē, -jē-\ *noun* (1807)
1 : literature dealing with venerated persons or writings
2 : a list of venerated figures
— **ha·gi·o·log·ic** \-gē-ə-'lä-jik, -jē-\ *or* **ha·gi·o·log·i·cal** \-ji-kəl\ *adjective*

ha·gio·scope \'ha-gē-ə-,skōp, 'hā-jē-\ *noun* (circa 1840)
: an opening in the interior walls of a cruciform church so placed as to afford a view of the altar to those in the transept
— **ha·gio·scop·ic** \,ha-gē-ə-'skä-pik, ,hā-, -jē-\ *adjective*

hag·ride \'hag-,rīd\ *transitive verb* **-rode** \-,rōd\; **-rid·den** \-,ri-dᵊn\ (1702)
: HARASS, TORMENT

hah *variant of* HA

¹ha–ha \(')hä-'hä\ *interjection* [Middle English, from Old English *ha ha*] (before 12th century)
— used to express amusement or derision

²ha–ha \'hä-,hä\ *noun* [French *haha*] (1749)
: SUNK FENCE

hahn·ium \'hä-nē-əm\ *noun* [New Latin, from Otto *Hahn*] (1970)
: UNNILPENTIUM

Hai·da \'hī-də\ *noun, plural* **Haida** *or* **Hai·das** (1841)

1 : a member of an American Indian people of the Queen Charlotte islands, British Columbia, and Prince of Wales island, Alaska
2 : the language of the Haida people

haik \'hīk\ *noun* [Arabic *ḥā'ik*] (1713)
: a voluminous piece of usually white cloth worn as an outer garment in northern Africa

hai·ku \'hī-(,)kü\ *noun, plural* **haiku** [Japanese] (1902)
: an unrhymed verse form of Japanese origin having three lines containing usually 5, 7, and 5 syllables respectively; *also* : a poem in this form usually having a seasonal reference — compare TANKA

¹hail \'hā(ə)l\ *noun* [Middle English, from Old English *hægl*; akin to Old High German *hagal* hail] (before 12th century)
1 : precipitation in the form of small balls or lumps usually consisting of concentric layers of clear ice and compact snow
2 : something that gives the effect of a shower of hail ⟨a *hail* of rifle fire⟩

²hail *intransitive verb* (before 12th century)
1 : to precipitate hail ⟨it was *hailing* hard⟩
2 : to pour down or strike like hail

³hail *interjection* [Middle English, from Old Norse *heill*, from *heill* healthy — more at WHOLE] (13th century)
1 *archaic* — used as a salutation
2 — used to express acclamation ⟨*hail* to the chief —Sir Walter Scott⟩

⁴hail (13th century)
transitive verb
1 a : SALUTE, GREET **b** : to greet with enthusiastic approval : ACCLAIM
2 : to greet or summon by calling ⟨*hail* a taxi⟩
intransitive verb
: to call out; *especially* : to call a greeting to a passing ship
— **hail·er** \'hā-lər\ *noun*
— **hail from** : to be or have been native to or a resident of

⁵hail *noun* (1500)
1 : an exclamation of greeting or acclamation
2 : a calling to attract attention
3 : hearing distance ⟨stayed within *hail*⟩

hail–fel·low \'hāl-,fe-(,)lō\ *adjective* (1580)
: HAIL-FELLOW-WELL-MET
— **hail–fellow** *noun*

hail–fel·low–well–met \-lō-,wel-'met, -lə-,wel-\ *adjective* [from the archaic salutation "Hail, fellow! Well met!"] (1581)
: heartily informal : COMRADELY
— **hail–fellow–well–met** *noun*

Hail Mary *noun* [translation of Medieval Latin *Ave, Maria*, from the opening words] (15th century)
: a Roman Catholic prayer to the Virgin Mary that consists of salutations and a plea for her intercession

hail·stone \'hā(ə)l-,stōn\ *noun* (before 12th century)
: a pellet of hail

hail·storm \-,stȯrm\ *noun* (15th century)
: a storm accompanied by hail

haik

hair \'har, 'her\ *noun, often attributive* [Middle English, from Old English *hær*; akin to Old High German *hār* hair] (before 12th century)
1 a : a slender thread-like outgrowth of the epidermis of an animal; *especially* : one of the usually pigmented filaments that form the characteristic coat of a mammal **b** : the hairy covering of

hair 1a: *1* shaft, *2* sebaceous gland, *3* epidermis, *4* dermis, *5* hair follicle, *6* bulb, *7* papilla

an animal or a body part; *especially* **:** the coating of hairs on a human head
2 : HAIRCLOTH
3 a : a minute distance or amount ⟨won by a *hair*⟩ **b :** a precise degree ⟨aligned to a *hair*⟩
4 *obsolete* **:** NATURE, CHARACTER
5 : a filamentous structure that resembles hair ⟨leaf *hair*⟩
— **hair·less** *adjective*
— **hair·less·ness** *noun*
— **hair·like** \-ˌlīk\ *adjective*
hair ball *noun* (1712)
: a compact mass of hair formed in the stomach especially of a shedding animal (as a cat) that cleanses its coat by licking
¹hair·breadth \'har-ˌbretth, 'her-, -ˌbreth, -ˌbredth\ *or* **hairs·breadth** \'harz-, 'herz-\ *noun* (1561)
: a very small distance or margin
²hairbreadth *adjective* (1604)
: very narrow **:** CLOSE ⟨a *hairbreadth* escape⟩
hair·brush \'har-ˌbrəsh, 'her-\ *noun* (1599)
: a brush for the hair
hair cell *noun* (circa 1890)
: a cell with hairlike processes; *especially* **:** one of the sensory cells in the auditory epithelium of the organ of Corti
hair·cloth \'har-ˌkloth, 'her-\ *noun* (1500)
: any of various stiff wiry fabrics especially of horsehair or camel hair used for upholstery or for stiffening in garments
hair·cut \-ˌkət\ *noun* (1899)
: the act, process, or result of cutting and shaping the hair
— **hair·cut·ter** \-ˌkə-tər\ *noun*
— **hair·cut·ting** \-ˌkə-tiŋ\ *noun*
hair·do \-ˌdü\ *noun, plural* **hairdos** (1932)
: a way of wearing the hair **:** COIFFURE
hair·dress·er \-ˌdre-sər\ *noun* (1770)
1 : one whose occupation is the dressing or cutting of hair
2 *British* **:** BARBER
hair·dress·ing \-ˌdre-siŋ\ *noun* (1771)
1 a : the action or process of washing, cutting, curling, or arranging the hair **b :** the occupation of a hairdresser
2 : a preparation for grooming and styling the hair
haired \'hard, 'herd\ *adjective* (14th century)
: having hair especially of a specified kind — usually used in combination ⟨dark-*haired*⟩
hair follicle *noun* (1838)
: the tubular epithelial sheath that surrounds the lower part of the hair shaft and encloses at the bottom a vascular papilla supplying the growing basal part of the hair with nourishment
hair·line \-ˈlīn\ *noun* (1846)
1 : a very slender line: as **a :** a tiny line or crack on a surface ⟨a *hairline* bone fracture⟩ **b :** a fine line connecting thicker strokes in a printed letter
2 : HAIRBREADTH
3 a : a textile design consisting of lengthwise or crosswise lines usually one thread wide **b :** a fabric with such a design
4 a : the outline of scalp hair especially on the forehead **b :** the way the hair frames the face
— **hairline** *adjective*
hair·piece \-ˌpēs\ *noun* (1926)
1 : supplementary hair (as a switch) used in some feminine coiffures
2 : TOUPEE 2
¹hair·pin \-ˌpin\ *noun* (1779)
1 : a pin to hold the hair in place; *specifically* **:** a long U-shaped pin
2 : something shaped like a hairpin; *specifically* **:** a sharp U-shaped turn in a road
²hairpin *adjective* (1887)
: having the shape of a hairpin ⟨a *hairpin* turn⟩; *also* **:** having hairpin turns ⟨a steep *hairpin* road⟩
hair·rais·er \'har-ˌrā-zər, 'her-\ *noun* (1897)
: THRILLER
hair–rais·ing \-ˌrā-ziŋ\ *adjective* (1900)

: causing terror, excitement, or astonishment
— **hair–rais·ing·ly** \-ziŋ-lē\ *adverb*
hair seal *noun* (1865)
: any of a family (Phocidae) of seals having a coarse hairy coat, the hind limbs reduced to swimming flippers, and no external ears — called also *true seal*; compare EARED SEAL
hair shirt *noun* (14th century)
1 : a shirt made of rough animal hair worn next to the skin as a penance
2 : one that irritates like a hair shirt
hair·split·ter \'har-ˌspli-tər, 'her-\ *noun* (1849)
: one that makes excessively fine distinctions in reasoning **:** QUIBBLER
— **hair·split·ting** \-ˌspli-tiŋ\ *adjective or noun*
hair·spring \-ˌspriŋ\ *noun* (1830)
: a slender spiraled recoil spring that regulates the motion of the balance wheel of a timepiece
hair·streak \-ˌstrēk\ *noun* (1816)
: any of a subfamily (Theclinae of the family Lycaenidae) of small butterflies usually having striped markings on the underside of the wings and thin filamentous projections from the hind wings
hair·style \'har-ˌstīl, 'her-\ *noun* (1913)
: HAIRDO
hair·styl·ing \-ˌstī-liŋ\ *noun* (1936)
: the work of a hairstylist
hair·styl·ist \-ˌstī-list\ *noun* (1935)
: HAIRDRESSER; *especially* **:** one who does creative styling of coiffures
hair–trigger *adjective* (1834)
1 : immediately responsive to the slightest stimulus ⟨a *hair-trigger* temper⟩
2 : delicately adjusted or easily disrupted
hair trigger *noun* (1806)
: a gun trigger so adjusted as to permit the firearm to be fired by a very slight pressure
hair·worm \'har-ˌwərm, 'her-\ *noun* (1658)
1 : any of a phylum (Nematomorpha) of elongated worms that have separate sexes, are parasitic in arthropods as larvae, and are free-living in water as adults — called also *horsehair worm*
2 : any of a genus (*Capillaria*) of nematode worms that include serious parasites of the alimentary tract of fowls and tissue and organ parasites of mammals
hairy \'har-ē, 'her-\ *adjective* **hair·i·er; -est** (14th century)
1 a : covered with hair or hairlike material **b :** having a downy fuzz on the stems and leaves
2 : made of or resembling hair
3 a : tending to cause nervous tension (as from danger) ⟨a *hairy* adventure⟩ **b :** difficult to deal with or comprehend ⟨a *hairy* math problem⟩
— **hair·i·ness** \'har-ē-nəs, 'her-\ *noun*
hairy cell leukemia *noun* (1979)
: a lymphocytic leukemia that is usually of B cell origin and is characterized by malignant cells with a ciliated appearance
hairy–chest·ed \-ˌches-təd\ *adjective* (circa 1937)
: characterized by especially exaggerated or stereotypical manliness
hairy vetch *noun* (1901)
: a Eurasian vetch (*Vicia villosa*) extensively cultivated as a cover and early forage crop
hairy woodpecker *noun* (circa 1728)
: a common North American woodpecker (*Picoides villosus*) closely resembling the downy woodpecker but larger with a longer bill
Hai·tian \'hā-shən *also* 'hā-tē-ən\ *noun* (1805)
1 : a native or inhabitant of Haiti
2 : HAITIAN CREOLE
— **Haitian** *adjective*
Haitian Creole *noun* (circa 1938)
: a French-based creole spoken by Haitians
hajj \'haj\ *noun* [Arabic *ḥajj*] (1673)
: the pilgrimage to Mecca prescribed as a religious duty for Muslims
hajji \'ha-jē\ *noun* [Arabic *ḥajjī*, from *ḥajj*] (1609)

: one who has made a pilgrimage to Mecca — often used as a title
hake \'hāk\ *noun* [Middle English] (14th century)
: any of several marine food fishes (as of the genera *Merluccius* and *Urophycis*) that are related to the common Atlantic cod
¹ha·kim \'hä-kəm\ *noun* [Arabic *ḥākim*] (1611)
: an administrator in a Muslim country
²ha·kim \hə-ˈkēm\ *noun* [Arabic *ḥakīm*, literally, wise one] (1638)
: a physician in a Muslim country
hal- *or* **halo-** *combining form* [French, from Greek, from *hals* — more at SALT]
1 : salt ⟨*halophyte*⟩
2 [International Scientific Vocabulary, from *halogen*] **:** halogen ⟨*halide*⟩
ha·la·kah *or* **ha·la·cha** \hä-ˈlä-kə, ˌhä-lə-ˈkä\ *noun, often capitalized* [Hebrew *halākhāh*, literally, way] (1856)
: the body of Jewish law supplementing the scriptural law and forming especially the legal part of the Talmud
— **ha·lak·ic** \hə-ˈlä-kik, hä-ˈlä-\ *adjective, often capitalized*
ha·la·la \hə-ˈlä-lə\ *noun, plural* **halala** *or* **halalas** [Arabic] (1970)
— see *riyal* at MONEY table
ha·la·tion \hā-ˈlā-shən\ *noun* [*halo* + *-ation*] (1859)
1 : the spreading of light beyond its proper boundaries in a developed photographic image
2 : a bright ring that sometimes surrounds a bright object on a television screen
hal·berd \'hal-bərd, 'hol-\ *also* **hal·bert** \-bərt\ *noun* [Middle English, from Middle French *hallebarde*, from Middle High German *helmbarte*, from *helm* handle (from Old High German *helmo*) + *barte* ax, from Old High German *barta* ax, akin to Old High German *bart* beard — more at HELM, BEARD] (15th century)
: a weapon especially of the 15th and 16th centuries consisting typically of a battle-ax and pike mounted on a handle about six feet long
¹hal·cy·on \'hal-sē-ən\ *noun* [Middle English *alceon*, from Latin *halcyon*, from Greek *alkyōn, halkyōn*] (14th century)
1 : a bird identified with the kingfisher and held in ancient legend to nest at sea about the time of the winter solstice and to calm the waves during incubation
2 : KINGFISHER ◆

◇ **WORD HISTORY**
halcyon According to Greek myth, Alkyone, the daughter of Aeolus, god of the winds, was so distraught on learning that her husband had been killed in a shipwreck that she threw herself into the sea and was changed into a kingfisher. Henceforth the bird was known to the Greeks as *alkyōn* or *halkyōn* (the latter by association with *hals*, meaning "sea"). Legend had it that the kingfisher built a floating nest on the sea every year before the winter solstice. For two weeks before and after the solstice Aeolus charmed the wind and the waves while the bird incubated its eggs, and *alkyonides hēmerai* (literally, "kingfisher days") became a proverbial expression for a time of peace and tranquility. The Romans borrowed the Greek word as *alcyon* or *halcyon*, and the Latin word found its way into Middle English as a poetic name for the kingfisher. Subsequently, *halcyon* has been used as an adjective meaning first "calm, tranquil" and later "happy" or "prosperous." It usually modifies *days* or another noun denoting a period of time.

\ə\ abut \ᵊ\ kitten \ər\ further \a\ ash \ā\ ace
\ä\ mop, mar \au̇\ out \ch\ chin \e\ bet \ē\ easy
\g\ go \i\ hit \ī\ ice \j\ job \ŋ\ sing \ō\ go
\ȯ\ law \ȯi\ boy \th\ thin \t͟h\ the \ü\ loot \u̇\ foot
\y\ yet \zh\ vision *see also* Guide to Pronunciation

²halcyon *adjective* (1540)
1 : of or relating to the halcyon or its nesting period
2 a : CALM, PEACEFUL **b :** HAPPY, GOLDEN **c :** PROSPEROUS, AFFLUENT

¹hale \ˈhā(ə)l\ *adjective* [partly from Middle English (northern) *hale*, from Old English *hāl*; partly from Middle English *hail*, from Old Norse *heill* — more at WHOLE] (before 12th century)
: free from defect, disease, or infirmity **:** SOUND; *also* **:** retaining exceptional health and vigor ⟨a *hale* and hearty old man⟩
synonym see HEALTHY

²hale *transitive verb* **haled; hal·ing** [Middle English *halen*, from Old French *haler* — more at HAUL] (13th century)
1 : HAUL, PULL
2 : to compel to go

ha·ler \ˈhä-lər, -ˌler\ *noun, plural* **ha·le·ru** \ˈhä-lə-ˌrü\ [Czech *haléř*, genitive plural *haléřů*] (circa 1934)
— see *koruna* at MONEY table

¹half \ˈhaf, ˈhàf\ *noun, plural* **halves** \ˈhavz, ˈhàvz\ [Middle English, from Old English *healf;* akin to Old High German *halb* half] (before 12th century)
1 a : either of two equal parts into which a thing is divisible; *also* **:** a part of a thing approximately equal to the remainder — often used without *of* ⟨*half* the distance⟩ **b :** half an hour — used in designation of time
2 : one of a pair: as **a :** PARTNER **b :** SEMESTER, TERM **c :** either of the two equal periods that together make up the playing time of some games (as football); *also* **:** the midpoint in playing time ⟨the score was tied at the *half*⟩
3 : HALF-DOLLAR
4 : HALFBACK
— **by half :** by a great deal
— **by halves :** in part: HALFHEARTEDLY
— **half again as :** one-and-a-half times as ⟨*half again as* many⟩
— **in half :** into two equal or nearly equal parts

²half *adjective* (before 12th century)
1 a : being one of two equal parts ⟨a *half* share⟩ ⟨a *half* sheet of paper⟩ **b (1) :** amounting to approximately half ⟨a *half* mile⟩ ⟨a *half* million⟩ **(2) :** falling short of the full or complete thing **:** PARTIAL ⟨*half* measures⟩ ⟨a *half* smile⟩
2 : extending over or covering only half ⟨a *half* window⟩ ⟨a *half* mask⟩
— **half·ness** *noun*

³half *adverb* (12th century)
1 a : in an equal part or degree ⟨the crowd was *half* jeering, *half* respectful⟩ **b :** not completely **:** PARTIALLY ⟨*half* persuaded⟩
2 : by any means **:** AT ALL ⟨her singing isn't *half* bad⟩

half-and-half \ˌhaf-ᵊn-ˈhaf, ˌhàf-ᵊn-ˈhàf\ *noun* (1756)
: something that is approximately half one thing and half another: as **a :** a mixture of two malt beverages (as dark and light beer) **b :** a mixture of cream and whole milk
— **half-and-half** *adjective or adverb*

half-assed \ˈhaf-ˈast, ˈhàf-ˈàst\ *adjective* (circa 1932)
1 : lacking significance, adequacy, or completeness — often considered vulgar
2 : lacking intelligence, character, or effectiveness — often considered vulgar
— **half-assed** *adverb*

half·back \ˈhaf-ˌbak, ˈhàf-\ *noun* (1882)
1 : one of the backs stationed near either flank in football
2 : a player stationed immediately behind the forward line (as in field hockey, soccer, or rugby)

half-baked \-ˈbākt\ *adjective* (1621)
1 a : lacking adequate planning or forethought ⟨a *half-baked* scheme for getting rich⟩ **b :** lacking in judgment, intelligence, or common sense

2 : imperfectly baked **:** UNDERDONE
half-beak \-ˌbēk\ *noun* (1880)
: any of various narrow-bodied fishes of warm waters that have an elongated lower jaw and are grouped with the flying fishes (family Exocoetidae) or placed in their own family (Hemiramphidae)

half-blood \-ˈbləd\ *or* **half-blood·ed** \-ˈblə-dəd\ *adjective* (1605)
: having half blood or being a half blood

half blood *noun* (1553)
1 a : the relation between persons having only one parent in common **b :** a person so related to another
2 : HALF-BREED
3 : GRADE 4

half boot *noun* (1787)
: a boot with a top reaching above the ankle and ending below the knee

half-bound \ˈhaf-ˌbaund, ˈhàf-\ *adjective* (1775)
of a book **:** bound in material of two qualities with the material of better quality on the spine and corners
— **half binding** *noun*

half-bred \-ˌbred\ *adjective* (1701)
: having one purebred parent
— **half-bred** *noun*

half-breed \-ˌbrēd\ *noun* (1760)
: the offspring of parents of different races; *especially* **:** the offspring of an American Indian and a white person — often used disparagingly
— **half-breed** *adjective*

half brother *noun* (14th century)
: a brother related through one parent only

half-caste \ˈhaf-ˌkast, ˈhàf-\ *noun* (1789)
: one of mixed racial descent **:** HALF-BREED
— **half-caste** *adjective*

half cock *noun* (1745)
1 : the position of the hammer of a firearm when about half retracted and held by the sear so that it cannot be operated by a pull on the trigger
2 *chiefly British* **:** a state of inadequate preparation or mental confusion ⟨go off at *half cock*⟩

half-cocked \ˈhaf-ˈkäkt, ˈhàf-\ *adjective* (1809)
1 : being at half cock
2 : lacking adequate preparation or forethought ⟨go off *half-cocked*⟩

half-court \ˈhaf-ˈkȯrt, -ˈkȯrt, ˈhàf-\ *noun* (1888)
: a dividing line that separates a playing court into equal halves (as in basketball); *also* **:** the area comprising each half

half crown *noun* (1542)
: a British coin worth two shillings and sixpence used as legal tender until 1970

half dime *noun* (1792)
: a silver 5-cent coin struck by the U.S. mint in 1792 and from 1794 to 1873

half disme *noun* (1792)
: a half dime struck in 1792

half-dol·lar \ˈhaf-ˈdä-lər, ˈhàf-\ *noun* (1786)
1 : a coin representing one half of a dollar
2 : the sum of 50 cents

half duplex *noun* (1950)
: a mode of communication especially with a computer via telephone line in which information can be sent in only one direction at a time — compare DUPLEX

half eagle *noun* (1786)
: a 5-dollar gold piece issued by the U.S. from 1795 to 1916 and in 1929

half-hardy *adjective* (1824)
of a plant **:** able to withstand a moderately low temperature but injured by severe freezing and surviving the winter in cold climates only if carefully protected

half-heart·ed \ˈhaf-ˈhär-təd, ˈhàf-\ *adjective* (15th century)
: lacking heart, spirit, or interest
— **half-heart·ed·ly** *adverb*
— **half-heart·ed·ness** *noun*

half hitch *noun* (1769)
: a simple knot tied by passing the end of a line around an object, across the main part of the line, and then through the resulting loop — see KNOT illustration

half hour *noun* (15th century)
1 : thirty minutes
2 : the middle point of an hour
— **half-hour·ly** \ˈhaf-ˈau̇(-ə)r-lē, ˈhàf-\ *adverb or adjective*

half-knot \ˈhaf-ˌnät, ˈhàf-\ *noun* (1933)
: a knot intertwining the ends of two cords and used in tying other knots

half-length \ˈhaf-ˈleŋ(k)th, ˈhàf-\ *noun* (1699)
: something (as a portrait) that is or represents only half the complete length

half-life \-ˌlīf\ *noun* (1907)
1 : the time required for half of something to undergo a process: as **a :** the time required for half of the atoms of a radioactive substance to become disintegrated **b :** the time required for half the amount of a substance (as a drug or radioactive tracer) in or introduced into a living system or ecosystem to be eliminated or disintegrated by natural processes
2 : a period of usefulness or popularity preceding decline or obsolescence ⟨slang usually has a short *half-life*⟩

half-light \-ˌlīt\ *noun* (1625)
: dim grayish light

half line *noun* (circa 1914)
: a straight line extending from a point indefinitely in one direction only

¹half-mast \-ˈmast\ *noun* (1627)
: a point some distance but not necessarily halfway down below the top of a mast or staff or the peak of a gaff

²half-mast *transitive verb* (1891)
: to cause to hang at half-mast ⟨*half-mast* a flag⟩

half-moon \ˈhaf-ˌmün, ˈhàf-\ *noun* (15th century)
1 : the moon when half its disk appears illuminated
2 : something shaped like a crescent
3 : the lunule of a fingernail
— **half-moon** *adjective*

half nelson *noun* (1889)
: a wrestling hold in which one arm is thrust under the corresponding arm of an opponent and the hand placed on the back of the opponent's neck — compare FULL NELSON

half note *noun* (1597)
: a musical note with the time value of ½ of a whole note — see NOTE illustration

half·pen·ny \ˈhāp-nē, ˈhā-pə-, US also ˈhaf-ˌpe-nē, ˈhàf-\ *noun* (13th century)
1 *plural* **halfpence** \ˈhā-pən(t)s, US also ˈhaf-ˌpen(t)s, ˈhàf-\ *or* **halfpennies :** a former British coin representing one half of a penny
2 : the sum of half a penny
3 : a small amount
— **halfpenny** *adjective*

¹half-pint \ˈhaf-ˌpīnt, ˈhàf-\ *noun* (1611)
1 : half a pint
2 : a short, small, or inconsequential person

²half-pint *adjective* (circa 1926)
: of less than average size **:** DIMINUTIVE

half plane *noun* (1891)
: the part of a plane on one side of an indefinitely extended straight line drawn in the plane

half rest *noun* (circa 1899)
: a musical rest corresponding in time value to a half note — see REST illustration

half shell *noun* (1860)
: either of the valves of a bivalve
— **on the half shell :** served in a half shell ⟨oysters *on the half shell*⟩

half sister *noun* (13th century)
: a sister related through one parent only

half-slip \ˈhaf-ˌslip, ˈhàf-\ *noun* (circa 1948)
: a topless slip with an elasticized waistband

half-sole *transitive verb* (1795)
: to put half soles on

half sole *noun* (1865)
: a shoe sole extending from the shank forward
half sovereign *noun* (circa 1504)
: a British gold coin worth 10 shillings
half–space \'haf-,spās, 'håf-\ *noun* (1962)
: the part of three-dimensional euclidean space lying on one side of a plane
half–staff \-'staf\ *noun* (1708)
: HALF-MAST
half step *noun* (1904)
1 : a walking step of 15 inches or in double time of 18 inches
2 : a musical interval (as E-F or B-C) equivalent to one twelfth of an octave — called also *semitone*
half–timber *or* **half–tim·bered** \'haf-'tim-bərd, 'håf-\ *adjective* (circa 1876)
of a building **:** constructed of wood framing with spaces filled with masonry
— **half–tim·ber·ing** \-b(ə-)riŋ\ *noun*
half·time \-,tīm\ *noun* (1871)
: an intermission between halves of a game or contest (as in football or basketball)
half–time *adjective* (1961)
: involving or working half the standard hours
— **half–time** *adverb*
half title *noun* (1879)
: the title of a book appearing alone on a right-hand page immediately preceding the title page; *also* **:** the page itself
half·tone \'haf-,tōn, 'håf-\ *noun* (1651)
1 : HALF STEP 2
2 a : any of the shades of gray between the darkest and the lightest parts of a photographic image **b :** a photoengraving made from an image photographed through a screen and then etched so that the details of the image are reproduced in dots
— **halftone** *adjective*
half–track \-,trak\ *noun* (1935)
1 : an endless chain-track drive system that propels a vehicle supported in front by a pair of wheels
2 : a motor vehicle propelled by half-tracks; *specifically* **:** one lightly armored for military use
— **half–track** *or* **half–tracked** \-,trakt\ *adjective*
half–truth \-,trüth\ *noun* (1658)
1 : a statement that is only partially true
2 : a statement that mingles truth and falsehood with deliberate intent to deceive
half volley *noun* (1843)
: a stroke of a ball (as in tennis) at the instant it rebounds from the ground
— **half–volley** *verb*
half·way \'haf-'wā, 'håf-\ *adjective* (1694)
1 : midway between two points
2 : PARTIAL
— **halfway** *adverb*
halfway house *noun* (1694)
1 a : a place to stop midway on a journey **b :** a halfway place in a progression
2 : a residence for formerly institutionalized individuals (as mental patients, drug addicts, or convicts) that is designed to facilitate their readjustment to private life
half–wit \'haf-,wit, 'håf-\ *noun* (1640)
: a foolish or imbecilic person
— **half–wit·ted** \-'wi-təd\ *adjective*
— **half–wit·ted·ness** *noun*
half–world \-,wərld\ *noun* (1870)
: DEMIMONDE
hal·i·but \'ha-lə-bət *also* 'hä-\ *noun, plural* **halibut** *also* **halibuts** [Middle English *halybutte,* from *haly, holy* holy + *butte* flatfish, from Middle Dutch or Middle Low German *but;* from its being eaten on holy days] (14th century)
: any of several marine flatfishes (especially *Hippoglossus hippoglossus* of the Atlantic and *H. stenolepis* of the Pacific) that are widely used for food and include some of the largest bony fishes
ha·lide \'ha-,līd, 'hā-\ *noun* (1876)

: a binary compound of a halogen with a more electropositive element or radical
hal·i·dom \'ha-lə-dəm\ *or* **hal·i·dome** \-lə-,dōm\ *noun* [Middle English, from Old English *hāligdōm,* from *hālig* holy + *-dōm* -dom] (before 12th century)
archaic **:** something held sacred
ha·lite \'ha-,līt, 'hā-\ *noun* (1868)
: ROCK SALT
hal·i·to·sis \,ha-lə-'tō-səs\ *noun* [New Latin, from Latin *halitus* breath, from *halare* to breathe — more at EXHALE] (1874)
: a condition of having fetid breath
hall \'hȯl\ *noun* [Middle English *halle,* from Old English *heall;* akin to Latin *cella* small room, *celare* to conceal — more at HELL] (before 12th century)
1 a : the castle or house of a medieval king or noble **b :** the chief living room in such a structure
2 : the manor house of a landed proprietor
3 : a large usually imposing building for public or semipublic purposes
4 a (1) **:** a building used by a college or university for some special purpose (2) **:** DORMITORY **b :** a college or a division of a college at some universities **c** (1) **:** the common dining room of an English college (2) **:** a meal served there
5 a : the entrance room of a building **:** LOBBY **b :** a corridor or passage in a building
6 : a large room for assembly **:** AUDITORIUM
7 : a place used for public entertainment
hal·lah \'kä-lə, 'hä-\ *variant of* CHALLAH
Hall effect \'hȯl-\ *noun* [Edwin H. *Hall* (died 1938) American physicist] (circa 1889)
: a potential difference observed between the edges of a conducting strip carrying a longitudinal current when placed in a magnetic field perpendicular to the plane of the strip
Hal·lel \hä-'lā(ə)l\ *noun* [Hebrew *hallēl* praise] (1702)
: a selection comprising Psalms 113–118 chanted during Jewish feasts (as the Passover)
¹hal·le·lu·jah \,ha-lə-'lü-yə\ *interjection* [Hebrew *hallĕlūyāh* praise (ye) the Lord] (1535)
— used to express praise, joy, or thanks
²hallelujah *noun* (1625)
: a shout or song of praise or thanksgiving
hal·liard *variant of* HALYARD
¹hall·mark \'hȯl-,märk\ *noun* [Goldsmiths' *Hall,* London, England, where gold and silver articles were assayed and stamped] (1721)
1 a : an official mark stamped on gold and silver articles in England to attest their purity **b :** a mark or device placed or stamped on an article of trade to indicate origin, purity, or genuineness
2 : a distinguishing characteristic, trait, or feature ⟨the dramatic flourishes which are the *hallmark* of the trial lawyer —Marion K. Sanders⟩
²hallmark *transitive verb* (1773)
: to stamp with a hallmark
hal·lo \hə-'lō, ha-\ *or* **hal·loo** \-'lü\ *variant of* HOLLO
Hall of Fame (circa 1909)
1 : a structure housing memorials to famous or illustrious individuals usually chosen by a group of electors
2 : a group of individuals in a particular category (as a sport) who have been selected as particularly illustrious
— **Hall of Fam·er** \-'fā-mər\
hal·low \'ha-(,)lō\ *transitive verb* [Middle English *halowen,* from Old English *hālgian,* from *hālig* holy — more at HOLY] (before 12th century)
1 : to make holy or set apart for holy use
2 : to respect greatly **:** VENERATE
synonym see DEVOTE
hal·lowed \'ha-(,)lōd, 'ha-ləd, *in the Lord's Prayer often* 'ha-lə-wəd\ *adjective* (before 12th century)
1 : HOLY, CONSECRATED
2 : SACRED, REVERED ⟨*hallowed* customs⟩

Hal·low·een *also* **Hal·low·e'en** \,ha-lə-'wēn, ,hä-\ *noun* [short for *All Hallow Even* (All Saints' Eve)] (circa 1700)
: October 31 observed especially with dressing up in disguise, trick-or-treating, and displaying jack-o'-lanterns during the evening □
Hal·low·mas \'ha-lō-,mas, 'ha-lə-, -məs\ *noun* [short for Middle English *Alholowmesse,* from Old English *ealra halgena mæsse,* literally, all saints' mass] (14th century)
: ALL SAINTS' DAY
halls of ivy [from the traditional training of ivy on the walls of older college buildings] (1965)
: UNIVERSITY, COLLEGE
Hall·statt *also* **Hall·stadt** \'hȯl-,stat; 'häl-,shtät, -,stät\ *adjective* [*Hallstatt,* Austria] (1899)
: of or relating to the earlier period of the Iron Age in Europe
hal·lu·ci·nate \hə-'lü-sⁿn-,āt\ *verb* **-nat·ed; -nat·ing** [Latin *hallucinatus,* past participle of *hallucinari, allucinari* to prate, dream, modification of Greek *alyein* to be distressed, to wander] (circa 1834)
transitive verb
1 : to affect with visions or imaginary perceptions
2 : to perceive or experience as an hallucination
intransitive verb
: to have hallucinations
— **hal·lu·ci·na·tor** \-,ā-tər\ *noun*
hal·lu·ci·na·tion \hə-,lü-sⁿn-'ā-shən\ *noun* (1629)
1 a : perception of objects with no reality usually arising from disorder of the nervous system or in response to drugs (as LSD) **b :** the object so perceived
2 : an unfounded or mistaken impression or notion **:** DELUSION
hal·lu·ci·na·to·ry \hə-'lü-sⁿn-ə-,tōr-ē, -'lüs-nə-, -,tȯr-\ *adjective* (1830)
1 : tending to produce hallucination ⟨*hallucinatory* drugs⟩
2 : resembling, involving, or being an hallucination ⟨*hallucinatory* dreams⟩ ⟨an *hallucinatory* figure⟩
hal·lu·ci·no·gen \hə-'lü-sⁿn-ə-jən\ *noun* [*hallucination* + *-o-* + *-gen*] (1954)
: a substance that induces hallucinations
— **hal·lu·ci·no·gen·ic** \-,lü-sⁿn-ə-'je-nik\ *adjective or noun*
hal·lu·ci·no·sis \hə-,lü-sⁿn-'ō-səs\ *noun* [New Latin] (1905)
: a pathological mental state characterized by hallucinations
hal·lux \'ha-ləks\ *noun, plural* **hal·lu·ces** \'ha-lə-,sēz, 'hal-yə-\ [New Latin, from Latin *hallus, hallux*] (1831)

□ USAGE
Halloween Nothing sends chills down the spine of some English speakers like the pronunciation \,hä-lə-'wēn\. The first half of the word, it is argued, comes from the verb *hallow,* whose first syllable is pronounced \'ha-\. In earlier centuries, though, *hallow* had a second pronunciation rhyming with *swallow,* and so \,hä-lə-'wēn\ is a natural pronunciation of the name of the October holiday. The disputed variant is common throughout the United States but not in Great Britain. Those who insist that the pronunciation of *Halloween* should be the sum of its parts should consider their own pronunciations of the first vowels of *Christmas* and *Michaelmas.*

\ə\ **abut** \ᵊ\ **kitten** \ər\ **further** \a\ **ash** \ā\ **ace**
\ä\ **mop, mar** \aů\ **out** \ch\ **chin** \e\ **bet** \ē\ **easy**
\g\ **go** \i\ **hit** \ī\ **ice** \j\ **job** \ŋ\ **sing** \ō\ **go**
\ȯ\ **law** \ȯi\ **boy** \th\ **thin** \th̷\ **the** \ü\ **loot** \ů\ **foot**
\y\ **yet** \zh\ **vision** *see also* Guide to Pronunciation

: the innermost digit (as the big toe) of a hind or lower limb

hall·way \\'hòl-ˌwā\ *noun* (1876)
1 : an entrance hall
2 : CORRIDOR

hal·ma \\'hal-mə\ *noun* [Greek *halma* leap, from *hallesthai* to leap — more at SALLY] (1889)
: a game played on a square board and having rules similar to those of Chinese checkers

¹**ha·lo** \\'hā-(ˌ)lō\ *noun, plural* **halos** *or* **haloes** [Latin *halos,* from Greek *halōs* threshing floor, disk, halo] (1603)
1 : a circle of light appearing to surround the sun or moon and resulting from refraction or reflection of light by ice particles in the atmosphere
2 : something resembling a halo: as **a** : NIMBUS **b** : a region of space surrounding a galaxy that is sparsely populated with luminous objects (as globular clusters) but is believed to contain a great deal of dark matter **c** : a differentiated zone surrounding a central zone or object
3 : the aura of glory, veneration, or sentiment surrounding an idealized person or thing

²**halo** *transitive verb* (1801)
: to form into or surround with a halo ⟨rainbows *haloed* the waterfalls —Michael Crawford⟩

halo- — see HAL-

hal·o·car·bon \\'ha-lə-ˌkär-bən\ *noun* (1950)
: any of various compounds (as fluorocarbon) of carbon and one or more halogens

hal·o·cline \\'ha-lə-ˌklīn\ *noun* (1960)
: a usually vertical gradient in salinity (as of the ocean)

halo effect *noun* (circa 1928)
: generalization from the perception of one outstanding personality trait to an overly favorable evaluation of the whole personality

hal·o·gen \\'ha-lə-jən\ *noun* [Swedish, from *hal-* + *-gen*] (1842)
: any of the five elements fluorine, chlorine, bromine, iodine, and astatine that form part of group VII A of the periodic table and exist in the free state normally as diatomic molecules
— **ha·log·e·nous** \ha-'lä-jə-nəs\ *adjective*

ha·lo·ge·nate \\'ha-lə-jə-ˌnāt, ha-'lä-jə-\ *transitive verb* **-nat·ed; -nat·ing** (1882)
: to treat or cause to combine with a halogen
— **ha·lo·ge·na·tion** \ˌha-lə-jə-'nā-shən, ha-ˌlä-jə-\ *noun*

hal·o·ge·ton \ˌha-lə-'jē-ˌtän\ *noun* [New Latin, from *hal-* + Greek *geitōn* neighbor] (1943)
: a coarse annual herb (*Halogeton glomeratus*) of the goosefoot family that is a noxious weed in western American ranges

hal·o·mor·phic \ˌha-lə-'mòr-fik\ *adjective* (circa 1938)
of a soil : developed in the presence of neutral or alkali salts or both

hal·o·per·i·dol \ˌha-lō-'per-ə-ˌdòl, -ˌdōl\ *noun* [*hal-* + pi*peri*dine + ¹*-ol*] (1960)
: a depressant $C_{21}H_{23}ClFNO_2$ of the central nervous system used especially as an antipsychotic drug

hal·o·phile \\'ha-lə-ˌfīl\ *noun* [International Scientific Vocabulary] (1923)
: an organism that flourishes in a salty environment
— **hal·o·phil·ic** \ˌha-lə-'fi-lik\ *adjective*

hal·o·phyte \\'ha-lə-ˌfīt\ *noun* [International Scientific Vocabulary] (circa 1886)
: a plant (as saltbush or sea lavender) that grows in salty soil and usually has a physiological resemblance to a true xerophyte
— **hal·o·phyt·ic** \ˌha-lə-'fi-tik\ *adjective*

hal·o·thane \\'ha-lə-ˌthān\ *noun* [*halo-* + *ethane*] (1957)
: a nonexplosive inhalational anesthetic $C_2HBrClF_3$

¹**halt** \\'hòlt\ *adjective* [Middle English, from Old English *healt;* akin to Old High German *halz* lame] (before 12th century)
: LAME

²**halt** *intransitive verb* (before 12th century)

1 : to walk or proceed lamely : LIMP
2 : to stand in perplexity or doubt between alternate courses : WAVER
3 : to display weakness or imperfection : FALTER

³**halt** *noun* [German, from Middle High German, from *halt,* imperative of *halten* to hold, from Old High German *haltan* — more at HOLD] (circa 1598)
: STOP

⁴**halt** (1656)
intransitive verb
1 : to cease marching or journeying
2 : DISCONTINUE, TERMINATE ⟨the project *halted* for lack of funds⟩
transitive verb
1 : to bring to a stop ⟨the strike *halted* subways and buses⟩
2 : to cause the discontinuance of : END

¹**hal·ter** \\'hòl-tər\ *noun* [Middle English, from Old English *hælftre;* akin to Old High German *halftra* halter, Old English *hielfe* helve] (before 12th century)
1 a : a rope or strap for leading or tying an animal **b** : a headstall usually with noseband and throatlatch to which a lead may be attached
2 : a rope for hanging criminals : NOOSE; *also* : death by hanging
3 : a woman's blouse that leaves the back, arms, and midriff bare and that is typically held in place by straps around the neck and across the back

halter 1b

²**halter** *transitive verb* **hal·tered; hal·ter·ing** \-t(ə-)riŋ\ (14th century)
1 a : to catch with or as if with a halter; *also* : to put a halter on **b** : HANG
2 : to put restraint upon : HAMPER

hal·ter·break \\'hòl-tər-ˌbrāk\ *transitive verb* **-broke** \-ˌbrōk\; **-bro·ken** \-ˌbrō-kən\; **-break·ing** (1837)
: to break (as a colt) to a halter

hal·tere \\'hòl-ˌtir, 'hal-\ *noun, plural* **hal·teres** \\'hòl-ˌtirz, 'hal-; hòl-'tir-ēz, hal-\ [New Latin *halter,* from Latin, jumping weight, from Greek *haltēr,* from *hallesthai* to leap — more at SALLY] (1823)
: one of a pair of club-shaped organs in a dipteran insect that are the modified second pair of wings and function as sensory flight stabilizers

halt·ing \\'hòl-tiŋ\ *adjective* (1585)
: marked by a lack of sureness or effectiveness ⟨spoke in a *halting* manner⟩
— **halt·ing·ly** \-tiŋ-lē\ *adverb*

hal·vah *or* **hal·va** \häl-'vä; 'häl-(ˌ)vä, -və\ *noun* [Yiddish *halva,* from Romanian, from Turkish *helva,* from Arabic *ḥalwā* sweetmeat] (1846)
: a flaky confection of crushed sesame seeds in a base of syrup (as of honey)

halve \\'hav, 'hàv\ *transitive verb* **halved; halv·ing** [Middle English, from *half* half] (13th century)
1 a : to divide into two equal parts **b** : to reduce to one half ⟨*halving* the present cost⟩ **c** : to share equally
2 : to play (as a hole in golf) in the same number of strokes as one's opponent

halv·ers \\'ha-vərz, 'hà-\ *noun plural* (1517)
: half shares : HALVES

halves *plural of* HALF

hal·yard \\'hal-yərd\ *noun* [Middle English *halier,* from *halen* to pull — more at HALE] (14th century)
: a rope or tackle for hoisting and lowering something (as sails)

¹**ham** \\'ham\ *noun* [Middle English *hamme,* from Old English *hamm;* akin to Old High German *hamma* ham, Greek *knēmē* shinbone, Old Irish *cnáim* bone] (before 12th century)

1 a : the hollow of the knee **b** : a buttock with its associated thigh — usually used in plural
2 : a cut of meat consisting of a thigh; *especially* : one from a hog
3 [short for *hamfatter,* from "The *Ham-fat* Man," minstrel song] **a** : a showy performer; *especially* : an actor performing in an exaggerated theatrical style **b** : a licensed operator of an amateur radio station
4 : a cushion used especially by tailors for pressing curved areas of garments
— **ham** *adjective*

²**ham** *verb* **hammed; ham·ming** (1933)
transitive verb
: to execute with exaggerated speech or gestures : OVERACT
intransitive verb
: to overplay a part

Ham \\'ham\ *noun* [Hebrew]
: a son of Noah held to be the progenitor of the Egyptians, Nubians, and Canaanites

hama·dry·ad \ˌha-mə-'drī-əd, -ˌad\ *noun* [Latin *hamadryad-, hamadryas,* from Greek, from *hama* together with + *dryad-, dryas* dryad — more at SAME] (14th century)
1 : WOOD NYMPH
2 : KING COBRA

hama·dry·as baboon \ˌha-mə-'drī-əs-\ *noun* [New Latin *hamadryas,* from Latin] (circa 1890)
: a baboon (*Papio hamadryas*) that has a reddish pink muzzle and a large bare patch of pink skin on each buttock and that was venerated by the ancient Egyptians — called also *sacred baboon*

ha·mal *also* **ham·mal** \hə-'mäl\ *noun* [Arabic *hammāl* porter] (circa 1760)
: a porter in eastern countries (as Turkey)

Ha·man \\'hā-mən\ *noun* [Hebrew *Hāmān*]
: an enemy of the Jews hanged according to the book of Esther for plotting their destruction

ha·man·tasch \\'hä-mən-ˌtäsh, 'hò-, -ˌtòsh\ *noun, plural* **-tasch·en** \-ˌtä-shən, -ˌtò-\ [Yiddish *homentash,* from *Homen* Haman + *tash* pocket, bag] (1927)
: a three-cornered pastry with a filling (as of poppy seeds or prunes) traditionally eaten during the Jewish holiday Purim

ha·mar·tia \ˌhä-ˌmär-'tē-ə\ *noun* [Greek, from *hamartanein* to miss the mark, err] (1927)
: TRAGIC FLAW

ha·mate \\'hā-ˌmāt\ *noun* [Latin *hamatus* hooked, from *hamus* hook] (1924)
: a bone on the inner side of the second row of the carpus in mammals

ham·burg·er \\'ham-ˌbər-gər\ *or* **ham·burg** \-ˌbərg\ *noun* [German *Hamburger* of Hamburg, Germany] (1884)
1 a : ground beef **b** : a patty of ground beef
2 : a sandwich consisting of a patty of hamburger in a split round bun

¹**hame** \\'hām\ *noun* [Middle English] (14th century)
: one of two curved supports attached to the collar of a draft horse to which the traces are fastened

²**hame** *Scottish variant of* HOME

ham-fist·ed \\'ham-ˌfis-təd\ *adjective* (1928)
: HAM-HANDED

ham-hand·ed \-ˌhan-dəd\ *adjective* (1918)
: lacking dexterity or grace : HEAVY-HANDED
— **ham-hand·ed·ly** \-lē\ *adverb*
— **ham-hand·ed·ness** \-dəd-nəs\ *noun*

Ham·il·to·ni·an \ˌha-məl-'tō-nē-ən\ *noun* [Sir William *Hamilton* (died 1865) Irish mathematician] (1933)
: a function that is used to describe a dynamic system (as the motion of a particle) in terms of components of momentum and coordinates of space and time and that is equal to the total energy of the system when time is not explicitly part of the function — compare LAGRANGIAN

Ham·il·to·ni·an·ism \-nē-ə-ˌni-zəm\ *noun* (1901)

: the political principles and ideas held by or associated with Alexander Hamilton that center around a belief in a strong central government, broad interpretation of the federal constitution, encouragement of an industrial and commercial economy, and a general distrust of the political capacity or wisdom of the common man

— Hamiltonian \-'tō-nē-ən\ *adjective*

Ham·ite \'ha-ˌmīt\ *noun* [*Ham*] (1854)
: a member of a Hamitic-speaking people

¹**Ham·it·ic** \ha-'mi-tik, hə-\ *adjective* (1844)
: of, relating to, or characteristic of the Hamites or one of the Hamitic languages

²**Hamitic** *noun* (circa 1890)
: HAMITIC LANGUAGES

Hamitic languages *noun plural* (circa 1890)
: any of various groupings of non-Semitic Afro-Asiatic languages (as Berber, Egyptian, and Cushitic) that were formerly thought to comprise a single branch of the Afro-Asiatic family

Ham·i·to-Se·mit·ic \ˌha-mə-(ˌ)tō-sə-'mi-tik, hə-'mi-tō-\ *adjective* (1901)
: of, relating to, or constituting the Afro-Asiatic languages

— Hamito–Semitic *noun*

ham·let \'ham-lət\ *noun* [Middle English, from Middle French *hamelet*, diminutive of *ham* village, of Germanic origin; akin to Old English *hām* village, home] (before 12th century)
: a small village

Ham·let \'ham-lət\ *noun*
: a legendary Danish prince and hero of Shakespeare's play *Hamlet*

¹**ham·mer** \'ha-mər\ *noun* [Middle English *hamer*, from Old English *hamor*; akin to Old High German *hamar* hammer, and perhaps to Old Church Slavonic *kamen-*, *kamy* stone, Greek *akmē* point, edge — more at EDGE] (before 12th century)
1 a : a hand tool consisting of a solid head set crosswise on a handle and used for pounding **b :** a power tool that often substitutes a metal block or a drill for the hammerhead
2 : something that resembles a hammer in form or action: as **a :** a lever with a striking head for ringing a bell or striking a gong **b** (1) : an arm that strikes the cap in a percussion lock to ignite the propelling charge (2) : a part of the action of a modern gun that strikes the primer of the cartridge in firing or that strikes the firing pin to ignite the cartridge **c :** MALLEUS **d :** GAVEL **e** (1) : a padded mallet in a piano action for striking a string (2) : a hand mallet for playing on various percussion instruments (as a xylophone)
3 : a metal sphere thrown for distance in the hammer throw
4 : ACCELERATOR b
— under the hammer : for sale at auction

²**hammer** *verb* **ham·mered; ham·mer·ing** \'ha-mər-iŋ, 'ham-riŋ\ (14th century)
intransitive verb
1 : to strike blows especially repeatedly with or as if with a hammer **:** POUND
2 : to make repeated efforts; *especially* **:** to reiterate an opinion or attitude ⟨the lectures all *hammered* away at the same points⟩
transitive verb
1 a : to beat, drive, or shape with repeated blows of a hammer **b :** to fasten or build with a hammer
2 : to strike or drive with a force suggesting a hammer blow or repeated blows ⟨*hammered* the ball over the fence⟩ ⟨tried to *hammer* me into submission⟩

— ham·mer·er \'ha-mər-ər\ *noun*

hammer and sickle *noun* (1921)
: an emblem consisting of a crossed hammer and sickle used especially as a symbol of Soviet Communism

hammer and tongs *adverb* (circa 1780)

: with great force, vigor, or violence ⟨went at it *hammer and tongs*⟩

— hammer–and–tongs *adjective*

hammer dulcimer *noun* (1953)
: DULCIMER 1 — called also *hammered dulcimer*

hammered *adjective* (1522)
: having surface indentations produced or appearing to have been produced by hammering ⟨*hammered* copper⟩

ham·mer·head \'ha-mər-ˌhed\ *noun* (1562)
1 : the striking part of a hammer
2 : BLOCKHEAD
3 : any of a family (Sphyrnidae) of active voracious medium-sized sharks that have the eyes at the ends of lateral extensions of the flattened head — see SHARK illustration

ham·mer·less \-ləs\ *adjective* (1875)
: having the hammer concealed ⟨a *hammerless* revolver⟩

ham·mer·lock \-ˌläk\ *noun* (1897)
: a wrestling hold in which an opponent's arm is held bent behind his back; *broadly* **:** a strong hold

hammer mill *noun* (1610)
: a grinder or crusher in which materials are broken up by hammers

hammer out *transitive verb* (circa 1632)
: to produce or bring about as if by repeated blows ⟨*hammered out* an agreement⟩

hammer throw *noun* (1898)
: a field event in which a usually 16-pound metal sphere attached to a flexible handle is thrown for distance

ham·mer·toe \'ha-mər-ˌtō\ *noun* (circa 1885)
: a deformed claw-shaped toe and especially the second that results from permanent angular flexion between one or both phalangeal joints

¹**ham·mock** \'ha-mək\ *noun* [Spanish *hamaca*, from Taino] (1555)
: a swinging couch or bed usually made of netting or canvas and slung by cords from supports at each end

²**hammock** *noun* [origin unknown] (1555)
1 : HUMMOCK
2 : a fertile area in the southern U.S. and especially Florida that is usually higher than its surroundings and that is characterized by hardwood vegetation and deep humus-rich soil

ham·my \'ha-mē\ *adjective* **ham·mi·er; -est** (1929)
: marked by exaggerated and usually self-conscious theatricality

— ham·mi·ly \'ha-mə-lē\ *adverb*
— ham·mi·ness \'ha-mē-nəs\ *noun*

¹**ham·per** \'ham-pər\ *transitive verb* **ham·pered; ham·per·ing** \-p(ə-)riŋ\ [Middle English] (14th century)
1 a : to restrict the movement of by bonds or obstacles **:** IMPEDE **b :** to interfere with the operation of **:** DISRUPT
2 a : CURB, RESTRAIN **b :** to interfere with **:** ENCUMBER ☆

²**hamper** *noun* [Middle English *hampere*, alteration of *hanaper*, literally, case to hold goblets, from Middle French *hanapier*, from *hanap* goblet, of Germanic origin; akin to Old English *hnæpp* bowl] (14th century)
: a large basket usually with a cover for packing, storing, or transporting articles (as food or laundry)

Hamp·shire \'ham(p)-ˌshir, -shər\ *noun* [*Hampshire*, England] (1918)
1 : any of a British breed of large hornless black-faced mutton-producing sheep — called also *Hampshire Down*
2 : any of an American breed of black white-belted swine

ham·ster \'ham(p)-stər\ *noun* [German, from Old High German *hamustro*, of Slavic origin; akin to Old Russian *choměstoru* hamster, of Iranian origin; akin to Avestan *hamaēstar-* oppressor] (1607)

: any of a subfamily (Cricetinae) of small Old World rodents having very large cheek pouches

¹**ham·string** \'ham-ˌstriŋ\ *noun* (1565)
1 a : either of two groups of tendons at the back of the human knee **b :** HAMSTRING MUSCLE
2 : a large tendon above and behind the hock of a quadruped

²**hamstring** *transitive verb* **-strung** \-ˌstrəŋ\; **-string·ing** \-ˌstriŋ-iŋ\ (1641)
1 : to make ineffective or powerless **:** CRIPPLE ⟨*hamstring* by guilt⟩
2 : to cripple by cutting the leg tendons

hamstring muscle *noun* (circa 1888)
: any of three muscles at the back of the thigh that function to flex and rotate the leg and extend the thigh

ham·u·lus \'ham-yə-ləs\ *noun, plural* **-u·li** \-ˌlī, -ˌlē\ [New Latin, from Latin, diminutive of *hamus* hook] (circa 1751)
: a hook or hooked process (as of a bone)

ham·za or **ham·zah** \'ham-zə, 'häm-\ *noun* [Arabic *hamzah*, literally, compression] (1938)
: the sign for a glottal stop in Arabic orthography usually represented in English by an apostrophe

Han \'hän\ *noun* [Chinese (Beijing) *Hàn*] (1736)
1 : a Chinese dynasty dated 207 B.C.–A.D. 220 and marked by centralized control through an appointive bureaucracy, a revival of learning, and the penetration of Buddhism
2 : the Chinese peoples especially as distinguished from non-Chinese (as Mongolian) elements in the population

¹**hand** \'hand\ *noun, often attributive* [Middle English, from Old English; akin to Old High German *hant* hand] (before 12th century)
1 a (1) : the terminal part of the vertebrate forelimb when modified (as in humans) as a grasping organ (2) : the forelimb segment (as the terminal section of a bird's wing) of a vertebrate higher than the fishes that corresponds to the hand irrespective of its form or functional specialization **b :** a part serving the function of or resembling a hand: as (1) : the hind foot of an ape (2) : the chela of a crustacean **c :** something resembling a hand: as (1) : an indicator or pointer on a dial ⟨the *hands* of a clock⟩ (2) : INDEX 5 (3) : a cluster of bananas developed from a single flower group (4) : a branched rootstock of ginger (5) : a bunch of large leaves (as of tobacco) tied together usually with another leaf
2 a : personal possession — usually used in plural ⟨the documents fell into the *hands* of

\ə\ abut	\ᵊ\ kitten	\ər\ further	\a\ ash	\ā\ ace	
\ä\ mop, mar	\aù\ out	\ch\ chin	\e\ bet	\ē\ easy	
\g\ go	\i\ hit	\ī\ ice	\j\ job	\ŋ\ sing	\ō\ go
\ò\ law	\òi\ boy	\th\ thin	\th\ the	\ü\ loot	\ù\ foot
\y\ yet	\zh\ vision	*see also* Guide to Pronunciation			

the enemy〉 **b :** CONTROL, SUPERVISION — usually used in plural 〈left the matter in her *hands*〉
3 a : SIDE, DIRECTION 〈men fighting on either *hand*〉 **b :** one of two sides or aspects of an issue or argument 〈on the one *hand* we can appeal for peace, and on the other, declare war〉
4 : a pledge especially of betrothal or bestowal in marriage
5 a : style of penmanship **:** HANDWRITING 〈wrote in a fancy *hand*〉 **b :** SIGNATURE
6 a : SKILL, ABILITY 〈tried her *hand* at sailing〉 **b :** an instrumental part 〈had a *hand* in the victory〉
7 : a unit of measure equal to 4 inches (10.2 centimeters) used especially for the height of horses
8 a : assistance or aid especially involving physical effort 〈lend a *hand*〉 **b :** PARTICIPATION, INTEREST **c :** a round of applause
9 a (1) **:** a player in a card game or board game (2) **:** the cards or pieces held by a player **b :** a single round in a game **c :** the force or solidity of one's position (as in negotiations)
10 a : a person who performs or executes a particular work 〈two portraits by the same *hand*〉 **b** (1) **:** a person employed at manual labor or general tasks 〈a ranch *hand*〉 (2) **:** WORKER, EMPLOYEE 〈employed over a hundred *hands*〉 **c :** a member of a ship's crew 〈all *hands* on deck〉 **d :** a person skilled in a particular action or pursuit **e :** a specialist or veteran in a usually designated activity or region 〈a China *hand*〉
11 a : HANDIWORK, DOINGS **b :** style of execution **:** WORKMANSHIP 〈the *hand* of a master〉 **c :** the feel of or tactile reaction to something (as silk or leather)
12 : a punch made with a specified hand 〈knocked him out with a good right *hand*〉
— **at hand 1 :** near in time or place **:** within reach 〈use whatever ingredients are *at hand*〉 **2 :** currently receiving or deserving attention 〈the business *at hand*〉
— **at the hands of** *also* **at the hand of :** by or through the action of
— **by hand 1 :** with the hands or a hand-worked implement (as a tool or pen) rather than with a machine **2 :** from one individual directly to another 〈deliver the document *by hand*〉
— **in hand 1 :** in one's possession or control **2 :** in preparation **3 :** under consideration
— **on all hands** *or* **on every hand :** EVERYWHERE
— **on hand 1 :** in present possession or readily available **2 :** about to appear **:** PENDING **3 :** in attendance **:** PRESENT
— **on one's hands :** in one's possession or care 〈too much time *on my hands*〉
— **out of hand 1 :** without delay or deliberation; *also* **:** in a summary or peremptory manner **2 :** done with **:** FINISHED **3 :** out of control **4 :** with the hands 〈fruit eaten *out of hand*〉
— **to hand 1 :** into possession **2 :** within reach

²hand *adverb* (before 12th century)
: with the hands rather than by machine

³hand *transitive verb* (15th century)
1 a *obsolete* **:** to touch or manage with the hands; *also* **:** to deal with **b :** FURL
2 : to lead, guide, or assist with the hand 〈*hand* a lady into a bus〉
3 a : to give, pass, or transmit with the hand 〈*hand* a letter to her〉 **b :** to present or provide with 〈*handed* him a surprise〉
— **hand it to :** to give credit to **:** concede the excellence of

hand and foot *adverb* (before 12th century)
: TOTALLY, ASSIDUOUSLY

hand ax *noun* (13th century)
1 : a short-handled ax intended for use with one hand
2 : a prehistoric stone tool having one end pointed for cutting and the other end rounded for holding in the hand

hand·bag \'han(d)-,bag\ *noun* (1862)
1 : SUITCASE
2 : a bag held in the hand or hung from a shoulder strap and used for carrying small personal articles and money
hand·ball \-,bȯl\ *noun* (1886)
1 : a game played in a walled court or against a single wall or board by two or four players who use their hands to strike the ball
2 : a small rubber ball used in handball
hand·bar·row \-,bar-(,)ō\ *noun* (15th century)
: a flat rectangular frame with handles at both ends that is carried by two persons
hand·bas·ket \-,bas-kət\ *noun* (15th century)
: a small portable basket — usually used in the phrase *to hell in a handbasket* denoting rapid and utter ruination
hand·bell \-,bel\ *noun* (before 12th century)
: a small bell with a handle; *especially* **:** one of a set tuned in a scale for musical performance
hand·bill \-,bil\ *noun* (1753)
: a small printed sheet to be distributed (as for advertising) by hand
hand·blown \-'blōn\ *adjective* (1925)
: made by glassblowing and molded by hand
hand·book \-,bu̇k\ *noun* (before 12th century)
1 a : a book capable of being conveniently carried as a ready reference **:** MANUAL **b :** a concise reference book covering a particular subject
2 a : a bookmaker's book of bets **b :** a place where bookmaking is carried on
hand·breadth \-,bretth, -,breth, -,bredth\ *noun* (before 12th century)
: any of various units of length varying from about 2½ to 4 inches based on the breadth of a hand
hand·car \'han(d)-,kär\ *noun* (1850)
: a small four-wheeled railroad car propelled by a hand-operated mechanism or by a small motor
hand·cart \-,kärt\ *noun* (1640)
: a cart drawn or pushed by hand
hand cheese *noun* (1890)
: a soft cheese with a sharp pungent odor and flavor that was originally molded by hand
hand·clasp \'han(d)-,klasp\ *noun* (1583)
: HANDSHAKE
¹hand·craft \-,kraft\ *noun* (before 12th century)
: HANDICRAFT
²handcraft *transitive verb* (1947)
: to fashion by handicraft
hand·crafts·man \-,kraf(t)-smən\ *noun* (15th century)
: a person who is skilled in handicraft
— **hand·crafts·man·ship** \-ship\ *noun*
¹hand·cuff \-,kəf\ *noun* (1695)
: a metal fastening that can be locked around a wrist and is usually connected by a chain or bar with another such fastening — usually used in plural
²handcuff *transitive verb* (1720)
1 : to apply handcuffs to **:** MANACLE
2 : to hold in check **:** make ineffective or powerless
hand down *transitive verb* (1692)
1 : to transmit in succession (as from father to son)
2 : to make official formulation of and express (the opinion of a court)
hand·ed \'han-dəd\ *adjective* (15th century)
1 : having a hand or hands especially of a specified kind or number — usually used in combination 〈a large-*handed* man〉
2 : using a specified hand or number of hands — used in combination 〈right-*handed*〉 〈a one-*handed* catch〉
hand·ed·ness \-nəs\ *noun* (1915)
1 : a tendency to use one hand rather than the other
2 a : the property of an object (as a molecule) of not being identical with its mirror image **b :** either of the two configurations of an object that may exist in forms which are nonidentical mirror images

hand·fast \'han(d)-,fast\ *noun* [Middle English, from Old English *handfæst*] (1611)
archaic **:** a contract or covenant especially of betrothal or marriage
hand–feed \'han(d)-'fēd\ *transitive verb* **-fed** \-'fed\; **-feed·ing** (1805)
: to feed (as animals) by hand
hand·ful \'han(d)-,fu̇l\ *noun, plural* **handfuls** \-,fu̇lz\ *also* **hands·ful** \'han(d)z-,fu̇l\ (before 12th century)
1 : as much or as many as the hand will grasp
2 : a small quantity or number
3 : as much as one can manage
hand glass *noun* (1882)
: a small mirror with a handle
hand–grip \'han(d)-,grip\ *noun* (before 12th century)
1 : a grasping with the hand
2 : HANDLE
3 *plural* **:** hand-to-hand combat
hand–gun \-,gən\ *noun* (15th century)
: a firearm (as a revolver or pistol) designed to be held and fired with one hand
hand–held \-,held, -'held\ *adjective* (1923)
: held in the hand; *especially* **:** designed to be operated while being held in the hand 〈*hand-held* computers〉
— **handheld** \-,held\ *noun*
hand–hold \'hand-,hōld\ *noun* (1643)
1 : HOLD, GRIP
2 : something to hold on to (as in mountain climbing)
hand–hold·ing \-,hōl-diŋ\ *noun* (1967)
: solicitous attention, support, or instruction (as in the use of new technology)
¹hand·i·cap \'han-di-,kap, -dē-\ *noun* [obsolete English *handicap* (a game in which forfeit money was held in a cap), from *hand in cap*] (1754)
1 a : a race or contest in which an artificial advantage is given or disadvantage imposed on a contestant to equalize chances of winning **b :** an advantage given or disadvantage imposed usually in the form of points, strokes, weight to be carried, or distance from the target or goal
2 a : a disadvantage that makes achievement unusually difficult **b :** a physical disability ◇
²handicap *transitive verb* **-capped; -capping** (1852)
1 a : to give a handicap to **b :** to assess the relative winning chances of (contestants) or the likely winner of (a contest)
2 : to put at a disadvantage

◇ WORD HISTORY
handicap *Handicap*, from *hand in cap*, was an old form of barter. Two people who wished to make an exchange asked a third to act as umpire. All three put forfeit money in a cap, into which each of the two barterers inserted a hand. The umpire described the goods to be traded and set the additional amount the owner of the less valuable article should pay the other in order that the exchange might be fair. The barterers withdrew their hands from the cap empty to signify the refusal of the umpire's decision, or full to indicate acceptance. If the hands of both barterers were full, the exchange was made and the umpire pocketed the forfeit money. If both barterers came up empty-handed, there was no exchange but the umpire took the money. Otherwise, each barterer kept his own property, and the one who had accepted the umpire's decision took the forfeit money as well. Later, a horse race arranged in accordance with the rules of handicap was called a *handicap race*. The umpire decided how much extra weight the better horse should carry. The word was eventually extended to other contests, and also came to signify the advantage or disadvantage imposed.

hand·i·capped *adjective* (1915)
: having a physical or mental disability that substantially limits activity especially in relation to employment or education; *also* : of or reserved for handicapped persons ⟨*handicapped* parking spaces⟩

hand·i·cap·per \-ˌka-pər\ *noun* (1754)
1 : a person who assigns handicaps
2 : a person who predicts the winners in a race (as a horse race)
3 : a person who competes with a (specified) handicap (as in golf) — usually used in combination ⟨a 5-*handicapper*⟩

hand·i·craft \'han-di-ˌkraft, -dē-\ *noun* [Middle English *handi-crafte,* alteration of *handcraft*] (13th century)
1 a : manual skill **b** : an occupation requiring skill with the hands
2 : the articles fashioned by those engaged in handicraft
— **hand·i·craft·er** \-ˌkraf-tər\ *noun*

hand·i·crafts·man \-ˌkraf(t)-smən\ *noun* (1551)
: a person who engages in a handicraft : ARTISAN

Hand·ie–Talk·ie \ˌhan-dē-ˈtȯ-kē\ *trademark*
— used for a small portable radio transmitter-receiver

hand·i·ly \'han-də-lē\ *adverb* (1719)
1 : in a dexterous manner
2 : EASILY ⟨defeated the other candidate *handily*⟩
3 : conveniently nearby

hand in *transitive verb* (1837)
: SUBMIT 2 ⟨*hand in* your homework⟩

hand in glove *or* **hand and glove** *adverb* (1680)
: in extremely close relationship or agreement ⟨working *hand in glove* with the police⟩

hand in hand *adverb* (15th century)
1 : with hands clasped (as in intimacy or affection)
2 : in close association : TOGETHER

hand·i·work \'han-di-ˌwərk, -dē-\ *noun* [Middle English *handiwerk,* from Old English *handgeweorc,* from *hand* + *geweorc,* from *ge-* (collective prefix) + *weorc* work — more at CO-] (before 12th century)
1 a : work done by the hands **b** : work done personally
2 : the product of handiwork

hand·ker·chief \'haŋ-kər-chəf, -ˌchif, -ˌchēf\ *noun, plural* **-chiefs** *also* **-chieves** \-chəfs, -ˌchifs, -ˌchēvz, -ˌchēfs, -chəvz, -ˌchivz\ (1530)
1 : a small usually square piece of cloth used for usually personal purposes (as blowing the nose) or as a clothing accessory
2 : KERCHIEF 1

¹han·dle \'han-d⁰l\ *noun* [Middle English *handel,* from Old English *handle;* akin to Old English *hand*] (before 12th century)
1 : a part that is designed especially to be grasped by the hand
2 : something that resembles a handle
3 a : TITLE 8 **b** : NAME; *also* : NICKNAME
4 : HAND 11c
5 : the total amount of money bet on a race, game, or event
6 : a means of understanding or controlling ⟨can't quite get a *handle* on things⟩
— **han·dled** \-d⁰ld\ *adjective*
— **han·dle·less** \-d⁰l-(l)əs\ *adjective*
— **off the handle** : into a state of sudden and violent anger — usually used with *fly*

²handle *verb* **han·dled; han·dling** \'han(d)-liŋ, 'han-d⁰l-iŋ\ (before 12th century)
transitive verb
1 a : to try or examine (as by touching, feeling, or moving) with the hand ⟨*handle* silk to judge its weight⟩ **b** : to manage with the hands ⟨*handle* a horse⟩
2 a : to deal with in writing or speaking or in the plastic arts **b** : to have overall responsibility for supervising or directing : MANAGE ⟨a

lawyer *handles* all my affairs⟩ **c** : to train and act as second for (a boxer) **d** : to put up with : STAND ⟨can't *handle* the heat⟩
3 : to act on or perform a required function with regard to ⟨*handle* the day's mail⟩
4 : to engage in the buying, selling, or distributing of (a commodity)
intransitive verb
: to act, behave, or feel in a certain way when handled or directed ⟨a car that *handles* well⟩
— **han·dle·able** \-d⁰l-ə-bəl\ *adjective*

han·dle·bar \'han-d⁰l-ˌbär\ *noun* (1886)
: a straight or bent bar with a handle at each end; *specifically* : one used to steer a bicycle or similar vehicle — usually used in plural

handlebar mustache *noun* (1933)
: a heavy mustache with long sections that curve upward at each end

hand lens *noun* (1930)
: a magnifying glass to be held in the hand

han·dler \'han(d)-lər, 'han-d⁰l-ər\ *noun* (14th century)
1 : one that handles something
2 a : a person in immediate physical charge of an animal; *especially* : a person who exhibits dogs at shows or field trials **b** : a person who trains or acts as second for a boxer **c** : a manager of a political figure or campaign

hand·less \'han(d)-ləs\ *adjective* (15th century)
1 : having no hands
2 : inefficient in manual tasks : CLUMSY

han·dling \'han(d)-liŋ, 'han-d⁰l-iŋ\ *noun* (before 12th century)
1 a : the action of one that handles something **b** : a process by which something is handled in a commercial transaction; *especially* : the packaging and shipping of an object or material (as to a consumer)
2 : the manner in which something is treated (as in a musical, literary, or art work)

hand·list \'han(d)-ˌlist\ *noun* (1859)
: a list (as of books) for purposes of reference or checking

hand·made \'han(d)-'mād\ *adjective* (1613)
: made by hand or by a hand process

hand·maid·en \-ˌmā-d⁰n\ *also* **hand·maid** \-ˌmād\ *noun* (13th century)
1 : a personal maid or female servant
2 : something whose essential function is to serve or assist ⟨criticism is not the enemy of art but rather its *handmaiden* —Gary Michael⟩

hand–me–down \'han(d)-mē-ˌdaủn\ *adjective* (1827)
1 : put in use by one person or group after being used, discarded, or handed down by another ⟨*hand-me-down* clothes⟩ ⟨*hand-me-down* anecdotes⟩
2 : ready-made and usually cheap and shoddy
— **hand–me–down** *noun*

hand off (1949)
transitive verb
: to hand (a football) to a nearby teammate on a play
intransitive verb
: to hand off a football
— **hand·off** \'han-ˌdȯf\ *noun*

hand on *transitive verb* (1865)
: HAND DOWN

hand organ *noun* (1796)
: a barrel organ operated by a hand crank

hand·out \'han-ˌdaủt\ *noun* (1882)
1 : a portion of food, clothing, or money given to or as if to a beggar
2 : a folder or circular of information for free distribution
3 : a prepared statement released to the news media

hand out *transitive verb* (1877)
1 a : to give without charge **b** : to give freely
2 : ADMINISTER ⟨*handed out* a severe punishment⟩

hand over *transitive verb* (1816)
: to yield control of
— **hand·over** \'han-ˌdō-vər\ *noun*

hand over fist *adverb* (1825)

: quickly and in large amounts

hand·pick \'han(d)-'pik\ *transitive verb* (1831)
1 : to pick by hand as opposed to a machine process
2 : to select personally or for personal ends

hand·press \-ˌpres\ *noun* (1679)
: a hand-operated press

hand·print \-ˌprint\ *noun* (1886)
: an impression of a hand on a surface

hand puppet *noun* (1947)
: PUPPET 1a

hand·rail \'han(d)-ˌrāl\ *noun* (1793)
: a narrow rail for grasping with the hand as a support

hand running *adverb* (1828)
dialect : in unbroken succession

hand·saw \'han(d)-ˌsȯ\ *noun* (14th century)
: a saw designed to be used with one hand

hands·breadth \'han(d)z-ˌbredth, -ˌbretth\
variant of HANDBREADTH

hands down \'han(d)z-ˈdaủn\ *adverb* (1867)
1 : without much effort : EASILY
2 : without question
— **hands–down** \'han(d)z-ˌdaủn\ *adjective*

¹hand·sel \'han(t)-səl\ *noun* [Middle English *hansell*] (14th century)
1 : a gift made as a token of good wishes or luck especially at the beginning of a new year
2 : something received first (as in a day of trading) and taken to be a token of good luck
3 a : a first installment : earnest money **b** : EARNEST, FORETASTE

²handsel *transitive verb* **-seled** *or* **-selled; -sel·ing** *or* **-sel·ling** \-s(ə-)liŋ\ (15th century)
1 : to give a handsel to
2 : to inaugurate with a token or gesture of luck or pleasure
3 : to use or do for the first time

hand·set \'han(d)-ˌset\ *noun* (circa 1919)
: a combined telephone transmitter and receiver mounted on a handle

hand·shake \-ˌshāk\ *noun* (1873)
: a clasping usually of right hands by two people (as in greeting or farewell)

hands–off \'han(d)-'zȯf\ *adjective* (1902)
: characterized by noninterference ⟨a *hands-off* policy toward the internal affairs of other nations⟩

hand·some \'han(t)-səm\ *adjective* **hand·som·er; -est** [Middle English *handsom* easy to manipulate] (1530)
1 *chiefly dialect* : APPROPRIATE, SUITABLE
2 : moderately large : SIZABLE ⟨a painting that commanded a *handsome* price⟩
3 : marked by skill or cleverness : ADROIT
4 : marked by graciousness or generosity : LIBERAL ⟨*handsome* contributions to charity⟩
5 : having a pleasing and usually impressive or dignified appearance
synonym see BEAUTIFUL
— **hand·some·ly** *adverb*
— **hand·some·ness** *noun*

hands–on \'han(d)-'zȯn, -'zän\ *adjective* (1969)
1 : relating to, being, or providing direct practical experience in the operation or functioning of something ⟨*hands-on* training⟩; *also* : involving or allowing use of or touching with the hands ⟨a *hands-on* museum display⟩
2 : characterized by active personal involvement ⟨a *hands-on* manager⟩

hand·spike \'han(d)-ˌspīk\ *noun* [by folk etymology from Dutch *handspaak,* from *hand* hand + *spaak* pole; akin to Old English *spāca* spoke] (1615)
: a bar used as a lever

hand·spring \-ˌspriŋ\ *noun* (1875)

\ə\ abut \ˌ⁰\ kitten \ər\ further \a\ ash \ā\ ace
\ä\ mop, mar \aủ\ out \ch\ chin \e\ bet \ē\ easy
\g\ go \i\ hit \ī\ ice \j\ job \ŋ\ sing \ō\ go
\ȯ\ law \ȯi\ boy \th\ thin \t̲h̲\ the \ü\ loot \ủ\ foot
\y\ yet \zh\ vision *see also* Guide to Pronunciation

: an acrobatic feat in which the body turns forward or backward in a full circle from a standing position and lands first on the hands and then on the feet

hand·stand \-,stand\ *noun* (1899)
: an act of supporting the body on the hands with the trunk and legs balanced in the air

hand–to–hand \'han-tə-'hand, -də-\ *adjective* (1836)
: involving physical contact or close enough range for physical contact ⟨*hand-to-hand* fighting⟩

hand to hand *adverb* (circa 1533)
: at very close range

hand–to–mouth \-'mauth\ *adjective* (1748)
: having or providing nothing to spare beyond basic necessities ⟨a *hand-to-mouth* existence⟩

hand truck *noun* (1920)
: a small hand-propelled truck; *especially* : TRUCK 3b

hand up *transitive verb* (1970)
of a jury : to deliver (an indictment) to a judge or higher judicial authority

hand·wheel \'han(d)-,(h)wēl\ *noun* (circa 1889)
: a wheel worked by hand

hand·work \'hand-,wərk\ *noun* (before 12th century)
: work done with the hands and not by machines : HANDIWORK
— **hand·work·er** \-,wər-kər\ *noun*

hand·wo·ven \-'wō-vən\ *adjective* (1880)
1 : produced on a hand-operated loom
2 : woven by hand ⟨*handwoven* baskets⟩

hand–wring·ing \-,riŋ-iŋ\ *noun* (1922)
: an overwrought expression of concern or guilt
— **hand·wring·er** *noun*

hand·write \-,rīt\ *transitive verb* **-wrote** \-,rōt\, **-writ·ten** \-,ri-t°n\, **-writ·ing** \-,rī-tiŋ\ [back-formation from *handwriting*] (circa 1853)
: to write by hand

hand·writ·ing \'hand-,rī-tiŋ\ *noun* (15th century)
1 : writing done by hand; *especially* : the form of writing peculiar to a particular person
2 : something written by hand
— **handwriting on the wall** : an omen of one's unpleasant future

hand·wrought \'hand-'rôt\ *adjective* (1876)
: fashioned by hand or chiefly by hand processes ⟨*handwrought* silver⟩

handy \'han-dē\ *adjective* **hand·i·er; -est** (1650)
1 a : conveniently near **b** : convenient for use **c** *of a ship* : easily handled
2 : clever in using the hands especially in a variety of useful ways ⟨*handy* with a hammer as well as with a paintbrush⟩
— **hand·i·ness** *noun*

handy·man \-dē-,man\ *noun* (1872)
1 : one who does odd jobs
2 : one competent in a variety of small skills or inventive or ingenious in repair or maintenance work — called also *handyperson*

¹hang \'haŋ\ *verb* **hung** \'həŋ\ *also* **hanged** \'haŋd\; **hang·ing** \'haŋ-iŋ\ [partly from Middle English *hon*, from Old English *hōn*, transitive verb; partly from Middle English *hangen*, from Old English *hangian*, intransitive verb & transitive verb; both akin to Old High German *hāhan*, transitive verb, to hang, *hangēn*, intransitive verb — more at CUNCTATION] (before 12th century)
transitive verb
1 a : to fasten to some elevated point without support from below : SUSPEND **b** : to suspend by the neck until dead — often *hanged* in the past; often used as a mild oath ⟨I'll be *hanged*⟩ **c** : to fasten so as to allow free motion within given limits around a point of suspension ⟨*hang* a door⟩ **d** : to adjust the hem of (a skirt) so as to hang evenly and at a proper height
2 : to furnish with hanging decorations (as flags or bunting)

3 : to hold or bear in a suspended or inclined manner ⟨*hung* his head in shame⟩
4 : to apply to a wall ⟨*hang* wallpaper⟩
5 : to display (pictures) in a gallery
6 : to throw (as a curveball) so that it fails to break properly
7 : to make (a turn) especially while driving ⟨*hang* a right⟩ ⟨*hung* a quick U-turn —Tom Clancy⟩
intransitive verb
1 a : to remain suspended or fastened to some point above without support from below : DANGLE **b** : to die by hanging — often *hanged* in the past ⟨he *hanged* for his crimes⟩
2 : to remain poised or stationary in the air ⟨clouds *hanging* low overhead⟩
3 : LINGER, PERSIST
4 : to be imminent : IMPEND ⟨doom *hung* over the nation⟩
5 : to fall or droop from a usually tense or taut position
6 : DEPEND ⟨election *hangs* on one vote⟩
7 a (1) : to take hold for support : CLING ⟨she *hung* on his arm⟩ (2) : to keep persistent contact ⟨dogs *hung* to the trail⟩ **b** : to be burdensome or oppressive ⟨time *hangs* on his hands⟩
8 : to be uncertain or in suspense ⟨the decision is still *hanging*⟩
9 : to lean, incline, or jut over or downward
10 : to be in a state of rapt attention ⟨*hung* on her every word⟩
11 : to fit or fall from the figure in easy lines ⟨the coat *hangs* loosely⟩
12 *of a thrown ball* : to fail to break or drop as intended ▫
— **hang·able** \'haŋ-ə-bəl\ *adjective*
— **hang fire 1** : to be slow in the explosion of a charge after its primer has been discharged **2** : DELAY, HESITATE **3** : to remain unsettled or unresolved
— **hang it up** : to cease an activity or effort
— **hang loose** : to remain calm or relaxed
— **hang one on 1** : to inflict a blow on **2** *slang* : to get very drunk
— **hang one's hat** : to situate oneself in (as a residence or place of employment)
— **hang tough** : to remain resolute in the face of adversity : HANG IN

²hang *noun* (circa 1797)
1 : the manner in which a thing hangs
2 : DECLIVITY, SLOPE; *also* : DROOP
3 : facility with or an understanding of something ⟨can't get the *hang* of this⟩
4 : a hesitation or slackening in motion or in a course
— **give a hang** *or* **care a hang** : to be the least bit concerned or worried

hang about *intransitive verb* (1849)
British : HANG AROUND

¹han·gar \'haŋ-ər, 'haŋ-gər\ *noun* [French] (1852)
: SHELTER, SHED; *especially* : a covered and usually enclosed area for housing and repairing aircraft

²hangar *transitive verb* (1943)
: to place or store in a hangar

hang around (1830)
intransitive verb
1 : to pass time or stay aimlessly : loiter idly
2 : to spend one's time in company
transitive verb
: to pass time or stay aimlessly in or at ⟨*hung around* the house all day⟩

hang back *intransitive verb* (1581)
1 : to drag behind others
2 : to be reluctant

¹hang·dog \'haŋ-,dôg\ *adjective* (1677)
1 : SAD, DEJECTED
2 : SHEEPISH

²hangdog *noun* (1687)
: a despicable or miserable person

hang·er \'haŋ-ər\ *noun* (15th century)
1 : one that hangs or causes to be hung or hanged

2 : something that hangs, overhangs, or is suspended: as **a** : a decorative strip of cloth **b** : a small sword formerly used by seamen **c** *chiefly British* : a small wood on steeply sloping land
3 : a device by which or to which something is hung or hangs: as **a** : a strap on a sword belt by which a sword or dagger can be suspended **b** : a loop by which a garment is hung **c** : a device that fits inside or around a garment for hanging from a hook or rod

hang·er–on \-,ôn, -,än\ *noun*, *plural* **hangers–on** (1542)
: one that hangs around a person, place, or institution especially for personal gain

hang glider *noun* (1930)
: a kitelike glider from which a harnessed rider hangs while gliding down from a cliff or hill
— **hang glid·ing** *noun*

hang glider

hang in *intransitive verb* (1966)
: to refuse to be discouraged or intimidated : show pluck ⟨*hang in* there⟩

¹hang·ing \'haŋ-iŋ\ *adjective* (12th century)
1 : situated or lying on steeply sloping ground
2 a : jutting out : OVERHANGING ⟨a *hanging* rock⟩ **b** : supported only by the wall on one side ⟨a *hanging* staircase⟩
3 *archaic* : downcast in appearance
4 : adapted for sustaining a hanging object
5 : deserving, likely to cause, or prone to inflict death by hanging

²hanging *noun* (14th century)
1 : an execution by strangling or breaking the neck by a suspended noose
2 : something hung: as **a** : CURTAIN **b** : a covering (as a tapestry) for a wall
3 : a downward slope : DECLIVITY

hanging indention *noun* (1904)
: indention of all the lines of a paragraph except the first

hang·man \'haŋ-mən\ *noun* (14th century)
: one who hangs a condemned person; *also* : a public executioner

hang·nail \-,nāl\ *noun* [by folk etymology from *agnail* (inflammation about the nail), from Middle English, corn on the foot or toe, from Old English *angnægl*, from *ang-* (akin to *enge* tight, painful) + *nægl* nail — more at ANGER] (1678)
: a bit of skin hanging loose at the side or root of a fingernail ◆

hang off *intransitive verb* (1641)
: HANG BACK

hang on *intransitive verb* (circa 1719)
1 : to keep hold : hold onto something
2 : to persist tenaciously ⟨a cold that *hung on* all spring⟩
3 : HOLD ON 2 ⟨*hang on* a second while I look it up⟩
— **hang on to** : to hold, grip, or keep tenaciously ⟨*hang on to* your money⟩

hang·out \'haŋ-,aut\ *noun* (circa 1893)

: a favorite place for spending time; *also* **:** a place frequented for entertainment or for socializing

hang out (14th century)
intransitive verb
1 : to protrude and droop
2 a *slang* **:** LIVE, RESIDE **b :** HANG AROUND
transitive verb
: to display outside as an announcement to the public — used chiefly in the phrase *hang out one's shingle*

hang·over \ˈhaŋ-ˌō-vər\ *noun* (1894)
1 : something (as a surviving custom) that remains from what is past
2 a : disagreeable physical effects following heavy consumption of alcohol or the use of drugs **b :** a letdown following great excitement or excess

hang·tag \ˈhaŋ-ˌtag\ *noun* (1952)
: a tag attached to an article of merchandise giving information about its material and proper care

hang time *noun* (1976)
: the amount of time a kicked football remains in the air; *also* **:** the length of time a leaping athlete is in the air

hang together *intransitive verb* (1551)
1 : to remain united **:** stand by one another
2 : to have unity **:** form a consistent or coherent whole

Hang·town fry \ˈhaŋ-ˌtaùn-\ *noun, often F capitalized* [*Hangtown*, nickname for Placerville, Calif.] (1949)
: an omelet or scrambled eggs containing oysters

han·gul \ˈhän-ˌgül\ *noun, often capitalized* [Korean *hangŭl*] (1946)
: the alphabetic script in which Korean is written

hang–up \ˈhaŋ-ˌəp\ *noun* (1959)
: a source of mental or emotional difficulty; *broadly* **:** PROBLEM

hang up (12th century)
transitive verb
1 a : to place on a hook or hanger designed for the purpose ⟨*hang up* your coat⟩ **b :** to replace (a telephone receiver) on the cradle so that the connection is broken
2 : to keep delayed, suspended, or held up
3 : to cause to stick or snag immovably ⟨the ship was *hung up* on a sandbar⟩
intransitive verb
1 : to break a telephone connection
2 : to become stuck or snagged so as to be immovable

ha·ni·wa \ˈhä-nə-ˌwä\ *noun plural, often capitalized* [Japanese] (1931)
: large hollow baked clay sculptures placed on ancient Japanese burial mounds

hank \ˈhaŋk\ *noun* [Middle English, of Scandinavian origin; akin to Old Norse *hǫnk* hank; akin to Old English *hangian* to hang] (14th century)
1 : COIL, LOOP; *specifically* **:** a coiled or looped bundle (as of yarn or rope) usually containing a definite yardage
2 : any of a series of rings or clips by which a jib or staysail is attached to a stay

han·ker \ˈhaŋ-kər\ *intransitive verb* **han·kered; han·ker·ing** \-k(ə-)riŋ\ [probably from Flemish *hankeren*, frequentative of *hangen* to hang; akin to Old English *hangian*] (1642)
: to have a strong or persistent desire **:** YEARN — often used with *for* or *after*
synonym see LONG
— **han·ker·er** \-kər-ər\ *noun*

han·kie *or* **han·ky** \ˈhaŋ-kē\ *noun, plural* **hankies** [*handkerchief* + *-ie*] (1895)
: HANDKERCHIEF

han·ky-pan·ky \ˌhaŋ-kē-ˈpaŋ-kē\ *noun* [origin unknown] (1841)
1 : questionable or underhanded activity
2 : sexual dalliance

¹Han·o·ve·ri·an \ˌha-nə-ˈvir-ē-ən, -ˈver-\ *adjective* [*Hanover*, Germany] (circa 1775)

1 : of, relating to, or supporting the German ducal house of Hanover
2 : of or relating to the British royal house that ruled from 1714 to 1901

²Hanoverian *noun* (1827)
: a member or supporter of the ducal or of the British royal Hanoverian house

Han·sa \ˈhan(t)-sə, ˈhän-ˌzä\ *or* **Hanse** \ˈhan(t)s, ˈhän-zə\ *noun* [*Hansa* from Medieval Latin, from Middle Low German *hanse; Hanse* from Middle English *Hanze*, from Middle French *hanse*, from Middle Low German] (15th century)
1 : a league originally constituted of merchants of various free German cities dealing abroad in the medieval period and later of the cities themselves and organized to secure greater safety and privileges in trading
2 : a medieval merchant guild or trading association

— **Han·se·at·ic** \ˌhan(t)-sē-ˈa-tik\ *noun or adjective*

Han·sard \ˈhan(t)-sərd, ˈhan-ˌsärd\ *noun* [Luke *Hansard*] (circa 1859)
: the official published report of debates in a Commonwealth parliament

han·sel *variant of* HANDSEL

Han·sen's disease \ˈhan(t)-sənz-\ *noun* [Armauer *Hansen* (died 1912) Norwegian physician] (1938)
: LEPROSY

han·som \ˈhan(t)-səm\ *noun* [Joseph A. *Hansom* (died 1882) English architect] (1847)
: a light 2-wheeled covered carriage with the driver's seat elevated behind — called also *hansom cab*

hant \ˈhant\ *dialect variant of* HAUNT

Ha·nuk·kah \ˈhä-nə-kə, ˈkä-\ *noun* [Hebrew *hănukkāh* dedication] (1891)

hansom

: an 8-day Jewish holiday beginning on the 25th of Kislev and commemorating the rededication of the Temple of Jerusalem after its defilement by Antiochus of Syria

hao \ˈhaù\ *noun, plural* **hao** [Vietnamese *hào*] (1948)
: a monetary unit of Vietnam equal to ¹⁄₁₀ dong

hao·le \ˈhaù-lē, -(ˌ)lä\ *noun* [Hawaiian] (1834)
: one who is not descended from the aboriginal Polynesian inhabitants of Hawaii; *especially* **:** WHITE — sometimes used disparagingly

¹hap \ˈhap\ *noun* [Middle English, from Old Norse *happ* good luck; akin to Old English *gehæp* suitable, Old Church Slavonic *kobĭ* lot, fate] (13th century)
1 : HAPPENING 1
2 : CHANCE, FORTUNE

²hap *intransitive verb* **happed; hap·ping** (14th century)
: HAPPEN

³hap *transitive verb* **happed; hap·ping** [Middle English *happen*] (14th century)
dialect **:** CLOTHE, COVER

⁴hap *noun* (1724)
dialect **:** something (as a bed quilt or cloak) that serves as a covering or wrap

ha·pa hao·le \ˌhä-pə-ˈhaù-lē, -(ˌ)lä\ *adjective* [Hawaiian, from *hapa* half (from English *half*) + *haole*] (1919)
: of part-white ancestry or origin; *especially* **:** of white and Hawaiian ancestry

ha·pax le·go·me·non \ˌha-ˌpaks-li-ˈgä-mə-ˌnän, ˌhä-ˌpäks-, -nən\ *noun, plural* **hapax le·go·me·na** \-nə\ [Greek, something said only once] (1882)
: a word or form occurring only once in a document or corpus

ha'·pen·ny \ˈhāp-nē, ˈhā-pə-\ *noun* [by contraction] (circa 1550)

: HALFPENNY

¹hap·haz·ard \(ˌ)hap-ˈha-zərd\ *noun* [¹*hap* + *hazard*] (1576)
: CHANCE

²haphazard *adjective* (1671)
: marked by lack of plan, order, or direction
synonym see RANDOM
— **haphazard** *adverb*
— **hap·haz·ard·ly** *adverb*
— **hap·haz·ard·ness** *noun*
— **hap·haz·ard·ry** \-zər-drē\ *noun*

hapl- *or* **haplo-** *combining form* [New Latin, from Greek, from *haploos*, from *ha-* one (akin to *homos* same) + *-ploos* multiplied by; akin to Latin *-plex* -fold — more at SAME, -FOLD]
1 : single ⟨*haplology*⟩
2 : haploid ⟨*haplont*⟩

hap·less \ˈha-pləs\ *adjective* (14th century)
: having no luck **:** UNFORTUNATE
— **hap·less·ly** *adverb*
— **hap·less·ness** *noun*

hap·loid \ˈha-ˌplȯid\ *adjective* [International Scientific Vocabulary, from Greek *haploeidēs* single, from *haploos*] (1908)
: having the gametic number of chromosomes or half the number characteristic of somatic cells — compare DIPLOID
— **haploid** *noun*
— **hap·loi·dy** \-ˌplȯi-dē\ *noun*

hap·lol·o·gy \ha-ˈplä-lə-jē\ *noun* (1895)
: contraction of a word by omission of one or more similar sounds or syllables (as in *mineralogy* for **mineralology* or \ˈprä-blē\ for *probably*)

hap·lont \ˈha-ˌplänt\ *noun* [International Scientific Vocabulary] (1920)
: an organism (as some primitive algae) having a diploid zygote that undergoes meiosis to produce haploid cells — compare DIPLONT
— **hap·lon·tic** \ha-ˈplän-tik\ *adjective*

hap·lo·type \ˈha-plō-ˌtīp\ *noun* (1969)
: a set of genes that determine different antigens but are closely enough linked to be inherited as a unit; *also* **:** the antigenic phenotype determined by a haplotype

hap·ly \ˈha-plē\ *adverb* (14th century)
: by chance, luck, or accident

hap·pen \ˈha-pən, -pᵊm\ *intransitive verb* **hap·pened; hap·pen·ing** \ˈhap-niŋ, ˈha-pə-\ [Middle English, from *hap*] (14th century)
1 : to occur by chance — often used with *it* ⟨it so *happens* I'm going your way⟩
2 : to come into being or occur as an event, process, or result ⟨mistakes will *happen*⟩ ⟨what good things *happened* to you?⟩

◇ **WORD HISTORY**
hangnail *Hangnail* is altered by folk etymology from *angnail* or *agnail*, which in its earliest sense did not mean what we now call a hangnail. In Old English *angnægl* was used to mean "corn on the foot," with the second element, *nægl*, referring not to a fingernail or toenail but rather to the nail we drive in with a hammer, the head of an iron nail being likened to a hard corn. By the 16th century the association of *-nail* with the body's nails led to a new sense, "a sore or inflammation around a fingernail or toenail." The first element *ang-* or *ag-*, which is related to an Old English adjective *enge*, meaning "tight, painful," had ceased to be interpretable since Old English. In the next century it was altered to *hang-*, and the dominant sense of both *hangnail* and *agnail* came to be "a bit of loose skin at the side or root of a fingernail."

\ə\ **abut** \ᵊ\ **kitten** \ər\ **further** \a\ **ash** \ā\ **ace**
\ä\ **mop, mar** \aù\ **out** \ch\ **chin** \e\ **bet** \ē\ **easy**
\g\ **go** \i\ **hit** \ī\ **ice** \j\ **job** \ŋ\ **sing** \ō\ **go**
\ȯ\ **law** \ȯi\ **boy** \th\ **thin** \t̲h̲\ **the** \ü\ **loot** \ù\ **foot**
\y\ **yet** \zh\ **vision** *see also* Guide to Pronunciation

3 : to do, encounter, or attain something by or as if by chance ⟨*happened* to overhear the plotters⟩
4 a : to meet or discover something by chance ⟨*happened* upon a system that worked —Richard Corbin⟩ **b :** to come or go casually **:** make a chance appearance ⟨he *happened* into the room just then⟩
5 : to come especially by way of injury or harm ⟨I promise nothing will *happen* to you⟩
hap·pen·chance \'ha-pən-ˌchan(t)s, 'ha-pᵊm-\ *noun* (1876)
: HAPPENSTANCE
hap·pen·ing *noun* (1551)
1 : something that happens **:** OCCURRENCE
2 : an event or series of events designed to evoke a spontaneous reaction to sensory, emotional, or spiritual stimuli
3 : something (as an event) that is particularly interesting, entertaining, or important
hap·pen·stance \'ha-pən-ˌstan(t)s, 'ha-pᵊm-\ *noun* [*happen* + circum*stance*] (1897)
: a circumstance especially that is due to chance
— **hap·pen·stance** *adjective*
hap·pi·ly \'ha-pə-lē\ *adverb* (14th century)
1 a : in a fortunate manner **b :** as it fortunately happens ⟨*happily*, some boyhood pleasures don't change —P. A. Witteman⟩
2 *archaic* **:** by chance
3 : in a happy manner or state ⟨lived *happily* ever after⟩
4 : in an adequate or fitting manner **:** SUCCESSFULLY
hap·pi·ness \'ha-pi-nəs\ *noun* (15th century)
1 *obsolete* **:** good fortune **:** PROSPERITY
2 a : a state of well-being and contentment **:** JOY **b :** a pleasurable or satisfying experience
3 : FELICITY, APTNESS
hap·py \'ha-pē\ *adjective* **hap·pi·er; -est** [Middle English, from *hap*] (14th century)
1 : favored by luck or fortune **:** FORTUNATE
2 : notably fitting, effective, or well adapted **:** FELICITOUS ⟨a *happy* choice⟩
3 a : enjoying or characterized by well-being and contentment **:** JOYOUS **b :** expressing or suggestive of happiness **:** PLEASANT **c :** GLAD, PLEASED **d :** having or marked by an atmosphere of good fellowship **:** FRIENDLY
4 a : characterized by a dazed irresponsible state ⟨a punch-*happy* boxer⟩ **b :** impulsively or obsessively quick to use or do something ⟨trigger-*happy*⟩ **c :** enthusiastic about something to the point of obsession **:** OBSESSED ⟨education-conscious and statistic-*happy* —Helen Rowen⟩
synonym see LUCKY, FIT
hap·py–go–lucky \ˌha-pē-gō-'lə-kē\ *adjective* (1856)
: blithely unconcerned **:** CAREFREE
happy hour *noun* (1961)
: a period of time during which the price of drinks (as at a bar) is reduced or hors d'oeuvres are served free
happy hunting ground *noun* (1837)
1 : the paradise of some American Indian tribes to which the souls of warriors and hunters pass after death to spend a happy hereafter in hunting and feasting
2 : a choice or profitable area of activity or exploitation
happy talk *noun* (1973)
: informal talk among the participants in a television news broadcast; *also* **:** a broadcast format featuring such talk
Haps·burg \'haps-ˌbərg, 'häps-ˌbu̇rg\ *adjective* [*Habsburg*, Aargau, Switzerland] (circa 1895)
: of or relating to the German royal house to which belong the rulers of Austria from 1278 to 1918, the rulers of Spain from 1516 to 1700, and many of the Holy Roman emperors
— **Hapsburg** *noun*
hap·ten \'hap-ˌten\ *noun* [German, from Greek *haptein* to fasten] (1921)
: a small separable part of an antigen that reacts specifically with an antibody but is inca-

pable of stimulating antibody production except in combination with a carrier protein molecule
— **hap·ten·ic** \hap-'te-nik\ *adjective*
hap·tic \'hap-tik\ *adjective* [International Scientific Vocabulary, from Greek *haptesthai* to touch] (circa 1890)
1 : relating to or based on the sense of touch
2 : characterized by a predilection for the sense of touch ⟨a *haptic* person⟩
hap·to·glo·bin \'hap-tə-ˌglō-bən\ *noun* [International Scientific Vocabulary, from Greek *haptein* + International Scientific Vocabulary hem*oglobin*] (1941)
: any of several carbohydrate-containing serum alpha globulins that can combine with free hemoglobin in the plasma
hara–kiri \ˌhar-i-'kir-ē, -'kar-ē\ *noun* [Japanese *harakiri*, from *hara* belly + *kiri* cutting] (1840)
1 : ritual suicide by disembowelment practiced by the Japanese samurai or formerly decreed by a court in lieu of the death penalty
2 : SUICIDE 1b
¹ha·rangue \hə-'raŋ\ *noun* [Middle English *arang*, from Middle French *arenge*, from Old Italian *aringa*, from *aringare* to speak in public, from *aringo* public assembly, of Germanic origin; akin to Old High German *hring* ring] (15th century)
1 : a speech addressed to a public assembly
2 : a ranting speech or writing
3 : LECTURE
²harangue *verb* **ha·rangued; ha·rangu·ing** (1660)
intransitive verb
: to make a harangue **:** DECLAIM
transitive verb
: to address in a harangue ⟨*haranguing* me . . . on the folly of my ways —Jay Jacobs⟩
— **ha·rangu·er** *noun*
ha·rass \hə-'ras, 'har-əs\ *transitive verb* [French *harasser*, from Middle French, from *harer* to set a dog on, from Old French *hare*, interjection used to incite dogs, of Germanic origin; akin to Old High German *hier* here — more at HERE] (1617)
1 a : EXHAUST, FATIGUE **b :** to annoy persistently
2 : to worry and impede by repeated raids ⟨*harassed* the enemy⟩ □
synonym see WORRY
— **ha·rass·er** *noun*
— **ha·rass·ment** \-mənt\ *noun*
¹har·bin·ger \'här-bən-jər\ *noun* [Middle English *herbergere*, from Middle French, host, from *herberge* hostelry, of Germanic origin; akin to Old High German *heriberga*] (14th century)
1 *archaic* **:** a person sent ahead to provide lodgings
2 a : one that pioneers in or initiates a major change **:** PRECURSOR **b :** one that presages or foreshadows what is to come ◇
synonym see FORERUNNER
²harbinger *transitive verb* (1646)
: to be a harbinger of **:** PRESAGE
¹har·bor \'här-bər\ *noun* [Middle English *herberge, herberwe*, from Old English *hereborg* military quarters, from *here* army (akin to Old High German *heri* army) + *beorg* refuge; akin to Old English *burg* fortified town — more at HARRY, BOROUGH] (12th century)
1 : a place of security and comfort **:** REFUGE
2 : a part of a body of water protected and deep enough to furnish anchorage; *especially* **:** one with port facilities
word history see HARBINGER
— **har·bor·ful** \-ˌfu̇l\ *noun*
— **har·bor·less** \-ləs\ *adjective*
²harbor *verb* **har·bored; har·bor·ing** \-b(ə-)riŋ\ (12th century)
transitive verb
1 a : to give shelter or refuge to **b :** to be the home or habitat of ⟨the ledges still *harbor* rattlesnakes⟩; *broadly* **:** CONTAIN 2

2 : to hold especially persistently in the mind **:** CHERISH ⟨*harbored* a grudge⟩
intransitive verb
1 : to take shelter in or as if in a harbor
2 : LIVE
— **har·bor·er** \-bər-ər\ *noun*
har·bor·age \-bə-rij\ *noun* (15th century)
: SHELTER, HARBOR
har·bor·mas·ter \'här-bər-ˌmas-tər\ *noun* (1769)
: an officer who executes the regulations respecting the use of a harbor
harbor seal *noun* (1766)
: a small seal (*Phoca vitulina*) that occurs along oceanic coasts of the northern hemisphere and often ascends rivers
har·bor·side \'här-bər-ˌsīd\ *adjective* (1924)
: located next to a harbor
har·bour *chiefly British variant of* HARBOR
¹hard \'härd\ *adjective* [Middle English, from Old English *heard;* akin to Old High German *hart* hard, Greek *kratos* strength] (before 12th century)
1 a : not easily penetrated **:** not easily yielding to pressure **b** *of cheese* **:** not capable of being spread **:** very firm
2 a *of liquor* (1) **:** having a harsh or acid taste (2) **:** strongly alcoholic **b :** characterized by the presence of salts (as of calcium or magnesium) that prevent lathering with soap ⟨*hard* water⟩
3 a : of or relating to radiation of relatively high penetrating power ⟨*hard* X rays⟩ **b :** having or producing relatively great photographic contrast ⟨a *hard* negative⟩
4 a : metallic as distinct from paper ⟨*hard* money⟩ **b** *of currency* **:** convertible into gold **:** stable in value **c :** usable as currency ⟨paid in *hard* cash⟩ **d** *of currency* **:** readily acceptable in international trade **e :** being high and firm ⟨*hard* prices⟩
5 a : firmly and closely twisted ⟨*hard* yarns⟩ **b :** having a smooth close napless finish ⟨a *hard* worsted⟩

6 a : physically fit ⟨in good *hard* condition⟩ **b :** resistant to stress (as disease) **c :** free of weakness or defects

7 a (1) : FIRM, DEFINITE ⟨reached a *hard* agreement⟩ **(2) :** not speculative or conjectural **:** FACTUAL ⟨*hard* evidence⟩ **(3) :** important or informative rather than sensational or entertaining ⟨*hard* news⟩ **b :** CLOSE, SEARCHING ⟨gave a *hard* look⟩ **c :** free from sentimentality or illusion **:** REALISTIC ⟨good *hard* sense⟩ **d :** lacking in responsiveness **:** OBDURATE, UNFEELING ⟨a *hard* heart⟩

8 a (1) : difficult to bear or endure ⟨*hard* luck⟩ ⟨*hard* times⟩ **(2) :** OPPRESSIVE, INEQUITABLE ⟨sales taxes are *hard* on the poor⟩ ⟨a *hard* restriction⟩ **b (1) :** lacking consideration, compassion, or gentleness **:** CALLOUS ⟨a *hard* greedy landlord⟩ **(2) :** INCORRIGIBLE, TOUGH ⟨a *hard* gang⟩ **c (1) :** harsh, severe, or offensive in tendency or effect ⟨said some *hard* things⟩ **(2) :** RESENTFUL ⟨*hard* feelings⟩ **(3) :** STRICT, UNRELENTING ⟨drives a *hard* bargain⟩ **d :** INCLEMENT ⟨*hard* winter⟩ **e (1) :** intense in force, manner, or degree ⟨*hard* blows⟩ **(2) :** demanding the exertion of energy **:** calling for stamina and endurance ⟨*hard* work⟩ **(3) :** performing or carrying on with great energy, intensity, or persistence ⟨a *hard* worker⟩ **f :** EXTREME 4a ⟨the *hard* political right⟩

9 a : characterized by sharp or harsh outline, rigid execution, and stiff drawing **b :** sharply defined **:** STARK ⟨*hard* shadows⟩ **c :** lacking in shading, delicacy, or resonance ⟨*hard* singing tones⟩ **d :** sounding as in *arcing* and *geese* respectively — used of *c* and *g* **e :** suggestive of toughness or insensitivity ⟨*hard* eyes⟩

10 a (1) : difficult to accomplish or resolve **:** TROUBLESOME ⟨*hard* problems⟩ ⟨the true story was *hard* to come by⟩ **(2) :** difficult to comprehend or explain ⟨a *hard* concept⟩ **b :** having difficulty in doing something ⟨*hard* of hearing⟩ **c :** difficult to magnetize or demagnetize

11 : being at once addictive and gravely detrimental to health ⟨such *hard* drugs as heroin⟩

12 : resistant to biodegradation ⟨*hard* detergents⟩ ⟨*hard* pesticides like DDT⟩

13 : being, schooled in, or using the methods of the natural sciences and especially of the physical sciences ⟨a *hard* scientist⟩ ☆

²hard *adverb* (before 12th century)

1 a : with great or utmost effort or energy **:** STRENUOUSLY ⟨were *hard* at work⟩ ⟨the children played *hard*⟩ **b :** in a violent manner **:** FIERCELY **c :** to the full extent — usually used in nautical directions ⟨steer *hard* aport⟩ **d :** to an immoderate degree ⟨hitting the bottle *hard*⟩ **e :** in a searching, close, or concentrated manner ⟨stared *hard* at me⟩

2 a : in such a manner as to cause hardship, difficulty, or pain **b :** with rancor, bitterness, or grief ⟨took the defeat *hard*⟩

3 : in a firm manner **:** TIGHTLY

4 : to the point of hardness ⟨frozen *hard*⟩

5 : close in time or space ⟨stands *hard* by the river⟩

hard–and–fast \ˌhär-dᵊn-ˈfast\ *adjective* (1867)

: not to be modified or evaded **:** STRICT ⟨a *hard-and-fast* rule⟩

hard–ass \ˈhärˌdas\ *noun* (1972)

: a tough, demanding, or uncompromising person — often considered vulgar

— hard–assed \ˌdast\ *adjective*

hard·back \ˈhärdˌbak\ *noun* (1952)

: a book bound in hard covers

hard·ball \ˌbȯl\ *noun* (circa 1883)

1 : BASEBALL

2 : forceful uncompromising methods employed to gain an end ⟨played political *hardball*⟩

hard–bit·ten \ˈbi-tᵊn\ *adjective* (1784)

1 : inclined to bite hard

2 : seasoned or steeled by difficult experience **:** TOUGH

hard·board \ˈhärdˌbōrd, -ˌbȯrd\ *noun* (1925)

: a very dense fiberboard usually having one smooth face

hard–boil \-ˈbȯi(ə)l\ *transitive verb* [back-formation from *hard-boiled*] (1895)

: to cook (an egg) in the shell until both white and yolk have solidified

hard–boiled \-ˈbȯi(ə)ld\ *adjective* (1886)

1 a : devoid of sentimentality **:** TOUGH ⟨a *hard-boiled* drill sergeant⟩ **b :** of, relating to, or being a detective story featuring a tough unsentimental protagonist and a matter-of-fact attitude towards violence

2 : HARDHEADED, PRACTICAL ⟨handle aid programs on a friendly but *hard-boiled* business basis —N.Y. Times⟩

hard·boot \-ˌbüt\ *noun* (1922)

: an especially small-time horseman

hard–bound \-ˌbau̇nd\ *adjective* (1926)

: HARDCOVER

hard candy *noun* (1925)

: a candy made of sugar and corn syrup boiled without crystallizing

hard–case \ˈhärdˌkās\ *adjective* (1896)

: HARD-BITTEN, TOUGH

hard case \-ˌkās\ *noun* (1836)

: a tough or hardened person

hard cheese *noun* (1861)

chiefly British **:** tough luck — often used interjectionally

hard cider *noun* (1789)

: fermented apple juice

hard clam *noun* (1846)

: a clam with a thick hard shell; *specifically* **:** QUAHOG

hard coal *noun* (1846)

: ANTHRACITE

hard–coat·ed \ˈhärdˈkō-təd\ *adjective* (circa 1898)

of a dog **:** having a crisp harsh-textured coat

hard copy *noun* (1954)

: a copy of textual or graphic information (as from microfilm or computer storage) produced on paper in normal size

hard–core \-ˈkōr, -ˈkȯr\ *adjective* (1940)

1 a : of, relating to, or being part of a hard core ⟨*hard-core* poverty⟩ ⟨the *hard-core* unemployed⟩ **b :** CONFIRMED, DIE-HARD ⟨*hard-core* rock fans⟩ ⟨a *hard-core* liberal⟩

2 *of pornography* **:** containing explicit descriptions of sex acts or scenes of actual sex acts — compare SOFT-CORE

3 : characterized by or being the purest or most basic form of something **:** FUNDAMENTAL ⟨a room gussied up in *hard-core* French provincial style —John Canaday⟩

hard core *noun* (1936)

1 : a central or fundamental and usually enduring group or part: as **a :** a relatively small enduring core of society marked by apparent resistance to change or inability to escape a persistent wretched condition (as poverty or chronic unemployment) **b :** a militant or fiercely loyal faction

2 *usually* **hard-core** \-ˌkōr, -ˌkȯr\ *chiefly British* **:** hard material in pieces (as broken bricks or stone) used as a bottom (as in making roads and in foundations)

hard·cov·er \ˈhärdˈkə-vər\ *adjective* (1949)

1 : having rigid boards on the sides covered in cloth or paper ⟨*hardcover* books⟩

2 : of or relating to hardcover books ⟨*hardcover* sales⟩

— hardcover *noun*

hard disk *noun* (1978)

: a rigid metal disk that is sealed against dust and is used as a high-capacity storage device for a microcomputer

hard drive *noun* (1983)

: a disk drive containing one or more hard disks

hard–edge \ˈhärdˈej\ *adjective* (1961)

: of or relating to abstract painting characterized by geometric forms with clearly defined boundaries

hard–edged \-ˈejd\ *adjective* (1954)

: having a tough, driving, or sharp quality ⟨*hard-edged* stories about life in the city⟩

hard·en \ˈhär-dᵊn\ *verb* **hard·ened; hard·en·ing** \ˈhärd-niŋ, ˈhär-dᵊn-iŋ\ (13th century)

transitive verb

1 : to make hard or harder

2 : to confirm in disposition, feelings, or action; *especially* **:** to make callous ⟨*hardened* his heart⟩

3 a : INURE, TOUGHEN ⟨*harden* troops⟩ **b :** to inure to unfavorable environmental conditions (as cold) — often used with *off* ⟨*harden off* plants⟩

4 : to protect from blast, heat, or radiation (as by a thick barrier or placement underground)

intransitive verb

1 : to become hard or harder

2 a : to become firm, stable, or settled **b :** to assume an appearance of harshness or severity ⟨her face *hardened* at the word⟩

hard·en·er \ˈhärd-nər, ˈhär-dᵊn-ər\ *noun* (1611)

: one that hardens; *especially* **:** a substance added (as to a paint or varnish) to harden the film

hard·en·ing *noun* (1953)

: SCLEROSIS ⟨*hardening* of the arteries⟩

hard·fist·ed \ˈhärdˈfis-təd\ *adjective* (circa 1656)

1 : STINGY, CLOSEFISTED

2 : HARDHANDED 2

hard goods *noun plural* (1934)

: DURABLES

hard·hack \ˈhärdˌhak\ *noun* (1814)

: a shrubby American spirea (*Spiraea tomentosa*) with dense terminal panicles of pink or occasionally white flowers and leaves having a hairy and yellow to rust-colored underside

hard·hand·ed \-ˈhan-dəd\ *adjective* (1590)

1 : having hands made hard by labor

2 : STRICT, OPPRESSIVE

— hard·hand·ed·ness *noun*

hard hat *usually* -ˈhat *for 1 and* -ˌhat *for 2 & 3*\ *noun* (1926)

1 a : a protective hat made of rigid material (as metal or fiberglass) and worn especially by construction workers **b :** a construction worker

2 : a conservative who is intolerant of opposing views

hard·head \ˈhärdˌhed\ *noun* (15th century)

1 a : a hardheaded person **b :** BLOCKHEAD

2 *plural* **hardheads** *also* **hardhead** **:** any of several fishes especially with a spiny or bony head; *especially* **:** ATLANTIC CROAKER

hard·head·ed \-ˈhe-dəd\ *adjective* (1583)

1 : STUBBORN, WILLFUL

2 : concerned with or involving practical considerations **:** SOBER, REALISTIC ⟨some *hardheaded* advice⟩ ⟨a *hardheaded* observer of winds and tides⟩

— hard·head·ed·ly *adverb*

— hard·head·ed·ness *noun*

hard–heart·ed \-ˈhär-təd\ *adjective* (13th century)

: lacking in sympathetic understanding **:** UNFEELING, PITILESS

☆ **SYNONYMS**

Hard, difficult, arduous mean demanding great exertion or effort. HARD implies the opposite of all that is easy ⟨farming is *hard* work⟩. DIFFICULT implies the presence of obstacles to be surmounted or puzzles to be resolved and suggests the need of skill, patience, or courage ⟨the *difficult* ascent of the main face of the mountain⟩. ARDUOUS stresses the need of laborious and persevering exertion ⟨the *arduous* task of rebuilding⟩.

\ə\ abut \ᵊ\ kitten \ər\ further \a\ ash \ā\ ace
\ä\ mop, mar \au̇\ out \ch\ chin \e\ bet \ē\ easy
\g\ go \i\ hit \ī\ ice \j\ job \ŋ\ sing \ō\ go
\ȯ\ law \ȯi\ boy \th\ thin \t̲h̲\ the \ü\ loot \u̇\ foot
\y\ yet \zh\ vision *see also* Guide to Pronunciation

— **hard–heart·ed·ly** adverb
— **hard–heart·ed·ness** noun

hard–hit·ting \-'hi-tiŋ\ adjective (1926)
: strikingly effective in force or result ⟨a hard-hitting exposé⟩ ⟨plain hard-hitting English⟩

har·di·hood \'här-dē-ˌhu̇d\ noun (1570)
1 a : resolute courage and fortitude **b** : resolute and self-assured audacity often carried to the point of impudent insolence
2 : VIGOR, ROBUSTNESS
synonym see TEMERITY

har·di·ment \-mənt\ noun [Middle English, from Middle French, from Old French, from hardi bold, hardy] (14th century)
1 archaic : HARDIHOOD
2 obsolete : a bold deed

har·ding·grass \'här-diŋ-ˌgras\ noun, often capitalized [R. R. Harding (flourished about 1900) Australian botanist] (1917)
: a perennial grass (Phalaris tuberosa variety stenoptera) widely used as a forage grass

hard knocks noun plural (1913)
: rough unsparing treatment (as in use or in life) — often used in the phrase school of hard knocks

hard labor noun (1841)
: compulsory labor of imprisoned criminals as a part of the prison discipline

hard–line \'härd-'līn\ adjective (1962)
: advocating or involving a rigidly uncompromising course of action
— **hard–lin·er** \-'lī-nər\ noun

hard lines noun plural (1824)
chiefly British : hard luck — often used interjectionally

hard·ly \'härd-lē\ adverb (before 12th century)
1 : with force : VIGOROUSLY
2 : in a severe manner : HARSHLY
3 : with difficulty : PAINFULLY
4 a — used to emphasize a minimal amount ⟨I hardly knew her⟩ ⟨almost new — hardly a scratch on it⟩ **b** — used to soften a negative ⟨you can't hardly tell who anyone is —G. B. Shaw⟩
5 : certainly not ⟨that news is hardly surprising⟩ □

hard maple noun (1790)
: SUGAR MAPLE

hard·mouthed \'härd-'mau̇thd, -'mau̇tht\ adjective (1617)
1 of a horse : not sensitive to the bit
2 : OBSTINATE, STUBBORN

hard·ness \-nəs\ noun (before 12th century)
1 : the quality or state of being hard
2 a : the cohesion of the particles on the surface of a mineral as determined by its capacity to scratch another or be itself scratched — compare MOHS' SCALE **b** : resistance of metal to indentation under a static load or to scratching

hard·nose \'härd-ˌnōz\ noun (circa 1960)
: a hard-nosed person

hard–nosed \'härd-'nōzd\ adjective (circa 1927)
1 : being tough, stubborn, or uncompromising
2 : HARDHEADED 2, TOUGH-MINDED

hard–of–hear·ing \ˌhär-də(v)-'hir-iŋ\ adjective (1564)
: of or relating to a defective but functional sense of hearing

hard–on \'här-ˌdȯn, -ˌdän\ noun, plural **hard–ons** (circa 1893)
: an erection of the penis — sometimes considered vulgar

hard palate noun (circa 1847)
: the bony anterior part of the palate forming the roof of the mouth

hard·pan \'härd-ˌpan\ noun (1817)
1 : a cemented or compacted and often clayey layer in soil that is impenetrable by roots
2 : a fundamental part : BEDROCK

hard pine noun (1884)
: a pine (as longleaf pine or pitch pine) that has hard wood and leaves usually in groups of two or three; also : the wood of a hard pine

hard–pressed \'härd-'prest\ adjective (1825)

: HARD PUT; also : being under financial strain
hard put adjective (1893)
: barely able : faced with difficulty or perplexity ⟨was hard put to find an explanation⟩

hard rock noun (1967)
: rock music marked by a heavy regular beat, high amplification, and usually frenzied performances

hard rubber noun (1860)
: a firm rubber or rubber product; especially : a normally black horny substance made by vulcanizing natural rubber with high percentages of sulfur

hard sauce noun (1880)
: a creamed mixture of butter and powdered sugar often with added cream and flavoring (as vanilla or rum)

hard·scrab·ble \'härd-ˌskra-bəl\ adjective (1804)
1 a : being or relating to a place of barren or barely arable soil ⟨a hardscrabble farm⟩ ⟨hardscrabble prairies⟩ **b** : getting a meager living from poor soil ⟨a hardscrabble farmer⟩
2 : marked by poverty ⟨a hardscrabble cotton town⟩ ⟨a hardscrabble childhood⟩

hard sell noun (1952)
: aggressive high-pressure salesmanship — compare SOFT SELL

hard–set \'härd-'set\ adjective (1813)
: RIGID, FIXED

hard–shell \-ˌshel\ or **hard–shelled** \-ˌsheld\ adjective (1838)
: FUNDAMENTAL 2b, FUNDAMENTALIST ⟨a hard-shell preacher⟩ ⟨hard-shell Baptists⟩; also : UNCOMPROMISING, HIDEBOUND ⟨a hard-shell conservative⟩

hard–shell clam noun (1799)
: QUAHOG — called also hard-shelled clam

hard–shell crab noun (1902)
: a crab that has not recently shed its shell — called also hard-shelled crab

hard·ship \'härd-ˌship\ noun (13th century)
1 : PRIVATION, SUFFERING
2 : something that causes or entails suffering or privation

hard·stand \-ˌstand\ noun (1944)
: a paved area for parking an airplane

hard·stand·ing \-ˌstan-diŋ\ noun (1944)
chiefly British : HARDSTAND; also : PARKING LOT

hard stone noun (1931)
: an opaque usually semiprecious stone that can be shaped or carved (as for jewelery or mosaics)

hard·tack \-ˌtak\ noun, plural **hardtack** or **hardtacks** (1836)
1 : a saltless hard biscuit, bread, or cracker
2 : any of several mountain mahoganies (especially Cercocarpus betuloides)

hard–times token noun (1922)
: any of the tokens issued during the controversy between the Jackson administration and the bank of the U.S.

hard·top \'härd-ˌtäp\ noun (1950)
: an automobile or a motorboat having a permanent rigid top; also : such an automobile styled to resemble a convertible

hard up adjective (1821)
1 : short of money
2 : poorly provided ⟨hard up for friends⟩

hard·ware \'härd-ˌwar, -ˌwer\ noun (circa 1515)
1 : ware (as fittings, cutlery, tools, utensils, or parts of machines) made of metal
2 : major items of equipment or their components used for a particular purpose ⟨educational hardware⟩: as **a** : military equipment **b** : the physical components (as electronic and electrical devices) of a vehicle (as a spacecraft) or an apparatus (as a computer)

hardware cloth noun (circa 1914)
: rugged galvanized screening

hard wheat noun (1812)
: a wheat with hard flinty kernels that are high in gluten and that yield a flour especially suitable for bread and macaroni

hard–wired \'härd-ˌwīrd\ adjective (1968)
: implemented in the form of permanent electronic circuits; also : having permanent electrical connections ⟨hardwired phone⟩

hard–won \-'wən\ adjective (circa 1843)
: gained by great effort

¹**hard·wood** \'härd-ˌwu̇d\ noun (1568)
1 : the wood of an angiospermous tree as distinguished from that of a coniferous tree
2 : a tree that yields hardwood

²**hardwood** adjective (circa 1817)
1 : having or made of hardwood ⟨hardwood floors⟩
2 : consisting of mature woody tissue ⟨hardwood cuttings⟩

hard·work·ing \'härd-'wər-kiŋ\ adjective (1774)
: INDUSTRIOUS

har·dy \'här-dē\ adjective **har·di·er; -est** [Middle English hardi, from Old French, from (assumed) Old French hardir to make hard, of Germanic origin; akin to Old English heard hard] (13th century)
1 : BOLD, BRAVE
2 : AUDACIOUS, BRAZEN
3 a : inured to fatigue or hardships : ROBUST **b** : capable of withstanding adverse conditions ⟨hardy outdoor furniture⟩ ⟨hardy plants⟩ ⟨hardy cattle⟩
— **har·di·ly** \'här-d°l-ē\ adverb
— **har·di·ness** \'här-dē-nəs\ noun

Har·dy–Wein·berg law \ˌhär-dē-'wīn-ˌbərg-\ noun [G. H. Hardy (died 1947) English mathematician and W. Weinberg, 20th century German scientist] (1950)
: a fundamental principle of population genetics: population gene frequencies and genotype frequencies remain constant from generation to generation if mating is random and if mutation, selection, immigration, and emigration do not occur — called also Hardy-Weinberg principle

¹**hare** \'har, 'her\ noun, plural **hare** or **hares** [Middle English, from Old English hara; akin to Old High German haso hare, Sanskrit śaśa, Old English hasu gray] (before 12th century)
: any of various swift long-eared lagomorph mammals (family Leporidae and especially genus Lepus) that are usually solitary or sometimes live in pairs and have the young openeyed and furred at birth — compare RABBIT 1A

²**hare** intransitive verb **hared; har·ing** (1719)
: to go swiftly : ³TEAR

hare and hounds noun (circa 1845)
: a game in which some of the players leave a trail and others try to follow the trail to find and catch them

hare·bell \'har-ˌbel, 'her-\ noun (1765)
: a slender blue-flowered herb (Campanula rotundifolia) with linear leaves on the stem

hare·brained \-'brānd\ adjective (1534)
: FOOLISH 1, 2a

Ha·re Krish·na \ˌhär-ē-'krish-nə, ˌhar-\ noun, plural **Hare Krishna** or **Hare Krishnas**

□ USAGE

hardly Hardly in sense 5 is used sometimes with not for emphasis (just another day at the office? Not hardly). In sense 4b with a negative verb (as can't, wouldn't, didn't) it does not make a double negative but softens the negative. In "you can't hardly find a red one," the sense is that you can find a red one, but only with difficulty; in "you can't find a red one," the sense is that red ones are simply not available. Use of hardly with a negative verb is a speech form; it is most commonly heard in Southern and Midland speech areas. In other speech areas and in all discursive prose, hardly is normally used with a positive (you can hardly find a red one).

[from *Hare Krishna*, phrase in a chant, from Hindi *hare Kṛṣṇa* O Krishna!] (1969)
: a member of a religious group dedicated to the worship of the Hindu god Krishna

hare·lip \'har-ˌlip, 'her-\ *noun* (1567)
: a congenital deformity characterized by a cleft upper lip resulting from failure of the embryonic parts of the lip to unite

har·em \'har-əm, 'her-\ *noun* [Arabic *ḥarīm*, literally, something forbidden & *ḥaram*, literally, sanctuary] (1623)
1 a : a usually secluded house or part of a house allotted to women in a Muslim household **b :** the wives, concubines, female relatives, and servants occupying a harem
2 : a group of women associated with one man
3 : a group of females associated with one male — used of polygamous animals

harem pants *noun* [from their oriental appearance] (1952)
: women's loose trousers that fit closely at the ankle

har·i·cot \'(h)ar-i-ˌkō\ *noun* [French] (1653)
: the ripe seed or the unripe pod of any of several beans (genus *Phaseolus* and especially *P. vulgaris*)

ha·ri·jan \ˌhär-i-'jän\ *noun, often capitalized* [Sanskrit *harijana* one belonging to the god Vishnu, from *Hari* Vishnu + *jana* person] (1931)
: a member of the outcaste group in India **:** UNTOUCHABLE

hari-kari \ˌhar-i-'kar-ē, -'kir-\ *variant of* HARA-KIRI

hark \'härk\ *intransitive verb* [Middle English *herkien;* akin to Old High German *hōrechen* to listen, Old English *hīeran* to hear] (14th century)
: to pay close attention **:** LISTEN

hark back *intransitive verb* (1829)
1 : to turn back to an earlier topic or circumstance
2 : to go back to something as an origin or source

harken *intransitive verb* (before 12th century)
1 : HEARKEN
2 : HARK BACK — usually used with *back*

har·le·quin \'här-li-k(w)ən\ *noun* [ultimately from Italian *arlecchino*, from Middle French *Helquin*, a demon] (1590)
1 a *capitalized* **:** a character in comedy and pantomime with a shaved head, masked face, variegated tights, and wooden sword **b :** BUFFOON
2 a : a variegated pattern (as of a textile) **b :** a combination of patches on a solid ground of contrasting color (as in the coats of some dogs)

har·le·quin·ade \ˌhär-li-k(w)ə-'nād\ *noun* (1790)
: a play or pantomime in which Harlequin has a leading role

Harlequin

har·lot \'här-lət\ *noun* [Middle English, from Old French *herlot* rogue] (15th century)
: PROSTITUTE

har·lot·ry \-lə-trē\ *noun, plural* **-ries** (14th century)
1 : sexual profligacy **:** PROSTITUTION
2 : an unprincipled or immoral woman ⟨he sups tonight with a *harlotry* —Shakespeare⟩

¹harm \'härm\ *noun* [Middle English, from Old English *hearm;* akin to Old High German *harm* injury, Old Church Slavonic *sramŭ* shame] (before 12th century)
1 : physical or mental damage **:** INJURY
2 : MISCHIEF, HURT

²harm *transitive verb* (before 12th century)
: to cause harm to
synonym see INJURE
— **harm·er** *noun*

har·mat·tan \ˌhär-mə-'tan, här-'ma-t°n\ *noun, often capitalized* [Twi *haramata*] (1671)

: a dust-laden wind on the Atlantic coast of Africa in some seasons

harm·ful \'härm-fəl\ *adjective* (14th century)
: of a kind likely to be damaging **:** INJURIOUS
— **harm·ful·ly** \-fə-lē\ *adverb*
— **harm·ful·ness** *noun*

harm·less \'härm-ləs\ *adjective* (14th century)
1 : free from harm, liability, or loss
2 : lacking capacity or intent to injure **:** INNOCUOUS
— **harm·less·ly** *adverb*
— **harm·less·ness** *noun*

¹har·mon·ic \här-'mä-nik\ *adjective* (1570)
1 : MUSICAL
2 : of or relating to musical harmony or a harmonic
3 : pleasing to the ear **:** HARMONIOUS
4 : of an integrated nature **:** CONGRUOUS
— **har·mon·i·cal·ly** \-ni-k(ə-)lē\ *adverb*

²harmonic *noun* (1777)
1 a : OVERTONE; *especially* **:** one whose vibration frequency is an integral multiple of that of the fundamental **b :** a flutelike tone produced on a stringed instrument by touching a vibrating string at a nodal point
2 : a component frequency of a complex wave (as of electromagnetic energy) that is an integral multiple of the fundamental frequency

har·mon·i·ca \här-'mä-ni-kə\ *noun* [Italian *armonica*, feminine of *armonico* harmonious] (1762)
1 : GLASS HARMONICA
2 : a small rectangular wind instrument with free reeds recessed in air slots from which tones are sounded by exhaling and inhaling
— **har·mon·i·cist** \-nə-sist\ *noun*

harmonic analysis *noun* (1867)
: the expression of a periodic function as a sum of sines and cosines and specifically by a Fourier series

harmonic mean *noun* (1856)
: the reciprocal of the arithmetic mean of the reciprocals of a finite set of numbers

harmonic motion *noun* (1867)
: a periodic motion (as of a sounding violin string or swinging pendulum) that has a single frequency or amplitude or a periodic motion that is composed of two or more such simple periodic motions

harmonic progression *noun* (1856)
: a sequence of numbers whose reciprocals form an arithmetic progression

harmonic series *noun* (1866)
: a series of the form

$$1 + \frac{1}{2^\alpha} + \frac{1}{3^\alpha} + \frac{1}{4^\alpha} \cdots$$

which diverges for $0 \leq \alpha \leq 1$ and converges for $\alpha > 1$

har·mo·ni·ous \här-'mō-nē-əs\ *adjective* (1530)
1 : musically concordant
2 : having the parts agreeably related **:** CONGRUOUS ⟨blended into a *harmonious* whole⟩
3 : marked by accord in sentiment or action
— **har·mo·ni·ous·ly** *adverb*
— **har·mo·ni·ous·ness** *noun*

har·mo·nise *British variant of* HARMONIZE

har·mo·ni·um \här-'mō-nē-əm\ *noun* [French, from Middle French *harmonie, armonie*] (1847)
: REED ORGAN

har·mo·nize \'här-mə-ˌnīz\ *verb* **-nized; -niz·ing** (15th century)
intransitive verb
1 : to play or sing in harmony
2 : to be in harmony
transitive verb
1 : to bring into consonance or accord
2 : to provide or accompany with harmony
— **har·mo·ni·za·tion** \ˌhär-mə-nə-'zā-shən\ *noun*
— **har·mo·niz·er** \'här-mə-ˌnī-zər\ *noun*

har·mo·ny \'här-mə-nē\ *noun, plural* **-nies** [Middle English *armony*, from Middle French *armonie*, from Latin *harmonia*, from Greek, joint, harmony, from *harmos* joint — more at ARM] (14th century)
1 *archaic* **:** tuneful sound **:** MELODY
2 a : the combination of simultaneous musical notes in a chord **b :** the structure of music with respect to the composition and progression of chords **c :** the science of the structure, relation, and progression of chords
3 a : pleasing or congruent arrangement of parts ⟨a painting exhibiting *harmony* of color and line⟩ **b :** CORRESPONDENCE, ACCORD ⟨lives in *harmony* with her neighbors⟩ **c :** internal calm **:** TRANQUILLITY
4 a : an interweaving of different accounts into a single narrative **b :** a systematic arrangement of parallel literary passages (as of the Gospels) for the purpose of showing agreement or harmony

harm's way *noun* (circa 1661)
: a dangerous place or situation ⟨was placed in *harm's way*⟩ ⟨got them out of *harm's way*⟩

¹har·ness \'här-nəs\ *noun* [Middle English *herneis* baggage, gear, from Old French] (14th century)
1 a : the gear other than a yoke of a draft animal **b :** GEAR, EQUIPMENT; *especially* **:** military equipment for a horse or man
2 a : occupational surroundings or routine ⟨get back into *harness* after a vacation⟩ **b :** close association ⟨ability to work in *harness* with others —R. P. Brooks⟩
3 a : something that resembles a harness (as in holding or fastening something) ⟨a parachute *harness*⟩ **b :** prefabricated wiring with insulation and terminals ready to be attached
4 : a part of a loom which holds and controls the heddles

²harness *transitive verb* (14th century)
1 a : to put a harness on **b :** to attach by means of a harness
2 : to tie together **:** YOKE
3 : UTILIZE ⟨*harness* the computer's potential⟩

harness horse *noun* (1861)
: a horse for racing or working in harness

harness racing *noun* (1901)
: the sport of racing standardbred horses harnessed to 2-wheeled sulkies

¹harp \'härp\ *noun* [Middle English, from Old English *hearpe;* akin to Old High German *harpha* harp] (before 12th century)
1 : a plucked stringed instrument consisting of a resonator, an arched or angled neck that may be supported by a post, and strings of graded length that are perpendicular to the soundboard
2 : something that resembles a harp
3 : HARMONICA 2
— **harp·ist** \'här-pist\ *noun*

²harp *intransitive verb* (before 12th century)
1 : to play on a harp
2 : to dwell on or recur to a subject tiresomely or monotonously — usually used with *on*

harp·er \'här-pər\ *noun* (before 12th century)
1 : a harp player
2 : one that harps

har·poon \här-'pün\ *noun* [probably from Dutch *harpoen*, from Old French *harpon* brooch, from *harper* to grapple] (1625)
: a barbed spear or javelin used especially in hunting large fish or whales
— **harpoon** *transitive verb*
— **har·poon·er** *noun*

harp 1

\ə\ abut \ᵊ\ kitten \ər\ further \a\ ash \ā\ ace \ä\ mop, mar \au̇\ out \ch\ chin \e\ bet \ē\ easy \g\ go \i\ hit \ī\ ice \j\ job \ŋ\ sing \ō\ go \ȯ\ law \ȯi\ boy \th\ thin \tẖ\ the \ü\ loot \u̇\ foot \y\ yet \zh\ vision *see also* Guide to Pronunciation

harp seal *noun* [from the shape of its markings] (1766)
: a dark-faced seal (*Phoca groenlandicus*) of the North Atlantic that is a variable light gray with the male usually having a dark crescent on its back and sides

harp·si·chord \'härp-si-ˌkȯrd\ *noun* [modification of Italian *arpicordo*, from *arpa* harp + *corda* string] (1611)
: a stringed instrument resembling a grand piano but usually having two keyboards and two or more strings for each note and producing tones by the plucking of strings with plectra
— **harp·si·chord·ist** \-ˌkȯr-dist\ *noun*

har·py \'här-pē\ *noun, plural* **harpies** [Latin *Harpyia*, from Greek] (1513)
1 *capitalized* : a foul malign creature in Greek mythology that is part woman and part bird
2 a : a predatory person : LEECH **b** : a shrewish woman

harpy eagle *noun* (1830)
: a large powerful crested eagle (*Harpia harpyja*) of Central and South America

har·que·bus \'här-kwi-(ˌ)bəs, -kə-bəs\ *noun* [Middle French *harquebuse, arquebuse*, modification of Middle Dutch *hakebusse*, from *hake* hook + *busse* tube, box, gun, from Late Latin *buxis* box] (1532)
: a matchlock gun invented in the 15th century which was portable but heavy and was usually fired from a support
— **har·que·bus·ier** \ˌhär-kwi-(ˌ)bə-'sir, -kə-bə-\ *noun*

har·ri·dan \'har-ə-dⁿn\ *noun* [perhaps modification of French *haridelle* old horse, gaunt woman] (circa 1700)
: SHREW 2

har·ried \'har-ēd\ *adjective* (circa 1915)
: beset by problems : HARASSED

¹har·ri·er \'har-ē-ər\ *noun* [irregular from ¹*hare*] (1542)
1 : any of a breed of hunting dogs resembling a small foxhound and originally bred for hunting rabbits
2 : a runner on a cross-country team

²harrier *noun* [alteration of *harrower*, from ¹*harrow*] (1556)
: any of a genus (*Circus*) of slender hawks having long angled wings and long legs and feeding chiefly on small mammals, reptiles, and insects

³harrier *noun* (1596)
: one that harries

¹har·row \'har-(ˌ)ō\ *transitive verb* [Middle English *harwen*, from Old English *hergian*] (before 12th century)
archaic : PILLAGE, PLUNDER

²harrow *noun* [Middle English *harwe*, probably of Scandinavian origin; akin to Old Norse *hervi* harrow] (14th century)
: a cultivating implement set with spikes, spring teeth, or disks and used primarily for pulverizing and smoothing the soil

³harrow *transitive verb* (14th century)
1 : to cultivate with a harrow
2 : TORMENT, VEX
— **har·row·er** \'har-ə-wər\ *noun*

har·rumph \hə-'rəm(p)f\ *intransitive verb* [imitative] (1942)
1 : to clear the throat in a pompous way
2 : to comment disapprovingly

har·ry \'har-ē\ *transitive verb* **har·ried; har·ry·ing** [Middle English *harien*, from Old English *hergian;* akin to Old High German *heriōn* to lay waste, *heri* army, Greek *koiranos* ruler] (before 12th century)
1 : to make a pillaging or destructive raid on : ASSAULT
2 : to force to move along by harassing ⟨*harrying* the terrified horses down out of the mountains —R. A. Sokolov⟩
3 : to torment by or as if by constant attack
synonym see WORRY

harsh \'härsh\ *adjective* [Middle English *harsk*, of Scandinavian origin; akin to Norwegian *harsk* harsh] (14th century)

1 : having a coarse uneven surface that is rough or unpleasant to the touch
2 a : causing a disagreeable or painful sensory reaction : IRRITATING **b** : physically discomforting : PAINFUL
3 : unduly exacting : SEVERE
4 : lacking in aesthetic appeal or refinement : CRUDE
synonym see ROUGH
— **harsh·ly** *adverb*
— **harsh·ness** *noun*

harsh·en \'här-shən\ *verb* **harsh·ened; harsh·en·ing** \-sh(ə-)niŋ\ (1824)
transitive verb
: to make (as a voice) harsh
intransitive verb
: to become harsh ⟨saw the grain of his skin *harshening* over face bones —Elizabeth Bowen⟩

hart \'härt\ *noun* [Middle English *hert*, from Old English *heort;* akin to Latin *cervus* hart, Greek *keras* horn — more at HORN] (before 12th century)
chiefly British : the male of the red deer especially when over five years old : STAG — compare HIND

harte·beest \'här-tə-ˌbēst\ *noun* [obsolete Afrikaans (now *hartbees*), from Dutch, from *hart* deer + *beest* beast] (1786)
: either of two large African antelopes (*Alcelaphus buselaphus* and *Sigmoceros lichtensteini*) with long faces and short annulate divergent horns; *also* : a smaller antelope (*Damaliscus hunteri* synonym *Beatragus hunteri*) of eastern Africa having a horizontal white line between the eyes

harts·horn \'härts-ˌhȯrn\ *noun* [from the earlier use of hart's horns as the chief source of ammonia] (1685)
: a preparation of ammonia used as smelling salts

har·um–scar·um \ˌhar-əm-'skar-əm, ˌher-əm-'sker-\ *adjective* [perhaps from archaic *hare* (to harass) + *scare*] (1751)
: RECKLESS, IRRESPONSIBLE
— **harum–scarum** *adverb*

ha·rus·pex \hə-'rəs-ˌpeks, 'har-əs-\ *noun, plural* **ha·rus·pi·ces** \hə-'rəs-pə-ˌsēz\ [Latin, from *haru-* (akin to *chordē* gut, cord) + *-spex*, from *specere* to look — more at YARN, SPY] (1584)
: a diviner in ancient Rome basing his predictions on inspection of the entrails of sacrificial animals

ha·rus·pi·ca·tion \hə-ˌrəs-pə-'kā-shən\ *noun* (1871)
chiefly British : an act or instance of foretelling something

¹har·vest \'här-vəst\ *noun, often attributive* [Middle English *hervest*, from Old English *hærfest;* akin to Latin *carpere* to pluck, gather, Greek *karpos* fruit] (before 12th century)
1 : the season for gathering in agricultural crops
2 : the act or process of gathering in a crop
3 a : a mature crop (as of grain or fruit) : YIELD **b** : the quantity of a natural product gathered in a single season ⟨deer *harvest*⟩ ⟨ice *harvest*⟩
4 : an accumulated store or productive result ⟨a fantastic revenue *harvest* from lower tax rates —Peter Passell⟩

²harvest (15th century)
transitive verb
1 a : to gather in (a crop) : REAP **b** : to gather, catch, hunt, or kill (as salmon, oysters, or deer) for human use, sport, or population control **c** : to remove or extract (as living cells, tissues, or organs) from culture or a living or recently deceased body especially for transplanting
2 a : to accumulate a store of ⟨has now *harvested* this new generation's scholarly labors —M. J. Wiener⟩ **b** : to win by achievement ⟨the team *harvested* several awards⟩

intransitive verb
: to gather in a crop especially for food
— **har·vest·able** \-və-stə-bəl\ *adjective*
— **har·vest·er** *noun*

harvest fly *noun* (circa 1753)
: CICADA

harvest home *noun* (1596)
1 : the gathering or the time of harvest
2 : a feast at the close of harvest
3 : a song sung by the reapers at the close of the harvest

har·vest·man \'här-vəs(t)-mən\ *noun* (1830)
: an arachnid (order Phalangida) that superficially resembles a true spider but has a small rounded body and very long slender legs — called also *daddy longlegs*

harvest mite *noun* (1873)
: CHIGGER 2

harvest moon *noun* (1706)
: the full moon nearest the time of the September equinox

har·vest·time \'här-vəs(t)-ˌtīm\ *noun* (14th century)
: the time during which an annual crop (as wheat) is harvested

has *present 3d singular of* HAVE

has–been \'haz-ˌbin, *chiefly British* -ˌbēn\ *noun* (1606)
: one that has passed the peak of effectiveness or popularity

ha·sen·pfef·fer \'hä-zⁿn-ˌ(p)fe-fər, 'hä-sⁿn-\ *noun* [German, from *Hase* hare + *Pfeffer* pepper] (1892)
: a highly seasoned stew made of marinated rabbit meat

¹hash \'hash\ *transitive verb* [French *hacher*, from Old French *hachier*, from *hache* battle-ax, of Germanic origin; akin to Old High German *hāppa* sickle; akin to Greek *koptein* to cut — more at CAPON] (1590)
1 a : to chop (as meat and potatoes) into small pieces **b** : CONFUSE, MUDDLE
2 : to talk about : REVIEW — often used with *over* or *out*

²hash *noun* (circa 1663)
1 : chopped food; *specifically* : chopped meat mixed with potatoes and browned
2 : a restatement of something that is already known
3 a : HODGEPODGE, JUMBLE **b** : a confused muddle ⟨made a *hash* of the whole project⟩

³hash *noun* (1959)
: HASHISH

hash browns *noun plural* (1951)
: boiled potatoes that have been diced, mixed with chopped onions and shortening, and fried usually until they form a browned cake — called also *hash brown potatoes, hashed brown potatoes, hashed browns*

Hash·em·ite *or* **Hash·im·ite** \'ha-shə-ˌmīt\ *noun* [*Hashim*, great-grandfather of Muhammad] (1697)
: a member of an Arab family having common ancestry with Muhammad and founding dynasties in countries of the eastern Mediterranean

hash house *noun* (1869)
: an inexpensive eating place

hash·ish \'ha-ˌshēsh, ha-'shēsh\ *noun* [Arabic *ḥashīsh*] (1598)
: the concentrated resin from the flowering tops of the female hemp plant (*Cannabis sativa*) that is smoked, chewed, or drunk for its intoxicating effect — called also *charas;* compare BHANG, MARIJUANA

hash mark *noun* (1907)
1 : SERVICE STRIPE
2 : INBOUNDS LINE

Ha·sid \'ha-səd, 'kä-\ *noun, plural* **Ha·si·dim** \'ha-sə-dəm, kä-'sē-\ [Hebrew *ḥāsīdh* pious] (1812)
1 : a member of a Jewish sect of the second century B.C. opposed to Hellenism and devoted to the strict observance of the ritual law

2 *also* **Has·sid :** a member of a Jewish mystical sect founded in Poland about 1750 in opposition to rationalism and ritual laxity
— **Ha·sid·ic** *also* **Has·sid·ic** \ha-'si-dik, hä-, kä-\ *adjective*

Ha·si·dism \'ha-sə-,di-zəm, 'hä-, 'kä-\ *noun* (1893)
1 : the practices and beliefs of the Hasidim
2 : the Hasidic movement

Has·mo·nae·an *or* **Has·mo·ne·an** \,haz-mə-'nē-ən\ *noun* [Late Latin *Asmonaeus* Hasmon, ancestor of the Maccabees, from Greek *Asamōnaios*] (1620)
: a member of the Maccabees
— **Hasmonaean** *or* **Hasmonean** *adjective*

hasn't \'ha-z³nt, -z³n\ (1746)
: has not

hasp \'hasp\ *noun* [Middle English, alteration from Old English *hæpse*; akin to Middle High German *haspe* hasp] (before 12th century)
: any of several devices for fastening; *especially* **:** a fastener especially for a door or lid consisting of a hinged metal strap that fits over a staple and is secured by a pin or padlock

hasp

— **hasp** *transitive verb*

¹has·sle \'ha-səl\ *noun* (1945)
1 : a heated often protracted argument **:** WRANGLE
2 : a violent skirmish **:** FIGHT
3 a : a state of confusion **:** TURMOIL **b :** an annoying or troublesome concern

²hassle *verb* **has·sled; has·sling** \-s(ə-)liŋ\ [perhaps blend of *harass* and *hustle*] (1951)
intransitive verb
: ARGUE, FIGHT ⟨*hassled* with the umpire⟩
transitive verb
: to annoy persistently or acutely **:** HARASS ⟨he gets *hassled* in the street because he dresses funny —William Kloman⟩

has·sock \'ha-sək\ *noun* [Middle English, sedge, from Old English *hassuc*] (before 12th century)
1 : TUSSOCK
2 a : a cushion for kneeling ⟨a church *hassock*⟩ **b :** a padded cushion or low stool that serves as a seat or leg rest

hast \'hast, (h)əst\ *archaic present 2d singular of* HAVE

has·tate \'has-,tāt\ *adjective* [New Latin *hastatus*, from Latin *hasta* spear — more at YARD] (1788)
1 : triangular with sharp basal lobes spreading away from the base of the petiole ⟨*hastate* leaves⟩ — see LEAF illustration
2 : shaped like a spear or the head of a spear ⟨a *hastate* spot of a bird⟩

¹haste \'hāst\ *noun* [Middle English, from Middle French, of Germanic origin; akin to Old English *hǣst* violence] (14th century)
1 : rapidity of motion **:** SWIFTNESS
2 : rash or headlong action **:** PRECIPITATENESS ⟨the beauty of speed uncontaminated by *haste* —*Harper's*⟩
3 : undue eagerness to act ☆

²haste *verb* **hast·ed; hast·ing** (14th century)
transitive verb
archaic **:** to urge on **:** HASTEN
intransitive verb
: to move or act swiftly

has·ten \'hā-s³n\ *verb* **has·tened; has·ten·ing** \'hās-niŋ, 'hā-s³n-iŋ\ (1568)
intransitive verb
: to move or act quickly
transitive verb
1 : to urge on ⟨*hastened* her to the door —A. J. Cronin⟩
2 : ACCELERATE ⟨*hasten* the coming of a new order —D. W. Brogan⟩

— **has·ten·er** \'hās-nər, 'hā-s³n-ər\ *noun*

hast·i·ly \'hā-stə-lē\ *adverb* (14th century)
: in haste **:** HURRIEDLY

hasty \'hā-stē\ *adjective* **hast·i·er; -est** (14th century)
1 a *archaic* **:** rapid in action or movement **:** SPEEDY **b :** done or made in a hurry **c :** fast and typically superficial ⟨made a *hasty* examination of the wound⟩
2 : EAGER, IMPATIENT
3 : PRECIPITATE, RASH
4 : prone to anger **:** IRRITABLE
synonym see FAST
— **hast·i·ness** *noun*

hasty pudding *noun* (1599)
1 *British* **:** a porridge of oatmeal or flour boiled in water
2 *New England* **a :** cornmeal mush **b :** INDIAN PUDDING

¹hat \'hat\ *noun* [Middle English, from Old English *hæt*; akin to Old High German *huot* head covering — more at HOOD] (before 12th century)
1 : a covering for the head usually having a shaped crown and brim
2 a : a distinctive head covering worn as a symbol of office **b :** an office, position, or role assumed by or as if by the wearing of a special hat
— **hat·less** \-ləs\ *adjective*

²hat *verb* **hat·ted; hat·ting** (15th century)
transitive verb
: to furnish or provide with a hat
intransitive verb
: to make or supply hats

hat·band \'hat-,band\ *noun* (15th century)
: a band (as of fabric, leather, or cord) around the crown of a hat just above the brim

hat·box \-,bäks\ *noun* (1794)
1 : a box for holding or storing a hat
2 : a usually round piece of luggage designed especially for carrying hats

¹hatch \'hach\ *noun* [Middle English *hache*, from Old English *hæc*; akin to Middle Dutch *hecke* trapdoor] (before 12th century)
1 : a small door or opening (as in an airplane or spaceship) ⟨an escape *hatch*⟩
2 a : an opening in the deck of a ship or in the floor or roof of a building **b :** the covering for such an opening **c :** HATCHWAY **d :** COMPARTMENT
3 : FLOODGATE

²hatch *verb* [Middle English *hacchen*; akin to Middle High German *hecken* to mate] (13th century)
intransitive verb
1 : to produce young by incubation
2 a : to emerge from an egg, chrysalis, or pupa **b :** to give forth young or imagoes
3 : to incubate eggs **:** BROOD
transitive verb
1 a : to produce (young) from an egg by applying natural or artificial heat **b :** INCUBATE 1
2 : to bring into being **:** ORIGINATE; *especially* **:** to concoct in secret
— **hatch·abil·i·ty** \,ha-chə-'bi-lə-tē\ *noun*
— **hatch·able** \'ha-chə-bəl\ *adjective*
— **hatch·er** *noun*

³hatch *noun* (1601)
1 : an act or instance of hatching
2 : a brood of hatched young

⁴hatch *transitive verb* [Middle English *hachen*, from Middle French *hacher* to inlay, chop up, from Old French *hachier* — more at HASH] (15th century)
1 : to inlay with narrow bands of distinguishable material ⟨a silver handle *hatched* with gold⟩
2 : to mark (as a drawing or engraving) with fine closely spaced lines

⁵hatch *noun* (1658)
: LINE; *especially* **:** one used to give the effect of shading

hatch·back \'hach-,bak\ *noun* (1970)

: an automobile the back of which consists of a hatch that opens upward; *also* **:** the back itself

hat·check \'hat-,chek\ *adjective* (1917)
: employed in checking hats and articles of outdoor clothing ⟨a *hatcheck* girl⟩

hatch·ery \'ha-chə-rē\ *noun, plural* **-er·ies** (1880)
: a place for hatching eggs (as of poultry or fish)

hatch·et \'ha-chət\ *noun* [Middle English *hachet*, from Middle French *hachette*, diminutive of *hache* battle-ax — more at HASH] (14th century)
1 : a short-handled ax often with a hammerhead to be used with one hand
2 : TOMAHAWK

hatchet face *noun* (circa 1666)
: a thin sharp face
— **hatch·et-faced** \'ha-chət-,fāst\ *adjective*

hatchet job *noun* (1944)
: a forceful or malicious verbal attack

hatchet man *noun* (1880)
1 : one hired for murder, coercion, or attack
2 a : a writer specializing in invective **b :** a person hired to perform underhanded or unscrupulous tasks (as ruin reputations)

hatchet work *noun* (1944)
: the work of a hatchet man

hatch·ing *noun* (1662)
: the engraving or drawing of fine lines in close proximity especially to give an effect of shading; *also* **:** the pattern so made

hatch·ling \'hach-liŋ\ *noun* (1899)
: a recently hatched animal

hatch·ment \'hach-mənt\ *noun* [perhaps alteration of *achievement*] (1548)
: a panel on which a coat of arms of a deceased person is temporarily displayed

hatch·way \'hach-,wā\ *noun* (1626)
: a passage giving access usually by a ladder or stairs to an enclosed space (as a cellar); *also* **:** HATCH 2a

¹hate \'hāt\ *noun, often attributive* [Middle English, from Old English *hete*; akin to Old High German *haz* hate, Greek *kēdos* care] (before 12th century)
1 a : intense hostility and aversion usually deriving from fear, anger, or sense of injury **b :** extreme dislike or antipathy **:** LOATHING ⟨had a great *hate* of hard work⟩
2 : an object of hatred ⟨a generation whose finest *hate* had been big business —F. L. Paxson⟩

²hate *verb* **hat·ed; hat·ing** (before 12th century)
transitive verb
1 : to feel extreme enmity toward ⟨*hates* his country's enemies⟩

\ə\ **abut** \³\ **kitten** \ər\ **further** \a\ **ash** \ā\ **ace**
\ä\ **mop, mar** \au̇\ **out** \ch\ **chin** \e\ **bet** \ē\ **easy**
\g\ **go** \i\ **hit** \ī\ **ice** \j\ **job** \ŋ\ **sing** \ō\ **go**
\ȯ\ **law** \ȯi\ **boy** \th\ **thin** \th\ **the** \ü\ **loot** \u̇\ **foot**
\y\ **yet** \zh\ **vision** *see also* Guide to Pronunciation

2 : to have a strong aversion to **:** find very distasteful ⟨*hated* to have to meet strangers⟩ ⟨*hate* hypocrisy⟩
intransitive verb
: to express or feel extreme enmity or active hostility ☆
— **hat·er** *noun*
— **hate one's guts :** to hate someone with great intensity

hate crime *noun* (1989)
: any of various crimes (as assault or defacement of property) when motivated by hostility to the victim as a member of a group (as one based on color, creed, gender, or sexual orientation)

hate·ful \'hāt-fəl\ *adjective* (14th century)
1 : full of hate **:** MALICIOUS
2 : deserving of or arousing hate
— **hate·ful·ly** \-fə-lē\ *adverb*
— **hate·ful·ness** *noun*

hath \'hath, (h)əth\ *archaic present 3d singular of* HAVE

hatha yo·ga \'hə-tə-'yō-gə, 'hä-\ *noun* [Sanskrit *haṭha* force + *yoga* yoga] (1890)
: a system of physical exercises for the control and perfection of the body that constitutes one of the four chief Hindu disciplines

hat in hand *adverb* (1851)
: in an attitude of respectful humility ⟨have to go *hat in hand* to apologize⟩

hat·mak·er \'hat-ˌmā-kər\ *noun* (15th century)
: one who makes hats

ha·tred \'hā-trəd\ *noun* [Middle English, from *hate* + Old English *rǣden* condition — more at KINDRED] (12th century)
1 : HATE
2 : prejudiced hostility or animosity ⟨old racial prejudices and national *hatreds* —Peter Thomson⟩

hat·ter \'ha-tər\ *noun* (14th century)
: one that makes, sells, or cleans and repairs hats

hat trick *noun* [probably from the former practice of rewarding the feat with the gift of a hat] (1877)
1 : the retiring of three batsmen with three consecutive balls by a bowler in cricket
2 : the scoring of three goals in one game (as of hockey or soccer) by a single player
3 : a succession of three victories, successes, or related accomplishments ⟨scored a *hat trick* when her three best steers corralled top honors —*People*⟩

hau·berk \'hȯ-(ˌ)bərk\ *noun* [Middle English, from Old French *hauberc,* of Germanic origin; akin to Old English *healsbeorg* neck armor] (14th century)
: a tunic of chain mail worn as defensive armor from the 12th to the 14th century

haugh \'hȯ(k)\ *noun* [Middle English (Scots) *halch,* from Old English *healh* corner of land; akin to Old English *holh* hole] (before 12th century)
Scottish **:** a low-lying meadow by the side of a river

haugh·ty \'hȯ-tē, 'hä-\ *adjective*
haugh·ti·er; -est [obsolete *haught,* from Middle English *haute,* from Middle French *haut,* literally, high, from Latin *altus* — more at OLD] (15th century)
: blatantly and disdainfully proud
synonym see PROUD
— **haugh·ti·ly** \'hȯ-tᵊl-ē, 'hä-\ *adverb*
— **haugh·ti·ness** \'hȯ-tē-nəs, 'hä-\ *noun*

¹haul \'hȯl\ *verb* [Middle English *halen* to pull, from Old French *haler* of Germanic origin; akin to Middle Dutch *halen* to pull; akin to Old English *geholian* to obtain] (13th century)
transitive verb
1 a : to exert traction on **:** DRAW ⟨*haul* a wagon⟩ **b :** to obtain or move by or as if by hauling ⟨was *hauled* to parties night after night by his wife⟩ **c :** to transport in a vehicle **:** CART

1 hauberk

2 : to change the course of (a ship) especially so as to sail closer to the wind
3 : to bring before an authority for interrogation or judgment **:** HALE ⟨*haul* traffic violators into court⟩
intransitive verb
1 : to exert traction **:** PULL
2 : to move along **:** PROCEED
3 : to furnish transportation
4 *of the wind* **:** SHIFT
— **haul ass :** to move quickly — often considered vulgar

²haul *noun* (1670)
1 a : the act or process of hauling **:** PULL **b :** a device for hauling
2 a : the result of an effort to obtain, collect, or win ⟨the burglar's *haul*⟩ **b :** the fish taken in a single draft of a net
3 a : transportation by hauling **b :** the length or course of a transportation route ⟨a long *haul*⟩ **c :** a quantity transported **:** LOAD

haul·age \'hȯ-lij\ *noun* (1826)
1 : the act or process of hauling
2 : a charge made for hauling

haul·er \'hȯ-lər\ *noun* (1674)
: one that hauls: as **a :** a commercial establishment or worker whose business is hauling **b :** an automotive vehicle for hauling goods or material

haul·ier \'hȯl-yər\ *British variant of* HAULER

haulm \'hȯm\ *noun* [Middle English *halm,* from Old English *healm;* akin to Old High German *halm* stem, Latin *culmus* stalk, Greek *kalamos* reed] (before 12th century)
: the stems or tops of crop plants (as peas or potatoes) especially after the crop has been gathered

haul off *intransitive verb* (1870)
: to get ready — used with *and* and a following verb describing a usually sudden and violent act ⟨I *hauled off* and hit him⟩

haunch \'hȯnch, 'hänch\ *noun* [Middle English *haunche,* from Old French *hanche,* of Germanic origin; akin to Middle Dutch *hanke* haunch] (13th century)
1 a : HIP **1a b :** HINDQUARTER 2 — usually used in plural
2 : HINDQUARTER 1
3 : either side of an arch between the springing and the crown
— **on one's haunches :** in a squatting position

¹haunt \'hȯnt, 'hänt\ *verb* [Middle English, from Old French *hanter,* probably from Old Norse *heimta* to lead home, pull, claim, from *heimr* home] (14th century)
transitive verb
1 a : to visit often **:** FREQUENT **b :** to continually seek the company of
2 a : to have a disquieting or harmful effect on **:** TROUBLE ⟨problems we ignore now will come back to *haunt* us⟩ **b :** to recur constantly and spontaneously to ⟨the tune *haunted* her⟩ **c :** to reappear continually in ⟨a sense of tension that *haunts* his writing⟩
3 : to visit or inhabit as a ghost
intransitive verb
1 : to stay around or persist **:** LINGER
2 : to appear habitually as a ghost
— **haunt·er** *noun*
— **haunt·ing·ly** \'hȯn-tiŋ-lē, 'hän-\ *adverb*

²haunt \'hȯnt, 'hänt, 2 is usually 'hant\ *noun* (14th century)
1 : a place habitually frequented
2 *chiefly dialect* **:** GHOST

Hau·sa \'haú-sə, -zə\ *noun, plural* **Hausa** *or* **Hausas** (1853)
1 : the Chadic language of the Hausa people widely used in western Africa as a trade language
2 : a member of a black people of northern Nigeria and southern Niger

haus·frau \'haús-ˌfraú\ *noun* [German, from *Haus* house + *Frau* woman, wife] (1798)
: HOUSEWIFE

haus·tel·lum \hȯ-'ste-ləm\ *noun, plural* **-la** \-lə\ [New Latin, diminutive of Latin *haustrum* scoop on a waterwheel, from *haurire* to drink, draw — more at EXHAUST] (1816)
: a proboscis (as of an insect) adapted to suck blood or juices of plants

haus·to·ri·al \hȯ-'stȯr-ē-əl, -'stȯr-\ *adjective* (1894)
: of, relating to, or having a haustorium

haus·to·ri·um \-ē-əm\ *noun, plural* **-ria** \-ē-ə\ [New Latin, from Latin *haurire*] (1875)
: a food-absorbing outgrowth of a plant organ (as a hypha or stem)

haut·bois *or* **haut·boy** \'(h)ō-ˌbȯi\ *noun, plural* **hautbois** \-ˌbȯiz\ *or* **haut·boys** [Middle French *hautbois,* from *haut* high + *bois* wood] (1575)
: OBOE

haute \'ōt, *also* haut \'ōt, 'ō\ *adjective* [French] (1787)
: FASHIONABLE, HIGH-CLASS ⟨*haute* interior decorators⟩ ⟨a store filled with *haute* kitsch⟩

haute cou·ture \ˌōt-kù-'tùr\ *noun* [French, literally, high sewing] (1908)
: the houses or designers that create exclusive and often trend-setting fashions for women; *also* **:** the fashions created

haute cui·sine \-kwi-'zēn\ *noun* [French, literally, high cooking] (1928)
: artful or elaborate cuisine; *especially* **:** traditionally elaborate French cuisine

haute école \-ā-'kȯl, -'kəl\ *noun* [French, literally, high school] (1858)
: a highly stylized form of classical riding
: advanced dressage

hau·teur \hȯ-'tər, (h)ō-\ *noun* [French, from *haut* high — more at HAUGHTY] (circa 1628)
: ARROGANCE, HAUGHTINESS

haut monde \ō-'mänd, ō-mō\ⁿd\ *also* **haute monde** \ōt-\ *noun* [French, literally, high world] (1864)
: high society

Ha·va·na \hə-'va-nə\ *noun* [probably from Spanish *habano,* from *habano* of Havana, from La *Habana* (Havana), Cuba] (1826)
1 : a cigar made from Cuban tobacco
2 : a tobacco originally grown in Cuba

Ha·var·ti \hə-'vär-tē\ *noun* [*Havarti,* locale in Denmark] (1957)
: a semisoft Danish cheese having a porous texture and usually a mild flavor

hav·da·lah *variant of* HABDALAH

¹have \'hav, (h)əv, v; *in* "have to" *meaning* "must" *usually* 'haf\ *verb* **had** \'had, (h)əd, d\; **hav·ing** \'ha-viŋ\; **has** \'haz, (h)əz, z, s; *in* "has to" *meaning* "must" *usually* 'has\ [Middle English, from Old English *habban;* akin to Old High German *habēn* to have, and perhaps to *hevan* to lift — more at HEAVE] (before 12th century)
transitive verb
1 a : to hold or maintain as a possession, privilege, or entitlement ⟨they *have* a new car⟩ ⟨I *have* my rights⟩ **b :** to hold in one's use, service, regard, or at one's disposal ⟨the group will *have* enough tickets for everyone⟩ ⟨we don't *have* time to stay⟩ **c :** to hold, include, or contain as a part or whole ⟨the car *has* power brakes⟩ ⟨April *has* 30 days⟩

☆ **SYNONYMS**
Hate, detest, abhor, abominate, loathe mean to feel strong aversion or intense dislike for. HATE implies an emotional aversion often coupled with enmity or malice ⟨*hated* the enemy with a passion⟩. DETEST suggests violent antipathy ⟨*detests* cowards⟩. ABHOR implies a deep often shuddering repugnance ⟨a crime *abhorred* by all⟩. ABOMINATE suggests strong detestation and often moral condemnation ⟨every society *abominates* incest⟩. LOATHE implies utter disgust and intolerance ⟨*loathed* self-appointed moral guardians⟩.

2 : to feel obligation in regard to — usually used with an infinitive with *to* ⟨we *have* things to do⟩ ⟨*have* a deadline to meet⟩
3 : to stand in a certain relationship to ⟨*has* three fine children⟩ ⟨we will *have* the wind at our backs⟩
4 a : to acquire or get possession of **:** OBTAIN ⟨these shoes are the best to be *had*⟩ **b :** RECEIVE ⟨*had* news⟩ **c :** ACCEPT; *specifically* **:** to accept in marriage **d :** to copulate with
5 a : to be marked or characterized by (a quality, attribute, or faculty) ⟨both *have* red hair⟩ ⟨*has* a way with words⟩ **b :** EXHIBIT, SHOW ⟨*had* the gall to refuse⟩ **c :** USE, EXERCISE ⟨*have* mercy on us⟩
6 a : to experience especially by submitting to, undergoing, or suffering ⟨I *have* a cold⟩ **b :** to make the effort to perform (an action) or engage in (an activity) ⟨*have* a look at that cut⟩ **c :** to entertain in the mind ⟨*have* an opinion⟩
7 a : to cause or command to do something — used with the infinitive without *to* ⟨*have* the children stay⟩ **b :** to cause to be in a certain place or state ⟨*has* people around at all times⟩
8 : ALLOW ⟨we'll *have* no more of that⟩
9 : to be competent in ⟨*has* only a little French⟩
10 a : to hold in a position of disadvantage or certain defeat ⟨we *have* him now⟩ **b :** to take advantage of **:** TRICK, FOOL ⟨been *had* by a partner⟩
11 : BEGET, BEAR ⟨*have* a baby⟩
12 : to partake of ⟨*have* dinner⟩ ⟨*have* a smoke⟩
13 : BRIBE, SUBORN ⟨can be *had* for a price⟩
verbal auxiliary
1 — used with the past participle to form the present perfect, past perfect, or future perfect ⟨*has* gone home⟩ ⟨*had* already eaten⟩ ⟨will *have* finished dinner by then⟩
2 : to be compelled, obliged, or required — used with an infinitive with *to* or *to* alone ⟨we *had* to go⟩ ⟨do what you *have* to⟩ ⟨it *has* to be said⟩
— **had better** *or* **had best :** would be wise to
— **have at :** to go at or deal with **:** ATTACK
— **have coming :** to deserve or merit what one gets, benefits by, or suffers ⟨he *had* that *coming*⟩
— **have done :** FINISH, STOP
— **have done with :** to bring to an end **:** have no further concern with ⟨let us *have done with* name-calling⟩
— **have had it 1 :** to have had or have done all one is going to be allowed to **2 :** to have experienced, endured, or suffered all one can
— **have it :** ASSERT, CLAIM ⟨rumor *has it* that he was drunk⟩
— **have it in for :** to intend to do harm to
— **have it out :** to settle a matter of contention by discussion or a fight
— **have none of :** to refuse to have anything to do with
— **have one's eye on 1 a :** to look at **b :** to watch constantly and attentively **2 :** to have as an objective
— **have to do with 1 :** to deal with ⟨the story *has to do with* real people —Alice M. Jordan⟩ **2 :** to have a specified relationship with or effect on ⟨the size of the brain *has* nothing *to do with* intelligence —Ruth Benedict⟩

²**have** \'hav\ *noun* (1836)
: one that is well-endowed especially in material wealth

have·lock \'hav-ˌläk, -lək\ *noun* [Sir Henry *Havelock*] (1861)
: a covering attached to a cap to protect the neck from the sun or bad weather

ha·ven \'hā-vən\ *noun* [Middle English, from Old English *hæfen*; akin to Middle High German *habene* harbor] (before 12th century)
1 : HARBOR, PORT

2 : a place of safety **:** ASYLUM
3 : a place offering favorable opportunities or conditions ⟨a tourist's *haven*⟩
— **haven** *transitive verb*

have-not \'hav-ˌnät, -'nät\ *noun* (1836)
: one that is poor especially in material wealth

haven't \'ha-vənt, 'ha-bᵊm(t)\ (1777)
: have not

have on *transitive verb* (before 12th century)
1 : WEAR ⟨*has on* a new suit⟩
2 *chiefly British* **:** to trick or deceive intentionally **:** PUT ON 5
3 : to have plans for ⟨what do you *have on* for tomorrow⟩

ha·ver \'hā-vər\ *intransitive verb* [origin unknown] (1866)
chiefly British **:** to hem and haw

hav·er·sack \'ha-vər-ˌsak\ *noun* [French *havresac*, from German *Habersack* bag for oats, from *Haber* oats + *Sack* bag] (1749)
: a bag similar to a knapsack but worn over one shoulder

ha·ver·sian canal \hə-'vər-zhən-\ *noun, often H capitalized* [Clopton *Havers* (died 1702) English physician & anatomist] (1842)
: any of the small canals through which the blood vessels ramify in bone

haversian system *noun, often H capitalized* (circa 1846)
: a haversian canal with the concentrically arranged laminae of bone that surround it

¹**hav·oc** \'ha-vək, -vik\ *noun* [Middle English *havok*, from Anglo-French, modification of Old French *havot* plunder] (15th century)
1 : wide and general destruction **:** DEVASTATION
2 : great confusion and disorder ⟨children can create *havoc* in a house⟩

²**havoc** *transitive verb* **hav·ocked; hav·ock·ing** (1577)
: to lay waste **:** DESTROY

¹**haw** \'hȯ\ *noun* [Middle English *hawe*, from Old English *haga* — more at HEDGE] (before 12th century)
1 : a hawthorn berry
2 : HAWTHORN

²**haw** *noun* [origin unknown] (15th century)
: NICTITATING MEMBRANE; *especially* **:** an inflamed nictitating membrane of a domesticated mammal

³**haw** *intransitive verb* [imitative] (1632)
1 : to utter the sound represented by *haw* ⟨hemmed and *hawed* before answering⟩
2 : EQUIVOCATE ⟨the administration hemmed and *hawed* over the students' demands⟩

⁴**haw** *interjection* (1679)
— often used to indicate a vocalized pause in speaking

⁵**haw** \'hȯ\ *verb* [origin unknown] (1777)
verb imperative
— used as a direction to turn to the left; compare GEE
intransitive verb
: to turn to the near or left side

Hawaii–Aleutian time *noun* (1983)
: the time of the 10th time zone west of Greenwich that includes the Hawaiian islands and the Aleutians west of the Fox group

Ha·wai·ian \hə-'wä-yən, -'wī-(y)ən, -'wȯ-yən\ *noun* (circa 1864)
1 : a native or resident of Hawaii; *especially* **:** one of Polynesian ancestry
2 : the Polynesian language of the Hawaiians
— **Hawaiian** *adjective*

Hawaiian goose *noun* (circa 1909)
: NENE

Hawaiian guitar *noun* (1928)
: a usually electric stringed instrument having a long fretted neck and six to eight steel strings that are plucked while being pressed with a movable steel bar for a glissando effect

Hawaiian shirt *noun* (1962)
: a usually short-sleeved sport shirt with a colorful pattern

haw·finch \'hȯ-ˌfinch\ *noun* [¹*haw*] (circa 1674)
: an Old World finch (*Coccothraustes coccothraustes*) with a large heavy bill and short thick neck and the male marked with black, white, and brown

¹**hawk** \'hȯk\ *noun* [Middle English *hauk*, from Old English *hafoc*; akin to Old High German *habuh* hawk, Russian *kobets* a falcon] (before 12th century)
1 : any of numerous diurnal birds of prey belonging to a suborder (Falcones of the order Falconiformes) and including all the smaller members of this group; *especially* **:** ACCIPITER — compare OWL
2 : a small board or metal sheet with a handle on the underside used to hold mortar
3 : one who takes a militant attitude and advocates immediate vigorous action; *especially* **:** a supporter of a war or warlike policy — compare DOVE
— **hawk·ish** \'hȯ-kish\ *adjective*
— **hawk·ish·ly** *adverb*
— **hawk·ish·ness** *noun*

²**hawk** (14th century)
intransitive verb
1 : to hunt birds by means of a trained hawk
2 : to soar and strike like a hawk
transitive verb
: to hunt on the wing like a hawk

³**hawk** *verb* [imitative] (1581)
transitive verb
: to raise by trying to clear the throat ⟨*hawk* up phlegm⟩
intransitive verb
: to utter a harsh guttural sound in or as if in hawking

⁴**hawk** *noun* (1604)
: an audible effort to force up phlegm from the throat

⁵**hawk** *transitive verb* [back-formation from ²*hawker*] (1713)
: to offer for sale by calling out in the street ⟨*hawking* newspapers⟩; *broadly* **:** SELL

¹**hawk·er** \'hȯ-kər\ *noun* [Middle English, from Old English *hafocere*, from *hafoc*] (before 12th century)
: FALCONER

²**hawker** *noun* [by folk etymology from Low German *höker*, from Middle Low German *höker*, from *höken* to peddle] (1512)
: one that hawks wares

Hawk·eye \'hȯ-ˌkī\ *noun* (1823)
: a native or resident of Iowa — used as a nickname

hawk·eyed \'hȯ-ˌkīd\ *adjective* (circa 1818)
: having keen sight

hawk·moth \'hȯ-ˌmȯth\ *noun* (1785)
: any of a family (Sphingidae) of stout-bodied moths with a long proboscis, long narrow more or less pointed forewings, and small hind wings — called also *sphinx*

hawks·bill \'hȯks-ˌbil\ *noun* (1712)
: a small brown or brown and yellow sea turtle (*Eretmochelys imbricata*) of warm waters that has a carapace of overlapping plates — compare TORTOISESHELL 1

hawksbill

hawk·shaw \'hȯk-ˌshȯ\ *noun* [from *Hawkshaw*, detective in the play *The Ticket of Leave Man* (1863) by Tom Taylor] (1888)
: DETECTIVE

hawk·weed \'hȯk-ˌwēd\ *noun* (1562)

\ə\ abut \ᵊ\ kitten \ər\ further \a\ ash \ā\ ace
\ä\ mop, mar \au̇\ out \ch\ chin \e\ bet \ē\ easy
\g\ go \i\ hit \ī\ ice \j\ job \ŋ\ sing \ō\ go
\ȯ\ law \ȯi\ boy \th\ thin \th\ the \ü\ loot \u̇\ foot
\y\ yet \zh\ vision *see also* Guide to Pronunciation

: any of a genus (*Hieracium*) of composite plants usually having flower heads with red or orange rays — compare ORANGE HAWKWEED

hawse \'hoz\ *noun* [alteration of Middle English *halse*, from Old Norse *hals* neck, hawse — more at COLLAR] (14th century)
1 a : the part of a ship's bow that contains the hawseholes **b :** HAWSEHOLE
2 : the distance between a ship's bow and her anchor

hawse·hole \-,hōl\ *noun* (1664)
: a hole in the bow of a ship through which a cable passes

haw·ser \'ho-zər\ *noun* [Middle English, from Anglo-French *hauceour*, from Middle French *haucier* to hoist, from (assumed) Vulgar Latin *altiare*, from Latin *altus* high — more at OLD] (13th century)
: a large rope for towing, mooring, or securing a ship

haw·ser–laid \'ho-zər-,lād\ *adjective* (1769)
: composed of three ropes laid together right‑handed with each containing three strands twisted together

haw·thorn \'ho-,thorn\ *noun* [Middle English *hawethorn*, from Old English *hagathorn*, from *haga* hawthorn + *thorn* — more at HEDGE] (before 12th century)
: any of a genus (*Crataegus*) of spring‑flowering spiny shrubs of the rose family with glossy and often lobed leaves, white or pink fragrant flowers, and small red fruits

Haw·thorne effect \'ho-,thorn-\ *noun* [from the *Hawthorne* Works of the Western Electric Co., Cicero, Ill., where its existence was established by experiment] (1962)
: the stimulation to output or accomplishment that results from the mere fact of being under observation; *also* : such an increase in output or accomplishment

¹hay \'hā\ *noun* [Middle English *hey*, from Old English *hīeg*; akin to Old High German *hewi* hay, Old English *hēawan* to hew] (before 12th century)
1 : herbage and especially grass mowed and cured for fodder
2 : REWARD
3 *slang* : BED
4 : a small sum of money ⟨a saving of . . . $14 million is not *hay* —H. C. Schonberg⟩

²hay (1556)
intransitive verb
: to cut, cure, and store hay
transitive verb
: to feed with hay

hay·cock \'hā-,käk\ *noun* (13th century)
: a somewhat rounded conical pile of hay

hay fever *noun* (1829)
: an acute allergic rhinitis and conjunctivitis; *especially* : POLLINOSIS

hay·lage \'hā-lij\ *noun* [*hay* + silage] (circa 1958)
: a stored forage that is essentially a grass silage wilted to 35 to 50 percent moisture

hay·loft \'hā-,loft\ *noun* (1573)
: a loft especially for storing hay

hay·mak·er \-,mā-kər\ *noun* (1912)
: a powerful blow

hay·mow \-,maù\ *noun* (15th century)
: a mow especially of or for hay

hay·rack \-,rak\ *noun* (1825)
1 : a feeding rack that holds hay for livestock
2 : a frame mounted on the running gear of a wagon and used especially in hauling hay or straw; *also* : a wagon equipped with a hayrack

hay·rick \-,rik\ *noun* (15th century)
: a relatively large sometimes thatched outdoor pile of hay : HAYSTACK

hay·ride \-,rīd\ *noun* (1896)
: a pleasure ride usually at night by a group in a wagon, sleigh, or open truck partly filled with straw or hay

hay–scent·ed fern \'hā-,sen-təd-\ *noun* (1915)

: a common fern (*Dennstaedtia punctilobula*) of eastern North America with fragrant finely divided pale green fronds

hay·seed \'hā-,sēd\ *noun, plural* **hayseed** or **hayseeds** (1577)
1 a : seed shattered from hay **b :** clinging bits of straw or chaff from hay
2 *plural* hayseeds : BUMPKIN, YOKEL

hay·stack \-,stak\ *noun* (15th century)
1 : a stack of hay
2 : a vertical standing wave in turbulent river waters

hay·wire \-,wīr\ *adverb or adjective* [from the use of baling wire for makeshift repairs] (1929)
1 : being out of order or having gone wrong ⟨the radio went *haywire*⟩
2 : emotionally or mentally upset or out of control : CRAZY ⟨is going *haywire* with grief⟩

ha·zan \kə-'zän, 'kä-z°n\ *noun, plural* **ha·za·nim** \kə-'zä-nəm\ [Late Hebrew *ḥazzān*] (1650)
1 : an official of a Jewish synagogue or community of the period when the Talmud was compiled
2 : CANTOR 2

¹haz·ard \'ha-zərd\ *noun* [Middle English, from Middle French *hasard*, from Arabic *az‑zahr* the die] (14th century)
1 : a game of chance like craps played with two dice
2 : a source of danger
3 a : CHANCE, RISK **b :** a chance event : ACCIDENT
4 *obsolete* : STAKE 3a
5 : a golf-course obstacle ◇
— **at hazard :** at stake

²hazard *transitive verb* (1530)
: VENTURE, RISK ⟨*hazard* a guess as to the outcome⟩

haz·ard·ous \'ha-zər-dəs\ *adjective* (1585)
1 : depending on hazard or chance
2 : involving or exposing one to risk (as of loss or harm) ⟨a *hazardous* occupation⟩ ⟨disposing of *hazardous* waste⟩
synonym see DANGEROUS
— **haz·ard·ous·ly** *adverb*
— **haz·ard·ous·ness** *noun*

¹haze \'hāz\ *noun* [probably back-formation from *hazy*] (1706)
1 a : fine dust, smoke, or light vapor causing lack of transparency of the air **b :** a cloudy appearance in a transparent liquid or solid; *also* : a dullness of finish (as on furniture)
2 : something suggesting atmospheric haze; *especially* : vagueness of mind or mental perception

²haze *verb* **hazed; haz·ing** (1801)
transitive verb
: to make hazy, dull, or cloudy
intransitive verb
: to become hazy or cloudy

³haze *transitive verb* **hazed; haz·ing** [origin unknown] (1840)
1 a : to harass by exacting unnecessary or disagreeable work **b :** to harass by banter, ridicule, or criticism
2 : to haze by way of initiation ⟨*haze* the fraternity pledges⟩
3 *West* : to drive (as cattle or horses) from horseback
— **haz·er** *noun*

¹ha·zel \'hā-zəl\ *noun* [Middle English *hasel*, from Old English *hæsel*; akin to Old High German *hasal* hazel, Latin *corulus*] (before 12th century)
1 : any of a genus (*Corylus* and especially the American *C. americana* and the European *C. avellana*) of shrubs or small trees of the birch family bearing nuts enclosed in a leafy involucre
2 : a light brown to strong yellowish brown

²hazel *adjective* (14th century)
1 : consisting of hazels or of the wood of the hazel
2 : of the color hazel

hazel hen *noun* (1661)
: a European woodland grouse (*Bonasa bonasia*) related to the ruffed grouse — called also *hazel grouse*

ha·zel·nut \'hā-zəl-,nət\ *noun* (before 12th century)
: the nut of a hazel

haz·ing \'hā-ziŋ\ *noun* (circa 1855)
: the action of hazing; *especially* : an initiation process involving harassment

hazy \'hā-zē\ *adjective* **haz·i·er; -est** [origin unknown] (1625)
1 : obscured or made dim or cloudy by or as if by haze
2 : VAGUE, INDEFINITE ⟨has only a *hazy* recollection⟩; *also* : UNCERTAIN ⟨I'm *hazy* on that point⟩
— **haz·i·ly** \-zə-lē\ *adverb*
— **haz·i·ness** \-zē-nəs\ *noun*

H–bomb \'āch-,bäm\ *noun* (1950)
: HYDROGEN BOMB

HDL \,āch-(,)dē-'el\ *noun* [high-density lipoprotein] (circa 1965)
: a cholesterol-poor protein-rich lipoprotein of blood plasma correlated with reduced risk of atherosclerosis — compare LDL

¹he \'hē, ē\ *pronoun* [Middle English, from Old English *hē*; akin to Old English *hēo* she, *hit* it, Old High German *hē* he, Latin *cis, citra* on this side, Greek *ekeinos* that person] (before 12th century)
1 : that male one who is neither speaker nor hearer ⟨*he* is my father⟩ — compare HIM, HIS, IT, SHE, THEY
2 — used in a generic sense or when the sex of the person is unspecified ⟨he that hath ears to hear, let him hear —Matthew 11:15 (Authorized Version)⟩ ⟨one should do the best *he* can⟩ □

²he \'hē\ *noun* (before 12th century)
1 : a male person or animal
2 : one that is strongly masculine or has strong masculine appeal — usually used in combination ⟨that's what I call *he*-literature —Sinclair Lewis⟩

³he \'hā\ *noun* [Hebrew *hē'*] (1639)
: the 5th letter of the Hebrew alphabet — see ALPHABET table

¹head \'hed\ *noun* [Middle English *hed*, from Old English *hēafod*; akin to Old High German *houbit* head, Latin *caput*] (before 12th century)
1 : the upper or anterior division of the animal body that contains the brain, the chief sense organs, and the mouth
2 a : the seat of the intellect : MIND ⟨two *heads* are better than one⟩ **b :** a person with respect to mental qualities ⟨let wiser *heads* prevail⟩ **c** : natural aptitude or talent ⟨a good *head* for figures⟩ **d :** mental or emotional control : POISE ⟨a level *head*⟩ **e :** HEADACHE
3 : the obverse of a coin — usually used in plural ⟨*heads*, I win⟩

◇ WORD HISTORY
hazard *Hazard* was once only a game played with dice. The French archbishop William of Tyre, writing his Latin history of the Crusades late in the 12th century, explained the origin of this hazard and its name (*hasard* in Old French). The game was invented, he said, to pass the time during the siege of a castle in Palestine called *Hazard* or *Azart*. Unfortunately for the credibility of William's theory, the name of the castle seems actually to have been '*Ain Zarba*, and the name of the game was certainly never that. The French word did not originate in the time of the Crusades, however, and most likely comes from post-classical Arabic *az‑zahr* "the die (one of the dice)." Old French *hasard* was borrowed into Middle English, and within a few centuries what had been a venture on the outcome of a throw of the dice could be any venture or risk.

4 a : PERSON, INDIVIDUAL 〈count *heads*〉 **b** *plural* **head :** one of a number (as of domestic animals)
5 a : the end that is upper or higher or opposite the foot 〈the *head* of the table〉 〈*head* of a sail〉 **b :** the source of a stream **c :** either end of something (as of a drum) whose two ends need not be distinguished
6 : DIRECTOR, LEADER: as **a :** HEADMASTER **b :** one in charge of a division or department in an office or institution 〈the *head* of the English department〉
7 a : CAPITULUM 2 **b :** the foliaged part of a plant especially when consisting of a compact mass of leaves or close fructification
8 a : the leading element of a military column or a procession **b :** HEADWAY
9 a : the uppermost extremity or projecting part of an object : TOP **b :** the striking part of a weapon, tool, or implement **c :** the rounded proximal end of a long bone (as the humerus) **d :** the end of a muscle nearest the origin — compare ORIGIN **e :** the oval part of a printed musical note
10 a : a body of water kept in reserve at a height; *also* : the containing bank, dam, or wall **b :** a mass of water in motion
11 a : the difference in elevation between two points in a body of fluid **b :** the resulting pressure of the fluid at the lower point expressible as this height; *broadly* : pressure of a fluid
12 a : the bow and adjacent parts of a ship **b :** a ship's toilet; *broadly* : TOILET
13 : the approximate length of the head of a horse 〈won by a *head*〉
14 : the place of leadership, honor, or command 〈at the *head* of her class〉
15 a (1) **:** a word or series of words often in larger letters placed at the beginning of a passage or at the top of a page in order to introduce or categorize (2) **:** a separate part or topic **b :** a portion of a page or sheet that is above the first line of printing
16 : the foam or scum that rises on a fermenting or effervescing liquid (as beer)
17 a : the part of a boil, pimple, or abscess at which it is likely to break **b :** culminating point of action : CRISIS 〈events came to a *head*〉
18 a : a part or attachment of a machine or machine tool containing a device (as a cutter or drill); *also* : the part of an apparatus that performs the chief function or a particular function **b :** an electromagnet used as a transducer in magnetic recording for recording on, reading, or erasing a magnetic medium (as tape)
19 : an immediate constituent of a construction that can have the same grammatical function as the whole (as *man* in "an old man", "a very old man", or "the man in the street")
20 a : one who uses a drug **b :** DEVOTEE 〈chili *heads*〉
21 : FELLATIO, CUNNILINGUS — usually used with *give;* often considered vulgar
— by the head : drawing the greater depth of water forward
— off one's head : CRAZY, DISTRACTED
— out of one's head : DELIRIOUS
— over one's head 1 : beyond one's comprehension or competence 〈the most awful intellectual detail, all of it *over my head* —E. B. White〉 **2 :** so as to pass over one's superior standing or authority 〈went *over my head* to complain〉

²**head** *adjective* (before 12th century)
1 : of, relating to, or intended for the head
2 : PRINCIPAL, CHIEF 〈*head* cook〉
3 : situated at the head
4 : coming from in front 〈*head* sea〉

³**head** (14th century)
transitive verb
1 : BEHEAD
2 a : to put a head on : fit a head to 〈*head* an arrow〉 **b :** to form the head or top of 〈tower *headed* by a spire〉
3 : to act as leader or head to 〈*head* a revolt〉

4 a : to get in front of so as to hinder, stop, or turn back **b :** to take a lead over (as a racehorse) : SURPASS **c :** to pass (a stream) by going round above the source
5 a : to put something at the head of (as a list) **b :** to stand as the first or leading member of 〈*heads* the list of heroes〉
6 : to set the course of 〈*head* a ship northward〉
7 : to drive (as a soccer ball) with the head
intransitive verb
1 : to form a head 〈this cabbage *heads* early〉
2 : to point or proceed in a certain direction 〈the fleet was *heading* out〉
3 : to have a source : ORIGINATE

head·ache \'he-ˌdāk\ *noun* (before 12th century)
1 : pain in the head
2 : a vexatious or baffling situation or problem
— head·achy \-ˌdā-kē\ *adjective*

head and shoulders *adverb* (circa 1864)
: beyond comparison : by far 〈*head and shoulders* above the competition〉

head·band \'hed-ˌband\ *noun* (1535)
1 : a band worn on or around the head
2 : a narrow strip of cloth sewn or glued by hand to a book at the extreme ends of the backbone

head·board \-ˌbōrd, -ˌbȯrd\ *noun* (1730)
: a board forming the head (as of a bed)

head·cheese \-ˌchēz\ *noun* (1841)
: a jellied loaf or sausage made from edible parts of the head, feet, and sometimes the tongue and heart especially of a pig

head cold *noun* (1937)
: a common cold centered in the nasal passages and adjacent mucous tissues

head·dress \'hed-ˌdres\ *noun* (1703)
: an often elaborate covering for the head

headdress

head·ed \'he-dəd\ *adjective* (13th century)
1 : having a head or a heading
2 : having a head or heads of a specified kind or number — used in combination 〈became light-*headed* from the fever〉 〈a round*headed* screw〉

head·er \'he-dər\ *noun* (15th century)
1 : one that removes heads; *especially* : a grain-harvesting machine that cuts off the grain heads and elevates them to a wagon
2 a : a brick or stone laid in a wall with its end toward the face of the wall **b :** a beam fitted at one side of an opening to support free ends of floor joists, studs, or rafters **c :** a horizontal structural or finish piece over an opening : LINTEL **d :** a conduit (as an exhaust pipe for a many-cylindered engine) into which a number of smaller conduits open **e :** a mounting plate through which electrical terminals pass from a sealed device (as a transistor)
3 : a fall or dive headfirst
4 : a shot or pass in soccer made by heading the ball
5 : HEAD 15a(1)

head·first \'hed-'fərst\ *adverb* (circa 1828)
: with the head foremost : HEADLONG 〈dove *headfirst* into the waves〉
— headfirst *adjective*

head·fore·most \-'fōr-ˌmōst, -'fȯr-\ *adverb* (1697)
: HEADFIRST

head·gate \'hed-ˌgāt\ *noun* (1832)
: a gate for controlling the water flowing into a channel (as an irrigation ditch)

head·gear \-ˌgir\ *noun* (15th century)
1 : a covering or protective device for the head
2 : a harness for a horse's head

head·hunt·er \-ˌhən-tər\ *noun* (1853)
1 : one that engages in head-hunting
2 : a recruiter of personnel especially at the executive level

head–hunt·ing \-ˌhən-tiŋ\ *noun* (1853)
1 : the act or custom of seeking out, decapitating, and preserving the heads of enemies as trophies
2 : a seeking to deprive usually political enemies of position or influence

head·ing \'he-diŋ\ *noun* (1676)
1 a : something that forms or serves as a head; *especially* : an inscription, headline, or title standing at the top or beginning (as of a letter or chapter) **b :** the address and date at the beginning of a letter showing its place and time of origin
2 : the compass direction in which the longitudinal axis of a ship or aircraft points; *broadly* : DIRECTION
3 : DRIFT 6

head·lamp \-ˌlamp\ *noun* (1885)
: HEADLIGHT

head·land \'hed-lənd, -ˌland\ *noun* (before 12th century)
1 : unplowed land at the ends of furrows or near a fence

\ə\ abut \ᵊ\ kitten \ər\ further \a\ ash \ā\ ace
\ä\ mop, mar \au̇\ out \ch\ chin \e\ bet \ē\ easy
\g\ go \i\ hit \ī\ ice \j\ job \ŋ\ sing \ō\ go
\ȯ\ law \ȯi\ boy \th\ thin \th̲\ the \ü\ loot \u̇\ foot
\y\ yet \zh\ vision *see also* Guide to Pronunciation

2 : a point of usually high land jutting out into a body of water **:** PROMONTORY

head·less \-ləs\ *adjective* (before 12th century)
1 a : having no head **b :** having the head cut off **:** BEHEADED
2 : having no chief
3 : lacking good sense or prudence **:** FOOLISH
— **head·less·ness** *noun*

head·light \-ˌlīt\ *noun* (1861)
1 : a light with a reflector and special lens mounted on the front of a vehicle to illuminate the road ahead; *also* **:** the beam cast by a headlight
2 : a light worn on the forehead (as of a miner or physician)

¹**head·line** \-ˌlīn\ *noun* (1824)
1 : words set at the head of a passage or page to introduce or categorize
2 a : a head of a newspaper story or article usually printed in large type and giving the gist of the story or article that follows **b** *plural* **:** front-page news ⟨the scandal made *headlines*⟩

²**headline** *transitive verb* (1891)
1 : to provide with a headline
2 : to publicize highly
3 : to be engaged as a leading performer in (a show)

head·lin·er \'hed-ˌlī-nər\ *noun* (1896)
1 : the principal performer in a show **:** STAR; *broadly* **:** PERSONALITY 4b
2 : fabric covering the inside of the roof of an automobile

head linesman *noun* (circa 1949)
: a football linesman

head·lock \'hed-ˌläk\ *noun* (1905)
: a hold in which a wrestler encircles his opponent's head with one arm

¹**head·long** \-'lȯŋ\ *adverb* [Middle English *hedlong*, alteration of *hedling*, from *hed* head] (14th century)
1 : HEADFIRST
2 : without deliberation **:** RECKLESSLY
3 : without pause or delay

²**head·long** \-ˌlȯŋ\ *adjective* (circa 1550)
1 *archaic* **:** STEEP, PRECIPITOUS
2 : lacking in calmness or restraint **:** PRECIPITATE ⟨a *headlong* torrent of emotion⟩
3 : plunging headforemost
synonym see PRECIPITATE

head louse *noun* (1547)
: one of a variety (*Pediculus humanus capitis*) of the common louse that lives on the human scalp

head·man *noun* (before 12th century)
1 a \'hed-'man\ **:** FOREMAN, OVERSEER **b** \-'man, -ˌman\ **:** a lesser chief of a primitive community
2 \-mən\ **:** HEADSMAN

head·mas·ter \'hed-ˌmas-tər, -'mas-\ *noun* (1576)
: a man heading the staff of a private school **:** PRINCIPAL
— **head·mas·ter·ship** \-ˌship\ *noun*

head·mis·tress \-ˌmis-trəs, -'mis-\ *noun* (1872)
: a woman heading the staff of a private school

head·most \'hed-ˌmōst\ *adjective* (1628)
: most advanced **:** LEADING

head·note \-ˌnōt\ *noun* (1855)
1 : a prefixed note of comment or explanation
2 : a note prefixed to the report of a decided legal case

head off *transitive verb* (1841)
: to turn back or turn aside **:** BLOCK, PREVENT ⟨*head* them *off* at the pass⟩ ⟨attempts to *head off* the imminent crisis⟩

¹**head–on** \'hed-'ȯn, -'än\ *adverb* (1840)
1 : with the head or front making the initial contact ⟨the cars collided *head-on*⟩
2 : in direct opposition, confrontation, or contradiction ⟨met the problem *head-on*⟩

²**head–on** *adjective* (1903)

1 : having the front facing in the direction of initial contact or line of sight ⟨a *head-on* collision⟩
2 : FRONTAL

head over heels *adverb* (1771)
1 a : in or as if in a somersault **:** HELTER-SKELTER **b :** UPSIDE DOWN
2 : very much **:** DEEPLY ⟨*head over heels* in love⟩

head·phone \'hed-ˌfōn\ *noun* (1914)
: an earphone held over the ear by a band worn on the head — usually used in plural

head·piece \-ˌpēs\ *noun* (1535)
1 a : a protective or defensive covering for the head **b :** an ornamental, ceremonial, or traditional covering for the head
2 : BRAINS, INTELLIGENCE
3 : an ornament especially at the beginning of a chapter

head·pin \-ˌpin\ *noun* (1927)
: a bowling pin that stands foremost in the arrangement of pins

head·quar·ter \'hed-ˌkwȯ(r)-tər, -ˌkȯr-, (ˌ)hed-'\ (1903)
transitive verb
: to place in headquarters
intransitive verb
: to make one's headquarters

head·quar·ters \-tərz\ *noun plural but singular or plural in construction* (1647)
1 : a place from which a commander performs the functions of command
2 : the administrative center of an enterprise

head·rest \-ˌrest\ *noun* (1853)
1 : a support for the head
2 : HEAD RESTRAINT

head restraint *noun* (1967)
: a resilient pad at the top of the back of an automobile seat especially for preventing whiplash injury

head rhyme *noun* (circa 1943)
: ALLITERATION

head·room \'hed-ˌrüm, -ˌrum\ *noun* (1851)
: vertical space in which to stand, sit, or move

head·sail \-ˌsāl, -səl\ *noun* (1627)
: a sail set forward of the foremast

head·set \-ˌset\ *noun* (1921)
1 : an attachment for holding an earphone and transmitter at one's head
2 : a pair of headphones

head·ship \-ˌship\ *noun* (1582)
: the position, office, or dignity of a head

head shop *noun* (1968)
: a shop specializing in articles (as hashish pipes and roach clips) of interest to drug users

head·shrink·er \-ˌshriŋ-kər, *especially Southern* -ˌsriŋ-\ *noun* (1950)
: SHRINK 3

heads·man \'hedz-mən\ *noun* (1601)
: one that beheads **:** EXECUTIONER

head·space \'hed-ˌspās\ *noun* (1936)
: the volume above a liquid or solid in a closed container

head·spring \'hed-ˌspriŋ\ *noun* (14th century)
: FOUNTAINHEAD, SOURCE

head·stall \-ˌstȯl\ *noun* (14th century)
: a part of a bridle or halter that encircles the head

head·stand \-ˌstand\ *noun* (circa 1934)
: the gymnastic feat of standing on one's head usually with support from the hands

head start *noun* (1886)
1 : an advantage granted or achieved at the beginning of a race, a chase, or a competition ⟨a 10-minute *head start*⟩
2 : a favorable or promising beginning

head·stock \'hed-ˌstäk\ *noun* (1731)
: a bearing or pedestal for a revolving or moving part; *specifically* **:** a part of a lathe that holds the revolving spindle and its attachments

head·stone \-ˌstōn\ *noun* (1775)
: a memorial stone at the head of a grave

head·stream \-ˌstrēm\ *noun* (14th century)
: a stream that is the source of a river

head·strong \-ˌstrȯŋ\ *adjective* (14th century)

1 : not easily restrained **:** impatient of control, advice, or suggestions
2 : directed by ungovernable will ⟨violent *headstrong* actions⟩
synonym see UNRULY

heads–up \'hed-'zəp\ *adjective* (1947)
: ALERT, RESOURCEFUL ⟨*heads-up* football⟩

heads up *interjection* (circa 1941)
— used as a warning to look out for danger especially overhead or to clear a passageway

head–to–head *adverb or adjective* (circa 1728)
: in a direct confrontation or encounter usually between individuals

head·wait·er \'hed-'wā-tər\ *noun* (1805)
: the head of the dining-room staff of a restaurant or hotel

head·wa·ter \-ˌwȯ-tər, -ˌwä-\ *noun* (1802)
: the source of a stream — usually used in plural

head·way \-ˌwā\ *noun* (1748)
1 a : motion or rate of motion in a forward direction **b :** ADVANCE, PROGRESS
2 : headroom (as under an arch) sufficient to allow passage
3 : the time interval between two vehicles traveling in the same direction on the same route

head·word \'hed-ˌwərd\ *noun* (circa 1823)
1 : a word or term placed at the beginning (as of a chapter or an entry in an encyclopedia)
2 : HEAD 19

head·work \-ˌwərk\ *noun* (1837)
: mental labor; *especially* **:** clever thinking

heady \'he-dē\ *adjective* **head·i·er; -est** (14th century)
1 a : WILLFUL, RASH ⟨*heady* opinions⟩ **b :** VIOLENT, IMPETUOUS
2 a : tending to intoxicate or make giddy or elated ⟨*heady* wine⟩ ⟨being in such distinguished company was a *heady* experience⟩ **b :** GIDDY, EXHILARATED ⟨*heady* with his success⟩ **c :** RICH ⟨a *heady* sauce⟩ ⟨a *heady* variety⟩ **d :** IMPRESSIVE ⟨a man of *heady* accomplishments⟩
3 a : marked by or showing good judgment **:** SHREWD, INTELLIGENT **b :** intellectually stimulating or demanding
— **head·i·ly** \'he-dᵊl-ē\ *adverb*
— **head·i·ness** \'he-dē-nəs\ *noun*

heal \'hē(ə)l\ *verb* [Middle English *helen*, from Old English *hǣlan*; akin to Old High German *heilen* to heal, Old English *hāl* whole — more at WHOLE] (before 12th century)
transitive verb
1 a : to make sound or whole ⟨*heal* a wound⟩ **b :** to restore to health
2 a : to cause (an undesirable condition) to be overcome **:** MEND ⟨the troubles . . . had not been forgotten, but they had been *healed* —William Power⟩ **b :** to patch up (a breach or division) ⟨*heal* a breach between friends⟩
3 : to restore to original purity or integrity ⟨*healed* of sin⟩
intransitive verb
: to return to a sound state

heal·er \'hē-lər\ *noun* (12th century)
1 : one that heals
2 : a Christian Science practitioner

health \'helth *also* 'helth\ *noun, often attributive* [Middle English *helthe*, from Old English *hǣlth*, from *hāl*] (before 12th century)
1 a : the condition of being sound in body, mind, or spirit; *especially* **:** freedom from physical disease or pain **b :** the general condition of the body ⟨in poor *health*⟩ ⟨enjoys good *health*⟩
2 a : flourishing condition **:** WELL-BEING ⟨defending the *health* of the beloved oceans —Peter Wilkinson⟩ **b :** general condition or state ⟨poor economic *health*⟩
3 : a toast to someone's health or prosperity

health food *noun* (1882)
: a food promoted as highly conducive to health

health·ful \'helth-fəl *also* 'heltth-\ *adjective* (14th century)
1 : beneficial to health of body or mind
2 : HEALTHY ⟨he felt incapable of looking into the girl's pretty, *healthful* face —Saul Bellow⟩
☆
usage see HEALTHY
— **health·ful·ness** *noun*
health insurance *noun* (1901)
: insurance against loss through illness of the insured; *especially* : insurance providing compensation for medical expenses
health maintenance organization *noun* (1973)
: HMO
health spa *noun* (1960)
: a commercial establishment (as a resort) providing facilities devoted to health and fitness
healthy \'hel-thē *also* 'helt-\ *adjective* **health·i·er; -est** (1552)
1 : enjoying health and vigor of body, mind, or spirit : WELL
2 : evincing health ⟨a *healthy* complexion⟩
3 : conducive to health ⟨walk three miles every day . . . a beastly bore, but *healthy* —G. S. Patton⟩
4 a : PROSPEROUS, FLOURISHING **b** : not small or feeble : CONSIDERABLE ☆ □
— **health·i·ly** \-thə-lē\ *adverb*
— **health·i·ness** \-thē-nəs\ *noun*
¹heap \'hēp\ *noun* [Middle English *heep,* from Old English *hēap;* akin to Old High German *houf* heap] (before 12th century)
1 : a collection of things thrown one on another : PILE
2 : a great number or large quantity : LOT
²heap *transitive verb* (before 12th century)
1 a : to throw or lay in a heap : pile or collect in great quantity ⟨his sole object was to *heap* up riches⟩ **b** : to form or round into a heap ⟨*heaped* the dirt into a mound⟩ **c** : to form a heap on : load heavily ⟨*heap* the plates with food⟩
2 : to accord or bestow lavishly or in large quantities ⟨*heaped* honors upon them⟩
hear \'hir\ *verb* **heard** \'hərd\; **hear·ing** \'hir-iŋ\ [Middle English *heren,* from Old English *hīeran;* akin to Old High German *hōren* to hear, and probably to Latin *cavēre* to be on guard, Greek *akouein* to hear] (before 12th century)
transitive verb
1 : to perceive or apprehend by the ear
2 : to gain knowledge of by hearing
3 a : to listen to with attention : HEED **b** : ATTEND ⟨*hear* mass⟩
4 a : to give a legal hearing to **b** : to take testimony from ⟨*hear* witnesses⟩
intransitive verb
1 : to have the capacity of apprehending sound
2 a : to gain information : LEARN **b** : to receive communication ⟨*heard* from her recently⟩
3 : to entertain the idea — used in the negative ⟨wouldn't *hear* of it⟩
4 — often used in the expression *Hear! Hear!* to express approval (as during a speech)
— **hear·er** \'hir-ər\ *noun*
hear·ing *noun* (13th century)
1 a : the process, function, or power of perceiving sound; *specifically* : the special sense by which noises and tones are received as stimuli **b** : EARSHOT
2 a : opportunity to be heard, to present one's side of a case, or to be generally known or appreciated **b** (1) : a listening to arguments (2) : a preliminary examination in criminal procedure **c** : a session (as of a legislative committee) in which testimony is taken from witnesses
3 *chiefly dialect* : a piece of news
hearing aid *noun* (1922)
: an electronic device usually worn by a person for amplifying sound before it reaches the receptor organs
hearing dog *noun* (1952)
: a dog trained to alert its deaf or hearing-

impaired owner to sounds (as of a doorbell, alarm, or telephone) — called also *hearing ear dog*
hear·ken \'här-kən\ *verb* **hear·kened; hear·ken·ing** \'härk-niŋ, 'här-kə-\ [Middle English *herknen,* from Old English *heorcnian;* akin to Old High German *hōrechen* to listen, Old English *hīeran* to hear] (before 12th century)
intransitive verb
1 : LISTEN
2 : to give respectful attention
transitive verb
archaic : to give heed to : HEAR
hearken back *intransitive verb* (1933)
: HARK BACK
hear·say \'hir-,sā\ *noun* (circa 1532)
: RUMOR
hearsay evidence *noun* (1753)
: evidence based not on a witness's personal knowledge but on another's statement not made under oath
¹hearse \'hərs\ *noun* [Middle English *herse,* from Middle French *herce* harrow, frame for holding candles, from Latin *hirpic-, hirpex* harrow] (14th century)
1 a : an elaborate framework erected over a coffin or tomb to which memorial verses or epitaphs are attached **b** : a triangular candelabrum for 15 candles used especially at Tenebrae
2 a *archaic* : COFFIN **b** *obsolete* : BIER 2
3 : a vehicle for conveying the dead to the grave ◆
²hearse *transitive verb* **hearsed; hears·ing** (1592)
1 a *archaic* : to place on or in a hearse **b** : to convey in a hearse
2 : BURY
¹heart \'härt\ *noun* [Middle English *hert,* from Old English *heorte;* akin to Old High German *herza* heart, Latin *cord-, cor,* Greek *kardia*] (before 12th century)
1 a : a hollow muscular organ of vertebrate animals that by its rhythmic contraction acts as a force pump maintaining the circulation of the blood **b** : a structure in an invertebrate animal functionally analogous to the vertebrate heart **c** : BREAST, BOSOM **d** : something resembling a heart in shape; *specifically* : a stylized representation of a heart
2 a : a playing card marked with a stylized figure of a red heart **b** *plural* : the suit comprising cards marked with hearts **c** *plural but singular or plural in construction* : a game in which the object is to avoid taking tricks containing hearts

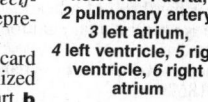
heart 1a: *1* aorta, *2* pulmonary artery, *3* left atrium, *4* left ventricle, *5* right ventricle, *6* right atrium

☆ SYNONYMS
Healthy, sound, wholesome, robust, hale, well mean enjoying or indicative of good health. HEALTHY implies full strength and vigor as well as freedom from signs of disease ⟨a *healthy* family⟩. SOUND emphasizes the absence of disease, weakness, or malfunction ⟨a *sound* heart⟩. WHOLESOME implies appearance and behavior indicating soundness and balance ⟨a face with a *wholesome* glow⟩. ROBUST implies the opposite of all that is delicate or sickly ⟨a lively, *robust* little boy⟩. HALE applies particularly to robustness in old age ⟨still *hale* at the age of eighty⟩. WELL implies nothing more than just freedom from disease or illness ⟨in her declining years she has never been a *well* person⟩.

□ USAGE
healthy Since 1881 usage writers have been trying to draw a distinction between *healthy* and *healthful. Healthy,* they say, should be used in the sense "enjoying health, evincing health" and *healthful* in the sense "conducive to health." And each word is used in the prescribed way part of the time. The problem is that both words are used in the latter sense ⟨on the high, *healthful* promontory on the right bank —David Levering Lewis⟩ ⟨on horseback, attending to my farm or other concerns, which I find *healthful* to my body —Thomas Jefferson⟩ ⟨prescribed the very *healthful* exercise of woodcutting —T. Coraghessan Boyle⟩ ⟨having been born & brought up in a mountainous & *healthy* country —Thomas Jefferson⟩ ⟨bastion of right thinking, vegetarianism and self-improvement, . . . the single *healthiest* spot on the planet —T. Coraghessan Boyle⟩ ⟨more genteel or *healthier* living habits —J. M. Richards⟩. The commentators would like to eliminate this use of *healthy* from the language, but as you can see from the second Thomas Jefferson quotation, this use had long been established when its first critic was writing. In fact, it first appeared in the middle of the 16th century. The distinction is simply a fabrication that one may observe or ignore and still be in good company.

◇ WORD HISTORY
hearse In medieval French the word *herce,* which literally meant "harrow," was applied to other things that were thought to resemble the toothed cultivating implement, such as a portcullis and a frame like a chandelier for holding candles. The latter sense when borrowed into Middle English as *herce* or *herse* was applied specifically to a framework for candles, statues or other objects that was placed over the coffin or tomb of a distinguished person. From this starting point the English word diverged further and further in meaning from its French source; its reference was transferred from the framework to the coffin itself or the stand on which the coffin was placed, and then to the vehicle that transports a coffin, which is the ordinary sense of the word today. Completely obscured for people today is the relation of *hearse* to *rehearse,* which comes from a medieval French verb meaning "to harrow again."

\ə\ abut \ᵊ\ kitten \ər\ **further** \a\ ash \ā\ ace
\ä\ mop, mar \au̇\ out \ch\ chin \e\ bet \ē\ easy
\g\ go \i\ hit \ī\ ice \j\ job \ŋ\ sing \ō\ go
\ȯ\ law \ȯi\ boy \th\ thin \th\ the \ü\ loot \u̇\ foot
\y\ yet \zh\ vision *see also* Guide to Pronunciation

3 a : PERSONALITY, DISPOSITION ⟨a cold *heart*⟩ **b** *obsolete* **:** INTELLECT
4 : the emotional or moral as distinguished from the intellectual nature: as **a :** generous disposition **:** COMPASSION ⟨a leader with *heart*⟩ **b :** LOVE, AFFECTIONS ⟨won her *heart*⟩ **c :** COURAGE, ARDOR ⟨never lost *heart*⟩
5 : one's innermost character, feelings, or inclinations ⟨knew it in his *heart*⟩ ⟨a man after my own *heart*⟩
6 a : the central or innermost part **:** CENTER **b :** the essential or most vital part of something **c :** the younger central compact part of a leafy rosette (as a head of lettuce)
— **at heart :** in essence **:** BASICALLY, ESSENTIALLY
— **by heart :** by rote or from memory
— **to heart :** with deep concern
²**heart** *transitive verb* (before 12th century)
1 *archaic* **:** HEARTEN
2 *archaic* **:** to fix in the heart
heart·ache \'härt-ˌāk\ *noun* (1602)
: anguish of mind **:** SORROW
heart attack *noun* (1928)
: an acute episode of heart disease (as myocardial infarction) due to insufficient blood supply to the heart muscle especially when caused by a coronary thrombosis or a coronary occlusion
heart·beat \'härt-ˌbēt\ *noun* (1850)
1 : one complete pulsation of the heart
2 : the vital center or driving impulse
heart block *noun* (1903)
: incoordination of the heartbeat in which the atria and ventricles beat independently and which is marked by decreased cardiac output
heart·break \'härt-ˌbrāk\ *noun* (14th century)
: crushing grief
heart·break·er \-ˌbrā-kər\ *noun* (1863)
: one that causes heartbreak
heart·break·ing \-ˌbrā-kiŋ\ *adjective* (1591)
1 a : causing intense sorrow or distress **b :** extremely trying or difficult
2 : producing an intense emotional reaction or response ⟨*heartbreaking* beauty⟩
— **heart·break·ing·ly** \-kiŋ-lē\ *adverb*
heart·bro·ken \-ˌbrō-kən\ *adjective* (circa 1586)
: overcome by sorrow
heart·burn \-ˌbərn\ *noun* (1597)
: a burning discomfort behind the lower part of the sternum usually related to spasm of the lower end of the esophagus or of the upper part of the stomach
heart·burn·ing \-ˌbər-niŋ\ *noun* (1513)
: intense or rancorous jealousy or resentment
heart disease *noun* (1864)
: an abnormal organic condition of the heart or of the heart and circulation
heart·ed \'här-təd\ *adjective* (13th century)
1 : having a heart especially of a specified kind — usually used in combination ⟨a faint-*hearted* leader⟩ ⟨a light*hearted* wanderer⟩
2 : seated in the heart
heart·en \'här-tᵊn\ *transitive verb* **heart·ened; heart·en·ing** \'härt-niŋ, 'har-tᵊn-iŋ\ (1526)
: to give heart to **:** CHEER
synonym see ENCOURAGE
— **heart·en·ing·ly** \-niŋ-lē, -tᵊn-iŋ-\ *adverb*
heart failure *noun* (1894)
1 : a condition in which the heart is unable to pump blood at an adequate rate or in adequate volume
2 : cessation of heartbeat **:** DEATH
heart·felt \'härt-ˌfelt\ *adjective* (1734)
: deeply felt **:** EARNEST
synonym see SINCERE
heart–free \'härt-ˌfrē\ *adjective* (1748)
: not in love
hearth \'härth\ *noun* [Middle English *herth*, from Old English *heorth;* akin to Old High German *herd* hearth, and probably to Sanskrit *kūdayāti* he scorches] (before 12th century)
1 a : a brick, stone, or cement area in front of

a fireplace **b :** the floor of a fireplace; *also* **:** FIREPLACE **c :** the lowest section of a furnace; *especially* **:** the section of a furnace on which the ore or metal is exposed to the flame or heat
2 : HOME
3 : a vital or creative center ⟨the central *hearth* of occidental civilization —A. L. Kroeber⟩
hearth·stone \-ˌstōn\ *noun* (14th century)
1 : stone forming a hearth
2 : HOME
heart·i·ly \'här-tᵊl-ē\ *adverb* (14th century)
1 : in a hearty manner
2 a : with all sincerity **:** WHOLEHEARTEDLY **b :** with zest or gusto
3 : WHOLLY, THOROUGHLY ⟨*heartily* sick of all this talk⟩
heart·land \'härt-ˌland\ *noun* (1904)
: a central area: as **a :** a central land area (as northern Eurasia) having strategic advantages **b :** a central geographical region especially of the U.S. in which mainstream or traditional values predominate
heart·less \-ləs\ *adjective* (14th century)
1 *archaic* **:** SPIRITLESS
2 : lacking feeling **:** CRUEL
— **heart·less·ly** *adverb*
— **heart·less·ness** *noun*
heart–lung machine *noun* (1953)
: a mechanical pump that maintains circulation during heart surgery by shunting blood away from the body, oxygenating it, and returning it to the body
heart·rend·ing \'härt-ˌren-diŋ\ *adjective* (1594)
: HEARTBREAKING 1a
— **heart·rend·ing·ly** \-diŋ-lē\ *adverb*
hearts·ease \'härts-ˌēz\ *noun* (15th century)
1 : peace of mind **:** TRANQUILLITY
2 : any of various violas; *especially* **:** JOHNNY-JUMP-UP
heart·sick \'härt-ˌsik\ *adjective* (1526)
: very despondent **:** DEPRESSED
— **heart·sick·ness** *noun*
heart·some \'hert-səm\ *adjective* (1596)
chiefly Scottish **:** giving spirit or vigor **:** ANIMATING, ENLIVENING
— **heart·some·ly** *adverb, chiefly Scottish*
heart·sore \'härt-ˌsōr, -ˌsȯr\ *adjective* (1591)
: HEARTSICK
heart·string \-ˌstriŋ\ *noun* (15th century)
1 *obsolete* **:** a nerve once believed to sustain the heart
2 : the deepest emotions or affections ⟨pulled at his *heartstrings*⟩
heart·throb \-ˌthräb\ *noun* (1839)
1 : the throb of a heart
2 a : sentimental emotion **:** PASSION **b :** SWEETHEART
¹**heart–to–heart** \'härt-tə-'härt\ *adjective* (1867)
: SINCERE, FRANK ⟨a *heart-to-heart* talk⟩
²**heart–to–heart** *noun* (1910)
: a frank, serious, and often intimate conversation
heart·warm·ing \'härt-ˌwȯr-miŋ\ *adjective* (1899)
: inspiring sympathetic feeling **:** CHEERING
— **heart–warm·er** *noun*
heart–whole \-ˌhōl\ *adjective* (1600)
1 : HEART-FREE
2 : SINCERE, GENUINE
heart·wood \-ˌwu̇d\ *noun* (1810)
: the older harder nonliving central wood of trees that is usually darker, denser, less permeable, and more durable than the surrounding sapwood
heart·worm \-ˌwərm\ *noun* (1888)
: a filarial worm (*Dirofilaria immitis*) that is a parasite especially in the right heart of dogs and is transmitted by mosquitoes; *also* **:** infestation or disease caused by the heartworm
¹**hearty** \'här-tē\ *adjective* **heart·i·er; -est** (14th century)
1 a : giving unqualified support ⟨a *hearty* en-

dorsement⟩ **b :** enthusiastically or exuberantly cordial **:** JOVIAL **c :** expressed unrestrainedly
2 a : exhibiting vigorous good health **b** (1) **:** having a good appetite (2) **:** abundant, rich, or flavorful enough to satisfy the appetite
3 : VIGOROUS, VEHEMENT ⟨a *hearty* pull⟩
synonym see SINCERE
— **heart·i·ness** *noun*
²**hearty** *noun, plural* **heart·ies** (1803)
: a hearty fellow; *also* **:** SAILOR
¹**heat** \'hēt\ *verb* [Middle English *heten*, from Old English *hǣtan;* akin to Old English *hāt* hot] (before 12th century)
intransitive verb
1 : to become warm or hot
2 : to start to spoil from heat
transitive verb
1 : to make warm or hot
2 : EXCITE
— **heat·able** \'hē-tə-bəl\ *adjective*
²**heat** *noun* [Middle English *hete*, from Old English *hǣte, hǣtu;* akin to Old English *hāt* hot] (before 12th century)
1 a (1) **:** a condition of being hot **:** WARMTH (2) **:** a marked or notable degree of hotness **b :** pathological excessive bodily temperature **c :** a hot place or situation **d** (1) **:** a period of heat (2) **:** a single complete operation of heating; *also* **:** the quantity of material so heated **e** (1) **:** added energy that causes substances to rise in temperature, fuse, evaporate, expand, or undergo any of various other related changes, that flows to a body by contact with or radiation from bodies at higher temperatures, and that can be produced in a body (as by compression) (2) **:** the energy associated with the random motions of the molecules, atoms, or smaller structural units of which matter is composed **f :** appearance, condition, or color of a body as indicating its temperature
2 a : intensity of feeling or reaction **:** PASSION **b :** the height or stress of an action or condition ⟨in the *heat* of battle⟩ **c :** sexual excitement especially in a female mammal; *specifically* **:** ESTRUS
3 : a single continuous effort: as **a :** a single round of a contest (as a race) having two or more rounds for each contestant **b :** one of several preliminary contests held to eliminate less competent contenders
4 : pungency of flavor
5 a *slang* (1) **:** the intensification of law-enforcement activity or investigation (2) **:** POLICE **b :** PRESSURE, COERCION **c :** ABUSE, CRITICISM ⟨took a lot of *heat*⟩
6 : SMOKE 8
— **heat·less** \'hēt-ləs\ *adjective*
— **heat·proof** \-'prüf\ *adjective*
heat cramps *noun plural* (1938)
: a condition that is marked by sudden development of cramps in skeletal muscles and that results from prolonged work in high temperatures accompanied by profuse perspiration with loss of sodium chloride from the body
heat·ed \'hē-təd\ *adjective* (1886)
: marked by anger ⟨a *heated* argument⟩
— **heat·ed·ly** *adverb*
heat engine *noun* (circa 1895)
: a mechanism (as an internal-combustion engine) for converting heat energy into mechanical or electrical energy
heat·er \'hē-tər\ *noun* (15th century)
1 : one that heats; *especially* **:** a device that imparts heat or holds something to be heated
2 : FASTBALL
heat exchanger *noun* (1902)
: a device (as an automobile radiator) for transferring heat from one fluid to another without allowing them to mix
heat exhaustion *noun* (1939)
: a condition marked by weakness, nausea, dizziness, and profuse sweating that results from physical exertion in a hot environment — called also *heat prostration;* compare HEAT-STROKE
heath \'hēth\ *noun* [Middle English *heth*, from

Old English *hæth;* akin to Old High German *heida* heather, Old Welsh *coit* forest] (before 12th century)
1 a : a tract of wasteland **b :** an extensive area of rather level open uncultivated land usually with poor coarse soil, inferior drainage, and a surface rich in peat or peaty humus
2 a : any of a family (Ericaceae, the heath family) of shrubby dicotyledonous and often evergreen plants that thrive on open barren usually acid and ill-drained soil; *especially* **:** an evergreen subshrub of either of two genera (*Erica* and *Calluna*) with whorls of needlelike leaves and clusters of small flowers **b :** any of various plants that resemble true heaths
— **heath·less** \-ləs\ *adjective*
— **heath·like** \-,līk\ *adjective*
— **heathy** \'hē-thē\ *adjective*
¹hea·then \'hē-thən\ *adjective* [Middle English *hethen,* from Old English *hǣthen;* akin to Old High German *heidan* heathen, and probably to Old English *hǣth* heath] (before 12th century)
1 : of or relating to heathens, their religions, or their customs
2 : STRANGE, UNCIVILIZED
²heathen *noun, plural* **heathens** *or* **heathen** (before 12th century)
1 : an unconverted member of a people or nation that does not acknowledge the God of the Bible
2 : an uncivilized or irreligious person
— **hea·then·dom** \-dəm\ *noun*
— **hea·then·ism** \-thə-,ni-zəm\ *noun*
— **hea·then·ize** \-thə-,nīz\ *transitive verb*
hea·then·ish \'hē-thə-nish\ *adjective* (1593)
: resembling or characteristic of heathens **:** BARBAROUS
— **hea·then·ish·ly** *adverb*
¹heath·er \'he-thər\ *noun* [Middle English (northern) *hather*] (14th century)
: HEATH 2a; *especially* **:** a common Eurasian heath (*Calluna vulgaris*) of northern and alpine regions that has small crowded sessile leaves and racemes of tiny usually purplish pink flowers and is naturalized in the northeastern U.S.
²heather *adjective* (1615)
: HEATHERY
heath·ery \'heth-rē, 'he-thə-\ *adjective* (1535)
1 : of, relating to, or resembling heather
2 : having flecks of various colors ⟨a soft *heathery* tweed⟩
heath hen *noun* (1644)
: a now extinct grouse (*Tympanuchus cupido cupido*) of the northeastern U.S. — compare PRAIRIE CHICKEN
heath·land \'hēth-,land\ *noun* (1819)
: HEATH 1
heat lightning *noun* (1834)
: vivid and extensive flashes of electric light without thunder seen near the horizon especially at the close of a hot day and ascribed to far-off lightning reflected by high clouds
heat prostration *noun* (1938)
: HEAT EXHAUSTION
heat pump *noun* (1894)
: an apparatus for heating or cooling a building by transferring heat by mechanical means from or to a reservoir (as the ground, water, or air) outside the building
heat rash *noun* (1887)
: PRICKLY HEAT
heat shield *noun* (1962)
: a barrier of ablative material to protect a space capsule from heat on its entry into an atmosphere
heat sink *noun* (1936)
: a substance or device for the absorption or dissipation of unwanted heat (as from a process or an electronic device)
heat·stroke \'hēt-,strōk\ *noun* (1874)
: a condition marked especially by cessation of sweating, extremely high body temperature, and collapse that results from prolonged exposure to high temperature — compare HEAT EXHAUSTION
heat–treat \'hēt-,trēt\ *transitive verb* (1907)
: to subject to heat; *especially* **:** to treat (as metals) by heating and cooling in a way that will produce desired properties
— **heat treater** *noun*
— **heat treatment** *noun*
heat wave *noun* (1893)
: a period of unusually hot weather
¹heave \'hēv\ *verb* **heaved** *or* **hove** \'hōv\; **heav·ing** [Middle English *heven,* from Old English *hebban;* akin to Old High German *hevan* to lift, Latin *capere* to take] (before 12th century)
transitive verb
1 *obsolete* **:** ELEVATE
2 : LIFT, RAISE
3 : THROW, CAST
4 a : to cause to swell or rise **b :** to displace (as a rock stratum) especially by a fault
5 : to utter with obvious effort or with a deep breath
6 : HAUL, DRAW
intransitive verb
1 : LABOR, STRUGGLE
2 : RETCH
3 a : to rise and fall rhythmically **b :** PANT
4 a : PULL, PUSH **b :** to move a ship in a specified direction or manner **c** *past usually* **hove :** to move in an indicated way — used of a ship
5 : to rise or become thrown or raised up
synonym see LIFT
— **heav·er** *noun*
— **heave to :** to bring a ship to a stop
²heave *noun* (circa 1571)
1 a : an effort to heave or raise **b :** HURL, CAST
2 : an upward motion **:** RISING; *especially* **:** a rhythmical rising
3 : horizontal displacement especially by the faulting of a rock
4 *plural but singular or plural in construction* **:** chronic pulmonary emphysema of the horse resulting in difficult expiration, heaving of the flanks, and a persistent cough
heave–ho \'hēv-'hō\ *noun* [from *heave ho!,* interjection used when heaving on a rope] (1947)
: DISMISSAL ⟨gave him the old *heave-ho*⟩
heav·en \'he-vən\ *noun* [Middle English *heven,* from Old English *heofon;* akin to Old High German *himil* heaven] (before 12th century)
1 : the expanse of space that seems to be over the earth like a dome **:** FIRMAMENT — usually used in plural
2 a *often capitalized* **:** the dwelling place of the Deity and the joyful abode of the blessed dead **b :** a spiritual state of everlasting communion with God
3 *capitalized* **:** GOD 1
4 : a place or condition of utmost happiness
5 *Christian Science* **:** a state of thought in which sin is absent and the harmony of divine Mind is manifest
heav·en·ly \-lē\ *adjective* (before 12th century)
1 : of or relating to heaven or the heavens **:** CELESTIAL ⟨the *heavenly* choirs⟩ ⟨use a telescope to study the *heavenly* bodies⟩
2 a : suggesting the blessed state of heaven **:** BEATIFIC ⟨*heavenly* peace⟩ **b :** DELIGHTFUL
— **heav·en·li·ness** *noun*
heav·en–sent \-,sent\ *adjective* (circa 1649)
: PROVIDENTIAL
heav·en·ward \-wərd\ *adverb or adjective* (13th century)
: toward heaven
heav·en·wards \-wərdz\ *adverb* (1650)
: HEAVENWARD
heavier–than–air *adjective* (1903)
: of greater weight than the air displaced
heavi·ly \'he-və-lē\ *adverb* (before 12th century)
1 : to a great degree **:** SEVERELY
2 : slowly and laboriously **:** DULLY
3 *archaic* **:** with sorrow **:** GRIEVOUSLY
4 : in a heavy manner
Heav·i·side layer \'he-vē-,sīd-\ *noun* [Oliver *Heaviside*] (1912)
: IONOSPHERE
¹heavy \'he-vē\ *adjective* **heavi·er; -est** [Middle English *hevy,* from Old English *hefig;* akin to Old High German *hebīc* heavy, Old English *hebban* to lift — more at HEAVE] (before 12th century)
1 a : having great weight; *also* **:** characterized by mass or weight ⟨how *heavy* is it?⟩ **b :** having a high specific gravity **:** having great weight in proportion to bulk **c** (1) *of an isotope* **:** having or being atoms of greater than normal mass for that element (2) *of a compound* **:** containing heavy isotopes
2 : hard to bear; *specifically* **:** GRIEVOUS, AFFLICTIVE ⟨a *heavy* sorrow⟩
3 : of weighty import **:** SERIOUS
4 : DEEP, PROFOUND
5 a : borne down by something oppressive **:** BURDENED **b :** PREGNANT; *especially* **:** approaching parturition
6 a : slow or dull from loss of vitality or resiliency **:** SLUGGISH **b :** lacking sparkle or vivacity **:** DRAB **c :** lacking mirth or gaiety **:** DOLEFUL **d :** characterized by declining prices
7 : dulled with weariness **:** DROWSY
8 : greater in quantity or quality than the average of its kind or class: as **a :** of unusually large size or amount ⟨a *heavy* turnout⟩ ⟨*heavy* traffic⟩ **b :** of great force ⟨*heavy* seas⟩ **c :** threatening to rain or snow **d** (1) **:** impeding motion (2) **:** full of clay and inclined to hold water **e :** coming as if from a depth **:** LOUD ⟨*heavy* breathing⟩ **f :** THICK, COARSE **g :** OPPRESSIVE ⟨*heavy* odor⟩ **h :** STEEP, ACUTE **i :** LABORIOUS, DIFFICULT ⟨*heavy* going⟩ **j :** IMMODERATE ⟨a *heavy* smoker⟩ **k :** more powerful than usual for its kind ⟨*heavy* cavalry⟩ ⟨*heavy* cruiser⟩ **l :** of large capacity or output
9 a : very rich and hard to digest ⟨*heavy* desserts⟩ **b :** not properly raised or leavened ⟨*heavy* bread⟩
10 : producing goods (as coal, steel, or chemicals) used in the production of other goods ⟨*heavy* industry⟩
11 a : having stress ⟨*heavy* rhythm⟩ — used especially of syllables in accentual verse **b :** being the strongest degree of stress in speech
12 : relating to theatrical parts of a grave or somber nature
13 : LONG 9 ⟨*heavy* on ideas⟩
14 : IMPORTANT, PROMINENT ⟨a *heavy* politician⟩ ☆
— **heavi·ness** *noun*
²heavy *adverb* (before 12th century)
: in a heavy manner **:** HEAVILY

☆ SYNONYMS
Heavy, weighty, ponderous, cumbrous, cumbersome mean having great weight. HEAVY implies that something has greater density or thickness than the average of its kind or class ⟨a *heavy* child for his age⟩. WEIGHTY suggests having actual and not just relative weight ⟨a load of *weighty* boxes⟩. PONDEROUS implies having great weight because of size and massiveness with resulting great inertia ⟨*ponderous* elephants in a circus parade⟩. CUMBROUS and CUMBERSOME imply heaviness and bulkiness that make for difficulty in grasping, moving, carrying, or manipulating ⟨wrestled with the *cumbrous* furniture⟩ ⟨early cameras were *cumbersome* and inconvenient⟩.

\ə\ abut	\ə\ kitten	\ər\ further	\a\ ash \ā\ ace
\ä\ mop, mar	\au̇\ out	\ch\ chin	\e\ bet \ē\ easy
\g\ go	\i\ hit	\ī\ ice	\j\ job \ŋ\ sing \ō\ go
\o̧\ law	\o̧i\ boy	\th\ thin	\t͟h\ the \ü\ loot \u̇\ foot
\y\ yet	\zh\ vision	*see also* Guide to Pronunciation	

³heavy *noun, plural* **heav·ies** (1897)
1 : HEAVYWEIGHT 2
2 a : a theatrical role of a dignified or somber character; *also* **:** an actor playing such a role **b :** VILLAIN 4 **c :** someone or something influential, serious, or important

heavy chain *noun* (1964)
: either of the two larger of the four polypeptide chains comprising antibodies — compare LIGHT CHAIN

heavy cream *noun* (1930)
: a cream that is markedly thick; *especially* **:** cream that by law contains not less than 36 percent butterfat

heavy–du·ty \'he-vē-'dü-tē, -'dyü-\ *adjective* (1914)
1 : able or designed to withstand unusual strain
2 : INTENSIVE ⟨*heavy-duty* bargaining⟩

heavy–foot·ed \-'fu̇-təd\ *adjective* (1625)
: heavy and slow in movement

heavy–hand·ed \-'han-dəd\ *adjective* (1647)
1 : CLUMSY
2 : OPPRESSIVE, HARSH
— **heavy–hand·ed·ly** *adverb*
— **heavy–hand·ed·ness** *noun*

heavy·heart·ed \-'här-təd\ *adjective* (14th century)
: DESPONDENT, SADDENED
— **heavy·heart·ed·ly** *adverb*
— **heavy·heart·ed·ness** *noun*

heavy hitter *noun* (1976)
: BIG SHOT, HEAVY

heavy hydrogen *noun* (1933)
: DEUTERIUM

heavy metal *noun* (1974)
: energetic and highly amplified electronic rock music having a hard beat

heavy·set \,he-vē-'set\ *adjective* (1922)
: stocky and compact and sometimes tending to stoutness in build

heavy water *noun* (1933)
1 : the compound D_2O composed of deuterium and oxygen — called also *deuterium oxide*
2 : water enriched in deuterium

heavy·weight \'he-vē-,wāt\ *noun* (1857)
1 : one that is above average in weight
2 : one in the usually heaviest class of contestants: as **a :** a boxer in an unlimited weight division — compare LIGHT HEAVYWEIGHT **b :** a weight lifter weighing more than 198 pounds
3 : BIG SHOT, HEAVY

heb·do·mad \'heb-də-,mad\ *noun* [Latin *hebdomad-, hebdomas,* from Greek, from *hebdomos* seventh, from *hepta* seven — more at SEVEN] (1545)
1 : a group of seven
2 : a period of seven days **:** WEEK

heb·dom·a·dal \heb-'dä-mə-dᵊl\ *adjective* (1711)
: WEEKLY
— **heb·dom·a·dal·ly** \-dᵊl-ē\ *adverb*

hebe \'hēb\ *noun, often capitalized* [short for *Hebrew*] (1932)
: JEW — usually taken to be offensive

He·be \'hē-bē\ *noun* [Latin, from Greek *Hēbē*]
: the Greek goddess of youth and a cupbearer to the gods

he·be·phre·nia \,hē-bə-'frē-nē-ə, -'fre-nē-\ *noun* [New Latin, irregular from Greek *hēbētēs* young adult (from *hēbē* youth) + English *-phrenia;* from the childish behavior which is often found with it] (1883)
: a form of schizophrenia characterized especially by incoherence, delusions lacking an underlying theme, and affect that is flat, inappropriate, or silly
— **he·be·phre·nic** \-'fre-nik, -'frē-nik\ *adjective or noun*

heb·e·tate \'he-bə-,tāt\ *transitive verb* **-tat·ed; -tat·ing** [Latin *hebetatus,* past participle of *hebetare,* from *hebet-, hebes* dull] (1574)
: to make dull or obtuse
— **heb·e·ta·tion** \,he-bə-'tā-shən\ *noun*

heb·e·tude \'he-bə-,tüd, -,tyüd\ *noun* [Late Latin *hebetudo,* from *hebēre* to be dull; akin to Latin *hebes* dull] (circa 1621)

: LETHARGY, DULLNESS
— **heb·e·tu·di·nous** \,he-bə-'tü-dᵊn-əs, -'tyü-\ *adjective*

He·bra·ic \hi-'brā-ik\ *adjective* [Middle English *Ebrayke,* from Late Latin *Hebraicus,* from Greek *Hebraikos,* from *Hebraios*] (14th century)
: of, relating to, or characteristic of the Hebrews or their language or culture
— **He·bra·i·cal·ly** \-'brā-ə-k(ə-)lē\ *adverb*

He·bra·ism \'hē-(,)brā-,i-zəm\ *noun* (1570)
1 : a characteristic feature of Hebrew occurring in another language
2 : the thought, spirit, or practice characteristic of the Hebrews
3 : a moral theory or emphasis attributed to the Hebrews

He·bra·ist \-,brā-ist\ *noun* (circa 1755)
: a specialist in Hebrew and Hebraic studies

He·bra·is·tic \,hē-brā-'is-tik\ *adjective* (1690)
1 : marked by Hebraisms
2 : HEBRAIC

he·bra·ize \'hē-brā-,īz\ *verb* **-ized; -iz·ing** *often capitalized* (1645)
intransitive verb
: to use Hebraisms
transitive verb
: to make Hebraic in character or form
— **he·bra·iza·tion** \,hē-,brā-ə-'zā-shən\ *noun, often capitalized*

He·brew \'hē-(,)brü\ *noun* [Middle English *Ebreu,* from Old French, from Late Latin *Hebraeus,* from Latin, adjective, from Greek *Hebraios,* from Aramaic *'Ebrai*] (13th century)
1 a : the Semitic language of the ancient Hebrews **b :** any of various later forms of this language
2 : a member of or descendant from one of a group of northern Semitic peoples including the Israelites; *especially* **:** ISRAELITE
— **Hebrew** *adjective*

He·brews \'hē-(,)brüz\ *noun plural but singular in construction*
: a theological treatise addressed to early Christians and included as a book in the New Testament — see BIBLE table

Hec·ate \'he-kə-tē, 'he-kət\ *noun* [Latin, from Greek *Hekatē*]
: a Greek goddess associated especially with the underworld, night, and witchcraft

hec·a·tomb \'he-kə-,tōm\ *noun* [Latin *hecatombe,* from Greek *hekatombē,* from *hekaton* hundred + *-bē;* akin to Greek *bous* cow — more at HUNDRED, COW] (circa 1592)
1 : an ancient Greek and Roman sacrifice of 100 oxen or cattle
2 : the sacrifice or slaughter of many victims

heck \'hek\ *noun* [euphemism] (1887)
: HELL ⟨a *heck* of a lot of money⟩

heck·le \'he-kəl\ *transitive verb* **heck·led; heck·ling** \-k(ə-)liŋ\ [Middle English *hekelen* to dress flax, scratch, from *heckele* hackle; akin to Old High German *hāko* hook — more at HOOK] (circa 1825)
: to harass and try to disconcert with questions, challenges, or gibes **:** BADGER
synonym see BAIT
— **heck·ler** \-k(ə-)lər\ *noun*

hect- *or* **hecto-** *combining form* [French, irregular from Greek *hekaton*]
: hundred ⟨*hectare*⟩

hect·are \'hek-,tar, -,ter, -,tär\ *noun* [French, from *hect-* + *are* ²are] (1810)
— see METRIC SYSTEM table

hec·tic \'hek-tik\ *adjective* [Middle English *etyk,* from Middle French *etique,* from Late Latin *hecticus,* from Greek *hektikos* habitual, consumptive, from *echein* to have — more at SCHEME] (14th century)
1 : of, relating to, or being a fluctuating but persistent fever (as in tuberculosis)
2 : having a hectic fever
3 : RED, FLUSHED
4 : characterized by activity, excitement, or confusion ⟨the *hectic* days before Christmas⟩
— **hec·ti·cal·ly** \-ti-k(ə-)lē\ *adverb*

hec·to·gram \'hek-tə-,gram\ *noun* [French *hectogramme,* from *hect-* + *gramme* gram] (1810)
— see METRIC SYSTEM table

hec·to·graph \-,graf\ *noun* [German *Hektograph,* from *hekto-* hect- + *-graph* -graph] (1880)
: a machine for making copies of a writing or drawing produced on a gelatin surface
— **hectograph** *transitive verb*

hec·to·li·ter \'hek-tə-,lē-tər\ *noun* [French *hectolitre,* from *hect-* + *litre* liter] (1810)
— see METRIC SYSTEM table

hec·to·me·ter \'hek-tə-,mē-tər, hek-'tä-mə-tər\ *noun* [French *hectomètre,* from *hect-* + *mètre* meter] (1810)
— see METRIC SYSTEM table

¹hec·tor \'hek-tər\ *noun* [Latin, from Greek *Hektōr*]
1 *capitalized* **:** a son of Priam, husband of Andromache, and Trojan champion slain by Achilles
2 : BULLY, BRAGGART ◆

²hector *verb* **hec·tored; hec·tor·ing** \-t(ə-)riŋ\ (1660)
intransitive verb
: to play the bully **:** SWAGGER
transitive verb
: to intimidate or harass by bluster or personal pressure
synonym see BAIT
— **hec·tor·ing·ly** \-t(ə-)riŋ-lē\ *adverb*

Hec·u·ba \'he-kyə-bə\ *noun* [Latin, from Greek *Hekabē*]
: the wife of Priam in Homer's *Iliad*

he'd \'hēd, ēd\ (circa 1600)
: he had **:** he would

hed·dle \'he-dᵊl\ *noun* [probably alteration of Middle English *helde,* from Old English *hefeld;* akin to Old Norse *hafald* heddle, Old English *hebban* to lift — more at HEAVE] (1513)
: one of the sets of parallel cords or wires that with their mounting compose the harness used to guide warp threads in a loom

he·der \'kā-dər, 'ke-\ *noun* [Yiddish *kheyder,* from Hebrew *hedher* room] (1882)
: an elementary Jewish school in which children are taught to read the Torah and other books in Hebrew

¹hedge \'hej\ *noun* [Middle English *hegge,* from Old English *hecg;* akin to Old English *haga* hedge, hawthorn] (before 12th century)
1 a : a fence or boundary formed by a dense row of shrubs or low trees **b :** BARRIER, LIMIT
2 : a means of protection or defense (as against financial loss)
3 : a calculatedly noncommittal or evasive statement

²hedge *verb* **hedged; hedg·ing** (14th century)

◇ **WORD HISTORY**
hector In Homer's account of the Trojan War, Hector, the great Trojan hero, is portrayed as the ideal warrior: fearless combatant, loving son and husband, steadfast friend. After his death at the hands of Achilles, he is buried with the highest honors. From the 14th century the name *Hector* has been used allusively in English literature for a valiant warrior. The word apparently acquired its pejorative sense in the latter half of the 17th century. At that time there appeared on the streets of London rowdy toughs who were known as *Hectors.* While they may have perceived themselves as gallant young blades, to the general populace they were blustering, swaggering bullies who brandished their swords, intimidated passersby, and engaged in vandalism. Thus *Hector* deteriorated into a synonym for a braggart and a bully. The conversion of *hector* into a verb soon followed.

transitive verb
1 : to enclose or protect with or as if with a hedge **:** ENCIRCLE
2 : to hem in or obstruct with or as if with a barrier **:** HINDER ⟨*hedged* about by special regulations and statutes —Sandi Rosenbloom⟩
3 : to protect oneself from losing or failing by a counterbalancing action ⟨*hedge* a bet⟩
intransitive verb
1 : to plant, form, or trim a hedge
2 : to evade the risk of commitment especially by leaving open a way of retreat **:** TRIM
3 : to protect oneself financially: as **a :** to buy or sell commodity futures as a protection against loss due to price fluctuation **b :** to minimize the risk of a bet
— **hedg·er** *noun*
— **hedg·ing·ly** \'he-jiŋ-lē\ *adverb*
³**hedge** *adjective* (14th century)
1 : of, relating to, or designed for a hedge
2 : born, living, or made near or as if near hedges **:** ROADSIDE
3 : INFERIOR 3
hedge fund *noun* (1967)
: an investing group usually in the form of a limited partnership that employs speculative techniques in the hope of obtaining large capital gains
hedge·hog \'hej-,hȯg, -,häg\ *noun* (15th century)

hedgehog 1a

1 a : any of a subfamily (Erinaceinae) of Old World nocturnal insectivores that have both hair and spines which they present outwardly by rolling themselves up when threatened **b :** any of several spiny mammals (as a porcupine)
2 a : a military defensive obstacle (as of barbed wire) **b :** a well-fortified military stronghold
hedge·hop \-,häp\ *intransitive verb* [back-formation from *hedgehopper*] (1926)
: to fly an airplane close to the ground and rise over obstacles as they appear
— **hedge·hop·per** *noun*
hedge·pig \-,pig\ *noun* (1605)
: HEDGEHOG
hedge·row \-,rō\ *noun* (before 12th century)
: a row of shrubs or trees enclosing or separating fields
he·don·ic \hi-'dä-nik\ *adjective* (1656)
1 : of, relating to, or characterized by pleasure
2 : of, relating to, or characterized by hedonism
— **he·don·i·cal·ly** \-ni-k(ə-)lē\ *adverb*
he·do·nism \'hē-d°n-,i-zəm\ *noun* [Greek *hēdonē* pleasure; akin to Greek *hēdys* sweet — more at SWEET] (1856)
1 : the doctrine that pleasure or happiness is the sole or chief good in life
2 : a way of life based on or suggesting the principles of hedonism
— **he·do·nist** \-d°n-ist\ *noun*
— **he·do·nis·tic** \,hē-d°n-'is-tik\ *adjective*
— **he·do·nis·ti·cal·ly** \-ti-k(ə-)lē\ *adverb*
-he·dral \'hē-drəl\ *adjective combining form* [New Latin *-hedron*]
: having (such) a surface or (such or so many) surfaces ⟨di*hedral*⟩
-he·dron \'hē-drən\ *noun combining form, plural* **-hedrons** *or* **-he·dra** \-drə\ [New Latin, from Greek *-edron*, from *hedra* seat — more at SIT]
: crystal or geometrical figure having a (specified) form or number of surfaces ⟨penta*hedron*⟩ ⟨trapezo*hedron*⟩
hee·bie–jee·bies \,hē-bē-'jē-bēz\ *noun plural* [coined by Billy DeBeck (died 1942) American cartoonist] (1923)
: JITTERS, CREEPS

¹**heed** \'hēd\ *verb* [Middle English, from Old English *hēdan*; akin to Old High German *huota* guard, Old English *hōd* hood] (before 12th century)
intransitive verb
: to pay attention
transitive verb
: to give consideration or attention to **:** MIND ⟨*heed* what he says⟩ ⟨*heed* the call⟩
²**heed** *noun* (14th century)
: ATTENTION, NOTICE
heed·ful \'hēd-fəl\ *adjective* (1548)
: taking heed **:** ATTENTIVE ⟨*heedful* of what they were doing⟩
— **heed·ful·ly** \-fə-lē\ *adverb*
— **heed·ful·ness** *noun*
heed·less \-ləs\ *adjective* (1579)
: not taking heed **:** INCONSIDERATE, THOUGHTLESS ⟨*heedless* follies of unbridled youth —John DeBruyn⟩
— **heed·less·ly** *adverb*
— **heed·less·ness** *noun*
hee–haw \'hē-,hȯ, -'hȯ\ *noun* [imitative] (1815)
1 : the bray of a donkey
2 : a loud rude laugh **:** GUFFAW
— **hee–haw** *intransitive verb*
¹**heel** \'hē(ə)l\ *noun* [Middle English, from Old English *hēla*; akin to Old Norse *hæll* heel, Old English *hōh* — more at HOCK] (before 12th century)
1 a : the back of the human foot below the ankle and behind the arch **b :** the part of the hind limb of other vertebrates that is homologous with the human heel
2 : an anatomical structure suggestive of the human heel; *especially* **:** the part of the palm of the hand nearest the wrist
3 : one of the crusty ends of a loaf of bread
4 a : the part (as of a shoe) that covers the human heel **b :** a solid attachment of a shoe or boot forming the back of the sole under the heel of the foot
5 : a rear, low, or bottom part: as **a :** the after end of a ship's keel or the lower end of a mast **b :** the base of a tuber or cutting of a plant used for propagation **c :** the base of a ladder
6 : a contemptible person
— **heel·less** \'hē(ə)l-ləs\ *adjective*
— **by the heels :** in a tight grip
— **down at heel** *or* **down at the heel :** in or into a run-down or shabby condition
— **on the heels of :** immediately following
— **to heel 1 :** close behind **2 :** into agreement or line
— **under heel :** under control or subjection
²**heel** (1605)
transitive verb
1 a : to furnish with a heel **b :** to supply especially with money
2 a : to exert pressure on, propel, or strike with the heel ⟨*heeled* her horse⟩ **b :** to urge (as a lagging animal) by following closely or by nipping at the heels ⟨dogs *heeling* cattle⟩
intransitive verb
: to move along at someone's heels
³**heel** *verb* [alteration of Middle English *heellen*, from Old English *hieldan*; akin to Old High German *hald* inclined, Lithuanian *šalis* side, region] (1575)
intransitive verb
: to lean to one side **:** TIP; *especially, of a boat or ship* **:** to lean temporarily (as from the action of wind or waves) — compare LIST
transitive verb
: to cause (a boat) to heel
⁴**heel** *noun* (1760)
: a tilt (as of a boat) to one side; *also* **:** the extent of such a tilt
heel–and–toe \,hē-lən-'tō\ *adjective* (1827)
: marked by a stride in which the heel of one foot touches the ground before the toe of the other foot leaves it ⟨*heel-and-toe* walking⟩
heel·ball \'hē(ə)l-,bȯl\ *noun* (1822)

: a composition of wax and lampblack used by shoemakers for polishing and by antiquarians for making rubbings of inscriptions
heel·er \'hē-lər\ *noun* (1665)
1 a : one that heels **b :** AUSTRALIAN CATTLE DOG
2 a : a henchman of a local political boss **b :** a worker for a local party organization; *especially* **:** WARD HEELER
heel fly *noun* (1878)
: CATTLE GRUB
heel·piece \'hē(ə)l-,pēs\ *noun* (1709)
: a piece designed for or forming the heel (as of a shoe)
heel·tap \-,tap\ *noun* (1780)
: a small quantity of alcoholic beverage remaining (as in a glass after drinking)
¹**heft** \'heft\ *noun* [from *heave*, after such pairs as *weave : weft*] (15th century)
1 a : WEIGHT, HEAVINESS **b :** IMPORTANCE, INFLUENCE
2 *archaic* **:** the greater part of something **:** BULK
²**heft** *transitive verb* (1661)
1 : to heave up **:** HOIST
2 : to test the weight of by lifting ⟨*hefting* the rod . . . to get the feel of it —*Consumer Reports*⟩
hefty \'hef-tē\ *adjective* **heft·i·er; -est** (1867)
1 : quite heavy
2 a : marked by bigness, bulk, and usually strength ⟨a *hefty* football player⟩ **b :** POWERFUL, MIGHTY **c :** impressively large **:** SUBSTANTIAL ⟨*hefty* portions⟩
— **heft·i·ly** \-tə-lē\ *adverb*
— **heft·i·ness** \-tē-nəs\ *noun*
he·gari \hi-'gar-ē, -'gar-ə, -'ger-; 'hī-,gir\ *noun* [Arabic dialect (Sudan) *hegiri*] (1919)
: any of several Sudanese grain sorghums having chalky white seeds including one grown in the southwestern U.S.
¹**He·ge·li·an** \hā-'gā-lē-ən, hi-\ *adjective* (1838)
: of, relating to, or characteristic of Hegel, his philosophy, or his dialectic method
²**Hegelian** *noun* (1843)
: a follower of Hegel **:** an adherent of Hegelianism
He·ge·li·an·ism \-lē-ə-,ni-zəm\ *noun* (1846)
: the philosophy of Hegel that places ultimate reality in ideas rather than in things and that uses dialectic to comprehend an absolute idea behind phenomena
he·ge·mo·ny \hi-'je-mə-nē, -'ge-; 'he-jə-,mō-nē\ *noun* [Greek *hēgemonia*, from *hēgemōn* leader, from *hēgeisthai* to lead — more at SEEK] (1567)
: preponderant influence or authority over others **:** DOMINATION
— **heg·e·mon·ic** \,he-jə-'mä-nik, ,he-gə-\ *adjective*
he·gi·ra *also* **he·ji·ra** \hi-'jī-rə, 'he-jə-rə\ *noun* [the *Hegira*, flight of Muhammad from Mecca in A.D. 622, from Medieval Latin, from Arabic *hijrah*, literally, flight] (1753)
: a journey especially when undertaken to escape from a dangerous or undesirable situation **:** EXODUS
Hei·del·berg man \,hī-d°l-,bərg-, -,berg-\ *noun* [*Heidelberg*, Germany] (1920)
: an early Pleistocene man known from a massive fossilized jaw with distinctly human dentition and now classified with the pithecanthropines
heif·er \'he-fər\ *noun* [Middle English *hayfare*, from Old English *hēahfore*] (before 12th century)
: a young cow; *especially* **:** one that has not had a calf

\ə\ abut	\°\ kitten	\ər\ further	\a\ ash \ā\ ace
\ä\ mop, mar	\aů\ out	\ch\ chin	\e\ bet \ē\ easy
\g\ go	\i\ hit	\ī\ ice	\j\ job \ŋ\ sing \ō\ go
\ȯ\ law	\ȯi\ boy	\th\ thin	\th\ the \ü\ loot \ů\ foot
\y\ yet	\zh\ vision	*see also* Guide to Pronunciation	

heigh–ho \'hī-'hō, 'hā-\ *interjection* (circa 1553)
— used typically to express boredom, weariness, or sadness or sometimes as a cry of encouragement

height \'hīt, ÷'hītth\ *noun* [Middle English *heighthe*, from Old English *hīehthu*; akin to Old High German *hōhida* height, Old English *hēah* high] (before 12th century)
1 a : the highest part **: SUMMIT b :** highest or most advanced point **: ZENITH** ⟨at the *height* of his powers⟩
2 a : the distance from the bottom to the top of something standing upright **b :** the extent of elevation above a level
3 : the condition of being tall or high
4 a : an extent of land rising to a considerable degree above the surrounding country **b :** a high point or position
5 *obsolete* **:** an advanced social rank ☆ ◇

height·en \'hī-t°n\ *verb* **height·ened; height·en·ing** \'hīt-niŋ, 'hī-t°n-iŋ\ (1523)
transitive verb
1 a : to increase the amount or degree of **: AUGMENT b :** to make brighter or more intense **: DEEPEN c :** to bring out more strongly **:** point up **d :** to make more acute **: SHARPEN**
2 a : to raise high or higher **: ELEVATE b :** to raise above the ordinary or trite
3 *obsolete* **: ELATE**
intransitive verb
1 *archaic* **: GROW, RISE**
2 a : to become great or greater in amount, degree, or extent **b :** to become brighter or more intense

height to paper (1771)
: the height of printing type standardized at 0.9186 inch (2.333 centimeters) in English-speaking countries

Heim·lich maneuver \'hīm-lik-\ *noun* [Henry J. *Heimlich* (born 1920) American surgeon] (1974)
: the manual application of sudden upward pressure on the upper abdomen of a choking victim to force a foreign object from the windpipe

hei·nie \'hī-nē\ *noun* [alteration of ²*hinder*] (1940)
slang **: BUTTOCKS**

hei·nous \'hā-nəs\ *adjective* [Middle English, from Middle French *haineus*, from *haine* hate, from *hair* to hate, of Germanic origin; akin to Old High German *haz* hate — more at HATE] (14th century)
: hatefully or shockingly evil **: ABOMINABLE**
— **hei·nous·ly** *adverb*
— **hei·nous·ness** *noun*

¹heir \'ar, 'er\ *noun* [Middle English, from Old French, from Latin *hered-, heres*; akin to Greek *chēros* bereaved] (13th century)
1 : one who inherits or is entitled to inherit property
2 : one who inherits or is entitled to succeed to a hereditary rank, title, or office ⟨*heir* to the throne⟩
3 : one who receives or is entitled to receive some endowment or quality from a parent or predecessor
— **heir·less** \-ləs\ *adjective*
— **heir·ship** \-,ship\ *noun*
²heir *transitive verb* (14th century)
chiefly dialect **: INHERIT**

heir apparent *noun, plural* **heirs apparent** (14th century)
1 : an heir whose right to an inheritance is indefeasible in law if he survives the legal ancestor
2 : HEIR PRESUMPTIVE
3 : one whose succession especially to a position or role appears certain under existing circumstances

heir at law (1729)
: an heir in whom an intestate's real property is vested by operation of law

heir·ess \'ar-əs, 'er-\ *noun* (1607)

: a female heir; *especially* **:** a female heir to great wealth

heir·loom \'ar-,lüm, 'er-\ *noun* [Middle English *heirlome*, from *heir* + *lome* implement — more at LOOM] (15th century)
1 : a piece of property that descends to the heir as an inseparable part of an inheritance of real property
2 : something of special value handed on from one generation to another

heir presumptive *noun, plural* **heirs presumptive** (circa 1737)
: an heir whose legal right to an inheritance may be defeated (as by the birth of a nearer relative)

Hei·sen·berg uncertainty principle \'hī-z°n-,bərg-, -,bərk-\ *noun* [Werner *Heisenberg*] (1939)
: UNCERTAINTY PRINCIPLE — called also *Heisenberg's uncertainty principle*

¹heist \'hīst\ *transitive verb* [variant of ¹*hoist*] (1865)
1 *chiefly dialect* **: HOIST**
2 *slang* **a :** to commit armed robbery on **b : STEAL 1a**
²heist *noun* (1930)
slang **:** armed robbery **: HOLDUP;** *also* **: THEFT**

Hel \'hel\ *noun* [Old Norse]
: the Norse goddess of the dead and queen of the underworld

hela cell \'he-lə-\ *noun, often H&1stL capitalized* [*Henrietta Lacks* (died 1951) patient from whom the cells were taken] (1953)
: a cell of a continuously cultured strain isolated from a human uterine cervical carcinoma in 1951 and used in biomedical research especially to culture viruses

held *past and past participle of* HOLD

hel·den·te·nor \'hel-dən-,tā-,nor, -,nor, -,te-nər\ *noun, often capitalized* [German, from *Held* hero + *Tenor* tenor] (circa 1903)
: a tenor with a powerful dramatic voice well suited to heroic (as Wagnerian) roles

Helen of Troy \,he-lə-nəv-'tròi\
: the wife of Menelaus whose abduction by Paris brings about the Trojan War

¹heli- *or* **helio-** *combining form* [Latin, from Greek *hēli-, hēlio-*, from *hēlios* — more at SOLAR]
: sun ⟨*heliocentric*⟩
²heli- *combining form* [by shortening]
: helicopter ⟨*heliport*⟩

he·li·a·cal \hi-'lī-ə-kəl\ *adjective* [Late Latin *heliacus*, from Greek *hēliakos*, from *hēlios*] (1545)
: relating to or near the sun — used especially of the last setting of a star before and its first rising after invisibility due to conjunction with the sun
— **he·li·a·cal·ly** \-k(ə-)lē\ *adverb*

helic- *or* **helico-** *combining form* [Greek *helik-, heliko-*, from *helik-, helix* spiral — more at HELIX]
: spiral ⟨*helical*⟩

he·li·cal \'he-li-kəl, 'hē-\ *adjective* (1591)
: of, relating to, or having the form of a helix; *broadly* **: SPIRAL 1a**
— **he·li·cal·ly** \-k(ə-)lē\ *adverb*

he·li·coid \'he-lə-,kòid, 'hē-\ *or* **he·li·coi·dal** \,he-lə-'kòi-d°l, ,hē-\ *adjective* (1704)
1 : forming or arranged in a spiral
2 : having the form of a flat coil or flattened spiral ⟨*helicoid* snail shell⟩

hel·i·con \'he-lə-,kän, -i-kən\ *noun* [probably from Greek *helik-, helix* + English -*on* (as in *bombardon*); from its tube's forming a spiral encircling the player's body] (1875)
: a large circular tuba similar to a sousaphone but lacking an adjustable bell

¹he·li·cop·ter \'he-lə-,käp-tər, 'hē-\ *noun* [French *hélicoptère*, from Greek *heliko-* + *pteron* wing — more at FEATHER] (1887)
: an aircraft whose lift is derived from the aerodynamic forces acting on one or more powered rotors turning about substantially vertical axes

²helicopter (1952)
intransitive verb
: to travel by helicopter
transitive verb
: to transport by helicopter

helicon

he·lio·cen·tric \,hē-lē-ō-'sen-trik\ *adjective* (1685)
1 : referred to or measured from the sun's center or appearing as if seen from it
2 : having or relating to the sun as center — compare GEOCENTRIC

he·lio·graph \-,graf\ *noun* [International Scientific Vocabulary] (1877)
: an apparatus for telegraphing by means of the sun's rays flashed from a mirror
— **heliograph** *transitive verb*

he·lio·graph·ic \,hē-lē-ə-'gra-fik\ *adjective* (1706)
: measured on the sun's disk ⟨*heliographic* latitude⟩

he·li·ol·a·try \,hē-lē-'ä-lə-trē\ *noun* (circa 1828)
: sun worship
— **he·li·ol·a·trous** \-trəs\ *adjective*

he·li·om·e·ter \,hē-lē-'ä-mə-tər\ *noun* [French *héliomètre*, from *hélio-* ¹*heli-* + *-mètre* -meter] (1753)
: a visual telescope that has a divided objective designed for measuring the apparent diameter of the sun but also used for measuring angles between celestial bodies or between points on the moon
— **he·lio·met·ric** \,hē-lē-ō-'me-trik\ *adjective*
— **he·lio·met·ri·cal·ly** \-tri-k(ə-)lē\ *adverb*

He·li·os \'hē-lē-əs, -(,)ōs\ *noun* [Greek *Hēlios*]

: the god of the sun in Greek mythology — compare SOL

he·lio·stat \'hē-lē-ə-ˌstat\ *noun* [New Latin *heliostata,* from ¹*heli-* + Greek *-statēs* -stat] (1747)

: an instrument consisting of a mirror mounted on an axis moved by clockwork by which a sunbeam is steadily reflected in one direction

he·lio·trope \'hē-lē-ə-ˌtrōp, 'hēl-yə-, *British also* 'hel-yə-\ *noun* [Latin *heliotropium,* from Greek *hēliotropion,* from *hēlio-* ¹*heli-* + *tropos* turn; from its flowers' turning toward the sun — more at TROPE] (circa 1626)

1 : any of a genus (*Heliotropium*) of herbs or shrubs of the borage family — compare GARDEN HELIOTROPE

2 : BLOODSTONE

3 : a variable color averaging a moderate to reddish purple

heliotrope 1

he·li·ot·ro·pism \ˌhē-lē-'ä-trə-ˌpi-zəm\ *noun* (circa 1854)

: phototropism in which sunlight is the orienting stimulus

— **he·lio·tro·pic** \-lē-ə-'trō-pik, -'trä-\ *adjective*

he·lio·zo·an \ˌhē-lē-ə-'zō-ən\ *noun* [New Latin *Heliozoa,* from ¹*heli-* + *-zoa*] (circa 1889)

: any of a class (Heliozoa) of free-living holozoic usually freshwater rhizopod protozoans that reproduce by binary fission or budding

he·li·pad \'he-lə-ˌpad, 'hē-\ *noun* (1960)

: HELIPORT

he·li·port \-ˌpōrt, -ˌpȯrt\ *noun* (1948)

: a landing and takeoff place for a helicopter

he·li·ski·ing \-ˌskē-iŋ\ *noun* (1976)

: downhill skiing on remote mountains reached by helicopter

he·li·um \'hē-lē-əm, 'hēl-yəm\ *noun* [New Latin, from Greek *hēlios*] (1872)

: a light colorless nonflammable gaseous element found especially in natural gases and used chiefly for inflating airships and balloons, for filling incandescent lamps, and for cryogenic research — see ELEMENT table

he·lix \'hē-liks\ *noun, plural* **he·li·ces** \'he-lə-ˌsēz, 'hē-\ *or* **he·lix·es** \'hē-lik-səz\ [Latin, from Greek; akin to Greek *eilyein* to roll, wrap — more at VOLUBLE] (1563)

1 : something spiral in form: as **a :** an ornamental volute **b :** a coil formed by winding wire around a uniform tube

2 : the incurved rim of the external ear

3 : a curve traced on a cylinder or cone by the rotation of a point crossing its right sections at a constant oblique angle; *broadly* : SPIRAL 1b

hell \'hel\ *noun* [Middle English, from Old English; akin to Old English *helan* to conceal, Old High German *helan,* Latin *celare,* Greek *kalyptein*] (before 12th century)

1 a (1) : a nether world in which the dead continue to exist : HADES (2) : the nether realm of the devil and the demons in which the damned suffer everlasting punishment — often used in curses ⟨go to *hell*⟩ or as a generalized term of abuse ⟨the *hell* with it⟩ **b** *Christian Science* : ERROR 2b, SIN

2 a : a place or state of misery, torment, or wickedness ⟨war is *hell* —W. T. Sherman⟩ **b** : a place or state of turmoil or destruction ⟨all *hell* broke loose⟩ **c :** a severe scolding ⟨got *hell* for coming in late⟩ **d :** unrestrained fun or sportiveness ⟨the kids were full of *hell*⟩ — often used in the phrase *for the hell of it* especially to suggest action on impulse or without a serious motive ⟨decided to go for the *hell* of it⟩

3 *archaic* : a tailor's receptacle

4 — used as an interjection ⟨*hell,* I don't know!⟩ or as an intensive ⟨hurts like *hell*⟩ ⟨funny as *hell*⟩; often used in the phrase *hell of*

a ⟨it was one *hell* of a good fight⟩ or *hell out of* ⟨scared the *hell* out of him⟩ or with *the* or *in* ⟨moved way the *hell* up north⟩ ⟨what in *hell* is wrong, now?⟩

— **from hell :** being the worst or most dreadful of its kind

— **hell on :** very hard on or destructive to ⟨the constant traveling is *hell on* your digestive system⟩

— **hell or high water :** difficulties of whatever kind or size ⟨will stand by her convictions come *hell or high water*⟩

— **hell to pay :** dire consequences ⟨if he's late there'll be *hell to pay*⟩

he'll \'hē(ə)l, 'hil, ēl, il\ (1588)

: he will : he shall

hel·la·cious \he-'lā-shəs\ *adjective* [*hell* + *-acious* (as in *audacious*)] (1943)

1 : exceptionally powerful or violent

2 : remarkably good

3 : extremely difficult

4 : extraordinarily large

— **hel·la·cious·ly** *adverb*

hell·ben·der \'hel-ˌben-dər\ *noun* (1812)

: a large aquatic usually gray salamander (*Cryptobranchus alleganiensis*) of the Ohio valley region

hell-bent \-ˌbent\ *adjective* (1835)

: stubbornly and often recklessly determined or intent ⟨*hell-bent* on winning⟩

— **hell-bent** *adverb*

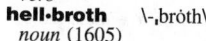

hellbender

hell·broth \-ˌbrȯth\ *noun* (1605)

: a brew for working black magic

hell·cat \-ˌkat\ *noun* (circa 1605)

1 : WITCH 2

2 : a violently temperamental person; *especially* : an ill-tempered woman

hel·le·bore \'he-lə-ˌbōr, -ˌbȯr\ *noun* [Middle English *elebre,* from Latin *elleborus, helleborus,* from Greek *helleboros*] (15th century)

1 : any of a genus (*Helleborus*) of poisonous herbs of the buttercup family having showy flowers with petaloid sepals; *also* : the dried rhizome or an extract or powder of this formerly used in medicine

2 : a poisonous herb (genus *Veratrum*) of the lily family; *also* : the dried rhizome of a hellebore (*Veratrum album* or *V. viride*) or a powder or extract of this containing alkaloids used as a cardiac and respiratory depressant and as an insecticide

Hel·lene \'he-ˌlēn\ *noun* [Greek *Hellēn*] (1662)

: GREEK 1a

¹Hel·len·ic \he-'le-nik, hə-\ *adjective* (1644)

: of or relating to Greece, its people, or its language; *specifically* : of or relating to ancient Greek history, culture, or art before the Hellenistic period

²Hellenic *noun* (1847)

: GREEK 2a

Hel·le·nism \'he-lə-ˌni-zəm\ *noun* (1609)

1 : GRECISM 1

2 : devotion to or imitation of ancient Greek thought, customs, or styles

3 : Greek civilization especially as modified in the Hellenistic period by oriental influences

4 : a body of humanistic and classical ideals associated with ancient Greece and including reason, the pursuit of knowledge and the arts, moderation, civic responsibility, and bodily development

Hel·le·nist \-nist\ *noun* (1613)

1 : a person living in Hellenistic times who was Greek in language, outlook, and way of life but was not Greek in ancestry; *especially* : a hellenized Jew

2 : a specialist in the language or culture of ancient Greece

Hel·le·nis·tic \ˌhe-lə-'nis-tik\ *adjective* (circa 1706)

1 : of or relating to Greek history, culture, or art after Alexander the Great

2 : of or relating to the Hellenists

— **Hel·le·nis·ti·cal·ly** \-ti-k(ə-)lē\ *adverb*

hel·le·nize \'he-lə-ˌnīz\ *verb* **-nized; -nizing** *often capitalized* (1613)

intransitive verb

: to become Greek or Hellenistic

transitive verb

: to make Greek or Hellenistic in form or culture

— **hel·le·ni·za·tion** \ˌhe-lə-nə-'zā-shən\ *noun, often capitalized*

hell·er \'he-lər\ *noun* (circa 1895)

: HELLION

hel·leri \'he-lə-ˌrī, -(ˌ)rē\ *noun, plural* **-ler·ies** [New Latin (specific epithet of *Xiphophorus helleri*), from C. *Heller,* 20th century tropical fish collector] (1931)

1 : SWORDTAIL

2 : any of various brightly colored aquarium fishes developed by hybridization of swordtails and platys

hell·fire \'hel-ˌfīr\ *noun* (before 12th century)

: the eternal fire of hell that tortures sinners

— **hellfire** *adjective*

¹hell-for-leather *adverb* (1889)

: in a hell-for-leather manner : at full speed ⟨rode *hell-for-leather* down the trail⟩

²hell-for-leather *adjective* (1920)

: marked by determined recklessness, great speed, or lack of restraint ⟨a cocky, *hell-for-leather* fighting man —H. H. Martin⟩

hell·gram·mite \'hel-grə-ˌmīt\ *noun* [origin unknown] (1866)

: a carnivorous aquatic North American insect larva that is the young form of a dobsonfly (especially *Corydalis cornutus*) and is used for fish bait

hell·hole \'hel-ˌhōl\ *noun* (1866)

: a place of extreme misery or squalor

hell·hound \-ˌhau̇nd\ *noun* (before 12th century)

1 : a dog represented in mythology as a guardian of the underworld

2 : a fiendish person

hel·lion \'hel-yən\ *noun* [probably alteration (influenced by *hell*) of *hallion* (scamp)] (1787)

: a troublesome or mischievous person

hell·ish \'he-lish\ *adjective* (circa 1530)

: of, resembling, or befitting hell; *broadly* : TERRIBLE

— **hell·ish·ly** *adverb*

— **hell·ish·ness** *noun*

hel·lo \hə-'lō, he-\ *noun, plural* **hellos** [alteration of *hollo*] (1889)

: an expression or gesture of greeting — used interjectionally in greeting, in answering the telephone, or to express surprise

hell-rais·er \'hel-ˌrā-zər\ *noun* (1914)

: one given to wild, boisterous, or intemperate behavior

— **hell-rais·ing** \-ˌrā-ziŋ\ *noun or adjective*

¹helm \'helm\ *noun* [Middle English, from Old English] (before 12th century)

: HELMET 1

²helm *transitive verb* (before 12th century)

: to cover or furnish with a helmet

³helm *noun* [Middle English *helme,* from Old English *helma;* akin to Old High German *helmo* tiller] (before 12th century)

1 a : a lever or wheel controlling the rudder of a ship for steering; *broadly* : the entire apparatus for steering a ship **b :** position of the helm with respect to the amidships position ⟨turn the *helm* hard alee⟩

2 : a position of control : HEAD ⟨a new dean is at the *helm* of the medical school⟩

\ə\ abut	\ᵊ\ kitten	\ər\ further	\a\ ash	\ā\ ace	
\ä\ mop, mar	\au̇\ out	\ch\ chin	\e\ bet	\ē\ easy	
\g\ go	\i\ hit	\ī\ ice	\j\ job	\ŋ\ sing	\ō\ go
\ȯ\ law	\ȯi\ boy	\th\ thin	\t͟h\ the	\ü\ loot	\u̇\ foot
\y\ yet	\zh\ vision		*see also* Guide to Pronunciation		

⁴helm *transitive verb* (1603)
: to direct with or as if with a helm : STEER

hel·met \'hel-mət\ *noun* [Middle French, diminutive of *helme* helmet, of Germanic origin; akin to Old English *helm* helmet, Old High German *helan* to conceal — more at HELL] (15th century)
1 : a covering or enclosing headpiece of ancient or medieval armor — see ARMOR illustration
2 : any of various protective head coverings usually made of a hard material to resist impact
3 : something resembling a helmet
— **hel·met·ed** \-mə-təd\ *adjective*
— **hel·met·like** \-mət-,līk\ *adjective*

hel·minth \'hel-,min(t)th\ *noun* [Greek *helminth-, helmis*] (1852)
: a parasitic worm (as a tapeworm, liver fluke, ascarid, or leech); *especially* : an intestinal worm
— **hel·min·thic** \hel-'min(t)-thik\ *adjective*

hel·min·thi·a·sis \hel-mən-'thī-ə-səs\ *noun, plural* **-a·ses** \-ə-,sēz\ [New Latin] (circa 1811)
: infestation with or disease caused by parasitic worms

hel·min·thol·o·gy \-'thä-lə-jē\ *noun* (1819)
: a branch of zoology concerned with helminths; *especially* : the study of parasitic worms

helms·man \'helmz-mən\ *noun* (1627)
: the person at the helm : STEERSMAN
— **helms·man·ship** \-,ship\ *noun*

he·lo \'hē-(,)lō\ *noun, plural* **helos** [by shortening & alteration] (1968)
: HELICOPTER

hel·ot \'he-lət\ *noun* [Latin *Helotes,* plural, from Greek *Heilōtes*] (1579)
1 *capitalized* : a member of a class of serfs in ancient Sparta
2 : SERF, SLAVE
— **hel·ot·ry** \'he-lə-trē\ *noun*

hel·ot·ism \'he-lə-,ti-zəm\ *noun* (circa 1900)
: the physiological relation existing in a lichen where a fungus appears to control an alga

¹help \'help; *Southern often* 'hep *also* 'heəp\ *verb* [Middle English, from Old English *helpan*; akin to Old High German *helfan* to help, and perhaps to Lithuanian *šelpti*] (before 12th century)
transitive verb
1 : to give assistance or support to ⟨*help* a child with homework⟩
2 a : to make more pleasant or bearable : IMPROVE, RELIEVE ⟨bright curtains will *help* the room⟩ ⟨took an aspirin to *help* her headache⟩ **b** *archaic* : RESCUE, SAVE
3 a : to be of use to : BENEFIT **b** : to further the advancement of : PROMOTE
4 a : to change for the better **b** : to refrain from : AVOID **c** : to keep from occurring : PREVENT ⟨they couldn't *help* the accident⟩ **d** : to restrain (oneself) from doing something ⟨knew they shouldn't go but couldn't *help* themselves⟩
5 : to serve with food or drink especially at a meal ⟨told the guests to *help* themselves⟩
6 : to appropriate something for (oneself) ⟨*helped* himself to the car keys⟩
intransitive verb
1 : give assistance or support — often used with *out*
2 : to be of use or benefit
synonym see IMPROVE
— **so help me** : upon my word : believe it or not

²help *noun* (before 12th century)
1 : AID, ASSISTANCE
2 : a source of aid ⟨printed *helps* to the memory —C. S. Braden⟩
3 : REMEDY, RELIEF ⟨there was no *help* for it⟩
4 a : one who serves or assists another (as in housework) : HELPER **b** : EMPLOYEE ⟨*help* wanted⟩ — often used collectively ⟨the hired *help*⟩

help·er *noun* (13th century)

: one that helps; *especially* : a relatively unskilled worker who assists a skilled worker usually by manual labor

helper T cell *noun* (1976)
: a T cell that participates in an immune response by recognizing a foreign antigen and secreting lymphokines to activate T cell and B cell proliferation, that usually carries CD4 molecular markers on its cell surface, and that is reduced to 20 percent or less of normal numbers in AIDS — called also *helper cell, T-helper cell*

help·ful \'help-fəl; *Southern often* 'hep- *also* 'heəp-\ *adjective* (14th century)
: of service or assistance : USEFUL
— **help·ful·ly** \-fə-lē\ *adverb*
— **help·ful·ness** *noun*

help·ing *noun* (1883)
: a portion of food : SERVING

helping hand *noun* (15th century)
: HAND 8a

helping verb *noun* (1711)
: an auxiliary verb

help·less \'hel-pləs; *Southern often* 'hep-ləs *also* 'heəp-\ *adjective* (before 12th century)
1 : lacking protection or support : DEFENSELESS
2 a : marked by an inability to act or react ⟨the crowd looked on in *helpless* horror —*Current Biography*⟩ **b** : not able to be controlled or restrained ⟨*helpless* laughter⟩
— **help·less·ly** *adverb*
— **help·less·ness** *noun*

help·mate \'help-,māt; *Southern often* 'hep- *also* 'heəp-\ *noun* [by folk etymology from *helpmeet*] (circa 1714)
: one who is a companion and helper; *especially* : WIFE

help·meet \-,mēt\ *noun* [²help + meet, adjective] (1673)
: HELPMATE

¹hel·ter–skel·ter \,hel-tər-'skel-tər\ *adverb* [perhaps from Middle English *skelten* to come, go] (1593)
1 : in undue haste, confusion, or disorder ⟨ran *helter-skelter,* getting in each other's way —F. V. W. Mason⟩
2 : in a haphazard manner

²helter–skelter *noun* (1713)
1 : a disorderly confusion : TURMOIL
2 *British* : a spiral slide around a tower at an amusement park

³helter–skelter *adjective* (1785)
1 : confusedly hurried : PRECIPITATE
2 : marked by a lack of order or plan : HAPHAZARD ⟨the *helter-skelter* arrangement of the papers, all mussed and frayed —Jean Stafford⟩

helve \'helv\ *noun* [Middle English, from Old English *hielfe;* probably akin to Old English *helma* helm] (before 12th century)
: a handle of a tool or weapon : HAFT

Hel·ve·tii \hel-'vē-shē-,ī\ *noun plural* [Latin] (1889)
: an early Celtic people in the area of western Switzerland at the time of Julius Caesar

¹hem \'hem\ *noun* [Middle English, from Old English; akin to Middle High German *hemmen* to hem in, Armenian *kamel* to press] (before 12th century)
1 : a border of a cloth article doubled back and stitched down
2 : RIM, MARGIN ⟨bright green *hem* of reeds about the ponds —R. M. Lockley⟩

²hem *verb* **hemmed; hem·ming** (14th century)
transitive verb
1 a : to finish with a hem **b** : BORDER, EDGE
2 : to surround in a restrictive manner : CONFINE — usually used with *in* ⟨*hemmed* in by enemy troops⟩
intransitive verb
: to make a hem in sewing
— **hem·mer** *noun*

³hem \'hem\ *intransitive verb* **hemmed; hem·ming** (15th century)
1 : to utter the sound represented by *hem* ⟨*hemmed* and hawed before answering⟩

2 : EQUIVOCATE ⟨the administration *hemmed* and hawed over the students' demands⟩

⁴hem *usually read as* 'hem\ *interjection* [imitative]
— often used to indicate a vocalized pause in speaking

hem- *or* **hemo-** *combining form* [Middle French *hemo-,* from Latin *haem-, haemo-,* from Greek *haim-, haimo-,* from *haima*]
: blood ⟨*hem*agglutination⟩ ⟨*hemo*flagellate⟩

hema- *combining form* [New Latin, from Greek *haima*]
: HEM- ⟨*hema*cytometer⟩

he·ma·cy·tom·e·ter \,hē-mə-sī-'tä-mə-tər\ *noun* (1877)
: an instrument for counting blood cells

hem·ag·glu·ti·na·tion \,hē-mə-,glü-tᵊn-'ā-shən\ *noun* (1907)
: agglutination of red blood cells
— **hem·ag·glu·ti·nate** \-'glü-tᵊn-,āt\ *transitive verb*

hem·ag·glu·ti·nin \-'glü-tᵊn-ən\ *noun* [International Scientific Vocabulary] (circa 1903)
: an agglutinin (as an antibody or viral capsid protein) that causes hemagglutination

he–man \'hē-,man\ *noun* (1832)
: a strong virile man

hem·an·gi·o·ma \,hē-,man-jē-'ō-mə\ *noun* [New Latin, from *hem-* + *angioma*] (circa 1890)
: a usually benign tumor made up of blood vessels that typically occurs as a purplish or reddish slightly elevated area of skin

hemat- *or* **hemato-** *combining form* [Latin *haemat-, haemato-,* from Greek *haimat-, haimato-,* from *haimat-, haima*]
: HEM- ⟨*hemato*genous⟩

he·ma·tin \'hē-mə-tən\ *noun* (1845)
: a brownish black or bluish black derivative $C_{34}H_{33}N_4O_5Fe$ of oxidized heme; *also* : any of several similar compounds

he·ma·tin·ic \,hē-mə-'ti-nik\ *noun* (1855)
: an agent that tends to stimulate blood cell formation or to increase the hemoglobin in the blood
— **hematinic** *adjective*

he·ma·tite \'hē-mə-,tīt\ *noun* (1540)
: a mineral constituting an important iron ore and occurring in crystals or in a red earthy form
— **he·ma·tit·ic** \,hē-mə-'ti-tik\ *adjective*

he·mat·o·crit \hi-'ma-tə-krət, -,krit\ *noun* [International Scientific Vocabulary *hemat-* + Greek *kritēs* judge, from *krinein* to judge — more at CERTAIN] (circa 1903)
1 : an instrument for determining usually by centrifugation the relative amounts of plasma and corpuscles in blood
2 : the ratio of the volume of packed red blood cells to the volume of whole blood as determined by a hematocrit

he·ma·tog·e·nous \,hē-mə-'tä-jə-nəs\ *adjective* (1886)
1 : producing blood
2 : involving, spread by, or arising in the blood ⟨*hematogenous* spread of infection⟩

he·ma·to·log·ic \,hē-mə-tᵊl-'ä-jik\ *also* **he·ma·to·log·i·cal** \-ji-kəl\ *adjective* (1854)
: of or relating to blood or to hematology

he·ma·tol·o·gy \,hē-mə-'tä-lə-jē\ *noun* (circa 1811)
: a medical science that deals with the blood and blood-forming organs
— **he·ma·tol·o·gist** \-jist\ *noun*

he·ma·to·ma \-'tō-mə\ *noun, plural* **-mas** *or* **-ma·ta** \-mə-tə\ [New Latin] (circa 1849)
: a mass of usually clotted blood that forms in a tissue, organ, or body space as a result of a broken blood vessel

he·ma·toph·a·gous \-'tä-fə-gəs\ *adjective* [International Scientific Vocabulary] (circa 1854)
: feeding on blood

he·ma·to·poi·e·sis \hi-,ma-tə-pȯi-'ē-səs, ,hē-mə-tō-\ *noun* [New Latin] (circa 1854)

: the formation of blood or of blood cells in the living body
— **he·ma·to·poi·et·ic** \-'e-tik\ *adjective*

he·ma·to·por·phy·rin \-'pȯr-fə-rən\ *noun* [International Scientific Vocabulary] (1885)
: any of several isomeric porphyrins $C_{34}H_{38}O_6N_4$ that are hydrated derivatives of protoporphyrins; *especially* **:** the deep red crystalline pigment obtained by treating hematin or heme with acid

he·ma·tox·y·lin \ˌhē-mə-'täk-sə-lən\ *noun* [International Scientific Vocabulary, from New Latin *Haematoxylon*, genus of plants] (circa 1847)
: a crystalline phenolic compound $C_{16}H_{14}O_6$ found in logwood and used chiefly as a biological stain

he·ma·tu·ria \-'tu̇r-ē-ə, -'tyu̇r-\ *noun* [New Latin] (circa 1811)
: the presence of blood or blood cells in the urine

heme \'hēm\ *noun* [International Scientific Vocabulary, from *hematin*] (1925)
: the deep red iron-containing prosthetic group $C_{34}H_{32}N_4O_4Fe$ of hemoglobin and myoglobin

hem·el·y·tron \he-'me-lə-ˌträn\ *noun, plural* **-tra** \-trä\ [New Latin, from *hemi-* + *elytron*] (circa 1889)
: one of the basally thickened anterior wings of various insects (as true bugs)

hem·ero·cal·lis \ˌhe-mə-rō-'ka-ləs\ *noun* [New Latin, from Greek *hēmerokalles*, from *hēmera* day + *kallos* beauty] (1625)
: DAYLILY

hem·er·y·thrin \hē-'mer-ə-thrən\ *noun* [*hem-* + *erythr-* + 1*-in*] (1903)
: an iron-containing respiratory pigment in the blood of various invertebrates (as some annelids)

hemi- *prefix* [Middle English, from Latin, from Greek *hēmi-* — more at SEMI-]
: half ⟨*hemi*hedral⟩

-hemia — see -EMIA

hemi·ac·e·tal \ˌhe-mē-'a-sə-ˌtal\ *noun* (1893)
: any of a class of compounds characterized by the grouping C(OH)(OR) where R is an alkyl group and usually formed as intermediates in the preparation of acetals from aldehydes or ketones

he·mic \'hē-mik\ *adjective* (1857)
: of, relating to, or produced by the blood or the circulation of blood ⟨a *hemic* murmur⟩

hemi·cel·lu·lose \ˌhe-mi-'sel-yə-ˌlōs, -ˌlōz\ *noun* [International Scientific Vocabulary] (1891)
: any of various plant polysaccharides less complex than cellulose and easily hydrolyzable to simple sugars and other products

hemi·chor·date \-'kȯr-dət, -'kȯr-ˌdāt\ *noun* [New Latin *Hemichordata*, from *hemi-* + *Chordata* chordates] (1885)
: any of a phylum (Hemichordata) of wormlike marine animals (as an acorn worm) that have in the proboscis an outgrowth of the pharyngeal wall which superficially resembles the notochord of chordates

hemi·cy·cle \'he-mi-ˌsī-kəl\ *noun* [French *hémicycle*, from Latin *hemicyclium*, from Greek *hēmikyklion*, from *hēmi-* + *kyklos* circle — more at CYCLE] (15th century)
: a curved or semicircular structure or arrangement

hemi·demi·semi·qua·ver \ˌhe-mi-ˌde-mi-'se-mi-ˌkwä-vər\ *noun* (1853)
: SIXTY-FOURTH NOTE

hemi·he·dral \ˌhe-mi-'hē-drəl\ *adjective* [*hemi-* + *-hedron*] (1837)
of a crystal **:** having half the faces required by complete symmetry — compare HOLOHEDRAL, TETARTOHEDRAL

hemi·hy·drate \-'hī-ˌdrāt\ *noun* (circa 1901)
: a hydrate (as plaster of paris) containing half a mole of water to one mole of the compound forming the hydrate
— **hemi·hy·drat·ed** \-ˌdrā-təd\ *adjective*

hemi·me·tab·o·lous \ˌhe-mi-mə-'ta-bə-ləs\ *adjective* (1870)
: characterized by incomplete metamorphosis ⟨*hemimetabolous* insects⟩ — compare HOLOMETABOLOUS

hemi·mor·phic \ˌhe-mi-'mȯr-fik\ *adjective* [International Scientific Vocabulary] (circa 1859)
of a crystal **:** having different crystalline forms at each end of a crystallographic axis
— **hemi·mor·phism** \-ˌfi-zəm\ *noun*

he·min \'hē-mən\ *noun* [International Scientific Vocabulary] (circa 1857)
: a red-brown to blue-black crystalline salt $C_{34}H_{32}N_4O_4FeCl$ derived from oxidized heme but usually obtained in a characteristic crystalline form from hemoglobin

hemi·o·la \ˌhe-mē-'ō-lə\ *noun* [Late Latin *hemiolia*, from Greek *hēmiolia* ratio of one and a half to one, from *hēmi-* + *holos* whole — more at SAFE] (circa 1934)
: a musical rhythmic alteration in which six equal notes may be heard as two groups of three or three groups of two

hemi·ple·gia \ˌhe-mi-'plē-j(ē-)ə\ *noun* [New Latin, from Middle Greek *hēmiplēgia* paralysis, from Greek *hēmi-* + *-plēgia* -plegia] (1600)
: total or partial paralysis of one side of the body that results from disease of or injury to the motor centers of the brain
— **hemi·ple·gic** \-jik\ *adjective or noun*

he·mip·ter·an \hi-'mip-tə-rən\ *noun* [ultimately from Greek *hēmi-* + *pteron* wing — more at FEATHER] (circa 1864)
: any of a large order (Hemiptera) of hemimetabolous insects (as the true bugs) that have hemelytra and mouthparts adapted to piercing and sucking
— **he·mip·ter·ous** \-rəs\ *adjective*

hemi·sphere \'he-mə-ˌsfir\ *noun* [Middle English *hemispere*, from Latin *hemisphaerium*, from Greek *hēmisphairion*, from *hēmi-* + *sphairion*, diminutive of *sphaira* sphere] (14th century)
1 a : a half of the celestial sphere divided into two halves by the horizon, the celestial equator, or the ecliptic **b :** half of a spherical or roughly spherical body (as a planet); *specifically* **:** the northern or southern half of the earth divided by the equator or the eastern or western half divided by a meridian **c :** the inhabitants of a terrestrial hemisphere
2 : REALM, PROVINCE
3 : one of two half spheres formed by a plane through the sphere's center
4 : a map or projection of a celestial or terrestrial hemisphere
5 : CEREBRAL HEMISPHERE
— **hemi·spher·ic** \ˌhe-mə-'sfir-ik, -'sfer-\ *or* **hemi·spher·i·cal** \-'sfir-i-kəl, -'sfer-\ *adjective*

hemi·stich \'he-mi-ˌstik\ *noun* [Latin *hemistichium*, from Greek *hēmistichion*, from *hēmi-* + *stichos* line, row; akin to Greek *steichein* to go — more at STAIR] (1575)
: half a poetic line of verse usually divided by a caesura

hemi·zy·gous \ˌhe-mi-'zī-gəs\ *adjective* (circa 1921)
: having or characterized by one or more genes (as in a genetic deficiency or in an X chromosome paired with a Y chromosome) that have no allelic counterparts

hem·line \'hem-ˌlīn\ *noun* (1923)
: the line formed by the lower edge of a dress, skirt, or coat

hem·lock \'hem-ˌläk\ *noun* [Middle English *hemlok*, from Old English *hemlic*] (before 12th century)
1 a : any of several poisonous herbs (as a poison hemlock or a water hemlock) of the carrot family having finely cut leaves and small white flowers **b :** a drug or lethal drink prepared from the poison hemlock (*Conium maculatum*)

2 : any of a genus (*Tsuga*) of evergreen coniferous trees of the pine family; *also* **:** the soft light splintery wood of a hemlock

hemo- — see HEM-

he·mo·chro·ma·to·sis \ˌhē-mə-ˌkrō-mə-'tō-səs\ *noun* [New Latin, from *hem-* + *chromat-* + *-osis*] (1899)
: a metabolic disorder involving the deposition of iron-containing pigments in the tissues and characterized by bronzing of the skin, diabetes, and weakness

he·mo·coel \'hē-mə-ˌsēl\ *noun* (1839)
: a body cavity (as in arthropods or some mollusks) that contains blood or hemolymph and functions as part of the circulatory system

he·mo·cy·a·nin \ˌhē-mō-'sī-ə-nən\ *noun* [International Scientific Vocabulary *hem-* + *cyan-* + 1*-in*] (1885)
: a colorless copper-containing respiratory pigment in the circulatory fluid of various arthropods and mollusks

he·mo·cyte \'hē-mə-ˌsīt\ *noun* [International Scientific Vocabulary] (circa 1903)
: a blood cell especially of an invertebrate animal

he·mo·cy·tom·e·ter \ˌhē-mə-sī-'tä-mə-tər\ *noun* [International Scientific Vocabulary] (1877)
: HEMACYTOMETER

he·mo·di·al·y·sis \ˌhē-mō-dī-'a-lə-səs\ *noun* (1947)
: the process of removing blood from an artery (as of a kidney patient), purifying it by dialysis, adding vital substances, and returning it to a vein

he·mo·di·lu·tion \-dī-'lü-shən, -də-\ *noun* (1939)
: decreased concentration of cells and solids in the blood resulting from gain of fluid

he·mo·dy·nam·ic \-dī-'na-mik, -də-\ *adjective* (1907)
1 : of, relating to, or involving hemodynamics
2 : relating to or functioning in the mechanics of blood circulation
— **he·mo·dy·nam·i·cal·ly** \-mi-k(ə-)lē\ *adverb*

he·mo·dy·nam·ics \-miks\ *noun plural but singular or plural in construction* (circa 1857)
1 : a branch of physiology that deals with the circulation of the blood
2 : the forces or mechanisms involved in circulation

he·mo·fla·gel·late \ˌhē-mō-'fla-jə-lət, -ˌlāt; -flə-'je-lət\ *noun* (1909)
: a flagellate (as a trypanosome) that is a blood parasite

he·mo·glo·bin \'hē-mə-ˌglō-bən\ *noun* [International Scientific Vocabulary, short for earlier *hematoglobulin*] (1869)
1 : an iron-containing respiratory pigment of vertebrate red blood cells that consists of a globin composed of four subunits each of which is linked to a heme molecule, that functions in oxygen transport to the tissues after conversion to oxygenated form in the gills or lungs, and that assists in carbon dioxide transport back to the gills or lungs after surrender of its oxygen
2 : any of numerous iron-containing respiratory pigments of invertebrates and some plants (as yeasts)

he·mo·glo·bin·op·a·thy \ˌhē-mə-ˌglō-bə-'nä-pə-thē\ *noun, plural* **-thies** (1957)
: a blood disorder (as sickle-cell anemia) caused by a genetically determined change in the molecular structure of hemoglobin

hemoglobin S *noun* (1954)
: an abnormal hemoglobin that occurs in the red blood cells in sickle-cell anemia and sickle-cell trait

\ə\ abut \ᵊ\ kitten \ər\ **further** \a\ **ash** \ā\ **ace**
\ä\ **mop, mar** \au̇\ **out** \ch\ **chin** \e\ **bet** \ē\ **easy**
\g\ **go** \i\ **hit** \ī\ **ice** \j\ **job** \ŋ\ **sing** \ō\ **go**
\ȯ\ **law** \ȯi\ **boy** \th\ **thin** \t̲h̲\ **the** \ü\ **loot** \u̇\ **foot**
\y\ **yet** \zh\ **vision** *see also* Guide to Pronunciation

he·mo·glo·bin·uria \ˌhē-mə-ˌglō-bə-'nùr-ē-ə, -'nyùr-\ *noun* [New Latin] (1866)
: the presence of free hemoglobin in the urine
— **he·mo·glo·bin·uric** \-'nùr-ik, -'nyùr-\ *adjective*

he·mo·lymph \'hē-mə-ˌlim(p)f\ *noun* (1885)
: the circulatory fluid of various invertebrate animals that is functionally comparable to the blood and lymph of vertebrates

he·mo·ly·sin \hē-mə-'lī-sᵊn\ *noun* [International Scientific Vocabulary] (1900)
: a substance that causes the dissolution of red blood cells

he·mo·ly·sis \hi-'mä-lə-səs, ˌhē-mə-'lī-səs\ *noun* [New Latin] (1890)
: lysis of red blood cells with liberation of hemoglobin
— **he·mo·lyt·ic** \ˌhē-mə-'li-tik\ *adjective*

hemolytic anemia *noun* (1938)
: anemia caused by excessive destruction (as in chemical poisoning, infection, or sickle-cell anemia) of red blood cells

hemolytic disease of the newborn (1948)
: ERYTHROBLASTOSIS FETALIS

he·mo·lyze \'hē-mə-ˌlīz\ *verb* **-lyzed; -lyzing** [irregular from *hemolysis*] (1902)
transitive verb
: to cause hemolysis of
intransitive verb
: to undergo hemolysis

he·mo·phil·ia \ˌhē-mə-'fi-lē-ə\ *noun* [New Latin] (1872)
: a sex-linked hereditary blood defect that occurs almost exclusively in males and is characterized by delayed clotting of the blood and consequent difficulty in controlling hemorrhage even after minor injuries

¹**he·mo·phil·i·ac** \-'fi-lē-ˌak\ *adjective* (1896)
: of, resembling, or affected with hemophilia

²**hemophiliac** *noun* (1897)
: one affected with hemophilia — called also *bleeder*

he·mo·phil·ic \-'fi-lik\ *noun or adjective* (1864)
: HEMOPHILIAC

he·mo·poi·e·sis \ˌhē-mə-pòi-'ē-səs\ *noun* [New Latin] (circa 1900)
: HEMATOPOIESIS
— **he·mo·poi·et·ic** \-'e-tik\ *adjective*

he·mo·pro·tein \-'prō-ˌtēn, -'prō-tē-ən\ *noun* (1948)
: a conjugated protein (as hemoglobin or cytochrome) whose prosthetic group is a porphyrin combined with iron

he·mop·ty·sis \hi-'mäp-tə-səs\ *noun* [New Latin, from *hem-* + Greek *ptysis* act of spitting, from *ptyein* to spit — more at SPEW] (1646)
: expectoration of blood from some part of the respiratory tract

¹**hem·or·rhage** \'hem-rij, 'he-mə-\ *noun* [Latin *haemorrhagia*, from Greek *haimorrhagia*, from *haimo-* hem- + *-rrhagia*] (1671)
: a copious discharge of blood from the blood vessels
— **hem·or·rhag·ic** \ˌhe-mə-'ra-jik\ *adjective*

²**hemorrhage** *verb* **-rhaged; -rhag·ing** (1928)
intransitive verb
: to undergo heavy or uncontrollable bleeding
transitive verb
: to lose rapidly and uncontrollably ⟨*hemorrhage* money⟩

hemorrhagic fever *noun* (1948)
: any of a diverse group of arthropod-borne virus diseases characterized by a sudden onset, fever, aching, bleeding in the internal organs, petechiae, and shock

hem·or·rhoid \'hem-ˌròid, 'he-mə-\ *noun* [Middle English *emeroides*, plural, from Middle French *hemorrhoides*, from Latin *haemorrhoidae*, from Greek *haimorrhoides*, from *haimorrhoos* flowing with blood, from *haimo-*

hem- + *rhein* to flow — more at STREAM] (14th century)
: a mass of dilated veins in swollen tissue at the margin of the anus or nearby within the rectum — usually used in plural; called also *piles*

¹**hem·or·rhoid·al** \ˌhem-'ròi-dᵊl, ˌhe-mə-\ *noun* (15th century)
: a hemorrhoidal part (as an artery or vein)

²**hemorrhoidal** *adjective* (1651)
1 : of, relating to, or involving hemorrhoids
2 : RECTAL

he·mo·sid·er·in \ˌhē-mō-'si-də-rən\ *noun* [International Scientific Vocabulary *hem-* + *sider-* + ¹-*in*] (circa 1885)
: a yellowish brown granular pigment that is formed in some phagocytic cells by the breakdown of hemoglobin and is probably essentially a denatured form of ferritin

he·mo·sta·sis \ˌhē-mə-'stā-səs\ *noun* [New Latin, from Greek *haimostasis* styptic, from *haimo-* hem- + *-stasis*] (1843)
: arrest of bleeding

he·mo·stat \'hē-mə-ˌstat\ *noun* (circa 1900)
: HEMOSTATIC; *especially* : an instrument for compressing a bleeding vessel

¹**he·mo·stat·ic** \ˌhē-mə-'sta-tik\ *noun* (circa 1706)
: a hemostatic agent

²**hemostatic** *adjective* (1834)
1 : of or caused by hemostasis
2 : serving to check bleeding

hemp \'hemp\ *noun* [Middle English, from Old English *hænep*; akin to Old High German *hanaf* hemp, Greek *kannabis*] (before 12th century)
1 a : a tall widely cultivated Asian herb (*Cannabis sativa*) of the mulberry family with tough bast fiber used especially for cordage **b** : the fiber of hemp **c** : a psychoactive drug (as marijuana or hashish) from hemp
2 : a fiber (as jute) from a plant other than the true hemp; *also* : a plant yielding such fiber

hemp·en \'hem-pən\ *adjective* (14th century)
: composed of hemp

hemp nettle *noun* (1801)
: any of a genus (*Galeopsis*) of coarse Old World herbs of the mint family; *especially* : a bristly Eurasian herb (*G. tetrahit*) naturalized in the U.S. as a weed

¹**hem·stitch** \'hem-ˌstich\ *transitive verb* (1839)
: to decorate (as a border) with hemstitch
— **hem·stitch·er** *noun*

²**hemstitch** *noun* (1853)
1 : decorative network similar to drawnwork that is used especially on or next to the stitching line of hems
2 : a stitch used in hemstitching

hemstitch

hen \'hen\ *noun* [Middle English, from Old English *henn*; akin to Old English *hana* rooster — more at CHANT] (before 12th century)
1 a : a female chicken especially over a year old; *broadly* : a female bird **b** : the female of various mostly aquatic animals (as lobsters or fish)
2 : WOMAN; *especially* : a fussy middle-aged woman

hen and chickens *noun* (1884)
: any of several plants having offsets, runners, or flowers that send out shoots; *especially* : HOUSELEEK

hen·bane \'hen-ˌbān\ *noun* (14th century)
: a poisonous fetid Old World herb (*Hyoscyamus niger*) of the nightshade family having sticky hairy dentate leaves and yellowish brown flowers and yielding hyoscyamine and scopolamine

hen·bit \'hen-ˌbit\ *noun* (1597)
: a Eurasian herb (*Lamium amplexicaule*) of the mint family that has scalloped reniform

leaves and purplish flowers and is naturalized in North America

hence \'hen(t)s\ *adverb* [Middle English *hennes, henne,* from Old English *heonan;* akin to Old High German *hinnan* away, Old English *hēr* here] (13th century)
1 : from this place : AWAY
2 a *archaic* : HENCEFORTH **b** : from this time
3 : because of a preceding fact or premise : THEREFORE
4 : from this source or origin
— **from hence** *archaic* : from this place : from this time

hence·forth \'hen(t)s-ˌfòrth, -ˌfòrth, hen(t)s-'\ *adverb* (14th century)
: from this point on

hence·for·ward \hen(t)s-'fòr-wərd\ *adverb* (14th century)
: HENCEFORTH

hench·man \'hench-mən\ *noun* [Middle English *henshman, hengestman* groom, from *hengest* stallion (from Old English) + *man;* akin to Old High German *hengist* gelding] (15th century)
1 *obsolete* : a squire or page to a person of high rank
2 a : a trusted follower : a right-hand man **b** : a political follower whose support is chiefly for personal advantage **c** : a member of a gang

hen·deca·syl·lab·ic \(ˌ)hen-ˌde-kə-sə-'la-bik\ *adjective* [Latin *hendecasyllabus,* from Greek *hendeka* eleven (from *hen-, heis* one + *deka* ten) + *syllabē* syllable — more at SAME, TEN] (circa 1751)
: consisting of 11 syllables or composed of verses of 11 syllables
— **hendecasyllabic** *noun*
— **hen·deca·syl·la·ble** \hen-'de-kə-ˌsi-lə-bəl, (ˌ)hen-ˌde-kə-'\ *noun*

hen·di·a·dys \hen-'dī-ə-dəs\ *noun* [Late Latin *hendiadys, hendiadyoin,* modification of Greek *hen dia dyoin,* literally, one through two] (circa 1577)
: the expression of an idea by the use of usually two independent words connected by *and* (as *nice and warm*) instead of the usual combination of independent word and its modifier (as *nicely warm*)

hen·e·quen \'he-ni-kən, ˌhe-ni-'ken\ *noun* [Spanish *henequén*] (1880)
: a strong yellowish or reddish hard fiber obtained from the leaves of a tropical American agave chiefly in Yucatán and used especially for binder twine; *also* : a plant (*Agave fourcroydes*) that yields henequen

hen·house \'hen-ˌhaùs\ *noun* (circa 1513)
: a house or shelter for fowl

Hen·le's loop \'hen-lēz-\ *noun* (circa 1890)
: LOOP OF HENLE

¹**hen·na** \'he-nə\ *noun* [Arabic *ḥinnā'*] (1600)
1 : a reddish brown dye obtained from leaves of the henna plant and used especially on hair
2 : an Old World tropical shrub or small tree (*Lawsonia inermis*) of the loosestrife family with small opposite leaves and axillary panicles of fragrant white flowers

²**henna** *transitive verb* (1919)
: to dye (as hair) with henna

hen·nery \'he-nə-rē\ *noun, plural* **-ner·ies** (1850)
: a poultry farm; *also* : an enclosure for poultry

heno·the·ism \'he-nə-(ˌ)thē-ˌi-zəm\ *noun* [German *Henotheismus,* from Greek *hen-, heis* one + *theos* god — more at SAME] (1860)
: the worship of one god without denying the existence of other gods
— **heno·the·ist** \-ˌthē-ist\ *noun*
— **heno·the·is·tic** \ˌhe-nə-thē-'is-tik\ *adjective*

hen party *noun* (circa 1885)
: a party for women only

hen·peck \'hen-ˌpek\ *transitive verb* (1688)
: to subject (one's husband) to persistent nagging and domination

hen·ry \'hen-rē\ *noun, plural* **henrys** *or* **henries** [Joseph *Henry*] (circa 1890)
: the practical meter-kilogram-second unit of inductance equal to the self-inductance of a circuit or the mutual inductance of two circuits in which the variation of one ampere per second results in an induced electromotive force of one volt

hent \'hent\ *transitive verb* [Middle English, from Old English *hentan* — more at HUNT] *archaic* (before 12th century)
: SEIZE

hen track *noun* (1907)
: an illegible or scarcely legible mark intended as handwriting — called also *hen scratch*

¹hep \'hep, 'həp, 'hət\ *interjection* [origin unknown] (1862)
— used to mark a marching cadence

²hep \'hep\ *adjective* [origin unknown] (1904)
: ⁴HIP

hep·a·rin \'he-pə-rən\ *noun* [International Scientific Vocabulary, from Greek *hēpar* liver] (1918)
: a mucopolysaccharide sulfuric acid ester that is found especially in liver, that prolongs the clotting time of blood, and that is used medically
— **hep·a·rin·ized** \-rə-ˌnīzd\ *adjective*

hepat- *or* **hepato-** *combining form* [Latin, from Greek *hēpat-, hēpato-*, from *hēpat-, hēp-ar*; akin to Latin *jecur* liver]
1 : liver ⟨*hepat*ectomy⟩ ⟨*hepato*toxic⟩
2 : hepatic and ⟨*hepato*cellular⟩

hep·a·tec·to·my \ˌhe-pə-'tek-tə-mē\ *noun, plural* **-mies** (circa 1890)
: excision of the liver or of part of the liver
— **hep·a·tec·to·mized** \-ˌmīzd\ *adjective*

¹he·pat·ic \hi-'pa-tik\ *adjective* [Latin *hepaticus*, from Greek *hēpatikos*, from *hēpat-, hēp-ar*] (1599)
: of, relating to, affecting, associated with, supplying, or draining the liver ⟨a *hepatic* complaint⟩ ⟨*hepatic* arteries⟩

²hepatic *noun* (1900)
: LIVERWORT

he·pat·i·ca \hi-'pa-ti-kə\ *noun* [New Latin, from Medieval Latin, liverwort, from Latin, feminine of *hepaticus*] (1578)
: any of a genus (*Hepatica*) of herbs of the buttercup family with lobed leaves and delicate flowers

hep·a·ti·tis \ˌhe-pə-'tī-təs\ *noun, plural* **-tit·i·des** \-'ti-tə-ˌdēz\ [New Latin] (circa 1751)
1 : inflammation of the liver
2 : a disease or condition (as hepatitis A or hepatitis B) marked by inflammation of the liver

hepatitis A *noun* (1972)
: an acute usually benign hepatitis caused by an RNA virus that does not persist in the blood serum and is transmitted especially in food and water contaminated with infected fecal matter — called also *infectious hepatitis*

hepatitis B *noun* (1972)
: a sometimes fatal hepatitis caused by a double-stranded DNA virus that tends to persist in the blood serum and is transmitted especially by contact with infected blood (as by transfusion) or blood products — called also *serum hepatitis*

he·pa·to·cel·lu·lar \ˌhe-pə-tō-'sel-yə-lər, hi-ˌpa-tə-'sel-\ *adjective* (1940)
: of or involving hepatocytes ⟨*hepatocellular* carcinoma⟩

he·pa·to·cyte \hi-'pa-tə-ˌsīt, 'he-pə-tə-\ *noun* (1965)
: an epithelial parenchymatous cell of the liver

hep·a·to·ma \ˌhe-pə-'tō-mə\ *noun, plural* **-mas** *or* **-ma·ta** \-mə-tə\ [New Latin] (circa 1923)
: a usually malignant tumor of the liver

he·pa·to·meg·a·ly \ˌhe-pə-tō-'me-gə-lē, hi-ˌpa-tə-'me-\ *noun, plural* **-lies** (circa 1901)
: enlargement of the liver

he·pa·to·pan·cre·as \-'paŋ-krē-əs, -'pan-\ *noun* (1884)
: a glandular structure (as of a crustacean) that combines the digestive functions of the vertebrate liver and pancreas

hep·a·to·tox·ic \-'täk-sik\ *adjective* (1926)
: relating to or causing injury to the liver ⟨*hepatotoxic* drugs⟩

hep·a·to·tox·ic·i·ty \-täk-'si-sə-tē\ *noun* (1952)
1 : a state of toxic damage to the liver
2 : a tendency or capacity to cause hepatotoxicity

hep·cat \'hep-ˌkat\ *noun* (1938)
: HIPSTER

He·phaes·tus \hi-'fes-təs, -'fēs-\ *noun* [Latin, from Greek *Hēphaistos*]
: the Greek god of fire and metalworking — compare VULCAN

hepped up *adjective* (1947)
: ENTHUSIASTIC

Hep·ple·white \'he-pəl-ˌhwīt, -ˌwīt\ *adjective* [George *Hepplewhite*] (1897)
: of, relating to, or imitating a style of furniture originating in late 18th century England

hepta- *or* **hept-** *combining form* [Greek, from *hepta* — more at SEVEN]
1 : seven ⟨*hepta*meter⟩
2 : containing seven atoms, groups, or equivalents ⟨*hepta*ne⟩

hep·ta·chlor \'hep-tə-ˌklȯr, -ˌklȯr\ *noun* [*hepta-* + *chlor*ine] (1949)
: a cyclodiene chlorinated hydrocarbon pesticide $C_{10}H_5Cl_7$ that causes liver disease in animals and is a suspected human carcinogen

hep·tad \'hep-ˌtad\ *noun* [Greek *heptad-, heptas*, from *hepta*] (1660)
: a group of seven

hep·ta·gon \'hep-tə-ˌgän\ *noun* [Greek *heptagōnos* heptagonal, from *hepta* + *gōnia* angle — more at -GON] (1570)
: a polygon of seven angles and seven sides
— **hep·tag·o·nal** \hep-'ta-gə-nᵊl\ *adjective*

hep·tam·e·ter \hep-'ta-mə-tər\ *noun* (circa 1898)
: a line of verse consisting of seven metrical feet

hep·tane \'hep-ˌtān\ *noun* (1877)
: any of several isomeric alkanes C_7H_{16}; *especially* : the liquid normal isomer occurring in petroleum and used especially as a solvent and in determining octane numbers

hep·tar·chy \'hep-ˌtär-kē\ *noun* (1576)
: a hypothetical confederacy of seven Anglo-Saxon kingdoms of the 7th and 8th centuries

Hep·ta·teuch \'hep-tə-ˌtük, -ˌtyük\ *noun* [Late Latin *heptateuchos*, from Greek, from *hepta* + *teuchos* book — more at PENTATEUCH] (1678)
: the first seven books of the canonical Jewish and Christian Scriptures

hep·tose \'hep-ˌtōs, -ˌtōz\ *noun* (1890)
: any of various monosaccharides $C_7H_{14}O_7$ containing seven carbon atoms in a molecule

¹her \(h)ər, 'hər\ *adjective* [Middle English *hire*, from Old English *hiere*, genitive of *hēo* she — more at HE] (before 12th century)
: of or relating to her or herself especially as possessor, agent, or object of an action ⟨*her* house⟩ ⟨*her* research⟩ ⟨*her* rescue⟩ — compare ¹SHE

²her *pronoun objective case of* SHE

He·ra \'hir-ə, 'hē-rə, 'her-ə\ *noun* [Greek *Hēra, Hērē*]
: the sister and consort of Zeus — compare JUNO

Her·a·cles \'her-ə-ˌklēz\ *noun* [Greek *Hērak-lēs*]
: HERCULES

¹her·ald \'her-əld\ *noun* [Middle English, from Middle French *hiraut*, from an (assumed) Germanic compound whose first component is akin to Old High German *heri* army, and whose second is akin to Old High German *waltan* to rule — more at HARRY, WIELD] (14th century)
1 a : an official at a tournament of arms with duties including the making of announcements and the marshaling of combatants **b** : an officer with the status of ambassador acting as official messenger between leaders especially in war **c** (1) : OFFICER OF ARMS (2) : an officer of arms ranking above a pursuivant and below a king of arms
2 : an official crier or messenger
3 a : one that precedes or foreshadows **b** : one that conveys news or proclaims : ANNOUNCER ⟨it was the lark, the *herald* of the morn —Shakespeare⟩ **c** : one who actively promotes or advocates : EXPONENT
synonym see FORERUNNER

²herald *transitive verb* (14th century)
1 : to give notice of : ANNOUNCE
2 a : to greet especially with enthusiasm : HAIL **b** : PUBLICIZE
3 : to signal the approach of : FORESHADOW

he·ral·dic \he-'ral-dik, hə-\ *adjective* (1772)
: of or relating to heralds or heraldry
— **he·ral·di·cal·ly** \-di-k(ə-)lē\ *adverb*

her·ald·ry \'her-əl-drē\ *noun, plural* **-ries** (1572)
1 : the practice of devising, blazoning, and granting armorial insignia and of tracing and recording genealogies
2 : an armorial ensign; *broadly* : INSIGNIA
3 : PAGEANTRY

herb \'ərb, *US also & British usually* 'hərb\ *noun, often attributive* [Middle English *herbe*, from Old French, from Latin *herba*] (14th century)
1 : a seed-producing annual, biennial, or perennial that does not develop persistent woody tissue but dies down at the end of a growing season
2 : a plant or plant part valued for its medicinal, savory, or aromatic qualities
3 *slang* : MARIJUANA 2
— **herb·like** \'(h)ər-ˌblīk\ *adjective*
— **herby** \'(h)ər-bē\ *adjective*

her·ba·ceous \ˌ(h)ər-'bā-shəs\ *adjective* (1646)
1 a : of, relating to, or having the characteristics of an herb **b** *of a stem* : having little or no woody tissue and persisting usually for a single growing season
2 : having the texture, color, or appearance of a leaf

herb·age \'(h)ər-bij\ *noun* (14th century)
1 : herbaceous vegetation (as grass) especially when used for grazing
2 : the succulent parts of herbaceous plants

¹herb·al \'(h)ər-bəl\ *noun* (1516)
1 : a book about plants especially with reference to their medicinal properties
2 *archaic* : HERBARIUM 1

²herbal *adjective* (1612)
: of, relating to, or made of herbs

herb·al·ist \'(h)ər-bə-list\ *noun* (1589)
1 : one who practices healing by the use of herbs
2 : one who collects or grows herbs

her·bar·i·um \ˌ(h)ər-'bar-ē-əm, -'ber-\ *noun, plural* **-ia** \-ē-ə\ (1776)
1 : a collection of dried plant specimens usually mounted and systematically arranged for reference
2 : a place that houses an herbarium

herb doctor *noun* (1828)
: HERBALIST 1

herbed \'(h)ərbd\ *adjective* (1950)
: seasoned with herbs

her·bi·cide \'(h)ər-bə-ˌsīd\ *noun* [Latin *herba* + International Scientific Vocabulary *-cide*] (1899)

\ə\ abut \ᵊ\ kitten \ər\ further \a\ ash \ā\ ace
\ä\ mop, mar \au̇\ out \ch\ chin \e\ bet \ē\ easy
\g\ go \i\ hit \ī\ ice \j\ job \ŋ\ sing \ō\ go
\ȯ\ law \ȯi\ boy \th\ thin \th\ the \ü\ loot \u̇\ foot
\y\ yet \zh\ vision *see also* Guide to Pronunciation

: an agent used to destroy or inhibit plant growth

— **her·bi·cid·al** \,(h)ər-bə-'sī-d°l\ *adjective*
— **her·bi·cid·al·ly** \-d°l-ē\ *adverb*

her·bi·vore \'(h)ər-bə-,vōr, -,vȯr\ *noun* [New Latin *Herbivora*, group of mammals, from neuter plural of *herbivorus*] (1854)
: a plant-eating animal

her·biv·o·rous \,(h)ər-'biv-rəs, -'biv-ə-\ *adjective* [New Latin *herbivorus*, from Latin *herba* grass + *-vorus* -vorous] (1661)
: feeding on plants

— **her·biv·o·ry** \-'biv-ə-rē\ *noun*

herb Rob·ert \'(h)ərb-'rä-bərt\ *noun* [Medieval Latin *herba Roberti*, probably from *Robertus* (Saint Robert) (died 1067) French ecclesiastic] (13th century)
: a sticky low geranium (*Geranium robertianum*) with small reddish purple flowers

Her·cu·le·an \,hər-kyə-'lē-ən, ,hər-'kyü-lē-\ *adjective* (1593)
1 : of, relating to, or characteristic of Hercules
2 *often not capitalized* : of extraordinary power, extent, intensity, or difficulty

Her·cu·les \'hər-kyə-,lēz\ *noun* [Latin, from Greek *Hēraklēs*]
1 : a mythical Greek hero renowned for his great strength and especially for performing 12 labors imposed on him by Hera
2 [Latin (genitive *Herculis*)] : a northern constellation between Corona Borealis and Lyra

Her·cu·les'-club \'hər-kyə-,lēz-,kləb\ *noun* (1847)
1 : a small prickly eastern U.S. tree (*Aralia spinosa*) of the ginseng family — called also *angelica tree*
2 : a small prickly southern U.S. tree (*Zanthoxylum clava-herculis*) of the rue family

¹herd \'hərd\ *noun* [Middle English, from Old English *heord;* akin to Old High German *herta* herd, Middle Welsh *cordd* troop, Lithuanian *kerdžius* shepherd] (before 12th century)
1 a : a number of animals of one kind kept together under human control **b** : a congregation of gregarious wild animals
2 a (1) : a group of people usually having a common bond (2) : a large assemblage of like things **b** : the undistinguished masses : CROWD ⟨isolate the individual prophets from the *herd* —Norman Cousins⟩

— **herd·like** \-,līk\ *adjective*

²herd (13th century)
transitive verb
1 a : to gather, lead, or drive as if in a herd ⟨seventy-five boys and girls were *herded* by six or eight teachers —W. A. White⟩ **b** : to keep or move (animals) together
2 : to place in a group
intransitive verb
1 : to assemble or move in a herd
2 : to place oneself in a group : ASSOCIATE

herd·er \'hər-dər\ *noun* (1635)
: one that herds; *specifically* : HERDSMAN 1

herds·man \'hərdz-mən\ *noun* (1603)
1 : a manager, breeder, or tender of livestock
2 *capitalized* : BOÖTES

¹here \'hir\ *adverb* [Middle English, from Old English *hēr;* akin to Old High German *hier* here, Old English *hē* he] (before 12th century)
1 a : in or at this place ⟨turn *here*⟩ — often used interjectionally in answering a roll call **b** : NOW ⟨*here* it's morning already⟩ **c** : in an arbitrary location ⟨a book *here*, a paper there⟩
2 : at or in this point, particular, or case ⟨*here* we agree⟩
3 : in the present life or state
4 : HITHER ⟨come *here*⟩
5 — used interjectionally in rebuke or encouragement

— **here goes** — used interjectionally to express resolution or resignation especially at the beginning of a difficult or unpleasant undertaking

— **neither here nor there** : having no interest or relevance : of no consequence ⟨comfort is *neither here nor there* to a real sailor⟩

²here *adjective* (15th century)
1 — used for emphasis especially after a demonstrative pronoun or after a noun modified by a demonstrative adjective ⟨this book *here*⟩
2 *nonstandard* — used for emphasis after a demonstrative adjective but before the noun modified ⟨this *here* book⟩

³here *noun* (1605)
: this place

here·abouts \'hir-ə-,baůts\ *or* **here·about** \-,baůt\ *adverb* (13th century)
: in this vicinity

¹here·af·ter \hir-'af-tər\ *adverb* (before 12th century)
1 : after this in sequence or in time
2 : in some future time or state

²hereafter *noun, often capitalized* (1546)
1 : FUTURE
2 : an existence beyond earthly life

³hereafter *adjective* (1591)
archaic : FUTURE

here and now *noun* (1829)
: the present time — used with *the* ⟨man's obligation is in the *here and now* —W. H. Whyte⟩

here and there *adverb* (14th century)
1 : in one place and another
2 : from time to time

here·away \'hir-ə-,wā\ *or* **here·aways** \-,wāz\ *adverb* (14th century)
dialect : HEREABOUTS

here·by \hir-'bī, 'hir-,\ *adverb* (13th century)
: by this means

here·dit·a·ment \,her-ə-'di-tə-mənt\ *noun* [Medieval Latin *hereditamentum*, from Late Latin *hereditare* to inherit, from Latin *hered-, heres*] (15th century)
: heritable property

he·red·i·tar·i·an \hə-,re-də-'ter-ē-ən\ *noun* (1881)
: an advocate of the theory that individual differences in human beings can be accounted for primarily on the basis of genetics

— **hereditarian** *adjective*

he·red·i·tary \hə-'re-də-,ter-ē\ *adjective* [Latin *hereditarius*, from *hereditas*] (15th century)
1 a : genetically transmitted or transmittable from parent to offspring **b** : characteristic of or fostered by one's predecessors
2 a : received or passing by inheritance or required to pass by inheritance or by reason of birth **b** : having title or possession through inheritance or by reason of birth
3 : of a kind established by tradition ⟨*hereditary* enemies⟩
4 : of or relating to inheritance or heredity
synonym see INNATE

— **he·red·i·tar·i·ly** \-,re-də-'ter-ə-lē\ *adverb*

he·red·i·ty \hə-'re-də-tē\ *noun* [Middle French *heredité*, from Latin *hereditat-, hereditas*, from *hered-, heres* heir — more at HEIR] (circa 1540)
1 a : INHERITANCE **b** : TRADITION
2 a : the sum of the qualities and potentialities genetically derived from one's ancestors **b** : the transmission of such qualities from ancestor to descendant through the genes

Her·e·ford \'hər-fərd *sometimes* 'her-ə-\ *noun* [*Hereford* former county in England] (1805)
: any of a breed of hardy red-coated beef cattle of English origin with white faces and markings

here·in \hir-'in\ *adverb* (before 12th century)
: in this

here·in·above \(,)hir-,in-ə-'bəv\ *adverb* (circa 1812)
: at a prior point in this writing or document

here·in·af·ter \,hir-ə-'naf-tər\ *adverb* (1590)
: in the following part of this writing or document

here·in·be·fore \(,)hir-,in-bi-'fȯr, -'fȯr\ *adverb* (1687)

: in the preceding part of this writing or document

here·in·be·low \-bi-'lō\ *adverb* (1946)
: at a subsequent point in this writing or document

here·of \hir-'əv, -'äv\ *adverb* (before 12th century)
: of this

here·on \-'ȯn, -'än\ *adverb* (12th century)
: on this

He·re·ro \hə-'rer-(,)ō, 'her-ə-,rō\ *noun, plural* **Herero** *or* **Hereros** (1880)
: a member of a Bantu people of central Namibia

he·re·si·arch \hə-'rē-zē-,ärk, 'her-ə-sē-\ *noun* [Late Latin *haeresiarcha*, from Late Greek *hairesiarchēs*, from *hairesis* + Greek *-archēs* -arch] (1624)
: an originator or chief advocate of a heresy

her·e·sy \'her-ə-sē\ *noun, plural* **-sies** [Middle English *heresie*, from Old French, from Late Latin *haeresis*, from Late Greek *hairesis*, from Greek, action of taking, choice, sect, from *hairein* to take] (13th century)
1 a : adherence to a religious opinion contrary to church dogma **b** : denial of a revealed truth by a baptized member of the Roman Catholic Church **c** : an opinion or doctrine contrary to church dogma
2 a : dissent or deviation from a dominant theory, opinion, or practice **b** : an opinion, doctrine, or practice contrary to the truth or to generally accepted beliefs or standards

her·e·tic \'her-ə-,tik\ *noun* (14th century)
1 : a dissenter from established church dogma; *especially* : a baptized member of the Roman Catholic Church who disavows a revealed truth
2 : one who dissents from an accepted belief or doctrine : NONCONFORMIST

he·ret·i·cal \hə-'re-ti-kəl\ *also* **he·re·tic** \'her-ə-,tik\ *adjective* (15th century)
1 : of, relating to, or characterized by heresy
2 : of, relating to, or characterized by departure from accepted beliefs or standards : UNORTHODOX

— **he·ret·i·cal·ly** \hə-'re-ti-k(ə-)lē\ *adverb*

here·to \hir-'tü\ *adverb* (12th century)
: to this writing or document

here·to·fore \'hir-tə-,fōr, -,fȯr, ,hir-tə-'\ *adverb* (13th century)
: up to this time : HITHERTO

here·un·der \hir-'ən-dər\ *adverb* (15th century)
: under or in accordance with this writing or document

here·un·to \hir-'ən-(,)tü, ,hir-(,)ən-'tü\ *adverb* (1509)
: to this

here·up·on \'hir-ə-,pȯn, -,pän, ,hir-ə-'\ *adverb* (12th century)
: on this : immediately after this

here·with \hir-'with, -'with\ *adverb* (before 12th century)
1 : with this communication : enclosed in this
2 : HEREBY

He·rez \hə-'rez\ *or* **He·riz** \-'riz\ *noun* [*Herez, Heriz,* town in Iran] (circa 1922)
: a Persian rug characterized by a large central geometric medallion and by angular floral designs

her·i·ot \'her-ē-ət\ *noun* [Middle English, from Old English *heregeatwe*, plural, military equipment, from *here* army (akin to Old High German *heri* army) + *geatwe* equipment — more at HARRY] (before 12th century)
: a feudal duty or tribute due under English law to a lord on the death of a tenant

her·i·ta·bil·i·ty \,her-ə-tə-'bi-lə-tē\ *noun* (1832)
1 : the quality or state of being heritable
2 : the proportion of observed variation in a particular trait (as intelligence) that can be attributed to inherited genetic factors in contrast to environmental ones

her·i·ta·ble \'her-ə-tə-bəl\ *adjective* (14th century)
1 : capable of being inherited or of passing by inheritance
2 : HEREDITARY

her·i·tage \'her-ə-tij\ *noun* [Middle English, from Middle French, from *heriter* to inherit, from Late Latin *hereditare,* from Latin *hered-, heres* heir — more at HEIR] (13th century)
1 : property that descends to an heir
2 a : something transmitted by or acquired from a predecessor **:** LEGACY, INHERITANCE **b :** TRADITION
3 : something possessed as a result of one's natural situation or birth **:** BIRTHRIGHT ⟨the nation's *heritage* of tolerance⟩

her·i·tor \'her-ə-tər\ *noun* (15th century)
: one that inherits **:** INHERITOR

herky–jerky \'hər-kē-'jər-kē\ *adjective* [reduplication of *jerky*] (1957)
: characterized by sudden, irregular, or unpredictable movement or style

herm \'hərm\ *noun* [Latin *hermes,* from Greek *hermēs* statue of Hermes, herm, from *Hermēs*] (circa 1580)
: a statue in the form of a square stone pillar surmounted by a bust or head especially of Hermes

her·ma \'hər-mə\ *noun, plural* **her·mae** \-,mē, -,mī\ *or* **her·mai** \-,mī\ (1638)
: HERM

her·maph·ro·dite \(,)hər-'ma-frə-,dīt\ *noun* [Middle English *hermofrodite,* from Latin *hermaphroditus,* from Greek *hermaphroditos,* from *Hermaphroditos*] (14th century)
1 : an animal or plant having both male and female reproductive organs
2 : something that is a combination of diverse elements
— hermaphrodite *adjective*
— her·maph·ro·dit·ic \(,)hər-,ma-frə-'di-tik\ *adjective*
— her·maph·ro·dit·ism \-'ma-frə-,dī-,ti-zəm\ *noun*

Her·maph·ro·di·tus \(,)hər-,ma-frə-'dī-təs\ *noun* [Latin, from Greek *Hermaphroditos,* from *Hermēs* + *Aphroditē* Aphrodite]
: a son of Hermes and Aphrodite who becomes joined in one body with a nymph while bathing

her·ma·typ·ic \,hər-mə-'ti-pik\ *adjective* [Greek *herma* prop, reef + *typtein* to strike, coin + English *-ic* — more at TYPE] (1950)
: building reefs ⟨*hermatypic* corals⟩

her·me·neu·ti·cal \,hər-mə-'nü-ti-kəl, -'nyü-\ *or* **her·me·neu·tic** \-tik\ *adjective* [Greek *hermēneutikos,* from *hermēneuein* to interpret, from *hermēneus* interpreter] (1678)
: of or relating to hermeneutics **:** INTERPRETATIVE
— her·me·neu·ti·cal·ly \-ti-k(ə-)lē\ *adverb*

her·me·neu·tics \-tiks\ *noun plural but singular or plural in construction* (1737)
: the study of the methodological principles of interpretation (as of the Bible)

Her·mes \'hər-(,)mēz\ *noun* [Latin, from Greek *Hermēs*]
: a Greek god of commerce, eloquence, invention, travel, and theft who serves as herald and messenger of the other gods — compare MERCURY

Hermes Tris·me·gis·tus \-,tris-mə-'jis-təs\ *noun* [Medieval Latin, from Greek *Hermēs trismegistos,* literally, Hermes thrice greatest]
: a legendary author of works embodying magical, astrological, and alchemical doctrines

her·met·ic \(,)hər-'me-tik\ *also* **her·met·i·cal** \-ti-kəl\ *adjective* [New Latin *hermeticus,* from *Hermet-, Hermes Trismegistus*] (1605)
1 *often capitalized* **:** of or relating to the Gnostic writings or teachings arising in the first three centuries A.D. and attributed to Hermes Trismegistus **b :** relating to or characterized by occultism or abstruseness **:** RECONDITE

2 [from the belief that Hermes Trismegistus invented a magic seal to keep vessels airtight]
a : AIRTIGHT ⟨*hermetic* seal⟩ **b :** impervious to external influence ⟨trapped inside the *hermetic* military machine —Jack Newfield⟩ **c :** RECLUSE, SOLITARY ⟨leads a *hermetic* life⟩ ◇
— her·met·i·cal·ly \-ti-k(ə-)lē\ *adverb*

her·met·i·cism \-'me-tə-,si-zəm\ *noun, often capitalized* (1897)
: HERMETISM

her·me·tism \'hər-mə-,ti-zəm\ *noun, often capitalized* (1897)
1 a : a system of ideas based on hermetic teachings **b :** adherence to or practice of hermetic doctrine
2 : the practice of being hermetically mysterious ⟨it is not . . . willful *hermetism,* if the message of their art is veiled and indirect —R. J. Goldwater⟩
— her·me·tist \-mə-tist\ *noun*

her·mit \'hər-mət\ *noun* [Middle English *eremite,* from Old French, from Late Latin *eremita,* from Late Greek *erēmitēs,* from Greek, adjective, living in the desert, from *erēmia* desert, from *erēmos* desolate] (12th century)
1 a : one that retires from society and lives in solitude especially for religious reasons **:** RECLUSE **b** *obsolete* **:** BEADSMAN
2 : a spiced molasses cookie
— her·mit·ism \'hər-mə-,ti-zəm\ *noun*

her·mit·age \'hər-mə-tij\ *noun* (14th century)
1 a : the habitation of a hermit **b :** a secluded residence or private retreat **:** HIDEAWAY **c :** MONASTERY
2 : the life or condition of a hermit

Her·mi·tage \,(h)er-mi-'täzh\ *noun* [Tain-l'*Ermitage,* commune in France] (1680)
: a red or white Rhone valley wine

hermit crab *noun* (1735)
: any of numerous chiefly marine decapod crustaceans (especially families Diogenidae, Paguridae, and Parapaguridae) having soft asymmetrical abdomens and occupying the empty shells of gastropods

hermit crab

Her·mi·tian matrix \er-'mē-shən-, ,hər-'mi-shən-\ *noun* [Charles *Hermite* (died 1901) French mathematician] (1935)
: a square matrix having the property that each pair of elements in the *i*th row and *j*th column and in the *j*th row and *i*th column are conjugate complex numbers

hern \'hern, 'hərn\ *dialect variant of* HERON

her·nia \'hər-nē-ə\ *noun, plural* **-ni·as** *or* **-ni·ae** \-nē-,ē, -nē-,ī\ [Latin — more at YARN] (14th century)
: a protrusion of an organ or part through connective tissue or through a wall of the cavity in which it is normally enclosed — called also *rupture*
— her·ni·al \-nē-əl\ *adjective*

her·ni·ate \'hər-nē-,āt\ *intransitive verb* **-at·ed; -at·ing** (circa 1922)
: to protrude through an abnormal body opening **:** RUPTURE
— her·ni·a·tion \,hər-nē-'ā-shən\ *noun*

he·ro \'hir-(,)ō, 'hē-(,)rō\ *noun, plural* **heroes** [Latin *heros,* from Greek *hērōs*] (14th century)
1 a : a mythological or legendary figure often of divine descent endowed with great strength or ability **b :** an illustrious warrior **c :** a man admired for his achievements and noble qualities **d :** one that shows great courage
2 a : the principal male character in a literary or dramatic work **b :** the central figure in an event, period, or movement
3 *plural usually* **heros :** SUBMARINE 2
4 : an object of extreme admiration and devotion **:** IDOL

Hero *noun* [Latin, from Greek *Hērō*]

: a legendary priestess of Aphrodite loved by Leander

¹he·ro·ic \hi-'rō-ik *also* her-'ō- *or* hē-'rō-\ *also* **he·ro·ical** \-i-kəl\ *adjective* (1549)
1 : of, relating to, or resembling heroes especially of antiquity
2 a : exhibiting or marked by courage and daring **b :** supremely noble or self-sacrificing
3 a : of impressive size, power, extent, or effect **:** POTENT ⟨*heroic* doses⟩ ⟨a *heroic* voice⟩ **b** (1) **:** of great intensity **:** EXTREME, DRASTIC ⟨*heroic* effort⟩ (2) **:** of a kind that is likely only to be undertaken to save a life ⟨*heroic* surgery⟩
4 : of, relating to, or constituting drama written during the Restoration in heroic couplets and concerned with a conflict between love and honor
— he·ro·ical·ly \-i-k(ə-)lē\ *adverb*

²heroic *noun* (1596)
1 : a heroic verse or poem
2 *plural* **a :** flamboyantly heroic language or action **b :** heroic action or behavior **c :** determined effort especially in the face of difficulty

heroic couplet *noun* (1889)
: a rhyming couplet in iambic pentameter

he·roi·com·ic \hi-,rō-i-'kä-mik\ *or* **he·roi·com·i·cal** \-'kä-mi-kəl\ *adjective* [French *héroïcomique,* from *héroïque* heroic + *comique* comic] (1756)
: comic by being ludicrously noble, bold, or elevated

heroic poem *noun* (1693)
: an epic or a poem in epic style

heroic stanza *noun* (circa 1922)
: a rhymed quatrain in heroic verse with a rhyme scheme of *abab* — called also *heroic quatrain*

heroic verse *noun* (1586)
1 : dactylic hexameter especially of epic verse of classical times — called also *heroic meter*
2 : the iambic pentameter used especially in English epic poetry during the 17th and 18th centuries — called also *heroic line, heroic meter*

her·o·in \'her-ə-wən\ *noun* [from *Heroin,* a trademark] (1898)
: a strongly physiologically addictive narcotic $C_{21}H_{23}NO_5$ that is made by acetylation of but is more potent than morphine and that is prohibited for medical use in the U.S. but is used illicitly for its euphoric effects
— her·o·in·ism \-wə-,ni-zəm\ *noun*

◇ WORD HISTORY
hermetic Thoth was an ancient Egyptian god of wisdom whose cult in the Nile valley endured for millennia. The Greeks who settled in Egypt after its conquest by Alexander the Great and created a blend of Egyptian and Hellenistic culture identified their god Hermes with Thoth, who was then renamed in Greek *Hermēs Trismegistos* "thrice-greatest Hermes," a rough translation of one of Thoth's Egyptian titles. Thoth-Hermes was the reputed author of a set of treatises, the *Hermetica,* containing revelation on mystical subjects as well as astrological and alchemical speculation, nearly all of which was Greek rather than Egyptian in origin. In medieval alchemical tradition Hermes Trismegistus, as his name was latinized, was the inventor of a seal that kept vessels airtight. From this tradition come the most common meanings of *hermetic* in English, "airtight" and by extension "impervious to external influence."

her·o·ine \'her-ə-wən, 'hir-\ *noun* [Latin *heroina*, from Greek *hērōinē*, feminine of *hērōs*] (1609)
1 a : a mythological or legendary woman having the qualities of a hero **b :** a woman admired and emulated for her achievements and qualities
2 a : the principal female character in a literary or dramatic work **b :** the central female figure in an event or period

her·o·ism \'her-ə-,wi-zəm *also* 'hir-\ *noun* (1717)
1 : heroic conduct especially as exhibited in fulfilling a high purpose or attaining a noble end
2 : the qualities of a hero

he·ro·ize \'hē-(,)rō-,īz, 'hir-(,)ō-; 'her-ə-,wīz\ *transitive verb* **-ized; -iz·ing** (1738)
: to make heroic

her·on \'her-ən\ *noun, plural* **herons** *also* **heron** [Middle English *heiroun*, from Middle French *hairon*, of Germanic origin; akin to Old High German *heigaro* heron] (14th century)
: any of various long-necked wading birds (family Ardeidae) with a long tapering bill, large wings, and soft plumage

her·on·ry \-ən-rē\ *noun, plural* **-ries** (1616)
: a heron rookery

hero–worship *transitive verb* (1884)
: to feel or express hero worship for
— **hero–worshiper** *noun*

hero worship *noun* (1774)
1 : veneration of a hero
2 : foolish or excessive adulation for an individual

her·pes \'hər-(,)pēz\ *noun* [Latin, from Greek *herpēs*, from *herpein* to creep — more at SERPENT] (14th century)
: any of several inflammatory virus diseases of the skin characterized by clusters of vesicles; *especially* **:** HERPES SIMPLEX
— **her·pet·ic** \(,)hər-'pe-tik\ *adjective*

her·pes sim·plex \-'sim-,pleks\ *noun* [New Latin, literally, simple herpes] (1907)
: either of two virus diseases marked in one case by groups of watery blisters on the skin or mucous membranes (as of the mouth and lips) above the waist and in the other by such blisters on the genitals

her·pes·vi·rus \-'vī-rəs\ *noun* (1925)
: any of a group of DNA-containing viruses that replicate in cell nuclei and produce herpes

herpes zos·ter \-'zäs-tər\ *noun* [New Latin, literally, girdle herpes] (1807)
: an acute viral inflammation of the sensory ganglia of spinal and cranial nerves associated with a vesicular eruption and neuralgic pains and caused by reactivation of the poxvirus causing chicken pox — called also *shingles*

her·pe·tol·o·gy \,hər-pə-'tä-lə-jē\ *noun* [Greek *herpeton* quadruped, reptile, from neuter of *herpetos* crawling, from *herpein*] (1824)
: a branch of zoology dealing with reptiles and amphibians
— **her·pe·to·log·i·cal** \-tə-'lä-ji-kəl\ *adjective*
— **her·pe·tol·o·gist** \,hər-pə-'tä-lə-jist\ *noun*

Herr \(,)her\ *noun, plural* **Her·ren** \,her-ən, (,)hern\ [German] (1653)
— used among German-speaking people as a title equivalent to *Mr.*

her·ren·volk \'her-ən-,fōk, -,fòlk\ *noun, often capitalized* [German] (1940)
: MASTER RACE

her·ring \'her-iŋ\ *noun, plural* **herring** *or* **herrings** [Middle English *hering*, from Old English *hæring*; akin to Old High German *hārinc* herring] (before 12th century)
1 : either of two clupeid food fishes (genus *Clupeus*): **a :** one (*C. harengus*) that is abundant in the temperate and colder parts of the North Atlantic and that in the adult state is preserved by smoking or salting and in the young state is extensively canned and sold as

sardines **b :** one (*C. pallasi* synonym *C. h. pallasi*) of the North Pacific harvested especially for its roe
2 : CLUPEID

¹her·ring·bone \'her-iŋ-,bōn\ *noun, often attributive* (1659)
1 : a pattern made up of rows of parallel lines which in any two adjacent rows slope in opposite directions
2 a : a twilled fabric with a herringbone pattern; *also* **:** a suit made of this fabric **b :** a herringbone arrangement (as of materials or parts)
3 : a method in skiing of ascending a slope by herringboning

herringbone 1

²herringbone (1787)
transitive verb
1 : to produce a herringbone pattern on
2 : to arrange in a herringbone pattern
intransitive verb
1 : to produce a herringbone pattern
2 : to ascend a slope by toeing out on skis and placing the weight on the inner side

herring gull *noun* (1857)
: a common large gull (*Larus argentatus*) of the northern hemisphere that as an adult is largely white with a gray mantle, dark wing tips, pink feet, and yellow bill

hers \'hərz\ *pronoun, singular or plural in construction*
: that which belongs to her — used without a following noun as a pronoun equivalent in meaning to the adjective *her*

her·self \(h)ər-'self, *Southern also* -'sef\ *pronoun* (before 12th century)
1 : that identical female one — compare ¹SHE; used reflexively, for emphasis, in absolute constructions, or in place of *her* especially when joined to another object ⟨she considers *herself* lucky⟩ ⟨she *herself* did it⟩ ⟨*herself* an orphan, she understood the situation⟩ ⟨accepted the award for her colleagues and *herself*⟩
2 : her normal, healthy, or sane condition or self
3 *chiefly Irish & Scottish* **:** a woman of consequence; *especially* **:** the mistress of the house

her·sto·ry \'hər-st(ə-)rē\ *noun, plural* **-ries** [blend of *her* and *history*] (1971)
: HISTORY; *specifically* **:** history considered or presented from a feminist viewpoint or with special attention to the experience of women

hertz \'hərts, 'herts\ *noun, plural* **hertz** [Heinrich R. *Hertz*] (circa 1928)
: a unit of frequency equal to one cycle per second — abbreviation *Hz*

he's \'hēz, ēz\ (1588)
: he is **:** he has

he/she \'hē-'shē; 'hē-ər-; 'hē-'slash-\ *pronoun* (1974)
: he or she — used in writing as a pronoun of common gender

Hesh·van \'kesh-vən\ *noun* [Hebrew *Ḥeshwān*] (circa 1769)
: the 2d month of the civil year or the 8th month of the ecclesiastical year in the Jewish calendar — see MONTH table

hes·i·tance \'he-zə-tən(t)s\ *noun* (1601)
: HESITANCY

hes·i·tan·cy \-tən(t)-sē\ *noun, plural* **-cies** (1617)
1 : the quality or state of being hesitant: as **a :** INDECISION **b :** RELUCTANCE ⟨took that drastic step only with the greatest *hesitancy*⟩
2 : HESITATION 1

hes·i·tant \'he-zə-tənt\ *adjective* (1647)
: tending to hesitate
synonym see DISINCLINED
— **hes·i·tant·ly** *adverb*

hes·i·tate \'he-zə-,tāt\ *verb* **-tat·ed; -tat·ing** [Latin *haesitatus*, past participle of *haesitare* to stick fast, hesitate, frequentative of *haerēre* to stick] (circa 1623)

intransitive verb
1 : to hold back in doubt or indecision
2 : to delay momentarily **:** PAUSE
3 : STAMMER
transitive verb
: to hold back from in doubt or uncertainty ⟨wouldn't *hesitate* to commit herself⟩ ☆
— **hes·i·tat·er** *noun*
— **hes·i·tat·ing·ly** \-,tā-tiŋ-lē\ *adverb*

hes·i·ta·tion \,he-zə-'tā-shən\ *noun* (14th century)
1 : an act or instance of hesitating
2 : a pausing or faltering in speech

Hes·pe·ri·an \he-'spir-ē-ən\ *adjective* [Latin *Hesperia*, the west, from Greek, from feminine of *hesperios* of the evening, western, from *hesperos* evening — more at WEST] (15th century)
: WESTERN, OCCIDENTAL

Hes·per·i·des \he-'sper-ə-,dēz\ *noun plural* [Latin, from Greek]
1 : the nymphs in classical mythology who guard with the aid of a dragon a garden in which golden apples grow
2 : a legendary garden at the western extremity of the world producing golden apples

hes·per·i·din \he-'sper-ə-dᵊn\ *noun* [New Latin *hesperidium* orange, from Latin *Hesperides*] (1838)
: a crystalline glycoside $C_{28}H_{34}O_{15}$ found in most citrus fruits and especially in orange peel

hes·per·id·i·um \,hes-pə-'ri-dē-əm\ *noun, plural* **-id·ia** \-dē-ə\ [New Latin] (circa 1866)
: a berry (as an orange or lime) having a leathery rind

Hes·per·us \'hes-p(ə-)rəs\ *noun* [Middle English, from Latin, from Greek *Hesperos*] (14th century)
: EVENING STAR 1

hes·sian \'he-shən\ *noun* (1729)
1 *capitalized* **a :** a native of Hesse **b :** a German mercenary serving in the British forces during the American Revolution; *broadly* **:** a mercenary soldier
2 *chiefly British* **:** BURLAP

Hessian boot *noun* (1809)
: a high boot that extends to just below the knee and is commonly ornamented with a tassel and that was introduced into England by the Hessians early in the 19th century

Hessian fly *noun* (1786)
: a small dipteran fly (*Mayetiola destructor*) that is destructive to wheat in the U.S.

hess·ite \'he-,sīt\ *noun* [German *Hessit*, from Henry *Hess* (died 1850) Swiss chemist] (1849)
: a mineral consisting of a lead-gray sectile silver telluride

hes·so·nite \'he-sᵊn-,īt\ *variant of* ESSONITE

hest \'hest\ *noun* [Middle English *hest, hes*, from Old English *hǣs*; akin to Old English *hātan* to command — more at HIGHT] (before 12th century)
archaic **:** COMMAND, PRECEPT

Hes·tia \'hes-tē-ə; 'hes-chə, 'hesh-\ *noun* [Greek]
: the Greek goddess of the hearth and chief goddess of domestic activity — compare VESTA

☆ **SYNONYMS**
Hesitate, waver, vacillate, falter mean to show irresolution or uncertainty. HESITATE implies a pause before deciding or acting or choosing ⟨*hesitated* before answering the question⟩. WAVER implies hesitation after seeming to decide and so connotes weakness or a retreat ⟨*wavered* in his support of the rebels⟩. VACILLATE implies prolonged hesitation from inability to reach a firm decision ⟨*vacillated* until events were out of control⟩. FALTER implies a wavering or stumbling and often connotes nervousness, lack of courage, or outright fear ⟨never once *faltered* during her testimony⟩.

he·tae·ra \hi-'tir-ə\ *or* **he·tai·ra** \-'tī-rə\ *noun, plural* **he·tae·rae** \-'tir-(ˌ)ē\ *or* **he·taeras** *or* **hetairas** *or* **he·tai·rai** \-'tī-ˌrī\ [Greek *hetaira*, literally, companion, feminine of *hetairos*] (1820)
1 : one of a class of highly cultivated courtesans in ancient Greece
2 : DEMIMONDAINE
heter- *or* **hetero-** *combining form* [Middle French or Late Latin; Middle French, from Late Latin, from Greek, from *heteros*; akin to Greek *heis* one — more at SAME]
1 : other than usual : other : different ⟨*heterophyllous*⟩
2 : containing atoms of different kinds ⟨*heterocyclic*⟩
het·ero \'he-tə-ˌrō\ *noun, plural* **-er·os** (1933)
: HETEROSEXUAL
— **hetero** *adjective*
het·er·at·om \'he-tə-rō-ˌa-təm\ *noun* (1900)
: an atom other than carbon in the ring of a heterocyclic compound
het·ero·aux·in \ˌhe-tə-rō-'ȯk-sən\ *noun* (1935)
: INDOLEACETIC ACID
het·ero·cer·cal \-'sər-kəl\ *adjective* (1838)
1 *of a fish tail fin* : having the upper lobe larger than the lower with the vertebral column extending into the upper lobe
2 : having or relating to a heterocercal tail fin
het·ero·chro·ma·tin \-'krō-mə-tən\ *noun* [German] (1932)
: densely staining chromatin that appears as nodules in or along chromosomes and contains relatively few genes
— **het·ero·chro·mat·ic** \-krə-'ma-tik\ *adjective*
¹het·ero·clite \'he-tə-rə-ˌklīt\ *noun* (1580)
1 : a word irregular in inflection; *especially* : a noun irregular in declension
2 : one that deviates from common rules or forms
²heteroclite *adjective* [Middle French or Late Latin; Middle French, from Late Latin *heteroclitus*, from Greek *heteroklitos*, from *heter-* + *klinein* to lean, inflect — more at LEAN] (1598)
: deviating from common forms or rules
het·ero·cy·clic \ˌhe-tə-rō-'sī-klik, -'si-\ *adjective* [International Scientific Vocabulary] (1899)
: relating to, characterized by, or being a ring composed of atoms of more than one kind
— **het·ero·cy·cle** \'he-tə-rō-ˌsī-kəl\ *noun*
— **heterocyclic** *noun*
het·ero·cyst \'he-tə-rō-ˌsist\ *noun* (1872)
: a large transparent thick-walled cell that is found in the filaments of some blue-green algae and is the site of nitrogen fixation
— **het·ero·cys·tous** \ˌhe-tə-rō-'sis-təs\ *adjective*
het·ero·dox \'he-tə-rə-ˌdäks, 'he-trə-\ *adjective* [Late Latin *heterodoxus*, from Greek *heterodoxos*, from *heter-* + *doxa* opinion — more at DOXOLOGY] (circa 1650)
1 : contrary to or different from an acknowledged standard, a traditional form, or an established religion : UNORTHODOX, UNCONVENTIONAL ⟨a *heterodox* book⟩ ⟨*heterodox* ideas⟩
2 : holding unorthodox opinions or doctrines
het·ero·doxy \-ˌdäk-sē\ *noun, plural* **-dox·ies** (1659)
1 : the quality or state of being heterodox
2 : a heterodox opinion or doctrine
het·ero·du·plex \ˌhe-tə-rō-'dü-ˌpleks, -'dyü-\ *noun* (1962)
: a nucleic-acid molecule composed of two chains with each derived from a different parent molecule
— **heteroduplex** *adjective*
¹het·ero·dyne \'he-tə-rə-ˌdīn, 'he-trə-\ *adjective* [*heter-* + *-dyne*, modification of Greek *dynamis* power — more at DYNAMIC] (1908)
: of or relating to the production of an electrical beat between two radio frequencies of which one usually is that of a received signal

carrying current and the other that of an uninterrupted current introduced into the apparatus; *also* : of or relating to the production of a beat between two optical frequencies
²heterodyne *transitive verb* **-dyned; -dyning** (1923)
: to combine (as a radio frequency) with a different frequency so that a beat is produced
het·er·oe·cious \ˌhe-tə-'rē-shəs\ *adjective* [*heter-* + Greek *oikia* house — more at VICINITY] (1882)
: passing through the different stages in the life cycle on alternate and often unrelated hosts ⟨*heteroecious* insects⟩
— **het·er·oe·cism** \-'rē-ˌsi-zəm\ *noun*
het·ero·ga·mete \ˌhe-tə-rō-'ga-ˌmēt *also* -gə-'mēt\ *noun* [International Scientific Vocabulary] (1897)
: either of a pair of gametes that differ in form, size, or behavior and occur typically as large nonmotile oogametes and small motile sperms
het·ero·ga·met·ic \-gə-'me-tik\ *adjective* (1910)
: forming two kinds of gametes of which one produces male offspring and the other female offspring ⟨the human male is *heterogametic*⟩
— **het·ero·gam·e·ty** \-'gam-ə-tē\ *noun*
het·er·og·a·mous \ˌhe-tə-'rä-gə-məs\ *adjective* (1839)
: having or characterized by fusion of unlike gametes — compare ANISOGAMOUS, ISOGAMOUS
het·er·og·a·my \-mē\ *noun* (circa 1894)
1 : sexual reproduction involving fusion of unlike gametes often differing in size, structure, and physiology
2 : the condition of reproducing by heterogamy
het·ero·ge·ne·ity \ˌhe-tə-rō-jə-'nē-ə-tē, ˌhetrō-\ *noun* (1641)
: the quality or state of being heterogeneous
het·ero·ge·neous \ˌhe-tə-rə-'jē-nē-əs, ˌhe-trə-, -nyəs\ *adjective* [Medieval Latin *heterogeneus*, from Greek *heterogenēs*, from *heter-* + *genos* kind — more at KIN] (1630)
: consisting of dissimilar or diverse ingredients or constituents : MIXED
— **het·ero·ge·neous·ly** *adverb*
— **het·ero·ge·neous·ness** *noun*
het·er·og·e·nous \ˌhe-tə-'rä-jə-nəs\ *adjective* (1695)
: HETEROGENEOUS
het·er·og·e·ny \-nē\ *noun* (1838)
: a heterogenous collection or group
het·er·og·o·ny \ˌhe-tə-'rä-gə-nē\ *noun* (circa 1887)
1 : ALTERNATION OF GENERATIONS; *especially* : alternation of a dioecious with a parthenogenetic generation
2 : ALLOMETRY
— **het·ero·gon·ic** \ˌhe-tə-rə-'gä-nik\ *adjective*
het·ero·graft \'he-tə-rō-ˌgraft\ *noun* (1923)
: a graft of tissue taken from a donor of one species and grafted into a recipient of another species — called also *xenograft*; compare HOMOGRAFT
het·ero·kary·on \ˌhe-tə-rō-'kar-ē-ˌän, -ən\ *noun* [New Latin, from *heter-* + *karyon, caryon* nucleus, from Greek *karyon* nut, kernel] (1941)
: a cell (as in the mycelium of a fungus) that contains two or more genetically unlike nuclei
het·ero·kary·o·sis \ˌhe-tə-rō-ˌkar-ē-'ō-səs\ *noun* [New Latin] (1916)
: the condition of having cells that are heterokaryons
— **het·ero·kary·ot·ic** \-ē-'ä-tik\ *adjective*
het·er·ol·o·gous \ˌhe-tə-'rä-lə-gəs\ *adjective* [*heter-* + *-logous* (as in *homologous*)] (1893)
: derived from a different species ⟨*heterologous* DNAs⟩ ⟨*heterologous* transplants⟩
— **het·er·ol·o·gous·ly** *adverb*
het·er·ol·y·sis \ˌhe-tə-'rä-lə-səs, -ə-rə-'lī-səs\ *noun* [New Latin] (1938)

: decomposition of a compound into two oppositely charged particles or ions
— **het·er·o·lyt·ic** \-ə-rə-'li-tik\ *adjective*
het·ero·mor·phic \ˌhe-tə-rə-'mȯr-fik\ *adjective* [International Scientific Vocabulary] (circa 1859)
1 : deviating from the usual form
2 : exhibiting diversity of form or forms ⟨*heteromorphic* pairs of chromosomes⟩
— **het·ero·mor·phism** \-ˌfi-zəm\ *noun*
het·er·on·o·mous \ˌhe-tə-'rä-nə-məs\ *adjective* (circa 1871)
: subject to external controls and impositions
het·er·on·o·my \-mē\ *noun* [*heter-* + *-nomy* (as in *autonomy*)] (1798)
: subjection to something else; *especially* : a lack of moral freedom or self-determination
het·er·o·nym \'he-tə-rə-ˌnim\ *noun* (circa 1889)
: one of two or more homographs (as a *bass* voice and *bass*, a fish) that differ in pronunciation and meaning
het·er·o·phile \'he-tə-rə-ˌfīl\ *or* **het·er·o·phil** \-ˌfil\ *adjective* (1920)
: relating to or being any of a group of antigens in organisms of different species that induce the formation of antibodies that will cross-react with the other antigens of the group; *also* : being or relating to any of these antibodies
het·er·oph·o·ny \ˌhe-tə-'rä-fə-nē\ *noun, plural* **-nies** [Greek *heterophōnia* diversity of note, from *heter-* + *-phōnia* -phony] (1919)
: independent variation on a single melody by two or more voices
het·ero·phyl·lous \ˌhe-tə-rō-'fi-ləs\ *adjective* (circa 1828)
: having the foliage leaves of more than one form on the same plant or stem
— **het·ero·phyl·ly** \'he-tə-rō-ˌfi-lē\ *noun*
het·ero·ploid \'he-tə-rə-ˌplȯid\ *adjective* [International Scientific Vocabulary] (1926)
: having a chromosome number that deviates from and is not an integral multiple of the number characteristic of a given species
— **heteroploid** *noun*
— **het·ero·ploi·dy** \-ˌplȯi-dē\ *noun*
het·er·op·ter·ous \ˌhe-tə-'räp-tə-rəs\ *adjective* [ultimately from Greek *heter-* + *pteron* wing — more at FEATHER] (1895)
: of or relating to an insect order or suborder (Heteroptera) comprising the true bugs
¹het·ero·sex·u·al \ˌhe-tə-rō-'sek-sh(ə-)wəl, -'sek-shəl\ *adjective* [International Scientific Vocabulary] (1892)
1 a : of, relating to, or characterized by a tendency to direct sexual desire toward the opposite sex **b** : of, relating to, or involving sexual intercourse between individuals of opposite sex
2 : of or relating to different sexes
— **het·ero·sex·u·al·i·ty** \-ˌsek-shə-'wa-lə-tē\ *noun*
— **het·ero·sex·u·al·ly** \-'sek-sh(ə-)wə-lē, -'sek-shə-lē\ *adverb*
²heterosexual *noun* (1920)
: a heterosexual person
het·er·o·sis \ˌhe-tə-'rō-səs\ *noun* [New Latin] (1914)
: the marked vigor or capacity for growth often exhibited by crossbred animals or plants — called also *hybrid vigor*
— **het·er·ot·ic** \-'rä-tik\ *adjective*
het·ero·spo·ry \'he-tə-rə-ˌspōr-ē, -ˌspȯr-; ˌhe-tə-'räs-pə-rē\ *noun* (1898)
: the production of microspores and megaspores (as in seed plants and some ferns)
— **het·ero·spo·rous** \ˌhe-tə-rə-'spōr-əs, -'spȯr-; -'räs-pə-rəs\ *adjective*

het·ero·thal·lic \ˌhe-tə-rō-'tha-lik\ *adjective* [*heter-* + *thallus* + *-ic*] (1904)
1 : having two or more morphologically similar haploid phases or types of which individuals from the same type are mutually sterile but individuals from different types are cross‑fertile ⟨*heterothallic* fungi⟩ ⟨*heterothallic* spores⟩
2 : DIOECIOUS
— **het·ero·thal·lism** \-'tha-ˌli-zəm\ *noun*
het·ero·top·ic \-rə-'tä-pik\ *adjective* [*heter-* + Greek *topos* place] (1878)
: occurring in an abnormal place ⟨*heterotopic* bone formation⟩ ⟨*heterotopic* liver transplantation⟩
het·ero·troph \'he-tə-rə-ˌtröf, -ˌträf\ *noun* (circa 1900)
: a heterotrophic individual
het·ero·tro·phic \ˌhe-tə-rə-'trō-fik\ *adjective* (1893)
: requiring complex organic compounds of nitrogen and carbon for metabolic synthesis
— **het·ero·tro·phi·cal·ly** \-fi-k(ə-)lē\ *adverb*
— **het·ero·tro·phy** \ˌhe-tə-'rä-trə-fē, 'he-tə-rə-ˌtrō-\ *noun*
het·ero·typ·ic \ˌhe-tə-rō-'ti-pik\ *adjective* (1889)
: different in kind, arrangement, or form
het·ero·zy·go·sis \-(ˌ)zī-'gō-səs\ *noun* [New Latin] (1902)
: HETEROZYGOSITY
het·ero·zy·gos·i·ty \-'gä-sə-tē\ *noun* (1912)
: the state of being heterozygous
het·ero·zy·gote \-'zī-ˌgōt\ *noun* (1902)
: a heterozygous individual
het·ero·zy·gous \-gəs\ *adjective* (1902)
: having the two alleles at corresponding loci on homologous chromosomes different for one or more loci
heth \'kät, 'käth, 'ket, 'keth\ *noun* [Hebrew *ḥēth*] (1823)
: the 8th letter of the Hebrew alphabet — see ALPHABET table
het·man \'het-mən\ *noun, plural* **hetmans** [Ukrainian *het'man*] (1710)
: a cossack leader
het up \'het-'əp\ *adjective* [*het,* dialect past of *heat*] (1909)
: highly excited : UPSET
heu·land·ite \'hyü-lən-ˌdīt\ *noun* [Henry *Heuland,* 19th century English mineral collector] (1822)
: a zeolite consisting of a hydrous aluminosilicate of sodium and calcium
¹heu·ris·tic \hyù-'ris-tik\ *adjective* [German *heuristisch,* from New Latin *heuristicus,* from Greek *heuriskein* to discover; akin to Old Irish *fo-fúair* he found] (1821)
: involving or serving as an aid to learning, discovery, or problem-solving by experimental and especially trial-and-error methods ⟨*heuristic* techniques⟩ ⟨a *heuristic* assumption⟩; *also*
: of or relating to exploratory problem-solving techniques that utilize self-educating techniques (as the evaluation of feedback) to improve performance ⟨a *heuristic* computer program⟩
— **heu·ris·ti·cal·ly** \-ti-k(ə-)lē\ *adverb*
²heuristic *noun* (1860)
1 : the study or practice of heuristic procedure
2 : heuristic argument
3 : a heuristic method or procedure
hew \'hyü\ *verb* **hewed; hewed** *or* **hewn** \'hyün\; **hew·ing** [Middle English, from Old English *hēawan;* akin to Old High German *houwan* to hew, Lithuanian *kauti* to forge, Latin *cudere* to beat] (before 12th century)
transitive verb
1 : to cut with blows of a heavy cutting instrument
2 : to fell by blows of an ax ⟨*hew* a tree⟩
3 : to give form or shape to with or as if with heavy cutting blows ⟨*hewed* their farms from the wilderness —J. T. Shotwell⟩
intransitive verb

1 : to make cutting blows
2 : CONFORM, ADHERE — often used in the phrase *hew to the line* ⟨no pressure . . . on newspapers to *hew* to the official line —*N.Y. Times Magazine*⟩
— **hew·er** *noun*
¹hex \'heks\ *verb* [Pennsylvania German *hexe,* from German *hexen,* from *Hexe* witch, from Old High German *hagzissa;* akin to Middle English *hagge* hag] (1830)
intransitive verb
: to practice witchcraft
transitive verb
1 : to put a hex on
2 : to affect as if by an evil spell : JINX ⟨giving in to an unscientific fear of *hexing* the whole project —Daniel Lang⟩
— **hex·er** *noun*
²hex *noun* (1856)
1 : a person who practices witchcraft : WITCH
2 : SPELL, JINX
³hex *adjective* (1924)
: HEXAGONAL ⟨a bolt with a *hex* head⟩
⁴hex *adjective or noun* (1970)
: HEXADECIMAL
hexa- *or* **hex-** *combining form* [Greek, from *hex* six — more at SIX]
1 : six ⟨*hexa*ploid⟩
2 : containing six atoms, groups, or equivalents ⟨*hexa*ne⟩
hexa·chlo·ro·eth·ane \ˌhek-sə-ˌklōr-ō-'e-ˌthān, -ˌklȯr-\ *or* **hexa·chlor·eth·ane** \-ˌklōr-'e-, -ˌklȯr-\ *noun* [International Scientific Vocabulary] (1898)
: a toxic crystalline compound C_2Cl_6 used especially in smoke bombs and in the control of liver flukes in ruminants
hexa·chlo·ro·phene \-'klōr-ə-ˌfēn, -'klȯr-\ *noun* [*hexa-* + *chlor-* + *phenol*] (1948)
: a powdered phenolic bacteria-inhibiting agent $C_{13}Cl_6H_6O_2$
hexa·chord \'hek-sə-ˌkȯrd\ *noun* [*hexa-* + Greek *chordē* string — more at YARN] (1730)
: a diatonic series of six tones having a semitone between the third and fourth tones
hexa·dec·i·mal \ˌhek-sə-'des-məl, -'de-sə-\ *adjective* (1954)
: of, relating to, or being a number system with a base of 16
— **hexadecimal** *noun*
hexa·gon \'hek-sə-ˌgän\ *noun* [Greek *hexagōnon,* neuter of *hexagōnos* hexagonal, from *hexa-* + *gōnia* angle — more at -GON] (1570)
: a polygon of six angles and six sides
hex·ag·o·nal \hek-'sa-gə-nᵊl\ *adjective* (1571)
1 : having six angles and six sides
2 : having a hexagon as section or base
3 : relating to or being a crystal system characterized by three equal lateral axes intersecting at angles of 60 degrees and a vertical axis of variable length at right angles
— **hex·ag·o·nal·ly** \-nᵊl-ē\ *adverb*
hexa·gram \'hek-sə-ˌgram\ *noun* [International Scientific Vocabulary] (1871)
: a plane figure that has the shape of a 6-pointed star, that consists of two intersecting congruent equilateral triangles having the same point as center and their sides parallel, and that can be formed by constructing external equilateral triangles on the sides of a regular hexagon — compare SOLOMON'S SEAL 2

hexagram

hexa·he·dron \ˌhek-sə-'hē-drən\ *noun, plural* **-drons** *also* **-dra** \-drə\ [Late Latin, from Greek *hexaedron,* from neuter of *hexaedros* of six surfaces, from *hexa-* + *hedra* seat — more at SIT] (1571)
: a polyhedron of six faces (as a cube)
hexa·hy·drate \-'hī-ˌdrāt\ *noun* (1908)
: a chemical compound with six molecules of water
hex·am·e·ter \hek-'sa-mə-tər\ *noun* [Latin, from Greek *hexametron,* from neuter of *hex-*

ametros having six measures, from *hexa-* + *metron* measure — more at MEASURE] (1546)
: a line of verse consisting of six metrical feet
hexa·me·tho·ni·um \ˌhek-sə-mə-'thō-nē-əm\ *noun* [*hexa-* + *meth-* + *-onium*] (1949)
: either of two compounds $C_{12}H_{30}Br_2N_2$ or $C_{12}H_{30}Cl_2N_2$ used as ganglionic blocking agents in the treatment of hypertension
hexa·meth·y·lene·tet·ra·mine \ˌhek-sə-ˌme-thə-ˌlēn-'te-trə-ˌmēn\ *noun* [International Scientific Vocabulary *hexa-* + *methylene* + *tetra-* + *amine*] (1888)
: a crystalline compound $C_6H_{12}N_4$ used especially as an accelerator in vulcanizing rubber and as a urinary antiseptic — compare METHENAMINE
hex·ane \'hek-ˌsān\ *noun* [International Scientific Vocabulary] (1877)
: any of several isomeric volatile liquid alkanes C_6H_{14} found in petroleum
hex·a·no·ic acid \ˌhek-sə-ˌnō-ik-\ *noun* [International Scientific Vocabulary *hexane* + *-oic*] (1926)
: CAPROIC ACID
hexa·ploid \'hek-sə-ˌplȯid\ *adjective* [International Scientific Vocabulary] (1912)
: having or being six times the monoploid chromosome number
— **hexaploid** *noun*
— **hexa·ploi·dy** \-ˌplȯi-dē\ *noun*
¹hexa·pod \'hek-sə-ˌpäd\ *noun* [Greek *hexapod-, hexapous* having six feet, from *hexa-* + *pod-, pous* foot — more at FOOT] (1668)
: INSECT 1b
²hexapod *adjective* (circa 1847)
1 : six-footed
2 : of or relating to insects
Hexa·teuch \'hek-sə-ˌtük, -ˌtyük\ *noun* [*hexa-* + Greek *teuchos* book — more at PENTATEUCH] (1878)
: the first six books of the Bible
hex·e·rei \ˌhek-sə-'rī\ *noun* [Pennsylvania German, from German, from *Hexe* witch] (1898)
: WITCHCRAFT
hexo·bar·bi·tal \ˌhek-sə-'bär-bə-ˌtȯl\ *noun* [*hexo-* (from *hexa-*) + *barbital*] (1941)
: a barbiturate $C_{12}H_{16}N_2O_3$ used as a sedative and hypnotic and in the form of its soluble sodium salt as an intravenous anesthetic of short duration
hexo·ki·nase \ˌhek-sə-'kī-ˌnās, -ˌnāz\ *noun* [*hexose* + *kinase*] (1930)
: any of a group of enzymes that accelerate the phosphorylation of hexoses (as in the formation of glucose-6-phosphate from glucose and ATP) in carbohydrate metabolism
hex·os·a·min·i·dase \ˌhek-ˌsä-sə-'mi-nə-ˌdās, -ˌdāz\ *noun* [*hexose* + *amino* + *-ide* + *-ase*] (1969)
: either of two hydrolytic enzymes that catalyze the splitting off of a hexose from a ganglioside and are deficient in some metabolic diseases (as a variant of Tay-Sachs disease)
hex·o·san \'hek-sə-ˌsan\ *noun* (1894)
: a polysaccharide yielding only hexoses on hydrolysis
hex·ose \'hek-ˌsōs, -ˌsōz\ *noun* [International Scientific Vocabulary] (1892)
: a monosaccharide (as glucose) containing six carbon atoms in the molecule
hex·yl \'hek-səl\ *noun* [International Scientific Vocabulary] (1869)
: an alkyl radical $C_6H_{13}-$ derived from a hexane
hex·yl·res·or·cin·ol \ˌhek-səl-rə-'zȯr-sᵊn-ˌȯl, -ˌōl\ *noun* (1924)
: a crystalline phenol $C_{12}H_{18}O_2$ used as an antiseptic and anthelmintic
hey \'hā\ *interjection* [Middle English] (13th century)
— used especially to call attention or to express interrogation, surprise, or exultation
¹hey·day \'hā-ˌdā\ *interjection* [irregular from *hey*] (1672)
archaic — used to express elation or wonder
²heyday *noun* (1590)

1 *archaic* : high spirits
2 : the period of one's greatest strength, vigor, or prosperity

hey presto \(')hā-'pres-(,)tō\ *interjection* (1731)
British : suddenly as if by magic

Hez·e·ki·ah \,he-zə-'kī-ə\ *noun* [Hebrew *Ḥizqīyāh*]
: a king of Judah under whom the kingdom underwent a ruinous Assyrian invasion at the end of the 8th century B.C.

hi \'hī(-ē)\ *interjection* [Middle English *hy*] (15th century)
— used especially as a greeting

hi·a·tal \hī-'ā-t²l\ *adjective* (1909)
: of, relating to, or involving a hiatus

hiatal hernia *noun* (circa 1944)
: a hernia in which an anatomical part (as the stomach) protrudes through the esophageal hiatus of the diaphragm — called also *hiatus hernia*

hi·a·tus \hī-'ā-təs\ *noun* [Latin, from *hiare* to yawn — more at YAWN] (1563)
1 a : a break in or as if in a material object : GAP ⟨the *hiatus* between the theory and the practice of the party —J. G. Colton⟩ **b** : a gap or passage in an anatomical part or organ
2 a : an interruption in time or continuity : BREAK **b** : the occurrence of two vowel sounds without pause or intervening consonantal sound

Hi·a·wa·tha \,hī-ə-'wò-thə, ,hē-ə-, -'wä-\ *noun*
: the Indian hero of Longfellow's poem *The Song of Hiawatha*

hi·ba·chi \hi-'bä-chē\ *noun* [Japanese] (1863)
: a charcoal brazier

hi·ber·nac·u·lum \,hī-bər-'na-kyə-ləm\ *noun*, *plural* **-la** \-lə\ [New Latin, from Latin, winter residence, from *hibernare*] (1789)
: a shelter occupied during the winter by a dormant animal (as an insect or reptile)

hi·ber·nal \hī-'bər-n²l\ *adjective* (1646)
: of, relating to, or occurring in winter

hi·ber·nate \'hī-bər-,nāt\ *intransitive verb* **-nat·ed; -nat·ing** [Latin *hibernatus*, past participle of *hibernare* to pass the winter, from *hibernus* of winter; akin to Latin *hiems* winter, Greek *cheimōn*] (circa 1802)
1 : to pass the winter in a torpid or resting state
2 : to be or become inactive or dormant
— **hi·ber·na·tion** \,hī-bər-'nā-shən\ *noun*
— **hi·ber·na·tor** \'hī-bər-,nā-tər\ *noun*

¹Hi·ber·ni·an \hī-'bər-nē-ən\ *adjective* [Latin *Hibernia* Ireland] (1632)
: of, relating to, or characteristic of Ireland or the Irish

²Hibernian *noun* (1709)
: a native or inhabitant of Ireland

Hi·ber·no- *combining form* [Latin *Hibernia*]
1 : Irish and ⟨*Hiberno*-British⟩
2 : Irish ⟨*Hiberno*-English⟩

Hiberno–English *noun* (1985)
: the English language spoken in Ireland

hi·bis·cus \hī-'bis-kəs, hə-\ *noun* [New Latin, from Latin, marshmallow] (1706)
: any of a large genus (*Hibiscus*) of herbs, shrubs, or small trees of the mallow family with large showy flowers and usually dentate leaves

¹hic·cup *also* **hic·cough** \'hi-(,)kəp\ *noun* [imitative] (circa 1580)
1 : a spasmodic inhalation with closure of the glottis accompanied by a peculiar sound
2 : an attack of hiccuping — usually used in plural but singular or plural in construction

²hiccup *also* **hiccough** *intransitive verb* **hic·cuped** *also* **hic·cupped; hic·cup·ing** *also* **hic·cup·ping** (circa 1580)
: to make a hiccup; *also* : to be affected with hiccups

hic ja·cet \'hik-'jā-sət, 'hēk-'yä-kət\ *noun* [Latin, literally, here lies] (1654)
: EPITAPH

¹hick \'hik\ *noun* [*Hick*, nickname for *Richard*] (circa 1690)

: an unsophisticated provincial person
— **hick·ish** \'hi-kish\ *adjective*

²hick *adjective* (1920)
: UNSOPHISTICATED, PROVINCIAL ⟨a *hick* town⟩

¹hick·ey \'hi-kē\ *noun*, *plural* **hickeys** [origin unknown] (1913)
: DEVICE, GADGET

²hickey *noun*, *plural* **hickeys** [origin unknown] (circa 1915)
1 a : PIMPLE **b** : a temporary red mark on the skin (as one produced by biting and sucking)
2 *plural also* **hick·ies** : a small imperfection in printing

hick·o·ry \'hi-k(ə-)rē\ *noun*, *plural* **-ries** [short for obsolete *pokahickory*, from Virginia Algonquian *pawcohiccora* food prepared from pounded nuts] (1670)
1 a : any of a genus (*Carya*) of North American hardwood trees of the walnut family that often have sweet edible nuts **b** : the usually tough wood of a hickory
2 : a switch or cane (as of hickory wood) used especially for punishing a child
— **hickory** *adjective*

hid \'hid\ *adjective* (12th century)
: HIDDEN

hi·dal·go \hi-'dal-(,)gō, ē-'thäl-\ *noun*, *plural* **-gos** *often capitalized* [Spanish, from Old Spanish *fijo dalgo*, literally, son of something] (1594)
: a member of the lower nobility of Spain

Hi·dat·sa \hi-'dät-sə\ *noun*, *plural* **Hidatsa** *also* **Hidatsas** (1873)
1 : a member of an American Indian people of the Missouri River valley in North Dakota
2 : the Siouan language of the Hidatsa

hid·den \'hi-d²n\ *adjective* (13th century)
1 : being out of sight or not readily apparent : CONCEALED
2 : OBSCURE, UNEXPLAINED, UNDISCLOSED
— **hid·den·ness** \-nəs\ *noun*

hidden agenda *noun* (1971)
: an ulterior motive

hid·den·ite \'hi-d²n-,īt\ *noun* [William E. *Hidden* (died 1918) American mineralogist] (1881)
: a transparent yellow to green spodumene valued as a gem

hidden tax *noun* (1936)
1 : a tax that is ultimately paid by someone other than the person on whom it is levied
2 : an economic inequity that reduces one's real income or buying power

¹hide \'hīd\ *noun* [Middle English, from Old English *hīgid, hīd*] (before 12th century)
: any of various old English units of land area; *especially* : a unit of 120 acres

²hide *verb* **hid** \'hid\; **hid·den** \'hi-d²n\ *or* **hid; hid·ing** \'hī-diŋ\ [Middle English *hiden*, from Old English *hȳdan*; akin to Greek *keuthein* to conceal] (before 12th century)
transitive verb
1 a : to put out of sight : SECRETE **b** : to conceal for shelter or protection : SHIELD
2 : to keep secret
3 : to screen from or as if from view : OBSCURE
4 : to turn (the eyes or face) away in shame or anger
intransitive verb
1 : to remain out of sight — often used with *out*
2 : to seek protection or evade responsibility
☆
— **hid·er** \'hī-dər\ *noun*

³hide *noun* (14th century)
chiefly British : BLIND 2

⁴hide *noun* [Middle English, from Old English *hȳd;* akin to Old High German *hūt* hide, Latin *cutis* skin, Greek *kytos* hollow vessel] (before 12th century)
1 : the skin of an animal whether raw or dressed — used especially of large heavy skins
2 : the life or physical well-being of a person ⟨betrayed his friend to save his own *hide*⟩

— **hide or hair** *or* **hide nor hair** : a vestige or trace of someone or something ⟨a wife he hadn't seen *hide or hair* of in over 20 years —H. L. Davis⟩

⁵hide *transitive verb* **hid·ed; hid·ing** (circa 1825)
: to give a beating to : FLOG

hide–and–seek \,hī-d²n-'sēk\ *noun* (circa 1727)
: a children's game in which one player does not look while others hide and then goes to find them

hide·away \'hī-də-,wā\ *noun* (1926)
: RETREAT, HIDEOUT

hide·bound \'hī-,baùnd\ *adjective* (1559)
1 *of a domestic animal* : having a dry skin lacking in pliancy and adhering closely to the underlying flesh
2 : having an inflexible or ultraconservative character

hid·eous \'hi-dē-əs\ *adjective* [alteration of Middle English *hidous*, from Middle French, from *hisde, hide* terror] (14th century)
1 : offensive to the senses and especially to sight : exceedingly ugly
2 : morally offensive : SHOCKING
— **hid·eos·i·ty** \,hi-dē-'ä-sə-tē\ *noun*
— **hid·eous·ly** *adverb*
— **hid·eous·ness** *noun*

hide·out \'hī-,daùt\ *noun* (1904)
: a place of refuge, retreat, or concealment

hid·ey–hole *or* **hidy–hole** \'hī-dē-,hōl\ *noun* [alteration of earlier *hiding-hole*] (1817)
: HIDEAWAY

hie \'hī\ *verb* **hied; hy·ing** *or* **hie·ing** [Middle English, from Old English *hīgian* to strive, hasten] (12th century)
intransitive verb
: to go quickly : HASTEN
transitive verb
: to cause (oneself) to go quickly

hi·er·arch \'hī-(ə-),rärk\ *noun* [Middle English *ierarchis*, plural, from Middle French or Medieval Latin; Middle French *hierarche*, from Medieval Latin *hierarcha*, from Greek *hierarchēs*, from *hieros* sacred + *-archēs* -arch] (15th century)
1 : a religious leader in a position of authority
2 : a person high in a hierarchy
— **hi·er·ar·chal** \,hī-(ə-)'rär-kəl\ *adjective*

hi·er·ar·chi·cal \,hī-(ə-)'rär-ki-kəl *also* hir-'är-\ *or* **hi·er·ar·chic** \-kik\ *adjective* (1561)
: of, relating to, or arranged in a hierarchy
— **hi·er·ar·chi·cal·ly** \-ki-k(ə-)lē\ *adverb*

hi·er·ar·chize \'hī-(ə-),rär-,kīz\ *transitive verb* **-chized; -chiz·ing** (1884)
: to arrange in a hierarchy

hi·er·ar·chy \'hī-(ə-),rär-kē *also* 'hi-(ə)r-,är-\ *noun*, *plural* **-chies** (14th century)
1 : a division of angels
2 a : a ruling body of clergy organized into orders or ranks each subordinate to the one above it; *especially* : the bishops of a province

☆ SYNONYMS
Hide, conceal, screen, secrete, bury mean to withhold or withdraw from sight. HIDE may or may not suggest intent ⟨*hide* in the closet⟩ ⟨a house *hidden* in the woods⟩. CONCEAL usually does imply intent and often specifically implies a refusal to divulge ⟨*concealed* the weapon⟩. SCREEN implies an interposing of something that prevents discovery ⟨a house *screened* by trees⟩. SECRETE suggests a depositing in a place unknown to others ⟨*secreted* the amulet inside his shirt⟩. BURY implies covering up so as to hide completely ⟨*buried* the treasure⟩.

or nation **b :** church government by a hierarchy

3 : a body of persons in authority

4 : the classification of a group of people according to ability or to economic, social, or professional standing; *also* **:** the group so classified

5 : a graded or ranked series ⟨Christian *hierarchy* of values⟩ ⟨a machine's *hierarchy* of responses⟩

hi·er·at·ic \,hī-(ə-)'ra-tik\ *adjective* [Latin *hieraticus* sacerdotal, from Greek *hieratikos,* from *hierasthai* to perform priestly functions, from *hieros* sacred; probably akin to Sanskrit *iṣara* vigorous] (1669)

1 : constituting or belonging to a cursive form of ancient Egyptian writing simpler than the hieroglyphic

2 : SACERDOTAL

3 : highly stylized or formal ⟨*hieratic* poses⟩
— **hi·er·at·i·cal·ly** \-ti-k(ə-)lē\ *adverb*

hi·ero·dule \'hī-(ə-)rō-,dü(ə)l, hī-'er-ə-, -,dyü(ə)l\ *noun* [Late Latin *hierodulus,* from Greek *hierodoulos,* from *hieron* temple + *doulos* slave] (1835)
: a slave or prostitute in the service of a temple (as in ancient Greece)

hi·ero·glyph \'hī-(ə-)rə-,glif\ *noun* [French *hiéroglyphe,* from Middle French, back-formation from *hieroglyphique*] (1598)

1 : a character used in a system of hieroglyphic writing

2 : something that resembles a hieroglyph

¹hi·ero·glyph·ic \,hī-(ə-)rə-'gli-fik\ *also* **hi·ero·glyph·i·cal** \-fi-kəl\ *adjective* [Middle French *hieroglyphique,* from Late Latin *hieroglyphicus,* from Greek *hieroglyphikos,* from *hieros* + *glyphein* to carve — more at CLEAVE] (1585)

1 : written in, constituting, or belonging to a system of writing mainly in pictorial characters

2 : inscribed with hieroglyphic

3 : resembling hieroglyphic in difficulty of decipherment
— **hi·ero·glyph·i·cal·ly** \-fi-k(ə-)lē\ *adverb*

²hieroglyphic *noun* (1586)

1 : HIEROGLYPH

2 : a system of hieroglyphic writing; *specifically* **:** the picture script

hieroglyphic 2

of the ancient Egyptian priesthood — often used in plural but singular or plural in construction

3 : something that resembles a hieroglyph especially in difficulty of decipherment

hi·ero·phant \'hī-(ə-)rə-,fant, hī-'er-ə-fənt\ *noun* [Late Latin *hierophanta,* from Greek *hierophantēs,* from *hieros* + *phainein* to show — more at FANCY] (1677)

1 : a priest in ancient Greece; *specifically* **:** the chief priest of the Eleusinian mysteries

2 a : EXPOSITOR **b :** ADVOCATE
— **hi·ero·phan·tic** \,hī-(ə-)rə-'fan-tik, (,)hī-,er-ə-\ *adjective*

hi·fa·lu·tin *variant of* HIGHFALUTIN

hi-fi \'hī-'fī\ *noun* (1950)

1 : HIGH FIDELITY

2 : equipment for reproduction of sound with high fidelity

hig·gle \'hi-gəl\ *intransitive verb* **hig·gled; hig·gling** \-g(ə-)liŋ\ [probably alteration of *haggle*] (1633)
: HAGGLE
— **hig·gler** \-g(ə-)lər\ *noun*

hig·gle·dy–pig·gle·dy \,hi-gəl-dē-'pi-gəl-dē\ *adverb* [origin unknown] (circa 1598)
: in a confused, disordered, or random manner ⟨tiny hovels piled *higgledy-piggledy* against each other —Edward Behr⟩
— **higgledy–piggledy** *adjective*

¹high \'hī\ *adjective* [Middle English, from Old English *hēah;* akin to Old High German *hōh* high, Lithuanian *kaukaras* hill] (before 12th century)

1 a : having large extension upward **:** taller than average, usual, or expected ⟨a *high* wall⟩ **b :** having a specified elevation **:** TALL ⟨six feet *high*⟩ — often used in combinations ⟨sky-*high*⟩ ⟨waist-*high*⟩

2 a (1) **:** advanced toward the acme or culmination ⟨*high* summer⟩ (2) **:** advanced toward the most active or culminating period ⟨on the Riviera during *high* season⟩ (3) **:** constituting the late, most fully developed, or most creative stage or period ⟨*high* Gothic⟩ (4) **:** advanced in complexity, development, or elaboration ⟨the *higher* apes⟩ ⟨*higher* mathematics⟩ **b :** verging on lateness — usually used in the phrase *high time* **c :** long past **:** REMOTE ⟨*high* antiquity⟩

3 : elevated in pitch ⟨a *high* note⟩

4 : relatively far from the equator ⟨*high* latitude⟩

5 : rich in quality **:** LUXURIOUS ⟨*high* living⟩

6 : slightly tainted ⟨*high* game⟩; *also* **:** MALODOROUS ⟨smelled rather *high*⟩

7 : exalted in character **:** NOBLE ⟨*high* purposes⟩

8 : of greater degree, amount, cost, value, or content than average, usual, or expected ⟨*high* prices⟩ ⟨food *high* in iron⟩ ⟨the *high* bid⟩

9 : of relatively great importance: as **a :** foremost in rank, dignity, or standing ⟨*high* officials⟩ **b :** SERIOUS, GRAVE ⟨*high* crimes⟩ **c :** observed with the utmost solemnity ⟨*high* religious observances⟩ **d :** CRITICAL, CLIMACTIC ⟨the *high* point of the novel⟩ **e :** intellectually or artistically of the first order ⟨*high* culture⟩ **f :** marked by sublime, heroic, or stirring events or subject matter ⟨*high* tragedy⟩ ⟨*high* adventure⟩

10 : FORCIBLE, STRONG ⟨*high* winds⟩

11 : stressing matters of doctrine and ceremony; *specifically* **:** HIGH CHURCH

12 a : filled with or expressing great joy or excitement ⟨*high* spirits⟩ **b :** INTOXICATED; *also* **:** excited or stupefied by or as if by a drug

13 : articulated with some part of the tongue close to the palate ⟨a *high* vowel⟩ ☆
— **high on :** enthusiastically in favor or support of

²high *adverb* (before 12th century)

1 : at or to a high place, altitude, level, or degree ⟨climbed *higher*⟩ ⟨passions ran *high*⟩

2 : WELL, LUXURIOUSLY — often used in the phrases *high off the hog* and *high on the hog*

³high *noun* (13th century)

1 : an elevated place or region: as **a :** HILL, KNOLL **b :** the space overhead **:** SKY — usually used with *on* **c :** HEAVEN — usually used with *on*

2 : a region of high barometric pressure — called also *anticyclone*

3 a : a high point or level **:** HEIGHT ⟨sales reached a new *high*⟩ **b :** the transmission gear of a vehicle (as an automobile) giving the highest speed of travel

4 a : an excited, euphoric, or stupefied state produced by or as if by a drug **b :** a state of elation or high spirits

high altar *noun* (before 12th century)
: the principal altar in a church

high analysis *adjective* (1949)
of a fertilizer **:** containing more than 20 percent of total plant nutrients

high and dry *adjective* (1822)

1 : being out of reach of the current or tide or out of the water

2 : being in a helpless or abandoned position

high and low *adverb* (14th century)
: EVERYWHERE

high-and-mighty *adjective* (1654)
: characterized by arrogance **:** IMPERIOUS

¹high·ball \'hī-,bol\ *noun* (1897)

1 : a railroad signal for a train to proceed at full speed

2 : an iced drink containing liquor (as whiskey) and water or a carbonated beverage and served in a tall glass

²highball *intransitive verb* (1912)
: to go at full or high speed ⟨a *highballing* express train⟩

high beam *noun* (1939)
: the long-range focus of a vehicle headlight

high·bind·er \'hī-,bīn-dər\ *noun* [the *Highbinders,* gang of ruffians in New York City (about 1806)] (1876)

1 : a professional killer operating in the Chinese quarter of an American city

2 : a corrupt politician

high blood pressure *noun* (1916)
: HYPERTENSION

high·born \'hī-'born\ *adjective* (13th century)
: of noble birth

high·boy \-,boi\ *noun* (1891)
: a tall chest of drawers with a legged base

high·bred \-'bred\ *adjective* (1674)
: coming from superior stock

high·brow \-,braù\ *noun* (circa 1903)
: a person who possesses or has pretensions to superior learning or culture
— **highbrow** *adjective*
— **high-browed** \-,braùd\ *adjective*
— **high·brow·ism** \-,braù-,i-zəm\ *noun*

high·bush \-'bùsh\ *adjective* (1805)
: forming a notably tall or erect bush; *also* **:** borne on a highbush plant

highboy

highbush blueberry *noun* (1913)
: a variable moisture-loving North American shrub (*Vaccinium corymbosum*) that is the source of most cultivated blueberries; *also* **:** its fruit

high chair *noun* (1848)
: a child's chair with long legs, a footrest, and usually a feeding tray

High Church *adjective* (1687)
: favoring especially in Anglican worship the sacerdotal, liturgical, ceremonial, and traditional elements in worship

High Churchman *noun* (1687)
: an Anglican who adheres to High Church elements in worship

high-class \'hī-'klas\ *adjective* (1864)
: of superior quality or status

high comedy *noun* (1895)
: comedy employing subtle characterizations and witty dialogue — compare LOW COMEDY

high command *noun* (1917)

1 : the supreme headquarters of a military force

2 : the highest leaders in an organization

high commissioner *noun* (1881)
: a principal or a high-ranking commissioner; *especially* **:** an ambassadorial representative of the government of one country stationed in another

high–con·cept \'hī-'kän-,sept\ *adjective* (1985)

: having or exploiting elements (as fast action, glamour, or suspense) that appeal to a wide audience ⟨*high-concept* movies⟩

high–count \'hī-ˌkaȧnt\ *adjective* (1926) **:** having a large number of warp and weft yarns to the square inch ⟨*high-count* percale sheeting⟩

high court *noun* (14th century) **:** SUPREME COURT

high–density lipoprotein *noun* (1960) **:** HDL

high–end \'hī-ˌend\ *adjective* (1980) **:** UPSCALE ⟨*high-end* boutiques⟩

high–energy *adjective* (1934) **1 a :** having such speed and kinetic energy as to exhibit relativistic departure from classical laws of motion — used especially of elementary particles whose velocity has been imparted by an accelerator **b :** of or relating to high-energy particles ⟨a *high-energy* reaction⟩ **2 :** yielding a relatively large amount of energy when undergoing hydrolysis ⟨*high-energy* phosphate bonds in ATP⟩

high–energy physics *noun* (1964) **:** PARTICLE PHYSICS

higher criticism *noun* (1836) **:** study of biblical writings to determine their literary history and the purpose and meaning of the authors — compare LOWER CRITICISM
— higher critic *noun*

higher education *noun* (1866) **:** education beyond the secondary level; *especially* **:** education provided by a college or university

higher law *noun* (1844) **:** a principle of divine or moral law that is considered to be superior to constitutions and enacted legislation

higher learning *noun* (1926) **:** education, learning, or scholarship on the collegiate or university level

high·er–up \ˌhī-ə-ˈrəp, ˈhī-ə-ˌ\ *noun* (1911) **:** a superior officer or official

high explosive *noun* (1877) **:** an explosive (as TNT) that generates gas with extreme rapidity and has a shattering effect

high·fa·lu·tin \ˌhī-fə-ˈlü-tᵊn\ *adjective* [perhaps from ²*high* + alteration of *fluting*, present participle of *flute*] (1839) **1 :** PRETENTIOUS **2 :** expressed in or marked by the use of high-flown bombastic language **:** POMPOUS

high fashion *noun* (1945) **1 :** HIGH STYLE **2 :** HAUTE COUTURE

high fidelity *noun* (1934) **:** the reproduction of an effect (as sound or an image) with a high degree of faithfulness to the original
— high–fidelity *adjective*

high five *noun* (1981) **:** a slapping of upraised right hands by two people (as in celebration)
— high–five *verb*

high·fli·er *or* **high·fly·er** \'hī-ˈflī(-ə)r\ *noun* (circa 1961) **1 :** a stock whose price rises much more rapidly than the market average **2 :** a company whose stock is a highflier **3 :** an ambitiously competitive person with high aspirations

high–flown \'hī-ˈflōn\ *adjective* (1647) **1 :** exceedingly or excessively high or favorable **2 :** having an excessively embellished or inflated character **:** PRETENTIOUS ⟨inflated rhetoric and *high-flown* vocabulary —James Yaffe⟩

high–fly·ing \-ˈflī-iŋ\ *adjective* (1581) **1 :** marked by extravagance, pretension, or excessive ambition **2 :** rising to considerable height

high frequency *noun* (1892) **:** a radio frequency between very high frequency and medium frequency — see RADIO FREQUENCY table

high gear *noun* (1896) **1 :** HIGH 3b **2 :** a state of intense or maximum activity — usually used with *in*

High German *noun* (1673) **1 :** German as natively used in southern and central Germany **2 :** GERMAN 3b

high–grade *adjective* (1878) **1 :** of superior grade or quality ⟨*high-grade* bonds⟩ **2 :** being near the upper or most favorable extreme of a specified range

high ground *noun* (1944) **:** a position of advantage or preeminence

high–hand·ed \-ˈhan-dəd\ *adjective* (1631) **:** having or showing no regard for the rights, concerns, or feelings of others **:** ARBITRARY, OVERBEARING
— high–hand·ed·ly *adverb*
— high–hand·ed·ness *noun*

high–hat \'hī-ˈhat\ *adjective* (1924) **:** SUPERCILIOUS, SNOBBISH
— high–hat *transitive verb*

high hat *noun* (1889) **1 :** ¹BEAVER 2 **2** *or* **hi–hat :** a pair of cymbals operated by a foot pedal

high heels *noun plural* (1671) **:** shoes with high heels

High Holiday *noun* (1946) **:** either of two important Jewish holidays: **a :** ROSH HASHANAH **b :** YOM KIPPUR

high horse *noun* (1721) **:** an arrogant and unyielding mood or attitude

high·jack \'hī-ˌjak\ *variant of* HIJACK

high jinks *noun plural* (1825) **:** boisterous or rambunctious carryings-on **:** carefree antics or horseplay

high jump *noun* (1895) **:** a jump for height over a horizontal bar in a track-and-field contest
— high jumper *noun*

¹high·land \'hī-lənd\ *noun* (before 12th century) **:** elevated or mountainous land

²highland *adjective* (15th century) **1 :** of or relating to a highland **2** *capitalized* **:** of or relating to the Highlands of Scotland

high·land·er \-lən-dər\ *noun* (1610) **1 :** an inhabitant of a highland **2** *capitalized* **:** an inhabitant of the Highlands of Scotland

Highland fling *noun* (1804) **:** a lively Scottish folk dance

high–lev·el \'hī-ˈle-vəl\ *adjective* (1876) **1 :** occurring, done, or placed at a high level **2 :** being of high importance or rank ⟨*high-level* diplomats⟩ **3 :** of, relating to, or being a computer programming language (as BASIC or Pascal) which is similar to a natural language (as English) and in which each statement is translated by a compiler usually into several machine language instructions

¹high·light \'hī-ˌlīt\ *noun* (circa 1889) **1 :** the lightest spot or area (as in a painting) **:** any of several spots in a modeled drawing or painting that receives the greatest amount of illumination **2 :** something (as an event or detail) that is of major significance or special interest

²highlight *transitive verb* **-light·ed; -light·ing** (1927) **1 :** to throw a strong light on **2 a :** to center attention on **b :** to constitute a highlight of

high–low–jack \ˌhī-ˌlō-ˈjak\ *noun* (1818) **:** an all-fours game in which scores are made by winning the highest trump, the lowest trump, the jack of trumps, and either the ten of trumps or the most points

high·ly \'hī-lē\ *adverb* (before 12th century) **1 :** in or to a high place, level, or rank **2 :** in or to a high degree or amount

3 : with approval **:** FAVORABLY

high mass *noun, often H&M capitalized* (12th century) **:** a mass marked by the singing of prescribed parts by the celebrant and the choir or congregation

high–mind·ed \'hī-ˈmīn-dəd\ *adjective* (1556) **:** marked by elevated principles and feelings; *also* **:** PRETENTIOUS ⟨too *high-minded* to read any fiction —Alfred Kazin⟩
— high–mind·ed·ly *adverb*
— high–mind·ed·ness *noun*

high–muck–a–muck \ˌhī-ˈmə-ki-ˌmək\ *or* **high–muck·e·ty–muck** \ˌhī-ˈmə-kə-tē-ˌmək\ *noun* [by folk etymology from Chinook Jargon *hayo makamak* plenty to eat] (1856) **:** an important and often arrogant person ◇

high·ness \'hī-nəs\ *noun* (before 12th century) **1 :** the quality or state of being high **2** — used as a title for a person of exalted rank (as a king or prince)

high noon *noun* (1523) **1 :** precisely noon **2 :** the most advanced, flourishing, or creative stage or period ⟨the *high noon* of her career⟩

high–octane *adjective* (1932) **1 :** having a high octane number and hence good antiknock properties ⟨*high-octane* gasoline⟩ **2 :** HIGH-POWERED

high–pitched \'hī-ˈpicht\ *adjective* (1748) **1 :** having a high pitch ⟨a *high-pitched* voice⟩ **2 :** marked by or exhibiting strong feeling **:** AGITATED ⟨a *high-pitched*, almost frantic campaign —Geoffrey Rice⟩

high place *noun* (14th century) **:** a temple or altar used by the ancient Semites and built usually on a hill or elevation

high polymer *noun* (1942) **:** a substance (as polystyrene) consisting of molecules that are large multiples of units of low molecular weight

high–pow·ered \'hī-ˈpaȯ(-ə)rd\ *also* **high–pow·er** \-ˈpaȯ(-ə)r\ *adjective* (1893) **1 :** having great drive, energy, or capacity **:** DYNAMIC ⟨a *high-powered* executive⟩

◇ WORD HISTORY

high–muck–a–muck Chinook Jargon was a pidgin spoken in the Pacific Northwest during the 19th century. Its vocabulary was drawn largely from lower Chinook, once spoken at the mouth of the Columbia River, and Nootka, spoken by an Indian people living on western Vancouver Island. A small number of words from Chinook Jargon have found their way into American and Canadian English, of which the most curious is the phrase *hayo makamak*, literally "plenty of food," both elements of which are Nootka in origin (*hayo*, literally, "ten" and *ma·ho·maq-* "eat"). Somehow this phrase was transplanted from the Northwest to central California, where it surfaced in 1856 as a colloquialism meaning not "plenty of food," but "big shot." Presumably the first syllable was transformed by folk-etymology into *high*, though how *makamak* came to be interpreted as "person" is unclear. Indians of local importance in Northwest Coast cultures would give potlatches at which *hayo makamak* would be distributed, but there is no evidence that the phrase was transferred from food to person in Chinook Jargon. At any rate, once established, further variants of *high-muck-a-muck* have proliferated, such as *high-muckety-muck*, *high-monkey-monk*, and—by a second round of folk-etymology—*high mogul*.

2 : having or conferring great influence ⟨a *high-powered* job⟩

¹high–pressure *adjective* (1824)
1 a : having or involving a high or comparatively high pressure especially greatly exceeding that of the atmosphere **b :** having a high barometric pressure
2 a : using or involving aggressive and insistent sales techniques **b :** imposing or involving severe strain or tension ⟨*high-pressure* occupations⟩

²high–pressure *transitive verb* (1926)
: to sell or influence by high-pressure tactics

high priest *noun* (14th century)
1 : a chief priest especially of the ancient Jewish Levitical priesthood traditionally traced from Aaron
2 : a priest of the Melchizedek priesthood in the Mormon Church
3 : the head of a movement or chief exponent of a doctrine or an art
— high priesthood *noun*

high priestess *noun* (1645)
: a chief priestess

high relief *noun* (circa 1828)
: sculptural relief in which at least half of the circumference of the modeled form projects

high–rise \'hī-'rīz\ *adjective* (1954)
1 : being multistory and equipped with elevators ⟨*high-rise* apartments⟩
2 : of, relating to, or characterized by high-rise buildings
— high–rise \'hī-,\ *noun*

high road *noun* (1709)
1 : HIGHWAY
2 : the easiest course
3 : an ethical course

high roller *noun* (1881)
1 : a person who spends freely in luxurious living
2 : a person who gambles recklessly or for high stakes
— high–rolling *adjective*

¹high school *noun* (1824)
: a school especially in the U.S. usually including grades 9–12 or 10–12
— high school·er \-'skü-lər\ *noun*

²high school *noun* [translation of French *haute école*] (1884)
: a system of advanced exercises in horsemanship

high sea *noun* (before 12th century)
: the open part of a sea or ocean especially outside territorial waters — usually used in plural

high sign *noun* (1902)
: a gesture used as a signal (as of approval or warning) — usually used in the phrase *give the high sign*

high–sound·ing \'hī-'saun-diŋ\ *adjective* (1784)
: POMPOUS, IMPOSING

high–speed \'hī-'spēd\ *adjective* (1873)
1 : operated or adapted for operation at high speed
2 : relating to the production of short-exposure photographs of rapidly moving objects or events of short duration

high–spir·it·ed \-'spir-ə-təd\ *adjective* (circa 1631)
: characterized by a bold or energetic spirit
— high–spir·it·ed·ly *adverb*
— high–spir·it·ed·ness *noun*

high·spot \'hī-,spät\ *noun* (1910)
: HIGHLIGHT 2

high–stick·ing \-,sti-kiŋ\ *noun* (1947)
: the act of carrying the blade of the stick at an illegal height in ice hockey

high street *noun* (before 12th century)
British **:** a main or principal street

high–strung \'hī-'strəŋ\ *adjective* (1748)
: having an extremely nervous or sensitive temperament

high style *noun* (1939)
: the newest style in fashion or design usually adopted by a limited number of people

hight \'hīt\ *adjective* [Middle English, past participle (earlier past) of *hoten* to command, call, be called, from Old English *hātan;* akin to Old High German *heizzan* to command, call] (15th century)
archaic **:** being called **:** NAMED

high table *noun* (1711)
: an elevated table in the dining room of a British college for use by the master and fellows and distinguished guests

high·tail \'hī-,tāl\ *intransitive verb* (1925)
: to move at full speed or rapidly often in making a retreat — usually used with *it*

high tea *noun* (1831)
: a fairly substantial late afternoon or early evening meal at which tea is served

high tech \-'tek\ *noun* (1973)
1 : HIGH TECHNOLOGY
2 : a style of interior design featuring industrial products, materials, or designs
— high–tech *adjective*

high technology *noun* (1968)
: scientific technology involving the production or use of advanced or sophisticated devices especially in the fields of electronics and computers

high–tension *adjective* (1905)
: having or using a high voltage

high–test *adjective* (1923)
: meeting a high standard; *also* **:** HIGH-OCTANE

high tide *noun* (1745)
1 : the tide when the water is at its greatest elevation
2 : culminating point **:** CLIMAX

high–toned \'hī-'tōnd\ *adjective* (1807)
1 : high in social, moral, or intellectual quality
2 : PRETENTIOUS, POMPOUS

high–top \'hī-,täp\ *adjective* (1966)
: extending up over the ankle ⟨*high-top* sneakers⟩
— high–tops *noun plural*

high treason *noun* (15th century)
: TREASON 2

high–volt·age \'hī-'vōl-tij\ *adjective* (1948)
: marked by great energy **:** ELECTRIC, DYNAMIC ⟨a *high-voltage* performance⟩

high–water *adjective* (1856)
: unusually short ⟨*high-water* pants⟩

high water *noun* (15th century)
: a high stage of the water in a river or lake; *also* **:** HIGH TIDE

high–water mark *noun* (1814)
: highest point **:** PEAK

high·way \'hī-,wā\ *noun* (before 12th century)
: a public way; *especially* **:** a main direct road

high·way·man \-mən\ *noun* (1649)
: a person who robs travelers on a road

highway robbery *noun* (1778)
1 : robbery committed on or near a public highway usually against travelers
2 : excessive profit or advantage derived from a business transaction

high–wire \'hī-,wī(-ə)r\ *adjective* (1956)
1 : involving great risk ⟨a financial *high-wire* act⟩
2 : DARING ⟨*high-wire* prose⟩

high–wrought \'hī-'rót\ *adjective* (1604)
: extremely agitated

high yellow *noun* (1923)
: a black person of light complexion — called also *high yal·ler* \-'ya-lər\; often taken to be offensive

hi–hat *variant of* HIGH HAT 2

hi·jack \'hī-,jak\ *transitive verb* [origin unknown] (1923)
1 a : to steal by stopping a vehicle on the highway **b :** to commandeer (a flying airplane) especially by coercing the pilot at gunpoint **c :** to stop and steal from (a vehicle in transit) **d :** KIDNAP
2 a : to steal or rob as if by hijacking **b :** to subject to extortion or swindling
— hijack *noun*
— hi·jack·er *noun*

hi·jinks \'hī-,jiŋks\ *variant of* HIGH JINKS

¹hike \'hīk\ *verb* **hiked; hik·ing** [perhaps akin to ¹*hitch*] (1804)
intransitive verb
1 a : to go on a hike **b :** to travel by any means
2 : to rise up; *especially* **:** to work upward out of place ⟨skirt had *hiked* up in back⟩
transitive verb
1 a : to move, pull, or raise with a sudden motion ⟨*hiked* himself onto the top bunk⟩ **b :** SNAP 6b **c :** to raise in amount sharply or suddenly ⟨*hike* rents⟩
2 : to take on a hike
— hik·er *noun*

²hike *noun* (1865)
1 : a long walk especially for pleasure or exercise
2 : an increase especially in quantity or amount ⟨a new wage *hike*⟩
3 : SNAP 11

hi·lar \'hī-lər\ *adjective* (circa 1859)
: of, relating to, or located near a hilum

hi·lar·i·ous \hi-'lar-ē-əs, hī-, -'ler-\ *adjective* [irregular from Latin *hilarus, hilaris* cheerful, from Greek *hilaros*] (circa 1840)
: marked by or affording hilarity
— hi·lar·i·ous·ly *adverb*
— hi·lar·i·ous·ness *noun*

hi·lar·i·ty \-ə-tē\ *noun* (15th century)
: high spirits that may be carried to the point of boisterous conviviality or merriment

Hil·bert space \'hil-bərt-\ *noun* [David *Hilbert*] (1939)
: a vector space for which a scalar product is defined and in which every Cauchy sequence composed of elements in the space converges to a limit in the space

hil·ding \'hil-diŋ\ *noun* [*hilding*, adjective (base)] (1592)
archaic **:** a base contemptible person

¹hill \'hil\ *noun* [Middle English, from Old English *hyll;* akin to Latin *collis* hill, *culmen* top] (before 12th century)
1 : a usually rounded natural elevation of land lower than a mountain
2 : an artificial heap or mound (as of earth)
3 : several seeds or plants planted in a group rather than a row
4 : SLOPE, INCLINE

²hill *transitive verb* (1581)
1 : to form into a heap
2 : to draw earth around the roots or base of
— hill·er *noun*

hill·bil·ly \'hil-,bi-lē\ *noun, plural* **-lies** [¹*hill* + *Billy,* nickname for *William*] (1900)
: a person from a backwoods area

hillbilly music *noun* (1943)
: COUNTRY MUSIC

hill climb *noun* (1905)
: a road race for automobiles or motorcycles in which competitors are individually timed up a hill

hill·crest \'hil-,krest\ *noun* (circa 1898)
: the top line of a hill

hill mynah *noun* (circa 1890)
: a largely black Asian mynah (*Gracula religiosa*) often tamed and taught to pronounce words

hill·ock \'hi-lək\ *noun* (14th century)
: a small hill
— hill·ocky \-lə-kē\ *adjective*

Hill reaction \'hil-\ *noun* [Robert *Hill* (died 1991) British biochemist] (1950)
: the light-dependent transfer of electrons by chloroplasts in photosynthesis that results in the cleavage of water molecules and liberation of oxygen

hill·side \-,sīd\ *noun* (14th century)
: a part of a hill between the top and the foot

hill·top \'hil-,täp\ *noun* (15th century)
: the highest part of a hill

hilly \'hi-lē\ *adjective* **hill·i·er; -est** (14th century)
: abounding in hills

hilt \'hilt\ *noun* [Middle English, from Old English; akin to Old High German *helza* hilt] (before 12th century)
: a handle especially of a sword or dagger
— **to the hilt** : to the very limit : COMPLETELY

hi·lum \'hī-ləm\ *noun, plural* **hi·la** \-lə\ [New Latin, from Latin, trifle] (circa 1753)
1 : a scar on a seed (as a bean) marking the point of attachment of the ovule
2 : a notch in or opening from a bodily part suggesting the hilum of a bean

him \im, 'him\ *pronoun objective case of* HE

Hi·ma·la·yan \ˌhi-mə-'lā-ən, hi-'mäl-yən, -'mä-lē-ən\ *noun* [*Himalaya* Mountains] (1949)
: any of a breed of domestic cats developed by crossing the Persian and the Siamese and having the stocky build and long thick coat of the former and the blue eyes and coat patterns of the latter

Himalayan

hi·mat·i·on \hi-'ma-tē-ˌän, -ən\ *noun* [Greek, diminutive of *heimat-, heima* garment; akin to Greek *hennynai* to clothe — more at WEAR] (1850)
: a rectangular cloth draped over the left shoulder and about the body and worn as a garment in ancient Greece

him/her \'him-'hər, 'hi-mər-, 'him-'slash-\ *pronoun objective case of* HE/SHE

him·self \(h)im-'self, *Southern also* -'sef\ *pronoun* (before 12th century)
1 a : that identical male one — compare [1]HE; used reflexively, for emphasis, in absolute constructions, and in place of *him* especially when joined to another object ⟨considers *himself* lucky⟩ ⟨he *himself* did it⟩ ⟨*himself* unhappy, he understood the situation⟩ ⟨a gift to his wife and *himself*⟩ **b** — used reflexively when the sex of the antecedent is unspecified ⟨everyone must fend for *himself*⟩
2 : his normal, healthy, or sane condition or self
3 *chiefly Irish & Scottish* : a man of consequence; *especially* : the master of the house

hin \'hin\ *noun* [Hebrew *hīn*, from Egyptian *hnw*] (14th century)
: an ancient Hebrew unit of liquid measure equal to about 1.5 gallons (5.7 liters)

Hi·na·ya·na \ˌhi-nə-'yä-nə, ˌhē-\ *noun* [Sanskrit *hīnayāna* lesser vehicle] (1868)
: THERAVADA
— **Hi·na·ya·nist** \-'yä-nist\ *noun*
— **Hi·na·ya·nis·tic** \-yä-'nis-tik\ *adjective*

[1]hind \'hīnd\ *noun, plural* **hinds** *also* **hind** [Middle English, from Old English; akin to Old High German *hinta* hind, Greek *kemas* young deer] (before 12th century)
1 : the female of the red deer — compare HART
2 : any of various spotted groupers (especially genus *Epinephelus*)

[2]hind *noun* [Middle English *hine* servant, farmhand, from Old English *hīna*, genitive of *hīwan*, plural, members of a household; akin to Old High German *hīwo* spouse, Latin *civis* fellow citizen, and probably to Old Irish *cóim* dear, Lithuanian *šeima* family] (1520)
1 : a British farm assistant
2 *archaic* : RUSTIC

[3]hind *adjective* [Middle English, probably back-formation from Old English *hinder*, adverb, behind; akin to Old High German *hintar*, preposition, behind] (14th century)
: of or forming the part that follows or is behind : REAR

hind·brain \'hīn(d)-ˌbrān\ *noun* (1888)

1 : the posterior of the three primary divisions of the developing vertebrate brain or the corresponding part of the adult brain that includes the cerebellum, the medulla oblongata, and in mammals the pons and that controls autonomic functions and equilibrium — called also *rhombencephalon*; compare METENCEPHALON, MYELENCEPHALON
2 : the posterior segment of the brain of an invertebrate

[1]hin·der \'hin-dər\ *verb* **hin·dered; hin·der·ing** \-d(ə-)riŋ\ [Middle English *hindren*, from Old English *hindrian*; akin to Old English *hinder* behind] (before 12th century)
transitive verb
1 : to make slow or difficult the progress of : HAMPER
2 : to hold back : CHECK
intransitive verb
: to delay, impede, or prevent action ☆
— **hin·der·er** \-dər-ər\ *noun*

[2]hind·er \'hīn-dər\ *adjective* [Middle English, from Old English *hinder*, adverb] (13th century)
: situated behind or in the rear : POSTERIOR

hind·gut \'hīn(d)-ˌgət\ *noun* (1878)
: the posterior part of the alimentary canal

Hin·di \'hin-(ˌ)dē\ *noun* [Hindi *hindī*, from *Hind* India, from Persian] (1801)
1 : a literary and official language of northern India
2 : a complex of Indo-Aryan languages and dialects of northern India for which Hindi is the usual literary language
— **Hindi** *adjective*

hind·most \'hīn(d)-ˌmōst\ *adjective* (14th century)
: farthest to the rear : LAST

hind·quar·ter \-ˌkwȯ(r)-tər, -ˌkȯ(r)-\ *noun* (1881)
1 : one side of the back half of the carcass of a quadruped including a leg and usually one or more ribs
2 *plural* : the hind pair of legs of a quadruped; *broadly* : all the structures of a quadruped that lie posterior to the attachment of the hind legs to the trunk

hin·drance \'hin-drən(t)s\ *noun* (1526)
1 : the state of being hindered
2 : IMPEDIMENT
3 : the action of hindering

hind·sight \'hīn(d)-ˌsīt\ *noun* (1866)
: perception of the nature of an event after it has happened

[1]Hin·du *also* **Hin·doo** \'hin-(ˌ)dü\ *noun* [Persian *Hindū* inhabitant of India, from *Hind* India] (1662)
1 : an adherent of Hinduism
2 : a native or inhabitant of India

[2]Hindu *also* **Hindoo** *adjective* (1698)
: of, relating to, or characteristic of the Hindus or Hinduism

Hindu–Arabic *adjective* (1925)
: relating to, being, or composed of Arabic numerals ⟨*Hindu-Arabic* numeration system⟩

Hindu calendar *noun* (circa 1909)
: a lunar calendar usually dating from 3101 B.C. and used especially in India

Hin·du·ism \'hin-(ˌ)dü-ˌi-zəm\ *noun* (1809)
: the dominant religion of India that emphasizes dharma with its resulting ritual and social observances and often mystical contemplation and ascetic practices

[1]Hin·du·stani *also* **Hin·do·stani** \ˌhin-dù-'sta-nē, -'stä-nē\ *noun* [Hindi *Hindūstānī*, from Persian *Hindūstān* India] (1808)
: a group of Indo-Aryan dialects of northern India of which literary Hindi and Urdu are considered diverse written forms

[2]Hindustani *also* **Hindostani** *adjective* (1800)
: of or relating to Hindustan or its people or Hindustani

hind wing *noun* (1899)
: either of the posterior wings of a 4-winged insect

[1]hinge \'hinj\ *noun* [Middle English *heng*; akin to Middle Dutch *henge* hook, Old English *hangian* to hang] (14th century)
1 a : a jointed or flexible device on which a door, lid, or other swinging part turns **b** : a flexible ligamentous joint **c** : a small piece of thin gummed paper used in fastening a postage stamp in an album
2 : a determining factor : TURNING POINT

[2]hinge *verb* **hinged; hing·ing** (1719)
intransitive verb
: to be contingent on a single consideration or point — used with *on* or *upon*
transitive verb
: to attach by or furnish with hinges

hinge joint *noun* (1802)
: a joint between bones (as at the elbow) that permits motion in only one plane

hin·ny \'hi-nē\ *noun, plural* **hinnies** [Latin *hinnus*, from Greek *innos*] (1688)
: a hybrid between a stallion and a female donkey — compare MULE

[1]hint \'hint\ *noun* [probably alteration of obsolete *hent* act of seizing, from *hent* verb] (1604)
1 *archaic* : OPPORTUNITY, TURN
2 a : a statement conveying by implication what it is preferred not to say explicitly **b** : an indirect or summary suggestion ⟨helpful *hints*⟩
3 : a slight indication of the existence, approach, or nature of something : CLUE
4 : a very small amount : SUGGESTION

[2]hint (1648)
transitive verb
: to convey indirectly and by allusion rather than explicitly ⟨a suspicion that she scarcely dared to *hint*⟩
intransitive verb
: to give a hint — usually used with *at*
synonym see SUGGEST
— **hint·er** *noun*

hin·ter·land \'hin-tər-ˌland, -lənd\ *noun* [German, from *hinter* hinder + *Land*] (1890)
1 : a region lying inland from a coast
2 a : a region remote from urban areas **b** : a region lying beyond major metropolitan or cultural centers

[1]hip \'hip\ *noun* [Middle English *hipe*, from Old English *hēope*; akin to Old High German *hiafo* hip] (before 12th century)
: ROSE HIP

[2]hip *noun* [Middle English, from Old English *hype*; akin to Old High German *huf* hip] (before 12th century)
1 a : the laterally projecting region of each side of the lower or posterior part of the mammalian trunk formed by the lateral parts of the pelvis and upper part of the femur together with the fleshy parts covering them **b** : HIP JOINT
2 : the external angle formed by the meeting of two sloping sides of a roof that have their wall plates running in different directions

☆ **SYNONYMS**
Hinder, impede, obstruct, block mean to interfere with the activity or progress of. HINDER stresses causing harmful or annoying delay or interference with progress ⟨rain *hindered* the climb⟩. IMPEDE implies making forward progress difficult by clogging, hampering, or fettering ⟨tight clothing that *impedes* movement⟩. OBSTRUCT implies interfering with something in motion or in progress by the sometimes intentional placing of obstacles in the way ⟨the view was *obstructed* by billboards⟩. BLOCK implies complete obstruction to passage or progress ⟨a landslide *blocked* the road⟩.

\ə\ abut \ᵊ\ kitten \ər\ further \a\ ash \ā\ ace
\ä\ mop, mar \aù\ out \ch\ chin \e\ bet \ē\ easy
\g\ go \i\ hit \ī\ ice \j\ job \ŋ\ sing \ō\ go
\ȯ\ law \ȯi\ boy \th\ thin \th\ the \ü\ loot \ù\ foot
\y\ yet \zh\ vision *see also* Guide to Pronunciation

³hip *interjection* [origin unknown] (1827)
— used in a cheer ⟨*hip hip* hooray⟩

⁴hip *adjective* **hip·per; hip·pest** [alteration of ²*hep*] (1904)
: characterized by a keen informed awareness of or involvement in the newest developments or styles

⁵hip *transitive verb* **hipped; hip·ping** (circa 1932)
: to make aware **:** TELL, INFORM

⁶hip *noun* (1952)
: HIPNESS

hip and thigh *adverb* (1560)
: in a fierce or ruthless manner **:** UNSPARINGLY

hip·bone \'hip-'bōn, -,bōn\ *noun* (12th century)
: INNOMINATE BONE

hip boot *noun* (1893)
: a waterproof boot reaching to the hips

hip–hop \'hip-,häp\ *noun, often attributive* [perhaps from ⁴*hip* + ¹*hop*] (1983)
: a subculture especially of inner-city youths whose amusements include rap music, graffiti, and break dancing; *also* **:** an element or art form prevalent within this subculture

hip joint *noun* (1794)
: the articulation between the femur and the innominate bone

hip–line \'hip-,līn\ *noun* (1907)
1 : an arbitrary line encircling the fullest part of the hips
2 : body circumference at the hips

hip·ness \'hip-nəs\ *noun* (1946)
: the quality or state of being hip

¹hipped \'hipt\ *adjective* (1508)
1 : having hips especially of a specified kind
— often used in combination ⟨a broad-*hipped* person⟩
2 : constructed with hips ⟨a *hipped* roof⟩

²hipped *adjective* [*hip* (hypochondria)] (circa 1710)
: DEPRESSED

³hipped *adjective* [⁵*hip*] (1920)
: extremely absorbed or interested ⟨*hipped* on astrology⟩

hip·pie *or* **hip·py** \'hi-pē\ *noun, plural* **hip·pies** [⁴*hip* + -*ie*] (1965)
: a usually young person who rejects the mores of established society (as by dressing unconventionally or favoring communal living) and advocates a nonviolent ethic; *broadly* **:** a long-haired unconventionally dressed young person
— **hip·pie·dom** \-pē-dəm\ *noun*
— **hip·pie·ness** *or* **hip·pi·ness** \-pē-nəs\ *noun*

hip·po \'hi-(,)pō\ *noun, plural* **hippos** (1872)
: HIPPOPOTAMUS

hip·po·cam·pus \,hi-pə-'kam-pəs\ *noun, plural* **-pi** \-,pī, -(,)pē\ [New Latin, from Greek *hippokampos* sea horse, from *hippos* horse + *kampos* sea monster — more at EQUINE] (1706)
: a curved elongated ridge that extends over the floor of the descending horn of each lateral ventricle of the brain and consists of gray matter covered on the ventricular surface with white matter
— **hip·po·cam·pal** \-pəl\ *adjective*

hip·po·cras \'hi-pə-,kras\ *noun* [Middle English *ypocras,* from *Ypocras* Hippocrates, to whom its invention was ascribed] (14th century)
: a mulled wine popular in medieval Europe

Hip·po·crat·ic \,hi-pə-'kra-tik\ *adjective* (circa 1620)
: of or relating to Hippocrates or to the school of medicine that took his name

Hippocratic oath *noun* (1747)
: an oath embodying a code of medical ethics usually taken by those about to begin medical practice

Hip·po·crene \'hi-pə-,krēn, ,hi-pə-'krē-nē\ *noun* [Latin, from Greek *Hippokrēnē*] (1605)

: a fountain on Mount Helicon sacred to the Muses and believed to be a source of poetic inspiration

hip·po·drome \'hi-pə-,drōm\ *noun* [Middle French, from Latin *hippodromos,* from Greek, from *hippos* + *dromos* racecourse — more at DROMEDARY] (1585)
1 : an oval stadium for horse and chariot races in ancient Greece
2 : an arena for equestrian performances

hip·po·griff \-,grif\ *noun* [French *hippogriffe,* from Italian *ippogrifo,* from *ippo-* (from Greek *hippos* horse) + *grifo* griffin, from Latin *gryphus*] (circa 1656)
: a legendary animal having the foreparts of a griffin and the body of a horse

Hip·pol·y·ta \hi-'pä-lə-tə\ *noun* [Latin, from Greek *Hippolytē*]
: a queen of the Amazons given in marriage to Theseus by Hercules

Hip·pol·y·tus \-ə-təs\ *noun* [Latin, from Greek *Hippolytos*]
: a son of Theseus falsely accused of amorous advances by his stepmother and killed by his father through the agency of Poseidon

Hip·pom·e·nes \hi-'pä-mə-nēz\ *noun* [Latin, from Greek *Hippomenēs*]
: the successful suitor of Atalanta in Greek mythology

hip·po·pot·a·mus \,hi-pə-'pä-tə-məs\ *noun, plural* **-mus·es** *or* **-mi** \-,mī, -(,)mē\ [Latin, from Greek *hippopotamos,* alteration of *hippos potamios,* literally, riverine horse] (1563)
: a very large herbivorous 4-toed chiefly aquatic artiodactyl mammal (*Hippopotamus amphibius*) of sub-Saharan Africa with an extremely large head and mouth,

hippopotamus

bare and very thick grayish skin, and short legs; *also* **:** a smaller closely related mammal (*Choeropsis liberiensis*) of western Africa ◆

hip·py \'hi-pē\ *adjective* (1919)
: having large hips

hip roof *noun* (circa 1741)
: a roof having sloping ends and sloping sides
— see ROOF illustration

hip–shoot·ing \'hip-,shü-tiŋ\ *noun* (1951)
: action or reaction that is quick and often reckless
— **hip shooter** *noun*

hip·ster \'hip-stər\ *noun* [⁴*hip*] (circa 1941)
: a person who is unusually aware of and interested in new and unconventional patterns (as in jazz or the use of stimulants)

hip·ster·ism \-stə-,ri-zəm\ *noun* (1958)
1 : HIPNESS
2 : the way of life characteristic of hipsters

hi·ra·ga·na \,hir-ə-'gä-nə\ *noun* [Japanese, from *hira-* ordinary + *kana* syllabary] (1859)
: the cursive script that is one of two sets of symbols of Japanese syllabic writing — compare KATAKANA

¹hire \'hī(-ə)r\ *noun* [Middle English, from Old English *hȳr;* akin to Old Saxon *hūria* hire] (before 12th century)
1 a : payment for the temporary use of something **b :** payment for labor or personal services **:** WAGES
2 a : the act or an instance of hiring **b :** the state of being hired **:** EMPLOYMENT
3 *British* **:** RENTAL — often used attributively
4 : one who is hired ⟨starting wage for the new *hires*⟩
— **for hire** *also* **on hire :** available for use or service in return for payment

²hire *verb* **hired; hir·ing** (before 12th century)
transitive verb
1 a : to engage the personal services of for a set sum ⟨*hire* a crew⟩ **b :** to engage the temporary use of for a fixed sum ⟨*hire* a hall⟩

2 : to grant the personal services of or temporary use of for a fixed sum ⟨*hire* themselves out⟩
3 : to get done for pay ⟨*hire* the mowing done⟩
intransitive verb
: to take employment ⟨*hire* out as a guide during the tourist season⟩ ☆
— **hir·er** *noun*

hired gun *noun* (1971)
: an expert hired to do a specific job; *especially* **:** HIRELING — often used disparagingly

hire·ling \'hī(-ə)r-liŋ\ *noun* (before 12th century)
: a person who serves for hire especially for purely mercenary motives

hire purchase *noun* (1895)
chiefly British **:** purchase on the installment plan

hiring hall *noun* (1934)
: a union-operated placement office where registered applicants are referred in rotation to jobs

hir·sute \'hər-,süt, 'hir-, ,hər-', hir-'\ *adjective* [Latin *hirsutus;* akin to Latin *horrēre* to bristle — more at HORROR] (1621)
: HAIRY 1; *especially* **:** covered with coarse stiff hairs ⟨*hirsute* leaf⟩
— **hir·sute·ness** *noun*

hir·sut·ism \'hər-sə-,ti-zəm, 'hir-\ *noun* (1927)
: excessive growth of hair of normal or abnormal distribution

hi·ru·din \hi-'rü-d³n, 'hir-(y)ə-\ *noun* [from *Hirudin,* a trademark] (1905)
: an anticoagulant extracted from the buccal glands of a leech

¹his \(h)iz, ,hiz\ *adjective* [Middle English, from Old English, genitive of *hē* he] (before 12th century)
: of or relating to him or himself especially as possessor, agent, or object of an action ⟨*his* house⟩ ⟨*his* writings⟩ ⟨*his* confirmation⟩ — compare ¹HE

☆ **SYNONYMS**
Hire, let, lease, rent, charter mean to engage or grant for use at a price. HIRE and LET, strictly speaking, are complementary terms. HIRE implying the act of engaging or taking for use and LET the granting of use (we *hired* a car for the summer) ⟨decided to *let* the cottage to a young couple⟩. LEASE strictly implies a letting under the terms of a contract but is often applied to hiring on a lease ⟨the diplomat *leased* an apartment for a year⟩. RENT stresses the payment of money for the full use of property and may imply either hiring or letting ⟨instead of buying a house, they decided to *rent*⟩ ⟨will not *rent* to families with children⟩. CHARTER applies to the hiring or letting of a vehicle usually for exclusive use ⟨*charter* a bus to go to the game⟩.

◇ **WORD HISTORY**
hippopotamus The bulky African mammal that spends its daytime hours submerged up to its eyes in a river owes its English name to the ancient Greeks. The historian Herodotus referred to this animal, which he may have seen in Egypt, as *ho hippos ho potamios* "the riverine horse." This epithet was reduced by later Greek writers to *hippopotamos* (which by normal rules of Greek compounding should mean "horse river"). Despite its name, the hippopotamus, which may weigh up to five tons, is more closely related to hogs than horses. Greek *hippos* "horse" was also applied to a species of marine fish that bore even less resemblance to a horse than a hippopotamus does—paralleling to some degree English *sea horse* (which resembles a horse) and *redhorse* (which does not).

²his \'hiz\ *pronoun, singular or plural in construction* (before 12th century)
: that which belongs to him — used without a following noun as a pronoun equivalent in meaning to the adjective *his*

his/her \'hiz-'hər, 'hi-zər-'hər, 'hiz-'slash-\ *adjective* (1952)
: his or her — used in writing as an adjective of common gender

His·pan·ic \hi-'spa-nik\ *adjective* [Latin *hispanicus*, from *Hispania* Iberian Peninsula, Spain] (circa 1889)
: of, relating to, or being a person of Latin American descent living in the U.S.; *especially* : one of Cuban, Mexican, or Puerto Rican origin
— **Hispanic** *noun*
— **His·pan·i·cism** \-'spa-nə-ˌsi-zəm\ *noun*
— **His·pan·i·cist** \-sist\ *noun*
— **His·pan·i·cize** \-ˌsīz\ *transitive verb*

his·pa·ni·dad \ˌis-ˌpa-ni-'thä(th)\ *noun* (1941)
: HISPANISM 1

his·pa·nism \'his-pə-ˌni-zəm\ *noun, often capitalized* (1940)
1 : a movement to reassert the cultural unity of Spain and Latin America
2 : a characteristic feature of Spanish occurring in another language

His·pa·nist \-nist\ *noun* (1786)
: a scholar specially informed in Spanish or Portuguese language, literature, linguistics, or civilization

His·pa·no \hi-'spa-(ˌ)nō, 'his-pə-ˌnō\ *noun, plural* **-nos** [American Spanish *hispano*, probably short for *hispanoamericano*, literally, Spanish-American] (1946)
: a native or resident of the southwestern U.S. descended from Spaniards settled there before annexation; *also* : MEXICAN 1

his·pid \'his-pəd\ *adjective* [Latin *hispidus*; akin to Latin *horrēre*] (1646)
: rough or covered with bristles, stiff hairs, or minute spines ⟨*hispid* leaf⟩

hiss \'his\ *verb* [Middle English, of imitative origin] (14th century)
intransitive verb
: to make a sharp sibilant sound ⟨the crowd *hissed* in disapproval⟩ ⟨*hissing* steam⟩
transitive verb
1 : to express disapproval of by hissing
2 : to utter or whisper angrily or threateningly and with a hiss
— **hiss** *noun*
— **hiss·er** *noun*

his·self \(h)i-'self, -'sef\ *pronoun* (12th century)
chiefly dialect : HIMSELF 1

hissy \'hi-sē\ *noun* [perhaps by shortening & alteration from *hysterical*] (circa 1934)
chiefly Southern & southern Midland : TANTRUM — called also *hissy fit*

¹hist \s *often prolonged and usually with p preceding and t following; often read as* 'hist\ *interjection* [origin unknown] (1592)
— used to attract attention

²hist \'hīst\ *dialect variant of* HOIST

hist- *or* **histo-** *combining form* [French, from Greek *histos* mast, loom beam, web, from *histanai* to cause to stand — more at STAND]
: tissue ⟨*histo*physiology⟩

his·ta·mi·nase \hi-'sta-mə-ˌnās, 'his-tə-mə-, -ˌnāz\ *noun* [International Scientific Vocabulary] (1930)
: a widely occurring flavoprotein enzyme that oxidizes histamine and various diamines

his·ta·mine \'his-tə-ˌmēn, -mən\ *noun* [International Scientific Vocabulary *hist-* + *amine*] (circa 1913)
: a compound $C_5H_9N_3$ especially of mammalian tissues that causes dilatation of capillaries, contraction of smooth muscle, and stimulation of gastric acid secretion, that is released during allergic reactions, and that is formed by decarboxylation of histidine

his·ta·min·er·gic \ˌhis-tə-mə-'nər-jik\ *adjective* [International Scientific Vocabulary] (1936)
of autonomic nerve fibers : liberating or activated by histamine ⟨*histaminergic* receptors⟩

his·ti·dine \'his-tə-ˌdēn\ *noun* [International Scientific Vocabulary *hist-* + *-idine*] (1896)
: a crystalline essential amino acid $C_6H_9N_3O_2$ formed by the hydrolysis of most proteins

his·tio·cyte \'his-tē-ə-ˌsīt\ *noun* [Greek *histion* web (diminutive of *histos*) + International Scientific Vocabulary *-cyte*] (1924)
: a nonmotile macrophage of extravascular tissues and especially connective tissue
— **his·tio·cyt·ic** \ˌhis-tē-ə-'si-tik\ *adjective*

his·to·chem·is·try \ˌhis-tō-'ke-mə-strē\ *noun* [International Scientific Vocabulary] (circa 1860)
: a science that combines the techniques of biochemistry and histology in the study of the chemical constitution of cells and tissues
— **his·to·chem·i·cal** \-'ke-mi-kəl\ *adjective*
— **his·to·chem·i·cal·ly** \-k(ə-)lē\ *adverb*

his·to·com·pat·i·bil·i·ty \'his-(ˌ)tō-kəm-ˌpa-tə-'bi-lə-tē\ *noun* (1948)
: a state of mutual tolerance that allows some tissues to be grafted effectively to others

his·to·gen·e·sis \ˌhis-tə-'je-nə-səs\ *noun* [New Latin] (circa 1854)
: the formation and differentiation of tissues
— **his·to·ge·net·ic** \-jə-'ne-tik\ *adjective*

his·to·gram \'his-tə-ˌgram\ *noun* [Greek *histos* mast, web + English *-gram*] (1891)
: a representation of a frequency distribution by means of rectangles whose widths represent class intervals and whose areas are proportional to the corresponding frequencies

his·tol·o·gy \his-'tä-lə-jē\ *noun, plural* **-gies** [French *histologie*, from *hist-* + *-logie* -logy] (circa 1847)
1 : a branch of anatomy that deals with the minute structure of animal and plant tissues as discernible with the microscope
2 : a treatise on histology
3 : tissue structure or organization
— **his·to·log·i·cal** \ˌhis-tə-'lä-ji-kəl\ *or* **his·to·log·ic** \-'lä-jik\ *adjective*
— **his·to·log·i·cal·ly** \-ji-k(ə-)lē\ *adverb*
— **his·tol·o·gist** \his-'tä-lə-jist\ *noun*

his·tol·y·sis \his-'tä-lə-səs\ *noun* [New Latin] (circa 1857)
: the breakdown of bodily tissues

his·tone \'his-ˌtōn\ *noun* [German *Histon*] (1885)
: any of various simple water-soluble proteins that are rich in the basic amino acids lysine and arginine and are complexed with DNA in the nucleosomes of eukaryotic chromatin

his·to·pa·thol·o·gy \ˌhis-tō-pə-'thä-lə-jē, -pa-\ *noun* [International Scientific Vocabulary] (1896)
1 : a branch of pathology concerned with the tissue changes characteristic of disease
2 : the tissue changes that affect a part or accompany a disease
— **his·to·path·o·log·ic** \-ˌpa-thə-'lä-jik\ *or* **his·to·path·o·log·i·cal** \-ji-kəl\ *adjective*
— **his·to·pa·thol·o·log·i·cal·ly** \-ji-k(ə-)lē\ *adverb*
— **his·to·pa·thol·o·gist** \-pə-'thä-lə-jist, -pa-\ *noun*

his·to·phys·i·ol·o·gy \-ˌfi-zē-'ä-lə-jē\ *noun* (circa 1886)
1 : a branch of physiology concerned with the function and activities of tissues
2 : structural and functional tissue organization
— **his·to·phys·i·o·log·i·cal** \-ē-ə-'lä-ji-kəl\ *or* **his·to·phys·i·o·log·ic** \-jik\ *adjective*

his·to·plas·mo·sis \ˌhis-tə-plaz-'mō-səs\ *noun* [New Latin, from *Histoplasma*, genus of fungi] (1907)
: a respiratory disease with symptoms like those of influenza that is caused by a fungus (*Histoplasma capsulatum*) and is marked by benign involvement of lymph nodes of the trachea and bronchi or by severe progressive generalized involvement of the lymph nodes and the reticuloendothelial system

his·to·ri·an \hi-'stōr-ē-ən, -'stòr-, -'stär-\ *noun* (15th century)
1 : a student or writer of history; *especially* : one that produces a scholarly synthesis
2 : a writer or compiler of a chronicle

his·tor·ic \hi-'stòr-ik, -'stär-\ *adjective* (1607)
: HISTORICAL: as **a** : famous or important in history ⟨*historic* battlefields⟩ **b** : having great and lasting importance ⟨an *historic* occasion⟩ **c** : known or established in the past ⟨*historic* interest rates⟩ **d** : dating from or preserved from a past time or culture ⟨*historic* buildings⟩ ⟨*historic* artifacts⟩

his·tor·i·cal \-i-kəl\ *adjective* (15th century)
1 **a** : of, relating to, or having the character of history **b** : based on history **c** : used in the past and reproduced in historical presentations
2 : famous in history : HISTORIC a
3 **a** : SECONDARY 1c **b** : DIACHRONIC ⟨*historical* grammar⟩
— **his·tor·i·cal·ness** \-i-kəl-nəs\ *noun*

his·tor·i·cal·ly \-i-k(ə-)lē\ *adverb* (1550)
1 : in accordance with or with respect to history ⟨an *historically* accurate account⟩
2 : in the past ⟨*historically*, stagnant cities seldom have recovered —Jane Jacobs⟩

historical materialism *noun* (1925)
: the Marxist theory of history and society that holds that ideas and social institutions develop only as the superstructure of a material economic base — compare DIALECTICAL MATERIALISM

historical present *noun* (1867)
: the present tense used in relating past events

his·tor·i·cism \hi-'stòr-ə-ˌsi-zəm, -'stär-\ *noun* (1895)
: a theory, doctrine, or style that emphasizes the importance of history: as **a** : a theory in which history is seen as a standard of value or as a determinant of events **b** : a style (as in architecture) characterized by the use of traditional forms and elements
— **his·tor·i·cist** \-sist\ *adjective or noun*

his·to·ric·i·ty \ˌhis-tə-'ri-sə-tē\ *noun* (1880)
: historical actuality

his·tor·i·cize \hi-'stòr-ə-ˌsīz, -'stär-\ *verb* **-cized; -ciz·ing** (1846)
transitive verb
: to make historical
intransitive verb
: to use historical material

his·to·ri·og·ra·pher \hi-ˌstòr-ē-'ä-grə-fər, -ˌstòr-\ *noun* [Middle French *historiographeur*, from Late Latin *historiographus*, from Greek *historiographos*, from *historia* + *graphein* to write — more at CARVE] (15th century)
: HISTORIAN

his·to·ri·og·ra·phy \-fē\ *noun* (1569)
1 **a** : the writing of history; *especially* : the writing of history based on the critical examination of sources, the selection of particulars from the authentic materials, and the synthesis of particulars into a narrative that will stand the test of critical methods **b** : the principles, theory, and history of historical writing ⟨a course in *historiography*⟩
2 : the product of historical writing : a body of historical literature
— **his·to·rio·graph·i·cal** \-ē-ə-'gra-fi-kəl\ *also* **his·to·rio·graph·ic** \-fik\ *adjective*
— **his·to·rio·graph·i·cal·ly** \-ē-ə-'gra-fi-k(ə-)lē\ *adverb*

his·to·ry \'his-t(ə-)rē\ *noun, plural* **-ries** [Latin *historia,* from Greek, inquiry, history, from *histōr, istōr* knowing, learned; akin to Greek *eidenai* to know — more at WIT] (14th century)
1 : TALE, STORY
2 a : a chronological record of significant events (as affecting a nation or institution) often including an explanation of their causes **b :** a treatise presenting systematically related natural phenomena **c :** an account of a patient's medical background **d :** an established record ⟨a prisoner with a *history* of violence⟩
3 : a branch of knowledge that records and explains past events ⟨medieval *history*⟩
4 a : events that form the subject matter of a history **b :** events of the past **c :** one that is finished or done for ⟨the winning streak was *history*⟩ ⟨you're *history*⟩ **d :** previous treatment, handling, or experience (as of a metal)
his·tri·on·ic \,his-trē-'ä-nik\ *adjective* [Late Latin *histrionicus,* from Latin *histrion-, histrio* actor] (1648)
1 : deliberately affected **:** THEATRICAL
2 : of or relating to actors, acting, or the theater
synonym *see* DRAMATIC
— **his·tri·on·i·cal·ly** \-ni-k(ə-)lē\ *adverb*
his·tri·on·ics \-niks\ *noun plural but singular or plural in construction* (1864)
1 : theatrical performances
2 : deliberate display of emotion for effect
¹hit \'hit\ *verb* **hit; hit·ting** [Middle English, from Old English *hittan,* from Old Norse *hitta* to meet with, hit] (before 12th century)
transitive verb
1 a : to reach with or as if with a blow **b :** to come in contact with ⟨the ball *hit* the window⟩
2 a : to cause to come into contact **b :** to deliver (as a blow) by action **c :** to apply forcefully or suddenly ⟨*hit* the brakes⟩
3 : to affect especially detrimentally ⟨farmers *hit* by drought⟩
4 : to make a request of ⟨*hit* his friend for 10 dollars⟩ — often used with *up*
5 : to discover or meet especially by chance
6 a : to accord with **:** SUIT **b :** REACH, ATTAIN ⟨prices *hit* a new high⟩ **c :** to arrive or appear at, in, or on ⟨*hit* town⟩ ⟨the best time to *hit* the stores⟩ **d :** of fish **:** to bite at or on **e :** to reflect accurately ⟨*hit* the right note⟩ **f :** to reach or strike (as a target) especially for a score in a game or contest ⟨couldn't seem to *hit* the basket⟩ **g :** BAT 2b
7 : to indulge in excessively ⟨*hit* the bottle⟩
intransitive verb
1 a : to strike a blow **b :** to arrive with a forceful effect like that of a blow ⟨the storm *hit*⟩
2 a : to come into contact with something **b :** ATTACK **c :** of a fish **:** STRIKE 11b **d :** BAT 1
3 : to succeed in attaining or coming up with something — often used with *on* or *upon* ⟨*hit* on a solution⟩
4 *obsolete* **:** to be in agreement **:** SUIT
5 *of an internal-combustion engine* **:** to fire the charge in the cylinders
— **hit·ter** *noun*
— **hit it big :** to achieve great success
— **hit it off :** to get along well **:** become friends ⟨they *hit it off* immediately⟩
— **hit on :** to make especially sexual overtures to
— **hit one's stride :** to reach one's best speed or highest potential
— **hit the books :** to study especially with intensity
— **hit the fan :** to have a major usually undesirable impact
— **hit the hay** *or* **hit the sack :** to go to bed
— **hit the high points** *or* **hit the high spots :** to touch on or at the most important points or places
— **hit the jackpot :** to become notably and unexpectedly successful

— **hit the nail on the head :** to be exactly right
— **hit the road :** LEAVE, TRAVEL; *also* **:** to set out
— **hit the roof** *or* **hit the ceiling :** to give vent to a burst of anger or angry protest
— **hit the spot :** to give complete or special satisfaction — used especially of food or drink
²hit *noun* (15th century)
1 : an act or instance of hitting or being hit ⟨more *hits* than misses⟩ ⟨took a financial *hit*⟩
2 a : a stroke of luck **b :** a great success
3 : a telling or critical remark
4 : BASE HIT
5 : a quantity of a narcotic drug ingested at one time
6 : a premeditated murder committed especially by a member of a crime syndicate
— **hit·less** \'hit-ləs\ *adjective*
hit–and–miss \,hi-tᵊn-'mis\ *adjective* (1897)
: sometimes successful and sometimes not **:** not reliably good or successful
¹hit–and–run \-'rən\ *adjective* (1899)
1 : being or relating to a hit-and-run in baseball
2 : being or involving a motor-vehicle driver who does not stop after being involved in an accident
3 : involving or intended for quick specific action or results
²hit–and–run *noun* (1904)
: a baseball play calling for a runner on first to begin running as a pitch is delivered and for the batter to attempt to hit the pitch
³hit–and–run *intransitive verb* (1966)
: to execute a hit-and-run play in baseball
¹hitch \'hich\ *verb* [Middle English *hytchen*] (14th century)
transitive verb
1 : to move by jerks or with a tug
2 a : to catch or fasten by or as if by a hook or knot ⟨*hitched* his horse to the fence post⟩ **b** (1) **:** to connect (a vehicle or implement) with a source of motive power ⟨*hitch* a rake to a tractor⟩ (2) **:** to attach (a source of motive power) to a vehicle or instrument ⟨*hitch* the horses to the wagon⟩ **c :** to join in marriage ⟨got *hitched*⟩
3 : HITCHHIKE
intransitive verb
1 : to move with halts and jerks **:** HOBBLE
2 a : to become entangled, made fast, or linked **b :** to become joined in marriage
3 : HITCHHIKE
— **hitch·er** *noun*
²hitch *noun* (1664)
1 : LIMP
2 : a sudden movement or pull **:** JERK ⟨gave his trousers a *hitch*⟩
3 a : a sudden halt **:** STOPPAGE **b :** a usually unforeseen difficulty or obstacle ⟨the plan went off without a *hitch*⟩
4 : the act or fact of catching hold
5 : a connection between a vehicle or implement and a detachable source of power (as a tractor or horse)
6 : a delimited period especially of military service
7 : any of various knots used to form a temporary noose in a line or to secure a line temporarily to an object
8 : LIFT 5b
hitch·hike \'hich-,hīk\ (1926)
intransitive verb
1 : to travel by securing free rides from passing vehicles
2 : to be carried or transported by chance or unintentionally ⟨destructive insects *hitchhiking* on ships⟩
transitive verb
: to solicit and obtain (a free ride) especially in a passing vehicle
— **hitch·hik·er** *noun*
hitch up *intransitive verb* (1817)
: to hitch a draft animal or team to a vehicle

hi–tech *variant of* HIGH-TECH
¹hith·er \'hi-thər\ *adverb* [Middle English *hider, hither,* from Old English *hider;* akin to Gothic *hidre* hither, Latin *citra* on this side — more at HE] (before 12th century)
: to this place
²hither *adjective* (14th century)
: being on the near or adjacent side
hith·er·most \-,mōst\ *adjective* (1563)
: nearest on this side
hith·er·to \-,tü, ,hi-thər-'tü\ *adverb* (13th century)
: up to this or that time
hith·er·ward \'hi-thə(r)-wərd\ *adverb* (before 12th century)
: HITHER
Hit·ler·ism \'hit-lə-,ri-zəm\ *noun* (1930)
: the principles and policies associated with Hitler
— **Hit·ler·ite** \-,rīt\ *noun or adjective*
hit list *noun* (1972)
: a list of persons or programs to be opposed or eliminated; *broadly* **:** a list of those targeted for special attention or treatment
hit man *noun* (1968)
1 : a professional assassin who works for a crime syndicate
2 : HATCHET MAN
hit–or–miss \,hit-ər-'mis\ *adjective* (1848)
: marked by a lack of care, forethought, system, or plan; *also* **:** HIT-AND-MISS
hit or miss *adverb* (1606)
: in a hit-or-miss manner **:** HAPHAZARDLY
hit parade *noun* (1929)
: a group or listing of the most popular or noteworthy items of a particular kind (as popular songs)
Hit·tite \'hi-,tīt\ *noun* [Hebrew *Ḥittī,* from Hittite *ḥatti*] (1608)
1 : a member of a conquering people in Asia Minor and Syria with an empire in the 2d millennium B.C.
2 : the extinct Indo-European language of the Hittites — see INDO-EUROPEAN LANGUAGES table
— **Hittite** *adjective*
HIV \,āch-,ī-'vē\ *noun* (1986)
: any of a group of retroviruses and especially HIV-1 that infect and destroy helper T cells of the immune system causing the marked reduction in their numbers that is diagnostic of AIDS — called also *AIDS virus, human immunodeficiency virus*
¹hive \'hīv\ *noun* [Middle English, from Old English *hȳf;* perhaps akin to Old Norse *hūfr* ship's hull, Latin *cūpa* tub, Sanskrit *kūpa* cave] (before 12th century)
1 : a container for housing honeybees
2 : a colony of bees
3 : a place swarming with activity
— **hive·less** \-ləs\ *adjective*
²hive *verb* **hived; hiv·ing** (14th century)
intransitive verb
1 *of bees* **:** to enter and take possession of a hive
2 : to reside in close association
transitive verb
1 : to collect into a hive
2 : to store up in or as if in a hive
hive off (circa 1856)
intransitive verb
chiefly British **:** to break away from or as if from a group **:** become separate
transitive verb
chiefly British **:** to make separate: as **a** **:** to remove from a group ⟨*hive off* the youngest campers into another room⟩ **b :** to assign (as assets or responsibilities) to another **c** **:** SPIN OFF
hives \'hīvz\ *noun plural but singular or plural in construction* [origin unknown] (circa 1500)
: URTICARIA
HIV–1 \-'wən\ *noun* (1986)
: a retrovirus that is the most common HIV

hiz·zon·er \hi-'zä-nər\ *noun, often capitalized* [alteration of *his honor*] (circa 1924)
— used as a title for a man holding the office of mayor

HLA \ˌāch-(ˌ)el-'ā\ *noun* [*human l*eukocyte *a*ntigen] (1968)
1 : the major histocompatibility complex in humans
2 : a genetic locus, gene, or antigen of HLA — often used with one or more letters to designate a locus or with letters and a number to designate an allele at the locus or the antigen corresponding to the locus and allele

HMO \ˌāch-(ˌ)em-'ō\ *noun* (1972)
: an organization that provides comprehensive health care to voluntarily enrolled individuals and families in a particular geographic area by member physicians with limited referral to outside specialists and that is financed by fixed periodic payments determined in advance — called also *health maintenance organization*

ho \'hō\ *interjection* [Middle English] (15th century)
— used especially to attract attention to something specified ⟨land *ho*⟩

hoa·gie *also* **hoa·gy** \'hō-gē\ *noun, plural* **hoagies** [origin unknown] (1955)
: SUBMARINE 2

¹hoar \'hōr, 'hȯr\ *adjective* [Middle English *hor*, from Old English *hār*; akin to Old High German *hēr* hoary] (before 12th century)
: HOARY

²hoar *noun* [Middle English *hor* hoariness, from *hor*, adjective] (1567)
: FROST 1c

¹hoard \'hōrd, 'hȯrd\ *noun* [Middle English *hord*, from Old English; akin to Gothic *huzd* treasure, Old English *hȳdan* to hide] (before 12th century)
: a supply or fund stored up and often hidden away

²hoard (before 12th century)
transitive verb
1 : to lay up a hoard of
2 : to keep (as one's thoughts) to oneself
intransitive verb
: to lay up a hoard
— **hoard·er** *noun*

hoard·ing \'hōr-diŋ, 'hȯr-\ *noun* [*hourd, hoard* (hoarding)] (circa 1823)
1 : a temporary board fence put about a building being erected or repaired — called also *hoard*
2 *British* : BILLBOARD

hoar·frost \'hōr-ˌfrȯst, 'hȯr-\ *noun* (14th century)
: FROST 1c

hoarse \'hōrs, 'hȯrs\ *adjective* **hoars·er; hoars·est** [Middle English *hos, hors*, probably from (assumed) Old Norse *hārs*; akin to Old English *hās* hoarse, Old High German *heis*] (before 12th century)
1 : rough or harsh in sound : GRATING ⟨a *hoarse* voice⟩
2 : having a hoarse voice ⟨shouted himself *hoarse*⟩
— **hoarse·ly** *adverb*
— **hoarse·ness** *noun*

hoars·en \'hōr-sᵊn, 'hȯr-\ *verb* **hoars·ened; hoars·en·ing** \'hōrs-niŋ, 'hȯrs-, 'hōr-sə-, 'hȯr-\ (1748)
transitive verb
: to make hoarse
intransitive verb
: to become hoarse

hoary \'hōr-ē, 'hȯr-\ *adjective* **hoar·i·er; -est** (1530)
1 : gray or white with or as if with age
2 : extremely old : ANCIENT ⟨*hoary* legends⟩
— **hoar·i·ness** *noun*

hoa·tzin \wät-'sēn\ *noun* [Nahuatl *huāctzin* the laughing falcon (*Herpetotheres cachinnans*)] (1661)
: a crested large South American bird (*Opisthocomos hoazin* synonym *O. hoatzin*) with

blue facial skin, red eyes, brown plumage marked with white above, and claws on the first and second digits of the wing when young

hoatzin

¹hoax \'hōks\ *transitive verb* [probably contraction of *hocus*] (circa 1796)
: to trick into believing or accepting as genuine something false and often preposterous
synonym see DUPE
— **hoax·er** *noun*

²hoax *noun* (1808)
1 : an act intended to trick or dupe : IMPOSTURE
2 : something accepted or established by fraud or fabrication

¹hob \'häb\ *noun* [Middle English *hobbe*, from *Hobbe*, nickname for Robert] (15th century)
1 *dialect English* : HOBGOBLIN, ELF
2 : MISCHIEF, TROUBLE — used with *play* and *raise* ⟨always raising *hob*⟩

²hob *noun* [origin unknown] (1511)
1 : a projection at the back or side of a fireplace on which something may be kept warm
2 : a cutting tool used for cutting the teeth of worm wheels or gears

³hob *transitive verb* **hobbed; hob·bing** (1799)
1 : to cut with a hob
2 : to furnish with hobnails

Hobbes·ian \'häb-zē-ən\ *adjective* (1776)
: of or relating to the English philosopher Thomas Hobbes or Hobbism

Hob·bism \'hä-ˌbi-zəm\ *noun* (1691)
: the philosophical system of Thomas Hobbes; *especially* : the Hobbesian theory that people have a fundamental right to self-preservation and to pursue selfish aims but will relinquish these rights to an absolute monarch in the interest of common safety and happiness
— **Hob·bist** \'hä-bist\ *noun or adjective*

hob·bit \'hä-bət\ *noun* [coined by J.R.R. Tolkien] (1937)
: a member of a fictitious peaceful and genial race of small humanlike creatures that dwell underground

¹hob·ble \'hä-bəl\ *verb* **hob·bled; hob·bling** \-b(ə-)liŋ\ [Middle English *hoblen*; akin to Middle Dutch *hobbelen* to turn, roll] (14th century)
intransitive verb
: to move along unsteadily or with difficulty; *especially* : to limp along
transitive verb
1 : to cause to limp : make lame : CRIPPLE
2 [probably alteration of *hopple* (to hobble)] **a** : to fasten together the legs of (as a horse) to prevent straying : FETTER **b** : to place under handicap : HAMPER, IMPEDE
— **hob·bler** \-b(ə-)lər\ *noun*

²hobble *noun* (1726)
1 : a hobbling movement
2 *archaic* : an awkward situation
3 : something used to hobble an animal

hob·ble·bush \'hä-bəl-ˌbu̇sh\ *noun* (circa 1818)
: a white-flowered shrubby viburnum (*Viburnum alnifolium*) of northeastern North America having serrate rounded leaves and red berries

hob·ble·de·hoy \'hä-bəl-di-ˌhȯi\ *noun* [origin unknown] (1540)
: an awkward gawky youth

hobble skirt *noun* (1911)
: a skirt constricted at the bottom

¹hob·by \'hä-bē\ *noun, plural* **hobbies** [Middle English *hoby*, from Middle French *hobé*] (15th century)
: a small Old World falcon (*Falco subbuteo*) formerly trained to catch small birds (as larks)

²hobby *noun, plural* **hobbies** [short for *hobbyhorse*] (1816)
: a pursuit outside one's regular occupation engaged in especially for relaxation

— **hob·by·ist** \-bē-ist\ *noun*

hob·by·horse \'hä-bē-ˌhȯrs\ *noun* [*hobby* (small light horse)] (1557)
1 a : a figure of a horse fastened about the waist in the morris dance **b** : a dancer wearing this figure
2 *obsolete* : BUFFOON
3 a : a stick having an imitation horse's head at one end that a child pretends to ride **b** : ROCKING HORSE **c** : a toy horse suspended by springs from a frame
4 a : a topic to which one constantly reverts **b** : ²HOBBY

hob·gob·lin \'häb-ˌgäb-lən\ *noun* (1530)
1 : a mischievous goblin
2 : BOGEY 2, BUGABOO

hob·nail \-ˌnāl\ *noun* [²hob] (1592)
: a short large-headed nail for studding shoe soles
— **hob·nailed** \-ˌnāld\ *adjective*

hob·nob \-ˌnäb\ *intransitive verb* **hob·nobbed; hob·nob·bing** [from the obsolete phrase *drink hobnob* (to drink alternately to one another)] (1763)
1 *archaic* : to drink sociably
2 : to associate familiarly ◇
— **hob·nob·ber** *noun*

¹ho·bo \'hō-(ˌ)bō\ *noun, plural* **hoboes** *also* **hobos** [origin unknown] (1889)
1 : a migratory worker
2 : a homeless and usually penniless person who wanders from place to place

²hobo *intransitive verb* (1906)
: to live or travel in the manner of a hobo

Hob·son's choice \'häb-sənz-\ *noun* [Thomas *Hobson* (died 1631) English liveryman, who required every customer to take the horse nearest the door] (1649)
: an apparently free choice when there is no real alternative

¹hock \'häk\ *noun* [Middle English *hoch, hough*, from Old English *hōh* heel; akin to Old Norse *hāsin* hock] (1540)
1 a : the tarsal joint or region in the hind limb of a digitigrade quadruped (as the horse) corresponding to the human ankle but elevated and bending backward — see HORSE illustration **b** : a joint of a fowl's leg that corresponds to the hock of a quadruped

◇ WORD HISTORY

hobnob *Hobnob*, which first appears in Shakespeare in this form, meant in various contexts "one way or another," "hit or miss," or "give and take." This linguistic Siamese twin appears originally to have been a phrase, because from its earliest appearance as *habbe or nhabbe* in 1542, *hob* is commonly separated from *nob* by an intervening word, as *hob or nob, hob a nob*, or *hob and nob*. The form *habnab*, attested earlier and probably older than *hobnob*, may descend from a joining of early Middle English *habbe*, a subjunctive form of *haven* "to have" and *nabbe*, the negative form of *habbe* (from Old English *nabban*, a contraction of *ne* "not" and *habban* "to have"). The original meaning of *habbe (or) nabbe* would thus have been "may he have or may he not have." In the 18th century, people drinking to each other's health began to use *hob and nob* and its variants—first with the verb *drink* and then as a verb itself—to suggest alternation, first one person and then another lifting a glass. To *hob-and-nob* or to *hobnob* with someone began in the 19th century to refer to simple social intercourse, with no implication of drinking.

2 : a small cut of meat from either the front or hind leg just above the foot 〈ham *hocks*〉

²hock *noun, often capitalized* [modification of German *Hochheimer,* from *Hochheim,* Germany] (circa 1625)
chiefly British **:** RHINE WINE 1

³hock *transitive verb* (1878)
: PAWN
— **hock·er** *noun*

⁴hock *noun* [Dutch *hok* pen, prison] (1883)
1 a : ²PAWN 2 〈got his watch out of *hock*〉 **b** **:** DEBT 3 〈in *hock* to the bank〉
2 : PRISON

hock·ey \'hä-kē\ *noun* [perhaps from Middle French *hoquet* shepherd's crook, diminutive of *hoc* hook, of Germanic origin; akin to Old English *hōc* hook] (1527)
1 : FIELD HOCKEY
2 : ICE HOCKEY

hock·shop \'häk-ˌshäp\ *noun* (1871)
: PAWNSHOP

ho·cus \'hō-kəs\ *transitive verb* **ho·cussed** *or* **ho·cused; ho·cus·sing** *or* **ho·cus·ing** [obsolete *hocus,* noun, short for *hocus-pocus*] (1675)
1 : to perpetrate a trick or hoax on **:** DECEIVE
2 : to befuddle often with drugged liquor; *also* **:** DOPE, DRUG 〈*hocussed* the favorite before the race〉

¹ho·cus-po·cus \ˌhō-kəs-'pō-kəs\ *noun* [probably from *hocus pocus,* imitation Latin phrase used by jugglers] (1647)
1 : SLEIGHT OF HAND
2 : nonsense or sham used especially to cloak deception

²hocus-pocus *transitive verb* **-cussed** *or* **-cused; -cus·sing** *or* **-cus·ing** (1774)
: to play tricks on

hod \'häd\ *noun* [probably from Middle Dutch *hodde;* akin to Middle High German *hotte* cradle] (1573)
1 : a tray or trough that has a pole handle and that is borne on the shoulder for carrying loads (as of mortar or brick)
2 : a coal scuttle

hod carrier *noun* (1771)
: a laborer employed in carrying supplies to bricklayers, stonemasons, cement finishers, or plasterers on the job

hodge·podge \'häj-ˌpäj\ *noun* [alteration of *hotchpotch*] (15th century)
: a heterogeneous mixture **:** JUMBLE

Hodg·kin's disease \'häj-kinz-\ *noun* [Thomas *Hodgkin* (died 1866) English physician] (1865)
: a neoplastic disease that is characterized by progressive enlargement of lymph nodes, spleen, and liver and by progressive anemia

ho·do·scope \'hä-də-ˌskōp, 'hō-\ *noun* [Greek *hodos* road, path + English *-scope*] (circa 1933)
: an instrument for tracing the paths of ionizing particles by means of ion counters in close array

¹hoe \'hō\ *noun* [Middle English *howe,* from Middle French *houe,* of Germanic origin; akin to Old High German *houwa* mattock, *houwan* to hew — more at HEW] (14th century)
1 : any of various implements for tilling, mixing, or raking; *especially* **:** an implement with a thin flat blade on a long handle used especially for cultivating, weeding, or loosening the earth around plants
2 : BACKHOE

²hoe *verb* **hoed; hoe·ing** (15th century)
intransitive verb
: to use a hoe **:** work with a hoe
transitive verb
1 : to weed, cultivate, or thin (a crop) with a hoe
2 : to remove (weeds) by hoeing

hod 1

3 : to dress or cultivate (land) by hoeing
— **ho·er** \'hō-(-ə)r\ *noun*

hoe·cake \'hō-ˌkāk\ *noun* (1745)
: a small cake made of cornmeal

hoe·down \-ˌdaůn\ *noun* (1841)
1 : SQUARE DANCE
2 : a gathering featuring hoedowns

¹hog \'hóg, 'häg\ *noun, plural* **hogs** *also* **hog** [Middle English *hogge,* from Old English *hogg*] (14th century)
1 : a domestic swine especially when weighing more than 120 pounds; *broadly* **:** any of various wild and domestic swine
2 *usually* **hogg** *British* **:** a young unshorn sheep; *also* **:** wool from such a sheep
3 a : a selfish, gluttonous, or filthy person **b** **:** one that uses something to excess 〈old cars that are gas *hogs*〉

²hog *verb* **hogged; hog·ging** (1769)
transitive verb
1 : to cut (a horse's mane) short **:** ROACH
2 : to cause to arch
3 : to take in excess of one's due 〈*hog* the credit〉
4 : to tear up or shred (as waste wood) into bits by machine
intransitive verb
: to become curved upward in the middle — used of a ship's bottom or keel

ho·gan \'hō-ˌgän\ *noun* [Navajo *hooghan*] (1871)
: a Navajo Indian dwelling usually made of logs and mud with a door traditionally facing east

hogan

hog·back \'hóg-ˌbak, 'häg-\ *noun* (1840)
: a ridge of land formed by the outcropping edges of tilted strata; *broadly*
: a ridge with a sharp summit and steeply sloping sides

hog cholera *noun* (1859)
: a highly infectious often fatal virus disease of swine characterized by fever, loss of appetite, weakness, erythematous lesions especially in light-skinned animals, and severe leukopenia

hog·fish \'hóg-ˌfish, 'häg-\ *noun* (1734)
: a large West Indian and Florida wrasse (*Lachnolaimus maximus*) often used for food

hog·get \'hä-gət, 'hó-\ *noun* [Middle English, from *hog* + *-et*] (15th century)
chiefly British **:** HOG 2

hog·gish \'hó-gish, 'hä-\ *adjective* (15th century)
: grossly selfish, gluttonous, or filthy
— **hog·gish·ly** *adverb*
— **hog·gish·ness** *noun*

hog heaven *noun* (1945)
: an extremely satisfying state or situation

Hog·ma·nay \ˌhäg-mə-'nā, 'häg-mə-ˌ\ *noun* [origin unknown] (circa 1680)
1 *Scottish* **:** the eve of New Year's Day
2 *Scottish* **:** a gift solicited or given at Hogmanay

hog·nose snake \'hóg-ˌnōz-, 'häg-\ *noun* (1736)
: any of a genus (*Heterodon*) of rather small harmless stout-bodied North American colubrid snakes with keeled scales and an upturned snout that seldom bite but hiss wildly and often play dead when disturbed — called also *hog-nosed snake, puff adder*

hog score *noun* [*hog* (curling stone that fails to reach the score)] (1685)
: a line which is marked across a curling rink seven yards from the tee and beyond which a stone must pass or be removed from the ice — called also *hog line*

hogs·head \'hógz-ˌhed, 'hägz-\ *noun* (14th century)

1 : a large cask or barrel
2 : any of various units of capacity; *especially*
: a U.S. unit equal to 63 gallons (238 liters)

hog sucker *noun* (1877)
: a North American sucker (*Hypentelium nigricans*) that is brassy olive marked with brown and is sometimes used for food

hog-tie \'hóg-ˌtī, 'häg-\ *transitive verb* (1894)
1 : to tie together the feet of
2 : to make helpless

hog·wash \-ˌwósh, -ˌwäsh\ *noun* (15th century)
1 : SWILL 2a, SLOP
2 : NONSENSE, BALDERDASH

hog-wild \-'wī(ə)ld\ *adjective* (1904)
: lacking in restraint of judgment or temper 〈*hog-wild* enthusiasm〉 〈would go *hog-wild* if unconfined by constitutional limitations —Leo Egan〉

¹Ho·hen·stau·fen \'hō-ən-ˌshtaů-fən, -ˌstaů-\ *noun* (circa 1895)
: a member of the Hohenstaufen family; *especially* **:** a Hohenstaufen monarch

²Hohenstaufen *adjective* (1921)
: of or relating to a princely German family that reigned over the Holy Roman Empire from 1138–1254 and over Sicily from 1194–1266

¹Ho·hen·zol·lern \ˌhō-ən-'zä-lərn, -'zó-\ *noun* (circa 1895)
: a member of the Hohenzollern family; *especially* **:** a Hohenzollern monarch

²Hohenzollern *adjective* (1924)
: of or relating to a princely German family that reigned in Prussia from 1701–1918 and in Germany from 1871–1918

Ho·ho·kam \ˌhō-hō-'käm\ *noun, plural* **Hohokam** [O'odham (Uto-Aztecan language of southern Arizona) *huhugam,* literally, those who have gone] (1884)
: a member of a prehistoric desert culture of the southwestern U.S. centering in the Gila Valley of Arizona and characterized especially by irrigated agriculture
— **Hohokam** *adjective*

ho-hum \'hō-'həm\ *adjective* (1969)
1 : ROUTINE, DULL 〈a *ho-hum* existence〉
2 : BORED, INDIFFERENT 〈a *ho-hum* reaction〉

ho hum *interjection* [imitative] (1924)
— used to express weariness, boredom, or disdain

hoick \'hóik\ *transitive verb* [probably alteration of ¹*hike*] (1898)
: to move or pull abruptly **:** YANK 〈was *hoicked* out of my job —Vincent Sheean〉

hoi pol·loi \ˌhói-pə-'lói\ *noun plural* [Greek, the many] (1837)
: the general populace **:** MASSES ☐

hoise \'hóiz\ *transitive verb* **hoised** \'hóizd\ *or* **hoist** \'hóist\; **hois·ing** \'hói-ziŋ\ [alteration of *hysse* to hoist, perhaps from Low German *hissen*] (1509)
: HOIST
— **hoist with one's own petard :** victimized or hurt by one's own scheme

¹hoist \'hóist, *chiefly dialect* 'hīst\ *verb* [alteration of *hoise*] (15th century)
transitive verb
1 : LIFT, RAISE; *especially* **:** to raise into position by or as if by means of tackle
2 : DRINK 1 〈*hoist* a few beers〉

intransitive verb
: to become hoisted **:** RISE
synonym see LIFT
— **hoist·er** *noun*

²**hoist** *noun* (1654)
1 : an act of hoisting **:** LIFT
2 : an apparatus for hoisting
3 : the height of a flag when viewed flying

¹**hoi·ty–toi·ty** \ˌhȯi-tē-ˈtȯi-tē, ˌhī-tē-ˈtī-tē\ *noun* [rhyming compound from English dialect *hoit* to play the fool] (1668)
: thoughtless giddy behavior

²**hoity–toity** *adjective* (1690)
1 : thoughtlessly silly or frivolous **:** FLIGHTY
2 : marked by an air of assumed importance **:** HIGHFALUTIN

hoke \ˈhōk\ *transitive verb* **hoked; hok·ing** [*hokum*] (1925)
: to give an impressive but false value or quality to **:** FAKE — usually used with *up* ⟨used parts of B-grade movies to *hoke* up a film —Robert Sherrill⟩

hok·ey \ˈhō-kē\ *adjective* **hok·i·er; -est** (1927)
1 : ¹CORNY 3 ⟨the usual *hokey* melodrama⟩
2 : obviously contrived **:** PHONY ⟨the plots are tricky but not *hokey* —Cleveland Amory⟩
— **hok·ey·ness** *or* **hok·i·ness** \ˈhō-kē-nəs\ *noun*
— **hok·i·ly** \ˈhō-kə-lē\ *adverb*

ho·key-po·key \ˌhō-kē-ˈpō-kē\ *noun* (circa 1878)
1 : HOCUS-POCUS 2
2 : ice cream sold by street vendors

hok·ku \ˈhȯ-(ˌ)kü\ *noun, plural* **hokku** [Japanese] (1898)
: HAIKU

ho·kum \ˈhō-kəm\ *noun* [probably blend of *hocus-pocus* and *bunkum*] (1917)
1 : a device used (as by showmen) to evoke a desired audience response
2 : pretentious nonsense **:** BUNKUM

hol- *or* **holo-** *combining form* [Middle English, from Old French, from Latin, from Greek, from *holos* whole — more at SAFE]
1 : complete **:** total ⟨*holo*hedral⟩
2 : completely **:** totally ⟨*hol*andric⟩

hol·an·dric \hō-ˈlan-drik, hä-\ *adjective* [International Scientific Vocabulary, from *hol-* + *andr-* + *-ic*] (1930)
: transmitted by a gene in the nonhomologous portion of the Y chromosome

Hol·arc·tic \hō-ˈlärk-tik, hä-, -ˈlär-tik\ *adjective* (1883)
: of, relating to, or being the biogeographic region including the northern parts of the Old and the New Worlds and comprising the Nearctic and Palearctic regions or subregions

¹**hold** \ˈhōld\ *verb* **held** \ˈheld\; **hold·ing** [Middle English, from Old English *healdan;* akin to Old High German *haltan* to hold, and perhaps to Latin *celer* rapid, Greek *klonos* agitation] (before 12th century)
transitive verb
1 a : to have possession or ownership of or have at one's disposal ⟨*holds* property worth millions⟩ ⟨the bank *holds* the title to the car⟩ **b :** to have as a privilege or position of responsibility ⟨*hold* a professorship⟩ **c :** to have as a mark of distinction ⟨*holds* the record for the 100-yard dash⟩ ⟨*holds* a PhD⟩
2 : to keep under restraint ⟨*hold* price increases to a minimum⟩: as **a :** to prevent free expression of ⟨*hold* your temper⟩ **b :** to prevent from some action ⟨ordered the troops to *hold* fire⟩ ⟨the only restraining motive which may *hold* the hand of a tyrant —Thomas Jefferson⟩ **c :** to keep back from use ⟨ask them to *hold* a room for us⟩ ⟨I'll have a hot dog, and *hold* the mustard⟩ **d :** to delay temporarily the handling of ⟨please *hold* all my calls⟩
3 : to make liable or accountable or bound to an obligation ⟨I'll *hold* you to your promise⟩
4 a : to have or maintain in the grasp ⟨*hold* my hand⟩ ⟨this is how you *hold* the racket⟩;

also **:** AIM, POINT ⟨*held* a gun on them⟩ **b :** to support in a particular position or keep from falling or moving ⟨*hold* me up so I can see⟩ ⟨*hold* the ladder steady⟩ ⟨a clamp *holds* the whole thing together⟩ ⟨*hold* your head up⟩ **c :** to bear the pressure of **:** SUPPORT ⟨can the roof *hold* all of that weight⟩
5 : to prevent from leaving or getting away ⟨*hold* the train⟩: as **a :** to avoid emitting or letting out ⟨how long can you *hold* your breath⟩ **b :** to restrain as or as if a captive ⟨the suspect was *held* without bail⟩ ⟨*held* them at gunpoint⟩; *also* **:** to have strong appeal to ⟨the book *held* my interest throughout⟩
6 a : to enclose and keep in a container or within bounds **:** CONTAIN ⟨the jug *holds* one gallon⟩ ⟨this corral will not *hold* all of the horses⟩ **b :** to be able to consume easily or without undue effect ⟨can't *hold* any more pie⟩; *especially* **:** to be able to drink (alcoholic beverages) without becoming noticeably drunk ⟨can't *hold* your liquor⟩ **c :** ACCOMMODATE ⟨the restaurant *holds* 400 diners⟩ **d :** to have as a principal or essential feature or attribute ⟨the book *holds* a number of surprises⟩; *also* **:** to have in store ⟨no one knows what the future *holds*⟩
7 a : to have in the mind or express as a judgment, opinion, or belief ⟨I *hold* the view that this is wrong⟩ ⟨*hold* a grudge⟩ ⟨*holding* that it is nobody's business but his —Jack Olsen⟩ — often used with *against* ⟨in America they *hold* everything you say against you —Paul McCartney⟩ **b :** to think of in a particular way **:** REGARD ⟨were *held* in high esteem⟩
8 a : to assemble for and carry on the activity of ⟨*held* a convention⟩ **b :** to cause to be carried on **:** CONDUCT ⟨will *hold* a seminar⟩ **c :** to produce or sponsor especially as a public exhibition ⟨will *hold* an art show⟩
9 a : to maintain occupation, control, or defense of ⟨the troops *held* the ridge⟩; *also* **:** to resist the offensive efforts or advance of ⟨*held* the opposing team to just two points⟩ **b :** to maintain (a certain condition, situation, or course of action) without change ⟨*hold* a course due east⟩
10 : to cover (a part of the body) especially for protection ⟨had to *hold* their ears because of the cold⟩
intransitive verb
1 a : to maintain position **:** refuse to give ground ⟨the defensive line is *holding*⟩ **b :** to continue in the same way or to the same degree **:** LAST ⟨hopes the weather will *hold*⟩ — often used with *up*
2 : to derive right or title — often used with *of* or *from*
3 : to be or remain valid **:** APPLY ⟨the rule *holds* in most cases⟩ — often used in the phrase *hold true*
4 : to maintain a grasp on something **:** remain fastened to something ⟨the anchor *held* in the rough sea⟩
5 : to go ahead as one has been going ⟨*held* south for several miles⟩
6 : to bear or carry oneself ⟨asked him to *hold* still⟩
7 : to forbear an intended or threatened action **:** HALT, PAUSE — often used as a command
8 : to stop counting during a countdown
9 *slang* **:** to have illicit drug material in one's possession
synonym see CONTAIN
— **hold a candle to :** to qualify for comparison with
— **hold court :** to be the center of attention among friends or admirers
— **hold forth :** to speak at length **:** EXPATIATE
— **hold hands :** to engage one's hand with another's especially as an expression of affection
— **hold one's horses :** to slow down or stop for a moment — usually used in the imperative

— **hold one's own :** to do well in the face of difficulty or opposition
— **hold one's tongue :** to keep silent
— **hold sway :** to have a dominant influence **:** RULE
— **hold the bag 1 :** to be left empty-handed **2 :** to bear alone a responsibility that should have been shared by others
— **hold the fort 1 :** to maintain a firm position **2 :** to take care of usual affairs ⟨is *holding the fort* until the manager returns⟩
— **hold the line :** to maintain the current position or situation ⟨*hold the line* on prices⟩
— **hold to :** to give firm assent to **:** adhere to strongly ⟨*holds to* his promise⟩
— **hold to account :** to hold responsible
— **hold water :** to stand up under criticism or analysis
— **hold with :** to agree with or approve of

²**hold** *noun* (14th century)
1 : STRONGHOLD 1
2 a : CONFINEMENT, CUSTODY **b :** PRISON
3 a (1) **:** the act or the manner of holding or grasping **:** GRIP ⟨released his *hold* on the handle⟩ (2) **:** a manner of grasping an opponent in wrestling **b :** a nonphysical bond that attaches, restrains, or constrains or by which something is affected, controlled, or dominated ⟨has lost its *hold* on the broad public —Oscar Cargill⟩ **c :** full comprehension ⟨get *hold* of exactly what is happening —J. P. Lyford⟩ **d :** full or immediate control **:** POSSESSION ⟨get *hold* of yourself⟩ ⟨wants to get *hold* of a road map⟩ **e :** TOUCH 14 — used with *of* ⟨tried to get *hold* of me⟩
4 : something that may be grasped as a support
5 a : FERMATA **b :** the time between the onset and the release of a vocal articulation
6 : a sudden motionless posture at the end of a dance
7 a : an order or indication that something is to be reserved or delayed **b :** a delay in a countdown (as in launching a spacecraft)
— **on hold 1 :** into a state of interruption during a telephone call when one party switches to another line without totally disconnecting the other party **2 :** into a state or period of indefinite suspension ⟨put our plans *on hold*⟩

³**hold** *noun* [alteration of *hole*] (1591)
1 : the interior of a ship below decks; *especially* **:** the cargo deck of a ship
2 : the cargo compartment of a plane

hold·all \ˈhōl-ˌdȯl\ *noun* (1851)
chiefly British **:** an often cloth traveling case or bag

hold·back \ˈhōl(d)-ˌbak\ *noun* (1581)
1 : something that retains or restrains
2 a : the act of holding back **b :** something held back

hold back (1535)
transitive verb
1 : to hinder the progress or achievement of **:** RESTRAIN
2 : to refrain from revealing or parting with
intransitive verb
1 : to keep oneself in check
2 : to refrain from revealing or parting with something

hold–down \ˈhōl-ˌdaun\ *noun* (1888)
1 : something used to fasten an object in place
2 a : an act of holding down **b :** LIMIT ⟨agreed to wage-rate *hold-downs*⟩

hold down *transitive verb* (1533)
1 : to keep within limits ⟨*hold* the noise *down*⟩
2 : to assume the responsibility for ⟨*holding down* two jobs⟩

hold·en \ˈhōl-dən\ *archaic past participle of* HOLD

hold·er \ˈhōl-dər\ *noun* (14th century)

1 : a person that holds: as **a** (1) : OWNER (2) : TENANT **b :** a person in possession of and legally entitled to receive payment of a bill, note, or check **2 :** a device that holds ⟨cigarette *holder*⟩

holder in due course (1882)
: one other than the original recipient who holds a legally effective negotiable instrument (as a promissory note) and who has a right to collect from and no responsibility toward the issuer

hold·fast \ˈhōl(d)-ˌfast\ *noun* (1566)
1 : something to which something else may be firmly secured **2 a :** a part by which a plant clings to a flat surface **b :** an organ by which a parasitic animal attaches itself to its host

¹hold·ing \ˈhōl-diŋ\ *noun* (15th century)
1 a : land held especially by a vassal or tenant **b :** property (as land or securities) owned — usually used in plural **2 :** a ruling of a court especially on an issue of law raised in a case — compare DICTUM **3 :** something that holds

²holding *adjective* (1568)
1 : having the effect of holding back or delaying something ⟨the [war] represented a *holding* action against the spread of world Communism —Sidney Offit⟩ **2 :** intended for usually temporary storage or retention ⟨a *holding* tank⟩

holding company *noun* (1906)
: a company whose primary business is holding a controlling interest in the securities of other companies — compare INVESTMENT COMPANY

holding pattern *noun* (circa 1952)
1 : the usually oval course flown (as over an airport) by aircraft awaiting clearance especially to land **2 :** a state of waiting or suspended activity or progress

hold off (15th century)
transitive verb
1 : to block from an objective : DELAY **2 :** to defer action on : POSTPONE **3 :** to fight to a standoff : WITHSTAND
intransitive verb
: to defer or temporarily stop doing something

hold on *intransitive verb* (13th century)
1 a : to maintain a condition or position : PERSIST **b :** to maintain a grasp on something : HANG ON **2 :** to await something (as a telephone connection) desired or requested; *broadly* : WAIT
— hold on to : to maintain possession of or adherence to

hold·out \ˈhōl-ˌdaut\ *noun* (1945)
: one that holds out (as in negotiations); *also* : an instance of holding out

hold out (1585)
intransitive verb
1 : to remain unsubdued or operative : continue to cope or function **2 :** to refuse to go along with others in a concerted action or to come to an agreement ⟨*holding out* for a shorter workweek⟩
transitive verb
1 : to present as something realizable : PROFFER **2 :** to represent to be
— hold out on : to withhold something (as information) from

hold·over \ˈhōl-ˌdō-vər\ *noun* (1893)
: one that is held over

hold over (1647)
intransitive verb
: to continue (as in office) for a prolonged period
transitive verb
1 a : POSTPONE, DEFER **b :** to retain in a condition or position from an earlier period **2 :** to prolong the engagement of ⟨the film was *held over* another week⟩

hold·up \ˈhōl-ˌdəp\ *noun* (1837)
1 : DELAY

2 : a robbery carried out at gunpoint

hold up (1851)
transitive verb
1 : to rob at gunpoint **2 :** DELAY, IMPEDE **3 :** to call attention to : single out ⟨his work was *held up* to ridicule⟩ ⟨*hold* this *up* as perfection —*Times Literary Supplement*⟩
intransitive verb
: to continue in the same condition without failing or losing effectiveness or force ⟨you seem to be *holding up* under the strain⟩

¹hole \ˈhōl\ *noun* [Middle English, from Old English *hol* (from neuter of *hol*, adjective, hollow) & *holh;* akin to Old High German *hol*, adjective, hollow; perhaps akin to Old English *helan* to conceal — more at HELL] (before 12th century)
1 a : an opening through something : PERFORATION ⟨have a *hole* in my coat⟩ **b :** an area where something is missing : GAP: as (1) : a serious discrepancy : FLAW, WEAKNESS ⟨there are *holes* in your logic⟩ (2) : an opening in a defensive formation; *especially* : the area of a baseball field between the positions of shortstop and third baseman (3) : a defect in a crystal (as of a semiconductor) that is due to an electron's having left its normal position in one of the crystal bonds and that is equivalent in many respects to a positively charged particle **2 :** a hollowed-out place: as **a :** a cave, pit, or well in the ground **b :** BURROW **c :** an unusually deep place in a body of water **3 :** a wretched or dreary place **4 a :** a shallow cylindrical hole in the putting green of a golf course into which the ball is played **b :** a part of the golf course from tee to putting green ⟨just beginning play on the third *hole*⟩; *also* : the play on such a hole as a unit of scoring ⟨won the *hole* by two strokes⟩ **5 a :** an awkward position or circumstance : FIX ⟨got the rebels out of a *hole* at the battle —Kenneth Roberts⟩ **b :** a position of owing or losing money ⟨$10 million in the *hole*⟩ ⟨raising money to get out of the *hole*⟩
— in the hole 1 : having a score below zero **2 :** at a disadvantage

²hole *verb* **holed; hol·ing** (before 12th century)
transitive verb
1 : to make a hole in **2 :** to drive or hit into a hole
intransitive verb
: to make a hole in something

hole–and–corner *adjective* (1835)
1 : being or carried on in a place away from public view : CLANDESTINE **2 :** INSIGNIFICANT

hole card *noun* (1908)
: a card in stud poker that is properly dealt facedown and that the holder need not expose before the showdown

hole in one (1925)
: ACE 4

hole–in–the–wall *noun, plural* **holes–in–the–wall** (1856)
: a small and often unpretentious out-of-the-way place (as a restaurant)

hole out *intransitive verb* (1857)
: to play one's ball into the hole in golf

hole up (1875)
intransitive verb
: to take refuge or shelter in or as if in a hole or cave
transitive verb
: to place in or as if in a refuge or hiding place

hol·ey \ˈhō-lē\ *adjective* (13th century)
: having holes

¹hol·i·day \ˈhä-lə-ˌdā, *British usually* ˈhä-lə-dē\ *noun* [Middle English, from Old English *hāligdæg*, from *hālig* holy + *dæg* day] (before 12th century)
1 : HOLY DAY

2 : a day on which one is exempt from work; *specifically* : a day marked by a general suspension of work in commemoration of an event **3** *chiefly British* : a period of relaxation : VACATION — often used in the phrase *on holiday;* often used in plural

²holiday *intransitive verb* (1869)
: to take or spend a holiday especially in travel or at a resort
— hol·i·day·er *noun*

hol·i·day·mak·er \ˈhä-lə-dē-ˌmā-kər, ˈhä-lə-ˌdā-\ *noun* (1836)
chiefly British : VACATIONER

hol·i·days \-ˌdāz, *British usually* -lə-dēz\ *adverb* (circa 1961)
: on holidays repeatedly : on any holiday

ho·li·er–than–thou \ˌhō-lē-ər-thən-ˈthau\ *adjective* (1859)
: marked by an air of superior piety or morality

¹ho·li·ness \ˈhō-lē-nəs\ *noun* (before 12th century)
1 : the quality or state of being holy — used as a title for various high religious dignitaries ⟨his *holiness* the pope⟩ **2 :** SANCTIFICATION 2

²holiness *adjective, often capitalized* (1888)
: emphasizing the doctrine of the second blessing; *specifically* : of or relating to a perfectionist movement arising in U.S. Protestantism in the late 19th century

ho·lism \ˈhō-ˌli-zəm\ *noun* [hol- + -ism] (1926)
1 : a theory that the universe and especially living nature is correctly seen in terms of interacting wholes (as of living organisms) that are more than the mere sum of elementary particles **2 :** a holistic study or method of treatment
— hol·ist \ˈhō-list\ *noun*

ho·lis·tic \hō-ˈlis-tik\ *adjective* (1926)
1 : of or relating to holism **2 :** relating to or concerned with wholes or with complete systems rather than with the analysis of, treatment of, or dissection into parts ⟨*holistic* medicine attempts to treat both the mind and the body⟩ ⟨*holistic* ecology views man and the environment as a single system⟩
— ho·lis·ti·cal·ly \-ti-k(ə-)lē\ *adverb*

hol·land \ˈhä-lənd\ *noun, often capitalized* [Middle English *holand*, from *Holand*, county in the Netherlands, from Middle Dutch *Holland*] (14th century)
: a cotton or linen fabric in plain weave usually heavily sized or glazed and used for window shades, bookbinding, and clothing

hol·lan·daise \ˌhä-lən-ˈdāz\ *noun* [French *sauce hollandaise*, literally, Dutch sauce] (1907)
: a rich sauce made basically of butter, egg yolks, and lemon juice or vinegar

Hol·lands \ˈhä-lən(d)z\ *noun* [Dutch *hollandsch*, from *hollandsch genever* Dutch gin] (1788)
: gin made in the Netherlands — called also *Holland gin*

¹hol·ler \ˈhä-lər\ *verb* **hol·lered; hol·ler·ing** \ˈhäl-riŋ, ˈhä-lə-\ [alteration of *hollo*] (1699)
intransitive verb
1 : to cry out (as to attract attention or in pain) : SHOUT **2 :** GRIPE, COMPLAIN
transitive verb
: to call out (a word or phrase)

²holler *noun* (1825)
1 : SHOUT, CRY **2 :** COMPLAINT **3 :** a freely improvised work song of black Americans ⟨field *hollers*⟩

³holler *chiefly dialect variant of* HOLLOW

Hol·ler·ith card \ˈhä-lə-rith-\ *noun* [Herman Hollerith (died 1929) American engineer] (1946)
: PUNCHED CARD

Hollerith code *noun* (1962)
: a system for encoding alphanumeric information on punched cards

¹**hol·lo** *also* **hol·loa** \'hä-(ˌ)lō\ *or* **hol·la** \'hä-lə\ (14th century)
intransitive verb
: to cry hollo : HOLLER
transitive verb
1 : to call or cry hollo to
2 : to utter loudly : HOLLER

²**hollo** *also* **holloa** *or* **holla** *noun, plural* **hollos** *also* **holloas** *or* **hollas** (15th century)
: an exclamation or call of hollo

³**hol·lo** \hä-'lō, hə-; 'hä-(ˌ)\ *also* **hol·loa** \hä-'lō, hə-\ *or* **hol·la** \hə-'lä, 'hä-(ˌ)\ *interjection* [origin unknown] (1588)
1 — used to attract attention (as when a fox is spied during a fox hunt)
2 — used as a call of encouragement or jubilation

¹**hollow** *noun* (before 12th century)
1 : an unfilled space : CAVITY, HOLE
2 : a depressed or low part of a surface; *especially* : a small valley or basin

²**hol·low** \'hä-(ˌ)lō\ *adjective* **hol·low·er** \'hä-lə-wər\; **hol·low·est** \-lə-wəst\ [Middle English *holw, holh,* from *holh* hole, den, from Old English *holh* hole, hollow — more at HOLE] (13th century)
1 : having an indentation or inward curve : CONCAVE, SUNKEN
2 : having a cavity within ⟨*hollow* tree⟩
3 : lacking in real value, sincerity, or substance : FALSE, MEANINGLESS ⟨*hollow* promises⟩ ⟨a victory over a weakling is *hollow* and without triumph —Ernest Beaglehole⟩
4 : reverberating like a sound made in or by beating on a large empty enclosure : MUFFLED
synonym *see* VAIN
— **hol·low·ly** \'hä-lō-lē, -lə-lē\ *adverb*
— **hol·low·ness** *noun*

³**hollow** (15th century)
transitive verb
1 : to make hollow
2 : to form by a hollowing action — usually used with *out* ⟨rain barrels *hollowed* out from trees —Robert Shaplen⟩
intransitive verb
: to become hollow

⁴**hollow** *adverb* (1601)
1 : so as to have a hollow sound
2 : COMPLETELY, THOROUGHLY ⟨an ongoing story that has the old cowboy-and-Indians genre beat *hollow* —Barbara Bannon⟩ — often used with *all*

hol·low·ware *or* **hol·lo·ware** \'hä-(ˌ)lō-ˌwar, -ˌwer\ *noun* (1682)
: vessels (as bowls, cups, or vases) usually of pottery, glass, or metal that have a significant depth and volume — compare FLATWARE

hol·ly \'hä-lē\ *noun, plural* **hollies** [Middle English *holin, holly,* from Old English *holen;* akin to Old High German *hulis* holly, Middle Irish *cuilenn*] (before 13th century)
1 : any of a genus (*Ilex* of the family Aquifoliaceae, the holly family) of trees and shrubs; *especially* : either of two (*I. opaca* of the eastern U.S. and *I. aquifolium* of Eurasia) with spiny-margined evergreen leaves and usually red berries often used for Christmas decorations
2 : the foliage or branches of the holly

hol·ly·hock \'hä-lē-ˌhäk, -ˌhôk\ *noun* [Middle English *holihoc* marshmallow, from *holi* holy + *hoc* mallow, from Old English] (1548)
: a tall widely cultivated perennial Chinese herb (*Alcea rosea* synonym *Althaea rosea*) of the mallow family with large coarse rounded leaves and tall spikes of showy flowers

hollyhock

¹**Hol·ly·wood** \'hä-lē-ˌwu̇d\ *noun* [Hollywood, district of Los Angeles, Calif.] (1923)
: the American motion-picture industry
— **Hol·ly·wood·ish** \-ˌwu̇-dish\ *adjective*

²**Hollywood** *adjective* (1935)
: of or characteristic of people in the American motion-picture industry ⟨*Hollywood* lifestyle⟩

Hollywood bed *noun* (1947)
: a mattress on a box spring supported by low legs and often having an upholstered headboard

holm \'hō(l)m\ *noun* [Middle English, from Old English, from Old Norse *hōlmr;* akin to Old English *hyll* hill] (before 12th century)
British : a small inland or inshore island; *also* : BOTTOMS

Holmes·ian \'hōm-zē-ən *also* 'hōlm-\ *adjective* [Sherlock *Holmes,* detective in stories by Sir Arthur Conan Doyle] (1929)
: of, characteristic of, or suggestive of the detective Sherlock Holmes

hol·mi·um \'hō(l)-mē-əm\ *noun* [New Latin, from *Holmia* Stockholm, Sweden] (1879)
: a metallic element of the rare-earth group that occurs with yttrium and forms highly magnetic compounds — see ELEMENT table

holm oak *noun* (1597)
: a southern European evergreen oak (*Quercus ilex*)

holo- — *see* HOL-

ho·lo·blas·tic \ˌhō-lə-'blas-tik, ˌhä-\ *adjective* [International Scientific Vocabulary] (1872)
: characterized by cleavage planes that divide the whole egg into distinct and separate though coherent blastomeres — compare MEROBLASTIC

ho·lo·caust \'hō-lə-ˌkȯst, 'hä- *also* -ˌkäst *or* 'hȯ-lə-kȯst\ *noun* [Middle English, from Old French *holocauste,* from Late Latin *holocaustum,* from Greek *holokauston,* from neuter of *holokaustos* burnt whole, from *hol-* + *kaustos* burnt, from *kaiein* to burn — more at CAUSTIC] (13th century)
1 : a sacrifice consumed by fire
2 : a thorough destruction involving extensive loss of life especially through fire ⟨a nuclear *holocaust*⟩
3 a *often capitalized* : the mass slaughter of European civilians and especially Jews by the Nazis during World War II — usually used with *the* **b** : a mass slaughter of people; *especially* : GENOCIDE ◇

Ho·lo·cene \'hō-lə-ˌsēn, 'hä-\ *adjective* [International Scientific Vocabulary] (1897)
: of, relating to, or being the present or post-Pleistocene geologic epoch — see GEOLOGIC TIME table
— **Holocene** *noun*

ho·lo·crine \-krən, -ˌkrīn, -ˌkrēn\ *adjective* [International Scientific Vocabulary *hol-* + Greek *krinein* to separate — more at CERTAIN] (circa 1905)
: producing or being a secretion resulting from lysis of secretory cells ⟨*holocrine* gland⟩

ho·lo·en·zyme \ˌhō-lō-'en-ˌzīm\ *noun* [International Scientific Vocabulary] (1943)
: a catalytically active enzyme consisting of an apoenzyme combined with its cofactor

Ho·lo·fer·nes \ˌhä-lə-'fər-(ˌ)nēz, ˌhō-\ *noun* [Late Latin, from Greek *Holophernēs*]
: a general of Nebuchadnezzar's who led an Assyrian army against Israel and was beheaded in his sleep by Judith

ho·lo·gram \'hō-lə-ˌgram, 'hä-\ *noun* (1949)
: a three-dimensional image reproduced from a pattern of interference produced by a split coherent beam of radiation (as a laser); *also* : the pattern of interference itself

ho·lo·graph \'hō-lə-ˌgraf, 'hä-\ *noun* [Late Latin *holographus,* from Late Greek *holographos,* from Greek *hol-* + *graphein* to write — more at CARVE] (circa 1623)
: a document wholly in the handwriting of its author; *also* : the handwriting itself ⟨a letter in the president's *holograph*⟩

— **holograph** *or* **ho·lo·graph·ic** \ˌhō-lə-'gra-fik, ˌhä-\ *adjective*

ho·log·ra·phy \hō-'lä-grə-fē\ *noun* (1964)
: the art or process of making or using a hologram
— **ho·lo·graph** \'hō-lə-ˌgraf, 'hä-\ *transitive verb*
— **ho·log·ra·pher** \hō-'lä-grə-fər\ *noun*
— **ho·lo·graph·ic** \ˌhō-lə-'gra-fik, ˌhä-\ *adjective*
— **ho·lo·graph·i·cal·ly** \-fi-k(ə-)lē\ *adverb*

ho·lo·he·dral \ˌhō-lə-'hē-drəl, ˌhä-\ *adjective* (1837)
of a crystal : having all the faces required by complete symmetry — compare HEMIHEDRAL, TETARTOHEDRAL

ho·lo·me·tab·o·lous \ˌhō-lō-mə-'ta-bə-ləs, ˌhä-\ *adjective* (1870)
: characterized by complete metamorphosis ⟨*holometabolous* insects⟩ — compare HEMIMETABOLOUS
— **ho·lo·me·tab·o·lism** \-ˌli-zəm\ *noun*

ho·lo·phras·tic \ˌhō-lə-'fras-tik, ˌhä-\ *adjective* [International Scientific Vocabulary *hol-* + *-phrastic* (from Greek *phrazein* to point out, declare)] (1860)
: expressing a complex of ideas in a single word or in a fixed phrase

ho·lo·phyt·ic \ˌhō-lə-'fi-tik\ *adjective* (1885)
: obtaining food after the manner of a green plant by photosynthetic activity

ho·lo·thu·ri·an \-'thu̇r-ē-ən, -'thyu̇r-\ *noun* [ultimately from Greek *holothourion* water polyp] (circa 1842)
: SEA CUCUMBER
— **holothurian** *adjective*

ho·lo·type \'hō-lə-ˌtīp, 'hä-\ *noun* (1897)
1 : the single specimen designated as the type of a species or lesser taxon at the time of establishing the group
2 : the type of a species or lesser taxon designated at a date later than that of establishing a group or by another person than the author of the taxon
— **ho·lo·typ·ic** \ˌhō-lə-'ti-pik, ˌhä-\ *adjective*

ho·lo·zo·ic \ˌhō-lə-'zō-ik, ˌhä-\ *adjective* (1885)
: characterized by food procurement after the manner of most animals by the ingestion of

◇ WORD HISTORY
holocaust The ancient Greek word *holokauston* meant literally "something completely burnt up." In the Septuagint, the Greek translation of Jewish scripture dating from the early centuries B.C., it renders the Hebrew word *kālil* "sacrifice consumed wholly on the altar." Borrowed from Greek through Latin, the English word *holocaust* by the 18th century had begun to lose as its primary sense "burnt offering" and to refer more generally to a destructive fire or any massive catastrophe, without implying sacrifice. It was the "catastrophe" sense of *holocaust* that Jewish historians writing in English adopted in the late 1950's when they used the word as a proper noun to refer to a single event, the Nazi slaughter of European Jews during World War II, in part to render Modern Hebrew *hurban* (literally, "destruction") or *shoa* (literally, "disaster, catastrophe"). *Holocaust* has in recent decades been applied to the mass murder of civilians at other times in history, and on occasion is virtually synonymous with *genocide*.

\ə\ abut \ᵊ\ kitten \ər\ further \a\ ash \ā\ ace
\ä\ mop, mar \au̇\ out \ch\ chin \e\ bet \ē\ easy
\g\ go \i\ hit \ī\ ice \j\ job \ŋ\ sing \ō\ go
\ȯ\ law \ȯi\ boy \th\ thin \ṯh\ the \ü\ loot \u̇\ foot
\y\ yet \zh\ vision *see also* Guide to Pronunciation

complex organic matter : HETEROTROPHIC ⟨*ho-lozoic* nutrition⟩

holp \'hō(l)p\ *chiefly dialect past of* HELP

hol·pen \'hō(l)-pən\ *chiefly dialect past participle of* HELP

hols \'hälz\ *noun plural* [short for *holidays*] (1905)
British : VACATION 2

Hol·stein \'hōl-ˌstēn, -ˌstīn\ *noun* [short for *Holstein-Friesian*] (1865)
: any of a breed of large usually black-and-white dairy cattle originally from northern Holland and Friesland that produce large quantities of comparatively low-fat milk

Hol·stein–Frie·sian \-'frē-zhən\ *noun* [*Holstein*, Germany, its later locality + *Friesian* (variant of *Frisian*)] (1889)
: HOLSTEIN

hol·ster \'hōl-stər\ *noun* [Dutch; akin to Old English *heolstor* cover, *helan* to conceal — more at HELL] (1663)
: a leather or fabric case for carrying a firearm on the person (as on the hip or chest), on a saddle, or in a vehicle

holt \'hōlt\ *noun* [Middle English, from Old English; akin to Old High German *holz* wood, Greek *klados* twig] (before 12th century)
archaic : a small woods : COPPICE

ho·lus-bo·lus \ˌhō-ləs-'bō-ləs\ *adverb* [probably reduplication of *bolus*] (1857)
: all at once

ho·ly \'hō-lē\ *adjective* **ho·li·er; -est** [Middle English, from Old English *hālig*; akin to Old English *hāl* whole — more at WHOLE] (before 12th century)
1 : exalted or worthy of complete devotion as one perfect in goodness and righteousness
2 : DIVINE ⟨for the Lord our God is *holy* —Psalms 99:9 (Authorized Version)⟩
3 : devoted entirely to the deity or the work of the deity ⟨a *holy* temple⟩ ⟨*holy* prophets⟩
4 a : having a divine quality ⟨*holy* love⟩ **b** : venerated as or as if sacred ⟨*holy* scripture⟩ ⟨a *holy* relic⟩ ⟨lampooning the *holy* conventions of playwriting —William Zinsser⟩
5 — used as an intensive ⟨this is a *holy* mess⟩ ⟨he was a *holy* terror when he drank —Thomas Wolfe⟩; often used in combination as a mild oath ⟨*holy* smoke⟩
— **ho·li·ly** \-lə-lē\ *adverb*

holy city *noun* (14th century)
: a city that is the center of religious worship and traditions

Holy Communion *noun* (1548)
: COMMUNION 2a

holy day *noun* (before 12th century)
: a day set aside for special religious observance

holy day of obligation (1909)
: a feast on which Roman Catholics are duty-bound to attend mass

Holy Father *noun* (15th century)
: POPE 1

Holy Ghost *noun* (before 12th century)
: the third person of the Trinity : HOLY SPIRIT

Holy Grail *noun* (1590)
: GRAIL

Holy Joe \'hō-lē-'jō\ *noun* (circa 1874)
slang : PARSON, CHAPLAIN

Holy Office *noun* (circa 1741)
: a congregation of the curia charged with protecting faith and morals

holy of holies [translation of Late Latin *sanctum sanctorum*, translation of Hebrew *qōdhesh haq-qŏdhāshīm*] (1641)
: the innermost and most sacred chamber of the Jewish tabernacle and temple

holy oil *noun* (14th century)
: olive oil blessed by a bishop for use in a sacrament or sacramental

holy order *noun, often H&O capitalized* (14th century)
1 a : MAJOR ORDER — usually used in plural **b** : one of the orders of the ministry in the Anglican or Episcopal church

2 : the rite or sacrament of ordination — usually used in plural

Holy Roller *noun* (1842)
: a member of one of the Protestant sects whose worship meetings are characterized by spontaneous expressions of emotional excitement — often taken to be offensive

Holy Roman Empire *noun* (1728)
: an empire consisting primarily of a loose confederation of German and Italian territories under the suzerainty of an emperor and existing from the 9th or 10th century to 1806

Holy Saturday *noun* (14th century)
: the Saturday before Easter

Holy See *noun* (1765)
: the see of the pope

Holy Spirit *noun* (14th century)
: the third person of the Christian Trinity

ho·ly·stone \'hō-lē-ˌstōn\ *noun* (circa 1823)
: a soft sandstone used to scrub a ship's decks
— **holystone** *transitive verb*

Holy Synod *noun* (1768)
: the governing body of a national Eastern church

Holy Thursday *noun* (13th century)
1 : ASCENSION DAY
2 : MAUNDY THURSDAY

holy war *noun* (1691)
: a war waged by religious partisans to propagate or defend their faith

holy water *noun* (before 12th century)
: water blessed by a priest and used as a purifying sacramental

Holy Week *noun* (1710)
: the week before Easter during which the last days of Christ's life are commemorated

holy writ *noun, often H&W capitalized* (before 12th century)
1 : BIBLE 1
2 : a writing or utterance having unquestionable authority ⟨its financial precepts were not necessarily *Holy Writ* —Herbert Stein⟩

Holy Year *noun* (1900)
: a Roman Catholic jubilee year

hom- *or* **homo-** *combining form* [Latin, from Greek, from *homos* — more at SAME]
1 : one and the same : similar : alike ⟨*homo*graph⟩ ⟨*homo*sporous⟩
2 : homosexual ⟨*homo*phobia⟩

hom·age \'ä-mij, 'hä-\ *noun* [Middle English, from Old French *hommage*, from *homme* man, vassal, from Latin *homin-, homo* human being; akin to Old English *guma* human being, Latin *humus* earth — more at HUMBLE] (14th century)
1 a : a feudal ceremony by which a man acknowledges himself the vassal of a lord **b** : the relationship between a feudal lord and his vassal **c** : an act done or payment made in meeting the obligations of vassalage
2 a : expression of high regard : RESPECT — often used with *pay* **b** : something that shows respect or attests to the worth or influence of another : TRIBUTE ⟨his long life filled with international *homages* to his unique musical talent —*People*⟩
synonym *see* HONOR
usage *see* HUMOR

hom·ag·er \'ä-mi-jər, 'hä-\ *noun* (15th century)
: VASSAL

hom·bre \'äm-brā, 'əm-, 'ōm-, -ˌbrē\ *noun* [Spanish, man, from Latin *homin-, homo*] (1846)
: GUY, FELLOW

hom·burg \'häm-ˌbərg\ *noun* [*Bad Homburg*, Germany] (1894)
: a man's felt hat with a stiff curled brim and a high crown creased lengthwise

¹home \'hōm\ *noun* [Middle English *hom*, from Old English *hām* village, home;

homburg

akin to Old High German *heim* home] (before 12th century)
1 a : one's place of residence : DOMICILE **b** : HOUSE
2 : the social unit formed by a family living together
3 a : a familiar or usual setting : congenial environment; *also* : the focus of one's domestic attention ⟨*home* is where the heart is⟩ **b** : HABITAT
4 a : a place of origin ⟨salmon returning to their *home* to spawn⟩; *also* : one's own country ⟨having troubles at *home* and abroad⟩ **b** : HEADQUARTERS 2 ⟨*home* of the dance company⟩
5 : an establishment providing residence and care for people with special needs ⟨*homes* for the elderly⟩ ⟨a *home* for unwed mothers⟩
6 : the objective in various games; *especially* : HOME PLATE
— **at home 1** : relaxed and comfortable : at ease ⟨felt completely *at home* on the stage⟩ **2** : in harmony with the surroundings **3** : on familiar ground : KNOWLEDGEABLE ⟨teachers *at home* in their subject fields⟩

²home *adverb* (before 12th century)
1 : to, from, or at one's home ⟨go *home*⟩ ⟨left *home* at the age of 12⟩
2 a : to a final, closed, or ultimate position ⟨drive a nail *home*⟩ **b** : to or at an ultimate objective (as a goal or finish line)
3 : to a vital sensitive core ⟨the truth struck *home*⟩
— **home free** : out of jeopardy : in a comfortable position with respect to some objective

³home *adjective* (1552)
1 : of, relating to, or being a home, place of origin, or base of operations ⟨*home* office⟩ ⟨checkers in position on their *home* squares⟩
2 : prepared, done, or designed for use in a home ⟨*home* remedies⟩ ⟨*home* cooking⟩ ⟨a *home* videotape system⟩
3 : operating or occurring in a home area ⟨the *home* team⟩ ⟨*home* games⟩

⁴home *verb* **homed; hom·ing** (1765)
intransitive verb
1 : to go or return home
2 *of an animal* : to return accurately to one's home or natal area from a distance
3 : to proceed to or toward a source of radiated energy used as a guide ⟨missiles *home* in on radar⟩
4 : to proceed or direct attention toward an objective ⟨science is *homing* in on the mysterious human process —Sam Glucksberg⟩
transitive verb
: to send to or provide with a home

home·body \'hōm-ˌbä-dē\ *noun* (1821)
: one whose life centers in the home

¹home·bound \'hōm-ˌbaund\ *adjective* [*home* + ¹*bound*] (circa 1625)
: going homeward : bound for home ⟨*homebound* travelers⟩

²homebound *adjective* [*home* + ⁵*bound*] (1882)
: confined to the home

home·boy \'hōm-ˌbȯi\ *noun* (1927)
1 : a boy or man from one's neighborhood, hometown, or region
2 : a fellow member of a youth gang

home·bred \'hōm-'bred\ *adjective* (1587)
: produced at home : INDIGENOUS

home brew *noun* (1853)
: an alcoholic beverage (as beer) made at home

home·built \'hōm-'bilt\ *adjective* (1676)
: HOMEMADE 1

home·com·ing \'hōm-ˌkə-miŋ\ *noun* (14th century)
1 : a return home
2 : the return of a group of people usually on a special occasion to a place formerly frequented or regarded as home; *especially* : an annual celebration for alumni at a college or university

home computer *noun* (1976)

: a small inexpensive microcomputer

home economics *noun plural but singular or plural in construction* (1899)
: the theory and practice of homemaking — called also *home ec* \-'ek\
— **home economist** *noun*

home fries *noun plural* (1951)
: potatoes that have usually been parboiled, sliced, and then fried — called also *home fried potatoes*

home front *noun* (1919)
: the sphere of civilian activity in war

home-grown \'hōm-'grōn\ *adjective* (1827)
1 : grown or produced at home or in a particular local area ⟨*homegrown* vegetables⟩ ⟨*homegrown* films⟩
2 : native to or characteristic of a particular area ⟨the festival will feature *homegrown* artists⟩

home-land \-,land *also* -lənd\ *noun* (1670)
1 : native land : FATHERLAND
2 : a state or area set aside to be a state for a people of a particular national, cultural, or racial origin; *especially* : BANTUSTAN

home-less \-ləs\ *adjective* (1615)
: having no home or permanent place of residence
— **home-less-ness** *noun*

home-like \'hōm-,līk\ *adjective* (1817)
: characteristic of a home

home-ly \'hōm-lē\ *adjective* **home-li-er; -est** (14th century)
1 : suggestive or characteristic of a home
2 : being something familiar with which one is at home ⟨satisfy themselves with houses, furniture, books and clothes that were worn and *homely* and friendly to the touch —Brendan Gill⟩
3 a : unaffectedly natural : SIMPLE **b** : not elaborate or complex ⟨*homely* virtues⟩
4 : plain or unattractive in appearance
— **home-li-ness** *noun*

home-made \'hō(m)-'mād\ *adjective* (circa 1659)
1 : made in the home, on the premises, or by one's own efforts
2 : of domestic manufacture

home-mak-er \'hōm-,mā-kər\ *noun* (1876)
: one who manages a household especially as a wife and mother
— **home-mak-ing** \-kiŋ\ *noun or adjective*

homeo- *or* **homoeo-** *or* **homoeo-** *also* **homoio-** *combining form* [Latin & Greek; Latin homoeo-, from Greek homoi-, homoio-, from homoios, from homos same — more at SAME]
: like : similar ⟨*homeo*stasis⟩ ⟨*homeo*thermic⟩
2 : homeotic ⟨*homeo*box⟩

ho-meo-box \'hō-mē-ə-,bäks\ *noun* (1984)
: a short usually highly conserved DNA sequence in various eukaryotic genes (as many homeotic genes) that codes for a peptide which may be a DNA-binding protein

ho-meo-mor-phism \,hō-mē-ə-'mȯr-,fi-zəm\ *noun* [International Scientific Vocabulary] (1854)
: a function that is a one-to-one mapping between sets such that both the function and its inverse are continuous and that in topology exists for geometric figures which can be transformed one into the other by an elastic deformation
— **ho-meo-mor-phic** \-'mȯr-fik\ *adjective*

ho-meo-path-ic \,hō-mē-ə-'pa-thik\ *adjective* (1830)
1 : of or relating to homeopathy
2 : of a diluted or insipid nature ⟨a *homeopathic* abolitionist —W. A. White⟩
— **ho-meo-path-i-cal-ly** \-thi-k(ə-)lē\ *adverb*

ho-me-op-a-thy \,hō-mē-'ä-pə-thē, ,hä-\ *noun* [German *Homöopathie*, from *homöo-* homeo- + *-pathie* -pathy] (1826)
: a system of medical practice that treats a disease especially by the administration of minute doses of a remedy that would in

healthy persons produce symptoms similar to those of the disease
— **ho-meo-path** \'hō-mē-ə-,path\ *noun*

ho-meo-sta-sis \,hō-mē-ō-'stā-səs\ *noun* [New Latin] (1926)
: a relatively stable state of equilibrium or a tendency toward such a state between the different but interdependent elements or groups of elements of an organism, population, or group
— **ho-meo-stat-ic** \-'sta-tik\ *adjective*

ho-meo-ther-mic \-'thər-mik\ *adjective* (1870)
: WARM-BLOODED 1
— **ho-meo-therm** \'hō-mē-ō-,thərm\ *noun*
— **ho-meo-ther-my** \-,thər-mē\ *noun*

ho-me-o-tic \,hō-mē-'ä-tik, ,hä-\ *adjective* [from *homeosis*, *homoeosis* a shift in structural development, from Greek *homoiōsis* assimilation, resemblance, from *homoioun* to make like, from *homoios*] (circa 1903)
: relating to or being a gene producing a usually major shift in structural development

home plate *noun* (1875)
: a 5-sided rubber slab at one corner of a baseball diamond at which a batter stands when batting and which must be touched by a base runner in order to score

home-port \'hōm-,pōrt, -,pȯrt\ *transitive verb* (1957)
: to provide with or assign to a home port

home port *noun* (circa 1891)
: the port from which a ship hails or from which it is documented

¹ho-mer \'hō-mər\ *noun* [Hebrew *ḥōmer*] (1535)
: an ancient Hebrew unit of capacity equal to about 10½ or later 11½ bushels or 100 gallons (378 liters)

²hom-er \'hō-mər\ *noun* [¹*home*] (1868)
1 : HOME RUN
2 : HOMING PIGEON

³hom-er *intransitive verb* (1940)
: to hit a home run

home range *noun* (1884)
: the area to which an animal usually confines its daily activities

Ho-mer-ic \hō-'mer-ik\ *adjective* (circa 1771)
1 : of, relating to, or characteristic of the Greek poet Homer, his age, or his writings
2 : of epic proportions : HEROIC ⟨*Homeric* feats of reporting —Stanley Walker⟩
— **Ho-mer-i-cal-ly** \-i-k(ə-)lē\ *adverb*

home-room \'hōm-,rüm, -,rüm\ *noun* (1915)
: a classroom where pupils report especially at the beginning of each school day

home rule *noun* (1860)
: self-government or limited autonomy in internal affairs by a dependent political unit (as a territory or municipality)

home run *noun* (1856)
: a hit in baseball that enables the batter to make a complete circuit of the bases and score a run

home-school \'hōm-,skül\ (1986)
intransitive verb
: to teach school subjects to one's children at home
transitive verb
: to teach (one's children) at home
— **home-school-er** \-,skü-lər\ *noun*

home screen *noun* (1968)
: TELEVISION 1

home-sick \'hōm-,sik\ *adjective* (1756)
: longing for home and family while absent from them
— **home-sick-ness** *noun*

home-site \-,sīt\ *noun* (1911)
: a location of or suitable for a home

¹home-spun \-,spən\ *adjective* (1591)
1 a : spun or made at home **b** : made of homespun
2 : SIMPLE, HOMELY ⟨*homespun* philosophy⟩

²homespun *noun* (1607)
: a loosely woven usually woolen or linen fabric originally made from homespun yarn

home stand *noun* (1965)
: a series of baseball games played at a team's home field

home-stay \'hōm-,stā\ *noun* (1956)
: a period during which a visitor in a foreign country lives with a local family

¹home-stead \'hōm-,sted, -stid\ *noun* (before 12th century)
1 a : the home and adjoining land occupied by a family **b** : an ancestral home **c** : HOUSE
2 : a tract of land acquired from U.S. public lands by filing a record and living on and cultivating the tract

²home-stead \-,sted\ (1872)
transitive verb
: to acquire or occupy as a homestead
intransitive verb
: to acquire or settle on land under a homestead law
— **home-stead-er** \-,ste-dər\ *noun*

homestead law *noun* (1850)
1 : a law exempting a homestead from attachment or sale under execution for general debts
2 : any of several legislative acts authorizing the sale of public lands in homesteads

home-stretch \'hōm-'strech\ *noun* (1841)
1 : the part of a racecourse between the last turn and the winning post
2 : a final stage (as of a project)

home-town \-'taun\ *noun, often attributive* (1912)
: the city or town where one was born or grew up; *also* : the place of one's principal residence

home truth *noun* (1711)
1 : an unpleasant fact that jars the sensibilities
2 : a statement of undisputed fact

¹home-ward \'hōm-wərd\ *or* **home-wards** \-wərdz\ *adverb* (before 12th century)
: toward home ⟨look *homeward*, angel —John Milton⟩

²homeward *adjective* (1566)
: being or going in the direction of home

home-work \'hōm-,wərk\ *noun* (circa 1683)
1 : piecework done at home for pay
2 : an assignment given to a student to be completed outside the regular class period
3 : preparatory reading or research (as for a discussion or a debate)

hom-ey \'hō-mē\ *adjective* **hom-i-er; -est** (1856)
: HOMELIKE ⟨a restaurant with a *homey* atmosphere⟩
— **hom-ey-ness** *or* **hom-i-ness** *noun*

ho-mi-cid-al \,hä-mə-'sī-d°l, ,hō-\ *adjective* (1725)
: of, relating to, or tending toward homicide
— **ho-mi-cid-al-ly** \-d°l-ē\ *adverb*

ho-mi-cide \'hä-mə-,sīd, 'hō-\ *noun* [in sense 1, from Middle English, from Middle French, from Latin *homicida*, from *homo* human being + *-cida* -cide; in sense 2, from Middle English, from Middle French, from Latin *homicidium*, from *homo* + *-cidium* -cide] (14th century)
1 : a person who kills another
2 : a killing of one human being by another

hom-i-let-ic \,hä-mə-'le-tik\ *or* **hom-i-let-i-cal** \-ti-kəl\ *adjective* [Late Latin *homileticus*, from Greek *homilētikos* of conversation, from *homilein*] (1644)
1 : of, relating to, or resembling a homily
2 : of or relating to homiletics; *also* : PREACHY

hom-i-let-ics \-tiks\ *noun plural but singular in construction* (1830)
: the art of preaching

hom-i-ly \'hä-mə-lē\ *noun, plural* **-lies** [Middle English *omelie*, from Middle French, from Late Latin *homilia*, from Late Greek, from Greek, conversation, discourse, from *homilein* to consort with, address, from *homilos* crowd,

\ə\ abut \ᵊ\ kitten \ər\ further \a\ ash \ā\ ace \ä\ mop, mar \au̇\ out \ch\ chin \e\ bet \ē\ easy \g\ go \i\ hit \ī\ ice \j\ job \ŋ\ sing \ō\ go \ȯ\ law \ȯi\ boy \th\ thin \th̶\ the \ü\ loot \u̇\ foot \y\ yet \zh\ vision *see also* Guide to Pronunciation

assembly; akin to Greek *homos* same — more at SAME] (14th century)
1 : a usually short sermon
2 : a lecture or discourse on or of a moral theme
3 : an inspirational catchphrase; *also* **:** PLATITUDE

homing pigeon *noun* (1886)
: a racing pigeon trained to return home

hom·i·nid \'hä-mə-nəd, -,nid\ *noun* [New Latin *Hominidae*, from *Homin-, Homo* + *-idae*] (circa 1889)
: any of a family (Hominidae) of erect bipedal primate mammals comprising recent humans together with extinct ancestral and related forms
— **hominid** *adjective*

hom·i·ni·za·tion \,hä-mə-nə-'zā-shən\ *noun* [Latin *homin-, homo* + English *-ization*] (1952)
: the evolutionary development of human characteristics that differentiate hominids from their primate ancestors

hom·i·noid \'hä-mə-,nȯid\ *noun* [New Latin *Hominoidea*, from *Homin-, Homo* + *-oidea*, suffix of higher taxa, from Latin *-oïdes* ²-oid] (1949)
: any of a superfamily (Hominoidea) of primates including recent hominids, gibbons, and pongids together with extinct ancestral and related forms (as of the genera *Proconsul* and *Dryopithecus*)
— **hominoid** *adjective*

hom·i·ny \'hä-mə-nē\ *noun* [Virginia Algonquian *-homen*, literally, that treated (in the way specified)] (1629)
: kernels of corn that have been soaked in a caustic solution (as of lye) and then washed to remove the hulls

hominy grits *noun plural but singular or plural in construction* (1879)
: GRITS

¹**ho·mo** \'hō-(,)mō\ *noun, plural* **homos** [New Latin *Homin-, Homo*, from Latin, human being — more at HOMAGE] (1596)
: any of a genus (*Homo*) of primate mammals that includes modern humans (*H. sapiens*) and several extinct related species

²**homo** *noun, plural* **homos** [by shortening] (1929)
: HOMOSEXUAL — often used disparagingly

homo- — see HOM-

ho·mo·cer·cal \,hō-mə-'sər-kəl, ,hä-\ *adjective* (1838)
1 *of a fish tail fin* **:** having the upper and lower lobes approximately symmetrical and the vertebral column ending at or near the middle of the base
2 : having or relating to a homocercal tail fin

homoe- — see HOMEO-

ho·mo·erot·ic \,hō-mō-i-'rä-tik\ *adjective* (1916)
: HOMOSEXUAL
— **ho·mo·erot·i·cism** \-'rä-tə-,si-zəm\ *noun*

ho·mo·ga·met·ic \,hō-mō-gə-'me-tik, ,hä-\ *adjective* (1910)
: forming gametes which all have the same type of sex chromosome

ho·mog·a·my \hō-'mä-gə-mē\ *noun* [German *Homogamie*, from *hom-* + *-gamie* -gamy] (1897)
: the mating of like with like
— **ho·mog·a·mous** \-məs\ *adjective*

ho·mog·e·nate \hō-'mä-jə-,nāt, hə-\ *noun* (1941)
: a product of homogenizing

ho·mo·ge·ne·i·ty \,hō-mə-jə-'nē-ə-tē, -'nā- *also* ÷-'nī-; *especially British* ,hä-\ *noun* (1625)
1 : the quality or state of being homogeneous
2 : the state of having identical distribution functions or values ⟨*homogeneity* of variances⟩

ho·mo·ge·neous \-'jē-nē-əs, -nyəs\ *adjective* [Medieval Latin *homogeneus, homogenus*,

from Greek *homogenēs*, from *hom-* + *genos* kind — more at KIN] (1641)
1 : of the same or a similar kind or nature
2 : of uniform structure or composition throughout ⟨a culturally *homogeneous* neighborhood⟩
3 : having the property that if each variable is replaced by a constant times that variable the constant can be factored out **:** having each term of the same degree if all variables are considered ⟨a *homogeneous* equation⟩
— **ho·mo·ge·neous·ly** *adverb*
— **ho·mo·ge·neous·ness** *noun*

ho·mog·e·ni·sa·tion, **ho·mog·e·nise**
British variant of HOMOGENIZATION, HOMOGENIZE

ho·mog·e·ni·za·tion \hō-,mä-jə-nə-'zā-shən, hə-\ *noun* (1908)
1 : the act or process of homogenizing
2 : the quality or state of being homogenized

ho·mog·e·nize \hō-'mä-jə-,nīz, hə-\ *verb* **-nized; -niz·ing** (1886)
transitive verb
1 a : to blend (diverse elements) into a uniform mixture **b :** to make homogeneous
2 a : to reduce to small particles of uniform size and distribute evenly usually in a liquid **b :** to reduce the particles of so that they are uniformly small and evenly distributed; *specifically* **:** to break up the fat globules of (milk) into very fine particles
intransitive verb
: to become homogenized
— **ho·mog·e·niz·er** *noun*

ho·mog·e·nous \-nəs\ *adjective* (1919)
1 : HOMOPLASTIC 2
2 : HOMOGENEOUS

ho·mo·graft \'hō-mə-,graft, 'hä-\ *noun* (1923)
: a graft of tissue taken from a donor of the same species as the recipient — compare HETEROGRAFT

ho·mo·graph \'hä-mə-,graf, 'hō-\ *noun* (1873)
: one of two or more words spelled alike but different in meaning or derivation or pronunciation (as the *bow* of a ship, a *bow* and arrow)
— **ho·mo·graph·ic** \,hä-mə-'gra-fik, ,hō-\ *adjective*

homoio- — see HOMEO-

ho·moio·therm, ho·moio·ther·mic *variant of* HOMEOTHERM, HOMEOTHERMIC

ho·moi·ou·si·an \,hō-,mȯi-'ü-zē-ən, hä-, -'ü-sē-\ *noun* [Late Greek *homoiousios* of like substance, from Greek *homoi-* homeo- + *ousia* essence, substance, from *ont-, ōn*, present participle of *einai* to be — more at IS] (1732)
: an adherent of an ecclesiastical party of the 4th century holding that the Son is essentially like the Father but not of the same substance

ho·mol·o·gate \hō-'mä-lə-,gāt, hə-\ *transitive verb* **-gat·ed; -gat·ing** [Medieval Latin *homologatus*, past participle of *homologare* to agree, from Greek *homologein*, from *homologos*] (1593)
: SANCTION, ALLOW; *especially* **:** to approve or confirm officially
— **ho·mol·o·ga·tion** \-,mä-lə-'gā-shən\ *noun*

ho·mo·log·i·cal \,hō-mə-'lä-ji-kəl, ,hä-\ *adjective* (circa 1847)
1 : HOMOLOGOUS
2 : of or relating to topological homology theory ⟨*homological* algebra⟩
— **ho·mo·log·i·cal·ly** \-ji-k(ə-)lē\ *adverb*

ho·mol·o·gize \hō-'mä-lə-,jīz, hə-\ *transitive verb* **-gized; -giz·ing** (1811)
1 : to make homologous
2 : to demonstrate the homology of
— **ho·mol·o·giz·er** *noun*

ho·mol·o·gous \hō-'mä-lə-gəs, hə-\ *adjective* [Greek *homologos* agreeing, from *hom-* + *legein* to say — more at LEGEND] (1660)
1 a : having the same relative position, value, or structure: as (1) **:** exhibiting biological homology (2) **:** having the same or allelic genes with genetic loci usually arranged in the same

order ⟨*homologous* chromosomes⟩ **b :** belonging to or consisting of a chemical series whose successive members have a regular difference in composition especially of one methylene group
2 : derived from or developed in response to organisms of the same species

ho·mo·logue *or* **ho·mo·log** \'hō-mə-,lȯg, 'hä-, -,läg\ *noun* (1848)
: something (as a chemical compound or a chromosome) homologous

ho·mol·o·gy \hō-'mä-lə-jē, hə-\ *noun, plural* **-gies** (circa 1656)
1 : a similarity often attributable to common origin
2 a : likeness in structure between parts of different organisms due to evolutionary differentiation from the same or a corresponding part of a remote ancestor — compare ANALOGY **b :** correspondence in structure between different parts of the same individual
3 : similarity of nucleotide or amino-acid sequence in nucleic acids, peptides, or proteins
4 : a branch of the theory of topology concerned with partitioning space into geometric components (as points, lines, and triangles) and with the study of the number and interrelationships of these components especially by the use of group theory — called also *homology theory*; compare COHOMOLOGY

ho·mo·lyt·ic \,hō-mə-'li-tik, ,hä-\ *adjective* (1941)
of a chemical compound **:** decomposing into two uncharged atoms or radicals
— **ho·mol·y·sis** \hō-'mä-lə-səs\ *noun*

ho·mo·mor·phism \,hō-mə-'mȯr-,fi-zəm, ,hä-\ *noun* [International Scientific Vocabulary] (1935)
: a mapping of a mathematical set (as a group, ring, or vector space) into or onto another set or itself in such a way that the result obtained by applying the operations to elements of the first set is mapped onto the result obtained by applying the corresponding operations to their respective images in the second set
— **ho·mo·mor·phic** \-fik\ *adjective*

ho·mo·nu·cle·ar \,hō-mə-'nü-klē-ər, ,hä-, -'nyü-, ÷-kyə-lər\ *adjective* (1930)
: of or relating to a molecule composed of identical nuclei

hom·onym \'hä-mə-,nim, 'hō-\ *noun* [Latin *homonymum*, from Greek *homōnymon*, from neuter of *homōnymos*] (1697)
1 a : HOMOPHONE **b :** HOMOGRAPH **c :** one of two or more words spelled and pronounced alike but different in meaning (as the noun *quail* and the verb *quail*)
2 : NAMESAKE
3 : a taxonomic designation rejected as invalid because the identical term has been used to designate another group of the same rank — compare SYNONYM
— **hom·onym·ic** \,hä-mə-'ni-mik, ,hō-\ *adjective*

hom·on·y·mous \hō-'mä-nə-məs\ *adjective* [Latin *homonymus* having the same name, from Greek *homōnymos*, from *hom-* + *onyma, onoma* name — more at NAME] (1621)
1 : AMBIGUOUS
2 : having the same designation
3 : of, relating to, or being homonyms **:** HOMONYMIC
— **hom·on·y·mous·ly** *adverb*

hom·on·y·my \-mē\ *noun* (1597)
: the quality or state of being homonymous

ho·mo·ou·si·an \,hō-,mō-'ü-zē-ən, hä-, -'ü-sē-\ *noun* [Late Greek *homoousios* of the same substance, from Greek *hom-* + *ousia* substance — more at HOMOIOUSIAN] (1565)
: an adherent of an ecclesiastical party of the 4th century holding to the doctrine of the Nicene Creed that the Son is of the same substance with the Father

ho·mo·phile \'hō-mə-,fīl\ *adjective* [*hom-* + ²-*phil*] (1960)
: GAY 4b

ho·mo·phobe \-ˌfōb\ *noun* (1975)
: a person characterized by homophobia
ho·mo·pho·bia \ˌhō-mə-ˈfō-bē-ə\ *noun* (1969)
: irrational fear of, aversion to, or discrimination against homosexuality or homosexuals
— **ho·mo·pho·bic** \-ˈfō-bik\ *adjective*
ho·mo·phone \ˈhä-mə-ˌfōn, ˈhō-\ *noun* [International Scientific Vocabulary] (1843)
1 : one of two or more words pronounced alike but different in meaning or derivation or spelling (as the words *to, too,* and *two*)
2 : a character or group of characters pronounced the same as another character or group
— **ho·moph·o·nous** \hō-ˈmä-fə-nəs\ *adjective*
ho·mo·phon·ic \ˌhä-mə-ˈfä-nik, ˌhō-, -ˈfō-\ *adjective* [Greek *homophōnos* being in unison, from *hom-* + *phōnē* sound — more at BAN] (circa 1879)
1 : CHORDAL
2 : of or relating to homophones
— **ho·moph·o·ny** \hō-ˈmä-fə-nē\ *noun*
ho·mo·plas·tic \ˌhō-mə-ˈplas-tik, ˌhä-\ *adjective* (1870)
1 : of or relating to homoplasy
2 : of, relating to, or derived from another individual of the same species ⟨*homoplastic* grafts⟩
ho·mo·pla·sy \ˈhō-mə-ˌplā-sē, ˈhä-, -ˌpla-; hō-ˈmä-plə-sē\ *noun* (1870)
: correspondence between parts or organs acquired as the result of parallel evolution or convergence
ho·mo·po·lar \ˌhō-mə-ˈpō-lər, ˌhä-\ *adjective* (1896)
1 *of a motor or generator* : using or producing direct current without the use of commutators
2 : of or relating to a union of atoms of like polarity : NONIONIC
ho·mo·pol·y·mer \-ˈpä-lə-mər\ *noun* (1946)
: a polymer (as polyethylene) consisting of identical monomer units
— **ho·mo·pol·y·mer·ic** \-ˌpä-lə-ˈmer-ik\ *adjective*
ho·mop·ter·an \hō-ˈmäp-tə-rən\ *noun* [ultimately from Greek *hom-* + *pteron* wing — more at FEATHER] (circa 1842)
: any of a large order or suborder (Homoptera) of insects (as cicadas, aphids, and scale insects) that have sucking mouthparts
— **homopteran** *adjective*
— **ho·mop·ter·ous** \-rəs\ *adjective*
homos *plural of* HOMO
Ho·mo sa·pi·ens \ˌhō-(ˌ)mō-ˈsā-pē-ˌenz, -ˌənz, *especially British* -ˈsa-pē-ənz\ *noun* [New Latin, species name, from *Homo,* genus name + *sapiens,* specific epithet, from Latin, wise, intelligent — more at HOMO. SAPIENT] (1802)
: HUMANKIND
ho·mo·sce·das·tic·i·ty \ˌhō-mō-si-das-ˈti-sə-tē, ˌhä-\ *noun* [*hom-* + Greek *skedastikos* able to disperse, from *skedannynai* to disperse] (1905)
: the property of having equal statistical variances
— **ho·mo·sce·das·tic** \-ˈdas-tik\ *adjective*
¹**ho·mo·sex·u·al** \ˌhō-mə-ˈsek-sh(ə-)wəl, -ˈsek-shəl\ *adjective* (1892)
1 : of, relating to, or characterized by a tendency to direct sexual desire toward another of the same sex
2 : of, relating to, or involving sexual intercourse between persons of the same sex
— **ho·mo·sex·u·al·ly** *adverb*
²**homosexual** *noun* (1902)
: a homosexual person and especially a male
ho·mo·sex·u·al·i·ty \ˌhō-mə-ˌsek-shə-ˈwa-lə-tē\ *noun* (1892)
1 : the quality or state of being homosexual
2 : erotic activity with another of the same sex
ho·mo·spo·rous \ˌhō-mə-ˈspōr-əs, ˌhä-, -ˈspór-; hō-ˈmäs-pə-rəs\ *adjective* (1887)
: producing asexual spores of one kind only

ho·mo·spo·ry \ˈhō-mə-ˌspōr-ē, ˈhä-, -ˌspór-; hō-ˈmäs-pə-rē\ *noun* (1903)
: the production by various plants (as the club mosses and horsetails) of asexual spores of only one kind
ho·mo·thal·lic \ˌhō-mō-ˈtha-lik\ *adjective* [*hom-* + Greek *thallein* to sprout, grow — more at THALLUS] (1904)
1 : having a haploid phase that produces two kinds of gametes capable of fusing to form a zygote — used especially of algae and fungi
2 : MONOECIOUS
— **ho·mo·thal·lism** \-ˈtha-ˌli-zəm\ *noun*
ho·mo·trans·plant \ˌhō-mō-ˈtran(t)s-ˌplant, ˌhä-\ *noun* (1927)
: HOMOGRAFT
— **ho·mo·trans·plan·ta·tion** \-ˌtran(t)s-ˌplan-ˈtā-shən\ *noun*
ho·mo·zy·go·sis \ˌhō-mə-zi-ˈgō-səs, ˌhä-\ *noun* [New Latin] (1905)
: HOMOZYGOSITY
ho·mo·zy·gos·i·ty \-ˈgä-sə-tē\ *noun* (1916)
: the state of being homozygous
ho·mo·zy·gote \-ˈzī-ˌgōt\ *noun* [International Scientific Vocabulary] (1902)
: a homozygous individual
ho·mo·zy·gous \-ˈzī-gəs\ *adjective* (1902)
: having the two genes at corresponding loci on homologous chromosomes identical for one or more loci
— **ho·mo·zy·gous·ly** *adverb*
ho·mun·cu·lus \hō-ˈmən-kyə-ləs\ *noun, plural* **-li** \-ˌlī, -ˌlē\ [Latin, diminutive of *homin-, homo* human being — more at HOMAGE] (1656)
1 : a little man : MANIKIN
2 : a miniature adult that in the theory of preformation is held to inhabit the germ cell and to produce a mature individual merely by an increase in size
homy *variant of* HOMEY
hon \ˈhən\ *noun* (circa 1906)
: HONEY 2a
hon·cho \ˈhän-(ˌ)chō\ *noun, plural* **honchos** [Japanese *hanchō* squad leader, from *han* squad + *chō* head, chief] (1947)
: BOSS, BIG SHOT; *also* : HOTSHOT ◇
¹**hone** \ˈhōn\ *noun* [Middle English, from Old English *hān* stone; akin to Old Norse *hein* whetstone, Latin *cot-, cos,* Sanskrit *śiśāti* he whets] (14th century)
: WHETSTONE
²**hone** *transitive verb* **honed; hon·ing** (1826)
1 : to sharpen or smooth with a whetstone
2 : to make more acute, intense, or effective : WHET ⟨helped her *hone* her comic timing —Patricia Bosworth⟩
— **hon·er** *noun*
³**hone** *intransitive verb* **honed; hon·ing** [Middle French *hoigner* to grumble] (1600)
1 *dialect* : YEARN — often used with *for* or *after*
2 *dialect* : GRUMBLE, MOAN
hone in *intransitive verb* [alteration of *home in*] (1965)
: to move toward or focus attention on an objective ⟨looking back for the ball *honing in* —George Plimpton⟩ ⟨a missile *honing in* on its target —Bob Greene⟩ ⟨*hones in* on the plights and victories of the common man —Lisa Russell⟩ □
¹**hon·est** \ˈä-nəst\ *adjective* [Middle English, from Middle French *honeste,* from Latin *honestus* honorable, from *honos, honor* honor] (14th century)
1 a : free from fraud or deception : LEGITIMATE, TRUTHFUL ⟨an *honest* plea⟩ **b** : GENUINE, REAL ⟨making *honest* stops at stop signs —*Christian Science Monitor*⟩ **c** : HUMBLE, PLAIN ⟨good *honest* food⟩
2 a : REPUTABLE, RESPECTABLE ⟨*honest* decent people⟩ **b** *chiefly British* : GOOD, WORTHY
3 : CREDITABLE, PRAISEWORTHY ⟨an *honest* day's work⟩

4 a : marked by integrity **b** : marked by free, forthright, and sincere expression : FRANK ⟨an *honest* appraisal⟩ **c** : INNOCENT, SIMPLE
synonym see UPRIGHT
²**honest** *adverb* (1596)
1 : in an honest manner : HONESTLY ⟨I have ever found thee *honest* true —Shakespeare⟩
2 : with all sincerity ⟨I didn't do it, *honest*⟩
honest broker *noun* (circa 1884)
: a neutral mediator
hon·est·ly \ˈä-nəst-lē\ *adverb* (14th century)
1 : in an honest manner: as **a** : without cheating ⟨counted the ballots *honestly*⟩ **b** : REALLY, GENUINELY ⟨was *honestly* scared⟩ **c** : without frills ⟨food *honestly* prepared⟩
2 : to be honest : to tell the truth ⟨*honestly,* I don't know⟩
hon·es·ty \ˈä-nəs-tē\ *noun, plural* **-ties** (14th century)
1 *obsolete* : CHASTITY
2 a : fairness and straightforwardness of conduct **b** : adherence to the facts : SINCERITY
3 : any of a genus (*Lunaria*) of European herbs of the mustard family with toothed leaves and flat disk-shaped siliques ☆

☆ SYNONYMS
Honesty, honor, integrity, probity mean uprightness of character or action. HONESTY implies a refusal to lie, steal, or deceive in any way. HONOR suggests an active or anxious regard for the standards of one's profession, calling, or position. INTEGRITY implies trustworthiness and incorruptibility to a degree that one is incapable of being false to a trust, responsibility, or pledge. PROBITY implies tried and proven honesty or integrity.

□ USAGE
hone in The few commentators who have noticed *hone in* consider it to be a mistake for *home in.* It may have arisen from *home in* by the weakening of the \m\ sound to \n\ or may perhaps simply be due to the influence of *hone.* Even though it seems to have established itself in American English (and its mention in a British usage book suggests it is used in British English too), your use of it especially in writing is likely to be called a mistake. *Home in* or in figurative use *zero in* is an easy alternative.

◇ WORD HISTORY
honcho *Honcho* is a relic of the large U.S. presence in Japan during the years following World War II, when the Japanese word *hanchō* "leader of the squad, section, or group" entered English. We are uncertain of the exact route by which this word found its way into American military argot in the mid-1950s, though it is known that the Japanese applied *hanchō* to British or Australian officers in charge of work parties in prisoner-of-war camps. Judging by the scarcity of print evidence, *honcho* was not well established in general colloquial English before the 1960s. By that time it had become part of American political jargon—an area where it continues to flourish in the 1990s. *Honcho* has occasionally been used as a verb meaning "to supervise," and in 1993 the cartoonist Garry Trudeau produced the derivative *honchette* to describe a female big shot—surely a sign of the naturalization of *honcho* in English.

\ə\ **abut** \ᵊ\ **kitten** \ər\ **further** \a\ **ash** \ā\ **ace** \ä\ **mop, mar** \aú\ **out** \ch\ **chin** \e\ **bet** \ē\ **easy** \g\ **go** \i\ **hit** \ī\ **ice** \j\ **job** \ŋ\ **sing** \ō\ **go** \ó\ **law** \ói\ **boy** \th\ **thin** \t̶h̶\ **the** \ü\ **loot** \ú\ **foot** \y\ **yet** \zh\ **vision** *see also* Guide to Pronunciation

¹hon·ey \'hə-nē\ *noun, plural* **honeys** [Middle English *hony*, from Old English *hunig*; akin to Old High German *honag* honey, Latin *canicae* bran] (before 12th century)
1 a : a sweet viscid material elaborated out of the nectar of flowers in the honey sac of various bees **b :** a sweet fluid resembling honey that is collected or elaborated by various insects
2 a : a loved one : SWEETHEART, DEAR **b :** a superlative example
3 : the quality or state of being sweet : SWEETNESS
²honey *verb* **hon·eyed** *also* **hon·ied** \'hə-nēd\; **hon·ey·ing** (14th century)
transitive verb
1 : to sweeten with or as if with honey
2 : to speak ingratiatingly to : FLATTER
intransitive verb
: to use blandishments or cajolery
³honey *adjective* (14th century)
1 : of, relating to, or resembling honey
2 : much loved : DEAR
hon·ey·bee \'hə-nē-,bē\ *noun* (15th century)
: a honey-producing bee (*Apis* and related genera); *especially* : a European bee (*A. mellifera*) introduced worldwide and kept in hives for the honey it produces

honeybees, left to right: worker, queen, drone

¹hon·ey·comb \-,kōm\ *noun* (before 12th century)
1 : a mass of hexagonal wax cells built by honeybees in their nest to contain their brood and stores of honey
2 : something that resembles a honeycomb in structure or appearance; *especially* : a strong lightweight cellular structural material
²honeycomb (1774)
transitive verb
1 a : to cause to be full of cavities like a honeycomb **b :** to make into a checkered pattern : FRET
2 a : to penetrate into every part : FILL **b :** SUBVERT, WEAKEN
intransitive verb
: to become pitted, checked, or cellular
hon·ey·creep·er \'hə-nē-,krē-pər\ *noun* (1872)
1 : any of numerous small bright-colored oscine birds (especially genera *Cyanerpes* and *Chlorophanes* of the family Coerebidae) of tropical America
2 : any of a family (Drepanididae) of oscine birds that are found only in Hawaii
hon·ey·dew \-,dü, -,dyü\ *noun* (1577)
: a saccharine deposit secreted on the leaves of plants usually by aphids or scale insects or sometimes by a fungus
honeydew melon *noun* (1916)
: a pale smooth-skinned winter melon with sweet greenish flesh
hon·ey·eat·er \-,ē-tər\ *noun* (1822)
: any of a family (Meliphagidae) of oscine birds chiefly of the South Pacific that have a long protrusible tongue adapted for extracting nectar and small insects from flowers
hon·ey·guide \-,gīd\ *noun* (1777)
: any of a family (Indicatoridae) of small plainly colored nonpasserine birds that inhabit Africa, the Himalayas, and the East Indies and that include some which lead people or animals to the nests of bees

honey locust *noun* (1743)
: a tall usually spiny North American leguminous tree (*Gleditsia triacanthos*) with very hard wood and long twisted pods containing a sweet edible pulp and seeds that resemble beans
hon·ey·moon \'hə-nē-,mün\ *noun* [from the idea that the first month of marriage is the sweetest] (1546)
1 : a period of harmony immediately following marriage
2 : a period of unusual harmony especially following the establishment of a new relationship
3 : a trip or vacation taken by a newly married couple
— **honeymoon** *intransitive verb*
— **hon·ey·moon·er** *noun*
honey sac *noun* (circa 1909)
: a distension of the esophagus of a bee in which honey is elaborated — called also *honey stomach*
hon·ey·suck·le \'hə-nē-,sə-kəl\ *noun* [Middle English *honysoukel* clover, alteration of *honysouke*, from Old English *hunisūce*, from *hunig* honey + *sūcan* to suck] (1548)
: any of a genus (*Lonicera* of the family Caprifoliaceae, the honeysuckle family) of shrubs with opposite leaves and often showy flowers rich in nectar; *broadly* : any of various plants (as a columbine or azalea) with tubular flowers rich in nectar

honeysuckle

hong \'häŋ, 'hòŋ\ *noun* [Chinese (Guangdong) *hòhng*, literally, row] (1726)
: a commercial establishment or house of foreign trade in China
¹honk \'häŋk, 'hòŋk\ *verb* [imitative] (circa 1835)
intransitive verb
1 : to make the characteristic cry of a goose
2 : to make a sound resembling the cry of a goose
transitive verb
: to cause (as a horn) to honk
— **honk·er** *noun*
²honk *noun* (1854)
: the characteristic cry of a goose; *also* : a similar sound
hon·ky *or* **hon·kie** *also* **hon·key** \'hòŋ-kē, 'häŋ-\ *noun, plural* **honkies** *also* **honkeys** [probably alteration of *Hunky*] (1967)
: a white person — usually used disparagingly
¹hon·ky–tonk \'häŋ-kē-,täŋk, 'hòŋ-kē-,tòŋk\ *noun* [origin unknown] (circa 1909)
1 : a usually tawdry nightclub or dance hall; *especially* : one that features country music
2 : a district marked by places of cheap entertainment
²honky–tonk *adjective* (circa 1920)
1 : of, used in, or being a form of ragtime piano playing performed typically on an upright piano
2 : marked by or characteristic of honky-tonks
¹hon·or \'ä-nər\ *noun* [Middle English, from Old French *honor*, from Latin *honos, honor*] (13th century)
1 a : good name or public esteem : REPUTATION **b :** a showing of usually merited respect : RECOGNITION ⟨pay *honor* to our founder⟩
2 : PRIVILEGE
3 : a person of superior standing — now used especially as a title for a holder of high office ⟨if Your *Honor* please⟩
4 : one whose worth brings respect or fame : CREDIT ⟨an *honor* to the profession⟩
5 : the center point of the upper half of an armorial escutcheon

6 : an evidence or symbol of distinction: as **a :** an exalted title or rank **b** (1) : BADGE, DECORATION (2) : a ceremonial rite or observance ⟨buried with full military *honors*⟩ **c :** an award in a contest or field of competition **d** *archaic* : a gesture of deference : BOW **e** *plural* (1) : an academic distinction conferred on a superior student (2) : a course of study for superior students supplementing or replacing a regular course
7 : CHASTITY, PURITY ⟨fought fiercely for her *honor* and her life —Barton Black⟩
8 a : a keen sense of ethical conduct : INTEGRITY **b :** one's word given as a guarantee of performance
9 *plural* : social courtesies or civilities extended by a host ⟨did the *honors* at the table⟩
10 a (1) : an ace, king, queen, jack, or ten especially of the trump suit in bridge (2) : the scoring value of honors held in bridge — usually used in plural **b :** the privilege of playing first from the tee in golf ☆
²honor *transitive verb* **hon·ored; hon·or·ing** \'ä-nə-riŋ, 'än-riŋ\ (13th century)
1 a : to regard or treat with honor or respect **b :** to confer honor on
2 a : to live up to or fulfill the terms of ⟨*honor* a commitment⟩ **b :** to accept as payment ⟨*honor* a credit card⟩
3 : to salute with a bow in square dancing
— **hon·or·ee** \,ä-nə-'rē\ *noun*
— **hon·or·er** \'ä-nər-ər\ *noun*
hon·or·able \'ä-nər-(ə-)bəl, 'än-rə-\ *adjective* (14th century)
1 : deserving of honor
2 a : of great renown : ILLUSTRIOUS **b :** entitled to honor — used as a title for the children of certain British noblemen and for various government officials
3 : performed or accompanied with marks of honor or respect
4 a : attesting to creditable conduct **b :** consistent with an untarnished reputation ⟨an *honorable* withdrawal⟩
5 : characterized by integrity : guided by a high sense of honor and duty
synonym see UPRIGHT
— **hon·or·abil·i·ty** \,än-rə-'bi-lə-tē, ,ä-nə-\ *noun*
— **hon·or·able·ness** \'än-rə-bəl-nəs, 'ä-nə-\ *noun*
— **hon·or·ably** \-blē\ *adverb*
honorable mention *noun* (1866)
: a distinction conferred (as in a contest or exhibition) on works or persons of exceptional merit but not deserving of top honors
hon·o·rar·i·um \,ä-nə-'rer-ē-əm\ *noun, plural* **-ia** \-ē-ə\ *also* **-i·ums** [Latin, from neuter of *honorarius*] (1658)
: a payment for a service (as making a speech) on which custom or propriety forbids a price to be set
hon·or·ary \'ä-nə-,rer-ē\ *adjective* [Latin *honorarius*, from *honor*] (1614)
1 a : having or conferring distinction **b :** COMMEMORATIVE
2 : dependent on honor for fulfillment

3 a : conferred or elected in recognition of achievement or service without the usual prerequisites or obligations ⟨an *honorary* degree⟩ ⟨an *honorary* member⟩ **b :** UNPAID, VOLUNTARY ⟨an *honorary* chairman⟩
— **hon·or·ari·ly** \ˌä-nə-ˈrer-ə-lē\ *adverb*
— **honorary** *noun*
honor guard *noun* (1925)
: a guard assigned to a ceremonial duty (as to accompany a casket at a military funeral)
hon·or·if·ic \ˌä-nə-ˈri-fik\ *adjective* (1650)
1 : conferring or conveying honor ⟨*honorific* titles⟩
2 : belonging to or constituting a class of grammatical forms used in speaking to or about a social superior
— **honorific** *noun*
— **hon·or·if·i·cal·ly** \-fi-k(ə-)lē\ *adverb*
honor roll *noun* (1909)
: a roster of names of persons deserving honor; *especially* **:** a list of students achieving academic distinction
honor society *noun* (1927)
: a society for the recognition of scholarly achievement especially of undergraduates
honor system *noun* (1904)
: a system (as at a college or prison) whereby persons are trusted to abide by the regulations (as for a code of conduct) without supervision or surveillance
hon·our, hon·our·able *chiefly British variant of* HONOR, HONORABLE
¹**hooch** \ˈhüch\ *noun* [short for *hoochinoo*, a distilled liquor made by the Hoochinoo (Hutsnuwu) Indians, a Tlingit tribe] (1897) *slang* **:** alcoholic liquor especially when inferior or illicitly made or obtained ◇
²**hooch** *or* **hootch** \ˈhüch\ *noun* [modification of Japanese *uchi* house] (1960) *slang* **:** a usually thatched hut; *broadly* **:** DWELLING
¹**hood** \ˈhu̇d\ *noun* [Middle English, from Old English *hōd;* akin to Old High German *huot* head covering, *huota* guard] (before 12th century)
1 a (1) **:** a flexible covering for the head and neck (2) **:** a protective covering for the head and face **b :** a covering for a hawk's head and eyes **c :** a covering for a horse's head; *also* **:** BLINDER
2 a : an ornamental scarf worn over an academic gown that indicates by its color the wearer's college or university **b :** a color marking or crest on the head of an animal or an expansion of the head that suggests a hood
3 a : something resembling a hood in form or use **b :** a cover for parts of mechanisms; *specifically* **:** the movable metal covering over the engine of an automobile **c** *chiefly British* **:** a top cover over the passenger section of a vehicle usually designed to be folded back **d :** an enclosure or canopy provided with a draft for carrying off disagreeable or noxious fumes, sprays, smokes, or dusts **e :** a covering for an opening (as a companion hatch) on a boat
— **hood** *transitive verb*
— **hood·like** \-ˌlīk\ *adjective*
²**hood** \ˈhu̇d, ˈhüd\ *noun* (1930) **:** HOODLUM
— **hoody** \ˈhu̇-dē, ˈhü-\ *adjective*
³**hood** \ˈhu̇d\ *noun* [by shortening] (1967) **:** NEIGHBORHOOD 4
-hood \ˌhu̇d\ *noun suffix* [Middle English *-hod*, from Old English *-hād;* akin to Old High German *-heit* state, Gothic *haidus* way, manner]
1 : state **:** condition **:** quality **:** character ⟨widowerhood⟩ ⟨hardihood⟩
2 : time **:** period ⟨childhood⟩
3 : instance of a (specified) state or quality ⟨falsehood⟩
4 : individuals sharing a (specified) state or character ⟨brotherhood⟩
hood·ed \ˈhu̇-dəd\ *adjective* (15th century)
1 : having a hood
2 : shaped like a hood ⟨*hooded* spathes⟩

3 a : having the head conspicuously different in color from the rest of the body ⟨*hooded* bird⟩ **b :** having a crest on the head that suggests a hood ⟨*hooded* seals⟩ **c :** having the skin at each side of the neck capable of expansion by movements of the ribs ⟨*hooded* cobra⟩
4 : half-closed ⟨*hooded* eyes⟩
— **hood·ed·ness** *noun*
hood·lum \ˈhu̇d-ləm, ˈhu̇d-\ *noun* [perhaps from German dialect (Swabia) *hudelum* disorderly] (1871)
1 : THUG; *especially* **:** one who commits acts of violence
2 : a young ruffian
— **hood·lum·ish** \-lə-mish\ *adjective*
— **hood·lum·ism** \-ˌmi-zəm\ *noun*
hood·man–blind \ˌhu̇d-mən-ˈblīnd\ *noun* (1565) *archaic* **:** BLINDMAN'S BUFF
¹**hoo·doo** \ˈhü-(ˌ)dü\ *noun, plural* **hoodoos** [of African origin; akin to Hausa *hu³du³ba¹* to arouse resentment] (1875)
1 : a body of practices of sympathetic magic traditional especially among blacks in the southern U.S.
2 : a natural column of rock in western North America often in fantastic form
3 : something that brings bad luck
— **hoo·doo·ism** \-ˌi-zəm\ *noun*
²**hoodoo** *transitive verb* (1886) **:** to cast a spell on; *broadly* **:** to be a source of misfortune to
hood·wink \ˈhu̇d-ˌwiŋk\ *transitive verb* [¹*hood* + *wink*] (1562)
1 *archaic* **:** BLINDFOLD
2 *obsolete* **:** HIDE
3 : to deceive by false appearance **:** DUPE
— **hood·wink·er** *noun*
hoo·ey \ˈhü-ē\ *noun* [origin unknown] (1924) **:** NONSENSE
¹**hoof** \ˈhu̇f, ˈhüf\ *noun, plural* **hooves** \ˈhüvz, ˈhu̇vz\ *also* **hoofs** [Middle English, from Old English *hōf;* akin to Old High German *huof* hoof, Sanskrit *śapha*] (before 12th century)
1 : a curved covering of horn that protects the front of or encloses the ends of the digits of an ungulate mammal and that corresponds to a nail or claw
2 : a hoofed foot especially of a horse
— **on the hoof** *of a meat animal* **:** before butchering **:** LIVING ⟨90¢ a pound *on the hoof*⟩

hoof 2: *1, 2, 3, 4* parts of wall (*1* toe, *2* side walls, *3* quarters, *4* buttresses), *5* bulbs, *6* sole, *7* white line, *8* frog

²**hoof** (1641) *transitive verb*
1 : WALK ⟨*hoofed* it to the lecture hall⟩
2 : KICK, TRAMPLE *intransitive verb*
: to move on the feet; *especially* **:** DANCE
hoof–and–mouth disease *noun* (1884) **:** FOOT-AND-MOUTH DISEASE
hoof·beat \ˈhu̇f-ˌbēt, ˈhüf-\ *noun* (1847)
: the sound of a hoof striking a hard surface (as the ground)
hoofed \ˈhu̇ft, ˈhüft, ˈhüvd, ˈhu̇vd\ *or* **hooved** \ˈhüvd, ˈhu̇vd\ *adjective* (1513)
: furnished with hooves **:** UNGULATE
hoof·er \ˈhu̇-fər, ˈhü-\ *noun* (circa 1918) **:** a professional dancer
hoof·print \ˈhu̇f-ˌprint, ˈhüf-\ *noun* (1804) **:** an impression or hollow made by a hoof
hoo–ha \ˈhü-ˌhä\ *noun* [probably from Yiddish *hu-ha* uproar, exclamation of surprise] (1931) **:** UPROAR
¹**hook** \ˈhu̇k\ *noun* [Middle English, from Old English *hōc;* akin to Middle Dutch *hoec* fishhook, corner, Lithuanian *kengė* hook] (before 12th century)

1 a : a curved or bent device for catching, holding, or pulling **b :** something intended to attract and ensnare
2 : something curved or bent like a hook; *especially, plural* **:** FINGERS
3 : a flight or course of a ball that deviates from straight in a direction opposite to the dominant hand of the player propelling it; *also* **:** a ball following such a course — compare SLICE
4 : a short blow delivered with a circular motion by a boxer while the elbow remains bent and rigid
5 : HOOK SHOT
6 : BUTTONHOOK
7 : quick or summary removal — used with *get* or *give* ⟨the pitcher got the *hook* after giving up three runs⟩
8 : a device especially in music or writing that catches the attention
9 : a selling point or marketing scheme
— **by hook or by crook :** by any means
— **off the hook 1 :** out of trouble **2 :** free of responsibility or accountability
— **on one's own hook :** by oneself **:** INDEPENDENTLY
²**hook** (13th century) *transitive verb*
1 : to form into a hook **:** CROOK
2 a : to seize or make fast by or as if by a hook **b :** to connect by or as if by a hook — often used with *up*
3 : STEAL, PILFER
4 : to make (as a rug) by drawing loops of yarn, thread, or cloth through a coarse fabric with a hook
5 : to hit or throw (a ball) so that a hook results
intransitive verb
1 : to form a hook **:** CURVE
2 : to become hooked
3 : to work as a prostitute
hoo·kah \ˈhu̇-kə, ˈhü-\ *noun* [Arabic *ḥuqqah* bottle of a water pipe] (1763) **:** WATER PIPE 2
hook and eye *noun* (circa 1626)

◇ WORD HISTORY
hooch The Tlingit Indians of the Alaskan panhandle, like indigenous peoples elsewhere in the world confronted with drastic cultural disruption, suffered from epidemic alcoholism in the 19th century. After Alaska was purchased from Russia in 1867, contact with U.S. troops, as well as an influx of American merchants ready to sell whiskey, greatly exacerbated the Indian drinking problem, to the point that the importation of distilled spirits into Alaska was banned in 1870. The Tlingit resourcefully responded by distilling their own liquor. Some Anglo-American, whose identity remains uncertain, introduced the Indians to a crude style of pot still, with mash made from potatoes, berries, and a crucial imported ingredient, molasses. The foul-tasting outcome was called by whites *hoochinoo* or *hoochenoo*, after the Hoochinoo or Hutsnuwu, a Tlingit tribe of Admiralty, Chichagof, and Baranof Islands. (The Tlingit name of the tribe, *xucnu·wú*, means literally "grizzly bear fort.") It is not clear that the Hutsnuwu drank or made more alcohol than their neighbors, but nonetheless *hoochinoo* became a common word for "illicit liquor" in Alaska, western Canada, and the western U.S. In the 1890s it was clipped to *hooch*, which in the Prohibition Era spread throughout American English.

: a 2-part fastening device (as on a garment or a door) consisting of a metal hook that catches over a bar or into a loop

hook and ladder truck *noun* (1865)
: a piece of mobile fire apparatus carrying ladders and usually other fire-fighting and rescue equipment — called also *hook and ladder*, *ladder truck*

hook check *noun* (circa 1939)
: an act or instance of attempting to knock the puck away from an opponent in ice hockey by hooking it with the stick

hooked \'hu̇kt, *1 is also* 'hu̇-kəd\ *adjective* (before 12th century)
1 : having the form of a hook
2 : provided with a hook
3 : made by hooking ⟨a *hooked* rug⟩
4 a : addicted to narcotics **b** : fascinated by or devoted to something ⟨*hooked* on skiing⟩

¹hook·er \'hu̇-kər\ *noun* (1567)
1 : one that hooks
2 : DRINK ⟨a *hooker* of Scotch⟩
3 : PROSTITUTE

²hooker *noun* [Dutch *hoeker*, alteration of Middle Dutch *hoecboot*, from *hoec* fishhook + *boot* boat] (1801)
: a one-masted fishing boat used on the English and Irish coasts; *also* : a small clumsy boat

Hooke's law \'hu̇ks-\ *noun* [Robert *Hooke*] (1853)
: a statement in physics: the stress within an elastic solid is proportional to the strain responsible for it

hook·let \'hu̇k-lət\ *noun* (circa 1839)
: a small hook

hook, line and sinker *adverb* [from analogy with a well-hooked fish] (1838)
: without hesitation or reservation : COMPLETELY ⟨fell for the story *hook, line and sinker*⟩

hook shot *noun* (circa 1932)
: a shot in basketball made usually while standing sideways to the basket by swinging the ball up in an arc with the far hand

hook·up \'hu̇k-,əp\ *noun* (1903)
1 : a state of cooperation or alliance
2 : an assemblage (as of circuits) used for a specific purpose (as radio transmission); *also* : the plan of such an assemblage
3 : an arrangement of mechanical parts; *also* : CONNECTION ⟨a campsite with electric, water, and sewer *hookups*⟩

hook up *intransitive verb* (1925)
: to become associated especially in a working or social relationship

hook·worm \'hu̇k-,wərm\ *noun* (1902)
1 : any of several parasitic nematode worms (family Ancylostomatidae) that have strong buccal hooks or plates for attaching to the host's intestinal lining and that include serious bloodsucking pests
2 : ANCYLOSTOMIASIS

hooky *or* **hook·ey** \'hu̇-kē\ *noun, plural* **hook·ies** *or* **hookeys** [probably from slang *hook, hook it* (to make off)] (circa 1848)
: TRUANT — used chiefly in the phrase *play hooky*

hoo·li·gan \'hü-li-gən\ *noun* [perhaps from Patrick *Hooligan* (flourished 1898) Irish hoodlum in Southwark, London] (1898)
: RUFFIAN, HOODLUM
— **hoo·li·gan·ism** \-gə-,ni-zəm\ *noun*

¹hoop \'hüp *also* 'hu̇p\ *noun, often attributive* [Middle English, from Old English *hōp*; akin to Middle Dutch *hoep* ring, hoop] (12th century)
1 : a circular strip used especially for holding together the staves of containers or as a plaything
2 a : a circular figure or object : RING **b** : the rim of a basketball goal; *broadly* : the entire goal
3 : a circle or series of circles of flexible material used to expand a woman's skirt
4 : BASKETBALL — usually used in plural
— **hoop·like** \-,līk\ *adjective*

²hoop *transitive verb* (15th century)
: to bind or fasten with or as if with a hoop
— **hoop·er** *noun*

hoop·la \'hü-,plä, 'hu̇-\ *noun* [French *houp-là*, interjection] (1877)
: excited commotion : TO-DO; *also* : BALLYHOO

hoo·poe \'hü-(,)pü, -(,)pō\ *noun* [alteration of obsolete *hoop*, from Middle French *huppe*, from Latin *upupa*, of imitative origin] (1668)
: a crested Old World nonpasserine bird (*Upupa epops* of the family Upupidae) having a slender decurved bill and barred black-and-white wings and tail

hoop·skirt \'hüp-,skərt *also* 'hu̇p-\ *noun* (1857)
: a skirt stiffened with or as if with hoops

hoo·rah \hu̇-'rä, -'rȯ\, **hoo·ray** \-'rā\ *variant of* HURRAH

hoose·gow \'hüs-,gau̇\ *noun* [Spanish *juzgado* panel of judges, courtroom, from past participle of *juzgar* to judge, from Latin *judicare* — more at JUDGE] (1909)
: JAIL

Hoo·sier \'hü-zhər\ *noun* [perhaps alteration of English dialect *hoozer* anything large of its kind] (1826)
: a native or resident of Indiana — used as a nickname
— **Hoosier** *adjective*

¹hoot \'hüt\ *verb* [Middle English *houten*, of imitative origin] (13th century)
intransitive verb
1 : to shout or laugh usually derisively
2 : to make the natural throat noise of an owl or a similar cry
3 : to make a loud clamorous mechanical sound
transitive verb
1 : to assail or drive out by hooting ⟨*hooted* down the speaker⟩
2 : to express or utter with hoots ⟨*hooted* their disapproval⟩
— **hoot·er** *noun*

²hoot *noun* (15th century)
1 : a sound of hooting; *especially* : the cry of an owl
2 : a minimum amount or degree : the least bit ⟨don't give a *hoot*⟩
3 : something or someone amusing ⟨the play is a real *hoot*⟩
— **hooty** \'hü-tē\ *adjective*

³hoot \'hüt\ *or* **hoots** \'hüts\ *interjection* [origin unknown] (1540)
chiefly Scottish — used to express impatience, dissatisfaction, or objection

hoo·te·nan·ny \'hü-t³n-,a-nē\ *noun, plural* **-nies** [origin unknown] (1925)
1 *chiefly dialect* : GADGET
2 : a gathering at which folksingers entertain often with the audience joining in

Hoo·ver·ville \'hü-vər-,vil\ *noun* [Herbert *Hoover* + *-ville*] (1933)
: a shantytown of temporary dwellings during the depression years in the U.S.; *broadly* : any similar area of temporary dwellings

¹hop \'häp\ *verb* **hopped; hop·ping** [Middle English *hoppen*, from Old English *hoppian*; probably akin to Old English *hype* hip] (before 12th century)
intransitive verb
1 : to move by a quick springy leap or in a series of leaps; *also* : to move as if by hopping ⟨*hop* in the car⟩
2 : to make a quick trip especially by air
transitive verb
1 : to jump over ⟨*hop* a fence⟩
2 : to ride on ⟨*hopped* a flight⟩; *also* : to ride surreptitiously and without authorization ⟨*hop* a freight train⟩

²hop *noun* (1508)
1 a : a short brisk leap especially on one leg **b** : BOUNCE, REBOUND ⟨shortstop scooped it up on the first *hop*⟩
2 : DANCE 3
3 a : a flight in an aircraft **b** : a short trip

³hop *noun* [Middle English *hoppe*, from Middle Dutch; akin to Old High German *hopfo* hop] (15th century)
1 *plural* : the ripe dried pistillate catkins of a hop used especially to impart a bitter flavor to malt liquors
2 : a twining vine (*Humulus lupulus*) of the mulberry family with 3-lobed or 5-lobed leaves and inconspicuous flowers of which the pistillate ones are in glandular cone-shaped catkins

⁴hop *transitive verb* **hopped; hop·ping** (1572)
: to impregnate with hops

¹hope \'hōp\ *verb* **hoped; hop·ing** [Middle English, from Old English *hopian*; akin to Middle High German *hoffen* to hope] (before 12th century)
intransitive verb
1 : to cherish a desire with anticipation ⟨*hopes* for a promotion⟩
2 *archaic* : TRUST
transitive verb
1 : to desire with expectation of obtainment
2 : to expect with confidence : TRUST
synonym see EXPECT
— **hop·er** *noun*
— **hope against hope** : to hope without any basis for expecting fulfillment

²hope *noun* (before 12th century)
1 *archaic* : TRUST, RELIANCE
2 a : desire accompanied by expectation of or belief in fulfillment ⟨came in *hopes* of seeing you⟩; *also* : expectation of fulfillment or success ⟨no *hope* of a cure⟩ **b** : someone or something on which hopes are centered ⟨our only *hope* for victory⟩ **c** : something hoped for

hope chest *noun* (1911)
: a young woman's accumulation of clothes and domestic furnishings (as silver and linen) kept in anticipation of her marriage; *also* : a chest for such an accumulation

¹hope·ful \'hōp-fəl\ *adjective* (1568)
1 : having qualities which inspire hope ⟨*hopeful* signs of economic recovery⟩
2 : full of hope : inclined to hope
— **hope·ful·ness** *noun*

²hopeful *noun* (1720)
: ASPIRANT ⟨Olympic *hopefuls*⟩

hope·ful·ly \'hōp-fə-lē\ *adverb* (circa 1639)
1 : in a hopeful manner
2 : it is hoped : I hope : we hope ☐

hope·less \'hō-pləs\ *adjective* (1534)
1 a : having no expectation of good or success : DESPAIRING **b** : not susceptible to remedy or cure **c** : incapable of redemption or improvement
2 a : giving no ground for hope : DESPERATE **b** : incapable of solution, management, or accomplishment : IMPOSSIBLE
synonym see DESPONDENT
— **hope·less·ness** *noun*

hope·less·ly \-lē\ *adverb* (1616)

☐ USAGE
hopefully In the early 1960s the second sense of *hopefully*, which had been in sporadic use since around 1932, underwent a surge of popular use. A surge of popular criticism followed in reaction, but the criticism took no account of the grammar of adverbs. *Hopefully* in its second sense is a member of a class of adverbs known as disjuncts. Disjuncts serve as a means by which the author or speaker can comment directly to the reader or hearer usually on the content of the sentence to which they are attached. Many other adverbs (as *interestingly, frankly, clearly, luckily, unfortunately*) are similarly used; most are so ordinary as to excite no comment or interest whatsoever. The second sense of *hopefully* is entirely standard.

: in a hopeless manner — used especially as an intensifier ⟨the formerly despised and *hopelessly* middle-class game of golf —Ejner Jensen⟩

hop·head \'häp-ˌhed\ *noun* (1911)
slang : a drug addict

hop hornbeam *noun* (1785)
: a chiefly eastern U.S. tree (*Ostrya virginiana*) of the birch family with fruiting clusters resembling hops

Ho·pi \'hō-(ˌ)pē\ *noun, plural* **Hopi** *or* **Hopis** [Hopi *hópi*, literally, good, peaceful] (1877)
1 : a member of an American Indian people of northeastern Arizona
2 : the Uto-Aztecan language of the Hopi people

hop·lite \'häp-ˌlīt\ *noun* [Greek *hoplitēs*, from *hoplon* tool, weapon, from *hepein* to care for, work at — more at SEPULCHRE] (circa 1741)
: a heavily armed infantry soldier of ancient Greece

hop–o'–my–thumb \ˌhä-pə-mə-'thəm\ *noun* [earlier *hop on my thumb*, imperative issued to one supposedly small enough to be held in the hand] (1530)
: a very small person

hopped–up \'häpt-'əp, -ˌəp\ *adjective* (circa 1924)
1 a : being under the influence of a narcotic **b** : full of enthusiasm or excitement; *also* : overly excited **c** : more exciting or attractive than normal or usual
2 : having more than usual power : being souped up

hop·per \'hä-pər\ *noun* (13th century)
1 a : one that hops **b** : a leaping insect; *specifically* : an immature hopping form of an insect (as a grasshopper or locust)
2 [from the shaking motion of hoppers used to feed grain into a mill] **a** : a usually funnel-shaped receptacle for delivering material (as grain or coal); *also* : any of various other receptacles for the temporary storage of material **b** : a freight car with a floor sloping to one or more hinged doors for discharging bulk materials — called also *hopper car* **c** : a box in which a bill to be considered by a legislative body is dropped **d** : a tank holding liquid and having a device for releasing its contents through a pipe

¹hop·ping \'hä-piŋ\ *adverb* (1675)
: EXTREMELY, VIOLENTLY — used in the phrase *hopping mad*

²hopping *adjective* (1785)
1 : intensely active : BUSY ⟨they kept us *hopping*⟩
2 : extremely angry

³hopping *noun* (1879)
: a going from one place to another of the same kind — usually used in combination ⟨gallery-*hopping*⟩

hopping John \ˌhä-pən-'jän, -piŋ-\ *or* **hoppin' John** \ˌhä-pən-\ *noun, often H capitalized* (1838)
: a dish made essentially of cowpeas, rice, and salt pork or bacon

hop·py \'hä-pē\ *adjective* **hop·pi·er; -est** (circa 1889)
: having the taste or aroma of hops — used especially of ale or beer

hop·sack \'häp-ˌsak\ *also* **hop·sack·ing** \-ˌsa-kiŋ\ *noun* [Middle English *hopsak* sack for hops, from *hoppe* ³hop + *sak* sack] (1888)
: a rough-surfaced loosely woven clothing fabric

¹hop·scotch \'häp-ˌskäch\ *noun* [¹hop + *scotch* (line)] (1801)
: a child's game in which a player tosses an object (as a stone) into areas of a figure outlined on the ground and hops through the figure and back to regain the object

²hopscotch *intransitive verb* (1918)
: to move as if by hopping ⟨*hopscotched* across Europe⟩

hop, skip, and jump *noun* (1760)
: a short distance

hop, step, and jump *noun* (circa 1719)
: TRIPLE JUMP

ho·ra *also* **ho·rah** \'hōr-ə, 'hȯr-ə\ *noun* [New Hebrew *hōrāh*, from Romanian *horǎ*] (1878)
: a circle dance of Romania and Israel

Ho·rae \'hōr-ē, 'hȯr-, -ˌī\ *noun plural* [Latin, from Greek *Hōrai*]
: the Greek goddesses of the seasons

ho·ra·ry \'hōr-ər-ē, 'hȯr-, 'här-\ *adjective* [Medieval Latin *horarius*, from Latin *hora* hour — more at HOUR] (1632)
: of or relating to an hour; *also* : HOURLY

Ho·ra·tio Al·ger \hə-'rā-shō-'al-jər\ *adjective* (1925)
: of, relating to, or resembling the fiction of Horatio Alger in which success is achieved through self-reliance and hard work

Ho·ra·tius \hə-'rā-sh(ē-)əs\ *noun* [Latin]
: a hero in Roman legend noted for his defense of a bridge over the Tiber against the Etruscans

horde \'hōrd, 'hȯrd\ *noun* [Middle French German, & Polish; Middle French & German, from Polish *horda*, from Ukrainian dialect *gorda*, alteration of Ukrainian *orda*, from Old Russian, from Turkic *orda, ordu* khan's residence] (1555)
1 a : a political subdivision of central Asian nomads **b** : a people or tribe of nomadic life
2 : a teeming crowd or throng : SWARM ◇
synonym see CROWD

hore·hound \'hōr-ˌhaund, 'hȯr-\ *noun* [Middle English *horhoune*, from Old English *hārhūne*, from *hār* hoary + *hūne* horehound — more at HOAR] (before 12th century)
1 a : a bitter mint (*Marrubium vulgare*) with downy leaves **b** : an extract or confection made from this plant
2 : any of several mints resembling the horehound

ho·ri·zon \hə-'rī-z°n\ *noun* [Middle English *orizon*, from Late Latin *horizont-, horizon*, from Greek *horizont-, horizōn*, from present participle of *horizein* to bound, define, from *horos* boundary; perhaps akin to Latin *urvum* curved part of a plow] (14th century)
1 a : the apparent junction of earth and sky **b** : the great circle on the celestial sphere formed by the intersection of a plane tangent to the earth's surface at an observer's position with the celestial sphere **c** : range of perception or experience **d** : something that might be attained ⟨new *horizons*⟩
2 a : the geological deposit of a particular time usually identified by distinctive fossils **b** : any of the reasonably distinct layers of soil or its underlying material in a vertical section of land **c** : a cultural area or level of development indicated by separated groups of artifacts
— **ho·ri·zon·al** \-'rī-z°n-əl\ *adjective*

ho·ri·zon·less \-ləs\ *adjective* (circa 1839)
1 a : having no horizon **b** : ENDLESS 1
2 : HOPELESS

hor·i·zon·tal \ˌhȯr-ə-'zän-t°l, ˌhär-\ *adjective* (1555)
1 a : of, relating to, or situated near the horizon **b** : parallel to, in the plane of, or operating in a plane parallel to the horizon or to a base line : LEVEL ⟨*horizontal* distance⟩ ⟨*horizontal* engine⟩
2 : relating to, directed toward, or consisting of individuals or entities of similar status or on the same level ⟨*horizontal* mergers⟩ ⟨*horizontal* hostility⟩
— **horizontal** *noun*
— **hor·i·zon·tal·i·ty** \-ˌzän-'ta-lə-tē\ *noun*
— **hor·i·zon·tal·ly** \-'zän-t°l-ē\ *adverb*

horizontal bar *noun* (1827)
1 : a steel bar supported in a horizontal position approximately eight feet above the floor and used for swinging feats in gymnastics
2 : an event in gymnastics competition in which the horizontal bar is used

hor·mo·go·ni·um \ˌhȯr-mə-'gō-nē-əm\ *noun, plural* **-nia** \-nē-ə\ [New Latin, from Greek *hormos* chain, necklace + New Latin *-gonium* — more at SERIES] (1880)
: a portion of a filament in many blue-green algae that becomes detached as a reproductive body

hor·mon·al \hȯr-'mō-n°l\ *adjective* (1926)
: of, relating to, or effected by hormones
— **hor·mon·al·ly** \-n°l-ē\ *adverb*

hor·mone \'hȯr-ˌmōn\ *noun* [Greek *hormōn*, present participle of *horman* to stir up, from *hormē* impulse, assault; akin to Greek *ornynai* to rouse — more at RISE] (1905)
1 : a product of living cells that circulates in body fluids or sap and produces a specific effect on the activity of cells remote from its point of origin; *especially* : one exerting a stimulatory effect on a cellular activity
2 : a synthetic substance that acts like a hormone
— **hor·mone·like** \-ˌlīk\ *adjective*

horn \'hȯrn\ *noun* [Middle English, from Old English; akin to Old High German *horn*, Latin *cornu*, Greek *keras*] (before 12th century)
1 a : one of the usually paired bony processes that arise from the head of many ungulates and that are found in some extinct mammals and reptiles: as (1) : one of the permanent paired hollow sheaths of keratin usually present in both sexes of cattle and their relatives that function chiefly for defense and arise from a bony core anchored to the skull — see COW illustration (2) : ANTLER (3) : a permanent solid horn of keratin that is attached to the nasal bone of a rhinoceros (4) : one of a pair of permanent bone protuberances from the skull of a giraffe or okapi that are covered with hairy skin **b** : a part like an animal's horn attributed especially to the devil **c** : a natural projection or excrescence from an animal resembling or suggestive of a horn **d** (1) : the tough fibrous material consisting chiefly of keratin that covers or forms the horns of cattle and related animals, hooves, or other horny parts (as claws or nails) (2) : a manufactured product (as a plastic) resembling horn **e** : a hollow horn used to hold something

◇ WORD HISTORY

horde In a 1985 novel, a young boy is described as owning "a horde of teddy bears." That *horde* can now be linked with something as innocuous as teddy bears demonstrates how far the word has strayed from its original application to divisions of the Mongols and Turks, whose forays beyond Central Asia in the Middle Ages terrified the world. The source of *horde* is ultimately Turkic *ordu* or *ordō*, meaning "royal camp" or "royal residence" in the earliest inscriptions. The word was borrowed from Turkic into Mongolian as *ordu* and after the division of Genghis Khan's empire following his death was associated with the field armies and encampments, such as the Golden Horde, that governed each part of the empire. The Turkic and Mongolian word was borrowed into Old Russian as *orda*, and, with the addition of a murmured \h\ in some forms of Ukrainian, was borrowed into Polish as *horda* and hence into Western European languages. The indistinct European image of a Central Asian army as a nomadic swarm led to the eventual generalization of the word *horde* to mean a large number of almost anything—even teddy bears.

\ə\ **abut** \ᵊ\ **kitten** \ər\ **further** \a\ **ash** \ā\ **ace** \ä\ **mop, mar** \au̇\ **out** \ch\ **chin** \e\ **bet** \ē\ **easy** \g\ **go** \i\ **hit** \ī\ **ice** \j\ **job** \ŋ\ **sing** \ō\ **go** \o̊\ **law** \o̊i\ **boy** \th\ **thin** \t͟h\ **the** \ü\ **loot** \u̇\ **foot** \y\ **yet** \zh\ **vision** *see also* Guide to Pronunciation

2 : something resembling or suggestive of a horn: as **a :** one of the curved ends of a crescent **b :** a sharp mountain peak **c :** a body of land or water shaped like a horn **d :** a beak-shaped part of an anvil **e :** a high pommel of a saddle **f :** CORNU
3 a : an animal's horn used as a wind instrument **b :** a brass wind instrument: as (1) : HUNTING HORN (2) : FRENCH HORN **c :** a wind instrument used in a jazz band; *especially* : TRUMPET **d :** a usually electrical device that makes a noise like that of a horn
4 : a source of strength
5 : one of the equally disadvantageous alternatives presented by a dilemma
6 *slang* : TELEPHONE
— **horn** *adjective*
— **horned** \'hȯrnd *also* 'hȯr-nəd\ *adjective*
— **horned·ness** \'hȯr-nəd-nəs, 'hȯrn(d)-nəs\ *noun*
— **horn·less** \'hȯrn-ləs\ *adjective*
— **horn·less·ness** *noun*
— **horn·like** \-,līk\ *adjective*
horn·beam \'hȯrn-,bēm\ *noun* (14th century)
: any of a genus (*Carpinus*) of trees of the birch family having smooth gray bark and hard white wood
horn·bill \-,bil\ *noun* (1773)
: any of a family (Bucerotidae) of large non-passerine Old World birds having enormous bills
horn·blende \-,blend\ *noun* [German] (1770)
: a mineral that is the common dark variety of aluminous amphibole; *broadly* : AMPHIBOLE 2
— **horn·blend·ic** \'hȯrn-'blen-dik\ *adjective*
horn·book \'hȯrn-,bȯk\ *noun* (circa 1595)
1 : a child's primer consisting of a sheet of parchment or paper protected by a sheet of transparent horn
2 : a rudimentary treatise
horned lizard *noun* (1806)
: HORNED TOAD
horned owl *noun* (14th century)
: any of various owls having conspicuous tufts of feathers on the head
horned pout *noun* (1837)
: a bullhead (genus *Ameiurus*); *especially* : a common bullhead (*A. nebulosus*) of the eastern U.S. that has been introduced into streams of the Pacific coast
horned toad \'hȯrnd-; 'hȯr-nəd-, -nət-\ *noun* (1806)
: any of several small harmless insectivorous lizards (genus *Phrynosoma*) of the western U.S. and Mexico having hornlike spines
horned viper *noun* (1767)
: CERASTES
hor·net \'hȯr-nət\ *noun* [Middle English *hernet*, from Old English *hyrnet;* akin to Old High German *hornaz* hornet, Latin *crabro*] (before 12th century)
: any of the larger social wasps (family Vespidae) — compare YELLOW JACKET
hornet's nest *noun* (circa 1740)
1 : a troublesome or hazardous situation
2 : an angry reaction ⟨must have known that his frank comments . . . would stir up a *hornet's nest* —*U.S. Investor*⟩
horn·fels \'hȯrn-,felz\ *noun* [German, from *Horn* horn + *Fels* cliff, rock] (1854)
: a fine-grained silicate rock produced by metamorphism especially of slate
horn fly *noun* (1708)
: a small black European fly (*Haematobia irritans*) that has been introduced into North America where it is a blood-sucking pest of cattle
horn in *intransitive verb* (1911)
: to participate without invitation or consent : INTRUDE
horn·ist \'hȯr-nist\ *noun* (1836)
: one who plays a French horn
horn-mad \'hȯrn-'mad\ *adjective* (1579)
: furiously enraged
horn of plenty (circa 1586)
: CORNUCOPIA

horn·pipe \'hȯrn-,pīp\ *noun* (15th century)
1 : a single-reed wind instrument consisting of a wooden or bone pipe with finger holes, a bell, and mouthpiece usually of horn
2 : a lively folk dance of the British Isles originally accompanied by hornpipe playing
horn-rims \-,rimz\ *noun plural* (1927)
: glasses with horn rims
horn·stone \'hȯrn-,stōn\ *noun* (1728)
: a mineral that is a variety of quartz much like flint but more brittle
horn·swog·gle \-,swä-gəl\ *transitive verb* **-swog·gled; -swog·gling** \-g(ə-)liŋ\ [origin unknown] (circa 1829)
slang : BAMBOOZLE, HOAX
horn·tail \-,tāl\ *noun* (1884)
: any of various hymenopterous insects (family Siricidae) related to the typical sawflies but having larvae that burrow in woody plants and on the females a stout hornlike ovipositor for depositing the egg
horn·worm \-,wərm\ *noun* (1676)
: a hawkmoth caterpillar having a hornlike tail process — compare TOMATO HORNWORM
horn·wort \-,wərt, -,wȯrt\ *noun* (circa 1805)
: any of a genus (*Ceratophyllum*) of rootless thin-stemmed aquatic herbs that have flowers with a sepaloid perianth and a single carpel
horny \'hȯr-nē\ *adjective* **horn·i·er; -est** (14th century)
1 a : of or made of horn **b :** HARD, CALLOUS ⟨*horny*-handed⟩ **c :** compact and homogeneous with a dull luster — used of a mineral
2 : having horns
3 [*horn* erect penis + [1]-*y*] **a :** desiring sexual gratification **b :** excited sexually
— **horn·i·ness** *noun*
hor·o·loge \'hȯr-ə-,lōj, 'här-\ *noun* [Middle English, from Middle French, from Latin *horologium*, from Greek *hōrologion*, from *hōra* hour + *legein* to gather — more at YEAR, LEGEND] (14th century)
: a timekeeping device
hor·o·log·i·cal \,hȯr-ə-'lä-ji-kəl\ *adjective* (15th century)
: of or relating to a horologe or horology
ho·rol·o·gist \hə-'rä-lə-jist\ *noun* (1798)
1 : a person skilled in the practice or theory of horology
2 : a maker of clocks or watches
ho·rol·o·gy \-jē\ *noun* [Greek *hōra* + English *-logy*] (1819)
1 : the science of measuring time
2 : the art of making instruments for indicating time
horo·scope \'hȯr-ə-,skōp, 'här-\ *noun* [Middle English *oruscope*, from Middle French *horoscope*, from Latin *horoscopus*, from Greek *hōroskopos*, from *hōra* + *skopos* watcher; akin to Greek *skopein* to look at — more at SPY] (14th century)
1 : a diagram of the relative positions of planets and signs of the zodiac at a specific time (as at one's birth) for use by astrologers in inferring individual character and personality traits and in foretelling events of a person's life
2 : an astrological forecast
hor·ren·dous \hȯ-'ren-dəs, hä-, hə-\ *adjective* [Latin *horrendus*, from gerundive of *horrēre*] (1659)
: perfectly horrid : DREADFUL ⟨the tax rate was *horrendous*⟩
— **hor·ren·dous·ly** *adverb*
hor·rent \'hȯr-ənt, 'här-\ *adjective* [Latin *horrent-, horrens*, present participle of *horrēre*] (1667)
1 *archaic* : covered with bristling points : BRISTLED
2 *archaic* : standing up like bristles : BRISTLING
hor·ri·ble \'hȯr-ə-bəl, 'här-\ *adjective* [Middle English *orrible, horrible*, from Middle French, from Latin *horribilis*, from *horrēre*] (14th century)
1 : marked by or conducive to horror

2 : extremely unpleasant or disagreeable
— **horrible** *noun*
— **hor·ri·ble·ness** *noun*
— **hor·ri·bly** \-blē\ *adverb*
hor·rid \'hȯr-əd, 'här-\ *adjective* [Latin *horridus*, from *horrēre*] (1590)
1 *archaic* : ROUGH, BRISTLING
2 : innately offensive or repulsive: **a :** inspiring horror : SHOCKING **b :** inspiring disgust or loathing : NASTY
— **hor·rid·ly** *adverb*
— **hor·rid·ness** *noun*
hor·rif·ic \hȯ-'ri-fik, hä-\ *adjective* (1653)
: having the power to horrify ⟨a *horrific* account of the tragedy⟩
— **hor·rif·i·cal·ly** \-fi-k(ə-)lē\ *adverb*
hor·ri·fy \'hȯr-ə-,fī, 'här-\ *transitive verb* **-fied; -fy·ing** (1791)
1 : to cause to feel horror
2 : to fill with distaste : SHOCK
synonym see DISMAY
— **hor·ri·fy·ing·ly** \-,fī-iŋ-lē\ *adverb*
[1]hor·ror \'hȯr-ər, 'här-\ *noun* [Middle English *horrour*, from Middle French *horror*, from Latin, action of bristling, from *horrēre* to bristle, shiver; akin to Sanskrit *harṣate* he is excited] (14th century)
1 a : painful and intense fear, dread, or dismay ⟨astonishment giving place to *horror* on the faces of the people about me —H. G. Wells⟩ **b :** intense aversion or repugnance
2 a : the quality of inspiring horror : repulsive, horrible, or dismal quality or character ⟨contemplating the *horror* of their lives —Liam O'Flaherty⟩ **b :** something that inspires horror
3 *plural* : a state of extreme depression or apprehension
[2]horror *adjective* (1797)
: calculated to inspire feelings of dread or horror : BLOODCURDLING ⟨a *horror* story⟩
hor·ror–struck \-,strək\ *adjective* (1814)
: struck with horror ⟨stood *horror-struck* as they watched . . . their own city destroyed —*Nashville Tennessean*⟩
hors de com·bat \,ȯr-də-kōⁿ-'bä\ *adverb or adjective* [French] (1757)
: out of combat : DISABLED
hors d'oeuvre \ȯr-'dərv\ *noun, plural* **hors d'oeuvres** *also* **hors d'oeuvre** \-'dərv(z)\ [French *hors-d'œuvre*, literally, outside of the work] (1714)
: any of various savory foods usually served as appetizers
[1]horse \'hȯrs\ *noun, plural* **hors·es** *also* **horse** [Middle English *hors*, from Old English; akin to Old High German *hros* horse] (before 12th century)

horse 1a(1): *1* forehead, *2* forelock, *3* poll, *4* mane, *5* withers, *6* back, *7* flank, *8* loin, *9* haunch, *10* croup, *11* point of hip, *12* tail, *13* hock, *14* cannon, *15* gaskin, *16* thigh, *17* stifle, *18* barrel, *19* chestnut, *20* fetlock, *21* pastern, *22* hoof, *23* coronet, *24* knee, *25* forearm, *26* chest, *27* shoulder, *28* neck, *29* throatlatch, *30* cheek

1 a (1) **:** a large solid-hoofed herbivorous mammal (*Equus caballus,* family Equidae, the horse family) domesticated since a prehistoric period and used as a beast of burden, a draft animal, or for riding (2) **:** RACEHORSE ⟨play the *horses*⟩ **b :** a male horse; *especially* **:** STALLION **c :** a recent or extinct animal (as a zebra, ass, or onager) of the horse family **2 a :** JACKSTAY **b :** a frame usually with legs used for supporting something (as planks or staging) **c** (1) **:** POMMEL HORSE (2) **:** VAULTING HORSE **3** *horse plural* **:** CAVALRY **4 :** a mass of the same geological character as the wall rock occurring within a vein **5 :** HORSEPOWER **6** *slang* **:** HEROIN **7 :** an athlete whose performance is consistently strong and reliable ⟨a team with the *horses* to win the pennant⟩ — **horse·less** \'hȯr-sləs\ *adjective* — **horse·like** \'hȯrs-ˌlīk\ *adjective* — **from the horse's mouth :** from the original source

²horse *verb* **horsed; hors·ing** (before 12th century) *transitive verb* **1 :** to provide with a horse **2 :** to move by brute force *intransitive verb* *of a mare* **:** to be in heat

³horse *adjective* (15th century) **1 a :** of or relating to a horse **b :** hauled or powered by a horse ⟨a *horse* barge⟩ **2 :** large or coarse of its kind **3 :** mounted on horses ⟨*horse* guards⟩

horse–and–buggy *adjective* (circa 1926) **1 :** of or relating to the era before the advent of certain socially revolutionizing inventions (as the automobile) **2 :** clinging to outdated attitudes or ideas **:** OLD-FASHIONED

horse around *intransitive verb* (circa 1928) **:** to engage in horseplay ⟨*horse around* together, joking and laughing and pushing each other —D. K. Shipler⟩; *also* **:** FOOL AROUND 1

¹horse·back \'hȯrs-ˌbak\ *noun* (14th century) **:** the back of a horse

²horseback *adverb* (1727) **:** on horseback

³horseback *adjective* (1879) **:** given without thorough consideration ⟨a *horseback* opinion⟩

horse·bean \'hȯrs-ˌbēn\ *noun* (1684) **1 :** BROAD BEAN **2 :** JERUSALEM THORN

horse·car \-ˌkär\ *noun* (1833) **1 :** a streetcar drawn by horses **2 :** a car fitted for transporting horses

horse chestnut *noun* (1597) **1 :** a large Asian tree (*Aesculus hippocastanum* of the family Hippocastanaceae, the horse-chestnut family) that has palmate leaves and erect conical clusters of showy flowers and is widely cultivated as an ornamental and shade tree and naturalized as an escape; *also* **:** BUCKEYE **2 :** the large glossy brown seed of a horse chestnut

horse coper *noun* (1614) *British* **:** COPER

horse·feath·ers \'hȯrs-ˌfe-thərz\ *noun plural* (1928) *slang* **:** NONSENSE, BALDERDASH

horse·flesh \-ˌflesh\ *noun* (15th century) **:** horses considered especially with reference to riding, driving, or racing

horse·fly \-ˌflī\ *noun* (14th century) **:** any of a family (Tabanidae) of swift usually large two-winged flies with bloodsucking females

horse gentian *noun* (1837) **:** FEVERWORT

horse·hair \'hȯrs-ˌhar, -ˌher\ *noun* (14th century) **1 :** the hair of a horse especially from the mane or tail **2 :** cloth made from horsehair

horsehair worm *noun* (circa 1753) **:** HAIRWORM 1 — called also *horsehair snake*

horse·hide \'hȯrs-ˌhīd\ *noun* (14th century) **1 :** the dressed or raw hide of a horse **2 :** the ball used in the game of baseball

horse latitudes *noun plural* (1777) **:** either of two belts or regions in the neighborhood of 30° N and 30° S latitude characterized by high pressure, calms, and light variable winds

horse·laugh \'hȯrs-ˌlaf, -ˌláf\ *noun* (1713) **:** a loud boisterous laugh **:** GUFFAW

horseless carriage *noun* (1895) **:** AUTOMOBILE

horse mackerel *noun* (circa 1705) **1 :** any of various large carangid food fishes; *especially* **:** JACK MACKEREL **2 :** BLUEFIN TUNA

horse·man \'hȯr-smən\ *noun* (14th century) **1 :** a rider or driver of horses; *especially* **:** one whose skill is exceptional **2 :** a person skilled in caring for or managing horses **3 :** a person who breeds or raises horses — **horse·man·ship** \-ˌship\ *noun*

horse·mint \'hȯrs-ˌmint\ *noun* (before 12th century) **:** any of various coarse mints; *especially* **:** MONARDA

horse nettle *noun* (circa 1818) **:** a coarse prickly weed (*Solanum carolinense*) of the nightshade family with bright yellow fruit resembling berries

horse opera *noun* (1927) **:** WESTERN 2

horse·play \'hȯrs-ˌplā\ *noun* (1589) **:** rough or boisterous play

horse·play·er \-ər\ *noun* (1947) **:** one who habitually bets on horse races

horse·pow·er \'hȯrs-ˌpau̇(-ə)r\ *noun* (1806) **1 :** the power that a horse exerts in pulling **2 :** a unit of power equal in the U.S. to 746 watts and nearly equivalent to the English gravitational unit of the same name that equals 550 foot-pounds of work per second **3 :** effective power ⟨intellectual *horsepower*⟩ ⟨computing *horsepower*⟩

horse race *noun* (1954) **:** a close contest (as in politics)

horse·rad·ish \'hȯrs-ˌra-dish, -ˌre-\ *noun* (1597) **1 :** a tall coarse white-flowered herb (*Armoracia lapathifolia*) of the mustard family **2 :** a condiment made from ground-up horseradish root

horse's ass \'hȯr-səz-\ *noun* (circa 1942) **:** a stupid or incompetent person **:** BLOCKHEAD — often considered vulgar

horse sense *noun* (1832) **:** COMMON SENSE

horse·shit \'hȯrs-ˌshit, 'hȯrsh-\ *noun* (1946) **:** NONSENSE, BUNK — usually considered vulgar

horse·shoe \'hȯrs-ˌshü, 'hȯrsh-\ *noun* (14th century) **1 :** a usually U-shaped band of iron fitted and nailed to the rim of a horse's hoof to protect it **2 :** something (as a valley) shaped like a horseshoe **3** *plural* **:** a game like quoits played with horseshoes or with horseshoe-shaped pieces of metal — **horseshoe** *transitive verb* — **horse·sho·er** \-ˌshü-ər\ *noun*

horseshoe arch *noun* (circa 1816) **:** an arch having an intrados that widens above the springing before narrowing to a rounded or pointed crown — see ARCH illustration

horseshoe crab *noun* (1797) **:** any of several closely related marine arthropods (order Xiphosura and class Merostomata) with a broad crescentic cephalothorax — called also *king crab*

horse show *noun* (1856) **:** an exhibition of horses that usually includes competition in riding, driving, and jumping

horse·tail \'hȯrs-ˌtāl\ *noun* (15th century) **:** EQUISETUM

horse trade *noun* (1846) **:** negotiation accompanied by shrewd bargaining and reciprocal concessions ⟨a political *horse trade*⟩ — **horse–trade** *intransitive verb* — **horse trader** *noun*

horse·weed \'hȯrs-ˌwēd\ *noun* (1790) **1 :** a common North American fleabane (*Conyza canadensis* synonym *Erigeron canadensis*) with linear leaves and small discoid heads of yellowish flowers **2 :** a coarse annual ragweed (*Ambrosia trifida*)

horse·whip \'hȯrs-ˌwip, 'hȯrs-ˌhwip\ *transitive verb* (1768) **:** to flog with or as if with a whip made to be used on a horse — **horse·whip·per** *noun*

horse·wom·an \'hȯrs-ˌwu̇m-ən\ *noun* (circa 1578) **1 :** a woman rider or driver of horses; *especially* **:** one whose skill is exceptional **2 :** a woman skilled in caring for or managing horses **3 :** a woman who breeds or raises horses

hors·ey *or* **horsy** \'hȯr-sē\ *adjective* **hors·i·er; -est** (1591) **1 :** of, relating to, or resembling a horse **2 :** having to do with horses or horse racing **3 :** characteristic of the manners, dress, or tastes of horsemen or horsewomen — **hors·i·ly** \-sə-lē\ *adverb* — **hors·i·ness** \-sē-nəs\ *noun*

horst \'hȯrst\ *noun* [German, literally, thicket] (1893) **:** a block of the earth's crust separated by faults from adjacent relatively depressed blocks

hor·ta·tive \'hȯr-tə-tiv\ *adjective* [Late Latin *hortativus,* from Latin *hortatus,* past participle of *hortari* to urge — more at YEARN] (1623) **:** giving exhortation **:** ADVISORY — **hor·ta·tive·ly** *adverb*

hor·ta·to·ry \'hȯr-tə-ˌtōr-ē, -ˌtȯr-\ *adjective* (1586) **:** HORTATIVE, EXHORTATORY

hor·ti·cul·ture \'hȯr-tə-ˌkəl-chər\ *noun* [Latin *hortus* garden + English *-i-* + *culture* — more at YARD] (1678) **:** the science and art of growing fruits, vegetables, flowers, or ornamental plants — **hor·ti·cul·tur·al** \ˌhȯr-tə-ˈkəl-chə-rəl\ *adjective* — **hor·ti·cul·tur·al·ly** \-rə-lē\ *adverb* — **hor·ti·cul·tur·ist** \-rist\ *noun*

Ho·rus \'hȯr-əs, 'hȯr-\ *noun* [Late Latin, from Greek *Hōros,* from Egyptian *Ḥr*] **:** the Egyptian god of light and the son of Osiris and Isis

ho·san·na *also* **ho·san·nah** \hō-ˈza-nə *also* -ˈzä-\ *interjection* [Middle English *osanna,* from Old English, from Late Latin, from Greek *hōsanna,* from Hebrew *hōshīʿāh-nnā* pray, save (us)!] (before 12th century) — used as a cry of acclamation and adoration — **hosanna** *noun*

HO scale \ˌ(ˈ)ā-ˈchō-\ *noun* [half + O (gauge)] (1939) **:** a scale of 3.5 millimeters to one foot used especially for model toys (as automobiles or trains)

¹hose \'hōz\ *noun, plural* **hose** *or* **hos·es** [Middle English, from Old English *hosa* stocking, husk; akin to Old High German *hosa* leg covering] (before 12th century)

¹hose *plural* **hose a** (1) **:** a cloth leg covering that sometimes covers the foot (2) **:** STOCKING, SOCK **b** (1) **:** a close-fitting garment covering the legs and waist that is usually attached to a doublet by points (2) **:** short breeches reaching to the knee **2 :** a flexible tube for conveying fluids (as from a faucet or hydrant)

²hose *transitive verb* **hosed; hos·ing** (1889) **1 :** to spray, water, or wash with a hose — often used with *down* ⟨*hose* down a stable floor⟩ **2** *slang* **a :** to deprive of something due or expected **:** TRICK, CHEAT **b :** to shoot with automatic weapons fire

Ho·sea \hō-'zā-ə, -'zē-\ *noun* [Hebrew *Hōshēaʿ*] **1 :** a Hebrew prophet of the 8th century B.C. **2 :** a prophetic book of canonical Jewish and Christian Scripture — see BIBLE table

ho·sel \'hō-zəl\ *noun* [diminutive of ¹*hose*] (1899) **:** a socket in the head of a golf club into which the shaft is inserted

hose·pipe \'hōz-,pīp\ *noun* (1835) *chiefly British* **:** HOSE 2

ho·siery \'hōzh-rē, 'hōz-; 'hō-zhə-rē, -zə-\ *noun* (1796) **1 :** HOSE 1a **2** *chiefly British* **:** KNITWEAR

hos·pice \'häs-pəs\ *noun* [French, from Latin *hospitium*, from *hospit-, hospes* host — more at HOST] (1818) **1 :** a lodging for travelers, young persons, or the underprivileged especially when maintained by a religious order **2 :** a facility or program designed to provide a caring environment for supplying the physical and emotional needs of the terminally ill

hos·pi·ta·ble \hä-'spi-tə-bəl, 'häs-(,)pi-\ *adjective* (circa 1570) **1 a :** given to generous and cordial reception of guests **b :** promising or suggesting generous and cordial welcome **c :** offering a pleasant or sustaining environment **2 :** readily receptive **:** OPEN ⟨*hospitable* to new ideas⟩ — **hos·pi·ta·bly** \-blē\ *adverb*

hos·pi·tal \'häs-(,)pi-t°l\ *noun, often attributive* [Middle English, from Middle French, from Medieval Latin *hospitale* hospice, guest house, from neuter of Latin *hospitalis* of a guest, from *hospit-, hospes*] (14th century) **1 :** a charitable institution for the needy, aged, infirm, or young **2 :** an institution where the sick or injured are given medical or surgical care — usually used in British English without an article after a preposition **3 :** a repair shop for specified small objects ⟨clock *hospital*⟩

hos·pi·tal·ise *British variant of* HOSPITALIZE

hos·pi·tal·i·ty \,häs-pə-'ta-lə-tē\ *noun, plural* **-ties** (14th century) **:** hospitable treatment, reception, or disposition

hospitality suite *noun* (1963) **:** a room or suite especially in a hotel set aside as a place for socializing especially for business purposes

hos·pi·tal·ize \'häs-,pi-t°l-,īz\ *transitive verb* **-ized; -iz·ing** (circa 1899) **:** to place in a hospital as a patient — **hos·pi·tal·iza·tion** \,häs-,pi-t°l-ə-'zā-shən\ *noun*

Hos·pi·tal·ler *or* **Hos·pi·tal·er** \-t°l-ər\ *noun* [Middle English *hospitalier*, from Middle French, from Medieval Latin *hospitalarius*, from Late Latin *hospitale*] (14th century) **:** a member of a religious military order established in Jerusalem in the 12th century

¹host \'hōst\ *noun* [Middle English, from Old French, from Late Latin *hostis*, from Latin, stranger, enemy — more at GUEST] (14th century) **1 :** ARMY **2 :** a very large number **:** MULTITUDE

²host *intransitive verb* (15th century) **:** to assemble in a host usually for a hostile purpose

³host *noun* [Middle English *hoste* host, guest, from Old French, from Latin *hospit-, hospes*, probably from *hostis*] (14th century) **1 a :** one that receives or entertains guests socially, commercially, or officially **b :** one that provides facilities for an event or function ⟨our college served as *host* for the basketball tournament⟩ **2 a :** a living animal or plant affording subsistence or lodgment to a parasite **b :** the larger, stronger, or dominant member of a commensal or symbiotic pair **c :** an individual into which a tissue, part, or embryo is transplanted from another **3 :** a mineral or rock that is older than the minerals or rocks in it; *also* **:** a substance that contains a usually small amount of another substance incorporated in its structure **4 :** a radio or television emcee **5 :** a computer that controls communications in a network that administers a database

⁴host *transitive verb* (15th century) **1 :** to serve as host to, at, or for ⟨*host* friends⟩ **2 :** EMCEE ⟨*hosted* a series of TV programs⟩

⁵host *noun, often capitalized* [Middle English *hoste, oste*, from Middle French *hoiste*, from Late Latin & Latin; Late Latin *hostia* Eucharist, from Latin, sacrifice] (14th century) **:** the eucharistic bread

hos·ta \'hō-stə, 'hä-\ *noun* [New Latin, from Nicolaus *Host* (died 1834) Austrian botanist] (1828) **:** PLANTAIN LILY

hos·tage \'häs-tij\ *noun* [Middle English, from Old French, from *hoste*] (13th century) **1 a :** a person held by one party in a conflict as a pledge that promises will be kept or terms met by the other party **b :** a person taken by force to secure the taker's demands **2 :** one that is involuntarily controlled by an outside influence

¹hos·tel \'häs-t°l\ *noun* [Middle English, from Old French, from Medieval Latin *hospitale* hospice] (14th century) **1 :** INN **2 a** *chiefly British* **:** a supervised institutional residence **b :** a supervised lodging for usually young travelers — called also *youth hostel*

²hostel *intransitive verb* **-teled** *or* **-telled; -tel·ing** *or* **-tel·ling** (14th century) **:** to stay at hostels overnight in the course of traveling

hos·tel·er *or* **hos·tel·ler** \'häs-tə-lər\ *noun* (14th century) **1 :** one that lodges guests or strangers **2 :** a traveler who stops at hostels overnight

hos·tel·ry \'häs-t°l-rē\ *noun, plural* **-ries** (14th century) **:** INN, HOTEL

¹host·ess \'hōs-təs\ *noun* (14th century) **1 :** a woman who entertains socially **2 a :** a woman in charge of a public dining room who seats diners **b :** a female employee on a public conveyance (as an airplane) who manages the provisioning of food and attends passengers **c :** a woman who acts as a dancing partner or companion to male patrons in a dance hall or bar

²hostess (1927) *intransitive verb* **:** to act as hostess *transitive verb* **:** to serve as hostess to

hos·tile \'häs-t°l, -,tīl\ *adjective* [Middle French or Latin; Middle French, from Latin *hostilis*, from *hostis*] (1580) **1 a :** of or relating to an enemy ⟨*hostile* fire⟩ **b :** marked by malevolence ⟨a *hostile* act⟩ **c :** openly opposed or resisting ⟨a *hostile* critic⟩ ⟨*hostile* to new ideas⟩ **d :** not hospitable ⟨a *hostile* environment⟩ **2 a :** of or relating to the opposing party in a legal controversy ⟨a *hostile* witness⟩ **b :** adverse to the interests of a property owner or corporation management ⟨a *hostile* takeover⟩ — **hostile** *noun* — **hos·tile·ly** \-t°l-(l)ē, -,tīl-lē\ *adverb*

hos·til·i·ty \hä-'sti-lə-tē\ *noun, plural* **-ties** (15th century) **1 a :** deep-seated usually mutual ill will **b** (1) **:** hostile action (2) *plural* **:** overt acts of warfare **:** WAR **2 :** conflict, opposition, or resistance in thought or principle *synonym* see ENMITY

hos·tler \'häs-lər, 'äs-\ *noun* [Middle English, innkeeper, hostler, from *hostel*] (14th century) **1 :** one who takes care of horses or mules **2 :** one who moves locomotives in and out of a roundhouse; *also* **:** one who services locomotives

host·ly \'hōst-lē\ *adjective* (1893) **:** of or appropriate to a host

¹hot \'hät\ *adjective* **hot·ter; hot·test** [Middle English, from Old English *hāt*; akin to Old High German *heiz* hot, Lithuanian *kaisti* to get hot] (before 12th century) **1 a :** having a relatively high temperature **b :** capable of giving a sensation of heat or of burning, searing, or scalding **c :** having heat in a degree exceeding normal body heat **2 a :** VIOLENT, STORMY ⟨a *hot* temper⟩ ⟨a *hot* battle⟩; *also* **:** ANGRY ⟨got *hot* about the remark⟩ **b :** sexually excited or receptive; *also* **:** SEXY **c :** EAGER, ZEALOUS ⟨*hot* for reform⟩ **d** *of jazz* **:** emotionally exciting and marked by strong rhythms and free melodic improvisations **3 :** having or causing the sensation of an uncomfortable degree of body heat ⟨*hot* and tired⟩ ⟨it's *hot* in here⟩ **4 a :** newly made **:** FRESH ⟨a *hot* scent⟩ ⟨*hot* off the press⟩ **b :** close to something sought ⟨*hot* on the trail⟩ **5 a :** suggestive of heat or of burning or glowing objects ⟨*hot* colors⟩ **b :** PUNGENT, PEPPERY **6 a :** of intense and immediate interest ⟨some *hot* gossip⟩ **b :** unusually lucky or favorable ⟨on a *hot* streak⟩ **c :** temporarily capable of unusual performance (as in a sport) **d :** currently popular or in demand ⟨a *hot* commodity⟩ **e :** very good ⟨a *hot* idea⟩ ⟨not feeling too *hot*⟩ **f :** ABSURD, UNBELIEVABLE ⟨wants to fight the champ? that's a *hot* one⟩ **7 a :** electrically energized especially with high voltage **b :** RADIOACTIVE; *also* **:** dealing with radioactive material **c** *of an atom or molecule* **:** being in an excited state **8 a :** recently and illegally obtained ⟨*hot* jewels⟩ **b :** wanted by the police; *also* **:** unsafe for a fugitive **9 :** FAST ⟨a *hot* new fighter plane⟩ ⟨a *hot* lap around the track⟩ — **hot·ness** *noun* — **hot·tish** \'hä-tish\ *adjective* — **hot under the collar :** extremely exasperated or angry

²hot *adverb* (before 12th century) **1 :** HOTLY **2 :** FAST, QUICKLY

³hot *noun* (13th century) **1 :** HEAT 1d(1) ⟨the *hot* of the day⟩ **2 :** one that is hot (as a hot meal or a horse just after a workout) **3** *plural* **:** strong sexual desire — used with *the*

⁴hot *transitive verb* **hot·ted; hot·ting** (1561) *chiefly Southern, southern Midland, & British* **:** HEAT, WARM — usually used with *up*

hot air *noun* (1873) **:** empty talk

hot·bed \'hät-,bed\ *noun* (1626)

1 : a bed of soil enclosed in glass, heated especially by fermenting manure, and used for forcing or for raising seedlings
2 : an environment that favors rapid growth or development ⟨a *hotbed* of activity⟩
hot·blood \-,bləd\ *noun* (1798)
1 : one that is hot-blooded; *especially* **:** one having strong passions or a quick temper
2 : THOROUGHBRED 1
hot–blood·ed \-'blə-dəd\ *adjective* (1598)
1 : easily excited **:** PASSIONATE
2 *of a horse* **:** having Arab or Thoroughbred ancestors
— **hot–blood·ed·ness** *noun*
hot·box \-,bäks\ *noun* (1848)
: a journal bearing (as of a railroad car) overheated by friction
hot button *noun* (1975)
: an emotional and usually controversial issue or concern that triggers immediate intense reaction
— **hot–button** *adjective*
hot·cake \-,kāk\ *noun* (1683)
: PANCAKE
— **like hotcakes :** at a rapid rate ⟨selling *like hotcakes*⟩
hotch \'häch\ *intransitive verb* [Middle English, probably from Middle French *hocher* to shake, from Old French *hochier*] (15th century)
1 *Scottish* **:** WIGGLE, FIDGET
2 *chiefly Scottish* **:** SWARM
hotch·pot \'häch-,pät\ *noun* [Anglo-French *hochepot*, from Old French, hotchpotch] (1552)
: the combining of properties into a common lot to ensure equality of division among heirs
hotch·potch \'häch-,päch\ *noun* [Middle English *hochepot*, from Middle French, from Old French, from *hochier* to shake + *pot*] (1583)
1 a : a thick soup or stew of vegetables, potatoes, and usually meat **b :** HODGEPODGE
2 : HOTCHPOT
hot comb *noun* (1970)
: a metal comb usually electrically heated for straightening or styling the hair
— **hot–comb** *transitive verb*
hot corner *noun* (1903)
: the fielding position of the third baseman in baseball
hot·dog \'hät-,dȯg\ *intransitive verb* [²*hot dog*] (1962)
: to perform in a conspicuous or often ostentatious manner; *especially* **:** to perform fancy stunts and maneuvers (as while surfing or skiing)
— **hot·dog·ger** \-,dȯ-gər\ *noun*
¹**hot dog** \'hät-,dȯg\ *noun* (circa 1900)
1 : FRANKFURTER; *especially* **:** a frankfurter heated and served in a long split roll
2 [perhaps from ²*hot dog*] **:** one that hotdogs; *also* **:** SHOW-OFF
²**hot dog** \'hät-,dȯg\ *interjection* (circa 1906)
— used to express approval or gratification
ho·tel \hō-'tel, 'hō-,\ *noun* [French *hôtel,* from Old French *hostel* hostel] (1765)
: an establishment that provides lodging and usually meals, entertainment, and various personal services for the public **:** INN
— **ho·tel·dom** \-dəm\ *noun*
Hotel (1952)
— a communications code word for the letter *h*
ho·te·lier \hō-'tel-yər; ,ō-t²l-'yā, ,ȯ-\ *noun* [French *hôtelier,* from Old French *hostelier,* from *hostel*] (1905)
: a proprietor or manager of a hotel
ho·tel·man \hō-'tel-,man, -mən\ *noun* (1920)
: one who is engaged in the hotel business especially in a supervisory or managerial capacity
hot flash *noun* (1910)
: a sudden brief flushing and sensation of heat caused by dilation of skin capillaries usually associated with menopausal endocrine imbalance — called also *hot flush*

¹**hot·foot** \'hät-,fu̇t\ *adverb* (14th century)
: in haste
²**hotfoot** *intransitive verb* (1896)
: to go hotfoot **:** HURRY — usually used with *it*
³**hotfoot** *noun, plural* **hotfoots** (1934)
: a practical joke in which a match is surreptitiously inserted between the upper and the sole of a victim's shoe and lighted
hot·head \'hät-,hed\ *noun* (1660)
: a hotheaded person
hot·head·ed \-'he-dəd\ *adjective* (1641)
: FIERY, IMPETUOUS
— **hot·head·ed·ly** *adverb*
— **hot·head·ed·ness** *noun*
¹**hot·house** \-,hau̇s\ *noun* (1511)
1 *obsolete* **:** BORDELLO
2 : a greenhouse maintained at a high temperature especially for the culture of tropical plants
3 : HOTBED 2
²**hothouse** *adjective* (1838)
1 : grown in a hothouse
2 : suggestive of growth and development in a hothouse ⟨a *hothouse* existence⟩; *also* **:** suggesting a hothouse ⟨a *hothouse* atmosphere⟩
hot line *noun* (1955)
1 : a direct telephone line in constant operational readiness so as to facilitate immediate communication
2 : a usually toll-free telephone service available to the public for some specific purpose ⟨a consumer *hot line*⟩
hot·ly \'hät-lē\ *adverb* (15th century)
: in a hot manner ⟨a *hotly* contested series⟩
hot–melt \'hät-,melt\ *noun* (1939)
: a fast-drying nonvolatile adhesive applied hot in the molten state
hot metal *noun* (1960)
: composition in which the type is cast from molten metal
hot money *noun* (1936)
: investment funds intended for the highest short-term rate of return
hot pepper *noun* (1945)
: any of various small and usually thin-walled capsicum fruits of marked pungency; *also* **:** a plant bearing hot peppers
hot plate *noun* (1845)
1 : a heated iron plate for cooking
2 : a simple portable appliance for heating or for cooking in limited spaces
hot pot *noun* (1851)
1 : a stew of meat and vegetables
2 : FIREPOT 2
hot potato *noun* (1846)
: a controversial question or issue that involves unpleasant or dangerous consequences for anyone dealing with it
hot pursuit *noun* (circa 1922)
: close continuous pursuit of a fleeing suspected lawbreaker or hostile military force especially across territorial lines
hot rod *noun* (1945)
: an automobile rebuilt or modified for high speed and fast acceleration
— **hot–rod** \'hät-'räd\ *verb*
— **hot–rod·der** \'hät-,rä-dər\ *noun*
hot seat *noun* (1925)
1 *slang* **:** ELECTRIC CHAIR
2 : a position of uneasiness, embarrassment, or anxiety
hot·shot \'hät-,shät\ *noun, often attributive* (circa 1925)
1 : a fast freight
2 : a person who is conspicuously talented or successful
hot spot *noun* (1929)
1 : a place of more than usual interest, activity, or action
2 : a place in the upper mantle of the earth at which hot magma from the lower mantle upwells to melt through the crust usually in the interior of a tectonic plate to form a volcanic feature; *also* **:** a place in the crust overlying a hot spot

hot spring *noun* (1669)
: a spring whose water issues at a temperature higher than that of its surroundings
hot stuff *noun* (1889)
: someone or something unusually good
Hot·ten·tot \'hä-t²n-,tät\ *noun* [Afrikaans] (1677)
1 : a member of any of a group of Khoisan-speaking pastoral peoples of southern Africa
2 : the group of Khoisan languages spoken by the Hottentots
hot ticket *noun* (1972)
: someone or something very popular **:** RAGE
hot tub *noun* (1975)
: a large usually wooden tub of hot water in which bathers soak and usually socialize
hot up (1878)
intransitive verb
chiefly British **:** to increase in intensity, pace, or excitement ⟨air raids began to *hot up* about the beginning of February —George Orwell⟩
transitive verb
chiefly British **:** to make livelier, speedier, or more intense
hot war *noun* (1947)
: a conflict involving actual fighting — compare COLD WAR
hot water *noun* (1537)
: TROUBLE 4, DIFFICULTY ⟨was in *hot water* with the authorities⟩
hot–wire \'hät-,wī(-ə)r\ *transitive verb* (1954)
: to start (as an automobile) by short-circuiting the ignition system
¹**hound** \'hau̇nd\ *noun* [Middle English, from Old English *hund;* akin to Old High German *hunt* dog, Latin *canis,* Greek *kyōn*] (before 12th century)
1 a : DOG **b :** a dog of any of various hunting breeds typically having large drooping ears and a deep voice and following their prey by scent
2 : a mean or despicable person
3 : DOGFISH
4 : a person who pursues like a hound; *especially* **:** one who avidly seeks or collects something ⟨autograph *hounds*⟩
²**hound** *transitive verb* (1528)
1 : to pursue with or as if with hounds
2 : to drive or affect by persistent harassing
synonym SEE BAIT
— **hound·er** *noun*
hounds \'hau̇n(d)z\ *noun plural* [Middle English *houne,* from Old Norse *hūnn* knob at the top of a masthead] (15th century)
: the framing at the masthead of a ship that supports the heel of the topmast and the upper parts of the lower rigging
hound's–tongue \'hau̇n(d)z-,təŋ\ *noun* (before 12th century)
: any of various coarse plants (genus *Cynoglossum,* especially *C. officinale*) of the borage family having tongue-shaped leaves and reddish flowers
hounds·tooth check *or* **hound's–tooth check** \'hau̇n(d)z-,tüth-\ *noun* (1937)
: a usually small broken-check textile pattern
hour \'au̇(-ə)r\ *noun* [Middle English, from Old French *heure,* from Late Latin & Latin; Late Latin *hora* canonical hour, from Latin, hour of the day, from Greek *hōra* — more at YEAR] (13th century)
1 : a time or office for daily liturgical devotion; *especially* **:** CANONICAL HOUR
2 : the 24th part of a day **:** 60 minutes

houndstooth check

3 a : the time of day reckoned in two 12-hour periods **b** *plural* **:** the time reckoned in one 24-hour period from midnight to midnight using a 4-digit number of which the first two digits indicate the hour and the last two digits indicate the minute ⟨in the military 4:30 p.m. is called 1630 *hours*⟩
4 a : a customary or particular time ⟨lunch *hour*⟩ ⟨in our *hour* of need⟩ **b** *plural* **:** time of going to bed ⟨keeps late *hours*⟩; *also* **:** time of working ⟨banker's *hours*⟩
5 : an angular unit of right ascension equal to 15 degrees measured along the celestial equator
6 : the work done or distance traveled at normal rate in an hour ⟨the city was two *hours* away⟩
7 a : a class session **b :** CREDIT HOUR, SEMESTER HOUR
— **after hours :** after the regular quitting or closing time

hour angle *noun* (circa 1837)
: the angle between the celestial meridian of an observer and the hour circle of a celestial object measured westward from the meridian

hour circle *noun* (1690)
: a circle on the celestial sphere that passes through both celestial poles

¹**hour·glass** \'aù(-ə)r-,glas\ *noun* (circa 1515)
: an instrument for measuring time consisting of a glass vessel having two compartments from the uppermost of which a quantity of sand, water, or mercury runs in an hour into the lower one

²**hourglass** *adjective* (circa 1834)
: shaped like an hourglass ⟨an *hourglass* figure⟩

hour hand *noun* (1669)
: the short hand that marks the hours on the face of a watch or clock

hou·ri \'hùr-ē, 'hü-rē\ *noun* [French, from Persian *hūri*, from Arabic *hūrīyah*] (1737)
1 : one of the beautiful maidens that in Muslim belief live with the blessed in paradise
2 : a voluptuously beautiful young woman

hour-long \'aù(-ə)r-'lòṅ\ *adjective* (1803)
: lasting an hour

¹**hour·ly** \'aù(-ə)r-lē\ *adverb* (15th century)
: at or during every hour; *also* **:** FREQUENTLY, CONTINUALLY

²**hourly** *adjective* (circa 1530)
1 a : occurring hour by hour ⟨*hourly* bus service⟩ **b :** FREQUENT, CONTINUAL ⟨in *hourly* expectation of the rain's stopping⟩
2 : computed in terms of an hour ⟨an *hourly* wage⟩
3 : paid by the hour ⟨*hourly* workers⟩

¹**house** \'haùs\ *noun, plural* **hous·es** \'haù-zəz *also* -səz\ *often attributive* [Middle English *hous*, from Old English *hūs*; akin to Old High German *hūs* house] (before 12th century)
1 : a building that serves as living quarters for one or a few families **:** HOME
2 a : (1) **:** a shelter or refuge (as a nest or den) of a wild animal (2) **:** a natural covering (as a test or shell) that encloses and protects an animal or a colony of zooids **b :** a building in which something is housed ⟨a carriage *house*⟩
3 a : one of the 12 equal sectors in which the celestial sphere is divided in astrology **b :** a zodiacal sign that is the seat of a planet's greatest influence
4 a : HOUSEHOLD **b :** a family including ancestors, descendants, and kindred ⟨the *house* of Tudor⟩
5 a : a residence for a religious community or for students **b :** the community or students in residence
6 a : a legislative, deliberative, or consultative assembly; *especially* **:** one constituting a divi-sion of a bicameral body **b :** the building or chamber where such an assembly meets **c :** a quorum of such an assembly
7 a : a place of business or entertainment **b** (1) **:** a business organization ⟨a publishing *house*⟩ (2) **:** a gambling establishment **c :** the audience in a theater or concert hall ⟨a full *house* on opening night⟩
8 : the circular area 12 feet in diameter surrounding the tee and within which a curling stone must rest in order to count
9 : a type of dance music mixed by a disc jockey that features overdubbing with a heavy repetitive drumbeat and repeated electronic melody lines
— **house·ful** \'haùs-,fùl\ *noun*
— **house·less** \'haù-sləs\ *adjective*
— **house·less·ness** *noun*
— **on the house :** without charge **:** FREE

²**house** \'haùz\ *verb* **housed; hous·ing** (before 12th century)
transitive verb
1 a : to provide with living quarters or shelter **b :** to store in a house
2 : to encase, enclose, or shelter as if by putting in a house
3 : to serve as shelter for **:** CONTAIN
intransitive verb
: to take shelter **:** LODGE

house arrest *noun* (1936)
: confinement often under guard to one's house or quarters instead of in prison

house·boat \'haùs-,bōt\ *noun* (1790)
: a boat fitted for use as a dwelling; *especially* **:** a pleasure craft with a broad beam, a usually shallow draft, and a large superstructure resembling a house
— **house·boat·er** \-,bō-tər\ *noun*

house·bound \'haùs-,baùnd\ *adjective* (1878)
: confined to the house

house·boy \-,bói\ *noun* (circa 1898)
: HOUSEMAN

house·break \-,brāk\ *transitive verb* **-broke** \-,brōk\; **-bro·ken** \-,brō-kən\; **-break·ing** [back-formation from *housebroken*] (1944)
1 : to make housebroken
2 a : to teach acceptable social manners to **b :** TAME, SUBDUE

house·break·ing \'haùs-,brā-kiṅ\ *noun* (1617)
: an act of breaking open and entering the dwelling house of another with a felonious purpose
— **house·break·er** \-,brā-kər\ *noun*

house·bro·ken \-,brō-kən\ *adjective* (1900)
1 : trained to excretory habits acceptable in indoor living — used of a household pet
2 : made tractable or polite

house call *noun* (1960)
: a visit (as by a doctor or a repair person) to a home to provide a requested service

house·carl \-,kär(-ə)l\ *noun* [Old English *hūscarl*, from Old Norse *hūskarl*, from *hūs* house + *karl* man; akin to Old English *ceorl* churl] (before 12th century)
: a member of the bodyguard of a Danish or early English king or noble

house cat *noun* (1607)
: CAT 1a

house·clean \'haùs-,klēn\ *verb* [back-formation from *housecleaning*] (1863)
intransitive verb
1 : to clean a house and its furniture
2 : to get rid of unwanted or undesirable items or people
transitive verb
1 : to clean the surfaces and furnishings of a house
2 : to improve or reform by ridding of undesirable people or practices
— **house·clean·ing** *noun*

house·coat \-,kōt\ *noun* (1913)
: a woman's often long-skirted informal garment for wear around the house

house cricket *noun* (1774)
: a widely distributed cricket (*Acheta domesticus*) usually living in or about dwellings

house detective *noun* (1898)
: a person who is employed (as by a hotel) to prevent disorderly or improper conduct of patrons

house·dress \'haùs-,dres\ *noun* (1897)
: a dress with simple lines that is suitable for housework and is made usually of a washable fabric

house·fa·ther \-,fä-thər, -,fä-\ *noun* (1901)
: a man in charge of a dormitory, hall, or hostel

house finch *noun* (1869)
: a small finch (*Carpodacus mexicanus*) that has a male with a red head, breast, and rump and that is native to Mexico and the western U.S. and has been introduced in the eastern U.S.

house·fly \'haùs-,flī\ *noun* (15th century)
: a cosmopolitan dipteran fly (*Musca domestica*) that is often about human habitations and may act as a mechanical vector of diseases (as typhoid fever); *also* **:** any of various flies of similar appearance or habitat

house·front \-,frənt\ *noun* (1838)
: the facade of a house

house girl *noun* (1835)
: HOUSEMAID

house·guest \'haùs-,gest\ *noun* (1917)
: GUEST 1a

¹**house·hold** \'haùs-,hōld, 'haù-,sōld\ *noun* (14th century)
: those who dwell under the same roof and compose a family; *also* **:** a social unit comprised of those living together in the same dwelling

²**household** *adjective* (14th century)
1 : of or relating to a household **:** DOMESTIC ⟨cooking and other *household* arts⟩
2 : FAMILIAR, COMMON ⟨a *household* name⟩

house·hold·er \'haùs-,hōl-dər, 'haù-,sōl-\ *noun* (14th century)
: a person who occupies a house or tenement alone or as the head of a household

household troops *noun plural* (1711)
: troops appointed to attend and guard a sovereign or the residence of a sovereign

house·hus·band \'haùs-,həz-bənd\ *noun* (1955)
: a husband who does housekeeping usually while his wife earns the family income

house·keep \'haùs-,kēp\ *intransitive verb* **-kept** \-,kept\; **-keep·ing** [back-formation from *housekeeper*] (1842)
: to perform the routine duties (as cooking and cleaning) of managing a house

house·keep·er \-,kē-pər\ *noun* (1607)
1 : a woman employed to keep house
2 : HOUSEWIFE 1

house·keep·ing \-piṅ\ *noun* (1550)
1 : the management of a house and home affairs
2 : the care and management of property and the provision of equipment and services (as for an industrial organization)
3 : the routine tasks that must be done in order for a system to function or to function efficiently

¹**hou·sel** \'haù-zəl\ *noun* [Middle English, from Old English *hūsel* sacrifice, Eucharist; akin to Gothic *hunsl* sacrifice] (before 12th century)
archaic **:** the Eucharist or the act of administering or receiving it

²**housel** *transitive verb* (before 12th century)
archaic **:** to administer communion to

house·leek \'haùs-,lēk\ *noun* (14th century)
: a pink-flowered thick-leaved European plant (*Sempervivum tectorum*) of the orpine family that tends to form clusters of rosettes and is often grown in rock gardens; *broadly* **:** SEMPERVIVUM

house·lights \'haùs-,līts\ *noun plural* (1920)
: the lights that illuminate the auditorium of a theater

house·maid \'haùs-,mād\ *noun* (circa 1694)
: a female servant employed to do housework

hourglass

housemaid's knee *noun* [so called from its occurrence among women who work a great deal on their knees] (1831)
: a swelling over the knee due to an enlargement of the bursa in the front of the patella

house·man \'haùs-mən, -ˌman\ *noun* (1920)
: a person who performs general work about a house or hotel

house·mas·ter \-ˌmas-tər\ *noun* (1884)
: a master in charge of a house in a boy's boarding school

house·mate \'haùs-ˌmāt\ *noun* (circa 1810)
: a person who lives in the same house with another

house·moth·er \'haùs-ˌmə-thər\ *noun* (1882)
: a woman acting as hostess, chaperon, and often housekeeper in a group residence

house mouse *noun* (1835)
: a common nearly cosmopolitan grayish-brown mouse (*Mus musculus*) that usually lives and breeds about buildings, may act as a vector of diseases, and is an important laboratory animal

house of assembly (1653)
: a legislative body or the lower house of a legislature (as in various British colonies, protectorates, and countries of the Commonwealth)

House of Burgesses (1658)
: the colonial representative assembly of Virginia

house of cards (1903)
: a structure, situation, or institution that is insubstantial, shaky, or in constant danger of collapse

House of Commons (1621)
: the lower house of the British and Canadian parliaments

house of correction (circa 1576)
: an institution where persons who have committed a minor offense and are considered capable of reformation are confined

house of delegates (1783)
: HOUSE 6a; *especially* : the lower house of the state legislature in Maryland, Virginia, and West Virginia

House of Lords (1818)
: the upper house of the British Parliament composed of the lords temporal and spiritual

house of representatives (1716)
: the lower house of a legislative body (as the U.S. Congress)

house of studies (1929)
: an educational institution serving scholars of a religious order — called also *house of study*

house organ *noun* (1907)
: a periodical distributed by a business concern among its employees, sales personnel, or customers

house·paint·er \'haùs-ˌpān-tər\ *noun* (1689)
: one whose business or occupation is painting houses

house·par·ent \-ˌpar-ənt, -ˌper-\ *noun*
: an adult in charge of a dormitory, hall, hostel, or group residence

house party *noun* (1876)
: a party lasting over one or more nights at a residence (as a home or fraternity house)

house·per·son \'haùs-ˌpər-sⁿn\ *noun* (1974)
: a person who does housekeeping

house·plant \'haùs-ˌplant\ *noun* (1871)
: a plant grown or kept indoors

house-proud \'haùs-ˌpraùd\ *adjective* (1849)
chiefly British : proud of one's house or housekeeping

hous·er \'haù-zər\ *noun* (1940)
: one that promotes or administers housing projects

house-rais·ing \'haùs-ˌrā-zin\ *noun* (1704)
: the joint erection of a house or its framework by a gathering of neighbors

house·room \-ˌrüm, -ˌrùm\ *noun* (1582)
: space for accommodation in or as if in a house ⟨given *houseroom* by a family all too eager to have a celebrity in their midst —Walter Kerr⟩

house rule *noun* (1947)
: a rule (as in a game) that applies only among a certain group or in a certain place

house seat *noun* (1948)
: a theater seat reserved by the management for a special guest

house sitter *noun* (1971)
: a person who occupies a dwelling to provide security and maintenance while the tenant is away
— **house-sit** \'haù(s)-ˌsit\ *intransitive verb*
— **house-sit·ting** \-ˌsi-tin\ *noun*

house sparrow *noun* (1674)
: a sparrow (*Passer domesticus*) native to Eurasia that has been introduced worldwide and is found especially in urban and agricultural areas — called also *English sparrow*

house–to–house \ˌhaùs-tə-'haùs\ *adjective* (1859)
: going or done by going from one building to the next ⟨*house-to-house* fighting⟩

house·top \'haùs-ˌtäp\ *noun* (1526)
: ROOF; *especially* : the level surface of a flat roof
— **from the housetops** : for all to hear : OPENLY ⟨shouting their grievances *from the housetops*⟩

house trailer *noun* (1937)
: MOBILE HOME

house–train \'haùs-ˌtrān\ *transitive verb* (1924)
chiefly British : HOUSEBREAK

house·wares \'haùs-ˌwarz, -ˌwerz\ *noun plural* (1921)
: furnishings for a house; *especially* : small articles of household equipment (as cooking utensils or small appliances)

house·warm·ing \'haùs-ˌwòr-min\ *noun* (1577)
: a party to celebrate the taking possession of a house or premises

house·wife \'haùs-ˌwīf; *especially 2 & in early poetry* 'hə-zəf *or* -səf\ *noun, plural* **house·wives** \'haùs-ˌwīvz *also* 'haùz-ˌwīvz; 'hə-zəfs, -zəvz, -səfs, -səvz\ (13th century)
1 : a married woman in charge of a household
2 : a pocket-size container for small articles (as thread)
— **house·wife·li·ness** \-lē-nəs\ *noun*
— **house·wife·ly** \-lē\ *adjective*
— **house·wif·ery** \-ˌwī-f(ə-)rē; *British* -(ˌ)wi-f(ə-)rē *also* 'hə-zə-frē\ *noun*
— **house·wif·ey** \'haùs-ˌwī-fē\ *adjective*

house·work \'haùs-ˌwərk\ *noun* (1841)
: the work of housekeeping

¹hous·ing \'haù-zin\ *noun* (14th century)
1 a : SHELTER, LODGING **b** : dwellings provided for people
2 a : a niche for a sculpture **b** : the space taken out of a structural member (as a timber) to admit the insertion of part of another
3 : something that covers or protects: as **a** : a case or enclosure (as for a mechanical part or an instrument) **b** : a casing (as an enclosed bearing) in which a shaft revolves **c** : a support (as a frame) for mechanical parts

²housing *noun* [Middle English, from *house* housing (from Middle French *houce*, of Germanic origin) + *-ing*; akin to Middle High German *hulft* covering] (15th century)
: CAPARISON 1

housing development *noun* (1951)
: a group of individual dwellings or apartment houses typically of similar design that are usually built and sold or leased by one management

housing estate *noun* (1920)
British : HOUSING DEVELOPMENT

housing project *noun* (circa 1937)
: a publicly supported and administered housing development planned usually for low-income families

Hou·yhn·hnm \'hwi-nəm, hü-'i-nəm\ *noun*
: a member of a race of horses endowed with reason in Swift's *Gulliver's Travels*

hove *past and past participle of* HEAVE

hov·el \'hə-vəl, 'hä-\ *noun* [Middle English] (15th century)
1 : an open shed or shelter
2 : TABERNACLE
3 : a small, wretched, and often dirty house : HUT

hov·er \'hə-vər, 'hä-\ *intransitive verb* **hov·ered; hov·er·ing** \-v(ə-)rin\ [Middle English *hoveren*, frequentative of *hoven* to hover] (15th century)
1 a : to hang fluttering in the air or on the wing **b** : to remain suspended over a place or object
2 a : to move to and fro near a place : fluctuate around a given point ⟨unemployment *hovered* around 10%⟩ **b** : to be in a state of uncertainty, irresolution, or suspense
— **hover** *noun*
— **hov·er·er** \-vər-ər\ *noun*

hov·er·craft \-vər-ˌkraft\ *noun* (1959)
: a vehicle that is supported above the surface of land or water by a cushion of air produced by downwardly directed fans

¹how \'haù\ *adverb* [Middle English, from Old English *hū*; akin to Old High German *hwuo* how, Old English *hwā* who — more at WHO] (before 12th century)
1 a : in what manner or way **b** : for what reason : WHY **c** : with what meaning : to what effect **d** : by what name or title ⟨*how* art thou called —Shakespeare⟩
2 : to what degree or extent
3 : in what state or condition ⟨*how* are you⟩
4 : at what price ⟨*how* a score of ewes now —Shakespeare⟩ □
— **how about** : what do you say to or think of ⟨*how about* it, are you going?⟩
— **how come** : how does it happen that : WHY

²how *conjunction* (before 12th century)
1 a : the way or manner in which ⟨remember *how* they fought⟩; *also* : the state or condition in which **b** : THAT ⟨told them *how* he had a situation —Charles Dickens⟩
2 : HOWEVER, AS ⟨a reader can shift his attention *how* he likes —William Empson⟩

³how \'haù\ *noun* (1533)
1 : a question about manner or method
2 : MANNER, METHOD

¹how·be·it \haù-'bē-ət\ *conjunction* (14th century)
: ALTHOUGH

²howbeit *adverb* (15th century)
: NEVERTHELESS

□ USAGE

how *How come* is a familiar phrase of obscure origin that first came to attention as an Americanism in the 19th century. It seems to scare writers on usage: most of them treat it as a highly informal or even slangy speech form and warn against its use in writing. But it is precisely in writing that the phrase surprises us—it is gaining improved status in print. It now appears commonly in the general prose of good writers ⟨if the car was going that fast, *how come* it wasn't more seriously damaged? —Calvin Trillin⟩ ⟨*how come* I never hear those sounds in the daytime? —Andy Rooney⟩ ⟨that's *how come* she knows about food —Harold Brodkey⟩ ⟨*The Tempest* begins with exactly the same *dramatis personae* as the *Mabinogi* *How come?* —Robert Graves⟩. This sort of use began about the end of World War II. The phrase is still not used in highly elevated prose.

\ə\ **abut** \ᵊ\ **kitten** \ər\ **further** \a\ **ash** \ā\ **ace**
\ä\ **mop, mar** \aù\ **out** \ch\ **chin** \e\ **bet** \ē\ **easy**
\g\ **go** \i\ **hit** \ī\ **ice** \j\ **job** \n\ **sing** \ō\ **go**
\ò\ **law** \òi\ **boy** \th\ **thin** \th\ **the** \ü\ **loot** \ù\ **foot**
\y\ **yet** \zh\ **vision** *see also* Guide to Pronunciation

how·dah \ˈhau̇-də\ *noun* [Hindi *hauda,* from Arabic *hawdaj*] (1774)
: a seat or covered pavilion on the back of an elephant or camel

how·dy \ˈhau̇-dē\ *interjection* [alteration of *how do ye*] (1712)
— used to express greeting
— **howdy** *verb*

howe \ˈhau̇, ˈhō\ *noun* [Middle English (northern) *holl* hollow place, from Old English *hol,* from *hol,* adjective, hollow — more at HOLE] (before 12th century)
Scottish : HOLLOW, VALLEY

¹**how·ev·er** \hau̇-ˈe-vər\ *conjunction* (14th century)
1 : in whatever manner or way ⟨will help *however* I can⟩
2 *archaic* : ALTHOUGH

²**however** *adverb* (14th century)
1 a : in whatever manner or way ⟨shall serve you, sir, truly, *however* else —Shakespeare⟩ **b** : to whatever degree or extent ⟨has done this for *however* many thousands of years —Emma Hawkridge⟩
2 : in spite of that : on the other hand ⟨still seems possible, *however,* that conditions will improve⟩ ⟨would like to go; *however,* I think I'd better not⟩
3 : how in the world ⟨*however* did you manage to do it⟩

howff *or* **howf** \ˈhau̇f, ˈhōf\ *noun* [Dutch *hof* enclosure; akin to Old English *hof* enclosure, and perhaps to *hufil* hill] (1711)
Scottish : HAUNT, RESORT

how·it·zer \ˈhau̇-ət-sər\ *noun* [Dutch *houwitser,* ultimately from Czech *houfnice ballista*] (1695)
: a short cannon used to fire projectiles at medium muzzle velocities and with relatively high trajectories

howl \ˈhau̇(ə)l\ *verb* [Middle English *houlen;* akin to Middle High German *hiulen* to howl] (14th century)
intransitive verb
1 : to emit a loud sustained doleful sound characteristic of members of the dog family
2 : to cry out loudly and without restraint under strong impulse (as pain, grief, or amusement)
3 : to go on a spree or rampage
transitive verb
1 : to utter with unrestrained outcry
2 : to drown out or cause to fail by adverse outcry — used especially with *down* ⟨howled down the speaker⟩
— **howl** *noun*

howl·er \ˈhau̇-lər\ *noun* (1800)
1 a : one that howls **b** : HOWLER MONKEY
2 : a humorous and ridiculous blunder

howler monkey *noun* (1932)
: any of a genus (*Alouatta*) of South and Central American monkeys that have a long prehensile tail and enlargement of the hyoid and laryngeal apparatus enabling them to make loud howling noises

howler monkey

howl·ing \ˈhau̇-liŋ\ *adjective* (1599)
1 : producing or marked by a sound resembling a sustained howl ⟨a *howling* storm⟩
2 : DESOLATE, WILD ⟨a *howling* wilderness⟩
3 : very great : PRONOUNCED ⟨a *howling* success⟩
— **howl·ing·ly** *adverb*

how·so·ev·er \ˌhau̇-sə-ˈwe-vər\ *adverb* (14th century)
1 : in whatever manner
2 : to whatever degree or extent

¹**how-to** \ˈhau̇-ˈtü\ *adjective* (1926)
: giving practical instruction and advice (as on a craft) ⟨*how-to* books on all sorts of hobbies —Harry Milt⟩

²**how-to** *noun* (1954)
: a practical method or instruction ⟨the *how-tos* of balancing a checkbook⟩

¹**hoy** \ˈhȯi\ *interjection* [Middle English] (14th century)
— used in attracting attention or in driving animals

²**hoy** *noun* [Middle English, from Middle Dutch *hoei*] (15th century)
1 : a small usually sloop-rigged coasting ship
2 : a heavy barge for bulky cargo

hoya \ˈhȯi-(y)ə\ *noun* [New Latin, from Thomas *Hoy* (died 1821) English gardener] (1851)
: any of a genus (*Hoya*) of climbing Asian and Australian evergreen shrubs of the milkweed family

hoy·den \ˈhȯi-dᵊn\ *noun* [perhaps from obsolete Dutch *heiden* country lout, from Middle Dutch, heathen; akin to Old English *hǣthen* heathen] (1676)
: a girl or woman of saucy, boisterous, or carefree behavior
— **hoy·den·ish** \-ish\ *adjective*

hoyle \ˈhȯi(ə)l\ *noun, often capitalized* [Edmond *Hoyle* (died 1769) English writer on games] (1906)
: an encyclopedia of the rules of indoor games and especially card games

Hsia \shē-ˈä\ *noun* [Chinese (Beijing) *Xià*] (circa 1909)
: the legendary first dynasty of Chinese history traditionally dated from about 2200–1766 B.C.

HTLV \ˌāch-(ˌ)tē-(ˌ)el-ˈvē\ *noun* [*human T-cell lymphotropic virus*] (1980)
: any of several retroviruses — often used with a number or Roman numeral to indicate type

HTLV–III \-(ˌ)vē-ˈthrē\ *noun* (1984)
: HIV-1

hua·ra·che \wə-ˈrä-chē, hə-\ *noun* [Mexican Spanish, from Tarascan *kʷaṛáči*] (1892)
: a low-heeled sandal having an upper made of interwoven leather strips

hub \ˈhəb\ *noun* [probably alteration of ²*hob*] (1649)
1 : the central part of a circular object (as a wheel or propeller)
2 a : a center of activity : FOCAL POINT **b** : an airport or city through which an airline routes most of its traffic
3 : a steel punch from which a working die for a coin or medal is made

hub-and-spoke *adjective* (1980)
: being or relating to a system of routing air traffic in which a major airport serves as a central point for coordinating flights to and from other airports

Hub·bard squash \ˈhə-bərd-\ *noun* [probably from the name *Hubbard*] (1868)
: any of various often large variably green winter squashes — called also *Hubbard*

hub·ble-bub·ble \ˈhə-bəl-ˌbə-bəl\ *noun* [reduplication of *bubble*] (1634)
1 : WATER PIPE 2
2 : a flurry of sound or activity : COMMOTION

hub·bub \ˈhə-ˌbəb\ *noun* [perhaps of Irish origin; akin to Scottish Gaelic *ub ub,* interjection of contempt] (1555)
1 : NOISE, UPROAR
2 : CONFUSION, TURMOIL

hub·by \ˈhə-bē\ *noun, plural* **hubbies** [by alteration] (1688)
: HUSBAND

hub·cap \ˈhəb-ˌkap\ *noun* (1903)
: a removable usually metal cap over the end of an axle; *especially* : one used on the wheel of a motor vehicle

hu·bris \ˈhyü-brəs\ *noun* [Greek *hybris*] (1884)
: exaggerated pride or self-confidence

— **hu·bris·tic** \hyü-ˈbris-tik\ *adjective*

huck \ˈhək\ *noun* (1851)
: HUCKABACK

huck·a·back \ˈhə-kə-ˌbak\ *noun* [origin unknown] (1690)
: an absorbent durable fabric of cotton, linen, or both used chiefly for towels

huck·le·ber·ry \ˈhə-kəl-ˌber-ē\ *noun* [perhaps alteration of *hurtleberry* (huckleberry)] (1670)
1 : any of a genus (*Gaylussacia*) of American shrubs of the heath family; *also* : the edible dark blue to black usually acid berry (especially of *G. baccata*) with 10 nutlets
2 : BLUEBERRY

¹**huck·ster** \ˈhək-stər\ *noun* [Middle English *hukster,* from Middle Dutch *hokester,* from *hoeken* to peddle] (13th century)
1 : HAWKER, PEDDLER
2 : one who produces promotional material for commercial clients especially for radio or television
— **huck·ster·ism** \-stə-ˌri-zəm\ *noun*

²**huckster** *verb* **huck·stered; huck·ster·ing** \-st(ə-)riŋ\ (1592)
intransitive verb
: HAGGLE
transitive verb
1 : to deal in or bargain over
2 : to promote by showmanship

¹**hud·dle** \ˈhə-dᵊl\ *verb* **hud·dled; hud·dling** \ˈhəd-liŋ, ˈhə-dᵊl-iŋ\ [probably from or akin to Middle English *hoderen* to huddle] (1579)
transitive verb
1 *British* : to arrange carelessly or hurriedly
2 a : to crowd together **b** : to draw (oneself) together : CROUCH
3 : to wrap closely in (as clothes)
intransitive verb
1 a : to gather in a close-packed group **b** : to curl up : CROUCH
2 a : to hold a consultation **b** : to gather in a huddle in football
— **hud·dler** \ˈhəd-lər, ˈhə-dᵊl-ər\ *noun*

²**huddle** *noun* (1586)
1 : a close-packed group : BUNCH ⟨*huddles* of children⟩ ⟨a *huddle* of cottages⟩
2 a : MEETING, CONFERENCE ⟨secret *huddles* were held by five leading Republicans —*Newsweek*⟩ **b** : a brief gathering of football players away from the line of scrimmage to receive instructions (as from the quarterback) for the next down

Hu·di·bras·tic \ˌhyü-də-ˈbras-tik\ *adjective* [irregular from *Hudibras,* satirical poem by Samuel Butler (died 1680)] (1712)
1 : written in humorous octosyllabic couplets
2 : MOCK-HEROIC
— **Hudibrastic** *noun*

hue \ˈhyü\ *noun* [Middle English *hewe,* from Old English *hīw;* akin to Old Norse *hȳ* plant down, Gothic *hiwi* form] (before 12th century)
1 : COMPLEXION, ASPECT ⟨political parties of every *hue* —Louis Wasserman⟩
2 a : COLOR **b** : gradation of color **c** : the attribute of colors that permits them to be classed as red, yellow, green, blue, or an intermediate between any contiguous pair of these colors — compare BRIGHTNESS 2, LIGHTNESS 2, SATURATION 4

hue and cry *noun* [*hue* (outcry)] (15th century)
1 a : a loud outcry formerly used in the pursuit of one who is suspected of a crime **b** : the pursuit of a suspect or a written proclamation for the capture of a suspect
2 : a clamor of alarm or protest
3 : HUBBUB

hued \ˈhyüd\ *adjective* (before 12th century)
: COLORED — usually used in combination ⟨green-*hued*⟩

¹**huff** \ˈhəf\ *verb* [imitative] (1583)
intransitive verb
1 : to emit puffs (as of breath or steam)

2 a : to make empty threats **:** BLUSTER **b :** to react or behave indignantly 〈*huffed* off in anger〉
transitive verb
1 : to puff up **:** INFLATE
2 *archaic* **:** to treat with contempt **:** BULLY
3 : to make angry
4 : to utter with indignation or scorn
²huff *noun* (1599)
: a usually peevish and transitory spell of anger or resentment 〈quit in a *huff*〉
synonym see OFFENSE
huff·ish \ˈhə-fish\ *adjective* (circa 1755)
: ARROGANT, SULKY
huffy \ˈhə-fē\ *adjective* **huff·i·er; -est** (1677)
1 : HAUGHTY, ARROGANT
2 a : roused to indignation **:** IRRITATED **b :** easily offended **:** TOUCHY
— **huff·i·ly** \ˈhə-fə-lē\ *adverb*
— **huff·i·ness** \-fē-nəs\ *noun*
hug \ˈhəg\ *transitive verb* **hugged; hug·ging** [perhaps of Scandinavian origin; akin to Old Norse *hugga* to soothe] (1567)
1 : to press tightly especially in the arms
2 a : CONGRATULATE **b :** to hold fast **:** CHERISH 〈*hugged* his miseries like a sulky child —John Buchan〉
3 : to stay close to 〈the road *hugs* the river〉
— **hug** *noun*
— **hug·ga·ble** \ˈhə-gə-bəl\ *adjective*
huge \ˈhyüj, ˈyüj\ *adjective* **hug·er; hug·est** [Middle English, from Old French *ahuge*] (12th century)
: very large or extensive: as **a :** of great size or area **b :** great in scale or degree 〈a *huge* deficit〉 **c :** great in scope or character 〈a man of *huge* talent〉
synonym see ENORMOUS
— **huge·ly** *adverb*
— **huge·ness** *noun*
huge·ous \ˈhyü-jəs, ˈyü-\ *adjective* (1519)
: HUGE
— **huge·ous·ly** *adverb*
¹hug·ger–mug·ger \ˈhə-gər-ˌmə-gər\ *noun* [origin unknown] (1529)
1 : SECRECY
2 : CONFUSION, MUDDLE
²hugger–mugger *adjective* (1692)
1 : SECRET
2 : of a confused or disorderly nature **:** JUMBLED
— **hugger–mugger** *adverb*
hug–me–tight \ˈhəg-mē-ˌtīt\ *noun* (1860)
: a woman's short usually knitted sleeveless close-fitting jacket
Hu·gue·not \ˈhyü-gə-ˌnät\ *noun* [Middle French, alteration of Middle French dialect *eyguenot*, adherent of a Swiss political movement, from German dialect *Eidgnosse* confederate] (1565)
: a member of the French Reformed communion especially of the 16th and 17th centuries
— **Hu·gue·not·ic** \ˌhyü-gə-ˈnä-tik\ *adjective*
— **Hu·gue·not·ism** \ˈhyü-gə-ˌnä-ˌti-zəm\ *noun*
huh \a grunt articulated as a syllabic m or n with a voiceless onset, or as the syllable ˈhə or ˈhəⁿ, often ending in a glottal stop, and uttered with a range of intonations; often read as ˈhə\ *interjection* [imitative of a grunt] (1608)
— used to express surprise, disbelief, or confusion, or as an inquiry inviting affirmative reply
Hui·chol \wē-ˈchōl\ *noun, plural* **Huichol** *or* **Hui·cho·les** [Mexican Spanish] (1900)
1 : a member of an American Indian people of the mountains between Zacatecas and Nayarit, Mexico
2 : the Uto-Aztecan language of the Huichol people
— **Huichol** *adjective*
hui·sa·che \wē-ˈsä-chē\ *noun* [Mexican Spanish, from Nahuatl *huixachi*, from *huitzli* thorn + *ixachi* a great amount, many] (1838)

: a widely cultivated thorny shrubby acacia (*Acacia farnesiana*) of the southern U.S. and tropical America
hu·la \ˈhü-lə\ *also* **hu·la–hu·la** \ˌhü-lə-ˈhü-lə\ *noun* [Hawaiian] (1825)
: a sinuous Polynesian dance characterized by rhythmic movement of the hips and mimetic gestures with the hands and often accompanied by chants and rhythmic drumming
hula hoop *noun* (1958)
: a plastic hoop that is twirled around the body
¹hulk \ˈhəlk\ *noun* [Middle English *hulke*, from Old English *hulc*, probably from Medieval Latin *holcas*, from Greek *holkas*, from *helkein* to pull — more at SULCUS] (before 12th century)
1 a : a heavy clumsy ship **b** (1) **:** the body of an old ship unfit for service (2) **:** a ship used as a prison — usually used in plural 〈every prisoner sent to the *hulks* —Kenneth Roberts〉 **c :** an abandoned wreck or shell (as of a building or automobile)
2 : one that is bulky or unwieldy 〈a big *hulk* of a man〉
²hulk *intransitive verb* (circa 1825)
1 *dialect English* **:** to move ponderously
2 : to appear impressively large or massive **:** LOOM
hulk·ing \ˈhəl-kiŋ\ *adjective* (1698)
: PONDEROUS, MASSIVE
¹hull \ˈhəl\ *noun* [Middle English, from Old English *hulu*; akin to Old High German *hala* hull, Old English *helan* to conceal — more at HELL] (before 12th century)
1 a : the outer covering of a fruit or seed **b :** the persistent calyx or involucre that subtends some fruits
2 a : the frame or body of a ship or boat exclusive of masts, yards, sails, and rigging **b :** the main body of a usually large or heavy craft or vehicle (as an airship or tank)
3 : COVERING, CASING
— **hull·less** \ˈhəl-ləs\ *adjective*
²hull *transitive verb* (14th century)
: to remove the hulls of **:** SHUCK
— **hull·er** *noun*
hul·la·ba·loo \ˈhə-lə-bə-ˌlü\ *noun, plural* **-loos** [perhaps from *hallo* + Scots *balloo*, interjection used to hush children] (1762)
: DIN; *also* **:** UPROAR
hull down *adverb or adjective* (1775)
of a ship **:** at such a distance that only the superstructure is visible
hulled corn *noun* (1788)
: whole grain corn from which the hulls have been removed by soaking or boiling in lye water
hul·lo \(ˌ)hə-ˈlō\ *chiefly British variant of* HELLO
¹hum \ˈhəm\ *verb* **hummed; hum·ming** [Middle English *hummen*; akin to Middle High German *hummen* to hum, Middle Dutch *hommel* bumblebee] (14th century)
intransitive verb
1 a : to utter a sound like that of the speech sound \m\ prolonged **b :** to make the natural noise of an insect in motion or a similar sound **:** DRONE **c :** to give forth a low continuous blend of sound
2 a : to be busily active 〈the museum *hummed* with visitors〉 **b :** to run smoothly 〈the business started to *hum*〉
transitive verb
1 : to sing with the lips closed and without articulation
2 : to affect or express by humming 〈*hummed* his displeasure〉
— **hum** *noun*
— **hum·ma·ble** \ˈhə-mə-bəl\ *adjective*
²hum *chiefly British variant of* HEM
¹hu·man \ˈhyü-mən, ˈyü-\ *adjective* [Middle English *humain*, from Middle French, from Latin *humanus*; akin to Latin *homo* human being — more at HOMAGE] (14th century)
1 : of, relating to, or characteristic of humans
2 : consisting of humans

3 a : having human form or attributes **b :** susceptible to or representative of the sympathies and frailties of human nature 〈such an inconsistency is very *human* —P. E. More〉
usage see HUMOR
— **hu·man·ness** \-mən-nəs\ *noun*
²human *noun* (circa 1533)
: a bipedal primate mammal (*Homo sapiens*) **:** MAN; *broadly* **:** any living or extinct member of the family (Hominidae) to which the primate belongs
— **hu·man·like** \-mən-ˌlīk\ *adjective*
human being *noun* (1800)
: HUMAN
hu·mane \hyü-ˈmān, yü-\ *adjective* [Middle English *humain*] (circa 1500)
1 : marked by compassion, sympathy, or consideration for humans or animals
2 : characterized by or tending to broad humanistic culture **:** HUMANISTIC 〈*humane* studies〉
— **hu·mane·ly** *adverb*
— **hu·mane·ness** \-ˈmān-nəs\ *noun*
human ecology *noun* (1907)
1 : a branch of sociology dealing especially with the spatial and temporal interrelationships between humans and their economic, social, and political organization
2 : the ecology of human communities and populations especially as concerned with preservation of environmental quality (as of air or water) through proper application of conservation and civil engineering practices
human engineering *noun* (1920)
1 : management of humans and their affairs especially in industry
2 : ERGONOMICS
human immunodeficiency virus *noun* (1986)
: HIV
hu·man·ism \ˈhyü-mə-ˌni-zəm, ˈyü-\ *noun* (1832)
1 a : devotion to the humanities **:** literary culture **b :** the revival of classical letters, individualistic and critical spirit, and emphasis on secular concerns characteristic of the Renaissance
2 : HUMANITARIANISM
3 : a doctrine, attitude, or way of life centered on human interests or values; *especially* **:** a philosophy that usually rejects supernaturalism and stresses an individual's dignity and worth and capacity for self-realization through reason
— **hu·man·ist** \-nist\ *noun or adjective*
— **hu·man·is·tic** \ˌhyü-mə-ˈnis-tik, ˌyü-\ *adjective*
— **hu·man·is·ti·cal·ly** \-ti-k(ə-)lē\ *adverb*
hu·man·i·tar·i·an \hyü-ˌma-nə-ˈter-ē-ən, yü-\ *noun* (1844)
: a person promoting human welfare and social reform **:** PHILANTHROPIST
— **humanitarian** *adjective*
— **hu·man·i·tar·i·an·ism** \-ē-ə-ˌni-zəm\ *noun*
hu·man·i·ty \hyü-ˈma-nə-tē, yü-\ *noun, plural* **-ties** (14th century)
1 : the quality or state of being humane
2 a : the quality or state of being human **b** *plural* **:** human attributes or qualities 〈his work has the ripeness of the 18th century, and its rough *humanities* —Pamela H. Johnson〉
3 *plural* **:** the branches of learning (as philosophy or languages) that investigate human constructs and concerns as opposed to natural processes (as in physics or chemistry)
4 : MANKIND 1
hu·man·ize \ˈhyü-mə-ˌnīz, ˈyü-\ *transitive verb* **-ized; -iz·ing** (1603)

1 a : to represent as human : attribute human qualities to **b** : to adapt to human nature or use **2** : to make humane
— **hu·man·iza·tion** \,hyü-mə-nə-'zā-shən, ,yü-\ noun
— **hu·man·iz·er** noun

hu·man·kind \'hyü-mən-,kīnd, 'yü-\ noun singular but singular or plural in construction (circa 1645)
: the human race

hu·man·ly \'hyü-mən-lē, 'yü-\ adverb (15th century)
1 a : with regard to human needs and emotions ⟨provide humanly for those who are not needed in the economy —E. F. Bacon⟩ **b** : with regard to or in keeping with human proneness to error or weakness ⟨humanly inaccurate⟩
2 a : from a human viewpoint ⟨humanly speaking, the process works . . . like this —Elizabeth Janeway⟩ **b** : within the range of human capacity ⟨did everything humanly possible⟩ **c** : by humans ⟨humanly made⟩

human nature noun
: the nature of humans; especially : the fundamental dispositions and traits of humans

hu·man·oid \'hyü-mə-,nȯid, 'yü-\ adjective (1918)
: having human form or characteristics ⟨humanoid dentition⟩ ⟨humanoid robots⟩
— **humanoid** noun

human relations noun plural but usually singular in construction (1946)
1 : a study of human problems arising from organizational and interpersonal relations (as in industry)
2 : a course, study, or program designed to develop better interpersonal and intergroup adjustments

human resources noun plural (1975)
: PERSONNEL 1a, 2 ⟨director of human resources⟩

human rights noun plural (1791)
: rights (as freedom from unlawful imprisonment, torture, and execution) regarded as belonging fundamentally to all persons

hu·mate \'hyü-,māt, 'yü-\ noun (1844)
: a salt or ester of a humic acid

¹**hum·ble** \'həm-bəl also chiefly Southern 'əm-\ adjective **hum·bler** \-b(ə-)lər\; **hum·blest** \-b(ə-)ləst\ [Middle English, from Old French, from Latin humilis low, humble, from humus earth; akin to Greek chthōn earth, chamai on the ground] (13th century)
1 : not proud or haughty : not arrogant or assertive
2 : reflecting, expressing, or offered in a spirit of deference or submission ⟨a humble apology⟩
3 a : ranking low in a hierarchy or scale : INSIGNIFICANT, UNPRETENTIOUS **b** : not costly or luxurious ⟨a humble contraption⟩
usage see HUMOR
— **hum·ble·ness** \-bəl-nəs\ noun
— **hum·bly** \-blē\ adverb

²**humble** transitive verb **hum·bled; humbling** \-b(ə-)liŋ\ (14th century)
1 : to make humble in spirit or manner
2 : to destroy the power, independence, or prestige of
— **hum·bler** \-b(ə-)lər\ noun
— **hum·bling·ly** \-b(ə-)liŋ-lē\ adverb

hum·ble·bee \'həm-bəl-,bē\ noun [Middle English humbylbee, from humbyl- (akin to Middle Dutch hommel bumblebee) + bee — more at HUM] (15th century)
: BUMBLEBEE

humble pie noun (1830)
: a figurative serving of humiliation usually in the form of a forced submission, apology, or retraction — often used in the phrase eat humble pie ◇

¹**hum·bug** \'həm-,bəg\ noun [origin unknown] (1751)

1 a : something designed to deceive and mislead **b** : a willfully false, deceptive, or insincere person
2 : an attitude or spirit of pretense and deception
3 : NONSENSE, DRIVEL
4 British : a hard usually mint-flavored candy
synonym see IMPOSTURE
— **hum·bug·gery** \-,bə-g(ə-)rē\ noun

²**humbug** verb **hum·bugged; hum·bugging** (1751)
transitive verb
: DECEIVE, HOAX
intransitive verb
: to engage in a hoax or deception

hum·ding·er \'həm-'diŋ-ər\ noun [probably alteration of hummer] (circa 1904)
: a striking or extraordinary person or thing

hum·drum \'həm-,drəm\ adjective [reduplication of hum] (1553)
: MONOTONOUS, DULL
— **humdrum** noun

hu·mec·tant \hyü-'mek-tənt\ noun [Latin humectant-, humectans, present participle of humectare to moisten, from humectus moist, from humēre to be moist — more at HUMOR] (circa 1857)
: a substance that promotes retention of moisture
— **humectant** adjective

hu·mer·al \'hyü-mə-rəl\ adjective (1615)
1 : of, relating to, or situated in the region of the humerus or shoulder
2 : of, relating to, or being a body part analogous to the humerus or shoulder
— **humeral** noun

humeral veil noun (1853)
: an oblong vestment worn around the shoulders and over the hands by a priest holding a sacred vessel

hu·mer·us \'hyü-mə-rəs\ noun, plural **hu·meri** \-,rī, -,rē\ [Middle English, from Latin humerus, umerus upper arm, shoulder; akin to Gothic ams shoulder, Greek ōmos] (15th century)
: the long bone of the upper arm or forelimb extending from the shoulder to the elbow

hu·mic \'hyü-mik, 'yü-\ adjective (1844)
: of, relating to, or derived at least in part from humus

humic acid noun (1844)
: any of various organic acids obtained from humus

hu·mid \'hyü-məd, 'yü-\ adjective [French or Latin; French humide, from Latin humidus, from humēre] (15th century)
: containing or characterized by perceptible moisture especially to the point of being oppressive
synonym see WET
— **hu·mid·ly** adverb

hu·mid·i·fi·er \hyü-'mid-ə-,fī(-ə)r, yü-\ noun (1884)
: a device for supplying or maintaining humidity

hu·mid·i·fy \-,fī\ transitive verb **-fied; -fying** (1885)
: to make humid
— **hu·mid·i·fi·ca·tion** \-,mi-də-fə-'kā-shən\ noun

hu·mid·i·stat \hyü-'mi-də-,stat, yü-\ noun (circa 1904)
: an instrument for regulating or maintaining the degree of humidity

hu·mid·i·ty \hyü-'mi-də-tē, yü-\ noun, plural **-ties** (15th century)
: a moderate degree of wetness especially of the atmosphere — compare RELATIVE HUMIDITY

hu·mi·dor \'hyü-mə-,dȯr, 'yü-\ noun [humid + -or (as in cuspidor)] (1903)
: a case or enclosure (as for storing cigars) in which the air is kept properly humidified

hu·mi·fi·ca·tion \,hyü-mə-fə-'kā-shən, ,yü-\ noun (1897)
: formation of or conversion into humus

hu·mi·fied \'hyü-mə-,fīd, 'yü-\ adjective (1906)
: converted into humus

hu·mil·i·ate \hyü-'mi-lē-,āt, yü-\ transitive verb **-at·ed; -at·ing** [Late Latin humiliatus, past participle of humiliare, from Latin humilis low — more at HUMBLE] (circa 1534)
: to reduce to a lower position in one's own eyes or others' eyes : MORTIFY
— **hu·mil·i·a·tion** \-,mi-lē-'ā-shən\ noun

hu·mil·i·at·ing \hyü-'mi-lē-,ā-tiŋ, yü-\ adjective (1757)
: extremely destructive to one's self-respect or dignity : HUMBLING
— **hu·mil·i·at·ing·ly** \-tiŋ-lē\ adverb

hu·mil·i·ty \hyü-'mi-lə-tē, yü-\ noun (14th century)
: the quality or state of being humble

hum·mer \'hə-mər\ noun (1605)
1 : one that hums
2 : HUMMINGBIRD
3 : HUMDINGER
4 : FASTBALL

hum·ming·bird \'hə-miŋ-,bərd\ noun (1637)
: any of a family (Trochilidae) of tiny brightly colored nonpasserine New World birds related to the swifts and like them having narrow wings with long primaries, a slender bill, and a very extensible tongue

hum·mock \'hə-mək\ noun [alteration of ²hammock] (1555)
1 : a rounded knoll or hillock
2 : a ridge of ice
3 : ²HAMMOCK 2
— **hummock** verb
— **hum·mocky** \-mə-kē\ adjective

hum·mus \'hə-məs, 'hu̇-\ noun [Arabic hummuṣ chickpeas] (1950)
: a paste of pureed chickpeas usually mixed with sesame oil or sesame paste and eaten as a dip or sandwich spread

hu·mon·gous \hyü-'məŋ-gəs, yü-, -'mäŋ-\ also **hu·mun·gous** \-'məŋ-gəs\ adjective [perhaps alteration of huge + monstrous] (circa 1967)
: extremely large : HUGE

¹**hu·mor** \'hyü-mər, 'yü-\ noun [Middle English humour, from Middle French humeur, from Medieval Latin & Latin; Medieval Latin humor, from Latin humor, umor moisture; akin to Old Norse vǫkr damp, Latin humēre to be moist, and perhaps to Greek hygros wet] (14th century)

1 a : a normal functioning bodily semifluid or fluid (as the blood or lymph) **b :** a secretion (as a hormone) that is an excitant of activity **2 a** *in medieval physiology* **:** a fluid or juice of an animal or plant; *specifically* **:** one of the four fluids entering into the constitution of the body and determining by their relative proportions a person's health and temperament **b :** characteristic or habitual disposition or bent **:** TEMPERAMENT ⟨of cheerful *humor*⟩ **c :** an often temporary state of mind imposed especially by circumstances ⟨was in no *humor* to listen⟩ **d :** a sudden, unpredictable, or unreasoning inclination **:** WHIM ⟨the uncertain *humors* of nature⟩ **3 a :** that quality which appeals to a sense of the ludicrous or absurdly incongruous **b :** the mental faculty of discovering, expressing, or appreciating the ludicrous or absurdly incongruous **c :** something that is or is designed to be comical or amusing □ ◇
synonym see WIT
— **out of humor :** out of sorts
²**humor** *transitive verb* **hu·mored; hu·mor·ing** \'hyüm-riŋ, 'yüm-, 'hyü-mə-, 'yü-\ (1588)
1 : to soothe or content by indulgence
2 : to adapt oneself to
synonym see INDULGE
hu·mor·al \'hyü-mə-rəl, 'yü-\ *adjective* (15th century)
1 : of, relating to, proceeding from, or involving a bodily humor (as a hormone)
2 : relating to or being the part of immunity or the immune response that involves antibodies secreted by B cells and circulating in bodily fluids
hu·mor·esque \,hyü-mə-'resk, ,yü-\ *noun* [German *Humoreske,* from *Humor,* from Medieval Latin] (1889)
: a typically whimsical or fanciful musical composition
hu·mor·ist \'hyü-mə-rist, 'yü-\ *noun* (1589)
1 *archaic* **:** a person subject to whims
2 : a person specializing in or noted for humor
hu·mor·is·tic \,hyü-mə-'ris-tik, ,yü-\ *adjective* (1818)
: HUMOROUS
hu·mor·less \'hyü-mər-ləs\ *adjective* (circa 1847)
1 : lacking a sense of humor
2 : lacking humorous characteristics
— **hu·mor·less·ly** \-lē\ *adverb*
— **hu·mor·less·ness** *noun*
hu·mor·ous \'hyüm-rəs, 'yüm-, 'hyü-mə-, 'yü-\ *adjective* (15th century)
1 *obsolete* **:** HUMID
2 a : full of or characterized by humor **:** JOCULAR **b :** indicating or expressive of a sense of humor
synonym see WITTY
— **hu·mor·ous·ly** *adverb*
— **hu·mor·ous·ness** *noun*
hu·mour *chiefly British variant of* HUMOR
¹**hump** \'həmp\ *noun* [akin to Middle Low German *hump* bump] (1709)
1 : a rounded protuberance: as **a :** HUMPBACK 1 **b :** a fleshy protuberance on the back of an animal (as a camel, bison, or whale) **c** (1) **:** MOUND, HUMMOCK (2) **:** MOUNTAIN, RANGE ⟨the Himalayan *hump*⟩
2 *British* **:** a fit of depression or sulking
3 : a difficult, trying, or critical phase or obstacle — often used in the phrase *over the hump*
— **humped** *adjective*
²**hump** (1835)
transitive verb
1 : to copulate with — often considered vulgar
2 : to exert (oneself) vigorously
3 : to make humpbacked **:** HUNCH
4 *chiefly British* **:** to put or carry on the back **:** LUG; *also* **:** TRANSPORT
intransitive verb
1 : to exert oneself **:** HUSTLE
2 : to move swiftly **:** RACE

hump·back \-,bak, *for 1 also* -'bak\ *noun* (1697)
1 : a humped or crooked back; *also* **:** KYPHOSIS
2 : HUNCHBACK 1
3 : HUMPBACK WHALE
4 : PINK SALMON
hump·backed \-'bakt\ *adjective* (1681)
1 : having a humped back
2 : convexly curved ⟨a *humpbacked* bridge⟩
humpback whale *noun* (1725)
: a large baleen whale (*Megaptera novaeangliae*) that is black above and white below and has very long flippers, and fleshy tubercles along the snout

humpback whale

¹**humph** \'həm(p)f\ (1814)
intransitive verb
: to utter a humph
transitive verb
: to utter (as a remark) in a tone suggestive of a humph
²**humph** \a snort articulated as a syllabic m or n with a voiceless onset and ending in a nasal h or a glottal stop; often read as 'həm(p)f\ *interjection* [imitative of a grunt] (1815)
— used to express doubt or contempt
hump·ty–dump·ty \,həm(p)-tē-'dəm(p)-tē\ *noun, plural* **-dumpties** *often H&D capitalized* [*Humpty-Dumpty,* egg-shaped nursery-rhyme character who fell from a wall and broke into bits] (1883)
: something that once broken is impossible or almost impossible to put back together
humpy \'həm-pē\ *adjective* **hump·i·er; -est** (1708)
1 : full of humps
2 : covered with humps
hu·mus \'hyü-məs, 'yü-\ *noun* [New Latin, from Latin, earth — more at HUMBLE] (1796)
: a brown or black complex variable material resulting from partial decomposition of plant or animal matter and forming the organic portion of soil
hum·vee \,həm-'vē, 'həm-,\ *noun* [from HMMWV (*High Mobility Multipurpose Wheeled Vehicle*)] (1982) *often capitalized*
: a diesel-powered multipurpose U.S. military vehicle that replaced the jeep
Hun \'hən\ *noun* [Middle English, from Old English *Hunas,* plural, from Late Latin *Hunni,* plural] (before 12th century)
1 : a member of a nomadic central Asian people gaining control of a large part of central and eastern Europe under Attila about A.D. 450
2 *often not capitalized* **:** a person who is wantonly destructive **:** VANDAL **b :** GERMAN; *especially* **:** a German soldier — usually used disparagingly
Hu·nan \'hü-'nän\ *or* **Hu·na·nese** \,hü-nə-'nēz, -'nēs\ *adjective* [*Hunan,* China] (1970)
: of, relating to, or being a hot and spicy style of Chinese cooking
¹**hunch** \'hənch\ *verb* [origin unknown] (1581)
transitive verb
1 : JOSTLE, SHOVE
2 : to thrust or bend over into a humped or crooked position
intransitive verb
1 : to thrust oneself forward
2 a : to assume a bent or crooked posture **b :** to draw oneself into a ball **:** curl up **c :** HUDDLE, SQUAT
²**hunch** *noun* (1630)
1 : an act or instance of hunching **:** PUSH
2 a : a thick piece **:** LUMP **b :** HUMP
3 : a strong intuitive feeling concerning especially a future event or result
hunch·back \'hənch-,bak\ *noun* (1712)
1 : a person with a humpback
2 : HUMPBACK 1
— **hunch·backed** \-'bakt\ *adjective*

hun·dred \'hən-drəd, -dərd\ *noun, plural* **hundreds** *or* **hundred** [Middle English, from Old English, from *hund* hundred + *-red* (akin to Gothic *rathjo* account, number); akin to Latin *centum* hundred, Greek he*katon,* Old English *tien* ten — more at TEN, REASON] (before 12th century)
1 — see NUMBER table
2 *hundreds plural* **a :** the numbers 100 to 999 **b :** a great number ⟨*hundreds* of times⟩
3 : a 100-dollar bill
4 : a subdivision of some English and American counties
— **hundred** *adj*
— **hun·dred·fold** \-,fōld\ *adjective or adverb*
— **hun·dredth** \-drədth, -drətth\ *adjective or noun*
hun·dred–per·cent·er \-pər-'sen-tər\ *noun* [hundred-percent (*American*)] (1921)
: a thoroughgoing nationalist
— **hun·dred–per·cent·ism** \-'sen-,ti-zəm\ *noun*
hundreds place *noun* (1937)
: the place three to the left of the decimal point in a number expressed in the Arabic system of notation
hun·dred·weight \'hən-drəd-,wāt, -dərd-,wāt\ *noun, plural* **hundredweight** *or* **hundredweights** (1577)

□ **USAGE**

humor Some speakers insist that in *humor* and similar words (as *human, humble, homage*) the *h* must be sounded. In the beginning, however, it was not so: these words were first brought into English without an *h* in the pronunciation or, in some cases, in the spelling. In time the literate classes adopted a spelling pronunciation of *humor,* sounding the *h* contrary to established usage. The *h*-less pronunciation came to be seen as a mark of poor education, and so even today critics advocate an initial \h\ in *humor.* Those who do not pronounce the \h\, however, have centuries of usage to vindicate their pronunciation.

◇ **WORD HISTORY**

humor A theory of physiology first articulated by the ancient Greeks and popular throughout the Middle Ages and Renaissance held that the composition of the human body included four fluids: yellow bile or choler, black bile or melancholy, blood, and phlegm. The proper proportion of these fluids determined both the physical and mental well-being of an individual. In Middle English these fluids were referred to as *humours,* ultimately from Latin *umor,* meaning "moisture" or "bodily fluid." If in a natural combination, a *humour* was *goode* and stimulated health and good spirits, but if unnatural or corrupted, a *humour* was *ille* and led to sickness and ill spirits. In the course of the 16th and 17th centuries, *good humour* and *ill humour* lost their original physiological senses and began to refer strictly to mental states, whether fixed disposition or passing mood, and we continue to use *humor* in this way. The use of *humors* to mean "whims" led to other common modern applications of *humor,* for a person's faculty for appreciating the ludicrous (as in *sense of humor*) and correspondingly, the quality that appeals to this faculty (as in *to see the humor in a situation*).

\ə\ abut \ᵊ\ kitten \ər\ further \a\ ash \ā\ ace
\ä\ mop, mar \au̇\ out \ch\ chin \e\ bet \ē\ easy
\g\ go \i\ hit \ī\ ice \j\ job \ŋ\ sing \ō\ go
\ȯ\ law \ȯi\ boy \th\ thin \t͟h\ the \ü\ loot \u̇\ foot
\y\ yet \zh\ vision *see also* Guide to Pronunciation

1 : a unit of weight equal to 100 pounds — called also *short hundredweight;* see WEIGHT table

2 *British* : a unit of weight equal to 112 pounds — called also *long hundredweight*

¹hung *past and past participle of* HANG

²hung *adjective* (1848)
: unable to reach a decision or verdict ⟨a *hung* jury⟩; *also, British* : not having a political party with an overall majority ⟨a *hung* parliament⟩

Hun·gar·i·an \ˌhəŋ-ˈger-ē-ən, -ˈgar-\ *noun* (1553)
1 a : a native or inhabitant of Hungary : MAGYAR **b** : a person of Hungarian descent **2** : the Finno-Ugric language of the Hungarians
— **Hungarian** *adjective*

¹hun·ger \ˈhəŋ-gər\ *noun* [Middle English, from Old English *hungor;* akin to Old High German *hungar* hunger, Lithuanian *kanka* torture] (before 12th century)
1 a : a craving or urgent need for food or a specific nutrient **b** : an uneasy sensation occasioned by the lack of food **c** : a weakened condition brought about by prolonged lack of food **2** : a strong desire : CRAVING
— **from hunger** : very bad or inept ⟨the jokes were *from hunger* —Mordecai Richler⟩

²hunger *verb* **hun·gered; hun·ger·ing** \-g(ə-)riŋ\ (before 12th century)
intransitive verb
1 : to feel or suffer hunger **2** : to have an eager desire
transitive verb
: to make hungry
synonym see LONG

hunger strike *noun* (1889)
: refusal (as by a prisoner) to eat enough to sustain life
— **hunger striker** *noun*

hung·over \ˈhəŋ-ˈō-vər\ *adjective* (1941)
: suffering from a hangover

hun·gry \ˈhəŋ-grē\ *adjective* **hun·gri·er; -est** [Middle English, from Old English *hungrig;* akin to Old English *hungor*] (before 12th century)
1 a : feeling hunger **b** : characterized by or characteristic of hunger or appetite **2 a** : EAGER, AVID ⟨*hungry* for affection⟩ **b** : strongly motivated (as by ambition) **3** : not rich or fertile : BARREN
— **hun·gri·ly** \-grə-lē\ *adverb*
— **hun·gri·ness** \-grē-nəs\ *noun*

hung up *adjective* (1948)
1 : delayed or detained for a time **2** : anxiously nervous **3** : being much involved with: as **a** : being infatuated **b** : ENTHUSIASTIC **c** : PREOCCUPIED

hunk \ˈhəŋk\ *noun* [Flemish *hunke*] (circa 1813)
1 : a large lump, piece, or portion ⟨a *hunk* of bread⟩ **2** : an attractive well-built man

hun·ker \ˈhəŋ-kər\ *intransitive verb* **hunkered; hun·ker·ing** \-k(ə-)riŋ\ [perhaps of Scandinavian origin; akin to Old Norse *hūka* to squat; akin to Middle Low German *hōken* to squat, peddle — more at HAWKER] (1720)
1 : CROUCH, SQUAT — usually used with *down* **2** : to settle in or dig in for a sustained period — used with *down* ⟨*hunker* down for a good long wait —*New Yorker*⟩

hun·kers \ˈhəŋ-kərz\ *noun plural* (1756)
: HAUNCHES

hunks \ˈhəŋ(k)s\ *noun plural but singular in construction* [origin unknown] (1602)
: a surly ill-natured person; *especially* : MISER

hunky \ˈhəŋ-kē\ *adjective* **hunk·i·er; -est** (1911)
: muscular and usually attractive ⟨*hunky* men⟩

Hun·ky *also* **Hun·kie** \ˈhəŋ-kē\ *noun, plural* **Hunkies** [alteration of *Hungarian*] (circa 1896)

: a person of central or east European birth or descent — usually used disparagingly

hun·ky-do·ry \ˌhəŋ-kē-ˈdōr-ē, -ˈdȯr-\ *adjective* [obsolete English dialect *hunk* (home base) + *-dory* (origin unknown)] (1866)
: quite satisfactory : FINE

Hun·nish \ˈhə-nish\ *adjective* (1820)
: relating to or resembling the Huns

¹hunt \ˈhənt\ *verb* [Middle English, from Old English *huntian;* akin to Old English *hentan* to seize] (before 12th century)
transitive verb
1 a : to pursue for food or in sport ⟨*hunt* buffalo⟩ **b** : to manage in the search for game ⟨*hunts* a pack of dogs⟩ **2 a** : to pursue with intent to capture ⟨*hunted* the escapees⟩ **b** : to search out : SEEK **3** : to drive or chase especially by harrying ⟨members . . . were *hunted* from their homes —J. T. Adams⟩ **4** : to traverse in search of prey ⟨*hunts* the woods⟩
intransitive verb
1 : to take part in a hunt **2** : to attempt to find something **3** : to oscillate alternately to each side (as of a neutral point) or to run alternately faster and slower — used especially of a device or machine

²hunt *noun* (14th century)
1 : the act, the practice, or an instance of hunting **2** : a group of mounted hunters and their hunting dogs

hunt-and-peck \ˌhənt-ᵊn-ˈpek\ *noun* (1939)
: a method of typing in which one looks at the keyboard and types using usually the forefingers

hunt·er \ˈhən-tər\ *noun* (13th century)
1 a : a person who hunts game **b** : a dog used or trained for hunting **c** : a horse used or adapted for use in hunting with hounds; *especially* : a fast strong horse trained for cross-country work and jumping **2** : one that searches for something **3** : a pocket watch with a hinged protective cover

hunt·er–gath·er·er \ˈhən-tər-ˈga-thər-ər\ *noun* (1977)
: a member of a culture in which food is obtained by hunting, fishing, and foraging rather than by agriculture or animal husbandry

hunter green *noun* (circa 1930)
: a dark yellowish green

hunt·ing *noun* (before 12th century)
1 : the act of one that hunts; *specifically* : the pursuit of game **2** : the process of hunting **3 a** : a periodic variation in speed of a synchronous electrical machine **b** : a self-induced and undesirable oscillation of a variable above and below the desired value in an automatic control system **c** : a continuous attempt by an automatically controlled system to find a desired equilibrium condition

hunting horn *noun* (1694)
: a signal horn used in the chase; *specifically* : a coiled circular horn with a flared bell and a cup-shaped mouthpiece

Hun·ting·ton's chorea \ˈhən-tiŋ-tənz-\ *noun* [George *Huntington* (died 1916) American physician] (1889)
: hereditary chorea usually developing in adult life and progressing to dementia — called also *Huntington's disease*

hunt·ress \ˈhən-trəs\ *noun* (14th century)
: a woman who hunts game; *also* : a female animal that hunts prey

hunts·man \ˈhən(t)s-smən\ *noun* (1567)
1 : HUNTER 1a **2** : a person who manages a hunt and looks after the hounds

hup \ˈhəp, ˈhət\ *interjection* [probably alteration of ¹*hep*] (1951)
— used to mark a marching cadence

hur·dies \ˈhər-dēz\ *noun plural* [origin unknown] (14th century)
dialect British : RUMP

¹hur·dle \ˈhər-dᵊl\ *noun* [Middle English *hurdel,* from Old English *hyrdel;* akin to Old High German *hurt* hurdle, Latin *cratis* wickerwork, hurdle] (before 12th century)

hurdle 2a

1 a : a portable panel usually of wattled withes and stakes used especially for enclosing land or livestock **b** : a frame or sled formerly used in England for dragging traitors to execution **2 a** : an artificial barrier over which racers must leap **b** *plural* : any of various track events in which a series of hurdles must be surmounted **3** : BARRIER, OBSTACLE

²hurdle *transitive verb* **hur·dled; hur·dling** \ˈhərd-liŋ, ˈhər-dᵊl-iŋ\ (1896)
1 : to leap over especially while running (as in a sporting competition) **2** : OVERCOME, SURMOUNT
— **hur·dler** \ˈhərd-lər, ˈhər-dᵊl-ər\ *noun*

hur·dy–gur·dy \ˌhər-dē-ˈgər-dē, ˈhər-dē-\ *noun, plural* **-gurdies** [probably imitative] (1749)
1 : a stringed instrument in which sound is produced by the friction of a rosined wheel turned by a crank against the strings and the pitches are varied by keys **2** : any of various mechanical musical instruments (as the barrel organ)

hurl \ˈhər(-ə)l\ *verb* **hurled; hurl·ing** \ˈhər-liŋ\ [Middle English] (13th century)
intransitive verb
1 : RUSH, HURTLE **2** : PITCH 5a, b
transitive verb
1 : to send or thrust with great vigor ⟨the forces that were to be *hurled* against the Turks —N. T. Gilroy⟩ **2** : to throw down with violence **3 a** : to throw forcefully : FLING ⟨*hurled* the manuscript into the fire⟩ ⟨*hurled* myself over the fence⟩ **b** : PITCH 2a **4** : to utter with vehemence ⟨*hurled* insults at the police⟩
synonym see THROW
— **hurl** *noun*
— **hurl·er** \ˈhər-lər\ *noun*

hurdy-gurdy 1

hurl·ing \ˈhər-liŋ\ *noun* (circa 1600)
: an Irish game resembling field hockey played between two teams of 15 players each

hur·ly \ˈhər-lē\ *noun* [probably short for *hurlyburly*] (1594)
: UPROAR, TUMULT

hur·ly–bur·ly \ˌhər-lē-ˈbər-lē\ *noun* [probably alteration & reduplication of *hurling,* gerund of *hurl*] (1539)
: UPROAR, TUMULT
— **hurly–burly** *adjective*

Hu·ron \ˈhyu̇r-ən, -ˌän\ *noun, plural* **Hurons** *or* **Huron** [French, literally, boor] (1658)
: a member of a confederacy of American Indian peoples formerly occupying the country between Georgian Bay and Lake Ontario

¹hur·rah \hu̇-ˈrȯ, -ˈrä, ˈhü-ˌ\ *noun* (1686)
1 a : EXCITEMENT, FANFARE **b** : CHEER 7 **2** : FUSS

²hur·rah \hu̇-ˈrȯ, -ˈrä\ *also* **hur·ray** \hu̇-ˈrā\ *interjection* [perhaps from German *hurra*] (1716)
— used to express joy, approbation, or encouragement

Hur·ri·an \ˈhu̇r-ē-ən\ *noun* (1911)
1 : a member of an ancient non-Semitic people of northern Mesopotamia, Syria, and eastern Asia Minor about 1500 B.C.
2 : the language of the Hurrian people
¹hur·ri·cane \ˈhər-ə-ˌkān, -i-kən, ˈhə-rə-, ˈhə-ri-\ *noun* [Spanish *huracán,* from Taino *hurakán*] (1555)
1 : a tropical cyclone with winds of 74 miles (118 kilometers) per hour or greater that occurs especially in the western Atlantic, that is usually accompanied by rain, thunder, and lightning, and that sometimes moves into temperate latitudes — see BEAUFORT SCALE table
2 : something resembling a hurricane especially in its turmoil
²hurricane *adjective* (1894)
: having or being a glass chimney providing protection from wind ⟨a *hurricane* lamp⟩
hur·ried \ˈhər-ēd, ˈhə-rēd\ *adjective* (1667)
1 : going or working at speed
2 : done in a hurry **:** HASTY
— **hur·ried·ly** \ˈhər-əd-lē, ˈhə-rəd-\ *adverb*
— **hur·ried·ness** \ˈhər-ēd-nəs, ˈhə-rēd-\ *noun*
¹hur·ry \ˈhər-ē, ˈhə-rē\ *verb* **hur·ried; hur·ry·ing** [perhaps from Middle English *horyen*] (1592)
transitive verb
1 a : to carry or cause to go with haste ⟨*hurry* them to the hospital⟩ **b :** to impel to rash or precipitate action
2 a : to impel to greater speed **:** PROD ⟨used spurs to *hurry* the horse⟩ **b :** EXPEDITE **c :** to perform with undue haste ⟨*hurry* a minuet⟩
intransitive verb
: to move or act with haste ⟨please *hurry* up⟩
— **hur·ri·er** *noun*
²hurry *noun* (1600)
1 : disturbed or disorderly activity **:** COMMOTION
2 a : agitated and often bustling or disorderly haste **b :** a state of eagerness or urgency **:** RUSH
synonym see HASTE
— **in a hurry :** without delay **:** as rapidly as possible ⟨the police got there *in a hurry*⟩
hur·ry–scur·ry *or* **hur·ry–skur·ry** \ˌhər-ē-ˈskər-ē, ˌhə-rē-ˈskə-rē\ *noun* [reduplication of ²*hurry*] (1754)
: a confused rush **:** TURMOIL
— **hurry–scurry** *adjective or adverb*
hur·ry–up \ˈhər-ē-ˌəp, ˈhə-rē-\ *adjective* (1902)
: speeded up **:** completed in a hurry ⟨a *hurry-up* dinner⟩
¹hurt \ˈhərt\ *verb* **hurt; hurt·ing** [Middle English, probably from Old French *hurter* to collide with, probably of Germanic origin; akin to Old Norse *hrūtr* male sheep] (13th century)
transitive verb
1 a : to inflict with physical pain **:** WOUND **b :** to do substantial or material harm to **:** DAMAGE ⟨the dry summer has *hurt* the land⟩
2 a : to cause emotional pain or anguish to **:** OFFEND **b :** to be detrimental to **:** HAMPER ⟨charges of graft *hurt* my chances of being elected⟩
intransitive verb
1 a : to suffer pain or grief **b :** to be in need — usually used with *for* ⟨*hurting* for money⟩
2 : to cause damage or distress ⟨hit where it *hurts*⟩
synonym see INJURE
— **hurt** *adjective*
— **hurt·er** *noun*
²hurt *noun* (13th century)
1 : a cause of injury or damage **:** BLOW
2 a : a bodily injury or wound **b :** mental distress or anguish **:** SUFFERING
3 : WRONG, HARM
hurt·ful \ˈhərt-fəl\ *adjective* (1526)
: causing injury, detriment, or suffering **:** DAMAGING
— **hurt·ful·ly** \-fə-lē\ *adverb*
— **hurt·ful·ness** *noun*
hur·tle \ˈhər-t²l\ *verb* **hur·tled; hur·tling** \ˈhərt-liŋ, ˈhər-t²l-iŋ\ [Middle English *hurtlen* to collide, frequentative of *hurten* to cause to strike, hurt] (14th century)

intransitive verb
: to move rapidly or forcefully
transitive verb
: HURL, FLING
— **hurtle** *noun*
hurt·less \ˈhərt-ləs\ *adjective* (1549)
: causing no pain or injury **:** HARMLESS
¹hus·band \ˈhəz-bənd\ *noun* [Middle English *husbonde,* from Old English *hūsbonda* master of a house, from Old Norse *hūsbōndi,* from *hūs* house + *bōndi* householder; akin to Old Norse *būa* to inhabit; akin to Old English *būan* to dwell — more at BOWER] (13th century)
1 : a male partner in a marriage
2 *British* **:** MANAGER, STEWARD
3 : a frugal manager
— **hus·band·ly** *adjective*
²husband *transitive verb* (15th century)
1 a : to manage prudently and economically **b :** to use sparingly **:** CONSERVE
2 *archaic* **:** to find a husband for **:** MATE
— **hus·band·er** *noun*
hus·band·man \ˈhəz-bən(d)-mən\ *noun* (14th century)
1 : one that plows and cultivates land **:** FARMER
2 : a specialist in a branch of farm husbandry
hus·band·ry \ˈhəz-bən-drē\ *noun* (14th century)
1 *archaic* **:** the care of a household
2 : the control or judicious use of resources **:** CONSERVATION
3 a : the cultivation or production of plants and animals **:** AGRICULTURE **b :** the scientific control and management of a branch of farming and especially of domestic animals
¹hush \ˈhəsh\ *verb* [back-formation from *husht* (hushed), from Middle English *hussht,* from *huissht,* interjection used to enjoin silence] (1546)
transitive verb
1 : CALM, QUIET ⟨*hushed* the children as they entered the library⟩
2 : to put at rest **:** MOLLIFY
3 : to keep from public knowledge **:** SUPPRESS ⟨*hush* the story up⟩
intransitive verb
: to become quiet
²hush *adjective* (1602)
1 *archaic* **:** SILENT, STILL
2 : intended to prevent the dissemination of certain information ⟨*hush* money⟩
³hush *noun* (1689)
: a silence or calm especially following noise **:** QUIET
hush–hush \ˈhəsh-ˌhəsh\ *adjective* (1916)
: SECRET, CONFIDENTIAL
hush puppy *noun* [from its occasional use as food for dogs] (circa 1918)
chiefly Southern & southern Midland **:** cornmeal dough shaped into small balls and fried in deep fat — usually used in plural
¹husk \ˈhəsk\ *noun* [Middle English] (14th century)
1 a : a usually dry or membranous outer covering (as a pod or hull or one composed of bracts) of various seeds and fruits; *also* **:** one of the constituent parts **b :** a carob pod
2 a : an outer layer **:** SHELL **b :** an emptied shell **:** REMNANT **c :** a supporting framework
²husk *transitive verb* (1562)
: to strip the husk from
— **husk·er** *noun*
husk·ing *noun* (1692)
: CORNHUSKING — called also *husking bee*
husk–tomato *noun* (1895)
: GROUND-CHERRY
¹husky \ˈhəs-kē\ *adjective* **husk·i·er; -est** (1552)
: resembling, containing, or full of husks
²hus·ky \ˈhəs-kē\ *adjective* **hus·ki·er; -est** [probably from *husk* (huskiness), from obsolete *husk* (to have a dry cough)] (circa 1722)
: hoarse with or as if with emotion
— **hus·ki·ly** \-kə-lē\ *adverb*
— **hus·ki·ness** \-kē-nəs\ *noun*

³hus·ky *noun, plural* **huskies** [shortening of *Huskemaw, Uskemaw* Eskimo, from Cree *aškimeˑw;* akin to Montagnais (Algonquian language of eastern Canada) *aiachkime8* Micmac, Eskimo — more at ESKIMO] (1852)
1 : a heavy-coated working dog of the New World arctic region
2 : SIBERIAN HUSKY
⁴hus·ky *noun, plural* **huskies** (1864)
: one that is husky
⁵hus·ky *adjective* **hus·ki·er; -est** [probably from ¹*husk*] (1869)
1 : BURLY, ROBUST
2 : LARGE
hus·sar \(ˌ)hə-ˈzär, -ˈsär\ *noun* [Hungarian *huszár* hussar, (obsolete) highway robber, from Serbo-Croatian *husar* pirate, from Medieval Latin *cursarius* — more at CORSAIR] (1532)
: a member of any of various European units originally modeled on the Hungarian light cavalry of the 15th century
Huss·ite \ˈhə-ˌsīt, ˈhu̇-\ *noun* [New Latin *Hussita,* from John *Huss*] (1532)
: a member of the Bohemian religious and nationalist movement originating with John Huss
— **Hussite** *adjective*
— **Huss·it·ism** \-ˌsī-ˌti-zəm\ *noun*
hus·sy \ˈhə-sē, -zē\ *noun, plural* **hussies** [alteration of Middle English *huswif* housewife, from *hus* house + *wif* wife, woman] (1505)
1 : a lewd or brazen woman
2 : a saucy or mischievous girl
hus·tings \ˈhəs-tiŋz\ *noun plural but singular or plural in construction* [Middle English, from Old English *hūsting,* from Old Norse *hūsthing,* from *hūs* house + *thing* assembly] (before 12th century)
1 a : a local court formerly held in various English municipalities and still held infrequently in London **b :** a local court in some cities in Virginia
2 a : a raised platform used until 1872 for the nomination of candidates for the British Parliament and for election speeches **b :** an election platform **:** STUMP **c :** the proceedings or locale of an election campaign ◇

◇ **WORD HISTORY**
hustings Hustings, now the haunt of politicians, were originally assemblies. Late Old English *hūsting,* the ancestor of modern *husting,* was a loan from Old Norse *hūsthing,* a compound of *hūs* "house" and *thing* "assembly"; the modifying *hūs* presumably signified that the assembly took place in a building rather than outdoors. After the Norman Conquest the *husting,* originally a sort of royal council, became a court hearing civil cases, especially one in London that met at the Guildhall, London's original seat of municipal government. *Hustings* was also apparently applied to a dais at one end of the Guildhall's Gothic meeting room, where the Court of Hustings met and where the lord mayor, sheriffs, and other officials were elected. At this point the history of *hustings* becomes murky, but it appears that about 1700, at a time when English electoral politics were taking something like their modern form, *hustings* was applied to any platform where a parliamentary seat was contested. In Hanoverian England this was typically a substantial structure erected in a large open space, where nomination speeches were made and the results of polling announced. Today in both Britain and the U.S. the hustings are usually the figurative rather than literal site of electioneering.

\ə\ **abut**	\ᵊ\ **kitten**	\ər\ **further** \a\ **ash** \ā\ **ace**
\ä\ **mop, mar**	\au̇\ **out**	\ch\ **chin** \e\ **bet** \ē\ **easy**
\g\ **go**	\i\ **hit**	\ī\ **ice** \j\ **job** \ŋ\ **sing** \ō\ **go**
\ȯ\ **law**	\ȯi\ **boy**	\th\ **thin** \th\ **the** \ü\ **loot** \u̇\ **foot**
\y\ **yet**	\zh\ **vision**	*see also* Guide to Pronunciation

hus·tle \'hə-səl\ *verb* **hus·tled; hus·tling** \'hə-s(ə-)liŋ\ [Dutch *husselen* to shake, from Middle Dutch *hutselen*, frequentative of *hutsen*] (1751)
transitive verb
1 a : JOSTLE, SHOVE **b :** to convey forcibly or hurriedly **c :** to urge forward precipitately
2 a : to obtain by energetic activity ⟨*hustle* up new customers⟩ **b :** to sell something to or obtain something from by energetic and especially underhanded activity ⟨*hustling* the suckers⟩ **c :** to sell or promote energetically and aggressively ⟨*hustling* a new product⟩ **d :** to lure less skillful players into competing against oneself at (a gambling game) ⟨*hustle* pool⟩
intransitive verb
1 : SHOVE, PRESS
2 : HASTEN, HURRY
3 a : to make strenuous efforts to obtain especially money or business **b :** to obtain money by fraud or deception **c :** to engage in prostitution
4 : to play a game or sport in an alert aggressive manner
— **hustle** *noun*
— **hus·tler** \'hə-slər\ *noun*

¹**hut** \'hət\ *noun* [Middle French *hutte*, of Germanic origin; akin to Old High German *hutta* hut; probably akin to Old English *hȳd* skin, hide] (1658)
1 : an often small and temporary dwelling of simple construction **:** SHACK
2 : a simple shelter from the elements
— **hut** *verb*

²**hut** \'hət, 'həp\ *interjection* [probably alteration of ¹*hep*] (1948)
— used to mark a marching cadence

hutch \'həch\ *noun* [Middle English *huche*, from Old French] (13th century)
1 a : a chest or compartment for storage **b :** a cupboard usually surmounted by open shelves
2 : a pen or coop for an animal
3 : SHACK, SHANTY

hut·ment \'hət-mənt\ *noun* (1889)
1 : a collection of huts **:** ENCAMPMENT
2 : HUT

Hut·ter·ite \'hə-tə-ˌrīt, 'hü-\ *noun* [Jakob *Hutter* (died 1536) Moravian Anabaptist] (1910)
: a member of a Mennonite sect of northwestern U.S. and Canada living communally and holding property in common
— **Hut·te·ri·an** \ˌhə-'tir-ē-ən, hü-\ *adjective*

Hu·tu \'hü-(ˌ)tü\ *noun, plural* **Hutu** *or* **Hutus** (1952)
: a member of a Bantu-speaking people of Rwanda and Burundi

hutz·pah *or* **hutz·pa** *variant of* CHUTZPAH

huz·zah *or* **huz·za** \(ˌ)hə-'zä\ *noun* [origin unknown] (1573)
: an expression or shout of acclaim — often used interjectionally to express joy or approbation

hy·a·cinth \'hī-ə-(ˌ)sin(t)th, -sən(t)th\ *noun* [Latin *hyacinthus*, a precious stone, a flowering plant, from Greek *hyakinthos*] (1553)
1 a : a precious stone of the ancients sometimes held to be the sapphire **b :** a gem zircon or essonite
2 a : a plant of the ancients held to be a lily, iris, larkspur, or gladiolus **b :** a bulbous herb (*Hyacinthus orientalis*) of the lily family that is native to the Mediterranean region but is widely grown for its dense spikes of fragrant flowers — compare GRAPE HYACINTH, WATER HYACINTH
3 : a light violet to moderate purple
— **hy·a·cin·thine** \ˌhī-ə-'sin(t)-thən\ *adjective*

Hy·a·cin·thus \ˌhī-ə-'sin(t)-thəs\ *noun* [Latin, from Greek *Hyakinthos*]

: a youth loved and accidentally killed by Apollo who memorializes him with a hyacinth growing from the youth's blood

Hy·a·des \'hī-ə-ˌdēz\ *noun plural* [Latin, from Greek] (14th century)
: a V-shaped cluster of stars in the head of the constellation Taurus held by the ancients to indicate rainy weather when they rise with the sun

hy·ae·na *variant of* HYENA

hyal- *or* **hyalo-** *combining form* [Late Latin, glass, from Greek, from *hyalos*]
: glass **:** glassy **:** hyaline ⟨*hyaluronic* acid⟩

¹**hy·a·line** \'hī-ə-lən, -,līn\ *adjective* [Late Latin *hyalinus*, from Greek *hyalinos*, from *hyalos*] (circa 1661)
: transparent or nearly so and usually homogeneous

²**hy·a·line** \'hī-ə-lən, -,līn, *in sense 2* -lən *or* -,lēn\ *noun* (1667)
1 : something (as the clear atmosphere) that is transparent
2 *or* **hy·a·lin** \-lən\ **:** any of several translucent nitrogenous substances related to chitin, found especially around cells, and readily stained by eosin

hyaline cartilage *noun* (1855)
: translucent bluish white cartilage with the cells embedded in an apparently homogeneous matrix present in joints and respiratory passages and forming most of the fetal skeleton

hy·a·lite \'hī-ə-,līt\ *noun* [German *Hyalit*, from Greek *hyalos*] (1794)
: a colorless opal that is clear as glass or sometimes translucent or whitish

hy·a·loid \-,lȯid\ *adjective* [Greek *hyaloeidēs*, from *hyalos*] (1835)
: GLASSY, TRANSPARENT

hy·a·lo·plasm \hī-'a-lə-,pla-zəm, 'hī-ə-lō-\ *noun* [probably from German *Hyaloplasma*, from *hyal-* + *-plasma* -plasm] (1886)
: CYTOSOL

hy·al·uron·ic acid \ˌhīl-yu̇-'rä-nik-, ˌhī-əl-yu̇-\ *noun* [International Scientific Vocabulary] (1934)
: a viscous mucopolysaccharide acid that occurs especially in the vitreous humor, the umbilical cord, and synovial fluid and as a cementing substance in the subcutaneous tissue

hy·al·uron·i·dase \-'rä-nə-,dās, -,dāz\ *noun* [International Scientific Vocabulary, from *hyaluronic* (acid) + *-idase* (as in *glucosidase*)] (1940)
: a mucolytic enzyme that facilitates the spread of fluids through tissues by lowering the viscosity of hyaluronic acid

hy·brid \'hī-brəd\ *noun* [Latin *hybrida*] (1601)
1 : an offspring of two animals or plants of different races, breeds, varieties, species, or genera
2 : a person whose background is a blend of two diverse cultures or traditions
3 a : something heterogeneous in origin or composition **:** COMPOSITE ⟨artificial *hybrids* of DNA and RNA⟩ ⟨a *hybrid* of medieval and Renaissance styles⟩ **b :** something (as a power plant, vehicle, or electronic circuit) that has two different types of components performing essentially the same function
— **hybrid** *adjective*
— **hy·brid·ism** \-brə-,di-zəm\ *noun*
— **hy·brid·i·ty** \hī-'bri-də-tē\ *noun*

hybrid computer *noun* (1968)
: a computer system consisting of a combination of analog and digital computer systems

hy·brid·ize \'hī-brə-,dīz\ *verb* **-ized; -iz·ing** (1845)
transitive verb
: to cause to produce hybrids **:** INTERBREED
intransitive verb
: to produce hybrids
— **hy·brid·iza·tion** \ˌhī-brə-də-'zā-shən\ *noun*
— **hy·brid·iz·er** *noun*

hy·brid·oma \ˌhī-brə-'dō-mə\ *noun* (1978)

: a hybrid cell produced by the fusion of an antibody-producing lymphocyte with a tumor cell and used to culture continuously a specific monoclonal antibody

hybrid tea rose *noun* (1926)
: any of numerous moderately hardy cultivated hybrid bush roses grown especially for their strongly recurrent bloom of large usually scentless flowers — called also *hybrid tea*

hybrid vigor *noun* (1918)
: HETEROSIS

hy·bris \'hī-brəs, 'hē-\ *variant of* HUBRIS

hy·da·thode \'hī-də-,thȯd\ *noun* [International Scientific Vocabulary, from Greek *hydat-, hydōr* water + *hodos* road] (1895)
: a specialized pore on the leaves of higher plants that functions in the exudation of water

hy·da·tid \'hī-də-təd, -,tid\ *noun* [Greek *hydatid-, hydatis* watery cyst, from *hydat-, hydōr*] (1683)
: the larval cyst of a tapeworm (genus *Echinococcus*) occurring as a fluid-filled sac containing daughter cysts in which scolices develop

hydr- *or* **hydro-** *combining form* [Middle English *ydr-, ydro-*, from Old French, from Latin *hydr-, hydro-*, from Greek, from *hydōr* — more at WATER]
1 a : water ⟨*hydrous*⟩ ⟨*hydro*electric⟩ **b :** liquid ⟨*hydrokinetic*⟩
2 : hydrogen **:** containing or combined with hydrogen ⟨*hydro*carbon⟩ ⟨*hydroxyl*⟩
3 : hydroid ⟨*hydromedusa*⟩

Hy·dra \'hī-drə\ *noun* [Middle English *Ydra*, from Latin *Hydra*, from Greek]
1 : a many-headed serpent or monster in Greek mythology that was slain by Hercules and each head of which when cut off was replaced by two others
2 *not capitalized* **:** a multifarious evil not to be overcome by a single effort
3 [Latin (genitive *Hydrae*), from Greek] **:** a southern constellation of great length that lies south of Cancer, Sextans, Corvus, and Virgo and is represented on old maps by a serpent
4 *not capitalized* [New Latin, from Latin, *Hydra*] **:** any of numerous small tubular freshwater hydrozoan polyps (*Hydra* and related genera) having at one end a mouth surrounded by tentacles

hy·dra–head·ed \ˌhī-drə-'he-dəd\ *adjective* (1599)
: having many centers or branches ⟨a *hydraheaded* organization⟩

hy·dral·azine \hī-'dra-lə-,zēn\ *noun* [*hydr-* + *phthalic* (acid) + *azine*] (1952)
: a vasodilator $C_8H_8N_4$ used in the treatment of hypertension

hy·dran·gea \hī-'drān-jə\ *noun* [New Latin, from *hydr-* + Greek *angeion* vessel — more at ANGI-] (circa 1753)
: any of a genus (*Hydrangea*) of shrubs and one woody vine of the saxifrage family with opposite leaves and showy clusters of usually sterile white or tinted flowers

hy·drant \'hī-drənt\ *noun* (1806)
1 : a discharge pipe with a valve and spout at which water may be drawn from a water main (as for fighting fires) — called also *fireplug*
2 : FAUCET

hy·dranth \'hī-,dran(t)th\ *noun* [International Scientific Vocabulary *hydr-* + Greek *anthos* flower — more at ANTHOLOGY] (1874)
: one of the nutritive zooids of a hydroid colony

hy·drase \'hī-,drās, -,drāz\ *noun* (1943)
: an enzyme that promotes the addition or removal of water to or from its substrate

¹**hy·drate** \'hī-,drāt\ *noun* (1802)
: a compound formed by the union of water with some other substance

²**hydrate** *verb* **hy·drat·ed; hy·drat·ing** (1850)
transitive verb
: to cause to take up or combine with water or the elements of water

intransitive verb
: to become a hydrate
— **hy·dra·tion** \hī-'drā-shən\ *noun*
— **hy·dra·tor** \'hī-,drā-tər\ *noun*

hy·drau·lic \hī-'dró-lik\ *adjective* [Latin *hydraulicus*, from Greek *hydraulikos*, from *hydraulis* hydraulic organ, from *hydr-* + *aulos* reed instrument — more at ALVEOLUS] (1661)
1 : operated, moved, or effected by means of water
2 a : of or relating to hydraulics ⟨*hydraulic* engineer⟩ **b** : of or relating to water or other liquid in motion ⟨*hydraulic* erosion⟩
3 : operated by the resistance offered or the pressure transmitted when a quantity of liquid (as water or oil) is forced through a comparatively small orifice or through a tube ⟨*hydraulic* brakes⟩
4 : hardening or setting under water ⟨*hydraulic* cement⟩
— **hy·drau·li·cal·ly** \-li-k(ə-)lē\ *adverb*

hy·drau·lics \hī-'dró-liks\ *noun plural but singular in construction* (1671)
: a branch of science that deals with practical applications (as the transmission of energy or the effects of flow) of liquid (as water) in motion

hy·dra·zide \'hī-drə-,zīd\ *noun* (1888)
: any of a class of compounds resulting from the replacement of hydrogen by an acid group in hydrazine or in one of its derivatives

hy·dra·zine \'hī-drə-,zēn\ *noun* [International Scientific Vocabulary] (1887)
: a colorless fuming corrosive strongly reducing liquid base N_2H_4 used especially in fuels for rocket and jet engines; *also* : an organic base derived from this compound

hy·dra·zo·ic acid \,hī-drə-'zō-ik-\ *noun* [*hydr-* + *azo-* + 1*-ic*] (1894)
: a colorless volatile poisonous explosive liquid HN_3 that has a foul odor and yields explosive salts of heavy metals

hy·dric \'hī-drik\ *adjective* (1926)
: characterized by, relating to, or requiring an abundance of moisture ⟨a *hydric* habitat⟩ ⟨a *hydric* plant⟩ — compare MESIC, XERIC

-hydric *adjective suffix*
: containing acid hydrogen ⟨mono*hydric*⟩

hy·dride \'hī-,drīd\ *noun* (1869)
: a compound of hydrogen with a more electropositive element or group

hy·dri·od·ic acid \,hī-drē-'ä-dik-\ *noun* [International Scientific Vocabulary] (1819)
: an aqueous solution of hydrogen iodide HI that is a strong acid resembling hydrochloric acid chemically and that is also a strong reducing agent

1**hy·dro** \'hī-(,)drō\ *noun, plural* **hydros** [short for *hydropathic establishment*] (1882)
British : an establishment offering hydropathic treatment (as for weight loss) : HEALTH SPA

2**hydro** *noun, often attributive* [short for *hydropower*] (1916)
: hydroelectric power

hy·dro·bi·ol·o·gy \,hī-drō-bī-'ä-lə-jē\ *noun* (1926)
: the biology of bodies or units of water; *especially* : LIMNOLOGY
— **hy·dro·bi·o·log·i·cal** \-,bī-ə-'lä-ji-kəl\ *adjective*
— **hy·dro·bi·ol·o·gist** \-bī-'ä-lə-jist\ *noun*

hy·dro·bro·mic acid \,hī-drə-'brō-mik-\ *noun* [International Scientific Vocabulary] (1836)
: an aqueous solution of hydrogen bromide HBr that is a strong acid resembling hydrochloric acid chemically, that is a weak reducing agent, and that is used especially for making bromides

hy·dro·car·bon \'hī-drō-,kär-bən\ *noun* (1826)
: an organic compound (as acetylene or butane) containing only carbon and hydrogen and often occurring in petroleum, natural gas, coal, and bitumens

hy·dro·cele \'hī-drə-,sēl\ *noun* [Latin, from Greek *hydrokēlē*, from *hydr-* + *kēlē* tumor — more at -CELE] (1597)
: an accumulation of serous fluid in a sacculated cavity (as the scrotum)

hy·dro·ce·phal·ic \,hī-drō-sə-'fa-lik\ *adjective* (1815)
: relating to, characterized by, or affected with hydrocephalus
— **hydrocephalic** *noun*

hy·dro·ceph·a·lus \-'se-fə-ləs\ *also* **hy·dro·ceph·a·ly** \-lē\ *noun* [New Latin *hydrocephalus*, from Late Latin, hydrocephalic, adjective, from Greek *hydrokephalos*, from *hydr-* + *kephalē* head — more at CEPHALIC] (1670)
: an abnormal increase in the amount of cerebrospinal fluid within the cranial cavity that is accompanied by expansion of the cerebral ventricles, enlargement of the skull and especially the forehead, and atrophy of the brain

hy·dro·chlo·ric acid \,hī-drə-'klōr-ik-, -'klór-\ *noun* [International Scientific Vocabulary] (circa 1828)
: an aqueous solution of hydrogen chloride HCl that is a strong corrosive irritating acid, is normally present in dilute form in gastric juice, and is widely used in industry and in the laboratory

hy·dro·chlo·ride \-'klōr-,īd, -'klór-\ *noun* (1826)
: a chemical complex composed of an organic base (as an alkaloid) in association with hydrogen chloride

hy·dro·chlo·ro·thi·a·zide \-,klōr-ə-'thī-ə-,zīd, -,klór-\ *noun* [*hydr-* + *chlor-* + *thiazine* + *-ide*] (1958)
: a diuretic and antihypertensive drug $C_7H_8ClN_3O_4S_2$

hy·dro·col·loid \,hī-drə-'kä-,lóid\ *noun* (1916)
: a substance that yields a gel with water
— **hy·dro·col·loi·dal** \-kə-'lói-d'l, -kä-\ *adjective*

hy·dro·cor·ti·sone \-'kór-tə-,sōn, -,zōn\ *noun* (1951)
: a glucocorticoid $C_{21}H_{30}O_5$ of the adrenal cortex that is a derivative of cortisone and is used in the treatment of rheumatoid arthritis — called also *cortisol*

hy·dro·crack·ing \'hī-drə-,kra-kiŋ\ *noun* (1940)
: the cracking of hydrocarbons in the presence of hydrogen
— **hy·dro·crack** \-,krak\ *transitive verb*
— **hy·dro·crack·er** *noun*

hy·dro·cy·an·ic acid \,hī-drō-sī-'a-nik-\ *noun* [International Scientific Vocabulary] (1819)
: an aqueous solution of hydrogen cyanide HCN that is a poisonous weak acid and is used chiefly in fumigating and in organic synthesis

hy·dro·dy·nam·ic \-dī-'na-mik\ *also* **hy·dro·dy·nam·i·cal** \-mi-kəl\ *adjective* [New Latin *hydrodynamicus*, from *hydr-* + *dynamicus* dynamic] (circa 1828)
: of, relating to, or involving principles of hydrodynamics
— **hy·dro·dy·nam·i·cal·ly** \-mi-k(ə-)lē\ *adverb*

hy·dro·dy·nam·ics \-miks\ *noun plural but singular in construction* (1779)
: a branch of physics that deals with the motion of fluids and the forces acting on solid bodies immersed in fluids and in motion relative to them — compare HYDROSTATICS
— **hy·dro·dy·nam·i·cist** \-'na-mə-sist\ *noun*

hy·dro·elec·tric \,hī-drō-i-'lek-trik\ *adjective* [International Scientific Vocabulary] (1884)
: of or relating to production of electricity by waterpower ⟨constructed a *hydroelectric* power plant at the dam site⟩
— **hy·dro·elec·tri·cal·ly** \-tri-k(ə-)lē\ *adverb*

— **hy·dro·elec·tric·i·ty** \-,lek-'tri-sə-tē, -'tris-tē\ *noun*

hy·dro·flu·or·ic acid \,hī-drō-'flōr-ik, -'flúr-\ *noun* [International Scientific Vocabulary] (circa 1872)
: an aqueous solution of hydrogen fluoride HF that is a weak poisonous acid, that resembles hydrochloric acid chemically but attacks silica and silicates, and that is used especially in finishing and etching glass

hy·dro·foil \'hī-drə-,fóil\ *noun* (1919)
1 : a body similar to an airfoil but designed for action in or on water
2 : a motorboat that has metal plates or fins attached by struts fore and aft for lifting the hull clear of the water as speed is attained

hydrofoil 2

hy·dro·gen \'hī-drə-jən, -dər-\ *noun* [French *hydrogène*, from *hydr-* + *-gène* -gen; from the fact that water is generated by its combustion] (1791)
: a nonmetallic element that is the simplest and lightest of the elements, is normally a colorless odorless highly flammable diatomic gas, and is used especially in synthesis — compare DEUTERIUM, TRITIUM; see ELEMENT table
— **hy·drog·e·nous** \hī-'drä-jə-nəs\ *adjective*

hy·drog·e·nase \hī-'drä-jə-,nās, -,nāz\ *noun* (1900)
: an enzyme of various microorganisms that promotes the formation and utilization of gaseous hydrogen

hy·dro·ge·nate \hī-'drä-jə-,nāt, 'hī-drə-\ *transitive verb* **-nat·ed; -nat·ing** (1809)
: to combine or treat with or expose to hydrogen; *especially* : to add hydrogen to the molecule of (an unsaturated organic compound)
— **hy·dro·ge·na·tion** \hī-,drä-jə-'nā-shən, ,hī-drə-\ *noun*

hydrogen bomb *noun* (1947)
: a bomb whose violent explosive power is due to the sudden release of atomic energy resulting from the fusion of light nuclei (as of hydrogen atoms) at very high temperature and pressure to form helium nuclei

hydrogen bond *noun* (1923)
: an electrostatic attraction between a hydrogen atom in one polar molecule (as of water) and a small electronegative atom (as of oxygen, nitrogen, or fluorine) in usually another molecule of the same or a different polar substance
— **hydrogen bonding** *noun*

hydrogen bromide *noun* (1885)
: a colorless irritating gas HBr that fumes in moist air and yields hydrobromic acid when dissolved in water

hydrogen chloride *noun* (1869)
: a colorless pungent poisonous gas HCl that fumes in moist air and yields hydrochloric acid when dissolved in water

hydrogen cyanide *noun* (1882)
1 : a poisonous usually gaseous compound HCN that has the odor of bitter almonds
2 : HYDROCYANIC ACID

hydrogen fluoride *noun* (1885)
: a colorless corrosive fuming usually gaseous compound HF that yields hydrofluoric acid when dissolved in water

hydrogen iodide *noun* (1885)
: an acrid colorless gas HI that fumes in moist air and yields hydriodic acid when dissolved in water

hydrogen ion *noun* (1896)
1 : the cation H⁺ of acids consisting of a hydrogen atom whose electron has been transferred to the anion of the acid
2 : HYDRONIUM

hydrogen peroxide *noun* (1872)
: an unstable compound H_2O_2 used especially as an oxidizing and bleaching agent, an antiseptic, and a propellant

hydrogen sulfide *noun* (1873)
: a flammable poisonous gas H_2S that has an odor suggestive of rotten eggs and is found especially in many mineral waters and in putrefying matter

hy·dro·graph·ic \ˌhī-drə-'gra-fik\ *adjective* [French *hydrographique*, from Middle French, from *hydr-* + *-graphique* -graphic] (1665)
1 : of or relating to the characteristic features (as flow or depth) of bodies of water
2 : relating to the charting of bodies of water
 — **hy·drog·ra·pher** \hī-'drä-grə-fər\ *noun*
 — **hy·drog·ra·phy** \-grə-fē\ *noun*

¹**hy·droid** \'hī-ˌdrȯid\ *adjective* [ultimately from New Latin *Hydra*] (circa 1864)
: of or relating to a hydrozoan; *especially* : resembling a typical hydra

²**hydroid** *noun* (1865)
: HYDROZOAN; *especially* : a hydrozoan polyp as distinguished from a medusa

hy·dro·ki·net·ic \ˌhī-drō-kə-'ne-tik, -(ˌ)kī-\ *adjective* (1876)
: of or relating to the motions of fluids or the forces which produce or affect such motions — compare HYDROSTATIC

hy·dro·lase \'hī-drə-ˌlās, -ˌlāz\ *noun* [International Scientific Vocabulary, from New Latin *hydrolysis* + International Scientific Vocabulary *-ase*] (1910)
: a hydrolytic enzyme

hydrologic cycle *noun* (1936)
: the sequence of conditions through which water passes from vapor in the atmosphere through precipitation upon land or water surfaces and ultimately back into the atmosphere as a result of evaporation and transpiration — called also *hydrological cycle*

hy·drol·o·gy \hī-'drä-lə-jē\ *noun* [New Latin *hydrologia*, from Latin *hydr-* + *-logia* -logy] (1762)
: a science dealing with the properties, distribution, and circulation of water on and below the earth's surface and in the atmosphere
 — **hy·dro·log·ic** \ˌhī-drə-'lä-jik\ *or* **hy·dro·log·i·cal** \-ji-kəl\ *adjective*
 — **hy·dro·log·i·cal·ly** \-ji-k(ə-)lē\ *adverb*
 — **hy·drol·o·gist** \hī-'drä-lə-jist\ *noun*

hy·dro·ly·sate \hī-'drä-lə-ˌsāt\ *also* **hy·dro·ly·zate** \-ˌzāt\ *noun* (1915)
: a product of hydrolysis

hy·dro·ly·sis \hī-'drä-lə-səs\ *noun* [New Latin] (1880)
: a chemical process of decomposition involving the splitting of a bond and the addition of the hydrogen cation and the hydroxide anion of water
 — **hy·dro·lyt·ic** \ˌhī-drə-'li-tik\ *adjective*
 — **hy·dro·lyt·i·cal·ly** \-ti-k(ə-)lē\ *adverb*

hy·dro·lyze \'hī-drə-ˌlīz\ *verb* **-lyzed; -lyz·ing** [International Scientific Vocabulary, from New Latin *hydrolysis*] (1880)
transitive verb
: to subject to hydrolysis
intransitive verb
: to undergo hydrolysis
 — **hy·dro·lyz·able** \-ˌlī-zə-bəl\ *adjective*

hy·dro·mag·net·ic \ˌhī-drō-mag-'ne-tik\ *adjective* (1943)
: MAGNETOHYDRODYNAMIC

hy·dro·man·cy \'hī-drə-ˌman(t)-sē\ *noun* [Middle English *ydromancie*, from Middle French, from Latin *hydromantia*, from *hydr-* + *-mantia* -mancy] (14th century)
: divination by the appearance or motion of liquids (as water)

hy·dro·me·chan·i·cal \ˌhī-drō-mi-'ka-ni-kəl\ *adjective* (1825)

: relating to a branch of mechanics that deals with the equilibrium and motion of fluids and of solid bodies immersed in them
 — **hy·dro·me·chan·ics** \-'ka-niks\ *noun plural but singular in construction*

hy·dro·me·du·sa \ˌhī-drō-mi-'dü-sə, -'dyü-, -zə\ *noun, plural* **-sae** \-ˌsē, -ˌzē\ [New Latin] (circa 1889)
: a medusa (as of the orders Anthomedusae and Leptomedusae) produced as a bud from a hydroid

hy·dro·met·al·lur·gy \ˌhī-drō-'me-t°l-ˌər-jē\ *noun* [International Scientific Vocabulary] (circa 1859)
: the treatment of ores by wet processes (as leaching)
 — **hy·dro·met·al·lur·gi·cal** \-ˌme-t°l-'ər-ji-kəl\ *adjective*
 — **hy·dro·met·al·lur·gist** \-'me-t°l-ˌər-jist\ *noun*

hy·dro·me·te·or \ˌhī-drō-'mē-tē-ər, -tē-ˌȯr\ *noun* [International Scientific Vocabulary] (1857)
: a product (as fog, rain, or hail) formed by the condensation of atmospheric water vapor

hy·dro·me·te·o·rol·o·gy \-ˌmē-tē-ə-'rä-lə-jē\ *noun* (circa 1859)
: a branch of meteorology that deals with water in the atmosphere especially as precipitation
 — **hy·dro·me·te·o·ro·log·i·cal** \-tē-ˌȯr-ə-'lä-ji-kəl, -ˌär-ə-, -ə-rə-\ *adjective*
 — **hy·dro·me·te·o·rol·o·gist** \-tē-ə-'rä-lə-jist\ *noun*

hy·drom·e·ter \hī-'drä-mə-tər\ *noun* (1675)
: an instrument for determining the specific gravity of a liquid (as battery acid or an alcohol solution) and hence its strength
 — **hy·dro·met·ric** \ˌhī-drə-'me-trik\ *adjective*

hy·dro·mor·phic \ˌhī-drə-'mȯr-fik\ *adjective* (1938)
of a soil : developed in the presence of an excess of moisture which tends to suppress aerobic factors in soil-building

hy·dron·ic \hī-'drä-nik\ *adjective* [*hydr-* + *-onic* (as in *electronic*)] (1946)
: of, relating to, or being a system of heating or cooling that involves transfer of heat by a circulating fluid (as water or vapor) in a closed system of pipes
 — **hy·dron·i·cal·ly** \-ni-k(ə-)lē\ *adverb*

hy·dro·ni·um \hī-'drō-nē-əm\ *noun* [International Scientific Vocabulary *hydr-* + *-onium*] (1908)
: a hydrated hydrogen ion H_3O^+

hy·drop·a·thy \hī-'drä-pə-thē\ *noun* [International Scientific Vocabulary] (1843)
: the empirical use of water in the treatment of disease — compare HYDROTHERAPY
 — **hy·dro·path·ic** \ˌhī-drə-'pa-thik\ *adjective*

hy·dro·per·ox·ide \ˌhī-drō-pə-'räk-ˌsīd\ *noun* (1937)
: a compound containing an O_2H group

hy·dro·phane \'hī-drə-ˌfān\ *noun* (1784)
: a semitranslucent opal that becomes translucent or transparent on immersion in water

hy·dro·phil·ic \ˌhī-drə-'fi-lik\ *adjective* [New Latin *hydrophilus*, from Greek *hydr-* + *-philos* -philous] (1916)
: of, relating to, or having a strong affinity for water ⟨*hydrophilic* proteins⟩
 — **hy·dro·phi·lic·i·ty** \ˌhī-drə-fi-'li-sə-tē\ *noun*

hy·dro·pho·bia \ˌhī-drə-'fō-bē-ə\ *noun* [Late Latin, from Greek, from *hydr-* + *-phobia* -phobia] (1547)
1 : RABIES
2 : a morbid dread of water

hy·dro·pho·bic \-'fō-bik\ *adjective* (1807)
1 : of, relating to, or suffering from hydrophobia
2 : lacking affinity for water
 — **hy·dro·pho·bic·i·ty** \-fō-'bi-sə-tē\ *noun*

hy·dro·phone \'hī-drə-ˌfōn\ *noun* (1860)

: an instrument for listening to sound transmitted through water

hy·dro·phyte \-ˌfīt\ *noun* [International Scientific Vocabulary] (1832)
1 : a perennial vascular aquatic plant having its overwintering buds under water
2 : a plant growing in water or in soil too waterlogged for most plants to survive
 — **hy·dro·phyt·ic** \ˌhī-drə-'fi-tik\ *adjective*

¹**hy·dro·plane** \'hī-drə-ˌplān\ *noun* (1904)
1 : a powerboat designed for racing that skims the surface of the water
2 : SEAPLANE

²**hydroplane** *intransitive verb* (1962)
: to skim on water; *especially, of a vehicle* : to skid on a wet surface (as pavement) because a film of water on the surface causes the tires to lose contact with it

hy·dro·pon·ics \ˌhī-drə-'pä-niks\ *noun plural but singular in construction* [*hydr-* + *-ponics* (as in *geoponics* agriculture)] (1937)
: the growing of plants in nutrient solutions with or without an inert medium to provide mechanical support
 — **hy·dro·pon·ic** \-nik\ *adjective*
 — **hy·dro·pon·i·cal·ly** \-ni-k(ə-)lē\ *adverb*

hy·dro·pow·er \'hī-drə-ˌpau̇(-ə)r\ *noun* (1933)
: hydroelectric power

hy·dro·qui·none \ˌhī-drō-kwi-'nōn, -'kwi-ˌnōn\ *noun* [International Scientific Vocabulary] (circa 1872)
: a white crystalline strongly reducing phenol $C_6H_6O_2$ used especially as a photographic developer and as an antioxidant and stabilizer

hy·dro·sere \'hī-drə-ˌsir\ *noun* (1920)
: an ecological sere originating in an aquatic habitat

hy·dro·sol \'hī-drə-ˌsäl, -ˌsȯl\ *noun* [*hydr-* + *-sol* (from *solution*)] (1864)
: a sol in which the liquid is water
 — **hy·dro·sol·ic** \ˌhī-drə-'säl-ik\ *adjective*

hy·dro·space \-ˌspās\ *noun* (1963)
: the regions beneath the surface of the ocean

hy·dro·sphere \-ˌsfir\ *noun* [International Scientific Vocabulary] (1887)
: the aqueous vapor of the atmosphere; *broadly* : the aqueous envelope of the earth including bodies of water and aqueous vapor in the atmosphere
 — **hy·dro·spher·ic** \ˌhī-drə-'sfir-ik, -'sfer-\ *adjective*

hy·dro·stat·ic \ˌhī-drə-'sta-tik\ *adjective* [probably from New Latin *hydrostaticus*, from *hydr-* + *staticus* static] (1666)
: of or relating to fluids at rest or to the pressures they exert or transmit — compare HYDROKINETIC
 — **hy·dro·stat·i·cal·ly** \-ti-k(ə-)lē\ *adverb*

hy·dro·stat·ics \-tiks\ *noun plural but singular in construction* (1660)
: a branch of physics that deals with the characteristics of fluids at rest and especially with the pressure in a fluid or exerted by a fluid on an immersed body — compare HYDRODYNAMICS

hy·dro·ther·a·py \ˌhī-drə-'ther-ə-pē\ *noun* [International Scientific Vocabulary] (1876)
: the use of water especially externally in the treatment of disease or disability

hy·dro·ther·mal \ˌhī-drə-'thər-məl\ *adjective* [International Scientific Vocabulary] (1849)
: of or relating to hot water — used especially of the formation of minerals by hot solutions rising from a cooling magma
 — **hy·dro·ther·mal·ly** \-mə-lē\ *adverb*

hy·dro·tho·rax \-'thōr-ˌaks, -'thȯr-\ *noun* [New Latin] (1793)
: an excess of serous fluid in the pleural cavity; *especially* : an effusion resulting from failing circulation (as in heart disease or from lung infection)

hy·drot·ro·pism \hī-'drä-trə-ˌpi-zəm\ *noun* [International Scientific Vocabulary] (circa 1882)
: a tropism (as in plant roots) in which water or water vapor is the orienting factor

— **hy·dro·tro·pic** \,hī-drə-'trō-pik, -'trä-\ *adjective*

hy·drous \'hī-drəs\ *adjective* (1826)
: containing water usually in chemical association (as in hydrates)

hy·drox·ide \hī-'dräk-,sīd\ *noun* [International Scientific Vocabulary] (1851)
1 : the univalent anion OH^- consisting of one atom of hydrogen and one of oxygen — called also *hydroxide ion*
2 : an ionic compound of hydroxide with an element or group

hy·droxy \hī-'dräk-sē\ *adjective* [International Scientific Vocabulary, from *hydroxyl*] (1812)
: being or containing hydroxyl; *especially* **:** containing hydroxyl especially in place of hydrogen — usually used in combination 〈*hydroxy*acetic acid〉

hy·droxy·ap·a·tite \hī-,dräk-sē-'a-pə-,tīt\ *or* **hy·drox·yl·ap·a·tite** \-sə-'la-pə-,tīt\ *noun* (1912)
: a complex phosphate of calcium $Ca_5(PO_4)_3OH$ that occurs as a mineral and is the chief structural element of vertebrate bone

hy·droxy·bu·tyr·ic acid \hī-,dräk-sē-byü-'tir-ik-\ *noun* (1879)
: a hydroxy derivative $C_4H_8O_3$ of butyric acid that is excreted in increased quantities in the urine in diabetes

hy·drox·yl \hī-'dräk-səl\ *noun* [*hydr-* + *ox-* + *-yl*] (1869)
1 : the chemical group or ion OH that consists of one atom of hydrogen and one of oxygen and is neutral or positively charged
2 : HYDROXIDE 1
— **hy·drox·yl·ic** \,hī-,dräk-'si-lik\ *adjective*

hy·drox·yl·amine \hī-'dräk-sə-lə-,mēn, ,hī-,dräk-'si-lə-,mēn\ *noun* [International Scientific Vocabulary] (1869)
: a colorless odorless nitrogenous base NH_3O that resembles ammonia in its reactions but is less basic and that is used especially as a reducing agent

hy·drox·y·lase \hī-'dräk-sə-,lās, -,lāz\ *noun* (1953)
: any of a group of enzymes that catalyze oxidation reactions in which one of the two atoms of molecular oxygen is incorporated into the substrate and the other is used to oxidize NADH or NADPH

hy·drox·yl·ate \hī-'dräk-sə-,lāt\ *transitive verb* **-at·ed; -at·ing** (circa 1909)
: to introduce hydroxyl into
— **hy·drox·yl·ation** \-,dräk-sə-'lā-shən\ *noun*

hy·droxy·pro·line \hī-,dräk-sē-'prō-,lēn\ *noun* (1905)
: an amino acid $C_5H_9NO_3$ that occurs naturally as a constituent of collagen

hy·droxy·tryp·ta·mine \-'trip-tə-,mēn\ *noun* (1949)
: SEROTONIN

hy·droxy·urea \-yü-'rē-ə\ *noun* (1949)
: a compound $CH_4N_2O_2$ used to treat some forms of leukemia

hy·droxy·zine \hī-'dräk-sə-,zēn\ *noun* [*hydroxy-* + pipera*zine*] (1956)
: a compound $C_{21}H_{27}ClN_2O_2$ used as an antihistaminic and tranquilizer

hy·dro·zo·an \,hī-drə-'zō-ən\ *noun* [ultimately from Greek *hydr-* + *zōion* animal — more at ZO-] (1877)
: any of a class (Hydrozoa) of coelenterates that includes simple and compound polyps and jellyfishes having no stomodeum or gastric tentacles
— **hydrozoan** *adjective*

hy·e·na \hī-'ē-nə\ *noun, plural* **hyenas** *also* **hyena** [Middle English *hyene*, from Latin *hyaena*, from Greek *hyaina*, from *hys* hog — more at SOW] (14th century)
: any of several large strong nocturnal carnivorous Old World mammals (family Hyaenidae) that usually feed as scavengers
— **hy·e·nic** \-'ē-nik, -'e-nik\ *adjective*

Hy·ge·ia \hī-'jē-ə\ *noun* [Latin, from Greek *Hygieia*]
: the goddess of health in Greek mythology

hy·giene \'hī-,jēn *also* hī-'\ *noun* [French *hygiène* & New Latin *hygieina*, from Greek, neuter plural of *hygieinos* healthful, from *hygiēs* healthy; akin to Sanskrit *su* well and to Latin *vivus* living — more at QUICK] (1671)
1 : a science of the establishment and maintenance of health
2 : conditions or practices (as of cleanliness) conducive to health
— **hy·gien·ic** \,hī-'jē-nik, -'je- *also* -jē-'e-nik\ *adjective*
— **hy·gien·i·cal·ly** \-ni-k(ə-)lē\ *adverb*
— **hy·gien·ist** \hī-'jē-nist, 'hī-,jē-, hī-'je-\ *noun*

hy·gien·ics \,hī-'jē-niks, -'je- *also* -jē-'e-niks\ *noun plural but singular in construction* (1855)
: HYGIENE 1

hygr- *also* **hygro-** *combining form* [Greek, from *hygros* wet — more at HUMOR]
: humidity **:** moisture 〈*hygro*phyte〉

hy·gro·graph \'hī-grə-,graf\ *noun* [International Scientific Vocabulary] (circa 1864)
: an instrument for recording automatically variations in atmospheric humidity

hy·grom·e·ter \hī-'grä-mə-tər\ *noun* [probably from French *hygromètre*, from *hygr-* + *-mètre* -meter] (1670)
: any of several instruments for measuring the humidity of the atmosphere
— **hy·gro·met·ric** \,hī-grə-'me-trik\ *adjective*

hy·groph·i·lous \hī-'grä-fə-ləs\ *adjective* (1863)
: living or growing in moist places

hy·gro·phyte \'hī-grə-,fīt\ *noun* [International Scientific Vocabulary] (1903)
: HYDROPHYTE
— **hy·gro·phyt·ic** \,hī-grə-'fi-tik\ *adjective*

hy·gro·scop·ic \,hī-grə-'skä-pik\ *adjective* [*hygroscope*, an instrument showing changes in humidity + *-ic*; from the use of such materials in the hygroscope] (1790)
1 : readily taking up and retaining moisture
2 : taken up and retained under some conditions of humidity and temperature 〈*hygroscopic* water in clay〉
— **hy·gro·scop·ic·i·ty** \-(,)skä-'pi-sə-tē\ *noun*

hying *present participle of* HIE

Hyk·sos \'hik-,säs, -,sōs\ *adjective* [Greek *Hyksōs*, dynasty ruling Egypt, perhaps from Egyptian *ḥqꜣ* ruler + *bꜣšt* foreign land] (1602)
: of or relating to a Semite dynasty that ruled Egypt from about the 18th to the 16th century B.C.

hy·la \'hī-lə\ *noun* [New Latin, from Latin *Hylas*, a companion of Hercules] (1842)
: any of a genus (*Hyla*) of tree frogs

hy·lo·zo·ism \,hī-lə-'zō-,i-zəm\ *noun* [Greek *hylē* matter, literally, wood + *zōos* alive, living; akin to Greek *zōē* life — more at QUICK] (1678)
: a doctrine held especially by early Greek philosophers that all matter has life
— **hy·lo·zo·ist** \-'zō-ist\ *noun*
— **hy·lo·zo·is·tic** \-zō-'is-tik\ *adjective*

hy·men \'hī-mən\ *noun* [Late Latin, from Greek *hymēn* membrane] (1615)
: a fold of mucous membrane partly closing the orifice of the vagina
— **hy·men·al** \-mə-n°l\ *adjective*

Hymen *noun* [Latin, from Greek *Hymēn*]
: the Greek god of marriage

¹hy·me·ne·al \,hī-mə-'nē-əl\ *adjective* [Latin *hymenaeus* wedding song, wedding, from Greek *hymenaios*, from *Hymēn*] (1602)
: NUPTIAL
— **hy·me·ne·al·ly** \-'nē-ə-lē\ *adverb*

²hymeneal *noun* (1655)
1 *plural, archaic* **:** NUPTIALS
2 *archaic* **:** a wedding hymn

hy·me·ni·um \hī-'mē-nē-əm\ *noun, plural* **-nia** \-nē-ə\ *or* **-niums** [New Latin, from Greek *hymēn*] (1830)
: a spore-bearing layer in fungi consisting of a group of asci or basidia often interspersed with sterile structures

hy·me·nop·ter·an \,hī-mə-'näp-tə-rən\ *noun* [New Latin *Hymenoptera*, from Greek, neuter plural of *hymenopteros* membrane-winged, from *hymēn* + *pteron* wing — more at FEATHER] (circa 1842)
: any of an order (Hymenoptera) of highly specialized insects with complete metamorphosis that include the bees, wasps, ants, ichneumon flies, sawflies, gall wasps, and related forms, often associate in large colonies with complex social organization, and have usually four membranous wings and the abdomen generally borne on a slender pedicel
— **hymenopteran** *adjective*
— **hy·me·nop·ter·ous** \-rəs\ *adjective*

hy·me·nop·ter·on \-tə-,rän, -rən\ *noun, plural* **-tera** \-rə\ *also* **-terons** [New Latin, from Greek, neuter of *hymenopteros*] (1877)
: HYMENOPTERAN

¹hymn \'him\ *noun* [Middle English *ymne*, from Old English *ymen*, from Latin *hymnus* song of praise, from Greek *hymnos*] (before 12th century)
1 a : a song of praise to God **b :** a metrical composition adapted for singing in a religious service
2 : a song of praise or joy
3 : something resembling a hymn **:** PAEAN

²hymn *verb* **hymned** \'himd\; **hymn·ing** \'hi-miŋ\ (1667)
transitive verb
: to praise or worship in or as if in hymns
intransitive verb
: to sing a hymn

hym·nal \'him-nəl\ *noun* [Middle English *hymnale*, from Medieval Latin, from Latin *hymnus*] (15th century)
: a collection of church hymns

hym·na·ry \'him-nə-rē\ *noun, plural* **-ries** (1888)
: HYMNAL

hymn·book \'him-,bük\ *noun* (before 12th century)
: HYMNAL

hym·no·dy \'him-nə-dē\ *noun* [Late Latin *hymnodia*, from Greek *hymnōidia*, from *hymnos* + *aeidein* to sing — more at ODE] (1711)
1 : hymn singing
2 : hymn writing
3 : the hymns of a time, place, or church

hym·nol·o·gy \him-'nä-lə-jē\ *noun* [Greek *hymnologia* singing of hymns, from *hymnos* + *-logia* -logy] (circa 1638)
1 : HYMNODY
2 : the study of hymns

hy·oid \'hī-,óid\ *adjective* [New Latin *hyoides* hyoid bone] (1842)
: of or relating to the hyoid bone

hyoid bone *noun* [New Latin *hyoides*, from Greek *hyoeidēs* shaped like the letter upsilon (Υ, υ), being the hyoid bone, from *y, hy* upsilon] (circa 1811)
: a bone or complex of bones situated at the base of the tongue and supporting the tongue and its muscles

hy·o·scine \'hī-ə-,sēn\ *noun* [International Scientific Vocabulary *hyosc*yamine + *-ine*] (1872)
: SCOPOLAMINE; *especially* **:** the levorotatory form of scopolamine

hy·o·scy·a·mine \,hī-ə-'sī-ə-,mēn\ *noun* [German *Hyoscyamin*, from New Latin *Hyoscyamus*, genus of herbs, from Latin, henbane, from Greek *hyoskyamos*, literally, swine's

bean, from *hyos* (genitive of *hys* swine) + *kyamos* bean — more at SOW] (1858)
: a poisonous crystalline alkaloid $C_{17}H_{23}NO_3$ of which atropine is a racemic mixture; *especially* : its levorotatory form found especially in the plants belladonna and henbane and used similarly to atropine

hyp- — see HYPO-

hyp·abys·sal \ˌhī-pə-'bi-səl, ˌhī-\ *adjective* [International Scientific Vocabulary] (1895)
: of or relating to a fine-grained igneous rock usually formed at a moderate distance below the surface
— **hyp·abys·sal·ly** \-sə-lē\ *adverb*

hy·pae·thral \hī-'pē-thrəl\ *adjective* [Latin *hypaethrus* exposed to the open air, from Greek *hypaithros,* from *hypo-* + *aithēr* ether, air — more at ETHER] (1794)
1 : having a roofless central space ⟨*hypaethral* temple⟩
2 : open to the sky

hy·pal·la·ge \hī-'pa-lə-jē, hi-\ *noun* [Latin, from Greek *hypallagē,* literally, interchange, from *hypallassein* to interchange, from *hypo-* + *allassein* to change, from *allos* other — more at ELSE] (1586)
: an interchange of two elements in a phrase or sentence from a more logical to a less logical relationship (as in "a mind is a terrible thing to waste" for "to waste a mind is a terrible thing")

hy·pan·thi·um \hī-'pan(t)-thē-əm\ *noun, plural* **-thia** \-thē-ə\ [New Latin, from *hypo-* + *anth-* + *-ium*] (circa 1855)
: an enlargement of the floral receptacle bearing on its rim the stamens, petals, and sepals and often enlarging and surrounding the fruits (as in the rose hip)

¹hype \'hīp\ *noun* [by shortening & alteration] (1924)
1 *slang* : a narcotics addict
2 *slang* : HYPODERMIC

²hype *transitive verb* **hyped; hyping** (1938)
1 : STIMULATE, ENLIVEN — usually used with *up*
2 : INCREASE
— **hyped–up** \'hīp-'dəp\ *adjective*

³hype *transitive verb* **hyped; hyp·ing** [origin unknown] (circa 1931)
1 : PUT ON, DECEIVE
2 : to promote or publicize extravagantly

⁴hype *noun* (1955)
1 : DECEPTION, PUT-ON
2 : PUBLICITY; *especially* : promotional publicity of an extravagant or contrived kind

hy·per \'hī-pər\ *adjective* [short for *hyperactive*] (1971)
1 : HIGH-STRUNG, EXCITABLE; *also* : highly excited
2 : extremely active

hyper- *prefix* [Middle English *iper-,* from Latin *hyper-,* from Greek, from *hyper* — more at OVER]
1 : above : beyond : SUPER- ⟨*hyper*market⟩
2 a : excessively ⟨*hyper*sensitive⟩ **b** : excessive ⟨*hyper*emia⟩
3 : that is or exists in a space of more than three dimensions ⟨*hyper*space⟩

hy·per·acu·ity
hy·per·acute
hy·per·aes·thet·ic
hy·per·ag·gres·sive
hy·per·alert
hy·per·arid
hy·per·arous·al
hy·per·aware
hy·per·aware·ness
hy·per·ca·tab·o·lism
hy·per·cau·tious
hy·per·charged
hy·per·civ·i·lized
hy·per·co·ag·u·la·bil·i·ty
hy·per·co·ag·u·la·ble
hy·per·com·pet·i·tive
hy·per·con·cen·tra·tion
hy·per·con·scious
hy·per·con·scious·ness
hy·per·de·vel·op·ment
hy·per·ef·fi·cient
hy·per·emo·tion·al
hy·per·emo·tion·al·i·ty
hy·per·en·dem·ic
hy·per·en·er·get·ic
hy·per·ex·cit·abil·i·ty
hy·per·ex·cit·able
hy·per·ex·cit·ed
hy·per·ex·cite·ment

hy·per·ex·cre·tion
hy·per·fas·tid·i·ous
hy·per·func·tion
hy·per·func·tion·al
hy·per·func·tion·ing
hy·per·im·mune
hy·per·im·mu·ni·za·tion
hy·per·im·mu·nize
hy·per·in·flat·ed
hy·per·in·ner·va·tion
hy·per·in·tel·lec·tu·al
hy·per·in·tel·li·gent
hy·per·in·tense
hy·per·in·vo·lu·tion
hy·per·ma·nia
hy·per·man·ic
hy·per·mas·cu·line
hy·per·met·a·bol·ic
hy·per·me·tab·o·lism
hy·per·mo·bil·i·ty
hy·per·mod·ern
hy·per·mod·ern·ist
hy·per·mu·ta·bil·i·ty
hy·per·mu·ta·ble
hy·per·na·tion·al·is·tic
hy·per·phys·i·cal
hy·per·pig·men·ta·tion
hy·per·pig·ment·ed

hy·per·pro·duc·er
hy·per·pro·duc·tion
hy·per·pure
hy·per·ra·tio·nal
hy·per·ra·tio·nal·i·ty
hy·per·re·ac·tive
hy·per·re·ac·tiv·i·ty
hy·per·re·ac·tor
hy·per·re·spon·sive
hy·per·ro·man·tic
hy·per·sa·line
hy·per·sa·lin·i·ty
hy·per·sal·i·va·tion
hy·per·se·cre·tion
hy·per·sen·si·ti·za·tion
hy·per·sen·si·tize
hy·per·som·no·lence
hy·per·stat·ic
hy·per·stim·u·late
hy·per·stim·u·la·tion
hy·per·sus·cep·ti·bil·i·ty
hy·per·sus·cep·ti·ble
hy·per·tense
hy·per·typ·i·cal
hy·per·vig·i·lance
hy·per·vig·i·lant
hy·per·vir·u·lent
hy·per·vis·cos·i·ty

hy·per·acid·i·ty \ˌhī-pər-ə-'si-də-tē\ *noun* (circa 1890)
: the condition of containing more than the normal amount of acid
— **hy·per·ac·id** \ˌhī-pər-'a-səd\ *adjective*

hy·per·ac·tive \ˌhī-pər-'ak-tiv\ *adjective* (1867)
: affected with or exhibiting hyperactivity; *broadly* : more active than is usual or desirable
— **hyperactive** *noun*

hy·per·ac·tiv·i·ty \-ˌak-'ti-və-tē\ *noun* (1888)
: the state or condition of being excessively or pathologically active; *especially* : ATTENTION DEFICIT DISORDER

hy·per·aes·the·sia *variant of* HYPERESTHESIA

hy·per·al·i·men·ta·tion \ˌhī-pər-ˌa-lə-mən-'tā-shən\ *noun* (1967)
: the administration of nutrients by intravenous feeding especially to patients who cannot ingest food through the alimentary tract

hy·per·bar·ic \ˌhī-pər-'bar-ik\ *adjective* [*hyper-* + *bar-* + *¹-ic*] (1962)
: of, relating to, or utilizing greater than normal pressure (as of oxygen) ⟨*hyperbaric* chamber⟩ ⟨*hyperbaric* medicine⟩
— **hy·per·bar·i·cal·ly** \-i-k(ə-)lē\ *adverb*

hy·per·bo·la \hī-'pər-bə-lə\ *noun, plural* **-las** *or* **-lae** \-(ˌ)lē\ [New Latin, from Greek *hyperbolē*] (1668)
: a plane curve generated by a point so moving that the difference of the distances from two fixed points is a constant : a curve formed by the intersection of a double right circular cone with a plane that cuts both halves of the cone

hyperbola: *AB, CD* axes; *F, F'* foci; *xy, zw* asymptotes; *h, h', h", h'''* hyperbola

hy·per·bo·le \hī-'pər-bə-(ˌ)lē\ *noun* [Latin, from Greek *hyperbolē* excess, hyperbole, hyperbola, from *hyperballein* to exceed, from *hyper-* + *ballein* to throw — more at DEVIL] (15th century)
: extravagant exaggeration (as "mile-high ice-cream cones")
— **hy·per·bo·list** \-list\ *noun*

¹hy·per·bol·ic \ˌhī-pər-'bä-lik\ *also* **hy·per·bol·i·cal** \-li-kəl\ *adjective* (15th century)
: of, relating to, or marked by hyperbole
— **hy·per·bol·i·cal·ly** \-li-k(ə-)lē\ *adverb*

²hyperbolic *adjective* (1646)
1 : of, relating to, or being analogous to a hyperbola
2 : of, relating to, or being a space in which more than one line parallel to a given line passes through a point ⟨*hyperbolic* geometry⟩

hyperbolic function *noun* (circa 1890)
: any of a set of six functions analogous to the trigonometric functions but related to the hyperbola in a way similar to that in which the trigonometric functions are related to a circle

hyperbolic paraboloid *noun* (1842)
: a saddle-shaped quadric surface whose sections by planes parallel to one coordinate plane are hyperbolas while those sections by planes parallel to the other two are parabolas if proper orientation of the coordinate axes is assumed

hy·per·bo·lize \hī-'pər-bə-ˌlīz\ *verb* **-lized; -liz·ing** (1599)
intransitive verb
: to indulge in hyperbole
transitive verb
: to exaggerate to a hyperbolic degree

hy·per·bo·loid \-ˌlȯid\ *noun* (1743)
: a quadric surface whose sections by planes parallel to one coordinate plane are ellipses while those sections by planes parallel to the other two are hyperbolas if proper orientation of the axes is assumed
— **hy·per·bo·loi·dal** \(ˌ)hī-ˌpər-bə-'lȯi-d°l\ *adjective*

¹hy·per·bo·re·an \ˌhī-pər-'bōr-ē-ən, -'bȯr-; -(ˌ)pər-bə-'rē-ən\ *noun* [Latin *Hyperborei* (plural), from Greek *Hyperboreoi,* from *hyper-* + *Boreas*] (15th century)
1 *often capitalized* : a member of a people held by the ancient Greeks to live beyond the north wind in a region of perpetual sunshine
2 : an inhabitant of a cool northern climate

²hyperborean *adjective* (1591)
1 : of or relating to an extreme northern region : FROZEN
2 : of or relating to any of the arctic peoples

hy·per·cal·ce·mia \ˌhī-pər-ˌkal-'sē-mē-ə\ *noun* [New Latin] (1925)
: an excess of calcium in the blood
— **hy·per·cal·ce·mic** \-'sē-mik\ *adjective*

hy·per·cap·nia \-'kap-nē-ə\ *noun* [New Latin, from *hyper-* + Greek *kapnos* smoke; probably akin to Lithuanian *Kvapas* breath] (1908)
: the presence of excessive amounts of carbon dioxide in the blood
— **hy·per·cap·nic** \-nik\ *adjective*

hy·per·cat·a·lex·is \-ˌka-tə-'lek-səs\ *noun, plural* **-lex·es** \-'lek-ˌsēz\ [New Latin] (circa 1890)
: the occurrence of an additional syllable after the final complete foot or dipody in a line of verse
— **hy·per·cat·a·lec·tic** \-'lek-tik\ *adjective*

hy·per·charge \'hī-pər-ˌchärj\ *noun* [short for *hyperonic charge,* from *hyperon*] (1956)
: a quantum characteristic of a group of subatomic particles governed by the strong force that is related to strangeness and is represented by a number equal to twice the average value of the electric charge of the group

hy·per·cho·les·ter·ol·emia \ˌhī-pər-kə-ˌles-tə-rə-'lē-mē-ə\ *noun* [New Latin] (circa 1894)
: the presence of excess cholesterol in the blood
— **hy·per·cho·les·ter·ol·emic** \-mik\ *adjective*

hy·per·com·plex \ˌhī-pər-'käm-ˌpleks\ *adjective* (circa 1889)
: of, relating to, or being the most general form of number that extends the complex number to an expression of the same type (as a quaternion) involving a finite number of units or components in which addition is by

components and multiplication does not have all of the properties of real or complex numbers

hy·per·cor·rect \ˌhī-pər-kə-ˈrekt\ *adjective* (1922)
: of, relating to, or characterized by the production of a nonstandard linguistic form or construction on the basis of a false analogy (as "badly" in "my eyes have gone badly" and "widely" in "open widely")
— **hy·per·cor·rec·tion** \-ˈrek-shən\ *noun*
— **hy·per·cor·rect·ly** \-ˈrek-(t)lē\ *adverb*
— **hy·per·cor·rect·ness** \-ˈrek(t)-nəs\ *noun*

hy·per·crit·ic \ˌhī-pər-ˈkri-tik\ *noun* [New Latin *hypercriticus,* from *hyper-* + Latin *criticus* critic] (1633)
: a carping or unduly censorious critic
— **hy·per·crit·i·cism** \-ˈkri-tə-ˌsi-zəm\ *noun*

hy·per·crit·i·cal \-ˈkri-ti-kəl\ *adjective* (1605)
: meticulously or excessively critical
synonym see CRITICAL
— **hy·per·crit·i·cal·ly** \-k(ə-)lē\ *adverb*

hy·per·cube \ˈhī-pər-ˌkyüb\ *noun* (1909)
1 : a geometric figure (as a tesseract) in Euclidean space of *n* dimensions that is analogous to a cube in three dimensions
2 : a computer architecture in which each processor is connected to *n* others based on analogy to a hypercube of *n* dimensions

hy·per·emia \ˌhī-pər-ˈē-mē-ə\ *noun* [New Latin] (circa 1839)
: excess of blood in a body part : CONGESTION
— **hy·per·emic** \-mik\ *adjective*

hy·per·es·the·sia \ˌhī-pər-es-ˈthē-zh(ē-)ə\ *noun* [New Latin, from *hyper-* + *-esthesia* (as in *anesthesia*)] (circa 1852)
: unusual or pathological sensitivity of the skin or of a particular sense
— **hy·per·es·thet·ic** \-ˈthe-tik\ *adjective*

hy·per·eu·tec·tic \ˌhī-pər-yù-ˈtek-tik\ *adjective* (1902)
: HYPEREUTECTOID

hy·per·eu·tec·toid \-ˌtóid\ *adjective* (1908)
: containing the minor component in excess of that contained in the eutectoid

hy·per·ex·tend \ˌhī-pər-ik-ˈstend\ *transitive verb* (1883)
: to extend so that the angle between bones of a joint is greater than normal ⟨a *hyperextended* elbow⟩
— **hy·per·ex·ten·sion** \-ˈsten(t)-shən\ *noun*

hy·per·fine \ˈhī-pər-ˌfīn\ *adjective* (1926)
: being or relating to a fine-structure multiplet occurring in an atomic spectrum that is due to interaction between electrons and nuclear spin

hy·per·fo·cal distance \ˌhī-pər-ˈfō-kəl-\ *noun* [International Scientific Vocabulary] (1905)
: the nearest distance upon which a photographic lens may be focused to produce satisfactory definition at infinity

hy·per·ga·my \hī-ˈpər-gə-mē\ *noun, plural* **-mies** (1883)
: marriage into an equal or higher caste or social group

hy·per·geo·met·ric distribution \ˌhī-pər-ˌjē-ə-ˈme-trik-\ *noun* (1950)
: a probability function that gives the probability of obtaining exactly *x* elements of one kind and *n* − *x* elements of another if *n* elements are chosen at random without replacement from a finite population containing *N* elements of which *M* are of the first kind and *N* − *M* are of the second kind and has the form

$$f(x) = \frac{\binom{M}{x}\binom{N-M}{n-x}}{\binom{N}{n}} \text{ where } \binom{M}{x} = \frac{M!}{x!(M-x)!}$$

hy·per·gly·ce·mia \ˌhī-pər-glī-ˈsē-mē-ə\ *noun* [New Latin] (1894)
: excess of sugar in the blood
— **hy·per·gly·ce·mic** \-mik\ *adjective*

hy·per·gol·ic \ˌhī-pər-ˈgä-lik\ *adjective* [German *Hypergol* a hypergolic fuel, probably from *hyper-* + *erg-* + *-ol* (hydrocarbon)] (1947)
1 : igniting upon contact of components without external aid (as a spark)
2 : of, relating to, or using hypergolic fuel
— **hy·per·gol·i·cal·ly** \-li-k(ə-)lē\ *adverb*

hy·per·hi·dro·sis \ˌhī-pər-hī-ˈdrō-səs\ *noun* [New Latin *hidrosis* perspiration, from Greek *hidrōsis,* from *hidroun* to sweat, from *hidrōs* sweat — more at SWEAT] (circa 1860)
: generalized or local excessive sweating

hy·per·in·fla·tion \ˌhī-pər-in-ˈflā-shən\ *noun* (1930)
: inflation growing at a very high rate in a very short time; *also* : a period of hyperinflation
— **hy·per·in·fla·tion·ary** \-shə-ˌner-ē\ *adjective*

hy·per·in·su·lin·ism \ˌhī-pə-ˈrin(t)-s(ə-)lə-ˌni-zəm\ *noun* [International Scientific Vocabulary] (1924)
: the presence of excess insulin in the body resulting in hypoglycemia

Hy·pe·ri·on \hī-ˈpir-ē-ən\ *noun* [Latin, from Greek *Hyperiōn*]
: a Titan and the father of Aurora, Selene, and Helios

hy·per·ir·ri·ta·bil·i·ty \ˌhī-pər-ˌir-ə-tə-ˈbi-lə-tē\ *noun* (1913)
: abnormally great or uninhibited response to stimuli
— **hy·per·ir·ri·ta·ble** \-ˈir-ə-tə-bəl\ *adjective*

hy·per·ker·a·to·sis \ˌhī-pər-ˌker-ə-ˈtō-səs\ *noun, plural* **-to·ses** \-ˈtō-ˌsēz\ [New Latin] (1841)
: hypertrophy of the corneous layer of the skin
— **hy·per·ker·a·tot·ic** \-ˈtä-tik\ *adjective*

hy·per·ki·ne·sia \-kə-ˈnē-zh(ē-)ə, -ˌkī-\ *noun* [New Latin, from *hyperkinesis*] (circa 1848)
: HYPERKINESIS

hy·per·ki·ne·sis \-ˈnē-səs\ *noun* [New Latin] (circa 1855)
1 : abnormally increased and sometimes uncontrollable activity or muscular movements
2 : a condition especially of childhood characterized by hyperactivity

hy·per·ki·net·ic \-ˈne-tik\ *adjective* (1888)
: of, relating to, or affected with hyperkinesis or hyperactivity ⟨the *hyperkinetic* child⟩; *also* : characterized by fast-paced or frenetic activity

hy·per·li·pe·mia \ˌhī-pər-lī-ˈpē-mē-ə\ *noun* [New Latin] (circa 1894)
: the presence of excess fat or lipids in the blood
— **hy·per·li·pe·mic** \-mik\ *adjective*

hy·per·lip·id·emia \-ˌli-pə-ˈdē-mē-ə\ *noun* [New Latin] (1961)
: HYPERLIPEMIA

hy·per·mar·ket \ˈhī-pər-ˌmär-kət\ *noun* (1970)
: a very large store that carries products found in a supermarket as well as merchandise commonly found in department stores

hy·per·me·ter \hī-ˈpər-mə-tər\ *noun* [Late Latin *hypermetrus* hypercatalectic, from Greek *hypermetros* beyond measure, beyond the meter, from *hyper-* + *metron* measure, meter] (circa 1656)
1 : a verse marked by hypercatalexis
2 : a period comprising more than two or three cola
— **hy·per·met·ric** \ˌhī-pər-ˈme-trik\ *or* **hy·per·met·ri·cal** \-tri-kəl\ *adjective*

hy·per·me·tro·pia \ˌhī-pər-mi-ˈtrō-pē-ə\ *noun* [New Latin, from Greek *hypermetros* + New Latin *-opia*] (1868)
: HYPEROPIA
— **hy·per·me·tro·pic** \-ˈtrō-pik, -ˈträ-\ *adjective*

hy·perm·ne·sia \ˌhī-(ˌ)pərm-ˈnē-zh(ē-)ə\ *noun* [New Latin, from *hyper-* + *-mnesia* (as in *amnesia*)] (1882)
: abnormally vivid or complete memory or recall of the past
— **hy·perm·ne·sic** \-ˈnē-zik, -sik\ *adjective*

hy·per·on \ˈhī-pə-ˌrän\ *noun* [probably from *hyper-* + [2]*-on*] (1953)
: a fundamental particle of the baryon group that is greater in mass than a proton or neutron

hy·per·opia \ˌhī-pə-ˈrō-pē-ə\ *noun* [New Latin] (1884)
: a condition in which visual images come to a focus behind the retina of the eye and vision is better for distant than for near objects — called also *farsightedness*
— **hy·per·opic** \-ˈrō-pik, -ˈrä-\ *adjective*

hy·per·os·to·sis \ˌhī-pər-ˌäs-ˈtō-səs\ *noun, plural* **-to·ses** \-ˈtō-ˌsēz\ [New Latin] (circa 1836)
: excessive growth or thickening of bone tissue
— **hy·per·os·tot·ic** \-ˈtä-tik\ *adjective*

hy·per·par·a·site \ˌhī-pər-ˈpar-ə-ˌsīt\ *noun* (circa 1889)
: a parasite that is parasitic upon another parasite
— **hy·per·par·a·sit·ic** \-ˌpar-ə-ˈsi-tik\ *adjective*
— **hy·per·par·a·sit·ism** \-ˈpar-ə-ˌsī-ˌti-zəm, -ˌpar-ə-sə-\ *noun*

hy·per·para·thy·roid·ism \-ˌpar-ə-ˈthī-ˌrói-ˌdi-zəm\ *noun* (1917)
: the presence of excess parathyroid hormone in the body resulting in disturbance of calcium metabolism with increase in serum calcium and decrease in inorganic phosphorus, loss of calcium from bone, and renal damage with frequent kidney-stone formation

hy·per·pha·gia \ˌhī-pər-ˈfā-j(ē-)ə\ *noun* [New Latin] (1941)
: abnormally increased appetite for consumption of food frequently associated with injury to the hypothalamus
— **hy·per·phag·ic** \-ˈfa-jik\ *adjective*

hy·per·pi·tu·i·ta·rism \-pə-ˈtü-ə-tə-ˌri-zəm, -ˈtü-ə-ˌtri-, -ˈtyü-\ *noun* [International Scientific Vocabulary] (1909)
: excessive production of growth hormones by the pituitary gland
— **hy·per·pi·tu·itary** \-ˈtü-ə-ˌter-ē, -ˈtyü-\ *adjective*

hy·per·plane \ˈhī-pər-ˌplān\ *noun* (1903)
: a figure in hyperspace corresponding to a plane in ordinary space

hy·per·pla·sia \ˌhī-pər-ˈplā-zh(ē-)ə\ *noun* [New Latin] (1861)
: an abnormal or unusual increase in the elements composing a part (as cells composing a tissue)
— **hy·per·plas·tic** \-ˈplas-tik\ *adjective*

hy·per·ploid \ˈhī-pər-ˌplóid\ *adjective* [International Scientific Vocabulary] (1930)
: having a chromosome number slightly greater than an exact multiple of the monoploid number
— **hyperploid** *noun*
— **hy·per·ploi·dy** \-ˌplói-dē\ *noun*

hy·per·pnea \ˌhī-pər-ˈnē-ə, -ˌpərp-ˈnē-\ *noun* [New Latin] (circa 1860)
: abnormally rapid or deep breathing
— **hy·per·pne·ic** \-ˈnē-ik\ *adjective*

hy·per·po·lar·ize \ˌhī-pər-ˈpō-lə-ˌrīz\ (1950) *transitive verb*
: to produce an increase in potential difference across (a biological membrane) ⟨a *hyperpolarized* nerve cell⟩

\ə\ abut \ᵊ\ kitten \ər\ further \a\ ash \ā\ ace \ä\ mop, mar \aù\ out \ch\ chin \e\ bet \ē\ easy \g\ go \i\ hit \ī\ ice \j\ job \ŋ\ sing \ō\ go \ò\ law \òi\ boy \th\ thin \t͟h\ the \ü\ loot \ù\ foot \y\ yet \zh\ vision *see also* Guide to Pronunciation

intransitive verb
: to undergo or produce an increase in potential difference across something
— **hy·per·po·lar·iza·tion** \-ˌpō-lə-rə-'zā-shən\ *noun*

hy·per·py·rex·ia \-pī-'rek-sē-ə\ *noun* [New Latin] (1875)
: exceptionally high fever (as in a particular disease)

hy·per·re·al·ism \ˌhī-pər-'rē-ə-ˌli-zəm, -'ri-ə-\ *noun* (1937)
: realism in painting characterized by depiction of real life in an unusual or striking manner — compare PHOTO-REALISM
— **hy·per·re·al·ist** \-list\ *adjective*
— **hy·per·re·al·is·tic** \-ˌrē-ə-'lis-tik, -ˌri-\ *adjective*

hy·per·sen·si·tive \ˌhī-pər-'sen(t)-s(ə-)tiv\ *adjective* (1871)
1 : excessively or abnormally sensitive
2 : abnormally susceptible physiologically to a specific agent (as a drug or antigen)
— **hy·per·sen·si·tive·ness** *noun*
— **hy·per·sen·si·tiv·i·ty** \-ˌsen(t)-sə-'ti-və-tē\ *noun*

hy·per·sex·u·al \-'sek-sh(ə-)wəl, -'sek-shəl\ *adjective* (1942)
: exhibiting unusual or excessive concern with or indulgence in sexual activity
— **hy·per·sex·u·al·i·ty** \-ˌsek-shə-'wa-lə-tē\ *noun*

hy·per·son·ic \-'sä-nik\ *adjective* [International Scientific Vocabulary] (1946)
1 : of or relating to speed five or more times that of sound in air — compare SONIC
2 : moving, capable of moving, or utilizing air currents that move at hypersonic speed ⟨*hypersonic* wind tunnel⟩
— **hy·per·son·i·cal·ly** \-ni-k(ə-)lē\ *adverb*

hy·per·space \'hī-pər-ˌspās\ *noun* (1867)
1 : space of more than three dimensions
2 : a fictional space held to support extraordinary events (as travel faster than the speed of light)

hy·per·sthene \'hī-pərs-ˌthēn\ *noun* [French *hypersthène,* from Greek *hyper-* + *sthenos* strength] (circa 1808)
: an orthorhombic grayish or greenish black or dark brown pyroxene
— **hy·per·sthe·nic** \ˌhī-pərs-'the-nik, -'thē-\ *adjective*

hy·per·sur·face \'hī-pər-ˌsər-fəs\ *noun* (circa 1909)
: a figure that is the analogue in hyperspace of a surface in three-dimensional space

hy·per·ten·sion \ˌhī-pər-'ten(t)-shən\ *noun* [International Scientific Vocabulary] (1893)
: abnormally high blood pressure and especially arterial blood pressure; *also* : the systemic condition accompanying high blood pressure
— **hy·per·ten·sive** \ˌhī-pər-'ten(t)-siv\ *adjective or noun*

hy·per·text \'hī-pər-ˌtekst\ *noun* (1986)
: a database format in which information related to that on a display can be accessed directly from the display

hy·per·ther·mia \ˌhī-pər-'thər-mē-ə\ *noun* [New Latin, from *hyper-* + *therm-* + *-ia*] (1887)
: exceptionally high fever especially when induced artificially for therapeutic purposes
— **hy·per·ther·mic** \-mik\ *adjective*

hy·per·thy·roid \-'thī-ˌrȯid\ *adjective* [back-formation from *hyperthyroidism*] (1916)
: of, relating to, or affected with hyperthyroidism

hy·per·thy·roid·ism \-ˌrȯi-ˌdi-zəm\ *noun* [International Scientific Vocabulary] (circa 1900)
: excessive functional activity of the thyroid gland; *also* : the resulting condition marked especially by increased metabolic rate, enlargement of the thyroid gland, rapid heart rate, and high blood pressure

hy·per·to·nia \ˌhī-pər-'tō-nē-ə\ *noun* (circa 1842)
: HYPERTONICITY

hy·per·ton·ic \-'tä-nik\ *adjective* [International Scientific Vocabulary] (1855)
1 : exhibiting excessive tone or tension ⟨a *hypertonic* baby⟩ ⟨a *hypertonic* bladder⟩
2 : having a higher osmotic pressure than a surrounding medium or a fluid under comparison

hy·per·to·nic·i·ty \-tə-'ni-sə-tē\ *noun* (1886)
: the quality or state of being hypertonic

¹**hy·per·tro·phy** \hī-'pər-trə-fē\ *noun, plural* **-phies** [probably from New Latin *hypertrophia,* from *hyper-* + *-trophia* -trophy] (1834)
1 : excessive development of an organ or part; *specifically* : increase in bulk (as by thickening of muscle fibers) without multiplication of parts
2 : exaggerated growth or complexity
— **hy·per·tro·phic** \ˌhī-pər-'trō-fik\ *adjective*

²**hypertrophy** *intransitive verb* **-phied; -phy·ing** (1883)
: to undergo hypertrophy

hy·per·ur·ban·ism \ˌhī-pər-'ər-bə-ˌni-zəm\ *noun* (1925)
: use of hypercorrect forms in language; *also* : such a form

hy·per·uri·ce·mia \ˌhī-pər-ˌyur-ə-'sē-mē-ə\ *noun* [New Latin] (circa 1894)
: excess uric acid in the blood

hy·per·ve·loc·i·ty \-və-'lä-sə-tē, -'läs-tē\ *noun* (1949)
: a high or relatively high velocity; *especially* : one greater than 10,000 feet (3048 meters) per second

hy·per·ven·ti·late \ˌhī-pər-'ven-t²l-ˌāt\ *intransitive verb* (1931)
: to breathe rapidly and deeply : undergo hyperventilation

hy·per·ven·ti·la·tion \-ˌven-t²l-'ā-shən\ *noun* (1928)
: excessive rate and depth of respiration leading to abnormal loss of carbon dioxide from the blood

hy·per·vi·ta·min·osis \-ˌvī-tə-mə-'nō-səs\ *noun, plural* **-oses** \-'nō-ˌsēz\ [New Latin] (1928)
: an abnormal state resulting from excessive intake of one or more vitamins

hy·pha \'hī-fə\ *noun, plural* **hy·phae** \-(ˌ)fē\ [New Latin, from Greek *hyphē* web; akin to Greek *hyphos* web — more at WEAVE] (1866)
: one of the threads that make up the mycelium of a fungus, increase by apical growth, and are coenocytic or transversely septate
— **hy·phal** \-fəl\ *adjective*

¹**hy·phen** \'hī-fən\ *noun* [Late Latin & Greek; Late Latin, from Greek, from *hyph' hen* under one, from *hypo* under + *hen,* neuter of *heis* one — more at UP, SAME] (circa 1620)
: a punctuation mark - used especially to divide or to compound words, word elements, or numbers
— **hy·phen·less** \-ləs\ *adjective*

²**hyphen** *transitive verb* (1814)
: HYPHENATE

¹**hy·phen·ate** \'hī-fə-ˌnāt\ *transitive verb* **-at·ed; -at·ing** (circa 1889)
: to connect (as two words) or divide (as a word at the end of a line of print) with a hyphen
— **hy·phen·ation** \ˌhī-fə-'nā-shən\ *noun*

²**hyphenate** *noun* [from the hyphens in the titles of such people, as *producer-director*] (1974)
: a person who performs more than one function (as on a filmmaking project)

hyphenated *adjective* [from the use of hyphenated words (as German-American) to designate foreign-born citizens of the U.S.] (circa 1893)
: of, relating to, or being an individual or unit of mixed or diverse background or composition ⟨*hyphenated* Americans⟩

hypn- *or* **hypno-** *combining form* [French, from Late Latin, from Greek, from *hypnos* — more at SOMNOLENT]

1 : sleep ⟨*hypno*pompic⟩
2 : hypnotism ⟨*hypno*therapy⟩

hyp·na·go·gic *also* **hyp·no·go·gic** \ˌhip-nə-'gä-jik, -'gō-\ *adjective* [French *hypnagogique,* from Greek *hypn-* + *-agōgos* leading, inducing, from *agein* to lead — more at AGENT] (1886)
: of, relating to, or associated with the drowsiness preceding sleep

hyp·noid \'hip-ˌnȯid\ *or* **hyp·noi·dal** \hip-'nȯi-d²l\ *adjective* (1898)
: of or relating to sleep or hypnosis

hyp·no·pom·pic \ˌhip-nə-'päm-pik\ *adjective* [*hypn-* + Greek *pompē* act of sending — more at POMP] (circa 1901)
: associated with the semiconsciousness preceding waking ⟨*hypnopompic* illusions⟩

Hyp·nos \'hip-nəs, -ˌnōs\ *noun* [Greek]
: the Greek god of sleep

hyp·no·sis \hip-'nō-səs\ *noun, plural* **-no·ses** \-ˌsēz\ [New Latin] (1876)
1 : a state that resembles sleep but is induced by a person whose suggestions are readily accepted by the subject
2 : any of various conditions that resemble sleep
3 : HYPNOTISM 1

hyp·no·ther·a·py \ˌhip-nō-'ther-ə-pē\ *noun* (1897)
1 : the treatment of disease by hypnotism
2 : psychotherapy that facilitates suggestion, reeducation, or analysis by means of hypnosis
— **hyp·no·ther·a·pist** \-pist\ *noun*

¹**hyp·not·ic** \hip-'nä-tik\ *adjective* [French or Late Latin; French *hypnotique,* from Late Latin *hypnoticus,* from Greek *hypnōtikos,* from *hypnoun* to put to sleep, from *hypnos*] (1625)
1 : tending to produce sleep : SOPORIFIC
2 a : of or relating to hypnosis or hypnotism **b** : readily holding the attention ⟨a *hypnotic* personality⟩ ⟨a simple *hypnotic* beat⟩
— **hyp·not·i·cal·ly** \-ti-k(ə-)lē\ *adverb*

²**hypnotic** *noun* (1681)
1 : a sleep-inducing agent : SOPORIFIC
2 : one that is or can be hypnotized

hyp·no·tism \'hip-nə-ˌti-zəm\ *noun* (1842)
1 : the study or act of inducing hypnosis — compare MESMERISM
2 : HYPNOSIS 1
— **hyp·no·tist** \-tist\ *noun*

hyp·no·tize \-ˌtīz\ *transitive verb* **-tized; -tiz·ing** (1843)
1 : to induce hypnosis in
2 : to dazzle or overcome by or as if by suggestion ⟨a voice that *hypnotizes* its hearers⟩ ⟨drivers *hypnotized* by speed⟩
— **hyp·no·tiz·abil·i·ty** \ˌhip-nə-ˌtī-zə-'bi-lə-tē\ *noun*
— **hyp·no·tiz·able** \'hip-nə-ˌtī-zə-bəl\ *adjective*

¹**hy·po** \'hī-(ˌ)pō\ *noun, plural* **hypos** (1711)
: HYPOCHONDRIA

²**hypo** *noun, plural* **hypos** [short for *hyposulfite* thiosulfate] (1855)
: SODIUM THIOSULFATE

³**hypo** *noun, plural* **hypos** (1925)
1 : HYPODERMIC SYRINGE
2 : HYPODERMIC INJECTION
3 : STIMULUS

⁴**hypo** *transitive verb* (1942)
: STIMULATE ⟨do everything possible to *hypo* the economy —Clem Morgello⟩

hypo- *or* **hyp-** *prefix* [Middle English *ypo-,* from Old French, from Late Latin *hypo-, hyp-,* from Greek, from *hypo* — more at UP]
1 : under : beneath : down ⟨*hypo*blast⟩ ⟨*hypo*dermic⟩
2 : less than normal or normally ⟨*hyp*esthesia⟩ ⟨*hypo*tension⟩
3 : in a lower state of oxidation : in a low and usually the lowest position in a series of compounds ⟨*hypo*chlorous acid⟩ ⟨*hypo*xanthine⟩

hy·po·al·ler·gen·ic \ˌhī-pō-ˌa-lər-'je-nik\ *adjective* (1940)

: having little likelihood of causing an allergic response ⟨*hypoallergenic* cosmetics⟩ ⟨*hypoallergenic* foods⟩

hy·po·blast \'hī-pə-ˌblast\ *noun* (1875)
: the endoderm of an embryo

hy·po·cal·ce·mia \ˌhī-pō-kal-'sē-mē-ə\ *noun* [New Latin] (1925)
: a deficiency of calcium in the blood
— **hy·po·cal·ce·mic** \-mik\ *adjective*

hy·po·caust \'hī-pə-ˌkȯst\ *noun* [Latin *hypocaustum*, from Greek *hypokauston*, from *hypokaiein* to light a fire under, from *hypo-* + *kaiein* to burn] (1678)
: an ancient Roman central heating system with underground furnace and tile flues to distribute the heat

hy·po·cen·ter \'hī-pə-ˌsen-tər\ *noun* (1905)
1 : the focus of an earthquake — compare EPICENTER 1
2 : the point on the earth's surface directly below the center of a nuclear bomb explosion
— **hy·po·cen·tral** \ˌhī-pə-'sen-trəl\ *adjective*

hy·po·chlo·rite \ˌhī-pə-'klōr-ˌīt, -'klȯr-\ *noun* (circa 1849)
: a salt or ester of hypochlorous acid

hy·po·chlo·rous acid \ˌhī-pə-'klōr-əs-, -'klȯr-\ *noun* [International Scientific Vocabulary] (1841)
: an unstable strongly oxidizing but weak acid HClO obtained in solution along with hydrochloric acid by reaction of chlorine with water and used especially in the form of salts as an oxidizing agent, bleaching agent, disinfectant, and chlorinating agent

hy·po·chon·dria \ˌhī-pə-'kän-drē-ə\ *noun* [New Latin, from Late Latin, plural, upper abdomen (formerly regarded as the seat of hypochondria), from Greek, literally, the parts under the cartilage (of the breastbone), from *hypo-* + *chondros* cartilage] (1668)
: extreme depression of mind or spirits often centered on imaginary physical ailments; *specifically* : HYPOCHONDRIASIS ◇

¹hy·po·chon·dri·ac \-drē-ˌak\ *adjective* [French *hypochondriaque*, from Greek *hypochondriakos*, from *hypochondria*] (1599)
1 : HYPOCHONDRIACAL
2 : of, relating to, or being the two regions of the abdomen lying on either side of the epigastric region and above the lumbar regions

²hypochondriac *noun* (1639)
: one affected by hypochondria

hy·po·chon·dri·a·cal \ˌhī-pə-kən-'drī-ə-kəl, -ˌkän-\ *adjective* (1621)
: affected or produced by hypochondria
— **hy·po·chon·dri·a·cal·ly** \-k(ə-)lē\ *adverb*

hy·po·chon·dri·a·sis \-'drī-ə-səs\ *noun, plural* **-a·ses** \-ˌsēz\ [New Latin] (1766)
: morbid concern about one's health especially when accompanied by delusions of physical disease

hy·po·chro·mic anemia \ˌhī-pə-'krō-mik-\ *noun* (1934)
: an anemia marked by deficient hemoglobin and usually microcytic red blood cells

hy·po·co·rism \hī-'pä-kə-ˌri-zəm; ˌhī-pə-'kōr-ˌi-, -'kȯr-\ *noun* [Late Latin *hypocorisma*, from Greek *hypokorisma*, from *hypokorizesthai* to call by pet names, from *hypo-* + *korizesthai* to caress, from *koros* boy, *korē* girl] (1850)
1 : a pet name
2 : the use of pet names
— **hy·po·co·ris·tic** \ˌhī-pə-kə-'ris-tik\ *or* **hy·po·co·ris·ti·cal** \-ti-kəl\ *adjective*
— **hy·po·co·ris·ti·cal·ly** \-ti-k(ə-)lē\ *adverb*

hy·po·cot·yl \'hī-pə-ˌkä-tᵊl\ *noun* [International Scientific Vocabulary *hypo-* + *cotyl*edon] (1880)
: the part of the axis of a plant embryo or seedling below the cotyledon — see PLUMULE illustration

hy·poc·ri·sy \hi-'pä-krə-sē *also* hī-\ *noun, plural* **-sies** [Middle English *ypocrisie*, from

Old French, from Late Latin *hypocrisis*, from Greek *hypokrisis* act of playing a part on the stage, hypocrisy, from *hypokrinesthai* to answer, act on the stage, from *hypo-* + *krinein* to decide — more at CERTAIN] (13th century)
1 : a feigning to be what one is not or to believe what one does not; *especially* : the false assumption of an appearance of virtue or religion
2 : an act or instance of hypocrisy

hyp·o·crite \'hi-pə-ˌkrit\ *noun* [Middle English *ypocrite*, from Old French, from Late Latin *hypocrita*, from Greek *hypokritēs* actor, hypocrite, from *hypokrinesthai*] (13th century)
: a person who puts on a false appearance of virtue or religion
— **hypocrite** *adjective*

hyp·o·crit·i·cal \ˌhi-pə-'kri-ti-kəl\ *adjective* (1561)
: characterized by hypocrisy; *also* : being a hypocrite
— **hyp·o·crit·i·cal·ly** \-k(ə-)lē\ *adverb*

hy·po·cy·cloid \ˌhī-pō-'sī-ˌklȯid\ *noun* (1843)
: a curve traced by a point on the circumference of a circle rolling internally on the circumference of a fixed circle

hy·po·der·mal \ˌhī-pə-'dər-məl\ *adjective* (1854)
1 : of or relating to a hypodermis
2 : lying beneath an outer skin or epidermis

¹hy·po·der·mic \-mik\ *adjective* [International Scientific Vocabulary] (1863)
1 : adapted for use in or administered by injection beneath the skin
2 : of or relating to the parts beneath the skin
3 : resembling a hypodermic injection in effect : STIMULATING
— **hy·po·der·mi·cal·ly** \-mi-k(ə-)lē\ *adverb*

²hypodermic *noun* (circa 1889)
1 : HYPODERMIC INJECTION
2 : HYPODERMIC SYRINGE

hypodermic injection *noun* (1868)
: an injection made into the subcutaneous tissues

hypodermic needle *noun* (circa 1909)
1 : NEEDLE 1c(1)
2 : a hypodermic syringe complete with needle

hypodermic syringe *noun* (1893)
: a small syringe used with a hollow needle for injection of material into or beneath the skin

hy·po·der·mis \ˌhī-pə-'dər-məs\ *noun* [New Latin] (circa 1866)
1 : the tissue immediately beneath the epidermis of a plant especially when modified to serve as a supporting and protecting layer
2 : the cellular layer that underlies and secretes the chitinous cuticle (as of an arthropod)
3 : SUPERFICIAL FASCIA

hy·po·dip·loid \ˌhī-pō-'di-ˌplȯid\ *adjective* (1962)
: having slightly fewer than the diploid number of chromosomes
— **hy·po·dip·loi·dy** \-ˌplȯi-dē\ *noun*

hy·po·eu·tec·toid \ˌhī-pō-yù-'tek-ˌtȯid\ *adjective* (1911)
: containing less of the minor component than is contained in the eutectoid

hy·po·gas·tric \ˌhī-pə-'gas-trik\ *adjective* [French *hypogastrique*, from *hypogastre* hypogastric region, from Greek *hypogastrion*, from *hypo-* + *gastr-, gastēr* belly — more at GASTRIC] (1656)
: of or relating to the lower median region of the abdomen

hy·po·ge·al \ˌhī-pə-'jē-əl\ *or* **hy·po·ge·an** \-'jē-ən\ *or* **hy·po·ge·ous** \-'jē-əs\ *adjective* [Late Latin *hypogeus* subterranean, from Greek *hypogaios*, from *hypo-* + *gaia* earth] (1686)
1 : growing or living below the surface of the ground
2 *of a cotyledon* : remaining below the ground while the epicotyl elongates

hy·po·gene \'hī-pə-ˌjēn\ *adjective* [*hypo-* + Greek *-genēs* born, produced — more at -GEN] (1831)
: formed, crystallized, or lying at depths below the earth's surface : PLUTONIC — used of various rocks

hy·po·ge·um \ˌhī-pə-'jē-əm\ *noun, plural* **-gea** \-'jē-ə\ [Latin, from Greek *hypogaion*, from neuter of *hypogaios*]
: the subterranean part of an ancient building; *also* : an ancient underground burial chamber

hy·po·glos·sal \ˌhī-pə-'glä-səl\ *adjective* (1831)
: of or relating to the hypoglossal nerves

hypoglossal nerve *noun* (1848)
: either of the 12th and final pair of cranial nerves which are motor nerves arising from the medulla oblongata and supplying muscles of the tongue in higher vertebrates — called also *hypoglossal*

hy·po·gly·ce·mia \ˌhī-pō-glī-'sē-mē-ə\ *noun* [New Latin] (circa 1894)
: abnormal decrease of sugar in the blood
— **hy·po·gly·ce·mic** \-mik\ *adjective or noun*

hy·pog·y·nous \hī-'pä-jə-nəs\ *adjective* (1821)
1 *of a floral organ* : inserted upon the receptacle or axis below the gynoecium and free from it
2 : having hypogynous floral organs
— **hy·pog·y·ny** \-nē\ *noun*

hy·po·ka·le·mia \ˌhī-pō-ˌkā-'lē-mē-ə\ *noun* [New Latin, from *hypo-* + *kalium* potassium (from *kali* alkali, from Arabic *qily* saltwort) + *-emia*] (1949)
: a deficiency of potassium in the blood
— **hy·po·ka·le·mic** \-mik\ *adjective*

hy·po·lim·ni·on \ˌhī-pō-'lim-nē-ˌän, -nē-ən\ *noun, plural* **-nia** \-nē-ə\ [New Latin, from *hypo-* + Greek *limnion*, diminutive of *limnē* lake — more at LIMNETIC] (1928)
: the part of a lake below the thermocline made up of water that is stagnant and of essentially uniform temperature except during the period of overturn

◇ **WORD HISTORY**

hypochondria A hypochondriac's ailment is deemed to be mental rather than physical, but etymologically hypochondria has nothing to do with the head. The ancient Greek noun *chondros* meant "cartilage," and the adjective *hypochondrios* meant "located under the cartilage of the breastbone and ribs." Formed from this adjective was the plural noun *hypochondria*, designating the area of the abdomen below the rib cartilage and above the navel. In Greek medical doctrine the spleen and kidneys, located in this part of the abdomen, secreted black bile, or melancholy, an excess of which caused low spirits, and the ancient physician Galen characterized depression as *hypochondriakon nosēma* "the ailment of the upper abdominal organs." The English adjective *hypochondriac*, borrowed from Greek through French, was used in the 17th century to mean "suffering from depression," and later in the century the noun *hypochondria* came into use, either as a Latinism created by removing the final letter from *hypochondriac*, or by construing the Greek and Latin neuter plural noun *hypochondria* as feminine singular. The narrowing of *hypochondria* to morbid concern about one's health—in more formal medical terminology *hypochondriasis*—dates from the late 18th and 19th centuries.

\ə\ abut \ᵊ\ kitten \ər\ **further** \a\ ash \ā\ ace
\ä\ mop, mar \au̇\ **out** \ch\ **chin** \e\ **bet** \ē\ **easy**
\g\ go \i\ hit \ī\ ice \j\ job \ŋ\ sing \ō\ go
\ȯ\ law \ȯi\ boy \th\ **thin** \ṯh\ the \ü\ loot \u̇\ foot
\y\ yet \zh\ vision *see also* Guide to Pronunciation

hy·po·mag·ne·se·mia \ˌhī-pə-ˌmag-nə-'sē-mē-ə\ *noun* [New Latin, from *hypo-* + *magnesium* + *-emia*] (1933)
: deficiency of magnesium in the blood especially of cattle

hy·po·ma·nia \ˌhī-pə-'mā-nē-ə, -nyə\ *noun* [New Latin] (1843)
: a mild mania especially when part of a manic-depressive cycle
— **hy·po·man·ic** \-'ma-nik\ *adjective*

hy·po·morph \'hī-pə-ˌmȯrf\ *noun* (1926)
: a mutant gene having a similar but weaker effect than the corresponding wild-type gene
— **hy·po·mor·phic** \ˌhī-pə-'mȯr-fik\ *adjective*

hy·po·para·thy·roid·ism \ˌhī-pō-ˌpar-ə-'thī-ˌrȯi-ˌdi-zəm\ *noun* (1910)
: deficiency of parathyroid hormone in the body; *also* : the resultant abnormal state marked by low serum calcium and a tendency to chronic tetany

hy·po·phar·ynx \-'far-iŋ(k)s, -'fer-\ *noun* [New Latin] (1826)
1 : an appendage or thickened fold on the floor of the mouth of many insects that resembles a tongue
2 : the laryngeal part of the pharynx extending from the hyoid bone to the lower margin of the cricoid cartilage

hy·po·phy·se·al *also* **hy·po·phy·si·al** \(ˌ)hī-ˌpä-fə-'sē-əl, ˌhī-pə-, -'zē-; ˌhī-pə-'fi-zē-əl\ *adjective* [irregular from New Latin *hypophysis*] (1882)
: of or relating to the hypophysis

hy·poph·y·sec·to·mize \(ˌ)hī-ˌpä-fə-'sek-tə-ˌmīz\ *transitive verb* **-mized; -miz·ing** (1910)
: to remove the pituitary gland from

hy·poph·y·sec·to·my \-mē\ *noun, plural* **-mies** (1909)
: surgical removal of the pituitary gland

hy·poph·y·sis \hī-'pä-fə-səs\ *noun, plural* **-y·ses** \-ˌsēz\ [New Latin, from Greek, attachment underneath, from *hypophyein* to grow beneath, from *hypo-* + *phyein* to grow, produce — more at BE] (1825)
: PITUITARY GLAND

hy·po·pi·tu·ita·rism \ˌhī-pō-pə-'tü-ə-tə-ˌri-zəm, -'tü-ə-ˌtri-, -'tyü-\ *noun* [International Scientific Vocabulary] (1909)
: deficient production of growth hormones by the pituitary gland
— **hy·po·pi·tu·itary** \-'tü-ə-ˌter-ē, -'tyü-\ *adjective*

hy·po·pla·sia \-'plā-zh(ē-)ə\ *noun* [New Latin] (1889)
: a condition of arrested development in which an organ or part remains below the normal size or in an immature state
— **hy·po·plas·tic** \-'plas-tik\ *adjective*

hy·po·ploid \'hī-pō-ˌplȯid\ *adjective* (1930)
: having a chromosome number slightly less than an exact multiple of the monoploid number
— **hypoploid** *noun*

hy·po·sen·si·ti·za·tion \ˌhī-pō-ˌsen(t)-sə-tə-'zā-shən, -ˌsen(t)-stə-'zā-\ *noun* (1922)
: the state or process of being reduced in sensitivity especially to an allergen : DESENSITIZATION
— **hy·po·sen·si·tize** \-'sen(t)-sə-ˌtīz\ *transitive verb*

hy·po·spa·di·as \ˌhī-pə-'spā-dē-əs\ *noun* [New Latin, from Greek, man with hypospadias, from *hypo-* + *-spadias*, from *-spad-, -spas* something torn, from *span* to tear, pluck off] (circa 1855)
: an abnormality of the penis in which the urethra opens on the undersurface

hy·pos·ta·sis \hī-'päs-tə-səs\ *noun, plural* **-ta·ses** \-ˌsēz\ [Late Latin, substance, sediment, from Greek, support, foundation, substance, sediment, from *hyphistasthai* to stand under, support, from *hypo-* + *histasthai* to be standing — more at STAND] (1590)

1 a : something that settles at the bottom of a fluid **b** : the settling of blood in the dependent parts of an organ or body
2 : PERSON 3
3 a : the substance or essential nature of an individual **b** : something that is hypostatized
4 [New Latin, from Late Latin] : failure of a gene to produce its usual effect when coupled with another gene that is epistatic toward it
— **hy·po·stat·ic** \ˌhī-pə-'sta-tik\ *adjective*
— **hy·po·stat·i·cal·ly** \-ti-k(ə-)lē\ *adverb*

hy·pos·ta·tize \hī-'päs-tə-ˌtīz\ *transitive verb* **-tized; -tiz·ing** [Greek *hypostatos* substantially existing, from *hyphistasthai*] (1829)
: to attribute real identity to (a concept)
— **hy·pos·ta·ti·za·tion** \-ˌpäs-tə-tə-'zā-shən\ *noun*

hy·po·stome \'hī-pə-ˌstōm\ *noun* [International Scientific Vocabulary *hypo-* + *-stome* (from Greek *stoma* mouth) — more at STOMACH] (circa 1862)
: any of several structures associated with the mouth: as **a** : the manubrium of a hydrozoan **b** : a rodlike organ that arises at the base of the beak in various mites and ticks

hy·po·style \'hī-pə-ˌstīl\ *adjective* [Greek *hypostylos,* from *hypo-* + *stylos* pillar — more at STEER] (1831)
: having the roof resting on rows of columns
— **hypostyle** *noun*

hy·po·tac·tic \ˌhī-pə-'tak-tik\ *adjective* [Greek *hypotaktikos,* from *hypotassein*] (1896)
: of or relating to hypotaxis

hy·po·tax·is \-'tak-səs\ *noun* [New Latin, from Greek, subjection, from *hypotassein* to arrange under, from *hypo-* + *tassein* to arrange] (1883)
: syntactic subordination (as by a conjunction)

hy·po·ten·sion \ˌhī-pō-'ten(t)-shən\ *noun* [International Scientific Vocabulary] (1893)
: abnormally low blood pressure

¹hy·po·ten·sive \ˌhī-pō-'ten(t)-siv\ *adjective* (1904)
1 : characterized by or due to hypotension
2 : causing low blood pressure or a lowering of blood pressure ⟨*hypotensive* drugs⟩

²hypotensive *noun* (1941)
: a person with hypotension

hy·pot·e·nuse \hī-'pä-tⁿn-ˌüs, -ˌyüz\ *also* **hy·poth·e·nuse** \-'pä-thən-\ *noun* [Latin *hypotenusa,* from Greek *hypoteinousa,* from feminine of *hypoteinōn,* present participle of *hypoteinein* to subtend, from *hypo-* + *teinein* to stretch — more at THIN] (1594)
1 : the side of a right-angled triangle that is opposite the right angle
2 : the length of a hypotenuse

hy·po·thal·am·ic \ˌhī-pō-thə-'la-mik\ *adjective* (1899)
: of or relating to the hypothalamus

ac hypotenuse

hy·po·thal·a·mus \-'tha-lə-məs\ *noun* [New Latin] (1896)
: a basal part of the diencephalon that lies beneath the thalamus on each side, forms the floor of the third ventricle, and includes vital autonomic regulatory centers

¹hy·poth·e·cate \hī-'pä-thə-ˌkāt, hī-\ *transitive verb* **-cat·ed; -cat·ing** [Medieval Latin *hypothecare* to pledge, from Late Latin *hypotheca* pledge, from Greek *hypothēkē,* from *hypotithenai* to put under, deposit as a pledge] (1681)
: to pledge as security without delivery of title or possession
— **hy·poth·e·ca·tion** \-ˌpä-thə-'kā-shən\ *noun*
— **hy·poth·e·ca·tor** \-'pä-thə-ˌkā-tər\ *noun*

²hy·poth·e·cate \hī-'pä-thə-ˌkāt\ *transitive verb* **-cat·ed; -cat·ing** [Greek *hypothēkē* suggestion, from *hypotithenai*] (1906)
: HYPOTHESIZE

hy·po·ther·mal \ˌhī-pō-'thər-məl\ *adjective* (1944)

: of or relating to a hydrothermal metalliferous ore vein deposited at high temperature

hy·po·ther·mia \-'thər-mē-ə\ *noun* [New Latin] (circa 1886)
: subnormal temperature of the body
— **hy·po·ther·mic** \-mik\ *adjective*

hy·poth·e·sis \hī-'pä-thə-səs\ *noun, plural* **-e·ses** \-ˌsēz\ [Greek, from *hypotithenai* to put under, suppose, from *hypo-* + *tithenai* to put — more at DO] (circa 1656)
1 a : an assumption or concession made for the sake of argument **b** : an interpretation of a practical situation or condition taken as the ground for action
2 : a tentative assumption made in order to draw out and test its logical or empirical consequences
3 : the antecedent clause of a conditional statement ☆

hy·poth·e·size \-ˌsīz\ *verb* **-sized; -siz·ing** (1738)
intransitive verb
: to make a hypothesis
transitive verb
: to adopt as a hypothesis

hy·po·thet·i·cal \ˌhī-pə-'the-ti-kəl\ *adjective* (1588)
: being or involving a hypothesis : CONJECTURAL ⟨*hypothetical* arguments⟩ ⟨a *hypothetical* situation⟩
— **hy·po·thet·i·cal·ly** \-ti-k(ə-)lē\ *adverb*

hy·po·thet·i·co-de·duc·tive \ˌhī-pə-ˌthe-ti-ˌkō-di-'dək-tiv\ *adjective* (1912)
: relating to, being, or making use of the method of proposing hypotheses and testing their acceptability or falsity by determining whether their logical consequences are consistent with observed data

hy·po·thy·roid \ˌhī-pō-'thī-ˌrȯid\ *adjective* (1909)
: of, relating to, or affected with hypothyroidism

hy·po·thy·roid·ism \-ˌrȯi-ˌdi-zəm\ *noun* [International Scientific Vocabulary] (1905)
: deficient activity of the thyroid gland; *also* : a resultant bodily condition characterized by lowered metabolic rate and general loss of vigor

hy·po·to·nia \ˌhī-pə-'tō-nē-ə, -pō-\ *noun* [New Latin] (circa 1886)
: the state of having hypotonic muscle tone

hy·po·ton·ic \ˌhī-pə-'tä-nik, -pō-\ *adjective* [International Scientific Vocabulary] (1895)
1 : having deficient tone or tension ⟨*hypotonic* children⟩
2 : having a lower osmotic pressure than a surrounding medium or a fluid under comparison ⟨*hypotonic* organisms⟩
— **hy·po·to·nic·i·ty** \-tə-'ni-sə-tē\ *noun*

hy·po·xan·thine \ˌhī-pō-'zan-ˌthēn\ *noun* [International Scientific Vocabulary] (circa 1857)
: a purine base $C_5H_4N_4O$ found in plant and animal tissues that yields xanthine on oxidation

hyp·ox·emia \ˌhi-ˌpäk-'sē-mē-ə, ˌhī-\ *noun* [New Latin] (circa 1886)
: deficient oxygenation of the blood
— **hyp·ox·emic** \-mik\ *adjective*

hyp·ox·ia \hi-'päk-sē-ə, hī-\ *noun* [New Latin] (1941)

☆ **SYNONYMS**
Hypothesis, theory, law mean a formula derived by inference from scientific data that explains a principle operating in nature. HYPOTHESIS implies insufficient evidence to provide more than a tentative explanation ⟨a *hypothesis* explaining the extinction of the dinosaurs⟩. THEORY implies a greater range of evidence and greater likelihood of truth ⟨the *theory* of evolution⟩. LAW implies a statement of order and relation in nature that has been found to be invariable under the same conditions ⟨the *law* of gravitation⟩.

: a deficiency of oxygen reaching the tissues of the body
— **hyp·ox·ic** \-sik\ *adjective*

hyp·som·e·ter \hip-'sä-mə-tər\ *noun* [International Scientific Vocabulary, from Greek *hypsos* height (akin to Old English *ūp* up) + International Scientific Vocabulary *-meter* — more at UP] (1927)
: any of various instruments for determining the height of trees by triangulation

hyp·so·met·ric \hip-sə-'me-trik\ *adjective* [Greek *hypsos*] (1845)
: of, relating to, or indicating elevation (as on a map) ⟨*hypsometric* curve⟩

hy·rax \'hī-,raks\ *noun, plural* **hy·rax·es** \-,rak-səz\ *also* **hy·ra·ces** \-rə-,sēz\ [Greek *hyrak-, hyrax* shrew] (1832)
: any of a family (Procaviidae) of small ungulate mammals of Africa and the Middle East characterized by thickset body with short legs and ears and rudimentary tail, feet with soft pads and broad nails, and teeth of which the molars resemble those of the rhinoceros and the incisors those of rodents — called also *coney, dassie*

hyrax

hy·son \'hī-s°n\ *noun* [Chinese (Guangdong) *héichēun*, literally, bright spring] (1740)
: a Chinese green tea made from thinly rolled and twisted leaves

hys·sop \'hi-səp\ *noun* [Middle English *ysop*, from Old English *ysope*, from Latin *hyssopus*, from Greek *hyssōpos*, of Semitic origin; akin to Hebrew *ēzōbh* hyssop] (before 12th century)
1 : a plant used in purificatory sprinkling rites by the ancient Hebrews
2 : a European mint (*Hyssopus officinalis*) that has highly aromatic and pungent leaves and is sometimes used as a potherb

hyster- *or* **hystero-** *combining form* [French or Latin; French *hystér-*, from Latin *hyster-*, from Greek, from *hystera*]
: womb ⟨*hyster*ectomy⟩

hys·ter·ec·to·my \,his-tə-'rek-tə-mē\ *noun, plural* **-mies** (circa 1886)
: surgical removal of the uterus
— **hys·ter·ec·to·mized** \-tə-,mīzd\ *adjective*

hys·ter·e·sis \,his-tə-'rē-səs\ *noun, plural* **-e·ses** \-,sēz\ [New Latin, from Greek *hysterēsis* shortcoming, from *hysterein* to be late, fall short, from *hysteros* later — more at OUT] (1881)
: a retardation of an effect when the forces acting upon a body are changed (as if from viscosity or internal friction); *especially* : a lagging in the values of resulting magnetization in a magnetic material (as iron) due to a changing magnetizing force
— **hys·ter·et·ic** \-'re-tik\ *adjective*

hys·te·ria \his-'ter-ē-ə, -'tir-\ *noun* [New Latin, from English *hysteric*, adjective, from Latin *hystericus*, from Greek *hysterikos*, from *hystera* womb; from the Greek notion that hysteria was peculiar to women and caused by disturbances of the uterus] (1801)
1 : a psychoneurosis marked by emotional excitability and disturbances of the psychic, sensory, vasomotor, and visceral functions
2 : behavior exhibiting overwhelming or unmanageable fear or emotional excess ⟨political *hysteria*⟩ ◇
— **hys·ter·ic** \-'ter-ik\ *noun*
— **hys·ter·i·cal** \-'ter-i-kəl\ *also* **hysteric** *adjective*
— **hys·ter·i·cal·ly** \-i-k(ə-)lē\ *adverb*

hys·ter·ics \-'ter-iks\ *noun plural but singular or plural in construction* (1721)
: a fit of uncontrollable laughter or crying

hys·ter·oid \'his-tə-,ròid\ *adjective* (circa 1855)
: resembling or tending toward hysteria

hys·ter·on prot·er·on \,his-tə-,rän-'prä-tə-,rän, -tə-rən-'prä-tə-rən, -'prò-\ *noun* [Late Latin, from Greek, literally, (the) later earlier, (the) latter first] (1565)
: a figure of speech consisting of the reversal of a natural or rational order (as in "then came the thunder and the lightning")

hys·ter·ot·o·my \,his-tə-'rä-tə-mē\ *noun, plural* **-mies** [New Latin *hysterotomia*, from *hyster-* + *-tomia* -tomy] (1801)
: surgical incision of the uterus; *especially* : CESAREAN SECTION

◇ WORD HISTORY

hysteria Since the earliest days of civilization physicians have attempted to treat psychological disorders that manifest themselves physically, through tics and tremors, seizures, and a variety of other symptoms, including what sufferers experience as numbness and partial paralysis. Following ancient Egyptian medical lore, Greek physicians from Hippocrates to Galen believed that these ailments were unique to women and resulted from disturbances in the uterus. The collective labeling of such symptoms in Greek as *hysterika pathē* "sufferings of the womb," rendered in Latin as *hysterica passio*, gave rise to the term *hysteria* in English around the end of the 18th century, with counterparts in other European languages, such as French *hystérie* and German *Hysterie*. The boundaries of what constitutes hysteria, its diverse expression in different cultures, and the difficulties in separating it from genuine neurological disease are all issues that still preoccupy psychiatrists. The word itself has gradually been slipping from the usage of medical professionals. Most of the phenomena traditionally called *hysteria* are now put under the rubric *conversion reaction*, based on Freud's German term *Konversionshysterie*, which embodies his hypothesis that psychic anxiety is "converted" into bodily expression.

\ə\ abut \ᵊ\ kitten \ər\ further \a\ ash \ā\ ace
\ä\ mop, mar \aú\ out \ch\ chin \e\ bet \ē\ easy
\g\ go \i\ hit \ī\ ice \j\ job \ŋ\ sing \ō\ go
\ò\ law \òi\ boy \th\ thin \t͟h\ the \ü\ loot \ú\ foot
\y\ yet \zh\ vision *see also* Guide to Pronunciation

I *is the ninth letter of the English alphabet and of most alphabets closely related to it. The character can be traced back through Latin, Etruscan and Greek (*iota*) to Phoenician* yōdh, *and probably ultimately to Egyptian. In Phoenician* i *represented a fricative (a consonant pronounced with air friction) articulated like the* y *in English* yet, *but it also had the value of a vowel in certain positions, and only the vowel pronunciation was taken over by the Greeks. In Latin and Old English,* i *had both vowel and consonant* y *sounds. Several hundred years later,* i *was used in English to spell both the vowel sound and the consonant sound* j *(as in modern* jewel). *By the 17th century, English used the* J *letter form (see* J*) exclusively for the consonant, and* I *exclusively for the vowel. Small* i *developed through a reduction in the size of the capital letter and the addition of an accent mark (later a dot) above the vertical stroke to distinguish it from adjacent letters (as* m, n, *and* u*) having identically formed strokes.*

i \'ī\ *noun, plural* **i's** *or* **is** \'īz\ *often capitalized, often attributive* (before 12th century)
1 a : the 9th letter of the English alphabet **b** **:** a graphic representation of this letter **c :** a speech counterpart of orthographic *i*
2 : ONE — see NUMBER table
3 : a graphic device for reproducing the letter *i*
4 : one designated *i* especially as the 9th in order or class
5 : something shaped like the letter I
6 : a unit vector parallel to the x-axis
7 [abbreviation for *incomplete*] **a :** a grade rating a student's work as incomplete **b :** one graded or rated with an I
8 : I FORMATION

¹**I** \'ī, ə\ *pronoun* [Middle English, from Old English *ic;* akin to Old High German *ih* I, Latin *ego,* Greek *egō*] (before 12th century)
: the one who is speaking or writing ⟨*I* feel fine⟩ — compare ME, MINE, MY, WE
usage see ME

²**I** \'ī\ *noun, plural* **I's** *or* **Is** \'īz\ (1539)
: someone aware of possessing a personal individuality **:** SELF

-i- [Middle English, from Old French, from Latin, thematic vowel of most nouns and adjectives in combination]
— used as a connective vowel to join word elements especially of Latin origin ⟨matr*i*lineal⟩ ⟨rat*i*cide⟩

¹**-ia** *noun suffix* [New Latin, from Latin & Greek, suffix forming feminine nouns]
1 : pathological condition ⟨hyster*ia*⟩
2 : genus of plants or animals ⟨Fuchs*ia*⟩
3 : territory **:** world **:** society ⟨suburb*ia*⟩

²**-ia** *noun plural suffix* [New Latin, from Latin (neuter plural of *-ius,* adjective ending) & Greek, neuter plural of *-ios,* adjective ending]
1 : higher taxon (as class or order) consisting of (such plants or animals) ⟨Saur*ia*⟩
2 : things derived from or relating to (something specified) ⟨militar*ia*⟩

³**-ia** *plural of* -IUM

Ia·go \ē-'ä-(,)gō\ *noun*
: the villain of Shakespeare's tragedy *Othello*

-ial *adjective suffix* [Middle English, from Middle French, from Latin *-ialis,* from *-i-* + *-alis* -al]
: ¹-AL ⟨manor*ial*⟩

iamb \'ī-,am(b)\ *or* **iam·bus** \ī-'am-bəs\ *noun, plural* **iambs** \'ī-,amz\ *or* **iam·bus·es** [Latin *iambus,* from Greek *iambos*] (1586)
: a metrical foot consisting of one short syllable followed by one long syllable or of one unstressed syllable followed by one stressed syllable (as in *above*)
— **iam·bic** \ī-'am-bik\ *adjective or noun*

-ian — see -AN

-iana — see -ANA

-iasis *noun suffix, plural* **-iases** [New Latin, from Latin, from Greek, suffix of action, from denominative verbs in *-ian, -iazein*]
: disease having characteristics of or produced by (something specified) ⟨onchocerc*iasis*⟩ ⟨ancylostom*iasis*⟩

-iatric *also* **-iatrical** *adjective combining form* [New Latin *-iatria*]
: of or relating to (such) medical treatment or healing ⟨ped*iatric*⟩

-iatrics *noun plural combining form but singular or plural in construction*
: medical treatment ⟨ped*iatrics*⟩

iat·ro·gen·ic \(,)ī,a-trə-'je-nik\ *adjective* [Greek *iatros* physician + English *-genic*] (1924)
: induced inadvertently by a physician or surgeon or by medical treatment or diagnostic procedures ⟨an *iatrogenic* rash⟩
— **iat·ro·gen·i·cal·ly** \-'je-ni-k(ə-)lē\ *adverb*

-iatry *noun combining form* [French *-iatrie,* from New Latin *-iatria,* from Greek *iatreia* art of healing, from *iatros* healer, from *iasthai* to heal]
: medical treatment **:** healing ⟨pod*iatry*⟩

I band \'ī-\ *noun* (1948)
: an isotropic band of a striated muscle fiber

I beam *noun* (circa 1889)
: an iron or steel beam that is I-shaped in cross section

¹**Ibe·ri·an** \ī-'bir-ē-ən\ *noun* [*Iberia,* ancient region of the Caucasus] (1601)
: a member of one or more peoples anciently inhabiting the Caucasus in Asia between the Black and Caspian seas
— **Iberian** *adjective*

²**Iberian** *noun* [*Iberia,* peninsula in Europe] (1611)
1 a : a member of one or more peoples anciently inhabiting parts of the peninsula comprising Spain and Portugal **b :** a native or inhabitant of Spain or Portugal or the Basque region
2 : one or more of the languages of the ancient Iberians
— **Iberian** *adjective*

ibex \'ī-,beks\ *noun, plural* **ibex** *or* **ibex·es** [Latin] (1607)
: any of several wild goats (genus *Capra,* especially *C. ibex*) living chiefly in high mountain areas of the Old World and having large recurved horns transversely ridged in front

ibi·dem \'i-bə-,dem; i-'bī-dəm, -'bē-\ *adverb* [Latin] (circa 1771)
: in the same place

-ibility — see -ABILITY

ibis \'ī-bəs\ *noun, plural* **ibis** *or* **ibis·es** [Middle English, from Latin, from Greek, from Egyptian *hb*] (14th century)
: any of various wading birds (family Threskiornithidae) related to the herons but distinguished by a long slender downwardly curved bill

ibis

Ibi·zan hound \i-'bē-zən-\ *noun* [*Ibiza* Island] (1960)
: any of a breed of slender agile medium-sized hunting dogs developed in the Balearic Islands with a short and smooth or a wire-haired coat

-ible — see -ABLE

Ibo \'ē-(,)bō\ *noun, plural* **Ibo** *or* **Ibos** (1732)
1 : a member of a people of the area around the lower Niger in Africa
2 : the language of the Ibo people

Ibizan hound

Ib·sen·ism \'ib-sə-,ni-zəm, 'ip-\ *noun* (1890)
1 : dramatic invention or construction characteristic of Ibsen
2 : championship of Ibsen's plays and ideas
— **Ib·sen·ite** \-,nīt\ *noun or adjective*

ibu·pro·fen \,ī-byü-'prō-fən *also* ī-'byü-prə-fən\ *noun* [*is-* + *bu*tyl + *pro*pionic acid + *-fen* (alteration of *phenyl*)] (1969)
: a nonsteroidal anti-inflammatory drug $C_{13}H_{18}O_2$ used to relieve pain and fever

¹**IC** \,ī-'sē\ *noun* (1947)
: IMMEDIATE CONSTITUENT

²**IC** *noun* (1966)
: INTEGRATED CIRCUIT

¹**-ic** *adjective suffix* [Middle English, from Old French & Latin; Old French *-ique,* from Latin *-icus* — more at -Y]
1 : having the character or form of **:** being ⟨panoram*ic*⟩ **:** consisting of ⟨run*ic*⟩
2 a : of or relating to ⟨alderman*ic*⟩ **b :** related to, derived from, or containing ⟨alcohol*ic*⟩
3 : in the manner of **:** like that of **:** characteristic of ⟨Byron*ic*⟩
4 : associated or dealing with ⟨Ved*ic*⟩ **:** utilizing ⟨electron*ic*⟩
5 : characterized by **:** exhibiting ⟨nostalg*ic*⟩ **:** affected with ⟨allerg*ic*⟩
6 : caused by ⟨amoeb*ic*⟩
7 : tending to produce ⟨analges*ic*⟩
8 : having a valence relatively higher than in compounds or ions named with an adjective ending in *-ous* ⟨ferr*ic* iron⟩

²**-ic** *noun suffix*
: one having the character or nature of **:** one belonging to or associated with **:** one exhibiting or affected by **:** one that produces

-ical *adjective suffix* [Middle English, from Late Latin *-icalis* (as in *clericalis* clerical, *radicalis* radical)]
: -IC ⟨symmetr*ical*⟩ ⟨geolog*ical*⟩ — sometimes differing from *-ic* in that adjectives formed with *-ical* have a wider or more transferred semantic range than corresponding adjectives in *-ic*

Ic·a·rus \'i-kə-rəs\ *noun* [Latin, from Greek *Ikaros*]
: the son of Daedalus who to escape imprisonment flies by means of artificial wings but falls into the sea and drowns when the wax of his wings melts as he flies too near the sun

ICBM \,ī-,sē-(,)bē-'em\ *noun, plural* **ICBM's** *or* **ICBMs** \-'emz\ (1955)
: an intercontinental ballistic missile

¹ice \ˈīs\ *noun, often attributive* [Middle English *is*, from Old English *īs;* akin to Old High German *īs* ice, Avestan *isu-* icy] (before 12th century)
1 a : frozen water **b :** a sheet or stretch of ice
2 : a substance resembling ice; *especially* : the solid state of a substance usually found as a gas or liquid ⟨ammonia *ice* in the rings of Saturn⟩
3 : a state of coldness (as from formality or reserve)
4 a : a frozen dessert containing a flavoring (as fruit juice); *especially* : one containing no milk or cream **b** *British* : a serving of ice cream
5 *slang* : DIAMONDS; *broadly* : JEWELRY
6 : an undercover premium paid to a theater employee for choice theater tickets
— **ice·less** \ˈī-sləs\ *adjective*
— **on ice 1 :** with every likelihood of being won or accomplished **2 :** in reserve or safekeeping

²ice *verb* **iced; ic·ing** (15th century)
transitive verb
1 a : to coat with or convert into ice **b :** to chill with ice **c :** to supply with ice
2 : to cover with or as if with icing
3 : to put on ice
4 : SECURE 1b ⟨made two free throws . . . to *ice* the win —Jack McCallum⟩
5 : to shoot (an ice hockey puck) the length of the rink and beyond the opponents' goal line
6 *slang* : KILL 1a
intransitive verb
1 : to become ice-cold
2 a : to become covered with ice — often used with *up* or *over* **b :** to have ice form inside ⟨the carburetor *iced* up⟩

ice age *noun* (1873)
1 : a time of widespread glaciation
2 *I&A capitalized* : the Pleistocene glacial epoch

ice ax *noun* (1820)
: a combination pick and adze with a spiked handle that is used in mountain climbing

ice bag *noun* (1883)
: a waterproof bag to hold ice for local application of cold to the body

ice·berg \ˈīs-ˌbərg\ *noun* [probably part translation of Danish or Norwegian *isberg*, from *is* ice + *berg* mountain] (1820)
1 : a large floating mass of ice detached from a glacier
2 : an emotionally cold person
3 : ICEBERG LETTUCE

ice ax

iceberg lettuce *noun* (1893)
: any of various crisp light green lettuces that when mature have the leaves arranged in a compact head

ice·blink \-ˌbliŋk\ *noun* (1817)
: a glare in the sky over an ice field

ice·boat \-ˌbōt\ *noun* (circa 1819)
: a skeleton boat or frame on runners propelled on ice usually by sails

ice·boat·ing \-ˌbō-tiŋ\ *noun* (1885)
: the sport of sailing in iceboats
— **ice·boat·er** \-ˌbō-tər\ *noun*

ice·bound \-ˌbaund\ *adjective* (1641)
: surrounded, obstructed, or covered by ice

ice·box \-ˌbäks\ *noun* (1846)
: REFRIGERATOR

ice·break·er \-ˌbrā-kər\ *noun* (1875)
1 : a ship equipped to make and maintain a channel through ice
2 : something that breaks the ice on a project or occasion; *especially* : MIXER 1c

ice cap *noun* (circa 1860)
1 : an ice bag shaped to the head
2 : a cover of perennial ice and snow; *specifically* : a glacier forming on an extensive area of relatively level land and flowing outward from its center

ice–cold \ˈīs-ˈkōld\ *adjective* (before 12th century)
: extremely cold

ice–cream *adjective* (1890)
: of a color similar to that of vanilla ice cream

ice cream \ˈīs-ˈkrēm, ˈīs-ˌ\ *noun* (1744)
: a sweet flavored frozen food containing cream or butterfat and usually eggs

ice–cream chair *noun* [from its use in ice cream parlors] (1949)
: a small armless chair with a circular seat for use at a table (as at a café)

ice–cream cone *noun* (1909)
: a thin crisp edible cone for holding ice cream; *also* : one filled with ice cream

ice dancing *noun* (1925)
: a sport in which ice-skating pairs perform to music routines similar to ballroom dances

ice·fall \ˈīs-ˌfȯl\ *noun* (1817)
1 : a frozen waterfall
2 : the mass of usually jagged blocks into which a glacier may break when it moves down a steep declivity

ice field *noun* (1694)
1 : an extensive sheet of sea ice
2 : ICE CAP 2

ice floe *noun* (1819)
: a usually large flat free mass of floating sea ice

ice fog *noun* (1856)
: a fog composed of ice particles

ice hockey *noun* (1883)
: a game played on an ice rink by two teams of six players on skates whose object is to drive a puck into the opponents' goal with a hockey stick

ice·house \ˈīs-ˌhaús, ˈī-ˌsaús\ *noun* (1687)
: a building in which ice is made or stored

¹Ice·lan·dic \ˌī-ˈslan-dik\ *adjective* (1674)
: of, relating to, or characteristic of Iceland, the Icelanders, or Icelandic

²Icelandic *noun* (circa 1824)
: the North Germanic language of Iceland

Ice·land moss \ˈī-slən(d)-, -ˌslan(d)-\ *noun* (1805)
: a lichen (*Cetraria islandica*) of mountainous and arctic regions sometimes used in medicine or as food

Iceland poppy *noun* (1884)
: a poppy (*Papaver nudicaule*) of holarctic regions often cultivated for its usually single showy flowers

Iceland spar *noun* (1771)
: a doubly refracting transparent calcite

ice·man \ˈīs-ˌman\ *noun* (1833)
1 : one who sells or delivers ice
2 : a man skilled in traveling on ice

ice milk *noun* (1947)
: a sweetened frozen food made of skim milk

Ice·ni \ī-ˈsē-ˌnī\ *noun plural* [Latin] (circa 1891)
: an ancient British people that under their queen Boudicca revolted against the Romans in A.D. 60
— **Ice·ni·an** \-ˈsē-nē-ən\ *or* **Ice·nic** \-ˈsē-nik, -ˈse-\ *adjective*

ice–out \ˈīs-ˌaút\ *noun* (1951)
: the disappearance of ice from the surface of a body of water (as a lake) as a result of thawing

ice pack *noun* (1853)
: an expanse of pack ice

ice pick *noun* (circa 1877)
: a hand tool ending in a spike for chipping ice

ice plant *noun* (1753)
: an Old World annual herb (*Mesembryanthemum crystallinum*) of the carpetweed family that has fleshy foliage covered with glistening papillate dots or vesicles and is widely naturalized in warm regions; *broadly* : FIG MARIGOLD

ice point *noun* (1903)
: the freezing point of water of 0° Celsius or 273.15 Kelvin at standard atmospheric pressure

ice sheet *noun* (1873)

: ICE CAP 2

ice show *noun* (1948)
: an entertainment consisting of various exhibitions by ice-skaters usually with musical accompaniment

ice–skate \ˈī(s)-ˌskāt\ *intransitive verb* (circa 1948)
: to skate on ice
— **ice–skat·er** \-ˌskā-tər\ *noun*

ice skate *noun* (1897)
: a shoe with a metal runner attached for ice-skating

ice storm *noun* (1876)
: a storm in which falling rain freezes on contact

ice water *noun* (1722)
: chilled or iced water especially served as a beverage

ich·neu·mon \ik-ˈnü-mən, -ˈnyü-\ *noun* [Middle English, from Latin, from Greek *ichneumōn*, literally, tracker, from *ichneuein* to track, from *ichnos* footprint] (15th century)
1 : a mongoose (*Herpestes ichneumon*) of Africa, southern Europe, and southwestern Asia
2 : ICHNEUMON FLY

ichneumon fly *noun* (1713)
: any of a large superfamily (Ichneumonoidea) of hymenopterous insects whose larvae are usually internal parasites of other insect larvae and especially of caterpillars

ichor \ˈī-ˌkȯr, -kər\ *noun* [Greek *ichōr*] (15th century)
1 : a thin watery or blood-tinged discharge
2 : an ethereal fluid taking the place of blood in the veins of the ancient Greek gods
— **ichor·ous** \ˈī-kə-rəs\ *adjective*

ichthy- *or* **ichthyo-** *combining form* [Latin, from Greek, from *ichthys;* akin to Armenian *jukn* fish, Lithuanian *žuvis*]
: fish ⟨*ichthy*ology⟩

ich·thyo·fau·na \ˌik-thē-ō-ˈfȯ-nə, -ˈfä-\ *noun* [New Latin] (1883)
: the fish life of a region
— **ich·thyo·fau·nal** \-ˈfȯ-n³l, -ˈfä-\ *adjective*

ich·thy·ol·o·gy \ˌik-thē-ˈä-lə-jē\ *noun* (1646)
: a branch of zoology that deals with fishes
— **ich·thy·o·log·i·cal** \-thē-ə-ˈlä-ji-kəl\ *adjective*
— **ich·thy·o·log·i·cal·ly** \-k(ə-)lē\ *adverb*
— **ich·thy·ol·o·gist** \-thē-ˈä-lə-jist\ *noun*

ich·thy·oph·a·gous \ˌik-thē-ˈä-fə-gəs\ *adjective* [Greek *ichthyophagos*, from *ichthy-* + *-phagos* -phagous] (circa 1828)
: eating or subsisting on fish

ich·thyo·saur \ˈik-thē-ə-ˌsȯr\ *noun* [ultimately from Greek *ichthy-* + *sauros* lizard] (1830)
: any of an order (Ichthyosauria) of extinct marine reptiles of the Mesozoic specialized for aquatic life by a streamlined body with a long snout, limbs reduced to small fins for steering, and a large lunate caudal fin
— **ich·thyo·sau·ri·an** \ˌik-thē-ə-ˈsȯr-ē-ən\ *adjective or noun*

-ician *noun suffix* [Middle English, from Old French *-icien*, from Latin *-ica* (as in *rhetorica* rhetoric) + Old French *-ien* -ian]
: specialist : practitioner ⟨beau*tician*⟩

ici·cle \ˈī-si-kəl\ *noun* [Middle English *isikel*, from *is* ice + *ikel* icicle, from Old English *gicel;* akin to Old High German *ihilla* icicle, Middle Irish *aig* ice] (14th century)
1 : a pendent mass of ice formed by the freezing of dripping water
2 : an emotionally cold person

3 : a long narrow strip (as of foil) used to decorate a Christmas tree ◇

¹ic·ing \ˈī-siŋ\ noun (1769)
1 : a sweet flavored usually creamy mixture used to coat baked goods (as cupcakes) — called also **frosting**
2 : something that adds to the interest, value, or appeal of an item or event — often used in the phrase *icing on the cake*

²icing noun (1948)
: an act by an ice-hockey player of shooting a puck from within the defensive zone or defensive half of the rink beyond the opponents' goal line but not into the goal

ick·er \ˈi-kər\ noun [(assumed) Middle English (Scots dialect), from Old English *ēar, eher* — more at EAR] (1513)
Scottish **:** a head of grain

icky \ˈi-kē\ adjective **ick·i·er; -est** [perhaps baby talk alteration of *sticky*] (1929)
: offensive to the senses or sensibilities **:** DISTASTEFUL ⟨put off by her *icky* triteness —Renata Adler⟩
— **ick·i·ness** \-nəs\ noun

icon \ˈī-ˌkän\ noun [Latin, from Greek *eikōn*, from *eikenai* to resemble] (1572)
1 : a usually pictorial representation **:** IMAGE
2 [Late Greek *eikōn*, from Greek] **:** a conventional religious image typically painted on a small wooden panel and used in the devotions of Eastern Christians
3 : an object of uncritical devotion **:** IDOL
4 : EMBLEM, SYMBOL ⟨the house became an *icon* of 1860's residential architecture —Paul Goldberger⟩
5 a : a sign (as a word or graphic symbol) whose form suggests its meaning **b :** a graphic symbol on a computer display screen that suggests the purpose of an available function
— **icon·ic** \ī-ˈkä-nik\ adjective
— **icon·i·cal·ly** \-ni-k(ə-)lē\ adverb

icon- or **icono-** combining form [Greek *eikon-, eikono-,* from *eikon-, eikōn*]
: image ⟨*iconolatry*⟩

ico·nic·i·ty \ˌī-kə-ˈni-sə-tē\ noun (1946)
: correspondence between form and meaning ⟨the *iconicity* of the Roman numeral III⟩

icon·o·clasm \ī-ˈkä-nə-ˌkla-zəm\ noun (1797)
: the doctrine, practice, or attitude of an iconoclast

icon·o·clast \-ˌklast\ noun [Medieval Latin *iconoclastes*, from Middle Greek *eikonoklastēs*, literally, image destroyer, from Greek *eikono-* + *klan* to break — more at CLAST] (1641)
1 : one who destroys religious images or opposes their veneration
2 : one who attacks settled beliefs or institutions
— **icon·o·clas·tic** \(ˌ)ī-ˌkä-nə-ˈklas-tik\ adjective
— **icon·o·clas·ti·cal·ly** \-ti-k(ə-)lē\ adverb

ico·nog·ra·pher \ˌī-kə-ˈnä-grə-fər\ noun (1888)
1 : a maker of figures or drawings especially of a conventional type
2 : a student of iconography

icon·o·graph·ic \(ˌ)ī-ˌkä-nə-ˈgra-fik\ or **icon·o·graph·i·cal** \-fi-kəl\ adjective (circa 1855)
1 : of or relating to iconography
2 : representing something by pictures or diagrams
— **icon·o·graph·i·cal·ly** \-fi-k(ə-)lē\ adverb

ico·nog·ra·phy \ˌī-kə-ˈnä-grə-fē\ noun, plural **-phies** [Medieval Latin *iconographia*, from Greek *eikonographia* sketch, description, from *eikonographein* to describe, from *eikon-* + *graphein* to write — more at CARVE] (1678)
1 : pictorial material relating to or illustrating a subject
2 : the traditional or conventional images or symbols associated with a subject and especially a religious or legendary subject

3 : the imagery or symbolism of a work of art, an artist, or a body of art
4 : ICONOLOGY

ico·nol·a·try \-ˈnä-lə-trē\ noun (1624)
: the worship of images or icons

ico·nol·o·gy \-ˈnä-lə-jē\ noun [French *iconologie*, from *icono-* icon- + *-logie* -logy] (circa 1736)
: the study of icons or artistic symbolism
— **icon·o·log·i·cal** \(ˌ)ī-ˌkä-nᵊl-ˈä-ji-kəl\ adjective

icon·o·scope \ī-ˈkä-nə-ˌskōp\ noun [from *Iconoscope*, a trademark] (1932)
: a camera tube containing an electron gun and a photoemissive mosaic screen of which each cell produces a charge proportional to the varying light intensity of the image focused on the screen

ico·nos·ta·sis \ˌī-kə-ˈnäs-tə-səs, (ˌ)ī-ˈkä-nə-ˌstä-səs\ noun, plural **-ta·ses** \-ˌsēz\ [modification of Middle Greek *eikonostasion*, from Late Greek, shrine, from Greek *eikono-* + *-stasion* (from *histanai* to stand) — more at STAND] (1833)
: a screen or partition with doors and tiers of icons that separates the bema from the nave in Eastern churches

ico·sa·he·dral \(ˌ)ī-ˌkō-sə-ˈhē-drəl, -ˌkä-\ adjective (circa 1828)
: of or having the form of an icosahedron

ico·sa·he·dron \-drən\ noun, plural **-drons** or **-dra** \-drä\ [Greek *eikosaedron*, from *eikosi* twenty + *-edron* -hedron — more at VIGESIMAL] (1570)
: a polyhedron having 20 faces

-ics noun plural suffix but singular or plural in construction [¹-ic + ²-s; translation of Greek *-ika,* from neuter plural of *-ikos* -ic]
1 : study **:** knowledge **:** skill **:** practice ⟨linguist*ics*⟩ ⟨electron*ics*⟩
2 : characteristic actions or activities ⟨acrobat*ics*⟩
3 : characteristic qualities, operations, or phenomena ⟨mechan*ics*⟩

ic·ter·ic \ik-ˈter-ik\ adjective (circa 1600)
: of, relating to, or affected with jaundice

ic·ter·us \ˈik-tə-rəs\ noun [New Latin, from Greek *ikteros*] (circa 1706)
: JAUNDICE

ic·tus \ˈik-təs\ noun [Latin, literally, blow, from *icere* to strike] (1752)
: the recurring stress or beat in a rhythmic or metrical series of sounds

icy \ˈī-sē\ adjective **ic·i·er; -est** (before 12th century)
1 a : covered with, abounding in, or consisting of ice **b :** intensely cold
2 : characterized by coldness **:** FRIGID ⟨an *icy* stare⟩; *also* **:** STEELY ⟨*icy* nerves⟩
— **ic·i·ly** \-sə-lē\ adverb
— **ic·i·ness** \-sē-nəs\ noun

id \ˈid\ noun [New Latin, from Latin, it] (1924)
: the one of the three divisions of the psyche in psychoanalytic theory that is completely unconscious and is the source of psychic energy derived from instinctual needs and drives — compare EGO, SUPEREGO

¹-id noun suffix [in sense 1, from Latin *-ides,* masculine patronymic suffix, from Greek *-idēs;* in sense 2, from Italian *-ide,* from Latin *-id-, -is,* feminine patronymic suffix, from Greek]
1 : one belonging to a (specified) dynastic line ⟨Abbas*id*⟩
2 : meteor associated with or radiating from a (specified) constellation or comet ⟨Perse*id*⟩

²-id noun suffix [probably from Latin *-id-, -is,* feminine patronymic suffix, from Greek]
: body **:** particle ⟨chromat*id*⟩

I'd \ˈīd\ (circa 1592)
: I would **:** I had **:** I should

-idae noun plural suffix [New Latin, from Latin, from Greek *-idai,* plural of *-idēs*]
: members of the family of — in names of zoological families ⟨Felid*ae*⟩

Ida·ho \ˈī-də-ˌhō\ noun, plural **Idahos** or **Idahoes** (1934)
: an elongated baking potato grown especially in the state of Idaho

ID card \ˈī-ˈdē-\ noun (circa 1945)
: a card bearing identifying data (as age or organizational membership) about the individual whose name appears thereon — called also **identification card, identity card**

-ide also **-id** noun suffix [German & French; German *-id,* from French *-ide* (as in *oxide*)]
1 : binary chemical compound — added to the contracted name of the nonmetallic or more electronegative element ⟨hydrogen sulf*ide*⟩ or group ⟨cyan*ide*⟩
2 : chemical compound derived from or related to another (usually specified) compound ⟨anhydr*ide*⟩ ⟨glucos*ide*⟩

idea \ī-ˈdē-ə also ˈī-(ˌ)dē-ə or ˈī-ˌdē\ noun [Middle English, from Latin, from Greek, from *idein* to see — more at WIT] (14th century)
1 a : a transcendent entity that is a real pattern of which existing things are imperfect representations **b :** a standard of perfection **:** IDEAL **c :** a plan for action **:** DESIGN
2 archaic **:** a visible representation of a conception **:** a replica of a pattern
3 a obsolete **:** an image recalled by memory **b :** an indefinite or unformed conception **c :** an entity (as a thought, concept, sensation, or image) actually or potentially present to consciousness
4 : a formulated thought or opinion
5 : whatever is known or supposed about something ⟨a child's *idea* of time⟩
6 : the central meaning or chief end of a particular action or situation
7 Christian Science **:** an image in Mind ☆

☆ **SYNONYMS**
Idea, concept, conception, thought, notion, impression mean what exists in the mind as a representation (as of something comprehended) or as a formulation (as of a plan). IDEA may apply to a mental image or formulation of something seen or known or imagined, to a pure abstraction, or to something assumed or vaguely sensed ⟨innovative *ideas*⟩ ⟨my *idea* of paradise⟩. CONCEPT may apply to the idea formed by consideration of instances of a species or genus or, more broadly, to any idea of what a thing ought to be ⟨a society with no *concept* of private property⟩. CONCEPTION is often interchangeable with CONCEPT; it may stress the process of imagining or formulating rather than the result ⟨our changing *conception* of what constitutes art⟩. THOUGHT is likely to suggest the result of reflecting, reasoning, or meditating rather than of imagining ⟨commit your *thoughts* to paper⟩. NOTION suggests an idea not much resolved by analysis or reflection and may suggest the capricious or accidental ⟨you have the oddest *notions*⟩. IMPRESSION applies to an idea or notion resulting immediately from some stimulation of the senses ⟨the first *impression* is of soaring height⟩.

◇ **WORD HISTORY**
icicle The Old English noun *gicel* is found as early as the first half of the 8th century translating Latin *stiria* "icicle." *Gicel* became Middle English *ikyl* or *ikel* and later Modern English *ickle*, which was still in use around the middle of this century in Derbyshire and Yorkshire. The word for ice in Old English was *is*, and in a manuscript of about the year 1000 we find *stiria* translated with seeming redundancy as *ises gicel*, that is, "icicle of ice." Some three hundred years later in Middle English appeared the compound that we know today as *icicle*, which means precisely what *ises gicel* meant a thousand years ago.

— **idea·less** \ī-'dē-ə-ləs\ *adjective*

¹ide·al \ī-'dē(-ə)l, 'ī-,\ *adjective* [Middle English *ydeall*, from Late Latin *idealis*, from Latin *idea*] (15th century)
1 : existing as an archetypal idea
2 a : existing as a mental image or in fancy or imagination only; *broadly* : lacking practicality **b** : relating to or constituting mental images, ideas, or conceptions
3 a : of, relating to, or embodying an ideal **b** : conforming exactly to an ideal, law, or standard : PERFECT ⟨an *ideal* gas⟩ — compare REAL 2b(3)
4 : of or relating to philosophical idealism

²ideal *noun* (15th century)
1 : a standard of perfection, beauty, or excellence
2 : one regarded as exemplifying an ideal and often taken as a model for imitation
3 : an ultimate object or aim of endeavor : GOAL
4 : a subset of a mathematical ring that is closed under addition and subtraction and contains the products of any given element of the subset with each element of the ring
synonym see MODEL
— **ide·al·less** \ī-'dē(-ə)l-ləs\ *adjective*

ide·al·ise *British variant of* IDEALIZE

ide·al·ism \ī-'dē-(ə-)liz-əm, 'ī-(,)dē-\ *noun* (1796)
1 a (1) : a theory that ultimate reality lies in a realm transcending phenomena (2) : a theory that the essential nature of reality lies in consciousness or reason **b** (1) : a theory that only the perceptible is real (2) : a theory that only mental states or entities are knowable
2 a : the practice of forming ideals or living under their influence **b** : something that is idealized
3 : literary or artistic theory or practice that affirms the preeminent value of imagination as compared with faithful copying of nature — compare REALISM

¹ide·al·ist \-(ə-)list\ *noun* (1701)
1 a : an adherent of a philosophical theory of idealism **b** : an artist or author who advocates or practices idealism in art or writing
2 : one guided by ideals; *especially* : one that places ideals before practical considerations

²idealist *adjective* (1875)
: IDEALISTIC

ide·al·is·tic \(,)ī-,dē-(ə-)'lis-tik, ,ī-dē-\ *adjective* (1829)
: of or relating to idealists or idealism
— **ide·al·is·ti·cal·ly** \-ti-k(ə-)lē\ *adverb*

ide·al·i·ty \,ī-dē-'al-ə-tē\ *noun, plural* **-ties**
1 a : the quality or state of being ideal **b** : existence only in idea
2 : something imaginary or idealized

ide·al·ize \ī-'dē-(ə-),līz\ *verb* **-ized; -iz·ing** (1786)
intransitive verb
1 : to form ideals
2 : to work idealistically
transitive verb
1 a : to give an ideal form or value to **b** : to attribute ideal characteristics to
2 : to treat idealistically
— **ide·al·i·za·tion** \-,dē-(ə-)lə-'zā-shən\ *noun*
— **ide·al·iz·er** \-'dē-(ə-),lī-zər\ *noun*

ide·al·ly \ī-'dē-ə-lē, -'dē(-ə)l-lē\ *adverb* (1598)
1 : in idea or imagination : MENTALLY
2 : in relation to an exemplar
3 a : conformably to or in respect to an ideal : PERFECTLY **b** : for best results ⟨*ideally*, the counselor should vary his techniques for each applicant —T. M. Martinez⟩ **c** : in accordance with an ideal or typical standard : CLASSICALLY

ideal point *noun* (1879)
: a point added to the plane or to space to eliminate special cases; *specifically* : the point at infinity added in projective geometry at the assumed intersection of two parallel lines

ide·ate \'ī-dē-,āt\ *verb* **-at·ed; -at·ing** (1610)

transitive verb
: to form an idea or conception of
intransitive verb
: to form an idea

ide·a·tion \,ī-dē-'ā-shən\ *noun* (1818)
: the forming of ideas (as of things not present to the senses)

ide·a·tion·al \-shnəl, -shə-nᵊl\ *adjective* (1853)
: of, relating to, or produced by ideation; *broadly* : of or relating to ideas
— **ide·a·tion·al·ly** *adverb*

idée fixe \(,)ē-,dā-'feks\ *noun, plural* **idées fixes** *same*\ [French, literally, fixed idea] (1836)
: an idea that dominates one's mind especially for a prolonged period : OBSESSION

idem \'ī-,dem, 'ē-, 'i-\ *pronoun* [Middle English, from Latin, same — more at IDENTITY] (14th century)
: something previously mentioned : SAME

idem·po·tent \'ī-dəm-,pō-t°nt\ *adjective* [Latin *idem* same + *potent-, potens* having power — more at POTENT] (1870)
: relating to or being a mathematical quantity which when applied to itself under a given binary operation (as multiplication) equals itself; *also* : relating to or being an operation under which a mathematical quantity is idempotent
— **idempotent** *noun*

iden·tic \ī-'den-tik, ə-\ *adjective* (1649)
: IDENTICAL: as **a** : constituting a diplomatic action or expression in which two or more governments follow precisely the same course or employ an identical form **b** : constituting an action or expression in which a government follows precisely the same course or employs identical forms with reference to two or more other governments

iden·ti·cal \ī-'den-ti-kəl, ə-\ *adjective* [probably from Medieval Latin *identicus*, from Late Latin *identitas*] (1599)
1 : being the same : SELFSAME ⟨the *identical* place we stopped before⟩
2 : having such close resemblance as to be essentially the same ⟨*identical* hats⟩ — often used with *to* or *with*
3 a : having the same cause or origin ⟨*identical* infections⟩ **b** : MONOZYGOTIC
synonym see SAME
— **iden·ti·cal·ly** \-k(ə-)lē\ *adverb*
— **iden·ti·cal·ness** \-kəl-nəs\ *noun*

iden·ti·fi·ca·tion \ī-,den-tə-fə-'kā-shən, ə-\ *noun* (1644)
1 a : an act of identifying : the state of being identified **b** : evidence of identity
2 a : psychological orientation of the self in regard to something (as a person or group) with a resulting feeling of close emotional association **b** : a largely unconscious process whereby an individual models thoughts, feelings, and actions after those attributed to an object that has been incorporated as a mental image

identification card *noun* (1908)
: ID CARD

iden·ti·fi·er \ī-'den-tə-,fī(-ə)r, ə-\ *noun* (1889)
: one that identifies

iden·ti·fy \ī-'den-tə-,fī, ə-\ *verb* **-fied; -fy·ing** (1644)
transitive verb
1 a : to cause to be or become identical **b** : to conceive as united (as in spirit, outlook, or principle) ⟨groups that are *identified* with conservation⟩
2 a : to establish the identity of **b** : to determine the taxonomic position of (a biological specimen)
intransitive verb
1 : to be or become the same
2 : to practice psychological identification ⟨*identify* with the hero of a novel⟩
— **iden·ti·fi·able** \-,den-tə-'fī-ə-bəl\ *adjective*
— **iden·ti·fi·ably** \-blē\ *adverb*

iden·ti·ty \ī-'den-tə-tē, ə-, -'de-nə-\ *noun, plural* **-ties** [Middle French *identité*, from Late Latin *identitat-, identitas*, probably from Latin *identidem* repeatedly, contraction of *idem et idem*, literally, same and same] (1570)
1 a : sameness of essential or generic character in different instances **b** : sameness in all that constitutes the objective reality of a thing : ONENESS
2 a : the distinguishing character or personality of an individual : INDIVIDUALITY **b** : the relation established by psychological identification
3 : the condition of being the same with something described or asserted ⟨establish the *identity* of stolen goods⟩
4 : an equation that is satisfied for all values of the symbols
5 : IDENTITY ELEMENT

identity card *noun* (1900)
: ID CARD

identity crisis *noun* (1954)
1 : personal psychosocial conflict especially in adolescence that involves confusion about one's social role and often a sense of loss of continuity to one's personality
2 : a state of confusion in an institution or organization regarding its nature or direction

identity element *noun* (1902)
: an element (as 0 in the set of all integers under addition or 1 in the set of positive integers under multiplication) that leaves any element of the set to which it belongs unchanged when combined with it by a specified operation

identity matrix *noun* (circa 1929)
: a square matrix that has numeral 1's along the principal diagonal and 0's elsewhere

ideo- *combining form* [French *idéo-*, from Greek *idea*]
: idea ⟨*ideogram*⟩

ideo·gram \'i-dē-ə-,gram, 'ī-\ *noun* (circa 1840)
1 : a picture or symbol used in a system of writing to represent a thing or an idea but not a particular word or phrase for it; *especially* : one that represents not the object pictured but some thing or idea that the object pictured is supposed to suggest
2 : LOGOGRAM
— **ideo·gram·ic** *or* **ideo·gram·mic** \,i-dē-ə-'gra-mik, ,ī-\ *adjective*
— **ideo·gram·mat·ic** \-dē-ō-grə-'ma-tik\ *adjective*

ideo·graph \'i-dē-ə-,graf, 'ī-\ *noun* (1835)
: IDEOGRAM
— **ideo·graph·ic** \,i-dē-ə-'gra-fik, ,ī-\ *adjective*
— **ideo·graph·i·cal·ly** \-fi-k(ə-)lē\ *adverb*

ide·og·ra·phy \,i-dē-'ä-grə-fē, ,ī-\ *noun* (1836)
1 : the use of ideograms
2 : the representation of ideas by graphic symbols

ideo·log·i·cal \,ī-dē-ə-'lä-ji-kəl, ,i-\ *also* **ideo·log·ic** \-'lä-jik\ *adjective* (1797)
1 : relating to or concerned with ideas
2 : of, relating to, or based on ideology
— **ideo·log·i·cal·ly** \-'lä-ji-k(ə-)lē\ *adverb*

ide·ol·o·gize \,ī-dē-'ä-lə-,jīz, ,i-\ *transitive verb* **-gized; -giz·ing** (1860)
: to give an ideological character or interpretation to; *especially* : to change or interpret in relation to a sociopolitical ideology often seen as biased or limited

ideo·logue *also* **idea·logue** \'ī-dē-ə-,lòg, -,läg\ *noun* [French *idéologue*, back-formation from *idéologie*] (1815)
1 : an impractical idealist : THEORIST
2 : an often blindly partisan advocate or adherent of a particular ideology

\ə\ abut \ᵊ\ kitten \ər\ further \a\ ash \ā\ ace
\ä\ mop, mar \aù\ out \ch\ chin \e\ bet \ē\ easy
\g\ go \i\ hit \ī\ ice \j\ job \ŋ\ sing \ō\ go
\ò\ law \òi\ boy \th\ thin \tẖ\ the \ü\ loot \ù\ foot
\y\ yet \zh\ vision *see also* Guide to Pronunciation

ide·ol·o·gy \ˌī-dē-'ä-lə-jē, ˌi-\ *also* **ide·al·o·gy** \-'ä-lə-jē, -'a-\ *noun, plural* **-gies** [French *idéologie,* from *idéo-* ideo- + *-logie* -logy] (1813)
1 : visionary theorizing
2 a : a systematic body of concepts especially about human life or culture **b :** a manner or the content of thinking characteristic of an individual, group, or culture **c :** the integrated assertions, theories and aims that constitute a sociopolitical program
— **ide·ol·o·gist** \-jist\ *noun*

ideo·mo·tor \ˌī-dē-ə-'mō-tər, ˌi-\ *adjective* [International Scientific Vocabulary] (1867)
: not reflex but motivated by an idea ⟨*ideomotor* muscular activity⟩

ides \'īdz\ *noun plural but singular or plural in construction* [Middle English, from Middle French, from Latin *idus*]
: the 15th day of March, May, July, or October or the 13th day of any other month in the ancient Roman calendar; *broadly* **:** this day and the seven days preceding it

-idin *or* **-idine** *noun suffix* [International Scientific Vocabulary *-ide* + *-in, -ine*]
: chemical compound related in origin or structure to another compound ⟨tolu*idine*⟩ ⟨guan*idine*⟩

idio- *combining form* [Greek, from *idios* — more at IDIOT]
: one's own **:** personal **:** separate **:** distinct ⟨*idio*blast⟩

id·i·o·blast \'i-dē-ə-ˌblast\ *noun* [International Scientific Vocabulary] (1822)
: a plant cell (as a sclereid) that differs markedly from neighboring cells
— **id·io·blas·tic** \ˌi-dē-ə-'blas-tik\ *adjective*

id·i·o·cy \'i-dē-ə-sē\ *noun, plural* **-cies** (circa 1529)
1 : extreme mental retardation commonly due to incomplete or abnormal development of the brain
2 : something notably stupid or foolish

id·i·o·graph·ic \ˌi-dē-ə-'gra-fik\ *adjective* [International Scientific Vocabulary] (circa 1890)
: relating to or dealing with something concrete, individual, or unique

id·i·o·lect \'i-dē-ə-ˌlekt\ *noun* [*idio-* + *-lect* (as in *dialect*)] (1948)
: the language or speech pattern of one individual at a particular period of life
— **id·io·lec·tal** \ˌi-dē-ə-'lek-t'l\ *adjective*

id·i·om \'i-dē-əm\ *noun* [Middle French & Late Latin; Middle French *idiome,* from Late Latin *idioma* individual peculiarity of language, from Greek *idiōmat-, idiōma,* from *idiousthai* to appropriate, from *idios*] (1588)
1 a : the language peculiar to a people or to a district, community, or class **:** DIALECT **b :** the syntactical, grammatical, or structural form peculiar to a language
2 : an expression in the usage of a language that is peculiar to itself either grammatically (as *no, it wasn't me*) or in having a meaning that cannot be derived from the conjoined meanings of its elements (as *Monday week* for "the Monday a week after next Monday")
3 : a style or form of artistic expression that is characteristic of an individual, a period or movement, or a medium or instrument ⟨the modern jazz *idiom*⟩; *broadly* **:** MANNER, STYLE ⟨a new culinary *idiom*⟩

id·i·o·mat·ic \ˌi-dē-ə-'ma-tik\ *adjective* (1712)
1 : of, relating to, or conforming to idiom
2 : peculiar to a particular group, individual, or style
— **id·i·o·mat·i·cal·ly** \-ti-k(ə-)lē\ *adverb*
— **id·i·o·mat·ic·ness** \-tik-nəs\ *noun*

id·i·o·mor·phic \ˌi-dē-ə-'mòr-fik\ *adjective* [Greek *idiomorphos,* from *idio-* + *-morphos* -morphous] (1887)
: having the proper form or shape — used of minerals whose crystalline growth has not been interfered with

id·i·o·path·ic \ˌi-dē-ə-'pa-thik\ *adjective* (1669)

1 : arising spontaneously or from an obscure or unknown cause **:** PRIMARY
2 : peculiar to the individual
— **id·i·o·path·i·cal·ly** \-'pa-thi-k(ə-)lē\ *adverb*

id·i·o·syn·cra·sy \ˌi-dē-ə-'siŋ-krə-sē\ *noun, plural* **-sies** [Greek *idiosynkrasia,* from *idio-* + *synkerannynai* to blend, from *syn-* + *kerannynai* to mingle, mix — more at CRATER] (1604)
1 a : a peculiarity of constitution or temperament **:** an individualizing characteristic or quality **b :** individual hypersensitiveness (as to a drug or food)
2 : characteristic peculiarity (as of temperament); *broadly* **:** ECCENTRICITY
— **id·i·o·syn·crat·ic** \ˌi-dē-ō-(ˌ)sin-'kra-tik\ *adjective*
— **id·i·o·syn·crat·i·cal·ly** \-'kra-ti-k(ə-)lē\ *adverb*

id·i·ot \'i-dē-ət\ *noun* [Middle English, from Latin *idiota* ignorant person, from Greek *idiōtēs* one in a private station, layman, ignorant person, from *idios* one's own, private; akin to Latin *suus* one's own — more at SUICIDE] (14th century)
1 : a person affected with idiocy; *especially* **:** a feebleminded person having a mental age not exceeding three years and requiring complete custodial care
2 : a foolish or stupid person ◇
— **idiot** *adjective*

idiot box *noun* (circa 1955)
: TELEVISION

id·i·ot·ic \ˌi-dē-'ä-tik\ *also* **id·i·ot·i·cal** \-'ä-ti-kəl\ *adjective* (1713)
1 : characterized by idiocy
2 : showing complete lack of thought or common sense **:** FOOLISH
— **id·i·ot·i·cal·ly** \-ti-k(ə-)lē\ *adverb*

¹id·i·o·tism \'i-dē-ə-ˌti-zəm\ *noun* [Middle French *idiotisme,* from Latin *idiotismus* common speech, from Greek *idiōtismos,* from *idiōtēs*] (1588)
1 *obsolete* **:** IDIOM 1
2 : IDIOM 2

²id·i·ot·ism \'i-dē-ə-(ˌ)ti-zəm\ *noun* [*idiot* + *-ism*] (circa 1611)
archaic **:** IDIOCY 2

idiot light *noun* (1966)
: a colored light on an instrument panel (as of an automobile) designed to give a warning (as of low oil pressure)

idiot sa·vant \'ē-ˌdyō-sä-'väⁿ, *or same as* IDIOT *and* SAVANT *for respective singular and plural forms*\ *noun, plural* **idiots savants** \-ˌdyō-sä-'väⁿ(z)\ *or* **idiot savants** \-'väⁿ(z)\ [French, literally, learned idiot] (1927)
1 : a mentally defective person who exhibits exceptional skill or brilliance in some limited field
2 : a person who is highly knowledgeable about one subject but knows little about anything else

-idium *noun suffix, plural* **-idiums** *or* **-idia** [New Latin, from Greek *-idion,* diminutive suffix]
: small one ⟨anther*idium*⟩

¹idle \'ī-d'l\ *adjective* **idler** \'īd-lər, 'ī-d'l-ər\; **idlest** \'īd-ləst, 'ī-d'l-əst\ [Middle English *idel,* from Old English *īdel;* akin to Old High German *ītal* worthless] (before 12th century)
1 : lacking worth or basis **:** VAIN ⟨*idle* chatter⟩ ⟨*idle* pleasure⟩
2 : not occupied or employed: as **a :** having no employment **:** INACTIVE ⟨*idle* workers⟩ **b :** not turned to normal or appropriate use ⟨*idle* funds⟩ ⟨*idle* farmland⟩ **c :** not scheduled to compete ⟨the team will be *idle* tomorrow⟩
3 a : SHIFTLESS, LAZY **b :** having no evident lawful means of support
synonym see VAIN, INACTIVE
— **idle·ness** \'ī-d'l-nəs\ *noun*
— **idly** \'īd-lē, 'ī-d'l-ē\ *adverb*

²idle *verb* **idled; idling** \'īd-liŋ, 'ī-d'l-iŋ\ (1592)

intransitive verb
1 a : to spend time in idleness **b :** to move idly
2 : to run at low power and often disconnected usually so that that power is not used for useful work ⟨the engine is *idling*⟩
transitive verb
1 : to pass in idleness
2 : to make idle ⟨workers *idled* by a strike⟩
3 : to cause to idle
— **idler** \'īd-lər, 'ī-d'l-ər\ *noun*

idler pulley *noun* (circa 1890)
: a guide or tightening pulley for a belt or chain

idler wheel *noun* (1805)
1 : a wheel, gear, or roller used to transfer motion or to guide or support something
2 : IDLER PULLEY

idler wheel 1

idlesse \'īd-ləs, 'īd-'les\ *noun* [Middle English, from *idle* + *-esse* (as in *richesse* wealth) — more at RICHES] (15th century)
: the quality or state of being idle **:** IDLENESS

ido·crase \'ī-də-ˌkrās, 'i-, -ˌkrāz\ *noun* [French, from Greek *eidos* form + *krasis* mixture, from *kerannynai* to mix — more at CRATER] (1804)
: a mineral that is a complex silicate of calcium, magnesium, iron, and aluminum

idol \'ī-d'l\ [Middle English, from Old French *idole,* from Late Latin *idolum,* from Greek *eidōlon* image, idol; akin to Greek *eidos* form — more at IDYLL] (13th century)
1 : a representation or symbol of an object of worship; *broadly* **:** a false god
2 a : a likeness of something **b** *obsolete* **:** PRETENDER, IMPOSTOR
3 : a form or appearance visible but without substance ⟨an enchanted phantom, a lifeless *idol* —P. B. Shelley⟩
4 : an object of extreme devotion ⟨a movie *idol*⟩; *also* **:** IDEAL 2
5 : a false conception **:** FALLACY

idol·a·ter *or* **idol·a·tor** \ī-'dä-lə-tər\ *noun* [Middle English *idolatrer,* from Middle French *idolatre,* from Late Latin *idololatres,* from Greek *eidōlolatrēs,* from *eidōlon* + *-latrēs* -later] (14th century)
1 : a worshiper of idols
2 : a person that admires intensely and often blindly one that is not usually a subject of worship

idol·a·trous \ī-'dä-lə-trəs\ *adjective* (1543)
1 : of or relating to idolatry
2 : having the character of idolatry ⟨the religion of *idolatrous* nationalism —Aldous Huxley⟩
3 : given to idolatry
— **idol·a·trous·ly** *adverb*

◇ WORD HISTORY
idiot To be called "one's own man" is usually to receive a compliment. To be called an *idiot* is a blatant insult. Surprisingly, there is an etymological equivalence in the two characterizations. In Greek *idiōtēs,* a derivative of *idios* "one's own," meant "a private person," that is, one who did not hold public office. Through a series of natural extensions, *idiōtēs* came to mean "a common man" and then "an ignorant person." The imputation of ignorance is more benign than one might suspect, for it implied a lack of book learning, not innate stupidity. The word became *idiota* in Latin, from whence it was borrowed into Middle English in the then-standard sense of "an ignorant person." By the 16th century, however, the meaning of *idiot* had deteriorated to the point where it no longer meant a lack of education but rather of basic intelligence.

— **idol·a·trous·ness** *noun*

idol·a·try \-trē\ *noun, plural* **-tries** (13th century)
1 : the worship of a physical object as a god
2 : immoderate attachment or devotion to something

idol·ize \'ī-d°l-,īz\ *verb* **-ized; -iz·ing** (1598)
transitive verb
: to worship as a god; *broadly* **:** to love or admire to excess ⟨the common people whom he so *idolized* —*Times Literary Supplement*⟩
intransitive verb
: to practice idolatry
— **idol·i·za·tion** \,ī-d°l-ə-'zā-shən\ *noun*
— **idol·iz·er** \'ī-d°l-,ī-zər\ *noun*

idyll *also* **idyl** \'ī-d°l, *British usually* 'i-(,)dil\ *noun* [Latin *idyllium*, from Greek *eidyllion*, from diminutive of *eidos* form; akin to Greek *idein* to see — more at WIT] (1586)
1 a : a simple descriptive work in poetry or prose that deals with rustic life or pastoral scenes or suggests a mood of peace and contentment **b :** a narrative poem (as Tennyson's *Idylls of the King*) treating an epic, romantic, or tragic theme
2 a : a lighthearted carefree episode that is a fit subject for an idyll **b :** a romantic interlude

idyl·lic \ī-'di-lik, *chiefly British* i-\ *adjective* (1856)
1 : of, relating to, or being an idyll
2 : pleasing or picturesque in natural simplicity
— **idyl·li·cal·ly** \-'di-li-k(ə-)lē\ *adverb*

-ie *also* **-y** *noun suffix* [Middle English]
1 : little one **:** dear little one ⟨bird*ie*⟩ ⟨sonny⟩
2 : one belonging to **:** one having to do with ⟨town*ie*⟩ **:** one who is ⟨preem*ie*⟩
3 : one of (such) a kind or quality ⟨cut*ie*⟩ ⟨tough*ie*⟩

-ier — see -ER

¹if \'if, əf\ *conjunction* [Middle English, from Old English *gif*; akin to Old High German *ibu* if] (before 12th century)
1 a : in the event that **b :** allowing that **c :** on the assumption that **d :** on condition that
2 : WHETHER ⟨asked *if* the mail had come⟩ ⟨I doubt *if* I'll pass the course⟩
3 — used as a function word to introduce an exclamation expressing a wish ⟨*if* it would only rain⟩
4 : even though ⟨an interesting *if* untenable argument⟩
— **if anything :** on the contrary even **:** perhaps even ⟨*if anything*, you ought to apologize⟩

²if \'if\ *noun* (1513)
1 : CONDITION, STIPULATION ⟨the question . . . depends on too many *ifs* to allow an answer —*Encounter*⟩
2 : SUPPOSITION

-iferous *adjective combining form* [Middle English, from Latin *-ifer*, from *-i-* + *-fer* -ferous]
: -FEROUS

iff \'if-°n(d)-'ōn-lē-,if; 'if, *sometimes read with a prolonged* f\ *conjunction* [alteration of ¹*if*] (1955)
: if and only if ⟨two figures are congruent *iff* one can be placed over the other so that they coincide⟩

if·fy \'i-fē\ *adjective* [¹*if*] (1937)
: abounding in contingencies or unknown qualities or conditions **:** UNCERTAIN ⟨an *iffy* proposition⟩
— **if·fi·ness** *noun*

-ification *noun suffix* [Middle English *-ificacioun*, from Middle French & Latin; Middle French *-ification*, from Latin *-ification-*, *-ificatio*, from *-i-* + *-ficatio* -fication]
: -FICATION ⟨desert*ification*⟩

-iform *adjective combining form* [Middle French & Latin; Middle French *-iforme*, from Latin *-iformis*, from *-i-* + *-formis* -form]
: -FORM ⟨patell*iform*⟩

I formation *noun* (1951)

: an offensive football formation in which the running backs line up in a line directly behind the quarterback — compare T FORMATION

-ify *verb suffix* [Middle English *-ifien*, from Old French *-ifier*, from Latin *-ificare*, from *-i-* + *-ficare* -fy]
: -FY

IgA \,ī-(,)jē-'ā\ *noun* [immunoglobulin] (1969)
: a class of immunoglobulins found in external bodily secretions (as saliva, tears, and sweat)

Ig·bo \'ig-(,)bō\ *variant of* IBO

IgE \,ī-(,)jē-'ē\ *noun* (1969)
: a class of immunoglobulins that function especially in allergic reactions

IgG \-'jē\ *noun* (1969)
: a class of immunoglobulins that includes the most common antibodies circulating in the blood

ig·loo \'i-(,)glü\ *noun, plural* **igloos** [Inuit *iglu* house] (1856)
1 : an Eskimo house usually made of sod, wood, or stone when permanent or of blocks of snow or ice in the shape of a dome when built for temporary purposes
2 : a building or structure shaped like a dome

igloo 1

IgM \,ī-(,)jē-'em\ *noun* (1969)
: a class of immunoglobulins that includes antibodies that appear early in the immune response

ig·ne·ous \'ig-nē-əs\ *adjective* [Latin *igneus*, from *ignis* fire; akin to Sanskrit *agni* fire] (1664)
1 : of, relating to, or resembling fire **:** FIERY
2 a : relating to, resulting from, or suggestive of the intrusion or extrusion of magma or volcanic activity **b :** formed by solidification of magma ⟨*igneous* rock⟩

ig·nes·cent \ig-'ne-s°nt\ *adjective* [Latin *ignescent-, ignescens*, present participle of *ignescere* to catch fire, from *ignis*] (circa 1828)
: VOLATILE

ig·nim·brite \'ig-nəm-,brīt\ *noun* [German *Ignimbrit*, from Latin *ignis* + *imbr-* (from *imber* rain) + German *-it* ¹-ite — more at IMBRICATE] (1932)
: a hard rock formed by solidification of chiefly fine deposits of volcanic ash

ig·nis fat·u·us \'ig-nəs-'fa-chə-wəs, -'fach-wəs\ *noun, plural* **ig·nes fat·ui** \-,nēz-'fa-chə-,wī\ [Medieval Latin, literally, foolish fire] (circa 1563)
1 : a light that sometimes appears in the night over marshy ground and is often attributable to the combustion of gas from decomposed organic matter
2 : a deceptive goal or hope

ig·nite \ig-'nīt\ *verb* **ig·nit·ed; ig·nit·ing** [Latin *ignitus*, past participle of *ignire* to ignite, from *ignis*] (1666)
transitive verb
1 : to subject to fire or intense heat; *especially* **:** to render luminous by heat
2 a : to set afire; *also* **:** KINDLE **b :** to cause (a fuel) to burn
3 : to heat up **:** EXCITE ⟨oppression that *ignited* the hatred of the people⟩
intransitive verb
1 : to catch fire
2 : to begin to glow
— **ig·nit·abil·i·ty** \ig-,nī-tə-'bi-lə-tē\ *noun*
— **ig·nit·able** *also* **ig·nit·ible** \-'nī-tə-bəl\ *adjective*
— **ig·nit·er** *also* **ig·ni·tor** \-'nī-tər\ *noun*

ig·ni·tion \ig-'ni-shən\ *noun* (1612)
1 : the act or action of igniting: as **a :** the starting of a fire **b :** the heating of a plasma to a temperature high enough to sustain nuclear fusion
2 : the process or means (as an electric spark) of igniting a fuel mixture

ig·ni·tron \ig-'nī-,trän\ *noun* [Latin *ignis* fire + English *-tron*] (1933)
: a mercury-containing rectifier tube in which the arc is struck again at the beginning of each cycle by a special electrode separately energized by an auxiliary circuit

ig·no·ble \ig-'nō-bəl\ *adjective* [Middle English, from Middle French, from Latin *ignobilis*, from *in-* + Old Latin *gnobilis* noble] (15th century)
1 : of low birth or common origin **:** PLEBEIAN
2 : characterized by baseness, lowness, or meanness
synonym see MEAN
— **ig·no·bil·i·ty** \,ig-nō-'bi-lə-tē\ *noun*
— **ig·no·ble·ness** \ig-'nō-bəl-nəs\ *noun*
— **ig·no·bly** \-blē *also* -bə-lē\ *adverb*

ig·no·min·i·ous \,ig-nə-'mi-nē-əs\ *adjective* (15th century)
1 : marked with or characterized by disgrace or shame **:** DISHONORABLE
2 : deserving of shame or infamy **:** DESPICABLE
3 : HUMILIATING, DEGRADING ⟨suffered an *ignominious* defeat⟩
— **ig·no·min·i·ous·ly** *adverb*
— **ig·no·min·i·ous·ness** *noun*

ig·no·mi·ny \'ig-nə-,mi-nē, -mə-nē *also* ig-'nä-mə-nē\ *noun, plural* **-nies** [Middle French or Latin; Middle French *ignominie*, from Latin *ignominia*, from *ig-* (as in *ignorare* to be ignorant of, ignore) + *nomin-, nomen* name, repute — more at NAME] (1540)
1 : deep personal humiliation and disgrace
2 : disgraceful or dishonorable conduct, quality, or action
synonym see DISGRACE

ig·no·ra·mus \,ig-nə-'rā-məs *also* -'ra-\ *noun, plural* **-mus·es** *also* **-mi** \-mē\ [*Ignoramus*, ignorant lawyer in *Ignoramus* (1615), play by George Ruggle, from Latin, literally, we are ignorant of] (circa 1616)
: an utterly ignorant person **:** DUNCE ◇

ig·no·rance \'ig-n(ə-)rən(t)s\ *noun* (13th century)
: the state or fact of being ignorant

ig·no·rant \'ig-n(ə-)rənt\ *adjective* (14th century)
1 a : destitute of knowledge or education ⟨an *ignorant* society⟩; *also* **:** lacking knowledge or comprehension of the thing specified ⟨parents

◇ WORD HISTORY

ignoramus *Ignoramus* was a Latin satire written by a Cambridge University tutor named George Ruggle (1575–1622) and first performed in 1615. The title character, whose name in Latin means literally "we do not know," was Ruggle's send-up of unlearned but crafty lawyers. He was inspired by a real attorney named Francis Brakin, who had won a court dispute between the town of Cambridge and the university and thus aroused the ire of local scholars. The success of the play, which was performed twice before King James I in 1615, led to the generic use of *ignoramus* in the 17th century for any woefully ignorant person. The character's name may have been suggested by the legal term *ignoramus*, written on bills of indictment when the evidence presented seemed to be insufficient to justify prosecution. In these cases *ignoramus* meant "we take no notice of (i.e., we do not recognize) the indictment." Such a reference would have been familiar to Ruggle's audience and appropriate to his satire of the legal profession.

ignorant of modern mathematics⟩ **b :** resulting from or showing lack of knowledge or intelligence ⟨*ignorant* errors⟩
2 : UNAWARE, UNINFORMED ☆
— **ig·no·rant·ly** *adverb*
— **ig·no·rant·ness** *noun*
ig·no·ra·tio elen·chi \ˌig-nə-ˈrä-tē-ˌō-i-ˈlen-ˌkē\ *noun* [Latin, literally, ignorance of proof] (1588)
: a fallacy in logic of supposing a point proved or disproved by an argument proving or disproving something not at issue
ig·nore \ig-ˈnōr, -ˈnȯr\ *transitive verb* **ig·nored; ig·nor·ing** [obsolete *ignore* to be ignorant of, from French *ignorer*, from Latin *ignorare*, from *ignarus* ignorant, unknown, from *in-* + *gnoscere*, *noscere* to know — more at KNOW] (1801)
1 : to refuse to take notice of
2 : to reject (a bill of indictment) as ungrounded
synonym see NEGLECT
— **ig·nor·able** \-ˈnōr-ə-bəl, -ˈnȯr-\ *adjective*
— **ig·nor·er** *noun*
Igo·rot \ˌē-gə-ˈrōt\ *noun, plural* **Igorot** or **Igorots** (1821)
1 : a member of any of several related peoples of northwestern Luzon, Philippines
2 : any of the Austronesian languages of the Igorot
Igraine \i-ˈgrān\ *noun*
: the wife of Uther and mother of King Arthur
igua·na \i-ˈgwä-nə\ *noun* [Spanish, from Arawak & Carib *iwana*] (1555)
: any of various large herbivorous typically dark-colored tropical American lizards (family Iguanidae) that have a serrated dorsal crest and are important as human food in their native habitat; *broadly* **:** any of various large lizards

iguana

iguan·odon \i-ˈgwä-nə-ˌdän\ *noun* [New Latin *Iguanodont-, Iguanodon*, from Spanish *iguana* + Greek *odōn* tooth, from *odont-, odous* — more at TOOTH] (1830)
: any of a genus (*Iguanodon*) of very large herbivorous dinosaurs of the early Cretaceous
IHS \ˌī-ˌäch-ˈes\ [Late Latin, part transliteration of Greek ΙΗΣ, abbreviation for ΙΗΣΟΥΣ *Iēsous* Jesus]
— used as a Christian symbol and monogram for *Jesus*
ikat \ˈē-ˌkät\ *noun* [Malay, tying] (1927)
: a fabric in which the yarns have been tie-dyed before weaving
ike·ba·na \ˌi-kā-ˈbä-nə, ˌi-ki-, ˌē-\ *noun* [Japanese, from *ikeru* to keep alive, arrange + *hana* flower] (1901)
: the Japanese art of flower arranging that emphasizes form and balance
ikon *variant of* ICON
il- — see IN-
ilang–ilang *variant of* YLANG-YLANG
¹-ile *adjective suffix* [Middle English, from Middle French, from Latin *-ilis*]
: tending to or capable of ⟨contract*ile*⟩
²-ile *noun suffix* [-*ile* (as in *quartile*, noun)]
: segment of a (specified) size in a frequency distribution ⟨dec*ile*⟩
ile·i·tis \ˌi-lē-ˈī-təs\ *noun* [New Latin] (circa 1855)
: inflammation of the ileum
ile·um \ˈi-lē-əm\ *noun, plural* **il·ea** \-lē-ə\ [New Latin, alteration of Latin *ilia*, plural, groin, viscera] (1682)
: the last division of the small intestine extending between the jejunum and large intestine
— **ile·al** \-lē-əl\ *adjective*
ile·us \ˈi-lē-əs\ *noun* [Latin, from Greek *eileos*, from *eilyein* to roll — more at VOLUBLE] (1693)

: mechanical or functional obstruction of the bowel
ilex \ˈī-ˌleks\ *noun* [Middle English, from Latin] (14th century)
1 : HOLM OAK
2 : HOLLY 1
il·i·ac \ˈi-lē-ˌak\ *also* **il·i·al** \ˈi-lē-əl\ *adjective* [Late Latin *iliacus*, from Latin *ilium*] (1541)
: of, relating to, or located near the ilium
Il·i·ad \ˈi-lē-əd, -ˌad\ *noun* [*Iliad*, ancient Greek epic poem attributed to Homer, from Latin *Iliad-, Ilias*, from Greek, from *Ilion* Troy] (1603)
1 a : a series of miseries or disastrous events
b : a series of exploits regarded as suitable for an epic
2 : a long narrative; *especially* **:** an epic in the Homeric tradition
— **Il·i·ad·ic** \ˌi-lē-ˈa-dik\ *adjective*
il·i·um \ˈi-lē-əm\ *noun, plural* **il·ia** \-lē-ə\ [New Latin, alteration of Latin *ilia*] (1706)
: the dorsal, upper, and largest one of the three bones composing either lateral half of the pelvis
¹ilk \ˈilk\ *pronoun* [Middle English, from Old English *ilca*, from a prehistoric compound whose constituents are akin respectively to Gothic *is* he (akin to Latin *is* he, that) and Old English *gelīc* like — more at ITERATE, LIKE] (before 12th century)
chiefly Scottish **:** SAME — used with *that* especially in the names of landed families
²ilk *noun* (1790)
: SORT, KIND ⟨the rejection of these books or others of like *ilk* —Kathleen Molz⟩
³ilk *pronoun* [Middle English, adjective & pronoun, from Old English *ylc, ælc* — more at EACH] (before 12th century)
chiefly Scottish **:** EACH
il·ka \ˈil-kə\ *adjective* [Middle English, from *ilk* + *a* (indefinite article)] (13th century)
chiefly Scottish **:** EACH, EVERY
¹ill \ˈil\ *adjective* **worse** \ˈwərs\; **worst** \ˈwərst\ [Middle English, from Old Norse *illr*] (12th century)
1 a *chiefly Scottish* **:** IMMORAL, VICIOUS **b :** resulting from, accompanied by, or indicative of an evil or malevolent intention ⟨*ill* deeds⟩ **c :** attributing evil or an objectionable quality ⟨held an *ill* opinion of his neighbors⟩
2 a : causing suffering or distress ⟨*ill* weather⟩ **b** *comparative also* **ill·er** (1) **:** not normal or sound ⟨*ill* health⟩ (2) **:** not in good health; *also* **:** NAUSEATED
3 a : not suited to circumstances or not to one's advantage **:** UNLUCKY ⟨an *ill* omen⟩ **b :** involving difficulty **:** HARD ⟨an *ill* man to please⟩
4 a : not meeting an accepted standard ⟨*ill* manners⟩ **b** *archaic* **:** notably unskillful or inefficient
5 : UNFRIENDLY, HOSTILE ⟨*ill* feeling⟩
²ill *adverb* **worse; worst** (13th century)
1 a : with displeasure or hostility **b :** in a harsh manner **c :** so as to reflect unfavorably ⟨spoke *ill* of the neighbors⟩
2 : in a reprehensible manner
3 : HARDLY, SCARCELY ⟨can *ill* afford such extravagances⟩
4 a : in an unfortunate manner **:** BADLY, UNLUCKILY ⟨*ill* fares the land . . . where wealth accumulates, and men decay —Oliver Goldsmith⟩ **b :** in a faulty, inefficient, insufficient, or unpleasant manner — often used in combination ⟨the methods used may be *ill*-adapted to the aims in view —R. M. Hutchins⟩
³ill *noun* (13th century)
1 : the reverse of good **:** EVIL
2 a : MISFORTUNE, DISTRESS **b** (1) **:** AILMENT, SICKNESS (2) **:** something that disturbs or afflicts **:** TROUBLE ⟨economic and social *ills*⟩
3 : something that reflects unfavorably ⟨spoke no *ill* of him⟩
I'll \ˈī(ə)l\ (1567)
: I will **:** I shall

ill–ad·vised \ˌi-ləd-ˈvīzd\ *adjective* (circa 1592)
: resulting from or showing lack of wise and sufficient counsel or deliberation ⟨an *ill-advised* decision⟩
— **ill–ad·vis·ed·ly** \-ˈvī-zəd-lē\ *adverb*
ill at ease *adjective* (14th century)
: not feeling easy **:** UNCOMFORTABLE
il·la·tion \i-ˈlā-shən\ *noun* [Late Latin *illation-, illatio*, from Latin, action of bringing in, from *inferre* (past participle *illatus*) to bring in, from *in-* + *ferre* to carry — more at TOLERATE, BEAR] (1533)
1 : the action of inferring **:** INFERENCE
2 : a conclusion inferred
¹il·la·tive \ˈi-lə-tiv, i-ˈlā-\ *noun* (1591)
1 : a word (as *therefore*) or phrase (as *as a consequence*) introducing an inference
2 : ILLATION 2
²illative *adjective* (1611)
: INFERENTIAL
— **il·la·tive·ly** *adverb*
il·laud·able \(ˌ)i(l)-ˈlȯ-də-bəl\ *adjective* [Latin *illaudabilis*, from *in-* + *laudabilis* laudable] (1589)
: deserving no praise
— **il·laud·ably** \-blē\ *adverb*
ill–be·ing \ˈil-ˈbē-iŋ\ *noun* (1840)
: a condition of being deficient in health, happiness, or prosperity
ill–bod·ing \-ˈbō-diŋ\ *adjective* (1591)
: boding evil **:** INAUSPICIOUS
ill–bred \-ˈbred\ *adjective* (1604)
: badly brought up or showing bad upbringing **:** IMPOLITE
¹il·le·gal \(ˌ)i(l)-ˈlē-gəl\ *adjective* [Middle French or Medieval Latin; Middle French *illegal*, from Medieval Latin *illegalis*, from Latin *in-* + *legalis* legal] (1538)
: not according to or authorized by law **:** UNLAWFUL, ILLICIT; *also* **:** not sanctioned by official rules (as of a game)
— **il·le·gal·i·ty** \ˌi-li-ˈga-lə-tē\ *noun*
— **il·le·gal·ly** \(ˌ)i(l)-ˈlē-gə-lē\ *adverb*
²illegal *noun* (1939)
: an illegal immigrant
il·le·gal·ize \(ˌ)i(l)-ˈlē-gə-ˌlīz\ *transitive verb* (circa 1818)
: to make or declare illegal
— **il·le·gal·i·za·tion** \-ˌlē-gə-lə-ˈzā-shən\ *noun*
il·leg·i·ble \(ˌ)i(l)-ˈle-jə-bəl\ *adjective* (1640)
: not legible **:** UNDECIPHERABLE ⟨*illegible* writing⟩
— **il·leg·i·bil·i·ty** \-ˌle-jə-ˈbi-lə-tē\ *noun*
— **il·leg·i·bly** \-jə-blē\ *adverb*
il·le·git·i·ma·cy \ˌi-li-ˈji-tə-mə-sē\ *noun* (1680)
1 : the quality or state of being illegitimate
2 : BASTARDY 2
il·le·git·i·mate \-ˈji-tə-mət\ *adjective* (1536)
1 : not recognized as lawful offspring; *specifically* **:** born of parents not married to each other
2 : not rightly deduced or inferred **:** ILLOGICAL

3 : departing from the regular **:** ERRATIC
4 a : not sanctioned by law **:** ILLEGAL **b :** not authorized by good usage **c** *of a taxon* **:** published but not in accordance with the rules of the relevant international code
— **il·le·git·i·mate·ly** *adverb*
ill–fat·ed \'il-'fā-təd\ *adjective* (1710)
1 : having or destined to a hapless fate **:** UN-FORTUNATE ⟨an *ill-fated* expedition⟩
2 : that causes or marks the beginning of misfortune
ill–fa·vored \-'fā-vərd\ *adjective* (circa 1530)
1 : unattractive in physical appearance; *especially* **:** having an ugly face
2 : OFFENSIVE, OBJECTIONABLE
ill–got·ten \-'gä-t°n\ *adjective* (1552)
: acquired by illicit or improper means ⟨*ill-gotten* gains⟩
ill–hu·mored \'il-'hyü-mərd, -'yü-\ *adjective* (1687)
: SURLY, IRRITABLE
— **ill–hu·mored·ly** *adverb*
il·lib·er·al \(,)i(l)-'li-b(ə-)rəl\ *adjective* [Middle French or Latin; Middle French, from Latin *illiberalis* ignoble, stingy, from Latin *in-* + *liberalis* liberal] (1535)
: not liberal: as **a** *archaic* **(1) :** lacking a liberal education **(2) :** lacking culture and refinement **b :** not requiring the background of a liberal arts education ⟨*illiberal* occupations⟩ **c** *archaic* **:** not generous **:** STINGY **d :** not broadminded **:** BIGOTED **e :** opposed to liberalism
— **il·lib·er·al·i·ty** \-,li-bə-'ra-lə-tē\ *noun*
— **il·lib·er·al·ly** \-'li-b(ə-)rə-lē\ *adverb*
— **il·lib·er·al·ness** \-b(ə-)rəl-nəs\ *noun*
il·lib·er·al·ism \-b(ə-)rə-,li-zəm\ *noun* (1839)
: opposition to or lack of liberalism
il·lic·it \(,)i(l)-'li-sət\ *adjective* [Latin *illicitus*, from *in-* + *licitus* lawful — more at LICIT] (1506)
: not permitted **:** UNLAWFUL
— **il·lic·it·ly** *adverb*
il·lim·it·able \(,)i(l)-'li-mə-tə-bəl\ *adjective* (1596)
: incapable of being limited or bounded **:** MEASURELESS ⟨the *illimitable* reaches of space and time⟩
— **il·lim·it·abil·i·ty** \-,li-mə-tə-'bi-lə-tē\ *noun*
— **il·lim·it·able·ness** \-'li-mə-tə-bəl-nəs\ *noun*
— **il·lim·it·ably** \-blē\ *adverb*
Il·li·nois \,i-lə-'nòi\ *also* -'nòiz\ *noun, plural* **Il·linois** [French, of Algonquian origin] (1703)
1 *plural* **:** a confederacy of American Indian peoples of Illinois, Iowa, and Wisconsin
2 : a member of any of the Illinois peoples
il·liq·uid \(,)i(l)-'lik-wəd\ *adjective* (1913)
1 : not being cash or readily convertible into cash ⟨*illiquid* holdings⟩
2 : deficient in liquid assets ⟨an *illiquid* bank⟩
— **il·li·quid·i·ty** \-,li-'kwi-də-tē\ *noun*
il·lite \'i-,līt\ *noun* [*Ill*inois, state of U.S. + [1]-*ite*] (1937)
: any of a group of clay minerals having essentially the crystal structure of muscovite
— **il·lit·ic** \i-'li-tik\ *adjective*
il·lit·er·a·cy \(,)i(l)-'li-t(ə)rə-sē\ *noun, plural* **-cies** (1660)
1 : the quality or state of being illiterate; *especially* **:** inability to read or write
2 : a mistake or crudity (as in speaking) typical of one who is illiterate
il·lit·er·ate \(,)i(l)-'li-t(ə-)rət\ *adjective* [Middle English, from Latin *illiteratus*, from *in-* + *litteratus* literate] (15th century)
1 : having little or no education; *especially* **:** unable to read or write
2 a : showing or marked by a lack of familiarity with language and literature **b :** violating approved patterns of speaking or writing
3 : showing or marked by a lack of acquaintance with the fundamentals of a particular field of knowledge
synonym see IGNORANT
— **illiterate** *noun*

— **il·lit·er·ate·ly** *adverb*
— **il·lit·er·ate·ness** *noun*
ill–man·nered \'il-'ma-nərd\ *adjective* (15th century)
: having bad manners **:** RUDE
ill–na·tured \-'nā-chərd\ *adjective* (1605)
1 : MALEVOLENT, SPITEFUL
2 : having a bad disposition **:** CROSS, SURLY
— **ill–na·tured·ly** *adverb*
ill·ness \'il-nəs\ *noun* (circa 1500)
1 *obsolete* **a :** WICKEDNESS **b :** UNPLEASANTNESS
2 a : an unhealthy condition of body or mind **b :** SICKNESS 2
il·lo·cu·tion·ary \,i-lə-'kyü-shə-,ner-ē, ,i(l)-lō-\ *adjective* [[2]*in-* + *locution*] (1955)
: relating to or being the communicative effect (as commanding or requesting) of an utterance ("There's a snake under you" may have the *illocutionary* force of a warning)
il·log·ic \(,)i(l)-'lä-jik\ *noun* [back-formation from *illogical*] (1856)
: the quality or state of being illogical **:** ILLOGICALITY
il·log·i·cal \-ji-kəl\ *adjective* (1588)
1 : not observing the principles of logic
2 : devoid of logic **:** SENSELESS
— **il·log·i·cal·i·ty** \-,lä-jə-'ka-lə-tē\ *noun*
— **il·log·i·cal·ly** \-'lä-ji-k(ə-)lē\ *adverb*
— **il·log·i·cal·ness** \-kəl-nəs\ *noun*
ill–sort·ed \'il-'sòr-təd\ *adjective* (1691)
1 : not well matched ⟨he and his wife were an *ill-sorted* pair —Lord Byron⟩
2 *Scottish* **:** much displeased
ill–starred \-'stärd\ *adjective* (1604)
: ILL-FATED, UNLUCKY ⟨an *ill-starred* venture⟩
ill–tem·pered \-'tem-pərd\ *adjective* (1601)
: ILL-NATURED, QUARRELSOME
— **ill–tem·pered·ly** \-lē\ *adverb*
ill–treat \-'trēt\ *transitive verb* (1689)
: to treat cruelly or improperly **:** MALTREAT
— **ill–treat·ment** \-mənt\ *noun*
il·lume \i-'lüm\ *transitive verb* **il·lumed; il·lum·ing** (1602)
: ILLUMINATE
il·lu·mi·nance \i-'lü-mə-nən(t)s\ *noun* (circa 1938)
: ILLUMINATION 2
il·lu·mi·nant \-nənt\ *noun* (1644)
: an illuminating device or substance
[1]**il·lu·mi·nate** \i-'lü-mə-nət\ *adjective* (15th century)
1 *archaic* **:** brightened with light
2 *archaic* **:** intellectually or spiritually enlightened
[2]**il·lu·mi·nate** \-,nāt\ *transitive verb* **-nat·ed; -nat·ing** [Middle English, from Latin *illuminatus*, past participle of *illuminare*, from *in-* + *luminare* to light up, from *lumin-*, *lumen* light — more at LUMINARY] (15th century)
1 a : to enlighten spiritually or intellectually **b (1) :** to supply or brighten with light **(2) :** to make luminous or shining **c** *archaic* **:** to set alight **d :** to subject to radiation
2 : to make clear **:** ELUCIDATE
3 : to make illustrious or resplendent
4 : to decorate (as a manuscript) with gold or silver or brilliant colors or with often elaborate designs or miniature pictures
— **il·lu·mi·nat·ing·ly** \-,nā-tiŋ-lē\ *adverb*
— **il·lu·mi·na·tor** \-,nā-tər\ *noun*
[3]**il·lu·mi·nate** \-nət\ *noun* (1600)
archaic **:** one having or claiming unusual enlightenment
il·lu·mi·na·ti \i-,lü-mə-'nä-tē\ *noun plural* [Italian & New Latin; Italian, from New Latin, from Latin, plural of *illuminatus*] (1599)
1 *capitalized* **:** any of various groups claiming special religious enlightenment
2 : persons who are or who claim to be unusually enlightened
il·lu·mi·na·tion \i-,lü-mə-'nā-shən\ *noun* (14th century)

1 : the action of illuminating or state of being illuminated: as **a :** spiritual or intellectual enlightenment **b (1) :** a lighting up **(2) :** decorative lighting or lighting effects **c :** decoration by the art of illuminating
2 : the luminous flux per unit area on an intercepting surface at any given point
3 : one of the decorative features used in the art of illuminating or in decorative lighting
il·lu·mi·na·tive \i-'lü-mə-,nā-tiv\ *adjective* (1644)
: of, relating to, or producing illumination **:** ILLUMINATING
il·lu·mine \i-'lü-mən\ *transitive verb* **-mined; -min·ing** (14th century)
: ILLUMINATE
— **il·lu·min·able** \-mə-nə-bəl\ *adjective*
il·lu·mi·nism \-mə-,ni-zəm\ *noun* (1798)
1 : belief in or claim to a personal enlightenment not accessible to mankind in general
2 *capitalized* **:** beliefs or claims viewed as forming doctrine or principles of Illuminati
— **il·lu·mi·nist** \-nist\ *noun*
ill–us·age \'il-'yü-sij, -zij\ *noun* (1593)
: harsh, unkind, or abusive treatment
ill–use \-'yüz\ *transitive verb* (1841)
: to use badly **:** MALTREAT, ABUSE
il·lu·sion \i-'lü-zhən\ *noun* [Middle English, from Middle French, from Late Latin *illusion-, illusio*, from Latin, action of mocking, from *illudere* to mock at, from *in-* + *ludere* to play, mock — more at LUDICROUS] (14th century)
1 a *obsolete* **:** the action of deceiving **b (1) :** the state or fact of being intellectually deceived or misled **:** MISAPPREHENSION **(2) :** an instance of such deception

illusion 2a(1): *a* and *b* are equal in length

2 a (1) : a misleading image presented to the vision **(2) :** something that deceives or misleads intellectually **b (1) :** perception of something objectively existing in such a way as to cause misinterpretation of its actual nature **(2) :** HALLUCINATION 1 **(3) :** a pattern capable of reversible perspective
3 : a fine plain transparent bobbinet or tulle usually made of silk and used for veils, trimmings, and dresses
— **il·lu·sion·al** \-'lüzh-nəl, -'lü-zhə-n°l\ *adjective*
il·lu·sion·ary \i-'lü-zhə-,ner-ē\ *adjective* (1886)
: ILLUSORY
il·lu·sion·ism \i-'lü-zhə-,ni-zəm\ *noun* (1911)
: the use of artistic techniques (as perspective or shading) to create the illusion of reality especially in a work of art
il·lu·sion·ist \i-'lüzh-nist, -'lü-zhə-\ *noun* (1850)
: one who produces illusory effects: as **a :** one (as an artist) whose work is marked by illusionism **b :** a sleight-of-hand performer or a magician
— **il·lu·sion·is·tic** \-,lü-zhə-'nis-tik\ *adjective*
— **il·lu·sion·is·ti·cal·ly** \-ti-k(ə-)lē\ *adverb*
il·lu·sive \i-'lü-siv, -ziv\ *adjective* (1606)
: ILLUSORY
— **il·lu·sive·ly** *adverb*
— **il·lu·sive·ness** *noun*
il·lu·so·ry \i-'lüs-rē, -'lüz-; -'lü-sə-, -zə-\ *adjective* (circa 1631)

\ə\ abut \°\ kitten \ər\ further \a\ ash \ā\ ace
\ä\ mop, mar \aů\ out \ch\ chin \e\ bet \ē\ easy
\g\ go \i\ hit \ī\ ice \j\ job \ŋ\ sing \ō\ go
\ò\ law \òi\ boy \th\ thin \t͟h\ the \ü\ loot \ů\ foot
\y\ yet \zh\ vision *see also* Guide to Pronunciation

: based on or producing illusion : DECEPTIVE ⟨*illusory* hopes⟩
synonym see APPARENT
— **il·lu·so·ri·ly** \-rə-lē\ *adverb*
— **il·lu·so·ri·ness** \-rē-nəs\ *noun*

il·lus·trate \'i-ləs-ˌtrāt *also* i-'ləs-\ *verb* **-trat·ed; -trat·ing** [Latin *illustratus*, past participle of *illustrare*, from *in-* + *lustrare* to purify, make bright — more at LUSTER] (1526)
transitive verb
1 *obsolete* **a :** ENLIGHTEN **b :** to light up
2 a *archaic* **:** to make illustrious **b** *obsolete* (1) **:** to make bright (2) **:** ADORN
3 a : to make clear **:** CLARIFY **b :** to make clear by giving or by serving as an example or instance **c :** to provide with visual features intended to explain or decorate ⟨*illustrate* a book⟩
4 : to show clearly **:** DEMONSTRATE
intransitive verb
: to give an example or instance
— **il·lus·tra·tor** \'i-ləs-ˌtrā-tər *also* i-'ləs-\ *noun*

il·lus·tra·tion \ˌi-ləs-'trā-shən *also* i-ˌləs-\ *noun* (14th century)
1 a : the action of illustrating **:** the condition of being illustrated **b** *archaic* **:** the action of making illustrious or honored or distinguished
2 : something that serves to illustrate: as **a :** an example or instance that helps make something clear **b :** a picture or diagram that helps make something clear or attractive
synonym see INSTANCE
— **il·lus·tra·tion·al** \-shnəl, -shə-nᵊl\ *adjective*

il·lus·tra·tive \i-'ləs-trə-tiv *also* 'i-lə-ˌstrā-\ *adjective* (1643)
: serving, tending, or designed to illustrate ⟨*illustrative* examples⟩
— **il·lus·tra·tive·ly** *adverb*

il·lus·tri·ous \i-'ləs-trē-əs\ *adjective* [Latin *illustris*, probably from *illustrare*] (1588)
1 : notably or brilliantly outstanding because of dignity or achievements or actions **:** EMINENT
2 *archaic* **a :** shining brightly with light **b :** clearly evident
synonym see FAMOUS
— **il·lus·tri·ous·ly** *adverb*
— **il·lus·tri·ous·ness** *noun*

il·lu·vi·al \i-'lü-vē-əl\ *adjective* (1924)
: of, relating to, or marked by illuviation or illuviated materials or areas

il·lu·vi·a·tion \i-ˌlü-vē-'ā-shən\ *noun* [²*in-* + -*luviation* (as in *eluviation*)] (1928)
: accumulation of dissolved or suspended soil materials in one area or horizon as a result of eluviation from another
— **il·lu·vi·at·ed** \i-'lü-vē-ˌā-təd\ *adjective*

ill will *noun* (14th century)
: unfriendly feeling
synonym see MALICE

ill-wish·er \'il-ˌwi-shər, -'wi-\ *noun* (1607)
: one that wishes ill to another

il·ly \'i(l)-lē\ *adverb* (15th century)
: not wisely or well **:** BADLY, ILL ⟨his *illy* concealed pride —Della Lutes⟩

Il·lyr·i·an \i-'lir-ē-ən\ *noun* (1584)
1 : a native or inhabitant of ancient Illyria
2 : the poorly attested Indo-European languages of the Illyrians — see INDO-EUROPEAN LANGUAGES table
— **Illyrian** *adjective*

il·men·ite \'il-mə-ˌnīt\ *noun* [German *Ilmenit*, from *Ilmen* range, Ural Mts., Russia] (circa 1827)
: a usually massive iron-black mineral composed of iron, titanium, and oxygen that is a titanium ore

Ilo·ca·no *or* **Ilo·ka·no** \ˌē-lə-'kä-(ˌ)nō, ˌi-\ *noun, plural* **Ilocano** *or* **Ilocanos** *or* **Ilokano** *or* **Ilokanos** (1898)
1 : a member of a major people of northern Luzon in the Philippines
2 : the Austronesian language of the Ilocano people

im- — see IN-
I'm \'īm\ (circa 1594)
: I am

¹im·age \'i-mij\ *noun* [Middle English, from Old French, short for *imagene*, from Latin *imagin-, imago;* perhaps akin to Latin *imitari* to imitate] (13th century)
1 : a reproduction or imitation of the form of a person or thing; *especially* **:** an imitation in solid form **:** STATUE
2 a : the optical counterpart of an object produced by an optical device (as a lens or mirror) or an electronic device **b :** a likeness of an object produced on a photographic material
3 a : exact likeness **:** SEMBLANCE ⟨God created man in his own *image* —Genesis 1:27 (Revised Standard Version)⟩ **b :** a person strikingly like another person ⟨she is the *image* of her mother⟩
4 a : a tangible or visible representation **:** INCARNATION ⟨the *image* of filial devotion⟩ **b** *archaic* **:** an illusory form **:** APPARITION
5 a (1) **:** a mental picture of something not actually present **:** IMPRESSION (2) **:** a mental conception held in common by members of a group and symbolic of a basic attitude and orientation ⟨a disorderly courtroom can seriously tarnish a community's *image* of justice —Herbert Brownell⟩ **b :** IDEA, CONCEPT
6 : a vivid or graphic representation or description
7 : FIGURE OF SPEECH
8 : a popular conception (as of a person, institution, or nation) projected especially through the mass media ⟨promoting a corporate *image* of brotherly love and concern —R. C. Buck⟩
9 : a set of values given by a mathematical function (as a homomorphism) that corresponds to a particular subset of the domain

²image *transitive verb* **im·aged; im·ag·ing** (14th century)
1 : to call up a mental picture of **:** IMAGINE
2 : to describe or portray in language especially in a vivid manner
3 a : to create a representation of; *also* **:** to form an image of **b :** to represent symbolically
4 a : REFLECT, MIRROR **b :** to make appear **:** PROJECT
— **im·ag·er** \'i-mi-jər\ *noun*

image orthicon *noun* (1945)
: a highly sensitive television image tube

im·ag·ery \'i-mij-rē, -mi-jə-\ *noun, plural* **-er·ies** (14th century)
1 a : the product of image makers **:** IMAGES; *also* **:** the art of making images **b :** pictures produced by an imaging system
2 : figurative language
3 : mental images; *especially* **:** the products of imagination

image tube *noun* (1936)
: an electron tube in which incident electromagnetic radiation (as light or infrared) produces a visible image on its fluorescent screen duplicating the original pattern of radiation — called also *image converter*

imag·in·able \i-'maj-nə-bəl, -'ma-jə-\ *adjective* (14th century)
: capable of being imagined **:** CONCEIVABLE
— **imag·in·able·ness** *noun*
— **imag·in·ably** \-blē\ *adverb*

¹imag·i·nal \i-'ma-jə-nᵊl\ *adjective* [*imagine* + ¹-*al*] (1647)
: of or relating to imagination, images, or imagery

²imag·i·nal \i-'ma-jə-nᵊl, -'mā-; -'mä-gə-\ *adjective* [New Latin *imagin-, imago*] (1877)
: of or relating to the insect imago

imag·i·nary \i-'ma-jə-ˌner-ē\ *adjective* (14th century)
1 a : existing only in imagination **:** lacking factual reality **b :** formed or characterized imaginatively or arbitrarily ⟨his canvases, chiefly *imaginary*, somber landscapes —*Current Biography*⟩
2 : containing or relating to the imaginary unit ⟨*imaginary* roots⟩ ☆

— **imag·i·nari·ly** \i-ˌma-jə-'ner-ə-lē\ *adverb*
— **imag·i·nari·ness** \i-'ma-jə-ˌner-ē-nəs\ *noun*

imaginary number *noun* (circa 1911)
: a complex number (as $2 + 3i$) in which the coefficient of the imaginary unit is not zero — called also *imaginary;* compare PURE IMAGINARY

imaginary part *noun* (circa 1929)
: the part of a complex number (as $3i$ in $2 + 3i$) that has the imaginary unit as a factor

imaginary unit *noun* (circa 1911)
: the positive square root of minus 1 denoted by i or $+\sqrt{-1}$

imag·i·na·tion \i-ˌma-jə-'nā-shən\ *noun* [Middle English, from Middle French, from Latin *imagination-, imaginatio*, from *imaginari*] (14th century)
1 : the act or power of forming a mental image of something not present to the senses or never before wholly perceived in reality
2 a : creative ability **b :** ability to confront and deal with a problem **:** RESOURCEFULNESS **c :** the thinking or active mind **:** INTEREST ⟨stories that fired the *imagination*⟩
3 a : a creation of the mind; *especially* **:** an idealized or poetic creation **b :** fanciful or empty assumption

imag·i·na·tive \i-'maj-nə-tiv; -'ma-jə-ˌnā-, -nə-\ *adjective* (14th century)
1 a : of, relating to, or characterized by imagination **b :** devoid of truth **:** FALSE
2 : given to imagining **:** having a lively imagination
3 : of or relating to images; *especially* **:** showing a command of imagery
— **imag·i·na·tive·ly** *adverb*
— **imag·i·na·tive·ness** *noun*

imag·ine \i-'ma-jən\ *verb* **imag·ined; imag·in·ing** \-'maj-niŋ, -'ma-jə-\ [Middle English, from Middle French *imaginer*, from Latin *imaginari*, from *imagin-, imago* image] (14th century)
transitive verb
1 : to form a mental image of (something not present)
2 *archaic* **:** PLAN, SCHEME
3 : SUPPOSE, GUESS ⟨I *imagine* it will rain⟩
4 : to form a notion of without sufficient basis **:** FANCY ⟨*imagines* himself to be a charming conversationalist⟩
intransitive verb
1 : to use the imagination
2 : BELIEVE 3
synonym see THINK

im·ag·ing \'i-mi-jiŋ\ *noun* (1967)
: the action or process of producing an image especially by means other than visible light ⟨acoustic *imaging*⟩ — compare MAGNETIC RESONANCE IMAGING

im·ag·ism \'i-mi-ˌji-zəm\ *noun, often capitalized* (1912)

: a 20th century movement in poetry advocating free verse and the expression of ideas and emotions through clear precise images
— **im·ag·ist** \-mi-jist\ *noun or adjective, often capitalized*
— **im·ag·is·tic** \,i-mi-'jis-tik\ *adjective*
— **im·ag·is·ti·cal·ly** \-ti-k(ə-)lē\ *adverb*

ima·go \i-'mä-(,)gō, -'mā-\ *noun, plural* **ima·goes** *or* **ima·gi·nes** \-'mā-gə-,nēz, -'mä-, -'mā-jə-, -'ma-\ [New Latin, from Latin, image] (circa 1797)
1 : an insect in its final, adult, sexually mature, and typically winged state
2 : an idealized mental image of another person or the self
word history see LARVA

imam \i-'mäm, ē-', -'mam\ *noun, often capitalized* [Arabic *imām*] (1613)
1 : the prayer leader of a mosque
2 : a Muslim leader of the line of Ali held by Shiites to be the divinely appointed, sinless, infallible successors of Muhammad
3 : any of various rulers that claim descent from Muhammad and exercise spiritual and temporal leadership over a Muslim region

imam·ate \i-'mä-,māt, -'ma-\ *noun, often capitalized* (circa 1741)
1 : the office of an imam
2 : the region or country ruled by an imam

ima·ret \i-'mär-ət\ *noun* [Turkish] (1613)
: an inn or hospice in Turkey

Ima·ri \i-'mär-ē\ *noun* [*Imari*, Japan] (1875)
: a multicolored Japanese porcelain usually characterized by elaborate floral designs
— **Imari** *adjective*

im·bal·ance \(,)im-'ba-lən(t)s\ *noun* (circa 1890)
: lack of balance : the state of being out of equilibrium or out of proportion ⟨a vitamin *imbalance*⟩ ⟨racial *imbalance* in schools⟩
— **im·bal·anced** \-lən(t)st\ *adjective*

im·be·cile \'im-bə-səl, -,sil\ *noun* [French *imbécile*, noun, from adjective, weak, weakminded, from Latin *imbecillus*] (1802)
1 : a mentally deficient person; *especially* : a feebleminded person having a mental age of three to seven years and requiring supervision in the performance of routine daily tasks of self-care
2 : FOOL, IDIOT
— **imbecile** *or* **im·be·cil·ic** \,im-bə-'si-lik\ *adjective*

im·be·cil·i·ty \,im-bə-'si-lə-tē\ *noun, plural* **-ties** (1533)
1 : the quality or state of being imbecile or an imbecile
2 a : utter foolishness; *also* : FUTILITY **b** : something that is foolish or nonsensical

im·bed *variant of* EMBED

im·bibe \im-'bīb\ *verb* **im·bibed; im·bib·ing** [in sense 1, from Middle English *enbiben*, from Middle French *embiber*, from Latin *imbibere* to drink in, conceive, from *in-* + *bibere* to drink; in other senses, from Latin *imbibere* — more at POTABLE] (14th century)
transitive verb
1 *archaic* : SOAK, STEEP
2 a : to receive into the mind and retain ⟨*imbibe* moral principles⟩ **b** : to assimilate or take into solution
3 a : DRINK **b** : to take in or up ⟨a sponge *imbibes* moisture⟩
intransitive verb
1 : DRINK 2
2 a : to take in liquid **b** : to absorb or assimilate moisture, gas, light, or heat
— **im·bib·er** *noun*

im·bi·bi·tion \,im-bə-'bi-shən\ *noun* (15th century)
: the act or action of imbibing; *especially* : the taking up of fluid by a colloidal system resulting in swelling
— **im·bi·bi·tion·al** \-'bish-nəl, -'bi-shə-nᵊl\ *adjective*

im·bit·ter *variant of* EMBITTER
im·bo·som *variant of* EMBOSOM

¹im·bri·cate \'im-bri-kət\ *adjective* [Late Latin *imbricatus*, past participle of *imbricare* to cover with pantiles, from Latin *imbric-, imbrex* pantile, from *imbr-, imber* rain; akin to Greek *ombros* rain] (circa 1610)
: lying lapped over each other in regular order ⟨*imbricate* scales⟩

²im·bri·cate \'im-brə-,kāt\ *transitive verb* **-cat·ed; -cat·ing** (1784)
: OVERLAP; *especially* : to overlap like roof tiles

im·bri·ca·tion \,im-brə-'kā-shən\ *noun* (1713)
1 : an overlapping of edges (as of tiles or scales)
2 : a decoration or pattern showing imbrication

im·bro·glio \im-'brōl-(,)yō\ *noun, plural* **-glios** [Italian, from *imbrogliare* to entangle, from Middle French *embrouiller* — more at EMBROIL] (1750)
1 : a confused mass
2 a : an intricate or complicated situation (as in a drama or novel) **b** : an acutely painful or embarrassing misunderstanding **c** : a violently confused or bitterly complicated altercation : EMBROILMENT

imbrication

im·brown *variant of* EMBROWN

im·brue \im-'brü\ *transitive verb* **im·brued; im·bru·ing** [Middle English *enbrewen*, probably from Middle French *abrevrer, embevrer* to soak, drench, ultimately from Latin *bibere* to drink — more at POTABLE] (15th century)
: STAIN

im·brute \im-'brüt\ *verb* **im·brut·ed; im·brut·ing** (1634)
intransitive verb
: to sink to the level of a brute
transitive verb
: to degrade to the level of a brute

im·bue \im-'byü\ *transitive verb* **im·bued; im·bu·ing** [Latin *imbuere*] (1555)
1 : to permeate or influence as if by dyeing ⟨the spirit that *imbues* the new constitution⟩
2 : to tinge or dye deeply
synonym see INFUSE

im·id·az·ole \,i-mə-'da-,zōl\ *noun* [International Scientific Vocabulary] (1892)
: a white crystalline heterocyclic base $C_3H_4N_2$ that is an antimetabolite related to histidine; *broadly* : any of various derivatives of this

im·ide \'i-,mīd\ *noun* [International Scientific Vocabulary, alteration of *amide*] (1857)
: a compound containing the NH group that is derived from ammonia by replacement of two hydrogen atoms by a metal or an equivalent of acid groups — compare AMIDE
— **im·id·ic** \i-'mi-dik\ *adjective*

im·i·do \'i-mə-,dō\ *adjective* (1881)
: relating to or containing the NH group or its substituted form NR united to one or two acid groups

im·ine \'i-,mēn\ *noun* [International Scientific Vocabulary, alteration of *amine*] (1883)
: a compound containing the NH group or its substituted form NR that is derived from ammonia by replacement of two hydrogen atoms by a hydrocarbon group or other nonacid organic group

im·i·no \'i-mə-,nō\ *adjective* (1903)
: relating to or containing the NH group or its substituted form NR united to a group other than an acid group

imip·ra·mine \i-'mi-prə-,mēn\ *noun* [*imide* + *propyl* + *amine*] (1958)
: a tricyclic antidepressant drug $C_{19}H_{24}N_2$

im·i·ta·ble \'i-mə-tə-bəl\ *adjective* (1550)
: capable or worthy of being imitated or copied

im·i·tate \'i-mə-,tāt\ *transitive verb* **-tat·ed; -tat·ing** [Latin *imitatus*, past participle of *imitari* — more at IMAGE] (1534)
1 : to follow as a pattern, model, or example
2 : to be or appear like : RESEMBLE
3 : to produce a copy of : REPRODUCE

4 : MIMIC, COUNTERFEIT ⟨can *imitate* his father's booming voice⟩
synonym see COPY
— **im·i·ta·tor** \-,tā-tər\ *noun*

¹im·i·ta·tion \,i-mə-'tā-shən\ *noun* (14th century)
1 : an act or instance of imitating
2 : something produced as a copy : COUNTERFEIT
3 : a literary work designed to reproduce the style of another author
4 : the repetition by one voice of a melody, phrase, or motive stated earlier in the composition by a different voice
5 : the quality of an object in possessing some of the nature or attributes of a transcendent idea
6 : the assumption of behavior observed in other individuals

²imitation *adjective* (1840)
: resembling something else that is usually genuine and of better quality : not real ⟨*imitation* leather⟩

im·i·ta·tive \'i-mə-,tā-tiv, *especially British* -tə-tiv\ *adjective* (1584)
1 a : marked by imitation ⟨acting is an *imitative* art⟩ **b** : reproducing or representing a natural sound : ONOMATOPOEIC ("hiss" is an *imitative* word) **c** : exhibiting mimicry
2 : inclined to imitate
3 : imitating something superior : COUNTERFEIT
— **im·i·ta·tive·ly** *adverb*
— **im·i·ta·tive·ness** *noun*

im·mac·u·la·cy \i-'ma-kyə-lə-sē\ *noun* (1799)
: the quality or state of being immaculate

im·mac·u·late \i-'ma-kyə-lət\ *adjective* [Middle English *immaculat*, from Latin *immaculatus*, from *in-* + *maculatus* stained — more at MACULATE] (15th century)
1 : having no stain or blemish : PURE
2 : containing no flaw or error
3 a : spotlessly clean **b** : having no colored spots or marks ⟨petals *immaculate*⟩
— **im·mac·u·late·ly** *adverb*

Immaculate Conception *noun* (1687)
1 : the conception of the Virgin Mary in which as decreed in Roman Catholic dogma her soul was preserved free from original sin by divine grace
2 : December 8 observed as a Roman Catholic feast in commemoration of the Immaculate Conception

im·mane \i-'mān\ *adjective* [Latin *immanis*, from *in-* + *manus* good — more at MATURE] (1602)
archaic : HUGE; *also* : monstrous in character

im·ma·nence \'i-mə-nən(t)s\ *noun* (1816)
: the quality or state of being immanent : INHERENCE

im·ma·nen·cy \-nən(t)-sē\ *noun* (1659)
: IMMANENCE

im·ma·nent \-nənt\ *adjective* [Late Latin *immanent-, immanens*, present participle of *immanēre* to remain in place, from Latin *in-* + *manēre* to remain — more at MANSION] (1535)
: remaining or operating within a domain of reality or realm of discourse : INHERENT; *specifically* : having existence or effect only within the mind or consciousness — compare TRANSCENDENT
— **im·ma·nent·ly** *adverb*

im·ma·nent·ism \-nən-,ti-zəm\ *noun* (1907)
: any of several theories according to which God or an abstract mind or spirit pervades the world
— **im·ma·nent·ist** \-nən-tist, -,nen-\ *noun or adjective*

im·ma·nent·is·tic \ˌi-mə-nən-'tis-tik\ *adjective*

Im·man·u·el \i-'man-yə-wəl, -yəl\ *noun* [Middle English *Emanuel*, from Late Latin *Emmanuel*, from Greek *Emmanouēl*, from Hebrew *'immānū'ēl*, literally, with us is God] (15th century)
: MESSIAH 1

im·ma·te·ri·al \ˌi-mə-'tir-ē-əl\ *adjective* [Middle English *immateriel*, from Middle French, from Late Latin *immaterialis*, from Latin *in-* + Late Latin *materialis* material] (14th century)
1 : not consisting of matter : INCORPOREAL
2 : of no substantial consequence : UNIMPORTANT

im·ma·te·ri·al·ism \-ē-ə-ˌli-zəm\ *noun* (1713)
: a philosophical theory that material things have no reality except as mental perceptions
— **im·ma·te·ri·al·ist** \-list\ *noun*
im·ma·te·ri·al·i·ty \ˌi-mə-ˌtir-ē-'a-lə-tē\ *noun, plural* **-ties** (1570)
1 : the quality or state of being immaterial
2 : something immaterial
im·ma·te·ri·al·ize \-'tir-ē-ə-ˌlīz\ *transitive verb* (1661)
: to make immaterial or incorporeal

im·ma·ture \ˌi-mə-'tùr, -'tyùr, -'chùr\ *adjective* [Latin *immaturus*, from *in-* + *maturus* mature] (1548)
1 *archaic* : PREMATURE
2 a : lacking complete growth, differentiation, or development ⟨a thin *immature* soil⟩ **b** : having the potential capacity to attain a definitive form or state : CRUDE, UNFINISHED ⟨a vigorous but *immature* school of art⟩ **c** : exhibiting less than an expected degree of maturity ⟨emotionally *immature* adults⟩
— **immature** *noun*
— **im·ma·ture·ly** *adverb*
— **im·ma·tu·ri·ty** \-'tùr-ə-tē, -'tyùr-, -'chùr-\ *noun*

im·mea·sur·able \(ˌ)i(m)-'mezh-rə-bəl, -'māzh-; -'me-zhə-rə-, -'mā-, -zhər-bəl\ *adjective* (14th century)
: incapable of being measured; *broadly* : indefinitely extensive
— **im·mea·sur·able·ness** *noun*
— **im·mea·sur·ably** \-blē\ *adverb*

im·me·di·a·cy \i-'mē-dē-ə-sē, *British often* -'mē-jə-sē\ *noun, plural* **-cies** (1605)
1 : the quality or state of being immediate
2 : something that is immediate — usually used in plural

im·me·di·ate \i-'mē-dē-ət, *British often* -'mē-jit\ *adjective* [Middle English, from Late Latin *immediatus*, from Latin *in-* + Late Latin *mediatus* intermediate — more at MEDIATE] (15th century)
1 a : acting or being without the intervention of another object, cause, or agency : DIRECT ⟨the *immediate* cause of death⟩ **b** : present to the mind independently of other states or factors ⟨*immediate* awareness⟩ **c** : involving or derived from a single premise ⟨an *immediate* inference⟩
2 : being next in line or relation ⟨the *immediate* family⟩
3 a : existing without intervening space or substance ⟨brought into *immediate* contact⟩ **b** : being near at hand ⟨the *immediate* neighborhood⟩
4 a : occurring, acting, or accomplished without loss or interval of time : INSTANT ⟨an *immediate* need⟩ **b** (1) : near to or related to the present ⟨the *immediate* past⟩ (2) : of or relating to the here and now : CURRENT ⟨too busy with *immediate* concerns to worry about the future⟩
5 : directly touching or concerning a person or thing ⟨the child's *immediate* world is the classroom⟩

immediate constituent *noun* (1933)
: any of the meaningful constituents directly forming a larger linguistic construction (as a phrase or sentence)

¹im·me·di·ate·ly \i-'mē-dē-ət-lē *also* -'mēdit-, *British often* -'mē-jət-\ *adverb* (15th century)
1 : in direct connection or relation : DIRECTLY ⟨the parties *immediately* involved in the case⟩ ⟨the house *immediately* beyond this one⟩
2 : without interval of time : STRAIGHTWAY
²immediately *conjunction* (1839)
chiefly British : AS SOON AS

im·me·di·ate·ness *noun* (1633)
: IMMEDIACY 1

im·med·i·ca·ble \(ˌ)i(m)-'me-di-kə-bəl\ *adjective* [Latin *immedicabilis*, from *in-* + *medicabilis* medicable] (1533)
: INCURABLE ⟨wounds *immedicable* —John Milton⟩
— **im·med·i·ca·bly** \-blē\ *adverb*

Im·mel·mann \'i-məl-mən\ *noun* [Max *Immelmann*] (1917)
: a maneuver in which an airplane reverses direction by executing half of a loop upwards followed by half of a roll — called also *Immelmann turn*

im·me·mo·ri·al \ˌi-mə-'mòr-ē-əl, -'mòr-\ *adjective* [probably from French *immémorial*, from Middle French, from Medieval Latin *immemorialis* lacking memory, from Latin *in-* + *memorialis* memorial] (1602)
: extending or existing since beyond the reach of memory, record, or tradition ⟨existing from time *immemorial*⟩
— **im·me·mo·ri·al·ly** \-ē-ə-lē\ *adverb*

im·mense \i-'men(t)s\ *adjective* [Middle English, from Middle French, from Latin *immensus* immeasurable, from *in-* + *mensus*, past participle of *metiri* to measure — more at MEASURE] (15th century)
1 : marked by greatness especially in size or degree; *especially* : transcending ordinary means of measurement ⟨the *immense* and boundless universe⟩
2 : supremely good : EXCELLENT
synonym see ENORMOUS
— **im·mense·ly** *adverb*
— **im·mense·ness** *noun*

im·men·si·ty \i-'men(t)-sə-tē\ *noun, plural* **-ties** (15th century)
1 : the quality or state of being immense
2 : something immense

im·men·su·ra·ble \(ˌ)i(m)-'men(t)s-rə-bəl, -'men(t)sh-; -'men(t)-sə-, -shə-\ *adjective* [Middle English, from Late Latin *immensurabilis*, from Latin *in-* + Late Latin *mensurabilis* measurable — more at MENSURABLE] (15th century)
: IMMEASURABLE

im·merge \i-'mərj\ *intransitive verb* **im·merged; im·merg·ing** [Latin *immergere*] (1706)
: to plunge into or immerse oneself in something

im·merse \i-'mərs\ *transitive verb* **im·mersed; im·mers·ing** [Middle English, from Latin *immersus*, past participle of *immergere*, from *in-* + *mergere* to merge] (15th century)
1 : to plunge into something that surrounds or covers; *especially* : to plunge or dip into a fluid
2 : ENGROSS, ABSORB ⟨completely *immersed* in his work⟩
3 : to baptize by immersion

im·mers·ible \i-'mər-sə-bəl\ *adjective* (circa 1846)
: capable of being totally submerged in water without damage to the heating element ⟨an *immersible* electric frying pan⟩

im·mer·sion \i-'mər-zhən, -shən\ *noun* (15th century)
: an act of immersing : a state of being immersed; *specifically* : baptism by complete submersion of the person in water

immersion heater *noun* (1914)
: a usually electric unit that heats the liquid in which it is immersed

im·mesh \i-'mesh\ *variant of* ENMESH

im·me·thod·i·cal \ˌi-mə-'thä-di-kəl\ *adjective* (1605)
: not methodical
— **im·me·thod·i·cal·ly** \-k(ə-)lē\ *adverb*

im·mi·grant \'i-mi-grənt\ *noun* (1789)
: one that immigrates: as **a** : a person who comes to a country to take up permanent residence **b** : a plant or animal that becomes established in an area where it was previously unknown
— **immigrant** *adjective*

im·mi·grate \'i-mə-ˌgrāt\ *verb* **-grat·ed; -grat·ing** [Latin *immigratus*, past participle of *immigrare* to remove, go in, from *in-* + *migrare* to migrate] (circa 1623)
intransitive verb
: to enter and usually become established; *especially* : to come into a country of which one is not a native for permanent residence
transitive verb
: to bring in or send as immigrants
— **im·mi·gra·tion** \ˌi-mə-'grā-shən\ *noun*
— **im·mi·gra·tion·al** \-shnəl, -shə-nᵊl\ *adjective*

im·mi·nence \'i-mə-nən(t)s\ *noun* (1606)
1 : something imminent; *especially* : impending evil or danger
2 : the quality or state of being imminent

im·mi·nen·cy \-nən-sē\ *noun* (1665)
: IMMINENCE 2

im·mi·nent \'i-mə-nənt\ *adjective* [Latin *imminent-, imminens*, present participle of *imminēre* to project, threaten, from *in-* + *-minēre* (akin to Latin *mont-, mons* mountain) — more at MOUNT] (1528)
: ready to take place; *especially* : hanging threateningly over one's head ⟨was in *imminent* danger of being run over⟩
— **im·mi·nent·ly** *adverb*

im·min·gle \i-'miŋ-gəl\ *verb* (1606)
: BLEND, INTERMINGLE

im·mis·ci·ble \(ˌ)i(m)-'mi-sə-bəl\ *adjective* (1671)
: incapable of mixing or attaining homogeneity
— **im·mis·ci·bil·i·ty** \-ˌmi-sə-'bi-lə-tē\ *noun*

im·mit·i·ga·ble \(ˌ)i(m)-'mi-ti-gə-bəl\ *adjective* [Late Latin *immitigabilis*, from Latin *in-* + *mitigare* to mitigate] (1576)
: not capable of being mitigated
— **im·mit·i·ga·bly** \-blē\ *adverb*

im·mit·tance \(ˌ)i(m)-'mi-tᵊn(t)s\ *noun* [*im*pedance + ad*mittance*] (circa 1948)
: electrical admittance or impedance

im·mix \i-'miks\ *transitive verb* [back-formation from *immixed* mixed in, from Middle English *immixte*, from Latin *immixtus*, past participle of *immiscēre*, from *in-* + *miscēre* to mix — more at MIX] (15th century)
: to mix intimately : COMMINGLE
— **im·mix·ture** \-'miks-chər\ *noun*

im·mo·bile \(ˌ)i(m)-'mō-bəl, -ˌbīl *also* -ˌbēl\ *adjective* [Middle English *in-mobill*, from Latin *immobilis*, from *in-* + *mobilis* mobile] (14th century)
1 : incapable of being moved : FIXED
2 : not moving : MOTIONLESS ⟨keep the patient *immobile*⟩
— **im·mo·bil·i·ty** \ˌi-(ˌ)mō-'bi-lə-tē\ *noun*

im·mo·bi·lism \i-'mō-bə-ˌli-zəm\ *noun* (1949)
: a policy of extreme conservatism and opposition to change

im·mo·bi·lize \i-'mō-bə-ˌlīz\ *transitive verb* (1871)
: to make immobile: as **a** : to prevent freedom of movement or effective use of ⟨the planes were *immobilized* by bad weather⟩ **b** : to reduce or eliminate motion of (the body or a part) by mechanical means or by strict bed rest **c** : to withhold (money or capital) from circulation
— **im·mo·bi·li·za·tion** \-ˌmō-bə-lə-'zā-shən\ *noun*
— **im·mo·bi·liz·er** \-'mō-bə-ˌlī-zər\ *noun*

im·mod·er·a·cy \(ˌ)i(m)-ˈmä-d(ə-)rə-sē\ *noun* (1682)
: lack of moderation

im·mod·er·ate \-d(ə-)rət\ *adjective* [Middle English *immoderat*, from Latin *immoderatus*, from *in-* + *moderatus*, past participle of *moderare* to moderate] (14th century)
: exceeding just, usual, or suitable bounds ⟨*immoderate* pride⟩ ⟨an *immoderate* appetite⟩
synonym see EXCESSIVE
— **im·mod·er·ate·ly** *adverb*
— **im·mod·er·ate·ness** *noun*
— **im·mod·er·a·tion** \(ˌ)i-ˌmä-də-ˈrā-shən\ *noun*

im·mod·est \(ˌ)i(m)-ˈmä-dəst\ *adjective* [Latin *immodestus*, from *in-* + *modestus* modest] (circa 1570)
: not modest; *specifically* : not conforming to the sexual mores of a particular time or place
— **im·mod·est·ly** *adverb*
— **im·mod·es·ty** \-də-stē\ *noun*

im·mo·late \ˈi-mə-ˌlāt\ *transitive verb* **-lat·ed; -lat·ing** [Latin *immolatus*, past participle of *immolare*, from *in-* + *mola* spelt grits; from the custom of sprinkling victims with sacrificial meal; akin to Latin *molere* to grind — more at MEAL] (1548)
1 : to offer in sacrifice; *especially* : to kill as a sacrificial victim
2 : to kill or destroy often by fire
— **im·mo·la·tor** \-ˌlā-tər\ *noun*

im·mo·la·tion \ˌi-mə-ˈlā-shən\ *noun* (15th century)
1 : the act of immolating : the state of being immolated
2 : something that is immolated

im·mor·al \(ˌ)i(m)-ˈmȯr-əl, -ˈmär-\ *adjective* (1660)
: not moral; *broadly* : conflicting with generally or traditionally held moral principles
— **im·mor·al·ly** \-ə-lē\ *adverb*

im·mor·al·ist \-ə-list\ *noun* (1697)
: an advocate of immorality
— **im·mor·al·ism** \-ˌli-zəm\ *noun*

im·mo·ral·i·ty \ˌi-(ˌ)mȯ-ˈra-lə-tē, ˌi-mə-\ *noun* (circa 1566)
1 : the quality or state of being immoral; *especially* : UNCHASTITY
2 : an immoral act or practice

¹**im·mor·tal** \(ˌ)i(m)-ˈmȯr-tᵊl\ *adjective* [Middle English, from Latin *immortalis*, from *in-* + *mortalis* mortal] (14th century)
1 : exempt from death ⟨the *immortal* gods⟩
2 : exempt from oblivion : IMPERISHABLE ⟨*immortal* fame⟩
3 : connected with or relating to immortality
— **im·mor·tal·ly** \-tᵊl-ē\ *adverb*

²**immortal** *noun* (1684)
1 a : one exempt from death **b** *plural, often capitalized* : the gods of the Greek and Roman pantheon
2 a : a person whose fame is lasting **b** *capitalized* : any of the 40 members of the Académie Française

im·mor·tal·ise *British variant of* IMMORTALIZE

im·mor·tal·i·ty \ˌi-ˌmȯr-ˈta-lə-tē\ *noun* (14th century)
: the quality or state of being immortal: **a** : unending existence **b** : lasting fame

im·mor·tal·ize \i-ˈmȯr-tᵊl-ˌīz\ *transitive verb* **-ized; -iz·ing** (circa 1566)
: to make immortal
— **im·mor·tal·i·za·tion** \-ˌmȯr-tᵊl-ə-ˈzā-shən\ *noun*
— **im·mor·tal·iz·er** \-ˈmȯr-tᵊl-ˌī-zər\ *noun*

im·mor·telle \ˌi-ˌmȯr-ˈtel\ *noun* [French, from feminine of *immortel* immortal, from Latin *immortalis*] (1832)
: EVERLASTING 3

im·mo·tile \(ˌ)i(m)-ˈmō-tᵊl, -ˌtīl\ *adjective* (1872)
: lacking motility

¹**im·mov·able** \(ˌ)i(m)-ˈmü-və-bəl\ *adjective* (14th century)
1 : incapable of being moved; *broadly* : not moving or not intended to be moved
2 a : STEADFAST, UNYIELDING **b** : not capable of being moved emotionally
— **im·mov·abil·i·ty** \-ˌmü-və-ˈbi-lə-tē\ *noun*
— **im·mov·able·ness** \-ˈmü-və-bəl-nəs\ *noun*
— **im·mov·ably** \-blē\ *adverb*

²**immovable** *noun* (1588)
1 : one that cannot be moved
2 *plural* : real property as opposed to movable property

im·mune \i-ˈmyün\ *adjective* [Middle English, from Latin *immunis*, from *in-* + *munia* services, obligations; akin to Latin *munus* service — more at MEAN] (15th century)
1 a : FREE, EXEMPT ⟨*immune* from further taxation⟩ **b** : marked by protection ⟨some criminal leaders are *immune* from arrest⟩
2 : not susceptible or responsive ⟨*immune* to all pleas⟩; *especially* : having a high degree of resistance to a disease ⟨*immune* to diphtheria⟩
3 a : having or producing antibodies or lymphocytes capable of reacting with a specific antigen ⟨an *immune* serum⟩ **b** : produced by, involved in, or concerned with immunity or an immune response ⟨*immune* agglutinins⟩ ⟨*immune* globulins⟩
— **immune** *noun*

immune response *noun* (1953)
: a bodily response to an antigen that occurs when lymphocytes identify the antigenic molecule as foreign and induce the formation of antibodies and lymphocytes capable of reacting with it and rendering it harmless — called also *immune reaction*

immune system *noun* (circa 1919)
: the bodily system that protects the body from foreign substances, cells, and tissues by producing the immune response and that includes especially the thymus, spleen, lymph nodes, special deposits of lymphoid tissue (as in the gastrointestinal tract and bone marrow), lymphocytes including the B cells and T cells, and antibodies

im·mu·ni·ty \i-ˈmyü-nə-tē\ *noun, plural* **-ties** (14th century)
: the quality or state of being immune; *especially* : a condition of being able to resist a particular disease especially through preventing development of a pathogenic microorganism or by counteracting the effects of its products

im·mu·nize \ˈi-myə-ˌnīz\ *transitive verb* **-nized; -niz·ing** (1892)
: to make immune
— **im·mu·ni·za·tion** \ˌi-myə-nə-ˈzā-shən *also* i-ˌmyü-nə-\ *noun*

immuno- *combining form* [International Scientific Vocabulary, from *immune*]
1 : physiological immunity ⟨*immuno*logy⟩
2 : immunologic ⟨*immuno*chemistry⟩ : immunologically ⟨*immuno*competent⟩ : immunology and ⟨*immuno*genetics⟩

im·mu·no·as·say \ˌi-myə-nō-ˈa-ˌsā, i-ˌmyü-nō-, -a-ˈsā\ *noun* (1959)
: the identification of a substance (as a protein) based on its capacity to act as an antigen
— **im·mu·no·as·say·able** \-a-ˈsā-ə-bəl\ *adjective*

im·mu·no·blot \ˈi-myə-nə-ˌblät, i-ˈmyü-(ˌ)nō-\ *noun* (1982)
: a blot in which a radioactively labeled antibody is used as the molecular probe
— **im·mu·no·blot·ting** \-ˌblä-tiŋ\ *noun*

im·mu·no·chem·is·try \ˌi-myə-nō-ˈke-mə-strē, i-ˌmyü-nō-\ *noun* [International Scientific Vocabulary] (1907)
: a branch of chemistry that deals with the chemical aspects of immunology
— **im·mu·no·chem·i·cal** \-ˈke-mi-kəl\ *adjective*
— **im·mu·no·chem·i·cal·ly** \-k(ə-)lē\ *adverb*
— **im·mu·no·chem·ist** \-ˈke-mist\ *noun*

im·mu·no·com·pe·tence \-ˈkäm-pə-tən(t)s\ *noun* (1967)
: the capacity for a normal immune response
— **im·mu·no·com·pe·tent** \-tənt\ *adjective*

im·mu·no·com·pro·mised \-ˈkäm-prə-ˌmīzd\ *adjective* (1979)
: having the immune system impaired or weakened (as by drugs or illness) ⟨*immunocompromised* patients⟩

im·mu·no·cy·to·chem·is·try \-ˌsī-tō-ˈke-mə-strē\ *noun* (1960)
: the application of biochemistry to cellular immunology
— **im·mu·no·cy·to·chem·i·cal** \-ˈkə-mi-kəl\ *adjective*
— **im·mu·no·cy·to·chem·i·cal·ly** \-ˈke-mi-k(ə-)lē\ *adverb*

im·mu·no·de·fi·cien·cy \-di-ˈfi-shən(t)-sē\ *noun* (1969)
: inability to produce a normal complement of antibodies or immunologically sensitized T cells especially in response to specific antigens
— **im·mu·no·de·fi·cient** \-shənt\ *adjective*

im·mu·no·di·ag·no·sis \-ˌdī-ig-ˈnō-səs, -əg-\ *noun* (1972)
: diagnosis (as of cancer) by immunological methods
— **im·mu·no·di·ag·nos·tic** \-ˈnäs-tik\ *adjective*

im·mu·no·dif·fu·sion \-di-ˈfyü-zhən\ *noun* (1959)
: any of several techniques for obtaining a precipitate between an antibody and its specific antigen by suspending one in a gel and letting the other migrate through it from a well or by letting both antibody and antigen migrate through the gel from separate wells to form an area of precipitation

im·mu·no·elec·tro·pho·re·sis \-ə-ˌlek-trə-fə-ˈrē-səs\ *noun, plural* **-re·ses** \-ˌsēz\ (1958)
: electrophoretic separation of proteins followed by identification by the formation of precipitates through specific immunologic reactions
— **im·mu·no·elec·tro·pho·ret·ic** \-ˈre-tik\ *adjective*
— **im·mu·no·elec·tro·pho·ret·i·cal·ly** \-ti-k(ə-)lē\ *adverb*

im·mu·no·flu·o·res·cence \-(ˌ)flȯ-ˈre-sᵊn(t)s, -(ˌ)flō-, -(ˌ)flu̇-(-ə)-\ *noun* (1960)
: the labeling of antibodies or antigens with fluorescent dyes especially for the purpose of demonstrating the presence of a particular antigen or antibody in a tissue preparation or smear
— **im·mu·no·flu·o·res·cent** \-sᵊnt\ *adjective*

im·mu·no·gen \i-ˈmyü-nə-jən, -ˌjen\ *noun* [from *Immunogen*, a trademark] (1959)
: an antigen that produces an immune response

im·mu·no·ge·net·ics \ˌi-myə-nō-jə-ˈne-tiks, i-ˌmyü-nō-\ *noun plural but singular in construction* (1936)
: a branch of immunology concerned with the interrelations of heredity, disease, and the immune system and its components (as antibodies)
— **im·mu·no·ge·net·ic** \-tik\ *adjective*
— **im·mu·no·ge·net·i·cal·ly** \-ti-k(ə-)lē\ *adverb*
— **im·mu·no·ge·net·i·cist** \-jə-ˈne-tə-sist\ *noun*

im·mu·no·gen·ic \ˌi-myə-nō-ˈje-nik, i-ˌmyü-nō-\ *adjective* (circa 1923)
: relating to or producing an immune response ⟨*immunogenic* substances⟩

\ə\ abut \ᵊ\ kitten \ər\ further \a\ ash \ā\ ace
\ä\ mop, mar \au̇\ out \ch\ chin \e\ bet \ē\ easy
\g\ go \i\ hit \ī\ ice \j\ job \ŋ\ sing \ō\ go
\ȯ\ law \ȯi\ boy \th\ thin \th\ the \ü\ loot \u̇\ foot
\y\ yet \zh\ vision *see also* Guide to Pronunciation

— **im·mu·no·gen·e·sis** \-'je-nə-səs\ *noun*
— **im·mu·no·ge·nic·i·ty** \-jə-'ni-sə-tē\ *noun*

im·mu·no·glob·u·lin \-'glä-byə-lən\ *noun* (1953)
: ANTIBODY

im·mu·no·he·ma·tol·o·gy \-,hē-mə-'tä-lə-jē\ *noun* (1950)
: a branch of immunology that deals with the immunologic properties of blood
— **im·mu·no·he·ma·to·log·ic** \-,hē-mə-tᵊl-'ä-jik\ *or* **im·mu·no·he·ma·to·log·i·cal** \-'ä-ji-kəl\ *adjective*
— **im·mu·no·he·ma·tol·o·gist** \-,hē-mə-'tä-lə-jist\ *noun*

im·mu·no·his·to·chem·i·cal \-,his-tō-'ke-mi-kəl\ *adjective* (1960)
: of or relating to the application of histochemical and immunologic methods to chemical analysis of living cells and tissues
— **im·mu·no·his·to·chem·is·try** \-'ke-mə-strē\ *noun*

im·mu·nol·o·gy \,i-myə-'nä-lə-jē\ *noun* [International Scientific Vocabulary] (1910)
: a science that deals with the immune system and the cell-mediated and humoral aspects of immunity and immune responses
— **im·mu·no·log·ic** \-nə-'lä-jik\ *or* **im·mu·no·log·i·cal** \-'lä-ji-kəl\ *adjective*
— **im·mu·no·log·i·cal·ly** \-ji-k(ə-)lē\ *adverb*
— **im·mu·nol·o·gist** \,i-myə-'nä-lə-jist\ *noun*

im·mu·no·mod·u·la·tor \,i-myə-nō-'mä-jə-,lā-tər, i-,myü-nō-\ *noun* (1977)
: a substance that affects the functioning of the immune system
— **im·mu·no·mod·u·la·to·ry** \-'mä-jə-lə-,tōr-ē, -,tòr-\ *adjective*

im·mu·no·pa·thol·o·gy \-pə-'thä-lə-jē, -pa-\ *noun* (1959)
: a branch of medicine that deals with immune responses associated with disease
— **im·mu·no·path·o·log·ic** \-,pa-thə-'lä-jik\ *or* **im·mu·no·path·o·log·i·cal** \-ji-kəl\ *adjective*
— **im·mu·no·pa·thol·o·gist** \-pə-'thä-lə-jist, -pa-\ *noun*

im·mu·no·pre·cip·i·ta·tion \-pri-,si-pə-'tā-shən\ *noun* (1966)
: precipitation of a complex of an antibody and its specific antigen
— **im·mu·no·pre·cip·i·tate** \-'si-pə-tət, -pə-,tāt\ *noun*
— **im·mu·no·pre·cip·i·tate** \-pə-,tāt\ *transitive verb*

im·mu·no·re·ac·tive \-rē-'ak-tiv\ *adjective* (1966)
: reacting to particular antigens or haptens ⟨*immunoreactive* lymphocytes⟩
— **im·mu·no·re·ac·tiv·i·ty** \-(,)rē-,ak-'ti-və-tē\ *noun*

im·mu·no·reg·u·la·to·ry \-'re-gyə-lə-,tōr-ē, -,tòr-\ *adjective* (1971)
: of or relating to the regulation of the immune system ⟨*immunoregulatory* T cells⟩
— **im·mu·no·reg·u·la·tion** \-,re-gyə-'lā-shən, -gə-\ *noun*

im·mu·no·sor·bent \-'sòr-bənt\ *adjective* (1966)
: relating to or using a substrate consisting of a specific antibody or antigen chemically combined with an insoluble substance (as cellulose) to selectively remove the corresponding specific antigen or antibody from solution
— **immunosorbent** *noun*

im·mu·no·sup·pres·sion \-sə-'pre-shən\ *noun* (1963)
: suppression (as by drugs) of natural immune responses
— **im·mu·no·sup·press** \-sə-'pres\ *transitive verb*
— **im·mu·no·sup·pres·sant** \-'pre-sᵊnt\ *noun or adjective*
— **im·mu·no·sup·pres·sive** \-'pre-siv\ *adjective*

im·mu·no·ther·a·py \-'ther-ə-pē\ *noun* [International Scientific Vocabulary] (circa 1911)
: treatment of or prophylaxis against disease by attempting to produce active or passive immunity
— **im·mu·no·ther·a·peu·tic** \-,ther-ə-'pyü-tik\ *adjective*

im·mure \i-'myúr\ *transitive verb* **im·mured; im·mur·ing** [Medieval Latin *immurare*, from Latin *in-* + *murus* wall — more at MUNITION] (1583)
1 a : to enclose within or as if within walls **b :** IMPRISON
2 : to build into a wall; *especially* : to entomb in a wall
— **im·mure·ment** \-'myúr-mənt\ *noun*

im·mu·ta·ble \(,)i(m)-'myü-tə-bəl\ *adjective* [Middle English, from Latin *immutabilis*, from *in-* + *mutabilis* mutable] (15th century)
: not capable of or susceptible to change
— **im·mu·ta·bil·i·ty** \-,myü-tə-'bi-lə-tē\ *noun*
— **im·mu·ta·ble·ness** \-'myü-tə-bəl-nəs\ *noun*
— **im·mu·ta·bly** \-blē\ *adverb*

¹imp \'imp\ *noun* [Middle English *impe*, from Old English *impa*, from *impian* to imp] (before 12th century)
1 *obsolete* : SHOOT, BUD; *also* : GRAFT
2 a : a small demon : FIEND **b :** a mischievous child : URCHIN ◆

²imp *transitive verb* [Middle English, from Old English *impian* to graft, from (assumed) Vulgar Latin *imputare*, from Late Latin *impotus* grafted shoot, from Greek *emphytos* implanted, from *emphyein* to implant, from *em-* ²*en-* + *phyein* to bring forth — more at BE] (15th century)
1 : to graft or repair (a wing, tail, or feather) with a feather to improve a falcon's flying capacity
2 : to equip with wings

¹im·pact \im-'pakt\ *verb* [Latin *impactus*, past participle of *impingere* to push against — more at IMPINGE] (1601)
transitive verb
1 a : to fix firmly by or as if by packing or wedging **b :** to press together
2 a : to have an impact on : impinge on **b :** to strike forcefully; *also* : to cause to strike forcefully
intransitive verb
1 : to have an impact
2 : to impinge or make contact especially forcefully
— **im·pac·tive** \im-'pak-tiv\ *adjective*
— **im·pac·tor** *also* **im·pact·er** \-tər\ *noun*

²im·pact \'im-,pakt\ *noun* (1781)
1 a : an impinging or striking especially of one body against another **b :** a forceful contact, collision, or onset; *also* : the impetus communicated in or as if in a collision
2 : the force of impression of one thing on another : a significant or major effect ⟨the *impact* of science on our society⟩ ⟨an environmental *impact* study⟩

impact crater *noun* (1895)
: CRATER 1b

im·pact·ed \im-'pak-təd\ *adjective* (circa 1616)
1 a : packed or wedged in **b :** deeply entrenched : not easily changed or removed
2 *of a tooth* : wedged between the jawbone and another tooth
3 : of, relating to, or being an area (as a school district) providing tax-supported services to a population having a large proportion of federal employees and especially those living or working on tax-exempt federal property ⟨aid to education in *impacted* areas⟩

im·pac·tion \im-'pak-shən\ *noun* (1739)
: the act of becoming or the state of being impacted; *especially* : lodgment of something (as feces) in a body passage or cavity

impact printer *noun* (1968)

: a printing device in which a printing element directly strikes a surface (as in a typewriter)

im·paint \im-'pānt\ *transitive verb* (1596)
obsolete : PAINT, DEPICT

im·pair \im-'par, -'per\ *transitive verb* [Middle English *empeiren*, from Middle French *empeirer*, from (assumed) Vulgar Latin *impejorare*, from Latin *in-* + Late Latin *pejorare* to make worse — more at PEJORATIVE] (14th century)
: to damage or make worse by or as if by diminishing in some material respect ⟨his health was *impaired* by overwork⟩ ⟨the strike seriously *impaired* community services⟩
synonym see INJURE
— **im·pair·er** *noun*
— **im·pair·ment** \-mənt\ *noun*

im·paired \-'pard, -'perd\ *adjective* (1605)
: being in a less than perfect or whole condition: as **a :** handicapped or functionally defective — often used in combination ⟨hearing-*impaired*⟩ **b** *chiefly Canadian* : DRUNK ⟨driving while *impaired*⟩

im·pa·la \im-'pa-lə, -'pä-\ *noun, plural* **impalas** *or* **impala** [Zulu] (1875)
: a large brownish African antelope (*Aepyceros melampus*) that in the male has slender lyrate horns

impala

im·pale \im-'pā(ə)l\ *transitive verb* **im·paled; im·pal·ing** [Middle French & Medieval Latin; Middle French *empaler*, from Medieval Latin *impalare*, from Latin *in-* + *palus* stake — more at POLE] (1605)
1 : to join (coats of arms) on a heraldic shield divided vertically by a pale
2 a : to pierce with or as if with something pointed; *especially* : to torture or kill by fixing on a sharp stake **b :** to fix in an inescapable or helpless position
— **im·pale·ment** \-mənt\ *noun*
— **im·pal·er** \-'pā-lər\ *noun*

im·pal·pa·ble \(,)im-'pal-pə-bəl\ *adjective* (1509)
1 a : incapable of being felt by touch : INTANGIBLE ⟨the *impalpable* aura of power that emanated from him —Osbert Sitwell⟩ **b :** so finely divided that no grains or grit can be felt ⟨rock worn to an *impalpable* powder⟩
2 : not readily discerned by the mind
— **im·pal·pa·bil·i·ty** \-,pal-pə-'bi-lə-tē\ *noun*
— **im·pal·pa·bly** \-'pal-pə-blē\ *adverb*

im·pan·el \im-'pa-nᵊl\ *transitive verb* (15th century)
: to enroll in or on a panel ⟨*impanel* a jury⟩

◇ **WORD HISTORY**
imp *Imp*, which now usually refers to either a small demon or a mischievous child, has its origin in the unlikely field of horticulture. Old English *impa* or *impe* meant "graft" or "young shoot of a plant" and was a derivative of the verb *impian* "to graft." By later Middle English *impe* could mean metaphorically "offspring" or "child," a sense that survived at least into the 19th century. The frequency of phrases such as *imp of the devil* (i.e., "offspring of the devil") and *imp of hell* led to the use of *imp* without qualification to denote a demon, the evil parentage of the offspring being understood. By the 18th century the demonic sense had, as had the words *demon* and *devil* themselves, given rise to a less forceful usage: *imp* could be applied to nothing more than a naughty child.

im·par·a·dise \im-'par-ə-ˌdīs, -ˌdīz\ *transitive verb* **-dised; -dis·ing** (1592)
: ENRAPTURE

im·par·i·ty \(ˌ)im-'par-ə-tē\ *noun, plural* **-ties** [Late Latin *imparitas,* from Latin *impar* unequal, from *in-* + *par* equal] (1563)
: INEQUALITY, DISPARITY

im·part \im-'pärt\ *transitive verb* [Middle French & Latin; Middle French *impartir,* from Latin *impartire,* from *in-* + *partire* to divide, part] (15th century)
1 : to give, convey, or grant from or as if from a store ⟨her experience *imparted* authority to her words⟩ ⟨the flavor *imparted* by herbs⟩
2 : to communicate the knowledge of **:** DISCLOSE ⟨*imparted* my scheme to no one⟩
— **im·par·ta·tion** \ˌim-ˌpär-'tā-shən\ *noun*
— **im·part·ment** \im-'pärt-mənt\ *noun*

im·par·tial \(ˌ)im-'pär-shəl\ *adjective* (1587)
: not partial or biased **:** treating or affecting all equally
synonym see FAIR
— **im·par·tial·i·ty** \-ˌpär-shē-'a-lə-tē, -ˌpär-'sha-\ *noun*
— **im·par·tial·ly** \-'pär-sh(ə-)lē\ *adverb*

im·par·ti·ble \(ˌ)im-'pär-tə-bəl\ *adjective* [Late Latin *impartibilis,* from Latin *in-* + Late Latin *partibilis* divisible, from Latin *partire*] (14th century)
: not partible **:** not subject to partition
— **im·par·ti·bly** \-blē\ *adverb*

im·pass·able \(ˌ)im-'pa-sə-bəl\ *adjective* (1568)
: incapable of being passed, traveled, crossed, or surmounted
— **im·pass·abil·i·ty** \-ˌpa-sə-'bi-lə-tē\ *noun*
— **im·pass·able·ness** \-'pa-sə-bəl-nəs\ *noun*
— **im·pass·ably** \-blē\ *adverb*

im·passe \'im-ˌpas, im-'\ *noun* [French, from *in-* + *passer* to pass] (1851)
1 a : a predicament affording no obvious escape **b :** DEADLOCK
2 : an impassable road or way **:** CUL-DE-SAC

im·pas·si·ble \(ˌ)im-'pa-sə-bəl\ *adjective* [Middle English, from Middle French or Late Latin; Middle French, from Late Latin *impassibilis,* from Latin *in-* + Late Latin *passibilis* passible] (14th century)
1 a : incapable of suffering or of experiencing pain **b :** inaccessible to injury
2 : incapable of feeling **:** IMPASSIVE
— **im·pas·si·bil·i·ty** \-ˌpa-sə-'bi-lə-tē\ *noun*
— **im·pas·si·bly** \-'pa-sə-blē\ *adverb*

im·pas·sion \im-'pa-shən\ *transitive verb* **im·pas·sioned; im·pas·sion·ing** \-sh(ə-)niŋ\ [probably from Italian *impassionare,* from *in-* (from Latin) + *passione* passion, from Late Latin *passion-, passio*] (1591)
: to arouse the feelings or passions of

impassioned *adjective* (1603)
: filled with passion or zeal **:** showing great warmth or intensity of feeling ☆

im·pas·sive \(ˌ)im-'pa-siv\ *adjective* (1605)
1 a *archaic* **:** unsusceptible to pain **b :** unsusceptible to physical feeling **:** INSENSIBLE **c :** unsusceptible to or destitute of emotion **:** APATHETIC
2 : giving no sign of feeling or emotion **:** EXPRESSIONLESS ☆
— **im·pas·sive·ly** *adverb*
— **im·pas·sive·ness** *noun*
— **im·pas·siv·i·ty** \ˌim-ˌpa-'si-və-tē\ *noun*

im·paste \im-'pāst\ *transitive verb* [Italian *impastare,* from *in-* (from Latin) + *pasta* paste, from Late Latin] (1576)
obsolete **:** to make into a paste or crust

im·pas·to \im-'pas-(ˌ)tō, -'päs-\ *noun, plural* **-tos** [Italian, from *impastare*] (1784)
1 : the thick application of a pigment to a canvas or panel in painting; *also* **:** the body of pigment so applied
2 : raised decoration on ceramic ware usually of slip or enamel

im·pas·toed \-(ˌ)tōd\ *adjective*

im·pa·tience \(ˌ)im-'pā-shən(t)s\ *noun* (13th century)
: the quality or state of being impatient

im·pa·tiens \im-'pā-shənz, -shən(t)s\ *noun* [New Latin, from Latin, impatient] (1885)
: any of a widely distributed genus (*Impatiens,* family Balsaminaceae) of annual herbs with irregular spurred or saccate flowers and dehiscent capsules — compare TOUCH-ME-NOT

im·pa·tient \(ˌ)im-'pā-shənt\ *adjective* [Middle English *impacient,* from Middle French, from Latin *impatient-, impatiens,* from *in-* + *patient-, patiens* patient] (14th century)
1 a : not patient **:** restless or short of temper especially under irritation, delay, or opposition **b :** INTOLERANT ⟨*impatient* of delay⟩
2 : prompted or marked by impatience ⟨an *impatient* reply⟩
3 : eagerly desirous **:** ANXIOUS ⟨*impatient* to get home⟩
— **im·pa·tient·ly** *adverb*

im·pawn \im-'pȯn, -'pän\ *transitive verb* (1596)
archaic **:** to put in pawn **:** PLEDGE

¹im·peach \im-'pēch\ *transitive verb* [Middle English *empechen,* from Middle French *empeechier* to hinder, from Late Latin *impedicare* to fetter, from Latin *in-* + *pedica* fetter, from *ped-, pes* foot — more at FOOT] (14th century)
1 a : to bring an accusation against **b :** to charge with a crime or misdemeanor; *specifically* **:** to charge (a public official) before a competent tribunal with misconduct in office
2 : to cast doubt on; *especially* **:** to challenge the credibility or validity of ⟨*impeach* the testimony of a witness⟩
3 : to remove from office especially for misconduct ☆
— **im·peach·able** \-'pē-chə-bəl\ *adjective*
— **im·peach·ment** \-'pēch-mənt\ *noun*

²impeach *noun* (1590)
obsolete **:** CHARGE, IMPEACHMENT

im·pearl \im-'pər(-ə)l\ *transitive verb* [probably from Middle French *emperler,* from *en-* + *perle* pearl] (15th century)
: to form into pearls; *also* **:** to form of or adorn with pearls

im·pec·ca·ble \(ˌ)im-'pek-ə-bəl\ *adjective* [Latin *impeccabilis,* from *in-* + *peccare* to sin] (1531)
1 : not capable of sinning or liable to sin
2 : free from fault or blame **:** FLAWLESS ⟨spoke *impeccable* French⟩
— **im·pec·ca·bil·i·ty** \-ˌpe-kə-'bi-lə-tē\ *noun*
— **im·pec·ca·bly** \-'pe-kə-blē\ *adverb*

im·pe·cu·nious \ˌim-pi-'kyü-nyəs, -nē-əs\ *adjective* [¹*in-* + obsolete English *pecunious* rich, from Middle English, from Latin *pecuniosus,* from *pecunia* money — more at FEE] (1596)
: having very little or no money usually habitually **:** PENNILESS
— **im·pe·cu·ni·os·i·ty** \-ˌkyü-nē-'ä-sə-tē\ *noun*
— **im·pe·cu·nious·ly** *adverb*
— **im·pe·cu·nious·ness** *noun*

im·ped·ance \im-'pē-dᵊn(t)s\ *noun* (1886)
: something that impedes HINDRANCE: as **a :** the apparent opposition in an electrical circuit to the flow of an alternating current that is analogous to the actual electrical resistance to a direct current and that is the ratio of effective electromotive force to the effective current **b :** the ratio of the pressure to the volume displacement at a given surface in a sound-transmitting medium

im·pede \im-'pēd\ *transitive verb* **im·ped·ed; im·ped·ing** [Latin *impedire,* from *in-* + *ped-, pes* foot — more at FOOT] (1605)
: to interfere with or slow the progress of
synonym see HINDER
— **im·ped·er** *noun*

im·ped·i·ment \im-'pe-də-mənt\ *noun* (14th century)
1 : something that impedes; *especially* **:** an organic obstruction to speech
2 : a bar or hindrance (as lack of sufficient age) to a lawful marriage

im·ped·i·men·ta \(ˌ)im-ˌpe-də-'men-tə\ *noun plural* [Latin, plural of *impedimentum* impediment, from *impedire*] (1600)
1 : APPURTENANCES, EQUIPMENT
2 : things that impede

im·pel \im-'pel\ *transitive verb* **im·pelled; im·pel·ling** [Latin *impellere,* from *in-* + *pellere* to drive — more at FELT] (15th century)
1 : to urge or drive forward or on by or as if by the exertion of strong moral pressure **:** FORCE
2 : to impart motion to **:** PROPEL
synonym see MOVE

☆ SYNONYMS
Impassioned, passionate, ardent, fervent, fervid, perfervid mean showing intense feeling. IMPASSIONED implies warmth and intensity without violence and suggests fluent verbal expression (an *impassioned* plea for justice). PASSIONATE implies great vehemence and often violence and wasteful diffusion of emotion (a *passionate* denunciation). ARDENT implies an intense degree of zeal, devotion, or enthusiasm (an *ardent* supporter of human rights). FERVENT stresses sincerity and steadiness of emotional warmth or zeal (*fervent* good wishes). FERVID suggests warmly and spontaneously and often feverishly expressed emotion (*fervid* love letters). PERFERVID implies the expression of exaggerated or overwrought feelings (*perfervid* expressions of patriotism).

Impassive, stoic, phlegmatic, apathetic, stolid mean unresponsive to something that might normally excite interest or emotion. IMPASSIVE stresses the absence of any external sign of emotion in action or facial expression (met the news with an *impassive* look). STOIC implies an apparent indifference to pleasure or especially to pain often as a matter of principle or self-discipline (was resolutely *stoic* even in adversity). PHLEGMATIC implies a temperament or constitution hard to arouse (a *phlegmatic* man unmoved by tears). APATHETIC may imply a puzzling or deplorable indifference or inertness (charitable appeals met an *apathetic* response). STOLID implies an habitual absence of interest, responsiveness, or curiosity (*stolid* workers wedded to routine).

□ USAGE
impeach Back in 1970 a newspaperman took an informal poll of people who worked for the paper and discovered that 10 out of 13 believed *impeach* meant "to remove from office" rather than "to charge with misconduct in office." This is a meaning many people know—our evidence goes back to before World War I—but seldom see in print. (It is sense 3 here.) But the strong presence of this meaning in people's minds can make many uses of *impeach* ambiguous ⟨(who, by the way, was later *impeached* for corruption!) —Julian Huxley⟩. Was he removed or merely charged with corruption? A writer must reckon with the sense "remove from office" when writing for the general public and take care to make the context clear.

\ə\ abut \ᵊ\ kitten \ər\ further \a\ ash \ā\ ace \ä\ mop, mar \au̇\ out \ch\ chin \e\ bet \ē\ easy \g\ go \i\ hit \ī\ ice \j\ job \ŋ\ sing \ō\ go \ȯ\ law \ȯi\ boy \th\ thin \t͟h\ the \ü\ loot \u̇\ foot \y\ yet \zh\ vision *see also* Guide to Pronunciation

im·pel·ler *also* **im·pel·lor** \im-'pe-lər\ *noun* (1685)
1 : one that impels
2 : ROTOR; *also* : a blade of a rotor

im·pend \im-'pend\ *intransitive verb* [Latin *impendēre,* from *in-* + *pendēre* to hang — more at PENDANT] (1599)
1 a : to hover threateningly : MENACE **b** : to be about to occur
2 *archaic* : to hang suspended

im·pen·dent \im-'pen-dənt\ *adjective* (1590)
: being near at hand : APPROACHING

im·pen·e·tra·bil·i·ty \(,)im-,pe-nə-trə-'bi-lə-tē\ *noun* (1665)
1 : the inability of two portions of matter to occupy the same space at the same time
2 : the quality or state of being impenetrable

im·pen·e·tra·ble \(,)im-'pe-nə-trə-bəl\ *adjective* [Middle English *impenetrabel,* from Middle French *impenetrable,* from Latin *impenetrabilis,* from *in-* + *penetrabilis* penetrable] (15th century)
1 a : incapable of being penetrated or pierced **b** : inaccessible to knowledge, reason, or sympathy : IMPERVIOUS
2 : incapable of being comprehended : INSCRUTABLE
— **im·pen·e·tra·bly** \-blē\ *adverb*

im·pen·i·tence \(,)im-'pe-nə-tən(t)s\ *noun* (1624)
archaic : the quality or state of being impenitent

im·pen·i·tent \-tənt\ *adjective* [Middle English, from Late Latin *impaenitent-, impaenitens,* from Latin *in-* + *paenitent-, paenitens* penitent] (15th century)
: not penitent
— **im·pen·i·tent·ly** *adverb*

¹**im·per·a·tive** \im-'per-ə-tiv\ *adjective* [Middle English *imperatyf,* from Late Latin *imperativus,* from Latin *imperatus,* past participle of *imperare* to command — more at EMPEROR] (15th century)
1 a : of, relating to, or constituting the grammatical mood that expresses the will to influence the behavior of another **b** : expressive of a command, entreaty, or exhortation **c** : having power to restrain, control, and direct
2 : not to be avoided or evaded : NECESSARY ⟨an *imperative* duty⟩
synonym SEE MASTERFUL
— **im·per·a·tive·ly** *adverb*
— **im·per·a·tive·ness** *noun*

²**imperative** *noun* (1530)
1 : the imperative mood or a verb form or verbal phrase expressing it
2 : something that is imperative: as **a** : COMMAND, ORDER **b** : RULE, GUIDE **c** : an obligatory act or duty **d** : an imperative judgment or proposition

im·pe·ra·tor \,im-pə-'rä-tər, -,tòr\ *noun* [Latin — more at EMPEROR] (circa 1580)
: a commander in chief or emperor of the ancient Romans
— **im·per·a·to·ri·al** \(,)im-,per-ə-'tòr-ē-əl, -'tòr-\ *adjective*

im·per·ceiv·able \,im-pər-'sē-və-bəl\ *adjective* (circa 1617)
archaic : IMPERCEPTIBLE

im·per·cep·ti·ble \,im-pər-'sep-tə-bəl\ *adjective* [Middle French, from Medieval Latin *imperceptibilis,* from Latin *in-* + Late Latin *perceptibilis* perceptible] (15th century)
: not perceptible by a sense or by the mind : extremely slight, gradual, or subtle
— **im·per·cep·ti·bly** \-'sep-tə-blē\ *adverb*

im·per·cep·tive \,im-pər-'sep-tiv\ *adjective* (1661)
: not perceptive
— **im·per·cep·tive·ness** *noun*

im·per·cip·i·ence \-'si-pē-ən(t)s\ *noun* (1891)
: the quality or state of being imperceptive
— **im·per·cip·i·ent** \-ənt\ *adjective*

¹**im·per·fect** \(,)im-'pər-fikt\ *adjective* [alteration of Middle English *imperfit,* from Middle French *imparfait,* from Latin *imperfectus,* from *in-* + *perfectus* perfect] (1570)
1 : not perfect: as **a** : DEFECTIVE **b** *of a flower* : having stamens or pistils but not both **c** : lacking or not involving sexual reproduction ⟨the *imperfect* stage of a fungus⟩
2 : of, relating to, or constituting a verb tense used to designate a continuing state or an incomplete action especially in the past
3 : not enforceable at law
— **im·per·fect·ly** \-fik(t)-lē\ *adverb*
— **im·per·fect·ness** \-fik(t)-nəs\ *noun*

²**imperfect** *noun* (1871)
: an imperfect tense; *also* : the verb form expressing it

imperfect fungus *noun* (circa 1895)
: any of various fungi (order Fungi Imperfecti synonym Deuteromycetes) of which only the conidial stage is known

im·per·fec·tion \,im-pər-'fek-shən\ *noun* (14th century)
: the quality or state of being imperfect; *also* : FAULT, BLEMISH

im·per·fec·tive \,im-pər-'fek-tiv\ *adjective* (1887)
of a verb form or aspect : expressing action as incomplete or without reference to completion or as reiterated — compare PERFECTIVE
— **imperfective** *noun*

im·per·fo·rate \(,)im-'pər-f(ə-)rət, -fə-,rāt\ *adjective* (1673)
1 : having no opening or aperture; *specifically* : lacking the usual or normal opening
2 *of a stamp or a sheet of stamps* : lacking perforations or roulettes

¹**im·pe·ri·al** \im-'pir-ē-əl\ *adjective* [Middle English, from Middle French, from Late Latin *imperialis,* from Latin *imperium* command, empire] (14th century)
1 a : of, relating to, befitting, or suggestive of an empire or an emperor **b** (1) : of or relating to the United Kingdom as distinguished from the constituent parts (2) : of or relating to the Commonwealth and British Empire
2 a : SOVEREIGN **b** : REGAL, IMPERIOUS
3 : of superior or unusual size or excellence
4 : belonging to the official British series of weights and measures — see WEIGHT table
— **im·pe·ri·al·ly** \-ə-lē\ *adverb*

²**imperial** *noun* (1524)
1 *capitalized* : an adherent or soldier of the Holy Roman emperor
2 : EMPEROR
3 [French *impériale;* from the beard worn by Napoléon III] : a pointed beard growing below the lower lip
4 : something of unusual size or excellence

im·pe·ri·al·ism \im-'pir-ē-ə-,li-zəm\ *noun* (1851)
1 : imperial government, authority, or system
2 : the policy, practice, or advocacy of extending the power and dominion of a nation especially by direct territorial acquisitions or by gaining indirect control over the political and economic life of other areas; *broadly* : the extension or imposition of power, authority, or influence ⟨union *imperialism*⟩
— **im·pe·ri·al·ist** \-list\ *noun or adjective*
— **im·pe·ri·al·is·tic** \-,pir-ē-ə-'lis-tik\ *adjective*
— **im·pe·ri·al·is·ti·cal·ly** \-ti-k(ə-)lē\ *adverb*

imperial moth *noun* (circa 1904)
: a large American saturniid moth (*Eacles imperialis*) marked with yellow and lilac or purplish brown

im·per·il \im-'per-əl\ *transitive verb* **-iled** *or* **-illed; -il·ing** *or* **-il·ling** (15th century)
: to bring into peril : ENDANGER

imperial moth

— **im·per·il·ment** \-mənt\ *noun*

im·pe·ri·ous \im-'pir-ē-əs\ *adjective* [Latin *imperiosus,* from *imperium*] (1540)
1 : befitting or characteristic of one of eminent rank or attainments : COMMANDING, DOMINANT ⟨an *imperious* manner⟩ **b** : marked by arrogant assurance : DOMINEERING
2 : intensely compelling : URGENT ⟨the *imperious* problems of the new age —J. F. Kennedy⟩
synonym SEE MASTERFUL
— **im·pe·ri·ous·ly** *adverb*
— **im·pe·ri·ous·ness** *noun*

im·per·ish·able \(,)im-'per-i-shə-bəl\ *adjective* (1648)
1 : not perishable or subject to decay
2 : enduring or occurring forever ⟨*imperishable* fame⟩
— **im·per·ish·abil·i·ty** \-,per-i-shə-'bi-lə-tē\ *noun*
— **imperishable** *noun*
— **im·per·ish·able·ness** \-'per-i-shə-bəl-nəs\ *noun*
— **im·per·ish·ably** \-blē\ *adverb*

im·pe·ri·um \im-'pir-ē-əm\ *noun* [Latin — more at EMPIRE] (1651)
1 a : supreme power or absolute dominion : CONTROL **b** : EMPIRE
2 : the right to command or to employ the force of the state : SOVEREIGNTY

im·per·ma·nence \(,)im-'pərm-nən(t)s, -'pər-mə-\ *noun* (1796)
: the quality or state of being impermanent

im·per·ma·nen·cy \-nən(t)-sē\ *noun* (1648)
: IMPERMANENCE

im·per·ma·nent \-nənt\ *adjective* (1653)
: not permanent : TRANSIENT
— **im·per·ma·nent·ly** *adverb*

im·per·me·able \(,)im-'pər-mē-ə-bəl\ *adjective* [Late Latin *impermeabilis,* from Latin *in-* + Late Latin *permeabilis* permeable] (1697)
: not permitting passage (as of a fluid) through its substance; *broadly* : IMPERVIOUS
— **im·per·me·abil·i·ty** \-,pər-mē-ə-'bi-lə-tē\ *noun*

im·per·mis·si·ble \,im-pər-'mi-sə-bəl\ *adjective* (1858)
: not permissible
— **im·per·mis·si·bil·i·ty** \-,mi-sə-'bi-lə-tē\ *noun*
— **im·per·mis·si·bly** \-'mi-sə-blē\ *adverb*

im·per·son·al \(,)im-'pərs-nəl, -'pər-sᵊn-əl\ *adjective* [Middle English, from Late Latin *impersonalis,* from Latin *in-* + Late Latin *personalis* personal] (15th century)
1 a : denoting the verbal action of an unspecified agent and hence used with no expressed subject (as *methinks*) or with a merely formal subject (as *rained* in *it rained*) **b** *of a pronoun* : INDEFINITE
2 a : having no personal reference or connection ⟨*impersonal* criticism⟩ **b** : not engaging the human personality or emotions ⟨the machine as compared with the hand tool is an *impersonal* agency —John Dewey⟩ **c** : not existing as a person : not having human qualities or characteristics
— **im·per·son·al·i·ty** \-,pər-sᵊn-'a-lə-tē\ *noun*
— **im·per·son·al·ly** \-'pərs-nə-lē, -'pər-sᵊn-ə-lē\ *adverb*

im·per·son·al·ize \(,)im-'pərs-nə-,līz, -'pər-sᵊn-ə-\ *transitive verb* (circa 1899)
: to make impersonal
— **im·per·son·al·i·za·tion** \-,pərs-nə-lə-'zā-shən, -,pər-sᵊn-ə-\ *noun*

im·per·son·ate \im-'pər-sᵊn-,āt\ *transitive verb* **-at·ed; -at·ing** (1715)
: to assume or act the character of : PERSONATE
— **im·per·son·a·tion** \-,pər-sᵊn-'ā-shən\ *noun*
— **im·per·son·a·tor** \-'pər-sᵊn-,ā-tər\ *noun*

im·per·ti·nence \(,)im-'pər-tᵊn-ən(t)s, -'pərt-nən(t)s\ *noun* (1603)
1 : the quality or state of being impertinent: as **a** : IRRELEVANCE, INAPPROPRIATENESS **b** : INCIVILITY, INSOLENCE

2 : an instance of impertinence

im·per·ti·nen·cy \-ən(t)-sē, -nən(t)-\ *noun, plural* **-cies** (1589)
: IMPERTINENCE

im·per·ti·nent \(ˌ)im-'pər-tⁿn-ənt, -'pərt-nənt\ *adjective* [Middle English, from Middle French, from Late Latin *impertinent-, impertinens*, from Latin *in- + pertinent-, pertinens*, present participle of *pertinēre* to pertain] (14th century)
1 : not pertinent **:** IRRELEVANT
2 a : not restrained within due or proper bounds especially of propriety or good taste ⟨*impertinent* curiosity⟩ **b :** given to or characterized by insolent rudeness ⟨an *impertinent* answer⟩ ☆
— **im·per·ti·nent·ly** *adverb*

im·per·turb·able \ˌim-pər-'tər-bə-bəl\ *adjective* [Middle English, from Late Latin *imperturbabilis*, from Latin *in- + perturbare* to perturb] (15th century)
: marked by extreme calm, impassivity, and steadiness **:** SERENE
synonym see COOL
— **im·per·turb·abil·i·ty** \-ˌtər-bə-'bi-lə-tē\ *noun*
— **im·per·turb·ably** \-'tər-bə-blē\ *adverb*

im·per·vi·ous \(ˌ)im-'pər-vē-əs\ *adjective* [Latin *impervius*, from *in- + pervius* pervious] (1650)
1 a : not allowing entrance or passage **:** IMPENETRABLE ⟨a coat *impervious* to rain⟩ **b :** not capable of being damaged or harmed ⟨a carpet *impervious* to rough treatment⟩
2 : not capable of being affected or disturbed ⟨*impervious* to criticism⟩
— **im·per·vi·ous·ly** *adverb*
— **im·per·vi·ous·ness** *noun*

im·pe·tig·i·nous \ˌim-pə-'ti-jə-nəs\ *adjective* (1620)
: of, relating to, or resembling impetigo ⟨*impetiginous* lesions⟩

im·pe·ti·go \ˌim-pə-'tē-(ˌ)gō, -'tī-\ *noun* [Latin, from *impetere* to attack — more at IMPETUS] (14th century)
: an acute contagious staphylococcal or streptococcal skin disease characterized by vesicles, pustules, and yellowish crusts

im·pe·trate \'im-pə-ˌtrāt\ *transitive verb* **-trat·ed; -trat·ing** [Latin *impetratus*, past participle of *impetrare*, from *in- + patrare* to accomplish — more at PERPETRATE] (circa 1534)
1 : to obtain by request or entreaty
2 : to ask for **:** ENTREAT
— **im·pe·tra·tion** \ˌim-pə-'trā-shən\ *noun*

im·pet·u·os·i·ty \im-ˌpe-chə-'wä-sə-tē\ *noun, plural* **-ties** (15th century)
1 : the quality or state of being impetuous
2 : an impetuous action or impulse

im·pet·u·ous \im-'pech-wəs, -'pe-chə-\ *adjective* [Middle English, from Middle French *impetueux*, from Late Latin *impetuosus*, from Latin *impetus*] (14th century)
1 : marked by impulsive vehemence or passion ⟨an *impetuous* temperament⟩
2 : marked by force and violence of movement or action ⟨an *impetuous* wind⟩
synonym see PRECIPITATE
— **im·pet·u·ous·ly** *adverb*
— **im·pet·u·ous·ness** *noun*

im·pe·tus \'im-pə-təs\ *noun* [Latin, assault, impetus, from *impetere* to attack, from *in- + petere* to go to, seek — more at FEATHER] (1641)
1 a (1) **:** a driving force **:** IMPULSE (2) **:** INCENTIVE, STIMULUS **b :** stimulation or encouragement resulting in increased activity
2 : the property possessed by a moving body in virtue of its mass and its motion — used of bodies moving suddenly or violently to indicate the origin and intensity of the motion

im·pi·e·ty \(ˌ)im-'pī-ə-tē\ *noun, plural* **-ties** (14th century)
1 : the quality or state of being impious **:** IRREVERENCE
2 : an impious act

im·pinge \im-'pinj\ *intransitive verb* **impinged; im·ping·ing** [Latin *impingere*, from *in- + pangere* to fasten, drive in — more at PACT] (1605)
1 : to strike or dash especially with a sharp collision ⟨I heard the rain *impinge* upon the earth —James Joyce⟩
2 : to have an effect **:** make an impression ⟨waiting for the germ of a new idea to *impinge* upon my mind —Phyllis Bentley⟩
3 : ENCROACH, INFRINGE ⟨*impinge* on other people's rights⟩
— **im·pinge·ment** \-'pinj-mənt\ *noun*

im·pi·ous \'im-pē-əs, (ˌ)im-'pī-\ *adjective* [Latin *impius*, from *in- + pius* pious] (1542)
: not pious **:** lacking in reverence or proper respect (as for God or one's parents) **:** IRREVERENT
— **im·pi·ous·ly** *adverb*

imp·ish \'im-pish\ *adjective* (1652)
: of, relating to, or befitting an imp; *especially* **:** MISCHIEVOUS
— **imp·ish·ly** *adverb*
— **imp·ish·ness** *noun*

im·pla·ca·ble \(ˌ)im-'pla-kə-bəl, -'plā-\ *adjective* [Middle French or Latin; Middle French, from Latin *implacabilis*, from *in- + placabilis* placable] (15th century)
: not placable **:** not capable of being appeased, significantly changed, or mitigated ⟨an *implacable* enemy⟩
— **im·pla·ca·bil·i·ty** \-ˌpla-kə-'bi-lə-tē, -ˌplā-\ *noun*
— **im·pla·ca·bly** \-'pla-kə-blē, -'plā-\ *adverb*

¹im·plant \im-'plant\ *transitive verb* (15th century)
1 a : to fix or set securely or deeply ⟨a ruby *implanted* in the idol's forehead⟩ **b :** to set permanently in the consciousness or habit patterns **:** INCULCATE
2 : to insert in a living site (as for growth, slow release, or formation of an organic union) ⟨subcutaneously *implanted* hormone pellets⟩ ☆
— **im·plant·able** \-'plan-tə-bəl\ *adjective*
— **im·plant·er** \-'plan-tər\ *noun*

²im·plant \'im-ˌplant\ *noun* (1890)
: something (as a graft or pellet) implanted in tissue

im·plan·ta·tion \ˌim-ˌplan-'tā-shən\ *noun* (1578)
1 a : the act or process of implanting something **b :** the state resulting from being implanted
2 *in placental mammals* **:** the process of attachment of the embryo to the maternal uterine wall

im·plau·si·ble \(ˌ)im-'plȯ-zə-bəl\ *adjective* (circa 1677)
: not plausible **:** provoking disbelief
— **im·plau·si·bil·i·ty** \-ˌplȯ-zə-'bi-lə-tē\ *noun*
— **im·plau·si·bly** \-'plȯ-zə-blē\ *adverb*

im·plead \im-'plēd\ *transitive verb* [Middle English *empleden*, from Middle French *emplaider*, from Old French *emplaidier*, from *en- + plaidier* to plead] (14th century)
: to sue or prosecute at law

¹im·ple·ment \'im-plə-mənt\ *noun* [Middle English, from Late Latin *implementum* action of filling up, from Latin *implēre* to fill up, from *in- + plēre* to fill — more at FULL] (15th century)
1 : an article serving to equip ⟨the *implements* of religious worship⟩
2 : a device used in the performance of a task
3 : one that serves as an instrument or tool ⟨the partnership agreement does not seem to be a very potent *implement* —H. B. Hoffman⟩ ☆

²im·ple·ment \-ˌment\ *transitive verb* (1806)
1 : CARRY OUT, ACCOMPLISH; *especially* **:** to give practical effect to and ensure of actual fulfillment by concrete measures
2 : to provide instruments or means of expression for

im·ple·men·ta·tion \ˌim-plə-mən-'tā-shən, -ˌmen-\ *noun*
— **im·ple·men·ter** *or* **im·ple·men·tor** \'im-plə-ˌmən-tər\ *noun*

im·pli·cate \'im-plə-ˌkāt\ *transitive verb* **-cat·ed; -cat·ing** [Middle English, to convey by implication, from Medieval Latin *implicatus*, past participle of *implicare*, from Latin, to entwine, involve — more at EMPLOY] (15th century)
1 : to involve as a consequence, corollary, or natural inference **:** IMPLY
2 *archaic* **:** to fold or twist together **:** ENTWINE
3 a : to bring into intimate or incriminating connection **b :** to involve in the nature or operation of something

im·pli·ca·tion \ˌim-plə-'kā-shən\ *noun* (15th century)
1 a : the act of implicating **:** the state of being implicated **b :** close connection; *especially* **:** an incriminating involvement

☆ **SYNONYMS**
Impertinent, officious, meddlesome, intrusive, obtrusive mean given to thrusting oneself into the affairs of others. IMPERTINENT implies exceeding the bounds of propriety in showing interest or curiosity or in offering advice ⟨resented their *impertinent* interference⟩. OFFICIOUS implies the offering of services or attentions that are unwelcome or annoying ⟨*officious* friends made the job harder⟩. MEDDLESOME stresses an annoying and usually prying interference in others' affairs ⟨a *meddlesome* landlord⟩. INTRUSIVE implies a tactless or otherwise objectionable thrusting into others' affairs ⟨tried to be helpful without being *intrusive*⟩. OBTRUSIVE stresses improper or offensive conspicuousness of interfering actions ⟨expressed an *obtrusive* concern for his safety⟩.

Implant, inculcate, instill, inseminate, infix mean to introduce into the mind. IMPLANT implies teaching that makes for permanence of what is taught ⟨*implanted* a love of reading in her students⟩. INCULCATE implies persistent or repeated efforts to impress on the mind ⟨tried to *inculcate* in him high moral standards⟩. INSTILL stresses gradual, gentle imparting of knowledge over a long period of time ⟨*instill* traditional values in your children⟩. INSEMINATE applies to a sowing of ideas in many minds so that they spread through a class or nation ⟨*inseminated* an unquestioning faith in technology⟩. INFIX stresses firmly inculcating a habit of thought ⟨*infixed* a chronic cynicism⟩.

Implement, tool, instrument, appliance, utensil mean a relatively simple device for performing work. IMPLEMENT may apply to anything necessary to perform a task ⟨crude stone *implements*⟩ ⟨farm *implements*⟩. TOOL suggests an implement adapted to facilitate a definite kind or stage of work and suggests the need of skill more strongly than IMPLEMENT ⟨a carpenter's *tools*⟩. INSTRUMENT suggests a device capable of delicate or precise work ⟨the dentist's *instruments*⟩. APPLIANCE refers to a tool or instrument utilizing a power source and suggests portability or temporary attachment ⟨household *appliances*⟩. UTENSIL applies to a device used in domestic work or some routine unskilled activity ⟨kitchen *utensils*⟩.

\ə\ **abut** \ᵊ\ **kitten** \ər\ **further** \a\ **ash** \ā\ **ace**
\ä\ **mop, mar** \au̇\ **out** \ch\ **chin** \e\ **bet** \ē\ **easy**
\g\ **go** \i\ **hit** \ī\ **ice** \j\ **job** \ŋ\ **sing** \ō\ **go**
\ȯ\ **law** \ȯi\ **boy** \th\ **thin** \th̲\ **the** \ü\ **loot** \u̇\ **foot**
\y\ **yet** \zh\ **vision** *see also* Guide to Pronunciation

2 a : the act of implying **:** the state of being implied **b** (1) **:** a logical relation between two propositions that fails to hold only if the first is true and the second is false (2) **:** a logical relationship between two propositions in which if the first is true the second is true (3) **:** a statement exhibiting a relation of implication **3 :** something implied: as **a :** SUGGESTION **b :** a possible significance ⟨the book has political *implications*⟩ — **im·pli·ca·tive** \'im-plə-ˌkā-tiv, im-'pli-kə-\ *adjective* — **im·pli·ca·tive·ly** *adverb* — **im·pli·ca·tive·ness** *noun*

im·plic·it \im-'pli-sət\ *adjective* [Latin *implicitus*, past participle of *implicare*] (1599) **1 a :** capable of being understood from something else though unexpressed **:** IMPLIED ⟨an *implicit* assumption⟩ **b :** involved in the nature or essence of something though not revealed, expressed, or developed **:** POTENTIAL ⟨a sculptor may see different figures *implicit* in a block of stone —John Dewey⟩ **c** *of a mathematical function* **:** defined by an expression in which the dependent variable and the one or more independent variables are not separated on opposite sides of an equation — compare EXPLICIT 4 **2 :** being without doubt or reserve **:** UNQUESTIONING — **im·plic·it·ly** *adverb* — **im·plic·it·ness** *noun*

implicit differentiation *noun* (circa 1889) **:** the process of finding the derivative of a dependent variable in an implicit function by differentiating each term separately, by expressing the derivative of the dependent variable as a symbol, and by solving the resulting expression for the symbol

im·plode \im-'plōd\ *verb* **im·plod·ed; im·plod·ing** [²*in-* + *-plode* (as in *explode*)] (1881) *intransitive verb* **1 a :** to burst inward ⟨a blow causing a vacuum tube to *implode*⟩ **b :** to undergo violent compression ⟨massive stars which *implode*⟩ **2 :** to collapse inward as if from external pressure; *also* **:** to become greatly reduced as if from collapsing *transitive verb* **:** to cause to implode

im·plore \im-'plōr, -'plȯr\ *transitive verb* **im·plored; im·plor·ing** [Middle French or Latin; Middle French *implorer*, from Latin *implorare*, from *in-* + *plorare* to cry out] (circa 1540) **1 :** to call upon in supplication **:** BESEECH **2 :** to call or pray for earnestly **:** ENTREAT *synonym* see BEG — **im·plor·ing·ly** *adverb*

im·plo·sion \im-'plō-zhən\ *noun* [²*in-* + *-plosion* (as in *explosion*)] (1877) **1 :** the inrush of air in forming a suction stop **2 :** the action of imploding **3 :** the act or action of bringing to or as if to a center; *also* **:** INTEGRATION ⟨this *implosion* of cultures makes realistic for the first time the age-old vision of a world culture —Kenneth Keniston⟩ — **im·plo·sive** \-'plō-siv, -ziv\ *adjective or noun*

im·ply \im-'plī\ *transitive verb* **im·plied; im·ply·ing** [Middle English *emplien*, from Middle French *emplier*, from Latin *implicare*] (14th century) **1** *obsolete* **:** ENFOLD, ENTWINE **2 :** to involve or indicate by inference, association, or necessary consequence rather than by direct statement ⟨rights *imply* obligations⟩ **3 :** to contain potentially **4 :** to express indirectly ⟨his silence *implied* consent⟩ *synonym* see SUGGEST *usage* see INFER

im·po·lite \ˌim-pə-'līt\ *adjective* [Latin *impolitus*, from *in-* + *politus* polite] (1739)

: not polite **:** RUDE — **im·po·lite·ly** *adverb* — **im·po·lite·ness** *noun*

im·pol·i·tic \(ˌ)im-'pä-lə-ˌtik\ *adjective* (circa 1600) **:** not politic **:** RASH — **im·po·lit·i·cal** \-pə-'li-ti-kəl\ *adjective* — **im·po·lit·i·cal·ly** \-'li-ti-k(ə-)lē\ *adverb* — **im·po·lit·ic·ly** \-'pä-lə-ˌti-klē\ *adverb*

im·pon·der·a·ble \(ˌ)im-'pän-d(ə-)rə-bəl\ *adjective* [Medieval Latin *imponderabilis*, from Latin *in-* + Late Latin *ponderabilis* ponderable] (1794) **:** not ponderable **:** incapable of being weighed or evaluated with exactness — **im·pon·der·a·bil·i·ty** \-ˌpän-d(ə-)rə-'bi-lə-tē\ *noun* — **imponderable** *noun* — **im·pon·der·a·bly** \-'pän-d(ə-)rə-blē\ *adverb*

im·pone \im-'pōn\ *transitive verb* **im·poned; im·pon·ing** [Latin *imponere* to put upon, from *in-* + *ponere* to put — more at POSITION] (circa 1623) *obsolete* **:** WAGER, BET

¹im·port \im-'pōrt, -'pȯrt, 'im-ˌ\ *verb* [Middle English *importen*, from Latin *importare* to bring into, from *in-* + *portare* to carry — more at FARE] (15th century) *transitive verb* **1 a :** to bear or convey as meaning or portent **:** SIGNIFY **b** *archaic* **:** EXPRESS, STATE **c :** IMPLY **2 :** to bring from a foreign or external source; *especially* **:** to bring (as merchandise) into a place or country from another country **3** *archaic* **:** to be of importance to **:** CONCERN *intransitive verb* **:** to be of consequence **:** MATTER — **im·port·able** \im-'pōr-tə-bəl, -'pȯr-, 'im-ˌ\ *adjective* — **im·port·er** *noun*

²im·port \'im-ˌpōrt, -ˌpȯrt\ *noun* (circa 1568) **1 :** IMPORTANCE; *especially* **:** relative importance ⟨it is hard to determine the *import* of this decision⟩ **2 :** PURPORT, SIGNIFICATION **3 :** something that is imported **4 :** IMPORTATION

im·por·tance \im-'pȯr-tᵊn(t)s, *especially Southern & New England* -tᵊn(t)s, -dᵊn(t)s\ *noun* (1508) **1 a :** the quality or state of being important **:** CONSEQUENCE **b :** an important aspect or bearing **:** SIGNIFICANCE **2** *obsolete* **:** IMPORT, MEANING **3** *obsolete* **:** IMPORTUNITY **4** *obsolete* **:** a weighty matter ☆

im·por·tan·cy \-tᵊn(t)-sē, -tᵊn(t)-, -dᵊn(t)-\ *noun* (1540) *archaic* **:** IMPORTANCE

im·por·tant \im-'pȯr-tᵊnt, *especially Southern & New England* -tᵊnt, -dᵊnt\ *adjective* [Middle English *importante*, from Medieval Latin *important-, importans*, present participle of *importare* to signify, from Latin, to bring into] (15th century) **1 :** marked by or indicative of significant worth or consequence **:** valuable in content or relationship **2** *obsolete* **:** IMPORTUNATE, URGENT **3 :** giving evidence of a feeling of self-importance *usage* see IMPORTANTLY

im·por·tant·ly \-lē\ *adverb* (1647) **1 :** in an important way ⟨contributed *importantly* to the language of the field —Ernst Mayr⟩ ⟨cleared his throat *importantly* and waited —E. K. Gann⟩ ⟨the real story is *importantly* different —Alexander Woollcott⟩ **2 :** it is important that ⟨more *importantly* he stands a chance of having his publication barred —H. L. Mencken⟩ ☐

im·por·ta·tion \ˌim-ˌpōr-'tā-shən, -ˌpȯr-, -pər-\ *noun* (1601) **1 :** the act or practice of importing **2 :** something imported

imported cabbageworm *noun* (1892) **:** a small cosmopolitan white butterfly (*Pieris rapae*) or its larva which is a pest of cruciferous plants and especially cabbage

imported fire ant *noun* (circa 1949) **:** either of two mound-building South American fire ants (*Solenopsis richteri* and *S. invicta*) introduced into the southeastern U.S. that are agricultural pests and can produce stings requiring medical attention

im·por·tu·nate \im-'pȯr-chə-nət, -tyú-nət\ *adjective* (1529) **1 :** troublesomely urgent **:** overly persistent in request or demand **2 :** TROUBLESOME — **im·por·tu·nate·ly** *adverb* — **im·por·tu·nate·ness** *noun*

¹im·por·tune \ˌim-pər-'tün, -'tyün; im-'pȯr-ˌ, -chən\ *adjective* [Middle English, from Middle French & Latin; Middle French *importun*, from Latin *importunus*, from *in-* + *-portunus* (as in *opportunus* fit) — more at OPPORTUNE] (15th century) **:** IMPORTUNATE — **im·por·tune·ly** *adverb*

²importune *verb* **-tuned; -tun·ing** (1530) *transitive verb* **1 a :** to press or urge with troublesome persistence **b** *archaic* **:** to request or beg for urgently **2 :** ANNOY, TROUBLE *intransitive verb* **:** to beg, urge, or solicit persistently or troublesomely *synonym* see BEG — **im·por·tun·er** *noun*

im·por·tu·ni·ty \ˌim-pər-'tü-nə-tē, -'tyü-\ *noun, plural* **-ties** (15th century) **1 :** the quality or state of being importunate **2 :** an importunate request or demand

☆ SYNONYMS
Importance, consequence, moment, weight, significance mean a quality or aspect having great worth or significance. IMPORTANCE implies a value judgment of the superior worth or influence of something or someone ⟨a region with no cities of *importance*⟩. CONSEQUENCE generally implies importance because of probable or possible effects ⟨the style you choose is of little *consequence*⟩. MOMENT implies conspicuous or self-evident consequence ⟨a decision of great *moment*⟩. WEIGHT implies a judgment of the immediate relative importance of something ⟨the argument carried no *weight* with the judge⟩. SIGNIFICANCE implies a quality or character that should mark a thing as important but that is not self-evident and may or may not be recognized ⟨the treaty's *significance*⟩.

☐ USAGE
importantly A number of commentators have objected to *importantly* as a sentence modifier (sense 2) and have recommended *important* instead. Actually both the adverb and the adjective are in reputable standard use in this function. *Important* is always used with *more* or *most* ⟨had bronze weapons and composite bows; more *important*, they utilized the horse and war chariot —Harry A. Gailey, Jr.⟩ ⟨second and most *important*, the book contains no important woman character —F. Scott Fitzgerald⟩. *Importantly* is somewhat more flexible in not requiring *more* or *most* ⟨sticks and, just as *importantly*, unsticks easily —Phoebe Hawkins⟩ ⟨*importantly*, the leaven in the mixture is quality —George O'Brien⟩.

im·pose \im-'pōz\ *verb* **im·posed; im·pos·ing** [Middle French *imposer,* from Latin *imponere,* literally, to put upon (perfect indicative *imposui*), from *in-* + *ponere* to put — more at POSITION] (1581)
transitive verb
1 a : to establish or apply by authority 〈*impose* a tax〉 〈*impose* new restrictions〉 〈*impose* penalties〉 **b :** to establish or bring about as if by force 〈those limits *imposed* by our own inadequacies —C. H. Plimpton〉
2 a : PLACE, SET **b :** to arrange (as pages) in the proper order for printing
3 : PASS OFF 〈*impose* fake antiques on the public〉
4 : to force into the company or on the attention of another 〈*impose* oneself on others〉
intransitive verb
: to take unwarranted advantage of something 〈*imposed* on his good nature〉
— **im·pos·er** *noun*
im·pos·ing \im-'pō-ziŋ\ *adjective* (1786)
: impressive in size, bearing, dignity, or grandeur
synonym see GRAND
— **im·pos·ing·ly** \-ziŋ-lē\ *adverb*
im·po·si·tion \ˌim-pə-'zi-shən\ *noun* (14th century)
1 : something imposed: as **a :** LEVY, TAX **b :** an excessive or uncalled-for requirement or burden
2 : the act of imposing
3 : DECEPTION
4 : the order of arrangement of imposed pages
im·pos·si·bil·i·ty \(ˌ)im-ˌpä-sə-'bi-lə-tē\ *noun* (14th century)
1 : the quality or state of being impossible
2 : something impossible
im·pos·si·ble \(ˌ)im-'pä-sə-bəl\ *adjective* [Middle English, from Middle French & Latin; Middle French, from Latin *impossibilis,* from *in-* + *possibilis* possible] (14th century)
1 a : incapable of being or of occurring **b :** felt to be incapable of being done, attained, or fulfilled **:** insuperably difficult
2 a : extremely undesirable **:** UNACCEPTABLE **b :** extremely awkward or difficult to deal with
— **im·pos·si·ble·ness** *noun*
im·pos·si·bly \-blē\ *adverb* (circa 1580)
1 : not possibly
2 : to an improbable degree **:** UNBELIEVABLY 〈an *impossibly* green lawn〉
¹im·post \'im-ˌpōst\ *noun* [Middle French, from Medieval Latin *impositum,* from Latin, neuter of *impositus,* past participle of *imponere*] (1568)
: something imposed or levied **:** TAX
²impost *noun* [French *imposte,* ultimately from Latin *impositus*] (1664)
: a block, capital, or molding from which an arch springs — see ARCH illustration
im·pos·tor *or* **im·pos·ter** \im-'päs-tər\ *noun* [Late Latin *impostor,* from Latin *imponere*] (1624)
: one that assumes false identity or title for the purpose of deception
im·pos·tume \im-'päs-ˌchüm\ *or* **im·pos·thume** \-ˌthüm, -ˌthyüm\ *noun* [Middle English *empostume,* ultimately from Greek *apostēma,* from *aphistanai* to remove, from *apo-* + *histanai* to cause to stand — more at STAND] (14th century)
archaic **:** ABSCESS
im·pos·ture \im-'päs-chər\ *noun* [Late Latin *impostura,* from Latin *impositus, impostus,* past participle of *imponere*] (1537)
1 : the act or practice of deceiving by means of an assumed character or name
2 : an instance of imposture ☆
im·po·tence \'im-pə-tən(t)s\ *noun* (15th century)
: the quality or state of being impotent
im·po·ten·cy \-tən(t)-sē\ *noun* (15th century)
: IMPOTENCE
im·po·tent \'im-pə-tənt\ *adjective* [Middle English, from Middle French & Latin; Middle

French, from Latin *impotent-, impotens,* from *in-* + *potent-, potens* potent] (14th century)
1 a : not potent **:** lacking in power, strength, or vigor **:** HELPLESS **b :** unable to copulate; *broadly* **:** STERILE — usually used of males
2 *obsolete* **:** incapable of self-restraint **:** UNGOVERNABLE
— **impotent** *noun*
— **im·po·tent·ly** *adverb*
im·pound \im-'paünd\ *transitive verb* (15th century)
1 a : to shut up in or as if in a pound **:** CONFINE
b : to seize and hold in the custody of the law
c : to take possession of 〈she was dismissed and her manuscript *impounded* —Jonathan Weiner〉
2 : to collect and confine (water) in or as if in a reservoir
im·pound·ment \-'paün(d)-mənt\ *noun* (circa 1665)
1 : the act of impounding **:** the state of being impounded
2 : a body of water formed by impounding
im·pov·er·ish \im-'päv-rish, -'pä-və-\ *transitive verb* [Middle English *enpoverisen,* from Middle French *empovriss-,* stem of *empovrir,* from *en-* + *povre* poor — more at POOR] (15th century)
1 : to make poor
2 : to deprive of strength, richness, or fertility by depleting or draining of something essential
synonym see DEPLETE
— **im·pov·er·ish·er** *noun*
— **im·pov·er·ish·ment** \-mənt\ *noun*
impoverished *adjective* (1950)
of a fauna or flora **:** represented by few species or individuals
im·prac·ti·ca·ble \(ˌ)im-'prak-ti-kə-bəl\ *adjective* (1653)
1 : IMPASSABLE 〈an *impracticable* road〉
2 : not practicable **:** incapable of being performed or accomplished by the means employed or at command
— **im·prac·ti·ca·bil·i·ty** \-ˌprak-ti-kə-'bi-lə-tē\ *noun*
— **im·prac·ti·ca·bly** \-'prak-ti-kə-blē\ *adverb*
im·prac·ti·cal \(ˌ)im-'prak-ti-kəl\ *adjective* (1865)
: not practical: as **a :** not wise to put into or keep in practice or effect **b :** incapable of dealing sensibly or prudently with practical matters **c :** IMPRACTICABLE **d :** IDEALISTIC
— **im·prac·ti·cal·i·ty** \-ˌprak-ti-'ka-lə-tē\ *noun*
— **im·prac·ti·cal·ly** \-'prak-ti-k(ə-)lē\ *adverb*
im·pre·cate \'im-pri-ˌkāt\ *verb* **-cat·ed; -cat·ing** [Latin *imprecatus,* past participle of *imprecari,* from *in-* + *precari* to pray — more at PRAY] (1613)
transitive verb
: to invoke evil on **:** CURSE
intransitive verb
: to utter curses
im·pre·ca·tion \ˌim-pri-'kā-shən\ *noun* (15th century)
1 : CURSE
2 : the act of imprecating
— **im·pre·ca·to·ry** \'im-pri-kə-ˌtōr-ē, im-'pre-kə-, -ˌtòr-\ *adjective*
im·pre·cise \ˌim-pri-'sīs\ *adjective* (1805)
: not precise **:** INEXACT, VAGUE
— **im·pre·cise·ly** *adverb*
— **im·pre·cise·ness** *noun*
— **im·pre·ci·sion** \-'si-zhən\ *noun*
im·preg·na·ble \im-'preg-nə-bəl\ *adjective* [Middle English *imprenable,* from Middle French, from *in-* + *prenable* vulnerable to capture, from *prendre* to take — more at PRIZE] (15th century)
1 : incapable of being taken by assault **:** UNCONQUERABLE
2 : UNASSAILABLE; *also* **:** IMPENETRABLE

— **im·preg·na·bil·i·ty** \(ˌ)im-ˌpreg-nə-'bi-lə-tē\ *noun*
— **im·preg·na·ble·ness** \im-'preg-nə-bəl-nəs\ *noun*
— **im·preg·na·bly** \-blē\ *adverb*
im·preg·nant \im-'preg-nənt\ *noun* (1926)
: a substance used for impregnating another substance
¹im·preg·nate \im-'preg-ˌnāt, 'im-ˌ\ *transitive verb* **-nat·ed; -nat·ing** [Late Latin *impraegnatus,* past participle of *impraegnare,* from Latin *in-* + *praegnas* pregnant] (1605)
1 a : to cause to be filled, imbued, permeated, or saturated **b :** to permeate thoroughly
2 : to make pregnant **:** FERTILIZE
synonym see SOAK
— **im·preg·na·tion** \(ˌ)im-ˌpreg-'nā-shən\ *noun*
— **im·preg·na·tor** \im-'preg-ˌnā-tər, 'im-ˌ\ *noun*
²im·preg·nate \im-'preg-nət\ *adjective* (1646)
: being filled or saturated
im·pre·sa \im-'prā-zə, -sə\ *noun* [Italian, literally, undertaking] (1588)
: a device with a motto used in the 16th and 17th centuries; *broadly* **:** EMBLEM
im·pre·sa·rio \ˌim-prə-'sär-ē-ˌō, -'sar-, -'zär-\ *noun, plural* **-ri·os** [Italian, from *impresa* undertaking, from *imprendere* to undertake, from (assumed) Vulgar Latin *imprehendere* — more at EMPRISE] (1746)
1 : the promoter, manager, or conductor of an opera or concert company
2 : a person who puts on or sponsors an entertainment (as a television show or sports event)
3 : MANAGER, DIRECTOR
¹im·press \im-'pres\ *verb* [Middle English, from Latin *impressus,* past participle of *imprimere,* from *in-* + *premere* to press — more at PRESS] (14th century)
transitive verb
1 a : to apply with pressure so as to imprint **b :** to produce (as a mark) by pressure **c :** to mark by or as if by pressure or stamping
2 a : to produce a vivid impression of **b :** to affect especially forcibly or deeply **:** INFLUENCE
3 : TRANSFER, TRANSMIT
intransitive verb
: to produce an impression
synonym see AFFECT
— **im·press·ibil·i·ty** \-ˌpre-sə-'bi-lə-tē\ *noun*
— **im·press·ible** \-'pre-sə-bəl\ *adjective*
²im·press \'im-ˌpres *also* im-'\ *noun* (1590)

\ə\ **abut** \ᵊ\ **kitten** \ər\ **further** \a\ **ash** \ā\ **ace** \ä\ **mop, mar** \aü\ **out** \ch\ **chin** \e\ **bet** \ē\ **easy** \g\ **go** \i\ **hit** \ī\ **ice** \j\ **job** \ŋ\ **sing** \ō\ **go** \ò\ **law** \òi\ **boy** \th\ **thin** \t͟h\ **the** \ü\ **loot** \u̇\ **foot** \y\ **yet** \zh\ **vision** *see also* Guide to Pronunciation

1 : a characteristic or distinctive mark **:** STAMP ⟨the *impress* of a fresh and vital intelligence is stamped . . . in his work —Lytton Strachey⟩ **2 :** IMPRESSION, EFFECT ⟨have an *impress* on history⟩ **3 :** the act of impressing **4 a :** a mark made by pressure **:** IMPRINT **b :** an image of something formed by or as if by pressure; *especially* **:** SEAL **c :** a product of pressure or influence

³**im·press** \im-'pres\ *transitive verb* [²*in-* + ³*press*] (1596) **1 :** to levy or take by force for public service; *especially* **:** to force into naval service **2 a :** to procure or enlist by forcible persuasion **b :** FORCE ⟨*impressed* him into a white coat for the Christmas festivities —Nancy Hale⟩

⁴**im·press** \'im-ˌpres *also* im-'\ *noun* (1602) **:** IMPRESSMENT

im·pres·sion \im-'pre-shən\ *noun* (14th century) **1 a :** a characteristic, trait, or feature resulting from some influence ⟨the *impression* on behavior produced by the social milieu⟩ **b :** an effect of alteration or improvement ⟨the settlement left little *impression* on the wilderness⟩ **c :** a telling image impressed on the senses or the mind **2 :** the effect produced by impressing: as **a :** a stamp, form, or figure resulting from physical contact **b :** an imprint of the teeth and adjacent portions of the jaw for use in dentistry **c :** an especially marked and often favorable influence or effect on feeling, sense, or mind **3 :** the act of impressing: as **a :** an affecting by stamping or pressing **b :** a communicating of a mold, trait, or character by an external force or influence **4 a :** the amount of pressure with which an inked printing surface deposits its ink on the paper **b :** one instance of the meeting of a printing surface and the material being printed; *also* **:** a single print or copy so made **c :** all the copies (as of a book) printed in one continuous operation from a single makeready **5 :** an often indistinct or imprecise notion or remembrance **6 a :** the first coat of color in painting **b :** a coat of paint for ornament or preservation **7 :** an imitation or representation of salient features in an artistic or theatrical medium; *especially* **:** an imitation in caricature of a noted personality as a form of theatrical entertainment

synonym see IDEA

im·pres·sion·able \im-'pre-sh(ə-)nə-bəl\ *adjective* (1836) **:** capable of being easily impressed
— **im·pres·sion·abil·i·ty** \-ˌpre-sh(ə-)nə-'bi-lə-tē\ *noun*

im·pres·sion·ism \im-'pre-shə-ˌni-zəm\ *noun* (1882) **1** *often capitalized* **:** a theory or practice in painting especially among French painters of about 1870 of depicting the natural appearances of objects by means of dabs or strokes of primary unmixed colors in order to simulate actual reflected light **2 a :** the depiction (as in literature) of scene, emotion, or character by details intended to achieve a vividness or effectiveness more by evoking subjective and sensory impressions than by recreating an objective reality **b :** a style of musical composition designed to create subtle moods and impressions

im·pres·sion·ist \im-'pre-sh(ə-)nist\ *noun* (1876) **1** *often capitalized* **:** one (as a painter) who practices or adheres to the theories of impressionism **2 :** an entertainer who does impressions

im·pres·sion·is·tic \(ˌ)im-ˌpre-shə-'nis-tik\ *adjective* (1886)

1 *or* **im·pres·sion·ist** \im-'pre-sh(ə-)nist\ *often capitalized* **:** of, relating to, or constituting impressionism **2 :** based on or involving impression as distinct from expertise or fact ⟨intuitions and *impressionistic* anecdotal accounts —Sidney Hook⟩
— **im·pres·sion·is·ti·cal·ly** \(ˌ)im-ˌpre-shə-'nis-ti-k(ə-)lē\ *adverb*

im·pres·sive \im-'pre-siv\ *adjective* (1598) **:** making or tending to make a marked impression **:** having the power to excite attention, awe, or admiration
synonym see MOVING
— **im·pres·sive·ly** *adverb*
— **im·pres·sive·ness** *noun*

im·press·ment \im-'pres-mənt\ *noun* (1787) **:** the act of seizing for public use or of impressing into public service

im·pres·sure \im-'pre-shər\ *noun* (1600) *archaic* **:** a mark made by pressure **:** IMPRESSION

im·prest \'im-ˌprest\ *noun* [obsolete *imprest* to lend, probably from Italian *imprestare*] (1568) **:** a loan or advance of money

im·pri·ma·tur \ˌim-prə-'mä-ˌtu̇r, im-'pri-mə-ˌtu̇r, -ˌtyu̇r\ *noun* [New Latin, let it be printed, from *imprimere* to print, from Latin, to imprint, impress — more at IMPRESS] (1640) **1 a :** a license to print or publish especially by Roman Catholic episcopal authority **b :** approval of a publication under circumstances of official censorship **2 a :** SANCTION, APPROVAL **b :** IMPRINT **c :** a mark of approval or distinction

im·pri·mis \im-'prī-məs, -'prē-\ *adverb* [Middle English *imprimis*, from Latin *in primis* among the first (things)] (15th century) **:** in the first place — used to introduce a list of items or considerations

¹**im·print** \im-'print, 'im-ˌ\ (14th century) *transitive verb* **1 :** to mark by or as if by pressure **:** IMPRESS **2 a :** to fix indelibly or permanently (as on the memory) **b :** to subject to or induce by imprinting ⟨an *imprinted* preference⟩ *intransitive verb* **:** to undergo imprinting
— **im·print·er** \-'prin-tər, -ˌprin-\ *noun*

²**im·print** \'im-ˌprint\ *noun* [Middle English *enpreent*, from Middle French *empreinte*, from feminine of *empreint*, past participle of *empreindre* to imprint, from Latin *imprimere*] (15th century) **:** something imprinted or printed: as **a :** a mark or depression made by pressure ⟨the fossil *imprint* of a dinosaur's foot⟩ **b :** an identifying name (as of a publisher) placed conspicuously on a product; *also* **:** the name under which a publisher issues books **c :** an indelible distinguishing effect or influence

im·print·ing \'im-ˌprin-tiŋ, im-'\ *noun* (1937) **:** a rapid learning process that takes place early in the life of a social animal (as a greylag goose) and establishes a behavior pattern (as recognition of and attraction to its own kind or a substitute)

im·pris·on \im-'pri-zᵊn\ *transitive verb* [Middle English, from Old French *emprisoner*, from *en-* + *prison* prison] (14th century) **:** to put in or as if in prison **:** CONFINE
— **im·pris·on·ment** \-mənt\ *noun*

im·prob·a·ble \(ˌ)im-'prä-bə-bəl, -'präb-bəl\ *adjective* [Middle French or Latin; Middle French, from Latin *improbabilis*, from *in-* + *probabilis* probable] (1598) **:** unlikely to be true or to occur; *also* **:** unlikely but real or true
— **im·prob·a·bil·i·ty** \-ˌprä-bə-'bi-lə-tē\ *noun*
— **im·prob·a·bly** \-'prä-bə-blē, -'präb-blē\ *adverb*

¹**im·promp·tu** \im-'präm(p)-ˌtü, -(ˌ)tyü\ *noun* [French, from *impromptu* extemporaneously, from Latin *in promptu* in readiness] (1683)

1 : something that is impromptu **2 :** a musical composition suggesting improvisation

²**impromptu** *adjective* (1764) **1 :** made, done, or formed on or as if on the spur of the moment **:** IMPROVISED **2 :** composed or uttered without previous preparation **:** EXTEMPORANEOUS
— **impromptu** *adverb*

im·prop·er \(ˌ)im-'prä-pər\ *adjective* [Middle English, from Middle French *impropre*, from Latin *improprius*, from *in-* + *proprius* proper] (15th century) **:** not proper: as **a :** not in accord with fact, truth, or right procedure **:** INCORRECT ⟨*improper* inference⟩ **b :** not regularly or normally formed or not properly so called **c :** not suited to the circumstances, design, or end ⟨*improper* medicine⟩ **d :** not in accord with propriety, modesty, good manners, or good taste
synonym see INDECOROUS
— **im·prop·er·ly** *adverb*
— **im·prop·er·ness** *noun*

improper fraction *noun* (1542) **:** a fraction whose numerator is equal to, larger than, or of equal or higher degree than the denominator

improper integral *noun* (circa 1942) **:** a definite integral whose region of integration is unbounded or includes a point at which the integrand is undefined or tends to infinity

im·pro·pri·e·ty \ˌim-p(r)ə-'prī-ə-tē\ *noun*, *plural* **-ties** [French or Late Latin; French *impropriété*, from Late Latin *improprietat-*, *improprietas*, from Latin *improprius*] (1607) **1 :** an improper or indecorous act or remark; *especially* **:** an unacceptable use of a word or of language **2 :** the quality or state of being improper

im·prove \im-'prüv\ *verb* **im·proved;** **im·prov·ing** [Anglo-French *emprouer* to invest profitably, from Old French *en-* + *prou* advantage, from Late Latin *prode* — more at PROUD] (circa 1529) *transitive verb* **1** *archaic* **:** EMPLOY, USE **2 a :** to enhance in value or quality **:** make better **b :** to increase the value of (land or property) by making it more useful for humans (as by cultivation or the erection of buildings) **c :** to grade and drain (a road) and apply surfacing material other than pavement **3 :** to use to good purpose *intransitive verb* **1 :** to advance or make progress in what is desirable **2 :** to make useful additions or amendments ☆
— **im·prov·abil·i·ty** \(ˌ)im-ˌprü-və-'bi-lə-tē\ *noun*
— **im·prov·able** \-'prü-və-bəl\ *adjective*
— **im·prov·er** *noun*

im·prove·ment \im-'prüv-mənt\ *noun* (circa 1550) **1 :** the act or process of improving **2 a :** the state of being improved; *especially* **:** enhanced value or excellence **b :** an instance of such improvement **:** something that enhances value or excellence

im·prov·i·dence \(,)im-'prä-və-dən(t)s, -,dén(t)s\ *noun* (15th century)
: the quality or state of being improvident

im·prov·i·dent \-dənt, -,dent\ *adjective* [Late Latin *improvident-, improvidens,* from Latin *in-* + *provident-, providens* provident] (1624)
: not provident : not foreseeing and providing for the future
— **im·prov·i·dent·ly** *adverb*

im·pro·vi·sa·tion \(,)im-,prä-və-'zā-shən, ,im-prə-və- *also* ,im-prə-(,)vī-\ *noun* (1786)
1 : the act or art of improvising
2 : something (as a musical or dramatic composition) improvised
— **im·pro·vi·sa·tion·al** \-shnəl, -shə-n°l\ *adjective*
— **im·pro·vi·sa·tion·al·ly** *adverb*

im·prov·i·sa·tor \im-'prä-və-,zā-tər\ *noun* (1795)
: one that improvises
— **im·prov·i·sa·to·ri·al** \(,)im-,prä-və-zə-'tōr-ē-əl, -'tor-\ *adjective*
— **im·prov·i·sa·to·ry** \im-'prä-və-zə-,tōr-ē, ,im-prə-'vī-zə-, -,tor-\ *adjective*

im·pro·vi·sa·to·re \(,)im-,prä-və-zə-'tōr-ē, ,im-prə-,vē-zə-, -'tor-\ *noun, plural* **-to·ri** \-'tōr-ē, -'tor-\ *or* **-tores** [Italian *improvvisatore,* from *improvvisare*] (1765)
: one that improvises (as verse) usually extemporaneously

im·pro·vise \'im-prə-,vīz *also* ,im-prə-'\ *verb* **-vised; -vis·ing** [French *improviser,* from Italian *improvvisare,* from *improvviso* sudden, from Latin *improvisus,* literally, unforeseen, from *in-* + *provisus,* past participle of *providēre* to see ahead — more at PROVIDE] (1826)
transitive verb
1 : to compose, recite, play, or sing extemporaneously
2 : to make, invent, or arrange offhand
3 : to fabricate out of what is conveniently on hand
intransitive verb
: to improvise something
— **im·pro·vis·er** *or* **im·pro·vi·sor** \-,vī-zər, -'vī-\ *noun*

im·pru·dence \(,)im-'prü-d°n(t)s\ *noun* (15th century)
1 : the quality or state of being imprudent
2 : an imprudent act

im·pru·dent \-d°nt\ *adjective* [Middle English, from Latin *imprudent-, imprudens,* from *in-* + *prudent-, prudens* prudent] (14th century)
: not prudent : lacking discretion
— **im·pru·dent·ly** *adverb*

im·pu·dence \'im-pyə-dən(t)s\ *noun* (14th century)
: the quality or state of being impudent

im·pu·dent \-dənt\ *adjective* [Middle English, from Latin *impudent-, impudens,* from *in-* + *pudent-, pudens,* present participle of *pudēre* to feel shame] (14th century)
1 *obsolete* : lacking modesty
2 : marked by contemptuous or cocky boldness or disregard of others : INSOLENT
— **im·pu·dent·ly** *adverb*

im·pu·dic·i·ty \,im-pyù-'di-sə-tē\ *noun* [Middle French *impudicité,* from Latin *impudicus* immodest, from *in-* + *pudicus* modest, from *pudēre*] (1528)
: lack of modesty : SHAMELESSNESS

im·pugn \im-'pyün\ *transitive verb* [Middle English, to assail, from Middle French *impugner,* from Latin *inpugnare,* from *in-* + *pugnare* to fight — more at PUNGENT] (14th century)
1 : to assail by words or arguments : oppose or attack as false or lacking integrity
2 *obsolete* **a** : ASSAIL **b** : RESIST
— **im·pugn·able** \-'pyü-nə-bəl\ *adjective*
— **im·pugn·er** \-nər\ *noun*

im·puis·sance \(,)im-'pwi-s°n(t)s, (,)im-'pyü-ə-sən(t)s; ,im-pyü-'i-s°n(t)s\ *noun* [Middle En-

glish, from Middle French, from *in-* + *puissance* puissance, power] (15th century)
: WEAKNESS, POWERLESSNESS

im·puis·sant \-s°nt, -sənt\ *adjective* [French] (1629)
: WEAK, POWERLESS

¹im·pulse \'im-,pəls, im-'\ *transitive verb* **im·pulsed; im·puls·ing** (1611)
: to give an impulse to

²im·pulse \'im-,pəls\ *noun* [Latin *impulsus,* from *impellere* to impel] (1647)
1 a : INSPIRATION, MOTIVATION **b** : a force so communicated as to produce motion suddenly **c** : INCENTIVE
2 a : the act of driving onward with sudden force : IMPULSION **b** : motion produced by such an impulsion : IMPETUS **c** : a wave of excitation transmitted through tissues and especially nerve fibers and muscles that results in physiological activity or inhibition
3 a : a sudden spontaneous inclination or incitement to some usually unpremeditated action **b** : a propensity or natural tendency usually other than rational
4 a : the product of the average value of a force and the time during which it acts : the change in momentum produced by the force **b** : PULSE 4a
synonym see MOTIVE

im·pul·sion \im-'pəl-shən\ *noun* (15th century)
1 a : the act of impelling : the state of being impelled **b** : an impelling force **c** : an onward tendency derived from an impulsion
2 : IMPULSE 3a
3 : COMPULSION 2

im·pul·sive \im-'pəl-siv\ *adjective* (15th century)
1 : having the power of or actually driving or impelling
2 : actuated by or prone to act on impulse
3 : acting momentarily
synonym see SPONTANEOUS
— **im·pul·sive·ly** *adverb*
— **im·pul·sive·ness** *noun*
— **im·pul·siv·i·ty** \-,pəl-'si-və-tē\ *noun*

im·pu·ni·ty \im-'pyü-nə-tē\ *noun* [Middle French or Latin; Middle French *impunité,* from Latin *impunitat-, impunitas,* from *impune* without punishment, from *in-* + *poena* punishment — more at PAIN] (1532)
: exemption or freedom from punishment, harm, or loss

im·pure \(,)im-'pyur\ *adjective* [Middle English, from Middle French & Latin; Middle French, from Latin *impurus,* from *in-* + *purus* pure] (15th century)
: not pure: as **a** : LEWD, UNCHASTE **b** : containing something unclean : FOUL ⟨*impure* water⟩ **c** : ritually unclean **d** : mixed or impregnated with an extraneous and usually unwanted substance ⟨an *impure* chemical⟩
— **im·pure·ly** *adverb*
— **im·pure·ness** *noun*

im·pu·ri·ty \(,)im-'pyùr-ə-tē\ *noun, plural* **-ties** (15th century)
1 : something that is impure or makes something else impure
2 : the quality or state of being impure

im·pu·ta·tion \,im-pyə-'tā-shən\ *noun* (1581)
1 : the act of imputing: as **a** : ATTRIBUTION, ASCRIPTION **b** : ACCUSATION **c** : INSINUATION
2 : something imputed
— **im·pu·ta·tive** \im-'pyü-tə-tiv\ *adjective*
— **im·pu·ta·tive·ly** *adverb*

im·pute \im-'pyüt\ *transitive verb* **im·put·ed; im·put·ing** [Middle English *inputen,* from Middle French *imputer,* from Latin *imputare,* from *in-* + *putare* to consider] (14th century)
1 : to lay the responsibility or blame for often falsely or unjustly
2 : to credit to a person or a cause : ATTRIBUTE ⟨our vices as well as our virtues have been *imputed* to bodily derangement —B. N. Cardozo⟩
synonym see ASCRIBE

— **im·put·abil·i·ty** \-,pyü-tə-'bi-lə-tē\ *noun*
— **im·put·able** \-'pyü-tə-bəl\ *adjective*

¹in \'in, ən, °n\ *preposition* [Middle English, from Old English; akin to Old High German *in* in, Latin *in,* Greek *en*] (before 12th century)
1 a — used as a function word to indicate inclusion, location, or position within limits ⟨*in* the lake⟩ ⟨wounded *in* the leg⟩ ⟨*in* the summer⟩ **b** : INTO ⟨went *in* the house⟩
2 — used as a function word to indicate means, medium, or instrumentality ⟨written *in* pencil⟩ ⟨bound *in* leather⟩
3 a — used as a function word to indicate limitation, qualification, or circumstance ⟨alike *in* some respects⟩ ⟨left *in* a hurry⟩ **b** : INTO 2a ⟨broke *in* pieces⟩
4 — used as a function word to indicate purpose ⟨said *in* reply⟩
5 — used as a function word to indicate the larger member of a ratio ⟨one *in* six is eligible⟩

²in \'in\ *adverb* (before 12th century)
1 a (1) : to or toward the inside especially of a house or other building ⟨come *in*⟩ (2) : to or toward some destination or particular place ⟨flew *in* on the first plane⟩ (3) : at close quarters : NEAR ⟨play close *in*⟩ **b** : so as to incorporate ⟨mix *in* the flour⟩ — often used in combination ⟨built-*in* bookcases⟩ **c** : to or at an appropriate place ⟨fit a piece *in*⟩
2 a : within a particular place; *especially* : within the customary place of residence or business ⟨the doctor is *in*⟩ **b** : in the position of participant, insider, or officeholder — often used with *on* ⟨*in* on the joke⟩ **c** (1) : on good terms (2) : in a specified relation ⟨*in* bad with the boss⟩ (3) : in a position of assured or definitive success **d** : in vogue or season **e** *of an oil well* : in production **f** : in one's presence, possession, or control ⟨after the crops are *in*⟩ **g** : from a condition of indistinguishability to one of clarity ⟨fade *in*⟩
— **in for** : certain to experience ⟨*in for* a rude awakening⟩

³in \'in\ *adjective* (1599)
1 a : that is located inside or within ⟨the *in* part⟩ **b** : that is in position, operation, or power ⟨the *in* party⟩ **c** : INSIDE 2
2 : that is directed or bound inward : INCOMING ⟨the *in* train⟩
3 a : extremely fashionable ⟨the *in* thing to do⟩ **b** : keenly aware of and responsive to what is new and smart ⟨the *in* crowd⟩

⁴in \'in\ *noun* (1764)
1 : one who is in office or power or on the inside ⟨a matter of *ins* versus outs⟩
2 : INFLUENCE, PULL ⟨enjoyed some sort of *in* with the commandant —Henriette Roosenburg⟩

¹in- *or* **il-** *or* **im-** *or* **ir-** *prefix* [Middle English, from Middle French, from Latin; akin to Old English *un-*]
: not : NON-, UN- — usually *il-* before *l* ⟨*il*logical⟩, *im-* before *b, m,* or *p* ⟨*im*balance⟩ ⟨*im*moral⟩ ⟨*im*practical⟩, *ir-* before *r* ⟨*ir*reducible⟩, and *in-* before other sounds ⟨*in*conclusive⟩

²in- *or* **il-** *or* **im-** *or* **ir-** *prefix* [Middle English, from Middle French, from Latin, from *in* in, into]
1 : in : within : into : toward : on — usually *il-* before *l* ⟨*il*luviation⟩, *im-* before *b, m,* or *p* ⟨*im*mingle⟩, *ir-* before *r* ⟨*ir*radiance⟩, and *in-* before other sounds ⟨*in*filtrate⟩
2 : ¹EN- ⟨*im*brute⟩ ⟨*im*peril⟩ ⟨*in*spirit⟩

¹-in *noun suffix* [French *-ine,* from Latin *-īna,* feminine of *-īnus* of or belonging to — more at -EN]
1 a : neutral chemical compound ⟨insul*in*⟩ **b** : enzyme ⟨pancreat*in*⟩ **c** : antibiotic ⟨penicill*in*⟩
2 : ²-INE 1a, b ⟨epinephr*in*⟩

\ə\ abut \°\ kitten \ər\ further \a\ ash \ā\ ace
\ä\ mop, mar \aù\ out \ch\ chin \e\ bet \ē\ easy
\g\ go \i\ hit \ī\ ice \j\ job \ŋ\ sing \ō\ go
\ò\ law \òi\ boy \th\ thin \th\ the \ü\ loot \ù\ foot
\y\ yet \zh\ vision *see also* Guide to Pronunciation

3 : pharmaceutical product ⟨niac*in*⟩

²-in *combining form* [sit-*in*]
: organized public protest by means of or in favor of : demonstration ⟨teach-*in*⟩ ⟨love-*in*⟩

in·a·bil·i·ty \ˌi-nə-ˈbi-lə-tē\ *noun* [Middle English *inabilite*, from Middle French *inhabilité*, from *in-* + *habilité* ability] (15th century)
: lack of sufficient power, resources, or capacity ⟨his *inability* to do math⟩

in ab·sen·tia \ˌin-ab-ˈsen(t)-sh(ē-)ə\ *adverb* [Latin] (1886)
: in absence ⟨gave him the award *in absentia*⟩

in·ac·ces·si·ble \ˌi-nik-ˈse-sə-bəl, (ˌ)i-ˌnak-\ *adjective* [Middle English, from Middle French or Late Latin; Middle French, from Late Latin *inaccessibilis*, from Latin *in-* + Late Latin *accessibilis* accessible] (15th century)
: not accessible
— **in·ac·ces·si·bil·i·ty** \-ˌse-sə-ˈbi-lə-tē\ *noun*
— **in·ac·ces·si·bly** \-ˈse-sə-blē\ *adverb*

in·ac·cu·ra·cy \(ˌ)i-ˈna-kyə-rə-sē, -k(ə-)rə-sē\ *noun, plural* **-cies** (circa 1755)
1 : the quality or state of being inaccurate
2 : MISTAKE, ERROR

in·ac·cu·rate \-ˈa-kyə-rət, -k(ə-)rət\ *adjective* (1738)
: not accurate : FAULTY
— **in·ac·cu·rate·ly** \-kyə-rət-lē, -k(ə-)rət-, -kyərt-\ *adverb*

in·ac·tion \(ˌ)i-ˈnak-shən\ *noun* (1707)
: lack of action or activity : IDLENESS

in·ac·ti·vate \(ˌ)i-ˈnak-tə-ˌvāt\ *transitive verb* (1906)
: to make inactive
— **in·ac·ti·va·tion** \-ˌnak-tə-ˈvā-shən\ *noun*

in·ac·tive \(ˌ)i-ˈnak-tiv\ *adjective* (1664)
: not active: as **a** (1) : SEDENTARY (2) : INDOLENT, SLUGGISH **b** (1) : being out of use (2) : relating to or being members of the armed forces who are not performing or available for military duties (3) *of a disease* : QUIESCENT **c** (1) : chemically inert (2) : optically neutral in polarized light **d** : biologically inert especially because of the loss of some quality (as infectivity or antigenicity) ☆
— **in·ac·tive·ly** *adverb*
— **in·ac·tiv·i·ty** \-ˌnak-ˈti-və-tē\ *noun*

in·ad·e·qua·cy \(ˌ)i-ˈna-di-kwə-sē\ *noun, plural* **-cies** (1787)
1 : the quality or state of being inadequate
2 : INSUFFICIENCY, DEFICIENCY

in·ad·e·quate \-kwət\ *adjective* (1671)
: not adequate : INSUFFICIENT; *also* : not capable
— **in·ad·e·quate·ly** *adverb*
— **in·ad·e·quate·ness** *noun*

in·ad·mis·si·ble \ˌi-nəd-ˈmi-sə-bəl\ *adjective* (1776)
: not admissible
— **in·ad·mis·si·bil·i·ty** \-ˌmi-sə-ˈbi-lə-tē\ *noun*
— **in·ad·mis·si·bly** \-ˈmi-sə-blē\ *adverb*

in·ad·ver·tence \ˌi-nəd-ˈvər-t°n(t)s\ *noun* [Middle English, from Medieval Latin *inadvertentia*, from Latin *in-* + *advertent-, advertens*, present participle of *advertere* to advert] (15th century)
1 : the fact or action of being inadvertent
2 : a result of inattention : OVERSIGHT

in·ad·ver·ten·cy \-t°n(t)-sē\ *noun, plural* **-cies** (1592)
: INADVERTENCE

in·ad·ver·tent \-t°nt\ *adjective* [back-formation from *inadvertence*] (1653)
1 : not focusing the mind on a matter : INATTENTIVE
2 : UNINTENTIONAL
— **in·ad·ver·tent·ly** *adverb*

in·ad·vis·able \ˌi-nəd-ˈvī-zə-bəl\ *adjective* (1870)
: not advisable
— **in·ad·vis·abil·i·ty** \-ˌvī-zə-ˈbi-lə-tē\ *noun*

-inae *noun plural suffix* [New Latin *-inae*, from Latin, feminine plural of *-īnus*]
: members of the subfamily of — in all names of zoological subfamilies in recent classifications ⟨Fel*inae*⟩

in·alien·able \(ˌ)i-ˈnāl-yə-nə-bəl, -ˈnā-lē-ə-nə-\ *adjective* [probably from French *inaliénable*, from *in-* + *aliénable* alienable] (circa 1645)
: incapable of being alienated, surrendered, or transferred ⟨*inalienable* rights⟩
— **in·alien·abil·i·ty** \-ˌnāl-yə-nə-ˈbi-lə-tē, -ˌnā-lē-ə-nə-\ *noun*
— **in·alien·ably** \-ˈnāl-yə-nə-blē, -ˈnā-lē-ə-nə-\ *adverb*

in·al·ter·able \(ˌ)i-ˈnȯl-t(ə-)rə-bəl\ *adjective* (1541)
: not alterable : UNALTERABLE
— **in·al·ter·abil·i·ty** \-ˌnȯl-t(ə-)rə-ˈbi-lə-tē\ *noun*
— **in·al·ter·able·ness** \-ˈnȯl-t(ə-)rə-bəl-nəs\ *noun*
— **in·al·ter·ably** \-blē\ *adverb*

in·amo·ra·ta \i-ˌna-mə-ˈrä-tə\ *noun* [Italian *innamorata*, from feminine of *innamorato*, past participle of *innamorare* to inspire with love, from *in-* (from Latin) + *amore* love, from Latin *amor* — more at AMOROUS] (1651)
: a woman with whom one is in love or has intimate relations

in–and–in \ˌin-ən(d)-ˈin\ *adverb or adjective* (1765)
: in repeated generations of the same or closely related stock ⟨families . . . of one blood through mating or marrying *in-and-in* —F. H. Giddings⟩ ⟨*in-and-in* breeding⟩

¹inane \i-ˈnān\ *adjective* **inan·er; -est** [Latin *inanis*] (1662)
1 : EMPTY, INSUBSTANTIAL
2 : lacking significance, meaning, or point : SILLY
synonym see INSIPID
— **inane·ly** *adverb*
— **inane·ness** \-ˈnān-nəs\ *noun*

²inane *noun* (1677)
: void or empty space ⟨a voyage into the limitless *inane* —V. G. Childe⟩

in·an·i·mate \(ˌ)i-ˈna-nə-mət\ *adjective* [Middle English, from Late Latin *inanimatus*, from Latin *in-* + *animatus*, past participle of *animare* to animate] (15th century)
1 : not animate: **a** : not endowed with life or spirit **b** : lacking consciousness or power of motion
2 : not animated or lively : DULL
— **in·an·i·mate·ly** *adverb*
— **in·an·i·mate·ness** *noun*

in·a·ni·tion \ˌi-nə-ˈni-shən\ *noun* (14th century)
: the quality or state of being empty: **a** : the loss of vitality that results from lack of food and water **b** : the absence or loss of social, moral, or intellectual vitality or vigor

inan·i·ty \i-ˈna-nə-tē\ *noun, plural* **-ties** (1603)
1 : the quality or state of being inane: as **a** : lack of substance : EMPTINESS **b** : vapid, pointless, or fatuous character : SHALLOWNESS
2 : something that is inane

in·ap·par·ent \ˌi-nə-ˈpar-ənt, -ˈper-\ *adjective* (1626)
: not apparent
— **in·ap·par·ent·ly** *adverb*

in·ap·peas·able \ˌi-nə-ˈpē-zə-bəl\ *adjective* (1803)
: UNAPPEASABLE

in·ap·pe·tence \(ˌ)i-ˈna-pə-tən(t)s\ *noun* (circa 1691)
: loss or lack of appetite

in·ap·pli·ca·ble \(ˌ)i-ˈna-pli-kə-bəl *also* ˌi-nə-ˈpli-kə-\ *adjective* (1656)
: not applicable : IRRELEVANT
— **in·ap·pli·ca·bil·i·ty** \-ˌna-pli-kə-ˈbi-lə-tē *also* ˌi-nə-ˌpli-kə-\ *noun*
— **in·ap·pli·ca·bly** \(ˌ)i-ˈna-pli-kə-blē *also* ˌi-nə-ˈpli-kə-\ *adverb*

in·ap·po·site \(ˌ)i-ˈna-pə-zət\ *adjective* (1661)
: not apposite
— **in·ap·po·site·ly** *adverb*
— **in·ap·po·site·ness** *noun*

in·ap·pre·cia·ble \ˌi-nə-ˈprē-shə-bəl, -ˈpri-sh(ē-)ə-bəl\ *adjective* [probably from French *inappréciable*, from Middle French *inappreciable*, from *in-* + *appreciable*] (1802)
: too small to be perceived
— **in·ap·pre·cia·bly** \-blē\ *adverb*

in·ap·pre·cia·tive \ˌi-nə-ˈprē-shə-tiv, -ˈpri- also -ˈprē-shē-, ˌā-\ *adjective* (1869)
: not appreciative
— **in·ap·pre·cia·tive·ly** *adverb*
— **in·ap·pre·cia·tive·ness** *noun*

in·ap·proach·able \ˌi-nə-ˈprō-chə-bəl\ *adjective* (circa 1828)
: not approachable : INACCESSIBLE

in·ap·pro·pri·ate \ˌi-nə-ˈprō-prē-ət\ *adjective* (1804)
: not appropriate : UNSUITABLE
— **in·ap·pro·pri·ate·ly** *adverb*
— **in·ap·pro·pri·ate·ness** *noun*

in·apt \(ˌ)i-ˈnapt\ *adjective* (circa 1670)
: not apt: **a** : not suitable **b** : INEPT
— **in·apt·ly** \-ˈnap(t)-lē\ *adverb*
— **in·apt·ness** \-nəs\ *noun*

in·ap·ti·tude \(ˌ)i-ˈnap-tə-ˌtüd, -ˌtyüd\ *noun* (1620)
: lack of aptitude

in·ar·gu·able \(ˌ)i-ˈnär-gyə-wə-bəl\ *adjective* (circa 1875)
: not arguable
— **in·ar·gu·ably** \-blē\ *adverb*

in·ar·tic·u·la·cy \ˌi-(ˌ)när-ˈti-kyə-lə-sē\ *noun* (1921)
: the quality or state of being inarticulate

¹in·ar·tic·u·late \-kyə-lət\ *adjective* [Late Latin *inarticulatus*, from Latin *in-* + *articulatus*, past participle of *articulare* to utter distinctly — more at ARTICULATE] (1603)
1 a *of a sound* : uttered or formed without the definite articulations of intelligible speech **b** (1) : incapable of speech especially under stress of emotion : MUTE (2) : incapable of being expressed by speech ⟨*inarticulate* fear⟩ (3) : not voiced or expressed : UNSPOKEN ⟨society functions on many *inarticulate* premises⟩
2 : incapable of giving coherent, clear, or effective expression to one's ideas or feelings
3 [New Latin *inarticulatus*, from Latin *in-* + New Latin *articulatus* articulate] : relating to, characteristic of, or being an inarticulate or its shell
— **in·ar·tic·u·late·ly** *adverb*
— **in·ar·tic·u·late·ness** *noun*

²inarticulate *noun* (1952)
: any of a class (Inarticulata) of brachiopods lacking a hinge connecting the two shell valves

in·ar·tis·tic \ˌi-när-ˈtis-tik\ *adjective* (1859)
1 : not conforming to the principles of art

☆ **SYNONYMS**
Inactive, idle, inert, passive, supine mean not engaged in work or activity. INACTIVE applies to anyone or anything not in action or in operation or at work ⟨on *inactive* status as an astronaut⟩ ⟨*inactive* accounts⟩. IDLE applies to persons that are not busy or occupied or to their powers or their implements ⟨workers were *idle* in the fields⟩. INERT as applied to things implies powerlessness to move or to affect other things; as applied to persons it suggests an inherent or habitual indisposition to activity ⟨*inert* ingredients in drugs⟩ ⟨an *inert* citizenry⟩. PASSIVE implies immobility or lack of normally expected response to an external force or influence and often suggests deliberate submissiveness or self-control ⟨*passive* resistance⟩. SUPINE applies only to persons and commonly implies abjectness or indolence ⟨a *supine* willingness to play the fool⟩.

2 : not appreciative of art
— **in·ar·tis·ti·cal·ly** \-ti-k(ə-)lē\ *adverb*

in·as·much as \ˌi-nəz-'mə-chəz, -'məch-ˌaz\ *conjunction* (14th century)
1 : in the degree that : INSOFAR AS
2 : in view of the fact that : SINCE

in·at·ten·tion \ˌi-nə-'ten(t)-shən\ *noun* (circa 1670)
: failure to pay attention

in·at·ten·tive \-'ten-tiv\ *adjective* (1692)
: not attentive
— **in·at·ten·tive·ly** *adverb*
— **in·at·ten·tive·ness** *noun*

in·au·di·ble \(ˌ)i-'nȯ-də-bəl\ *adjective* [Late Latin *inaudibilis*, from Latin *in-* + Late Latin *audibilis* audible] (1601)
: not audible
— **in·au·di·bil·i·ty** \(ˌ)i-ˌnȯ-də-'bi-lə-tē\ *noun*
— **in·au·di·bly** \(ˌ)i-'nȯ-də-blē\ *adverb*

¹**in·au·gu·ral** \i-'nȯ-gyə-rəl, -g(ə-)rəl\ *adjective* (1689)
1 : of or relating to an inauguration
2 : marking a beginning : first in a projected series

²**inaugural** *noun* (1832)
1 : an inaugural address
2 : INAUGURATION

in·au·gu·rate \i-'nȯ-gyə-ˌrāt, -gə-ˌrāt\ *transitive verb* **-rat·ed; -rat·ing** [Latin *inauguratus*, past participle of *inaugurare*, literally, to practice augury, from *in-* + *augurare* to augur; from the rites connected with augury] (1606)
1 : to induct into an office with suitable ceremonies
2 a : to dedicate ceremoniously : observe formally the beginning of **b :** to bring about the beginning of
synonym see BEGIN
— **in·au·gu·ra·tor** \-ˌrā-tər\ *noun*

in·au·gu·ra·tion \-ˌnȯ-gyə-'rā-shən, -gə-\ *noun* (1569)
: an act of inaugurating; *especially* : a ceremonial induction into office

Inauguration Day *noun* (1829)
: January 20 following a presidential election on which the president of the U.S. is inaugurated

in·aus·pi·cious \ˌi-ˌnȯ-'spi-shəs\ *adjective* (1592)
: not auspicious
— **in·aus·pi·cious·ly** *adverb*
— **in·aus·pi·cious·ness** *noun*

in·au·then·tic \ˌi-ˌnȯ-'then-tik\ *adjective* (1860)
: not authentic
— **in·au·then·tic·i·ty** \ˌi-ˌnȯ-ˌthen-'ti-sə-tē, -thən-\ *noun*

in·be·tween \ˌin-bi-'twēn\ *adjective or noun* (1815)
: INTERMEDIATE

in between *adverb or preposition* (1892)
: BETWEEN

¹**in·board** \'in-ˌbȯrd, -ˌbȯrd\ *adverb* (1830)
1 : inside the line of a ship's bulwarks or hull
2 : toward the center line of a vehicle or craft (as a ship or aircraft)

²**inboard** *adjective* (1847)
1 : located inboard ⟨an *inboard* engine⟩ ⟨an *inboard* spoiler⟩
2 *of a boat* **:** having an inboard engine

³**inboard** *noun* (1950)
: a boat with an inboard motor

in·born \'in-'bȯrn\ *adjective* (1513)
1 : present from or as if from birth
2 : HEREDITARY, INHERITED
synonym see INNATE

in·bound \'in-ˌbaund\ *adjective* (1894)
: inward bound

in·bounds \'in-'baun(d)z\ *adjective* (1968)
: involving putting a basketball in play by passing it onto the court from out of bounds

inbounds line *noun* (circa 1961)
: either of two broken lines running the length of a football field at right angles to the yard lines

in·breathe \'in-ˌbrēth\ *transitive verb* (14th century)
: to breathe (something) in : INHALE

in·bred \'in-'bred\ *adjective* (circa 1592)
1 : rooted and ingrained in one's nature as deeply as if implanted by heredity ⟨an *inbred* love of freedom⟩
2 [from past participle of *inbreed*] **:** subjected to or produced by inbreeding
synonym see INNATE
— **in·bred** \'in-ˌbred\ *noun*

in·breed \'in-'brēd\ *verb* **-bred** \-'bred\; **-breed·ing** (1599)
transitive verb
: to subject to inbreeding
intransitive verb
: to engage in inbreeding

in·breed·ing \'in-ˌbrē-diŋ\ *noun* (circa 1842)
1 : the interbreeding of closely related individuals especially to preserve and fix desirable characters of and to eliminate unfavorable characters from a stock
2 : confinement to a narrow range or a local or limited field of choice

in·built \'in-'bilt\ *adjective* (1923)
chiefly British **:** BUILT-IN

In·ca \'iŋ-kə\ *noun* [Spanish, from Quechua *inka* ruler of the Inca empire] (1594)
1 a : a member of the Quechuan peoples of Peru maintaining an empire until the Spanish conquest **b :** a king or noble of the Inca empire
2 : a member of any people under Inca influence
— **In·ca·ic** \in-'kā-ik\ *adjective*
— **In·can** \'iŋ-kən\ *adjective*

in·cal·cu·la·ble \(ˌ)in-'kal-kyə-lə-bəl\ *adjective* (1795)
: not capable of being calculated: as **a :** very great **b :** not predictable : UNCERTAIN
— **in·cal·cu·la·bil·i·ty** \-ˌkal-kyə-lə-'bi-lə-tē\ *noun*
— **in·cal·cu·la·bly** \-'kal-kyə-lə-blē\ *adverb*

in·ca·les·cence \ˌin-kə-'le-sᵊn(t)s, -iŋ-\ *noun* [Latin *incalescere* to become warm, from *in-* + *calēre* to become warm, inchoative of *calēre* to be warm — more at LEE] (1646)
: a growing warm or ardent
— **in·ca·les·cent** \-sᵊnt\ *adjective*

in camera *adverb* [New Latin, literally, in a chamber] (1882)
: in private : SECRETLY

in·can·desce \ˌin-kən-'des *also* -(ˌ)kan-\ *intransitive verb* **-desced; -desc·ing** [Latin *incandescere*] (1874)
: to be or become incandescent

in·can·des·cence \ˌin-kən-'de-sᵊn(t)s *also* -(ˌ)kan-\ *noun* (1656)
: the quality or state of being incandescent; *especially* **:** emission by a hot body of radiation that makes it visible

in·can·des·cent \-sᵊnt\ *adjective* [probably from French, from Latin *incandescent-, incandescens*, present participle of *incandescere* to become hot, from *in-* + *candescere* to become hot, from *candēre* to glow — more at CANDID] (1794)
1 a : white, glowing, or luminous with intense heat **b :** strikingly bright, radiant, or clear **c :** marked by brilliance especially of expression ⟨*incandescent* wit⟩ **d :** characterized by glowing zeal : ARDENT ⟨*incandescent* affection⟩
2 a : of, relating to, or being light produced by incandescence **b :** producing light by incandescence
— **in·can·des·cent·ly** *adverb*

incandescent lamp *noun* (1881)
: an electric lamp in which a filament gives off light when heated to incandescence by an electric current — called also *incandescent, incandescent bulb, incandescent lightbulb, lightbulb*

in·cant \in-'kant\ *intransitive verb* [Latin *incantare*] (1945)
: RECITE, UTTER

in·can·ta·tion \ˌin-ˌkan-'tā-shən\ *noun* [Middle English *incantacioun*, from Middle French *incantation*, from Late Latin *incantation-, incantatio*, from Latin *incantare* to enchant — more at ENCHANT] (14th century)
: a use of spells or verbal charms spoken or sung as a part of a ritual of magic; *also* **:** a written or recited formula of words designed to produce a particular effect
— **in·can·ta·tion·al** \-shnəl, -shə-nᵊl\ *adjective*
— **in·can·ta·to·ry** \in-ˈkan-tə-ˌtōr-ē, -ˌtȯr-\ *adjective*

incandescent lamp:
1 bulb containing gas, *2* filament, *3* connecting and supporting wires, *4* exhaust tube, *5* screw base, *6* base contact

in·ca·pa·ble \(ˌ)in-ˈkā-pə-bəl\ *adjective* [Middle French, from *in-* + *capable* capable] (1594)
1 : lacking capacity, ability, or qualification for the purpose or end in view: as **a** *archaic* **:** not able to take in, hold, or keep **b** *archaic* **:** not receptive **c :** not being in a state or of a kind to admit : INSUSCEPTIBLE **d :** not able or fit for the doing or performance : INCOMPETENT
2 : lacking legal qualification or power (as by reason of mental incompetence) : DISQUALIFIED
— **in·ca·pa·bil·i·ty** \-ˌkā-pə-'bi-lə-tē\ *noun*
— **in·ca·pa·ble·ness** \-'kā-pə-bəl-nəs\ *noun*
— **in·ca·pa·bly** \-blē\ *adverb*

in·ca·pac·i·tate \ˌin-kə-'pa-sə-ˌtāt\ *transitive verb* **-tat·ed; -tat·ing** (1657)
1 : to make legally incapable or ineligible
2 : to deprive of capacity or natural power : DISABLE
— **in·ca·pac·i·ta·tion** \-ˌpa-sə-'tā-shən\ *noun*

in·ca·pac·i·ty \ˌin-kə-'pa-sə-tē, -'pas-tē\ *noun*, *plural* **-ties** [French *incapacité*, from Middle French, from *in-* + *capacité* capacity] (1611)
: the quality or state of being incapable; *especially* **:** lack of physical or intellectual power or of natural or legal qualifications

in·car·cer·ate \in-'kär-sə-ˌrāt\ *transitive verb* **-at·ed; -at·ing** [Latin *incarceratus*, past participle of *incarcerare*, from *in-* + *carcer* prison] (1560)
1 : to put in prison
2 : to subject to confinement
— **in·car·cer·a·tion** \(ˌ)in-ˌkär-sə-'rā-shən\ *noun*

in·car·di·na·tion \(ˌ)in-ˌkär-dᵊn-'ā-shən\ *noun* [Late Latin *incardination-, incardinatio*, from *incardinare* to ordain as chief priest, from Latin *in-* ²*in-* + Late Latin *cardinalis* principal — more at CARDINAL] (1897)
: the formal acceptance by a diocese of a clergyman from another diocese

¹**in·car·na·dine** \in-'kär-nə-ˌdīn, -ˌdēn, -dən\ *adjective* [Middle French *incarnadin*, from Old Italian *incarnadino*, from *incarnato* flesh-colored, from Late Latin *incarnatus*] (1591)
1 : having the pinkish color of flesh
2 : RED; *especially* **:** BLOODRED

²**incarnadine** *transitive verb* **-dined; -din·ing** (1605)
: to make incarnadine : REDDEN

¹**in·car·nate** \in-'kär-nət, -ˌnāt\ *adjective* [Middle English *incarnat*, from Late Latin *incarnatus*, past participle of *incarnare* to incarnate, from Latin *in-* + *carn-, caro* flesh — more at CARNAL] (14th century)

1 a : invested with bodily and especially human nature and form **b :** made manifest or comprehensible **:** EMBODIED ⟨a fiend *incarnate*⟩ **2 :** INCARNADINE ⟨*incarnate* clover⟩

²in·car·nate \in-'kär-ˌnāt, 'in-ˌ\ *transitive verb* **-nat·ed; -nat·ing** (1533) **:** to make incarnate: as **a :** to give bodily form and substance to **b** (1) **:** to give a concrete or actual form to **:** ACTUALIZE (2) **:** to constitute an embodiment or type of ⟨no one culture *incarnates* every important human value —Denis Goulet⟩

in·car·na·tion \ˌin-(ˌ)kär-'nā-shən\ *noun* (14th century) **1 a** (1) **:** the embodiment of a deity or spirit in some earthly form (2) *capitalized* **:** the union of divinity with humanity in Jesus Christ **b :** a concrete or actual form of a quality or concept; *especially* **:** a person showing a trait or typical character to a marked degree ⟨she is the *incarnation* of goodness⟩ **2 :** the act of incarnating **:** the state of being incarnate **3 :** a particular physical form or state **:** VERSION ⟨in another *incarnation* he might be a first vice-president —Walter Teller⟩ ⟨TV and movie *incarnations* of the story⟩

in·case *variant of* ENCASE

in case *conjunction* (14th century) **1 :** IF ⟨*in case* we are surprised, keep by me —Washington Irving⟩ **2 :** as a precaution against the event that ⟨carries a gun *in case* he is attacked⟩

in·cau·tion \(ˌ)in-'kȯ-shən\ *noun* (circa 1720) **:** lack of caution **:** HEEDLESSNESS

in·cau·tious \-shəs\ *adjective* (circa 1703) **:** lacking in caution **:** CARELESS
— **in·cau·tious·ly** *adverb*
— **in·cau·tious·ness** *noun*

in·cen·di·a·rism \in-'sen-dē-ə-ˌri-zəm\ *noun* (circa 1710) **:** incendiary action or behavior

¹in·cen·di·ary \in-'sen-dē-ˌer-ē; -'sen-də-rē, -dyə-\ *noun, plural* **-ar·ies** [Middle English, from Latin *incendiarius,* from *incendium* conflagration, from *incendere*] (15th century) **1 a :** a person who deliberately sets fire to a building or other property **b :** an incendiary agent (as a bomb) **2 :** a person who excites factions, quarrels, or sedition **:** AGITATOR

²incendiary *adjective* (15th century) **1 :** of, relating to, or involving a deliberate burning of property **2 :** tending to excite or inflame **:** INFLAMMATORY ⟨*incendiary* speeches⟩ **3 a :** igniting combustible materials spontaneously **b :** of, relating to, or being a weapon (as a bomb) designed to start fires

¹in·cense \'in-ˌsen(t)s\ *noun* [Middle English *encens,* from Old French, from Late Latin *incensum,* from Latin, neuter of *incensus,* past participle of *incendere* to set on fire, from *in-* + *-cendere* to burn; akin to Latin *candēre* to glow — more at CANDID] (13th century) **1 :** material used to produce a fragrant odor when burned **2 :** the perfume exhaled from some spices and gums when burned; *broadly* **:** a pleasing scent **3 :** pleasing attention **:** FLATTERY

²incense *transitive verb* **in·censed; in·cens·ing** (13th century) **1 :** to apply or offer incense to **2 :** to perfume with incense

³in·cense \in-'sen(t)s\ *transitive verb* **in·censed; in·cens·ing** [Middle English *encensen,* from Middle French *incenser,* from Latin *incensus*] (15th century) **1** *archaic* **:** to cause (a passion or emotion) to become aroused **2 :** to arouse the extreme anger or indignation of

in·cen·ter \'in-ˌsen-tər\ *noun* [*inscribe* + ¹*center*] (circa 1890)

: the single point in which the three bisectors of the interior angles of a triangle intersect and which is the center of the inscribed circle

in·cen·tive \in-'sen-tiv\ *noun* [Middle English, from Late Latin *incentivum,* from neuter of *incentivus* stimulating, from Latin, setting the tune, from *incentus,* past participle of *incinere* to set the tune, from *in-* + *canere* to sing — more at CHANT] (15th century) **:** something that incites or has a tendency to incite to determination or action
synonym see MOTIVE
— **incentive** *adjective*

in·cep·tion \in-'sep-shən\ *noun* [Middle English *incepcion,* from Latin *inception-, inceptio,* from *incipere* to begin, from *in-* + *capere* to take] (15th century) **:** an act, process, or instance of beginning **:** COMMENCEMENT
synonym see ORIGIN

¹in·cep·tive \in-'sep-tiv\ *noun* (1612) **:** an inchoative verb

²inceptive *adjective* (1656) **1 :** INCHOATIVE 2 **2 :** of or relating to a beginning
— **in·cep·tive·ly** *adverb*

in·cer·ti·tude \(ˌ)in-'sər-tə-ˌtüd, -ˌtyüd\ *noun* [Middle English, from Middle French, from Late Latin *incertitudo,* from Latin *in-* + Late Latin *certitudo* certitude] (15th century) **:** UNCERTAINTY: **a :** absence of assurance or confidence **:** DOUBT **b :** the quality or state of being unstable or insecure

in·ces·san·cy \(ˌ)in-'se-sᵊn(t)-sē\ *noun* (1615) **:** the quality or state of being incessant

in·ces·sant \(ˌ)in-'se-sᵊnt\ *adjective* [Middle English *incessaunt,* from Late Latin *incessant-, incessans,* from Latin *in-* + *cessant-, cessans,* present participle of *cessare* to delay — more at CEASE] (15th century) **:** continuing or following without interruption **:** UNCEASING
synonym see CONTINUAL
— **in·ces·sant·ly** *adverb*

in·cest \'in-ˌsest\ *noun* [Middle English, from Latin *incestus* sexual impurity, from *incestus* impure, from *in-* + *castus* pure — more at CASTE] (13th century) **:** sexual intercourse between persons so closely related that they are forbidden by law to marry; *also* **:** the statutory crime of such a relationship

in·ces·tu·ous \in-'ses-chə-wəs, -'sesh-\ *adjective* (1532) **1 :** constituting or involving incest **2 :** guilty of incest
— **in·ces·tu·ous·ly** *adverb*
— **in·ces·tu·ous·ness** *noun*

¹inch \'inch\ *noun* [Middle English, from Old English *ynce,* from Latin *uncia* — more at OUNCE] (before 12th century) **1 :** a unit of length equal to 1/36 yard — see WEIGHT table **2 :** a small amount, distance, or degree ⟨is like cutting a dog's tail off by *inches* —Milton Friedman⟩ **3** *plural* **:** STATURE, HEIGHT **4 a :** a fall (as of rain or snow) sufficient to cover a surface or to fill a gauge to the depth of one inch **b :** a degree of atmospheric or other pressure sufficient to balance the weight of a column of liquid (as mercury) one inch high in a barometer or manometer
— **every inch :** to the utmost degree ⟨looks *every inch* a winner⟩
— **within an inch of :** almost to the point of

²inch (1599)
intransitive verb **:** to move by small degrees **:** progress slowly ⟨the long line of people *inching* up the stairs⟩
transitive verb **:** to cause to move slowly ⟨sooner or later they begin *inching* prices back up —*Forbes*⟩

³inch *noun* [Middle English (Scots dialect), from Scottish Gaelic *innis*] (15th century) *chiefly Scottish* **:** ISLAND

inched \'incht\ *adjective* (1605) **:** measuring a specified number of inches

-inch·er \'in-chər\ *noun combining form* **:** one that has a dimension of a specified number of inches ⟨a four-*incher*⟩

inch·meal \'inch-ˌmēl, -'mē(ə)l\ *adverb* [¹*inch* + *-meal* (as in *piecemeal*)] (1530) **:** LITTLE BY LITTLE, GRADUALLY

in·cho·ate \in-'kō-ət, 'in-kə-ˌwāt\ *adjective* [Latin *inchoatus,* past participle of *inchoare* to start work on, perhaps from *in-* + *cohum* part of a yoke to which the beam of a plow is fitted] (1534) **:** being only partly in existence or operation; *especially* **:** imperfectly formed or formulated **:** FORMLESS ⟨misty, *inchoate* suspicions that all is not well with the nation —J. M. Perry⟩
— **in·cho·ate·ly** *adverb*
— **in·cho·ate·ness** *noun*

in·cho·a·tive \in-'kō-ə-tiv\ *adjective* (circa 1631) **1 :** INITIAL, FORMATIVE ⟨the *inchoative* stages⟩ **2 :** denoting the beginning of an action, state, or occurrence — used of verbs
— **inchoative** *noun*
— **in·cho·a·tive·ly** *adverb*

inch·worm \'inch-ˌwərm\ *noun* (circa 1861) **:** LOOPER 1

in·ci·dence \'in(t)-sə-dən(t)s, -ˌden(t)s\ *noun* (1626) **1 a :** ANGLE OF INCIDENCE **b :** the arrival of something (as a projectile or a ray of light) at a surface **2 a :** an act or the fact or manner of falling upon or affecting **:** OCCURRENCE **b :** rate of occurrence or influence ⟨a high *incidence* of crime⟩

¹in·ci·dent \'in(t)-sə-dənt, -ˌdent\ *noun* [Middle English, from Middle French, from Medieval Latin *incident-, incidens,* from Latin, present participle of *incidere* to fall into, from *in-* + *cadere* to fall — more at CHANCE] (15th century) **1 :** something dependent on or subordinate to something else of greater or principal importance **2 a :** an occurrence of an action or situation that is a separate unit of experience **:** HAPPENING **b :** an accompanying minor occurrence or condition **:** CONCOMITANT **3 :** an action likely to lead to grave consequences especially in diplomatic matters ⟨a serious border *incident*⟩
synonym see OCCURRENCE

²incident *adjective* (15th century) **1 :** occurring or likely to occur especially as a minor consequence or accompaniment ⟨the confusion *incident* to moving day⟩ **2 :** dependent on or relating to another thing in law **3 :** falling or striking on something ⟨*incident* light rays⟩

¹in·ci·den·tal \ˌin(t)-sə-'den-tᵊl\ *adjective* (1616) **1 :** being likely to ensue as a chance or minor consequence ⟨social obligations *incidental* to the job⟩ **2 :** occurring merely by chance or without intention or calculation

²incidental *noun* (1707) **1** *plural* **:** minor items (as of expense) that are not particularized **2 :** something that is incidental

in·ci·den·tal·ly \-'den-tᵊl-ē, *especially for 2* -'dent-lē\ *adverb* (1665) **1 :** in an incidental manner **:** not intentionally ⟨the arrant nonsense of some of his statements is *incidentally* hilarious —John Lahr⟩ **2 :** by way of interjection or digression **:** by the way ⟨fortunate in having a good teacher . . . —still living, *incidentally* —John Fischer⟩

incidental music *noun* (1864)
: descriptive music played during a play to project a mood or to accompany stage action

in·cin·er·ate \in-'si-nə-ˌrāt\ *transitive verb* **-at·ed; -at·ing** [Medieval Latin *incineratus*, past participle of *incinerare*, from Latin *in-* + *ciner-, cinis* ashes; akin to Greek *konis* dust, ashes] (1555)
: to cause to burn to ashes
— **in·cin·er·a·tion** \-ˌsi-nə-'rā-shən\ *noun*

in·cin·er·a·tor \in-'si-nə-ˌrā-tər\ *noun* (1883)
: one that incinerates; *especially* : a furnace or a container for incinerating waste materials

in·cip·i·ence \in-'si-pē-ən(t)s\ *noun* (circa 1864)
: INCIPIENCY

in·cip·i·en·cy \-ən(t)-sē\ *noun* (1817)
: the state or fact of being incipient : BEGINNING

in·cip·i·ent \-ənt\ *adjective* [Latin *incipient-, incipiens*, present participle of *incipere* to begin — more at INCEPTION] (1669)
: beginning to come into being or to become apparent ⟨an *incipient* solar system⟩ ⟨evidence of *incipient* racial tension⟩
— **in·cip·i·ent·ly** *adverb*

in·cip·it \'in(t)-sə-pət, 'iŋ-kə-ˌpit; in-'si-pət, -'ki-\ *noun* [Latin, it begins, from *incipere*] (1897)
: the first part : BEGINNING; *specifically* : the opening words of a text of a medieval manuscript or early printed book

in·ci·sal \in-'sī-zəl, -səl\ *adjective* (1903)
: relating to, involving, or being the cutting edge or surface of a tooth (as an incisor)

in·cise \in-'sīz, -'sīs\ *transitive verb* **in·cised; in·cis·ing** [Middle French or Latin; Middle French *inciser*, from Latin *incisus*, past participle of *incidere*, from *in-* + *caedere* to cut] (1567)
1 : to cut into
2 a : to carve figures, letters, or devices into : ENGRAVE b : to carve (as an inscription) into a surface

incised *adjective* (15th century)
1 : cut in : ENGRAVED; *especially* : decorated with incised figures
2 : having a margin that is deeply and sharply notched ⟨an *incised* leaf⟩

in·ci·sion \in-'si-zhən\ *noun* (14th century)
1 a : CUT, GASH; *specifically* : a wound made especially in surgery by incising the body b : a marginal notch (as in a leaf)
2 : an act of incising something
3 : the quality or state of being incisive

in·ci·sive \in-'sī-siv\ *adjective* (circa 1850)
: impressively direct and decisive (as in manner or presentation)
— **in·ci·sive·ly** *adverb*
— **in·ci·sive·ness** *noun*

in·ci·sor \in-'sī-zər\ *noun* (1666)
: a front tooth typically adapted for cutting; *especially* : one of the cutting teeth in mammals located between the canines when canines are present — see TOOTH illustration

in·ci·ta·tion \ˌin-ˌsī-'tā-shən, ˌin(t)-sə-\ *noun* (15th century)
1 : an act of inciting : STIMULATION
2 : something that incites to action : INCENTIVE

in·cite \in-'sīt\ *transitive verb* **in·cit·ed; in·cit·ing** [Middle French *inciter*, from Latin *incitare*, from *in-* + *citare* to put in motion — more at CITE] (15th century)
: to move to action : stir up : spur on : urge on ☆
— **in·cit·ant** \-'sī-tᵊnt\ *noun*
— **in·cite·ment** \-'sīt-mənt\ *noun*
— **in·cit·er** *noun*

in·ci·vil·i·ty \ˌin(t)-sə-'vi-lə-tē\ *noun* [Middle French *incivilité*, from Late Latin *incivilitat-, incivilitas*, from *incivilis*, from Latin *in-* + *civilis* civil] (1584)
1 : the quality or state of being uncivil
2 : a rude or discourteous act

in·clem·en·cy \(ˌ)in-'kle-mən(t)-sē\ *noun* (1559)
: the quality or state of being inclement

in·clem·ent \(ˌ)in-'kle-mənt, 'in-klə-\ *adjective* [Latin *inclement-, inclemens*, from *in-* + *clement-, clemens* clement] (1621)
: lacking mildness: as a *archaic* : severe in temper or action : UNMERCIFUL b : physically severe ⟨STORMY ⟨*inclement* weather⟩
— **in·clem·ent·ly** *adverb*

in·clin·able \in-'klī-nə-bəl\ *adjective* (15th century)
: having a tendency or inclination; *also* : disposed to favor or think well of

in·cli·na·tion \ˌin-klə-'nā-shən, ˌiŋ-\ *noun* (14th century)
1 a *obsolete* : natural disposition : CHARACTER b : a particular disposition of mind or character : PROPENSITY; *especially* : LIKING ⟨had little *inclination* for housekeeping⟩
2 : an act or the action of bending or inclining: as a : BOW, NOD b : a tilting of something
3 a : a deviation from the true vertical or horizontal : SLANT; *also* : the degree of such deviation b : an inclined surface : SLOPE c (1) : the angle determined by two lines or planes (2) : the angle made by a line with the x-axis measured counterclockwise from the positive direction of that axis
4 : a tendency to a particular aspect, state, character, or action ⟨the clutch has an *inclination* to slip⟩
— **in·cli·na·tion·al** \-shnəl, -shə-nᵊl\ *adjective*

¹**in·cline** \in-'klīn\ *verb* **in·clined; in·clin·ing** [Middle English, from Middle French *incliner*, from Latin *inclinare*, from *in-* + *clinare* to lean — more at LEAN] (14th century)
intransitive verb
1 : to bend the head or body forward : BOW
2 : to lean, tend, or become drawn toward an opinion or course of conduct
3 : to deviate from a line, direction, or course; *specifically* : to deviate from the vertical or horizontal
transitive verb
1 : to cause to stoop or bow : BEND
2 : to have influence on : PERSUADE ⟨his love of books *inclined* him toward a literary career⟩
3 : to give a bend or slant to ☆
— **in·clin·er** *noun*

²**in·cline** \'in-ˌklīn\ *noun* (1846)
: an inclined plane : GRADE, SLOPE

in·clined \in-'klīnd, 2 *also* 'in-ˌ\ *adjective* (14th century)
1 : having inclination, disposition, or tendency
2 a : having a leaning or slope b : making an angle with a line or plane

inclined plane *noun* (1710)
: a plane surface that makes an oblique angle with the plane of the horizon

in·clin·ing \in-'klī-niŋ\ *noun* (14th century)
1 : INCLINATION
2 *archaic* : PARTY, FOLLOWING

in·cli·nom·e·ter \ˌin-klə-'nä-mə-tər, ˌiŋ-; ˌin-ˌklī-\ *noun* (1852)
: an instrument for indicating the inclination to the horizontal of an axis (as of an airplane)

in·clip \in-'klip\ *transitive verb* (1608)
archaic : CLASP, ENCLOSE

inclose, inclosure *variant of* ENCLOSE, ENCLOSURE

in·clude \in-'klüd\ *transitive verb* **in·clud·ed; in·clud·ing** [Middle English, from Latin *includere*, from *in-* + *claudere* to close — more at CLOSE] (15th century)
1 : to shut up : ENCLOSE
2 : to take in or comprise as a part of a whole
3 : to contain between or within ⟨two sides and the *included* angle⟩ ☆
— **in·clud·able** *or* **in·clud·ible** \-'klü-də-bəl\ *adjective*

in·clu·sion \in-'klü-zhən\ *noun* [Latin *inclusion-, inclusio*, from *includere*] (1600)
1 : the act of including : the state of being included
2 : something that is included: as a : a gaseous, liquid, or solid foreign body enclosed in a mass (as of a mineral) b : a passive usually temporary product of cell activity (as a starch grain) within the cytoplasm or nucleus
3 : a relation between two classes that exists when all members of the first are also members of the second — compare MEMBERSHIP 3

inclusion body *noun* (circa 1919)
: an inclusion, abnormal structure, or foreign cell within a cell; *specifically* : an intracellular body that is characteristic of some virus diseases and that is the site of virus multiplication

in·clu·sive \in-'klü-siv, -ziv\ *adjective* (15th century)
1 : comprehending stated limits or extremes ⟨from Monday to Friday *inclusive*⟩
2 a : broad in orientation or scope b : covering or intended to cover all items, costs, or services
— **in·clu·sive·ly** *adverb*
— **in·clu·sive·ness** *noun*

inclusive disjunction *noun* (1942)
: a complex sentence in logic that is true when either or both of its constituent propositions are true — see TRUTH TABLE table

inclusive of *preposition* (1709)
: including or taking into account ⟨the cost of building *inclusive of* materials⟩

in·co·erc·ible \ˌin-kō-'ər-sə-bəl\ *adjective* (1710)

☆ **SYNONYMS**

Incite, instigate, abet, foment mean to spur to action. INCITE stresses a stirring up and urging on, and may or may not imply initiating ⟨*inciting* a riot⟩. INSTIGATE definitely implies responsibility for initiating another's action and often connotes underhandedness or evil intention ⟨*instigated* a conspiracy⟩. ABET implies both assisting and encouraging ⟨aiding and *abetting* the enemy⟩. FOMENT implies persistence in goading ⟨*fomenting* rebellion⟩.

Incline, bias, dispose, predispose mean to influence one to have or take an attitude toward something. INCLINE implies a tendency to favor one of two or more actions or conclusions ⟨I *incline* to agree⟩. BIAS suggests a settled and predictable leaning in one direction and connotes unfair prejudice ⟨the experience *biased* him against foreigners⟩. DISPOSE suggests an affecting of one's mood or temper so as to incline one toward something ⟨her nature *disposes* her to trust others⟩. PREDISPOSE implies the operation of a disposing influence well in advance of the opportunity to manifest itself ⟨does fictional violence *predispose* them to accept real violence?⟩.

Include, comprehend, embrace, involve mean to contain within as part of the whole. INCLUDE suggests the containment of something as a constituent, component, or subordinate part of a larger whole ⟨the price of dinner *includes* dessert⟩. COMPREHEND implies that something comes within the scope of a statement or definition ⟨his system *comprehends* all history⟩. EMBRACE implies a gathering of separate items within a whole ⟨her faith *embraces* both Christian and non-Christian beliefs⟩. INVOLVE suggests inclusion by virtue of the nature of the whole, whether by being its natural or inevitable consequence ⟨the new job *involves* a lot of detail⟩.

\ə\ abut \ᵊ\ kitten \ər\ further \a\ ash \ā\ ace
\ä\ mop, mar \au̇\ out \ch\ chin \e\ bet \ē\ easy
\g\ go \i\ hit \ī\ ice \j\ job \ŋ\ sing \ō\ go
\ȯ\ law \ȯi\ boy \th\ thin \t̶h\ the \ü\ loot \u̇\ foot
\y\ yet \zh\ vision *see also* Guide to Pronunciation

: incapable of being controlled, checked, or confined

in·cog·i·tant \in-'kä-jə-tənt\ *adjective* [Latin *incogitant-, incogitans,* from *in-* + *cogitant-, cogitans,* present participle of *cogitare* to cogitate] (1628)
: THOUGHTLESS, INCONSIDERATE

in·cog·ni·ta \ˌin-ˌkäg-'nē-tə *also* in-'käg-nə-tə\ *adverb or adjective* [Italian, feminine of *incognito*] (1638)
: INCOGNITO — used only of a woman
— **incognita** *noun*

¹in·cog·ni·to \ˌin-ˌkäg-'nē-(ˌ)tō *also* in-'käg-nə-ˌtō\ *adverb or adjective* [Italian, from Latin *incognitus* unknown, from *in-* + *cognitus,* past participle of *cognoscere* to know — more at COGNITION] (1635)
: with one's identity concealed

²incognito *noun, plural* **-tos** (1638)
1 : one appearing or living incognito
2 : the state or assumed identity of one living or traveling incognito or incognita

in·cog·ni·zant \(ˌ)in-'käg-nə-zənt\ *adjective* (1837)
: lacking awareness or consciousness
— **in·cog·ni·zance** \-zən(t)s\ *noun*

in·co·her·ence \ˌin-kō-'hir-ən(t)s, -'her-\ *noun* (1611)
1 : the quality or state of being incoherent
2 : something that is incoherent

in·co·her·ent \-ənt\ *adjective* (1626)
1 : lacking coherence: as **a** : lacking cohesion : LOOSE **b** : lacking orderly continuity, arrangement, or relevance : INCONSISTENT
2 : lacking clarity or intelligibility : INCOMPREHENSIBLE
— **in·co·her·ent·ly** *adverb*

in·com·bus·ti·ble \ˌin-kəm-'bəs-tə-bəl\ *adjective* [Middle English, probably from Middle French, from *in-* + *combustible* combustible] (15th century)
: not combustible : incapable of being burned
— **in·com·bus·ti·bil·i·ty** \-ˌbəs-tə-'bi-lə-tē\ *noun*
— **incombustible** *noun*

in·come \'in-ˌkəm *also* 'in-kəm *or* 'iŋ-kəm\ *noun* (14th century)
1 : a coming in : ENTRANCE, INFLUX ⟨fluctuations in the nutrient *income* of a body of water⟩
2 : a gain or recurrent benefit usually measured in money that derives from capital or labor; *also* : the amount of such gain received in a period of time ⟨has an *income* of $20,000 a year⟩

income account *noun* (1869)
: a financial statement of a business showing the details of revenues, costs, expenses, losses, and profits for a given period — called also *income statement*

income bond *noun* (circa 1864)
: a bond that pays interest at a rate based on the issuer's earnings

income tax *noun* (1799)
: a tax on the net income of an individual or a business

¹in·com·ing \'in-ˌkə-miŋ\ *noun* (14th century)
1 : the act of coming in : ARRIVAL
2 : INCOME — usually used in plural

²incoming *adjective* (1753)
1 : coming in : ARRIVING ⟨an *incoming* ship⟩ ⟨*incoming* mail⟩
2 : taking a new place or position especially as part of a succession ⟨the *incoming* president⟩
3 : just starting or beginning ⟨the *incoming* year⟩

in·com·men·su·ra·ble \ˌin-kə-'men(t)s-rə-bəl, -'men(t)sh-; -'men(t)s-ə-, -shə-\ *adjective* (1570)
: not commensurable; *broadly* : lacking a basis of comparison in respect to a quality normally subject to comparison
— **in·com·men·su·ra·bil·i·ty** \-ˌmen(t)s-rə-'bi-lə-tē, -ˌmen(t)sh-; -ˌmen(t)s-ə-, -shə-\ *noun*
— **incommensurable** *noun*

in·com·men·su·ra·bly \-'men(t)s-rə-blē, -'men(t)sh-; -'men(t)-sə-, -shə-\ *adverb*

in·com·men·su·rate \-'men(t)s-rət, -'men(t)sh-; -'men(t)s-ə-, -shə-\ *adjective* (1650)
a : not commensurate: as **a** : INCOMMENSURABLE **b** : INADEQUATE **c** : DISPROPORTIONATE

in·com·mode \ˌin-kə-'mōd\ *transitive verb* **-mod·ed; -mod·ing** [Middle French *incommoder,* from Latin *incommodare,* from *incommodus* inconvenient, from *in-* + *commodus* convenient — more at COMMODE] (1598)
: to give inconvenience or distress to : DISTURB

in·com·mo·di·ous \ˌin-kə-'mō-dē-əs\ *adjective* (1551)
: not commodious : INCONVENIENT
— **in·com·mo·di·ous·ly** *adverb*
— **in·com·mo·di·ous·ness** *noun*

in·com·mod·i·ty \-'mä-də-tē\ *noun* (15th century)
: a source of inconvenience : DISADVANTAGE

in·com·mu·ni·ca·ble \ˌin-kə-'myü-ni-kə-bəl\ *adjective* [Middle French or Late Latin; Middle French, from Late Latin *incommunicabilis,* from Latin *in-* + Late Latin *communicabilis* communicable] (1568)
: not communicable: as **a** : incapable of being communicated or imparted **b** : UNCOMMUNICATIVE
— **in·com·mu·ni·ca·bil·i·ty** \-ˌmyü-ni-kə-'bi-lə-tē\ *noun*
— **in·com·mu·ni·ca·bly** \-'myü-ni-kə-blē\ *adverb*

in·com·mu·ni·ca·do \-ˌmyü-nə-'kä-(ˌ)dō\ *adverb or adjective* [Spanish *incomunicado,* from past participle of *incomunicar* to deprive of communication, from *in-* (from Latin) + *comunicar* to communicate, from Latin *communicare*] (1844)
: without means of communication; *also* : in solitary confinement

in·com·mu·ni·ca·tive \-'myü-nə-ˌkā-tiv, -ni-kə-tiv\ *adjective* (1670)
: UNCOMMUNICATIVE

in·com·mut·able \ˌin-kə-'myü-tə-bəl\ *adjective* [Middle English, from Latin *incommutabilis,* from *in-* + *commutabilis* commutable] (15th century)
: not commutable: as **a** : not interchangeable **b** : UNCHANGEABLE
— **in·com·mut·ably** \-blē\ *adverb*

in·com·pa·ra·ble \(ˌ)in-'käm-p(ə-)rə-bəl, ÷in-kəm-'par-ə-\ *adjective* [Middle English, from Middle French, from Latin *incomparabilis,* from *in-* + *comparabilis* comparable] (15th century)
1 : eminent beyond comparison : MATCHLESS
2 : not suitable for comparison
— **in·com·pa·ra·bil·i·ty** \(ˌ)in-ˌkäm-p(ə-)rə-'bi-lə-tē, ÷in-kəm-,par-ə-\ *noun*
— **in·com·pa·ra·bly** \(ˌ)in-'käm-p(ə-)rə-blē, ÷in-kəm-'par-ə-\ *adverb*

in·com·pat·i·bil·i·ty \ˌin-kəm-ˌpa-tə-'bi-lə-tē\ *noun, plural* **-ties** (1611)
1 a : the quality or state of being incompatible
b : lack of interfertility between two plants
2 *plural* : mutually antagonistic things or qualities

in·com·pat·i·ble \ˌin-kəm-'pa-tə-bəl\ *adjective* [Middle English, from Middle French & Medieval Latin; Middle French, from Medieval Latin *incompatibilis,* from Latin *in-* + Medieval Latin *compatibilis* compatible] (15th century)
1 : incapable of being held by one person at one time — used of offices that make conflicting demands on the holder
2 : not compatible: as **a** : incapable of association or harmonious coexistence ⟨*incompatible* colors⟩ **b** : unsuitable for use together because of undesirable chemical or physiological effects ⟨*incompatible* drugs⟩ **c** : not both true ⟨*incompatible* propositions⟩ **d** : incapable of blending into a stable homogeneous mixture
— **incompatible** *noun*
— **in·com·pat·i·bly** \-blē\ *adverb*

in·com·pe·tence \(ˌ)in-'käm-pə-tən(t)s\ *noun* (1663)
: the state or fact of being incompetent

in·com·pe·ten·cy \-tən(t)-sē\ *noun* (1611)
: INCOMPETENCE

in·com·pe·tent \(ˌ)in-'käm-pə-tənt\ *adjective* [Middle French *incompétent,* from *in-* + *compétent* competent] (1597)
1 : not legally qualified
2 : inadequate to or unsuitable for a particular purpose
3 a : lacking the qualities needed for effective action **b** : unable to function properly ⟨*incompetent* heart valves⟩
— **incompetent** *noun*
— **in·com·pe·tent·ly** *adverb*

in·com·plete \ˌin-kəm-'plēt\ *adjective* [Middle English *incompleet,* from Late Latin *incompletus,* from Latin *in-* + *completus* complete] (14th century)
1 : not complete : UNFINISHED: as **a** : lacking a part; *especially* : lacking one or more sets of floral organs **b** *of insect metamorphosis* : characterized by the absence of a pupal stage between the immature stages and the adult of an insect in which the young usually resemble the adult — compare COMPLETE 5
2 *of a football pass* : not legally caught
— **in·com·plete·ly** *adverb*
— **in·com·plete·ness** *noun*

in·com·pli·ant \ˌin-kəm-'plī-ənt\ *adjective* (1647)
: not compliant or pliable

in·com·pre·hen·si·ble \(ˌ)in-ˌkäm-pri-'hen(t)-sə-bəl\ *adjective* [Middle English, from Latin *incomprehensibilis,* from *in-* + *comprehensibilis* comprehensible] (14th century)
1 *archaic* : having or subject to no limits
2 : impossible to comprehend : UNINTELLIGIBLE
— **in·com·pre·hen·si·bil·i·ty** \-ˌhen(t)-sə-'bi-lə-tē\ *noun*
— **in·com·pre·hen·si·ble·ness** *noun*
— **in·com·pre·hen·si·bly** \-'hen(t)-sə-blē\ *adverb*

in·com·pre·hen·sion \-'hen(t)-shən\ *noun* (1605)
: lack of comprehension or understanding

in·com·press·ible \ˌin-kəm-'pre-sə-bəl\ *adjective* (circa 1736)
: incapable of or resistant to compression

in·com·put·able \ˌin-kəm-'pyü-tə-bəl\ *adjective* (1606)
: not computable : very great
— **in·com·put·ably** \-blē\ *adverb*

in·con·ceiv·able \ˌin-kən-'sē-və-bəl\ *adjective* (circa 1631)
: not conceivable: as **a** : impossible to comprehend **b** : UNBELIEVABLE
— **in·con·ceiv·abil·i·ty** \-ˌsē-və-'bi-lə-tē\ *noun*
— **in·con·ceiv·able·ness** \-'sē-və-bəl-nəs\ *noun*
— **in·con·ceiv·ably** \-blē\ *adverb*

in·con·cin·ni·ty \ˌin-kən-'si-nə-tē\ *noun* [Latin *inconcinnitas,* from *in-* + *concinnitas* concinnity] (circa 1616)
: lack of suitability or congruity : INELEGANCE

in·con·clu·sive \ˌin-kən-'klü-siv, -ziv\ *adjective* (1707)
: leading to no conclusion or definite result
— **in·con·clu·sive·ly** *adverb*
— **in·con·clu·sive·ness** *noun*

in·con·dite \in-'kän-dət, -ˌdīt\ *adjective* [Latin *inconditus,* from *in-* + *conditus,* past participle of *condere* to put together, from *com-* + *-dere* to put — more at DO] (1539)
: badly put together : CRUDE

in·con·for·mi·ty \ˌin-kən-'fȯr-mə-tē\ *noun* (1594)
: NONCONFORMITY

in·con·gru·ence \ˌin-kən-'grü-ən(t)s, (ˌ)in-'käŋ-grə-wən(t)s\ *noun* (1610)
: INCONGRUITY

in·con·gru·ent \-ənt, -wənt\ *adjective* [Middle English, from Latin *incongruent-, incongruens,* from *in-* + *congruent-, congruens* congruent] (15th century)
: not congruent ⟨*incongruent* triangles⟩
— **in·con·gru·ent·ly** *adverb*

in·con·gru·i·ty \ˌin-kən-ˈgrü-ə-tē, -ˌkän-\ *noun, plural* **-ties** (circa 1532)
1 : the quality or state of being incongruous
2 : something that is incongruous

in·con·gru·ous \(ˌ)in-ˈkäŋ-grə-wəs\ *adjective* [Late Latin *incongruus,* from Latin *in-* + *congruus* congruous] (1611)
: lacking congruity: as **a** : not harmonious : INCOMPATIBLE ⟨*incongruous* colors⟩ **b** : not conforming : DISAGREEING ⟨conduct *incongruous* with principle⟩ **c** : inconsistent within itself ⟨an *incongruous* story⟩ **d** : lacking propriety ⟨*incongruous* manners⟩
— **in·con·gru·ous·ly** *adverb*
— **in·con·gru·ous·ness** *noun*

in·con·scient \(ˌ)in-ˈkän(t)-shənt\ *adjective* [probably from French, from *in-* + *conscient* mindful, from Latin *conscient-, consciens,* present participle of *conscire* to be conscious — more at CONSCIENCE] (1885)
: UNCONSCIOUS, MINDLESS

in·con·sec·u·tive \ˌin-kən-ˈse-kyə-tiv, -kə-tiv\ *adjective* (1831)
: not consecutive

in·con·se·quence \(ˌ)in-ˈkän(t)-sə-ˌkwen(t)s, -si-kwən(t)s\ *noun* (1588)
: the quality or state of being inconsequent

in·con·se·quent \-ˌkwent, -kwənt\ *adjective* [Late Latin *inconsequent-, inconsequens,* from Latin *in-* + *consequent-, consequens* consequent] (1579)
1 a : lacking reasonable sequence : ILLOGICAL **b** : INCONSECUTIVE
2 : INCONSEQUENTIAL 2
3 : IRRELEVANT
— **in·con·se·quent·ly** *adverb*

in·con·se·quen·tial \(ˌ)in-ˌkän(t)-sə-ˈkwen(t)-shəl\ *adjective* (1621)
1 a : ILLOGICAL **b** : IRRELEVANT
2 : of no significance : UNIMPORTANT
— **in·con·se·quen·ti·al·i·ty** \-ˌkwen(t)-shē-ˈa-lə-tē\ *noun*
— **in·con·se·quen·tial·ly** \-ˈkwen(t)-shlē, -ˈkwen(t)-shə-\ *adverb*

in·con·sid·er·able \ˌin-kən-ˈsi-dər-(ə-)bəl, -ˈsi-drə-bəl\ *adjective* [French, from *in-* + *considerable* considerable, from Medieval Latin *considerabilis*] (1637)
: not considerable : TRIVIAL
— **in·con·sid·er·able·ness** *noun*
— **in·con·sid·er·ably** \-blē\ *adverb*

in·con·sid·er·ate \ˌin-kən-ˈsi-d(ə-)rət\ *adjective* [Middle English *inconsyderatt,* from Latin *inconsideratus,* from *in-* + *consideratus* considerate] (15th century)
1 a : HEEDLESS, THOUGHTLESS **b** : careless of the rights or feelings of others
2 : not adequately considered : ILL-ADVISED
— **in·con·sid·er·ate·ly** *adverb*
— **in·con·sid·er·ate·ness** *noun*
— **in·con·sid·er·ation** \-ˌsi-də-ˈrā-shən\ *noun*

in·con·sis·tence \ˌin-kən-ˈsis-tən(t)s\ *noun* (1643)
: INCONSISTENCY

in·con·sis·ten·cy \ˌin-kən-ˈsis-tən(t)-sē\ *noun* (1647)
1 : an instance of being inconsistent
2 : the quality or state of being inconsistent

in·con·sis·tent \-tənt\ *adjective* (1646)
: lacking consistency: as **a** : not compatible with another fact or claim ⟨*inconsistent* statements⟩ **b** : containing incompatible elements ⟨an *inconsistent* argument⟩ **c** : incoherent or illogical in thought or actions : CHANGEABLE **d** : not satisfiable by the same set of values for the unknowns ⟨*inconsistent* equations⟩ ⟨*inconsistent* inequalities⟩
— **in·con·sis·tent·ly** *adverb*

in·con·sol·able \ˌin-kən-ˈsō-lə-bəl\ *adjective* [Latin *inconsolabilis,* from *in-* + *consolabilis* consolable] (1596)
: incapable of being consoled : DISCONSOLATE
— **in·con·sol·able·ness** *noun*
— **in·con·sol·ably** \-blē\ *adverb*

in·con·so·nance \(ˌ)in-ˈkän(t)-s(ə-)nən(t)s\ *noun* (circa 1811)
: lack of consonance or harmony : DISAGREEMENT

in·con·so·nant \-s(ə-)nənt\ *adjective* (1658)
: not consonant : DISCORDANT

in·con·spic·u·ous \ˌin-kən-ˈspi-kyə-wəs\ *adjective* [Latin *inconspicuus,* from *in-* + *conspicuus* conspicuous] (1648)
: not readily noticeable
— **in·con·spic·u·ous·ly** *adverb*
— **in·con·spic·u·ous·ness** *noun*

in·con·stan·cy \(ˌ)in-ˈkän(t)-stən(t)-sē\ *noun* (1526)
: the quality or state of being inconstant

in·con·stant \-stənt\ *adjective* [Middle English, from Middle French, from Latin *inconstant-, inconstans,* from *in-* + *constant-, constans* constant] (15th century)
: likely to change frequently without apparent or cogent reason ☆
— **in·con·stant·ly** *adverb*

in·con·sum·able \ˌin-kən-ˈsü-mə-bəl\ *adjective* (1646)
: not capable of being consumed
— **in·con·sum·ably** \-blē\ *adverb*

in·con·test·able \ˌin-kən-ˈtes-tə-bəl\ *adjective* [French, from *in-* + *contestable,* from *contester* to contest] (1673)
: not contestable : INDISPUTABLE
— **in·con·test·abil·i·ty** \-ˌtes-tə-ˈbi-lə-tē\ *noun*
— **in·con·test·ably** \-ˈtes-tə-blē\ *adverb*

in·con·ti·nence \(ˌ)in-ˈkän-tᵊn-ən(t)s\ *noun* (14th century)
: the quality or state of being incontinent: as **a** : failure to restrain sexual appetite : UNCHASTITY **b** : inability of the body to control the evacuative functions

in·con·ti·nen·cy \-ən(t)-sē\ *noun* (15th century)
: INCONTINENCE

¹in·con·ti·nent \(ˌ)in-ˈkän-tᵊn-ənt\ *adjective* [Middle English, from Middle French or Latin; Middle French, from Latin *incontinent-, incontinens,* from *in-* + *continent-, continens* continent] (14th century)
: not continent: as **a** (1) : lacking self-restraint (2) : not being under control **b** : unable to retain a bodily discharge (as urine) voluntarily

²incontinent *adverb* [Middle English, from Middle French, from Late Latin *in continenti*] (15th century)
: ¹INCONTINENTLY

¹in·con·ti·nent·ly *adverb* (15th century)
: without delay : IMMEDIATELY

²incontinently *adverb* (circa 1552)
: in an incontinent or unrestrained manner: as **a** : without moral restraint : LEWDLY **b** : without due or reasonable consideration

in·con·trol·la·ble \ˌin-kən-ˈtrō-lə-bəl\ *adjective* (1599)
: UNCONTROLLABLE

in·con·tro·vert·ible \(ˌ)in-ˌkän-trə-ˈvər-tə-bəl\ *adjective* (1646)
: not open to question : INDISPUTABLE ⟨*incontrovertible* evidence⟩
— **in·con·tro·vert·ibly** \-blē\ *adverb*

¹in·con·ve·nience \ˌin-kən-ˈvē-nyən(t)s\ *noun* [Middle English, harm, damage, from Late Latin *inconvenientia,* from Latin *inconvenient-, inconveniens*] (1547)
1 : something that is inconvenient
2 : the quality or state of being inconvenient

²inconvenience *transitive verb* **-nienced; -nienc·ing** (circa 1656)
: to subject to inconvenience : put to trouble

in·con·ve·nien·cy \ˌin-kən-ˈvē-nyən(t)-sē\ *noun, plural* **-cies** (circa 1552)
: INCONVENIENCE

in·con·ve·nient \ˌin-kən-ˈvē-nyənt\ *adjective* [Middle English, from Middle French, from Latin *inconvenient-, inconveniens,* from *in-* + *convenient-, conveniens* convenient] (1651)
: not convenient especially in giving trouble or annoyance : INOPPORTUNE
— **in·con·ve·nient·ly** *adverb*

in·con·vert·ible \-ˈvər-tə-bəl\ *adjective* [probably from Late Latin *inconvertibilis,* from Latin *in-* + *convertibilis* convertible] (1646)
: not convertible: as **a** *of paper money* : not exchangeable for coin **b** *of a currency* : not exchangeable for a foreign currency
— **in·con·vert·ibil·i·ty** \-ˌvər-tə-ˈbi-lə-tē\ *noun*
— **in·con·vert·ibly** \-ˈvər-tə-blē\ *adverb*

in·con·vin·ci·ble \ˌin-kən-ˈvin(t)-sə-bəl\ *adjective* (1674)
: incapable of being convinced

in·co·or·di·na·tion \-(ˌ)kō-ˌȯr-dᵊn-ˈā-shən\ *noun* (1876)
: lack of coordination especially of muscular movements resulting from loss of voluntary control

¹in·cor·po·rate \in-ˈkȯr-pə-ˌrāt\ *verb* **-rat·ed; -rat·ing** [Middle English, from Late Latin *incorporatus,* past participle of *incorporare,* from Latin *in-* + *corpor-, corpus* body — more at MIDRIFF] (14th century)
transitive verb
1 a : to unite or work into something already existent so as to form an indistinguishable whole **b** : to blend or combine thoroughly
2 a : to form into a legal corporation **b** : to admit to membership in a corporate body
3 : to give material form to : EMBODY
intransitive verb
1 : to unite in or as one body
2 : to form or become a corporation
— **in·cor·po·ra·ble** \-p(ə-)rə-bəl\ *adjective*
— **in·cor·po·ra·tion** \-ˌkȯr-pə-ˈrā-shən\ *noun*
— **in·cor·po·ra·tive** \-ˈkȯr-pə-ˌrā-tiv, -p(ə-)rə-tiv\ *adjective*
— **in·cor·po·ra·tor** \-pə-ˌrā-tər\ *noun*

²in·cor·po·rate \in-ˈkȯr-p(ə-)rət\ *adjective* (14th century)
: INCORPORATED

in·cor·po·rat·ed \-pə-ˌrā-təd\ *adjective* (1599)
1 : united in one body
2 : formed into a legal corporation

in·cor·po·re·al \ˌin-(ˌ)kȯr-ˈpȯr-ē-əl, -ˈpȯr-\ *adjective* [Middle English *incorporealle,* from Latin *incorporeus,* from *in-* + *corporeus* corporeal] (15th century)

☆ **SYNONYMS**
Inconstant, fickle, capricious, mercurial, unstable mean lacking firmness or steadiness (as in purpose or devotion). IN-CONSTANT implies an incapacity for steadiness and an inherent tendency to change ⟨an *inconstant* friend⟩. FICKLE suggests unreliability because of perverse changeability and incapacity for steadfastness ⟨performers discover how *fickle* fans can be⟩. CAPRICIOUS suggests motivation by sudden whim or fancy and stresses unpredictability ⟨an utterly *capricious* critic⟩. MERCURIAL implies a rapid changeability in mood ⟨made anxious by her boss's *mercurial* temperament⟩. UNSTABLE implies an incapacity for remaining in a fixed position or steady course and applies especially to a lack of emotional balance ⟨too *unstable* to hold a job⟩.

\ə\ abut \ᵊ\ kitten \ər\ further \a\ ash \ā\ ace
\ä\ mop, mar \au̇\ out \ch\ chin \e\ bet \ē\ easy
\g\ go \i\ hit \ī\ ice \j\ job \ŋ\ sing \ō\ go
\ȯ\ law \ȯi\ boy \th\ thin \t͟h\ the \ü\ loot \u̇\ foot
\y\ yet \zh\ vision *see also* Guide to Pronunciation

1 : not corporeal **:** having no material body or form
2 : of, relating to, or constituting a right that is based on property (as bonds or patents) which has no intrinsic value
— **in·cor·po·re·al·ly** \-ə-lē\ *adverb*
in·cor·po·re·ity \(,)in-,kȯr-pə-'rē-ə-tē\ *noun* (1601)
: the quality or state of being incorporeal **:** IMMATERIALITY
in·cor·rect \,in-kə-'rekt\ *adjective* [Middle English, from Middle French or Latin; Middle French, from Latin *incorrectus,* from *in-* + *correctus* correct] (15th century)
1 *obsolete* **:** not corrected or chastened
2 a : INACCURATE, FAULTY **b :** not true **:** WRONG
3 : UNBECOMING, IMPROPER
— **in·cor·rect·ly** \-'rek(t)-lē\ *adverb*
— **in·cor·rect·ness** \-nəs\ *noun*
in·cor·ri·gi·ble \(,)in-'kȯr-ə-jə-bəl, -'kär-\ *adjective* [Middle English, from Late Latin *incorrigibilis,* from Latin *in-* + *corrigere* to correct — more at CORRECT] (14th century)
: incapable of being corrected or amended: as
a (1) **:** not reformable **:** DEPRAVED (2) **:** DELINQUENT **b :** not manageable **:** UNRULY **c :** UNALTERABLE, INVETERATE
— **in·cor·ri·gi·bil·i·ty** \-,kȯr-ə-jə-'bi-lə-tē, -,kär-\ *noun*
— **incorrigible** *noun*
— **in·cor·ri·gi·ble·ness** \-'kȯr-ə-jə-bəl-nəs, -'kär-\ *noun*
— **in·cor·ri·gi·bly** \-blē\ *adverb*
in·cor·rupt \,in-kə-'rəpt\ *also* **in·cor·rupt·ed** \-'rəp-təd\ *adjective* [Middle English, from Latin *incorruptus,* from *in-* + *corruptus* corrupt] (14th century)
: free from corruption: as **a** *obsolete* **:** not affected with decay **b :** not defiled or depraved **c :** UPRIGHT **c :** free from error
— **in·cor·rupt·ly** \-'rəp(t)-lē\ *adverb*
— **in·cor·rupt·ness** \-nəs\ *noun*
in·cor·rupt·ible \,in-kə-'rəp-tə-bəl\ *adjective* (14th century)
: incapable of corruption: as **a :** not subject to decay or dissolution **b :** incapable of being bribed or morally corrupted
— **in·cor·rupt·ibil·i·ty** \-,rəp-tə-'bi-lə-tē\ *noun*
— **incorruptible** *noun*
— **in·cor·rupt·ibly** \-'rəp-tə-blē\ *adverb*
in·cor·rup·tion \,in-kə-'rəp-shən\ *noun* (14th century)
archaic **:** the quality or state of being free from physical decay
¹in·crease \in-'krēs, 'in-,\ *verb* **in·creased;** **in·creas·ing** [Middle English *encresen,* from Middle French *encreistre,* from Latin *increscere,* from *in-* + *crescere* to grow — more at CRESCENT] (14th century)
intransitive verb
1 : to become progressively greater (as in size, amount, number, or intensity)
2 : to multiply by the production of young
transitive verb
1 : to make greater **:** AUGMENT
2 *obsolete* **:** ENRICH ☆
— **in·creas·able** \-'krē-sə-bəl, -,krē-\ *adjective*
— **in·creas·er** *noun*
²in·crease \'in-,krēs, in-'\ *noun* (14th century)
1 : the act or process of increasing: as **a :** addition or enlargement in size, extent, or quantity **b** *obsolete* **:** PROPAGATION
2 : something that is added to an original stock or amount by augmentation or growth (as offspring, produce, profit)
in·creas·ing·ly \in-'krē-siŋ-lē, 'in-,krē-\ *adverb* (14th century)
: to an increasing degree
in·cre·ate \,in-krē-'āt, in-'krē-ət\ *adjective* [Middle English *increat,* from Late Latin *increatus,* from Latin *in-* + *creatus,* past participle of *creare* to create] (15th century)
: UNCREATED

in·cred·i·ble \(,)in-'kre-də-bəl\ *adjective* [Middle English, from Latin *incredibilis,* from *in-* + *credibilis* credible] (15th century)
1 : too extraordinary and improbable to be believed; *also* **:** hard to believe
— **in·cred·i·bil·i·ty** \-,kre-də-'bi-lə-tē\ *noun*
— **in·cred·i·ble·ness** \-'kre-də-bəl-nəs\ *noun*
— **in·cred·i·bly** \-blē\ *adverb* (circa 1500)
1 : in an incredible manner
2 : EXTREMELY ⟨*incredibly* difficult⟩
in·cre·du·li·ty \,in-kri-'dü-lə-tē, -'dyü-\ *noun* (15th century)
: the quality or state of being incredulous **:** DISBELIEF
in·cred·u·lous \(,)in-'kre-jə-ləs, -dyə-ləs\ *adjective* [Latin *incredulus,* from *in-* + *credulus* credulous] (1579)
1 : unwilling to admit or accept what is offered as true **:** not credulous **:** SKEPTICAL
2 : INCREDIBLE
3 : expressing incredulity □
— **in·cred·u·lous·ly** *adverb*
in·cre·ment \'iŋ-krə-mənt, 'in-\ *noun* [Middle English, from Latin *incrementum,* from *increscere* to increase] (15th century)
1 : the action or process of increasing especially in quantity or value **:** ENLARGEMENT
2 a : something gained or added **b :** one of a series of regular consecutive additions **c :** a minute increase in quantity
3 : the amount or degree by which something changes; *especially* **:** the amount of positive or negative change in the value of one or more of a set of variables
— **in·cre·men·tal** \,iŋ-krə-'men-tᵊl, ,in-\ *adjective*
— **in·cre·men·tal·ly** \-tᵊl-ē\ *adverb*
in·cre·men·tal·ism \,iŋ-krə-'men-tᵊl-,i-zəm\ *noun* (1966)
: a policy or advocacy of a policy of political or social change by degrees **:** GRADUALISM
— **in·cre·men·tal·ist** \-tᵊl-ist\ *noun*
incremental repetition *noun* (1918)
: repetition in each stanza (as of a ballad) of part of the preceding stanza usually with a slight change in wording for dramatic effect
in·cres·cent \in-'kre-sᵊnt\ *adjective* [Latin *increscent-, increscens,* present participle of *increscere*] (circa 1658)
: becoming gradually greater **:** WAXING ⟨the *increscent* moon⟩
in·crim·i·nate \in-'kri-mə-,nāt\ *transitive verb* **-nat·ed; -nat·ing** [Late Latin *incriminatus,* past participle of *incriminare,* from Latin *in-* + *crimin-, crimen* crime] (circa 1736)
: to charge with or show evidence or proof of involvement in a crime or fault
— **in·crim·i·na·tion** \-,kri-mə-'nā-shən\ *noun*
— **in·crim·i·na·to·ry** \-'krim-nə-,tōr-ē, -'kri-mə-, -,tȯr-\ *adjective*
incrust *variant of* ENCRUST
in·crus·ta·tion \,in-,krəs-'tā-shən\ *noun* [Latin *incrustation-, incrustatio,* from *incrustare* to encrust] (1644)
1 a : a crust or hard coating **b :** a growth or accumulation (as of habits, opinions, or customs) resembling a crust
2 : the act of encrusting **:** the state of being encrusted
3 a : OVERLAY **b :** INLAY
in·cu·bate \'iŋ-kyə-,bāt, 'in-\ *verb* **-bat·ed; -bat·ing** [Latin *incubatus,* past participle of *incubare,* from *in-* + *cubare* to lie] (circa 1721)
transitive verb
1 : to sit on (eggs) so as to hatch by the warmth of the body; *also* **:** to maintain (as an embryo or a chemically active system) under conditions favorable for hatching, development, or reaction
2 : to cause (as an idea) to develop
intransitive verb
1 : to sit on eggs

2 : to undergo incubation
— **in·cu·ba·tive** \-,bā-tiv\ *adjective*
— **in·cu·ba·to·ry** \-kyə-bə-,tōr-ē, -,tȯr-; -,bā-tə-rē\ *adjective*
in·cu·ba·tion \,iŋ-kyə-'bā-shən, ,in-\ *noun* (1646)
1 : the act or process of incubating
2 : INCUBATION PERIOD
incubation period *noun* (1879)
: the period between the infection of an individual by a pathogen and the manifestation of the disease it causes
in·cu·ba·tor \'iŋ-kyə-,bā-tər, 'in-\ *noun* (1857)
: one that incubates: as **a :** an apparatus by which eggs are hatched artificially **b :** an apparatus with a chamber used to provide controlled environmental conditions especially for the cultivation of microorganisms or the care and protection of premature or sick babies
in·cu·bus \'iŋ-kyə-bəs, 'in-\ *noun, plural* **-bi** \-,bī, -,bē\ *also* **-bus·es** [Middle English, from Late Latin, from Latin *incubare*] (13th century)
1 : an evil spirit that lies on persons in their sleep; *especially* **:** one that has sexual intercourse with women while they are sleeping — compare SUCCUBUS
2 : NIGHTMARE 2
3 : one that oppresses or burdens like a nightmare
in·cul·cate \in-'kəl-,kāt, 'in-(,)\ *transitive verb* **-cat·ed; -cat·ing** [Latin *inculcatus,* past participle of *inculcare,* literally, to tread on, from *in-* + *calcare* to trample, from *calc-, calx* heel] (1550)
: to teach and impress by frequent repetitions or admonitions
synonym see IMPLANT
— **in·cul·ca·tion** \,in-(,)kəl-'kā-shən\ *noun*
— **in·cul·ca·tor** \in-'kəl-,kā-tər, 'in-(,)\ *noun*
in·cul·pa·ble \(,)in-'kəl-pə-bəl\ *adjective* (15th century)
: free from guilt **:** BLAMELESS
in·cul·pate \in-'kəl-,pāt, 'in-(,)\ *transitive verb* **-pat·ed; -pat·ing** [Late Latin *inculpatus,* from Latin *in-* + *culpatus,* past participle of *culpare* to blame, from *culpa* guilt] (1799)
: INCRIMINATE
— **in·cul·pa·tion** \,in-(,)kəl-'pā-shən\ *noun*
— **in·cul·pa·to·ry** \in-'kəl-pə-,tōr-ē, -,tȯr-\ *adjective*
in·cult \in-'kəlt\ *adjective* [Latin *incultus,* from *in-* + *cultus,* past participle of *colere* to cultivate — more at WHEEL] (1599)

☆ **SYNONYMS**
Increase, enlarge, augment, multiply mean to make or become greater. INCREASE used intransitively implies progressive growth in size, amount, or intensity ⟨his waistline *increased* with age⟩; used transitively it may imply simple not necessarily progressive addition ⟨*increased* her landholdings⟩. ENLARGE implies expansion or extension that makes greater in size or capacity ⟨*enlarged* the kitchen⟩. AUGMENT implies addition to what is already well grown or well developed ⟨the inheritance *augmented* his fortune⟩. MULTIPLY implies increase in number by natural generation or by indefinite repetition of a process ⟨with each attempt the problems *multiplied*⟩.

□ **USAGE**
incredulous Sense 2 has been revived in this century after a couple of centuries of disuse. Although it is a sense with good literary precedent—among others Shakespeare used it—many people think it is a result of confusion with *incredible,* which is still the usual word in this sense.

: COARSE, UNCULTURED

in·cum·ben·cy \in-'kəm-bən(t)-sē\ *noun, plural* **-cies** (circa 1608)
1 : something that is incumbent : DUTY
2 : the quality or state of being incumbent
3 : the sphere of action or period of office of an incumbent
¹**in·cum·bent** \in-'kəm-bənt\ *noun* [Middle English, from Latin *incumbent-, incumbens,* present participle of *incumbere* to lie down on, from *in-* + *-cumbere* to lie down; akin to *cubare* to lie] (15th century)
1 : the holder of an office or ecclesiastical benefice
2 : OCCUPANT
²**incumbent** *adjective* (1567)
1 : imposed as a duty : OBLIGATORY
2 : having the status of an incumbent; *especially* : occupying a specified office
3 : lying or resting on something else
4 : bent over so as to rest on or touch an underlying surface
incumber *variant of* ENCUMBER
in·cu·na·ble \in-'kyü-nə-bəl\ *noun* [French, from New Latin *incunabulum*] (1886)
: INCUNABULUM
in·cu·nab·u·lum \,in-kyə-'na-byə-ləm, ,iŋ-\ *noun, plural* **-la** \-lə\ [New Latin, from Latin *incunabula,* plural, bands holding the baby in a cradle, from *in-* + *cunae* cradle] (circa 1859)
1 : a book printed before 1501
2 : a work of art or of industry of an early period
in·cur \in-'kər\ *transitive verb* **in·curred; in·cur·ring** [Middle English *incurren,* from Latin *incurrere,* literally, to run into, from *in-* + *currere* to run — more at CAR] (15th century)
: to become liable or subject to : bring down upon oneself ⟨*incur* expenses⟩
in·cur·able \(,)in-'kyúr-ə-bəl\ *adjective* [Middle English, from Middle French or Late Latin; Middle French, from Late Latin *incurabilis,* from Latin *in-* + *curabilis* curable] (14th century)
: not curable ⟨an *incurable* disease⟩; *broadly* : not likely to be changed or corrected ⟨*incurable* optimism⟩
— **incurable** *noun*
— **in·cur·ably** \-blē\ *adverb*
in·cu·ri·ous \(,)in-'kyúr-ē-əs\ *adjective* [Latin *incuriosus,* from *in-* + *curiosus* curious] (circa 1618)
: lacking a normal or usual curiosity : UNINTERESTED ⟨a blank *incurious* stare⟩
synonym see INDIFFERENT
— **in·cu·ri·os·i·ty** \-,kyúr-ē-'ä-sə-tē\ *noun*
— **in·cu·ri·ous·ly** \-'kyúr-ē-əs-lē\ *adverb*
— **in·cu·ri·ous·ness** *noun*
in·cur·rence \in-'kər-ən(t)s, -'kə-rən(t)s\ *noun* (circa 1656)
: the act or process of incurring
in·cur·rent \-ənt, -rənt\ *adjective* [Latin *incurrent-, incurrens,* present participle of *incurrere*] (circa 1856)
: giving passage to a current that flows inward
in·cur·sion \in-'kər-zhən\ *noun* [Middle English, from Middle French or Latin; Middle French, from Latin *incursion-, incursio,* from *incurrere*] (15th century)
1 : a hostile entrance into a territory : RAID
2 : an entering in or into (as an activity or undertaking) ⟨his only *incursion* into the arts⟩
in·cur·vate \'in-,kər-,vāt, (,)in-'kər-\ *transitive verb* **-vat·ed; -vat·ing** (1578)
: to cause to curve inward : BEND
— **in·cur·vate** \'in-,kər-,vāt, (,)in-'kər-vət\ *adjective*
— **in·cur·va·tion** \,in-,kər-'vā-shən\ *noun*
— **in·cur·va·ture** \(,)in-'kər-və-,chúr, -chər, -,tyúr-, -,túr\ *noun*
in·curve \(,)in-'kərv, 'in-,\ *transitive verb* [Latin *incurvare,* from *in-* + *curvare* to curve, from *curvus* curved — more at CURVE] (1610)
: to bend so as to curve inward

in·cus \'iŋ-kəs\ *noun, plural* **in·cu·des** \iŋ-'kyü-(,)dēz, 'iŋ-kyə-,dēz\ [New Latin, from Latin, anvil, from *incudere*] (1669)
: the middle bone of a chain of three small bones in the ear of a mammal — called also *anvil;* see EAR illustration
in·cuse \in-'kyüz, -'kyüs\ *adjective* [Latin *incusus,* past participle of *incudere* to stamp, strike, from *in-* + *cudere* to beat — more at HEW] (1818)
: formed by stamping or punching in — used chiefly of old coins or features of their design
Ind \'ind, 'īnd\ *noun* (13th century)
1 *archaic* : India
2 *obsolete* : Indies
ind- *or* **indo-** *combining form* [International Scientific Vocabulary, from Latin *indicum* — more at INDIGO]
1 : indigo ⟨*indoxyl*⟩
2 : resembling indigo (as in color) ⟨*indophenol*⟩
in·da·ba \in-'dä-bə\ *noun* [Zulu *indaba* affair] (1827)
chiefly South African : CONFERENCE, PARLEY
in·da·gate \'in-də-,gāt\ *transitive verb* **-gat·ed; -gat·ing** [Latin *indagatus,* past participle of *indagare,* from *indago* ring of hunters encircling game, act of searching, from Old Latin *indu* in + Latin *agere* to drive — more at END-, AGENT] (circa 1623)
: to search into : INVESTIGATE
— **in·da·ga·tion** \,in-də-'gā-shən\ *noun*
— **in·da·ga·tor** \'in-də-,gā-tər\ *noun*
in·debt·ed \in-'de-təd\ *adjective* [Middle English *indetted,* from Old French *endeté,* past participle of *endeter* to involve in debt, from *en-* + *dete* debt] (13th century)
1 : owing gratitude or recognition to another : BEHOLDEN
2 : owing money
in·debt·ed·ness *noun* (1647)
1 : the condition of being indebted
2 : something (as an amount of money) that is owed
in·de·cen·cy \(,)in-'dē-s²n(t)-sē\ *noun* (1589)
1 : the quality or state of being indecent
2 : something (as a word or action) that is indecent
in·de·cent \-s²nt\ *adjective* [Middle French or Latin; Middle French *indécent,* from Latin *indecent-, indecens,* from *in-* + *decent-, decens* decent] (1587)
: not decent; *especially* : grossly unseemly or offensive to manners or morals
— **in·de·cent·ly** *adverb*
indecent assault *noun* (1861)
: an immoral act or series of acts exclusive of rape committed against another person without consent
indecent exposure *noun* (1851)
: intentional exposure of part of one's body (as the genitals) in a place where such exposure is likely to be an offense against the generally accepted standards of decency
in·de·ci·pher·able \,in-di-'sī-f(ə-)rə-bəl\ *adjective* (1802)
: incapable of being deciphered
in·de·ci·sion \,in-di-'si-zhən\ *noun* [French *indécision,* from *indécis* undecided, from Late Latin *indecisus,* from Latin *in-* + *decisus,* past participle of *decidere* to decide] (circa 1763)
: a wavering between two or more possible courses of action : IRRESOLUTION
in·de·ci·sive \,in-di-'sī-siv\ *adjective* (1726)
1 : not decisive : INCONCLUSIVE
2 : marked by or prone to indecision : IRRESOLUTE
3 : not clearly marked out : INDEFINITE
— **in·de·ci·sive·ly** *adverb*
— **in·de·ci·sive·ness** *noun*
in·de·clin·able \,in-di-'klī-nə-bəl\ *adjective* [Middle English, from Middle French, from Late Latin *indeclinabilis,* from Latin *in-* + Late Latin *declinabilis* capable of being inflected, from Latin *declinare* to inflect — more at DECLINE] (14th century)

: having no grammatical inflections
in·de·com·pos·able \,in-,dē-kəm-'pō-zə-bəl\ *adjective* (1807)
: not capable of being separated into component parts or elements
in·de·co·rous \(,)in-'de-k(ə-)rəs; ,in-di-'kōr-əs, -'kór-\ *adjective* [Latin *indecorus,* from *in-* + *decorus* decorous] (1682)
: not decorous : conflicting with accepted standards of good conduct or good taste ☆
— **in·de·co·rous·ly** *adverb*
— **in·de·co·rous·ness** *noun*
in·de·co·rum \,in-di-'kōr-əm, -'kór-\ *noun* [Latin, neuter of *indecorus*] (1575)
1 : something that is indecorous
2 : lack of decorum : IMPROPRIETY
in·deed \in-'dēd\ *adverb* (14th century)
1 : without any question : TRULY, UNDENIABLY — often used interjectionally to express irony or disbelief or surprise
2 : in reality
3 : all things considered : as a matter of fact
in·de·fat·i·ga·ble \,in-di-'fa-ti-gə-bəl\ *adjective* [Middle French, from Latin *indefatigabilis,* from *in-* + *defatigare* to fatigue, from *de-* + *fatigare* to fatigue] (1611)
: incapable of being fatigued : UNTIRING
— **in·de·fat·i·ga·bil·i·ty** \-,fa-ti-gə-'bi-lə-tē\ *noun*
— **in·de·fat·i·ga·ble·ness** \-'fa-ti-gə-bəl-nəs\ *noun*
— **in·de·fat·i·ga·bly** \-blē\ *adverb*
in·de·fea·si·ble \-'fē-zə-bəl\ *adjective* (1548)
: not capable of being annulled or voided or undone ⟨an *indefeasible* right⟩
— **in·de·fea·si·bil·i·ty** \-,fē-zə-'bi-lə-tē\ *noun*
— **in·de·fea·si·bly** \-'fē-zə-blē\ *adverb*
in·de·fec·ti·ble \-'fek-tə-bəl\ *adjective* (1659)
1 : not subject to failure or decay : LASTING
2 : free of faults : FLAWLESS
— **in·de·fec·ti·bil·i·ty** \-,fek-tə-'bi-lə-tē\ *noun*
— **in·de·fec·ti·bly** \-'fek-tə-blē\ *adverb*
in·de·fen·si·ble \-'fen(t)-sə-bəl\ *adjective* (1529)
1 a : incapable of being maintained as right or valid : UNTENABLE **b** : incapable of being justified or excused : INEXCUSABLE
2 : incapable of being protected against physical attack
— **in·de·fen·si·bil·i·ty** \-,fen(t)-sə-'bi-lə-tē\ *noun*
— **in·de·fen·si·bly** \-'fen(t)-sə-blē\ *adverb*
in·de·fin·able \-'fī-nə-bəl\ *adjective* (1810)
: incapable of being precisely described or analyzed

☆ **SYNONYMS**
Indecorous, improper, unseemly, unbecoming, indelicate mean not conforming to what is accepted as right, fitting, or in good taste. INDECOROUS suggests a violation of accepted standards of good manners ⟨*indecorous* behavior⟩. IMPROPER applies to a broader range of transgressions of rules not only of social behavior but of ethical practice or logical procedure or prescribed method ⟨*improper* use of campaign contributions⟩. UNSEEMLY adds a suggestion of special inappropriateness to a situation or an offensiveness to good taste ⟨remarked with *unseemly* haste⟩. UNBECOMING suggests behavior or language that does not suit one's character or status ⟨conduct *unbecoming* to an officer⟩. INDELICATE implies a lack of modesty or of tact or of refined perception of feeling ⟨*indelicate* expressions for bodily functions⟩.

\ə\ **abut** \ᵊ\ **kitten** \ər\ **further** \a\ **ash** \ā\ **ace**
\ä\ **mop, mar** \aú\ **out** \ch\ **chin** \e\ **bet** \ē\ **easy**
\g\ **go** \i\ **hit** \ī\ **ice** \j\ **job** \ŋ\ **sing** \ō\ **go**
\ó\ **law** \ói\ **boy** \th\ **thin** \t̲h̲\ **the** \ü\ **loot** \ú\ **foot**
\y\ **yet** \zh\ **vision** *see also* Guide to Pronunciation

— **in·de·fin·abil·i·ty** \-,fī-nə-'bi-lə-tē\ *noun*
— **indefinable** *noun*
— **in·de·fin·able·ness** \-'fī-nə-bəl-nəs\ *noun*
— **in·de·fin·ably** \-blē\ *adverb*

in·def·i·nite \(,)in-'def-nət, -'de-fə-\ *adjective* [Latin *indefinitus*, from *in-* + *definitus* definite] (1530)
: not definite: as **a** : typically designating an unidentified, generic, or unfamiliar person or thing (the *indefinite* articles *a* and *an*) (*indefinite* pronouns) **b** : not precise : VAGUE **c** : having no exact limits **d** *of floral organs* : numerous and difficult to ascertain in number
— **indefinite** *noun*
— **in·def·i·nite·ly** *adverb*
— **in·def·i·nite·ness** *noun*

indefinite integral *noun* (circa 1877)
: any function whose derivative is a given function

in·de·his·cent \,in-di-'hi-sᵊnt\ *adjective* (1832)
: remaining closed at maturity (*indehiscent* fruits)
— **in·de·his·cence** \-sᵊn(t)s\ *noun*

in·del·i·ble \in-'de-lə-bəl\ *adjective* [Middle English *indelyble*, from Medieval Latin *indelibilis*, alteration of Latin *indelebilis*, from *in-* + *delēre* to delete] (15th century)
1 a : that cannot be removed, washed away, or erased **b** : making marks that cannot easily be removed (an *indelible* pencil)
2 a : LASTING (*indelible* memories) **b** : UNFORGETTABLE, MEMORABLE (an *indelible* performance)
— **in·del·i·bil·i·ty** \(,)in-,de-lə-'bi-lə-tē\ *noun*
— **in·del·i·bly** \in-'de-lə-blē\ *adverb*

in·del·i·ca·cy \(,)in-'de-li-kə-sē\ *noun* (1712)
1 : the quality or state of being indelicate
2 : something that is indelicate

in·del·i·cate \-li-kət\ *adjective* (1742)
: not delicate: **a** : lacking in or offending against propriety : IMPROPER (2) : verging on the indecent : COARSE **b** : marked by a lack of feeling for the sensibilities of others : TACTLESS
synonym see INDECOROUS
— **in·del·i·cate·ly** *adverb*
— **in·del·i·cate·ness** *noun*

in·dem·ni·fi·ca·tion \in-,dem-nə-fə-'kā-shən\ *noun* (1732)
1 a : the action of indemnifying **b** : the condition of being indemnified
2 : INDEMNITY 2b

in·dem·ni·fy \in-'dem-nə-,fī\ *transitive verb* **-fied; -fy·ing** [Latin *indemnis* unharmed, from *in-* + *damnum* damage] (circa 1611)
1 : to secure against hurt, loss, or damage
2 : to make compensation to for incurred hurt, loss, or damage
synonym see PAY
— **in·dem·ni·fi·er** \-,fī(-ə)r\ *noun*

in·dem·ni·ty \in-'dem-nə-tē\ *noun, plural* **-ties** (15th century)
1 a : security against hurt, loss, or damage **b** : exemption from incurred penalties or liabilities
2 a : INDEMNIFICATION 1 **b** : something that indemnifies

in·de·mon·stra·ble \,in-di-'män(t)-strə-bəl, (,)in-'dem-ən-strə-\ *adjective* (1570)
: incapable of being demonstrated : not subject to proof
— **in·de·mon·stra·bly** \-blē\ *adverb*

¹in·dent \in-'dent\ *verb* [Middle English, from Middle French *endenter*, from Old French, from *en-* + *dent* tooth, from Latin *dent-, dens* — more at TOOTH] (14th century)
transitive verb
1 a : to divide (a document) so as to produce sections with irregular edges that can be matched for authentication **b** : to draw up (as a deed) in two or more exactly corresponding copies
2 : to notch the edge of : make jagged
3 : INDENTURE

4 : to set (as a line of a paragraph) in from the margin
5 *chiefly British* : to order by an indent
intransitive verb
1 *obsolete* : to make a formal or express agreement
2 : to form an indentation
3 *chiefly British* : to make out an indent for something
— **in·dent·er** *noun*
— **indent on 1** *chiefly British* : to make a requisition on **2** *chiefly British* : to draw on

²in·dent \in-'dent, 'in-,\ *noun* (15th century)
1 a : INDENTURE 1 **b** : a certificate issued by the U.S. at the close of the American Revolution for the principal or interest on the public debt
2 *chiefly British* **a** : an official requisition **b** : a purchase order for goods especially when sent from a foreign country
3 : INDENTION

³in·dent \in-'dent\ *transitive verb* [Middle English *endenten*, from *en-* + *denten* to dent] (15th century)
1 : to force inward so as to make a depression
2 : to form a dent in
— **in·dent·er** *noun*

⁴in·dent \in-'dent, 'in-,\ *noun* (1596)
: INDENTATION

in·den·ta·tion \,in-,den-'tā-shən\ *noun* (circa 1728)
1 a : an angular cut in an edge : NOTCH **b** : a recess in a surface
2 : the action of indenting : the condition of being indented
3 : DENT
4 : INDENTION 2b

in·den·tion \in-'den(t)-shən\ *noun* (1763)
1 *archaic* : INDENTATION 1
2 a : the action of indenting : the condition of being indented **b** : the blank space produced by indenting

¹in·den·ture \in-'den(t)-shər\ *noun* [Middle English *endenture*, from Middle French, from *endenter*] (14th century)
1 a (1) : a document or a section of a document that is indented (2) : a formal or official document usually executed in two or more copies (3) : a contract binding one person to work for another for a given period of time — usually used in plural **b** : a formal certificate (as an inventory or voucher) prepared for purposes of control **c** : a document stating the terms under which a security (as a bond) is issued
2 : INDENTATION 1
3 [³*indent*] : DENT

²indenture *transitive verb* **in·den·tured; in·den·tur·ing** \-'den(t)-shriŋ, -'den(t)-shə-riŋ\ (1676)
: to bind (as an apprentice) by or as if by indentures

indentured servant *noun* (1723)
: a person who signs and is bound by indentures to work for another for a specified time especially in return for payment of travel expenses and maintenance

in·de·pen·dence \,in-də-'pen-dən(t)s\ *noun* (1640)
1 : the quality or state of being independent
2 *archaic* : COMPETENCE 1

Independence Day *noun* (1791)
: a civil holiday for the celebration of the anniversary of the beginnings of national independence; *specifically* : July 4 observed as a legal holiday in the U.S. in commemoration of the adoption of the Declaration of Independence in 1776

in·de·pen·den·cy \,in-də-'pen-dən(t)-sē\ *noun* (circa 1611)
1 : INDEPENDENCE 1
2 *capitalized* : the Independent polity or movement
3 : an independent political unit

¹in·de·pen·dent \,in-də-'pen-dənt\ *adjective* (1611)

1 : not dependent: as **a** (1) : not subject to control by others : SELF-GOVERNING (2) : not affiliated with a larger controlling unit **b** (1) : not requiring or relying on something else : not contingent (an *independent* conclusion) (2) : not looking to others for one's opinions or for guidance in conduct (3) : not bound by or committed to a political party **c** (1) : not requiring or relying on others (as for care or livelihood) (*independent* of her parents) (2) : being enough to free one from the necessity of working for a living (a man of *independent* means) **d** : showing a desire for freedom (an *independent* manner) **e** (1) : not determined by or capable of being deduced or derived from or expressed in terms of members (as axioms or equations) of the set under consideration; *especially* : having linear independence (an *independent* set of vectors) (2) : having the property that the joint probability (as of events or samples) or the joint probability density function (as of random variables) equals the product of the probabilities or probability density functions of separate occurrence
2 *capitalized* : of or relating to the Independents
3 a : MAIN 5 (an *independent* clause) **b** : neither deducible from nor incompatible with another statement (*independent* postulates)
synonym see FREE
— **in·de·pen·dent·ly** *adverb*

²independent *noun* (1644)
1 *capitalized* : a sectarian of an English religious movement for congregational autonomy originating in the late 16th century, giving rise to Congregationalists, Baptists, and Friends, and forming one of the major political groupings of the period of Cromwell
2 : one that is independent; *especially, often capitalized* : one that is not bound by or definitively committed to a political party

independent assortment *noun* (circa 1948)
: formation of random combinations of chromosomes in meiosis and of genes on different pairs of homologous chromosomes by the passage according to the laws of probability of one of each diploid pair of homologous chromosomes into each gamete independently of each other pair

independent variable *noun* (1852)
: a mathematical variable whose value is specified first and determines the value of one or more other values in an expression or function

in–depth \('\)in-'depth\ *adjective* (1965)
: COMPREHENSIVE, THOROUGH (an *in-depth* study)

in·de·scrib·able \,in-di-'skrī-bə-bəl\ *adjective* (1794)
1 : that cannot be described (an *indescribable* sensation)
2 : surpassing description (*indescribable* joy)
— **in·de·scrib·able·ness** *noun*
— **in·de·scrib·ably** \-blē\ *adverb*

in·de·struc·ti·ble \-'strək-tə-bəl\ *adjective* [probably from Late Latin *indestructibilis*, from Latin *in-* + *destructus*, past participle of *destruere* to tear down — more at DESTROY] (1667)
: incapable of being destroyed, ruined, or rendered ineffective
— **in·de·struc·ti·bil·i·ty** \-,strək-tə-'bi-lə-tē\ *noun*
— **in·de·struc·ti·ble·ness** \-'strək-tə-bəl-nəs\ *noun*
— **in·de·struc·ti·bly** \-blē\ *adverb*

in·de·ter·min·able \,in-di-'tərm-nə-bəl, -'tər-mə-\ *adjective* (15th century)
1 : incapable of being definitely decided or settled
2 : incapable of being definitely fixed or ascertained
— **in·de·ter·min·ably** \-blē\ *adverb*

in·de·ter·mi·na·cy \-nə-sē\ *noun* (1649)

: the quality or state of being indeterminate

indeterminacy principle *noun* (circa 1928)
: UNCERTAINTY PRINCIPLE

in·de·ter·mi·nate \,in-di-'tərm-nət, -'tər-mə-\ *adjective* [Middle English *indeterminat,* from Late Latin *indeterminatus,* from Latin *in-* + *determinatus,* past participle of *determinare* to determine] (14th century)
1 a : not definitely or precisely determined or fixed **:** VAGUE **b :** not known in advance **c :** not leading to a definite end or result
2 : having an infinite number of solutions ⟨a system of *indeterminate* equations⟩
3 : being one of the seven undefined mathematical expressions

$$\frac{0}{0},\ \frac{\infty}{\infty},\ \infty \cdot 0,\ 1^{\infty},\ 0^{0},\ \infty^{0},\ \infty - \infty$$

4 : characterized by sequential flowering from the lateral or basal buds to the central or uppermost buds; *also* **:** characterized by growth in which the main stem continues to elongate indefinitely without being limited by a terminal inflorescence — compare DETERMINATE 4
— **in·de·ter·mi·nate·ly** *adverb*
— **in·de·ter·mi·nate·ness** *noun*
— **in·de·ter·mi·na·tion** \-,tər-mə-'nā-shən\ *noun*

in·de·ter·min·ism \-'tər-mə-,ni-zəm\ *noun* (1874)
1 a : a theory that the will is free and that deliberate choice and actions are not determined by or predictable from antecedent causes **b :** a theory that holds that not every event has a cause
2 : the quality or state of being indeterminate; *especially* **:** UNPREDICTABILITY
— **in·de·ter·min·ist** \-'tərm-nist, -'tər-mə-\ *noun*
— **in·de·ter·min·is·tic** \-,tər-mə-'nis-tik\ *adjective*

¹in·dex \'in-,deks\ *noun, plural* **in·dex·es** *or* **in·di·ces** \-də-,sēz\ [Latin *indic-, index,* from *indicare* to indicate] (1571)
1 a : a device (as the pointer on a scale or the gnomon of a sundial) that serves to indicate a value or quantity **b :** something (as a physical feature or a mode of expression) that leads one to a particular fact or conclusion **:** INDICATION
2 : a list (as of bibliographical information or citations) to a body of literature) arranged usually in alphabetical order of some specified datum (as author, subject, or keyword): as **a :** a list of items (as topics or names) treated in a printed work that gives for each item the page number where it may be found **b :** THUMB INDEX **c :** a bibliographical analysis of groups of publications that is usually published periodically
3 : a list of restricted or prohibited material; *specifically, capitalized* **:** a list of books the reading of which is prohibited or restricted for Roman Catholics by the church authorities
4 *plural usually* **indices :** a number or symbol or expression (as an exponent) associated with another to indicate a mathematical operation to be performed or to indicate use or position in an arrangement
5 : a character ☞ used to direct attention to a note or paragraph — called also *fist*
6 a : a number (as a ratio) derived from a series of observations and used as an indicator or measure; *specifically* **:** INDEX NUMBER **b :** the ratio of one dimension of a thing (as an anatomical structure) to another dimension

²index (1720)
transitive verb
1 a : to provide with an index **b :** to list in an index ⟨all persons and places mentioned are carefully *indexed*⟩
2 : to serve as an index of
3 : to regulate (as wages, prices, or interest rates) by indexation

intransitive verb
: to index something
— **in·dex·er** *noun*

in·dex·ation \,in-dek-'sā-shən\ *noun* (1960)
: a system of economic control in which certain variables (as wages and interest) are tied to a cost-of-living index so that both rise or fall at the same rate and the detrimental effect of inflation is theoretically eliminated

index finger *noun* (1849)
: FOREFINGER

index fossil *noun* (1900)
: a fossil usually with a narrow time range and wide spatial distribution that used in the identification of related geologic formations

¹in·dex·i·cal \(,)in-'dek-si-kəl\ *adjective* (circa 1828)
1 : of or relating to an index
2 a : varying in reference with the individual speaker ⟨the *indexical* words *I, here, now*⟩ **b :** associated with or identifying an individual speaker ⟨*indexical* features of speech⟩

²indexical *noun* (1971)
: an indexical word, sign, or feature

indexing *noun* (1957)
: INDEXATION

index number *noun* (circa 1896)
: a number used to indicate change in magnitude (as of cost or price) as compared with the magnitude at some specified time usually taken as 100

index of refraction (1829)
: the ratio of the speed of radiation (as light) in one medium (as a vacuum) to that in another medium

indi- — see IND-

In·dia \'in-dē-ə\ (circa 1952)
— a communications code word for the letter *i*

india ink *noun, often 1st I capitalized* (1665)
1 : a solid black pigment (as specially prepared lampblack) used in drawing and lettering
2 : a fluid ink consisting usually of a fine suspension of india ink in a liquid

In·dia·man \'in-dē-ə-mən\ *noun* (1709)
: a merchant ship formerly used in trade with India; *especially* **:** a large sailing ship used in this trade

In·di·an \'in-dē-ən, *dialect* -jən *or* -din\ *noun* (14th century)
1 a : a native or inhabitant of India or of the East Indies **b :** a person of Indian descent
2 a [from the belief held by Columbus that the lands he discovered were part of Asia] **:** AMERICAN INDIAN **b :** one of the native languages of American Indians
— **Indian** *adjective*
— **In·di·an·ness** *noun*

Indian agent *noun* (1807)
: an official representative of the U.S. federal government to American Indian tribes especially on reservations

Indian club *noun* (1857)
: a usually wooden club shaped like a large bottle or tenpin that is swung for gymnastic exercise

Indian corn *noun* (1617)
1 : a tall widely cultivated American cereal grass (*Zea mays*) bearing seeds on elongated ears
2 : the ears of Indian corn; *also* **:** its edible seeds

Indian elephant *noun* (1607)
: ELEPHANT 1b

Indian file *noun* (1758)
: SINGLE FILE

Indian giver *noun* (circa 1848)
: a person who gives something to another and then takes it back or expects an equivalent in return
— **Indian giving** *noun*

Indian hemp *noun* (1619)
1 : an American dogbane (*Apocynum cannabinum*) with milky juice, tough fibrous bark, and an emetic and cathartic root

2 : HEMP 1

In·di·an·ism \'in-dē-ə-,ni-zəm\ *noun* (1651)
1 : the qualities or culture distinctive of American Indians
2 : policy designed to further the interests or culture of American Indians
— **In·di·an·ist** \-nist\ *adjective or noun*

In·di·an·ize \'in-dē-ə-,nīz\ *transitive verb* **-ized; -izing** (1702)
1 : to cause to acquire or conform to the characteristics, culture, or usage of American Indians or of India
2 : to bring (as a region) under the cultural or political influence or control of India
— **In·di·an·i·za·tion** \,in-dē-ə-(,)nī-'zā-shən\ *noun*

Indian licorice *noun* (circa 1890)
: ROSARY PEA 1

Indian meal *noun* (1609)
: CORNMEAL

Indian paintbrush *noun* (circa 1892)
1 : any of a genus (*Castilleja*) of herbaceous plants of the snapdragon family that have brightly colored bracts — called also *painted cup*
2 : ORANGE HAWKWEED

Indian pipe *noun* (circa 1818)
: a waxy white saprophytic herb (*Monotropa uniflora* of the family Monotropaceae, the Indian-pipe family) of Asia and North America having leaves reduced to scales

Indian paintbrush

Indian pudding *noun* (1722)
: a baked pudding made chiefly of cornmeal, milk, and molasses

Indian red *noun* (circa 1753)
1 : any of various usually dark red pigments consisting chiefly of iron oxide
2 : a strong or moderate reddish brown

Indian pipe

Indian sign *noun* (1910)
: HEX, SPELL

Indian summer *noun* (1778)
1 : a period of warm or mild weather in late autumn or early winter
2 : a happy or flourishing period occurring toward the end of something ⟨life in the *Indian summer* of Czarist Russia —John Davenport⟩

Indian tobacco *noun* (circa 1618)
1 : an American wild lobelia (*Lobelia inflata*) with small blue or white flowers
2 : a wild tobacco (*Nicotiana bigelovii*) found in dry valleys from southern California to southern Oregon

In·di·an–wres·tle \'in-dē-ən-,re-səl, -,ra-\ *intransitive verb* [back-formation from *Indian wrestling*] (1938)
: to engage in Indian wrestling

Indian wrestling *noun* (1913)
1 : wrestling in which two people lie side by side on their backs in reversed position locking their near arms and raising and locking the corresponding legs and attempt to force each other's leg down and turn the other wrestler facedown
2 : wrestling in which two people stand face to face gripping usually their right hands and setting the outsides of the corresponding feet together and attempt to force each other off balance
3 : ARM WRESTLING

India paper *noun* (1768)

\ə\ abut	\ᵊ\ kitten	\ər\ further	\a\ ash	\ā\ ace	
\ä\ mop, mar	\aù\ out	\ch\ chin	\e\ bet	\ē\ easy	
\g\ go	\i\ hit	\ī\ ice	\j\ job	\ŋ\ sing	\ō\ go
\ò\ law	\òi\ boy	\th\ thin	\th̲\ the	\ü\ loot	\ù\ foot
\y\ yet	\zh\ vision		*see also* Guide to Pronunciation		

1 : a thin absorbent paper used especially for proving inked intaglio surfaces (as steel engravings)
2 : a thin tough opaque printing paper
india rubber *noun, often I capitalized* (1790)
: ¹RUBBER 2a
In·dic \'in-dik\ *adjective* (1877)
1 : of or relating to the subcontinent of India **:** INDIAN
2 : of, relating to, or constituting the Indo-Aryan branch of the Indo-European languages
— **Indic** *noun*
in·di·can \'in-də-ˌkan\ *noun* [Latin *indicum* indigo — more at INDIGO] (1859)
1 : an indigo-forming substance $C_8H_7NO_4S$ found as a salt in urine and other animal fluids; *also* **:** its potassium salt $C_8H_6KNO_4S$
2 : a glucoside $C_{14}H_{17}NO_6$ occurring especially in the indigo plant and being a source of natural indigo
in·di·cant \'in-di-kənt\ *noun* (1623)
: something that serves to indicate
in·di·cate \'in-də-ˌkāt\ *transitive verb* **-cat·ed; -cat·ing** [Latin *indicatus,* past participle of *indicare,* from *in-* + *dicare* to proclaim, dedicate — more at DICTION] (circa 1609)
1 a : to point out or point to **b :** to be a sign, symptom, or index of ⟨the high fever *indicates* a serious condition⟩ **c :** to demonstrate or suggest the necessity or advisability of ⟨*indicated* the need for a new school⟩
2 : to state or express briefly ⟨*indicated* a desire to cooperate⟩
in·di·ca·tion \ˌin-də-'kā-shən\ *noun* (15th century)
1 a : something that serves to indicate **b :** something that is indicated as advisable or necessary
2 : the action of indicating
— **in·di·ca·tion·al** \-shnəl, -shə-nᵊl\ *adjective*
¹in·dic·a·tive \in-'di-kə-tiv\ *adjective* (15th century)
1 : of, relating to, or constituting a verb form or set of verb forms that represents the denoted act or state as an objective fact ⟨the *indicative* mood⟩
2 : serving to indicate ⟨actions *indicative* of fear⟩
— **in·dic·a·tive·ly** *adverb*
²indicative *noun* (1530)
1 : the indicative mood of a language
2 : a form in the indicative mood
in·di·ca·tor \'in-də-ˌkā-tər\ *noun* (1666)
1 : one that indicates: as **a :** an index hand (as on a dial) **:** POINTER **b** (1) **:** GAUGE 2b, DIAL 4a (2) **:** an instrument for automatically making a diagram that indicates the pressure in and volume of the working fluid of an engine throughout the cycle
2 a : a substance (as litmus) used to show visually (as by change of color) the condition of a solution with respect to the presence of a particular material (as a free acid or alkali) **b :** TRACER 4b
3 : an organism or ecological community so strictly associated with particular environmental conditions that its presence is indicative of the existence of these conditions
4 : any of a group of statistical values (as level of employment) that taken together give an indication of the health of the economy
— **in·dic·a·to·ry** \in-'di-kə-ˌtȯr-ē, -ˌtȯr-\ *adjective*
indices *plural of* INDEX
in·di·cia \in-'di-sh(ē-)ə\ *noun plural* [Latin, plural of *indicium* sign, from *indicare*] (circa 1626)
1 : distinctive marks **:** INDICATIONS
2 : postal markings often imprinted on mail or on labels to be affixed to mail
in·dict \in-'dīt\ *transitive verb* [alteration of earlier *indite,* from Middle English *inditen,* from Anglo-French *enditer,* from Old French, to write down — more at INDITE] (circa 1626)

1 : to charge with a fault or offense **:** CRITICIZE, ACCUSE
2 : to charge with a crime by the finding or presentment of a jury (as a grand jury) in due form of law
— **in·dict·er** *or* **in·dict·or** \-'dī-tər\ *noun*
in·dict·able \-'dī-tə-bəl\ *adjective* (circa 1706)
1 : subject to being indicted **:** liable to indictment
2 : making one liable to indictment ⟨an *indictable* offense⟩
in·dic·tion \in-'dik-shən\ *noun* [Middle English *indiccioun,* from Late Latin *indiction-, indictio,* from Latin, proclamation, from *indicere* to proclaim, from *in-* + *dicere* to say — more at DICTION] (14th century)
: a 15-year cycle used as a chronological unit in several ancient and medieval systems
in·dict·ment \in-'dīt-mənt\ *noun* (14th century)
1 a : the action or the legal process of indicting **b :** the state of being indicted
2 : a formal written statement framed by a prosecuting authority and found by a jury (as a grand jury) charging a person with an offense
3 : an expression of strong disapproval ⟨an *indictment* of contemporary morality⟩
in·die \'in-dē\ *noun* [by shortening & alteration from *independent*] (1928)
: something (as an unaffiliated record or motion-picture production company) independent
— **indie** *adjective*
in·dif·fer·ence \in-'di-fərn(t)s, -f(ə-)rən(t)s\ *noun* (15th century)
1 : the quality, state, or fact of being indifferent
2 a *archaic* **:** lack of difference or distinction between two or more things **b :** absence of compulsion to or toward one thing or another
in·dif·fer·en·cy \-fərn(t)-sē, -f(ə-)rən(t)-sē\ *noun* (15th century)
archaic **:** INDIFFERENCE
in·dif·fer·ent \in-'di-fərnt, -f(ə-)rənt\ *adjective* [Middle English, from Middle French or Latin; Middle French, regarded as neither good nor bad, from Latin *indifferent-, indifferens,* from *in-* + *different-, differens,* present participle of *differre* to be different — more at DIFFER] (14th century)
1 : marked by impartiality **:** UNBIASED
2 a : that does not matter one way or the other **b :** of no importance or value one way or the other
3 a : marked by no special liking for or dislike of something ⟨*indifferent* about which task he was given⟩ **b :** marked by a lack of interest, enthusiasm, or concern for something **:** APATHETIC ⟨*indifferent* to suffering and poverty⟩
4 : being neither excessive nor inadequate **:** MODERATE ⟨hills of *indifferent* size⟩
5 a : being neither good nor bad **:** MEDIOCRE ⟨does *indifferent* work⟩ **b :** being neither right nor wrong
6 : characterized by lack of active quality **:** NEUTRAL
7 a : not differentiated **b :** capable of development in more than one direction; *especially* **:** not yet embryologically determined ☆
— **in·dif·fer·ent·ly** *adverb*
in·dif·fer·ent·ism \-fərn-ˌti-zəm, -f(ə-)rən-\ *noun* (1827)
: INDIFFERENCE; *specifically* **:** belief that all religions are equally valid
— **in·dif·fer·ent·ist** \-fərn-tist, -f(ə-)rən-\ *noun*
in·di·gence \'in-di-jən(t)s\ *noun* (14th century)
: a level of poverty in which real hardship and deprivation are suffered and comforts of life are wholly lacking
synonym see POVERTY
in·di·gene \'in-də-ˌjēn\ *also* **in·di·gen** \-di-jən, -də-ˌjen\ *noun* [Latin *indigena*] (1598)
: NATIVE

in·dig·e·nize \in-'di-jə-ˌnīz\ *transitive verb* **-nized; -niz·ing** (1951)
: to cause to have indigenous characteristics
— **in·dig·e·ni·za·tion** \-ˌdi-jə-nə-'zā-shən, -ˌnī-'\ *noun*
in·dig·e·nous \in-'di-jə-nəs\ *adjective* [Late Latin *indigenus,* from Latin *indigena,* noun, native, from Old Latin *indu, endo* in, within + Latin *gignere* to beget — more at END-, KIN] (1646)
1 : having originated in and being produced, growing, living, or occurring naturally in a particular region or environment
2 : INNATE, INBORN
synonym see NATIVE
— **in·dig·e·nous·ly** *adverb*
— **in·dig·e·nous·ness** *noun*
in·di·gent \'in-di-jənt\ *adjective* [Middle English, from Middle French, from Latin *indigent-, indigens,* present participle of *indigēre* to need, from Old Latin *indu* + Latin *egēre* to need; perhaps akin to Old High German *ekrōdi* thin] (15th century)
1 : suffering from indigence **:** IMPOVERISHED
2 a *archaic* **:** DEFICIENT **b** *archaic* **:** totally lacking in something specified
— **indigent** *noun*
in·di·gest·ed \ˌin-(ˌ)dī-'jes-təd, -də-\ *adjective* (1587)
: not carefully thought out or arranged **:** FORMLESS
in·di·gest·ible \-'jes-tə-bəl\ *adjective* [Middle English, from Late Latin *indigestibilis,* from Latin *in-* + Late Latin *digestibilis* digestible] (15th century)
: not digestible **:** not easily digested
— **in·di·gest·ibil·i·ty** \-ˌjes-tə-'bi-lə-tē\ *noun*
— **indigestible** *noun*
in·di·ges·tion \-'jes-chən, -'jesh-\ *noun* (14th century)
1 : inability to digest or difficulty in digesting something
2 : a case or attack of indigestion
in·dign \in-'dīn\ *adjective* [Middle English *indigne,* from Middle French, from Latin *indignus*] (14th century)
1 *archaic* **:** UNWORTHY, UNDESERVING
2 *obsolete* **:** UNBECOMING, DISGRACEFUL
in·dig·nant \in-'dig-nənt\ *adjective* [Latin *indignant-, indignans,* present participle of *indignari* to be indignant, from *indignus* unworthy, from *in-* + *dignus* worthy — more at DECENT] (1590)
: filled with or marked by indignation ⟨became *indignant* at the accusation⟩
— **in·dig·nant·ly** *adverb*
in·dig·na·tion \ˌin-dig-'nā-shən\ *noun* (14th century)

: anger aroused by something unjust, unworthy, or mean

synonym see ANGER

in·dig·ni·ty \in-'dig-nə-tē\ noun, plural **-ties** [Latin indignitat-, indignitas, from indignus] (1584)

1 a : an act that offends against a person's dignity or self-respect **:** INSULT **b :** humiliating treatment

2 obsolete **:** lack or loss of dignity or honor

in·di·go \'in-di-ˌgō\ noun, plural **-gos** or **-goes** [Italian dialect, from Latin indicum, from Greek indikon, from neuter of indikos Indic, from Indos India] (1555)

1 a : a blue vat dye obtained from plants (as indigo plants) **b :** the principal coloring matter $C_{16}H_{10}N_2O_2$ of natural indigo usually synthesized as a blue powder with a coppery luster

2 : INDIGO PLANT

3 : a deep reddish blue

indigo bunting noun (1783)

: a common small American finch (Passerina cyanea) of which the male is largely indigo‣ blue in spring and summer

indigo plant noun (1757)

: a plant that yields indigo; especially **:** any of a genus (Indigofera) of leguminous herbs

indigo snake noun (circa 1885)

: a large blue-black or brownish colubrid snake (Drymarchon corais) of the southeastern U.S. and Texas to Argentina — called also gopher snake

in·di·go·tin \in-'di-gə-tən, ˌin-di-'gō-tᵊn\ noun [French indigotine, irregular from indigo indigo] (1838)

: INDIGO 1b

in·di·rect \ˌin-də-'rekt, -(ˌ)dī-\ adjective [Middle English, from Medieval Latin indirectus, from Latin in- + directus direct — more at DRESS] (14th century)

: not direct: as **a** (1) **:** deviating from a direct line or course **:** ROUNDABOUT (2) **:** not going straight to the point ⟨an indirect accusation⟩ (3) **:** being or involving proof of a proposition or theorem by demonstration that its negation leads to an absurdity or contradiction **b :** not straightforward and open **:** DECEITFUL **c :** not directly aimed at or achieved ⟨indirect consequences⟩ **d :** stating what a real or supposed original speaker said with changes in wording that conform the statement grammatically to the sentence in which it is included ⟨indirect discourse⟩ ⟨an indirect question⟩ **e :** not effected by the action of the people or the electorate ⟨indirect government representation⟩

— **in·di·rect·ly** \-'rek(t)-lē\ adverb
— **in·di·rect·ness** \-nəs\ noun

indirect cost noun (circa 1909)

: a cost that is not identifiable with a specific product, function, or activity

indirect evidence noun (1824)

: evidence that establishes immediately collateral facts from which the main fact may be inferred **:** CIRCUMSTANTIAL EVIDENCE

in·di·rec·tion \ˌin-də-'rek-shən, -(ˌ)dī-\ noun (1590)

1 a : indirect action or procedure **b :** lack of direction **:** AIMLESSNESS

2 a : lack of straightforwardness and openness **:** DECEITFULNESS **b :** something (as an act or statement) marked by lack of straightforwardness ⟨hated diplomatic indirections —Review of Reviews⟩

indirect lighting noun (1922)

: lighting in which the light emitted by a source is diffusely reflected (as by the ceiling)

indirect object noun (1879)

: a grammatical object representing the secondary goal of the action of its verb (as her in "I gave her the book")

in·dis·cern·ible \ˌin-di-'sər-nə-bəl, -'zər-\ adjective (1635)

: incapable of being discerned **:** not recognizable as distinct

in·dis·ci·plin·able \(ˌ)in-ˌdi-sə-'pli-nə-bəl; -'di-sə-plə-\ adjective (1600)

: not subject to or capable of being disciplined

in·dis·ci·pline \(ˌ)in-'di-sə-plən\ noun (1783)

: lack of discipline

— **in·dis·ci·plined** \-plənd, -(ˌ)plind\ adjective

in·dis·cov·er·able \ˌin-dis-'kəv-rə-bəl, -'kə-və-\ adjective (1640)

: not discoverable

in·dis·creet \ˌin-di-'skrēt\ adjective [Middle English indiscrete, from Middle French & Late Latin; Middle French indiscret, from Late Latin indiscretus, from Latin, indistinguishable, from in- + discretus, past participle of discernere to separate — more at DISCERN] (15th century)

: not discreet **:** IMPRUDENT

— **in·dis·creet·ly** adverb
— **in·dis·creet·ness** noun

in·dis·cre·tion \ˌin-dis-'kre-shən\ noun (14th century)

1 : lack of discretion **:** IMPRUDENCE ⟨dietary indiscretion⟩

2 a : something (as an act or remark) marked by lack of discretion **b :** an act at variance with the accepted morality of a society ⟨resigned because of financial indiscretions⟩

in·dis·crim·i·nate \ˌin-dis-'krim-nət, -'kri-mə-\ adjective (circa 1598)

1 a : not marked by careful distinction **:** deficient in discrimination and discernment ⟨indiscriminate reading habits⟩ ⟨indiscriminate mass destruction⟩ **b :** HAPHAZARD, RANDOM ⟨indiscriminate application of a law⟩

2 a : PROMISCUOUS, UNRESTRAINED ⟨indiscriminate sexual behavior⟩ **b :** HETEROGENEOUS, MOTLEY ⟨an indiscriminate collection⟩

— **in·dis·crim·i·nate·ly** adverb
— **in·dis·crim·i·nate·ness** noun

in·dis·crim·i·nat·ing \-'kri-mə-ˌnā-tiŋ\ adjective (circa 1767)

: not discriminating

— **in·dis·crim·i·nat·ing·ly** \-tiŋ-lē\ adverb

in·dis·crim·i·na·tion \-ˌkri-mə-'nā-shən\ noun (1649)

: lack of discrimination

in·dis·pens·able \ˌin-di-'spen(t)-sə-bəl\ adjective (1653)

1 : not subject to being set aside or neglected ⟨an indispensable obligation⟩

2 : absolutely necessary **:** ESSENTIAL ⟨an indispensable member of the staff⟩

— **in·dis·pens·abil·i·ty** \-ˌspen(t)-sə-'bi-lə-tē\ noun
— **indispensable** noun
— **in·dis·pens·able·ness** \-'spen(t)-sə-bəl-nəs\ noun
— **in·dis·pens·ably** \-blē\ adverb

in·dis·pose \ˌin-di-'spōz\ transitive verb **-posed; -pos·ing** [probably back-formation from indisposed] (1657)

1 a : to make unfit **:** DISQUALIFY **b :** to make averse **:** DISINCLINE

2 archaic **:** to cause to be in poor physical health

in·dis·posed \-'spōzd\ adjective (15th century)

1 : slightly ill

2 : AVERSE

in·dis·po·si·tion \(ˌ)in-ˌdis-pə-'zi-shən\ noun (15th century)

: the condition of being indisposed: **a :** DISINCLINATION **b :** a usually slight illness

in·dis·put·able \ˌin-di-'spyü-tə-bəl, (ˌ)in-'dis-pyə-\ adjective [Late Latin indisputabilis, from Latin in- + disputabilis disputable] (1551)

: not disputable **:** UNQUESTIONABLE ⟨indisputable proof⟩

— **in·dis·put·able·ness** noun
— **in·dis·put·ably** \-blē\ adverb

in·dis·so·cia·ble \ˌin-di-'sō-sh(ē-)ə-bəl, -sē-ə-\ adjective (1855)

: not dissociated **:** INSEPARABLE

— **in·dis·so·cia·bly** \-blē\ adverb

in·dis·sol·u·ble \ˌin-di-'säl-yə-bəl\ adjective (1542)

: not dissoluble; especially **:** incapable of being annulled, undone, or broken **:** PERMANENT ⟨an indissoluble contract⟩

— **in·dis·sol·u·bil·i·ty** \-ˌsäl-yə-'bi-lə-tē\ noun
— **in·dis·sol·u·ble·ness** \-'säl-yə-bəl-nəs\ noun
— **in·dis·sol·u·bly** \-blē\ adverb

in·dis·tinct \ˌin-di-'stiŋ(k)t\ adjective [Latin indistinctus, from in- + distinctus distinct] (1526)

: not distinct: as **a :** not sharply outlined or separable **:** BLURRED ⟨indistinct figures in the fog⟩ **b :** FAINT, DIM ⟨an indistinct light in the distance⟩ **c :** not clearly recognizable or understandable **:** UNCERTAIN

— **in·dis·tinct·ly** \-'stiŋ(k)t-lē, -'stiŋ-klē\ adverb
— **in·dis·tinct·ness** \-'stiŋ(k)t-nəs, -'stiŋk-nəs\ noun

in·dis·tinc·tive \-'stiŋ(k)-tiv\ adjective (1846)

: lacking distinctive qualities

in·dis·tin·guish·able \ˌin-di-'stiŋ-gwi-shə-bəl, -'stiŋ-wi-\ adjective (1606)

: not distinguishable: as **a :** indeterminate in shape or structure **b :** not clearly recognizable or understandable **c :** lacking identifying or individualizing qualities

— **in·dis·tin·guish·abil·i·ty** \-ˌstiŋ-gwi-shə-'bi-lə-tē, -ˌstiŋ-wi-\ noun
— **in·dis·tin·guish·able·ness** \-'stiŋ-gwi-shə-bəl-nəs, -'stiŋ-wi-\ noun
— **in·dis·tin·guish·ably** \-blē\ adverb

in·dite \in-'dīt\ transitive verb **in·dit·ed; in·dit·ing** [Middle English enditen, from Old French enditer to write down, proclaim, from (assumed) Vulgar Latin indictare to proclaim, frequentative of Latin indicere to proclaim, from in- + dicere to say — more at DICTION] (14th century)

1 a : MAKE UP, COMPOSE ⟨indite a poem⟩ **b :** to give literary or formal expression to **c :** to put down in writing ⟨indite a message⟩

2 obsolete **:** DICTATE

— **in·dit·er** noun

in·di·um \'in-dē-əm\ noun [International Scientific Vocabulary ind- + New Latin -ium] (1864)

: a malleable fusible silvery metallic element that is chiefly trivalent, occurs especially in sphalerite ores, and is used as a plating for bearings, in alloys having a low melting point, and in the making of transistors — see ELEMENT table

indium antimonide noun (1957)

: a synthetic compound InSb of indium and antimony that is a semiconducting and photosensitive material and is used especially in infrared photodetectors

¹in·di·vid·u·al \ˌin-də-'vij-wəl, -'vi-jə-wəl, -'vi-jəl\ adjective [Medieval Latin individualis, from Latin individuus indivisible, from in- + dividuus divided, from dividere to divide] (15th century)

1 obsolete **:** INSEPARABLE

2 a : of, relating to, or distinctively associated with an individual ⟨an individual effort⟩ **b :** being an individual or existing as an indivisible whole **c :** intended for one person ⟨an individual serving⟩

3 : existing as a distinct entity **:** SEPARATE

4 : having marked individuality ⟨an individual style⟩

synonym see SPECIAL, CHARACTERISTIC

— **in·di·vid·u·al·ly** adverb

²individual noun (1605)

1 a : a particular being or thing as distinguished from a class, species, or collection: as

(1) **:** a single human being as contrasted with a social group or institution ⟨a teacher who works with *individuals*⟩ (2) **:** a single organism as distinguished from a group **b :** a particular person ⟨are you the *individual* I spoke with on the telephone?⟩
2 : an indivisible entity
3 : the reference of a name or variable of the lowest logical type in a calculus

in·di·vid·u·al·ise *British variant of* INDIVIDU-ALIZE

in·di·vid·u·al·ism \,in-də-'vij-wə-,li-zəm, -'vi-jə-wə-, -'vi-jə-,li-\ *noun* (1827)
1 a (1) **:** a doctrine that the interests of the individual are or ought to be ethically paramount; *also* **:** conduct guided by such a doctrine (2) **:** the conception that all values, rights, and duties originate in individuals **b :** a theory maintaining the political and economic independence of the individual and stressing individual initiative, action, and interests; *also* **:** conduct or practice guided by such a theory **2 a :** INDIVIDUALITY **b :** an individual peculiarity **:** IDIOSYNCRASY

in·di·vid·u·al·ist \-list\ *noun* (1840)
1 : one that pursues a markedly independent course in thought or action
2 : one that advocates or practices individualism
— **individualist** *or* **in·di·vid·u·al·is·tic** \-,vij-wə-'lis-tik, -,vi-jə-wə-, -,vi-jə-'lis-\ *adjective*
— **in·di·vid·u·al·is·ti·cal·ly** \-'lis-ti-k(ə-)lē\ *adverb*

in·di·vid·u·al·i·ty \-,vi-jə-'wa-lə-tē\ *noun,* *plural* **-ties** (1614)
1 a : total character peculiar to and distinguishing an individual from others **b :** PERSONALITY
2 *archaic* **:** the quality or state of being indivisible
3 : separate or distinct existence
4 : INDIVIDUAL, PERSON

in·di·vid·u·al·ize \-'vij-wə-,līz, -'vi-jə-wə-, -'vi-jə-,līz\ *transitive verb* **-ized; -iz·ing** (1637)
1 : to make individual in character
2 : to treat or notice individually **:** PARTICULARIZE
3 : to adapt to the needs or special circumstances of an individual ⟨*individualize* teaching according to student ability⟩
— **in·di·vid·u·al·i·za·tion** \-,vij-wə-lə-'zā-shən, -,vi-jə-wə-, -,vi-jə-lə-\ *noun*

individual medley *noun* (circa 1949)
: a swimming race in which each contestant swims each part of the course with a different stroke

individual retirement account *noun* (1974)
: IRA

in·di·vid·u·ate \,in-də-'vi-jə-,wāt\ *transitive verb* **-at·ed; -at·ing** (1614)
1 : to give individuality to
2 : to form into a distinct entity

in·di·vid·u·a·tion \-,vi-jə-'wā-shən\ *noun* (1628)
1 : the act or process of individuating: as **a** (1) **:** the development of the individual from the universal (2) **:** the determination of the individual in the general **b :** the process by which individuals in society become differentiated from one another **c :** regional differentiation along a primary embryonic axis
2 : the state of being individuated; *specifically* **:** INDIVIDUALITY

in·di·vis·i·ble \,in-də-'vi-zə-bəl\ *adjective* [Middle English, from Late Latin *indivisibilis,* from Latin *in-* + Late Latin *divisibilis* divisible] (14th century)
: not divisible
— **in·di·vis·i·bil·i·ty** \-,vi-zə-'bi-lə-tē\ *noun*
— **indivisible** *noun*
— **in·di·vis·i·bly** \-'vi-zə-blē\ *adverb*

indo- — see IND-

Indo- *combining form* [Greek, from *Indos* India]
1 : India or the East Indies ⟨*Indo*-Pakistani⟩
2 : Indo-European ⟨*Indo*-Hittite⟩

In·do-Ar·y·an \,in-dō-'ar-ē-ən, -'er-; -'är-yən\ *noun* (1881)
1 : a member of one of the peoples of the Indian subcontinent speaking an Indo-European language
2 : one of the early Indo-European invaders of southern Asia
3 : a branch of the Indo-European language family that includes Hindi, Bengali, Punjabi, and other languages spoken primarily in India, Pakistan, Bangladesh, and Sri Lanka — see INDO-EUROPEAN LANGUAGES table
— **Indo-Aryan** *adjective*

In·do-Chi·nese \-,chī-'nēz, -'nēs\ *noun* (circa 1934)
1 : a native or inhabitant of Indochina
2 : SINO-TIBETAN
— **Indo-Chinese** *adjective*

in·doc·ile \(,)in-'dä-səl *also* -,sīl, *especially British* -'dō-,sīl\ *adjective* [Middle French, from Latin *indocilis,* from *in-* + *docilis* docile] (1603)
: unwilling or indisposed to be taught or disciplined **:** INTRACTABLE
— **in·do·cil·i·ty** \,in-dä-'si-lə-tē, -dō-\ *noun*

in·doc·tri·nate \in-'däk-trə-,nāt\ *transitive verb* **-nat·ed; -nat·ing** [probably from Middle English *endoctrinen,* from Middle French *endoctriner,* from Old French, from *en-* + *doctrine* doctrine] (1626)
1 : to instruct especially in fundamentals or rudiments **:** TEACH
2 : to imbue with a usually partisan or sectarian opinion, point of view, or principle
— **in·doc·tri·na·tion** \(,)in-,däk-trə-'nā-shən\ *noun*
— **in·doc·tri·na·tor** \in-'däk-trə-,nā-tər\ *noun*

¹In·do-Eu·ro·pe·an \,in-dō-,yùr-ə-'pē-ən\ *adjective* (1814)
: of, relating to, or constituting the Indo-European languages

²Indo-European *noun* (1864)
1 : INDO-EUROPEAN LANGUAGES
2 a : an unrecorded prehistoric language from which the Indo-European languages are descended **b :** a member of the people speaking this language

In·do-Eu·ro·pe·an·ist \-,yùr-ə-'pē-ə-nist\ *noun* (1926)
: a specialist in Indo-European linguistics

Indo-European languages *noun plural* (1864)
: a family of languages comprising those spoken in most of Europe and in the parts of the world colonized by Europeans since 1500 and also in Persia, the subcontinent of India, and some other parts of Asia

In·do-Ger·man·ic \,in-dō-jər-'ma-nik\ *adjective* (1835)
: INDO-EUROPEAN LANGUAGES
— **Indo-Germanic** *noun*

In·do-Hit·tite \-'hi-,tīt\ *noun* (1930)
1 : a hypothetical parent language of Indo-European and Anatolian
2 : a language family including Indo-European and Anatolian
— **Indo-Hittite** *adjective*

In·do-Ira·ni·an \-ir-'ä-nē-ən\ *adjective* (1876)
: of, relating to, or constituting a subfamily of the Indo-European languages that consists of the Indo-Aryan and the Iranian branches — see INDO-EUROPEAN LANGUAGES table
— **Indo-Iranian** *noun*

in·dole \'in-,dōl\ *noun* [International Scientific Vocabulary *ind-* + *-ole*] (1869)
: a crystalline compound C_8H_7N that is a decomposition product of proteins containing tryptophan, that can be made synthetically, and that is used in perfumes; *also* **:** a derivative of indole

in·dole·ace·tic acid \,in-(,)dō-lə-'sē-tik-\ *noun* (1937)
: a crystalline plant hormone $C_{10}H_9NO_2$ that is a naturally occurring auxin promoting growth and rooting of plants — called also *heteroauxin*

in·dole·bu·tyr·ic acid \,in-(,)dōl-byü-'tir-ik-\ *noun* (1936)
: a crystalline acid $C_{12}H_{13}NO_2$ similar to indoleacetic acid in its effects on plants

in·do·lence \'in-də-lən(t)s\ *noun* (1710)
: inclination to laziness **:** SLOTH

in·do·lent \-lənt\ *adjective* [Late Latin *indolent-, indolens* insensitive to pain, from Latin *in-* + *dolent-, dolens,* present participle of *dolēre* to feel pain] (1663)
1 a : causing little or no pain **b :** slow to develop or heal
2 a : averse to activity, effort, or movement **:** habitually lazy **b :** conducing to or encouraging laziness ⟨*indolent* heat⟩ **c :** exhibiting indolence ⟨an *indolent* sigh⟩
synonym see LAZY
— **in·do·lent·ly** *adverb*

In·dol·o·gy \(,)in-'dä-lə-jē\ *noun* (1888)
: the study of India and its people
— **In·dol·o·gist** \-jist\ *noun*

in·do·meth·a·cin \,in-dō-'me-thə-sən\ *noun* [*indole* + *meth-* + *acetic acid* + *¹-in*] (1963)
: a nonsteroidal drug $C_{19}H_{16}ClNO_4$ with antiinflammatory, analgesic, and antipyretic properties used especially in treating arthritis

in·dom·i·ta·ble \in-'dä-mə-tə-bəl\ *adjective* [Late Latin *indomitabilis,* from Latin *in-* + *domitare* to tame — more at DAUNT] (1830)
: incapable of being subdued **:** UNCONQUERABLE ⟨*indomitable* courage⟩
— **in·dom·i·ta·bil·i·ty** \(,)in-,dä-mə-tə-'bi-lə-tē\ *noun*
— **in·dom·i·ta·ble·ness** \in-'dä-mə-tə-bəl-nəs\ *noun*
— **in·dom·i·ta·bly** \-blē\ *adverb*

In·do·ne·sian \,in-də-'nē-zhən, -shən\ *noun* (1850)
1 : a native or inhabitant of the Malay Archipelago
2 a : a native or inhabitant of the Republic of Indonesia **b :** the language based on Malay that is the national language of the Republic of Indonesia
— **Indonesian** *adjective*

in·door \'in-'dór, -'dòr\ *adjective* (1711)
1 : of or relating to the interior of a building
2 : living, located, or carried on within a building ⟨an *indoor* sport⟩

in·doors \'in-'dórz, (,)in-, -'dòrz\ *adverb* (1832)
: in or into a building

in·do·phe·nol \,in-dō-'fē-,nōl, -,nòl, ,in-(,)dō-fi-'\ *noun* [International Scientific Vocabulary] (circa 1881)
: any of various blue or green dyes

in·dorse, in·dorse·ment *variant of* ENDORSE, ENDORSEMENT

in·dox·yl \in-'däk-səl\ *noun* [International Scientific Vocabulary *ind-* + *hydroxyl*] (circa 1886)
: a crystalline compound C_8H_7NO found in plants and animals or synthesized as a step in indigo manufacture

in·draft \'in-,draft, -,dråft\ *noun* (1594)
1 : an inward flow or current (as of air or water)
2 : a drawing or pulling in

in·drawn \'in-'dròn\ *adjective* (1751)
1 : ALOOF, RESERVED
2 : drawn in

in·dri \'in-drē\ *noun, plural* **indris** [French, from Malagasy *indry* look!] (1839)
: a large black-and-white Madagascan lemur (*Indri indri*) that is about two feet long with a rudimentary tail

in·du·bi·ta·ble \(,)in-'dü-bə-tə-bəl, -'dyü-\ *adjective* [Middle English *indubitabyll,* from Latin *indubitabilis,* from *in-* + *dubitabilis* dubitable] (15th century)

INDO-EUROPEAN LANGUAGES

BRANCH	GROUP	LANGUAGES AND MAJOR DIALECTS[1] — ANCIENT	MEDIEVAL	MODERN	PROVENIENCE
Anatolian		*Hittite, Lydian, Lycian Luwian, Palaic* / *Hieroglyphic Luwian*			ancient Asia Minor
INDO-IRANIAN — Kafiri (Nuristani)				languages of eastern Afghanistan	Afghanistan
INDO-IRANIAN / Indo-Aryan	Sanskritic	Sanskrit, Pali / *Prakrits*	*Prakrits*		India
				Shina, Khowar	Upper Indus valley
				Kashmiri	Kashmir
				Lahnda	western Punjab
				Sindhi	Sind
				Panjabi	Punjab
				Rajasthani	Rajasthan
				Gujarati	Gujarat
				Marathi	western India
				Konkani	western India
				Oriya	Orissa
				Bengali	Bangladesh, West Bengal
				Assamese	Assam
				Bhojpuri	Bihar, Uttar Pradesh
				Hindi	northern India
				Urdu	Pakistan, India
				Nepali	Nepal
				Sinhalese	Sri Lanka
				Romany	uncertain
Iranian	West	*Old Persian*	*Pahlavi*		Persia
			Persian	Persian	Iran
				Kurdish	Iran, Iraq, Turkey
				Baluchi	Pakistan
				Tajiki	Tajikistan
	East	*Avestan*			ancient Persia
			Sogdian, Khotanese		central Asia
				Pashto	Afghanistan, Pakistan
				Ossetic	Caucasus
Armenian			Armenian	Armenian	Asia Minor, Caucasus
Greek or Hellenic		Greek	Greek	Greek	Greece, the eastern Mediterranean
BALTO-SLAVIC / Baltic			*Old Prussian*		East Prussia
				Lithuanian	Lithuania
				Latvian	Latvia
Slavic	South		*Old Church Slavonic*		
				Slovene	Slovenia
				Serbo-Croatian	Croatia, Bosnia and Herzegovina, Serbia, Montenegro
				Macedonian	Macedonia
				Bulgarian	Bulgaria
	West			Czech, Slovak	Czechoslovakia
				Polish, Kashubian	Poland
				Wendish, *Polabian*	Germany
	East		*Old Russian*	Russian	Russia
				Ukrainian	Ukraine
				Belorussian	Belarus
Albanian				Albanian	Albania, Serbia, Macedonia
Scantily recorded and of uncertain affinities within Indo-European		*Ligurian, Messapian, Illyrian, Thracian, Phrygian*			ancient Italy / Balkans / Asia Minor
Tocharian			*Tocharian A* / *Tocharian B*		central Asia
GERMANIC	East		*Gothic*		eastern Europe
	North		*Old Norse*	Icelandic	Iceland
				Faeroese	Faeroe Islands
				Norwegian	Norway
				Swedish	Sweden
				Danish	Denmark
	West		*Old High German* / *Middle High German*	German	Germany, Switzerland, Austria
				Yiddish	Germany, eastern Europe
			Old Saxon / *Middle Low German*	Low German	northern Germany
			Middle Dutch	Dutch	Netherlands
				Afrikaans	South Africa
				Flemish	Belgium
			Old Frisian	Frisian	Netherlands, Germany
			Old English / *Middle English*	English	England
ITALIC		*Venetic, Oscan, Umbrian, Faliscan* / Latin			ancient Italy
				Portuguese	Portugal
				Spanish	Spain
				Judeo-Spanish	Mediterranean lands
				Catalan	Spain (Catalonia)
			Old Provençal	Provençal	southern France
			Old French / *Middle French*	French	France, Belgium, Switzerland
				Italian	Italy, Switzerland
				Rhaeto-Romance	Switzerland, Italy
				Sardinian	Sardinia
				Dalmation	Adriatic coast
				Romanian	Romania, Balkans
CELTIC	Continental	*Gaulish*			Gaul
	Goidelic		*Old Irish* / *Middle Irish*	Irish	Ireland
				Scottish Gaelic	Scotland
				Manx	Isle of Man
	Brythonic		*Old Welsh* / *Middle Welsh*	Welsh	Wales
			Old Cornish	*Cornish*	Cornwall
			Old Breton	Breton	Brittany

[1]Italics denote dead languages. Languages listed in roman type in the ancient or medieval column survive only in some special use, as in literary composition or liturgy.

: too evident to be doubted **:** UNQUESTIONABLE
— **in·du·bi·ta·bil·i·ty** \-,dü-bə-tə-'bi-lə-tē, -,dyü-\ *noun*
— **in·du·bi·ta·ble·ness** \-'dü-bə-tə-bəl-nəs, -'dyü-\ *noun*
— **in·du·bi·ta·bly** \-blē\ *adverb*
in·duce \in-'düs, -'dyüs\ *transitive verb* **in·duced; in·duc·ing** [Middle English, from Latin *inducere,* from *in-* + *ducere* to lead — more at TOW] (14th century)
1 a : to move by persuasion or influence **b :** to call forth or bring about by influence or stimulation
2 a : EFFECT, CAUSE **b :** to cause the formation of **c :** to produce (as an electric current) by induction
3 : to determine by induction; *specifically* **:** to infer from particulars
in·duce·ment \in-'düs-mənt, -'dyüs-\ *noun* (1594)
1 : a motive or consideration that leads one to action or to additional or more effective actions
2 : the act or process of inducing
3 : matter presented by way of introduction or background to explain the principal allegations of a legal cause, plea, or defense
synonym see MOTIVE
in·duc·er \-'dü-sər, -'dyü-\ *noun* (1554)
: one that induces; *especially* **:** a substance that is capable of activating a structural gene by combining with and inactivating a genetic repressor
in·duc·ible \in-'dü-sə-bəl, -'dyü-\ *adjective* (circa 1677)
: capable of being induced; *especially* **:** formed by a cell in response to the presence of its substrate (*inducible* enzymes) — compare CONSTITUTIVE
— **in·duc·ibil·i·ty** \-,dü-sə-'bi-lə-tē, -,dyü-\ *noun*
in·duct \in-'dəkt\ *transitive verb* [Middle English, from Medieval Latin *inductus,* past participle of *inducere,* from Latin] (14th century)
1 : to put in formal possession (as of a benefice or office) **:** INSTALL (was *inducted* as president of the college)
2 a : to admit as a member (*inducted* into a scholastic society) **b :** INTRODUCE, INITIATE **c :** to enroll for military training or service (as under a selective service act)
3 : LEAD, CONDUCT
in·duc·tance \in-'dək-tən(t)s\ *noun* (1886)
1 a : a property of an electric circuit by which an electromotive force is induced in it by a variation of current either in the circuit itself or in a neighboring circuit **b :** the measure of this property that is equal to the ratio of the induced electromotive force to the rate of change of the inducing current
2 : a circuit or a device possessing inductance
in·duct·ee \(,)in-,dək-'tē, in-'dək-,\ *noun* (1940)
: one who is inducted
in·duc·tion \in-'dək-shən\ *noun* (14th century)
1 a : the act or process of inducting (as into office) **b :** an initial experience **:** INITIATION **c :** the formality by which a civilian is inducted into military service
2 a (1) **:** inference of a generalized conclusion from particular instances — compare DEDUCTION 2a (2) **:** a conclusion arrived at by induction **b :** mathematical demonstration of the validity of a law concerning all the positive integers by proving that it holds for the integer 1 and that if it holds for all the integers preceding a given integer it must hold for the next following integer
3 : a preface, prologue, or introductory scene especially of an early English play
4 a : the act of bringing forward or adducing (as facts or particulars) **b :** the act of causing or bringing on or about **c :** the process by which an electrical conductor becomes electrified when near a charged body, by which a magnetizable body becomes magnetized when

in a magnetic field or in the magnetic flux set up by a magnetomotive force, or by which an electromotive force is produced in a circuit by varying the magnetic field linked with the circuit **d :** the inspiration of the fuel-air charge from the carburetor into the combustion chamber of an internal-combustion engine **e :** the sum of the processes by which the fate of embryonic cells is determined and morphogenetic differentiation brought about
induction coil *noun* (1837)
: an apparatus for obtaining intermittent high voltage consisting of a primary coil through which the direct current flows, an interrupter, and a secondary coil of a larger number of turns in which the high voltage is induced
induction heating *noun* (1919)
: heating of material by means of an electric current that is caused to flow through the material or its container by electromagnetic induction
induction motor *noun* (1897)
: an alternating-current motor in which torque is produced by the reaction between a varying magnetic field generated in the stator and the current induced in the coils of the rotor
in·duc·tive \in-'dək-tiv\ *adjective* (15th century)
1 : leading on **:** INDUCING
2 : of, relating to, or employing mathematical or logical induction (*inductive* reasoning)
3 : of or relating to inductance or electrical induction
4 : INTRODUCTORY
5 : involving the action of an embryological inductor **:** tending to produce induction
— **in·duc·tive·ly** *adverb*
in·duc·tor \in-'dək-tər\ *noun* (1652)
1 : one that inducts
2 a : a part of an electrical apparatus that acts upon another or is itself acted upon by induction **b :** REACTOR 2
3 : ORGANIZER 2
in·due *variant of* ENDUE
in·dulge \in-'dəlj\ *verb* **in·dulged; in·dulg·ing** [Latin *indulgēre* to be complaisant] (circa 1623)
transitive verb
1 a : to give free rein to **b :** to take unrestrained pleasure in **:** GRATIFY
2 a : to yield to the desire of **:** HUMOR **b :** to treat with excessive leniency, generosity, or consideration
intransitive verb
: to indulge oneself ☆
— **in·dulg·er** *noun*
in·dul·gence \in-'dəl-jən(t)s\ *noun* (14th century)
1 : remission of part or all of the temporal and especially purgatorial punishment that according to Roman Catholicism is due for sins whose eternal punishment has been remitted and whose guilt has been pardoned (as through the sacrament of reconciliation)
2 : the act of indulging **:** the state of being indulgent
3 a : an indulgent act **b :** an extension of time for payment or performance granted as a favor
4 a : the act of indulging in something; *especially* **:** SELF-INDULGENCE **b :** something indulged in (walk off gastronomic *indulgences* —Barbara L. Michaels)
in·dul·gent \in-'dəl-jənt\ *adjective* [Latin *indulgent-, indulgens,* present participle of *indulgēre*] (1509)
: indulging or characterized by indulgence; *especially* **:** LENIENT
— **in·dul·gent·ly** *adverb*
in·dult \'in-,dəlt, in-'\ *noun* [Middle English (Scots), from Medieval Latin *indultum,* from Late Latin, grant, from Latin, neuter of *indultus,* past participle of *indulgēre*] (15th century)
: a special often temporary dispensation granted in the Roman Catholic Church

¹in·du·rate \'in-də-rət, -dyə-; in-'dur-ət, -'dyur-\ *adjective* (14th century)
: physically or morally hardened
²in·du·rate \'in-də-,rāt, -dyə-\ *verb* **-rat·ed; -rat·ing** [Latin *induratus,* past participle of *indurare,* from *in-* + *durare* to harden, from *durus* hard — more at DURING] (1538)
transitive verb
1 : to make unfeeling, stubborn, or obdurate
2 : to make hardy **:** INURE
3 : to make hard (great heat *indurates* clay)
4 : to establish firmly **:** CONFIRM
intransitive verb
1 : to grow hard **:** HARDEN
2 : to become established
in·du·rat·ed \-,rā-təd\ *adjective* (1604)
: having become firm or hard especially by increase of fibrous elements (*indurated* tissue)
in·du·ra·tion \,in-də-'rā-shən, -dyə-\ *noun* (14th century)
: the process of or condition produced by growing hard; *specifically* **:** sclerosis especially when associated with inflammation
— **in·du·ra·tive** \'in-də-,rā-tiv, -dyə-; in-'dür-ə-, -'dyür-\ *adjective*
in·du·si·um \in-'dü-zē-əm, -'dyü-, -zhē-\ *noun, plural* **-sia** \-zē-ə, -zhē-\ [New Latin, from Latin, tunic] (1807)
: an investing outgrowth or membrane: as **a :** an outgrowth of a fern frond that invests the sori **b :** the annulus of a fungus especially when large and full
¹in·dus·tri·al \in-'dəs-trē-əl\ *adjective* (15th century)
1 : of or relating to industry
2 : derived from human industry (*industrial* wealth)
3 : engaged in industry (the *industrial* classes)
4 : used in or developed for use in industry (*industrial* diamonds); *also* **:** HEAVY-DUTY (an *industrial* zipper)
5 : characterized by highly developed industries (an *industrial* nation)
— **in·dus·tri·al·ly** \-trē-ə-lē\ *adverb*
²industrial *noun* (1865)
1 a : one that is employed in industry **b :** a company engaged in industrial production or service
2 : a stock or bond issued by an industrial corporation or enterprise
industrial action *noun* (circa 1931)
British **:** JOB ACTION
industrial archaeology *noun* (1951)
: the study of the buildings, machinery, and equipment of the industrial revolution
— **industrial archaeologist** *noun*
industrial arts *noun plural but singular in construction* (circa 1925)
: a subject taught in elementary and secondary schools that aims at developing manual skill and familiarity with tools and machines
industrial engineering *noun* (circa 1924)

☆ **SYNONYMS**
Indulge, pamper, humor, spoil, baby, mollycoddle mean to show undue favor to a person's desires and feelings. INDULGE implies excessive compliance and weakness in gratifying another's or one's own desires (*indulged* myself with food at the slightest excuse). PAMPER implies inordinate gratification of desire for luxury and comfort with consequent enervating effect (*pampered* by the amenities of modern living). HUMOR stresses a yielding to a person's moods or whims (*humored* him by letting him tell the story). SPOIL stresses the injurious effects on character by indulging or pampering (foolish parents *spoil* their children). BABY suggests excessive care, attention, or solicitude (*babying* students by grading too easily). MOLLYCODDLE suggests an excessive degree of care and attention to another's health or welfare (refused to *mollycoddle* her malingering son).

: engineering that deals with the design, improvement, and installation of integrated systems (as of people, materials, and energy) in industry
— **industrial engineer** *noun*

in·dus·tri·al·ise *British variant of* INDUSTRIALIZE

in·dus·tri·al·ism \in-'dəs-trē-ə-,li-zəm\ *noun* (1831)
: social organization in which industries and especially large-scale industries are dominant

in·dus·tri·al·ist \-list\ *noun* (1864)
: one owning or engaged in the management of an industry **:** MANUFACTURER

in·dus·tri·al·ize \in-'dəs-trē-ə-,līz\ *verb* **-ized; -iz·ing** (1882)
transitive verb
: to make industrial ⟨*industrialize* an agricultural region⟩
intransitive verb
: to become industrial
— **in·dus·tri·al·i·za·tion** \-,dəs-trē-ə-lə-'zā-shən\ *noun*

industrial melanism *noun* (1943)
: genetically determined melanism as a population phenomenon especially in moths in which the proportion of dark individuals tends to increase due to differential predation especially by birds which more easily find and eat lighter-colored individuals in habitats darkened by industrial pollution

industrial psychology *noun* (1917)
: the application of the findings and methods of experimental, clinical, and social psychology to industrial concerns
— **industrial psychologist** *noun*

industrial relations *noun plural* (1904)
: the dealings or relationships of a usually large business or industrial enterprise with its own workers, with labor in general, with governmental agencies, or with the public

industrial revolution *noun* (1848)
: a rapid major change in an economy (as in England in the late 18th century) marked by the general introduction of power-driven machinery or by an important change in the prevailing types and methods of use of such machines

industrial school *noun* (1853)
: a school specializing in the teaching of industrial arts; *specifically* **:** one for juvenile delinquents

industrial sociology *noun* (1948)
: sociological analysis directed at institutions and social relationships within and largely controlled or affected by industry

in·dus·tri·al–strength \in-'dəs-trē-əl-'stren(k)th, -'stren(t)th\ *adjective* (1976)
: of industrial quality; *also* **:** marked by more than usual power or durability ⟨*industrial-strength* boots⟩ ⟨an *industrial-strength* voice⟩

industrial union *noun* (1902)
: a labor union open to workers in an industry irrespective of their occupation or craft — compare CRAFT UNION

in·dus·tri·ous \in-'dəs-trē-əs\ *adjective* (15th century)
1 *obsolete* **:** SKILLFUL, INGENIOUS
2 : persistently active **:** ZEALOUS
3 : constantly, regularly, or habitually occupied **:** DILIGENT
synonym see BUSY
— **in·dus·tri·ous·ly** *adverb*
— **in·dus·tri·ous·ness** *noun*

in·dus·try \'in-(,)dəs-trē\ *noun, plural* **-tries** [Middle English *industrie* skill, employment involving skill, from Middle French, from Latin *industria* diligence, from *industrius* diligent, from Old Latin *indostruus*, perhaps from *indu* in + *-struus* (akin to Latin *struere* to build) — more at END-, STREW] (15th century)
1 : diligence in an employment or pursuit; *especially* **:** steady or habitual effort
2 a : systematic labor especially for some useful purpose or the creation of something of

value **b :** a department or branch of a craft, art, business, or manufacture; *especially* **:** one that employs a large personnel and capital especially in manufacturing **c :** a distinct group of productive or profit-making enterprises ⟨the banking *industry*⟩ **d :** manufacturing activity as a whole ⟨the nation's *industry*⟩
3 : work devoted to the study of a particular subject or author ⟨the Shakespeare *industry*⟩
synonym see BUSINESS

in·dwell \in-'dwel, 'in-,\ (14th century)
intransitive verb
: to exist as an inner activating spirit, force, or principle
transitive verb
: to exist within as an activating spirit, force, or principle
— **in·dwell·er** *noun*

in·dwell·ing \'in-,dwe-liŋ\ *adjective* (1646)
1 : being an inner activating or guiding force
2 : left within a bodily organ or passage especially to promote drainage — used of an implanted tube (as a catheter)

¹-ine *adjective suffix*
1 [Middle English *-in*, *-ine*, from Middle French & Latin; Middle French *-in*, from Latin *-īnus* — more at -EN] **:** of or relating to ⟨estuar*ine*⟩
2 [Middle English *-in*, *-ine*, from Middle French & Latin; Middle French *-in*, from Latin *-īnus*, from Greek *-inos* — more at -EN] **:** made of **:** like ⟨opal*ine*⟩

²-ine *noun suffix* [Middle English *-ine*, *-in*, from Middle French & Latin; Middle French *-ine*, from Latin *-īna*, from feminine of *-īnus*, adjective suffix]
1 : chemical substance: as **a :** halogen element ⟨chlor*ine*⟩ **b :** basic or base-containing carbon compound that contains nitrogen ⟨quin*ine*⟩ ⟨cyst*ine*⟩ **c :** mixture of compounds (as of hydrocarbons) ⟨gasol*ine*⟩ **d :** hydride ⟨ars*ine*⟩
2 : -IN 1a
3 : commercial product or material ⟨glass*ine*⟩

in·ebri·ant \i-'nē-brē-ənt\ *noun* (1819)
: INTOXICANT

¹in·ebri·ate \i-'nē-brē-,āt\ *transitive verb* **-at·ed; -at·ing** [Latin *inebriatus*, past participle of *inebriare*, from *in-* + *ebriare* to intoxicate, from *ebrius* drunk] (15th century)
1 : to exhilarate or stupefy as if by liquor
2 : to make drunk **:** INTOXICATE
— **in·ebri·a·tion** \-,nē-brē-'ā-shən\ *noun*

²in·ebri·ate \i-'nē-brē-ət, -,āt\ *adjective* (15th century)
1 : affected by alcohol **:** DRUNK
2 : addicted to excessive drinking

³in·ebri·ate \-ət\ *noun* (circa 1796)
: one who is drunk; *especially* **:** DRUNKARD

in·ebri·at·ed \-brē-,ā-təd\ *adjective* (1609)
: exhilarated or confused by or as if by alcohol **:** INTOXICATED

in·ebri·ety \,i-ni-'brī-ə-tē\ *noun* [probably blend of *inebriation* and *ebriety* drunkenness] (1801)
: the state of being inebriated **:** DRUNKENNESS

in·ed·i·ble \(,)i-'ne-də-bəl\ *adjective* (circa 1834)
: not fit to be eaten

in·ed·u·ca·ble \(,)i-'ne-jə-kə-bəl\ *adjective* (1884)
: incapable of being educated
— **in·ed·u·ca·bil·i·ty** \-,ne-jə-kə-'bi-lə-tē\ *noun*

in·ef·fa·ble \(,)i-'ne-fə-bəl\ *adjective* [Middle English, from Middle French, from Latin *ineffabilis*, from *in-* + *effabilis* capable of being expressed, from *effari* to speak out, from *ex-* + *fari* to speak — more at BAN] (14th century)
1 a : incapable of being expressed in words **:** INDESCRIBABLE ⟨*ineffable* joy⟩ **b :** UNSPEAKABLE ⟨*ineffable* disgust⟩
2 : not to be uttered **:** TABOO ⟨the *ineffable* name of Jehovah⟩
— **in·ef·fa·bil·i·ty** \-,ne-fə-'bi-lə-tē\ *noun*
— **in·ef·fa·ble·ness** \-'ne-fə-bəl-nəs\ *noun*
— **in·ef·fa·bly** \-blē\ *adverb*

in·ef·face·able \,i-nə-'fā-sə-bəl\ *adjective* [probably from French *ineffaçable*, from Middle French, from *in-* + *effaçable* effaceable] (1804)
: not effaceable **:** INERADICABLE
— **in·ef·face·abil·i·ty** \-,fā-sə-'bi-lə-tē\ *noun*
— **in·ef·face·ably** \-'fā-sə-blē\ *adverb*

in·ef·fec·tive \,i-nə-'fek-tiv\ *adjective* (1649)
1 : not producing an intended effect **:** INEFFECTUAL ⟨*ineffective* lighting⟩
2 : not capable of performing efficiently or as expected **:** INCAPABLE ⟨an *ineffective* executive⟩
— **in·ef·fec·tive·ly** *adverb*
— **in·ef·fec·tive·ness** *noun*

in·ef·fec·tu·al \,i-nə-'fek-chə(-wə)l, -'feksh-wəl\ *adjective* (15th century)
1 : not producing the proper or intended effect **:** FUTILE
2 : INEFFECTIVE 2
— **in·ef·fec·tu·al·i·ty** \-,fek-chə-'wa-lə-tē\ *noun*
— **in·ef·fec·tu·al·ly** \-'fek-chə(-wə)-lē, -'feksh-wə-\ *adverb*
— **in·ef·fec·tu·al·ness** *noun*

in·ef·fi·ca·cious \(,)i-,ne-fə-'kā-shəs\ *adjective* (1658)
: lacking the power to produce a desired effect **:** INEFFECTIVE
— **in·ef·fi·ca·cious·ly** *adverb*
— **in·ef·fi·ca·cious·ness** *noun*

in·ef·fi·ca·cy \(,)i-'ne-fi-kə-sē\ *noun* [Late Latin *inefficacia*, from Latin *inefficac-, inefficax* inefficacious, from *in-* + *efficac-, efficax* efficacious] (circa 1615)
: lack of power to produce a desired effect

in·ef·fi·cien·cy \,i-nə-'fi-shən(t)-sē\ *noun, plural* **-cies** (1749)
1 : the quality or state of being inefficient
2 : something that is inefficient

in·ef·fi·cient \-'fi-shənt\ *adjective* (1750)
: not efficient: as **a :** not producing the effect intended or desired **b :** wasteful of time or energy ⟨*inefficient* operating procedures⟩ **c :** INCAPABLE, INCOMPETENT ⟨an *inefficient* worker⟩
— **inefficient** *noun*
— **in·ef·fi·cient·ly** *adverb*

in·egal·i·tar·i·an \,i-ni-,ga-lə-'ter-ē-ən\ *adjective* (1940)
: marked by disparity in social and economic standing

in·elas·tic \,i-nə-'las-tik\ *adjective* (1748)
: not elastic: as **a :** slow to react or respond to changing conditions **b :** INFLEXIBLE, UNYIELDING
— **in·elas·tic·i·ty** \,i-ni-,las-'ti-s(ə-)tē, (,)i-,nē-,las-\ *noun*

inelastic collision *noun* (1937)
: a collision in which part of the kinetic energy of the colliding particles changes into another form of energy (as radiation)

inelastic scattering *noun* (1938)
: a scattering of particles as the result of inelastic collision in which the total kinetic energy of the colliding particles changes

in·el·e·gance \(,)i-'ne-li-gən(t)s\ *noun* (1726)
: lack of elegance

in·el·e·gant \-gənt\ *adjective* [Middle French, from Latin *inelegant-, inelegans*, from *in-* + *elegant-, elegans* elegant] (circa 1570)
: lacking in refinement, grace, or good taste
— **in·el·e·gant·ly** *adverb*

in·el·i·gi·ble \(,)i-'ne-lə-jə-bəl\ *adjective* [French *inéligible*, from *in-* + *éligible* eligible] (1770)
: not eligible: as **a :** not qualified for an office or position **b :** not permitted under football rules to catch a forward pass
— **in·el·i·gi·bil·i·ty** \-,ne-lə-jə-'bi-lə-tē\ *noun*

— **ineligible** *noun*
in·el·o·quent \(,)i-'ne-lə-kwənt\ *adjective*
(circa 1530)
: not eloquent
— **in·el·o·quent·ly** *adverb*
in·eluc·ta·ble \,i-ni-'lək-tə-bəl\ *adjective*
[Latin *ineluctabilis,* from *in-* + *eluctari* to
struggle clear of, from *ex-* + *luctari* to strug-
gle, wrestle; akin to Latin *luxus* dislocated —
more at LOCK] (circa 1623)
: not to be avoided, changed, or resisted : IN-
EVITABLE
— **in·eluc·ta·bil·i·ty** \-,lək-tə-'bi-lə-tē\
noun
— **in·eluc·ta·bly** \-'lək-tə-blē\ *adverb*
in·elud·ible \,i-ni-'lü-də-bəl\ *adjective* (1662)
: INESCAPABLE
in·enar·ra·ble \,i-ni-'nar-ə-bəl\ *adjective*
[Middle English, from Middle French, from
Latin *inenarrabilis,* from *in-* + *enarrare* to ex-
plain in detail, from *e-* + *narrare* to narrate]
(15th century)
: incapable of being narrated : INDESCRIBABLE
in·ept \i-'nept\ *adjective* [Middle French *in-
epte,* from Latin *ineptus,* from *in-* + *aptus* apt]
(1542)
1 : lacking in fitness or aptitude : UNFIT
2 : lacking sense or reason : FOOLISH
3 : not suitable to the time, place, or occasion
: inappropriate often to an absurd degree
4 : generally incompetent : BUNGLING
synonym see AWKWARD
— **in·ept·ly** \-'nep(t)-lē\ *adverb*
— **in·ept·ness** \-nəs\ *noun*
in·ep·ti·tude \(,)i-'nep-tə-,tüd, -,tyüd\ *noun*
[Latin *ineptitudo,* from *ineptus*] (1615)
: the quality or state of being inept; *especially*
: INCOMPETENCE
in·equal·i·ty \,i-ni-'kwä-lə-tē\ *noun* [Middle
English *inequalite,* from Middle French *in-
equalité,* from Latin *inaequalitat-, inaequali-
tas,* from *inaequalis* unequal, from *in-* +
aequalis equal] (15th century)
1 : the quality of being unequal or uneven: as
a : lack of evenness **b** : social disparity **c**
: disparity of distribution or opportunity **d**
: the condition of being variable : CHANGE-
ABLENESS
2 : an instance of being unequal
3 : a formal statement of inequality between
two quantities usually separated by a sign of
inequality (as <, >, or ≠ signifying respective-
ly *is less than, is greater than,* or *is not equal
to*)
in·eq·ui·ta·ble \(,)i-'ne-kwə-tə-bəl\ *adjective*
(1667)
: not equitable : UNFAIR
— **in·eq·ui·ta·bly** \-blē\ *adverb*
in·eq·ui·ty \(,)i-'ne-kwə-tē\ *noun* (1556)
1 : INJUSTICE, UNFAIRNESS
2 : an instance of injustice or unfairness
in·equi·valve \,i-ni-'nē-kwə-,valv\ *also* **in-
equi·valved** \-,valvd\ *adjective* (1776)
: having the valves unequal in size and form
— used of a bivalve mollusk or shell
in·erad·i·ca·ble \,i-ni-'ra-di-kə-bəl\ *adjective*
(1818)
: incapable of being eradicated
— **in·erad·i·ca·bil·i·ty** \-,ra-di-kə-'bi-lə-
tē\ *noun*
— **in·erad·i·ca·bly** \-'ra-di-kə-blē\ *adverb*
in·er·ran·cy \(,)i-'ner-ən(t)-sē\ *noun* (circa
1834)
: exemption from error : INFALLIBILITY ⟨the
question of biblical *inerrancy*⟩
in·er·rant \-ənt\ *adjective* [Latin *inerrant-, in-
errans,* from *in-* + *errant-, errans,* present par-
ticiple of *errare* to err] (1837)
: free from error
in·ert \i-'nərt\ *adjective* [Latin *inert-, iners* un-
skilled, idle, from *in-* + *art-, ars* skill —
more at ARM] (1647)
1 : lacking the power to move
2 : very slow to move or act : SLUGGISH

3 : deficient in active properties; *especially*
: lacking a usual or anticipated chemical or bi-
ological action
synonym see INACTIVE
— **inert** *noun*
— **in·ert·ly** *adverb*
— **in·ert·ness** *noun*
inert gas *noun* (1898)
: NOBLE GAS
in·er·tia \i-'nər-shə, -shē-ə\ *noun* [New Latin,
from Latin, lack of skill, from *inert-, iners*]
(1713)
1 a : a property of matter by which it remains
at rest or in uniform motion in the same
straight line unless acted upon by some exter-
nal force **b** : an analogous property of other
physical quantities (as electricity)
2 : indisposition to motion, exertion, or
change : INERTNESS
— **in·er·tial** \-shəl\ *adjective*
— **in·er·tial·ly** \-'nər-sh(ə-)lē\ *adverb*
inertial guidance *noun* (circa 1948)
: guidance (as of an aircraft or spacecraft) by
means of self-contained automatically control-
ling devices that respond to inertial forces —
called also *inertial navigation*
in·es·cap·able \,i-nə-'skā-pə-bəl\ *adjective*
(1792)
: incapable of being avoided, ignored, or de-
nied : INEVITABLE
— **in·es·cap·ably** \-blē\ *adverb*
in·es·sen·tial \,i-nə-'sen(t)-shəl\ *adjective*
(1677)
1 : having no essence
2 : not essential : UNESSENTIAL
— **inessential** *noun*
in·es·ti·ma·ble \(,)i-'nes-tə-mə-bəl\ *adjective*
[Middle English, from Middle French, from
Latin *inaestimabilis,* from *in-* + *aestimabilis*
estimable] (14th century)
1 : incapable of being estimated or computed
⟨storms caused *inestimable* damage⟩
2 : too valuable or excellent to be measured or
appreciated ⟨has performed an *inestimable* ser-
vice for his country⟩
— **in·es·ti·ma·bly** \-blē\ *adverb*
in·ev·i·ta·ble \i-'ne-və-tə-bəl\ *adjective* [Mid-
dle English, from Latin *inevitabilis,* from *in-* +
evitabilis evitable] (14th century)
: incapable of being avoided or evaded
— **in·ev·i·ta·bil·i·ty** \-,ne-və-tə-'bi-lə-tē\
noun
— **in·ev·i·ta·ble·ness** \-'ne-və-tə-bəl-nəs\
noun
— **in·ev·i·ta·bly** \-blē\ *adverb* (15th century)
1 : in an inevitable way
2 : as is to be expected ⟨*inevitably,* it rained⟩
in·ex·act \,i-nig-'zakt\ *adjective* [French, from
in- + *exact* exact] (circa 1828)
1 : not precisely correct or true : INACCURATE
⟨an *inexact* translation⟩
2 : not rigorous and careful ⟨an *inexact* think-
er⟩
— **in·ex·act·ly** \-'zak(t)-lē\ *adverb*
— **in·ex·act·ness** \-nəs\ *noun*
in·ex·ac·ti·tude \(,)i-,nig-'zak-tə-,tüd, -,tyüd\
noun [French, from *inexact*] (1782)
1 : lack of exactitude or precision
2 : an instance of inexactness
in ex·cel·sis \,in-ik-'sel-səs *also* -'chel-\ *ad-
verb* [Late Latin, on high] (1602)
: in the highest degree
in·ex·cus·able \,i-nik-'skyü-zə-bəl\ *adjective*
[Middle English, from Latin *inexcusabilis,*
from *in-* + *excusabilis* excusable] (15th centu-
ry)
: being without excuse or justification
— **in·ex·cus·able·ness** *noun*
— **in·ex·cus·ably** \-blē\ *adverb*
in·ex·haust·ible \,i-nig-'zȯ-stə-bəl\ *adjective*
(1601)
: not exhaustible: as **a** : incapable of being
used up ⟨*inexhaustible* riches⟩ **b** : incapable of
being wearied or worn out ⟨an *inexhaustible*
hiker⟩

— **in·ex·haust·ibil·i·ty** \-,zȯ-stə-'bi-lə-tē\
noun
— **in·ex·haust·ible·ness** \-'zȯ-stə-bəl-
nəs\ *noun*
— **in·ex·haust·ibly** \-blē\ *adverb*
in·ex·is·tence \,i-nig-'zis-tən(t)s\ *noun* (circa
1623)
: absence of existence : NONEXISTENCE
in·ex·is·tent \-tənt\ *adjective* [Late Latin
inexsistent-, inexsistens, from Latin *in-* +
exsistent-, exsistens, present participle of *ex-
sistere* to exist] (1646)
: not having existence : NONEXISTENT
in·ex·o·ra·ble \(,)i-'neks-rə-bəl, -'nek-sə-,
-'neg-zə-rə-\ *adjective* [Latin *inexorabilis,*
from *in-* + *exorabilis* pliant, from *exorare* to
prevail upon, from *ex-* + *orare* to speak —
more at ORATION] (1553)
: not to be persuaded or moved by entreaty
: RELENTLESS
— **in·ex·o·ra·bil·i·ty** \(,)i-,neks-rə-'bi-lə-tē,
-,nek-sə-, -,neg-zə-\ *noun*
— **in·ex·o·ra·ble·ness** \-'neks-rə-bəl-nəs,
-'nek-sə-, -'neg-zə-\ *noun*
— **in·ex·o·ra·bly** \-blē\ *adverb*
in·ex·pe·di·ence \,i-nik-'spē-dē-ən(t)s\ *noun*
(1608)
: INEXPEDIENCY
in·ex·pe·di·en·cy \-ən(t)-sē\ *noun* (1641)
: the quality or fact of being inexpedient
in·ex·pe·di·ent \-ənt\ *adjective* (1608)
: not expedient : INADVISABLE
— **in·ex·pe·di·ent·ly** *adverb*
in·ex·pen·sive \,i-nik-'spen(t)-siv\ *adjective*
(circa 1846)
: reasonable in price : CHEAP
— **in·ex·pen·sive·ly** *adverb*
— **in·ex·pen·sive·ness** *noun*
in·ex·pe·ri·ence \,i-nik-'spir-ē-ən(t)s\ *noun*
[Middle French, from Late Latin *inexperien-
tia,* from Latin *in-* + *experientia* experience]
(1598)
1 : lack of practical experience
2 : lack of knowledge of the ways of the
world
— **in·ex·pe·ri·enced** \-ən(t)st\ *adjective*
in·ex·pert \(,)i-'nek-,spərt, ,i-nik-'\ *adjective*
[Middle English, from Middle French, from
Latin *inexpertus,* from *in-* + *expertus* expert]
(15th century)
: not expert : UNSKILLED
— **in·ex·pert** \-'nek-,spərt\ *noun*
— **in·ex·pert·ly** \-'nek-,spərt-lē, ,i-nik-'\
adverb
— **in·ex·pert·ness** *noun*
in·ex·pi·a·ble \(,)i-'nek-spē-ə-bəl\ *adjective*
[Middle English *inexpyable,* from Latin *inex-
piabilis,* from *in-* + *expiare* to expiate] (15th
century)
1 : not capable of being atoned for
2 *obsolete* : IMPLACABLE, UNAPPEASABLE
— **in·ex·pi·a·bly** \-blē\ *adverb*
in·ex·plain·able \,i-nik-'splā-nə-bəl\ *adjec-
tive* (circa 1923)
: INEXPLICABLE
in·ex·pli·ca·ble \,i-nik-'spli-kə-bəl, (,)i-'nek-
(,)spli-\ *adjective* [Middle English, from Mid-
dle French, from Latin *inexplicabilis,* from *in-*
+ *explicabilis* explicable] (15th century)
: incapable of being explained, interpreted, or
accounted for
— **in·ex·pli·ca·bil·i·ty** \,i-nik-,spli-kə-'bi-
lə-tē, (,)i-,nek-(,)spli-\ *noun*
— **in·ex·pli·ca·ble·ness** \,i-nik-'spli-kə-
bəl-nəs, (,)i-'nek-(,)spli-\ *noun*
— **in·ex·pli·ca·bly** \-blē\ *adverb*
in·ex·plic·it \,i-nik-'spli-sət\ *adjective* (circa
1812)
: not explicit
in·ex·press·ible \-'spre-sə-bəl\ *adjective*
(1625)
: not capable of being expressed : INDESCRIB-
ABLE
— **in·ex·press·ibil·i·ty** \-,spre-sə-'bi-lə-tē\
noun

— **in·ex·press·ible·ness** \-'spre-sə-bəl-nəs\ *noun*

— **in·ex·press·ibly** \-blē\ *adverb*

in·ex·pres·sive \-'spre-siv\ *adjective* (1652)
1 *archaic* : INEXPRESSIBLE
2 : lacking expression or meaning ⟨an *inexpressive* face⟩
— **in·ex·pres·sive·ly** *adverb*
— **in·ex·pres·sive·ness** *noun*

in·ex·pug·na·ble \,i-nik-'spəg-nə-bəl, -'spyü-nə-\ *adjective* [Middle English *in-expungnabull*, from Middle French, from Latin *inexpugnabilis*, from *in-* + *expugnare* to take by storm, from *ex-* + *pugnare* to fight — more at PUNGENT] (15th century)
1 : incapable of being subdued or overthrown : IMPREGNABLE ⟨an *inexpugnable* position⟩
2 : STABLE, FIXED ⟨*inexpugnable* hatred⟩
— **in·ex·pug·na·ble·ness** *noun*
— **in·ex·pug·na·bly** \-blē\ *adverb*

in·ex·pung·ible \,i-nik-'spən-jə-bəl\ *adjective* [*in-* + *expunge*] (1888)
: incapable of being obliterated

in ex·ten·so \,in-ik-'sten(t)-(,)sō\ *adverb* [Medieval Latin] (1826)
: at full length ⟨the passage was quoted *in extenso*⟩

in·ex·tin·guish·able \,i-nik-'stiŋ-gwi-shə-bəl, -'stiŋ-wi-\ *adjective* (15th century)
: not extinguishable : UNQUENCHABLE ⟨an *inextinguishable* flame⟩ ⟨an *inextinguishable* longing⟩
— **in·ex·tin·guish·ably** \-blē\ *adverb*

in ex·tre·mis \,in-ik-'strē-məs, -'strā-\ *adverb* [Latin] (circa 1530)
: in extreme circumstances; *especially* : at the point of death

in·ex·tri·ca·ble \,i-nik-'stri-kə-bəl, (,)i-nek-(,)stri-\ *adjective* [Middle English, from Middle French or Latin; Middle French, from Latin *inextricabilis*, from *in-* + *extricabilis* extricable] (15th century)
1 : forming a maze or tangle from which it is impossible to get free
2 a : incapable of being disentangled or untied ⟨an *inextricable* knot⟩ **b** : not capable of being solved
— **in·ex·tri·ca·bil·i·ty** \,i-nik-,stri-kə-'bi-lə-tē, (,)i-,nek-(,)stri-\ *noun*
— **in·ex·tri·ca·bly** \,i-nik-'stri-kə-blē, (,)i-'nek-(,)stri-\ *adverb*

in·fal·li·ble \(,)in-'fa-lə-bəl\ *adjective* [Middle English, from Medieval Latin *infallibilis*, from Latin *in-* + Late Latin *fallibilis* fallible] (15th century)
1 : incapable of error : UNERRING ⟨an *infallible* memory⟩
2 : not liable to mislead, deceive, or disappoint : CERTAIN ⟨an *infallible* remedy⟩
3 : incapable of error in defining doctrines touching faith or morals
— **in·fal·li·bil·i·ty** \-,fa-lə-'bi-lə-tē\ *noun*
— **in·fal·li·bly** \-'fa-lə-blē\ *adverb*

in·fall·ing \'in-,fȯ-liŋ\ *adjective* (1964)
: moving under the influence of gravity toward a celestial object (as a black hole)
— **in·fall** \-,fȯl\ *noun*

in·fa·mous \'in-fə-məs\ *adjective* [Middle English, from Latin *infamis*, from *in-* + *fama* fame] (14th century)
1 : having a reputation of the worst kind
2 : causing or bringing infamy : DISGRACEFUL
3 : convicted of an offense bringing infamy
— **in·fa·mous·ly** *adverb*

in·fa·my \-mē\ *noun, plural* **-mies** (15th century)
1 : evil reputation brought about by something grossly criminal, shocking, or brutal
2 a : an extreme and publicly known criminal or evil act **b** : the state of being infamous
synonym see DISGRACE

in·fan·cy \'in-fən(t)-sē\ *noun, plural* **-cies** (14th century)
1 : early childhood
2 : a beginning or early period of existence
3 : the legal status of an infant

¹in·fant \'in-fənt\ *noun* [Middle English *enfaunt*, from Middle French *enfant*, from Latin *infant-, infans*, from *infant-, infans*, adjective, incapable of speech, young, from *in-* + *fant-, fans*, present participle of *fari* to speak — more at BAN] (14th century)
1 : a child in the first period of life
2 : a person who is not of full age : MINOR ◇

²infant *adjective* (circa 1586)
1 : intended for young children
2 : being in an early stage of development
3 : of, relating to, or being in infancy

in·fan·ta \in-'fan-tə, -'fän-\ *noun* [Spanish & Portuguese, feminine of *infante*] (1593)
: a daughter of a Spanish or Portuguese monarch

in·fan·te \in-'fan-tē, -'fän-(,)tā\ *noun* [Spanish & Portuguese, literally, infant, from Latin *infant-, infans*] (1555)
: a younger son of a Spanish or Portuguese monarch

in·fan·ti·cide \in-'fan-tə-,sīd\ *noun* [Late Latin *infanticidium*, from Latin *infant-, infans* + *-i-* + *-cidium* -cide] (circa 1656)
1 : the killing of an infant
2 [Late Latin *infanticida*, from Latin *infant-, infans* + *-i-* + *-cida* -cide] : one who kills an infant
— **in·fan·ti·ci·dal** \-,fan-tə-'sī-d³l\ *adjective*

in·fan·tile \'in-fən-,tīl, -t³l, -,tēl, -(,)til\ *adjective* (1696)
1 : of or relating to infants or infancy
2 : suitable to or characteristic of an infant; *especially* : very immature
— **in·fan·til·i·ty** \,in-fən-'ti-lə-tē\ *noun*

infantile paralysis *noun* (1843)
: POLIOMYELITIS

in·fan·til·ism \'in-fən-,tī-,li-zəm, -tə-,li-; in-'fan-t³l-,i-\ *noun* (1895)
1 : retention of childish physical, mental, or emotional qualities in adult life; *especially* : failure to attain sexual maturity
2 : an act or expression that indicates lack of maturity

in·fan·til·ize \'in-fən-,tī-,līz, -fən-t³l-,īz; in-'fan-t³l-,īz\ *transitive verb* **-ized; -iz·ing** (1943)
1 : to make or keep infantile
2 : to treat as if infantile
— **in·fan·til·i·za·tion** \,in-fən-,tī-lə-'zā-shən, -fən-t³l-ə-; in-,fan-t³l-ə-\ *noun*

in·fan·tine \'in-fən-,tīn, -,tēn\ *adjective* (1603)
: INFANTILE, CHILDISH

in·fan·try \'in-fən-trē\ *noun, plural* **-tries** [Middle French & Old Italian; Middle French *infanterie*, from Old Italian *infanteria*, from *infante* boy, foot soldier, from Latin *infant-, infans*] (1579)
1 a : soldiers trained, armed, and equipped to fight on foot **b** : a branch of an army composed of these soldiers
2 : an infantry regiment or division ◇

in·fan·try·man \-trē-mən\ *noun* (1883)
: an infantry soldier

infant school *noun* (1824)
British : a school for children aged five to seven or eight

in·farct \'in-,färkt, in-'\ *noun* [Latin *infarctus*, past participle of *infarcire* to stuff, from *in-* + *farcire* to stuff] (1873)
: an area of necrosis in a tissue or organ resulting from obstruction of the local circulation by a thrombus or embolus
— **in·farct·ed** \in-'färk-təd\ *adjective*
— **in·farc·tion** \in-'färk-shən\ *noun*

in·fare \'in-,far, -,fer\ *noun* [Middle English, entrance, from Old English *infær*, from *in* + *fær* way, from *faran* to go — more at FARE] (1595)
chiefly dialect : a reception for a newly married couple

¹in·fat·u·ate \in-'fa-chə-wət\ *adjective* (15th century)
: being in an infatuated state or condition

²in·fat·u·ate \-,wāt\ *transitive verb* **-at·ed; -at·ing** [Latin *infatuatus*, past participle of *infatuare*, from *in-* + *fatuus* fatuous] (1533)
1 : to cause to be foolish : deprive of sound judgment
2 : to inspire with a foolish or extravagant love or admiration
— **in·fat·u·a·tion** \-,fa-chə-'wā-shən\ *noun*

in·fau·na \'in-,fȯ-nə, -,fä-\ *noun* [New Latin, from *²in-* + *fauna*] (1914)
: benthic fauna living in the substrate and especially in a soft sea bottom — compare EPIFAUNA
— **in·fau·nal** \-,fȯ-n³l, -,fä-\ *adjective*

in·fea·si·ble \(,)in-'fē-zə-bəl\ *adjective* (1533)
: not feasible : IMPRACTICABLE
— **in·fea·si·bil·i·ty** \-,fē-zə-'bi-lə-tē\ *noun*

in·fect \in-'fekt\ *transitive verb* [Middle English, from Latin *infectus*, past participle of *inficere*, from *in-* + *facere* to make, do — more at DO] (14th century)
1 : to contaminate with a disease-producing substance or agent (as bacteria)
2 a : to communicate a pathogen or a disease to **b** *of a pathogenic organism* : to invade (an individual or organ) usually by penetration **c** *of a computer virus* : to become transmitted and copied to (as a computer)

◇ WORD HISTORY

infant To the frustrated parent of a sick, bawling infant incapable of saying just where it hurts, the etymology of *infant* must seem especially apt. In Latin the adjective *infans* literally meant "not speaking, incapable of speech." The noun *infans* designated a very young child who had not yet learned to talk. Later, however, the scope of *infans* was broadened to include any child, no matter how talkative. When the word was adopted into the Romance languages, the broader usage was carried over also. Like French, from which it had directly borrowed the word, English originally used *infant* for any child. Over time, English reverted to the earlier Latin sense, restricting *infant* to a child still young enough to be called a baby.

infantry In the 20th century U.S. Army, the infantry's training film epithet is "queen of battle," and the combat infantryman's badge is a coveted mark of honor, though colloquialisms such as *dogface* and *grunt* express another viewpoint about the status of the ordinary foot soldier. The history of the word *infantry*, moreover, reveals a rather lowly origin for this branch of arms. The Italian word *fante*, descended from Latin *infans* "infant, child," originally meant "child," later "youth, boy," and then "servant." In the early 14th century, *fante* also took on the sense "foot soldier." In the High Middle Ages he was typically a lowly figure, who was often no more than a servant in a horseman's retinue and of little value on the battlefield. But in the 15th and 16th centuries the situation changed, as foot soldiers equipped first with longbows and crossbows and then with pikes and matchlock guns achieved dominance over mounted troops in cumbersome armor. The *fanteria*, that is, the *fanti* or foot soldiers collectively, became a significant branch of arms, and the Italian word, in the more Latinate form *infanteria*, was borrowed into French as *infanterie* in the 1500s and later in the same century into English as *infantry*.

3 a : CONTAMINATE, CORRUPT ⟨the inflated writing that *infects* such stories⟩ **b :** to work upon or seize upon so as to induce sympathy, belief, or support ⟨trying to *infect* their salespeople with their enthusiasm⟩
— **in·fec·tor** \-'fek-tər\ *noun*
in·fec·tion \in-'fek-shən\ *noun* (14th century)
1 : the act or result of affecting injuriously
2 : an infective agent or material contaminated with an infective agent
3 a : the state produced by the establishment of an infective agent in or on a suitable host **b :** a disease resulting from infection
4 : an act or process of infecting; *also* : the establishment of a pathogen in its host after invasion
5 : the communication of emotions or qualities through example or contact
in·fec·tious \-shəs\ *adjective* (1542)
1 a : capable of causing infection **b :** communicable by infection — compare CONTAGIOUS
2 : that corrupts or contaminates
3 : spreading or capable of spreading rapidly to others ⟨their enthusiasm was *infectious*⟩ ⟨an *infectious* grin⟩
— **in·fec·tious·ly** *adverb*
— **in·fec·tious·ness** *noun*
infectious hepatitis *noun* (circa 1941)
: HEPATITIS A
infectious mononucleosis *noun* (1920)
: an acute infectious disease associated with Epstein-Barr virus and characterized by fever, swelling of lymph nodes, and lymphocytosis
in·fec·tive \in-'fek-tiv\ *adjective* (14th century)
1 : producing or capable of producing infection
2 : affecting others : INFECTIOUS
— **in·fec·tiv·i·ty** \(,)in-,fek-'ti-və-tē\ *noun*
in·fe·lic·i·tous \,in-fi-'li-sə-təs\ *adjective* (1835)
: not appropriate in application or expression
— **in·fe·lic·i·tous·ly** *adverb*
in·fe·lic·i·ty \-sə-tē\ *noun, plural* **-ties** [Middle English *infelicite* unhappiness, from Latin *infelicitas*, from *infelic-, infelix* unhappy, from *in-* + *felic-, felix* fruitful — more at FEMININE] (1617)
1 : the quality or state of being infelicitous
2 : something that is infelicitous
in·fer \in-'fər\ *verb* **in·ferred; in·fer·ring** [Middle French or Latin; Middle French *inferer*, from Latin *inferre*, literally, to carry or bring into, from *in-* + *ferre* to carry — more at BEAR] (1528)
transitive verb
1 : to derive as a conclusion from facts or premises ⟨we see smoke and *infer* fire —L. A. White⟩ — compare IMPLY
2 : GUESS, SURMISE ⟨your letter . . . allows me to *infer* that you are as well as ever —O. W. Holmes (died 1935)⟩
3 a : to involve as a normal outcome of thought **b :** to point out : INDICATE ⟨this doth *infer* the zeal I had to see him —Shakespeare⟩
4 : SUGGEST, HINT ⟨another survey . . . *infers* that two-thirds of all present computer installations are not paying for themselves —H. R. Chellman⟩
intransitive verb
: to draw inferences ⟨men . . . have observed, *inferred*, and reasoned . . . to all kinds of results —John Dewey⟩ ☆ ▢
— **in·fer·able** *also* **in·fer·ri·ble** \in-'fər-ə-bəl\ *adjective*
— **in·fer·rer** \-'fər-ər\ *noun*
in·fer·ence \'in-f(ə-)rən(t)s, -fərn(t)s\ *noun* (1594)
1 : the act or process of inferring: as **a :** the act of passing from one proposition, statement, or judgment considered as true to another whose truth is believed to follow from that of the former **b :** the act of passing from statistical sample data to generalizations (as of the value of population parameters) usually with calculated degrees of certainty

2 : something that is inferred; *especially* : a proposition arrived at by inference
3 : the premises and conclusion of a process of inferring
in·fer·en·tial \,in-fə-'ren(t)-shəl\ *adjective* [Medieval Latin *inferentia*, from Latin *inferent-, inferens*, present participle of *inferre*] (1657)
1 : relating to, involving, or resembling inference
2 : deduced or deducible by inference
in·fer·en·tial·ly \-'ren(t)-sh(ə-)lē\ *adverb* (1691)
: by way of inference : through inference
in·fe·ri·or \in-'fir-ē-ər\ *adjective* [Middle English, from Latin, comparative of *inferus* lower — more at UNDER] (15th century)
1 : situated lower down : LOWER
2 a : of low or lower degree or rank **b :** of poor quality : MEDIOCRE
3 : of little or less importance, value, or merit ⟨always felt *inferior* to his older brother⟩
4 a : situated below another and especially another similar superior part of an upright body **b :** situated in a relatively low posterior or ventral position in a quadrupedal body **c** (1) : situated below another plant part or organ (2) : ABAXIAL
5 : relating to or being a subscript
— **inferior** *noun*
— **in·fe·ri·or·i·ty** \(,)in-,fir-ē-'òr-ə-tē, -'är-\ *noun*
— **in·fe·ri·or·ly** \in-'fir-ē-ər-lē\ *adverb*
inferior conjunction *noun* (1833)
: a conjunction of an inferior planet with the sun in which the planet is aligned between the earth and the sun
inferiority complex *noun* (1922)
1 : an acute sense of personal inferiority often resulting either in timidity or through overcompensation in exaggerated aggressiveness
2 : a collective sense of cultural, regional, or national inferiority
inferior planet *noun* (1658)
: either of the planets Mercury and Venus whose orbits lie within that of the earth
in·fer·nal \in-'fər-n°l\ *adjective* [Middle English, from Middle French, from Late Latin *infernalis*, from *infernus* hell, from Latin, lower, from *inferus*] (14th century)
1 : of or relating to a nether world of the dead
2 a : of or relating to hell **b :** HELLISH, DIABOLICAL
3 : DAMNABLE ⟨an *infernal* nuisance⟩
— **in·fer·nal·ly** \-n°l-ē\ *adverb*
infernal machine *noun* (1810)
: a machine or apparatus maliciously designed to explode and destroy life or property; *especially* : a concealed or disguised bomb
in·fer·no \in-'fər-(,)nō\ *noun, plural* **-nos** [Italian, hell, from Late Latin *infernus*] (1834)
: a place or a state that resembles or suggests hell ⟨the *inferno* of war⟩; *also* : intense heat ⟨the roaring *inferno* of the blast furnace⟩
in·fer·tile \(')in-'fər-t°l\ *adjective* [Middle French, from Late Latin *infertilis*, from Latin *in-* + *fertilis* fertile] (1597)
: not fertile or productive ⟨*infertile* eggs⟩ ⟨*infertile* fields⟩
— **in·fer·til·i·ty** \,in-(,)fər-'ti-lə-tē\ *noun*
in·fest \in-'fest\ *transitive verb* [French *infester*, from Latin *infestare*, from *infestus* hostile] (1602)
1 : to spread or swarm in or over in a troublesome manner ⟨a slum *infested* with crime⟩ ⟨shark-*infested* waters⟩
2 : to live in or on as a parasite
— **in·fes·tant** \-'fes-tənt\ *noun*
— **in·fes·ta·tion** \,in-,fes-'tā-shən\ *noun*
— **in·fest·er** \in-'fes-tər\ *noun*
in·fi·del \'in-fə-d°l, -fə-,del\ *noun* [Middle English *infidele*, from Middle French, from Late Latin *infidelis* unbelieving, from Latin, unfaithful, from *in-* + *fidelis* faithful — more at FIDELITY] (15th century)

1 : one who is not a Christian or who opposes Christianity
2 a : an unbeliever with respect to a particular religion **b :** one who acknowledges no religious belief
3 : a disbeliever in something specified or understood
— **infidel** *adjective*
in·fi·del·i·ty \,in-fə-'de-lə-tē, -(,)fī-\ *noun, plural* **-ties** (15th century)
1 : lack of belief in a religion
2 a : unfaithfulness to a moral obligation : DISLOYALTY **b :** marital unfaithfulness or an instance of it
in·field \'in-,fēld\ *noun* (1606)
1 : a field near a farmhouse
2 a : the area of a baseball field enclosed by the three bases and home plate **b :** the defensive positions comprising first base, second base, shortstop, and third base; *also* : the players who play these positions
3 : the area enclosed by a racetrack or running track
in·field·er \-,fēl-dər\ *noun* (1867)
: a baseball player who plays in the infield
infield hit *noun* (1912)
: a base hit on a ball that does not leave the infield
infield out *noun* (1926)
: a ground ball on which the batter is put out by an infielder
in·fight·ing \'in-,fī-tiŋ\ *noun* (1816)

☆ **SYNONYMS**
Infer, deduce, conclude, judge, gather mean to arrive at a mental conclusion. IN-FER implies arriving at a conclusion by reasoning from evidence; if the evidence is slight, the term comes close to *surmise* ⟨from that remark, I *inferred* that they knew each other⟩. DEDUCE often adds to INFER the special implication of drawing a particular inference from a generalization ⟨denied we could *deduce* anything important from human mortality⟩. CONCLUDE implies arriving at a necessary inference at the end of a chain of reasoning ⟨*concluded* that only the accused could be guilty⟩. JUDGE stresses a weighing of the evidence on which a conclusion is based ⟨*judge* people by their actions⟩. GATHER suggests an intuitive forming of a conclusion from implications ⟨*gathered* their desire to be alone without a word⟩.

▢ **USAGE**
infer Sir Thomas More is the first writer known to have used both *infer* and *imply* in their approved senses (1528). He is also the first to have used *infer* in a sense close in meaning to *imply* (1533). Both of these uses of *infer* coexisted without comment until some time around the end of World War I. Since then, senses 3 and 4 of *infer* have been frequently condemned as an undesirable blurring of a useful distinction. The actual blurring has been done by the commentators. Sense 3, descended from More's use of 1533, does not occur with a personal subject. When objections arose, they were to a use with a personal subject (now sense 4). Since dictionaries did not recognize this use specifically, the objectors assumed that sense 3 was the one they found illogical, even though it had been in respectable use for four centuries. The actual usage condemned was a spoken one never used in logical discourse. At present sense 4 is found in print chiefly in letters to the editor and other informal prose, not in serious intellectual writing. The controversy over sense 4 has apparently reduced the frequency of use of sense 3.

1 : fighting or boxing at close quarters
2 : rough-and-tumble fighting
3 : prolonged and often bitter dissension or rivalry among members of a group or organization ⟨bureaucratic *infighting*⟩
— **in·fight** \'in-ˌfīt\ *intransitive verb*
— **in·fight·er** \-ˌfī-tər\ *noun*
in·fil·trate \in-'fil-ˌtrāt, 'in-(ˌ)\ *verb* **-trat·ed; -trat·ing** (1758)
transitive verb
1 : to cause (as a liquid) to permeate something by penetrating its pores or interstices
2 : to pass into or through (a substance) by filtering or permeating
3 : to pass (troops) singly or in small groups through gaps in the enemy line
4 : to enter or become established in gradually or unobtrusively usually for subversive purposes ⟨the intelligence staff had been *infiltrated* by spies⟩
intransitive verb
: to enter, permeate, or pass through a substance or area by filtering or by insinuating gradually
— **infiltrate** *noun*
— **in·fil·tra·tion** \ˌin-(ˌ)fil-'trā-shən\ *noun*
— **in·fil·tra·tive** \'in-(ˌ)fil-ˌtrā-tiv, in-'fil-trə-\ *adjective*
— **in·fil·tra·tor** \in-'fil-ˌtrā-tər, 'in-(ˌ)\ *noun*
¹**in·fi·nite** \'in-fə-nət\ *adjective* [Middle English *infinit*, from Middle French or Latin; Middle French, from Latin *infinitus*, from *in- + finitus* finite] (14th century)
1 : extending indefinitely : ENDLESS ⟨*infinite* space⟩
2 : immeasurably or inconceivably great or extensive : INEXHAUSTIBLE ⟨*infinite* patience⟩
3 : subject to no limitation or external determination
4 a : extending beyond, lying beyond, or being greater than any preassigned finite value however large ⟨*infinite* number of positive numbers⟩ **b** : extending to infinity ⟨*infinite* plane surface⟩ **c** : characterized by an infinite number of elements or terms ⟨an *infinite* set⟩ ⟨an *infinite* series⟩
— **in·fi·nite·ly** *adverb*
— **in·fi·nite·ness** *noun*
²**infinite** *noun* (1535)
: something that is infinite (as in extent, duration, or number)
¹**in·fin·i·tes·i·mal** \(ˌ)in-ˌfi-nə-'te-sə-məl, -zə-məl\ *noun* [New Latin *infinitesimus* infinite in rank, from Latin *infinitus*] (1706)
: an infinitesimal quantity or variable
²**infinitesimal** *adjective* (1710)
1 : taking on values arbitrarily close to but greater than zero
2 : immeasurably or incalculably small
— **in·fin·i·tes·i·mal·ly** \-mə-lē\ *adverb*
infinitesimal calculus *noun* (1801)
: CALCULUS 1b
in·fin·i·ti·val \(ˌ)in-ˌfi-nə-'tī-vəl\ *adjective* (1869)
: relating to the infinitive
¹**in·fin·i·tive** \in-'fi-nə-tiv\ *adjective* [Middle English *infinityf*, from Late Latin *infinitivus*, from Latin *infinitus*] (15th century)
: formed with the infinitive
— **in·fin·i·tive·ly** *adverb*
²**infinitive** *noun* (1530)
: a verb form normally identical in English with the first person singular that performs some functions of a noun and at the same time displays some characteristics of a verb and that is used with *to* (as in "I asked him *to go*") except with auxiliary and various other verbs (as in "no one saw him *leave*")
in·fin·i·tude \in-'fi-nə-ˌtüd, -ˌtyüd\ *noun* (1641)
1 : the quality or state of being infinite : INFINITENESS
2 : something that is infinite especially in extent
3 : an infinite number or quantity
in·fin·i·ty \in-'fi-nə-tē\ *noun, plural* **-ties** (14th century)

1 a : the quality of being infinite **b** : unlimited extent of time, space, or quantity : BOUNDLESSNESS
2 : an indefinitely great number or amount ⟨an *infinity* of stars⟩
3 a : the limit of the value of a function or variable when it tends to become numerically larger than any preassigned finite number **b** : a part of a geometric magnitude that lies beyond any part whose distance from a given reference position is finite ⟨do parallel lines ever meet if they extend to *infinity*⟩ **c** : a transfinite number (as aleph-null)
4 : a distance so great that the rays of light from a point source at that distance may be regarded as parallel
in·firm \in-'fərm\ *adjective* [Middle English, from Latin *infirmus*, from *in- + firmus* firm] (14th century)
1 : of poor or deteriorated vitality; *especially* : feeble from age
2 : weak of mind, will, or character : IRRESOLUTE, VACILLATING
3 : not solid or stable : INSECURE
synonym see WEAK
— **in·firm·ly** *adverb*
in·fir·ma·ry \in-'fər-mə-rē, -'fər-mə-\ *noun, plural* **-ries** (15th century)
: a place where the infirm or sick are lodged for care and treatment
in·fir·mi·ty \in-'fər-mə-tē\ *noun, plural* **-ties** (14th century)
1 a : the quality or state of being infirm **b** : the condition of being feeble : FRAILTY
2 : DISEASE, MALADY
3 : a personal failing : FOIBLE ⟨one of the besetting *infirmities* of living creatures is egotism —A. J. Toynbee⟩
¹**in·fix** \'in-ˌfiks, in-'\ *transitive verb* [Latin *infixus*, past participle of *infigere*, from *in- + figere* to fasten — more at FIX] (1502)
1 : to fasten or fix by piercing or thrusting in
2 : to impress firmly in the consciousness or disposition
3 : to insert (as a sound or letter) as an infix
synonym see IMPLANT
— **in·fix·a·tion** \ˌin-(ˌ)fik-'sā-shən\ *noun*
²**in·fix** \'in-ˌfiks\ *noun* (1881)
: a derivational or inflectional affix appearing in the body of a word (as Sanskrit *-n-* in *vindami* "I know" as contrasted with *vid* "to know")
³**in·fix** *same as* ²\ *adjective* (1971)
: characterized by placement of a binary operator between the operands ⟨*a + b* is expressed in *infix* notation⟩ — compare POSTFIX, PREFIX
in fla·gran·te de·lic·to \ˌin-flə-ˌgrän-tē-di-'lik-(ˌ)tō, -ˌgran-\ *adverb* (1772)
: FLAGRANTE DELICTO
in·flame \in-'flām\ *verb* **in·flamed; in·flam·ing** [Middle English *enflamen*, from Middle French *enflamer*, from Latin *inflammare*, from *in- + flamma* flame] (14th century)
transitive verb
1 a : to excite to excessive or uncontrollable action or feeling **b** : to make more heated or violent : INTENSIFY ⟨insults served only to *inflame* the feud⟩
2 : to set on fire : KINDLE
3 : to cause to redden or grow hot from anger or excitement
4 : to cause inflammation in (bodily tissue)
intransitive verb
1 : to burst into flame
2 : to become excited or angered
3 : to become affected with inflammation
— **in·flam·er** *noun*
in·flam·ma·ble \in-'fla-mə-bəl\ *adjective* [French, from Medieval Latin *inflammabilis*, from Latin *inflammare*] (1605)
1 : FLAMMABLE
2 : easily inflamed, excited, or angered : IRASCIBLE
— **in·flam·ma·bil·i·ty** \-ˌfla-mə-'bi-lə-tē\ *noun*
— **inflammable** *noun*

— **in·flam·ma·ble·ness** \-'fla-mə-bəl-nəs\ *noun*
— **in·flam·ma·bly** \-blē\ *adverb*
in·flam·ma·tion \ˌin-flə-'mā-shən\ *noun* (15th century)
1 : a local response to cellular injury that is marked by capillary dilatation, leukocytic infiltration, redness, heat, and pain and that serves as a mechanism initiating the elimination of noxious agents and of damaged tissue
2 : the act of inflaming : the state of being inflamed
in·flam·ma·to·ry \in-'fla-mə-ˌtōr-ē, -ˌtor-\ *adjective* (circa 1711)
1 : tending to excite anger, disorder, or tumult : SEDITIOUS
2 : tending to inflame or excite the senses
3 : accompanied by or tending to cause inflammation
— **in·flam·ma·to·ri·ly** \-ˌfla-mə-'tōr-ə-lē, -'tor-\ *adverb*
in·flat·able \in-'flā-tə-bəl\ *adjective* (1878)
: capable of being inflated ⟨an *inflatable* boat⟩
— **inflatable** *noun*
in·flate \in-'flāt\ *verb* **in·flat·ed; in·flat·ing** [Middle English, from Latin *inflatus*, past participle of *inflare*, from *in- + flare* to blow — more at BLOW] (15th century)
transitive verb
1 : to swell or distend with air or gas
2 : to puff up : ELATE
3 : to expand or increase abnormally or imprudently
intransitive verb
: to become inflated
synonym see EXPAND
— **in·fla·tor** *or* **in·flat·er** \-'flā-tər\ *noun*
inflated *adjective* (1652)
1 : elaborated or heightened by artificial or empty means ⟨an *inflated* style of writing⟩
2 : distended with air or gas
3 : expanded to an abnormal or unjustifiable volume or level ⟨*inflated* prices⟩
4 : being hollow and enlarged or distended
in·fla·tion \in-'flā-shən\ *noun* (14th century)
1 : an act of inflating : a state of being inflated: as **a** : DISTENSION **b** : a hypothetical extremely brief period of very rapid expansion of the universe immediately following the big bang **c** : empty pretentiousness : POMPOSITY
2 : an increase in the volume of money and credit relative to available goods and services resulting in a continuing rise in the general price level
in·fla·tion·ary \-shə-ˌner-ē\ *adjective* (1920)
: of, characterized by, or productive of inflation
inflationary spiral *noun* (1931)
: a continuous rise in prices that is sustained by the tendency of wage increases and cost increases to react on each other
in·fla·tion·ism \in-'flā-shə-ˌni-zəm\ *noun* (1919)
: the policy of economic inflation
— **in·fla·tion·ist** \-sh(ə-)nist\ *noun or adjective*
in·flect \in-'flekt\ *verb* [Middle English, from Latin *inflectere*, from *in- + flectere* to bend] (15th century)
transitive verb
1 : to turn from a direct line or course : CURVE
2 : to vary (a word) by inflection : DECLINE, CONJUGATE
3 : to change or vary the pitch of (as the voice)
intransitive verb
: to become modified by inflection
— **in·flect·able** \-'flek-tə-bəl\ *adjective*
— **in·flec·tive** \-'flek-tiv\ *adjective*

\ə\ abut \ᵊ\ kitten \ər\ further \a\ ash \ā\ ace
\ä\ mop, mar \au̇\ out \ch\ chin \e\ bet \ē\ easy
\g\ go \i\ hit \ī\ ice \j\ job \ŋ\ sing \ō\ go
\o̊\ law \o̊i\ boy \th\ thin \t̲h̲\ the \ü\ loot \u̇\ foot
\y\ yet \zh\ vision *see also* Guide to Pronunciation

in·flec·tion \in-'flek-shən\ *noun* (1531)
1 : the act or result of curving or bending **:** BEND
2 : change in pitch or loudness of the voice
3 a : the change of form that words undergo to mark such distinctions as those of case, gender, number, tense, person, mood, or voice **b :** a form, suffix, or element involved in such variation **c :** ACCIDENCE
4 a : change in curvature of an arc or curve from concave to convex or conversely **b :** INFLECTION POINT
in·flec·tion·al \-shnəl, -shə-nᵊl\ *adjective* (1832)
: of, relating to, or characterized by inflection ⟨an *inflectional* suffix⟩
— **in·flec·tion·al·ly** *adverb*
inflection point *noun* (circa 1721)
: a point on a curve that separates an arc concave upward from one concave downward and vice versa
in·flexed \'in-,flekst\ *adjective* [Latin *inflexus,* past participle of *inflectere*] (1661)
: bent or turned abruptly inward or downward or toward the axis ⟨*inflexed* petals⟩
in·flex·i·ble \(,)in-'flek-sə-bəl\ *adjective* [Middle English, from Latin *inflexibilis,* from *in-* + *flexibilis* flexible] (14th century)
1 : rigidly firm in will or purpose **:** UNYIELDING
2 : not readily bent **:** lacking or deficient in suppleness
3 : incapable of change **:** UNALTERABLE ☆
— **in·flex·i·bil·i·ty** \-,flek-sə-'bi-lə-tē\ *noun*
— **in·flex·i·ble·ness** \-'flek-sə-bəl-nəs\ *noun*
— **in·flex·i·bly** \-blē\ *adverb*
in·flex·ion *chiefly British variant of* INFLECTION
in·flict \in-'flikt\ *transitive verb* [Latin *inflictus,* past participle of *infligere,* from *in-* + *fligere* to strike — more at PROFLIGATE] (1566)
1 : AFFLICT
2 a : to give by or as if by striking ⟨*inflict* pain⟩ **b :** to cause (something unpleasant) to be endured ⟨*inflict* my annual message upon the church —Mark Twain⟩
— **in·flict·er** *or* **in·flic·tor** \-'flik-tər\ *noun*
— **in·flic·tive** \-tiv\ *adjective*
in·flic·tion \in-'flik-shən\ *noun* (1534)
1 : the act of inflicting
2 : something (as punishment or suffering) that is inflicted
in·flight \'in-'flīt\ *adjective* (1944)
: made, carried out, or provided for use or enjoyment while in flight ⟨*in-flight* movies⟩
in·flo·res·cence \,in-flə-'re-sᵊn(t)s\ *noun* [New Latin *inflorescentia,* from Late Latin *inflorescent-, inflorescens,* present participle of *inflorescere* to begin to bloom, from Latin *in-* + *florescere* to begin to bloom — more at FLORESCENCE] (1760)
1 a (1) **:** the mode of development and arrangement of flowers on an axis (2) **:** a floral axis with its appendages; *also* **:** a flower cluster **b :** a cluster of reproductive organs on a moss usually subtended by a bract

inflorescence 1a(1): *1* raceme, *2* corymb, *3* umbel, *4* compound umbel, *5* capitulum, *6* spike, *7* compound spike, *8* panicle, *9* cyme

2 : the budding and unfolding of blossoms **:** FLOWERING
in·flow \'in-,flō\ *noun* (1839)
: a flowing in ⟨the *inflow* of air⟩ ⟨an *inflow* of funds⟩
¹in·flu·ence \'in-,flü-ən(t)s, *especially Southern* in-'\ *noun* [Middle English, from Middle French, from Medieval Latin *influentia,* from Latin *influent-, influens,* present participle of *influere* to flow in, from *in-* + *fluere* to flow — more at FLUID] (14th century)
1 a : an ethereal fluid held to flow from the stars and to affect the actions of humans **b :** an emanation of occult power held to derive from stars
2 : an emanation of spiritual or moral force
3 a : the act or power of producing an effect without apparent exertion of force or direct exercise of command **b :** corrupt interference with authority for personal gain
4 : the power or capacity of causing an effect in indirect or intangible ways **:** SWAY
5 : one that exerts influence ☆
— **under the influence :** affected by alcohol **:** DRUNK ⟨was arrested for driving *under the influence*⟩
²influence *transitive verb* **-enced; -encing** (1658)
1 : to affect or alter by indirect or intangible means **:** SWAY
2 : to have an effect on the condition or development of **:** MODIFY
synonym *see* AFFECT
— **in·flu·ence·able** \-ən(t)-sə-bəl\ *adjective*
¹in·flu·ent \'in-,flü-ənt, in-'\ *adjective* (15th century)
: flowing in
²influent *noun* (1859)
1 : something that flows in: as **a :** a tributary stream **b :** fluid input into a reservoir or process
2 : a factor (as a particular animal) modifying the balance and stability of an ecological community
¹in·flu·en·tial \,in-(,)flü-'en(t)-shəl\ *adjective* (1570)
: exerting or possessing influence
— **in·flu·en·tial·ly** \-'en(t)-sh(ə-)lē\ *adverb*
²influential *noun* (1831)
: one who has great influence
in·flu·en·za \,in-(,)flü-'en-zə\ *noun* [Italian, literally, influence, from Medieval Latin *influentia;* from the belief that epidemics were due to the influence of the stars] (1743)
1 : an acute highly contagious virus disease caused by various strains of a myxovirus (family Orthomyxoviridae) and characterized by sudden onset, fever, prostration, severe aches and pains, and progressive inflammation of the respiratory mucous membrane; *broadly* **:** a human respiratory infection of undetermined cause
2 : any of numerous febrile usually virus diseases of domestic animals marked by respiratory symptoms, inflammation of mucous membranes, and often systemic involvement ◇
— **in·flu·en·zal** \-zəl\ *adjective*
in·flux \'in-,fləks\ *noun* [Medieval Latin *influxus,* from Latin *influere*] (1626)
: a coming in ⟨an *influx* of tourists⟩
in·fo \'in-(,)fō\ *noun* (1913)
: INFORMATION
in·fold \in-'fōld\ (15th century)
transitive verb
: ENFOLD, ENVELOP
intransitive verb
: to fold inward or toward one another
in·fo·mer·cial \'in-(,)fō-,mər-shəl, -fə-\ *noun* [*information* + ²*commercial*] (1981)
: a television program that is an extended advertisement often including a discussion or demonstration

in·form \in-'fòrm\ *verb* [Middle English, from Middle French *enformer,* from Latin *informare,* from *in-* + *forma* form] (14th century)
transitive verb
1 *obsolete* **:** to give material form to
2 a : to give character or essence to ⟨the principles which *inform* modern teaching⟩ **b :** to be the characteristic quality of **:** ANIMATE ⟨the compassion that *informs* her work⟩
3 *obsolete* **:** GUIDE, DIRECT
4 *obsolete* **:** to make known
5 : to communicate knowledge to ⟨*inform* a prisoner of his rights⟩
intransitive verb
1 : to impart information or knowledge
2 : to give information (as of another's wrongdoing) to an authority ☆

in·for·mal \(ˌ)in-ˈfȯr-məl\ *adjective* (1585)
1 : marked by the absence of formality or ceremony ⟨an *informal* meeting⟩ ⟨an *informal* group⟩
2 : characteristic of or appropriate to ordinary, casual, or familiar use ⟨*informal* English⟩ ⟨*informal* clothes⟩
— **in·for·mal·i·ty** \-(ˌ)fȯr-ˈma-lə-tē, -fər-\ *noun*
— **in·for·mal·ly** \-ˈfȯr-mə-lē\ *adverb*
in·for·mant \in-ˈfȯr-mənt\ *noun* (1693)
: a person who gives information: as **a :** IN-FORMER **b :** one who supplies cultural or linguistic data in response to interrogation by an investigator
in for·ma pau·pe·ris \ˌin-ˈfȯr-mə-ˈpȯ-pə-rəs, -ˈpau̇-\ *adjective or adverb* [Latin, in the form of a pauper] (1592)
: as a poor person
in·for·mat·ics \ˌin-fər-ˈma-tiks\ *noun plural but singular in construction* [International Scientific Vocabulary *informa*tion + *-ics*] (circa 1967)
chiefly British **:** INFORMATION SCIENCE
in·for·ma·tion \ˌin-fər-ˈmā-shən\ *noun* (14th century)
1 : the communication or reception of knowledge or intelligence
2 a (1) **:** knowledge obtained from investigation, study, or instruction (2) **:** INTELLIGENCE, NEWS (3) **:** FACTS, DATA **b :** the attribute inherent in and communicated by one of two or more alternative sequences or arrangements of something (as nucleotides in DNA or binary digits in a computer program) that produce specific effects **c** (1) **:** a signal or character (as in a communication system or computer) representing data (2) **:** something (as a message, experimental data, or a picture) which justifies change in a construct (as a plan or theory) that represents physical or mental experience or another construct **d :** a quantitative measure of the content of information; *specifically* **:** a numerical quantity that measures the uncertainty in the outcome of an experiment to be performed
3 : the act of informing against a person
4 : a formal accusation of a crime made by a prosecuting officer as distinguished from an indictment presented by a grand jury
— **in·for·ma·tion·al** \-shnəl, -shə-nᵊl\ *adjective*
— **in·for·ma·tion·al·ly** *adverb*
information retrieval *noun* (1950)
: the techniques of storing and recovering and often disseminating recorded data especially through the use of a computerized system
information science *noun* (1960)
: the collection, classification, storage, retrieval, and dissemination of recorded knowledge treated both as a pure and as an applied science
information theory *noun* (1950)
: a theory that deals statistically with information, with the measurement of its content in terms of its distinguishing essential characteristics or by the number of alternatives from which it makes a choice possible, and with the efficiency of processes of communication between humans and machines
in·for·ma·tive \in-ˈfȯr-mə-tiv\ *adjective* (1655)
: imparting knowledge **:** INSTRUCTIVE
— **in·for·ma·tive·ly** *adverb*
— **in·for·ma·tive·ness** *noun*
in·for·ma·to·ry \-mə-ˌtōr-ē, -ˌtȯr-\ *adjective* (circa 1879)
: conveying information
— **in·for·ma·to·ri·ly** \ˌin-ˌfȯr-mə-ˈtōr-ə-lē, -ˈtȯr-\ *adverb*
in·formed \in-ˈfȯrmd\ *adjective* (15th century)
1 a : having information ⟨*informed* sources⟩ ⟨*informed* observers⟩ **b :** based on possession of information ⟨an *informed* opinion⟩

2 : EDUCATED, KNOWLEDGEABLE ⟨what the *informed* person should know⟩
— **in·formed·ly** \-ˈfȯrmd-lē, -ˈfȯr-məd-lē\ *adverb*
informed consent *noun* (circa 1967)
: consent to surgery by a patient or to participation in a medical experiment by a subject after achieving an understanding of what is involved
in·form·er \in-ˈfȯr-mər\ *noun* (14th century)
1 : one that imparts knowledge or news
2 : one that informs against another; *specifically* **:** one who makes a practice especially for a financial reward of informing against others for violations of penal laws
in·fo·tain·ment \ˌin-(ˌ)fō-ˈtān-mənt\ *noun* [*in*formation + enter*tainment*] (1982)
: a television program that presents information (as news) in a manner intended to be entertaining
in·fra \ˈin-frə *also* -ˌfrä\ *adverb* [Latin] (circa 1740)
: later in this writing **:** BELOW ⟨for additional examples see *infra*⟩
infra- *prefix* [Latin *infra* — more at UNDER]
1 : below ⟨*infra*human⟩ ⟨*infra*sonic⟩
2 : within ⟨*infra*specific⟩
3 : below in a scale or series ⟨*infra*red⟩
in·frac·tion \in-ˈfrak-shən\ *noun* [Middle English, from Medieval Latin *infraction-, infractio*, from Latin, subduing, from *infringere* to break — more at INFRINGE] (15th century)
: the act of infringing **:** VIOLATION
— **in·fract** \in-ˈfrakt\ *transitive verb*
in·fra dig \ˈin-frə-ˈdig, -(ˌ)frä-\ *adjective* [short for Latin *infra dignitatem*] (1824)
: being beneath one's dignity **:** UNDIGNIFIED ⟨while his work . . . was financially profitable, it was just a bit *infra dig* —John McCarten⟩
in·fra·hu·man \ˌin-frə-ˈhyü-mən, -(ˌ)frä-, -ˈyü-\ *adjective* (1847)
: less or lower than human ⟨*infrahuman* primates⟩
— **infrahuman** *noun*
in·fran·gi·ble \(ˌ)in-ˈfran-jə-bəl\ *adjective* [Middle French, from Late Latin *infrangibilis*, from Latin *in-* + *frangere* to break — more at BREAK] (1597)
1 : not capable of being broken or separated into parts
2 : not to be infringed or violated
— **in·fran·gi·bil·i·ty** \-ˌfran-jə-ˈbi-lə-tē\ *noun*
— **in·fran·gi·bly** \-ˈfran-jə-blē\ *adverb*
in·fra·red \ˌin-frə-ˈred, -(ˌ)frä-, -fə-\ *adjective* (1881)
1 : situated outside the visible spectrum at its red end — used of radiation having a wavelength between about 700 nanometers and 1 millimeter
2 : relating to, producing, or employing infrared radiation ⟨*infrared* therapy⟩
3 : sensitive to infrared radiation ⟨*infrared* photographic film⟩
— **infrared** *noun*
in·fra·son·ic \ˌin-frə-ˈsä-nik, -(ˌ)frä-\ *adjective* (1927)
1 : having or relating to a frequency below the audibility range of the human ear
2 : utilizing or produced by infrasonic waves or vibrations
in·fra·spe·cif·ic \-spi-ˈsi-fik\ *adjective* (1939)
: included within a species ⟨*infraspecific* variability⟩
in·fra·struc·ture \ˈin-frə-ˌstrək-chər, -(ˌ)frä-\ *noun* (1927)
1 : the underlying foundation or basic framework (as of a system or organization)
2 : the permanent installations required for military purposes
3 : the system of public works of a country, state, or region; *also* **:** the resources (as personnel, buildings, or equipment) required for an activity

in·fre·quence \(ˌ)in-ˈfrē-kwən(t)s\ *noun* (1644)
: INFREQUENCY
in·fre·quen·cy \-kwən(t)-sē\ *noun* (1677)
: rarity of occurrence
in·fre·quent \(ˌ)in-ˈfrē-kwənt\ *adjective* [Latin *infrequent-, infrequens*, from *in-* + *frequent-, frequens* frequent] (1531)
1 : seldom happening or occurring **:** RARE
2 : placed or occurring at wide intervals in space or time ⟨a slope scattered with *infrequent* pines⟩ ⟨*infrequent* visits⟩ ☆
— **in·fre·quent·ly** *adverb*
in·fringe \in-ˈfrinj\ *verb* **in·fringed; in·fring·ing** [Medieval Latin *infringere*, from Latin, to break, crush, from *in-* + *frangere* to break — more at BREAK] (1533)
transitive verb
1 : to encroach upon in a way that violates law or the rights of another ⟨*infringe* a patent⟩
2 *obsolete* **:** DEFEAT, FRUSTRATE
intransitive verb
: ENCROACH — used with *on* or *upon* ⟨*infringe* on our rights⟩
synonym see TRESPASS
— **in·fring·er** *noun*
in·fringe·ment \in-ˈfrinj-mənt\ *noun* (1628)
1 : the act of infringing **:** VIOLATION
2 : an encroachment or trespass on a right or privilege
in·fun·dib·u·lar \ˌin-(ˌ)fən-ˈdi-byə-lər\ *adjective* (1795)
1 : INFUNDIBULIFORM
2 : of, relating to, or having an infundibulum
in·fun·dib·u·li·form \-lə-ˌfȯrm\ *adjective* [New Latin *infundibulum* + English *-iform*] (1752)
: having the form of a funnel or cone
in·fun·dib·u·lum \ˌin-(ˌ)fən-ˈdi-byə-ləm\ *noun, plural* **-la** \-lə\ [New Latin, from Latin, funnel — more at FUNNEL] (1543)
: any of various funnel-shaped organs or parts: as **a :** the hollow conical process of gray matter by which the pituitary gland is continuous with the brain **b :** the calyx of a kidney **c :** the abdominal opening of a fallopian tube
¹**in·fu·ri·ate** \in-ˈfyu̇r-ē-ˌāt\ *transitive verb* **-at·ed; -at·ing** [Medieval Latin *infuriatus*,

☆ **SYNONYMS**
Inform, acquaint, apprise, notify mean to make one aware of something. INFORM implies the imparting of knowledge especially of facts or occurrences ⟨*informed* us of the crisis⟩. ACQUAINT lays stress on introducing to or familiarizing with ⟨*acquaint* yourself with the keyboard⟩. APPRISE implies communicating something of special interest or importance ⟨keep us *apprised* of the situation⟩. NOTIFY implies sending notice of something requiring attention or demanding action ⟨*notified* the witness when to appear⟩.

Infrequent, uncommon, scarce, rare, sporadic mean not common or abundant. INFREQUENT implies occurrence at wide intervals in space or time ⟨*infrequent* family visits⟩. UNCOMMON suggests a frequency below normal expectation ⟨smallpox is now *uncommon* in many countries⟩. SCARCE implies falling short of a standard or required abundance ⟨jobs were *scarce* during the Depression⟩. RARE suggests extreme scarcity or infrequency and often implies consequent high value ⟨*rare* first editions⟩. SPORADIC implies occurrence in scattered instances or isolated outbursts ⟨*sporadic* cases of influenza⟩.

\ə\ **abut** \ᵊ\ **kitten** \ər\ **further** \a\ **ash** \ā\ **ace**
\ä\ **mop, mar** \au̇\ **out** \ch\ **chin** \e\ **bet** \ē\ **easy**
\g\ **go** \i\ **hit** \ī\ **ice** \j\ **job** \ŋ\ **sing** \ō\ **go**
\ȯ\ **law** \ȯi\ **boy** \th\ **thin** \th\ **the** \ü\ **loot** \u̇\ **foot**
\y\ **yet** \zh\ **vision** *see also* Guide to Pronunciation

past participle of *infuriare,* from Latin *in-* + *furia* fury] (1667)
: to make furious
— **in·fu·ri·at·ing·ly** \-ˌā-tiŋ-lē\ *adverb*
— **in·fu·ri·a·tion** \-ˌfyuṙ-ē-ˈā-shən\ *noun*
²**in·fu·ri·ate** \in-ˈfyu̇r-ē-ət\ *adjective* (1667)
: furiously angry
in·fuse \in-ˈfyüz\ *transitive verb* **in·fused;**
in·fus·ing [Middle English, to pour in, from
Middle French & Latin; Middle French *infu-
ser,* from Latin *infusus,* past participle of *in-
fundere* to pour in, from *in-* + *fundere* to pour
— more at FOUND] (1526)
1 a : to cause to be permeated with something
(as a principle or quality) that alters usually
for the better ⟨*infuse* the team with confi-
dence⟩ **b :** INTRODUCE, INSINUATE ⟨a new spirit
was *infused* into American art —*American
Guide Series: New York*⟩
2 : INSPIRE, ANIMATE ⟨the sense of purpose that
infuses scientific research⟩
3 : to steep in liquid (as water) without boiling
so as to extract the soluble constituents or
principles ☆
— **in·fus·er** *noun*
in·fus·ible \ˌ(ˌ)in-ˈfyü-zə-bəl\ *adjective* (1555)
: incapable of being fused : very difficult to
fuse
— **in·fus·ibil·i·ty** \-ˌfyü-zə-ˈbi-lə-tē\ *noun*
— **in·fus·ible·ness** \-ˈfyü-zə-bəl-nəs\ *noun*
in·fu·sion \in-ˈfyü-zhən\ *noun* (15th century)
1 : the act or process of infusing
2 : a product obtained by infusing
3 : the continuous slow introduction of a solu-
tion especially into a vein
in·fu·so·ri·al earth \ˌin-fyü-ˈzōr-ē-əl-, -ˈsōr-,
-ˈzȯr-, -ˈsȯr-\ *noun* (1882)
: KIESELGUHR
in·fu·so·ri·an \-ē-ən\ *noun* [ultimately from
Latin *infusus*] (1859)
: any of a heterogeneous group of minute or-
ganisms found especially in decomposing in-
fusions of organic matter; *especially* : a ciliat-
ed protozoan
— **infusorian** *adjective*
¹**-ing** \iŋ\ *also* ēŋ; *in some dialects & in other
dialects informally* in, ən *also* ēn; *after certain
consonants* ᵊn, ᵊm, ᵊŋ\ *noun suffix* [Middle En-
glish, from Old English *-ung, -ing,* suffix
forming nouns from verbs; akin to Old High
German *-ung,* suffix forming nouns from
verbs]
1 : action or process ⟨runn*ing*⟩ ⟨sleep*ing*⟩ : in-
stance of an action or process ⟨a meet*ing*⟩
2 a : product or result of an action or process
⟨an engrav*ing*⟩ — often in plural ⟨earn*ings*⟩ **b**
: something used in an action or process ⟨a
bed cover*ing*⟩ ⟨the lin*ing* of a coat⟩
3 : action or process connected with (a speci-
fied thing) ⟨boat*ing*⟩
4 : something connected with, consisting of,
or used in making (a specified thing) ⟨scaf-
fold*ing*⟩ ⟨shirt*ing*⟩
5 : something related to (a specified concept)
⟨off*ing*⟩
²**-ing** *noun suffix* [Middle English, from Old
English *-ing, -ung;* akin to Old High German
-ing one of a (specified) kind]
: one of a (specified) kind ⟨sweet*ing*⟩
³**-ing** *verb suffix or adjective suffix* [Middle En-
glish, probably from ¹*-ing*]
— used to form the present participle ⟨sail*ing*⟩
and sometimes to form an adjective resem-
bling a present participle but not derived from
a verb ⟨swashbuckl*ing*⟩ □
in·gath·er \ˈin-ˌga-thər, -ˌge-\ (1557)
transitive verb
: to gather in
intransitive verb
: ASSEMBLE
— **in·gath·er·ing** \-ˌgath-riŋ, -ˌgeth-; -ˌga-
thə-, -ˌge-\ *noun*
in·ge·nious \in-ˈjēn-yəs\ *adjective* [Middle
English *ingenyous,* from Middle French *in-*

genieux, from Latin *ingeniosus,* from *inge-
nium* natural capacity — more at ENGINE]
(15th century)
1 *obsolete* : showing or calling for intelli-
gence, aptitude, or discernment
2 : marked by especial aptitude at discovering,
inventing, or contriving
3 : marked by originality, resourcefulness, and
cleverness in conception or execution ⟨an *in-
genious* contraption⟩
synonym see CLEVER
— **in·ge·nious·ly** *adverb*
— **in·ge·nious·ness** *noun*
in·ge·nue *or* **in·gé·nue** \ˈan-jə-ˌnü, ˈän-; ˈaⁿ-
zhə-, ˈäⁿ-\ *noun* [French *ingénue,* feminine of
ingénu ingenuous, from Latin *ingenuus*] (1848)
1 : a naive girl or young woman
2 : the stage role of an ingenue; *also* : an ac-
tress playing such a role
in·ge·nu·i·ty \ˌin-jə-ˈnü-ə-tē, -ˈnyü-\ *noun,
plural* **-ties** (circa 1592)
1 *obsolete* : CANDOR, INGENUOUSNESS
2 a : skill or cleverness in devising or combin-
ing : INVENTIVENESS **b :** cleverness or aptness
of design or contrivance
3 : an ingenious device or contrivance
¹**in·gen·u·ous** \in-ˈjen-yə-wəs\ *adjective* [by
alteration] (1588)
obsolete : INGENIOUS
²**ingenuous** *adjective* [Latin *ingenuus* native,
free born, from *in-* + *gignere* to beget —
more at KIN] (1588)
1 *obsolete* : NOBLE, HONORABLE
2 a : showing innocent or childlike simplicity
and candidness **b :** lacking craft or subtlety
synonym see NATURAL
— **in·gen·u·ous·ly** *adverb*
— **in·gen·u·ous·ness** *noun*
in·gest \in-ˈjest\ *transitive verb* [Latin *inges-
tus,* past participle of *ingerere* to carry in,
from *in-* + *gerere* to bear] (1620)
: to take in or as if for digestion
— **in·gest·ible** \-ˈjes-tə-bəl\ *adjective*
— **in·ges·tion** \-ˈjes-chən, -ˈjesh-\ *noun*
— **in·ges·tive** \-ˈjes-tiv\ *adjective*
in·ges·ta \in-ˈjes-tə\ *noun plural* [New Latin,
from Latin, neuter plural of *ingestus*] (1727)
: material taken into the body by way of the
digestive tract
in·gle \ˈiŋ-gəl, ˈiŋ-əl\ *noun* [Scottish Gaelic
aingeal] (1508)
1 : a fire in a fireplace
2 : FIREPLACE
3 : CORNER, ANGLE
in·gle·nook \-ˌnu̇k\ *noun* (1772)
: a nook by a large open fireplace; *also* : a
bench or settle occupying this nook
in·glo·ri·ous \ˌ(ˌ)in-ˈglōr-ē-əs, -ˈglȯr-\ *adjec-
tive* [Latin *inglorius,* from *in-* + *gloria* glory]
(1573)
1 : SHAMEFUL, IGNOMINIOUS
2 : not glorious : lacking fame or honor
— **in·glo·ri·ous·ly** *adverb*
— **in·glo·ri·ous·ness** *noun*
in·got \ˈiŋ-gət\ *noun* [Middle English, perhaps
modification of Middle French *lingot* ingot of
metal, incorrectly divided as *l'ingot,* as if from
le the, from Latin *ille* that] (14th century)
1 : a mold in which metal is cast
2 : a mass of metal cast into a convenient
shape for storage or transportation to be later
processed
ingot iron *noun* (1877)
: iron containing only small proportions of im-
purities (as less than 0.05 percent carbon)
¹**in·grain** \ˌ(ˌ)in-ˈgrān\ *transitive verb* (circa
1641)
: to work indelibly into the natural texture or
mental or moral constitution
synonym see INFUSE
²**in·grain** \ˈin-ˌgrān\ *adjective* (1766)
1 a : made of fiber that is dyed before being
spun into yarn **b :** made of yarn that is dyed
before being woven or knitted
2 : thoroughly worked in : INNATE
³**in·grain** \ˈin-ˌgrān\ *noun* (circa 1890)

: innate quality or character
in·grained \ˈin-ˌgrānd, ˌ(ˌ)in-ˈ\ *adjective* (1599)
1 : worked into the grain or fiber
2 : forming a part of the essence or inmost be-
ing : DEEP-SEATED ⟨*ingrained* prejudice⟩
— **in·grained·ly** \ˈin-ˌgrā-nəd-lē, ˈin-
ˌgrānd-lē, ˌ(ˌ)in-ˈ\ *adverb*
in·grate \ˈin-ˌgrāt\ *noun* [Latin *ingratus* un-
grateful, from *in-* + *gratus* grateful — more
at GRACE] (1622)
: an ungrateful person
in·gra·ti·ate \in-ˈgrā-shē-ˌāt\ *transitive verb*
-at·ed; -at·ing [²*in-* + Latin *gratia* grace]
(1622)
: to gain favor or favorable acceptance for by
deliberate effort — usually used with *with*
⟨*ingratiate* themselves with the community
leaders —William Attwood⟩
— **in·gra·ti·a·tion** \-ˌgrā-shē-ˈā-shən\ *noun*
— **in·gra·tia·to·ry** \-ˈgrā-sh(ē-)ə-ˌtōr-ē,
-ˌtȯr-\ *adjective*
ingratiating *adjective* (1655)
1 : capable of winning favor : PLEASING ⟨an *in-
gratiating* smile⟩
2 : intended or adopted in order to gain favor
: FLATTERING
— **in·gra·ti·at·ing·ly** \-ˈgrā-shē-ˌā-tiŋ-lē\
adverb
in·grat·i·tude \ˌ(ˌ)in-ˈgra-tə-ˌtüd, -ˌtyüd\ *noun*
[Middle English, from Middle French, from
Medieval Latin *ingratitudo,* from Latin *in-* +
Late Latin *gratitudo* gratitude] (14th century)
: forgetfulness of or poor return for kindness
received : UNGRATEFULNESS

☆ **SYNONYMS**
**Infuse, suffuse, imbue, ingrain, inoc-
ulate, leaven** mean to introduce one thing
into another so as to affect it throughout. IN-
FUSE implies a pouring in of something that
gives new life or significance ⟨new members
infused enthusiasm into the club⟩. SUFFUSE
implies a spreading through of something
that gives an unusual color or quality ⟨a room
suffused with light⟩. IMBUE implies the intro-
duction of a quality that fills and permeates
the whole being ⟨*imbue* students with intel-
lectual curiosity⟩. INGRAIN, used only in the
passive or past participle, suggests the deep
implanting of a quality or trait ⟨clung to *in-
grained* habits⟩. INOCULATE implies an imbu-
ing or implanting with a germinal idea and
often suggests surreptitiousness or subtlety
⟨an electorate *inoculated* with dangerous
ideas⟩. LEAVEN implies introducing something
that enlivens, tempers, or markedly alters the
total quality ⟨a serious play *leavened* with
comic moments⟩.

□ **USAGE**
-ing Though the pronunciation of *-ing* with
the consonant \n\, misleadingly referred to as
"dropping the *g,*" is often deprecated, this
pronunciation is frequently heard. It is not
known for certain why the Middle English
present participle ending *-ende* was replaced
by *-ing.* Analogy with the earlier noun suffix
-ing probably had something to do with it. In
early Modern English, present participles
were regularly formed with *-ing* pronounced
\ŋ\ (as can still be heard in a few dialects)
and later \n\. Evidence also shows that some
speakers used \n\ and by the 18th century
this pronunciation became widespread.
Though teachers (with some success) cam-
paigned against it, \n\ remained a feature of
the speech of many of the best speakers in
Britain and the U.S. well into this century. It
has by now lost its respectability, at least
when attention is drawn to it, but throughout
the U.S. it persists largely unnoticed and in
some dialects it predominates over \ŋ\.

in·gre·di·ent \in-'grē-dē-ənt\ *noun* [Middle English, from Latin *ingredient-, ingrediens,* present participle of *ingredi* to go into, from *in-* + *gradi* to go — more at GRADE] (15th century)
: something that enters into a compound or is a component part of any combination or mixture : CONSTITUENT
synonym see ELEMENT
— **ingredient** *adjective*

in·gress \'in-ˌgres\ *noun* [Middle English, from Latin *ingressus,* from *ingredi*] (15th century)
1 : the act of entering : ENTRANCE
2 : the power or liberty of entrance or access
— **in·gres·sion** \in-'gre-shən\ *noun*

in·gres·sive \in-'gre-siv\ *adjective* (1649)
1 : of, relating to, or involving ingress; *especially* : produced by ingress of air into the vocal tract ⟨*ingressive* sounds⟩
2 : INCHOATIVE 2
— **ingressive** *noun*
— **in·gres·sive·ness** *noun*

in-group \'in-ˌgrüp\ *noun* (1907)
1 : a group with which one feels a sense of solidarity or community of interests — compare OUT-GROUP
2 : CLIQUE

in·grow·ing \'in-ˌgrō-iŋ\ *adjective* (1869)
: growing or tending inward

in·grown \-ˌgrōn\ *adjective* (1670)
1 : grown in; *specifically* : having the free tip or edge embedded in the flesh ⟨an *ingrown* toenail⟩
2 : having the direction of growth or activity or interest inward rather than outward : WITHDRAWN
— **in·grown·ness** \(ˌ)in-'grōn-nəs\ *noun*

in·growth \'in-ˌgrōth\ *noun* (1870)
1 : a growing inward (as to fill a void)
2 : something that grows in or into a space

in·gui·nal \'iŋ-gwə-n°l\ *adjective* [Middle English *inguynale,* from Latin *inguinalis,* from *inguin-, inguen* groin — more at ADEN-] (15th century)
: of, relating to, or situated in the region of the groin or in either of the lowest lateral regions of the abdomen ⟨*inguinal* hernia⟩

in·gur·gi·tate \in-'gər-jə-ˌtāt\ *transitive verb* **-tat·ed; -tat·ing** [Latin *ingurgitatus,* past participle of *ingurgitare,* from *in-* + *gurgit-, gurges* whirlpool — more at VORACIOUS] (circa 1570)
: to swallow greedily or in large quantities : GUZZLE
— **in·gur·gi·ta·tion** \(ˌ)in-ˌgər-jə-'tā-shən\ *noun*

in·hab·it \in-'ha-bət\ *verb* [Middle English *enhabiten,* from Middle French & Latin; Middle French *enhabiter,* from Latin *inhabitare,* from *in-* + *habitare* to dwell, frequentative of *habēre* to have — more at GIVE] (14th century)
transitive verb
1 : to occupy as a place of settled residence or habitat : live in ⟨*inhabit* a small house⟩
2 : to be present in or occupy in any manner or form ⟨the human beings who *inhabit* this tale —Al Newman⟩
intransitive verb
archaic : to have residence in a place : DWELL
— **in·hab·it·able** \-bə-tə-bəl\ *adjective*
— **in·hab·it·er** *noun*

in·hab·i·tan·cy \in-'ha-bə-tən(t)-sē\ *noun* (1681)
: INHABITATION

in·hab·i·tant \in-'ha-bə-tənt\ *noun* (15th century)
: one that occupies a particular place regularly, routinely, or for a period of time ⟨*inhabitants* of large cities⟩ ⟨the tapeworm is an *inhabitant* of the intestine⟩

in·hab·i·ta·tion \in-ˌha-bə-'tā-shən\ *noun* (15th century)
: the act of inhabiting : the state of being inhabited

inhabited *adjective* (15th century)
: having inhabitants

in·hal·ant \in-'hā-lənt\ *noun* (circa 1834)
: something (as an allergen or medication) that is inhaled
— **inhalant** *adjective*

in·ha·la·tion \ˌin-hə-'lā-shən, ˌi-n°l-'ā-\ *noun* (circa 1623)
1 : the act or an instance of inhaling
2 : material (as medication) to be taken in by inhaling
— **in·ha·la·tion·al** \-shnəl, -shə-n°l\ *adjective*

in·ha·la·tor \'in-hə-ˌlā-tər, 'i-n°l-ˌā-\ *noun* (1925)
: a device providing a mixture of oxygen and carbon dioxide for breathing that is used especially in conjunction with artificial respiration

in·hale \in-'hā(ə)l\ *verb* **in·haled; in·hal·ing** [*in-* + *exhale*] (1725)
transitive verb
1 : to draw in by breathing
2 : to take in eagerly or greedily ⟨*inhaled* about four meals at once —Ring Lardner⟩
intransitive verb
: to breathe in
— **in·hale** \in-', -'in-,\ *noun*

in·hal·er \in-'hā-lər\ *noun* (1778)
1 : a device by means of which medicinal material is inhaled
2 : one that inhales

in·har·mon·ic \ˌin-(ˌ)här-'mä-nik\ *adjective* (circa 1828)
: not harmonic

in·har·mo·ni·ous \-'mō-nē-əs\ *adjective* (1711)
1 : not harmonious : DISCORDANT
2 : not fitting or congenial : CONFLICTING
— **in·har·mo·ni·ous·ly** *adverb*
— **in·har·mo·ni·ous·ness** *noun*

in·har·mo·ny \(ˌ)in-'här-mə-nē\ *noun* (1799)
: DISCORD

in·here \in-'hir\ *intransitive verb* **in·hered; in·her·ing** [Latin *inhaerēre,* from *in-* + *haerēre* to adhere] (14th century)
: to be inherent

in·her·ence \in-'hir-ən(t)s, -'her-\ *noun* (1577)
: the quality, state, or fact of inhering

in·her·ent \-ənt\ *adjective* [Latin *inhaerent-, inhaerens,* present participle of *inhaerēre*] (1581)
: involved in the constitution or essential character of something : belonging by nature or habit : INTRINSIC
— **in·her·ent·ly** *adverb*

in·her·it \in-'her-ət\ *verb* [Middle English *enheriten* to make one an heir, inherit, from Middle French *enheriter* to make one an heir, from Late Latin *inhereditare,* from Latin *in-* + *hereditas* inheritance — more at HEREDITY] (14th century)
transitive verb
1 : to come into possession of or receive especially as a right or divine portion ⟨and every one who has left houses or brothers or sisters . . . for my name's sake, will receive a hundredfold, and *inherit* eternal life —Matthew 19:29 (Revised Standard Version)⟩
2 a : to receive from an ancestor as a right or title descendible by law at the ancestor's death **b** : to receive as a devise or legacy
3 : to receive from ancestors by genetic transmission ⟨*inherit* a strong constitution⟩
4 : to have in turn or receive as if from an ancestor ⟨*inherited* the problem from his predecessor⟩
intransitive verb
: to take or hold a possession or rights by inheritance
— **in·her·i·tor** \-ə-tər\ *noun*
— **in·her·i·tress** \-ə-trəs\ *or* **in·her·i·trix** \-ə-(ˌ)triks\ *noun*

in·her·it·able \in-'her-ə-tə-bəl\ *adjective* (15th century)
1 : capable of being inherited : TRANSMISSIBLE
2 : capable of taking by inheritance

— **in·her·it·abil·i·ty** \-ˌher-ə-tə-'bi-lə-tē\ *noun*
— **in·her·it·able·ness** \-'her-ə-tə-bəl-nəs\ *noun*

in·her·i·tance \in-'her-ə-tən(t)s\ *noun* (14th century)
1 a : the act of inheriting property **b** : the reception of genetic qualities by transmission from parent to offspring **c** : the acquisition of a possession, condition, or trait from past generations
2 : something that is or may be inherited
3 a : TRADITION **b** : a valuable possession that is a common heritage from nature
4 *obsolete* : POSSESSION

inheritance tax *noun* (1841)
1 : an excise in the form of a percentage of the value of the property received that is levied on the privilege of an heir to inherit property
2 : DEATH TAX; *especially* : ESTATE TAX

in·hib·in \in-'hi-bən\ *noun* [Latin *inhibēre* to inhibit + English ¹*-in*] (1932)
: a human hormone that is secreted by Sertoli cells in the male and granulosa cells in the female and that inhibits the secretion of follicle-stimulating hormone

in·hib·it \in-'hi-bət\ *verb* [Middle English, from Latin *inhibitus,* past participle of *inhibēre,* from *in-* ²*in-* + *habēre* to have — more at HABIT] (15th century)
transitive verb
1 : to prohibit from doing something
2 a : to hold in check : RESTRAIN **b** : to discourage from free or spontaneous activity especially through the operation of inner psychological impediments or of social controls
intransitive verb
: to cause inhibition
synonym see FORBID
— **in·hib·i·tive** \-bə-tiv\ *adjective*
— **in·hib·i·to·ry** \-bə-ˌtōr-ē, -ˌtȯr-\ *adjective*

in·hi·bi·tion \ˌin-hə-'bi-shən, ˌi-nə-\ *noun* (14th century)
1 a : the act of inhibiting : the state of being inhibited **b** : something that forbids, debars, or restricts
2 : an inner impediment to free activity, expression, or functioning: as **a** : a psychic activity imposing restraint upon another activity **b** : a restraining of the function of a bodily organ or an agent (as an enzyme)

in·hib·i·tor \in-'hi-bə-tər\ *noun* (circa 1611)
: one that inhibits; *especially* : an agent that slows or interferes with a chemical action

in·hold·ing \'in-ˌhōl-diŋ\ *noun* (1947)
: privately owned land inside the boundary of a national park

in·ho·mo·ge·ne·i·ty \(ˌ)in-ˌhō-mə-jə-'nē-ə-tē, -'nā- *also* -'nī-; *especially British* -ˌhä-mə-\ *noun, plural* **-ties** (1899)
1 : the condition of not being homogeneous
2 : a part that is not homogeneous with the larger uniform mass in which it occurs; *especially* : a localized collection of matter in the universe
— **in·ho·mo·ge·neous** \-'jē-nē-əs, -nyəs\ *adjective*

in·hos·pi·ta·ble \ˌin-(ˌ)hä-'spi-tə-bəl, (ˌ)in-'häs-(ˌ)pi-\ *adjective* (circa 1570)
1 : not showing hospitality : not friendly or receptive
2 : providing no shelter or sustenance
— **in·hos·pi·ta·ble·ness** *noun*
— **in·hos·pi·ta·bly** \-blē\ *adverb*

in·hos·pi·tal·i·ty \(ˌ)in-ˌhäs-pə-'ta-lə-tē\ *noun* (circa 1576)
: the quality or state of being inhospitable

in-house \'in-ˌhaus, -'haus\ *adjective* (circa 1956)

: existing, originating, or carried on within a group or organization or its facilities : not outside ⟨an *in-house* publication⟩ ⟨a company's *in-house* staff⟩

— **in–house** *adverb*

in·hu·man \(,)in-'hyü-mən, -'yü-\ *adjective* [Middle English *inhumayne*, from Middle French & Latin; Middle French *inhumain*, from Latin *inhumanus*, from *in-* + *humanus* human] (15th century)
1 a : lacking pity, kindness, or mercy : SAVAGE ⟨an *inhuman* tyrant⟩ **b :** COLD, IMPERSONAL ⟨his usual quiet, almost *inhuman* courtesy —F. Tennyson Jesse⟩ **c :** not worthy of or conforming to the needs of human beings ⟨*inhuman* living conditions⟩
2 : of or suggesting a nonhuman class of beings

— **in·hu·man·ly** *adverb*
— **in·hu·man·ness** \-mən-nəs\ *noun*

in·hu·mane \,in-(,)hyü-'mān, -(,)yü-\ *adjective* [Middle French *inhumain* & Latin *inhumanus*] (1599)
: not humane : INHUMAN 1

— **in·hu·mane·ly** *adverb*

in·hu·man·i·ty \-'ma-nə-tē\ *noun, plural* **-ties** (15th century)
1 a : the quality or state of being cruel or barbarous **b :** a cruel or barbarous act
2 : absence of warmth or geniality : IMPERSONALITY

in·hume \in-'hyüm\ *transitive verb* **in·humed; in·hum·ing** [probably from French *inhumer*, from Medieval Latin *inhumare*, from Latin *in-* + *humus* earth — more at HUMBLE] (1604)
: BURY, INTER

— **in·hu·ma·tion** \,in-hyü-'mā-shən\ *noun*

in·im·i·cal \i-'ni-mi-kəl\ *adjective* [Late Latin *inimicalis*, from Latin *inimicus* enemy — more at ENEMY] (1573)
1 : being adverse often by reason of hostility or malevolence
2 a : having the disposition of an enemy : HOSTILE **b :** reflecting or indicating hostility : UNFRIENDLY

— **in·im·i·cal·ly** \-mi-k(ə-)lē\ *adverb*

in·im·i·ta·ble \(,)i-'ni-mə-tə-bəl\ *adjective* [Middle English, from Middle French or Latin; Middle French, from Latin *inimitabilis*, from *in-* + *imitabilis* imitable] (15th century)
: not capable of being imitated : MATCHLESS

— **in·im·i·ta·ble·ness** *noun*
— **in·im·i·ta·bly** \-blē\ *adverb*

in·i·on \'i-nē-,än, -ən\ *noun* [New Latin, from Greek, back of the head, diminutive of *in-*, is sinew, tendon] (circa 1811)
: the external occipital protuberance of the skull

in·iq·ui·tous \i-'ni-kwə-təs\ *adjective* (1726)
: characterized by iniquity

synonym see VICIOUS

— **in·iq·ui·tous·ly** *adverb*
— **in·iq·ui·tous·ness** *noun*

in·iq·ui·ty \-kwə-tē\ *noun, plural* **-ties** [Middle English *iniquite*, from Middle French *iniquité*, from Latin *iniquitat-, iniquitas*, from *iniquus* uneven, from *in-* + *aequus* equal] (14th century)
1 : gross injustice : WICKEDNESS
2 : a wicked act or thing : SIN

¹ini·tial \i-'ni-shəl\ *adjective* [Middle French & Latin; Middle French, from Latin *initialis*, from *initium* beginning, from *inire* to go into, from *in-* + *ire* to go — more at ISSUE] (1526)
1 : of or relating to the beginning : INCIPIENT
2 : placed at the beginning : FIRST

— **ini·tial·ly** \i-'ni-sh(ə-)lē\ *adverb*
— **ini·tial·ness** \i-'ni-shəl-nəs\ *noun*

²initial *noun* (1627)
1 a : the first letter of a name **b** *plural* **:** the first letter of each word in a full name ⟨found that their *initials* were identical⟩
2 : a large letter beginning a text or a division or paragraph

3 : ANLAGE, PRECURSOR; *specifically* **:** a meristematic cell

³initial *transitive verb* **ini·tialed** *or* **ini·tialled; ini·tial·ing** *or* **ini·tial·ling** \i-'ni-sh(ə-)liŋ\ (circa 1864)
1 : to affix an initial to
2 : to authenticate or give preliminary approval to by affixing the initials of an authorizing representative

ini·tial·ism \i-'ni-shə-,li-zəm\ *noun* (1899)
: an acronym formed from initial letters

ini·tial·ize \-,līz\ *transitive verb* **-ized; -iz·ing** (1957)
: to set (as a computer program counter) to a starting position, value, or configuration

— **ini·tial·i·za·tion** \i-,ni-sh(ə-)lə-'zā-shən\ *noun*

initial rhyme *noun* (1838)
: ALLITERATION

initial side *noun* (1957)
: a stationary straight line that contains a point about which another straight line is rotated to form an angle — compare TERMINAL SIDE

¹ini·ti·ate \i-'ni-shē-,āt\ *transitive verb* **-at·ed; -at·ing** [Late Latin *initiatus*, past participle of *initiare*, from Latin, to induct, from *initium*] (circa 1573)
1 : to cause or facilitate the beginning of : set going ⟨*initiate* a program of reform⟩ ⟨enzymes that *initiate* fermentation⟩
2 : to induct into membership by or as if by special rites
3 : to instruct in the rudiments or principles of something : INTRODUCE

synonym see BEGIN

— **ini·ti·a·tor** \-,ā-tər\ *noun*

²ini·ti·ate \i-'ni-shē-(ē-)ət\ *adjective* (1605)
1 *obsolete* **:** relating to an initiate
2 a : initiated or properly admitted (as to membership or an office) **b :** instructed in some secret knowledge

³ini·tiate \i-'ni-shē-(ē-)ət\ *noun* (1811)
1 : a person who is undergoing or has undergone an initiation
2 : a person who is instructed or adept in some special field

ini·ti·a·tion \i-,ni-shē-'ā-shən\ *noun* (1583)
1 a : the act or an instance of initiating **b :** the process of being initiated **c :** the rites, ceremonies, ordeals, or instructions with which one is made a member of a sect or society or is invested with a particular function or status
2 : the condition of being initiated into some experience or sphere of activity : KNOWLEDGEABLENESS

¹ini·tia·tive \i-'ni-shə-tiv *also* -shē-ə-tiv\ *adjective* (1795)
: of or relating to initiation : INTRODUCTORY, PRELIMINARY

²initiative *noun* (1793)
1 : an introductory step ⟨took the *initiative* in attempting to settle the issue⟩
2 : energy or aptitude displayed in initiation of action : ENTERPRISE ⟨showed great *initiative*⟩
3 a : the right to initiate legislative action **b** **:** a procedure enabling a specified number of voters by petition to propose a law and secure its submission to the electorate or to the legislature for approval — compare REFERENDUM 1

— **on one's own initiative :** at one's own discretion : independently of outside influence or control

ini·tia·to·ry \i-'ni-shē-(ē-)ə-,tōr-ē, -,tòr-\ *adjective* (circa 1615)
1 : constituting a beginning
2 : tending or serving to initiate

in·ject \in-'jekt\ *transitive verb* [Latin *injectus*, past participle of *inicere*, from *in-* + *jacere* to throw — more at JET] (1601)
1 a : to introduce into something forcefully ⟨*inject* fuel into an engine⟩ **b :** to force a fluid into (as for medical purposes)
2 : to introduce as an element or factor in or into some situation or subject ⟨condemning

any attempt to *inject* religious bigotry into the campaign —*Current Biography*⟩
— **in·ject·able** \-'jek-tə-bəl\ *adjective or noun*
— **in·jec·tor** \-'jek-tər\ *noun*

in·jec·tant \-'jek-tənt\ *noun* (1950)
: a substance that is injected into something

in·jec·tion \in-'jek-shən\ *noun* (15th century)
1 a : an act or instance of injecting **b :** the placing of an artificial satellite or a spacecraft into an orbit or on a trajectory; *also* **:** the time or place at which injection occurs
2 : something (as a medication) that is injected
3 : a mathematical function that is a one-to-one mapping — compare BIJECTION, SURJECTION

injection molding *noun* (1932)
: a method of forming articles (as of plastic) by heating the molding material until it can flow and injecting it into a mold
— **injection–molded** *adjective*

in·jec·tive \in-'jek-tiv\ *adjective* (1952)
: being a one-to-one mathematical function

in–joke \'in-,jōk, -'jōk\ *noun* (1964)
: a joke for or about a select group of people

in·ju·di·cious \,in-jù-'di-shəs\ *adjective* (1649)
: not judicious : INDISCREET, UNWISE
— **in·ju·di·cious·ly** *adverb*
— **in·ju·di·cious·ness** *noun*

in·junc·tion \in-'jəŋ(k)-shən\ *noun* [Middle English *injunccion*, from Middle French & Late Latin; Middle French *injonction*, from Late Latin *injunction-, injunctio*, from Latin *injungere* to enjoin — more at ENJOIN] (15th century)
1 : the act or an instance of enjoining : ORDER, ADMONITION
2 : a writ granted by a court of equity whereby one is required to do or to refrain from doing a specified act
— **in·junc·tive** \-'jəŋ(k)-tiv\ *adjective*

in·jure \'in-jər\ *transitive verb* **in·jured; in·jur·ing** \'inj-riŋ, 'in-jə-\ [Middle English *enjuren*, from Middle French *enjurier*, from Late Latin *injuriare*, from Latin *injuria* injury] (15th century)
1 a : to do an injustice to : WRONG **b :** to harm, impair, or tarnish the standing of **c :** to give pain to ⟨*injure* a person's pride⟩
2 a : to inflict bodily hurt on **b :** to impair the soundness of **c :** to inflict material damage or loss on ☆
— **in·jur·er** \'in-jər-ər\ *noun*

in·ju·ri·ous \in-'jùr-ē-əs\ *adjective* (15th century)
1 : inflicting or tending to inflict injury : DETRIMENTAL ⟨*injurious* to health⟩
2 : ABUSIVE, DEFAMATORY ⟨speak not *injurious* words —George Washington⟩
— **in·ju·ri·ous·ly** *adverb*
— **in·ju·ri·ous·ness** *noun*

☆ **SYNONYMS**
Injure, harm, hurt, damage, impair, mar mean to affect injuriously. INJURE implies the inflicting of anything detrimental to one's looks, comfort, health, or success ⟨badly *injured* in an accident⟩. HARM often stresses the inflicting of pain, suffering, or loss ⟨careful not to *harm* the animals⟩. HURT implies inflicting a wound to the body or to the feelings ⟨*hurt* by their callous remarks⟩. DAMAGE suggests injury that lowers value or impairs usefulness ⟨a table *damaged* in shipping⟩. IMPAIR suggests a making less complete or efficient by deterioration or diminution ⟨years of smoking had *impaired* his health⟩. MAR applies to injury that spoils perfection (as of a surface) or causes disfigurement ⟨the text is *marred* by many typos⟩.

in·ju·ry \'in-jə-rē, 'in-jə-\ *noun, plural* **-ries** [Middle English *injurie*, from Latin *injuria*, from *injurius* injurious, from *in-* + *jur-, jus* right] (14th century) **1 a :** an act that damages or hurts **b :** a more at JUST (14th century) **1 a :** an act that damages or hurts : WRONG **b :** violation of another's rights for which the law allows an action to recover damages **2 :** hurt, damage, or loss sustained

synonym see INJUSTICE

in·jus·tice \(,)in-'jəs-təs\ *noun* [Middle English, from Middle French, from Latin *injustitia*, from *injustus* unjust, from *in-* + *justus* just] (14th century) **1 :** absence of justice : violation of right or of the rights of another **2 :** an unjust act : WRONG

1ink \'iŋk\ *noun* [Middle English *enke*, from Old French, from Late Latin *encaustum*, from neuter of Latin *encaustus*, verbal of *encaien* to burn in, from Greek *enkaustos*, verbal of *enkaiein* to burn in — more at ENCAUSTIC] (13th century) **1 :** a colored usually liquid material for writing and printing **2 :** the black protective secretion of a cephalopod

3 : *slang* : PUBLICITY 2d

— **ink·i·ness** \'iŋ-kē-nəs\ *noun*

— **inky** \'iŋ-kē\ *adjective*

2ink *transitive verb* (1562) **1 :** to put ink on *(ink a pen); also* **:** to draw or write on in ink

2 a : SIGN 2a *(inked a new contract)* **b :** SIGN 4 **3 :** to rub, beat, or fuse [as wire] into an incision in metal, wood, or stone

ink·ber·ry \'iŋk-,ber-ē\ *noun* [from the use of the berries for making ink] (1765) **1 a :** a holly *(Ilex glabra)* of eastern North America with evergreen oblong leathery leaves and small usually black berries **b :** POKEWEED **2 :** the fruit of an inkberry

ink·blot test \'iŋk-,blät-\ *noun* (1928) **:** any of several psychological tests (as a Rorschach test) based on the interpretation of irregular figures (as blots of ink)

1ink·horn \'iŋk-,ho(ə)rn\ *noun* (14th century) **:** a small portable bottle (as of horn) for holding ink

2inkhorn *adjective* (1543) **:** ostentatiously learned : PEDANTIC *(inkhorn terms)*

ink·ling \'iŋ-kliŋ\ *noun* [Middle English *yngkiling* whisper, mention, probably from *inclen* to hint at; akin to Old English *inca* suspicion] (1513) **1 :** a slight indication or suggestion : HINT, CLUE *(there was no path—no inkling even of a track —New Yorker)* **2 :** a slight knowledge or vague notion *(had not the faintest inkling of what it was all about —H. W. Carter)*

ink·jet \'iŋk-'jet\ *adjective* (1976) **:** of, relating to, or being a dot matrix printer in which electrically charged droplets of ink are projected onto the paper

in·kle \'iŋ-kəl\ *noun* [origin unknown] (1541) **:** a colored linen tape or braid woven on a very narrow loom and used for trimming; *also* **:** the thread used

ink·stand \'iŋk-,stand\ *noun* (1773) **1 :** INKWELL; *also* : a stand with fittings for holding ink and pens

ink·stone \'iŋk-,stōn\ *noun* (circa 1889) **:** a stone used in Chinese art and calligraphy on which dry ink and water are mixed

ink·well \'iŋk-,wel\ *noun* (circa 1875) **:** a container (as in a desk) for ink

inky cap *noun* (1923) **:** a mushroom (genus *Coprinus*, especially *C. atramentarius*) whose pileus deliquesces into an inky fluid after the spores have matured — called also *ink cap*

in·laid \'in-'lād\ *adjective* (1598) **1 a :** set into a surface in a decorative design *(tables with inlaid marble)* **b :** decorated with a design or material set into a surface (a table with an *inlaid* top) **2** *of linoleum* **:** having a design that goes all the way through to the backing

1in·land \'in-land, -lənd\ *adjective* (1546) **1** *chiefly British* **:** not foreign : DOMESTIC **2 :** of or relating to the interior of a country

2inland *noun* (1573) **:** the interior part of a country **in·land·er** \'in-lan-dər, -lən-\ *noun* **:** one who lives inland

3inland \'in-lənd, -,land\ *adverb* (1596) **:** into or toward the interior

in-law \'in-,lo\ *noun* [mother-in-law, etc.] (1894) **:** a relative by marriage

1in·lay \(,)in-'lā, 'in-,\ *transitive verb* (1599) **1 a :** to set into a surface or ground material **b :** to adorn with insertions **c :** to insert (as a color plate) into a mat or other reinforcement **2 :** a tooth filling shaped to fit a cavity and then cemented into place

2in·lay \'in-,lā\ *noun* (1667) **1 :** inlaid work or a decorative inlaid pattern

— **in·lay·ing** \-,lā-iŋ\ *noun*

in·let \'in-,let, -lət\ *noun* [from its letting water in] (circa 1576) **1 a :** a bay or recess in the shore of a sea, lake, or river; *also* **:** CREEK **b :** a narrow water passage between peninsulas or through a barrier island leading to a bay or lagoon **2 :** a way of entering; *especially* **:** an opening for intake

in·li·er \'in-,lī(-ə)r\ *noun* [*in* + *outlier*] (circa 1859) **1 :** a mass of rock whose outcrop is surrounded by rock of younger age **2 :** a distinct area or formation completely surrounded by another; *also* **:** ENCLAVE

in-line \'in-'līn, -in-\ *adjective or adverb* (1929) **:** having the parts or units arranged in a straight line; *also* **:** being so arranged

in-line engine \(,)in-'līn-, 'in-,\ *noun* (1929) **:** an internal combustion engine in which the cylinders are arranged in one or more straight lines

in-line skate *noun* (1989) **:** a roller skate whose four wheels are set in-line for greater speed and maneuverability

— **in-line skating** *noun*

1in lo·co pa·ren·tis \in-,lō-kō-pə-'ren-təs\ *adverb* [Latin] (1828) **:** in the place of a parent

2in loco parentis *noun* (1968) **:** regulation or supervision by an administrative body (as at a university) acting in loco parentis

in·ly \'in-lē\ *adverb* (before 12th century) **1 :** INWARDLY **2 :** in a manner suggesting great depth of knowledge or understanding : THOROUGHLY

in·mate \'in-,māt\ *noun* (1589) **1 :** any of a group occupying a single place of residence; *especially* **:** a person confined (as in a prison or hospital)

in me·di·as res \in-'mē-dē-as-'rās, -'mē-dē-as-'rēz\ *adverb* [Latin, literally, into the midst of things] (1786) **:** in or into the middle of a narrative or plot

in me·mo·ri·am \,in-mə-'mōr-ē-əm, -'mor-\ *preposition* [Latin] (1850) **:** in memory of — used especially in epitaphs

in·mi·grant \'in-,mī-grənt\ *noun* (1942) **:** one that in-migrates

in·mi·grate \'in-,mī-grāt\ *intransitive verb* (1942) **:** to move into or come to live in a region or community especially as part of a large-scale and continuing movement of population — compare OUT-MIGRATE

— **in-mi·gra·tion** \,in-mī-'grā-shən\ *noun*

in·most \'in-,mōst\ *adjective* [Middle English, from Old English *innemest*, superlative of *inne, adverb, in, within, from in, adverb*] (before 12th century) **:** deepest within : farthest from the outside

1inn \'in\ *noun* [Middle English, from Old English *inn* dwelling, inn, from Old English *in*, adverb] (before 12th century) **1 :** an establishment for the lodging and entertaining of travelers **b :** TAVERN **2 :** a residence formerly provided for British students in London and especially for students of law

2inn *intransitive verb* (14th century) **:** to put up at an inn

in·nards \'i-nərdz\ *noun plural* [alteration of *inwards*] (circa 1825) **1 :** the internal organs of a human being or animal; *especially* **:** VISCERA **2 :** the internal parts of a structure or mechanism

in·nate \i-'nāt, 'i-,\ *adjective* [Middle English *innat*, from Latin *innatus*, past participle of *innasci* to be born in, from *in-* + *nasci* to be born — more at NATION] (15th century) **1 :** existing in, belonging to, or determined by factors present in an individual from birth **2 :** belonging to the essential nature of something : INHERENT **3 :** originating in or derived from the mind or the constitution of the intellect rather than from experience

— **in·nate·ly** *adverb*

— **in·nate·ness** *noun*

inky cap

☆ SYNONYMS

Injustice, injury, wrong, grievance mean an act that inflicts undeserved hurt. INJUSTICE applies to any act that involves unfairness to another or violation of his rights (the *injustices* suffered by the lower classes). INJURY applies in law specifically to an injustice for which one may sue to recover compensation (*libel* constitutes a legal *injury*). WRONG applies also in law to any act punishable according to the criminal code; it may apply more generally to any flagrant injustice (determined to right society's *wrongs*). GRIEVANCE applies to any circumstance or condition that constitutes an injustice to the sufferer and gives ground for complaint (investigating employee *grievances*).

Innate, inborn, inbred, congenital, hereditary mean not acquired after birth. INNATE applies to qualities or characteristics that are part of one's inner essential nature (an *innate* sense of fair play). INBORN suggests a quality or tendency either actually present at birth or so marked and deep-seated as to seem so (her *inborn* love of nature). INBRED suggests something either acquired from parents by heredity or so deeply rooted and ingrained as to seem acquired that way (*inbred* political loyalties). CONGENITAL and HEREDITARY refer to what is acquired before or at birth, the former to things acquired during fetal development and the latter to things transmitted from one's ancestors (a *congenital* heart murmur) (eye color is hereditary).

\ə\ abut	\ə\ kitten	\ər\ further	\a\ ash	\ā\ ace	
\ä\ mop, mar	\au\ out	\ch\ chin	\e\ bet	\ē\ easy	
\g\ go	\i\ hit	\ī\ ice	\j\ job		
\ŋ\ sing	\ō\ go	\o\ law	\oi\ boy	\th\ thin	
\th\ the	\ü\ loot	\u\ foot			
\y\ yet	\zh\ vision			*see also* Guide to Pronunciation	

in·ner \'i-nər\ *adjective* [Middle English, from Old English *innera*, comparative of *inne* within] (before 12th century) **1 a :** situated farther in (the *inner* bark) **b :** being near a center especially of influence (the *inner* circles of political power) **2 :** of or relating to the mind or spirit (the *inner* life)
— **inner** *noun*
— **in·ner·ly** *adverb*

inner city *noun* (1961) **:** the usually older, poorer, and more densely populated central section of a city
— **inner-city** *adjective*

in·ner-di·rect·ed \'i-nər-də-'rek-təd, -(,)di-\ *adjective* (1950) **:** directed in thought and action by one's own scale of values as opposed to external norms

inner ear *noun* (circa 1923) **:** the essential organ of hearing and equilibrium that is located in the temporal bone, is innervated by the auditory nerve, and includes the vestibule, the semicircular canals, and the cochlea

inner light *noun, often I&L capitalized* (1856) **:** a divine presence held (as in Quaker doctrine) to enlighten and guide the soul

¹in·ner·most \'i-nər-,mōst\ *adjective* (14th century)
: farthest inward **:** INMOST

²innermost *noun* (14th century) **:** the inmost part

inner planet *noun* (1951) **:** any of the planets Mercury, Venus, Earth, and Mars whose orbits are within the asteroid belt

inner product *noun* (circa 1911) **:** SCALAR PRODUCT

in·ner·sole \'i-nər-'sōl\ *noun* (circa 1892) **:** INSOLE

inner space *noun* (1958) **1 :** space at or near the earth's surface and especially under the sea **2 :** one's inner self

in·ner·spring \'i-nər-'spriŋ\ *adjective* (1928) **:** having coil springs inside a padded casing (*innerspring* mattress)

inner tube *noun* (1895) **:** an airtight rubber tube inside a pneumatic tire to hold air under pressure

in·ner·vate \i-'nər-,vāt, 'i-(,)nər-\ *transitive verb* **-vat·ed; -vat·ing** (1870) **:** to supply with nerves
— **in·ner·va·tion** \,i-(,)nər-'vā-shən, i-,nər-\ *noun*

in·ning \'i-niŋ\ *noun* [²in + ¹-ing] (1735) **1 a** *plural but singular or plural in construction* **:** a division of a cricket match **b :** a division of a baseball game consisting of a turn at bat for each team; *also* **:** a baseball team's turn at bat ending with the third out **c :** a player's turn (as in horseshoes, pool, or croquet) **2 :** a chance or opportunity for action or accomplishment — usually used in plural but singular or plural in construction (that momentous *innings* which was to project him into world politics —*Times Literary Supplement*)

inn·keep·er \'in-,kē-pər\ *noun* (15th century) **1 :** a proprietor of an inn **2 :** HOTELMAN

in·no·cence \'i-nə-sən(t)s\ *noun* (14th century) **1 a :** freedom from guilt or sin through being unacquainted with evil **:** BLAMELESSNESS **b :** CHASTITY **c :** freedom from legal guilt of a particular crime or offense **d** (1) **:** freedom from guile or cunning **:** SIMPLICITY (2) **:** lack of worldly experience or sophistication **e :** lack of knowledge **:** IGNORANCE (written in entire *innocence* of the Italian language —E. R. Bentley) **2 :** one that is innocent **3 :** BLUET

in·no·cen·cy \-sən(t)-sē\ *noun, plural* **-cies** (14th century) **:** INNOCENCE; *also* **:** an innocent action or quality

in·no·cent \'i-nə-sənt\ *adjective* [Middle English, from Middle French, from Latin *innocent-, innocens*, from *in- + nocent-, nocens* wicked, from present participle of *nocēre* to harm — more at NOXIOUS] (14th century) **1 a :** free from guilt or sin especially through lack of knowledge of evil **:** BLAMELESS (an *innocent* child) **b :** harmless in effect or intention (searching for a hidden motive in even the most *innocent* conversation —Leonard Wibberley); *also* **:** CANDID (gave me an *innocent* gaze) **c :** free from legal guilt or fault; *also* **:** LAWFUL (a wholly *innocent* transaction) **2 a :** lacking or reflecting a lack of sophistication, guile, or self-consciousness **:** ARTLESS, INGENUOUS **b :** IGNORANT (almost entirely *innocent* of Latin —C. L. Wrenn); *also* **:** UNAWARE (perfectly *innocent* of the confusion he had created —B. R. Haydon) **3 :** lacking or deprived of something (her face *innocent* of cosmetics —Marcia Davenport)
— **innocent** *noun*
— **in·no·cent·ly** *adverb*

in·noc·u·ous \i-'nä-kyə-wəs\ *adjective* [Latin *innocuus*, from *in- + nocēre*] (1598) **1 :** producing no injury **:** HARMLESS **2 :** not likely to give offense or to arouse strong feelings or hostility **:** INOFFENSIVE, INSIPID
— **in·noc·u·ous·ly** *adverb*
— **in·noc·u·ous·ness** *noun*

in·nom·i·nate \i-'nä-mə-nət\ *adjective* [Late Latin *innominatus*, from Latin *in- + nominatus*, past participle of *nominare* to nominate] (1638) **:** having no name **:** UNNAMED; *also* **:** ANONYMOUS

innominate artery *noun* (1870) **:** BRACHIOCEPHALIC ARTERY

innominate bone *noun* (1866) **:** the large flaring bone that constitutes a lateral half of the pelvis in mammals and is composed of the ilium, ischium, and pubis which are fused into one bone in the adult

innominate vein *noun* (1876) **:** BRACHIOCEPHALIC VEIN

in·no·vate \'i-nə-,vāt\ *verb* **-vat·ed; -vat·ing** [Latin *innovatus*, past participle of *innovare*, from *in- + novus* new — more at NEW] (1548) *transitive verb* **1 :** to introduce as or as if new **2** *archaic* **:** to effect a change in (the dictates of my father were . . . not to be altered, *innovated*, or even discussed —Sir Walter Scott) *intransitive verb*
: to make changes **:** do something in a new way
— **in·no·va·tor** \-,vā-tər\ *noun*
— **in·no·va·to·ry** \'i-nə-və-,tōr-ē, -,tȯr-; 'i-nə-,vā-tə-rē\ *adjective*

in·no·va·tion \,i-nə-'vā-shən\ *noun* (15th century) **1 :** the introduction of something new **2 :** a new idea, method, or device **:** NOVELTY
— **in·no·va·tion·al** \-shnəl, -shə-nᵊl\ *adjective*

in·no·va·tive \'i-nə-,vā-tiv\ *adjective* (1608) **:** characterized by, tending to, or introducing innovations
— **in·no·va·tive·ly** *adverb*
— **in·no·va·tive·ness** *noun*

Inns of Court (15th century) **1 :** the four sets of buildings in London belonging to four societies of students and practitioners of the law **2 :** the four societies that alone admit to practice at the English bar

in·nu·en·do \,in-yə-'wen-(,)dō\ *noun, plural* **-dos** *or* **-does** [Latin, by hinting, from *innuere* to nod, from *in- + nuere* to nod — more at NUMEN] (1678) **1 a :** an oblique allusion **:** HINT, INSINUATION; *especially* **:** a veiled or equivocal reflection on character or reputation **b :** the use of such allusions (resorting to *innuendo*) **2 :** a parenthetical explanation introduced into the text of a legal document ◆

In·nu·it *variant of* INUIT

in·nu·mer·a·ble \i-'nüm-rə-bəl, -'n(y)üm-; -'n(y)ü-mə-\ *adjective* [Middle English, from Latin *innumerabilis*, from *in- + numerabilis* numerable] (14th century) **:** too many to be numbered **:** COUNTLESS; *also* **:** very many
— **in·nu·mer·a·bly** \-blē\ *adverb*

in·nu·mer·ate \-rət\ *adjective* (1959) **:** marked by an ignorance of mathematics and the scientific approach
— **in·nu·mer·a·cy** \-rə-sē\ *noun*
— **innumerate** *noun*

in·nu·mer·ous \-rəs\ *adjective* [Latin *innumerus*, from *in- + numerus* number] (1531) **:** INNUMERABLE

in·ob·ser·vance \,i-nəb-'zər-vən(t)s\ *noun* [French & Latin; French, from Latin *inobservantia*, from *in- + observantia* observance] (1611) **1 :** lack of attention **:** HEEDLESSNESS **2 :** failure to fulfill **:** NONOBSERVANCE
— **in·ob·ser·vant** \-vənt\ *adjective*

in·oc·u·lant \i-'nä-kyə-lənt\ *noun* (1898) **:** INOCULUM

in·oc·u·late \i-'nä-kyə-,lāt\ *transitive verb* **-lat·ed; -lat·ing** [Middle English, to insert a bud in a plant, from Latin *inoculatus*, past participle of *inoculare*, from *in- + oculus* eye, bud — more at EYE] (1721) **1 a :** to introduce a microorganism into (*inoculate* mice with anthrax) (beans *inoculated* with nitrogen-fixing bacteria) **b :** to introduce (as a microorganism) into a suitable situation for growth **c :** to introduce immunologically active material (as an antibody or antigen) into especially in order to treat or prevent a disease (*inoculate* children against diphtheria) **2 :** to introduce something into the mind of **3 :** to protect as if by inoculation ◆

synonym see INFUSE
— **in·oc·u·la·tive** \-ˌlā-tiv\ *adjective*
— **in·oc·u·la·tor** \-ˌlā-tər\ *noun*
in·oc·u·la·tion \i-ˌnä-kyə-'lā-shən\ *noun* (1714)
1 : the act or process or an instance of inoculating; *especially* **:** the introduction of a pathogen or antigen into a living organism to stimulate the production of antibodies
2 : INOCULUM
in·oc·u·lum \i-'nä-kyə-ləm\ *noun, plural* **-la** \-lə\ [New Latin, from Latin *inoculare*] (1902)
: material used for inoculation
in·of·fen·sive \ˌi-nə-'fen(t)-siv\ *adjective* (1646)
1 : causing no harm or injury
2 a : giving no provocation **:** PEACEABLE **b :** not objectionable to the senses
— **in·of·fen·sive·ly** *adverb*
— **in·of·fen·sive·ness** *noun*
in·op·er·a·ble \(ˌ)i-'nä-p(ə-)rə-bəl\ *adjective* [probably from French *inopérable*] (1886)
1 : not treatable or remediable by surgery ⟨*inoperable* cancer⟩
2 : INOPERATIVE
in·op·er·a·tive \-'nä-p(ə-)rə-tiv, -'nä-pə-ˌrā-\ *adjective* (circa 1631)
: not operative: as **a :** not functioning ⟨an *inoperative* clock⟩ **b :** having no effect or force ⟨an *inoperative* law⟩
— **in·op·er·a·tive·ness** *noun*
in·oper·cu·late \ˌi-nō-'pər-kyə-lət\ *adjective* (circa 1836)
: having no operculum
— **inoperculate** *noun*
in·op·por·tune \(ˌ)i-ˌnä-pər-'tün, -'tyün\ *adjective* [Latin *inopportunus*, from *in-* + *opportunus* opportune] (circa 1507)
: INCONVENIENT, UNSEASONABLE
— **in·op·por·tune·ly** *adverb*
— **in·op·por·tune·ness** \-'t(y)ün-nəs\ *noun*
in order that *conjunction* (1711)
: THAT 2a(1)
in·or·di·nate \i-'nȯr-d°n-ət, -'nȯrd-nət\ *adjective* [Middle English *inordinat*, from Latin *inordinatus*, from *in-* + *ordinatus*, past participle of *ordinare* to arrange — more at ORDAIN] (14th century)
1 *archaic* **:** DISORDERLY, UNREGULATED
2 : exceeding reasonable limits **:** IMMODERATE
synonym see EXCESSIVE
— **in·or·di·nate·ly** *adverb*
— **in·or·di·nate·ness** *noun*
in·or·gan·ic \ˌi-(ˌ)nȯr-'ga-nik\ *adjective* (1794)
1 a (1) **:** being or composed of matter other than plant or animal **:** MINERAL (2) **:** forming or belonging to the inanimate world **b :** of, relating to, or dealt with by a branch of chemistry concerned with substances not usually classed as organic
2 : not arising from natural growth **:** ARTIFICIAL; *also* **:** lacking structure, character, or vitality ⟨dull *inorganic* things, without individuality or prestige —John Buchan⟩
— **in·or·gan·i·cal·ly** \-ni-k(ə-)lē\ *adverb*
in·os·cu·late \i-'näs-kyə-ˌlāt\ *verb* **-lat·ed; -lat·ing** [²*in-* + *osculate*] (1671)
: JOIN, UNITE
— **in·os·cu·la·tion** \(ˌ)i-ˌnäs-kyə-'lā-shən\ *noun*
ino·si·tol \i-'nō-sə-ˌtȯl, ī-'nō-, -ˌtōl\ *noun* [International Scientific Vocabulary, from *inosite*, from Greek *in-*, *is* sinew + International Scientific Vocabulary ²-*ose* + ¹-*ite*] (1891)
: any of several crystalline stereoisomeric cyclic alcohols $C_6H_{12}O_6$; *especially* **:** MYOINOSITOL
ino·tro·pic \ˌē-nə-'trō-pik, ˌī-nə-, -'trä-\ *adjective* [International Scientific Vocabulary *ino-* (from Greek *in-*, *is* sinew) + -*tropic*] (1903)
: relating to or influencing the force of muscular contractions
in·pa·tient \'in-ˌpā-shənt\ *noun* (1760)

: a hospital patient who receives lodging and food as well as treatment — compare OUTPATIENT
in per·so·nam \ˌin-pər-'sō-ˌnam, -ˌnäm\ *adverb or adjective* [Late Latin, against a person] (circa 1860)
: against a person for the purpose of imposing a liability or obligation — used especially of legal actions, judgments, or jurisdiction; compare IN REM
in pet·to \in-'pe-(ˌ)tō\ *adverb or adjective* [Italian, literally, in the breast] (circa 1674)
1 : in private **:** SECRETLY
2 : in miniature
in·pour·ing \'in-ˌpōr-iŋ, -ˌpȯr-\ *noun* (1721)
: INRUSH
in–print \'in-'print\ *adjective* (1950)
: being in print
in–pro·cess \(ˌ)in-'prä-ˌses, -'prō-, -səs\ *adjective* (1925)
: of, relating to, or being goods in manufacture as distinguished from raw materials or from finished products
in pro·pria per·so·na \in-'prō-prē-ə-pər-'sō-nə\ *adverb* [Medieval Latin] (1654)
: in one's own person or character **:** PERSONALLY; *especially* **:** without the assistance of an attorney
¹in·put \'in-ˌpu̇t\ *noun* (1753)
1 : something that is put in: as **a :** an amount put in ⟨increased *input* of fertilizer increases crop yield⟩ **b :** power or energy put into a machine or system for storage, conversion in kind, or conversion of characteristics usually with the intent of sizable recovery in the form of output **c :** a component of production (as land, labor, or raw materials) **d :** information fed into a data processing system or computer **e :** ADVICE, OPINION, COMMENT
2 : the means by which or the point at which an input (as of energy, material, or data) is made
3 : the act or process of putting in
²input *transitive verb* **in·put·ted** *or* **input; in·put·ting** (1946)
: to enter (as data) into a computer or data processing system
in·quest \'in-ˌkwest\ *noun* [Middle English, from Old French *enqueste*, from (assumed) Vulgar Latin *inquaesta*, feminine of *inquaestus*, past participle of *inquaerere* to inquire] (13th century)
1 a : a judicial or official inquiry or examination especially before a jury ⟨a coroner's *inquest*⟩ **b :** a body of people (as a jury) assembled to hold such an inquiry **c :** the finding of the jury upon such inquiry or the document recording it
2 : INQUIRY, INVESTIGATION
in·qui·etude \(ˌ)in-'kwī-ə-ˌtüd, -ˌtyüd\ *noun* [Middle English, from Middle French or Late Latin; Middle French, from Late Latin *inquietudo*, from Latin *inquietus* disturbed, from *in-* + *quietus* quiet] (15th century)
: disturbed state **:** DISQUIETUDE
in·qui·line \'in-kwə-ˌlīn, -ˌlən\ *noun* [Latin *inquilinus* tenant, lodger, from *in-* + *colere* to cultivate, dwell — more at WHEEL] (1879)
: an animal that lives habitually in the nest or abode of some other species
in·quire \in-'kwīr\ *verb* **in·quired; in·quir·ing** [Middle English *enquiren*, from Old French *enquerre*, from (assumed) Vulgar Latin *inquaerere*, alteration of Latin *inquirere*, from *in-* + *quaerere* to seek] (13th century)
transitive verb
1 : to ask about ⟨some kindred spirit shall *inquire* thy fate —Thomas Gray⟩
2 : to search into **:** INVESTIGATE
intransitive verb
1 : to put a question **:** seek for information by questioning ⟨*inquired* about the horses⟩
2 : to make investigation or inquiry — often used with *into*
synonym see ASK
— **in·quir·er** *noun*

— **in·quir·ing·ly** \-'kwī-riŋ-lē\ *adverb*
— **inquire after :** to ask about the health of
in·qui·ry \in-'kwīr-ē, -'in-ˌ; 'in-kwə-rē, 'iŋ-; 'in-ˌkwir-ē\ *noun, plural* **-ries** (15th century)
1 : examination into facts or principles **:** RESEARCH
2 : a request for information
3 : a systematic investigation often of a matter of public interest
in·qui·si·tion \ˌin-kwə-'zi-shən, ˌiŋ-\ *noun* [Middle English *inquisicioun*, from Middle French *inquisition*, from Latin *inquisition-*, *inquisitio*, from *inquirere*] (14th century)
1 : the act of inquiring **:** EXAMINATION
2 : a judicial or official inquiry or examination usually before a jury; *also* **:** the finding of the jury
3 a *capitalized* **:** a former Roman Catholic tribunal for the discovery and punishment of heresy **b :** an investigation conducted with little regard for individual rights **c :** a severe questioning
— **in·qui·si·tion·al** \-'zi-sh(ə-)n°l\ *adjective*
in·quis·i·tive \in-'kwi-zə-tiv\ *adjective* (14th century)
1 : given to examination or investigation
2 : inclined to ask questions; *especially* **:** inordinately or improperly curious about the affairs of others
synonym see CURIOUS
— **in·quis·i·tive·ly** *adverb*
— **in·quis·i·tive·ness** *noun*
in·quis·i·tor \in-'kwi-zə-tər\ *noun* (1504)
: one who inquires or makes inquisition; *especially* **:** one who is unduly harsh, severe, or hostile in making an inquiry
— **in·quis·i·to·ri·al** \-ˌkwi-zə-'tōr-ē-əl, -'tȯr-\ *adjective*
— **in·quis·i·to·ri·al·ly** \-ē-ə-lē\ *adverb*
in re \in-'rā, -'rē\ *preposition* [Latin] (1877)
: in the matter of **:** CONCERNING, RE — often used in the title or name of a law case
in rem \in-'rem\ *adverb or adjective* [Late Latin] (circa 1860)
: against a thing (as a right, status, or property) — used especially of legal actions, judgments, or jurisdiction; compare IN PERSONAM
in–residence *adjective* (1845)
: being officially associated with an organization in a specified capacity — usually used in combination ⟨writer-*in-residence* at the university⟩
in·ro \'in-(ˌ)rō\ *noun, plural* **inro** [Japanese *inrō*] (1617)
: a small compartmented and usually ornamented container hung from an obi to hold small objects (as medicines and perfumes)
in·road \'in-ˌrōd\ *noun* (1548)
1 : a sudden hostile incursion **:** RAID
2 : an advance or penetration often at the expense of someone or something — usually used in plural
in·rush \'in-ˌrəsh\ *noun* (1817)
: a crowding or flooding in
in·sa·lu·bri·ous \ˌin-sə-'lü-brē-əs\ *adjective* [Latin *insalubris*, from *in-* + *salubris* healthful — more at SAFE] (1615)
: not conducive to health **:** UNWHOLESOME ⟨an *insalubrious* climate⟩
— **in·sa·lu·bri·ty** \-brə-tē\ *noun*
ins and outs \ˌin-zən(d)-'au̇ts\ *noun plural* (circa 1670)
1 : characteristic peculiarities or technicalities
2 : RAMIFICATIONS
in·sane \(ˌ)in-'sān\ *adjective* [Latin *insanus*, from *in-* + *sanus* sane] (circa 1550)
1 : mentally disordered **:** exhibiting insanity
2 : used by, typical of, or intended for insane persons ⟨an *insane* asylum⟩

\ə\ abut \°\ kitten \ər\ further \a\ ash \ā\ ace
\ä\ mop, mar \au̇\ out \ch\ chin \e\ bet \ē\ easy
\g\ go \i\ hit \ī\ ice \j\ job \ŋ\ sing \ō\ go
\ȯ\ law \ȯi\ boy \th\ thin \th\ the \ü\ loot \u̇\ foot
\y\ yet \zh\ vision *see also* Guide to Pronunciation

3 : ABSURD ⟨an *insane* scheme for making money⟩
— **in·sane·ly** *adverb*
— **in·sane·ness** \-'sān-nəs\ *noun*
in·san·i·tary \(ˌ)in-'sa-nə-ˌter-ē\ *adjective* (1874)
: unclean enough to endanger health **:** CONTAMINATED
— **in·san·i·ta·tion** \in-ˌsa-nə-'tā-shən\ *noun*
in·san·i·ty \in-'sa-nə-tē\ *noun, plural* **-ties** (1590)
1 a : a deranged state of the mind usually occurring as a specific disorder (as schizophrenia) and usually excluding such states as mental retardation, psychoneurosis, and various character disorders **b :** a mental disorder
2 : such unsoundness of mind or lack of understanding as prevents one from having the mental capacity required by law to enter into a particular relationship, status, or transaction or as removes one from criminal or civil responsibility
3 a : extreme folly or unreasonableness **b :** something utterly foolish or unreasonable
in·sa·tia·ble \(ˌ)in-'sā-shə-bəl\ *adjective* [Middle English *insaciable*, from Middle French, from Latin *insatiabilis*, from *in-* + *satiare* to satisfy — more at SATIATE] (15th century)
: incapable of being satisfied **:** QUENCHLESS ⟨had an *insatiable* desire for wealth⟩
— **in·sa·tia·bil·i·ty** \(ˌ)in-ˌsā-shə-'bi-lə-tē\ *noun*
— **in·sa·tia·ble·ness** \(ˌ)in-'sā-shə-bəl-nəs\ *noun*
— **in·sa·tia·bly** \-blē\ *adverb*
in·sa·tiate \(ˌ)in-'sā-sh(ē-)ət\ *adjective* (15th century)
: INSATIABLE
— **in·sa·tiate·ly** *adverb*
— **in·sa·tiate·ness** *noun*
in·scribe \in-'skrīb\ *transitive verb* [Middle English, from Latin *inscribere*, from *in-* + *scribere* to write — more at SCRIBE] (15th century)
1 a : to write, engrave, or print as a lasting record **b :** to enter on a list **:** ENROLL
2 a : to write, engrave, or print characters upon **b :** to autograph or address (a book) as a gift
3 : to dedicate to someone
4 : to draw within a figure so as to touch in as many places as possible ⟨a regular polygon *inscribed* in a circle⟩
5 *British* **:** to register the name of the holder of (a security)
— **in·scrib·er** *noun*
in·scrip·tion \in-'skrip-shən\ *noun* [Middle English *inscripcioun*, from Latin *inscription-, inscriptio*, from *inscribere*] (14th century)
1 a : something that is inscribed; *also* **:** SUPERSCRIPTION **b :** EPIGRAPH 2 **c :** the wording on a coin, medal, seal, or currency note
2 : the dedication of a book or work of art
3 a : the act of inscribing **b :** the entering of a name on or as if on a list **:** ENROLLMENT
4 *British* **a :** the act of inscribing securities **b** *plural* **:** inscribed securities
— **in·scrip·tion·al** \-shnəl, -shə-nᵊl\ *adjective*
in·scrip·tive \in-'skrip-tiv\ *adjective* (1740)
: relating to or constituting an inscription
— **in·scrip·tive·ly** *adverb*
in·scroll \in-'skrōl\ *transitive verb* (1596)
archaic **:** to write on a scroll **:** RECORD
in·scru·ta·ble \in-'skrü-tə-bəl\ *adjective* [Middle English, from Late Latin *inscrutabilis*, from Latin *in-* + *scrutari* to search — more at SCRUTINY] (15th century)
: not readily investigated, interpreted, or understood **:** MYSTERIOUS
— **in·scru·ta·bil·i·ty** \-ˌskrü-tə-'bi-lə-tē\ *noun*
— **in·scru·ta·ble·ness** \-'skrü-tə-bəl-nəs\ *noun*

— **in·scru·ta·bly** \-blē\ *adverb*
in·sculp \in-'skəlp\ *transitive verb* [Middle English, from Latin *insculpere*, from *in-* + *scalpere* to scratch, carve — more at SHELF] (15th century)
archaic **:** ENGRAVE, SCULPTURE
in·seam \'in-ˌsēm\ *noun* (1886)
: the seam on the inside of the leg of a pair of pants; *also* **:** the length of this seam
in·sect \'in-ˌsekt\ *noun* [Latin *insectum*, from neuter of *insectus*, past participle of *insecare* to cut into, from *in-* + *secare* to cut — more at SAW] (1601)
1 a : any of numerous small invertebrate animals (as spiders or centipedes) that are more or less obviously segmented **b :** any of a class (Insecta) of arthropods (as bugs or bees) with well-defined head, thorax, and abdomen, only three pairs of legs, and typically one or two pairs of wings
2 : a trivial or contemptible person ◇
— **insect** *adjective*

insect 1b: *1* labial palpus, *2* maxillary palpus, *3* simple eye, *4* antenna, *5* compound eye, *6* prothorax, *7* tympanum, *8* wing, *9* ovipositor, *10* spiracles, *11* abdomen, *12* metathorax, *13* mesothorax

in·sec·ta·ry \'in-ˌsek-tə-rē, in-'\ *noun, plural* **-ries** (1888)
: a place for the keeping or rearing of living insects
in·sec·ti·cid·al \(ˌ)in-ˌsek-tə-'sī-dᵊl\ *adjective* (1857)
1 : destroying or controlling insects
2 : of or relating to an insecticide
— **in·sec·ti·cid·al·ly** \-dᵊl-ē\ *adverb*
in·sec·ti·cide \in-'sek-tə-ˌsīd\ *noun* [International Scientific Vocabulary] (1865)
: an agent that destroys insects
in·sec·tile \(ˌ)in-'sek-tᵊl, -ˌtīl, -(ˌ)til\ *adjective* (circa 1626)
: being or suggestive of an insect
in·sec·ti·vore \in-'sek-tə-ˌvōr, -ˌvȯr\ *noun* [New Latin *Insectivora*, from Latin *insectum* + *-vorus* -vorous] (1840)
1 : any of an order (Insectivora) of mammals comprising forms (as moles, shrews, and hedgehogs) that are mostly small, insectivorous, and nocturnal
2 : an insectivorous plant or animal
in·sec·tiv·o·rous \ˌin-ˌsek-'tiv-rəs, -'ti-və-\ *adjective* (1661)
: depending on insects as food
in·se·cure \ˌin-si-'kyur\ *adjective* [Medieval Latin *insecurus*, from Latin *in-* + *securus* secure] (1649)
1 : not confident or sure **:** UNCERTAIN ⟨feeling somewhat *insecure* of his reception⟩
2 : not adequately guarded or sustained **:** UNSAFE ⟨an *insecure* investment⟩
3 : not firmly fastened or fixed **:** SHAKY ⟨the hinge is loose and *insecure*⟩
4 a : not highly stable or well-adjusted ⟨an *insecure* marriage⟩ **b :** deficient in assurance **:** beset by fear and anxiety ⟨always felt *insecure* in a group of strangers⟩
— **in·se·cure·ly** *adverb*
— **in·se·cure·ness** *noun*
— **in·se·cu·ri·ty** \-'kyur-ə-tē\ *noun*
in·sel·berg \'in(t)-səl-ˌbərg, 'in-zəl-, -ˌberg\ *noun, plural* **-bergs** *also* **-ber·ge** \-ˌbər-gə, -ˌber-\ [German, from *Insel* island + *Berg* mountain] (1913)

: an isolated mountain
in·sem·i·nate \in-'se-mə-ˌnāt\ *transitive verb* **-nat·ed; -nat·ing** [Latin *inseminatus*, past participle of *inseminare*, from *in-* + *semin-, semen* seed — more at SEMEN] (circa 1623)
1 : SOW
2 : to introduce semen into the genital tract of (a female)
synonym see IMPLANT
— **in·sem·i·na·tion** \-ˌse-mə-'nā-shən\ *noun*
in·sem·i·na·tor \-'se-mə-ˌnā-tər\ *noun* (1944)
: one that inseminates cattle artificially
in·sen·sate \(ˌ)in-'sen-ˌsāt, -sət\ *adjective* [Late Latin *insensatus*, from Latin *in-* + Late Latin *sensatus* having sense, from Latin *sensus* sense] (15th century)
1 : lacking sense or understanding; *also* **:** FOOLISH
2 : lacking animate awareness or sensation
3 : lacking humane feeling **:** BRUTAL
— **in·sen·sate·ly** *adverb*
in·sen·si·ble \(ˌ)in-'sen(t)-sə-bəl\ *adjective* [Middle English, from Middle French & Latin; Middle French, from Latin *insensibilis*, from *in-* + *sensibilis* sensible] (14th century)
1 : IMPERCEPTIBLE ⟨dampened by an *insensible* dew⟩; *broadly* **:** SLIGHT, GRADUAL ⟨*insensible* motion⟩
2 : incapable or bereft of feeling or sensation: as **a :** not endowed with life or spirit **:** INSENTIENT ⟨*insensible* earth⟩ **b :** UNCONSCIOUS ⟨knocked *insensible* by a sudden blow⟩ **c :** lacking sensory perception or ability to react ⟨*insensible* to pain⟩
3 a : lacking emotional response **:** APATHETIC, INDIFFERENT ⟨*insensible* to fear⟩ **b :** UNAWARE ⟨*insensible* of their danger⟩
4 *archaic* **:** STUPID, SENSELESS
5 : not intelligible **:** MEANINGLESS
6 : lacking delicacy or refinement
— **in·sen·si·bil·i·ty** \(ˌ)in-ˌsen(t)-sə-'bi-lə-tē\ *noun*
— **in·sen·si·ble·ness** \(ˌ)in-'sen(t)-sə-bəl-nəs\ *noun*
— **in·sen·si·bly** \-blē\ *adverb*
in·sen·si·tive \(ˌ)in-'sen(t)-s(ə-)tiv\ *adjective* (1834)
1 a : not responsive or susceptible ⟨*insensitive* to the demands of the public⟩ **b :** lacking feeling or tact ⟨so *insensitive* as to laugh at someone in pain⟩
2 : not physically or chemically sensitive
— **in·sen·si·tive·ly** *adverb*
— **in·sen·si·tive·ness** *noun*
— **in·sen·si·tiv·i·ty** \(ˌ)in-ˌsen(t)-sə-'ti-və-tē\ *noun*
in·sen·tient \(ˌ)in-'sen(t)-sh(ē-)ənt\ *adjective* (1764)
: lacking perception, consciousness, or animation
— **in·sen·tience** \-sh(ē-)ən(t)s\ *noun*
in·sep·a·ra·ble \(ˌ)in-'se-p(ə-)rə-bəl\ *adjective* [Middle English, from Latin *inseparabilis*, from *in-* + *separabilis* separable] (14th century)

: incapable of being separated or disjoined
— **in·sep·a·ra·bil·i·ty** \(͵)in-͵se-p(ə-)rə-'bi-lə-tē\ *noun*
— **inseparable** *noun*
— **in·sep·a·ra·ble·ness** \(͵)in-'se-p(ə-)rə-bəl-nəs\ *noun*
— **in·sep·a·ra·bly** \-blē\ *adverb*

¹**in·sert** \in-'sərt\ *verb* [Latin *insertus,* past participle of *inserere,* from *in-* + *serere* to join — more at SERIES] (1529)
transitive verb
1 : to put or thrust in ⟨*insert* the key in the lock⟩ ⟨*insert* a spacecraft into orbit⟩
2 : to put or introduce into the body of something **:** INTERPOLATE ⟨*insert* a change in a manuscript⟩
3 : to set in and make fast; *especially* **:** to insert by sewing between two cut edges
4 : to place into action (as in a game) ⟨*insert* a new pitcher⟩
intransitive verb
of a muscle **:** to be in attachment to the part to be moved
synonym see INTRODUCE
— **in·sert·er** *noun*
²**in·sert** \'in-͵sərt\ *noun* (circa 1889)
: something that is inserted or is for insertion; *especially* **:** written or printed material inserted (as between the leaves of a book)
in·ser·tion \in-'sər-shən\ *noun* (1539)
1 : something that is inserted: as **a :** the part of a muscle that inserts **b :** the mode or place of attachment of an organ or part **c :** embroidery or needlework inserted as ornament between two pieces of fabric **d :** a section of genetic material that is inserted into an existing gene sequence
2 a : the act or process of inserting **b :** the mutational process producing a genetic insertion
— **in·ser·tion·al** \-shnəl, -shə-nᵊl\ *adjective*
in-ser·vice \'in-'sər-vəs\ *adjective* (1928)
1 : going on or continuing while one is fully employed ⟨*in-service* teacher education workshops⟩
2 : of, relating to, or being one that is fully employed ⟨*in-service* police officers⟩
¹**in·set** \'in-͵set\ *noun* (1559)
1 a : a place where something flows in **:** CHANNEL **b :** a setting or flowing in
2 : something that is inset: as **a :** a small graphic representation (as a map or picture) set within a larger one **b :** a piece of cloth set into a garment (as for decoration) **c :** a part or section of a utensil that fits into an outer part
²**in·set** \'in-͵set, in-'\ *transitive verb* **inset** *or* **in·set·ted; in·set·ting** (1658)
1 : SET IN; *especially* **:** to insert within something else in such a way as to be visible
2 : to provide with an inset
¹**in·shore** \'in-͵shōr, -'shȯr\ *adjective* (1701)
1 : situated, living, or carried on near shore
2 : moving toward shore ⟨an *inshore* current⟩
²**inshore** *adverb* (1748)
: to or toward shore ⟨boats driven *inshore* by the storm⟩
¹**in·side** \(͵)in-'sīd, 'in-\ *noun* (14th century)
1 a : an interior or internal part or place **:** the part within **b :** inward nature, thoughts, or feeling **c :** VISCERA, ENTRAILS — usually used in plural
2 : an inner side or surface
3 a : a position of power, trust, or familiarity ⟨only someone on the *inside* could have told⟩ **b :** confidential information ⟨has the *inside* on what happened at the convention⟩
4 : the area nearest a specified or implied point of reference: as **a :** the side of home plate nearest the batter **b :** the middle portion of a playing area **c :** the area near or underneath the basket in basketball
²**inside** *adverb* (15th century)
1 : on the inner side
2 : in or into the interior
3 : to or on the inside
4 : in prison
³**inside** *adjective* (1611)

1 : of, relating to, or being on or near the inside ⟨an *inside* pitch⟩
2 a : relating or known to a select group ⟨*inside* information⟩ **b :** BEHIND-THE-SCENES
⁴**inside** *preposition* (1791)
1 a : in or into or as if in or into the interior of
b : on the inner side of
2 : WITHIN ⟨*inside* an hour⟩
inside address *noun* (circa 1941)
: ADDRESS 5c
inside of *preposition* (1839)
: INSIDE
inside out *adverb* (circa 1600)
1 : in such a manner that the inner surface becomes the outer ⟨turned the shirt *inside out*⟩
2 : to a thorough degree ⟨knows the subject *inside out*⟩
3 : in or into a state of disarray often involving drastic reorganization ⟨turned the business *inside out*⟩
in·sid·er \(͵)in-'sī-dər, 'in-͵\ *noun* (1848)
: a person recognized or accepted as a member of a group, category, or organization: as **a :** a person who is in a position of power or has access to confidential information **b :** one (as an officer or director) who is in a position to have special knowledge of the affairs of or to influence the decisions of a company
insider trading *noun* (1966)
: the illegal use of insider information for profit in financial trading
inside track *noun* (1857)
: an advantageous competitive position ⟨the owner's son has the *inside track* for the job⟩
in·sid·i·ous \in-'si-dē-əs\ *adjective* [Latin *insidiosus,* from *insidiae* ambush, from *insidēre* to sit in, sit on, from *in-* + *sedēre* to sit — more at SIT] (1545)
1 a : awaiting a chance to entrap **:** TREACHEROUS **b :** harmful but enticing **:** SEDUCTIVE ⟨*insidious* drugs⟩
2 a : having a gradual and cumulative effect **:** SUBTLE ⟨the *insidious* pressures of modern life⟩ **b** *of a disease* **:** developing so gradually as to be well established before becoming apparent
— **in·sid·i·ous·ly** *adverb*
— **in·sid·i·ous·ness** *noun*
in·sight \'in-͵sīt\ *noun* (13th century)
1 : the power or act of seeing into a situation **:** PENETRATION
2 : the act or result of apprehending the inner nature of things or of seeing intuitively
synonym see DISCERNMENT
in·sight·ful \'in-͵sīt-fəl, in-'\ *adjective* (1907)
: exhibiting or characterized by insight
— **in·sight·ful·ly** *adverb*
in·sig·nia \in-'sig-nē-ə\ *or* **in·sig·ne** \-(͵)nē\ *noun, plural* **-nia** *or* **-ni·as** [Latin *insignia,* plural of *insigne* mark, badge, from neuter of *insignis* marked, distinguished, from *in-* + *signum* mark — more at SIGN] (1648)
1 : a badge of authority or honor
2 : a distinguishing mark or sign
in·sig·nif·i·cance \͵in(t)-sig-'ni-fi-kən(t)s\ *noun* (1699)
: the quality or state of being insignificant
in·sig·nif·i·can·cy \-kən(t)-sē\ *noun, plural* **-cies** (1651)
1 : INSIGNIFICANCE
2 : an insignificant thing or person
in·sig·nif·i·cant \-kənt\ *adjective* (1651)
: not significant: as **a :** lacking meaning or import **:** INCONSEQUENTIAL **b :** not worth considering **:** UNIMPORTANT **c :** lacking weight, position, or influence **:** CONTEMPTIBLE **d :** small in size, quantity, or number
— **in·sig·nif·i·cant·ly** *adverb*
in·sin·cere \͵in-sin-'sir, -sən-\ *adjective* [Latin *insincerus,* from *in-* + *sincerus* sincere] (1634)
: not sincere **:** HYPOCRITICAL
— **in·sin·cere·ly** *adverb*
— **in·sin·cer·i·ty** \-'ser-ə-tē *also* -'sir-\ *noun*
in·sin·u·ate \in-'sin-yə-͵wāt\ *verb* **-at·ed; -at·ing** [Latin *insinuatus,* past participle of

insinuare, from *in-* + *sinuare* to bend, curve, from *sinus* curve] (1529)
transitive verb
1 a : to introduce (as an idea) gradually or in a subtle, indirect, or covert way ⟨*insinuate* doubts into a trusting mind⟩ **b :** to impart or communicate with artful or oblique reference
2 : to introduce (as oneself) by stealthy, smooth, or artful means
intransitive verb
1 *archaic* **:** to enter gently, slowly, or imperceptibly **:** CREEP
2 *archaic* **:** to ingratiate oneself
synonym see INTRODUCE, SUGGEST
— **in·sin·u·a·tive** \-͵wā-tiv\ *adjective*
— **in·sin·u·a·tor** \-͵wā-tər\ *noun*
insinuating *adjective* (1591)
1 : winning favor and confidence by imperceptible degrees **:** INGRATIATING
2 : tending gradually to cause doubt, distrust, or change of outlook often in a slyly subtle manner ⟨*insinuating* remarks⟩
— **in·sin·u·at·ing·ly** *adverb*
in·sin·u·a·tion \(͵)in-͵sin-yə-'wā-shən\ *noun* (1526)
1 : the act or process of insinuating
2 : something that is insinuated; *especially* **:** a sly, subtle, and usually derogatory utterance
in·sip·id \in-'si-pəd\ *adjective* [French & Late Latin; French *insipide,* from Late Latin *insipidus,* from Latin *in-* + *sapidus* savory, from *sapere* to taste — more at SAGE] (1609)
1 : lacking taste or savor **:** TASTELESS
2 : lacking in qualities that interest, stimulate, or challenge **:** DULL, FLAT ☆
— **in·si·pid·i·ty** \͵in-sə-'pi-də-tē\ *noun*
— **in·sip·id·ly** \in-'si-pəd-lē\ *adverb*
in·sist \in-'sist\ *verb* [Middle French or Latin; Middle French *insister,* from Latin *insistere* to stand upon, persist, from *in-* + *sistere* to take a stand; akin to Latin *stare* to stand — more at STAND] (1586)
intransitive verb
1 : to be emphatic, firm, or resolute about something intended, demanded, or required ⟨they *insist* on going⟩
2 *archaic* **:** PERSIST
transitive verb
: to maintain in a persistent or positive manner ⟨*insisted* that the story was true⟩
in·sis·tence \in-'sis-tən(t)s\ *noun* (15th century)
1 : the act or an instance of insisting
2 : the quality or state of being insistent **:** URGENCY
in·sis·ten·cy \-tən(t)-sē\ *noun, plural* **-cies** (1859)
: INSISTENCE

☆ **SYNONYMS**
Insipid, vapid, flat, jejune, banal, inane mean devoid of qualities that make for spirit and character. INSIPID implies a lack of sufficient taste or savor to please or interest ⟨an *insipid* romance with platitudes on every page⟩. VAPID suggests a lack of liveliness, force, or spirit ⟨an exciting story given a *vapid* treatment⟩. FLAT applies to things that have lost their sparkle or zest ⟨although well-regarded in its day, the novel now seems *flat*⟩. JEJUNE suggests a lack of rewarding or satisfying substance ⟨a *jejune* and gassy speech⟩. BANAL stresses the complete absence of freshness, novelty, or immediacy ⟨a *banal* tale of unrequited love⟩. INANE implies a lack of any significant or convincing quality ⟨an *inane* interpretation of the play⟩.

\ə\ abut \ᵊ\ kitten \ər\ further \a\ ash \ā\ ace
\ä\ mop, mar \au̇\ out \ch\ chin \e\ bet \ē\ easy
\g\ go \i\ hit \ī\ ice \j\ job \ŋ\ sing \ō\ go
\ȯ\ law \ȯi\ boy \th\ thin \t͟h\ the \ü\ loot \u̇\ foot
\y\ yet \zh\ vision *see also* Guide to Pronunciation

in·sis·tent \in-'sis-tənt\ *adjective* [Latin *insistent-, insistens,* present participle of *insistere*] (1868)
1 : disposed to insist : PERSISTENT
2 : compelling attention ⟨the *insistent* pounding of the waves⟩
— **in·sis·tent·ly** *adverb*
in si·tu \(ˌ)in-'sī-(ˌ)tü, -'si-, -(ˌ)tyü *also* -'sē-, -(ˌ)chü\ *adverb or adjective* [Latin, in position] (1740)
: in the natural or original position or place
in·so·bri·ety \ˌin-sə-'brī-ə-tē, -sō-\ *noun* (circa 1611)
: lack of sobriety or moderation; *especially* : intemperance in drinking
in·so·cia·ble \(ˌ)in-'sō-shə-bəl\ *adjective* [Latin *insociabilis,* from *in-* + *sociabilis* sociable] (1588)
: not sociable
— **in·so·cia·bil·i·ty** \-(ˌ)sō-shə-'bi-lə-tē\ *noun*
— **in·so·cia·bly** \-'sō-shə-blē\ *adverb*
in·so·far \ˌin-sə-'fär\ *adverb* (1596)
: to such extent or degree
insofar as *conjunction* (15th century)
: to the extent or degree that
in·so·la·tion \ˌin-(ˌ)sō-'lā-shən\ *noun* [French or Latin; French, from Latin *insolation-, insolatio,* from *insolare* to expose to the sun, from *in-* + *sol* sun — more at SOLAR] (1617)
1 : exposure to the sun's rays
2 : SUNSTROKE
3 a : solar radiation that has been received **b** : the rate of delivery of direct solar radiation per unit of horizontal surface; *broadly* : that relating to total solar radiation
in·sole \'in-ˌsōl\ *noun* (circa 1861)
1 : an inside sole of a shoe
2 : a loose thin strip placed inside a shoe for warmth or comfort
in·so·lence \'in(t)-s(ə-)lən(t)s\ *noun* (14th century)
1 : the quality or state of being insolent
2 : an instance of insolent conduct or treatment
in·so·lent \-s(ə-)lənt\ *adjective* [Middle English, from Latin *insolent-, insolens* unaccustomed, overbearing, from *in-* + *solens,* present participle of *solēre* to be accustomed; perhaps akin to Latin *sodalis* comrade — more at SIB] (14th century)
1 : insultingly contemptuous in speech or conduct : OVERBEARING
2 : exhibiting boldness or effrontery : IMPUDENT
synonym see PROUD
— **insolent** *noun*
— **in·so·lent·ly** *adverb*
in·sol·u·bi·lize \(ˌ)in-'säl-yə-bə-ˌlīz\ *transitive verb* (1897)
: to make insoluble
— **in·sol·u·bi·li·za·tion** \-ˌsäl-yə-bə-lə-'zā-shən\ *noun*
in·sol·u·ble \(ˌ)in-'säl-yə-bəl\ *adjective* [Middle English *insolible,* from Latin *insolubilis,* from *in-* + *solvere* to free, dissolve — more at SOLVE] (14th century)
1 : not soluble: as **a** *archaic* : INDISSOLUBLE **b** : having or admitting of no solution or explanation **c** : incapable of being dissolved in a liquid; *also* : soluble only with difficulty or to a slight degree
— **in·sol·u·bil·i·ty** \-ˌsäl-yə-'bi-lə-tē\ *noun*
— **insoluble** *noun*
— **in·sol·u·ble·ness** \-'säl-yə-bəl-nəs\ *noun*
— **in·sol·u·bly** \-blē\ *adverb*
in·solv·able \(ˌ)in-'säl-və-bəl, -'sȯl-\ *adjective* (1693)
: admitting no solution ⟨an apparently *insolvable* problem⟩
— **in·solv·ably** \-blē\ *adverb*
in·sol·vent \(ˌ)in-'säl-vənt, -'sȯl-\ *adjective* (1591)

1 a (1) : unable to pay debts as they fall due in the usual course of business (2) : having liabilities in excess of a reasonable market value of assets held **b** : insufficient to pay all debts ⟨an *insolvent* estate⟩ **c** : not up to a normal standard or complement : IMPOVERISHED
2 : relating to or for the relief of insolvents
— **in·sol·ven·cy** \-vən(t)-sē\ *noun*
— **insolvent** *noun*
in·som·nia \in-'säm-nē-ə\ *noun* [Latin, from *insomnis* sleepless, from *in-* + *somnus* sleep — more at SOMNOLENT] (circa 1623)
: prolonged and usually abnormal inability to obtain adequate sleep
— **in·som·ni·ac** \-nē-ˌak\ *adjective or noun*
in·so·much as \ˌin(t)-sō-'məch-\ *conjunction* (14th century)
: INASMUCH AS
insomuch that *conjunction* (14th century)
: SO 1
in·sou·ci·ance \in-'sü-sē-ən(t)s, aⁿ-'süs-yäⁿs\ *noun* [French, from *in-* + *soucier* to trouble, disturb, from Latin *sollicitare* — more at SOLICIT] (1799)
: lighthearted unconcern : NONCHALANCE
— **in·sou·ci·ant** \in-'sü-sē-ənt, aⁿ-'süs-yäⁿ\ *adjective*
— **in·sou·ci·ant·ly** \in-'sü-sē-ənt-lē\ *adverb*
in·soul *variant of* ENSOUL
in·span \in-'span, 'in-ˌ\ *verb* [Afrikaans, from Dutch *inspannen*] (circa 1827)
chiefly South African : YOKE, HARNESS
in·spect \in-'spekt\ *verb* [Latin *inspectus,* past participle of *inspicere,* from *in-* + *specere* to look — more at SPY] (circa 1623)
transitive verb
1 : to view closely in critical appraisal : look over
2 : to examine officially ⟨*inspects* the barracks every Friday⟩
intransitive verb
: to make an inspection
synonym see SCRUTINIZE
— **in·spec·tive** \-'spek-tiv\ *adjective*
in·spec·tion \in-'spek-shən\ *noun* (14th century)
1 a : the act of inspecting **b** : recognition of a familiar pattern leading to immediate solution of a mathematical problem ⟨solve an equation by *inspection*⟩
2 : a checking or testing of an individual against established standards
inspection arms *noun* [from the command *inspection arms!*] (circa 1884)
: a position in the manual of arms in which the rifle is held at port arms with the chamber open for inspection; *also* : a command to assume this position
in·spec·tor \in-'spek-tər\ *noun* (1602)
1 : a person employed to inspect something
2 a : a police officer who is in charge of usually several precincts and ranks below a superintendent or deputy superintendent **b** : a person appointed to oversee a polling place
— **in·spec·tor·ship** \-ˌship\ *noun*
in·spec·tor·ate \in-'spek-t(ə-)rət\ *noun* (1762)
1 : the office, position, work, or district of an inspector
2 : a body of inspectors
inspector general *noun* (1702)
: a person who heads an inspectorate or a system of inspection (as of an army)
in·sphere *variant of* ENSPHERE
in·spi·ra·tion \ˌin(t)-spə-'rā-shən, -(ˌ)spi-\ *noun* (14th century)
1 a : a divine influence or action on a person believed to qualify him or her to receive and communicate sacred revelation **b** : the action or power of moving the intellect or emotions **c** : the act of influencing or suggesting opinions
2 : the act of drawing in; *specifically* : the drawing of air into the lungs

3 a : the quality or state of being inspired **b** : something that is inspired ⟨a scheme that was pure *inspiration*⟩
4 : an inspiring agent or influence
— **in·spi·ra·tion·al** \-shnəl, -shə-nᵊl\ *adjective*
— **in·spi·ra·tion·al·ly** *adverb*
in·spi·ra·tor \'in(t)-spə-ˌrā-tər, -(ˌ)spi-\ *noun* (1624)
: one that inspires ⟨teachers who are *inspirators* of the young⟩
in·spi·ra·to·ry \in-'spī-rə-ˌtȯr-ē, 'in(t)-sp(ə-)rə-, -ˌtȯr-\ *adjective* (1773)
: of, relating to, used for, or associated with inspiration
in·spire \in-'spīr\ *verb* **in·spired; in·spir·ing** [Middle English, from Middle French & Latin; Middle French *inspirer,* from Latin *inspirare,* from *in-* + *spirare* to breathe] (14th century)
transitive verb
1 a : to influence, move, or guide by divine or supernatural inspiration **b** : to exert an animating, enlivening, or exalting influence on ⟨was particularly *inspired* by the Romanticists⟩ **c** : to spur on : IMPEL, MOTIVATE ⟨threats don't necessarily *inspire* people to work⟩ **d** : AFFECT ⟨seeing the old room again *inspired* him with nostalgia⟩
2 a : to breathe or blow into or upon **b** *archaic* : to infuse (as life) by breathing
3 a : to communicate to an agent supernaturally **b** : to draw forth or bring out ⟨thoughts *inspired* by a visit to the cathedral⟩
4 : INHALE 1
5 a : BRING ABOUT, OCCASION ⟨the book was *inspired* by his travels in the Far East⟩ **b** : INCITE
6 : to spread (rumor) by indirect means or through the agency of another
intransitive verb
: INHALE
— **in·spir·er** *noun*
inspired *adjective* (15th century)
: outstanding or brilliant in a way or to a degree suggestive of divine inspiration ⟨gave an *inspired* performance⟩
inspiring *adjective* (1717)
: having an animating or exalting effect
in·spir·it \in-'spir-ət\ *transitive verb* (15th century)
: to fill with spirit
synonym see ENCOURAGE
— **in·spir·it·ing·ly** \-ə-tiŋ-lē\ *adverb*
in·spis·sate \in-'spi-ˌsāt, 'in(t)-spə-ˌsāt\ *transitive verb* **-sat·ed; -sat·ing** [Late Latin *inspissatus,* past participle of *inspissare,* from Latin *in-* + *spissus* slow, dense; akin to Greek *spidnos* compact, Lithuanian *spisti* to form a swarm] (1626)
: to make thick or thicker
— **in·spis·sa·tion** \ˌin(t)-spə-'sā-shən, (ˌ)in-ˌspi-'sā-\ *noun*
— **in·spis·sa·tor** \in-'spi-ˌsā-tər, 'in(t)-spə-ˌsā-\ *noun*
in·spis·sat·ed \in-'spi-ˌsā-təd, 'in(t)-spə-ˌsā-\ *adjective* (1603)
: thickened in consistency; *broadly* : made or having become thick, heavy, or intense
in·sta·bil·i·ty \ˌin(t)-stə-'bi-lə-tē\ *noun* (15th century)
: the quality or state of being unstable; *especially* : lack of emotional or mental stability
in·sta·ble \(ˌ)in-'stā-bəl\ *adjective* [Middle French or Latin; Middle French, from Latin *instabilis,* from *in-* + *stabilis* stable] (15th century)
: UNSTABLE
in·stall *also* **in·stal** \in-'stȯl\ *transitive verb* **in·stalled; in·stall·ing** [Middle English, from Middle French *installer,* from Medieval Latin *installare,* from Latin *in-* + Medieval Latin *stallum* stall, from Old High German *stal*] (15th century)

1 a : to place in an office or dignity by seating in a stall or official seat **b** : to induct into an office, rank, or order ⟨*installed* the new president⟩
2 : to establish in an indicated place, condition, or status ⟨*installing* herself in front of the fireplace⟩
3 : to set up for use or service ⟨had an exhaust fan *installed* in the kitchen⟩
— **in·stall·er** *noun*

in·stal·la·tion \ˌin(t)-stə-ˈlā-shən\ *noun* (15th century)
1 : the act of installing : the state of being installed
2 : something that is installed for use
3 : a military camp, fort, or base

¹in·stall·ment *also* **in·stal·ment** \in-ˈstól-mənt\ *noun* (1589)
: INSTALLATION 1

²installment *also* **instalment** *noun* [alteration of earlier *estallment* payment by installment, derivative of Old French *estaler* to place, fix, from *estal* place, of Germanic origin; akin to Old High German *stal* place, stall] (1776)
1 : one of the parts into which a debt is divided when payment is made at intervals
2 a : one of several parts (as of a publication) presented at intervals **b** : one part of a serial story
— **installment** *adjective*

installment plan *noun* (1876)
: a system of paying for goods by installments

¹in·stance \ˈin(t)-stən(t)s\ *noun* (14th century)
1 a *archaic* : urgent or earnest solicitation **b** : INSTIGATION, REQUEST ⟨am writing to you at the *instance* of my client⟩ **c** *obsolete* : an impelling cause or motive
2 a *archaic* : EXCEPTION **b** : an individual illustrative of a category or brought forward in support or disproof of a generalization **c** *obsolete* : TOKEN, SIGN
3 : the institution and prosecution of a lawsuit : SUIT
4 : a step, stage, or situation viewed as part of a process or series of events ⟨prefers, in this *instance*, to remain anonymous —*Times Literary Supplement*⟩ ☆
— **for in·stance** \fə-ˈrin(t)-stən(t)s, ˈfrin(t)-\ : as an instance or example ⟨older people like my grandmother, *for instance*⟩

²instance *transitive verb* **in·stanced; in·stanc·ing** (1601)
1 : to illustrate or demonstrate by an instance
2 : to mention as a case or example : CITE

in·stan·cy \ˈin(t)-stən(t)-sē\ *noun, plural* **-cies** (1515)
1 : URGENCY, INSISTENCE
2 : nearness of approach : IMMINENCE
3 : immediacy of occurrence or action : INSTANTANEOUSNESS

¹in·stant \ˈin(t)-stənt\ *noun* [Middle English, from Medieval Latin *instant-, instans,* from *instant-, instans,* adjective, instant, from Latin] (14th century)
1 : an infinitesimal space of time; *especially* : a point in time separating two states ⟨at the *instant* of death⟩
2 : the present or current month

²instant *adjective* [Middle English, from Middle French or Latin; Middle French, from Latin *instant-, instans,* from present participle of *instare* to stand upon, urge, from *in-* + *stare* to stand — more at STAND] (15th century)
1 : IMPORTUNATE, URGENT
2 a : PRESENT, CURRENT ⟨previous felonies not related to the *instant* crime⟩ **b** : of or occurring in the present month
3 : IMMEDIATE, DIRECT ⟨the play was an *instant* success⟩
4 a (1) : premixed or precooked for easy final preparation ⟨*instant* pudding⟩ (2) : appearing in or as if in ready-to-use form ⟨*instant* culture⟩ **b** : immediately soluble in water ⟨*instant* coffee⟩

5 : produced or occurring with or as if with extreme rapidity and ease
— **in·stant·ness** *noun*

in·stan·ta·neous \ˌin(t)-stən-ˈtā-nē-əs, -nyəs\ *adjective* [Medieval Latin *instantaneus,* from *instant-, instans,* noun] (1651)
1 : done, occurring, or acting without any perceptible duration of time ⟨death was *instantaneous*⟩
2 : done without any delay being purposely introduced ⟨took *instantaneous* action to correct the abuse⟩
3 : occurring or present at a particular instant ⟨*instantaneous* velocity⟩
— **in·stan·ta·ne·ity** \ˌin-ˌstan-tˀn-ˈē-ə-tē, ˌin(t)-stən-tə-ˈnē-\ *noun*
— **in·stan·ta·neous·ly** \ˌin(t)-stən-ˈtā-nē-əs-lē, -nyəs-lē\ *adverb*
— **in·stan·ta·neous·ness** *noun*

in·stan·ter \in-ˈstan-tər\ *adverb* [Medieval Latin, from *instant-, instans*] (1688)
: at once

in·stan·ti·ate \in-ˈstan(t)-shē-ˌāt\ *transitive verb* **-at·ed; -at·ing** (1949)
: to represent (an abstraction) by a concrete instance ⟨heroes *instantiate* ideals —W. J. Bennett⟩
— **in·stan·ti·a·tion** \-ˌstan(t)-shē-ˈā-shən\ *noun*

¹in·stant·ly \ˈin(t)-stənt-lē\ *adverb* (15th century)
1 : with importunity : URGENTLY
2 : without the least delay : IMMEDIATELY

²instantly *conjunction* (1793)
: as soon as ⟨he ran across the grass *instantly* he perceived his mother —W. M. Thackeray⟩

instant replay *noun* (1966)
: a videotape recording of an action (as a play in football) that can be played back (as in slow motion) immediately after the action has been completed; *also* : the playing of such a recording

in·star \ˈin-ˌstär\ *noun* [New Latin, from Latin, equivalent] (1895)
: a stage in the life of an arthropod (as an insect) between two successive molts; *also* : an individual in a specified instar

in·state \in-ˈstāt\ *transitive verb* (1603)
1 *obsolete* **a** : INVEST, ENDOW **b** : BESTOW, CONFER
2 : to set or establish in a rank or office : INSTALL

in sta·tu quo \in-ˌstā-tə-(ˌ)tü-ˈkwō, -ˌsta-; -ˌsta-(ˌ)chü-\ *adverb* [New Latin, literally, in the state in which] (1602)
: in the former or same state

in·stau·ra·tion \ˌin-ˌstó-ˈrā-shən, ˌin(t)-stə-\ *noun* [Latin *instauration-, instauratio,* from *instaurare* to renew, restore — more at STORE] (circa 1603)
1 : restoration after decay, lapse, or dilapidation
2 : an act of instituting or establishing something

in·stead \in-ˈsted\ *adverb* (1667)
1 : as a substitute or equivalent ⟨was going to write but called *instead*⟩
2 : as an alternative to something expressed or implied : RATHER ⟨longed *instead* for a quiet country life⟩

in·stead of \in-ˈste-də(v), -ˈsti-\ *preposition* [Middle English *in sted of*] (13th century)
: in place of : as a substitute for or alternative to

in·step \ˈin-ˌstep\ *noun* (15th century)
1 : the arched middle portion of the human foot in front of the ankle joint; *especially* : its upper surface
2 : the part of a shoe or stocking that fits over the instep

instep 1

in·sti·gate \ˈin(t)-stə-ˌgāt\ *transitive verb* **-gat·ed; -gat·ing** [Latin *instigatus,* past participle of *instigare* — more at STICK] (1542)
: to goad or urge forward : PROVOKE
synonym see INCITE
— **in·sti·ga·tion** \ˌin(t)-stə-ˈgā-shən\ *noun*
— **in·sti·ga·tive** \ˈin(t)-stə-ˌgā-tiv\ *adjective*
— **in·sti·ga·tor** \-ˌgā-tər\ *noun*

in·still *also* **in·stil** \in-ˈstil\ *transitive verb* **in·stilled; in·still·ing** [Middle English, from Middle French & Latin; Middle French *instiller,* from Latin *instillare,* from *in-* + *stillare* to drip, from *stilla* drop] (15th century)
1 : to cause to enter drop by drop ⟨*instill* medication into the infected eye⟩
2 : to impart gradually ⟨*instilling* a love of learning in children⟩
synonym see IMPLANT
— **in·stil·la·tion** \ˌin(t)-stə-ˈlā-shən, -(ˌ)sti-\ *noun*
— **in·still·er** \in-ˈsti-lər\ *noun*
— **in·still·ment** \-mənt\ *noun*

¹in·stinct \ˈin-ˌstiŋ(k)t\ *noun* [Middle English, from Latin *instinctus* impulse, from *instinguere* to incite; akin to Latin *instigare* to instigate] (15th century)
1 : a natural or inherent aptitude, impulse, or capacity ⟨had an *instinct* for the right word⟩
2 a : a largely inheritable and unalterable tendency of an organism to make a complex and specific response to environmental stimuli without involving reason **b** : behavior that is mediated by reactions below the conscious level
— **in·stinc·tu·al** \in-ˈstiŋ(k)-chə-wəl, -chəl, -shwəl\ *adjective*
— **in·stinc·tu·al·ly** *adverb*

²in·stinct \in-ˈstiŋ(k)t, ˈin-\ *adjective* (1667)
1 *obsolete* : impelled by an inner or animating or exciting agency
2 : profoundly imbued : INFUSED ⟨my mood, *instinct* with romance —S. J. Perelman⟩

in·stinc·tive \in-ˈstiŋ(k)-tiv\ *adjective* (15th century)
1 : of, relating to, or being instinct
2 : prompted by natural instinct or propensity : arising spontaneously ⟨an *instinctive* fear of innovation —V. L. Parrington⟩
synonym see SPONTANEOUS
— **in·stinc·tive·ly** *adverb*

¹in·sti·tute \ˈin(t)-stə-ˌtüt, -ˌtyüt\ *transitive verb* **-tut·ed; -tut·ing** [Middle English, from

\ə\ abut \ᵊ\ kitten \ər\ further \a\ ash \ā\ ace
\ä\ mop, mar \aù\ out \ch\ chin \e\ bet \ē\ easy
\g\ go \i\ hit \ī\ ice \j\ job \ŋ\ sing \ō\ go
\ò\ law \òi\ boy \th\ thin \th\ the \ü\ loot \ù\ foot
\y\ yet \zh\ vision *see also* Guide to Pronunciation

Latin *institutus,* past participle of *instituere,* from *in- + statuere* to set up — more at STATUTE] (14th century)
1 : to establish in a position or office
2 a : to originate and get established **:** ORGANIZE ⟨*instituted* reading clinics⟩ **b :** to set going **:** INAUGURATE ⟨*instituting* an investigation of the charges⟩
— **in·sti·tut·er** *or* **in·sti·tu·tor** \-,tü-tər, -,tyü-\ *noun*

²**institute** *noun* (1546)
: something that is instituted: as **a** (1) **:** an elementary principle recognized as authoritative (2) *plural* **:** a collection of such principles and precepts; *especially* **:** a legal compendium **b :** an organization for the promotion of a cause **:** ASSOCIATION ⟨a research *institute*⟩ ⟨an *institute* for the blind⟩ **c :** an educational institution and especially one devoted to technical fields **d :** a usually brief intensive course of instruction on selected topics relating to a particular field ⟨an urban studies *institute*⟩

in·sti·tu·tion \,in(t)-stə-'tü-shən, -'tyü-\ *noun* (14th century)
1 : an act of instituting **:** ESTABLISHMENT
2 a : a significant practice, relationship, or organization in a society or culture ⟨the *institution* of marriage⟩; *also* **:** something or someone firmly associated with a place or thing ⟨she has become an *institution* in the theater⟩ **b :** an established organization or corporation (as a college or university) especially of a public character; *also* **:** ASYLUM 4
— **in·sti·tu·tion·al** \-shnəl, -shə-n⁰l\ *adjective*
— **in·sti·tu·tion·al·ly** *adverb*
— **in·sti·tu·tion·al·ise** *British variant of* INSTITUTIONALIZE

in·sti·tu·tion·al·ism \-shnə-,li-zəm, -shə-n⁰l-,i-zəm\ *noun* (1862)
1 : emphasis on organization (as in religion) at the expense of other factors
2 : public institutional care of handicapped, delinquent, or dependent persons
3 : an economic school of thought that emphasizes the role of social institutions in influencing economic behavior
— **in·sti·tu·tion·al·ist** \-shnə-list, -shə-n⁰l-ist\ *noun*

in·sti·tu·tion·al·ize \-shnə-,līz, -shə-n⁰l-,īz\ *transitive verb* **-ized; -iz·ing** (1865)
1 : to make into an institution **:** give character of an institution to ⟨*institutionalized* housing⟩; *especially* **:** to incorporate into a structured and often highly formalized system ⟨*institutionalized* values⟩
2 : to put in the care of an institution ⟨*institutionalize* alcoholics⟩
— **in·sti·tu·tion·al·i·za·tion** \-,tü-shnə-lə-'zā-shən, -shə-n⁰l-ə-'zā-\ *noun*

in-store \'in-,stōr, -'stòr\ *adjective* (1961)
: relating to or being an operation or activity located or taking place inside a store ⟨*in-store* consumer survey⟩

in·struct \in-'strəkt\ *transitive verb* [Middle English, from Latin *instructus,* past participle of *instruere,* from *in- + struere* to build — more at STRUCTURE] (15th century)
1 : to give knowledge to **:** TEACH, TRAIN
2 : to provide with authoritative information or advice ⟨the judge *instructed* the jury⟩
3 : to give an order or command to **:** DIRECT
synonym *see* TEACH, COMMAND

in·struc·tion \in-'strək-shən\ *noun* (15th century)
1 a : PRECEPT ⟨prevailing cultural *instructions*⟩ **b :** a direction calling for compliance **:** ORDER — usually used in plural ⟨had *instructions* not to admit strangers⟩ **c** *plural* **:** an outline or manual of technical procedure **:** DIRECTIONS **d :** a code that tells a computer to perform a particular operation
2 : the action, practice, or profession of teaching
— **in·struc·tion·al** \-shnəl, -shə-n⁰l\ *adjective*

in·struc·tive \in-'strək-tiv\ *adjective* (1611)
: carrying a lesson **:** ENLIGHTENING
— **in·struc·tive·ly** *adverb*
— **in·struc·tive·ness** *noun*

in·struc·tor \in-'strək-tər\ *noun* (15th century)
: one that instructs **:** TEACHER; *especially* **:** a college teacher below professorial rank
— **in·struc·tor·ship** \-,ship\ *noun*

in·struc·tress \-'strək-trəs\ *noun* (1630)
: a woman who is an instructor

¹**in·stru·ment** \'in(t)-strə-mənt\ *noun* [Middle English, from Latin *instrumentum,* from *in-struere* to arrange, instruct] (14th century)
1 : a device used to produce music
2 a : a means whereby something is achieved, performed, or furthered **b :** one used by another as a means or aid **:** DUPE, TOOL
3 : IMPLEMENT; *especially* **:** one designed for precision work
4 : a formal legal document (as a deed, bond, or agreement)
5 a : a measuring device for determining the present value of a quantity under observation **b :** an electrical or mechanical device used in navigating an airplane; *especially* **:** such a device used as the sole means of navigating
synonym *see* IMPLEMENT

²**in·stru·ment** \-,ment\ *transitive verb* (1752)
1 : to address a legal instrument to
2 : to score for musical performance **:** ORCHESTRATE
3 : to equip with instruments especially for measuring and recording data ⟨an *instrumented* spacecraft⟩

in·stru·men·tal \,in(t)-strə-'men-t⁰l\ *adjective* (14th century)
1 a : serving as a means, agent, or tool ⟨was *instrumental* in organizing the strike⟩ **b :** of, relating to, or done with an instrument or tool
2 : relating to, composed for, or performed on a musical instrument
3 : of, relating to, or being a grammatical case or form expressing means or agency
4 : of or relating to instrumentalism
5 : OPERANT 3 ⟨*instrumental* learning⟩ ⟨*instrumental* conditioning⟩
— **instrumental** *noun*
— **in·stru·men·tal·ly** \-t⁰l-ē\ *adverb*

in·stru·men·tal·ism \-,i-zəm\ *noun* (1909)
: a doctrine that ideas are instruments of action and that their usefulness determines their truth

in·stru·men·tal·ist \-ist\ *noun* (1823)
1 : a player on a musical instrument
2 : an exponent of instrumentalism
— **instrumentalist** *adjective*

in·stru·men·tal·i·ty \,in(t)-strə-mən-'ta-lə-tē, -,men-\ *noun, plural* **-ties** (1651)
1 : the quality or state of being instrumental
2 : MEANS, AGENCY

in·stru·men·ta·tion \,in(t)-strə-mən-'tā-shən, -,men-\ *noun* (1845)
1 : the arrangement or composition of music for instruments especially for a band or orchestra
2 : the use or application of instruments (as for observation, measurement, or control)
3 : instruments for a particular purpose; *also* **:** a selection or arrangement of instruments

instrument flying *noun* (1928)
: navigation of an airplane by instruments only

instrument landing *noun* (1938)
: a landing made with limited visibility by means of instruments and by ground radio direction

instrument panel *noun* (1922)
: a panel on which instruments are mounted; *especially* **:** DASHBOARD 2

in·sub·or·di·nate \,in(t)-sə-'bòr-d⁰n-ət, -'bòrd-nət\ *adjective* (circa 1828)
: disobedient to authority
— **insubordinate** *noun*
— **in·sub·or·di·nate·ly** *adverb*
— **in·sub·or·di·na·tion** \-,bòr-d⁰n-'ā-shən\ *noun*

in·sub·stan·tial \,in(t)-səb-'stan(t)-shəl\ *adjective* [probably from French *insubstantiel,* from Late Latin *insubstantialis,* from Latin *in- + Late Latin substantialis* substantial] (1607)
: not substantial: as **a :** lacking substance or material nature **b :** lacking firmness or solidity **:** FLIMSY
— **in·sub·stan·ti·al·i·ty** \-,stan(t)-shē-'a-lə-tē\ *noun*

in·suf·fer·able \(,)in-'sə-f(ə-)rə-bəl\ *adjective* (15th century)
: not to be endured **:** INTOLERABLE ⟨an *insufferable* bore⟩
— **in·suf·fer·able·ness** *noun*
— **in·suf·fer·ably** \-blē\ *adverb*

in·suf·fi·cien·cy \,in(t)-sə-'fi-shən(t)-sē\ *noun, plural* **-cies** (1526)
1 : the quality or state of being insufficient: as **a :** lack of mental or moral fitness **:** INCOMPETENCE ⟨the *insufficiency* of this person for public office⟩ **b :** lack of adequate supply ⟨*insufficiency* of provisions⟩ **c :** lack of physical power or capacity; *specifically* **:** inability of an organ or body part to function normally
2 : something that is insufficient or falls short of expectations

in·suf·fi·cient \,in(t)-sə-'fi-shənt\ *adjective* [Middle English, from Middle French, from Late Latin *insufficient-, insufficiens,* from Latin *in- + sufficient-, sufficiens* sufficient] (14th century)
: not sufficient **:** INADEQUATE; *especially* **:** lacking adequate power, capacity, or competence
— **in·suf·fi·cient·ly** *adverb*

in·suf·fla·tion \,in(t)-sə-'flā-shən, in-,sə-'flā-\ *noun* [Middle English *insufflacion,* from Middle French *insufflation,* from Late Latin *insufflation-, insufflatio,* from *insufflare* to blow upon, from Latin *in- + sufflare* to inflate, from *sub- + flare* to blow — more at BLOW] (15th century)
: an act or the action of blowing on, into, or in: as **a :** a Christian ceremonial rite of exorcism performed by breathing on a person **b :** the act of blowing something (as a gas, powder, or vapor) into a body cavity
— **in·suf·flate** \'in(t)-sə-,flāt, in-'sə-,flāt\ *transitive verb*
— **in·suf·fla·tor** \-,flā-tər\ *noun*

in·su·lant \'in(t)-sə-lənt\ *noun* (circa 1929)
chiefly British **:** INSULATION 2

in·su·lar \'in(t)-sü-lər, -syü-, 'in-shə-lər\ *adjective* [Late Latin *insularis,* from Latin *insula* island] (1611)
1 a : of, relating to, or constituting an island **b :** dwelling or situated on an island ⟨*insular* residents⟩
2 : characteristic of an isolated people; *especially* **:** being, having, or reflecting a narrow provincial viewpoint
3 : of or relating to an island of cells or tissue
— **in·su·lar·ism** \-lə-,ri-zəm\ *noun*
— **in·su·lar·i·ty** \,in(t)-sü-'lar-ə-tē, -syü-, ,in-shə-'lar-\ *noun*
— **in·su·lar·ly** \'in(t)-sü-lər-lē, -syü-, 'in-shə-\ *adverb*

in·su·late \'in(t)-sə-,lāt\ *transitive verb* **-lat·ed; -lat·ing** [Latin *insula*] (circa 1741)
: to place in a detached situation **:** ISOLATE; *especially* **:** to separate from conducting bodies by means of nonconductors so as to prevent transfer of electricity, heat, or sound

in·su·la·tion \,in(t)-sə-'lā-shən\ *noun* (1798)
1 a : the action of insulating **b :** the state of being insulated
2 : material used in insulating

in·su·la·tor \'in(t)-sə-,lā-tər\ *noun* (1801)
: one that insulates: as **a :** a material that is a poor conductor (as of electricity or heat) — compare SEMICONDUCTOR **b :** a device made of an electrical insulating material and used for separating or supporting conductors

in·su·lin \'in(t)-s(ə-)lən\ *noun* [New Latin *insula* islet (of Langerhans), from Latin, island] (1914)

: a protein pancreatic hormone secreted by the islets of Langerhans that is essential especially for the metabolism of carbohydrates and is used in the treatment and control of diabetes mellitus

insulin shock *noun* (1925)
: hypoglycemia associated with the presence of excessive insulin in the system and characterized by progressive development of coma

¹**in·sult** \in-'səlt\ *verb* [Middle French or Latin; Middle French *insulter*, from Latin *insultare*, literally, to spring upon, from *in-* + *saltare* to leap — more at SALTATION] (1540)
intransitive verb
archaic **:** to behave with pride or arrogance **:** VAUNT
transitive verb
: to treat with insolence, indignity, or contempt **:** AFFRONT; *also* **:** to affect offensively or damagingly ⟨doggerel that *insults* the reader's intelligence⟩
synonym see OFFEND
— **in·sult·er** *noun*
— **in·sult·ing·ly** \in-'səl-tiŋ-lē\ *adverb*
²**in·sult** \'in-,səlt\ *noun* (1671)
1 : a gross indignity
2 : injury to the body or one of its parts; *also* **:** something that causes or has a potential for causing such insult ⟨pollution and other environmental *insults*⟩

in·su·per·a·ble \(,)in-'sü-p(ə-)rə-bəl\ *adjective* [Middle English, from Middle French & Latin; Middle French, from Latin *insuperabilis*, from *in-* + *superare* to surmount, from *super* over — more at OVER] (14th century)
: incapable of being surmounted, overcome, passed over, or solved ⟨*insuperable* difficulties⟩
— **in·su·per·a·bly** \-blē\ *adverb*

in·sup·port·able \,in(t)-sə-'pōr-tə-bəl, -'pȯr-\ *adjective* [Middle French or Late Latin; Middle French, from Late Latin *insupportabilis*, from Latin *in-* + *supportare* to support] (circa 1530)
: not supportable: **a :** more than can be endured ⟨*insupportable* pain⟩ **b :** impossible to justify ⟨*insupportable* charges⟩
— **in·sup·port·ably** \-blē\ *adverb*

in·sup·press·ible \,in(t)-sə-'pre-sə-bəl\ *adjective* (1610)
: IRREPRESSIBLE

in·sur·able \in-'shùr-ə-bəl\ *adjective* (1810)
: that may be insured
— **in·sur·abil·i·ty** \-,shùr-ə-'bi-lə-tē\ *noun*

¹**in·sur·ance** \in-'shùr-ən(t)s *also* 'in-,\ *noun* (1651)
1 a : the business of insuring persons or property **b :** coverage by contract whereby one party undertakes to indemnify or guarantee another against loss by a specified contingency or peril **c :** the sum for which something is insured
2 : a means of guaranteeing protection or safety ⟨the contract is your *insurance* against price changes⟩
²**insurance** *adjective* (1954)
: being a score that adds to a team's lead and makes it impossible for the opposing team to tie the game with its next score ⟨*insurance* run⟩

in·sure \in-'shùr\ *verb* **in·sured; in·sur·ing** [Middle English, to assure, probably alteration of *assuren*] (1635)
transitive verb
1 : to provide or obtain insurance on or for
2 : to make certain especially by taking necessary measures and precautions
intransitive verb
: to contract to give or take insurance
synonym see ENSURE

insured *noun* (1681)
: a person whose life or property is insured

in·sur·er \in-'shùr-ər\ *noun* (1654)
: one that insures; *specifically* **:** an insurance underwriter

in·sur·gence \in-'sər-jən(t)s\ *noun* (1847)

: an act or the action of being insurgent **:** INSURRECTION

in·sur·gen·cy \-jən(t)-sē\ *noun, plural* **-cies** (1803)
1 : the quality or state of being insurgent; *specifically* **:** a condition of revolt against a government that is less than an organized revolution and that is not recognized as belligerency
2 : INSURGENCE

¹**in·sur·gent** \-jənt\ *noun* [Latin *insurgent-, insurgens*, present participle of *insurgere* to rise up, from *in-* + *surgere* to rise — more at SURGE] (1765)
1 : a person who revolts against civil authority or an established government; *especially* **:** a rebel not recognized as a belligerent
2 : one who acts contrary to the policies and decisions of one's own political party
²**insurgent** *adjective* (1814)
: rising in opposition to civil authority or established leadership **:** REBELLIOUS
— **in·sur·gent·ly** *adverb*

in·sur·mount·able \,in(t)-sər-'maùn-tə-bəl\ *adjective* (1690)
: incapable of being surmounted **:** INSUPERABLE ⟨*insurmountable* problems⟩
— **in·sur·mount·ably** \-blē\ *adverb*

in·sur·rec·tion \,in(t)-sə-'rek-shən\ *noun* [Middle English, from Middle French, from Late Latin *insurrection-, insurrectio,* from *insurgere*] (15th century)
: an act or instance of revolting against civil authority or an established government
synonym see REBELLION
— **in·sur·rec·tion·al** \-shnəl, -shə-nᵊl\ *adjective*
— **in·sur·rec·tion·ary** \-shə-,ner-ē\ *adjective or noun*
— **in·sur·rec·tion·ist** \-sh(ə-)nist\ *noun*

in·sus·cep·ti·ble \,in(t)-sə-'sep-tə-bəl\ *adjective* (1603)
: not susceptible ⟨*insusceptible* to flattery⟩
— **in·sus·cep·ti·bil·i·ty** \-,sep-tə-'bi-lə-tē\ *noun*
— **in·sus·cep·ti·bly** \,in(t)-sə-'sep-tə-blē\ *adverb*

in·tact \in-'takt\ *adjective* [Middle English *intacte,* from Latin *intactus,* from *in-* + *tactus,* past participle of *tangere* to touch — more at TANGENT] (15th century)
1 : untouched especially by anything that harms or diminishes **:** ENTIRE, UNINJURED
2 *of a living body or its parts* **:** having no relevant component removed or destroyed: **a :** physically virginal **b :** not castrated
synonym see PERFECT
— **in·tact·ness** \-'tak(t)-nəs\ *noun*

in·ta·glio \in-'tal-(,)yō, -'täl-; -'ta-glē-,ō, -'tä-\ *noun, plural* **-glios** [Italian, from *intagliare* to engrave, cut, from Medieval Latin *intaliare,* from Latin *in-* + Late Latin *taliare* to cut — more at TAILOR] (1644)
1 a : an engraving or incised figure in stone or other hard material depressed below the surface so that an impression from the design yields an image in relief **b :** the art or process of executing intaglios **c :** printing (as in die stamping and gravure) done from a plate in which the image is sunk below the surface
2 : something (as a gem) carved in intaglio

intaglio 1a

in·take \'in-,tāk\ *noun* (15th century)
1 : an opening through which fluid enters an enclosure
2 a : a taking in **b** (1) **:** the amount taken in (2) **:** something (as energy) taken in **:** INPUT

¹**in·tan·gi·ble** \(,)in-'tan-jə-bəl\ *adjective* [French or Medieval Latin; French, from Medieval Latin *intangibilis,* from Latin *in-* + Late Latin *tangibilis* tangible] (1640)
: not tangible **:** IMPALPABLE

— **in·tan·gi·bil·i·ty** \-,tan-jə-'bi-lə-tē\ *noun*
— **in·tan·gi·ble·ness** \-'tan-jə-bəl-nəs\ *noun*
— **in·tan·gi·bly** \-blē\ *adverb*
²**intangible** *noun* (1914)
: something intangible; *specifically* **:** an asset (as goodwill) that is not corporeal

in·tar·sia \in-'tär-sē-ə\ *noun* [German, modification of Italian *intarsio*] (1867)
1 : a mosaic usually of wood fitted into a support; *also* **:** the art or process of making such a mosaic
2 : a colored design knitted on both sides of a fabric (as in a sweater)

in·te·ger \'in-ti-jər\ *noun* [Latin, adjective, whole, entire — more at ENTIRE] (1571)
1 : any of the natural numbers, the negatives of these numbers, or zero
2 : a complete entity

in·te·gra·ble \'in-ti-grə-bəl\ *adjective* (circa 1741)
: capable of being integrated ⟨*integrable* functions⟩
— **in·te·gra·bil·i·ty** \,in-ti-grə-'bi-lə-tē\ *noun*

¹**in·te·gral** \'in-ti-grəl (*usually so in mathematics*); in-'te-grəl *also* -'tē- *also* ÷'in-trə-gəl\ *adjective* (1551)
1 a : essential to completeness **:** CONSTITUENT ⟨an *integral* part of the curriculum⟩ **b** (1) **:** being, containing, or relating to one or more mathematical integers (2) **:** relating to or concerned with mathematical integrals or integration **c :** formed as a unit with another part ⟨a seat with *integral* headrest⟩
2 : composed of integral parts
3 : lacking nothing essential **:** ENTIRE
— **in·te·gral·i·ty** \,in-tə-'gra-lə-tē\ *noun*
— **in·te·gral·ly** \'in-ti-grə-lē; in-'te-grə-also -'tē-\ *adverb*
²**integral** *noun* (circa 1741)
: the result of a mathematical integration — compare DEFINITE INTEGRAL, INDEFINITE INTEGRAL

integral calculus *noun* (circa 1741)
: a branch of mathematics concerned with the theory and applications (as in the determination of lengths, areas, and volumes and in the solution of differential equations) of integrals and integration

integral domain *noun* (1937)
: a mathematical ring in which multiplication is commutative, which has a multiplicative identity element, and which contains no pair of nonzero elements whose product is zero ⟨the integers under the operations of addition and multiplication form an *integral domain*⟩

in·te·grand \'in-tə-,grand\ *noun* [Latin *integrandus,* gerundive of *integrare*] (1897)
: a mathematical expression to be integrated

in·te·grate \'in-tə-,grāt\ *verb* **-grat·ed; -grat·ing** [Latin *integratus,* past participle of *integrare,* from *integr-, integer*] (1638)
transitive verb
1 : to form, coordinate, or blend into a functioning or unified whole **:** UNITE
2 : to find the integral of (as a function or equation)
3 a : to unite with something else **b :** to incorporate into a larger unit
4 a : to end the segregation of and bring into equal membership in society or an organization **b :** DESEGREGATE ⟨*integrate* school districts⟩
intransitive verb
: to become integrated

integrated *adjective* (1922)
1 : marked by the unified control of all aspects of industrial production from raw materials

\ə\ abut \ᵊ\ kitten \ər\ further \a\ ash \ā\ ace
\ä\ mop, mar \aù\ out \ch\ chin \e\ bet \ē\ easy
\g\ go \i\ hit \ī\ ice \j\ job \ŋ\ sing \ō\ go
\ȯ\ law \ȯi\ boy \th\ thin \th\ the \ü\ loot \ù\ foot
\y\ yet \zh\ vision *see also* Guide to Pronunciation

2 : marked by or expressive of great zeal, energy, determination, or concentration ⟨*intense* effort⟩
3 a : exhibiting strong feeling or earnestness of purpose ⟨an *intense* student⟩ **b :** deeply felt
— **in·tense·ly** *adverb*
— **in·tense·ness** *noun*

in·ten·si·fi·er \in-'ten(t)-sə-ˌfī(-ə)r\ *noun* (1835)
: one that intensifies; *especially* **:** INTENSIVE

in·ten·si·fy \in-'ten(t)-sə-ˌfī\ *verb* **-fied; -fy·ing** (1817)
transitive verb
1 : to make intense or more intensive **:** STRENGTHEN
2 a : to increase the density and contrast of (a photographic image) by chemical treatment **b :** to make more acute **:** SHARPEN
intransitive verb
: to become intense or more intensive **:** grow stronger or more acute
— **in·ten·si·fi·ca·tion** \-ˌten(t)s-fə-'kā-shən, -ˌten(t)-sə-\ *noun*

in·ten·sion \in-'ten(t)-shən\ *noun* (1604)
1 : INTENSITY
2 : CONNOTATION 3
— **in·ten·sion·al** \-'tench-nəl, -'ten(t)-shə-nᵊl\ *adjective*
— **in·ten·sion·al·i·ty** \-ˌten(t)-shə-'na-lə-tē\ *noun*
— **in·ten·sion·al·ly** \-'tench-nə-lē, -'ten(t)-shə-nᵊl-ē\ *adverb*

in·ten·si·ty \in-'ten(t)-sə-tē\ *noun, plural* **-ties** (1665)
1 : the quality or state of being intense; *especially* **:** extreme degree of strength, force, energy, or feeling
2 : the magnitude of a quantity (as force or energy) per unit (as of area, charge, mass, or time)
3 : SATURATION 4a

¹in·ten·sive \in-'ten(t)-siv\ *adjective* (15th century)
: of, relating to, or marked by intensity or intensification: as **a :** highly concentrated ⟨*intensive* study⟩ **b :** tending to strengthen or increase; *especially* **:** tending to give force or emphasis ⟨*intensive* adverb⟩ **c :** constituting or relating to a method designed to increase productivity by the expenditure of more capital and labor rather than by increase in scope ⟨*intensive* farming⟩
— **in·ten·sive·ly** *adverb*
— **in·ten·sive·ness** *noun*

²intensive *noun* (1813)
: an intensive linguistic element

intensive care *noun* (1963)
: special medical equipment and services for taking care of seriously ill patients ⟨heart patients in *intensive care*⟩ ⟨an *intensive care* unit⟩

¹in·tent \in-'tent\ *noun* [Middle English *entent,* from Old French, from Late Latin *intentus,* from Latin, act of stretching out, from *intendere*] (13th century)
1 a : the act or fact of intending **:** PURPOSE; *especially* **:** the design or purpose to commit a wrongful or criminal act ⟨admitted wounding him with *intent*⟩ **b :** the state of mind with which an act is done **:** VOLITION
2 : a usually clearly formulated or planned intention **:** AIM
3 a : MEANING, SIGNIFICANCE **b :** CONNOTATION 3
synonym see INTENTION

²intent *adjective* [Latin *intentus,* from past participle of *intendere*] (14th century)
1 : directed with strained or eager attention **:** CONCENTRATED
2 : having the mind, attention, or will concentrated on something or some end or purpose ⟨*intent* on their work⟩
— **in·tent·ly** *adverb*
— **in·tent·ness** *noun*

in·ten·tion \in-'ten(t)-shən\ *noun* (14th century)

1 : a determination to act in a certain way **:** RESOLVE
2 : IMPORT, SIGNIFICANCE
3 a : what one intends to do or bring about **b :** the object for which a prayer, mass, or pious act is offered
4 : a process or manner of healing of incised wounds
5 : CONCEPT; *especially* **:** a concept considered as the product of attention directed to an object of knowledge
6 *plural* **:** purpose with respect to marriage ☆

in·ten·tion·al \in-'tench-nəl, -'ten(t)-shə-nᵊl\ *adjective* (circa 1727)
1 : done by intention or design **:** INTENDED ⟨*intentional* damage⟩
2 a : of or relating to epistemological intention **b :** having external reference
synonym see VOLUNTARY
— **in·ten·tion·al·i·ty** \-ˌten(t)-shə-'na-lə-tē\ *noun*
— **in·ten·tion·al·ly** \in-'tench-nə-lē, -'ten(t)-shə-nᵊl-ē\ *adverb*

in·ter \in-'tər\ *transitive verb* **in·terred; in·ter·ring** [Middle English *enteren,* from Middle French *enterrer,* from (assumed) Vulgar Latin *interrare,* from *in-* + Latin *terra* earth — more at TERRACE] (14th century)
: to deposit (a dead body) in the earth or in a tomb

inter- *prefix* [Middle English *inter-, enter-,* from Middle French & Latin; Middle French *inter-, entre-,* from Latin *inter-,* from *inter;* akin to Old High German *untar* among, Greek *enteron* intestine, Old English *in* in]
1 : between **:** among **:** in the midst ⟨*inter*crop⟩ ⟨*inter*penetrate⟩ ⟨*inter*stellar⟩
2 : reciprocal ⟨*inter*relation⟩ **:** reciprocally ⟨*inter*marry⟩
3 : located between ⟨*inter*face⟩
4 : carried on between ⟨*inter*national⟩
5 : occurring between ⟨*inter*borough⟩ **:** intervening ⟨*inter*glacial⟩
6 : shared by, involving, or derived from two or more ⟨*inter*faith⟩
7 : between the limits of **:** within ⟨*inter*tropical⟩
8 : existing between ⟨*inter*communal⟩ ⟨*inter*company⟩

in·ter–Af·ri·can
in·ter·agen·cy
in·ter·al·le·lic
in·ter–Amer·i·can
in·ter·an·i·ma·tion
in·ter·an·nu·al
in·ter·as·so·ci·a·tion
in·ter·atom·ic
in·ter·avail·abil·i·ty
in·ter·bank
in·ter·ba·sin
in·ter·bed
in·ter·be·hav·ior
in·ter·be·hav·ior·al
in·ter·bor·ough
in·ter·branch
in·ter·cal·i·bra·tion
in·ter·cam·pus
in·ter·caste
in·ter·cell
in·ter·cel·lu·lar
in·ter·chain
in·ter·chan·nel
in·ter·chro·mo·som·al
in·ter·church
in·ter·city
in·ter·clan
in·ter·class
in·ter·club
in·ter·clus·ter
in·ter·coast·al
in·ter·co·lo·nial
in·ter·com·mu·nal
in·ter·com·mu·ni·ty
in·ter·com·pa·ny

in·ter·com·pare
in·ter·com·par·i·son
in·ter·com·pre·hen·si·bil·i·ty
in·ter·cor·po·rate
in·ter·cor·re·late
in·ter·cor·re·la·tion
in·ter·cor·ti·cal
in·ter·coun·try
in·ter·coun·ty
in·ter·cou·ple
in·ter·cra·ter
in·ter·crys·tal·line
in·ter·cul·tur·al
in·ter·cul·tur·al·ly
in·ter·cul·ture
in·ter·deal·er
in·ter·de·nom·i·na·tion·al
in·ter·de·part·men·tal
in·ter·de·part·men·tal·ly
in·ter·de·pend
in·ter·de·pen·dence
in·ter·de·pen·den·cy
in·ter·de·pen·dent
in·ter·de·pen·dent·ly
in·ter·di·a·lec·tal
in·ter·dis·trict
in·ter·di·vi·sion·al
in·ter·do·min·ion
in·ter·elec·trode
in·ter·elec·tron
in·ter·elec·tron·ic
in·ter·ep·i·dem·ic
in·ter·eth·nic

in·ter·fac·ul·ty
in·ter·fa·mil·ial
in·ter·fam·i·ly
in·ter·fi·ber
in·ter·firm
in·ter·flow
in·ter·flu·vi·al
in·ter·fold
in·ter·fra·ter·ni·ty
in·ter·gang
in·ter·gen·er·a·tion
in·ter·gen·er·a·tion·al
in·ter·gen·er·ic
in·ter·graft
in·ter·gran·u·lar
in·ter·group
in·ter·hemi·spher·ic
in·ter·in·di·vid·u·al
in·ter·in·dus·try
in·ter·in·flu·ence
in·ter·in·sti·tu·tion·al
in·ter·in·volve
in·ter·ion·ic
in·ter·is·land
in·ter·ju·ris·dic·tion·al
in·ter·la·cus·trine
in·ter·lam·i·nar
in·ter·lay
in·ter·lay·er
in·ter·lend
in·ter·li·brary
in·ter·lin·er
in·ter·lob·u·lar
in·ter·lo·cal
in·ter·male
in·ter·mar·gin·al
in·ter·mem·brane
in·ter·men·stru·al
in·ter·min·is·te·ri·al
in·ter·mi·tot·ic
in·ter·mo·lec·u·lar
in·ter·mo·lec·u·lar·ly
in·ter·moun·tain
in·ter·nu·cle·ar
in·ter·nu·cle·on
in·ter·nu·cle·o·tide
in·ter·ob·serv·er

in·ter·ocean
in·ter·oce·an·ic
in·ter·of·fice
in·ter·op·er·a·tive
in·ter·or·bit·al
in·ter·or·gan
in·ter·or·ga·ni·za·tion·al
in·ter·pan·dem·ic
in·ter·par·ish
in·ter·pa·ro·chi·al
in·ter·par·ox·ys·mal
in·ter·par·ti·cle
in·ter·par·ty
in·ter·per·cep·tu·al
in·ter·per·me·ate
in·ter·pha·lan·ge·al
in·ter·plan·e·tary
in·ter·plu·vi·al
in·ter·point
in·ter·pop·u·la·tion
in·ter·pop·u·la·tion·al
in·ter·pro·fes·sion·al
in·ter·pro·vin·cial
in·ter·psy·chic
in·ter·re·gion·al
in·ter·re·li·gious
in·ter·re·nal
in·ter·row
in·ter·school
in·ter·sec·tion·al
in·ter·seg·ment
in·ter·seg·men·tal
in·ter·sen·so·ry
in·ter·so·ci·etal
in·ter·so·ci·ety
in·ter·stage
in·ter·sta·tion
in·ter·stim·u·la·tion
in·ter·stim·u·lus
in·ter·strain
in·ter·strand
in·ter·strat·i·fi·ca·tion
in·ter·strat·i·fy
in·ter·sub·sti·tut·abil·i·ty
in·ter·sub·sti·tut·able
in·ter·sys·tem
in·ter·term

☆ SYNONYMS
Intention, intent, purpose, design, aim, end, object, objective, goal mean what one intends to accomplish or attain. INTENTION implies little more than what one has in mind to do or bring about ⟨announced his *intention* to marry⟩. INTENT suggests clearer formulation or greater deliberateness ⟨the clear *intent* of the statute⟩. PURPOSE suggests a more settled determination ⟨being successful was her *purpose* in life⟩. DESIGN implies a more carefully calculated plan ⟨the order of events came by accident, not *design*⟩. AIM adds to these implications of effort directed toward attaining or accomplishing ⟨her *aim* was to raise film to an art form⟩. END stresses the intended effect of action often in distinction or contrast to the action or means as such ⟨willing to use any means to achieve his *end*⟩. OBJECT may equal END but more often applies to a more individually determined wish or need ⟨his constant *object* was the achievement of pleasure⟩. OBJECTIVE implies something tangible and immediately attainable ⟨their *objective* is to seize the oil fields⟩. GOAL suggests something attained only by prolonged effort and hardship ⟨worked years to reach her *goals*⟩.

in·ter·ter·mi·nal
in·ter·ter·ri·to·ri·al
in·ter·trans·lat·able
in·ter·tri·al
in·ter·trib·al
in·ter·troop
in·ter·union
in·ter·unit
in·ter·uni·ver·si·ty
in·ter·ur·ban
in·ter·val·ley

in·ter·ven·tric·u·lar
in·ter·ver·te·bral
in·ter·vil·lage
in·ter·vis·i·bil·i·ty
in·ter·vis·i·ble
in·ter·vis·i·ta·tion
in·ter·war
in·ter·work
in·ter·work·ing
in·ter·zon·al
in·ter·zone

in·ter·a·bang *variant of* INTERROBANG
in·ter·act \,in-tə-'rakt\ *intransitive verb* (1839)
: to act upon one another
in·ter·ac·tant \-'rak-tənt\ *noun* (1949)
: one that interacts
in·ter·ac·tion \,in-tə-'rak-shən\ *noun* (1832)
: mutual or reciprocal action or influence
— **in·ter·ac·tion·al** \-shnəl, -shə-n°l\ *adjective*
in·ter·ac·tive \-'rak-tiv\ *adjective* (1832)
1 : mutually or reciprocally active
2 : of, relating to, or being a two-way electronic communication system (as a telephone, cable television, or a computer) that involves a user's orders (as for information or merchandise) or responses (as to a poll)
— **in·ter·ac·tive·ly** *adverb*
in·ter alia \,in-tər-'ā-lē-ə, -'ä-\ *adverb* [Latin] (1665)
: among other things
in·ter ali·os \-lē-,ōs\ *adverb* [Latin] (circa 1670)
: among other persons
in·ter·al·lied \,in-tər-'a,-līd, -ə-'līd\ *adjective* (1917)
: relating to, composed of, or involving allies
in·ter·breed \,in-tər-'brēd\ *verb* **-bred** \-'bred\; **-breed·ing** (1859)
intransitive verb
: to breed together: as **a** : CROSSBREED **b** : to breed within a closed population
transitive verb
: to cause to breed together
in·ter·ca·la·ry \in-'tər-kə-,ler-ē, ,in-tər-'ka-lə-rē\ *adjective* [Latin *intercalarius*, from *intercalare*] (1614)
1 a : inserted in a calendar ⟨an *intercalary* day⟩ **b** *of a year* : containing an intercalary period (as a day or month)
2 : inserted between other things or parts : INTERPOLATED
in·ter·ca·late \in-'tər-kə-,lāt\ *transitive verb* **-lat·ed; -lat·ing** [Latin *intercalatus*, past participle of *intercalare*, from *inter-* + *calare* to proclaim, call — more at LOW] (1603)
1 : to insert (as a day) in a calendar
2 : to insert between or among existing elements or layers
synonym see INTRODUCE
— **in·ter·ca·la·tion** \-,tər-kə-'lā-shən\ *noun*
in·ter·cede \,in-tər-'sēd\ *intransitive verb* **-ced·ed; -ced·ing** [Latin *intercedere*, from *inter-* + *cedere* to go] (1597)
: to intervene between parties with a view to reconciling differences : MEDIATE
synonym see INTERPOSE
— **in·ter·ced·er** *noun*
in·ter·cen·sal \,in-tər-'sen(t)-səl\ *adjective* (1887)
: occurring between censuses ⟨*intercensal* estimates⟩ ⟨*intercensal* period⟩
¹in·ter·cept \,in-tər-'sept\ *transitive verb* [Middle English, from Latin *interceptus*, past participle of *intercipere*, from *inter-* + *capere* to take, seize — more at HEAVE] (15th century)
1 *obsolete* : PREVENT, HINDER
2 a : to stop, seize, or interrupt in progress or course or before arrival **b** : to receive (a communication or signal directed elsewhere) usually secretly
3 *obsolete* : to interrupt communication or connection with

4 : to include (part of a curve, surface, or solid) between two points, curves, or surfaces ⟨the part of a circumference *intercepted* between two radii⟩
5 a : to gain possession of (an opponent's pass) **b** : to intercept a pass thrown by (an opponent)
²in·ter·cept \'in-tər-,sept\ *noun* (1821)
1 : the distance from the origin to a point where a graph crosses a coordinate axis
2 : INTERCEPTION; *especially* : the interception of a missile by an interceptor or of a target by a missile
3 : a message, code, or signal that is intercepted (as by monitoring radio communications)
in·ter·cep·tion \,in-tər-'sep-shən\ *noun* (15th century)
1 a : the action of intercepting **b** : the state of being intercepted
2 : something that is intercepted; *especially* : an intercepted forward pass
in·ter·cep·tor *also* **in·ter·cept·er** \,in-tər-'sep-tər\ *noun* (1598)
: one that intercepts; *specifically* : a light high-speed fast-climbing fighter plane or missile designed for defense against raiding bombers or missiles
in·ter·ces·sion \,in-tər-'se-shən\ *noun* [Middle English, from Middle French or Latin; Middle French, from Latin *intercession-, intercessio*, from *intercedere*] (15th century)
1 : the act of interceding
2 : prayer, petition, or entreaty in favor of another
— **in·ter·ces·sion·al** \-'sesh-nəl, -'se-shə-n°l\ *adjective*
— **in·ter·ces·sor** \-'se-sər\ *noun*
— **in·ter·ces·so·ry** \-'ses-rē, -'se-sə-rē\ *adjective*
¹in·ter·change \,in-tər-'chānj\ *verb* [Middle English *entrechaungen*, from Middle French *entrechangier*, from Old French, from *entre-* inter- + *changier* to change] (14th century)
transitive verb
1 : to put each of (two things) in the place of the other
2 : EXCHANGE
intransitive verb
: to change places mutually
— **in·ter·chang·er** *noun*
²in·ter·change \'in-tər-,chānj\ *noun* (15th century)
1 : the act, process, or an instance of interchanging : EXCHANGE
2 : a junction of two or more highways by a system of separate levels that permit traffic to pass from one to another without the crossing of traffic streams
in·ter·change·able \,in-tər-'chān-jə-bəl\ *adjective* (14th century)
: capable of being interchanged; *especially* : permitting mutual substitution ⟨*interchange-able* parts⟩
— **in·ter·change·abil·i·ty** \-,chān-jə-'bi-lə-tē\ *noun*
— **in·ter·change·able·ness** \-'chān-jə-bəl-nəs\ *noun*
— **in·ter·change·ably** \-blē\ *adverb*
in·ter·col·le·giate \,in-tər-kə-'lē-jət, -jē-ət\ *adjective* (circa 1874)
: existing, carried on, or participating in activities between colleges ⟨*intercollegiate* athletics⟩
in·ter·co·lum·ni·a·tion \,in-tər-kə-,ləm-nē-'ā-shən\ *noun* [Latin *intercolumnium* space between two columns, from *inter-* + *columna* column] (1624)
1 : the clear space between the columns of a series
2 : the system of spacing of the columns of a colonnade
in·ter·com \'in-tər-,käm\ *noun* [short for *intercommunication system*] (1940)
: a two-way communication system with a microphone and loudspeaker at each station for localized use

in·ter·com·mu·ni·cate \,in-tər-kə-'myü-nə-,kāt\ *intransitive verb* (1586)
1 : to exchange communication with one another
2 : to afford passage from one to another
— **in·ter·com·mu·ni·ca·tion** \-,myü-nə-'kā-shən\ *noun*
intercommunication system *noun* (1911)
: INTERCOM
in·ter·com·mu·nion \,in-tər-kə-'myü-nyən\ *noun* (1921)
: interdenominational participation in communion
in·ter·con·nect \,in-tər-kə-'nekt\ (1865)
transitive verb
: to connect with one another
intransitive verb
: to be or become mutually connected
— **in·ter·con·nec·tion** \-'nek-shən\ *noun*
interconnected *adjective* (1865)
1 : mutually joined or related ⟨*interconnected* highways⟩ ⟨*interconnected* political issues⟩
2 : having internal connections between the parts or elements
— **in·ter·con·nec·ted·ness** *noun*
in·ter·con·ti·nen·tal \,in-tər-,kän-t°n-'en-t°l\ *adjective* (circa 1855)
1 : extending among continents or carried on between continents
2 : capable of traveling between continents ⟨*intercontinental* ballistic missile⟩
in·ter·con·ver·sion \,in-tər-kən-'vər-zhən, -shən\ *noun* (1865)
: mutual conversion ⟨*interconversion* of chemical compounds⟩
— **in·ter·con·vert** \-'vərt\ *transitive verb*
— **in·ter·con·vert·ibil·i·ty** \-,vər-tə-'bi-lə-tē\ *noun*
— **in·ter·con·vert·ible** \-'vər-tə-bəl\ *adjective*
in·ter·cool·er \,in-tər-'kü-lər\ *noun* (1899)
: a device for cooling a fluid (as air) between successive heat-generating processes
in·ter·cos·tal \,in-tər-'käs-t°l\ *adjective* [New Latin *intercostalis*, from Latin *inter-* + *costa* rib — more at COAST] (1597)
: situated or extending between the ribs ⟨*intercostal* spaces⟩ ⟨*intercostal* muscles⟩
— **intercostal** *noun*
in·ter·course \'in-tər-,kōrs, -,kȯrs\ *noun* [Middle English *intercurse*, probably from Middle French *entrecours*, from Medieval Latin *intercursus*, from Latin, act of running between, from *intercurrere* to run between, from *inter-* + *currere* to run — more at CAR] (15th century)
1 : connection or dealings between persons or groups
2 : exchange especially of thoughts or feelings : COMMUNION
3 : physical sexual contact between individuals that involves the genitalia of at least one person ⟨heterosexual *intercourse*⟩ ⟨anal *intercourse*⟩ ⟨oral *intercourse*⟩; *especially* : SEXUAL INTERCOURSE 1
in·ter·crop \,in-tər-'kräp, 'in-tər-,\ (1898)
transitive verb
: to grow a crop in between (another)
intransitive verb
: to grow two or more crops simultaneously (as in alternate rows) on the same plot
— **in·ter·crop** \'in-tər-,kräp\ *noun*
¹in·ter·cross \,in-tər-'krȯs\ *verb* (1711)
: CROSS
²in·ter·cross \'in-tər-,krȯs\ *noun* (1859)
: an instance or a product of crossbreeding
in·ter·cur·rent \,in-tər-'kər-ənt, -'kə-rənt\ *adjective* [Latin *intercurrent-, intercurrens*, present participle of *intercurrere*] (1611)
: occurring during and modifying the course of another disease ⟨an *intercurrent* infection⟩
in·ter·cut \,in-tər-'kət\ (1938)
transitive verb
1 : to insert (a contrasting camera shot) into a take by cutting

2 : to insert a contrasting camera shot into (a take) by cutting
intransitive verb
: to alternate contrasting camera shots by cutting

in·ter·den·tal \ˌin-tər-ˈden-tᵊl\ *adjective* (circa 1874)
1 : situated or intended for use between the teeth
2 : formed with the tip of the tongue between the upper and lower front teeth
— **in·ter·den·tal·ly** \-tᵊl-ē\ *adverb*

¹in·ter·dict \ˈin-tər-ˌdikt\ *noun* [Middle English, alteration of *entredit*, from Old French, from Latin *interdictum* prohibition, from neuter of *interdictus*, past participle of *interdicere* to interpose, forbid, from *inter-* + *dicere* to say — more at DICTION] (15th century)
1 : a Roman Catholic ecclesiastical censure withdrawing most sacraments and Christian burial from a person or district
2 : a prohibitory decree : PROHIBITION

²in·ter·dict \ˌin-tər-ˈdikt\ *transitive verb* (15th century)
1 : to lay under or prohibit by an interdict
2 : to forbid in a usually formal or authoritative manner
3 : to destroy, damage, or cut off (as an enemy line of supply) by firepower to stop or hamper an enemy
synonym see FORBID
— **in·ter·dic·tion** \-ˈdik-shən\ *noun*
— **in·ter·dic·tive** \-ˈdik-tiv\ *adjective*
— **in·ter·dic·tor** \-tər\ *noun*
— **in·ter·dic·to·ry** \-t(ə-)rē\ *adjective*

in·ter·dif·fu·sion \-di-ˈfyü-zhən\ *noun* (circa 1872)
: the process of diffusing and mixing freely so as to approach a homogeneous mixture
— **in·ter·dif·fuse** \-ˈfyüz\ *transitive verb*

in·ter·dig·i·tate \-ˈdi-jə-ˌtāt\ *intransitive verb* **-tat·ed; -tat·ing** [*inter-* + Latin *digitus* finger — more at TOE] (circa 1849)
: to become interlocked like the fingers of folded hands
— **in·ter·dig·i·ta·tion** \-ˌdi-jə-ˈtā-shən\ *noun*

in·ter·dis·ci·plin·ary \-ˈdi-sə-plə-ˌner-ē\ *adjective* (1926)
: involving two or more academic, scientific, or artistic disciplines

¹in·ter·est \ˈin-t(ə-)rəst; ˈin-tə-ˌrest, -ˌtrest; ˈin-tərst\ *noun* [Middle English, probably alteration of earlier *interesse*, from Anglo-French & Medieval Latin; Anglo-French, from Medieval Latin, from Latin, to be between, make a difference, concern, from *inter-* + *esse* to be — more at IS] (15th century)
1 a (1) **:** right, title, or legal share in something (2) **:** participation in advantage and responsibility **b :** BUSINESS, COMPANY
2 a : a charge for borrowed money generally a percentage of the amount borrowed **b :** an excess above what is due or expected ⟨returned the insults with *interest*⟩
3 : ADVANTAGE, BENEFIT; *also* : SELF-INTEREST
4 : SPECIAL INTEREST
5 a : a feeling that accompanies or causes special attention to an object or class of objects : CONCERN **b :** something that arouses such attention **c :** a quality in a thing arousing interest

²interest *transitive verb* (1608)
1 : to induce or persuade to participate or engage
2 : to engage the attention or arouse the interest of

in·ter·est·ed *adjective* (1602)
1 : having the attention engaged ⟨*interested* listeners⟩
2 : being affected or involved ⟨*interested* parties⟩
— **in·ter·est·ed·ly** *adverb*
interest group *noun* (1908)

: a group of persons having a common identifying interest that often provides a basis for action

in·ter·est·ing \ˈin-t(ə-)rəs-tiŋ; ˈin-tə-ˌres-, ˈin-ˌtres-; ˈin-tərs-\ *adjective* (1768)
: holding the attention : arousing interest
— **in·ter·est·ing·ness** *noun*

in·ter·est·ing·ly \-lē\ *adverb* (1811)
1 : in an interesting manner
2 : as a matter of interest

¹in·ter·face \ˈin-tər-ˌfās\ *noun* (1882)
1 : a surface forming a common boundary of two bodies, spaces, or phases ⟨an oil-water *interface*⟩
2 a : the place at which independent and often unrelated systems meet and act on or communicate with each other ⟨the man-machine *interface*⟩ **b :** the means by which interaction or communication is achieved at an interface
— **in·ter·fa·cial** \ˌin-tər-ˈfā-shəl\ *adjective*

²interface (1962)
transitive verb
1 : to connect by means of an interface ⟨*interface* a machine with a computer⟩
2 : to serve as an interface for
intransitive verb
1 : to become interfaced
2 : to interact or coordinate harmoniously

in·ter·fac·ing \-ˈfā-siŋ\ *noun* (1942)
: fabric sewn between the facing and the outside of a garment (as in a collar or cuff) for stiffening and shape retention

in·ter·faith \ˌin-tər-ˈfāth\ *adjective* (1932)
: involving persons of different religious faiths

in·ter·fere \ˌin-tə(r)-ˈfir\ *intransitive verb* **-fered; -fer·ing** [Middle English *enterferen*, from Middle French (*s'*)*entreferir* to strike one another, from Old French, from *entre-* inter- + *ferir* to strike, from Latin *ferire* — more at BORE] (15th century)
1 : to interpose in a way that hinders or impedes : come into collision or be in opposition
2 : to strike one foot against the opposite foot or ankle in walking or running — used especially of horses
3 : to enter into or take a part in the concerns of others
4 : to act reciprocally so as to augment, diminish, or otherwise affect one another — used of waves
synonym see INTERPOSE
— **in·ter·fer·er** *noun*

in·ter·fer·ence \-ˈfir-ən(t)s\ *noun* (1783)
1 a : the act or process of interfering **b :** something that interferes : OBSTRUCTION
2 : the mutual effect on meeting of two wave trains (as of light or sound) that constitutes alternating areas of increased and decreased amplitude (as light and dark lines or louder and softer sound)
3 a : the legal blocking of an opponent in football to make way for the ballcarrier **b :** the illegal hindering of an opponent in sports
4 : partial or complete inhibition or sometimes facilitation of other genetic crossovers in the vicinity of a chromosomal locus where a preceding crossover has occurred
5 a : confusion of a received radio signal due to the presence of noise (as atmospherics) or signals from two or more transmitters on a single frequency **b :** something that produces such confusion
6 : the disturbing effect of new learning on the performance of previously learned behavior with which it is inconsistent
— **in·ter·fer·en·tial** \-fə-ˈren(t)-shəl, -ˌfir-ˈen(t)-\ *adjective*

in·ter·fer·o·gram \ˌin-tə(r)-ˈfir-ə-ˌgram\ *noun* (1921)
: a photographic record made by an apparatus for recording optical interference phenomena

in·ter·fer·om·e·ter \ˌin-tə(r)-fə-ˈrä-mə-tər, -ˌfi-ˈrä-\ *noun* [International Scientific Vocabulary] (1897)

: an instrument that utilizes the interference of waves (as of light) for precise determinations (as of distance or wavelength)
— **in·ter·fer·o·met·ric** \-ˌfir-ə-ˈme-trik\ *adjective*
— **in·ter·fer·o·met·ri·cal·ly** \-tri-k(ə-)lē\ *adverb*
— **in·ter·fer·om·e·try** \-fə-ˈrä-mə-trē, -ˌfi-ˈrä-\ *noun*

in·ter·fer·on \ˌin-tə(r)-ˈfir-ˌän\ *noun* [*interfere* + ²*-on*] (1957)
: any of a group of heat-stable soluble basic antiviral glycoproteins of low molecular weight that are produced usually by cells exposed to the action of a virus, sometimes to the action of another intracellular parasite (as a bacterium), or experimentally to the action of some chemicals

in·ter·fer·tile \ˌin-tər-ˈfər-tᵊl\ *adjective* (1899)
: capable of interbreeding
— **in·ter·fer·til·i·ty** \-(ˌ)fər-ˈti-lə-tē\ *noun*

in·ter·file \ˌin-tər-ˈfī(ə)l\ *transitive verb* (1950)
: to arrange in or add to a file : FILE

in·ter·fluve \ˈin-tər-ˌflüv\ *noun* [*inter-* + Latin *fluvius* river — more at FLUVIAL] (1895)
: the area between adjacent streams flowing in the same direction

in·ter·fuse \ˌin-tər-ˈfyüz\ *verb* [Latin *interfusus*, past participle of *interfundere* to pour between, from *inter-* + *fundere* to pour — more at FOUND] (1593)
transitive verb
1 : to combine by fusing : BLEND
2 : to add as if by fusing : INFUSE
intransitive verb
: BLEND, FUSE
— **in·ter·fu·sion** \-ˈfyü-zhən\ *noun*

in·ter·ga·lac·tic \ˌin-tər-gə-ˈlak-tik\ *adjective* (1928)
1 : situated in or relating to the spaces between galaxies
2 : of, relating to, or occurring in outer space ⟨*intergalactic* battles⟩

in·ter·gla·cial \-ˈglā-shəl\ *noun* (1867)
: a warm period between glacial epochs
— **interglacial** *adjective*

in·ter·gov·ern·men·tal \-ˌgə-vər(n)-ˈmen-tᵊl\ *adjective* (1927)
: existing or occurring between two or more governments or levels of government

in·ter·gra·da·tion \-grā-ˈdā-shən, -grə-\ *noun* (1874)
: the condition of an individual or population that intergrades
— **in·ter·gra·da·tion·al** \-shnəl, -shə-nᵊl\ *adjective*

¹in·ter·grade \ˌin-tər-ˈgrād\ *intransitive verb* (1874)
: to merge gradually one with another through a continuous series of intermediate forms

²in·ter·grade \ˈin-tər-ˌgrād\ *noun* (1888)
: an intermediate form

in·ter·growth \ˈin-tər-ˌgrōth\ *noun* (1844)
: a growing between or together; *also* : the product of such growth

¹in·ter·im \ˈin-tə-rəm\ *noun* [Latin, adverb, meanwhile, from *inter* between — more at INTER-] (circa 1580)
: an intervening time : INTERVAL

²interim *adjective* (1604)
: done, made, appointed, or occurring for an interim

¹in·te·ri·or \in-ˈtir-ē-ər\ *adjective* [Middle French & Latin; Middle French, from Latin, comparative of (assumed) Old Latin *interus* inward, on the inside; akin to Latin *inter*] (15th century)
1 : lying, occurring, or functioning within the limiting boundaries : INNER ⟨an *interior* point of a triangle⟩

2 : belonging to mental or spiritual life ⟨a simple *interior* piety⟩
3 : belonging to the inner constitution or concealed nature of something ⟨*interior* meaning of a poem⟩
4 : lying away or remote from the border or shore
— **in·te·ri·or·ly** \in-'tir-ē-ər-lē\ *adverb*

²interior *noun* (1596)
1 : the inner or spiritual nature **:** CHARACTER
2 : the interior part (as of a country or island)
3 : the internal or inner part of a thing **:** INSIDE
4 : the internal affairs of a state or nation
5 : a representation (as in a play or movie) of the interior of a building

interior angle *noun* (1756)
1 : the inner of the two angles formed where two sides of a polygon come together
2 : any of the four angles formed in the area between a pair of parallel lines when a third line cuts them

agh, bgh, ghd, ghc
interior angle 2

interior decoration *noun* (1807)
: INTERIOR DESIGN

interior decorator *noun* (1867)
: INTERIOR DESIGNER, DECORATOR

interior design *noun* (1927)
: the art or practice of planning and supervising the design and execution of architectural interiors and their furnishings

interior designer *noun* (1938)
: one who specializes in interior design

in·te·ri·or·ise *British variant of* INTERIORIZE

in·te·ri·or·i·ty \(,)in-,tir-ē-'ȯr-ə-tē, -'är-\ *noun* (1701)
: interior quality or character; *also* **:** inner life or substance ⟨characters that lack *interiority*⟩

in·te·ri·or·ize \in-'tir-ē-ə-,rīz\ *transitive verb* **-ized; -iz·ing** (1906)
: to make interior; *especially* **:** to make a part of one's own inner being or mental structure
— **in·te·ri·or·i·za·tion** \-,tir-ē-ə-rə-'zā-shən\ *noun*

interior monologue *noun* (1922)
: a usually extended representation in monologue of a fictional character's thought and feeling

in·ter·ject \in-tər-'jekt\ *transitive verb* [Latin *interjectus*, past participle of *intericere*, from *inter-* + *jacere* to throw — more at JET] (1588)
: to throw in between or among other things **:** INTERPOLATE ⟨*interject* a remark⟩
synonym see INTRODUCE
— **in·ter·jec·tor** \-'jek-tər\ *noun*
— **in·ter·jec·to·ry** \-t(ə-)rē\ *adjective*

in·ter·jec·tion \,int-ər-'jek-shən\ *noun* (15th century)
1 a : the act of uttering exclamations **:** EJACULATION **b :** the act of putting in between **:** INTERPOSITION
2 : an ejaculatory utterance usually lacking grammatical connection: as **a :** a word or phrase used in exclamation ⟨as *Heavens! Dear me!*⟩ **b :** a cry or inarticulate utterance ⟨as *Alas! ouch! phooey! ugh!*⟩ expressing an emotion
3 : something that is interjected or that interrupts

in·ter·jec·tion·al \-shnəl, -shə-nᵊl\ *adjective* (1761)
1 : of, relating to, or constituting an interjection **:** EJACULATORY
2 : thrown in between other words **:** PARENTHETICAL
— **in·ter·jec·tion·al·ly** *adverb*

in·ter·lace \,in-tər-'lās\ *verb* [Middle English *entrelacen*, from Middle French *entrelacer*, from Old French *entrelacier*, from *entre-* inter- + *lacier* to lace] (14th century)
transitive verb

1 : to unite by or as if by lacing together **:** INTERWEAVE
2 : to vary by alternation or intermixture **:** INTERSPERSE ⟨narrative *interlaced* with anecdotes⟩
intransitive verb
: to cross one another as if woven together **:** INTERTWINE
— **in·ter·lace·ment** \-mənt\ *noun*

in·ter·lard \,in-tər-'lärd\ *transitive verb* [Middle French *entrelarder*, from Old French, from *entre* inter- + *larder* to lard, from *lard,* noun] (circa 1587)
: to vary by intermixture **:** INTERSPERSE, INTERLACE

in·ter·leave \,in-tər-'lēv\ *transitive verb* **-leaved; -leav·ing** (1668)
: to arrange in or as if in alternate layers

in·ter·leu·kin \,in-tər-'lü-kən\ *noun* [*inter-* + *leuk-* + ¹*-in*] (1979)
: any of several compounds of low molecular weight that are produced by lymphocytes, macrophages, and monocytes and that function especially in regulation of the immune system and especially cell-mediated immunity

in·ter·leu·kin–1 \-'wən\ *noun* (1979)
: an interleukin produced especially by monocytes and macrophages that regulates immune responses by activating lymphocytes and mediates other biological processes (as the onset of fever) usually associated with infection and inflammation

in·ter·leu·kin–2 \-'tü\ *noun* (1979)
: an interleukin produced by antigen-stimulated helper T cells in the presence of interleukin-1 that induces proliferation of immune cells (as T cells and B cells) and is used experimentally especially in treating certain cancers

¹in·ter·line \,in-tər-'līn\ *transitive verb* [Middle English *enterlinen*, from Medieval Latin *interlineare*, from Latin *inter-* + *linea* line] (15th century)
: to insert between lines already written or printed
— **in·ter·lin·e·a·tion** \-,li-nē-'ā-shən\ *noun*

²interline *transitive verb* [Middle English, from *inter-* + *linen* to line] (15th century)
: to provide (a garment) with an interlining

³interline *adjective* (1897)
: relating to, involving, or carried by two or more transportation lines

¹in·ter·lin·ear \,in-tər-'li-nē-ər\ *adjective* [Middle English *interliniare*, from Medieval Latin *interlinearis*, from Latin *inter-* + *linea* line] (15th century)
1 : inserted between lines already written or printed
2 : written or printed in different languages or texts in alternate lines
— **in·ter·lin·ear·ly** *adverb*

²interlinear *noun* (1850)
: a book having interlinear matter; *especially* **:** a book in a foreign language with interlinear translation

in·ter·lin·ing \'in-tər-,lī-niŋ\ *noun* (1881)
: a lining (as of a coat) sewn between the ordinary lining and the outside fabric

in·ter·link \,in-tər-'liŋk\ *transitive verb* (1587)
: to link together
— **in·ter·link** \'in-tər-,liŋk\ *noun*

¹in·ter·lock \,in-tər-'läk\ (1632)
intransitive verb
: to become locked together or interconnected
transitive verb
1 : to lock together **:** UNITE
2 : to connect so that the motion or operation of any part is constrained by another

²in·ter·lock \'in-tər-,läk\ *noun* (1874)
1 : the quality, state, sense, or an instance of being interlocked
2 : an arrangement in which the operation of one part or mechanism automatically brings about or prevents the operation of another ⟨a safety *interlock*⟩

3 a : a stretchable fabric made on a circular knitting machine and consisting of two ribbed fabrics joined by interlocking **b :** a garment made of interlock

in·ter·loc·u·tor \,in-tər-'lä-kyə-tər\ *noun* [Latin *interloqui* to speak between, issue an interlocutory decree, from *inter-* + *loqui* to speak] (1514)
1 : one who takes part in dialogue or conversation
2 : a man in the middle of the line in a minstrel show who questions the end men and acts as leader

in·ter·loc·u·to·ry \-kyə-,tōr-ē, -,tȯr-\ *adjective* (15th century)
: pronounced during the progress of a legal action and having only provisional force ⟨*interlocutory* decree⟩

in·ter·lope \,in-tər-'lōp, 'in-tər-,\ *intransitive verb* **-loped; -lop·ing** [probably back-formation from *interloper*, from *inter-* + *-loper* (akin to Middle Dutch *lopen* to run, Old English *hlēapan* to leap) — more at LEAP] (1615)
1 : to encroach on the rights (as in trade) of others
2 : INTRUDE, INTERFERE

in·ter·lop·er \,in-tər-'lō-pər, 'in-tər-,\ *noun* (circa 1590)
: one that interlopes: as **a :** an illegal or unlicensed trader **b :** one that intrudes in a place or sphere of activity

in·ter·lude \'in-tər-,lüd\ *noun* [Middle English *enterlude*, from Medieval Latin *interludium*, from Latin *inter-* + *ludus* play — more at LUDICROUS] (14th century)
1 : a usually short simple play or dramatic entertainment
2 : an intervening or interruptive period, space, or event **:** INTERVAL
3 : a musical composition inserted between the parts of a longer composition, a drama, or a religious service

in·ter·lu·nar \,in-tər-'lü-nər\ *also* **in·ter·lu·na·ry** \-nə-rē\ *adjective* [probably from Middle French *interlunaire*, from Latin *interlunium* interlunar period, from *inter-* + *luna* moon — more at LUNAR] (1598)
: relating to the interval between old and new moon when the moon is invisible

in·ter·mar·riage \,in-tər-'mar-ij\ *noun* (1579)
1 : ENDOGAMY
2 : marriage between members of different groups

in·ter·mar·ry \-'mar-ē\ *intransitive verb* (1574)
1 a : to marry each other **b :** to marry within a group
2 : to become connected by intermarriage

in·ter·med·dle \,in-tər-'me-dᵊl\ *intransitive verb* [Middle English *entermedlen*, from Middle French *entremedler*, from Old French, from *entre-* inter- + *medler* to mix — more at MEDDLE] (15th century)
: to meddle impertinently and officiously and usually so as to interfere
— **in·ter·med·dler** \-'med-lər, -'me-dᵊl-ər\ *noun*

in·ter·me·di·a·cy \,in-tər-'mē-dē-ə-sē\ *noun* (1713)
1 : the act or action of intermediating
2 : the quality or state of being intermediate

¹in·ter·me·di·ary \,in-tər-'mē-dē-,er-ē\ *adjective* (1788)
1 : INTERMEDIATE
2 : acting as a mediator ⟨an *intermediary* agent⟩ ⟨an *intermediary* particle⟩

²intermediary *noun, plural* **-ar·ies** (1791)
1 a : MEDIATOR, GO-BETWEEN **b :** MEDIUM, MEANS
2 : an intermediate form, product, or stage

¹in·ter·me·di·ate \,in-tər-'mē-dē-ət\ *adjective* [Medieval Latin *intermediatus*, from Latin *intermedius*, from *inter-* + *medius* mid, middle — more at MID] (15th century)

1 : being or occurring at the middle place, stage, or degree or between extremes
2 : of or relating to an intermediate school ⟨an *intermediate* curriculum⟩
— **in·ter·me·di·ate·ly** *adverb*
— **in·ter·me·di·ate·ness** *noun*
²intermediate *noun* (1650)
1 : one that is intermediate
2 : MEDIATOR, GO-BETWEEN
3 a : a chemical compound synthesized from simpler compounds and usually intended to be used in later syntheses of more complex products **b :** a usually short-lived chemical species formed in a reaction as an intermediate step between the starting material and the final product
4 : an automobile larger than a compact but smaller than a full-sized automobile
³in·ter·me·di·ate \-dē-ˌāt\ *intransitive verb* [Medieval Latin *intermediatus*, past participle of *intermediare*, from Latin *inter-* + Late Latin *mediare* to mediate] (1610)
1 : INTERVENE, INTERPOSE
2 : to act as an intermediate
intermediate host *noun* (1878)
1 : a host which is normally used by a parasite in the course of its life cycle and in which it may multiply asexually but not sexually — compare DEFINITIVE HOST
2 a : RESERVOIR **3 b :** VECTOR
intermediate school *noun* (1842)
1 : JUNIOR HIGH SCHOOL
2 : a school usually comprising grades 4 to 6
intermediate vector boson *noun* (1968)
: any of three particles that mediate the weak force — called also *intermediate boson*; compare W PARTICLE, Z PARTICLE
in·ter·me·di·a·tion \ˌin-tər-ˌmē-dē-ˈā-shən\ *noun* (1602)
: the act of coming between : INTERVENTION, MEDIATION
in·ter·me·din \ˌin-tər-ˈmē-dᵊn\ *noun* (1932)
: MELANOCYTE-STIMULATING HORMONE
in·ter·ment \in-ˈtər-mənt\ *noun* (14th century)
: the act or ceremony of interring
in·ter·mesh \ˌin-tər-ˈmesh\ (circa 1903)
intransitive verb
: INTERLOCK
transitive verb
: to mesh together **:** INTERLOCK
in·ter·me·tal·lic \ˌin-tər-mə-ˈta-lik\ *adjective* (1900)
: composed of two or more metals or of a metal and a nonmetal; *especially* **:** being an alloy having a characteristic crystal structure and usually a definite composition ⟨*intermetallic* compound⟩
— **intermetallic** *noun*
in·ter·mez·zo \ˌin-tər-ˈmet-(ˌ)sō, -ˈmed-(ˌ)zō\ *noun, plural* **-zi** \-(ˌ)sē, -(ˌ)zē\ *or* **-zos** [Italian, ultimately from Latin *intermedius* intermediate] (1771)
1 : a short light entr'acte
2 a : a movement coming between the major sections of an extended musical work (as an opera) **b :** a short independent instrumental composition
3 : a usually brief interlude or diversion
in·ter·mi·na·ble \(ˌ)in-ˈtərm-nə-bəl, -ˈtər-mə-\ *adjective* [Middle English, from Late Latin *interminabilis*, from Latin *in-* + *terminare* to terminate] (15th century)
: having or seeming to have no end; *especially* **:** wearisomely protracted ⟨an *interminable* sermon⟩
— **in·ter·mi·na·ble·ness** *noun*
— **in·ter·mi·na·bly** \-blē\ *adverb*
in·ter·min·gle \ˌin-tər-ˈmiŋ-gəl\ *verb* (15th century)
: INTERMIX
in·ter·mis·sion \ˌin-tər-ˈmi-shən\ *noun* [Middle English *intermyssyown*, from Latin *intermission-, intermissio*, from *intermittere*] (15th century)
1 : the act of intermitting **:** the state of being intermitted

2 : an interval between the parts of an entertainment (as the acts of a play)
— **in·ter·mis·sion·less** *adjective*
in·ter·mit \-ˈmit\ *verb* **-mit·ted; -mit·ting** [Latin *intermittere*, from *inter-* + *mittere* to send] (circa 1542)
transitive verb
: to cause to cease for a time or at intervals **:** DISCONTINUE
intransitive verb
: to be intermittent
— **in·ter·mit·ter** *noun*
in·ter·mit·tence \-ˈmi-tən(t)s\ *noun* (1796)
: the quality or state of being intermittent
in·ter·mit·ten·cy \-ˈmi-tən(t)-sē\ *noun* (1662)
: INTERMITTENCE
in·ter·mit·tent \-ˈmi-tᵊnt\ *adjective* [Latin *intermittent-, intermittens*, present participle of *intermittere*] (1601)
: coming and going at intervals **:** not continuous ⟨*intermittent* rain⟩; *also* **:** OCCASIONAL ⟨*intermittent* trips abroad⟩
— **in·ter·mit·tent·ly** *adverb*
in·ter·mix \ˌin-tər-ˈmiks\ *verb* [back-formation from obsolete *intermixt* intermingled, from Latin *intermixtus*, past participle of *intermiscēre* to intermix, from *inter-* + *miscēre* to mix — more at MIX] (1542)
transitive verb
: to mix together
intransitive verb
: to become mixed together
— **in·ter·mix·ture** \-ˈmiks-chər\ *noun*
in·ter·mod·al \-ˈmō-dəl\ *adjective* (1963)
1 : being or involving transportation by more than one form of carrier during a single journey
2 : used for intermodal transport
in·ter·mod·u·la·tion \-ˌmä-jə-ˈlā-shən\ *noun* [International Scientific Vocabulary] (1931)
: the production in an electrical device of currents having frequencies equal to the sums and differences of frequencies supplied to the device or of their harmonics
in·ter·mon·tane \ˌin-tər-ˈmän-ˌtān\ *or* **in·ter·mont** \ˈin-tər-ˌmänt\ *adjective* [Latin *mont-, mons* mount] (1807)
: situated between mountains ⟨an *intermontane* basin⟩
¹in·tern *or* **in·terne** \ˈin-ˌtərn, ˈin-ˌ\ *adjective* [Middle French *interne*, from Latin *internus*] (circa 1500)
archaic **:** INTERNAL
²in·tern \ˈin-ˌtərn, in-ˈ\ *transitive verb* (1866)
: to confine or impound especially during a war ⟨intern enemy aliens⟩
— **in·tern·ee** \(ˌ)in-ˌtər-ˈnē\ *noun*
— **in·tern·ment** \in-ˈtərn-mənt, ˈin-ˌ\ *noun*
³in·tern *also* **in·terne** \ˈin-ˌtərn\ *noun* [French *interne*, from *interne*, adjective] (circa 1879)
: an advanced student or graduate usually in a professional field (as medicine or teaching) gaining supervised practical experience (as in a hospital or classroom)
— **in·tern·ship** \-ˌship\ *noun*
⁴in·tern \ˈin-ˌtərn\ *intransitive verb* (circa 1928)
: to act as an intern
in·ter·nal \in-ˈtər-nᵊl, ˈin-ˌ\ *adjective* [Middle English *internalle*, from Late Latin *internus*; akin to Latin *inter* between] (15th century)
1 : existing or situated within the limits or surface of something: as **a** (1) **:** situated near the inside of the body (2) **:** situated on the side toward the median plane of the body **b :** of, relating to, or occurring within the confines of an organized structure (as a club, company, or state) ⟨*internal* affairs⟩
2 : relating or belonging to or existing within the mind
3 : INTRINSIC, INHERENT ⟨*internal* evidence of forgery in a document⟩
4 : present or arising within an organism or one of its parts ⟨*internal* stimulus⟩

5 : applied or intended for application through the stomach by being swallowed ⟨an *internal* remedy⟩
— **in·ter·nal·i·ty** \ˌin-ˌtər-ˈna-lə-tē\ *noun*
— **in·ter·nal·ly** \in-ˈtər-nᵊl-ē\ *adverb*
internal combustion engine *noun* (1884)
: a heat engine in which the combustion that generates the heat takes place inside the engine proper instead of in a furnace
in·ter·nal·ise *British variant of* INTERNALIZE
in·ter·nal·ize \in-ˈtər-nᵊl-ˌīz\ *transitive verb* **-ized; -iz·ing** (1884)
: to give a subjective character to; *specifically* **:** to incorporate (as values or patterns of culture) within the self as conscious or subconscious guiding principles through learning or socialization
— **in·ter·nal·i·za·tion** \-ˌtər-nᵊl-ə-ˈzā-shən\ *noun*
internal medicine *noun* (circa 1904)
: a branch of medicine that deals with the diagnosis and treatment of diseases not requiring surgery
internal respiration *noun* (circa 1890)
: an exchange of gases between the cells of the body and the blood by way of the fluid bathing the cells — compare EXTERNAL RESPIRATION
internal rhyme *noun* (1903)
: rhyme between a word within a line and another either at the end of the same line or within another line
internal secretion *noun* (1895)
: HORMONE
¹in·ter·na·tion·al \ˌin-tər-ˈnash-nəl, -ˈna-shə-nᵊl\ *adjective* (1780)
1 : of, relating to, or affecting two or more nations ⟨*international* trade⟩
2 : of, relating to, or constituting a group or association having members in two or more nations ⟨*international* movement⟩
3 : active, known, or reaching beyond national boundaries ⟨an *international* reputation⟩
— **in·ter·na·tion·al·i·ty** \-ˌna-shə-ˈna-lə-tē\ *noun*
— **in·ter·na·tion·al·ly** \-ˈnash-nə-lē, -ˈna-shə-nᵊl-ē\ *adverb*
²international *noun* (1870)
: one that is international; *especially* **:** an organization of international scope
international date line *noun* (circa 1909)
: an arbitrary line approximately along the 180th meridian designated as the place where each calendar day begins
in·ter·na·tion·al·ise *British variant of* INTERNATIONALIZE
in·ter·na·tion·al·ism \-ˈnash-nə-ˌli-zəm, -ˈna-shə-nᵊl-ˌi-zəm\ *noun* (1851)
1 : international character, principles, interests, or outlook
2 a : a policy of cooperation among nations **b :** an attitude or belief favoring such a policy
— **in·ter·na·tion·al·ist** \-list, -ist\ *noun or adjective*
in·ter·na·tion·al·ize \ˌin-tər-ˈnash-nə-ˌlīz, -ˈna-shə-nᵊl-ˌīz\ *transitive verb* (circa 1864)
: to make international; *also* **:** to place under international control ⟨a proposal to *internationalize* the city⟩
— **in·ter·na·tion·al·i·za·tion** \-ˌnash-nə-lə-ˈzā-shən, -ˌna-shə-nᵊl-ə-\ *noun*
international law *noun* (circa 1828)
: a body of rules that control or affect the rights of nations in their relations with each other
International Phonetic Alphabet *noun* (1898)
: IPA
international pitch *noun* (1904)

: a tuning standard of 440 vibrations per second for A above middle C

international relations *noun plural but singular in construction* (1951)
: a branch of political science concerned with relations between nations and primarily with foreign policies

International Scientific Vocabulary *noun* (circa 1959)
: a part of the vocabulary of the sciences and other specialized studies that consists of words or other linguistic forms current in two or more languages and differing from New Latin in being adapted to the structure of the individual languages in which they appear

International Style *noun* (1932)
1 : a style in European art of the 14th and early 15th centuries marked by sinuous line, rich color, and decorative surface detail
2 : a style in architecture developed in the 1920s that uses modern materials (as steel, glass, and reinforced concrete), expresses structure directly, and eliminates nonstructural ornament

International System of Units *noun* (1961)
: a system of units based on the metric system and developed and refined by international convention especially for scientific work

international unit *noun* (1922)
: a quantity of a biologic (as a vitamin) that produces a particular biological effect agreed upon as an international standard

in·ter·ne·cine \,in-tər-'ne-,sēn, -'nē-s°n, -'nē-,sīn, -nə-'sēn; in-'tər-nə-,sēn\ *adjective* [Latin *internecinus*, from *internecare* to destroy, kill, from *inter-* + *necare* to kill, from *nec-*, *nex* violent death — more at NOXIOUS] (1663)
1 : marked by slaughter **:** DEADLY; *especially* **:** mutually destructive
2 : of, relating to, or involving conflict within a group ⟨bitter *internecine* feuds⟩ ◆

in·ter·neu·ron \,in-tər-'nùr-,än, -'nyùr-\ *noun* (1939)
: an internuncial neuron
— **in·ter·neu·ro·nal** \-'nùr-ə-n°l, -'nyùr-; -nù-'rō-, -nyù-'\ *adjective*

in·ter·nist \'in-,tər-nist\ *noun* (1904)
: a specialist in internal medicine

in·ter·node \'in-tər-,nōd\ *noun* [Latin *internodium*, from *inter-* + *nodus* knot] (1667)
: an interval or part between two nodes (as of a stem)
— **in·ter·nod·al** \,in-tər-'nō-d°l\ *adjective*

in·ter·nun·ci·al \,in-tər-'nən(t)-sē-əl, -'nùn(t)-\ *adjective* (1845)
1 : of or relating to an internuncio
2 : serving to link sensory and motor neurons

in·ter·nun·cio \,in-tər-'nən(t)-sē-,ō, -'nùn(t)-\ *noun* [Italian *internunzio*, from Latin *internuntius*, *internuncius*, from *inter-* + *nuntius*, *nuncius* messenger] (1641)
1 : a messenger between two parties **:** GO-BETWEEN
2 : a papal legate of lower rank than a nuncio

in·ter·o·cep·tive \,in-tə-rō-'sep-tiv\ *adjective* [*interior* + *-o-* + *-ceptive* (as in *receptive*)] (circa 1921)
: of, relating to, or being stimuli arising within the body and especially in the viscera

in·ter·o·cep·tor \-tər\ *noun* (1906)
: a sensory receptor excited by interoceptive stimuli

in·ter·op·er·a·bil·i·ty \,in-tə-,rä-p(ə-)rə-'bi-lə-tē\ *noun* (1977)
: ability of a system (as a weapons system) to use the parts or equipment of another system
— **in·ter·op·er·a·ble** \-'rä-p(ə-)rə-bəl\ *adjective*

in·ter·pel·late \in-tər-'pe-,lāt, -pə-'lāt\ *transitive verb* **-lat·ed; -lat·ing** [Latin *interpellatus*, past participle of *interpellare* to interrupt, from *inter-* + *-pellare* (from *pellere* to drive) — more at FELT] (1874)

: to question (as a foreign minister) formally concerning an official action or policy or personal conduct
— **in·ter·pel·la·tion** \-pə-'lā-shən\ *noun*
— **in·ter·pel·la·tor** \-'pe-,lā-tər, -pə-'lā-\ *noun*

in·ter·pen·e·trate \,in-tər-'pe-nə-,trāt\ (circa 1810)
intransitive verb
: to penetrate mutually
transitive verb
: to penetrate between, within, or throughout **:** PERMEATE
— **in·ter·pen·e·tra·tion** \-,pe-nə-'trā-shən\ *noun*

in·ter·per·son·al \-'pərs-nəl, -'pər-s°n-əl\ *adjective* (1842)
: being, relating to, or involving relations between persons
— **in·ter·per·son·al·ly** *adverb*

in·ter·phase \'in-tər-,fāz\ *noun* (1913)
: the interval between the end of one mitotic or meiotic division and the beginning of another

in·ter·plant \,in-tər-'plant\ *transitive verb* (1911)
: to plant a crop between (plants of another kind); *also* : to set out young trees among (existing growth)

in·ter·play \'in-tər-,plā\ *noun* (1862)
: INTERACTION ⟨the *interplay* of opposing forces⟩
— **in·ter·play** \,in-tər-', 'in-tər-,\ *intransitive verb*

in·ter·plead \,in-tər-'plēd\ *intransitive verb* [Anglo-French *enterpleder*, from *enter-* inter- + *pleder* to plead, from Old French *plaidier* — more at PLEAD] (1567)
: to go to trial with each other in order to determine a right on which the action of a third party depends

¹**in·ter·plead·er** \-'plē-dər\ *noun* [Anglo-French *enterpleder*, from *enterpleder*, verb] (1567)
: a proceeding to enable a person to compel parties making the same claim against him to litigate the matter between themselves

²**interpleader** *noun* (circa 1846)
: one that interpleads

in·ter·po·late \in-'tər-pə-,lāt\ *verb* **-lat·ed; -lat·ing** [Latin *interpolatus*, past participle of *interpolare* to refurbish, alter, interpolate, from *inter-* + *-polare* (from *polire* to polish)] (1612)
transitive verb
1 a : to alter or corrupt (as a text) by inserting new or foreign matter **b :** to insert (words) into a text or into a conversation
2 : to insert between other things or parts **:** INTERCALATE
3 : to estimate values of (a function) between two known values
intransitive verb
: to make insertions (as of estimated values)
synonym see INTRODUCE
— **in·ter·po·la·tion** \-,tər-pə-'lā-shən\ *noun*
— **in·ter·po·la·tive** \-'tər-pə-,lā-tiv\ *adjective*
— **in·ter·po·la·tor** \-,lā-tər\ *noun*

in·ter·pose \,in-tər-'pōz\ *verb* **-posed; -pos·ing** [Middle French *interposer*, from Latin *interponere* (perfect indicative *interposui*), from *inter-* + *ponere* to put — more at POSITION] (1582)
transitive verb
1 a : to place in an intervening position **b :** to put (oneself) between **:** INTRUDE
2 : to put forth by way of interference or intervention
3 : to introduce or throw in between the parts of a conversation or argument
intransitive verb
1 : to be or come between
2 : to step in between parties at variance **:** INTERVENE

3 : INTERRUPT ☆
— **in·ter·pos·er** *noun*

in·ter·po·si·tion \-pə-'zi-shən\ *noun* (14th century)
1 a : the act of interposing **b :** the action of a state whereby its sovereignty is placed between its citizens and the federal government
2 : something interposed

in·ter·pret \in-'tər-prət, -pət\ *verb* [Middle English, from Middle French & Latin; Middle French *interpreter*, from Latin *interpretari*, from *interpret-*, *interpres* agent, negotiator, interpreter] (14th century)
transitive verb
1 : to explain or tell the meaning of **:** present in understandable terms
2 : to conceive in the light of individual belief, judgment, or circumstance **:** CONSTRUE
3 : to represent by means of art **:** bring to realization by performance or direction ⟨*interprets* a role⟩
intransitive verb
: to act as an interpreter between speakers of different languages
synonym see EXPLAIN
— **in·ter·pret·abil·i·ty** \-,tər-prə-tə-'bi-lə-tē, -pə-tə-\ *noun*
— **in·ter·pret·able** \-'tər-prə-tə-bəl, -pə-tə-\ *adjective*

in·ter·pre·ta·tion \in-,tər-prə-'tā-shən, -pə-\ *noun* (14th century)
1 : the act or the result of interpreting **:** EXPLANATION
2 : a particular adaptation or version of a work, method, or style
3 : a teaching technique that combines factual with stimulating explanatory information ⟨natural history *interpretation* program⟩

☆ **SYNONYMS**
Interpose, interfere, intervene, mediate, intercede mean to come or go between. INTERPOSE often implies no more than this ⟨*interposed* herself between him and the door⟩. INTERFERE implies hindering ⟨noise *interfered* with my concentration⟩. INTERVENE may imply an occurring in space or time between two things or a stepping in to stop a conflict ⟨quarreled until the manager *intervened*⟩. MEDIATE implies intervening between hostile factions ⟨*mediated* between the parties⟩. INTERCEDE implies acting in behalf of an offender in begging mercy or forgiveness ⟨*interceded* on our behalf⟩. See in addition INTRODUCE.

◇ **WORD HISTORY**
internecine In Latin the verb *necare* meant "to kill" and the verb *internecare* "to kill without exception, massacre." In this instance the familiar Latin prefix *inter-* did not mean "between" but served to signify the completion of an action. The derivative adjective *internecinus* thus had the meaning of "fought to the death, devastating." In 1755, when Samuel Johnson published his great dictionary, it became clear that he had apparently interpreted the *inter-* of *internecine* as meaning "between" and so had defined the word as "endeavouring mutual destruction." In 1828, when Noah Webster defined *internecine*, he gave only the original sense of "deadly, destructive"; the Johnsonian sense of "mutually destructive" was not added until later revisions. Ironically, the invented Johnsonian sense won favor among the learned and superseded the original meaning entirely. In the 20th century the meaning of *internecine* was extended to include bitter—but bloodless—conflict within a group, and this has become the dominant sense.

— **in·ter·pre·ta·tion·al** \-shnəl, -shə-n°l\ *adjective*

— **in·ter·pre·ta·tive** \in-'tər-prə-ˌtā-tiv *also* -prə-tə-tiv\ *adjective*

— **in·ter·pre·ta·tive·ly** *adverb*

— **in·ter·pre·tive** \-'tər-prə-tiv, -pə-\ *adjective*

— **in·ter·pre·tive·ly** *adverb*

in·ter·pret·er \in-'tər-prə-tər, -pə-\ *noun* (14th century)
1 : one that interprets: as **a** : one who translates orally for parties conversing in different languages **b** : one who explains or expounds
2 a : a machine that prints on punched cards the symbols recorded in them by perforations **b** : a computer program that translates an instruction into machine language and executes it before going to the next instruction

in·ter·prox·i·mal \ˌin-tər-'präk-sə-məl\ *adjective* (1897)
: situated or used in the areas between adjoining teeth 〈*interproximal* space〉

in·ter·pu·pil·lary \in-tər-'pyü-pə-ˌler-ē\ *adjective* (circa 1904)
: extending between the pupils of the eyes; *also* : extending between the centers of a pair of spectacle lenses 〈*interpupillary* distance〉

in·ter·ra·cial \-'rā-shəl\ *adjective* (1888)
: of, involving, or designed for members of different races
— **in·ter·ra·cial·ly** \-shə-lē\ *adverb*

interred *past and past participle of* INTER

in·ter·reg·num \ˌin-tə-'reg-nəm\ *noun, plural* **-nums** *or* **-na** \-nə\ [Latin, from *inter-* + *regnum* reign — more at REIGN] (1590)
1 : the time during which a throne is vacant between two successive reigns or regimes
2 : a period during which the normal functions of government or control are suspended
3 : a lapse or pause in a continuous series

in·ter·re·late \ˌin-tə(r)-ri-'lāt\ (1888)
transitive verb
: to bring into mutual relation
intransitive verb
: to have mutual relationship
— **in·ter·re·la·tion** \-'lā-shən\ *noun*
— **in·ter·re·la·tion·ship** \-ˌship\ *noun*

in·ter·re·lat·ed \-'lā-təd\ *adjective* (1827)
: having a mutual or reciprocal relation
— **in·ter·re·lat·ed·ly** *adverb*
— **in·ter·re·lat·ed·ness** *noun*

interring *present participle of* INTER

in·ter·ro·bang \in-'ter-ə-ˌbaŋ\ *noun* [*interrogation* (point) + *bang* (printers' slang for *exclamation* point)] (1967)
: a punctuation mark ‽ designed for use especially at the end of an exclamatory rhetorical question

in·ter·ro·gate \in-'ter-ə-ˌgāt\ *transitive verb* **-gat·ed; -gat·ing** [Latin *interrogatus*, past participle of *interrogare*, from *inter-* + *rogare* to ask — more at RIGHT] (15th century)
1 : to question formally and systematically
2 : to give or send out a signal to (as a transponder or computer) for triggering an appropriate response
synonym see ASK
— **in·ter·ro·ga·tee** \-ˌter-ə-(ˌ)gā-'tē\ *noun*
— **in·ter·ro·ga·tion** \-ˌter-ə-'gā-shən\ *noun*
— **in·ter·ro·ga·tion·al** \-shnəl, -shə-n°l\ *adjective*

interrogation point *noun* (circa 1864)
: QUESTION MARK

¹in·ter·rog·a·tive \ˌin-tə-'rä-gə-tiv\ *adjective* (15th century)
1 a : used in a question **b** : having the form or force of a question
2 : INQUISITIVE, QUESTIONING
— **in·ter·rog·a·tive·ly** *adverb*

²interrogative *noun* (1522)
1 : a word (as *who, what, which*) or a particle (as Latin *-ne*) used in asking questions
2 : QUESTION 1a

in·ter·ro·ga·tor \in-'ter-ə-ˌgā-tər\ *noun* (1751)
1 : one that interrogates

2 : a radio transmitter and receiver for sending out a signal that triggers a transponder and for receiving and displaying the reply

¹in·ter·rog·a·to·ry \ˌin-tə-'rä-gə-ˌtōr-ē, -ˌtȯr-\ *noun, plural* **-ries** (1533)
: a formal question or inquiry; *especially* : a written question required to be answered under direction of a court

²interrogatory *adjective* (1576)
: INTERROGATIVE

in·ter·ro·gee \in-ˌter-ə-'gē\ *noun* (1919)
: one who is interrogated

¹in·ter·rupt \ˌin-tə-'rəpt\ *verb* [Middle English, from Latin *interruptus*, past participle of *interrumpere*, from *inter-* + *rumpere* to break — more at REAVE] (15th century)
transitive verb
1 : to stop or hinder by breaking in
2 : to break the uniformity or continuity of
intransitive verb
: to break in upon an action; *especially* : to break in with questions or remarks while another is speaking
— **in·ter·rupt·ible** \-'rəp-tə-bəl\ *adjective*
— **in·ter·rup·tion** \-'rəp-shən\ *noun*
— **in·ter·rup·tive** \-'rəp-tiv\ *adverb*

²in·ter·rupt \ˌin-tə-'rəpt, 'in-tə-ˌ\ *noun* (1957)
: a feature of a computer that permits the execution of a program to be interrupted in order to perform a special set of operations; *also* : the interruption itself

in·ter·rupt·er *or* **in·ter·rup·tor** \ˌin-tə-'rəp-tər\ *noun* (circa 1512)
: one that interrupts; *especially* : a device for interrupting an electric current usually automatically

in·ter·scho·las·tic \ˌin-tər-skə-'las-tik\ *adjective* (1879)
: existing or carried on between schools 〈*interscholastic* athletics〉

in·ter se \ˌin-tər-'sā, -'sē\ *adverb or adjective* [Latin] (1845)
: among or between themselves

in·ter·sect \ˌin-tər-'sekt\ *verb* [Latin *intersectus*, past participle of *intersecare*, from *inter-* + *secare* to cut — more at SAW] (1615)
transitive verb
: to pierce or divide by passing through or across : CROSS
intransitive verb
1 : to meet and cross at a point
2 : to share a common area : OVERLAP

in·ter·sec·tion \ˌin-tər-'sek-shən, *especially in sense 2* 'in-tər-ˌ\ *noun* (1559)
1 : the act or process of intersecting
2 : a place or area where two or more things (as streets) intersect
3 a : the set of elements common to two or more sets; *especially* : the set of points common to two geometric configurations **b** : the operation of finding the intersection of two or more sets

a intersection 3a

in·ter·ser·vice \ˌin-tər-'sər-vəs\ *adjective* (1946)
: existing between or relating to two or more of the armed services 〈*interservice* rivalry〉

in·ter·ses·sion \'in-tər-ˌse-shən\ *noun* (1932)
: a period between two academic sessions or terms sometimes utilized for brief concentrated courses

in·ter·sex \'in-tər-ˌseks\ *noun* [International Scientific Vocabulary] (1910)
: an intersexual individual

in·ter·sex·u·al \ˌin-tər-'sek-shə-wəl, -shwəl, -shəl\ *adjective* [International Scientific Vocabulary] (circa 1866)
1 : existing between sexes 〈*intersexual* hostility〉
2 : intermediate in sexual characters between a typical male and a typical female
— **in·ter·sex·u·al·i·ty** \-ˌsek-shə-'wa-lə-tē\ *noun*

— **in·ter·sex·u·al·ly** \-'sek-shə-wə-lē, -shwə-lē, -shə-lē\ *adverb*

¹in·ter·space \'in-tər-ˌspās\ *noun* (15th century)
: an intervening space : INTERVAL

²in·ter·space \ˌin-tər-'spās\ *transitive verb* (1685)
: to occupy or fill the space between

in·ter·spe·cif·ic \ˌin-tər-spi-'si-fik\ *also* **in·ter·spe·cies** \-'spē-(ˌ)shēz, -(ˌ)sēz\ *adjective* (1889)
: existing, occurring, or arising between species 〈*interspecific* hybrid〉

in·ter·sperse \ˌin-tər-'spərs\ *transitive verb* **-spersed; -spers·ing** [Latin *interspersus* interspersed, from *inter-* + *sparsus*, past participle of *spargere* to scatter — more at SPARK] (1566)
1 : to place something at intervals in or among
2 : to insert at intervals among other things 〈*interspersing* drawings throughout the text〉
— **in·ter·sper·sion** \-'spər-zhən, -shən\ *noun*

in·ter·sta·di·al \ˌin-tər-'stä-dē-əl\ *noun* [International Scientific Vocabulary *inter-* + New Latin *stadium* stage, phase, from Latin — more at STADIUM] (1914)
: a subdivision within a glacial stage marking a temporary retreat of the ice

¹in·ter·state \ˌin-tər-'stāt\ *adjective* (1844)
: of, connecting, or existing between two or more states especially of the U.S. 〈*interstate* commerce〉

²in·ter·state \'in-tər-ˌstāt\ *noun* (1968)
: any of a system of expressways connecting most major U.S. cities — called also *interstate highway*

in·ter·stel·lar \-'ste-lər\ *adjective* (1626)
: located, taking place, or traveling among the stars especially of the Milky Way galaxy

in·ter·ster·ile \-'ster-əl, *chiefly British* -ˌīl\ *adjective* (1916)
: incapable of producing offspring by interbreeding
— **in·ter·ste·ril·i·ty** \-stə-'ri-lə-tē\ *noun*

in·ter·stice \in-'tər-stəs\ *noun, plural* **-stic·es** \-stə-ˌsēz, -stə-səz\ [Middle English, from Latin *interstitium*, from *inter-* + *-stit-*, *-stes* standing (as in *superstes* standing over) — more at SUPERSTITION] (15th century)
1 a : a space that intervenes between things; *especially* : one between closely spaced things **b** : a gap or break in something generally continuous 〈the *interstices* of society〉 〈passages of genuine literary merit in the *interstices* of the ludicrous . . . plots —Joyce Carol Oates〉
2 : a short space of time between events

in·ter·sti·tial \ˌin-tər-'sti-shəl\ *adjective* (1646)
1 : relating to or situated in the interstices
2 a : situated within but not restricted to or characteristic of a particular organ or tissue — used especially of fibrous tissue **b** : affecting the interstitial tissues of an organ or part
3 : being or relating to a crystalline compound in which usually small atoms or ions of a nonmetal occupy holes between the larger metal atoms or ions in the crystal lattice
— **in·ter·sti·tial·ly** \-shə-lē\ *adverb*

in·ter·sub·jec·tive \ˌin-tər-səb-'jek-tiv\ *adjective* (1899)
1 : involving or occurring between separate conscious minds 〈*intersubjective* communication〉
2 : accessible to or capable of being established for two or more subjects : OBJECTIVE
— **in·ter·sub·jec·tive·ly** *adverb*
— **in·ter·sub·jec·tiv·i·ty** \-(ˌ)səb-ˌjek-'ti-və-tē\ *noun*

\ə\ **abut** \ə\ **kitten** \ər\ **further** \a\ **ash** \ā\ **ace**
\ä\ **mop, mar** \aů\ **out** \ch\ **chin** \e\ **bet** \ē\ **easy**
\g\ **go** \i\ **hit** \ī\ **ice** \j\ **job** \ŋ\ **sing** \ō\ **go**
\ȯ\ **law** \ȯi\ **boy** \th\ **thin** \th̲\ **the** \ü\ **loot** \ů\ **foot**
\y\ **yet** \zh\ **vision** *see also* Guide to Pronunciation

in·ter·tes·ta·men·tal \-,tes-tə-'men-t°l\ *adjective* (1929)
: of, relating to, or forming the period of two centuries between the composition of the last book of the Old Testament and the first book of the New Testament

in·ter·tid·al \-'tī-d°l\ *adjective* (1883)
: of, relating to, or being the part of the littoral zone above low-tide mark
— **in·ter·tid·al·ly** \-d°l-ē\ *adverb*

in·ter·tie \'in-tər-,tī\ *noun* (1951)
: an interconnection permitting passage of current between two or more electric utility systems

in·ter·till \,in-tər-'til\ *transitive verb* (1912)
: to cultivate between the rows of (a crop)
— **in·ter·till·age** \-'ti-lij\ *noun*

in·ter·trop·i·cal \-'trä-pi-kəl\ *adjective* (1794)
1 : situated between or within the tropics
2 : relating to regions within the tropics : TROPICAL

in·ter·twine \-'twīn\ (1641)
transitive verb
: to unite by twining one with another
intransitive verb
: to twine about one another; *also* : to become mutually involved
— **in·ter·twine·ment** \-mənt\ *noun*

in·ter·twist \-'twist\ *verb* (circa 1659)
: INTERTWINE
— **in·ter·twist** \'in-tər-,twist\ *noun*

in·ter·val \'in-tər-vəl\ *noun* [Middle English *intervalle*, from Middle French, from Latin *intervallum* space between ramparts, interval, from *inter-* + *vallum* rampart — more at WALL] (14th century)
1 a : a space of time between events or states **b** *British* : INTERMISSION
2 a : a space between objects, units, points, or states **b** : difference in pitch between tones
3 : a set of real numbers between two numbers either including or excluding one or both of them
4 : one of a series of fast-paced runs interspersed with jogging for training (as of a runner)
— **in·ter·val·ic** \,in-tər-'va-lik\ *adjective*

in·ter·vale \'in-tər-vəl, -,vāl\ *noun* [obsolete *intervale* interval] (1647)
chiefly New England : BOTTOMLAND

in·ter·val·om·e·ter \,in-tər-və-'lä-mə-tər\ *noun* (1933)
: a device that operates a control (as for a camera shutter) at regular intervals

in·ter·vene \,in-tər-'vēn\ *intransitive verb* **-vened; -ven·ing** [Latin *intervenire* to come between, from *inter-* + *venire* to come — more at COME] (1587)
1 : to occur, fall, or come between points of time or events
2 : to enter or appear as an irrelevant or extraneous feature or circumstance
3 : to come in or between by way of hindrance or modification ⟨*intervene* to stop a fight⟩
4 : to occur or lie between two things
5 a : to become a third party to a legal proceeding begun by others for the protection of an alleged interest **b** : to interfere usually by force or threat of force in another nation's internal affairs especially to compel or prevent an action or to maintain or alter a condition
synonym see INTERPOSE
— **in·ter·ven·tion** \-'ven(t)-shən\ *noun*
— **in·ter·ve·nor** \-'vē-nər, -,nȯr\ *or* **in·ter·ven·er** \-'vē-nər\ *noun* (1621)
: one who intervenes; *especially* : one who intervenes as a third party in a legal proceeding

in·ter·ven·tion·ism \-'ven(t)-shə-,ni-zəm\ *noun* (1923)
: the theory or practice of intervening; *specifically* : governmental interference in economic affairs at home or in political affairs of another country
— **in·ter·ven·tion·ist** \-'vench-nist, -'ven(t)-shə-nist\ *noun or adjective*

in·ter·ver·te·bral disk \,in-tər-'vər-tə-brəl-, -(,)vər-'tē-\ *noun* (circa 1860)
: any of the tough elastic disks that are interposed between the centra of adjoining vertebrae and that consist of an outer fibrous ring enclosing an inner pulpy nucleus

in·ter·view \'in-tər-,vyü\ *noun* [Middle French *entrevue*, from *(s')entrevoir* to see one another, meet, from *entre-* inter- + *voir* to see — more at VIEW] (1514)
1 : a formal consultation usually to evaluate qualifications (as of a prospective student or employee)
2 a : a meeting at which information is obtained (as by a reporter, television commentator, or pollster) from a person **b** : a report or reproduction of information so obtained
3 : INTERVIEWEE
— **interview** *verb*
— **in·ter·view·er** *noun*

in·ter·view·ee \,in-tər-(,)vyü-'ē\ *noun* (1884)
: one who is interviewed

in·ter vi·vos \'in-tər-'vē-,vōs, -'vī-\ *adverb or adjective* [Late Latin] (1837)
: between living persons ⟨transaction *inter vivos*⟩; *especially* : from one living person to another ⟨*inter vivos* gifts⟩ ⟨property transferred *inter vivos*⟩

in·ter·vo·cal·ic \,in-tər-vō-'ka-lik\ *adjective* (1887)
: immediately preceded and immediately followed by a vowel
— **in·ter·vo·cal·i·cal·ly** \-li-k(ə-)lē\ *adverb*

in·ter·weave \,in-tər-'wēv\ *verb* **-wove** \-'wōv\ *also* **-weaved; -wo·ven** \-'wō-vən\ *also* **-weaved; -weav·ing** (1598)
transitive verb
1 : to weave together
2 : to mix or blend together ⟨*interweaving* his own insights . . . with letters and memoirs —Phoebe Adams⟩
intransitive verb
: INTERTWINE, INTERMINGLE
— **in·ter·weave** \'in-tər-,wēv\ *noun*
— **in·ter·wo·ven** \,in-tər-'wō-vən\ *adjective*

in·tes·ta·cy \in-'tes-tə-sē\ *noun* (1767)
: the quality or state of being or dying intestate

¹in·tes·tate \in-'tes-,tāt, -tət\ *adjective* [Middle English, from Latin *intestatus*, from *in-* + *testatus* testate] (14th century)
1 : having made no valid will ⟨died *intestate*⟩
2 : not disposed of by will ⟨an *intestate* estate⟩

²intestate *noun* (1658)
: one who dies intestate

in·tes·ti·nal \in-'tes-tə-n°l, -'tes(t)-nəl, -'tes°n-əl, *British often* ,in-(,)tes-'tī-n°l\ *adjective* (15th century)
1 : affecting or occurring in the intestine; *also* : living in the intestine
2 : of, relating to, or being the intestine
— **in·tes·ti·nal·ly** *adverb*

intestinal fortitude *noun* [euphemism for *guts*] (circa 1937)
: COURAGE, STAMINA

¹in·tes·tine \in-'tes-tən\ *adjective* [Middle English, from Middle French or Latin; Middle French *intestin*, from Latin *intestinus*, from *intus* within — more at ENT-] (15th century)
: INTERNAL; *specifically* : of or relating to the internal affairs of a state or country ⟨*intestine* war⟩

²intestine *noun* [Middle English, from Middle French *intestin*, from Latin *intestinum*, from neuter of *intestinus*] (15th century)

intestine: *A* large intestine, *B* small intestine

: the tubular part of the alimentary canal that extends from the stomach to the anus

in·ti \'in-tē\ *noun* [Quechua, sun] (1985)
: the basic monetary unit of Peru from 1985 to 1990

in·ti·ma \'in-tə-mə\ *noun, plural* **-mae** \-,mē, -,mī\ *or* **-mas** [New Latin, from Latin, feminine of *intimus*] (1873)
: the innermost coat of an organ (as a blood vessel) consisting usually of an endothelial layer backed by connective tissue and elastic tissue
— **in·ti·mal** \-məl\ *adjective*

in·ti·ma·cy \'in-tə-mə-sē\ *noun, plural* **-cies** (1641)
1 : the state of being intimate : FAMILIARITY
2 : something of a personal or private nature

¹in·ti·mate \'in-tə-,māt\ *transitive verb* **-mat·ed; -mat·ing** [Late Latin *intimatus*, past participle of *intimare* to put in, announce, from Latin *intimus* innermost, superlative of (assumed) Old Latin *interus* inward — more at INTERIOR] (1522)
1 : to make known especially publicly or formally : ANNOUNCE
2 : to communicate delicately and indirectly : HINT
synonym see SUGGEST
— **in·ti·mat·er** *noun*
— **in·ti·ma·tion** \,in-tə-'mā-shən\ *noun*

²in·ti·mate \'in-tə-mət\ *adjective* [alteration of obsolete *intime*, from Latin *intimus*] (1632)
1 a : INTRINSIC, ESSENTIAL **b** : belonging to or characterizing one's deepest nature
2 : marked by very close association, contact, or familiarity ⟨*intimate* knowledge of the law⟩
3 a : marked by a warm friendship developing through long association **b** : suggesting informal warmth or privacy ⟨*intimate* clubs⟩
4 : of a very personal or private nature
— **in·ti·mate·ly** *adverb*
— **in·ti·mate·ness** *noun*

³in·ti·mate \'in-tə-mət\ *noun* (1659)
: an intimate friend or confidant

in·tim·i·date \in-'ti-mə-,dāt\ *transitive verb* **-dat·ed; -dat·ing** [Medieval Latin *intimidatus*, past participle of *intimidare*, from Latin *in-* + *timidus* timid] (1646)
: to make timid or fearful : FRIGHTEN; *especially* : to compel or deter by or as if by threats ☆
— **in·tim·i·dat·ing·ly** \-,dā-tiŋ-lē\ *adverb*
— **in·tim·i·da·tion** \-,ti-mə-'dā-shən\ *noun*
— **in·tim·i·da·tor** \-'ti-mə-,dā-tor\ *noun*

in·tim·i·da·to·ry \-'ti-mə-də-,tōr-ē, -,tȯr-\ *adjective* (circa 1846)
: tending to intimidate

in·tinc·tion \in-'tiŋ(k)-shən\ *noun* [Late Latin *intinction-, intinctio* baptism, from Latin *intingere* to dip in, from *in-* + *tingere* to dip, moisten — more at TINGE] (1872)
: the administration of the sacrament of Communion by dipping the bread in the wine and giving both together to the communicant

in·tine \'in-ˌtēn\ noun [probably from German, from Latin intus within + New Latin in- fibrous tissue, from Greek in-, is tendon] (1835) : the inner mostly cellulose wall of a spore (as a pollen grain)

in·tit·ule \in-'ti-(ˌ)chü(ə)l\ transitive verb **-uled; -ul·ing** [Middle French intituler, from Late Latin intitulare, from Latin in- + titulus title] (15th century) British : to furnish (as a legislative act) with a title or designation

in·to \'in-(ˌ)tü, -tə\ preposition [Middle English, from Old English intō, from ²in + tō to] (before 12th century) 1 — used as a function word to indicate entry, introduction, insertion, superposition, or inclusion ⟨came into the house⟩ ⟨enter into an alliance⟩ 2 a : to the state, condition, or form of ⟨got into trouble⟩ b : to the occupation, action, or possession of ⟨go into farming⟩ c : involved with or interested in ⟨into hard drugs⟩ ⟨into Latin epigrammatists⟩ 3 — used as a function word to indicate a period of time or an extent of space part of which is passed or occupied ⟨far into the night⟩ 4 : in the direction of ⟨looking into the sun⟩ 5 : to a position of contact with : AGAINST ⟨ran into a wall⟩ 6 — used as a function word to indicate the dividend in division ⟨dividing 3 into 6 gives 2⟩

in·tol·er·a·ble \(ˌ)in-'täl-rə-bəl, -'tä-lə-rə-, -'tä-lər-bəl\ adjective [Middle English, from Latin intolerabilis, from in- + tolerabilis tolerable] (15th century) 1 : not tolerable : UNBEARABLE ⟨intolerable pain⟩ 2 : EXCESSIVE — **in·tol·er·a·bil·i·ty** \-ˌtäl-rə-'bi-lə-tē, -ˌtä-lə-rə-, -ˌtä-lər-\ noun — **in·tol·er·a·ble·ness** \-'täl-rə-bəl-nəs, -'tä-lə-rə-, -'tä-lər-bəl-\ noun — **in·tol·er·a·bly** \-blē\ adverb

in·tol·er·ance \(ˌ)in-'täl-rən(t)s, -'tä-lə-\ noun (1765) : the quality or state of being intolerant; especially : exceptional sensitivity (as to a drug)

in·tol·er·ant \-rənt\ adjective (circa 1735) 1 : unable or unwilling to endure ⟨a plant intolerant of direct sunlight⟩ ⟨intolerant of criticism⟩ 2 a : unwilling to grant equal freedom of expression especially in religious matters b : unwilling to grant or share social, political, or professional rights : BIGOTED — **in·tol·er·ant·ly** adverb — **in·tol·er·ant·ness** noun

in·to·nate \'in-tə-ˌnāt, -(ˌ)tō-\ transitive verb **-nat·ed; -nat·ing** (1795) : INTONE, UTTER

in·to·na·tion \ˌin-tə-'nā-shən, -(ˌ)tō-\ noun (1620) 1 : the act of intoning and especially of chanting 2 : something that is intoned; specifically : the opening tones of a Gregorian chant 3 : the ability to play or sing notes in tune 4 : manner of utterance; specifically : the rise and fall in pitch of the voice in speech — **in·to·na·tion·al** \-shnəl, -shə-nᵊl\ adjective

in·tone \in-'tōn\ verb **in·toned; in·ton·ing** [Middle English entonen, from Middle French entoner, from Medieval Latin intonare, from Latin in- + tonus tone] (15th century) transitive verb : to utter in musical or prolonged tones : recite in singing tones or in a monotone intransitive verb : to utter something in singing tones or in monotone — **in·ton·er** noun

in to·to \in-'tō-(ˌ)tō\ adverb [Latin, on the whole] (1796) : TOTALLY, ENTIRELY

in·tox·i·cant \in-'täk-si-kənt\ noun (1863) : something that intoxicates; especially : an alcoholic drink — **intoxicant** adjective

¹**in·tox·i·cate** \-si-kət\ adjective (15th century) archaic : INTOXICATED

²**in·tox·i·cate** \-sə-ˌkāt\ transitive verb **-cat·ed; -cat·ing** [Middle English, from Medieval Latin intoxicatus, past participle of intoxicare, from Latin in- + toxicum poison — more at TOXIC] (15th century) 1 : POISON 2 a : to excite or stupefy by alcohol or a drug especially to the point where physical and mental control is markedly diminished b : to excite or elate to the point of enthusiasm or frenzy

in·tox·i·cat·ed \-sə-ˌkā-təd\ adjective (1576) : affected by or as if by alcohol : DRUNK — **in·tox·i·cat·ed·ly** \-ˌkā-təd-lē\ adverb

in·tox·i·ca·tion \in-ˌtäk-sə-'kā-shən\ noun (15th century) 1 : an abnormal state that is essentially a poisoning ⟨intestinal intoxication⟩ 2 a : the condition of being drunk : INEBRIATION b : a strong excitement or elation

in·tra- \'in-trə, -(ˌ)trä\ prefix [Late Latin, from Latin intra, from (assumed) Old Latin interus, adjective, inward — more at INTERIOR] 1 a : within ⟨intragalactic⟩ b : during ⟨intraday⟩ c : between layers of ⟨intradermal⟩ 2 : INTRO- ⟨an intramuscular injection⟩

in·tra-ar·te·ri·al \-är-'tir-ē-əl\ adjective (1897) : situated or occurring within, administered into, or involving entry by way of an artery — **in·tra-ar·te·ri·al·ly** \-ē-ə-lē\ adverb

in·tra·ar·tic·u·lar \-är-'ti-kyə-lər\ adjective (circa 1888) : situated within, occurring within, or administered by entry into a joint

in·tra·car·di·ac \-'kär-dē-ˌak\ also **in·tra·car·di·al** \-dē-əl\ adjective (1876) : situated or occurring within or introduced or involving entry into the heart ⟨intracardiac surgery⟩ ⟨an intracardiac catheter⟩ — **in·tra·car·di·al·ly** \-dē-ə-lē\ adverb

in·tra·cel·lu·lar \-'sel-yə-lər\ adjective (1876) : existing, occurring, or functioning within a cell ⟨intracellular parasites⟩ — **in·tra·cel·lu·lar·ly** adverb

in·tra·ce·re·bral \-sə-'rē-brəl, -'ser-ə-\ adjective (1881) : situated in, introduced into, or made into the cerebrum ⟨intracerebral injections⟩ ⟨intracerebral bleeding⟩ — **in·tra·ce·re·bral·ly** \-brə-lē\ adverb

in·tra·com·pa·ny \-'kəmp-nē, -'kəm-pə-\ adjective (1926) : occurring within or taking place between branches or employees of a company ⟨intracompany income⟩

in·tra·cra·ni·al \-'krā-nē-əl\ adjective (circa 1849) : existing or occurring within the cranium; also : affecting or involving intracranial structures — **in·tra·cra·ni·al·ly** \-nē-ə-lē\ adverb

in·trac·ta·ble \(ˌ)in-'trak-tə-bəl\ adjective [Latin intractabilis, from in- + tractabilis tractable] (1531) 1 : not easily governed, managed, or directed : OBSTINATE 2 : not easily manipulated or wrought ⟨intractable metal⟩ 3 : not easily relieved or cured ⟨intractable pain⟩ synonym see UNRULY — **in·trac·ta·bil·i·ty** \(ˌ)in-ˌtrak-tə-'bi-lə-tē\ noun — **in·trac·ta·bly** \-blē\ adverb

in·tra·cu·ta·ne·ous \ˌin-trə-kyù-'tā-nē-əs, -(ˌ)trä-\ adjective (1885) : INTRADERMAL — **in·tra·cu·ta·ne·ous·ly** adverb

in·tra·day \'in-trə-ˌdā, -(ˌ)trä-\ adjective (1950) : occurring in the course of a single day ⟨the market showed wide intraday fluctuations⟩

in·tra·der·mal \ˌin-trə-'dər-məl, -(ˌ)trä-\ adjective (circa 1900) : situated, occurring, or done within or between the layers of the skin; also : administered by entering the skin ⟨intradermal injections⟩ — **in·tra·der·mal·ly** \-mə-lē\ adverb

intradermal test noun (1916) : a test for immunity or hypersensitivity made by injecting a minute amount of diluted antigen into the skin

in·tra·dos \'in-trə-ˌdäs, -ˌdō; in-'trä-ˌdäs\ noun, plural **-dos** \-ˌdōz, -ˌdäs\ or **-dos·es** \-ˌdä-səz\ [French, from Latin intra within + French dos back — more at DOSSIER] (1772) : the interior curve of an arch — see ARCH illustration

in·tra·ga·lac·tic \ˌin-trə-gə-'lak-tik, -(ˌ)trä-\ adjective (1964) : situated or occurring within the confines of a single galaxy

in·tra·gen·ic \-'je-nik\ adjective (1937) : being or occurring within a gene ⟨intragenic recombination⟩ ⟨intragenic mutation⟩

in·tra·mo·lec·u·lar \-mə-'le-kyə-lər\ adjective [International Scientific Vocabulary] (1884) : existing or acting within the molecule; also : formed by reaction between different parts of the same molecule — **in·tra·mo·lec·u·lar·ly** adverb

in·tra·mu·ral \-'myúr-əl\ adjective (1846) 1 a : being or occurring within the limits usually of a community, organization, or institution b : competed only within the student body ⟨intramural sports⟩ 2 : situated or occurring within the substance of the walls of an organ — **in·tra·mu·ral·ly** \-ə-lē\ adverb

in·tra·mus·cu·lar \-'məs-kyə-lər\ adjective [International Scientific Vocabulary] (1874) : situated in, occurring in, or administered by entering a muscle — **in·tra·mus·cu·lar·ly** adverb

in·tra·na·sal \-'nā-zəl\ adjective (1886) : lying within or administered by way of the nasal structures — **in·tra·na·sal·ly** \-'nāz-lē, -'nā-zə-\ adverb

in·tran·si·geance \in-'tran(t)s-ə-jən(t)s, -'tran-zə-\ noun [French] (1899) : INTRANSIGENCE — **in·tran·si·geant** \-jənt\ adjective or noun — **in·tran·si·geant·ly** adverb

in·tran·si·gence \-jən(t)s\ noun (1882) : the quality or state of being intransigent

in·tran·si·gent \-jənt\ adjective [Spanish intransigente, from in- + transigente, present participle of transigir to compromise, from Latin transigere to come to an agreement — more at TRANSACT] (circa 1879) 1 a : refusing to compromise or to abandon an extreme position or attitude : UNCOMPROMISING b : IRRECONCILABLE 2 : characteristic of an intransigent person — **intransigent** noun — **in·tran·si·gent·ly** adverb

in·tran·si·tive \(ˌ)in-'tran(t)-sə-tiv, -'tran-zə-; -'tran(t)s-tiv\ adjective [Late Latin intransitivus, from Latin in- + Late Latin transitivus transitive] (1612) : not transitive; especially : characterized by not having or containing a direct object ⟨an intransitive verb⟩ — **in·tran·si·tive·ly** adverb

— **in·tran·si·tive·ness** noun
— **in·tran·si·tiv·i·ty** \(,)in-,tran(t)-sə-'ti-və-tē, -,tran-zə-\ noun
in·tra·oc·u·lar \,in-trə-'ä-kyə-lər, -(,)trä-\ adjective [International Scientific Vocabulary] (1826)
: implanted in, occurring in, or administered by entering the eyeball
— **in·tra·oc·u·lar·ly** adverb
in·tra·per·i·to·ne·al \,in-trə-,per-ə-tᵊn-'ē-əl\ adjective (circa 1836)
: existing within or administered by entering the peritoneum
— **in·tra·per·i·to·ne·al·ly** \-'ē-ə-lē\ adverb
in·tra·per·son·al \-'pərs-nəl, -'pər-sᵊn-əl\ adjective (1909)
: occurring within the individual mind or self ⟨intrapersonal concerns of the aged⟩
in·tra·plate \'in-trə-,plāt, -(,)trä-\ adjective (1973)
: relating to or occurring within the interior of a tectonic plate ⟨an intraplate earthquake⟩
in·tra·pop·u·la·tion \'in-trə-,pä-pyə-'lā-shən, -(,)trä-\ adjective (1959)
: occurring within or taking place between members of a population
in·tra·pre·neur \,in-trə-prə-'nər, -'nủr, -'nyủr\ noun [intra- + entrepreneur] (1982)
: a corporate executive who develops new enterprises within the corporation
— **in·tra·pre·neur·ial** \-'nər-ē-əl, -'n(y)ủr-\ adjective
in·tra·psy·chic \,in-trə-'sī-kik, -(,)trä-\ adjective (1917)
: being or occurring within the psyche, mind, or personality
— **in·tra·psy·chi·cal·ly** \-ki-k(ə-)lē\ adverb
in·tra·spe·cies \-'spē-(,)shēz, -(,)sēz\ adjective (1927)
: INTRASPECIFIC
in·tra·spe·cif·ic \-spi-'si-fik\ adjective (1919)
: occurring within a species or involving members of one species
in·tra·state \-'stāt\ adjective (1903)
: existing or occurring within a state
in·tra·the·cal \-'thē-kəl\ adjective (1887)
: introduced into or occurring in the space under the arachnoid membrane of the brain or spinal cord
— **in·tra·the·cal·ly** \-k(ə-)lē\ adverb
in·tra·tho·rac·ic \-thə-'ra-sik\ adjective [International Scientific Vocabulary] (1862)
: situated or occurring within the thorax ⟨intrathoracic pressure⟩
— **in·tra·tho·rac·i·cal·ly** adverb
in·tra·uter·ine \-'yü-tə-rən, -,rīn\ adjective [International Scientific Vocabulary] (circa 1836)
: situated, used, or occurring within the uterus; also : involving the part of development that takes place in the uterus
intrauterine device noun (1964)
: a device inserted and left in the uterus to prevent effective conception — called also intrauterine contraceptive device, IUD
in·tra·vas·cu·lar \,in-trə-'vas-kyə-lər, -(,)trä-\ adjective (1876)
: situated in, occurring in, or administered by entry into a blood vessel ⟨intravascular thrombosis⟩ ⟨an intravascular injection⟩
— **in·tra·vas·cu·lar·ly** adverb
in·tra·ve·nous \,in-trə-'vē-nəs\ adjective [International Scientific Vocabulary] (circa 1849)
: situated, performed, or occurring within or entering by way of a vein; also : used in intravenous procedures
— **in·tra·ve·nous·ly** adverb
in·tra·ven·tric·u·lar \,in-trə-ven-'tri-kyə-lər, -(,)trä-\ adjective (1882)
: situated within, occurring within, or administered into a ventricle
— **in·tra·ven·tric·u·lar·ly** adverb

in·tra·vi·tal \-'vī-tᵊl\ adjective [International Scientific Vocabulary] (circa 1890)
1 : performed upon or found in a living subject
2 : having or utilizing the property of staining cells without killing them — compare SUPRAVITAL
— **in·tra·vi·tal·ly** \-tᵊl-ē\ adverb
in·tra·vi·tam \-'vī-,tam, -'wē-,täm\ adjective [New Latin intra vitam during life] (1881)
: INTRAVITAL
in·tra·zon·al \,in-trə-'zō-nᵊl, -(,)trä-\ adjective (1927)
: of, relating to, or being a soil or a major soil group marked by relatively well-developed characteristics that are determined primarily by essentially local factors (as the parent material) rather than climate and vegetation — compare AZONAL, ZONAL
intreat archaic variant of ENTREAT
intrench variant of ENTRENCH
in·trep·id \in-'tre-pəd\ adjective [Latin intrepidus, from in- + trepidus alarmed — more at TREPIDATION] (1697)
: characterized by resolute fearlessness, fortitude, and endurance
— **in·tre·pid·i·ty** \,in-trə-'pi-də-tē\ noun
— **in·trep·id·ly** \in-'tre-pəd-lē\ adverb
— **in·trep·id·ness** noun
in·tri·ca·cy \'in-tri-kə-sē\ noun, plural **-cies** (1602)
1 : the quality or state of being intricate
2 : something intricate ⟨the intricacies of a plot⟩
in·tri·cate \'in-tri-kət\ adjective [Middle English, from Latin intricatus, past participle of intricare to entangle, from in- + tricae trifles, complications] (15th century)
1 : having many complexly interrelating parts or elements : COMPLICATED
2 : difficult to resolve or analyze
synonym see COMPLEX
— **in·tri·cate·ly** adverb
— **in·tri·cate·ness** noun
in·tri·gant or **in·tri·guant** \,in-trē-'gänt, ,an-, -'gänⁿ\ noun [French intrigant, from Italian intrigante, present participle of intrigare] (1781)
: one that intrigues
¹**in·trigue** \in-'trēg\ verb **in·trigued; in·trigu·ing** [French intriguer, from Italian intrigare, from Latin intricare] (1612)
transitive verb
1 : CHEAT, TRICK
2 : to accomplish by intrigue ⟨intrigued myself into the club⟩
3 obsolete : ENTANGLE
4 : to arouse the interest, desire, or curiosity of ⟨intrigued by the tale⟩
intransitive verb
: to carry on an intrigue; especially : PLOT, SCHEME
— **in·trigu·er** noun
²**in·trigue** \'in-,trēg, in-'\ noun (1647)
1 a : a secret scheme : MACHINATION **b** : the practice of engaging in intrigues
2 : a clandestine love affair
synonym see PLOT
in·trigu·ing \in-'trē-giŋ\ adjective (1909)
: engaging the interest to a marked degree : FASCINATING
— **in·trigu·ing·ly** \-giŋ-lē\ adverb
in·trin·sic \in-'trin-zik, -'trin(t)-sik\ adjective [Middle French intrinsèque internal, from Late Latin intrinsecus, from Latin, adverb, inwardly; akin to Latin intra within — more at INTRA-] (1642)
1 a : belonging to the essential nature or constitution of a thing ⟨the intrinsic worth of a gem⟩ ⟨the intrinsic brightness of a star⟩ **b** : being or relating to a semiconductor in which the concentration of charge carriers is characteristic of the material itself instead of the content of any impurities it contains
2 a : originating or due to causes within a body, organ, or part ⟨an intrinsic metabolic

disease⟩ **b** : originating and included wholly within an organ or part ⟨intrinsic muscles⟩ — compare EXTRINSIC 1b
— **in·trin·si·cal·ly** \-zi-k(ə-)lē, -si-\ adverb
in·trin·si·cal \-zi-kəl, -si-\ adjective (circa 1548)
archaic : INTRINSIC
intrinsic factor noun (1930)
: a substance produced by normal gastrointestinal mucosa that facilitates absorption of vitamin B_{12}
in·tro \'in-(,)trō\ noun, plural **intros** (circa 1899)
: INTRODUCTION
intro- prefix [Middle English, from Middle French, from Latin, from intro inside, to the inside, from (assumed) Old Latin interus, adjective, inward]
1 : in : into ⟨introjection⟩
2 : inward : within ⟨introvert⟩ — compare EXTRO-
in·tro·duce \,in-trə-'düs, -'dyüs\ transitive verb **-duced; -duc·ing** [Middle English, from Latin introducere, from intro- + ducere to lead — more at TOW] (15th century)
1 : to lead or bring in especially for the first time
2 a : to bring into play **b** : to bring into practice or use : INSTITUTE
3 : to lead to or make known by a formal act, announcement, or recommendation: as **a** : to cause to be acquainted **b** : to present formally at court or into society **c** : to present or announce formally or officially or by an official reading **d** : to make preliminary explanatory or laudatory remarks about **e** : to bring (as an actor or singer) before the public for the first time
4 : PLACE, INSERT
5 : to bring to a knowledge of something ☆
— **in·tro·duc·er** noun
in·tro·duc·tion \,in-trə-'dək-shən\ noun [Middle English introduccioun act of introducing, from Middle French introduction, from Latin introduction-, introductio, from introducere] (14th century)
1 : something that introduces: as **a** (1) : a part of a book or treatise preliminary to the main portion (2) : a preliminary treatise or course of study **b** : a short introductory musical passage
2 : the act or process of introducing : the state of being introduced
3 : a putting in : INSERTION
4 : something introduced; specifically : a new or exotic plant or animal
in·tro·duc·to·ry \,in-trə-'dək-t(ə-)rē\ adjective (1605)
: of, relating to, or being a first step that sets something going or in proper perspective ⟨an introductory course in calculus⟩

☆ **SYNONYMS**
Introduce, insert, insinuate, interpolate, intercalate, interpose, interject mean to put between or among others. IN-TRODUCE is a general term for bringing or placing a thing or person into a group or body already in existence ⟨introduced a new topic into the conversation⟩. INSERT implies putting into a fixed or open space between or among ⟨inserted a clause in the contract⟩. INSINUATE implies introducing gradually or by gentle pressure ⟨insinuated himself into the group⟩. INTERPOLATE applies to the inserting of something extraneous or spurious ⟨interpolated her own comments into the report⟩. INTERCALATE suggests an intrusive inserting of something in an existing series or sequence ⟨new chapters intercalated with the old⟩. INTERPOSE suggests inserting an obstruction or cause of delay ⟨interpose barriers to communication⟩. INTERJECT implies an abrupt or forced introduction ⟨interjected a question⟩.

— **in·tro·duc·to·ri·ly** \-t(ə-)rə-lē\ *adverb*

in·tro·gres·sion \ˌin-trə-'gre-shən\ *noun* [*intro-* + *-gression* (as in *regression*)] (1938)
: the entry or introduction of a gene from one gene complex into another
— **in·tro·gres·sant** \-'gre-sᵊnt\ *adjective or noun*
— **in·tro·gres·sive** \-'gre-siv\ *adjective*

in·troit \'in-ˌtroit, -ˌtrō-ət, in-'\ *noun* [Middle English, from Middle French *introite*, from Medieval Latin *introitus*, from Latin, entrance, from *introire* to go in, from *intro-* + *ire* to go — more at ISSUE] (15th century)
1 *often capitalized* : the first part of the traditional proper of the Mass consisting of an antiphon, verse from a psalm, and the Gloria Patri
2 : a piece of music sung or played at the beginning of a worship service

in·tro·ject \ˌin-trə-'jekt\ *transitive verb* [back-formation from *introjection*, from International Scientific Vocabulary *intro-* + pro*jection*] (1925)
: to incorporate (attitudes or ideas) into one's personality unconsciously
— **in·tro·jec·tion** \-'jek-shən\ *noun*

in·tro·mis·sion \ˌin-trə-'mi-shən\ *noun* [French, from Middle French, from Medieval Latin *intromission-, intromissio*, from Latin *intromittere*] (1601)
: the act or process of intromitting; *especially* : the insertion or period of insertion of the penis in the vagina in copulation

in·tro·mit \-'mit\ *transitive verb* **-mit·ted; -mit·ting** [Latin *intromittere*, from *intro-* + *mittere* to send] (circa 1588)
: to send or put in : INSERT
— **in·tro·mit·tent** \-'mi-tᵊnt\ *adjective*
— **in·tro·mit·ter** \-tər\ *noun*

in·tron \'in-ˌträn\ *noun* [*intervening* sequence + ²-*on*] (1978)
: a polynucleotide sequence in a nucleic acid that does not code information for protein synthesis and is removed before translation of messenger RNA — compare EXON

in·trorse \'in-ˌtrors\ *adjective* [Latin *introrsus*, adverb, inward, from *intro-* + *versus* toward, from past participle of *vertere* to turn — more at WORTH] (1842)
: facing toward or toward the axis of growth ⟨an *introrse* anther⟩

in·tro·spec·tion \ˌin-trə-'spek-shən\ *noun* [Latin *introspicere* to look inside, past participle of *introspicere* to look inside, from *intro-* + *specere* to look — more at SPY] (circa 1677)
: a reflective looking inward : an examination of one's own thoughts and feelings
— **in·tro·spect** \-'spekt\ *verb*
— **in·tro·spec·tion·al** \-'spek-shnəl, -shə-nᵊl\ *adjective*
— **in·tro·spec·tive** \-'spek-tiv\ *adjective*
— **in·tro·spec·tive·ly** *adverb*
— **in·tro·spec·tive·ness** *noun*

in·tro·spec·tion·ism \-shə-ˌni-zəm\ *noun* (1922)
: a doctrine that psychology must be based essentially on data derived from introspection — compare BEHAVIORISM
— **in·tro·spec·tion·ist** \-sh(ə-)nist\ *or* **in·tro·spec·tion·is·tic** \-ˌspek-shə-'nis-tik\ *adjective*

— **introspectionist** *noun*

in·tro·ver·sion \ˌin-trə-'vər-zhən, -shən\ *noun* [*intro-* + *-version* (as in *diversion*)] (1654)
1 : the act of introverting : the state of being introverted
2 : the state or tendency toward being wholly or predominantly concerned with and interested in one's own mental life
— **in·tro·ver·sive** \-'vər-siv, -ziv\ *adjective*
— **in·tro·ver·sive·ly** *adverb*

¹**in·tro·vert** \'in-trə-ˌvərt\ *transitive verb* [*intro-* + *-vert* (as in *divert*)] (1669)
: to turn inward or in upon itself: as **a** : to concentrate or direct upon oneself **b** : to produce psychological introversion in

²**introvert** *noun* (1883)

1 : something (as the retractile proboscis of some worms) that is or can be drawn in especially by invagination
2 : one whose personality is characterized by introversion; *broadly* : a reserved or shy person

in·trude \in-'trüd\ *verb* **in·trud·ed; in·trud·ing** [Middle English, from Latin *intrudere* to thrust in, from *in-* + *trudere* to thrust — more at THREAT] (15th century)
intransitive verb
1 : to thrust oneself in without invitation, permission, or welcome
2 : to enter as a geological intrusion
transitive verb
1 : to thrust or force in or upon someone or something especially without permission, welcome, or fitness
2 : to cause to enter as if by force
— **in·trud·er** *noun*

in·tru·sion \in-'trü-zhən\ *noun* [Middle English, from Middle French, from Medieval Latin *intrusion-, intrusio*, from Latin *intruder*] (15th century)
1 : the act of intruding or the state of being intruded; *especially* : the act of wrongfully entering upon, seizing, or taking possession of the property of another
2 : the forcible entry of molten rock or magma into or between other rock formations; *also* : the intruded magma

in·tru·sive \in-'trü-siv, -ziv\ *adjective* (15th century)
1 a : characterized by intrusion **b** : intruding where one is not welcome or invited
2 a : projecting inward ⟨an *intrusive* arm of the sea⟩ **b** (1) *of a rock* : having been forced while in a plastic state into cavities or between layers (2) : PLUTONIC
3 : having nothing that corresponds to a sound or letter in orthography or etymon ⟨*intrusive* \t\ in \'mints\ for *mince*⟩
synonym see IMPERTINENT
— **intrusive** *noun*
— **in·tru·sive·ly** *adverb*
— **in·tru·sive·ness** *noun*

intrust *variant of* ENTRUST

in·tu·ba·tion \ˌin-(ˌ)tü-'bā-shən, -(ˌ)tyü-, -tə-\ *noun* (1887)
: the introduction of a tube into a hollow organ (as the trachea)
— **in·tu·bate** \'in-(ˌ)tü-ˌbāt, -(ˌ)tyü-, -tə-\ *transitive verb*

in·tu·it \in-'tü-ət, -'tyü-\ *transitive verb* (1855)
: to apprehend by intuition
— **in·tu·it·able** \-ə-tə-bəl\ *adjective*

in·tu·i·tion \ˌin-tü-'wi-shən, -tyü-\ *noun* [Middle English *intuycyon*, from Late Latin *intuition-, intuitio* act of contemplating, from Latin *intuēri* to look at, contemplate, from *in-* + *tuēri* to look at] (15th century)
1 : quick and ready insight
2 a : immediate apprehension or cognition **b** : knowledge or conviction gained by intuition **c** : the power or faculty of attaining to direct knowledge or cognition without evident rational thought and inference
— **in·tu·i·tion·al** \-'wish-nəl, -'wi-shə-nᵊl\ *adjective*

in·tu·i·tion·ism \ˌin-tü-'wi-shə-ˌni-zəm\ *noun* (1847)
1 a : a doctrine that objects of perception are intuitively known to be real **b** : a doctrine that there are basic truths intuitively known
2 : a doctrine that right or wrong or fundamental principles about what is right and wrong can be intuited
3 : a philosophical thesis that human beings have a direct intuitive understanding of mathematics and that rejects the principle that every mathematical statement must be true or false
— **in·tu·i·tion·ist** \-sh(ə-)nist\ *adjective or noun*

in·tu·i·tive \in-'tü-ə-tiv, -'tyü-\ *adjective* (1621)

1 a : known or perceived by intuition : directly apprehended ⟨had an *intuitive* awareness of his sister's feelings⟩ **b** : knowable by intuition
2 : knowing or perceiving by intuition
3 : possessing or given to intuition or insight ⟨an *intuitive* mind⟩
— **in·tu·i·tive·ly** *adverb*
— **in·tu·i·tive·ness** *noun*

in·tu·mes·cence \ˌin-tü-'me-sᵊn(t)s, -tyü-\ *noun* [French, from Latin *intumescere* to swell up, from *in-* + *tumescere* to swell — more at TUMESCENCE] (circa 1656)
: a swollen or enlarged part of a plant or animal; *also* : the process of swelling up or enlarging
— **in·tu·mes·cent** \-sᵊnt\ *adjective* (1953)
of paint : swelling and charring when exposed to flame

in·tus·sus·cept \ˌin-tə-sə-'sept\ *verb* [back-formation from *intussusception*] (1802)
transitive verb
: to take in by or cause to undergo intussusception; *especially* : INVAGINATE
intransitive verb
: to undergo intussusception

in·tus·sus·cep·tion \-'sep-shən\ *noun* [Latin *intus* within + *susception-, susceptio* action of undertaking, from *suscipere* to take up — more at SUSCEPTIBLE] (1707)
: a drawing in of something from without: as **a** : INVAGINATION; *especially* : the slipping of a length of intestine into an adjacent portion usually producing obstruction **b** : the assimilation of new material and its dispersal among preexistent matter
— **in·tus·sus·cep·tive** \-'sep-tiv\ *adjective*

In·u·it \'i-nü-wət, -nyü-\ *noun* [Inuit *inuit*, plural of *inuk* person] (1765)
1 *plural* **Inuit** *or* **Inuits a** (1) : the Eskimo people of North America and Greenland (2) : the Eskimo people of Canada **b** : a member of such people
2 a : ESKIMO 2 **b** : the group of Eskimo dialects spoken from northwestern Canada to Greenland

Inuk·ti·tut \i-'nük-tə-ˌtüt\ *noun* (1974)
: the group of Eskimo dialects spoken by the Inuit of central and eastern arctic Canada

in·u·lin \'in-yə-lən\ *noun* [probably from German *Inulin*, from Latin *inula* elecampane] (1813)
: a tasteless white polysaccharide found especially dissolved in the sap of the roots and rhizomes of composite plants

in·unc·tion \i-'nən(k)-shən\ *noun* [Middle English, from Latin *inunction-, inunctio*, from *inunguere* to anoint — more at ANOINT] (15th century)
: an act of applying oil or ointment : ANOINTING

in·un·date \'i-(ˌ)nən-ˌdāt\ *transitive verb* **-dat·ed; -dat·ing** [Latin *inundatus*, past participle of *inundare*, from *in-* + *unda* wave — more at WATER] (1590)
1 : to cover with a flood : OVERFLOW
2 : OVERWHELM
— **in·un·da·tion** \ˌi-(ˌ)nən-'dā-shən\ *noun*
— **in·un·da·tor** \'i-(ˌ)nən-ˌdā-tər\ *noun*
— **in·un·da·to·ry** \i-'nən-də-ˌtōr-ē, -ˌtor-\ *adjective*

In·u·pi·at \i-'nü-pē-ˌät, -nyü-\ *also* **In·u·pi·aq** \-ˌäk\ *noun* [Inupiat *inᵘpiaq*, plural *inᵘpiat*, literally, real person] (1967)
1 *plural* **Inupiat** *or* **Inupiats** *also* **Inupiaq** *or* **Inupiaqs** : a member of the Eskimo people of northern Alaska
2 : the language of the Inupiat people

in·ure \i-'nur, -'nyur\ *verb* **in·ured; in·ur·ing** [Middle English *enuren*, from *en-* + *ure*, noun,

\ə\ abut \ᵊ\ kitten \ər\ further \a\ ash \ā\ ace
\ä\ mop, mar \aú\ out \ch\ chin \e\ bet \ē\ easy
\g\ go \i\ hit \ī\ ice \j\ job \ŋ\ sing \ō\ go
\ó\ law \ói\ boy \th\ thin \th\ the \ü\ loot \ú\ foot
\y\ yet \zh\ vision *see also* Guide to Pronunciation

use, custom, from Middle French *uevre* work, practice, from Latin *opera* work — more at OPERA] (15th century)
transitive verb
: to accustom to accept something undesirable
intransitive verb
: to become of advantage
— **in·ure·ment** \-mənt\ *noun*
in·urn \i-'nərn\ *transitive verb* (1602)
1 : ENTOMB
2 : to place (as cremated remains) in an urn
in utero \in-'yü-tə-,rō\ *adverb or adjective* [Latin] (1713)
: in the uterus : before birth ⟨a disease acquired *in utero*⟩ ⟨an *in utero* diagnosis⟩
in·utile \(,)in-'yü-t²l, -,tīl\ *adjective* [Middle English, from Middle French, from Latin *inutilis,* from *in-* + *utilis* useful — more at UTILITY] (15th century)
: USELESS, UNUSABLE
— **in·util·i·ty** \,in-yù-'ti-lə-tē\ *noun*
in vac·uo \in-'va-kyə-,wō\ *adverb* [New Latin] (1660)
: in a vacuum
in·vade \in-'vād\ *transitive verb* **in·vad·ed; in·vad·ing** [Middle English, from Latin *invadere,* from *in-* + *vadere* to go — more at WADE] (15th century)
1 : to enter for conquest or plunder
2 : to encroach upon : INFRINGE
3 a : to spread over or into as if invading : PERMEATE ⟨doubts *invade* his mind⟩ **b** : to affect injuriously and progressively ⟨gangrene *invades* healthy tissue⟩
synonym see TRESPASS
— **in·vad·er** *noun*
in·vag·i·nate \in-'va-jə-,nāt\ *verb* **-nat·ed; -nat·ing** [Medieval Latin *invaginatus,* past participle of *invaginare,* from Latin *in-* + *vagina* sheath] (circa 1656)
transitive verb
1 : ENCLOSE, SHEATHE
2 : to fold in so that an outer becomes an inner surface
intransitive verb
: to undergo invagination
in·vag·i·na·tion \-,va-jə-'nā-shən\ *noun* (circa 1658)
1 : an act or process of invaginating; *especially* : the formation of a gastrula by an infolding of part of the wall of the blastula
2 : an invaginated part
¹in·val·id \(,)in-'va-ləd\ *adjective* [Latin *invalidus* weak, from *in-* + *validus* strong — more at VALID] (1542)
: not valid: **a** : being without foundation or force in fact, truth, or law **b** : logically inconsequent
— **in·val·id·ly** \-lē\ *adverb*
²in·va·lid \'in-və-ləd, *British usually* -,lēd\ *adjective* [Latin & French; French *invalide,* from Latin *invalidus*] (1642)
1 : suffering from disease or disability : SICKLY
2 : of, relating to, or suited to one that is sick
³invalid *same as* ²\ *noun* (1709)
: one that is sickly or disabled
⁴in·va·lid \'in-və-ləd, -,lid, *British usually* -,lēd or ,in-və-'lēd\ *transitive verb* (1787)
1 : to remove from active duty by reason of sickness or disability
2 : to make sickly or disabled
in·val·i·date \(,)in-'va-lə-,dāt\ *transitive verb* (1649)
: to make invalid; *especially* : to weaken or destroy the cogency of
synonym see NULLIFY
— **in·val·i·da·tion** \-,va-lə-'dā-shən\ *noun*
— **in·val·i·da·tor** \in-'va-lə-,dā-tər\ *noun*
in·va·lid·ism \'in-və-lə-,di-zəm\ *noun* (1794)
: a chronic condition of being an invalid
in·val·id·i·ty \,in-və-'li-də-tē, -va-\ *noun, plural* **-ties** (circa 1550)
1 : lack of validity or cogency
2 : incapacitating bodily disability; *also* : INVALIDISM

in·valu·able \(,)in-'val-yə-bəl, -yə-wə-bəl\ *adjective* [¹*in-* + *value,* verb + *-able*] (1576)
: valuable beyond estimation : PRICELESS
— **in·valu·able·ness** *noun*
— **in·valu·ably** \-blē\ *adverb*
in·var \'in-,vär\ *noun, often capitalized* [from *Invar,* a trademark] (1902)
: an iron-nickel alloy that expands little on heating
in·vari·able \(,)in-'ver-ē-ə-bəl, -'var-\ *adjective* (15th century)
: not changing or capable of change : CONSTANT
— **in·vari·abil·i·ty** \-,ver-ē-ə-'bi-lə-tē, -,var-\ *noun*
— **invariable** *noun*
— **in·vari·ably** \-blē\ *adverb*
in·vari·ance \(,)in-'ver-ē-ən(t)s, -'var-\ *noun* (1878)
: the quality or state of being invariant
in·vari·ant \-ənt\ *adjective* (1874)
: CONSTANT, UNCHANGING; *specifically* : unchanged by specified mathematical or physical operations or transformations ⟨*invariant* factor⟩
— **invariant** *noun*
in·va·sion \in-'vā-zhən\ *noun* [Middle English *invasioune,* from Middle French *invasion,* from Late Latin *invasion-, invasio,* from Latin *invadere* to invade] (15th century)
1 : an act of invading; *especially* : incursion of an army for conquest or plunder
2 : the incoming or spread of something usually hurtful
in·va·sive \-siv, -ziv\ *adjective* (1598)
1 : of, relating to, or characterized by military aggression
2 : tending to spread; *especially* : tending to invade healthy tissue ⟨*invasive* cancer cells⟩
3 : tending to infringe
4 : involving entry into the living body (as by incision or by insertion of an instrument) ⟨*invasive* diagnostic techniques⟩
— **in·va·sive·ness** *noun*
¹in·vec·tive \in-'vek-tiv\ *adjective* [Middle English *invectif,* from Middle French, from Latin *invectivus,* from *invectus,* past participle of *invehere*] (15th century)
: of, relating to, or characterized by insult or abuse
— **in·vec·tive·ly** *adverb*
— **in·vec·tive·ness** *noun*
²invective *noun* (1523)
1 : an abusive expression or speech
2 : insulting or abusive language : VITUPERATION
synonym see ABUSE
in·veigh \in-'vā\ *intransitive verb* [Latin *invehi* to attack, inveigh, passive of *invehere* to carry in, from *in-* + *vehere* to carry — more at WAY] (1529)
: to protest or complain bitterly or vehemently : RAIL
— **in·veigh·er** *noun*
in·vei·gle \in-'vā-gəl *sometimes* -'vē-\ *transitive verb* **in·vei·gled; in·vei·gling** \-g(ə-)liŋ\ [modification of Middle French *aveugler* to blind, hoodwink, from Old French *avogler,* from *avogle* blind, from Medieval Latin *ab oculis,* literally, lacking eyes] (1539)
1 : to win over by wiles : ENTICE
2 : to acquire by ingenuity or flattery ◇
synonym see LURE
— **in·vei·gle·ment** \-gəl-mənt\ *noun*
— **in·vei·gler** \-g(ə-)lər\ *noun*
in·vent \in-'vent\ *transitive verb* [Middle English, from Latin *inventus,* past participle of *invenire* to come upon, find, from *in-* + *venire* to come — more at COME] (15th century)
1 *archaic* : FIND, DISCOVER
2 : to devise by thinking : FABRICATE
3 : to produce (as something useful) for the first time through the use of the imagination or of ingenious thinking and experiment
— **in·ven·tor** \-'ven-tər\ *noun*
— **in·ven·tress** \-'ven-trəs\ *noun*

in·ven·tion \in-'ven(t)-shən\ *noun* (14th century)
1 : DISCOVERY, FINDING
2 : productive imagination : INVENTIVENESS
3 a : something invented: as (1) : a product of the imagination; *especially* : a false conception (2) : a device, contrivance, or process originated after study and experiment **b** : a short keyboard composition featuring two or three part counterpoint
4 : the act or process of inventing
in·ven·tive \in-'ven-tiv\ *adjective* (15th century)
1 : adept or prolific at producing inventions : CREATIVE
2 : characterized by invention
— **in·ven·tive·ly** *adverb*
— **in·ven·tive·ness** *noun*
¹in·ven·to·ry \'in-vən-,tōr-ē, -,tòr-\ *noun, plural* **-ries** (1523)
1 a : an itemized list of current assets: as (1) : a catalog of the property of an individual or estate (2) : a list of goods on hand **b** : a survey of natural resources **c** : a list of traits, preferences, attitudes, interests, or abilities used to evaluate personal characteristics or skills
2 : the quantity of goods or materials on hand : STOCK
3 : the act or process of taking an inventory
— **in·ven·to·ri·al** \,in-vən-'tōr-ē-əl\ *adjective*
— **in·ven·to·ri·al·ly** \-ē-ə-lē\ *adverb*
²inventory *transitive verb* **-ried; -ry·ing** (1602)
: to make an inventory of : CATALOG
in·ver·ness \,in-vər-'nes\ *noun* [*Inverness,* Scotland] (1863)
: a loose belted coat having a cape with a close-fitting round collar

inverness

¹in·verse \(,)in-'vərs, 'in-,\ *adjective* [Latin *inversus,* from past participle of *invertere*] (15th century)
1 : opposite in order, nature, or effect
2 : being an inverse function ⟨*inverse* sine⟩
²inverse *noun* (circa 1681)
1 : something of a contrary nature or quality : OPPOSITE, REVERSE
2 : a proposition or theorem formed by contradicting both the subject and predicate or both the hypothesis and conclusion

◇ WORD HISTORY
inveigle To inveigle is not to blind, yet when we permit ourselves to be inveigled we are, in a sense, blinded by our tempter's wiles. The ancestor of our word *inveigle* is probably a phrase meaning "blind" in the Latin spoken around the time of the Roman Empire's fall. Literally, Latin *orbus ab oculis* would have meant "deprived of eyes," and in a text of the 5th or 6th century A.D. *ab oculis* occurs by itself with the meaning "blind." This phrase is the most likely source of French *aveugle* "blind," from which was derived *aveugler* "to blind." Although *aveugler* was used both literally and figuratively, only the figurative sense was borrowed by English in the late 15th century. English *inveigle* originally meant "to blind or delude in judgment." This sense is now obsolete, but the present meaning, "to win over by wiles," is not far removed. The substitution of *in-* for *a-,* taken to be a prefix, was probably based on Anglo-French usage, in which forms such as *aveogler* and *enveegler* were employed indiscriminately.

of a given proposition or theorem ⟨the *inverse* of "if A then B" is "if not-A then not-B"⟩ — compare CONTRAPOSITIVE

3 a : INVERSE FUNCTION; *also* **:** an operation (as subtraction) that undoes the effect of another operation **b :** a set element that is related to another element in such a way that the result of applying a given binary operation to them is an identity element of the set

inverse function *noun* (1816)
: a function that is derived from a given function by interchanging the two variables — compare LOGARITHMIC FUNCTION

in·verse·ly \'in-,vərs-lē, (,)in-'\ *adverb* (1660)
1 : in an inverse order or manner
2 : in the manner of inverse variation ⟨varies *inversely*⟩

inversely proportional *adjective* (circa 1890)
: related by inverse variation — compare DIRECTLY PROPORTIONAL

inverse square law *noun* (1921)
: a statement in physics: a given physical quantity (as illumination) varies with the distance from the source inversely as the square of the distance

inverse variation *noun* (1936)
1 : mathematical relationship between two variables which can be expressed by an equation in which the product of two variables is equal to a constant
2 : an equation or function expressing inverse variation — compare DIRECT VARIATION

in·ver·sion \in-'vər-zhən, -shən\ *noun* (1586)
1 : a reversal of position, order, form, or relationship: as **a** (1) **:** a change in normal word order; *especially* **:** the placement of a verb before its subject (2) **:** the process or result of changing or reversing the relative positions of the notes of a musical interval, chord, or phrase **b :** the condition of being turned inward or inside out **c :** a breaking off of a chromosome section and its subsequent reattachment in inverted position; *also* **:** a chromosomal section that has undergone this process
2 : the act or process of inverting
3 a : a change in the order of the terms of a mathematical proportion effected by inverting each ratio **b :** the operation of forming the inverse of a magnitude, a function, an operation, or an element
4 a : the conversion of dextrorotatory sucrose into a levorotatory mixture of glucose and fructose **b :** a change from one stereochemical figuration at a chiral center in a usually organic molecule to the opposite configuration that is brought about by a reaction in which a substitution of one group is made for a different group
5 : HOMOSEXUALITY
6 : an increase of temperature with height through a layer of air

in·ver·sive \-'vər-siv, -ziv\ *adjective* (1875)
: marked by inversion

¹in·vert \in-'vərt\ *transitive verb* [Latin *invertere*, from *in-* + *vertere* to turn — more at WORTH] (1533)
1 a : to reverse in position, order, or relationship **b :** to subject to inversion
2 a : to turn inside out or upside down **b :** to turn inward
3 : to find the mathematical reciprocal of ⟨to divide using fractions, *invert* the divisor and multiply⟩
synonym see REVERSE

²in·vert \'in-,vərt\ *noun* (1838)
: one characterized by inversion; *especially* **:** HOMOSEXUAL

in·ver·tase \in-'vər-,tās, -,tāz; 'in-vər-,\ *noun* [International Scientific Vocabulary] (1887)
: an enzyme that catalyzes the hydrolysis of sucrose

in·ver·te·brate \(,)in-'vər-tə-brət, -,brāt\ *adjective* [New Latin *invertebratus*, from Latin *in-* + New Latin *vertebratus* vertebrate] (1838)

1 : lacking a spinal column; *also* **:** of or relating to invertebrate animals
2 : lacking in strength or vitality **:** WEAK
— **invertebrate** *noun*

inverted comma *noun* (1789)
chiefly British **:** QUOTATION MARK

in·vert·er \in-'vər-tər\ *noun* (1611)
1 : one that inverts
2 : a device for converting direct current into alternating current

in·vert·ible \in-'vər-tə-bəl\ *adjective* (1881)
: capable of being inverted or subjected to inversion ⟨an *invertible* matrix⟩

invert sugar *noun* (1880)
: a mixture of dextrose and levulose found in fruits or produced artificially by the inversion of sucrose

¹in·vest \in-'vest\ *transitive verb* [Latin *investire* to clothe, surround, from *in-* + *vestis* garment — more at WEAR] (circa 1534)
1 [Medieval Latin *investire*, from Latin, to clothe] **a :** to array in the symbols of office or honor **b :** to furnish with power or authority **c :** to grant someone control or authority over **:** VEST
2 : to cover completely **:** ENVELOP
3 : CLOTHE, ADORN
4 [Middle French *investir*, from Old Italian *investire*, from Latin, to surround] **:** to surround with troops or ships so as to prevent escape or entry
5 : to endow with a quality **:** INFUSE

²invest *verb* [Italian *investire* to clothe, invest money, from Latin, to clothe] (1613)
transitive verb
1 : to commit (money) in order to earn a financial return
2 : to make use of for future benefits or advantages
intransitive verb
: to make an investment
— **in·vest·able** \-'ves-tə-bəl\ *adjective*
— **in·ves·tor** \-tər\ *noun*

in·ves·ti·gate \in-'ves-tə-,gāt\ *verb* **-gat·ed; -gat·ing** [Latin *investigatus*, past participle of *investigare* to track, investigate, from *in-* + *vestigium* footprint, track] (circa 1510)
transitive verb
: to observe or study by close examination and systematic inquiry
intransitive verb
: to make a systematic examination; *especially* **:** to conduct an official inquiry
— **in·ves·ti·ga·tion** \-,ves-tə-'gā-shən\ *noun*
— **in·ves·ti·ga·tion·al** \-shnəl, -shə-nᵊl\ *adjective*
— **in·ves·ti·ga·tive** \-'ves-tə-,gā-tiv\ *adjective*
— **in·ves·ti·ga·tor** \-,gā-tər\ *noun*
— **in·ves·ti·ga·to·ry** \-'ves-ti-gə-,tōr-ē, -,tōr-\ *adjective*

in·ves·ti·ture \in-'ves-tə-,chùr, -chər, -,tyùr, -,tùr\ *noun* [Middle English, from Medieval Latin *investitura*, from *investitus*, past participle of *investire*] (14th century)
1 : the act of establishing in office or ratifying
2 : something that covers or adorns

¹in·vest·ment \in-'ves(t)-mənt\ *noun* [¹*invest*] (1597)
1 a *archaic* **:** VESTMENT **b :** an outer layer **:** ENVELOPE
2 : INVESTITURE 1
3 : BLOCKADE, SIEGE

²investment *noun* [²*invest*] (1615)
: the outlay of money usually for income or profit **:** capital outlay; *also* **:** the sum invested or the property purchased

investment company *noun* (circa 1917)
: a company whose primary business is holding securities of other companies purely for investment purposes — compare HOLDING COMPANY

in·vet·er·a·cy \in-'ve-t(ə-)rə-sē\ *noun* [*inveterate* + *-cy*] (circa 1719)

: the quality or state of being obstinate or persistent **:** TENACITY

in·vet·er·ate \in-'ve-t(ə-)rət\ *adjective* [Middle English, from Latin *inveteratus*, from past participle of *inveterare* to age (transitive verb), from *in-* + *veter-*, *vetus* old — more at WETHER] (14th century)
1 : firmly established by long persistence ⟨the *inveterate* tendency to overlook the obvious⟩
2 : confirmed in a habit **:** HABITUAL ⟨an *inveterate* liar⟩ ☆
— **in·vet·er·ate·ly** *adverb*

in·vi·a·ble \(,)in-'vī-ə-bəl\ *adjective* [International Scientific Vocabulary] (1918)
: incapable of surviving especially because of a deleterious genetic constitution
— **in·vi·a·bil·i·ty** \-,vī-ə-'bi-lə-tē\ *noun*

in·vid·i·ous \in-'vi-dē-əs\ *adjective* [Latin *invidiosus* envious, invidious, from *invidia* envy — more at ENVY] (1606)
1 : tending to cause discontent, animosity, or envy ⟨the *invidious* task of arbitration⟩
2 : ENVIOUS
3 a : of an unpleasant or objectionable nature **:** OBNOXIOUS ⟨*invidious* remarks⟩ **b :** of a kind to cause harm or resentment ⟨an *invidious* comparison⟩
synonym see REPUGNANT
— **in·vid·i·ous·ly** *adverb*
— **in·vid·i·ous·ness** *noun*

in·vig·i·late \in-'vi-jə-,lāt\ *verb* **-lat·ed; -lat·ing** [Latin *invigilatus*, past participle of *invigilare* to stay awake, be watchful, from *in-* + *vigilare* to stay awake — more at VIGILANT] (1553)
intransitive verb
: to keep watch; *especially, British* **:** to supervise students at an examination
transitive verb
: SUPERVISE, MONITOR
— **in·vig·i·la·tion** \-,vi-jə-'lā-shən\ *noun*
— **in·vig·i·la·tor** \-'vi-jə-,lā-tər\ *noun*

in·vig·o·rate \in-'vi-gə-,rāt\ *transitive verb* **-rat·ed; -rat·ing** [probably from *in-* + *vigor*] (1646)
: to give life and energy to **:** ANIMATE; *also* **:** STIMULATE 1
— **in·vig·o·rat·ing·ly** \-,rā-tiŋ-lē\ *adverb*
— **in·vig·o·ra·tion** \-,vi-gə-'rā-shən\ *noun*
— **in·vig·o·ra·tor** \-'vi-gə-,rā-tər\ *noun*

in·vin·ci·ble \(,)in-'vin(t)-sə-bəl\ *adjective* [Middle English, from Middle French, from Late Latin *invincibilis*, from Latin *in-* + *vincere* to conquer — more at VICTOR] (15th century)
: incapable of being conquered, overcome, or subdued
— **in·vin·ci·bil·i·ty** \-,vin(t)-sə-'bi-lə-tē\ *noun*
— **in·vin·ci·ble·ness** \-'vin(t)-sə-bəl-nəs\ *noun*
— **in·vin·ci·bly** \-blē\ *adverb*

☆ **SYNONYMS**
Inveterate, confirmed, chronic mean firmly established. INVETERATE applies to a habit, attitude or feeling of such long existence as to be practically ineradicable or unalterable ⟨an *inveterate* smoker⟩. CONFIRMED implies a growing stronger and firmer with time so as to resist change or reform ⟨a *confirmed* bachelor⟩. CHRONIC suggests something that is persistent or endlessly recurrent and troublesome ⟨a *chronic* complainer⟩.

\ə\ abut \ᵊ\ kitten \ər\ further \a\ ash \ā\ ace \ä\ mop, mar \aù\ out \ch\ chin \e\ bet \ē\ easy \g\ go \i\ hit \ī\ ice \j\ job \ŋ\ sing \ō\ go \ò\ law \òi\ boy \th\ thin \th\ the \ü\ loot \ù\ foot \y\ yet \zh\ vision *see also* Guide to Pronunciation

in·vi·o·la·ble \(ˌ)in-'vī-ə-lə-bəl\ *adjective* [Middle English, from Middle French or Latin; Middle French, from Latin *inviolabilis*, from *in-* + *violare* to violate] (15th century)
1 : secure from violation or profanation
2 : secure from assault or trespass : UNASSAILABLE
— **in·vi·o·la·bil·i·ty** \-ˌvī-ə-lə-'bi-lə-tē\ *noun*
— **in·vi·o·la·ble·ness** \-'vī-ə-lə-bəl-nəs\ *noun*
— **in·vi·o·la·bly** \-blē\ *adverb*
in·vi·o·la·cy \(ˌ)in-'vī-ə-lə-sē\ *noun* (circa 1846)
: the quality or state of being inviolate
in·vi·o·late \-'vī-ə-lət\ *adjective* (15th century)
: not violated or profaned; *especially* : PURE
— **in·vi·o·late·ly** *adverb*
— **in·vi·o·late·ness** *noun*
in·vis·cid \(ˌ)in-'vi-səd\ *adjective* (circa 1889)
1 : having zero viscosity
2 : of or relating to an inviscid fluid ⟨*inviscid* flow⟩
in·vis·i·ble \(ˌ)in-'vi-zə-bəl\ *adjective* [Middle English, from Middle French, from Latin *invisibilis*, from *in-* + *visibilis* visible] (14th century)
1 a : incapable by nature of being seen **b** : inaccessible to view : HIDDEN
2 : IMPERCEPTIBLE, INCONSPICUOUS
3 a : not appearing in published financial statements **b** : not reflected in statistics
— **in·vis·i·bil·i·ty** \-ˌvi-zə-'bi-lə-tē\ *noun*
— **invisible** *noun*
— **in·vis·i·ble·ness** \-'vi-zə-bəl-nəs\ *noun*
— **in·vis·i·bly** \-blē\ *adverb*
in·vi·ta·tion \ˌin-və-'tā-shən\ *noun* (15th century)
1 a : the act of inviting **b** : an often formal request to be present or participate
2 : INCENTIVE, INDUCEMENT
in·vi·ta·tion·al \-shnəl, -shə-nᵊl\ *adjective* (1922)
1 : prepared or entered in response to a request ⟨an *invitational* article⟩
2 : limited to invited participants ⟨an *invitational* tournament⟩
— **invitational** *noun*
¹in·vi·ta·to·ry \in-'vī-tə-ˌtōr-ē, -ˌtȯr-\ *adjective* (14th century)
: containing an invitation
²invitatory *noun, plural* **-ries** (14th century)
: an invitatory psalm or antiphon
¹in·vite \in-'vīt\ *transitive verb* **in·vit·ed; in·vit·ing** [Middle French or Latin; Middle French *inviter*, from Latin *invitare*] (1533)
1 a : to offer an incentive or inducement to : ENTICE **b** : to increase the likelihood of
2 a : to request the presence or participation of **b** : to request formally **c** : to urge politely : WELCOME
— **in·vit·er** *noun*
²in·vite \'in-ˌvīt\ *noun* (1659)
: INVITATION 1
in·vi·tee \ˌin-və-'tē, -ˌvī-\ *noun* (1803)
: an invited person
inviting \in-'vī-tiŋ\ *adjective* (1604)
: ATTRACTIVE, TEMPTING
— **in·vit·ing·ly** \-tiŋ-lē\ *adverb*
in vi·tro \in-'vē-(ˌ)trō, -'vi-\ *adverb or adjective* [New Latin, literally, in glass] (circa 1894)
: outside the living body and in an artificial environment
in vi·vo \in-'vē-(ˌ)vō\ *adverb or adjective* [New Latin, literally, in the living] (1901)
: in the living body of a plant or animal
in·vo·cate \'in-və-ˌkāt\ *transitive verb* (1526)
archaic : INVOKE
in·vo·ca·tion \ˌin-və-'kā-shən\ *noun* [Middle English *invocacioun*, from Middle French *invocation*, from Latin *invocation-, invocatio*, from *invocare*] (14th century)
1 a : the act or process of petitioning for help or support; *specifically, often capitalized* : a

prayer of entreaty (as at the beginning of a service of worship) **b** : a calling upon for authority or justification
2 : a formula for conjuring : INCANTATION
3 : an act of legal or moral implementation : ENFORCEMENT
— **in·vo·ca·tion·al** \-shnəl, -shə-nᵊl\ *adjective*
— **in·voc·a·to·ry** \in-'vä-kə-ˌtōr-ē, -ˌtȯr-\ *adjective*
¹in·voice \'in-ˌvȯis\ *noun* [modification of Middle French *envois*, plural of *envoi* message — more at ENVOI] (1560)
1 : an itemized list of goods shipped usually specifying the price and the terms of sale : BILL
2 : a consignment of merchandise
²invoice *transitive verb* **in·voiced; in·voic·ing** (1698)
: to send an invoice for or to
in·voke \in-'vōk\ *transitive verb* **in·voked; in·vok·ing** [Middle English, from Middle French *invoquer*, from Latin *invocare*, from *in-* + *vocare* to call, from *voc-, vox* voice — more at VOICE] (15th century)
1 a : to petition for help or support **b** : to appeal to or cite as authority
2 : to call forth by incantation : CONJURE
3 : to make an earnest request for : SOLICIT
4 : to put into effect or operation : IMPLEMENT
5 : BRING ABOUT, CAUSE
— **in·vok·er** *noun*
in·vo·lu·cre \'in-və-ˌlü-kər\ *noun* [French, from New Latin *involucrum*] (1794)
: one or more whorls of bracts situated below and close to a flower, flower cluster, or fruit
— **in·vo·lu·cral** \ˌin-və-'lü-krəl\ *adjective*
— **in·vo·lu·crate** \-krət, -ˌkrāt\ *adjective*
in·vo·lu·crum \ˌin-və-'lü-krəm\ *noun, plural* **-cra** \-krə\ [New Latin, sheath, involucre, from Latin, wrapper, from *involvere* to wrap] (circa 1677)
: a surrounding envelope or sheath
in·vol·un·tary \(ˌ)in-'vä-lən-ˌter-ē\ *adjective* [Middle English *involuntari*, from Late Latin *involuntarius*, from Latin *in-* + *voluntarius* voluntary] (15th century)
1 : done contrary to or without choice
2 : COMPULSORY
3 : not subject to control of the will : REFLEX
— **in·vol·un·tari·ly** \-ˌvä-lən-'ter-ə-lē\ *adverb*
— **in·vol·un·tari·ness** \-'vä-lən-ˌter-ē-nəs\ *noun*
involuntary manslaughter *noun* (circa 1879)
: manslaughter resulting from the failure to perform a legal duty expressly required to safeguard human life, from the commission of an unlawful act not constituting a felony, or from the commission of a lawful act in a negligent or improper manner
involuntary muscle *noun* (1840)
: muscle governing reflex functions and not under direct voluntary control; *especially* : SMOOTH MUSCLE
¹in·vo·lute \'in-və-ˌlüt\ *adjective* [Latin *involutus* concealed, from past participle of *involvere*] (1661)
1 a : curled spirally **b** (1) : curled or curved inward (2) : having the edges rolled over the upper surface toward the midrib ⟨an *involute* leaf⟩ **c** : having the form of an involute ⟨a gear with *involute* teeth⟩
2 : INVOLVED, INTRICATE
²involute *noun* (circa 1796)
: a curve traced by a point on a thread kept taut as it is unwound from another curve ⟨*involute* of a circle⟩
³in·vo·lute \ˌin-və-'lüt\ *intransitive verb* **-lut·ed; -lut·ing** (1816)
1 : to become involute
2 a : to return to a former condition **b** : to become cleared up : DISAPPEAR

in·vo·lu·tion \ˌin-və-'lü-shən\ *noun* [Latin *involution-, involutio*, from *involvere*] (circa 1611)
1 a (1) : the act or an instance of enfolding or entangling : INVOLVEMENT (2) : an involved grammatical construction usually characterized by the insertion of clauses between the subject and predicate **b** : COMPLEXITY, INTRICACY
2 : EXPONENTIATION
3 a : an inward curvature or penetration **b** : the formation of a gastrula by ingrowth of cells formed at the dorsal lip
4 : a shrinking or return to a former size
5 : the regressive alterations of a body or its parts characteristic of the aging process; *specifically* : decline marked by a decrease of bodily vigor and in women by menopause
— **in·vo·lu·tion·al** \-shnəl, -shə-nᵊl\ *adjective*
in·volve \in-'välv, -'vȯlv *also* -'väv *or* -'vȯv\ *transitive verb* **in·volved; in·volv·ing** [Middle English, to roll up, wrap, from Latin *involvere*, from *in-* + *volvere* to roll — more at VOLUBLE] (14th century)
1 *archaic* : to enfold or envelop so as to encumber
2 a : to engage as a participant ⟨workers *involved* in building a house⟩ **b** : to oblige to take part ⟨right of Congress to *involve* the nation in war⟩ **c** : to occupy (as oneself) absorbingly; *especially* : to commit (as oneself) emotionally ⟨was *involved* with a married man⟩
3 : to surround as if with a wrapping : ENVELOP
4 a *archaic* : to wind, coil, or wreathe about **b** : to relate closely : CONNECT
5 a : to have within or as part of itself : INCLUDE **b** : to require as a necessary accompaniment : ENTAIL **c** : to have an effect on
synonym see INCLUDE
— **in·volve·ment** \-'välv-mənt, -'vȯlv-\ *noun*
— **in·volv·er** *noun*
in·volved \-'välvd, -'vȯlvd *also* -'vävd *or* -'vȯvd\ *adjective* (15th century)
1 : INVOLUTE, TWISTED
2 a : marked by extreme and often needless or excessive complexity **b** : difficult to deal with because of complexity or disorder
3 : being affected or implicated
synonym see COMPLEX
— **in·volv·ed·ly** \-'väl-vəd-lē, -'vȯl- *also* -'vä-vəd- *or* -'vȯ-\ *adverb*
in·vul·ner·a·ble \(ˌ)in-'vəl-n(ə-)rə-bəl, -nər-bəl\ *adjective* [Latin *invulnerabilis*, from *in-* + *vulnerare* to wound — more at VULNERABLE] (1595)
1 : incapable of being wounded, injured, or harmed
2 : immune to or proof against attack : IMPREGNABLE
— **in·vul·ner·a·bil·i·ty** \-ˌvəl-n(ə-)rə-'bi-lə-tē\ *noun*
— **in·vul·ner·a·ble·ness** \-'vəl-n(ə-)rə-bəl-nəs, -nər-bəl-\ *noun*
— **in·vul·ner·a·bly** \-blē\ *adverb*
¹in·ward \'in-wərd\ *adjective* [Middle English, from Old English *inweard* (akin to Old High German *inwert*), from *in* + *-weard* ward] (before 12th century)
1 : situated on the inside : INNER
2 a : of or relating to the mind or spirit ⟨*inward* peace⟩ **b** : absorbed in one's own mental or spiritual life : INTROSPECTIVE
3 : marked by close acquaintance : FAMILIAR
4 : directed toward the interior
²inward *or* **in·wards** \-wərdz\ *adverb* (before 12th century)

involute *a, p, p, p, p* traced by any point *p* of the thread *t* unwinding from curve *c*

1 : toward the inside, center, or interior
2 : toward the inner being
³**inward** *noun* (before 12th century)
1 : something that is inward
2 in·wards \'in-ərdz, -wərdz\ *plural* : IN-
WARDS
Inward Light *noun* (1706)
: INNER LIGHT
in·ward·ly \'in-wərd-lē\ *adverb* (before 12th
century)
1 : in the innermost being : MENTALLY, SPIRITU-
ALLY
2 a : beneath the surface : INTERNALLY ⟨bled
inwardly⟩ **b :** to oneself : PRIVATELY ⟨cursed
inwardly⟩
in·ward·ness *noun* (14th century)
1 : internal quality or substance
2 : close acquaintance : FAMILIARITY
3 : fundamental nature : ESSENCE
4 : absorption in one's own mental or spiritual
life
in·weave \(,)in-'wēv\ *transitive verb* **-wove**
\-'wōv\ *also* **-weaved; -wo·ven** \-'wō-vən\
also **-weaved; -weav·ing** (15th century)
: INTERWEAVE, INTERLACE
in–wrought \(,)in-'rȯt, 'in-,\ *adjective* (1637)
1 : having decoration worked in : ORNAMENT-
ED; *especially* : decorated with embroidery
2 : worked in especially as decoration
in–your–face *adjective* (1982)
: characterized by or being bold and often ar-
rogant aggressiveness ⟨*in-your-face* basket-
ball⟩
Io \'ī-(,)ō\ *noun* [Latin, from Greek *Īō*]
: a maiden loved by Zeus and changed by him
into a heifer so that she might escape the jeal-
ous rage of Hera
iod- *or* **iodo-** *combining form* [French *iode*]
: iodine ⟨*iod*ize⟩ ⟨*iodo*form⟩
io·date \'ī-ə-,dāt, -dət\ *noun* [French, from
iode] (1826)
: a salt of iodic acid
iod·ic acid \ī-'ä-dik-\ *noun* [French *iodique*,
from *iode*] (1826)
: a crystalline oxidizing solid HIO_3 formed by
oxidation of iodine
io·dide \'ī-ə-,dīd\ *noun* [International Scientific
Vocabulary] (1822)
: a salt of hydriodic acid; *also* : the univalent
anion I^- of such a salt
io·din·ate \'ī-ə-də-,nāt\ *transitive verb* **-at-
ed; -at·ing** (1908)
: to treat or cause to combine with iodine or a
compound of iodine
— **io·din·ation** \,ī-ə-də-'nā-shən\ *noun*
io·dine \'ī-ə-,dīn, -dᵊn, -,dēn\ *noun, often at-
tributive* [French *iode*, from Greek *ioeidēs* vi-
olet colored, from *ion* violet] (1814)
1 : a nonmetallic halogen element obtained
usually as heavy shining blackish gray crystals
and used especially in medicine, photography,
and analysis — see ELEMENT table
2 : a tincture of iodine used especially as a
topical antiseptic
io·dise *British variant of* IODIZE
io·dize \'ī-ə-,dīz\ *transitive verb* **io·dized; io-
diz·ing** (1841)
: to treat with iodine or an iodide ⟨*iodized* salt⟩
io·do·form \ī-'ō-də-,fȯrm, -'ä-\ *noun* [Interna-
tional Scientific Vocabulary iod- + -form (as
in *chloroform*)] (1838)
: a yellow crystalline volatile compound CHI_3
with a penetrating persistent odor that is used
as an antiseptic dressing
io·do·phor \-,fȯr\ *noun* [iod- + Greek -*phoros*
carrier — more at -PHORE] (1952)
: a complex of iodine and a surface-active
agent that releases iodine gradually and serves
as a disinfectant
io·dop·sin \,ī-ə-'däp-sən\ *noun* [iod- (from
Greek *ioeidēs* violet colored) + Greek *opsis*
sight, vision + English -*in* — more at OPTIC]
(1938)
: a photosensitive violet pigment in the retinal
cones that is similar to rhodopsin but more la-

bile, is formed from vitamin A, and is impor-
tant in daylight vision
io moth \'ī-(,)ō-\ *noun* [Latin *Io*] (1870)
: a chiefly North American saturniid moth
(*Automeris io*) having a large circular eyelike
spot on the upper surface of each hind wing
and a larva with stinging spines
ion \'ī-ən, 'ī-,än\ *noun* [Greek, neuter of *iōn*,
present participle of *ienai* to go — more at IS-
SUE] (circa 1834)
1 : an atom or group of atoms that carries a
positive or negative electric charge as a result
of having lost or gained one or more electrons
2 : a charged subatomic particle (as a free
electron)
-ion *noun suffix* [Middle English -*ioun*, -*ion*,
from Old French -*ion*, from Latin -*ion-*, -*io*]
1 a : act or process ⟨valida*tion*⟩ **b :** result of an
act or process ⟨regula*tion*⟩
2 : state or condition ⟨hydra*tion*⟩
ion engine *noun* (1958)
: a reaction engine deriving thrust from the
ejection of a stream of ionized particles
ion exchange *noun* (1923)
: a reversible interchange of one kind of ion
present on an insoluble solid with another of
like charge present in a solution surrounding
the solid with the reaction being used especial-
ly for softening or demineralizing water, the
purification of chemicals, or the separation of
substances
— **ion exchanger** *noun*
ion exchange resin *noun* (1943)
: an insoluble material of high molecular
weight that contains groups which can be ex-
changed with ions in a solution with which it
is in contact
Io·ni·an \ī-'ō-nē-ən\ *noun* [*Ionia*, Asia Minor]
(1550)
1 : a member of any of the Greek peoples who
settled on the islands of the Aegean Sea and
the western shore of Asia Minor toward the
end of the second millennium B.C.
2 : a native or inhabitant of Ionia
— **Ionian** *adjective*
ion·ic \ī-'ä-nik\ *adjective* [International Scien-
tific Vocabulary] (1890)
1 : of, relating to, existing as, or characterized
by ions ⟨*ionic* gases⟩ ⟨the *ionic* charge⟩
2 : based on or functioning by means of ions
⟨*ionic* conduction⟩ ⟨an *ionic* lattice⟩
— **ion·ic·i·ty** \,ī-ə-'ni-sə-tē\ *noun*
¹**Ion·ic** \ī-'ä-nik\ *adjective* [Latin & Middle
French; Middle French *ionique*, from Latin
ionicus, from Greek *iōnikos*, from *Iōnia* Ionia]
(1585)
1 : of or relating to the ancient Greek architec-
tural order distinguished especially by fluted
columns on bases and scroll volutes in its cap-
itals — see ORDER illustration
2 : of or relating to Ionia or the Ionians
²**Ionic** *noun* (1668)
: a dialect of ancient Greek spoken especially
in Ionia and the Cyclades
ionic bond *noun* (1939)
: a chemical bond formed between oppositely
charged species because of their mutual elec-
trostatic attraction
ion·ise *British variant of* IONIZE
io·ni·um \ī-'ō-nē-əm\ *noun* [*ion;* from its ion-
izing action] (1907)
: a natural radioactive isotope of thorium hav-
ing a mass number of 230
ionization chamber *noun* (1904)
: a partially evacuated tube provided with
electrodes so that its conductivity due to the
ionization of the residual gas reveals the pres-
ence of ionizing radiation
ion·ize \'ī-ə-,nīz\ *verb* **ion·ized; ion·iz·ing**
[International Scientific Vocabulary] (1898)
transitive verb
: to convert wholly or partly into ions
intransitive verb
: to become ionized
— **ion·iz·able** \-,nī-zə-bəl\ *adjective*
— **ion·i·za·tion** \,ī-ə-nə-'zā-shən\ *noun*

— **ion·iz·er** \'ī-ə-,nī-zər\ *noun*
ion·o·phore \ī-'ä-nə-,fōr, -,fȯr\ *noun* (circa
1955)
: a compound that facilitates transmission of
an ion (as of calcium) across a lipid barrier (as
in a cell membrane) by combining with the
ion or by increasing the permeability of the
barrier to it
ion·o·sphere \ī-'ä-nə-,sfir\ *noun* (1926)
: the part of the earth's atmosphere in which
ionization of atmospheric gases affects the
propagation of radio waves, which extends
from about 30 miles (50 kilometers) to the ex-
osphere, which is divided into regions of one
or more layers whose altitudes and degrees of
ionization vary with time of day, season, and
solar cycle, and which is contiguous with the
upper portion of the mesosphere and the ther-
mosphere; *also* : a comparable region of
charged particles surrounding another celestial
body (as Venus)
— **ion·o·spher·ic** \,ī-,ä-nə-'sfir-ik, -'sfer-\
adjective
— **ion·o·spher·i·cal·ly** \-i-k(ə-)lē\ *adverb*
ion·to·pho·re·sis \(,)ī-,än-tə-fə-'rē-səs\ *noun,
plural* **-re·ses** \-,sēz\ [New Latin, from *ionto-*
ion (from Greek *iont-*, *iōn*, present participle
of *ienai*) + -*phoresis*] (1909)
: the introduction of an ionized substance (as a
drug) through intact skin by the application of
a direct electric current
— **ion·to·pho·ret·ic** \-'re-tik\ *adjective*
— **ion·to·pho·ret·i·cal·ly** \-ti-k(ə-)lē\ *ad-
verb*
io·ta \ī-'ō-tə\ *noun* [Latin, from Greek *iōta*, of
Semitic origin; akin to Hebrew *yōdh* yod]
(1607)
1 : the 9th letter of the Greek alphabet — see
ALPHABET table
2 : an infinitesimal amount : JOT
IOU \,ī-(,)ō-'yü\ *noun* [from the pronunciation
of *I owe you*] (1795)
1 : a paper that has on it the letters IOU, a
stated sum, and a signature and that is given as
an acknowledgment of debt
2 : DEBT, OBLIGATION
-ious *adjective suffix* [Middle English, partly
from Old French -*ious*, -*ieux*, from Latin
-*iosus*, from -*i-*, penultimate vowel of some
noun stems + -*osus* -ous; partly from Latin
-*ius*, adjective suffix]
: -OUS ⟨edac*ious*⟩
IPA \,ī-(,)pē-'ā\ *noun* [International Phonetic
Alphabet] (1933)
: an alphabet designed to represent each hu-
man speech sound with a unique symbol
ip·e·cac \'i-pi-,kak\ *or* **ipe·ca·cu·an·ha** \,i-
pi-,ka-kyə-'wä-nə, -nyə\ *noun* [Portuguese *ipe-
cacuanha*, from Tupi *ipekaaguéne*] (1682)
1 : the dried rhizome and roots of either of
two tropical American plants (*Cephaelis
acuminata* and *C. ipecacuanha*) of the madder
family used especially as a source of emetine;
also : either of these plants
2 : an emetic and expectorant drug that con-
tains emetine and is prepared from ipecac es-
pecially as a syrup for use in treating acciden-
tal poisoning
Iph·i·ge·nia \,i-fə-jə-'nī-ə\ *noun* [Latin, from
Greek *Iphigeneia*]
: a daughter of Agamemnon nearly sacrificed
by him to Artemis but saved by her and made
a priestess
ipro·ni·a·zid \,ī-prə-'nī-ə-zəd\ *noun* [blend of
isoniazid and *propyl*] (1952)
: a derivative $C_9H_{13}N_3O$ of isoniazid that is
used as a monoamine oxidase inhibitor and
was formerly used in treating tuberculosis
ip·se dix·it \'ip-sē-'dik-sət\ *noun* [Latin, he
himself said it] (15th century)

\ə\ abut \ᵊ\ kitten \ər\ further \a\ ash \ā\ ace
\ä\ mop, mar \au̇\ out \ch\ chin \e\ bet \ē\ easy
\g\ go \i\ hit \ī\ ice \j\ job \ŋ\ sing \ō\ go
\ȯ\ law \ȯi\ boy \th\ thin \t̲h̲\ the \ü\ loot \u̇\ foot
\y\ yet \zh\ vision *see also* Guide to Pronunciation

ip·si·lat·er·al \ˌip-si-ˈla-t(ə-)rəl\ *adjective* [International Scientific Vocabulary, from Latin *ipse* self, himself + *later-, latus* side] (1907)
: situated or appearing on or affecting the same side of the body
— **ip·si·lat·er·al·ly** \-t(ə-)rə-lē\ *adverb*

ip·sis·si·ma ver·ba \ip-ˈsi-sə-mə-ˈvər-bə\ *noun plural* [New Latin, literally, the selfsame words] (1807)
: the exact language used by someone quoted

ip·so fac·to \ˈip-(ˌ)sō-ˈfak-(ˌ)tō\ *adverb* [New Latin, literally, by the fact itself] (1548)
: by that very fact or act : as an inevitable result

IQ \ˌī-ˈkyü\ *noun* (1920)
: INTELLIGENCE QUOTIENT

ir- — see IN-

IRA \ˌī-(ˌ)är-ˈā; ˈī-rə\ *noun, plural* **IRAs** [*i*ndividual *r*etirement *a*ccount] (1974)
: a savings account in which a person may deposit up to a stipulated amount each year with the deposits deductible from taxable income and both deposits and interest taxable after the person's retirement

Ira·ni·an \i-ˈrä-nē-ən, -ˈra-, -ˈrä-; ī-ˈ\ *noun* (1789)
1 : a native or inhabitant of Iran
2 : a branch of the Indo-European family of languages that includes Persian — see INDO-EUROPEAN LANGUAGES table
— **Iranian** *adjective*

iras·ci·ble \i-ˈra-sə-bəl\ *adjective* [Middle French, from Late Latin *irascibilis*, from Latin *irasci* to become angry, be angry, from *ira*] (circa 1530)
: marked by hot temper and easily provoked anger
— **iras·ci·bil·i·ty** \-ˌra-sə-ˈbi-lə-tē\ *noun*
— **iras·ci·ble·ness** \i-ˈra-sə-bəl-nəs\ *noun*
— **iras·ci·bly** \-blē\ *adverb*

irate \ī-ˈrāt, ˈī-ˌ, i-ˈrāt\ *adjective* (1838)
1 : roused to ire ⟨an *irate* taxpayer⟩
2 : arising from anger ⟨*irate* words⟩
— **irate·ly** *adverb*
— **irate·ness** *noun*

ire \ˈī(ə)r\ *noun* [Middle English, from Middle French, from Latin *ira;* perhaps akin to Greek *oistros* gadfly, frenzy] (14th century)
: intense and usually openly displayed anger
synonym see ANGER
— **ire** *transitive verb*
— **ire·ful** \-fəl\ *adjective*

ire·nic \ī-ˈre-nik, -ˈrē-\ *adjective* [Greek *eirēnikos*, from *eirēnē* peace] (circa 1864)
: favoring, conducive to, or operating toward peace, moderation, or conciliation
— **ire·ni·cal·ly** \-ni-k(ə-)lē, -rē-\ *adverb*

irid- *or* **irido-** *combining form*
1 [Latin *irid-, iris*] : rainbow ⟨*irid*escent⟩
2 [New Latin *irid-, iris*] : iris of the eye ⟨*irid*ology⟩

ir·i·des·cence \ˌir-ə-ˈde-s⁵n(t)s\ *noun* (1804)
1 : a lustrous rainbowlike play of color caused by differential refraction of light waves (as from an oil slick, soap bubble, or fish scales) that tends to change as the angle of view changes
2 : a lustrous or attractive quality or effect ⟨the agglomeration of power which . . . gives them a certain *iridescence* of glamor and superiority —Margaret Landon⟩

ir·i·des·cent \-s⁵nt\ *adjective* (1791)
: having or exhibiting iridescence
— **ir·i·des·cent·ly** *adverb*

irid·ic \i-ˈri-dik, ī-ˈri-dik\ *adjective* (circa 1890)
: of or relating to the iris of the eye

irid·i·um \i-ˈri-dē-əm\ *noun* [New Latin, from Latin *irid-, iris;* from the colors produced by its dissolving in hydrochloric acid] (1804)
: a silver-white hard brittle very heavy metallic element — see ELEMENT table

ir·i·dol·o·gy \ˌī-rə-ˈdä-lə-jē\ *noun, plural* **-gies** (circa 1923)
: the study of the iris of the eye for indications of bodily health and disease

— **ir·i·dol·o·gist** \-jist\ *noun*

ir·id·os·mine \ˌir-ə-ˈdäz-ˌmēn\ *noun* [German, from New Latin *iridium + osmium*] (1827)
: a mineral that is a native iridium osmium alloy usually containing some rhodium and platinum

¹**iris** \ˈī-rəs\ *noun, plural* **iris·es** *or* **iri·des** \ˈī-rə-ˌdēz, ˈir-ə-\ [Middle English, from Latin *irid-, iris* rainbow, iris plant, from Greek, rainbow, iris plant, iris of the eye — more at WIRE] (15th century)
1 : RAINBOW
2 [New Latin *irid-, iris*, from Greek] **a** : the opaque contractile diaphragm perforated by the pupil and forming the colored portion of the eye — see EYE illustration **b** : IRIS DIAPHRAGM; *also* : a similar device with a circular opening that can be varied in size
3 *or plural* **iris** [New Latin *Irid-, Iris*, genus name, from Latin] : any of a large genus (*Iris* of the family Iridaceae, the iris family) of perennial herbaceous plants with linear usually basal leaves and large showy flowers

²**iris** *transitive verb* (1816)
: to make iridescent

Iris \ˈī-rəs\ *noun* [Latin, from Greek]
: the Greek goddess of the rainbow and a messenger of the gods

iris diaphragm *noun* (1867)
: an adjustable diaphragm of thin opaque plates that can be turned by a ring so as to change the diameter of a central opening usually to regulate the aperture of a lens

iris diaphragm

Irish \ˈī-rish\ *noun* [Middle English, from (assumed) Old English *Īrisc*, from *Īras* Irishmen, of Celtic origin; akin to Old Irish *Ériu* Ireland] (13th century)
1 *plural in construction* : natives or inhabitants of Ireland or their descendants especially when of Celtic speech or culture
2 a : the Celtic language of Ireland especially as used since the later medieval period **b** : English spoken by the Irish
3 : IRISH WHISKEY
— **Irish** *adjective*

Irish bull *noun* (1802)
: an incongruous statement (as "it was hereditary in his family to have no children")

Irish coffee *noun* (1950)
: hot sugared coffee and Irish whiskey topped with whipped cream

Irish confetti *noun* (1922)
: a rock or brick used as a missile

Irish Gaelic *noun* (1891)
: IRISH 2a

Irish·ism \ˈī-ri-ˌshi-zəm\ *noun* (1734)
1 : a word, phrase, or expression characteristic of the Irish
2 : IRISH BULL

Irish·ly \ˈī-rish-lē\ *adverb* (1571)
: in a manner characteristic of the Irish

Irish mail *noun* (1908)
: a 3- or 4-wheeled toy vehicle activated by a hand lever

Irish·man \ˈī-rish-mən\ *noun* (13th century)
1 : a native or inhabitant of Ireland
2 : one that is of Irish descent

Irish moss *noun* (1845)
1 : the dried and bleached plants of a red alga (especially *Chondrus crispus*) used as an agent for thickening or emulsifying or as a demulcent
2 : a red alga that is a source of Irish moss — called also *carrageen*

Irish·ness \ˈī-rish-nəs\ *noun* (1804)
: the fact or quality of being Irish

Irish potato *noun* (1664)
: POTATO 2b

Irish·ry \ˈī-rish-rē\ *noun, plural* **-ries** (14th century)
1 : IRISH 1
2 a : Irish quality or character **b** : an Irish peculiarity or trait

Irish setter *noun* (1866)
: any of a breed of bird dogs generally comparable to English setters but with a mahogany red coat

Irish stew *noun* (1814)
: a stew having as its principal ingredients meat (as lamb), potatoes, and onions in a thick gravy

Irish terrier *noun* (1857)
: any of a breed of active medium-sized terriers developed in Ireland and characterized by a dense close usually reddish wiry coat

Irish water spaniel *noun* (1885)
: any of a breed of large retrievers characterized by a topknot, a heavy curly coat which is dark liver in color, and a short-haired tail

Irish whiskey *noun* (1798)
: whiskey made in Ireland chiefly of barley

Irish wolfhound *noun* (1880)
: any of a breed of very tall heavily built hounds having a rough wiry coat

Irish·wom·an \ˈī-rish-ˌwů-mən\ *noun* (15th century)
: a woman born in Ireland or of Irish descent

Irish wolfhound

iri·tis \ī-ˈrī-təs\ *noun* [New Latin, irregular from *iris*] (1818)
: inflammation of the iris of the eye

¹**irk** \ˈərk\ *transitive verb* [Middle English] (15th century)
: to make weary, irritated, or bored
synonym see ANNOY

²**irk** *noun* (circa 1570)
1 : the fact of being annoying
2 : a source of annoyance

irk·some \ˈərk-səm\ *adjective* (15th century)
: tending to irk : TEDIOUS ⟨an *irksome* task⟩
— **irk·some·ly** *adverb*
— **irk·some·ness** *noun*

iro·ko \ə-ˈrō-(ˌ)kō\ *noun* [Yoruba *ìrokò*] (1890)
: a large tropical western African tree (*Chlorophora excelsa*) of the mulberry family having strong streaky insect-resistant wood which is often used as a teak substitute; *also* : this wood

¹**iron** \ˈī(-ə)rn\ *noun* [Middle English, from Old English *īsern, īren;* akin to Old High German *īsarn* iron] (before 12th century)
1 : a heavy malleable ductile magnetic silver-white metallic element that readily rusts in moist air, occurs native in meteorites and combined in most igneous rocks, is the most used of metals, and is vital to biological processes — see ELEMENT table
2 : something made of iron: as **a** *plural* : shackles for the hands or legs **b** : a heated metal implement used for branding or cauterizing **c** : a household device usually with a flat metal base that is heated to smooth, finish, or press (as cloth) **d** : STIRRUP — usually used in plural **e** : any of a series of numbered golf clubs having relatively thin metal heads — compare WOOD
3 : great strength, hardness, or determination
usage see ASK
— **iron in the fire 1** : a matter requiring close attention **2** : a prospective course of action

²**iron** *adjective* (before 12th century)
1 : of, relating to, or made of iron
2 : resembling iron
3 a : strong and healthy : ROBUST **b** : INFLEXIBLE, UNRELENTING ⟨*iron* determination⟩ **c** : holding or binding fast ⟨an *iron* grip⟩
— **iron·ness** \ˈī(-ə)rn-nəs\ *noun*

³**iron** (15th century)
transitive verb
1 : to furnish or cover with iron

2 : to shackle with irons
3 a : to smooth with or as if with a heated iron ⟨*iron* a shirt⟩ **b :** to remove (as wrinkles) by ironing
intransitive verb
: to smooth or press cloth or clothing with a heated iron
Iron Age *noun* (1879)
: the period of human culture characterized by the smelting of iron and its use in industry beginning somewhat before 1000 B.C. in western Asia and Egypt
iron·bark \ˈī(-ə)rn-ˌbärk\ *noun* (1799)
: any of several Australian eucalypti having hard gray bark and heavy hard durable wood used especially in heavy construction; *also* **:** this wood
iron·bound \-ˈbau̇nd\ *adjective* (14th century)
: bound with or as if with iron: as **a :** HARSH, RUGGED ⟨*ironbound* coast⟩ **b :** STERN, RIGOROUS ⟨*ironbound* traditions⟩
¹iron·clad \-ˈklad\ *adjective* (circa 1847)
1 : sheathed in iron armor — used especially of naval vessels
2 : so firm or secure as to be unbreakable: as **a :** BINDING ⟨an *ironclad* oath⟩ **b :** having no obvious weakness ⟨an *ironclad* case against the defendant⟩
²iron·clad \-ˌklad\ *noun* (1862)
: an armored naval vessel especially of the mid to late nineteenth century
iron curtain *noun* (1819)
1 : an impenetrable barrier ⟨the *iron curtain* between the ego and the unconscious —C. J. Rolo⟩
2 : a political, military, and ideological barrier that cuts off and isolates an area; *specifically, often capitalized* **:** one isolating an area under Soviet control
iron·er \ˈī(-ə)r-nər\ *noun* (1773)
: one that irons; *specifically* **:** MANGLE
iron·fisted \ˈī(-ə)rn-ˈfis-təd\ *adjective* (1599)
1 : STINGY, MISERLY
2 : being both harsh and ruthless ⟨*ironfisted* methods⟩
iron gray *noun* (before 12th century)
: a slightly greenish dark gray
iron hand *noun* (1703)
: stern or rigorous control ⟨ruled with an *iron hand*⟩
— **iron·hand·ed** \ˈī(-ə)rn-ˈhan-dəd\ *adjective*
iron·heart·ed \ˈī(-ə)rn-ˈhär-təd\ *adjective* (1600)
: CRUEL, HARD-HEARTED
iron horse *noun* (1840)
: LOCOMOTIVE 1; *especially* **:** a steam locomotive
iron·ic \ī-ˈrä-nik *also* i-ˈrä-\ *or* **iron·i·cal** \-ni-kəl\ *adjective* (1576)
1 : relating to, containing, or constituting irony
2 : given to irony
synonym see SARCASTIC
— **iron·i·cal·ness** \-ni-kəl-nəs\ *noun*
iron·i·cal·ly \-ni-k(ə-)lē\ *adverb* (1576)
1 : in an ironic manner
2 : it is ironic, curious, or surprising
iron·ing \ˈī(-ə)r-niŋ\ *noun* (circa 1710)
1 : the action or process of smoothing or pressing with or as if with a heated iron
2 : clothes ironed or to be ironed
ironing board *noun* (1843)
: a flat padded cloth-covered surface on which clothes are ironed
iro·nist \ˈī-rə-nist\ *noun* (1727)
: one who uses irony especially in the development of a literary work or theme
iro·nize \-ˌnīz\ *verb* **-nized; -niz·ing** (1602)
transitive verb
: to make ironic in appearance or effect
intransitive verb
: to use irony **:** speak or behave ironically
iron lung *noun* (1932)
: a device for artificial respiration in which rhythmic alternations in the air pressure in a

chamber surrounding a patient's chest force air into and out of the lungs
iron maiden *noun* (circa 1895)
: a supposed medieval torture device consisting of a hollow iron statue or coffin in the shape of a woman that is lined with spikes which impale the enclosed victim
iron man *noun* (1914)
: a man of unusual physical endurance
iron·mas·ter \ˈī(-ə)rn-ˌmas-tər\ *noun* (1674)
: a manufacturer of iron
iron·mon·ger \-ˌməŋ-gər, -ˌmäŋ-\ *noun* (14th century)
British **:** a dealer in iron and hardware
iron·mon·gery \-g(ə-)rē\ *noun* (1711)
: something made of metal; *especially, British* **:** HARDWARE 1
iron out *transitive verb* (1870)
1 : to make smooth or flat by or as if by pressing
2 : to resolve or work out a solution to ⟨*ironed out* their differences⟩
iron oxide *noun* (1885)
: any of several oxides of iron: as **a :** FERRIC OXIDE **b :** FERROUS OXIDE
iron pyrites *noun* (circa 1817)
: PYRITE — called also *iron pyrite*
iron ration *noun* (1876)
: an emergency ration
iron·side \-ˌsīd\ *noun* (13th century)
: a man of great strength or bravery
iron·stone \ˈī(-ə)rn-ˌstōn\ *noun* (1522)
1 : a hard sedimentary rock rich in iron; *especially* **:** a siderite in a coal region
2 : IRONSTONE CHINA
ironstone china *noun* (1825)
: a hard heavy durable white pottery developed in England early in the 19th century
iron sulfide *noun* (1885)
: any of several sulfides of iron
iron·ware \ˈī(-ə)rn-ˌwar, -ˌwer\ *noun* (15th century)
: articles made of iron
iron·weed \-ˌwēd\ *noun* (1819)
: any of several mostly weedy American composite plants (genus *Vernonia*) usually having alternate leaves and perfect red, purple, or white tubular flowers in terminal cymose heads
iron·wood \-ˌwu̇d\ *noun* (1657)
1 : any of numerous trees and shrubs (as a hornbeam or hop hornbeam) with exceptionally tough or hard wood
2 : the wood of an ironwood
iron·work \-ˌwərk\ *noun* (15th century)
1 : work in iron; *also* **:** something made of iron
2 *plural but singular or plural in construction* **:** a mill or building where iron or steel is smelted or heavy iron or steel products are made
— **iron·work·er** \-ˌwər-kər\ *noun*
iro·ny \ˈī-rə-nē *also* ˈī(-ə)r-nē\ *noun, plural* **-nies** [Latin *ironia*, from Greek *eirōnia*, from *eirōn* dissembler] (1502)
1 : a pretense of ignorance and of willingness to learn from another assumed in order to make the other's false conceptions conspicuous by adroit questioning — called also *Socratic irony*
2 a : the use of words to express something other than and especially the opposite of the literal meaning **b :** a usually humorous or sardonic literary style or form characterized by irony **c :** an ironic expression or utterance
3 a (1) **:** incongruity between the actual result of a sequence of events and the normal or expected result (2) **:** an event or result marked by such incongruity **b :** incongruity between a situation developed in a drama and the accompanying words or actions that is understood by the audience but not by the characters in the play — called also *dramatic irony, tragic irony*
synonym see WIT
Ir·o·quoi·an \ˌir-ə-ˈkwȯi-ən\ *noun* (1697)

1 : a member of any of the peoples constituting the Iroquois
2 : an American Indian language family of eastern North America including Cayuga, Cherokee, Mohawk, Onondaga, Oneida, Seneca, and Tuscarora
— **Iroquoian** *adjective*
Ir·o·quois \ˈir-ə-ˌkwȯi *also* -ˌkwä\ *noun, plural* **Iroquois** \-ˌkwȯi(z), -ˌkwä(z)\ [French, probably of Algonquian origin] (1666)
1 *plural* **:** an American Indian confederacy originally of New York consisting of the Cayuga, Mohawk, Oneida, Onondaga, and Seneca and later including the Tuscarora
2 : a member of any of the Iroquois peoples
ir·ra·di·ance \i-ˈrā-dē-ən(t)s\ *noun* (1667)
1 : RADIANCE 1
2 : the density of radiation incident on a given surface usually expressed in watts per square centimeter or square meter
ir·ra·di·ate \i-ˈrā-dē-ˌāt\ *verb* **-at·ed; -at·ing** [Latin *irradiatus*, past participle of *irradiare*, from *in-* + *radius* ray] (1603)
transitive verb
1 a : to cast rays of light upon **:** ILLUMINATE **b :** to enlighten intellectually or spiritually **c :** to affect or treat by radiant energy (as heat); *specifically* **:** to treat by exposure to radiation
2 : to emit like rays of light **:** RADIATE ⟨*irradiating* strength and comfort⟩
intransitive verb
archaic **:** to emit rays **:** SHINE
— **ir·ra·di·a·tive** \-ˌā-tiv\ *adjective*
— **ir·ra·di·a·tor** \-ˌā-tər\ *noun*
ir·ra·di·a·tion \i-ˌrā-dē-ˈā-shən\ *noun* (1901)
1 : exposure to radiation (as X rays or alpha particles)
2 : application of radiation (as X rays or ultraviolet light) especially for therapeutic purposes
ir·rad·i·ca·ble \i-ˈra-di-kə-bəl, ˌi(r)-\ *adjective* [Medieval Latin *irradicabilis*, from Latin *in-* + *radic-, radix* root — more at ROOT] (1728)
: impossible to eradicate **:** DEEP-ROOTED
— **ir·rad·i·ca·bly** \-blē\ *adverb*
¹ir·ra·tio·nal \i-ˈra-sh(ə-)nəl, ˌi(r)-\ *adjective* [Middle English, from Latin *irrationalis*, from *in-* + *rationalis* rational] (14th century)
: not rational: as **a** (1) **:** not endowed with reason or understanding (2) **:** lacking usual or normal mental clarity or coherence **b :** not governed by or according to reason ⟨*irrational* fears⟩ **c** *Greek & Latin prosody* (1) *of a syllable* **:** having a quantity other than that required by the meter (2) *of a foot* **:** containing such a syllable **d** (1) **:** being an irrational number ⟨an *irrational* root of an equation⟩ (2) **:** having a numerical value that is an irrational number ⟨a length that is *irrational*⟩
— **ir·ra·tio·nal·i·ty** \-ˌra-shə-ˈna-lə-tē\ *noun*
— **ir·ra·tio·nal·ly** \-ˈra-sh(ə-)nə-lē\ *adverb*
²irrational *noun* (1646)
1 : an irrational being
2 : IRRATIONAL NUMBER
ir·ra·tio·nal·ism \-ˈra-sh(ə-)nə-ˌli-zəm\ *noun* (1811)
1 : a system emphasizing intuition, instinct, feeling, or faith rather than reason or holding that the universe is governed by irrational forces
2 : the quality or state of being irrational
— **ir·ra·tio·nal·ist** \-list\ *noun or adjective*
— **ir·ra·tio·nal·is·tic** \-ˌra-sh(ə-)nə-ˈlis-tik\ *adjective*
irrational number *noun* (1551)
: a number that can be expressed as an infinite decimal with no set of consecutive digits repeating itself indefinitely and that cannot be expressed as the quotient of two integers

\ə\ **abut** \ᵊ\ **kitten** \ər\ **further** \a\ **ash** \ā\ **ace**
\ä\ **mop, mar** \au̇\ **out** \ch\ **chin** \e\ **bet** \ē\ **easy**
\g\ **go** \i\ **hit** \ī\ **ice** \j\ **job** \ŋ\ **sing** \ō\ **go**
\ȯ\ **law** \ȯi\ **boy** \th\ **thin** \th̲\ **the** \ü\ **loot** \u̇\ **foot**
\y\ **yet** \zh\ **vision** *see also* Guide to Pronunciation

ir·re·al \i-'rē(-ə)l, ,i(r)-, -'ri(-ə)l\ *adjective* (1944)
: not real

ir·re·al·i·ty \,ir-ē-'a-lə-tē\ *noun* (1803)
: UNREALITY

ir·re·claim·able \,ir-i-'klā-mə-bəl\ *adjective* (1662)
: incapable of being reclaimed
— **ir·re·claim·ably** \-blē\ *adverb*

¹**ir·rec·on·cil·able** \i-,re-kən-'sī-lə-bəl, -'re-kən-,, ,i(r)-\ *adjective* (1599)
: impossible to reconcile
— **ir·rec·on·cil·abil·i·ty** \-,re-kən-,sī-lə-'bi-lə-tē\ *noun*
— **ir·rec·on·cil·able·ness** \-,re-kən-'sī-lə-bəl-nəs, -'re-kən-,\ *noun*
— **ir·rec·on·cil·ably** \-blē\ *adverb*

²**irreconcilable** *noun* (1748)
: one that is irreconcilable; *especially* : a member of a group (as a political party) opposing compromise or collaboration

ir·re·cov·er·able \,ir-i-'kəv-rə-bəl, -'kə-və-\ *adjective* (15th century)
: not capable of being recovered or rectified : IRREPARABLE
— **ir·re·cov·er·able·ness** *noun*
— **ir·re·cov·er·ably** \-blē\ *adverb*

ir·re·cu·sa·ble \,ir-i-'kyü-zə-bəl\ *adjective* [Late Latin *irrecusabilis,* from Latin *in-* + *recusare* to reject, refuse — more at RECUSANT] (1776)
: not subject to exception or rejection
— **ir·re·cu·sa·bly** \-blē\ *adverb*

ir·re·deem·able \,ir-i-'dē-mə-bəl\ *adjective* (1609)
1 : not redeemable: as **a** : not terminable by payment of the principal ⟨*irredeemable* bond⟩ **b** : INCONVERTIBLE a
2 : being beyond remedy : HOPELESS ⟨*irredeemable* mistakes⟩
— **ir·re·deem·ably** \-blē\ *adverb*

ir·re·den·ta \,ir-i-'den-tə\ *noun* [Italian *Italia irredenta,* literally, unredeemed Italy, Italian-speaking territory not incorporated in Italy] (1914)
: a territory historically or ethnically related to one political unit but under the political control of another

ir·re·den·tism \-'den-,ti-zəm\ *noun* (1883)
: a political principle or policy directed toward the incorporation of irredentas within the boundaries of their historically or ethnically related political unit
— **ir·re·den·tist** \-'den-tist\ *noun or adjective*

ir·re·duc·ible \,ir-i-'dü-sə-bəl, -'dyü-\ *adjective* (1633)
: impossible to transform into or restore to a desired or simpler condition ⟨an *irreducible* matrix⟩; *specifically* : incapable of being factored into polynomials of lower degree with coefficients in some given field (as the rational numbers) or integral domain (as the integers) ⟨an *irreducible* equation⟩
— **ir·re·duc·ibil·i·ty** \-,dü-sə-'bi-lə-tē, -,dyü-\ *noun*
— **ir·re·duc·ibly** \-'dü-sə-blē, -'dyü-\ *adverb*

ir·re·flex·ive \,ir-i-'flek-siv\ *adjective* (circa 1890)
: being a relation for which the reflexive property does not hold for any element of a given set

ir·re·form·able \,ir-i-'fȯr-mə-bəl\ *adjective* (1609)
1 : incapable of being reformed : INCORRIGIBLE
2 : not subject to revision or alteration ⟨*irreformable* dogma⟩
— **ir·re·form·abil·i·ty** \-,fȯr-mə-'bi-lə-tē\ *noun*

ir·re·fra·ga·ble \i-'re-frə-gə-bəl, ,i(r)-; ,ir-i-'fra-gə-\ *adjective* [Late Latin *irrefragabilis,* from Latin *in-* + *refragari* to oppose, from *re-* + *-fragari* (as in *suffragari* to vote for); akin to Latin *suffragium* suffrage] (1533)

1 : impossible to refute ⟨*irrefragable* arguments⟩
2 : impossible to break or alter ⟨*irrefragable* rules⟩
— **ir·re·fra·ga·bil·i·ty** \i-,re-frə-gə-'bi-lə-tē, ,i(r)-; ,ir-i-,fra-gə-\ *noun*
— **ir·ref·ra·ga·bly** \i-'re-frə-gə-blē, ,i(r)-; ,ir-i-'fra-gə-\ *adverb*

ir·re·fut·able \,ir-i-'fyü-tə-bəl; i-'re-fyə-tə-, ,i(r)-\ *adjective* [Late Latin *irrefutabilis,* from Latin *in-* + *refutare* to refute] (1620)
: impossible to refute : INCONTROVERTIBLE ⟨*irrefutable* proof⟩
— **ir·re·fut·abil·i·ty** \,ir-i-,fyü-tə-'bi-lə-tē; i-,re-fyə-tə-, ,i(r)-\ *noun*
— **ir·re·fut·ably** \,ir-i-'fyü-tə-blē; i-'re-fyə-tə-, ,i(r)-\ *adverb*

ir·re·gard·less \,ir-i-'gärd-ləs\ *adverb* [probably blend of *irrespective* and *regardless*] (circa 1912)
nonstandard : REGARDLESS □

¹**ir·reg·u·lar** \i-'re-gyə-lər, ,i(r)-\ *adjective* [Middle English *irreguler,* from Middle French, from Late Latin *irregularis* not in accordance with rule, from Latin *in-* + *regularis* regular] (14th century)
1 a : not being or acting in accord with laws, rules, or established custom ⟨*irregular* conduct⟩ **b** : not conforming to the usual pattern of inflection ⟨*irregular* verbs⟩; *specifically* : STRONG 16 **c** : not following a usual or prescribed procedure; *especially, British* : celebrated without either proclamation of the banns or publication of intention to marry ⟨*irregular* marriage⟩
2 : not belonging to or a part of a regular organized group; *specifically* : not belonging to a regular army but raised for a special purpose ⟨*irregular* troops⟩
3 a : lacking perfect symmetry or evenness ⟨an *irregular* coastline⟩ **b** : ZYGOMORPHIC ⟨*irregular* flowers⟩
4 : lacking continuity or regularity especially of occurrence or activity ⟨*irregular* employment⟩ ☆
— **ir·reg·u·lar·ly** *adverb*

²**irregular** *noun* (15th century)
: one that is irregular: as **a** : a soldier who is not a member of a regular military force **b** *plural* : merchandise that has minor defects or that falls next below the manufacturer's standard for firsts

ir·reg·u·lar·i·ty \i-,re-gyə-'la-rə-tē, ,i(r)-\ *noun, plural* **-ties** [Middle English *irregularite,* from Middle French *irregularité,* from Medieval Latin *irregularitat-, irregularitas,* from Late Latin *irregularis*] (14th century)
1 : something that is irregular (as improper or dishonest conduct) ⟨alleged *irregularities* in the city government⟩
2 : the quality or state of being irregular
3 : CONSTIPATION

ir·rel·a·tive \-'re-lə-tiv\ *adjective* (1640)
: not relative: **a** : not related **b** : IRRELEVANT
— **ir·rel·a·tive·ly** *adverb*

ir·rel·e·vance \-'re-lə-vən(t)s\ *noun* (1847)
1 : the quality or state of being irrelevant
2 : something irrelevant

ir·rel·e·van·cy \-vən(t)-sē\ *noun, plural* **-cies** (1592)
: IRRELEVANCE

ir·rel·e·vant \-vənt\ *adjective* (1786)
: not relevant : INAPPLICABLE ⟨that statement is *irrelevant* to your argument⟩
— **ir·rel·e·vant·ly** *adverb*

ir·re·li·gion \,ir-i-'li-jən\ *noun* [Middle French or Late Latin; Middle French, from Late Latin *irreligion-, irreligio,* from Latin *in-* + *religion-, religio* religion] (1598)
: the quality or state of being irreligious
— **ir·re·li·gion·ist** \-'lij-nist, -'li-jə-\ *noun*

ir·re·li·gious \-'li-jəs\ *adjective* (15th century)
1 : neglectful of religion : lacking religious emotions, doctrines, or practices ⟨so *irreligious* that they exploit popular religion for professional purposes —G. B. Shaw⟩

2 : indicating lack of religion
— **ir·re·li·gious·ly** *adverb*

ir·re·me·able \i-'rē-mē-ə-bəl, ,i(r)-\ *adjective* [Latin *irremeabilis,* from *in-* + *remeare* to go back, from *re-* + *meare* to go — more at PERMEATE] (1569)
: offering no possibility of return

ir·re·me·di·a·ble \,ir-i-'mē-dē-ə-bəl\ *adjective* [Middle English, from Latin *irremediabilis,* from *in-* + *remediabilis* remediable] (15th century)
: not remediable; *specifically* : INCURABLE
— **ir·re·me·di·a·ble·ness** *noun*
— **ir·re·me·di·a·bly** \-blē\ *adverb*

ir·re·mov·able \-'mü-və-bəl\ *adjective* (1598)
: not removable
— **ir·re·mov·abil·i·ty** \-,mü-və-'bi-lə-tē\ *noun*
— **ir·re·mov·ably** \-'mü-və-blē\ *adverb*

ir·rep·a·ra·ble \i-'re-p(ə-)rə-bəl, ,i(r)- *also* ÷,ir-(r)ə-'par-ə-bəl\ *adjective* [Middle English, from Middle French, from Latin *irreparabilis,* from *in-* + *reparabilis* reparable] (15th century)
: not reparable : IRREMEDIABLE ⟨*irreparable* damage⟩
— **ir·rep·a·ra·ble·ness** *noun*
— **ir·rep·a·ra·bly** \-blē\ *adverb*

ir·re·peal·able \,ir-i-'pē-lə-bəl\ *adjective* (1633)
: not repealable
— **ir·re·peal·abil·i·ty** \-,pē-lə-'bi-lə-tē\ *noun*

ir·re·place·able \-'plā-sə-bəl\ *adjective* (1807)
: not replaceable
— **ir·re·place·abil·i·ty** \-,plā-sə-'bi-lə-tē\ *noun*
— **ir·re·place·able·ness** \-'plā-sə-bəl-nəs\ *noun*
— **ir·re·place·ably** \-blē\ *adverb*

ir·re·press·ible \-'pre-sə-bəl\ *adjective* (1811)
: impossible to repress, restrain, or control ⟨*irrepressible* curiosity⟩
— **ir·re·press·ibil·i·ty** \-,pre-sə-'bi-lə-tē\ *noun*
— **ir·re·press·ibly** \-'pre-sə-blē\ *adverb*

ir·re·proach·able \-'prō-chə-bəl\ *adjective* (1634)

: not reproachable : BLAMELESS, IMPECCABLE ⟨*irreproachable* conduct⟩

— **ir·re·proach·abil·i·ty** \-ˌprō-chə-'bi-lə-tē\ *noun*

— **ir·re·proach·able·ness** \-'prō-chə-bəl-nəs\ *noun*

— **ir·re·proach·ably** \-blē\ *adverb*

ir·re·pro·duc·ible \ˌi-ˌrē-prə-'dü-sə-bəl, ˌi(r)-, -'dyü-\ *adjective* (1868)

: not reproducible

— **ir·re·pro·duc·ibil·i·ty** \-ˌdü-sə-'bi-lə-tē, -ˌdyü-\ *noun*

ir·re·sist·ible \ˌir-i-'zis-tə-bəl\ *adjective* (1597)

: impossible to resist ⟨an *irresistible* attraction⟩

— **ir·re·sist·ibil·i·ty** \-ˌzis-tə-'bi-lə-tē\ *noun*

— **ir·re·sist·ible·ness** \-'zis-tə-bəl-nəs\ *noun*

— **ir·re·sist·ibly** \-blē\ *adverb*

ir·re·sol·u·ble \-'zäl-yə-bəl\ *adjective* [Latin *irresolubilis,* from *in-* + *resolvere* to resolve] (1666)

1 *archaic* : INDISSOLUBLE

2 : having or admitting of no solution or explanation

ir·res·o·lute \i-'re-zə-ˌlüt, ˌi(r)-, -lət\ *adjective* (1579)

: uncertain how to act or proceed : VACILLATING

— **ir·res·o·lute·ly** \-ˌlüt-lē, -lət-; -ˌre-zə-'lüt-\ *adverb*

— **ir·res·o·lute·ness** \-ˌlüt-nəs, -lət-, -'lüt-\ *noun*

— **ir·res·o·lu·tion** \-ˌre-zə-'lü-shən\ *noun*

ir·re·solv·able \ˌir-i-'zäl-və-bəl, -'zȯl-\ *adjective* (1660)

: incapable of being resolved; *also* : not analyzable

ir·re·spec·tive of \ˌir-i-'spek-tiv-\ *preposition* (1839)

: REGARDLESS OF ⟨free public schools open to all *irrespective of* race, color, or creed —J. B. Conant⟩

¹**ir·re·spon·si·ble** \ˌir-i-'spän(t)-sə-bəl\ *adjective* (1648)

: not responsible: as **a** : not answerable to higher authority ⟨an *irresponsible* dictatorship⟩ **b** : said or done with no sense of responsibility ⟨*irresponsible* accusations⟩ **c** : lacking a sense of responsibility **d** : unable especially mentally or financially to bear responsibility

— **ir·re·spon·si·bil·i·ty** \ˌir-i-ˌspän(t)-sə-'bi-lə-tē\ *noun*

— **ir·re·spon·si·ble·ness** \ˌir-i-'spän(t)-sə-bəl-nəs\ *noun*

— **ir·re·spon·si·bly** \-blē\ *adverb*

²**irresponsible** *noun* (1894)

: one that is irresponsible

ir·re·spon·sive \ˌir-i-'spän(t)-siv\ *adjective* (circa 1846)

: not responsive; *especially* : not able, ready, or inclined to respond

— **ir·re·spon·sive·ness** *noun*

ir·re·triev·able \ˌir-i-'trē-və-bəl\ *adjective* (1702)

: not retrievable : impossible to regain or recover

— **ir·re·triev·abil·i·ty** \-ˌtrē-və-'bi-lə-tē\ *noun*

— **ir·re·triev·ably** \ˌir-i-'trē-və-blē\ *adverb*

ir·rev·er·ence \i-'rev-rən(t)s, ˌi(r)-, -'re-və-, -'re-vərn(t)s\ *noun* (14th century)

1 : lack of reverence

2 : an irreverent act or utterance

ir·rev·er·ent \-rənt; -vərnt\ *adjective* [Middle English, from Latin *irreverent-, irreverens,* from *in-* + *reverent-, reverens* reverent] (15th century)

: lacking proper respect or seriousness; *also* : SATIRIC

— **ir·rev·er·ent·ly** *adverb*

ir·re·vers·ible \ˌir-i-'vər-sə-bəl\ *adjective* (1630)

: not reversible

— **ir·re·vers·ibil·i·ty** \-ˌvər-sə-'bi-lə-tē\ *noun*

— **ir·re·vers·ibly** \-'vər-sə-blē\ *adverb*

ir·rev·o·ca·ble \i-'re-və-kə-bəl, ˌi(r)-\ *also* **-some·times** \ˌir-(r)ə-'vō-kə-\ *adjective* [Middle English, from Latin *irrevocabilis,* from *in-* + *revocabilis* revocable] (14th century)

: not possible to revoke : UNALTERABLE ⟨an *irrevocable* decision⟩

— **ir·rev·o·ca·bil·i·ty** \-ˌre-və-kə-'bi-lə-tē, ˌir-(r)ə-ˌvō-kə-\ *noun*

— **ir·rev·o·ca·ble·ness** \-'re-və-kə-bəl-nəs, ˌir-(r)ə-'vō-kə-\ *noun*

— **ir·rev·o·ca·bly** \-blē\ *adverb*

ir·ri·den·ta *variant of* IRREDENTA

ir·ri·gate \'ir-ə-ˌgāt\ *verb* **-gat·ed; -gat·ing** [Latin *irrigatus,* past participle of *irrigare,* from *in-* + *rigare* to water; perhaps akin to Old High German *regan* rain — more at RAIN] (1615)

transitive verb

1 : WET, MOISTEN: as **a** : to supply (as land) with water by artificial means **b** : to flush (a body part) with a stream of liquid (as in removing a foreign body or medicating)

2 : to refresh as if by watering

intransitive verb

: to practice irrigation

— **ir·ri·ga·tion** \ˌir-ə-'gā-shən\ *noun*

— **ir·ri·ga·tor** \'ir-ə-ˌgā-tər\ *noun*

ir·ri·ta·bil·i·ty \ˌir-ə-tə-'bi-lə-tē\ *noun, plural* **-ties** (1755)

1 : the property of protoplasm and of living organisms that permits them to react to stimuli

2 : the quality or state of being irritable: as **a** : quick excitability to annoyance, impatience, or anger : PETULANCE **b** : abnormal or excessive excitability of an organ or part of the body

ir·ri·ta·ble \'ir-ə-tə-bəl\ *adjective* (1662)

: capable of being irritated: as **a** : easily exasperated or excited **b** : responsive to stimuli

— **ir·ri·ta·ble·ness** *noun*

— **ir·ri·ta·bly** \-blē\ *adverb*

¹**ir·ri·tant** \'ir-ə-tənt\ *adjective* (1636)

: causing irritation; *specifically* : tending to produce physical irritation

²**irritant** *noun* (1802)

: something that irritates or excites

ir·ri·tate \'ir-ə-ˌtāt\ *verb* **-tat·ed; -tat·ing** [Latin *irritatus,* past participle of *irritare*] (1598)

transitive verb

1 : to provoke impatience, anger, or displeasure in : ANNOY

2 : to induce irritability in or of

intransitive verb

: to cause or induce displeasure or irritation ☆

— **ir·ri·tat·ing·ly** \-ˌtā-tiŋ-lē\ *adverb*

irritated *adjective* (1595)

: subjected to irritation; *especially* : roughened, reddened, or inflamed by an irritant ⟨*irritated* eyes⟩

ir·ri·ta·tion \ˌir-ə-'tā-shən\ *noun* (15th century)

1 a : the act of irritating **b** : something that irritates **c** : the state of being irritated

2 : a condition of irritability, soreness, roughness, or inflammation of a bodily part

ir·ri·ta·tive \'ir-ə-ˌtā-tiv\ *adjective* (1644)

1 : serving to excite : IRRITATING

2 : accompanied with or produced by irritation ⟨*irritative* coughing⟩

ir·ro·ta·tion·al \ˌir-(r)ō-'tā-shnəl, -shə-nᵊl\ *adjective* (1875)

1 : not rotating or involving rotation ⟨an *irrotational* electric field⟩

2 : free of vortices ⟨*irrotational* flow⟩

ir·rupt \i-'rəpt\ *intransitive verb* [Latin *irruptus,* past participle of *irrumpere,* from *in-* + *rumpere* to break — more at REAVE] (1886)

1 : to rush in forcibly or violently

2 *of a natural population* : to undergo a sudden upsurge in numbers especially when natural ecological balances and checks are disturbed

3 : ERUPT 1c ⟨the crowd *irrupted* in a fervor of patriotism —*Time*⟩

— **ir·rup·tion** \-'rəp-shən\ *noun*

ir·rup·tive \-'rəp-tiv\ *adjective* (1593)

: irrupting or tending to irrupt

— **ir·rup·tive·ly** *adverb*

is [Middle English, from Old English; akin to Old High German *ist* is (from *sīn* to be), Latin *est* (from *esse* to be), Greek *esti* (from *einai* to be)] *present 3d singular of* BE, *dialect present 1st & 2d singular of* BE, *substandard present plural of* BE

is- *or* **iso-** *combining form* [Late Latin, from Greek, from *isos* equal]

1 : equal : homogeneous : uniform ⟨*isentropic*⟩

2 : isomeric ⟨*isocyanate*⟩

3 : for or from different individuals of the same species ⟨*isoagglutinin*⟩

Isaac \'ī-zik, -zək\ *noun* [Late Latin, from Hebrew *Yiṣḥāq*]

: the son of Abraham and father of Jacob according to the account in Genesis

Isa·iah \ī-'zā-ə, *chiefly British* -'zī-\ *noun* [Hebrew *Yĕsha ʿáyāhū*]

1 : a major Hebrew prophet in Judah about 740 to 701 B.C.

2 : a prophetic book of canonical Jewish and Christian Scripture — see BIBLE table

Isa·ias \-əs\ *noun* [Late Latin, from Greek *Ēsaias,* from Hebrew *Yĕsha ʿáyāhū*]

: ISAIAH

is·al·lo·bar \(ˌ)ī-'sa-lə-ˌbär\ *noun* [International Scientific Vocabulary *is-* + *all-* + *-bar* (as in *isobar*)] (1909)

: an imaginary line or a line on a chart connecting the places of equal change of atmospheric pressure within a specified time

— **is·al·lo·bar·ic** \ˌī-ˌsa-lə-'bär-ik, -'bar-\ *adjective*

is·chae·mia *chiefly British variant of* ISCHEMIA

is·che·mia \is-'kē-mē-ə\ *noun* [New Latin *ischaemia,* from *ischaemus* styptic, from Greek *ischaimos,* from *ischein* to restrain (akin to Greek *echein* to hold) + *haima* blood — more at SCHEME] (circa 1860)

: localized tissue anemia due to obstruction of the inflow of arterial blood

— **is·che·mic** \-mik\ *adjective*

is·chi·um \'is-kē-əm\ *noun, plural* **is·chia** \-ə\ [Latin, hip joint, from Greek *ischion*] (1646)

: the dorsal and posterior of the three principal bones composing either half of the pelvis

— **is·chi·al** \-əl\ *adjective*

-ise *verb suffix, chiefly British*

: -IZE

☆ **SYNONYMS**

Irritate, exasperate, nettle, provoke, rile, peeve mean to excite a feeling of anger or annoyance. IRRITATE implies an often gradual arousing of angry feelings that may range from mere impatience to rage ⟨constant nagging that *irritated* me greatly⟩. EXASPERATE suggests galling annoyance and the arousing of extreme impatience ⟨his *exasperating* habit of putting off needed decisions⟩. NETTLE suggests a sharp but passing annoyance or stinging ⟨your pompous attitude *nettled* several people⟩. PROVOKE implies an arousing of strong annoyance that may excite to action ⟨remarks made solely to *provoke* her⟩. RILE implies inducing an angry or resentful agitation ⟨the new work schedules *riled* the employees⟩. PEEVE suggests arousing fretful often petty or querulous irritation ⟨a toddler *peeved* at being refused a cookie⟩.

\ə\ abut \ᵊ\ kitten \ər\ further \a\ ash \ā\ ace
\ä\ mop, mar \au̇\ out \ch\ chin \e\ bet \ē\ easy
\g\ go \i\ hit \ī\ ice \j\ job \ŋ\ sing \ō\ go
\ȯ\ law \ȯi\ boy \th\ thin \t͟h\ the \ü\ loot \u̇\ foot
\y\ yet \zh\ vision *see also* Guide to Pronunciation

is·en·tro·pic \ˌī-sᵊn-ˈtrō-pik, -ˈträ-\ *adjective* (1873)
: of or relating to equal or constant entropy; *especially* : taking place without change of entropy
— **is·en·tro·pi·cal·ly** \-ˈtrō-pi-k(ə-)lē, -ˈträ-\ *adverb*

Iseult \is-ˈült, iz-\ *noun* [Old French *Isolt, Iseut*]
: ISOLDE

-ish *adjective suffix* [Middle English, from Old English *-isc;* akin to Old High German *-isc,* -ish, Greek *-iskos,* diminutive suffix]
1 : of, relating to, or being — chiefly in adjectives indicating nationality or ethnic group ⟨Finn*ish*⟩
2 a : characteristic of ⟨boy*ish*⟩ ⟨Pollyanna*ish*⟩ **b** : inclined or liable to ⟨book*ish*⟩ ⟨qualm*ish*⟩
3 a : having a touch or trace of ⟨purpl*ish*⟩ : somewhat ⟨dark*ish*⟩ **b** : having the approximate age of ⟨forty*ish*⟩

Ish·ma·el \ˈish-(ˌ)mā-əl, -mē-\ *noun* [Hebrew *Yishmāʽēl*]
1 : the outcast son of Abraham and Hagar according to the account in Genesis
2 a : a social outcast

Ish·ma·el·ite \-ə-ˌlīt\ *noun* (14th century)
1 : a descendant of Ishmael
2 : ISHMAEL 2
— **Ish·ma·el·it·ish** \-ˌlī-tish\ *adjective*
— **Ish·ma·el·it·ism** \-ˌlī-ˌti-zəm\ *noun*

isin·glass \ˈī-zᵊn-ˌglas, ˈī-ziŋ-\ *noun* [probably by folk etymology from obsolete Dutch *huizenblas,* from Middle Dutch *huusblase,* from *huus* sturgeon + *blase* bladder] (1545)
1 : a semitransparent whitish very pure gelatin prepared from the air bladders of fishes (as sturgeons) and used especially as a clarifying agent and in jellies and glue
2 : MICA

Isis \ˈī-səs\ *noun* [Latin *Isid-, Isis,* from Greek, from Egyptian *ʼst*]
: an Egyptian nature goddess and wife and sister of Osiris

Is·lam \is-ˈläm, iz-, -ˈlam, ˈis-, ˈiz-\ *noun* [Arabic *islām* submission (to the will of God)] (1817)
1 : the religious faith of Muslims including belief in Allah as the sole deity and in Muhammad as his prophet
2 a : the civilization erected upon Islamic faith **b** : the group of modern nations in which Islam is the dominant religion
— **Is·lam·ic** \is-ˈlä-mik, iz-, -ˈla-\ *adjective*
— **Is·lam·ics** \-miks\ *noun plural but singular or plural in construction*

Islamic calendar *noun* (1974)
: a lunar calendar reckoned from the Hegira in A.D. 622 and organized in cycles of 30 years — see MONTH table

Islamic era *noun* (1975)
: the era used in Muslim countries for numbering Islamic calendar years since the Hegira

Is·lam·ism \is-ˈlä-ˌmi-zəm, iz-, -ˈla-; ˈiz-lə-\ *noun* (1747)
: the faith, doctrine, or cause of Islam
— **Is·lam·ist** \-mist\ *noun*

Is·lam·ize \ˈiz-lə-ˌmīz; is-ˈlä-ˌmīz, iz-, -ˈla-\ *transitive verb* **-ized; -iz·ing** (circa 1846)
: to make Islamic; *especially* : to convert to Islam
— **Is·lam·i·za·tion** \ˌiz-lə-mə-ˈzā-shən; is-ˌlä-mə-, iz-, -ˌla-\ *noun*

¹is·land \ˈī-lənd\ *noun* [alteration (influenced by Old French *isle*) of earlier *iland,* from Middle English, from Old English *igland* (akin to Old Norse *eyland*), from *ig* island (akin to Old English *ēa* river, Latin *aqua* water) + *land* land] (before 12th century)
1 : a tract of land surrounded by water and smaller than a continent
2 : something resembling an island especially in its isolated or surrounded position: as **a** : a usually raised area within a thoroughfare, parking lot, or driveway used especially to separate or direct traffic **b** : a superstructure on the deck of a ship (as an aircraft carrier) **c** : a kitchen counter that is approachable from all sides
3 : an isolated group or area; *especially* : an isolated ethnological group

²island *transitive verb* (1661)
1 a : to make into or as if into an island **b** : to dot with or as if with islands
2 : ISOLATE

is·land·er \ˈī-lən-dər\ *noun* (circa 1550)
: a native or inhabitant of an island

is·land–hop \ˈī-lənd-ˌhäp\ *intransitive verb* (1944)
: to travel from island to island in a chain

island universe *noun* (1867)
: a galaxy other than the Milky Way

¹isle \ˈī(ə)l\ *noun* [Middle English, from Old French, from Latin *insula*] (13th century)
: ISLAND; *especially* : ISLET

²isle *transitive verb* **isled; isl·ing** (circa 1576)
1 : to make an isle of
2 : to place on or as if on an isle

is·let \ˈī-lət\ *noun* (1538)
: a little island

islet of Lang·er·hans \-ˈläŋ-ər-ˌhänz, -ˌhän(t)s\ [Paul *Langerhans* (died 1888) German physician] (1896)
: any of the groups of small slightly granular endocrine cells that form anastomosing trabeculae among the tubules and alveoli of the pancreas and secrete insulin and glucagon — called also *islet*

ism \ˈi-zəm\ *noun* [*-ism*] (1680)
: a distinctive doctrine, cause, or theory

-ism *noun suffix* [Middle English *-isme,* from Middle French & Latin; Middle French, partly from Latin *-isma* (from Greek) & partly from Latin *-ismus,* from Greek *-ismos;* Greek *-isma* & *-ismos,* from verbs in *-izein* -ize]
1 a : act : practice : process ⟨critic*ism*⟩ ⟨plagiar*ism*⟩ **b** : manner of action or behavior characteristic of a (specified) person or thing ⟨animal*ism*⟩ **c** : prejudice or discrimination on the basis of a (specified) attribute ⟨rac*ism*⟩ ⟨sex*ism*⟩
2 a : state : condition : property ⟨barbarian*ism*⟩ **b** : abnormal state or condition resulting from excess of a (specified) thing ⟨alcohol*ism*⟩ or marked by resemblance to (such) a person or thing ⟨mongol*ism*⟩
3 a : doctrine : theory : cult ⟨Buddh*ism*⟩ **b** : adherence to a system or a class of principles ⟨stoic*ism*⟩
4 : characteristic or peculiar feature or trait ⟨colloquial*ism*⟩

isn't \ˈi-zᵊnt, -ᵊn, *dialect also* ˈi-dᵊn(t) *or* ˈin(t)\ (1710)
: is not

iso- — see IS-

iso·ag·glu·ti·nin \ˌī-(ˌ)sō-ə-ˈglü-tᵊn-ən\ *noun* (circa 1903)
: an agglutinin from one individual that is specific for a cell type (as of red blood cells) possessed by some individuals of the same species

iso·al·lox·a·zine \-ə-ˈläk-sə-ˌzēn\ *noun* [*is-* + *all*antoic + *oxalic* + *azine*]
: a yellow solid $C_{10}H_6N_4O_2$ that is the precursor of various flavins (as riboflavin)

iso·an·ti·body \-ˈan-ti-ˌbä-dē\ *noun* (1919)
: ALLOANTIBODY

iso·an·ti·gen \-ˈan-ti-jən\ *noun* [International Scientific Vocabulary] (1936)
: ALLOANTIGEN
— **iso·an·ti·gen·ic** \ˌī-(ˌ)sō-ˌan-ti-ˈje-nik\ *adjective*

iso·bar \ˈī-sə-ˌbär\ *noun* [International Scientific Vocabulary *is-* + *-bar* (from Greek *baros* weight); akin to Greek *barys* heavy — more at GRIEVE] (circa 1864)
1 : an imaginary line or a line on a map or chart connecting or marking places on the surface of the earth where the height of the barometer reduced to sea level is the same either at a given time or for a certain period
2 : one of two or more atoms or elements having the same atomic weights or mass numbers but different atomic numbers

iso·bar·ic \ˌī-sə-ˈbär-ik, -ˈbar-\ *adjective* [International Scientific Vocabulary] (1878)
1 : of or relating to an isobar
2 : characterized by constant or equal pressure ⟨an *isobaric* process⟩

iso·bu·tane \ˌī-sō-ˈbyü-ˌtān\ *noun* [International Scientific Vocabulary] (1876)
: a gaseous branched-chain hydrocarbon $(CH_3)_3CH$ isomeric with normal butane that is used especially as a fuel

iso·bu·tyl·ene \-ˈbyü-tᵊl-ˌēn\ *noun* [International Scientific Vocabulary] (1872)
: a gaseous butylene C_4H_8 used especially in making butyl rubber and gasoline components

iso·ca·lo·ric \-kə-ˈlȯr-ik, -ˈlōr-, -ˈlär-; -ˈka-lə-rik\ *adjective* (1922)
: having similar caloric values ⟨*isocaloric* diets⟩

iso·car·box·az·id \-ˌkär-ˈbäk-sə-zəd\ *noun* [*is-* + *carb-* + *ox-* + hydra*zide*] (1959)
: an antidepressant drug $C_{12}H_{13}N_3O_2$

iso·chro·mo·some \ˌī-sə-ˈkrō-mə-ˌsōm, -ˌzōm\ *noun* (1939)
: a chromosome produced by transverse splitting of the centromere so that both arms are derived from the dyad on one side of the centromere of the parental chromosome and each arm has identical genes arranged in the same order counting away from the centromere

iso·chron \ˈī-sə-ˌkrän\ *or* **iso·chrone** \-ˌkrōn\ *noun* [International Scientific Vocabulary *is-* + *-chron* (from Greek *chronos* time)] (1881)
: an imaginary line or a line on a chart connecting points at which an event occurs simultaneously or which represents the same time or time difference

iso·chro·nal \ī-ˈsä-krə-nᵊl, ˌī-sə-ˈkrō-\ *adjective* [Greek *isochronos,* from *is-* + *chronos* time] (1680)
: uniform in time : having equal duration : recurring at regular intervals
— **iso·chro·nal·ly** \-nᵊl-ē\ *adverb*
— **iso·chro·nism** \ī-ˈsä-krə-ˌni-zəm, ˌī-sə-ˈkrō-\ *noun*

iso·chro·nous \ī-ˈsä-krə-nəs, ˌī-sə-ˈkrō-\ *adjective* [Greek *isochronos*] (1706)
: ISOCHRONAL
— **iso·chro·nous·ly** *adverb*

iso·cit·ric acid \ˌī-sə-ˈsi-trik-\ *noun* (1869)
: a crystalline isomer of citric acid that occurs especially as an intermediate stage in the Krebs cycle

iso·cy·a·nate \ˌī-sə-ˈsī-ə-ˌnāt, -nət\ *noun* [International Scientific Vocabulary] (1872)
: an ester of isomeric cyanic acid used especially in plastics and adhesives

iso·cy·clic \-ˈsī-klik, -ˈsi-\ *adjective* [International Scientific Vocabulary] (1900)
: having or being a ring composed of atoms of only one element; *especially* : CARBOCYCLIC

iso·di·a·met·ric \-ˌdī-ə-ˈme-trik\ *adjective* [International Scientific Vocabulary] (circa 1879)
: having equal diameters

iso·dose \ˈī-sə-ˌdōs\ *adjective* [International Scientific Vocabulary] (1922)
: of or relating to points or zones in a medium that receive equal doses of radiation

iso·elec·tric \ˌī-sō-i-ˈlek-trik\ *adjective* [International Scientific Vocabulary] (1877)
1 : having or representing zero difference of electric potential
2 : being the pH at which the electrolyte will not migrate in an electrical field ⟨the *isoelectric* point of a protein⟩

isoelectric focusing *noun* (1971)
: an electrophoretic technique for separating proteins by causing them to migrate under the

influence of an electric field through a medium (as a gel) having a pH gradient to locations with pH values corresponding to their isoelectric points

iso·elec·tron·ic \ˌī-i-ˌlek-'trä-nik\ adjective [International Scientific Vocabulary] (1926) : having the same number of electrons or valence electrons

— **iso·elec·tron·i·cal·ly** \-ni-k(ə-)lē\ adverb

iso·en·zyme \-'en-ˌzīm\ noun (1960) : any of two or more chemically distinct but functionally similar enzymes

— **iso·en·zy·mat·ic** \-ˌen-zə-'ma-tik, -zī-\ adjective

— **iso·en·zy·mic** \-en-'zī-mik\ adjective

iso·ga·mete \-'ga-ˌmēt also -gə-'mēt\ noun [International Scientific Vocabulary] (1891) : a gamete indistinguishable in form or size or behavior from another gamete with which it can unite to form a zygote

— **iso·ga·met·ic** \-gə-'me-tik\ adjective

isog·a·mous \ī-'sä-gə-məs\ adjective [probably from (assumed) New Latin isogamus, from is- + -gamous -gamous] (1887) : having or involving isogametes — compare HETEROGAMOUS

— **isog·a·my** \-mē\ noun

iso·ge·ne·ic \ˌī-sō-jə-'nē-ik, -'nā-\ adjective [alteration of isogenic] (1963) : SYNGENEIC ⟨an isogeneic graft⟩

iso·gen·ic \-'je-nik\ adjective [is- + gene + ¹-ic] (circa 1931) : characterized by essentially identical genes ⟨identical twins are isogenic⟩

iso·gloss \'ī-sə-ˌgläs, -ˌglòs\ noun [International Scientific Vocabulary is- + Greek glōssa language — more at GLOSS] (1925) **1** : a boundary line between places or regions that differ in a particular linguistic feature **2** : a line on a map representing an isogloss

— **iso·gloss·al** \ˌī-sə-'glä-səl, -'glò-\ adjective

— **iso·gloss·ic** \-'glä-sik, -'glò-\ adjective

iso·gon·ic \ˌī-sə-'gä-nik\ adjective [isogony, from is- + -gony] (1924) : exhibiting equivalent relative growth of parts such that size relations remain constant

— **isog·o·ny** \ī-'sä-gə-nē\ noun

isogonic line (circa 1859) : an imaginary line or a line on a map joining points on the earth's surface at which the magnetic declination is the same — called also isogonal

iso·graft \'ī-sə-ˌgraft\ noun (1958) : a homograft between genetically identical or nearly identical individuals

— **isograft** transitive verb

iso·gram \'ī-sə-ˌgram\ noun (1889) : ISOLINE

iso·hy·et \ˌī-sō-'hī-ət\ noun [International Scientific Vocabulary is- + Greek hyetos rain, from hyein to rain; probably akin to Tocharian B swese rain] (1899) : a line on a map or chart connecting areas of equal rainfall

— **iso·hy·et·al** \-ə-təl\ adjective

iso·la·ble \'ī-sə-lə-bəl also 'i-\ also **iso·lat·able** \ˌī-sə-'lā-tə-bəl also ˌi-\ adjective (circa 1855) : capable of being isolated

¹**iso·late** \'ī-sə-ˌlāt also 'i-\ transitive verb **-lat·ed; -lat·ing** [back-formation from isolated set apart, from French isolé, from Italian isolato, from isola island, from Latin insula] (1807) **1** : to set apart from others; also : QUARANTINE **2** : to select from among others; especially : to separate from another substance so as to obtain pure or in a free state **3** : INSULATE

— **iso·la·tor** \-ˌlā-tər\ noun

²**iso·late** \-lət\ adjective (1819) : being alone : SOLITARY, ISOLATED

³**iso·late** \-lət, -ˌlāt\ noun (1890)

1 : a product of isolating : an individual, population, or kind obtained by or resulting from selection or separation **2** : an individual socially withdrawn or removed from society

isolated adjective (1763) **1** : occurring alone or once : UNIQUE **2** : SPORADIC

iso·la·tion \ˌī-sə-'lā-shən also ˌi-\ noun (1833) : the action of isolating : the condition of being isolated

synonym see SOLITUDE

iso·la·tion·ism \-shə-ˌni-zəm\ noun (1922) : a policy of national isolation by abstention from alliances and other international political and economic relations

— **iso·la·tion·ist** \-sh(ə-)nist\ noun or adjective

Isol·de \i-'zōl-də, -'sōl-\ noun [German, from Old French Isolt, Iseut] **1** : an Irish princess married to King Mark of Cornwall and loved by Tristram **2** : the daughter of the King of Brittany and wife of Tristram

iso·leu·cine \ˌī-sō-'lü-ˌsēn\ noun [International Scientific Vocabulary] (1903) : a crystalline essential amino acid $C_6H_{13}NO_2$ isomeric with leucine

iso·line \'ī-(ˌ)sō-ˌlīn\ noun (1944) : a line on a map or chart along which there is a constant value (as of temperature or rainfall)

iso·mer \'ī-sə-mər\ noun [International Scientific Vocabulary, back-formation from isomeric] (1866) **1** : one of two or more compounds, radicals, or ions that contain the same number of atoms of the same elements but differ in structural arrangement and properties **2** : a nuclide isomeric with one or more others

isom·er·ase \ī-'sä-mə-ˌrās, -ˌrāz\ noun (1927) : an enzyme that catalyzes the conversion of its substrate to an isomeric form

iso·mer·ic \ˌī-sə-'mer-ik\ adjective [German isomerisch, from Greek isomerēs equally divided, from is- + meros part — more at MERIT] (1838) : of, relating to, or exhibiting isomerism

isom·er·ism \ī-'sä-mə-ˌri-zəm\ noun (1839) **1** : the relationship of two or more chemical species that are isomers **2** : the relation of two or more nuclides with the same mass numbers and atomic numbers but different energy states and rates of radioactive decay

isom·er·ize \ī-'sä-mə-ˌrīz\ verb **-ized; -iz·ing** (1891) intransitive verb : to become changed into an isomeric form transitive verb : to cause to isomerize

— **isom·er·i·za·tion** \-ˌsä-mə-rə-'zā-shən\ noun

iso·met·ric \ˌī-sə-'me-trik\ adjective (circa 1855) **1** : of, relating to, or characterized by equality of measure; especially : relating to or being a crystallographic system characterized by three equal axes at right angles **2** : of, relating to, involving, or being muscular contraction (as in isometrics) against resistance, without significant shortening of muscle fibers, and with marked increase in muscle tone — compare ISOTONIC

— **iso·met·ri·cal·ly** \-tri-k(ə-)lē\ adverb

isometric line noun (circa 1911) **1** : a line representing changes of pressure or temperature under conditions of constant volume **2** : a line (as a contour line) drawn on a map and indicating a true constant value throughout its extent

iso·met·rics \ˌī-sə-'me-triks\ noun plural but singular or plural in construction (1962) : exercise or a system of exercises in which opposing muscles are so contracted that there

is little shortening but great increase in tone of muscle fibers involved

isom·e·try \ī-'sä-mə-trē\ noun, plural **-tries** (1941) : a mapping of a metric space onto another or onto itself so that the distance between any two points in the original space is the same as the distance between their images in the second space ⟨rotation and translation are isometries of the plane⟩

iso·mor·phic \ˌī-sə-'mòr-fik\ adjective (1862) **1 a** : being of identical or similar form, shape, or structure ⟨isomorphic crystals⟩ **b** : having sporophytic and gametophytic generations alike in size and shape **2** : related by an isomorphism ⟨isomorphic mathematical rings⟩

— **iso·mor·phi·cal·ly** \-fi-k(ə-)lē\ adverb

iso·mor·phism \ˌī-sə-'mòr-ˌfi-zəm\ noun [International Scientific Vocabulary] (circa 1828) **1** : the quality or state of being isomorphic: as **a** : similarity in organisms of different ancestry resulting from convergence **b** : similarity of crystalline form between chemical compounds **2** : a one-to-one correspondence between two mathematical sets; especially : a homomorphism that is one-to-one — compare ENDOMORPHISM

iso·mor·phous \ˌī-sə-'mòr-fəs\ adjective (circa 1828) : ISOMORPHIC 1a

— **iso·morph** \'ī-sə-ˌmòrf\ noun

iso·ni·a·zid \ˌī-sə-'nī-ə-zəd\ noun [is- + nicotinic acid + hydrazide] (1952) : a crystalline compound $C_6H_7N_3O$ used in treating tuberculosis

iso·oc·tane \ˌī-sō-'äk-ˌtān\ noun [International Scientific Vocabulary] (1909) : an octane of branched-chain structure or a mixture of such octanes; especially : a flammable liquid octane used in determining the octane number of fuels

iso·pach \'ī-sə-ˌpak\ noun [is- + -pach (from Greek pachys thick) — more at PACHYDERM] (circa 1918) : an isoline that connects points of equal thickness of a geological stratum formation or group of formations

iso·phote \'ī-sə-ˌfōt\ noun [International Scientific Vocabulary is- + -phote (from Greek phōt-, phōs light) — more at FANCY] (circa 1909) : a curve on a chart joining points of equal light intensity from a given source

— **iso·phot·al** \ˌī-sə-'fō-təl\ adjective

iso·pi·es·tic \ˌī-sō-pē-'es-tik, -pī-\ adjective [is- + Greek piestos, verbal of piezein to press — more at PIEZO-] (1873) : of, relating to, or marked by equal pressure

iso·pleth \'ī-sə-ˌpleth\ noun [International Scientific Vocabulary is- + Greek plēthos quantity; akin to Greek plēthein to be full — more at FULL] (1908) **1** : an isoline on a graph showing the occurrence or frequency of a phenomenon as a function of two variables **2** : a line on a map connecting points at which a given variable has a specified constant value

— **iso·pleth·ic** \ˌī-sə-'ple-thik\ adjective

iso·pod \'ī-sə-ˌpäd\ noun [ultimately from Greek is- + pod-, pous foot — more at FOOT] (circa 1835) : any of a large order (Isopoda) of small sessile-eyed crustaceans with the body composed of seven free thoracic segments each bearing a pair of similar legs

— **isopod** adjective

iso·pren·a·line \ˌī-sə-'pre-nᵊl-ən\ noun [probably from isopropyl + adrenaline] (1951)

\ə\ abut \ᵊ\ kitten \ər\ further \a\ ash \ā\ ace
\ä\ mop, mar \aù\ out \ch\ chin \e\ bet \ē\ easy
\g\ go \i\ hit \ī\ ice \j\ job \ŋ\ sing \ō\ go
\ò\ law \òi\ boy \th\ thin \t̷h\ the \ü\ loot \ù\ foot
\y\ yet \zh\ vision see also Guide to Pronunciation

: ISOPROTERENOL

iso·prene \ˈī-sə-ˌprēn\ *noun* [probably from *is-* + *propyl* + *-ene*] (1860)
: a flammable liquid unsaturated hydrocarbon C_5H_8 used especially in synthetic rubber

iso·pren·oid \ˌī-sə-ˈprē-ˌnȯid\ *adjective* (1940)
: relating to, containing, or being a branched-chain grouping characteristic of isoprene

iso·pro·pyl \ˌī-sə-ˈprō-pəl\ *noun, often attributive* [International Scientific Vocabulary] (1866)
: the alkyl radical isomeric with normal propyl — often used in combination

isopropyl alcohol *noun* (1872)
: a volatile flammable alcohol C_3H_8O used especially as a solvent and rubbing alcohol

iso·pro·ter·e·nol \ˌī-sə-prō-ˈter-ə-ˌnȯl, -ˌnōl\ *noun* [*isopropyl* + ar*terenol* norepinephrine, from *Arterenol*, a trademark] (1957)
: a drug $C_{11}H_{17}NO_3$ used in the treatment of asthma

iso·pyc·nic \ˌī-sō-ˈpik-nik\ *adjective* [*is-* + Greek *pyknos* dense] (circa 1890)
1 : of, relating to, or marked by equal or constant density
2 : being or produced by a technique (as centrifugation) in which the components of a mixture are separated on the basis of differences in density

isos·ce·les \ī-ˈsäs-ˌlēz, -ˈsä-sə-\ *adjective* [Late Latin *isosceles* having two equal sides, from Greek *isoskelēs*, from *is-* + *skelos* leg; perhaps akin to Old English *sceol* wry] (1551)
1 *of a triangle* : having two equal sides — see TRIANGLE illustration
2 *of a trapezoid* : having the two nonparallel sides equal

is·os·mot·ic \ˌī-ˌsäz-ˈmä-tik, -ˌsäs-\ *adjective* [International Scientific Vocabulary] (1895)
: of, relating to, or exhibiting equal osmotic pressure ⟨*isosmotic* solutions⟩
— **is·os·mot·i·cal·ly** \-ˈmä-ti-k(ə-)lē\ *adverb*

iso·spin \ˈī-sə-ˌspin\ *noun* (1961)
: a quantum characteristic of a group of closely related subatomic particles (as a proton and a neutron) handled mathematically like ordinary spin with the possible orientations in a hypothetical space specifying the number of particles of differing electric charge comprising the group — called also *isotopic spin*

isos·ta·sy \ī-ˈsäs-tə-sē\ *noun* [International Scientific Vocabulary *is-* + Greek *-stasia* condition of standing, from *histanai* to cause to stand — more at STAND] (1889)
1 : general equilibrium in the earth's crust maintained by a yielding flow of rock material beneath the surface under gravitative stress
2 : the quality or state of being subjected to equal pressure from every side
— **iso·stat·ic** \ˌī-sə-ˈsta-tik\ *adjective*
— **iso·stat·i·cal·ly** \-ˈsta-ti-k(ə-)lē\ *adverb*

iso·tach \ˈī-sə-ˌtak\ *noun* [International Scientific Vocabulary *is-* + *-tach* (from Greek *tachys* quick)] (1947)
: a line on a map or chart connecting points of equal wind speed

iso·tac·tic \ˌī-sə-ˈtak-tik\ *adjective* (1955)
: having or relating to a stereochemical regularity of structure in the repeating units of a polymer — compare ATACTIC

iso·therm \ˈī-sə-ˌthərm\ *noun* [French *isotherme*, adjective] (1859)
1 : a line on a map or chart of the earth's surface connecting points having the same temperature at a given time or the same mean temperature for a given period
2 : a line on a chart representing changes of volume or pressure under conditions of constant temperature

iso·ther·mal \ˌī-sə-ˈthər-məl\ *adjective* [French *isotherme*, from *is-* + *-therme* (from Greek *thermos* hot) — more at THERM] (1826)
1 : of, relating to, or marked by equality of temperature

2 : of, relating to, or marked by changes of volume or pressure under conditions of constant temperature
— **iso·ther·mal·ly** \-mə-lē\ *adverb*

iso·ton·ic \ˌī-sə-ˈtä-nik\ *adjective* [International Scientific Vocabulary] (1891)
1 : of, relating to, or being muscular contraction in the absence of significant resistance, with marked shortening of muscle fibers, and without great increase in muscle tone — compare ISOMETRIC
2 : ISOSMOTIC — used of solutions
— **iso·ton·i·cal·ly** \-ni-k(ə-)lē\ *adverb*
— **iso·to·nic·i·ty** \-tō-ˈni-sə-tē\ *noun*

iso·tope \ˈī-sə-ˌtōp\ *noun* [*is-* + Greek *topos* place] (1913)
1 : any of two or more species of atoms of a chemical element with the same atomic number and nearly identical chemical behavior but with differing atomic mass or mass number and different physical properties
2 : NUCLIDE
— **iso·to·pic** \ˌī-sə-ˈtä-pik, -ˈtō-\ *adjective*
— **iso·to·pi·cal·ly** \-ˈtä-pi-k(ə-)lē, -ˈtō-\ *adverb*

isotopic spin *noun* (1937)
: ISOSPIN

iso·tro·pic \ˌī-sə-ˈtrō-pik, -ˈträ-\ *adjective* [International Scientific Vocabulary] (circa 1860)
: exhibiting properties (as velocity of light transmission) with the same values when measured along axes in all directions ⟨an *isotropic* crystal⟩
— **isot·ro·py** \ī-ˈsä-trə-pē\ *noun*

iso·zyme \ˈī-sə-ˌzīm\ *noun* (1959)
: ISOENZYME
— **iso·zy·mic** \ˌī-sə-ˈzī-mik\ *adjective*

Is·ra·el \ˈiz-rē-əl, -(ˌ)rā- *also* ˈis- *or* ˈiz-rəl\ *noun* [Middle English, from Old English, from Late Latin, from Greek *Israēl*, from Hebrew *Yiśrāʾēl*]
1 : JACOB 2
2 : the Jewish people
3 : a people chosen by God
— **Israel** *adjective*

¹Is·rae·li \iz-ˈrā-lē *also* ˌiz-rə-ˈā-lē\ *adjective* [New Hebrew *yiśrĕʾēlī*, from Hebrew, Israelite, noun & adjective, from *Yiśrāʾēl*] (1948)
: of or relating to the people or the republic of Israel

²Israeli *noun, plural* **Israelis** *also* **Israeli** (1948)
: a native or inhabitant of the republic of Israel

¹Is·ra·el·ite \ˈiz-r(ē-)ə-ˌlīt\ *noun* [Middle English, from Late Latin *Israelita*, from Greek *Israēlitēs*, from *Israēl*] (14th century)
: a descendant of the Hebrew patriarch Jacob; *specifically* : a native or inhabitant of the ancient northern kingdom of Israel

²Israelite *adjective* (1851)
: of or relating to Israel or to the Israelites

Is·sa·char \ˈi-sə-ˌkär\ *noun* [Late Latin, from Greek, from Hebrew *Yiśśākhār*]
: a son of Jacob and the traditional eponymous ancestor of one of the tribes of Israel

is·sei \(ˌ)ē-ˈsä, ˈē-ˌsä\ *noun, plural* **issei** *often capitalized* [Japanese, literally, first generation] (1937)
: a Japanese immigrant especially to the U.S.

is·su·able \ˈi-shü-ə-bəl\ *adjective* (circa 1570)
1 : open to contest, debate, or litigation
2 : authorized for issue ⟨bonds *issuable* under the merger terms⟩
3 : possible as a result or consequence
— **is·su·ably** \-blē\ *adverb*

is·su·ance \ˈi-shə-wən(t)s\ *noun* (1863)
: ISSUE 2, 9a

is·su·ant \-wənt\ *adjective* (1610)
1 *of a heraldic animal* : rising with only the upper part visible
2 *archaic* : coming forth : EMERGING

¹is·sue \ˈi-(ˌ)shü, *chiefly Southern* ˈi-shə, *chiefly British* ˈis-(ˌ)yü\ *noun* [Middle English, exit, proceeds, from Middle French, from Old French, from *issir* to come out, go out, from Latin *exire* to go out, from *ex-* + *ire* to go;

akin to Gothic *iddja* he went, Greek *ienai* to go, Sanskrit *eti* he goes] (14th century)
1 *plural* : proceeds from a source of revenue (as an estate)
2 : the action of going, coming, or flowing out : EGRESS, EMERGENCE
3 : a means or place of going out : EXIT, OUTLET
4 : OFFSPRING, PROGENY ⟨died without *issue*⟩
5 a : a final outcome that usually constitutes a solution (as of a problem) or resolution (as of a difficulty) b *obsolete* : a final conclusion or decision about something arrived at after consideration c *archaic* : TERMINATION, END ⟨hope that his enterprise would have a prosperous *issue* —T. B. Macaulay⟩
6 a : a matter that is in dispute between two or more parties b : the point at which an unsettled matter is ready for a decision ⟨brought the matter to an *issue*⟩
7 : a discharge (as of blood) from the body
8 a : something coming forth from a specified source ⟨*issues* of a disordered imagination⟩ b *obsolete* : DEED
9 a : the act of publishing or officially giving out or making available ⟨the next *issue* of commemorative stamps⟩ ⟨*issue* of supplies by the quartermaster⟩ b : the thing or the whole quantity of things given out at one time ⟨read the latest *issue*⟩
— **is·sue·less** \ˈi-shü-ləs\ *adjective*
— **at issue** 1 : in a state of controversy : in disagreement 2 *also* **in issue** : under discussion or in dispute

²issue *verb* **is·sued**; **is·su·ing** (14th century)
intransitive verb
1 a : to go, come, or flow out b : to come forth : EMERGE c : to come to an issue of law or fact in pleading
2 : ACCRUE ⟨profits *issuing* from the sale of the stock⟩
3 : to descend from a specified parent or ancestor
4 : to be a consequence or final outcome : EMANATE, RESULT
5 : to appear or become available through being officially put forth or distributed
6 : EVENTUATE, TERMINATE
transitive verb
1 : to cause to come forth : DISCHARGE, EMIT
2 a : to put forth or distribute usually officially ⟨government *issued* a new airmail stamp⟩ ⟨*issue* orders⟩ b : to send out for sale or circulation : PUBLISH c *British* : PROVIDE 2b, SUPPLY
synonym see SPRING
— **is·su·er** *noun*

¹-ist *noun suffix* [Middle English *-iste*, from Old French & Latin; Old French *-iste*, from Latin *-ista*, *-istes*; from Greek *-istēs*, from verbs in *-izein* *-ize*]
1 a : one that performs a (specified) action ⟨cycl*ist*⟩ : one that makes or produces a (specified) thing ⟨novel*ist*⟩ b : one that plays a (specified) musical instrument ⟨harp*ist*⟩ c : one that operates a (specified) mechanical instrument or contrivance ⟨automobil*ist*⟩
2 : one that specializes in a (specified) art or science or skill ⟨geolog*ist*⟩ ⟨ventriloqu*ist*⟩
3 : one that adheres to or advocates a (specified) doctrine or system or code of behavior ⟨social*ist*⟩ ⟨royal*ist*⟩ ⟨hedon*ist*⟩ or that of a (specified) individual ⟨Calvin*ist*⟩ ⟨Darwin*ist*⟩

²-ist *adjective suffix*
: of, relating to, or characteristic of ⟨elit*ist*⟩

¹isth·mi·an \ˈis-mē-ən\ *noun* (1601)
1 : a native or inhabitant of an isthmus
2 *capitalized* : a native or inhabitant of the Isthmus of Panama

²isthmian *adjective* (1603)
: of, relating to, or situated in or near an isthmus: as a *often capitalized* : of or relating to the Isthmus of Corinth in Greece or the games

held there in ancient times **b** *often capitalized* **:** of or relating to the Isthmus of Panama connecting the North American and South American continents

isth·mic \'is-mik\ *adjective* (1585)
: of or relating to an anatomical isthmus

isth·mus \'is-məs\ *noun* [Latin, from Greek *isthmos*] (1555)
1 : a narrow strip of land connecting two larger land areas
2 : a narrow anatomical part or passage connecting two larger structures or cavities

is·tle \'ist-lē\ *noun* [American Spanish *ixtle*, from Nahuatl *īchtli*] (1883)
: a strong fiber (as for cordage or basketwork) from various tropical American plants (as of the genus *Agave*)

¹it \'it, ət\ *pronoun* [Middle English, from Old English *hit* — more at HE] (before 12th century)
1 : that one — used as subject or direct object or indirect object of a verb or object of a preposition usually in reference to a lifeless thing ⟨took a quick look at the house and noticed *it* was very old⟩, a plant ⟨there is a rosebush near the fence and *it* is now blooming⟩, a person or animal whose sex is unknown or disregarded ⟨don't know who *it* is⟩, a group of individuals or things, or an abstract entity ⟨beauty is everywhere and *it* is a source of joy⟩; compare HE, ITS, SHE, THEY
2 — used as subject of an impersonal verb that expresses a condition or action without reference to an agent ⟨*it* is raining⟩
3 a — used as anticipatory subject or object of a verb ⟨*it* is necessary to repeat the whole thing⟩; often used to shift emphasis to a part of a statement other than the subject ⟨*it* was in this city that the treaty was signed⟩ **b** — used with many verbs as a direct object with little or no meaning ⟨footed *it* back to camp⟩
4 — used to refer to an explicit or implicit state of affairs or circumstances ⟨how is *it* going⟩
5 : a crucial or climactic point ⟨this is *it*⟩

²it \'it\ *noun* (1842)
: the player in a game who performs the principal action of the game (as trying to find others in hide-and-seek)

it·a·con·ic acid \,i-tə-'kä-nik-\ *noun* [International Scientific Vocabulary, anagram of *aconitic acid*, C₃H₃(COOH)₃, from *aconite*] (circa 1872)
: a crystalline dicarboxylic acid $C_5H_6O_4$ obtained usually by fermentation of sugars with molds (genus *Aspergillus*) and used as a monomer for polymers and polyesters

¹Ital·ian \ə-'tal-yən, i- *also* ,ī-\ *noun* (14th century)
1 a : a native or inhabitant of Italy **b :** a person of Italian descent
2 : the Romance language of the Italians

²Italian *adjective* (15th century)
: of, relating to, or characteristic of Italy, the Italians, or Italian

ital·ian·ate \-yə-,nāt\ *transitive verb* **-at·ed; -at·ing** *often capitalized* (1553)
: ITALIANIZE

Ital·ian·ate \-nət, -,nāt\ *adjective* (1572)
: Italian in quality or characteristics

Italian dressing *noun* (circa 1902)
: a salad dressing flavored especially with garlic and oregano

Italian grey·hound *noun* (1743)
: any of a breed of toy dogs resembling the standard greyhound in miniature

ital·ian·ise *often capitalized, British variant of* ITALIANIZE

Italian greyhound

Ital·ian·ism \ə-'tal-yə-,ni-zəm, i- *also* ī-\ *noun* (1594)
1 a : a quality characteristic of Italy or the Italian people **b :** a characteristic feature of Italian occurring in another language
2 a : specialized interest in or emulation of Italian qualities or achievements **b :** promotion or love of Italian policies or ideals

ital·ian·ize \ə-'tal-yə-,nīz, i- *also* ī-\ *verb* **-ized; -iz·ing** *often capitalized* (circa 1611)
intransitive verb
: to act Italian; *specifically* **:** to follow the style or technique of recognized Italian painters
transitive verb
: to make Italian (as in appearance or behavior)
— Ital·ian·i·za·tion \-,tal-yə-nə-'zā-shən\ *noun*

Italian sandwich *noun* (circa 1953)
: SUBMARINE 2

Italian sonnet *noun* (1879)
: a sonnet consisting of an octave rhyming *abba abba* and a sestet rhyming in any of various patterns (as *cde cde* or *cdc dcd*) — called also *Petrarchan sonnet*

¹ital·ic \ə-'ta-lik, i-, ī-\ *adjective* (1612)
1 a : of or relating to a type style with characters that slant upward to the right (as in "*these words are italic*") — compare ROMAN **b :** of or relating to a style of slanted cursive handwriting developed in the 15th and 16th centuries
2 *capitalized* **:** of or relating to ancient Italy, its peoples, or their Indo-European languages

²italic *noun* (1676)
1 : an italic character or type
2 *capitalized* **:** a branch of the Indo-European language family that includes Latin, Oscan, and Umbrian — see INDO-EUROPEAN LANGUAGES table

ital·i·cise *British variant of* ITALICIZE

ital·i·cize \ə-'ta-lə-,sīz, i-, ī-\ *transitive verb* **-cized; -ciz·ing** (1795)
1 : to print in italics or underscore with a single line
2 : EMPHASIZE ⟨the microphone *italicizes* every curdled top note —P. G. Davis⟩
— ital·i·ci·za·tion \-,ta-lə-sə-'zā-shən\ *noun*

Ita·lo- \i-'ta-lō *also* 'i-t°l-ō\ *combining form*
1 : Italian ⟨*Italo*phile⟩
2 : Italian and ⟨*Italo*-Austrian⟩

Ita·lo·phile \i-'ta-lə-,fīl\ *adjective* (circa 1902)
: friendly to or favoring what is Italian
— Italophile *noun*

¹itch \'ich\ *verb* [Middle English *icchen*, from Old English *giccan*; akin to Old High German *jucchen* to itch] (before 12th century)
intransitive verb
1 a : to have an itch ⟨her arm *itched*⟩ **b :** to produce an itchy sensation ⟨long underwear that *itches*⟩
2 : to have a restless desire or hankering for something ⟨were *itching* to go outside⟩
transitive verb
1 : to cause to itch
2 : VEX, IRRITATE

²itch *noun* (before 12th century)
1 a : an uneasy irritating sensation in the upper surface of the skin usually held to result from mild stimulation of pain receptors **b :** a skin disorder accompanied by such a sensation; *especially* **:** a contagious eruption caused by a mite (*Sarcoptes scabiei*) that burrows in the skin and causes intense itching
2 a : a restless usually constant often compulsive desire ⟨an *itch* to travel⟩ **b :** LUST, PRURIENCE
— itch·i·ness \'i-chē-nəs\ *noun*
— itchy \'i-chē\ *adjective*

it'd \'i-təd, ,id\ (1859)
: it had **:** it would

¹-ite *noun suffix* [Middle English, from Old French & Latin; Old French, from Latin *-ita*, *-ites*, from Greek *-itēs*]
1 a : native **:** resident ⟨Brooklyn*ite*⟩ **b :** descendant ⟨Ephraim*ite*⟩ **c :** adherent **:** follower ⟨Jacob*ite*⟩ ⟨Pusey*ite*⟩

2 a (1) **:** product ⟨metabol*ite*⟩ (2) **:** commercially manufactured product ⟨ebon*ite*⟩ **b :** -ITOL ⟨mann*ite*⟩
3 [New Latin *-ites*, from Latin] **:** fossil ⟨ammon*ite*⟩
4 : mineral ⟨erythr*ite*⟩ **:** rock ⟨anorthos*ite*⟩
5 [French, from Latin *-ita*, *-ites*] **:** segment or constituent part of a body or of a bodily part ⟨som*ite*⟩ ⟨dendr*ite*⟩

²-ite *noun suffix* [French, alteration of *-ate* -ate, from New Latin *-atum*]
: salt or ester of an acid with a name ending in *-ous* ⟨nitr*ite*⟩

¹item \'ī-,tem, 'ī-təm\ *adverb* [Middle English, from Latin, from *ita* thus] (14th century)
: and in addition **:** ALSO — used to introduce each article in a list or enumeration

²item \'ī-təm\ *noun* (1571)
1 *obsolete* **:** WARNING, HINT
2 : a distinct part in an enumeration, account, or series **:** ARTICLE
3 : an object of attention, concern, or interest
4 : a separate piece of news or information
5 : a couple in a romantic or sexual relationship ☆

³item \'ī-təm\ *transitive verb* (1601)
1 *archaic* **:** COMPUTE, RECKON
2 *archaic* **:** to set down the particular details of

item·ise *British variant of* ITEMIZE

item·i·za·tion \,ī-tə-mə-'zā-shən\ *noun* (1894)
: the act of itemizing; *also* **:** an itemized list

item·ize \'ī-tə-,mīz\ *transitive verb* **-ized; -iz·ing** (1857)
: to set down in detail or by particulars **:** LIST ⟨*itemized* all expenses⟩

it·er·ance \'i-tə-rən(t)s\ *noun* (1604)
: REPETITION

it·er·ant \-rənt\ *adjective* (1626)
: marked by repetition, reiteration, or recurrence ⟨*iterant* echoes⟩

it·er·ate \'i-tə-,rāt\ *transitive verb* **-at·ed; -at·ing** [Latin *iteratus*, past participle of *iterare*, from *iterum* again; akin to Latin *is* he, that, *ita* thus, Sanskrit *itara* the other, *iti* thus] (1533)
: to say or do again or again and again **:** REITERATE

it·er·a·tion \,i-tə-'rā-shən\ *noun* (15th century)
1 : the action or a process of iterating or repeating: as **a :** a procedure in which repetition of a sequence of operations yields results successively closer to a desired result **b :** the repetition of a sequence of computer instructions a specified number of times or until a condition is met — compare RECURSION
2 : one execution of a sequence of operations or instructions in an iteration

it·er·a·tive \'i-tə-,rā-tiv, -rə-\ *adjective* (15th century)
: involving repetition: as **a :** expressing repetition of a verbal action **b :** relating to or being iteration of an operation or procedure
— it·er·a·tive·ly *adverb*

☆ SYNONYMS
Item, detail, particular mean one of the distinct parts of a whole. ITEM applies to each thing specified separately in a list or in a group of things that might be listed or enumerated ⟨every *item* on the list⟩. DETAIL applies to one of the small component parts of a larger whole such as a task, building, painting, narration, or process ⟨leave the *details* to others⟩. PARTICULAR stresses the smallness, singleness, and especially the concreteness of a detail or item ⟨a description that included few *particulars*⟩.

\ə\ **abut** \ᵊ\ **kitten** \ər\ **further** \a\ **ash** \ā\ **ace**
\ä\ **mop, mar** \aù\ **out** \ch\ **chin** \e\ **bet** \ē\ **easy**
\g\ **go** \i\ **hit** \ī\ **ice** \j\ **job** \ŋ\ **sing** \ō\ **go**
\ò\ **law** \òi\ **boy** \th\ **thin** \th\ **the** \ü\ **loot** \ù\ **foot**
\y\ **yet** \zh\ **vision** *see also* Guide to Pronunciation

ithy·phal·lic \ˌi-thi-'fa-lik\ *adjective* [Late Latin *ithyphallicus,* from Greek *ithyphallikos,* from *ithyphallos* erect phallus, from *ithys* straight + *phallos* phallus] (1795)
1 : of or relating to the phallus carried in procession in ancient festivals of Bacchus
2 a : having a erect penis — usually used of figures in an art representation **b :** OBSCENE, LEWD

itin·er·an·cy \ī-'ti-nə-rən(t)-sē\ *noun* (1789)
1 : a system (as in the Methodist Church) of rotating ministers who itinerate
2 a : the act of itinerating **b :** the state of being itinerant

itin·er·ant \-rənt\ *adjective* [Late Latin *itinerant-, itinerans,* present participle of *itinerari* to journey, from Latin *itiner-, iter* journey, way; akin to Hittite *itar* way, Latin *ire* to go — more at ISSUE] (circa 1576)
: traveling from place to place; *especially* **:** covering a circuit ⟨*itinerant* preacher⟩
— **itinerant** *noun*
— **itin·er·ant·ly** *adverb*

itin·er·ary \ī-'ti-nə-ˌrer-ē, ə-, *chiefly British* ÷-'ti-nə-rē\ *noun, plural* **-ar·ies** (15th century)
1 : the route of a journey or tour or the proposed outline of one
2 : a travel diary
3 : a traveler's guidebook
— **itinerary** *adjective*

itin·er·ate \ī-'ti-nə-ˌrāt, ə-\ *intransitive verb* **-at·ed; -at·ing** (1775)
: to travel a preaching or judicial circuit
— **itin·er·a·tion** \-ˌti-nə-'rā-shən\ *noun*

-itious *adjective suffix* [Latin *-icius, -itius*]
: of, relating to, or having the characteristics of ⟨excrement*itious*⟩

-itis *noun suffix, plural* **-itises** *also* **-itides** *or* **-ites** [New Latin, from Latin & Greek; Latin, from Greek, from feminine of *-itēs* -ite]
1 : disease or inflammation ⟨bronch*itis*⟩
2 *plural usually* **-itises :** condition likened to a disease — chiefly in nonce formations ⟨television*itis*⟩

it'll \'i-t²l\ (1824)
: it will **:** it shall

-itol *noun suffix* [International Scientific Vocabulary ¹-*ite* + ¹-*ol*]
: polyhydroxy alcohol usually related to a sugar ⟨mann*itol*⟩

its \'its, əts\ *adjective* (1598)
: of or relating to it or itself especially as possessor, agent, or object of an action ⟨going to *its* kennel⟩ ⟨a child proud of *its* first drawings⟩ ⟨*its* final enactment into law⟩

it's \'its, əts\ (circa 1555)
: it is **:** it has

it·self \it-'self, ət-, *Southern also* -'sef\ *pronoun* (before 12th century)
1 : that identical one — compare IT 1; used reflexively ⟨watched the cat giving *itself* a bath⟩, for emphasis ⟨the letter *itself* was missing⟩, or in absolute constructions ⟨*itself* a splendid specimen of classic art, it has been exhibited throughout the world⟩
2 : its normal, healthy, or sane condition
— **in itself :** in its own nature **:** INTRINSICALLY ⟨was not *in itself* bad⟩

it·ty-bit·ty \'i-tē-'bi-tē\ *or* **it·sy-bit·sy** \'it-sē-'bit-sē\ *adjective* [probably from baby talk for *little bit*] (1938)
: extremely small **:** TINY

-ity *noun suffix, plural* **-ities** [Middle English *-ite,* from Old French or Latin; Old French *-ité,* from Latin *-itat-, -itas,* from *-i-* (stem vowel of adjectives) + *-tat-, -tas* -ity; akin to Greek *-tēt-, -tēs* -ity]
: quality **:** state **:** degree ⟨alkalin*ity*⟩ ⟨theatrical*ity*⟩

IUD \ˌī-(ˌ)yü-'dē\ *noun* (1965)
: INTRAUTERINE DEVICE

-ium *noun suffix*
1 [New Latin, from Latin, ending of some neuter nouns] **a :** a chemical element ⟨sod*ium*⟩ **b :** cation ⟨tetrazol*ium*⟩

2 *plural* **-iums** *or* **-ia** [New Latin, from Latin, from Greek *-ion*] **:** small one **:** mass — especially in botanical terms ⟨polli*nium*⟩

IV \ˌī-'vē\ *noun, plural* **IVs** [intravenous] (circa 1955)
: an apparatus used to administer an intravenous injection or feeding; *also* **:** such an injection or feeding

-ive *adjective suffix* [Middle English *-if, -ive,* from Middle French & Latin; Middle French *-if,* from Latin *-ivus*]
: that performs or tends toward an (indicated) action ⟨amus*ive*⟩

I've \'īv\ (1586)
: I have

iver·mec·tin \ˌī-vər-'mek-tən\ *noun* [perhaps from d*i-* + New Latin a*vermitilis* (specific epithet of *Streptomyces avermitilis,* bacterium from which it is derived) + English *-ect-* (of unknown origin) + ¹-*in*] (1981)
: a drug mixture of two structurally similar semisynthetic lactones that is used in veterinary medicine as an anthelmintic, acaricide, and insecticide and in human medicine to treat onchocerciasis

ivied \'ī-vēd\ *adjective* (circa 1771)
1 : overgrown with ivy
2 : ACADEMIC

ivo·ry \'īv-rē, 'ī-və-rē\ *noun, plural* **-ries** [Middle English *ivorie,* from Old French *ivoire,* from Latin *eboreus* of ivory, from *ebor-, ebur* ivory, from Egyptian *ꜣbw, ꜣbw* elephant, ivory] (13th century)
1 a : the hard creamy-white modified dentine that composes the tusks of a tusked mammal (as an elephant, walrus, or narwhal) **b :** a tusk that yields ivory
2 : a variable color averaging a pale yellow
3 *slang* **:** TOOTH
4 : something (as a piano key) made of ivory or of a similar substance
— **ivory** *adjective*

ivo·ry-bill \-ˌbil\ *noun* (1787)
: IVORY-BILLED WOODPECKER

ivo·ry-billed woodpecker \-'bild-\ *noun* (1811)
: a very large black-and-white woodpecker (*Campephilus principalis*) of the southeastern U.S. and Cuba that has a showy red crest in the male and is presumed extinct in the U.S.

ivory-billed
woodpecker

ivory black *noun* (1634)
: a fine black pigment made by calcining ivory

ivory nut *noun* (circa 1847)
: the nutlike seed of a South American palm (*Phytelephas macrocarpa*) containing a very hard endosperm used for carving and turning — compare VEGETABLE IVORY

ivory tower *noun* [translation of French *tour d'ivoire*] (1911)
1 : an impractical often escapist attitude marked by aloof lack of concern with or interest in practical matters or urgent problems
2 : a secluded place that affords the means of treating practical issues with an impractical often escapist attitude; *especially* **:** a place of learning
— **ivory-tower** *adjective*
— **ivo·ry-tow·er·ish** \-'taù-(ə-)rish\ *adjective*

ivo·ry-tow·ered \-'taù(-ə)rd\ *adjective* (1937)
: divorced from reality and practical matters ⟨an *ivory-towered* recluse⟩

¹ivy \'ī-vē\ *noun, plural* **ivies** [Middle English, from Old English *īfig;* akin to Old High German *ebah* ivy] (before 12th century)
1 : a widely cultivated ornamental climbing or prostrate or sometimes shrubby chiefly Eurasian vine (*Hedera helix*) of the ginseng fami-

ly with evergreen leaves, small yellowish flowers, and black berries
2 : POISON IVY
3 *often capitalized* **:** an Ivy League college

ivy 1

²ivy *adjective* [from the prevalence of ivy-covered buildings on the campuses of older U.S. colleges] (1933)
1 : ACADEMIC
2 : IVY LEAGUE

Ivy League *adjective* (1939)
1 : of, relating to, or characteristic of a group of long-established eastern U.S. colleges widely regarded as high in scholastic and social prestige
2 : of, relating to, or characteristic of the students of Ivy League colleges

Ivy Leaguer *noun* (1943)
: a student at or a graduate of an Ivy League college

iwis \ē-'wis, ī-\ *adverb* [Middle English, from Old English *gewis* certain; akin to Old High German *giwisso* certainly, Old English *witan* to know — more at WIT] (12th century)
archaic **:** SURELY

Ix·i·on \ik-'sī-ən\ *noun* [Latin, from Greek *Ixīōn*]
: a Thessalian king bound by Zeus to a burning wheel in Tartarus for attempting to seduce Hera

ix·o·did \'ik-sə-ˌdid, ik-'sō-dəd\ *adjective* [ultimately from Greek *ixōdēs* sticky, from *ixos* birdlime] (circa 1909)
: of, relating to, or being a typical tick (family Ixodidae)
— **ixodid** *noun*

Iyar \'ē-ˌyär\ *noun* [Hebrew *Iyyār*] (1737)
: the 8th month of the civil year or the 2d month of the ecclesiastical year in the Jewish calendar — see MONTH table

-iza·tion \ə-'zā-shən *also* (ˌ)ī-'zā-\ *noun suffix*
: action, process, or result of making ⟨social*ization*⟩

-ize *verb suffix* [Middle English *-isen,* from Old French *-iser,* from Late Latin *-izare,* from Greek *-izein*]
1 a (1) **:** cause to be or conform to or resemble ⟨system*ize*⟩ ⟨American*ize*⟩ **:** cause to be formed into ⟨union*ize*⟩ (2) **:** subject to a (specified) action ⟨plagiar*ize*⟩ (3) **:** impregnate or treat or combine with ⟨alumin*ize*⟩ **b :** treat like ⟨idol*ize*⟩ **c :** treat according to the method of ⟨bowdler*ize*⟩
2 a : become **:** become like ⟨crystall*ize*⟩ **b :** be productive in or of ⟨hypothes*ize*⟩ **:** engage in a (specified) activity ⟨philosoph*ize*⟩ **c :** adopt or spread the manner of activity or the teaching of ⟨Platon*ize*⟩ ▢

iz·zard \'i-zərd\ *noun* [alteration of earlier *ezod, ezed,* probably from Middle French *et zede* and Z] (circa 1726)
chiefly dialect **:** the letter z

▢ USAGE
-ize The suffix *-ize* has been productive in English since the time of Thomas Nashe (1567–1601), who claimed credit for introducing it into English to remedy the surplus of monosyllabic words. Almost any noun or adjective can be made into a verb by adding *-ize* ⟨hospital*ize*⟩ ⟨familiar*ize*⟩; many technical terms are coined this way ⟨oxid*ize*⟩ as well as verbs of ethnic derivation ⟨American*ize*⟩ and verbs derived from proper names ⟨bowdler*ize*⟩ ⟨mesmer*ize*⟩. Nashe noted in 1591 that his coinages in *-ize* were being complained about, and to this day new words in *-ize* ⟨final*ize*⟩ ⟨prioritize*ize*⟩ are sure to draw critical fire.

J

J is the tenth letter of the English alphabet. In Latin i was used for either a vowel sound or for a consonant sound like the y in English yet. The letter form j was developed as a lengthened form of i during the Middle Ages and was used in certain positions, such as at the beginning of a word as in jet, or as an equivalent for the shorter form. In those positions it had exactly the same value as i. Because the initial i was usually consonantal, the j that so often took its place gradually became differentiated from i in sound as well as form. It was not, however, until the 17th century that the distinction of j as a consonant and i as a vowel was fully established and the capital form J introduced. In English, what is now the regular sound of j, as in jet, dates from the 11th century. It came with the Normans from the continent, where it was the consonant sound of i and j in French.

j \ˈjā\ *noun, plural* **j's** *or* **js** \ˈjāz\ *often capitalized, often attributive* (15th century) **1 a :** the 10th letter of the English alphabet **b :** a speech counterpart of orthographic j **2 :** a graphic device for reproducing the letter j **b :** a unit vector parallel to the y-axis **3 :** one designated j especially as the 10th in order or class **4 :** something shaped like the letter J

1jab \ˈjab\ *verb* **jabbed; jab·bing** [alteration of *job* to strike] (1827) *transitive verb* **1 a :** to pierce with or as if with a sharp object **b :** to poke quickly or abruptly : THRUST **2 :** to strike with a short straight blow *intransitive verb* **1 :** to make quick or abrupt thrusts with a sharp object **2 :** to strike a person with a short straight blow

2jab *noun* (1872) **1 :** an act of jabbing; *especially* **:** a short straight boxing punch delivered with the leading hand

1jab·ber \ˈja-bər\ *verb* **jab·bered; jab·ber·ing** \-b(ə-)riŋ\ [Middle English *jaberen*, of imitative origin] (15th century) *intransitive verb* **:** to talk rapidly, indistinctly, or unintelligibly *transitive verb* **:** to speak rapidly or indistinctly — **jab·ber·er** \ˈja-bər-ər\ *noun*

2jabber *noun* (1727) **:** GIBBERISH, CHATTER

jab·ber·wocky \ˈja-bər-ˌwä-kē\ *noun* [*Jabberwocky*, nonsense poem by Lewis Carroll] (1908) **:** meaningless speech or writing

jabi·ru \ˌzha-bə-ˈrü\ *noun* [Portuguese, from Tupi & Guarani *jabirú*] (1774) **:** any of several large tropical storks

jab·o·ran·di \ˌzha-bə-ˈran-ˌdē, -ˈran-dē\ *noun* [Portuguese, from Tupi *yaborandi*] (circa 1875) **1 :** the dried leaves of two South American shrubs (*Pilocarpus jaborandi* and *P. microphyllus*) of the rue family that are a source of pilocarpine

jab·ot \zha-ˈbō, ˈja-ˌbō\ *noun* [French] (1823) **1 :** a fall of lace or cloth attached to the front of a neckband and worn especially by men in the 18th century **2 :** a pleated frill of cloth or lace attached down the center front of a woman's blouse or dress

jab·o·ti·ca·ba \ˌzha-bü-ti-ˈkä-bə\ *noun* [Portuguese, from Tupi] (1824) **:** a Brazilian tree (*Myciaria cauliflora*) of the myrtle family cultivated in warm regions for its edible usually purplish fruit

jabot 1

ja·cal \hə-ˈkäl\ *noun, plural* **ja·ca·les** \-ˈkä-(ˌ)lās\ *also* **jacals** [Mexican Spanish, from Nahuatl *xahcalli*] (1838) **:** a hut in Mexico and southwestern U.S. with a thatched roof and walls made of upright poles or sticks covered and chinked with mud or clay

jac·a·mar \ˈzha-kə-ˌmär\ *noun* [French, from Tupi *jacamá-ciri*] (1825) **:** any of a family (Galbulidae) of usually iridescent green or bronze insectivorous birds of Central and South American tropical forests

ja·ca·na \ˌjə-kä-ˈna, ˌzha-sᵊ-ˈaⁿ\ *noun* [Portuguese *jaçaná*, from Tupi & Guarani] (circa 1753) **:** any of a family (Jacanidae) of long-legged and long-toed tropical wading birds that frequent coastal freshwater marshes and ponds

jac·a·ran·da \ˌja-kə-ˈran-də\ *noun* [New Latin, from Portuguese *jacarandá*, a tree of this genus, from Tupi] (1753) **:** any of a genus (*Jacaranda*) of pinnate-leaved tropical American trees of the trumpet-creeper family with showy usually blue flowers in panicles

ja·cinth \ˈja-sᵊⁿth, ˈja-\ *noun* [Middle English *jacinct*, from Old French *jacinthe*, from Latin *hyacinthus*, a flowering plant, a gem] (13th century) **1 :** HYACINTH **2 :** a gem more nearly orange in color than a hyacinth

1jack \ˈjak\ *noun* [Middle English *Jacke*, familiar term of address (from a nickname for *Johan* John] (1548) **1 a :** MAN — usually used as an intensive in such phrases as *every man jack* **b :** *often capitalized* **:** SAILOR **c** (1) **:** SERVANT, LABORER (2) **2 :** any of various usually mechanical devices: **a :** a device for turning a spit **b :** a usually portable mechanism or device for exerting pressure or lifting a heavy body a short distance **3 :** something that supports or holds in position: as **a :** an iron bar at a topgallant masthead to support a royal mast and spread the royal shrouds **b :** a wooden brace fastened behind a scenic unit in a stage set to prop it up **4 :** any of several fishes; *especially* **:** any of various carangids **b :** a male donkey **c :** JACKRABBIT **d :** any of several birds (as a jackdaw) **5 a :** a small white target ball in lawn bowling **b :** a small national flag flown by a ship **c** (1) **:** a playing card carrying the figure of a soldier or servant usually below the queen **b :** JACKPOT 1a(2) **6 a :** a small 6-pointed metal object used in the game of jacks **b :** *plural but singular in construction* **:** a game played with a set of small objects that are tossed, caught, and moved in various figures (2) **:** a small 6-pointed metal object used in the game of jacks **7** *slang* **:** MONEY

8 : a female fitting in an electric circuit used with a plug to make a connection with another circuit **9 a :** APPLEJACK **b :** BRANDY **10 :** JACKKNIFE 2 **11 :** MONTEREY JACK

2jack (circa 1841) *intransitive verb* **1 :** to hunt or fish at night with a jacklight **2 a :** to move or lift by or as if by a jack **b :** to raise the level of — *usually used with up* ⟨*jack* up the price⟩ **c :** to take to task — **jack·er** *noun*

jack·al \ˈja-kal *also* -ˌkȯl\ *noun* [Turkish *çakal*, from Persian *shagāl*, of Indo-Aryan origin; akin to Sanskrit *sṛgāla* jackal] (1603) **1 :** any of several small omnivorous canids (as *Canis aureus*) of Africa and Asia having large ears, long legs, and bushy tails **2 a :** a person who performs routine or menial tasks for another **b :** a person who serves or collaborates with another especially in the commission of base acts

Jack-a-Lent \ˈjak-ə-ˌlent\ *noun* [*jack* + *a*] (1598) **1 :** a small stuffed puppet set up to be pelted for fun in Lent **2 :** a simple or insignificant person

jack-a-napes \ˈja-kə-ˌnāps\ *noun* [Middle English *Jack Napis*, nickname for William de la Pole (1450) duke of Suffolk] (1526) **1 :** MONKEY, APE **2 :** an impudent or conceited fellow **b :** a saucy or mischievous child

jack·ass \ˈjak-ˌas\ *noun* (1727) **1 :** DONKEY; *especially* **:** a male donkey **2 :** a stupid person : FOOL

jack·ass·ery \ˈjak-ə-sə-rē, -ˌas-rē\ *noun, plural* **-er·ies** (1833) **:** foolish action or behavior

jack bean *noun* (1885) **:** a bushy annual tropical American legume (genus *Canavalia*); *especially* **:** a plant (*C. ensiformis*) grown especially for forage

jack·boot \ˈjak-ˌbüt\ *noun* (1686) **1 :** a heavy military boot made of glossy black leather extending above the knee and worn especially during the 17th and 18th centuries **2 :** the spirit or policy of militarism or totalitarianism **3 :** a laceless military boot reaching to the calf

jack·boot·ed \-ˌbü-təd\ *adjective* (1846) **1 :** wearing jackboots **2 :** ruthlessly and violently oppressive ⟨*jack-booted force*⟩

◆ **WORD HISTORY** **jabberwocky** Lewis Carroll's poem "Jabberwocky," published in *Through the Looking-Glass*, the second of his *Alice-in-Wonderland* books, is a wonderful example of nonsense verse. In the opening lines "Twas brillig and the slithy toves/Did gyre and gimble in the wabe," the words appear to be English, and we can tell which are nouns, adjectives, and verbs, but as evocative as they are they mean nothing. Lewis Carroll simply created them for the purposes of the poem. The word *jabberwocky*, a mock derivative of *Jabberwock*, the fantastic monster in the poem, has become a generic term for words (or sometimes acts) that seem but do not. In one bound *jabberwocky* has leapt from nonsense to metalanguage (language we use to talk about language).

\ə\ about \ə'\ kitten \ər\ further \a\ ash \ā\ ace \ä\ mop, mar \au̇\ out \ch\ chin \e\ bet \ē\ easy \g\ go \i\ hit \ī\ ice \j\ job \ŋ\ sing \ō\ go \o\̇ law \ȯi\ boy \th\ thin \tẖ\ the \ü\ loot \u̇\ foot \y\ yet \zh\ vision *see also* Guide to Pronunciation

jack cheese *noun, often J capitalized* [alteration of David *Jacks*, 19th century California landowner] (1912) **:** MONTEREY JACK

jack crevalle *noun* (1948) **:** a carangid fish (*Caranx hippos*) that is an important food fish along the west coast of Florida

jack-daw \'jak-ˌdȯ\ *noun* (1543) **1 :** a common black and gray bird (*Corvus monedula*) of Eurasia and northern Africa that is related to but smaller than the common crow **2 :** GRACKLE 1

¹**jack-et** \'ja-kət\ *noun* [Middle English *jaket*, from Middle French *jaquet*, diminutive of *jaque* short jacket, from *jacque* peasant, from the name *Jacques* James] (15th century) **1 a : a** : a garment for the upper body usually having a front opening, collar, lapels, sleeves, and pockets **b :** something worn or fastened around the body but not for use as clothing **2 a** (1) **:** the natural covering of an animal (2) **:** the fur or wool of a mammal **b :** the skin of a potato **3 :** an outer covering or casing: as **a** (1) **:** a thermally nonconducting cover (2) **:** a covering that encloses an intermediate space through which a temperature-controlling fluid circulates (3) **:** a tough cold-worked metal casing that forms the outer shell of a built-up bullet **b** (1) **:** a wrapper or open envelope for a document (2) **:** an envelope for enclosing registered mail during delivery from one post office to another **c** (1) **:** a detachable protective cover for a book (2) **:** a paper or paperboard envelope for a phonograph record
— **jack-et-less** \-ləs\ *adjective*

²**jacket** *transitive verb* (1856) **:** to put a jacket on **:** enclose in or with a jacket

Jack Frost *noun* (1826) **:** frost or frosty weather personified

jack-fruit \'jak-ˌfrüt\ *noun* [Portuguese *jaca* jackfruit, from Malayalam *cakka*] (1830) **:** a large tropical Asian tree (*Artocarpus heterophyllus*) related to the breadfruit that yields a fine-grained yellow wood and immense fruits which contain an edible pulp and nutritious seeds; *also* **:** its fruit

jack-ham-mer \'jak-ˌha-mər\ *noun* (1916) **1 :** a pneumatically operated percussive rock-drilling tool usually held in the hands **2 :** a device in which a tool (as a chisel for breaking up pavements) is driven percussively by compressed air
— **jackhammer** *verb*

jack-in-the-box \'ja-kən-thə-ˌbäks\ *noun, plural* **jack-in-the-box-es** *or* **jacks-in-the-box** (1702) **:** a toy consisting of a small box out of which a figure (as of a clown's head) springs when the lid is raised

jack-in-the-pul-pit \ˌja-kən-thə-ˈpul-pit, -pət *also* -ˈpäl-\ *noun, plural* **jack-in-the-pulpits** *or* **jacks-in-the-pulpit** (1837) **:** an American spring-flowering woodland herb (*Arisaema triphyllum* synonym *A. atrorubens*) of the arum family having an upright club-shaped spadix arched over by a green and purple spathe

¹**jack-knife** \'jak-ˌnif\ *noun* (1711) **1 :** a large strong pocket-knife **2 : a** dive executed in which the diver bends from the waist and touches the ankles while holding the knees unbent and then straightens out

²**jackknife** *verb* (1806)
transitive verb
1 : to cut with a jackknife **2 :** to cause to double up like a jackknife
intransitive verb
1 : to double up like a jackknife **2 :** to turn and form an angle of 90 degrees or less with each other — used especially of a tractor-trailer combination

jack-leg \'jak-ˌleg, -ˌlāg\ *adjective* [*jack* + *-leg* (as in *blackleg*)] (1850) **1 a :** lacking skill or training **:** AMATEUR ⟨a *jackleg* carpenter⟩ **b :** characterized by unscrupulousness, dishonesty, or lack of professional standards ⟨a *jackleg* lawyer⟩ **2 :** designed as a temporary expedient **:** MAKESHIFT
— **jackleg** *noun*

jack-light \-ˌlīt\ *noun* (circa 1841) **:** a light used especially in hunting or fishing at night

jack mackerel *noun* (1882) **:** a California carangid food fish (*Trachurus symmetricus*) that is iridescent green or bluish above and silvery below

jack-of-all-trades \ˌja-kə-ˌvȯl-ˈtrādz\ *noun, plural* **jacks-of-all-trades** (1618) **:** a person who can do passable work at various tasks **:** a handy versatile person

jack off *verb* [probably alteration of *jerk off*] (1959)
: MASTURBATE — usually considered vulgar

jack-o'-lan-tern \'ja-kə-ˌlan-tərn\ *noun* (1750)
1 : IGNIS FATUUS **2 :** a lantern made of a pumpkin cut to look like a human face **3 :** a large orangish gill fungus (*Omphalotus olearius* synonym *Clitocybe illudens*) that is poisonous and luminescent

jack pine *noun* (1883) **:** a slender pine (*Pinus banksiana*) of northern North America that has two stout needles in each fascicle and wood used especially for pulpwood

jack plane *noun* (circa 1816) **:** a medium-sized general-purpose plane used in carpentry and joinery

jack-pot \'jak-ˌpät\ *noun* (1881) **1 a** (1) **:** a hand or game of draw poker in which a pair of jacks or better is required to open (2) **:** a large pot (as in poker) formed by the accumulation of stakes from previous play **b** (1) **:** a combination on a slot machine that wins a top prize or all the coins available for paying out (2) **:** the sum so won **c : a** large fund of money or other reward formed by the accumulation of unwon prizes **2 :** an impressive often unexpected success or reward

³ *chiefly West* **:** a tight spot **:** JAM

jack-rab-bit \-ˌra-bət\ *noun* [*'jack* (jackass) + *rabbit*; from its long ears] (1863) **:** any of several large hares (genus *Lepus*) of western North America having very long ears and long hind legs

Jack Russell terrier \'jak-ˈrə-səl-\ *noun* [Jack (John) *Russell* (died 1883) English clergyman & dog breeder] (1961) **:** any of a breed of small terriers having a usually white coat with brown, black, or tricolor markings — called also *Jack Russell*

jack salmon *noun* (1871)
1 : WALLEYE 3 **2 :** GRILSE

jack-screw \'jak-ˌskrü\ *noun* (1769) **:** SCREW JACK

jack-smelt \-ˌsmelt\ *noun* (1949) **:** a large silversides (*Atherinopsis californiensis*) of the Pacific coast of North America that is the chief commercial smelt of the California markets

jack-son Day \'jak-sən-\ *noun* [Andrew *Jackson*; from his defense of New Orleans] (1885) **:** January 8 celebrated as a legal holiday in Louisiana to commemorate the successful defense of New Orleans in 1815

jack stand *noun* (1968) **:** a stand whose height may be adjusted and fixed by a pin and which is used to support an automobile that has been raised by a jack

jack-stay \-ˌstā\ *noun* (circa 1840) **1 :** an iron rod, wooden bar, or wire rope along a yard of a ship to which the sails are fastened **2 :** a support of wood, iron, or rope running up a mast on which the parrel of a yard travels

jack-straw \'jak-ˌstrȯ\ *noun* (1801) **1** *plural but singular in construction* **:** a game in which a set of straws or thin strips is let fall in a heap with each player in turn trying to remove one at a time without disturbing the rest **2 :** one of the pieces used in the game jackstraws

jack-tar \-'tär\ *noun, often capitalized* (1781) **:** SAILOR

jack-up \-ˌəp\ *noun* (1965) **:** a drilling rig used in offshore drilling whose drilling platform is a barge from which legs are lowered to the bottom when over the drill site and which is raised above the water and supported on the legs to conduct drilling operations

Ja-cob \'jā-kəb\ *noun* [Late Latin, from Greek *Iakōb*, from Hebrew *Ya'ăqōbh*] **1 :** a son of Isaac and Rebekah, the twin brother of Esau, and heir of God's promise of blessing to Abraham **2 :** the ancient Hebrew nation

Ja-co-be-an \ˌja-kə-ˈbē-ən\ *adjective* [New Latin *Jacobaeus*, from *Jacobus* James] (1844) **:** of, relating to, or characteristic of James I of England or his age
— **Jacobean** *noun*

Jacobean lily *noun, often J capitalized* [Late Latin *Jacobus* (Saint James)] (circa 1774) **:** a Mexican bulbous herb (*Sprekelia formosissima*) of the amaryllis family cultivated for its bright red solitary flower

Ja-co-bi-an \jə-ˈkō-bē-ən, yä-\ *noun* [K. G. J. *Jacobi* (died 1851) German mathematician] (1881) **:** a determinant defined for a finite number of functions of the same number of variables in which each row consists of the first partial derivatives of the same function with respect to each of the variables

Jac-o-bin \'ja-kə-bən\ *noun* [Middle English, from Middle French, from Medieval Latin *Jacobinus*, from Late Latin *Jacobus* (Saint James); from the location of the first Dominican convent in the street of Saint James, Paris] (14th century)
1 : DOMINICAN
2 [French, from *Jacobin* Dominican; from the group's founding in the Dominican convent in Paris] **:** a member of an extremist or radical political group; *especially* **:** a member of such a group advocating egalitarian democracy and engaging in terrorist activities during the French Revolution of 1789

Jac-o-bin-ic \ˌja-kə-ˈbi-nik\ *or* **Jac-o-bin-i-cal** \-ni-kəl\ *adjective*
— **Jac-o-bin-ism** \'ja-kə-bə-ˌni-zəm\ *noun*

¹**Jac-o-bite** \'ja-kə-ˌbīt\ *noun* [Middle English, from Medieval Latin *Jacobita*, from *Jacobus* (Jacob Baradai) (died 578) Syrian monk] (15th century) **:** a member of any of various Monophysite Eastern churches; *especially* **:** a member of the Monophysite Syrian church

²**Jacobite** *noun* [*Jacobus* (James II)] (1689) **:** a partisan of James II of England or of the Stuarts after the revolution of 1688
— **Jac-o-bit-i-cal** \ˌja-kə-ˈbi-ti-kəl\ *adjective*
— **Jac-o-bit-ism** \'ja-kə-bə-ˌti-zəm\ *noun*

Ja-cob's ladder \ˌjā-kəbz-\ *noun* [from the ladder seen in a dream by Jacob in Genesis 28:12] (1733) **1 :** any of a genus (*Polemonium*) of herbs of the phlox family that have pinnate leaves, an herbaceous calyx, a bell-shaped corolla with stamens with their filaments bent downward,

and a several-seeded capsule; *especially* **:** a perennial (*P. caeruleum*) of European origin with bright blue or occasionally white flowers **2 :** a marine ladder of rope or chain with wooden or iron rungs

Ja·cob·son's organ \'jā-kəb-sənz-\ *noun* [Ludvig L. *Jacobson* (died 1843) Danish anatomist] (1885)
: either of a pair of small pits that are situated one on either side of the nasal septum (as in higher vertebrates) or in the buccal cavity and that are rudimentary in humans but developed in reptiles, amphibians, and some mammals as chemoreceptors

Ja·co·bus \jə-'kō-bəs\ *noun* [*Jacobus* (James I), during whose reign unites were coined] (1612)
: UNITE

jac·o·net \'ja-kə-ˌnet\ *noun* [modification of Urdu *jagannāthī*] (1769)
: a lightweight cotton cloth used for clothing and bandages

jac·quard \'ja-ˌkärd\ *noun, often capitalized, often attributive* [Joseph *Jacquard*] (1841)
1 a : the control mechanism of a Jacquard loom **b :** JACQUARD LOOM
2 : a fabric of intricate variegated weave or pattern

Jacquard loom *noun* (1851)
: a loom designed to weave fabrics of intricate design whose control mechanism makes use of cards with holes punched in them

jac·que·rie \ˌzhä-kə-'rē, ˌzha-\ *noun, often capitalized* [Middle French, from the French peasant revolt in 1358, from *jacque* peasant — more at JACKET] (1523)
: a peasants' revolt

jac·ti·ta·tion \ˌjak-tə-'tā-shən\ *noun* [Late Latin *jactitation-, jactitatio*, from *jactitare*, frequentative of Latin *jactare* to throw — more at JET] (1665)
: a tossing to and fro or jerking and twitching of the body

Ja·cuz·zi \jə-'kü-zē\ *trademark*
— used for a whirlpool bath and a recreational bathing tub or pool

¹jade \'jād\ *noun* [Middle English] (14th century)
1 : a broken-down, vicious, or worthless horse
2 a : a disreputable woman **b :** a flirtatious girl

²jade *verb* **jad·ed; jad·ing** (1598)
transitive verb
1 a : to wear out by overwork or abuse **b :** to tire or dull through repetition or excess
2 *obsolete* **:** to make ridiculous
intransitive verb
: to become weary or dulled
synonym *see* TIRE

³jade *noun* [French, from obsolete Spanish (*piedra de la*) *ijada*, literally, loin stone, ultimately from Latin *ilia*, plural, flanks; from the belief that jade cures renal colic] (1657)
1 : either of two tough compact typically green gemstones that take a high polish: **a :** JADEITE **b :** NEPHRITE
2 : a sculpture or artifact of jade
3 : JADE GREEN ◆

jaded *adjective* (1600)
1 : fatigued by overwork **:** EXHAUSTED
2 : dulled by experience or by surfeit
— **jad·ed·ly** *adverb*
— **jad·ed·ness** *noun*

jade green *noun* (1892)
: a light bluish green

jade·ite \'jā-ˌdīt\ *noun* [French] (1865)
: a monoclinic mineral that is a silicate of sodium and aluminum and is a jade
— **ja·dit·ic** \jā-'di-tik\ *adjective*

jade plant *noun* (1944)
: any of several succulent plants (genus *Crassula*) of the orpine family cultivated as foliage plants

jae·ger \'yā-gər\ *noun* [German *Jäger*] (1809)

1 a : HUNTER, HUNTSMAN **b :** one attending a person of rank or wealth and wearing hunter's costume
2 : any of several large dark-colored birds (genus *Stercorarius* of the family Stercorariidae) of northern seas that are strong fliers and that tend to harass weaker birds until they drop or disgorge their prey

¹jag \'jag\ *verb* **jagged; jag·ging** [Middle English *jaggen*] (15th century)
transitive verb
1 *chiefly dialect* **:** PRICK, STAB
2 : to cut indentations into; *also* **:** to form teeth on (a saw) by cutting indentations
intransitive verb
1 : PRICK, THRUST
2 : to move in jerks
— **jag·ger** *noun*

²jag *noun* (1578)
: a sharp projecting part **:** BARB

³jag *noun* [origin unknown] (1597)
1 : a small load
2 a : a state or feeling of exhilaration or intoxication usually induced by liquor **b :** SPREE ⟨a crying *jag*⟩

jag·ged \'ja-gəd\ *adjective* (1577)
1 : having a sharply uneven edge or surface
2 : having a harsh, rough, or irregular quality
— **jag·ged·ly** *adverb*
— **jag·ged·ness** *noun*

jag·gery \'ja-gə-rē\ *noun* [Portuguese *jágara*, probably from Malayalam *chakkara* sugar] (1598)
: an unrefined brown sugar made from palm sap

jag·gy \'ja-gē\ *adjective* (1717)
: JAGGED, NOTCHED

jag·uar \'ja-ˌgwär, -gyə-ˌwär, -gwər, *especially British* 'ja-gyə-wər\ *noun* [Spanish *yaguar* & Portuguese *jaguar*, from Guarani *yaguara* & Tupi *jaguara*] (1604)
: a large cat (*Panthera onca* synonym *Felis onca*) chiefly of Central and South America that is larger and stockier than the leopard and is brownish yellow or buff with black spots

jaguar

jag·ua·run·di \ˌzha-gwə-'rən-dē\ *also* **jag·ua·ron·di** \-'rän-\ *noun* [American Spanish, from Guarani *yaguarundi*] (circa 1885)
: a slender long-tailed short-legged black, gray, or reddish wildcat (*Felis yagouaroundi*) chiefly of Central and South America

Jah \'jä\ *noun* [Hebrew *Yāh*] (1975)
: the Supreme Being of Rastafarianism

Jah·veh \'yä-(ˌ)vä\ *variant of* YAHWEH

jai alai \'hī-ˌlī, ˌhī-ə-'lī\ *noun* [Spanish, from Basque, from *jai* festival + *alai* merry] (1903)
: a court game somewhat like handball played usually by two or four players with a ball and a long curved wicker basket strapped to the wrist

¹jail \'jā(ə)l\ *noun* [Middle English *jaiole*, from Old French, from Late Latin *caveola*, diminutive of Latin *cavea* cage — more at CAGE] (13th century)
1 : a place of confinement for persons held in lawful custody; *specifically* **:** such a place under the jurisdiction of a local government (as a county) for the confinement of persons awaiting trial or those convicted of minor crimes — compare PRISON
2 : confinement in a jail

²jail *transitive verb* (1604)
: to confine in or as if in a jail

jail·bait \'jā(ə)l-ˌbāt\ *noun* (1930)
: a girl under the age of consent with whom sexual intercourse is unlawful and constitutes statutory rape

jail·bird \-ˌbərd\ *noun* (1603)

: a person confined in jail; *specifically* **:** an habitual criminal

jail·break \-ˌbrāk\ *noun* (1910)
: a forcible escape from jail

jail·er *or* **jail·or** \'jā-lər\ *noun* (13th century)
1 : a keeper of a jail
2 : one that restricts another's liberty as if by imprisonment

jail·house \'jā(ə)l-ˌhaus\ *noun* (1812)
: JAIL 1

jailhouse lawyer *noun* (1969)
: a prison inmate self-taught in the law who tries to gain release through legal maneuvers or who advises fellow inmates on their legal problems

Jain \'jīn\ *or* **Jai·na** \'jī-nə\ *noun* [Hindi *Jain*, from Sanskrit *Jaina*] (1805)
: an adherent of Jainism

Jain·ism \'jī-ˌni-zəm\ *noun* (1858)
: a religion of India originating in the 6th century B.C. and teaching liberation of the soul by right knowledge, right faith, and right conduct

jake \'jāk\ *adjective* [origin unknown] (1914) *slang* **:** ALL RIGHT, FINE

jake leg \'jāk-ˌleg, -ˌlāg\ *noun* [*jake* grain alcohol flavored with an alcoholic extract of ginger] (1932)
: a paralysis caused by drinking improperly distilled or contaminated liquor

jakes \'jāks\ *noun plural but singular or plural in construction* [perhaps from French *Jacques* James] (1538)
: PRIVY 1

jal·ap \'ja-ləp, 'jä-\ *noun* [French & Spanish; French *jalap*, from Spanish *jalapa*, from *Jalapa*, Mexico] (1644)
1 a : the dried tuberous root of a Mexican plant (*Ipomoea purga* synonym *Exogonium purga*) of the morning-glory family; *also* **:** a powdered purgative drug prepared from it that contains resinous glycosides **b :** the root or derived drug of plants related to the one supplying jalap
2 : a plant yielding jalap

ja·la·pe·ño *also* **ja·la·pe·no** \ˌhä-lə-'pā-(ˌ)nyō, ˌha-, -'pā-(ˌ)nō, -'pē-(ˌ)nō\ *noun, plural* **-ños** *also* **-nos** [Mexican Spanish, from *jalapeño*, adjective, of Jalapa] (1939)
: a small plump dark green Mexican hot pepper — called also *jalapeño pepper*

ja·lopy \jə-'lä-pē\ *noun, plural* **ja·lop·ies** [origin unknown] (1928)
: a dilapidated old vehicle (as an automobile)

jal·ou·sie \'ja-lə-sē\ *noun* [French, literally, jealousy, from Old French *jelous* jealous] (1766)

◇ **WORD HISTORY**

jade Gemstones were once believed to have magical and medicinal properties. Jade was supposed to be especially effective in combating kidney disorders, and it owes its name to this belief. The green gemstone was known as *piedra de la ijada* or "loin stone" to the 16th century Spanish who brought it home from the New World. Not only in Spain but throughout western Europe jade became popular both as an ornament and as a cure or preventive for internal disorders. English *jade* was borrowed from French, in which *jade* had developed from earlier *ejade*, through construing *l'ejade*, the form of the word when preceded by the definite article, as *le jade*; *ejade*, in turn, was borrowed from Spanish *ijada*, taken to be the name of the stone.

\ə\ **abut** \ᵊ\ **kitten** \ər\ **further** \a\ **ash** \ā\ **ace**
\ä\ **mop, mar** \aù\ **out** \ch\ **chin** \e\ **bet** \ē\ **easy**
\g\ **go** \i\ **hit** \ī\ **ice** \j\ **job** \ŋ\ **sing** \ō\ **go**
\ò\ **law** \òi\ **boy** \th\ **thin** \ṯh\ **the** \ü\ **loot** \ù\ **foot**
\y\ **yet** \zh\ **vision** *see also* Guide to Pronunciation

1 : a blind with adjustable horizontal slats for admitting light and air while excluding direct sun and rain
2 : a window made of adjustable glass louvers that control ventilation

¹jam \'jam\ *verb* **jammed; jam·ming** [origin unknown] (1706)
intransitive verb
1 a : to become blocked or wedged **b :** to become unworkable through the jamming of a movable part
2 : to force one's way into a restricted space
3 : to take part in a jam session
transitive verb
1 a : to press into a close or tight position ⟨*jam* his hat on⟩ **b** (1) **:** to cause to become wedged so as to be unworkable ⟨*jam* the typewriter keys⟩ (2) **:** to make unworkable by jamming **c :** to block passage of **:** OBSTRUCT **d :** to fill often to excess **:** PACK ⟨the crowd *jammed* the theater⟩
2 : to push forcibly; *especially* **:** to apply (brakes) suddenly and forcibly — used with *on*
3 : CRUSH, BRUISE
4 a : to make unintelligible by sending out interfering signals or messages **b :** to make (as a radar apparatus) ineffective by jamming signals or by causing reflection of radar waves
5 : to pitch inside to (a batter)
— **jam·mer** \'ja-mər\ *noun*

²jam *noun* (1805)
1 a : an act or instance of jamming **b :** a crowded mass that impedes or blocks ⟨a traffic *jam*⟩
2 a : the quality or state of being jammed **b :** the pressure or congestion of a crowd **:** CRUSH
3 : a difficult state of affairs **:** FIX ⟨got into a *jam*⟩
4 : JAM SESSION
5 : DUNK SHOT

³jam *noun* [probably from ¹*jam*] (circa 1736)
: a food made by boiling fruit and sugar to a thick consistency
— **jam·my** \'ja-mē\ *adjective*

Jamaica rum *noun* (circa 1900)
: a heavy-bodied rum made by slow fermentation and marked by a pungent bouquet

jamb \'jam\ *noun* [Middle English *jambe*, from Middle French, literally, leg, from Late Latin *gamba* — more at GAMBIT] (14th century)
1 : an upright piece or surface forming the side of an opening (as for a door, window, or fireplace)
2 : a projecting columnar part or mass

jam·ba·laya \ˌjəm-bə-'lī-ə\ *noun* [Louisiana French, from Provençal *jambalaia*] (1872)
1 : rice cooked usually with ham, sausage, chicken, shrimp, or oysters and seasoned with herbs
2 : a mixture of diverse elements ⟨curious *jambalayas* of competing elements —Neil Hickey⟩

jam·beau \'jam-(ˌ)bō\ *noun, plural* **jam·beaux** \-(ˌ)bōz\ [Middle English, from (assumed) Anglo-French, from Middle French *jambe*] (14th century)
: a piece of medieval armor for the leg below the knee — see ARMOR illustration

jam·bo·ree \ˌjam-bə-'rē\ *noun* [origin unknown] (1864)
1 : a noisy or unrestrained carouse
2 a : a large festive gathering **b :** a national or international camping assembly of Boy Scouts
3 : a long mixed program of entertainment

James \'jāmz\ *noun* [Middle English, from Middle French, from (assumed) Vulgar Latin *Jacomus*, alteration of Late Latin *Jacobus, Jacob* Jacob]
1 : an apostle, son of Zebedee, and brother of the apostle John according to the Gospel accounts
2 : an apostle and son of Alphaeus according to the Gospel accounts — called also *James the Less*

3 : a brother of Jesus traditionally held to be the author of the New Testament Epistle of James
4 : a moral lecture addressed to early Christians and included as a book in the New Testament — see BIBLE table

jam·mies \'ja-mēz\ *noun plural* [by shortening & alteration] (1973)
: PAJAMAS 2

jam–pack \'jam-'pak\ *transitive verb* (1924)
: to pack tightly or to excess

Jams \'jamz\ *trademark*
— used for knee-length loose-fitting swim trunks

jam session *noun* [²*jam*] (1933)
: an often impromptu performance by a group especially of jazz musicians that is characterized by improvisation

Jam·shid *or* **Jam·shyd** \jam-'shēd\ *noun* [Persian *Jamshīd*]
: an early legendary king of Persia who reigned for 700 years

jam–up \'jam-ˌəp\ *noun* (1941)
: JAM 1

Jane Doe \'jān-'dō\ *noun* (1936)
: a female party to legal proceedings whose true name is unknown

Jane–ite \'jā-ˌnīt\ *noun* (1896)
: an enthusiastic admirer of Jane Austen's writings

¹jan·gle \'jaŋ-gəl\ *verb* **jan·gled; jan·gling** \-g(ə)liŋ\ [Middle English, from Middle French *jangler*, of Germanic origin; akin to Middle Dutch *jangelen* to grumble] (14th century)
intransitive verb
1 : to talk idly
2 : to quarrel verbally
3 : to make a harsh or discordant often ringing sound ⟨keys *jangling* in my pocket⟩
transitive verb
1 : to utter or sound in a discordant, babbling, or chattering way
2 a : to cause to sound harshly or inharmoniously **b :** to excite to tense irritation ⟨*jangled* nerves⟩
— **jan·gler** \-g(ə-)lər\ *noun*

²jangle *noun* (14th century)
1 : idle talk
2 : noisy quarreling
3 : a discordant often ringing sound **:** DISCORD

jan·gly \'jaŋ-g(ə)lē\ *adjective* (1892)
: marked by jangling **:** having a jangling quality ⟨*jangly* earrings⟩ ⟨*jangly* guitar music⟩

jan·is·sary *or* **jan·i·zary** \'ja-nə-ˌser-ē, -ˌzer-\ *noun, plural* **-sar·ies** *or* **-zar·ies** [Italian *gianizzero*, from Turkish *yeniçeri*, from *yeni* new + *çeri* soldier] (1529)
1 *often capitalized* **:** a soldier of an elite corps of Turkish troops organized in the 14th century and abolished in 1826
2 : a member of a group of loyal or subservient troops, officials, or supporters

jan·i·tor \'ja-nə-tər\ *noun* [Latin, from *janus* arch, gate] (1629)
1 : DOORKEEPER
2 : one who keeps the premises of a building (as an apartment or office) clean, tends the heating system, and makes minor repairs
— **jan·i·to·ri·al** \ˌja-nə-'tōr-ē-əl, -'tor-\ *adjective*

Jan·sen·ism \'jan(t)-sə-ˌni-zəm\ *noun* [French *jansénisme*, from Cornelis *Jansen*] (circa 1656)
1 : a system of doctrine based on moral determinism, defended by various reformist factions among 17th and 18th century western European Roman Catholic clergy, religious, and scholars, and condemned as heretical by papal authority
2 : a puritanical attitude (as toward sex)
— **Jan·sen·ist** \-nist\ *noun*
— **Jan·sen·is·tic** \ˌjan(t)-sə-'nis-tik\ *adjective*

Jan·u·ary \'jan-yə-ˌwer-ē\ *noun, plural* **-ar·ies** *or* **-ar·ys** [Middle English *Januarie*, from Latin *Januarius*, 1st month of the ancient Roman year, from *Janus*] (14th century)
: the 1st month of the Gregorian calendar

Ja·nus \'jā-nəs\ *noun* [Latin]
: a Roman god that is identified with doors, gates, and all beginnings and that is represented artistically with two opposite faces

Janus–faced \-ˌfāst\ *adjective* (1682)
: having two contrasting aspects; *especially* **:** DUPLICITOUS, TWO-FACED

Janus green *noun* [probably from *Janus*, a trademark] (1898)
: a basic azine dye used especially as a biological stain (as for mitochondria)

Jap \'jap\ *noun or adjective* (1886)
: JAPANESE — usually used disparagingly

JAP \'jap\ *noun* (circa 1973)
: JEWISH AMERICAN PRINCESS — usually used disparagingly

¹ja·pan \jə-'pan\ *adjective* (1673)
: of, relating to, or originating in Japan **:** of a kind or style characteristic of Japanese workmanship

²japan *noun* (1688)
1 a : any of several varnishes yielding a hard brilliant finish **b :** a hard dark coating containing asphalt and a drier that is used especially on metal and fixed by heating — called also *japan black*
2 : work (as lacquer ware) finished and decorated in the Japanese manner

³japan *transitive verb* **ja·panned; ja·pan·ning** (1688)
1 : to cover with or as if with a coat of japan
2 : to give a high gloss to
— **ja·pan·ner** *noun*

Jap·a·nese \ˌja-pə-'nēz, -'nēs\ *noun, plural* **Japanese** (1604)
1 a : a native or inhabitant of Japan **b :** a person of Japanese descent
2 : the language of the Japanese
— **Japanese** *adjective*

Japanese an·drom·e·da \-ˌan-'drä-mə-də\ *noun* [New Latin *Andromeda*, genus of plants, from Latin *Andromeda*, Ethiopian princess, from Greek *Andromedē*] (1948)
: a shrubby evergreen Asian heath (*Pieris japonica*) with glossy leaves and drooping clusters of usually whitish flowers

Japanese beetle *noun* (1900)
: a small metallic green and brown scarab beetle (*Popillia japonica*) that has been introduced into America from Japan and as a grub feeds on the roots of grasses and decaying vegetation and as an adult eats foliage and fruits

Japanese cedar *noun* (circa 1880)
: a large evergreen tree (*Cryptomeria japonica*) grown especially in China and Japan for its valuable soft wood

Japanese iris *noun* (1883)
: any of various beardless garden irises (especially *Iris kaempferi*) with very large showy flowers

Japanese lacquer *noun* (1876)
: LACQUER 1b

Japanese maple *noun* (1898)
: a maple (*Acer palmatum*) of Japan, China, and Korea with purple flowers and usually deeply parted leaves that is widely cultivated as a shrub or small tree

Japanese millet *noun* (1900)
: a coarse annual grass (*Echinochloa frumentacea*) cultivated especially in Asia for its edible seeds

Japanese plum *noun* (1893)
: a tree (*Prunus salicina*) native to China and cultivated in Japan that bears Japanese plums; *also* **:** the large usually yellow to light red fruit of a Japanese plum

Japanese quail *noun* (1963)
: a quail (*Coturnix japonica* synonym *C. coturnix japonica*) from China and Japan that is often used in laboratory research

Japanese quince *noun* (1900)
: a hardy Chinese ornamental shrub (*Chaenomeles speciosa* synonym *C. lagenaria*) of the rose family with scarlet, pink, or white flowers

Japanese spurge *noun* (1924)
: a low Japanese herb or subshrub (*Pachysandra terminalis*) of the box family often used as a ground cover

Jap·a·nize \'ja-pə-ˌnīz\ *transitive verb* **-nized; -niz·ing** (1890)
1 : to make Japanese
2 : to bring (as an area or industry) under the influence of Japan
— **Jap·a·ni·za·tion** \ˌja-pə-nə-'zā-shən\ *noun*

Japan wax *noun* (1859)
: a yellowish fat obtained from the berries of several sumacs (as *Rhus verniciflua* and *R. succedanea*) and used chiefly in polishes

¹jape \'jāp\ *verb* **japed; jap·ing** [Middle English] (14th century)
intransitive verb
: to say or do something jokingly or mockingly
transitive verb
: to make mocking fun of
— **jap·er** \'jā-pər\ *noun*
— **jap·ery** \'jā-p(ə-) rē\ *noun*

²jape *noun* (14th century)
: something designed to arouse amusement or laughter: as **a :** an amusing literary or dramatic production **b :** GIBE

Ja·pheth \'jā-fəth\ *noun* [Latin *Japheth* or Greek *Iapheth*, from Hebrew *Yepheth*]
: a son of Noah held to be the progenitor of the Medes and Greeks

ja·po·nais·e·rie \zhà-pò-ne-zà-'rē, -nez-'rē\ *noun, often capitalized* [French, from *japonais* Japanese] (1896)
: a style in art reflecting Japanese qualities or motifs; *also* **:** an object or decoration in this style

ja·pon·i·ca \jə-'pä-ni-kə\ *noun* [New Latin, from feminine of *Japonicus* Japanese, from *Japonia* Japan] (1819)
: JAPANESE QUINCE

¹jar \'jär\ *verb* **jarred; jar·ring** [probably of imitative origin] (1526)
intransitive verb
1 a : to make a harsh or discordant sound **b :** to have a harshly disagreeable or disconcerting effect **c :** to be out of harmony; *specifically* **:** BICKER
2 : to undergo severe vibration
transitive verb
: to cause to jar: as **a :** to affect disagreeably **:** UNSETTLE **b :** to make unstable **:** SHAKE
— **jar·ring·ly** \'jär-iŋ-lē\ *adverb*

²jar *noun* (1537)
1 a : a state or manifestation of discord or conflict **b :** a harsh grating sound
2 a : a sudden or unexpected shake **b :** an unsettling shock **c :** an unpleasant break or conflict in rhythm, flow, or transition

³jar *noun* [Middle French *jarre*, from Old Provençal *jarra*, from Arabic *jarrah* earthen water vessel] (1592)
1 : a widemouthed container made typically of earthenware or glass
2 : as much as a jar will hold
— **jar·ful** \-ˌfúl\ *noun*

⁴jar *noun* [alteration of earlier *char* turn, from Middle English — more at CHARE] (1674)
archaic **:** the position of being ajar — usually used in the phrase *on the jar*

jar·di·niere *or* **jar·di·nière** \ˌjär-dⁿ-'ir, ˌzhär-dⁿ-'yer, -'er\ *noun* [French *jardinière*, literally, female gardener] (1841)
1 a : an ornamental stand for plants or flowers **b :** a large usually ceramic flowerpot holder
2 : a garnish for meat consisting of several cooked vegetables cut into pieces

¹jar·gon \'jär-gən, -ˌgän\ *noun* [Middle English, from Middle French] (14th century)
1 a : confused unintelligible language **b :** a strange, outlandish, or barbarous language or dialect **c :** a hybrid language or dialect simplified in vocabulary and grammar and used for communication between peoples of different speech
2 : the technical terminology or characteristic idiom of a special activity or group
3 : obscure and often pretentious language marked by circumlocutions and long words
— **jar·gon·ish** \-gə-nish\ *adjective*
— **jar·gon·is·tic** \ˌjär-gə-'nis-tik\ *adjective*

²jargon *intransitive verb* (14th century)
1 : TWITTER, WARBLE
2 : JARGONIZE

jar·gon·ize \'jär-gə-ˌnīz\ *verb* **-ized; -iz·ing** (1803)
intransitive verb
: to speak or write jargon
transitive verb
1 : to express in jargon
2 : to make into jargon

jar·goon \jär-'gün\ *or* **jar·gon** \-'gän\ *noun* [French *jargon* — more at ZIRCON] (1769)
: a colorless, pale yellow, or smoky zircon

jar·head \'jär-ˌhed\ *noun* (circa 1960)
slang **:** MARINE 2

jarl \'yär(-ə)l\ *noun* [Old Norse — more at EARL] (1820)
: a Scandinavian noble ranking immediately below the king

jar·rah \'jar-ə\ *noun* [Nyungar (Australian aboriginal language of southwest Western Australia) *jarily*] (circa 1866)
: a eucalyptus (*Eucalyptus marginata*) of western Australia with rough bark and alternate leaves; *also* **:** its wood

jas·mine \'jaz-mən\ *noun* [French *jasmin*, from Arabic *yāsamīn*, from Persian] (1562)
1 a : any of numerous often climbing shrubs (genus *Jasminum*) of the olive family that usually have extremely fragrant flowers; *especially* **:** a tall-climbing semievergreen Asian shrub (*J. officinale*) with fragrant white flowers from which oil is extracted for use in perfumes **b :** any of numerous plants having sweet-scented flowers; *especially* **:** YELLOW JESSAMINE
2 : a light yellow

jasmine 1a

Ja·son \'jā-sⁿn\ *noun* [Latin *Iason*, from Greek *Iasōn*]
: a legendary Greek hero distinguished for his successful quest of the Golden Fleece

jas·per \'jas-pər\ *noun* [Middle English *jaspre*, from Middle French, from Latin *jaspis*, from Greek *iaspis*, of Semitic origin; akin to Hebrew *yāshĕpheh* jasper] (14th century)
1 : an opaque cryptocrystalline quartz of any of several colors; *especially* **:** green chalcedony
2 : colored stoneware with raised white decoration
3 : a blackish green
— **jas·pery** \-pə-rē\ *adjective*

jas·per·ware \'jas-pər-ˌwar, -ˌwer\ *noun* (1863)
: JASPER 2

jas·sid \'ja-səd\ *noun* [ultimately from Greek *Iasos*, town in Asia Minor] (1892)
: any of numerous small leafhoppers that include many economically significant pests of cultivated plants; *broadly* **:** LEAFHOPPER

Jat \'jät\ *noun* [Hindi *Jāṭ*] (1622)
: a member of an Indo-Aryan people of the Punjab and Uttar Pradesh

jaunce \'jon(t)s, 'jän(t)s\ *intransitive verb* [origin unknown] (1593)
archaic **:** PRANCE

jaun·dice \'jon-dəs, 'jän-\ *noun* [Middle English *jaundis*, from Middle French *jaunisse*, from *jaune* yellow, from Latin *galbinus* greenish yellow] (14th century)
1 : yellowish pigmentation of the skin, tissues, and body fluids caused by the deposition of bile pigments
2 : a disease or abnormal condition characterized by jaundice
3 : a state or attitude characterized by satiety, distaste, or hostility

jaun·diced \-dəst\ *adjective* (1640)
1 : affected with or as if with jaundice
2 : exhibiting or influenced by envy, distaste, or hostility ⟨a *jaundiced* eye⟩

¹jaunt \'jont, 'jänt\ *intransitive verb* [origin unknown] (1575)
1 *archaic* **:** to trudge about
2 : to make a usually short journey for pleasure

²jaunt *noun* (1592)
1 *archaic* **:** a tiring trip
2 : an excursion undertaken especially for pleasure

jaunting car *noun* (1801)
: a light 2-wheeled open horse-drawn vehicle used especially in Ireland with lengthwise seats placed face-to-face or back to back

jaun·ty \'jon-tē, 'jän-\ *adjective* **jaun·ti·er; -est** [modification of French *gentil*] (1662)
1 *archaic* **a :** GENTEEL **b :** STYLISH
2 : sprightly in manner or appearance **:** LIVELY
— **jaun·ti·ly** \'jon-tⁿl-ē, 'jän-\ *adverb*
— **jaun·ti·ness** \'jon-tē-nəs, 'jän-\ *noun*

ja·va \'ja-və, 'jä-, -vē\ *noun, often capitalized* [*Java*, island of Indonesia] (1850)
: COFFEE

Ja·va man \'jä-və-, 'ja-\ *noun* (1911)
: a Pleistocene hominid known from fragmentary skeletons found in Trinil and Djetis, Java and now classified with the pithecanthropines

Ja·va·nese \ˌja-və-'nēz, ˌjä-, -'nēs\ *noun, plural* **Javanese** [*Java* + *-nese* (as in *Japanese*)] (1704)
1 : a member of an Indonesian people inhabiting the island of Java
2 : an Austronesian language of the Javanese people
— **Javanese** *adjective*

jav·e·lin \'jav-lən, 'ja-və-\ *noun* [Middle English *chafeveleyn*, from Middle French *javeline*, alteration of *javelot*, of Celtic origin; akin to Old Irish *gabul* forked stick] (15th century)
1 : a light spear thrown as a weapon of war or in hunting
2 : a slender usually metal shaft at least 260 centimeters long that is thrown for distance in a field event

ja·ve·li·na \ˌhä-və-'lē-nə\ *noun* [American Spanish *jabalina*, from Spanish, feminine of *jabalí* wild boar, from Arabic *jabalīy*] (1822)
: PECCARY

Ja·velle water \zha-'vel, zhə-\ *noun* [*Javel*, former village in France] (1890)
: an aqueous solution of sodium hypochlorite used as a disinfectant or a bleaching agent

¹jaw \'jo\ *noun* [Middle English] (14th century)
1 a : either of two complex cartilaginous or bony structures in most vertebrates that border the mouth, support the soft parts enclosing it, usually bear teeth on their oral margin, and are an upper that is more or less firmly fused with the skull and a lower that is hinged, movable, and articulated with the temporal bone of either side **b :** the parts constituting the walls of the mouth and serving to open and close it —

usually used in plural **c :** any of various organs of invertebrates that perform the function of the vertebrate jaws
2 : something resembling the jaw of an animal: as **a :** one of the sides of a narrow pass or channel **b :** either of two or more opposable parts that open and close for holding or crushing something between them
3 a : a space lying between or as if between open jaws ⟨escaped from out of the *jaws* of the whale⟩ **b :** a position or situation in which one is threatened ⟨rode into the *jaws* of danger⟩
4 : a friendly chat

²**jaw** (1748)
intransitive verb
: to talk especially abusively, indignantly, or long-windedly
transitive verb
: to talk to in a scolding or boring manner

jaw·bone \'jȯ-ˌbōn\ *noun* (15th century)
: JAW 1a; *especially* **:** MANDIBLE

jaw·bon·ing \-ˌbō-niŋ\ *noun* (1969)
: the use of public appeals (as by a president) to influence the actions especially of business and labor leaders; *broadly* **:** the use of spoken persuasion
— **jaw·bone** \-ˌbōn\ *transitive verb*

jaw·break·er \-ˌbrā-kər\ *noun* (1839)
1 : a word difficult to pronounce
2 : a round hard candy

jawed \'jȯd\ *adjective* (circa 1529)
: having jaws ⟨*jawed* fishes⟩ — usually used in combination ⟨square-*jawed*⟩ ⟨a 3-*jawed* chuck⟩

jaw·less fish \'jȯ-ləs-\ *noun* (circa 1941)
: any of the taxonomic group (Agnatha) of primitive vertebrates without jaws including cyclostomes and extinct related forms — compare BONY FISH, CARTILAGINOUS FISH

jaw·line \'jȯ-ˌlīn\ *noun* (1924)
: the outline of the lower jaw

¹**jay** \'jā\ *noun* [Middle English, from Middle French *jai*, from Late Latin *gaius*] (14th century)
1 a : a predominantly fawn-colored Old World bird (*Garrulus glandarius*) of the crow family with a black-and-white crest and wings marked with black, white, and blue **b :** any of various usually crested and largely blue chiefly New World birds that are related to the common Old World jay and have roving habits and harsh voices
2 a : an impertinent chatterer **b :** DANDY 1 **c :** GREENHORN
3 : a moderate blue

²**jay** *noun* (circa 1889)
1 : the letter *j*
2 : JOINT 4

jay·bird \'jā-ˌbərd\ *noun* (1661)
: ¹JAY 1, 2

Jay·cee \ˌjā-'sē\ *noun* [from the initials of *Junior Citizens*, former name of the organization] (1938)
: a member of a major national and international civic organization

jay·gee \'jā-jē\ *noun* [*junior grade*] (1943)
: LIEUTENANT JUNIOR GRADE

jay·hawk·er \'jā-ˌhȯ-kər\ *noun* (1858)
1 a *often capitalized* **:** a member of a band of antislavery guerrillas in Kansas and Missouri before and during the Civil War **b :** BANDIT
2 *capitalized* **:** a native or resident of Kansas — used as a nickname

jay·vee \ˌjā-'vē\ *noun* [*junior varsity*] (1937)
1 : JUNIOR VARSITY
2 : a member of a junior varsity team

jay·walk \'jā-ˌwȯk\ *intransitive verb* (1919)
: to cross a street carelessly or in an illegal manner so as to be endangered by traffic
— **jay·walk·er** *noun*

¹**jazz** \'jaz\ *noun, often attributive* [origin unknown] (1913)
1 a : American music developed especially from ragtime and blues and characterized by propulsive syncopated rhythms, polyphonic

ensemble playing, varying degrees of improvisation, and often deliberate distortions of pitch and timbre **b :** popular dance music influenced by jazz and played in a loud rhythmic manner
2 : empty talk **:** HUMBUG ⟨spouted all the scientific *jazz* —Pete Martin⟩
3 : similar but unspecified things **:** STUFF ⟨that wind, and the waves, and all that *jazz* —John Updike⟩
— **jazz·like** \-ˌlīk\ *adjective*

²**jazz** (1917)
transitive verb
1 a : ENLIVEN — usually used with *up* **b :** ACCELERATE
2 : to play in the manner of jazz
intransitive verb
1 : to go here and there **:** GAD
2 : to dance to or play jazz

jazz·man \'jaz-ˌman, -mən\ *noun* (1926)
: a jazz musician

jazz–rock \-'räk\ *noun* (1968)
: a blend of jazz and rock music

jazzy \'ja-zē\ *adjective* **jazz·i·er; -est** (1919)
1 : having the characteristics of jazz
2 : marked by unrestraint, animation, or flashiness
— **jazz·i·ly** \'ja-zə-lē\ *adverb*
— **jazz·i·ness** \'ja-zē-nəs\ *noun*

J–bar lift \'jā-ˌbär-\ *noun* (1954)
: a ski lift having a series of J-shaped bars each of which pulls one skier

jeal·ous \'je-ləs\ *adjective* [Middle English *jelous*, from Old French, from (assumed) Vulgar Latin *zelosus*, from Late Latin *zelus* zeal — more at ZEAL] (13th century)
1 a : intolerant of rivalry or unfaithfulness **b :** disposed to suspect rivalry or unfaithfulness
2 : hostile toward a rival or one believed to enjoy an advantage
3 : vigilant in guarding a possession ⟨new colonies were *jealous* of their new independence —Scott Buchanan⟩
— **jeal·ous·ly** *adverb*
— **jeal·ous·ness** *noun*

jeal·ou·sy \'je-lə-sē\ *noun, plural* **-sies** (13th century)
1 : a jealous disposition, attitude, or feeling
2 : zealous vigilance

jean \'jēn\ *noun* [short for *jean fustian*, from Middle English *Gene* Genoa, Italy + *fustian*] (1577)
1 : a durable twilled cotton cloth used especially for sportswear and work clothes
2 : pants that are usually close-fitting and made especially of jean or denim — usually used in plural

¹**jeep** \'jēp\ *noun* [probably from *g. p.* (abbreviation of *general purpose*)] (1940)
: a small general-purpose motor vehicle with 80-inch wheelbase, ¼-ton capacity, and four-wheel drive used by the U.S. army in World War II; *also* **:** a similar but larger and more powerful U.S. army vehicle ◆

²**jeep** *intransitive verb* (1942)
: to travel by jeep

Jeep *trademark*
— used for a civilian automotive vehicle

jee·pers \'jē-pərz\ *also* **jee·pers cree·pers** \-'krē-pərz\ *interjection* [*jeepers*, euphemism for *Jesus*; *jeepers creepers*, euphemism for *Jesus Christ*] (1927)
— used as a mild oath

jeep·ney \'jēp-nē\ *noun* [*jeep* + *jitney*] (circa 1949)
: a Philippine jitney bus converted from a jeep

¹**jeer** \'jir\ *verb* [origin unknown] (1561)
intransitive verb
: to speak or cry out with derision or mockery
transitive verb
: to deride with jeers **:** TAUNT
synonym see SCOFF
— **jeer·er** *noun*
— **jeer·ing·ly** \-iŋ-lē\ *adverb*

²**jeer** *noun* (1625)
: a jeering remark or sound **:** TAUNT

jeez \'jēz\ *interjection* [euphemism for *Jesus*] (1923)
— used as a mild oath or introductory expletive (as to express surprise)

je·fe \'hā-(ˌ)fā, 'he-; 'he-fē\ *noun* [Spanish, from French *chef*, from Middle French *chief* — more at CHIEF] (1903)
: CHIEF, LEADER

Jef·fer·son Da·vis's Birthday \'je-fər-sən-'dā-və-səz-\ *noun* (1929)
: the first Monday in June observed as a legal holiday in many Southern states

Jef·fer·son Day \'je-fər-sən-\ *noun* (1936)
: April 13 observed as a holiday in Alabama in commemoration of Thomas Jefferson's birthday

Jef·frey pine \'je-frē-\ *noun* [John *Jeffrey* (died 1854) Scottish botanical explorer] (1858)
: a pine (*Pinus jeffreyi*) of the western U.S. having long needles in groups of three

je·had *variant of* JIHAD

Je·hosh·a·phat \ji-'hä-sə-ˌfat, -shə-\ *noun* [Hebrew *Yĕhōshāphāt*]
: a king of Judah who brought Judah into an alliance with the northern kingdom of Israel in the 9th century B.C.

Je·ho·vah \ji-'hō-və\ *noun* [New Latin, reading (as *Yĕhōwāh*) of Hebrew *yhwh* Yahweh with the vowel points of *'adhōnāy* my lord] (1530)
: GOD 1

Jehovah's Witness *noun* (1932)
: a member of a group that witness by distributing literature and by personal evangelism to beliefs in the theocratic rule of God, the sinfulness of organized religions and governments, and an imminent millennium

je·hu \'jē-(ˌ)hyü, -(ˌ)hü\ *noun* [Hebrew *Yēhū*]
1 *capitalized* **:** a king of Israel in the 9th century B.C. who according to the account in II Kings had Jezebel killed in accordance with Elijah's prophecy
2 : a driver of a coach or cab

je·ju·nal \ji-'jü-nᵊl\ *adjective* (circa 1887)
: of or relating to the jejunum

je·june \ji-'jün\ *adjective* [Latin *jejunus* empty of food, hungry, meager] (1646)
1 : lacking nutritive value ⟨*jejune* diets⟩
2 : devoid of significance or interest **:** DULL ⟨*jejune* lectures⟩

◇ WORD HISTORY

jeep A common etymology of *jeep* claims that the word was vocalized from *g.p.* (general purpose), stenciled on military vehicles. Whatever merit this hypothesis has, *jeep* in its early days saw a wide range of applications. Perhaps the progenitor of all of them was a character named Eugene the Jeep that first appeared in March 1936 in Elzie C. Segar's comic strip *Thimble Theater*, featuring Popeye. In a short story of 1938, *jeep* means "nerd," a direction that seems to have been continued by the sense "trainee," U.S. Army slang during World War II. In 1936 *jeep* was applied to an oil company's recording device, and in 1940 to an agricultural tractor converted to military use. In the same year, a wire-service article defined *jeep* as Army vernacular for "any very small plane, helicopter, or gadget." To the Air Corps, *jeep* was a small trainer, and to the Navy an escort carrier. The now familiar use of *jeep* for a 1/4-ton military vehicle was first noted in February 1941, but in the early years of the war, some soldiers applied *jeep* to a now forgotten 3/4-ton command car, while the 1/4-ton vehicle was known as a *peep*.

3 : JUVENILE, PUERILE ⟨*jejune* reflections on life and art⟩ □ ◆
synonym see INSIPID
— **je·june·ly** *adverb*
— **je·june·ness** \-'jün-nəs\ *noun*

je·ju·num \ji-'jü-nəm\ *noun* [Middle English, from Medieval Latin, from neuter of Latin *jejunus*] (14th century)
: the section of the small intestine that comprises the first two fifths beyond the duodenum and that is larger, thicker-walled, and more vascular and has more circular folds than the ileum

Je·kyll and Hyde \'je-kə-lən-'hīd *also* 'jē- *or* 'jā-\ *noun* [Dr. *Jekyll* & Mr. *Hyde*, representing the two-sided personality of the protagonist in *The Strange Case of Dr. Jekyll and Mr. Hyde* (1886) by R. L. Stevenson] (circa 1922)
: one having a two-sided personality one side of which is good and the other evil

jell \'jel\ *verb* [back-formation from *jelly*] (1869)
intransitive verb
1 : to come to the consistency of jelly **:** CONGEAL, SET
2 : to take shape and achieve distinctness **:** become cohesive
transitive verb
: to cause to jell

jellied gasoline *noun* (1944)
: NAPALM

Jell-O \'je-(,)lō\ *trademark*
— used for a gelatin dessert usually with the flavor and color of fruit

¹jel·ly \'je-lē\ *noun, plural* **jellies** [Middle English *gelly*, from Middle French *gelee*, from feminine of *gelé*, past participle of *geler* to freeze, congeal, from Latin *gelare* — more at COLD] (14th century)
1 : a soft somewhat elastic food product made usually with gelatin or pectin; *especially* **:** a fruit product made by boiling sugar and the juice of fruit
2 : a substance resembling jelly in consistency
3 : a state of fear or irresolution
4 : a shapeless structureless mass **:** PULP
— **jel·ly·like** \-,līk\ *adjective*

²jelly *verb* **jel·lied; jel·ly·ing** (1590)
intransitive verb
1 : JELL
2 : to make jelly
transitive verb
: to bring to the consistency of jelly

jelly bean *noun* (1905)
: a sugar-glazed bean-shaped candy

jel·ly·fish \'je-lē-,fish\ *noun* (1841)
1 a : a free-swimming marine coelenterate that is the sexually reproducing form of a hydrozoan or scyphozoan and has a nearly transparent saucer-shaped body and extensile marginal tentacles studded with stinging cells **b :** SIPHONOPHORE **c :** CTENOPHORE
2 : a person lacking backbone or firmness

jelly roll *noun* (1895)
: a thin sheet of sponge cake spread with jelly and rolled up

jel·u·tong \'je-lə-,tȯŋ\ *noun* [Malay *jĕlutong*] (circa 1836)
1 : any of several trees (genus *Dyera*) of the dogbane family
2 : the resinous rubbery latex of a jelutong (especially *Dyera costulata*) used especially as a chicle substitute

jem·my \'je-mē\ *noun, plural* **jemmies** [from the name *Jemmy*] (circa 1811)
British **:** JIMMY

je ne sais quoi \zhə-nə-,sā-'kwä\ *noun* [French, literally, I know not what] (circa 1656)
: something that cannot be adequately described or expressed

jen·net \'he-nā, 'je-nət\ *noun* [Middle English *genett*, from Middle French *genet*, from Catalan, Zenete (member of a Berber people), horse] (15th century)
1 : a small Spanish horse

2 a : a female donkey **b :** HINNY

jen·ny \'je-nē\ *noun, plural* **jennies** [from the name *Jenny*] (1600)
1 a : a female bird ⟨*jenny* wren⟩ **b :** a female donkey
2 : SPINNING JENNY

je·on \(,)jā-'ȯn\ *noun, plural* **jeon** [Korean *chŏn*] (circa 1969)
: the chon of South Korea

jeop·ard \'je-pərd\ *transitive verb* [Middle English, back-formation from *jeopardie*] (14th century)
: JEOPARDIZE

jeop·ar·dise *British variant of* JEOPARDIZE

jeop·ar·dize \'je-pər-,dīz\ *transitive verb* **-dized; -diz·ing** (1582)
: to expose to danger or risk **:** IMPERIL

jeop·ar·dy \'je-pər-dē\ *noun* [Middle English *jeopardie*, from Anglo-French *juparti*, from Old French *jeu parti* alternative, literally, divided game] (14th century)
1 : exposure to or imminence of death, loss, or injury **:** DANGER
2 : the danger that an accused person is subjected to when on trial for a criminal offense

je·quir·i·ty bean \jə-'kwir-ə-tē-\ *noun* [French *jékwirity*] (circa 1889)
1 : the poisonous scarlet and black seed of the rosary pea often used for beads
2 : ROSARY PEA 1

jer·boa \jər-'bō-ə, jer-\ *noun* [New Latin, from Arabic *yarbū'*] (1662)
: any of several social nocturnal Old World jumping rodents (family Dipodidae) with long hind legs and long tail

jer·e·mi·ad \,jer-ə-'mī-əd, -,ad\ *noun* [French *jérémiade*, from *Jérémie* Jeremiah, from Late Latin *Jeremias*] (1780)
: a prolonged lamentation or complaint; *also* **:** a cautionary or angry harangue ◆

Jer·e·mi·ah \-'mī-ə\ *noun* [Late Latin *Jeremias*, from Greek *Hieremias*, from Hebrew *Yirmĕyāh*]
1 : a major Hebrew prophet of the 6th and 7th centuries B.C.
2 : one who is pessimistic about the present and foresees a calamitous future
3 : a prophetic book of canonical Jewish and Christian Scripture — see BIBLE table

Jer·e·mi·as \-'mī-əs\ *noun* [Late Latin]
: JEREMIAH

¹jerk \'jərk\ *noun* [probably alteration of *yerk*] (1575)
1 : a single quick motion of short duration
2 a : jolting, bouncing, or thrusting motions **b :** a tendency to produce spasmodic motions
3 a : an involuntary spasmodic muscular movement due to reflex action **b** *plural* **:** involuntary twitchings due to nervous excitement
4 : an annoyingly stupid or foolish person
5 : the pushing of a weight from shoulder height to a position overhead in weight lifting

²jerk (1589)
transitive verb
1 : to give a quick suddenly arrested push, pull, or twist to
2 : to propel or move with or as if with a quick suddenly arrested motion
3 : to mix and serve (as sodas) behind a soda fountain
intransitive verb
1 : to make a sudden spasmodic motion
2 : to move in short abrupt motions or with frequent jolts
— **jerk·er** *noun*

³jerk *transitive verb* [back-formation from *¹jerky*] (1707)
: to preserve (meat) in long sun-dried slices

jerk around *transitive verb* (1941)
: to treat badly especially by being underhanded or inconsistent

\ə\ abut \ʰ\ kitten \ər\ further \a\ ash \ā\ ace
\ä\ mop, mar \aú\ out \ch\ chin \e\ bet \ē\ easy
\g\ go \i\ hit \ī\ ice \j\ job \ŋ\ sing \ō\ go
\ȯ\ law \ȯi\ boy \th\ thin \th\ the \ü\ loot \ú\ foot
\y\ yet \zh\ vision *see also* Guide to Pronunciation

jer·kin \'jər-kən\ *noun* [origin unknown] (1519)
: a close-fitting hip-length usually sleeveless jacket

jerk off *verb* (circa 1904)
: MASTURBATE — usually considered vulgar

jerk·wa·ter \'jərk-ˌwȯ-tər, -ˌwä-\ *adjective* [from *jerkwater* rural train] (1888)
1 : remote and unimportant ⟨*jerkwater* towns⟩
2 : TRIVIAL

¹**jer·ky** \'jər-kē\ *noun* [Spanish *charqui*, from Quechua *ch'arki*] (1850)
: jerked meat

²**jerky** \'jər-kē\ *adjective* **jerk·i·er; -est** (1858)
1 a : moving along with or marked by fits and starts **b** : characterized by abrupt transitions
2 : INANE, FOOLISH
— **jerk·i·ly** \-kə-lē\ *adverb*
— **jerk·i·ness** \-kē-nəs\ *noun*

jer·o·bo·am \ˌjer-ə-'bō-əm\ *noun* [*Jeroboam* I (died about 912 B.C.) king of the northern kingdom of Israel] (1816)
: an oversize wine bottle holding about three liters

jer·ri·can *or* **jerry can** \'jer-ē-ˌkan\ *noun* [*Jerry* + *can*; from its German design] (1943)
: a narrow flat-sided liquid container holding five gallons (about 19 liters)

Jer·ry \'jer-ē\ *noun, plural* **Jerries** [by shortening & alteration] (1898)
chiefly British : GERMAN

jer·ry–build \'jer-ē-ˌbild\ *transitive verb* **-built** \-ˌbilt\; **-build·ing** [back-formation from *jerry-built*] (1885)
: to build cheaply and flimsily
— **jer·ry–build·er** *noun*

jer·ry–built *adjective* [origin unknown] (1869)
1 : built cheaply and unsubstantially
2 : carelessly or hastily put together

jer·sey \'jər-zē\ *noun, plural* **jerseys** [*Jersey*, one of the Channel Islands] (1587)
1 : a plain weft-knitted fabric made of wool, cotton, nylon, rayon, or silk and used especially for clothing
2 : any of various close-fitting usually circular-knitted garments especially for the upper body
3 *often capitalized* : any of a breed of small short-horned predominantly yellowish brown or fawn dairy cattle noted for their rich milk

Jersey pine *noun* (1743)
: VIRGINIA PINE

Je·ru·sa·lem artichoke \jə-'rü-s(ə-)ləm-, -'rüz-ləm-, -'rü-zə-\ *noun* [*Jerusalem* by folk etymology from Italian *girasole* girasole] (1641)
: a perennial American sunflower (*Helianthus tuberosus*) widely cultivated for its tubers that are used as a vegetable and as a livestock food

Jerusalem cherry *noun* [*Jerusalem*, Palestine] (1788)
: either of two plants (*Solanum pseudocapsicum* and *S. capsicastrum*) of the nightshade family cultivated as ornamental houseplants for their orange to red berries

Jerusalem cricket *noun* (1947)
: a large-headed burrowing nocturnal orthopteran insect (*Stenopelmatus fuscus*) of the southwestern U.S.

Jerusalem thorn *noun* (1866)
: a tropical American leguminous

Jerusalem cricket

spiny shrub or shrubby tree (*Parkinsonia aculeata*) with pinnate leaves and showy racemose yellow flowers that is widely cultivated

jess \'jes\ *noun* [Middle English *ges*, from Middle French *gies*, from plural of *jet* throw, from *jeter* to throw — more at JET] (14th century)

: a short strap secured on the leg of a hawk and usually provided with a ring for attaching a leash
— **jessed** \'jest\ *adjective*

jes·sa·mine \'jes-mən, 'je-sə-\ *variant of* JASMINE

Jes·se \'je-sē\ *noun* [Hebrew *Yishay*]
: the father of David, king of Israel, according to the account in I Samuel

jest \'jest\ *noun* [Middle English *geste* idle tale, story in verse, from Old French, from Latin *gesta* deeds, from neuter plural of *gestus*, past participle of *gerere* to bear, wage] (circa 1548)
1 : an utterance (as a jeer or quip) intended to be taken as mockery or humor
2 a : PRANK **b** : a ludicrous circumstance or incident
3 a : a frivolous mood or manner ⟨spoken in *jest*⟩ **b** : gaiety and merriment
4 : LAUGHINGSTOCK
synonym see FUN
— **jest** *verb*

jest·er \'jes-tər\ *noun* (14th century)
1 : FOOL 2a
2 : one given to jests

Je·su·it \'je-zü-ət, -zhü- *also* -zyü-\ *noun* [New Latin *Jesuita*, from Late Latin *Jesus*] (1559)
1 : a member of the Roman Catholic Society of Jesus founded by Saint Ignatius Loyola in 1534 and devoted to missionary and educational work
2 : one given to intrigue or equivocation
— **je·su·it·ic** \ˌje-zü-'(w)i-tik, -zhü-, -zyü-\ *or* **je·su·it·i·cal** \-ti-kəl\ *adjective, often capitalized*
— **je·su·it·i·cal·ly** \-ti-k(ə-)lē\ *adverb, often capitalized*
— **je·su·it·ism** \'je-zü-ə-ˌti-zəm, -zhü-, -zyü-\ *or* **je·su·it·ry** \-ə-trē\ *noun, often capitalized*

Je·sus \'jē-zəs, -zəz *also* -ˌzəs *and* -ˌzəz\ *noun* [Late Latin, from Greek *Iēsous*, from Hebrew *Yēshūa'*]
1 : the Jewish religious teacher whose life, death, and resurrection as reported by the Evangelists are the basis of the Christian message of salvation — called also *Jesus Christ*
2 *Christian Science* : the highest human corporeal concept of the divine idea rebuking and destroying error and bringing to light man's immortality

¹**jet** \'jet\ *noun* [Middle English, from Middle French *jaiet*, from Latin *gagates*, from Greek *gagatēs*, from *Gagas*, town and river in Asia Minor] (14th century)
1 : a compact velvet-black coal that takes a good polish and is often used for jewelry
2 : an intense black

²**jet** *adjective* (1716)
: of the color jet

³**jet** *verb* **jet·ted; jet·ting** [French *jeter*, literally, to throw, from Middle French, from Latin *jactare* to throw, frequentative of *jacere* to throw; akin to Greek *hienai* to send] (1692)
intransitive verb
: to spout forth : GUSH
transitive verb
: to emit in a stream : SPOUT

⁴**jet** *noun* (circa 1696)
1 a (1) : a usually forceful stream of fluid (as water or gas) discharged from a narrow opening or a nozzle (2) : a narrow stream of material (as plasma) emanating or appearing to emanate from a celestial object (as a radio galaxy) **b** : a nozzle for a jet of fluid
2 : something issuing as if in a jet ⟨talk poured from her in a brilliant *jet* —*Time*⟩
3 a : JET ENGINE **b** : an airplane powered by one or more jet engines
4 : a long narrow current of high-speed winds (as a jet stream)
— **jet·like** \-ˌlīk\ *adjective*

⁵**jet** *intransitive verb* **jet·ted; jet·ting** (1949)
1 : to travel by jet airplane

2 : to move or progress by or as if by jet propulsion

jet·bead \'jet-ˌbēd\ *noun* (circa 1930)
: a shrub (*Rhodotypos scandens*) that has black shining fruit and is used as an ornamental

jet–black \-'blak\ *adjective* (15th century)
: black as jet

je·té \zhə-'tā\ *noun* [French, from past participle of *jeter*] (1830)
: a springing jump in ballet made from one foot to the other in any direction

jet engine *noun* (1943)
: an engine that produces motion as a result of the rearward discharge of a jet of fluid; *specifically* : an airplane engine that uses atmospheric oxygen to burn fuel and produces a rearward discharge of heated air and exhaust gases — see AIRPLANE illustration

jet lag *noun* (1969)
: a condition that is characterized by various psychological and physiological effects (as fatigue and irritability), occurs following long flight through several time zones, and probably results from disruption of circadian rhythms in the human body
— **jet–lagged** \'jet-ˌlagd\ *adjective*

jet·lin·er \'jet-ˌlī-nər\ *noun* (1949)
: a jet-propelled airliner

jet·port \'jet-ˌpȯrt, -ˌpȯrt\ *noun* (1961)
: an airport designed to handle jet airplanes

jet–pro·pelled \ˌjet-prə-'peld\ *adjective* (1877)
1 : moving by jet propulsion
2 : suggestive of the speed and force of a jet airplane

jet propulsion *noun* (1867)
: propulsion of a body produced by the forwardly directed forces of the reaction resulting from the rearward discharge of a jet of fluid; *especially* : propulsion of an airplane by jet engines

jet·sam \'jet-səm\ *noun* [alteration of *jettison*] (1570)
1 : the part of a ship, its equipment, or its cargo that is cast overboard to lighten the load in time of distress and that sinks or is washed ashore
2 : FLOTSAM 2

jet set *noun* (1951)
: an international social group of wealthy individuals who frequent fashionable resorts
— **jet–set·ter** \-ˌse-tər\ *noun*
— **jet–set·ting** \-ˌse-tin\ *adjective*

jet stream *noun* (1947)
: a long narrow meandering current of high-speed winds near the tropopause blowing from a generally westerly direction and often exceeding a speed of 250 miles (402 kilometers) per hour

¹**jet·ti·son** \'je-tə-sən, -zən\ *noun* [Middle English *jetteson*, from Anglo-French *getteson*, from Old French *getaison* action of throwing, from Latin *jactation-, jactatio*, from *jactare* — more at JET] (15th century)
: a voluntary sacrifice of cargo to lighten a ship's load in time of distress

²**jettison** *transitive verb* (1848)
1 : to make jettison of
2 : to get rid of as superfluous or encumbering : DISCARD
3 : to drop from an airplane or spacecraft in flight
— **jet·ti·son·able** \-sə-nə-bəl, -zə-\ *adjective*

¹**jet·ty** \'je-tē\ *noun, plural* **jetties** [Middle English *jette*, from Middle French *jetee*, from feminine of *jeté*, past participle of *jeter* to throw — more at JET] (15th century)
1 a : a structure extended into a sea, lake, or river to influence the current or tide or to protect a harbor **b** : a protecting frame of a pier
2 : a landing wharf

²**jetty** *intransitive verb* **jet·tied; jet·ty·ing** (1598)
: PROJECT, JUT

³**jetty** *adjective* (1586)
: black as jet

jeu d'es·prit \zhœ-des-prē\ *noun, plural* **jeux d'esprit** *same*\ [French, literally, play of the mind] (1712)
: a witty comment or composition

jeu·nesse do·rée \zhœ-nes-dò-rā\ *noun* [French, gilded youth] (1836)
: young people of wealth and fashion

Jew \'jü\ *noun* [Middle English, from Old French *gyu*, from Latin *Judaeus*, from Greek *Ioudaios*, from Hebrew *Yĕhūdhī*, from *Yĕhūdhāh* Judah, Jewish kingdom] (13th century)
1 a : a member of the tribe of Judah **b :** ISRAELITE
2 : a member of a nation existing in Palestine from the 6th century B.C. to the 1st century A.D.
3 : a person belonging to a continuation through descent or conversion of the ancient Jewish people
4 : one whose religion is Judaism

¹**jew·el** \'jü-əl, 'jül *also* 'jù(ə)l\ *noun, often attributive* [Middle English *juel*, from Old French, probably diminutive of *jeu* game, play, from Latin *jocus* game, joke — more at JOKE] (13th century)
1 : an ornament of precious metal often set with stones or decorated with enamel and worn as an accessory of dress
2 : one that is highly esteemed
3 : a precious stone **:** GEM
4 : a bearing for a pivot (as in a watch) made of crystal, glass, or a gem
— **jew·el·like** \-,līk\ *adjective*

²**jewel** *transitive verb* **-eled** *or* **-elled; -el·ing** *or* **-el·ling** (1601)
1 : to adorn or equip with jewels
2 : to give beauty to as if with jewels **:** EMBELLISH

jewel box *noun* (1831)
1 : a small box or case designed to hold jewelry
2 : something small and exquisite
3 : a clear plastic case for a compact disc

jew·el·er *or* **jew·el·ler** \'jü-ə-lər, 'jül-lər *also* 'jù(-ə)-lər\ *noun* (14th century)
1 : one who makes or repairs jewelry
2 : one who deals in jewelry, precious stones, watches, and usually silverware and china

jew·el·lery *chiefly British variant of* JEWELRY

jew·el·ry \'jü-əl-rē, 'jül-rē, 'jù(-ə)l-\ *noun* (14th century)
: JEWELS; *especially* **:** objects of precious metal often set with gems and worn for personal adornment

jew·el·weed \-,wēd\ *noun* (1818)
: TOUCH-ME-NOT

Jew·ess \'jü-əs\ *noun* (14th century)
: a Jewish girl or woman — sometimes taken to be offensive

jew·fish \'jü-,fish\ *noun* (1679)
: any of various large groupers (especially *Epinephelus itajara*) that are usually dusky green, brown, or blackish, thickheaded, and rough-scaled

Jew·ish \'jü-ish\ *adjective* (circa 1546)
: of, relating to, or characteristic of the Jews; *also* **:** being a Jew
— **Jew·ish·ly** *adverb*
— **Jew·ish·ness** *noun*

Jewish American Princess *noun* (1979)
: a stereotypical well-to-do or spoiled American Jewish girl or woman — called also *Jewish Princess*; often used disparagingly

Jewish calendar *noun* (circa 1888)
: a calendar in use among Jewish peoples that is reckoned from the year 3761 B.C. and dates in its present form from about A.D. 360 — see MONTH table

Jew·ry \'jù(-ə)r-ē, 'jü-rē\ *noun* (14th century)
1 *plural* **Jewries :** a community of Jews
2 : the Jewish people

JEWISH YEARS 5754–5773

JEWISH YEAR		A.D.
5754	begins	September 16, 1993
5755	begins	September 6, 1994
5756	begins	September 25, 1995
5757	begins	September 14, 1996
5758	begins	October 2, 1997
5759	begins	September 21, 1998
5760	begins	September 11, 1999
5761	begins	September 30, 2000
5762	begins	September 18, 2001
5763	begins	September 7, 2002
5764	begins	September 27, 2003
5765	begins	September 16, 2004
5766	begins	October 4, 2005
5767	begins	September 23, 2006
5768	begins	September 13, 2007
5769	begins	September 30, 2008
5770	begins	September 19, 2009
5771	begins	September 9, 2010
5772	begins	September 29, 2011
5773	begins	September 17, 2012

Jew's harp *or* **Jews' harp** \'jüz-,härp, 'jüs-\ *noun* (1595)
: a small lyre-shaped instrument that when held between the teeth gives tones from a metal tongue struck by the finger

Jew's harp

Jez·e·bel \'je-zə-,bel\ *noun* [Hebrew *Izebhel*]
1 : the Phoenician wife of Ahab who according to the account in I and II Kings pressed the cult of Baal on the Israelite kingdom but was finally killed in accordance with Elijah's prophecy
2 *often not capitalized* **:** an impudent, shameless, or morally unrestrained woman

JHVH *variant of* YHWH

jiao \jē-'aù\ *noun* [Chinese (Beijing) *jiǎo*] (1949)
: a monetary unit of the People's Republic of China equal to ¹⁄₁₀ yuan

¹**jib** \'jib\ *noun* [origin unknown] (1661)
: a triangular sail set on a stay extending usually from the head of the foremast to the bowsprit or the jibboom; *also* **:** the small triangular headsail on a sloop — see SAIL illustration

²**jib** *noun* [probably by shortening & alteration from *gibbet*] (1764)
1 : the projecting arm of a crane
2 : a derrick boom

³**jib** *intransitive verb* **jibbed; jib·bing** [probably from *jib* to shift from one side of a ship to the other, perhaps from ¹*jib*] (1811)
: to refuse to proceed further **:** BALK
— **jib·ber** *noun*

jib·boom \'ji(b)-'büm\ *noun* [¹*jib* + *boom*] (1748)
: a spar that forms an extension of the bowsprit

¹**jibe** \'jīb\ *variant of* GIBE

²**jibe** *verb* **jibed; jib·ing** [perhaps modification of Dutch *gijben*] (1693)
intransitive verb
1 : to shift suddenly and forcibly from one side to the other — used of a fore-and-aft sail
2 : to change a vessel's course when sailing with the wind so that as the stern passes through the eye of the wind the boom swings to the opposite side
transitive verb
: to cause to jibe

³**jibe** *intransitive verb* **jibed; jib·ing** [origin unknown] (1813)
: to be in accord **:** AGREE

ji·ca·ma \'hē-kə-mə\ *noun* [Mexican Spanish *jícama*, from Nahuatl *xīcamatl*] (circa 1909)

: an edible starchy tuberous root of a leguminous tropical American vine (*Pachyrhizus erosus*)

Ji·ca·ril·la \,hē-kə-'rē-yə\ *noun, plural* **Jicarilla** *or* **Jicarillas** [American Spanish *apaches de la xicarilla*, literally, gourd-cup Apaches, from *Cerro de la Xicarilla*, literally, gourd-cup peak, unidentified mountain in Jicarilla territory] (1850)
1 : a member of an Apache people originally of southeastern Colorado, northern New Mexico, and adjacent areas and now living chiefly in northern New Mexico
2 : the language of the Jicarilla people

jiff \'jif\ *noun* (1797)
: JIFFY

jif·fy \'ji-fē\ *noun, plural* **jiffies** [origin unknown] (1779)
: MOMENT, INSTANT ⟨ready in a *jiffy*⟩

¹**jig** \'jig\ *noun* [perhaps from Middle French *giguer* to frolic, from *gigue* fiddle, of Germanic origin; akin to Old High German *gīga* fiddle; akin to Old Norse *geiga* to turn aside] (circa 1560)
1 a : any of several lively springy dances in triple rhythm **b :** music to which a jig may be danced
2 : TRICK, GAME — used chiefly in the phrase *the jig is up*
3 a : any of several fishing devices that are jerked up and down or drawn through the water **b :** a device used to maintain mechanically the correct positional relationship between a piece of work and the tool or between parts of work during assembly **c :** a device in which crushed ore is concentrated or coal is cleaned by agitating in water
— **in jig time :** in a short time **:** QUICKLY

²**jig** *verb* **jigged; jig·ging** (1604)
intransitive verb
1 a : to move with rapid jerky motions **b :** to dance a jig
2 : to fish with a jig
transitive verb
1 : to dance in the rapid lively manner of a jig
2 a : to give a rapid jerky motion to **b :** to separate (a mineral or ore from waste) with a jig
3 : to catch (a fish) with a jig
4 : to machine by means of a jig-controlled tool operation

³**jig** *noun* [short for *jigaboo* black person] (1927)
: BLACK 4 — usually taken to be offensive

¹**jig·ger** \'ji-gər\ *noun* (1675)
1 : one that jigs or operates a jig
2 : any of several sails
3 : JIG 3a
4 a (1) **:** a mechanical device usually with a jerky reciprocating motion (2) **:** a mold or a machine incorporating a revolving mold on which ceramic items (as plates) are formed **b :** GADGET, DOODAD
5 : a measure used in mixing drinks that usually holds 1 to 2 ounces (30 to 60 milliliters)

²**jigger** *noun* [perhaps from Wolof *jiga* insect] (1781)
: CHIGGER

³**jigger** *verb* [frequentative of ²*jig*] (1867)
intransitive verb
: to jerk up and down
transitive verb
: to alter or rearrange especially by manipulating ⟨*jigger* an election district⟩

jig·gery–pok·ery \'ji-gər-ē-'pō-kər-ē\ *noun* [probably alteration of Scots *joukery-pawkery*, from *jouk* to dodge, cheat + *pawk* trick, wile] (circa 1892)
: underhanded manipulation or dealings **:** TRICKERY

jig·gle \'ji-gəl\ *verb* **jig·gled; jig·gling** \-g(ə-)liŋ\ [frequentative of ²*jig*] (1836) *transitive verb* : to cause to move with quick little jerks or oscillating motions *intransitive verb* : to move from or as if from being jiggled — **jiggle** *noun* — **jig·gly** \-g(ə-)lē\ *adjective*

¹jig·saw \'jig-,sȯ\ *noun* (1873) **1** : a machine saw with a narrow vertically reciprocating blade for cutting curved and irregular lines or ornamental patterns in openwork **2** : SCROLL SAW 1 **3** : JIGSAW PUZZLE

²jigsaw *transitive verb* (1873) **1** : to cut or form by or as if by a jigsaw **2** : to arrange or place in an intricate or interlocking way

³jigsaw *adjective* (1884) : suggesting a jigsaw puzzle or its separate pieces

jigsaw puzzle *noun* (1919) : a puzzle consisting of small irregularly cut pieces that are to be fitted together to form a picture; *also* : something suggesting a jigsaw puzzle

ji·had \ji-'häd, *chiefly British* -'had\ *noun* [Arabic *jihād*] (1869) **1** : a holy war waged on behalf of Islam as a religious duty **2** : a crusade for a principle or belief

jil·lion \'jil-yən\ *noun* [*j* + *-illion* (as in *million*)] (circa 1942) : an indeterminately large number — **jillion** *adjective*

¹jilt \'jilt\ *transitive verb* (1673) : to drop (a lover) capriciously or unfeelingly — **jilt·er** *noun*

²jilt *noun* [alteration of *jillet* flirtatious girl] (circa 1674) : one who jilts a lover

jim crow \'jim-'krō\ *noun, often J&C capitalized* [*Jim Crow*, stereotype black man in a 19th century song-and-dance act] (1838) **1** : BLACK 4 — usually taken to be offensive **2** : ethnic discrimination especially against blacks by legal enforcement or traditional sanctions — **jim crow** *adjective, often J&C capitalized* — **jim crow·ism** \-,i-zəm\ *noun, often J&C capitalized*

jim—dan·dy \'jim-'dan-dē\ *noun* [from the name *Jim*] (1887) : something excellent of its kind

jim-jams \'jim-,jamz\ *noun plural* [perhaps alteration of *delirium tremens*] (1852) : JITTERS

jim·mies \'ji-mēz\ *noun plural* [origin unknown] (circa 1947) : tiny rod-shaped bits of usually chocolate-flavored candy often sprinkled on ice cream

¹jim·my \'ji-mē\ *noun, plural* **jimmies** [from the name *Jimmy*] (1848) : a short crowbar

²jimmy *transitive verb* **jim·mied; jim·my·ing** (1893) : to force open with or as if with a jimmy ⟨the burglar *jimmied* a window⟩

jim·son·weed \'jim(p)-sən-,wēd\ *noun, often capitalized* [*Jamestown*, Va.] (1832) : a poisonous tall coarse annual weed (*Datura stramonium*) of the nightshade family with rank-smelling foliage and large white or violet trumpet-shaped flowers succeeded by globose prickly fruits

¹jin·gle \'jiŋ-gəl\ *verb* **jin·gled; jin·gling** \-g(ə-)liŋ\ [Middle English *ginglen*, of imitative origin] (14th century) *intransitive verb* **1** : to make a light clinking or tinkling sound **2** : to rhyme or sound in a catchy repetitious manner *transitive verb* : to cause to jingle

— **jin·gler** \-g(ə-)lər\ *noun*

²jingle *noun* (1599) **1 a** : a light clinking or tinkling sound **b** : a catchy repetition of sounds in a poem **2 a** : something that jingles **b** : a short verse or song marked by catchy repetition — **jin·gly** \-g(ə-)lē\ *adjective*

¹jin·go \'jiŋ-(,)gō\ *interjection* [probably euphemism for *Jesus*] (1694) — used as a mild oath usually in the phrase *by jingo*

²jingo *noun, plural* **jingoes** [from the fact that the phrase *by jingo* appeared in the refrain of a chauvinistic song] (1878) : one characterized by jingoism — **jin·go·ish** \-ish\ *adjective*

jin·go·ism \'jiŋ-(,)gō-,i-zəm\ *noun* (1878) : extreme chauvinism or nationalism marked especially by a belligerent foreign policy ◇ — **jin·go·ist** \-ist\ *noun or adjective* — **jin·go·is·tic** \,jiŋ-gō-'is-tik\ *adjective* — **jin·go·is·ti·cal·ly** \-ti-k(ə-)lē\ *adverb*

¹jink \'jiŋk\ *intransitive verb* [origin unknown] (1785) : to move quickly or unexpectedly with sudden turns and shifts (as in dodging)

²jink *noun* (1786) **1** : a quick evasive turn : SLIP **2** *plural* : PRANKS, FROLICS; *especially* : HIGH JINKS

jin·ni \'jē-nē, 'ji-, jə-'nē\ *or* **jinn** \'jin\ *noun, plural* **jinn** *or* **jinns** [Arabic *jinnīy* demon] (1684) **1** : one of a class of spirits that according to Muslim demonology inhabit the earth, assume various forms, and exercise supernatural power **2** : GENIE 2

jin·rick·sha *or* **jin·rik·i·sha** \jin-'rik-,shȯ\ *noun* [Japanese] (1874) : RICKSHA

¹jinx \'jiŋ(k)s\ *noun* [perhaps alteration of *jynx* wryneck; from the use of wrynecks in witchcraft] (1911) : one that brings bad luck; *also* : the state or spell of bad luck brought on by a jinx

²jinx *transitive verb* (1917) : to foredoom to failure or misfortune : bring bad luck to

ji·pi·ja·pa \,hē-pē-'hä-pə\ *noun* [Spanish, from *Jipijapa*, Ecuador] (1858) **1** : a Central and South American plant (*Carludovica palmata* of the family Cyclanthaceae) resembling a palm **2** : PANAMA

jit·ney \'jit-nē\ *noun, plural* **jitneys** [origin unknown] (1903) **1** *slang* : NICKEL 2a(1) **2** [from the original 5 cent fare] : BUS 1a; *especially* : a small bus that carries passengers over a regular route on a flexible schedule

¹jit·ter \'ji-tər\ *noun* [origin unknown] (1929) **1** *plural* : a sense of panic or extreme nervousness ⟨had a bad case of the *jitters* before his performance⟩ **2** : the state of mind or the movement of one that jitters **3** : irregular random movement (as of a pointer or an image on a television screen); *also* : vibratory motion

²jitter *intransitive verb* (1931) **1** : to be nervous or act in a nervous way **2** : to make continuous fast repetitive movements

¹jit·ter·bug \'ji-tər-,bəg\ *noun* (1938) **1** : a jazz variation of the two-step in which couples swing, balance, and twirl in standardized patterns and often with vigorous acrobatics **2** : one who dances the jitterbug

²jitterbug *intransitive verb* (1939) **1** : to dance the jitterbug **2** : to move around or back and forth with quick often jerky movements especially to confuse or disconcert an opponent in sports

jit·tery \'ji-tə-rē\ *adjective* (1931)

1 : suffering from the jitters **2** : marked by jittering movements — **jit·ter·i·ness** \-nəs\ *noun*

jiu·jit·su, jiu·jut·su *variant of* JUJITSU

¹jive \'jīv\ *noun* [origin unknown] (1928) **1** : swing music or the dancing performed to it **2 a** : glib, deceptive, or foolish talk **b** : the jargon of hipsters **c** : a special jargon of difficult or slang terms — **jivey** \'jī-vē\ *adjective*

²jive *verb* **jived; jiv·ing** (1928) *transitive verb* **1** : TEASE 3, CAJOLE **2** : SWING 5 *intransitive verb* **1** : KID **2** : to dance to or play jive

³jive *adjective* (1953) *slang* : PHONY

jo \'jō\ *noun, plural* **joes** [alteration of *joy*] (circa 1529) *chiefly Scottish* : SWEETHEART, DEAR

¹job \'jäb\ *noun* [perhaps from obsolete English *job* lump] (circa 1627) **1 a** : a piece of work; *especially* : a small miscellaneous piece of work undertaken on order at a stated rate **b** : the object or material on which work is being done **c** : something produced by or as if by work ⟨do a better *job* next time⟩ **d** : an example of a usually specified type : ITEM ⟨this *job* is round-necked and sleeveless —Lois Long⟩ **2 a** : something done for private advantage ⟨suspected the whole incident was a put-up *job*⟩ **b** : a criminal enterprise; *specifically* : ROBBERY **c** : a damaging or destructive bit of work ⟨did a *job* on him⟩ **3 a** (1) : something that has to be done : TASK (2) : an undertaking requiring unusual exertion ⟨it was a real *job* to talk over that noise⟩ **b** : a specific duty, role, or function **c** : a regular remunerative position **d** *chiefly British* : state of affairs — used with *bad* or *good* ⟨it was a good *job* you didn't hit the old man —E. L. Thomas⟩ **synonym** see TASK — **on the job** : at work

²job *verb* **jobbed; job·bing** (1694) *intransitive verb* **1** : to do odd or occasional pieces of work for hire **2** : to carry on public business for private gain **3** : to carry on the business of a middleman or wholesaler *transitive verb*

◇ WORD HISTORY

jingoism The word *jingoism* grew out of an issue that bedeviled 19th century European diplomats, the Eastern Question. As the Ottoman Empire, "the sick man of Europe," gradually collapsed, the other major European powers came into constant conflict on when and how to carve it up among themselves. Britain's policy was to support Turkey in order to prevent any other single power from overwhelming it, and pursuit of this aim led to war with Russia in 1854–55 and a near-war in 1878, when Russian troops, in support of their Slavic coreligionists fighting Ottoman rule in the Balkans, reached the outskirts of Constantinople. With the dispatch of the British fleet to Constantinople, anti-Russian sentiment mounted and the words of a music-hall song expressed the patriotic fervor of some Britons: "We don't want to fight, yet by jingo if we do, we've got the ships, we've got the men, we've got the money too." The song made *jingo* a catchword for a militant patriot. War never came, and the Eastern Question was temporarily settled by an international conference in Berlin, but *jingoism* has remained in English as a byword for excessive patriotism.

1 : to buy and sell (as stock) for profit **:** SPEC-
ULATE
2 : to hire or let by the job or for a period of
service
3 : to get, deal with, or effect by jobbery
4 : to do or cause to be done by separate por-
tions or lots **:** SUBCONTRACT
5 : to penalize or deprive unfairly
³**job** adjective (1710)
1 British **:** that is for hire for a given service
or period
2 : used in, engaged in, or done as job work ⟨a
job shop⟩
3 : of or relating to a job or to employment ⟨a
guarantee of job security⟩
Job \'jōb\ noun [Latin, from Greek Iōb, from
Hebrew Iyyōbh]
1 : the hero of the book of Job who endures
afflictions with fortitude and faith
2 : a narrative and poetic book of canonical
Jewish and Christian Scripture — see BIBLE
table
job action noun (circa 1968)
: a temporary action (as a slowdown) by
workers as a protest and means of forcing
compliance with demands
job·ber \'jä-bər\ noun (1670)
: one that jobs: as **a** (1) **:** WHOLESALER; specif-
ically **:** a wholesaler who operates on a small
scale or who sells only to retailers and institu-
tions (2) **:** STOCKJOBBER a **b :** a person who
works by the job
job·bery \'jä-b(ə-)rē\ noun (1832)
: the act or practice of jobbing; especially
: corruption in public office
job·hold·er \'jäb-ˌhōl-dər\ noun (1904)
: a person having a regular job
job·hop·ping \-ˌhä-piŋ\ noun (circa 1952)
: the practice of moving from job to job
— **job·hop·per** \-ˌhä-pər\ noun
job·less \'jäb-ləs\ adjective (1919)
1 : having no job
2 : of or relating to those having no job
— **job·less·ness** noun
job lot noun (1851)
1 : a miscellaneous collection of goods for
sale as a lot usually to a retailer
2 : a miscellaneous and usually inferior col-
lection or group
Job's comforter \'jōbz-\ noun [from the tone
of the speeches made to Job by his friends]
(1738)
: a person who discourages or depresses while
seemingly giving comfort and consolation
Job's tears noun plural (1597)
1 : hard pearly white seeds of-
ten used as beads
2 singular in construction **:** an
Asian grass (Coix lacryma-
jobi) whose seeds are Job's tears
Jo·cas·ta \jō-'kas-tə\ noun
[Latin, from Greek Iokastē]
: a queen of Thebes who mar-
ries Oedipus not knowing that
he is her son
¹**jock** \'jäk\ noun (1826)
1 : JOCKEY
2 : DISC JOCKEY
²**jock** noun [jockstrap] (1922)
1 : ATHLETIC SUPPORTER
2 : ATHLETE; especially **:** a col-
lege athlete
¹**jock·ey** \'jä-kē\ noun, plural
jockeys [Jockey, Scots nick-
name for John] (1670)

Job's tears 2

1 : a person who rides or drives a horse espe-
cially as a professional in a race
2 : a person who operates or works with a
specified vehicle, device, or object **:** OPERATOR
⟨an accountant, a pencil jockey — with almost
no association with the out-of-doors —James
Selder⟩
²**jockey** verb **jock·eyed; jock·ey·ing**
(1708)
transitive verb
1 : to deal shrewdly or fraudulently with

2 a : to ride or drive (a horse) as a jockey **b**
: DRIVE, OPERATE
3 a : to maneuver or manipulate by adroit or
devious means ⟨was jockeyed out of the job⟩ **b**
: to change the position of by a series of
movements ⟨jockey a truck into position⟩
intransitive verb
1 : to act as a jockey
2 : to maneuver for advantage — often used
in the phrase jockey for position
jockey club noun (1775)
: an association for the promotion and regula-
tion of horse racing
jock itch noun [²jock] (1950)
: ringworm of the crotch **:** TINEA CRURIS
jock·strap \'jäk-ˌstrap\ noun [English slang
jock penis + English strap] (1886)
: ATHLETIC SUPPORTER
jo·cose \jō-'kōs, jə-\ adjective [Latin jocosus,
from jocus joke] (1673)
1 : given to joking **:** MERRY
2 : characterized by joking **:** HUMOROUS
synonym see WITTY
— **jo·cose·ly** adverb
— **jo·cose·ness** noun
— **jo·cos·i·ty** \jō-'kä-sə-tē, jə-\ noun
joc·u·lar \'jä-kyə-lər\ adjective [Latin jocu-
laris, from joculus, diminutive of jocus]
(1626)
1 : given to jesting **:** habitually jolly or jocund
2 : characterized by jesting **:** PLAYFUL
synonym see WITTY
— **joc·u·lar·i·ty** \ˌjä-kyə-'lar-ə-tē\ noun
— **joc·u·lar·ly** \'jä-kyə-lər-lē\ adverb
jo·cund \'jä-kənd also 'jō-(ˌ)kənd\ adjective
[Middle English, from Late Latin jocundus, al-
teration of Latin jucundus, from juvare to
help] (14th century)
: marked by or suggestive of high spirits and
lively mirthfulness ⟨a poet could not but be
gay, in such a jocund company —William
Wordsworth⟩
synonym see MERRY
— **jo·cun·di·ty** \jō-'kən-də-tē, jä-\ noun
— **jo·cund·ly** \'jä-kənd-lē, 'jō-(ˌ)\ adverb
jodh·pur \'jäd-(ˌ)pər\ noun [Jodhpur, India]
(1899)
1 plural **:** riding breeches cut full through the
hips and close-fitting from knee to ankle
2 : an ankle-high boot fastened with a strap
that is buckled at the side — called also jodh-
pur boot
joe \'jō\ noun, often capitalized [from Joe,
nickname for Joseph] (1846)
: FELLOW, GUY ⟨an average joe⟩
Jo·el \'jō(-ə)l\ noun [Latin, from Greek Iōēl,
from Hebrew Yō'ēl]
1 : the traditionally assumed author of the
book of Joel
2 : a narrative and apocalyptic book of canon-
ical Jewish and Christian Scripture — see BI-
BLE table
joe–pye weed \'jō-ˌpī-\ noun [origin un-
known] (circa 1818)
: any of several tall American perennial com-
posite herbs (especially Eupatorium macula-
tum and E. purpureum) with whorled leaves
and corymbose heads of typically purple tubu-
lar flowers
jo·ey \'jō-ē\ noun [origin unknown] (1839)
Australian **:** a baby animal; especially **:** a baby
kangaroo
¹**jog** \'jäg, 'jȯg\ verb **jogged; jog·ging** [prob-
ably alteration of shog] (1548)
transitive verb
1 : to give a slight shake or push to **:** NUDGE
2 : to rouse to alertness ⟨jogged his memory⟩
3 : to cause (as a horse) to go at a jog
4 : to align the edges of (piled sheets of paper)
by hitting or shaking against a flat surface
intransitive verb
1 : to move up and down or about with a short
heavy motion ⟨his . . . holster jogging against
his hip —Thomas Williams⟩
2 a : to run or ride at a slow trot **b :** to go at a
slow, leisurely, or monotonous pace **:** TRUDGE

²**jog** noun (1635)
1 : a slight shake **:** PUSH
2 a : a movement, pace, or instance of jogging
(as for exercise) **b :** a horse's slow measured
trot
³**jog** noun [probably alteration of ²jag] (1715)
1 a : a projecting or retreating part (as of a
line or surface) **b :** the space in the angle of a
jog
2 : a brief abrupt change in direction
⁴**jog** intransitive verb **jogged; jog·ging**
(1953)
: to make a jog ⟨the road jogs to the right⟩
jog·ger \'jä-gər, 'jȯ-\ noun (circa 1700)
1 : one that jogs
2 : a device for jogging piled sheets of paper
¹**jog·gle** \'jä-gəl\ verb **jog·gled; jog·gling**
\-g(ə-)liŋ\ [frequentative of ¹jog] (1513)
transitive verb
: to shake slightly
intransitive verb
: to move shakily or jerkily
— **jog·gler** \-g(ə-)lər\ noun
²**joggle** noun (circa 1727)
: ²JOG 2a
³**joggle** noun [diminutive of ³jog] (1793)
1 : a notch or tooth in a joining surface (as of
a piece of building material) to prevent slip-
ping
2 : a dowel for joining two adjacent blocks of
masonry
⁴**joggle** transitive verb **jog·gled; jog·gling**
\'jä-g(ə-)liŋ\ (1820)
: to join by means of a joggle so as to prevent
sliding apart
jog trot noun (1796)
1 : ²JOG 2b
2 : a routine habit or course of action
Jo·han·nine \jō-'ha-ˌnīn, -nən\ adjective [Late
Latin Johannes John] (1861)
: of, relating to, or characteristic of the apostle
John or the New Testament books ascribed to
him
Jo·han·nis·berg Riesling \yō-'hä-nəs-
ˌberg-\ noun [Johannisberg, village in Germa-
ny] (1976)
: a Riesling produced in the U.S. (as in Cali-
fornia)
john \'jän\ noun [from the name John] (1856)
1 : TOILET
2 : a prostitute's client
John \'jän\ noun [Late Latin Johannes, from
Greek Iōannēs, from Hebrew Yōḥānān]
1 : a Jewish prophet who according to Gospel
accounts foretold Jesus's messianic ministry
and baptized him — called also John the
Baptist
2 : an apostle who according to various Chris-
tian traditions wrote the fourth Gospel, the
three Johannine Epistles, and the Book of
Revelation
3 : the fourth Gospel in the New Testament
— see BIBLE table
4 : any of three short didactic letters addressed
to early Christians and included in the New
Testament — see BIBLE table
John Barleycorn noun (circa 1620)
: alcoholic liquor personified
john·boat \'jän-ˌbōt\ noun [from the name
John] (1905)
: a narrow flat-bottomed square-ended boat
usually propelled by a pole or paddle and used
on inland waterways
John Bull \-'bu̇l\ noun [John Bull, character
typifying the English nation in The History of
John Bull (1712) by John Arbuthnot] (1778)
1 : the English nation personified **:** the English
people
2 : a typical Englishman
— **John Bull·ish** \-'bu̇-lish\ adjective

— **John Bull·ish·ness** *noun*
— **John Bull·ism** \-,li-zəm\ *noun*
John Doe \-'dō\ *noun* (1768)
1 : a party to legal proceedings whose true name is unknown
2 : an average man
John Do·ry \-'dōr-ē, -'dȯr-\ *noun, plural* **John Dories** [earlier *dory,* from Middle English *dorre,* from Middle French *doree,* literally, gilded one] (1754)
: a common yellow to olive food fish (*Zeus faber*) of Europe and Africa with an oval compressed body, long dorsal spines, and a dark spot on each side; *also* **:** a closely related and possibly identical fish (*Z. capensis*) widely distributed in southern seas
Joh·ne's disease \'yō-nəz-\ *noun* [Heinrich A. *Johne* (died 1910) German bacteriologist] (1907)
: a chronic often fatal contagious enteritis of ruminants and especially of cattle that is caused by a bacterium (*Mycobacterium paratuberculosis*) and is characterized by persistent diarrhea and gradual emaciation
John Han·cock \'jän-'han-,käk\ *noun* [*John Hancock;* from the prominence of his signature on the Declaration of Independence] (1903)
: an autograph signature
John Hen·ry \-'hen-rē\ *noun* [from the name *John Henry,* from confusion with *John Hancock*] (1914)
: an autograph signature
John Mark *noun*
: MARK 1a
john·ny \'jä-nē\ *noun, plural* **johnnies** [from the name *Johnny*] (1673)
1 *often capitalized* **:** FELLOW, GUY
2 : a short-sleeved collarless gown that is open in the back and is worn by persons (as hospital patients) undergoing medical examination or treatment
john·ny·cake \'jä-nē-,käk\ *noun* [probably from the name *Johnny*] (1739)
: a bread made with cornmeal
John·ny–come–late·ly \'jä-nē-(,)kəm-'lāt-lē\ *noun, plural* **Johnnies–come–latelies** *or* **Johnnies–come–lately** (1839)
1 : a late or recent arrival **:** NEWCOMER
2 : UPSTART ⟨established families tend to hold themselves above the *Johnny-come-latelies* —William Zeckendorf (died 1976)⟩
John·ny–jump–up \,jä-nē-'jəmp-,əp\ *noun* (1842)
1 : a common and long-cultivated European viola (*Viola tricolor*) which has short-spurred flowers usually blue or purple mixed with white and yellow and from which most of the garden pansies are derived; *broadly* **:** any of various small-flowered cultivated pansies
2 : any of various American violets
John·ny–on–the–spot \'jä-nē-,ȯn-thə-'spät, -,än-\ *noun* (1896)
: a person who is on hand and ready to perform a service or respond to an emergency
Johnny Reb \-'reb\ *noun* [from the name *Johnny* + *reb* rebel] (1865)
: a Confederate soldier
John·son·ese \,jän(t)-sə-'nēz, -'nēs\ *noun* [Samuel *Johnson*] (1843)
: a literary style characterized by balanced phraseology and Latinate diction
john·son·grass \'jän(t)-sən-,gras\ *noun, often capitalized* [William *Johnson* (died 1859) American agriculturist] (1884)
: a tall perennial sorghum (*Sorghum halepense*) originally of the Mediterranean region that is widely used for forage in warm areas and often becomes naturalized
joie de vi·vre \,zhwä-də-'vēvrᵊ\ *noun* [French, literally, joy of living] (1889)
: keen or buoyant enjoyment of life
¹join \'jȯin\ *verb* [Middle English, from Old French *joindre,* from Latin *jungere* — more at YOKE] (13th century)
transitive verb

1 a : to put or bring together so as to form a unit ⟨*join* two blocks of wood with glue⟩ **b :** to connect (as points) by a line **c :** ADJOIN
2 : to put or bring into close association or relationship ⟨*joined* in marriage⟩
3 : to engage in (battle)
4 a : to come into the company of ⟨*joined* us for lunch⟩ **b :** to associate oneself with ⟨*joined* the church⟩
intransitive verb
1 a : to come together so as to be connected ⟨nouns *join* to form compounds⟩ **b :** ADJOIN ⟨the two estates *join*⟩
2 : to come into close association or relationship: as **a :** to form an alliance **b :** to become a member of a group **c :** to take part in a collective activity ⟨*join* in singing⟩ ☆
— **join·able** \'jȯi-nə-bəl\ *adjective*
²join *noun* (1825)
1 : JOINT
2 : UNION 2d
join·der \'jȯin-dər\ *noun* [French *joindre* to join, from Old French] (1601)
1 : CONJUNCTION 1
2 a (1) **:** a joining of parties as plaintiffs or defendants in a suit (2) **:** a joining of causes of action or defense **b :** acceptance of an issue tendered
join·er \'jȯi-nər\ *noun* (14th century)
: one that joins: as **a :** a person whose occupation is to construct articles by joining pieces of wood **b :** a gregarious or civic-minded person who joins many organizations
join·ery \'jȯi-nə-rē, 'jȯin-rē\ *noun* (1678)
1 : the art or trade of a joiner
2 : work done by a joiner
join·ing \'jȯi-niŋ\ *noun* (14th century)
1 : the act or an instance of joining one thing to another **:** JUNCTURE
2 a : the place or manner of being joined together **b :** something that joins two things together
¹joint \'jȯint\ *noun* [Middle English *jointe,* from Old French, from *joindre*] (13th century)
1 a (1) **:** the point of contact between elements of an animal skeleton with the parts that surround and support it (2) **:** NODE 5b **b :** a part or space included between two articulations, knots, or nodes **c :** a large piece of meat for roasting
2 a : a place where two things or parts are joined **b :** a space between the adjacent surfaces of two bodies joined and held together (as by cement or mortar) **c :** a fracture or crack in rock not accompanied by dislocation **d :** the flexing part of a cover along either backbone edge of a book **e :** the junction of two or more members of a framed structure **f :** a union formed by two abutting rails in a track including the elements (as bars and bolts) necessary to hold the abutting rails together **g :** an area at which two ends, surfaces, or edges are attached
3 a : a shabby or disreputable place of entertainment **b :** PLACE, ESTABLISHMENT **c** *slang* **:** PRISON 2
4 : a marijuana cigarette
— **joint·ed** \'jȯin-təd\ *adjective*
— **joint·ed·ly** *adverb*
— **joint·ed·ness** *noun*
— **out of joint 1 a** *of a bone* **:** having the head slipped from its socket **b :** at variance **2 a :** DISORDERED 2a **b :** being out of humor **:** DISSATISFIED
²joint *adjective* [Middle English, from Middle French, from past participle of *joindre,* from Old French] (14th century)
1 : UNITED, COMBINED ⟨the *joint* influences of culture and climate⟩
2 : common to two or more: as **a** (1) **:** involving the united activity of two or more ⟨a *joint* effort⟩ (2) **:** constituting an activity, operation, or organization in which elements of more than one armed service participate ⟨*joint* maneuvers⟩ (3) **:** constituting an action or expression of two or more governments ⟨*joint* peace

talks⟩ **b :** shared by or affecting two or more ⟨a *joint* fine⟩
3 : united, joined, or sharing with another (as in a right or status) ⟨*joint* heirs⟩
4 : being a function of or involving two or more variables and especially random variables
— **joint·ly** *adverb*
³joint *verb* [¹*joint*] (1530)
transitive verb
1 : to separate the joints of (as meat)
2 a : to unite by a joint **:** fit together **b :** to provide with a joint **:** ARTICULATE **c :** to prepare (as a board) for joining by planing the edge
intransitive verb
1 : to fit as if by joints ⟨the stones *joint* neatly⟩
2 : to form joints as a stage in growth — used especially of small grains
Joint Chiefs of Staff (1946)
: a military advisory group composed of the chiefs of staff of the army and air force, the chief of naval operations, and sometimes the commandant of the marine corps
joint·er \'jȯin-tər\ *noun* (1678)
: one that joints; *especially* **:** any of various tools used in making joints
joint grass *noun* (1835)
: a coarse creeping grass (*Paspalum distichum*) with jointed stems that is used for fodder and for erosion control
joint resolution *noun* (1838)
: a resolution passed by both houses of a legislative body that has the force of law when signed by or passed over the veto of the executive
join·tress \'jȯin-trəs\ *noun* (1602)
: a woman having a legal jointure
joint–stock company *noun* (1776)
: a company or association consisting of individuals organized to conduct a business for gain and having a joint stock of capital represented by shares owned individually by the members and transferable without the consent of the group
join·ture \'jȯin-chər\ *noun* (14th century)
1 a : an act of joining **:** the state of being joined **b :** JOINT
2 a : an estate settled on a wife to be taken by her in lieu of dower **b :** a settlement on the wife of a freehold estate for her lifetime
joint·worm \'jȯint-,wərm\ *noun* (1851)
: the larva of any of several small chalcid wasps (genus *Harmolita*) that attacks the stems of grain and causes swellings like galls at or just above the first joint
joist \'jȯist\ *noun* [Middle English *joiste,* from Middle French *giste,* from (assumed) Vulgar

☆ **SYNONYMS**
Join, combine, unite, connect, link, associate, relate mean to bring or come together into some manner of union. JOIN implies a bringing into contact or conjunction of any degree of closeness ⟨*joined* forces in an effort to win⟩. COMBINE implies some merging or mingling with corresponding loss of identity of each unit ⟨*combined* jazz and rock to create a new music⟩. UNITE implies somewhat greater loss of separate identity ⟨the colonies *united* to form a republic⟩. CONNECT suggests a loose or external attachment with little or no loss of identity ⟨a mutual defense treaty *connected* the two nations⟩. LINK may imply strong connection or inseparability of elements still retaining identity ⟨a name forever *linked* with liberty⟩. ASSOCIATE stresses the mere fact of frequent occurrence or existence together in space or in logical relation ⟨opera is popularly *associated* with high society⟩. RELATE suggests the existence of a real or presumed logical connection ⟨*related* what he observed to what he already knew⟩.

Latin *jacitum,* from Latin *jacēre* to lie — more at ADJACENT] (15th century)
: any of the small timbers or metal beams ranged parallel from wall to wall in a structure to support a floor or ceiling

joists

jo·jo·ba \hə-'hō-bə\ *noun* [Mexican Spanish] (1923)
: a shrub or small tree (*Simmondsia chinensis* synonym *S. californica*) of the box family of southwestern North America with edible seeds that yield a valuable liquid wax

¹joke \'jōk\ *noun* [Latin *jocus;* perhaps akin to Old High German *gehan* to say, Sanskrit *yācati* he asks] (1670)
1 a : something said or done to provoke laughter; *especially* : a brief oral narrative with a climactic humorous twist **b** (1) : the humorous or ridiculous element in something (2) : an instance of jesting : KIDDING ⟨can't take a *joke*⟩ **c :** PRACTICAL JOKE **d :** LAUGHINGSTOCK
2 : something not to be taken seriously : a trifling matter ⟨consider his skiing a *joke* —Harold Callender⟩ — often used in negative construction ⟨it is no *joke* to be lost in the desert⟩

²joke *verb* **joked; jok·ing** (1670)
intransitive verb
: to make jokes : JEST
transitive verb
: to make the object of a joke : KID
— **jok·ing·ly** \'jō-kiŋ-lē\ *adverb*

jok·er \'jō-kər\ *noun* (1729)
1 a : a person given to joking : WAG **b :** FELLOW, GUY; *especially* : an insignificant, obnoxious, or incompetent person ⟨a shame to let a *joker* like this win —Harold Robbins⟩
2 : a playing card added to a pack as a wild card or as the highest-ranking card
3 a (1) : an ambiguous or apparently immaterial clause inserted in a legislative bill to make it inoperative or uncertain in some respect (2) : an unsuspected, misleading, or misunderstood clause, phrase, or word in a document that nullifies or greatly alters it **b :** something (as an expedient or stratagem) held in reserve to gain an end or escape from a predicament **c :** an unsuspected or not readily apparent fact, factor, or condition that thwarts or nullifies a seeming advantage

jok·ey *also* **joky** \'jō-kē\ *adjective* **jok·i·er; -est** (circa 1825)
1 : given to joking
2 : HUMOROUS, COMICAL
3 : amusingly ridiculous : LAUGHABLE
— **jok·i·ly** \-kə-lē\ *adverb*
— **jok·i·ness** \-kē-nəs\ *noun*

jol·li·fi·ca·tion \,jä-li-fə-'kā-shən\ *noun* (1809)
: FESTIVITY, MERRYMAKING

jol·li·ty \'jä-lə-tē\ *noun, plural* **-ties** (14th century)
1 : the quality or state of being jolly : MERRIMENT
2 *British* : a festive gathering

¹jol·ly \'jä-lē\ *adjective* **jol·li·er; -est** [Middle English *joli,* from Old French] (14th century)
1 a (1) : full of high spirits : JOYOUS (2) : given to conviviality : JOVIAL **b :** expressing, suggesting, or inspiring gaiety : CHEERFUL
2 : extremely pleasant or agreeable : SPLENDID
synonym see MERRY

²jolly *adverb* (1549)
: VERY ⟨would . . . do as they were *jolly* well told —John Stockbridge⟩

³jolly *verb* **jol·lied; jol·ly·ing** (1610)
intransitive verb
: to engage in good-natured banter
transitive verb
: to put or try to put in good humor especially to gain an end

⁴jolly *noun, plural* **jollies** (1905)
1 *chiefly British* : a good time : JOLLIFICATION

2 *plural* : KICKS ⟨get their *jollies* by reenacting famous murders —H. F. Waters⟩

jol·ly boat \'jä-lē-\ *noun* [origin unknown] (circa 1741)
: a ship's boat of medium size used for general-purpose work

Jol·ly Rog·er \'jä-lē-'rä-jər\ *noun* [probably from ¹*jolly* + the name *Roger*] (circa 1785)
: a black flag with a white skull and crossbones formerly used by pirates as their ensign

¹jolt \'jōlt\ *verb* [probably blend of obsolete *joll* to strike and *jot* to bump] (1596)
transitive verb
1 : to cause to move with a sudden jerky motion
2 : to give a knock or blow to; *specifically* : to jar with a quick or hard blow
3 a : to disturb the composure of ⟨crudely *jolted* out of that mood —Virginia Woolf⟩ **b :** to interfere with roughly, abruptly, and disconcertingly ⟨determination to pursue his own course was *jolted* badly —F. L. Paxson⟩
intransitive verb
: to move with a sudden jerky motion
— **jolt·er** *noun*

²jolt *noun* (1599)
1 : an abrupt sharp jerky blow or movement
2 a (1) : a sudden feeling of shock, surprise, or disappointment (2) : an event or development causing such a feeling ⟨the defeat was quite a *jolt*⟩ **b :** a serious check or reverse ⟨a severe financial *jolt*⟩
3 : a small potent or bracing portion ⟨a *jolt* of horseradish⟩
— **jolty** \'jōl-tē\ *adjective*

jolt–wag·on \'jōlt-,wa-gən\ *noun* (1886)
Midland : a farm wagon

Jo·nah \'jō-nə, *3 is also* -nər\ *noun* [Hebrew *Yōnāh*]
1 : an Israelite prophet who according to the account in the book of Johah resisted a divine call to preach repentance to the people of Nineveh, was swallowed and vomited by a great fish, and eventually carried out his mission
2 : a narrative book of canonical Jewish and Christian Scripture — see BIBLE table
3 : one believed to bring bad luck

Jo·nas \'jō-nəs\ *noun* [Late Latin, from Hebrew *Yōnāh*]
: JONAH

Jon·a·than \'jä-nə-thən\ *noun* [Hebrew *Yōnāthān*]
1 : a son of Saul and friend of David according to the account in I Samuel
2 : AMERICAN; *especially* : a New Englander
3 : any of a variety of red-skinned apple

jon·gleur \zhōⁿ-'glər\ *noun* [French, from Old French *jogleour* — more at JUGGLER] (1779)
: an itinerant medieval entertainer proficient in juggling, acrobatics, music, and recitation

jon·quil \'jän-kwəl, 'jäŋ-\ *noun* [French *jonquille,* from Spanish *junquillo,* diminutive of *junco* reed, from Latin *juncus*] (1629)
: a Mediterranean perennial bulbous herb (*Narcissus jonquilla*) of the amaryllis family with long linear leaves that is widely cultivated for its yellow or white fragrant short-tubed clustered flowers — compare DAFFODIL

Jor·dan almond \'jȯr-dⁿn-\ *noun* [Middle English *jardin almande,* from Middle French *jardin* garden + Middle English *almande* almond] (1615)
: a large Spanish almond especially when salted or coated with sugar of various colors

Jor·dan curve \zhȯr-'däⁿ-, 'jȯr-dⁿn-\ *noun* [Camille *Jordan* (died 1922) French mathematician] (1900)
: SIMPLE CLOSED CURVE

Jordan curve theorem *noun* (1947)
: a fundamental theorem of topology: every simple closed curve divides the plane into two regions for which it is the common boundary

jo·rum \'jȯr-əm, 'jōr-\ *noun* [perhaps from *Joram* in the Bible who "brought with him vessels of silver" (2 Samuel 8:10—Authorized Version)] (1730)

: a large drinking vessel or its contents

jo·seph \'jō-zəf *also* -səf\ *noun* [Latin, from Greek *Iōsēph,* from Hebrew *Yōsēph*]
1 *capitalized* **a :** a son of Jacob who according to the account in Genesis rose to high political office in Egypt after being sold into slavery by his brothers **b :** the husband of Mary the mother of Jesus according to the Gospel accounts
2 : a long cloak worn especially by women in the 18th century

Jo·seph·ite \-zə-,fīt, -sə-\ *noun* (1890)
: a member of Saint Joseph's Society of the Sacred Heart founded in 1871 in Baltimore, Md. and devoted to missionary work among black Americans

Joseph of Ar·i·ma·thea \-,ar-ə-mə-'thē-ə\
: a rich councillor of the Sanhedrin who according to the Gospel accounts placed the body of Jesus in his own tomb and according to medieval legend took the Holy Grail to England

Jo·seph·son junction \'jō-zəf-sən- *also* -səf-sən-\ *noun* [Brian D. *Josephson*] (1965)
: an electronic fast-switching device that consists of two layers of superconducting metal separated by a thin layer of insulator through which low current flows but increased current causes the insulator to block the flow

¹josh \'jäsh\ *verb* [origin unknown] (1852)
transitive verb
: to tease good-naturedly : KID
intransitive verb
: to engage in banter : JOKE
— **josh·er** *noun*

²josh *noun* (1878)
: a good-humored joke : JEST

Josh·ua \'jä-sh(ə-)wə\ *noun* [Hebrew *Yěhōshūaʿ*]
1 : the divinely commissioned successor of Moses and military leader of the Israelites during the conquest of Canaan according to the account in the book of Joshua
2 : a mainly narrative book of canonical Jewish and Christian Scripture — see BIBLE table

Joshua tree *noun* (1884)
: a tall branched arborescent yucca (*Yucca brevifolia*) of the southwestern U.S. that has clustered greenish white flowers

joss \'jäs, 'jȯs\ *noun* [Chinese Pidgin English, from Portuguese *deus* god, from Latin — more at DEITY] (1711)
: a Chinese idol or cult image

Joshua tree

joss house *noun* (1771)
: a Chinese temple or shrine

joss stick *noun* (1845)
: a slender stick of incense burned in front of a joss

¹jos·tle \'jä-səl\ *verb* **jos·tled; jos·tling** \-s(ə-)liŋ\ [alteration of *justle,* frequentative of ¹*joust*] (1546)
intransitive verb
1 a : to come in contact or into collision **b :** to make one's way by pushing and shoving **c :** to exist in close proximity
2 : to vie in gaining an objective : CONTEND
transitive verb
1 a : to come in contact or into collision with **b :** to force by pushing : ELBOW **c :** to stir up : AGITATE **d :** to exist in close proximity with
2 : to vie with in attaining an objective

²jostle *noun* (1611)
1 : a jostling encounter or experience

2 : the state of being crowded or jostled together

Jos·ue \'jä-shü-(ˌ)ē\ *noun* [Late Latin, from Hebrew *Yĕhōshūaʿ*]
: JOSHUA

¹jot \'jät\ *noun* [Latin *iota, jota* iota] (1500)
: the least bit **:** IOTA ◆

²jot *transitive verb* **jot·ted; jot·ting** (1721)
: to write briefly or hurriedly **:** set down in the form of a note ⟨*jot* this down⟩

jotting *noun* (1814)
: a brief note **:** MEMORANDUM

Jo·tun *also* **Jo·tunn** \'yō-tʰn, -ˌtùn\ *noun* [Old Norse *jǫtunn*]
: a member of a race of giants in Norse mythology

Jo·tun·heim *also* **Jo·tunn·heim** \-ˌhīm, -ˌhäm\ *noun* [Old Norse *Jǫtunheimar*]
: the home of the Jotuns in Norse mythology

jou·al \zhü-'al, -'äl, -'ål\ *noun* [Canadian French, rendering of a nonstandard pronunciation of French *cheval* horse] (1962)
: spoken Canadian French; *especially* **:** the local forms of the spoken French of Quebec that differ the most from prescribed forms

joule \'jü(ə)l *also* ÷'jaù(ə)l\ *noun* [James P. *Joule*] (1882)
: a unit of work or energy equal to the work done by a force of one newton acting through a distance of one meter

¹jounce \'jaùn(t)s\ *verb* **jounced; jounc·ing** [Middle English] (15th century)
intransitive verb
: to move in an up-and-down manner **:** BOUNCE
transitive verb
: to cause to jounce

²jounce *noun* (circa 1787)
: JOLT

jouncy \'jaùn(t)-sē\ *adjective* **jounc·i·er; -est** (1943)
: marked by a jouncing motion or effect

jour·nal \'jər-nʰl\ *noun* [Middle English, service book containing the day hours, from Middle French, from *journal*, adjective, daily, from Latin *diurnalis,* from *diurnus* of the day, from *dies* day — more at DEITY] (15th century)
1 a : a record of current transactions; *especially* **:** a book of original entry in double-entry bookkeeping **b :** an account of day-to-day events **c :** a record of experiences, ideas, or reflections kept regularly for private use **d :** a record of transactions kept by a deliberative or legislative body **e :** LOG 3, 4
2 a : a daily newspaper **b :** a periodical dealing especially with matters of current interest
3 : the part of a rotating shaft, axle, roll, or spindle that turns in a bearing

journal box *noun* (circa 1859)
: a metal housing to support and protect a journal bearing

jour·nal·ese \ˌjər-nʰl-'ēz, -'ēs\ *noun* (1882)
: a style of writing held to be characteristic of newspapers

jour·nal·ism \'jər-nʰl-ˌi-zəm\ *noun* (1833)
1 a : the collection and editing of news for presentation through the media **b :** the public press **c :** an academic study concerned with the collection and editing of news or the management of a news medium
2 a : writing designed for publication in a newspaper or magazine **b :** writing characterized by a direct presentation of facts or description of events without an attempt at interpretation **c :** writing designed to appeal to current popular taste or public interest

jour·nal·ist \-nʰl-ist\ *noun* (1693)
1 a : a person engaged in journalism; *especially* **:** a writer or editor for a news medium **b :** a writer who aims at a mass audience
2 : a person who keeps a journal

jour·nal·is·tic \ˌjər-nʰl-'is-tik\ *adjective* (1829)
: of, relating to, or characteristic of journalism or journalists
— jour·nal·is·ti·cal·ly \-ti-k(ə-)lē\ *adverb*

jour·nal·ize \'jər-nʰl-ˌīz\ *verb* **-ized; -iz·ing** (1766)
transitive verb
: to record in a journal
intransitive verb
1 : to keep a journal in accounting
2 : to keep a personal journal
— jour·nal·iz·er *noun*

¹jour·ney \'jər-nē\ *noun, plural* **journeys** [Middle English, from Old French *journee* day's journey, from *jour* day, from Late Latin *diurnum,* from Latin, neuter of *diurnus*] (13th century)
1 : travel or passage from one place to another **:** TRIP
2 : *chiefly dialect* **:** a day's travel
3 : something suggesting travel or passage from one place to another ⟨the *journey* from youth to maturity⟩ ⟨a *journey* through time⟩

²journey *verb* **jour·neyed; jour·ney·ing** (14th century)
intransitive verb
: to go on a journey **:** TRAVEL
transitive verb
: to travel over or through
— jour·ney·er *noun*

jour·ney·man \-mən\ *noun* [Middle English, from *journey* journey, a day's labor + *man*] (15th century)
1 : a worker who has learned a trade and works for another person usually by the day
2 : an experienced reliable worker or performer especially as distinguished from one who is brilliant or colorful ⟨a good *journeyman* trumpeter —*New Yorker*⟩ ⟨a *journeyman* outfielder⟩

jour·ney·work \-ˌwərk\ *noun* (1601)
1 : work done by a journeyman
2 : HACKWORK

¹joust \'jaùst *sometimes* 'jəst *or* 'jüst\ *intransitive verb* [Middle English, from Middle French *juster* to unite, joust, from (assumed) Vulgar Latin *juxtare,* from Latin *juxta* near; akin to Latin *jungere* to join — more at YOKE] (14th century)
1 a : to fight on horseback as a knight or man-at-arms **b :** to engage in combat with lances on horseback
2 : to engage in personal combat or competition
— joust·er *noun*

²joust *noun* (14th century)
1 a : a combat on horseback between two knights with lances especially as part of a tournament **b** *plural* **:** TOURNAMENT
2 : a personal combat or competition **:** STRUGGLE

Jove \'jōv\ *noun* [Latin *Jov-, Juppiter*]
: JUPITER — often used interjectionally to express surprise or agreement especially in the phrase *by Jove*

jo·vial \'jō-vē-əl, -vyəl\ *adjective* (1592)
1 *capitalized* **:** of or relating to Jove
2 : markedly good-humored especially as evidenced by jollity and conviviality
synonym see MERRY
— jo·vi·al·i·ty \ˌjō-vē-'a-lə-tē\ *noun*
— jo·vi·al·ly \'jō-vē-ə-lē, -vyə-\ *adverb*

Jo·vi·an \'jō-vē-ən\ *adjective* (1530)
: of, relating to, or characteristic of the god or planet Jupiter

jow \'jaù\ *noun* [Middle English *jollen* to knock] (1515)
chiefly Scottish **:** STROKE, TOLL

jo·war \jə-'wär\ *noun* [Hindi *joār, juwār,* from Sanskrit *yavākāra* barley-shaped, from *yava* barley + *karoti* he makes] (1800)
: DURRA

¹jowl \'jaù(ə)l *sometimes* 'jōl\ *noun* [alteration of Middle English *choll*] (15th century)
: a cut of fish consisting of the head and usually adjacent parts

²jowl *noun* [alteration of Middle English *cholle,* probably from Old English *ceole* throat — more at GLUTTON] (1591)
: usually slack flesh (as a dewlap, wattle, or the pendulous part of a double chin) associated with the cheeks, lower jaw, or throat

³jowl *noun* [alteration of Middle English *chavel,* from Old English *ceafl;* akin to Middle High German *kivel* jaw, Avestan *zafar-* mouth] (1598)
1 a : JAW; *especially* **:** MANDIBLE **b :** one of the lateral halves of the mandible
2 a : CHEEK 1 **b :** the cheek meat of a hog ⟨a dinner of boiled *jowls*⟩

jowly \'jaù-lē *sometimes* 'jō-\ *adjective* **jowl·i·er; -est** (circa 1873)
: having marked jowls **:** having full or saggy flesh about the lower cheeks and jaw area ⟨elderly man with a disillusioned *jowly* face —John Dos Passos⟩

¹joy \'jòi\ *noun* [Middle English, from Old French *joie,* from Latin *gaudia,* plural of *gaudium,* from *gaudēre* to rejoice; probably akin to Greek *gēthein* to rejoice] (13th century)
1 a : the emotion evoked by well-being, success, or good fortune or by the prospect of possessing what one desires **:** DELIGHT **b :** the expression or exhibition of such emotion **:** GAIETY
2 : a state of happiness or felicity **:** BLISS
3 : a source or cause of delight
— joy·less \-ləs\ *adjective*
— joy·less·ly *adverb*
— joy·less·ness *noun*

²joy (14th century)
intransitive verb
: to experience great pleasure or delight **:** REJOICE
transitive verb
1 *archaic* **:** GLADDEN
2 *archaic* **:** ENJOY

joy·ance \'jòi-ən(t)s\ *noun* (circa 1586)
archaic **:** DELIGHT, ENJOYMENT

joy·ful \'jòi-fəl\ *adjective* (13th century)
: experiencing, causing, or showing joy **:** HAPPY
— joy·ful·ly \-fə-lē\ *adverb*
— joy·ful·ness *noun*

joy·ous \'jòi-əs\ *adjective* (14th century)
: JOYFUL
— joy·ous·ly *adverb*
— joy·ous·ness *noun*

joy·pop \'jòi-ˌpäp\ *intransitive verb* (1953)
: to use habit-forming drugs occasionally or irregularly without becoming addicted
— joy·pop·per *noun*

joy·ride \'jòi-ˌrīd\ *noun* (1909)
1 : a ride taken for pleasure (as in a car or aircraft); *especially* **:** an automobile ride marked by reckless driving (as in a stolen car)
2 : conduct or action resembling a joyride especially in disregard of cost or consequences
— joyride *intransitive verb*
— joy·rid·er \-ˌrī-dər\ *noun*
— joy·rid·ing *noun*

◇ WORD HISTORY
jot "Till heaven and earth pass, one jot or one tittle shall in no wise pass from the law, till all be fulfilled." These are the words, in the King James Version, of Christ's assurance (Matthew 5:18) that He had not "come to destroy the law or the prophets." Not the smallest letter, not even a single stroke of a letter, we are told, will be lost. The word *jot* first appeared in English in William Tyndale's translation of Matthew's Gospel, in 1526. Tyndale simply put in an anglicized form the Latin word *jota* (or *iota*), itself simply a transliteration of the Greek name of the ninth letter in the Greek alphabet. The Gospel writer may have had in mind *yōdh,* the smallest letter in the Hebrew alphabet. The transfer across language boundaries was easily made because the Greek equivalent, *iōta,* was also the smallest letter in its alphabet. A *jot* is now simply "a very small part."

joy·stick \-,stik\ *noun* [perhaps from English slang *joystick* penis] (1910)
1 : a lever in an airplane that operates the elevators by a fore-and-aft motion and the ailerons by a side-to-side motion
2 : a control for any of various devices (as a computer display) that resembles an airplane's joystick especially in being capable of motion in two or more directions

J/psi particle \,jā-'sī-, -'psī-\ *noun* (1977)
: an unstable neutral fundamental particle of the meson group that has a mass about 6000 times the mass of an electron — called also *J particle, psi particle*

ju·ba \'jü-bə\ *noun* [origin unknown] (1834)
: a dance of Southern plantation blacks accompanied by complexly rhythmic hand clapping and slapping of the knees and thighs

Ju·bal \'jü-bəl\ *noun* [Hebrew *Yūbhāl*]
: a descendant of Cain who according to the account in Genesis is the father of those who play the harp and organ

ju·bi·lance \'jü-bə-lən(t)s\ *noun* (1864)
: JUBILATION 1

ju·bi·lant \'jü-bə-lənt\ *adjective* (1667)
: EXULTANT
— **ju·bi·lant·ly** *adverb*

ju·bi·lar·i·an \,jü-bə-'ler-ē-ən, -'lar-\ *noun* (1782)
: one celebrating a jubilee

ju·bi·late \'jü-bə-,lāt\ *intransitive verb* **-lat·ed; -lat·ing** [Latin *jubilatus,* past participle of *jubilare;* akin to Middle High German *jū* (exclamation of joy), Greek *iygē* shout] (circa 1641)
: REJOICE

Ju·bi·la·te \,yü-bə-'lä-,tā, ,jü-\ *noun* [Latin, 2d person plural imperative of *jubilare*] (1549)
1 a : the 100th Psalm in the Authorized Version **b** *not capitalized* : a joyous song or outburst
2 : the third Sunday after Easter

ju·bi·la·tion \,jü-bə-'lā-shən\ *noun* (14th century)
1 : an act of rejoicing : the state of being jubilant
2 : an expression of great joy

¹ju·bi·lee \'jü-bə-(,)lē, ,jü-bə-'lē\ *noun* [Middle English, from Middle French & Late Latin; Middle French *jubilé,* from Late Latin *jubilaeus,* modification of Late Greek *iōbēlaios,* from Hebrew *yōbhēl* ram's horn, jubilee] (14th century)
1 *often capitalized* : a year of emancipation and restoration provided by ancient Hebrew law to be kept every 50 years by the emancipation of Hebrew slaves, restoration of alienated lands to their former owners, and omission of all cultivation of the land
2 a : a special anniversary; *especially* : a 50th anniversary **b** : a celebration of such an anniversary
3 a : a period of time proclaimed by the Roman Catholic pope ordinarily every 25 years as a time of special solemnity **b** : a special plenary indulgence granted during a year of jubilee to Roman Catholics who perform certain specified works of repentance and piety
4 a : JUBILATION **b** : a season of celebration
5 : an Afro-American religious song usually referring to a time of future happiness ◇

²jubilee *adjective, often capitalized* (1951)
: FLAMBÉ ⟨cherries *jubilee*⟩

Ju·dah \'jü-də\ *noun* [Hebrew *Yĕhūdhāh*]
: a son of Jacob and the traditional eponymous ancestor of one of the tribes of Israel

Ju·da·ic \jü-'dā-ik\ *also* **Ju·da·ical** \-'dā-ə-kəl\ *adjective* [Middle English *Judeical,* from Latin *judaicus,* from Greek *ioudaikos,* from *Ioudaios* Jew — more at JEW] (15th century)
: of, relating to, or characteristic of Jews or Judaism

Ju·da·ica \-'dā-ə-kə\ *noun plural* [Latin, neuter plural of *Judaicus*] (1923)
: literary or historical materials relating to Jews or Judaism

Ju·da·ism \'jü-də-,i-zəm, 'jü-dē-, 'jü-(,)dā-, British also 'jü-,di-zəm\ *noun* (14th century)
1 : a religion developed among the ancient Hebrews and characterized by belief in one transcendent God who has revealed himself to Abraham, Moses, and the Hebrew prophets and by a religious life in accordance with Scriptures and rabbinic traditions
2 : conformity to Jewish rites, ceremonies, and practices
3 : the cultural, social, and religious beliefs and practices of the Jews
4 : the whole body of Jews : the Jewish people

Ju·da·ist \'jü-də-ist, 'jü-dē-, jü-'dā-\ *noun* (circa 1846)
: one that believes in or practices Judaism
— **Ju·da·is·tic** \,jü-də-'is-tik, ,jü-dē-, ,jü-(,)dā-\ *adjective*

Ju·da·ize \'jü-də-,īz, 'jü-dē-, 'jü-(,)dā-\ *verb* **-ized; -iz·ing** (1582)
intransitive verb
: to adopt the customs, beliefs, or character of a Jew
transitive verb
: to make Jewish
— **Ju·da·i·za·tion** \,jü-də-ə-'zā-shən, ,jü-dē-ə-, ,jü-(,)dā-ə-\ *noun*
— **Ju·da·iz·er** \'jü-də-,īz-ər, 'jü-dē-, 'jü-(,)dā-\ *noun*

Ju·das \'jü-dəs\ *noun* [Late Latin, from Greek *Ioudas,* from Hebrew *Yĕhūdhāh*]
1 a : the apostle who in the Gospel accounts betrayed Jesus **b** : a son of James and one of the twelve apostles
2 : TRAITOR; *especially* : one who betrays under the guise of friendship
3 *not capitalized* : PEEPHOLE — called also *judas hole, judas window*

Judas Is·car·i·ot \-is-'kar-ē-ət\ *noun* [Late Latin *Judas Iscariotes,* from Greek *Ioudas Iskariōtēs*]
: JUDAS 1a

Judas tree *noun* [from the belief that Judas Iscariot hanged himself from a tree of this kind] (1668)
: any of a genus (*Cercis*) of leguminous trees and shrubs (as a redbud) often cultivated for their showy flowers; *especially* : a Eurasian tree (*C. siliquastrum*) with purplish rosy flowers

¹jud·der \'jə-dər\ *intransitive verb* [probably alteration of *shudder*] (1931)
chiefly British : to vibrate with intensity ⟨the engine stalled and kept *juddering* —Roy Spicer⟩

²judder *noun* (1935)
chiefly British : the action or sound of juddering

Jude \'jüd\ *noun* [Late Latin *Judas*]
1 : the author of the New Testament Epistle of Jude
2 : a short hortatory epistle addressed to early Christians and included as a book in the New Testament — see BIBLE table

Ju·deo–Chris·tian \jü-,dā-ō-'kris-chən, -'krish-\ *also* \,jü-dē-ō- *or* jü-,dē-ō-\ *adjective* [Latin *Judaeus* Jew — more at JEW] (1899)
: having historical roots in both Judaism and Christianity

Ju·deo–Span·ish \-'spa-nish\ *noun* (1851)
: the Romance language of Sephardic Jews especially in the Balkans and Asia Minor

¹judge \'jəj\ *verb* **judged; judg·ing** [Middle English *juggen,* from Old French *jugier,* from Latin *judicare,* from *judic-, judex* judge, from *jus* right, law + *dicere* to decide, say — more at JUST, DICTION] (13th century)
transitive verb
1 : to form an opinion about through careful weighing of evidence and testing of premises
2 : to sit in judgment on : TRY
3 : to determine or pronounce after inquiry and deliberation
4 : GOVERN, RULE — used of a Hebrew tribal leader

5 : to form an estimate or evaluation of; *especially* : to form a negative opinion about ⟨shouldn't *judge* him because of his accent⟩
6 : to hold as an opinion : GUESS, THINK ⟨I *judge* she knew what she was doing⟩
intransitive verb
1 : to form an opinion
2 : to decide as a judge
synonym see INFER
— **judg·er** *noun*

²judge *noun* [Middle English *juge,* from Middle French, from Latin *judex*] (14th century)
: one who judges: as **a** : a public official authorized to decide questions brought before a court **b** *often capitalized* : a tribal hero exercising leadership among the Hebrews after the death of Joshua **c** : one appointed to decide in a contest or competition : UMPIRE **d** : one who gives an authoritative opinion **e** : CRITIC
— **judge·ship** \-,ship\ *noun*

judge advocate *noun* (1748)
1 : an officer assigned to the judge advocate general's corps or department
2 : a staff officer serving as legal adviser to a military commander

judge advocate general *noun* (1862)
: the senior legal officer and chief legal adviser in the army, air force, or navy

Judg·es \'jə-jəz\ *noun*
: a narrative and historical book of Jewish and Christian Scripture — see BIBLE table

judg·mat·ic \,jəj-'ma-tik\ *or* **judg·mat·i·cal** \-ti-kəl\ *adjective* [probably irregular from *judgment*] (1826)
: JUDICIOUS
— **judg·mat·i·cal·ly** \-ti-k(ə-)lē\ *adverb*

judg·ment *or* **judge·ment** \'jəj-mənt\ *noun* (13th century)
1 a : a formal utterance of an authoritative opinion **b** : an opinion so pronounced
2 a : a formal decision given by a court **b** (1) : an obligation (as a debt) created by the decree of a court (2) : a certificate evidencing such a decree
3 a *capitalized* : the final judging of mankind by God **b** : a divine sentence or decision; *specifically* : a calamity held to be sent by God
4 a : the process of forming an opinion or evaluation by discerning and comparing **b** : an opinion or estimate so formed
5 a : the capacity for judging : DISCERNMENT **b** : the exercise of this capacity
6 : a proposition stating something believed or asserted
synonym see SENSE

◇ WORD HISTORY
jubilee Ancient Hebrew law established every 50th year as a year of emancipation and restoration. All Hebrew slaves were freed; lands were restored to their former owners; fields were left uncultivated. This year took its name, *yōbhēl,* from the ram's horn trumpets sounded to proclaim its advent. Since neither the Greeks nor the Romans held comparable celebrations, when the Hebrew scriptures were translated into Greek and later into Latin, the Hebrew name for this joyful time was retained. The Greeks simply put *yōbhēl* into Greek form as *iōbēlaios.* Under the influence of the Latin verb *jubilare,* which meant "to let out joyful shouts," *iōbēlaios* became *jubilaeus* in Late Latin. Since its introduction into English, in John Wycliffe's translation of the Bible, *jubilee* has broadened in meaning considerably. It is now used for any 50th anniversary and even for other special anniversaries.

\ə\ abut \ᵊ\ kitten \ər\ further \a\ ash \ā\ ace
\ä\ mop, mar \au̇\ out \ch\ chin \e\ bet \ē\ easy
\g\ go \i\ hit \ī\ ice \j\ job \ŋ\ sing \ō\ go
\ȯ\ law \ȯi\ boy \th\ thin \t͟h\ the \ü\ loot \u̇\ foot
\y\ yet \zh\ vision *see also* Guide to Pronunciation

judg·men·tal \,jəj-'men-t°l\ *adjective* (1909)
1 : of, relating to, or involving judgment
2 : characterized by a tendency to judge harshly
— **judg·men·tal·ly** \-ē\
judgment day *noun* (1591)
1 *J&D capitalized* : the day of God's judgment of mankind at the end of the world according to various theologies
2 : a day of final judgment
ju·di·ca·to·ry \'jü-di-kə-,tōr-ē, -,tór-\ *noun*, *plural* **-ries** (circa 1575)
1 : JUDICIARY 1a
2 : JUDICATURE 2
ju·di·ca·ture \'jü-di-kə-,chùr, -chər, -,tyùr, -,tùr\ *noun* [Middle French, from Medieval Latin *judicatura*, from Latin *judicatus*, past participle of *judicare* (circa 1530)
1 : the action of judging : the administration of justice
2 : a court of justice
3 : JUDICIARY 1
ju·di·cial \jù-'di-shəl\ *adjective* [Middle English, from Latin *judicialis*, from *judicium* judgment, from *judex*] (14th century)
1 a : of or relating to a judgment, the function of judging, the administration of justice, or the judiciary ⟨*judicial* processes⟩ **b** : belonging to the branch of government that is charged with trying all cases that involve the government and with the administration of justice within its jurisdiction — compare EXECUTIVE, LEGISLATIVE
2 : ordered or enforced by a court ⟨*judicial* decisions⟩
3 : of, characterized by, or expressing judgment : CRITICAL 1b
4 : arising from a judgment of God
5 : belonging or appropriate to a judge or the judiciary
— **ju·di·cial·ly** \-'di-sh(ə-)lē\ *adverb*
judicial review *noun* (circa 1924)
1 : REVIEW 5
2 : a constitutional doctrine that gives to a court system the power to annul legislative or executive acts which the judges declare to be unconstitutional
ju·di·cia·ry \jù-'di-shē-,er-ē, -'di-shə-rē\ *noun* [*judiciary*, adjective, from Latin *judiciarius* judicial, from *judicium*] (1787)
1 a : a system of courts of law **b** : the judges of these courts
2 : a branch of government in which judicial power is vested
— **judiciary** *adjective*
ju·di·cious \jù-'di-shəs\ *adjective* (1598)
: having, exercising, or characterized by sound judgment : DISCREET
synonym see WISE
— **ju·di·cious·ly** *adverb*
— **ju·di·cious·ness** *noun*
Ju·dith \'jü-dəth\ *noun* [Late Latin, from Greek *Ioudith*, from Hebrew *Yĕhūdhīth*]
1 : the Jewish heroine who saves the city of Bethulia in the book of Judith
2 : a book of Scripture included in the Roman Catholic canon of the Old Testament and in the Protestant Apocrypha — see BIBLE table
ju·do \'jü-(,)dō\ *noun* [Japanese *jūdō*, from *jū* weakness, gentleness + *dō* art] (1889)
: a sport developed from jujitsu that emphasizes the use of quick movement and leverage to throw an opponent
— **ju·do·ist** \-,ō-ist\ *noun*
¹**jug** \'jəg\ *noun* [perhaps from *Jug*, nickname for *Joan*] (1538)
1 a *chiefly British* : a small pitcher **b** (1) : a large deep usually earthenware or glass container with a narrow mouth and a handle (2) : the contents of such a container : JUGFUL
2 : JAIL, PRISON
²**jug** *transitive verb* **jugged; jug·ging** (1747)
1 : to stew (as a hare) in an earthenware vessel
2 : JAIL, IMPRISON
ju·gate \'jü-,gāt, -gət\ *adjective* [New Latin *jugum* yoke] (circa 1887)

1 : having parts arranged in pairs : PAIRED
2 : having a jugum
jug band *noun* (circa 1933)
: a band that uses primitive or improvised instruments (as jugs, washboards, and kazoos) to play blues, jazz, and folk music
jug·ful \'jəg-,fùl\ *noun* (1831)
1 : as much as a jug will hold
2 : a great deal — used in the phrase *not by a jugful*
jug·ger·naut \'jə-gər-,nòt, -,nät\ *noun* [Hindi *Jagannāth*, literally, lord of the world, title of Vishnu] (1841)
1 *chiefly British* : a large heavy truck
2 : a massive inexorable force, campaign, movement, or object that crushes whatever is in its path ⟨an advertising *juggernaut*⟩ ⟨a political *juggernaut*⟩ ◆
¹**jug·gle** \'jə-gəl\ *verb* **jug·gled; jug·gling** \-g(ə-)lin\ [Middle English *jogelen*, from Middle French *jogler* to joke, from Latin *joculari*, from *joculus*, diminutive of *jocus* joke] (15th century)
intransitive verb
1 : to perform the tricks of a juggler
2 : to engage in manipulation especially in order to achieve a desired end
transitive verb
1 a : to practice deceit or trickery on : BEGUILE
b : to manipulate or rearrange especially in order to achieve a desired end ⟨*juggle* an account to hide a loss⟩
2 a : to toss in the manner of a juggler **b** : to hold or balance precariously
3 : to handle or deal with usually several things (as obligations) at one time so as to satisfy often competing requirements ⟨*juggle* the responsibilities of family life and full-time job —Jane S. Gould⟩
²**juggle** *noun* (1664)
: an act or instance of juggling: **a** : a trick of magic **b** : a show of manual dexterity **c** : an act of manipulation especially to achieve a desired end
jug·gler \'jə-g(ə-)lər\ *noun* [Middle English *jogelour*, from Old English *geogelere* jester, from Old French *jogleour*, from Latin *joculator*, from *joculari*] (14th century)
1 a : one who performs tricks or acts of magic or deftness **b** : one skilled in keeping several objects in motion in the air at the same time by alternately tossing and catching them
2 : one who manipulates especially in order to achieve a desired end
jug·glery \'jə-glə-rē\ *noun* (14th century)
1 : the art or practice of a juggler
2 : manipulation or trickery especially to achieve a desired end
¹**jug·u·lar** \'jə-gyə-lər *also* 'jü- *also* -g(ə-)lər\ *adjective* [Late Latin *jugularis*, from Latin *jugulum* collarbone, throat, from *jugum* yoke] (1597)
1 : of or relating to the throat or neck
2 : of or relating to the jugular vein
²**jugular** *noun* (1615)
1 : JUGULAR VEIN
2 : the most vital or vulnerable part of something ⟨showed an instinct for the *jugular* in competition⟩
jugular vein *noun* (1597)
: any of several veins of each side of the neck that return blood from the head
ju·gum \'jü-gəm\ *noun*, *plural* **ju·ga** \-gə\ *or* **jugums** [New Latin, from Latin, yoke — more at YOKE] (1893)
: the most posterior and basal region of an insect's wing modified in some lepidopterans into a lobe that couples the fore and hind wings during flight
jug wine *noun* (1972)
: table wine sold in large bottles
¹**juice** \'jüs\ *noun* [Middle English *jus*, from Old French, broth, juice, from Latin; akin to Old Norse *ostr* cheese, Greek *zymē* leaven, Sanskrit *yūṣa* broth] (14th century)

1 : the extractable fluid contents of cells or tissues
2 a *plural* : the natural fluids of an animal body **b** : the liquid or moisture contained in something
3 a : the inherent quality of a thing : ESSENCE **b** : STRENGTH, VIGOR, VITALITY
4 : a medium (as electricity or gasoline) that supplies power
5 *slang* : LIQUOR
6 *slang* : exorbitant interest exacted of a borrower under the threat of violence
7 *slang* : INFLUENCE, CLOUT
8 : a motivating, inspiring, or enabling force or factor ⟨creative *juices*⟩
— **juice·less** \'jüs-ləs\ *adjective*
²**juice** *transitive verb* **juiced; juic·ing** (1603)
1 : to add juice to
2 : to extract the juice of
juiced \'jüst\ *adjective* (1592)
1 : containing juice — usually used in combination ⟨precious-*juiced* flowers —Shakespeare⟩
2 : DRUNK 1a
juice·head \'jüs-,hed\ *noun* (1955)
slang : ALCOHOLIC
juic·er \'jü-sər\ *noun* (1938)
1 : an appliance for extracting juice from fruit or vegetables
2 *slang* : a heavy or habitual drinker
juice up *transitive verb* (1955)
: to give life, energy, or spirit to
juicy \'jü-sē\ *adjective* **juic·i·er; -est** (15th century)
1 : having much juice : SUCCULENT
2 : rewarding or profitable especially financially : FAT ⟨*juicy* contract⟩ ⟨a *juicy* dramatic role⟩
3 a : rich in interest : COLORFUL ⟨*juicy* details⟩ **b** : SENSATIONAL, RACY ⟨a *juicy* scandal⟩ **c** : full of vitality : LUSTY
— **juic·i·ly** \-sə-lē\ *adverb*
— **juic·i·ness** \-sē-nəs\ *noun*
ju·jit·su *or* **ju·jut·su** \jü-'jit-(,)sü\ *noun* [Japanese *jūjutsu*, from *jū* weakness, gentleness + *jutsu* art, skill] (1875)
: an art of weaponless fighting employing holds, throws, and paralyzing blows to subdue or disable an opponent
ju·ju \'jü-(,)jü\ *noun* [of West African origin; akin to Hausa *jùju* fetish] (1894)
1 : a fetish, charm, or amulet of West African peoples
2 : the magic attributed to or associated with jujus

◇ **WORD HISTORY**

juggernaut *Jagannātha* (meaning "world-lord" in Sanskrit) is a form of the Hindu deity Krishna worshipped mainly in northeastern India. The god's chief annual festival involves a procession in which his image is mounted on an enormous wooden chariot, about 35 feet square and 45 feet high, which is wheeled from his temple at Puri, in the state of Orissa, to his nearby country house. Accounts by western travelers dating back to the Middle Ages claimed that some of Jagannātha's devotees would allow themselves to be crushed beneath the wheels of the chariot in sacrifice to their god. British officials in the 19th century determined that these reports were greatly exaggerated; occasionally people with painful illnesses or suicidal tendencies would throw themselves in front of the chariot, but most deaths during the celebration resulted accidentally, through the crush of thousands of pilgrims striving to touch the god's vehicle. Despite the spuriousness of the belief, the English form *juggernaut* began to be used in the 19th century to denote a massive, inexorable force or object that crushes everything in its path.

ju·jube \'jü-ˌjüb, *especially for 2* 'jü-jù-ˌbē\ *noun* [Middle English, from Medieval Latin *jujuba,* alteration of Latin *zizyphum,* from Greek *zizyphon*] (14th century)
1 a : an edible drupaceous fruit of any of several trees (genus *Ziziphus*) of the buckthorn family; *especially* **:** one of an Asian tree (*Z. jujuba*) **b :** a tree producing this fruit
2 : a fruit-flavored gumdrop or lozenge

juke \'jük\ *verb* **juked; juk·ing** [probably alteration of English dialect *jouk* to cheat, deceive] (1967)
transitive verb
: to fake out of position (as in football)
intransitive verb
: to juke someone

juke·box \'jük-ˌbäks\ *noun* [*juke* brothel, akin to Gullah *juke* disorderly, of West African origin; akin to Bambara *dzugu* wicked] (1939)
: a coin-operated phonograph or compact-disc player that automatically plays recordings selected from its list

juke joint *noun* (1937)
: a small inexpensive establishment for eating, drinking, or dancing to the music of a jukebox

ju·lep \'jü-ləp\ *noun* [Middle English, from Middle French, from Arabic *julāb,* from Persian *gulāb,* from *gul* rose + *āb* water] (14th century)
1 : a drink consisting of sweet syrup, flavoring, and water
2 : a drink consisting of a liquor (as bourbon or brandy) and sugar poured over crushed ice and garnished with mint

Ju·lian calendar \'jül-yən-\ *noun* [Latin *julianus,* from Gaius *Julius* Caesar] (circa 1771)
: a calendar introduced in Rome in 46 B.C. establishing the 12-month year of 365 days with each fourth year having 366 days and the months each having 31 or 30 days except for February which has 28 or in leap years 29 days — compare GREGORIAN CALENDAR

¹ju·li·enne \ˌjü-lē-'en, ˌzhü-\ *noun* [French, short for *potage à la julienne,* probably from *Julienne* woman's name] (1841)
1 : a consommé containing julienned vegetables
2 a : food (as meat or vegetables) that has been julienned **b :** a preparation or garnish of julienned food ⟨a *julienne* of leeks⟩
— julienne *adjective*

²julienne *transitive verb* **-enned; -en·ning** (circa 1930)
: to slice into thin strips the size of matchsticks ⟨wash and *julienne* the carrots⟩

Ju·liet \'jül-yət; ˌjü-lē-'et, 'jü-lē-ˌ\ *noun*
: the heroine of Shakespeare's tragedy *Romeo and Juliet* who dies for love of Romeo

Ju·li·ett \ˌjü-lē-'et\ [probably irregular from *Juliet*] (1952)
— a communications code word for the letter *j*

Ju·ly \jù-'lī\ *noun* [Middle English *Julie,* from Old English *Julius,* from Latin, from Gaius *Julius* Caesar] (13th century)
: the 7th month of the Gregorian calendar

Ju·ma·da \jù-'ma-də\ *noun* [Arabic *Jumāda*] (1771)
: either of two months of the Islamic year: **a :** the 5th month **b :** the 6th month — see MONTH table

¹jum·ble \'jəm-bəl\ *verb* **jum·bled; jum·bling** \-b(ə-)liŋ\ [perhaps imitative] (circa 1529)
intransitive verb
: to move in a confused or disordered manner
transitive verb
: to mix into a confused or disordered mass — often used with *up*

²jumble *noun* (1661)
1 a : a mass of things mingled together without order or plan **:** HODGEPODGE **b :** a state of confusion
2 *British* **:** articles for a rummage sale

³jumble *noun* [origin unknown] (1615)
: a small thin usually ring-shaped sugared cookie or cake

jumble sale *noun* (1898)
British **:** RUMMAGE SALE

jum·bo \'jəm-(ˌ)bō\ *noun, plural* **jumbos** [*Jumbo,* a huge elephant exhibited by P. T. Barnum] (1883)
: a very large specimen of its kind
— jumbo *adjective*

¹jump \'jəmp\ *verb* [probably akin to Low German *gumpen* to jump] (1530)
intransitive verb
1 a : to spring into the air **:** LEAP; *especially* **:** to spring free from the ground or other base by the muscular action of feet and legs **b :** to move suddenly or involuntarily **:** START **c :** to move over a position occupied by an opponent's piece in a board game often thereby capturing the piece **d :** to undergo a vertical or lateral displacement owing to improper alignment of the film on a projector mechanism **e :** to start out or forward **:** BEGIN — usually used with *off* ⟨*jump* off to a big lead⟩ **f :** to move energetically **:** HUSTLE **g :** to go from one sequence of instructions in a computer program to another ⟨*jump* to a subroutine⟩
2 : COINCIDE, AGREE
3 a : to move haphazardly or irregularly **:** shift abruptly ⟨*jumped* from job to job⟩ **b :** to change or abandon employment especially in violation of contract **c :** to rise suddenly in rank or status **d :** to undergo a sudden sharp change in value ⟨prices *jumped*⟩ **e :** to make a jump in bridge **f :** to make a hurried judgment ⟨*jump* to conclusions⟩ **g :** to show eagerness ⟨*jumped* at the chance⟩ **h :** to enter eagerly ⟨*jump* on the bandwagon⟩
4 : to make a sudden physical or verbal attack ⟨*jumped* on him for his criticism⟩
5 : to bustle with activity ⟨the bar was *jumping* with young people⟩
transitive verb
1 a : to leap over ⟨*jump* a hurdle⟩ **b :** to move over (a piece) in a board game **c :** to act, move, or begin before (as a signal) ⟨*jump* the green light⟩ **d :** to leap aboard ⟨*jump* a freight⟩
2 *obsolete* **:** RISK, HAZARD
3 a : to escape from **:** AVOID **b :** to leave hastily or in violation of contract ⟨*jump* town without paying their bills —Hamilton Basso⟩ **c :** to depart from (a normal course) ⟨*jump* the track⟩
4 a : to make a sudden physical or verbal attack on **b :** to occupy illegally ⟨*jump* a mining claim⟩
5 a (1) **:** to cause to leap (2) **:** to cause (game) to break cover **:** START, FLUSH **b :** to elevate in rank or status **c :** to raise (a bridge partner's bid) by more than one rank **d :** to increase suddenly and sharply
— jump bail : to abscond after being released from prison on bail
— jump ship 1 : to leave the company of a ship without authority **2 :** to desert a cause or party especially abruptly **:** DEFECT
— jump the gun 1 : to start in a race before the starting signal **2 :** to act, move, or begin something before the proper time
— jump the queue *British* **:** to advance directly to or as if to the head of a line

²jump *adverb* (1539)
obsolete **:** EXACTLY, PAT

³jump *noun* (circa 1552)
1 a (1) **:** an act of jumping **:** LEAP (2) **:** any of several sports competitions featuring a leap, spring, or bound (3) **:** a space cleared or covered by a leap (4) **:** an obstacle to be jumped over or from **b :** a sudden involuntary movement **:** START **c :** a move made in a board game by jumping **d :** a transfer from one sequence of instructions in a computer program to a different sequence of instructions ⟨conditional *jump*⟩
2 *obsolete* **:** VENTURE
3 a (1) **:** a sharp sudden increase (2) **:** a bid in bridge of more tricks than are necessary to overcall the preceding bid — compare SHIFT

b : an abrupt change or transition **c** (1) **:** a quick short journey (2) **:** one in a series of moves from one place to another
4 : an advantage at the start ⟨desirous of getting the *jump* on the competition —Elmer Davis⟩

jump ball *noun* (1924)
: a method of putting a basketball into play by tossing it into the air between two opponents who jump up and attempt to tap the ball to a teammate

jump boot *noun* (1942)
: a boot worn especially by paratroopers

jump cut *noun* (1948)
: a sudden often jarring cut from one shot or scene to another without intervening devices (as fade-outs or dissolves); *broadly* **:** an abrupt transition (as in a narrative)
— jump–cut \'jəmp-ˌkət\ *verb*

¹jump·er \'jəm-pər\ *noun* (1611)
1 : a person who jumps
2 a : any of various devices operating with a jumping motion **b :** any of several sleds **c :** a short wire used to close a break or cut out part of a circuit
3 : any of several jumping animals; *especially* **:** a saddle horse trained to jump obstacles
4 : JUMP SHOT

²jum·per \'jəm-pər\ *noun* [probably from English dialect *jump* jumper] (1853)
1 : a loose blouse or jacket worn by workmen
2 : a sleeveless one-piece dress worn usually with a blouse
3 : a child's coverall — usually used in plural
4 *chiefly British* **:** SWEATER 2

jumper cables *noun plural* (circa 1926)
: a pair of heavy-duty electrical cables with alligator clamps used to make a connection for jump-starting a vehicle

jump hook *noun* (1982)
: a hook shot in which the player jumps before releasing the ball

jumping bean *noun* (circa 1889)
: a seed of any of several Mexican shrubs (genera *Sebastiania* and *Sapium*) of the spurge family that tumbles about because of the movements of the larva of a small moth (*Carpocapsa saltitans*) inside it

jumping jack *noun* (1883)
1 : a toy figure of a man jointed and made to jump or dance by means of strings or a sliding stick
2 : a conditioning exercise performed from a standing position by jumping to a position with legs spread and hands touching overhead and then to the original position — called also *side-straddle hop*

jumping mouse *noun* (1826)
: any of several small hibernating North American rodents (family Zapodidae) with long hind legs and tail and no cheek pouches

jumping–off place \ˌjəm-piŋ-'of-\ *noun* (1826)
1 : a remote or isolated place
2 : a place or point from which an enterprise, investigation, or discussion is launched — called also *jumping-off point*

jumping plant louse *noun* (circa 1901)
: any of numerous plant lice (family Psyllidae) with the femurs thickened and adapted for leaping

jumping spider *noun* (1813)
: any of a family (Salticidae) of small spiders that stalk and leap upon their prey

jump jet *noun* (1964)
: a military jet aircraft with vertical takeoff and landing capability

jump-off \'jəm-ˌpof\ *noun* (1917)
1 : the start of a race or an attack

\ə\ abut \ᵊ\ kitten \ər\ further \a\ ash \ā\ ace
\ä\ mop, mar \aù\ out \ch\ chin \e\ bet \ē\ easy
\g\ go \i\ hit \ī\ ice \j\ job \ŋ\ sing \ō\ go
\ò\ law \òi\ boy \th\ thin \t̲h̲\ the \ü\ loot \ù\ foot
\y\ yet \zh\ vision *see also* Guide to Pronunciation

2 : a jumping competition to break a tie at the end of regular competition (as in a horse show)

jump pass *noun* (circa 1948)
: a pass made by a player (as in football or basketball) while jumping

jump rope *noun* (1834)
: a rope used for exercises and children's games that involve jumping over the usually twirling rope each time it reaches its lowest point; *also* **:** a game played with a jump rope

jump seat *noun* (circa 1864)
1 : a movable carriage seat
2 : a folding seat between the front and rear seats of a passenger automobile

jump shot *noun* (1948)
: a shot in basketball made by jumping into the air and releasing the ball with one or both hands at the peak of the jump

jump–start \'jəmp-'stärt\ *transitive verb* (1973)
1 : to start (an engine or vehicle) by temporary connection to an external power source (as another vehicle's battery)
2 a : to get off to a speedy start ⟨advertising can *jump-start* a political campaign⟩ **b :** to impart fresh or renewed energy to **:** ENERGIZE ⟨a plan to *jump-start* the stagnant economy⟩
— jump start *noun*

jump·suit \'jəmp-,süt\ *noun* (1944)
1 : a coverall worn by parachutists for jumping
2 : a one-piece garment consisting of a blouse or shirt with attached trousers or shorts

jumpy \'jəm-pē\ *adjective* **jump·i·er; -est** (1869)
1 : characterized by jumps or sudden variations
2 : NERVOUS, JITTERY
— jump·i·ness *noun*

jun \'jən\ *noun, plural* **jun** [Korean *chŏn*] (1966)
: the chon of North Korea

jun·co \'jəŋ-(,)kō\ *noun, plural* **juncos** *or* **juncoes** [New Latin, from Spanish, reed — more at JONQUIL] (1887)
: any of a genus (*Junco*) of small widely distributed American finches usually having a pink bill, ashy gray head and back, and conspicuous white lateral tail feathers

junc·tion \'jəŋ(k)-shən\ *noun* [Latin *junction-, junctio*, from *jungere* to join — more at YOKE] (1711)
1 : an act of joining **:** the state of being joined
2 a : a place or point of meeting **b :** an intersection of roads especially where one terminates **c :** a point (as in a thermocouple) at which dissimilar metals make contact **d :** an interface in a semiconductor device between regions with different electrical characteristics
3 : something that joins
— junc·tion·al \-shnəl, -shə-n°l\ *adjective*

junc·tur·al \'jəŋ(k)-chə-rəl, 'jəŋ(k)-shrəl\ *adjective* (1942)
: of or relating to phonetic juncture

junc·ture \'jəŋ(k)-chər\ *noun* (14th century)
1 a : JOINT, CONNECTION **b :** the manner of transition or mode of relationship between two consecutive sounds in speech
2 : an instance of joining **:** UNION, JUNCTION
3 : a point of time; *especially* **:** one made critical by a concurrence of circumstances ☆

June \'jün\ *noun* [Middle English, from Middle French & Latin; Middle French *Juin*, from Latin *Junius*] (14th century)
: the 6th month of the Gregorian calendar

June·ber·ry \'jün-,ber-ē\ *noun* (circa 1810)
: SERVICEBERRY

june bug *noun, often J capitalized* (1829)
: any of numerous rather large leaf-eating scarab beetles (subfamily Melolonthinae) that fly chiefly in late spring and have larvae that are white grubs which live in soil and feed chiefly on the roots of grasses and other plants — called also *june beetle*

Jung·ian \'yu̇ŋ-ē-ən\ *adjective* (circa 1930)

: of, relating to, or characteristic of C. G. Jung or his psychological doctrines
— Jungian *noun*

jun·gle \'jəŋ-gəl\ *noun, often attributive* [Hindi *jaṅgal* forest, from Sanskrit *jaṅgala* desert region] (1776)
1 a : an impenetrable thicket or tangled mass of tropical vegetation **b :** a tract overgrown with thickets or masses of vegetation
2 : a hobo camp
3 a (1) **:** a confused or disordered mass of objects **:** JUMBLE (2) **:** something that baffles or frustrates by its tangled or complex character **:** MAZE ⟨the *jungle* of housing laws —Bernard Taper⟩ **b :** a place of ruthless struggle for survival ⟨the city is a *jungle* where no one is safe after dark —Stuart Chase⟩
— jun·gle·like \-gə(l)-,līk\ *adjective*
— jun·gly \-g(ə-)lē\ *adjective*

jun·gled \-gəld\ *adjective* (1842)
: abounding in jungle ⟨a *jungled* island⟩

jungle fowl *noun* (circa 1825)
: any of several Asian wild birds (genus *Gallus*) related to the pheasants; *especially* **:** a bird (*G. gallus*) of southeastern Asia from which domestic fowls have probably descended

jungle gym *noun* [from *Junglegym*, a trademark] (1923)
: a structure of vertical and horizontal bars for use by children at play

¹ju·nior \'jün-yər\ *adjective* [Latin, comparative of *juvenis* young — more at YOUNG] (13th century)
1 a : less advanced in age **:** YOUNGER — used chiefly to distinguish a son with the same given name as his father **b** (1) **:** YOUTHFUL (2) **:** designed for young people and especially adolescents **c :** of more recent date and therefore inferior or subordinate ⟨a *junior* lien⟩
2 a : lower in standing or rank ⟨*junior* partners⟩ **b :** duplicating or suggesting on a smaller scale something typically large or powerful ⟨a *junior* gale⟩
3 : of or relating to juniors or the class of juniors at an educational institution ⟨the *junior* prom⟩

²junior *noun* [Latin, noun & adjective] (1526)
1 a (1) **:** a person who is younger than another ⟨a man six years my *junior*⟩ (2) **:** a male child **:** SON (3) **:** a young person **b :** a clothing size for women and girls with slight figures
2 a : a person holding a lower position in a hierarchy of ranks **b :** a student in the next-to-the-last year before graduating from an educational institution
3 *capitalized* **:** a member of a program of the Girl Scouts for girls in the third through sixth grades in school

ju·nior·ate \'jün-yə-,rāt, -rət\ *noun* (1845)
1 : a course of high school or college study for candidates for the priesthood, brotherhood, or sisterhood; *specifically* **:** one preparatory to the course in philosophy
2 : a seminary for juniorate training

junior college *noun* (1899)
: an educational institution that offers two years of studies corresponding to those in the first two years of a four-year college and that often offers technical, vocational, and liberal studies to the adults of a community

junior high school *noun* (1909)
: a school usually including grades 7 to 9 — called also *junior high*

Junior Leaguer *noun* (1938)
: a member of a league of young women organized for volunteer service to civic and social organizations

junior miss *noun* (1927)
1 : an adolescent girl
2 : JUNIOR 1b

junior varsity *noun* (1949)
: a team composed of members lacking the experience or qualification required for the varsity

ju·ni·per \'jü-nə-pər\ *noun* [Middle English *junipere*, from Latin *juniperus*] (14th century)
1 : any of numerous shrubs or trees (genus *Juniperus*) of the cypress family with leaves resembling needles or scales and female cones usually resembling berries
2 : any of several coniferous trees resembling true junipers

juniper oil *noun* (circa 1889)
: an acrid essential oil obtained from the fruit of a common juniper (*Juniperus communis*) and used especially in gin and liqueurs

juniper tar *noun* (circa 1930)
: a tarry liquid used locally in treating skin diseases and obtained by distillation from the wood of a Eurasian juniper (*Juniperus oxycedrus*) — called also *cade oil, juniper tar oil*

¹junk \'jəŋk\ *noun* [Middle English *jonke*] (14th century)
1 : pieces of old cable or cordage used especially to make gaskets, mats, swabs, or oakum
2 a (1) **:** old iron, glass, paper, or other waste that may be used again in some form (2) **:** secondhand, worn, or discarded articles (3) **:** CLUTTER 1b **b :** something of poor quality **:** TRASH **c :** something of little meaning, worth, or significance
3 *slang* **:** NARCOTICS; *especially* **:** HEROIN
4 : JUNK BOND
5 : baseball pitches other than fastballs (as curveballs or change-ups)
— junky \'jəŋ-kē\ *adjective*

²junk *transitive verb* (1916)
: to get rid of as worthless **:** SCRAP
synonym *see* DISCARD

³junk *noun* [Portuguese *junco*, from Javanese *joṅ*] (1613)
: any of various ships of Chinese waters with bluff lines, a high poop and overhanging stem, little or no keel, high pole masts, and a deep rudder

junk

junk art *noun* (1962)
: three-dimensional art made from discarded material (as metal, mortar, glass, or wood)
— junk artist *noun*

junk bond *noun* (1976)
: a high-risk bond that offers a high yield and is often issued to finance a takeover of a company

junk·er \'jəŋ-kər\ *noun* [¹*junk* + ²-*er*] (1944)
: something (as an automobile) of such age and condition as to be ready for scrapping

☆ **SYNONYMS**
Juncture, exigency, emergency, contingency, pinch, straits, crisis mean a critical or crucial time or state of affairs. JUNCTURE stresses the significant concurrence or convergence of events ⟨an important *juncture* in our country's history⟩. EXIGENCY stresses the pressure of restrictions or urgency of demands created by a special situation ⟨provide for *exigencies*⟩. EMERGENCY applies to a sudden unforeseen situation requiring prompt action to avoid disaster ⟨the presence of mind needed to deal with *emergencies*⟩. CONTINGENCY implies an emergency or exigency that is regarded as possible but uncertain of occurrence ⟨*contingency* plans⟩. PINCH implies urgency or pressure for action to a less intense degree than EXIGENCY or EMERGENCY ⟨come through in a *pinch*⟩. STRAITS applies to a troublesome situation from which escape is extremely difficult ⟨in dire *straits*⟩. CRISIS applies to a juncture whose outcome will make a decisive difference ⟨a *crisis* of confidence⟩.

Jun·ker \'yùŋ-kər\ *noun* [German, from Old High German *junchêrro*, literally, young lord] (1554)
: a member of the Prussian landed aristocracy
— **Jun·ker·dom** \-kər-dəm\ *noun*
— **Jun·ker·ism** \-kə-,ri-zəm\ *noun*

¹**jun·ket** \'jəŋ-kət\ *noun* [Middle English *ioncate*, ultimately from (assumed) Vulgar Latin *juncata*, from Latin *juncus* rush] (15th century)
1 : a dessert of sweetened flavored milk set with rennet
2 a : a festive social affair **b** : TRIP, JOURNEY; *especially* : a trip made by an official at public expense ◆

²**junket** *intransitive verb* (1555)
1 : FEAST, BANQUET
2 : to go on a junket
— **jun·ke·teer** \,jəŋ-kə-'tir\ *or* **jun·ket·er** \'jəŋ-kə-tər\ *noun*

junk food *noun* (1971)
1 : food that is high in calories but low in nutritional content
2 : something that is appealing or enjoyable but of little or no real value ⟨the ultimate in *junk food* for young minds —Cleveland Amory⟩

junk·ie *also* **junky** \'jəŋ-kē\ *noun, plural* **junk·ies** (1923)
1 *slang* **a** : a narcotics peddler or addict **b** : a person who derives inordinate pleasure from or who is dependent on something ⟨sugar *junkie*⟩ ⟨television news *junkie*⟩
2 : a junk dealer

junk mail *noun* (1954)
: third-class mail (as advertising circulars) that is often addressed to "occupant" or "resident"

junk sculpture *noun* (1965)
: JUNK ART

junk·yard \'jəŋk-,yärd\ *noun* (1880)
: a yard used to store sometimes resalable junk

Ju·no \'jü-(,)nō\ *noun*
: the wife of Jupiter, queen of heaven, and goddess of light, birth, women, and marriage
— compare HERA

Ju·no·esque \,jü-(,)nō-'esk\ *adjective* (1888)
: marked by stately beauty

jun·ta \'hùn-tə, 'jən-, 'hən-\ *noun* [Spanish, from feminine of *junto* joined, from Latin *junctus*, past participle of *jungere* to join — more at YOKE] (1622)
1 : a council or committee for political or governmental purposes; *especially* : a group of persons controlling a government especially after a revolutionary seizure of power
2 : JUNTO

jun·to \'jən-(,)tō\ *noun, plural* **juntos** [probably alteration of *junta*] (1623)
: a group of persons joined for a common purpose

Ju·pi·ter \'jü-pə-tər\ *noun* [Latin]
1 : the chief Roman god, husband of Juno, and god of light, of the sky and weather, and of the state and its welfare and its laws — compare ZEUS
2 : the largest of the planets and fifth in order from the sun — see PLANET table

ju·ral \'jùr-əl\ *adjective* [Latin *jur-, jus* law] (1635)
1 : of or relating to law
2 : of or relating to rights or obligations
— **ju·ral·ly** \-ə-lē\ *adverb*

Ju·ras·sic \jù-'ra-sik\ *adjective* [French *jurassique*, from *Jura* mountain range] (1831)
: of, relating to, or being the period of the Mesozoic era between the Triassic and the Cretaceous or the corresponding system of rocks marked by the presence of dinosaurs and the first appearance of birds — see GEOLOGIC TIME table
— **Jurassic** *noun*

ju·rat \'jùr-,at\ *noun* [short for Latin *juratum* (*est*) it has been sworn, 3d singular perfect passive of *jurare* to swear — more at JURY] (1796)

: a certificate added to an affidavit stating when, before whom, and where it was made

ju·rel \hü-'rel\ *noun* [Spanish] (1772)
: any of several food fishes (family Carangidae) of warm seas

ju·rid·i·cal \jù-'ri-di-kəl\ *also* **ju·rid·ic** \-dik\ *adjective* [Latin *juridicus*, from *jur-, jus* + *dicere* to say — more at DICTION] (1502)
1 : of or relating to the administration of justice or the office of a judge
2 : of or relating to law or jurisprudence : LEGAL
— **ju·rid·i·cal·ly** \-di-k(ə-)lē\ *adverb*

ju·ris·con·sult \,jùr-əs-'kän-,səlt, -kən-'\ *noun* [Latin *jurisconsultus*, from *juris* (genitive of *jus*) + *consultus*, past participle of *consulere* to consult] (1605)
: JURIST; *especially* : one learned in international and public law

ju·ris·dic·tion \,jùr-əs-'dik-shən\ *noun* [Middle English *jurisdiccioun*, from Middle French & Latin; Middle French *juridiction*, from Latin *jurisdiction-, jurisdictio*, from *juris* + *diction-, dictio* act of saying — more at DICTION] (14th century)
1 : the power, right, or authority to interpret and apply the law
2 a : the authority of a sovereign power to govern or legislate **b** : the power or right to exercise authority : CONTROL
3 : the limits or territory within which authority may be exercised
synonym see POWER
— **ju·ris·dic·tion·al** \-shnəl, -shə-n°l\ *adjective*
— **ju·ris·dic·tion·al·ly** *adverb*

Ju·ris Doctor \'jùr-əs-\ *noun* [Latin, doctor of law] (1969)
: a degree equivalent to bachelor of laws

ju·ris·pru·dence \,jùr-əs-'prü-d°n(t)s\ *noun* (circa 1656)
1 a : a system or body of law **b** : the course of court decisions
2 : the science or philosophy of law
3 : a department of law ⟨medical *jurisprudence*⟩
— **ju·ris·pru·den·tial** \-prü-'den(t)-shəl\ *adjective*
— **ju·ris·pru·den·tial·ly** \-'den(t)-sh(ə-)lē\ *adverb*

ju·ris·pru·dent \-'prü-d°nt\ *noun* [Late Latin *jurisprudent-, jurisprudens*, from Latin *juris* + *prudent-, prudens* skilled, prudent] (1628)
: JURIST

ju·rist \'jùr-ist\ *noun* [Middle French *juriste*, from Medieval Latin *jurista*, from Latin *jur-, jus*] (15th century)
: one having a thorough knowledge of law; *especially* : JUDGE

ju·ris·tic \jù-'ris-tik\ *adjective* (1831)
1 : of or relating to a jurist or jurisprudence
2 : of, relating to, or recognized in law
— **ju·ris·ti·cal·ly** \-ti-k(ə-)lē\ *adverb*

ju·ror \'jùr-ər, 'jùr-,òr\ *noun* (14th century)
1 a : a member of a jury **b** : a person summoned to serve on a jury
2 : a person who takes an oath (as of allegiance)

¹**ju·ry** \'jùr-ē\ *noun, plural* **juries** [Middle English *jure*, from Anglo-French *juree*, from Old French *jurer* to swear, from Latin *jurare*, from *jur-, jus*] (15th century)
1 : a body of persons sworn to give a verdict on some matter submitted to them; *especially* : a body of persons legally selected and sworn to inquire into any matter of fact and to give their verdict according to the evidence
2 : a committee for judging and awarding prizes at a contest or exhibition
3 : one (as the public or test results) that will decide — used especially in the phrase *the jury is still out*

²**jury** *adjective* [origin unknown] (1616)
: improvised for temporary use especially in an emergency : MAKESHIFT ⟨a *jury* mast⟩ ⟨a *jury* rig⟩

³**jury** *transitive verb* **jur·ied; jury·ing** (1947)
: to select material as appropriate for exhibition in (as an art show) — used chiefly as a participle ⟨a *juried* show⟩

ju·ry-rig \'jùr-ē-,rig, -'rig\ *transitive verb* [²*jury*] (1788)
: to erect, construct, or arrange in a makeshift fashion

jus gen·ti·um \'yüs-'gen-tē-əm\ *noun* [Latin, law of nations] (1548)
: INTERNATIONAL LAW

jus san·gui·nis \-'säŋ-gwə-nəs\ *noun* [Latin, right of blood] (1902)
: a rule that a child's citizenship is determined by its parents' citizenship

jus·sive \'jə-siv\ *noun* [Latin *jussus*, past participle of *jubēre* to order; akin to Greek *hysminē* battle] (1846)
: a word, form, case, or mood expressing command
— **jussive** *adjective*

jus so·li \'yüs-'sō-,lē\ *noun* [Latin, right of the soil] (1902)
: a rule that the citizenship of a child is determined by the place of its birth

¹**just** \'jəst, 'jüst\ *variant of* JOUST

²**just** \'jəst\ *adjective* [Middle English, from Middle French & Latin; Middle French *juste*, from Latin *justus*, from *jus* right, law; akin to Sanskrit *yos* welfare] (14th century)
1 a : having a basis in or conforming to fact or reason : REASONABLE ⟨a *just* but not a generous decision⟩ **b** *archaic* : faithful to an original **c** : conforming to a standard of correctness : PROPER ⟨*just* proportions⟩
2 a (1) : acting or being in conformity with what is morally upright or good : RIGHTEOUS ⟨a *just* war⟩ (2) : being what is merited : DESERVED ⟨a *just* punishment⟩ **b** : legally correct : LAWFUL ⟨*just* title to an estate⟩
synonym see FAIR, UPRIGHT
— **just·ly** *adverb*
— **just·ness** \'jəs(t)-nəs\ *noun*

³**just** \'jəst, 'jist, 'jest *also without* t\ *adverb* (15th century)
1 a : EXACTLY, PRECISELY ⟨*just* right⟩ **b** : very recently ⟨the bell *just* rang⟩
2 a : by a very small margin : BARELY ⟨*just* too late⟩ **b** : IMMEDIATELY, DIRECTLY ⟨*just* west of here⟩

◇ WORD HISTORY
junket *Juncus* is the Latin word for "rush." The stems of that marsh plant have long been the source of plaiting for mats and baskets. French inherited *juncus* as *jonc*, and derivatives of *jonc* in the medieval French of Normandy came to denote rush baskets, as well as soft, unripened cheeses made in such baskets. One such derivative is presumed to be the source of Middle English *ioncate* (with the suffix perhaps influenced by Medieval Latin *juncata*), a name for a sweetened dish of curds and cream; in the form *junket* this word is still applied to desserts made from sweetened milk or cream. Back in the 16th century, however, we find that *junket* embarked on a long semantic journey away from desserts. Its meaning was extended from any sweet dish to a feast or banquet that presumably featured such dishes, and then to any banquet, a usage that lasted at least into the 19th century. In the U.S. *junket* became a picnic or pleasure trip, and by the later 19th century the word had entered the political vocabulary as a derogatory expression for a politician's trip at taxpayers' expense.

3 a : ONLY, SIMPLY 〈*just* last year〉 〈*just* be yourself〉 **b :** QUITE, VERY 〈*just* wonderful〉 **4 :** PERHAPS, POSSIBLY 〈it *just* might work〉
— **just about :** ALMOST 〈the work is *just about* done〉

just-folks \'jəs(t)-'fōks\ *adjective* (1952)
: marked by the absence of formality or sophistication **:** UNPRETENTIOUS 〈her *just-folks* manner〉

jus·tice \'jəs-təs\ *noun* [Middle English, from Old English & Old French; Old English *justice,* from Old French *justice,* from Latin *justitia,* from *justus*] (12th century)
1 a : the maintenance or administration of what is just especially by the impartial adjustment of conflicting claims or the assignment of merited rewards or punishments **b :** JUDGE **c :** the administration of law; *especially* **:** the establishment or determination of rights according to the rules of law or equity
2 a : the quality of being just, impartial, or fair **b** (1) **:** the principle or ideal of just dealing or right action (2) **:** conformity to this principle or ideal **:** RIGHTEOUSNESS **c :** the quality of conforming to law
3 : conformity to truth, fact, or reason **:** CORRECTNESS

justice of the peace (15th century)
: a local magistrate empowered chiefly to administer summary justice in minor cases, to commit for trial, and to administer oaths and perform marriages

jus·ti·cia·ble \ˌjə-'sti-sh(ē-)ə-bəl\ *adjective* (15th century)
1 : liable to trial in a court of justice 〈a *justiciable* offense〉
2 : capable of being decided by legal principles or by a court of justice
— **jus·ti·cia·bil·i·ty** \ˌjə-ˌsti-sh(ē-)ə-'bi-lə-tē\ *noun*

jus·ti·ci·ar \jə-'sti-shē-ər, -ˌär\ *noun* [Middle English, from Medieval Latin *justitiarius,* from Latin *justitia*] (1580)
: the chief political and judicial officer of the Norman and later kings of England until the 13th century

jus·ti·fi·able \'jəs-tə-ˌfī-ə-bəl\ *adjective* (1561)
: capable of being justified **:** EXCUSABLE 〈*justifiable* family pride —*Current Biography*〉
— **jus·ti·fi·abil·i·ty** \ˌjəs-tə-ˌfī-ə-'bi-lə-tē\ *noun*
— **jus·ti·fi·ably** \'jəs-tə-ˌfī-ə-blē\ *adverb*

jus·ti·fi·ca·tion \ˌjəs-tə-fə-'kā-shən\ *noun* (14th century)
1 : the act, process, or state of being justified by God
2 a : the act or an instance of justifying **:** VINDICATION **b :** something that justifies
3 : the process or result of justifying lines of text

jus·ti·fi·ca·tive \'jəs-tə-fə-ˌkā-tiv\ *adjective* (1611)
: JUSTIFICATORY

jus·ti·fi·ca·to·ry \ˌjəs-'ti-fi-kə-ˌtōr-ē, -ˌtȯr-; 'jəs-tə-fə-ˌkā-tə-rē\ *adjective* (1579)

: tending or serving to justify **:** VINDICATORY

jus·ti·fy \'jəs-tə-ˌfī\ *verb* **-fied; -fy·ing** [Middle English *justifien,* from Middle French or Late Latin; Middle French *justifier,* from Late Latin *justificare,* from Latin *justus*] (14th century)
transitive verb
1 a : to prove or show to be just, right, or reasonable **b** (1) **:** to show to have had a sufficient legal reason (2) **:** to qualify (oneself) as a surety by taking oath to the ownership of sufficient property
2 a *archaic* **:** to administer justice to **b** *archaic* **:** ABSOLVE **c :** to judge, regard, or treat as righteous and worthy of salvation
3 : to space (as lines of text) so that the lines come out even at the margin **b :** to make even by justifying 〈*justified* margins〉
intransitive verb
1 a : to show a sufficient lawful reason for an act done **b :** to qualify as bail or surety
2 : to justify lines of text
synonym see MAINTAIN
— **jus·ti·fi·er** \-ˌfī(-ə)r\ *noun*

just–in–time *noun, often attributive* (1981)
: a manufacturing strategy wherein parts are produced or delivered only as needed

¹**jut** \'jət\ *verb* **jut·ted; jut·ting** [perhaps short for ²*jutty*] (circa 1573)
intransitive verb
: to extend out, up, or forward **:** PROJECT 〈mountains *jutting* into the sky〉 〈a *jutting* jaw〉
transitive verb
: to cause to project

²**jut** *noun* (1786)
: something that juts **:** PROJECTION

jute \'jüt\ *noun* [Bengali *jhuṭo*] (1746)
: the glossy fiber of either of two East Indian plants (*Corchorus olitorius* and *C. capsularis*) of the linden family used chiefly for sacking, burlap, and twine; *also* **:** a plant producing jute

Jute \'jüt\ *noun* [Middle English, from Medieval Latin *Jutae* Jutes, of Germanic origin; akin to Old English *Eotenas* Jutes] (14th century)
: a member of a Germanic people invading England from the Continent and settling in Kent in the 5th century
— **Jut·ish** \'jü-tish\ *adjective*

¹**jut·ty** \'jə-tē\ *noun, plural* **jutties** [Middle English] (15th century)
1 *archaic* **:** JETTY
2 : a projecting part of a building

²**jutty** *transitive verb* **jut·tied; jut·ty·ing** (1599)
obsolete **:** to project beyond

ju·ve·nes·cence \ˌjü-və-'ne-sᵊn(t)s\ *noun* (1800)
: the state of being youthful or of growing young
— **ju·ve·nes·cent** \-sᵊnt\ *adjective*

¹**ju·ve·nile** \'jü-və-ˌnīl, -nᵊl\ *adjective* [French or Latin; French *juvénile,* from Latin *juvenilis,* from *juvenis* young person — more at YOUNG] (1625)

1 a : physiologically immature or undeveloped **:** YOUNG **b :** derived from sources within the earth and coming to the surface for the first time — used especially of water and gas
2 : of, relating to, characteristic of, or suitable for children or young people 〈*juvenile* books〉
3 : reflecting psychological or intellectual immaturity **:** CHILDISH

²**juvenile** *noun* (1733)
1 a : a young person **:** YOUTH **b :** a book for children or young people
2 : a young individual resembling an adult of its kind except in size and reproductive activity: as **a :** a fledged bird not yet in adult plumage **b :** a 2-year-old racehorse
3 : an actor or actress who plays youthful parts

juvenile court *noun* (1899)
: a court that has special jurisdiction over delinquent and dependent children usually up to the age of 18

juvenile delinquency *noun* (1816)
1 : conduct by a juvenile characterized by antisocial behavior that is beyond parental control and therefore subject to legal action
2 : a violation of the law committed by a juvenile and not punishable by death or life imprisonment
— **juvenile delinquent** *noun*

juvenile hormone *noun* (1940)
: an insect hormone that is secreted by the corpora allata, inhibits maturation to the imago, and plays a role in reproduction

juvenile officer *noun* (1954)
: a police officer charged with the detection, prosecution, and care of juvenile delinquents

ju·ve·nil·ia \ˌjü-və-'ni-lē-ə\ *noun plural* [Latin, neuter plural of *juvenilis*] (1622)
1 : compositions produced in the artist's or author's youth
2 : artistic or literary compositions suited to or designed for the young

ju·ve·nil·i·ty \ˌjü-və-'ni-lə-tē\ *noun, plural* **-ties** (circa 1623)
1 : the quality or state of being juvenile **:** YOUTHFULNESS
2 a : immaturity of thought or conduct **b :** an instance of being juvenile

jux·ta·pose \'jək-stə-ˌpōz\ *transitive verb* **-posed; -pos·ing** [probably back-formation from *juxtaposition*] (1851)
: to place side by side 〈*juxtapose* unexpected combinations of colors, shapes and ideas —J. F. T. Bugental〉

juxtaposed *adjective* (1855)
: placed side by side **:** being in juxtaposition
synonym see ADJACENT

jux·ta·po·si·tion \ˌjək-stə-pə-'zi-shən\ *noun* [Latin *juxta* near + English *position* — more at JOUST] (1654)
: the act or an instance of placing two or more things side by side; *also* **:** the state of being so placed
— **jux·ta·po·si·tion·al** \-'zish-nəl, -'zi-shə-nᵊl\ *adjective*

K *is the eleventh letter of the English alphabet. It came through Latin, via Etruscan, from Greek, where it was called* kappa; *Greek took it from the Phoenician* kaph. *In all these languages* k *represented practically the same sound as in English, but in Latin, the Romance languages, and Old English it was largely replaced by* c. *Eventually, however, the phonetic ambiguity of that letter, which stood for both the* g *and* k *sounds in Latin and presented other problems of interpretation in Romance and Old English, led to the revival of the old letter for the sound* k. *This is true in English especially before* e *and* i *(as in* kine, *plural for* cow), *before* n *(as in* knife, *from Old English* cnīf), *and more recently in loan words from many sources (such as* kugel *from German,* karaoke *from Japanese, and* Koran *from Arabic). In many words (for example,* knead, knight, *and* know) k *has become silent before* n, *though once it was pronounced. It is frequent also after short vowels in the combination* ck, *which is pronounced like simple* k, *as in* black. *The small form of* k *developed through a downsizing of the capital form.*

k \'kā\ *noun, plural* **k's** *or* **ks** \'kāz\ *often capitalized, often attributive* (before 12th century) **1 a :** the 11th letter of the English alphabet **b :** a graphic representation of this letter **c :** a speech counterpart of orthographic *k* **2 :** a graphic device for reproducing the letter *k* **3 :** one designated *k* especially as the 11th in order or class **4 :** something shaped like the letter K **5 :** a unit vector parallel to the z-axis **6** [*kilo-*] **:** THOUSAND ⟨a salary of $24*K*⟩ **7** [*kilo-*] **:** a unit of computer storage capacity equal to 1024 bytes ⟨a computer memory of 64*K*⟩ **8** *capitalized* **:** STRIKEOUT

Kaa·ba \'kä-bə\ *noun* [Arabic *ka'bah*, literally, cubic building] (1734) **:** a small stone building in the court of the Great Mosque at Mecca that contains a sacred black stone and is the goal of Islamic pilgrimage and the point toward which Muslims turn in praying

ka·ba·la *or* **kab·ba·la** *or* **kab·ba·lah** *variant of* CABALA

ka·bob \kə-'bäb *also* 'kā-,\ *noun* [Persian, Hindi, Arabic & Turkish; Persian & Hindi *kabāb*, from Arabic, from Turkish *kebap*] (1673) **:** cubes of meat (as lamb or beef) marinated and cooked with vegetables (as onions, tomatoes, and green peppers) usually on a skewer

Ka·bu·ki \kə-'bü-kē, 'kä-bù-(,)kē\ *noun* [Japanese] (1899) **:** traditional Japanese popular drama with singing and dancing performed in a highly stylized manner

Ka·byle \kə-'bī(ə)l\ *noun* [Arabic *qabā'il*, plural of *qabīlah* tribe] (1738) **1 :** a member of a Berber people living in the mountainous coastal area east of Algiers **2 :** the Berber language of the Kabyles

ka·chi·na \kə-'chē-nə\ *noun* [Hopi *qacína*] (1888) **1 :** one of the deified ancestral spirits believed among the Hopi and other Pueblo Indians to visit the pueblos at intervals **2 :** one of the elaborately masked kachina impersonators that dance at agricultural ceremonies **3 :** a doll representing a kachina

kad·dish \'kä-dish\ *noun, often capitalized* [Aramaic *qaddish* holy] (1613) **:** a Jewish prayer recited in the daily ritual of the synagogue and by mourners at public services after the death of a close relative

kaf·fee·klatsch \'kò-fē-,klach, 'kä-,fē-, -,kläch, -,klòch\ *noun, often capitalized* [German, from *Kaffee* coffee + *Klatsch* gossip] (1888) **:** an informal social gathering for coffee and conversation

Kaf·fir *or* **Kaf·ir** \'ka-fər\ *noun* [Arabic *kāfir* infidel] (1778) **1** *archaic* **:** a member of a group of southern African Bantu-speaking peoples **2** *often not capitalized, chiefly South African* **:** a black African — usually used disparagingly

kaf·fi·yeh \kə-'fē-ə\ *noun* [Arabic *kūfīyah, kaffīyah*, from al-*Kufah* Al Kufa, town in Iraq] (circa 1817) **:** an Arab headdress consisting of a square of cloth folded to form a triangle and held on by a cord

kaf·ir \'ka-fər\ *noun* (circa 1785) **:** a grain sorghum (*Sorghum caffrorum*) with stout short-jointed somewhat juicy stalks and erect heads

Kaf·ir \'ka-fər\ *noun* [Arabic *kāfir*] (1759) **:** a member of a group of peoples of the Hindu Kush in northeastern Afghanistan

Kaf·iri \'ka-fə-rē\ *noun* (1901) **:** the group of languages spoken by the Kafirs that constitutes a distinct branch of Indo-Iranian — see INDO-EUROPEAN LANGUAGES table

Kaf·ka·esque \,käf-kə-'esk, ,kaf-\ *adjective* (1946) **:** of, relating to, or suggestive of Franz Kafka or his writings; *especially* **:** having a nightmarishly complex, bizarre, or illogical quality ⟨*Kafkaesque* bureaucratic delays⟩

kaf·tan *variant of* CAFTAN

ka·hu·na \kə-'hü-nə\ *noun* [Hawaiian] (1886) **:** a Hawaiian witch doctor

kai·nite \'kī-,nīt, 'kā-\ *also* **kai·nit** \kī-'nēt\ *noun* [German *Kainit*, from Greek *kainos* new — more at RECENT] (1868) **:** a natural salt KMg(SO₄)Cl·3H₂O consisting of a hydrous sulfate and chloride of magnesium and potassium that is used as a fertilizer and as a source of potassium and magnesium compounds

kai·ser \'kī-zər\ *noun* [Middle English, from Old Norse *keisari*; akin to Old High German *keisur* emperor; both from a prehistoric Germanic word borrowed from Latin *Caesar*, cognomen of the Emperor Augustus] (13th century) **:** EMPEROR; *especially* **:** the ruler of Germany from 1871 to 1918 ◆

— **kai·ser·dom** \-zər-dəm\ *noun*

— **kai·ser·ism** \-zə-,ri-zəm\ *noun*

kai·se·rin \'kī-zə-rən\ *noun* [German, feminine of *Kaiser*] (circa 1888) **:** the wife of a kaiser

kaiser roll *noun* (circa 1898) **:** a crusty roll often used for sandwiches

ka·ka \'kä-kə\ *noun* [Maori] (circa 1774) **:** an olive brown New Zealand parrot (*Nestor meridionalis*) with gray and red markings

ka·ka·po \,kä-kə-'pō\ *noun, plural* **-pos** [Maori] (1843) **:** a large chiefly nocturnal burrowing New Zealand parrot (*Strigops habroptilus*) that has green and brown barred plumage and well-developed wings with little power of flight

ka·ke·mo·no \,kä-ki-'mō-(,)nō\ *noun, plural* **-nos** [Japanese] (1890) **:** a vertical Japanese ornamental pictorial or calligraphic scroll

ka·ki·e·mon \,kä-kē-'ā-,män\ *noun, often capitalized* [Sakaida *Kakiemon* (flourished 1650) Japanese potter] (1890) **:** a Japanese porcelain decorated with enamel

ka·la-azar \,kä-lə-ə-'zär, ,ka-\ *noun* [Hindi *kālā-āzār* black disease, from Hindi *kālā* black + Persian *āzār* disease] (1882) **:** a severe infectious disease chiefly of tropical areas that is marked by fever, progressive anemia, leukopenia, and enlargement of the spleen and liver and caused by a flagellate (*Leishmania donovani*) transmitted by the bite of sand flies

ka·lan·choe \,ka-lən-'kō-ē *also* kə-'laŋ-kə-(,)wē *or* 'ka-lən-,chō\ *noun* [New Latin] (1830) **:** any of a genus (*Kalanchoe*) of chiefly African tropical succulent herbs or shrubs of the orpine family that are cultivated as ornamentals — compare BRYOPHYLLUM

kale \'kā(ə)l\ *noun* [Scots, from Middle English (northern) *cal*, from Old English *cāl* — more at COLE] (14th century) **1 a :** COLE **b :** a hardy cabbage (*Brassica oleracea acephala*) with curled often finely incised leaves that do not form a dense head **2** *slang* **:** MONEY

◇ WORD HISTORY

kaiser Augustus, the man whom history regards as the first Roman emperor, was born Gaius Octavius; but when he was adopted by his great uncle Julius Caesar in the latter's will, he took the new name Gaius Julius Caesar Octavianus. Subsequent Roman emperors preserved *Caesar* as part of their full name, and the word was used generically in Latin with the meaning "emperor." Several early Germanic languages borrowed the word in this sense. Old English *cāsere* passed into Old Scots and northern dialects of Middle English as *casere* or *kasere*, but this word was displaced in Middle English and early Modern English by forms such as *cayser* and *keyser*, borrowed from Old Norse *keisari*. Although the latter words were occasionally resurrected by later authors as deliberate archaisms, Modern English *kaiser* is borrowed from Modern German *Kaiser*, used to denote the Holy Roman Emperor and (after the demise of the Holy Roman Empire in 1806) his successor, the emperor of Austria. *Kaiser* is most closely associated in English with the three emperors of Germany's Second Reich (1871–1918). Since the abdication of the Austrian and German emperors at the end of World War I, *kaiser* has become purely a historical term.

\ə\ abut \ᵊ\ kitten \ər\ **further** \a\ ash \ā\ ace \ä\ mop, mar \aù\ out \ch\ chin \e\ bet \ē\ easy \g\ go \i\ hit \ī\ ice \j\ job \ŋ\ sing \ō\ go \ò\ law \òi\ boy \th\ thin \th\ the \ü\ loot \ù\ foot \y\ yet \zh\ vision *see also* Guide to Pronunciation

ka·lei·do·scope \kə-'lī-də-ˌskōp\ *noun* [Greek *kalos* beautiful + *eidos* form + English *-scope* — more at IDYLL] (1817)
1 : an instrument containing loose bits of colored material (as glass or plastic) between two flat plates and two plane mirrors so placed that changes of position of the bits of material are reflected in an endless variety of patterns
2 : something resembling a kaleidoscope: as **a :** a variegated changing pattern or scene ⟨the lake a *kaleidoscope* of changing colors — Robert Gibbings⟩ **b :** a succession of changing phases or actions ⟨a . . . *kaleidoscope* of shifting values, information, fashions —Frank McLaughlin⟩
— **ka·lei·do·scop·ic** \-ˌlī-də-'skä-pik\ *adjective*
— **ka·lei·do·scop·i·cal·ly** \-pi-k(ə-)lē\ *adverb*
ka·lends *variant of* CALENDS
kal·li·din \'ka-lə-dən\ *noun* [German, from *Kalli*krein + Pept*id* peptide + *-in*] (1950)
: either of two vasodilator kinins formed from blood plasma globulin by the action of kallikrein: **a :** BRADYKININ **b :** one with a terminal lysine amino-acid residue added to bradykinin
kal·li·kre·in \ˌka-lə-'krē-ən, kə-'li-krē-ən\ *noun* [German, from Greek *kallikreas* sweetbread, pancreas, from *kalli-* beautiful (from *kallos* beauty) + *kreas* flesh — more at RAW] (1930)
: a hypotensive protease that liberates kinins from blood plasma proteins and is used therapeutically for vasodilation
Kal·muck *or* **Kal·muk** \'kal-ˌmək, kal-'\ *or* **Kal·myk** \kal-'mik\ *noun* [Russian *kalmyk*, from Volga Tatar *kalmïk*] (1613)
1 : a member of a Buddhist Mongol people originally of Dzungaria living mainly northwest of the Caspian Sea in Russia
2 : the Mongolian language of the Kalmucks
Ka·ma \'kä-mə\ *noun* [Sanskrit *Kāma*, from *kāma* love]
: the Hindu god of love
ka·ma·ai·na \ˌkä-mə-'ī-nə\ *noun* [Hawaiian *kama'āina*, from *kama* child + *'āina* land] (1903)
: one who has lived in Hawaii for a long time
kame \'kām\ *noun* [Scots, name, comb, from Middle English (northern) *camb* comb, from Old English] (1795)
: a short ridge, hill, or mound of stratified drift deposited by glacial meltwater
Ka·me·ha·me·ha Day \kə-ˌmā-ə-'mā-(ˌ)hä-\ *noun* (1925)
: June 11 observed as a holiday in Hawaii in commemoration of the birthday of Kamehameha I
¹ka·mi·ka·ze \ˌkä-mi-'kä-zē\ *noun* [Japanese, literally, divine wind] (1945)
1 : a member of a Japanese air attack corps in World War II assigned to make a suicidal crash on a target (as a ship)
2 : an airplane containing explosives to be flown in a suicide crash on a target ◇
²kamikaze *adjective* (1945)
1 : of, relating to, being, or resembling a kamikaze
2 : having or showing reckless disregard for safety or personal welfare
kam·pong \'käm-ˌpȯŋ, 'kam-\ *noun* [Malay] (1844)
: a hamlet or village in a Malay-speaking country
ka·na \'kä-nə\ *noun, plural* **kana** *often attributive* [Japanese] (1727)
: a Japanese system of syllabic writing having characters that can be used exclusively for writing foreign words or in combination with kanji (as for indicating pronunciations or grammatical inflections); *also* **:** a single character belonging to the kana system — compare HIRAGANA, KATAKANA
Ka·nak \kə-'näk, -'nak\ *noun* [French *canaque*, probably from English *Kanaka* South Sea islander, from Hawaiian *person*] (1910)
: a native Melanesian inhabitant of New Caledonia
kana·my·cin \ˌka-nə-'mī-sᵊn\ *noun* [New Latin *kanamyceticus*, specific epithet of *Streptomyces kanamyceticus*] (1957)
: a broad-spectrum antibiotic from a Japanese soil streptomyces (*Streptomyces kanamyceticus*)
Kan·a·rese \ˌka-nə-'rēz, -'rēs\ *noun, plural* **Kanarese** [*Kanara*, India] (1847)
1 : KANNADA
2 : a member of a Kannada-speaking people of Karnataka, southern India
kan·ban \'kän-ˌbän\ *noun, often attributive* [Japanese, sign, placard; from the cards used on assembly lines to signal that parts are needed] (1982)
: JUST-IN-TIME
kan·ga·roo \ˌkaŋ-gə-'rü\ *noun, plural* **-roos** [Guugu Yimidhirr (Australian aboriginal language of northern Queensland) *gaŋurru*] (1770)
: any of various herbivorous leaping marsupial mammals (family Macropodidae) of Australia, New Guinea, and adjacent islands with a small head, large ears, long powerful hind legs, a long thick tail used as a support and in balancing, and rather small forelegs not used in progression ◇

kangaroo

kangaroo court *noun* (1853)
1 : a mock court in which the principles of law and justice are disregarded or perverted
2 : a court characterized by irresponsible, unauthorized, or irregular status or procedures
3 : judgment or punishment given outside of legal procedure
kangaroo rat *noun* (1867)
: any of a genus (*Dipodomys*) of pouched nocturnal burrowing rodents of arid parts of the western U.S. and Mexico
kan·ji \'kän-(ˌ)jē\ *noun, plural* **kanji** *often attributive* [Japanese] (1920)
: a Japanese system of writing that utilizes characters borrowed or adapted from Chinese writing; *also* **:** a single character belonging to the kanji system — compare KANA

kangaroo rat

Kan·na·da \'kä-nə-də *also* 'ka-\ *noun* [Kannada *kannaḍa*] (1856)
: the major Dravidian language of Karnataka, southern India
kan·te·le \'kän-tə-lə\ *noun* [Finnish] (circa 1903)
: a traditional Finnish zither originally having five strings but now having as many as thirty
ka·o·lin \'kā-ə-lən\ *noun* [French *kaolin*, from *Gaoling* hill in China] (circa 1741)
: a fine usually white clay that is used in ceramics and refractories, as a filler or extender, and in medicine especially as an adsorbent in the treatment of diarrhea
— **ka·o·lin·ite** \-lə-ˌnīt\ *noun* (1867)
: a mineral consisting of a hydrous silicate of aluminum that constitutes the principal mineral in kaolin
— **ka·o·lin·it·ic** \ˌkā-ə-lə-'ni-tik\ *adjective*
ka·on \'kā-ˌän\ *noun* [International Scientific Vocabulary *ka* kay (from *K-meson*, its earlier name) + ²-*on*] (1958)
: an unstable meson that occurs in both charged and neutral forms and is about 970 times more massive than an electron
ka·pell·mei·ster \kə-'pel-ˌmī-stər, kä-\ *noun, often capitalized* [German, from *Kapelle* choir + *Meister* master] (1838)
: the director of a choir or orchestra

kaph \'käf, 'kȯf\ *noun* [Hebrew, literally, palm of the hand] (circa 1823)
: the 11th letter of the Hebrew alphabet — see ALPHABET table
ka·pok \'kā-ˌpäk\ *noun* [Malay] (circa 1750)
: a mass of silky fibers that clothe the seeds of the ceiba tree and are used especially as a filling for mattresses, life preservers, and sleeping bags and as insulation
Ka·po·si's sarcoma \'ka-pə-sēz- *also* -shēz-, kə-'pō-sēz-\ *noun* [Moritz *Kaposi* (died 1902) Hungarian dermatologist] (1916)
: a neoplastic disease associated especially with AIDS, affecting especially the skin and mucous membranes, and characterized usually by the formation of pink to reddish-brown or bluish plaques, macules, papules, or nodules
kap·pa \'ka-pə\ *noun* [Middle English, from Greek, of Semitic origin; akin to Hebrew *kaph*] (15th century)
: the 10th letter of the Greek alphabet — see ALPHABET table
ka·putt *also* **ka·putt** \kə-'pút, kä-, -'pút\ *adjective* [German *kaputt*, from French *capot* not having made a trick at piquet] (1895)
1 : utterly finished, defeated, or destroyed

2 : unable to function **:** USELESS ⟨my battery went *kaput* —Henry James Jr.⟩
3 : hopelessly outmoded ◇
kar·a·bi·ner *variant of* CARABINER
Kara·ism \'kar-ə-ˌi-zəm\ *noun* [Late Hebrew *qěrāīm* Karaites, from Hebrew *qārā* to read] (circa 1883)
: a Jewish doctrine originating in Baghdad in the 8th century that rejects rabbinism and talmudism and bases its tenets on Scripture alone
— **Kara·ite** \-ˌīt\ *noun*
kar·a·kul \'kar-ə-kəl\ *noun* [*Karakul,* village in Uzbekistan] (1853)
1 *often capitalized* **:** any of a breed of hardy fat-tailed sheep from Uzbekistan with a narrow body and coarse wiry fur
2 : the tightly curled glossy coat of the newborn lamb of a karakul valued as fur

karakul 1

kar·a·o·ke \ˌkar-'ō-kē, kə-ˈrō-kē, ˌkä-rä-ˈō-(ˌ)kā\ *noun* [Japanese, from *kara* empty + *ōke,* short for *ōkesutora* orchestra] (1982)
: a device that plays instrumental accompaniments for a selection of songs to which the user sings along and that records the user's singing with the music
kar·at \'kar-ət\ *noun* [Middle English, probably from Middle French *carat,* from Medieval Latin *carratus* unit of weight for precious stones — more at CARAT] (15th century)
: a unit of fineness for gold equal to ¹⁄₂₄ part of pure gold in an alloy
ka·ra·te \kə-ˈrä-tē\ *noun* [Japanese, from *kara* empty + *te* hand] (1955)
: an Oriental art of self-defense in which an attacker is disabled by crippling kicks and punches
— **ka·ra·te·ist** \-tē-ist\ *noun*
ka·ra·ya gum \kə-ˈrī-ə-\ *noun* [Hindi *karāyal* resin] (1916)
: any of several vegetable gums similar to tragacanth and often used as substitutes for it that are obtained from tropical Asian trees (genera *Sterculia* of the family Sterculiaceae and *Cochlospermum* of the family Bixaceae); *especially* **:** one derived from an Indian tree (*S. urens*)
Ka·re·lian \kə-ˈrē-lē-ən, -ˈrēl-yən\ *noun* (1855)
1 : a native or inhabitant of Karelia
2 : the Finno-Ugric language of the Karelians
— **Karelian** *adjective*
Ka·ren \kə-ˈren\ *noun, plural* **Karen** *or* **Ka·rens** (1833)
1 : a member of a group of peoples of eastern and southern Myanmar
2 a : a group of languages spoken by the Karen peoples **b :** a language of this group
kar·ma \'kär-mə *also* 'kər-\ *noun* [Sanskrit *karma* fate, work] (1827)
1 *often capitalized* **:** the force generated by a person's actions held in Hinduism and Buddhism to perpetuate transmigration and in its ethical consequences to determine the nature of the person's next existence
2 : VIBRATION 4
— **kar·mic** \-mik\ *adjective*
ka·roo *or* **kar·roo** \kə-ˈrü\ *noun, plural* **ka·roos** *or* **kar·roos** [Afrikaans *karo*] (1789)
: a dry tableland of southern Africa
ka·ross \kə-ˈräs\ *noun* [Afrikaans *karos*] (1785)
: a simple garment or rug of skins used especially by native tribesmen of southern Africa
karst \'kärst\ *noun* [German] (1902)
: an irregular limestone region with sinks, underground streams, and caverns
— **karst·ic** \'kär-stik\ *adjective*
kart \'kärt\ *noun* [probably from *GoKart,* a trademark] (1959)

: a miniature motorcar used especially in racing
— **kart·ing** *noun*
kary- *or* **karyo-** *also* **cary-** *or* **caryo-** *combining form* [New Latin, from Greek *karyon* nut — more at CAREEN]
1 : nucleus of a cell ⟨*karyo*kinesis⟩
2 : nut : kernel ⟨*caryo*psis⟩
kar·y·og·a·my \ˌkar-ē-ˈä-gə-mē\ *noun, plural* **-mies** (1891)
: the fusion of cell nuclei (as in fertilization)
kar·y·o·ki·ne·sis \ˌkar-ē-ō-kə-ˈnē-səs, -kī-\ *noun* [New Latin] (1882)
1 : the nuclear phenomena characteristic of mitosis
2 : the whole process of mitosis
— **kar·y·o·ki·net·ic** \-ˈne-tik\ *adjective*
kar·y·ol·o·gy \ˌkar-ē-ˈä-lə-jē\ *noun* [International Scientific Vocabulary] (1895)
1 : the minute cytological characteristics of the cell nucleus especially with regard to the chromosomes
2 : a branch of cytology concerned with the karyology of cell nuclei
— **kar·y·o·log·i·cal** \-ē-ə-ˈlä-ji-kəl\ *also* **kar·y·o·log·ic** \-jik\ *adjective*
kar·y·o·lymph \'kar-ē-ə-ˌlim(p)f\ *noun* [International Scientific Vocabulary] (1899)
: NUCLEAR SAP
kar·y·o·some \'kar-ē-ə-ˌsōm\ *noun* [International Scientific Vocabulary] (1889)
: a mass of chromatin in a cell nucleus that resembles a nucleolus
¹**kar·y·o·type** \'kar-ē-ə-ˌtīp\ *noun* [International Scientific Vocabulary] (1929)
: the chromosomal characteristics of a cell; *also* **:** the chromosomes themselves or a representation of them
— **kar·y·o·typ·ic** \ˌkar-ē-ə-ˈti-pik\ *adjective*
— **kar·y·o·typ·i·cal·ly** \-pi-k(ə-)lē\ *adverb*
²**karyotype** *transitive verb*
: to determine the karyotype of
Kas·bah *variant of* CASBAH
ka·sha \'kä-shə, 'ka-\ *noun* [Russian] (1808)
1 : a porridge made usually from buckwheat groats
2 : kasha grain before cooking
Ka·shan \kə-ˈshän\ *noun* [*Kashan,* Iran] (1920)
: an Oriental rug with floral motifs in soft colors
Kash·mir *variant of* CASHMERE
Kash·miri \kash-ˈmir-ē, kazh-\ *noun, plural* **Kashmiris** *or* **Kashmiri** (1880)
1 : an Indo-Aryan language spoken in Kashmir
2 : a native or inhabitant of Kashmir
kash·ruth *or* **kash·rut** \kä-ˈshrüt, -'shrüth\ *noun* [Hebrew *kashrūth,* literally, fitness] (1907)
1 : the Jewish dietary laws
2 : the state of being kosher
Ka·shu·bi·an \kə-ˈshü-bē-ən\ *noun* [*Kashube* a member of a Slavic people] (1919)
: a Slavic language spoken in the vicinity of Gdansk
kat *variant of* KHAT
ka·ta \'kä-(ˌ)tä\ *noun, plural* **kata** *or* **katas** [Japanese, literally, model, pattern] (1945)
: a set combination of positions and movements (as in karate) performed as an exercise
kat·a·bat·ic \ˌka-tə-ˈba-tik\ *adjective* [Greek *katabatos* descending, verbal of *katabainein* to go down, from *kata-* cata- + *bainein* to go — more at COME] (1918)
: relating to or being a wind produced by the flow of cold dense air down a slope (as of a mountain or glacier) in an area subject to radiational cooling
ka·ta·ka·na \ˌkä-tə-ˈkä-nə\ *noun* [Japanese, from *kata* part + *kana* kana] (1727)
: the form of Japanese syllabic writing used especially for scientific terms, official documents, and words adopted from other languages — compare HIRAGANA
ka·tchi·na *or* **ka·tci·na** *variant of* KACHINA

Ka·tha·re·vu·sa \ˌkä-thə-ˈre-və-ˌsä\ *noun* [New Greek *kathareuousa,* from Greek, feminine of *kathareuōn,* present participle of *kathareuein* to be pure, from *katharos* pure] (1936)
: modern Greek conforming to classic Greek usage
ka·thar·sis *variant of* CATHARSIS
ka·ty·did \'kā-tē-ˌdid\ *noun* [imitative] (1784)
: any of several large green American long-horned grasshoppers usually having stridulating organs on the forewings of the males that produce a loud shrill sound
kat·zen·jam·mer \'kat-sən-ˌja-mər\ *noun* [German, from *Katze* cat + *Jammer* distress] (1849)
1 : HANGOVER
2 : DISTRESS 2
3 : a discordant clamor
kau·ri \'kaù(-ə)r-ē\ *noun* [Maori *kawri*] (1823)
1 : any of various trees (genus *Agathis*) of the araucaria family; *especially* **:** a tall timber tree (*A. australis*) of New Zealand having fine white straight-grained wood
2 : a light-colored to brown resin from the kauri tree found as a fossil in the ground or collected from living trees and used especially in varnishes and linoleum — called also *kauri gum, kauri resin*
ka·va \'kä-və\ *noun* [Tongan & Marquesan, literally, bitter] (1810)
1 : an Australasian shrubby pepper (*Piper methysticum*) from whose crushed root an intoxicating beverage is made
2 : the beverage made from kava
kay \'kā\ *noun* (14th century)
: the letter *k*
Kay \'kā\ *noun*
: a boastful overbearing knight of the Round Table who is foster brother and seneschal of King Arthur
kay·ak \'kī-ˌak\ *noun* [Inuit *qayaq*] (1757)
1 : an Eskimo canoe made of a frame covered with skins except for a small opening in the center and propelled by a double-bladed paddle
2 : a portable boat styled like an Eskimo kayak
— **kay·ak·er** \-ˌa-kər\ *noun*
— **kay·ak·ing** \-kiŋ\ *noun*
¹**kayo** \(ˌ)kā-'ō, 'kā-(ˌ)ō\ *noun* [pronunciation of *KO,* abbreviation] (1920)
: KNOCKOUT
²**kayo** *transitive verb* **kay·oed; kayo·ing** (1923)
: KNOCK OUT
Ka·zak \kə-ˈzak, -ˈzäk\ *noun* [*Kazak* (Kazakh), town in Azerbaijan] (1900)
: an Oriental rug in bold colors with geometric designs or stylized plant and animal forms

◇ WORD HISTORY

kaput To win all of the tricks in the card game piquet is *faire capot* "to make capot" in French, while *être capot* "to be capot" is to have lost all of the tricks in a game. In German *capot* was borrowed as *kaput,* and from the sense of having lost a game *kaput* developed the meanings "finished" and "broken." *Kaput* began to appear in English writing in the late 19th century, generally in contexts where a German word would be appropriate or else printed in italics or glossed to show that it was not yet a fully anglicized word. However, during and after World War II *kaput* gained greater currency in English in the senses "utterly finished," "useless," or "hopelessly outmoded" and is now completely established in our language.

\ə\ **abut** \ᵊ\ **kitten** \ər\ **further** \a\ **ash** \ā\ **ace**
\ä\ **mop, mar** \aù\ **out** \ch\ **chin** \e\ **bet** \ē\ **easy**
\g\ **go** \i\ **hit** \ī\ **ice** \j\ **job** \ŋ\ **sing** \ō\ **go**
\ò\ **law** \òi\ **boy** \th\ **thin** \tẖ\ **the** \ü\ **loot** \ù\ **foot**
\y\ **yet** \zh\ **vision** *see also* Guide to Pronunciation

Ka·zakh \kə-'zak, -'zäk\ noun [Russian *kazakh*, from Kazakh *kazak*] (1832)
1 : a member of a Turkic people of Kazakhstan and other countries of central Asia
2 : the language of the Kazakhs

ka·zoo \kə-'zü\ noun, plural **kazoos** [imitative] (1884)
: an instrument that imparts a buzzing quality to the human voice and that usually consists of a small metal or plastic tube with a side hole covered by a thin membrane

K–band \'kā-\ noun (circa 1948)
: a segment of the radio spectrum that lies between 10.9 GHz and 36.0 GHz and spans the upper superhigh-frequency and lower extremely-high-frequency bands and that is used especially for police radars, satellite communication, and astronomical observation

kea \'kē-ə\ noun [Maori] (1862)
: a large mostly dull green New Zealand parrot (*Nestor notabilis*) that is normally insectivorous but sometimes destroys sheep by slashing the back to feed on the kidney fat

ke·bab or **ke·bob** variant of KABOB

keb·buck or **keb·bock** \'ke-bək\ noun [Middle English (Scots dialect) *cabok*, from Scottish Gaelic *ceapag*] (15th century)
dialect British **:** a whole wheel or ball of cheese

¹kedge \'kej\ transitive verb **kedged; kedging** [Middle English *caggen*] (1627)
: to move (a ship) by means of a line attached to a kedge dropped at the distance and in the direction desired

²kedge noun (circa 1769)
: a small anchor used especially in kedging

ked·ge·ree \'ke-jə-rē\ noun [Hindi *khicaṛī*, from Sanskrit *khiccā*] (1662)
1 : an Indian dish of seasoned rice, beans, lentils, and sometimes smoked fish
2 : cooked or smoked fish, rice, hard-boiled eggs, and seasoning heated in cream

¹keek \'kēk\ intransitive verb [Middle English *kiken*] (14th century)
chiefly Scottish **:** PEEP, LOOK

²keek noun (1721)
chiefly Scottish **:** PEEP, LOOK

¹keel \'kē(ə)l\ verb [Middle English *kelen*, from Old English *cēlan*, from *cōl* cool] (before 12th century)
chiefly dialect **:** COOL

²keel noun [Middle English *kele*, from Middle Dutch *kiel*; akin to Old English *cēol* ship] (14th century)
: a flat-bottomed barge used especially on the Tyne to carry coal

³keel noun [Middle English *kele*, from Old Norse *kjǫlr*; akin to Old English *ceole* throat, beak of a ship — more at GLUTTON] (14th century)
1 a : the chief structural member of a boat or ship that extends longitudinally along the center of its bottom and that often projects from the bottom; *also* **:** this projection **b :** SHIP
2 : a projection suggesting a keel; *especially* **:** CARINA
— **keeled** \'kē(ə)ld\ adjective
— **keel·less** \'kē(ə)l-ləs\ adjective

⁴keel intransitive verb (1832)
1 : to fall in or as if in a faint — usually used with *over*
2 : to heel or lean precariously

⁵keel noun [Middle English (Scots dialect) *keyle*] (15th century)
chiefly dialect **:** RED OCHER

keel·boat \'kē(ə)l-ˌbōt\ noun (1695)
: a shallow covered keeled riverboat that is usually rowed, poled, or towed and that is used for freight

keel·haul \-ˌhȯl\ transitive verb [Dutch *kielhalen*, from *kiel* keel + *halen* to haul] (1666)
1 : to haul under the keel of a ship as punishment or torture
2 : to rebuke severely

keel·son \'kel-sən, 'kē(ə)l-\ noun [Middle English *kelswayn*, probably of Scandinavian origin; akin to Swedish *kölsvin* keelson] (1598)
: a longitudinal structure running above and fastened to the keel of a ship in order to stiffen and strengthen its framework

¹keen \'kēn\ adjective [Middle English *kene* brave, sharp, from Old English *cēne* brave; akin to Old High German *kuoni* brave] (13th century)
1 a : having a fine edge or point **:** SHARP ⟨a *keen* sword⟩ **b :** affecting one as if by cutting ⟨*keen* sarcasm⟩ **c :** pungent to the sense ⟨a *keen* scent⟩
2 a (1) **:** showing a quick and ardent responsiveness **:** ENTHUSIASTIC ⟨a *keen* swimmer⟩ (2) **:** EAGER ⟨was *keen* to begin⟩ **b** of emotion or feeling **:** INTENSE ⟨the *keen* delight in the chase —F. W. Maitland⟩
3 a : intellectually alert **:** having or characteristic of a quick penetrating mind ⟨a *keen* student⟩ ⟨a *keen* awareness of the problem⟩; *also* **:** shrewdly astute ⟨*keen* bargainers⟩ **b :** sharply contested ⟨*keen* debate⟩ **c :** extremely sensitive in perception ⟨*keen* eyes⟩
4 : WONDERFUL, EXCELLENT
synonym see SHARP, EAGER
— **keen·ly** adverb
— **keen·ness** \'kēn-nəs\ noun

²keen noun (1830)
: a lamentation for the dead uttered in a loud wailing voice or sometimes in a wordless cry

³keen verb [Irish *caoinim* I lament] (1845)
intransitive verb
1 a : to lament with a keen **b :** to make a sound suggestive of a keen
2 : to lament, mourn, or complain loudly
transitive verb
: to utter by keening
— **keen·er** noun

¹keep \'kēp\ verb **kept** \'kept\; **keep·ing** [Middle English *kepen*, from Old English *cēpan*; perhaps akin to Old High German *chapfēn* to look] (before 12th century)
transitive verb
1 : to take notice of by appropriate conduct **:** FULFILL: as **a :** to be faithful to ⟨*keep* a promise⟩ **b :** to act fittingly in relation to ⟨*keep* the Sabbath⟩ **c :** to conform to in habits or conduct ⟨*keep* late hours⟩ **d :** to stay in accord with (a beat) ⟨*keep* time⟩
2 : PRESERVE, MAINTAIN: as **a :** to watch over and defend ⟨*keep* us from harm⟩ **b** (1) **:** to take care of **:** TEND ⟨*keep* a garden⟩ (2) **:** SUPPORT (3) **:** to maintain in a good, fitting, or orderly condition — usually used with *up* **c :** to continue to maintain ⟨*keep* watch⟩ **d** (1) **:** to cause to remain in a given place, situation, or condition ⟨*keep* him waiting⟩ (2) **:** to preserve (food) in an unspoiled condition **e :** to have or maintain in one's service or at one's disposal ⟨*keep* a mistress⟩ — often used with *on* ⟨*kept* the cook on⟩; *also* **:** to lodge or feed for pay ⟨*keep* boarders⟩ **f** (1) **:** to maintain a record in ⟨*keep* a diary⟩ (2) **:** to enter in a book ⟨*keep* records⟩ **g :** to have customarily in stock for sale
3 a : to restrain from departure or removal **:** DETAIN ⟨*keep* children in after school⟩ **b :** HOLD BACK, RESTRAIN ⟨*keep* them from going⟩ ⟨*kept* him back with difficulty⟩ **c :** SAVE, RESERVE ⟨*keep* some for later⟩ ⟨*kept* some out for a friend⟩ **d :** to refrain from revealing ⟨*keep* a secret⟩
4 a : to retain in one's possession or power ⟨*kept* the money we found⟩ **b :** to refrain from granting, giving, or allowing ⟨*kept* the news back⟩ **c :** to have in control ⟨*keep* your temper⟩
5 : to confine oneself to ⟨*keep* my room⟩
6 a : to stay or continue in ⟨*keep* the path⟩ ⟨*keep* your seat⟩ **b :** to stay or remain on or in usually against opposition **:** HOLD ⟨*kept* her ground⟩
7 : CONDUCT, MANAGE ⟨*keep* a tearoom⟩
intransitive verb
1 *chiefly British* **:** LIVE, LODGE

2 a : to maintain a course, direction, or progress ⟨*keep* to the right⟩ **b :** to continue usually without interruption ⟨*keep* talking⟩ ⟨*keep* quiet⟩ ⟨*keep* on smiling⟩ **c :** to persist in a practice ⟨*kept* bothering them⟩ ⟨*kept* on smoking in spite of warnings⟩
3 : STAY, REMAIN ⟨*keep* out of the way⟩ ⟨*keep* off the grass⟩: as **a :** to stay even — usually used with *up* ⟨*keep* up with the Joneses⟩ **b :** to remain in good condition ⟨meat will *keep* in the freezer⟩ **c :** to remain secret ⟨the secret would *keep*⟩ **d :** to call for no immediate action ⟨the matter will *keep* until morning⟩
4 : ABSTAIN, REFRAIN ⟨can't *keep* from talking⟩
5 : to be in session ⟨school will *keep* through the winter —W. M. Thayer⟩
6 of a quarterback **:** to retain possession of a football especially after faking a handoff ☆☆
— **keep an eye on :** WATCH
— **keep at :** to persist in doing or concerning oneself with
— **keep company :** to go together as frequent companions or in courtship
— **keep house :** to manage a household
— **keep one's distance** or **keep at a distance :** to stay aloof **:** maintain a reserved attitude
— **keep one's eyes open** or **keep one's eyes peeled :** to be on the alert **:** be watchful
— **keep one's hand in :** to keep in practice
— **keep pace :** to stay even; *also* **:** KEEP UP
— **keep step :** to keep in step
— **keep to 1 a :** to stay in **b :** to limit oneself to **2 :** to abide by
— **keep to oneself 1 :** to keep secret ⟨*kept* the facts *to myself*⟩ **2 :** to remain solitary or apart from other people

²keep noun (1579)
1 a archaic **:** CUSTODY, CHARGE **b :** MAINTENANCE
2 : one that keeps or protects: as **a :** FORTRESS, CASTLE; *specifically* **:** the strongest and securest part of a medieval castle **b :** one whose job is to keep or tend **c :** PRISON, JAIL
3 : the means or provisions by which one is kept ⟨earned his *keep*⟩
4 : KEEPER 4

☆ **SYNONYMS**

Keep, observe, celebrate, commemorate mean to notice or honor a day, occasion, or deed. KEEP stresses the idea of not neglecting or violating ⟨*kept* the Sabbath by refraining from work⟩. OBSERVE suggests marking the occasion by ceremonious performance ⟨not all holidays are *observed* nationally⟩. CELEBRATE suggests acknowledging an occasion by festivity ⟨traditionally *celebrates* Thanksgiving with a huge dinner⟩. COMMEMORATE suggests that an occasion is marked by observances that remind one of the origin and significance of the day ⟨*commemorate* Memorial Day with the laying of wreaths⟩.

Keep, retain, detain, withhold, reserve mean to hold in one's possession or under one's control. KEEP may suggest a holding securely in one's possession, custody, or control ⟨*keep* this while I'm gone⟩. RETAIN implies continued keeping, especially against threatened seizure or forced loss ⟨managed to *retain* their dignity even in poverty⟩. DETAIN suggests a delay in letting go ⟨*detained* them for questioning⟩. WITHHOLD implies restraint in letting go or a refusal to let go ⟨*withheld* information from the authorities⟩. RESERVE suggests a keeping in store for future use ⟨*reserve* some of your energy for the last mile⟩.

— for keeps 1 a : with the provision that one keep what one has won ⟨played marbles *for keeps*⟩ **b :** with deadly seriousness **2 :** for an indefinitely long time **:** PERMANENTLY **3 :** with the result of ending the matter

keep back *intransitive verb* (1837)
: to refrain from approaching or advancing near something ⟨police asked the spectators to *keep back*⟩

keep down *transitive verb* (1581)
1 : to keep in control ⟨*keep* expenses *down*⟩
2 : to prevent from growing, advancing, or succeeding

keep·er \'kē-pər\ *noun* (14th century)
1 : one that keeps: as **a :** PROTECTOR **b :** GAME-KEEPER **c :** WARDEN **d :** CUSTODIAN **e** *chiefly British* **:** CURATOR
2 : any of various devices for keeping something in position
3 a : one fit or suitable for keeping; *especially* **:** a fish large enough to be legally caught and kept **b :** a domestic animal considered with respect to how easy it is to care for ⟨an easy *keeper*⟩
4 : an offensive football play in which the quarterback runs with the ball

keep·ing \'kē-piŋ\ *noun* (14th century)
1 : the act of one that keeps: as **a :** CUSTODY, MAINTENANCE **b :** OBSERVANCE **c :** a reserving or preserving for future use
2 a : the means by which something is kept **:** SUPPORT, PROVISION **b :** the state of being kept or the condition in which something is kept ⟨the house is in good *keeping*⟩
3 : CONFORMITY ⟨in *keeping* with good taste⟩ ⟨out of *keeping* with the decor⟩

keep·sake \'kēp-ˌsāk\ *noun* [¹*keep* + -*sake* (as in *namesake*)] (1790)
: something kept or given to be kept as a memento

keep up (15th century)
transitive verb
: to persist or persevere in ⟨*kept up* the good work⟩; *also* **:** MAINTAIN, SUSTAIN ⟨*keep* standards *up*⟩
intransitive verb
1 : to keep adequately informed or up-to-date ⟨*keep up* on international affairs⟩
2 : to continue without interruption ⟨rain *kept up* all night⟩
3 : to maintain contact or relations with ⟨*keep up* with old friends⟩

kees·hond \'kās-ˌhȯnt\ *noun, plural* **kees·hon·den** \-ˌhȯn-dən\ [Dutch, probably from *Kees,* nickname for *Cornelis* Cornelius + *hond* dog, from Middle Dutch; akin to Old English *hund* hound] (1926)
: any of a Dutch breed of compact medium-sized dogs that have a dense heavy grayish coat and a foxy head

kef \'kēf, 'kef, 'kāf\ *noun* [Arabic *kayf* pleasure] (1808)
1 : a state of dreamy tranquillity
2 : a smoking material (as marijuana) that produces kef

kef·fi·yeh *variant of* KAFFIYEH

ke·fir \ke-'fir; 'kē-fər, 'ke-\ *noun* [Russian] (1884)
: a beverage of fermented cow's milk

keg \'keg, *dialect* 'kag, 'kāg\ *noun* [Middle English *kag,* of Scandinavian origin; akin to Old Norse *kaggi* keg] (circa 1632)
1 : a small cask or barrel having a capacity of 30 gallons (136.4 liters) or less
2 : the contents of a keg

keg·ler \'ke-glər, 'kā-\ *noun* [German, from *kegeln* to bowl, from *Kegel* bowling pin, from Old High German *kegil* stake, peg] (1932)
: ¹BOWLER

keg·ling \'ke-gliŋ, 'kā-\ *noun* (1938)
: BOWLING

keis·ter \'kēs-tər, 'kīs-\ *or* **kees·ter** \'kēs-\ *noun* [English slang *keister* satchel] (1931)
slang **:** BUTTOCKS

ke·lim *variant of* KILIM

kel·ly green \'ke-lē-\ *noun, often K capitalized* [from the common Irish name *Kelly;* from the association of Ireland with the color green] (circa 1935)
: a strong yellowish green

ke·loid \'kē-ˌlȯid\ *noun* [French *kéloïde,* from Greek *chēlē* claw] (1854)
: a thick scar resulting from excessive growth of fibrous tissue
— keloid *adjective*
— ke·loi·dal \kē-'lȯi-dᵊl\ *adjective*

kelp \'kelp\ *noun* [Middle English *culp*] (14th century)
1 a : any of various large brown seaweeds (order Laminariales) **b :** a mass of large seaweeds
2 : the ashes of seaweed used especially as a source of iodine

kelp bass *noun* (circa 1936)
: a mottled sea bass (*Paralabrax clathratus*) that occurs along the Pacific coast of the U.S. and is an important sport fish

¹kel·pie \'kel-pē\ *noun* [perhaps from Scottish Gaelic *cailpeach, colpach* heifer, colt] (1747)
: a water sprite of Scottish folklore that delights in or brings about the drowning of wayfarers

²kelpie *noun* [*Kelpie,* name of a dog of this breed] (1903)
: any of a breed of energetic working dogs developed in Australia from British sheepdogs

Kelt \'kelt\, **Kelt·ic** \'kel-tik\ *variant of* CELT, CELTIC

kel·vin \'kel-vən\ *noun* (1968)
: the base unit of temperature in the International System of Units that is equal to 1/273.16 of the Kelvin scale temperature of the triple point of water

Kelvin *adjective* [William Thomson, Lord *Kelvin*] (1908)
: relating to, conforming to, or having a thermometric scale on which the unit of measurement equals the Celsius degree and according to which absolute zero is 0 K, the equivalent of $-273.15°C$

kemp \'kemp\ *noun* [Middle English *kempe* coarse hair, probably of Scandinavian origin; akin to Old Norse *kampr* mustache; akin to Old English *cenep* mustache] (1641)
: a coarse fiber especially of wool that is usually short, wavy, and white, has little affinity for dye, and is used in mixed wools

Kemp's ridley \'kemps-\ *noun* [Richard M. *Kemp* (flourished 1873) American amateur naturalist] (1979)
: RIDLEY a

kempt \'kem(p)t\ *adjective* [back-formation from *unkempt*] (1929)
: neatly kept **:** TRIM

¹ken \'ken\ *verb* **kenned; ken·ning** [Middle English *kennen,* from Old English *cennan* to make known & Old Norse *kenna* to perceive; both akin to Old English *can* know — more at CAN] (13th century)
transitive verb
1 *archaic* **:** SEE
2 *chiefly dialect* **:** RECOGNIZE
3 *chiefly Scottish* **:** KNOW
intransitive verb
chiefly Scottish **:** KNOW

²ken *noun* (1590)
1 a : the range of vision **b :** SIGHT, VIEW ⟨'tis double death to drown in *ken* of shore —Shakespeare⟩
2 : the range of perception, understanding, or knowledge ⟨abstract words that are beyond the *ken* of young children —Lois M. Rettie⟩

ke·naf \kə-'naf\ *noun* [Persian] (1891)
: an African hibiscus (*Hibiscus cannabinus*) widely cultivated for its fiber; *also* **:** the fiber used especially for cordage

Ken·dal green \'ken-dᵊl-\ *noun* [*Kendal,* England] (1514)
: a green woolen cloth resembling homespun or tweed

ken·do \'ken-(ˌ)dō\ *noun* [Japanese *kendō,* from *ken* sword + *dō* art] (1921)
: a Japanese sport of fencing with bamboo swords

¹ken·nel \'ke-nᵊl\ *noun* [Middle English *kenel,* ultimately from (assumed) Vulgar Latin *canile,* from Latin *canis* dog — more at HOUND] (14th century)
1 a : a shelter for a dog or cat **b :** an establishment for the breeding or boarding of dogs or cats
2 : a pack of dogs

²kennel *verb* **-neled** *or* **-nelled; -nel·ing** *or* **-nel·ling** (1552)
intransitive verb
: to take shelter in or as if in a kennel
transitive verb
: to put or keep in or as if in a kennel

³kennel *noun* [alteration of *cannel* gutter] (15th century)
: a gutter in a street

¹ken·ning \'ke-niŋ\ *noun* [Middle English, sight, view, from gerund of *kennen*] (1786)
chiefly Scottish **:** a perceptible but small amount

²kenning *noun* [Old Norse, from *kenna*] (1883)
: a metaphorical compound word or phrase (as *swan-road* for *ocean*) used especially in Old English and Old Norse poetry

ke·no \'kē-(ˌ)nō\ *noun* [French *quine,* set of five winning numbers in a lottery + English -*o* (as in *lotto*)] (1814)
: a game resembling bingo

ken·speck·le \'ken-ˌspe-kəl\ *adjective* [probably of Scandinavian origin; akin to Norwegian *kjennspak* quick to recognize] (1616)
chiefly Scottish **:** CONSPICUOUS

kent·ledge \'kent-lij\ *noun* [origin unknown] (1607)
: pig iron or scrap metal used as ballast

Ken·tucky bluegrass \kən-'tə-kē-\ *noun* [*Kentucky,* state of U.S.] (1849)
: a valuable Old World pasture and meadow grass (*Poa pratensis*) naturalized in America — called also *bluegrass*

Kentucky coffee tree *noun* (1785)
: a tall North American leguminous tree (*Gymnocladus dioica*) with bipinnate leaves and large woody brown pods whose seeds have been used as a substitute for coffee

Kentucky rifle *noun* (1832)
: a muzzle-loading long-barreled flintlock rifle developed in the 18th century in Pennsylvania and used extensively on the American frontier

Ke·ogh plan \'kē-(ˌ)ō-\ *noun* [Eugene James *Keogh* (died 1989) American politician] (1974)
: an individual retirement account for the self-employed

ke·pi \'kā-pē, 'ke-\ *also* **ké·pi** \'kā-\ *noun* [French *képi,* from German dialect (Switzerland) *käppi* cap] (1861)
: a military cap with a round flat top sloping toward the front and a visor

kept *past and past participle of* KEEP

kerat- *or* **kerato-** *combining form* [International Scientific Vocabulary, from Greek *kerato-, keras* horn — more at HORN]
: cornea ⟨*kerat*itis⟩

ker·a·tin \'ker-ə-tᵊn\ *noun* [International Scientific Vocabulary] (circa 1849)
: any of various sulfur-containing fibrous proteins that form the chemical basis of horny epidermal tissues (as hair and nails)
— ke·ra·ti·nous \kə-'ra-tᵊn-əs\ *adjective*

ke·ra·ti·ni·za·tion \ˌker-ə-tə-nə-'zā-shən, kə-ˌra-tᵊn-ə-\ *noun* (circa 1887)
: conversion into keratin or keratinous tissue
— ke·ra·ti·nize \'ker-ə-tə-ˌnīz, kə-'ra-tᵊn-ˌīz\ *verb*

ke·ra·ti·no·phil·ic \ˌker-ə-tə-nə-'fi-lik, kə-ˌra-tᵊn-ə-\ *adjective* (1946)

: exhibiting affinity for keratin (as in hair, skin, feathers, or horns) — used chiefly of fungi capable of growing on such materials

ker·a·ti·tis \,ker-ə-'tī-təs\ *noun, plural* **-tit·i·des** \-'ti-tə-,dēz\ [New Latin] (1858)
: inflammation of the cornea of the eye

ker·a·to·con·junc·ti·vi·tis \'ker-ə-(,)tō-kən-,jən(k)-tə-'vī-təs\ *noun* [New Latin] (1887)
: combined inflammation of the cornea and conjunctiva

ker·a·to·plas·ty \'ker-ə-tō-,plas-tē\ *noun, plural* **-ties** (circa 1857)
: plastic surgery on the cornea; *especially*
: corneal grafting

ker·a·to·sis \,ker-ə-'tō-səs\ *noun, plural* **-to·ses** \-,sēz\ [New Latin] (1885)
: an area of skin marked by overgrowth of horny tissue
— **ker·a·tot·ic** \-'tä-tik\ *adjective*

kerb \'kərb\ *noun* (1805)
British : CURB 5

ker·chief \'kər-chəf, -,chēf\ *noun, plural* **ker·chiefs** \-chəfs, -,chēfs\ *also* **ker·chieves** \-,chēvz\ [Middle English *courchef*, from Old French *cuevrechief*, from *covrir* to cover + *chief* head — more at CHIEF] (13th century)
1 : a square of cloth used as a head covering or worn as a scarf around the neck
2 : HANDKERCHIEF 1
— **ker·chiefed** \-chəft, -,chēft\ *adjective*

kerf \'kərf\ *noun* [Middle English, action of cutting, from Old English *cyrf*; akin to Old English *ceorfan* to carve — more at CARVE] (1523)
1 : a slit or notch made by a saw or cutting torch
2 : the width of cut made by a saw or cutting torch

ker·fuf·fle \kər-'fə-fəl\ *noun* [alteration of *carfuffle*, from Scots *car-* (probably from Scottish Gaelic *cearr* wrong, awkward) + *fuffle* to become disheveled] (1946)
chiefly British : DISTURBANCE, FUSS

Ker·man \kər-'män, ker-\ *variant of* KIRMAN

ker·mes \'kər-(,)mēz\ *noun* [French *kermès*, from Arabic *qirmiz*] (1603)
: the dried bodies of the females of various scale insects (genus *Kermes*) that are found on a Mediterranean oak (*Quercus coccifera*) and constitute a red dyestuff; *also* : the dye

ker·mis \'kər-məs\ *or* **ker·mess** \-məs, -,mes\ *or* **ker·messe** \-məs, -,mes\ *noun* [Dutch *kermis*, from Middle Dutch *kercmisse*, from *kerc, kerke* church + *misse* mass, church festival] (1577)
1 : an outdoor festival of the Low Countries
2 : a fair held usually for charitable purposes

¹kern *or* **kerne** \'kərn, 'kern\ *noun* [Middle English *kerne*, from Middle Irish *cethern* band of soldiers] (15th century)
1 : a light-armed foot soldier of medieval Ireland or Scotland
2 : YOKEL

²kern \'kərn\ *noun* [French *carne* corner, from French dialect, from Latin *cardin-, cardo* hinge] (1683)
: a part of a typeset letter that projects beyond its side bearings

ker·nel \'kər-n²l\ *noun* [Middle English, from Old English *cyrnel*, diminutive of *corn*] (before 12th century)
1 *chiefly dialect* : a fruit seed
2 : the inner softer part of a seed, fruit stone, or nut
3 : a whole seed of a cereal ⟨a *kernel* of corn⟩
4 : a central or essential part : GERM ⟨like many stereotypes . . . this one too contains some *kernels* of truth —S. M. Lyman⟩
5 : a subset of the elements of one set (as a group) that a function (as a homomorphism) maps onto an identity element of another set

kern·ite \'kər-,nīt\ *noun* [*Kern* Co., Calif.] (1927)
: a mineral that consists of a hydrous borate of sodium and is an important source of borax

ker·o·gen \'ker-ə-jən\ *noun* [Greek *kēros* wax + English *-gen* — more at CERUMEN] (1906)
: bituminous material occurring in shale and yielding oil when heated

ker·o·sene *or* **ker·o·sine** \'ker-ə-,sēn, ,ker-ə-', 'kar-, ,kar-\ *noun* [Greek *kēros* + English *-ene* (as in *camphene*)] (1854)
: a flammable hydrocarbon oil usually obtained by distillation of petroleum and used for a fuel and as a solvent and thinner

ker·ria \'ker-ē-ə\ *noun* [New Latin, from William *Kerr* (died 1814) English gardener] (1823)
: a shrub (*Kerria japonica*) of the rose family that is native to China and Japan and has solitary yellow and often double flowers

ker·ry \'ker-ē\ *noun, plural* **kerries** *often capitalized* [County *Kerry*, Ireland] (1829)
: any of an Irish breed of small hardy black dairy cattle

Kerry blue terrier *noun* (1922)
: any of an Irish breed of medium-sized terriers with a long squarish head, deep chest, and silky bluish coat

ker·sey \'kər-zē\ *noun, plural* **kerseys** [Middle English, from *Kersey*, England] (14th century)
1 a : a coarse ribbed woolen cloth for hose and work clothes **b** : a heavy wool or wool and cotton fabric used especially for uniforms and coats
2 : a garment of kersey

ker·sey·mere \'kər-zē-,mir\ *noun* [alteration of *cassimere*] (1798)
: a fine woolen fabric with a close nap made in fancy twill weaves

ke·ryg·ma \kə-'rig-mə\ *noun* [Greek *kērygma*, from *kēryssein* to proclaim, from *kēryx* herald — more at CADUCEUS] (1889)
: the apostolic proclamation of salvation through Jesus Christ
— **ke·ryg·mat·ic** \,ker-ig-'ma-tik\ *adjective*

kes·trel \'kes-trəl\ *noun* [Middle English *castrel*, from Middle French *crecerelle*, from *crecelle* rattle; from its cry] (15th century)
: any of various small chiefly Old World falcons (genus *Falco*) that usually hover in the air while searching for prey: as **a** : a common Eurasian falcon (*F. tinnunculus*) **b** : an American falcon (*F. sparverius*) having a reddish brown back and tail and bluish gray wings

ket- *or* **keto-** *combining form* [International Scientific Vocabulary]
: ketone ⟨*ketosis*⟩

ketch \'kech\ *noun* [alteration of *catch*, from Middle English *cache*] (circa 1649)
: a fore-and-aft rigged vessel similar to a yawl but with a larger mizzen and with the mizzenmast stepped farther forward

ketch·up \'ke-chəp, 'ka-\ *noun* [Malay *kēchap* fish sauce] (circa 1690)
: a seasoned pureed condiment usually made from tomatoes

ke·tene \'kē-,tēn\ *noun* [International Scientific Vocabulary] (1907)
: a colorless poisonous gas C_2H_2O of penetrating odor used especially as an acetylating agent; *also* : any of various derivatives of this compound

ke·to \'kē-(,)tō\ *adjective* [ket-] (1891)
: of or relating to a ketone; *also* : containing a ketone group

ke·to·gen·e·sis \,kē-tō-'je-nə-səs\ *noun* [New Latin] (1915)
: the production of ketone bodies (as in diabetes)
— **ke·to·gen·ic** \-'je-nik\ *adjective*

ke·to·glu·tar·ic acid \-glü-'tar-ik-\ *noun* (1908)
: either of two crystalline keto derivatives $C_5H_6O_5$ of glutaric acid; *especially* : the alpha keto isomer formed in various metabolic processes (as the Krebs cycle)

ke·tone \'kē-,tōn\ *noun* [German *Keton*, alteration of *Aceton* acetone] (1851)
: an organic compound (as acetone) with a carbonyl group attached to two carbon atoms
— **ke·ton·ic** \kē-'tä-nik\ *adjective*

ketone body *noun* (1915)
: any of the three compounds acetoacetic acid, acetone, and beta-hydroxybutyric acid which are normal intermediates in lipid metabolism and accumulate in the blood and urine in abnormal amounts in conditions of impaired metabolism (as diabetes mellitus)

ke·tose \'kē-,tōs, -,tōz\ *noun* [International Scientific Vocabulary] (1902)
: a sugar (as fructose) containing one ketone group per molecule

ke·to·sis \kē-'tō-səs\ *noun* [New Latin] (1917)
: an abnormal increase of ketone bodies in the body
— **ke·tot·ic** \-'tä-tik\ *adjective*

ke·to·ste·roid \,kē-tō-'stir-,oid *also* -'ster-\ *noun* [International Scientific Vocabulary] (1939)
: a steroid (as cortisone or estrone) containing a ketone group

ket·tle \'ke-t²l\ *noun* [Middle English *ketel*, from Old Norse *ketill* (akin to Old English *cietel* kettle), both from a prehistoric Germanic word borrowed from Latin *catillus*, diminutive of *catinus* bowl] (13th century)
1 : a metallic vessel usually used for boiling liquids; *especially* : TEAKETTLE
2 : KETTLEDRUM
3 a : POTHOLE 1b **b** : a steep-sided hollow without surface drainage especially in a deposit of glacial drift

ket·tle·drum \-,drəm\ *noun* (1602)
: a percussion instrument that consists of a hollow brass, copper, or fiberglass hemisphere with a calfskin or plastic head whose tension can be changed to vary the pitch

kettledrum

kettle of fish (1742)
1 : a bad state of affairs : MESS
2 : something to be considered or reckoned with : MATTER ⟨books and discs . . . were two very different *kettles of fish* —Roland Gelatt⟩

Kew·pie \'kyü-pē\ *trademark*
— used for a small chubby doll with a topknot of hair

¹key \'kē\ *noun* [Middle English, from Old English *cæg*; akin to Old Frisian *kēi* key] (before 12th century)
1 a : a usually metal instrument by which the bolt of a lock is turned **b** : any of various devices having the form or function of such a key
2 a : a means of gaining or preventing entrance, possession, or control **b** : an instrumental or deciding factor
3 a : something that gives an explanation or identification or provides a solution ⟨the *key* to a riddle⟩ **b** : a list of words or phrases giving an explanation of symbols or abbreviations **c** : an aid to interpretation or identification : CLUE **d** : an arrangement of the salient characters of a group of plants or animals or of taxa designed to facilitate identification **e** : a map legend
4 a (1) : COTTER PIN (2) : COTTER **b** : a keystone in an arch **c** : a small piece of wood or metal used as a wedge or for preventing motion between parts

5 a : one of the levers of a keyboard musical instrument that actuates the mechanism and produces the tones **b :** a lever that controls a vent in the side of a woodwind instrument or a valve in a brass instrument **c :** a part to be depressed by a finger that serves as one unit of a keyboard
6 : SAMARA
7 : a system of tones and harmonies generated from a hierarchical scale of seven tones based on a tonic ⟨the *key* of G major⟩
8 a : characteristic style or tone **b :** the tone or pitch of a voice **c :** the predominant tone of a photograph with respect to its lightness or darkness
9 : a decoration or charm resembling a key
10 : a small switch for opening or closing an electric circuit ⟨a telegraph *key*⟩
11 : the set of instructions governing the encipherment and decipherment of messages
12 : a free-throw area in basketball
— **keyed** \'kēd\ *adjective*
— **key·less** \'kē-ləs\ *adjective*
²**key** (14th century)
transitive verb
1 : to lock with or as if with a key : FASTEN: as
a : to secure (as a pulley on a shaft) by a key
b : to finish off (an arch) by inserting a keystone
2 : to regulate the musical pitch of
3 : to bring into harmony or conformity : make appropriate : ATTUNE ⟨remarks *keyed* to a situation⟩
4 : to identify (a biological specimen) by a key
5 : to provide with identifying or explanatory cross-references ⟨instructions *keyed* to accompanying drawings —John Gartner⟩
6 : to make nervous, tense, or excited — usually used with *up* ⟨was *keyed* up over her impending operation⟩
7 : KEYBOARD — often used with *in*
intransitive verb
1 : to use a key
2 : to observe the position or movement of an opposing player in football in order to anticipate the play — usually used with *on*
3 : KEYBOARD
³**key** *adjective* (1913)
: IMPORTANT, FUNDAMENTAL ⟨*key* issues⟩
⁴**key** *noun* [Spanish *cayo,* from Taino] (1697)
: a low island or reef; *specifically* **:** any of the coral islets off the southern coast of Florida
⁵**key** *noun* [by shortening & alteration from *kilo*] (1968)
slang **:** a kilogram especially of marijuana or heroin
¹**key·board** \'kē-,bȯrd, -,bȯrd\ *noun* (1819)
1 : a bank of keys on a musical instrument (as a piano) that usually consists of seven white and five raised black keys to the octave
2 : an assemblage of systematically arranged keys by which a machine or device is operated
3 : a board on which keys for locks are hung
²**keyboard** (1961)
transitive verb
: to capture or set (as data or text) by means of a keyboard
intransitive verb
: to operate a machine (as for typesetting) by means of a keyboard
— **key·board·er** *noun*
key·board·ist \'kē-,bȯr-dist, -,bȯr-\ *noun* (1973)
: a person who plays a keyboard musical instrument
key·but·ton \'kē-bə-t²n\ *noun* (circa 1920)
: KEY 5c
key club *noun* [from the key to the premises provided to each member] (1962)
: an informal private club serving liquor and providing entertainment
key deer *noun, often K capitalized* (1950)
: a very small rare white-tailed deer (*Odocoileus virginianus clavium*) native to the Florida Keys

key grip \-,kē-\ *noun* (1979)
: the technician in charge of moving and setting up camera tracks and scenery in a motion-picture or television production
¹**key·hole** \'kē-,hōl\ *noun* (circa 1592)
1 : a hole for receiving a key
2 : KEY 12
²**keyhole** *adjective* (1937)
1 : revealingly intimate ⟨a *keyhole* report⟩
2 : intent on revealing intimate details ⟨*keyhole* columnists⟩
keyhole saw *noun* (1777)
: a narrow pointed fine-toothed handsaw used for cutting curves of short radius
key light *noun* (circa 1937)
: the main light illuminating a photographic subject
key lime *noun, often K capitalized* (1929)
: a lime grown especially in the Florida Keys and adjacent areas
key lime pie *noun, often K capitalized* (1954)
: a usually meringue-topped lime-custard pie traditionally made from key limes
Keynes·ian·ism \'kān-zē-ə-,ni-zəm\ *noun* (1946)
: the economic theories and programs ascribed to John M. Keynes and his followers; *specifically* **:** the advocacy of monetary and fiscal programs by government to increase employment and spending
— **Keynes·ian** \'kān-zē-ən\ *noun or adjective*
¹**key·note** \'kē-,nōt\ *noun* (1776)
1 : the first and harmonically fundamental tone of a scale
2 : the fundamental or central fact, idea, or mood ⟨sadness is the *keynote* of this little collection —*Books Abroad*⟩
²**keynote** *transitive verb* (1914)
1 : to set the keynote of
2 : to deliver the keynote address at
— **key·not·er** *noun*
keynote address *noun* (circa 1908)
: an address designed to present the issues of primary interest to an assembly (as a political convention) and often to arouse unity and enthusiasm — called also *keynote speech*
keynote speaker *noun* (1950)
: one who delivers a keynote address
key·pad \'kē-,pad\ *noun* (1975)
: a small often handheld keyboard
¹**key·punch** \'kē-,pənch\ *noun* (1918)
: a machine with a keyboard used to cut holes or notches in punched cards
²**keypunch** *transitive verb* (1959)
: to enter (data) on punched cards with a keypunch
— **key·punch·er** *noun*
key signature *noun* (1875)
: the sharps or flats placed after a clef in music to indicate the key
key·stone \'kē-,stōn\ *noun* (circa 1637)
1 : the wedge-shaped piece at the crown of an arch that locks the other pieces in place — see ARCH illustration
2 : something on which associated things depend for support ⟨determination, a *keystone* of the puritan ethic —L. S. Lewis⟩
¹**key·stroke** \-,strōk\ *noun* (circa 1910)
: the act or an instance of depressing a key on a keyboard
²**keystroke** *transitive verb* (1966)
: KEYBOARD
key·way \-,wā\ *noun* (circa 1864)
1 : a groove or channel for a key
2 : the aperture for the key in a lock having a flat metal key
key word *noun* (1859)
: a word that is a key: as **a :** a word exemplifying the meaning or value of a letter or symbol **b** *usually* **key·word** \-,wərd\ **:** a significant word from a title or document used as an index to content
khad·dar \'kä-dər\ *or* **kha·di** \'kä-dē\ *noun* [Hindi *khādar, khādī*] (circa 1885)
: homespun cotton cloth of India

kha·ki \'ka-kē, 'kä-, *Canadian often* 'kär-\ *noun* [Hindi *khākī* dust-colored, from *khāk* dust, from Persian] (1857)
1 : a light yellowish brown
2 a : a khaki-colored cloth made usually of cotton or wool and used especially for military uniforms **b :** a garment of this cloth; *especially* **:** a military uniform — usually used in plural ◇
— **khaki** *adjective*
Khal·kha \'kal-kə, 'kal-kə\ *noun* (1873)
1 : a member of a Mongol people of Outer Mongolia
2 : the language of the Khalkha people used as the official language of the Mongolian People's Republic
kham·sin \kam-'sēn\ *noun* [Arabic *rīḥ al-khamsīn* the wind of the fifty (days between Easter and Pentecost)] (1685)
: a hot southerly Egyptian wind
¹**khan** \'kän *also* 'kan\ *noun* [Middle English *caan,* from Middle French, of Turkic origin; akin to Turkish *han* prince] (15th century)
1 : a medieval sovereign of China and ruler over the Turkish, Tatar, and Mongol tribes
2 : a local chieftain or man of rank in some countries of central Asia
²**khan** *noun* [Arabic *khān*] (1614)
: a caravansary or rest house in some Asian countries
khan·ate \'kä-,nāt *also* 'ka-\ *noun* (1799)
: the state or jurisdiction of a khan
khap·ra beetle \'ka-prə-, 'kä-\ *noun* [Hindi *khaprā,* literally, destroyer] (1928)
: a dermestid beetle (*Trogoderma granarium*) that is native to the Indian subcontinent and is now a serious pest of stored grain in most parts of the world
khat \'kät\ *noun* [Arabic *qāt*] (1858)
: a shrub (*Catha edulis*) cultivated in the Middle East and Africa for its leaves and buds that are the source of an habituating stimulant when chewed or used as a tea
khe·dive \kə-'dēv\ *noun* [French *khédive,* from Turkish *hidiv*] (1867)
: a ruler of Egypt from 1867 to 1914 governing as a viceroy of the sultan of Turkey
— **khe·div·i·al** \-'dē-vē-əl\ *or* **khe·div·al** \-'dē-vəl\ *adjective*

◇ WORD HISTORY
khaki *Khaki,* like *bungalow, cot,* and *shampoo,* is a by-product of British rule in India, though for the average user of English these words have lost all association with the Raj. The Hindi word *khākī* "dust-colored, brown" was applied to the color of a uniform cloth used by units of Britain's Indian Army in the mid-19th century. Dull brown field uniforms were most likely originally adopted for their ease of maintenance on dirty trails, though as the range of a rifle increased and battlefield tactics changed in the later 19th century, it was doubtless realized that drab clothing was valuable as camouflage. By the time of the South African War (1899–1902), all colonial units of the British Army were dressed in the color, and *khaki* became linked with support for the army and a militaristic foreign policy. (The vote of 1900, when patriotic Britons returned to Parliament the same Conservatives who had started the war with the Boers, went down in history as the "Khaki Election.") Contemporary retailers in the U.S., however, to judge by their advertising, associate khaki clothing with fashionable casualness and a summery look rather than with military uniforms or British India.

\ə\ abut \ᵊ\ kitten \ər\ further \a\ ash \ā\ ace
\ä\ mop, mar \au̇\ out \ch\ chin \e\ bet \ē\ easy
\g\ go \i\ hit \ī\ ice \j\ job
\ŋ\ sing \ō\ go \ȯ\ law \ȯi\ boy \th\ thin \th\ the \ü\ loot \u̇\ foot
\y\ yet \zh\ vision *see also* Guide to Pronunciation

Khmer \kə-'mer\ *noun, plural* **Khmer** *or* **Khmers** (1876)
1 : a member of an aboriginal people of Cambodia
2 : the Mon-Khmer language of the Khmer people that is the official language of Cambodia
— **Khmer** *adjective*

Khoi·khoi \'kȯi-ˌkȯi\ *noun, plural* **Khoikhoi** (1791)
: HOTTENTOT

Khoi·san \'kȯi-ˌsän, -'sän\ *noun* [*Khoi*khoi + *San*] (1930)
1 : a group of African peoples speaking Khoisan languages
2 : a family of African languages comprising principally Hottentot and the Bushman languages

khoum \'küm, 'k̇üm\ *noun* [modification of Arabic *khums,* literally, one fifth] (1973)
— see *ouguiya* at MONEY table

Kho·war \'kō-ˌwär\ *noun* (1882)
: an Indo-Aryan language of northwest Pakistan

ki·ang \kē-'äŋ\ *noun* [Tibetan *rkyaṅ*] (1869)
: an Asian wild ass (*Equus hemionus kiang* synonym *E. kiang*) usually with reddish back and sides and white underparts, muzzle, and legs

kiaugh \'kyȧk\ *noun* [origin unknown] (1786)
Scottish : TROUBLE, ANXIETY

kib·be *or* **kib·beh** *or* **kib·bi** \'ki-bē\ *noun* [Arabic *kubbah*] (1937)
: a Near Eastern dish of ground lamb and bulgur that is eaten cooked or raw

¹**kib·ble** \'ki-bəl\ *transitive verb* **kib·bled; kib·bling** \-b(ə-)liŋ\ [origin unknown] (circa 1790)
: to grind coarsely ⟨*kibbled* dog biscuit⟩ ⟨*kibbled* grain⟩

²**kibble** *noun* (1942)
: coarsely ground meal or grain (as for animal feed)

kib·butz \ki-'bu̇ts, -'bu̇ts\ *noun, plural* **kib·but·zim** \-ˌbu̇t-'sēm, -ˌbu̇t-\ [New Hebrew *qibbūṣ*] (1944)
: a communal farm or settlement in Israel

kib·butz·nik \-'bu̇t-snik, -'bu̇t-\ *noun* [Yiddish *kibutsnik,* from *kibuts* kibbutz (from New Hebrew *qibbūṣ*) + *-nik,* agent suffix] (1947)
: a member of a kibbutz

kibe \'kīb\ *noun* [Middle English] (14th century)
: an ulcerated chilblain especially on the heel

ki·bitz *also* **kib·bitz** \'ki-bəts, kə-'bits\ *verb* [Yiddish *kibetsn*] (1927)
intransitive verb
: to act as a kibitzer
transitive verb
: to observe as a kibitzer; *especially* : to be a kibitzer at ⟨*kibitz* a card game⟩

ki·bitz·er *also* **kib·bitz·er** \'ki-bət-sər, kə-'bit-\ *noun* (1922)
: one who looks on and often offers unwanted advice or comment especially at a card game; *broadly* : one who offers opinions

ki·bosh \'kī-ˌbäsh, kī-'; ki-'bäsh\ *noun* [origin unknown] (1836)
: something that serves as a check or stop ⟨put the *kibosh* on that⟩ ◇
— **kibosh** *transitive verb*

¹**kick** \'kik\ *verb* [Middle English *kiken*] (14th century)
intransitive verb
1 a : to strike out with the foot or feet **b** : to make a kick in football
2 a : to show opposition : RESIST, REBEL **b** : to protest strenuously or urgently : express grave discontent; *broadly* : COMPLAIN
3 : to function with vitality and energy ⟨alive and *kicking*⟩
4 *of a firearm* : to recoil when fired
5 : to go from one place to another as circumstance or whim dictates
6 : to run at a faster speed during the last part of a race

transitive verb
1 a : to strike, thrust, or hit with the foot **b** : to strike suddenly and forcefully as if with the foot **c** : to remove from a position or status ⟨*kicked* him off the team⟩
2 : to score by kicking a ball
3 : to heap reproaches upon (oneself) ⟨*kicked* themselves for not going⟩
4 : to free oneself of (as a drug habit)
— **kick·able** \'ki-kə-bəl\ *adjective*
— **kick ass** : to kick butt — often considered vulgar
— **kick butt** : to use forceful or coercive measures in order to achieve a purpose; *also* : to succeed or win overwhelmingly
— **kick over the traces** : to cast off restraint, authority, or control
— **kick the bucket** : DIE
— **kick up one's heels 1** : to show sudden delight **2** : to have a lively time
— **kick upstairs** : to promote to a higher but less desirable position

²**kick** *noun* (1530)
1 a : a blow or sudden forceful thrust with the foot; *specifically* : a sudden propelling of a ball with the foot **b** : the power to kick **c** : a rhythmic motion of the legs used in swimming **d** : a burst of speed in racing
2 : a sudden forceful jolt or thrust suggesting a kick; *especially* : the recoil of a gun
3 : POCKET, WALLET
4 a : a feeling or expression of opposition or objection ⟨a *kick* against the administration⟩ **b** : the grounds for objection
5 a : an effect suggestive of a kick ⟨chili with a *kick*⟩ **b** : a stimulating or pleasurable effect or experience **c** : pursuit of an absorbing or obsessive new interest ⟨a skiing *kick*⟩
6 : a sudden and striking surprise, revelation, or turn of events

kick around (1839)
intransitive verb
1 : to wander or pass time aimlessly
2 : to lie about mostly unnoticed or forgotten
transitive verb
1 : to treat in an inconsiderate or high-handed fashion
2 : to consider, examine, or discuss from various angles

kick–ass \'kik-ˌas\ *adjective* (1970)
: strikingly tough, aggressive, or uncompromising — often considered vulgar

kick·back \'kik-ˌbak\ *noun* (1920)
1 : a sharp violent reaction
2 : a return of a part of a sum received often because of confidential agreement or coercion ⟨every city contract had been let with a ten percent *kickback* to city officials —D. K. Shipler⟩

kick·board \-ˌbȯrd, -ˌbȯrd\ *noun* (1949)
: a buoyant rectangular board held by a swimmer while developing kicking techniques

kick·box·ing \-ˌbäk-siŋ\ *noun* (1971)
: boxing in which boxers are permitted to kick with bare feet as in karate
— **kick·box·er** \-sər\ *noun*

kick·er *noun* (circa 1580)
1 : one that kicks or kicks something
2 : KICK 6

kick in (1908)
transitive verb
: CONTRIBUTE
intransitive verb
1 *slang* : DIE
2 : to make a contribution

kick·off \'kik-ˌȯf\ *noun* (1857)
1 : a kick that puts the ball into play in a football or soccer game
2 : COMMENCEMENT 1 ⟨the campaign *kickoff*⟩

kick off (1857)
intransitive verb
1 : to start or resume play in football by a placekick
2 : to begin proceedings
3 *slang* : DIE

transitive verb
: to mark the beginning of

kick out *transitive verb* (1697)
: to dismiss or eject forcefully or summarily

kick over (1951)
intransitive verb
: to begin to fire — used of an internal combustion engine
transitive verb
: TURN OVER 1b

kick pleat *noun* (1926)
: a short inverted pleat (as at the bottom of a skirt) used to give breadth

kick·shaw \'kik-ˌshȯ\ *noun* [by folk etymology from French *quelque chose* something] (1597)
1 : a fancy dish : DELICACY
2 : TRINKET, GEWGAW

kick·stand \'kik-ˌstand\ *noun* [from its being put in position by a kick] (1947)
: a swiveling metal bar or rod for holding up a 2-wheeled vehicle (as a bicycle) when not in use

kick turn *noun* (1910)
: a standing half turn in skiing made by swinging one ski high with a jerk and planting it in the desired direction and then lifting the other ski into a parallel position

kick-up \'kik-ˌəp\ *noun* (circa 1793)
: a noisy quarrel : ROW

kick up (1756)
transitive verb
1 : to stir up : PROVOKE ⟨*kick up* a fuss⟩
2 : to cause to rise upward ⟨clouds of dust *kicked up* by passing cars⟩
intransitive verb
: to give evidence of disorder

kicky \'ki-kē\ *adjective* (1966)
: providing a kick or thrill : EXCITING; *also* : excitingly fashionable

¹**kid** \'kid\ *noun* [Middle English *kide,* of Scandinavian origin; akin to Old Norse *kith* kid] (13th century)
1 a : a young goat **b** : a young individual of various animals related to the goat
2 a : the flesh, fur, or skin of a kid **b** : something made of kid
3 : a young person; *especially* : CHILD — often used as a generalized reference to one especially younger or less experienced ⟨the *kid* on the pro golf tour⟩ ⟨poor *kid*⟩
— **kid·dish** \'ki-dish\ *adjective*

²**kid** *intransitive verb* **kid·ded; kid·ding** (15th century)

◇ WORD HISTORY
kibosh The word *kibosh* is first recorded in 1836 in an early sketch by Charles Dickens (spelled *kye-bosk,* with a perhaps erroneous final *k*). Nine years later *kye-bosh* resurfaces in a dictionary of British underworld argot defined as "eighteen pence," the connection between this and the more familiar "check" or "stop" sense is unclear. For over a century this peculiar colloquialism has taxed the ingenuity of etymologists, with minimal results: beyond the fact that it was prominent enough in lower-class London speech to attract Dickens's attention in the 1830s we know nothing for certain. Claims were once made that the word was Yiddish, though no remotely plausible Yiddish source has ever been produced. Another hypothesis is that its source is Irish *caidhp bháis,* literally, "coif (or cap) of death," variously explained as headgear a judge put on when pronouncing a death sentence, or—somewhat more plausibly—as a covering pulled over the face of a dead person when a coffin was closed. But evidence for any metaphorical use of this phrase in Irish appears to be lacking, and *kibosh* is not recorded in English as spoken in Ireland until decades after Dickens must have heard it in London.

: to bring forth young — used of a goat or an antelope

³kid verb **kid·ded; kid·ding** [probably from ¹kid] (1902)
transitive verb
1 : to deceive as a joke ⟨it's the truth; I wouldn't kid you⟩
2 : to make fun of
intransitive verb
: to engage in good-humored fooling or horseplay — often used with around
— **kid·der** noun
— **kid·ding·ly** \'ki-diŋ-lē\ adverb

Kid·der·min·ster \'ki-dər-,min(t)-stər\ noun [Kidderminster, England] (1836)
: an ingrain carpet — called also Kidderminster carpet

kid·die or **kid·dy** \'ki-dē\ noun, plural **kiddies** often attributive [¹kid] (1889)
: a small child

kid·dush \'ki-dəsh, -dish; ki-'düsh\ noun [Late Hebrew qiddūsh sanctification] (1753)
: a ceremonial blessing pronounced over wine or bread in a Jewish home or synagogue on a holy day (as the Sabbath)

kid–glove \'kid-'gləv\ adjective (1888)
: marked by extreme care or deference ⟨kid-glove treatment⟩

kid glove noun (1832)
: a dress glove made of kid leather
— **kid–gloved** \'kid-'gləvd\ adjective
— **with kid gloves** : with special consideration

kid leather noun (1687)
1 : a soft pliable leather made from kidskin
2 : a glove leather made from lambskin or goatskin

kid·nap \'kid-,nap\ transitive verb **-napped** or **-naped** \-,napt\; **-nap·ping** or **-nap·ing** [probably back-formation from kidnapper, from kid + obsolete napper thief] (1682)
: to seize and detain or carry away by unlawful force or fraud and often with a demand for ransom
— **kid·nap·pee** or **kid·nap·ee** \,kid-,na-'pē\ noun
— **kid·nap·per** or **kid·nap·er** noun

kid·ney \'kid-nē\ noun, plural **kidneys** [Middle English] (14th century)
1 a : one of a pair of vertebrate organs situated in the body cavity near the spinal column that excrete waste products of metabolism, in humans are bean-shaped organs about 4½ inches (11½ centimeters) long lying behind the peritoneum in a mass of fatty tissue, and consist chiefly of nephrons by which urine is secreted, collected, and discharged into a main cavity whence it is conveyed by the ureter to the bladder **b** : any of various excretory organs of invertebrate animals
2 : the kidney of an animal eaten as food
3 : sort or kind especially with regard to temperament ⟨a nice helpful guy, of a different kidney entirely from the . . . Secret Police —Paula Lecler⟩

kidney bean noun (1548)
1 : an edible and nutritious seed of any cultivated bean of the common species (Phaseolus vulgaris); especially : a large dark red bean seed
2 : a plant bearing kidney beans

kidney stone noun (1946)
: a calculus in the kidney

kid·skin \'kid-,skin\ noun (14th century)
: the skin of a young or sometimes a mature goat; also : KID LEATHER

kid stuff noun (1929)
1 : something befitting or appropriate only to children
2 : something extremely simple or easy

kiel·ba·sa \kēl-'bä-sə, kil- also ki-'bä-sə\ noun, plural **-basas** also **-ba·sy** \-'bä-sē\ [Polish kiełbasa] (circa 1939)
: a smoked sausage of Polish origin

kie·sel·guhr \'kē-zəl-,gùr\ noun [German Kieselgur] (1875)
: loose or porous diatomite

kie·ser·ite \'kē-zə-,rīt\ noun [German Kieserit, from Dietrich Kieser (died 1862) German physician] (1862)
: a mineral that is a white hydrous magnesium sulfate

kif \'kif, 'kēf\ variant of KEF

kike \'kīk\ noun [origin unknown] (1904)
: JEW — usually taken to be offensive

Ki·ku·yu \kē-'kü-(,)yü\ noun, plural **Kikuyu** or **Kikuyus** (1894)
1 : a member of a Bantu-speaking people of Kenya
2 : the Bantu language of the Kikuyu people

kil·der·kin \'kil-dər-kən\ noun [Middle English, from Middle Dutch kindekijn, from Medieval Latin quintale quintal] (14th century)
1 : an English unit of capacity equal to ½ barrel
2 : CASK

ki·lim \kē-'lēm\ noun [Turkish, from Persian kilīm] (1881)
: a pileless handwoven reversible rug or covering made in Turkey, Kurdistan, the Caucasus, Iran, and western Turkestan

¹kill \'kil\ verb [Middle English, perhaps from (assumed) Old English cyllan; akin to Old English cwellan to kill — more at QUELL] (14th century)
transitive verb
1 a : to deprive of life **b** (1) : to slaughter (as a hog) for food (2) : to convert a food animal into (a kind of meat) by slaughtering
2 a : to put an end to ⟨kill competition⟩ **b** : DEFEAT, VETO ⟨killed the amendment⟩ **c** : to mark for omission; also : DELETE
3 a : to destroy the vital or essential quality of ⟨killed the pain with drugs⟩ **b** : to cause to stop ⟨kill the motor⟩ **c** : to check the flow of current through
4 : to make a markedly favorable impression on ⟨she killed the audience⟩
5 : to get through uneventfully ⟨kill time⟩; also : to get through (the time of a penalty) without being scored on ⟨kill a penalty⟩
6 a : to cause extreme pain to **b** : to tire almost to the point of collapse
7 : to hit (a shot) so hard in various games that a return is impossible
8 : to consume (as a drink) totally
intransitive verb
1 : to deprive one of life
2 : to make a markedly favorable impression ⟨was dressed to kill⟩ ☆

²kill noun (1814)
1 : an act or instance of killing
2 : something killed: as **a** (1) : an animal shot in a hunt (2) : animals killed in a hunt, season, or particular period of time **b** : an enemy unit (as an airplane or ship) destroyed by military action **c** : a return shot in any of various games (as badminton, handball, or table tennis) that is too hard for an opponent to handle

³kill noun, often capitalized [Dutch kil] (1669)
: CHANNEL, CREEK — used chiefly in place names in Delaware, Pennsylvania, and New York

kill·deer \'kil-,dir\ noun, plural **killdeers** or **killdeer** [imitative] (1731)
: an American plover (Charadrius vociferus) characterized by two black breast bands and a plaintive penetrating cry

¹kill·er \'ki-lər\ noun (15th century)
1 : one that kills
2 : KILLER WHALE
3 a : one that has a forceful, violent, or striking impact **b** : one that is extremely difficult to deal with

killdeer

²killer adjective (1951)
1 : strikingly impressive or effective ⟨a killer smile⟩ ⟨a killer résumé⟩

2 : extremely difficult to deal with ⟨a killer fastball⟩; also : causing death or devastation ⟨a killer tornado⟩

killer bee noun (1976)
: AFRICANIZED BEE

killer cell noun (1972)
: a T cell that functions in cell-mediated immunity by destroying a cell (as a tumor cell) having a specific antigenic molecule on its surface — called also killer T cell

killer instinct noun (1931)
: an aggressive tenacious urge for domination in a struggle to attain a set goal

killer whale noun (1884)
: a small gregarious whale (Orcinus orca) that is black with a white ventral side and white oval-shaped patches behind the eyes and attains a length of 20 to 30 feet (6.1 to 9.1 meters) — called also orca

kil·li·fish \'ki-li-,fish\ noun [killie killifish (perhaps from ³kill) + fish] (1836)
1 : any of a family (Cyprinodontidae) of numerous small oviparous fishes much used as bait and in mosquito control
2 : any of a family (Poeciliidae) of livebearers

¹kill·ing \'ki-liŋ\ noun (15th century)
1 : the act of one that kills
2 : KILL 2a
3 : a sudden notable gain or profit

²killing adjective (15th century)
1 : that kills or relates to killing
2 : highly amusing
3 : extremely difficult to deal with ⟨the suspense is killing⟩; also : calling for great strength, stamina, or endurance ⟨a killing schedule⟩
— **kill·ing·ly** \-lē\ adverb

kill·joy \'kil-,jòi\ noun (1776)
: one who spoils the pleasure of others

kill off transitive verb (1607)
: to destroy in large numbers or totally

kiln \'kiln, 'kil\ noun [Middle English kilne, from Old English cyln, from Latin culina kitchen, from coquere to cook — more at COOK] (before 12th century)
: an oven, furnace, or heated enclosure used for processing a substance by burning, firing, or drying
— **kiln** transitive verb

ki·lo \'kē-(,)lō also 'ki-\ noun, plural **kilos** (1870)
: KILOGRAM

Kilo (1952)
: a communications code word for the letter k

kilo- combining form [French, modification of Greek chilioi]
: thousand ⟨kiloton⟩

☆ **SYNONYMS**
Kill, slay, murder, assassinate, dispatch, execute mean to deprive of life. KILL merely states the fact of death caused by an agency in any manner ⟨killed in an accident⟩ ⟨frost killed the plants⟩. SLAY is a chiefly literary term implying deliberateness and violence but not necessarily motive ⟨slew thousands of the Philistines⟩. MURDER specifically implies stealth and motive and premeditation and therefore full moral responsibility ⟨convicted of murdering a rival⟩. ASSASSINATE applies to deliberate killing openly or secretly often for political motives ⟨terrorists assassinated the Senator⟩. DISPATCH stresses quickness and directness in putting to death ⟨dispatched the sentry with one bullet⟩. EXECUTE stresses putting to death as a legal penalty ⟨executed by lethal gas⟩.

\ə\ abut \ᵊ\ kitten \ər\ further \a\ ash \ā\ ace
\ä\ mop, mar \aù\ out \ch\ chin \e\ bet \ē\ easy
\g\ go \i\ hit \ī\ ice \j\ job \ŋ\ sing
\ò\ law \òi\ boy \th\ thin \t͟h\ the \ü\ loot \ù\ foot
\y\ yet \zh\ vision see also Guide to Pronunciation

ki·lo·bar \'kē-lə-,bär, 'ki-lə-\ *noun* [International Scientific Vocabulary] (1926)
: a unit of pressure equal to 1000 bars

ki·lo·base \-,bās\ *noun* (1975)
: a unit of measure of the length of a nucleic-acid chain that equals one thousand base pairs

ki·lo·bit \-,bit\ *noun* [International Scientific Vocabulary] (1961)
1 : 1000 bits
2 : 1024 bits

ki·lo·byte \-,bīt\ *noun* [from the fact that 1024 (2^{10}) is the power of 2 closest to 1000] (1970)
: 1024 bytes

ki·lo·cal·o·rie \-,ka-lə-rē, -'kal-rē\ *noun* [International Scientific Vocabulary] (1894)
: CALORIE 1b

kilo·cy·cle \'ki-lə-,sī-kəl\ *noun* [International Scientific Vocabulary] (1921)
: 1000 cycles; *especially* : KILOHERTZ

ki·lo·gauss \'kē-lə-,gaůs, 'ki-lə-\ *noun* [International Scientific Vocabulary] (1895)
: 1000 gauss

ki·lo·gram \-,gram\ *noun* [French *kilogramme*, from *kilo-* + *gramme* gram] (1797)
1 : the base unit of mass in the International System of Units that is equal to the mass of a prototype agreed upon by international convention and that is nearly equal to the mass of 1000 cubic centimeters of water at the temperature of its maximum density — see METRIC SYSTEM table
2 : a unit of force equal to the weight of a kilogram mass under a gravitational attraction equal to that of the earth

kilogram–meter *noun* (1886)
: the meter-kilogram-second gravitational unit of work and energy equal to the work done by a kilogram force acting through a distance of one meter in the direction of the force : about 7.235 foot-pounds

ki·lo·hertz \'ki-lə-,hərts, 'kē-lə-, -,herts\ *noun* [International Scientific Vocabulary] (1929)
: 1000 hertz

ki·lo·joule \-,jü(ə)l\ *noun* [International Scientific Vocabulary] (circa 1889)
: 1000 joules

kilo·li·ter \'ki-lə-,lē-tər\ *noun* [French *kilolitre*, from *kilo-* + *litre* liter] (1810)
— see METRIC SYSTEM table

ki·lo·me·ter \÷kə-'lä-mə-tər, 'ki-; 'ki-lə-,mē-tər\ *noun* [French *kilomètre*, from *kilo-* + *mètre* meter] (1810)
— see METRIC SYSTEM table □

ki·lo·par·sec \'ki-lə-,pär-,sek, 'ki-lə-\ *noun* (1922)
: 1000 parsecs

ki·lo·pas·cal \,ki-lə-,pas-'kal\ *noun* (1978)
: 1000 pascals

ki·lo·rad \'ki-lə-,rad\ *noun* [International Scientific Vocabulary] (1965)
: 1000 rads

ki·lo·ton \-,tən *also* -,tän\ *noun* (1950)
1 : 1000 tons
2 : an explosive force equivalent to that of 1000 tons of TNT

ki·lo·volt \-,vōlt\ *noun* [International Scientific Vocabulary] (circa 1898)
: a unit of potential difference equal to 1000 volts

kilo·watt \'ki-lə-,wät\ *noun* [International Scientific Vocabulary] (1884)
: 1000 watts

kilowatt–hour *noun* (1892)
: a unit of work or energy equal to that expended by one kilowatt in one hour or to 3.6 million joules

¹kilt \'kilt\ *verb* [Middle English, of Scandinavian origin; akin to Old Norse *kjalta* lap, fold of a gathered skirt] (14th century)
transitive verb
1 *chiefly dialect* : to tuck up (as a skirt)
2 : to equip with a kilt
intransitive verb
: to move nimbly

²kilt *noun* (circa 1730)
1 : a knee-length pleated skirt usually of tartan worn by men in Scotland and by Scottish regiments in the British armies
2 : a garment that resembles a Scottish kilt

kil·ter \'kil-tər\ *noun* [origin unknown] (1628)
: proper or usual state or condition : ORDER ⟨out of *kilter*⟩

kilt·ie \'kil-tē\ *noun* (1842)
1 *or* **kilty** : one who wears a kilt
2 : a shoe with a long slashed tongue that folds over the instep; *also* : such a tongue

kim·ber·lite \'kim-bər-,līt\ *noun* [*Kimberley*, South Africa + ¹-*ite*] (1887)
: an agglomerate biotite-peridotite that occurs in pipes especially in southern Africa and that often contains diamonds

Kim·bun·du \kim-'bùn-(,)dü\ *noun* (circa 1895)
: a Bantu language of northern Angola

kim·chi *also* **kim·chee** \'kim-chē\ *noun* [Korean *kimch'i*] (1898)
: a vegetable pickle seasoned with garlic, red pepper, and ginger that is the national dish of Korea

ki·mo·no \kə-'mō-(,)nō, -nə\ *noun, plural* **-nos** [Japanese, clothes, from *ki* wearing + *mono* thing] (1886)
1 : a long robe with wide sleeves traditionally worn with a broad sash as an outer garment by the Japanese
2 : a loose dressing gown or jacket
— **ki·mo·noed** \-(,)nōd, -nəd\ *adjective*

kimono 1

¹kin \'kin\ *noun* [Middle English, akin to Old High German *cynn*; akin to Old High German *chunni* race, Latin *genus* birth, race, kind, Greek *genos*, Latin *gignere* to beget, Greek *gignesthai* to be born] (before 12th century)
1 : a group of persons of common ancestry : CLAN
2 a : one's relatives : KINDRED **b** : KINSMAN ⟨he wasn't any *kin* to you —Jean Stafford⟩
3 *archaic* : KINSHIP

²kin *adjective* (1597)
: KINDRED, RELATED

-kin \kən\ *also* **-kins** \kənz\ *noun suffix* [Middle English, from Middle Dutch *-kin*; akin to Old High German *-chīn*, diminutive suffix]
: little ⟨*catkin*⟩ ⟨*babykins*⟩

ki·na \'kē-nə\ *noun* [New Guinea Pidgin, literally, a kind of shell] (1975)
— see MONEY table

ki·nase \'kī-,nās, -,nāz\ *noun* [International Scientific Vocabulary, from *kinetic*] (1947)
: an enzyme that catalyzes the transfer of phosphate groups from a high-energy phosphate-containing molecule (as ATP) to a substrate

¹kind \'kīnd\ *noun* [Middle English *kinde*, from Old English *cynd*; akin to Old English *cynn* kin] (before 12th century)
1 a *archaic* : NATURE **b** *archaic* : FAMILY, LINEAGE
2 *archaic* : MANNER
3 : fundamental nature or quality : ESSENCE
4 a : a group united by common traits or interests : CATEGORY **b** : a specific or recognized variety ⟨what *kind* of car do you drive⟩ **c** : a doubtful or barely admissible member of a category ⟨a *kind* of gray⟩
5 a : goods or commodities as distinguished from money ⟨payment in *kind*⟩ **b** : the equivalent of what has been offered or received
synonym see TYPE
— **all kinds of 1** : MANY ⟨likes *all kinds of* sports⟩ **2** : plenty of ⟨has *all kinds of* time⟩

²kind *adjective* (14th century)
1 *chiefly dialect* : AFFECTIONATE, LOVING
2 a : of a sympathetic or helpful nature **b** : of a forbearing nature : GENTLE **c** : arising from or characterized by sympathy or forbearance ⟨a *kind* act⟩
3 : of a kind to give pleasure or relief

kin·der·gar·ten \'kin-də(r)-,gär-t°n, -,d°n\ *noun* [German, from *Kinder* children + *Garten* garden] (1852)
: a school or class for children usually from four to six years old

kin·der·gart·ner \-,gärt-nər, -,gärd-\ *also* **kin·der·gar·ten·er** \-,gär-t°n-ər, -,d°n-\ *noun* (1889)
1 : a teacher at a kindergarten
2 : a child attending or of an age to attend kindergarten

kind·heart·ed \,kīnd-'här-təd\ *adjective* (1535)
: marked by a sympathetic nature
— **kind·heart·ed·ly** *adverb*
— **kind·heart·ed·ness** *noun*

¹kin·dle \'kin-d°l\ *verb* **kin·dled; kin·dling** \'kin(d)-liŋ, 'kin-d°l-iŋ\ [Middle English, probably modification of Old Norse *kynda*; akin to Old High German *cuntesal* fire] (13th century)
transitive verb
1 : to start (a fire) burning : LIGHT
2 a : to stir up : AROUSE ⟨*kindle* interest⟩ **b** : to bring into being : START
3 : to cause to glow : ILLUMINATE
intransitive verb
1 : to catch fire
2 a : to flare up **b** : to become animated
3 : to become illuminated
— **kin·dler** \'kin(d)-lər, 'kin-d°l-ər\ *noun*

²kindle *verb* **kin·dled; kin·dling** [Middle English, from *kindle* young animal, probably from *kinde*, noun, kind] (13th century)
transitive verb
: BEAR — used especially of a rabbit
intransitive verb
: to bring forth young — used especially of a rabbit

kind·less \'kīn(d)-ləs\ *adjective* (13th century)
1 *obsolete* : INHUMAN
2 : DISAGREEABLE, UNCONGENIAL
— **kind·less·ly** *adverb*

kind·li·ness \'kīn(d)-lē-nəs\ *noun* (15th century)
1 : the quality or state of being kindly
2 : a kindly deed

kin·dling \'kin(d)-liŋ, 'kin-lən\ *noun* (1513)
: easily combustible material for starting a fire

¹kind·ly \'kīn(d)-lē\ *adjective* **kind·li·er; -est** [Middle English, from Old English *cyndelīc*, from *cynd*] (before 12th century)
1 a *obsolete* : NATURAL **b** *archaic* : LAWFUL
2 : of an agreeable or beneficial nature : PLEASANT ⟨*kindly* climate⟩

3 : of a sympathetic or generous nature
²**kindly** *adverb* (before 12th century)
1 a : in the normal way **:** NATURALLY ⟨old wounds which had healed *kindly* —*American Mercury*⟩ **b :** READILY ⟨did not take *kindly* to suggestions⟩
2 a : in a kind manner **:** SYMPATHETICALLY **b :** as a gesture of goodwill ⟨would take it *kindly* if you would put in a good word⟩ **c :** in a gracious manner **:** COURTEOUSLY ⟨they *kindly* invited us along⟩ **d :** as a matter of courtesy **:** PLEASE ⟨would you *kindly* order me a cab⟩
3 *chiefly Southern* **:** SOMEWHAT, KIND OF ⟨it's *kindly* embarrassing —Walter Davis⟩
kind·ness \'kīn(d)-nəs\ *noun* (13th century)
1 : a kind deed **:** FAVOR
2 a : the quality or state of being kind **b** *archaic* **:** AFFECTION
kind of *adverb* (1775)
1 : to a moderate degree **:** SOMEWHAT ⟨it's *kind of* late to begin⟩
2 : in a way that approximates **:** MORE OR LESS ⟨*kind of* sneaked up on us⟩
¹**kin·dred** \'kin-drəd\ *noun* [Middle English, from *kin* + Old English *rǣden* condition, from *rǣdan* to advise, read] (12th century)
1 a : a group of related individuals **b :** one's relatives
2 : family relationship **:** KINSHIP
²**kindred** *adjective* (14th century)
1 : of a similar nature or character **:** LIKE
2 : of the same ancestry
kine \'kīn\ *archaic plural of* COW
kin·e·ma \'ki-nə-mə\ *British variant of* CINEMA
ki·ne·mat·ics \,ki-nə-'ma-tiks *also* ,kī-\ *noun plural but singular in construction* [French *cinématique*, from Greek *kinēmat-*, *kinēma* motion, from *kinein* to move] (1840)
: a branch of dynamics that deals with aspects of motion apart from considerations of mass and force
— **ki·ne·mat·ic** \-tik\ *or* **ki·ne·mat·i·cal** \-ti-kəl\ *adjective*
— **ki·ne·mat·i·cal·ly** \-ti-k(ə-)lē\ *adverb*
¹**ki·ne·scope** \'ki-nə-,skōp *also* 'kī-\ *noun* [from *Kinescope*, a trademark] (1930)
1 : PICTURE TUBE
2 : a motion picture made from an image on a picture tube
²**kinescope** *transitive verb* **-scoped; -scop·ing** (1949)
: to make a kinescope of
ki·ne·sics \kə-'nē-siks, kī-, -ziks\ *noun plural but singular in construction* [Greek *kinēsis* motion + English *-ics*] (1952)
: a systematic study of the relationship between nonlinguistic body motions (as blushes, shrugs, or eye movement) and communication
ki·ne·si·ol·o·gy \kə-,nē-sē-'ä-lə-jē, kī-, -zē-\ *noun* [Greek *kinēsis*] (1894)
: the study of the principles of mechanics and anatomy in relation to human movement
ki·ne·sis \kə-'nē-səs, kī-\ *noun, plural* **ki·ne·ses** \-,sēz\ [New Latin, from Greek *kinēsis*] (1905)
: a movement that lacks directional orientation and depends upon the intensity of stimulation
-kinesis *noun combining form, plural* **-kineses** [New Latin, from Greek *kinēsis*, from *kinein* to move; akin to Latin *ciēre* to move]
1 : division ⟨karyo*kinesis*⟩
2 : production of motion ⟨tele*kinesis*⟩
kin·es·the·sia \,ki-nəs-'thē-zh(ē-)ə, ,kī-\ *or* **kin·es·the·sis** \-'thē-səs\ *noun, plural* **-the·sias** *or* **-the·ses** \-,sēz\ [New Latin, from Greek *kinein* + *aisthēsis* perception — more at ANESTHESIA] (1880)
: a sense mediated by end organs located in muscles, tendons, and joints and stimulated by bodily movements and tensions; *also* **:** sensory experience derived from this sense
— **kin·es·thet·ic** \-'the-tik\ *adjective*
— **kin·es·thet·i·cal·ly** \-ti-k(ə-)lē\ *adverb*

kinet- *or* **kineto-** *combining form* [Greek *ki-nētos* moving]
: movement **:** motion ⟨*kineto*some⟩
ki·net·ic \kə-'ne-tik *also* kī-\ *adjective* [Greek *kinētikos*, from *kinētos*, from *kinein*] (1864)
1 : of or relating to the motion of material bodies and the forces and energy associated therewith
2 a : ACTIVE, LIVELY **b :** DYNAMIC, ENERGIZING
3 : of or relating to kinetic art
— **ki·net·i·cal·ly** \-ti-k(ə-)lē\ *adverb*
kinetic art *noun* (1961)
: art (as sculpture or assemblage) having mechanical parts which can be set in motion
— **kinetic artist** *noun*
kinetic energy *noun* (1870)
: energy associated with motion
ki·net·i·cist \kə-'ne-tə-sist *also* kī-\ *noun* (1960)
1 : a specialist in kinetics
2 : a person who works in kinetic art **:** KINETIC ARTIST
ki·net·ics \kə-'ne-tiks *also* kī-\ *noun plural but singular or plural in construction* (circa 1859)
1 a : a branch of science that deals with the effects of forces upon the motions of material bodies or with changes in a physical or chemical system **b :** the rate of change in such a system
2 : the mechanism by which a physical or chemical change is effected
kinetic theory *noun* (1864)
: either of two theories in physics based on the fact that the minute particles of a substance are in vigorous motion: **a :** a theory that the particles of a gas move in straight lines with high average velocity, continually encounter one another and thus change their individual velocities and directions, and cause pressure by their impact against the walls of a container — called also *kinetic theory of gases* **b :** a theory that the temperature of a substance increases with an increase in either the average kinetic energy of the particles or the average potential energy of separation (as in fusion) of the particles or in both when heat is added — called also *kinetic theory of heat*
ki·ne·tin \'kī-nə-tən\ *noun* (1955)
: a cytokinin $C_{10}H_9N_5O$ that increases mitosis and callus formation
ki·net·o·chore \kə-'ne-tə-,kōr, kī-, -,kȯr\ *noun* [*kinet-* + Greek *chōros* place] (1934)
: CENTROMERE
ki·net·o·plast \kə-'ne-tə-,plast, kī-\ *noun* [International Scientific Vocabulary] (1925)
: an extranuclear cell organelle within a mitochondrion especially of trypanosomes that contains DNA
ki·net·o·scope \kə-'ne-tə-,skōp, kī-\ *noun* [from *Kinetoscope*, a trademark] (1894)
: a device for viewing through a magnifying lens a sequence of pictures on an endless band of film moved continuously over a light source and a rapidly rotating shutter that creates an illusion of motion
ki·net·o·some \-,sōm\ *noun* (1912)
: BASAL BODY
kin·folk \'kin-,fōk\ *or* **kinfolks** *noun plural* (1873)
: RELATIVES
king \'kiŋ\ *noun* [Middle English, from Old English *cyning;* akin to Old High German *kuning* king, Old English *cynn* kin] (before 12th century)
1 a : a male monarch of a major territorial unit; *especially* **:** one whose position is hereditary and who rules for life **b :** a paramount chief
2 *capitalized* **:** GOD, CHRIST
3 : one that holds a preeminent position; *especially* **:** a chief among competitors
4 : the principal piece of each color in chess having the power to move ordinarily one square in

any direction and to capture opposing pieces but being obliged never to enter or remain in check
5 : a playing card marked with a stylized figure of a king
6 : a checker that has been crowned
king·bird \-,bərd\ *noun* (1778)
: any of various American tyrant flycatchers (genus *Tyrannus*)
king·bolt \-,bōlt\ *noun* (1825)
: a vertical bolt by which the forward axle and wheels of a vehicle or the trucks of a railroad car are connected with the other parts
King Charles spaniel \-'chär(-ə)lz-\ *noun* [*Charles* II of England] (1833)
: an English toy spaniel having a black and tan coat
king cobra *noun* (1894)
: a large cobra (*Ophiophagus hannah* synonym *Naja hannah*) of southeastern Asia and the Philippines that may attain a length of 18 feet (5.5 meters)

king cobra

king crab *noun* (1698)
1 : HORSESHOE CRAB
2 : any of several very large crabs; *especially* **:** one (*Paralithoides camtschaticus*) of the North Pacific caught commercially for food
king·craft \'kiŋ-,kraft\ *noun* (1643)
: the art of governing as a king
king·cup \-,kəp\ *noun* (1538)
: any of several plants of the buttercup family; *especially* **:** MARSH MARIGOLD
king·dom \'kiŋ-dəm\ *noun* (before 12th century)
1 *archaic* **:** KINGSHIP
2 : a politically organized community or major territorial unit having a monarchical form of government headed by a king or queen
3 *often capitalized* **a :** the eternal kingship of God **b :** the realm in which God's will is fulfilled
4 a : a realm or region in which something is dominant **b :** an area or sphere in which one holds a preeminent position
5 a : one of the three primary divisions into which natural objects are commonly classified — compare ANIMAL KINGDOM, MINERAL KINGDOM, PLANT KINGDOM **b :** a major category (as Plantae or Protista) in biological taxonomy that ranks above the phylum and is the highest and most encompassing group
kingdom come *noun* [from the phrase "Thy kingdom come" (Matthew 6:10)] (1785)
: the next world **:** HEAVEN
king·fish \'kiŋ-,fish\ *noun* (1750)
1 : any of several marine croakers (family Sciaenidae) **a :** any of three fishes (*Menticirrhus americanus, M. littoralis,* and *M. saxatilis*) of shallow coastal waters of the Atlantic Ocean **b :** a small silvery food and sport fish (*Genyonemus lineatus*) of inshore waters especially of California — called also *white croaker*
2 : KING MACKEREL
3 : an undisputed master in an area or group
king·fish·er \-,fi-shər\ *noun* (15th century)
: any of numerous nonpasserine birds (family Alcedinidae) that are usually crested and bright-colored with a short tail and a long stout sharp bill
King James Version \-'jāmz-\ *noun* [*James* I of England] (circa 1889)
: AUTHORIZED VERSION
king·let \'kiŋ-lət\ *noun* (1603)

1 : a weak or petty king
2 : any of several small birds (genus *Regulus*) that are related to the gnatcatchers

king·ly \'kiŋ-lē\ *adjective* **king·li·er; -est** (14th century)
1 : having royal rank
2 : of, relating to, or befitting a king
3 MONARCHICAL
— **king·li·ness** *noun*
— **kingly** *adverb*

king mackerel *noun* (circa 1930)
: a mackerel (*Scomberomorus cavalla*) that is noted especially as a fighting sport fish

king·mak·er \'kiŋ-,mā-kər\ *noun* (1599)
: one having great influence over the choice of candidates for political office

king of arms (15th century)
: an officer of arms of the highest rank

king penguin *noun* (1885)
: a large penguin (*Aptenodytes patagonica*) chiefly of subantarctic regions

king·pin \'kiŋ-,pin\ *noun* (1801)
1 : any of several bowling pins: as **a** : HEADPIN **b** : the pin that stands in the middle of a triangular arrangement of bowling pins
2 : the chief person in a group or undertaking
3 a : KINGBOLT **b** : a pin connecting the two parts of a knuckle joint (as in an automobile steering linkage)

king post *noun* (1776)
: a vertical member connecting the apex of a triangular truss (as of a roof) with the base

Kings \'kiŋz\ *noun plural but singular in construction*
1 : either of two narrative and historical books of canonical Jewish and Christian Scripture — see BIBLE table
2 : any of four narrative and historical books in the former Roman Catholic canon of the Old Testament

king salmon *noun* (1881)
: CHINOOK SALMON

King's Bench *noun* (14th century)
: a division in the English superior courts system that hears civil and criminal cases

King's Counsel *noun* (1689)
: a barrister selected to serve as counsel to the British crown

King's English *noun* (1553)
: standard, pure, or correct English speech or usage

king's evil *noun, often K&E capitalized* [from the former belief that it could be healed by a king's touch] (14th century)
: SCROFULA

king·ship \'kiŋ-,ship\ *noun* (14th century)
1 : the position, office, or dignity of a king
2 : the personality of a king
3 : government by a king

king·side \-,sīd\ *noun* (1941)
: the side of a chessboard containing the file on which the king sits at the beginning of the game

king–size \-,sīz\ *or* **king–sized** \-,sīzd\ *adjective* (1942)
1 : longer than the regular or standard size ⟨a *king-size* cigarette⟩
2 : unusually large
3 a : having dimensions of approximately 76 inches by 80 inches (about 1.9 by 2.0 meters) — used of a bed; compare FULL-SIZE, QUEEN-SIZE, TWIN-SIZE **b** : of a size that fits a king-size bed ⟨*king-size* sheets⟩

king snake *noun* (1709)
: any of numerous brightly marked colubrid snakes (genus *Lampropeltis*) chiefly of North and Central America

king's ransom *noun* (circa 1590)
: a very large sum

king·wood \-,wu̇d\ *noun* (circa 1851)
: the wood of any of several tropical American leguminous trees (especially genus *Dalbergia*); *especially* : the wood of a Brazilian tree (*D. cearensis*) used especially for furniture

ki·nin \'kī-nən\ *noun* [Greek *kinein* to move, stimulate + English ¹*-in* — more at -KINESIS] (1954)
1 : any of various polypeptide hormones that are formed locally in the tissues and cause dilation of blood vessels and contraction of smooth muscle
2 : CYTOKININ

¹**kink** \'kiŋk\ *noun* [Dutch; akin to Middle Low German *kinke* kink] (1678)
1 : a short tight twist or curl caused by a doubling or winding of something upon itself
2 a : a mental or physical peculiarity : ECCENTRICITY, QUIRK **b** : WHIM
3 : a clever unusual way of doing something
4 : a cramp in some part of the body
5 : an imperfection likely to cause difficulties in the operation of something

²**kink** (1697)
intransitive verb
: to form a kink
transitive verb
: to make a kink in

kin·ka·jou \'kiŋ-kə-,jü\ *noun* [French, alteration of *quincajou* wolverine, of Algonquian origin; akin to Ojibwa *kwiˑnkwaˀaˑkeˑ* wolverine] (1796)
: a nocturnal arboreal omnivorous mammal (*Potos flavus*) found from Mexico to South America that is related to the raccoon and has a long prehensile tail, large eyes, and yellowish brown fur

kinky \'kiŋ-kē\ *adjective* **kink·i·er; -est** (1844)
1 : closely twisted or curled
2 : relating to, having, or appealing to unconventional tastes especially in sex; *also* : sexually deviant
3 : OUTLANDISH, FAR-OUT
— **kink·i·ly** \'kiŋ-kə-lē\ *adverb*
— **kink·i·ness** \'kiŋ-kē-nəs\ *noun*

kin·ni·kin·nick \,ki-ni-kə-'nik, 'ki-ni-kə-,\ *noun* [of Algonquian origin; akin to Massachuset *kinukkinuk* mixture] (1799)
: a mixture of dried leaves and bark and sometimes tobacco smoked by the Indians and pioneers especially in the Ohio valley; *also* : a plant (as a sumac or dogwood) used in it

-kins — see -KIN

kins·folk \'kinz-,fōk\ *noun plural* (15th century)
: RELATIVES

kin·ship \'kin-,ship\ *noun* (1833)
: the quality or state of being kin : RELATIONSHIP

kins·man \'kinz-mən\ *noun* (12th century)
: RELATIVE; *specifically* : a male relative

kins·wom·an \-,wu̇-mən\ *noun* (14th century)
: a female relative

ki·osk \'kē-,äsk\ *noun* [Turkish *köşk*, from Persian *kūshk* portico] (1625)
1 : an open summerhouse or pavilion
2 : a small structure with one or more open sides that is used to vend merchandise (as newspapers) or services (as film developing)

Ki·o·wa \'kī-ə-,wò, -wä, -,wā\ *noun, plural* **Kiowa** *or* **Kiowas** (1808)
1 : a member of an American Indian people of what are now Colorado, Kansas, New Mexico, Oklahoma, and Texas
2 : the language of the Kiowa people

¹**kip** \'kip\ *noun* [obsolete Dutch; akin to Middle Low German *kip* bundle of hides] (circa 1525)
: a bundle of undressed hides of young or small animals; *also* : one of the hides

²**kip** *noun* [perhaps from Danish *kippe* cheap tavern] (1879)
1 : BED ⟨ready for the *kip* after this screwball day —K. M. Dodson⟩
2 *chiefly British* : SLEEP, NAP ⟨roused the . . . family from their *kip* —Sylvia Margolis⟩

³**kip** *intransitive verb* **kipped; kip·ping** (circa 1889)
British : SLEEP — sometimes used with *down* ⟨*kip* down on a spare bed —Alice Glenday⟩

⁴**kip** *noun* [*kilo-* + *pound*] (1914)
: a unit of weight equal to 1000 pounds (4448 newtons) used to express deadweight load

⁵**kip** \'kip, 'gip\ *noun, plural* **kip** *or* **kips** [Lao *kìːp*, literally, ingot] (1955)
— see MONEY table

¹**kip·per** \'ki-pər\ *noun* [Middle English *kypre*, from Old English *cypera*; akin to Old English *coper* copper] (before 12th century)
1 : a male salmon or sea trout during or after the spawning season
2 : a kippered herring or salmon

²**kipper** *transitive verb* **kip·pered; kip·per·ing** \-p(ə-)riŋ\ (1773)
: to cure (split dressed fish) by salting and smoking
— **kip·per·er** \-pər-ər\ *noun*

Kir·ghiz \kir-'gēz\ *noun, plural* **Kirghiz** *or* **Kir·ghiz·es** [Kirghiz *kırğız*] (1600)
1 : a member of a Turkic people of Kyrgyzstan and adjacent areas of central Asia
2 : the language of the Kirghiz

kirk \'kirk, 'kərk\ *noun* [Middle English (northern dialect), from Old Norse *kirkja*, from Old English *cirice* — more at CHURCH] (12th century)
1 *chiefly Scottish* : CHURCH
2 *capitalized* : the national church of Scotland as distinguished from the Church of England or the Episcopal Church in Scotland

Kir·li·an photography \'kir-lē-ən-\ *noun* [Semyon D. & Valentina K. *Kirlian* (flourished 1939) Soviet inventors] (1972)
: a process in which an image is obtained by application of a high-frequency electric field to an object so that it radiates a characteristic pattern of luminescence that is recorded on photographic film
— **Kirlian photograph** *noun*

Kir·man \kər-'män, kir-\ *noun* [*Kirman*, province in Iran] (1876)
: a Persian carpet or rug characterized by elaborate fluid designs and soft colors

kir·mess \'kər-məs\ *variant of* KERMIS

kirsch \'kirsh\ *noun* [German, short for *Kirschwasser*, from *Kirsche* cherry + *Wasser* water] (1869)
: a dry colorless brandy distilled from the fermented juice of the black morello cherry

Kirt·land's warbler \'kərt-lən(d)z-\ *noun* [Jared P. *Kirtland* (died 1877) American naturalist] (1858)
: a rare warbler (*Dendroica kirtlandii*) of northeastern North America that breeds in Michigan and winters in the Bahamas

kir·tle \'kər-tᵊl\ *noun* [Middle English *kirtel*, from Old English *cyrtel*, from (assumed) Old English *curt* short, from Latin *curtus* shortened — more at SHEAR] (before 12th century)
1 : a tunic or coat worn by men especially in the Middle Ages
2 : a long gown or dress worn by women

kish·ke *also* **kish·ka** \'kish-kə\ *noun* [Yiddish *kishke* gut, sausage, of Slavic origin; akin to Polish *kiszka* gut, sausage] (circa 1936)
: beef or fowl casing stuffed (as with meat, flour, and spices) and cooked

Kis·lev \'kis-ləf\ *noun* [Hebrew *Kislēw*] (14th century)
: the 3d month of the civil year or the 9th month of the ecclesiastical year in the Jewish calendar — see MONTH table

kis·met \'kiz-,met, -mət\ *noun, often capitalized* [Turkish, from Arabic *qismah* portion, lot] (1834)
: FATE 1, 2a

¹**kiss** \'kis\ *verb* [Middle English, from Old English *cyssan*; akin to Old High German *kussen* to kiss] (before 12th century)
transitive verb
1 : to touch with the lips especially as a mark of affection or greeting

2 : to touch gently or lightly ⟨wind gently *kissing* the trees⟩
intransitive verb
1 : to salute or caress one another with the lips
2 : to come in gentle contact
— **kiss·able** \'ki-sə-bəl\ *adjective*
— **kiss ass :** to act obsequiously especially to gain favor — usually considered vulgar
— **kiss good–bye 1 :** LEAVE **2 :** to resign oneself to the loss of
²kiss *noun* (before 12th century)
1 : a caress with the lips
2 : a gentle touch or contact
3 a : a small drop cookie made of meringue **b :** a bite-size piece of candy often wrapped in paper or foil
4 : an expression of affection ⟨sent him *kisses* in her letter⟩
kiss–and–tell \'kis-ᵊn(d)-'tel\ *adjective* (1949)
: telling details of private matters ⟨*kiss-and-tell* autobiographies⟩
kiss·er \'ki-sər\ *noun* (1537)
1 : one that kisses
2 *slang* **a :** MOUTH **b :** FACE
kissing bug *noun* (1899)
: CONENOSE
kissing cousin *noun* (1941)
1 : a person and especially a relative whom one knows well enough to kiss more or less formally upon meeting
2 : one that is closely related in kind to something else
kissing disease *noun* [from the belief that it is frequently transmitted by kissing] (1962)
: INFECTIOUS MONONUCLEOSIS
kiss of death [from the kiss with which Judas betrayed Jesus (Mark 14:44–46)] (1943)
: something (as an act or association) ultimately causing ruin
kiss off *transitive verb* (circa 1935)
: to dismiss lightly ⟨*kisses* the other performers *off* as mere amateurs⟩
— **kiss–off** \'ki-,sof\ *noun*
kiss of life (1961)
chiefly British **:** artificial respiration by the mouth-to-mouth method
kiss of peace (circa 1898)
: a ceremonial kiss, embrace, or handclasp used in Christian liturgies and especially the Eucharist as a sign of fraternal unity
kist \'kist\ *noun* [Middle English *kiste*, from Old Norse *kista*, ultimately from Latin *cista* — more at CHEST] (14th century)
chiefly Scottish & South African **:** CHEST 1b
¹kit \'kit\ *noun* [Middle English] (14th century)
1 *dialect British* **:** a wooden tub
2 a (1) **:** a collection of articles usually for personal use ⟨a travel *kit*⟩ (2) **:** a set of tools or implements ⟨a carpenter's *kit*⟩ (3) **:** a set of parts to be assembled or worked up ⟨model airplane *kit*⟩ (4) **:** a packaged collection of related material ⟨convention *kit*⟩ (5) *chiefly British* **:** GEAR ⟨run over to my billet and get some overnight *kit* —Lionel Shapiro⟩ **b :** a container for any of such sets or collections
3 : a group of persons or things — usually used in the phrase *the whole kit and caboodle*
²kit *transitive verb* **kit·ted; kit·ting** (1919)
chiefly British **:** EQUIP, OUTFIT — often used with *up* or *out*
³kit *noun* [origin unknown] (1519)
: a small narrow violin
⁴kit *noun* (1562)
1 : KITTEN
2 : a young or undersized fur-bearing animal; *also* **:** its pelt
kit bag *noun* [¹*kit*] (1893)
1 : KNAPSACK
2 : a suitcase usually with sides that fasten at the top or open to the full width of the bag
kitch·en \'ki-chən\ *noun* [Middle English *kichene*, from Old English *cycene*, from Late Latin *coquina*, from Latin *coquere* to cook — more at COOK] (before 12th century)
1 : a place (as a room) with cooking facilities

2 : the personnel that prepares, cooks, and serves food
3 : CUISINE
kitchen cabinet *noun* (1832)
1 : an informal group of advisers to one in a position of power (as the head of a government)
2 : a cupboard with drawers and shelves for use in a kitchen
kitch·en·ette \,ki-chə-'net\ *noun* (1903)
: a small kitchen or an alcove containing cooking facilities
kitchen garden *noun* (1580)
: a garden in which plants (as vegetables or herbs) for use in the kitchen are cultivated
kitchen midden *noun* (1863)
: a refuse heap; *specifically* **:** a mound marking the site of a primitive human habitation
kitchen police *noun* (circa 1917)
1 : KP
2 : the work of KPs
kitch·en–sink \-'siŋk\ *adjective* (1941)
1 *chiefly British* **:** portraying or emphasizing the squalid aspects of modern life ⟨the *kitchen-sink* realism of contemporary British drama —*Current Biography*⟩
2 : being or made up of a hodgepodge of disparate elements or ingredients
kitch·en·ware \-,war, -,wer\ *noun* (1722)
: utensils and appliances for use in a kitchen
¹kite \'kīt\ *noun* [Middle English, from Old English *cȳta*; akin to Middle High German *kūze* owl] (before 12th century)
1 : any of various usually small hawks (family Accipitridae) with long narrow wings and often a notched or forked tail
2 : a person who preys on others
3 : a light frame covered usually with paper or cloth, often provided with a balancing tail, and designed to be flown in the air at the end of a long string
4 : a check drawn against uncollected funds in a bank account or fraudulently raised before cashing
5 : a light sail used in a light breeze usually in addition to the regular working sails; *especially* **:** SPINNAKER
— **kite·like** *adjective*
²kite *verb* **kit·ed; kit·ing** (1839)
transitive verb
1 : to use (a bad check) to get credit or money
2 : to cause to soar ⟨*kited* the prices they charged wealthy clients⟩
intransitive verb
1 a : to go in a rapid, carefree, or flighty manner **b :** to rise rapidly **:** SOAR ⟨the prices of necessities continue to *kite*⟩
2 : to get money or credit by a kite
kit fox *noun* [⁴*kit*] (1805)
1 a : SWIFT FOX **b :** a fox (*Vulpes macrotis*) of the southwestern U.S. and Mexico with exceptionally large ears and a black tip on the tail
2 : the fur or pelt of a kit fox
kith \'kith\ *noun* [Middle English, from Old English *cȳthth*; akin to *cūth* known — more at UNCOUTH] (before 12th century)
: familiar friends, neighbors, or relatives ⟨*kith* and kin⟩
kith·a·ra \'ki-thə-rə\ *noun* [Middle English *cithara*, from Latin, from Greek *kithara*] (14th century)
: an ancient Greek stringed instrument similar to but larger than the lyre and having a box-shaped resonator
kithe \'kīth\ *verb* **kithed; kith·ing** [Middle English, from Old English *cȳthan*, from *cūth*] (before 12th century)
transitive verb
chiefly Scottish **:** to make known
intransitive verb
chiefly Scottish **:** to become known
kitsch \'kich\ *noun* [German, *kitsch*, trash] (1925)
: something that appeals to popular or lowbrow taste and is often of poor quality
— **kitsch** *adjective*

— **kitschy** \'ki-chē\ *adjective*
¹kit·ten \'ki-tᵊn\ *noun* [Middle English *kitoun*, from (assumed) Old North French *caton*, diminutive of *cat*, from Late Latin *cattus*] (14th century)
: a young cat; *also* **:** an immature individual of various other small mammals
²kitten *intransitive verb* **kit·tened; kit·tening** \'kit-niŋ, 'ki-tᵊn-iŋ\ (15th century)
: to give birth to kittens
kit·ten·ish \'kit-nish, 'ki-tᵊn-ish\ *adjective* (1754)
: resembling a kitten; *especially* **:** coyly playful
— **kit·ten·ish·ly** *adverb*
— **kit·ten·ish·ness** *noun*
kit·ti·wake \'ki-tē-,wāk\ *noun* [imitative] (1661)
: either of two cliff-nesting gulls (*Rissa tridactyla* and *R. brevirostris*) that winter on the open ocean
¹kit·tle \'ki-tᵊl\ *transitive verb* **kit·tled; kit·tling** \'kit-liŋ, 'ki-tᵊl-iŋ\ [Middle English (northern dialect) *kytyllen*] (before 12th century)
1 *chiefly Scottish* **:** TICKLE
2 *chiefly Scottish* **:** PERPLEX
²kittle *adjective* (1568)
chiefly Scottish **:** TICKLISH 2, TOUCHY
¹kit·ty \'ki-tē\ *noun, plural* **kitties** (1719)
: CAT 1a; *especially* **:** KITTEN
²kitty *noun, plural* **kitties** [¹*kit*] (circa 1887)
1 : a fund in a poker game made up of contributions from each pot
2 : a sum of money or collection of goods often made up of small contributions **:** POOL
kit·ty–cor·ner *or* **kit·ty–cor·nered** *variant of* CATERCORNER
ki·va \'kē-və\ *noun* [Hopi *kíva*] (1871)
: a Pueblo Indian ceremonial structure that is usually round and partly underground
Ki·wa·ni·an \kə-'wä-nē-ən\ *noun* [*Kiwanis* (Club)] (1921)
: a member of a major national and international service club
ki·wi \'kē-(,)wē\ *noun* [Maori] (1835)
1 : any of a small genus (*Apteryx*) of flightless New Zealand birds with rudimentary wings, stout legs, a long bill, and grayish brown hairlike plumage
2 *capitalized* **:** a native or resident of New Zealand — used as a nickname
3 : KIWIFRUIT

kiwi 1

ki·wi·fruit \-,früt\ *noun* (1966)
: the fruit of a Chinese gooseberry
Klam·ath weed \'kla-məth-\ *noun* [*Klamath* (River)] (1922)
: a European yellow-flowered perennial Saint-John's-wort (*Hypericum perforatum*) that is naturalized in North America especially in rangelands
Klan \'klan\ *noun* [(*Ku Klux*) *Klan*] (1867)
: an organization of Ku Kluxers; *also* **:** a subordinate unit of such an organization
— **Klan·ism** \-,i-zəm\ *noun*
— **Klans·man** \'klanz-mən\ *noun*
klatch *or* **klatsch** \'klach, 'kläch\ *noun* [German *Klatsch* gossip] (1941)
: a gathering characterized usually by informal conversation
klav·ern \'kla-vərn\ *noun, often capitalized* [blend of *Klan* and *cavern*] (circa 1924)
: a local unit of the Klan

\ə\ abut \ᵊ\ kitten \ər\ further \a\ ash \ā\ ace
\ä\ mop, mar \aú\ out \ch\ chin \e\ bet \ē\ easy
\g\ go \i\ hit \ī\ ice \j\ job \ŋ\ sing \ō\ go
\ò\ law \òi\ boy \th\ thin \t̲h̲\ the \ü\ loot \ú\ foot
\y\ yet \zh\ vision *see also* Guide to Pronunciation

Klax·on \'klak-sən\ *trademark*
— used for an electrically operated horn or warning signal

kleb·si·el·la \,kleb-zē-'e-lə\ *noun* [New Latin, from Edwin *Klebs* (died 1913) German pathologist] (1928)
: any of a genus (*Klebsiella*) of nonmotile gram-negative frequently encapsulated bacterial rods

Klee·nex \'klē-,neks\ *trademark*
— used for a cleansing tissue

Klein bottle \'klīn-\ *noun* [Felix *Klein* (died 1925) German mathematician] (1941)
: a one-sided surface that is formed by passing the narrow end of a tapered tube through the side of the tube and flaring this end out to join the other end

klepht \'kleft\ *noun, often capitalized* [New Greek *klephtēs*, literally, robber, from Greek *kleptēs*, from *kleptein*] (1820)
: a Greek belonging to any of several independent guerrilla communities formed after the Turkish conquest of Greece
— **kleph·tic** \'klef-tik\ *adjective, often capitalized*

klepto- *combining form* [Greek, from *kleptein* to steal; akin to Gothic *hlifan* to steal, Latin *clepere*]
: stealing : theft ⟨*klepto*mania⟩

klep·to·ma·nia \,klep-tə-'mā-nē-ə, -nyə\ *noun* [New Latin] (1830)
: a persistent neurotic impulse to steal especially without economic motive

klep·to·ma·ni·ac \-nē-,ak\ *noun* (1861)
: a person evidencing kleptomania

klez·mer \'klez-mər\ *noun, plural* **klez·mo·rim** \(,)klez-'mòr-əm\ [Yiddish, from Hebrew *kĕlēy zemer* musical instruments] (1949)
1 : a Jewish instrumentalist especially of traditional eastern European music
2 : the music played by klezmorim

klieg light *or* **kleig light** \'klēg-\ *noun* [John H. *Kliegl* (died 1959) & Anton T. *Kliegl* (died 1919) German-born American lighting experts] (1919)
: a carbon arc lamp used especially in making motion pictures

Kline·fel·ter's syndrome \'klīn-,fel-tərz-\ *noun* [Harry F. *Klinefelter* (born 1912) American physician] (1950)
: an abnormal condition in a male characterized by usually two X and one Y chromosomes, infertility, and smallness of the testicles

klis·ter \'klis-tər\ *noun* [Norwegian, literally, paste, from Middle Low German *klīster*] (1936)
: a soft wax used on skis

kloof \'klüf\ *noun* [Afrikaans] (1731)
South African : a deep glen : RAVINE

kludge \'klüj\ *or* **kluge** \'klüj, 'klü-jē\ *noun* [origin unknown] (1962)
: a system and especially a computer system made up of poorly matched components

klutz \'kləts\ *noun* [Yiddish *klots*, literally, wooden beam, from Middle High German *kloz* lumpy mass — more at CLOUT] (1960)
: a clumsy person
— **klutz·i·ness** \'klət-sē-nəs\ *noun*
— **klutzy** \'klət-sē\ *adjective*

kly·stron \'klī-,strän\ *noun* [from *Klystron*, a trademark] (1939)
: an electron tube in which bunching of electrons is produced by electric fields and which is used for the generation and amplification of ultrahigh-frequency current

K–me·son \'kā-\ *noun* (1951)
: KAON

knack \'nak\ *noun* [Middle English *knak*] (14th century)
1 a : a clever trick or stratagem **b** : a clever way of doing something
2 : a special ready capacity that is hard to analyze or teach

3 *archaic* : an ingenious device; *broadly* : TOY, KNICKKNACK
synonym see GIFT

knack·er \'na-kər\ *noun* [probably from English dialect, saddlemaker] (1812)
1 *British* : a buyer of worn-out domestic animals or their carcasses for use especially as animal food or fertilizer
2 *British* : a buyer of old structures for their constituent materials

knack·ered \'na-kərd\ *adjective* [English slang *knacker* to kill, tire, perhaps from *knacker*, noun] (1886)
British : TIRED, EXHAUSTED

knack·wurst *variant of* KNOCKWURST

¹knap \'nap\ *noun* [Middle English, from Old English *cnæp*; akin to Old English *cnotta* knot] (before 12th century)
1 *chiefly dialect* : a crest of a hill : SUMMIT
2 *chiefly dialect* : a small hill

²knap *transitive verb* **knapped; knap·ping** [Middle English *knappen*, of imitative origin] (15th century)
1 *dialect British* : ²RAP 1
2 : to break with a quick blow; *especially* : to shape (as flints) by breaking off pieces
3 *dialect British* : SNAP, CROP
4 *dialect British* : CHATTER
— **knap·per** *noun*

knap·sack \'nap-,sak\ *noun* [Low German *knappsack* or Dutch *knapzak*, from Low German & Dutch *knappen* to make a snapping noise, eat + Low German *sack* or Dutch *zak* sack] (1603)
: a bag (as of canvas or nylon) strapped on the back and used for carrying supplies or personal belongings
— **knap·sacked** \-,sakt\ *adjective*

knap·weed \-,wēd\ *noun* [Middle English *knopwed*, from *knop* knop + *wed* weed] (15th century)
: any of various weedy centaureas; *especially* : a widely naturalized European perennial (*Centaurea nigra*) with tough wiry stems and knobby heads of purple flowers

knave \'nāv\ *noun* [Middle English, from Old English *cnafa*; akin to Old High German *knabo* boy] (before 12th century)
1 *archaic* **a** : a boy servant **b** : a male servant **c** : a man of humble birth or position
2 : a tricky deceitful fellow
3 : JACK 6a

knav·ery \'nā-və-rē, 'nāv-rē\ *noun, plural* **-er·ies** (1528)
1 a : RASCALITY **b** : a roguish or mischievous act
2 *obsolete* : roguish mischief

knav·ish \'nā-vish\ *adjective* (14th century)
: of, relating to, or characteristic of a knave; *especially* : DISHONEST
— **knav·ish·ly** *adverb*

knead \'nēd\ *transitive verb* [Middle English *kneden*, from Old English *cnedan*; akin to Old High German *knetan* to knead] (before 12th century)
1 a : to work and press into a mass with or as if with the hands ⟨*kneading* dough⟩ **b** : to manipulate or massage with a kneading motion ⟨*kneaded* sore neck muscles⟩
2 : to form or shape by or as if by kneading
— **knead·able** \'nē-də-bəl\ *adjective*
— **knead·er** *noun*

¹knee \'nē\ *noun, often attributive* [Middle English, from Old English *cnēow*; akin to Old High German *kneo* knee, Latin *genu*, Greek *gony*] (before 12th century)
1 a : a joint in the middle part of the human leg that is the articulation between the femur, tibia, and patella; *also* : the part of the leg that includes this joint **b** (1) : the joint in the hind leg of a four-footed vertebrate that corresponds to the human knee (2) : the carpal joint of the foreleg of a four-footed vertebrate **c** : the tarsal joint of a bird **d** : the joint between the femur and tibia of an insect

2 : something resembling the human knee: as **a** : a piece of timber naturally or artificially bent for use in supporting structures coming together at an angle (as the deck beams of a ship) **b** : a rounded or conical process rising from the roots of various swamp-growing trees ⟨cypress *knee*⟩
3 : the part of a garment covering the knee
4 : a blow with the bent knee
— **kneed** \'nēd\ *adjective*
— **to one's knees** : into a state of submission or defeat

²knee *transitive verb* **kneed; knee·ing** (before 12th century)
1 *archaic* : to bend the knee to
2 : to strike with the knee

knee breeches *noun plural* (1833)
: BREECH 1a

knee·cap \'nē-,kap\ *noun* (1869)
: PATELLA

knee·cap·ping \'nē-,ka-piŋ\ *noun* (1974)
: the terroristic act or practice of maiming a person's knees (as by gunshot)
— **kneecap** *transitive verb*

knee–deep \-'dēp\ *adjective* (15th century)
1 a : sunk to the knees ⟨*knee-deep* in mud⟩ **b** : deeply engaged or occupied ⟨*knee-deep* in work⟩
2 : KNEE-HIGH

knee–high \-'hī\ *adjective* (1743)
: rising or reaching upward to the knees ⟨*knee-high* stockings⟩
— **knee–high** \-,hī\ *noun*

knee·hole \-,hōl\ *noun* (1893)
: an open space (as under a desk) for the knees

knee–jerk \'nē-,jərk, -'jərk\ *adjective* (1951)
: readily predictable : AUTOMATIC ⟨*knee-jerk* reactions⟩; *also* : reacting in a readily predictable way ⟨*knee-jerk* liberals⟩

knee jerk *noun* (1876)
: an involuntary forward kick produced by a light blow on the tendon below the patella

kneel \'nē(ə)l\ *intransitive verb* **knelt** \'nelt\ *or* **kneeled; kneel·ing** [Middle English *knelen*, from Old English *cnēowlian*; akin to Old English *cnēow* knee] (before 12th century)
: to bend the knee : fall or rest on the knees

kneel·er \'nē-lər\ *noun* (14th century)
1 : one that kneels
2 : something (as a cushion or board) to kneel on

knee·pan \'nē-,pan\ *noun* (15th century)
: PATELLA

knee–slap·per \-,sla-pər\ *noun* (1966)
: an extremely funny joke, line, or story

knee·sock \-,säk\ *noun* (1964)
: a knee-high sock

¹knell \'nel\ *verb* [Middle English, from Old English *cnyllan*; akin to Middle High German *erknellen* to toll] (before 12th century)
transitive verb
: to summon or announce by or as if by a knell
intransitive verb
1 : to ring especially for a death, funeral, or disaster : TOLL
2 : to sound in an ominous manner or with an ominous effect

²knell *noun* (before 12th century)
1 : a stroke or sound of a bell especially when rung slowly (as for a death, funeral, or disaster)
2 : an indication of the end or the failure of something ⟨sounded the death *knell* for our hopes⟩

knew *past of* KNOW

knick·er·bock·er \'ni-kə(r)-,bä-kər\ *noun* [Diedrich *Knickerbocker*, fictitious author of *History of New York* (1809) by Washington Irving] (1848)
1 *capitalized* : a descendant of the early Dutch settlers of New York; *broadly* : a native or resident of the city or state of New York — used as a nickname

2 *plural* : KNICKERS ◆

knick·ers \'ni-kərz\ *noun plural* [short for *knickerbockers*] (1881)
1 : loose-fitting short pants gathered at the knee
2 *chiefly British* : UNDERPANTS
word history see KNICKERBOCKER

knick·knack \'nik-ˌnak\ *noun* [reduplication of *knack*] (1682)
: a small trivial article usually intended for ornament

¹knife \'nīf\ *noun, plural* **knives** \'nīvz\ *often attributive* [Middle English *knif*, from Old English *cnīf*, perhaps from Old Norse *knīfrom*; akin to Middle Low German *knīf* knife] (before 12th century)
1 a : a cutting instrument consisting of a sharp blade fastened to a handle **b** : a weapon resembling a knife
2 : a sharp cutting blade or tool in a machine
3 : SURGERY 4 — usually used in the phrase *under the knife*
— **knife·like** \'nīf-ˌlīk\ *adjective*

²knife *verb* **knifed; knif·ing** (1865)
transitive verb
1 : to use a knife on; *specifically* : to stab, slash, or wound with a knife
2 : to cut, mark, or spread with a knife
3 : to try to defeat by underhanded means
4 : to move like a knife in ⟨birds *knifing* the autumn sky⟩
intransitive verb
: to cut a way with or as if with a knife blade ⟨the cruiser *knifed* through the heavy seas⟩

knife–edge \'nīf-ˌej\ *noun* (1818)
1 : a sharp wedge of steel or other hard material used as a fulcrum for a lever beam in a precision instrument
2 : a sharp narrow knifelike edge

knife·point \-ˌpóint\ *noun* (circa 1911)
: the point of a knife
— **at knifepoint** : under a threat of being knifed

¹knight \'nīt\ *noun* [Middle English, from Old English *cniht* man-at-arms, boy, servant; akin to Old High German *kneht* youth, military follower] (before 12th century)
1 a (1) : a mounted man-at-arms serving a feudal superior; *especially* : a man ceremonially inducted into special military rank usually after completing service as page and squire (2) : a man honored by a sovereign for merit and in Great Britain ranking below a baronet (3) : a person of antiquity equal to a knight in rank **b** : a man devoted to the service of a lady as her attendant or champion **c** : a member of an order or society
2 : either of two pieces of the same color in a set of chessmen having the power to make an L-shaped move of two squares in one row and one square in a perpendicular row over squares that may be occupied

²knight *transitive verb* (13th century)
: to make a knight of

knight–er·rant \'nīt-'er-ənt\ *noun, plural* **knights–errant** (14th century)
: a knight traveling in search of adventures in which to exhibit military skill, prowess, and generosity

knight–er·rant·ry \-'er-ən-trē\ *noun, plural* **knight–errantries** (1654)
1 : the practice or actions of a knight-errant
2 : quixotic conduct

knight·hood \'nīt-ˌhùd\ *noun* (13th century)
1 : the rank, dignity, or profession of a knight
2 : the qualities befitting a knight : CHIVALRY
3 : knights as a class or body

knight·ly \'nīt-lē\ *adjective* (14th century)
1 : of, relating to, or characteristic of a knight
2 : made up of knights
— **knight·li·ness** *noun*
— **knightly** *adverb*

Knight of Co·lum·bus \-kə-'ləm-bəs\ *noun, plural* **Knights of Columbus** [Christopher Columbus] (1882)

: a member of a benevolent and fraternal society of Roman Catholic men

Knight of Pyth·i·as \-'pi-thē-əs\ *noun, plural* **Knights of Pythias** (1869)
: a member of a secret benevolent and fraternal order

Knight of the Mac·ca·bees \-'ma-kə-ˌbēz\ *noun, plural* **Knights of the Maccabees** (1922)
: a member of a secret benevolent society

Knight Templar *noun, plural* **Knights Templars** *or* **Knights Templar** (1610)
1 : TEMPLAR 1
2 : a member of an order of Freemasonry conferring three orders in the York rite

knish \kə-'nish\ *noun* [Yiddish, from Polish *knysz*] (1916)
: a small round or square of dough stuffed with a filling (as potato) and baked or fried

¹knit \'nit\ *verb* **knit** *or* **knit·ted; knit·ting** [Middle English *knitten*, from Old English *cnyttan*; akin to Old English *cnotta* knot] (before 12th century)
transitive verb
1 *chiefly dialect* : to tie together
2 a : to link firmly or closely ⟨*knitted* my hands⟩ **b** : to cause to grow together ⟨time and rest will *knit* a fractured bone⟩ **c** : to contract into wrinkles ⟨*knitted* her brow⟩
3 : to form by interlacing yarn or thread in a series of connected loops with needles
intransitive verb
1 : to make knitted fabrics or objects
2 a : to become compact **b** : to grow together
c : to become drawn together
— **knit·ter** *noun*

²knit *noun* (1596)
1 : KNIT STITCH; *also* : a knit fabric

knit stitch *noun* (circa 1885)
: a basic knitting stitch usually made with the yarn at the back of the work by inserting the right needle into the front part of a loop on the left needle from the left side, catching the yarn with the point of the right needle, and bringing it through the first loop to form a new loop — compare PURL STITCH

knit·ting *noun* (15th century)
1 : the action or method of one that knits
2 : work done or being done by one that knits

knit·wear \'nit-ˌwar, -ˌwer\ *noun* (1926)
: knitted clothing

knob \'näb\ *noun* [Middle English *knobbe*; akin to Middle Low German *knubbe* knob] (before 12th century)
1 a : a rounded protuberance : LUMP **b** : a small rounded ornament or handle
2 : a rounded usually isolated hill or mountain
— **knobbed** \'näbd\ *adjective*
— **knob·by** \'nä-bē\ *adjective*

knob·bly \'nä-b(ə-)lē\ *adjective* (1859)
: having very small knobs ⟨a *knobbly* mattress⟩

knob·ker·rie \'näb-ˌker-ē\ *noun* [Afrikaans *knopkierie*, from *knop* knob + *kierie* club] (1844)
: a short wooden club with a knob at one end used as a missile or in close attack especially by Zulus of southern Africa

¹knock \'näk\ *verb* [Middle English *knoken*, from Old English *cnocian*; akin to Middle High German *knochen* to press] (before 12th century)
intransitive verb
1 : to strike something with a sharp blow
2 : to collide with something
3 a : BUSTLE ⟨heard them *knocking* around in the kitchen⟩ **b** : WANDER ⟨*knocked* about Europe all summer⟩
4 a : to make a pounding noise **b** : to have engine knock
5 : to find fault
transitive verb
1 a (1) : to strike sharply (2) : to drive, force, or make by or as if by so striking **b** : to set forcibly in motion with a blow
2 : to cause to collide
3 : to find fault with ⟨never *knocks* a friend⟩

— **knock cold** : KNOCK OUT 2a(1)
— **knock dead** : to move strongly especially to admiration or applause ⟨a comedian who really *knocks* them *dead*⟩
— **knock for a loop 1 a** : OVERCOME ⟨*knocked* my opponent *for a loop*⟩ **b** : DEMOLISH ⟨*knocked* our idea *for a loop*⟩ **2** : DUMBFOUND, AMAZE ⟨the news *knocked* them *for a loop*⟩
— **knock one's socks off** : to overwhelm or amaze one ⟨a performance that will *knock your socks off*⟩
— **knock together** : to make or assemble especially hurriedly or in a makeshift way ⟨*knocked together* my own bookcase⟩

²knock *noun* (14th century)
1 a : a sharp blow : RAP, HIT ⟨a loud *knock* on the door⟩ **b** (1) : a severe misfortune or hardship (2) : SETBACK, REVERSAL
2 a : a pounding noise **b** : a sharp repetitive metallic noise caused by abnormal ignition in an automobile engine
3 : a harsh and often petty criticism ⟨likes praise but can't stand the *knocks*⟩

knock·about \'nä-kə-ˌbaùt\ *adjective* (1880)
1 : suitable for rough use ⟨*knockabout* clothing⟩
2 a : being noisy and rough : BOISTEROUS ⟨*knockabout* games⟩ **b** : characterized by boisterous antics and often extravagant burlesque ⟨*knockabout* comedy⟩
3 *of a sailing vessel* : having a simplified rig marked by absence of bowsprit and topmast ⟨a *knockabout* sloop⟩
— **knockabout** *noun*

knock back *transitive verb* (circa 1931)
: DRINK, SWALLOW; *specifically* : to toss down (an alcoholic beverage)

¹knock·down \'näk-ˌdaùn\ *adjective* (1690)
1 : having such force as to strike down or overwhelm ⟨a bewildering assortment of *knockdown* arguments —J. W. Krutch⟩
2 : that can easily be assembled or disassembled ⟨a *knockdown* table⟩
3 *chiefly British* : extremely low : REDUCED ⟨*knockdown* prices⟩

²knockdown *noun* (1809)
1 : the action of knocking down

◆ **WORD HISTORY**
knickerbocker In 1809 Washington Irving published *A History of New York,* a supposed work of the fictitious historian Diedrich Knickerbocker, as a genial satire of the early Dutch settlers of the New Netherlands. Irving most likely chose the name *Knickerbocker* for his fictional alter ego in humorous allusion to his friend Herman Knickerbocker, who was of Dutch descent. *Knickerbocker's History of New York* (as the work came to be known) had such an enduring popularity that by the middle of the 19th century New Yorkers of Dutch descent had taken to calling themselves "genuine Knickerbockers." *Knickerbocker* then went on to become a nickname for any native or resident of New York city or state. The use of *knickerbockers* as a term for knee breeches stems from an edition of Irving's work published in the 1850s with illustrations by English caricaturist George Cruikshank. Cruikshank depicted Diedrich Knickerbocker and his fellow Dutch burghers as wearing loose-fitting breeches gathered just below the knee. A coincidental revival of the fashion for knee breeches at that time prompted the adoption of *knickerbockers* for the garment. The shortened form *knickers* soon followed.

\ə\ abut \ᵊ\ kitten \ər\ further \a\ ash \ā\ ace
\ä\ mop, mar \aù\ out \ch\ chin \e\ bet \ē\ easy
\g\ go \i\ hit \ī\ ice \j\ job \ŋ\ sing \ō\ go
\ò\ law \òi\ boy \th\ thin \th\ the \ü\ loot \ù\ foot
\y\ yet \zh\ vision *see also* Guide to Pronunciation

2 : something (as a blow) that strikes down or overwhelms
3 : something (as a piece of furniture) that can be easily assembled or disassembled

knock down \-'daún\ *transitive verb* (15th century)
1 : to strike to the ground with or as if with a sharp blow : FELL
2 : to dispose of (an item) to a bidder at an auction sale
3 : to take apart : DISASSEMBLE
4 : to receive as income or salary : EARN ⟨positions where they were able to *knock down* good money —*Infantry Journal*⟩
5 : REDUCE

knock–down–drag–out *or* **knock–down–and–drag–out** *adjective* (1834)
: marked by extreme violence or bitterness and by the showing of no mercy ⟨*knock-down-drag-out* political debates⟩
— **knock–down–drag–out** *noun*

knock·er \'nä-kər\ *noun* (14th century)
1 : one that knocks: as **a** : a metal ring, bar, or hammer hinged to a door for use in knocking **b** : a persistently pessimistic critic
2 : BREAST — usually used in plural; often considered vulgar

knock–knee \'näk-'nē, -,nē\ *noun* (1879)
: a condition in which the legs curve inward at the knees
— **knock–kneed** \-'nēd\ *adjective*

knock–off \'näk-,óf\ *noun* (1966)
: a copy that sells for less than the original; *broadly* : a copy or imitation of someone or something popular

knock off (1649)
intransitive verb
: to stop doing something
transitive verb
1 : to do hurriedly or routinely ⟨*knocked off* one painting after another⟩
2 : DISCONTINUE, STOP ⟨*knocked off* work at five⟩
3 : DEDUCT ⟨*knocked off* a little to make the price more attractive⟩
4 a : KILL ⟨*knocked off* two men . . . on mercenary grounds —Lewis Baker⟩ **b** : OVERCOME, DEFEAT ⟨*knocked off* each center of rebellion⟩
5 : ROB ⟨*knocked off* a couple of banks⟩
6 : to make a knockoff of : COPY, IMITATE ⟨*knocks off* popular dress designs⟩

knock·out \'näk-,aút\ *noun* (1887)
1 a : the act of knocking out : the condition of being knocked out **b** (1) : the termination of a boxing match when one boxer has been knocked down and is unable to rise and resume boxing within a specified time (2) : TECHNICAL KNOCKOUT **c** : a blow that knocks out an opponent
2 : something sensationally striking, appealing, or attractive
— **knockout** *adjective*

knock out *transitive verb* (1856)
1 : to produce roughly or hastily
2 a (1) : to defeat (a boxing opponent) by a knockout (2) : to make unconscious ⟨the drug *knocked* him *out*⟩ **b** : to make inoperative or useless ⟨electricity was *knocked out* by the storm⟩ **c** : to get rid of : ELIMINATE ⟨*knocked out* illegal gambling⟩
3 : to tire out : EXHAUST ⟨*knocked* themselves *out* with work⟩
4 : to cause (an opposing pitcher) to be removed from a baseball game by a batting rally

knockout drops *noun plural* (1895)
: drops of a solution of a drug (as chloral hydrate) put into a drink to produce unconsciousness or stupefaction

knock over *transitive verb* (circa 1814)
1 a (1) : to strike to the ground : FELL (2) : OVERWHELM ⟨was *knocked over* by the news⟩ **b** : ELIMINATE ⟨*knocked over* every difficulty⟩
2 a : STEAL; *especially* : HIJACK ⟨*knocks over* a truckload of merchandise —J. B. Martin⟩ **b** : ROB ⟨*knocking over* a bank⟩

knock up *transitive verb* (1663)

1 *British* : ROUSE, SUMMON
2 : to make pregnant — sometimes considered vulgar

knock·wurst \'näk-(,)wərst *also* -,vú(r)st, *sometimes* -,vúsht\ *noun* [German *Knackwurst*, from *knacken* to crackle (of imitative origin) + *Wurst* wurst] (circa 1929)
: a short thick heavily seasoned sausage

¹knoll \'nōl\ *noun* [Middle English *knol*, from Old English *cnoll*; akin to Old Norse *knollr* mountaintop] (before 12th century)
: a small round hill : MOUND

²knoll *verb* [Middle English, probably alteration of *knellen* to knell] (15th century)
archaic : KNELL

knop \'näp\ *noun* [Middle English, from Old English *-cnoppa* knob] (before 12th century)
: a usually ornamental knob
— **knopped** \'näpt\ *adjective*

¹knot \'nät\ *noun* [Middle English, from Old English *cnotta*; akin to Old High German *knoto* knot] (before 12th century)
1 a : an interlacement of the parts of one or more flexible bodies forming a lump or knob **b** : the lump or knob so formed **c** : a tight constriction or the sense of constriction ⟨my stomach was all in *knots*⟩
2 : something hard to solve : PROBLEM ⟨a matter full of legal *knots*⟩
3 : a bond of union; *especially* : the marriage bond
4 a : a protuberant lump or swelling in tissue ⟨a *knot* in a gland⟩ **b** : the base of a woody branch enclosed in the stem from which it arises; *also* : its section in lumber
5 : a cluster of persons or things : GROUP
6 : an ornamental bow of ribbon : COCKADE
7 a : a division of the log's line serving to measure a ship's speed **b** (1) : one nautical mile per hour (2) : one nautical mile — not used technically ☐

knot 1b: *1* Blackwall hitch, *2* carrick bend, *3* clove hitch, *4* cat's-paw, *5* figure eight, *6* granny knot, *7* bowline, *8* overhand knot, *9* fisherman's bend, *10* half hitch, *11* square knot, *12* slip knot, *13* stevedore knot, *14* true lover's knot, *15* surgeon's knot, *16* Turk's head, *17* sheet bend, *18* timber hitch, *19* seizing, *20* rolling hitch, *21* sheepshank

²knot *verb* **knot·ted; knot·ting** (1547)
transitive verb
1 : to tie in or with a knot : form knots in
2 : to unite closely or intricately : ENTANGLE
3 : TIE 4b ⟨*knotted* the score⟩
intransitive verb
: to form knots
— **knot·ter** *noun*

³knot *noun, plural* **knots** *or* **knot** [Middle English *knott*] (15th century)
: either of two sandpipers (*Calidris canutus* and *C. tenuirostris*) that breed in the Arctic and winter in temperate or warm parts of the New and Old World

knot garden *noun* (1519)
: an elaborately designed garden especially of flowers or herbs

knot·grass \'nät-,gras\ *noun* (1538)
1 : a cosmopolitan weed (*Polygonum aviculare*) of the buckwheat family with jointed

stems, prominent sheathing stipules, and minute flowers; *broadly* : any of several congeneric plants
2 : any of several grasses with markedly jointed stems; *especially* : JOINT GRASS

knot·hole \-,hōl\ *noun* (1726)
: a hole in a board or tree trunk where a knot or branch has come out

knot·ted \'nä-təd\ *adjective* (12th century)
1 : tied in or with a knot
2 : full of knots : GNARLED
3 : KNOTTY
4 : ornamented with knots or knobs

knot·ty \'nä-tē\ *adjective* **knot·ti·er; -est** (13th century)
: marked by or full of knots; *especially* : so full of difficulties and complications as to be likely to defy solution ⟨a *knotty* problem⟩
synonym see COMPLEX
— **knot·ti·ness** *noun*

knotty pine *noun* (circa 1898)
: pine wood that has a decorative distribution of knots and is used especially for interior finish

knot·weed \'nät-,wēd\ *noun* (1884)
: any of several herbs (genus *Polygonum*) of the buckwheat family with leaves and bracts jointed and having a very short petiole; *broadly* : POLYGONUM

knout \'naút, *sometimes* 'nüt\ *noun* [Russian *knut*, of Scandinavian origin; akin to Old Norse *knútr* knot; akin to Old English *cnotta*] (1716)
: a whip used for flogging
— **knout** *transitive verb*

¹know \'nō\ *verb* **knew** \'nü *also* 'nyü\; **known** \'nōn\; **know·ing** [Middle English, from Old English *cnāwan*; akin to Old High German *bichnāan* to recognize, Latin *gnoscere, noscere* to come to know, Greek *gignōskein*] (before 12th century)
transitive verb
1 a (1) : to perceive directly : have direct cognition of (2) : to have understanding of ⟨importance of *knowing* oneself⟩ (3) : to recognize the nature of : DISCERN **b** (1) : to recognize as being the same as something previously known (2) : to be acquainted or familiar with (3) : to have experience of
2 a : to be aware of the truth or factuality of : be convinced or certain of **b** : to have a practical understanding of ⟨*knows* how to write⟩
3 *archaic* : to have sexual intercourse with
intransitive verb
1 : to have knowledge
2 : to be or become cognizant — sometimes used interjectionally with *you* especially as a filler in informal speech
— **know·able** \'nō-ə-bəl\ *adjective*
— **know·er** \'nō(-ə)r\ *noun*
— **know from** : to have knowledge of ⟨didn't *know from* sibling rivalry —Penny Marshall⟩

²know *noun* (1592)

: KNOWLEDGE
— **in the know** : in possession of exclusive knowledge or information; *broadly* : WELL-INFORMED

know–all \'nō-,ȯl\ *noun* (circa 1864) *chiefly British* : KNOW-IT-ALL

know–how \'nō-,haů\ *noun* (1838) : knowledge of how to do something smoothly and efficiently : EXPERTISE

¹**know·ing** \'nō-iŋ\ *noun* (14th century) : ACQUAINTANCE, COGNIZANCE

²**knowing** *adjective* (14th century)
1 : having or reflecting knowledge, information, or intelligence
2 a : shrewdly and keenly alert : ASTUTE **b** : indicating possession of exclusive inside knowledge or information ⟨a *knowing* smile⟩
3 : COGNITIVE
4 : DELIBERATE ⟨*knowing* interference in the affairs of another⟩
— **know·ing·ly** *adverb*
— **know·ing·ness** *noun*

know–it–all \'nō-ət-,ȯl\ *noun* (1895) : one who claims to know everything; *also* : one who disdains advice
— **know–it–all** *adjective*

knowl·edge \'nä-lij\ *noun* [Middle English *knowlege*, from *knowlechen* to acknowledge, irregular from *knowen*] (14th century)
1 *obsolete* : COGNIZANCE
2 a (1) : the fact or condition of knowing something with familiarity gained through experience or association (2) : acquaintance with or understanding of a science, art, or technique **b** (1) : the fact or condition of being aware of something (2) : the range of one's information or understanding ⟨answered to the best of my *knowledge*⟩ **c** : the circumstance or condition of apprehending truth or fact through reasoning : COGNITION **d** : the fact or condition of having information or of being learned ⟨a man of unusual *knowledge*⟩
3 *archaic* : SEXUAL INTERCOURSE
4 a : the sum of what is known : the body of truth, information, and principles acquired by mankind **b** *archaic* : a branch of learning ☆

knowl·edge·able \'nä-lij-ə-bəl\ *adjective* (1829)
: having or exhibiting knowledge or intelligence
— **knowl·edge·abil·i·ty** \,nä-li-jə-'bi-lə-tē\ *noun*
— **knowl·edge·able·ness** *noun*
— **knowl·edge·ably** \-blē\ *adverb*

knowledge engineering *noun* (1980) : a branch of artificial intelligence that emphasizes the development and use of expert systems
— **knowledge engineer** *noun*

known \'nōn\ *adjective* (13th century) : familiar : generally recognized ⟨a *known* authority on art⟩

know–noth·ing \'nō-,nə-thiŋ\ *noun* (1827)
1 a : IGNORAMUS **b** : AGNOSTIC
2 *K&N capitalized* : a member of a 19th century secret American political organization hostile to the political influence of recent immigrants and Roman Catholics

know–noth·ing·ism \-thiŋ-,i-zəm\ *noun* (1854)
1 *K&N capitalized* : the principles and policies of the Know-Nothings
2 : the condition of knowing nothing or desiring to know nothing or the conviction that nothing can be known with certainty especially in religion or morality
3 *often K&N capitalized* : a mid-twentieth century political attitude characterized by anti-intellectualism, exaggerated patriotism, and fear of foreign subversive influences

knub·by *variant of* NUBBY

¹**knuck·le** \'nə-kəl\ *noun* [Middle English *knokel*; akin to Middle High German *knöchel* knuckle] (14th century)
1 a : the rounded prominence formed by the ends of the two adjacent bones at a joint —

used especially of those at the joints of the fingers **b** : the joint of a knuckle
2 : a cut of meat consisting of the tarsal or carpal joint with the adjoining flesh
3 : something resembling a knuckle: as **a** (1) : one of the joining parts of a hinge through which a pin or rivet passes (2) : KNUCKLE JOINT **b** : the meeting of two surfaces at a sharp angle (as in a roof) **c** : a pivotal point
4 *plural* : a set of metal finger rings or guards attached to a transverse piece and worn over the front of the doubled fist for use as a weapon — called also *brass knuckles*
— **knuck·led** *adjective*

²**knuckle** *verb* **knuck·led; knuck·ling** \'nə-k(ə-)liŋ\ (1740)
intransitive verb
: to place the knuckles on the ground in shooting a marble
transitive verb
: to press or rub with the knuckles

knuck·le·ball \'nə-kəl-,bȯl\ *noun* (1910) : a baseball pitch in which the ball is gripped with the knuckles or the tips of the fingers pressed against the top and thrown with little speed or spin
— **knuck·le·ball·er** \-,bȯ-lər\ *noun*

knuck·le·bone \'nək-əl-,bōn\ *noun* (1577)
1 : a bone (as a metatarsus or metacarpus of a sheep) used in games and formerly in divination
2 *plural but singular in construction* : a game played with knucklebones or jacks

knuckle down *intransitive verb* (circa 1864) : to apply oneself earnestly

knuck·le·dust·er \'nə-kəl-,dəs-tər\ *noun* (1858)
: KNUCKLE 4

knuck·le·head \-,hed\ *noun* (1942) : DUMBBELL 2
— **knuck·le·head·ed** \-,hed-əd\ *adjective*

knuckle joint *noun* (circa 1864) : a hinge joint in which a projection with an eye on one piece enters a jaw between two corresponding projections with eyes on another piece and is retained by a pin or rivet

knuckle joint

knuck·ler \'nə-k(ə-)lər\ *noun* (1928) : KNUCKLEBALL

knuckle under *intransitive verb* (1869) : GIVE IN, SUBMIT

knur \'nər\ *noun* [Middle English *knorre*; akin to Middle High German *knorre* burl] (14th century) : a hard excrescence (as on a tree trunk) : GNARL

knurl \'nər(-ə)l\ *noun* [probably blend of *knur* and *gnarl*] (1608)
1 : a small protuberance, excrescence, or knob
2 : one of a series of small ridges or beads on a metal surface to aid in gripping
— **knurled** \'nər(-ə)ld\ *adjective*
— **knurly** \'nər-lē\ *adjective*

¹**KO** \(,)kā-'ō, 'kā-(,)ō\ *noun* [*knock out*] (1911) : KNOCKOUT

²**KO** *transitive verb* **KO'd** \kā-'ōd, 'kā-(,)ōd\; **KO'·ing** \-'ō-iŋ, -(,)ō-\ (1926) : to knock out (as in boxing)

koa \'kō-ə\ *noun* [Hawaiian] (1850)
1 : a Hawaiian timber tree (*Acacia koa*) with crescent-shaped leaves and white flowers borne in small round heads
2 : the fine-grained red wood of the koa used especially for furniture

ko·ala \kə-'wä-lə, kō-'ä-\ *noun* [Dharuk (Australian aboriginal language of the Port Jackson area) *gulawaṇ*] (1803) : an Australian arboreal marsupial (*Phascolarctos cinereus*) that has a broad head, large hairy ears, dense gray fur, and sharp claws and feeds on eucalyptus leaves — called also *koala bear*

ko·an \'kō-,än\ *noun* [Japanese *kōan*, from *kō* public + *an* proposition] (1945) : a paradox to be meditated upon that is used to train Zen Buddhist monks to abandon ultimate dependence on reason and to force them into gaining sudden intuitive enlightenment

koala

ko·bo \'kō-(,)bō\ *noun, plural* **kobo** [alteration of ¹*copper*] (1972) — see *naira* at MONEY table

ko·bold \'kō-,bȯld\ *noun* [German — more at COBALT] (1830)
1 : a gnome that in German folklore inhabits underground places
2 : an often mischievous domestic spirit of German folklore

Ko·di·ak bear \'kō-dē-,ak-\ *noun* [Kodiak Island, Alaska] (1899) : a large brown bear of the southern coast of Alaska and adjacent islands

kohl \'kōl\ *noun* [Arabic *kuhl*] (1799) : a preparation used especially in Arabia and Egypt to darken the edges of the eyelids

kohl·ra·bi \kōl-'rä-bē *also* -'ra-\ *noun, plural* -**bies** [German, from Italian *cavolo rapa*, from *cavolo* cabbage + *rapa* turnip] (1807) : any of a race of cabbages (*Brassica oleracea gongylodes*) having a greatly enlarged, fleshy, turnip-shaped edible stem

koi \'kȯi\ *noun, plural* **koi** [Japanese] (1727) : a carp (*Cyprinus carpio*) bred especially in Japan for large size and a variety of colors and often stocked in ornamental ponds

koi·ne *also* **koi·né** \kȯi-'nā, 'kȯi-,; kē-'nē\ *noun* [Greek *koinē*, from feminine of *koinos* common] (1909)
1 *capitalized* : the Greek language commonly spoken and written in eastern Mediterranean countries in the Hellenistic and Roman periods
2 : a dialect or language of a region that has become the common or standard language of a larger area

ko·kan·ee \kō-'ka-nē\ *noun* [perhaps from Shuswap (Salishan language of British Columbia) *kəknáéxʷ*] (1875) : a small landlocked sockeye salmon — called also *kokanee salmon*

kok–sa·ghyz *or* **kok–sa·gyz** \,kōk-sə-'gēz, ,käk-, -'giz\ *noun* [Russian *kok-sagyz*] (1932)

☆ **SYNONYMS**
Knowledge, learning, erudition, scholarship mean what is or can be known by an individual or by mankind. KNOWLEDGE applies to facts or ideas acquired by study, investigation, observation, or experience ⟨rich in the *knowledge* of human nature⟩. LEARNING applies to knowledge acquired especially through formal, often advanced, schooling ⟨a book that demonstrates vast *learning*⟩. ERUDITION strongly implies the acquiring of profound, recondite, or bookish learning ⟨an *erudition* unusual even in a scholar⟩. SCHOLARSHIP implies the possession of learning characteristic of the advanced scholar in a specialized field of study or investigation ⟨a work of first-rate literary *scholarship*⟩.

: a perennial Asian dandelion (*Taraxacum kok-saghyz*) cultivated for its fleshy roots that have a high rubber content

ko·la *variant of* COLA

ko·la nut \'kō-lə-\ *noun* [*kola*, perhaps modification of Malinke *kolo* kola nut] (1868)
: the bitter caffeine-containing chestnut-sized seed of a kola tree used especially as a masticatory and in beverages

kola tree *noun* (1937)
: an African tree (genus *Cola*, especially *C. nitida* and *C. acuminata* of the family Sterculiaceae) cultivated in various tropical areas for its kola nuts

ko·lin·sky \kə-'lin(t)-skē\ *noun, plural* **-skies** [origin unknown] (1851)
1 : any of several Asian minks (especially *Mustela siberica*)
2 : the fur or pelt of a kolinsky

kol·khoz \käl-'kóz, -'kòs\ *noun, plural* **kol·kho·zy** \-'kó-zē\ *or* **kol·khoz·es** \-'kó-zəz\ [Russian, from *kollektivnoe khozyaĭstvo* collective farm] (1921)
: a collective farm of the U.S.S.R.

kol·khoz·nik \käl-'kóz-nik\ *noun, plural* **-ni·ki** \-ni-kē\ *or* **-niks** [Russian, from *kolkhoz* + *-nik*, agent suffix] (1944)
: a member of a kolkhoz

Kol Ni·dre \kōl-'ni-(,)drā, kól-, -drə; -ni-'drā\ *noun* [Aramaic *kol nidhrē* all the vows; from the opening phrase of the prayer] (1881)
: a formula for the annulment of private vows chanted in the synagogue on the eve of Yom Kippur

ko·lo \'kō-(,)lō\ *noun, plural* **kolos** [Serbo-Croatian, literally, circle, wheel; akin to Greek *kyklos* circle — more at WHEEL] (1910)
: a central European folk dance in which dancers form a circle and progress slowly to right or left while one or more dancers perform elaborate steps in the center

ko·mat·ik \'kō-'ma-tik\ *noun* [Inuit *qamutik*] (circa 1824)
: an Eskimo sledge with wooden runners and crossbars lashed with rawhide

Ko·mo·do dragon \kə-'mō-dō-\ *noun* [*Komodo* Island, Indonesia] (1927)
: an Indonesian monitor lizard (*Varanus komodoensis*) that is the largest of all known lizards and may attain a length of 10 feet (3 meters)

ko·mon·dor \'kä-mən-,dór, 'kō-\ *noun, plural* **-dors** *or* **-dor·ok** \-,dór-ək\ [Hungarian] (1931)
: any of a breed of large powerful shaggy-coated white dogs of Hungarian origin that are used to guard sheep

Kom·so·mol \'käm-sə-,mól, -,mōl\ *noun* [Russian, from *Kommunisticheskiĭ Soyuz Molodezhi* Communist Union of Youth] (1925)
: a Russian Communist youth organization

Kon·go \'käŋ-(,)gō\ *noun, plural* **Kongo** *or* **Kongos** (circa 1902)
1 : a member of a Bantu people of the lower Congo river
2 : the Bantu language of the Kongo people

Kon·ka·ni \'käŋ-kə-(,)nē\ *noun* [Marathi *Koṅkaṇī*] (1873)
: an Indo-Aryan language of the west coast of India

koo·doo *variant of* KUDU

kook \'kük\ *noun* [by shortening & alteration from *cuckoo*] (1960)
: one whose ideas or actions are eccentric, fantastic, or insane : SCREWBALL

kook·a·bur·ra \'ku-kə-,bər-ə, -,bə-rə\ *noun* [Wiradhuri (Australian aboriginal language of central New South Wales) *gugubarra*] (1834)
: a brownish kingfisher (*Dacelo novaeguineae* synonym *D. gigas*) of Australia that is about the size of a crow and has a call resembling loud laughter — called also *laughing jackass*

kooky *also* **kook·ie** \'kü-kē\ *adjective* **kook·i·er; -est** (1959)
: having the characteristics of a kook : CRAZY, OFFBEAT
— **kook·i·ness** *noun*

ko·peck *or* **ko·pek** \'kō-,pek\ *noun* [Russian *kopeĭka*] (1698)
— see *ruble* at MONEY table

koph *variant of* QOPH

kop·je *or* **kop·pie** \'kä-pē\ *noun* [Afrikaans *koppie*] (1848)
: a small hill especially on the African veld

kor *variant of* COR

Ko·ran \kə-'ran, -'rän; 'kór-,an, 'kór-\ *noun* [Arabic *qur'ān*] (circa 1615)
: the book composed of sacred writings accepted by Muslims as revelations made to Muhammad by Allah through the angel Gabriel
— **Ko·ran·ic** \kə-'ra-nik\ *adjective*

Ko·rat \kō-'rät, kó-\ *noun* [*Korat* province, Thailand] (1967)
: any of a breed of shorthaired domestic cats originating in Thailand and having a heart-shaped face, a silver-blue coat, and green eyes

ko·re \'kó-(,)rā, 'kō-\ *noun, plural* **ko·rai** \-,rī, -(,)rā\ [Greek *korē* girl; akin to Greek *koros* boy — more at CRESCENT] (1920)
: an ancient Greek statue of a clothed young woman standing with feet together

Ko·re·an \kə-'rē-ən, *especially Southern* (,)kō-\ *noun* (1600)
1 : a native or inhabitant of Korea
2 : the language of the Korean people
— **Korean** *adjective*

ko·ru·na \'kór-ə-,nä, 'kär-\ *noun, plural* **ko·ru·ny** \-ə-nē\ *or* **korunas** *or* **ko·run** \'kór-ən, 'kär-\ [Czech, literally, crown, from Latin *corona* — more at CROWN] (1930)
— see MONEY table

¹ko·sher \'kō-shər\ *adjective* [Yiddish, from Hebrew *kāshēr* fit, proper] (1851)
1 a : sanctioned by Jewish law; *especially* : ritually fit for use ⟨*kosher* meat⟩ **b** : selling or serving food ritually fit according to Jewish law ⟨a *kosher* restaurant⟩
2 : being proper, acceptable, or satisfactory ⟨found things going on that were not *kosher* —Homer Bigart⟩

²kosher *transitive verb* **ko·shered; ko·sher·ing** \-sh(ə-)riŋ\ (1871)
: to make kosher

³kosher *noun* (1886)
: the observance of kosher practices — used in the phrase *keep kosher*

ko·to \'kō-(,)tō\ *noun* [Japanese] (1795)
: a long Japanese zither having 13 silk strings

kou·miss \'kü-,mis, 'kü-məs\ *noun* [Russian *kumys*, of Turkic origin; akin to Turkish *kımız* koumiss] (1598)
: a beverage of fermented mare's milk made originally by the nomadic peoples of central Asia

kou·prey \'kü-,prā\ *noun* [Khmer *ko:prey*] (1940)
: a short-haired ox (*Bos sauveli*) of forests of Cambodia, Thailand, and Vietnam having a large dewlap

kou·ros \'kü-,rós\ *noun, plural* **kou·roi** \-(,)rói\ [Greek *kouros, koros* boy — more at CRESCENT] (1920)
: an ancient Greek statue of a nude male youth standing with the left leg forward and arms at the sides

¹kow·tow \(,)kaü-'taü, 'kaü-,\ *noun* [Chinese (Beijing) *kòutóu*, from *kòu* to knock + *tóu* head] (1804)
: an act of kowtowing

²kowtow *intransitive verb* (1826)
1 : to show obsequious deference : FAWN
2 : to kneel and touch the forehead to the ground in token of homage, worship, or deep respect

KP \,kā-'pē\ *noun* [*kitchen police*] (1918)
1 : an enlisted man detailed to assist the cooks in a military mess
2 : the work of KPs

¹kraal \'król, 'kräl\ *noun* [Afrikaans, from Portuguese *curral* pen for cattle, enclosure, from (assumed) Vulgar Latin *currale* enclosure for vehicles — more at CORRAL] (1731)
1 a : a village of southern African natives **b** : the native village community
2 : an enclosure for animals especially in southern Africa

²kraal *transitive verb* (1827)
: to pen in a kraal

kraft \'kräft, 'kraft\ *noun, often attributive* [German, literally, strength, from Old High German — more at CRAFT] (1906)
: a strong paper or paperboard made from wood pulp produced from wood chips boiled in an alkaline solution containing sodium sulfate

krait \'krīt\ *noun* [Hindi *karait*] (1874)
: any of a genus (*Bungarus*) of brightly banded extremely venomous nocturnal elapid snakes of Pakistan, India, southeastern Asia, and adjacent islands

kra·ken \'krä-kən\ *noun* [Norwegian dialect] (1755)
: a fabulous Scandinavian sea monster

kra·ter \'krā-tər, 'krä-ter\ *noun* [Greek *kratēr* — more at CRATER] (circa 1736)
: a jar or vase of classical antiquity having a large round body and a wide mouth and used for mixing wine and water

K ration \'kā-\ *noun* [A. B. *Keys* (born 1904) American physiologist] (circa 1940)
: a lightweight packaged ration of emergency foods developed for the U.S. armed forces in World War II

kraut \'kraüt\ *noun* [German, cabbage, from Old High German *krūt*] (1855)
1 : SAUERKRAUT
2 *often capitalized* : GERMAN — usually used disparagingly

Krebs cycle \'krebz-\ *noun* [H. A. *Krebs*] (1941)
: a sequence of reactions in the living organism in which oxidation of acetic acid or acetyl equivalent provides energy for storage in phosphate bonds (as in ATP) — called also *citric acid cycle, tricarboxylic acid cycle*

krem·lin \'krem-lən\ *noun* [obsolete German *Kremelien* the citadel of Moscow, ultimately from Old Russian *kremlĭ*] (1662)
1 : the citadel of a Russian city
2 *capitalized* [the *Kremlin*, citadel of Moscow and seat of government of Russia and formerly of the U.S.S.R.] : the Russian government

krem·lin·ol·o·gy \,krem-lə-'nä-lə-jē\ *noun, often capitalized* (1958)
: the study of the policies and practices of the Soviet government
— **krem·lin·ol·o·gist** \-jist\ *noun, often capitalized*

krep·lach \'krep-lək, -,läk\ *noun* [Yiddish *kreplekh*, plural of *krepl* filled dumpling] (circa 1892)
: square or triangular dumplings filled with ground meat or cheese, boiled or fried, and usually served in soup

kreu·zer \'króit-sər\ *noun* [German, from *Kreuz* cross; from its markings] (1547)
: a small coin formerly used in Austria and Germany

krill \'kril\ *noun* [Norwegian *kril* fry of fish] (1907)
: planktonic crustaceans and larvae (order Euphausiacea) that constitute the principal food of baleen whales

krim·mer \'kri-mər\ *noun* [German, from *Krim* Crimea] (1834)
: a gray fur made from the pelts of young lambs of the Crimean Peninsula region

Krio \'krē-ō\ *noun* [Krio, speaker of Krio, Krio language, perhaps from Yoruba *Kiriyó* Christian, ultimately from Portuguese *crioulo* Creole] (1955)
: an English-based creole spoken in Sierra Leone

kris \'krēs\ *noun* [Malay *kĕris*] (circa 1580)
: a Malay or Indonesian dagger with a ridged serpentine blade

Krish·na \'krish-nə, 'krēsh-\ *noun* [Sanskrit *Kṛṣṇa*] (1864)

: a deity or deified hero of later Hinduism worshiped as an incarnation of Vishnu

Krish·na·ism \-ˌi-zəm\ *noun* (1885)
: a widespread form of Hindu religion characterized by the worship of Krishna

Kriss Krin·gle \ˈkris-ˈkriŋ-gəl\ *noun* [modification of German *Christkindl* Christ child, Christmas gift, diminutive of *Christkind* Christ child] (1830)
: SANTA CLAUS

¹**kro·na** \ˈkrō-nə\ *noun, plural* **kro·nor** \-ˌnȯr, -nər\ [Swedish, literally, crown] (1875)
— see MONEY table

²**kro·na** \ˈkrō-nə\ *noun, plural* **kro·nur** \-nər\ [Icelandic *krōna*, literally, crown] (1886)
— see MONEY table

¹**kro·ne** \ˈkrō-nə\ *noun, plural* **kro·ner** \-nər\ [Danish, literally, crown] (1885)
— see MONEY table

²**kro·ne** \ˈkrō-nə\ *noun, plural* **kro·nen** \-nən\ [German, literally, crown] (1895)
1 : the basic monetary unit of Austria from 1892 to 1925
2 : a coin representing one krone

Kro·neck·er delta \ˈkrō-ˌne-kər-\ *noun* [Leopold *Kronecker* (died 1891) German mathematician] (1926)
: a function of two variables that is 1 when the variables have the same value and is 0 when they have different values

Kru·ger·rand \ˈkrü-gə(r)-ˌrand, -ˌränd, -ˌränt\ *noun* [S.J.P. *Kruger* + *rand*] (1967)
: a one-ounce gold coin of the Republic of South Africa

krumm·holz \ˈkrüm-ˌhōlts\ *noun, plural* **krummholz** [German, from *krumm* crooked + *Holz* wood] (1903)
: stunted forest characteristic of timberline

krumm·horn *also* **krum·horn** \ˈkrəm-ˌhȯrn\ *noun* [German *Krummhorn*, from *krumm* curved + *Horn* horn] (circa 1696)
: a Renaissance double-reed woodwind instrument consisting of a curved boxwood tube and having a pierced cap covering the reed

kryp·ton \ˈkrip-ˌtän\ *noun* [Greek, neuter of *kryptos* hidden — more at CRYPT] (1898)
: a colorless relatively inert gaseous element found in air at about one part per million and used especially in electric lamps — see ELEMENT table

Ksha·tri·ya \ˈksha-trē-ə, ˈcha-\ *noun* [Sanskrit *kṣatriya*, from *kṣatra* dominion — more at CHECK] (1794)
: a Hindu of an upper caste traditionally assigned to governing and military occupations

Ku·che·an \kü-ˈchē-ən\ *noun* [*Kuche, Kucha,* Sinkiang, China] (circa 1934)
: TOCHARIAN B

ku·chen \ˈkü-kən, -kən\ *noun, plural* **kuchen** [German, cake, from Old High German *kuocho* — more at CAKE] (1854)
: any of various coffee cakes made from sweet yeast dough

ku·do \ˈkü-(ˌ)dō, ˈkyü-\ *noun, plural* **kudos** [back-formation from *kudos* (taken as a plural)] (1926)
1 : AWARD, HONOR ⟨a score of honorary degrees and . . . other *kudos* —*Time*⟩
2 : COMPLIMENT, PRAISE ⟨to all three should go some kind of special *kudo* for refusing to succumb —Al Hine⟩ □

ku·dos \ˈkü-ˌdäs, ˈkyü-, -ˌdōs\ *noun* [Greek *kydos*] (1831)
1 : fame and renown resulting from an act or achievement : PRESTIGE
2 : praise given for achievement

ku·du \ˈkü-(ˌ)dü\ *noun, plural* **kudu** *or* **kudus** [Afrikaans *koedoe*] (1777)
: a large grayish brown African antelope (*Tragelaphus strepsiceros*) with large annulated spirally twisted horns; *also* : a related antelope (*T. imberbis*)

kud·zu \ˈkùd-(ˌ)zü, ˈkəd-\ *noun* [Japanese *kuzu*] (1876)
: an Asian leguminous vine (*Pueraria lobata* synonym *P. thunbergiana*) that is used for for-

age and erosion control and that is often a serious weed in the southeastern U.S.

ku·gel \ˈkü-gəl\ *noun* [Yiddish *kugl*, from Middle High German *kugel* — more at CUDGEL] (1846)
: a baked pudding (as of potatoes or noodles) usually served as a side dish

Ku Klux·er \ˈkü-ˈklək-sər *also* ˈkyü- *or* ˈklü-\ *noun* (1880)
: a member of the Ku Klux Klan

— **Ku Klux·ism** \-ˈklək-ˌsi-zəm\ *noun*

Ku Klux Klan \ˈkü-ˈkləks-ˈklan *also* ˈkyü- *or* ˈklü-\ *noun* (1867)
1 : a post-Civil War secret society advocating white supremacy
2 : a 20th century secret fraternal group held to confine its membership to American-born white Christians

ku·lak \ˈkü-ˌlak, -ˌläk, kü-ˈ\ *noun* [Russian, literally, fist] (1877)
1 : a prosperous or wealthy peasant farmer in 19th century Russia
2 : a farmer characterized by Communists as having excessive wealth

kul·tur \kùl-ˈtùr\ *noun, often capitalized* [German, from Latin *cultura* culture] (1914)
1 : CULTURE 5
2 : culture emphasizing practical efficiency and individual subordination to the state
3 : German culture held to be superior especially by militant Nazi and Hohenzollern expansionists

Kul·tur·kampf \-ˌkäm(p)f\ *noun* [German, from *Kultur* + *Kampf* conflict] (1879)
: conflict between civil government and religious authorities especially over control of education and church appointments

ku·miss *variant of* KOUMISS

küm·mel \ˈki-məl\ *noun* [German, literally, caraway seed, from Old High German *kumīn* cumin] (1864)
: a colorless liqueur flavored principally with caraway seeds

kum·quat \ˈkəm-ˌkwät\ *noun* [Chinese (Guangdong) *gām-gwāt,* from *gām* gold + *gwāt* citrus fruit] (1699)
: any of several small yellow to orange citrus fruits with sweet spongy rind and somewhat acid pulp that are used chiefly for preserves; *also* : a tree or shrub (genus *Fortunella*) of the rue family that bears kumquats

kun·da·li·ni \ˌkùn-də-ˈlē-nē, ˌkən-\ *noun, often capitalized* [Sanskrit *kuṇḍalinī*, from feminine of *kuṇḍalin* circular, coiled, from *kuṇḍala* ring] (1903)
: the yogic life force that is held to lie coiled at the base of the spine until it is aroused and sent to the head to trigger enlightenment

Kung \ˈkùŋ, ˈküŋ; *in* !*Kung the initial sound is a type of click*\ *noun, plural* **Kung** (1926)
1 : a member of a people of southern Africa — usually preceded in writing by !
2 : the Khoisan language of the !Kung people — usually preceded in writing by !

kung fu \ˌkəŋ-ˈfü, ˌkùŋ-\ *noun* [Chinese (Beijing) *gōngfu* skill, art] (1966)
: any of various Chinese arts of self-defense like karate

kunz·ite \ˈkùn(t)-ˌsīt\ *noun* [G. F. *Kunz* (died 1932) American gem expert] (1903)
: a spodumene that occurs in pinkish lilac crystals and is used as a gem

Kurd \ˈkùrd, ˈkərd\ *noun* (1595)
: a member of a pastoral and agricultural people who inhabit a plateau region in adjoining parts of Turkey, Iran, Iraq, Syria, Armenia, and Azerbaijan

— **Kurd·ish** \ˈkùr-dish, ˈkər-\ *adjective*

kudu

Kurdish *noun* (1813)
: the Iranian language of the Kurds

Kur·di·stan \ˌkùr-də-ˈstan, ˌkər-\ *noun* [*Kurdistan,* Asia] (1904)
: an Oriental rug woven by the Kurds and noted for fine colors

kur·gan \kùr-ˈgän, -ˈgan\ *noun* [Russian, of Turkic origin; akin to Turkish *kurgan* fortress, castle] (1889)
: a burial mound of eastern Europe or Siberia

kur·ra·jong \ˈkər-ə-ˌjȯŋ, ˈkə-rə-, -ˌjäŋ\ *noun* [Dharuk (Australian aboriginal language of the Port Jackson area) *garajuŋ*] (1823)
: any of several Australian trees or shrubs (family Sterculiaceae) having strong bast fiber used by Australian aborigines; *especially* : a widely branched shelter and forage tree (*Brachychiton populneum*)

kur·to·sis \(ˌ)kər-ˈtō-səs\ *noun* [Greek *kyrtōsis* convexity, from *kyrtos* convex — more at CURVE] (1905)
: the peakedness or flatness of the graph of a frequency distribution especially with respect to the concentration of values near the mean as compared with the normal distribution

ku·ru \ˈkùr-(ˌ)ü\ *noun* [Fore (language of eastern highland Papua New Guinea)] (1957)
: a rare progressive fatal encephalopathy that is caused by a slow virus, resembles Creutzfeldt-Jakob disease, and occurs among tribesmen in eastern New Guinea

ku·rus \kə-ˈrüsh\ *noun, plural* **kurus** [Turkish *kuruş*] (1882)
— see lira at MONEY table

Ku·te·nai \ˈkü-tᵊn-ˌā, -ˌē\ *noun, plural* **Kutenai** *or* **Kutenais** (1801)
1 : a member of an American Indian people of the Rocky Mountains in both the U.S. and Canada
2 : the language of the Kutenai people

kvass \ˈkväs, ˈkfäs\ *noun* [Russian *kvas*] (circa 1553)
: a slightly alcoholic beverage of eastern Europe made from fermented mixed cereals and often flavored

¹**kvetch** \ˈkvech, ˈkfech\ *intransitive verb* [Yiddish *kvetshn*, literally, to squeeze, pinch, from Middle High German *quetschen*] (circa 1952)
: to complain habitually : GRIPE

²**kvetch** *noun* (1964)
1 : an habitual complainer
2 : COMPLAINT 1

— **kvetchy** \ˈkve-chē, ˈkfe-\ *adjective*

Kwa \ˈkwä\ *noun* (1857)
: a branch of the Niger-Congo language family that is spoken along the African coast and its hinterland from the Ivory Coast to southwestern Nigeria

kwa·cha \ˈkwä-chə\ *noun, plural* **kwacha** [Bemba or Chichewa (Bantu language of Malawi), literally, it dawns] (1966)

□ USAGE

kudo Some commentators hold that since *kudos* is a singular word it cannot be used as a plural and that the word *kudo* is impossible. But *kudo* does exist; it is simply one of the most recent words created by back-formation from another word misunderstood as a plural. *Kudos* was introduced into English in the 19th century; it was used in contexts where a reader unfamiliar with Greek could not be sure whether it was singular or plural. By the 1920s it began to appear as a plural, and about 25 years later *kudo* began to appear. It may have begun as a misunderstanding, but then so did *cherry* and *pea*.

— see MONEY table

Kwa·ki·utl \ˌkwä-kē-ˈyü-t⁀l, ˌkwä-ˈkyü-\ *noun, plural* **Kwakiutl** (1848)
1 : a member of an American Indian people of the Canadian Pacific coast
2 : the language of the Kwakiutl people

kwan·za \ˈkwän-zə\ *noun, plural* **kwanzas** *or* **kwanza** [*Kwanza* (Cuanza), river in Angola] (1978)
— see MONEY table

Kwan·za *or* **Kwan·zaa** \ˈkwän-zə\ *noun* [Swahili *kwanza* first] (1972)
: an African-American festival held in late December

kwash·i·or·kor \ˌkwä-shē-ˈôr-kər, -ôr-ˈkôr\ *noun* [Ga (Kwa language of coastal Ghana) *kwàṣìɔkɔ́* influence a child is said to be under when a second child comes] (1935)
: severe malnutrition in infants and children that is caused by a diet high in carbohydrate and low in protein

KWIC \ˈkwik\ *noun* [keyword *in* context] (1959)

: a computer-generated index alphabetized on a keyword that appears within a brief context

ky·ack \ˈkī-ˌak\ *noun* [origin unknown] (1901)
: a packsack to be swung on either side of a packsaddle

ky·a·nite \ˈkī-ə-ˌnīt\ *noun* [German *Zyanit*, from Greek *kyanos* dark blue enamel, lapis lazuli] (1794)
: an aluminum silicate Al_2SiO_5 that occurs usually in blue thin-bladed triclinic crystals and crystalline aggregates and is sometimes used as a gemstone

kyat \ˈchät\ *noun* [Burmese *cʸat*] (1952)
— see MONEY table

ky·bosh *chiefly British variant of* KIBOSH

ky·mo·gram \ˈkī-mə-ˌgram\ *noun* [International Scientific Vocabulary] (1923)
: a record made by a kymograph

ky·mo·graph \-ˌgraf\ *noun* [Greek *kyma* wave + International Scientific Vocabulary *-graph* — more at CYME] (1872)
: a device which graphically records motion or pressure (as of blood)

— **ky·mo·graph·ic** \ˌkī-mə-ˈgra-fik\ *adjective*
— **ky·mog·ra·phy** \kī-ˈmä-grə-fē\ *noun*

Kym·ric *variant of* CYMRIC

ky·pho·sis \kī-ˈfō-səs\ *noun* [New Latin, from Greek *kyphōsis*, from *kyphos* humpbacked] (1847)
: abnormal backward curvature of the spine
— **ky·phot·ic** \-ˈfä-tik\ *adjective*

ky·rie \ˈkir-ē-ˌā\ *noun, often capitalized* [Middle English, from Medieval Latin, from Late Latin *kyrie eleison*, transliteration of Greek *kyrie eleēson* Lord, have mercy] (14th century)
: a short liturgical prayer that begins with or consists of the words "Lord, have mercy"

ky·rie elei·son \ˈkir-ē-ˌā-ə-ˈlā-(ə-),sän, -(ə-)sən *also* ˈkir-ē-ə-ˈlā-\ *noun, often K&E capitalized* (13th century)
: KYRIE

kyte \ˈkīt\ *noun* [probably from Low German *küt* bowel] (circa 1540)
chiefly Scottish : BELLY 1, 2

kythe *variant of* KITHE

L

L *is the twelfth letter of the English alphabet. It came to Latin from Etruscan, and there from Greek, where it was called* lambda; *Greek, in turn, took its letter from Phoenician* lāmadh. *Throughout these migrations* L *has not varied greatly either in form or in value. In English it normally represents a lateral continuant, a sound produced by the free flow of air through the sides of the mouth when the center of the tongue touches the palate.* L *is also described as a liquid consonant, that is, one produced without air friction and capable of being prolonged like a vowel. In unaccented syllables the sound often forms a syllable by itself without a vowel sound, as in* medal, little. *It is silent in some words, especially after* a *or* o *and before* k, m, *or* f, *as in* talk, yolk, calm, *and* half. *The small* l *came into being when scribes replaced the horizontal stroke at the foot of the capital letter with a curved hook.*

l \'el\ *noun, plural* **l's** *or* **ls** \'elz\ *often capitalized, often attributive* (before 12th century)
1 a : the 12th letter of the English alphabet **b :** a graphic representation of this letter **c :** a speech counterpart of orthographic *l*
2 : fifty — see NUMBER table
3 : a graphic device for reproducing the letter *l*
4 : one designated *l* especially as the 12th in order or class
5 : something shaped like the letter L; *specifically* : ²ELL 1
6 : ²EL

l- *prefix* [International Scientific Vocabulary, from *lev-*]
1 \,lē-(,)vō, ,el, 'el\ **:** levorotatory ⟨*l*-tartaric acid⟩
2 \,el, 'el\ **:** having a similar configuration at a selected carbon atom to the configuration of levorotatory glyceraldehyde — usually printed as a small capital ⟨L-fructose⟩

¹la \'lò, 'lä\ *interjection* [Middle English (northern dialect), from Old English *lā*] (before 12th century)
chiefly dialect — used for emphasis or expressing surprise

²la \'lä\ *noun* [Middle English, from Medieval Latin, from the syllable sung to this note in a medieval hymn to Saint John the Baptist] (14th century)
: the 6th tone of the diatonic scale in solmization

laa·ger \'lä-gər\ *noun* [obsolete Afrikaans *lager* (now *laer*), from German *Lager*, from Old High German *legar* couch — more at LAIR] (1850)
1 *South African* **:** CAMP; *especially* : an encampment protected by a circle of wagons or armored vehicles
2 : a defensive position, policy, or attitude
— **laager** *intransitive verb*

laa·ri \'lä-(,)rē\ *noun, plural* **laari** [probably from Divehi (Indo-Aryan language of the Maldive Islands), from Persian *lārī* piece of silver wire used as currency] (1983)
— see *rufiyaa* at MONEY table

lab \'lab\ *noun* (circa 1895)
: LABORATORY

Lab \'lab\ *noun* (1957)
: LABRADOR RETRIEVER

la·ba·no·ta·tion \,lä-bə-nō-'tā-shən, ,la-; ,bä-(,)nō-\ *noun* [Rudolf *Laban* (died 1958) Hungarian dance theorist + English *notation*] (1952)
: a method of recording bodily movement (as in dance) on a staff by means of symbols (as of direction) that can be aligned with musical accompaniment

lab·a·rum \'la-bə-rəm\ *noun* [Late Latin] (1606)
: an imperial standard of the later Roman emperors resembling the vexillum; *especially*

: the standard bearing the Chi-Rho adopted by Constantine after his conversion to Christianity

lab·da·num \'lab-də-nəm\ *noun* [Medieval Latin *lapdanum*] (14th century)
: a soft dark fragrant bitter oleoresin derived from various rockroses (genus *Cistus*) and used in making perfumes

¹la·bel \'lā-bəl\ *noun* [Middle English, from Middle French] (14th century)
1 *archaic* **:** BAND, FILLET; *specifically* : one attached to a document to hold an appended seal
2 : a heraldic charge that consists of a narrow horizontal band with usually three pendants
3 a : a slip (as of paper or cloth) inscribed and affixed to something for identification or description **b :** written or printed matter accompanying an article to furnish identification or other information **c :** a descriptive or identifying word or phrase : as (1) **:** EPITHET (2) **:** a word or phrase used with a dictionary definition to provide additional information **d :** a usually radioactive isotope used in labeling
4 : an adhesive stamp (as for postage or revenue)
5 a (1) **:** a brand of commercial recordings issued under a usually trademarked name (2) **:** a recording so issued (3) **:** a company issuing such recordings **b :** the brand name of a retail store selling clothing, a clothing manufacturer, or a fashion designer

²label *transitive verb* **la·beled** *or* **la·belled; la·bel·ing** *or* **la·bel·ling** \'lā-b(ə-)liŋ\ (1601)
1 a : to affix a label to **b :** to describe or designate with or as if with a label
2 a : to distinguish (an element or atom) by using an isotope distinctive in some manner (as in mass or radioactivity) **b :** to distinguish (as a compound or cell) by introducing a traceable constituent (as a dye or labeled atom)
— **la·bel·able** \'lā-bə-lə-bəl\ *adjective*
— **la·bel·er** \'lā-b(ə-)lər\ *noun*

la·bel·lum \lə-'be-ləm\ *noun, plural* **la·bel·la** \-lə\ [New Latin, from Latin, diminutive of *labrum* lip — more at LIP] (1830)
1 : the median and usually most morphologically distinct member of the corolla of an orchid
2 : a terminal part of the labium or labrum of various insects

labia *plural of* LABIUM

¹la·bi·al \'lā-bē-əl\ *adjective* [Medieval Latin *labialis*, from Latin *labium* lip] (1594)
1 : uttered with the participation of one or both lips ⟨the *labial* sounds \f\, \p\, and \ü\⟩
2 : of, relating to, or situated near the lips or labia
— **la·bi·al·ly** \-ə-lē\ *adverb*

²labial *noun* (1668)
: a labial consonant

la·bi·al·ize \'lā-bē-ə-,līz\ *transitive verb* **-ized; -iz·ing** (1867)
: to make labial : ROUND 1b(2)
— **la·bi·al·i·za·tion** \,lā-bē-ə-lə-'zā-shən, -byə-lə-\ *noun*

la·bia ma·jo·ra \'lā-bē-ə-mə-'jòr-ə, -'jòr-\ *noun plural* [New Latin, literally, larger lips] (1838)
: the outer fatty folds of the vulva bounding the vestibule

labia mi·no·ra \-mə-'nòr-ə, -'nòr-\ *noun plural* [New Latin, literally, smaller lips] (1838)
: the inner highly vascular largely connective-tissue folds of the vulva bounding the vestibule

¹la·bi·ate \'lā-bē-ət, -bē-,āt\ *adjective* [New Latin *labiatus*, from Latin *labium*] (1706)
1 : having the limb of a tubular corolla or calyx divided into two unequal parts projecting one over the other like lips ⟨mints and the snapdragon are *labiate*⟩
2 : of or relating to the mint family

²labiate *noun* (1845)
: a plant of the mint family

la·bile \'lā-,bīl, -bəl\ *adjective* [French, from Middle French, prone to err, from Late Latin *labilis*, from Latin *labi* to slip — more at SLEEP] (1603)
1 : readily or continually undergoing chemical, physical, or biological change or breakdown : UNSTABLE ⟨a *labile* mineral⟩
2 : readily open to change
— **la·bil·i·ty** \lā-'bi-lə-tē\ *noun*

labio- *combining form* [Latin *labium*]
: labial and ⟨*labio*dental⟩

la·bio·den·tal \,lā-bē-ō-'den-t³l\ *adjective* (1669)
: uttered with the participation of the lip and teeth ⟨the *labiodental* sounds \f\ and \v\⟩
— **labiodental** *noun*

la·bio·ve·lar \-'vē-lər\ *adjective* [International Scientific Vocabulary] (1894)
: both labial and velar ⟨the *labiovelar* sound \w\⟩
— **labiovelar** *noun*

la·bi·um \'lā-bē-əm\ *noun, plural* **la·bia** \-ə\ [New Latin, from Latin, lip — more at LIP] (1634)
1 : any of the folds at the margin of the vulva — compare LABIA MAJORA, LABIA MINORA
2 : the lower lip of a labiate corolla
3 a : a lower mouthpart of an insect that is formed by the second pair of maxillae united in the middle line **b :** a liplike part of various invertebrates

¹la·bor \'lā-bər\ *noun* [Middle English, from Middle French, from Latin *labor*; perhaps akin to Latin *labare* to totter, *labi* to slip — more at SLEEP] (14th century)
1 a : expenditure of physical or mental effort especially when difficult or compulsory **b** (1) **:** human activity that provides the goods or services in an economy (2) **:** the services performed by workers for wages as distinguished from those rendered by entrepreneurs for profits **c :** the physical activities involved in giving birth; *also* : the period of such labor
2 : an act or process requiring labor : TASK
3 : a product of labor
4 a : an economic group comprising those who do manual labor or work for wages **b** (1) **:** workers employed in an establishment (2) **:** workers available for employment **c :** the organizations or officials representing groups of workers
5 *usually Labour* **:** the Labour party of the United Kingdom or of another nation of the Commonwealth
synonym see WORK

\ə\ **abut** \ᵊ\ **kitten** \ər\ **further** \a\ **ash** \ā\ **ace**
\ä\ **mop, mar** \au̇\ **out** \ch\ **chin** \e\ **bet** \ē\ **easy**
\g\ **go** \i\ **hit** \ī\ **ice** \j\ **job** \ŋ\ **sing** \ō\ **go**
\ò\ **law** \òi\ **boy** \th\ **thin** \t̲h̲\ **the** \ü\ **loot** \u̇\ **foot**
\y\ **yet** \zh\ **vision** *see also* Guide to Pronunciation

²**labor** *verb* **la·bored; la·bor·ing** \-b(ə-)riŋ\ (14th century)
intransitive verb
1 : to exert one's powers of body or mind especially with painful or strenuous effort : WORK
2 : to move with great effort ⟨the truck *labored* up the hill⟩
3 : to be in the labor of giving birth
4 : to suffer from some disadvantage or distress ⟨*labor* under a delusion⟩
5 *of a ship* : to pitch or roll heavily
transitive verb
1 *archaic* **a** : to spend labor on or produce by labor **b** : to strive to effect or achieve
2 : to treat or work out in often laborious detail ⟨*labor* the obvious⟩
3 : DISTRESS, BURDEN
4 : to cause to labor

³**labor** *adjective* (1640)
1 : of or relating to labor
2 *capitalized* : of, relating to, or constituting a political party held to represent the interests of workers or made up largely of organized labor groups

lab·o·ra·to·ry \'la-b(ə-)rə-,tōr-ē, -,tòr- *sometimes* 'la-bə(r)-, *or* lə-'bòr-ə-, *British usually* lə-'bär-ə-t(ə-)rē\ *noun, plural* **-ries** *often attributive* [Medieval Latin *laboratorium*, from Latin *laborare* to labor, from *labor*] (1605)
1 a : a place equipped for experimental study in a science or for testing and analysis; *broadly* : a place providing opportunity for experimentation, observation, or practice in a field of study **b** : a place like a laboratory for testing, experimentation, or practice ⟨the *laboratory* of the mind⟩
2 : an academic period set aside for laboratory work

labor camp *noun* (1900)
1 : a penal colony where forced labor is performed
2 : a camp for migratory laborers

Labor Day *noun* (1886)
: a day set aside for special recognition of working people: as **a** : the first Monday in September observed in the U.S. and Canada as a legal holiday **b** : May 1 in many countries

la·bored \'lā-bərd\ *adjective* (1608)
: produced or performed with labor ⟨*labored* breathing⟩; *also* : lacking ease of expression ⟨a *labored* speech⟩

la·bor·er \-bər-ər\ *noun* (14th century)
: one that labors; *specifically* : a person who does unskilled physical work for wages

labor force *noun* (1911)
: WORK FORCE

la·bor–in·ten·sive \'lā-bər-in-,ten(t)-siv\ *adjective* (1953)
: having high labor costs per unit of output; *especially* : requiring greater expenditure on labor than in capital

la·bo·ri·ous \lə-'bōr-ē-əs, -'bòr-\ *adjective* (14th century)
1 : devoted to labor : INDUSTRIOUS
2 : involving or characterized by hard or toilsome effort : LABORED
— **la·bo·ri·ous·ly** *adverb*
— **la·bo·ri·ous·ness** *noun*

la·bor·ite \'lā-bə-,rīt\ *noun* (1889)
1 : a member of a group favoring the interests of labor
2 *capitalized* **a** : a member of a political party devoted chiefly to the interests of labor **b** *usually* **La·bour·ite** : a member of the British Labour party

la·bor·sav·ing \'lā-bər-,sā-viŋ\ *adjective* (circa 1779)
: adapted to replace or decrease human and especially manual labor

labor union *noun* (1866)
: an organization of workers formed for the purpose of advancing its members' interests in respect to wages, benefits, and working conditions

la·bour *chiefly British variant of* LABOR

lab·ra·dor·ite \'la-brə-,dòr-,īt\ *noun* [*Labrador* Peninsula, Canada] (1814)
: a triclinic feldspar showing a play of several colors

Lab·ra·dor retriever \'la-brə-,dòr-\ *noun* [*Labrador*, Newfoundland] (1910)
: any of a breed of compact, strongly built retrievers largely developed in England from stock originating in Newfoundland and having a short dense black, yellow, or chocolate coat — called also *Lab, Labrador*

Labrador tea *noun* (1767)
: a low-growing ericaceous evergreen shrub (*Ledum groenlandicum*) chiefly of northern North America with white or creamy bell-shaped flowers and leaves sometimes used in making tea; *also* : a related Rocky Mountain shrub (*L. glandulosum*)

la·bret \'lā-brət\ *noun* [Latin *labrum*] (1857)
: an ornament worn in a perforation of the lip

la·brum \'lā-brəm\ *noun* [New Latin, from Latin, lip, edge — more at LIP] (1826)
: an upper or anterior mouthpart of an arthropod consisting of a single median piece in front of or above the mandibles

la·bur·num \lə-'bər-nəm\ *noun* [New Latin, from Latin] (1567)
: any of a small genus (*Laburnum* and especially *L. anagyroides*) of poisonous leguminous shrubs and trees of Eurasia with pendulous racemes of bright yellow flowers

lab·y·rinth \'la-bə-,rin(t)th, -rən(t)th\ *noun* [Middle English *laborintus*, from Latin *labyrinthus*, from Greek *labyrinthos*] (14th century)
1 a : a place constructed of or full of intricate passageways and blind alleys **b** : a maze (as in a garden) formed by paths separated by high hedges
2 : something extremely complex or tortuous in structure, arrangement, or character : INTRICACY, PERPLEXITY ⟨a *labyrinth* of swamps and channels⟩ ⟨guided them through the *labyrinths* of city life —Paul Blanshard⟩
3 : a tortuous anatomical structure; *especially* : the internal ear or its bony or membranous part

lab·y·rin·thi·an \,la-bə-'rin(t)-thē-ən\ *adjective* (1588)
: LABYRINTHINE

lab·y·rin·thine \-'rin(t)-thən; -'rin-,thīn, -,thēn\ *adjective* (1632)
1 : of, relating to, or resembling a labyrinth : INTRICATE, INVOLVED
2 : of, relating to, affecting, or originating in the internal ear ⟨*labyrinthine* lesions⟩

lab·y·rin·tho·dont \-'rin(t)-thə-,dänt\ *noun* [New Latin *Labyrinthodontia*, from Greek *labyrinthos* + *odont-, odous* tooth — more at TOOTH] (circa 1852)
: any of a superorder (Labyrinthodontia) of extinct amphibians of the Late Paleozoic and Early Mesozoic typically having bodies resembling salamanders or crocodiles and considered to be the earliest tetrapod vertebrates
— **labyrinthodont** *adjective*

lac \'lak\ *noun* [Persian *lak* & Hindi *lākh*, from Sanskrit *lākṣā*] (1598)
: a resinous substance secreted by a scale insect (*Laccifer lacca*) and used chiefly in the form of shellac

lac·co·lith \'la-kə-,lith\ *noun* [Greek *lakkos* pond, reservoir + English *-lith* — more at LAKE] (1879)
: a mass of igneous rock that is intruded between sedimentary beds and produces a domical bulging of the overlying strata
— **lac·co·lith·ic** \,la-kə-'li-thik\ *adjective*

¹**lace** \'lās\ *verb* **laced; lac·ing** [Middle English, from Old French *lacier*, from Latin *laqueare* to ensnare, from *laqueus*] (13th century)
transitive verb
1 : to draw together the edges of by or as if by a lace passed through eyelets

2 : to draw or pass (as a lace) through something (as eyelets)
3 : to confine or compress by tightening laces of a garment
4 a : to adorn with or as if with lace **b** : to mark with streaks of color
5 : BEAT, LASH
6 a : to add a dash of liquor to **b** : to add to something to impart pungency, savor, or zest ⟨a sauce *laced* with garlic⟩ ⟨conversation *laced* with sarcasm⟩ **c** : to adulterate with a substance ⟨*laced* a guard's coffee with a sedative⟩
intransitive verb
: to admit of being tied or fastened with a lace
— **lac·er** *noun*

²**lace** *noun* [Middle English, from Middle French *laz*, from Latin *laqueus* snare] (14th century)
1 : a cord or string used for drawing together two edges (as of a garment or a shoe)
2 : an ornamental braid for trimming coats or uniforms
3 : an openwork usually figured fabric made of thread or yarn and used for trimmings, household coverings, and entire garments
— **laced** \'lāst\ *adjective*
— **lace·less** \'lās-ləs\ *adjective*
— **lace·like** \'lās-,līk\ *adjective*

lace–curtain *adjective* (1934)
: copying middle-class attributes : aspiring to middle-class standing

¹**lac·er·ate** \'la-sə-,rāt\ *transitive verb* **-at·ed; -at·ing** [Middle English, from Latin *laceratus*, past participle of *lacerare* to tear; akin to Greek *lakis* tear] (15th century)
1 : to tear or rend roughly
2 : to cause sharp mental or emotional pain to : DISTRESS
— **lac·er·a·tive** \-,rā-tiv\ *adjective*

²**lac·er·ate** \-rət, -,rāt\ *or* **lac·er·at·ed** \-,rā-təd\ *adjective* (1542)
1 a : torn jaggedly : MANGLED **b** : extremely harrowed or distracted
2 : having the edges deeply and irregularly cut ⟨a *lacerate* petal⟩

lac·er·a·tion \,la-sə-'rā-shən\ *noun* (1597)
1 : the act of lacerating
2 : a torn and ragged wound

lace·wing \'lās-,wiŋ\ *noun* (1854)
: any of various neuropterous insects (as genera *Chrysopa* and *Hemerobius*) having delicate lace-like wing venation, usually long antennae, and often brilliant eyes — called also *lacewing fly*

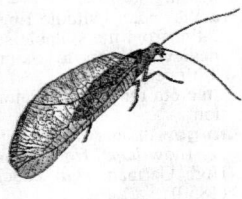
lacewing

lace·work \'lās-,wərk\ *noun* (1849)
: objects or patterns consisting of or resembling lace

lac·ey *variant of* LACY

lach·es \'la-chəz, 'lā-\ *noun, plural* **laches** [Middle English *lachesse*, from Middle French *laschesse*, from Old French *lasche* lax, ultimately from Latin *laxare* to loosen — more at LEASE] (14th century)
: negligence in the observance of duty or opportunity; *specifically* : undue delay in asserting a legal right or privilege

lach·ry·mal *or* **lac·ri·mal** \'la-krə-məl\ *adjective* [Middle French or Medieval Latin; Middle French *lacrymal*, from Medieval Latin *lacrimalis*, from Latin *lacrima* tear, from Old Latin *dacrima*, probably from Greek *dakry* — more at TEAR] (15th century)
1 *usually* **lacrimal** : of, relating to, or being glands that produce tears
2 : of, relating to, or marked by tears

lach·ry·mose \-,mōs\ *adjective* [Latin *lacrimosus*, from *lacrima*] (circa 1727)
1 : given to tears or weeping : TEARFUL
2 : tending to cause tears : MOURNFUL

— **lach·ry·mose·ly** *adverb*
— **lach·ry·mos·i·ty** \ˌla-krə-'mä-sə-tē\ *noun*

lac·ing \'lā-siŋ\ *noun* (14th century)
1 : the action of one that laces
2 : something that laces : LACE
3 : a contrasting marginal band of color (as on a feather)
4 a : a dash of liquor in a food or beverage **b** : a trace or sprinkling that adds spice or flavor
5 : a decisive defeat

la·cin·i·ate \lə-'si-nē-ət, -ˌāt\ *adjective* [Latin *lacinia* flap; akin to Latin *lacerare*] (circa 1760)
: bordered with a fringe; *especially* : cut into deep irregular usually pointed lobes ⟨*laciniate* petals⟩
— **la·cin·i·a·tion** \-ˌsi-nē-'ā-shən\ *noun*

¹lack \'lak\ (13th century)
intransitive verb
1 : to be deficient or missing ⟨time is *lacking* for a full explanation⟩
2 : to be short or have need of something ⟨he will not *lack* for advisers⟩
transitive verb
: to stand in need of : suffer from the absence or deficiency of ⟨*lack* the necessities of life⟩

²lack *noun* [Middle English *lak*; akin to Middle Dutch *lak* lack, Old Norse *lakr* defective] (14th century)
1 : the fact or state of being wanting or deficient
2 : something that is lacking or is needed

lack·a·dai·si·cal \ˌla-kə-'dā-zi-kəl\ *adjective* [irregular from *lackaday* + -ical] (1768)
: lacking life, spirit, or zest : LANGUID
— **lack·a·dai·si·cal·ly** \-k(ə-)lē\ *adverb*

lack·a·day \'la-kə-ˌdā\ *interjection* [by alteration & shortening from *alack the day*] (1695)
archaic — used to express regret or deprecation

¹lack·ey \'la-kē\ *noun, plural* **lackeys** [Middle French *laquais*] (1523)
1 a : FOOTMAN 2, SERVANT **b** : someone who does menial tasks or runs errands for another
2 : a servile follower : TOADY

²lackey *verb* **lack·eyed; lack·ey·ing** (1568)
intransitive verb
obsolete : to act as a lackey : TOADY
transitive verb
: to wait upon or serve obsequiously

lack·lus·ter \'lak-ˌləs-tər\ *adjective* (1600)
: lacking in sheen, brilliance, or vitality : DULL, MEDIOCRE
— **lackluster** *noun*

la·con·ic \lə-'kä-nik\ *adjective* [Latin *laconicus* Spartan, from Greek *lakōnikos;* from the Spartan reputation for terseness of speech] (1589)
: using or involving the use of a minimum of words : concise to the point of seeming rude or mysterious
synonym see CONCISE
— **la·con·i·cal·ly** \-ni-k(ə-)lē\ *adverb*

lac·o·nism \'la-kə-ˌni-zəm\ *noun* (1570)
1 : brevity or terseness of expression or style
2 : a laconic expression

¹lac·quer \'la-kər\ *noun* [Portuguese *lacré* sealing wax, from *laca* lac, from Arabic *lakk*, from Persian *lak* — more at LAC] (1592)
1 a : a spirit varnish (as shellac) **b** : any of various durable natural varnishes; *especially* : a varnish obtained from an Asian sumac (*Rhus verniciflua*) — called also *Japanese lacquer*
2 : any of various clear or colored synthetic organic coatings that typically dry to form a film by evaporation of the solvent; *especially* : a solution of a cellulose derivative (as nitrocellulose)

²lacquer *transitive verb* **lac·quered; lac·quer·ing** \-k(ə-)riŋ\ (1688)
1 : to coat with or as if with lacquer
2 : to give a smooth finish or appearance to : make glossy

— **lac·quer·er** \-kər-ər\ *noun*

lac·quer·ware \-ˌwar, -ˌwer\ *noun* (1697)
: a decorative article usually made of wood and coated with lacquer; *also* : such articles or ware collectively

lac·quer·work \-ˌwərk\ *noun* (circa 1901)
: LACQUERWARE

lac·ri·ma·tion \ˌla-krə-'mā-shən\ *noun* (1572)
: the secretion of tears especially when abnormal or excessive

lac·ri·ma·tor *or* **lach·ry·ma·tor** \'la-krə-ˌmā-tər\ *noun* [Latin *lacrimare* to weep, from *lacrima* tear — more at LACHRYMAL] (1918)
: a tear-producing substance (as tear gas)

la·crosse \lə-'krȯs\ *noun* [Canadian French *la crosse*, literally, the crosier] (1718)
: a goal game in which players use a long-handled stick that has a triangular head with a mesh pouch for catching, carrying, and throwing the ball

lact- *or* **lacti-** *or* **lacto-** *combining form* [French & Latin; French, from Latin, from *lact-, lac*] — more at GALAXY]
1 : milk ⟨*lacto*globulin⟩
2 a : lactic acid ⟨*lactate*⟩ **b** : lactose ⟨*lactase*⟩

lact·al·bu·min \ˌlak-ˌtal-'byü-mən\ *noun* [International Scientific Vocabulary] (circa 1857)
: an albumin that is obtained from whey and is similar to serum albumin

lac·tase \'lak-ˌtās, -ˌtāz\ *noun* [International Scientific Vocabulary] (1891)
: an enzyme that hydrolyzes beta-galactosides (as lactose) and occurs especially in the intestines of young mammals and in yeasts

¹lac·tate \'lak-ˌtāt\ *noun* (circa 1794)
: a salt or ester of lactic acid

²lactate *intransitive verb* **lac·tat·ed; lac·tat·ing** [Latin *lactatus*, past participle of *lactare*, from *lact-, lac*] (circa 1889)
: to secrete milk
— **lac·ta·tion** \lak-'tā-shən\ *noun*
— **lac·ta·tion·al** \-shnəl, -shə-nᵊl\ *adjective*

¹lac·te·al \'lak-tē-əl\ *adjective* [Latin *lacteus* of milk, from *lact-, lac*] (circa 1658)
1 : relating to, consisting of, producing, or resembling milk
2 a : conveying or containing a milky fluid **b** : of or relating to the lacteals

²lacteal *noun* (1680)
: any of the lymphatic vessels arising from the villi of the small intestine and conveying chyle to the thoracic duct

lac·tic \'lak-tik\ *adjective* (1790)
1 a : of or relating to milk **b** : obtained from sour milk or whey
2 : involving the production of lactic acid

lactic acid *noun* (1790)
: a hygroscopic organic acid $C_3H_6O_3$ present normally in tissue, produced in carbohydrate matter usually by bacterial fermentation, and used especially in food and medicine and in industry

lac·tif·er·ous \lak-'ti-f(ə-)rəs\ *adjective* [French or Late Latin; French *lactifère*, from Late Latin *lactifer*, from Latin *lact-, lac* + -*fer*] (circa 1674)
1 : yielding a milky juice ⟨*lactiferous* plants⟩
2 : secreting or conveying milk

lac·to·ba·cil·lus \ˌlak-tō-bə-'si-ləs\ *noun* [New Latin] (1924)
: any of a genus (*Lactobacillus*) of lactic-acid-forming bacteria

lac·to·gen·ic \ˌlak-tə-'je-nik\ *adjective* (1933)
: inducing lactation ⟨*lactogenic* hormones⟩

lac·to·glob·u·lin \-'glä-byə-lən\ *noun* (1885)
: a crystalline protein fraction that is obtained from the whey of milk

lac·tone \'lak-ˌtōn\ *noun* [International Scientific Vocabulary] (1880)
: any of various cyclic esters formed from hydroxy acids
— **lac·ton·ic** \lak-'tä-nik\ *adjective*

lac·tose \'lak-ˌtōs, -ˌtōz\ *noun* [International Scientific Vocabulary] (1858)
: a disaccharide sugar $C_{12}H_{22}O_{11}$ that is present in milk and yields glucose and galac-

tose upon hydrolysis and yields especially lactic acid upon fermentation

la·cu·na \lə-'kü-nə, -'kyü-\ *noun, plural* **la·cu·nae** \lə-'kü-(ˌ)nē, -'kü-ˌnī\ *or* **la·cu·nas** \-'kü-nəz, -'kyü-\ [Latin, pool, pit, gap — more at LAGOON] (1652)
1 : a blank space or a missing part : GAP
2 : a small cavity, pit, or discontinuity in an anatomical structure
— **la·cu·nar** \-'kü-nər, -'kyü-\ *also* **la·cu·nate** \lə-'kü-nət, -'kyü-, -ˌnāt; 'la-kyə-ˌnāt\ *adjective*

la·cus·trine \lə-'kəs-trən\ *adjective* [French or Italian *lacustre*, from Latin *lacus* lake] (1830)
: of, relating to, formed in, living in, or growing in lakes ⟨*lacustrine* deposits⟩ ⟨*lacustrine* faunas⟩

lacy \'lā-sē\ *adjective* **lac·i·er; -est** (1804)
: resembling or consisting of lace

lad \'lad\ *noun* [Middle English *ladde*] (14th century)
1 : a male person of any age between early boyhood and maturity : BOY, YOUTH
2 : FELLOW, CHAP

lad·a·num \'la-dᵊn-əm, 'lad-nəm\ *variant of* LABDANUM

lad·der \'la-dər\ *noun, often attributive* [Middle English, from Old English *hlæder*; akin to Old High German *leitara* ladder, Old English *hlinian* to lean — more at LEAN] (before 12th century)
1 : a structure for climbing up or down that consists essentially of two long sidepieces joined at intervals by crosspieces on which one may step
2 : something that resembles or suggests a ladder in form or use; *especially* : RUN 11a
3 : a series of usually ascending steps or stages : SCALE ⟨climbing up the corporate *ladder*⟩
— **lad·der·like** \-ˌlīk\ *adjective*

lad·der-back \-ˌbak\ *adjective* (1908)
of furniture : having a back consisting of two upright posts connected by horizontal slats

ladder truck *noun* (1889)
: HOOK AND LADDER TRUCK

lad·die \'la-dē\ *noun* (1546)
: a young lad

lade \'lād\ *verb* **lad·ed; lad·ed** *or* **lad·en** \'lā-dᵊn\; **lad·ing** [Middle English, from Old English *hladan;* akin to Old High German *hladan* to load, Old Church Slavonic *klasti* to place] (before 12th century)
transitive verb
1 a : to put a load or burden on or in : LOAD **b** : to put or place as a load especially for shipment : SHIP **c** : to load heavily or oppressively
2 : DIP, LADLE
intransitive verb
1 : to take on cargo : LOAD
2 : to take up or convey a liquid by dipping

¹lad·en \'lā-dᵊn\ *transitive verb* **lad·ened; lad·en·ing** \'lād-niŋ, 'lā-dᵊn-iŋ\ (1514)
: LADE

²laden *adjective* (before 12th century)
: carrying a load or burden

la·di·da \ˌlä-dē-'dä\ *also* **la·de·da** *adjective* [perhaps alteration of *lardy-dardy* foppish] (1895)
: affectedly refined in manners or tastes : PRETENTIOUS, ELEGANT

la·dies \'lā-dēz\ *noun plural but singular or plural in construction* (1918)
chiefly British : LADIES' ROOM

ladies' man *also* **lady's man** *noun* (1784)
: a man who shows a marked fondness for the company of women or is especially attentive to women

ladies' room *noun* (1870)
: a room equipped with lavatories and toilets for the use of women

ladies' tresses *noun plural but singular or plural in construction* (1548)
: any of a widely distributed genus (*Spiranthes*) of terrestrial orchids with slender often twisted spikes of white irregular flowers

La·din \lə-ˈdēn\ *noun* [Rhaeto-Romance, from Latin *Latinum* Latin] (1877)
1 a : a Rhaeto-Romance dialect of Alto Adige in northern Italy **b** : the Rhaeto-Romance dialects of the Engadine Valley in Switzerland
2 : one speaking Ladin as a mother tongue

lad·ing \ˈlā-diŋ\ *noun* (1500)
1 a : LOADING 1 **b** : an act of bailing, dipping, or ladling
2 : CARGO, FREIGHT

la·di·no \lə-ˈdē-(ˌ)nō\ *noun, plural* **-nos** [Spanish, literally, Latin, from Latin *latinus*] (1877)
1 *often capitalized* [American Spanish] : a westernized Spanish-speaking Latin American; *especially* : MESTIZO
2 *capitalized* [Judeo-Spanish, from Old Spanish] : JUDEO-SPANISH

la·di·no clover \lə-ˈdī-(ˌ)nō-, -nə-\ *noun* [perhaps irregular from *Lodi*, Italy + Italian *-ino*, adjective suffix] (1924)
: a large nutritious rapidly growing clover that is a variety of white clover and is widely planted especially for forage — called also *ladino*

¹la·dle \ˈlā-dᵊl\ *noun* [Middle English *ladel*, from Old English *hlædel*, from *hladan*] (before 12th century)
1 : a deep-bowled long-handled spoon used especially for dipping up and conveying liquids
2 : something resembling a ladle in form or function

²ladle *transitive verb* **la·dled; la·dling** \ˈlād-liŋ, ˈlā-dᵊl-iŋ\ (1525)
: to take up and convey in or as if in a ladle

la dol·ce vi·ta \(ˌ)lä-ˈdōl-(ˌ)chä-ˈvē-(ˌ)tä\ *variant of* DOLCE VITA

la·dy \ˈlā-dē\ *noun, plural* **ladies** *often attributive* [Middle English, from Old English *hlǣfdige*, from *hlāf* bread + *-dige* (akin to *dǣge* kneader of bread) — more at LOAF, DAIRY] (before 12th century)
1 a : a woman having proprietary rights or authority especially as a feudal superior **b** : a woman receiving the homage or devotion of a knight or lover
2 *capitalized* : VIRGIN MARY — usually used with *Our*
3 a : a woman of superior social position **b** : a woman of refinement and gentle manners **c** : WOMAN, FEMALE — often used in a courteous reference ⟨show the *lady* to a seat⟩ or usually in the plural in address ⟨*ladies* and gentlemen⟩
4 a : WIFE **b** : GIRLFRIEND, MISTRESS
5 a : any of various titled women in Great Britain — used as the customary title of (1) a marchioness, countess, viscountess, or baroness or (2) the wife of a knight, baronet, member of the peerage, or one having the courtesy title of *lord* and used as a courtesy title for the daughter of a duke, marquess, or earl **b** : a female member of an order of knighthood — compare DAME ◇

la·dy·bug \ˈlā-dē-ˌbəg\ *noun* [Our *Lady*, the Virgin Mary] (1699)
: any of numerous small nearly hemispherical often brightly colored beetles (family Coccinellidae) of temperate and tropical regions that usually feed both as larvae and adults on other insects — called also *lady beetle, ladybird, ladybird beetle*

ladybug

lady chapel *noun, often L&C capitalized* (15th century)
: a chapel dedicated to the Virgin Mary

Lady Day *noun* (13th century)
: ANNUNCIATION 1

la·dy·fin·ger \ˈlā-dē-ˌfiŋ-gər\ *noun* (1820)
: a small finger-shaped sponge cake

la·dy·fish \-ˌfish\ *noun* (1712)
1 : BONEFISH 1
2 : a large silvery food and sport fish (*Elops saurus*) that resembles a herring but is related to the tarpon

la·dy–in–wait·ing \ˈlā-dē-in-ˈwā-tiŋ\ *noun*, *plural* **ladies–in–waiting** (1862)
: a lady of a queen's or a princess's household appointed to wait on her

la·dy–kill·er \ˈlā-dē-ˌki-lər\ *noun* (circa 1810)
: a man who is extremely attractive to women

la·dy·kin \ˈlā-dē-kən\ *noun* (1853)
: a little lady

la·dy·like \-ˌlīk\ *adjective* (1586)
1 : becoming or suitable to a lady
2 : resembling a lady in appearance or manners : WELL-BRED
3 a : feeling or showing too much concern about elegance or propriety ⟨*ladylike* embarrassment at not being the wife of a real doctor —Lewis Vogler⟩ **b** : lacking in strength, force, or virility

la·dy·love \ˈlā-dē-ˌləv, ˌlā-dē-\ *noun* (1733)
: SWEETHEART, MISTRESS

lady of the house (1816)
: the chief female in a household

Lady of the Lake (15th century)
: VIVIAN

la·dy·ship \ˈlā-dē-ˌship\ *noun* (13th century)
: the condition of being a lady : rank of lady — used as a title for a woman having the rank of lady ⟨her *Ladyship* is not at home⟩ ⟨if your *Ladyship* please⟩

lady's slipper *noun* (1597)
: any of several North American temperate-zone orchids (as of the genus *Cypripedium*) having flowers whose shape suggests a slipper — called also *lady slipper*

la·dy's–smock \-ˌsmäk\ *noun* (1588)
: CUCKOOFLOWER 1

lady's thumb *noun* (1837)
: a widely distributed weedy annual herb (*Polygonum persicaria*) that has large lanceolate leaves often with a blackish blotch suggesting a thumbprint

La·er·tes \lā-ˈər-tēz\ *noun* [Latin, from Greek *Laertēs*]
1 : the father of Odysseus in Greek mythology
2 : the son of Polonius and brother of Ophelia in Shakespeare's *Hamlet*

Lae·ta·re Sunday \lā-ˈtär-ē-, -ˈtar-\ *noun* [Latin *laetare*, singular imperative of *laetari* to rejoice] (circa 1870)
: the fourth Sunday in Lent

la·e·trile \ˈlā-ə-(ˌ)tril, -trəl\ *noun, often capitalized* [*lae*vorotary (levorotary) + *nitrile*] (1953)
: a drug derived especially from apricot pits that contains amygdalin and has been used in the treatment of cancer although of unproved effectiveness

¹lag \ˈlag\ *noun* [probably of Scandinavian origin; akin to Norwegian dialect *lagga* to go slowly] (1514)
1 : one that lags or is last
2 a : the act or the condition of lagging **b** : comparative slowness or retardation **c** (1) : an amount of lagging or the time during which lagging continues (2) : a space of time especially between related events or phenomena : INTERVAL
3 : the action of lagging for opening shot (as in marbles or billiards)

²lag *verb* **lagged; lag·ging** (1530)
intransitive verb

lady's slipper

1 a : to stay or fall behind : LINGER, LOITER **b** : to move, function, or develop with comparative slowness **c** : to become retarded in attaining maximum value
2 : to slacken or weaken gradually : FLAG
3 : to toss or roll a marble toward a line or a cue ball toward the head cushion to determine order of play
transitive verb
1 : to lag behind ⟨current that *lags* the voltage⟩
2 : to pitch or shoot (as a coin or marble) at a mark

synonym SEE DELAY
— **lag·ger** *noun*

³lag *adjective* (1552)
: LAST, HINDMOST

⁴lag *noun* [probably of Scandinavian origin; akin to Old Norse *lǫgg* rim of a barrel] (1672)
1 : a barrel stave
2 : a stave, slat, or strip (as of wood or asbestos) forming part of a covering for a cylindrical object

⁵lag *transitive verb* **lagged; lag·ging** (1870)
: to cover or provide with lags

⁶lag *transitive verb* **lagged; lag·ging** [origin unknown] (circa 1812)
1 *slang chiefly British* : to transport or jail for crime
2 *slang chiefly British* : ARREST

⁷lag *noun* (circa 1812)
1 *slang chiefly British* **a** : a person transported for crime **b** : CONVICT **c** : an ex-convict
2 *slang chiefly British* : a jail sentence : STRETCH

lag·an \ˈla-gən\ *also* **lag·end** \-gənd\ *noun* [Middle French *lagan* or Medieval Latin *laganum* debris washed up from the sea] (1641)
: goods thrown into the sea with a buoy attached so that they may be found again

Lag b'Omer \ˈläg-ˈbō-mər, ˌläg-bə-ˈō-\ *noun* [Hebrew, 33d in Omer] (circa 1904)
: a Jewish holiday falling on the 33d day of the Omer and commemorating the heroism of Bar Kokhba and Akiba ben Joseph

la·ger \ˈlä-gər\ *noun* [German *Lagerbier* beer made for storage, from *Lager* storehouse + *Bier* beer] (circa 1853)
: a light beer brewed by slow fermentation and matured under refrigeration

¹lag·gard \ˈla-gərd\ *adjective* (1702)
: lagging or tending to lag : DILATORY
— **lag·gard·ly** *adverb or adjective*
— **lag·gard·ness** *noun*

²lag·gard *noun* (1808)
: one that lags or lingers

lag·ging \'la-giŋ\ *noun* (1794)
: a lag or material used for making lags: as **a** : material for thermal insulation especially around a cylindrical object **b** : planking used especially for preventing cave-ins in earthwork or for supporting an arch during construction

la·gniappe \'lan-,yap, lan-'\ *noun* [American French, from American Spanish *la ñapa* the lagniappe] (1849)
: a small gift given a customer by a merchant at the time of a purchase; *broadly* : something given or obtained gratuitously or by way of good measure

lago·morph \'la-gə-,mȯrf\ *noun* [ultimately from Greek *lagōs* hare + *morphē* form] (1882)
: any of an order (Lagomorpha) of gnawing herbivorous mammals having two pairs of incisors in the upper jaw one behind the other and comprising the rabbits, hares, and pikas

la·goon \lə-'gün\ *noun* [French & Italian; French *lagune*, from Italian *laguna*, from Latin *lacuna* pit, pool, from *lacus* lake] (1673)
1 : a shallow sound, channel, or pond near or communicating with a larger body of water
2 : a shallow artificial pool or pond (as for the processing of sewage or storage of a liquid)
— **la·goon·al** \-'gü-nᵊl\ *adjective*

La·grang·ian \lə-'grän-jē-ən, -'grä̈n-zhē-\ *noun* [Joseph-Louis *Lagrange*] (1938)
: a function that describes the state of a dynamic system in terms of position coordinates and their time derivatives and that is equal to the difference between the potential energy and kinetic energy — compare HAMILTONIAN

la·har \'lä-,här\ *noun* [Javanese] (1929)
: a mudflow composed of volcanic debris and water

lah–de–dah, lah–dee–dah, lah–di–dah *variant of* LA-DI-DA

Lahn·da \'län-də\ *noun* (1901)
: an Indo-Aryan language of eastern Pakistan

la·ical \'lā-ə-kəl\ *or* **la·ic** \'lā-ik\ *adjective* [Late Latin *laicus*, from Late Greek *laïkos*, from Greek, of the people, from *laos* people] (circa 1587)
: of or relating to the laity : SECULAR
— **laic** *noun*
— **la·ical·ly** \'lā-ə-k(ə-)lē\ *adverb*

la·i·cism \'lā-ə-,si-zəm\ *noun* (circa 1909)
: a political system characterized by the exclusion of ecclesiastical control and influence

la·i·cize \'lā-ə-,sīz\ *transitive verb* **la·i·cized; la·i·ciz·ing** (1870)
1 : to reduce to lay status
2 : to put under the direction of or open to the laity
— **la·i·ci·za·tion** \,lā-ə-sə-'zā-shən\ *noun*

laid *past and past participle of* LAY

laid–back \'lād-'bak, ,lād-\ *adjective* (1969)
: having a relaxed style or character ⟨*laid-back* music⟩
— **laid–back·ness** \-nəs\ *noun*

laid paper \'lād-\ *noun* (1810)
: paper watermarked with fine lines running across the grain — compare WOVE PAPER

laigh \'lāk\ *Scottish variant of* LOW

lain *past participle of* LIE

¹lair \'lar, 'ler\ *noun* [Middle English, from Old English *leger*; akin to Old High German *legar* bed, Old English *licgan* to lie — more at LIE] (before 12th century)
1 *dialect British* : a resting or sleeping place : BED
2 a : the resting or living place of a wild animal : DEN **b** : a refuge or place for hiding

²lair *verb* [Scots *lair* mire] (circa 1560)
transitive verb
chiefly Scottish : to cause to sink in mire
intransitive verb
chiefly Scottish : WALLOW

laird \'lard, 'lerd\ *noun* [Middle English (northern dialect) *lord, lard* lord] (14th century)
chiefly Scottish : a landed proprietor
— **laird·ly** \-lē\ *adjective*

lais·ser–faire *chiefly British variant of* LAISSEZ-FAIRE

lais·ser–pas·ser *chiefly British variant of* LAISSEZ-PASSER

lais·sez–faire \,le-,sā-'far, ,lā-, -,zā-, -'fer\ *noun* [French *laissez faire*, imperative of *laisser faire* to let (people) do (as they choose)] (1825)
1 : a doctrine opposing governmental interference in economic affairs beyond the minimum necessary for the maintenance of peace and property rights
2 : a philosophy or practice characterized by a usually deliberate abstention from direction or interference especially with individual freedom of choice and action
— **laissez–faire** *adjective*

lais·sez–pas·ser \-,pa-'sā\ *noun* [French, from *laissez passer* let (someone) pass] (1914)
: PERMIT, PASS

lai·tance \'lā-tᵊn(t)s\ *noun* [French, from *lait* milk, from Latin *lact-, lac* — more at GALAXY] (circa 1902)
: an accumulation of fine particles on the surface of fresh concrete due to an upward movement of water (as when excessive mixing water is used)

la·ity \'lā-ə-tē\ *noun* [⁵*lay*] (15th century)
1 : the people of a religious faith as distinguished from its clergy
2 : the mass of the people as distinguished from those of a particular profession or those specially skilled

La·ius \'lā-əs, 'lī-əs\ *noun* [Latin, from Greek *Laïos*]
: a king of Thebes slain by his son Oedipus in fulfillment of an oracle

¹lake \'lāk\ *noun, often attributive* [Middle English, from Old French *lac* lake, from Latin *lacus*; akin to Old English *lagu* sea, Greek *lakkos* pond] (12th century)
: a considerable inland body of standing water; *also* : a pool of other liquid (as lava, oil, or pitch)
— **lake·like** \-,līk\ *adjective*

²lake *noun* [French *laque* lac, from Old Provençal *laca*, from Arabic *lakk* — more at LACQUER] (1598)
1 a : a purplish red pigment prepared from lac or cochineal **b** : any of numerous usually bright translucent organic pigments composed essentially of a soluble dye absorbed on or combined with an inorganic carrier
2 : CARMINE 2
— **laky** \'lā-kē\ *adjective*

³lake *verb* **laked; lak·ing** (1903)
transitive verb
: to cause (blood) to undergo a physiological change in which the hemoglobin becomes dissolved in the plasma
intransitive verb
of blood : to undergo the process by which hemoglobin becomes dissolved in the plasma

lake dwelling *noun* (1863)
: a dwelling built on piles in a lake; *specifically* : one built in prehistoric times
— **lake dweller** *noun*

lake·front \'lāk-,frənt\ *noun* (1880)
: an area fronting on a lake

lake herring *noun* (1842)
: a cisco (*Coregonus artedii*) found from Lake Memphremagog to Lake Superior and northward and important as a commercial food fish

Lake·land terrier \'lāk-lənd-, -,land-\ *noun* [*Lakeland*, England] (1926)
: any of an English breed of rather small harsh-coated terriers

lak·er \'lā-kər\ *noun* (1823)
: one associated with a lake; *especially* : a fish living in or taken from a lake

lake·shore \'lāk-,shȯr, -,shȯr\ *noun* (1798)
: the shore of a lake; *also* : LAKEFRONT

lake·side \-,sīd\ *noun* (1560)
: LAKEFRONT

lake trout *noun* (1668)
: any of various trout and salmon found in lakes; *especially* : MACKINAW TROUT

lakh \'läk, 'lak\ *noun* [Hindi *lākh*] (1599)
1 : one hundred thousand ⟨50 *lakhs* of rupees⟩
2 : a great number
— **lakh** *adjective*

La·ko·ta \lə-'kō-tə\ *noun, plural* **Lakota** *also* **Lakotas** (1927)
1 : a member of a western division of the Dakota peoples
2 : a dialect of Dakota

-lalia *noun combining form* [New Latin, from Greek *lalia* chatter, from *lalein* to chat]
: speech disorder (of a specified type) ⟨echolalia⟩

lal·lan \'la-lən\ *or* **lal·land** \-lən(d)\ *Scottish variant of* LOWLAND

Lal·lans \'la-lənz\ *noun* (1785)
: Scots as spoken and written in the lowlands of Scotland

Lal·ly \'lä-lē\ *trademark*
— used for a concrete-filled cylindrical steel structural column

lal·ly·gag *variant of* LOLLYGAG

¹lam \'lam\ *verb* **lammed; lam·ming** [of Scandinavian origin; akin to Old Norse *lemja* to thrash; akin to Old English *lama* lame] (1595)
transitive verb
: to beat soundly : THRASH
intransitive verb
1 : STRIKE, THRASH
2 : to flee hastily : SCRAM

²lam *noun* (1897)
: sudden or hurried flight especially from the law ⟨on the *lam*⟩

la·ma \'lä-mə\ *noun* [Tibetan *blama*] (1654)
: a Lamaist monk

La·ma·ism \'lä-mə-,i-zəm\ *noun* (1817)
: the Mahayana Buddhism of Tibet and Mongolia marked by tantric and shamanistic ritual and a dominant monastic hierarchy headed by the Dalai Lama
— **La·ma·ist** \-mə-ist\ *noun or adjective*
— **La·ma·is·tic** \,lä-mə-'is-tik\ *adjective*

La·marck·ism \lə-'märk-,ki-zəm\ *noun* [J.-B. de Monet de *Lamarck*] (1884)
: a theory of organic evolution asserting that environmental changes cause structural changes in animals and plants that are transmitted to offspring
— **La·marck·ian** \-kē-ən\ *adjective*

la·ma·sery \'lä-mə-,ser-ē\ *noun, plural* **-ser·ies** [French *lamaserie*, from *lama* + Persian *sarāi* palace] (1849)
: a monastery of lamas

La·maze \lə-'mäz\ *adjective* [Fernand *Lamaze* (died 1957) French obstetrician] (1965)
: relating to or being a method of childbirth that involves psychological and physical preparation by the mother in order to suppress pain and facilitate delivery without drugs

¹lamb \'lam\ *noun* [Middle English, from Old English; akin to Old High German *lamb* lamb] (before 12th century)
1 a : a young sheep; *especially* : one that is less than one year old or without permanent teeth **b** : the young of various animals (as the smaller antelopes) other than sheep
2 a : a gentle or weak person **b** : DEAR, PET **c** : a person easily cheated or deceived especially in trading securities

\ə\ abut \ᵊ\ kitten \ər\ further \a\ ash \ā\ ace
\ä\ mop, mar \au̇\ out \ch\ chin \e\ bet \ē\ easy
\g\ go \i\ hit \ī\ ice \j\ job \ŋ\ sing \ō\ go
\ȯ\ law \ȯi\ boy \th\ thin \t͟h\ the \ü\ loot \u̇\ foot
\y\ yet \zh\ vision *see also* Guide to Pronunciation

3 a : the flesh of a lamb used as food **b** : LAMBSKIN
— **lamb·like** \-,līk\ *adjective*
— **lamby** \'la-mē\ *adjective*
²**lamb** (1611)
intransitive verb : to bring forth a lamb
transitive verb
1 : to bring forth (a lamb)
2 : to tend (ewes) at lambing time
— **lamb·er** \'la-mər\ *noun*

lam·baste *or* **lam·bast** \(,)lam-'bāst, -'bast; 'lam-,\ *transitive verb* [probably from ¹*lam* + *baste*] (1637)
1 : to assault violently : BEAT, WHIP
2 : to attack verbally : CENSURE

lamb·da \'lam-də\ *noun* [Middle English, from Greek, of Semitic origin; akin to Hebrew *lāmedh* lamed] (15th century)
1 : the 11th letter of the Greek alphabet — see ALPHABET table
2 : an uncharged unstable elementary particle that has a mass 2183 times that of an electron and that decays typically into a nucleon and a pion

lam·ben·cy \'lam-bən(t)-sē\ *noun, plural* **-cies** (1817) : the quality, state, or an instance of being lambent

lam·bent \'lam-bənt\ *adjective* [Latin *lambent-, lambens*, present participle of *lambere* to lick — more at LAP] (1647)
1 : playing lightly on or over a surface : FLICKERING
2 : softly bright or radiant
3 : marked by lightness or brilliance especially of expression
— **lam·bent·ly** *adverb*

lam·bert \'lam-bərt\ *noun* [Johann H. *Lambert* (died 1777) German physicist & philosopher] (1915) : the centimeter-gram-second unit of brightness equal to the brightness of a perfectly diffusing surface that radiates or reflects one lumen per square centimeter

lamb·kill \'lam-,kil\ *noun* (1790) : SHEEP LAUREL

lam·bre·quin \'lam-bər-kən, -bri-kən\ *noun* [French] (circa 1725)
1 : a scarf used to cover a knight's helmet
2 : a short decorative drapery for a shelf edge or for the top of a window casing : VALANCE

Lam·brus·co \lam-'brü-(,)skō, -'brù-\ *noun* [Italian, from Latin *labruscum* fruit of the wild grape *Vitis labrusca*] (1943) : a fruity and fizzy red Italian table wine

lamb's ears *noun plural but usually singular in construction* (1930) : a widely cultivated perennial herb (*Stachys byzantina* synonym *S. olympica*) of the mint family that occurs in southwestern Asia and has leaves covered with densely matted hairs

lamb·skin \'lam-,skin\ *noun* (14th century) : a lamb's skin or a small fine-grade sheepskin or the leather made from either; *specifically* : such a skin dressed with the wool on and used especially for winter clothing

lamb's lettuce *noun* (1597) : CORN SALAD

lamb's–quar·ter \'lamz-,kwȯ(r)-tər, -,kȯ(r)-\ *noun* (1773)

1 : a goosefoot (*Chenopodium album*) having glaucous foliage that is sometimes used as greens — usually used in plural but singular or plural in construction
2 : any of several oraches — usually used in plural but singular or plural in construction

¹**lame** \'lām\ *adjective* **lam·er; lam·est** [Middle English, from Old English *lama*; akin to Old High German *lam* lame, Lithuanian *limti* to break down] (before 12th century)
1 a : having a body part and especially a limb so disabled as to impair freedom of movement **b** : marked by stiffness and soreness ⟨a lame shoulder⟩
2 : lacking needful or desirable substance : WEAK, INEFFECTUAL ⟨a lame excuse⟩
3 *slang* : not being in the know : SQUARE
— **lame·ly** *adverb*
— **lame·ness** *noun*

²**lame** *transitive verb* **lamed; lam·ing** (14th century)
1 : to make lame : CRIPPLE
2 : to make weak or ineffective : DISABLE

³**lame** *noun* (1959) *slang* : a person who is not in the know : SQUARE

⁴**lame** \'lām, 'lam\ *noun* [Middle French, from Latin *lamina*] (1586)
1 : a thin plate especially of metal : LAMINA
2 *plural* : small overlapping steel plates joined to slide on one another (as in medieval armor)

la·mé \lä-'mā, la-\ *noun* [French] (1922) : a brocaded clothing fabric made from any of various fibers combined with tinsel filling threads

lame·brain \'lām-,brān\ *noun* (1944) : a dull-witted person : DOLT
— **lamebrain** *or* **lame·brained** \-'brānd\ *adjective*

la·med \'lä-,med\ *noun* [Hebrew *lāmedh*, literally, ox goad] (1665) : the 12th letter of the Hebrew alphabet — see ALPHABET table

lame duck *noun* (1761)
1 : one that is weak or that falls behind in ability or achievement; *especially, chiefly British* : an ailing company
2 : an elected official or group continuing to hold office during the period between the election and the inauguration of a successor
3 : one whose position or term of office will soon end
— **lame–duck** \'lām-,dək\ *adjective*

lamell- *or* **lamelli-** *combining form* [New Latin, from *lamella*] : lamella ⟨*lamelliform*⟩

la·mel·la \lə-'me-lə\ *noun, plural* **la·mel·lae** \-'me-(,)lē, -,lī\ *also* **lamellas** [New Latin, from Latin, diminutive of *lamina* thin plate] (1678) : a thin flat scale, membrane, or layer: as **a** : one of the thin plates composing the gills of a bivalve mollusk **b** : a gill of a mushroom

la·mel·lar \lə-'me-lər\ *adjective* (1794)
1 : composed of or arranged in lamellae
2 : LAMELLIFORM

la·mel·late \lə-'me-lət, 'la-mə-,lāt\ *adjective* (1826)
1 : composed of or furnished with lamellae
2 : LAMELLIFORM
— **la·mel·late·ly** *adverb*

la·mel·li·branch \lə-'me-lə-,braŋk\ *noun, plural* **-branchs** [New Latin *Lamellibranchia*, from *lamell-* + Latin *branchia* gill] (1855) : any of a class (Lamellibranchia) of bivalve mollusks (as clams, oysters, and mussels) that have the body bilaterally symmetrical, compressed, and enclosed within the mantle and that build up a shell whose right and left parts are connected by a hinge over the animal's back
— **lamellibranch** *adjective*

la·mel·li·corn \lə-'me-lə-,kȯrn\ *adjective* [ultimately from New Latin *lamella* + Latin *cornu* horn — more at HORN] (circa 1842)

: of, relating to, or belonging to a superfamily (Scarabaeoidea synonym Lamellicornia) of beetles (as a scarab or stag beetle) characterized by 5-jointed tarsi and club-tipped antennae often angled like an elbow
— **lamellicorn** *noun*

la·mel·li·form \-,fȯrm\ *adjective* (1819) : having the form of a thin plate

¹**la·ment** \lə-'ment\ *verb* [Middle English *lementen*, from Middle French & Latin; Middle French *lamenter*, from Latin *lamentari*, from *lamentum*, noun, lament] (15th century)
intransitive verb : to mourn aloud : WAIL
transitive verb
1 : to express sorrow, mourning, or regret for often demonstratively : MOURN
2 : to regret strongly
synonym see DEPLORE

²**lament** *noun* (1591)
1 : a crying out in grief : WAILING
2 : DIRGE, ELEGY
3 : COMPLAINT

la·men·ta·ble \'la-mən-tə-bəl, ÷lə-'men-\ *adjective* (15th century)
1 : that is to be regretted or lamented : DEPLORABLE
2 : expressing grief : MOURNFUL
— **la·men·ta·ble·ness** *noun*
— **la·men·ta·bly** \-blē\ *adverb*

lam·en·ta·tion \,la-mən-'tā-shən\ *noun* (14th century) : an act or instance of lamenting

Lam·en·ta·tions \-shənz\ *noun plural but singular in construction* : a poetic book on the fall of Jerusalem in canonical Jewish and Christian Scripture — see BIBLE table

la·ment·ed \lə-'men-təd\ *adjective* (1611) : mourned for
— **la·ment·ed·ly** *adverb*

la·mia \'lā-mē-ə\ *noun* [Middle English, from Latin, from Greek, devouring monster; akin to Greek *lamyros* gluttonous] (14th century) : a female demon : VAMPIRE

lamin- *combining form* : lamina ⟨*laminar*⟩

lam·i·na \'la-mə-nə\ *noun, plural* **-nae** \-,nē, -,nī\ *or* **-nas** [Latin] (circa 1656)
1 : a thin plate or scale : LAYER
2 : the expanded part of a foliage leaf
3 : one of the narrow thin parallel plates of soft vascular sensitive tissue that cover the flesh within the wall of a hoof

lam·i·nal \'la-mə-nᵊl\ *adjective* (1825)
1 : LAMINAR
2 : produced with the blade of the tongue (as \sh\, \zh\, \ch\, \j\, or \y\) — compare APICAL

lamina pro·pria \-'prō-prē-ə\ *noun, plural* **laminae pro·pri·ae** \-,prē-,ē, -,ī\ [New Latin, literally, proper lamina] (1937) : a highly vascular layer of connective tissue under the basement membrane lining a layer of epithelium

lam·i·nar \'la-mə-nər\ *adjective* (1811) : arranged in, consisting of, or resembling laminae

laminar flow *noun* (1935) : streamline flow in a fluid near a solid boundary — compare TURBULENT FLOW

lam·i·nar·ia \,la-mə-'ner-ē-ə, -'nar-\ *noun* [New Latin, from Latin *lamina*] (1848) : any of a genus (*Laminaria*) of large chiefly perennial kelps with an unbranched cylindrical or flattened stipe and a smooth or convoluted blade; *broadly* : any of various related kelps (order Laminariales)
— **lam·i·nar·i·an** \-ē-ən\ *adjective or noun*

lam·i·nar·in \,la-mə-'ner-ən, -'nar-\ *noun* [International Scientific Vocabulary *laminar-* (from New Latin *Laminaria*) + ¹*-in*] (circa 1931) : a polysaccharide found in various brown algae that yields only glucose on hydrolysis

¹**lam·i·nate** \'la-mə-,nāt\ *verb* **-nat·ed; -nat·ing** (1665)

lamb 3a: *A* wholesale cuts: *1* leg, *2* loin, *3* rack, *4* breast, *5* shank, *6* shoulder; *B* retail cuts: *a* leg, *b* sirloin chops and roast, *c* loin chops, rolled loin roast, *d* patties and chopped roast, *e* rib chops, crown roast, *f* riblets, stew, and stuffed or rolled breast, *g* shoulder roast, shoulder chops, *h* neck slices, *i* shanks, *j* blade chops, *k* arm chops

transitive verb
1 : to roll or compress into a thin plate
2 : to separate into laminae
3 a : to make (as a windshield) by uniting superposed layers of one or more materials **b :** to unite (layers of material) by an adhesive or other means
intransitive verb
: to divide into laminae
— **lam·i·na·tor** \-,nā-tər\ *noun*
²**lam·i·nate** \-nət, -,nāt\ *adjective* (1668)
1 : consisting of laminae
2 : bearing or covered with laminae
³**lam·i·nate** \-nət, -,nāt\ *noun* (1939)
: a product made by laminating
lam·i·nat·ed \-,nā-təd\ *adjective* (1665)
1 : LAMINATE 1
2 a : composed of layers of firmly united material **b :** made by bonding or impregnating superposed layers (as of paper, wood, or fabric) with resin and compressing under heat
lam·i·na·tion \,la-mə-'nā-shən\ *noun* (circa 1676)
1 : the process of laminating
2 : the state of being laminated
3 : a laminated structure
4 : LAMINA
lam·i·ni·tis \,la-mə-'nī-təs\ *noun* [New Latin] (1843)
: inflammation of the laminae especially in the hoof of a horse — called also *founder*
Lam·mas \'la-məs\ *noun* [Middle English *Lammasse*, from Old English *hlāfmæsse*, from *hlāf* loaf, bread + *mæsse* mass; from the fact that formerly loaves from the first ripe grain were consecrated on this day] (before 12th century)
1 : August 1 originally celebrated in England as a harvest festival — called also *Lammas Day*
2 : the time of the year around Lammas Day
Lam·mas·tide \-,tīd\ *noun* (14th century)
: LAMMAS 2
lam·mer·gei·er *or* **lam·mer·gey·er** \'la-mər-,gī(-ə)r\ *noun* [German *Lämmergeier*, from *Lämmer* lambs + *Geier* vulture] (1817)
: a large Old World vulture (*Gypaetus barbatus*) that occurs in mountain regions and in flight resembles a huge falcon
lamp \'lamp\ *noun* [Middle English, from Old French *lampe*, from Latin *lampas*, from Greek, from *lampein* to shine; akin to Hittite *lap-* to burn] (13th century)
1 a : any of various devices for producing light or sometimes heat: as (1) **:** a vessel with a wick for burning an inflammable liquid (as oil) to produce light (2) **:** a glass bulb or tube that emits light produced by electricity (as an incandescent lamp or fluorescent lamp) **b :** a decorative appliance housing a lamp that is usually covered by a shade
2 : a celestial body
3 : a source of intellectual or spiritual illumination
4 : EYE 1a — usually used in plural
lamp·black \-,blak\ *noun* (1598)
: a finely powdered black soot deposited in incomplete combustion of carbonaceous materials and used chiefly as a pigment (as in paints, enamels, and printing inks)
lamp·brush chromosome \'lamp-,brəsh-\ *noun* (1911)
: a greatly enlarged diplotene chromosome that has apparently filamentous granular loops extending from the chromomeres and is characteristic of some animal oocytes
lamp·light \'lamp-,līt\ *noun* (14th century)
: the light of a lamp
lamp·light·er \-,lī-tər\ *noun* (1750)
: one that lights a lamp
¹**lam·poon** \lam-'pün\ *noun* [French *lampon*] (1645)
: SATIRE 1; *specifically* **:** a harsh satire usually directed against an individual
²**lampoon** *transitive verb* (circa 1657)
: to make the subject of a lampoon **:** RIDICULE
— **lam·poon·er** *noun*

— **lam·poon·ery** \-'pü-nə-rē, -'pün-rē\ *noun*
lamp·post \'lam(p)-,pōst\ *noun* (1790)
: a post supporting a usually outdoor lamp or lantern
lam·prey \'lam-prē, -,prā\ *noun, plural* **lampreys** [Middle English, from Old French *lampreie*, from Medieval Latin *lampreda*] (14th century)
: any of a family (Petromyzontidae) of eel-shaped freshwater or anadromous jawless fishes that include those cyclostomes having well-developed eyes and a large disk-shaped suctorial mouth armed with horny teeth — called also *lamprey eel*
lamp·shell \'lamp-,shel\ *noun* [from the resemblance of the shell and its protruding peduncle to an ancient oil lamp with the wick protruding] (1854)
: BRACHIOPOD
lam·ster \'lam(p)-stər\ *also* **lam·is·ter** \'la-mə-stər\ *noun* [²*lam* + -*ster*] (1904)
: a fugitive especially from the law
LAN \'lan, ,el-(,)ā-'en\ *noun* (1982)
: LOCAL AREA NETWORK
la·nai \lə-'nī, lä-\ *noun* [Hawaiian *lānai*] (1823)
: PORCH, VERANDA
Lan·ca·shire \'laŋ-kə-,shir, -shər\ *noun* [*Lancashire*, England] (1896)
: a moist crumbly white English cheese that is used especially in cooking
Lan·cas·tri·an \lan-'kas-trē-ən, laŋ-\ *adjective* [John of Gaunt, duke of *Lancaster*] (1612)
: of or relating to the English royal house that ruled from 1399 to 1461
¹**lance** \'lan(t)s\ *noun* [Middle English, from Old French, from Latin *lancea*] (14th century)
1 : a steel-tipped spear carried by mounted knights or light cavalry
2 : any of various sharp objects suggestive of a lance: as **a :** LANCET **b :** a spear used for killing whales or fish
3 : LANCER 1b
²**lance** *verb* **lanced; lanc·ing** [Middle English *launcen*, from Middle French *lancer*, from Late Latin *lanceare*, from Latin *lancea*] (14th century)
transitive verb
1 a : to pierce with or as if with a lance **b :** to open with or as if with a lancet 〈*lance* a boil〉
2 : to throw forward **:** HURL
intransitive verb
: to move forward quickly
lance corporal *noun* [*lance* (as in obsolete *lancepesade* lance corporal, from Middle French *lancepessade*)] (1786)
: an enlisted man in the marine corps ranking above a private first class and below a corporal
lance·let \'lan(t)-slət\ *noun* (circa 1836)
: any of a subphylum (Cephalochordata) of small translucent marine primitive chordate animals that are fishlike in appearance and usually live partially buried on the ocean floor — called also *amphioxus*
Lan·ce·lot \'lan(t)-sə-,lät, 'län(t)-, -s(ə-)lət\ *noun*
: a knight of the Round Table and lover of Queen Guinevere
lan·ce·o·late \'lan(t)-sē-ə-,lāt\ *adjective* [Late Latin *lanceolatus*, from Latin *lanceola*, diminutive of *lancea*] (circa 1760)
: shaped like a lance head; *specifically* **:** tapering to a point at the apex and sometimes at the base 〈*lanceolate* leaves〉 〈*lanceolate* prisms〉
— see LEAF illustration
lanc·er \'lan(t)-sər\ *noun* (1590)
1 a : one who carries a lance **b :** a member of a military unit formerly composed of light cavalry armed with lances
2 *plural but singular in construction* **a :** a set of five quadrilles each in a different meter **b :** the music for such dances
lan·cet \'lan(t)-sət\ *noun* (15th century)
1 : a sharp-pointed and commonly 2-edged

surgical instrument used to make small incisions
2 a : LANCET WINDOW **b :** LANCET ARCH
lancet arch *noun* (circa 1823)
: an acutely pointed arch — see ARCH illustration
lan·cet·ed \'lan(t)-sə-təd\ *adjective* (1855)
: having a lancet arch or lancet windows
lancet window *noun* (1781)
: a high narrow window with an acutely pointed head and without tracery
lance·wood \'lan(t)s-,wúd\ *noun* (1697)
: a tough elastic wood used especially for shafts, fishing rods, and bows; *also* **:** a tree (especially *Oxandra lanceolata*) yielding this wood
lan·ci·nat·ing \'lan(t)-sə-,nā-tiŋ\ *adjective* [*lancinate* to pierce, from Latin *lancinatus*, past participle of *lancinare*; akin to Latin *lacerare* to rend — more at LACERATE] (1762)
: characterized by piercing or stabbing sensations 〈*lancinating* pain〉
¹**land** \'land\ *noun, often attributive* [Middle English, from Old English; akin to Old High German *lant* land, Middle Irish *lann*] (before 12th century)
1 a : the solid part of the surface of the earth; *also* **:** a corresponding part of a celestial body (as the moon) **b :** ground or soil of a specified situation, nature, or quality 〈dry *land*〉 **c :** the surface of the earth and its natural resources
2 : a portion of the earth's solid surface distinguishable by boundaries or ownership 〈bought *land* in the country〉: as **a :** COUNTRY 〈campaigned across the *land*〉 **b :** a rural area characterized by farming or ranching; *also* **:** farming or ranching as a way of life 〈wanted to move back to the *land*〉
3 : REALM, DOMAIN 〈in the *land* of dreams〉 — sometimes used in combination 〈movie*land*〉
4 : the people of a country 〈the *land* rose in rebellion〉
5 : an area of a partly machined surface that is left without machining
— **land·less** \'land-ləs\ *adjective*
— **land·less·ness** \-nəs\ *noun*
²**land** (13th century)
transitive verb
1 : to set or put on shore from a ship **:** DISEMBARK
2 a : to set down after conveying **b :** to cause to reach or come to rest in a particular place 〈never *landed* a punch〉 **c :** to bring to a specified condition 〈his carelessness *landed* him in trouble〉 **d :** to bring (as an airplane) to a landing
3 a : to catch and bring in (as a fish) **b :** GAIN, SECURE 〈*land* a job〉
intransitive verb
1 a : to go ashore from a ship **:** DISEMBARK **b** *of a ship or boat* **:** to touch at a place on shore
2 a : to come to the end of a course or to a stage in a journey **:** ARRIVE 〈took the wrong subway and *landed* on the other side of town〉 **b :** to come to be in a condition or situation 〈*landed* in jail〉 **c :** to strike or meet a surface (as after a fall) 〈*landed* on my head〉 **d :** to alight on a surface
lan·dau \'lan-,daú, -,dò\ *noun* [*Landau*, Bavaria, Germany] (1743)
: a four-wheel carriage with a top divided into two sections that can be let down, thrown back, or removed and with a raised seat outside for the driver

landau

\ə\ **abut** \ᵊ\ **kitten** \ər\ **further** \a\ **ash** \ā\ **ace**
\ä\ **mop, mar** \aú\ **out** \ch\ **chin** \e\ **bet** \ē\ **easy**
\g\ **go** \i\ **hit** \ī\ **ice** \j\ **job** \ŋ\ **sing** \ō\ **go**
\ò\ **law** \òi\ **boy** \th\ **thin** \t͟h\ **the** \ü\ **loot** \ú\ **foot**
\y\ **yet** \zh\ **vision** *see also* Guide to Pronunciation

lan·dau·let \,lan-dᵊl-'et\ *noun* (1794)
: a small landau

land bank *noun* (1696)
: a bank that provides financing for land development and for farm mortgages

land·ed \'lan-dəd\ *adjective* (15th century)
1 : having an estate in land ⟨*landed* proprietors⟩
2 : consisting in or derived from land or real estate ⟨*landed* wealth⟩

land·er \'lan-dər\ *noun* (1859)
: one that lands; *especially* : a space vehicle that is designed to land on a celestial body (as the moon or a planet)

land·fall \'lan(d)-,fȯl\ *noun* (1627)
1 : a sighting or making of land after a voyage or flight
2 : the land first sighted on a voyage or flight

land·fill \-,fil\ *noun* (1942)
1 : a system of trash and garbage disposal in which the waste is buried between layers of earth to build up low-lying land — called also *sanitary landfill*
2 : an area built up by landfill

land·form \-,fȯrm\ *noun* (1893)
: a natural feature of a land surface

land·grab \-,grab\ *noun* (1860)
: a usually swift acquisition of land often by fraud or force
— **land·grab·ber** \-,gra-bər\ *noun*

land grant *noun* (1862)
: a grant of land made by the government especially for roads, railroads, or agricultural colleges

land·hold·er \'land-,hōl-dər\ *noun* (15th century)
: a holder or owner of land

land·hold·ing \-,hōl-din\ *noun* (circa 1890)
1 : the state or fact of holding or owning land
2 : property in land
— **landholding** *adjective*

land·ing *noun* (15th century)
1 : an act or process of one that lands; *especially* : a going or bringing to a surface (as land or shore) after a voyage or flight
2 : a place for discharging and taking on passengers and cargo
3 : a level part of a staircase (as at the end of a flight of stairs)

landing craft *noun* (1940)
: any of numerous naval craft designed for conveying troops and equipment from a transport to a beach in an amphibious assault

landing field *noun* (circa 1920)
: a field where aircraft may land and take off

landing gear *noun* (1911)
: the part that supports the weight of an airplane or spacecraft when in contact with the land or water

landing strip *noun* (1930)
: AIRSTRIP

land·la·dy \'land-,lā-dē\ *noun* (circa 1536)
: a woman who is a landlord

land·line \-,līn\ *noun* (1865)
: a line of communication (as by telephone cable) on land

land·locked \-,läkt\ *adjective* (1622)
1 : enclosed or nearly enclosed by land ⟨a *landlocked* country⟩
2 : confined to fresh water by some barrier ⟨*landlocked* salmon⟩

land·lord \-,lȯrd\ *noun* (before 12th century)
1 : the owner of property (as land, houses, or apartments) that is leased or rented to another
2 : the master of an inn or lodging house : INNKEEPER

land·lord·ism \-,lȯr-,di-zəm\ *noun* (1844)
: an economic system or practice by which ownership of land is vested in one who leases it to cultivators

land·lub·ber \-,lə-bər\ *noun* (circa 1700)
: LANDSMAN 2 ⟨clumsy *landlubbers* learning to sail⟩
— **land·lub·ber·li·ness** \-bər-lē-nəs\ *noun*
— **land·lub·ber·ly** \-bər-lē\ *adjective*
— **land·lub·bing** \-bin\ *adjective*

land·mark \-,märk\ *noun* (before 12th century)
1 : an object (as a stone or tree) that marks the boundary of land
2 a : a conspicuous object on land that marks a locality **b** : an anatomical structure used as a point of orientation in locating other structures
3 : an event or development that marks a turning point or a stage
4 : a structure (as a building) of unusual historical and usually aesthetic interest; *especially* : one that is officially designated and set aside for preservation

land·mass \-,mas\ *noun* (1856)
: a large area of land ⟨continental *landmasses*⟩

land mine *noun* (1890)
1 : a mine placed on or just below the surface of the ground and designed to be exploded by the weight of vehicles or troops passing over it
2 : BOOBY TRAP 1

land office *noun* (1681)
: a government office in which entries upon and sales of public land are registered

land–office business *noun* (1839)
: extensive and rapid business ⟨money changers . . . did a *land-office business* on payday —F. J. Haskin⟩

land·own·er \'land-,ō-nər\ *noun* (circa 1733)
: an owner of land
— **land·own·er·ship** \-,ship\ *noun*
— **land·own·ing** \-,ō-nin\ *adjective or noun*

land–poor \'lan(d)-,pu̇r\ *adjective* (1873)
: owning so much unprofitable or encumbered land as to lack funds to develop the land or pay the charges due on it

Land·ra·ce \'län(d)-,rä-sə\ *noun* [Danish, from *land* + *race*] (1935)
: a swine of any of several breeds locally developed in northern Europe

land reform *noun* (1846)
: measures designed to effect a more equitable distribution of agricultural land especially by governmental action; *also* : the resulting redistribution

¹land·scape \'lan(d)-,skāp\ *noun, often attributive* [Dutch *landschap*, from *land* + *-schap* -ship] (1598)
1 a : a picture representing a view of natural inland scenery **b** : the art of depicting such scenery
2 a : the landforms of a region in the aggregate **b** : a portion of territory that can be viewed at one time from one place **c** : a particular area of activity : SCENE ⟨political *landscape*⟩
3 *obsolete* : VISTA, PROSPECT ◇

²landscape *verb* **land·scaped; land·scap·ing** (1914)
transitive verb
: to modify or ornament (a natural landscape) by altering the plant cover
intransitive verb
: to engage in landscape gardening
— **land·scap·er** *noun*

landscape architect *noun* (1863)
: one who develops land for human use and enjoyment through effective placement of structures, vehicular and pedestrian ways, and plantings
— **landscape architecture** *noun*

landscape gardener *noun* (circa 1763)
: one who is engaged in the development and decorative planting of gardens and grounds
— **landscape gardening** *noun*

land·scap·ist \'lan(d)-,skā-pist\ *noun* (1843)
: a painter of landscapes

¹land·slide \'lan(d)-,slīd\ *noun* (1838)
1 : the usually rapid downward movement of a mass of rock, earth, or artificial fill on a slope; *also* : the mass that moves down
2 a : a great majority of votes for one side **b** : an overwhelming victory

²landslide *intransitive verb* **-slid** \-,slid\; **-slid·ing** \-,slī-din\ (1926)
1 : to produce a landslide

2 : to win an election by a heavy majority

land·slip \-,slip\ *noun* (1679)
: LANDSLIDE 1

Lands·mål *or* **Lands·maal** \'län(t)s-,mȯl\ *noun* [Norwegian, from *land* country + *mål* speech] (1886)
: NYNORSK

lands·man \'lan(d)z-mən\ *noun* (1598)
1 : a fellow countryman
2 : one who lives on the land; *especially* : one who knows little or nothing of the sea or seamanship

land·ward \'land-wərd\ *adverb or adjective* (15th century)
: to or toward the land

land yacht *noun* (1928)
: a 3-wheel wind-driven recreation vehicle consisting usually of a bare-frame structure and a single sail and used especially on areas of firmly packed sand

¹lane \'lān\ *noun* [Middle English, from Old English *lanu*; akin to Middle Dutch *lane* lane] (before 12th century)
1 : a narrow passageway between fences or hedges
2 : a relatively narrow way or track: as **a** : an ocean route used by or prescribed for ships **b** : a strip of roadway for a single line of vehicles **c** : AIR LANE **d** : any of several parallel courses on a track or swimming pool in which a competitor must stay during a race **e** : an unmarked lengthwise division of a playing area which defines the playing zone of a particular player **f** : a narrow hardwood surface having pins at one end and a shallow channel along each side that is used in bowling **g** : FREE THROW LANE

²lane *Scottish variant of* LONE

lane·way \'lān-,wā\ *noun* (1882)
British : LANE

lang·bein·ite \'laŋ-,bī-,nīt\ *noun* [German *Langbeinit*, from A. *Langbein*, 19th century German chemist] (circa 1897)
: a mineral that is a double sulfate of potassium and magnesium used in the fertilizer industry

lang·lauf \'läŋ-,lau̇f\ *noun* [German, from *lang* long + *Lauf* race] (1927)
: cross-country running or racing on skis
— **lang·lauf·er** \-,lau̇-fər\ *noun*

lang·ley \'laŋ-lē\ *noun, plural* **langleys** [Samuel P. *Langley*] (1947)
: a unit of solar radiation equivalent to one gram calorie per square centimeter of irradiated surface

Lan·go·bard \'laŋ-gə-,bärd\ *noun* [Latin *Langobardus*] (1788)
: LOMBARD 1a
— **Lan·go·bar·dic** \,laŋ-gə-'bär-dik\ *adjective*

lan·gouste \lä⁼-'güst\ *noun* [French, grasshopper, lobster, from Old French *languste*,

◇ **WORD HISTORY**
landscape The word *landscape* is appropriately enough a loan from the language of the Dutch, who pioneered in making landscape a distinct genre of painting in the 17th century. Traditionally views of natural scenery in a painting were no more than background to the portrait or episode of mythology or history that occupied the foreground. But the figures got smaller and of less significance, and the natural scene became the true subject of the painting in the work of artists such as Jacob van Ruisdael and Meindert Hobbema. In the 18th century the meaning of *landscape* was extended from a painted view of natural scenery to the landforms themselves, a usage that still remains common. The element *-scape* has detached itself from *landscape* and become something like a suffix, forming words such as *seascape*, *streetscape*, and *moonscape*.

from Old Provençal *langosta*, from (assumed) Vulgar Latin *lacusta*, alteration of Latin *locusta*] (1832)

: SPINY LOBSTER

lan·gous·tine \ˌlaŋ-gə-'stēn\ *also* **lan·gos·ti·no** \ˌlaŋ-gə-'stē-(ˌ)nō\ *noun, plural* **-tines** *also* **-ti·nos** [*langoustine*, from French, diminutive of *langouste*; *langostino*, from Spanish, diminutive of *langosta* spiny lobster, locust, from (assumed) Vulgar Latin *lacusta*] (1915)

: any of several small lobsters (genera *Nephropsis* and *Metanephrops* of the family Nephropidae) widely used for food

¹lang syne \(ˌ)laŋ-'zīn, -'sīn\ *adverb* [Middle English (Scots), from *lang* long + *syne* since] (15th century)

chiefly Scottish **:** at a distant time in the past

²lang syne *noun* (1694)

chiefly Scottish **:** times past ⟨should auld acquaintance be forgot, and days o' auld *lang syne* —Robert Burns⟩

lan·guage \'laŋ-gwij, -wij\ *noun* [Middle English, from Old French, from *langue* tongue, language, from Latin *lingua* — more at TONGUE] (14th century)

1 a : the words, their pronunciation, and the methods of combining them used and understood by a community **b** (1) **:** audible, articulate, meaningful sound as produced by the action of the vocal organs (2) **:** a systematic means of communicating ideas or feelings by the use of conventionalized signs, sounds, gestures, or marks having understood meanings (3) **:** the suggestion by objects, actions, or conditions of associated ideas or feelings ⟨*language* in their very gesture —Shakespeare⟩ (4) **:** the means by which animals communicate (5) **:** a formal system of signs and symbols (as FORTRAN or a calculus in logic) including rules for the formation and transformation of admissible expressions (6) **:** MACHINE LANGUAGE 1 **2 a :** form or manner of verbal expression; *specifically* **:** STYLE **b :** the vocabulary and phraseology belonging to an art or a department of knowledge **c :** PROFANITY **3 :** the study of language especially as a school subject

language arts *noun plural* (1948)

: the subjects (as reading, spelling, literature, and composition) that aim at developing the student's comprehension and capacity for use of written and oral language

langue \läⁿg\ *noun* [French, literally, language] (1924)

: language viewed abstractly as a system of forms and conventions used for communication in a community; *also* **:** COMPETENCE 3 — compare PAROLE

langue d'oc \läⁿ-'dȯk, läⁿg-dȯk\ *noun* [French, from Old French, literally, language of *oc*; from the Provençal use of the word *oc* for "yes"] (1703)

: PROVENÇAL 2

langue d'oïl \läⁿ-'dȯi(ə)l, -'dȯi; läⁿg-dȯ-ēl, -dȯi\ *noun* [French, from Old French, literally, language of *oïl*; from the French use of the word *oil* for "yes"] (1703)

: FRENCH 1

lan·guet \'laŋ-gwət, laŋ-'gwet\ *noun* [Middle English, from Middle French *languete*, diminutive of *langue*] (15th century)

: something resembling the tongue in form or function

lan·guid \'laŋ-gwəd\ *adjective* [Middle French *languide*, from Latin *languidus*, from *languēre* to languish — more at SLACK] (1597)

1 : drooping or flagging from or as if from exhaustion **:** WEAK **2 :** sluggish in character or disposition **:** LISTLESS **3 :** lacking force or quickness of movement **:** SLOW

— **lan·guid·ly** *adverb*
— **lan·guid·ness** *noun*

HOME LANGUAGES WITH OVER FORTY MILLION SPEAKERS[1]

LANGUAGE	MILLIONS
Mandarin Chinese	865
English	334
Spanish	283
Arabic	197
Bengali	181
Hindi and Urdu	172
Portuguese	161
Russian	156
Japanese	125
German	104
Wu Chinese	94
Panjabi	76
Javanese	76
Telugu	72
Cantonese	70
Korean	70
Marathi	68
Italian	68
Tamil	65
French	65
Vietnamese	61
Awadhi[2]	61
Bhojpuri	58
Southern Min Chinese[3]	55
Turkish	52
Ukrainian	50
Thai and Lao	47
Polish	42
Gujarati	41
Persian	40

[1]Compiled by William W. Gage, using information supplied in *Ethnologue: Languages of the World*, 11th ed. (Dallas: Summer Institute of Linguistics, 1988). Home language used here means the language usually spoken at home.

[2]Indo-Aryan language of eastern and central Uttar Pradesh.

[3]Group of Chinese dialects especially of Xiamen, Shantou, and Taiwan.

lan·guish \'laŋ-gwish\ *intransitive verb* [Middle English, from Middle French *languiss-*, stem of *languir*, from (assumed) Vulgar Latin *languire*, from Latin *languēre*] (14th century)

1 a : to be or become feeble, weak, or enervated **b :** to be or live in a state of depression or decreasing vitality **2 a :** to become dispirited **:** PINE ⟨*languishing* in prison⟩ **b :** to suffer neglect ⟨the bill *languished* in the Senate for eight months⟩ **3 :** to assume an expression of grief or emotion appealing for sympathy

— **lan·guish·er** *noun*
— **lan·guish·ing·ly** \-gwi-shiŋ-lē\ *adverb*
— **lan·guish·ment** \-gwish-mənt\ *noun*

lan·guor \'laŋ-gər *also* -ər\ *noun* [Middle English, from Middle French, from Latin, from *languēre*] (14th century)

1 : weakness or weariness of body or mind **2 :** listless indolence or inertia

synonym see LETHARGY

lan·guor·ous \'laŋ-gə-rəs, -grəs *also* -ə-rəs\ *adjective* (15th century)

1 : producing or tending to produce languor ⟨a *languorous* climate⟩ **2 :** full of or characterized by languor

— **lan·guor·ous·ly** *adverb*

lan·gur \läŋ-'gùr\ *noun* [Hindi *lāgūr*] (1825)

: any of several slender long-tailed Asian monkeys (subfamily Colobinae)

lank \'laŋk\ *adjective* [Middle English, from Old English *hlanc*; akin to Old

langur

High German *hlanca* loin] (before 12th century)

1 : not well filled out **:** SLENDER, THIN ⟨*lank* cattle⟩ **2 :** insufficient in quantity, degree, or extent ⟨*lank* grass⟩ **3 :** hanging straight and limp without spring or curl ⟨*lank* hair⟩

synonym see LEAN

— **lank·ly** *adverb*
— **lank·ness** *noun*

lanky \'laŋ-kē\ *adjective* **lank·i·er; -est** (1818)

: ungracefully tall and thin

synonym see LEAN

— **lank·i·ly** \-kə-lē\ *adverb*
— **lank·i·ness** \-kē-nəs\ *noun*

lan·ner \'la-nər\ *noun* [Middle English *laner*, from Middle French *lanier*] (14th century)

: a falcon (*Falco biarmicus*) of southern Europe, southwestern Asia, and Africa; *specifically* **:** a female lanner

lan·ner·et \ˌla-nə-'ret\ *noun* (15th century)

: a male lanner

lan·o·lin \'la-nᵊl-ən\ *noun* [Latin *lana* wool + International Scientific Vocabulary ³*-ol* + ¹*-in*] (1885)

: wool grease especially when refined for use in ointments and cosmetics

lan·ta·na \lan-'tä-nə\ *noun* [New Latin, from Italian dialect, viburnum] (1791)

: any of a genus (*Lantana*) of tropical shrubs of the vervain family with showy heads of small bright flowers

lan·tern \'lan-tərn\ *noun, often attributive* [Middle English *lanterne*, from Old French, from Latin *lanterna*, from Greek *lamptēr*, from *lampein* to shine — more at LAMP] (13th century)

1 : a usually portable protective case for a light with transparent openings — compare CHINESE LANTERN **2 a** *obsolete* **:** LIGHTHOUSE **b :** the chamber in a lighthouse containing the light **c :** a structure with glazed or open sides above an opening in a roof for light or ventilation **d :** a small tower or cupola or one stage of a cupola **3 :** PROJECTOR 2b

lantern fish *noun* (circa 1753)

: any of a family (Myctophidae) of small deep-sea bony fishes that have a large mouth, large eyes, and usually numerous photophores

lantern fly *noun* (circa 1753)

: any of several large brightly marked homopterous insects (family Fulgoridae) having the front of the head prolonged into a hollow structure

lantern jaw *noun* (1711)

: an undershot jaw

— **lan·tern–jawed** \'lan-tərn-ˌjȯd\ *adjective*

lantern pinion *noun* (circa 1859)

: a gear pinion having cylindrical bars instead of teeth

lan·tha·nide \'lan(t)-thə-ˌnīd\ *noun* [International Scientific Vocabulary] (1926)

: any in a series of elements of increasing atomic numbers beginning with lanthanum (57) or cerium (58) and ending with lutetium (71) — see PERIODIC TABLE table

lan·tha·num \-nəm\ *noun* [New Latin, from Greek *lanthanein* to escape notice — more at LATENT] (1841)

: a white soft malleable metallic element that occurs in rare-earth minerals — see ELEMENT table

lant·horn \'lan-tərn\ *noun* (1587)

chiefly British **:** LANTERN

la·nu·gi·nous \lə-'nü-jə-nəs, -'nyü-\ *adjective* [Latin *lanuginosus*, from *lanugin-*, *lanugo*] (1575)

\ə\ abut \ᵊ\ kitten \ər\ further \a\ ash \ā\ ace \ä\ mop, mar \au̇\ out \ch\ chin \e\ bet \ē\ easy \g\ go \i\ hit \ī\ ice \j\ job \ŋ\ sing \ō\ go \ȯ\ law \ȯi\ boy \th\ thin \tẖ\ the \ü\ loot \ u̇\ foot \y\ yet \zh\ vision *see also* Guide to Pronunciation

: covered with down or fine soft hair : DOWNY

la·nu·go \lə-'nü-(,)gō, -'nyü-\ *noun* [Latin, down, from *lana* wool — more at WOOL] (15th century)
: a dense cottony or downy growth; *specifically* : the soft woolly hair that covers the fetus of some mammals

lan·yard \'lan-yərd\ *noun* [Middle English *lanyer* thong, strap, from Middle French *laniere*] (1626)
1 : a piece of rope or line for fastening something in a ship; *especially* : one of the pieces passing through deadeyes to extend shrouds or stays
2 a : a cord or strap to hold something (as a knife or a whistle) and usually worn around the neck **b** : a cord worn as a symbol of a military citation
3 : a strong line used to activate a system (as in firing a cannon or sounding a whistle)

Lao \'laü\ *noun, plural* **Lao** *or* **Laos** \'laüz\ (1808)
1 : a member of a Buddhist people living in Laos and adjacent parts of northeastern Thailand
2 : the Thai language of the Lao people
— **Lao** *adjective*

La·oc·o·ön \lā-'ä-kə-,wän\ *noun* [Latin, from Greek *Laokoōn*]
: a Trojan priest killed with his sons by two sea serpents after warning the Trojans against the wooden horse

La·od·i·ce·an \lā-,ä-də-'sē-ən, ,lā-ō-də-\ *adjective* [from the reproach to the church of the Laodiceans in Revelation 3:15–16] (1633)
: lukewarm or indifferent in religion or politics
— **Laodicean** *noun*

Lao·tian \lā-'ō-shən, 'laü-shən\ *noun* [probably from French *laotien*, adjective & noun, from *Lao*] (1847)
: LAO
— **Laotian** *adjective*

¹lap \'lap\ *noun* [Middle English *lappe*, from Old English *læppa*; akin to Old High German *lappa* flap] (before 12th century)
1 a : a loose overlapping or hanging panel or flap especially of a garment **b** *archaic* : the skirt of a coat or dress
2 a : the clothing that lies on the knees, thighs, and lower part of the trunk when one sits **b** : the front part of the lower trunk and thighs of a seated person
3 : responsible custody : CONTROL ⟨going to drop the whole thing in your *lap* —Hamilton Basso⟩
— **lap·ful** \'lap-,fül\ *noun*
— **the lap of luxury** : an environment of great ease, comfort, and wealth ⟨was reared in the *lap of luxury*⟩

²lap *verb* **lapped; lap·ping** (14th century)
transitive verb
1 a : to fold over or around something : WIND **b** : to envelop entirely : SWATHE
2 : to fold over especially into layers
3 : to hold protectively in or as if in the lap : CUDDLE
4 a : to place over and cover a part of : OVERLAP ⟨*lap* shingles on a roof⟩ **b** : to join (as two boards) by a lap joint
5 a : to dress, smooth, or polish (as a metal surface) to a high degree of refinement or accuracy **b** : to shape or fit by working two surfaces together with or without abrasives until a very close fit is produced
6 a : to overtake and thereby lead or increase the lead over (another contestant) by a full circuit of a racecourse **b** : to complete the circuit of (a racecourse)
intransitive verb
1 : FOLD, WIND
2 a : to project beyond or spread over something **b** : to lie partly over or alongside of something or of one another : OVERLAP
3 : to traverse a course
— **lap·per** *noun*

³lap *noun* (1800)

1 a : the amount by which one object overlaps or projects beyond another **b** : the part of an object that overlaps another
2 : a smoothing and polishing tool usually consisting of a piece of wood, leather, felt, or soft metal in a special shape used with or without an embedded abrasive
3 : a doubling or layering of a flexible substance (as fibers or paper)
4 a : the act or an instance of traversing a course (as a racing track or swimming pool); *also* : the distance covered **b** : one segment of a larger unit (as a journey) **c** : one complete turn (as of a rope around a drum)

⁴lap *verb* **lapped; lap·ping** [Middle English, from Old English *lapian*; akin to Old High German *laffan* to lick, Latin *lambere*, Greek *laphyssein* to devour] (before 12th century)
intransitive verb
1 : to take in food or drink with the tongue
2 a : to make a gentle intermittent splashing sound **b** : to move in little waves : WASH
transitive verb
1 a : to take in (food or drink) with the tongue **b** : to take in or absorb eagerly or quickly — used with *up* ⟨the crowd *lapped* up every word he said⟩
2 : to flow or splash against in little waves
— **lap·per** *noun*

⁵lap *noun* (14th century)
1 a : an act or instance of lapping **b** : the amount that can be carried to the mouth by one lick or scoop of the tongue
2 : a thin or weak beverage or food
3 : a gentle splashing sound

laparo- *combining form* [Greek *lapara* flank, from *laparos* slack]
: abdominal wall ⟨*laparo*tomy⟩

lap·a·ro·scope \'la-p(ə-)rə-,skōp\ *noun* [International Scientific Vocabulary] (circa 1923)
: a fiberoptic instrument inserted through an incision in the abdominal wall and used to examine visually the interior of the peritoneal cavity

lap·a·ros·co·py \,la-pə-'räs-kə-pē\ *noun, plural* **-pies** (1916)
1 : visual examination of the abdomen by means of a laparoscope
2 : an operation involving laparoscopy; *especially* : one for sterilization of the female or for removal of ova that involves use of a laparoscope to guide surgical procedures within the abdomen
— **lap·a·ro·scop·ic** \-rə-'skä-pik\ *adjective*
— **lap·a·ros·co·pist** \,la-pə-'räs-kə-pist\ *noun*

lap·a·rot·o·my \,la-pə-'rä-tə-mē\ *noun, plural* **-mies** (1878)
: surgical section of the abdominal wall

lap belt *noun* (1952)
: a seat belt that fastens across the lap

lap·board \'lap-,bōrd, -,bȯrd\ *noun* (1804)
: a board used on the lap as a table or desk

lap·dog \-,dȯg\ *noun* (1645)
1 : a small dog that may be held in the lap
2 : a servile dependent or follower

la·pel \lə-'pel\ *noun* [diminutive of ¹lap] (1789)
: the part of a garment that is turned back; *specifically* : the fold of the front of a coat that is usually a continuation of the collar
— **la·pelled** *or* **la·peled** *adjective*

lap·i·dar·i·an \,la-pə-'der-ē-ən\ *adjective* (1683)
: LAPIDARY 1

¹lap·i·dary \'la-pə-,der-ē\ *noun, plural* **-dar·ies** (14th century)
1 : a cutter, polisher, or engraver of precious stones usually other than diamonds
2 : the art of cutting gems

²lapidary *adjective* [Latin *lapidarius* of stone, from *lapid-, lapis* stone] (1724)
1 : having the elegance and precision associated with inscriptions on monumental stone ⟨the *lapidary* phrasing . . . and subtle condensa-

tions of emotions . . . reward attentive reading —G. A. Cardwell⟩
2 a : sculptured in or engraved on stone **b** : of or relating to precious stones or the art of cutting them

la·pil·lus \lə-'pi-ləs\ *noun, plural* **-li** \-,lī, -,(,)lē\ [Latin, diminutive of *lapis*] (1747)
: a small stony or glassy fragment of lava ejected in a volcanic eruption

lap·in \'la-pən\ *noun* [French] (1905)
1 : RABBIT; *specifically* : a castrated male rabbit
2 : rabbit fur usually sheared and dyed

la·pis la·zu·li \,lap-əs-'la-zə-lē, -'la-zhə-\ *noun* [Middle English, from Medieval Latin, from Latin *lapis* + Medieval Latin *lazuli*, genitive of *lazulum* lapis lazuli, from Arabic *lāzaward* — more at AZURE] (15th century)
: a semiprecious stone that is usually rich azure blue and is essentially a complex silicate often with spangles of iron pyrites — called also *lapis*

lap joint *noun* (1823)
: a joint made by overlapping two ends or edges and fastening them together
— **lap–joint·ed** \'lap-,jȯin-təd\ *adjective*

La·place transform \lə-'pläs-, -'plas-\ [Pierre Simon, Marquis de *Laplace*] (1942)
: a transformation of a function $f(x)$ into the function

$$g(t) = \int_0^\infty e^{-xt} f(x) dx$$

that is useful especially in reducing the solution of an ordinary linear differential equation with constant coefficients to the solution of a polynomial equation

Lapp \'lap\ *noun* [Swedish] (1859)
1 : a member of a people of northern Scandinavia, Finland, and the Kola Peninsula of northern Russia who are traditionally fishermen, nomadic herders of caribou, and hunters of sea mammals
2 : any or all of the closely related Finno-Ugric languages of the Lapps
— **Lapp·ish** *adjective or noun*

lap·pet \'la-pət\ *noun* (1573)
1 : a fold or flap on a garment or headdress
2 : a flat overlapping or hanging piece

lap robe *noun* (circa 1866)
: a covering (as a blanket) for the legs, lap, and feet especially of a passenger in a car or carriage

Lap·sang souchong \'läp-,sän-, 'lap-,saŋ-\ *noun* [origin unknown] (circa 1878)
: a souchong tea having a pronounced smoky flavor and aroma

¹lapse \'laps\ *noun* [Latin *lapsus*, from *labi* to slip — more at SLEEP] (1526)
1 a : a slight error typically due to forgetfulness or inattention ⟨a *lapse* in table manners⟩ **b** : a temporary deviation or fall especially from a higher to a lower state ⟨a *lapse* from grace⟩
2 : a becoming less : DECLINE
3 a (1) : the termination of a right or privilege through neglect to exercise it within some limit of time (2) : termination of coverage for nonpayment of premiums **b** : INTERRUPTION, DISCONTINUANCE ⟨returned to college after a *lapse* of several years⟩
4 : an abandonment of religious faith : APOSTASY
5 : a passage of time; *also* : INTERVAL
synonym see ERROR

²lapse *verb* **lapsed; laps·ing** (1611)
intransitive verb
1 a : to fall from an attained and usually high level (as of morals or manners) to one much lower; *also* : to depart from an accepted pattern or standard **b** : to sink or slip gradually : SUBSIDE ⟨*lapsed* into unconsciousness⟩
2 : to go out of existence : CEASE ⟨after a few polite exchanges, the conversation *lapsed*⟩

3 : to pass from one proprietor to another or from an original owner by omission or negligence (allowed the insurance policy to *lapse*) **4 a :** to glide along **:** PASS ⟨time *lapses*⟩ *transitive verb* **:** to let slip **:** FORFEIT ⟨all of those who have *lapsed* their membership —*AAUP Bulletin*⟩ — **laps·er** *noun*

lapsed *adjective* (1638) *of a person* **:** having given up or allowed the lapse of a former position, relationship, or commitment ⟨a *lapsed* Catholic⟩

lapse rate *noun* (1918) **:** the adiabatic rate of decrease of atmospheric temperature with increasing altitude

lap·strake \'lap-ˌstrāk\ *adjective* (1771) **:** CLINKER-BUILT

lap·top \'lap-ˌtäp\ *adjective* (1984) **:** of a size and design that makes operation and use on one's lap convenient ⟨a *laptop* personal computer⟩ — compare DESKTOP — **laptop** *noun*

La·pu·tan \lə-'pyü-t³n\ *noun* **:** an inhabitant of a flying island in Swift's *Gulliver's Travels* characterized by a neglect of useful occupations and a devotion to visionary projects — **Laputan** *adjective*

lap·wing \'lap-ˌwiŋ\ *noun* [Middle English, by folk etymology from Old English *hlēape-wince*; akin to Old English *hlēapan* to leap and to Old English *wincian* to wink] (14th century) **:** a crested Old World plover (*Vanellus vanellus*) noted for its slow irregular flapping flight and shrill wailing cry; *also* **:** any of several related plovers

Lar \'lär\ *noun, plural* **Lar·es** \'lar-(ˌ)ēz, 'ler-\ [Latin — more at LARVA] **:** a tutelary god or spirit associated with Vesta and the Penates as a guardian of the household by the ancient Romans

lar·board \'lär-bərd\ *noun* [Middle English *ladeborde*] (14th century) **:** ⁵PORT

word history see STARBOARD — **larboard** *adjective*

lar·ce·ner \'lärs-nər, 'lär-s³n-ər\ *noun* (circa 1635) **:** LARCENIST

lar·ce·nist \-nist, -s³n-ist\ *noun* (1803) **:** a person who commits larceny

lar·ce·nous \-nəs, -s³n-əs\ *adjective* (1742) **1 :** having the character of or constituting larceny **2 :** committing larceny — **lar·ce·nous·ly** *adverb*

lar·ce·ny \-nē, -s³n-ē\ *noun, plural* **-nies** [Middle English, from Middle French *larcin* theft, from Latin *latrocinium* robbery, from *latron-, latro* mercenary soldier, probably from (assumed) Greek *latrōn*, from Greek *latron* pay] (15th century) **:** the unlawful taking of personal property with intent to deprive the rightful owner of it permanently

larch \'lärch\ *noun* [probably from German *Lärche*, from Middle High German *lerche*, from Latin *laric-, larix*] (1548) **:** any of a genus (*Larix*) of trees of the pine family with short fascicled deciduous leaves; *also* **:** the wood of a larch

larch

¹lard \'lärd\ *transitive verb* (14th century) **1 a :** to dress (meat) for cooking by inserting or covering with something (as strips of fat) **b :** to cover or soil with grease **2 :** to decorate or intersperse with something ⟨the book is *larded* with anecdotes⟩

3 *obsolete* **:** to make rich with or as if with fat

²lard *noun* [Middle English, from Middle French *lard*, from Latin *lardum, laridum*; perhaps akin to Greek *larinos* fat] (14th century) **:** a soft white solid or semisolid fat obtained by rendering fatty tissue of the hog — **lardy** \'lär-dē\ *adjective*

lar·der \'lär-dər\ *noun* [Middle English, from Middle French *lardier*, from *lard*] (14th century) **1 :** a place where food is stored **:** PANTRY **2 :** a supply of food

lar·doon \lär-'dün\ *or* **lar·don** \'lär-ˌdän\ *noun* [Middle English, from Middle French *lardon* piece of fat pork, from *lard*] (14th century) **:** a strip (as of salt pork) with which meat is larded

lares and penates *see* LAR, PENATES\ *noun plural* (1775) **1 :** household gods **2 :** personal or household effects

¹large \'lärj\ *adjective* **larg·er; larg·est** [Middle English, from Old French, from Latin *largus*] (12th century) **1** *obsolete* **:** LAVISH **2** *obsolete* **a :** AMPLE, ABUNDANT **b :** EXTENSIVE, BROAD **3 :** having more than usual power, capacity, or scope **:** COMPREHENSIVE ⟨take the *large* view⟩ ⟨will take a *larger* role in the negotiations⟩ **4 a :** exceeding most other things of like kind especially in quantity or size **:** BIG **b :** dealing in great numbers or quantities ⟨a *large* and highly profitable business⟩ **5** *obsolete* **a** *of language or expression* **:** COARSE, VULGAR **b :** lax in conduct **:** LOOSE **6** *of a wind* **:** FAVORABLE **7 :** EXTRAVAGANT, BOASTFUL ⟨*large* talk⟩ — **large·ness** *noun* — **larg·ish** \'lär-jish\ *adjective*

²large *adverb* (14th century) **1** *obsolete* **:** in abundance **:** AMPLY, LIBERALLY **2 :** with the wind abaft the beam

³large *noun* (14th century) *obsolete* **:** LIBERALITY, GENEROSITY — **at large 1 a :** free of restraint or confinement ⟨the escaped prisoner is still *at large*⟩ **b :** without a specific subject or assignment ⟨critic *at large*⟩ **2 :** at length **3 :** in a general way **4 :** as a whole ⟨society *at large*⟩ **5 :** as the political representative of or to a whole area rather than of one of its subdivisions — used in combination with a preceding noun ⟨a congressman-*at-large*⟩ — **in the large :** on a large scale **:** in general

large calorie *noun* (circa 1909) **:** CALORIE 1b

large·heart·ed \ˌlärj-'här-təd\ *adjective* (1645) **:** having a generous disposition **:** SYMPATHETIC — **large·heart·ed·ness** *noun*

large intestine *noun* (1823) **:** the more terminal division of the vertebrate intestine that is wider and shorter than the small intestine, typically divided into cecum, colon, and rectum, and concerned especially with the resorption of water and the formation of feces

large·ly \'lärj-lē\ *adverb* (13th century) **:** in a large manner; *especially* **:** to a large extent **:** MOSTLY, PRIMARILY

large–mind·ed \ˌlärj-'mīn-dəd\ *adjective* (1725) **:** generous or comprehensive in outlook, range, or capacity — **large–mind·ed·ly** *adverb* — **large–mind·ed·ness** *noun*

large–mouth bass \'lärj-ˌmauth-\ *noun* (1941) **:** a large black bass (*Micropterus salmoides*) that is blackish green above and lighter below and has the maxillary bones of the upper jaw extending behind the eyes — called also *largemouth, largemouth black bass*

large–print \-'print\ *adjective* (1968)

: being set in a large size of type (as 14 point or larger) especially for use by the partially sighted ⟨*large-print* books⟩

larger–than–life *adjective* (1950) **:** of the sort legends are made of ⟨*larger-than-life* heroes⟩

large–scale integration *noun* (1966) **:** the process of placing a large number of circuits on a small chip

lar·gesse *or* **lar·gess** \lär-'zhes, lär-'jes *also* 'lär-ˌjes\ *noun* [Middle English *largesse*, from Old French, from *large*] (13th century) **1 :** liberal giving (as of money) to or as if to an inferior; *also* **:** something so given **2 :** GENEROSITY

¹lar·ghet·to \lär-'ge-(ˌ)tō\ *noun, plural* **-tos** (circa 1724) **:** a movement played larghetto

²larghetto *adverb or adjective* [Italian, somewhat slow, from *largo*] (circa 1801) **:** slower than andante but not so slow as largo — used as a direction in music

¹lar·go \'lär-(ˌ)gō\ *adverb or adjective* [Italian, slow, broad, from Latin *largus* abundant] (1683) **:** at a very slow tempo — used as a direction in music

²largo *noun, plural* **largos** (circa 1724) **:** a largo movement

lar·i·at \'lar-ē-ət, 'ler-\ *noun* [American Spanish *la reata* the lasso, from Spanish *la* the (feminine of *el*, from Latin *ille* that) + American Spanish *reata* lasso, from Spanish *reatar* to tie again, from *re- + atar* to tie, from Latin *aptare* to fit — more at ADAPT] (1832) **:** a long light rope (as of hemp or leather) used with a running noose to catch livestock or with or without the noose to tether grazing animals **:** LASSO

¹lark \'lärk\ *noun* [Middle English *laveroc, laverke*, from Old English *lāwerce*; akin to Old High German *lērihha* lark] (before 12th century) **:** any of a family (Alaudidae) of chiefly Old World songbirds that are usually brownish in color; *especially* **:** SKYLARK — compare MEADOWLARK

²lark *noun* [³*lark*] (circa 1811) **:** something done solely for fun or adventure ⟨ran for office on a *lark*⟩

³lark *intransitive verb* [probably alteration of *lake* to frolic] (1813) **:** to engage in harmless fun or mischief — often used with *about* — **lark·er** *noun*

lark·spur \'lärk-ˌspər\ *noun* (1578) **1 :** DELPHINIUM **2 :** any of the delphiniums that are annuals, have the upper two petals of the corolla united and the bottom two missing, are now often placed in a separate genus (*Consolida*), and include several widely cultivated forms

larky \'lär-kē\ *adjective* **lark·i·er; -est** (1841) **1 :** given to or ready for larking **:** SPORTIVE **2 :** resulting from a lark — **lark·i·ness** \-nəs\ *noun*

lar·ri·gan \'lar-i-gən\ *noun* [origin unknown] (1886) **:** an oil-tanned moccasin with a leg often reaching the knee

lar·ri·kin \'lar-i-kən\ *noun* [origin unknown] (1868) *chiefly Australian* **:** HOODLUM, ROWDY — **larrikin** *adjective*

¹lar·rup \'lar-əp\ *noun* [origin unknown] (circa 1820) *dialect* **:** ⁵BLOW

²larrup (circa 1823) *transitive verb* **1** *dialect* **:** to flog soundly **:** WHIP

\ə\ abut \ᵊ\ kitten \ər\ further \a\ ash \ā\ ace \ä\ mop, mar \aú\ out \ch\ chin \e\ bet \ē\ easy \g\ go \i\ hit \ī\ ice \j\ job \ŋ\ sing \ō\ go \ó\ law \ói\ boy \th\ thin \th\ the \ü\ loot \ú\ foot \y\ yet \zh\ vision *see also* Guide to Pronunciation

2 *dialect* **:** to defeat decisively **:** TROUNCE
intransitive verb
dialect **:** to move indolently or clumsily

la·rum \'lär-əm, 'lar-\ *noun* [short for *alarum*] (15th century)
archaic **:** ALARM

lar·va \'lär-və\ *noun, plural* **lar·vae** \-(,)vē, -,vī\ *also* **larvas** [New Latin, from Latin, specter, mask; akin to Latin *lar* Lar] (1768)
1 : the immature, wingless, and often worm-like feeding form that hatches from the egg of many insects, alters chiefly in size while passing through several molts, and is finally transformed into a pupa or chrysalis from which the adult emerges
2 : the early form of an animal (as a frog or sea urchin) that at birth or hatching is fundamentally unlike its parent and must metamorphose before assuming the adult characters ◇
— **lar·val** \-vəl\ *adjective*

lar·vi·cide \'lär-və-,sīd\ *noun* (circa 1888)
: an agent for killing larval pests
— **lar·vi·cid·al** \,lär-və-'sī-dᵊl\ *adjective*

laryng- *or* **laryngo-** *combining form* [New Latin, from Greek, from *laryng-, larynx*]
: larynx ⟨*laryngitis*⟩

¹la·ryn·ge·al \lə-'rin-jəl *also* -jē-əl; ,lar-ən-'jē-əl\ *adjective* (1795)
1 : of, relating to, or used on the larynx
2 : produced by or with constriction of the larynx ⟨*laryngeal* articulation of sounds⟩

²laryngeal *noun* (circa 1902)
1 : an anatomical part (as a nerve or artery) that supplies or is associated with the larynx
2 a : a laryngeal sound **b :** any of a set of several conjectured phonemes reconstructed for Proto-Indo-European chiefly on indirect evidence

lar·yn·gec·to·mee \,lar-ən-,jek-tə-'mē\ *noun* (1956)
: a person who has undergone laryngectomy

lar·yn·gec·to·my \-'jek-tə-mē\ *noun, plural* **-mies** (circa 1888)
: surgical removal of all or part of the larynx
— **lar·yn·gec·to·mized** \-tə-,mīzd\ *adjective*

lar·yn·gi·tis \,lar-ən-'jī-təs\ *noun* [New Latin] (circa 1834)
: inflammation of the larynx
— **lar·yn·git·ic** \-'ji-tik\ *adjective*

lar·yn·gol·o·gy \,lar-ən-'gä-lə-jē\ *noun* [International Scientific Vocabulary] (circa 1842)
: a branch of medicine dealing with diseases of the larynx and nasopharynx

la·ryn·go·scope \lə-'riŋ-gə-,skōp, -'rin-jə-\ *noun* [International Scientific Vocabulary] (1860)
: an instrument for examining the interior of the larynx
— **lar·yn·gos·co·py** \,lar-ən-'gäs-kə-pē\ *noun*

lar·ynx \'lar-iŋ(k)s\ *noun, plural* **la·ryn·ges** \lə-'rin-(,)jēz\ *or* **lar·ynx·es** [New Latin *laryng-, larynx*, from Greek] (1578)
: the modified upper part of the trachea of air-breathing vertebrates that in humans, most other mammals, and a few lower forms contains the vocal cords

la·sa·gna \lə-'zän-yə\ *noun* [Italian *lasagna*, from (assumed) Vulgar Latin *lasania* cooking pot, its contents, from Latin *lasanum* chamber pot, from Greek *lasanon*] (1846)
1 *also* **la·sa·gne** \-yə\ **:** pasta in the form of broad often ruffled ribbons
2 : a baked dish consisting chiefly of layers of boiled lasagna, cheese, and a seasoned sauce of tomatoes and usually meat

las·car \'las-kər\ *noun* [Hindi *lashkar* army] (1615)
: an Indian sailor, army servant, or artilleryman

las·civ·i·ous \lə-'si-vē-əs\ *adjective* [Late Latin *lasciviosus*, from Latin *lascivia* wantonness, from *lascivus* wanton — more at LUST] (15th century)
: LEWD, LUSTFUL

— **las·civ·i·ous·ly** *adverb*
— **las·civ·i·ous·ness** *noun*

lase \'lāz\ *intransitive verb* **lased; las·ing** [back-formation from *laser*] (1962)
: to emit coherent light

la·ser \'lā-zər\ *noun, often attributive* [*light amplification* by *stimulated emission* of *radiation*] (1960)
: a device that utilizes the natural oscillations of atoms or molecules between energy levels for generating coherent electromagnetic radiation usually in the ultraviolet, visible, or infrared regions of the spectrum

laser disc *noun* (1980)
: OPTICAL DISK; *especially* **:** one on which programs are recorded for playback on a television set

laser printer *noun* (1979)
: a high-resolution printer for computer output that xerographically prints an image formed by a laser

¹lash \'lash\ *verb* [Middle English] (14th century)
intransitive verb
1 : to move violently or suddenly **:** DASH
2 : to thrash or beat violently ⟨rain *lashed* at the windowpanes⟩
3 : to make a verbal attack or retort — usually used with *out*
transitive verb
1 a : to whip or fling about violently ⟨the big cat *lashed* its tail about threateningly⟩ **b :** to strike or beat with or as if with a whip ⟨waves *lashed* the shore⟩
2 a : to assail with stinging words **b :** DRIVE, WHIP ⟨*lashed* them to fury with his speech⟩
— **lash·er** *noun*

²lash *noun* (14th century)
1 a (1) **:** a stroke with or as if with a whip (2) **:** the flexible part of a whip; *also* **:** WHIP **b :** punishment by whipping
2 : a beating, whipping, or driving force
3 : a stinging rebuke
4 : EYELASH
5 : the clearance or play between adjacent movable mechanical parts

³lash *transitive verb* [Middle English *lasschyn* to lace, from Middle French *lacier* — more at LACE] (1624)
: to bind with or as if with a line
— **lash·er** *noun*

lash·ing *noun* (1669)
: something used for binding, wrapping, or fastening

lash·ings \'la-shiŋz, -shənz\ *also* **lash-ins** \-shənz\ *noun plural* [from gerund of ¹*lash*] (1829)
chiefly British **:** a great plenty **:** ABUNDANCE ⟨piles of bread and butter and *lashings* of tea —Molly Weir⟩

lash–up \'lash-,əp\ *noun* [³*lash*] (1898)
1 : something hastily put together or improvised
2 : OUTFIT 3

L–as·par·a·gi·nase \'el-as-'par-ə-jə-,nās, -,nāz\ *noun* (1962)
: an enzyme that breaks down the physiologically commoner form of asparagine, is obtained especially from bacteria, and is used especially to treat leukemia

lass \'las\ *noun* [Middle English *las*] (14th century)
1 : a young woman **:** GIRL
2 : SWEETHEART

Las·sa fever \'la-sə-\ *noun* [*Lassa*, village in Nigeria] (1970)
: a virus disease especially of Africa that is characterized by a high fever, headaches, mouth ulcers, muscle aches, small hemorrhages under the skin, heart and kidney failure, and a high mortality rate

lass·ie \'la-sē\ *noun* (1725)
: LASS 1

las·si·tude \'la-sə-,tüd, -,tyüd\ *noun* [Middle French, from Latin *lassitudo*, from *lassus* wea-

ry; probably akin to Old English *læt* late — more at LATE] (15th century)
1 : a condition of weariness or debility **:** FATIGUE
2 : a condition of listlessness **:** LANGUOR
synonym see LETHARGY

¹las·so \'la-(,)sō, la-'sü\ *transitive verb* (1807)
: to capture with or as if with a lasso **:** ROPE
— **las·so·er** *noun*

²lasso *noun, plural* **lassos** *or* **lassoes** [Spanish *lazo*, from Latin *laqueus* snare] (1808)
: a rope or long thong of leather with a noose used especially for catching horses and cattle **:** LARIAT

¹last \'last\ *verb* [Middle English, from Old English *læstan* to last, follow; akin to Old English *lāst* footprint] (before 12th century)
intransitive verb
1 : to continue in time
2 a : to remain fresh or unimpaired **:** ENDURE **b :** to manage to continue (as in a course of action) **c :** to continue to live
transitive verb
1 : to continue in existence or action as long as or longer than — often used with *out* ⟨couldn't *last* out the training program⟩
2 : to be enough for the needs of ⟨the supplies will *last* them a week⟩
synonym see CONTINUE
word history see LEARN

²last *noun* [Middle English, from Old English *lāste*, from *lāst* footprint; akin to Old High German *leist* shoemaker's last, Latin *lira* furrow — more at LEARN] (before 12th century)
: a form (as of metal or plastic) which is shaped like the human foot and over which a shoe is shaped or repaired
word history see LEARN

³last *transitive verb* (circa 1859)
: to shape with a last
— **last·er** *noun*

⁴last *adverb* [Middle English, from Old English *latost*, superlative of *læt* late] (before 12th century)
1 : after all others **:** at the end ⟨came *last* and left first⟩
2 : most lately ⟨saw him *last* in Rome⟩
3 : in conclusion ⟨*last*, let's consider the social aspect⟩

⁵last *adjective* (13th century)
1 a : following all the rest ⟨he was the *last* one out⟩ **b :** being the only remaining ⟨our *last* dollar⟩
2 a : belonging to the final stage (as of life) ⟨his *last* hours on earth⟩ **b :** administered to the seriously sick or dying ⟨the *last* rites of the church⟩
3 a : next before the present **:** most recent ⟨*last* week⟩ ⟨his *last* book was a failure⟩ **b :** most up-to-date **:** LATEST ⟨it's the *last* thing in fashion⟩

◇ WORD HISTORY
larva The designations *larva, pupa,* and *imago* for the three post-egg stages of an insect's life cycle are usually credited to Carolus Linnaeus, the founder of modern biological taxonomy. Biologists of the 18th century saw the adult as the only genuine form of the insect, and hence called it the *imago,* the proper "image" or representation of the creature as it actually is. The preceding stages were considered somehow unreal, or at best misleading, and so were named with the Latin words *pupa* "doll" and *larva,* which in classical Latin was a sort of ghostlike demon or a mask representing a demon. Although to modern biology larval stages such as caterpillars are as real and taxonomically valid as adults, the traditional terminology remains with us.

4 a : lowest in rank or standing; *also* : WORST **b** : farthest from a specified quality, attitude, or likelihood 〈would be the *last* person to fall for flattery〉 **5 a** : CONCLUSIVE 〈there is no *last* answer to the problem〉 **b** : highest in degree : SUPREME, ULTIMATE **c** : DISTINCT, SEPARATE — used as an intensive 〈ate every *last* piece of food〉 ☆ — **last·ly** *adverb*

⁶last *noun* (13th century) : something that is last — **at last** *or* **at long last** : at the end of a period of time : FINALLY 〈*at last* you've come home〉

last–ditch \'las(t)-ˌdich, -'dich\ *adjective* (1937) **1** : fought or conducted from the last ditch : waged with desperation or unyielding defiance 〈*last-ditch* resistance〉 **2** : made as a final effort especially to avert disaster 〈a *last-ditch* attempt to raise the money〉

last ditch *noun* (circa 1715) : a place of final defense or resort

last–gasp \'las(t)-'gasp\ *adjective* (1921) : done or coming at the very end — **last gasp** *noun*

last hurrah *noun* [from *The Last Hurrah* (1956) by Edwin O'Connor (died 1968) American novelist] (1966) : a final often valedictory effort, production, or appearance 〈his unsuccessful Senate run was his *last hurrah* —R. W. Daly〉

last–in first–out *adjective* (1940) : of, relating to, or being a method of inventory accounting that values stock on hand according to costs at the time of acquisition and not according to the cost of replacement

¹last·ing *adjective* (12th century) : existing or continuing a long while : ENDURING ☆ — **last·ing·ly** \'las-tiŋ-lē\ *adverb* — **last·ing·ness** *noun*

²lasting *noun* (15th century) **1** *archaic* : long life **2** : a sturdy cotton or worsted cloth used especially in shoes and luggage

Last Judgment *noun* (14th century) : the judgment of mankind before God at the end of the world

last minute *noun* (1920) : the moment just before some climactic, decisive, or disastrous event

last name *noun* (1897) : SURNAME 2

last rites *noun* (1922) : EXTREME UNCTION

last straw *noun* [from the fable of the last straw that broke the camel's back when added to its burden] (1848) : the last of a series (as of events or indignities) that brings one beyond the point of endurance

Last Supper *noun* (14th century) : the supper eaten by Jesus and his disciples on the night of his betrayal

Last Things *noun plural* [translation of Medieval Latin *Novissima*] (1522) : events (as the resurrection and divine judgment of all humankind) marking the end of the world : eschatological happenings

last word *noun* (1563) **1** : the final remark in a verbal exchange **2 a** : the power of final decision **b** : a definitive statement or treatment 〈this study will surely be the *last word* on the subject for many years〉 **3** : the most advanced, up-to-date, or fashionable exemplar of its kind 〈the *last word* in sports cars〉

lat \'lat\ *noun* [Latvian *lats*, from *Latvija* Latvia] (1923) — see MONEY table

lat·a·kia \ˌla-tə-'kē-ə\ *noun* [*Latakia*, seaport in Syria] (1833) : a highly aromatic Turkish smoking tobacco

¹latch \'lach\ *intransitive verb* [Middle English *lachen*, from Old English *læccan*; perhaps akin to Greek *lambanein* to take, seize] (13th century) **1** : to lay hold with or as if with the hands or arms — used with *on* or *onto* **2** : to associate oneself intimately and often artfully — used with *on* or *onto* 〈*latched* onto a rich widow〉

²latch *noun* (13th century) : any of various devices in which mating mechanical parts engage to fasten but usually not to lock something: **a** : a fastener (as for a door) consisting essentially of a pivoted bar that falls into a notch **b** : a fastener (as for a door) in which a spring slides a bolt into a hole; *also* : NIGHT LATCH

³latch *transitive verb* (15th century) : to make fast with or as if with a latch

latch·et \'la-chət\ *noun* [Middle English *lachet*, from Middle French, shoestring, from *laz* snare, from Latin *laqueus*] (15th century) : a narrow leather strap, thong, or lace that fastens a shoe or sandal on the foot

latch·key \'lach-ˌkē\ *noun* (1825) : a key to an outside and especially a front door

latchkey child *noun* (1944) : a young child of working parents who must spend part of the day unsupervised (as at home) — called also *latchkey kid*

latch·string \-ˌstriŋ\ *noun* (1791) : a string on a latch that may be left hanging outside the door to permit the raising of the latch from the outside or drawn inside to prevent intrusion

¹late \'lāt\ *adjective* **lat·er; lat·est** [Middle English, late, slow, from Old English *læt*; akin to Old High German *laz* slow, Old English *lǣtan* to let] (before 12th century) **1 a** (1) : coming or remaining after the due, usual, or proper time 〈a *late* spring〉 (2) : of, relating to, or imposed because of tardiness **b** : of or relating to an advanced stage in point of time or development 〈the *late* Middle Ages〉; *especially* : far advanced toward the close of the day or night 〈*late* hours〉 **2 a** : living comparatively recently — used of persons 〈the *late* John Doe〉 and often with reference to a specific relationship or status 〈his *late* wife〉 **b** : being something or holding some position or relationship recently but not now 〈the *late* belligerents〉 **c** : made, appearing, or happening just previous to the present time especially as the most recent of a succession 〈our *late* quarrel〉 □ *synonym* see DEAD — **late·ness** *noun*

²late *adverb* **lat·er; lat·est** (before 12th century) **1 a** : after the usual or proper time 〈got to work *late*〉 **b** : at or to an advanced point of time **2** : not long ago : RECENTLY 〈a man *late* of Chicago〉 — **of late** : in the period shortly or immediately preceding : RECENTLY 〈has been sick *of late*〉

late blight *noun* (1900) : a disease of solanaceous plants (as the potato and tomato) that is caused by a fungus (*Phytophthora infestans*) and is characterized by decay of stems, leaves, and in the potato also of tubers

late·com·er \'lāt-ˌkə-mər\ *noun* (1892) : one that arrives late; *also* : a recent arrival

lat·ed \'lā-təd\ *adjective* (circa 1592) : BELATED

¹la·teen \lə-'tēn\ *adjective* [French (*voile*) *latine*, literally, Latin (Mediterranean) sail] (circa 1741) : being or relating to a rig used especially on the north coast of Africa and characterized by a triangular sail extended by a long spar slung to a low mast

²lateen *noun* (circa 1775) **1** *also* **la·teen·er** \-'tē-nər\ : a lateen-rigged ship **2** : a lateen sail

Late Greek *noun* (circa 1889) : the Greek language as used in the 3d to 6th centuries

Late Hebrew *noun* (1951) : the Hebrew language used by writers from about the 2d century B.C. to the early Middle Ages

Late Latin *noun* (1888) : the Latin language used by writers in the 3d to 6th centuries

☆ **SYNONYMS**

Last, final, terminal, eventual, ultimate mean following all others (as in time, order, or importance). LAST applies to something that comes at the end of a series but does not always imply that the series is completed or stopped 〈*last* page of a book〉 〈*last* news we had of him〉. FINAL applies to that which definitely closes a series, process, or progress 〈*final* day of school〉. TERMINAL may indicate a limit of extension, growth, or development 〈*terminal* phase of a disease〉. EVENTUAL applies to something that is bound to follow sooner or later as the final effect of causes already operating 〈*eventual* defeat of the enemy〉. ULTIMATE implies the last degree or stage of a long process beyond which further progress or change is impossible 〈the *ultimate* collapse of the system〉.

Lasting, permanent, durable, stable mean enduring for so long as to seem fixed or established. LASTING implies a capacity to continue indefinitely 〈a book that left a *lasting* impression on me〉. PERMANENT adds usually the implication of being designed or planned to stand or continue indefinitely 〈*permanent* living arrangements〉. DURABLE implies power to resist destructive agencies 〈*durable* fabrics〉. STABLE implies lastingness because of resistance to being overturned or displaced 〈a *stable* government〉.

□ **USAGE**

late The definition of sense 2a above contains the words "comparatively recently." One of the hardest things for the user of this sense of *late* to decide is how long the word applies. The commentators—mostly newspaper editors—who have given the subject some thought have reached no consensus; their advice runs from "within the preceding decade" to "half a century." This certainly gives you some latitude, and our evidence shows that writers have in general taken advantage of that latitude. Two strictures are placed on the use of *late* by various critics. The first is that *late* should not be used of famous people everyone knows are dead; a couple of instances will show how little this is observed 〈the *late* Henry Ford —*N.Y. Times*〉 〈the *late* President John F. Kennedy —*Current Biography*〉. The other is that *late* should not be used if the person was alive at the time referred to; this too is little observed 〈the Senate Select Intelligence Committee, then . . . headed by the *late* Senator Frank Church —David Burnham〉 〈my *late* sister Lucy at one time decided to be on the safe side —George Bernard Shaw〉.

\ə\ **abut** \ᵊ\ **kitten** \ər\ **further** \a\ **ash** \ā\ **ace** \ä\ **mop, mar** \au̇\ **out** \ch\ **chin** \e\ **bet** \ē\ **easy** \g\ **go** \i\ **hit** \ī\ **ice** \j\ **job** \ŋ\ **sing** \ō\ **go** \ȯ\ **law** \ȯi\ **boy** \th\ **thin** \t͟h\ **the** \ü\ **loot** \u̇\ **foot** \y\ **yet** \zh\ **vision** *see also* Guide to Pronunciation

late·ly \'lāt-lē\ *adverb* (15th century)
: of late : RECENTLY ⟨has been friendlier *lately*⟩

lat·en \'lā-t'n\ *verb* **lat·ened; lat·en·ing** \'lāt-niŋ, 'lā-t'n-iŋ\ (1880)
intransitive verb
: to grow late
transitive verb
: to cause to grow late

la·ten·cy \'lā-t'n(t)-sē\ *noun, plural* **-cies** (circa 1638)
1 : the quality or state of being latent : DORMANCY
2 : something latent
3 : a stage of personality development that extends from about the age of five to the beginning of puberty and during which sexual urges often appear to lie dormant
4 : LATENT PERIOD 2

latency period *noun* (1910)
1 : LATENCY 3
2 : LATENT PERIOD

La Tène \lä-'ten, -'tān\ *adjective* [*La Tène*, shallows of the Lake of Neuchâtel, Switzerland] (1901)
: of or relating to the later period of the Iron Age in Europe assumed to date from 500 B.C. to A.D. 1

la·ten·si·fi·ca·tion \lā-,ten(t)-sə-fə-'kā-shən, lə-\ *noun* [blend of ¹*latent* and *intensification*] (1940)
: intensification of a latent photographic image by chemical treatment or exposure to light of low intensity

¹la·tent \'lā-t'nt\ *adjective* [Middle English, from Latin *latent-, latens,* from present participle of *latēre* to lie hidden; akin to Greek *lanthanein* to escape notice] (15th century)
: present and capable of becoming though not now visible, obvious, or active ⟨a *latent* infection⟩ ☆
— **la·tent·ly** *adverb*

²latent *noun* (1923)
: a fingerprint (as at the scene of a crime) that is scarcely visible but can be developed for study

latent heat *noun* (circa 1757)
: heat given off or absorbed in a process (as fusion or vaporization) other than a change of temperature

latent period *noun* (1837)
1 : the incubation period of a disease
2 : the interval between stimulation and response

latent root *noun* (1883)
: an eigenvalue of a matrix

lat·er \'lā-tər\ *adverb* (13th century)
: at some time subsequent to a given time : SUBSEQUENTLY, AFTERWARD ⟨four months *later*⟩ ⟨they *later* regretted their decision⟩ — often used with *on* ⟨experience that will be useful *later on*⟩

-later *noun combining form* [Middle English *-latrer,* from Middle French *-latre,* from Late Latin *-latres,* from Greek *-latrēs;* akin to Greek *latron* pay]
: worshiper ⟨biblio*later*⟩

lat·er·ad \'la-tə-,rad\ *adverb* [Latin *later-, latus*] (1814)
: toward the side

¹lat·er·al \'la-tə-rəl *also* 'la-trəl\ *adjective* [Middle English *laterale,* from Latin *lateralis,* from *later-, latus* side] (15th century)
1 : of or relating to the side
2 : situated on, directed toward, or coming from the side
3 : extending from side to side ⟨*lateral* axis of an airplane⟩
4 : produced with passage of breath around the side of a constriction formed with the tongue ⟨\l\ is *lateral*⟩
— **lat·er·al·ly** *adverb*

²lateral *noun* (1851)
1 : a branch from the main part (as in an irrigation or electrical system)

2 : a pass in football thrown parallel to the line of scrimmage or in a direction away from the opponent's goal
3 : a lateral speech sound

³lateral *intransitive verb* (1944)
: to throw a lateral

lateral bud *noun* (circa 1892)
: a bud that develops in the axil between a petiole and a stem

lat·er·al·i·za·tion \,la-tə-rə-lə-'zā-shən, ,la-trə-\ *noun* (circa 1899)
: localization of function or activity (as of verbal processes in the brain) on one side of the body in preference to the other
— **lat·er·al·ize** \'la-tə-rə-,līz, 'la-trə-\ *transitive verb*

lateral line *noun* (1870)
: a canal along the side of a fish containing pores that open into tubes supplied with sense organs sensitive to low vibrations; *also* : one of these tubes or sense organs

lat·er·ite \'la-tə-,rīt\ *noun* [Latin *later* brick] (1807)
: a residual product of rock decay that is red in color and has a high content in the oxides of iron and hydroxide of aluminum
— **lat·er·it·ic** \,la-tə-'ri-tik\ *adjective*

lat·er·i·za·tion \,la-tə-rə-'zā-shən\ *noun* (circa 1882)
: the process of conversion of rock to laterite

¹lat·est \'lā-təst\ *adjective* (1588)
1 *archaic* : LAST
2 : most recent ⟨the *latest* news⟩ ⟨the *latest* style⟩

²latest *noun* (1884)
1 : the latest acceptable time — usually used in the phrase *at the latest*
2 : something that is the most recent or currently fashionable ⟨the *latest* in diving techniques⟩

late·wood \'lāt-,wu̇d\ *noun* (circa 1933)
: SUMMERWOOD

la·tex \'lā-,teks\ *noun, plural* **la·ti·ces** \'lā-tə-,sēz, 'la-\ *or* **la·tex·es** [New Latin *latic-, latex,* from Latin, fluid] (1835)
1 : a milky usually white fluid that is produced by cells of various seed plants (as of the milkweed, spurge, and poppy families) and is the source of rubber, gutta-percha, chicle, and balata
2 : a water emulsion of a synthetic rubber or plastic obtained by polymerization and used especially in coatings (as paint) and adhesives

lath \'lath *also* 'lȧth\ *noun, plural* **laths** *or* **lath** [Middle English, from (assumed) Old English *læthth-;* akin to Old High German *latta* lath, Welsh *llath* yard] (13th century)
1 : a thin narrow strip of wood nailed to rafters, joists, or studding as a groundwork for slates, tiles, or plaster
2 : a building material in sheets used as a base for plaster
3 : a quantity of laths
— **lath** *transitive verb*

¹lathe \'lāth\ *noun* [probably from Middle English *lath* supporting stand] (circa 1611)
: a machine in which work is rotated about a horizontal axis and shaped by a fixed tool

²lathe *transitive verb* **lathed; lath·ing** (circa 1903)
: to cut or shape with a lathe

¹lath·er \'la-thər\ *noun* [(assumed) Middle English, from Old English *lēathor;* akin to Latin *lavere* to wash — more at LYE] (before 12th century)
1 a : a foam or froth formed when a detergent (as soap) is agitated in water **b** : foam or froth from profuse sweating (as on a horse)
2 : an agitated or overwrought state : DITHER
— **lath·ery** \-thə-)rē\ *adjective*

²lather *verb* **lath·ered; lath·er·ing** \-th(ə-)riŋ\ (before 12th century)
transitive verb
1 : to spread lather over
2 : to beat severely : FLOG

intransitive verb
: to form a lather or a froth like lather
— **lath·er·er** \-thər-ər\ *noun*

lath·y·rism \'la-thə-,ri-zəm\ *noun* [New Latin *Lathyrus,* from Greek *lathyros,* a type of pea] (circa 1888)
: a diseased condition of humans, domestic animals, and especially horses that results from poisoning by a substance found in some legumes (genus *Lathyrus* and especially *L. sativus*) and is characterized especially by spastic paralysis of the hind or lower limbs

lath·y·rit·ic \,la-thə-'ri-tik\ *adjective* (1960)
: of, relating to, affected with, or characteristic of lathyrism ⟨*lathyritic* rats⟩ ⟨*lathyritic* cartilage⟩

latices *plural of* LATEX

la·tic·i·fer \lā-'ti-sə-fər\ *noun* [International Scientific Vocabulary *latici-* (from New Latin *latic-, latex*) + *-fer*] (circa 1928)
: a plant cell or vessel that contains latex

la·ti·fun·dio \,la-tə-'fün-dē-,ō\ *noun, plural* **-di·os** [Spanish, from Latin *latifundium*] (circa 1902)
: a latifundium in Spain or Latin America

lat·i·fun·di·um \,la-tə-'fən-dē-əm\ *noun, plural* **-dia** \-dē-ə\ [Latin, from *latus* wide + *fundus* piece of landed property, foundation, bottom — more at BOTTOM] (1630)
: a great landed estate with primitive agriculture and labor often in a state of partial servitude

lat·i·go \'la-ti-,gō\ *noun, plural* **-gos** *also* **-goes** [Spanish *látigo*] (1873)
chiefly West : a long strap on a saddletree of a western saddle to adjust the cinch

¹Lat·in \'la-t'n\ *adjective* [Middle English, from Old English, from Latin *Latinus,* from *Latium,* ancient country of Italy] (before 12th century)
1 a : of, relating to, or composed in Latin **b** : ROMANCE
2 : of or relating to Latium or the Latins
3 : of or relating to the part of the Catholic Church that until recently used a Latin rite and forms the patriarchate of the pope
4 : of or relating to the peoples or countries using Romance languages; *specifically* : of or relating to the peoples or countries of Latin America

²Latin *noun* (before 12th century)
1 : the Italic language of ancient Latium and of Rome and until modern times the dominant language of school, church, and state in western Europe — see INDO-EUROPEAN LANGUAGES table
2 : a member of the people of ancient Latium
3 : a Catholic of the Latin rite
4 : a member of one of the Latin peoples; *specifically* : a native or inhabitant of Latin America
5 : LATIN ALPHABET

Latin alphabet *noun* (1823)
: an alphabet that was used for writing Latin and that has been modified for writing many modern languages

Latin Americanist *noun* (1972)
: a specialist in Latin American civilization

Lat·in·ate \'la-t'n-,āt\ *adjective* (1904)

☆ **SYNONYMS**
Latent, dormant, quiescent, potential mean not now showing signs of activity or existence. LATENT applies to a power or quality that has not yet come forth but may emerge and develop ⟨a *latent* desire for success⟩. DORMANT suggests the inactivity of something (as a feeling or power) as though sleeping ⟨their passion had lain *dormant*⟩. QUIESCENT suggests a usually temporary cessation of activity ⟨the disease was *quiescent*⟩. POTENTIAL applies to what does not yet have existence or effect but is likely soon to have ⟨a *potential* disaster⟩.

: of, relating to, resembling, or derived from Latin

Latin cross *noun* (1797)
: a figure of a cross having a long upright shaft and a shorter crossbar traversing it above the middle — see CROSS illustration

Lat·in·ism \'la-t⁼n-ˌi-zəm\ *noun* (circa 1570)
1 : a characteristic feature of Latin occurring in another language
2 : Latin quality or character

Lat·in·ist \'la-t⁼n-ist, 'lat-nist\ *noun* (15th century)
: a specialist in the Latin language or Roman culture

la·tin·i·ty \la-'ti-nə-tē, lə-\ *noun, often capitalized* (1619)
1 : a manner of speaking or writing Latin
2 : LATINISM 2

lat·in·ize \'la-t⁼n-ˌīz\ *verb* **-ized; -iz·ing** *often capitalized* (1589)
transitive verb
1 *a obsolete* : to translate into Latin **b** : to give a Latin form to **c** : to introduce Latinisms into **d** : ROMANIZE 2
2 : to make Latin or Italian in doctrine, ideas, or traits; *specifically* : to cause to resemble the Roman Catholic Church
intransitive verb
1 : to use Latinisms
2 : to exhibit the influence of the Romans or of the Roman Catholic Church
— **lat·in·i·za·tion** \ˌla-t⁼n-ə-'zā-shən, ˌlat-nə-\ *noun*

La·ti·no \lə-'tē-(ˌ)nō\ *noun, plural* **-nos** [American Spanish, probably short for *latinoamericano* Latin American] (1946)
1 : a native or inhabitant of Latin America
2 : a person of Latin-American origin living in the U.S.
— **Latino** *adjective*

Latin square *noun* (1890)
: a square array which contains *n* different elements with each element occurring *n* times but with no element occurring twice in the same column or row and which is used especially in the statistical design of experiments (as in agriculture)

lat·ish \'lā-tish\ *adjective* (1611)
: somewhat late

lat·i·tude \'la-tə-ˌtüd, -ˌtyüd\ *noun* [Middle English, from Latin *latitudin-, latitudo*, from *latus* wide; akin to Old Church Slavonic *postŭlati* to spread] (14th century)
1 *archaic* : extent or distance from side to side : WIDTH
2 : angular distance from some specified circle or plane of reference: as **a** : angular distance north or south from the earth's equator measured through 90 degrees **b** : angular distance of a celestial body from the ecliptic **c** : a region or locality as marked by its latitude

latitude 2a: hemisphere marked with parallels of latitude

3 a *archaic* : SCOPE, RANGE **b** : the range of exposures within which a film or plate will produce a negative or positive of satisfactory quality
4 : freedom of action or choice
— **lat·i·tu·di·nal** \ˌla-tə-'tüd-nəl, -'tyüd-; -'tü-d⁼n-əl, -'tyü-\ *adjective*
— **lat·i·tu·di·nal·ly** *adverb*

lat·i·tu·di·nar·i·an \ˌla-tə-ˌtü-d⁼n-'er-ē-ən, -ˌtyü-\ *noun* (1662)
: a person who is broad and liberal in standards of religious belief and conduct
— **latitudinarian** *adjective*
— **lat·i·tu·di·nar·i·an·ism** \-ē-ə-ˌni-zəm\ *noun*

lat·ke \'lät-kə\ *noun* [Yiddish, pancake, from Ukrainian *oladka*] (1927)
: POTATO PANCAKE

lat·o·sol \'la-tə-ˌsȯl\ *noun* [irregular from Latin *later* brick + English *-sol* (as in *podsol*, variant of *podzol*)] (1949)
: a leached red and yellow tropical soil
— **lat·o·sol·ic** \ˌla-tə-'sȯ-lik\ *adjective*

la·trine \lə-'trēn\ *noun* [French, from Latin *latrina*, contraction of *lavatrina*, from *lavare* to wash — more at LYE] (1642)
1 : a receptacle (as a pit in the earth) for use as a toilet
2 : TOILET

-latry *noun combining form* [Middle English *-latrie*, from Old French, from Late Latin *-latria*, from Greek, from *latreia; akin to* Greek *latron* pay]
: worship ⟨helio*latry*⟩

lat·te \'lä-(ˌ)tā\ *noun* (1991)
: CAFFE LATTE

lat·ten \'la-t⁼n\ *noun* [Middle English *laton*, from Middle French] (14th century)
: a yellow alloy identical to or resembling brass typically hammered into thin sheets and formerly much used for church utensils

lat·ter \'la-tər\ *adjective* [Middle English, from Old English *lætra*, comparative of *læt* late] (before 12th century)
1 a : belonging to a subsequent time or period : more recent ⟨the *latter* stages of growth⟩ **b** : of or relating to the end ⟨in their *latter* days⟩ **c** : RECENT, PRESENT ⟨affected by *latter* calamities⟩
2 : of, relating to, or being the second of two groups or things or the last of several groups or things referred to ⟨of ham and beef the *latter* meat is cheaper today⟩ ⟨of ham and beef the *latter* is cheaper today⟩

lat·ter-day \'la-tər-ˌdā\ *adjective* (1850)
1 : of present or recent times ⟨*latter-day* prophets⟩
2 : of a later or subsequent time

Latter-day Saint *noun, often D capitalized* (1834)
: a member of any of several religious bodies tracing their origin to Joseph Smith in 1830 and accepting the Book of Mormon as divine revelation : MORMON

lat·ter·ly *adverb* (1734)
1 : LATER
2 : of late : RECENTLY

lat·tice \'la-təs\ *noun* [Middle English *latis*, from Middle French *lattis*] (14th century)
1 a : a framework or structure of crossed wood or metal strips **b** : a window, door, or gate having a lattice **c** : a network or design resembling a lattice
2 : a regular geometrical arrangement of points or objects over an area or in space; *specifically* : the arrangement of atoms in a crystal
3 : a mathematical set that has some elements ordered and that is such that for any two elements there exists a greatest element in the subset of all elements less than or equal to both and a least element in the subset of all elements greater than or equal to both
— **lattice** *transitive verb*
— **lat·ticed** \-tist\ *adjective*

lattice girder *noun* (1852)
: a girder with top and bottom flanges connected by a latticework web

lat·tice·work \'la-təs-ˌwərk\ *noun* (15th century)
: a lattice or work made of lattices

la·tus rec·tum \ˌla-təs-'rek-təm\ *noun* [New Latin, literally, straight side] (1702)
: a chord of a conic section (as an ellipse) that passes through a focus and is parallel to the directrix

Lat·vi·an \'lat-vē-ən\ *noun* (1924)
1 : the Baltic language of the Latvian people
2 : a native or inhabitant of Latvia
— **Latvian** *adjective*

lau·an \'lü-ˌän, lü-'; laù-'än\ *noun* [Tagalog *lawaan*] (1894)
: any of various Philippine timbers (as of the genera *Shorea* and *Parashorea*) that are light

yellow to reddish brown or brown and include some which enter commerce as Philippine mahogany

¹laud \'lȯd\ *noun* [Middle English *laudes* (plural), from Medieval Latin, from Latin, plural of *laud-, laus* praise] (14th century)
1 *plural but singular or plural in construction, often capitalized* : an office of solemn praise to God forming with matins the first of the canonical hours
2 : PRAISE, ACCLAIM

²laud *transitive verb* [Latin *laudare*, from *laud-, laus*] (14th century)
: PRAISE, EXTOL

laud·able \'lȯ-də-bəl\ *adjective* (15th century)
: worthy of praise : COMMENDABLE
— **laud·able·ness** \'lȯ-də-bəl-nəs\ *noun*
— **laud·ably** \-blē\ *adverb*

lau·da·num \'lȯd-nəm, 'lȯ-d⁼n-əm\ *noun* [New Latin] (circa 1603)
1 : any of various formerly used preparations of opium
2 : a tincture of opium

lau·da·tion \lȯ-'dā-shən\ *noun* (15th century)
: the act of praising : EULOGY

lau·da·tive \'lȯ-də-tiv\ *adjective* (15th century)
: LAUDATORY

lau·da·to·ry \'lȯ-də-ˌtȯr-ē, -ˌtȯr-\ *adjective* (1555)
: of, relating to, or expressing praise

¹laugh \'laf, 'laf\ *verb* [Middle English, from Old English *hliehhan;* akin to Old High German *lachēn* to laugh] (before 12th century)
intransitive verb
1 a : to show mirth, joy, or scorn with a smile and chuckle or explosive sound **b** : to find amusement or pleasure in something ⟨*laughed* at his own clumsiness⟩ **c** : to become amused or derisive ⟨a very skeptical public *laughed* at our early efforts —Graenum Berger⟩
2 a : to produce the sound or appearance of laughter ⟨a *laughing* brook⟩ **b** : to be of a kind that inspires joy
transitive verb
1 : to influence or move by laughter ⟨*laughed* the bad singer off the stage⟩
2 : to utter with a laugh
— **laugh·ing·ly** \'la-fiŋ-lē, 'lä-\ *adverb*

²laugh *noun* (1690)
1 : the act of laughing
2 a : a cause for derision or merriment : JOKE **b** : an expression of scorn or mockery : JEER
3 *plural* : DIVERSION, SPORT ⟨play baseball just for *laughs*⟩

laugh·able \'la-fə-bəl, 'lä-\ *adjective* (1596)
: of a kind to provoke laughter or sometimes derision : amusingly ridiculous ☆
— **laugh·able·ness** *noun*
— **laugh·ably** \-blē\ *adverb*

laugh·er \'la-fər, 'lä-\ *noun* (15th century)
1 : one that laughs

☆ **SYNONYMS**
Laughable, ludicrous, ridiculous, comic, comical mean provoking laughter or mirth. LAUGHABLE applies to anything occasioning laughter (*laughable* attempts at waterskiing). LUDICROUS suggests absurdity or preposterousness that excites both laughter and scorn (a spy thriller with a *ludicrous* plot). RIDICULOUS suggests extreme absurdity, foolishness, or contemptibility (a *ridiculous* portrayal of wartime combat). COMIC applies especially to that which arouses thoughtful amusement (a *comic* character). COMICAL applies to that which arouses spontaneous hilarity (you looked *comical*).

2 : something (as a game) that is easily won or handled

laughing gas *noun* (circa 1842)
: NITROUS OXIDE

laughing gull *noun* (1789)
: an American gull (*Larus atricilla*) having a black head in breeding plumage and black wing tips blending into the gray upper side of the wings

laughing jackass *noun* (1798)
: KOOKABURRA

laughing matter *noun* (circa 1583)
: something not to be taken seriously — usually used in the phrase *no laughing matter*

laugh·ing·stock \'la-fiŋ-ˌstäk, 'lä-\ *noun* (1533)
: an object of ridicule

laugh off *transitive verb* (1715)
: to minimize by treating as amusingly or absurdly trivial

laugh·ter \'laf-tər, 'läf-\ *noun* [Middle English, from Old English *hleahtor*; akin to Old English *hliehhan*] (before 12th century)
1 : a sound of or as if of laughing
2 *archaic* : a cause of merriment

laugh track *noun* (1962)
: laughter to accompany dialogue or action (as of a television program)

launce \'lon(t)s, 'län(t)s\ *noun* [probably from ¹*lance*] (1623)
: SAND LANCE

¹launch \'lonch, 'länch\ *verb* [Middle English, from Old North French *lancher*, from Late Latin *lanceare* to wield a lance — more at LANCE] (14th century)
transitive verb
1 a : to throw forward : HURL **b** : to release, catapult, or send off (a self-propelled object) ⟨*launch* a rocket⟩
2 a : to set (a boat or ship) afloat **b** : to give (a person) a start ⟨*launched* in a new career⟩ **c** (1) : to originate or set in motion : INITIATE, INTRODUCE (2) : to get off to a good start
intransitive verb
1 a : to spring forward : TAKE OFF **b** : to throw oneself energetically : PLUNGE
2 a *archaic* : to slide down the ways **b** : to make a start

²launch *noun* (1749)
: an act or instance of launching

³launch *noun* [Spanish or Portuguese; Spanish *lancha*, from Portuguese] (1697)
1 : a large boat that operates from a ship
2 : a small motorboat that is open or that has the forepart of the hull covered

launch·er \'lon-chər, 'län-\ *noun* (1911)
: one that launches: as **a** : a device for firing grenades **b** : a device for launching a missile **c** : LAUNCH VEHICLE

launching pad *noun* (1951)
1 : LAUNCHPAD
2 : SPRINGBOARD 2

launch·pad \'lonch-ˌpad, 'länch-\ *noun* (1958)
: a nonflammable platform from which a rocket, launch vehicle, or guided missile can be launched

launch vehicle *noun* (circa 1960)
: a rocket used to launch a satellite or spacecraft

launch window *noun* (1962)
: WINDOW 8

¹laun·der \'lon-dər, 'län-\ *verb* **laun·dered; laun·der·ing** \-d(ə-)riŋ\ [Middle English *launder*, noun] (1664)
transitive verb
1 : to wash (as clothes) in water
2 : to make ready for use by washing and ironing ⟨a freshly *laundered* shirt⟩
3 : to transfer (as illegally obtained money or investments) through an outside party to conceal the true source
intransitive verb
: to wash or wash and iron clothing or household linens
— **laun·der·er** \-dər-ər\ *noun*

²launder *noun* [Middle English, launderer, from Middle French *lavandier*, from Medieval Latin *lavandarius*, from Latin *lavandus*, gerundive of *lavare* to wash — more at LYE] (1667)
: TROUGH; *especially* : a box conduit conveying particulate material suspended in water in ore dressing

laun·der·ette \ˌlon-də-'ret, ˌlän-\ *also* **laun·drette** \-'dret\ *noun* [from *Launderette*, a service mark] (circa 1948)
: a self-service laundry

laun·dress \'lon-drəs, 'län-\ *noun* (1550)
: a woman who is a laundry worker

Laun·dro·mat \'lon-drə-ˌmat, 'län-\ *service mark*
— used for a self-service laundry

laun·dry \'lon-drē, 'län-\ *noun, plural* **laun·dries** (14th century)
1 a : a room for doing the family wash **b** : a commercial laundering establishment
2 : clothes or linens that have been or are to be laundered

laundry list *noun* (1958)
: a usually long list of items ⟨the *laundry list* of new consumer-protection bills —N. C. Miller⟩

laun·dry·man \-mən\ *noun* (1708)
: a man who is a laundry worker

Laun·fal \'lon-fal, 'län-\ *noun*
: a knight of the Round Table in late Arthurian legend

lau·ra \'läv-rə\ *noun* [Late Greek, from Greek, lane] (circa 1752)
: a monastery of an Eastern church

¹lau·re·ate \'lor-ē-ət, 'lär-\ *noun* [Middle English, crowned with laurel as a distinction, from Latin *laureatus*, from *laurea* laurel wreath, from feminine of *laureus* of laurel, from *laurus*] (circa 1529)
: the recipient of honor or recognition for achievement in an art or science; *specifically* : POET LAUREATE
— **laureate** *adjective*
— **lau·re·ate·ship** \-ˌship\ *noun*

²lau·re·ate \'lor-ē-ˌāt, 'lär-\ *transitive verb* **-at·ed; -at·ing** (circa 1610)
1 : to crown with or as if with a laurel wreath for excellence or achievement
2 : to appoint to the office of poet laureate
— **lau·re·ation** \ˌlor-ē-'ā-shən, ˌlär-\ *noun*

¹lau·rel \'lor-əl, 'lär-\ *noun* [Middle English *lorel*, from Old French *lorier*, from *lor* laurel, from Latin *laurus*] (14th century)
1 : any of a genus (*Laurus* of the family Lauraceae) of evergreen trees that have alternate entire leaves, small tetramerous flowers surrounded by bracts, and fruits that are ovoid berries; *specifically* : a tree (*L. nobilis*) of southern Europe with foliage used by the ancient Greeks to crown victors in the Pythian games
2 : a tree or shrub that resembles the true laurel; *especially* : MOUNTAIN LAUREL
3 : a crown of laurel : HONOR — usually used in plural

laurel 1

²laurel *transitive verb* **-reled** *or* **-relled; -rel·ing** *or* **-rel·ling** (1631)
: to deck or crown with laurel

lau·ric acid \'lor-ik-, 'lär-\ *noun* [International Scientific Vocabulary, from Latin *laurus*] (1873)
: a crystalline fatty acid $C_{12}H_{24}O_2$ found especially in coconut oil and used in making soaps, esters, and lauryl alcohol

lau·ryl alcohol \'lor-əl-, 'lär-\ *noun* (1922)

: a compound $C_{12}H_{26}O$; *also* : a liquid mixture of this and other alcohols used especially in making detergents

la·va \'lä-və, 'la-\ *noun* [Italian, ultimately from Latin *labes* fall; akin to Latin *labi* to slide — more at SLEEP] (1759)
: molten rock that issues from a volcano or from a fissure in the earth's surface; *also* : such rock that has cooled and hardened
— **la·va·like** \-ˌlīk\ *adjective*

la·va·bo \lə-'vä-(ˌ)bō\ *noun, plural* **-bos** [Latin, I shall wash, from *lavare*] (circa 1858)
1 *often capitalized* : a ceremony at Mass in which the celebrant washes his hands after offering the oblations and says Psalm 25:6–12 (Douay Version)
2 a : a washbasin and a tank with a spigot that are fastened to a wall **b** : this combination used as a planter

la·vage \lə-'väzh, *British usually* 'la-vij\ *noun* [French, from Middle French, from *laver* to wash, from Latin *lavare*] (circa 1895)
: WASHING; *especially* : the therapeutic washing out of an organ

la·va-la·va \ˌlä-və-'lä-və\ *noun* [Samoan, clothing] (circa 1891)
: a rectangular cloth of cotton print worn like a kilt or skirt in Polynesia and especially in Samoa

la·va·liere *or* **la·val·liere** \ˌlä-və-'lir, ˌla-\ *noun* [French *lavallière* necktie with a large knot] (1906)
: a pendant on a fine chain that is worn as a necklace

la·va·lier microphone \ˌlä-və-'lir-, ˌla-\ *or* **lavaliere microphone** *same*\ *noun* (circa 1962)
: a small microphone hung around the neck of the user

la·va·tion \lā-'vā-shən\ *noun* [Latin *lavation-, lavatio*, from *lavare*] (15th century)
: the act or an instance of washing or cleansing

lav·a·to·ry \'la-və-ˌtōr-ē, -ˌtor-, *British* -və-t(ə-)rē\ *noun, plural* **-ries** [Middle English *lavatorie*, from Medieval Latin *lavatorium*, from Latin *lavare* to wash — more at LYE] (14th century)
1 : a vessel (as a basin) for washing; *especially* : a fixed bowl or basin with running water and drainpipe for washing
2 : a room with conveniences for washing and usually with one or more toilets
3 : TOILET 3b
— **lavatory** *adjective*

¹lave \'lāv\ *noun* [Middle English (northern dialect), from Old English *lāf*; akin to Old English be*lītan* to remain — more at LEAVE] (before 12th century)
chiefly dialect : something that is left : RESIDUE

²lave *verb* **laved; lav·ing** [Middle English, from Old English *lafian*, from Latin *lavare*] (before 12th century)
transitive verb
1 a : WASH, BATHE **b** : to flow along or against
2 : POUR
intransitive verb
archaic : to wash oneself : BATHE

¹lav·en·der \'la-vən-dər\ *noun* [Middle English *lavendre*, from Anglo-French, from Medieval Latin *lavandula*] (13th century)
1 a : a Mediterranean mint (*Lavandula angustifolia* synonym *L. officinalis*) widely cultivated for its narrow aromatic leaves and spikes of lilac-purple flowers which are dried and used in sachets **b** : any of several plants congeneric with true lavender and used similarly but often considered inferior
2 : a pale purple

²lavender *transitive verb* **lav·en·dered; lav·en·der·ing** \-d(ə-)riŋ\ (1820)
: to sprinkle or perfume with lavender

¹la·ver \'lā-vər\ *noun* [Middle English *lavour*, from Middle French *lavoir*, from Medieval Latin *lavatorium*] (1535)

: a large basin used for ceremonial ablutions in the ancient Jewish Tabernacle and Temple worship

²**la·ver** \'lā-vər, 'lä-\ *noun* [New Latin, from Latin, a water plant] (1611)
: any of several common red algae (genus *Porphyra*) with fronds used for stewing or pickling

La·vin·ia \lə-'vi-nē-ə\ *noun* [Latin]
: a daughter of King Latinus in Virgil's *Aeneid* who is betrothed to Turnus but marries Aeneas

¹**lav·ish** \'la-vish\ *adjective* [Middle English *lavas* abundance, from Middle French *lavasse* downpour of rain, from *laver* to wash — more at LAVAGE] (15th century)
1 : expending or bestowing profusely : PRODIGAL
2 a : expended or produced in abundance **b** : marked by profusion or excess
synonym see PROFUSE
— **lav·ish·ly** *adverb*
— **lav·ish·ness** *noun*

²**lavish** *transitive verb* (1542)
: to expend or bestow with profusion : SQUANDER

lav·rock \'lav-rək, 'lav-\ *or* **la·ver·ock** \'la-və-\ *noun* [Middle English *laverok*, from Old English *lāwerce*] (14th century)
chiefly Scottish : LARK

¹**law** \'lò\ *noun* [Middle English, from Old English *lagu*, of Scandinavian origin; akin to Old Norse *lǫg* law; akin to Old English *licgan* to lie — more at LIE] (before 12th century)
1 a (1) : a binding custom or practice of a community : a rule of conduct or action prescribed or formally recognized as binding or enforced by a controlling authority (2) : the whole body of such customs, practices, or rules (3) : COMMON LAW **b** (1) : the control brought about by the existence or enforcement of such law (2) : the action of laws considered as a means of redressing wrongs; *also* : LITIGATION (3) : the agency of or an agent of established law **c** : a rule or order that it is advisable or obligatory to observe **d** : something compatible with or enforceable by established law **e** : CONTROL, AUTHORITY
2 a *often capitalized* : the revelation of the will of God set forth in the Old Testament **b** *capitalized* : the first part of the Jewish scriptures : PENTATEUCH, TORAH — see BIBLE table
3 : a rule of construction or procedure ⟨the *laws* of poetry⟩
4 : the whole body of laws relating to one subject
5 a : the legal profession **b** : law as a department of knowledge : JURISPRUDENCE **c** : legal knowledge
6 a : a statement of an order or relation of phenomena that so far as is known is invariable under the given conditions **b** : a general relation proved or assumed to hold between mathematical or logical expressions ☆ ◇
— **at law** : under or within the provisions of the law ⟨enforceable *at law*⟩

²**law** (circa 1550)
intransitive verb
: LITIGATE
transitive verb
chiefly dialect : to sue or prosecute at law

law–abid·ing \'lò-ə-,bī-diŋ\ *adjective* (1834)
: abiding by or obedient to the law
— **law–abid·ing·ness** *noun*

law·break·er \'lò-,brā-kər\ *noun* (15th century)
: one who violates the law
— **law·break·ing** \-kiŋ\ *adjective or noun*

law·ful \'lò-fəl\ *adjective* (14th century)
1 a : being in harmony with the law ⟨a *lawful* judgment⟩ **b** : constituted, authorized, or established by law : RIGHTFUL ⟨*lawful* institutions⟩
2 : LAW-ABIDING ⟨*lawful* citizens⟩ ☆
— **law·ful·ly** \-f(ə-)lē\ *adverb*
— **law·ful·ness** \-fəl-nəs\ *noun*

law·giv·er \'lò-,gi-vər\ *noun* (14th century)
1 : one who gives a code of laws to a people
2 : LEGISLATOR

law·less \'lò-ləs\ *adjective* (12th century)
1 : not regulated by or based on law
2 a : not restrained or controlled by law : UNRULY **b** : ILLEGAL
— **law·less·ly** *adverb*
— **law·less·ness** *noun*

law·mak·er \-,mā-kər\ *noun* (14th century)
: one that makes laws : LEGISLATOR
— **law·mak·ing** \-,kiŋ\ *noun*

law·man \'lò-mən\ *noun* (1944)
: a law-enforcement officer (as a sheriff or marshal)

law merchant *noun*, *plural* **laws merchant** (15th century)
: the legal rules formerly applied to cases arising in commercial transactions

¹**lawn** \'lòn, 'län\ *noun* [Middle English *launde*, from Middle French *lande* heath, of Celtic origin; akin to Middle Irish *lann* land — more at LAND] (14th century)
1 *archaic* : an open space between woods : GLADE
2 : ground (as around a house or in a garden or park) that is covered with grass and is kept mowed
3 : a relatively even layer of bacteria covering the surface of a culture medium
— **lawn** *or* **lawny** \'lò-nē, 'lä-\ *adjective*

²**lawn** *noun* [Middle English, from *Laon*, France] (15th century)
: a fine sheer linen or cotton fabric of plain weave that is thinner than cambric
— **lawny** *adjective*

lawn bowling *noun* (circa 1929)
: a bowling game played on a green with wooden balls which are rolled at a jack

lawn mower *noun* (1869)
: a machine for cutting grass on lawns

lawn tennis *noun* (1874)
: TENNIS 2

law of averages (circa 1929)
: the commonsense observation that probability influences everyday life so that over the long term the possible outcomes of a repeated event occur with specific frequencies

law of definite proportions (circa 1909)
: a statement in chemistry: every definite compound always contains the same elements in the same proportions by weight

law of dominance (1942)
: MENDEL'S LAW 3

law of independent assortment (1943)
: MENDEL'S LAW 2

law of large numbers (1911)
: a theorem in mathematical statistics: the probability that the absolute value of the difference between the mean of a population sample and the mean of the population from which it is drawn is greater than an arbitrarily small amount approaches zero as the size of the sample approaches infinity

Law of Moses (14th century)
: PENTATEUCH, TORAH

law of nations (circa 1548)
: INTERNATIONAL LAW

law of parsimony (1837)
: OCCAM'S RAZOR

law of segregation (circa 1909)
: MENDEL'S LAW 1

law of war (1947)
: the code that governs or one of the rules that govern the rights and duties of belligerents in international war

law·ren·ci·um \lò-'ren(t)-sē-əm\ *noun* [New Latin, from Ernest O. *Lawrence*] (1961)
: a short-lived radioactive element that is produced artificially from californium — see ELEMENT table

law·suit \'lò-,süt\ *noun* (1624)
: a suit in law : a case before a court

law·yer \'lò-yər, 'lòi-ər\ *noun* (14th century)
: one whose profession is to conduct lawsuits for clients or to advise as to legal rights and obligations in other matters

— **law·yer·like** \-,līk\ *adjective*
— **law·yer·ly** \-lē\ *adjective*

law·yer·ing \'lò-yə-riŋ, 'lòi-\ *noun* (1676)
: the profession or work of a lawyer

☆ SYNONYMS

Law, rule, regulation, precept, statute, ordinance, canon mean a principle governing action or procedure. LAW implies imposition by a sovereign authority and the obligation of obedience on the part of all subject to that authority ⟨obey the *law*⟩. RULE applies to more restricted or specific situations ⟨the *rules* of the game⟩. REGULATION implies prescription by authority in order to control an organization or system ⟨*regulations* affecting nuclear power plants⟩. PRECEPT commonly suggests something advisory and not obligatory communicated typically through teaching ⟨the *precepts* of effective writing⟩. STATUTE implies a law enacted by a legislative body ⟨a *statute* requiring the use of seat belts⟩. ORDINANCE applies to an order governing some detail of procedure or conduct enforced by a limited authority such as a municipality ⟨a city *ordinance*⟩. CANON suggests in nonreligious use a principle or rule of behavior or procedure commonly accepted as a valid guide ⟨the *canons* of good taste⟩. See in addition HYPOTHESIS.

Lawful, legal, legitimate, licit mean being in accordance with law. LAWFUL may apply to conformity with law of any sort (as natural, divine, common, or canon) ⟨the *lawful* sovereign⟩. LEGAL applies to what is sanctioned by law or in conformity with the law, especially as it is written or administered by the courts ⟨*legal* residents of the state⟩. LEGITIMATE may apply to a legal right or status but also, in extended use, to a right or status supported by tradition, custom, or accepted standards ⟨a perfectly *legitimate* question about finances⟩. LICIT applies to a strict conformity to the provisions of the law and applies especially to what is regulated by law ⟨the *licit* use of the drug by hospitals⟩.

◇ WORD HISTORY

law The word *law* is part of the English language's abundant heritage from medieval Scandinavia. It was borrowed into late Old English from an unrecorded Old Norse noun *lagu* (whose existence is inferred from the linguistically later Old Icelandic form *log*). *Lagu* is the plural of *lag* "something laid, layer, stratum." The image of the law as a sort of edifice built up of past decisions and decrees is fairly natural. Other languages have resorted to similar metaphors, using derivatives of verbs meaning "to put or place" or "to erect" in order to express the notion of a law. Hence, for example, we have Greek *thesmos* "law, ordinance" (from *tithenai* "to place"), Latin *statutum* "ordinance, statute" (from *statuere* "to set upright, erect"), and German *Gesetz* "law" (from *setzen* "to put, set"). Old English did not lack an earlier word for "law"; this was *æ* or *æw*, which also meant "custom"—appropriately enough, since law and custom in preliterate societies typically overlap. This word may be akin to Latin *jus* "what is sanctioned, law," the ultimate source of English *jury*, *perjury*, *injury*, and a host of other words.

lax \'laks\ *adjective* [Middle English, from Latin *laxus* loose — more at SLACK] (14th century)
1 a *of the bowels* **:** LOOSE, OPEN **b :** having loose bowels
2 : deficient in firmness **:** not stringent ⟨*lax* control⟩ ⟨a *lax* foreman⟩
3 a : not tense, firm, or rigid **:** SLACK ⟨a *lax* rope⟩ **b :** having an open or loose texture **c :** having the constituents spread apart ⟨a *lax* flower cluster⟩
4 : articulated with the muscles involved in a relatively relaxed state (as the vowel \i\ in contrast with the vowel \ē\)
synonym see NEGLIGENT
— **lax·a·tion** \lak-'sā-shən\ *noun*
— **lax·ly** \'laks-lē\ *adverb*
— **lax·ness** *noun*

¹lax·a·tive \'lak-sə-tiv\ *adjective* [Middle English *laxatif*, from Medieval Latin *laxativus*, from Latin *laxatus*, past participle of *laxare* to loosen, from *laxus*] (14th century)
: having a tendency to loosen or relax; *specifically* **:** relieving constipation

²laxative *noun* (14th century)
: a usually mild laxative drug

lax·ity \'lak-sə-tē\ *noun* (1528)
: the quality or state of being lax

¹lay \'lā\ *verb* **laid** \'lād\; **lay·ing** [Middle English *leyen*, from Old English *lecgan; akin to* Old English *licgan* to lie — more at LIE] (before 12th century)
transitive verb
1 : to beat or strike down with force
2 a : to put or set down **b :** to place for rest or sleep; *especially* **:** BURY
3 : to bring forth and deposit (an egg)
4 : CALM, ALLAY ⟨*lay* the dust⟩
5 : BET, WAGER
6 : to press down giving a smooth and even surface
7 a : to dispose or spread over or on a surface ⟨*lay* track⟩ ⟨*lay* plaster⟩ **b :** to set in order or position ⟨*lay* a table for dinner⟩ ⟨*lay* brick⟩ **c :** to put (strands) in place and twist to form a rope, hawser, or cable; *also* **:** to make by so doing ⟨*lay* up rope⟩
8 a : to impose as a duty, burden, or punishment ⟨*lay* a tax⟩ **b :** to put as a burden of reproach ⟨*laid* the blame on her⟩ **c :** to advance as an accusation **:** IMPUTE ⟨the disaster was *laid* to faulty inspection⟩
9 : to place (something immaterial) on something ⟨*lay* stress on grammar⟩
10 : PREPARE, CONTRIVE ⟨a well-*laid* plan⟩
11 a : to bring against or into contact with something **:** APPLY ⟨*laid* the watch to his ear⟩ **b :** to prepare or position for action or operation ⟨*lay* a fire in the fireplace⟩; *also* **:** to adjust (a gun) to the proper direction and elevation
12 : to bring to a specified condition ⟨*lay* waste the land⟩
13 a : ASSERT, ALLEGE ⟨*lay* claim to an estate⟩ **b :** to submit for examination and judgment ⟨*laid* her case before the commission⟩
14 : to copulate with — sometimes considered vulgar
intransitive verb
1 : to produce and deposit eggs
2 *nonstandard* **:** ¹LIE
3 : WAGER, BET
4 *dialect* **:** PLAN, PREPARE
5 a : to apply oneself vigorously ⟨*laid* to his oars⟩ **b :** to proceed to a specified place or position on a ship ⟨*lay* aloft⟩ □
— **lay on the table 1 :** to remove (a parliamentary motion) from consideration indefinitely **2** *British* **:** to put (as legislation) on the agenda

²lay *noun* (1590)
1 : COVERT, LAIR
2 : something (as a layer) that lies or is laid
3 a : line of action **:** PLAN **b :** line of work **:** OCCUPATION

4 a : terms of sale or employment **:** PRICE **b :** share of profit (as on a whaling voyage) paid in lieu of wages
5 a : the amount of advance of any point in a rope strand for one turn **b :** the nature of a fiber rope as determined by the amount of twist, the angle of the strands, and the angle of the threads in the strands
6 : the way in which a thing lies or is laid in relation to something else ⟨the *lay* of the land⟩
7 : the state of one that lays eggs ⟨hens coming into *lay*⟩
8 a : a partner in sexual intercourse — usually considered vulgar **b :** SEXUAL INTERCOURSE — usually considered vulgar

³lay *past of* LIE

⁴lay *noun* [Middle English, from Old French *lai*] (13th century)
1 : a simple narrative poem **:** BALLAD
2 : MELODY, SONG

⁵lay *adjective* [Middle English, from Middle French *lai*, from Late Latin *laicus*, from Greek *laikos* of the people, from *laos* people] (15th century)
1 : of or relating to the laity **:** not ecclesiastical
2 : of or relating to members of a religious house occupied with domestic or manual work ⟨a *lay* brother⟩
3 : not of a particular profession ⟨the *lay* public⟩; *also* **:** lacking extensive knowledge of a particular subject

lay·about \'lā-ə-ˌbaut\ *noun* (1932)
: a lazy shiftless person **:** IDLER

lay·away \'lā-ə-ˌwā\ *noun* (1944)
: a purchasing agreement by which a retailer agrees to hold merchandise secured by a deposit until the price is paid in full by the customer

lay away *transitive verb* (circa 1928)
: to put aside for future use or delivery

lay–by \'lā-ˌbī\ *noun* (1939)
1 *British* **:** TURNOUT 4b
2 : the final operation (as a last cultivating) in the growing of a field crop

lay by *transitive verb* (15th century)
1 : to lay aside **:** DISCARD
2 : to store for future use **:** SAVE
3 : to cultivate (as corn) for the last time

lay day *noun* (1845)
1 : one of the days allowed by the charter for loading or unloading a vessel
2 : a day of delay in port

lay down (13th century)
transitive verb
1 : to give up **:** SURRENDER ⟨*lay down* your arms⟩
2 a : ESTABLISH, PRESCRIBE ⟨*lay down* a scale for a map⟩ **b :** to assert or command dogmatically ⟨*lay down* the law⟩
3 : STORE, PRESERVE
4 a : to direct toward a target ⟨*lay down* a barrage⟩ **b :** to hit along the ground ⟨*laid down* a sacrifice bunt⟩
intransitive verb
nonstandard **:** to lie down

¹lay·er \'lā-ər\ *noun* (13th century)
1 : one that lays (as a worker who lays brick or a hen that lays eggs)
2 a : one thickness, course, or fold laid or lying over or under another **b :** STRATUM **c :** HORIZON 2
3 a : a branch or shoot of a plant that roots while still attached to the parent plant **b :** a plant developed by layering
— **lay·ered** \'lā-ərd, 'le(-ə)rd\ *adjective*

²layer (1832)
transitive verb
1 : to propagate (a plant) by means of layers
2 a : to place as a layer **b :** to place a layer on top of **c :** to form or arrange in layers
intransitive verb
1 a : to separate into layers **b :** to form out of superimposed layers
2 *of a plant* **:** to form roots where a stem comes in contact with the ground

lay·er·age \'lā-ə-rij, 'le-ə-\ *noun* (1902)
: the practice, art, or process of rooting plants by layering

lay·ette \lā-'et\ *noun* [French, from Middle French, diminutive of *laye* box, from Middle Dutch *lade; akin to* Old English *hladan* to load — more at LADE] (1839)
: a complete outfit of clothing and equipment for a newborn infant

lay figure *noun* [obsolete English *layman* lay figure, from Dutch *leeman*] (1795)
1 : a jointed model of the human body used by artists to show the disposition of drapery
2 : a person likened to a dummy or puppet

lay in *transitive verb* (1579)
: LAY BY, SAVE

laying on of hands (15th century)
: the act of laying hands on a person's head to confer a spiritual blessing (as in Christian ordination, confirmation, or faith healing)

lay·man \'lā-mən\ *noun* (15th century)
1 : a person who is not a member of the clergy
2 : a person who does not belong to a particular profession or who is not expert in some field

lay·off \'lā-ˌof\ *noun* (1889)
1 : a period of inactivity or idleness
2 : the act of laying off an employee or a workforce; *also* **:** SHUTDOWN

lay off (1748)
transitive verb
1 : to mark or measure off
2 : to cease to employ (a worker) often temporarily
3 *of a bookie* **:** to place all or part of (an accepted bet) with another bookie to reduce the risk
4 a : to leave undisturbed **b :** AVOID, QUIT
intransitive verb
1 : to stop doing or taking something
2 : to leave one alone ⟨wish you'd just *lay off*⟩

lay on (1600)
transitive verb
1 a : to apply by or as if by spreading on a surface ⟨*laying* it *on* thick⟩ **b :** PROVIDE, ARRANGE ⟨food *laid on* in abundance⟩ **c :** HAND OUT ⟨*laid on* awards⟩
2 *chiefly British* **:** HIRE
intransitive verb
: ATTACK, BEAT

lay·out \'lā-ˌaut\ *noun* (1852)
1 : the plan or design or arrangement of something that is laid out: as **a :** DUMMY 5b **b :** final arrangement of matter to be reproduced especially by printing
2 : the act or process of planning or laying out in detail

3 a : something that is laid out ⟨a model train *layout*⟩ **b :** land or structures or rooms used for a particular purpose ⟨a cattle-ranching *layout*⟩; *also :* PLACE **c :** a set or outfit especially of tools

lay out *transitive verb* (15th century)
1 : DISPLAY, EXHIBIT
2 : SPEND
3 a : to prepare (a corpse) for viewing **b :** to knock flat or unconscious
4 : to plan in detail ⟨*lay out* a campaign⟩
5 : ARRANGE, DESIGN
6 : to mark (work) for drilling, machining, or filing

lay·over \'lā-,ō-vər\ *noun* (1873)
: STOPOVER

lay over (1838)
transitive verb
: POSTPONE
intransitive verb
: to make a stopover

lay·peo·ple \'lā-,pē-pəl\ *noun plural* (15th century)
: LAYPERSONS

lay·per·son \-,pər-sᵊn\ *noun* (1972)
: a member of the laity

lay reader *noun* (1751)
: an Anglican or Roman Catholic layman authorized to conduct parts of the church services not requiring a clergyman

lay to (1796)
intransitive verb
: LIE TO
transitive verb
: to bring (a ship) into the wind and hold stationary

lay·up \'lā-,əp\ *noun* (1925)
1 : the action of laying up or the condition of being laid up
2 : a shot in basketball made from near the basket usually by playing the ball off the backboard

lay up *transitive verb* (14th century)
1 : to store up **:** LAY BY
2 : to disable or confine with illness or injury
3 : to take out of active service

lay·wom·an \'lā-,wu̇-mən\ *noun* (1529)
: a woman who is a member of the laity

la·zar \'la-zər, 'lā-\ *noun* [Middle English, from Medieval Latin *lazarus*, from Late Latin *Lazarus*] (14th century)
: a person afflicted with a repulsive disease; *specifically :* LEPER

laz·a·ret·to \,la-zə-'re-(,)tō\ *or* **laz·a·ret** \-'ret\ *also* **laz·a·rette** \-'ret\ *noun, plural* **-rettos** *or* **-rets** *also* **-rettes** [Italian *lazzaretto*, alteration of *Nazaretto*, quarantine station in Venice, from *Santa Maria di Nazareth*, church on the island where it was located] (1549)
1 *usually* lazaretto **:** an institution (as a hospital) for those with contagious diseases
2 : a building or a ship used for detention in quarantine
3 *usually* lazaret **:** a space in a ship between decks used as a storeroom

La·za·rist \'la-zə-rist, lə-'zär-ist\ *noun* [College of Saint Lazare, Paris, former home of the congregation] (1747)
: VINCENTIAN

Laz·a·rus \'laz-rəs, 'la-zə-\ *noun* [Late Latin, from Greek *Lazaros*, from Hebrew *El'āzār*]
1 : a brother of Mary and Martha raised from the dead by Jesus according to the account in John 11
2 : the diseased beggar in the parable of the rich man and the beggar found in Luke 16

laze \'lāz\ *verb* **lazed; laz·ing** [back-formation from *lazy*] (circa 1592)
intransitive verb
: to act or lie lazily **:** IDLE
transitive verb
: to pass (time) in idleness or relaxation
— **laze** *noun*

la·zu·lite \'la-zyü-,līt, -zhə-\ *noun* [German *Lazulith*, from Medieval Latin *lazulum* lapis lazuli] (1807)
: an often crystalline azure-blue mineral that is a hydrous phosphate of aluminum, iron, and magnesium

¹la·zy \'lā-zē\ *adjective* **la·zi·er; -est** [perhaps from Middle Low German *lasich* feeble; akin to Middle High German er*leswen* to become weak] (1549)
1 a : disinclined to activity or exertion **:** not energetic or vigorous **b :** encouraging inactivity or indolence ⟨a *lazy* summer day⟩
2 : moving slowly **:** SLUGGISH
3 : DROOPY, LAX ⟨a rabbit with *lazy* ears⟩
4 : placed on its side ⟨*lazy* E livestock brand⟩
5 : not rigorous or strict ⟨*lazy* scholarship⟩ ☆
— **la·zi·ly** \-zə-lē\ *adverb*
— **la·zi·ness** \-zē-nəs\ *noun*
— **la·zy·ish** \-zē-ish\ *adjective*

²lazy *intransitive verb* **la·zied; la·zy·ing** (1612)
: to move or lie lazily **:** LAZE

la·zy·bones \'lā-zē-,bōnz\ *noun plural but singular or plural in construction* (1592)
: a lazy person

lazy eye *noun* (1939)
: AMBLYOPIA; *also :* an eye affected with amblyopia

lazy Su·san \-'sü-zᵊn\ *noun* (1917)
: a revolving tray used for serving food, condiments, or relishes

lazy tongs *noun plural* (1836)
: a series of jointed and pivoted bars capable of great extension used to pick up or handle something at a distance

lazy tongs

LCD \,el-(,)sē-'dē\ *noun* [*l*iquid *c*rystal *d*isplay] (1973)
: a constantly operating display (as of the time in a digital watch) that consists of segments of a liquid crystal whose reflectivity varies according to the voltage applied to them

LD₅₀ \,el-,dē-'fif-tē\ *noun* [*l*ethal *d*ose] (1942)
: the amount of a toxic agent (as a poison, virus, or radiation) that is sufficient to kill 50% of a population of animals usually within a certain time

LDL \,el-(,)dē-'el\ *noun* [*l*ow-*d*ensity *l*ipoprotein] (1976)
: a cholesterol-rich protein-poor lipoprotein of blood plasma correlated with increased risk of atherosclerosis — compare HDL

L-do·pa \'el-'dō-pə\ *noun* (1939)
: the levorotatory form of dopa that is obtained especially from broad beans or prepared synthetically, stimulates the production of dopamine in the brain, and is used in treating Parkinson's disease

lea *or* **ley** \'lē, 'lā\ *noun* [Middle English *leye*, from Old English *lēah*; akin to Old High German *lōh* thicket, Latin *lucus* grove, *lux* light — more at LIGHT] (before 12th century)
1 : GRASSLAND, PASTURE
2 *usually* ley **:** arable land used temporarily for hay or grazing

¹leach \'lēch\ *variant of* LEECH

²leach *verb* [*leach* vessel through which water is passed to extract lye] (1796)
transitive verb
1 : to dissolve out by the action of a percolating liquid ⟨*leach* out alkali from ashes⟩
2 : to subject to the action of percolating liquid (as water) in order to separate the soluble components
3 a : to remove (nutritive or harmful elements) from soil by percolation **b :** to draw out or remove as if by percolation ⟨all meaning has been *leached* from my life⟩
intransitive verb
: to pass out or through by percolation
— **leach·abil·i·ty** \,lē-chə-'bi-lə-tē\ *noun*
— **leach·able** \'lē-chə-bəl\ *adjective*
— **leach·er** *noun*

leach·ate \'lē-,chāt\ *noun* (1934)
: a solution or product obtained by leaching

¹lead \'lēd\ *verb* **led** \'led\; **lead·ing** [Middle English *leden*, from Old English *lǣdan*; akin to Old High German *leiten* to lead, Old English *līthan* to go] (before 12th century)
transitive verb
1 a : to guide on a way especially by going in advance **b :** to direct on a course or in a direction **c :** to serve as a channel for ⟨a pipe *leads* water to the house⟩
2 : to go through **:** LIVE ⟨*lead* a quiet life⟩
3 a (1) **:** to direct the operations, activity, or performance of ⟨*lead* an orchestra⟩ (2) **:** to have charge of ⟨*lead* a campaign⟩ (3) **:** to suggest to (a witness) the answer desired by asking leading questions **b** (1) **:** to go at the head of ⟨*lead* a parade⟩ (2) **:** to be first in or among ⟨*lead* the league⟩ (3) **:** to have a margin over ⟨*led* his opponent⟩
4 : to bring to some conclusion or condition ⟨*led* to believe otherwise⟩
5 : to begin play with ⟨*lead* trumps⟩
6 a : to aim in front of (a moving object) ⟨*lead* a duck⟩ **b :** to pass a ball or puck just in front of (a moving teammate)
intransitive verb
1 a : to guide someone or something along a way **b :** to lie, run, or open in a specified place or direction ⟨path *leads* uphill⟩ **c :** to guide a dance partner through the steps of a dance
2 a : to be first **b** (1) **:** BEGIN, OPEN (2) **:** to play the first card of a trick, round, or game
3 : to tend toward or have a result ⟨study *leading* to a degree⟩
4 : to direct the first of a series of blows at an opponent in boxing □
synonym see GUIDE
— **lead one down the garden path** *also* **lead one up the garden path** **:** HOODWINK, DECEIVE

²lead *noun* (15th century)
1 a (1) **:** LEADERSHIP (2) **:** EXAMPLE, PRECEDENT **b** (1) **:** position at the front **:** VANGUARD (2) **:** INITIATIVE (3) **:** the act or privilege of leading in cards; *also :* the card or suit led **c :** a margin or measure of advantage or superiority or position in advance
2 : one that leads: as **a :** LODE 1 **b :** a channel of water especially through a field of ice **c :** INDICATION, CLUE **d :** a principal role in a dramatic production; *also :* one who plays such a role **e :** LEASH 1 **f** (1) **:** an introductory section of a news story (2) **:** a news story of chief importance

☆ **SYNONYMS**
Lazy, indolent, slothful mean not easily aroused to activity. LAZY suggests a disinclination to work or to take trouble ⟨convenience foods for *lazy* cooks⟩. INDOLENT suggests a love of ease and a settled dislike of movement or activity ⟨the heat made us all *indolent*⟩. SLOTHFUL implies a temperamental inability to act promptly or speedily when action or speed is called for ⟨fired for being *slothful* about filling orders⟩.

□ **USAGE**
lead The past tense and past participle of *lead* is spelled *led*. Many people—perhaps influenced by the pronunciation of the metal *lead* or by the past tense of the verb *read*—tend to spell it *lead*. This is a common mistake in casual writing and is to be avoided.

\ə\ abut \ᵊ\ kitten \ər\ further \a\ ash \ā\ ace
\ä\ mop, mar \au̇\ out \ch\ chin \e\ bet \ē\ easy
\g\ go \i\ hit \ī\ ice \j\ job \ŋ\ sing \ō\ go
\ȯ\ law \ȯi\ boy \th\ thin \t͟h\ the \ü\ loot \u̇\ foot
\y\ yet \zh\ vision *see also* Guide to Pronunciation

3 : an insulated electrical conductor connected to an electrical device
4 : the course of a rope from end to end
5 : the amount of axial advance of a point accompanying a complete turn of a thread (as of a screw or worm)
6 : a position taken by a base runner off a base toward the next
7 : the first punch of a series or an exchange of punches in boxing
— **lead·less** \-ləs\ *adjective*

³**lead** *adjective* (1828)
: acting or serving as a lead or leader ⟨a *lead* article⟩

⁴**lead** \'led\ *noun, often attributive* [Middle English *leed*, from Old English *lēad;* akin to Middle High German *lōt* lead] (before 12th century)
1 : a heavy soft malleable ductile plastic but inelastic bluish white metallic element found mostly in combination and used especially in pipes, cable sheaths, batteries, solder, and shields against radioactivity — see ELEMENT table
2 a : a plummet for sounding at sea **b** *plural, British* : a usually flat lead roof **c** *plural* : lead framing for panes in windows **d** : a thin strip of metal used to separate lines of type in printing
3 a : a thin stick of marking substance in or for a pencil **b** : WHITE LEAD
4 : BULLETS, PROJECTILES
5 : TETRAETHYL LEAD
— **lead·less** \-ləs\ *adjective*

⁵**lead** \'led\ *transitive verb* (14th century)
1 : to cover, line, or weight with lead
2 : to fix (window glass) in position with leads
3 : to put space between the lines of (typeset matter)
4 : to treat or mix with lead or a lead compound ⟨*leaded* gasoline⟩

lead acetate *noun* (1885)
: an acetate of lead; *especially* : a poisonous soluble salt $PbC_4H_6O_4 \cdot 3H_2O$

lead arsenate *noun* (circa 1903)
: an arsenate of lead: as **a** : an acid salt $PbHAsO_4$ used especially as an insecticide **b** : a neutral salt $Pb_3(AsO_4)_2$ used especially as an insecticide

lead azide *noun* (1918)
: a crystalline explosive compound $Pb(N_3)_2$ used as a detonating agent

lead carbonate *noun* (1873)
: a carbonate of lead; *especially* : a poisonous basic salt $Pb_3(OH)_2(CO_3)_2$ used especially as a white pigment

lead chromate *noun* (circa 1885)
: a chromate of lead; *especially* : CHROME YELLOW

lead dioxide *noun* (1885)
: a poisonous compound PbO_2 used especially as an oxidizing agent and as an electrode in batteries

lead·en \'le-dᵊn\ *adjective* (before 12th century)
1 a : made of lead **b** : of the color of lead : dull gray
2 a : oppressively heavy **b** : SLUGGISH **c** : lacking spirit or animation
— **lead·en·ly** *adverb*
— **lead·en·ness** \-dᵊn-(n)əs\ *noun*

lead·er \'le-dər\ *noun* (14th century)
1 : something that leads: as **a** : a primary or terminal shoot of a plant **b** : TENDON, SINEW **c** *plural* : dots or hyphens (as in an index) used to lead the eye horizontally : ELLIPSIS **2 d** *chiefly British* : a newspaper editorial **e** (1) : something for guiding (often into a trap) (2) : a short length of material for attaching the end of a fishing line to a lure or hook **f** : LOSS LEADER **g** : something that ranks first **h** : a blank section at the beginning or end of a reel of film or recorded tape

2 : a person who leads: as **a** : GUIDE, CONDUCTOR **b** (1) : a person who directs a military force or unit (2) : a person who has commanding authority or influence **c** (1) : the principal officer of a British political party (2) : a party member chosen to manage party activities in a legislative body (3) : such a party member presiding over the whole legislative body when the party constitutes a majority **d** (1) : CONDUCTOR **c** (2) : a first or principal performer of a group
3 : a horse placed in advance of the other horses of a team
— **lead·er·less** \-ləs\ *adjective*

leader of the opposition (1771)
: the principal member of the opposition party in a British legislative body who is given the status of a salaried government official and an important role in organizing the business of the house

lead·er·ship \'le-dər-,ship\ *noun* (1821)
1 : the office or position of a leader
2 : capacity to lead
3 : the act or an instance of leading
4 : LEADERS

lead glass *noun* (1856)
: glass containing a high proportion of lead oxide and having extraordinary clarity and brilliance

lead-in \'led-,in\ *noun* (1913)
: something that leads into something else ⟨a *lead-in* to the commercial⟩
— **lead-in** *adjective*

lead·ing \'le-diŋ\ *adjective* (1597)
1 : coming or ranking first : FOREMOST
2 : exercising leadership
3 : providing direction or guidance ⟨a *leading* question⟩
4 : given most prominent display ⟨the *leading* story⟩

leading edge \'le-diŋ-\ *noun* (1877)
1 : the foremost edge of an airfoil
2 : the forward part of something that moves or seems to move

leading lady *noun* (1874)
: an actress who plays the leading female role (as in a play or movie)

leading man *noun* (1827)
: an actor who plays the leading male role (as in a play or movie)

leading tone *noun* (circa 1889)
: the seventh tone of a diatonic scale — called also *leading note*

lead line \'led-\ *noun* (15th century)
: SOUNDING LINE

lead·man \'led-,man, -mən\ *noun* (1939)
: a worker in charge of other workers

lead monoxide *noun* (circa 1909)
: a yellow to brownish red poisonous compound PbO used in rubber manufacture and glassmaking

lead-off \'led-,òf\ *noun* (circa 1886)
1 : a beginning or leading action
2 : one that leads off
— **leadoff** *adjective*

lead off \'led-\ (1817)
transitive verb
1 : to make a start on : OPEN
2 : to bat first for a baseball team in (an inning)
intransitive verb
: BEGIN; *also* : to come on or perform first

lead on *transitive verb* (1598)
: to entice or induce to proceed in a course especially when unwise or mistaken

lead oxide *noun* (circa 1926)
: any of several oxides of lead; *especially* : LEAD MONOXIDE

lead pencil \'led-\ *noun* (1688)
: a pencil using graphite as the marking material

lead-pipe \'led-'pīp\ *adjective* (1898)
: CERTAIN, GUARANTEED ⟨a *lead-pipe* cinch⟩

lead-plant \'led-,plant\ *noun* (circa 1833)

: a leguminous shrub (*Amorpha canescens*) of the western U.S. that has hoary pinnate leaves and bears dull-colored racemose flowers

lead poisoning *noun* (circa 1842)
: chronic intoxication that is produced by the absorption of lead into the system and is characterized by severe colicky pains, a dark line along the gums, and local muscular paralysis

lead-screw \'led-,skrü\ *noun* (circa 1889)
: a threaded rod on which a mechanism travels and can be positioned precisely

leads·man \'ledz-mən\ *noun* (1857)
: a man who uses a sounding lead to determine depth of water

lead sulfide *noun* (circa 1898)
: an insoluble black compound PbS that occurs naturally as galena and is used in photoconductive cells

lead time \'led-\ *noun* (1944)
: the time between the beginning of a process or project and the appearance of its results

lead-up \'led-,əp\ *noun* (1942)
: something that leads up to or prepares the way for something else

lead up \'led-\ *intransitive verb* (1861)
1 : to prepare the way
2 : to make a gradual or indirect approach to a topic

lead·work \'led-,wərk\ *noun* (1641)
: articles made of or work done in lead

leady \'le-dē\ *adjective* **lead·i·er; -est** (14th century)
: containing or resembling lead

¹**leaf** \'lēf\ *noun, plural* **leaves** \'lēvz\ *also* **leafs** \'lēfs\ *often attributive* [Middle English *leef*, from Old English *lēaf;* akin to Old High German *loub* leaf] (before 12th century)
1 a (1) : a lateral outgrowth from a plant stem that is typically a flattened expanded variably shaped greenish organ, constitutes a unit of the foliage, and functions primarily in food manufacture by photosynthesis (2) : a modified leaf primarily engaged in functions other than food manufacture **b** (1) : FOLIAGE ⟨trees in full *leaf*⟩ (2) : the leaves of a plant as an article of commerce
2 : something suggestive of a leaf: as **a** : a part of a book or folded sheet containing a page on each side **b** (1) : a part (as of window shutters, folding doors, or gates) that slides or is hinged (2) : the movable parts of a table top **c** (1) : a thin sheet or plate of any substance : LAMINA (2) : metal (as gold or silver) in sheets usually thinner than foil (3) : one of the plates of a leaf spring
— **leaf·less** \'lēf-ləs\ *adjective*
— **leaf·like** \'lēf-,līk\ *adjective*

²**leaf** (1611)
intransitive verb
1 : to shoot out or produce leaves
2 : to turn over pages ⟨*leaf* through a book⟩

forms of leaf 1a(1): **1** needle-shaped, **2** linear, **3** lanceolate, **4** elliptical, **5** ensiform, **6** oblong, **7** oblanceolate with acuminate tip, **8** ovate with acute tip, **9** obovate, **10** spatulate, **11** fiddle-shaped, **12** cuneate, **13** deltoid, **14** cordate, **15** reniform, **16** orbiculate, **17** runcinate, **18** lyrate, **19** peltate, **20** hastate, **21** sagittate, **22** odd-pinnate, **23** abruptly pinnate, **24** trifoliolate, **25, 26** palmate

transitive verb
: to turn over the pages of
leaf·age \ˈlē-fij\ *noun* (1599)
1 : FOLIAGE 2
2 : the representation of leafage (as in architecture)
leaf bud *noun* (1664)
: a bud that develops into a leafy shoot and does not produce flowers
leaf butterfly *noun* (1882)
: any of a genus (*Kallima*) of nymphalid butterflies of southern Asia and the East Indies that mimic leaves
leaf curl *noun* (1899)
: a plant disease caused by a fungus (genus *Taphrina*) or virus and characterized by curling of leaves; *especially* : PEACH LEAF CURL
leafed \ˈlēft\ *adjective* (1552)
: LEAVED
leaf fat *noun* (circa 1725)
: the fat that lines the abdominal cavity and encloses the kidneys; *especially* : that of a hog used in the manufacture of lard
leaf·hop·per \ˈlēf-ˌhä-pər\ *noun* (1852)
: any of a family (Cicadellidae) of small leaping homopterous insects that suck the juices of plants
leaf lard *noun* (circa 1847)
: high-quality lard made from leaf fat
¹leaf·let \ˈlēf-lət\ *noun* (1787)
1 a : one of the divisions of a compound leaf **b** : a small or young foliage leaf
2 : a leaflike organ or part
3 : a usually folded printed sheet intended for free distribution
²leaflet *verb* **-let·ed** *or* **-let·ted; -let·ing** *or* **-let·ting** (1962)
intransitive verb
: to hand out leaflets
transitive verb
: to hand out leaflets to
— **leaf·le·teer** \ˌlēf-lə-ˈtir\ *noun*
leaf miner *noun* (1830)
: any of various small insects (as moths or dipteran flies) that in the larval stages burrow in and eat the parenchyma of leaves
leaf mold *noun* (1845)
1 : a compost or layer composed chiefly of decayed vegetable matter
2 : a mold or mildew that affects foliage
leaf roll *noun* (1916)
: a virus disease of the potato that is transmitted by aphids and is characterized by an upward rolling of the leaf margins, smaller tubers, and netlike necrotic areas in the phloem
leaf roller *noun* (1830)
: any of various lepidopterans whose larvae make a nest by rolling up plant leaves
leaf rust *noun* (1865)
: a rust disease of plants and especially of wheat that affects primarily the leaves
leaf scar *noun* (1835)
: the mark left on a stem after a leaf falls
leaf scorch *noun* (circa 1909)
: any of various plant diseases characterized by a burned or scorched appearance of the foliage
leaf spot *noun* (circa 1895)
: any of various plant diseases characterized by discolored often circular spots on the leaves
leaf spring *noun* (circa 1893)
: a spring made of superposed strips or leaves
leaf·stalk \ˈlēf-ˌstȯk\ *noun* (circa 1776)
: PETIOLE
leaf trace *noun* [³*trace*] (1875)
: a trace associated with a leaf
leafy \ˈlē-fē\ *adjective* **leaf·i·er; -est** (15th century)
1 a : furnished with or abounding in leaves ⟨*leafy* woodlands⟩ **b** : having broad-bladed leaves ⟨mosses, grasses, and *leafy* plants⟩ **c** : consisting chiefly of leaves ⟨*leafy* vegetables⟩
2 : resembling a leaf; *specifically* : LAMINATE
leafy liverwort *noun* (1922)

: any of an order (Jungermanniales) of usually epiphytic liverworts with a leafy gametophyte that has one ventral and two dorsal rows of leaves on the stem
leafy spurge *noun* (circa 1889)
: a tall perennial European herb (*Euphorbia esula*) that is naturalized in the northern U.S. and Canada
¹league \ˈlēg\ *noun* [Middle English *leuge, lege,* from Late Latin *leuga*] (14th century)
1 : any of various units of distance from about 2.4 to 4.6 statute miles (3.9 to 7.4 kilometers)
2 : a square league
²league *noun* [Middle English (Scots) *ligg,* from Middle French *ligue,* from Old Italian *liga,* from *ligare* to bind, from Latin — more at LIGATURE] (15th century)
1 a : an association of nations or other political entities for a common purpose **b** (1) : an association of persons or groups united by common interests or goals (2) : a group of sports teams that regularly play one another **c** : an informal alliance
2 : CLASS, CATEGORY
³league *verb* **leagued; leagu·ing** (1604)
transitive verb
: to unite in a league
intransitive verb
: to form a league
¹lea·guer \ˈlē-gər\ *noun* [Dutch *leger;* akin to Old High German *legar* bed — more at LAIR] (1577)
1 : a military camp
2 : SIEGE
²leaguer *transitive verb* (circa 1720)
archaic : BESIEGE, BELEAGUER
³leagu·er \ˈlē-gər\ *noun* [²*league*] (1591)
: a member of a league
¹leak \ˈlēk\ *verb* [Middle English *leken,* from Old Norse *leka;* akin to Old English *leccan* to moisten, Middle Irish *legaid* it melts] (14th century)
intransitive verb
1 a : to enter or escape through an opening usually by a fault or mistake ⟨fumes *leak* in⟩ **b** : to let a substance or light in or out through an opening
2 a : to become known despite efforts at concealment **b** : to be the source of an information leak
transitive verb
1 : to permit to enter or escape through or as if through a leak
2 : to give out (information) surreptitiously ⟨*leaked* the story to the press⟩
— **leak·er** \ˈlē-kər\ *noun*
²leak *noun* (15th century)
1 a : a crack or hole that usually by mistake admits or lets escape **b** : something that permits the admission or escape of something else usually with prejudicial effect
2 : the act, process, or an instance of leaking
3 : an act of urinating — used especially in the phrase *take a leak; sometimes considered vulgar*
— **leak·proof** \ˈlēk-ˌprüf\ *adjective*
leak·age \ˈlē-kij\ *noun* (15th century)
1 a : the act or process or an instance of leaking **b** : loss of electricity especially due to faulty insulation
2 : something or the amount that leaks
leaky \ˈlē-kē\ *adjective* **leak·i·er; -est** (15th century)
: permitting fluid to leak in or out
— **leak·i·ly** \-kə-lē\ *adverb*
— **leak·i·ness** \-kē-nəs\ *noun*
leal \ˈlē(ə)l\ *adjective* [Middle English *leel,* from Middle French *leial, leel* — more at LOYAL] (14th century)
chiefly Scottish : LOYAL, TRUE
— **leal·ly** \ˈlē-ə(l)-lē, ˈlēl-lē\ *adverb*
¹lean \ˈlēn\ *verb* **leaned** \ˈlēnd, *chiefly British* ˈlent\; **lean·ing** \ˈlē-niŋ\ [Middle English *lenen,* from Old English *hleonian;* akin to Old High German *hlinēn* to lean, Greek *klinein,* Latin *clinare*] (before 12th century)

intransitive verb
1 a : to incline, deviate, or bend from a vertical position **b** : to cast one's weight to one side for support
2 : to rely for support or inspiration
3 : to incline in opinion, taste, or desire
transitive verb
: to cause to lean : INCLINE
— **lean on** : to apply pressure to
²lean *noun* (1776)
: the act or an instance of leaning : INCLINATION
³lean *adjective* [Middle English *lene,* from Old English *hlæne*] (before 12th century)
1 a : lacking or deficient in flesh **b** : containing little or no fat
2 : lacking richness, sufficiency, or productiveness
3 : deficient in an essential or important quality or ingredient: as **a** *of ore* : containing little valuable mineral **b** : low in combustible component — used especially of fuel mixtures
4 : characterized by economy (as of style, expression, or operation) ☆
— **lean·ly** *adverb*
— **lean·ness** \ˈlēn-nəs\ *noun*
⁴lean *transitive verb* (before 12th century)
: to make lean
⁵lean *noun* (15th century)
: the part of meat that consists principally of lean muscle
Le·an·der \lē-ˈan-dər\ *noun* [Latin, from Greek *Leandros*]
: a youth in Greek mythology who swims the Hellespont nightly to visit Hero and who ultimately drowns in one of the crossings
lean·ing \ˈlē-niŋ\ *noun* (15th century)
: a definite but not decisive attraction or tendency — often used in plural ☆
leant \ˈlent\ *chiefly British past of* LEAN
¹lean-to \ˈlēn-ˌtü\ *noun, plural* **lean-tos** \-ˌtüz\ (15th century)

\ə\ abut \ᵊ\ kitten \ər\ further \a\ ash \ā\ ace
\ä\ mop, mar \au̇\ out \ch\ chin \e\ bet \ē\ easy
\g\ go \i\ hit \ī\ ice \j\ job \ŋ\ sing \ō\ go
\o̍\ law \ȯi\ boy \th\ thin \t͟h\ the \ü\ loot \u̇\ foot
\y\ yet \zh\ vision *see also* Guide to Pronunciation

1 : a wing or extension of a building having a lean-to roof
2 : a rough shed or shelter with a lean-to roof
²**lean–to** *adjective* (1649)
: having only one slope or pitch ⟨*lean-to* roof⟩
— see ROOF illustration
¹**leap** \'lēp\ *verb* **leaped** *or* **leapt** \'lept *also* 'lēpt\; **leap·ing** \'lē-piŋ\ [Middle English *lepen,* from Old English *hlēapan;* akin to Old High German *hlouffan* to run] (before 12th century)
intransitive verb
1 : to spring free from or as if from the ground : JUMP ⟨*leap* over a fence⟩ ⟨a fish *leaps* out of the water⟩
2 a : to pass abruptly from one state or topic to another **b :** to act precipitately ⟨*leaped* at the chance⟩
transitive verb
: to pass over by leaping
— **leap·er** \'lē-pər\ *noun*
²**leap** *noun* (before 12th century)
1 a : an act of leaping : SPRING, BOUND **b** (1) **:** a place leaped over or from (2) **:** the distance covered by a leap
2 a : a sudden passage or transition ⟨a great *leap* forward⟩ **b :** a choice made in an area of ultimate concern ⟨a *leap* of faith⟩
— **by leaps and bounds :** with extraordinary rapidity
¹**leap·frog** \'lep-ˌfrog, -ˌfräg\ *noun* (1599)
: a game in which one player bends down and is vaulted over by another player
²**leapfrog** *verb* **leap·frogged; leap·frog·ging** (1872)
intransitive verb
: to leap or progress in or as if in leapfrog
transitive verb
1 : to go ahead of (each other) in turn; *specifically* **:** to advance (two military units) by keeping one unit in action while moving the other unit past it to a position farther in front
2 : to evade by or as if by a bypass
leap second *noun* (1971)
: an intercalary second added to Coordinated Universal Time to compensate for the slowing of the earth's rotation and keep Coordinated Universal Time in synchrony with solar time
leap year *noun* (14th century)
1 : a year in the Gregorian calendar containing 366 days with February 29 as the extra day
2 : an intercalary year in any calendar
Lear \'lir\ *noun*
: a legendary king of Britain and hero of Shakespeare's tragedy *King Lear*
learn \'lərn\ *verb* **learned** \'lərnd, 'lərnt\; **learn·ing** [Middle English *lernen,* from Old English *leornian;* akin to Old High German *lernēn* to learn, Old English *last* footprint, Latin *lira* furrow, track] (before 12th century)
transitive verb
1 a (1) **:** to gain knowledge or understanding of or skill in by study, instruction, or experience ⟨*learn* a trade⟩ (2) MEMORIZE ⟨*learn* the lines of a play⟩ **b :** to come to be able ⟨*learn* to dance⟩ **c :** to come to realize ⟨*learned* that honesty paid⟩
2 a *nonstandard* **:** TEACH **b** *obsolete* **:** to inform of something
3 : to come to know : HEAR ⟨we just *learned* that he was ill⟩
intransitive verb
: to acquire knowledge or skill or a behavioral tendency ▢ ◆
synonym see DISCOVER
— **learn·able** \'lər-nə-bəl\ *adjective*
— **learn·er** *noun*
learned *adjective* (14th century)
1 \'lər-nəd\ **:** characterized by or associated with learning : ERUDITE
2 \'lərnd, 'lərnt\ **:** acquired by learning ⟨*learned* behavior⟩
— **learn·ed·ly** \'lər-nəd-lē\ *adverb*
— **learn·ed·ness** \-nəd-nəs\ *noun*
learn·ing *noun* (before 12th century)
1 : the act or experience of one that learns

2 : knowledge or skill acquired by instruction or study
3 : modification of a behavioral tendency by experience (as exposure to conditioning)
synonym see KNOWLEDGE
learning curve *noun* (1922)
: a curve plotting performance against practice; *especially* **:** one graphing decline in unit costs with cumulative output
learning disabled *adjective* (1973)
: having difficulty in learning a basic scholastic skill because of a disorder (as dyslexia or attention deficit disorder) that interferes with the learning process
— **learning disability** *noun*
learnt \'lərnt\ *chiefly British past and past participle of* LEARN
leary *variant of* LEERY
¹**lease** \'lēs\ *noun* [Middle English *les,* from Anglo-French, from *lesser*] (14th century)
1 : a contract by which one conveys real estate, equipment, or facilities for a specified term and for a specified rent; *also* **:** the act of such conveyance or the term for which it is made
2 : a piece of land or property that is leased
3 : a continuance or opportunity for continuance ⟨a new *lease* on life⟩
²**lease** *transitive verb* **leased; leas·ing** [Anglo-French *lesser,* from Old French *laissier* to let go, from Latin *laxare* to loosen, from *laxus* slack — more at SLACK] (circa 1570)
1 : to grant by lease
2 : to hold under a lease
synonym see HIRE
— **leas·able** \'lē-sə-bəl\ *adjective*
lease·back \'lēs-ˌbak\ *noun* (1947)
: the sale of property with the understanding that the seller can lease it from the new owner
lease·hold \'lēs-ˌhōld\ *noun* (1720)
1 : a tenure by lease
2 : property held by lease
— **lease·hold·er** *noun*
leash \'lēsh\ *noun* [Middle English *lees, leshe,* from Middle French *laisse,* from Old French *laissier*] (14th century)
1 a : a line for leading or restraining an animal **b :** something that restrains
2 a : a set of three animals (as greyhounds, foxes, bucks, or hares) **b :** a set of three
— **leash** *transitive verb*
leash law *noun* (1966)
: an ordinance requiring dogs to be restrained when not confined to their owner's property
leas·ing \'lē-siŋ, -ziŋ\ *noun* [Middle English *lesing,* from Old English *lēasung,* from *lēasian* to lie, from *lēas* false] (before 12th century)
archaic **:** the act of lying; *also* **:** LIE, FALSEHOOD
¹**least** \'lēst\ *adjective superlative of* ¹LITTLE [Middle English *leest,* from Old English *lǣst,* superlative of *lǣssa* less] (before 12th century)
1 : lowest in importance or position
2 a : smallest in size or degree **b :** being a member of a kind distinguished by diminutive size ⟨*least* bittern⟩ **c :** smallest possible : SLIGHTEST
²**least** *noun* (12th century)
: one that is least
— **at least 1 :** at the minimum **2 :** in any case
³**least** *adverb superlative of* ²LITTLE (13th century)
: in the smallest or lowest degree
— **least of all :** especially not ⟨no one, *least of all* the children, paid attention⟩
least common denominator *noun* (1875)
: the least common multiple of two or more denominators
least common multiple *noun* (1823)
1 : the smallest common multiple of two or more numbers
2 : the common multiple of lowest degree of two or more polynomials

least squares *noun plural* (1825)
: a method of fitting a curve to a set of points representing statistical data in such a way that the sum of the squares of the distances of the points from the curve is a minimum
least·ways \'lēst-ˌwāz\ *adverb* (14th century)
dialect **:** at least
least·wise \-ˌwīz\ *adverb* (15th century)
: at least
¹**leath·er** \'le-thər\ *noun* [Middle English *lether,* from Old English *lether-;* akin to Old High German *leder* leather, Old Irish *lethar*] (13th century)
1 : animal skin dressed for use
2 : the flap of the ear of a dog — see DOG illustration
3 : something wholly or partly made of leather
— **leather** *adjective*
— **leath·er·like** \-ˌlīk\ *adjective*
²**leather** *transitive verb* **leath·ered; leath·er·ing** \'le-thə-riŋ, 'leth-riŋ\ (13th century)
1 : to cover with leather
2 : to beat with a strap : THRASH
leath·er·back \'le-thər-ˌbak\ *noun* (circa 1855)
: the largest existing sea turtle (*Dermochelys coriacea*) distinguished by its flexible carapace composed of a mosaic of small bones embedded in a thick leathery skin

leatherback

leath·er·ette \ˌle-thə-'ret\ *noun, often attributive* [from *Leatherette,* a trademark] (circa 1879)
: simulated leather
leath·er·leaf \'le-thər-ˌlēf\ *noun* (circa 1818)

: a north temperate ericaceous bog shrub (*Chamaedaphne calyculata*) with evergreen coriaceous leaves and small white cylindrical flowers

leath·ern \'le-thərn\ *adjective* (before 12th century)
: made of, consisting of, or resembling leather

leath·er·neck \-thər-,nek\ *noun* [from the leather collar formerly part of the uniform] (circa 1914)
: a member of the U.S. Marine Corps

leath·er·wood \'le-thər-,wu̇d\ *noun* (1743)
1 : a small tree (*Dirca palustris*) of the mezereon family with pliant stems and yellow flowers
2 : a small tree (*Cyrilla racemiflora*) of the southeastern U.S. related to the titi

leath·ery \'le-thə-rē, 'leth-rē\ *adjective* (circa 1552)
: resembling leather in appearance or consistency

¹leave \'lēv\ *verb* **left** \'left\; **leav·ing** [Middle English *leven*, from Old English *lǣfan;* akin to Old High German ver*leiben* to leave, Old English be*līfan* to be left over, and perhaps to Lithuanian *lipti* to adhere, Greek *lipos* grease, fat] (before 12th century)
transitive verb
1 a (1) : BEQUEATH, DEVISE ⟨*left* a fortune to his son⟩ (2) : to have remaining after one's death ⟨*leaves* a widow and two children⟩ **b** : to cause to remain as a trace or aftereffect ⟨oil *leaves* a stain⟩ ⟨the wound *left* an ugly scar⟩
2 a : to cause or allow to be or remain in a specified condition ⟨*leave* the door open⟩ ⟨his manner *left* me cold⟩ **b** : to fail to include or take along ⟨*left* the notes at home⟩ ⟨the movie *leaves* a lot out⟩ **c** : to have as a remainder ⟨4 from 7 *leaves* 3⟩ **d** : to permit to be or remain subject to another's action or control ⟨just *leave* everything to me⟩ **e** : LET **f** : to cause or allow to be or remain available ⟨*leave* room for expansion⟩ ⟨wanted to *leave* himself an out⟩
3 a : to go away from : DEPART ⟨*leave* the room⟩ **b** : DESERT, ABANDON ⟨*left* his wife⟩ **c** : to terminate association with : withdraw from ⟨*left* school before graduation⟩
4 : to put, deposit, or deliver before or in the process of departing ⟨someone *left* a package for you⟩
intransitive verb
: SET OUT, DEPART □
— **leav·er** *noun*
— **leave alone** : to refrain from bothering or using

²leave *noun* [Middle English *leve,* from Old English *lēaf;* akin to Middle High German *loube* permission, Old English a*lȳfan* to allow — more at BELIEVE] (before 12th century)
1 a : permission to do something **b** : authorized especially extended absence from duty or employment
2 : an act of leaving : DEPARTURE

³leave *intransitive verb* **leaved; leav·ing** [Middle English *leven,* from *leef* leaf] (14th century)
: LEAF

leaved *adjective* (13th century)
: having leaves — usually used in combination ⟨palmate-*leaved*⟩ ⟨a four-*leaved* clover⟩

¹leav·en \'le-vən\ *noun* [Middle English *levain,* from Middle French, from (assumed) Vulgar Latin *levamen,* from Latin *levare* to raise — more at LEVER] (14th century)
1 a : a substance (as yeast) used to produce fermentation in dough or a liquid; *especially* : SOURDOUGH **b** : a material (as baking powder) used to produce a gas that lightens dough or batter
2 : something that modifies or lightens

²leaven *transitive verb* **leav·ened; leav·en·ing** \'lev-niŋ, 'le-və-\ (15th century)
1 : to raise (as bread) with a leaven

2 : to mingle or permeate with some modifying, alleviating, or vivifying element
synonym see INFUSE

leavening *noun* (circa 1626)
: a leavening agent : LEAVEN

leave of absence (1771)
1 : permission to be absent from duty or employment
2 : LEAVE 1b

leave off *verb* (14th century)
: STOP, CEASE

leaves *plural of* LEAF

leave–tak·ing \'lēv-,tā-kiŋ\ *noun* (14th century)
: DEPARTURE, FAREWELL

leav·ings \'lē-viŋz\ *noun plural* (14th century)
: REMNANTS, RESIDUE

le·bens·raum \'lā-bənz-,rau̇m, -bən(t)s-\ *noun, often capitalized* [German, from *Leben* living, life + *Raum* space] (1905)
1 : territory believed especially by Nazis to be necessary for national existence or economic self-sufficiency
2 : space required for life, growth, or activity

¹lech \'lech\ *noun* (circa 1830)
1 : LETCH, LUST
2 : LECHER

²lech *intransitive verb* (1911)
: LUST

lech·er \'le-chər\ *noun* [Middle English *lechour,* from Old French *lecheor,* from *lechier* to lick, live in debauchery, of Germanic origin; akin to Old High German *leckōn* to lick — more at LICK] (13th century)
: a man who engages in lechery

lech·er·ous \'le-chə-rəs, 'lech-rəs\ *adjective* (14th century)
: given to or suggestive of lechery
— **lech·er·ous·ly** *adverb*
— **lech·er·ous·ness** *noun*

lech·ery \-rē\ *noun* (13th century)
: inordinate indulgence in sexual activity : LASCIVIOUSNESS

le·chwe \'lēch-wē\ *noun, plural* **lechwe** *or* **lechwes** [probably from Sesotho *lets'a*] (1857)
: an antelope (*Kobus leche*) that inhabits wetlands of southern Africa; *also* : a related antelope (*K. megaceros*) of the Nile Valley in Sudan and Ethiopia

lec·i·thin \'le-sə-thən\ *noun* [International Scientific Vocabulary, from Greek *lekithos* yolk of an egg] (1861)
: any of several waxy hygroscopic phospholipids that are widely distributed in animals and plants, form colloidal solutions in water, and have emulsifying, wetting, and antioxidant properties; *also* : a mixture of or substance rich in lecithins

lec·i·thin·ase \-thə-,nās, -,nāz\ *noun* (1910)
: PHOSPHOLIPASE

lec·tern \'lek-tərn\ *noun* [Middle English *lettorne,* from Middle French *letrun,* from Medieval Latin *lectorinum,* from Latin *lector* reader, from *legere* to read — more at LEGEND] (14th century)
: a stand used to support a book in a convenient position for a standing reader; *especially* : one from which scripture lessons are read in a church service
usage see PODIUM

lec·tion \'lek-shən\ *noun* [Late Latin *lection-, lectio,* from Latin, act of reading — more at LESSON] (1608)
1 : a liturgical lesson for a particular day
2 [New Latin *lection-, lectio,* from Latin] : a variant reading of a text

lec·tion·ary \'lek-shə-,ner-ē\ *noun, plural* **-ar·ies** (1780)
: a book or list of lections for the church year

lec·tor \'lek-tər, -,tȯr\ *noun* [Middle English, from Late Latin, reader of the lessons in a church service, from Latin, reader, from *legere*] (14th century)
: one who assists at a worship service chiefly by reading a lesson

lec·to·type \'lek-tə-,tīp\ *noun* [Greek *lektos* chosen (from *legein* to gather, choose) + English *type* — more at LEGEND] (circa 1905)
: a specimen chosen as the type of a species or subspecies if the author of the name fails to designate a type

¹lec·ture \'lek-chər, -shər\ *noun* [Middle English, act of reading, from Late Latin *lectura,* from Latin *lectus,* past participle of *legere*] (15th century)
1 : a discourse given before an audience or class especially for instruction
2 : a formal reproof
— **lec·ture·ship** \-,ship\ *noun*

²lecture *verb* **lec·tured; lec·tur·ing** \'lek-chə-riŋ, 'lek-shriŋ\ (circa 1590)
intransitive verb
: to deliver a lecture or a course of lectures
transitive verb
1 : to deliver a lecture to
2 : to reprove formally
— **lec·tur·er** \-chər-ər, -shrər\ *noun*

led *past and past participle of* LEAD

LED \,el-(,)ē-'dē\ *noun* [*l*ight-*e*mitting *d*iode] (1968)
: a semiconductor diode that emits light when a voltage is applied to it and that is used in an electronic display (as for a digital watch)

Le·da \'lē-də\ *noun* [Latin, from Greek *Lēda*]
: the mother of Clytemnestra and Castor by her husband Tyndareus and of Helen and Pollux by Zeus who comes to her in the form of a swan

le·der·ho·sen \'lā-dər-,hō-z³n\ *noun plural* [German, from Middle High German *lederhose,* from *leder* leather + *hose* trousers] (1936)
: leather shorts often with suspenders worn especially in Bavaria

ledge \'lej\ *noun* [Middle English *legge* bar of a gate] (1535)
1 : a raised or projecting edge or molding intended to protect or check ⟨a window *ledge*⟩
2 : an underwater ridge or reef especially near the shore
3 a : a narrow flat surface or shelf; *especially* : one that projects from a wall of rock **b** : rock that is solid or continuous enough to form ledges : BEDROCK ⟨the field was full of *ledge*⟩
4 : LODE, VEIN
— **ledgy** \'le-jē\ *adjective*

led·ger \'le-jər\ *noun* [Middle English *legger,* probably from *leyen, leggen* to lay] (1588)
1 : a book containing accounts to which debits and credits are posted from books of original entry
2 : a horizontal timber secured to the uprights of scaffolding to support the putlog

ledger line *noun* (1700)
: a short line added above or below a musical staff to extend its range

¹lee \'lē\ *noun* [Middle English, from Old English *hlēo;* perhaps akin to Old High German *lāo* lukewarm, Latin *calēre* to be warm] (before 12th century)
1 : protecting shelter
2 : the side (as of a ship) that is sheltered from the wind

²lee *adjective* (15th century)

□ **USAGE**
leave *Leave* (sense 2e) with the infinitive but without *to* (*leave* it be) is a mostly spoken idiom used in writing especially for humorous effect. It is not often criticized in British English, but American commentators, adhering to an opinion first expressed in 1881, still dislike it.

\ə\ **abut** \ᵊ\ **kitten** \ər\ **further** \a\ **ash** \ā\ **ace**
\ä\ **mop, mar** \au̇\ **out** \ch\ **chin** \e\ **bet** \ē\ **easy**
\g\ **go** \i\ **hit** \ī\ **ice** \j\ **job** \ŋ\ **sing** \ō\ **go**
\ȯ\ **law** \ȯi\ **boy** \th\ **thin** \t͟h\ **the** \ü\ **loot** \u̇\ **foot**
\y\ **yet** \zh\ **vision** *see also* Guide to Pronunciation

1 : of or relating to the side sheltered from the wind — compare WEATHER
2 : facing in the direction of motion of an overriding glacier — used especially of a hillside

lee·board \'lē-ˌbōrd, -ˌbȯrd\ *noun* (1691)
: either of the wood or metal planes attached outside the hull of a sailboat to prevent leeway

¹leech \'lēch\ *noun* [Middle English *leche*, from Old English *lǣce*; akin to Old High German *lāhhi* physician] (before 12th century)
1 *archaic* : PHYSICIAN, SURGEON
2 [from its former use by physicians for bleeding patients] : any of numerous carnivorous or bloodsucking usually freshwater annelid worms (class Hirudinea) that have typically a flattened lanceolate segmented body with a sucker at each end
3 : a hanger-on who seeks advantage or gain
synonym see PARASITE
— **leech·like** \-ˌlīk\ *adjective*

²leech (1828)
transitive verb
1 : to bleed by the use of leeches
2 : to drain the substance of : EXHAUST
intransitive verb
: to attach oneself to a person as a leech

³leech *noun* [Middle English *leche*, from Middle Low German *līk* boltrope — more at LIGATURE] (15th century)
1 : either vertical edge of a square sail
2 : the after edge of a fore-and-aft sail

leek \'lēk\ *noun* [Middle English, from Old English *lēac*; akin to Old High German *louh* leek] (before 12th century)
: a biennial garden herb (*Allium ampeloprasum porrum*) of the lily family grown for its mildly pungent succulent linear leaves and especially for its thick cylindrical stalk

leek

¹leer \'lir\ *intransitive verb* [probably from obsolete *leer* cheek] (1530)
: to cast a sidelong glance; *especially* : to give a leer
— **leer·ing·ly** \-iŋ-lē\ *adverb*

²leer *noun* (1598)
: a lascivious, knowing, or wanton look

leery \'lir-ē\ *adjective* (1718)
: SUSPICIOUS, WARY — often used with *of*

lees \'lēz\ *noun plural* [Middle English *lie*, from Middle French, from Medieval Latin *lia*] (14th century)
: the sediment of a liquor (as wine) during fermentation and aging : DREGS

Lee's Birthday \'lēz-\ *noun* [Robert E. *Lee*] (1910)
: January 19 or the third Monday in January observed as a legal holiday in many southern states

lee shore *noun* (circa 1580)
: a shore lying off a ship's leeward side and constituting a severe danger in storm

¹lee·ward \'lē-wərd, *especially nautical* 'lü-ərd\ *noun* (1549)
: the lee side

²leeward *adjective* (1666)
: being in or facing the direction toward which the wind is blowing; *also* : being the side opposite the windward

lee·way \'lē-ˌwā\ *noun* (1669)
1 a : off-course lateral movement of a ship when under way **b :** the angle between the heading and the track of an airplane
2 : an allowable margin of freedom or variation : TOLERANCE

¹left \'left\ *adjective* [Middle English, from Old English, weak; akin to Middle Low German *lucht* left; from the left hand's being the weaker in most individuals] (13th century)
1 a : of, relating to, situated on, or being the side of the body in which the heart is mostly

located **b :** located nearer to the left hand than to the right **c (1) :** located on the left of an observer facing in the same direction as the object specified ⟨stage *left*⟩ **(2) :** located on the left when facing downstream ⟨the *left* bank of a river⟩
2 *often capitalized* : of, adhering to, or constituted by the left especially in politics
— **left** *adverb*

²left *noun* (13th century)
1 a : the left hand **b :** the location or direction of the left side **c :** the part on the left side
2 a : LEFT FIELD **b :** a blow struck with the left fist
3 *often capitalized* **a :** the part of a legislative chamber located to the left of the presiding officer **b :** the members of a continental European legislative body occupying the left as a result of holding more radical political views than other members
4 *capitalized* **a :** those professing views usually characterized by desire to reform or overthrow the established order especially in politics and usually advocating change in the name of the greater freedom or well-being of the common man **b :** a radical as distinguished from a conservative position

³left *past and past participle of* LEAVE

left–bank *adjective, often L&B capitalized* (1929)
: of, relating to, situated in, or characteristic of the bohemian district of Paris on the left bank of the Seine River

left field *noun* (1857)
1 : the position of the player defending left field
2 : the part of the baseball outfield to the left looking out from the plate
3 : a state or position far from the mainstream (as of prevailing opinion) ⟨they were really out in *left field* with that idea⟩ : a source of the unexpected or illogical ⟨that question came out of *left field*⟩
— **left fielder** *noun*

left–hand \'left-'hand, 'lef-'tand\ *adjective* (1598)
1 : situated on the left
2 : LEFT-HANDED

left–hand·ed \-'han-dəd, -'tan-\ *adjective* (14th century)
1 : using the left hand habitually or more easily than the right; *also* : swinging from left to right ⟨a *left-handed* batter⟩
2 : relating to, designed for, or done with the left hand
3 : MORGANATIC
4 a : CLUMSY, AWKWARD **b :** INSINCERE, BACKHANDED, DUBIOUS ⟨a *left-handed* compliment⟩
5 a : having a direction contrary to that of the hands of a watch viewed from in front : COUNTERCLOCKWISE **b :** having a spiral structure or form that ascends or advances to the left ⟨a *left-handed* rope⟩
— **left–handed** *adverb*
— **left–hand·ed·ly** *adverb*
— **left–hand·ed·ness** *noun*

left–hand·er \-'han-dər, -'tan-\ *noun* (1881)
: a left-handed person

left·ish \'lef-tish\ *adjective* (1934)
: showing leftist tendencies

left·ism \'lef-ˌti-zəm\ *noun* (1920)
1 : the principles and views of the Left; *also* : the movement embodying these principles
2 : advocacy of or adherence to the doctrines of the Left
— **left·ist** \-tist\ *noun or adjective*

¹left·over \'left-ˌō-vər\ *noun* (1891)
1 : something that remains unused or unconsumed; *especially* : leftover food served at a later meal — usually used in plural
2 : an anachronistic survival : VESTIGE

²left·over *adjective* (1897)
: not consumed or used ⟨*leftover* food⟩ ⟨*leftover* space⟩

left shoulder arms *noun* [from the command *left shoulder arms!*] (circa 1918)

: a position in the manual of arms in which the butt of the rifle is held in the left hand with the barrel resting on the left shoulder; *also* : a command to assume this position

left·ward \'left-wərd\ *adjective or adverb* (15th century)
: being toward or on the left

left wing *noun* (1884)
1 : the leftist division of a group (as a political party)
2 : LEFT 4a
— **left–wing** *adjective*
— **left–wing·er** \'left-'wiŋ-ər\ *noun*

lefty \'lef-tē\ *noun, plural* **left·ies** (1886)
1 : LEFT-HANDER
2 : an advocate of leftism
— **lefty** *adjective*

¹leg \'leg *also* 'lāg\ *noun* [Middle English, from Old Norse *leggr*] (14th century)
1 : a limb of an animal used especially for supporting the body and for walking: as **a (1) :** one of the paired vertebrate limbs that in bipeds extend from the top of the thigh to the foot **(2) :** the part of such a limb between the knee and foot **b :** the back half of a hindquarter of a meat animal **c :** one of the rather generalized segmental appendages of an arthropod used in walking and crawling
2 a : a pole or bar serving as a support or prop ⟨the *legs* of a tripod⟩ **b :** a branch of a forked or jointed object ⟨the *legs* of a compass⟩
3 a : the part of an article of clothing that covers the leg **b :** the part of the upper (as of a boot) that extends above the ankle
4 : OBEISANCE, BOW — used chiefly in the phrase *to make a leg*
5 : a side of a right triangle that is not the hypotenuse; *also* : a side of an isosceles triangle that is not the base
6 a : the course and distance sailed by a boat on a single tack **b :** a portion of a trip : STAGE **c :** one section of a relay race **d :** one of several events or games necessary to be won to decide a competition ⟨won the first two *legs* of horse racing's Triple Crown⟩
7 : a branch or part of an object or system
— **leg·less** \-ləs\ *adjective*
— **a leg to stand on** : SUPPORT; *especially* : a basis for one's position in a controversy
— **on one's last legs** : at or near the end of one's resources : on the verge of failure, exhaustion, or ruin

²leg *intransitive verb* **legged; leg·ging** (1601)
: to use the legs in walking; *especially* : RUN

leg·a·cy \'le-gə-sē\ *noun, plural* **-cies** [Middle English *legacie* office of a legate, bequest, from Middle French or Medieval Latin; Middle French, office of a legate, from Medieval Latin *legatia*, from Latin *legatus*] (15th century)
1 : a gift by will especially of money or other personal property : BEQUEST
2 : something transmitted by or received from an ancestor or predecessor or from the past ⟨the *legacy* of the ancient philosophers⟩

¹le·gal \'lē-gəl\ *adjective* [Middle French, from Latin *legalis*, from *leg-, lex* law] (circa 1500)
1 : of or relating to law
2 a : deriving authority from or founded on law : DE JURE **b :** having a formal status derived from law often without a basis in actual fact : TITULAR ⟨a corporation is a *legal* but not a real person⟩ **c :** established by law; *especially* : STATUTORY
3 : conforming to or permitted by law or established rules
4 : recognized or made effective by a court of law as distinguished from a court of equity
5 : of, relating to, or having the characteristics of the profession of law or of one of its members
6 : created by the constructions of the law ⟨a *legal* fiction⟩
synonym see LAWFUL
— **le·gal·ly** \-gə-lē\ *adverb*

²legal *noun* (1526)
: one that conforms to rules or the law

legal age *noun* (circa 1904)
: the age at which a person enters into full adult legal rights and responsibilities (as of making contracts or wills)

legal aid *noun* (1890)
: aid provided by an organization established especially to serve the legal needs of the poor

legal eagle *noun* (1942)
: LAWYER

le·gal·ese \ˌlē-gə-'lēz, -'lēs\ *noun* (1914)
: the specialized language of the legal profession ⟨replaced *legalese* with plain talk —Steve Weinberg⟩

legal holiday *noun* (1867)
: a holiday established by legal authority and marked by restrictions on work and transaction of official business

le·gal·ise *British variant of* LEGALIZE

le·gal·ism \'lē-gə-ˌli-zəm\ *noun* (1838)
1 : strict, literal, or excessive conformity to the law or to a religious or moral code ⟨the institutionalized *legalism* that restricts free choice⟩
2 : a legal term or rule

le·gal·ist \-list\ *noun* (1646)
1 : an advocate or adherent of moral legalism
2 : one that views things from a legal standpoint; *especially* **:** one that places primary emphasis on legal principles or on the formal structure of governmental institutions
— **le·gal·is·tic** \ˌlē-gə-'lis-tik\ *adjective*
— **le·gal·is·ti·cal·ly** \-ti-k(ə-)lē\ *adverb*

le·gal·i·ty \li-'ga-lə-tē\ *noun, plural* **-ties** (15th century)
1 : attachment to or observance of law
2 : the quality or state of being legal **:** LAWFULNESS
3 *plural* **:** obligations imposed by law

le·gal·ize \'lē-gə-ˌlīz\ *transitive verb* **-ized; -iz·ing** (circa 1716)
: to make legal; *especially* **:** to give legal validity or sanction to
— **le·gal·i·za·tion** \ˌlē-gə-lə-'zā-shən\ *noun*
— **le·gal·iz·er** \'lē-gə-ˌlī-zər\ *noun*

legal pad *noun* (1967)
: a writing tablet of ruled yellow paper that is usually 8.5 by 14 inches (22 by 36 centimeters)

legal reserve *noun* (circa 1902)
: the minimum amount of bank deposits or life insurance company assets required by law to be kept as reserves

legal tender *noun* (1739)
: money that is legally valid for the payment of debts and that must be accepted for that purpose when offered

¹leg·ate \'le-gət\ *noun* [Middle English, from Middle French & Latin; Middle French *legat*, from Latin *legatus* deputy, emissary, from past participle of *legare* to depute, send as emissary, bequeath, from *leg-, lex*] (12th century)
: a usually official emissary
— **leg·ate·ship** \-ˌship\ *noun*

²le·gate \li-'gāt\ *transitive verb* **le·gat·ed; le·gat·ing** [*legatus*, past participle of *legare* to bequeath] (15th century)
: BEQUEATH 1
— **le·ga·tor** \-'gā-tər\ *noun*

leg·a·tee \ˌle-gə-'tē\ *noun* (circa 1688)
: one to whom a legacy is bequeathed or a devise is given

leg·a·tine \'le-gə-ˌtēn, -ˌtīn\ *adjective* (1611)
: of, headed by, or enacted under the authority of a legate

le·ga·tion \li-'gā-shən\ *noun* (14th century)
1 : the sending forth of a legate
2 : a body of deputies sent on a mission; *specifically* **:** a diplomatic mission in a foreign country headed by a minister
3 : the official residence and office of a diplomatic minister in a foreign country

¹le·ga·to \li-'gä-(ˌ)tō\ *adverb or adjective* [Italian, literally, tied] (circa 1811)

: in a manner that is smooth and connected (as between successive tones) — used especially as a direction in music

²legato *noun* (1885)
: a smooth and connected manner of performance (as of music); *also* **:** a passage of music so performed

leg·end \'le-jənd\ *noun* [Middle English *legende*, from Middle French & Medieval Latin; Middle French *legende*, from Medieval Latin *legenda*, from Latin, feminine of *legendus*, gerundive of *legere* to gather, say, read; akin to Greek *legein* to gather, say, *logos* speech, word, reason] (14th century)
1 a : a story coming down from the past; *especially* **:** one popularly regarded as historical although not verifiable **b :** a body of such stories ⟨a place in the *legend* of the frontier⟩ **c :** a popular myth of recent origin **d :** a person or thing that inspires legends **e :** the subject of a legend ⟨its violence was *legend* even in its own time —William Broyles Jr.⟩
2 a : an inscription or title on an object (as a coin) **b :** CAPTION 2b **c :** an explanatory list of the symbols on a map or chart ◇

leg·end·ary \'le-jən-ˌder-ē\ *adjective* (circa 1587)
1 : of, relating to, or characteristic of legend or a legend
2 : WELL-KNOWN, FAMOUS
synonym see FICTITIOUS
— **leg·end·ari·ly** \ˌle-jən-'der-ə-lē\ *adverb*

leg·end·ry \'le-jən-drē\ *noun* (1849)
: a body of legends

leg·er \'le-jər\ *variant of* LEDGER

leg·er·de·main \ˌle-jər-də-'mān\ *noun* [Middle English, from Middle French *leger de main* light of hand] (15th century)
1 : SLEIGHT OF HAND
2 : a display of skill or adroitness

le·ger·i·ty \lə-'jer-ə-tē, le-\ *noun* [Middle French *legereté*, from Old French *leger* light, from (assumed) Vulgar Latin *leviarius*, from Latin *levis* — more at LIGHT] (1561)
: alert facile quickness of mind or body

leger line *noun* (circa 1775)
: LEDGER LINE

leges *plural of* LEX

leg·ged \'le-gəd *also* 'lā-, *British usually* 'legd\ *adjective* (15th century)
: having a leg or legs especially of a specified kind or number — often used in combination ⟨a four-*legged* animal⟩

leg·ging *or* **leg·gin** \'le-gən *also* 'lā-, -gin\ *noun* (1751)
: a covering (as of leather or cloth) for the leg — usually used in plural; *also* **:** TIGHTS

leg·gy \'le-gē *also* 'lā-\ *adjective* **leg·gi·er; -est** (1787)
1 : having disproportionately long legs
2 : having long and attractive legs
3 : SPINDLY — used of a plant
— **leg·gi·ness** \-nəs\ *noun*

leg-hold trap \'leg-ˌhōld-\ *noun* (1973)
: a jawed usually steel trap that is used to hold a wild mammal and operates by springing closed and clamping onto the leg of the animal that steps on it

leg·horn \'leg-ˌhorn; 'le-ˌgorn, -gərn\ *noun* [*Leghorn*, Italy] (1740)
1 a : a fine plaited straw made from an Italian wheat **b :** a hat of this straw
2 : any of a Mediterranean breed of small hardy fowls noted for their large production of white eggs

leg·i·ble \'le-jə-bəl\ *adjective* [Middle English, from Late Latin *legibilis*, from Latin *legere* to read] (14th century)
1 : capable of being read or deciphered **:** PLAIN
2 : capable of being discovered or understood
— **leg·i·bil·i·ty** \ˌle-jə-'bi-lə-tē\ *noun*
— **leg·i·bly** \'le-jə-blē\ *adverb*

¹le·gion \'lē-jən\ *noun* [Middle English, from Old French, from Latin *legion-, legio*, from *legere* to gather — more at LEGEND] (13th century)
1 : the principal unit of the Roman army comprising 3000 to 6000 foot soldiers with cavalry
2 : a large military force; *especially* **:** ARMY 1a
3 : a very large number **:** MULTITUDE
4 : a national association of ex-servicemen

²legion *adjective* (1678)
: MANY, NUMEROUS ⟨the problems are *legion*⟩

¹le·gion·ary \'lē-jə-ˌner-ē\ *adjective* [Latin *legionarius*, from *legion-, legio*] (15th century)
: of, relating to, or constituting a legion

²legionary *noun, plural* **-ar·ies** (1598)
: LEGIONNAIRE

le·gion·naire \ˌlē-jə-'nar, -'ner\ *noun* [French *légionnaire*, from Latin *legionarius*] (1818)
: a member of a legion

Legionnaires' disease \-'narz-, -'nerz-\ *also* **Legionnaire's disease** *noun* [from its first recognized occurrence at an American Legion convention in 1976] (1976)
: a lobar pneumonia caused by a bacterium (*Legionella pneumophila*)

Legion of Honor (1827)
: a French order conferred as a reward for civil or military merit

Legion of Merit (1943)
: a U.S. military decoration awarded for exceptionally meritorious conduct in the performance of outstanding services

leg·is·late \'le-jəs-ˌlāt\ *verb* **-lat·ed; -lat·ing** [back-formation from *legislator*] (1805)
intransitive verb
: to perform the function of legislation; *specifically* **:** to make or enact laws
transitive verb
: to cause, create, provide, or bring about by or as if by legislation

leg·is·la·tion \ˌle-jəs-'lā-shən\ *noun* (circa 1655)
1 : the action of legislating; *specifically* **:** the exercise of the power and function of making rules (as laws) that have the force of authority by virtue of their promulgation by an official organ of a state or other organization
2 : the enactments of a legislator or a legislative body
3 : a matter of business for or under consideration by a legislative body

¹leg·is·la·tive \'le-jəs-ˌlā-tiv, -lə-\ *adjective* (circa 1641)
1 a : having the power or performing the function of legislating **b :** belonging to the branch of government that is charged with

◇ WORD HISTORY
legend The literal meaning of the Latin verb *legere* was "to gather," but it acquired extended senses such as "to pick out (sights or sounds)," "to make one's way over" and finally "to read." In Medieval Latin *legenda*, the gerundive of *legere*, meaning literally "a thing to be read," was used in specific reference to the story of the life of a saint. One of the most popular books of the later Middle Ages was the *Legenda Aurea* ("Golden Legend") of Jacobus de Voragine, a collection of saints' lives that incorporated a generous measure of fanciful material along with fact. When the word was borrowed, via French, into Middle English as *legende*, it continued to be used with specific reference to a saint's story. By the 17th century, however, *legend* had come to be applied to any story handed down from earlier times that, like the traditional saints' lives, was at best unverifiable.

such powers as making laws, levying and collecting taxes, and making financial appropriations — compare EXECUTIVE, JUDICIAL
2 a : of or relating to a legislature ⟨*legislative* committees⟩ **b :** composed of members of a legislature ⟨*legislative* caucus⟩ **c :** created by a legislature especially as distinguished from an executive or judicial body **d :** designed to assist a legislature or its members ⟨a *legislative* research agency⟩
3 : of, concerned with, or created by legislation
— **leg·is·la·tive·ly** *adverb*

²legislative *noun* (1642)
: the body or department exercising the power and function of legislating **:** LEGISLATURE

legislative assembly *noun, often L&A capitalized* (1836)
1 : a bicameral legislature (as in an American state)
2 : the lower house of a bicameral legislature
3 : a unicameral legislature; *especially* **:** one in a Canadian province

legislative council *noun, often L&C capitalized* (1787)
1 : a permanent committee chosen from both houses that meets between sessions of a state legislature to study state problems and plan a legislative program
2 : a unicameral legislature (as in a British colony)
3 : the upper house of a British bicameral legislature

leg·is·la·tor \'le-jəs-ˌlā-tȯr, -ˌlā-tər *also* ˌle-jəs-'lā-ˌtȯr\ *noun* [Latin *legis lator*, literally, proposer of a law, from *legis* (genitive of *lex* law) + *lator* proposer, from *ferre* (past participle *latus*) to carry, propose — more at TOLERATE, BEAR] (1603)
: one that makes laws especially for a political unit; *especially* **:** a member of a legislative body
— **leg·is·la·to·ri·al** \ˌle-jəs-lə-'tȯr-ē-əl, -'tȯr-\ *adjective*
— **leg·is·la·tor·ship** \'le-jəs-ˌlā-tər-ˌship\ *noun*

leg·is·la·ture \'le-jəs-ˌlā-chər *also* ˌle-jəs-\, *British often* 'le-jəs-lə-\ *noun* (circa 1676)
: a body of persons having the power to legislate; *specifically* **:** an organized body having the authority to make laws for a political unit

le·gist \'lē-jist\ *noun* [Middle English, from Middle French *legiste*, from Medieval Latin *legista*, from Latin *leg-, lex*] (15th century)
: a specialist in law; *especially* **:** one learned in Roman or civil law

le·git \li-'jit\ *adjective* (1908)
slang **:** LEGITIMATE

le·git·i·ma·cy \li-'ji-tə-mə-sē\ *noun* (1691)
: the quality or state of being legitimate

¹le·git·i·mate \li-'ji-tə-mət\ *adjective* [Middle English *legitimat*, from Medieval Latin *legitimatus*, past participle of *legitimare* to legitimate, from Latin *legitimus* legitimate, from *leg-, lex* law] (15th century)
1 a : lawfully begotten; *specifically* **:** born in wedlock **b :** having full filial rights and obligations by birth ⟨a *legitimate* child⟩
2 : being exactly as purposed **:** neither spurious nor false ⟨*legitimate* grievance⟩ ⟨a *legitimate* practitioner⟩
3 a : accordant with law or with established legal forms and requirements ⟨a *legitimate* government⟩ **b :** ruling by or based on the strict principle of hereditary right ⟨a *legitimate* king⟩
4 : conforming to recognized principles or accepted rules and standards ⟨*legitimate* advertising expenditure⟩ ⟨*legitimate* inference⟩
5 : relating to plays acted by professional actors but not including revues, burlesque, or some forms of musical comedy ⟨the *legitimate* theater⟩
synonym see LAWFUL
— **le·git·i·mate·ly** *adverb*

²le·git·i·mate \-ˌmāt\ *transitive verb* **-mated; -mat·ing** (1531)
: to make legitimate: **a** (1) **:** to give legal status or authorization to (2) **:** to show or affirm to be justified **b :** to put (a bastard) in the state of a legitimate child before the law by legal means
— **le·git·i·ma·tion** \-ˌji-tə-'mā-shən\ *noun*
— **le·git·i·mat·or** \-'ji-tə-ˌmā-tər\ *noun*

le·git·i·ma·tize \li-'ji-tə-mə-ˌtīz\ *transitive verb* **-tized; -tiz·ing** (1791)
: LEGITIMATE

le·git·i·mise *British variant of* LEGITIMIZE

le·git·i·mism \li-'ji-tə-ˌmi-zəm\ *noun, often capitalized* (1877)
: adherence to the principles of political legitimacy or to a person claiming legitimacy
— **le·git·i·mist** \-mist\ *noun, often capitalized*
— **legitimist** *adjective*

le·git·i·mize \-ˌmīz\ *transitive verb* **-mized; -miz·ing** (1848)
: LEGITIMATE
— **le·git·i·mi·za·tion** \-ˌji-tə-mə-'zā-shən\ *noun*
— **le·git·i·miz·er** \-'ji-tə-ˌmī-zər\ *noun*

leg·man \'leg-ˌman *also* 'lāg-\ *noun* (1923)
1 : a reporter assigned usually to gather information
2 : an assistant who performs various subordinate tasks (as gathering information or running errands)

leg–of–mut·ton *or* **leg–o'–mut·ton** \ˌle-gə(v)-'mə-tᵊn *also* ˌlāg-\ *adjective* (1840)
: having the approximately triangular shape or outline of a leg of mutton ⟨*leg-of-mutton* sleeve⟩ ⟨*leg-of-mutton* sail⟩

leg out *transitive verb* (1965)
: to make (as a base hit) by fast running

leg–pull \'leg-ˌpu̇l *also* 'lāg-\ *noun* [from the phrase *to pull one's leg*] (1915)
: a humorous deception or hoax

leg·room \-ˌrüm, -ˌru̇m\ *noun* (1926)
: space in which to extend the legs while seated

le·gume \'le-ˌgyüm, li-'gyüm\ *noun* [French *légume*, from Latin *legumin-, legumen* leguminous plant, from *legere* to gather — more at LEGEND] (1676)
1 a : the fruit or seed of leguminous plants (as peas or beans) used for food **b :** a vegetable used for food
2 : any of a large family (Leguminosae synonym Fabaceae) of dicotyledonous herbs, shrubs, and trees having fruits that are legumes (sense 3) or loments, bearing nodules on the roots that contain nitrogen-fixing bacteria, and including important food and forage plants (as peas, beans, or clovers)
3 : a dry dehiscent one-celled fruit developed from a simple superior ovary and usually dehiscing into two valves with the seeds attached to the ventral suture **:** POD

le·gu·mi·nous \li-'gyü-mə-nəs, le-\ *adjective* (15th century)
1 : of, relating to, or consisting of plants that are legumes
2 : resembling a legume

leg up *noun* (1837)
1 : a helping hand **:** BOOST
2 : HEAD START

leg warmer *noun* (1974)
: a usually knitted covering for the leg

leg·work \'leg-ˌwərk *also* 'lāg-\ *noun* (1891)
: active physical work (as in gathering information) that forms the basis of more creative or mentally exacting work (as writing a book)

le·hua \lā-'hü-ə\ *noun* [Hawaiian] (1888)
: a common very showy chiefly Polynesian tree (*Metrosideros collinus*) of the myrtle family having bright red flowers and a hard wood; *also* **:** its flower

¹lei \'lā, 'lā-ˌē\ *noun* [Hawaiian] (1843)
: a wreath or necklace usually of flowers or leaves

²lei \'lā\ *plural of* LEU

Leices·ter \'les-tər\ *noun* [*Leicester*, county in England] (1798)
1 : an individual of either of two English breeds of white-faced long-wool sheep raised especially for mutton
2 : a hard usually orange-colored cheese similar to cheddar

leish·ma·nia \lēsh-'ma-nē-ə\ *noun* [New Latin, from Sir W. B. *Leishman* (died 1926) British medical officer] (1914)
: any of a genus (*Leishmania*) of flagellate protozoans that are parasitic in the tissues of vertebrates; *broadly* **:** an organism resembling the leishmanias that is included in the family (Trypanosomatidae) to which they belong
— **leish·man·i·al** \-nē-əl\ *adjective*

leish·man·i·a·sis \ˌlēsh-mə-'nī-ə-səs\ *noun* [New Latin] (1912)
: infection with or disease caused by leishmanias

leis·ter \'lēs-tər\ *noun* [of Scandinavian origin; akin to Old Norse *ljōstr* leister] (circa 1534)
: a spear armed with three or more barbed prongs for catching fish

lei·sure \'lē-zhər, 'le-, 'lā-\ *noun* [Middle English *leiser*, from Middle French *leisir*, from *leisir* to be permitted, from Latin *licēre*] (14th century)
1 : freedom provided by the cessation of activities; *especially* **:** time free from work or duties
2 : EASE, LEISURELINESS
— **leisure** *adjective*
— **at leisure** *or* **at one's leisure** **:** in one's leisure time **:** at one's convenience ⟨read the book *at her leisure*⟩

lei·sured \-zhərd\ *adjective* (1631)
: having leisure **:** LEISURELY

¹lei·sure·ly \-zhər-lē\ *adverb* (15th century)
: without haste **:** DELIBERATELY

²leisurely *adjective* (1604)
: characterized by leisure **:** UNHURRIED
— **lei·sure·li·ness** *noun*

leisure suit *noun* (1975)
: a suit consisting of a shirt jacket and matching trousers for informal wear

leit·mo·tiv *or* **leit·mo·tif** \'līt-mō-ˌtēf\ *noun* [German *Leitmotiv*, from *leiten* to lead + *Motiv* motive] (circa 1876)
1 : an associated melodic phrase or figure that accompanies the reappearance of an idea, person, or situation especially in a Wagnerian music drama
2 : a dominant recurring theme

¹lek \'lek\ *noun* [Swedish, short for *lekställe* mating ground, from *lek* mating, sport + *ställe* place] (1871)
: an assembly area where animals (as the prairie chicken) carry on display and courtship behavior

²lek *noun, plural* **leks** *or* **le·ke** \'le-kə\ *also* **lek** *or* **le·ku** \'le-(ˌ)kü\ [Albanian] (1927)
— see MONEY table

lek·var \'lek-ˌvär\ *noun* [Hungarian *lekvár* jam] (circa 1958)
: a prune butter used as a pastry filling

le·man \'le-mən, 'lē-\ *noun* [Middle English *lefman, leman*, from *lef* lief] (13th century)
archaic **:** SWEETHEART, LOVER; *especially* **:** MISTRESS

¹lem·ma \'le-mə\ *noun, plural* **lemmas** *or* **lem·ma·ta** \-mə-tə\ [Latin, from Greek *lēmma* thing taken, assumption, from *lambanein* to take — more at LATCH] (1570)
1 : an auxiliary proposition used in the demonstration of another proposition
2 : the argument or theme of a composition prefixed as a title or introduction; *also* **:** the heading or theme of a comment or note on a text
3 : a glossed word or phrase

²lemma *noun* [Greek, husk, from *lepein* to peel — more at LEPER] (1906)
: the lower of the two bracts enclosing the flower in the spikelet of grasses

lem·ming \'le-miŋ\ *noun* [Norwegian] (1713)
: any of various small short-tailed furry-footed rodents (as genera *Lemmus* and *Dicrostonyx*) of circumpolar distribution that are notable for the recurrent mass migrations of a European form (*L. lemmus*) which often continue into the sea where vast numbers are drowned
— **lem·ming-like** \-,līk\ *adjective*

lem·nis·cate \lem-'nis-kət\ *noun* [New Latin *lemniscata*, from feminine of Latin *lemniscatus* with hanging ribbons, from *lemniscus*] (circa 1781)
: a figure-eight shaped curve whose equation in polar coordinates is $\rho^2=a^2 \cos 2\theta$ or $\rho^2=a^2 \sin 2\theta$

lem·nis·cus \lem-'nis-kəs\ *noun, plural* **-nis·ci** \-'nis-,kī -,kē; -'ni-,sī\ [New Latin, from Latin, ribbon, from Greek *lēmniskos*] (circa 1905)
: a band of fibers and especially nerve fibers
— **lem·nis·cal** \-kəl\ *adjective*

¹lem·on \'le-mən\ *noun* [Middle English *lymon*, from Middle French *limon*, from Medieval Latin *limon-, limo*, from Arabic *laymūn*] (15th century)
1 a : an acid fruit that is botanically a many-seeded pale yellow oblong berry and is produced by a small thorny tree (*Citrus limon*) **b** : a tree that bears lemons
2 : one (as an automobile) that is unsatisfactory or defective
— **lem·ony** \'le-mə-nē\ *adjective*

lemon 1: branch with fruit and flowers

²lemon *adjective* (1598)
1 : of the color lemon yellow
2 a : containing lemon **b** : having the flavor or scent of lemon

lem·on·ade \,le-mə-'nād\ *noun* (1604)
: a beverage of sweetened lemon juice mixed with water

lemon balm *noun* (circa 1888)
: a bushy perennial Old World mint (*Melissa officinalis*) often cultivated for its fragrant lemon-flavored leaves

lem·on·grass \'le-mən-,gras\ *noun* (1801)
: a grass (*Cymbopogon citratus*) of robust habit that grows in tropical regions, is used as an herb, and is the source of an essential oil with an odor of lemon or verbena

lemon law *noun* (1982)
: a law offering car buyers relief (as by repair, replacement, or refund) for defects detected during a specified period after purchase

lemon shark *noun* (1942)
: a medium-sized requiem shark (*Negaprion brevirostris*) of the warm Atlantic that is yellowish brown to gray above with yellow or greenish sides

lemon sole *noun* (1876)
: any of several flatfishes and especially flounders: as **a** : a bottom-dwelling flounder (*Microstomus kitt*) of the northeastern Atlantic that is an important food fish **b** : WINTER FLOUNDER

lemon yellow *noun* (1807)
: a brilliant greenish yellow color

lem·pi·ra \lem-'pir-ə\ *noun* [American Spanish, from *Lempira*, 16th century Indian chief] (circa 1934)
— see MONEY table

le·mur \'lē-mər\ *noun* [New Latin, from Latin *lemures*, plural, ghosts] (1795)
: any of various arboreal chiefly nocturnal mammals that were formerly widespread but are now largely confined to Madagascar, are related to the monkeys but are usually regarded as constituting a distinct superfamily (Lemuroidea), and usually have a muzzle like a fox, large eyes, very soft woolly fur, and a long furry tail ◆

le·mu·res \'le-mə-,rās, 'lem-yə-,rēz\ *noun plural* [Latin] (1555)
: spirits of the unburied dead exorcised from homes in early Roman religious rites

lend \'lend\ *verb* **lent** \'lent\; **lend·ing** [Middle English *lenen, lenden*, from Old English *lænan*, from *læn* loan — more at LOAN] (before 12th century)
transitive verb
1 a : to give for temporary use on condition that the same or its equivalent be returned **b** : to let out (money) for temporary use on condition of repayment with interest
2 a : to give the assistance or support of : AFFORD, FURNISH ⟨a dispassionate and scholarly manner which *lends* great force to his criticisms —*Times Literary Supplement*⟩ **b** : to adapt or apply (oneself) readily : ACCOMMODATE ⟨a topic that *lends* itself admirably to class discussion⟩
intransitive verb
: to make a loan
usage see LOAN
— **lend·able** \'len-də-bəl\ *adjective*
— **lend·er** *noun*

lending library *noun* (1708)
: a library from which materials are lent; *especially* : RENTAL LIBRARY

lend–lease \'lend-'lēs\ *noun* [U.S. *Lend-Lease Act* (1941)] (1941)
: the transfer of goods and services to an ally to aid in a common cause with payment made by a return of the original items or their use in the cause or by a similar transfer of other goods and services
— **lend–lease** *transitive verb*

length \'leŋ(k)th, 'len(t)th\ *noun, plural* **lengths** \'leŋ(k)ths, 'len(t)ths, 'leŋ(k)s\ [Middle English *lengthe*, from Old English *lengthu*, from *lang* long] (before 12th century)
1 a : the longer or longest dimension of an object **b** : a measured distance or dimension ⟨10 feet in *length*⟩ — see METRIC SYSTEM table, WEIGHT table **c** : the quality or state of being long
2 a : duration or extent in time **b** : relative duration or stress of a sound
3 a : distance or extent in space **b** : the length of something taken as a unit of measure ⟨his horse led by a *length*⟩
4 : the degree to which something (as a course of action or a line of thought) is carried — often used in plural ⟨went to great *lengths* to learn the truth⟩
5 a : a long expanse or stretch **b** : a piece constituting or usable as part of a whole or of a connected series : SECTION ⟨a *length* of pipe⟩
6 : a vertical dimension of an article of clothing
— **at length 1** : FULLY, COMPREHENSIVELY **2** : at last : FINALLY

length·en \'leŋ(k)-thən, 'len(t)-\ *verb* **length·ened; length·en·ing** \'leŋ(k)th-niŋ, 'len(t)th-; 'leŋ(k)th-thə-, 'len(t)th-\ (14th century)
transitive verb
: to make longer
intransitive verb
: to grow longer
synonym see EXTEND
— **length·en·er** \'leŋ(k)th-nər, 'len(t)th-; 'leŋ(k)th-thə-, 'len(t)-\ *noun*

length·ways \'leŋ(k)th-,wāz, 'len(t)th-\ *adverb* (1599)
: LENGTHWISE

length·wise \-,wīz\ *adverb* (circa 1580)
: in the direction of the length : LONGITUDINALLY
— **lengthwise** *adjective*

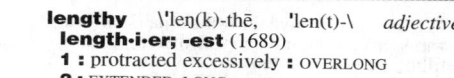
lemur

lengthy \'leŋ(k)-thē, 'len(t)-\ *adjective* **length·i·er; -est** (1689)
1 : protracted excessively : OVERLONG
2 : EXTENDED, LONG
— **length·i·ly** \-thə-lē\ *adverb*
— **length·i·ness** \-thē-nəs\ *noun*

le·nience \'lē-nyən(t)s, -nē-ən(t)s\ *noun* (1796)
: LENIENCY

le·nien·cy \'lē-nē-ən(t)-sē, -nyən(t)-sē\ *noun, plural* **-cies** (1780)
1 : the quality or state of being lenient
2 : a lenient disposition or practice
synonym see MERCY

le·nient \'lē-nē-ənt, -nyənt\ *adjective* [Latin *lenient-, leniens*, present participle of *lenire* to soften, soothe, from *lenis* soft, mild; probably akin to Lithuanian *lėnas* tranquil — more at LET] (1652)
1 : exerting a soothing or easing influence : relieving pain or stress
2 : of mild and tolerant disposition; *especially* : INDULGENT
— **le·nient·ly** *adverb*

Leni–Len·a·pe *or* **Len·ni–Len·a·pe** \,le-nē-'le-nə-pē, -lə-'nä-pē\ *noun* [Delaware (Unami dialects) *lèni-lənáp'e*] (circa 1782)
: DELAWARE 1

Le·nin·ism \'le-nə-,ni-zəm\ *noun* (1918)
: the political, economic, and social principles and policies advocated by Lenin; *especially* : the theory and practice of communism developed by or associated with Lenin
— **Le·nin·ist** \-nist\ *noun or adjective*
— **Le·nin·ite** \-,nīt\ *noun or adjective*

le·nis \'lē-nəs, 'lā-\ *adjective* [New Latin, from Latin, mild, smooth] (circa 1897)
: produced with an articulation that is lax in relation to another speech sound ⟨\t\ in *gutter* is lenis, \t\ in *toe* is fortis⟩

len·i·tion \lə-'ni-shən\ *noun* [Latin *lenire*] (1912)
: the change from fortis to lenis articulation

len·i·tive \'le-nə-tiv\ *adjective* [Middle English *lenitif*, from Middle French, from Medieval Latin *lenitivus*, from Latin *lenitus*, past participle of *lenire*] (15th century)
: alleviating pain or harshness : SOOTHING
— **lenitive** *noun*
— **len·i·tive·ly** *adverb*

len·i·ty \'le-nə-tē\ *noun* (1548)
: the quality or state of being lenient : CLEMENCY

le·no \'lē-(,)nō\ *noun* [perhaps from French *linon* linen fabric, lawn, from Middle French *lin* flax, linen, from Latin *linum* flax] (1821)

◇ WORD HISTORY
lemur In ancient Roman belief the *lemures* were the spirits of dead people who returned at night to disturb the living. They were placated by a ritual performed by the male head of a household on midnight of the *Lemuria*, three days in May during which temples were closed and marriages forbidden. In the late 17th and 18th centuries visitors to the island of Madagascar encountered some strange-looking creatures. Arboreal and nocturnal, these big-eyed, monkeylike mammals presented a strikingly eerie appearance to their first European observers. Specimens of the ring-tailed lemur (*Lemur catta*) were fittingly dubbed in scientific Latin *lemures* by the Swedish biologist Linnaeus, after the Roman ghosts. This word has been borrowed into English as *lemur*.

\ə\ abut \ᵊ\ kitten \ər\ further \a\ ash \ā\ ace \ä\ mop, mar \au̇\ out \ch\ chin \e\ bet \ē\ easy \g\ go \i\ hit \ī\ ice \j\ job \ŋ\ sing \ō\ go \ȯ\ law \ȯi\ boy \th\ thin \t͟h\ the \ü\ loot \u̇\ foot \y\ yet \zh\ vision *see also* Guide to Pronunciation

1 : an open weave in which pairs of warp yarns cross one another and thereby lock the filling yarn in position
2 : a fabric made with a leno weave

¹lens *also* **lense** \'lenz\ *noun* [New Latin *lent-, lens,* from Latin, lentil; from its shape] (1693)
1 a : a piece of transparent material (as glass) that has two opposite regular surfaces either both curved or one curved and the other plane and that is used either singly or combined in an optical instrument for forming an image by focusing rays of light **b :** a combination of two or more simple lenses **c :** a piece of glass or plastic used (as in safety goggles or sunglasses) to protect the eye
2 : a device for directing or focusing radiation other than light (as sound waves, radio microwaves, or electrons)
3 : something shaped like a double-convex optical lens ⟨*lens* of sandstone⟩
4 : a highly transparent biconvex lens-shaped or nearly spherical body in the eye that focuses light rays (as upon the retina) — see EYE illustration
5 : something that facilitates and influences perception, comprehension, or evaluation ⟨the author's own *lens* seems blurred by bias —Seymour Topping⟩
— **lensed** \'lenzd\ *adjective*
— **lens·less** \'lenz-ləs\ *adjective*

²lens *transitive verb* (1942)
: to make a motion picture of **:** FILM

lens·man \-mən, -ˌman\ *noun* (1938)
: PHOTOGRAPHER

Lent \'lent\ *noun* [Middle English *lente* springtime, Lent, from Old English *lencten;* akin to Old High German *lenzin* spring] (13th century)
: the 40 weekdays from Ash Wednesday to Easter observed by the Roman Catholic, Eastern, and some Protestant churches as a period of penitence and fasting

len·ta·men·te \ˌlen-tə-'men-(ˌ)tā\ *adverb or adjective* [Italian, from *lento* slow] (1724)
: LENTO

len·tan·do \len-'tän-(ˌ)dō\ *adverb or adjective* [Italian] (circa 1847)
: becoming slower — used as a direction in music

Lent·en \'len-t°n\ *adjective* (before 12th century)
: of, relating to, or suitable for Lent; *especially* **:** MEAGER ⟨*Lenten* fare⟩

len·tic \'len-tik\ *adjective* [Latin *lentus* sluggish] (circa 1938)
: of, relating to, or living in still waters (as lakes, ponds, or swamps) — compare LOTIC

len·ti·cel \'len-tə-ˌsel\ *noun* [New Latin *lenticella,* diminutive of Latin *lent-, lens* lentil] (circa 1864)
: a loose aggregation of cells which penetrates the surface (as of a stem) of a woody plant and through which gases are exchanged between the atmosphere and the underlying tissues

len·tic·u·lar \len-'ti-kyə-lər\ *adjective* [Middle English, from Latin *lenticularis* lentil-shaped, from *lenticula* lentil] (15th century)
1 : having the shape of a double-convex lens
2 : of or relating to a lens
3 : provided with or utilizing lenticules ⟨a *lenticular* screen⟩

len·ti·cule \'len-tə-ˌkyü(ə)l\ *noun* [Latin *lenticula*] (1942)
1 : any of the minute lenses on the base side of a film used in stereoscopic or color photography
2 : any of the tiny corrugations or grooves molded or embossed into the surface of a projection screen

len·til \'len-t°l\ *noun* [Middle English, from Old French *lentille,* from Latin *lenticula,* diminutive of *lent-, lens*] (13th century)
1 : a widely cultivated Eurasian annual leguminous plant (*Lens culinaris*) with flattened edible seeds and leafy stalks used as fodder

2 : the seed of the lentil

len·tis·si·mo \len-'ti-sə-ˌmō\ *adverb or adjective* [Italian, superlative of *lento*] (circa 1903)
: at a very slow tempo — used as a direction in music

len·ti·vi·rus \ˌlen-tə-'vī-rəs\ *noun* [New Latin, from Latin *lentus* slow + New Latin *virus*] (1982)
: any of a group of retroviruses that cause slowly progressive often fatal animal diseases

len·to \'len-(ˌ)tō\ *adverb or adjective* [Italian, from *lento,* adjective, slow, from Latin *lentus* pliant, sluggish, slow — more at LITHE] (circa 1724)
: at a slow tempo — used especially as a direction in music

Leo \'lē-(ˌ)ō\ *noun* [Latin (genitive *Leonis*), literally, lion — more at LION]
1 : a northern constellation east of Cancer
2 a : the 5th sign of the zodiac in astrology — see ZODIAC table **b :** one born under this sign

— **Le·o·nine** \'lē-ə-ˌnīn\ *adjective*

le·one \lē-'ōn\ *noun, plural* **leones** *or* **leone** [*Sierra Leone*] (1964)
— see MONEY table

Le·o·nid \'lē-ə-nid\ *noun, plural* **Leonids** *or* **Le·on·i·des** \lē-'ä-nə-ˌdēz\ [Latin *Leon-, Leo;* from their appearing to radiate from a point in Leo] (1876)
: any of the meteors in a meteor shower occurring every year about November 14

le·o·nine \'lē-ə-ˌnīn\ *adjective* [Middle English, from Latin *leoninus,* from *leon-, leo*] (14th century)
: of, relating to, suggestive of, or resembling a lion

leop·ard \'le-pərd\ *noun* [Middle English, from Old French *leupart,* from Late Latin *leopardus,* from Greek *leopardos,* from *leōn* lion + *pardos* leopard] (13th century)
1 : a large strong cat (*Panthera pardus*) of southern Asia and Africa that is adept at climbing and is usually tawny or buff with black spots arranged in rosettes — called *also* panther
2 : a heraldic representation of a lion passant guardant

leopard 1

— **leop·ard·ess** \-pər-dəs\ *noun*

leopard frog *noun* (1839)
: a common North American frog (*Rana pipiens*) that is bright green or brown with large black white-margined blotches on the back; *also* **:** a similar frog (*R. sphenocephala*) of the southeastern U.S.

leopard seal *noun* (1893)
: a spotted slate gray seal (*Hydrurga leptonyx*) of the southern Atlantic to the southern Pacific that often feeds on other seals

le·o·tard \'lē-ə-ˌtärd\ *noun* [Jules *Léotard,* (died 1870) French aerial gymnast] (1886)
: a close-fitting one-piece garment worn especially by dancers, acrobats, and aerialists; *also* **:** TIGHTS — often used in plural
— **le·o·tard·ed** \-ˌtär-dəd\ *adjective*

Lep·cha \'lep-chə\ *noun, plural* **Lepcha** *or* **Lepchas** (1819)
1 : a member of a people of Sikkim, India
2 : the Tibeto-Burman language of the Lepcha people

lep·er \'le-pər\ *noun* [Middle English, from *lepre* leprosy, from Middle French, from Late Latin *lepra,* from Greek, from *lepein* to peel; perhaps akin to Lithuanian *lopas* piece, scrap] (14th century)
1 : a person affected with leprosy
2 : a person shunned for moral or social reasons

lepid- *or* **lepido-** *combining form* [New Latin, from Greek, from *lepid-, lepis* scale, from *lepein*]
: flake **:** scale ⟨*Lepidoptera*⟩

le·pid·o·lite \li-'pi-d°l-ˌīt\ *noun* [German *Lepidolith,* from *lepid-* + *-lith*] (circa 1796)
: a variable mineral that consists of a mica containing lithium and is used especially in glazes and enamels

lep·i·dop·tera \ˌle-pə-'däp-tə-rə\ *noun plural* (circa 1773)
: insects that are lepidopterans

lep·i·dop·ter·an \-rən\ *noun* [New Latin *Lepidoptera,* from *lepid-* + Greek *pteron* wing — more at FEATHER] (circa 1901)
: any of a large order (Lepidoptera) of insects comprising the butterflies, moths, and skippers that as adults have four broad or lanceolate wings usually covered with minute overlapping and often brightly colored scales and that as larvae are caterpillars
— **lepidopteran** *adjective*
— **lep·i·dop·ter·ous** \-tə-rəs\ *adjective*

lep·i·dop·ter·ist \-t°-rist\ *noun* (1826)
: a specialist in lepidopterology

lep·i·dop·ter·ol·o·gy \-ˌdäp-tə-'rä-lə-jē\ *noun* (1898)
: a branch of entomology concerned with lepidopterans
— **lep·i·dop·ter·o·log·i·cal** \-tə-rə-'lä-ji-kəl\ *adjective*
— **lep·i·dop·ter·ol·o·gist** \-tə-'rä-lə-jist\ *noun*

lep·i·dote \'le-pə-ˌdōt\ *noun* [Greek *lepidōtos* scaly, from *lepid-, lepis*] (circa 1836)
: a rhododendron covered with scurf or scurfy scales

lep·re·chaun \'lep-rə-ˌkän, -ˌkòn\ *noun* [Irish *leipreachán*] (1604)
: a mischievous elf of Irish folklore usually believed to reveal the hiding place of treasure if caught
— **lep·re·chaun·ish** \-ˌkä-nish, -ˌkò-\ *adjective*

le·pro·ma·tous \lə-'prä-mə-təs, -'prō-\ *adjective* [New Latin *lepromat-, leproma* leprous lesion, from Late Latin *lepra*] (1898)
: characterized by, exhibiting, or being leprosy with infective superficial granulomatous nodules

lep·ro·sar·i·um \ˌle-prə-'ser-ē-əm\ *noun, plural* **-i·ums** *or* **-ia** \-ē-ə\ [Medieval Latin, from Late Latin *leprosus*] (circa 1846)
: a hospital for leprosy patients

lep·ro·sy \'le-prə-sē\ *noun* [Middle English *lepruse,* from *leprous*] (15th century)
1 : a chronic disease caused by a bacillus (*Mycobacterium leprae*) and characterized by the formation of nodules or of macules that enlarge and spread accompanied by loss of sensation with eventual paralysis, wasting of muscle, and production of deformities and mutilations
2 : a morally or spiritually harmful influence
— **lep·rot·ic** \le-'prä-tik\ *adjective*

lep·rous \'le-prəs\ *adjective* [Middle English, from Late Latin *leprosus* leprous, from *lepra* leprosy — more at LEPER] (13th century)
1 a : infected with leprosy **b :** of, relating to, or resembling leprosy or a leper
2 : SCALY, SCURFY
— **lep·rous·ly** *adverb*

-lepsy *noun combining form* [Middle French *-lepsie,* from Late Latin *-lepsia,* from Greek *-lēpsia,* from *lēpsis,* from *lambanein* to take, seize — more at LATCH]
: taking **:** seizure ⟨narco*lepsy*⟩

lep·to·ceph·a·lus \ˌlep-tə-'se-fə-ləs\ *noun, plural* **-li** \-ˌlī, -ˌlē\ [New Latin, from Greek *leptos* + *kephalē* head — more at CEPHALIC] (1769)
: a long thin small-headed transparent pelagic first larva of various eels

¹lep·ton \lep-'tän\ *noun, plural* **lep·ta** \-'tä\ [New Greek, from Greek, a small coin, from

neuter of *leptos* peeled, slender, small, from *lepein* to peel — more at LEPER] (circa 1741) — see *drachma* at MONEY table

²**lep·ton** \'lep-ˌtän\ *noun* [Greek *leptos* + English ²*-on*] (circa 1929)
: any of a family of particles (as electrons, muons, and neutrinos) that have spin quantum number ½ and that experience no strong forces
— **lep·ton·ic** \lep-'tä-nik\ *adjective*

lep·to·some \'lep-tə-ˌsōm\ *adjective* [German *Leptosom*, from Greek *leptos* + *sōma* body] (1931)
: ECTOMORPHIC
— **leptosome** *noun*

lep·to·spire \-ˌspīr\ *noun* [New Latin *Leptospira*, from Greek *leptos* + Latin *spira* coil — more at SPIRE] (1952)
: any of a genus (*Leptospira*) of slender aerobic spirochetes that are free-living or parasitic in mammals
— **lep·to·spir·al** \ˌlep-tə-ˈspī-rəl\ *adjective*

lep·to·spi·ro·sis \ˌlep-tə-spī-'rō-səs\ *noun*, *plural* **-ro·ses** \-ˌsēz\ [New Latin] (circa 1926)
: any of several diseases of humans and domestic animals that are caused by infection with leptospires

lep·to·tene \'lep-tə-ˌtēn\ *noun* [International Scientific Vocabulary] (1912)
: a stage of meiotic prophase immediately preceding synapsis in which the chromosomes appear as fine discrete threads
— **leptotene** *adjective*

¹**les·bi·an** \'lez-bē-ən\ *adjective*, *often capitalized* (1591)
1 : of or relating to Lesbos
2 [from the reputed homosexual band associated with Sappho of Lesbos] : of or relating to homosexuality between females

²**lesbian** *noun*, *often capitalized* (circa 1890)
: a female homosexual

les·bi·an·ism \'lez-bē-ə-ˌni-zəm\ *noun* (1870)
: female homosexuality

lèse–ma·jes·té *or* **lese maj·es·ty** \ˌläz-ˈma-jə-stē, ˌlez-, -ˌstā, -ˌlēz-\ *noun* [Middle French *lese majesté*, from Latin *laesa majestas*, literally, injured majesty] (1536)
1 a : a crime (as treason) committed against a sovereign power **b** : an offense violating the dignity of a ruler as the representative of a sovereign power
2 : a detraction from or affront to dignity or importance

le·sion \'lē-zhən\ *noun* [Middle English, from Middle French, from Latin *laesion-*, *laesio*, from *laedere* to injure] (15th century)
1 : INJURY, HARM
2 : an abnormal change in structure of an organ or part due to injury or disease; *especially* : one that is circumscribed and well defined
— **le·sioned** \-zhənd\ *adjective*

les·pe·de·za \ˌles-pə-'dē-zə\ *noun* [New Latin, irregular from V. M. de *Zespedes* (flourished 1785) Spanish governor of East Florida] (1891)
: any of a genus (*Lespedeza*) of herbaceous or shrubby leguminous plants including some widely used for forage, soil improvement, and especially hay

¹**less** \'les\ *adjective comparative of* ¹LITTLE [Middle English, partly from Old English *lǣs*, adverb & noun; partly from *lǣssa*, adjective; akin to Old Frisian *lēs* less] (before 12th century)
1 : constituting a more limited number ⟨*less* than three⟩
2 : of lower rank, degree, or importance ⟨no *less* a person than the president himself⟩
3 a : of reduced size, extent, or degree **b** : more limited in quantity ⟨in *less* time⟩ ☐

²**less** *adverb comparative of* ²LITTLE (before 12th century)
: to a lesser extent or degree
— **less and less** : to a progressively smaller extent or size

— **less than** : by no means : not at all ⟨*less than* honest in his replies⟩

³**less** *noun*, *plural* **less** (before 12th century)
1 : a smaller portion or quantity
2 : something of less importance

⁴**less** *preposition* (15th century)
: diminished by : MINUS

-less *adjective suffix* [Middle English *-les*, *-lesse*, from Old English *-lēas*, from *lēas* devoid, false; akin to Old High German *lōs* loose, Old English *losian* to get lost — more at LOSE]
1 : destitute of : not having ⟨wit*less*⟩ ⟨child*less*⟩
2 : unable to be acted on or to act (in a specified way) ⟨daunt*less*⟩ ⟨fade*less*⟩

les·see \le-'sē\ *noun* [Middle English, from Anglo-French, from *lessé*, past participle of *lesser* to lease — more at LEASE] (15th century)
: one that holds real or personal property under a lease

less·en \'le-sᵊn\ *verb* **less·ened; less·en·ing** \'les-niŋ, 'le-sᵊn-iŋ\ (13th century)
intransitive verb
: to shrink in size, number, or degree : DECREASE
transitive verb
1 : to reduce in size, extent, or degree
2 a *archaic* : to represent as of little value **b** : to lower in status or dignity : DEGRADE
synonym see DECREASE

¹**less·er** \'le-sər\ *adjective*, *comparative of* ¹LITTLE (13th century)
: of less size, quality, degree, or significance : of lower status

²**lesser** *adverb* (1539)
: LESS ⟨*lesser*-known⟩

lesser celandine *noun* (circa 1890)
: a yellow-flowered Eurasian perennial herb (*Ranunculus ficaria*) of the buttercup family naturalized in North America

lesser cornstalk borer *noun* (circa 1925)
: a pyralid moth (*Elasmopalpus lignosellus*) having slender greenish larvae that burrow in the stalk especially of Indian corn near ground level

lesser peach tree borer *noun* (circa 1924)
: a moth (*Synanthedon pictipes* family Aegeriidae) whose larva is a borer in the forks and crotches of stone-fruit trees and especially the peach

lesser yellowlegs *noun plural but singular or plural in construction* (circa 1903)
: a common American marsh and shore bird (*Tringa flavipes*) that closely resembles the greater yellowlegs in color and markings but is smaller with a shorter more slender bill

¹**les·son** \'le-sᵊn\ *noun* [Middle English, from Old French *leçon*, from Late Latin *lection-*, *lectio*, from Latin, act of reading, from *legere* to read — more at LEGEND] (13th century)
1 : a passage from sacred writings read in a service of worship
2 a : a piece of instruction **b** : a reading or exercise to be studied by a pupil **c** : a division of a course of instruction
3 a : something learned by study or experience ⟨his years of travel had taught him valuable *lessons*⟩ **b** : an instructive example ⟨the *lessons* of history⟩ **c** : REPRIMAND

²**lesson** *transitive verb* **les·soned; les·son·ing** \'le-sə-niŋ, 'les-niŋ\ (1555)
1 : to give a lesson to : INSTRUCT
2 : LECTURE, REBUKE

les·sor \'le-ˌsȯr, le-'sȯr\ *noun* [Middle English *lessour*, from Anglo-French, from *lesser* to lease] (14th century)
: one that conveys property by lease

lest \'lest\ *conjunction* [Middle English *les the*, *leste*, from Old English *thȳ lǣs the*, from *thȳ* (instrumental of *thæt* that) + *lǣs* + *the*, relative particle] (before 12th century)

: for fear that — used after an expression denoting fear or apprehension ⟨worried *lest* she should be late⟩ ⟨hesitant to speak out *lest* he be fired⟩

¹**let** \'let\ *transitive verb* **let·ted; letted** *or* **let; let·ting** [Middle English *letten*, from Old English *lettan* to delay, hinder; akin to Old High German *lezzen* to delay, hurt, Old English *lǣt* late] (before 12th century)
archaic : HINDER, PREVENT

²**let** *noun* (12th century)
1 : something that impedes : OBSTRUCTION
2 : a shot or point in racket games that does not count and must be replayed

³**let** *verb* **let; let·ting** [Middle English *leten*, from Old English *lǣtan*; akin to Old High German *lāzzan* to permit, and perhaps to Lithuanian *lénas* tranquil] (before 12th century)
transitive verb
1 : to cause to : MAKE ⟨*let* me know⟩
2 a : to offer or grant for rent or lease ⟨*let* rooms⟩ **b** : to assign especially after bids ⟨*let* a contract⟩
3 a : to give opportunity to or fail to prevent ⟨live and *let* live⟩ ⟨a break in the clouds *let* us see the summit⟩ ⟨*let* the opportunity slip⟩ **b** — used in the imperative to introduce a request or proposal ⟨*let* us pray⟩ **c** — used as an auxiliary to express a warning ⟨*let* him try⟩
4 : to free from or as if from confinement ⟨*let* out a scream⟩ ⟨*let* blood⟩
5 : to permit to enter, pass, or leave ⟨*let* them through⟩ ⟨*let* them off with a warning⟩
6 : to make an adjustment to ⟨*let* out the waist⟩
intransitive verb
1 : to become rented or leased
2 : to become awarded to a contractor
synonym see HIRE
— **let alone** : to leave undisturbed; *also* : to leave to oneself
— **let fly** : to hurl an object
— **let go** : to dismiss from employment ⟨the firm *let* him *go* at the end of the month⟩
— **let it all hang out** : to reveal one's true feelings : act without dissimulation
— **let one have it** : to subject to vigorous assault
— **let rip 1** : to utter or release without restraint ⟨*let* 'er *rip*⟩ **2** : to do or utter something without restraint ⟨*let rip* at the press⟩
— **let the cat out of the bag** : to give away a secret

-let *noun suffix* [Middle English, from Middle French *-elet*, from *-el*, diminutive suffix (from Latin *-ellus*) + *-et*]
1 : small one ⟨book*let*⟩
2 : article worn on ⟨wrist*let*⟩

let alone *conjunction* (1812)
: to say nothing of : not to mention — used to add an example of narrower range by way

☐ **USAGE**

less The traditional view is that *less* applies to matters of degree, value, or amount and modifies collective nouns, mass nouns, or nouns denoting an abstract whole while *fewer* applies to matters of number and modifies plural nouns. *Less* has been used to modify plural nouns since the days of King Alfred and the usage, though roundly decried, appears to be increasing. *Less* is more likely than *fewer* to modify plural nouns when distances, sums of money, and a few fixed phrases are involved ⟨*less* than 100 miles⟩ ⟨an investment of *less* than $2000⟩ ⟨in 25 words or *less*⟩ and as likely as *fewer* to modify periods of time ⟨in *less* (or *fewer*) than four hours⟩.

\ə\ **abut** \ᵊ\ **kitten** \ər\ **further** \a\ **ash** \ā\ **ace**
\ä\ **mop, mar** \au̇\ **out** \ch\ **chin** \e\ **bet** \ē\ **easy**
\g\ **go** \i\ **hit** \ī\ **ice** \j\ **job** \ŋ\ **go**
\ȯ\ **law** \ȯi\ **boy** \th\ **thin** \th̷\ **the** \ü\ **loot** \u̇\ **foot**
\y\ **yet** \zh\ **vision** *see also* Guide to Pronunciation

of contrast especially in negative contexts ⟨believed that he would never walk again *let alone* play golf —*Sports Illustrated*⟩ ⟨great to read but bloody to speak, *let alone* sing —Robertson Davies⟩

letch \'lech\ *noun* [back-formation from *letcher*, alteration of *lecher*] (circa 1796)
: CRAVING; *specifically* : sexual desire

let-down \'let-,daủn\ *noun* (1768)
1 a : DISCOURAGEMENT, DISAPPOINTMENT **b** : a slackening of effort : RELAXATION
2 : the descent of an aircraft or spacecraft to the point at which a landing approach is begun

let down *transitive verb* (12th century)
1 : to allow to descend gradually
2 a : to fail to support ⟨felt her parents had *let* her *down*⟩ **b** : to fall short of the expectations of ⟨the plot *lets* you *down* at the end⟩

¹le·thal \'lē-thəl\ *adjective* [Latin *letalis, lethalis,* from *letum* death] (1604)
1 a : of, relating to, or causing death ⟨death by *lethal* injection⟩ **b** : capable of causing death ⟨*lethal* chemicals⟩
2 : gravely damaging or destructive : DEVASTATING ⟨a *lethal* attack on his reputation⟩
synonym see DEADLY
— **le·thal·i·ty** \lē-'tha-lə-tē\ *noun*
— **le·thal·ly** \'lē-thə-lē\ *adverb*

²lethal *noun* (1917)
1 : an abnormality of genetic origin causing the death of the organism possessing it
2 : LETHAL GENE

lethal gene *noun* (1939)
: a gene that in some (as homozygous) conditions may prevent development or cause the death of an organism or its germ cells — called also *lethal factor, lethal mutant, lethal mutation*

le·thar·gic \lə-'thär-jik, le-\ *adjective* (14th century)
1 : of, relating to, or characterized by lethargy : SLUGGISH
2 : INDIFFERENT, APATHETIC
— **le·thar·gi·cal·ly** \-ji-k(ə-)lē\ *adverb*

leth·ar·gy \'le-thər-jē\ *noun* [Middle English *litargie,* from Medieval Latin *litargia,* from Late Latin *lethargia,* from Greek *lēthargia,* from *lēthargos* forgetful, lethargic, irregular from *lēthē*] (14th century)
1 : abnormal drowsiness
2 : the quality or state of being lazy, sluggish, or indifferent ☆

le·the \'lē-thē\ *noun* [Latin, from Greek *Lēthē,* from *lēthē* forgetfulness; akin to Greek *lanthanein* to escape notice, *lanthanesthai* to forget — more at LATENT]
1 *capitalized* : a river in Hades whose waters cause drinkers to forget their past
2 : OBLIVION, FORGETFULNESS
— **le·the·an** \'lē-thē-ən, li-'thē-\ *adjective,* often capitalized

let on *intransitive verb* (1725)
1 : to make acknowledgment : ADMIT ⟨knows more than he *lets on*⟩
2 : to reveal a secret ⟨nobody *let on* about the surprise party⟩
3 : PRETEND ⟨*let on* to being a stranger⟩

let out *intransitive verb* (1888)
: to conclude a session or performance ⟨school *let out* in June⟩

let's \'lets, *in rapid speech* 'les\ (1573)
: let us

Lett \'let\ *noun* [German *Lette,* ultimately from Latvian *latvis*] (1589)
: LATVIAN 2

¹let·ter \'le-tər\ *noun* [Middle English, from Old French *lettre,* from Latin *littera* letter of the alphabet, *litterae,* plural, epistle, literature] (13th century)
1 : a symbol usually written or printed representing a speech sound and constituting a unit of an alphabet
2 a : a direct or personal written or printed message addressed to a person or organization **b** : a written communication containing a grant — usually used in plural

3 *plural but singular or plural in construction*
a : LITERATURE, BELLES LETTRES **b** : LEARNING
4 : the strict or outward sense or significance ⟨the *letter* of the law⟩
5 a : a single piece of type **b** : a style of type
6 : the initial of a school awarded to a student for achievement usually in athletics

²letter (1668)
transitive verb
1 : to set down in letters : PRINT
2 : to mark with letters
intransitive verb
: to win an athletic letter
— **let·ter·er** \-tər-ər\ *noun*

³let·ter \'le-tər\ *noun* (1552)
: one that rents or leases

let·ter·boxed \'le-tər-,bäkst\ *adjective* [perhaps from the resemblance of the picture on the TV screen or the bands above and below the picture to slots in a mailbox] (1989)
of a video recording : formatted so as to display the full rectangular frame of a wide-screen motion picture
— **let·ter·box·ing** \-,bäk-siŋ\ *noun*

letter carrier *noun* (circa 1552)
: a person who delivers mail

let·tered \'le-tərd\ *adjective* (14th century)
1 a : LEARNED, EDUCATED **b** : of, relating to, or characterized by learning : CULTURED
2 : inscribed with or as if with letters

let·ter·form \'le-tər-,fȯrm\ *noun* (1908)
: the shape of a letter of an alphabet especially from the standpoint of design or development

let·ter·head \-,hed\ *noun* (circa 1887)
1 : a sheet of stationery printed or engraved usually with the name and address of an organization
2 : the heading at the top of a letterhead

let·ter·ing \'le-tə-riŋ\ *noun* (1811)
: letters used in an inscription

let·ter·man \'le-tər-mən\ *noun* (1926)
: an athlete who has earned a letter in a school sport

letter missive *noun, plural* **letters missive** [Middle English, from Middle French *lettre missive* letter intended to be sent] (15th century)
: a letter from a superior authority conveying a command, recommendation, permission, or invitation

letter of credence (14th century)
: a formal document attesting to the power of a diplomatic agent to act for the issuing government — called also *letters of credence*

letter of credit (1645)
1 : a letter addressed by a banker to a correspondent certifying that a person named therein is entitled to draw on the writer's credit up to a certain sum
2 : a letter addressed by a banker to a person to whom credit is given authorizing drafts on the issuing bank or on a bank in the person's country up to a certain sum and guaranteeing to accept the drafts if duly made

letter of intent (circa 1942)
: a written statement of the intention to enter into a formal agreement

let·ter–per·fect \'le-tər-'pər-fikt\ *adjective* (1845)
: correct to the smallest detail; *especially* : VERBATIM

let·ter·press \'le-tər-,pres\ *noun* (circa 1765)
1 : the process of printing from an inked raised surface especially when the paper is impressed directly upon the surface
2 *chiefly British* : text (as of a book) distinct from pictorial illustrations

letters close \-'klōs\ *noun plural* (1903)
: letters issued by a government or sovereign to a private person in a private matter

letter sheet *noun* (1851)
: a sheet of stationery that can be folded and sealed with the message inside to form its own envelope

letters of administration (15th century)

: a letter evidencing the right of an administrator to administer the goods or estate of a deceased person

letters of marque \-'märk\ (15th century)
: written authority granted to a private person by a government to seize the subjects of a foreign state or their goods; *specifically* : a license granted to a private person to fit out an armed ship to plunder the enemy

let·ter·spac·ing \'le-tər-,spā-siŋ\ *noun* (1917)
: insertion of space between the letters of a word

letters patent *noun plural* (14th century)
: a writing (as from a sovereign) that confers on a designated person a grant in a form open for public inspection

¹Lett·ish \'le-tish\ *adjective* (1831)
: of or relating to the Latvians or their language

²Lettish *noun* (1841)
: LATVIAN 1

let·tre de ca·chet \'le-trə-də-,ka-'shā\ *noun, plural* **lettres de cachet** \-trə(z)-\ [French, literally, letter with a seal] (1718)
: a letter bearing an official seal and usually authorizing imprisonment without trial of a named person

let·tuce \'le-təs\ *noun* [Middle English *letuse,* from Middle French *laitues,* plural of *laitue,* from Latin *lactuca,* from *lact-, lac* milk; from its milky juice — more at GALAXY] (14th century)
: any of a genus (*Lactuca*) of composite plants; *especially* : a common garden vegetable (*L. sativa*) whose succulent leaves are used especially in salads ◇

let·up \'let-,əp\ *noun* (1837)
: a lessening of effort or intensity

let up *intransitive verb* (1787)
1 a : to diminish or slow down : SLACKEN **b** : CEASE, STOP
2 : to become less severe — used with *on*

leu \'leủ\ *noun, plural* **lei** \'lā\ [Romanian, literally, lion, from Latin *leo* — more at LION] (1879)
— see MONEY table

leuc- *or* **leuco-** *chiefly British variant of* LEUK-

☆ **SYNONYMS**
Lethargy, languor, lassitude, stupor, torpor mean physical or mental inertness. LETHARGY implies such drowsiness or aversion to activity as is induced by disease, injury, or drugs ⟨months of *lethargy* followed my accident⟩. LANGUOR suggests inertia induced by an enervating climate or illness or love ⟨*languor* induced by a tropical vacation⟩. LASSITUDE stresses listlessness or indifference resulting from fatigue or poor health ⟨a depression marked by *lassitude*⟩. STUPOR implies a deadening of the mind and senses by shock, narcotics, or intoxicants ⟨lapsed into an alcoholic *stupor*⟩. TORPOR implies a state of suspended animation as of hibernating animals but may suggest merely extreme sluggishness ⟨a once alert mind now in a *torpor*⟩.

◇ **WORD HISTORY**
lettuce Many types of lettuce have a milky white juice, and it is to this property that the vegetable owes its name. The earliest known Middle English form, *letuse,* is apparently borrowed from Old French *laitues,* the plural of *laitue.* The Old French word is descended in turn from *lactuca,* the Latin word that is still used as the scientific name for the vegetable. *Lactuca* is a derivative of *lac,* the Latin word for "milk."

leu·cine \'lü-ˌsēn\ *noun* [French, from *leuc-* leuk-] (1826)
: a white crystalline essential amino acid $C_6H_{13}NO_2$ obtained by the hydrolysis of most dietary proteins

leu·cite \'lü-ˌsīt\ *noun* [German *Leuzit,* from *leuz-* leuk-] (1799)
: a white or gray mineral consisting of a silicate of potassium and aluminum and occurring in igneous rocks
— **leu·cit·ic** \lü-'si-tik\ *adjective*

leu·co·ci·din \ˌlü-kə-'sī-d°n\ *noun* [International Scientific Vocabulary *leuc-* + *-cide* + 1*-in*] (1894)
: a bacterial substance that destroys white blood cells

leu·co·plast \'lü-kə-ˌplast\ *noun* [International Scientific Vocabulary] (1886)
: a colorless plastid especially in the cytoplasm of interior plant tissues that is potentially capable of developing into a chloroplast

leuk- *or* **leuko-** *combining form* [New Latin *leuc-, leuco-,* from Greek *leuk-, leuko-,* from *leukos* — more at LIGHT]
1 : white **:** colorless **:** weakly colored ⟨*leuko*cyte⟩ ⟨*leuk*orrhea⟩
2 : leukocyte ⟨*leuk*emia⟩
3 : white matter of the brain ⟨*leuko*tomy⟩

leu·kae·mia *chiefly British variant of* LEUKEMIA

leu·kae·mo·gen·e·sis *chiefly British variant of* LEUKEMOGENESIS

leu·ke·mia \lü-'kē-mē-ə\ *noun* [New Latin] (circa 1855)
: an acute or chronic disease in humans and other warm-blooded animals characterized by an abnormal increase in the number of white blood cells in the tissues and often in the blood
— **leu·ke·mic** \-mik\ *adjective or noun*

leu·ke·mo·gen·e·sis \lü-ˌkē-mə-'je-nə-səs\ *noun* (1942)
: induction or production of leukemia
— **leu·ke·mo·gen·ic** \-'je-nik\ *adjective*

leu·ke·moid \-ˌmȯid\ *adjective* (1926)
: resembling leukemia but not involving the same changes in the blood-forming organs

leu·ko·cyte \'lü-kə-ˌsīt\ *noun* [International Scientific Vocabulary] (1870)
: WHITE BLOOD CELL
— **leu·ko·cyt·ic** \ˌlü-kə-'si-tik\ *adjective*

leu·ko·cy·to·sis \ˌlü-kə-sī-'tō-səs, -kə-sə-\ *noun* [New Latin] (1866)
: an increase in the number of white blood cells in the circulating blood

leu·ko·dys·tro·phy \ˌlü-kō-'dis-trə-fē\ *noun, plural* **-phies** (1962)
: any of several genetically determined diseases characterized by degeneration of the white matter of the brain

leu·ko·pe·nia \ˌlü-kə-'pē-nē-ə\ *noun* [New Latin] (1898)
: a condition in which the number of white blood cells circulating in the blood is abnormally low
— **leu·ko·pe·nic** \-nik\ *adjective*

leu·ko·pla·kia \ˌlü-kō-'plā-kē-ə\ *noun* [New Latin, from *leuk-* + Greek *plak-, plax* flat surface — more at FLUKE] (circa 1888)
: an abnormal condition in which thickened white patches of epithelium occur on the mucous membranes (as of the mouth or vulva); *also* **:** a lesion or lesioned area of leukoplakia
— **leu·ko·pla·kic** \-'plā-kik\ *adjective*

leu·ko·poi·e·sis \-ˌpȯi-'ē-səs\ *noun* [New Latin] (circa 1913)
: the formation of white blood cells
— **leu·ko·poi·et·ic** \-'e-tik\ *adjective*

leu·kor·rhea \ˌlü-kə-'rē-ə\ *noun* [New Latin] (circa 1797)
: a whitish viscid discharge from the vagina resulting from inflammation or congestion of the mucous membrane
— **leu·kor·rhe·al** \-'rē-əl\ *adjective*

leu·ko·sis \lü-'kō-səs\ *noun, plural* **-ko·ses** \-ˌsēz\ [New Latin] (1922)

: LEUKEMIA; *especially* **:** any of various leukemic diseases of poultry

leu·kot·o·my \lü-'kä-tə-mē\ *noun, plural* **-mies** (1937)
: LOBOTOMY

leu·ko·tri·ene \ˌlü-kō-'trī-ˌēn\ *noun* (1980)
: any of a group of eicosanoids that participate in allergic responses

lev \'lef\ *noun, plural* **le·va** \'le-və\ [Bulgarian, literally, lion] (circa 1900)
— see MONEY table

lev- *or* **levo-** *combining form* [French *lévo-,* from Latin *laevus* left; akin to Greek *laios* left]
1 : levorotatory ⟨*levo*lose⟩
2 : to the left ⟨*levo*rotatory⟩

Le·val·loi·si·an \ˌle-və-'lȯi-zē-ən, lə-ˌval-'wä-zē-\ *adjective* [*Levallois*-Perret, suburb of Paris, France] (1932)
: of or relating to a Middle Paleolithic culture characterized by a technique of manufacturing tools by striking flakes from a flint nodule

le·vant \lə-'vant\ *intransitive verb* [perhaps from Spanish *levantar* to break camp, ultimately from Latin *levare*] (1797)
chiefly British **:** to run away from a debt

le·vant·er \lə-'van-tər\ *noun* (1668)
1 *capitalized* **:** a native or inhabitant of the Levant
2 : a strong easterly Mediterranean wind

Le·vant storax \lə-'vant-\ *noun* (1937)
: STORAX 1a

le·va·tor \li-'vā-tər\ *noun, plural* **lev·a·to·res** \ˌle-və-'tōr-(ˌ)ēz\ *or* **le·va·tors** \li-'vā-tərz\ [New Latin, from Latin *levare* to raise — more at LEVER] (1615)
: a muscle that serves to raise a body part — compare DEPRESSOR

¹le·vee \'le-vē; lə-'vē, -'vā\ *noun* [French *lever,* from Middle French, act of arising, from (*se*) *lever* to rise] (1672)
1 : a reception held by a person of distinction on rising from bed
2 : an afternoon assembly at which the British sovereign or his or her representative receives only men
3 : a reception usually in honor of a particular person

²lev·ee \'le-vē\ *noun* [French *levée,* from Old French, act of raising, from *lever* to raise — more at LEVER] (circa 1720)
1 a : an embankment for preventing flooding **b :** a river landing place **:** PIER
2 : a continuous dike or ridge (as of earth) for confining the irrigation areas of land to be flooded

³lev·ee \'le-vē\ *transitive verb* **lev·eed; lev·ee·ing** (1832)
: to provide with a levee

¹lev·el \'le-vəl\ *noun* [Middle English, plumb line, from Middle French *livel,* from (assumed) Vulgar Latin *libellus,* alteration of Latin *libella,* from diminutive of *libra* weight, balance] (14th century)
1 : a device for establishing a horizontal line or plane by means of a bubble in a liquid that shows adjustment to the horizontal by movement to the center of a slightly bowed glass tube
2 : a measurement of the difference of altitude of two points by means of a level
3 : horizontal condition; *especially* **:** equilibrium of a fluid marked by a horizontal surface of even altitude ⟨water seeks its own *level*⟩
4 a : an approximately horizontal line or surface taken as an index of altitude **b :** a practically horizontal surface or area (as of land)
5 : a position in a scale or rank ⟨funded at the national *level*⟩
6 a : a line or surface that cuts perpendicularly all plumb lines that it meets and hence would everywhere coincide with a surface of still water **b :** the plane of the horizon or a line in it
7 : a horizontal passage in a mine intended for regular working and transportation

8 : a concentration of a constituent especially of a body fluid (as blood)
9 : the magnitude of a quantity considered in relation to an arbitrary reference value; *broadly* **:** MAGNITUDE, INTENSITY ⟨a high *level* of hostility⟩
— **on the level :** BONA FIDE, HONEST

²level *verb* **-eled** *or* **-elled; -el·ing** *or* **-el·ling** \'le-və-liŋ, 'lev-liŋ\ (15th century)
transitive verb
1 : to make (a line or surface) horizontal **:** make flat or level ⟨*level* a field⟩ ⟨*level* off a house lot⟩
2 a : to bring to a horizontal aiming position **b :** AIM, DIRECT ⟨*leveled* a charge of fraud⟩
3 : to bring to a common level or plane **:** EQUALIZE ⟨love *levels* all ranks —W. S. Gilbert⟩
4 a : to lay level with or as if with the ground **:** RAZE **b :** to knock down ⟨*leveled* him with one punch⟩
5 : to make (as color) even or uniform
6 : to find the heights of different points in (a piece of land) especially with a surveyor's level
intransitive verb
1 : to attain or come to a level ⟨the plane *leveled* off at 10,000 feet⟩
2 : to aim a gun or other weapon horizontally
3 : to bring persons or things to a level
4 : to deal frankly and openly

³level *adjective* (15th century)
1 a : having no part higher than another **:** conforming to the curvature of the liquid parts of the earth's surface **b :** parallel with the plane of the horizon **:** HORIZONTAL
2 a : even or unvarying in height **b :** equal in advantage, progression, or standing **c :** proceeding monotonously or uneventfully **d** (1) **:** STEADY, UNWAVERING ⟨gave him a *level* look⟩ (2) **:** CALM, UNEXCITED ⟨spoke in *level* tones⟩
3 : REASONABLE, BALANCED ⟨arrive at a justly proportional and *level* judgment on this affair —Sir Winston Churchill⟩
4 : distributed evenly ⟨*level* stress⟩
5 : being a surface perpendicular to all lines of force in a field of force **:** EQUIPOTENTIAL
6 : suited to a particular rank or plane of ability or achievement ⟨top-*level* thinking⟩
7 : of or relating to the spreading out of a cost or charge in even payments over a period of time ☆
— **lev·el·ly** \'le-və(l)-lē\ *adverb*
— **lev·el·ness** \-vəl-nəs\ *noun*
— **level best :** very best

level crossing *noun* (circa 1841)
British **:** GRADE CROSSING

lev·el·er *or* **lev·el·ler** \'le-və-lər, 'lev-lər\ *noun* (1598)

☆ **SYNONYMS**
Level, flat, plane, even, smooth mean having a surface without bends, curves, or irregularities. LEVEL applies to a horizontal surface that lies on a line parallel with the horizon ⟨the vast prairies are nearly *level*⟩. FLAT applies to a surface devoid of noticeable curvatures, prominences, or depressions ⟨the work surface must be *flat*⟩. PLANE applies to any real or imaginary flat surface in which a straight line between any two points on it lies wholly within that surface ⟨the *plane* sides of a crystal⟩. EVEN applies to a surface that is noticeably flat or level or to a line that is observably straight ⟨trim the hedge so it is *even*⟩. SMOOTH applies especially to a polished surface free of irregularities ⟨a *smooth* skating rink⟩.

\ə\ abut \ᵊ\ kitten \ər\ further \a\ ash \ā\ ace
\ä\ mop, mar \aü\ out \ch\ chin \e\ bet \ē\ easy
\g\ go \i\ hit \ī\ ice \j\ job \ŋ\ sing
\ō\ law \ȯi\ boy \th\ thin \th\ the \ü\ loot \u̇\ foot
\y\ yet \zh\ vision *see also* Guide to Pronunciation

1 : one that levels
2 a *capitalized* **:** one of a group of radicals arising during the English Civil War and advocating equality before the law and religious toleration **b :** one favoring the removal of political, social, or economic inequalities **c :** something that tends to reduce or eliminate differences among individuals
lev·el·head·ed \ˌle-vəl-ˈhe-dəd\ *adjective* (1879)
: having sound judgment **:** SENSIBLE
— **lev·el·head·ed·ness** *noun*
leveling rod *noun* (circa 1889)
: a graduated rod used in measuring the vertical distance between a point on the ground and the line of sight of a surveyor's level
level off *intransitive verb* (1919)
: to approach or reach a steady rate, volume, or amount **:** STABILIZE ⟨expect prices to *level off*⟩
level of significance (1925)
: the probability of rejecting the null hypothesis in a statistical test when it is true — called also *significance level*
¹**le·ver** \ˈle-vər, ˈlē-\ *noun* [Middle English, from Middle French *levier*, from *lever* to raise, from Latin *levare*, from *levis* light in weight — more at LIGHT] (14th century)
1 a : a bar used for prying or dislodging something **b :** an inducing or compelling force **:** TOOL ⟨use food as a political *lever* —*Time*⟩
2 a : a rigid piece that transmits and modifies force or motion when forces are applied at two points and it turns about a third; *specifically* **:** a rigid bar used to exert a pressure or sustain a weight at one point of its length by the application of a force at a second and turning at a third on a fulcrum **b :** a projecting piece by which a mechanism is operated or adjusted
²**lever** *transitive verb* **le·vered; le·ver·ing** \ˈle-və-riŋ, ˈlē-; ˈlev-riŋ, ˈlēv-\ (1876)
1 : to pry, raise, or move with or as if with a lever
2 : to operate (a device) in the manner of a lever
¹**le·ver·age** \ˈle-və-rij, ˈlē-; ˈlev-rij, ˈlēv-\ *noun* (1830)
1 : the action of a lever or the mechanical advantage gained by it
2 : POWER, EFFECTIVENESS ⟨trying to gain more political *leverage*⟩
3 : the use of credit to enhance one's speculative capacity
²**leverage** *transitive verb* **-aged; -ag·ing** (1937)
: to provide (as a corporation) or supplement (as money) with leverage; *also* **:** to enhance as if by supplying with financial leverage
lev·er·aged \ˈle-və-rijd, ˈlē-; ˈlev-rijd, ˈlēv-\ *adjective* (1953)
1 : having a high proportion of debt relative to equity
2 *of the purchase of a company* **:** made with borrowed money that is secured by the assets of the company bought ⟨a *leveraged* buyout⟩
lev·er·et \ˈle-və-rət, ˈlev-rət\ *noun* [Middle English, from (assumed) Middle French *levret*, from Middle French *levre* hare, from Latin *lepor-, lepus*] (15th century)
: a hare in its first year
Le·vi \ˈlē-ˌvī\ *noun* [Late Latin, from Hebrew *Lēwī*]
: a son of Jacob and the traditional eponymous ancestor of the priestly tribe of Levi
levi·able \ˈle-vē-ə-bəl\ *adjective* (15th century)
: capable of being levied or levied upon
le·vi·a·than \li-ˈvī-ə-thən\ *noun* [Middle English, from Late Latin, from Hebrew *liwyāthān*]
1 a *often capitalized* **:** a sea monster defeated by Yahweh in various scriptural accounts **b :** a large sea animal
2 *capitalized* **:** the political state; *especially* **:** a totalitarian state having a vast bureaucracy
3 : something large or formidable

— **leviathan** *adjective*
levi·er \ˈle-vē-ər\ *noun* (15th century)
: one that levies
lev·i·gate \ˈle-və-ˌgāt\ *transitive verb* **-gat·ed; -gat·ing** [Latin *levigatus*, past participle of *levigare* to make smooth, from *levis* smooth (akin to Greek *leios* smooth and perhaps to Latin *linere* to smear) + *-igare* (akin to *agere* to drive) — more at LIME, AGENT] (1612)
1 : POLISH, SMOOTH
2 a : to grind to a fine smooth powder while in moist condition **b :** to separate (fine powder) from coarser material by suspending in a liquid
— **lev·i·ga·tion** \ˌle-və-ˈgā-shən\ *noun*
lev·in \ˈle-vən\ *noun* [Middle English *levene*] (13th century)
archaic **:** LIGHTNING
le·vi·rate \ˈle-və-rət, ˈlē-, -ˌrāt\ *noun* [Latin *levir* husband's brother; akin to Old English *tācor* husband's brother, Greek *daēr*] (1725)
: the sometimes compulsory marriage of a widow to a brother of her deceased husband
— **lev·i·rat·ic** \ˌle-və-ˈra-tik, ˌlē-\ *adjective*
Le·vi's \ˈlē-ˌvīz\ *trademark*
— used especially for blue denim jeans
lev·i·tate \ˈle-və-ˌtāt\ *verb* **-tat·ed; -tat·ing** [*levity*] (1673)
intransitive verb
: to rise or float in the air especially in seeming defiance of gravitation
transitive verb
: to cause to levitate
lev·i·ta·tion \ˌle-və-ˈtā-shən\ *noun* (1668)
: the act or process of levitating; *especially* **:** the rising or lifting of a person or thing by means held to be supernatural
— **lev·i·ta·tion·al** \-shnəl, -shə-nᵊl\ *adjective*
Le·vite \ˈlē-ˌvīt\ *noun* (14th century)
: a member of the priestly Hebrew tribe of Levi; *specifically* **:** a Levite of non-Aaronic descent assigned to lesser ceremonial offices under the Levitical priests of the family of Aaron
Le·vit·i·cal \li-ˈvi-ti-kəl\ *adjective* [Late Latin *Leviticus*] (1535)
: of or relating to the Levites or to Leviticus
Le·vit·i·cus \-kəs\ *noun* [Late Latin, literally, of the Levites)
: the third book of canonical Jewish and Christian Scripture consisting mainly of priestly legislation — see BIBLE table
lev·i·ty \ˈle-və-tē\ *noun* [Latin *levitat-, levitas*, from *levis* light in weight — more at LIGHT] (1564)
1 : excessive or unseemly frivolity
2 : lack of steadiness **:** CHANGEABLENESS
le·vo \ˈlē-(ˌ)vō\ *adjective* (1938)
: LEVOROTATORY
levo- — see LEV-
levo·do·pa \ˌle-və-ˈdō-pə\ *noun* (1969)
: L-DOPA
le·vo·ro·ta·to·ry \-ˈrō-tə-ˌtōr-ē, -ˌtȯr-\ *or* **le·vo·ro·ta·ry** \-ˈrō-tə-rē\ *adjective* (1873)
: turning toward the left or counterclockwise; *especially* **:** rotating the plane of polarization of light to the left — compare DEXTROROTATORY
lev·u·lose \ˈlev-yə-ˌlōs, -ˌlōz\ *noun* [International Scientific Vocabulary, irregular from *lev-* + ²*-ose*] (1871)
: FRUCTOSE 2
¹**levy** \ˈle-vē\ *noun, plural* **lev·ies** [Middle English, from Old French *levee*, act of raising — more at LEVEE] (13th century)
1 a : the imposition or collection of an assessment **b :** an amount levied
2 a : the enlistment or conscription of men for military service **b :** troops raised by levy
²**levy** *verb* **lev·ied; levy·ing** (14th century)
transitive verb
1 a : to impose or collect by legal authority ⟨*levy* a tax⟩ **b :** to require by authority
2 : to enlist or conscript for military service
3 : to carry on (war) **:** WAGE

intransitive verb
: to seize property
lewd \ˈlüd\ *adjective* [Middle English *lewed* vulgar, from Old English *lǣwede* laical, ignorant] (14th century)
1 *obsolete* **:** EVIL, WICKED
2 a : sexually unchaste or licentious **b :** OBSCENE, VULGAR
— **lewd·ly** *adverb*
— **lewd·ness** *noun*
lew·is \ˈlü-əs\ *noun* [probably from the name *Lewis*] (1743)
: an iron dovetailed tenon that is made in sections, can be fitted into a dovetail mortise, and is used in hoisting large stones
Lew·is acid \ˈlü-əs-\ *noun* [Gilbert N. *Lewis* (died 1946) American chemist] (1944)
: a substance that is capable of accepting an unshared pair of electrons from a base to form a covalent bond
lew·is·ite \ˈlü-ə-ˌsīt\ *noun* [Winford L. *Lewis* (died 1943) American chemist] (1919)
: a colorless or brown vesicant liquid $C_2H_2AsCl_3$ developed as a poison gas for war use
lex \ˈleks\ *noun, plural* **le·ges** \ˈlā-(ˌ)gās\ [Latin *leg-, lex*] (circa 1775)
: LAW
lex·eme \ˈlek-ˌsēm\ *noun* [Greek *lexis* word, speech + English *-eme*] (1940)
: a meaningful linguistic unit that is an item in the vocabulary of a language
— **lex·em·ic** \lek-ˈsē-mik\ *adjective*
lex·i·cal \ˈlek-si-kəl\ *adjective* (1836)
1 : of or relating to words or the vocabulary of a language as distinguished from its grammar and construction
2 : of or relating to a lexicon or to lexicography
— **lex·i·cal·i·ty** \ˌlek-sə-ˈka-lə-tē\ *noun*
— **lex·i·cal·ly** \ˈlek-si-k(ə-)lē\ *adverb*
lex·i·cal·i·sa·tion *British variant of* LEXICALIZATION
lex·i·cal·i·za·tion \ˌlek-si-kə-lə-ˈzā-shən\ *noun* (1949)
1 : the realization of a meaning in a single word or morpheme rather than in a grammatical construction
2 : the treatment of a formerly freely composed, grammatically regular, and semantically transparent phrase or inflected form as a formally or semantically idiomatic expression
— **lex·i·cal·ize** \ˈlek-si-kə-ˌlīz\ *transitive verb*
lexical meaning *noun* (1933)
: the meaning of the base (as the word *play*) in a paradigm (as *plays, played, playing*) — compare GRAMMATICAL MEANING
lex·i·cog·ra·pher \ˌlek-sə-ˈkä-grə-fər\ *noun* [Late Greek *lexikographos*, from *lexikon* + Greek *-graphos* writer, from *graphein* to write] (1658)
: an author or editor of a dictionary
lex·i·cog·ra·phy \ˌlek-sə-ˈkä-grə-fē\ *noun* (1680)
1 : the editing or making of a dictionary
2 : the principles and practices of dictionary making
— **lex·i·co·graph·i·cal** \ˌlek-si-kō-ˈgra-fi-kəl\ *or* **lex·i·co·graph·ic** \-fik\ *adjective*
— **lex·i·co·graph·i·cal·ly** \-fi-k(ə-)lē\ *adverb*
lex·i·col·o·gy \ˌlek-sə-ˈkä-lə-jē\ *noun* [French *lexicologie*, from *lexico-* (from Late Greek *lexiko-*, from *lexikon*) + *-logie* -logy] (circa 1828)
: a branch of linguistics concerned with the signification and application of words
— **lex·i·col·o·gist** \-jist\ *noun*
lex·i·con \ˈlek-sə-ˌkän *also* -kən\ *noun, plural* **lex·i·ca** \-kə\ *or* **lexicons** [Late Greek *lexikon*, from neuter of *lexikos* of words, from Greek *lexis* word, speech, from *legein* to say — more at LEGEND] (1603)

1 : a book containing an alphabetical arrangement of the words in a language and their definitions **:** DICTIONARY
2 a : the vocabulary of a language, an individual speaker or group of speakers, or a subject **b :** the total stock of morphemes in a language
3 : REPERTOIRE, INVENTORY

lex·is \'lek-səs\ *noun, plural* **lex·es** \-ˌsēz\ [Greek, speech, word] (1960)
: LEXICON 2a

ley *variant of* LEA

Ley·den jar \'lī-dᵊn-\ *noun* [Leiden, Leyden, Netherlands] (1825)
: an electrical capacitor consisting of a glass jar coated inside and outside with metal foil and having the inner coating connected to a conducting rod passed through the insulating stopper

L–form \'el-ˌfȯrm\ *noun* [Lister Institute, London, where it was first isolated] (1948)
: a variant bacterium formed especially under stressful conditions and usually lacking a cell wall

Lha·sa ap·so \'lä-sə-'äp-(ˌ)sō, 'lä-sə-'ap-\ *noun, plural* **Lhasa apsos** *often A capitalized* [*Lhasa,* Tibet + Tibetan *apso*] (1935)
: any of a Tibetan breed of small dogs that have a dense coat of long hard straight hair, a heavy fall over the eyes, heavy whiskers and beard, and a well-feathered tail curled over the back — called also *Lhasa*

Lhasa apso

li·a·bil·i·ty \ˌlī-ə-'bi-lə-tē\ *noun, plural* **-ties** (circa 1809)
1 a : the quality or state of being liable **b :** PROBABILITY
2 : something for which one is liable; *especially* **:** pecuniary obligation **:** DEBT — usually used in plural
3 : one that acts as a disadvantage **:** DRAWBACK

li·a·ble \'lī-ə-bəl, *especially in sense 2 often* 'lī-bəl\ *adjective* [Middle English *lyable,* from (assumed) Anglo-French, from Old French *lier* to bind, from Latin *ligare* — more at LIGATURE] (15th century)
1 a : obligated according to law or equity **:** RESPONSIBLE **b :** subject to appropriation or attachment
2 a : being in a position to incur — used with *to* ⟨*liable* to a fine⟩ **b :** exposed or subject to some usually adverse contingency or action ⟨watch out or you're *liable* to fall⟩ ☆ ▢

li·aise \lē-'āz\ *intransitive verb* **li·aised; li·ais·ing** [back-formation from *liaison*] (1928) *chiefly British*
1 : to establish liaison
2 : to act as a liaison officer

li·ai·son \'lē-ə-ˌzän, lē-ā-, ÷'lā-ə-\ *noun* [French, from Middle French, from *lier,* from Old French] (1759)
1 : a binding or thickening agent used in cooking
2 a : a close bond or connection **:** INTERRELATIONSHIP **b :** an illicit sexual relationship **:** AFFAIR 3a
3 a : communication for establishing and maintaining mutual understanding and cooperation (as between parts of an armed force) **b :** one that establishes and maintains liaison
4 : the pronunciation of an otherwise absent consonant sound at the end of the first of two consecutive words the second of which begins with a vowel sound and follows without pause

li·a·na \lē-'ä-nə, -'a-\ *also* **li·ane** \-'än, -'an\ *noun* [French *liane*] (1796)
: any of various usually woody vines especially of tropical rain forests that root in the ground

li·ar \'lī-(-ə)r\ *noun* [Middle English, from Old English *lēogere,* from *lēogan* to lie — more at LIE] (before 12th century)

: one that tells lies

Li·as \'lī-əs\ *adjective* [*Lias,* division of the European Jurassic, from French, from English, a limestone rock] (1813)
chiefly British **:** LIASSIC

Li·as·sic \lī-'a-sik\ *adjective* [modification of French *liasique,* from *Lias*] (1833)
: of, relating to, or being a subdivision of the European Jurassic

lib \'lib\ *noun* (1970)
: LIBERATION 2

li·ba·tion \lī-'bā-shən\ *noun* [Latin *libation-, libatio,* from *libare* to pour as an offering; akin to Greek *leibein* to pour] (14th century)
1 a : an act of pouring a liquid as a sacrifice (as to a deity) **b :** a liquid (as wine) used in a libation
2 a : an act or instance of drinking often ceremoniously **b :** BEVERAGE; *especially* **:** a drink containing alcohol
— **li·ba·tion·ary** \-shə-ˌner-ē\ *adjective*

lib·ber \'li-bər\ *noun* [*lib*] (1971)
: a person who supports a liberation movement especially for women — often used disparagingly

li·bec·cio \li-'be-chē-ˌō, -'be-chō\ *or* **li·bec·chio** \-'be-kē-ˌō\ *noun* [Italian *libeccio*] (1667)
: a southwest wind in Italy

¹li·bel \'lī-bəl\ *noun* [Middle English, written declaration, from Middle French, from Latin *libellus,* diminutive of *liber* book] (14th century)
1 a : a written statement in which a plaintiff in certain courts sets forth the cause of action or the relief sought **b** *archaic* **:** a handbill especially attacking or defaming someone
2 a : a written or oral defamatory statement or representation that conveys an unjustly unfavorable impression **b** (1) **:** a statement or representation published without just cause and tending to expose another to public contempt (2) **:** defamation of a person by written or representational means (3) **:** the publication of blasphemous, treasonable, seditious, or obscene writings or pictures (4) **:** the act, tort, or crime of publishing such a libel ◆

²libel *verb* **-beled** *or* **-belled; -bel·ing** *or* **-bel·ling** \-b(ə-)liŋ\ (1570)
intransitive verb
: to make libelous statements
transitive verb
: to make or publish a libel against
— **li·bel·er** \-b(ə-)lər\ *noun*
— **li·bel·ist** \-bə-list\ *noun*

li·bel·ant *or* **li·bel·lant** \'lī-bə-lənt\ *noun* (1726)
: one that institutes a suit by a libel

li·bel·ee *or* **li·bel·lee** \ˌlī-bə-'lē\ *noun* (circa 1856)
: one against whom a libel has been filed in a court

li·bel·ous *or* **li·bel·lous** \'lī-b(ə-)ləs\ *adjective* (1619)
: constituting or including a libel **:** DEFAMATORY ⟨a *libelous* statement⟩

Li·be·ra \'lē-bə-ˌrä, 'lē-brə\ *noun* [Latin, literally, deliver, imperative of *liberare* to liberate; from the first word of the responsory] (circa 1903)
: a Roman Catholic funeral responsory

¹lib·er·al \'li-b(ə-)rəl\ *adjective* [Middle English, from Middle French, from Latin *liberalis* suitable for a freeman, generous, from *liber* free; perhaps akin to Old English *lēodan* to grow, Greek *eleutheros* free] (14th century)
1 a : of, relating to, or based on the liberal arts ⟨*liberal* education⟩ **b** *archaic* **:** of or befitting a man of free birth
2 a : marked by generosity **:** OPENHANDED ⟨a *liberal* giver⟩ **b :** given or provided in a generous and openhanded way ⟨a *liberal* meal⟩ **c :** AMPLE, FULL

3 *obsolete* **:** lacking moral restraint **:** LICENTIOUS
4 : not literal or strict **:** LOOSE ⟨a *liberal* translation⟩
5 : BROAD-MINDED; *especially* **:** not bound by authoritarianism, orthodoxy, or traditional forms
6 a : of, favoring, or based upon the principles of liberalism **b** *capitalized* **:** of or constituting a political party advocating or associated with the principles of political liberalism; *especially* **:** of or constituting a political party in the United Kingdom associated with ideals of individual especially economic freedom, greater individual participation in government, and

constitutional, political, and administrative re-
forms designed to secure these objectives ☆
— **lib·er·al·ly** \-b(ə-)rə-lē\ *adverb*
— **lib·er·al·ness** *noun*

²**liberal** *noun* (1820)
: a person who is liberal: as **a** : one who is
open-minded or not strict in the observance of
orthodox, traditional, or established forms or
ways **b** *capitalized* : a member or supporter of
a liberal political party **c** : an advocate or ad-
herent of liberalism especially in individual
rights

liberal arts *noun plural* (14th century)
1 : the medieval studies comprising the
trivium and quadrivium
2 : the studies (as language, philosophy, histo-
ry, literature, abstract science) in a college or
university intended to provide chiefly general
knowledge and to develop the general intellec-
tual capacities (as reason and judgment) as op-
posed to professional or vocational skills

lib·er·al·ism \'li-b(ə-)rə-li-zəm\ *noun* (1819)
1 : the quality or state of being liberal
2 *often capitalized* : a movement in modern
Protestantism emphasizing intellectual liberty
and the spiritual and ethical content of Chris-
tianity **b** : a theory in economics emphasizing
individual freedom from restraint and usually
based on free competition, the self-regulating
market, and the gold standard **c** : a political
philosophy based on belief in progress, the es-
sential goodness of the human race, and the
autonomy of the individual and standing for
the protection of political and civil liberties **d**
capitalized : the principles and policies of a
Liberal party
— **lib·er·al·ist** \-b(ə-)rə-list\ *noun or adjec-
tive*
— **lib·er·al·is·tic** \,li-b(ə-)rə-'lis-tik\ *adjec-
tive*

lib·er·al·ise *British variant of* LIBERALIZE
lib·er·al·i·ty \,li-bə-'ra-lə-tē\ *noun, plural*
-ties (14th century)
: the quality or state of being liberal; *also* : an
instance of this

lib·er·al·ize \'li-b(ə-)rə-,līz\ *verb* **-ized; -iz-
ing** (1774)
transitive verb
: to make liberal or more liberal
intransitive verb
: to become liberal or more liberal
— **lib·er·al·iza·tion** \,li-b(ə-)rə-lə-'zā-
shən\ *noun*
— **lib·er·al·iz·er** \'li-b(ə-)rə-,lī-zər\ *noun*

lib·er·ate \'li-bə-,rāt\ *transitive verb* **-at·ed;
-at·ing** [Latin *liberatus,* past participle of *lib-
erare,* from *liber*] (circa 1623)
1 : to set at liberty : FREE; *specifically* : to free
(as a country) from domination by a foreign
power
2 : to free from combination ⟨*liberate* the gas
by adding acid⟩
3 : to take or take over illegally or unjustly
⟨material *liberated* from a nearby construction
site —Thorne Dreyer⟩
synonym see FREE
— **lib·er·a·tor** \-,ā-tər\ *noun*

liberated *adjective* (1946)
: freed from or opposed to traditional social
and sexual attitudes or roles ⟨a *liberated* wom-
an⟩ ⟨a *liberated* marriage⟩

lib·er·a·tion \,li-bə-'rā-shən\ *noun* (15th cen-
tury)
1 : the act of liberating : the state of being lib-
erated
2 : a movement seeking equal rights and status
for a group ⟨women's *liberation*⟩
— **lib·er·a·tion·ist** \-sh(ə-)nist\ *noun*

liberation theology *noun* (1972)
: a religious movement especially among Ro-
man Catholic clergy in Latin America that
combines political philosophy usually of a
Marxist orientation with a theology of salva-
tion as liberation from injustice
— **liberation theologian** *noun*

lib·er·tar·i·an \,li-bər-'ter-ē-ən\ *noun* (1789)
1 : an advocate of the doctrine of free will
2 a : a person who upholds the principles of
absolute and unrestricted liberty especially of
thought and action **b** *capitalized* : a member
of a political party advocating libertarian prin-
ciples
— **libertarian** *adjective*
— **lib·er·tar·i·an·ism** \-ē-ə-,ni-zəm\ *noun*

lib·er·tin·age \'li-bər-,tē-nij\ *noun* (1611)
: LIBERTINISM

lib·er·tine \'li-bər-,tēn\ *noun* [Middle English
libertyn freedman, from Latin *libertinus,* from
libertinus, adjective, of a freedman, from *lib-
ertus* freedman, from *liber*] (1577)
1 : a freethinker especially in religious matters
— usually used disparagingly
2 : a person who is unrestrained by convention
or morality; *specifically* : one leading a disso-
lute life
— **libertine** *adjective*

lib·er·tin·ism \'li-bər-,tē-,ni-zəm, -tə-\ *noun*
(1611)
: the quality or state of being libertine : the be-
havior of a libertine

lib·er·ty \'li-bər-tē\ *noun, plural* **-ties** [Middle
English, from Middle French *liberté,* from
Latin *libertat-, libertas,* from *liber* free —
more at LIBERAL] (14th century)
1 : the quality or state of being free: **a** : the
power to do as one pleases **b** : freedom from
physical restraint **c** : freedom from arbitrary
or despotic control **d** : the positive enjoyment
of various social, political, or economic rights
and privileges **e** : the power of choice
2 a : a right or immunity enjoyed by prescrip-
tion or by grant : PRIVILEGE **b** : permission es-
pecially to go freely within specified limits
3 : an action going beyond normal limits: as **a**
: a breach of etiquette or propriety : FAMILIAR-
ITY **b** : RISK, CHANCE ⟨took foolish *liberties*
with his health⟩ **c** : a violation of rules or a de-
viation from standard practice **d** : a distortion
of fact
4 : a short authorized absence from naval duty
usually for less than 48 hours
synonym see FREEDOM
— **at liberty 1** : FREE **2** : at leisure : UNOC-
CUPIED

liberty cap *noun* (1803)
: a close-fitting conical cap used as a symbol
of liberty by the French revolutionists and in
the U.S. before 1800

liberty pole *noun* (1770)
: a tall flagstaff surmounted by a liberty cap or
the flag of a republic and set up as a symbol of
liberty

li·bid·i·nal \lə-'bi-d⁰n-əl, -'bid-n⁰l\ *adjective*
(1922)
: of or relating to the libido
— **li·bid·i·nal·ly** *adverb*

li·bid·i·nous \-d⁰n-əs, -'bid-nəs\ *adjective*
[Middle English, from Middle French *li-
bidineus,* from Latin *libidinosus,* from *libidin-,
libido*] (15th century)
1 : having or marked by lustful desires : LAS-
CIVIOUS
2 : LIBIDINAL
— **li·bid·i·nous·ly** *adverb*
— **li·bid·i·nous·ness** *noun*

li·bi·do \lə-'bē-(,)dō *also* 'li-bə-,dō\ *noun, plu-
ral* **-dos** [New Latin *libidin-, libido,* from Lat-
in, desire, lust, from *libēre* to please — more
at LOVE] (1909)
1 : emotional or psychic energy that in psy-
choanalytic theory is derived from primitive
biological urges and that is usually goal-
directed
2 : sexual drive

Li·bra \'lē-brə, *sometimes* 'lī-brə, *for
2b* 'lē-brə *or* 'lēv-rə\ *noun* [Middle English,
from Latin (genitive *Librae*), literally, scales,
pound] (before 12th century)
1 *capitalized* **a** : a southern zodiacal constella-
tion between Virgo and Scorpio represented

by a pair of scales **b** (1) : the 7th sign of the
zodiac in astrology — see ZODIAC table (2)
: one born under the sign of Libra
2 a *plural* **li·brae** \'lī-,brē, 'lē-,brī\ [Latin]
: an ancient Roman unit of weight equal to
327.45 grams **b** [Spanish & Portuguese, from
Latin] : any of various Spanish, Portuguese,
Colombian, or Venezuelan units of weight

Li·bran \'lē-brən, 'lī-\ *noun* (1911)
: LIBRA 1b(2)

li·brar·i·an \lī-'brer-ē-ən\ *noun* (1703)
: a specialist in the care or management of a
library
— **li·brar·i·an·ship** \-,ship\ *noun*

li·brary \'lī-,brer-ē; *British usually & US some-
times* -brər-ē; *US sometimes* -brē, ÷-,ber-ē\
noun, plural **-brar·ies** [Middle English, from
Medieval Latin *librarium,* from Latin, neuter
of *librarius* of books, from *libr-, liber* inner
bark, rind, book] (14th century)
1 a : a place in which literary, musical, artis-
tic, or reference materials (as books, manu-
scripts, recordings, or films) are kept for use
but not for sale **b** : a collection of such materi-
als
2 a : a collection resembling or suggesting a
library ⟨a *library* of computer programs⟩ ⟨wine
library⟩ **b** : MORGUE 2
3 a : a series of related books issued by a pub-
lisher **b** : a collection of publications on the
same subject
4 : a collection of sequences of DNA and es-
pecially recombinant DNA that are maintained
in a suitable cellular environment and that rep-
resent the genetic material of a particular or-
ganism or tissue □

library paste *noun* (1953)
: a thick white adhesive made from starch

library science *noun* (circa 1904)
: the study of the principles and practices of li-
brary care and administration

li·bra·tion \lī-'brā-shən\ *noun* [Latin *libra-
tion-, libratio,* from *librare* to balance, from *li-
bra* scales] (1669)
: an oscillation in the apparent aspect of a sec-
ondary body (as a planet or a satellite) as seen
from the primary object around which it re-
volves
— **li·bra·tion·al** \-shnəl, -shə-n⁰l\ *adjective*
— **li·bra·to·ry** \'lī-brə-,tōr-ē, -,tór-\ *adjec-
tive*

☆ SYNONYMS
**Liberal, generous, bountiful, munifi-
cent** mean giving or given freely and un-
stintingly. LIBERAL suggests openhandedness
in the giver and largeness in the thing or
amount given (a teacher *liberal* with her
praise). GENEROUS stresses warmhearted
readiness to give more than size or impor-
tance of the gift (a *generous* offer of help).
BOUNTIFUL suggests lavish, unremitting giv-
ing or providing (children spoiled by *bountiful*
presents). MUNIFICENT suggests a scale of
giving appropriate to lords or princes (a
munificent foundation grant).

□ USAGE
library While the pronunciation \'lī-,brer-ē\
is the most frequent variant in the U.S., the
other variants are not uncommon. The con-
traction \'lī-brē\ and the dissimilated form \'lī-
,ber-ē\ result from the relative difficulty of re-
peating \r\ in successive syllables; our files
contain citations for these variants from edu-
cated speakers, including college presidents
and professors, as well as with somewhat
greater frequency from less educated
speakers.

libration point *noun* (1962)
: any of five positions in the plane of a celestial system consisting of one massive body orbiting another at which the gravitational influences of the two bodies are approximately equal

li·bret·tist \lə-'bre-tist\ *noun* (1862)
: the writer of a libretto

li·bret·to \lə-'bre-(,)tō\ *noun, plural* **-tos** *or* **-ti** \-(,)tē\ [Italian, diminutive of *libro* book, from Latin *libr-, liber*] (1742)
1 : the text of a work (as an opera) for the musical theater
2 : the book containing a libretto

li·bri·form \'lī-brə-,fòrm\ *adjective* [Latin *libr-, liber* + International Scientific Vocabulary *-iform*] (1877)
: resembling phloem fibers

Lib·ri·um \'li-brē-əm\ *trademark*
— used for a preparation of chlordiazepoxide

Lib·y·an \'li-bē-ən\ *noun* (15th century)
1 : a native or inhabitant of Libya
2 : a language of ancient North Africa probably ancestral to Berber dialects
— **Libyan** *adjective*

lice *plural of* LOUSE

¹li·cense *or* **li·cence** \'lī-s⁸n(t)s\ *noun* [Middle English, from Middle French *licence*, from Latin *licentia*, from *licent-, licens*, present participle of *licēre* to be permitted] (14th century)
1 a : permission to act **b** : freedom of action
2 a : a permission granted by competent authority to engage in a business or occupation or in an activity otherwise unlawful **b** : a document, plate, or tag evidencing a license granted
3 a : freedom that allows or is used with irresponsibility **b** : disregard for standards of personal conduct : LICENTIOUSNESS
4 : deviation from fact, form, or rule by an artist or writer for the sake of the effect gained
synonym *see* FREEDOM

²license *also* **licence** *transitive verb* **licensed; li·cens·ing** (15th century)
1 a : to issue a license to **b** : to permit or authorize especially by formal license
2 : to give permission or consent to
— **li·cens·able** \-s⁸n(t)-sə-bəl\ *adjective*
— **li·cens·er** \-sər\ *or* **li·cen·sor** \-sər, ,lī-s⁸n-'sòr\ *noun*

licensed practical nurse *noun* (1951)
: a person who has undergone training and obtained a license (as from a state) conferring authorization to provide routine care for the sick

li·cens·ee \,lī-s⁸n(t)-'sē\ *noun* (circa 1864)
: one that is licensed

license plate *noun* (1926)
: a plate or tag (as of metal) attesting that a license has been secured and usually bearing a registration number

li·cen·sure \'lī-s⁸n-shər, -,shùr\ *noun* (circa 1846)
: the granting of licenses especially to practice a profession; *also* : the state of being licensed

licente *plural of* SENTE

li·cen·ti·ate \lī-'sen(t)-shē-ət, *especially in sense 2* li-\ *noun* [Medieval Latin *licentiatus*, from past participle of *licentiare* to allow, from Latin *licentia*] (1555)
1 : one who has a license granted especially by a university to practice a profession
2 : an academic degree ranking below that of doctor given by some European universities

li·cen·tious \lī-'sen(t)-shəs\ *adjective* [Latin *licentiosus*, from *licentia*] (1535)
1 : lacking legal or moral restraints; *especially* : disregarding sexual restraints
2 : marked by disregard for strict rules of correctness
— **li·cen·tious·ly** *adverb*
— **li·cen·tious·ness** *noun*

li·chee *variant of* LITCHI

li·chen \'lī-kən, *British also* 'li-chən\ *noun* [Latin, from Greek *leichēn, lichēn*, from *leichein* to lick] (circa 1657)

1 : any of several skin diseases characterized by a papular eruption
2 : any of numerous complex thallophytic plants made up of an alga and a fungus growing in symbiotic association on a solid surface (as a rock)
— **li·chened** \-kənd\ *adjective*
— **li·chen·ous** \-kə-nəs\ *adjective*

li·chen·ol·o·gy \,lī-kə-'nä-lə-jē\ *noun* [International Scientific Vocabulary] (1855)
: the study of lichens
— **li·chen·o·log·i·cal** \,lī-kə-nə-'lä-ji-kəl\ *adjective*
— **li·chen·ol·o·gist** \,lī-kə-'nä-lə-jist\ *noun*

lich–gate *variant of* LYCH-GATE

licht \'likt\ *Scottish variant of* LIGHT

lic·it \'li-sət\ *adjective* [Middle English, from Middle French *licite*, from Latin *licitus*, from past participle of *licēre* to be permitted — more at LICENSE] (15th century)
: conforming to the requirements of the law
: not forbidden by law : PERMISSIBLE
synonym *see* LAWFUL
— **lic·it·ly** *adverb*

¹lick \'lik\ *verb* [Middle English, from Old English *liccian;* akin to Old High German *leckōn* to lick, Latin *lingere*, Greek *leichein*] (before 12th century)
transitive verb
1 a (1) : to draw the tongue over ⟨*lick* a stamp⟩ (2) : to flicker over like a tongue **b** : to take into the mouth with the tongue : LAP
2 a : to strike repeatedly : THRASH **b** : to get the better of : OVERCOME, DEFEAT ⟨has *licked* every problem⟩
intransitive verb
1 : to lap with or as if with the tongue
2 : to dart like a tongue ⟨flames *licking* out of windows⟩
— **lick into shape** : to put into proper form or condition
— **lick one's wounds** : to recover from defeat or disappointment

²lick *noun* (1603)
1 a : an act or instance of licking **b** : a small amount : BIT ⟨couldn't swim a *lick*⟩ **c** : a hasty careless effort
2 a : a sharp hit : BLOW **b** : a directed effort : CRACK — usually used in plural; usually used in the phrase *get in one's licks*
3 a : a natural salt deposit (as a salt spring) that animals lick **b** : a block of often medicated saline preparation given to livestock to lick
4 : a musical figure; *specifically* : an interpolated and usually improvised figure or flourish
5 : a critical thrust : DIG, BARB
— **lick and a promise** : a perfunctory performance of a task

lick·er·ish \'li-k(ə-)rish\ *adjective* [alteration of *lickerous*, from Middle English *likerous, likerous*, from (assumed) Old North French, from Old North French *leckeur* lecher] (14th century)
1 : GREEDY, DESIROUS
2 *obsolete* : tempting to the appetite
3 : LECHEROUS
— **lick·er·ish·ly** *adverb*
— **lick·er·ish·ness** *noun*

lick·e·ty–split \,li-kə-tē-'split\ *adverb* [probably irregular from ¹*lick* + *split*] (circa 1859)
: at great speed

lick·ing *noun* (1756)
1 : a sound thrashing : DRUBBING
2 : DEFEAT

lick·spit·tle \'lik-,spi-t⁸l\ *noun* (1825)
: a fawning subordinate : TOADY

lic·o·rice \'li-k(ə-)rish, -k(ə-)rəs\ *noun* [Middle English *licorice*, from Old French, from Late Latin *liquiritia*, alteration of Latin *glycyrrhiza*, from Greek *glykyrrhiza*, from *glykys* sweet + *rhiza* root — more at DULCET, ROOT] (13th century)
1 a : the dried root of a European leguminous plant (*Glycyrrhiza glabra*) with pinnate leaves and spikes of blue flowers; *also* : an extract of this used especially in medicine, liquors, and

confectionery **b** : a candy flavored with licorice
2 : a plant yielding licorice

lic·tor \'lik-tər\ *noun* [Middle English *littour*, from Latin *lictor*] (14th century)
: an ancient Roman officer who bore the fasces as the insignia of his office and whose duties included accompanying the chief magistrates in public appearances

¹lid \'lid\ *noun* [Middle English, from Old English *hlid;* akin to Old High German *hlit* cover, and probably to Old English *hlinian* to lean — more at LEAN] (before 12th century)
1 : a movable cover for the opening of a hollow container (as a vessel or box)
2 : EYELID
3 : the operculum in mosses
4 *slang* : HAT
5 : something that confines, limits, or suppresses : CHECK, RESTRAINT
6 : an ounce of marijuana

²lid *transitive verb* **lid·ded; lid·ding** (13th century)
: to cover or supply with a lid

li·dar \'lī-,där\ *noun* [*light* + ra*dar*] (1963)
: a device that is similar in operation to radar but emits pulsed laser light instead of microwaves

lidded *adjective* (before 12th century)
1 : having or covered with a lid ⟨a *lidded* tureen⟩
2 : having lids especially of a specified kind — usually used in combination ⟨heavy-*lidded* eyes⟩

lid·less \'lid-ləs\ *adjective* (14th century)
1 : having no lid
2 *archaic* : WATCHFUL

li·do \'lē-(,)dō\ *noun, plural* **lidos** [*Lido*, Italy] (1860)
: a fashionable beach resort

li·do·caine \'lī-də-,kān\ *noun* [acetanil*id* + -*o-* + -*caine*] (circa 1949)
: a crystalline compound $C_{14}H_{22}N_2O$ that is used in the form of its hydrochloride as a local anesthetic and as an antiarrhythmic agent

¹lie \'lī\ *intransitive verb* **lay** \'lā\; **lain** \'lān\; **ly·ing** \'lī-iŋ\ [Middle English, from Old English *licgan;* akin to Old High German *ligen* to lie, Latin *lectus* bed, Greek *lechos*] (before 12th century)
1 a : to be or to stay at rest in a horizontal position : be prostrate : REST, RECLINE ⟨*lie* motionless⟩ ⟨*lie* asleep⟩ **b** : to assume a horizontal position — often used with *down* **c** *archaic* : to reside temporarily : stay for the night : LODGE **d** : to have sexual intercourse — used with *with* **e** : to remain inactive (as in concealment) ⟨*lie* in wait⟩
2 : to be in a helpless or defenseless state ⟨the town *lay* at the mercy of the invaders⟩
3 *of an inanimate thing* : to be or remain in a flat or horizontal position upon a broad support ⟨books *lying* on the table⟩
4 : to have direction : EXTEND ⟨the route *lay* to the west⟩
5 a : to occupy a certain relative place or position ⟨hills *lie* behind us⟩ **b** : to have a place in relation to something else ⟨the real reason *lies* deeper⟩ **c** : to have an effect through mere presence, weight, or relative position ⟨remorse *lay* heavily on him⟩ **d** : to be sustainable or admissible
6 : to remain at anchor or becalmed
7 a : to have place : EXIST ⟨the choice *lay* between fighting or surrendering⟩ **b** : CONSIST, BELONG ⟨the success of the book *lies* in its direct style⟩ ⟨responsibility *lay* with the adults⟩
8 : REMAIN; *especially* : to remain unused, unsought, or uncared for
usage *see* LAY

— **li·er** \\'lī(-ə)r\\ *noun*
— **lie low 1 :** to lie prostrate, defeated, or disgraced **2 :** to stay in hiding **:** strive to avoid notice **3 :** to bide one's time **:** remain secretly ready for action

²lie *noun* (1697)
1 *chiefly British* **:** LAY 6
2 : the position or situation in which something lies ⟨a golf ball in a difficult *lie*⟩
3 : the haunt of an animal (as a fish) **:** COVERT
4 *British* **:** an act or instance of lying or resting

³lie *verb* **lied; ly·ing** \\'lī-iŋ\\ [Middle English, from Old English *lēogan;* akin to Old High German *liogan* to lie, Old Church Slavonic *lŭgati*] (before 12th century)
intransitive verb
1 : to make an untrue statement with intent to deceive
2 : to create a false or misleading impression
transitive verb
: to bring about by telling lies ⟨*lied* his way out of trouble⟩ ☆

⁴lie *noun* [Middle English *lige, lie,* from Old English *lyge;* akin to Old High German *lugī,* Old English *lēogan* to lie] (before 12th century)
1 a : an assertion of something known or believed by the speaker to be untrue with intent to deceive **b :** an untrue or inaccurate statement that may or may not be believed true by the speaker
2 : something that misleads or deceives
3 : a charge of lying

lieb·frau·milch \\'lēp-,fraů-,milk, 'lēb-, -,milk, -,milsh\\ *noun* [German, alteration of *Liebfrauenmilch,* from *Liebfrauenstift,* religious foundation in Worms, Germany + *Milch* milk] (1833)
: a fruity white Rhine wine

lie by *intransitive verb* (1613)
: to remain inactive **:** REST

lied \\'lēt\\ *noun, plural* **lie·der** \\'lē-dər\\ [German, song, from Old High German *liod*] (1852)
: a German art song especially of the 19th century

Lie·der·kranz \\'lē-dər-,kran(t)s, -,krän(t)s\\ *trademark*
— used for a pungent surface-ripened cheese

lie detector *noun* (1909)
: an instrument for detecting physiological evidence of the tension that accompanies lying

lie down *intransitive verb* (1888)
1 : to submit meekly or abjectly to defeat, disappointment, or insult ⟨won't take that criticism *lying down*⟩
2 : to fail to perform or to neglect one's part deliberately ⟨*lying down* on the job⟩

¹lief \\'lēf, 'lēv\\ *adjective* [Middle English *lief, lef,* from Old English *lēof;* akin to Old English *lufu* love] (before 12th century)
1 *archaic* **:** DEAR, BELOVED
2 *archaic* **:** WILLING, GLAD

²lief \\'lēv, 'lēf\\ *adverb* (13th century)
: SOON, GLADLY ⟨I'd as *lief* go as not⟩

¹liege \\'lēj\\ *adjective* [Middle English, from Old French, from Late Latin *laeticus,* from *laetus* serf, of Germanic origin; akin to Old Frisian *let* serf] (14th century)
1 a : having the right to feudal allegiance or service ⟨his *liege* lord⟩ **b :** obligated to render feudal allegiance and service
2 : FAITHFUL, LOYAL

²liege *noun* (14th century)
1 a : a vassal bound to feudal service and allegiance **b :** a loyal subject
2 : a feudal superior to whom allegiance and service are due

liege man *noun* (14th century)
1 : VASSAL
2 : a devoted follower

lie–in \\'lī-,in\\ *noun* (1963)
: an act of lying down (as in a public place) in organized protest or as a means of forcing compliance with demands

lien \\'lēn, 'lē-ən\\ *noun* [Middle French, tie, band, from Latin *ligamen,* from *ligare* to bind — more at LIGATURE] (1531)
1 : a charge upon real or personal property for the satisfaction of some debt or duty ordinarily arising by operation of law
2 : the security interest created by a mortgage

lie off *intransitive verb* (1573)
1 : to hold back in the early part of a race
2 : to keep a little away from the shore or another ship
3 : to cease work for a time

lie over *intransitive verb* (circa 1847)
: to await disposal or attention at a later time

li·erne \\lē-'ərn, -'ern\\ *noun* [French, from Middle French, probably from *lier* to bind, from Latin *ligare*] (1842)
: a rib in Gothic vaulting that passes from one intersection of the principal ribs to another

lie to *intransitive verb* (1711)
of a ship **:** to stay stationary with head to windward

lieu \\'lü\\ *noun* [Middle English *lieu,* from Old French *lieu,* from Latin *locus* — more at STALL] (14th century)
archaic **:** PLACE, STEAD
— **in lieu :** INSTEAD
— **in lieu of :** in the place of **:** instead of

lie up *intransitive verb* (1699)
1 : to go into or remain in a dock
2 : to stay in bed or at rest

lieu·ten·an·cy \\lü-'te-nən(t)-sē, *British* le(f)-'ten(t)-\\ *noun* (15th century)
: the office, rank, or commission of a lieutenant

lieu·ten·ant \\-'te-nənt\\ *noun* [Middle English, from Middle French, from *lieu* + *tenant* holding, from *tenir* to hold, from Latin *tenēre* — more at THIN] (14th century)
1 a : an official empowered to act for a higher official **b :** an aide or representative of another in the performance of duty **:** ASSISTANT
2 a (1) **:** FIRST LIEUTENANT (2) **:** SECOND LIEUTENANT **b :** a commissioned officer in the navy or coast guard ranking above a lieutenant junior grade and below a lieutenant commander **c :** a fire or police department officer ranking below a captain

lieutenant colonel *noun* (1598)
: a commissioned officer in the army, air force, or marine corps ranking above a major and below a colonel

lieutenant commander *noun* (1839)
: a commissioned officer in the navy or coast guard ranking above a lieutenant and below a commander

lieutenant general *noun* (1589)
: a commissioned officer in the army, air force, or marine corps who ranks above a major general and whose insignia is three stars

lieutenant governor *noun* (1595)
: a deputy or subordinate governor: as **a :** an elected official serving as deputy to the governor of an American state **b :** the formal head of the government of a Canadian province appointed by the federal government as the representative of the crown
— **lieutenant governorship** *noun*

lieutenant junior grade *noun, plural* **lieutenants junior grade** (circa 1909)
: a commissioned officer in the navy or coast guard ranking above an ensign and below a lieutenant

¹life \\'līf\\ *noun, plural* **lives** \\'līvz\\ [Middle English *lif,* from Old English *līf;* akin to Old English *libban* to live — more at LIVE] (before 12th century)
1 a : the quality that distinguishes a vital and functional being from a dead body **b :** a principle or force that is considered to underlie the distinctive quality of animate beings — compare VITALISM 1 **c :** an organismic state characterized by capacity for metabolism, growth, reaction to stimuli, and reproduction
2 a : the sequence of physical and mental experiences that make up the existence of an individual **b :** one or more aspects of the process of living ⟨sex *life* of the frog⟩
3 : BIOGRAPHY 1
4 : spiritual existence transcending physical death
5 a : the period from birth to death **b :** a specific phase of earthly existence ⟨adult *life*⟩ **c :** the period from an event until death ⟨a judge appointed for *life*⟩ **d :** a sentence of imprisonment for the remainder of a convict's life
6 : a way or manner of living
7 : LIVELIHOOD
8 : a vital or living being; *specifically* **:** PERSON ⟨many *lives* were lost in the disaster⟩
9 : an animating and shaping force or principle
10 : SPIRIT, ANIMATION ⟨there was no *life* in her dancing⟩
11 : the form or pattern of something existing in reality ⟨painted from *life*⟩
12 : the period of duration, usefulness, or popularity of something ⟨the expected *life* of flashlight batteries⟩
13 : the period of existence (as of a subatomic particle) — compare HALF-LIFE
14 : a property (as resilience or elasticity) of an inanimate substance or object resembling the animate quality of a living being
15 : living beings (as of a particular kind or environment) ⟨forest *life*⟩
16 a : human activities **b :** animate activity and movement ⟨stirrings of *life*⟩ **c :** the activities of a given sphere, area, or time ⟨the political *life* of the country⟩
17 : one providing interest and vigor ⟨*life* of the party⟩
18 : an opportunity for continued viability ⟨gave the patient a new *life*⟩
19 *capitalized, Christian Science* **:** GOD 1b
20 : something resembling animate life ⟨a grant saved the project's *life*⟩

²life *adjective* (13th century)
1 : of or relating to animate being
2 : LIFELONG ⟨a *life* member⟩
3 : using a living model ⟨a *life* class⟩
4 : of, relating to, or provided by life insurance ⟨a *life* policy⟩

life–and–death *also* **life–or–death** *adjective* (1822)
: involving or culminating in life or death **:** vitally important as if involving life or death

life belt *noun* (circa 1858)
1 *chiefly British* **:** a life preserver in the form of a buoyant belt
2 : SAFETY BELT

life·blood \\'līf-'bləd, -,bləd\\ *noun* (1579)
1 : blood regarded as the seat of vitality
2 : a vital or life-giving force ⟨freedom of inquiry is the *lifeblood* of a university⟩

life·boat \\-,bōt\\ *noun* (1801)
: a sturdy buoyant boat (as one carried by a ship) for use in an emergency and especially in saving lives at sea

life buoy *noun* (1801)
: a ring-shaped life preserver

☆ **SYNONYMS**
Lie, prevaricate, equivocate, palter, fib mean to tell an untruth. LIE is the blunt term, imputing dishonesty ⟨*lied* about where he had been⟩. PREVARICATE softens the bluntness of LIE by implying quibbling or confusing the issue ⟨during the hearings the witness did his best to *prevaricate*⟩. EQUIVOCATE implies using words having more than one sense so as to seem to say one thing but intend another ⟨*equivocated* endlessly in an attempt to mislead her inquisitors⟩. PALTER implies making unreliable statements of fact or intention or insincere promises ⟨a swindler *paltering* with his investors⟩. FIB applies to a telling of a trivial untruth ⟨*fibbed* about the price of the new suit⟩.

life-care \'līf-,kar, -,ker\ *adjective* (1980)
: of, relating to, or being a residential complex for elderly people that provides an apartment, personal and social services, and health care for life

life cycle *noun* (1873)
1 : the series of stages in form and functional activity through which an organism passes between successive recurrences of a specified primary stage
2 : LIFE HISTORY 2
3 : a series of stages through which something (as an individual, culture, or manufactured product) passes during its lifetime

life expectancy *noun* (1935)
: the average life span of an individual

life force *noun* (1896)
: ÉLAN VITAL

life–form \'līf-'form, -,form\ *noun* (1899)
: the body form that characterizes a kind of organism (as a species) at maturity; *also* : a kind of organism

life-ful \'līf-fəl\ *adjective* (13th century)
archaic : full of or giving vitality

life–giv-ing \-,gi-viŋ\ *adjective* (1596)
: giving or having power to give life and spirit
— INVIGORATING

life-guard \-,gärd\ *noun* (1896)
: a usually expert swimmer employed (as at a beach or a pool) to safeguard other swimmers
— **lifeguard** *intransitive verb*

life history *noun* (1870)
1 : the history of an individual or thing
2 : a history of the changes through which an organism passes in its development from the primary stage to its natural death

life insurance *noun* (1809)
: insurance providing for payment of a stipulated sum to a designated beneficiary upon death of the insured

life jacket *noun* (1883)
: a life preserver in the form of a buoyant vest

life-less \'līf-ləs\ *adjective* (before 12th century)
: having no life: **a** : DEAD **b** : INANIMATE **c** : lacking qualities expressive of life and vigor : INSIPID **d** : destitute of living beings
— **life-less-ly** *adverb*
— **life-less-ness** *noun*

life-like \'līf-,līk\ *adjective* (14th century)
: accurately representing or imitating real life ⟨a *lifelike* portrait⟩
— **life-like-ness** *noun*

life-line \'līf-,līn\ *noun* (1700)
1 : a line (as a rope) used for saving or preserving life: as **a** : a line along the outer edge of the deck of a boat or ship **b** : a line used to keep contact with a person (as a diver or astronaut) in a dangerous or potentially dangerous situation
2 : something regarded as indispensable for the maintaining or protection of life

life list *noun* (1960)
: a record kept of all birds sighted and identified by a birder

life-long \'līf-,loŋ\ *adjective* (1855)
1 : lasting or continuing through life
2 : LONG-STANDING

life-man-ship \'līf-mən-,ship\ *noun* (1949)
: the skill or practice of achieving superiority or an appearance of superiority over others (as in conversation) by perplexing and demoralizing them

life net *noun* (circa 1904)
: a strong net or sheet (as of canvas) used (as by firefighters) to catch a person jumping from a burning building

life of Ri-ley *also* **life of Reil-ly** \-'rī-lē\ [from the name *Riley* or *Reilly*] (1923)
: a carefree comfortable way of living

life peer *noun* (1869)
: a British peer whose title is not hereditary
— **life peerage** *noun*

life preserver *noun* (1804)
1 : a device (as a life jacket or life buoy) designed to save a person from drowning by providing buoyancy in water
2 *chiefly British* : BLACKJACK 3

lif-er \'lī-fər\ *noun* (1827)
1 : a person sentenced to imprisonment for life
2 : a person who makes a career of one of the armed forces
3 : a person who has made a lifelong commitment (as to a way of life)

life raft *noun* (1819)
: a raft usually made of wood or an inflatable material and designed for use by people forced into the water

life ring *noun* (circa 1909)
: LIFE BUOY

life-sav-er \'līf-,sā-vər\ *noun* (1887)
1 : one trained to save lives of drowning persons
2 : one that is at once timely and effective in time of distress or need

¹life-sav-ing \-viŋ\ *adjective* (1858)
: designed for or used in saving lives ⟨*lifesaving* drugs⟩

²lifesaving *noun* (1919)
: the skill or practice of saving or protecting the lives especially of drowning persons

life science *noun* (1941)
: a branch of science (as biology, medicine, anthropology, or sociology) that deals with living organisms and life processes — usually used in plural
— **life scientist** *noun*

life-size \'līf-'sīz\ *or* **life-sized** \-'sīzd\ *adjective* (1841)
: of natural size : of the size of the original ⟨a *life-size* statue⟩

life span *noun* (1918)
1 : the duration of existence of an individual
2 : the average length of life of a kind of organism or of a material object especially in a particular environment or under specified circumstances

life-style \'līf-,stī(ə)l, -,stī(ə)l\ *noun* (1939)
: the typical way of life of an individual, group, or culture

life-sup-port \-,sə-pōrt, -,pȯrt\ *adjective* (1965)
: providing support necessary to sustain life; *especially* : of or relating to a system providing such support ⟨*life-support* equipment⟩

life support *noun* (1975)
: medical life-support equipment ⟨the patient was placed on *life support*⟩

life-sup-port system *noun* (1959)
: an artificial or natural system that provides all or some of the items (as oxygen, food, water, control of temperature and pressure, disposition of carbon dioxide and body wastes) necessary for maintaining life or health

life table *noun* (circa 1859)
: MORTALITY TABLE

¹life-time \'līf-,tīm\ *noun* (13th century)
1 a : the duration of the existence of a living being or a thing (as a star or a subatomic particle) **b** : LIFE 12
2 : an amount accumulated or experienced in a lifetime ⟨a *lifetime* of regrets⟩

²lifetime *adjective* (1904)
1 : LIFELONG
2 : measured or achieved over the span of a career ⟨a baseball player's *lifetime* batting average⟩

life vest *noun* (1939)
: LIFE JACKET

life-way \-,wā\ *noun* (1948)
: LIFE 6

life-work \-'wərk\ *noun* (1871)
: the entire or principal work of one's lifetime; *also* : a work extending over a lifetime

life zone *noun* (1901)
: a region characterized by specific plants and animals

¹lift \'lift\ *noun* [Middle English, from Old English *lyft*] (before 12th century)
chiefly Scottish : HEAVENS, SKY

²lift *verb* [Middle English, from Old Norse *lypta*; akin to Old English *lyft* air — more at LOFT] (14th century)
transitive verb
1 a : to raise from a lower to a higher position : ELEVATE **b** : to raise in rank or condition **c** : to raise in rate or amount
2 : to put an end to (a blockade or siege) by withdrawing or causing the withdrawal of investing forces
3 : REVOKE, RESCIND ⟨*lift* an embargo⟩
4 a : STEAL ⟨had her purse *lifted*⟩ **b** : PLAGIARIZE **c** : to take out of normal setting ⟨*lift* a word out of context⟩
5 : to take up (as a root crop or transplants) from the ground
6 : to pay off (an obligation) ⟨*lift* a mortgage⟩
7 : to move from one place to another (as by aircraft) : TRANSPORT
8 : to take up (a fingerprint) from a surface
intransitive verb
1 a : ASCEND, RISE ⟨the rocket *lifted* off⟩ **b** : to appear elevated (as above surrounding objects)
2 *of inclement weather* : to dissipate and clear
☆
— **lift-able** \'lif-tə-bəl\ *adjective*
— **lift-er** *noun*

³lift *noun* (14th century)
1 : the amount that may be lifted at one time : LOAD
2 a : the action or an instance of lifting **b** : the action or an instance of rising **c** : elevated carriage (as of a body part) **d** : the lifting up (as of a dancer) usually by a partner
3 : a device (as a handle or latch) for lifting
4 : an act of stealing : THEFT
5 a : ASSISTANCE, HELP **b** : a ride especially along one's way
6 : a layer in the heel of a shoe
7 : a rise or advance in position or condition
8 : a slight rise or elevation
9 : the distance or extent to which something rises
10 : an apparatus or machine used for hoisting: as **a** : a set of pumps used in a mine **b** *chiefly British* : ELEVATOR 1b **c** : an apparatus for raising an automobile (as for repair) **d** : SKI LIFT
11 a : an elevating influence **b** : an elevation of the spirit
12 a : the component of the total aerodynamic force acting on an airplane or airfoil that is perpendicular to the relative wind and that for an airplane constitutes the upward force that

☆ **SYNONYMS**
Lift, raise, rear, elevate, hoist, heave, boost mean to move from a lower to a higher place or position. LIFT usually implies exerting effort to overcome resistance of weight ⟨*lift* the chair while I vacuum⟩. RAISE carries a stronger implication of bringing up to the vertical or to a high position ⟨scouts *raising* a flagpole⟩. REAR may add an element of suddenness to RAISE ⟨suddenly *reared* itself up on its hind legs⟩. ELEVATE may replace LIFT or RAISE especially when exalting or enhancing is implied ⟨*elevated* the taste of the public⟩. HOIST implies lifting something heavy especially by mechanical means ⟨*hoisted* the cargo on board⟩. HEAVE implies lifting and throwing with great effort or strain ⟨*heaved* the heavy crate inside⟩. BOOST suggests assisting to climb or advance by a push ⟨*boosted* his brother over the fence⟩.

opposes the pull of gravity **b** : an updraft that can be used to increase altitude (as of a sailplane)
13 : an organized movement of people, equipment, or supplies by some form of transportation; *especially* : AIRLIFT
lift·gate \'lift-ˌgāt\ *noun* (1953)
: a rear panel (as on a station wagon) that opens upward
lift·man \-ˌman\ *noun* (1883)
British : an elevator operator
lift–off \-ˌȯf\ *noun* (circa 1956)
: a vertical takeoff by an aircraft or a rocket vehicle or missile
lift truck *noun* (1926)
: a small truck for lifting and transporting loads
lig·a·ment \'li-gə-mənt\ *noun* [Middle English, from Medieval Latin & Latin; Medieval Latin *ligamentum*, from Latin, band, tie, from *ligare*] (14th century)
1 : a tough band of tissue connecting the articular extremities of bones or supporting an organ in place
2 : a connecting or unifying bond ⟨the law of nations, the great *ligament* of mankind —Edmund Burke⟩
— **lig·a·men·tous** \-'men-təs\ *adjective*
li·gand \'li-gənd, 'lī-\ *noun* [Latin *ligandus*, gerundive of *ligare*] (1949)
: a group, ion, or molecule coordinated to a central atom or molecule in a complex
li·gase \'lī-ˌgās, -ˌgāz\ *noun* [International Scientific Vocabulary *lig-* (from Latin *ligare*) + *-ase*] (1961)
: SYNTHETASE
li·gate \'lī-ˌgāt, lī-'\ *transitive verb* **li·gat·ed; li·gat·ing** [Latin *ligatus*] (1599)
: to tie with a ligature
li·ga·tion \lī-'gā-shən\ *noun* (1597)
1 : an act of ligating
2 : something that binds : LIGATURE
lig·a·ture \'li-gə-ˌchu̇r, -chər, -ˌtu̇r, -ˌtyu̇r\ *noun* [Middle English, from Middle French, from Late Latin *ligatura*, from Latin *ligatus*, past participle of *ligare* to bind, tie; akin to Middle Low German *līk* band, boltrope, Albanian *lidh* I tie] (14th century)
1 a : something that is used to bind; *specifically* : a filament (as a thread) used in surgery **b** : something that unites or connects : BOND
2 : the action of binding or tying
3 : a compound note in mensural notation indicating a group of musical notes to be sung to one syllable
4 : a printed or written character (as æ or ff) consisting of two or more letters or characters joined together
¹light \'līt\ *noun* [Middle English, from Old English *lēoht*; akin to Old High German *lioht* light, Latin *luc-, lux* light, *lucēre* to shine, Greek *leukos* white] (before 12th century)
1 a : something that makes vision possible **b** : the sensation aroused by stimulation of the visual receptors **c** : an electromagnetic radiation in the wavelength range including infrared, visible, ultraviolet, and X rays and traveling in a vacuum with a speed of about 186,281 miles (300,000 kilometers) per second; *specifically* : the part of this range that is visible to the human eye
2 a : DAYLIGHT **b** : DAWN
3 : a source of light: as **a** : a celestial body **b** : CANDLE **c** : an electric light
4 *archaic* : SIGHT 4a
5 a : spiritual illumination **b** : INNER LIGHT **c** : ENLIGHTENMENT **d** : TRUTH
6 a : public knowledge ⟨facts brought to *light*⟩ **b** : a particular aspect or appearance presented to view ⟨saw the matter in a different *light*⟩
7 : a particular illumination
8 : something that enlightens or informs ⟨shed some *light* on the problem⟩
9 : a medium (as a window) through which light is admitted

10 *plural* : a set of principles, standards, or opinions ⟨worship according to one's *lights* —Adrienne Koch⟩
11 : a noteworthy person in a particular place or field
12 : a particular expression of the eye
13 a : LIGHTHOUSE, BEACON **b** : TRAFFIC LIGHT
14 : the representation of light in art
15 : a flame for lighting something
— **in the light of 1** : from the point of view of **2** *or* **in light of** : in view of
²light *adjective* (before 12th century)
1 : having light : BRIGHT ⟨a *light* airy room⟩
2 a : not dark, intense, or swarthy in color or coloring : PALE **b** *of colors* : medium in saturation and high in lightness ⟨*light* blue⟩
3 *of coffee* : served with extra milk or cream
³light *verb* **lit** \'lit\ *or* **light·ed; light·ing** (before 12th century)
intransitive verb
1 : to become light : BRIGHTEN — usually used with *up* ⟨her face *lit* up⟩
2 : to take fire
3 : to ignite something (as a cigarette) — often used with *up*
transitive verb
1 : to set fire to
2 a : to conduct with a light : GUIDE **b** : ILLUMINATE ⟨rockets *light* up the sky⟩ **c** : ANIMATE, BRIGHTEN ⟨a smile *lit* up her face⟩
⁴light *adjective* [Middle English, from Old English *lēoht*; akin to Old High German *līhti* light, Latin *levis*, Greek *elachys* small] (before 12th century)
1 a : having little weight : not heavy **b** : designed to carry a comparatively small load ⟨a *light* truck⟩ **c** : having relatively little weight in proportion to bulk ⟨aluminum is a *light* metal⟩ **d** : containing less than the legal, standard, or usual weight ⟨a *light* coin⟩
2 a : of little importance : TRIVIAL **b** : not abundant ⟨*light* rain⟩
3 a : easily disturbed ⟨a *light* sleeper⟩ **b** : exerting a minimum of force or pressure : GENTLE ⟨a *light* touch⟩ **c** : resulting from a very slight pressure : FAINT ⟨*light* print⟩
4 a : easily endurable ⟨a *light* illness⟩ **b** : requiring little effort ⟨*light* work⟩
5 : capable of moving swiftly or nimbly ⟨*light* on his feet⟩
6 a : FRIVOLOUS 1a ⟨*light* conduct⟩ **b** : lacking in stability : CHANGEABLE ⟨*light* opinions⟩ **c** : sexually promiscuous
7 : free from care : CHEERFUL
8 : less powerful but usually more mobile than usual for its kind ⟨*light* cavalry⟩
9 a : made with a lower calorie content or with less of some ingredient (as salt, fat, or alcohol) than usual ⟨*light* beer⟩ ⟨*light* salad dressing⟩ **b** : having a relatively mild flavor
10 a : easily digested ⟨a *light* soup⟩ **b** : well leavened ⟨a *light* crust⟩
11 : coarse and sandy or easily pulverized ⟨*light* soil⟩
12 : DIZZY, GIDDY ⟨felt *light* in the head⟩
13 : intended chiefly to entertain ⟨*light* verse⟩ ⟨*light* comedy⟩
14 a : carrying little or no cargo ⟨the ship returned *light*⟩ **b** : producing goods for direct consumption by the consumer ⟨*light* industry⟩
15 : not bearing a stress or accent ⟨a *light* syllable⟩
16 : having a clear soft quality ⟨a *light* voice⟩
17 : being in debt to the pot in a poker game ⟨three chips *light*⟩
18 : SHORT 5d ⟨*light* on experience⟩
synonym see EASY
— **light·ish** \'lī-tish\ *adjective*
⁵light *adverb* (before 12th century)
1 : LIGHTLY
2 : with little baggage ⟨travel *light*⟩
⁶light *intransitive verb* **lit** \'lit\ *or* **light·ed; light·ing** [Middle English, from Old English *līhtan*; akin to Old English *lēoht* light in weight] (before 12th century)
1 : DISMOUNT

2 : SETTLE, ALIGHT ⟨a bird *lit* on the lawn⟩
3 : to fall unexpectedly — usually used with *on* or *upon*
4 : to arrive by chance : HAPPEN — usually used with *on* or *upon* ⟨*lit* upon a solution⟩
— **light into** : to attack forcefully ⟨I *lit into* that food until I'd finished off the heel of the loaf —Helen Eustis⟩
light adaptation *noun* (1900)
: the process including contraction of the pupil and decrease in visual purple by which the eye adapts to conditions of increased illumination
light–adapt·ed \'līt-ə-ˌdap-təd\ *adjective* (1900)
: adjusted for vision in bright light : having undergone light adaptation
light air *noun* (circa 1881)
: wind having a speed of 1 to 3 miles (1.6 to 4.8 kilometers) per hour — see BEAUFORT SCALE table
light bread \'līt-ˌbred\ *noun* [²*light*] (1821)
chiefly Southern & Midland : bread in loaves made from white flour leavened with yeast
light breeze *noun* (circa 1881)
: wind having a speed of 4 to 7 miles (6.4 to 11 kilometers) per hour — see BEAUFORT SCALE table
light·bulb \'līt-ˌbəlb\ *noun* (1884)
: INCANDESCENT LAMP
light chain *noun* (1964)
: either of the two smaller of the four polypeptide chains comprising antibodies — compare HEAVY CHAIN
light curve *noun* (1890)
: a graph showing the variation in brightness of a celestial object (as a variable star) over a period of time
light–emitting diode *noun* (1970)
: LED
¹light·en \'lī-tᵊn\ *verb* **light·ened; light·en·ing** \'līt-niŋ, 'lī-tᵊn-iŋ\ [Middle English *lightenen*, from *light*] (14th century)
transitive verb
1 : to make light or clear : ILLUMINATE
2 *archaic* : ENLIGHTEN
3 : to make (as a color) lighter
intransitive verb
1 a *archaic* : to shine brightly **b** : to grow lighter : BRIGHTEN
2 : to give out flashes of lightning
— **light·en·er** \'līt-nər, 'lī-tᵊn-ər\ *noun*
²lighten *verb* **light·ened; light·en·ing** \'līt-niŋ, 'lī-tᵊn-iŋ\ (14th century)
transitive verb
1 a : to relieve of a burden in whole or in part ⟨the news *lightened* his mind⟩ **b** : to reduce in weight or quantity : LESSEN ⟨*lighten* her duties⟩ **c** : to make less wearisome : ALLEVIATE ⟨*lighten* our sorrow⟩
2 : CHEER, GLADDEN
intransitive verb
1 : to become lighter or less burdensome
2 : to become more cheerful
synonym see RELIEVE
— **light·en·er** \'līt-nər, 'lī-tᵊn-ər\ *noun*
lighten up *intransitive verb* (circa 1968)
: to take things less seriously
¹ligh·ter \'lī-tər\ *noun* [Middle English, from (assumed) Middle Dutch *lichter*, from Middle Dutch *lichten* to unload; akin to Old English *lēoht* light in weight] (14th century)
: a large usually flat-bottomed barge used especially in unloading or loading ships
²lighter *transitive verb* (1840)
: to convey by a lighter
³light·er \'lī-tər\ *noun* (1553)
1 : one that lights or sets a fire
2 : a device for lighting a fire; *especially* : a mechanical or electrical device used for lighting cigarettes, cigars, or pipes
light·er·age \'lī-tə-rij\ *noun* (15th century)
1 : the loading, unloading, or transportation of goods by means of a lighter
2 : a price paid for lightering
lighter–than–air *adjective* (1903)
: of less weight than the air displaced

light·face \'līt-ˌfās\ *noun* (circa 1871)
: a typeface having comparatively light thin lines; *also* **:** printing in lightface
— **light·faced** \-ˌfāst\ *adjective*

light–fast \-ˌfast\ *adjective* (1950)
: resistant to light and especially to sunlight; *especially* **:** colorfast to light
— **light–fast·ness** \-ˌfas(t)-nəs\ *noun*

light–fin·gered \-ˌfiŋ-gərd\ *adjective* (1547)
1 : showing adroitness in stealing or a tendency to steal especially by picking pockets or shoplifting
2 : having a light and dexterous touch **:** NIMBLE
— **light–fin·gered·ness** *noun*

light–foot·ed \-ˌfu̇-təd\ *also* **light–foot** \-ˌfu̇t\ *adjective* (15th century)
1 : having a light and springy step
2 : moving gracefully and nimbly

light guide *noun* (1951)
: an optical fiber used especially for telecommunication

light–hand·ed \'līt-ˌhan-dəd\ *adjective* (15th century)
: having a light or delicate touch **:** FACILE
— **light–hand·ed·ness** *noun*

light–head·ed \-ˌhe-dəd\ *adjective* (1537)
1 : mentally disoriented **:** DIZZY
2 : lacking in maturity or seriousness **:** FRIVOLOUS
— **light–head·ed·ly** *adverb*
— **light–head·ed·ness** *noun*

light·heart·ed \-ˌhär-təd\ *adjective* (15th century)
1 : free from care, anxiety, or seriousness **:** GAY
2 : cheerfully optimistic and hopeful **:** EASYGOING
— **light·heart·ed·ly** *adverb*
— **light·heart·ed·ness** *noun*

light heavyweight *noun* (1903)
: a boxer in a weight division having a maximum limit of 175 pounds for professionals and 178 pounds for amateurs — compare HEAVYWEIGHT, MIDDLEWEIGHT

light·house \'līt-ˌhau̇s\ *noun* (1622)
1 : a structure (as a tower) with a powerful light that gives a continuous or intermittent signal to navigators
2 : BEACON 3

light housekeeping *noun* (1904)
1 : domestic work restricted to the less laborious duties
2 : housekeeping in quarters with limited facilities for cooking

light·ing \'līt-iŋ\ *noun* (before 12th century)
1 a : ILLUMINATION **b :** IGNITION
2 : an artificial supply of light or the apparatus providing it

light·less \'līt-ləs\ *adjective* (before 12th century)
1 : receiving no light **:** DARK
2 : giving no light

light·ly \'līt-lē\ *adverb* (before 12th century)
: in a light manner: as **a :** with little weight or force **:** GENTLY **b :** with indifference or carelessness **:** UNCONCERNEDLY ⟨the problem should not be passed over *lightly* —Shelly Halpern⟩ **c :** with little difficulty **:** EASILY **d :** GAILY, CHEERFULLY **e :** in an agile manner **:** NIMBLY, SWIFTLY **f :** in a small degree or amount ⟨*lightly* salted food⟩

light meter *noun* (1921)
: a small and often portable device for measuring illumination; *especially* **:** EXPOSURE METER

light–mind·ed \'līt-ˌmīn-dəd\ *adjective* (1611)
: lacking in seriousness **:** FRIVOLOUS
— **light–mind·ed·ly** *adverb*
— **light–mind·ed·ness** *noun*

¹light·ness \-nəs\ *noun* (before 12th century)
1 : the quality or state of being illuminated **:** ILLUMINATION
2 : the attribute of object colors by which the object appears to reflect or transmit more or less of the incident light — compare BRIGHTNESS 2, HUE 2c, SATURATION 4

²lightness *noun* (12th century)
1 : the quality or state of being light especially in weight
2 : lack of seriousness and stability of character often accompanied by casual heedlessness
3 a : the quality or state of being nimble **b :** an ease and gaiety of style or manner
4 : lack of weightiness or force **:** DELICACY

¹light·ning \'līt-niŋ\ *noun* [Middle English, from gerund of *lightenen* to lighten] (13th century)
1 : the flashing of light produced by a discharge of atmospheric electricity; *also* **:** the discharge itself
2 : a sudden stroke of fortune

²lightning *adjective* (1640)
: having or moving with or as if with the speed and suddenness of lightning ⟨a *lightning* assault⟩

³lightning *intransitive verb* **light·ninged; lightning** (1903)
: to discharge a flash of lightning

lightning arrester *noun* (1860)
: a device for protecting an electrical apparatus from damage by lightning

lightning bug *noun* (1778)
: FIREFLY

lightning rod *noun* (1789)
1 : a grounded metallic rod set up on a structure (as a building) to protect it from lightning
2 : one that serves to divert attack from another or as a frequent target of criticism

light–o'–love \ˌlīt-ə-'ləv\ *also* **light–of–love** \-əv-'\ *noun, plural* **light–o'–loves** *also* **lights–of–love** (1589)
1 : PROSTITUTE
2 : LOVER, PARAMOUR

light opera *noun* (1882)
: OPERETTA

light out *intransitive verb* [⁶light] (1866)
1 : to leave in a hurry ⟨*lit out* for home at once⟩
2 : SET OFF

light pen *noun* (1958)
: a pen-shaped device for direct interaction with a computer through a cathode-ray tube display

light pipe *noun* (1950)
: an optical fiber or a solid transparent plastic rod for transmitting light lengthwise

light·plane \'līt-ˌplān\ *noun* (1923)
: a small and comparatively lightweight airplane; *especially* **:** a privately owned passenger airplane

light pollution *noun* (1971)
: artificial skylight (as from city lights) that interferes with astronomical observations

light·proof \'līt-ˌprüf\ *adjective* (1923)
: impenetrable by light

light quantum *noun* (1925)
: PHOTON; *especially* **:** one of luminous radiation

light–rail \'līt-ˌrā(ə)l\ *noun, often attributive* (1975)
: a means of urban railway transportation using trolley cars

light reaction *noun* (circa 1929)
: the phase of photosynthesis that requires the presence of light and that involves photophosphorylation

lights \'līts\ *noun plural* [Middle English *lightes*, from *light* light in weight] (12th century)
: the lungs especially of a slaughtered animal

light·ship \'līt-ˌship\ *noun* (1837)
: a ship equipped with a brilliant light and moored at a place dangerous to navigation

light show *noun* (1966)
: a kaleidoscopic display of colored lights, slides, and film loops

¹light·some \'līt-səm\ *adjective* (14th century)
1 : free from care **:** LIGHTHEARTED
2 : AIRY, NIMBLE
— **light·some·ly** *adverb*
— **light·some·ness** *noun*

²lightsome *adjective* (15th century)
1 : well lighted **:** BRIGHT
2 : giving light

lights–out \'līts-'au̇t\ *noun* (1868)
1 : a command or signal for putting out lights
2 : a prescribed bedtime for persons living under discipline

light table *noun* (circa 1948)
: a device that projects even light through a flat translucent surface over which films or tracings may be spread out and viewed

light·tight \'līt-ˌtīt\ *adjective* (1884)
: LIGHTPROOF

light trap *noun* (1906)
1 : a device that allows movement of a sliding part or passage of a person (as into a darkroom) but excludes light
2 : a device for collecting or destroying insects that consists of a bright light in association with a trapping or killing medium

light water *noun* (1933)
: WATER 1a — compare HEAVY WATER

¹light·weight \'līt-ˌwāt\ *noun* (1773)
1 : one of less than average weight; *specifically* **:** a boxer in a weight division having a maximum limit of 135 pounds for professionals and 132 pounds for amateurs
2 : one of little consequence or ability ⟨shows up its author as a *lightweight* —C. J. Rolo⟩

²lightweight *adjective* (1809)
1 : lacking in earnestness, ability, or profundity **:** INCONSEQUENTIAL
2 : having less than average weight
3 : of, relating to, or characteristic of a lightweight ⟨the *lightweight* championship⟩

light·wood \'līt-ˌwu̇d, 'lī-təd\ *noun* (1685)
chiefly Southern **:** wood used for kindling; *especially* **:** coniferous wood abounding in pitch

light–year \'līt-ˌyir\ *noun* (1888)
1 : a unit of length in astronomy equal to the distance that light travels in one year in a vacuum or about 5.88 trillion miles (9.46 trillion kilometers)
2 : an extremely large measure of comparison (as of distance, time, or quality) ⟨seems like *light-years* ago⟩ ⟨has *light-years* more talent⟩ ⟨two minutes and yet *light-years* away from the crowded village —Suzanne Patterson⟩ □

lign- *or* **ligni-** *or* **ligno-** *combining form* [Latin *lign-*, *ligni-*, from *lignum*]
: wood ⟨*lignin*⟩ ⟨*ligno*cellulose⟩

lig·ne·ous \'lig-nē-əs\ *adjective* [Latin *ligneus*, from *lignum* wood, probably from *legere* to gather — more at LEGEND] (1626)
: of or resembling wood

lig·ni·fy \'lig-nə-ˌfī\ *verb* **-fied; -fy·ing** [French *lignifier*, from Latin *lignum*] (circa 1828)
transitive verb
: to convert into wood or woody tissue

□ **USAGE**
light–year Although some commentators insist that *light-year* is a measure of distance only—literal or figurative—and not a measure of time, there is evidence that in general (though, not scientific) prose it is fairly commonly used for time ⟨cramming a . . . *light-year*'s thought into three calendar months —Flann O'Brien⟩ ⟨events and circumstances that had seemed *light-years* gone —Brent Staples⟩ ⟨it seems more like a thousand days, and a *light-year* since Father died —James Clavell⟩ ⟨a thousand *light-years* ago, I thought —Dick Francis⟩. This extension of meaning should cause no surprise: how many people think of *year* as denoting distance?

\ə\ abut \ə\ kitten \ər\ further \a\ ash \ā\ ace
\ä\ mop, mar \au̇\ out \ch\ chin \e\ bet \ē\ easy
\g\ go \i\ hit \ī\ ice \j\ job \ŋ\ sing \ō\ go
\ȯ\ law \ȯi\ boy \th\ thin \t͟h\ the \ü\ loot \u̇\ foot
\y\ yet \zh\ vision *see also* Guide to Pronunciation

intransitive verb
: to become wood or woody
— **lig·ni·fi·ca·tion** \,lig-nə-fə-'kā-shən\ *noun*

lig·nin \'lig-nən\ *noun* (1822)
: an amorphous polymer related to cellulose that provides rigidity and together with cellulose forms the woody cell walls of plants and the cementing material between them

lig·nite \'lig-,nīt\ *noun* [French, from Latin *lignum*] (circa 1808)
: a usually brownish black coal intermediate between peat and bituminous coal; *especially*
: one in which the texture of the original wood is distinct — called also *brown coal*
— **lig·nit·ic** \lig-'nit-ik\ *adjective*

lig·no·cel·lu·lose \,lig-nō-'sel-yə-,lōs, -,lōz\ *noun* [International Scientific Vocabulary] (1900)
: any of several closely related substances constituting the essential part of woody cell walls of plants and consisting of cellulose intimately associated with lignin
— **lig·no·cel·lu·los·ic** \-,sel-yə-'lō-sik, -zik\ *adjective*

lig·no·sul·fo·nate \-'səl-fə-,nāt\ *noun* (1908)
: any of various compounds produced from the spent sulfite liquor in the pulping of softwood in papermaking and used especially for binders and dispersing agents

lig·num vi·tae \,lig-nəm-'vī-tē\ *noun, plural* **lignum vitaes** [New Latin, literally, wood of life] (1594)
1 : the very hard heavy wood of any of several tropical American guaiacums
2 : a tree yielding lignum vitae

lig·u·la \'li-gyə-lə\ *noun, plural* **-lae** \-,lē, -,lī\ *also* **-las** [New Latin] (circa 1760)
1 : LIGULE
2 : the distal lobed part of the labium of an insect

lig·u·late \'li-gyə-lət, -,lāt\ *adjective* (1760)
1 : furnished with ligules, ligulae, or ligulate corollas
2 [Latin *ligula*] : shaped like a strap ⟨*ligulate* corolla of a ray flower⟩

lig·ule \'li-(,)gyü(ə)l\ *noun* [New Latin *ligula*, from Latin, small tongue, strap, from *lingere* to lick — more at LICK] (circa 1847)
: a scalelike projection especially on a plant: as **a** : a thin appendage of a foliage leaf and especially of the sheath of a blade of grass **b** : a ligulate corolla of a ray floret in a composite head

lig·ure \'li-,gyùr, -gyər\ *noun* [Middle English *lygire*, from Late Latin *ligurius*, from Greek *ligyrion*] (13th century)
: a traditional precious stone that is probably the jacinth

lik·able *or* **like·able** \'lī-kə-bəl\ *adjective* (1730)
: having qualities that bring about a favorable regard : PLEASANT, AGREEABLE
— **lik·abil·i·ty** \,lī-kə-'bi-lə-tē\ *noun*
— **lik·able·ness** *noun*

¹like \'līk\ *verb* **liked; lik·ing** [Middle English, from Old English *līcian*; akin to Old English *gelīc* alike] (before 12th century)
transitive verb
1 *chiefly dialect* : to be suitable or agreeable to ⟨I like onions but they don't *like* me⟩
2 a : to feel attraction toward or take pleasure in : ENJOY ⟨*likes* baseball⟩ **b** : to feel toward : REGARD ⟨how would you *like* a change⟩
3 : to wish to have : WANT ⟨would *like* a drink⟩
4 : to do well in ⟨this plant *likes* dry soil⟩ ⟨my car does not *like* cold weather⟩
intransitive verb
1 *dialect* : APPROVE
2 : to feel inclined : CHOOSE, PREFER ⟨leave any time you *like*⟩

²like *noun* (1851)
1 : LIKING, PREFERENCE
2 : something that one likes

³like *adjective* [Middle English, alteration of *ilich*, from Old English *gelīc* like, alike, from

ge-, associative prefix + *līc* body; akin to Old High German *gilīh* like, alike, Lithuanian *lygus* like — more at CO-] (13th century)
1 a : the same or nearly the same (as in appearance, character, or quantity) ⟨suits of *like* design⟩ — formerly used with *as, unto, of* ⟨it behoved him to be made *like* unto his brethren —Hebrews 2:17(Authorized Version)⟩ **b** *chiefly British* : closely resembling the subject or original ⟨the portrait is very *like*⟩
2 : LIKELY ⟨the importance of statistics as the one discipline *like* to give accuracy of mind —H. J. Laski⟩

⁴like *preposition* (13th century)
1 a : having the characteristics of : similar to ⟨his house is *like* a barn⟩ ⟨it's *like* when we were kids⟩ **b** : typical of ⟨was *like* him to do that⟩ **c** : comparable to : APPROXIMATING ⟨costs something *like* fifty cents⟩
2 : in the manner of : similarly to ⟨acts *like* a fool⟩
3 : as though there would be ⟨looks *like* rain⟩
4 : such as ⟨a subject *like* physics⟩
5 — used to form intensive or ironic phrases ⟨fought *like* hell⟩ ⟨*like* fun he did⟩ ⟨laughed *like* anything⟩

⁵like *noun* (13th century)
1 a : one that is similar : COUNTERPART, EQUAL ⟨have . . . never seen the *like* before —Sir Winston Churchill⟩ **b** : KIND 4a ⟨put him and his *like* to some job —J. R. R. Tolkien⟩ — used with *the* and often followed by *of* and a substantive, or with a preceding possessive
2 : one of many that are similar to each other — used chiefly in proverbial expressions ⟨*like* breeds *like*⟩
— **and the like** : ET CETERA
— **the likes of 1** : such people as : such things as ⟨reads *the likes of* Austen and Browning⟩ **2** : such a one as and perhaps others similar to — often used with a singular object and usually with disparaging overtones ⟨have no use for *the likes of* you⟩

⁶like *adverb* (14th century)
1 *archaic* : EQUALLY
2 : LIKELY, PROBABLY ⟨you'll try it, some day, *like* enough —Mark Twain⟩
3 a : to some extent : RATHER, ALTOGETHER ⟨saunter over nonchalantly *like* —Walter Karig⟩ **b** — used interjectionally in informal speech often to emphasize a word or phrase (as in "He was, like, gorgeous") or for an apologetic, vague, or unassertive effect (as in "I need to, like, borrow some money")
4 : NEARLY : APPROXIMATELY ⟨the actual interest is more *like* 18 percent⟩ — used interjectionally in informal speech with expressions of measurement ⟨it was, like, five feet long⟩ ⟨goes there every day, *like*⟩
— **as like as not** *or* **like as not** : PROBABLY

⁷like *conjunction* (14th century)
1 a : AS IF ⟨middle-aged men who looked *like* they might be out for their one night of the year —Norman Mailer⟩ **b** — used in intensive phrases ⟨drove *like* mad⟩ ⟨hurts *like* crazy⟩
2 : in the same way that : AS ⟨they raven down scenery *like* children do sweetmeats —John Keats⟩
3 a : in the way or manner that ⟨the violin sounds *like* an old masterpiece should⟩ ⟨did it *like* you told me⟩ **b** — used interjectionally in informal speech often with the verb *be* to introduce a quotation, paraphrase, or thought expressed by or imputed to the subject of the verb, or with *it's* to report a generally held opinion ⟨so I'm *like*, "Give me a break"⟩ ⟨it's *like*, "Who cares what they think?"⟩
4 : such as ⟨a bag *like* a doctor carries⟩ ⟨when your car has trouble — *like* when it won't start⟩ — used interjectionally in informal speech ⟨often stays up late, until *like* three in the morning⟩ □

⁸like *or* **liked** \'līkt\ *verbal auxiliary* (15th century)

chiefly dialect : came near : was near ⟨so loud I *like* to fell out of bed —Helen Eustis⟩

-like *adjective combining form*
: resembling or characteristic of ⟨bell-*like*⟩ ⟨lady*like*⟩

like·li·hood \'lī-klē-,hùd\ *noun* (14th century)
: PROBABILITY ⟨a strong *likelihood* that he is correct —T. D. Anderson⟩

¹like·ly \'lī-klē\ *adjective* **like·li·er; -est** [Middle English, from Old Norse *glīkligr*, from *glīkr* like; akin to Old English *gelīc*] (14th century)
1 : having a high probability of occurring or being true : very probable ⟨rain is *likely* today⟩
2 : apparently qualified : SUITABLE ⟨a *likely* place⟩
3 : RELIABLE, CREDIBLE ⟨a *likely* enough story⟩
4 : PROMISING ⟨a *likely* candidate⟩
5 : ATTRACTIVE ⟨a *likely* child⟩

²likely *adverb* (14th century)
: in all probability : PROBABLY ⟨those who seek power will most *likely* wind up exercising it —Halton Arp⟩

like–mind·ed \'līk-'mīn-dəd\ *adjective* (1526)
: having a like disposition or purpose : of the same mind or habit of thought
— **like–mind·ed·ly** *adverb*
— **like–mind·ed·ness** *noun*

lik·en \'lī-kən\ *transitive verb* **lik·ened; lik·en·ing** \'lī-kə-niŋ, 'līk-niŋ\ (14th century)
: COMPARE

like·ness \'līk-nəs\ *noun* (before 12th century)
1 : COPY, PORTRAIT
2 : APPEARANCE, SEMBLANCE
3 : the quality or state of being like : RESEMBLANCE ☆

like·wise \'līk-,wīz\ *adverb* (15th century)
1 : in like manner : SIMILARLY ⟨go and do like*wise*⟩

☆ **SYNONYMS**
Likeness, similarity, resemblance, similitude, analogy mean agreement or correspondence in details. LIKENESS implies a closer correspondence than SIMILARITY which often implies that things are merely somewhat alike ⟨a remarkable *likeness* to his late father⟩ ⟨some *similarity* between the two cases⟩. RESEMBLANCE implies similarity chiefly in appearance or external qualities ⟨statements that bear little *resemblance* to the truth⟩. SIMILITUDE applies chiefly to correspondence between abstractions ⟨two schools of social thought showing points of *similitude*⟩. ANALOGY implies likeness or parallelism in relations rather than in appearance or qualities ⟨pointed out *analogies* to past wars⟩.

□ **USAGE**
like *Like* has been used as a conjunction since the 14th century. In the 14th, 15th, and 16th centuries it was used in serious literature, but not often; in the 17th and 18th centuries it grew more frequent but less literary. It became markedly more frequent in literary use again in the 19th century. By mid-century it was coming under critical fire, but not from grammarians, oddly enough, who were wrangling over whether it could be called a preposition or not. There is no doubt that, after 600 years of use, conjunctive *like* is firmly established. It has been used by many prestigious literary figures of the past, though perhaps not in their most elevated works; in modern use it may be found in literature, journalism, and scholarly writing. While the present objection to it is perhaps more heated than rational, someone writing in a formal prose style may well prefer to use *as, as if, such as,* or an entirely different construction instead.

2 : in addition

3 : similarly so with me ⟨answered *"likewise"* to "Pleased to meet you"⟩

lik·ing \'lī-kiŋ\ *noun* (14th century)
: favorable regard **:** FONDNESS, TASTE ⟨had a greater *liking* for law —E. M. Coulter⟩ ⟨took a *liking* to the newcomer⟩

li·ku·ta \li-'kü-tə\ *noun, plural* **ma·ku·ta** \mä-\ [of Bantu origin] (1967)
— see *zaire* at MONEY table

li·lac \'lī-,läk, -,lak, -lək\ *noun* [obsolete French (now *lilas*), from Arabic *līlak*, from Persian *nīlak* bluish, from *nīl* blue, from Sanskrit *nīla* dark blue] (1625)
1 a : a European shrub (*Syringa vulgaris*) of the olive family that is often an escape in North America and has cordate ovate leaves and large panicles of fragrant pink-purple or white flowers **b :** a tree or shrub congeneric with the lilac
2 : a variable color averaging a moderate purple

lil·an·ge·ni \,li-lən-'ge-nē\ *noun, plural* **em·a·lan·ge·ni** \,e-mə-lən-'ge-nē\ [Swazi] (circa 1976)
— see MONEY table

lil·ied \'li-lēd\ *adjective* (1614)
1 *archaic* **:** resembling a lily in fairness
2 : full of or covered with lilies

Lil·ith \'li-ləth\ *noun* [Late Hebrew *līlīth*, from Hebrew, a female demon]
1 : a female figure who in rabbinic legend is Adam's first wife, is supplanted by Eve, and becomes an evil spirit
2 : a famous witch in medieval demonology

Lil·li·put \'li-li-(,)pət\ *noun*
: an island in Swift's *Gulliver's Travels* where the inhabitants are six inches tall

lil·li·pu·tian \,li-lə-'pyü-shən\ *adjective, often capitalized* (1726)
1 : of, relating to, or characteristic of the Lilliputians or the island of Lilliput
2 a : SMALL, MINIATURE **b :** PETTY

Lilliputian *noun*
1 : an inhabitant of Lilliput
2 *often not capitalized* **:** one resembling a Lilliputian; *especially* **:** an undersized individual

¹lilt \'lilt\ *noun* (circa 1680)
1 : a spirited and usually cheerful song or tune
2 : a rhythmical swing, flow, or cadence
3 : a springy buoyant movement

²lilt *verb* [Middle English *lulten* to sound an alarm] (1722)
transitive verb
: to sing or play in a lively cheerful manner
intransitive verb
1 : to sing or speak rhythmically and with fluctuating pitch
2 : to move in a lively springy manner

lilt·ing \'lil-tiŋ\ *adjective* (1800)
1 : characterized by a rhythmical swing or cadence ⟨a *lilting* stride⟩
2 : CHEERFUL, BUOYANT ⟨a *lilting* comedy⟩
— **lilt·ing·ly** \-lē\ *adverb*
— **lilt·ing·ness** *noun*

¹lily \'li-lē\ *noun, plural* **lil·ies** [Middle English *lilie*, from Old English, from Latin *lilium*] (before 12th century)
1 : any of a genus (*Lilium* of the family Liliaceae, the lily family) of erect perennial leafy-stemmed bulbous herbs that are native to the northern hemisphere and are widely cultivated for their showy flowers; *broadly* **:** any of various plants of the lily family or of the related amaryllis or iris families
2 : any of various plants with showy flowers: as **a :** a scarlet anemone (*Anemone coronaria*) of the Mediterranean region **b :** WATER LILY **c :** CALLA LILY
3 : FLEUR-DE-LIS 2

²lily *adjective* (circa 1553)
: resembling a lily in fairness, purity, or fragility ⟨my lady's *lily* hand —John Keats⟩

lily-liv·ered \'li-lē-'li-vərd\ *adjective* (1605)
: lacking courage **:** COWARDLY ◇

lily of the valley (1563)

: a low perennial herb (*Convallaria majalis*) of the lily family that has usually two large oblong lanceolate leaves and a raceme of fragrant nodding bell-shaped white flowers

lily pad *noun* (1814)
: a floating leaf of a water lily

¹lily–white \'li-lē-'hwīt, -'wīt\ *adjective* (14th century)
1 : white as a lily
2 : characterized by or favoring the exclusion of blacks especially from politics
3 : IRREPROACHABLE, PURE

²lily–white *noun* (circa 1903)
: a member of a lily-white political organization

Li·ma \'lē-mə\ (circa 1952)
— a communications code word for the letter *l*

li·ma bean \'lī-mə-\ *noun* [*Lima*, Peru] (1756)
1 a : a bushy or tall-growing tropical American bean (*Phaseolus limensis*) that is widely cultivated for its flat edible usually pale green or whitish seeds **b :** SIEVA BEAN
2 : the seed of a lima bean

li·ma·çon \,lē-mə-'sōⁿ\ *noun* [French, literally, snail, from Old French, diminutive of *limaz* slug, snail, from Latin *limax;* akin to Russian *slimak* snail and probably to Old English *līm* birdlime — more at LIME] (1874)
: a curve that is the locus of a variable point on a line as the line revolves about a fixed point of intersection with a circle while the variable point is always a fixed distance along the line from its second and variable point of intersection with the circle

¹limb \'lim\ *noun* [Middle English *lim*, from Old English; akin to Old Norse *limr* limb and perhaps to Old English *lith* limb] (before 12th century)
1 a : one of the projecting paired appendages (as wings) of an animal body used especially for movement and grasping but sometimes modified into sensory or sexual organs **b :** a leg or arm of a human being
2 : a large primary branch of a tree
3 : an active member or agent
4 : EXTENSION, BRANCH
5 : a mischievous child
— **limb·less** \'lim-ləs\ *adjective*
— **limby** \'li-mē\ *adjective*
— **out on a limb :** in an exposed or dangerous position with little chance of retreat

²limb *transitive verb* (1674)
1 : DISMEMBER
2 : to cut off the limbs of (a felled tree)

³limb *noun* [Latin *limbus* border] (circa 1677)
1 : the outer edge of the apparent disk of a celestial body
2 : the expanded portion of an organ or structure; *especially* **:** the spreading upper portion of a gamopetalous corolla as distinguished from the lower tubular portion

lim·ba \'lim-bə\ *noun* [origin unknown] (1943)
1 : a tall whitish-trunked West African tree (*Terminalia superba*) with straight-grained wood
2 : the wood of a limba

lim·beck \'lim-,bek\ *noun* [Middle English *lembike*, from Medieval Latin *alembicum*] (14th century)
: ALEMBIC

limbed \'limd\ *adjective* (14th century)
: having limbs especially of a specified kind or number — usually used in combination ⟨strong-*limbed*⟩

¹lim·ber \'lim-bər\ *noun* [Middle English *lymour*] (15th century)
: a two-wheeled vehicle to which a gun or caisson may be attached

²limber *adjective* [origin unknown] (1565)
1 : capable of being shaped **:** FLEXIBLE
2 : having a supple and resilient quality (as of mind or body) **:** AGILE, NIMBLE
— **lim·ber·ly** *adverb*
— **lim·ber·ness** *noun*

³limber *verb* **lim·bered; lim·ber·ing** \-b(ə-)riŋ\ (1748)
transitive verb
: to cause to become limber ⟨*limber* up his fingers⟩
intransitive verb
: to become limber ⟨*limber* up by running⟩

lim·bic \'lim-bik\ *adjective* [New Latin *limbicus* of a border or margin, from Latin *limbus*] (1882)
: of, relating to, or being the limbic system of the brain

limbic system *noun* (1952)
: a group of subcortical structures (as the hypothalamus, the hippocampus, and the amygdala) of the brain that are concerned especially with emotion and motivation

¹lim·bo \'lim-(,)bō\ *noun, plural* **limbos** [Middle English, from Medieval Latin, ablative of *limbus* limbo, from Latin, border] (14th century)
1 *often capitalized* **:** an abode of souls that are according to Roman Catholic theology barred from heaven because of not having received Christian baptism
2 a : a place or state of restraint or confinement **b :** a place or state of neglect or oblivion ⟨proposals kept in *limbo*⟩ **c :** an intermediate or transitional place or state **d :** a state of uncertainty

²limbo *noun, plural* **limbos** [English of Trinidad & Barbados; akin to Jamaican English *limba* to bend, from English ³*limber*] (circa 1950)
: a West Indian acrobatic dance originally for men that involves bending over backwards and passing under a horizontal pole lowered slightly for each successive pass

Lim·burg·er \'lim-,bər-gər\ *noun* [Flemish, one from Limburg, from *Limburg*, Belgium] (1817)
: a pungent semisoft surface-ripened cheese

lim·bus \'lim-bəs\ *noun* [Latin, border] (1877)
: the marginal region of the cornea of the eye by which it is continuous with the sclera

¹lime \'līm\ *noun* [Middle English *līm;* akin to Old High German *līm* birdlime, Latin *limus* mud, slime, and perhaps to Latin *linere* to smear] (before 12th century)
1 : BIRDLIME
2 a : a caustic highly infusible solid that consists of calcium oxide often together with magnesium oxide, that is obtained by calcining forms of calcium carbonate (as shells or limestone), and that is used in building (as in mortar and plaster) and in agriculture — called also *quicklime* **b :** a dry white powder consisting essentially of calcium hydroxide that is made by treating quicklime with water **c :** CALCIUM ⟨carbonate of *lime*⟩

◇ WORD HISTORY
lily-livered The basis of the word *lily-livered* lies in the former belief that a person's health and temperament are the product of a balance or imbalance of four bodily fluids, or humors: blood, phlegm, black bile, and yellow bile. It was thought that a deficiency of yellow bile or choler, the humor that governed anger, spirit, and courage, would leave a person's liver colorless or white. Someone with this deficiency, and so white-livered, would be spiritless and a coward. *Lily-livered* and *white-livered* have been used synonymously since the 16th century; but *lily-livered*, probably because of its alliteration, is now the more common expression. See in addition CHOLERA, HUMOR.

²**lime** *transitive verb* **limed; lim·ing** (13th century)
1 : to smear with a sticky substance (as birdlime)
2 : to entangle with or as if with birdlime
3 : to treat or cover with lime ⟨*lime* the lawn in the spring⟩

³**lime** *adjective* (15th century)
: of, relating to, or containing lime or limestone

⁴**lime** *noun* [alteration of Middle English *lind*, from Old English; akin to Old High German *linta* linden] (1625)
: LINDEN 1a

⁵**lime** *noun* [French, from Spanish *lima*, from Arabic *līma*, *līm*] (1638)
1 : the small globose yellowish green fruit of a lime with an acid juicy pulp used as a flavoring agent and as a source of vitamin C
2 : a spiny tropical citrus tree (*Citrus aurantifolia*) with elliptical oblong narrowly winged leaves

lime·ade \ˌlīm-ˈād, ˈlī-ˌmād\ *noun* (1892)
: a beverage of sweetened lime juice mixed with plain or carbonated water

lime glass *noun* (circa 1909)
: glass containing a substantial proportion of lime

lime-juic·er \ˈlīm-ˌjü-sər\ *noun* [from the use of lime juice on British ships as a beverage to prevent scurvy] (1859)
1 *slang* : ENGLISHMAN
2 *slang* **a** : a British ship **b** : a British sailor

lime-kiln \-ˌkil, -ˌkiln\ *noun* (13th century)
: a kiln or furnace for reducing limestone or shells to lime by burning

¹**lime·light** \-ˌlīt\ *noun* (1826)
1 a : a stage lighting instrument producing illumination by means of an oxyhydrogen flame directed on a cylinder of lime and usually equipped with a lens to concentrate the light in a beam **b** : the white light produced by such an instrument **c** *British* : SPOTLIGHT
2 : the center of public attention

²**limelight** *transitive verb* (1909)
: to center attention on : SPOTLIGHT

li·men \ˈlī-mən\ *noun* [Latin *limin-*, *limen* transverse beam in a door frame, threshold; probably akin to Latin *limus* transverse] (1895)
: THRESHOLD 3a

lim·er·ick \ˈli-mə-rik, ˈlim-rik\ *noun* [*Limerick*, Ireland] (1896)
: a light or humorous verse form of 5 chiefly anapestic verses of which lines 1, 2, and 5 are of 3 feet and lines 3 and 4 are of 2 feet with a rhyme scheme of *aabba*

lime·stone \ˈlīm-ˌstōn\ *noun* (14th century)
: a rock that is formed chiefly by accumulation of organic remains (as shells or coral), consists mainly of calcium carbonate, is extensively used in building, and yields lime when burned

lime-twig \ˈlīm-ˌtwig\ *noun* (15th century)
1 : a twig covered with birdlime to catch birds
2 : SNARE

lime-wa·ter \-ˌwȯ-tər, -ˌwä-\ *noun* (circa 1500)
: an alkaline water solution of calcium hydroxide used as an antacid

¹**lim·ey** \ˈlī-mē\ *noun, plural* **limeys** *often capitalized* [*lime-juicer* + ⁴*-y*] (1918)
1 *slang* : a British sailor
2 *slang* : ENGLISHMAN

²**limey** *variant of* LIMY

lim·i·nal \ˈli-mə-nᵊl\ *adjective* [Latin *limin-*, *limen* threshold] (1884)
1 : of or relating to a sensory threshold
2 : barely perceptible

¹**lim·it** \ˈli-mət\ *noun* [Middle English, from Middle French *limite*, from Latin *limit-*, *limes* boundary] (14th century)
1 a : something that bounds, restrains, or confines **b** : the utmost extent

2 a : a geographical or political boundary **b** *plural* : the place enclosed within a boundary
: BOUNDS
3 : LIMITATION
4 : a determining feature or differentia in logic
5 : a prescribed maximum or minimum amount, quantity, or number: as **a** : the maximum quantity of game or fish that may be taken legally in a specified period **b** : a maximum established for a gambling bet, raise, or payoff
6 a : a number whose numerical difference from a mathematical function is arbitrarily small for all values of the independent variables that are sufficiently close to but not equal to given prescribed numbers or that are sufficiently large positively or negatively **b** : a number that for an infinite sequence of numbers is such that ultimately each of the remaining terms of the sequence differs from this number by less than any given positive amount
7 : something that is exasperating or intolerable
— **lim·it·less** \-ləs\ *adjective*
— **lim·it·less·ly** *adverb*
— **lim·it·less·ness** *noun*

²**limit** *transitive verb* (14th century)
1 : to assign certain limits to : PRESCRIBE ⟨reserved the right to *limit* use of the land⟩
2 a : to restrict the bounds or limits of ⟨the specialist can no longer *limit* himself to his specialty⟩ **b** : to curtail or reduce in quantity or extent ⟨we must *limit* the power of aggressors⟩ ☆
— **lim·it·able** \-mə-tə-bəl\ *adjective*
— **lim·it·er** *noun*

lim·i·tary \ˈli-mə-ˌter-ē\ *adjective* (1620)
1 *archaic* : subject to limits
2 a *archaic* : of or relating to a boundary **b** : LIMITING, ENCLOSING

lim·i·ta·tion \ˌli-mə-ˈtā-shən\ *noun* (14th century)
1 : an act or instance of limiting
2 : the quality or state of being limited
3 : something that limits : RESTRAINT
4 : a certain period limited by statute after which actions, suits, or prosecutions cannot be brought in the courts
— **lim·i·ta·tion·al** \-shnəl, -shə-nᵊl\ *adjective*

lim·i·ta·tive \ˈli-mə-ˌtā-tiv\ *adjective* (1530)
: LIMITING, RESTRICTIVE

lim·it·ed *adjective* (1610)
1 a : confined within limits : RESTRICTED ⟨*limited* success⟩ **b** *of a train* : offering faster service especially by making a limited number of stops
2 : characterized by enforceable limitations prescribed (as by a constitution) upon the scope or exercise of powers ⟨a *limited* monarchy⟩
3 : lacking breadth and originality ⟨a bit *limited*; a bit thick in the head —Virginia Woolf⟩
— **lim·it·ed·ly** *adverb*
— **lim·it·ed·ness** *noun*

limited–access *adjective* (1944)
of a road : having access restricted to a relatively small number of points

limited edition *noun* (1903)
: an issue of something collectible (as books, prints, or medals) that is advertised to be limited to a relatively small number of copies

limited liability *noun* (1855)
: liability (as of a stockholder or shipowner) limited by statute or treaty

limited partner *noun* (1907)
: a partner in a venture who has no management authority and whose liability is restricted to the amount of his investment — compare GENERAL PARTNER
— **limited partnership** *noun*

limited war *noun* (1939)
: a war whose objective is less than the total defeat of the enemy

lim·it·ing *adjective* (1849)

1 a : functioning as a limit : RESTRICTIVE ⟨*limiting* value⟩ **b** : being an environmental factor (as a nutrient) that limits the population size of an organism
2 : serving to specify the application of the modified noun ⟨*this* in "this book" is a *limiting* word⟩
— **lim·it·ing·ly** *adverb*

limit point *noun* (1905)
: a point that is related to a set of points in such a way that every neighborhood of the point no matter how small contains another point belonging to the set — called also *point of accumulation*

lim·i·trophe \ˈli-mə-ˌtrōf, -ˌtrȯf\ *adjective* [French, from Late Latin *limitrophus* bordering upon, literally, providing subsistence for frontier troops, irregular from Latin *limit-*, *limes* boundary + Greek *trophos* feeder, from *trephein* to nourish] (1763)
: situated on a border or frontier : ADJACENT

lim·mer \ˈli-mər\ *noun* [Middle English (Scots)] (15th century)
1 *chiefly Scottish* : SCOUNDREL
2 *chiefly Scottish* : PROSTITUTE

limn \ˈlim\ *transitive verb* **limned; limn·ing** \ˈli-miŋ, ˈlim-niŋ\ [Middle English *luminen*, *limnen* to illuminate (a manuscript), from Middle French *enluminer*, from Latin *illuminare* to illuminate] (1592)
1 : to draw or paint on a surface
2 : to outline in clear sharp detail : DELINEATE
3 : DESCRIBE
— **limn·er** \ˈli-mər, ˈlim-nər\ *noun*

lim·net·ic \lim-ˈne-tik\ *adjective* [International Scientific Vocabulary, from Greek *limnē* pool, marshy lake; perhaps akin to Latin *limus* mud — more at LIME] (1899)
: of, relating to, or inhabiting the open water of a body of fresh water ⟨*limnetic* environment⟩

lim·nol·o·gy \lim-ˈnä-lə-jē\ *noun* [Greek *limnē* + International Scientific Vocabulary *-logy*] (circa 1888)
: the scientific study of bodies of fresh water (as lakes)
— **lim·no·log·i·cal** \ˌlim-nə-ˈlä-ji-kəl\ *also* **lim·no·log·ic** \-ˈlä-jik\ *adjective*
— **lim·nol·o·gist** \lim-ˈnä-lə-jist\ *noun*

limo \ˈli-(ˌ)mō\ *noun, plural* **lim·os** (1968)
: LIMOUSINE

Li·moges \li-ˈmōzh\ *noun* [*Limoges*, France] (1844)
: enamelware or porcelain made at Limoges

lim·o·nene \ˈli-mə-ˌnēn\ *noun* [International Scientific Vocabulary, from French *limon* lemon, from Middle French] (1845)
: a widely distributed terpene hydrocarbon $C_{10}H_{16}$ that occurs in essential oils (as of oranges or lemons) and has a lemon odor

li·mo·nite \ˈlī-mə-ˌnīt\ *noun* [German *Limonit*, from Greek *leimōn* wet meadow; akin to Greek *limnē* pool] (1823)
: a native hydrous ferric oxide of variable composition that is a major ore of iron
— **li·mo·nit·ic** \ˌlī-mə-ˈni-tik\ *adjective*

☆ **SYNONYMS**
Limit, restrict, circumscribe, confine mean to set bounds for. LIMIT implies setting a point or line (as in time, space, speed, or degree) beyond which something cannot or is not permitted to go ⟨visits are *limited* to 30 minutes⟩. RESTRICT suggests a narrowing or tightening or restraining within or as if within an encircling boundary ⟨laws intended to *restrict* the freedom of the press⟩. CIRCUMSCRIBE stresses a restriction on all sides and by clearly defined boundaries ⟨the work of the investigating committee was carefully *circumscribed*⟩. CONFINE suggests severe restraint and a resulting cramping, fettering, or hampering ⟨our freedom of choice was *confined* by finances⟩.

Lim·ou·sin \li-'mü-sin, 'li-mə-ˌzēn, lē-mü-'za"\ *noun* [*Limousin*, France] (1920)
: any of a French breed of medium-sized yellow-red cattle bred especially for meat

lim·ou·sine \'li-mə-ˌzēn, ˌli-mə-'\ *noun* [French, literally, cloak, from *Limousin*, France] (1902)
1 : a large luxurious often chauffeur-driven sedan that sometimes has a glass partition separating the driver's seat from the passenger compartment
2 : a large vehicle for transporting passengers to and from an airport

limousine liberal *noun* (1969)
: a wealthy political liberal

¹limp \'limp\ *intransitive verb* [probably from Middle English *lympen* to fall short; akin to Old English *limpan* to happen, *lemp*healt lame] (circa 1570)
1 a : to walk lamely; *especially* : to walk favoring one leg **b** : to go unsteadily : FALTER
2 : to proceed slowly or with difficulty ⟨the ship *limped* back to port⟩
— **limp·er** *noun*

²limp *noun* (1818)
: a limping movement or gait

³limp *adjective* [akin to ¹*limp*] (circa 1706)
1 a : lacking firm texture, substance, or structure ⟨*limp* curtains⟩ ⟨her hair hung *limp* about her shoulders⟩ **b** : not stiff or rigid ⟨a book in a *limp* binding⟩
2 a : WEARY, EXHAUSTED ⟨*limp* with fatigue⟩ **b** : lacking in strength, vigor, or firmness : SPIRITLESS
— **limp·ly** *adverb*
— **limp·ness** *noun*

lim·pa \'lim-pə\ *noun* [Swedish] (1948)
: rye bread made with molasses or brown sugar

lim·pet \'lim-pət\ *noun* [Middle English *lempet*, from Old English *lempedu*, from Medieval Latin *lampreda* lamprey] (before 12th century)
1 : a marine gastropod mollusk (especially families Acmaeidae and Patellidae) that has a low conical shell broadly open beneath, browses over rocks or timbers in the littoral area, and clings very tightly when disturbed

limpet 1

2 : one that clings tenaciously to someone or something
3 : an explosive device designed to cling magnetically to a metallic surface (as the hull of a ship)

lim·pid \'lim-pəd\ *adjective* [French or Latin; French *limpide*, from Latin *limpidus*, perhaps from *lympha* water — more at LYMPH] (1613)
1 a : marked by transparency : PELLUCID ⟨*limpid* streams⟩ **b** : clear and simple in style ⟨*limpid* prose⟩
2 : absolutely serene and untroubled
synonym see CLEAR
— **lim·pid·i·ty** \lim-'pi-də-tē\ *noun*
— **lim·pid·ly** \'lim-pəd-lē\ *adverb*
— **lim·pid·ness** *noun*

limp·kin \'lim(p)-kən\ *noun* [perhaps from ¹*limp*] (1871)
: a large brown wading bird (*Aramus guarauna*) of southern Georgia, Florida, and Central and South America that resembles a bittern but has a longer slightly curved bill, longer neck and legs, and white stripes on head and neck

limp–wrist·ed \'limp-ˌris-təd\ *adjective* (circa 1960)
1 : EFFEMINATE
2 : WEAK

lim·u·lus \'lim-yə-ləs\ *noun, plural* **-li** \-ˌlī, -ˌlē\ [New Latin, genus name, from Latin *limus* oblique, transverse — more at LIMEN] (1837)
: HORSESHOE CRAB

limy \'lī-mē\ *adjective* **lim·i·er; -est** (circa 1552)
1 : smeared with or consisting of lime : VISCOUS
2 : containing lime or limestone
3 : resembling or having the qualities of lime

lin·ac \'li-ˌnak\ *noun* (1950)
: LINEAR ACCELERATOR

lin·age \'lī-nij\ *noun* (1884)
: the number of lines of printed or written matter

lin·al·o·ol \lə-'na-lə-ˌwȯl, lī-, -ˌwȯl\ *noun* [International Scientific Vocabulary, from Mexican Spanish *lináloe*, tree yielding perfume, from Medieval Latin *lignum aloes*, literally, wood of the aloe] (1891)
: a fragrant liquid alcohol $C_{10}H_{18}O$ that occurs both free and in the form of esters in many essential oils and is used in perfumes, soaps, and flavoring materials

linch·pin \'linch-ˌpin\ *noun* [Middle English *lynspin*, from *lyns* linchpin (from Old English *lynis*) + *pin*; akin to Middle High German *luns* linchpin] (13th century)
1 : a locking pin inserted crosswise (as through the end of an axle or shaft)
2 : one that serves to hold together the elements of a complex ⟨the *linchpin* in the defense's case⟩

Lin·coln \'liŋ-kən\ *noun* [*Lincoln*shire, England] (1837)
: any of an English breed of long-wooled mutton-type sheep

Lin·coln·i·a·na \ˌ(ˌ)liŋ-ˌkō-nē-'ä-nə, -'a-nə, -'ā-nə\ *noun plural* (1921)
: materials relating to Abraham Lincoln

Lincoln's Birthday \'liŋ-kənz-\ *noun* (1898)
1 : February 12 observed as a legal holiday in many states of the U.S.
2 : the first Monday in February observed as a legal holiday by some states of the U.S.

lin·co·my·cin \ˌliŋ-kə-'mī-s°n\ *noun* [New Latin *lincolnensis* (specific epithet of *Streptomyces lincolnensis*) + English -*mycin*] (1963)
: an antibiotic obtained from an actinomycete (*Streptomyces lincolnensis*) and effective especially against gram-positive bacteria

lin·dane \'lin-ˌdān\ *noun* [T. van der *Lind*en, 20th century Dutch chemist] (circa 1949)
: an insecticide that consists chiefly of the gamma isomer of BHC and is biodegraded very slowly

lin·den \'lin-dən\ *noun* [Middle English, made of linden wood, from Old English, from *lind* linden tree; probably akin to Old English *līthe* gentle — more at LITHE] (1577)
1 : any of a genus (*Tilia* of the family Tiliaceae, the linden family) of trees of temperate regions that are planted as shade trees and are distinguished by having cordate leaves and a winglike bract attached to the peduncle of the flower and fruit: as **a** : a European tree (*T. europaea*) much used for ornamental planting **b** : a tall forest tree (*T. americana*) chiefly of the central and eastern U.S. — called also *basswood, whitewood*

linden 1: branch with bract and fruit

2 : the light fine-grained white wood of a linden; *especially* : BASSWOOD 2

lin·dy \'lin-dē\ *noun* [probably from *Lindy*, nickname of Charles A. Lindbergh] (1931)
: a jitterbug dance originating in Harlem and later developing many local variants

¹line \'līn\ *noun, often attributive* [Middle English; partly from Old French *ligne*, from Latin *linea*, from feminine of *lineus* made of flax, from *linum* flax; partly from Old English *līne*; akin to Old English *līn* flax — more at LINEN] (before 12th century)
1 a : THREAD, STRING, CORD, ROPE: as (1) : a comparatively strong slender cord (2) : CLOTHESLINE (3) : a rope used on shipboard **b** (1) : a device for catching fish consisting of a cord with hooks and other fishing gear (2) : scope for activity : ROPE **c** : a length of material used in measuring and leveling **d** : piping for conveying a fluid (as steam) **e** (1) : a wire or pair of wires connecting one telegraph or telephone station with another or a whole system of such wires; *also* : any circuit in an electronic communication system (2) : a telephone connection ⟨tried to get a *line*⟩; *also* : an individual telephone extension ⟨a call on *line* 2⟩ (3) : the principal circuits of an electric power system
2 a (1) : a horizontal row of written or printed characters; *also* : a blank row in lieu of such characters (2) : a unit in the rhythmic structure of verse formed by the grouping of a number of the smallest units of the rhythm (as metrical feet) : an often numbered section of a computer program containing a single command or a small number of commands **b** : a short letter : NOTE **c** *plural* : a certificate of marriage **d** : the words making up a part in a drama — usually used in plural **e** : any of the successive horizontal rows of picture elements on the screen of a cathode-ray tube (as a television screen)
3 a : something (as a ridge or seam) that is distinct, elongated, and narrow **b** : a narrow crease (as on the face) : WRINKLE **c** : the course or direction of something in motion : ROUTE **d** (1) : a state of agreement or conformity : ACCORDANCE (2) : a state of order, control, or obedience ⟨you're getting out of *line*⟩ **e** : a boundary of an area ⟨the state *line*⟩ **f** : the track and roadbed of a railway **g** : an amount of cocaine that is arranged in a line to be inhaled through the nose
4 a : a course of conduct, action, or thought **b** : a field of activity or interest **c** : a glib often persuasive way of talking
5 a : LIMIT, RESTRAINT **b** *archaic* : position in life : LOT
6 a (1) : FAMILY, LINEAGE (2) : a strain produced and maintained especially by selective breeding or biological culture (3) : a chronological series **b** : dispositions made to cover extended military positions and presenting a front to the enemy — usually used in plural **c** : a military formation in which the different elements are abreast of each other **d** : naval ships arranged in a regular order **e** (1) : the combatant forces of an army distinguished from the staff corps and supply services (2) : the force of a regular navy **f** (1) : officers of the navy eligible for command at sea distinguished from officers of the staff (2) : officers of the army belonging to a combatant branch **g** : an arrangement or placement of persons or objects of one kind in an orderly series ⟨a *line* of trees⟩ ⟨stand on *line*⟩ ⟨waiting in *line*⟩; *also* : the persons or objects so positioned ⟨the *line* moved slowly at the bank⟩ **h** (1) : a group of public conveyances plying regularly under one management over a route (2) : a system of transportation together with its equipment, routes, and appurtenances; *also* : the company owning or operating it **i** : a succession of musical notes especially considered in melodic

phrases **j** (1) **:** an arrangement of operations in manufacturing permitting sequential occurrence on various stages of production (2) **:** the personnel of an organization that are responsible for its stated objective **k** (1) **:** the 7 players including center, 2 guards, 2 tackles, and 2 ends who in offensive football play line up on or within one foot of the line of scrimmage (2) **:** the players who in defensive play line up within one yard of the line of scrimmage
7 : a narrow elongated mark drawn or projected: as **a** (1) **:** a circle of latitude or longitude on a map (2) **:** EQUATOR **b :** a mark (as on a map) recording a boundary, division, or contour **c :** any of the horizontal parallel strokes on a music staff on or between which notes are placed — compare SPACE **d :** a mark (as by pencil) that forms part of the formal design of a picture distinguished from the shading or color **e :** a division on a bridge score dividing the score for bonuses from that for tricks **f** (1) **:** a demarcation of a limit with reference to which the playing of some game or sport is regulated — usually used in combination (2) **:** a marked or imaginary line across a playing area (as a football field) parallel to the end line (3) **:** LINE OF SCRIMMAGE
8 : a straight or curved geometric element that is generated by a moving point and that has extension only along the path of the point **:** CURVE
9 a : a defining outline **:** CONTOUR **b :** a general plan **:** MODEL — usually used in plural
10 a chiefly British **:** PICA — used to indicate the size of large type **b :** the unit of fineness of halftones expressed as the number of screen lines to the linear inch
11 : merchandise or services of the same general class for sale or regularly available
12 a : a source of information **:** INSIGHT **b :** betting odds offered by a bookmaker especially on a sporting event
13 : a complete game of 10 frames in bowling — called also *string*
14 : LINE DRIVE
— **liny** also **lin·ey** \'lī-nē\ *adjective*
— **between the lines 1 :** by implication **:** in an indirect way **2 :** by way of inference
— **down the line :** all the way **:** FULLY
— **in line for :** due or in a position to receive
— **on line :** in or into operation
— **on the line 1 :** in complete commitment and at great risk ⟨puts his future *on the line* by backing that policy⟩ **2 :** on the border between two categories **3 :** IMMEDIATELY ⟨paid cash *on the line*⟩
²**line** *verb* **lined; lin·ing** (1530)
transitive verb
1 : to mark or cover with a line or lines ⟨*lined* paper⟩
2 : to depict with lines **:** DRAW
3 : to place or form a line along ⟨pedestrians *line* the walks⟩
4 : to form into a line or lines **:** ALIGN ⟨*line* up troops⟩
5 : to hit (as a baseball) hard and in a usually straight line
intransitive verb
1 : to hit a line drive in baseball
2 : to come into the correct relative position **:** ALIGN
³**line** *transitive verb* **lined; lin·ing** [Middle English, from *line* flax, from Old English *līn*] (14th century)
1 : to cover the inner surface of ⟨*line* a cloak with silk⟩
2 : to put something in the inside of **:** FILL
3 : to serve as the lining of ⟨tapestries *lined* the walls⟩
4 obsolete **:** FORTIFY
— **line one's pockets :** to take money freely and especially dishonestly
¹**lin·e·age** \'li-nē-ij also 'li-nij\ *noun* (14th century)

1 a : descent in a line from a common progenitor **b :** DERIVATION
2 : a group of individuals tracing descent from a common ancestor; *especially* **:** such a group of persons whose common ancestor is regarded as its founder
²**line·age** \'lī-nij\ *variant of* LINAGE
lin·e·al \'li-nē-əl\ *adjective* (14th century)
1 : LINEAR
2 : composed of or arranged in lines
3 a : consisting of or being in a direct male or female line of ancestry — compare COLLATERAL 2 **b :** relating to or derived from ancestors **:** HEREDITARY **c :** descended in a direct line
4 a : belonging to one lineage ⟨*lineal* relatives⟩ **b :** of, relating to, or dealing with a lineage
— **lin·e·al·i·ty** \,li-nē-'a-lə-tē\ *noun*
— **lin·e·al·ly** \'li-nē-ə-lē\ *adverb*
lin·e·a·ment \'li-nē-ə-mənt\ *noun* [Middle English, from Latin *lineamentum,* from *lineare* to draw a line, from *linea*] (15th century)
1 a : an outline, feature, or contour of a body or figure and especially of a face — usually used in plural **b :** a linear topographic feature (as of the earth or a planet) that reveals a characteristic (as a fault or the subsurface structure)
2 : a distinguishing or characteristic feature — usually used in plural
— **lin·e·a·men·tal** \,li-nē-ə-'men-t°l\ *adjective*
lin·e·ar \'li-nē-ər\ *adjective* (circa 1656)
1 a : of, relating to, resembling, or having a graph that is a line and especially a straight line **:** STRAIGHT (2) **:** involving a single dimension **b** (1) **:** of the first degree with respect to one or more variables (2) **:** of, relating to, based on, or being linear equations, linear differential equations, linear functions, linear transformations, or linear algebra **c** (1) **:** characterized by an emphasis on line ⟨*linear* art⟩ (2) **:** composed of simply drawn lines with little attempt at pictorial representation ⟨*linear* script⟩ **d :** consisting of a straight chain of atoms
2 : elongated with nearly parallel sides ⟨*linear* leaf⟩ — see LEAF illustration
3 : having or being a response or output that is directly proportional to the input
4 : of, relating to, or based or depending on sequential development ⟨*linear* thinking⟩ ⟨a *linear* narrative⟩
— **lin·e·ar·i·ty** \,li-nē-'ar-ə-tē\ *noun*
— **lin·e·ar·ly** \'li-nē-ər-lē\ *adverb*
Linear A \-'ā\ *noun* (1948)
: a linear form of writing used in Crete from the 18th to the 15th centuries B.C.
linear accelerator *noun* (1945)
: a device in which charged particles are accelerated in a straight line by successive impulses from a series of electric fields
linear algebra *noun* (circa 1884)
: a branch of mathematics that is concerned with mathematical structures closed under the operations of addition and scalar multiplication and that includes the theory of systems of linear equations, matrices, determinants, vector spaces, and linear transformations
Linear B \-'bē\ *noun* (1950)
: a linear form of writing employing syllabic characters and used at Knossos on Crete and on the Greek mainland from the 15th to the 12th centuries B.C. for documents in the Mycenaean language
linear combination *noun* (1960)
: a mathematical entity (as $4x + 5y + 6z$) which is composed of sums and differences of elements (as variables, matrices, or functions) especially when the coefficients are not all zero
linear dependence *noun* (1955)
: the property of one set (as of matrices or vectors) of having at least one linear combination of its elements equal to zero when the co-

efficients are taken from another given set and at least one of its coefficients is not equal to zero
— **linearly dependent** *adjective*
linear equation *noun* (1816)
: an equation of the first degree in any number of variables
linear function *noun* (circa 1889)
1 : a mathematical function in which the variables appear only in the first degree, are multiplied by constants, and are combined only by addition and subtraction
2 : LINEAR TRANSFORMATION
linear independence *noun* (1967)
: the property of a set (as of matrices or vectors) of having no linear combination of all its elements equal to zero when coefficients are taken from a given set unless the coefficient of each element is zero
— **linearly independent** *adjective*
lin·e·ar·ise *British variant of* LINEARIZE
lin·e·ar·ize \'li-nē-ə-,rīz\ *transitive verb* **-ized; -iz·ing** (1895)
: to give a linear form to; *also* **:** to project in linear form
— **lin·e·ar·i·za·tion** \,li-nē-ə-rə-'zā-shən\ *noun*
linear measure *noun* (circa 1890)
1 : a measure of length
2 : a system of measures of length
linear motor *noun* (1957)
: a motor that produces thrust in a straight line by direct induction rather than with the use of gears — called also *linear induction motor*
linear perspective *noun* (circa 1656)
: PERSPECTIVE 1a
linear programming *noun* (1949)
: a mathematical method of solving practical problems (as the allocation of resources) by means of linear functions where the variables involved are subject to constraints
linear space *noun* (circa 1889)
: VECTOR SPACE
linear transformation *noun* (circa 1889)
1 : a transformation in which the new variables are linear functions of the old variables
2 : a function that maps the vectors of one vector space onto the vectors of the same or another vector space with the same field of scalars in such a way that the image of the sum of two vectors equals the sum of their images and the image of the product of a scalar and a vector equals the product of the scalar and the image of the vector
lin·e·a·tion \,li-nē-'ā-shən\ *noun* [Middle English *lineacion* outline, from Latin *lineation-, lineatio,* from *lineare* to mark with lines, from *linea*] (14th century)
1 a : the action of marking with lines **:** DELINEATION **b :** OUTLINE
2 : an arrangement of lines
line·back·er \'līn-,ba-kər\ *noun* (1949)
: a defensive football player who lines up immediately behind the line of scrimmage to make tackles on running plays through the line or defend against short passes
line·back·ing \-,ba-kiŋ\ *noun* (1953)
: the action or art of playing linebacker
line·breed·ing \-,brē-diŋ\ *noun* (circa 1879)
: the interbreeding of individuals within a particular line of descent usually to perpetuate desirable characters
— **line·bred** \-,bred\ *adjective*
line·cast·er \-,kas-tər\ *noun* (1964)
: a machine that casts metal type in lines
— **line·cast·ing** \-tiŋ\ *noun*
line-cut \'līn-,kət\ *noun* (circa 1909)
: a photoengraving of a line drawing
line drawing *noun* (1891)
: a drawing made in solid lines
line drive *noun* (1912)
: a batted baseball hit in a nearly straight line usually not far above the ground
line engraving *noun* (1802)
: an engraving cut by hand directly in the plate

line graph *noun* (circa 1924)
: a graph in which points representing values of a variable for suitable values of an independent variable are connected by a broken line

line-haul \'līn-,hȯl\ *noun* (circa 1923)
: the transporting of items or persons between terminals

line item *noun* (1962)
: an appropriation that is itemized on a separate line in a budget
— **line–item** \'līn-'ī-təm\ *adjective*

line judge *noun* (1970)
: a football linesman whose duties include keeping track of the official time for the game

line-man \'līn-mən\ *noun* (1876)
1 : one who sets up or repairs electric wire communication or power lines — called also *linesman*
2 : a player in the forward line of a team; *specifically* : a football player in the line

¹lin-en \'li-nən\ *adjective* [Middle English, from Old English *līnen*, from *līn* flax, from Latin *linum* flax; akin to Greek *linon* flax, thread] (before 12th century)
1 : made of flax
2 : made of or resembling linen

²linen *noun* (14th century)
1 a : cloth made of flax and noted for its strength, coolness, and luster **b** : thread or yarn spun from flax
2 : clothing or household articles made of linen cloth or similar fabric
3 : paper made from linen fibers or with a linen finish

line of credit (1917)
: the maximum credit allowed a buyer or borrower

line of duty (circa 1918)
: all that is authorized, required, or normally associated with some field of responsibility

line officer *noun* (1850)
: a commissioned officer assigned to the line of the army or navy — compare STAFF OFFICER

line of force (1873)
: a line in a field of force (as a magnetic or electric field) whose tangent at any point gives the direction of the field at that point

line of scrimmage (circa 1909)
: an imaginary line in football that is parallel to the goal lines and tangent to the nose of the ball laid on the ground and that marks the position of the ball at the start of each down

line of sight (1559)
1 : a line from an observer's eye to a distant point
2 : the straight path between a radio or television transmitting antenna and receiving antenna when unobstructed by the horizon

line out (1618)
transitive verb
1 : to indicate with or as if with lines : OUTLINE ⟨*line out* a route⟩
2 : to arrange in an extended line
3 : BELT ⟨*line out* a song⟩
intransitive verb
1 : to move rapidly ⟨*lined out* for home⟩
2 : to make an out by hitting a baseball in a line drive that is caught

line printer *noun* (1955)
: a high-speed printing device (as for a computer) that prints each line as a unit rather than character by character

¹lin-er \'lī-nər\ *noun* (15th century)
1 : one that makes, draws, or uses lines
2 a : a ship belonging to a regular line **b** : an airplane belonging to an airline
3 : LINE DRIVE
4 : something with which lines are made

²liner *noun* (1611)
1 : one that lines or is used to line or back something
2 : JACKET 3c(2)
— **lin-er-less** \-ləs\ *adjective*

li-ner-board \'lī-nər-,bōrd, -,bȯrd\ *noun* (1948)
: a thin paperboard used for the flat facings of corrugated containerboard

liner notes *noun plural* (1955)
: comments or explanatory notes about a recording printed on the jacket or an insert

line score *noun* (1946)
: a score of a baseball game giving the runs, hits, and errors made by each team — compare BOX SCORE

lines-man \'līnz-mən\ *noun* (1883)
1 : LINEMAN 1
2 : an official who assists a referee in various games (as football or hockey) especially in determining if a ball, puck, or player is out-of-bounds or offside

line squall *noun* (1887)
: a squall or thunderstorm occurring along a cold front

line storm *noun* (1850)
: an equinoctial storm

line-up \'lī-,nəp\ *noun* (1889)
1 a : a list of players taking part in a game (as of baseball) **b** : the players on such a list
2 a : an alignment (as in entertainment or politics) of persons or things having a common purpose, distinction, or bond ⟨the show's star-studded *lineup*⟩ **b** : LINE 11 **c** : a television programming schedule
3 : a line of persons arranged especially for inspection or for identification by police

line up (1864)
intransitive verb
1 : to assume an orderly linear arrangement ⟨*line up* for inspection⟩
2 : to align oneself ⟨he *lined up* with the liberals against the bill⟩
transitive verb
1 : to put into alignment
2 : to arrange for ⟨*line up* support for a candidate⟩

¹ling \'liŋ\ *noun* [Middle English; akin to Dutch *leng* ling, Old English *lang* long] (13th century)
1 : any of various fishes (as a hake or burbot) of the cod family
2 : LINGCOD

²ling *noun* [Middle English, from Old Norse *lyng*] (13th century)
: a heath plant; *especially* : a common Old World heather (*Calluna vulgaris*)

¹-ling *noun suffix* [Middle English, from Old English, akin to Old English *-ing*]
1 : one connected with or having the quality of ⟨hire*ling*⟩
2 : young, small, or inferior one ⟨duck*ling*⟩

²-ling *or* **-lings** *adverb suffix* [Middle English *-ling* (from Old English), *-linges* (from *-ling* + *-es* -s); akin to Old High German *-lingūn* -ling, Old English *lang* long]
: in (such) a direction or manner ⟨side*ling*⟩ ⟨flat*ling*⟩

Lin-ga-la \liŋ-'gä-lə\ *noun* (1922)
: a Bantu language widely used in trade and public affairs in the Congo River area

lin-gam \'liŋ-gəm\ *or* **lin-ga** \-gə\ *noun* [Sanskrit *liṅga* (nominative *liṅgam*), literally, characteristic] (1719)
: a stylized phallic symbol of the masculine cosmic principle and of the Hindu god Siva — compare YONI

Lin-ga-yat \liŋ-'gä-yət\ *noun* [Kannada *liṅgāyta*] (1901)
: a member of a Saiva sect of southern India marked by wearing of the lingam and characterized by denial of caste distinctions

ling-cod \'liŋ-,käd\ *noun* (1940)
: a large greenish-fleshed fish (*Ophiodon elongatus*) of the Pacific coast of North America that is an important food and sport fish and belongs to the same family as the greenlings

lin-ger \'liŋ-gər\ *verb* **lin-gered; lin-ger-ing** \-g(ə-)riŋ\ [Middle English (northern dialect) *lengeren* to dwell, frequentative of *lengen* to prolong, from Old English *lengan*; akin to Old English *lang* long] (14th century)
intransitive verb
1 : to be slow in parting or in quitting something : TARRY
2 a : to remain alive although gradually dying
b : to remain existent although often waning in strength, importance, or influence ⟨*lingering* doubts⟩
3 : to be slow to act : PROCRASTINATE
4 : to move slowly : SAUNTER
transitive verb
1 *obsolete* : DELAY
2 : to pass (as a period of time) slowly
— **lin-ger-er** \-gər-ər\ *noun*
— **lin-ger-ing-ly** \-g(ə-)riŋ-lē\ *adverb*

lin-ge-rie \,län-jə-'rā, ,läⁿ-zhə-, -'rē; 'laⁿ-zhə-(,)rē, 'län-jə-, 'läⁿ-zhə-, -,rā\ *noun* [French, from Middle French, from *linge* linen, from Latin *lineus* made of linen — more at LINE] (1835)
1 *archaic* : linen articles or garments
2 : women's intimate apparel
— **lingerie** *adjective*

lin-go \'liŋ-(,)gō\ *noun, plural* **lingoes** [probably from Lingua Franca, language, tongue, from Provençal, from Latin *lingua* — more at TONGUE] (1660)
: strange or incomprehensible language or speech: as **a** : a foreign language **b** : the special vocabulary of a particular field of interest **c** : language characteristic of an individual

ling-on-ber-ry \'liŋ-ən-,ber-ē\ *noun* [Swedish *lingon* mountain cranberry; akin to Old Norse *lyng* ling] (1920)
: the fruit of the mountain cranberry; *also* : MOUNTAIN CRANBERRY

lin-gua \'liŋ-gwə\ *noun, plural* **lin-guae** \-,gwē, -,gwī\ [Latin — more at TONGUE] (circa 1826)
: a tongue or an organ resembling a tongue

lin-gua fran-ca \'liŋ-gwə-'fraŋ-kə\ *noun, plural* **lingua francas** *or* **lin-guae fran-cae** \-,gwē-'fraŋ-(,)kē\ [Italian, literally, Frankish language] (1619)
1 *often capitalized* : a common language consisting of Italian mixed with French, Spanish, Greek, and Arabic that was formerly spoken in Mediterranean ports
2 : any of various languages used as common or commercial tongues among peoples of diverse speech
3 : something resembling a common language

lin-gual \'liŋ-gwəl *also* 'liŋ-gyə-wəl\ *adjective* [Latin *lingua*] (1650)
1 a : of, relating to, or resembling the tongue
b : lying near or next to the tongue; *especially* : relating to or being the surface of tooth next to the tongue **c** : produced with the tongue
2 : LINGUISTIC
— **lin-gual-ly** *adverb*

lin-gui-ne *or* **lin-gui-ni** \liŋ-'gwē-nē\ *noun* [Italian, plural of *linguina*, diminutive of *lingua* tongue, from Latin] (circa 1948)
: narrow flat pasta

lin-guist \'liŋ-gwist\ *noun* [Latin *lingua* language, tongue] (1591)
1 : a person accomplished in languages; *especially* : one who speaks several languages
2 : a person who specializes in linguistics

lin-guis-tic \liŋ-'gwis-tik\ *also* **lin-guis-ti-cal** \-ti-kəl\ *adjective* (1846)
: of or relating to language or linguistics
— **lin-guis-ti-cal-ly** \-ti-k(ə-)lē\ *adverb*

linguistic atlas *noun* (1923)
: a publication containing a set of maps on which speech variations are recorded — called also *dialect atlas*

linguistic form *noun* (1921)
: a meaningful unit of speech (as a morpheme, word, or sentence) — called also *speech form*

\ə\ abut \ᵊ\ kitten \ər\ further \a\ ash \ā\ ace \ä\ mop, mar \au̇\ out \ch\ chin \e\ bet \ē\ easy \g\ go \i\ hit \ī\ ice \j\ job \ŋ\ go \ȯ\ law \ȯi\ boy \th\ thin \t͟h\ the \ü\ loot \u̇\ foot \y\ yet \zh\ vision *see also* Guide to Pronunciation

linguistic geography *noun* (1926)
: local or regional variations of a language or dialect studied as a field of knowledge — called also *dialect geography*
— **linguistic geographer** *noun*

lin·guis·ti·cian \ˌliŋ-gwə-'sti-shən\ *noun* (1895)
: LINGUIST 2

lin·guis·tics \liŋ-'gwis-tiks\ *noun plural but singular in construction* (circa 1847)
: the study of human speech including the units, nature, structure, and modification of language

lin·i·ment \'li-nə-mənt\ *noun* [Middle English, from Late Latin *linimentum*, from Latin *linere* to smear — more at LIME] (15th century)
: a liquid or semiliquid preparation that is applied to the skin as an anodyne or a counterirritant

lin·ing \'lī-niŋ\ *noun* (14th century)
1 : material that lines or that is used to line especially the inner surface of something (as a garment)
2 : the act or process of providing something with a lining

¹**link** \'liŋk\ *noun* [Middle English, of Scandinavian origin; akin to Old Norse *hlekkr* chain; akin to Old English *hlanc* lank] (15th century)
1 : a connecting structure: as **a** (1) : a single ring or division of a chain (2) : one of the standardized divisions of a surveyor's chain that is 7.92 inches (20.1 centimeters) long and serves as a measure of length **b** : CUFF LINK **c** : BOND 3c **d** : an intermediate rod or piece for transmitting force or motion; *especially* : a short connecting rod with a hole or pin at each end **e** : the fusible member of an electrical fuse
2 : something analogous to a link of chain: as **a** : a segment of sausage in a chain **b** : a connecting element or factor ⟨found a *link* between smoking and cancer⟩ **c** : a unit in a communication system **d** : an identifier attached to an element (as an index term) in a system in order to indicate or permit connection with other similarly identified elements

²**link** (15th century)
transitive verb
: to couple or connect by or as if by a link
intransitive verb
: to become connected by or as if by a link
synonym see JOIN
— **link·er** *noun*

³**link** *noun* [perhaps modification of Medieval Latin *linchinus* candle, alteration of Latin *lychnus*, from Greek *lychnos;* akin to Greek *leukos* white — more at LIGHT] (1526)
: a torch formerly used to light a person's way through the streets

⁴**link** *intransitive verb* [origin unknown] (1715)
Scottish : to skip smartly along

link·age \'liŋ-kij\ *noun* (1874)
1 : the manner or style of being united: as **a** : the manner in which atoms or radicals are linked in a molecule **b** : BOND 3c
2 : the quality or state of being linked; *especially* : the relationship between genes on the same chromosome that causes them to be inherited together — compare MENDEL'S LAW 2
3 : a system of links; *especially* : a system of links or bars which are jointed together and more or less constrained by having a link or links fixed and by means of which straight or nearly straight lines or other point paths may be traced
4 : LINK 2b

linkage group *noun* (1921)
: a set of linked genes at different loci on the same chromosome

link·boy \'liŋk-ˌbȯi\ *noun* (1660)
: an attendant formerly employed to bear a light for a person on the streets at night

linked \'liŋ(k)t\ *adjective* (15th century)
1 : marked by linkage and especially genetic linkage ⟨*linked* genes⟩
2 : having or provided with links ⟨a *linked* list⟩

linking verb *noun* (1923)
: a word or expression (as a form of *be, become, feel,* or *seem*) that links a subject with its predicate

link·man \'liŋk-mən\ *noun* (1716)
1 : LINKBOY
2 *British* : a broadcasting moderator or anchorman

links \'liŋ(k)s\ *noun plural* [Middle English, from Old English *hlincas*, plural of *hlinc* ridge; akin to Old English *hlanc* lank] (15th century)
1 *Scottish* : sand hills especially along the seashore
2 : GOLF COURSE

links·man \'liŋ(k)s-mən\ *noun* (1937)
: one who plays golf

link·up \'liŋ-ˌkəp\ *noun* (1945)
1 : establishment of contact : MEETING ⟨the *linkup* of two spacecraft⟩
2 a : something that serves as a linking device or factor **b** : a functional whole resulting from the linking up of separate elements ⟨an instructional TV *linkup*⟩

linn \'lin\ *noun* [Scottish Gaelic *linne* pool] (1513)
1 *chiefly Scottish* : WATERFALL
2 *chiefly Scottish* : PRECIPICE

Lin·nae·an *or* **Lin·ne·an** \lə-'nē-ən, -'nā-, 'li-nē-\ *adjective* [Carolus *Linnaeus*] (1753)
: of, relating to, or following the systematic methods of the Swedish botanist Linnaeus who established the system of binomial nomenclature

lin·net \'li-nət\ *noun* [Middle French *linette*, from *lin* flax, from Latin *linum;* from its feeding on flax seeds] (circa 1530)
: a common small brownish Old World finch (*Acanthis cannabina*) of which the male has red on the breast and crown during breeding season

li·no \'lī-(ˌ)nō\ *noun, plural* **linos** (1907)
chiefly British : LINOLEUM

li·no·cut \'lī-nō-ˌkət\ *noun* (1907)
: a print made from a design cut into a mounted piece of linoleum

li·no·le·ate \lə-'nō-lē-ˌāt\ *noun* (circa 1865)
: a salt or ester of linoleic acid

lin·o·le·ic acid \ˌli-nə-'lē-ik-, -'lā-\ *noun* [Greek *linon* flax + International Scientific Vocabulary *oleic (acid)*] (1857)
: a liquid unsaturated fatty acid $C_{18}H_{32}O_2$ found especially in semidrying oils (as peanut oil) and essential for the nutrition of some animals

lin·o·le·nic acid \-'lē-nik-, -'lā-\ *noun* [International Scientific Vocabulary, irregular from *linoleic*] (1887)
: a liquid unsaturated fatty acid $C_{18}H_{30}O_2$ found especially in drying oils (as linseed oil) and essential for the nutrition of some animals

li·no·leum \lə-'nō-lē-əm, -'nōl-yəm\ *noun, often attributive* [Latin *linum* flax + *oleum* oil — more at OIL] (1878)
1 : a floor covering made by laying on a burlap or canvas backing a mixture of solidified linseed oil with gums, cork dust or wood flour or both, and usually pigments
2 : a material similar to linoleum

Li·no·type \'lī-nə-ˌtīp\ *trademark*
— used for a keyboard-operated typesetting machine that uses circulating matrices and produces each line of type in the form of a solid metal slug

lin·sang \'lin-ˌsaŋ\ *noun* [Javanese *lingsang*] (1821)
: either of two nocturnal chiefly forest-dwelling Asian mammals (*Prionodon pardicolor* and *P. linsang*) that resemble and are related to the mongooses, civets, and genets; *also* : a related mammal (*Poiana richardsoni*) of Africa

lin·seed \'lin-ˌsēd\ *noun* [Middle English, from Old English *līnsǣd*, from *līn* flax + *sǣd* seed — more at LINEN] (before 12th century)
: FLAXSEED

linseed oil *noun* (15th century)
: a yellowish drying oil obtained from flaxseed and used especially in paint, varnish, printing ink, and linoleum

lin·sey–wool·sey \ˌlin-zē-'wu̇l-zē\ *noun* [Middle English *lynsy wolsye*] (15th century)
: a coarse sturdy fabric of wool and linen or cotton

lin·stock \'lin-ˌstäk\ *noun* [Dutch *lontstok*, from *lont* match + *stok* stick] (1575)
: a staff having a pointed foot (as for sticking into the ground) and a forked tip and formerly used to hold a lighted match for firing cannon

lint \'lint\ *noun* [Middle English] (14th century)
1 a : a soft fleecy material made from linen usually by scraping **b** : fuzz consisting especially of fine ravelings and short fibers of yarn and fabric
2 : a fibrous coat of thick convoluted hairs borne by cotton seeds that yields the cotton staple
— **linty** \'lin-tē\ *adjective*

lin·tel \'lin-tᵊl\ *noun* [Middle English, from Middle French, from Late Latin *limitaris* threshold, from Latin, constituting a boundary, from *limit-, limes* boundary] (14th century)
: a horizontal architectural member spanning and usually carrying the load above an opening

lint·er \'lin-tər\ *noun* (circa 1889)
1 : a machine for removing linters
2 *plural* : the fuzz of short fibers that adheres to cottonseed after ginning

1 lintel

lint·white \'lint-ˌhwīt, -ˌwīt\ *noun* [alteration of Middle English *lynkwhyt*, by folk etymology from Old English *līnetwige*] (1513)
: LINNET

li·on \'lī-ən\ *noun, plural* **lions** [Middle English, from Old French, from Latin *leon-, leo,* from Greek *leōn*] (12th century)
1 a *or plural* **lion** : a large heavily-built social cat (*Panthera leo* synonym *Leo leo*) of open or rocky areas chiefly of sub-Saharan Africa though once widely distributed throughout Africa and southern Asia that has a tawny body with a tufted tail and a shaggy blackish or dark brown mane in the male **b** : any of several large wildcats; *especially* : COUGAR **c** *capitalized* : LEO
2 a : a person felt to resemble a lion (as in courage or ferocity) **b** : a person of outstanding interest or importance
3 *capitalized* [*Lions* (*club*)] : a member of a major national and international service club
— **li·on·like** \-ˌlīk\ *adjective*

li·on·ess \'lī-ə-nəs\ *noun* (14th century)
: a female lion
usage see -ESS

li·on·fish \'lī-ən-ˌfish\ *noun* (circa 1907)
: any of several scorpion fishes (genus *Pterois*) of the Indian Ocean and the tropical Pacific that are brilliantly striped and barred with elongated fins and venomous dorsal spines

li·on·heart·ed \'lī-ən-ˌhär-təd\ *adjective* (1708)
: COURAGEOUS, BRAVE

li·on·ise *British variant of* LIONIZE

li·on·ize \'lī-ə-ˌnīz\ *transitive verb* **-ized; -iz·ing** (1809)
1 : to treat as an object of great interest or importance
2 *British* : to show the sights of a place to
— **li·on·i·za·tion** \ˌlī-ə-nə-'zā-shən\ *noun*
— **li·on·iz·er** \'lī-ə-ˌnī-zər\ *noun*

lion's share *noun* (1790)
: the largest portion ⟨received the *lion's share* of the research money⟩

¹**lip** \'lip\ *noun* [Middle English, from Old English *lippa;* akin to Old High German *leffur* lip and probably to Latin *labium, labrum* lip] (before 12th century)

1 : either of two fleshy folds that surround the mouth in humans and many other vertebrates and are the organs of human speech; *also* : the red or pinkish margin of the human lip
2 *slang* : BACK TALK
3 a : a fleshy edge or margin (as of a wound) **b** : LABIUM **c** : LABELLUM 1 **d** : a limb of a labiate corolla
4 a : the edge of a hollow vessel or cavity **b** : a projecting edge: as (1) : the beveled upper edge of the mouth of an organ flue pipe (2) : the sharp cutting edge on the end of a tool (as an auger) (3) : a short spout (as on a pitcher)
5 : EMBOUCHURE
— **lip·less** \-ləs\ *adjective*
— **lip·like** \-ˌlīk\ *adjective*
²**lip** *adjective* (1558)
1 : INSINCERE ⟨*lip* praise⟩
2 : produced with the participation of the lips : LABIAL ⟨*lip* consonants⟩
³**lip** *transitive verb* **lipped; lip·ping** (1604)
1 : to touch with the lips; *especially* : KISS
2 : UTTER
3 : to lap against : LICK
4 : to hit (a putt) so that the ball hits the edge of the cup but fails to drop in
lip- or **lipo-** *combining form* [New Latin, from Greek, from *lipos* — more at LEAVE]
: fat : fatty tissue : fatty ⟨*lipoid*⟩ ⟨*lipo*protein⟩
li·pase \'lī-ˌpās, -ˌpāz\ *noun* [International Scientific Vocabulary] (1897)
: an enzyme that hydrolyzes glycerides
lip·id \'li-pəd\ *also* **lip·ide** \-ˌpīd\ *noun* [International Scientific Vocabulary] (1912)
: any of various substances that are soluble in nonpolar organic solvents (as chloroform and ether), that with proteins and carbohydrates constitute the principal structural components of living cells, and that include fats, waxes, phosphatides, cerebrosides, and related and derived compounds
— **li·pid·ic** \li-'pi-dik\ *adjective*
Lip·iz·zan \ˌli-pət-'sän\ *or* **Lip·iz·zan·er** \-'sä-nər\ *also* **Lip·pi·zan** \-'sän\ *or* **Lip·pi·zan·er** \-'sä-nər\ *noun* [German *Lipizzaner, Lippizaner,* from *Lipizza, Lippiza,* former site of the Austrian Imperial Stud near Trieste, Italy] (1928)
: any of a breed of spirited horses developed from Spanish, Italian, Danish, and Arab stock that are usually born with a dark coat that lightens to white with age
li·po·gen·e·sis \ˌlī-pə-'je-nə-səs\ *noun* [New Latin] (1882)
: the formation of fatty acids from acetyl coenzyme A in the living body
li·po·ic acid \lī-'pō-ik-, li-\ *noun* [*lip-, lipo-*] (circa 1951)
: any of several microbial growth factors; *especially* : a crystalline compound $C_8H_{14}O_2S_2$ that is essential for the oxidation of alpha-keto acids (as pyruvic acid) in metabolism
¹**li·poid** \'lī-ˌpȯid, 'li-\ *or* **li·poi·dal** \lī-'pȯid°l, li-\ *adjective* [International Scientific Vocabulary] (1876)
: resembling fat
²**lipoid** *noun* [International Scientific Vocabulary] (1906)
: LIPID
li·pol·y·sis \lī-'pä-lə-səs, li-\ *noun* [New Latin] (circa 1903)
: the hydrolysis of fat
— **li·po·lyt·ic** \ˌlī-pə-'li-tik, ˌli-\ *adjective*
li·po·ma \lī-'pō-mə, li-\ *noun, plural* **-mas** *or* **-ma·ta** \-mə-tə\ [New Latin] (1830)
: a tumor of fatty tissue
— **li·po·ma·tous** \-mə-təs\ *adjective*
li·po·phil·ic \ˌlī-pə-'fi-lik, ˌli-\ *adjective* (1939)
: having an affinity for lipids (as fats) ⟨a *lipophilic* metabolite⟩
li·po·poly·sac·cha·ride \ˌlī-pō-ˌpä-li-'sa-kə-ˌrīd, ˌli-\ *noun* (1950)
: a large molecule consisting of lipids and sugars joined by chemical bonds

li·po·pro·tein \-'prō-ˌtēn, -'prō-tē-ən\ *noun* (1909)
: a conjugated protein that is a complex of protein and lipid
li·po·some \'lī-pə-ˌsōm, 'li-\ *noun* (1968)
: a vesicle composed of one or more concentric phospholipid bilayers and used medically especially to deliver a drug into the body
— **li·po·so·mal** \ˌlī-pə-'sō-məl, ˌli-\ *adjective*
li·po·suc·tion \'li-pə-ˌsək-shən, 'lī-\ *noun* (1986)
: surgical removal of local fat deposits (as in the thighs) especially for cosmetic purposes
li·po·tro·pic \ˌlī-pō-'trō-pik, ˌli-, -'trä-\ *adjective* [International Scientific Vocabulary] (1935)
: promoting the physiological utilization of fat ⟨*lipotropic* dietary factors⟩
li·po·tro·pin \-'trō-pən\ *noun* (1964)
: either of two protein hormones of the pituitary gland that function in the mobilization of fat reserves
lipped \'lipt\ *adjective* (14th century)
: having a lip or lips especially of a specified kind or number — often used in combination ⟨tight-*lipped*⟩
lip·pen \'li-pən\ *verb* [Middle English *lipnien*] (12th century)
intransitive verb
chiefly Scottish : TRUST, RELY
transitive verb
chiefly Scottish : ENTRUST
Lippes loop \'li-pəs-, -ˌpēz-\ *noun* [Jack Lippes (born 1924) American physician] (1964)
: an S-shaped plastic intrauterine device
lip·ping \'li-piŋ\ *noun* (1894)
1 : outgrowth of bone in liplike form at a joint margin
2 : a piece of wood set in an archer's bow where a flaw has been cut out
3 : EMBOUCHURE 1
lip·py \'li-pē\ *adjective* **lip·pi·er; -est** (circa 1875)
: given to back talk
lip–read \'lip-ˌrēd\ *verb* **-read** \-ˌred\; **-read·ing** \-ˌrē-diŋ\ (1892)
transitive verb
: to understand by lipreading
intransitive verb
: to use lipreading
— **lip–read·er** \-ˌrē-dər\ *noun*
lipreading *noun* (1874)
: the interpreting of speech by watching the speaker's lip and facial movements without hearing the voice
lip service *noun* (1644)
: an avowal of advocacy, adherence, or allegiance expressed in words but not backed by deeds — usually used with *pay*
lip·stick \'lip-ˌstik\ *noun* (1880)
: a waxy solid usually colored cosmetic in stick form for the lips; *also* : a stick of such cosmetic with its case
— **lip·sticked** *adjective*
lip–synch *or* **lip–sync** \'lip-ˌsiŋk\ (circa 1961)
transitive verb
: to pretend to sing or say in synchronization with recorded sound
intransitive verb
: to lip-synch something
— **lip sync** *noun*
li·quate \'lī-ˌkwāt\ *transitive verb* **li·quat·ed; li·quat·ing** [Latin *liquatus,* past participle of *liquare* to make liquid; akin to Latin *liquēre*] (circa 1859)
: to cause (a more fusible substance) to separate out of a combination or mixture by the application of heat ⟨*liquate* metallic lead from its ore⟩
— **li·qua·tion** \lī-'kwā-shən\ *noun*
liq·ue·fac·tion \ˌli-kwə-'fak-shən\ *noun* [Middle English, from Late Latin *liquefaction-, liquefactio,* from Latin *liquefacere,* from

liquēre to be fluid + *facere* to make — more at DO] (15th century)
1 : the process of making or becoming liquid
2 : the state of being liquid
liquefied petroleum gas *noun* (1925)
: a compressed gas that consists of flammable hydrocarbons (as propane and butane) and is used especially as fuel or as raw material for chemical synthesis
liq·ue·fy *also* **liq·ui·fy** \'li-kwə-ˌfī\ *verb* **-fied; -fy·ing** [Middle English *liquefien,* from Middle French *liquefier,* from Latin *liquefacere*] (15th century)
transitive verb
: to reduce to a liquid state
intransitive verb
: to become liquid
— **liq·ue·fi·er** \-ˌfī-(-ə)r\ *noun*
li·ques·cent \li-'kwe-s°nt\ *adjective* [Latin *liquescent-, liquescens,* present participle of *liquescere* to become fluid, inchoative of *liquēre*] (circa 1727)
: being or tending to become liquid : MELTING
li·queur \li-'kər, -'kúr, -'kyúr\ *noun* [French, from Old French *licour* liquid — more at LIQUOR] (1729)
: a usually sweetened alcoholic liquor (as brandy) flavored with fruit, spices, nuts, herbs, or seeds
¹**liq·uid** \'li-kwəd\ *adjective* [Middle English, from Middle French *liquide,* from Latin *liquidus,* from *liquēre* to be fluid; akin to Latin *lixa* water, lye, and perhaps to Old Irish *fliuch* damp] (14th century)
1 : flowing freely like water
2 : having the properties of a liquid : being neither solid nor gaseous
3 a : shining and clear ⟨large *liquid* eyes⟩ **b** : being musical and free of harshness in sound **c** : smooth and unconstrained in movement **d** : articulated without friction and capable of being prolonged like a vowel ⟨a *liquid* consonant⟩
4 : consisting of or capable of ready conversion into cash ⟨*liquid* assets⟩
— **li·quid·i·ty** \li-'kwi-də-tē\ *noun*
— **liq·uid·ly** \'li-kwəd-lē\ *adverb*
— **liq·uid·ness** *noun*
²**liquid** *noun* (1530)
1 : a liquid consonant
2 : a fluid (as water) that has no independent shape but has a definite volume and does not expand indefinitely and that is only slightly compressible
liq·uid·am·bar \ˌli-kwə-'dam-bər\ *noun* [New Latin, from Latin *liquidus* + Medieval Latin *ambar, ambra* amber] (circa 1577)
1 : any of a genus (*Liquidambar*) of trees of the witch-hazel family with monoecious flowers and a globose fruit of many woody carpels
2 : STORAX 1b
liq·ui·date \'li-kwə-ˌdāt\ *verb* **-dat·ed; -dat·ing** [Late Latin *liquidatus,* past participle of *liquidare* to melt, from Latin *liquidus*] (circa 1575)
transitive verb
1 a (1) : to determine by agreement or by litigation the precise amount of (indebtedness, damages, or accounts) (2) : to determine the liabilities and apportion assets toward discharging the indebtedness of **b** : to settle (a debt) by payment or other settlement
2 *archaic* : to make clear
3 : to do away with
4 : to convert (assets) into cash
intransitive verb
1 : to liquidate debts, damages, or accounts
2 : to determine liabilities and apportion assets toward discharging indebtedness
— **liq·ui·da·tion** \ˌli-kwə-'dā-shən\ *noun*

\ə\ abut \ᵊ\ kitten \ər\ further \a\ ash \ā\ ace
\ä\ mop, mar \aú\ out \ch\ chin \e\ bet \ē\ easy
\g\ go \i\ hit \ī\ ice \j\ job \ŋ\ sing \ō\ go
\ȯ\ law \ȯi\ boy \th\ thin \t͟h\ the \ü\ loot \ú\ foot
\y\ yet \zh\ vision *see also* Guide to Pronunciation

liq·ui·da·tor \'li-kwə-ˌdā-tər\ *noun* (circa 1828)
: one that liquidates; *especially* : an individual appointed by law to liquidate assets

liquid crystal *noun* (1891)
: an organic liquid whose physical properties resemble those of a crystal in the formation of loosely ordered molecular arrays similar to a regular crystalline lattice and the anisotropic refraction of light

liquid crystal display *noun* (1968)
: LCD

liq·uid·ize \'li-kwə-ˌdīz\ *transitive verb* **-ized; -iz·ing** (1837)
: to cause to be liquid

liquid measure *noun* (circa 1855)
: a unit or series of units for measuring liquid capacity — see METRIC SYSTEM table, WEIGHT table

¹li·quor \'li-kər\ *noun* [Middle English *licour*, from Old French, from Latin *liquor*, from *liquēre*] (13th century)
: a liquid substance: as **a** : a usually distilled rather than fermented alcoholic beverage **b** : a watery solution of a drug **c** : BATH 2b(1)

²liquor *verb* **li·quored; li·quor·ing** \'li-k(ə-)riŋ\ (1502)
transitive verb
1 : to dress (as leather) with oil or grease
2 : to make drunk with alcoholic liquor — usually used with *up*
intransitive verb
: to drink alcoholic liquor especially to excess — usually used with *up*

li·quo·rice *chiefly British variant of* LICORICE

¹li·ra \'lir-ə, 'lē-rə\ *noun, plural* **li·re** \'lē-(ˌ)rā\ *also* **liras** [Italian, from Latin *libra*, a unit of weight] (1617)
— see MONEY table

²lira *noun, plural* **liras** [Turkish, from Italian] (1871)
— see MONEY table

³lira *noun, plural* **li·roth** *or* **li·rot** \lē-'rōt, -ˌrōth\ [New Hebrew, from Italian] (circa 1946)
: the former Israeli pound

⁴lira *noun, plural* **li·ri** \'lē-(ˌ)rē\ [Maltese, from Italian] (circa 1985)
— see MONEY table

lir·i·pipe \'lir-ə-ˌpīp\ *noun* [Medieval Latin *liripipium*] (1614)
: a pendent part of a tippet; *also* : TIPPET, SCARF

lisente *plural of* SENTE

lisle \'līl\ *noun, often attributive* [*Lisle* Lille, France] (1851)
: a smooth tightly twisted thread usually made of long-staple cotton

¹lisp \'lisp\ *verb* [Middle English, from Old English *-wlyspian;* akin to Old High German *lispen* to lisp] (before 12th century)
intransitive verb
1 : to pronounce the sibilants \s\ and \z\ imperfectly especially by turning them into \th\ and \th\
2 : to speak falteringly, childishly, or with a lisp
transitive verb
: to utter falteringly or with a lisp
— **lisp·er** *noun*

²lisp *noun* (circa 1625)
1 : a speech defect or affectation characterized by lisping
2 : a sound resembling a lisp

LISP \'lisp\ *noun* [*list* processing] (1959)
: a computer programming language that is designed for easy manipulation of data strings and is used extensively for work in artificial intelligence

lis·some *also* **lis·som** \'li-səm\ *adjective* [alteration of *lithesome*] (circa 1800)
1 a : easily flexed **b** : LITHE 2
2 : NIMBLE
— **lis·some·ly** *adverb*
— **lis·some·ness** *noun*

¹list \'list\ *verb* [Middle English *lysten*, from Old English *lystan;* akin to Old English *lust* desire, lust] (before 12th century)
transitive verb
archaic : PLEASE, SUIT
intransitive verb
archaic : WISH, CHOOSE

²list *noun* [Middle English, probably from *lysten*] (13th century)
archaic : INCLINATION, CRAVING

³list *verb* [Middle English, from Old English *hlystan*, from *hlyst* hearing; akin to Old English *hlysnan* to listen] (before 12th century)
intransitive verb
archaic : LISTEN
transitive verb
archaic : to listen to : HEAR

⁴list *noun* [Middle English, from Old English *līste;* akin to Old High German *līsta* edge, Albanian *leth*] (before 12th century)
1 : a band or strip of material: as **a** : LISTEL **b** : SELVAGE **c** : a narrow strip of wood cut from the edge of a board
2 *plural but singular or plural in construction* **a** : an arena for combat (as jousting) **b** : a field of competition or controversy
3 *obsolete* : LIMIT, BOUNDARY
4 : STRIPE

⁵list *transitive verb* (1635)
1 : to cut away a narrow strip from the edge of
2 : to prepare or plant (land) in ridges and furrows with a lister

⁶list *noun* [French *liste*, from Italian *lista*, of Germanic origin; akin to Old High German *līsta* edge] (1602)
1 a : a simple series of words or numerals (as the names of persons or objects) ⟨a guest *list*⟩ **b** : an official roster : ROLL
2 : CATALOG, CHECKLIST
3 : the total number to be considered or included ⟨a situation that heads their *list* of troubles⟩

⁷list (1614)
transitive verb
1 a : to make a list of : ENUMERATE **b** : to include on a list : REGISTER
2 : to place (oneself) in a specified category ⟨*lists* himself as a political liberal⟩
3 *archaic* : RECRUIT
intransitive verb
1 *archaic* : ENLIST
2 : to become entered in a catalog with a selling price ⟨a car that *lists* for $12,000⟩
— **list·ee** \li-'stē\ *noun*

⁸list *verb* [origin unknown] (1626)
intransitive verb
: to tilt to one side; *especially, of a boat or ship* : to lean to one side in a state of equilibrium (as from an unbalanced load) — compare HEEL
transitive verb
: to cause to list

⁹list *noun* (1633)
: a deviation from the vertical : TILT; *also* : the extent of such a deviation

lis·tel \'lis-t³l, lis-'tel\ *noun* [French, from Italian *listello*, diminutive of *lista* fillet, roster] (1598)
: a narrow band in architecture : FILLET

¹lis·ten \'li-s³n\ *verb* **lis·tened; lis·ten·ing** \'lis-niŋ, 'li-s³n-iŋ\ [Middle English *listnen*, from Old English *hlysnan;* akin to Sanskrit *śroṣati* he hears, Old English *hlūd* loud] (before 12th century)
transitive verb
archaic : to give ear to : HEAR
intransitive verb
1 : to pay attention to sound ⟨*listen* to music⟩
2 : to hear something with thoughtful attention : give consideration ⟨*listen* to a plea⟩
3 : to be alert to catch an expected sound ⟨*listen* for his step⟩
— **lis·ten·er** \'lis-nər, 'li-s³n-ər\ *noun*

²listen *noun* (1788)
: an act of listening

lis·ten·able \'lis-nə-bəl, 'li-s³n-ə-\ *adjective* (1942)
: agreeable to listen to

lis·ten·er·ship \'lis-nər-ˌship, 'li-s³n-ər-\ *noun* (1943)
: the audience for a radio program or recording; *also* : the number or kind of that audience

listen in *intransitive verb* (1905)
1 : to tune in to or monitor a broadcast
2 : to listen to a conversation without participating in it; *especially* : EAVESDROP
— **lis·ten·er-in** \ˌlis-nər-'in, ˌli-s³n-ər-\ *noun*

listening post *noun* (1942)
: a center for monitoring electronic communications (as of an enemy)

¹list·er \'lis-tər\ *noun* (1682)
: one that lists or catalogs

²lister *noun* [⁵*list*] (1887)
: a double-moldboard plow often equipped with a subsoiling attachment and used mainly where rainfall is limited

lis·te·ri·o·sis \lis-ˌtir-ē-'ō-səs\ *noun, plural* **-o·ses** \-ˌsēz\ [New Latin, from *Listeria*, from Joseph *Lister*] (1941)
: a serious commonly fatal encephalitic disease of a great variety of wild and domestic mammals and birds and occasionally humans that is caused by a bacterium (*Listeria monocytogenes*)

list·ing *noun* (1659)
1 : an act or instance of making or including in a list
2 : something that is listed

list·less \'list-ləs\ *adjective* [Middle English *listles*, from ²*list*] (15th century)
: characterized by lack of interest, energy, or spirit : LANGUID ⟨a *listless* melancholy attitude⟩
— **list·less·ly** *adverb*
— **list·less·ness** *noun*

list price *noun* (1871)
: the basic price of an item as published in a catalog, price list, or advertisement before any discounts are taken

¹lit \'lit\ *past and past participle of* LIGHT

²lit *noun* [by shortening] (1850)
: LITERATURE

³lit *adjective* [past participle of ³*light*] (1904)
: affected by alcohol : DRUNK

lit·a·ny \'li-t³n-ē, 'lit-nē\ *noun, plural* **-nies** [Middle English *letanie*, from Old French & Late Latin; Old French, from Late Latin *litania*, from Late Greek *litaneia*, from Greek, entreaty, from *litanos* suppliant] (13th century)
1 : a prayer consisting of a series of invocations and supplications by the leader with alternate responses by the congregation
2 a : a resonant or repetitive chant ⟨a *litany* of cheering phrases —Herman Wouk⟩ **b** : a usually lengthy recitation or enumeration ⟨a familiar *litany* of complaints⟩

li·tchi \'lē-(ˌ)chē, 'lī-\ *noun* [Chinese (Beijing) *lìzhī*] (1588)
1 : the oval fruit of a tree (*Litchi chinensis*) of the soapberry family having a hard scaly reddish outer covering and sweet whitish edible flesh that surrounds a single large seed — called also *litchi nut*
2 : a tree bearing litchis

lit crit \'lit-ˌkrit\ *noun* (1963)
: literary criticism

lite \'līt\ *variant of* ⁴LIGHT 9a

-lite *noun combining form* [French, alteration of *-lithe*, from Greek *lithos* stone]
: mineral ⟨rhodo*lite*⟩ : rock ⟨aero*lite*⟩ : fossil ⟨stromato*lite*⟩

li·ter \'lē-tər\ *noun* [French *litre*, from Medieval Latin *litra*, a measure, from Greek, a weight] (1797)
: a metric unit of capacity equal to one cubic decimeter — see METRIC SYSTEM table

lit·er·a·cy \'li-t(ə-)rə-sē\ *noun* (1883)
: the quality or state of being literate

¹lit·er·al \'li-t(ə-)rəl\ *adjective* [Middle English, from Middle French, from Medieval En-
glish, from Middle French, from Medieval

Latin *litteralis*, from Latin, of a letter, from *littera* letter] (14th century) **1 a :** according with the letter of the scriptures **b :** adhering to fact or to the ordinary construction or primary meaning of a term or expression **:** ACTUAL ⟨liberty in the *literal* sense is impossible —B. N. Cardozo⟩ **c :** free from exaggeration or embellishment ⟨the *literal* truth⟩ **d :** characterized by a concern mainly with facts ⟨a very *literal* man⟩ **2 :** of, relating to, or expressed in letters **3 :** reproduced word for word **:** EXACT, VERBATIM ⟨a *literal* translation⟩
— **lit·er·al·i·ty** \ˌli-tə-'ra-lə-tē\ *noun*
— **lit·er·al·ness** \'li-t(ə-)rəl-nəs\ *noun*
²**literal** *noun* (1622)
: a small error usually of a single letter (as in writing)
lit·er·al·ism \'li-t(ə-)rə-ˌliz-əm\ *noun* (1644)
1 : adherence to the explicit substance of an idea or expression ⟨biblical *literalism*⟩
2 : fidelity to observable fact **:** REALISM
— **lit·er·al·ist** \-list\ *noun*
— **lit·er·al·is·tic** \ˌli-t(ə-)rə-'lis-tik\ *adjective*
lit·er·al·ize \'li-t(ə-)rə-ˌlīz\ *transitive verb* **-ized; -iz·ing** (1826)
: to make literal
— **lit·er·al·i·za·tion** \ˌli-t(ə-)rə-lə-'zā-shən\ *noun*
lit·er·al·ly \'li-tə-rə-lē, 'li-trə-lē, 'li-tər-lē\ *adverb* (1533)
1 : in a literal sense or manner **:** ACTUALLY ⟨took the remark *literally*⟩ ⟨was *literally* insane⟩
2 : in effect **:** VIRTUALLY ⟨will *literally* turn the world upside down to combat cruelty or injustice —Norman Cousins⟩ □
lit·er·ary \'li-tə-ˌrer-ē\ *adjective* (1749)
1 a : of, relating to, or having the characteristics of humane learning or literature **b :** BOOKISH 2 **c :** of or relating to books
2 a : WELL-READ **b :** of or relating to authors or scholars or to their profession
— **lit·er·ar·i·ly** \ˌli-tə-'rer-ə-lē\ *adverb*
— **lit·er·ar·i·ness** \'li-tə-ˌrer-ē-nəs\ *noun*
literary executor *noun* (1868)
: a person entrusted with the management of the papers and unpublished works of a deceased author
¹**lit·er·ate** \'li-tə-rət *also* 'li-trət\ *adjective* [Middle English *literat*, from Latin *litteratus* marked with letters, literate, from *litterae* letters, literature, from plural of *littera*] (15th century)
1 a : EDUCATED, CULTURED **b :** able to read and write
2 a : versed in literature or creative writing **:** LITERARY **b :** LUCID, POLISHED ⟨a *literate* essay⟩ **c :** having knowledge or competence ⟨computer-*literate*⟩ ⟨politically *literate*⟩
— **lit·er·ate·ly** *adverb*
— **lit·er·ate·ness** *noun*
²**literate** *noun* (circa 1550)
1 : an educated person
2 : a person who can read and write
li·te·ra·ti \ˌli-tə-'rä-(ˌ)tē\ *noun plural* [obsolete Italian *litterati*, from Latin, plural of *litteratus*] (1621)
1 : the educated class; *also* **:** INTELLIGENTSIA
2 : persons interested in literature or the arts
lit·er·a·tim \ˌli-tə-'rä-təm, -'rä-\ *adverb or adjective* [Medieval Latin, from Latin *littera*] (1643)
: letter for letter ⟨printed *literatim* from the manuscript —I. A. Gordon⟩
lit·er·a·tion \ˌli-tə-'rä-shən\ *noun* [Latin *littera* + English *-ation*] (circa 1889)
: the representation of sound or words by letters
lit·er·a·tor \'li-tə-ˌrä-tər, ˌli-tə-'rä-ˌtör\ *noun* (1791)
: LITTERATEUR
lit·er·a·ture \'li-tə-rə-ˌchûr, 'li-trə-ˌchûr, 'li-tə(r)-ˌchûr, -chər, -ˌtyûr, -ˌtûr\ *noun* [Middle

English, from Latin *litteratura* writing, grammar, learning, from *litteratus*] (14th century)
1 *archaic* **:** literary culture
2 : the production of literary work especially as an occupation
3 a (1) **:** writings in prose or verse; *especially* **:** writings having excellence of form or expression and expressing ideas of permanent or universal interest (2) **:** an example of such writings ⟨what came out, though rarely *literature*, was always a roaring good story —*People*⟩ **b :** the body of written works produced in a particular language, country, or age **c :** the body of writings on a particular subject ⟨scientific *literature*⟩ **d :** printed matter (as leaflets or circulars) ⟨campaign *literature*⟩
4 : the aggregate of a usually specified type of musical compositions ⟨Brahms piano *literature*⟩
lit·er·a·tus \ˌli-tə-'rä-təs\ *noun* [New Latin, back-formation from English *literati* (taken as Latin)] (1704)
: a member of the literati
lith- *or* **litho-** *combining form* [Latin, from Greek, from *lithos*]
: stone ⟨*lithology*⟩
-lith *noun combining form* [New Latin *-lithus* & French *-lithe*, from Greek *lithos*]
1 : structure or implement of stone ⟨mega*lith*⟩ ⟨eo*lith*⟩
2 : calculus ⟨uro*lith*⟩
3 : -LITE ⟨lacco*lith*⟩
li·tharge \'li-ˌthärj, li-'\ *noun* [Middle English, from Middle French, from Latin *lithargyrus*, from Greek *lithargyros*, from *lithos* + *argyros* silver — more at ARGENT] (14th century)
: a fused lead monoxide; *broadly* **:** LEAD MONOXIDE
lithe \'līth, 'līth\ *adjective* [Middle English, from Old English *līthe* gentle; akin to Old High German *lindi* gentle, Latin *lentus* slow] (14th century)
1 : easily bent or flexed ⟨*lithe* steel⟩ ⟨a *lithe* vine⟩
2 : characterized by easy flexibility and grace ⟨a *lithe* dancer⟩ ⟨treading with a *lithe* silent step⟩; *also* **:** athletically slim ⟨the most *lithe* and graspable of waists —R. P. Warren⟩
— **lithe·ly** *adverb*
— **lithe·ness** *noun*
lithe·some \'līth-səm, 'līth-\ *adjective* (circa 1774)
: LISSOME
li·thi·a·sis \li-'thī-ə-səs\ *noun, plural* **-a·ses** \-ˌsēz\ [New Latin, from Greek, from *lithos*] (circa 1657)
: the formation of stony concretions in the body (as in the gallbladder)
lith·ic \'li-thik\ *adjective* [Greek *lithikos*, from *lithos*] (1797)
1 : STONY 1
2 : of, relating to, or being a stone tool
-lithic *adjective combining form* [*lithic*]
: relating to or characteristic of a (specified) stage in humankind's use of stone as a cultural tool ⟨Neo*lithic*⟩
lith·i·fy \'li-thə-ˌfī\ *verb* **-fied; -fy·ing** (1877)
transitive verb
: to change to stone **:** PETRIFY; *especially* **:** to convert (unconsolidated sediment) into solid rock
intransitive verb
: to become changed into stone
— **lith·i·fi·ca·tion** \ˌli-thə-fə-'kā-shən\ *noun*
lith·i·um \'li-thē-əm\ *noun* [New Latin, from *lithia* oxide of lithium, from Greek *lithos*] (1818)
1 : a soft silver-white element of the alkali metal group that is the lightest metal known and that is used in chemical synthesis and storage batteries — see ELEMENT table
2 : a salt of lithium (as lithium carbonate) used in psychiatric medicine

lithium carbonate *noun* (1873)
: a crystalline salt Li_2CO_3 used in the glass and ceramic industries and in medicine in the treatment of manic-depressive psychosis
lithium fluoride *noun* (1944)
: a crystalline salt LiF used especially in making prisms and ceramics and as a flux
lithium ni·o·bate \-'nī-ə-ˌbāt\ *noun* [*niobium* + *-ate*] (1966)
: a crystalline material $LiNbO_3$ whose physical properties change in response to pressure or the presence of an electric field and which is used in fiber optics and as a synthetic gemstone
litho \'lī-(ˌ)thō\ *noun, plural* **lith·os** (circa 1889)
1 : LITHOGRAPH
2 : LITHOGRAPHY 1
¹**lith·o·graph** \'li-thə-ˌgraf\ *transitive verb* (1825)
: to produce, copy, or portray by lithography
— **li·tho·gra·pher** \li-'thä-grə-fər, 'li-thə-ˌgra-fər\ *noun*
²**lithograph** *noun* (1828)
: a print made by lithography
— **lith·o·graph·ic** \ˌli-thə-'gra-fik\ *adjective*
— **lith·o·graph·i·cal·ly** \-fi-k(ə-)lē\ *adverb*
li·thog·ra·phy \li-'thä-grə-fē\ *noun* [German *Lithographie*, from *lith-* + *-graphie* -graphy] (1813)
1 : the process of printing from a plane surface (as a smooth stone or metal plate) on which the image to be printed is ink-receptive and the blank area ink-repellent
2 : the process of producing patterns on semiconductor crystals for use as integrated circuits
li·thol·o·gy \li-'thä-lə-jē\ *noun, plural* **-gies** (1716)
1 : the study of rocks
2 : the character of a rock formation; *also* **:** a rock formation having a particular set of characteristics
— **lith·o·log·ic** \ˌli-thə-'lä-jik\ *or* **lith·o·log·i·cal** \-ji-kəl\ *adjective*
— **lith·o·log·i·cal·ly** \-ji-k(ə-)lē\ *adverb*
lith·o·phane \'li-thə-ˌfān\ *noun* [probably from German *Lithophan*, from Greek *lithos* + German *diaphan* diaphanous] (circa 1889)
: porcelain impressed with figures that are made distinct by transmitted light; *also* **:** an object of this material
lith·o·phyte \'li-thə-ˌfīt\ *noun* [French, from *lith-* + *-phyte*] (1774)
: a plant that grows on rock
lith·o·pone \'li-thə-ˌpōn\ *noun* [International Scientific Vocabulary *lith-* + Greek *ponos* work] (circa 1884)
: a white pigment consisting essentially of zinc sulfide and barium sulfate
lith·o·sol \'li-thə-ˌsäl, -ˌsȯl\ *noun* [*lith-* + Latin *solum* soil] (circa 1938)
: any of a group of shallow azonal soils consisting of imperfectly weathered rock fragments
lith·o·sphere \'li-thə-ˌsfir\ *noun* [International Scientific Vocabulary] (1887)

□ USAGE
literally Since some people take sense 2 to be the opposite of sense 1, it has been frequently criticized as a misuse. Instead, the use is pure hyperbole intended to gain emphasis, but it often appears in contexts where no additional emphasis is necessary.

: the solid part of a celestial body (as the earth); *specifically* : the outer part of the solid earth composed of rock essentially like that exposed at the surface and usually considered to be about 50 miles (80 kilometers) in thickness

— **lith·o·spher·ic** \,li-thə-'sfir-ik, -'sfer-\ *adjective*

li·thot·o·my \li-'thä-tə-mē\ *noun, plural* **-mies** [Late Latin *lithotomia,* from Greek, from *lithotomein* to perform a lithotomy, from *lith-* + *temnein* to cut — more at TOME] (1721)

: surgical incision of the urinary bladder for removal of a stone

lith·o·trip·sy \'li-thə-,trip-sē\ *noun, plural* **-sies** [*lith-* + Greek *tripsis* a rubbing, from *tribein* to rub — more at THROW] (1834)

: the breaking of a stone (as by shock waves or crushing with a surgical instrument) in the urinary system into pieces small enough to be voided or washed out

lith·o·trip·ter *also* **lith·o·trip·tor** \'li-thə-,trip-tər\ *noun* [alteration of *lithontriptor,* from *lithontriptic* breaking up bladder stones, modification of Greek (*pharmaka tōn*) *lithōn thryptika* (drugs) capable of pulverizing stones] (1825)

: a device for performing lithotripsy; *especially* : a noninvasive device that pulverizes stones by focusing shock waves on a patient immersed in a water bath

Lith·u·a·nian \,li-thə-'wā-nē-ən, -nyən, *chiefly British* ,lith-yü-\ *noun* (1607)

1 : a native or inhabitant of Lithuania

2 : the Baltic language of the Lithuanian people

— **Lithuanian** *adjective*

lit·i·gant \'li-ti-gənt\ *noun* (1659)

: one engaged in a lawsuit

— **litigant** *adjective*

lit·i·gate \'li-tə-,gāt\ *verb* **-gat·ed; -gat·ing** [Latin *litigatus,* past participle of *litigare,* from *lit-, lis* lawsuit + *agere* to drive — more at AGENT] (1615)

intransitive verb

: to carry on a legal contest by judicial process

transitive verb

1 *archaic* : DISPUTE

2 : to contest in law

— **lit·i·ga·ble** \'li-ti-gə-bəl\ *adjective*

— **lit·i·ga·tion** \,li-tə-'gā-shən\ *noun*

— **lit·i·ga·tor** \'li-tə-,gā-tər\ *noun*

li·ti·gious \lə-'ti-jəs, li-\ *adjective* [Middle English, from Middle French *litigieux,* from Latin *litigiosus,* from *litigium* dispute, from *litigare*] (14th century)

1 a : DISPUTATIOUS, CONTENTIOUS **b** : prone to engage in lawsuits

2 : subject to litigation

3 : of, relating to, or marked by litigation

— **li·ti·gious·ly** *adverb*

— **li·ti·gious·ness** *noun*

lit·mus \'lit-məs\ *noun* [Middle English *litmose,* of Scandinavian origin; akin to Old Norse *litmosi* herbs used in dyeing, from *litr* color (akin to Old English *wlite* brightness) + *mosi* moss; akin to Old English *mōs* moss] (14th century)

1 : a coloring matter from lichens that turns red in acid solutions and blue in alkaline solutions and is used as an acid-base indicator

2 : the critical factor in a litmus test; *also* : LITMUS TEST

litmus paper *noun* (1803)

: unsized paper colored with litmus and used as an indicator

litmus test *noun* (1952)

: a test in which a single factor (as an attitude, event, or fact) is decisive

li·to·tes \'lī-tə-,tēz, 'li-, lī-'tō-,tēz\ *noun, plural* **litotes** [Greek *litotēs,* from *litos* simple, perhaps from *lit-, lis* linen cloth] (1589)

: understatement in which an affirmative is expressed by the negative of the contrary (as in "not a bad singer" or "not unhappy")

li·tre \'lē-tər\ *variant of* LITER

lit·ten \'li-t³n\ *adjective* [alteration of *lit,* past participle of *light*] (circa 1849)

archaic : being lighted

¹**lit·ter** \'li-tər\ *noun* [Middle English, from Middle French *litiere,* from *lit* bed, from Latin *lectus* — more at LIE] (14th century)

1 a : a covered and curtained couch provided with shafts and used for carrying a single passenger **b** : a device (as a stretcher) for carrying a sick or injured person

litter 1a

2 a (1) : material used as bedding for animals (2) : material used to absorb the urine and feces of animals **b** : the uppermost slightly decayed layer of organic matter on the forest floor

3 : the offspring at one birth of a multiparous animal

4 a : trash, wastepaper, or garbage lying scattered about ⟨trying to clean up the roadside *litter*⟩ **b** : an untidy accumulation of objects ⟨a shabby writing-desk covered with a *litter* of yellowish dusty documents —Joseph Conrad⟩

— **lit·tery** \-tə-rē\ *adjective*

²**litter** (14th century)

transitive verb

1 : BED 1a

2 : to give birth to a litter of (young)

3 a : to strew with scattered articles **b** : to scatter about in disorder **c** : to lie about in disorder ⟨their upside-down hats *littered* the top of the bar —Michael Chabon⟩ **d** : to mark with objects scattered at random ⟨a book *littered* with misprints⟩

intransitive verb

1 : to give birth to a litter

2 : to strew litter

lit·te·rae hu·ma·ni·o·res \'li-tə-,rī-hü-,mä-nē-'ōr-,ās, -'ȯr-\ *noun plural* [Medieval Latin, literally, more humane letters] (1747)

: HUMANITIES

lit·ter·a·teur *or* **lit·té·ra·teur** \,li-tə-rə-'tər, ,li-trə-, -'tu̇r\ *noun* [French *littérateur,* from Latin *litterator* critic, from *litterae* letters, literature] (1806)

: a literary person; *especially* : a professional writer

lit·ter·bag \'li-tər-,bag\ *noun* (1955)

: a bag used (as in an automobile) for temporary refuse disposal

lit·ter·bug \-,bəg\ *noun* (1947)

: one who litters a public area

lit·ter·er \'li-tər-ər\ *noun* (1928)

: LITTERBUG

lit·ter·mate \'li-tər-,māt\ *noun* (1921)

: one of the offspring in a litter in relation to the others

¹**lit·tle** \'li-t³l\ *adjective* **lit·tler** \'li-t³l-ər, 'lit-lər\ *or* **less** \'les\ *or* **less·er** \'le-sər\; **lit·tlest** \'li-t³l-əst, 'lit-ləst\ *or* **least** \'lēst\ [Middle English *littel,* from Old English *lȳtel;* akin to Old High German *luzzil* little] (before 12th century)

1 : not big: as **a** : small in size or extent : TINY ⟨has *little* feet⟩ **b** : YOUNG ⟨was too *little* to remember⟩ **c** *of a plant or animal* : small in comparison with related forms — used in vernacular names **d** : small in number **e** : small in condition, distinction, or scope ⟨big business trampling on the *little* fellow⟩ **f** : NARROW, MEAN ⟨the pettiness of *little* minds⟩ **g** : pleasingly small ⟨a cute *little* thing⟩ — used as an intensive ⟨why, you *little* devil!⟩

2 : not much: as **a** : existing only in a small amount or to a slight degree ⟨has *little* money⟩

b : short in duration : BRIEF **c** : existing to an appreciable though not extensive degree or amount — used with *a* ⟨had a *little* money in the bank⟩

3 : small in importance or interest : TRIVIAL

synonym see SMALL

— **lit·tle·ness** \'li-t³l-nəs\ *noun*

²**little** *adverb* **less** \'les\; **least** \'lēst\ (before 12th century)

1 a : in only a small quantity or degree : SLIGHTLY ⟨facts that were *little* known at the time⟩ **b** : not at all ⟨cared *little* for their neighbors⟩

2 : RARELY, INFREQUENTLY

³**little** *noun* (before 12th century)

1 : a small amount, quantity, or degree; *also* : practically nothing ⟨*little* has changed⟩

2 a : a short time **b** : a short distance

— **a little** : SOMEWHAT, RATHER ⟨found the play a *little* dull⟩

— **in little** : on a small scale; *especially* : in miniature

Little Bear *noun*

: URSA MINOR

little bitty *adjective* (1905)

: SMALL, TINY

little bluestem *noun* (circa 1898)

: a forage grass (*Schizachyrium scoparium* synonym *Andropogon scoparius*) of eastern and central North America

little brown bat *noun* (1842)

: a small widely distributed insectivorous North American bat (*Myotis lucifugus*) with brown fur

little by little *adverb* (15th century)

: by small degrees or amounts : GRADUALLY

Little Dipper *noun*

: the seven principal stars in Ursa Minor

little finger *noun* (before 12th century)

: the fourth and smallest finger of the hand counting the forefinger as the first

little guy *noun* (1863)

: LITTLE MAN

Little Hours *noun plural* (circa 1872)

: the offices of prime, terce, sext, and none forming part of the canonical hours

little leaf *noun* (1916)

: a plant disorder characterized by small and often chlorotic and distorted foliage: as **a** : a zinc-deficiency disease of deciduous woody plants (as grape, peach, and pecan) **b** : a destructive disease of unknown cause that affects southern pines and especially the shortleaf pine — called also *little-leaf disease*

Little League *noun* (1952)

: a commercially sponsored baseball league for boys and girls from 8 to 12 years old

— **Little Leaguer** *noun*

◇ WORD HISTORY

litter The diverse senses of the word *litter* all grew out of the basic notion "bed." In Old French *litiere,* a derivative of *lit* "bed," could refer to a sleeping place in a general way, but it was usually applied more narrowly either to a curtained portable couch or to straw spread on the ground as a sleeping place for animals. In borrowing the word, English retained both usages and added new ones. The "bedding for animals" sense was extended to the offspring of an animal such as a dog or cat that gives birth to a number of young at once. In a different direction, *litter* became not just straw for animal bedding but straw or similar material used for any purpose, and by the 18th century any odds and ends of rubbish lying scattered about, and hence a near-synonym for "trash" or "refuse." A much more recent development, presumably arising from euphemism, has extended *litter* to absorbent clay that a cat is trained to use not for sleeping or giving birth but for depositing its feces and urine.

little magazine *noun* (1900)
: a literary usually noncommercial magazine that features works especially of writers who are not well-known

little man *noun* (1933)
: the ordinary individual

lit·tle·neck \'li-t³l-,nek\ *noun* [*Littleneck* Bay, Long Island, N.Y.] (1883)
: a young quahog suitable to be eaten raw — called also *littleneck clam*

Little Office *noun* (circa 1872)
: an office in honor of the Virgin Mary like but shorter than the Divine Office

little people *noun plural* (circa 1731)
1 : tiny imaginary beings (as fairies, elves, and leprechauns) of folklore
2 : CHILDREN
3 : MIDGETS
4 : common people

little slam *noun* (circa 1897)
: the winning of all tricks except one in bridge

little theater *noun* (1812)
: a small theater for low-cost dramatic productions designed for a relatively limited audience

little toe *noun* (before 12th century)
: the outermost and smallest digit of the foot

little woman *noun* (1795)
: WIFE

¹lit·to·ral \'li-tə-rəl; ,li-tə-'ral, -'räl\ *adjective* [Latin *litoralis,* from *litor-, litus* seashore] (circa 1656)
: of, relating to, or situated or growing on or near a shore especially of the sea

²littoral *noun* (1828)
: a coastal region; *especially* : the shore zone between high and low watermarks

lit up *adjective* (circa 1914)
: DRUNK 1a

li·tur·gi·cal \lə-'tər-ji-kəl, li-\ *adjective* (1641)
1 : of, relating to, or having the characteristics of liturgy
2 : using or favoring the use of liturgy ⟨*liturgical* churches⟩
— **li·tur·gi·cal·ly** \-k(ə-)lē\ *adverb*

li·tur·gics \-jiks\ *noun plural but singular or plural in construction* (circa 1855)
: the practice or study of formal public worship

li·tur·gi·ol·o·gist \-,tər-jē-'ä-lə-jist\ *noun* (1866)
: LITURGIST 2

li·tur·gi·ol·o·gy \-jē\ *noun* (1863)
: LITURGICS

lit·ur·gist \'li-tər-jist\ *noun* (1649)
1 : one who adheres to, compiles, or leads a liturgy
2 : a specialist in liturgics

lit·ur·gy \'li-tər-jē\ *noun, plural* **-gies** [Late Latin *liturgia,* from Greek *leitourgia* public service, from Greek (Attic) *leiton* public building (from Greek *laos* — Attic *leōs* — people) + *-ourgia* -urgy] (1560)
1 *often capitalized* : a eucharistic rite
2 : a rite or body of rites prescribed for public worship
3 : a customary repertoire of ideas, phrases, or observances

liv·abil·i·ty *also* **live·abil·i·ty** \,li-və-'bi-lə-tē\ *noun* (1914)
1 : survival expectancy : VIABILITY — used especially of poultry and livestock
2 : suitability for human living

liv·able *also* **live·able** \'li-və-bəl\ *adjective* (1814)
1 : suitable for living in or with
2 : ENDURABLE
— **liv·able·ness** *noun*

¹live \'liv\ *verb* **lived; liv·ing** [Middle English, from Old English *libban;* akin to Old High German *lebēn* to live] (before 12th century)
intransitive verb
1 : to be alive : have the life of an animal or plant
2 : to continue alive
3 : to maintain oneself : SUBSIST

4 : to occupy a home : DWELL ⟨*living* in a shabby room⟩ ⟨they had always *lived* in the country⟩
5 : to attain eternal life ⟨though he die, yet shall he *live* —John 11:25 (Revised Standard Version)⟩
6 : to conduct or pass one's life ⟨*lived* only for his work⟩
7 : to remain in human memory or record ⟨the past *lives* in us all —W. R. Inge⟩
8 : to have a life rich in experience
9 : COHABIT
transitive verb
1 : to pass through or spend the duration of ⟨*lived* their lives alone⟩
2 : ACT OUT, PRACTICE — often used with *out* ⟨to *live* out their fantasies⟩
3 : to exhibit vigor, gusto, or enthusiasm in ⟨*lived* life to the fullest⟩
— **live it up** : to live with gusto and usually fast and loose ⟨*lived it up* with wine and song —*Newsweek*⟩
— **live up to** : to act or be in accordance with ⟨had no intention of *living up to* his promise⟩

²live \'līv\ *adjective* [short for *alive*] (1542)
1 : having life : LIVING
2 : exerting force or containing energy: as **a** : AFIRE, GLOWING ⟨*live* coals⟩ **b** : connected to electric power **c** : charged with explosives and containing shot or a bullet ⟨*live* ammunition⟩; *also* : armed but not exploded ⟨a *live* bomb⟩ **d** : imparting or driven by power ⟨a *live* axle⟩ **e** : being in operation ⟨a *live* microphone⟩
3 : abounding with life : VIVID
4 : being in a pure native state
5 : of bright vivid color
6 : of continuing or current interest ⟨*live* issues⟩
7 a : not yet printed from or plated ⟨*live* type⟩ **b** : not yet typeset ⟨*live* copy⟩
8 a : of or involving a presentation (as a play or concert) in which both the performers and an audience are physically present ⟨a *live* record album⟩ ⟨a nightclub with *live* entertainment⟩ **b** : broadcast directly at the time of production ⟨a *live* radio program⟩
9 : being in play ⟨a *live* ball⟩

³live \'līv\ *adverb* (1946)
: at the actual time of occurrence : during, from, or at a live production ⟨the programming originated *live* from New York City —*Current Biography*⟩

live·bear·er \'līv-,bar-ər, -,ber-\ *noun* (1934)
: a fish that brings forth living young rather than eggs; *especially* : any of a family (Poeciliidae) of numerous small surface-feeding fishes

live-box \-,bäks\ *noun* (1862)
: a box or pen suspended in water to keep aquatic animals alive

-lived \'līvd, 'livd\ *adjective combining form* [Middle English, from *lif* life]
: having a life of a specified kind or length ⟨long-*lived*⟩

lived-in \'liv-,din\ *adjective* (1873)
: of or suggesting long-term human habitation or use : COMFORTABLE

live down *transitive verb* (1842)
: to live so as to wipe out the memory or effects of ⟨made a mistake and couldn't *live it down*⟩

live-for-ev-er \'liv-fə-,re-vər\ *noun* (1597)
: SEDUM

live-in \'liv-,in\ *adjective* (1953)
1 : living in one's place of employment ⟨a *live-in* maid⟩
2 : involving or involved with cohabitation ⟨a *live-in* relationship⟩ ⟨a *live-in* partner⟩
— **live-in** *noun*

live in *intransitive verb* (1890)
: to live in one's place of employment : live in another's home

live·li·hood \'līv-lē-,húd\ *noun* [alteration of Middle English *livelode* course of life, from

Old English *līflād,* from *līf* + *lād* course — more at LODE] (15th century)
1 : means of support or subsistence
2 *obsolete* : the quality or state of being lively

live load *noun* (1866)
: the load to which a structure is subjected in addition to its own weight

live·long \'liv-,lòn\ *adjective* [Middle English *lef long,* from *lef* dear + *long* — more at LIEF] (15th century)
: WHOLE, ENTIRE ⟨the *livelong* day⟩

live·ly \'līv-lē\ *adjective* **live·li·er; -est** [Middle English, from Old English *līflīc,* from *līf* life] (before 12th century)
1 *obsolete* : LIVING
2 : briskly alert and energetic : VIGOROUS, ANIMATED ⟨a *lively* discussion⟩ ⟨*lively* children racing for home⟩
3 : ACTIVE, INTENSE ⟨takes a *lively* interest in politics⟩
4 : BRILLIANT, FRESH ⟨a *lively* wit⟩
5 : imparting spirit or vivacity : STIMULATING ⟨many a peer of England brews *livelier* liquor than the Muse —A. E. Housman⟩
6 : quick to rebound : RESILIENT
7 : responding readily to the helm ⟨a *lively* boat⟩
8 : full of life, movement, or incident ⟨*lively* streets at carnival time⟩ ☆
— **live·li·ly** \'līv-lə-lē\ *adverb*
— **live·li·ness** \'līv-lē-nəs\ *noun*
— **lively** *adverb*

liv·en \'lī-vən\ *verb* **liv·ened; liv·en·ing** \'lī-və-niŋ, 'līv-niŋ\ (1884)
transitive verb
: ENLIVEN — often used with *up* ⟨he . . . *livened* up the editorial page —*Current Biography*⟩
intransitive verb
: to become lively

live oak *noun* (1610)
: any of several American evergreen oaks: as **a** : a medium-sized oak (*Quercus virginiana*) of southeastern North America often cultivated as a shelter and shade tree and noted for its extremely hard tough durable wood **b** : any of several oaks of the western U.S. with evergreen foliage and hard durable wood

¹liv·er \'li-vər\ *noun* [Middle English, from Old English *lifer;* akin to Old High German *lebra* liver] (before 12th century)
1 a : a large very vascular glandular organ of vertebrates that secretes bile and causes important changes in many of the substances contained in the blood (as by converting sugars into glycogen which it stores up until required and by forming urea) **b** : any of various large compound glands associated with the digestive tract of invertebrate animals and probably concerned with the secretion of digestive enzymes
2 *archaic* : a determinant of the quality or temper of a man

☆ SYNONYMS
Lively, animated, vivacious, sprightly, gay mean keenly alive and spirited. LIVELY suggests briskness, alertness, or energy ⟨a *lively* debate on the issues⟩. ANIMATED applies to what is spirited and active ⟨an *animated* discussion of current events⟩. VIVACIOUS suggests an activeness of gesture and wit, often playful or alluring ⟨a *vivacious* party host⟩. SPRIGHTLY suggests lightness and spirited vigor of manner or wit ⟨a tuneful, *sprightly* musical⟩. GAY stresses complete freedom from care and overflowing spirits ⟨the *gay* spirit of Paris in the 1920s⟩.

\ə\ **abut** \ᵊ\ **kitten** \ər\ **further** \a\ **ash** \ā\ **ace**
\ä\ **mop, mar** \aú\ **out** \ch\ **chin** \e\ **bet** \ē\ **easy**
\g\ **go** \i\ **hit** \ī\ **ice** \j\ **job** \ŋ\ **sing** \ō\ **go**
\ò\ **law** \òi\ **boy** \th\ **thin** \th̲\ **the** \ü\ **loot** \ú\ **foot**
\y\ **yet** \zh\ **vision** *see also* Guide to Pronunciation

3 : the liver of an animal (as a calf or chicken) eaten as food
4 : a grayish reddish brown — called also *liver brown, liver maroon*
²**liv·er** \'li-vər\ *noun* (14th century)
1 : one that lives especially in a specified way ⟨a fast *liver*⟩
2 : RESIDENT
-livered *adjective combining form*
: expressing vigor or courage considered suggestive of one with (such) a liver ⟨chicken-*livered*⟩ ⟨lily-*livered*⟩
liver fluke *noun* (circa 1798)
: any of various trematode worms (as *Fasciola hepatica*) that invade the mammalian liver
liv·er·ied \'li-və-rēd, 'liv-rēd\ *adjective* (1634)
: wearing a livery ⟨a *liveried* chauffeur⟩
liv·er·ish \'li-və-rish, 'liv-rish\ *adjective* (1740)
1 : resembling liver especially in color
2 a : suffering from liver disorder **:** BILIOUS **b :** PEEVISH, IRASCIBLE
— **liv·er·ish·ness** *noun*
liver sausage *noun* (1855)
: a sausage containing cooked ground liver and pork trimmings — called also *liver pudding*
liver spots *noun plural* (circa 1859)
: spots of dark pigmentation on the skin (as from exposure to sun) occurring especially among older people
liv·er·wort \'li-vər-,wərt, -,wȯrt\ *noun* (before 12th century)
1 : any of a class (Hepaticae) of bryophytic plants characterized by a thalloid gametophyte or sometimes an upright leafy gametophyte that resembles a moss
2 : HEPATICA
liv·er·wurst \'li-və(r)-,wərst *also* -,vu̇(r)st; *sometimes* -,vu̇sht\ *noun* [part translation of German *Leberwurst,* from *Leber* liver + *Wurst* sausage] (1869)
: LIVER SAUSAGE
¹**liv·ery** \'li-və-rē, 'liv-rē\ *noun, plural* **-er·ies** [Middle English, from Middle French *livree,* literally, delivery, from *livrer* to deliver, from Latin *liberare* to free — more at LIBERATE] (14th century)
1 *archaic* **:** the apportioning of provisions especially to servants **:** ALLOWANCE
2 a : the distinctive clothing or badge formerly worn by the retainers of a person of rank **b :** a servant's uniform **c :** distinctive dress **:** GARB **d** *chiefly British* **:** an identifying design (as on a vehicle) that designates ownership
3 *archaic* **a :** one's retainers or retinue **b :** the members of a British livery company
4 : the act of delivering legal possession of property
5 a : the feeding, stabling, and care of horses for pay **b :** LIVERY STABLE **c :** a concern offering vehicles (as boats) for rent
²**livery** *adjective* (1778)
1 : resembling liver
2 : suggesting liver disorder
livery company *noun* (1766)
: any of various London craft or trade associations that are descended from medieval guilds
liv·ery·man \'li-və-rē-mən, 'liv-rē-\ *noun* (1682)
1 : a freeman of the City of London entitled to wear the livery of the company to which he belongs
2 *archaic* **:** a liveried retainer
3 : the keeper of a vehicle-rental service
livery stable *noun* (1705)
: a stable where horses and vehicles are kept for hire and where stabling is provided — called also *livery barn*
lives *plural of* LIFE
live steam *noun* (circa 1875)
: steam direct from a boiler and under full pressure
live·stock \'līv-,stäk\ *noun* (1742)
: animals kept or raised for use or pleasure; *especially* **:** farm animals kept for use and profit

live-trap \-,trap\ *transitive verb* (1944)
: to capture (an animal) in a live trap
live trap *noun* (circa 1875)
: a trap for catching an animal alive and uninjured
live wire *noun* (1903)
: an alert, active, or aggressive person
liv·id \'li-vəd\ *adjective* [French *livide,* from Latin *lividus,* from *livēre* to be blue; akin to Welsh *lliw* color and probably to Russian *sliva* plum] (1622)
1 : discolored by bruising **:** BLACK-AND-BLUE ⟨the *livid* traces of the sharp scourges —Abraham Cowley⟩
2 : ASHEN, PALLID ⟨this cross, thy *livid* face, thy pierced hands and feet —Walt Whitman⟩
3 : REDDISH ⟨a fan of gladiolas blushed *livid* under the electric letters —Truman Capote⟩
4 : very angry **:** ENRAGED ⟨was *livid* at his son's disobedience⟩
— **li·vid·i·ty** \li-'vi-də-tē\ *noun*
— **liv·id·ness** \'li-vəd-nəs\ *noun*
¹**liv·ing** \'li-viŋ\ *adjective* (before 12th century)
1 a : having life **b :** ACTIVE, FUNCTIONING ⟨*living* languages⟩
2 a : exhibiting the life or motion of nature **:** NATURAL ⟨the wilderness is a *living* museum . . . of natural history —*NEA Journal*⟩ **b :** ²LIVE 2a
3 a : full of life or vigor **b :** true to life **:** VIVID ⟨televised in *living* color⟩ **c :** suited for living ⟨the *living* area⟩
4 : involving living persons
5 : VERY — used as an intensive ⟨scared the *living* daylights out of me⟩
— **liv·ing·ness** *noun*
²**living** *noun* (14th century)
1 : the condition of being alive
2 a : means of subsistence **:** LIVELIHOOD ⟨earning a *living*⟩ **b** *archaic* **:** ESTATE, PROPERTY **c** *British* **:** BENEFICE 1
3 : conduct or manner of life ⟨the collegiate way of *living* —J. B. Conant⟩
living death *noun* (1671)
: life emptied of joys and satisfactions
living fossil *noun* (1922)
: an organism (as a horseshoe crab or a ginkgo tree) that has remained essentially unchanged from earlier geologic times and whose close relatives are usually extinct
liv·ing·ly \'li-viŋ-lē\ *adverb* (15th century)
: in a vital manner **:** REALISTICALLY
living room *noun* (1857)
1 : a room in a residence used for the common social activities of the occupants
2 : LEBENSRAUM — called also *living space*
living standard *noun* (1944)
: STANDARD OF LIVING
living unit *noun* (circa 1937)
: an apartment or house for use by one family
living wage *noun* (1888)
1 : a subsistence wage
2 : a wage sufficient to provide the necessities and comforts essential to an acceptable standard of living
living will *noun* (1972)
: a document in which the signer requests to be allowed to die rather than be kept alive by artificial means if disabled beyond a reasonable expectation of recovery
liv·re \'lēvrə\ *noun* [French, from Latin *libra,* a unit of weight] (1553)
1 : an old French monetary unit equal to 20 sols
2 : a coin representing one livre
3 : the pound of Lebanon
lix·iv·i·ate \lik-'si-vē-,āt\ *transitive verb* **-at·ed; -at·ing** [Latin *lixivium* lye, from *lixivius* made of lye, from *lixa* lye — more at LIQUID] (1758)
: to extract a soluble constituent from (a solid mixture) by washing or percolation
— **lix·iv·i·a·tion** \(,)lik-,si-vē-'ā-shən\ *noun*
liz·ard \'li-zərd\ *noun* [Middle English *liserd,* from Middle French *laisarde,* from Latin *lacerta*] (14th century)

1 : any of a suborder (Lacertilia) of reptiles distinguished from the snakes by a fused inseparable lower jaw, a single temporal opening, two pairs of well differentiated functional limbs which may be lacking in burrowing forms, external ears, and eyes with movable lids; *broadly* **:** any relatively long-bodied reptile (as a crocodile or dinosaur) with legs and tapering tail
2 : leather made from lizard skin
lizard's tail *noun* (circa 1753)
: a perennial herb (*Saururus cernuus* of the family Saururaceae) of North American wetlands having spikes of tiny white flowers
¹**'ll** \l, əl, ᵊl\ *verb* (1578)
: WILL ⟨you'll be late⟩
lla·ma \'lä-mə, 'yä-mə\ *noun* [Spanish, from Quechua] (1600)
: any of a genus (*Lama*) of wild or domesticated South American ruminants related to the camels but smaller and without a hump; *especially* **:** the domesticated guanaco used especially in the Andes as a pack animal and a source of wool
lla·no \'lä-(,)nō, 'la-\ *noun, plural* **llanos** [Spanish, plain, from Latin *planum* — more at PLAIN] (1604)
: an open grassy plain in Spanish America or the southwestern U.S.

llama

lo \'lō\ *interjection* [Middle English, from Old English *lā*] (before 12th century)
— used to call attention or to express wonder or surprise ⟨*lo* these many years⟩
loach \'lōch\ *noun* [Middle English *loche,* from Middle French] (14th century)
: any of a family (Cobitidae) of small Old World freshwater fishes related to the carps
¹**load** \'lōd\ *noun* [Middle English *lod,* from Old English *lād* support, carrying — more at LODE] (12th century)
1 a : the quantity that can be carried at one time by a specified means; *especially* **:** a measured quantity of a commodity fixed for each type of carrier — often used in combination ⟨a boat*load* of tourists⟩ **b :** whatever is put on a person or pack animal to be carried **:** PACK **c :** whatever is put in a ship or vehicle or airplane for conveyance **:** CARGO; *especially* **:** a quantity of material assembled or packed as a shipping unit
2 a : a mass or weight supported by something ⟨branches bent low by their *load* of fruit⟩ **b :** the forces to which a structure is subjected due to superposed weight or to wind pressure on the vertical surfaces; *broadly* **:** the forces to which a given object is subjected
3 a : something that weighs down the mind or spirits ⟨took a *load* off her mind⟩ **b :** a burdensome or laborious responsibility ⟨always carried his share of the *load*⟩
4 *slang* **:** an intoxicating amount of liquor drunk
5 : a large quantity **:** LOT — usually used in plural
6 a : a charge for a firearm **b :** the quantity of material loaded into a device at one time
7 : external resistance overcome by a machine or prime mover
8 a : power output (as of a power plant) or power consumption (as by a device) **b :** a device to which power is delivered
9 a (1) : the amount of work that a person carries or is expected to carry **(2) :** the amount of authorized work to be performed by a machine, a group, a department, or a factory **b :** the demand on the operating resources of a

system (as a telephone exchange or a refrigerating apparatus)
10 *slang* : EYEFUL — used in the phrase *get a load of*
11 : an amount added (as to the price of a security or the net premium in insurance) to represent selling expense and profit to the distributor
12 : the decrease in capacity for survival of the average individual in a population due to the presence of deleterious genes in the gene pool 〈the mutational *load* is the genetic *load* caused by mutation〉
²**load** (15th century)
transitive verb
1 a : to put a load in or on 〈*load* a truck〉 **b** : to place in or on a means of conveyance 〈*load* freight〉
2 a : to encumber or oppress with something heavy, laborious, or disheartening : BURDEN 〈a company *loaded* down with debts〉 **b** : to place as a burden or obligation 〈*load* more work on him〉
3 a : to increase the weight of by adding something heavy **b** : to add a conditioning substance (as a mineral salt) to for body **c** : to weight or shape (dice) to fall unfairly **d** : to pack with one-sided or prejudicial influences : BIAS **e** : to charge with multiple meanings (as emotional associations or hidden implications)
f : to weight (as a test) with factors influencing validity or outcome
4 a : to supply in abundance or excess : HEAP, PACK **b** : to put runners on (first, second, and third bases) in baseball
5 a : to put a load or charge in (a device or piece of equipment) 〈*load* a gun〉 **b** : to place or insert especially as a load in a device or piece of equipment 〈*load* film in a camera〉 〈*load* a program into a computer〉
6 : to alter (as an alcoholic drink) by adding an adulterant or drug
7 a : to add a load to (an insurance premium) **b** : to add a sum to after profits and expenses are accounted for 〈*loaded* prices〉
intransitive verb
1 : to receive a load
2 : to put a load on or in a carrier, device, or container; *especially* : to insert the charge or cartridge in the chamber of a firearm
3 : to go or go in as a load 〈sightseers *loading* onto a bus〉
— **load·er** *noun*
load·ed *adjective* (1886)
1 *slang* : HIGH 12b
2 : having a large amount of money
load factor *noun* (1943)
: the percentage of available seats paid for and occupied in an aircraft
load·ing *noun* (15th century)
1 : a cargo, weight, or stress placed on something
2 : LOAD 11
3 : material used to load something : FILLER
load line *noun* (circa 1859)
: the line on a ship indicating the depth to which it sinks in the water when properly loaded — see PLIMSOLL MARK illustration
load·mas·ter \'lōd-ˌmas-tər\ *noun* (1961)
: a crew member of a transport aircraft who is in charge of the cargo
load·star *variant of* LODESTAR
load·stone *variant of* LODESTONE
¹**loaf** \'lōf\ *noun, plural* **loaves** \'lōvz\ [Middle English *lof*, from Old English *hlāf*; akin to Old High German *hleib* loaf] (before 12th century)
1 : a shaped or molded mass of bread
2 : a shaped or molded often symmetrical mass of food
3 *slang British* : HEAD, MIND
²**loaf** *intransitive verb* [probably back-formation from *loafer*] (1835)
: to spend time in idleness

loaf·er \'lō-fər\ *noun* [perhaps short for *landloafer*, from German *Landläufer* tramp, from *Land* + *Läufer* runner] (1830)
: one that loafs : IDLER
Loafer *trademark*
— used for a low step-in shoe
loam \'lōm, *chiefly Northern & Midland* 'lüm, *New England also* 'lüm\ *noun* [Middle English *lom*, from Old English *lām*, mud; akin to Old English *līm* lime] (12th century)
1 a : a mixture (as for plastering) composed chiefly of moistened clay **b** : a coarse molding sand used in founding
2 : SOIL; *specifically* : a soil consisting of a friable mixture of varying proportions of clay, silt, and sand
— **loamy** \'lō-mē, -lü-, -lù-\ *adjective*
¹**loan** \'lōn\ *noun* [Middle English *lon*, from Old Norse *lān*; akin to Old English *lǣn* loan, *lēon* to lend, Latin *linquere* to leave, Greek *leipein*] (12th century)
1 a : money lent at interest **b** : something lent usually for the borrower's temporary use
2 a : the grant of temporary use **b** : the temporary duty of a person transferred to another job for a limited time
3 : LOANWORD
²**loan** *transitive verb* (13th century)
: LEND ▢
— **loan·able** \'lō-nə-bəl\ *adjective*
lo and behold *interjection* (1808)
— used to express wonder or surprise
loan·er \'lō-nər\ *noun* (1926)
: one (as a car or a watch) that is lent especially as a replacement for something being repaired
loan·ing \'lō-niŋ\ *noun* [Middle English *loning*, from *lone*, alteration of *lane*] (14th century)
1 *dialect British* : LANE
2 *dialect British* : a milking yard
loan shark *noun* (1905)
: one who lends money to individuals at exorbitant rates of interest
loan–shark·ing \-ˌshär-kiŋ\ *noun* (1914)
: the practice of lending money at exorbitant rates of interest
loan translation *noun* (circa 1933)
: a compound, derivative, or phrase that is introduced into a language through translation of the constituents of a term in another language (as *superman* from German *Übermensch*)
loan·word \'lōn-ˌwərd\ *noun* (1874)
: a word taken from another language and at least partly naturalized
loath \'lōth, 'lōth\ *also* **loathe** \'lōth, 'lōth\ *adjective* [Middle English *loth*, from Old English *lāth*; akin to Old High German *leid* loathsome, Old Irish *lius* loathing] (12th century)
: unwilling to do something contrary to one's ways of thinking : RELUCTANT
synonym see DISINCLINED
— **loath·ness** *noun*
loathe \'lōth\ *transitive verb* **loathed; loath·ing** [Middle English *lothen*, from Old English *lāthian* to dislike, be hateful, from *lāth*] (12th century)
: to dislike greatly and often with disgust or intolerance : DETEST
synonym see HATE
— **loath·er** *noun*
loathing *noun* (14th century)
: extreme disgust : DETESTATION
¹**loath·ly** \'lōth-lē, 'lōth-\ *adjective* (before 12th century)
: LOATHSOME, REPULSIVE
²**loath·ly** \'lōth-lē, 'lōth-\ *adverb* (15th century)
: not willingly : RELUCTANTLY
loath·some \'lōth-səm, 'lōth-\ *adjective* [Middle English *lothsum*, from *loth* evil, from Old English *lāth*, from *lāth*, adjective] (14th century)
: giving rise to loathing : DISGUSTING
— **loath·some·ly** *adverb*

— **loath·some·ness** *noun*
¹**lob** \'läb\ *noun* [probably of Low German origin; akin to Low German *lubbe* coarse person] (1508)
dialect British : a dull heavy person : LOUT
²**lob** *verb* **lobbed; lob·bing** [*lob* a loosely hanging object] (1599)
transitive verb
1 : to let hang heavily : DROOP
2 : to throw, hit, or propel easily or in a high arc
intransitive verb
1 a : to move slowly and heavily **b** : to move in an arc
2 : to hit a tennis ball easily in a high arc
³**lob** *noun* (1851)
: a soft high-arching shot, throw, or kick
lob- *or* **lobo-** *combining form* [*lobe*]
: lobe 〈*lobar*〉 〈*lobo*tomy〉
lo·bar \'lō-bər, -ˌbär\ *adjective* (circa 1856)
: of or relating to a lobe
lo·bate \'lō-ˌbāt\ *also* **lo·bat·ed** \-ˌbā-təd\ *adjective* [New Latin *lobatus*, from Late Latin *lobus*] (circa 1760)
1 : LOBED
2 : resembling a lobe
— **lo·ba·tion** \lō-'bā-shən\ *noun*
¹**lob·by** \'lä-bē\ *noun, plural* **lobbies** [Medieval Latin *lobium* gallery, of Germanic origin; akin to Old High German *louba* porch] (1593)
1 : a corridor or hall connected with a larger room or series of rooms and used as a passageway or waiting room: as **a** : an anteroom of a legislative chamber; *especially* : one of two anterooms of a British parliamentary chamber to which members go to vote during a division **b** : a large hall serving as a foyer (as of a hotel or theater)
2 : a group of persons engaged in lobbying especially as representatives of a particular interest group
²**lobby** *verb* **lob·bied; lob·by·ing** (1837)
intransitive verb
: to conduct activities aimed at influencing public officials and especially members of a legislative body on legislation
transitive verb
1 : to promote (as a project) or secure the passage of (as legislation) by influencing public officials
2 : to attempt to influence or sway (as a public official) toward a desired action
— **lob·by·er** *noun*
— **lob·by·ism** \-ˌi-zəm\ *noun*
— **lob·by·ist** \-ist\ *noun*
lob·by·gow \'lä-bē-ˌgaů\ *noun* [origin unknown] (1906)

▢ USAGE
loan The verb *loan* is one of the words English settlers brought to America and continued to use after it had died out in Britain. Its use was soon noticed by British visitors and somewhat later by the New England literati, who considered it a bit provincial. It was flatly declared wrong in 1870 by a popular commentator, who based his objection on etymology. A later scholar showed that the commentator was ignorant of Old English and thus unsound in his objection, but by then it was too late, as the condemnation had been picked up by many other commentators. Although a surprising number of critics still voice objections, *loan* is entirely standard as a verb. You should note that it is used only literally; *lend* is the verb used for figurative expressions, such as "lending a hand" or "lending enchantment."

\ə\ abut \ᵊ\ kitten \ər\ **further** \a\ ash \ā\ ace
\ä\ mop, mar \au̇\ **out** \ch\ **chin** \e\ bet \ē\ **easy**
\g\ go \i\ hit \ī\ ice \j\ job \ŋ\ sing \ō\ go
\ȯ\ law \ȯi\ boy \th\ thin \t͟h\ the \ü\ loot \u̇\ foot
\y\ yet \zh\ vision *see also* Guide to Pronunciation

: an errand boy

lobe \'lōb\ *noun* [Middle French, from Late Latin *lobus,* from Greek *lobos*] (1541)
: a curved or rounded projection or division; *specifically* : a usually somewhat rounded projection or division of a bodily organ or part

lo·bec·to·my \lō-'bek-tə-mē\ *noun, plural* **-mies** [International Scientific Vocabulary] (circa 1911)
: surgical removal of a lobe of an organ (as a lung) or gland (as the thyroid)

lobed \'lōbd\ *adjective* (1787)
: having lobes ⟨palmately *lobed* leaves⟩

lobe–fin \'lōb-ˌfin\ *noun* (1941)
— CROSSOPTERYGIAN
— **lobe–finned** \-ˈfind\ *adjective*

lo·be·lia \lō-'bēl-yə, -'bē-lē-ə\ *noun* [New Latin, from Matthias de *Lobel* (died 1616) Flemish botanist] (1739)
1 : any of a genus (*Lobelia* of the family Lobeliaceae, the lobelia family) of widely cultivated plants having terminal clusters of showy lipped flowers
2 : the leaves and tops of Indian tobacco

lo·be·line \'lō-bə-ˌlēn\ *noun* [New Latin *Lobelia* + English ²*-ine*] (1852)
: a crystalline alkaloid $C_{22}H_{27}NO_2$ that is obtained from Indian tobacco and is used chiefly as a respiratory stimulant and as a smoking deterrent

lob·lol·ly \'läb-ˌlä-lē\ *noun, plural* **-lies** [probably from English dialect *lob* to boil + obsolete English dialect *lolly* broth] (1597)
1 *dialect* **a** : a thick gruel **b** : MIRE, MUDHOLE
2 *dialect* : LOUT
3 : LOBLOLLY PINE

loblolly pine *noun* (1760)
: a pine (*Pinus taeda*) of the southeastern U.S. with flaky bark, long needles in groups of three, and cones having spine-tipped scales; *also* : its coarse-grained wood

lo·bo \'lō-(ˌ)bō\ *noun, plural* **lobos** [Spanish, wolf, from Latin *lupus* — more at WOLF] (1839)
: GRAY WOLF

lo·bot·o·mise *British variant of* LOBOTOMIZE

lo·bot·o·mize \lō-'bä-tə-ˌmīz\ *transitive verb* **-mized; -miz·ing** (1943)
1 : to perform a lobotomy on
2 : to deprive of sensitivity, intelligence, or vitality ⟨fear of prosecution was causing the press to *lobotomize* itself —Tony Eprile⟩

lo·bot·o·my \lō-'bä-tə-mē\ *noun, plural* **-mies** [International Scientific Vocabulary] (1936)
: surgical severance of nerve fibers connecting the frontal lobes to the thalamus for the relief of some mental disorders

lob·scouse \'läb-ˌskaús\ *noun* [origin unknown] (1706)
: a sailor's dish of stewed or baked meat with vegetables and hardtack

lob·ster \'läb-stər\ *noun, often attributive* [Middle English, from Old English *loppestre,* from *loppe* spider] (before 12th century)
1 : any of a family (Nephropidae and especially *Homarus americanus*) of large edible marine decapod crustaceans that have stalked eyes, a pair of large claws, and a long abdomen and that include species from coasts on both sides of the North Atlantic and from the Cape of Good Hope
2 : SPINY LOBSTER
— **lob·ster·like** \-ˌlīk\ *adjective*

lobster 1

lob·ster·ing \'läb-st(ə-)riŋ\ *noun* (1881)
: the activity or business of catching lobsters

lob·ster·man \-mən\ *noun* (1881)
: one whose business is lobstering

lobster pot *noun* (1764)
: an oblong case with slat sides and a funnel-shaped net used to trap lobsters — called also *lobster trap*

lobster pot

lobster shift *noun* (circa 1933)
: a work shift (as on a newspaper) that covers the late evening and early morning hours — called also *lobster trick*

lobster ther·mi·dor \-'thər-mə-ˌdór\ *noun* [*thermidor,* from French, from *Thermidor,* drama (1891) by Victorien Sardou] (1930)
: cooked lobster meat in a rich wine sauce stuffed into a lobster shell and browned

lob·u·lar \'lä-byə-lər\ *adjective* (1826)
: of, relating to, affecting, or resembling a lobule

lob·u·lat·ed \'lä-byə-ˌlā-təd\ *also* **lob·u·late** \-ˌlāt\ *adjective* (1783)
: made up of or having lobules ⟨the pancreas is a *lobulated* organ⟩
— **lob·u·la·tion** \ˌlä-byə-'lā-shən\ *noun*

lob·ule \'lä-(ˌ)byü(ə)l\ *noun* (1682)
: a small lobe; *also* : a subdivision of a lobe

¹lo·cal \'lō-kəl\ *adjective* [Middle English *locale,* from Middle French *local,* from Late Latin *localis,* from Latin *locus* place — more at STALL] (15th century)
1 : characterized by or relating to position in space : having a definite spatial form or location
2 a : of, relating to, or characteristic of a particular place : not general or widespread **b** : of, relating to, or applicable to part of a whole
3 a : primarily serving the needs of a particular limited district **b** *of a public conveyance* : making all the stops on a route
4 : involving or affecting only a restricted part of the organism : TOPICAL
5 : of or relating to telephone communication within a specified area

²local *noun* (circa 1824)
: a local person or thing: as **a** : a local public conveyance (as a train or an elevator) **b** : a local or particular branch, lodge, or chapter of an organization (as a labor union) **c** *British* : a nearby or neighborhood pub

local area network *noun* (1981)
: a network of personal computers in a small area (as an office) that are linked by cable, can communicate directly with other devices in the network, and can share resources

local color *noun* (1884)
: the presentation of the features and peculiarities of a particular locality and its inhabitants in writing

lo·cale \lō-'kal\ *noun* [modification of French *local,* from *local,* adjective] (1772)
1 : a place or locality especially when viewed in relation to a particular event or characteristic
2 : SITE, SCENE ⟨the *locale* of a story⟩

local government *noun* (1844)
: the government of a specific local area constituting a subdivision of a major political unit (as a nation or state); *also* : the body of persons constituting such a government

lo·cal·ise *British variant of* LOCALIZE

lo·cal·ism \'lō-kə-ˌli-zəm\ *noun* (1823)
1 a : a local idiom **b** : a local peculiarity of speaking or acting
2 : affection or partiality for a particular place : SECTIONALISM

lo·cal·ite \'lō-kə-ˌlīt\ *noun* (1951)
: a native or resident of the locality under consideration : LOCAL

lo·cal·i·ty \lō-'ka-lə-tē\ *noun, plural* **-ties** (1628)
1 : the fact or condition of having a location in space or time

2 : a particular place, situation, or location

lo·cal·ize \'lō-kə-ˌlīz\ *verb* **-ized; -iz·ing** (1792)
transitive verb
1 : to make local : orient locally
2 : to assign to or keep within a definite locality
intransitive verb
: to accumulate in or be restricted to a specific or limited area ⟨an infection that *localizes* in the ear⟩
— **lo·cal·iz·abil·i·ty** \ˌlō-kə-ˌlī-zə-'bi-lə-tē\ *noun*
— **lo·cal·iz·able** \'lō-kə-ˌlī-zə-bəl\ *adjective*
— **lo·cal·i·za·tion** \ˌlō-kə-lə-'zā-shən\ *noun*

lo·cal·ly \'lō-k(ə-)lē\ *adverb* (15th century)
1 : with respect to a particular place or situation
2 : NEARBY
3 : in the region of origin

local option *noun* (1878)
: the power granted by a legislature to a political subdivision to determine by popular vote the local applicability of a law on a controversial issue (as the sale of liquor)

local time *noun* (1833)
: time based on the meridian through a particular place as contrasted with that of a time zone

lo·cate \'lō-ˌkāt, lō-'\ *verb* **lo·cat·ed; lo·cat·ing** [Latin *locatus,* past participle of *locare* to place, from *locus*] (1652)
intransitive verb
: to establish oneself or one's business : SETTLE
transitive verb
1 : to determine or indicate the place, site, or limits of
2 : to set or establish in a particular spot : STATION
3 : to seek out and determine the location of
4 : to find or fix the place of especially in a sequence : CLASSIFY
— **lo·cat·able** \-ˌkā-tə-bəl, -'kā-\ *adjective*

lo·ca·tion \lō-'kā-shən\ *noun* (1597)
1 a : a position or site occupied or available for occupancy or marked by some distinguishing feature : SITUATION **b** (1) : a tract of land designated for a purpose (2) *Australian* : FARM, STATION **c** : a place outside a motion-picture studio where a picture or part of it is filmed — usually used in the phrase *on location*
2 : the act or process of locating
— **lo·ca·tion·al** \-shnəl, -shə-nᵊl\ *adjective*
— **lo·ca·tion·al·ly** *adverb*

¹loc·a·tive \'lä-kə-tiv\ *noun* [Latin *locus* + English *-ative* (as in *vocative*)] (1804)
: the locative case; *also* : a word in that case

²locative *adjective* (1841)
: of or being a grammatical case that denotes place or the place where or wherein

lo·ca·tor *also* **lo·cat·er** \'lō-ˌkā-tər, lō-'\ *noun* (1784)
: one that locates something (as a mining claim or the course of a road)

loch \'läk, 'läḵ\ *noun* [Middle English (Scots) *louch,* from Scottish Gaelic *loch;* akin to Latin *lacus* lake — more at LAKE] (14th century)
1 *Scottish* : LAKE
2 *Scottish* : a bay or arm of the sea especially when nearly landlocked

loch·an \'lä-kən\ *noun* [Scottish Gaelic, diminutive of *loch*] (1670)
Scottish : a small lake

loci *plural of* LOCUS

¹lock \'läk\ *noun* [Middle English *lok,* from Old English *locc;* akin to Old High German *loc* lock, Greek *lygos* withe, Latin *luxus* dislocated] (before 12th century)
1 a : a tuft, tress, or ringlet of hair **b** *plural* : the hair of the head
2 : a cohering bunch (as of wool, cotton, or flax) : TUFT

²lock *noun* [Middle English *lok,* from Old English *loc;* akin to Old High German *loh* enclosure and perhaps to Old English *locc* lock of hair] (before 12th century)
1 a : a fastening (as for a door) operated by a key or a combination **b :** the mechanism for exploding the charge or cartridge of a firearm
2 a : an enclosure (as in a canal) with gates at each end used in raising or lowering boats as they pass from level to level **b :** AIR LOCK
3 a : a locking or fastening together **b :** an intricate mass of objects impeding each other (as in a traffic jam) **c :** a hold in wrestling secured on one part of the body; *broadly* **:** a controlling hold ⟨his paper . . . had a *lock* on a large part of the state —John Corry⟩
4 : one that is assured of success or favorable outcome

³lock (14th century)
transitive verb
1 a : to fasten the lock of **b :** to make fast with or as if with a lock ⟨*lock* up the house⟩
2 a : to fasten in or out or to make secure or inaccessible by or as if by means of locks ⟨*locked* himself away from the curious world⟩ ⟨*locked* her husband out⟩ **b :** to fix in a particular situation or method of operation ⟨a team firmly *locked* in last place⟩
3 a : to make fast, motionless, or inflexible especially by the interlacing or interlocking of parts ⟨*lock* wheels⟩ ⟨*lock* a knee⟩ **b :** to hold in a close embrace **c :** to grapple in combat; *also* **:** to bind closely ⟨administration and students were *locked* in conflict⟩
4 : to invest (capital) without assurance of easy convertibility into money
5 : to move or permit to pass (as a ship) by raising or lowering in a lock
intransitive verb
1 a : to become locked **b :** to be capable of being locked
2 : INTERLACE, INTERLOCK
3 : to go or pass by means of a lock (as in a canal)
— **lock·able** \ˈlä-kə-bəl\ *adjective*
— **lock horns :** to come into conflict
— **lock on** *also* **lock onto :** to sight and follow (a target) automatically using a sensor (as radar)

lock·box \ˈläk-ˌbäks\ *noun* (1872)
: a box (as a post-office box, strongbox, or safe-deposit box) that locks

lock·down \-ˌdau̇n\ *noun* (1977)
: the confinement of prisoners to their cells for all or most of the day as a temporary security measure

locked–in \ˈläkt-ˈin\ *adjective* (1952)
1 : not subject to adjustment **:** FIXED ⟨*locked-in* interest rates⟩
2 : unable or unwilling to shift invested funds because of the tax effect of realizing capital gains

lock·er \ˈlä-kər\ *noun* (14th century)
1 a : a drawer, cupboard, or compartment that may be closed with a lock; *especially* **:** one for individual storage use **b :** a chest or compartment on shipboard for compact stowage of articles **c :** a refrigerated compartment or room for the storage of fresh or frozen foods ⟨a meat *locker*⟩
2 : one that locks

lock·er–room \ˈlä-kə(r)-ˌrüm\ *adjective* (1946)
: of, relating to, or suitable for use in a locker room; *especially* **:** of an earthy or sexual nature ⟨*locker-room* talk⟩

locker room *noun* (circa 1896)
: a room for changing clothes and for storing clothing and equipment in lockers; *especially* **:** one for use by sports players

lock·et \ˈlä-kət\ *noun* [Middle French *loquet* latch, from Middle Dutch *loke;* akin to Old English *loc*] (1679)
: a small case usually of precious metal that has space for a memento and that is worn typically suspended from a chain or necklace

lock·jaw \ˈläk-ˌjȯ\ *noun* (1803)
: an early symptom of tetanus characterized by spasm of the jaw muscles and inability to open the jaws; *also* **:** TETANUS

lock·keep·er \ˈläk-ˌkē-pər\ *noun* (1794)
: a person in charge of a lock (as on a canal)

lock·nut \-ˌnət\ *noun* (circa 1864)
1 : a nut screwed down hard on another to prevent it from slacking back
2 : a nut so constructed that it locks itself when screwed tight against another part

lock·out \ˈläk-ˌau̇t\ *noun* (1854)
: the withholding of employment by an employer and the whole or partial closing of his business establishment in order to gain concessions from or resist demands of employees

lock out *transitive verb* (1868)
: to subject (a body of employees) to a lockout

lock·ram \ˈlä-krəm\ *noun* [Middle English *lokerham,* from *Locronan,* town in Brittany] (14th century)
: a coarse plain-woven linen formerly used in England

lock·smith \ˈläk-ˌsmith\ *noun* (13th century)
: a person who makes or repairs locks

lock·smith·ing \-ˌsmi-thiŋ\ *noun* (circa 1909)
: the work or business of a locksmith

lock·step \ˈläk-ˌstep\ *noun* (circa 1802)
1 : a mode of marching in step by a body of men going one after another as closely as possible
2 : a standard method or procedure that is mindlessly adhered to or that minimizes individuality
— **lockstep** *adjective*
— **in lockstep :** in perfect or rigid often mindless conformity or unison ⟨politicians marching *in lockstep* with the party line⟩

lock·stitch \ˈläk-ˌstich\ *noun* (circa 1859)
: a sewing machine stitch formed by the looping together of two threads one on each side of the material being sewn
— **lockstitch** *verb*

lock, stock, and barrel *adverb* [from the principal parts of a flintlock] (1842)
: WHOLLY, COMPLETELY ⟨the only thing which had not been sold *lock, stock, and barrel* with the . . . house was this piano —Marcia Davenport⟩

lock·up \ˈläk-ˌəp\ *noun* (1839)
1 : JAIL; *especially* **:** a local jail where persons are detained prior to court hearing
2 : an act of locking **:** the state of being locked

¹lo·co \ˈlō-(ˌ)kō\ *adverb or adjective* [Italian dialect, there, from Latin *in loco* in the place] (circa 1801)
: in the register as written — used as a direction in music

²loco *noun, plural* **locos** *or* **locoes** [Mexican Spanish, from Spanish, crazy] (1844)
1 : LOCOWEED
2 : LOCOISM

³loco *transitive verb* (1884)
1 : to poison with locoweed
2 : to make frenzied or crazy

⁴loco *adjective* [Spanish] (1887)
slang **:** mentally disordered **:** CRAZY, FRENZIED

Lo·co·fo·co \ˌlō-kə-ˈfō-(ˌ)kō\ *noun, plural* **-focos** [*locofoco,* a kind of friction match, probably from ¹*loco*motive + Italian *fuoco, foco* fire, from Latin *focus* hearth] (1835)
1 : a member of a radical group of New York Democrats organized in 1835 in opposition to the regular party organization
2 : DEMOCRAT 2

lo·co·ism \ˈlō-(ˌ)kō-ˌi-zəm\ *noun* (1900)
: a disease of horses, cattle, and sheep caused by chronic poisoning with locoweeds

lo·co·mote \ˈlō-kə-ˌmōt\ *intransitive verb* **-mot·ed; -mot·ing** [back-formation from *locomotion*] (1834)
: to move about

lo·co·mo·tion \ˌlō-kə-ˈmō-shən\ *noun* [Latin *locus* + English *motion*] (1646)
1 : an act or the power of moving from place to place

2 : TRAVEL ⟨interest in free *locomotion* and choice of occupation —Zechariah Chafee Jr.⟩

¹lo·co·mo·tive \ˌlō-kə-ˈmō-tiv\ *adjective* (1612)
1 : LOCOMOTORY
2 : of or relating to travel
3 : of, relating to, or being a machine that moves about by operation of its own mechanism

²locomotive *noun* (1829)
1 : a self-propelled vehicle that runs on rails and is used for moving railroad cars
2 : a school or college cheer characterized by a slow beginning and a progressive increase in speed

lo·co·mo·tor \ˌlō-kə-ˈmō-tər\ *adjective* (1870)
1 : of, relating to, or functioning in locomotion
2 : affecting or involving the locomotor organs

locomotor ataxia *noun* (1878)
: TABES DORSALIS

lo·co·mo·to·ry \ˌlō-kə-ˈmō-tə-rē\ *adjective* (circa 1836)
1 : LOCOMOTOR ⟨*locomotory* appendages⟩
2 : capable of moving independently from place to place ⟨*locomotory* animals⟩

lo·co·weed \ˈlō-(ˌ)kō-ˌwēd\ *noun* (1879)
: any of several leguminous plants (genera *Astragalus* and *Oxytropis*) of western North America that cause locoism in livestock

loc·u·lar \ˈlä-kyə-lər\ *adjective* (1784)
: having or composed of loculi — often used in combination ⟨uni*locular*⟩

loc·ule \ˈlä-(ˌ)kyü(ə)l\ *noun* [French, from Latin *loculus*] (circa 1888)
: LOCULUS; *especially* **:** any of the cells of a compound ovary of a plant
— **loc·uled** \-(ˌ)kyü(ə)ld\ *adjective*

loc·u·li·ci·dal \ˌlä-kyə-lə-ˈsī-dᵊl\ *adjective* [New Latin *loculus* + Latin *-cidere* to cut, from *caedere*] (circa 1819)
: dehiscing longitudinally so as to bisect each loculus ⟨*loculicidal* fruit⟩

loc·u·lus \ˈlä-kyə-ləs\ *noun, plural* **-li** \-ˌlī, -ˌlē\ [New Latin, from Latin, diminutive of *locus*] (1858)
: a small chamber or cavity especially in a plant or animal body

lo·cum \ˈlō-kəm\ *noun* (1901)
chiefly British **:** LOCUM TENENS

locum te·nens \-ˈtē-ˌnenz, -ˈte-, -nənz\ *noun, plural* **locum te·nen·tes** \-ti-ˈnen-ˌtēz\ [Medieval Latin, literally, (one) holding a place] (1641)
: one filling an office for a time or temporarily taking the place of another — used especially of a doctor or clergyman

lo·cus \ˈlō-kəs\ *noun, plural* **lo·ci** \ˈlō-ˌsī, -ˌkī, -ˌkē\ [Latin — more at STALL] (1715)
1 a : the place where something is situated or occurs **:** SITE, LOCATION ⟨was the culture of medicine in the beginning dispersed from a single focus or did it arise in several *loci*? —S. C. Harvey⟩ **b :** a center of activity, attention, or concentration ⟨in democracy the *locus* of power is in the people —H. G. Rickover⟩
2 : the set of all points whose location is determined by stated conditions
3 : the position in a chromosome of a particular gene or allele

locus clas·si·cus \-ˈkla-si-kəs\ *noun, plural* **loci clas·si·ci** \-ˈkla-sə-ˌsī, -ˌkī, -ˌkē\ [New Latin] (1853)
1 : a passage that has become a standard for the elucidation of a word or subject
2 : a classic case or example

locus coe·ru·le·us *also* **locus ce·ru·le·us** \-si-ˈrü-lē-əs\ *noun* [New Latin, literally, dark blue place] (circa 1889)

\ə\ abut \ᵊ\ kitten \ər\ further \a\ ash \ā\ ace
\ä\ mop, mar \au̇\ out \ch\ chin \e\ bet \ē\ easy
\g\ go \i\ hit \ī\ ice \j\ job \ŋ\ sing \ō\ go
\ȯ\ law \ȯi\ boy \th\ thin \th\ the \ü\ loot \u̇\ foot
\y\ yet \zh\ vision *see also* Guide to Pronunciation

: a blue area of the brain stem with many norepinephrine-containing neurons

lo·cust \'lō-kəst\ *noun* [Middle English, from Latin *locusta*] (14th century)
1 : SHORT-HORNED GRASSHOPPER; *especially* **:** a migratory grasshopper often traveling in vast swarms and stripping the areas passed of all vegetation
2 : CICADA
3 a : any of various leguminous trees: as (1) **:** CAROB 1 (2) **:** BLACK LOCUST (3) **:** HONEY LOCUST **b :** the wood of a locust tree

locust bean *noun* (1847)
: CAROB

lo·cu·tion \lō-'kyü-shən\ *noun* [Middle English *locucioun*, from Latin *locution-*, *locutio*, from *loqui* to speak] (15th century)
1 : a particular form of expression or a peculiarity of phrasing; *especially* **:** a word or expression characteristic of a region, group, or cultural level
2 : style of discourse **:** PHRASEOLOGY

lode \'lōd\ *noun* [Middle English, from Old English *lād* course, support; akin to Old English *līthan* to go — more at LEAD] (before 12th century)
1 *dialect English* **:** WATERWAY
2 : an ore deposit
3 : something that resembles a lode **:** an abundant store

lo·den \'lō-dᵊn\ *noun* [German, from Old High German *lodo* coarse cloth; akin to Old English *lotha* mantle] (1911)
1 : a thick woolen cloth used for outer clothing
2 : a variable color averaging a dull grayish green

lode·star \'lōd-ˌstär\ *noun* [Middle English *lode sterre*, from *lode* course, from Old English *lād*] (14th century)
1 *archaic* **:** a star that leads or guides; *especially* **:** NORTH STAR
2 : one that serves as an inspiration, model, or guide

lode·stone \-ˌstōn\ *noun* [obsolete *lode* course, from Middle English] (circa 1515)
1 : magnetite possessing polarity
2 : something that strongly attracts

¹lodge \'läj\ *verb* **lodged; lodg·ing** (13th century)
transitive verb
1 a (1) **:** to provide temporary quarters for (2) **:** to rent lodgings to **b :** to establish or settle in a place
2 : to serve as a receptacle for **:** CONTAIN
3 : to beat (as a crop) flat to the ground
4 : to bring to an intended or a fixed position (as by throwing or thrusting)
5 : to deposit for safeguard or preservation
6 : to place or vest especially in a source, means, or agent
7 : to lay (as a complaint) before a proper authority **:** FILE
intransitive verb
1 a : to occupy a place temporarily **:** SLEEP **b** (1) **:** to have a residence **:** DWELL (2) **:** to be a lodger
2 : to come to a rest
3 : to fall or lie down — used especially of hay or grain crops

²lodge *noun* [Middle English *loge*, from Old French, of Germanic origin; akin to Old High German *louba* porch] (13th century)
1 *chiefly dialect* **:** a rude shelter or abode
2 a : a house set apart for residence in a particular season (as the hunting season) **b :** a resort hotel **:** INN
3 a : a house on an estate originally for the use of a gamekeeper, caretaker, or porter **b :** a shelter for an employee (as a gatekeeper)
4 : a den or lair especially of gregarious animals
5 a : the meeting place of a branch of an organization and especially a fraternal organization **b :** the body of members of such a branch

6 a : WIGWAM **b :** a family of North American Indians

lodge·pole pine \'läj-ˌpōl-\ *noun* (1859)
: either of two pines of western North America with needles in pairs and short ovoid usually asymmetric cones: **a :** a scrubby chiefly coastal pine (*Pinus contorta*) with thick deeply furrowed bark and hard strong coarse-grained medium-light wood **b :** a tall straight pine (*P. contorta* variety *latifolia* synonym *P. murrayana*) with thin and little furrowed bark and soft weak fine-grained lightweight wood

lodg·er \'lä-jər\ *noun* (1596)
: ROOMER

lodging *noun* (14th century)
1 a : a place to live **:** DWELLING **b :** LODGMENT 3b
2 a (1) **:** sleeping accommodations ⟨found *lodging* in the barn⟩ (2) **:** a temporary place to stay ⟨a *lodging* for the night⟩ **b :** a room in the house of another used as a residence — usually used in plural
3 : the act of lodging

lodging house *noun* (1766)
: ROOMING HOUSE

lodg·ment *or* **lodge·ment** \'läj-mənt\ *noun* (1598)
1 a : a lodging place **:** SHELTER **b :** ACCOMMODATIONS, LODGINGS ⟨found *lodgment* in the city⟩
2 a : the act, fact, or manner of lodging ⟨a hut for temporary *lodgment* of cattlemen⟩ **b :** a placing, depositing, or coming to rest
3 a : an accumulation or collection deposited in a place or remaining at rest **b :** a place of rest or deposit

lod·i·cule \'lä-di-ˌkyü(ə)l\ *noun* [Latin *lodicula*, diminutive of *lodic-*, *lodix* cover] (1864)
: one of usually two delicate membranous hyaline scales at the base of the ovary of a grass that by their swelling assist in anthesis

loess \'les, 'ləs, 'lō-əs, 'lərs\ *noun* [German *Löss*] (1833)
: an unstratified usually buff to yellowish brown loamy deposit found in North America, Europe, and Asia and believed to be chiefly deposited by the wind
— loess·ial \'le-sē-əl, 'lə-, lō-'e-, 'lər-\ *adjective*

¹loft \'lóft\ *noun* [Middle English, from Old English, air, sky, from Old Norse *lopt*; akin to Old High German *luft* air] (13th century)
1 : an upper room or floor **:** ATTIC
2 a : a gallery in a church or hall **b :** one of the upper floors of a warehouse or business building especially when not partitioned ⟨living in a converted *loft*⟩ **c :** HAYLOFT
3 a : the backward slant of the face of a golf-club head **b :** the act of lofting
4 : the thickness of a fabric or insulating material (as goose down)
— loft·like \-ˌlīk\ *adjective*

²loft (1518)
transitive verb
1 : to place, house, or store in a loft
2 : to propel through the air or into space ⟨*lofted* a long hit to center⟩ ⟨instruments *lofted* by a powerful rocket⟩
3 : to lay out a full-sized working drawing of the lines and contours of (as a ship's hull)
intransitive verb
1 : to propel a ball high into the air
2 : to rise high

lofty \'lóf-tē\ *adjective* **loft·i·er; -est** (15th century)
1 a : elevated in character and spirit **:** NOBLE **b :** elevated in status **:** SUPERIOR
2 : having a haughty overbearing manner **:** SUPERCILIOUS
3 a : rising to a great height **:** impressively high ⟨*lofty* mountains⟩ **b :** REMOTE, ESOTERIC
synonym see HIGH
— loft·i·ly \-tə-lē\ *adverb*
— loft·i·ness \-tē-nəs\ *noun*

¹log \'lóg, 'läg\ *noun, often attributive* [Middle English *logge*, probably from Scandinavian ori-

gin; akin to Old Norse *lāg* fallen tree; akin to Old English *licgan* to lie — more at LIE] (14th century)
1 : a usually bulky piece or length of unshaped timber; *especially* **:** a length of a tree trunk ready for sawing and over six feet (1.8 meters) long
2 : an apparatus for measuring the rate of a ship's motion through the water that consists of a block fastened to a line and run out from a reel
3 a : the record of the rate of a ship's speed or of her daily progress; *also* **:** the full nautical record of a ship's voyage **b :** the full record of a flight by an aircraft
4 : a record of performance, events, or day-to-day activities ⟨a computer *log*⟩

²log *verb* **logged; log·ging** (1699)
transitive verb
1 a : to cut (trees) for lumber **b :** to clear (land) of trees in lumbering — often used with *off*
2 : to make a note or record of **:** enter details of or about in a log
3 a : to move (an indicated distance) or attain (an indicated speed) as noted in a log **b** (1) **:** to sail a ship or fly an airplane for (an indicated distance or period of time) (2) **:** to have (an indicated record) to one's credit **:** ACHIEVE
intransitive verb
: ³LUMBER 1

³log *noun, often attributive* [by shortening] (1631)
: LOGARITHM

log- *or* **logo-** *combining form* [Greek, from *logos* — more at LEGEND]
: word **:** thought **:** speech **:** discourse ⟨*logogram*⟩ ⟨*logorrhea*⟩

-log — see -LOGUE

lo·gan·ber·ry \'lō-gən-ˌber-ē\ *noun* [James H. Logan (died 1928) American lawyer + English *berry*] (1893)
: a red-fruited upright-growing dewberry regarded as a variety (*Rubus ursinus loganobaccus*) of a western dewberry or as a hybrid of a western dewberry and a red raspberry; *also* **:** its berry

log·a·oe·dic \ˌlä-gə-'ē-dik\ *adjective* [Late Latin *logaoedicus*, from Late Greek *logaoidikos*, from Greek *log-* + *aeidein* to sing; from the resemblance of such rhythm to prose — more at ODE] (1844)
: marked by the mixture of several meters; *specifically* **:** having a rhythm that uses both dactyls and trochees or anapests and iambs
— logaoedic *noun*

log·a·rithm \'lò-gə-ˌri-thəm, 'lä-\ *noun* [New Latin *logarithmus*, from *log-* + Greek *arithmos* number — more at ARITHMETIC] (circa 1616)
: the exponent that indicates the power to which a number is raised to produce a given number ⟨the *logarithm* of 100 to the base 10 is 2⟩
— log·a·rith·mic \ˌlò-gə-'rith-mik, ˌlä-\ *adjective*
— log·a·rith·mi·cal·ly \-mi-k(ə-)lē\ *adverb*

logarithmic function *noun* (1927)
: a function (as $y = \log_a x$ or $y = \ln x$) that is the inverse of an exponential function (as $y = a^x$ or $y = e^x$) so that the independent variable appears in a logarithm

log·book \'lòg-ˌbùk, 'läg-\ *noun* (circa 1679)
: LOG 3, 4

loge \'lōzh\ *noun* [French, from Old French, a shelter — more at LODGE] (1749)
1 a : a small compartment **:** BOOTH **b :** a box in a theater
2 a : a small partitioned area **b :** a separate forward section of a theater mezzanine or balcony

logged \'lògd, 'lägd\ *adjective* (circa 1820)
1 : HEAVY, SLUGGISH
2 : sodden especially with water

log·ger \'lȯ-gər, 'lä-\ *noun* (1732)
: one engaged in logging

log·ger·head \'lȯ-gər-ˌhed, 'lä-\ *noun* [probably from English dialect *logger* block of wood + English *head*] (1588)
1 *chiefly dialect* **a** : BLOCKHEAD **b** : HEAD; *especially* : a disproportionately large head
2 a : a very large carnivorous sea turtle (*Caretta caretta*) of subtropical and temperate waters **b** : ALLIGATOR SNAPPER
3 : an iron tool consisting of a long handle terminating in a ball or bulb that is heated and used to melt tar or to heat liquids
— **at loggerheads** : in or into a state of quarrelsome disagreement

log·gets *or* **log·gats** \'lȯ-gəts, 'lä-\ *noun plural but singular or plural in construction* [probably from ¹*log* + -*et*] (1581)
: a game formerly played in England in which participants throw pieces of wood at a stake

log·gia \'lȯ-jē-ə, 'lȯ-(ˌ)jä\ *noun, plural* **log·gias** \'lȯ-jē-əz, 'lȯ-(ˌ)jäz\ *also* **log·gie** \'lȯ-(ˌ)jä\ [Italian, from Old French *loge* lodge] (1742)
: a roofed open gallery especially at an upper story overlooking an open court

log·ic \'lä-jik\ *noun* [Middle English *logik*, from Middle French *logique*, from Latin *logica*, from Greek *logikē*, from feminine of *logikos* of reason, from *logos* reason — more at LEGEND] (12th century)
1 a (1) : a science that deals with the principles

1 loggia

and criteria of validity of inference and demonstration : the science of the formal principles of reasoning (2) : a branch or variety of logic ⟨modal *logic*⟩ ⟨Boolean *logic*⟩ (3) : a branch of semiotic; *especially* : SYNTACTICS (4) : the formal principles of a branch of knowledge **b** (1) : a particular mode of reasoning viewed as valid or faulty (2) : RELEVANCE, PROPRIETY **c** : interrelation or sequence of facts or events when seen as inevitable or predictable **d** : the arrangement of circuit elements (as in a computer) needed for computation; *also* : the circuits themselves
2 : something that forces a decision apart from or in opposition to reason ⟨the *logic* of war⟩
— **lo·gi·cian** \lō-'ji-shən\ *noun*

log·i·cal \'lä-ji-kəl\ *adjective* (15th century)
1 a (1) : of, relating to, involving, or being in accordance with logic (2) : skilled in logic **b** : formally true or valid : ANALYTIC, DEDUCTIVE
2 : capable of reasoning or of using reason in an orderly cogent fashion ⟨a *logical* thinker⟩
— **log·i·cal·i·ty** \ˌlä-jə-'ka-lə-tē\ *noun*
— **log·i·cal·ly** \'lä-ji-k(ə-)lē\ *adverb*
— **log·i·cal·ness** \-kəl-nəs\ *noun*

logical positivism *noun* (1931)
: a 20th century philosophical movement that holds characteristically that all meaningful statements are either analytic or conclusively verifiable or at least confirmable by observation and experiment and that metaphysical theories are therefore strictly meaningless — called also *logical empiricism*
— **logical positivist** *noun*

log in *intransitive verb* (1962)
: LOG ON
— **log–in** \'lȯg-ˌin, 'läg-\ *noun*

lo·gi·on \'lō-gē-ˌän\ *noun, plural* **lo·gia** \-gē-ˌä\ *or* **logions** [Greek, diminutive of *logos*] (1875)
: SAYING; *especially* : a saying attributed to Jesus

¹**lo·gis·tic** \lō-'jis-tik, lə-\ *or* **lo·gis·ti·cal** \-ti-kəl\ *adjective* (1628)
1 a : of or relating to symbolic logic **b** : of or relating to the philosophical attempt to reduce mathematics to logic

2 : of or relating to logistics
3 *logistic* : of, represented by, or relating to a logistic curve ⟨a *logistic* process⟩
— **lo·gis·ti·cal·ly** \-ti-k(ə-)lē\ *adverb*

²**logistic** *noun* (1905)
: SYMBOLIC LOGIC

logistic curve *noun* (circa 1903)
: an S-shaped curve that represents an exponential function and is used in mathematical models of growth processes

lo·gis·ti·cian \ˌlō-jəs-'ti-shən\ *noun* (1932)
: a specialist in logistics

lo·gis·tics \lō-'jis-tiks, lə-\ *noun plural but singular or plural in construction* [French *logistique* art of calculating, logistics, from Greek *logistikē* art of calculating, from feminine of *logistikos* of calculation, from *logizein* to calculate, from *logos* reason] (circa 1861)
1 : the aspect of military science dealing with the procurement, maintenance, and transportation of military matériel, facilities, and personnel
2 : the handling of the details of an operation

log·jam \'lȯg-ˌjam, 'läg-\ *noun* (1885)
1 : a jumble of logs jammed together in a watercourse
2 a : DEADLOCK, IMPASSE ⟨trying to break the *logjam* in negotiations⟩ **b** : BLOCKAGE

log·nor·mal \ˌlȯg-'nȯr-məl, ˌläg-\ *adjective* (1945)
: relating to or being a normal distribution that is the distribution of the logarithm of a random variable; *also* : relating to or being such a random variable
— **log·nor·mal·i·ty** \-nȯr-'ma-lə-tē\ *noun*
— **log·nor·mal·ly** \-'nȯr-mə-lē\ *adverb*

logo \'lō-(ˌ)gō\ *also* 'lä-\ *noun, plural* **log·os** \-(ˌ)gōz\ (1937)
1 : LOGOTYPE
2 : an identifying statement : MOTTO

Lo·go \'lō-(ˌ)gō\ *noun* [modification of Greek *logos* word] (1972)
: a computer programming language that employs simple English commands and is used especially for introducing school children to computers

logo- — see LOG-

logo·gram \'lȯ-gə-ˌgram, 'lä-\ *noun* (1840)
: a letter, symbol, or sign used to represent an entire word
— **logo·gram·mat·ic** \ˌlȯ-gə-grə-'ma-tik, ˌlä-\ *adjective*

logo·graph \'lȯ-gə-ˌgraf, 'lä-\ *noun* (circa 1888)
: LOGOGRAM
— **logo·graph·ic** \ˌlȯ-gə-'gra-fik, ˌlä-\ *adjective*
— **logo·graph·i·cal·ly** \-fi-k(ə-)lē\ *adverb*

logo·griph \'lȯ-gə-ˌgrif, 'lä-\ *noun* [*log-* + Greek *griphos* reed basket, riddle — more at CRIB] (circa 1598)
: a word puzzle (as an anagram)

lo·gom·a·chy \lō-'gä-mə-kē\ *noun, plural* **-chies** [Greek *logomachia*, from *log-* + *machesthai* to fight] (1569)
1 : a dispute over or about words
2 : a controversy marked by verbiage

log on *intransitive verb* (1977)
: to establish communication and initiate interaction with a time-shared computer or network — often used with *on*
— **log–on** \'lȯg-ˌȯn, 'läg-ˌän\ *noun*

log·or·rhea \ˌlȯ-gə-'rē-ə, ˌlä-\ *noun* [New Latin] (circa 1892)
: excessive and often incoherent talkativeness or wordiness
— **log·or·rhe·ic** \-'rē-ik\ *adjective*

Lo·gos \'lō-ˌgäs, -ˌgōs\ *noun, plural* **Lo·goi** \-ˌgȯi\ [Greek, speech, word, reason — more at LEGEND] (1587)
1 : the divine wisdom manifest in the creation, government, and redemption of the world and often identified with the second person of the Trinity

2 : reason that in ancient Greek philosophy is the controlling principle in the universe

logo·type \'lȯ-gə-ˌtīp, 'lä-\ *noun* (circa 1816)
1 : a single piece of type or a single plate faced with a term (as the name of a newspaper or a trademark)
2 : an identifying symbol (as for advertising)

log·roll \'lȯg-ˌrōl, 'läg-\ *verb* [back-formation from *logrolling*] (1835)
intransitive verb
: to take part in logrolling
transitive verb
: to promote passage of by logrolling
— **log·roll·er** *noun*

log·roll·ing \-ˌrō-liŋ\ *noun* (1812)
1 [from a former American custom of neighbors assisting one another in rolling logs into a pile for burning] : the exchanging of assistance or favors; *specifically* : the trading of votes by legislators to secure favorable action on projects of interest to each one
2 : the rolling of logs in water by treading; *also* : a sport in which contestants treading logs try to dislodge one another

-logue *or* **-log** *noun combining form* [Middle English *-logue*, from Old French, from Latin *-logus*, from Greek *-logos*, from *legein* to speak — more at LEGEND]
1 : discourse : talk ⟨duo*logue*⟩
2 : student : specialist ⟨sino*logue*⟩

log·wood \'lȯg-ˌwu̇d, 'läg-\ *noun* (1581)
1 a : a Mexican and West Indian leguminous tree (*Haematoxylon campechianum*) **b** : the very hard brown or brownish red heartwood of logwood
2 : a dye extracted from the heartwood of logwood — compare HEMATOXYLIN

lo·gy \'lō-gē\ *also* **log·gy** \'lȯ-gē, 'lä-\ *adjective* **lo·gi·er; -est** [perhaps from Dutch *log* heavy; akin to Middle Low German *luggich* lazy] (1847)
: marked by sluggishness and lack of vitality : GROGGY

-logy *noun combining form* [Middle English *-logie*, from Old French, from Latin *-logia*, from Greek, from *logos* word]
1 : oral or written expression ⟨phrase*ology*⟩
2 : doctrine : theory : science ⟨ethn*ology*⟩

Lo·hen·grin \'lō-ən-ˌgrin\ *noun* [German]
: a son of Parsifal and knight of the Holy Grail in Germanic legend

loin \'lȯin\ *noun* [Middle English *loyne*, from Middle French *loigne*, from (assumed) Vulgar Latin *lumbea*, from Latin *lumbus*; akin to Old English *lendenu* loins, Old Church Slavonic *lędviję*] (14th century)
1 a : the part of a human being or quadruped on each side of the spinal column between the hipbone and the false ribs **b** : a cut of meat comprising this part of one or both sides of a carcass with the adjoining half of the vertebrae included but without the flank
2 *plural* **a** : the upper and lower abdominal regions and the region about the hips **b** (1) : the pubic region (2) : the generative organs

loin·cloth \-ˌklȯth\ *noun* (1859)
: a cloth worn about the loins often as the sole article of clothing in warm climates

loi·ter \'lȯi-tər\ *intransitive verb* [Middle English] (14th century)
1 : to delay an activity with aimless idle stops and pauses : DAWDLE
2 a : to remain in an area for no obvious reason **b** : to lag behind
synonym see DELAY
— **loiter** *noun*
— **loi·ter·er** \-tər-ər\ *noun*

Lo·ki \'lō-kē\ *noun* [Old Norse]
: a Norse god who contrives evil and mischief for his fellow gods

Lo·li·ta \lō-ˈlē-tə\ *noun* [from *Lolita*, character in the novel *Lolita* (1955) by Vladimir Nabokov] (1959)
: a precociously seductive girl

¹loll \ˈläl\ *verb* [Middle English] (14th century)
intransitive verb
1 : to hang loosely or laxly : DROOP
2 : to act or move in a lax, lazy, or indolent manner : LOUNGE
transitive verb
: to let droop or dangle
— **loll·er** \ˈlä-lər\ *noun*

²loll *noun* (1709)
archaic : the act of lolling : a relaxed posture

Lol·lard \ˈlä-lərd\ *noun* [Middle English, from Middle Dutch *lollaert*, from *lollen* to mutter] (14th century)
: one of the followers of Wycliffe who traveled in the 14th and 15th centuries as lay preachers throughout England and Scotland
— **Lol·lard·ism** \-lər-ˌdi-zəm\ *noun*
— **Lol·lardy** \-lər-dē\ *noun*

lol·li·pop *or* **lol·ly·pop** \ˈlä-li-ˌpäp\ *noun* [perhaps from English dialect *lolly* tongue + ²*pop*] (1784)
1 : a lump of hard candy on the end of a stick
2 *British* : a round stop sign on a pole used to stop traffic (as at a school crossing)

lol·lop \ˈlä-ləp\ *intransitive verb* [¹*loll* + -*op* (as in *gallop*)] (1745)
1 *dialect English* : LOLL
2 : to proceed with a bounding or bobbing motion

lol·ly \ˈlä-lē\ *noun, plural* **lollies** [short for *lollipop*] (1854)
1 *British* : a piece of candy; *especially* : HARD CANDY
2 *British* : MONEY

lol·ly·gag \ˈlä-lē-ˌgag\ *intransitive verb* **-gagged; -gag·ging** [origin unknown] (1868)
: FOOL AROUND 1 : DAWDLE

Lom·bard \ˈläm-ˌbärd, -bərd\ *noun* [Middle English *Lumbarde*, from Middle French *lombard*, from Old Italian *lombardo*, from Latin *Langobardus*] (14th century)
1 a : a member of a Germanic people that invaded Italy in A.D. 568, settled in the Po valley, and established a kingdom **b** : a native or inhabitant of Lombardy
2 [from the prominence of Lombards as moneylenders] : BANKER, MONEYLENDER
— **Lom·bar·di·an** \läm-ˈbär-dē-ən\ *adjective*
— **Lom·bar·dic** \läm-ˈbär-dik\ *adjective*

Lom·bar·dy poplar \ˈläm-ˌbär-dē-, -bər-\ *noun* [*Lombardy*, Italy] (1766)
: a poplar of a staminate variety (*Populus nigra italica*) of European poplar having a columnar shape and strongly ascending branches

lo mein \ˈlō-ˈmān, ˌlō-\ *noun* [Chinese (Guangdong) *lòu-mihn* stirred noodles] (1970)
: a Chinese dish consisting of sliced vegetables, soft noodles, and usually meat or shrimp in bite-size pieces stir-fried in a seasoned sauce

lo·ment \ˈlō-ˌment, -mənt\ *noun* [New Latin *lomentum*, from Latin, wash made from bean meal, from *lavere* to wash — more at LYE] (circa 1830)
: a dry indehiscent one-celled fruit that is produced from a single superior ovary and breaks transversely into numerous segments at maturity

Lon·don broil \ˈlən-dən-\ *noun* [*London*, England] (1946)
: a boneless cut of beef (as from the shoulder or flank) usually served sliced diagonally across the grain

lone \ˈlōn\ *adjective* [Middle English, short for *alone*] (14th century)
1 a : having no company : SOLITARY **b** : preferring solitude
2 : ONLY, SOLE
3 : situated by itself : ISOLATED
synonym see ALONE

— **lone·ness** \ˈlōn-nəs\ *noun*

lone·li·ness \ˈlōn-lē-nəs\ *noun* (circa 1586)
: the quality or state of being lonely

lone·ly \ˈlōn-lē\ *adjective* **lone·li·er; -est** (1607)
1 a : being without company : LONE **b** : cut off from others : SOLITARY
2 : not frequented by human beings : DESOLATE
3 : sad from being alone : LONESOME
4 : producing a feeling of bleakness or desolation
synonym see ALONE
— **lone·li·ly** \-lə-lē\ *adverb*

lonely hearts *adjective* (1931)
: of or relating to lonely persons who are seeking companions or spouses

lon·er \ˈlō-nər\ *noun* (1947)
: one that avoids others; *especially* : INDIVIDUALIST

lone ranger *noun, often L&R capitalized* [*Lone Ranger*, hero of an American radio and television western] (1969)
: one who acts alone and without consultation or the approval of others; *broadly* : LONER

¹lone·some \ˈlōn(t)-səm\ *adjective* (1647)
1 a : sad or dejected as a result of lack of companionship or separation from others ⟨don't be *lonesome* while we are gone⟩ **b** : causing a feeling of loneliness ⟨the empty house seemed so *lonesome*⟩
2 a : REMOTE, UNFREQUENTED ⟨look down, look down that *lonesome* road —Gene Austin⟩ **b** : LONE
synonym see ALONE
— **lone·some·ly** *adverb*
— **lone·some·ness** *noun*

²lonesome *noun* (1899)
: SELF ⟨sat all by his *lonesome*⟩

lone wolf *noun* (1909)
: a person who prefers to work, act, or live alone

¹long \ˈlòn\ *adjective* **lon·ger** \ˈlòn-gər *also* -ər\; **lon·gest** \ˈlòn-gəst *also* -əst\ [Middle English *long, lang*, from Old English; akin to Old High German *lang* long, Latin *longus*] (before 12th century)
1 a : extending for a considerable distance **b** : having greater length than usual **c** : having greater height than usual : TALL **d** : having a greater length than breadth : ELONGATED **e** : having a greater length than desirable or necessary **f** : FULL-LENGTH ⟨*long* pants⟩
2 a : having a specified length ⟨six feet *long*⟩ **b** : forming the chief linear dimension ⟨the *long* side of the room⟩
3 a : extending over a considerable time ⟨a *long* friendship⟩ **b** : having a specified duration ⟨two hours *long*⟩ **c** : prolonged beyond the usual time ⟨a *long* look⟩
4 a : containing many items in a series ⟨a *long* list⟩ **b** : having a specified number of units ⟨300 pages *long*⟩ **c** : consisting of a greater number or amount than usual : LARGE
5 a *of a speech sound* : having a relatively long duration **b** : being the member of a pair of similarly spelled vowel or vowel-containing sounds that is descended from a vowel long in duration ⟨*long* a in *fate*⟩ ⟨*long* i in *sign*⟩ **c** *of a syllable in prosody* (1) : of relatively extended duration (2) : bearing a stress or accent
6 : having the capacity to reach, extend, or travel a considerable distance ⟨a *long* left jab⟩ ⟨tried to hit the *long* ball⟩
7 : larger or longer than the standard ⟨a *long* count by the referee⟩
8 a : extending far into the future ⟨the thoughts of youth are *long, long* thoughts —H. W. Longfellow⟩ **b** : extending beyond what is known ⟨a *long* guess⟩ **c** : payable after a considerable period ⟨a *long* note⟩
9 : possessing a high degree or a great deal of something specified : STRONG ⟨*long* on common sense⟩
10 a : of an unusual degree of difference between the amounts wagered on each side ⟨*long*

odds⟩ **b** : of or relating to the larger amount wagered ⟨take the *long* end of the bet⟩
11 : subject to great odds
12 : owning or accumulating securities or goods especially in anticipation of an advance in prices ⟨they are now *long* on wheat⟩ ⟨take a *long* position in steel⟩
— **long·ness** \ˈlòn-nəs\ *noun*
— **before long** : in a short time : SOON
— **long in the tooth** : past one's best days : OLD
— **not long for** : having little time left to do or enjoy something

²long *adverb* (before 12th century)
1 : for or during a long time ⟨*long* a popular hangout⟩
2 : at or to a long distance : FAR ⟨*long*-traveled⟩
3 : for the duration of a specified period
4 : at a point of time far before or after a specified moment or event ⟨was excited *long* before the big day⟩
5 : after or beyond a specified or implied time ⟨didn't stay *longer* than midnight⟩ ⟨said it was no *longer* possible⟩
6 : for a considerable distance ⟨faded back and threw the ball *long*⟩
7 : in or into a long position (as on a market)
— **so long** : GOOD-BYE

³long *noun* (before 12th century)
1 : a long period of time
2 : a long syllable
3 : one taking a long position especially in a security or commodity market
4 a *plural* : long trousers **b** : a size in clothing for tall men
— **the long and short** *or* **the long and the short** : GIST

⁴long *intransitive verb* **longed; long·ing** \ˈlòn-in\ [Middle English, from Old English *langian*; akin to Old High German *langēn* to long, Old English *lang* long] (before 12th century)
: to feel a strong desire or craving especially for something not likely to be attained ⟨they *long* for peace but are driven to war⟩ ☆
— **long·er** \ˈlòn-ər\ *noun*

⁵long *intransitive verb* [Middle English, from *along* (on) because (of)] (13th century)
archaic : to be suitable or fitting

long–ago \ˈlòn-ə-ˈgō\ *adjective* (circa 1834)
: of or relating to the past ⟨*long-ago* leaders⟩

long ago *noun* (1851)
: the distant past

lon·gan \ˈlòn-gən, -ən\ *noun* [Chinese (Beijing) *lóngyǎn*, literally, dragon's eye] (1732)
1 : a pulpy fruit related to the litchi and produced by an Indian evergreen tree (*Euphoria longana*)
2 : a tree that bears the longan

lon·ga·nim·i·ty \ˌlòn-gə-ˈni-mə-tē\ *noun* [Middle English *longanymyte*, from Late Latin *longanimitat-, longanimitas*, from *longanimis* patient, from Latin *longus* long + *animus* soul — more at ANIMATE] (15th century)

: a disposition to bear injuries patiently : FOR-BEARANCE

long·boat \'lȯṅ-ˌbōt\ *noun* (15th century)
: a large oared boat usually carried by a merchant sailing ship

long bone *noun* (circa 1860)
: any of the elongated bones supporting a vertebrate limb and consisting of an essentially cylindrical shaft that contains marrow and ends in enlarged heads for articulation with other bones

long·bow \'lȯṅ-ˌbō\ *noun* (14th century)
: a hand-drawn wooden bow held vertically and used especially by medieval English archers

long·bow·man \-mən\ *noun* (1925)
: an archer who uses a longbow

long–case clock \'lȯṅ-ˌkās-\ *noun* (1892)
: GRANDFATHER CLOCK

long–chain *adjective* (1930)
: having a relatively long chain of atoms and especially carbon atoms in the molecule ⟨*long-chain* hydrocarbons⟩

long–day *adjective* (1920)
: responding to or relating to a long photoperiod — used especially of a plant; compare DAY-NEUTRAL, SHORT-DAY

¹**long–distance** *adjective* (1884)
1 : of or relating to telephone communication with a distant point
2 a : situated a long distance away **b** : going or covering a long distance ⟨*long-distance* roads⟩ ⟨a *long-distance* runner⟩ **c** : conducted or effective over long distance ⟨a *long-distance* courtship⟩ ⟨*long-distance* listening devices⟩

²**long–distance** *adverb* (circa 1961)
1 : by long-distance telephone
2 : over or from a long distance

long distance *noun* (1904)
1 : communication by long-distance telephone
2 : a telephone operator or exchange that gives long-distance connections

long division *noun* (1827)
: arithmetical division in which the several steps involved in the division are indicated in detail

long–drawn–out *or* **long–drawn** *adjective* (1646)
: extended to a great length

lon·ge·ron \'län-jə-ˌrän\ *noun* [French] (1912)
: a fore-and-aft framing member of an airplane fuselage

lon·gev·i·ty \län-'je-və-tē, lȯn-\ *noun* [Late Latin *longaevitas*, from Latin *longaevus* long-lived, from *longus* long + *aevum* age — more at AYE] (1615)
1 a : a long duration of individual life **b** : length of life ⟨a study of *longevity*⟩
2 : long continuance : PERMANENCE, DURABILITY

lon·ge·vous \-'jē-vəs\ *adjective* (1680)
: LONG-LIVED

long face *noun* (1786)
: a facial expression of sadness or melancholy

long green *noun* (circa 1891)
slang : MONEY

long–hair \'lȯṅ-ˌhar, -ˌher\ *noun* (1920)
1 : an impractical intellectual
2 : a person of artistic gifts or interests; *especially* : a lover of classical music
3 : a person with long hair; *especially* : HIPPIE
4 : a domestic cat having long outer fur
— **long–haired** \-'hard, -'herd\ *or* **long–hair** *adjective*

long·hand \-ˌhand\ *noun* (1666)
: HANDWRITING: **a** : characters or words written out fully by hand **b** : cursive writing

long haul *noun* (1936)
1 : a long distance
2 : a considerable period of time; *especially* : LONG RUN
— **long–haul** *adjective*

long–head \'lȯṅ-ˌhed\ *noun* (1650)
: a dolichocephalic person

long–head·ed \-ˌhe-dəd\ *adjective* (circa 1700)
1 : having unusual foresight
2 : DOLICHOCEPHALIC
— **long–head·ed·ness** *noun*

long–horn \-ˌhȯrn\ *noun* (1834)
1 a : any of the long-horned cattle of Spanish derivation formerly common in southwestern U.S. **b** : TEXAS LONGHORN 2
2 : a firm-textured usually mild cheese (as cheddar or Colby)

long–horned beetle \-ˌhȯrn(d)-\ *noun* (1840)
: any of a family (Cerambycidae synonym Longicornia) of beetles usually distinguished by their very long antennae — called also *longhorn beetle*

long–horned grasshopper *noun* (1893)
: any of various grasshoppers (family Tettigoniidae) distinguished by their very long antennae

long horse *noun* (circa 1934)
: VAULTING HORSE

long·house \'lȯṅ-ˌhaús, -ˌhaús\ *noun* (1643)
: a long communal dwelling of some North American Indians (as the Iroquois)

long hundredweight *noun* (circa 1934)
British : HUNDREDWEIGHT 2

lon·gi·corn \'län-jə-ˌkȯrn\ *adjective* [ultimately from Latin *longus* long + *cornu* horn — more at HORN] (circa 1848)
1 : of, relating to, or being long-horned beetles
2 : having long antennae
— **longicorn** *noun*

long·ing \'lȯṅ-iṅ\ *noun* (before 12th century)
: a strong desire especially for something unattainable : CRAVING
— **long·ing·ly** \-iṅ-lē\ *adverb*

long·ish \'lȯṅ-ish\ *adjective* (1611)
: somewhat long : moderately long

lon·gi·tude \'län-jə-ˌtüd, -ˌtyüd, *British also* 'läṅ-gə-\ *noun* [Middle English, from Latin *longitudin-, longitudo*, from *longus*] (14th century)
1 a : angular distance measured on a great circle of reference from the intersection of the adopted zero meridian with this reference circle to the similar intersection of the meridian passing through the object **b** : the arc or portion of the earth's equator intersected between the meridian of a given place and the prime meridian and expressed either in degrees or in time
2 *archaic* : long duration

longitude 1a:
hemisphere marked
with meridians
of longitude

lon·gi·tu·di·nal \ˌlän-jə-'tüd-nəl, -'tyüd-, -'t(y)ü-d°n-əl, *British also* ˌläṅ-gə-\ *adjective* (15th century)
1 : placed or running lengthwise
2 : of or relating to length or the lengthwise dimension
3 : involving the repeated observation or examination of a set of subjects over time with respect to one or more study variables
— **lon·gi·tu·di·nal·ly** *adverb*

longitudinal wave *noun* (circa 1931)
: a wave (as a sound wave) in which the particles of the medium vibrate in the direction of the line of advance of the wave

long johns \'lȯṅ-ˌjänz\ *noun plural* (1943)
: long underwear

long jump *noun* (1882)
: a track-and-field event in which a jump for distance is made usually from a running start
— **long jumper** *noun*

long·leaf pine \'lȯṅ-ˌlēf-\ *noun* (1796)
: a tall pine (*Pinus palustris*) of the southeastern U.S. with long needles in bundles of three and long cones that is a major timber tree; *also* : its tough coarse-grained reddish orange wood

long–leaved pine \-ˌlēv(d)-\ *noun* (1765)
: LONGLEAF PINE

long·line \'lȯṅ-ˌlīn, -'līn\ *noun* (1876)
: a heavy fishing line that may be several miles long and that has baited hooks in series

long–lin·er \-ˌlī-nər\ *noun* (1909)
: one that fishes with a longline; *also* : a fishing vessel used in long-lining

long–lin·ing \-ˌlī-niṅ\ *noun* (1877)
: fishing with a longline

long–lived \'lȯṅ-'līvd *also* -'līvd\ *adjective* (14th century)
1 : having a long life : characterized by long life ⟨a *long-lived* family⟩
2 : lasting a long time : ENDURING □

long meter *noun* (1718)
: a quatrain in iambic tetrameter in which the second and fourth lines and often the first and third lines rhyme — called also *long measure*

Lon·go·bard \'lȯṅ-gə-ˌbärd, 'läṅ-\ *noun, plural* **Longobards** *also* **Lon·go·bar·di** \ˌlȯṅ-gə-'bär-ˌdī, ˌläṅ-, -dē\ [Middle English *Longobardes*, plural, from Latin *Langobardi, Longobardi*] (14th century)
: LOMBARD 1a
— **Lon·go·bar·dic** \ˌlȯṅ-gə-'bär-dik, ˌläṅ-\ *adjective*

long play *noun* (1952)
: a long-playing record

long–play·ing \'lȯṅ-'plā-iṅ\ *adjective* (1929)
: designed to be played at 33⅓ revolutions per minute — used of a microgroove record

long–range \-'rānj\ *adjective* (1854)
1 : relating to or fit for long distances ⟨*long-range* rockets⟩
2 : involving or taking into account a long period of time ⟨*long-range* planning⟩

long run *noun* (1627)
: a relatively long period of time — usually used in the phrase *in the long run*
— **long–run** \'lȯṅ-'rən\ *adjective*

long·shore·man \'lȯṅ-'shȯr-mən, -ˌshȯr-, ˌlȯṅ-\ *noun* [*longshore*, short for *alongshore*] (1811)
: a person who loads and unloads ships at a seaport

long·shor·ing \'lȯṅ-ˌshȯr-iṅ, -ˌshȯr-, ˌlȯṅ-\ *noun* (1926)
: the act or occupation of working as a longshoreman

long shot \'lȯṅ-ˌshät\ *noun* (1867)
1 : a venture involving great risk but promising a great reward if successful; *also* : a venture unlikely to succeed
2 : an entry (as in a horse race) given little chance of winning

□ USAGE
long–lived Americans were once split almost evenly between the \-'livd\ and the \-'līvd\ variants of *long-lived* and *short-lived*, but today the preference in American and British speech is for \-'līvd\. Objections to this variant have surfaced over the years, though. Some critics contend that the *-lived* element is formed from the noun *life* plus the suffix *-ed*, and so *-lived* should have the \ī\ vowel of *life*. In modern English, though, *-lived* has been reanalyzed as the past participle of the verb *live*. Different kinds of reanalysis have shaped English over the centuries, bringing about for example the second *r* in *bridegroom* and the *n* in *newt* and *notch*, as a check of their etymologies will reveal. The pronunciations of such reanalyzed forms, as in the case of *-lived*, have become fully acceptable over time.

\ə\ abut \ᵊ\ kitten \ər\ further \a\ ash \ā\ ace
\ä\ mop, mar \au̇\ out \ch\ chin \e\ bet \ē\ easy
\g\ go \i\ hit \ī\ ice \j\ job \ṅ\ sing \ō\ go
\ȯ\ law \ȯi\ boy \th\ thin \tẖ\ the \ü\ loot \u̇\ foot
\y\ yet \zh\ vision *see also* Guide to Pronunciation

3 : a bet in which the chances of winning are slight but the possible winnings great
— **by a long shot** : by a great deal
long·sight·ed \-ˌsī-təd\ *adjective* (circa 1790)
: FARSIGHTED
— **long·sight·ed·ness** *noun*
long since *adverb* (14th century)
1 : long ago ⟨promises *long since* forgotten⟩
2 : for a long time ⟨has *long since* been a devoted friend⟩
long·some \'lȯn-səm\ *adjective* (before 12th century)
: tediously long
— **long·some·ly** *adverb*
— **long·some·ness** *noun*
long·spur \'lȯn-ˌspər\ *noun* (1831)
: any of several long-clawed finches (especially genus *Calcarius*) of the arctic regions and the Great Plains of North America
long–stand·ing \-'stan-diŋ\ *adjective* (1814)
: of long duration
long–suf·fer·ing \-ˌsə-f(ə-)riŋ, -'sə-\ *noun* (1526)
: long and patient endurance of offense
— **long–suffering** *adjective*
— **long–suf·fer·ing·ly** \-lē\ *adverb*
long suit *noun* (circa 1876)
1 : a holding of more than the average number of cards in a suit
2 : the activity or quality in which one excels
long–term \'lȯn-'tərm\ *adjective* (1904)
1 : occurring over or involving a relatively long period of time
2 a : of, relating to, or constituting a financial operation or obligation based on a considerable term and especially one of more than 10 years ⟨*long-term* bonds⟩ **b** : generated by assets held for longer than six months ⟨a *long-term* capital gain⟩
long·time \'lȯn-ˌtīm\ *adjective* (1584)
: having been so for a long time : LONG-STANDING ⟨a *longtime* friend⟩ ⟨a *longtime* friendship⟩
Long Tom \'lȯn-'täm\ *noun* [from the name *Tom*] (1832)
1 : a large land gun having a long range
2 : a trough for washing gold-bearing earth
long ton *noun* (1829)
— see WEIGHT table
lon·gueur \lōⁿ-'gœr\ *noun, plural* **longueurs** \-'gœr(z)\ [French, literally, length] (1791)
: a dull and tedious passage or section (as of a book)
long view *noun* (1912)
: an approach to a problem or situation that emphasizes long-range factors
long–wind·ed \ˌlȯn-'win-dəd, 'lȯn-ˌwin-\ *adjective* (1589)
1 : tediously long in speaking or writing
2 : not easily subject to loss of breath
— **long–wind·ed·ly** *adverb*
— **long–wind·ed·ness** *noun*
¹loo \'lü\ *noun* [short for obsolete English *lanterloo*, from French *lanturelu* twaddle] (1675)
1 : an old card game in which the winner of each trick or a majority of tricks takes a portion of the pool while losing players are obligated to contribute to the next pool
2 : money staked at loo
²loo *transitive verb* (1680)
: to obligate to contribute to a new pool at loo for failing to win a trick
³loo *noun* [origin unknown] (1940)
chiefly British : TOILET 3
loo·by \'lü-bē\ *noun, plural* **loobies** [Middle English *loby*] (14th century)
: an awkward clumsy fellow : LUBBER
loo·fah \'lü-fä\ *noun* [New Latin *luffa*, from Arabic *lūf*] (1887)
1 : any of a genus (*Luffa*) of Old World tropical plants of the gourd family with large fruits; *also* : its fruit
2 : a sponge consisting of the fibrous skeleton of the fruit of a loofah (especially *Luffa aegyptiaca*)
¹look \'lu̇k\ *verb* [Middle English, from Old

English *lōcian*; akin to Old Saxon *lōcōn* to look] (before 12th century)
transitive verb
1 : to make sure or take care (that something is done)
2 : to ascertain by the use of one's eyes
3 a : to exercise the power of vision upon : EXAMINE **b** *archaic* : to search for
4 a : EXPECT, ANTICIPATE ⟨we *look* to have a good year⟩ **b** : to have in mind as an end ⟨*looking* to win back some lost profits⟩
5 *archaic* : to bring into a place or condition by the exercise of the power of vision
6 : to express by the eyes or facial expression
7 : to have an appearance that befits or accords with
intransitive verb
1 a : to exercise the power of vision : SEE **b** : to direct one's attention ⟨*look* upon the future with hope⟩ **c** : to direct the eyes
2 : to have the appearance or likelihood of being : SEEM ⟨it *looks* unlikely⟩ ⟨*looks* to be hard work⟩
3 : to have a specified outlook ⟨the house *looked* east⟩
4 : to gaze in wonder or surprise : STARE
5 : to show a tendency ⟨the evidence *looks* to acquittal⟩ □
synonym see EXPECT
— **look after** : to take care of
— **look at** : CONSIDER 1 ⟨*looking at* the possibility of relocating⟩
— **look down one's nose** : to view something with arrogance, disdain, or disapproval
— **look for** : to await with hope or anticipation
— **look forward** : to anticipate with pleasure or satisfaction ⟨*looking forward* to your visit⟩
— **look into** : EXPLORE 1a
— **look the other way** : to direct one's attention away from something unpleasant or troublesome
— **look to** 1 : to direct one's attention to ⟨*looking to* the future⟩ **2** : to rely upon ⟨*looks to* reading for relaxation⟩
²look *noun* (13th century)
1 a : the act of looking **b** : GLANCE
2 a : the expression of the countenance **b** : physical appearance; *especially* : attractive physical appearance — usually used in plural **c** : a combination of design features giving a unified appearance ⟨a new *look* in design⟩
3 : the state or form in which something appears
look–alike \'lu̇-kə-ˌlīk\ *noun* (1947)
: one that looks like another : DOUBLE
— **look–alike** *adjective*
look·down \'lu̇k-ˌdau̇n\ *noun* (circa 1882)
: a silvery carangid fish (*Selene vomer*) chiefly of the Atlantic having a laterally compressed deep body and steeply sloping facial profile
look down *intransitive verb* (14th century)
1 : to be in a position that affords a downward view
2 : to regard with contempt : DESPISE — used with *on* or *upon*
look·er \'lu̇-kər\ *noun* (14th century)
1 : one that looks
2 a : one having an appearance of a specified kind **b** : one that has an attractive appearance : BEAUTY
look·er–on \ˌlu̇-kər-'ȯn, -'än\ *noun, plural* **lookers–on** (1539)
: ONLOOKER
look–in \'lu̇k-ˌin\ *noun* (1870)
1 : a chance of success
2 : a quick pass in football to a receiver running diagonally toward the center of the field
looking glass *noun* (1562)
: MIRROR
look·out \'lu̇k-ˌau̇t\ *noun* (1699)
1 : one engaged in keeping watch : WATCHMAN
2 : an elevated place or structure affording a wide view for observation

3 : a careful looking or watching ⟨on the *lookout*⟩
4 : VIEW, OUTLOOK
5 : a matter of care or concern
look out *intransitive verb* (1602)
: to take care or concern oneself — used with *for* ⟨*looking out* for number one⟩
look over *transitive verb* (14th century)
: to inspect or examine especially in a cursory way
look–see \'lu̇k-'sē, -ˌsē\ *noun* (1883)
: a general survey : EVALUATION, INSPECTION
look·up \'lu̇k-ˌəp\ *noun* (1936)
: the process or an instance of looking something up; *especially* : the process of matching by computer the words of a text with material stored in memory
look up (14th century)
intransitive verb
1 : to cheer up ⟨*look up*—things are not all bad⟩
2 : to improve in prospects or conditions ⟨business is *looking up*⟩
transitive verb
1 : to search for in or as if in a reference work ⟨*look up* a phone number⟩
2 : to seek out especially for a brief visit
¹loom \'lüm\ *noun* [Middle English *lome* tool, loom, from Old English *gelōma* tool; akin to Middle Dutch *allame* tool] (15th century)
: a frame or machine for interlacing at right angles two or more sets of threads or yarns to form a cloth
²loom *intransitive verb* [origin unknown] (circa 1541)
1 : to come into sight in enlarged or distorted and indistinct form often as a result of atmospheric conditions
2 a : to appear in an impressively great or exaggerated form ⟨deficits *loomed* large⟩ **b** : to take shape as an impending occurrence
³loom *noun* (1836)
: the indistinct and exaggerated appearance of something seen on the horizon or through fog or darkness; *also* : a looming shadow or reflection
¹loon \'lün\ *noun* [Middle English *loun*] (15th century)
1 : LOUT, IDLER
2 *chiefly Scottish* : BOY
3 a : a crazy person **b** : SIMPLETON
²loon *noun* [of Scandinavian origin; akin to Old Norse *lōmr* loon] (1634)

□ USAGE

look Some people are offended or made uneasy by the construction in which *look* is followed by *to* and an infinitive. This construction, usually expressing expectation (*transitive verb* sense 4a), has been in use since the 17th century ⟨good morrow . . . I *look'd* to have found you with your headache and morning qualms —Thomas Shadwell⟩ ⟨is elderly now and . . . *looks* to be gathered to his fathers before the times get any worse —Rudyard Kipling⟩. In the 19th century the present participle began to turn up in this construction ⟨two lovers *looking* to be wed —A. E. Housman⟩. These uses carry the notion of purpose and are the beginning of sense 4b. This construction is very common at present ⟨had been *looking* to change jobs for several years —Curry Kirkpatrick⟩ ⟨*looking* to blaze her own trails as an actress —*Town & Country*⟩ ⟨a number of states are now *looking* to circumvent the national limit —Daniel Seligman⟩. The linking verb sense of *look* (*intransitive verb* sense 2) is commonly followed by *to be* ⟨sure *looked* to be the hero of this game —Rick Telander⟩ ⟨the baby *looks* to be about nine or ten months old —Léon Bing⟩. All of these constructions are standard.

: any of several large birds (genus *Gavia*) of Holarctic regions that feed on fish by diving and have their legs placed far back under the body for optimal locomotion underwater

loo·ny *also* **loo·ney** \'lü-nē\ *adjective* **loo·ni·er; -est** [by shortening & alteration from *lunatic*] (1872)
: CRAZY, FOOLISH
— **loo·ni·ness** *noun*
— **loony** *noun*

loony bin *noun* (1919)
: an insane asylum : MADHOUSE

¹**loop** \'lüp\ *noun* [Middle English *loupe;* perhaps akin to Middle Dutch *lupen* to watch, peer] (14th century)
archaic : LOOPHOLE 1a

²**loop** *noun* [Middle English *loupe,* of unknown origin] (14th century)
1 a : a curving or doubling of a line so as to form a closed or partly open curve within itself through which another line can be passed or into which a hook may be hooked **b :** such a fold of cord or ribbon serving as an ornament
2 a : something shaped like a loop **b :** a circular airplane maneuver executed in the vertical plane
3 : a ring or curved piece used to form a fastening, handle, or catch
4 : a closed electric circuit
5 : a piece of film or magnetic tape whose ends are spliced together so as to project or play back the same material continuously
6 : a series of instructions (as for a computer) that is repeated until a terminating condition is reached
7 : a sports league
8 : a select well-informed inner circle that is influential in decision making ⟨out of the policy *loop*⟩
— **for a loop :** into a state of amazement, confusion, or distress

³**loop** (1832)
intransitive verb
1 : to make or form a loop
2 : to execute a loop in an airplane
3 : to move in loops or in an arc
transitive verb
1 a : to make a loop in, on, or about **b :** to fasten with a loop
2 : to join (two courses of loops) in knitting
3 : to connect (electric conductors) so as to complete a loop
4 : to cause to move in an arc

looped \'lüpd\ *adjective* (1513)
1 : having, formed in, or characterized by loops ⟨*looped* fabrics⟩
2 : DRUNK 1a

loop·er \'lü-pər\ *noun* (1731)
1 : any of the usually rather small hairless caterpillars that are mostly larvae of moths (families Geometridae and Noctuidae) and move with a looping movement in which the anterior legs and the posterior prolegs are alternately made fast and released — called also *inchworm*
2 : one that loops

¹**loop·hole** \'lüp-,hōl\ *noun* [¹*loop*] (1591)
1 a : a small opening through which small arms may be fired **b :** a similar opening to admit light and air or to permit observation
2 : a means of escape; *especially* **:** an ambiguity or omission in the text through which the intent of a statute, contract, or obligation may be evaded

²**loophole** *transitive verb* (1664)
: to make loopholes in

loop of Hen·le \-'hen-lē\ [F. G. J. *Henle* (died 1885) German pathologist] (1890)
: a U-shaped part of the nephron of birds and mammals that lies between and is continuous with the proximal and distal convoluted tubules and that functions in water resorption

loopy \'lü-pē\ *adjective* **loop·i·er; -est** (1856)
1 : having or characterized by loops
2 : CRAZY, BIZARRE

¹**loose** \'lüs\ *adjective* **loos·er; loos·est** [Middle English *lous,* from Old Norse *lauss;* akin to Old High German *lōs* loose — more at -LESS] (13th century)
1 a : not rigidly fastened or securely attached **b** (1) **:** having worked partly free from attachments ⟨a *loose* tooth⟩ (2) **:** having relative freedom of movement **c :** produced freely and accompanied by raising of mucus ⟨a *loose* cough⟩ **d :** not tight-fitting
2 a : free from a state of confinement, restraint, or obligation ⟨a lion *loose* in the streets⟩ ⟨spend *loose* funds wisely⟩ **b :** not brought together in a bundle, container, or binding **c** *archaic* **:** DISCONNECTED, DETACHED
3 : not dense, close, or compact in structure or arrangement
4 a : lacking in restraint or power of restraint ⟨a *loose* tongue⟩ ⟨*loose* bowels⟩ **b :** lacking moral restraint : UNCHASTE
5 a : not tightly drawn or stretched : SLACK **:** being flexible or relaxed ⟨stay *loose*⟩
6 a : lacking in precision, exactness, or care ⟨*loose* brushwork⟩ ⟨*loose* usage⟩ **b :** permitting freedom of interpretation
7 : not in the possession of either of two competing teams ⟨a *loose* ball⟩ ⟨a *loose* puck⟩
— **loose·ly** *adverb*
— **loose·ness** *noun*

²**loose** *verb* **loosed; loos·ing** (13th century)
transitive verb
1 a : to let loose : RELEASE **b :** to free from restraint
2 : to make loose : UNTIE ⟨*loose* a knot⟩
3 : to cast loose : DETACH
4 : to let fly : DISCHARGE
5 : to make less rigid, tight, or strict : RELAX
intransitive verb
: to let fly a missile (as an arrow) : FIRE

³**loose** *adverb* (15th century)
: in a loose manner : LOOSELY

loose box *noun* (1849)
British : BOX STALL

loose cannon *noun* (1981)
: a dangerously uncontrollable person or thing

loose end *noun* (1546)
1 : something left hanging loose
2 : a fragment of unfinished business — usually used in plural

loose–joint·ed \'lüs-'join-təd\ *adjective* (1859)
1 : having joints apparently not closely articulated
2 : characterized by unusually free movements
— **loose–joint·ed·ness** *noun*

loose–leaf \'lüs-'lēf\ *adjective* (1902)
1 : having leaves secured in book form in a cover whose backbone may be opened for adding, arranging, or removing leaves ⟨*loose-leaf* notebook⟩
2 : of, relating to, or used with a loose-leaf binding ⟨*loose-leaf* paper⟩

loos·en \'lü-s°n\ *verb* **loos·ened; loos·en·ing** \'lüs-niŋ, 'lü-s°n-iŋ\ (14th century)
transitive verb
1 : to release from restraint
2 : to make looser
3 : to relieve (the bowels) of constipation
4 : to cause or permit to become less strict — often used with *up*
intransitive verb
: to become loose or looser

loosen up *intransitive verb* (1938)
: to become less tense : RELAX

loose sentence *noun* (circa 1890)
: a sentence in which the principal clause comes first and subordinate modifiers or trailing elements follow

loose smut *noun* (1890)
: a smut disease of grains in which the entire head is transformed into a dusty mass of spores

loose·strife \'lü(s)-,strīf\ *noun* [intended as translation of Greek *lysimacheios* loosestrife (as if from *lysis* act of loosing + *machesthai* to fight) — more at LYSIS] (1548)

1 : any of a genus (*Lysimachia*) of plants of the primrose family with leafy stems and usually yellow or white flowers
2 : any of a genus (*Lythrum,* family Lythraceae, the loosestrife family) of herbs having entire leaves and including some with showy spikes of purple flowers; *especially* **:** PURPLE LOOSESTRIFE

loos·ey–goos·ey \,lü-sē-'gü-sē\ *adjective* (1964)
: notably loose or relaxed : not tense

¹**loot** \'lüt\ *noun* [Hindi *lūṭ;* akin to Sanskrit *luṇṭati* he plunders] (circa 1788)
1 : goods usually of considerable value taken in war : SPOILS
2 : something held to resemble goods of value seized in war: as **a :** something appropriated illegally often by force or violence **b :** illicit gains by public officials **c :** MONEY
3 : the action of looting
synonym see SPOIL

²**loot** (1845)
transitive verb
1 a : to plunder or sack in war **b :** to rob especially on a large scale and usually by violence or corruption
2 : to seize and carry away by force especially in war
intransitive verb
: to engage in robbing or plundering especially in war
— **loot·er** *noun*

¹**lop** \'läp\ *noun* [Middle English *loppe*] (14th century)
: material cut away from a tree; *especially* **:** parts discarded in lumbering

²**lop** *transitive verb* **lopped; lop·ping** (1519)
1 a (1) **:** to cut off branches or twigs from (2) **:** to sever from a woody plant **b** (1) *archaic* **:** to cut off the head or limbs of (2) **:** to cut from a person
2 a : to remove superfluous parts from **b :** to eliminate as unnecessary or undesirable — usually used with *off*
— **lop·per** *noun*

³**lop** *intransitive verb* **lopped; lop·ping** [perhaps imitative] (1578)
: to hang downward : DROOP

¹**lope** \'lōp\ *noun* [Middle English *loup, lope* leap, from Old Norse *hlaup;* akin to Old English *hlēapan* to leap — more at LEAP] (1809)
1 : an easy natural gait of a horse resembling a canter
2 : an easy usually bounding gait capable of being sustained for a long time

²**lope** *intransitive verb* **loped; lop·ing** (circa 1825)
: to move or ride at a lope
— **lop·er** *noun*

lop–eared \'läp-,ird\ *adjective* (1687)
: having ears that droop

loph·o·phore \'lä-fə-,fōr, -,fȯr\ *noun* [Greek *lophos* crest + English *-phore*] (1850)
: a circular or horseshoe-shaped organ about the mouth especially of a brachiopod or bryozoan that bears tentacles and functions especially in food-getting

lop·sid·ed \'läp-,sī-dəd\ *adjective* (1711)
1 : leaning to one side
2 : lacking in balance, symmetry, or proportion : disproportionately heavy on one side ⟨a *lopsided* vote of 99–1⟩
— **lop·sid·ed·ly** *adverb*
— **lop·sid·ed·ness** *noun*

lo·qua·cious \lō-'kwā-shəs\ *adjective* [Latin *loquac-, loquax,* from *loqui* to speak] (1667)
1 : given to fluent or excessive talk : GARRULOUS
2 : full of excessive talk : WORDY
synonym see TALKATIVE

\ə\ abut \ᵊ\ kitten \ər\ further \a\ ash \ā\ ace
\ä\ mop, mar \au̇\ out \ch\ chin \e\ bet \ē\ easy
\g\ go \i\ hit \ī\ ice \j\ job \ŋ\ sing \ō\ go
\ȯ\ law \ȯi\ boy \th\ thin \t͟h\ the \ü\ loot \u̇\ foot
\y\ yet \zh\ vision *see also* Guide to Pronunciation

— **lo·qua·cious·ly** *adverb*
— **lo·qua·cious·ness** *noun*
lo·quac·i·ty \-'kwa-sə-tē\ *noun* (13th century)
: the quality or state of being very talkative
lo·quat \'lō-,kwät\ *noun* [Chinese (Guangdong) *làuh-gwât*] (1820)
: an Asian evergreen tree (*Eriobotrya japonica*) of the rose family often cultivated for its fruit; *also* : its small yellow edible fruit used especially for preserves
lo·ran \'lōr-,an, 'lôr-\ *noun* [*long-range navigation*] (1932)
: a system of long-range navigation in which pulsed signals sent out by two pairs of radio stations are used to determine the geographical position of a ship or an airplane
¹lord \'lôrd\ *noun* [Middle English *loverd, lord,* from Old English *hlāford,* from *hlāf* loaf + *weard* keeper — more at LOAF, WARD] (before 12th century)
1 : one having power and authority over others: **a** : a ruler by hereditary right or preeminence to whom service and obedience are due **b** : one of whom a fee or estate is held in feudal tenure **c** : an owner of land or other real property **d** *obsolete* : the male head of a household **e** : HUSBAND **f** : one that has achieved mastery or that exercises leadership or great power in some area ⟨a drug *lord*⟩
2 *capitalized* **a** : GOD 1 **b** : JESUS
3 : a man of rank or high position: as **a** : a feudal tenant whose right or title comes directly from the king **b** : a British nobleman: as (1) : BARON 2a (2) : an hereditary peer of the rank of marquess, earl, or viscount (3) : the son of a duke or a marquess or the eldest son of an earl (4) : a bishop of the Church of England **c** *plural, capitalized* : HOUSE OF LORDS
4 — used as a British title: as **a** — used as part of an official title ⟨*Lord* Advocate⟩ **b** — used informally in place of the full title for a marquess, earl, or viscount **c** — used for a baron **d** — used by courtesy before the name and surname of a younger son of a duke or a marquess
5 : a person chosen to preside over a festival

²lord *intransitive verb* (14th century)
: to act like a lord; *especially* : to put on airs — usually used with *it* ⟨*lords* it over his friends⟩
lord chancellor *noun, plural* **lords chancellor** (15th century)
: a British officer of state who presides over the House of Lords in both its legislative and judicial capacities, serves as the head of the British judiciary, and is usually a leading member of the cabinet
lord·ing \'lôr-diŋ\ *noun* (13th century)
1 *archaic* : LORD
2 *obsolete* : LORDLING
lord·ling \'lôrd-liŋ\ *noun* (13th century)
: a little or insignificant lord
lord·ly \-lē\ *adjective* **lord·li·er; -est** (before 12th century)
1 a : of, relating to, or having the characteristics of a lord : DIGNIFIED **b** : GRAND, NOBLE
2 : exhibiting such pride and assurance as could only be felt as appropriate to one of the highest birth or rank
synonym see PROUD
— **lord·li·ness** *noun*
— **lordly** *adverb*
lord of misrule (15th century)
: a master of Christmas revels in England especially in the 15th and 16th centuries
lor·do·sis \lôr-'dō-səs\ *noun* [New Latin, from Greek *lordōsis,* from *lordos* curving forward; akin to Old English be*lyrtan* to deceive] (1704)
1 : abnormal curvature of the spine forward
2 : a mating posture of some sexually receptive female mammals (as rats) in which the head and rump are raised and the back is arched downward
— **lor·dot·ic** \-'dä-tik\ *adjective*

Lord Protector of the Commonwealth (circa 1653)
: PROTECTOR 2b
Lord's day *noun, often D capitalized* (12th century)
: SUNDAY
lord·ship \'lôrd-,ship\ *noun* (before 12th century)
1 a : the rank or dignity of a lord — used as a title **b** : the authority or power of a lord : DOMINION
2 : the territory under the jurisdiction of a lord : SEIGNIORY
Lord's Prayer *noun* (circa 1549)
: the prayer with variant versions in Matthew and Luke that according to the Lucan account Christ taught his disciples
Lord's Supper *noun* (14th century)
: COMMUNION 2a
Lord's table *noun, often T capitalized* (1535)
: ALTAR 2
Lordy \'lôr-dē\ *interjection* [¹lord (God) + ⁴-y] (1853)
— used to express surprise or strength of feeling
¹lore \'lōr, 'lôr\ *noun* [Middle English, from Old English *lār;* akin to Old High German *lēra* doctrine, Old English *leornian* to learn] (before 12th century)
1 *archaic* : something that is taught : LESSON
2 : something that is learned: **a** : knowledge gained through study or experience **b** : traditional knowledge or belief
3 : a particular body of knowledge or tradition
word history see LEARN
²lore *noun* [New Latin *lorum,* from Latin, thong, rein; akin to Greek *eulēra* reins] (1828)
: the space between the eye and bill in a bird or the corresponding region in a reptile or fish
— **lo·re·al** \'lōr-ē-əl, 'lôr-\ *adjective*
Lo·re·lei \'lōr-ə-,lī, 'lôr-\ *noun* [German]
: a siren of Germanic legend whose singing lures Rhine River boatmen to destruction on a reef
lor·gnette \lôrn-'yet\ *noun* [French, from *lorgner* to take a sidelong look at, from Middle French, from *lorgne* squinting] (1803)
: a pair of eyeglasses or opera glasses with a handle
lor·gnon \lôrn-'yō^n\ *noun* [French, from *lorgner*] (1846)
: LORGNETTE
lo·ri·ca \lə-'rī-kə\ *noun, plural* **-cae** \-kē, -,sē\ [Latin] (circa 1706)
1 : a Roman cuirass of leather or metal
2 [New Latin, from Latin] : a hard protective case or shell (as of a rotifer)
lor·i·keet \'lôr-ə-,kēt, 'lär-\ *noun* [*lory* + *-keet* (as in *parakeet*)] (1770)
: any of numerous small arboreal chiefly Australasian parrots (family Loriidae) that usually have long slender tongue papillae which form an organ resembling a brush
lo·ris \'lōr-əs, 'lôr-\ *noun* [French, probably from obsolete Dutch *loeris* simpleton] (1774)
: any of several nocturnal slow-moving tailless arboreal primates (family Lorisidae): as **a** : a slim-bodied primate (*Loris tardigradus*) of southern India and Sri Lanka **b** : either of two larger related primates (*Nycticebus pygmaeus* or *N. coucang*) of southeastern Asia that are heavier limbed and slower moving

loris a

lorn \'lôrn\ *adjective* [Middle English, from *loren,* past participle of *lesen* to lose, from Old English *lēosan* — more at LOSE] (14th century)
: DESOLATE, FORSAKEN
Lor·raine cross \lə-'rān-, lô-\ *noun* (1898)

: CROSS OF LORRAINE
lor·ry \'lôr-ē, 'lär-\ *noun, plural* **lorries** [origin unknown] (1908)
chiefly British : MOTORTRUCK
lo·ry \'lōr-ē, 'lôr-\ *noun, plural* **lories** [Dutch, from Malay *nuri, luri*] (1682)
: any of numerous parrots (family Loriidae) of Australia, New Guinea, and adjacent islands related to the lorikeets and usually having the tongue papillose at the tip and the mandibles less toothed than in other parrots
lose \'lüz\ *verb* **lost** \'lôst\; **los·ing** \'lü-ziŋ\ [Middle English, from Old English *losian* to perish, lose, from *los* destruction; akin to Old English *lēosan* to lose; akin to Old Norse *losa* to loosen, Latin *luere* to atone for, Greek *lyein* to loosen, dissolve, destroy] (before 12th century)
transitive verb
1 a : to bring to destruction — used chiefly in passive construction ⟨the ship was *lost* on the reef⟩ **b** : DAMN ⟨if he shall gain the whole world and *lose* his own soul —Matthew 16:26 (Authorized Version)⟩
2 : to miss from one's possession or from a customary or supposed place
3 : to suffer deprivation of : part with especially in an unforeseen or accidental manner
4 a : to suffer loss through the death and removal of or final separation from (a person) **b** : to fail to keep control of or allegiance of ⟨*lose* votes⟩ ⟨*lost* his temper⟩
5 a : to fail to use : let slip by : WASTE ⟨*lose* the tide⟩ **b** (1) : to fail to win, gain, or obtain ⟨*lose* a prize⟩ ⟨*lose* a contest⟩ (2) : to undergo defeat in ⟨*lose* every battle⟩ **c** : to fail to catch with the senses or the mind ⟨*lost* part of what she said⟩
6 : to cause the loss of ⟨one careless statement *lost* him the election⟩
7 : to fail to keep, sustain, or maintain ⟨*lost* my balance⟩
8 a : to cause to miss one's way or bearings ⟨*lost* himself in the maze of streets⟩ **b** : to make (oneself) withdrawn from immediate reality ⟨*lost* herself in daydreaming⟩
9 a : to wander or go astray from ⟨*lost* his way⟩ **b** : to draw away from : OUTSTRIP ⟨*lost* his pursuers⟩
10 : to fail to keep in sight or in mind
11 : to free oneself from : get rid of ⟨dieting to *lose* some weight⟩
intransitive verb
1 : to undergo deprivation of something of value
2 : to undergo defeat ⟨*lose* with good grace⟩
3 *of a timepiece* : to run slow
— **los·able** \'lü-zə-bəl\ *adjective*

◇ WORD HISTORY
lord *Hlāford,* the Old English predecessor of *lord,* contains the word *hlāf* "bread, loaf," as does *hlǣfdige,* the ancestor of *lady.* The second element of *hlāford* was *weard* "keeper, guard" (hence Modern English *ward*), and the fuller form *hlāfweard* is actually found in one Old English manuscript. At first this compound undoubtedly alluded to the head of a household in his role as "the keeper of the bread," the provider for his family, servants, and retainers, but at a relatively early period it was applied more broadly to anyone in a position of power or authority, from king on down. This generalization may have contributed to the phonetic attrition of *-weard* to *-ord,* as the original sense of the compound lost relevance. Early Middle English *loverd* became *lord* through loss of the second vowel and merger of the \v\ into the preceding vowel; words that underwent a similar alteration include Modern English *head, hawk, auger,* and *lark,* from Old English *hēafod, hafoc, nafogār,* and *lāwerce.* See in addition LADY.

— **los·able·ness** *noun*

— **lose ground** : to suffer loss or disadvantage : fail to advance or improve

— **lose one's heart** : to fall in love

lo·sel \'lō-zəl\ *noun* [Middle English, from *losen* (past participle of *lesen* to lose), alteration of *loren* — more at LORN] (14th century)
: a worthless person

lose out *intransitive verb* (circa 1858)
: to fail to win in competition : fail to receive an expected reward or gain

los·er \'lü-zər\ *noun* (1548)
1 : one that loses especially consistently
2 : one who is incompetent or unable to succeed; *also* : something doomed to fail or disappoint

loss \'lòs\ *noun* [Middle English *los,* probably back-formation from *lost,* past participle of *losen* to lose] (13th century)
1 : DESTRUCTION, RUIN
2 a : the act of losing possession **b** : the harm or privation resulting from loss or separation **c** : an instance of losing
3 : a person or thing or an amount that is lost: as **a** *plural* : killed, wounded, or captured soldiers **b** : the power diminution of a circuit or circuit element corresponding to conversion of electrical energy into heat by resistance
4 a : failure to gain, win, obtain, or utilize **b** : an amount by which the cost of an article or service exceeds the selling price
5 : decrease in amount, magnitude, or degree
6 : the amount of an insured's financial detriment by death or damage that the insurer becomes liable for

— **at a loss** : UNCERTAIN, PUZZLED

— **for a loss** : into a state of distress

loss leader *noun* (1917)
: something (as merchandise) sold at a loss in order to draw customers

— **loss–leader** *adjective*

loss ratio *noun* (1926)
: the ratio between insurance losses incurred and premiums earned during a given period

lossy \'lò-sē\ *adjective* (1946)
: causing attenuation or dissipation of electrical energy ⟨a *lossy* transmission line⟩ ⟨a *lossy* dielectric⟩

lost \'lòst\ *adjective* [past participle of *lose*] (15th century)
1 : not made use of, won, or claimed
2 a : no longer possessed **b** : no longer known
3 : ruined or destroyed physically or morally : DESPERATE
4 a : taken away or beyond reach or attainment : DENIED ⟨regions *lost* to the faith⟩ **b** : INSENSIBLE, HARDENED ⟨*lost* to shame⟩
5 a : unable to find the way **b** : no longer visible **c** : lacking assurance or self-confidence : HELPLESS
6 : RAPT, ABSORBED ⟨*lost* in reverie⟩
7 : not appreciated or understood : WASTED ⟨their jokes were *lost* on me⟩

— **lost·ness** \'lòs(t)-nəs\ *noun*

lost wax *noun* (1909)
: a process used in metal casting that consists of making a wax model, coating it with a refractory to form a mold, heating until the wax melts and runs out of the mold, and then pouring metal into the vacant mold

¹**lot** \'lät\ *noun* [Middle English, from Old English *hlot;* akin to Old High German *hlōz*] (before 12th century)
1 : an object used as a counter in determining a question by chance
2 a : the use of lots as a means of deciding something **b** : the resulting choice
3 a : something that comes to one upon whom a lot has fallen : SHARE **b** : one's way of life or worldly fate : FORTUNE
4 a : a portion or parcel of land **b** : a measured parcel of land having fixed boundaries and designated on a plot or survey **c** : a motion-picture studio and its adjoining property

5 a : a number of units of an article, a single article, or a parcel of articles offered as one item (as in an auction sale) **b** : all the members of a present group, kind, or quantity — used with *the*
6 a : a number of associated persons : SET **b** : KIND, SORT
7 : a considerable quantity or extent ⟨a *lot* of money⟩ ⟨*lots* of friends⟩ □

synonym see FATE

— **a lot 1** : to a considerable degree or extent ⟨this is a *lot* nicer⟩ **2** : OFTEN, FREQUENTLY ⟨runs *a lot* every day⟩ **3** : LOTS

²**lot** *transitive verb* **lot·ted; lot·ting** (15th century)
1 : ALLOT, APPORTION
2 : to form or divide into lots

Lot \'lät\ *noun* [Hebrew *Lōt*]
: a nephew of Abraham who according to the account in Genesis escaped from the doomed city of Sodom with his wife who turned into a pillar of salt when she looked back

lo·ta *also* **lo·tah** \'lō-tə\ *noun* [Hindi *loṭā*] (1809)
: a small usually spherical water vessel of brass or copper used in India

loth \'lōth, 'lōth\ *variant of* LOATH

lo·thar·io \lō-'thar-ē-ō, -'ther-, -'thär-\ *noun, plural* **-i·os** *often capitalized* [*Lothario,* seducer in the play *The Fair Penitent* (1703) by Nicholas Rowe] (1756)
: a man whose chief interest is seducing women ◇

lo·ti \'lō-tē\ *noun, plural* **ma·lo·ti** \mə-'lō-tē\ [Sesotho] (1980)
— see MONEY table

lo·tic \'lō-tik\ *adjective* [Latin *lotus,* past participle of *lavere*] (1916)
: of, relating to, or living in actively moving water ⟨a *lotic* habitat⟩ — compare LENTIC

lo·tion \'lō-shən\ *noun* [Middle English *loscion,* from Latin *lotion-, lotio* act of washing, from *lavere* to wash — more at LYE] (14th century)
: a liquid preparation for cosmetic or external medicinal use

lots \'läts\ *adverb* [plural of ¹*lot*] (1891)
: MUCH ⟨feeling *lots* better⟩

lotte \'lät, 'lòt\ *noun* [French, from Middle French] (1977)
: MONKFISH

lot·tery \'lä-tə-rē\ *also* \'lä-trē\ *noun, plural* **-ter·ies** *often attributive* [Middle French *loterie,* from Middle Dutch, from *lot* lot; akin to Old English *hlot* lot] (1567)
1 a : a drawing of lots in which prizes are distributed to the winners among persons buying a chance **b** : a drawing of lots used to decide something
2 : an event or affair whose outcome is or seems to be determined by chance

lot·to \'lä-(ˌ)tō\ *noun* [Italian, lottery, lotto, from French *lot* lot, of Germanic origin; akin to Old English *hlot* lot] (1778)
: a game of chance resembling bingo

lo·tus \'lō-təs\ *noun* [Latin & Greek; Latin *lotus,* from Greek *lōtos*] (circa 1541)
1 *also* **lo·tos** \'lō-təs\
: a fruit eaten by the lotus-eaters and considered to cause indolence and dreamy contentment; *also* : a tree (as *Zizyphus lotus* of the buckthorn family) reputed to bear this fruit
2 : any of various water lilies including several represented in ancient Egyptian and Hindu art and religious symbolism
3 [New Latin, from Latin] **a** : any of a genus (*Lotus*) of widely distributed upright leguminous herbs or subshrubs **b** : SWEET CLOVER

lotus 2

lo·tus–eat·er \-ˌē-tər\ *noun* (1832)
1 : any of a people in Homer's *Odyssey* subsisting on the lotus and living in the dreamy indolence it induces
2 : an indolent person

lo·tus·land \-ˌland\ *noun* [from the Homeric land of lotus-eaters] (1842)
1 : a place inducing contentment especially through offering an idyllic living situation
2 : a state or an ideal marked by contentment often achieved through self-indulgence

lotus position *noun* [from the supposed resemblance of the position to a lotus blossom] (1953)
: a cross-legged sitting position used in yoga in which the right foot is on the left thigh and the left foot is on the right thigh

louche \'lüsh\ *adjective* [French, literally, cross-eyed, squint-eyed, from Latin *luscus* blind in one eye] (1819)
: not reputable or decent

loud \'laúd\ *adjective* [Middle English, from Old English *hlūd;* akin to Old High German *hlūt* loud, Latin in*clutus* famous, Greek *klytos,* Sanskrit *śṛnoti* he hears] (before 12th century)
1 a : marked by intensity or volume of sound
b : producing a loud sound
2 : CLAMOROUS, NOISY

□ **USAGE**

lot The phrases *a lot of* and *lots of* have been stigmatized as colloquial and unworthy of being used in writing since at least Ambrose Bierce did it in 1909. A surprising number of handbooks are still repeating his opinion even though the expressions are clearly well established and standard on all levels of usage except perhaps the most elevated. Literary use is common ⟨a *lot* of my old St. Louis chums will be out in the Spring —Mark Twain⟩ ⟨the Seurat paintings want a *lot* of seeing to appreciate —Arnold Bennett⟩ ⟨there were *lots* of people in Oxford like that —John Galsworthy⟩ ⟨I have sat around in bars with a *lot* of other ex-newspapermen —James Thurber⟩. Similarly the adverbial uses of *a lot* and *lots* are standard ⟨gave him something *a lot* more important —William Faulkner⟩ ⟨I hope you're *lots* better now —F. Scott Fitzgerald⟩. The spelling *alot* is rare in print and is generally considered a mistake, especially by editors and English teachers, who, along with computer spelling checkers, are evidently responsible for its rarity in print. It is by all accounts very common in spontaneously produced writing—notes, letters, drafts, memoranda, and the like. And it is well attested in the world of interactive computer networks, where no editors or spelling checkers are found.

◇ **WORD HISTORY**

lothario The word *lothario* derives from a character in a now seldom-performed tragedy, *The Fair Penitent* (1703) by Nicholas Rowe (1674–1718). In the play Lothario is a notorious seducer who is described as "haughty, gallant, and gay." He seduces Calista, an unfaithful wife and later the fair penitent of the title. Rowe's Lothario became a pattern for later characterizations in English literature, most notably Lovelace in Samuel Richardson's novel *Clarissa* (1747–48). Since the 18th century *lothario* has been used generically for a foppish, unscrupulous rake.

\ə\ abut \ᵊ\ kitten \ər\ further \a\ ash \ā\ ace
\ä\ mop, mar \aú\ out \ch\ chin \e\ bet \ē\ easy
\g\ go \i\ hit \ī\ ice \j\ job \ŋ\ sing \ō\ go
\ò\ law \òi\ boy \th\ thin \th\ the \ü\ loot \ú\ foot
\y\ yet \zh\ vision *see also* Guide to Pronunciation

3 : obtrusive or offensive in appearance or smell : OBNOXIOUS ☆
— **loud** *adverb*
— **loud·ly** *adverb*
loud·en \'laů-d°n\ *verb* **loud·ened; loud·en·ing** \'laů-niŋ, 'laů-d°n-iŋ\ (circa 1848)
intransitive verb
: to become loud
transitive verb
: to make loud
loud–hail·er \,laůd-'hā-lər\ *noun* (1941)
chiefly British : BULLHORN
loud·mouth \'laůd-,maůth\ *noun* (1914)
: a loudmouthed person
loud·mouthed \-,maůthd, -,maůtht\ *adjective* (1628)
: given to loud offensive talk
loud·ness *noun* (before 12th century)
: the attribute of a sound that determines the magnitude of the auditory sensation produced and that primarily depends on the amplitude of the sound wave involved
loud·speak·er \'laůd-,spē-kər\ *noun* (1920)
: a device that changes electrical signals into sounds loud enough to be heard at a distance
Lou Geh·rig's disease \,lü-'ger-igz-, -'gar-\ *noun* [*Lou Gehrig* (died 1941) American baseball player who suffered from the disease] (1958)
: AMYOTROPHIC LATERAL SCLEROSIS
lough \'läk, 'läk\ *noun* [Middle English, of Celtic origin; akin to Old Irish *loch* lake; akin to Latin *lacus* lake — more at LAKE] (14th century)
1 *chiefly Irish* : LAKE
2 *chiefly Irish* : a bay or inlet of the sea
lou·is d'or \,lü-ē-'dór\ *noun, plural* **louis d'or** [French, from *Louis* XIII of France + *d'or* of gold] (1665)
1 : a French gold coin first struck in 1640 and issued up to the Revolution
2 : the French 20-franc gold piece issued after the Revolution
Lou·is Qua·torze \,lü-ē-kə-'tórz\ *adjective* [French, Louis XIV] (1848)
: of, relating to, or characteristic of the architecture or furniture of the reign of Louis XIV of France
Louis Quinze \-'kaⁿz\ *adjective* [French, Louis XV] (1855)
: of, relating to, or characteristic of the architecture or furniture of the reign of Louis XV of France
Louis Seize \-'sāz, -'sez\ *adjective* [French, Louis XVI] (1882)
: of, relating to, or characteristic of the architecture or furniture of the reign of Louis XVI of France
Louis Treize \-'trāz, -'trez\ *adjective* [French, Louis XIII] (1883)
: of, relating to, or characteristic of the architecture or furniture of the reign of Louis XIII of France
¹lounge \'laůnj\ *verb* **lounged; loung·ing** [origin unknown] (1508)
intransitive verb
: to act or move idly or lazily : LOAF
transitive verb
: to pass (time) idly
²lounge *noun* (1775)
1 : a place for lounging: as **a** : a room in a private home or public building for leisure occupations : LIVING ROOM; *also* : LOBBY **b** : a room in a usually public building or vehicle often combining lounging, smoking, and toilet facilities
2 : a long couch
lounge car *noun* (1947)
: CLUB CAR
lounge lizard *noun* (1918)
1 : LADIES' MAN
2 : FOP
3 : a social parasite
loung·er \'laůn-jər\ *noun* (1508)
1 : one that lounges; *especially* : IDLER

2 : an article of clothing or furniture designed for comfort and leisure use
lounge suit *noun* (1901)
chiefly British : BUSINESS SUIT
lounge·wear \'laůnj-,war, -,wer\ *noun* (circa 1957)
: informal clothing usually designed to be worn at home
loup \'laůp, 'lōp\ *verb* [Middle English, from Old Norse *hlaupa*; akin to Old English *hlēapan* to leap — more at LEAP] (14th century)
chiefly Scottish : LEAP
— **loup** *noun*
loupe \'lüp\ *noun* [French] (circa 1775)
: a small magnifier used especially by jewelers and watchmakers
loup–ga·rou \,lü-gə-'rü\ *noun, plural* **loups–garous** \,lü-gə-'rü(z)\ [Middle French, from Old French *leu garoul*, from *leu* (from Latin *lupus*) wolf + *garoul* werewolf, of Germanic origin; akin to Old High German *werwolf* werewolf] (circa 1580)
: WEREWOLF
lour \'laů(-ə)r\, **loury** \'laů(ə)r-ē\ *variant of* LOWER, LOWERY
¹louse \'laůs\ *noun* [Middle English *lous*, from Old English *lūs*; akin to Old High German *lūs* louse, Welsh *llau* lice] (before 12th century)
1 *plural* **lice** \'līs\ **a** : any of various small wingless usually flattened insects (orders Anoplura and Mallophaga) parasitic on warm-blooded animals **b** : a small usually sluggish arthropod that lives on other animals or on plants and sucks their juices or blood — usually used in combination (plant *louse*) **c** : any of several small arthropods that are not parasitic — usually used in combination (book *louse*) (wood *louse*)
2 *plural* **lous·es** \'laů-səz\ : a contemptible person : HEEL
²louse \'laůs, 'laůz\ *transitive verb* **loused; lous·ing** (14th century)
: to pick lice from : DELOUSE
louse up (1934)
transitive verb
: FOUL UP, SNARL
intransitive verb
: to make a mess
louse·wort \'laůs-,wərt, -,wórt\ *noun* (1597)
: any of a genus (*Pedicularis*) of herbs of the snapdragon family typically having pinnatifid leaves and bilabiate flowers in terminal spikes
lousy \'laů-zē\ *adjective* **lous·i·er; -est** (14th century)
1 : infested with lice
2 a : totally repulsive : CONTEMPTIBLE **b** : miserably poor or inferior (got *lousy* grades) (felt *lousy* after dinner) **c** : amply supplied : REPLETE (*lousy* with money)
3 *of silk* : fuzzy and specked because of splitting of the fiber
— **lous·i·ly** \-zə-lē\ *adverb*
— **lous·i·ness** \-zē-nəs\ *noun*
¹lout \'laůt\ *intransitive verb* [Middle English, from Old English *lūtan*; akin to Old Norse *lūta* to bow down] (before 12th century)
1 : to bow in respect
2 : SUBMIT, YIELD
²lout *noun* [perhaps from Old Norse *lūtr* bent down, from *lūta*] (1542)
: an awkward brutish person
³lout *transitive verb* (circa 1530)
: to treat as a lout : SCORN
lout·ish \'laů-tish\ *adjective* (1542)
: resembling or befitting a lout
synonym see BOORISH
— **lout·ish·ly** *adverb*
— **lout·ish·ness** *noun*
lou·ver *or* **lou·vre** \'lü-vər\ *noun* [Middle English *lover*, from Middle French *lovier*] (14th century)
1 : a roof lantern or turret often with slatted apertures for escape of smoke or admission of light in a medieval building
2 a : an opening provided with one or more slanted fixed or movable fins to allow flow of

air but to exclude rain or sun or to provide privacy **b** : a finned or vaned device for controlling a flow of air or the radiation of light **c** : a fin or shutter of a louver
— **lou·vered** *also* **lou·vred** \-vərd\ *adjective*
lov·able *also* **love·able** \'lə-və-bəl\ *adjective* (14th century)
: having qualities that attract affection
— **lov·abil·i·ty** \,lə-və-'bi-lə-tē\ *noun*
— **lov·able·ness** *noun*
— **lov·ably** \-blē\ *adverb*
lov·age \'lə-vij\ *noun* [Middle English *lo-vache*, from Anglo-French, from Late Latin *levisticum*, alteration of Latin *ligusticum*, from neuter of *ligusticus* Ligurian, from *Ligur-, Ligus*, noun, Ligurian] (14th century)
: any of several aromatic perennial herbs of the carrot family; *especially* : a European herb (*Levisticum officinale*) sometimes cultivated as a domestic remedy, flavoring agent, or potherb
lov·a·stat·in \'lō-və-,sta-tən, 'lə-; ,lō-və-', ,lə-\ *noun* [*lov-* (perhaps from *mevinolin*, an earlier name) + connective *-a-* + *-stat* + ¹*-in*] (1987)
: a drug $C_{24}H_{36}O_5$ used to lower cholesterol levels in the blood
lov·at \'lə-vət\ *noun* [probably from T. A. Fraser, Lord *Lovat* (died 1875) Scottish nobleman who popularized muted tweeds] (1907)
: a predominantly dusty color mixture (as of green) in fabrics
¹love \'ləv\ *noun* [Middle English, from Old English *lufu*; akin to Old High German *luba* love, Old English *lēof* dear, Latin *lubēre, libēre* to please] (before 12th century)
1 a (1) : strong affection for another arising out of kinship or personal ties (maternal *love* for a child) (2) : attraction based on sexual desire : affection and tenderness felt by lovers (3) : affection based on admiration, benevolence, or common interests (*love* for his old schoolmates) **b** : an assurance of love (give her my *love*)
2 : warm attachment, enthusiasm, or devotion (*love* of the sea)
3 a : the object of attachment, devotion, or admiration (baseball was his first *love*) **b** (1) : a beloved person : DARLING — often used as a term of endearment (2) *British* — used as an informal term of address
4 a : unselfish loyal and benevolent concern for the good of another: as (1) : the fatherly concern of God for humankind (2) : brotherly concern for others **b** : a person's adoration of God
5 : a god or personification of love
6 : an amorous episode : LOVE AFFAIR
7 : the sexual embrace : COPULATION
8 : a score of zero (as in tennis)
9 *capitalized, Christian Science* : GOD
— **at love** : holding one's opponent scoreless in tennis
— **in love** : inspired by affection
²love *verb* **loved; lov·ing** (before 12th century)
transitive verb
1 : to hold dear : CHERISH

2 a : to feel a lover's passion, devotion, or tenderness for **b** (1) **:** CARESS (2) **:** to fondle amorously (3) **:** to copulate with
3 : to like or desire actively **:** take pleasure in ⟨*loved* to play the violin⟩
4 : to thrive in ⟨the rose *loves* sunlight⟩ *intransitive verb*
: to feel affection or experience desire
love affair *noun* (1591)
1 : a romantic attachment or episode between lovers
2 : a lively enthusiasm ⟨America's *love affair* with baseball⟩
love apple *noun* [probably translation of French *pomme d'amour*] (1578)
: TOMATO
love beads *noun plural* (1968)
: beads worn as a symbol of love and peace
love·bird \'ləv-,bərd\ *noun* (1595)
: any of various small usually gray or green parrots (especially genus *Agapornis* of Africa) that show great affection for their mates
love-bug \-,bəg\ *noun* [from the fact that it is usually seen copulating] (circa 1966)
: a small black fly (*Plecia nearctica*) with a red thorax that swarms along highways in the Gulf states of the U.S.
love child *noun* (1805)
: an illegitimate child
love feast *noun* (1580)
1 : a meal eaten in common by a Christian congregation in token of brotherly love
2 : a gathering held to promote reconciliation and good feeling or show someone affectionate honor
love grass *noun* (1702)
: any of a genus (*Eragrostis*) of grasses that resemble the bluegrasses but have flattened spikelets and deciduous lemmas
love handles *noun plural* (1975)
: fatty bulges along the sides at the waist
love-in \'ləv-,in\ *noun* (1967)
: a gathering of people especially for the expression of their mutual love
love-in-a-mist \'ləv-ə-nə-,mist\ *noun* (circa 1760)
: a European and African annual herb (*Nigella damascena*) of the buttercup family having whitish flowers enveloped in numerous finely dissected bracts
love knot *noun* (14th century)
: a stylized knot sometimes used as an emblem of love
love·less \'ləv-ləs\ *adjective* (14th century)
1 : having no love
2 : not loved
— **love·less·ly** *adverb*
— **love·less·ness** *noun*
love·lock \-,läk\ *noun* (1592)
: a long lock of hair variously worn (as over the front of the shoulder) especially by men in the 17th and 18th centuries
love·lorn \-,lorn\ *adjective* (1634)
: bereft of love or of a lover
— **love·lorn·ness** \-,lorn-nəs\ *noun*
¹love·ly \'ləv-lē\ *adjective* **love·li·er; -est** (before 12th century)
1 *obsolete* **:** LOVABLE
2 : delightful for beauty, harmony, or grace **:** ATTRACTIVE
3 : GRAND, SWELL
4 : eliciting love by moral or ideal worth
synonym see BEAUTIFUL
— **love·li·ly** \'ləv-lə-lē\ *adverb*
— **love·li·ness** \'ləv-lē-nəs\ *noun*
— **lovely** *adverb*
²lovely *noun, plural* **lovelies** (1652)
1 : a beautiful woman
2 : a lovely object
love·mak·ing \'ləv-,mā-kiŋ\ *noun* (15th century)
1 : COURTSHIP
2 : sexual activity; *especially* **:** COPULATION
lov·er \'lə-vər\ *noun* (13th century)
1 a : a person in love; *especially* **:** a man in

love with a woman **b** *plural* **:** two persons in love with each other
2 : an affectionate or benevolent friend
3 : DEVOTEE
4 a : PARAMOUR **b :** a person with whom one has sexual relations
lov·er·ly \-lē\ *adjective* (1875)
: resembling or befitting a lover
love seat *noun* (1904)
: a double chair, sofa, or settee for two persons
love·sick \'ləv-,sik\ *adjective* (15th century)
1 : languishing with love **:** YEARNING
2 : expressing a lover's longing
— **love·sick·ness** *noun*
love·some \-səm\ *adjective* (before 12th century)
1 : WINSOME, LOVELY
2 : AFFECTIONATE, AMOROUS
lovey–dovey \,lə-vē-'də-vē\ *adjective* (1886)
: expressing much love or sentimentality; *also* **:** MUSHY
— **lovey–dovey·ness** \-nəs\ *noun*
lov·ing \'lə-viŋ\ *adjective* (before 12th century)
1 : AFFECTIONATE
2 : PAINSTAKING
— **lov·ing·ly** \-viŋ-lē\ *adverb*
— **lov·ing·ness** *noun*
loving cup *noun* [from its former use in ceremonial drinking] (1812)
1 : a large ornamental drinking vessel with two or more handles
2 : a loving cup given as a token or trophy
lov·ing–kind·ness \,lə-viŋ-'kīn(d)-nəs\ *noun* (1535)
: tender and benevolent affection
¹low \'lō\ *intransitive verb* [Middle English *loowen*, from Old English *hlōwan*; akin to Old High German *hluoen* to moo, Latin *calare* to call, summon, Greek *kalein*] (before 12th century)
: MOO
²low *noun* (1549)
: the deep sustained sound characteristic especially of a cow
³low *adjective* **low·er** \'lō-(ə)r\; **low·est** \'lō-əst\ [Middle English *lah, low*, from Old Norse *lāgr*; akin to Middle High German *læge* low, flat; probably akin to Old English *licgan* to lie] (12th century)
1 a : having a small upward extension or elevation ⟨a *low* wall⟩ **b :** situated or passing little above a reference line, point, or plane ⟨*low* bridges⟩ **c** (1) **:** having a low-cut neckline (2) **:** not extending as high as the ankle ⟨*low* oxfords⟩
2 a : situated or passing below the normal level, surface, or base of measurement, or the mean elevation ⟨*low* ground⟩ **b :** marking a nadir or bottom ⟨the *low* point of his career⟩
3 : DEAD — used as a predicate adjective
4 a : not loud **:** SOFT **b :** FLAT 8a **c :** characterized by being toward the bottom of the range of pitch attainable (as by an instrument)
5 a : being near the equator ⟨*low* northern latitudes⟩ **b :** being near the horizon
6 : socially or economically humble in character or status ⟨*low* birth⟩
7 a : lacking strength, health, or vitality **:** WEAK, PROSTRATE ⟨very *low* with pneumonia⟩ **b :** lacking spirit or vivacity **:** DEPRESSED ⟨a *low* frame of mind⟩
8 a : of lesser degree, size, or amount than average or ordinary ⟨*low* energy⟩ **b** (1) **:** small in number or amount ⟨*low* level of employment⟩ ⟨a *low* income group⟩ (3) **:** CHEAP ⟨*low* prices⟩ (4) **:** SHORT, DEPLETED ⟨oil is in *low* supply⟩ **c :** of lesser position, rank, or order
9 : falling short of some standard: as **a :** lacking dignity or elevation ⟨a *low* style of writing⟩ **b :** morally reprehensible **:** BASE ⟨a *low* trick⟩ **c :** COARSE, VULGAR ⟨*low* language⟩
10 a : not advanced in complexity, development, or elaboration ⟨*low* organisms⟩ **b** *often capitalized* **:** LOW CHURCH

11 : UNFAVORABLE, DISPARAGING ⟨had a *low* opinion of him⟩
12 : designed for slow and usually the slowest speed ⟨*low* gear⟩
13 : articulated with a wide opening between the relatively flat tongue and the palate **:** OPEN ⟨\ä\ is a *low* vowel⟩
14 : intended to attract little attention ⟨kept a *low* profile⟩
synonym see BASE
— **low** *adverb*
— **low·ness** *noun*
⁴low *noun* (12th century)
1 : something that is low: as **a :** DEPTH **b :** a region of low barometric pressure
2 : the transmission gear of an automotive vehicle giving the lowest ratio of driveshaft to crankshaft speed
⁵low *or* **lowe** \'lō\ *noun* [Middle English, from Old Norse *logi, log*; akin to Old English *lēoht* light — more at LIGHT] (13th century) *chiefly Scottish* **:** FLAME, BLAZE
⁶low *or* **lowe** *verb* **lowed; low·ing** (14th century) *Scottish* **:** FLAME, BLAZE
low·ball \'lō-,bol\ *transitive verb* (circa 1961)
: to give a (customer) a deceptively low price or cost estimate
— **lowball** *noun*
low beam *noun* (circa 1952)
: the short-range focus of a vehicle headlight
low blood pressure *noun* (1924)
: HYPOTENSION
low blow *noun* (1952)
: an unprincipled attack ⟨gossip column that landed one *low blow* after another —James Fallows⟩
low·born \'lō-'born\ *adjective* (13th century)
: born in a low condition or rank
low·boy \-,boi\ *noun* (circa 1891)
: a chest or side table about three feet (one meter) high with drawers and usually with cabriole legs
low·bred \-'bred\ *adjective* (1757)
: RUDE, VULGAR
low·brow \-,brau\ *noun* (1906)
: a person with little taste or intellectual interest

lowboy

— **lowbrow** *adjective*
Low Church *adjective* (1710)
: tending especially in Anglican worship to minimize emphasis on the priesthood, sacraments, and ceremonial in worship and often to emphasize evangelical principles
Low Churchman *noun* (1702)
: a person holding or advocating Low Church views
low comedy *noun* (1608)
: comedy employing burlesque, horseplay, or the representation of low life — compare HIGH COMEDY
low country *noun, often L&C capitalized* (15th century)
: a low-lying country or region; *especially* **:** the part of a southern state extending from the seacoast inland to the fall line
— **low–country** *adjective, often L&C capitalized*
low–density lipoprotein *noun* (1951)
: LDL
low·down \'lō-,daun\ *noun* (1915)
: the inside facts **:** DOPE
low–down \'lō-(,)daun\ *adjective* (1850)
1 : CONTEMPTIBLE, BASE
2 : deeply emotional ⟨*low-down* blues⟩

\ə\ **abut** \ə\ **kitten** \ər\ **further** \a\ **ash** \ā\ **ace** \ä\ **mop, mar** \au\ **out** \ch\ **chin** \e\ **bet** \ē\ **easy** \g\ **go** \i\ **hit** \ī\ **ice** \j\ **job** \ŋ\ **sing** \ō\ **go** \ò\ **law** \òi\ **boy** \th\ **thin** \t̲h̲\ **the** \ü\ **loot** \ú\ **foot** \y\ **yet** \zh\ **vision** *see also* Guide to Pronunciation

low earth orbit *noun* (1963)
: a usually circular orbit from about 90 to 600 miles (144 to 960 kilometers) above the earth

low–end \'lō-,end\ *adjective* (1926)
: of, relating to, or being the lowest priced merchandise in a manufacturer's line

¹**low·er** \'laù(-ə)r, 'lō(-ə)r\ *intransitive verb* [Middle English *louren*; akin to Middle High German *lūren* to lie in wait] (13th century)
1 : to look sullen : FROWN
2 : to be or become dark, gloomy, and threatening

²**lower** *noun* (14th century)
: FROWN

³**low·er** \'lō(-ə)r\ *adjective* [³*low*] (13th century)
1 : relatively low in position, rank, or order
2 : SOUTHERN ⟨*lower* New York State⟩
3 : less advanced in the scale of evolutionary development
4 a : situated or held to be situated beneath the earth's surface **b** *capitalized* : being an earlier epoch or series of the period or series named ⟨*Lower* Cretaceous⟩ ⟨*Lower* Paleolithic⟩
5 : constituting the popular and often the larger and more representative branch of a bicameral legislative body ⟨*lower* house⟩

⁴**low·er** \'lō(-ə)r\ (1606)
intransitive verb
: to move down : DROP; *also* : DIMINISH
transitive verb
1 a : to let descend : LET DOWN **b** : to depress as to direction ⟨*lower* your aim⟩ **c** : to reduce the height of
2 a : to reduce in value, number, or amount **b** (1) : to bring down in quality or character : DEGRADE (2) : ABASE, HUMBLE **c** : to reduce the objective of

¹**low·er·case** \,lō(-ə)r-'kās\ *adjective* [from the compositor's practice of keeping such types in the lower of a pair of type cases] (1683)
of a letter : having as its typical form a f g or b n i rather than A F G or B N I
— **lowercase** *noun*

²**lowercase** *transitive verb* **-cased; -casing** (1908)
: to print or set in lowercase letters

low·er–class \,lō(-ə)r-'klas\ *adjective* (1892)
1 : of, relating to, or characteristic of the lower class
2 : being an inferior or low-ranking specimen of its kind

lower class *noun* (1772)
: a social class occupying a position below the middle class and having the lowest status in a society

lower criticism *noun* (circa 1889)
: criticism concerned with the recovery of original texts especially of Scripture through collation of extant manuscripts — compare HIGHER CRITICISM

lower fungus *noun* (1900)
: a fungus with hyphae absent or rudimentary and nonseptate

low·er·ing \'laù-(ə-)riŋ, 'lō-\ *adjective* (15th century)
: dark and threatening : GLOOMY

low·er·most \'lō(-ə)r-,mōst\ *adjective* (1547)
: LOWEST

low·ery \'laù-(ə-)rē, 'lō-\ *adjective* (15th century)
: GLOOMY, LOWERING

lowest common denominator *noun* (1924)
1 : LEAST COMMON DENOMINATOR
2 : something of small intellectual content designed to appeal to a lowbrow audience; *also* : such an audience

lowest common multiple *noun* (circa 1924)
: LEAST COMMON MULTIPLE

lowest terms *noun plural* (1806)
: the form of a fraction in which the numerator and denominator have no factor in common except 1 ⟨reduce a fraction to *lowest terms*⟩

low frequency *noun* (circa 1868)
: a radio frequency between medium frequency and very low frequency — see RADIO FREQUENCY table

Low German *noun* (1838)
1 : the German dialects of northern Germany especially as used since the end of the medieval period : PLATTDEUTSCH
2 : the West Germanic languages other than High German

low–grade \'lō-'grād\ *adjective* (1878)
1 : of inferior grade or quality
2 : being near that extreme of a specified range which is lowest, least intense, or least competent ⟨a *low-grade* fever⟩ ⟨a *low-grade* infection⟩

low-key \-'kē\ *also* **low-keyed** \-'kēd\ *adjective* (1907)
1 : having or producing dark tones only with little contrast
2 : of low intensity

¹**low·land** \'lō-lənd, -,land\ *noun* (15th century)
: low or level country

²**lowland** *adjective* (1508)
1 *capitalized* : of or relating to the Lowlands of Scotland
2 : of or relating to a lowland

low·land·er \-lən-dər, -,lan-\ *noun* (1692)
1 *capitalized* : an inhabitant of the Lowlands of Scotland
2 : a native or inhabitant of a lowland region

Low Latin *noun* (1872)
: postclassical Latin in its later stages

low–lev·el \'lō-'le-vəl\ *adjective* (1881)
1 : occurring, done, or placed at a low level
2 : being of low importance or rank

low·life \'lō-,līf\ *noun, plural* **low·lifes** \-,līfs\ *also* **low·lives** \-,līvz\ (1911)
1 : a person of low social status
2 : a person of low moral character
— **low-life** *adjective*

low·light \'lō-,līt\ *noun* (1941)
: a particularly bad or unpleasant event, detail, or part

low·li·head \'lō-lē-,hed\ *noun* [Middle English *lowliheed*, from *lowly* + *-hed* -hood; akin to Middle English *-hod* -hood] (15th century)
archaic : lowly state

¹**low·ly** \'lō-lē\ *adverb* (14th century)
1 : in a humble or meek manner
2 : in a low position, manner, or degree
3 : not loudly

²**lowly** *adjective* **low·li·er; -est** (14th century)
1 : humble in manner or spirit : free from self-assertive pride
2 : not lofty or sublime : PROSAIC
3 : ranking low in some hierarchy
4 : of or relating to a low social or economic rank
5 : low in the scale of biological or cultural evolution
— **low·li·ness** *noun*

low–ly·ing \'lō-'lī-iŋ\ *adjective* (1856)
1 : rising relatively little above the base of measurement ⟨*low-lying* hills⟩
2 : lying below the normal level, surface, or the base of measurement or mean elevation ⟨*low-lying* clouds⟩

low mass *noun, often L&M capitalized* (1568)
: a mass that is recited without singing by the celebrant, without a deacon, subdeacon, or choir assisting the celebrant, and without the use of incense

low–mind·ed \'lō-'mīn-dəd\ *adjective* (circa 1746)
: inclined to low or unworthy things
— **low–mind·ed·ly** *adverb*
— **low–mind·ed·ness** *noun*

lown \'laùn, 'lün\ *adjective* [Middle English (Scots) *lowne*] (15th century)
dialect : CALM, QUIET

low–pres·sure \'lō-'pre-shər\ *adjective* (1827)
1 : having, exerting, or operating under a relatively small pressure

2 : EASYGOING

low relief *noun* (1711)
: BAS-RELIEF

low–rent \'lō-'rent\ *adjective* (1957)
: low in character, cost, or prestige ⟨*low-rent* thugs⟩ ⟨a *low-rent* movie⟩ ⟨a *low-rent* literary form⟩

low–rise \'lō-'rīz\ *adjective* (1957)
1 : having few stories and not equipped with elevators ⟨a *low-rise* classroom building⟩
2 : of, relating to, or characterized by low-rise buildings ⟨a *low-rise* housing development⟩

low–slung \'lō-'sləŋ\ *adjective* (1943)
: relatively low to the ground or floor ⟨a *low-slung* convertible⟩ ⟨a *low-slung* modern building⟩ ⟨a *low-slung* sofa⟩

low–spir·it·ed \'lō-'spir-ə-təd\ *adjective* (1693)
: DEJECTED, DEPRESSED
— **low–spir·it·ed·ly** *adverb*
— **low–spir·it·ed·ness** *noun*

Low Sunday *noun* (15th century)
: the Sunday following Easter

low–tech \'lō-'tek\ *adjective* (1981)
: technologically simple or unsophisticated ⟨*low-tech* industries⟩

low tide *noun* (1843)
: the farthest ebb of the tide

low water *noun* (15th century)
: a low stage of the water in a river or lake; *also* : LOW TIDE

¹**lox** \'läks\ *noun* [liquid *ox*ygen] (1923)
: liquid oxygen

²**lox** *noun, plural* **lox** *or* **lox·es** [Yiddish *laks*, from Middle High German *lahs* salmon, from Old High German; akin to Old English *leax* salmon] (1941)
: smoked salmon

lox·o·drome \'läk-sə-,drōm\ *noun* [back-formation from *loxodromic* of a rhumb line, from French *loxodromique*, from Greek *loxos* oblique + *dromos* course — more at DROMEDARY] (1880)
: RHUMB LINE

loy·al \'lòi(-ə)l\ *adjective* [Middle French, from Old French *leial*, *leel*, from Latin *legalis* legal] (1531)
1 : unswerving in allegiance: as **a** : faithful in allegiance to one's lawful sovereign or government **b** : faithful to a private person to whom fidelity is due **c** : faithful to a cause, ideal, custom, institution, or product
2 : showing loyalty
3 *obsolete* : LAWFUL, LEGITIMATE
synonym see FAITHFUL
— **loy·al·ly** \'lòi-ə-lē\ *adverb*

loy·al·ist \'lòi-ə-list\ *noun* (1647)
: one who is or remains loyal especially to a political cause, party, government, or sovereign

loy·al·ty \'lòi-(ə)l-tē\ *noun, plural* **-ties** [Middle English *loyaltee*, from Middle French *loialté*, from Old French *leialté*, from *leial*] (15th century)
: the quality or state or an instance of being loyal
synonym see FIDELITY

loz·enge \'lä-z°nj\ *also* -s°nj\ *noun* [Middle English *losenge*, from Middle French *losange*] (14th century)
1 : a figure with four equal sides and two acute and two obtuse angles : DIAMOND
2 : something shaped like a lozenge
3 : a small often medicated candy

LP \el-'pē\ *noun* [long-*p*laying] (1948)
: a microgroove phonograph record designed to be played at 33⅓ revolutions per minute

LPN \,el-(,)pē-'en\ *noun* (1948)
: LICENSED PRACTICAL NURSE

LSD \,el-(,)es-'dē\ *noun* [German *Lysergsäure-Diäthylamid* lysergic acid diethylamide] (1950)
: an organic compound $C_{20}H_{25}N_3O$ that induces psychotic symptoms similar to those of schizophrenia — called also *lysergic acid diethylamide*

lu·au \'lü-ˌau̇\ *noun* [Hawaiian *lūʻau*] (1853)
: an Hawaiian feast
Lu·ba·vitch·er \'lü-bə-ˌvi-chər, lü-'bä-\ *noun* [Yiddish *lyubavitsher*, from *Lyubavitsh*, town in Belarus] (1954)
: a member of a Hasidic sect founded by Schneour Zalman of Lyady in the late 18th century
— **Lubavitcher** *adjective*
lub·ber \'lə-bər\ *noun* [Middle English *lobre, lobur*] (14th century)
1 : a big clumsy fellow
2 : a clumsy seaman
— **lub·ber·li·ness** \-lē-nəs\ *noun*
— **lub·ber·ly** \-lē\ *adjective or adverb*
lubber line *noun* (1889)
: a fixed line on the compass of a ship or airplane that is aligned with the longitudinal axis of the vehicle
lubber's hole *noun* (circa 1784)
: a hole in a square-rigger's top near the mast through which one may go farther aloft without going over the rim by the futtock shrouds
lube \'lüb\ *noun* [short for *lubricating oil*] (1926)
1 : LUBRICANT
2 : an application of a lubricant : LUBRICATION
lu·bric \'lü-brik\ *adjective* [Middle French *lubrique*, from Medieval Latin *lubricus*] (15th century)
archaic : LUBRICIOUS
— **lu·bri·cal** \-bri-kəl\ *adjective*
lu·bri·cant \'lü-bri-kənt\ *noun* (circa 1828)
1 : a substance (as grease) capable of reducing friction, heat, and wear when introduced as a film between solid surfaces
2 : something that lessens or prevents friction or difficulty
— **lubricant** *adjective*
lu·bri·cate \'lü-brə-ˌkāt\ *verb* **-cat·ed; -cat·ing** [Latin *lubricatus*, past participle of *lubricare*, from *lubricus* slippery — more at SLEEVE] (circa 1623)
transitive verb
1 : to make smooth or slippery
2 : to apply a lubricant to
intransitive verb
: to act as a lubricant
— **lu·bri·ca·tion** \ˌlü-brə-'kā-shən\ *noun*
— **lu·bri·ca·tive** \'lü-brə-ˌkā-tiv\ *adjective*
— **lu·bri·ca·tor** \-ˌkā-tər\ *noun*
lu·bri·cious \lü-'bri-shəs\ *or* **lu·bri·cous** \'lü-bri-kəs\ *adjective* [Medieval Latin *lubricus*, from Latin, slippery, easily led astray] (1535)
1 : marked by wantonness : LECHEROUS; *also* : SALACIOUS
2 [Latin *lubricus*] : having a smooth or slippery quality ⟨a *lubricious* skin⟩
— **lu·bri·cious·ly** *adverb*
lu·bric·i·ty \lü-'bri-sə-tē\ *noun, plural* **-ties** (15th century)
: the property or state of being lubricious; *also* : the capacity for reducing friction
Lu·can \'lü-kən\ *adjective* [Late Latin *lucanus*, from *Lucas* Luke, from Greek *Loukas*] (1890)
: of or relating to Luke or the Gospel ascribed to him
lu·carne \lü-'kärn\ *noun* [French] (circa 1825)
: DORMER
Lu·ca·yo \lü-'kī-(ˌ)ō\ *also* **Lu·ca·yan** \-'kī-ən\ *noun* (1929)
: a member of an Arawakan people of the Bahamas
lu·cen·cy \'lü-sᵊn(t)-sē\ *noun* (1656)
: the quality or state of being lucent
lu·cent \'lü-sᵊnt\ *adjective* [Middle English, from Latin *lucent-, lucens*, present participle of *lucēre* to shine — more at LIGHT] (15th century)
1 : glowing with light : LUMINOUS
2 : marked by clarity or translucence : CLEAR
— **lu·cent·ly** *adverb*
lu·cern *noun* [probably modification of German *lüchsern* of a lynx, from *Luchs* lynx] (circa 1533)

obsolete : LYNX
lu·cerne *also* **lu·cern** \lü-'sərn\ *noun* [French *luzerne*, from Provençal *luserno*] (1626)
chiefly British : ALFALFA
lu·cid \'lü-səd\ *adjective* [Latin *lucidus*, from *lucēre*] (1591)
1 a : suffused with light : LUMINOUS b : TRANSLUCENT
2 : having full use of one's faculties : SANE
3 : clear to the understanding : INTELLIGIBLE
synonym see CLEAR
— **lu·cid·ly** *adverb*
— **lu·cid·ness** *noun*
lu·cid·i·ty \lü-'si-də-tē\ *noun* (1851)
1 : clearness of thought or style
2 : a presumed capacity to perceive the truth directly and instantaneously : CLAIRVOYANCE
Lu·ci·fer \'lü-sə-fər\ *noun* [Middle English, the morning star, a fallen rebel archangel, the Devil, from Old English, from Latin, the morning star, from *lucifer* light-bearing, from *luc-, lux* light + *-fer* -ferous — more at LIGHT] (before 12th century)
1 — used as a name of the devil
2 : the planet Venus when appearing as the morning star
3 *not capitalized* : a friction match having as active substances antimony sulfide and potassium chlorate
— **Lu·ci·fe·ri·an** \ˌlü-sə-'fir-ē-ən\ *adjective*
lu·cif·er·ase \lü-'si-fə-ˌrās, -ˌrāz\ *noun* [International Scientific Vocabulary, from *luciferin*] (1888)
: an enzyme that catalyzes the oxidation of luciferin
lu·cif·er·in \-f(ə-)rən\ *noun* [International Scientific Vocabulary, from Latin *lucifer* light-bearing] (1888)
: any of various organic substances in luminescent organisms (as fireflies) that upon oxidation produce a virtually heatless light
lu·cif·er·ous \lü-'si-f(ə-)rəs\ *adjective* [Latin *lucifer*] (1648)
: bringing light or insight : ILLUMINATING
Lu·ci·na \lü-'sī-na\ *noun* [Latin, Roman goddess of childbirth] (1658)
archaic : MIDWIFE
Lu·cite \'lü-ˌsīt\ *trademark*
— used for an acrylic resin or plastic consisting essentially of polymerized methyl methacrylate
¹**luck** \'lək\ *noun* [Middle English *lucke*, from Middle Dutch *luc*; akin to Middle High German *gelücke* luck] (15th century)
1 a : a force that brings good fortune or adversity b : the events or circumstances that operate for or against an individual
2 : favoring chance : SUCCESS
— **luck·less** \-ləs\ *adjective*
²**luck** *intransitive verb* (circa 1584)
1 : to prosper or succeed especially through chance or good fortune — usually used with *out*
2 : to come upon something desirable by chance — usually used with *out, on, onto,* or *into*
luck·i·ly \'lə-kə-lē\ *adverb* (1530)
1 : in a lucky manner
2 : FORTUNATELY 2 ⟨*luckily*, we were on time⟩
usage see HOPEFULLY
lucky \'lə-kē\ *adjective* **luck·i·er; -est** (15th century)
1 : having good luck
2 : happening by chance : FORTUITOUS
3 : producing or resulting in good by chance : FAVORABLE
4 : seeming to bring good luck ⟨a *lucky* rabbit's foot⟩ ☆
— **luck·i·ness** \'lə-kē-nəs\ *noun*
lucky dip *noun* (1925)
British : GRAB BAG
lu·cra·tive \'lü-krə-tiv\ *adjective* [Middle English *lucratif*, from Middle French, from Latin *lucrativus*, from *lucratus*, past participle of *lucrari* to gain, from *lucrum*] (15th century)
: producing wealth : PROFITABLE

— **lu·cra·tive·ly** *adverb*
— **lu·cra·tive·ness** *noun*
lu·cre \'lü-kər\ *noun* [Middle English, from Latin *lucrum*; probably akin to Old English *lēan* reward, Old High German *lōn*, Greek *apolauein* to enjoy] (14th century)
: monetary gain : PROFIT; *also* : MONEY
lu·cu·bra·tion \ˌlü-kyə-'brā-shən, ˌlü-kə-\ *noun* [Latin *lucubration-, lucubratio* study by night, work produced at night, from *lucubrare* to work by lamplight; akin to Latin *luc-, lux*] (1595)
: laborious or intensive study; *also* : the product of such study — usually used in plural
lu·cu·lent \'lü-kyə-lənt\ *adjective* [Latin *luculentus*, from *luc-, lux* light] (circa 1548)
: clear in thought or expression : LUCID
— **lu·cu·lent·ly** *adverb*
Lu·cul·lan \lü-'kə-lən\ *also* **Lu·cul·li·an** \-'kə-lē-ən\ *adjective* [Latin *lucullanus* of Licinius *Lucullus*; from his reputation for luxurious banquets] (1861)
: LAVISH, LUXURIOUS ⟨a *Lucullan* feast⟩
Lud·dite \'lə-ˌdīt\ *noun* [perhaps from Ned *Ludd*, 18th century Leicestershire workman who destroyed machinery] (1811)
: one of a group of early 19th century English workmen destroying laborsaving machinery as a protest; *broadly* : one who is opposed to especially technological change ◊

☆ **SYNONYMS**
Lucky, fortunate, happy, providential mean meeting with unforeseen success. LUCKY stresses the agency of chance in bringing about a favorable result (won because of a *lucky* bounce). FORTUNATE suggests being rewarded beyond one's deserts ⟨*fortunate* in my investments⟩. HAPPY combines the implications of LUCKY and FORTUNATE with stress on being blessed ⟨a series of *happy* accidents⟩. PROVIDENTIAL more definitely implies the help or intervention of a higher power ⟨a *providential* change in the weather⟩.

◊ **WORD HISTORY**
Luddite Since *Luddite* first appeared in the fall of 1811, it has never gone out of use as a label for those opposed to new technology and its consequences. But introduction of labor-saving machinery was only one of the origins of the rampages in the Midlands and North of England that gave rise to the word. The initial attacks by discontented stocking and lace makers in Nottinghamshire, when the possibly fictitious Ned Ludd's name first appears in anonymous letters as the movement's leader, were directed against stocking-making frames of a type dating back to Elizabethan times. The first Luddites' raids were a labor protest at a time when trade unions were proscribed by law and sabotage of machinery, whether old or new, was an available form of collective action. Moreover, the disturbances took place against a background of crop failures and economic depression caused by Britain's blockade of continental Europe during the Napoleonic Wars. Concerning the origin of the name Ned Ludd, nothing is known for certain. Tradition holds that Ned Ludd (or Ludlam) was a Leicestershire knitter who out of anger at his employer destroyed his knitting frame, and that subsequently his name was proverbially connected with frame-breaking.

\ə\ abut \ᵊ\ kitten \ər\ further \a\ ash \ā\ ace
\ä\ mop, mar \au̇\ out \ch\ chin \e\ bet \ē\ easy
\g\ go \i\ hit \ī\ ice \j\ job \ŋ\ sing \ō\ go
\o̊\ law \o̊i\ boy \th\ thin \t͟h\ the \ü\ loot \u̇\ foot
\y\ yet \zh\ vision *see also* Guide to Pronunciation

— **Luddite** *adjective*

lu·dic \'lü-dik\ *adjective* [French *ludique*, from Latin *ludus*] (1940)
: of, relating to, or characterized by play : PLAYFUL ⟨*ludic* behavior⟩ ⟨a *ludic* novel⟩

lu·di·crous \'lü-də-krəs\ *adjective* [Latin *ludicrus*, from *ludus* play, sport; perhaps akin to Greek *loidoros* abusive] (1782)
1 : amusing or laughable through obvious absurdity, incongruity, exaggeration, or eccentricity
2 : meriting derisive laughter or scorn as absurdly inept, false, or foolish
synonym see LAUGHABLE
— **lu·di·crous·ly** *adverb*
— **lu·di·crous·ness** *noun*

lu·es \'lü-(,)ēz\ *noun, plural* **lues** [New Latin, from Latin, plague; akin to Greek *lyein* to loosen, destroy — more at LOSE] (1634)
: SYPHILIS
— **lu·et·ic** \lü-'e-tik\ *adjective*

¹luff \'ləf\ *noun* [Middle English, weather side of a ship, luff, from Middle French *lof* weather side of ship] (14th century)
1 : the act of sailing a ship nearer the wind
2 : the forward edge of a fore-and-aft sail

²luff *intransitive verb* (14th century)
: to turn the head of a ship toward the wind

luf·fa *variant of* LOOFAH

luft·mensch \'lùft-,men(t)sh\ *noun, plural* **luft·mensch·en** \-,men(t)-shən\ [Yiddish *luftmentsh*, from *luft* air + *mentsh* human being] (1907)
: an impractical contemplative person having no definite business or income

¹lug \'ləg\ *verb* **lugged; lug·ging** [Middle English *luggen* to pull by the hair or ear, drag, probably of Scandinavian origin; akin to Norwegian *lugga* to pull by the hair] (14th century)
transitive verb
1 : DRAG, PULL
2 : to carry laboriously
3 : to introduce in a forced manner ⟨*lugs* my name into the argument⟩
intransitive verb
1 : to pull with effort : TUG
2 : to move heavily or by jerks ⟨the car *lugs* on hills⟩
3 *of a racehorse* : to swerve from the course toward or away from the inside rail

²lug *noun* (1616)
1 *archaic* **a** : an act of lugging **b** : something that is lugged **c** : a shipping container for produce
2 : LUGSAIL
3 *plural* : superior airs or affectations ⟨put on *lugs*⟩
4 *slang* : an exaction of money — used in the phrase *put the lug on*

³lug *noun* [Middle English (Scots) *lugge*, perhaps from Middle English *luggen*] (15th century)
1 : something (as a handle) that projects like an ear: as **a** : a leather loop on a harness saddle through which the shaft passes **b** : a metal fitting to which electrical wires are soldered or connected
2 *chiefly British* : EAR
3 : a ridge (as on the bottom of a shoe) to increase traction
4 : a nut used to secure a wheel on an automotive vehicle — called also *lug nut*
5 : BLOCKHEAD, LOUT

Lu·gan·da \lü-'gän-də, -'gan-\ *noun* (1889)
: the Bantu language of the Ganda people

luge \'lüzh\ *noun* [French] (1905)
: a small sled that is ridden in a supine position and used especially in competition; *also* : the competition itself
— **luge** *intransitive verb*
— **lug·er** \'lü-zhər\ *noun*

lug·gage \'lə-gij\ *noun* (1596)
: something that is lugged; *especially* : suitcases for a traveler's belongings : BAGGAGE

lug·ger \'lə-gər\ *noun* [*lugsail*] (1757)
: a small fishing or coasting boat that carries one or more lugsails

lug·sail \'ləg-,sāl, -səl\ *noun* [perhaps from ³*lug*] (1677)
: a 4-sided sail bent to an obliquely hanging yard that is hoisted and lowered with the sail

lugger

lu·gu·bri·ous \lù-'gü-brē-əs *also* -'gyü-\ *adjective* [Latin *lugubris*, from *lugēre* to mourn; akin to Greek *lygros* mournful] (1601)
1 : MOURNFUL; *especially* : exaggeratedly or affectedly mournful ⟨dark, dramatic and *lugubrious* brooding —V. S. Pritchett⟩
2 : DISMAL ⟨a *lugubrious* landscape⟩
— **lu·gu·bri·ous·ly** *adverb*
— **lu·gu·bri·ous·ness** *noun*

lug·worm \'ləg-,wərm\ *noun* [origin unknown] (1802)
: any of a genus (*Arenicola*) of marine polychaete worms that have a row of tufted gills along each side of the back and are used for bait

Luk·an \'lü-kən\ *variant of* LUCAN

Luke \'lük\ *noun* [Latin *Lucas*, from Greek *Loukas*]
1 : a Gentile physician and companion of the apostle Paul traditionally identified as the author of the third Gospel in the New Testament and of the book of Acts
2 : the third Gospel in the New Testament — see BIBLE table

luke·warm \'lük-'wòrm\ *adjective* [Middle English, from *luke* lukewarm + *warm*; probably akin to Old High German *lāo* lukewarm — more at LEE] (14th century)
1 : moderately warm : TEPID
2 : lacking conviction : HALFHEARTED
— **luke·warm·ly** *adverb*
— **luke·warm·ness** *noun*

¹lull \'ləl\ *transitive verb* [Middle English; probably of imitative origin] (14th century)
1 : to cause to sleep or rest : SOOTHE
2 : to cause to relax vigilance

²lull *noun* (1719)
1 *archaic* : something that lulls; *especially* : LULLABY
2 : a temporary pause or decline in activity ⟨the early morning *lull* in urban noise⟩: as **a** : a temporary calm before or during a storm **b** : a temporary drop in business activity

¹lul·la·by \'lə-lə-,bī\ *noun, plural* **-bies** [obsolete English *lulla*, interjection used to lull a child (from Middle English) + *bye*, interjection used to lull a child, from Middle English *by*] (1588)
: a soothing refrain; *specifically* : a song to quiet children or lull them to sleep

²lullaby *transitive verb* **-bied; -by·ing** (1592)
: to quiet with or as if with a lullaby

lu·lu \'lü-(,)lü\ *noun* [probably from *Lulu*, nickname from *Louise*] (1886)
slang : one that is remarkable or wonderful

lum \'ləm\ *noun* [origin unknown] (circa 1628)
chiefly Scottish : CHIMNEY

lum·ba·go \,ləm-'bā-(,)gō\ *noun* [Latin, from *lumbus*] (circa 1693)
: usually painful muscular rheumatism involving the lumbar region

lum·bar \'ləm-bər, -,bär\ *adjective* [New Latin *lumbaris*, from Latin *lumbus* loin — more at LOIN] (circa 1656)
: of, relating to, or constituting the loins or the vertebrae between the thoracic vertebrae and sacrum ⟨*lumbar* region⟩

¹lum·ber \'ləm-bər\ *intransitive verb* **lumbered; lum·ber·ing** \-b(ə-)riŋ\ [Middle English *lomeren*] (14th century)
1 : to move ponderously
2 : RUMBLE

²lumber *noun* [perhaps from *Lombard*; from the use of pawnshops as storehouses of disused property] (1552)
1 : surplus or disused articles (as furniture) that are stored away
2 a : timber or logs especially when dressed for use **b** : any of various structural materials prepared in a form similar to lumber
— **lumber** *adjective*

³lumber *verb* **lum·bered; lum·ber·ing** \-b(ə-)riŋ\ (1642)
transitive verb
1 : to clutter with or as if with lumber : ENCUMBER
2 : to heap together in disorder
3 : to log and saw the timber of
intransitive verb
1 : to cut logs for lumber
2 : to saw logs into lumber for the market
— **lum·ber·er** \-bər-ər\ *noun*

lum·ber·jack \'ləm-bər-,jak\ *noun* (1831)
: LOGGER

lum·ber·man \-mən\ *noun* (circa 1817)
: a person who is engaged in or oversees the business of cutting, processing, and marketing lumber

lumber room *noun* (1741)
: STOREROOM 1

lum·ber·yard \-,yärd\ *noun* (1786)
: a yard where a stock of lumber is kept for sale

lum·bo·sa·cral \,ləm-bō-'sa-krəl, -'sā-\ *adjective* (1840)
: relating to the lumbar and sacral regions or parts

lu·men \'lü-mən\ *noun, plural* **lumens** *also* **lu·mi·na** \-mə-nə\ [New Latin *lumin-, lumen*, from Latin, light, air shaft, opening] (1873)
1 : the cavity of a tubular organ ⟨the *lumen* of a blood vessel⟩
2 : the bore of a tube (as of a hollow needle or catheter)
3 : a unit of luminous flux equal to the light emitted in a unit solid angle by a uniform point source of one candle intensity
— **lu·mi·nal** *also* **lu·men·al** \-mə-n²l\ *adjective*

lumin- *or* **lumini-** *combining form* [Middle English *lumin-*, from Latin *lumin-, lumen*]
: light ⟨*lumini*ferous⟩

lu·mi·naire \,lü-mə-'nar, -'ner\ *noun* [French, lamp, lighting] (1921)
: a complete lighting unit

lu·mi·nance \'lü-mə-nən(t)s\ *noun* (1880)
1 : the quality or state of being luminous
2 : the luminous intensity of a surface in a given direction per unit of projected area

lu·mi·nar·ia \,lü-mə-'ner-ē-ə\ *noun, plural* **-nar·i·as** [Spanish, decorative light, from Late Latin] (1949)
: a traditional Mexican Christmas lantern originally consisting of a candle set in sand inside a paper bag

lu·mi·nary \'lü-mə-,ner-ē\ *noun, plural* **-nar·ies** [Middle English *luminarye*, from Middle French & Late Latin; Middle French *luminaire* lamp, from Late Latin *luminaria*, plural of *luminare* lamp, heavenly body, from Latin, window, from *lumin-, lumen* light; akin to Latin *lucēre* to shine — more at LIGHT] (15th century)
1 : a person of prominence or brilliant achievement
2 : a body that gives light; *especially* : one of the celestial bodies
— **luminary** *adjective*

lu·mi·nesce \,lü-mə-'nes\ *intransitive verb* **-nesced; -nesc·ing** [back-formation from *luminescent*] (1896)
: to exhibit luminescence

lu·mi·nes·cence \-'ne-s°n(t)s\ *noun* (1889)
: the low-temperature emission of light (as by a chemical or physiological process); *also*
: light produced by luminescence
— **lu·mi·nes·cent** \-s°nt\ *adjective*

lu·mi·nif·er·ous \,lü-mə-'ni-f(ə-)rəs\ *adjective* (1801)
: transmitting, producing, or yielding light

lu·mi·nism \'lü-mə-,ni-zəm\ *noun, often capitalized* (circa 1974)
: a theory or practice of realist landscape and seascape painting developed in the U.S. in the mid 19th century and concerned with the study and depiction of effects of light and atmosphere
— **lu·mi·nist** \-nist\ *noun, often capitalized*

lu·mi·nos·i·ty \,lü-mə-'nä-sə-tē\ *noun, plural* **-ties** (1634)
1 a : the quality or state of being luminous **b** : something luminous
2 a : the relative quantity of light **b** : relative brightness of something
3 : the relative quantity of radiation emitted by a celestial source (as a star)

lu·mi·nous \'lü-mə-nəs\ *adjective* [Middle English, from Latin *luminosus*, from *lumin-, lumen*] (15th century)
1 a : emitting or reflecting usually steady, suffused, or glowing light **b :** of or relating to light or to luminous flux
2 : bathed in or exposed to steady light ⟨*luminous* with sunlight⟩
3 : CLEAR, ENLIGHTENING
synonym see BRIGHT
— **lu·mi·nous·ly** *adverb*
— **lu·mi·nous·ness** *noun*

luminous energy *noun* (circa 1931)
: energy transferred in the form of visible radiation

luminous flux *noun* (1925)
: radiant flux in the visible-wavelength range usually expressed in lumens instead of watts

luminous paint *noun* (circa 1889)
: a paint containing a phosphor (as zinc sulfide activated with copper) and so able to glow in the dark

lum·mox \'lə-məks, -miks\ *noun* [origin unknown] (circa 1825)
: a clumsy person

¹lump \'ləmp\ *noun* [Middle English] (14th century)
1 : a piece or mass of indefinite size and shape
2 a : AGGREGATE, TOTALITY ⟨taken in the *lump*⟩ **b :** MAJORITY
3 : PROTUBERANCE; *especially* **:** an abnormal swelling
4 : a person who is heavy and awkward; *also* : one who is stupid or dull
5 *plural* **a :** BEATINGS, BRUISES ⟨had taken a lot of *lumps* growing up in the city⟩ **b :** DEFEAT, LOSS ⟨can cheerfully take his *lumps* on losers, because the payout is big on the winners —Martin Mayer⟩
— **lump in one's throat** : a constriction of the throat caused by emotion

²lump (1624)
transitive verb
1 : to group indiscriminately
2 : to make into lumps; *also* : to make lumps on or in
3 : to move noisily and clumsily
intransitive verb
1 : to become formed into lumps
2 : to move oneself noisily and clumsily

³lump *adjective* (circa 1700)
: not divided into parts : ENTIRE ⟨*lump* sum⟩

⁴lump *transitive verb* [origin unknown] (1791)
: to put up with ⟨like it or *lump* it⟩

lump·ec·to·my \,ləm-'pek-tə-mē\ *noun, plural* **-mies** (1972)
: excision of a breast tumor with a limited amount of associated tissue

¹lum·pen \'lùm-pən, 'ləm-\ *adjective* [German *Lumpenproletariat* degraded section of the proletariat, from *Lump* contemptible person (from *Lumpen* rags) + *Proletariat*] (1936)
: of or relating to dispossessed and uprooted individuals cut off from the economic and social class with which they might normally be identified ⟨*lumpen* proletariat⟩ ⟨*lumpen* intellectuals⟩

²lumpen *noun, plural* **lumpen** *also* **lumpens** (1941)
: a member of the crude and uneducated lowest class of society

lump·er \'ləm-pər\ *noun* (circa 1785)
1 : a laborer employed to handle freight or cargo
2 : one who classifies organisms into large often variable taxonomic groups based on major characters — compare SPLITTER

lump·fish \'ləmp-,fish\ *noun* [obsolete English *lump* lumpfish (probably from Dutch *lomp* blenny, loach) + English *fish*] (circa 1620)
: a northern Atlantic usually greenish fish (*Cyclopterus lumpus* of the family Cyclopteridae) having rows of nodules on the body and eggs used as a caviar

lump·ish \'ləm-pish\ *adjective* (1528)
1 : DULL, SLUGGISH
2 *obsolete* **:** low in spirits
3 : HEAVY, AWKWARD
4 : LUMPY 1a
5 : tediously slow or dull : BORING; *also* : LUMPY 3
— **lump·ish·ly** *adverb*
— **lump·ish·ness** *noun*

lumpy \'ləm-pē\ *adjective* **lump·i·er; -est** (1707)
1 : filled or covered with lumps **b :** characterized by choppy waves
2 : having a heavy clumsy appearance
3 : uneven and often crude in style
— **lump·i·ly** \-pə-lē\ *adverb*
— **lump·i·ness** \-pē-nəs\ *noun*

lumpy jaw *noun* (1890)
: ACTINOMYCOSIS; *especially* : actinomycosis of the head in cattle

lu·na·cy \'lü-nə-sē\ *noun, plural* **-cies** [*lunatic*] (1541)
1 : any of various forms of insanity: as **a :** intermittent insanity once believed to be related to phases of the moon **b :** insanity amounting to lack of capacity or of responsibility in the eyes of the law
2 : wild foolishness : extravagant folly
3 : a foolish act

lu·na moth \'lü-nə-\ *noun* [New Latin *luna* (specific epithet of *Actias luna*), from Latin, moon] (1869)
: a large mostly pale green American saturniid moth (*Actias luna*) with long tails on the hind wings

luna moth

lu·nar \'lü-nər *also* -,när\ *adjective* [Middle English, from Latin *lunaris*, from *luna* moon; akin to Latin *lucēre* to shine — more at LIGHT] (15th century)
1 : CRESCENT, LUNATE
2 a : of or relating to the moon **b :** designed for use on the moon ⟨*lunar* vehicles⟩
3 : measured by the moon's revolution ⟨*lunar* month⟩

lunar caustic *noun* [obsolete *luna* silver, from Medieval Latin, from Latin, moon] (1771)
: silver nitrate especially when fused and molded into sticks for use as a caustic

lunar eclipse *noun* (circa 1737)
: an eclipse in which the moon near the full phase passes partially or wholly through the umbra of the earth's shadow — see ECLIPSE illustration

lunar module *noun* (1967)
: a space vehicle module designed to carry astronauts from the command module to the surface of the moon and back — called also *lunar excursion module*; abbreviation *LEM*

lu·nate \'lü-,nāt\ *adjective* [Latin *lunatus*, past participle of *lunare* to bend in a crescent, from *luna*] (circa 1777)
: shaped like a crescent

lu·na·tic \'lü-nə-,tik\ *adjective* [Middle English *lunatik*, from Old French or Late Latin; Old French *lunatique*, from Late Latin *lunaticus*, from Latin *luna*; from the belief that lunacy fluctuated with the phases of the moon] (14th century)
1 a : affected with lunacy : INSANE **b :** designed for the care of insane persons ⟨*lunatic* asylum⟩
2 : wildly foolish ◆
— **lunatic** *noun*

lunatic fringe *noun* (1913)
: the members of a usually political or social movement espousing extreme, eccentric, or fanatical views

lu·na·tion \lü-'nā-shən\ *noun* [Middle English *lunacioun*, from Medieval Latin *lunation-, lunatio*, from Latin *luna*] (14th century)
: the period of time averaging 29 days, 12 hours, 44 minutes, and 2.8 seconds elapsing between two successive new moons

¹lunch \'lənch\ *noun* [probably short for *luncheon*] (1812)
1 : a usually light meal; *especially* : one taken in the middle of the day
2 : the food prepared for a lunch
— **out to lunch** *slang* : out of touch with reality

²lunch (1823)
intransitive verb
: to eat lunch
transitive verb
: to treat to lunch
— **lunch·er** *noun*

lunch counter *noun* (1869)
1 : a long counter at which lunches are sold
2 : LUNCHEONETTE

lun·cheon \'lən-chən\ *noun* [perhaps alteration of *nuncheon* light snack] (circa 1652)
: LUNCH; *especially* : a formal usually midday meal as part of a meeting or for entertaining a guest

lun·cheon·ette \,lən-chə-'net\ *noun* (1924)
: a small restaurant serving light lunches

◇ WORD HISTORY

lunatic The word *lunatic* is based ultimately on an old folk-medical belief, that human behavior is affected by the phases of the moon. The full moon, in particular, was once thought to trigger phenomena as diverse as epilepsy and schizophrenia. Greek authors of late antiquity and the early Middle Ages used the adjectives *selēnoblēktos* or *selēnoplēktos*, literally, "moonstruck," to describe people influenced by the moon. (The word *moonstruck* is itself probably a loan translation of these words, introduced into English in the 17th century.) The Late Latin adjective *lunaticus*, a derivative of Latin *luna* "moon" (with the suffix of *fanaticus* "fanatic"), was coined to express the same notion. *Lunaticus* was borrowed into Old French as *lunatique* and from there into Middle English as *lunatik*. One peculiarity of *lunatic* that is due to its early appearance in English is its stress, which falls on the first syllable. All other English words ending in *-atic* are stressed on the *a*. Some words that were once stressed on the first syllable such as *phlegmatic* and *schismatic* have, in the last two centuries, joined the common pattern, so that *lunatic* now remains alone.

\ə\ **abut** \ᵊ\ **kitten** \ər\ **further** \a\ **ash** \ā\ **ace**
\ä\ **mop, mar** \aù\ **out** \ch\ **chin** \e\ **bet** \ē\ **easy**
\g\ **go** \i\ **hit** \ī\ **ice** \j\ **job** \ŋ\ **sing** \ō\ **go**
\ò\ **law** \òi\ **boy** \th\ **thin** \th\ **the** \ü\ **loot** \ù\ **foot**
\y\ **yet** \zh\ **vision** *see also* Guide to Pronunciation

lunch·room \'lənch-ˌrüm, -ˌr.m\ *noun* (1830)
1 : LUNCHEONETTE
2 : a room (as in a school) where lunches supplied on the premises or brought from home may be eaten

lunch·time \-ˌtīm\ *noun* (1859)
: the time at which lunch is usually eaten : NOON

lune \'lün\ *noun* [Latin *luna* moon — more at LUNAR] (circa 1704)
: the part of a plane surface bounded by two intersecting arcs or of a spherical surface bounded by two great circles

lunes \'lünz\ *noun plural* [French, plural of *lune* crazy whim, from Middle French, moon, crazy whim, from Latin *luna*] (1602)
: fits of lunacy

lu·nette \lü-'net\ *noun* [French, from Old French *lunete* small object shaped like the moon, from *lune* moon] (circa 1673)
1 : something that has the shape of a crescent or half-moon: as **a** : an opening in a vault especially for a window **b** : the surface at the upper part of a wall that is partly surrounded by a vault which the wall intersects and that is often filled by windows or by mural painting **c** : a low crescentic mound (as of sand) formed by the wind
2 : the figure or shape of a crescent moon

lung \'ləŋ\ *noun* [Middle English *lunge*, from Old English *lungen*; akin to Old High German *lungun* lung, *līhti* light in weight — more at LIGHT] (before 12th century)
1 a : one of the usually paired compound saccular thoracic organs that constitute the basic respiratory organ of air-breathing vertebrates **b** : any of various respiratory organs of invertebrates
2 a : a device enabling individuals abandoning a submarine to rise to the surface **b** : a mechanical device for regularly introducing fresh air into and withdrawing stale air from the lung : RESPIRATOR
— **lung·ful** \-ˌfúl\ *noun*

¹lunge \'lənj\ *noun* [modification of French *allonge* extension, reach, from Old French *alonge*, from *alongier* to lengthen, from (assumed) Vulgar Latin *allongare*, from Latin *ad-* ad- + Late Latin *longare*, from Latin *longus* long] (1748)
1 : a quick thrust or jab (as of a sword) usually made by leaning or striding forward
2 : a sudden forward rush or reach ⟨made a *lunge* to catch the ball⟩

²lunge *verb* **lunged; lung·ing** (1821)
intransitive verb
: to make a lunge : move with or as if with a lunge
transitive verb
: to thrust or propel (as a blow) in a lunge

lunged \'lənd\ *adjective* (1693)
1 : having lungs : PULMONATE
2 : having a lung or lungs of a specified kind or number — used in combination ⟨one-*lunged*⟩

¹lung·er \'lən-jər\ *noun* (1842)
: one that lunges

²lung·er \'ləŋ-ər\ *noun* (1893)
: a person suffering from a chronic disease of the lungs; *especially* : one who is tubercular

lung·fish \'ləŋ-ˌfish\ *noun* (1883)
: any of a subclass (Dipneusti) of bony fishes that breathe by a modified swim bladder as well as gills

lung·worm \-ˌwərm\ *noun* (1882)
: any of various nematodes that infest the lungs and air passages of mammals

lung·wort \-ˌwərt, -ˌwòrt\ *noun* (before 12th century)
: any of several plants (as a mullein) formerly used in the treatment of respiratory disorders; *especially* : a European herb (*Pulmonaria officinalis*) of the borage family with hispid leaves and usually bluish flowers

lu·ni·so·lar \ˌlü-ni-'sō-lər *also* -ˌlär\ *adjective* [Latin *luna* moon + English *-i-* + *solar*] (1691)

: relating or attributed to the moon and the sun

lun·ker \'lən-kər\ *noun* [origin unknown] (1912)
: something large of its kind — used especially of a game fish

lunk·head \'ləŋk-ˌhed\ *noun* [probably alteration of *lump* + *head*] (1852)
: a stupid person : DOLT
— **lunk·head·ed** \-ˌhe-dəd\ *adjective*

lu·nule \'lü-(ˌ)nyü(ə)l\ *noun* [New Latin *lunula*, from Latin, crescent-shaped ornament, from diminutive of *luna* moon] (1828)
: a crescent-shaped body part or marking (as the whitish mark at the base of a fingernail)

lu·ny \'lü-nē\ *variant of* LOONY

lu·pa·nar \lü-'pä-nər, -'pä-\ *noun* [Latin, from *lupa* prostitute, literally, she-wolf, feminine of *lupus*] (1864)
: BROTHEL

Lu·per·ca·lia \ˌlü-pər-'kā-lē-ə, -'kāl-yə\ *noun* [Latin, plural, from *Lupercus*, god of flocks] (1600)
: an ancient Roman festival celebrated February 15 to ensure fertility for the people, fields, and flocks
— **Lu·per·ca·lian** \-'kā-lē-ən, -'kāl-yən\ *adjective*

¹lu·pine *also* **lu·pin** \'lü-pən\ *noun* [Middle English, from Latin *lupinus, lupinum*, from *lupinus*, adjective] (14th century)
: any of a genus (*Lupinus*) of leguminous herbs including some poisonous forms and others cultivated for their long showy racemes of usually blue, purple, white, or yellow flowers or for green manure, fodder, or their edible seeds; *also* : an edible lupine seed

²lu·pine \-ˌpīn\ *adjective* [Latin *lupinus*, from *lupus* wolf — more at WOLF] (1660)
: WOLFISH

lu·pus \'lü-pəs\ *noun* [Middle English, from Medieval Latin, from Latin, wolf] (14th century)
: any of several diseases characterized by skin lesions; *especially* : SYSTEMIC LUPUS ERYTHEMATOSUS

lupus er·y·the·ma·to·sus \-ˌer-ə-ˌthē-mə-'tō-səs\ *noun* [New Latin, literally, erythematous lupus] (1860)
: a disorder characterized by skin inflammation; *especially* : SYSTEMIC LUPUS ERYTHEMATOSUS

¹lurch \'lərch\ *verb* [Middle English *lorchen*, probably alteration of *lurken* to lurk] (15th century)
intransitive verb
dialect chiefly English : to loiter about a place furtively : PROWL
transitive verb
1 *obsolete* : STEAL
2 *archaic* : CHEAT

²lurch *noun* [Middle French *lourche*, adjective, defeated by a lurch, deceived] (1598)
: a decisive defeat in which an opponent wins a game by more than double the defeated player's score especially in cribbage
— **in the lurch** : in a vulnerable and unsupported position

³lurch *transitive verb* (circa 1651)
1 *archaic* : to leave in the lurch
2 : to defeat by a lurch (as in cribbage)

⁴lurch *noun* [origin unknown] (1819)
1 : a sudden roll of a ship to one side
2 : a jerking or swaying movement; *also* : STAGGER 3

⁵lurch *intransitive verb* (circa 1828)
: to roll or tip abruptly : PITCH; *also* : STAGGER

lurch·er \'lər-chər\ *noun* [¹*lurch*] (1528)
1 *archaic* : a petty thief : PILFERER
2 *British* : a crossbred dog; *especially* : one that resembles a greyhound
3 *archaic* : one who lurks; *also* : SPY

lur·dane \'lər-dən\ *noun* [Middle English *lurdan*, from Middle French *lourdin* dullard, from *lourd* dull, stupid, from Latin *luridus* lurid] (14th century)

archaic : a lazy stupid person
— **lurdane** *adjective*

¹lure \'lúr\ *noun* [Middle English, from Middle French *loire*, of Germanic origin; akin to Middle High German *luoder* bait; perhaps akin to Old English *lathian* to invite, Old High German *ladōn*] (14th century)
1 : an object usually of leather or feathers attached to a long cord and used by a falconer to recall or exercise a hawk
2 a : an inducement to pleasure or gain : ENTICEMENT **b** : APPEAL, ATTRACTION
3 : a decoy for attracting animals to capture: as **a** : artificial bait used for catching fish **b** : an often luminous structure on the head of pediculate fishes that is used to attract prey

²lure *transitive verb* **lured; lur·ing** (14th century)
1 : to recall or exercise (a hawk) by means of a lure
2 : to draw with a hint of pleasure or gain : attract actively and strongly ☆

Lur·ex \'lùr-eks\ *trademark*
— used for metallic yarn or thread

lu·rid \'lùr-əd\ *adjective* [Latin *luridus* pale yellow, sallow] (circa 1656)
1 a : wan and ghastly pale in appearance **b** : of any of several light or medium grayish colors ranging in hue from yellow to orange
2 : shining with the red glow of fire seen through smoke or cloud
3 a : causing horror or revulsion : GRUESOME **b** : MELODRAMATIC, SENSATIONAL; *also* : SHOCKING ⟨paperbacks in the usual *lurid* covers —T. R. Fyvel⟩
synonym see GHASTLY
— **lu·rid·ly** *adverb*
— **lu·rid·ness** *noun*

lurk \'lərk\ *intransitive verb* [Middle English; akin to Middle High German *lūren* to lie in wait — more at LOWER] (14th century)
1 a : to lie in wait in a place of concealment especially for an evil purpose **b** : to move furtively or inconspicuously **c** : to persist in staying
2 a : to be concealed but capable of being discovered; *specifically* : to constitute a latent threat **b** : to lie hidden ☆
— **lurk·er** *noun*

lus·cious \'lə-shəs\ *adjective* [Middle English *lucius*, perhaps alteration of *licius*, short for *delicious*] (15th century) **1 a** : having a delicious taste or smell : SWEET **b** *archaic* : excessively sweet : CLOYING **2** : sexually attractive : SEDUCTIVE, SEXY **3 a** : richly luxurious or appealing to the senses **b** : excessively ornate — **lus·cious·ly** *adverb* — **lus·cious·ness** *noun*

¹lush \'ləsh\ *adjective* [Middle English *lusch* soft, tender] (1610) **1 a** : growing vigorously especially with luxuriant foliage ⟨*lush* grass⟩ **b** : lavishly productive : as (1) : FERTILE (2) : THRIVING (3) : characterized by abundance : PLENTIFUL (4) : PROSPEROUS, PROFITABLE **2 a** : SAVORY, DELICIOUS **b** : appealing to the senses ⟨the *lush* sounds of the orchestra⟩ **c** : OPULENT, SUMPTUOUS **synonym** see PROFUSE — **lush·ly** *adverb* — **lush·ness** *noun*

²lush *noun* [origin unknown] (circa 1790) **1** *slang* : intoxicating liquor : DRINK **2** : an habitual heavy drinker : DRUNKARD

³lush *verb* (circa 1811) *slang* : DRINK

Lu·so- \'lü-(,)sō\ *combining form* [Portuguese, from *lusitano* Portuguese, from Latin *Lusitanus* of Lusitania (ancient region corresponding approximately to modern Portugal)] : Portuguese and ⟨*Luso*-Brazilian⟩

¹lust \'ləst\ *noun* [Middle English, from Old English; akin to Old High German *lust* pleasure and perhaps to Latin *lascivus* wanton] (before 12th century) **1** *obsolete* **a** : PLEASURE, DELIGHT **b** : personal inclination : WISH **2** : usually intense or unbridled sexual desire : LASCIVIOUSNESS **3 a** : an intense longing : CRAVING **b** : ENTHUSIASM, EAGERNESS

²lust *intransitive verb* (12th century) : to have an intense desire or need : CRAVE *specifically* : to have a sexual urge

¹lus·ter *or* **lus·tre** \'ləs-tər\ *noun* [Middle English *lustre*, from Latin *lustrum*] (14th century) : a period of five years : LUSTRUM 2

²luster *or* **lustre** *noun* [Middle French *lustre*, from Old Italian *lustro*, from *lustrare* to brighten, from Latin, to purify ceremonially, from *lustrum*] (circa 1522) **1** : a glow of reflected light : SHEEN; *specifically* : the appearance of the surface of a mineral dependent upon its reflecting qualities **2 a** : a glow of light from within : LUMINOSITY **b** : an inner beauty : RADIANCE **3** : a superficial attractiveness or appearance of excellence **4 a** : a glass pendant used especially to ornament a candlestick or chandelier **b** : a decorative object (as a chandelier) hung with glass pendants **5** *chiefly British* : a fabric with cotton warp and a filling of wool, mohair, or alpaca **6** : LUSTERWARE — **lus·ter·less** \-tər-ləs\ *adjective*

³luster *or* **lustre** *verb* **lus·tered** *or* **lus·tred**; **lus·ter·ing** *or* **lus·tring** \-t(ə-)riŋ\ (1582) *intransitive verb* : to have luster : GLEAM *transitive verb* **1** : to give luster or distinction to **2** : to coat or treat with a substance that imparts luster

lus·ter·ware \'ləs-tər-,war, -,wer\ *noun* (1825) : pottery with an iridescent metallic sheen in the glaze

lust·ful \'ləst-fəl\ *adjective* (14th century) : excited by lust : LECHEROUS — **lust·ful·ly** \-fə-lē\ *adverb* — **lust·ful·ness** *noun*

lust·i·hood \'ləs-tē-,hud\ *noun* (1599) **1** : vigor of body or spirit : ROBUSTNESS **2** : sexual inclination or capacity

lus·tral \'ləs-trəl\ *adjective* [Latin *lustralis*, from *lustrum*] (1533) : PURIFICATORY

lus·trate \'ləs-,trāt\ *transitive verb* **lus·trat·ed**; **lus·trat·ing** [Latin *lustratus*, past participle of *lustrare*] (1653) : to purify ceremonially — **lus·tra·tion** \,ləs-'trā-shən\ *noun*

¹lus·tring \'ləs-triŋ\ *noun* [modification of Italian *lustrino*] (1697) *archaic* : LUTESTRING

²lus·tring \'ləs-t(ə-)riŋ\ *noun* [*lustring*, gerund of ³*luster*] (circa 1889) : a finishing process (as calendering) for giving a gloss to yarns and cloth

lus·trous \'ləs-trəs\ *adjective* (1601) **1** : reflecting light evenly and efficiently without glitter or sparkle ⟨a *lustrous* satin⟩ ⟨the *lustrous* glow of an opal⟩ **2** : radiant in character or reputation : ILLUSTRIOUS **synonym** see BRIGHT — **lus·trous·ly** *adverb* — **lus·trous·ness** *noun*

lus·trum \'ləs-trəm\ *noun, plural* **lustrums** *or* **lus·tra** \-trə\ [Latin] (1590) **1** : a period of five years **2 a** : a purification of the whole Roman people made in ancient times after the census every five years **b** : the Roman census

lusty \'ləs-tē\ *adjective* **lust·i·er; -est** (13th century) **1** *archaic* : MERRY, JOYOUS **2** : LUSTFUL ⟨*lusty* passion⟩ **3 a** : full of strength and vitality : HEALTHY, VIGOROUS ⟨a young, *lusty*, growing country —Helen Harris⟩ **b** : HEARTY, ROBUST ⟨a *lusty* beef stew⟩ **c** : ENTHUSIASTIC, ROUSING ⟨a *lusty* rendition of the song⟩ **synonym** see VIGOROUS — **lust·i·ly** \-tə-lē\ *adverb* — **lust·i·ness** \-tē-nəs\ *noun*

¹lute \'lüt\ *noun* [Middle English, from Middle French *lut*, from Old Provençal *laut*, from Arabic *al-'ūd*, literally, the wood] (13th century) : a stringed instrument having a large pear-shaped body, a vaulted back, a fretted fingerboard, and a head with tuning pegs which is often angled backward from the neck

²lute *transitive verb* **lut·ed; lut·ing** [Middle English, from Latin *lutare*, from *lutum* mud — more at POLLUTE] (14th century) : to seal or cover (as a joint or surface) with lute

³lute *noun* (15th century) : a substance (as cement or clay) for packing a joint or coating a porous surface to make it impervious to gas or liquid

lute

lute- *or* **luteo-** *combining form* [New Latin (*corpus*) *luteum*] : corpus luteum ⟨*luteal*⟩

lu·te·al \'lü-tē-əl\ *adjective* (1920) : of, relating to, characterized by, or involving the corpus luteum ⟨the *luteal* phase of the menstrual cycle⟩

lute·fisk \'lüt-,fisk, 'lü-tə-\ *noun* [Norwegian, from *lute* to wash in lye solution + *fisk* fish] (1924) : dried codfish that has been soaked in a water and lye solution before cooking

lu·tein \'lü-tē-ən, 'lü-,tēn\ *noun* (1869) : an orange xanthophyll $C_{40}H_{56}O_2$ occurring in plants, animal fat, egg yolk, and the corpus luteum

lu·tein·i·za·tion \,lü-tē-ə-nə-'zā-shən, ,lü-tē-nə-\ *noun* (1929) : the process of forming corpora lutea — **lu·tein·ize** \'lü-tē-ə-,nīz, 'lü-,tē-,nīz\ *verb*

luteinizing hormone *noun* (1931) : a hormone from the anterior lobe of the pituitary gland that in the female stimulates especially the development of corpora lutea and in the male the development of interstitial tissue in the testis

luteinizing hormone–releasing hormone *noun* (1970) : a hormone secreted by the hypothalamus that stimulates the pituitary gland to release gonadotropins (as luteinizing hormone and follicle-stimulating hormone) — called also *luteinizing hormone-releasing factor*

lu·te·nist *or* **lu·ta·nist** \'lü-tᵊn-ist, 'lüt-nist\ *noun* [Medieval Latin *lutanista*, from *lutana* lute, probably from Middle French *lut* lute] (1600) : a lute player

lu·teo·tro·pic \,lü-tē-ə-'trō-pik, -'trä-\ *or* **lu·teo·tro·phic** \-'trō-fik, -'trä-\ *adjective* (1941) : acting on the corpora lutea

luteotropic hormone *or* **luteotrophic hormone** *noun* (1949) : PROLACTIN

lu·teo·tro·pin \,lü-tē-ə-'trō-pən\ *or* **lu·teo·tro·phin** \-fən\ *noun* (1941) : PROLACTIN

lu·te·ous \'lü-tē-əs\ *adjective* [Latin *luteus* yellow, from *lutum*, a plant (*Reseda luteola*) used for dyeing yellow] (1657) : yellow tinged with green or brown

lute-string \'lüt-(,)striŋ\ *noun* [by folk etymology from Italian *lustrino* glossy fabric, from *lustro* luster] (1661) : a plain glossy silk formerly much used for women's dresses and ribbons

lu·te·tium *also* **lu·te·cium** \lü-'tē-sh(ē-)əm\ *noun* [New Latin, from Latin *Lutetia*, ancient name of Paris] (1907) : a metallic element of the rare-earth group — see ELEMENT table

¹Lu·ther·an \'lü-th(ə-)rən\ *noun* (1521) : a member of a Lutheran church

²Lutheran *adjective* (1530) **1** : of or relating to religious doctrines (as justification by faith alone) developed by Martin Luther or his followers **2** : of or relating to the Protestant churches adhering to Lutheran doctrines, liturgy, and polity — **Lu·ther·an·ism** \-rə-,ni-zəm\ *noun*

lu·thi·er \'lü-tē-ər, -the-ər\ *noun* [French, from *luth* lute (from Middle French *lut*)] (1879) : one who makes stringed musical instruments (as violins or guitars)

lutz \'ləts\ *noun* [probably irregular from Gustave *Lussi* (born 1898) Swiss figure skater] (1938) : a figure-skating jump from the outer edge of one skate with a full turn in the air and a return to the outer edge of the other skate

Lu·wi·an \'lü-ē-ən\ *noun* [*Luwi*, an ancient people of the southern coast of Asia Minor] (1924) : an Anatolian language of the Indo-European language family — see INDO-EUROPEAN LANGUAGES table — **Luwian** *adjective*

lux \'ləks\ *noun, plural* **lux** *or* **lux·es** [Latin, light — more at LIGHT] (1889) : a unit of illumination equal to the direct illumination on a surface that is everywhere one meter from a uniform point source of one candle intensity or equal to one lumen per square meter

lux·a·tion \,lək-'sā-shən\ *noun* [Late Latin *luxation-, luxatio*, from Latin *luxare* to dislocate, from *luxus* dislocated — more at LOCK] (1552)

\ə\ **abut** \ᵊ\ **kitten** \ər\ **further** \a\ **ash** \ā\ **ace** \ä\ **mop, mar** \aù\ **out** \ch\ **chin** \e\ **bet** \ē\ **easy** \g\ **go** \i\ **hit** \ī\ **ice** \j\ **job** \ŋ\ **sing** \ō\ **go** \ò\ **law** \òi\ **boy** \th\ **thin** \th\ **the** \ü\ **loot** \ù\ **foot** \y\ **yet** \zh\ **vision** *see also* Guide to Pronunciation

luxe : dislocation of an anatomical part (as a bone at a joint or the lens of the eye)

luxe \'lùks, 'ləks, 'lüks\ *noun* [French, from Latin *luxus* — more at LUXURY] (1558)
: LUXURY
— **luxe** *adjective*

lux·u·ri·ance \(,)ləg-'zhùr-ē-ən(t)s, (,) lək-'shùr-\ *noun* (circa 1746)
: the quality or state of being luxuriant

lux·u·ri·ant \-ē-ənt\ *adjective* (circa 1540)
1 a : yielding abundantly : FERTILE, FRUITFUL **b** : characterized by abundant growth : LUSH
2 : abundantly and often extravagantly rich and varied : PROLIFIC
3 : characterized by luxury : LUXURIOUS
synonym see PROFUSE
— **lux·u·ri·ant·ly** *adverb*

lux·u·ri·ate \-ē-,āt\ *intransitive verb* **-at·ed; -at·ing** [Latin *luxuriatus*, past participle of *luxuriare*, from *luxuria*] (1621)
1 a : to grow profusely : THRIVE **b** : to develop extensively
2 : to indulge oneself luxuriously : REVEL

lux·u·ri·ous \(,)ləg-'zhùr-ē-əs, (,)lək-'shùr-\ *adjective* (14th century)
1 : LECHEROUS
2 : marked by or given to self-indulgence ⟨*luxurious* tastes⟩ ⟨*luxurious* feeling⟩
3 : of, relating to, or marked by luxury ⟨*luxurious* accommodations⟩
4 : of the finest and richest kind ⟨*luxurious* cashmeres⟩ ⟨a *luxurious* chocolate sauce⟩
synonym see SENSUOUS
— **lux·u·ri·ous·ly** *adverb*
— **lux·u·ri·ous·ness** *noun*

lux·u·ry \'lək-sh(ə-)rē, -zh(ə-)rē\ *noun, plural* **-ries** [Middle English *luxurie*, from Middle French, from Latin *luxuria* rankness, luxury, excess; akin to Latin *luxus* luxury, excess] (14th century)
1 *archaic* : LECHERY, LUST
2 : a condition of abundance or great ease and comfort : sumptuous environment ⟨lived in *luxury*⟩
3 a : something adding to pleasure or comfort but not absolutely necessary **b** : an indulgence in something that provides pleasure, satisfaction, or ease ⟨had the *luxury* of rejecting a handful of job offers . . . before accepting a choice assignment —Terri Minsky⟩
— **luxury** *adjective*

lwei \lə-'wä\ *noun, plural* **lwei** *also* **lweis** [probably from *Lwei* (Lué), name of several rivers in Angola] (circa 1979)
— see *kwanza* at MONEY table

ly- *or* **lyo-** *combining form* [International Scientific Vocabulary, from Greek *lyein* to loosen, dissolve — more at LOSE]
1 : degrading : reduction ⟨*ly*ase⟩
2 : dispersed state : dispersion ⟨*ly*ophilic⟩

¹-ly \lē\ *in some dialects, especially British, Southern, New England, often* li *but not shown at individual entries\ adjective suffix* [Middle English, from Old English *-līc, -lic;* akin to Old High German *-līh, -lic,* Old English *līc* body — more at LIKE]
1 : like in appearance, manner, or nature : having the characteristics of ⟨queen*ly*⟩ ⟨father*ly*⟩
2 : characterized by regular recurrence in (specified) units of time : every ⟨hour*ly*⟩

²-ly *adverb suffix* [Middle English, from Old English *-līce, -lice,* from *-līc,* adjective suffix]
1 a : in a (specified) manner ⟨slow*ly*⟩ **b** : at a (specified) time interval ⟨annual*ly*⟩
2 : from a (specified) point of view ⟨eschatological*ly*⟩
3 : with respect to ⟨part*ly*⟩
4 : to a (specified) degree ⟨relative*ly*⟩
5 : in a (specified) place in a series ⟨second*ly*⟩

ly·am–hound \'lī-əm-,haùnd\ *or* **lyme–hound** \'līm-,haùnd\ *noun* [obsolete *lyam* leash] (1527)
archaic : BLOODHOUND

ly·art \'lī-ərt\ *adjective* [Middle English, from Middle French *liart*] (14th century) *chiefly Scottish* : streaked with gray : GRAY

ly·ase \'lī-,ās, -,āz\ *noun* (1965)
: an enzyme (as a decarboxylase) that forms double bonds by removing groups from a substrate other than by hydrolysis or that adds groups to double bonds

ly·can·thro·py \lī-'kan(t)-thrə-pē\ *noun* [New Latin *lycanthropia,* from Greek *lykanthrōpia,* from *lykanthrōpos* werewolf, from *lykos* wolf + *anthrōpos* human being — more at WOLF] (1594)
1 : a delusion that one has become a wolf
2 : the assumption of the form and characteristics of a wolf held to be possible by witchcraft or magic

ly·cée \lē-'sā\ *noun* [French, from Middle French, *lyceum,* from Latin *Lyceum*] (1865)
: a French public secondary school that prepares students for the university

ly·ce·um \lī-'sē-əm, 'lī-sē-\ *noun* [Latin *Lyceum,* gymnasium near Athens where Aristotle taught, from Greek *Lykeion,* from neuter of *lykeios,* epithet of Apollo] (1786)
1 : a hall for public lectures or discussions
2 : an association providing public lectures, concerts, and entertainments
3 : LYCÉE

ly·chee *variant of* LITCHI

lych–gate \'lich-,gāt\ *noun* [Middle English *lycheyate,* from *lich* body, corpse (from Old English *līc*) + *gate, yate* gate] (15th century)
: a roofed gate in a churchyard under which a bier rests during the initial part of the burial service

lych·nis \'lik-nəs\ *noun* [New Latin, from Latin, a red flower, from Greek; akin to Greek *lychnos* lamp, Latin *lux* light — more at LIGHT] (1601)
: any of a genus (*Lychnis*) of herbs of the pink family with terminal cymes of showy mostly red or white flowers having 5 or rarely 4 styles

Ly·cian \'li-sh(ē-)ən\ *noun* (1598)
1 : a native or inhabitant of Lycia
2 : an Anatolian language of the Indo-European language family — see INDO-EUROPEAN LANGUAGES table
— **Lycian** *adjective*

ly·co·pene \'lī-kə-,pēn\ *noun* [International Scientific Vocabulary *lycop-* (from New Latin *Lycopersicon,* genus of herbs) + *-ene*] (circa 1929)
: a carotenoid pigment $C_{40}H_{56}$ that is the red coloring matter of the tomato

ly·co·pod \'lī-kə-,päd\ *noun* [New Latin *Lycopodium*] (1861)
: LYCOPODIUM 1; *broadly* : CLUB MOSS

ly·co·po·di·um \,lī-kə-'pō-dē-əm\ *noun* [New Latin, from Greek *lykos* wolf + *podion,* diminutive of *pod-, pous* foot — more at FOOT] (circa 1706)
1 : any of a large genus (*Lycopodium*) of erect or creeping club mosses with reduced or scale-like evergreen leaves
2 : a fine yellowish flammable powder composed of lycopodium spores and used especially in pharmacy

Ly·cra \'lī-krə\ *trademark*
— used for a spandex synthetic fiber

lydd·ite \'li-,dīt\ *noun* [*Lydd,* England] (1888)
: a high explosive composed chiefly of picric acid

Lyd·i·an \'li-dē-ən\ *noun* (15th century)
1 : a native or inhabitant of Lydia
2 : an Anatolian language of the Indo-European language family — see INDO-EUROPEAN LANGUAGES table
— **Lydian** *adjective*

lye \'lī\ *noun* [Middle English, from Old English *lēag;* akin to Old High German *louga* lye, Latin *lavare, lavere* to wash, Greek *louein*] (before 12th century)
1 : a strong alkaline liquor rich in potassium carbonate leached from wood ashes and used especially in making soap and washing; *broadly* : a strong alkaline solution (as of sodium hydroxide or potassium hydroxide)
2 : a solid caustic (as sodium hydroxide)

ly·gus bug \'lī-gəs-\ *noun* [New Latin *Lygus*] (1940)
: any of various small sucking bugs (genus *Lygus*) including some pests of cultivated plants

¹ly·ing \'lī-in\ *present participle of* LIE

²lying *adjective* [Middle English *leghynge,* present participle of *lien* to lie] (14th century)
: marked by or containing falsehoods : FALSE ⟨a *lying* account of the accident⟩

ly·ing–in \,lī-in-'in\ *noun, plural* **lyings–in** *or* **lying–ins** (15th century)
: the state attending and consequent to childbirth : CONFINEMENT

Lyme disease \'līm-\ *noun* [*Lyme,* Connecticut, where it was first reported] (1980)
: an acute inflammatory disease that is caused by a spirochete (*Borrelia burgdorferi*) transmitted by ticks (genus *Ixodes* and especially *I. dammini*), that is often characterized initially by a spreading red annular skin lesion at the site of the infection, fever, and chills, and that may result in joint pain, arthritis, and cardiac and neurological disorders

lymph \'lim(p)f\ *noun* [Latin *lympha,* water goddess, water, perhaps modification of Greek *nymphē* nymph — more at NUPTIAL] (circa 1673)
1 *archaic* : the sap of plants
2 [New Latin *lympha,* from Latin, water] : a pale coagulable fluid that bathes the tissues, passes into lymphatic channels and ducts, is discharged into the blood by way of the thoracic duct, and consists of a liquid portion resembling blood plasma and containing white blood cells but normally no red blood cells

lymph- *or* **lympho-** *combining form* [New Latin *lympha*]
: lymph : lymphatic tissue ⟨*lympho*granuloma⟩

lymph·ad·e·ni·tis \,lim-,fa-d°n-'ī-təs\ *noun* [New Latin, from *lymphaden* lymph gland, from *lymph-* + Greek *adēn* gland — more at ADEN-] (1860)
: inflammation of lymph nodes

lymph·ade·nop·a·thy \,lim-,fa-d°n-'ä-pə-thē\ *noun, plural* **-thies** (1920)
: abnormal enlargement of the lymph nodes

lymph·an·gi·og·ra·phy \,lim-,fan-jē-'ä-grə-fē\ *noun* (circa 1941)
: X-ray depiction of lymph vessels and nodes after use of a radiopaque material — called also *lymphography*
— **lymph·an·gio·gram** \(,)lim-'fan-jē-ə-,gram\ *noun*
— **lymph·an·gio·graph·ic** \,lim-,fan-jē-ə-'gra-fik\ *adjective*

¹lym·phat·ic \lim-'fa-tik\ *adjective* (1649)
1 a : of, relating to, or produced by lymph, lymphoid tissue, or lymphocytes **b** : conveying lymph
2 : lacking physical or mental energy : SLUGGISH
— **lym·phat·i·cal·ly** \-ti-k(ə-)lē\ *adverb*

²lymphatic *noun* (1667)
: a vessel that contains or conveys lymph — called also *lymph vessel*

lymph gland *noun* (circa 1858)
: LYMPH NODE

lymph node *noun* (1892)
: any of the rounded masses of lymphoid tissue that are surrounded by a capsule of connective tissue, are distributed along the lymphatic vessels, and contain numerous lymphocytes which filter the flow of lymph

lym·pho·blast \'lim(p)-fə-,blast\ *noun* [International Scientific Vocabulary] (circa 1909)
: a lymphocyte that has enlarged following stimulation by an antigen, has the capacity to recognize the stimulating antigen, and is undergoing proliferation and differentiation either to an effector state in which it functions to eliminate the antigen or to a memory state in which it functions to recognize the future reappearance of the antigen

— lym·pho·blas·tic \,lim(p)-fə-'blas-tik\ *adjective*

lym·pho·cyte \'lim(p)-fə-,sīt\ *noun* [International Scientific Vocabulary] (1890)
: any of the colorless weakly motile cells originating from stem cells and differentiating in lymphoid tissue (as of the thymus or bone marrow) that are the typical cellular elements of lymph, include the cellular mediators of immunity, and constitute 20 to 30 percent of the leukocytes of normal human blood — compare B CELL, T CELL

— lym·pho·cyt·ic \,lim(p)-fə-'si-tik\ *adjective*

lymphocytic cho·rio·men·in·gi·tis \-,kȯr-ē-ō-,me-nən-'jī-təs\ *noun* [New Latin *choriomeningitis* cerebral meningitis, from *chorio-* of a membrane resembling the chorion] (1934)
: an acute virus disease that is characterized by fever, nausea and vomiting, headache, stiff neck, and slow pulse, is marked by the presence of numerous lymphocytes in the cerebrospinal fluid, and is transmitted especially by rodents and bloodsucking insects

lym·pho·cy·to·sis \,lim(p)-fə-,sī-'tō-səs, -fə-sə-\ *noun* [New Latin, from International Scientific Vocabulary *lymphocyte*] (1896)
: an increase in the number of lymphocytes in the blood usually associated with chronic infections or inflammations

lym·pho·gran·u·lo·ma \'lim(p)-fō-,gran-yə-'lō-mə\ *noun, plural* **-mas** *or* **-ma·ta** \-mə-tə\ [New Latin] (1924)
: LYMPHOGRANULOMA VENEREUM

lymphogranuloma in·gui·na·le \-,iŋ-gwə-'nä-lē, -'na-, -'nä-\ *noun* [New Latin, inguinal lymphogranuloma] (1932)
: LYMPHOGRANULOMA VENEREUM

lym·pho·gran·u·lo·ma·to·sis \-,lō-mə-'tō-səs\ *noun, plural* **-to·ses** \-,sēz\ [New Latin *lymphogranulomat-*, *lymphogranuloma* + *-osis*] (1911)
: the development of benign or malignant nodular swellings of lymph nodes in various parts of the body; *also* : a condition characterized by these

lymphogranuloma ve·ne·re·um \-və-'nir-ē-əm\ *noun* [New Latin, venereal lymphogranuloma] (1938)
: a contagious venereal disease caused by various strains of a chlamydia (*Chlamydia trachomatis*) and marked by swelling and ulceration of lymphatic tissue in the iliac and inguinal regions

lym·phog·ra·phy \lim-'fä-grə-fē\ *noun* (circa 1935)
: LYMPHANGIOGRAPHY

— lym·pho·gram \'lim(p)-fə-,gram\ *noun*
— lym·pho·graph·ic \,lim-fə-'gra-fik\ *adjective*

lym·phoid \'lim-,fȯid\ *adjective* (1867)
1 : of, relating to, or being tissue (as of the lymph nodes or thymus) containing lymphocytes
2 : of, relating to, or resembling lymph

lym·pho·kine \'lim(p)-fə-,kīn\ *noun* [*lymph-* + -kine, from Greek *kinein* to move about — more at -KINESIS] (1969)
: any of various substances (as interleukin-2) of low molecular weight that are not immunoglobulins, are secreted by T cells in response to stimulation by antigens, and have a role (as the activation of macrophages or the enhancement or inhibition of antibody production) in cell-mediated immunity

lym·pho·ma \lim-'fō-mə\ *noun, plural* **-mas** *or* **-ma·ta** \-mə-tə\ [New Latin] (1873)
: a tumor of lymphoid tissue
— lym·pho·ma·tous \-mə-təs\ *adjective*

lym·pho·ma·to·sis \(,)lim-,fō-mə-'tō-səs\ *noun, plural* **-to·ses** \-,sēz\ [New Latin *lymphomat-*, *lymphoma* + *-osis*] (circa 1900)
: the presence of multiple lymphomas in the body

lym·pho·sar·co·ma \,lim(p)-fə-sär-'kō-mə\ *noun, plural* **-mas** *or* **-ma·ta** \-mə-tə\ [New Latin] (1874)
: a malignant lymphoma that tends to metastasize freely especially along the regional lymphatic drainage

lynch \'linch\ *transitive verb* [lynch law] (1836)
: to put to death (as by hanging) by mob action without legal sanction ◇
— lynch·er *noun*

lynch law *noun* [William *Lynch* (died 1820) American vigilante] (1811)
: the punishment of presumed crimes or offenses usually by death without due process of law

lynch·pin *variant of* LINCHPIN

lynx \'liŋ(k)s\ *noun, plural* **lynx** *or* **lynx·es** [Middle English, from Latin, from Greek; akin to Old English *lox* lynx and probably to Greek *leukos* white — more at LIGHT] (14th century)
: any of several wildcats (genus *Lynx*) with relatively long legs, a short stubby tail, mottled coat, and often tufted ears: as **a** : a lynx (*L. lynx*) of northern Europe and Asia **b** : BOBCAT **c** : a North American lynx (*L. canadensis*) distinguished from the bobcat by its larger size, longer tufted ears, and wholly black tail tip — called also *Canadian lynx*

lynx–eyed \'liŋ(k)s-,īd\ *adjective* (1597)
: SHARP-SIGHTED

lyo- — see LY-

ly·on·naise \,lī-ə-'nāz\ *adjective* [French (*à la*) *lyonnaise* in the manner of Lyons, France] (1846)
: prepared with onions ⟨*lyonnaise* potatoes⟩

Ly·on·nesse \,lī-ə-'nes\ *noun*
: a country that according to Arthurian legend was contiguous to Cornwall before sinking beneath the sea

lyo·phile \'lī-ə-,fīl\ *adjective* [International Scientific Vocabulary] (1934)
1 : of or relating to freeze-drying
2 *or* **lyo·philed** \-,fīld\ : obtained by freeze-drying

lyo·phil·ic \,lī-ə-'fi-lik\ *adjective* (1911)
: marked by strong affinity between a dispersed phase and the liquid in which it is dispersed ⟨a *lyophilic* colloid⟩

ly·oph·i·lise *British variant of* LYOPHILIZE

ly·oph·i·lize \lī-'ä-fə-,līz\ *transitive verb* **-lized; -liz·ing** (1938)
: FREEZE-DRY
— ly·oph·i·li·za·tion \-,ä-fə-lə-'zā-shən\ *noun*
— ly·oph·i·liz·er \-'ä-fə-,lī-zər\ *noun*

lyo·pho·bic \,lī-ə-'fō-bik\ *adjective* (1911)
: marked by lack of strong affinity between a dispersed phase and the liquid in which it is dispersed ⟨a *lyophobic* colloid⟩

Ly·ra \'lī-rə\ *noun* [Latin (genitive *Lyrae*), literally, lyre]
: a northern constellation representing the lyre of Orpheus or Mercury and containing Vega

ly·rate \'lī-,rāt\ *adjective* (circa 1760)
: having or suggesting the shape of a lyre ⟨the *lyrate* horns of the impala⟩

lyre \'līr\ *noun* [Middle English *lire*, from Old French, from Latin *lyra*, from Greek] (13th century)
1 : a stringed instrument of the harp class used by the ancient Greeks especially to accompany song and recitation
2 *capitalized* : LYRA

lyre 1

lyre·bird \-,bərd\ *noun* (1834)
: either of two Australian passerine birds (genus *Menura*) distinguished in the male by very long tail feathers displayed in the shape of a lyre during courtship

¹lyr·ic \'lir-ik\ *noun* (1581)
1 : a lyric composition; *specifically* : a lyric poem
2 : the words of a song — often used in plural

²lyric *adjective* [Middle French or Latin; Middle French *lyrique*, from Latin *lyricus*, from Greek *lyrikos*, from *lyra*] (1589)
1 a : suitable for singing to the lyre or for being set to music and sung **b** : of, relating to, or being drama set to music; *especially* : OPERATIC ⟨*lyric* stage⟩
2 a : expressing direct usually intense personal emotion especially in a manner suggestive of song ⟨*lyric* poetry⟩ **b** : EXUBERANT, RHAPSODIC
3 *of an opera singer* : having a light voice and a melodic style — compare DRAMATIC

lyr·i·cal \'lir-i-kəl\ *adjective* (1581)
: LYRIC
— lyr·i·cal·ly \-i-k(ə-)lē\ *adverb*
— lyr·i·cal·ness \-kəl-nəs\ *noun*

lyr·i·cism \'lir-ə-,si-zəm\ *noun* (1760)
1 : the quality or state of being lyric : SONGFULNESS
2 a : an intense personal quality expressive of feeling or emotion in an art (as poetry or music) **b** : EXUBERANCE ⟨the sort of author who inspires *lyricism* or invective, not judicious interpretation —*Time*⟩

lyr·i·cist \-sist\ *noun* (1881)
: a writer of lyrics

lyr·ism \'lir-,i-zəm\ *noun* (1859)
: LYRICISM

lyr·ist *noun* (circa 1656)
1 \'līr-ist\ : a player on the lyre
2 \'lir-ist\ : LYRICIST

lys- *or* **lysi-** *or* **lyso-** *combining form* [New Latin, from Greek *lys-*, *lysi-* loosening, from *lysis*]
: lysis ⟨*lysin*⟩

ly·sate \'lī-,sāt\ *noun* (1922)
: a product of lysis

lyse \'līs, 'līz\ *verb* **lysed; lys·ing** [back-formation from New Latin *lysis*] (1924)
transitive verb
: to cause to undergo lysis
intransitive verb
: to undergo lysis

-lyse *chiefly British variant of* -LYZE

Ly·sen·ko·ism \lə-'seŋ-kō-,i-zəm\ *noun* [Trofim *Lysenko*] (1948)
: a biological doctrine asserting the fundamental influence of somatic and environmental factors on heredity in contradiction of orthodox genetics

◇ **WORD HISTORY**
lynch Despite the claims made on behalf of numerous other Lynches, the weight of evidence for the eponymous word *lynch* falls on the side of Captain William Lynch (1742–1820). Lynch served with the Virginia militia and presided over a self-created tribunal that was organized to rid Pittsylvania County of a band of troublesome ruffians that had eluded the civil authorities. On 22 September 1780, Lynch and others entered into a compact stating their goals, reasons, and methods. Captain Lynch and his vigilantes became known as "lynch-men," and by 1782 their judicial code had become known as *lynch's law* and subsequently *lynch law*. By 1836 *lynch law* had given rise to the verb *lynch* in its modern meaning.

\ə\ abut \ᵊ\ kitten \ər\ further \a\ ash \ā\ ace \ä\ mop, mar \aú\ out \ch\ chin \e\ bet \ē\ easy \g\ go \i\ hit \ī\ ice \j\ job \ŋ\ sing \ō\ go \ȯ\ law \ȯi\ boy \th\ thin \th\ the \ü\ loot \ú\ foot \y\ yet \zh\ vision *see also* Guide to Pronunciation

ly·ser·gic acid \lə-'sər-jik-, (,)lī-\ *noun* [*lys-* + *ergot*] (1934)
: a crystalline acid $C_{16}H_{16}N_2O_2$ from ergotic alkaloids; *also* : LSD

lysergic acid di·eth·yl·am·ide \-,dī-,e-thə-'la-,mīd\ *noun* (1944)
: LSD

ly·sim·e·ter \lī-'si-mə-tər\ *noun* (1879)
: a device for measuring the percolation of water through soils and for determining the soluble constituents removed in the drainage
— **ly·si·met·ric** \,lī-sə-'me-trik\ *adjective*

ly·sin \'lī-sᵊn\ *noun* (1900)
: a substance (as an antibody) capable of causing lysis

ly·sine \'lī-,sēn\ *noun* (1892)
: a crystalline essential amino acid $C_6H_{14}N_2O_2$ obtained from the hydrolysis of various proteins

ly·sis \'lī-səs\ *noun, plural* **ly·ses** \-,sēz\ [New Latin, from Greek, act of loosening, dissolution, remission of fever, from *lyein* to loosen — more at LOSE] (1543)
1 : the gradual decline of a disease process (as fever)
2 : a process of disintegration or dissolution (as of cells)

-lysis *noun combining form, plural* **-lyses** [New Latin, from Latin & Greek; Latin, loosening, from Greek, from *lysis*]
1 : decomposition ⟨electro*lysis*⟩
2 : disintegration : breaking down ⟨auto*lysis*⟩

ly·so·gen \'lī-sə-jən\ *noun* (circa 1934)
: a lysogenic bacterium or bacterial strain

ly·so·gen·ic \,lī-sə-'je-nik\ *adjective* [from the capacity of the prophage to lyse other bacteria] (1899)
1 : harboring a prophage as hereditary material ⟨*lysogenic* bacteria⟩
2 : TEMPERATE 3 ⟨*lysogenic* viruses⟩
— **ly·so·ge·nic·i·ty** \-jə-'ni-sə-tē\ *noun*

ly·sog·e·nise *British variant of* LYSOGENIZE

ly·sog·e·nize \lī-'sä-jə-,nīz\ *transitive verb* **-nized; -niz·ing** (1953)
: to render lysogenic
— **ly·sog·e·ni·za·tion** \-,sä-jə-nə-'zā-shən\ *noun*

ly·sog·e·ny \lī-'sä-jə-nē\ *noun* (1956)
: the state of being lysogenic

ly·so·lec·i·thin \,lī-sə-'le-sə-thən\ *noun* (1923)
: a hydrolytic substance formed by the enzymatic hydrolysis (as by some snake venoms) of a lecithin

ly·so·some \'lī-sə-,sōm\ *noun* [International Scientific Vocabulary *lys-* + ³*-some*] (1955)
: a saclike cellular organelle that contains various hydrolytic enzymes — see CELL illustration
— **ly·so·som·al** \,lī-sə-'sō-məl\ *adjective*

ly·so·zyme \'lī-sə-,zīm\ *noun* (1922)
: a basic bacteriolytic protein that hydrolyzes peptidoglycan and is present in egg white and in human tears and saliva

-lyte *noun combining form* [Greek *lytos* that may be untied, soluble, from *lyein*]
: substance capable of undergoing (such) decomposition ⟨electro*lyte*⟩

lyt·ic \'li-tik\ *adjective* [Greek *lytikos* able to loose, from *lyein*] (1889)
: of or relating to lysis or a lysin; *also* : productive of or effecting lysis (as of cells)
— **ly·ti·cal·ly** \-ti-k(ə-)lē\ *adverb*

-lytic *adjective suffix* [Greek *lytikos*]
: of, relating to, or effecting (such) decomposition ⟨hydro*lytic*⟩

-lyze *verb combining form* **-lyzed; -lyzing** [International Scientific Vocabulary, probably irregular from New Latin *-lysis*]
: produce or undergo lytic disintegration or dissolution ⟨electro*lyze*⟩

M

M *is the thirteenth letter of the English alphabet. It comes through the Latin, via Etruscan, from the Greek* mu, *which took it from the Phoenician* mêm. *Its sound is that of a bilabial continuant, a sound formed by stopping the oral passage of air at the lips and allowing it to continue through the nose, giving the sound a nasal resonance. (For this reason* M *is also classified as a nasal consonant).* M *is silent only when initial before* n *in several words from Greek, as* mnemonic. *In related languages, English* m *corresponds to German* m, *Latin* m *or* n, *Greek* m *or* n, *and Sanskrit* m, *as in English* mouse, *German* Maus, *Latin* mus, *Greek* mys, *Sanskrit* mus; *and English* come, *German* kommen, *Latin* venire, *Greek* bainein, *Sanskrit* gamati *(goes). Small* m *developed by a rounding of the sharp angles and a reduction in size of the capital form of the letter.*

m \'em\ *noun, plural* **m's** *or* **ms** \'emz\ *often capitalized, often attributive* (before 12th century)
1 a : the 13th letter of the English alphabet **b :** a graphic representation of this letter **c :** a speech counterpart of orthographic *m*
2 : one thousand — see NUMBER table
3 : a graphic device for reproducing the letter *m*
4 : one designated *m* especially as the 13th in order or class
5 : something shaped like the letter M
6 a : EM 2 **b :** PICA 2
'm \m\ *verb* (circa 1594)
: AM ⟨I'*m* going⟩
ma \'mä, 'mò\ *noun* [short for *mama*] (1829)
: MOTHER
ma'am \'mam, *after* "yes" *often* əm\ *noun* (1668)
: MADAM
ma–and–pa \,mä-ən-'pä, ,mò-ən-'pò\ *adjective* (1965)
: MOM-AND-POP
Mab \'mab\ *noun*
: a queen of fairies in English literature
mabe pearl \'mäb-\ *noun* [origin unknown] (1952)
: a cultured pearl essentially hemispherical in form — called also **mabe**
mac \'mak\ *noun* (1901)
British **:** MACKINTOSH
Mac \'mak\ *noun* [*Mac-, Mc-,* patronymic prefix in Scottish and Irish surnames] (circa 1937)
: FELLOW — used informally to address a man whose name is not known
ma·ca·bre \mə-'käb; -'kä-brə, -bər; -'käbr°\ *adjective* [French, from (*danse*) *macabre* dance of death, from Middle French (*danse de*) *Macabré*] (1889)
1 : having death as a subject **:** comprising or including a personalized representation of death
2 : dwelling on the gruesome
3 : tending to produce horror in a beholder
synonym see GHASTLY
mac·ad·am \mə-'ka-dəm\ *noun* [John L. *McAdam* (died 1836) British engineer] (1824)
: macadamized roadway or pavement especially with a bituminous binder ◇
mac·a·da·mia nut \,ma-kə-'dä-mē-ə-\ *noun* [New Latin *Macadamia,* from John *Macadam* (died 1865) Australian chemist] (1929)
: a hard-shelled nut somewhat resembling a filbert and produced by an Australian evergreen tree (*Macadamia integrifolia*) of the protea family that is cultivated extensively in Hawaii — called also **macadamia**
mac·ad·am·ize \mə-'ka-də-,mīz\ *transitive verb* **-ized; -iz·ing** (1826)

: to construct or finish (a road) by compacting into a solid mass a layer of small broken stone on a convex well-drained roadbed and using a binder (as cement or asphalt) for the mass
ma·caque \mə-'kak, -'käk\ *noun* [French, from Portuguese *macaco*] (1757)
: any of a genus (*Macaca*) of chiefly Asian monkeys typically having a sturdy build and including some short-tailed or tailless forms; *especially* **:** RHESUS MONKEY
mac·a·ro·ni \,ma-kə-'rō-nē\ *noun* [Italian *maccheroni,* plural of *maccherone,* from Italian dialect *maccarone* dumpling, macaroni] (1599)
1 : pasta made from semolina and shaped in the form of slender tubes
2 *plural* **macaronis** *or* **macaronies a :** a member of a class of traveled young Englishmen of the late 18th and early 19th centuries who affected foreign ways **b :** an affected young man **:** FOP
mac·a·ron·ic \-'rä-nik\ *adjective* [New Latin *macaronicus,* from Italian dialect *maccarone* macaroni] (1638)
1 : characterized by a mixture of vernacular words with Latin words or with non-Latin words having Latin endings
2 : characterized by a mixture of two languages
— **macaronic** *noun*
mac·a·roon \,ma-kə-'rün\ *noun* [French *macaron,* from Italian dialect *maccarone*] (circa 1611)
: a small cookie composed chiefly of egg whites, sugar, and ground almonds or coconut
ma·caw \mə-'kò\ *noun* [Portuguese *macau*] (1668)
: any of numerous parrots (especially genus *Ara*) of South and Central America including some of the largest and showiest of parrots

macaw

Mac·beth \mək-'beth, mak-\ *noun*
: a Scottish general who is the protagonist of Shakespeare's tragedy *Macbeth*
Mac·ca·bees \'ma-kə-(,)bēz\ *noun plural* [Greek *Makkabaioi,* from plural of *Makkabaios,* surname of Judas Maccabaeus 2d century B.C. Jewish patriot] (1702)
1 : a priestly family leading a Jewish revolt begun in 168 B.C. against Hellenism and Syrian rule and reigning over Palestine from 142 B.C. to 63 B.C.
2 *singular in construction* **:** either of two narrative and historical books included in the Ro-

man Catholic canon of the Old Testament and in the Protestant Apocrypha — see BIBLE table
— **Mac·ca·be·an** \,ma-kə-'bē-ən\ *adjective*
¹mace \'mās\ *noun* [Middle English, from Middle French *macis,* from Latin *macir,* an East Indian spice, from Greek *makir*] (13th century)
: an aromatic spice consisting of the dried external fibrous covering of a nutmeg
²mace *noun* [Middle English, from Old French, from (assumed) Vulgar Latin *mattia;* akin to Latin *mateola* mallet] (14th century)
1 a : a heavy often spiked staff or club used especially in the Middle Ages for breaking armor **b :** a club used as a weapon
2 a : an ornamental staff borne as a symbol of authority before a public official or a legislative body **b :** one who carries a mace
³mace *transitive verb* **maced; mac·ing** (1968)
: to attack with the liquid Mace
Mace \'mās\ *trademark*
— used for a temporarily disabling liquid usually used as a spray
ma·cé·doine \,ma-sə-'dwän\ *noun* [French, from *Macédoine* Macedonia; perhaps from the mixture of ethnic groups in Macedonia] (1820)
1 : a confused mixture **:** MEDLEY
2 : a mixture of fruits or vegetables served as a salad or cocktail or in a jellied dessert or used in a sauce or as a garnish
Mac·e·do·nian \,ma-sə-'dō-nyən, -nē-ən\ *noun* (1582)
1 : a native or inhabitant of Macedonia
2 : the Slavic language of modern Macedonia
3 : the language of ancient Macedonia of uncertain affinity but generally assumed to be Indo-European
mac·er·ate \'ma-sə-,rāt\ *verb* **-at·ed; -at·ing** [Latin *maceratus,* past participle of *macerare* to soften, steep] (1547)
transitive verb
1 : to cause to waste away by or as if by excessive fasting
2 : to cause to become soft or separated into constituent elements by or as if by steeping in fluid; *broadly* **:** STEEP, SOAK
intransitive verb
: to soften and wear away especially as a result of being wetted or steeped
— **mac·er·a·tion** \,ma-sə-'rā-shən\ *noun*
— **mac·er·a·tor** \'ma-sə-,rā-tər\ *noun*

◇ **WORD HISTORY**
macadam *Macadam* is named after the Scottish engineer John Loudon McAdam (1756–1836). Concerned about the poor condition of Scotland's roads at the end of the 18th century, McAdam studied the problem for a decade and a half. He concluded that roads constructed of small, similarly sized fragments of stone could withstand years of heavy traffic. Upon his appointment as surveyor-general of roads in Bristol in 1815, he began to put his theories into practice. By 1823 the superiority of his paving process was generally recognized, and four years later he was named surveyor-general of roads for Great Britain and was even offered a knighthood. His name evolved into a lowercase, generic noun, the spelling eventually undergoing alteration to produce a more conventional-looking word. McAdam's name also survives, albeit rather covertly, in *tarmac,* shortened from *tarmacadam,* which designates a road surfacing that incorporates a tar binder.

\ə\ **abut** \ə\ **kitten** \ər\ **further** \a\ **ash** \ā\ **ace**
\ä\ **mop, mar** \aú\ **out** \ch\ **chin** \e\ **bet** \ē\ **easy**
\g\ **go** \i\ **hit** \ī\ **ice** \j\ **job** \ŋ\ **sing** \ō\ **go**
\ò\ **law** \òi\ **boy** \th\ **thin** \t͟h\ **the** \ü\ **loot** \ú\ **foot**
\y\ **yet** \zh\ **vision** *see also* Guide to Pronunciation

Mach \'mäk\ *noun* [*Mach number*] (1946)
: a usually high speed expressed by a Mach number ⟨an airplane flying at *Mach* 2⟩

Mach·a·bees \'ma-kə-(,)bēz\ *noun plural but singular in construction* [Middle English, from Late Latin *Machabaei*, modification of Greek *Makkabaioi*] (14th century)
: MACCABEES

mâche \'mäsh\ *noun* [French, perhaps alteration of French dialect *pomache*, from (assumed) Vulgar Latin *pomasca*, from Latin *pomum* fruit] (1961)
: CORN SALAD

ma·chete \mə-'she-tē, -'che-; -'shet\ *noun* [Spanish] (1598)
: a large heavy knife used for cutting sugarcane and underbrush and as a weapon

Ma·chi·a·vel·lian \,ma-kē-ə-'ve-lē-ən, -'vel-yən\ *adjective* [Niccolo *Machiavelli*] (1579)
1 : of or relating to Machiavelli or Machiavellianism
2 : suggesting the principles of conduct laid down by Machiavelli; *specifically* : marked by cunning, duplicity, or bad faith
— **Machiavellian** *noun*

Ma·chi·a·vel·lian·ism \-'ve-lē-ə-,ni-zəm, -'vel-yə-,ni-zəm\ *noun* (1626)
: the political theory of Machiavelli; *especially* : the view that politics is amoral and that any means however unscrupulous can justifiably be used in achieving political power

ma·chic·o·la·tion \mə-,chi-kə-'lā-shən\ *noun* [Medieval Latin *machicolare* to furnish with machicolations, from Middle French *machicoller*, from *machicoleis* machicolation, from *macher* to crush + *col* neck, from Latin *collum* — more at COLLAR] (1788)
1 a : an opening between the corbels of a projecting parapet or in the floor of a gallery or roof of a portal for discharging missiles upon assailants below — see BATTLEMENT illustration **b** : a gallery or parapet containing such openings
2 : construction imitating medieval machicolation
— **ma·chic·o·lat·ed** \mə-'chi-kə-,lā-təd\ *adjective*

mach·i·nate \'ma-kə-,nāt, 'ma-shə-\ *verb* **-nat·ed; -nat·ing** [Latin *machinatus*, past participle of *machinari*, from *machina* machine, contrivance] (1600)
intransitive verb
: to plan or plot especially to do harm
transitive verb
: to scheme or contrive to bring about : PLOT
— **mach·i·na·tor** \-,nā-tər\ *noun*

mach·i·na·tion \,ma-kə-'nā-shən, ,ma-shə-\ *noun* (15th century)
1 : an act of machinating
2 : a scheming or crafty action or artful design intended to accomplish some usually evil end ⟨backstage *machinations* and power plays that have dominated the film industry —Peter Bogdanovich⟩
synonym see PLOT

¹ma·chine \mə-'shēn\ *noun, often attributive* [Middle French, from Latin *machina*, from Greek *mēchanē* (Doric dialect *machana*), from *mēchos* means, expedient — more at MAY] (circa 1545)
1 a *archaic* : a constructed thing whether material or immaterial **b** : CONVEYANCE, VEHICLE; *especially* : AUTOMOBILE **c** *archaic* : a military engine **d** : any of various apparatuses formerly used to produce stage effects **e** (1) : an assemblage of parts that transmit forces, motion, and energy one to another in a predetermined manner (2) : an instrument (as a lever) designed to transmit or modify the application of power, force, or motion **f** : a mechanically, electrically, or electronically operated device for performing a task ⟨a calculating *machine*⟩ ⟨a card-sorting *machine*⟩ **g** : a coin-operated device ⟨a cigarette *machine*⟩ **h** : MACHINERY — used with *the* or in plural

2 a : a living organism or one of its functional systems **b** : a person or organization that resembles a machine (as in being methodical, tireless, or unemotional) **c** (1) : a combination of persons acting together for a common end along with the agencies they use (2) : a highly organized political group under the leadership of a boss or small clique
3 : a literary device or contrivance introduced for dramatic effect

²machine *transitive verb* **ma·chined; ma·chin·ing** (circa 1864)
: to process by or as if by machine; *especially* : to reduce or finish by or as if by turning, shaping, planing, or milling by machine-operated tools
— **ma·chin·abil·i·ty** *also* **ma·chine·abil·i·ty** \-,shē-nə-'bi-lə-tē\ *noun*
— **ma·chin·able** *also* **ma·chine·able** \-'shē-nə-bəl\ *adjective*

ma·chine–gun \mə-'shēn-,gən\ *adjective* (1906)
: characterized by rapidity and sharpness : RAPID-FIRE ⟨a comic's *machine-gun* delivery⟩

machine gun *noun* (1870)
: a gun for sustained rapid fire that uses bullets; *broadly* : an automatic weapon
— **machine–gun** *verb*
— **machine gun·ner** *noun*

machine language *noun* (1949)
1 : the set of symbolic instruction codes usually in binary form that is used to represent operations and data in a machine (as a computer)
2 : ASSEMBLY LANGUAGE

ma·chine·like \mə-'shēn-,līk\ *adjective* (circa 1712)
: resembling a machine especially in regularity of action or stereotyped uniformity of product

machine pistol *noun* (1940)
: a usually small submachine gun

machine–readable *adjective* (1961)
: directly usable by a computer ⟨*machine-readable* text⟩

ma·chin·ery \mə-'shē-nə-rē, -'shēn-rē\ *noun, plural* **-er·ies** (1687)
1 a : machines in general or as a functioning unit **b** : the working parts of a machine
2 : the means or system by which something is kept in action or a desired result is obtained ⟨the *machinery* of government⟩ ⟨genetic *machinery* of cells⟩

machine shop *noun* (1827)
: a workshop in which work is machined to size and assembled

machine tool *noun* (1861)
: a machine designed for shaping solid work

ma·chin·ist \mə-'shē-nist\ *noun* (circa 1706)
1 a : a worker who fabricates, assembles, or repairs machinery **b** : a craftsman skilled in the use of machine tools **c** : one who operates a machine
2 *archaic* : a person in charge of the mechanical aspects of a theatrical production
3 : a warrant officer who supervises machinery and engine operation

ma·chis·mo \mä-'chēz-(,)mō, mə-, -'kēz-, -'kiz-, -'chiz-\ *noun* [Spanish, from *macho*] (1948)
1 : a strong sense of masculine pride : an exaggerated masculinity
2 : an exaggerated or exhilarating sense of power or strength

Mach number \'mäk-\ *noun* [Ernst *Mach* (died 1916) Austrian physicist] (1937)
: a number representing the ratio of the speed of a body (as an aircraft) to the speed of sound in a surrounding medium (as air)

¹ma·cho \'mä-(,)chō\ *adjective* [Spanish, literally, male, from Latin *masculus* — more at MASCULINE] (1928)
: characterized by machismo : aggressively virile

²macho *noun, plural* **machos** (1951)
1 : one who exhibits machismo
2 : MACHISMO

mack *variant of* MAC

mack·er·el \'ma-k(ə-)rəl\ *noun, plural* **mackerel** *or* **mackerels** [Middle English *makerel*, from Middle French] (14th century)
1 : a scombroid bony fish (*Scomber scombrus*) of the North Atlantic that is green above with dark blue bars and silvery below and is one of the most important food fishes
2 : any of a family (Scombridae) of fishes including the common mackerel; *especially* : a comparatively small member of this group as distinguished from a bonito or tuna

mackerel 1

mackerel shark *noun* (1819)
: any of a family (Lamnidae) of large pelagic sharks including the great white shark and mako sharks; *especially* : PORBEAGLE

mackerel sky *noun* (1669)
: a sky covered with rows of altocumulus or cirrocumulus clouds resembling the patterns on a mackerel's back

mack·i·naw \'ma-kə-,nȯ\ *noun* [*Mackinaw* (Mackinac), trading post at site of Mackinaw City, Michigan] (1836)
1 : a heavy woolen blanket formerly distributed by the U.S. government to the Indians
2 a : a heavy cloth of wool or wool and other fibers often with a plaid design and usually heavily napped and felted **b** : a short coat of mackinaw or similar heavy fabric

Mackinaw trout *noun* (1840)
: a large dark North American char (*Salvelinus namaycush*) that is an important commercial food fish in northern lakes

mack·in·tosh *also* **mac·in·tosh** \'ma-kən-,täsh\ *noun* [Charles *Macintosh* (died 1843) Scottish chemist & inventor] (1836)
1 *chiefly British* : RAINCOAT
2 : a lightweight waterproof fabric originally of rubberized cotton

Mac·lau·rin's series \mə-'klȯr-ən(z)-\ *noun* [Colin *Maclaurin* (died 1746) Scottish mathematician] (circa 1909)
: a Taylor's series of the form

$$f(x) = f(0) + \frac{f'(0)}{1!}x + \frac{f''(0)}{2!}x^2 + \ldots + \frac{f^{[n]}(0)}{n!}x^n + \ldots$$

in which the expansion is about the reference point zero — called also *Maclaurin series*

ma·cle \'ma-kəl\ *noun* [French, wide-meshed net, lozenge voided, macle, from Old French, mesh, lozenge voided, of Germanic origin; akin to Old High German *masca* mesh — more at MESH] (1801)
1 : a twin crystal
2 : a flat often triangular diamond that is usually a twin crystal
— **ma·cled** \'ma-kəld\ *adjective*

ma·con *also* **mâ·con** \mä-'kōⁿ\ *noun, often capitalized* [French *mâcon*, from *Mâcon*, France] (1863)
: a dry red or white wine produced in the area around Mâcon, France

Mac·Pher·son strut \mək-'fir-s^ən, -'fər-\ *noun* [Earle S. *MacPherson* (died 1960) American engineer] (1975)
: a component of an automobile suspension consisting of a shock absorber mounted within a coil spring

macr- *or* **macro-** *combining form* [French & Latin, from Greek *makr-, makro-* long, from *makros* — more at MEAGER]
1 : long ⟨*macrobiotic*⟩
2 : large ⟨*macromolecule*⟩

mac·ra·mé *also* **mac·ra·me** \'ma-krə-,mā\ *noun* [French or Italian; French *macramé*,

from Italian *macramè,* from Turkish *makrama* napkin, towel, from Arabic *miqramah* coverlet] (1869)

: a coarse lace or fringe made by knotting threads or cords in a geometrical pattern; *also* : the art of tying knots in patterns

¹**mac·ro** \'ma-(,)krō\ *adjective* [*macr-*] (1923)

1 : being large, thick, or exceptionally prominent

2 a : of, involving, or intended for use with relatively large quantities or on a large scale **b** : of or relating to macroeconomics

3 : GROSS 1c

²**macro** *noun, plural* **macros** [short for *macroinstruction*] (1959)

: a single computer instruction that stands for a sequence of operations

mac·ro·ag·gre·gate \,ma-krō-'a-gri-gət\ *noun* (1926)

: a relatively large particle (as of soil or a protein)

— **mac·ro·ag·gre·gat·ed** \-,gā-təd\ *adjective*

mac·ro·bi·ot·ic \-bī-'ä-tik, -bē-\ *adjective* (1965)

: of, relating to, or being an extremely restricted diet (as one containing chiefly whole grains) that is held by its advocates to promote health and well-being although it may actually be deficient in essential nutrients (as fats)

mac·ro·cosm \'ma-krə-,kä-zəm\ *noun* [French *macrocosme,* from Medieval Latin *macrocosmos,* from Latin *macr-* + Greek *kosmos* order, universe] (1600)

1 : the great world : UNIVERSE

2 : a complex that is a large-scale reproduction of one of its constituents

— **mac·ro·cos·mic** \,ma-krə-'käz-mik\ *adjective*

— **mac·ro·cos·mi·cal·ly** \-mi-k(ə-)lē\ *adverb*

mac·ro·cy·clic \,ma-krō-'sī-klik, -'sī-\ *adjective* (1936)

: containing or being a chemical ring that consists usually of 15 or more atoms

mac·ro·cyte \'ma-krə-,sīt\ *noun* [International Scientific Vocabulary] (circa 1889)

: an exceptionally large red blood cell occurring chiefly in anemias

— **mac·ro·cyt·ic** \,ma-krə-'si-tik\ *adjective*

mac·ro·cy·to·sis \,ma-krə-sī-'tō-səs, -krə-sə-\ *noun, plural* **-to·ses** \-,sēz\ [New Latin] (circa 1893)

: the occurrence of macrocytes in the blood

mac·ro·eco·nom·ics \'ma-krō-,e-kə-'nä-miks, -,ē-kə-\ *noun plural but usually singular in construction* (1948)

: a study of economics in terms of whole systems especially with reference to general levels of output and income and to the interrelations among sectors of the economy — compare MICROECONOMICS

— **mac·ro·eco·nom·ic** \-mik\ *adjective*

mac·ro·evo·lu·tion \'ma-krō-,e-və-'lü-shən *also* -,ē-və-\ *noun* (1939)

: evolution that results in relatively large and complex changes (as in species formation)

— **mac·ro·evo·lu·tion·ary** \-shə-,ner-ē\ *adjective*

mac·ro·fos·sil \'ma-krō-,fä-səl\ *noun* (1937)

: a fossil large enough to be observed by direct inspection

mac·ro·ga·mete \,ma-krō-'ga-,mēt *also* -gə-'mēt\ *noun* [International Scientific Vocabulary] (1899)

: the larger and usually female gamete of a heterogamous organism

mac·ro·glob·u·lin \-'glä-byə-lən\ *noun* [International Scientific Vocabulary] (1952)

: a highly polymerized globulin (as IgM) of high molecular weight

mac·ro·glob·u·li·ne·mia \-,glä-byə-lə-'nē-mē-ə\ *noun* [New Latin] (1949)

: a disorder characterized by increased blood serum viscosity and the presence of macroglobulins in the serum

— **mac·ro·glob·u·li·ne·mic** \-mik\ *adjective*

mac·ro·in·struc·tion \,ma-krō-in-'strək-shən\ *noun* (1959)

: MACRO

macro lens *noun* [*macr-,* from the fact that the focal length is greater than normal] (1961)

: a camera lens designed to focus at very short distances with up to life-size magnification of the image

mac·ro·lep·i·dop·tera \'ma-krō-,le-pə-'däp-tə-rə\ *noun plural* [New Latin] (1882)

: lepidoptera (as butterflies, skippers, saturniids, noctuids, and geometrids) that include most of the large forms and none of the minute ones

mac·ro·mere \'ma-krə-,mir\ *noun* (1877)

: a large blastomere — see BLASTULA illustration

mac·ro·mol·e·cule \,ma-krō-'mä-li-,kyü(ə)l\ *noun* [International Scientific Vocabulary] (circa 1929)

: a very large molecule (as of a protein or rubber)

— **mac·ro·mo·lec·u·lar** \-mə-'le-kyə-lər\ *adjective*

ma·cron \'mā-,krän, 'ma-, -krən\ *noun* [Greek *makron,* neuter of *makros* long] (1851)

: a mark ⁻ placed over a vowel to indicate that the vowel is long or placed over a syllable or used alone to indicate a stressed or long syllable in a metrical foot

mac·ro·nu·cle·us \,ma-krō-'nü-klē-əs, -'nyü-\ *noun* [New Latin] (1892)

: a relatively large densely staining nucleus of most ciliate protozoans that is derived from micronuclei and controls various nonreproductive functions

— **mac·ro·nu·cle·ar** \,mak-rō-'nü-klē-ər, -'nyü-, ÷-kyə-lər\ *adjective*

mac·ro·nu·tri·ent \-'nü-trē-ənt, -'nyü-\ *noun* (1942)

: a chemical element (as nitrogen, phosphorus, or potassium) of which relatively large quantities are essential to the growth and health of a plant

mac·ro·phage \'ma-krə-,fāj\ *noun* [International Scientific Vocabulary] (1890)

: a phagocytic tissue cell of the reticuloendothelial system that may be fixed or freely motile, is derived from a monocyte, and functions in the protection of the body against infection and noxious substances — called also *histiocyte*

— **mac·ro·phag·ic** \,ma-krə-'fa-jik\ *adjective*

mac·ro·pho·tog·ra·phy \,ma-krō-fə-'tä-grə-fē\ *noun* (1889)

: the making of photographs in which the object is either unmagnified or slightly magnified up to a limit often of about 10 diameters

— **mac·ro·pho·to·graph** \-'fō-tə-,graf\ *noun*

mac·ro·phyte \'ma-krə-,fīt\ *noun* (circa 1909)

: a member of the macroscopic plant life especially of a body of water

— **mac·ro·phyt·ic** \,ma-krə-'fi-tik\ *adjective*

mac·rop·ter·ous \ma-'kräp-tə-rəs\ *adjective* [Greek *makropteros,* from *makr-* + *pteron* wing — more at FEATHER] (circa 1836)

: having long or large wings

mac·ro·scale \'ma-krō-,skāl\ *noun* (1931)

: a large often macroscopic scale

mac·ro·scop·ic \,ma-krō-'skä-pik\ *adjective* [International Scientific Vocabulary *macr-* + *-scopic* (as in *microscopic*)] (1872)

1 : large enough to be observed by the naked eye

2 : considered in terms of large units or elements

— **mac·ro·scop·i·cal·ly** \-pi-k(ə-)lē\ *adverb*

mac·ro·struc·ture \'ma-krō-,strək-chər\ *noun* (circa 1899)

: the structure (as of metal, a body part, or the soil) revealed by visual examination with little or no magnification

— **mac·ro·struc·tur·al** \,ma-krō-'strək-chə-rəl, -'strək-shə-rəl\ *adjective*

mac·u·la \'ma-kyə-lə\ *noun, plural* **-lae** \-,lē, -,lī\ *also* **-las** [Middle English, from Latin] (14th century)

1 : SPOT, BLOTCH; *especially* : MACULE

2 : an anatomical structure (as the macula lutea) having the form of a spot differentiated from surrounding tissues

— **mac·u·lar** \-lər\ *adjective*

macula lu·tea \-'lü-tē-ə\ *noun, plural* **mac·ulae lu·te·ae** \-tē-,ē, -tē-,ī\ [New Latin, literally, yellow spot] (1848)

: a small yellowish area lying slightly lateral to the center of the retina that constitutes the region of maximum visual acuity — called also *yellow spot*

mac·u·late \'ma-kyə-lət\ *or* **mac·u·lat·ed** \-,lā-təd\ *adjective* [Latin *maculatus,* past participle of *maculare* to stain, from *macula*] (15th century)

1 : marked with spots : BLOTCHED

2 : IMPURE, BESMIRCHED

mac·u·la·tion \,ma-kyə-'lā-shən\ *noun* (15th century)

1 *archaic* : the state of being spotted

2 a : a blemish in the form of a discrete spot ⟨acne scars and *maculations*⟩ **b** : the arrangement of spots and markings on an animal or plant

mac·ule \'ma-(,)kyü(ə)l\ *noun* [French, from Latin *macula*] (1863)

: a patch of skin that is altered in color but usually not elevated and that is a characteristic feature of various diseases (as smallpox)

ma·cum·ba \mə-'küm-bə\ *noun* [Brazilian Portuguese] (1939)

: a polytheistic religion of African origin involving syncretistic elements and practiced mainly by Brazilian blacks in urban areas

¹**mad** \'mad\ *adjective* **mad·der; mad·dest** [Middle English *medd, madd,* from Old English *gemǣd,* past participle of (assumed) *gemǣdan* to madden, from *gemād* silly, mad; akin to Old High German *gimeit* foolish, crazy] (before 12th century)

1 : disordered in mind : INSANE

2 a : completely unrestrained by reason and judgment ⟨driven *mad* by the pain⟩ **b** : incapable of being explained or accounted for ⟨a *mad* decision⟩

3 : carried away by intense anger : FURIOUS ⟨*mad* at myself⟩ ⟨*mad* about the delay⟩

4 : carried away by enthusiasm or desire ⟨*mad* about horses⟩ ⟨*mad* for the boy next door⟩

5 : affected with rabies : RABID

6 : marked by wild gaiety and merriment : HILARIOUS

7 : intensely excited : FRANTIC ⟨*mad* with jealousy⟩

8 : marked by intense and often chaotic activity : WILD ⟨a *mad* scramble⟩

— **mad·dish** \'ma-dish\ *adjective*

²**mad** *verb* **mad·ded; mad·ding** (14th century)

: MADDEN

³**mad** *noun* (1834)

1 : a fit or mood of bad temper

2 : ANGER, FURY

Mad·a·gas·car periwinkle \,ma-də-'gas-kər-\ *noun* [*Madagascar,* Africa] (1821)

: ¹PERIWINKLE 1b

mad·am \'ma-dəm\ *noun, plural* **madams** [Middle English, from Middle French *ma dame,* literally, my lady] (14th century)

\ə\ abut \ᵊ\ kitten \ər\ further \a\ ash \ā\ ace
\ä\ mop, mar \au̇\ out \ch\ chin \e\ bet \ē\ easy
\g\ go \i\ hit \ī\ ice \j\ job \ŋ\ sing \ō\ go
\ȯ\ law \ȯi\ boy \th\ thin \th\ the \ü\ loot \u̇\ foot
\y\ yet \zh\ vision *see also* Guide to Pronunciation

1 *plural* **mes·dames** \mā-'däm, -'dam\ : LA-DY — used without a name as a form of respectful or polite address to a woman **2** : MISTRESS 1 — used as a title formerly with the given name but now with the surname or especially with a designation of rank or office ⟨*Madam* Chairman⟩ ⟨*Madam* President⟩ **3** : the female head of a house of prostitution **4** : the female head of a household : WIFE

ma·dame \mə-'dam, ma-', *before a surname also* 'ma-dəm\ *noun* [French, from Old French *ma dame*] (1674) **1** *plural* **mes·dames** \mā-'däm, -'dam\ — used as a title equivalent to *Mrs.* for a married woman not of English-speaking nationality **2** *plural* **madames** : MADAM 3

mad–brained \'mad-'brānd\ *adjective* (1562) : RASH, HOTHEADED

mad·cap \'mad-,kap\ *adjective* (1588) : marked by capriciousness, recklessness, or foolishness
— **madcap** *noun*

mad·den \'ma-d³n\ *verb* **mad·dened; mad·den·ing** \'mad-niŋ, 'ma-d³n-iŋ\ (1735) *intransitive verb* : to become or act as if mad *transitive verb* **1** : to drive mad : CRAZE **2** : to make intensely angry : ENRAGE

maddening *adjective* (1822) **1** : tending to craze **2 a** : tending to infuriate **b** : tending to vex : IRRITATING
— **mad·den·ing·ly** \-lē\ *adverb*

mad·der \'ma-dər\ *noun* [Middle English, from Old English *mædere*; akin to Old High German *matara* madder] (before 12th century) **1** : a Eurasian herb (*Rubia tinctorum* of the family Rubiaceae, the madder family) with whorled leaves and small yellowish panicled flowers succeeded by berries; *broadly* : any of several related herbs (genus *Rubia*) **2 a** : the root of the Eurasian madder used formerly in dyeing; *also* : an alizarin dye prepared from it **b** : a moderate to strong red

mad·ding \'ma-din\ *adjective* (1579) : acting in a frenzied manner ⟨the *madding* crowd⟩

made \'mād\ *adjective* [Middle English, from past participle of *maken* to make] (14th century) **1 a** : FICTITIOUS, INVENTED ⟨a *made* excuse⟩ **b** : artificially produced **c** : put together of various ingredients ⟨a *made* dish⟩ **2** : assured of success ⟨a *made* man⟩ — usually used in the phrase *have it made*

Ma·dei·ra \mə-'dir-ə, -'der-\ *noun* [Portuguese, from *Madeira* Islands] (1596) : an amber-colored fortified wine from Madeira; *also* : a similar wine made elsewhere

mad·e·leine \'ma-d³l-ən, ma-d³l-'ān\ *noun* [French, perhaps from *Madeleine* Paumier, 19th century French pastry cook] (1845) **1** : a small rich shell-shaped cake **2** : one that evokes a memory

ma·de·moi·selle \,mad-mwə-'zel, ,ma-də-, -mə-'zel, *sometimes* mam-'zel\ *noun, plural* **ma·de·moi·selles** \-'zelz\ *or* **mes·de·moi·selles** \,mād-mwə-'zel, ,mā-də-, -mə-'zel\ [Middle English *madamoiselle*, from Middle French, from Old French *ma damoisele*, literally, my (young) lady] (15th century) **1** : an unmarried French girl or woman — used as a title equivalent to *Miss* for an unmarried woman not of English-speaking nationality **2** : a French governess **3** : SILVER PERCH a

made–to–order *adjective* (circa 1908) **1** : produced to supply a special or an individual demand : CUSTOM-MADE **2** : ideally suited (as to a particular purpose) ⟨a ground ball *made-to-order* for a double play⟩

made–up \'mā-'dəp\ *adjective* (1607) **1** : fancifully conceived or falsely devised

2 : fully manufactured **3** : marked by the use of makeup

mad·house \'mad-,haủs\ *noun* (1687) **1** : a place where insane persons are detained and treated **2** : a place of uproar or confusion

Mad·i·son Avenue \'ma-də-sən-\ *noun* [*Madison Avenue,* New York City, former center of the American advertising business] (1952) : the American advertising industry

mad·ly \'mad-lē\ *adverb* (13th century) **1** : in a mad manner **2** : to an extreme or excessive degree ⟨*madly* in love⟩

mad·man \'mad-,man, -mən\ *noun* (14th century) : a man who is or acts as if insane

mad money *noun* (1922) : money that a woman carries to pay her fare home in case a date ends in a quarrel; *also* : money set aside for an emergency or personal use

mad·ness \'mad-nəs\ *noun* (14th century) **1** : the quality or state of being mad: as **a** : RAGE **b** : INSANITY **c** : extreme folly **d** : ECSTASY, ENTHUSIASM **2** : any of several ailments of animals marked by frenzied behavior; *specifically* : RABIES

Ma·don·na \mə-'dä-nə\ *noun* [Italian, from Old Italian *ma donna,* literally, my lady] (1584) **1** *archaic* : LADY — used as a form of respectful address **2** *obsolete* : an Italian lady **3 a** : VIRGIN MARY **b** : an artistic depiction (as a painting or statue) of the Virgin Mary

Madonna lily *noun* (1877) : a widely cultivated lily (*Lilium candidum*) with bell-shaped to broad funnel-shaped white flowers

ma·dras \'ma-drəs; mə-'dras, -'dräs\ *noun* [*Madras,* India] (circa 1830) **1** : a large silk or cotton kerchief usually of bright colors that is often worn as a turban **2 a** : a fine plain-woven shirting and dress fabric usually of cotton with varied designs (as plaid) in bright colors or in white **b** : a light open usually cotton fabric with a heavy design used for curtains

mad·re·pore \'ma-drə-,pōr, -,pòr\ *noun* [French *madrépore,* from Italian *madrepora,* from *madre* mother (from Latin *mater*) + *poro* pore (from Latin *porus*) — more at MOTHER] (1751) : any of various stony reef-building corals (order Madreporaria) of tropical seas that assume a variety of branching, encrusting, or massive forms
— **mad·re·po·ri·an** \,ma-drə-'pōr-ē-ən, -'pòr-\ *adjective or noun*
— **mad·re·por·ic** \-'pōr-ik, -'pòr-\ *adjective*

mad·re·por·ite \'ma-drə-,pōr-,īt, -,pòr-\ *noun* [International Scientific Vocabulary *madrepore* + ¹-*ite* (segment); from the resemblances of the perforations to those of a madrepore] (1877) : a perforated or porous body that is situated at the distal end of the stone canal in echinoderms

mad·ri·gal \'ma-dri-gəl\ *noun* [Italian *madrigale,* probably from Medieval Latin *matricale,* from neuter of (assumed) *matricalis* simple, from Late Latin, of the womb, from Latin *matric-, matrix* womb, from *mater* mother] (1588) **1** : a medieval short lyrical poem in a strict poetic form **2 a** : a complex polyphonic unaccompanied vocal piece on a secular text developed especially in the 16th and 17th centuries **b** : PART-SONG; *especially* : GLEE
— **mad·ri·gal·ian** \,ma-drə-'ga-lē-ən, -'gä-\ *adjective*
— **mad·ri·gal·ist** \'ma-dri-gə-list\ *noun*

ma·dri·lene \,ma-drə-'len, -'län\ *noun* [French (*consommé*) *madrilène,* literally, Madrid consommé] (1907) : a consommé flavored with tomato

ma·dro·na *or* **ma·dro·ne** *or* **ma·dro·no** \mə-'drō-nə\ *noun* [Spanish *madroño*] (1841) : any of several evergreen trees (genus *Arbutus*) of the heath family; *especially* : one (*A. menziesii*) of the Pacific coast of North America with smooth bark, thick shining leaves, and edible red berries

ma·du·ro \mə-'dùr-(,)ō\ *noun, plural* **-ros** [Spanish, from *maduro* ripe, from Latin *maturus* — more at MATURE] (1850) : a dark-colored relatively strong cigar

mad·wom·an \'mad-,wù-mən\ *noun* (15th century) : a woman who is or acts as if insane

mad·wort \-,wərt, -,wòrt\ *noun* (1597) **1** : ALYSSUM 1 **2** : a low hairy annual herb (*Asperugo procumbens*) of the borage family with blue flowers and a root used as a substitute for madder

Mae·ce·nas \mi-'sē-nəs\ *noun* [Latin, from Gaius *Maecenas* (died 8 B.C.) Roman statesman & patron of literature] (1542) : a generous patron especially of literature or art

mael·strom \'mā(ə)l-strəm, -,sträm\ *noun* [obsolete Dutch (now *maalstroom*), from *malen* to grind + *strom* stream] (1682) **1** : a powerful often violent whirlpool sucking in objects within a given radius **2** : something resembling a maelstrom in turbulence

mae·nad \'mē-,nad\ *noun* [Latin *maenad-, maenas,* from Greek *mainad-, mainas,* from *mainesthai* to be mad; akin to Greek *menos* spirit — more at MIND] (1579) **1** : a woman participant in orgiastic Dionysian rites : BACCHANTE **2** : an unnaturally excited or distraught woman
— **mae·nad·ic** \mē-'na-dik\ *adjective*

mae·sto·so \mī-'stō-(,)sō, -(,)zō\ *adjective or adverb* [Italian, from Latin *majestosus,* from *majestas* majesty] (circa 1724) : majestic and stately — used as a direction in music

mae·stro \'mī-(,)strō\ *noun, plural* **mae·stros** *or* **mae·stri** \-,strē\ [Italian, literally, master, from Latin *magister* — more at MASTER] (1724) : a master usually in an art; *especially* : an eminent composer, conductor, or teacher of music

Mae West \'mā-'west\ *noun* [*Mae West* (died 1980) American actress noted for her full figure] (1940) : an inflatable life jacket in the form of a collar extending down the chest that was worn by fliers in World War II

maf·fick \'ma-fik\ *intransitive verb* [back-formation from *Mafeking Night,* English celebration of the lifting of the siege of Mafeking, South Africa, May 17, 1900] (1900) : to celebrate with boisterous rejoicing and hilarious behavior

Ma·fia \'mä-fē-ə, 'ma-\ *noun* [*Mafia, Maffia,* a Sicilian secret criminal society, from Italian dialect (Sicily)] (1875) **1 a** : a secret criminal society of Sicily or Italy **b** : a similarly conceived criminal organization in the U.S.; *also* : a similar organization elsewhere ⟨the Japanese *Mafia*⟩ **c** : a criminal organization associated with a particular traffic ⟨the cocaine *Mafia*⟩ **2** *often not capitalized* : a group of people likened to the Mafia; *especially* : a group of people of similar interests or backgrounds prominent in a particular field or enterprise : CLIQUE

maf·ic \'ma-fik\ *adjective* [New Latin *magnesium* + Latin *ferrum* iron + English -*ic*] (1912) : of, relating to, or being a group of usually dark-colored minerals rich in magnesium and iron

ma·fi·o·so \,mä-fē-'ō-(,)sō, ,ma-, -(,)zō\ *noun*, *plural* **-si** \-(,)sē, -(,)zē\ [Italian, from *Mafia*] (1875)
: a member of the Mafia or a mafia

mag \'mag\ *noun* (1796)
: MAGAZINE

mag·a·zine \'ma-gə-,zēn, ,ma-gə-'-\ *noun* [Middle French, from Old Provençal, from Arabic *makhāzin*, plural of *makhzan* storehouse] (1583)
1 : a place where goods or supplies are stored : WAREHOUSE
2 : a room in which powder and other explosives are kept in a fort or a ship
3 : the contents of a magazine: as **a** : an accumulation of munitions of war **b** : a stock of provisions or goods
4 a : a periodical containing miscellaneous pieces (as articles, stories, poems) often illustrated **b** : a similar section of a newspaper usually appearing on Sunday **c** : a radio or television program presenting usually several short segments on a variety of topics
5 : a supply chamber: as **a** : a holder in or on a gun for cartridges to be fed into the gun chamber **b** : a lightproof chamber for films or plates on a camera or for film on a motion-picture projector ◇

mag·a·zin·ist \-,zē-nist, -'zē-\ *noun* (1821)
: a person who writes for or edits a magazine

mag·da·len \'mag-də-lən\ *or* **mag·da·lene** \-,lēn\ *noun*, *often capitalized* [Mary *Magdalen* or *Magdalene* woman healed by Jesus of evil spirits (Luke 8:2), considered identical with a reformed prostitute (Luke 7:36–50)] (1697)
1 : a reformed prostitute
2 : a house of refuge or reformatory for prostitutes

Mag·da·le·ni·an \,mag-də-'lē-nē-ən\ *adjective* [French *magdalénien*, from *La Madeleine*, rock shelter in southwest France] (1885)
: of or relating to an Upper Paleolithic culture characterized by flint, bone, and ivory implements, carving, and paintings

mage \'māj\ *noun* [Middle English, from Latin *magus*] (14th century)
: MAGUS

Mag·el·lan·ic Cloud \,ma-jə-'la-nik-, *chiefly British* ,ma-gə-\ *noun* [Ferdinand *Magellan*] (circa 1686)
: either of the two small galaxies that appear as conspicuous patches of light near the south celestial pole and are companions to the Milky Way galaxy

Ma·gen Da·vid \'mò-gən-'dò-vid, -'də-; 'mō-gən-'dā-vəd\ *noun* [Hebrew *māghēn Dāwīdh*, literally, shield of David] (circa 1904)
: a hexagram used as a symbol of Judaism

ma·gen·ta \mə-'jen-tə\ *noun* [*Magenta*, Italy] (1860)
1 : FUCHSIN
2 : a deep purplish red

mag·got \'ma-gət\ *noun* [Middle English *mathek*, *magotte*, of Scandinavian origin; akin to Old Norse *mathkr* maggot; akin to Old English *matha* maggot] (14th century)
1 : a soft-bodied legless grub that is the larva of a dipterous insect (as the housefly)
2 : a fantastic or eccentric idea : WHIM
— **mag·goty** \-gə-tē\ *adjective*

magi *plural of* MAGUS

¹**Ma·gi·an** \'mā-jē-ən\ *noun* (1578)
: MAGUS

²**Ma·gi·an** \-jē-ən, -,jī-\ *adjective* (1716)
: of or relating to the Magi
— **Ma·gi·an·ism** \-ə-,ni-zəm\ *noun*

¹**mag·ic** \'ma-jik\ *noun* [Middle English *magique*, from Middle French, from Latin *magice*, from Greek *magikē*, feminine of *magikos* Magian, magical, from *magos* magus, sorcerer, of Iranian origin; akin to Old Persian *maguš* sorcerer] (14th century)
1 a : the use of means (as charms or spells) believed to have supernatural power over natural forces **b** : magic rites or incantations

2 a : an extraordinary power or influence seemingly from a supernatural source **b** : something that seems to cast a spell : ENCHANTMENT
3 : the art of producing illusions by sleight of hand

²**magic** *adjective* (14th century)
1 : of or relating to magic
2 a : having seemingly supernatural qualities or powers **b** : giving a feeling of enchantment
— **mag·i·cal** \'ma-ji-kəl\ *adjective*
— **mag·i·cal·ly** \-ji-k(ə-)lē\ *adverb*

³**magic** *transitive verb* **mag·icked; mag·ick·ing** (1906)
: to produce, remove, or influence by magic

magic bullet *noun* (1940)
: a substance or therapy capable of destroying pathogens (as bacteria or cancer cells) without deleterious side effects

ma·gi·cian \mə-'ji-shən\ *noun* (14th century)
1 : one skilled in magic ; *especially* : SORCERER
2 : one who performs tricks of illusion and sleight of hand

magic lantern *noun* (1696)
: an early form of optical projector of still pictures using a transparent slide

Magic Marker *trademark*
— used for a felt-tipped pen

magic realism *noun* (1954)
: painting in a meticulously realistic style of imaginary or fantastic scenes or images
— **magic realist** *noun*

magic square *noun* (circa 1704)
: a square containing a number of integers arranged so that the sum of the numbers is the same in each row, column, and main diagonal and often in some or all of the other diagonals

magic squares

Ma·gi·not Line \'ma-zhə-,nō-, 'ma-jə-\ *noun* [André *Maginot* (died 1932) French minister of war] (1936)
: a line of defensive fortifications built before World War II to protect the eastern border of France but easily outflanked by German invaders

mag·is·te·ri·al \,ma-jə-'stir-ē-əl\ *adjective* [Late Latin *magisterialis* of authority, from *magisterium* office of a master, from *magister*] (1632)
1 a (1) : of, relating to, or having the characteristics of a master or teacher : AUTHORITATIVE (2) : marked by an overbearingly dignified or assured manner or aspect **b** : of, relating to, or required for a master's degree
2 : of or relating to a magistrate or a magistrate's office or duties
synonym see DICTATORIAL
— **mag·is·te·ri·al·ly** \-ē-ə-lē\ *adverb*

mag·is·te·ri·um \,ma-jə-'stir-ē-əm\ *noun* [Latin] (1866)
: teaching authority especially of the Roman Catholic Church

mag·is·tra·cy \'ma-jə-strə-sē\ *noun*, *plural* **-cies** (circa 1585)
1 : the state of being a magistrate
2 : the office, power, or dignity of a magistrate
3 : a body of magistrates
4 : the district under a magistrate

ma·gis·tral \'ma-jə-strəl, mə-'jis-trəl\ *adjective* [Late Latin *magistralis*, from Latin *magistr-, magister*] (1605)
: MAGISTERIAL 1a
— **ma·gis·tral·ly** \-ē\ *adverb*

mag·is·trate \'ma-jə-,strāt, -strət\ *noun* [Middle English *magestrat*, from Latin *magistratus* magistracy, magistrate, from *magistr-, magister* master, political superior — more at MASTER] (14th century)
: an official entrusted with administration of the laws: as **a** : a principal official exercising governmental powers over a major political

unit (as a nation) **b** : a local official exercising administrative and often judicial functions **c** : a local judiciary official having limited original jurisdiction especially in criminal cases
— **mag·is·trat·i·cal** \,ma-jə-'stra-ti-kəl\ *adjective*
— **mag·is·trat·i·cal·ly** \-k(ə-)lē\ *adverb*

magistrate's court *noun* (1867)
1 : POLICE COURT
2 : a court that has minor civil and criminal jurisdiction

mag·is·tra·ture \'ma-jə-,strā-chər, -strə-,chùr\ *noun* (1672)
: MAGISTRACY

mag·lev \'mag-lev\ *noun*, *often attributive* [*magnetic levitation*] (1969)
1 : the use of the physical properties of magnetic fields generated by superconducting magnets to cause an object (as a vehicle) to float above a solid surface
2 : a train utilizing maglev technology

mag·ma \'mag-mə\ *noun* [Middle English, from Latin *magmat-*, *magma*, from Greek, thick unguent, from *massein* to knead — more at MINGLE] (15th century)
1 *archaic* : DREGS, SEDIMENT
2 : a thin pasty suspension (as of a precipitate in water)
3 : molten rock material within the earth from which igneous rock results by cooling
— **mag·mat·ic** \mag-'ma-tik\ *adjective*

Mag·na Car·ta *or* **Mag·na Char·ta** \'mag-nə-'kär-tə\ *noun* [Middle English, from Medieval Latin, literally, great charter] (15th century)
1 : a charter of liberties to which the English barons forced King John to give his assent in June 1215 at Runnymede
2 : a document constituting a fundamental guarantee of rights and privileges

mag·na cum lau·de \'mäg-nə-(,)kùm-'laù-də-, 'mäg-nə-,kəm-'lò-də\ *adverb or adjective* [Latin] (1900)
: with great distinction ⟨graduated *magna cum laude*⟩ — compare CUM LAUDE, SUMMA CUM LAUDE

mag·na·nim·i·ty \,mag-nə-'ni-mə-tē\ *noun*, *plural* **-ties** (14th century)
1 : the quality of being magnanimous : loftiness of spirit enabling one to bear trouble

◇ WORD HISTORY
magazine In Arabic *makhzan* denotes a storehouse. From the plural form *makhāzin* medieval French borrowed *magasin* in the 14th century, most likely via Old Provençal. English in turn borrowed the word from French in the 16th century, in the same sense. The term then underwent various specializations of meaning, depending on what was being stored. An early development was the application of the word to storage places for weapons or gunpowder; a further extension applied *magazine* not to a building but to a chamber or clip to hold cartridges in a firearm. *Magazine* was also used in the titles of books with the implication "storehouse of knowledge." The word was thus used in 1731 for the first issue of *The Gentleman's Magazine: or, Monthly Intelligencer*, the suggestion being that the publication would present the general reader each month with a collection or "storehouse" of stories and articles. Other periodical publications began using *magazine* in their titles, and the word was soon used generically for a certain kind of periodical.

\ə\ abut \ᵊ\ kitten \ər\ further \a\ ash \ā\ ace
\ä\ mop, mar \aù\ out \ch\ chin \e\ bet \ē\ easy
\g\ go \i\ hit \ī\ ice \j\ job \ŋ\ sing \ō\ go
\ò\ law \òi\ boy \th\ thin \th\ the \ü\ loot \ù\ foot
\y\ yet \zh\ vision *see also* Guide to Pronunciation

calmly, to disdain meanness and pettiness, and to display a noble generosity **2** : a magnanimous act

mag·nan·i·mous \mag-'na-nə-məs\ *adjective* [Latin *magnanimus*, from *magnus* great + *animus* spirit — more at MUCH, ANIMATE] (1584) **1** : showing or suggesting a lofty and courageous spirit ⟨the irreproachable lives and *magnanimous* sufferings of their followers — Joseph Addison⟩ **2** : showing or suggesting nobility of feeling and generosity of mind ⟨too sincere for dissimulation, too *magnanimous* for resentment —Ellen Glasgow⟩ — **mag·nan·i·mous·ly** *adverb* — **mag·nan·i·mous·ness** *noun*

mag·nate \'mag-ˌnāt, -nət\ *noun* [Middle English *magnates*, plural, from Late Latin, from Latin *magnus*] (15th century) : a person of rank, power, influence, or distinction often in a specified area

mag·ne·sia \mag-'nē-shə, -zhə\ *noun* [New Latin, from *magnes carneus*, a white earth, literally, flesh magnet] (1755) : MAGNESIUM OXIDE — compare MILK OF MAGNESIA — **mag·ne·sian** \-shən, -zhən\ *adjective*

mag·ne·site \'mag-nə-ˌsīt\ *noun* (1815) : native magnesium carbonate used especially in making refractories and magnesium oxide

mag·ne·sium \mag-'nē-zē-əm, -zhəm\ *noun* [New Latin, from *magnesia*] (1812) : a silver-white light malleable ductile metallic element that occurs abundantly in nature and is used in metallurgical and chemical processes, in photography, signaling, and pyrotechnics because of the intense white light it produces on burning, and in construction especially in the form of light alloys — see ELEMENT table

magnesium carbonate *noun* (1903) : a carbonate of magnesium; *especially* : a white crystalline salt $MgCO_3$ that occurs naturally as dolomite and magnesite

magnesium chloride *noun* (circa 1910) : a bitter deliquescent salt $MgCl_2$ used especially as a source of magnesium metal

magnesium hydroxide *noun* (circa 1909) : a slightly alkaline crystalline compound $Mg(OH)_2$ used especially as a laxative and gastric antacid

magnesium oxide *noun* (circa 1909) : a white highly infusible compound MgO used especially in refractories, cements, insulation, and fertilizers, in rubber manufacture, and in medicine as an antacid and mild laxative

magnesium sulfate *noun* (circa 1890) : a sulfate of magnesium: as **a** : a white salt $MgSO_4$ used in medicine and in industry **b** : EPSOM SALTS

mag·net \'mag-nət\ *noun* [Middle English *magnete*, from Middle French, from Latin *magnet-*, *magnes*, from Greek *magnēs* (*lithos*), literally, stone of Magnesia, ancient city in Asia Minor] (15th century) **1 a** : LODESTONE **b** : a body having the property of attracting iron and producing a magnetic field external to itself; *specifically* : a mass of iron, steel, or alloy that has this property artificially imparted **2** : something that attracts ⟨a box-office *magnet*⟩

magnet- *or* **magneto-** *combining form* [Latin *magnet-*, *magnes*] **1** : magnetic force ⟨*magnet*ometer⟩ **2** : magnetism : magnetic ⟨*magneto*electric⟩ ⟨*magneto*n⟩ **3** : magnetoelectric ⟨*magneto*resistance⟩ **4** : magnetosphere ⟨*magneto*pause⟩

¹mag·net·ic \mag-'ne-tik\ *adjective* (1611) **1** : possessing an extraordinary power or ability to attract ⟨a *magnetic* personality⟩

2 a : of or relating to a magnet or to magnetism **b** : of, relating to, or characterized by the earth's magnetism **c** : magnetized or capable of being magnetized **d** : actuated by magnetic attraction — **mag·net·i·cal·ly** \-ti-k(ə-)lē\ *adverb*

²magnetic *noun* (1654) : a magnetic substance

magnetic bubble *noun* (1969) : a tiny movable magnetized cylindrical volume in a thin amorphous or crystalline magnetic material that along with other like volumes can be used to represent a bit of information (as in a computer)

magnetic disk *noun* (circa 1960) : DISK 4c

magnetic equator *noun* (1832) : an imaginary line roughly parallel to the geographical equator and passing through those points where a magnetic needle has no dip

magnetic field *noun* (1845) : the portion of space near a magnetic body or a current-carrying body in which the magnetic forces due to the body or current can be detected

magnetic flux *noun* (1896) : lines of force used to represent magnetic induction

magnetic mirror *noun* (1952) : a magnetic field that confines a plasma by reflecting ions of the plasma back toward the main plasma concentration

magnetic moment *noun* (1865) : a vector quantity that is a measure of the torque exerted on a magnetic system (as a bar magnet or dipole) when placed in a magnetic field and that for a magnet is the product of the distance between its poles and the strength of either pole

magnetic north *noun* (1812) : the northerly direction in the earth's magnetic field indicated by the north-seeking pole of a compass needle

magnetic pole *noun* (1701) **1** : either of two small regions which are located respectively in the polar areas of the northern and southern hemispheres and toward which a compass needle points from any direction throughout adjacent regions; *also* : either of two comparable regions on a celestial body **2** : either of the poles of a magnet

magnetic quantum number *noun* (1923) : an integer that expresses the component of the quantized angular momentum of an electron, atom, or molecule in the direction of an externally applied magnetic field

magnetic recording *noun* (1945) : the process of recording sound, data (as for a computer), or a television program by producing varying local magnetization of a moving tape or disc — **magnetic recorder** *noun*

magnetic resonance *noun* (1903) : the response of electrons, atoms, molecules, or nuclei to various discrete radiation frequencies as a result of space quantization in a magnetic field

magnetic resonance imaging *noun* (1984) : a noninvasive diagnostic technique that produces computerized images of internal body tissues and is based on nuclear magnetic resonance of atoms within the body induced by the application of radio waves — abbreviation *MRI*

magnetic storm *noun* (1860) : a marked temporary disturbance of the earth's magnetic field held to be related to sunspots

magnetic tape *noun* (1937) : a thin ribbon (as of plastic) coated with a magnetic material on which information (as sound or television images) may be stored

mag·ne·tise *British variant of* MAGNETIZE

mag·ne·tism \'mag-nə-ˌti-zəm\ *noun* (1616)

1 a : a class of physical phenomena that include the attraction for iron observed in lodestone and a magnet, are inseparably associated with moving electricity, are exhibited by both magnets and electric currents, and are characterized by fields of force **b** : a science that deals with magnetic phenomena **2** : an ability to attract or charm

mag·ne·tite \'mag-nə-ˌtīt\ *noun* (1851) : a black isometric mineral of the spinel group that is an oxide of iron and an important iron ore

mag·ne·ti·za·tion \ˌmag-nə-tə-'zā-shən\ *noun* (1801) : an instance of magnetizing or the state of being magnetized; *also* : the degree to which a body is magnetized

mag·ne·tize \'mag-nə-ˌtīz\ *transitive verb* **-tized; -tiz·ing** (1801) **1** : to induce magnetic properties in **2** : to attract like a magnet : CHARM — **mag·ne·tiz·able** \-ˌtī-zə-bəl\ *adjective* — **mag·ne·tiz·er** *noun*

mag·ne·to \mag-'nē-(ˌ)tō\ *noun, plural* **-tos** (1882) : a magnetoelectric machine; *especially* : an alternator with permanent magnets used to generate current for the ignition in an internal-combustion engine

mag·ne·to·elec·tric \-ˌnē-tō-ə-'lek-trik, -ˌne-\ *adjective* (1831) : relating to or characterized by electromotive forces developed by magnetic means

mag·ne·to·flu·id·dy·nam·ics \-ˌnē-tō-ˌflü-ə-dī-'na-miks, -ˌne-, -də-'\ *noun plural but singular or plural in construction* (1962) : the study of magnetohydrodynamic phenomena

mag·ne·to·graph \-ˌgraf\ *noun* (1847) : an automatic instrument for recording measurements of a magnetic field (as of the earth or the sun)

mag·ne·to·hy·dro·dy·nam·ic \mag-ˌnē-tō-ˌhī-drə-dī-'na-mik, -ˌne-, -də-'\ *adjective* (1943) : of, relating to, or being phenomena arising from the motion of electrically conducting fluids (as plasmas) in the presence of electric and magnetic fields — **mag·ne·to·hy·dro·dy·nam·ics** \-miks\ *noun plural but singular or plural in construction*

mag·ne·tom·e·ter \ˌmag-nə-'tä-mə-tər\ *noun* (1827) : an instrument used to detect the presence of a metallic object or to measure the intensity of a magnetic field — **mag·ne·to·met·ric** \mag-ˌnē-tə-'me-trik, -ˌne-\ *adjective* — **mag·ne·tom·e·try** \ˌmag-nə-'tä-mə-trē\ *noun*

mag·ne·to·mo·tive force \mag-ˌnē-tə-'mō-tiv-, -ˌne-\ *noun* (1883) : a force that is the cause of a flux of magnetic induction

mag·ne·ton \'mag-nə-ˌtän\ *noun* [International Scientific Vocabulary *magnet-* + *²-on*] (1911) : a unit of the quantized magnetic moment of a particle (as an atom)

mag·ne·to·op·tic \mag-ˌnē-tō-'äp-tik, -ˌne-\ *also* **mag·ne·to·op·ti·cal** \-ti-kəl\ *adjective* (1848) : of or relating to the influence of a magnetic field upon light — **mag·ne·to·op·tics** \-tiks\ *noun plural but singular or plural in construction*

mag·ne·to·pause \mag-'nē-tə-ˌpȯz, -'ne-\ *noun* (1962) : the outer boundary of a magnetosphere

mag·ne·to·re·sis·tance \-ˌnē-tō-ri-'zis-tən(t)s, -ˌne-\ *noun* (1927) : a change in electrical resistance due to the presence of a magnetic field

mag·ne·to·sphere \mag-'nē-tə-ˌsfir, -'ne-\ *noun* (1959)

: a region of space surrounding a celestial object (as the earth or a star) that is dominated by the object's magnetic field so that charged particles are trapped in it

— **mag·ne·to·spher·ic** \-ˌnē-tə-ˈsfir-ik, -ˈsfer-\ *adjective*

mag·ne·to·stat·ic \mag-ˌnē-tō-ˈsta-tik, -ˌne-\ *adjective* (1893)
: of, relating to, or being a stationary magnetic field

mag·ne·to·stric·tion \-ˈstrik-shən\ *noun* [International Scientific Vocabulary *magnet-* + *-striction* (as in *constriction*)] (1896)
: the change in the dimensions of a ferromagnetic body caused by a change in its state of magnetization

— **mag·ne·to·stric·tive** \-ˈstrik-tiv\ *adjective*

— **mag·ne·to·stric·tive·ly** *adverb*

mag·ne·tron \ˈmag-nə-ˌträn\ *noun* [blend of *magnet* and *-tron*] (1924)
: a diode vacuum tube in which the flow of electrons is controlled by an externally applied magnetic field to generate power at microwave frequencies

magnet school *noun* (1968)
: a school with superior facilities and staff and specialized curricula designed to attract pupils from all segments of the community

mag·nif·ic \mag-ˈni-fik\ *adjective* [Middle French *magnifique*, from Latin *magnificus*] (15th century)
1 : MAGNIFICENT 2
2 : imposing in size or dignity
3 a : SUBLIME, EXALTED **b** : characterized by grandiloquence : POMPOUS ⟨commenced the conversation in the most *magnific* style —S. T. Coleridge⟩

— **mag·nif·i·cal** \-fi-kəl\ *adjective*

— **mag·nif·i·cal·ly** \-k(ə-)lē\ *adverb*

mag·nif·i·cat \mag-ˈni-fi-ˌkat, -ˌkät; män-ˈyi-fi-ˌkät\ *noun* [Middle English, from Latin, magnifies, from *magnificare* to magnify; from the first word of the canticle] (13th century)
1 *capitalized* **a** : the canticle of the Virgin Mary in Luke 1:46–55 **b** : a musical setting for the Magnificat
2 : an utterance of praise

mag·ni·fi·ca·tion \ˌmag-nə-fə-ˈkā-shən\ *noun* (15th century)
1 : the act of magnifying
2 a : the state of being magnified **b** : the apparent enlargement of an object by an optical instrument — called also *power*

mag·nif·i·cence \mag-ˈni-fə-sən(t)s, məg-\ *noun* [Middle English, from Middle French, from Latin *magnificentia*, from *magnificus* noble in character, magnificent, from *magnus* great — more at MUCH] (14th century)
1 : the quality or state of being magnificent
2 : splendor of surroundings

mag·nif·i·cent \-sənt\ *adjective* (15th century)
1 : great in deed or exalted in place — used only of former famous rulers ⟨Lorenzo the *Magnificent*⟩
2 : marked by stately grandeur and lavishness ⟨a *magnificent* way of life⟩
3 : sumptuous in structure and adornment ⟨a *magnificent* cathedral⟩; *broadly* : strikingly beautiful or impressive ⟨a *magnificent* physique⟩
4 : impressive to the mind or spirit : SUBLIME ⟨*magnificent* prose⟩
5 : exceptionally fine ⟨a *magnificent* day⟩
synonym see GRAND

— **mag·nif·i·cent·ly** *adverb*

mag·nif·i·co \mag-ˈni-fi-ˌkō\ *noun, plural* **-coes** *or* **-cos** [Italian, from *magnifico*, adjective, magnificent, from Latin *magnificus*] (1573)
1 : a nobleman of Venice
2 : a person of high position

mag·ni·fi·er \ˈmag-nə-ˌfī(-ə)r\ *noun* (1550)

: one that magnifies; *especially* : a lens or combination of lenses that makes something appear larger

mag·ni·fy \ˈmag-nə-ˌfī\ *verb* **-fied; -fy·ing** [Middle English *magnifien*, from Middle French *magnifier*, from Latin *magnificare*, from *magnificus*] (14th century)
transitive verb
1 a : EXTOL, LAUD **b** : to cause to be held in greater esteem or respect
2 a : to increase in significance : INTENSIFY **b** : EXAGGERATE
3 : to enlarge in fact or in appearance
intransitive verb
: to have the power of causing objects to appear larger than they are

mag·nil·o·quence \mag-ˈni-lə-kwən(t)s\ *noun* [Latin *magniloquentia*, from *magniloquus* magniloquent, from *magnus* + *loqui* to speak] (circa 1623)
: the quality or state of being magniloquent

mag·nil·o·quent \-kwənt\ *adjective* [back-formation from *magniloquence*] (circa 1656)
: speaking in or characterized by a high-flown often bombastic style or manner

— **mag·nil·o·quent·ly** *adverb*

mag·ni·tude \ˈmag-nə-ˌtüd, -ˌtyüd\ *noun* [Middle English, from Latin *magnitudo*, from *magnus*] (15th century)
1 a : great size or extent **b** (1) : spatial quality : SIZE (2) : QUANTITY, NUMBER
2 : the importance, quality, or caliber of something
3 : a number representing the intrinsic or apparent brightness of a celestial body on a logarithmic scale in which an increase of one unit corresponds to a reduction in the brightness of light by a factor of 2.512
4 : a numerical quantitative measure expressed usually as a multiple of a standard unit

mag·no·lia \mag-ˈnōl-yə\ *noun* [New Latin, from Pierre *Magnol* (died 1715) French botanist] (1748)
: any of a genus (*Magnolia* of the family Magnoliaceae, the magnolia family) of American and Asian shrubs and trees with entire evergreen or deciduous leaves and usually showy white, yellow, rose, or purple flowers usually appearing in early spring

magnolia

mag·num \ˈmag-nəm\ *noun* [Latin, neuter of *magnus* great] (1788)
: a large wine bottle holding about 1.5 liters

mag·num opus \ˈmag-nəm-ˈō-pəs\ *noun* [Latin] (1791)
: a great work; *especially* : the greatest achievement of an artist or writer

¹**mag·pie** \ˈmag-ˌpī\ *noun* [*Mag* (nickname for *Margaret*) + ¹*pie*] (1598)
1 : any of various birds (especially *Pica pica*) related to the jays but having a long graduated tail and black-and-white or brightly colored plumage
2 : a person who chatters noisily
3 : one who collects indiscriminately

²**magpie** *adjective* (1808)
1 : collected indiscriminately : MISCELLANEOUS ⟨*magpie* compilations of unrelated tidbits —Helen R. Cross⟩
2 : given to indiscriminate collecting : ACQUISITIVE ⟨what possible *magpie* instinct had impelled me to retain them —S. J. Perelman⟩

mag tape \ˈmag-\ *noun* (1966)
: MAGNETIC TAPE

ma·guey \mə-ˈgā\ *noun* [Spanish, from Taino] (1589)
1 : any of various fleshy-leaved agaves (as the century plant)
2 : any of several hard fibers derived from magueys; *especially* : CANTALA

ma·gus \ˈmā-gəs\ *noun, plural* **ma·gi** \ˈmā-ˌjī\ [Latin, from Greek *magos* — more at MAGIC] (1621)
1 a : a member of a hereditary priestly class among the ancient Medes and Persians **b** *often capitalized* : one of the traditionally three wise men from the East paying homage to the infant Jesus
2 : MAGICIAN, SORCERER

Mag·yar \ˈmag-ˌyär, ˈmäg-; ˈmä-ˌjär\ *noun* [Hungarian] (1797)
1 : a member of the dominant people of Hungary
2 : HUNGARIAN 2

— **Magyar** *adjective*

ma·ha·ra·ja *or* **ma·ha·ra·jah** \ˌmä-hə-ˈrä-jə, -ˈrä-zhə\ *noun* [Sanskrit *mahārāja*, from *mahat* great + *rājan* raja; akin to Latin *rex* king — more at MUCH, ROYAL] (1698)
: a Hindu prince ranking above a raja

ma·ha·ra·ni *or* **ma·ha·ra·nee** \-ˈrä-nē\ *noun* [Hindi *mahārānī*, from *mahā* great (from Sanskrit *mahat*) + *rānī* rani] (circa 1855)
1 : the wife of a maharaja
2 : a Hindu princess ranking above a rani

ma·ha·ri·shi \ˌmä-hə-ˈrē-shē, -hä-, -ˈri-\ *noun* [Sanskrit *mahārṣi*, from *mahat* + *ṛṣi* sage and poet] (1785)
: a Hindu teacher of mystical knowledge

ma·hat·ma \mə-ˈhät-mə, -ˈhat-\ *noun* [Sanskrit *mahātman*, from *mahātman* great-souled, from *mahat* + *ātman* soul — more at ATMAN] (1923)
1 : a person to be revered for high-mindedness, wisdom, and selflessness
2 : a person of great prestige in a field of endeavor

Ma·ha·ya·na \ˌmä-hə-ˈyä-nə\ *noun* [Sanskrit *mahāyāna*, literally, great vehicle] (1855)
: a liberal and theistic branch of Buddhism comprising sects chiefly in China and Japan, recognizing a large body of scripture in addition to the Pali canon, and teaching social concern and universal salvation — compare THERAVADA

— **Ma·ha·ya·nist** \-ˈyä-nist\ *noun or adjective*

— **Ma·ha·ya·nis·tic** \-ˈyä-ˈnis-tik\ *adjective*

Mah·di \ˈmä-dē\ *noun* [Arabic *mahdīy*, literally, one rightly guided] (1800)
1 : the expected messiah of Muslim tradition
2 : a Muslim leader who assumes a messianic role

— **Mah·dism** \ˈmä-ˌdi-zəm\ *noun*

— **Mah·dist** \ˈmä-dist\ *noun*

Ma·hi·can \mə-ˈhē-kən\ *noun, plural* **Mahican** *or* **Mahicans** [Mahican] (circa 1614)
1 : a member of an American Indian people of the upper Hudson River valley
2 : the extinct Algonquian language of the Mahican people

ma·hi·ma·hi \ˌmä-hē-ˈmä-(ˌ)hē\ *noun* [Hawaiian, Tahitian, & Marquesan] (1943)
: the flesh of a dolphin (*Coryphaena hippurus*) used for food; *also* : the fish

mah·jongg *or* **mah·jong** \ˌmä-ˈzhäŋ, -ˈjäŋ, -ˈzhȯŋ, -ˈjȯŋ, ˈmä-,\ *noun* [from *Mah-Jongg*, a trademark] (1920)
: a game of Chinese origin usually played by four persons with 144 tiles that are drawn and discarded until one player secures a winning hand

mahl·stick \ˈmȯl-\ *variant of* MAULSTICK

ma·hoe \mə-ˈhō, ˈmä-ˌ\ *noun* [French *maho*, from Taino] (1666)
: either of two tropical hibiscus trees (*Hibiscus elatus* and *H. tiliaceus*)

ma·hog·a·ny \mə-ˈhä-gə-nē\ *noun, plural* **-nies** [origin unknown] (circa 1660)

1 : the wood of any of various chiefly tropical trees (family Meliaceae, the mahogany family): **a** (1) : the durable yellowish brown to reddish brown usually moderately hard and heavy wood of a West Indian tree (*Swietenia mahagoni*) that is widely used for cabinetwork and fine finish work (2) : a wood similar to mahogany from a congeneric tree (especially *S. macrophylla*) **b** (1) : the rather hard heavy usually odorless wood of any of several African trees (genus *Khaya*) (2) : the rather lightweight cedar-scented wood of any of several African trees (genus *Entandrophragma*) that varies in color from pinkish to deep reddish brown
2 : any of various woods resembling or substituted for mahogany obtained from trees of the mahogany family
3 : a tree that yields mahogany
4 : a moderate reddish brown
ma·ho·nia \mə-'hō-nē-ə\ *noun* [New Latin, from Bernard Mc*Mahon* (died 1816) American botanist] (1829)
: any of a genus (*Mahonia*) of American and Asian shrubs (as the Oregon grape) of the barberry family
ma·hout \mə-'haủt\ *noun* [Hindi *mahāwat, mahāut*] (1662)
: a keeper and driver of an elephant
Mah·rat·ta *variant of* MARATHA
maid \'mād\ *noun* [Middle English *maide*, short for *maiden*] (13th century)
1 : an unmarried girl or woman especially when young : VIRGIN
2 a : MAIDSERVANT **b** : a woman or girl employed to do domestic work
¹**maid·en** \'mā-dⁿn\ *noun* [Middle English, from Old English *mægden, mæden*, diminutive of *mægeth*; akin to Old High German *magad* maiden, Old Irish *mug* serf] (before 12th century)
1 : an unmarried girl or woman : MAID
2 : a former Scottish beheading device resembling the guillotine
3 : a horse that has never won a race
²**maiden** *adjective* (14th century)
1 a (1) : not married ⟨*maiden* aunt⟩ (2) : VIRGIN **b** *of a female animal* (1) : never yet mated (2) : never having borne young
2 : of, relating to, or befitting a maiden
3 : FIRST, EARLIEST ⟨*maiden* voyage⟩ ⟨*maiden* flight of a spacecraft⟩
maid·en·hair fern \-,har-, -,her-\ *noun* (1833)
: any of a genus (*Adiantum*) of ferns with delicate palmately branched fronds — called also *maidenhair*
maidenhair tree *noun* (1773)
: GINKGO
maid·en·head \'mā-dⁿn-,hed\ *noun* [Middle English *maidenhed*, from *maiden* + *-hed* -hood; akin to Middle English *-hod* -hood] (13th century)
1 : the quality or state of being a maiden : VIRGINITY
2 : HYMEN
maid·en·hood \-,hủd\ *noun* (before 12th century)
: the quality, state, or time of being a maiden
maid·en·li·ness \-lē-nəs\ *noun* (1555)
: conduct or traits befitting a maiden
maid·en·ly \-lē\ *adjective* (15th century)
: of, resembling, or suitable to a maiden
maiden name *noun* (1689)
: the surname of a woman before she marries
maid·hood \'mād-,hủd\ *noun* (before 12th century)
: MAIDENHOOD
maid–in–wait·ing \'mā-dⁿn-'wā-tiŋ\ *noun, plural* **maids–in–wait·ing** \'mādz-\ (1953)

: a young woman of a queen's or princess's household appointed to attend her
Maid Mar·i·an \-'mer-ē-ən, -'mar-\ *noun*
: a companion of Robin Hood in some forms of his legend
maid of honor (circa 1586)
1 : an unmarried lady usually of noble birth whose duty it is to attend a queen or a princess
2 : a bride's principal unmarried wedding attendant
maid·ser·vant \'mād-,sər-vənt\ *noun* (14th century)
: a female servant
ma·ieu·tic \mā-'yü-tik, mī-\ *adjective* [Greek *maieutikos* of midwifery] (1655)
: relating to or resembling the Socratic method of eliciting new ideas from another
¹**mail** \'mā(ə)l\ *noun* [Middle English *male, maille*, from Old English *māl* agreement, pay, from Old Norse *māl* speech, agreement; akin to Old English *mǣl* speech] (before 12th century)
chiefly Scottish : PAYMENT, RENT
²**mail** *noun, often attributive* [Middle English *male*, from Old French, of Germanic origin; akin to Old High German *malaha* bag] (13th century)
1 *chiefly Scottish* : BAG, WALLET
2 a : something sent or carried in the postal system **b** : a conveyance that transports mail **c** : messages sent electronically to an individual (as through a computer system)
3 : a nation's postal system — often used in plural
³**mail** *transitive verb* (1827)
: to send by mail : POST
— **mail·abil·i·ty** \,mā-lə-'bi-lə-tē\ *noun*
— **mail·able** \'mā-lə-bəl\ *adjective*
⁴**mail** *noun* [Middle English *maille*, from Middle French, from Latin *macula* spot, mesh] (14th century)
1 : armor made of metal links or sometimes plates
2 : a hard enclosing covering of an animal (as a tortoise)
— **mailed** \'mā(ə)ld\ *adjective*
mail·bag \'mā(ə)l-,bag\ *noun* (1812)
1 : a letter carrier's shoulder bag
2 : a pouch used in the shipment of mail
mail·box \-,bäks\ *noun* (1872)
1 : a public box for deposit of outgoing mail
2 : a box at or near a dwelling for the occupant's mail
3 : a computer file in which electronic mail is collected
mail carrier *noun* (1790)
: LETTER CARRIER
mail drop *noun* (1945)
1 : an address used in transmitting secret communications
2 : a receptacle or a slot for deposit of mail
mai·le \'mī-lē\ *noun* [Hawaiian] (1903)
: a Pacific island vine (*Alyxia olivaeformis*) of the dogbane family with fragrant leaves and bark that are used for decoration and in Hawaii for leis
mailed fist *noun* (1897)
: a threat of armed or overbearing force
mail·er \'mā-lər\ *noun* (1884)
1 : one that mails
2 : a container for mailing something
3 : something (as an advertisement) sent by mail
Mail·gram \'māl-,gram\ *trademark*
— used for a message sent by wire to a post office that delivers it to the addressee
mail·ing \'mā-liŋ\ *noun* (1946)
: the mail dispatched at one time by a sender
mail·lot \mī-'ō, mä-'yō\ *noun* [French] (1888)
1 : tights for dancers or gymnasts
2 : JERSEY 2
3 : a woman's one-piece bathing suit
mail·man \'mā(ə)l-,man\ *noun* (1881)
: a man who delivers mail — called also *postman*
mail order *noun* (1867)

: an order for goods that is received and filled by mail
— **mail–or·der** \-,ȯr-dər\ *adjective*
¹**maim** \'mām\ *transitive verb* [Middle English *maynhen, maymen*, from Old French *maynier* — more at MAYHEM] (14th century)
1 : to commit the felony of mayhem upon
2 : to mutilate, disfigure, or wound seriously ☆
— **maim·er** *noun*
²**maim** *noun* (14th century)
1 *obsolete* : serious physical injury; *especially* : loss of a member of the body
2 *obsolete* : a serious loss
¹**main** \'mān\ *noun* [in sense 1, from Middle English, from Old English *mægen*; akin to Old High German *magan* strength, Old English *magan* to be able; in other senses, from ²*main* or by shortening — more at MAY] (before 12th century)
1 : physical strength : FORCE — used in the phrase *with might and main*
2 a : MAINLAND **b** : HIGH SEA
3 : the chief part : essential point ⟨they are in the *main* well-trained⟩
4 : a pipe, duct, or circuit which carries the combined flow of tributary branches of a utility system
5 a : MAINMAST **b** : MAINSAIL
²**main** *adjective* [Middle English, from Old English *mægen-*, from *mægen* strength] (15th century)
1 : CHIEF, PRINCIPAL ⟨the *main* idea⟩
2 : fully exerted : SHEER ⟨*main* force⟩ ⟨by *main* strength⟩
3 *obsolete* : of or relating to a broad expanse (as of sea)
4 : connected with or located near the mainmast or mainsail
5 : expressing the chief predication in a complex sentence ⟨the *main* clause⟩
main chance *noun* (1584)
: the best chance for personal or financial gain ⟨kept an eye on the *main chance*⟩
Maine coon *noun* (1935)
: any of a breed of large long-haired domestic cats that have a very full tapered tail — called also *coon cat, Maine cat*
main·frame \'mān-,frām\ *noun* (circa 1964)
: a computer with its cabinet and internal circuits; *also* : a large fast computer that can handle multiple tasks concurrently

Maine coon

main·land \'mān-,land, -lənd\ *noun* (14th century)
: a continent or the main part of a continent as distinguished from an offshore island or sometimes from a cape or peninsula

maidenhair fern

— **main·land·er** \-ˌlan-dər, -lən-\ *noun*

¹**main·line** \ˈmān-ˌlīn\ (1938)
transitive verb
slang **:** to take by or as if by injecting into a principal vein
intransitive verb
slang **:** to mainline a narcotic drug

²**mainline** *adjective* (1941)
: being part of an established group; *also* **:** being in the mainstream

main line *noun* (1841)
1 : a principal highway or railroad line
2 *slang* **:** a principal vein of the circulatory system

main·ly \ˈmān-lē\ *adverb* (13th century)
1 *obsolete* **:** in a forceful manner
2 : for the most part **:** CHIEFLY

main man *noun* (1967)
1 : best male friend
2 : a man whose character or work is most admired
3 : the most reliable or effective performer

main·mast \ˈmān-ˌmast, -məst\ *noun* (15th century)
: a sailing ship's principal mast usually second from the bow

mains \ˈmānz\ *adjective* (circa 1927)
British **:** of or relating to utility distribution mains ⟨*mains* voltage⟩ ⟨*mains* water⟩

main·sail \ˈmān-ˌsāl, ˈmān(t)-səl\ *noun* (15th century)
: the principal sail on the mainmast — see SAIL illustration

main sequence *noun* (1925)
: the group of stars that on a graph of spectrum versus luminosity forms a band comprising 90% of stellar types and that includes stars believed to be representative of the stages a normal star passes through for the majority of its lifetime

main·sheet \ˈmān-ˌshēt\ *noun* (15th century)
: a rope by which the mainsail is trimmed and secured

main·spring \ˈmān-ˌspriŋ\ *noun* (1591)
1 : the chief spring in a mechanism especially of a watch or clock
2 : the chief or most powerful motive, agent, or cause

main squeeze *noun* (circa 1968)
slang **:** one's principal romantic partner

main·stay \ˈmān-ˌstā\ *noun* (15th century)
1 : a ship's stay extending from the maintop forward usually to the foot of the foremast
2 : a chief support

main stem *noun* (1832)
: a main trunk or channel: as **a :** the main course of a river or stream **b :** the main street of a city or town

¹**main·stream** \ˈmān-ˌstrēm\ *noun* (1831)
: a prevailing current or direction of activity or influence
— **mainstream** *adjective*

²**main·stream** \ˈmān-ˈstrēm\ *transitive verb* (1974)
: to place (as a handicapped child) in regular school classes

Main Street *noun* (circa 1743)
1 : the principal street of a small town
2 a : the sections of a country centering about its small towns **b :** a place or environment characterized by materialistic self-complacent provincialism **c :** MIDDLE AMERICA 3
— **Main Street·er** \ˈmān-ˌstrē-tər\ *noun*

main·tain \mān-ˈtān, mən-\ *transitive verb* [Middle English *mainteinen*, from Old French *maintenir*, from Medieval Latin *manutenēre*, from Latin *manu tenēre* to hold in the hand] (14th century)
1 : to keep in an existing state (as of repair, efficiency, or validity) **:** preserve from failure or decline ⟨*maintain* machinery⟩
2 : to sustain against opposition or danger **:** uphold and defend ⟨*maintain* a position⟩
3 : to continue or persevere in **:** CARRY ON, KEEP UP ⟨couldn't *maintain* his composure⟩

4 a : to support or provide for ⟨has a family to *maintain*⟩ **b :** SUSTAIN ⟨enough food to *maintain* life⟩
5 : to affirm in or as if in argument **:** ASSERT ⟨*maintained* that the earth is flat⟩ ☆
— **main·tain·abil·i·ty** \-ˌtā-nə-ˈbi-lə-tē\ *noun*
— **main·tain·able** \-ˈtā-nə-bəl\ *adjective*
— **main·tain·er** *noun*

main·te·nance \ˈmānt-nən(t)s, ˈmān-tᵊn-ən(t)s\ *noun* [Middle English, from Middle French, from Old French, from *maintenir*] (14th century)
1 : the act of maintaining **:** the state of being maintained **:** SUPPORT
2 : something that maintains
3 : the upkeep of property or equipment
4 : an officious or unlawful intermeddling in a legal suit by assisting either party with means to carry it on

main·top \ˈmān-ˌtäp\ *noun* (15th century)
: a platform about the head of the mainmast of a square-rigged ship

main–top·mast \mān-ˈtäp-ˌmast, -məst\ *noun* (15th century)
: a mast next above the mainmast

main yard *noun* (15th century)
: the yard of a mainsail

mair \ˈmār\ *chiefly Scottish variant of* MORE

mai·son·ette \ˌmā-zᵊn-ˈet, -sᵊn-\ *noun* [French *maisonnette*, from Old French, diminutive of *maison* house, from Latin *mansion-, mansio* dwelling place — more at MANSION] (1793)
1 : a small house
2 : an apartment often on two floors

mai·tre d' *or* **mai·tre d'** \ˌmā-trə-ˈdē, ˌme-, -tər-\ *noun, plural* **maître d's** *or* **maître d's** \-ˈdēz\ (1950)
: MAÎTRE D'HÔTEL

mai·tre d'hô·tel \ˌmā-trə-(ˌ)dō-ˈtel, ˌme-; ˌmāt-dō-, -met-\ *noun, plural* **maîtres d'hôtel** \same\ [French, literally, master of house] (1538)
1 a : MAJORDOMO **b :** HEADWAITER
2 : a sauce of butter, parsley, salt, pepper, and lemon juice — called also *maître d'hôtel butter*

maize \ˈmāz\ *noun* [Spanish *maíz*, from Taino *mahiz*] (1555)
: INDIAN CORN

ma·jes·tic \mə-ˈjes-tik\ *adjective* (1601)
: having or exhibiting majesty **:** STATELY
synonym see GRAND
— **ma·jes·ti·cal·ly** \-ti-k(ə-)lē\ *adverb*

maj·es·ty \ˈma-jə-stē\ *noun, plural* **-ties** [Middle English *maieste*, from Middle French *majesté*, from Latin *majestat-, majestas*; akin to Latin *major* greater] (14th century)
1 : sovereign power, authority, or dignity
2 — used in addressing or referring to reigning sovereigns and their consorts ⟨Your *Majesty*⟩ ⟨Her *Majesty's* Government⟩
3 a : royal bearing or aspect **:** GRANDEUR **b :** greatness or splendor of quality or character

ma·jol·i·ca \mə-ˈjä-li-kə\ *also* **ma·iol·i·ca** \-ˈyä-\ *noun* [Italian *maiolica*, from Old Italian *Maiolica, Maiorica* Majorca] (1555)
1 : earthenware covered with an opaque tin glaze and decorated on the glaze before firing; *especially* **:** an Italian ware of this kind
2 : a 19th century earthenware modeled in naturalistic shapes and glazed in lively colors

¹**ma·jor** \ˈmā-jər\ *adjective* [Middle English *maiour*, from Latin *major*, comparative of *magnus* great, large — more at MUCH] (15th century)
1 : greater in dignity, rank, importance, or interest ⟨one of the *major* poets⟩
2 : greater in number, quantity, or extent ⟨the *major* part of his work⟩
3 : having attained majority
4 : notable or conspicuous in effect or scope **:** CONSIDERABLE ⟨a *major* improvement⟩
5 : involving grave risk **:** SERIOUS ⟨a *major* illness⟩

6 : of or relating to a subject of academic study chosen as a field of specialization
7 a : having half steps between the third and fourth and the seventh and eighth degrees ⟨*major* scale⟩ **b :** based on a major scale ⟨*major* key⟩ **c :** equivalent to the distance between the keynote and another tone (except the fourth and fifth) of a major scale ⟨*major* third⟩ **d :** having a major third above the root ⟨*major* triad⟩

²**major** *noun* (1616)
1 : a person who has attained majority
2 a : one that is superior in rank, importance, size, or performance ⟨economic power of the oil *majors*⟩ **b :** a major musical interval, scale, key, or mode
3 : a commissioned officer in the army, air force, or marine corps ranking above a captain and below a lieutenant colonel
4 a : an academic subject chosen as a field of specialization **b :** a student specializing in such a field ⟨a history *major*⟩
5 *plural* **:** major league baseball — used with *the*

³**major** *intransitive verb* (1913)
: to pursue an academic major

major axis *noun* (1854)
: the axis passing through the foci of an ellipse

ma·jor·do·mo \ˌmā-jər-ˈdō-(ˌ)mō\ *noun, plural* **-mos** [Spanish *mayordomo* or obsolete Italian *maiordomo*, from Medieval Latin *major domus*, literally, chief of the house] (1589)
1 : a head steward of a large household (as a palace)
2 : BUTLER, STEWARD
3 : a person who speaks, makes arrangements, or takes charge for another

ma·jor·ette \ˌmā-jə-ˈret\ *noun* (1940)
: DRUM MAJORETTE 2

major general *noun* [French *major général*, from *major*, noun + *général*, adjective, general] (1642)
: a commissioned officer in the army, air force, or marine corps who ranks above a brigadier general and whose insignia is two stars

major histocompatibility complex *noun* (1975)
: a group of genes in mammals that function especially in determining the histocompatibility antigens found on cell surfaces

ma·jor·i·tar·i·an \mə-ˌjȯr-ə-ˈter-ē-ən, -ˌjär-\ *noun* (1942)
: a person who believes in or advocates majoritarianism
— **majoritarian** *adjective*

ma·jor·i·tar·i·an·ism \-ē-ə-ˌni-zəm\ *noun* (1942)
: the philosophy or practice according to which decisions of an organized group should be made by a numerical majority of its members

☆ **SYNONYMS**
Maintain, assert, defend, vindicate, justify mean to uphold as true, right, just, or reasonable. MAINTAIN stresses firmness of conviction (steadfastly *maintained* his innocence). ASSERT suggests determination to make others accept one's claim (*asserted* her rights). DEFEND implies maintaining in the face of attack or criticism (*defended* his voting record). VINDICATE implies successfully defending (his success *vindicated* our faith in him). JUSTIFY implies showing to be true, just, or valid by appeal to a standard or to precedent (the action was used to *justify* military intervention).

\ə\ **abut** \ᵊ\ **kitten** \ər\ **further** \a\ **ash** \ā\ **ace**
\ä\ **mop, mar** \au̇\ **out** \ch\ **chin** \e\ **bet** \ē\ **easy**
\g\ **go** \i\ **hit** \ī\ **ice** \j\ **job** \ŋ\ **sing** \ō\ **go**
\ȯ\ **law** \ȯi\ **boy** \th\ **thin** \t̲h̲\ **the** \ü\ **loot** \u̇\ **foot**
\y\ **yet** \zh\ **vision** *see also* Guide to Pronunciation

ma·jor·i·ty \mə-ˈjȯr-ə-tē, -ˈjär-\ *noun, plural* **-ties** (1552)
1 *obsolete* **:** the quality or state of being greater
2 a : the age at which full civil rights are accorded **b :** the status of one who has attained this age
3 a : a number greater than half of a total **b :** the excess of a majority over the remainder of the total **:** MARGIN **c :** the preponderant quantity or share
4 : the group or political party whose votes preponderate
5 : the military office, rank, or commission of a major
— **majority** *adjective*

majority leader *noun* (1952)
: a leader of the majority party in a legislative body (as the U.S. Senate)

majority rule *noun* (1893)
: a political principle providing that a majority usually constituted by fifty percent plus one of an organized group will have the power to make decisions binding upon the whole

major league *noun* (1906)
1 : a league of highest classification in U.S. professional baseball; *broadly* **:** a league of major importance in any of various sports
2 : BIG TIME 2
— **major–league** *adjective*

ma·jor·ly \ˈmā-jər-lē\ *adverb* (1956)
: in a major way **a :** PRIMARILY 1 ⟨was *majorly* a poet⟩ **b :** EXTREMELY 1 ⟨was *majorly* annoyed⟩

major–medical *adjective* (circa 1955)
: of, relating to, or being a form of insurance designed to pay all or part of the medical bills of major illnesses usually after deduction of a fixed initial sum

major order *noun* (circa 1741)
: one of the Roman Catholic or Eastern clerical orders that are sacramentally conferred and have a sacred character that implies major religious obligations (as clerical celibacy) — usually used in plural; compare MINOR ORDER

major party *noun* (1950)
: a political party having electoral strength sufficient to permit it to win control of a government usually with comparative regularity and when defeated to constitute the principal opposition to the party in power

major penalty *noun* (circa 1936)
: a 5-minute suspension of a player in ice hockey or lacrosse

major premise *noun* (1860)
: the premise of a syllogism containing the major term

major seminary *noun* (1945)
: a Roman Catholic seminary giving usually the entire six years of senior college and theological training required for major orders

major suit *noun* (1916)
: either of the suits hearts or spades having superior scoring value in bridge

major term *noun* (1847)
: the term of a syllogism constituting the predicate of the conclusion

ma·jus·cule \ˈma-jəs-ˌkyü(ə)l, mə-ˈjəs-\ *noun* [French, from Latin *majusculus* rather large, diminutive of *major*] (circa 1825)
: a large letter (as a capital)
— **ma·jus·cu·lar** \mə-ˈjəs-kyə-lər\ *adjective*
— **majuscule** *adjective*

mak·able *or* **make·able** \ˈmā-kə-bəl\ *adjective* (15th century)
: capable of being made

mak·ar \ˈmä-kər, ˈmā-\ *noun* [Middle English *maker*] (14th century)
chiefly Scottish **:** POET

¹make \ˈmāk\ *verb* **made** \ˈmād\; **mak·ing** [Middle English, from Old English *macian*; akin to Old High German *mahhōn* to prepare, make, Greek *magēnai* to be kneaded, Old Church Slavonic *mazati* to anoint, smear] (before 12th century)

transitive verb
1 a *obsolete* **:** BEHAVE, ACT **b :** to seem to begin (an action) ⟨*made* to go⟩
2 a : to cause to happen to or be experienced by someone ⟨*made* trouble for us⟩ **b :** to cause to exist, occur, or appear **:** CREATE ⟨*make* a disturbance⟩ **c :** to favor the growth or occurrence of ⟨haste *makes* waste⟩ **d :** to fit, intend, or destine by or as if by creating ⟨was *made* to be an actor⟩
3 a : to bring into being by forming, shaping, or altering material **:** FASHION ⟨*make* a dress⟩ **b :** COMPOSE, WRITE ⟨*make* verses⟩ **c :** to lay out and construct ⟨*make* a road⟩
4 : to frame or formulate in the mind ⟨*make* plans⟩
5 : to put together from components **:** CONSTITUTE ⟨houses *made* of stone⟩
6 a : to compute or estimate to be **b :** to form and hold in the mind ⟨*make* no doubt of it⟩
7 a : to assemble and set alight the materials for (a fire) **b :** to set in order ⟨*make* beds⟩ **:** PREPARE, FIX ⟨*make* dinner⟩ **d :** to shuffle (a deck of cards) in preparation for dealing
8 : to prepare (hay) by cutting, drying, and storing
9 a : to cause to be or become ⟨*made* them happy⟩ **b :** APPOINT ⟨*made* him bishop⟩
10 a : ENACT, ESTABLISH ⟨*make* laws⟩ **b :** to execute in an appropriate manner ⟨*make* a will⟩ **c :** SET, NAME ⟨*make* a price⟩
11 *chiefly dialect* **:** SHUT ⟨the doors are *made* against you —Shakespeare⟩ **b :** to cause (an electric circuit) to be completed
12 a : to conclude as to the nature or meaning of something ⟨what do you *make* of this development?⟩ **b :** to regard as being ⟨not the fool some *make* him⟩
13 a : to carry out (an action indicated or implied by the object) ⟨*make* war⟩ ⟨*make* a speech⟩ **b :** to perform with a bodily movement ⟨*make* a sweeping gesture⟩ **c :** to achieve by traversing ⟨*make* a detour⟩ ⟨*making* the rounds⟩
14 a : to produce as a result of action, effort, or behavior with respect to something ⟨*make* a mess of the job⟩ ⟨tried to *make* a thorough job of it⟩ **b** *archaic* **:** to turn into another language by translation
15 : to cause to act in a certain way **:** COMPEL ⟨*make* her give it back⟩
16 : to cause or assure the success or prosperity of ⟨can either *make* you or break you⟩
17 a : to amount to in significance ⟨*makes* a great difference⟩ **b :** to form the essential being of ⟨clothes *make* the man⟩ **c :** to form by an assembling of individuals ⟨*make* a quorum⟩ **d :** to count as ⟨that *makes* the third time you've said it⟩
18 a : to be or be capable of being changed or fashioned into ⟨rags *make* the best paper⟩ **b :** to develop into ⟨she will *make* a fine judge⟩ **c :** FORM 6b
19 a : REACH, ATTAIN — often used with *it* ⟨you'll never *make* it that far⟩; *also* **:** SURVIVE ⟨half the cubs won't *make* it through their first year⟩ **b :** to gain the rank of ⟨*make* major⟩ **c :** to gain a place on or in ⟨*make* the team⟩ ⟨the story *made* the papers⟩
20 : to gain (as money) by working, trading, or dealing ⟨*make* a living⟩
21 a : to act so as to win or acquire ⟨*makes* friends easily⟩ **b :** to score (points) in a game or sport **c :** to convert (a split) into a spare in bowling
22 a : to fulfill (a contract) in a card game **b :** to win a trick with (a card)
23 a : to include in a route or itinerary ⟨*make* New York on the return trip⟩ ⟨*make* it to the party⟩ **b :** CATCH 6b ⟨*made* the bus just in time⟩
24 : to persuade to consent to sexual intercourse **:** SEDUCE
25 : to provide the most enjoyable or satisfying experience of ⟨meeting the star of the show really *made* our day⟩
intransitive verb

1 *archaic* **:** to compose poetry
2 a : BEHAVE, ACT **b :** to begin or seem to begin a certain action ⟨*made* as though to hand it to me⟩ **c :** to act so as to be or to seem to be ⟨*make* merry⟩ **d** *slang* **:** to play a part — usually used with *like*
3 : SET OUT, HEAD ⟨*made* after the fox⟩ ⟨*made* straight for home⟩
4 : to increase in height or size ⟨the tide is *making* now⟩
5 : to reach or extend in a certain direction
6 : to have considerable effect ⟨courtesy *makes* for safer driving⟩
7 : to undergo manufacture or processing ⟨the silk *makes* up beautifully⟩
— **make a face :** to distort one's features **:** GRIMACE
— **make a mountain out of a molehill :** to treat a trifling matter as of great importance
— **make away with 1 :** to carry off **:** STEAL **2 :** KILL
— **make believe :** PRETEND, FEIGN
— **make bold :** VENTURE, DARE
— **make book :** to accept bets at calculated odds on all the entrants in a race or contest
— **make common cause :** to unite to achieve a shared goal
— **make do :** to get along or manage with the means at hand
— **make ends meet :** to make one's means adequate to one's needs
— **make eyes :** OGLE
— **make fun of :** to make an object of amusement or laughter **:** RIDICULE, MOCK
— **make good 1 :** to make valid or complete: as **a :** to make up for (a deficiency) **b :** INDEMNIFY ⟨*make good* the loss⟩ **c :** to carry out successfully ⟨*made good* his promise⟩ ⟨*made good* their escape⟩ **d :** PROVE ⟨*made good* a charge⟩ **2 :** to prove to be capable; *also* **:** SUCCEED
— **make hay :** to make use of offered opportunity especially in gaining an early advantage
— **make head 1 :** to make progress especially against resistance **2 :** to rise in armed revolt
— **make it 1 :** to be successful ⟨trying to *make it* in the big time as a fashion photographer —Joe Kane⟩ ⟨the crème brûlée didn't quite *make it*⟩ **2 :** to have sexual intercourse
— **make light of :** to treat as of little account
— **make love 1 :** WOO, COURT **2 a :** NECK, PET **b :** to engage in sexual intercourse
— **make much of 1 :** to treat as of importance **2 :** to treat with obvious affection or special consideration
— **make no bones :** to be straightforward, unhesitating, or sure ⟨*makes no bones* about the seriousness of the matter⟩
— **make one's mark :** to achieve success or fame
— **make public :** DISCLOSE
— **make sail 1 :** to raise or spread sail **2 :** to set out on a voyage
— **make shift :** to manage with difficulty
— **make sport of :** RIDICULE, MOCK
— **make the grade :** to measure up to some standard **:** be successful
— **make the most of :** to show or use to the best advantage
— **make the scene :** to be present at or participate in a usually specified activity or event
— **make time 1 :** to travel fast **2 :** to gain time **3 :** to make progress toward winning favor ⟨trying to *make time* with the waitress⟩
— **make tracks 1 :** to proceed at a walk or run **2 :** to go in a hurry **:** RUN AWAY, FLEE
— **make use of :** to put to use **:** EMPLOY
— **make water 1** *of a boat* **:** LEAK **2 :** URINATE
— **make waves :** to create a stir or disturbance

— **make way 1 :** to give room for passing, entering, or occupying **2 :** to make progress
— **make with** *slang* **:** PRODUCE, PERFORM — usually used with *the*

²**make** *noun* (14th century)
1 a : the manner or style in which a thing is constructed **b :** BRAND 4a
2 : the physical, mental, or moral constitution of a person ⟨men of his *make* are rare⟩
3 a : the action of producing or manufacturing **b :** the actual yield or amount produced over a specified period **:** OUTPUT
4 : the act of shuffling cards; *also* **:** turn to shuffle
— **on the make 1 :** in the process of forming, growing, or improving **2 :** in quest of a higher social or financial status **3 :** in search of sexual adventure

make·bate \'māk-ˌbāt\ *noun* [¹make + obsolete *bate* strife] (1529)
archaic **:** one that excites contention and quarrels

¹**make–be·lieve** \'māk-bə-ˌlēv\ *also* **make–be·lief** \-ˌlēf\ *noun* (1811)
: a pretending to believe

²**make–believe** *adjective* (1824)
: IMAGINARY, PRETENDED

make–do \'māk-ˈdü\ *adjective* (1923)
: MAKESHIFT
— **make–do** *noun*

make·fast \-ˌfast\ *noun* (1898)
: something (as a post or buoy) to which a boat can be fastened

make off *intransitive verb* (1709)
: to leave in haste
— **make off with :** to take away; *especially* **:** GRAB, STEAL

make–or–break \'mā-kər-ˈbrāk\ *adjective* (1919)
: allowing no middle ground between success and failure

make out (15th century)
transitive verb
1 : to complete (as a printed form) by supplying required information ⟨*make out* a check⟩
2 : to find or grasp the meaning of ⟨tried to *make out* what had really happened⟩
3 : to form an opinion or idea about **:** CONCLUDE ⟨how do you *make* that *out*⟩
4 a : to represent as being ⟨*made* them *out* to be losers⟩ **b :** to pretend to be true ⟨*made out* that he had never heard of me⟩
5 : to represent or delineate in detail
6 : to see and identify with difficulty or effort **:** DISCERN ⟨*make out* a ship through the fog⟩
intransitive verb
1 : GET ALONG, FARE ⟨how are you *making out* with the new job⟩
2 a : to engage in sexual intercourse **b :** NECK 1

make·over \'mā-ˌkō-vər\ *noun* (1927)
: an act or instance of making over; *especially* **:** a changing of a person's appearance (as by the use of cosmetics or a different hairdo)

make over *transitive verb* (1546)
1 : to transfer the title of (property)
2 : REMAKE, REMODEL ⟨*made* the whole house *over*⟩

mak·er \'mā-kər\ *noun* (14th century)
: one that makes: as **a** *capitalized* **:** GOD 1 **b** *archaic* **:** POET **c :** a person who borrows money on a promissory note **d :** MANUFACTURER

make·ready \'māk-ˌre-dē\ *noun, plural* **-readies** (1887)
: final preparation (as of a form on a printing press) for running

make·shift \'māk-ˌshift\ *noun* (circa 1812)
: a usually crude and temporary expedient **:** SUBSTITUTE
synonym see RESOURCE
— **makeshift** *adjective*

make–up \'mā-ˌkəp\ *noun* (1821)
1 a : the way in which the parts or ingredients of something are put together **:** COMPOSITION **b** **:** physical, mental, and moral constitution

2 a : the operation of making up especially pages for printing **b :** design or layout of printed matter
3 a (1) **:** cosmetics used to color and beautify the face (2) **:** a cosmetic applied to other parts of the body **b :** materials (as wigs and cosmetics) used in making up or in special costuming (as for a play)
4 : REPLACEMENT; *specifically* **:** material added (as in a manufacturing process) to replace material that has been used up ⟨*makeup* water⟩
5 : a special examination in which a student may make up for absence or previous failure

make up (14th century)
transitive verb
1 a : to form by fitting together or assembling ⟨*make up* a train of cars⟩ **b :** to arrange typeset matter in (as pages) for printing
2 a : to combine to produce (a sum or whole) **b :** CONSTITUTE, COMPOSE ⟨10 chapters *make up* this volume⟩
3 : to make good (a deficiency)
4 : SETTLE, DECIDE ⟨*made up* my mind to depart⟩
5 : to wrap or fasten up ⟨*make* the books *up* into a parcel⟩
6 a : to prepare in physical appearance for a role **b :** to apply cosmetics to
7 a : INVENT, IMPROVISE ⟨*make up* a story⟩ **b** **:** to set in order ⟨rooms are *made up* daily⟩
intransitive verb
1 : to become reconciled ⟨quarreled but later *made up*⟩
2 a : to act ingratiatingly and flatteringly ⟨*made up* to his aunt for a new bicycle⟩ **b :** to make advances **:** COURT
3 : COMPENSATE ⟨*make up* for lost time⟩
4 a : to put on costumes or makeup (as for a play) **b :** to apply cosmetics

make·weight \'māk-ˌwāt\ *noun* (1695)
1 a : something thrown into a scale to bring the weight to a desired value **b :** something of little independent value thrown in to fill a gap
2 : COUNTERWEIGHT, COUNTERPOISE

make–work \'māk-ˌwərk\ *noun* (1923)
: work assigned or done chiefly to keep one busy

ma·ki·mo·no \ˌmä-ki-ˈmō-(ˌ)nō\ *noun, plural* **-nos** [Japanese, scroll, from *maki* roll + *mono* thing] (1882)
: a horizontal Japanese ornamental pictorial or calligraphic scroll

mak·ing \'mā-kiŋ\ *noun* [Middle English, from Old English *macung*, from *macian* to make] (12th century)
1 : the act or process of forming, causing, doing, or coming into being ⟨spots problems in the *making*⟩
2 : a process or means of advancement or success
3 : something made; *especially* **:** a quantity produced at one time **:** BATCH
4 a : POTENTIALITY — often used in plural ⟨had the *makings* of a great artist⟩ **b** *plural* **:** the material from which something is to be made; *especially* \usually ⟨'mā-kənz\ **:** paper and tobacco for rolling cigarettes by hand

ma·ko shark \'mä-(ˌ)kō-, 'mä-\ *noun* [Maori *mako* mako shark] (1926)
: either of two mackerel sharks (*Isurus paucus* and *I. oxyrinchus*) that are notable sport fish and are considered dangerous to humans — called also *mako*; see SHARK illustration

makuta *plural of* LIKUTA

mal- *combining form* [Middle English, Middle French, from Old French, from *mal* bad (from Latin *malus*) & *mal* badly, from Latin *male*, from *malus*]
1 a : bad ⟨*mal*practice⟩ **b :** badly ⟨*mal*odorous⟩
2 a : abnormal ⟨*mal*formation⟩ **b :** abnormally ⟨*mal*formed⟩
3 a : inadequate ⟨*mal*adjustment⟩ **b :** inadequately ⟨*mal*nourished⟩

mal·ab·sorp·tion \ˌma-ləb-ˈsȯrp-shən, -ˈzȯrp-\ *noun* (circa 1929)

: faulty absorption especially of nutrient materials from the alimentary canal

ma·lac·ca \mə-ˈla-kə\ *adjective* [*Malacca*, Malaya] (1844)
: made or comprised of the cane of an Asian rattan palm (*Calamus rotang*) ⟨an umbrella with a *malacca* handle⟩
— **malacca** *noun*

Mal·a·chi \'ma-lə-ˌkī\ *noun* [Hebrew *Mal'ākhī*]
1 — used as the conventional name for the unidentified 5th century B.C. writer of the book of Malachi
2 : a prophetic book of canonical Jewish and Christian Scripture — see BIBLE table

Mal·a·chi·as \ˌma-lə-ˈkī-əs\ *noun* [Late Latin, from Greek, from Hebrew *Mal'ākhī*]
: MALACHI

mal·a·chite \'ma-lə-ˌkīt\ *noun* [alteration of Middle English *melochites*, from Latin *molochites*, from Greek *molochītēs*, from *molochē*, *malachē* mallow] (1656)
: a mineral that is a green basic carbonate of copper used as an ore and for making ornamental objects

mal·a·col·o·gy \ˌma-lə-ˈkä-lə-jē\ *noun* [French *malacologie*, contraction of *malacozoologie*, from New Latin *Malacozoa*, zoological group including soft-bodied animals (from Greek *malakos* soft + New Latin *-zoa*) + French *-logie* -logy] (1836)
: a branch of zoology dealing with mollusks
— **mal·a·co·log·i·cal** \ˌma-lə-kə-ˈlä-ji-kəl\ *adjective*
— **mal·a·col·o·gist** \ˌma-lə-ˈkä-lə-jist\ *noun*

mal·a·cos·tra·can \ˌma-lə-ˈkäs-tri-kən\ *noun* [ultimately from Greek *malakostrakos* soft-shelled, from *malakos* soft + *ostrakon* shell — more at MOLLIFY, OYSTER] (1835)
: any of a large subclass (Malacostraca) of crustaceans having a thorax consisting of eight segments usually covered by a carapace and including the decapods and isopods
— **malacostracan** *adjective*

mal·ad·ap·ta·tion \ˌma-la-ˌdap-ˈtā-shən\ *noun* (1877)
: poor or inadequate adaptation

mal·adapt·ed \ˌma-lə-ˈdap-təd\ *adjective* (1943)
: unsuited or poorly suited (as to a particular use, purpose, or situation)

mal·adap·tive \-ˈtiv\ *adjective* (1931)
1 : marked by poor or inadequate adaptation
2 : not conducive to adaptation

mal·ad·just·ed \ˌma-lə-ˈjəs-təd\ *adjective* (1886)
: poorly or inadequately adjusted; *specifically* **:** lacking harmony with one's environment from failure to adjust one's desires to the conditions of one's life

mal·ad·jus·tive \-ˈjəs-tiv\ *adjective* (1928)
: not conducive to adjustment

mal·ad·just·ment \-ˈjəs(t)-mənt\ *noun* (1833)
: poor, faulty, or inadequate adjustment

mal·ad·min·is·tra·tion \ˌma-ləd-ˌmi-nə-ˈstrā-shən\ *noun* (1644)
: administration that is corrupt or incompetent (as that of a public office) or incorrect (as that of a drug)
— **mal·ad·min·is·ter** \-ˈmi-nə-stər\ *transitive verb*

mal·adroit \ˌma-lə-ˈdrȯit\ *adjective* [French, from Middle French, from *mal-* + *adroit*] (1685)
: lacking adroitness **:** INEPT
synonym see AWKWARD
— **mal·adroit·ly** *adverb*
— **mal·adroit·ness** *noun*

mal·a·dy \'ma-lə-dē\ *noun, plural* **-dies** [Middle English *maladie*, from Old French, from *malade* sick, from Latin *male habitus* in bad condition] (13th century)
1 : a disease or disorder of the animal body
2 : an unwholesome or disordered condition

ma·la fi·de \,ma-lə-'fī-dē, -də\ *adverb or adjective* [Late Latin] (1561)
: with or in bad faith

Mal·a·ga \'ma-lə-gə\ *noun* (1608)
: a sweet brown fortified wine from Málaga, Spain; *also* : a similar wine made elsewhere

Mal·a·gasy \,ma-lə-'ga-sē; ,mä-lə-'gä-sē, -shē\ *noun, plural* **Malagasy** *also* **Mal·a·gas·ies** (1839)
1 : a member of a people of Indonesian and African origin who inhabit Madagascar
2 : the Austronesian language of the Malagasy people
— **Malagasy** *adjective*

ma·la·gue·na \,ma-lə-'gān-yə, ,mä-\ *noun* [Spanish *malagueña*, from feminine of *malagueño* of Málaga, from *Málaga*] (circa 1883)
1 : a folk tune native to Málaga that is similar to a fandango
2 : a Spanish dance for couples that is similar to a fandango

mal·aise \mə-'lāz, ma-, -'lez\ *noun* [French *malaise*, from Old French, from *mal-* + *aise* comfort — more at EASE] (circa 1768)
1 : an indefinite feeling of debility or lack of health often indicative of or accompanying the onset of an illness
2 : a vague sense of mental or moral ill-being ⟨a *malaise* of cynicism and despair —Malcolm Boyd⟩

mal·a·mute \'ma-lə-,myüt, -,müt\ *noun* [*Malemute*, an Alaskan Eskimo people] (1898)
: a sled dog of northern North America; *especially* : ALASKAN MALAMUTE

mal·a·pert \,ma-lə-'pərt\ *adjective* [Middle English, from Middle French, unskillful, from *mal-* + *apert* skillful, literally, open — more at PERT] (14th century)
: impudently bold : SAUCY
— **mal·a·pert·ly** *adverb*
— **mal·a·pert·ness** *noun*

mal·ap·por·tioned \,ma-lə-'pōr-shənd, -'pȯr-\ *adjective* (1965)
: characterized by an inequitable or unsuitable apportioning of representatives to a legislative body
— **mal·ap·por·tion·ment** \-shən-mənt\ *noun*

¹mal·a·prop \'ma-lə-,präp\ *noun* [Mrs. *Malaprop*] (1823)
: an example of malapropism ⟨was famed for *malaprops*: he always said "polo bears" and "Remember Pearl Island" and "neon stockings" —*Time*⟩

²malaprop *or* **mal·a·prop·ian** \,ma-lə-'prä-pē-ən\ *adjective* (1840)
: using or marked by the use of malapropisms

mal·a·prop·ism \'ma-lə-,prä-,pi-zəm\ *noun* [Mrs. *Malaprop*, character noted for her misuse of words in R. B. Sheridan's comedy *The Rivals* (1775)] (1849)
1 : the usually unintentionally humorous misuse or distortion of a word or phrase; *especially* : the use of a word sounding somewhat like the one intended but ludicrously wrong in the context
2 : MALAPROP
— **mal·a·prop·ist** \-,prä-pist\ *noun*

mal·ap·ro·pos \,ma-,la-prə-'pō\ *adverb* [French *mal à propos*] (1668)
: in an inappropriate or inopportune way
— **malapropos** *adjective*

¹ma·lar \'mā-lər, -,lär\ *adjective* [New Latin *malaris*, from Latin *mala* jawbone, cheek] (1782)
: of or relating to the cheek or the side of the head

²malar *noun* (circa 1828)
: ZYGOMATIC BONE — called also *malar bone*

ma·lar·ia \mə-'ler-ē-ə\ *noun* [Italian, from *mala aria* bad air] (1740)
1 *archaic* : air infected with a noxious substance capable of causing disease; *especially* : MIASMA
2 a : a human disease that is caused by sporozoan parasites (genus *Plasmodium*) in the red blood cells, is transmitted by the bite of anopheline mosquitoes, and is characterized by periodic attacks of chills and fever **b** : any of various diseases of birds and mammals caused by blood protozoans
— **ma·lar·i·al** \-əl\ *adjective*
— **ma·lar·i·ous** \-əs\ *adjective*

ma·lar·i·ol·o·gy \-,ler-ē-'ä-lə-jē\ *noun* (circa 1923)
: the scientific study of malaria
— **ma·lar·i·ol·o·gist** \-jist\ *noun*

ma·lar·key *also* **ma·lar·ky** \mə-'lär-kē\ *noun* [origin unknown] (1929)
: insincere or foolish talk : BUNKUM

ma·late \'ma-,lāt, 'mā-\ *noun* (1794)
: a salt or ester of malic acid

mal·a·thi·on \,ma-lə-'thī-ən, -,än\ *noun* [from *Malathion*, a trademark] (1953)
: an insecticide $C_{10}H_{19}O_6PS_2$ with a lower mammalian toxicity than parathion

Ma·lay \mə-'lā, 'mā-(,)lā\ *noun* [obsolete Dutch *Malayo* (now *Maleier*), from Malay *Mělayu*] (1598)
1 : a member of a people of the Malay Peninsula, eastern Sumatra, parts of Borneo, and some adjacent islands
2 : the Austronesian language of the Malays
— **Malay** *adjective*
— **Ma·lay·an** \mə-'lā-ən, mā-; 'mā-,lā-\ *noun or adjective*

Mal·a·ya·lam \,ma-lə-'yä-ləm, ,mä-\ *noun* (1837)
: the Dravidian language of Kerala, southwest India, closely related to Tamil

¹mal·con·tent \,mal-kən-'tent\ *noun* (1581)
: a discontented person: **a** : one who bears a grudge from a sense of grievance or thwarted ambition **b** : one who is in active opposition to an established order or government : REBEL

²malcontent *adjective* [Middle French, from Old French, from *mal-* + *content* content] (1586)
: dissatisfied with the existing state of affairs : DISCONTENTED

mal·con·tent·ed \-'ten-təd\ *adjective* (1586)
: MALCONTENT
— **mal·con·tent·ed·ly** *adverb*
— **mal·con·tent·ed·ness** *noun*

mal de mer \,mal-də-'mer\ *noun* [French] (1778)
: SEASICKNESS

mal·dis·tri·bu·tion \,mal-,dis-trə-'byü-shən\ *noun* (1895)
: bad or faulty distribution : undesirable inequality or unevenness of placement or apportionment (as of population, resources, or wealth) over an area or among members of a group

¹male \'mā(ə)l\ *noun* [Middle English, from Middle French *masle*, *male*, adjective & noun, from Latin *masculus* — more at MASCULINE] (14th century)
1 a : a male person : a man or a boy **b** : an individual that produces small usually motile gametes (as spermatozoa or spermatozoids) which fertilize the eggs of a female
2 : a staminate plant

²male *adjective* (14th century)
1 a (1) : of, relating to, or being the sex that produces gametes which fertilize the eggs of a female (2) : STAMINATE; *especially* : having only staminate flowers and not producing fruit or seeds ⟨a *male* holly⟩ **b** (1) : of, relating to, or characteristic of the male sex ⟨a deep *male* voice⟩ (2) : made up of usually adult male individuals ⟨a *male* choir⟩
2 : MASCULINE 3a

3 : designed for fitting into a corresponding female part ⟨*male* hose coupling⟩
— **male·ness** \-nəs\ *noun*

male alto *noun* (circa 1879)
: COUNTERTENOR

ma·le·ate \'mā-lē-,āt, -lē-ət\ *noun* (1853)
: a salt or ester of maleic acid

¹mal·e·dict \,ma-lə-'dikt\ *adjective* [Late Latin *maledictus*] (circa 1550)
archaic : ACCURSED

²maledict *transitive verb* (1623)
: CURSE, EXECRATE

mal·e·dic·tion \,ma-lə-'dik-shən\ *noun* [Middle English *malediccioun*, from Late Latin *malediction-, maledictio*, from *maledicere* to curse, from Latin, to speak evil of, from *male* badly + *dicere* to speak, say — more at MAL-, DICTION] (14th century)
: CURSE, EXECRATION
— **mal·e·dic·to·ry** \-'dik-t(ə-)rē\ *adjective*

mal·e·fac·tion \,ma-lə-'fak-shən\ *noun* (15th century)
: an evil deed : CRIME

mal·e·fac·tor \'ma-lə-,fak-tər\ *noun* [Middle English *malefactour*, from Latin *malefactor*, from *malefacere* to do evil, from *male* + *facere* to do — more at DO] (15th century)
1 : one who commits an offense against the law; *especially* : FELON
2 : one who does ill toward another

male fern *noun* (1562)
: a fern (*Dryopteris filix-mas*) producing an oleoresin used in expelling tapeworms

ma·lef·ic \mə-'le-fik\ *adjective* [Latin *maleficus* wicked, mischievous, from *male* + *-ficus* -fic] (1652)
1 : having malignant influence : BALEFUL
2 : MALICIOUS

ma·lef·i·cence \mə-'le-fə-sən(t)s\ *noun* [Italian *maleficenza*, from Latin *maleficentia*, from *maleficus*] (1598)
1 a : the act of committing harm or evil **b** : a harmful or evil act
2 : the quality or state of being maleficent

ma·lef·i·cent \-sənt\ *adjective* [back-formation from *maleficence*] (1678)
: working or productive of harm or evil : BALEFUL

ma·le·ic acid \mə-'lē-ik-, -'lā-\ *noun* [French *acide maléique*, alteration of *acide malique* malic acid; from its formation by dehydration of malic acid] (1857)
: a crystalline dicarboxylic acid $C_4H_4O_4$ that is isomeric with fumaric acid and is used especially in organic synthesis

maleic anhydride *noun* (1857)
: a caustic crystalline cyclic anhydride $C_4H_2O_3$ used especially in making resins

maleic hydrazide *noun* (1949)
: a crystalline cyclic hydrazide $C_4H_4N_2O_2$ used to retard plant growth

male·mute *variant of* MALAMUTE

male–ster·ile \'mā(ə)l-'ster-əl\ *adjective* (1921)
: having male gametes lacking or nonfunctional

ma·lev·o·lence \mə-'le-və-lən(t)s\ *noun* (15th century)
1 : the quality or state of being malevolent
2 : malevolent behavior
synonym *see* MALICE

ma·lev·o·lent \-lənt\ *adjective* [Latin *malevolent-, malevolens*, from *male* badly + *volent-, volens*, present participle of *velle* to wish — more at MAL-, WILL] (1509)
1 : having, showing, or arising from intense often vicious ill will, spite, or hatred
2 : productive of harm or evil
— **ma·lev·o·lent·ly** *adverb*

mal·fea·sance \,mal-'fē-z²n(t)s\ *noun* [*mal-* + obsolete *feasance* doing, execution] (1696)
: wrongdoing or misconduct especially by a public official

mal·for·ma·tion \,mal-fòr-'mā-shən, -fər-\ *noun* (1800)
: irregular, anomalous, abnormal, or faulty formation or structure

mal·formed \,mal-'fòrmd\ *adjective* (1817)
: characterized by malformation : badly or imperfectly formed : MISSHAPEN

mal·func·tion \,mal-'fən(k)-shən\ *intransitive verb* (1928)
: to function imperfectly or badly : fail to operate normally
— **malfunction** *noun*

mal·gré \mal-'grā, 'mal-\ *preposition* [French, from Old French *maugré* — more at MAUGRE] (1608)
: DESPITE

ma·lic \'ma-lik, 'mā-\ *adjective* (circa 1909)
: involved in and especially catalyzing a reaction in which malic acid participates ⟨*malic* dehydrogenase⟩

malic acid *noun* [French *acide malique*, ultimately from Latin *malum* apple, from Greek *mēlon, malon*] (1797)
: a crystalline dicarboxylic acid $C_4H_6O_5$; especially : the optical isomer of malic acid that is found in various fruits (as apples) and is formed as an intermediate in the Krebs cycle

mal·ice \'ma-ləs\ *noun* [Middle English, from Middle French, from Latin *malitia*, from *malus* bad] (14th century)
1 : desire to cause pain, injury, or distress to another
2 : intent to commit an unlawful act or cause harm without legal justification or excuse ☆

ma·li·cious \mə-'li-shəs\ *adjective* (13th century)
: given to, marked by, or arising from malice
— **ma·li·cious·ly** *adverb*
— **ma·li·cious·ness** *noun*

malicious mischief *noun* (1769)
: willful, wanton, or reckless damage to or destruction of another's property

¹ma·lign \mə-'līn\ *adjective* [Middle English *maligne*, from Middle French, from Latin *malignus*, from *male* badly + *gignere* to beget — more at MAL-, KIN] (14th century)
1 a : evil in nature, influence, or effect : INJURIOUS **b** : MALIGNANT, VIRULENT
2 : having or showing intense often vicious ill will : MALEVOLENT
synonym see SINISTER
— **ma·lign·ly** *adverb*

²malign *transitive verb* [Middle English, from Middle French *maligner* to act maliciously, from Late Latin *malignari*, from Latin *malignus*] (15th century)
: to utter injuriously misleading or false reports about : speak evil of ☆

ma·lig·nance \mə-'lig-nən(t)s\ *noun* (circa 1604)
: MALIGNANCY

ma·lig·nan·cy \-nən(t)-sē\ *noun, plural* **-cies** (1601)
1 : the quality or state of being malignant
2 a : exhibition (as by a tumor) of malignant qualities : VIRULENCE **b** : a malignant tumor

ma·lig·nant \mə-'lig-nənt\ *adjective* [Late Latin *malignant-, malignans*, present participle of *malignari*] (circa 1545)
1 a *obsolete* : MALCONTENT, DISAFFECTED **b** : evil in nature, influence, or effect : INJURIOUS **c** : passionately and relentlessly malevolent : aggressively malicious
2 : tending to produce death or deterioration ⟨*malignant* malaria⟩; *especially* : tending to infiltrate, metastasize, and terminate fatally ⟨*malignant* tumor⟩
— **ma·lig·nant·ly** *adverb*

ma·lig·ni·ty \mə-'lig-nə-tē\ *noun* (14th century)
1 : MALIGNANCY, MALEVOLENCE
2 : an instance of malignant or malicious behavior or nature
synonym see MALICE

ma·li·hi·ni \,mä-li-'hē-nē\ *noun* [Hawaiian] (1914)

: a newcomer or stranger among the people of Hawaii

ma·lines \mə-'lēn\ *noun, plural* **ma·lines** \-'lēn(z)\ [French, from *Malines* (Mechelen), Belgium] (1833)
1 : MECHLIN
2 *also* **ma·line** : a fine stiff net with a hexagonal mesh that is usually made of silk or rayon and that is often used for veils

ma·lin·ger \mə-'liŋ-gər\ *intransitive verb* **ma·lin·gered; ma·lin·ger·ing** \-g(ə-)riŋ\ [French *malingre* sickly] (1820)
: to pretend incapacity (as illness) so as to avoid duty or work
— **ma·lin·ger·er** \-gər-ər\ *noun*

Ma·lin·ke \mə-'liŋ-kē\ *noun, plural* **Malinke** *or* **Malinkes** (1883)
1 : a member of a people of Mandingo affiliation widespread in the western part of Africa
2 : the language of the Malinke people

Ma·li·nois \,ma-lən-'wä\ *noun* [French, one from Malines, from *Malines* (Mechelen), Belgium] (1929)
: BELGIAN MALINOIS

mal·i·son \'ma-lə-sən, -zən\ *noun* [Middle English, from Old French *maleïçon*, from Late Latin *malediction-, maledictio*] (13th century)
: CURSE, MALEDICTION

mal·kin \'mò(l)-kən, 'mal-\ *noun* [Middle English *malkyn* servant woman, from *Malkyn*, diminutive of the name *Maud*] (1586)
1 *dialect chiefly British* : an untidy woman : SLATTERN
2 *dialect chiefly British* **a** : CAT **b** : HARE

¹mall \'mòl\ *variant of* MAUL

²mall \'mòl, *especially British & for 1* 'mal\ *noun* [short for obsolete *pall-mall* mallet used in pall-mall] (1644)
1 : an alley used for pall-mall
2 [The *Mall*, promenade in London, originally a pall-mall alley] **a** : a usually public area often set with shade trees and designed as a promenade or as a pedestrian walk **b** : a usually paved or grassy strip between two roadways
3 a : an urban shopping area featuring a variety of shops surrounding a usually open-air concourse reserved for pedestrian traffic **b** : a usually large suburban building or group of buildings containing various shops with associated passageways ◇

mal·lard \'ma-lərd\ *noun, plural* **mallard** *or* **mallards** [Middle English, from Middle French *mallart*] (14th century)
: a common and widely distributed wild duck (*Anas platyrhynchos*) of the northern hemisphere the males of which have a green head and white-ringed neck and which is the source of the domestic ducks

mallard

mal·lea·ble \'ma-lē-ə-bəl, 'mal-yə-bəl, 'ma-lə-bəl\ *adjective* [Middle English *malliable*, from Middle French or Medieval Latin; Middle French *malleable*, from Medieval Latin *malleabilis*, from *malleare* to hammer, from Latin *malleus* hammer — more at MAUL] (14th century)
1 : capable of being extended or shaped by beating with a hammer or by the pressure of rollers
2 a : capable of being altered or controlled by outside forces or influences **b** : having a capacity for adaptive change
synonym see PLASTIC
— **mal·lea·bil·i·ty** \,ma-lē-ə-'bi-lə-tē, ,mal-yə-, ,ma-lə-\ *noun*

mal·lee \'ma-lē\ *noun* [Wuywurung (Australian aboriginal language of the Melbourne area, Victoria) *mali*] (1845)
1 : any of various low-growing shrubby Aus-

tralian eucalypts (as *Eucalyptus dumosa* and *E. oleosa*)
2 : a dense thicket or growth of mallees; *also* : land covered by such growth

\ə\ **abut** \ᵊ\ **kitten** \ər\ **further** \a\ **ash** \ā\ **ace**
\ä\ **mop, mar** \au̇\ **out** \ch\ **chin** \e\ **bet** \ē\ **easy**
\g\ **go** \i\ **hit** \ī\ **ice** \j\ **job** \ŋ\ **sing** \ō\ **go**
\ȯ\ **law** \ȯi\ **boy** \th\ **thin** \t̲h\ **the** \ü\ **loot** \u̇\ **foot**
\y\ **yet** \zh\ **vision** *see also* Guide to Pronunciation

mal·let \'ma-lət\ *noun* [Middle English *mail-let*, from Middle French, from Old French, diminutive of *mail* maul — more at MAUL] (15th century)
: a hammer with a typically barrel-shaped head: as **a** : a tool with a large head for driving another tool or for striking a surface without marring it **b** : a long-handled wooden implement used for striking a ball (as in polo or croquet) **c** : a light hammer with a small rounded or spherical usually padded head used in playing certain musical instruments (as a vibraphone)

mal·le·us \'ma-lē-əs\ *noun, plural* **mal·lei** \-lē-,ī, -lē-,ē\ [New Latin, from Latin, hammer] (1669)
: the outermost of a chain of three small bones of the mammalian middle ear — see EAR illustration

mal·low \'ma-(,)lō\ *noun* [Middle English *malwe*, from Old English *mealwe*, from Latin *malva*] (before 12th century)
: any of a genus (*Malva* of the family Malvaceae, the mallow family) of herbs with palmately lobed or dissected leaves, usually showy flowers, and a disk-shaped fruit

malm·sey \'mäm-zē, 'mälm-, *New England also* 'mäm-\ *noun, often capitalized* [Middle English *malmesey*, from Medieval Latin *Malmasia* Monemvasia, village in Greece where a sweet wine was produced] (15th century)
: the sweetest variety of Madeira wine

mal·nour·ished \,mal-'nər-isht, -'nə-risht\ *adjective* (1927)
: UNDERNOURISHED

mal·nu·tri·tion \,mal-nù-'tri-shən, -nyú-\ *noun* (1862)
: faulty or inadequate nutrition

mal·oc·clu·sion \,ma-lə-'klü-zhən\ *noun* (1888)
: improper occlusion; *especially* : abnormality in the coming together of teeth

mal·odor \,mal-'ō-dər\ *noun* (1825)
: an offensive odor

mal·odor·ous \-'ō-də-rəs\ *adjective* (1850)
1 : having a bad odor
2 : highly improper ⟨*malodorous* practices and chicanery in high financial places —*New Republic*⟩ ☆
— **mal·odor·ous·ly** *adverb*
— **mal·odor·ous·ness** *noun*

ma·lo·lac·tic \,ma-lō-'lak-tik, ,mā-\ *adjective* [*malic* + *-o-* + *lactic*] (1965)
: relating to or involved in the bacterial conversion of malic acid to lactic acid in wine ⟨*malolactic* fermentation⟩

maloti *plural of* LOTI

Mal·pi·ghi·an corpuscle \mal-'pi-gē-ən-, -'pē-\ *noun* [Marcello *Malpighi*] (1848)
: the part of a nephron that consists of a glomerulus and Bowman's capsule — called also *Malpighian body*

Malpighian layer *noun* (1878)
: the deeper part of the epidermis consisting of cells whose protoplasm has not yet changed into horny material

Malpighian tubule *noun* (1877)
: any of a group of long blind vessels opening into the posterior part of the alimentary canal in most insects and some other arthropods and functioning primarily as excretory organs — called also *Malpighian tube*

mal·po·si·tion \,mal-pə-'zi-shən\ *noun* (circa 1839)
: wrong or faulty position

mal·prac·tice \,mal-'prak-təs\ *noun* (1671)
1 : a dereliction from professional duty or a failure to exercise an accepted degree of professional skill or learning by one (as a physician) rendering professional services which results in injury, loss, or damage : MALFEASANCE
2 : an injurious, negligent, or improper practice

mal·prac·ti·tio·ner \,mal-prak-'ti-sh(ə-)nər\ *noun* (1800)
: one who engages in or commits malpractice

¹malt \'mȯlt\ *noun* [Middle English, from Old English *mealt;* akin to Old High German *malz* malt, Old English *meltan* to melt] (before 12th century)
1 : grain (as barley) softened by steeping in water, allowed to germinate, and used especially in brewing and distilling
2 : MALT LIQUOR
3 : MALTED MILK
— **malty** \'mȯl-tē\ *adjective*

²malt (15th century)
transitive verb
1 : to convert into malt
2 : to make or treat with malt or malt extract
intransitive verb
1 : to become malt
2 : to make grain into malt

malt·ase \'mȯl-,tās, -,tāz\ *noun* (1890)
: an enzyme that catalyzes the hydrolysis of maltose to glucose

malted milk *noun* (1887)
1 : a soluble powder prepared from dried milk and malted cereals
2 : a beverage made by dissolving malted milk in milk and usually adding ice cream and flavoring — called also *malted*

Mal·tese \mȯl-'tēz, -'tēs\ *noun, plural* **Maltese** (1615)
1 : a native or inhabitant of Malta
2 : the Semitic language of the Maltese people
3 : any of a breed of toy dogs with a long silky white coat, a black nose, and very dark eyes
— **Maltese** *adjective*

Maltese 3

Maltese cross *noun* (1877)
1 a : a cross formée **b** : a cross that resembles the cross formée but has the outer face of each arm indented in a V — see CROSS illustration
2 : a Eurasian perennial (*Lychnis chalcedonica*) having scarlet or rarely white flowers in dense terminal heads

Mal·thu·sian \mal-'thü-zhən, mȯl-, -'thyü-\ *adjective* [Thomas R. *Malthus*] (1821)
: of or relating to Malthus or to his theory that population tends to increase at a faster rate than its means of subsistence and that unless it is checked by moral restraint or disaster (as disease, famine, or war) widespread poverty and degradation inevitably result
— **Malthusian** *noun*
— **Mal·thu·sian·ism** \-zhə-,ni-zəm\ *noun*

malt liquor *noun* (1693)
: a fermented liquor (as beer) made with malt

malt·ose \'mȯl-,tōs, -,tōz\ *noun* [French, from English ¹*malt*] (1862)
: a crystalline dextrorotatory fermentable sugar $C_{12}H_{22}O_{11}$ formed especially from starch by amylase

mal·treat \,mal-'trēt\ *transitive verb* [part translation of French *maltraiter*, from Middle French, from *mal-* + *traiter* to treat, from Old French *traitier* — more at TREAT] (1708)
: to treat cruelly or roughly : ABUSE
— **mal·treat·er** \-'trē-tər\ *noun*
— **mal·treat·ment** \-'trēt-mənt\ *noun*

malt·ster \'mȯlt-stər\ *noun* (14th century)
: a maker of malt

malt sugar *noun* (1862)
: MALTOSE

malt whiskey *noun* (circa 1839)
: SCOTCH 3

mal·ver·sa·tion \,mal-vər-'sā-shən\ *noun* [Middle French, from *malverser* to be corrupt, from *mal* + *verser* to turn, handle, from Latin *versare*, frequentative of *vertere* to turn — more at WORTH] (1549)
1 : misbehavior and especially corruption in an office, trust, or commission
2 : corrupt administration

ma·ma *or* **mam·ma** \'mä-mə, *chiefly British* mə-'mȧ\ *noun* [baby talk] (1579)
1 : MOTHER
2 *slang* : WIFE, WOMAN

mama's boy *noun* (1850)
: a usually polite or timid boy or man who is extremely or excessively close to and solicitous of his mother

mam·ba \'mäm-bə, 'mam-\ *noun* [Zulu *imamba*] (1862)
: any of several chiefly arboreal venomous green or black elapid snakes (genus *Dendroaspis* synonym *Dendraspis*) of sub-Saharan Africa

mam·bo \'mäm-(,)bō\ *noun, plural* **mambos** [American Spanish] (1948)
: a ballroom dance of Cuban origin that resembles the rumba and the cha-cha; *also* : the music for this dance
— **mambo** *intransitive verb*

ma·mey \ma-'mē\ *noun* [Spanish, from Taino] (1604)
: a tropical American tree (*Mammea americana* of the family Guttiferae) having an ovoid fruit with thick russet leathery rind and yellow or reddish juicy sweet flesh; *also* : the fruit

Mam·luk \'mam-,lük\ *or* **Mam·e·luke** \'ma-mə-,lük\ *noun* [Arabic *mamlūk*, literally, slave] (circa 1506)
1 : a member of a politically powerful Egyptian military class occupying the sultanate from 1250 to 1517
2 *often not capitalized* : a white or east Asian slave in Muslim countries

mam·ma \'ma-mə\ *noun, plural* **mam·mae** \'ma-,mē, -,mī\ [Latin, mother, breast, of baby-talk origin] (circa 1693)
: a mammary gland and its accessory parts

mam·mal \'ma-məl\ *noun* [New Latin *Mammalia*, from Late Latin, neuter plural of *mammalis* of the breast, from Latin *mamma* breast] (1826)
: any of a class (Mammalia) of warm-blooded higher vertebrates (as placentals, marsupials, or monotremes) that nourish their young with milk secreted by mammary glands, have the skin usually more or less covered with hair, and include humans
— **mam·ma·li·an** \mə-'mā-lē-ən, ma-\ *adjective or noun*

mam·mal·o·gy \mə-'ma-lə-jē, ma-'mä-, -'mä-\ *noun* [International Scientific Vocabulary, blend of *mammal* and *-logy*] (1835)
: a branch of zoology dealing with mammals
— **mam·mal·o·gist** \-jist\ *noun*

mam·ma·ry \'ma-mə-rē\ *adjective* (1682)
: of, relating to, lying near, or affecting the mammae

mammary gland *noun* (1831)
: any of the large compound modified sebaceous glands that in female mammals are modified to secrete milk, are situated ventrally in pairs, and usually terminate in a nipple

mam·mer *intransitive verb* [Middle English *mameren* to stammer, of imitative origin] (circa 1555)
obsolete : WAVER, HESITATE

mam·mil·la·ry \'ma-mə-,ler-ē, ma-'mi-lə-rē\ *adjective* [Latin *mammilla* breast, nipple, diminutive of *mamma*] (1669)
1 : of, relating to, or resembling the breasts
2 : studded with breast-shaped protuberances

mam·mil·lat·ed \'ma-mə-,lā-təd\ *adjective* [Late Latin *mammillatus*, from Latin *mammilla*] (1741)
1 : having nipples or small protuberances
2 : having the form of a bluntly rounded protuberance

¹mam·mock \'ma-mək\ *noun* [origin unknown] (circa 1529)
chiefly dialect : a broken piece : SCRAP

²mammock *transitive verb* (1607)
chiefly dialect : to tear into fragments : MANGLE

mam·mo·gram \'ma-mə-,gram\ *noun* [Latin *mamma* + English *-o-* + *-gram*] (1937)
: a photograph of the breasts made by X rays

mam·mog·ra·phy \ma-'mä-grə-fē\ *noun* (1937)
: X-ray examination of the breasts (as for early detection of cancer)
— **mam·mo·graph·ic** \,ma-mə-'gra-fik\ *adjective*

mam·mon \'ma-mən\ *noun, often capitalized* [Late Latin *mammona*, from Greek *mamōna*, from Aramaic *māmōnā* riches] (15th century)
: material wealth or possessions especially as having a debasing influence ⟨you cannot serve God and *mammon* —Matthew 6:24 (Revised Standard Version)⟩
— **mam·mon·ism** \-mə-,ni-zəm\ *noun*

mam·mon·ist \-mə-nist\ *noun* (1550)
archaic : one devoted to the ideal or pursuit of wealth

¹mam·moth \'ma-məth\ *noun* [Russian *mamont*, *mamot*] (1706)
1 : any of a genus (*Mammuthus*) of extinct Pleistocene elephants distinguished from recent elephants by highly ridged molars, usually large size, very long tusks that curve upward, and well-developed body hair
2 : something immense of its kind : GIANT ⟨a company that is a *mammoth* of the industry⟩

²mammoth *adjective* (1802)
: of very great size
synonym see ENORMOUS

mam·my \'ma-mē\ *noun, plural* **mammies** [alteration of *mamma*] (1523)
1 : MAMA
2 : a black woman serving as a nurse to white children especially formerly in the southern U.S.

¹man \'man, *in compounds* ,man *or* mən\ *noun, plural* **men** \'men, *in compounds* ,men *or* mən\ [Middle English, from Old English *man*, *mon* human being, male human; akin to Old High German *man* human being, Sanskrit *manu*] (before 12th century)
1 a (1) : an individual human; *especially* : an adult male human (2) : a man belonging to a particular category (as by birth, residence, membership, or occupation) — usually used in combination ⟨council*man*⟩ (3) : HUSBAND (4) : LOVER **b** : the human race : MANKIND **c** : a bipedal primate mammal (*Homo sapiens*) that is anatomically related to the great apes but distinguished especially by notable development of the brain with a resultant capacity for articulate speech and abstract reasoning, is usually considered to form a variable number of freely interbreeding races, and is the sole representative of a natural family (Hominidae), and is the sole representative of this family **d** (1) : one possessing in high degree the qualities considered distinctive of manhood (2) *obsolete* : the quality or state of being manly : MANLINESS **e** : FELLOW, CHAP **f** — used interjectionally to express intensity of feeling ⟨*man*, what a game⟩

2 a : INDIVIDUAL, PERSON ⟨a *man* could get killed here⟩ **b** : the individual who can fulfill or who has been chosen to fulfill one's requirements ⟨she's your *man*⟩
3 a : a feudal tenant : VASSAL **b** : an adult male servant **c** *plural* : the working force as distinguished from the employer and usually the management
4 a : one of the distinctive objects moved by each player in various board games **b** : one of the players on a team
5 : an alumnus of or student at a college or university ⟨a Bowdoin *man*⟩
6 *Christian Science* : the compound idea of infinite Spirit : the spiritual image and likeness of God : the full representation of Mind
7 *often capitalized* : POLICE ⟨when I heard the siren, I knew it was the *Man* —*American Speech*⟩
8 *often capitalized* : the white establishment : white society ⟨surprise that any black . . . should take on so about The *Man* —Peter Goldman⟩
9 : one extremely fond of or devoted to something specified ⟨a real vanilla ice cream *man*⟩
— **man·less** \'man-ləs\ *adjective*
— **man·like** \-,līk\ *adjective*
— **as one man** : with the agreement and consent of all : UNANIMOUSLY
— **one's own man** : free from interference or control : INDEPENDENT
— **to a man** : without exception

²man *transitive verb* **manned; man·ning** (12th century)
1 a : to supply with people (as for service) ⟨*man* a fleet⟩ **b** : to station members of a ship's crew at ⟨*man* the capstan⟩ **c** : to serve in the force or complement of ⟨we'll *man* the concession stand while you sell tickets⟩
2 : to accustom (as a hawk) to humans and the human environment
3 : to furnish with strength or powers of resistance : BRACE

ma·na \'mä-nə\ *noun* [of Polynesian origin; akin to Hawaiian & Maori *mana* mana] (circa 1843)
1 : the power of the elemental forces of nature embodied in an object or person
2 : moral authority : PRESTIGE

man–about–town \,man-ə-,baút-'taún\ *noun, plural* **men–about–town** \,men-\ (1734)
: a worldly and socially active man

¹man·a·cle \'ma-ni-kəl\ *noun* [Middle English *manicle*, from Middle French, from Latin *manicula*, diminutive of *manus* hand — more at MANUAL] (14th century)
1 : a shackle for the hand or wrist : HANDCUFF — usually used in plural
2 : something used as a restraint

²manacle *transitive verb* **man·a·cled; man·a·cling** \-k(ə-)liŋ\ (14th century)
1 : to confine (the hands) with manacles
2 : to make fast or secure : BIND; *broadly* : to restrain from movement, progress, or action
synonym see HAMPER

¹man·age \'ma-nij\ *verb* **man·aged; man·ag·ing** [Italian *maneggiare*, from *mano* hand, from Latin *manus*] (1561)
transitive verb
1 : to handle or direct with a degree of skill: as **a** : to make and keep compliant ⟨can't *manage* her child⟩ **b** : to treat with care : HUSBAND ⟨*managed* his resources carefully⟩ **c** : to exercise executive, administrative, and supervisory direction of ⟨*manage* a business⟩ ⟨*manage* a bond issue⟩ ⟨*manage* a baseball team⟩
2 : to work upon or try to alter for a purpose ⟨*manage* the press⟩ ⟨*manage* stress⟩
3 : to succeed in accomplishing : CONTRIVE ⟨*managed* to escape from prison⟩
4 : to direct the professional career of ⟨an agency that *manages* entertainers⟩
intransitive verb
1 a : to direct or carry on business or affairs; *also* : to direct a baseball team **b** : to admit of being carried on

2 : to achieve one's purpose
synonym see CONDUCT

²manage *noun* [Italian *maneggio* management, training of a horse, from *maneggiare*] (circa 1587)
1 a *archaic* : the action and paces of a trained riding horse **b** : the schooling or handling of a horse **c** : a riding school
2 *obsolete* : MANAGEMENT

man·age·able \'ma-ni-jə-bəl\ *adjective* (1598)
: capable of being managed
— **man·age·abil·i·ty** \,ma-ni-jə-'bi-lə-tē\ *noun*
— **man·age·able·ness** \'ma-ni-jə-bəl-nəs\ *noun*
— **man·age·ably** \-blē\ *adverb*

man·age·ment \'ma-nij-mənt\ *noun* (1598)
1 : the act or art of managing : the conducting or supervising of something (as a business)
2 : judicious use of means to accomplish an end
3 : the collective body of those who manage or direct an enterprise
— **man·age·men·tal** \,ma-nij-'men-t³l\ *adjective*

man·ag·er \'ma-ni-jər\ *noun* (1588)
: one that manages: as **a** : a person who conducts business or household affairs **b** : a person whose work or profession is management **c** (1) : a person who directs a team or athlete (2) : a student who in scholastic or collegiate sports supervises equipment and records under the direction of a coach
— **man·a·ge·ri·al** \,ma-nə-'jir-ē-əl\ *adjective*
— **man·a·ge·ri·al·ly** \-ē-ə-lē\ *adverb*
— **man·ag·er·ship** \'ma-ni-jər-,ship\ *noun*

man·ag·er·ess \'ma-ni-jə-rəs\ *noun* (1797)
: a woman who is a manager
usage see -ESS

managing editor *noun* (1865)
: an editor in executive and supervisory charge of all editorial activities of a publication (as a newspaper)

¹ma·ña·na \mən-'yä-nə\ *noun* [Spanish, literally, tomorrow, from (assumed) Vulgar Latin *maneana*, from feminine of *maneanus* early, from Latin *mane* early in the morning] (1845)
: an indefinite time in the future

²mañana *adverb* (1879)
: at an indefinite time in the future

man ape *noun* (circa 1864)
1 : GREAT APE
2 : any of various fossil primates intermediate in characters between recent humans and the great apes

Ma·nas·seh \mə-'na-sə\ *noun* [Hebrew *Měnashsheh*]
1 : a son of Joseph and the traditional eponymous ancestor of one of the tribes of Israel
2 : a king of Judah reigning in the 7th century B.C. and noted for his attempt to establish polytheism

man–at–arms \,man-ət-'ärmz\ *noun, plural* **men–at–arms** \,men-\ (1581)
: SOLDIER; *especially* : a heavily armed and usually mounted soldier

manatee

man·a·tee \'ma-nə-,tē\ *noun* [Spanish *manatí*] (1555)
: any of a genus (*Trichechus*) of chiefly tropical aquatic herbivorous mammals that differ from the related dugong especially in having the tail rounded

Man·ches·ter terrier \'man-,ches-tər-, -chə-stər-\ noun [Manchester, England] (1891)
: any of a breed of small short-haired black-and-tan terriers developed in England

man–child \'man-,chīld\ noun, plural **men-chil·dren** \'men-,chil-drən, -dərn\ (14th century)
: a male child : SON

man·chi·neel \,man-chə-'nē(ə)l\ noun [French mancenille, from Spanish manzanilla, from diminutive of manzana apple] (1630)
: a poisonous tropical American tree (Hippomane mancinella) of the spurge family having a blistering milky juice and apple-shaped fruit

Man·chu \'man-(,)chü, man-'\ noun, plural **Manchu** or **Manchus** (1697)
1 : a member of an indigenous people of Manchuria who conquered China and established a dynasty there in 1644
2 : the Tungusic language of the Manchu people
— **Manchu** adjective

man·ci·ple \'man(t)-sə-pəl\ noun [Middle English, from Medieval Latin mancipium office of steward, from Latin, act of purchase, from mancip-, manceps purchaser — more at EMANCIPATE] (13th century)
: a steward or purveyor especially for a college or monastery

-mancy noun combining form [Middle English -mancie, from Old French, from Latin -mantia, from Greek -manteia, from manteia, from mantis diviner, prophet — more at MANTIS]
: divination ⟨oneiromancy⟩

Man·dae·an \man-'dē-ən\ noun [Mandaean mandayyā having knowledge] (1875)
1 : a member of a Gnostic sect of the lower Tigris and Euphrates regions
2 : a form of Aramaic found in documents written by Mandaeans
— **Mandaean** adjective

man·da·la \'mən-də-lə\ noun [Sanskrit maṇḍala circle] (1859)
1 : a Hindu or Buddhist graphic symbol of the universe; specifically : a circle enclosing a square with a deity on each side
2 : a graphic and often symbolic pattern usually in the form of a circle divided into four separate sections or bearing a multiple projection of an image
— **man·dal·ic** \,mən-'da-lik\ adjective

man·da·mus \man-'dā-məs\ noun [Latin, we enjoin, from mandare] (1535)
: a writ issued by a superior court commanding the performance of a specified official act or duty

Man·dan \'man-,dan, -dən\ noun, plural **Mandan** or **Mandans** (1805)
1 : a member of an American Indian people of the Missouri River Valley in North Dakota
2 : the Siouan language of the Mandans

¹man·da·rin \'man-d(ə-)rən\ noun [Portuguese mandarim, from Malay mĕntĕri, from Sanskrit mantrin counselor, from mantra counsel — more at MANTRA] (1589)
1 a : a public official in the Chinese Empire of any of nine superior grades b (1) : a pedantic official (2) : BUREAUCRAT c : a person of position and influence often in intellectual or literary circles; especially : an elder and often traditionalist or reactionary member of such a circle
2 capitalized a : a form of spoken Chinese used by the court and the official classes of the Empire b : the group of closely related Chinese dialects that are spoken in about four fifths of the country and have a standard variety centering about Beijing
3 [French mandarine, from Spanish mandarina, probably from mandarín mandarin, from Portuguese mandarim; probably from the color or of a mandarin's robes] a : a small spiny orange tree (Citrus reticulata) of southeastern Asia with yellow to reddish orange loose-rinded fruits; also : a derivative of this tree developed in cultivation by artificial selection or hybridization b : the fruit of a mandarin
— **man·da·rin·ic** \,man-də-'ri-nik\ adjective
— **man·da·rin·ism** \'man-d(ə-)rə-,ni-zəm\ noun

²mandarin adjective (1604)
1 : of, relating to, or typical of a mandarin ⟨mandarin graces⟩
2 : marked by polished ornate complexity of language ⟨mandarin prose⟩

man·da·rin·ate \'man-d(ə-)rə-,nāt\ noun [probably from French mandarinat, from mandarin mandarin, from Portuguese mandarim] (circa 1741)
1 : the office or status of a mandarin
2 : a body of mandarins
3 : rule by mandarins

mandarin collar noun (1947)
: a narrow stand-up collar usually open in front

mandarin orange noun (1771)
: MANDARIN 3

man·da·tary \'man-də-,ter-ē\ noun, plural **-tar·ies** (15th century)
: MANDATORY

¹man·date \'man-,dāt\ noun [Middle French & Latin; Middle French mandat, from Latin mandatum, from neuter of mandatus, past participle of mandare to entrust, enjoin, probably irregular from manus hand + -dere to put — more at MANUAL, DO] (1501)
1 : an authoritative command; especially : a formal order from a superior court or official to an inferior one
2 : an authorization to act given to a representative ⟨accepted the mandate of the people⟩
3 a : an order or commission granted by the League of Nations to a member nation for the establishment of a responsible government over a former German colony or other conquered territory b : a mandated territory

²mandate transitive verb **man·dat·ed; man·dat·ing** (1919)
1 : to administer or assign (as a territory) under a mandate
2 : to make mandatory : ORDER; also : DIRECT, REQUIRE

man·da·tor \'man-,dā-tər\ noun (1681)
: one that gives a mandate

¹man·da·to·ry \'man-də-,tōr-ē, -,tȯr-\ adjective (1576)
1 : containing or constituting a command : OBLIGATORY ⟨mandatory retirement age⟩
2 : of, by, relating to, or holding a League of Nations mandate
— **man·da·tor·i·ly** \-,tōr-ə-lē, -,tȯr-\ adverb

²mandatory noun, plural **-ries** (1661)
: one given a mandate; especially : a nation holding a mandate from the League of Nations

man–day \'man-'dā\ noun (1925)
: a unit of one day's work by one person

Man·de \'män-,dā, män-'\ noun (1883)
1 : MANDINGO
2 : a branch of the Niger-Congo language family spoken primarily in Sierra Leone, Liberia, Guinea, Ivory Coast, Mali, and Burkina Faso

man·di·ble \'man-də-bəl\ noun [Middle French, from Late Latin mandibula, from Latin mandere to chew; probably akin to Greek masasthai to chew] (15th century)
1 a : JAW 1a; especially : a lower jaw consisting of a single bone or of completely fused bones b : the lower jaw with its investing soft parts c : either the upper or lower segment of the bill of a bird
2 : any of various invertebrate mouthparts serving to hold or bite food materials; especially : either member of the anterior pair of mouth appendages of an arthropod often forming strong biting jaws
— **man·dib·u·lar** \man-'di-byə-lər\ adjective
— **man·dib·u·late** \-lət\ adjective

Man·din·go \man-'diŋ-(,)gō\ noun, plural **Mandingo** or **Mandingoes** or **Mandingos** (1623)
1 : a member of a people of western Africa centering in the area of the upper Niger valley
2 : the language of the Mandingo people

Man·din·ka \man-'diŋ-kə\ noun, plural **Mandinka** or **Mandinkas** (1939)
: MALINKE

man·di·o·ca \,man-dē-'ō-kə\ variant of MANIOC

man·do·la \man-'dō-lə\ noun [Italian, from French mandore, modification of Late Latin pandura 3-stringed lute — more at BANDORE] (1758)
: a 16th and 17th century lute that is the ancestor of the smaller mandolin

man·do·lin \,man-də-'lin, 'man-d°l-ən\ also **man·do·line** \,man-də-'lēn, 'man-d°l-ən\ noun [Italian mandolino, diminutive of mandola] (1707)
1 : a musical instrument of the lute family that has a usually pear-shaped body and fretted neck and four to six pairs of strings
2 usually mandoline [French, from Italian mandolino mandolin] : a kitchen utensil with a blade for slicing and shredding
— **man·do·lin·ist** \,man-də-'li-nist\ noun

mandolin 1

man·drag·o·ra \man-'dra-gə-rə\ noun [Middle English, from Old English, from Latin mandragoras, from Greek] (before 12th century)
: MANDRAKE 1

man·drake \'man-,drāk\ noun [Middle English, probably alteration of mandragora] (14th century)
1 a : a Mediterranean herb (Mandragora officinarum) of the nightshade family with ovate leaves, yellowish or purple flowers, and a large forked root traditionally credited with human attributes b : the root of a mandrake formerly used especially to promote conception, as a cathartic, or as a narcotic and soporific
2 : MAYAPPLE

mandrake 1

man·drel also **man·dril** \'man-drəl\ noun [probably modification of French mandrin] (1665)
1 a : a usually tapered or cylindrical axle, spindle, or arbor inserted into a hole in a piece of work to support it during machining b : a metal bar that serves as a core around which material (as metal) may be cast, molded, forged, bent, or otherwise shaped
2 : the shaft and bearings on which a tool (as a circular saw) is mounted

man·drill \'man-drəl\ noun [probably from ¹man + ³drill] (1744)
: a large baboon (Papio sphinx synonym Mandrillus sphinx) of central Africa west of the Congo River with the male having a bright red and blue muzzle

mandrill

mane \'mān\ noun [Middle English, from Old English manu; akin to Old High German mana mane, Latin monile necklace] (before 12th century)
1 : long and heavy hair growing about the neck and head of some mammals (as a horse or lion)
2 : long heavy hair on a person's head

— **maned** \'mānd\ *adjective*

man–eat·er \'man-ˌē-tər\ *noun* (1600)
: one that has or is thought to have an appetite for human flesh: as **a** : CANNIBAL **b** : MACKEREL SHARK; *especially* : GREAT WHITE SHARK — called also *man-eater shark, man-eating shark* **c** : a large feline (as a lion or tiger) that has acquired the habit of feeding on human flesh
— **man–eat·ing** \-ˌē-tiŋ\ *adjective*

maned wolf *noun* (1903)
: a yellowish red wild canid (*Chrysocyon brachyurus*) inhabiting South American grasslands and having black coloration on the nape and lower legs

ma·nège *also* **ma·nege** \ma-'nezh, mə-, -'näzh\ *noun* [French *manège*, from Italian *maneggio* training of a horse — more at MANAGE] (1644)
1 : a school for teaching horsemanship and for training horses
2 : the art of horsemanship or of training horses
3 : the movements or paces of a trained horse

ma·nes \'mä-ˌnās, 'mā-ˌnēz\ *noun plural* [Latin]
1 *often capitalized* : the deified spirits of the ancient Roman dead honored with graveside sacrifices
2 : the venerated or appeased spirit of a dead person

¹**ma·neu·ver** \mə-'nü-vər, -'nyü-\ *noun* [French *manœuvre*, from Old French *maneuvre* work done by hand, from Medieval Latin *manuopera*, from Latin *manu operare* to work by hand] (1758)
1 a : a military or naval movement **b** : an armed forces training exercise; *especially* : an extended and large-scale training exercise involving military and naval units separately or in combination — often used in plural
2 : a procedure or method of working usually involving expert physical movement
3 a : evasive movement or shift of tactics **b** : an intended and controlled variation from a straight and level flight path in the operation of an airplane
4 a : an action taken to gain a tactical end **b** : an adroit and clever management of affairs often using trickery and deception
synonym see TRICK

²**maneuver** *verb* **ma·neu·vered; ma·neu·ver·ing** \-'nü-və-riŋ, -'nyü-; -'n(y)üv-riŋ\ (1777)
intransitive verb
1 a : to perform a movement in military or naval tactics in order to secure an advantage **b** : to make a series of changes in direction and position for a specific purpose
2 : to use stratagems : SCHEME
transitive verb
1 : to cause to execute tactical movements
2 : to manage into or out of a position or condition : MANIPULATE
3 a : to guide with adroitness and design **b** : to bring about or secure as a result of skillful management ◇
— **ma·neu·ver·abil·i·ty** \-ˌnü-və-rə-'bi-lə-tē, -ˌnyü-; -ˌn(y)üv-rə-\ *noun*
— **ma·neu·ver·able** \-'nü-və-rə-bəl, -'nyü-; -'n(y)üv-rə-\ *adjective*
— **ma·neu·ver·er** \-'nü-vər-ər, -'nyü-\ *noun*

man–for–man \ˌman-fər-'man\ *adjective* (circa 1949)
: MAN-TO-MAN 2

man Friday *noun* [*Friday*, servant in *Robinson Crusoe* (1719), novel by Daniel Defoe] (1887)
: an efficient and devoted aide or employee : a right-hand man

man·ful \'man-fəl\ *adjective* (14th century)
: having or showing courage and resolution
— **man·ful·ly** \-fə-lē\ *adverb*
— **man·ful·ness** *noun*

man·ga·bey \'maŋ-gə-(ˌ)bē\ *noun, plural* **-beys** [French, from *Mangabey*, region of Madagascar] (1774)
: any of a genus (*Cercocebus*) of slender long-tailed African monkeys

mangan- *combining form* [German *Mangan*, from French *manganèse*]
: manganese 〈*manganate*〉

man·ga·nate \'maŋ-gə-ˌnāt\ *noun* (1839)
1 : a salt containing manganese in the anion MnO₄
2 : MANGANITE

man·ga·nese \'maŋ-gə-ˌnēz, -ˌnēs\ *noun* [French *manganèse*, from Italian *manganese* manganese dioxide] (1783)
: a grayish white usually hard and brittle metallic element that resembles iron but is not magnetic — see ELEMENT table
— **man·ga·ne·sian** \ˌmaŋ-gə-'nē-zhən, -shən\ *adjective*

manganese dioxide *noun* (1882)
: a dark insoluble compound MnO₂ used especially as an oxidizing agent, as a depolarizer of dry cells, and in making glass and ceramics

man·gan·ic \man-'ga-nik, maŋ-\ *adjective* (circa 1828)
: of, relating to, or derived from manganese; *especially* : containing this element with a valence of three or six

man·ga·nite \'maŋ-gə-ˌnīt\ *noun* (1827)
1 : an ore of manganese MnO(OH) that is a hydroxide of manganese usually in brilliant gray crystals
2 : any of various unstable salts made by reaction of manganese dioxide with a base

man·ga·nous \-nəs\ *adjective* (1842)
: of, relating to, or derived from manganese; *especially* : containing this element with a valence of two

mange \'mānj\ *noun* [alteration of Middle English *manjewe*, from Middle French *mangene* itching, from *mangier* to eat] (1540)
: any of various persistent contagious skin diseases marked especially by eczematous inflammation and loss of hair, affecting domestic animals or sometimes humans, and caused by a minute parasitic mite — compare SARCOPTIC MANGE

man·gel \'maŋ-gəl\ *noun* [short for *mangelwurzel*] (1877)
: a large coarse yellow to reddish orange beet extensively grown as food for cattle

man·gel–wur·zel \-ˌwər-zəl\ *noun* [German, alteration of *Mangoldwurzel*, from *Mangold* beet + *Wurzel* root] (1767)
: MANGEL

man·ger \'mān-jər\ *noun* [Middle English *mangeour, manger,* from Middle French *maingeure,* from *mangier* to eat, from Latin *manducare* to chew, devour, from *manducus* glutton, from *mandere* to chew — more at MANDIBLE] (14th century)
: a trough or open box in a stable designed to hold feed or fodder for livestock

¹**man·gle** \'maŋ-gəl\ *transitive verb* **mangled; man·gling** \-g(ə-)liŋ\ [Middle English, from Anglo-French *mangler*] (15th century)
1 : to injure with deep disfiguring wounds by cutting, tearing, or crushing 〈people . . . *mangled* by sharks —V. G. Heiser〉
2 : to spoil, injure, or make incoherent especially through ineptitude 〈a story *mangled* beyond recognition〉
synonym see MAIM
— **man·gler** \-g(ə-)lər\ *noun*

²**mangle** *noun* [Dutch *mangel,* from German, from Middle High German, diminutive of *mange* mangonel, mangle, from Latin *manganum*] (1774)
: a machine for ironing laundry by passing it between heated rollers

³**mangle** *transitive verb* **man·gled; man·gling** \-g(ə-)liŋ\ (1775)
: to press or smooth (as damp linen) with a mangle

— **man·gler** \-g(ə-)lər\ *noun*

man·go \'maŋ-(ˌ)gō\ *noun, plural* **mangoes** *also* **mangos** [Portuguese *manga,* probably from Malayalam *māṅṅa*] (1582)
1 : a tropical fruit commonly with a firm yellowish red skin, hard central stone, and juicy aromatic pulp; *also* : an evergreen tree (*Mangifera indica*) of the cashew family that bears mangoes
2 : SWEET PEPPER

man·go·nel \'maŋ-gə-ˌnel\ *noun* [Middle English, from Old French, probably from Medieval Latin *manganellus,* diminutive of Late Latin *manganum* philter, mangonel, from Greek *manganon*] (13th century)
: a military engine formerly used to throw missiles

man·go·steen \'maŋ-gə-ˌstēn\ *noun* [modification of Malay *manggisutan*] (1598)
: a dark reddish brown fruit of southeastern Asia with a thick rind and juicy flesh having a flavor suggestive of both peach and pineapple; *also* : a tree (*Garcinia mangostana*) of the Saint-John's-wort family that bears mangosteens

man·grove \'man-ˌgrōv, 'maŋ-\ *noun* [probably from Portuguese *mangue* mangrove (from Spanish *mangle,* probably from Taino) + English *grove*] (1613)
1 : any of a genus (*Rhizophora,* especially *R. mangle* of the family Rhizophoraceae) of tropical maritime trees or shrubs that send out many prop roots and form dense masses important in coastal land building
2 : any of numerous trees (as of the genera *Avicennia* of the vervain family or *Sonneratia* of the family Sonneratiaceae) with growth habits like those of the true mangroves

mangy \'mān-jē\ *adjective* **mang·i·er; -est** (1540)
1 : affected with or resulting from mange
2 : having many worn or bare spots : SEEDY, SHABBY
— **man·gi·ness** \-jē-nəs\ *noun*

man·han·dle \'man-ˌhan-d°l\ *transitive verb* (circa 1865)
1 : to handle roughly
2 : to move or manage by human force 〈*manhandled* the posts into place〉

man·hat·tan \man-'ha-t°n, mən-\ *noun, often capitalized* [*Manhattan,* borough of New York City] (1890)

◇ WORD HISTORY

maneuver As peculiar as the connection seems, we owe both *maneuver* and *manure* to the same French source. The Old French verb *manovrer,* meaning "to work" or "to place with the hand," developed from *manu operare,* literally, "to work by hand," in the spoken Latin of Gaul. From an Anglo-French variant of this Old French verb such as *meinourer,* Middle English adopted *maynouren* or *manouren,* which had the senses "to take in hand, manage" and "to cultivate (land)." In the 16th century English derived on the basis of the latter sense the noun *manure,* meaning "material that fertilizes land." In the meantime, *manovrer* continued to go its own way in French. By the middle of the 18th century, its Modern French outcome *manœuvrer* (influenced in form by the noun *manœuvre*) had developed a new specific meaning "to perform a movement in military or naval tactics" and English reborrowed the word, quickly adapting it to several nonmilitary uses as well.

\ə\ abut \ᵊ\ kitten \ər\ further \a\ ash \ā\ ace
\ä\ mop, mar \aú\ out \ch\ chin \e\ bet \ē\ easy
\g\ go \i\ hit \ī\ ice \j\ job \ŋ\ sing \ō\ go
\ó\ law \ói\ boy \th\ thin \th\ the \ü\ loot \ú\ foot
\y\ yet \zh\ vision *see also* Guide to Pronunciation

: a cocktail consisting of vermouth, whiskey, and sometimes a dash of bitters

man·hole \'man-,hōl\ *noun* (1793)
: a hole through which one may go especially to gain access to an underground or enclosed structure

man·hood \'man-,hůd\ *noun* (13th century)
1 : the condition of being a human being
2 : qualities associated with men
3 : the condition of being an adult male as distinguished from a child or female
4 : adult males **:** MEN

man–hour \'man-'aů(-ə)r\ *noun* (1912)
: a unit of one hour's work by one person that is used especially as a basis for cost accounting and wages

man·hunt \'man-,hənt\ *noun* (1846)
: an organized and usually intensive hunt for a person and especially for one charged with a crime

ma·nia \'mā-nē-ə, -nyə\ *noun* [Middle English, from Late Latin, from Greek, from *mainesthai* to be mad; akin to Greek *menos* spirit — more at MIND] (14th century)
1 : excitement manifested by mental and physical hyperactivity, disorganization of behavior, and elevation of mood; *specifically* : the manic phase of manic-depressive psychosis
2 : excessive or unreasonable enthusiasm ⟨a *mania* for saving things⟩; *also* : the object of such enthusiasm

ma·ni·ac \'mā-nē-,ak\ *noun* [Late Latin *maniacus* maniacal, from Greek *maniakos*, from *mania*] (circa 1763)
1 : MADMAN, LUNATIC
2 : a person characterized by an inordinate or ungovernable enthusiasm for something

ma·ni·a·cal \mə-'nī-ə-kəl\ *also* **ma·ni·ac** \'mā-nē-,ak\ *adjective* (1604)
1 : affected with or suggestive of madness
2 : characterized by ungovernable excitement or frenzy : FRANTIC
— **ma·ni·a·cal·ly** \mə-'nī-ə-k(ə-)lē\ *adverb*

man·ic \'ma-nik\ *adjective* (1902)
: affected with, relating to, or resembling mania
— **manic** *noun*
— **man·i·cal·ly** \-ni-k(ə-)lē\ *adverb*

man·ic–de·pres·sive \,ma-nik-di-'pre-siv\ *adjective* (1902)
: characterized either by mania or by psychotic depression or by alternating mania and depression
— **manic–depressive** *noun*

Man·i·chae·an *or* **Man·i·che·an** \,ma-nə-'kē-ən\ *or* **Man·i·chee** \'ma-nə-,kē\ *noun* [Late Latin *manichaeus*, from Late Greek *manichaios*, from *Manichaios* Manes (died about 276 A.D.) Persian founder of the sect] (1556)
1 : a believer in a syncretistic religious dualism originating in Persia in the 3d century A.D. and teaching the release of the spirit from matter through asceticism
2 : a believer in religious or philosophical dualism
— **Manichaean** *adjective*
— **Man·i·chae·an·ism** \,ma-nə-'kē-ə-,ni-zəm\ *noun*
— **Man·i·chae·ism** \'ma-nə-(,)kē-,i-zəm\ *noun*

man·i·cot·ti \,ma-nə-'kä-tē\ *noun, plural* **manicotti** [Italian, plural of *manicotto* muff, from *manica* sleeve, from Latin, from *manus* hand] (1948)
: tubular pasta shells that may be stuffed with ricotta or a meat mixture; *also* : a dish of stuffed manicotti usually with tomato sauce

¹man·i·cure \'ma-nə-,kyůr\ *noun* [French, from Latin *manus* hand + French *-icure* (as in *pédicure* pedicure) — more at MANUAL] (1880)
1 : MANICURIST
2 : a treatment for the care of the hands and fingernails

²manicure *transitive verb* **-cured; -cur·ing** (circa 1890)
1 : to do manicure work on; *especially* : to trim and polish the fingernails of
2 a : to trim closely and evenly ⟨*manicured* lawns⟩ **b** : GROOM 2 ⟨*manicured* flower beds⟩

man·i·cur·ist \-,kyůr-ist\ *noun* (1889)
: a person who gives manicures

¹man·i·fest \'ma-nə-,fest\ *adjective* [Middle English, from Middle French or Latin; Middle French *manifeste*, from Latin *manifestus* caught in the act, flagrant, obvious, perhaps from *manus* + *-festus* (akin to Latin in*festus* hostile)] (14th century)
1 : readily perceived by the senses and especially by the sight
2 : easily understood or recognized by the mind : OBVIOUS
synonym see EVIDENT
— **man·i·fest·ly** *adverb*

²manifest *transitive verb* (14th century)
: to make evident or certain by showing or displaying
synonym see SHOW
— **man·i·fest·er** *noun*

³manifest *noun* (1561)
1 : MANIFESTATION, INDICATION
2 : MANIFESTO
3 : a list of passengers or an invoice of cargo for a vehicle (as a ship or plane)

man·i·fes·tant \'ma-nə-'fes-tənt\ *noun* (1880)
: one who makes or participates in a manifestation

man·i·fes·ta·tion \,ma-nə-fə-'stā-shən, -,fe-'stā-\ *noun* (15th century)
1 a : the act, process, or an instance of manifesting **b** : something that manifests or is manifest **c** : one of the forms in which an individual is manifested **d** : an occult phenomenon; *specifically* : MATERIALIZATION
2 : a public demonstration of power and purpose

manifest destiny *noun, often M&D capitalized* (1845)
: a future event accepted as inevitable ⟨in the mid-19th century expansion to the Pacific was regarded as the *Manifest Destiny* of the United States⟩; *broadly* : an ostensibly benevolent or necessary policy of imperialistic expansion

¹man·i·fes·to \,ma-nə-'fes-(,)tō\ *noun, plural* **-tos** *or* **-toes** [Italian, denunciation, manifest, from *manifestare* to manifest, from Latin, from *manifestus*] (1647)
: a written statement declaring publically the intentions, motives, or views of its issuer

²manifesto *intransitive verb* (1748)
: to issue a manifesto

¹man·i·fold \'ma-nə-,fōld\ *adjective* [Middle English, from Old English *manigfeald*, from *manig* many + *-feald* -fold] (before 12th century)
1 a : marked by diversity or variety **b** : MANY
2 : comprehending or uniting various features : MULTIFARIOUS
3 : rightfully so-called for many reasons ⟨a *manifold* liar⟩
4 : consisting of or operating many of one kind combined ⟨a *manifold* bellpull⟩
— **man·i·fold·ly** \-,fōl(d)-lē\ *adverb*
— **man·i·fold·ness** \-,fōl(d)-nəs\ *noun*

²manifold *adverb* (before 12th century)
: many times : a great deal ⟨will increase your blessings *manifold*⟩

³manifold (before 12th century)
transitive verb
1 : to make manifold : MULTIPLY
2 : to make several or many copies of
intransitive verb
: to make several or many copies

⁴manifold *noun* (1855)
: something that is manifold: as **a** : a whole that unites or consists of many diverse elements ⟨the *manifold* of aspirations, passions, frustrations —Harry Slochower⟩ **b** : a pipe fitting with several lateral outlets for connecting one pipe with others; *also* : a fitting on an

internal-combustion engine that directs a fuel and air mixture to or receives the exhaust gases from several cylinders **c** : SET 21 **d** : a topological space in which every point has a neighborhood that is homeomorphic to the interior of a sphere in Euclidean space of the same number of dimensions

man·i·kin *or* **man·ni·kin** \'ma-ni-kən\ *noun* [Dutch *mannekijn* little man, from Middle Dutch, diminutive of *man*; akin to Old English *man*] (circa 1536)
1 : MANNEQUIN
2 : a little man : DWARF, PYGMY

ma·nila *also* **ma·nil·la** \mə-'ni-lə\ *adjective* (1834)
1 *capitalized* : made from Manila hemp
2 : made of manila paper
— **manila** *noun*

Manila hemp *noun* [*Manila*, Philippine Islands] (circa 1847)
: ABACA

manila paper *noun, often M capitalized* (1873)
: a strong and durable paper of a brownish or buff color and smooth finish made originally from Manila hemp

ma·nille \mə-'nil\ *noun* [modification of Spanish *malilla*] (1674)
: the second highest trump in various card games (as ombre)

man in the street (1831)
: an average or ordinary person

man·i·oc \'ma-nē-,äk\ *noun* [French *manioc* & Spanish & Portuguese *mandioca*, from Tupi *manioca*] (1568)
: CASSAVA

man·i·ple \'ma-nə-pəl\ *noun* [Middle English, from Medieval Latin *manipulus*, from Latin, handful, from *manus* hand + *-pulus* (perhaps akin to Latin *plēre* to fill); from its having been originally held in the hand — more at MANUAL, FULL] (15th century)
1 : a long narrow strip of silk worn at mass over the left arm by clerics of or above the order of subdeacon
2 [Latin *manipulus*, from *manipulus* handful] : a subdivision of the Roman legion consisting of either 120 or 60 men

ma·nip·u·la·ble \mə-'ni-pyə-lə-bəl\ *adjective* (1881)
: capable of being manipulated
— **ma·nip·u·la·bil·i·ty** \-,ni-pyə-lə-'bi-lə-tē\ *noun*

ma·nip·u·lar \mə-'ni-pyə-lər\ *adjective* (1623)
1 : of or relating to the ancient Roman maniple
2 : of, relating to, or performed by manipulation : MANIPULATIVE

ma·nip·u·late \mə-'ni-pyə-,lāt\ *transitive verb* **-lat·ed; -lat·ing** [back-formation from *manipulation*, from French, from *manipuler* to handle an apparatus in chemistry, ultimately from Latin *manipulus*] (1831)
1 : to treat or operate with the hands or by mechanical means especially in a skillful manner
2 a : to manage or utilize skillfully **b** : to control or play upon by artful, unfair, or insidious means especially to one's own advantage
3 : to change by artful or unfair means so as to serve one's purpose : DOCTOR
— **ma·nip·u·lat·able** \-,lā-tə-bəl\ *adjective*
— **ma·nip·u·la·tion** \-,ni-pyə-'lā-shən\ *noun*
— **ma·nip·u·la·tive** \-'ni-pyə-,lā-tiv, -lə-\ *adjective*
— **ma·nip·u·la·tive·ly** *adverb*
— **ma·nip·u·la·tive·ness** *noun*
— **ma·nip·u·la·tor** \-,lā-tər\ *noun*
— **ma·nip·u·la·to·ry** \-lə-,tōr-ē, -,tȯr-\ *adjective*

man·i·tou *or* **man·i·tu** \'ma-nə-,tü\ *also* **man·i·to** \-,tō\ *noun* [Ojibwa *manito'*] (1671)
: a supernatural force that according to an Algonquian conception pervades the natural world

man jack \'man-'jak\ *noun* (1840)
: individual man ⟨every *man jack*⟩
man·kind *noun singular but singular or plural in construction* (13th century)
1 \'man-'kīnd, -,kīnd\ : the human race : the totality of human beings
2 \-,kīnd\ : men especially as distinguished from women
¹man·ly \'man-lē\ *adverb* (before 12th century)
: in a manly manner
²manly *adjective* **man·li·er; -est** (13th century)
1 : having qualities generally associated with a man : STRONG, VIRILE
2 : appropriate in character to a man ⟨*manly* sports⟩
— **man·li·ness** *noun*
man–made \'man-'mād, -,mād\ *adjective* (circa 1718)
: manufactured, created, or constructed by human beings; *specifically* : SYNTHETIC ⟨*man-made* fibers⟩
man·na \'ma-nə\ *noun* [Middle English, from Old English, from Late Latin, from Greek, from Hebrew *mān*] (before 12th century)
1 a : food miraculously supplied to the Israelites in their journey through the wilderness **b** : divinely supplied spiritual nourishment **c** : a usually sudden and unexpected source of gratification, pleasure, or gain
2 a : the sweetish dried exudate of a European ash (especially *Fraxinus ornus*) that contains mannitol and has been used as a laxative and demulcent **b** : a similar product excreted by a scale insect (*Trabutina mannipara*) feeding on the tamarisk
manna grass *noun* (1597)
: any of a genus (*Glyceria*) of chiefly North American perennial grasses of wetland or aquatic habitats
man·nan \'ma-,nan, -nən\ *noun* [International Scientific Vocabulary *mann*ose + ³-*an*] (1895)
: any of several polysaccharides that are polymers of mannose and occur especially in plant cell walls
manned \'mand\ *adjective* (1617)
: carrying or performed by a human being ⟨*manned* space-flight⟩
man·ne·quin \'ma-ni-kən\ *noun* [French, from Dutch *mannekijn* little man — more at MANIKIN] (1730)
1 : an artist's, tailor's, or dressmaker's lay figure; *also* : a form representing the human figure used especially for displaying clothes
2 : one employed to model clothing
man·ner \'ma-nər\ *noun* [Middle English *manere*, from Old French *maniere* way of acting, from (assumed) Vulgar Latin *manuaria*, from Latin, feminine of *manuarius* of the hand, from *manus* hand — more at MANUAL] (12th century)
1 a : KIND, SORT ⟨what *manner* of man is he⟩ **b** : KINDS, SORTS ⟨all *manner* of problems⟩
2 a (1) : a characteristic or customary mode of acting : CUSTOM (2) : a mode of procedure or way of acting : FASHION (3) : method of artistic execution or mode of presentation : STYLE **b** *plural* : social conduct or rules of conduct as shown in the prevalent customs ⟨Victorian *manners*⟩ **c** : characteristic or distinctive bearing, air, or deportment ⟨his poised gracious *manner*⟩ **d** *plural* (1) : habitual conduct or deportment : BEHAVIOR ⟨mind your *manners*⟩ (2) : good manners **e** : a distinguished or stylish air
synonym see BEARING, METHOD
— **man·ner·less** \-ləs\ *adjective*
man·nered \'ma-nərd\ *adjective* (14th century)
1 : having manners of a specified kind ⟨well-*mannered*⟩
2 a : having or displaying a particular manner **b** : having an artificial or stilted character ⟨passages . . . so *mannered* as to be unintelligible —R. G. G. Price⟩

man·ner·ism \'ma-nə-,ri-zəm\ *noun* (1803)
1 a : exaggerated or affected adherence to a particular style or manner : ARTIFICIALITY, PRECIOSITY ⟨refined almost to the point of *mannerism* —Winthrop Sargeant⟩ : an art style in late 16th century Europe characterized by spatial incongruity and excessive elongation of the human figures
2 : a characteristic and often unconscious mode or peculiarity of action, bearing, or treatment
synonym see POSE
— **man·ner·ist** \-rist\ *noun*
— **man·ner·is·tic** \,ma-nə-'ris-tik\ *adjective*
man·ner·ly \'ma-nər-lē\ *adjective* (circa 1529)
: showing good manners
— **man·ner·li·ness** *noun*
— **mannerly** *adverb*
man·nish \'ma-nish\ *adjective* (14th century)
1 : resembling or suggesting a man rather than a woman
2 : generally associated with or characteristic of a man rather than a woman ⟨her *mannish* clothes⟩
— **man·nish·ly** *adverb*
— **man·nish·ness** *noun*
man·nite \'ma-,nīt\ *noun* [French, from *manna*, from Late Latin] (1830)
: MANNITOL
man·ni·tol \'ma-nə-,tol, -,tōl\ *noun* [International Scientific Vocabulary] (1879)
: a slightly sweet crystalline alcohol $C_6H_{14}O_6$ found in many plants and used especially as a diuretic and in testing kidney function
man·nose \'ma-,nōs, -,nōz\ *noun* [International Scientific Vocabulary *mann*ite + ²-*ose*] (1888)
: an aldose $C_6H_{12}O_6$ whose dextrorotatory enantiomorph occurs especially as a structural unit of mannans from which it can be recovered by hydrolysis
ma·no \'mä-(,)nō\ *noun, plural* **manos** [Spanish, literally, hand, from Latin *manus* — more at MANUAL] (circa 1892)
: a stone used as the upper millstone for grinding foods (as Indian corn) by hand in a metate
ma·noeu·vre *chiefly British variant of* MANEUVER
man of God (1748)
: CLERGYMAN
man of letters (1645)
1 : SCHOLAR
2 : AUTHOR
man of straw (1624)
: STRAW MAN
man of the house (circa 1904)
: the chief male in a household
man of the world (15th century)
: a practical or worldly-wise man of wide experience
man–of–war \,ma-nə(v)-'wòr\ *noun, plural* **men–of–war** \,men-\ (15th century)
: a combatant warship of a recognized navy
ma·nom·e·ter \mə-'nä-mə-tər\ *noun* [French *manomètre*, from Greek *manos* sparse, loose, rare (akin to Armenian *manr* small) + French *-mètre*] (circa 1730)
1 : an instrument (as a pressure gauge) for measuring the pressure of gases and vapors
2 : SPHYGMOMANOMETER
— **man·o·met·ric** \,ma-nə-'me-trik\ *adjective*
— **man·o·met·ri·cal·ly** \-tri-k(ə-)lē\ *adverb*
— **ma·nom·e·try** \mə-'nä-mə-trē\ *noun*
man on horseback (1860)
1 : a usually military figure whose ambitions and popularity mark him as a potential dictator
2 : DICTATOR
man·or \'ma-nər\ *noun* [Middle English *maner*, from Old French *manoir*, from *manoir* to sojourn, dwell, from Latin *manēre* — more at MANSION] (14th century)
1 a : the house or hall of an estate : MANSION **b** : a landed estate

2 a : a unit of English rural territorial organization; *especially* : such a unit in the Middle Ages consisting of an estate under a lord enjoying a variety of rights over land and tenants including the right to hold court **b** : a tract of land in North America occupied by tenants who pay a fixed rent in money or kind to the proprietor
— **ma·no·ri·al** \mə-'nōr-ē-əl, -'nòr-\ *adjective*
— **ma·no·ri·al·ism** \-ə-,li-zəm\ *noun*
manor house *noun* (1575)
: the house of the lord of a manor
man–o'–war bird \,ma-nə-'wòr-\ *noun* (1707)
: FRIGATE BIRD
man–pack \'man-,pak\ *adjective* (1965)
: designed to be carried by one person
man power *noun* (1862)
1 : power available from or supplied by the physical effort of human beings
2 *usually* **man·pow·er** : the total supply of persons available and fitted for service
man·qué \mäⁿ-'kā\ *adjective* [French, from past participle of *manquer* to lack, fail, from Italian *mancare*, from *manco* lacking, left-handed, from Latin, having a crippled hand, probably from *manus*] (1778)
: short of or frustrated in the fulfillment of one's aspirations or talents — used postpositively ⟨a poet *manqué*⟩
man·rope \'man-,rōp\ *noun* (1769)
: a side rope (as to a ship's gangway or ladder) used as a handrail
man·sard \'man-,särd, -sərd\ *noun* [French *mansarde*, from François *Mansart* (died 1666) French architect] (circa 1734)
: a roof having two slopes on all sides with the lower slope steeper than the upper one — see ROOF illustration
— **man·sard·ed** \-,sär-dəd, -sər-\ *adjective*
manse \'man(t)s\ *noun* [Middle English *manss*, from Medieval Latin *mansa, mansus, mansum*, from Latin *mansus* lodging, from *manēre*] (15th century)
1 *archaic* : the dwelling of a householder
2 : the residence of a clergyman; *especially* : the house of a Presbyterian clergyman
3 : a large imposing residence
man·ser·vant \'man-,sər-vənt\ *noun, plural* **men·ser·vants** \'men-,sər-vən(t)s\ (14th century)
: a male servant
-manship *noun suffix* [-*man* + -*ship* (as in *horsemanship*)]
1 : art or practice of a competitive nature ⟨brink*manship*⟩
2 : skilled engagement in a competitive activity ⟨grants*manship*⟩
word history see GAMESMANSHIP
man·sion \'man(t)-shən\ *noun* [Middle English, from Middle French, from Latin *mansion-, mansio*, from *manēre* to remain, dwell; akin to Greek *menein* to remain] (14th century)
1 a *obsolete* : the act of remaining or dwelling : STAY **b** *archaic* : DWELLING, ABODE
2 a (1) : the house of the lord of a manor (2) : a large imposing residence **b** : a separate apartment or lodging in a large structure
3 a : HOUSE 3b **b** : one of the 28 parts into which the moon's monthly course through the heavens is divided
man–size \'man-,sīz\ *or* **man–sized** \-,sīzd\ *adjective* (1913)
1 : suitable for or requiring a man ⟨a *man-size* job⟩
2 : larger than others of its kind ⟨constructed a *man-size* model⟩
man·slaugh·ter \'man-,slò-tər\ *noun* (15th century)

: the unlawful killing of a human being without express or implied malice

man·slay·er \-,slā-ər\ *noun* (14th century)
: one who commits homicide

man's man *noun* (1897)
: a man noted or admired for traditionally masculine interests and activities

man·sue·tude \'man(t)-swi-,tüd, man-'sü-ə-, -,tyüd\ *noun* [Middle English, from Latin *mansuetudo,* from *mansuescere* to tame, from *manus* hand + *suescere* to accustom; akin to Greek *ēthos* custom — more at MANUAL, SIB] (14th century)
: the quality or state of being gentle : MEEKNESS, TAMENESS

man·ta \'man-tə\ *noun* [Spanish, alteration of *manto* cloak, from Late Latin *mantus,* probably back-formation from Latin *mantellum* mantle] (1697)
1 : a square piece of cloth or blanket used in southwestern U.S. and Latin America usually as a cloak or shawl
2 [American Spanish, from Spanish; from its shape] : DEVILFISH 1

man–tai·lored \'man-,tā-lərd\ *adjective* (1922)
: made with the severe simplicity associated with men's coats and suits

manta ray *noun* (1936)
: DEVILFISH 1

man·teau \man-'tō, 'man-,\ *noun* [French, from Old French *mantel*] (1671)
: a loose cloak, coat, or robe

man·tel \'man-t°l\ *noun* [Middle English, from Middle French, from Old French, mantle] (15th century)
1 a : a beam, stone, or arch serving as a lintel to support the masonry above a fireplace **b** : the finish around a fireplace
2 : a shelf above a fireplace

man·tel·et \'mant-lət, 'man-t°l-ət, ,man-t°l-'et\ *noun* [Middle English, from Middle French *mantlet,* diminutive of *mantel*] (14th century)
1 : a very short cape or cloak
2 *or* **mant·let** \'mant-lət\ : a movable shelter formerly used by besiegers as a protection when attacking

man·tel·piece \'man-t°l-,pēs\ *noun* (1686)
1 : a mantel with its side elements
2 : MANTEL 2

man·tel·shelf \-,shelf\ *noun* (circa 1828)
: MANTEL 2

man·tic \'man-tik\ *adjective* [Greek *mantikos,* from *mantis*] (1850)
: of or relating to the faculty of divination : PROPHETIC

man·ti·core \'man-ti-,kōr, -,kȯr\ *noun* [Middle English, from Latin *mantichora,* from Greek *mantichōras*] (14th century)
: a legendary animal with the head of a man, the body of a lion, and the tail of a dragon or scorpion

man·tid \'man-təd\ *noun* [New Latin *Mantidae,* group name, from *Mantis,* genus name] (1895)
: MANTIS

man·til·la \man-'tē-yə, -'ti-lə\ *noun* [Spanish, diminutive of *manta*] (1717)
1 : a light scarf worn over the head and shoulders especially by Spanish and Latin American women
2 : a short light cape or cloak

man·tis \'man-təs\ *noun, plural* **man·tis·es** *or* **man·tes** \'man-,tēz\ [New Latin, from Greek, literally, diviner, prophet; akin to Greek *mainesthai* to be mad — more at MANIA] (1658)
: any of an order or suborder (Mantodea and especially family Mantidae) of large usually green insects that feed on other insects and clasp their prey in forelimbs held up as if in prayer

man·tis·sa \man-'ti-sə\ *noun* [Latin *mantisa, mantissa* makeweight, from Etruscan] (circa 1847)

: the part of a logarithm to the right of the decimal point

¹man·tle \'man-t°l\ *noun* [Middle English *mantel,* from Old French, from Latin *mantellum*] (13th century)
1 a : a loose sleeveless garment worn over other clothes : CLOAK **b** : a mantle regarded as a symbol of preeminence or authority ⟨invested his people with the *mantle* of universal champions of justice —Denis Goulet⟩
2 a : something that covers, enfolds, or envelops **b** (1) : a fold or lobe or pair of lobes of the body wall of a mollusk or brachiopod that in shell-bearing forms lines the shell and bears shell-secreting glands — see CLAM illustration (2) : the soft external body wall that lines the test or shell of a tunicate or barnacle **c** : the outer wall and casing of a blast furnace above the hearth; *broadly* : an insulated support or casing in which something is heated
3 : the back, scapulars, and wings of a bird
4 : a lacy hood or sheath of some refractory material that gives light by incandescence when placed over a flame
5 a : REGOLITH **b** : the part of the interior of a terrestrial planet and especially the earth that lies beneath the lithosphere and above the central core
6 : MANTEL

mantis

²mantle *verb* **man·tled; man·tling** \'mant-liŋ, 'man-t°l-iŋ\ (13th century)
transitive verb
: to cover with or as if with a mantle : CLOAK ⟨the encroaching jungle growth that *mantled* the building —Sanka Knox⟩
intransitive verb
1 : to become covered with a coating
2 : to spread over a surface
3 : BLUSH ⟨her rich face *mantling* with emotion —Benjamin Disraeli⟩

man–to–man \'man-tə-'man\ *adjective* (1902)
1 : characterized by frankness and honesty ⟨a *man-to-man* talk⟩
2 : of, relating to, or being a system of defense (as in football or basketball) in which each defensive player guards a specified opponent

Man·toux test \,man-'tü-, ,mä°-\ *noun* [Charles *Mantoux* (died 1947) French physician] (circa 1923)
: an intracutaneous test for hypersensitivity to tuberculin that indicates past or present infection with tubercle bacilli

man·tra \'män-trə *also* 'man- *or* 'mən-\ *noun* [Sanskrit, sacred counsel, formula, from *manyate* he thinks; akin to Latin *mens* mind — more at MIND] (1808)
: a mystical formula of invocation or incantation (as in Hinduism); *also* : WATCHWORD 2
— **man·tric** \-trik\ *adjective*

man·trap \'man-,trap\ *noun* (1788)
: a trap for catching humans : SNARE

man·tua \'man(t)-sh(ə-)wə, 'man-tə-wə\ *noun* [modification of French *manteau* mantle] (1678)
: a usually loose-fitting gown worn especially in the 17th and 18th centuries

Manu \'ma-(,)nü\ *noun* [Sanskrit]
: the progenitor of the human race and giver of the religious laws of Manu according to Hindu mythology

¹man·u·al \'man-yə-wəl, -yəl\ *adjective* [Middle English *manuel,* from Middle French, from Latin *manualis,* from *manus* hand; akin to Old English *mund* hand and perhaps to Greek *marē* hand] (15th century)

1 a : of, relating to, or involving the hands ⟨*manual* dexterity⟩ **b** : worked or done by hand and not by machine ⟨a *manual* transmission⟩ ⟨*manual* computation⟩ ⟨*manual* indexing⟩
2 : requiring or using physical skill and energy ⟨*manual* labor⟩ ⟨*manual* workers⟩
— **man·u·al·ly** *adverb*

²manual *noun* (15th century)
1 : a book that is conveniently handled; *especially* : HANDBOOK
2 : the prescribed movements in the handling of a weapon or other military item during a drill or ceremony ⟨the *manual* of arms⟩
3 a : a keyboard for the hands; *specifically* : one of the several keyboards of an organ or harpsichord that controls a separate division of the instrument **b** : a device or apparatus intended for manual operation

manual alphabet *noun* (circa 1864)
: an alphabet especially for the deaf in which the letters are represented by finger positions

manual alphabet

manual training *noun* (1880)
: a course of training to develop skill in using the hands and to teach practical arts (as woodworking and metalworking)

ma·nu·bri·um \mə-'nü-brē-əm, -'nyü-\ *noun, plural* **-bria** \-brē-ə\ *also* **-bri·ums** [New Latin, from Latin, handle, from *manus*] (circa 1848)
: an anatomical process or part shaped like a handle: as **a** : the cephalic segment of the sternum of humans and many other mammals **b** : the process that bears the mouth of a hydrozoan : HYPOSTOME

man·u·fac·to·ry \,man-yə-'fak-t(ə-)rē, ,ma-nə-\ *noun* (1647)
: FACTORY 2a

¹man·u·fac·ture \,man-yə-'fak-chər, ,ma-nə-\ *noun* [Middle French, from Medieval Latin *manufactura,* from Latin *manu factus,* literally, made by hand] (1567)
1 : something made from raw materials by hand or by machinery
2 a : the process of making wares by hand or by machinery especially when carried on systematically with division of labor **b** : a productive industry using mechanical power and machinery
3 : the act or process of producing something

²manufacture *verb* **-tured; -tur·ing** \-'fak-chə-riŋ, -'fak-shriŋ\ (1683)
transitive verb
1 : to make into a product suitable for use
2 a : to make from raw materials by hand or by machinery **b** : to produce according to an organized plan and with division of labor
3 : INVENT, FABRICATE

4 : to produce as if by manufacturing **:** CREATE ⟨writers who *manufacture* stories for television⟩
intransitive verb
: to engage in manufacture
— **manufacturing** *noun*
man·u·fac·tur·er \-'fak-chər-ər, -'fak-shrər\ *noun* (1719)
: one that manufactures; *especially* **:** an employer of workers in manufacturing
man·u·mis·sion \ˌman-yə-'mi-shən\ *noun* [Middle English, from Middle French, from Latin *manumission-, manumissio,* from *manumittere*] (15th century)
: the act or process of manumitting; *especially* **:** formal emancipation from slavery
man·u·mit \ˌman-yə-'mit\ *transitive verb* **-mit·ted; -mit·ting** [Middle English *manumitten,* from Middle French *manumitter,* from Latin *manumittere,* from *manus* hand + *mittere* to let go, send] (15th century)
: to release from slavery
synonym see FREE
¹ma·nure \mə-'nůr, -'nyůr\ *transitive verb* **ma·nured; ma·nur·ing** [Middle English *manouren,* from Middle French *manouvrer,* literally, to do work by hand, from Latin *manu operare*] (15th century)
1 *obsolete* **:** CULTIVATE
2 : to enrich (land) by the application of manure
word history see MANEUVER
— **ma·nur·er** *noun*
²manure *noun* (1549)
: material that fertilizes land; *especially* **:** refuse of stables and barnyards consisting of livestock excreta with or without litter
— **ma·nu·ri·al** \-'n(y)ůr-ē-əl\ *adjective*
ma·nus \'mā-nəs, 'mä-\ *noun, plural* **ma·nus** \-nəs, -ˌnüs\ [New Latin, from Latin, hand] (1826)
: the distal segment of the vertebrate forelimb from carpus to terminus
¹man·u·script \'man-yə-ˌskript\ *adjective* [Latin *manu scriptus*] (1597)
: written by hand or typed ⟨*manuscript* letters⟩
²manuscript *noun* (1600)
1 : a written or typewritten composition or document as distinguished from a printed copy; *also* **:** a document submitted for publication
2 : writing as opposed to print
¹Manx \'maŋ(k)s\ *adjective* [alteration of *Maniske,* from (assumed) Old Norse *manskr,* from *Mana* Isle of Man] (1630)
: of, relating to, or characteristic of the Isle of Man, its people, or the Manx language
²Manx *noun* (1672)
1 : the Celtic language of the Manx people almost completely displaced by English
2 *plural in construction* **:** the people of the Isle of Man
3 : MANX CAT
Manx cat *noun* (1859)
: any of a breed of shorthaired tailless domestic cats
¹many \'me-nē\ *adjective* **more** \'mōr, 'mȯr\; **most** \'mōst\ [Middle English, from Old English *manig;* akin to Old High German *manag* many, Old Church Slavonic *mŭnogŭ* much] (before 12th century)
1 : consisting of or amounting to a large but indefinite number ⟨worked for *many* years⟩
2 : being one of a large but indefinite number ⟨*many* a man⟩ ⟨*many* another student⟩
— **as many :** the same in number ⟨saw three plays in *as many* days⟩
²many *pronoun, plural in construction* (before 12th century)
: a large number of persons or things ⟨*many* are called⟩
³many *noun, plural in construction* (12th century)
1 : a large but indefinite number ⟨a good *many* of them⟩
2 : the great majority of people ⟨the *many*⟩

man–year \'man-ˌyir\ *noun* (1916)
: a unit of the work done by one person in a year composed of a standard number of working days
many·fold \ˌme-nē-'fōld\ *adverb* (14th century)
: by many times ⟨aid to research has increased *manyfold*⟩
many–sid·ed \ˌme-nē-'sī-dəd\ *adjective* (1570)
1 : having many sides or aspects
2 : having many interests or aptitudes
— **many–sid·ed·ness** *noun*
many–val·ued \ˌme-nē-'val-(ˌ)yüd, -yəd\ *adjective* (1934)
1 : possessing more than the customary two truth-values of truth and falsehood
2 : MULTIPLE-VALUED
Man·za·nil·la \ˌman-zə-'nē-yə, -'ni-lə\ *noun* [Spanish, diminutive of *manzana* apple] (1843)
: a pale very dry Spanish sherry
man·za·ni·ta \ˌman-zə-'nē-tə\ *noun* [American Spanish, diminutive of Spanish *manzana* apple] (1846)
: any of various western North American evergreen shrubs (genus *Arctostaphylos*) of the heath family with alternate leaves
Mao·ism \'maů-ˌi-zəm\ *noun* (1950)
: the theory and practice of Marxism-Leninism developed in China chiefly by Mao Tse-tung
— **Mao·ist** \'maů-ist\ *noun or adjective*
Mao·ri \'maů(ə)r-ē\ *noun, plural* **Maori** or **Maoris** (1843)
1 : a member of a Polynesian people native to New Zealand
2 : the Austronesian language of the Maori
mao–tai \'maů-'tī, -'dī\ *noun* [*Maotai,* town in China] (1943)
: a strong Chinese liquor made from sorghum
¹map \'map\ *noun* [Medieval Latin *mappa,* from Latin, napkin, towel] (1527)
1 a : a representation usually on a flat surface of the whole or a part of an area **b :** a representation of the celestial sphere or a part of it
2 : something that represents with a clarity suggestive of a map
3 : the arrangement of genes on a chromosome — called also *genetic map*
4 : FUNCTION 5a
— **map·like** \-ˌlīk\ *adjective*
— **on the map :** in a position of prominence or fame ⟨had put the fledgling university *on the map* —Lon Tinkle⟩
²map *verb* **mapped; map·ping** (1586)
transitive verb
1 a : to make a map of ⟨*map* the surface of the moon⟩ **b :** to delineate as if on a map ⟨sorrow was *mapped* on her face⟩ **c :** to make a survey of for or as if for the purpose of making a map **d :** to assign (as a set or element) in a mathematical correspondence ⟨*map* a set onto itself⟩ ⟨*map* picture elements to video memory⟩
2 : to plan in detail — often used with *out* ⟨*map* out a program⟩
3 : to locate (a gene) on a chromosome
intransitive verb
of a gene **:** to be located
— **map·pa·ble** \'ma-pə-bəl\ *adjective*
— **map·per** *noun*
ma·ple \'mā-pəl\ *noun* [Middle English, from Old English *mapul-;* akin to Old Norse *mǫpurr* maple] (14th century)
: any of a genus (*Acer* of the family Aceraceae, the maple family) of chiefly deciduous trees or shrubs with opposite leaves and a fruit of two united samaras; *also* **:** the hard light-colored close-grained wood of a maple used especially for flooring and furniture
maple sugar *noun* (1720)
: sugar made by boiling maple syrup
maple syrup *noun* (1849)
: syrup made by concentrating the sap of maple trees and especially the sugar maple
map·mak·er \'map-ˌmā-kər\ *noun* (1775)
: CARTOGRAPHER

— **map·mak·ing** \-kiŋ\ *noun*
map·ping \'ma-piŋ\ *noun* (circa 1775)
1 : the act or process of making a map
2 : FUNCTION 5a ⟨a one-to-one continuous *mapping*⟩
ma·quette \ma-'ket\ *noun* [French, from Italian *macchietta* sketch, diminutive of *macchia,* ultimately from Latin *macula* spot] (1903)
: a usually small preliminary model (as of a sculpture or a building)
ma·qui·la·do·ra \mə-ˌkē-lə-'dōr-ə, -'thōr-\ *noun* [Mexican Spanish (*planta*) *maquiladora,* from *maquilar* to process ore for a fee, from *maquila* processing fee, multure, from Spanish, multure, from Arabic dialect *makīla* measure of grain] (1976)
: a foreign-owned factory in Mexico at which imported parts are assembled by lower-paid workers into products for export
ma·quil·lage \ˌma-kē-'yäzh\ *noun* [French] (1892)
: MAKEUP 3
ma·quis \ma-'kē, mä-\ *noun, plural* **ma·quis** \-'kē(z)\ [French, from Italian *macchie,* plural of *macchia* thicket, sketch, spot] (1858)
1 : thick scrubby underbrush of Mediterranean shores and especially of the island of Corsica; *also* **:** an area of such underbrush
2 *often capitalized* **a :** a guerrilla fighter in the French underground during World War II **b :** a band of maquis
¹mar \'mär\ *transitive verb* **marred; mar·ring** [Middle English *marren,* from Old English *mierran* to obstruct, waste; akin to Old High German *merren* to obstruct] (before 12th century)
1 : to detract from the perfection or wholeness of **:** SPOIL
2 *archaic* **a :** to inflict serious bodily harm on **b :** DESTROY
synonym see INJURE
²mar *noun* (1551)
: something that mars **:** BLEMISH
mar·a·bou *also* **mar·a·bout** \'mar-ə-ˌbü\ *noun* [French *marabout,* literally, marabout] (1823)

marabou 1b

1 a : a soft feathery fluffy material prepared from turkey feathers or the coverts of marabous and used especially for trimming women's hats or clothes **b** *marabou* **:** a large dark gray African stork (*Leptoptilos crumeniferus*) that has a distensible pouch of pink skin at the front of the neck and feeds especially on carrion — called also *marabou stork*
2 a : a thrown silk usually dyed in the gum **b :** a fabric made of this silk
mar·a·bout \'mar-ə-ˌbü\ *noun, often capitalized* [French, from Portuguese *marabuto,* from Arabic *murābiṭ*] (1621)
: a dervish in Muslim Africa believed to have supernatural power
ma·ra·ca \mə-'rä-kə, -'ra-\ *noun* [Portuguese *maracá,* from Tupi] (1824)
: a rattle usually made from a gourd that is used as a percussion instrument
mar·ag·ing steel \'mär-ˌā-jiŋ-\ *noun* [*martensite* + *aging*] (1962)
: a strong tough low-carbon martensitic steel which contains up to 25 percent nickel and in which hardening precipitates are formed by aging

\ə\ abut \ᵊ\ kitten \ər\ further \a\ ash \ā\ ace \ä\ mop, mar \aů\ out \ch\ chin \e\ bet \ē\ easy \g\ go \i\ hit \ī\ ice \j\ job \ŋ\ sing \ō\ go \ȯ\ law \ȯi\ boy \th\ thin \th\ the \ü\ loot \ů\ foot \y\ yet \zh\ vision *see also* Guide to Pronunciation

mar·a·schi·no \,mar-ə-'skē-(,)nō, -'shē-\ *noun, plural* **-nos** *often capitalized* [Italian, from *marasca* bitter wild cherry, alteration of *amarasca*, from *amaro* bitter — more at AMARETTO] (circa 1793)
1 : a sweet liqueur distilled from the fermented juice of a bitter wild cherry
2 : a usually large cherry preserved in true or imitation maraschino

ma·ras·mus \mə-'raz-məs\ *noun* [Late Latin, from Greek *marasmos*, from *marainein* to waste away] (1656)
: a condition of chronic undernourishment occurring especially in children and usually caused by a diet deficient in calories and proteins
— **ma·ras·mic** \-'raz-mik\ *adjective*

Ma·ra·tha \mə-'rä-tə\ *noun* [Marathi *Mārāṭhā* & Hindi *Marhaṭṭā*, from Sanskrit *Mahārāṣṭra* Maharashtra] (1748)
: a member of a people of the south central part of the subcontinent of India

Ma·ra·thi \mə-'rä-tē\ *noun* [Marathi *marāṭhī*] (1698)
: the chief Indo-Aryan language of the state of Maharashtra in India

mar·a·thon \'mar-ə-,thän\ *noun, often attributive* [*Marathon*, Greece, site of a victory of Greeks over Persians in 490 B.C., the news of which was carried to Athens by a long-distance runner] (1896)
1 : a long-distance race: **a** : a footrace run on an open course usually of 26 miles 385 yards (42.2 kilometers) **b** : a race other than a footrace marked especially by great length
2 a : an endurance contest **b** : something (as an event, activity, or session) characterized by great length or concentrated effort ◇

mar·a·thon·er \-,thä-nər\ *noun* (1923)
: one (as a runner) who takes part in a marathon
— **mar·a·thon·ing** \-niŋ\ *noun*

ma·raud \mə-'röd\ *verb* [French *marauder*] (1711)
intransitive verb
: to roam about and raid in search of plunder
transitive verb
: RAID, PILLAGE
— **ma·raud·er** *noun*

¹mar·ble \'mär-bəl\ *noun* [Middle English, from Old French *marbre*, from Latin *marmor*, from Greek *marmaros*] (12th century)
1 a : limestone that is more or less crystallized by metamorphism, that ranges from granular to compact in texture, that is capable of taking a high polish, and that is used especially in architecture and sculpture **b** : something (as a piece of sculpture) composed of or made from marble **c** : something suggesting marble (as in hardness, coldness, or smoothness) ⟨a heart of *marble*⟩
2 a : a little ball made of a hard substance (as glass) and used in various games **b** *plural but singular in construction* : any of several games played with these little balls
3 : MARBLING
4 *plural* : elements of common sense; *especially* : SANITY ⟨persons who are born without all their *marbles* —Arthur Miller⟩
— **marble** *adjective*

²marble *transitive verb* **mar·bled; mar·bling** \-b(ə-)liŋ\ (1683)
: to give a veined or mottled appearance to ⟨*marble* the edges of a book⟩

marble cake *noun* (1871)
: a cake made with light and dark batter so as to have a mottled appearance

mar·bled \'mär-bəld\ *adjective* (1599)
1 [¹*marble*] **a** : made of or covered with marble or marbling **b** : marked by an extensive use of marble as an architectural or decorative feature ⟨ancient *marbled* cities⟩
2 [²*marble*] : marked by an intermixture of fat and lean ⟨well-*marbled* beef⟩

mar·ble·ise *British variant of* MARBLEIZE

mar·ble·ize \'mär-bə-,līz\ *transitive verb* **-ized; -iz·ing** (circa 1859)
: MARBLE

marbling *noun* (circa 1752)
1 : the action or process of making like marble especially in coloration
2 : coloration or markings resembling or suggestive of marble
3 : an intermixture of fat and lean especially in a cut of meat when evenly distributed

mar·bly \-b(ə-)lē\ *adjective* (15th century)
: resembling or suggestive of marble

marc \'märk\ *noun* [French, from Middle French, from *marchier* to trample, march] (1601)
1 : the residue remaining after a fruit has been pressed; *broadly* : the organic residue from an extraction process ⟨the protein-rich cottonseed *marc*⟩
2 : brandy made from the residue of wine grapes after pressing

mar·ca·site \'mär-kə-,sīt, -,zīt; ,mär-kə-'zēt\ *noun* [Middle English *marchasite*, from Medieval Latin *marcasita*] (15th century)
1 a : crystallized iron pyrites : a mineral of the same composition and appearance as iron pyrites but of different crystalline organization and lower specific gravity
2 : a piece of marcasite used in jewelry

mar·ca·to \mär-'kä-(,)tō\ *adverb or adjective* [Italian, past participle of *marcare* to mark, accent, of Germanic origin; akin to Old High German *marcōn* to mark] (circa 1840)
: with strong accentuation — used as a direction in music

¹mar·cel \mär-'sel\ *noun* [*Marcel* Grateau (died 1936) French hairdresser] (1895)
: a deep soft wave made in the hair by the use of a heated curling iron

²marcel *verb* **mar·celled; mar·cel·ling** (1906)
transitive verb
: to make a marcel in
intransitive verb
: to make a marcel

¹march \'märch\ *noun* [Middle English *marche*, from Old French, of Germanic origin; akin to Old High German *marha* boundary — more at MARK] (14th century)
: a border region : FRONTIER; *especially* : a district originally set up to defend a boundary — usually used in plural

²march *intransitive verb* (14th century)
: to have common borders or frontiers ⟨a region that *marches* with Canada in the north and the Pacific in the west⟩

³march \'märch, *imperatively often* 'härch *in the military*\ *verb* [Middle English, from Middle French *marchier* to trample, march, from Old French, to trample, probably of Germanic origin; akin to Old High German *marcōn* to mark] (15th century)
intransitive verb
1 : to move along steadily usually with a rhythmic stride and in step with others
2 a : to move in a direct purposeful manner : PROCEED **b** : to make steady progress : ADVANCE ⟨time *marches* on⟩
3 : to stand in orderly array suggestive of marching
transitive verb
1 : to cause to march ⟨*marched* the children off to bed⟩
2 : to cover by marching : TRAVERSE ⟨*marched* 10 miles⟩

⁴march \'märch\ *noun* (circa 1572)
1 : a musical composition that is usually in duple or quadruple time with a strongly accentuated beat and that is designed or suitable to accompany marching
2 a (1) : the action of marching (2) : the distance covered within a specific period of time by marching (3) : a regular measured stride or rhythmic step used in marching **b** : forward movement : PROGRESS ⟨the *march* of a movie toward the climax⟩
3 : an organized procession of demonstrators who are supporting or protesting something
— **march·like** \-,līk\ *adjective*
— **on the march** : moving steadily : ADVANCING

March \'märch\ *noun* [Middle English, from Old French, from Latin *martius*, from *martius* of Mars, from *Mart-, Mars*] (13th century)
: the 3d month of the Gregorian calendar

mär·chen \'mer-kən\ *noun, plural* **märchen** [German] (1871)
: TALE; *especially* : FOLKTALE

¹march·er \'mär-chər\ *noun* (14th century)
: one who inhabits a border region

²marcher *noun* (1589)
: one that marches; *especially* : one that marches for a specific cause ⟨a peace *marcher*⟩

mar·che·sa \mär-'kā-zə\ *noun, plural* **-se** \-(,)zā\ [Italian, feminine of *marchese*] (1797)
: an Italian woman holding the rank of a marchese : MARCHIONESS

mar·che·se \-(,)zā\ *noun, plural* **-si** \-(,)zē\ [Italian, from Medieval Latin *marcensis*, from *marca* border region, of Germanic origin; akin to Old High German *marha*] (1517)
: an Italian nobleman next in rank above a count : MARQUIS

marching orders *noun plural* (1780)
: authoritative orders or instructions especially to set out on or as if on a march

mar·chio·ness \'mär-sh(ə-)nəs\ *noun* [Medieval Latin *marchionissa*, from *marchion-, marchio* marquess, from *marca*] (circa 1599)
1 : the wife or widow of a marquess
2 : a woman who holds the rank of marquess in her own right

march·pane \'märch-,pān\ *noun* [Middle French *marcepain*, from Italian *marzapane*] (circa 1556)
: MARZIPAN

march–past \'märch-,past\ *noun* (circa 1876)
: a filing by : PROCESSION

Mar·cion·ism \'mär-shə-,ni-zəm, -sē-ə-, -shē-ə-\ *noun* [*Marcion* 2d century A.D. Christian Gnostic] (1882)
: the doctrinal system of a sect of the 2d and 3d centuries A.D. accepting some parts of the New Testament but denying Christ's corporality and humanity and condemning the Creator God of the Old Testament
— **Mar·cion·ite** \-,nīt\ *noun*

Mar·co·ni \mär-'kō-nē\ *adjective* [probably from the resemblance of the complex arrangement of stays and struts to that used to support

the antennae used in wireless telegraphy, invented by Guglielmo *Marconi*] (1912)
: of, having, or being a Bermuda rig

Mar·di Gras \'mär-dē-ˌgrä, *in New Orleans commonly* -ˌgrȯ\ *noun* [French, literally, fat Tuesday] (1699)
1 a : Shrove Tuesday often observed (as in New Orleans) with parades and festivities **b** : a carnival period climaxing on Shrove Tuesday
2 : a festive occasion resembling a pre-Lenten Mardi Gras

¹mare *noun* [Middle English, from Old English; akin to Old High German *mara* incubus, Serbo-Croatian *mora* nightmare] (before 12th century)
obsolete : an evil preternatural being causing nightmares

²mare \'mar, 'mer\ *noun* [Middle English, from Old English *mere;* akin to Old High German *merha* mare, Old English *mearh* horse, Welsh *march*] (before 12th century)
: a female horse or other equine animal especially when fully mature or of breeding age

³ma·re \'mär-(ˌ)ā\ *noun, plural* **ma·ria** \'mär-ē-ə\ *also* **ma·res** \'mär-(ˌ)āz\ [New Latin, from Latin, sea — more at MARINE] (1860)
: any of several mostly flat dark areas of considerable extent on the surface of the moon or Mars

ma·re clau·sum \'mär-(ˌ)ā-'klau̇-səm, -'klȯ-\ *noun* [New Latin, literally, closed sea] (1652)
: a navigable body of water (as a sea) that is under the jurisdiction of one nation and is closed to other nations

Mar·ek's disease \'mar-iks-, 'mer-\ *noun* [József *Marek* (died 1952) Hungarian veterinarian] (1947)
: a highly contagious viral disease of poultry that is characterized especially by proliferation of lymphoid cells and is caused by a herpesvirus

ma·re li·be·rum \'mär-(ˌ)ā-'lē-bə-ˌru̇m\ *noun* [New Latin, literally, free sea] (1652)
1 : a navigable body of water (as a sea) that is open to all nations
2 : FREEDOM OF THE SEAS

ma·ren·go \mə-'reŋ-(ˌ)gō\ *adjective, often capitalized* [French, from *Marengo*, village in northwest Italy] (circa 1924)
: of, consisting of, or served with a sauce of mushrooms, tomatoes, olives, oil, and wine ⟨*veal marengo*⟩

ma·re no·strum \'mär-(ˌ)ā-'nōs-trəm\ *noun* [New Latin, literally, our sea] (1941)
: a navigable body of water (as a sea) that belongs to a single nation or is mutually shared by two or more nations

mare's nest *noun, plural* **mare's nests** *or* **mares' nests** (1576)
1 : a false discovery, illusion, or deliberate hoax
2 : a place, condition, or situation of great disorder or confusion ⟨a *mare's nest* of spurious ambiguities to bewilder the simpleminded —J. H. Sledd⟩

mare's tail *noun, plural* **mare's tails** *or* **mares' tails** (circa 1762)
1 a : a common aquatic plant (*Hippuris vulgaris* of the family Hippuridaceae) with elongated shoots having dense whorls of narrow finely tapered leaves **b** : HORSEWEED 1
2 : a cirrus cloud that has a long slender flowing appearance

Mar·fan's syndrome \'mär-ˌfanz-\ *noun* [Antonin Bernard Jean *Marfan* (died 1942) French pediatrician] (circa 1923)
: a hereditary disorder of connective tissue that is characterized by abnormal elongation of the bones and often by ocular and circulatory defects — called also *Mar·fan syndrome* \'mär-ˌfan-\

mar·ga·rine \'mär-jə-rən, -ˌrēn; 'märj-rən\ *noun* [French, ultimately from Greek *margaron* pearl, probably back-formation from *margarītēs*] (1873)

: a food product made usually from vegetable oils churned with ripened skim milk to a smooth emulsion and used like butter

mar·ga·ri·ta \ˌmär-gə-'rē-tə\ *noun* [from the Spanish feminine name *Margarita*] (1963)
: a cocktail consisting of tequila, lime or lemon juice, and an orange-flavored liqueur

mar·ga·rite \'mär-gə-ˌrīt\ *noun* [Middle English, from Middle French, from Latin *margarita*, from Greek *margarītēs*] (13th century)
archaic : PEARL

mar·gay \'mär-ˌgā, mär-'\ *noun* [French, from Tupi *maracaja*] (1781)
: a small American spotted cat (*Felis wiedii*) resembling the ocelot and ranging from southernmost Texas to Argentina

margay

¹marge \'märj\ *noun* [Middle French, from Latin *margo*] (1551)
archaic : MARGIN

²marge *noun* (1922)
British : MARGARINE

mar·gent \'mär-jənt\ *noun* (15th century)
archaic : MARGIN

¹mar·gin \'mär-jən\ *noun* [Middle English, from Latin *margin-, margo* border — more at MARK] (14th century)
1 : the part of a page or sheet outside the main body of printed or written matter
2 : the outside limit and adjoining surface of something : EDGE ⟨at the *margin* of the woods⟩ ⟨continental *margin*⟩
3 a : a spare amount or measure or degree allowed or given for contingencies or special situations ⟨left no *margin* for error⟩ **b** (1) : a bare minimum below which or an extreme limit beyond which something becomes impossible or is no longer desirable ⟨on the *margin* of good taste⟩ (2) : the limit below which economic activity cannot be continued under normal conditions
4 a : the difference which exists between net sales and the cost of merchandise sold and from which expenses are usually met or profit derived **b** : the excess market value of collateral over the face of a loan **c** (1) : cash or collateral that is deposited by a client with a commodity or securities broker to protect the broker from loss on a contract (2) : the client's equity in securities bought with the aid of credit obtained specifically (as from a broker) for that purpose **d** : a range about a specified figure within which a purchase is to be made
5 : measure or degree of difference ⟨the bill passed by a one-vote *margin*⟩
— **mar·gined** \-jənd\ *adjective*

²margin *transitive verb* (1715)
1 a : to provide with an edging or border **b** : to form a margin to : BORDER
2 a : to add margin to ⟨*margin* up an account⟩ **b** (1) : to use as margin ⟨*margin* bonds to buy stock⟩ (2) : to provide margin for ⟨*margin* a transaction⟩ **c** : to buy (securities) on margin

mar·gin·al \'märj-nəl, 'mär-jə-n°l\ *adjective* [Medieval Latin *marginalis*, from Latin *margin-, margo*] (1573)
1 : written or printed in the margin of a page or sheet ⟨*marginal* notes⟩
2 a : of, relating to, or situated at a margin or border **b** : not of central importance ⟨regards violence as a *marginal* rather than a central problem⟩ **c** (1) : occupying the borderland of a relatively stable territorial or cultural area ⟨*marginal* tribes⟩ (2) : characterized by the incorporation of habits and values from two divergent cultures and by incomplete assimilation in either ⟨the *marginal* cultural habits of

new immigrant groups⟩ (3) : excluded from or existing outside the mainstream of society, a group, or a school of thought ⟨*marginal* voters⟩
3 : located at the fringe of consciousness ⟨*marginal* sensations⟩
4 a : close to the lower limit of qualification, acceptability, or function : barely exceeding the minimum requirements ⟨a semiliterate person of *marginal* ability⟩ **b** (1) : having a character or capacity fitted to yield a supply of goods which when marketed at existing price levels will barely cover the cost of production ⟨*marginal* land⟩ (2) : of, relating to, or derived from goods produced and marketed with such result ⟨*marginal* profits⟩
5 : relating to or being a function of a random variable that is obtained from a function of several random variables by integrating or summing over all possible values of the other variables ⟨a *marginal* probability function⟩
— **mar·gin·al·i·ty** \ˌmär-jə-'na-lə-tē\ *noun*
— **mar·gin·al·ly** \'märj-nə-lē, 'mär-jə-n°l-ē\ *adverb*

mar·gi·na·lia \ˌmär-jə-'nā-lē-ə\ *noun plural* [New Latin, from Medieval Latin, neuter plural of *marginalis*] (1832)
1 : marginal notes (as in a book)
2 : nonessential items ⟨the meat and *marginalia* of American politics —*Saturday Review*⟩

mar·gin·al·ize \'märj-nə-ˌlīz, 'mär-jə-n°l-ˌīz\ *transitive verb* **-ized; -iz·ing** (1970)
: to relegate to a marginal position within a society or group
— **mar·gin·al·i·za·tion** \ˌmärj-nə-lə-'zā-shən, ˌmär-jə-n°l-ə-\ *noun*

marginal utility *noun* (1890)
: the amount of additional utility provided by an additional unit of an economic good or service

mar·gin·ate \'mär-jə-ˌnāt\ *transitive verb* **-at·ed; -at·ing** (1623)
1 : MARGIN 1, 2a
2 : MARGINALIZE
— **mar·gin·ation** \ˌmär-jə-'nā-shən\ *noun*

mar·gin·at·ed \-ˌnā-təd\ *adjective* (circa 1727)
: having a distinct margin

mar·gra·vate \'mär-grə-ˌvāt\ *or* **mar·gra·vi·ate** \mär-'grā-vē-ət, -ˌāt\ *noun* (1802)
: the territory of a margrave

mar·grave \'mär-ˌgrāv\ *noun* [Dutch *markgraaf*, from Middle Dutch *marcgrave;* akin to Old High German *marha* boundary and to Old High German *grāvo* count — more at MARK] (1551)
1 : the military governor especially of a German border province
2 : a member of the German nobility corresponding in rank to a British marquess
— **mar·gra·vi·al** \mär-'grā-vē-əl\ *adjective*

mar·gra·vine \'mär-grə-ˌvēn, ˌmär-grə-'\ *noun* (1692)
: the wife of a margrave

mar·gue·rite \ˌmär-gə-'rēt, -gyə-\ *noun* [French, from Middle French *margarite* pearl, daisy — more at MARGARITE] (circa 1866)
1 : DAISY 1b
2 : any of various single-flowered chrysanthemums; *especially* : a chrysanthemum (*Chrysanthemum frutescens*) of the Canary Islands

maria *plural of* MARE

ma·ri·a·chi \ˌmär-ē-'ä-chē, ˌmar-\ *noun* [Mexican Spanish, perhaps modification of French *mariage* marriage] (1927)
1 : a Mexican street band; *also* : a musician belonging to such a band
2 : the music performed by a mariachi

Mar·i·an \'mer-ē-ən, 'mar-ē-, 'mā-rē-\ *adjective* (1608)

\ə\ abut \ᵊ\ kitten \ər\ further \a\ ash \ā\ ace \ä\ mop, mar \au̇\ out \ch\ chin \e\ bet \ē\ easy \g\ go \i\ hit \ī\ ice \j\ job \ŋ\ sing \ō\ go \ȯ\ law \ȯi\ boy \th\ thin \t̶h̶\ the \ü\ loot \u̇\ foot \y\ yet \zh\ vision *see also* Guide to Pronunciation

1 : of or relating to Mary Tudor or her reign
2 : of or relating to the Virgin Mary
Mar·i·an·ist \-ə-nist\ *noun* (circa 1899)
: a member of the Roman Catholic Society of Mary of Paris founded by William Joseph Chaminade in France in 1817 and devoted especially to education
Ma·ria The·re·sa dollar \mə-ˈrē-ə-tə-ˈrā-sə-, -ˈrā-zə-\ *noun* (circa 1883)
: a 1780 silver trade coin used in the Middle East
mari·cul·ture \ˈmar-ə-ˌkəl-chər\ *noun* [Latin *mare* sea + English *-culture* (as in *agriculture*)] (circa 1909)
: the cultivation of marine organisms in their natural environment
— **mari·cul·tur·ist** \ˌmar-ə-ˈkəl-chə-rist, -ˈkəlch-rist\ *noun*
mari·gold \ˈmar-ə-ˌgōld, ˈmer-\ *noun* [Middle English, from *Mary*, mother of Jesus + Middle English *gold*] (14th century)
1 : POT MARIGOLD
2 : any of a genus (*Tagetes*) of composite herbs with showy yellow, orange, or maroon flower heads
mari·jua·na *also* **mari·hua·na** \ˌmar-ə-ˈwä-nə *also* -ˈhwä-\ *noun* [Mexican Spanish *mariguana, marihuana*] (1894)
1 : HEMP 1a, c
2 : the dried leaves and flowering tops of the pistillate hemp plant that yield THC and are smoked in cigarettes for their intoxicating effect — compare BHANG, CANNABIS, HASHISH
ma·rim·ba \mə-ˈrim-bə\ *noun* [of Bantu origin; akin to Kimbundu *marimba* xylophone] (1704)
: a xylophone of southern Africa and Central America with resonators beneath each bar; *also* **:** a modern form of this instrument
— **ma·rim·bist** \-bist\ *noun*
ma·ri·na \mə-ˈrē-nə\ *noun* [Italian & Spanish, seashore, from feminine of *marino*, adjective, marine, from Latin *marinus*] (1924)
: a dock or basin providing secure moorings for pleasure boats and often offering supply, repair, and other facilities
¹mar·i·nade \ˌmar-ə-ˈnād\ *noun* [French, from *mariner* to pickle, marinate, probably from Italian *marinare*] (1725)
: a savory usually acidic sauce in which meat, fish, or a vegetable is soaked to enrich its flavor or to tenderize it
²marinade *transitive verb* **-nad·ed; -nad·ing** (1727)
: MARINATE
mar·i·na·ra \ˌmar-ə-ˈnar-ə, ˌmer-ə-ˈner-, -ˈnär-\ *adjective* [Italian (*alla*) *marinara*, literally, in sailor style] (circa 1948)
: made with tomatoes, onions, garlic, and spices ⟨*marinara* sauce⟩; *also* **:** served with marinara sauce ⟨spaghetti *marinara*⟩
mar·i·nate \ˈmar-ə-ˌnāt\ *verb* **-nat·ed; -nat·ing** [probably from Italian *marinato*, past participle of *marinare* to marinate, from *marino*] (circa 1645)
transitive verb
: to steep (meat, fish, or vegetables) in a marinade
intransitive verb
: to become marinated
— **mar·i·na·tion** \ˌmar-ə-ˈnā-shən\ *noun*
¹ma·rine \mə-ˈrēn\ *adjective* [Middle English, from Latin *marinus*, from *mare* sea; akin to Old English *mere* sea, pool, Old High German *meri* sea, Old Church Slavonic *morje*] (15th century)
1 a : of or relating to the sea ⟨*marine* life⟩ **b :** of or relating to the navigation of the sea **:** NAUTICAL ⟨a *marine* chart⟩ **c :** of or relating to the commerce of the sea **:** MARITIME ⟨*marine* law⟩ **d :** depicting the sea, seashore, or ships ⟨a *marine* painter⟩
2 : of or relating to marines ⟨*marine* barracks⟩
²marine *noun* (1669)

1 a : the mercantile and naval shipping of a country **b :** seagoing ships especially in relation to nationality or class
2 : one of a class of soldiers serving on shipboard or in close association with a naval force; *specifically* **:** a member of the U.S. Marine Corps
3 : an executive department (as in France) having charge of naval affairs
4 : a marine picture **:** SEASCAPE
marine architect *noun* (1949)
: NAVAL ARCHITECT
— **marine architecture** *noun*
mar·i·ner \ˈmar-ə-nər\ *noun* [Middle English, from Anglo-French *marinier*, from Medieval Latin *marinarius*, from *marinus*] (14th century)
: a person who navigates or assists in navigating a ship **:** SEAMAN, SAILOR
mariner's compass *noun* (1627)
: a compass used in navigation that consists of parallel magnetic needles or bundles of needles permanently attached to a card marked to indicate direction and degrees of a circle
Mar·i·ol·a·try \ˌmer-ē-ˈä-lə-trē, ˌmar-ē-, ˌmā-rē-\ *noun* (1612)
: excessive veneration of the Virgin Mary
— **Mar·i·ol·a·ter** \-ˈä-lə-tər\ *noun*
Mar·i·ol·o·gy \-ˈä-lə-jē\ *noun* (1857)
: study or doctrine relating to the Virgin Mary
— **Mar·i·o·log·i·cal** \-ə-ˈlä-ji-kəl\ *adjective*
mar·i·o·nette \ˌmar-ē-ə-ˈnet, ˌmer-\ *noun* [French *marionnette*, from Middle French *maryonete*, from *Marion*, diminutive of *Marie* Mary] (circa 1620)
: a small-scale usually wooden figure (as of a person) with jointed limbs that is moved from above by manipulation of the attached strings or wires ◇
mar·i·po·sa lily \ˌmar-ə-ˈpō-zə-, -sə-\ *noun* [probably from American Spanish *mariposa*, from Spanish, butterfly] (1882)
: any of a genus (*Calochortus*) of western North American plants of the lily family with showy flowers having three petals and three sepals — called also *mariposa tulip*; compare SEGO LILY
mar·ish \ˈmar-ish\ *noun* (15th century)
archaic **:** MARSH
Mar·ist \ˈmar-ist, ˈmer-\ *noun* [French *mariste*, from *Marie* Mary] (circa 1872)
: a member of the Roman Catholic Society of Mary founded by Jean Claude Colin in France in 1816 and devoted to education
mar·i·tal \ˈmar-ə-tᵊl\ *adjective* [Latin *maritalis*, from *maritus* married] (1603)
1 : of or relating to marriage or the married state ⟨*marital* vows⟩
2 : of or relating to a husband and his role in marriage
— **mar·i·tal·ly** \-tᵊl-ē\ *adverb*
mar·i·time \ˈmar-ə-ˌtīm\ *adjective* [Latin *maritimus*, from *mare*] (1550)
1 : of, relating to, or bordering on the sea ⟨a *maritime* province⟩
2 : of or relating to navigation or commerce on the sea
3 : having the characteristics of a mariner
mar·jo·ram \ˈmär-jə-rəm, ˈmärj-rəm\ *noun* [alteration of Middle English *mageram, majorane*, from Middle French *majorane*, from Medieval Latin *majorana*] (circa 1550)
: any of various usually fragrant and aromatic Old World mints (genus *Origanum*) often used in cookery
¹mark \ˈmärk\ *noun* [Middle English, from Old English *mearc* boundary, march, sign; akin to Old High German *marha* boundary, Latin *margo*] (before 12th century)
1 : a boundary land
2 a (1) **:** a conspicuous object serving as a guide for travelers (2) **:** something (as a line, notch, or fixed object) designed to record position **b :** one of the bits of leather or colored bunting placed on a sounding line at intervals

c : TARGET **d :** the starting line or position in a track event **e** (1) **:** GOAL, OBJECT (2) **:** an object of attack, ridicule, or abuse; *specifically* **:** a victim or prospective victim of a swindle (3) **:** the point under discussion (4) **:** condition of being correct or accurate ⟨her observations are on the *mark*⟩ **f :** a standard of performance, quality, or condition **:** NORM ⟨not feeling up to the *mark* lately⟩
3 a (1) **:** SIGN, INDICATION ⟨gave her the necklace as a *mark* of his esteem⟩ (2) **:** an impression (as a scratch, scar, or stain) made on something (3) **:** a distinguishing trait or quality **:** CHARACTERISTIC ⟨the *marks* of an educated person⟩ **b :** a symbol used for identification or indication of ownership **c :** a cross made in place of a signature **d** (1) **:** TRADEMARK (2) *capitalized* — used with a numeral to designate a particular model of a weapon or machine ⟨*Mark* II⟩ **e :** a written or printed symbol (as a comma or colon) **f :** POSTMARK **g :** a symbol used to represent a teacher's estimate of a student's work or conduct; *especially* **:** GRADE **h :** a figure registering a point or level reached or achieved ⟨the halfway *mark* in the first period of play⟩; *especially* **:** RECORD
4 a : ATTENTION, NOTICE ⟨nothing worthy of *mark*⟩ **b :** IMPORTANCE, DISTINCTION ⟨stands out as a person of *mark*⟩ **c :** a lasting or strong impression ⟨worked at several jobs but didn't make much of a *mark*⟩ **d :** an assessment of merits **:** RATING ⟨got high *marks* for honesty⟩
synonym see SIGN
²mark *verb* [Middle English, from Old English *mearcian*; akin to Old High German *marcōn* to mark, determine the boundaries of, Old English *mearc* boundary] (before 12th century)
transitive verb
1 a (1) **:** to fix or trace out the bounds or limits of (2) **:** to plot the course of **:** CHART **b :** to set apart by or as if by a line or boundary — usually used with *off*
2 a (1) **:** to designate as if by a mark ⟨*marked* for greatness⟩ (2) **:** to make or leave a mark on (3) **:** to furnish with natural marks ⟨wings *marked* with white⟩ (4) **:** to label so as to indicate price or quality (5) **:** to make notations in or on **b** (1) **:** to make note of in writing **:** JOT ⟨*marking* the date in his journal⟩ (2) **:** to indicate by a mark or symbol ⟨*mark* an accent⟩ (3) **:** REGISTER, RECORD (4) **:** to determine the value of by means of marks or symbols **:** GRADE ⟨*mark* term papers⟩ **c :** CHARACTERIZE, DISTINGUISH ⟨the flamboyance that *marks* her stage appearance⟩ (2) **:** SIGNALIZE ⟨this year *marks* our 50th anniversary⟩
3 : to take notice of **:** OBSERVE ⟨*mark* my words⟩

◇ WORD HISTORY
marionette Puppet shows have been widespread in the world since ancient times, but the elaborately jointed and intricately wired figure known as the marionette was not perfected until the 19th century. At the time the word entered English in the 17th century, French *marionnette* denoted a much more rudimentary hand- or string-operated puppet. Nonetheless performances involving these figures were quite popular in France in the 16th century, when *marionnette* is first attested in this sense in French. Puppet plays were performed in particular at the Feast of the Assumption of the Virgin Mary. This led to the puppets being called by a diminutive form of *Marie*, the French name of the Virgin Mary. (*Marionette* may be altered from a diminutive form of *mariole*, itself a diminutive of *Marie*, or formed directly from another diminutive, *Marion*.) Similar derivatives, such as *mariotte* and *mariole*, had been used to designate other objects associated with the Virgin, such as a 15th century coin bearing her image.

4 : to pick up (one's golf ball) from a putting green and substitute a marker
intransitive verb
: to take careful notice
— **mark time 1 :** to keep the time of a marching step by moving the feet alternately without advancing **2 :** to maintain a static state of readiness ⟨the House was *marking time* while the Senate talked —F. L. Paxson⟩

³mark *noun* [Middle English, from Old English *marc*, probably of Scandinavian origin; akin to Old Norse *mǫrk* mark; akin to Old English *mearc* sign] (before 12th century)
1 : any of various old European units of weight used especially for gold and silver; *especially* **:** a unit equal to about 8 ounces (248 grams)
2 : a unit of value: **a :** an old English unit equal to 13s 4d **b :** any one of various old Scandinavian or German units of value; *specifically* **:** a unit and corresponding silver coin of the 16th century worth ½ taler **c** (1) **:** DEUTSCHE MARK (2) **:** the basic monetary unit of East Germany replaced in 1990 by the West German deutsche mark **d :** MARKKA

Mark \'märk\ *noun* [Latin *Marcus*]
1 a : an early Jewish Christian traditionally identified as the writer of the Gospel of Mark — called also *John Mark* **b :** the second Gospel in the New Testament — see BIBLE table
2 : a king of Cornwall, uncle of Tristram, and husband of Isolde

mark·down \'märk-ˌdau̇n\ *noun* (1880)
1 : a lowering of price
2 : the amount by which an original selling price is reduced

mark down *transitive verb* (1859)
: to put a lower price on

marked \'märkt\ *adjective* (before 12th century)
1 : having an identifying mark ⟨a *marked* card⟩
2 \or 'mär-kəd\ **:** having a distinctive or emphasized character **:** NOTICEABLE ⟨has a *marked* drawl⟩
3 a : enjoying fame or notoriety **b :** being an object of attack, suspicion, or vengeance ⟨a *marked* man⟩
4 : overtly signaled by a linguistic feature ⟨with most English nouns the plural is the *marked* number⟩
— **mark·ed·ly** \'mär-kəd-lē\ *adverb*
— **mark·ed·ness** \'mär-kəd-nəs\ *noun*

mark·er \'mär-kər\ *noun* (15th century)
1 : one that marks
2 : something used for marking
3 : SCORE 7; *specifically* **:** RUN
4 : PROMISSORY NOTE, IOU
5 : GENETIC MARKER

¹mar·ket \'mär-kət\ *noun, often attributive* [Middle English, from Old North French, from Latin *mercatus* trade, marketplace, from *mercari* to trade, from *merc-, merx* merchandise] (12th century)
1 a (1) **:** a meeting together of people for the purpose of trade by private purchase and sale and usually not by auction (2) **:** the people assembled at such a meeting **b** (1) **:** a public place where a market is held; *especially* **:** a place where provisions are sold at wholesale ⟨a farmers' *market*⟩ (2) **:** a retail establishment usually of a specified kind ⟨a fish *market*⟩
2 *archaic* **:** the act or an instance of buying and selling
3 : the rate or price offered for a commodity or security
4 a (1) **:** a geographical area of demand for commodities or services ⟨the foreign *market* for consulting firms⟩ (2) **:** a specified category of potential buyers ⟨the youth *market*⟩ **b :** the course of commercial activity by which the exchange of commodities is effected **:** extent of demand ⟨the *market* is dull⟩ **c** (1) **:** an opportunity for selling ⟨a good *market* for used cars⟩ (2) **:** the available supply of or potential demand for specified goods or services ⟨the la-

bor *market*⟩ **d :** the area of economic activity in which buyers and sellers come together and the forces of supply and demand affect prices ⟨producing goods for *market* rather than for consumption⟩
— **in the market :** in the position of being a potential buyer ⟨*in the market* for a house⟩
— **on the market :** available for purchase; *also* **:** up for sale ⟨put their house *on the market*⟩

²market (1635)
intransitive verb
: to deal in a market
transitive verb
1 : to expose for sale in a market
2 : SELL

mar·ket·able \'mär-kə-tə-bəl\ *adjective* (1600)
1 a : fit to be offered for sale in a market ⟨food that is not *marketable*⟩ **b :** wanted by purchasers or employers **:** SALABLE ⟨*marketable* securities⟩ ⟨*marketable* skills⟩
2 : of or relating to buying or selling
— **mar·ket·abil·i·ty** \ˌmär-kə-tə-'bi-lə-tē\ *noun*

market basket *noun* (1943)
: a variety of consumer goods and services used to calculate a consumer price index

mar·ke·teer \ˌmär-kə-'tir\ *noun* (1832)
: a specialist in promoting or selling a product or service

mar·ket·er \'mär-kə-tər\ *noun* (1787)
: one that deals in a market; *specifically* **:** one that promotes or sells a product or service

market garden *noun* (1811)
British **:** TRUCK FARM
— **market gardener** *noun, British*
— **market gardening** *noun, British*

mar·ket·ing *noun* (1561)
1 a : the act or process of selling or purchasing in a market **b :** the process or technique of promoting, selling, and distributing a product or service
2 : an aggregate of functions involved in moving goods from producer to consumer

marketing research *noun* (circa 1937)
: research into the means of promoting, selling, and distributing a product or service

market order *noun* (circa 1920)
: an order to buy or sell securities or commodities immediately at the best price obtainable in the market

mar·ket·place \'mär-kət-ˌplās\ *noun* (14th century)
1 a : an open square or place in a town where markets or public sales are held **b :** MARKET ⟨the *marketplace* is the interpreter of supply and demand⟩
2 : the world of trade or economic activity **:** the everyday world ⟨a conviction that religion belongs in the *marketplace* —Current Biography⟩
3 : a sphere in which intangible values compete for acceptance ⟨the *marketplace* of ideas⟩

market price *noun* (15th century)
: a price actually given in current market dealings

market research *noun* (1926)
: research into the size, location, and makeup of a product market
— **market researcher** *noun*

market share *noun* (1970)
: the percentage of the market for a product or service that a company supplies

mark·ing *noun* (14th century)
1 : the act, process, or an instance of making or giving a mark
2 a : a mark made **b :** arrangement, pattern, or disposition of marks

mark·ka \'mär-ˌkä\ *noun, plural* **mark·kaa** \'mär-ˌkä\ *also* **mark·kas** \-ˌkäz\ [Finnish, from Swedish *mark*, a unit of value; akin to Old Norse *mǫrk* mark] (circa 1896)
— see MONEY table

Markov chain *noun* [A. A. *Markov* (died 1922) Russian mathematician] (1942)

: a usually discrete stochastic process (as a random walk) in which the probabilities of occurrence of various future states depend only on the present state of the system or on the immediately preceding state and not on the path by which the present state was achieved — called also *Markov chain*

Mar·kov·ian \mär-'kō-vē-ən, -'kȯ-\ *or* **Mar·kov** \'mär-ˌkȯf, -ˌkȯv\ *also* **Mar·koff** \'mär-ˌkȯf\ *adjective* (1950)
: of, relating to, or resembling a Markov process or Markov chain especially by having probabilities defined in terms of transition from the possible existing states to other states

Markov process *noun* (1939)
: a stochastic process (as Brownian motion) that resembles a Markov chain except that the states are continuous; *also* **:** MARKOV CHAIN — called also *Markoff process*

marks·man \'märks-mən\ *noun* (1660)
: a person skilled in shooting at a mark or target
— **marks·man·ship** \-ˌship\ *noun*

marks·wom·an \'märks-ˌwu̇-mən\ *noun* (1802)
: a woman skilled in shooting at a mark or target

mark·up \'mär-ˌkəp\ *noun* (1916)
1 : an amount added to the cost price to determine the selling price; *broadly* **:** PROFIT
2 : a U.S. Congressional committee session at which a bill is put into final form before it is reported out

mark up *transitive verb* (1869)
: to put a markup on

marl \'mär(-ə)l\ *noun* [Middle English, from Middle French *marle*, from Medieval Latin *margila*, diminutive of Latin *marga* marl, from Gaulish] (14th century)
: a loose or crumbling earthy deposit (as of sand, silt, or clay) that contains a substantial amount of calcium carbonate and is used especially as a fertilizer for soils deficient in lime
— **marly** \'mär-lē\ *adjective*

mar·lin \'mär-lən\ *noun* [short for *marlinspike*; from the appearance of its beak] (1917)
: any of several large marine billfishes (genera *Makaira* and *Tetrapturus*) that are notable sport fishes

mar·line *also* **mar·lin** \'mär-lən\ *noun* [Middle English *merlyn*, probably from Middle Low German *marlinc, merlinc*, from *mēren* to tie, moor] (15th century)
: a small usually tarred line of two strands twisted loosely left-handed that is used especially for seizing and as a covering for wire rope

mar·line·spike *also* **mar·lin·spike** \'mär-lən-ˌspīk\ *noun* (1626)
: a tool (as of wood or iron) that tapers to a point and is used to separate strands of rope or wire (as in splicing)

marl·stone \'mär(-ə)l-ˌstōn\ *noun* (circa 1839)
: a rock that consists of a mixture of clay materials and calcium carbonate and often contains kerogen

mar·ma·lade \'mär-mə-ˌlād\ *noun* [Portuguese *marmelada* quince conserve, from *marmelo* quince, from Latin *melimelum*, a sweet apple, from Greek *melimēlon*, from *meli* honey + *mēlon* apple — more at MELLIFLUOUS] (1524)
: a clear sweetened jelly in which pieces of fruit and fruit rind are suspended

mar·mo·re·al \mär-'mȯr-ē-əl, -'mȯr-\ *also* **mar·mo·re·an** \-ē-ən\ *adjective* [Latin *marmoreus*, from *marmor* marble] (1656)
: of, relating to, or suggestive of marble or a marble statue especially in coldness or aloofness

\ə\ abut \ᵊ\ kitten \ər\ further \a\ ash \ā\ ace
\ä\ mop, mar \au̇\ out \ch\ chin \e\ bet \ē\ easy
\g\ go \i\ hit \ī\ ice \j\ job \ŋ\ sing \ō\ go
\ȯ\ law \ȯi\ boy \th\ thin \th\ the \ü\ loot \u̇\ foot
\y\ yet \zh\ vision *see also* Guide to Pronunciation

— **mar·mo·re·al·ly** \-ē-ə-lē\ *adverb*

mar·mo·set \'mär-mə-,set, -,zet\ *noun* [Middle English *marmusette* kind of monkey, from Middle French *marmoset* grotesque figure, from *marmouser* to mumble, of imitative origin] (1679) : any of numerous small soft-furred South and Central American monkeys (family Callithricidae) with claws instead of nails on all the digits except the great toe

marmoset

mar·mot \'mär-mət\ *noun* [French *marmotte*] (1607) : any of a genus (*Marmota*) of stout-bodied short-legged chiefly herbivorous burrowing rodents with coarse fur, a short bushy tail, and very small ears — compare WOODCHUCK

marmot

mar·o·cain \'mar-ə-,kān\ *noun* [French (*crêpe*) *marocain*, literally, Moroccan crepe] (1922) : a ribbed crepe fabric used in women's clothing

Mar·o·nite \'mar-ə-,nīt\ *noun* [Medieval Latin *maronita*, from *Maron-*, *Maro* 5th century A.D. Syrian monk] (circa 1511) : a member of a Uniate church chiefly in Lebanon having a Syriac liturgy and married clergy

¹ma·roon \mə-'rün\ *noun* [French *maron*, *marron*, modification of American Spanish *cimarrón*, from *cimarrón* wild, savage] (1666) **1** *capitalized* : a fugitive black slave of the West Indies and Guiana in the 17th and 18th centuries; *also* : a descendant of such a slave **2** : a person who is marooned ◇

²maroon *transitive verb* (circa 1709) **1** : to put ashore on a desolate island or coast and leave to one's fate **2** : to place or leave in isolation or without hope of ready escape

³maroon *noun* [French *marron* Spanish chestnut] (1791) : a dark red

mar·plot \'mär-,plät\ *noun* (1764) : one who frustrates or ruins a plan or undertaking by meddling

¹marque \'märk\ *noun* [Middle English, from Middle French, from Old Provençal *marca*, from *marcar* to mark, seize as pledge, of Germanic origin; akin to Old High German *marcōn* to mark] (15th century) **1** *obsolete* : REPRISAL, RETALIATION **2** : LETTERS OF MARQUE

²marque *noun* [French, mark, brand, from Middle French, from *marquer* to mark, of Germanic origin; akin to Old High German *marcōn* to mark] (1906) : a brand or make of a product (as a sports car)

mar·quee \mär-'kē\ *noun* [modification of French *marquise*, literally, marchioness] (1690) **1** *chiefly British* : a large tent set up for an outdoor party, reception, or exhibition **2** : a permanent canopy often of metal and glass projecting over an entrance (as of a hotel or theater) **3** : BOX OFFICE 2 ⟨*marquee* value⟩

Mar·que·san \mär-'kā-z°n\ *noun* (1799) **1** : a native or inhabitant of the Marquesas Islands **2** : the Austronesian language of the Marquesans

— **Marquesan** *adjective*

mar·quess \'mär-kwəs\ *or* **mar·quis** \'mär-kwəs, mär-'kē\ *noun, plural* **mar·quess·es** *or* **mar·quis·es** \-kwə-səz\ *or* **mar·quis** \-'kē(z)\ [Middle English *marquis, markis*, from Middle French *marquis*, alteration of *marchis*, from *marche* march] (14th century) **1** : a nobleman of hereditary rank in Europe and Japan **2** : a member of the British peerage ranking below a duke and above an earl

— **mar·quess·ate** \'mär-kwə-sət\ *or* **mar·quis·ate** \'mär-kwə-zət, -sət\ *noun*

mar·que·try *also* **mar·que·terie** \'mär-kə-trē\ *noun* [Middle French *marqueterie*, from *marqueter* to checker, inlay, from *marque* mark] (1563) : decorative work in which elaborate patterns are formed by the insertion of pieces of material (as wood, shell, or ivory) into a wood veneer that is then applied to a surface (as of a piece of furniture)

mar·quise \mär-'kēz\ *noun, plural* **mar·quises** \-'kēz, -'kē-zəz\ [French, feminine of *marquis*] (1783) **1** : MARQUEE **2** : MARCHIONESS **3** : a gem or a ring setting or bezel usually elliptical in shape but with pointed ends

mar·qui·sette \,mär-kwə-'zet, -kə-\ *noun* [*marquise* + *-ette*] (1908) : a sheer meshed fabric used for clothing, curtains, and mosquito nets

mar·ram grass \'mar-əm-\ *noun* [of Scandinavian origin; akin to Old Norse *maralmr*, a beach grass] (1834) : any of several beach grasses (genus *Ammophila* and especially *A. arenaria*)

Mar·ra·no \mə-'rä-(,)nō\ *noun, plural* **-nos** [Spanish, literally, pig] (1583) : a Christianized Jew of medieval Spain

mar·riage \'mar-ij *also* 'mer-\ *noun* [Middle English *mariage*, from Old French, from *marier* to marry] (14th century) **1 a** : the state of being married **b** : the mutual relation of husband and wife : WEDLOCK **c** : the institution whereby men and women are joined in a special kind of social and legal dependence for the purpose of founding and maintaining a family **2** : an act of marrying or the rite by which the married status is effected; *especially* : the wedding ceremony and attendant festivities or formalities **3** : an intimate or close union ⟨the *marriage* of painting and poetry —J. T. Shawcross⟩

— **mar·riage·abil·i·ty** \,mar-i-jə-'bi-lə-tē *also* ,mer-\ *noun*

— **mar·riage·able** \'mar-i-jə-bəl *also* 'mer-\ *adjective*

marriage of convenience (1711) : a marriage contracted for social, political, or economic advantage rather than for mutual affection; *broadly* : a union or cooperation formed solely for pragmatic reasons

¹mar·ried \'mar-ēd *also* 'mer-\ *adjective* (14th century) **1 a** : being in the state of matrimony : WEDDED **b** : of or relating to marriage : CONNUBIAL **2** : UNITED, JOINED

²married *noun, plural* **marrieds** *or* **married** (1890) : a married person ⟨young *marrieds* are paid undue . . . attention —Paul Goodman⟩

mar·ron \ma-'rō°n\ *noun* [French] (1594) **1** : a large Mediterranean chestnut (*Castanea sativa*) or its sweet edible nut — called also *Spanish chestnut* **2** **mar·rons** \-'rō°(z)\ *plural* : chestnuts preserved in vanilla-flavored syrup

mar·rons gla·cés \ma-'rō°-gla-'sā\ *noun plural* [French, literally, glazed marrons] (1871) : MARRON 2

¹mar·row \'mar-(,)ō\ *noun* [Middle English *marowe*, from Old English *mearg*; akin to Old High German *marag* marrow, Sanskrit *majjan*] (before 12th century) **1 a** : a soft highly vascular modified connective tissue that occupies the cavities and cancellous part of most bones — compare RED MARROW **b** : the substance of the spinal cord **2 a** : the choicest of food **b** : the seat of animal vigor **c** : the inmost, best, or essential part : CORE ⟨personal liberty is the *marrow* of the American tradition —Clinton Rossiter⟩ **3** *chiefly British* : VEGETABLE MARROW

— **mar·rowy** \'mar-ə-wē\ *adjective*

²marrow *noun* [Middle English *marwe, marrow*] (1516) *chiefly Scottish* : one of a pair

mar·row·bone \'mar-ə-,bōn, -ō-,bōn\ *noun* (14th century) **1** : a bone (as a shinbone) rich in marrow **2** *plural* : KNEES

mar·row·fat \-ə-,fat, -ō-,fat\ *noun* (1733) : any of several wrinkled-seeded garden peas

¹mar·ry \'mar-ē *also* 'mer-\ *verb* **mar·ried; mar·ry·ing** [Middle English *marien*, from Old French *marier*, from Latin *maritare*, from *maritus* married] (14th century) *transitive verb* **1 a** : to join as husband and wife according to law or custom **b** : to give in marriage ⟨*married* his daughter to his partner's son⟩ **c** : to take as spouse : WED ⟨*married* the girl next door⟩ **d** : to perform the ceremony of marriage for ⟨a priest will *marry* them⟩ **e** : to obtain by marriage ⟨*marry* wealth⟩ **2** : to unite in close and usually permanent relation *intransitive verb* **1** : to take a spouse : WED **2** : COMBINE, UNITE ⟨seafood *marries* with other flavors⟩

— **marry into** : to become a member of by marriage ⟨*married into* a prominent family⟩

²marry *interjection* [Middle English *marie*, from *Marie*, the Virgin Mary] (14th century) *archaic* — used for emphasis and especially to express amused or surprised agreement

Mars \'märz\ *noun* [Latin *Mart-, Mars*] **1** : the Roman god of war — compare ARES **2** : the planet fourth in order from the sun and conspicuous for its red color — see PLANET table

mar·sa·la \mär-'sä-lə\ *noun, often capitalized* [*Marsala*, town in Sicily] (1806) : a fortified Sicilian wine that varies from dry to sweet

marse \'märs\ *noun* [by shortening & alteration] (1869) *Southern* : MASTER

Mar·seilles \mär-'sā(ə)lz\ *noun* [*Marseilles*, France] (1762)

◇ WORD HISTORY

maroon The modern Maroons of the Caribbean region are descendants of African slaves who fled from servitude into remote areas, such as the Cockpit Country of Jamaica and the interior of Suriname. In the 17th and 18th centuries, however, the word *maron* or *maroon* was used more or less generically to mean "fugitive slave." It is a loan from *maron* or *marron* in the local French of the Caribbean, originally used of a domestic animal and meaning "escaped into the wild." The French word in its turn was borrowed, directly or indirectly, from Spanish *cimarrón* "wild, savage," also applied in the 16th century to both animals and humans. In the late 17th century, the verbal form *marooned* was used by the English buccaneer William Dampier to mean "lost," and early in the next century *maroon* first clearly appears in the still-surviving sense "to put ashore on a desolate island or coast." In effect, the word now meant to reduce someone to the status of a fugitive slave, dependent on wits and knowledge of the wilderness for survival.

: a firm cotton fabric that is similar to piqué

¹marsh \'märsh\ *noun, often attributive* [Middle English *mersh*, from Old English *merisc, mersc;* akin to Middle Dutch *mersch* marsh, Old English *mere* sea, pool — more at MA-RINE] (before 12th century)
: a tract of soft wet land usually characterized by monocotyledons (as grasses or cattails)

¹mar·shal *also* **mar·shall** \'mär-shəl\ *noun* [Middle English, from Old French *mareschal,* of Germanic origin; akin to Old High German *marahscalc* marshal, from *marah* horse + *scalc* servant] (13th century)
1 a : a high official in the household of a medieval king, prince, or noble originally having charge of the cavalry but later usually in command of the military forces **b :** a person who arranges and directs the ceremonial aspects of a gathering
2 a : FIELD MARSHAL **b :** a general officer of the highest military rank
3 a : an officer having charge of prisoners **b** (1) **:** a ministerial officer appointed for a judicial district (as of the U.S.) to execute the process of the courts and perform various duties similar to those of a sheriff (2) **:** a city law officer entrusted with particular duties **c :** the administrative head of a city police department or fire department ◆
— **mar·shal·cy** \-sē\ *noun*
— **mar·shal·ship** \-,ship\ *noun*

²marshal *also* **marshall** *verb* **-shaled** *or* **-shalled; -shal·ing** *or* **-shal·ling** \'märsh-(ə-)liŋ\ (15th century)
transitive verb
1 : to place in proper rank or position ⟨*marshaling* the troops⟩
2 : to bring together and order in an appropriate or effective way ⟨*marshal* arguments⟩
3 : to lead ceremoniously or solicitously : USHER ⟨*marshaling* her little group of children down the street⟩
intransitive verb
: to take form or order ⟨ideas *marshaling* neatly⟩
synonym see ORDER

marshal of the Royal Air Force (1947)
: the highest ranking officer in the British air force

marsh elder *noun* (circa 1775)
: any of a genus (*Iva*) of coarse shrubby composite plants of moist areas in eastern and central North America

marsh gas *noun* (1848)
: METHANE

marsh hawk *noun* (1772)
: NORTHERN HARRIER

marsh hen *noun* (1709)
1 : any of various American rails
2 : BITTERN

marsh·land \'märsh-,land\ *noun* (12th century)
: a marshy tract or area : MARSH

marsh·mal·low \'märsh-,me-lō, -,ma-\ *noun* (before 12th century)
1 : a pink-flowered European perennial herb (*Althaea officinalis*) of the mallow family that is naturalized in the eastern U.S. and has a mucilaginous root sometimes used in confectionery and in medicine
2 : a confection made from the root of the marshmallow or from corn syrup, sugar, albumen, and gelatin beaten to a light spongy consistency; *also* : a piece of partially dried marshmallow ⟨a bag of *marshmallows*⟩
— **marsh·mal·lowy** \-,me-lə-wē, -,ma-\ *adjective*

marsh marigold *noun* (1578)
: a swamp herb (*Caltha palustris*) of the buttercup family that occurs in Europe and North America and has bright yellow flowers — called also *cowslip, kingcup*

marshy \'mär-shē\ *adjective* **marsh·i·er; -est** (14th century)
1 : resembling or constituting a marsh ⟨*marshy* ground⟩

2 : relating to or occurring in marshes ⟨*marshy* vegetation⟩
— **marsh·i·ness** *noun*

¹mar·su·pi·al \mär-'sü-pē-əl\ *adjective* (1819)
1 : of, relating to, or being a marsupial
2 : of, relating to, or forming a marsupium

²marsupial *noun* [New Latin *Marsupialia,* from *marsupium*] (circa 1835)
: any of an order (Marsupialia) of mammals comprising kangaroos, wombats, bandicoots, opossums, and related animals that do not develop a true placenta and that usually have a pouch on the abdomen of the female which covers the teats and serves to carry the young

mar·su·pi·um \mär-'sü-pē-əm\ *noun, plural* **-pia** \-pē-ə\ [New Latin, from Latin, purse, pouch, from Greek *marsypion*] (1698)
1 : an abdominal pouch that is formed of a fold of the skin and encloses the mammary glands of most marsupials
2 : any of several structures in various invertebrates (as a bryozoan or mollusk) for enclosing or carrying eggs or young

¹mart \'märt\ *noun* [Middle English, from Middle Dutch *marct, mart,* probably from Old North French *market*] (15th century)
1 *archaic* : a coming together of people to buy and sell ⟨ ⁵FAIR 1
2 *obsolete* : the activity of buying and selling; *also* : BARGAIN
3 : MARKET

²mart *transitive verb* (1589)
: to deal in : SELL

mar·tel·lo tower \mär-'te-lō-\ *noun, often M capitalized* [Cape *Mortella,* Corsica] (1803)
: a circular masonry fort or blockhouse

mar·ten \'mär-tᵊn\ *noun, plural* **marten** *or* **martens** [Middle English *martryn,* from Middle French *martrine* marten fur, from Old French, from *martre* marten, of Germanic origin; akin to Old English *mearth* marten] (13th century)
1 : any of several semiarboreal slender-bodied carnivorous mammals (genus *Martes*) chiefly of the northern hemisphere that are larger than the related weasels
2 : the fur or pelt of a marten

mar·tens·ite \'mär-tᵊn-,zīt\ *noun* [Adolf *Martens* (died 1914) German metallurgist] (1898)
: the hard constituent that is the chief component of quenched steel
— **mar·tens·it·ic** \,mar-tᵊn-'zi-tik, -'si-\ *adjective*
— **mar·tens·it·i·cal·ly** \-ti-k(ə-)lē\ *adverb*

Mar·tha \'mär-thə\ *noun* [Late Latin, from Greek]
: a sister of Lazarus and Mary and friend of Jesus

mar·tial \'mär-shəl\ *adjective* [Middle English, from Latin *martialis* of Mars, from *Mart-, Mars*] (14th century)
1 : of, relating to, or suited for war or a warrior
2 : relating to an army or to military life
3 : experienced in or inclined to war : WARLIKE
— **mar·tial·ly** \-shə-lē\ *adverb*

martial art *noun* (1933)
: any of several arts of combat and self-defense (as karate and judo) that are widely practiced as sport
— **martial artist** *noun*

martial law *noun* (1568)
1 : the law applied in occupied territory by the military authority of the occupying power
2 : the law administered by military forces that is invoked by a government in an emergency when the civilian law enforcement agencies are unable to maintain public order and safety

mar·tian \'mär-shən\ *adjective, often capitalized* (1880)

: of or relating to the planet Mars or its hypothetical inhabitants
— **martian** *noun, often capitalized*

mar·tin \'mär-tᵊn\ *noun* [probably from Saint *Martin*] (1589)
1 : a small Eurasian swallow (*Delichon urbica*) with a forked tail, bluish black head and back, and white rump and underparts
2 : any of various swallows and flycatchers other than the martin

mar·ti·net \,mär-tᵊn-'et\ *noun* [Jean *Martinet,* 17th century French army officer] (1779)
1 : a strict disciplinarian
2 : a person who stresses a rigid adherence to the details of forms and methods

mar·tin·gale \'mär-tᵊn-,gāl, -tiŋ-\ *noun* [Middle French] (1589)
1 : a device for steadying a horse's head or checking its upward movement that typically consists of a strap fastened to the girth, passing between the forelegs, and bifurcating to end in two rings through which the reins pass

martingale 1

2 a : a lower stay of rope or chain for the jibboom used to sustain the strain of the forestays and fastened to or rove through the dolphin striker **b :** DOLPHIN STRIKER
3 : any of several systems of betting in which a player increases the stake usually by doubling each time a bet is lost

mar·ti·ni \mär-'tē-nē\ *noun* [probably alteration of *Martinez* (cocktail), from the name *Martinez*] (1894)
: a cocktail made of gin and dry vermouth; *also* : VODKA MARTINI

Mar·tin Lu·ther King Day \'mär-tᵊn-'lü-thər-'kiŋ-\ *noun* (1977)
: the third Monday in January observed as a legal holiday in some states of the U.S.

Mar·tin·mas \'mär-tᵊn-məs, -,mas\ *noun* [Middle English *martinmasse,* from Saint *Martin* + Middle English *masse* mass] (14th century)

\ə\ **abut** \ᵊ\ **kitten** \ər\ **further** \a\ **ash** \ā\ **ace** \ä\ **mop, mar** \aú\ **out** \ch\ **chin** \e\ **bet** \ē\ **easy** \g\ **go** \i\ **hit** \ī\ **ice** \j\ **job** \ŋ\ **sing** \ō\ **go** \ò\ **law** \òi\ **boy** \th\ **thin** \th\ **the** \ü\ **loot** \ú\ **foot** \y\ **yet** \zh\ **vision** *see also* Guide to Pronunciation

: November 11 celebrated as the feast of Saint Martin

mart·let \'märt-lət\ *noun* [alteration of *martinet*, from Middle French, probably from Saint *Martin*] (1538)
: MARTIN 1

¹**mar·tyr** \'mär-tər\ *noun* [Middle English, from Old English, from Late Latin, from Greek *martyr-, martys*, literally, witness] (before 12th century)
1 : a person who voluntarily suffers death as the penalty of witnessing to and refusing to renounce a religion
2 : a person who sacrifices something of great value and especially life itself for the sake of principle
3 : VICTIM; *especially* : a great or constant sufferer ⟨a *martyr* to asthma all his life —A. J. Cronin⟩
— **mar·tyr·i·za·tion** \,mär-tə-rə-'zā-shən\ *noun*
— **mar·tyr·ize** \'mär-tə-,rīz\ *transitive verb*

²**martyr** *transitive verb* (before 12th century)
1 : to put to death for adhering to a belief, faith, or profession
2 : to inflict agonizing pain on : TORTURE

mar·tyr·dom \'mär-tər-dəm\ *noun* (before 12th century)
1 : the suffering of death on account of adherence to a cause and especially to one's religious faith
2 : AFFLICTION, TORTURE

mar·tyr·ol·o·gist \,mär-tə-'rä-lə-jist\ *noun* (1676)
: a writer of or a specialist in martyrology

mar·tyr·ol·o·gy \-jē\ *noun* (1599)
1 : a catalog of Roman Catholic martyrs and saints arranged by the dates of their feasts
2 : ecclesiastical history treating the lives and sufferings of martyrs

mar·tyry \'mär-tə-rē\ *noun, plural* **-tyr·ies** [Late Latin *martyrium*, from Late Greek *martyrion*, from Greek *martyr-, martys*] (circa 1722)
: a shrine erected in honor of a martyr

¹**mar·vel** \'mär-vəl\ *noun* [Middle English *mervel*, from Old French *merveille*, from Late Latin *mirabilia* marvels, from Latin, neuter plural of *mirabilis* wonderful, from *mirari* to wonder] (14th century)
1 : something that causes wonder or astonishment
2 : intense surprise or interest : ASTONISHMENT

²**marvel** *verb* **mar·veled** *or* **mar·velled**; **mar·vel·ing** *or* **mar·vel·ling** \'märv-liŋ, 'mär-və-\ (14th century)
intransitive verb
: to become filled with surprise, wonder, or amazed curiosity ⟨*marveled* at the magician's skill⟩
transitive verb
: to feel astonishment or perplexity at or about ⟨*marveled* that they had escaped⟩

mar·vel·ous *or* **mar·vel·lous** \'märv-(ə-)ləs\ *adjective* (14th century)
1 : causing wonder : ASTONISHING
2 : MIRACULOUS, SUPERNATURAL ⟨Gothic tales of the *marvelous* and the bizarre⟩
3 : of the highest kind or quality : notably superior ⟨has a *marvelous* way with children⟩
— **mar·vel·ous·ly** *adverb*
— **mar·vel·ous·ness** *noun*

Marx·ian \'märk-sē-ən\ *adjective* (1887)
: of, developed by, or influenced by the doctrines of Marx ⟨*Marxian* socialism⟩

Marx·ism \'märk-,si-zəm\ *noun* (1897)
: the political, economic, and social principles and policies advocated by Marx; *especially* : a theory and practice of socialism including the labor theory of value, dialectical materialism, the class struggle, and dictatorship of the proletariat until the establishment of a classless society
— **Marx·ist** \-sist\ *noun or adjective*

Marx·ism–Le·nin·ism \'märk-,si-zəm-'le-nə-,ni-zəm\ *noun* (1932)

: a theory and practice of communism developed by Lenin from doctrines of Marx
— **Marx·ist–Len·in·ist** \'märk-sist-'le-nə-nist\ *noun or adjective*

Mary \'mer-ē, 'mar-ē, 'mā-rē\ *noun* [Late Latin *Maria*, from Greek *Mariam, Maria*, from Hebrew *Miryām* Miriam]
1 : the mother of Jesus
2 : a sister of Lazarus and Martha and a friend of Jesus

Mary Jane \-'jān\ *noun* [by folk etymology (influenced by Spanish *Juana* Jane)] (1928)
slang : MARIJUANA

Mary·knoll·er \-,nō-lər\ *noun* (1943)
: a member of the Catholic Foreign Mission Society of America founded by T. F. Price and J. A. Walsh at Maryknoll, N.Y. in 1911

Mary Mag·da·lene \-'mag-də-lən, -,lēn; -,mag-də-'lē-nē\ *noun* [Late Latin *Magdalene*, from Greek *Magdalēnē*]
: a woman who was healed of evil spirits by Jesus and who saw the risen Christ near his sepulchre

mar·zi·pan \'märt-sə-,pän, -,pan; 'mär-zə-,pan\ *noun* [German, from Italian *marzapane*] (1542)
: a confection of crushed almonds or almond paste, sugar, and egg whites that is often shaped into various forms

Ma·sai \mä-'sī, 'mä-,\ *noun, plural* **Masai** *or* **Masais** (1857)
1 : a member of a pastoral and hunting people of Kenya and Tanzania
2 : the Nilotic language of the Masai people

mas·ca·ra \ma-'skar-ə\ *noun* [probably from Italian *maschera* mask] (1886)
: a cosmetic especially for coloring the eyelashes

mas·car·po·ne \,mas-kär-'pō-(,)nā\ *noun* [Italian, from Italian dialect (Lombardy) *mascarpón*, augmentative of *mascarpa* cream cheese] (1932)
: an Italian cream cheese

mas·con \'mas-,kän\ *noun* [²*mass* + *concentration*] (1968)
: any of the high-density regions below the surface of lunar maria that are held to perturb the motion of spacecraft in lunar orbit

mas·cot \'mas-,kät *also* -kət\ *noun* [French *mascotte*, from Provençal *mascoto*, from *masco* witch, from Medieval Latin *masca*] (1881)
: a person, animal, or object adopted by a group as a symbolic figure especially to bring them good luck ⟨the team had a mountain lion as their *mascot*⟩ ◇

¹**mas·cu·line** \'mas-kyə-lən\ *adjective* [Middle English *masculin*, from Middle French, from Latin *masculinus*, from *masculus*, noun, male, diminutive of *mas* male] (14th century)
1 a : MALE **b** : having qualities appropriate to or usually associated with a man
2 : of, relating to, or constituting the gender that ordinarily includes most words or grammatical forms referring to males
3 a : having or occurring in a stressed final syllable ⟨*masculine* rhyme⟩ **b** : having the final chord occurring on a strong beat ⟨*masculine* cadence⟩
4 : of or forming the formal, active, or generative principle of the cosmos
— **mas·cu·line·ly** *adverb*
— **mas·cu·lin·i·ty** \,mas-kyə-'li-nə-tē\ *noun*

²**masculine** *noun* (14th century)
1 : the masculine gender
2 : a noun, pronoun, adjective, or inflectional form or class of the masculine gender
3 : a male person

mas·cu·lin·ise *British variant of* MASCULINIZE

mas·cu·lin·ize \'mas-kyə-lə-,nīz\ *transitive verb* **-ized; -iz·ing** (1912)
: to give a chiefly masculine character to; *especially* : to cause (a female) to take on male characteristics

— **mas·cu·lin·i·za·tion** \,mas-kyə-lə-nə-'zā-shən\ *noun*

ma·ser \'mā-zər\ *noun* [*m*icrowave *a*mplification by *s*timulated *e*mission of *r*adiation] (1955)
: a device or object that emits coherent microwave radiation produced by the natural oscillations of atoms or molecules between energy levels

¹**mash** \'mash\ *transitive verb* (13th century)
1 a : to reduce to a soft pulpy state by beating or pressure **b** : CRUSH, SMASH ⟨*mash* a finger⟩
2 : to subject (as crushed malt) to the action of water with heating and stirring in preparing wort

²**mash** *noun* [Middle English *mash-*, from Old English *māx-*; akin to Middle High German *meisch* mash] (1577)
1 : a mixture of ground feeds for livestock
2 : crushed malt or grain meal steeped and stirred in hot water to ferment (as for the production of beer or whiskey)
3 : a soft pulpy mass
4 *British* : mashed potatoes

³**mash** *transitive verb* [origin unknown] (1879)
: to flirt with or seek the affection of

⁴**mash** *noun* (1880)
: CRUSH 4

¹**mash·er** \'ma-shər\ *noun* (circa 1500)
: one that mashes ⟨a potato *masher*⟩

²**masher** *noun* (1875)
: a man who makes passes at women

¹**mask** \'mask\ *noun* [Middle French *masque*, from Old Italian *maschera*] (1534)
1 a (1) : a cover or partial cover for the face used for disguise (2) : a person wearing a mask : MASKER **b** (1) : a figure of a head worn on the stage in antiquity to identify the character and project the voice (2) : a grotesque false face worn at carnivals or in rituals **c** : an often grotesque carved head or face used as an ornament (as on a keystone) **d** : a sculptured face or a copy of a face made by means of a mold
2 a : something that serves to conceal or disguise : PRETENSE, CLOAK ⟨aware of the *masks*, facades and defenses people erect to protect themselves —Kenneth Keniston⟩ **b** : something that conceals from view **c** : a translucent or opaque screen to cover part of the sensitive surface in taking or printing a photograph **d** : a pattern of opaque material used to shield selected areas of a surface (as of a semiconductor) in deposition or etching (as in producing an integrated circuit)

◇ WORD HISTORY
mascot The spoken Latin of Gaul, northern Italy, and the Iberian Peninsula had a root *mask-*, unattested in classical Latin. It overlapped two semantic fields, the color black and malevolent magic, that were strongly associated with each other in popular superstition. One outcome of this root in Occitan or Provençal, the Romance speech of southern France, was a feminine noun *masco* "sorceress, witch." *Mascoto* "enchantment, charm," a derivative of *masco*, was borrowed into French as *mascotte* and shortly thereafter provided English with the word *mascot*. Contemporary with the root *mask-* in spoken Latin was an extended form *maskar-*, which appears on the one hand in words such as Catalan *mascara* "lampblack, soot," and on the other in medieval Italian *maschera* "mask." The Italian word is the ultimate source of English *mask* and *masquerade*, both borrowed directly from French, and probably also of our *mascara*, which was originally theater argot.

3 a : a protective covering for the face **b :** GAS MASK **c :** a device covering the mouth and nose to facilitate inhalation **d :** a comparable device to prevent exhalation of infective material **e :** a cosmetic preparation for the skin of the face that produces a tightening effect as it dries
4 a : the head or face of an animal (as a fox or dog) **b :** an area (as the one around the eyes) of an animal's face that is distinguished by usually darker coloring

²**mask** (circa 1562)
intransitive verb
1 : to take part in a masquerade
2 a : to assume a mask **b :** to disguise one's true character or intentions
transitive verb
1 : to provide or conceal with a mask: as **a :** to conceal from view ⟨*mask* a gun battery⟩ **b :** to make indistinct or imperceptible (*masks* undesirable flavors) **c :** to cover up ⟨*masked* his real purpose⟩
2 : to cover for protection
3 : to modify the size or shape of (as a photograph) by means of an opaque border
synonym see DISGUISE
— **mask·like** \-ˌlīk\ *adjective*
masked \'maskt\ *adjective* (1585)
1 : marked by the use of masks ⟨a *masked* ball⟩
2 : failing to present or produce the usual symptoms **:** LATENT ⟨*masked* infection⟩ ⟨a *masked* virus⟩
mask·er \'mas-kər\ *noun* (circa 1548)
: a person who wears a mask; *especially* **:** a participant in a masquerade
mask·ing tape \'mas-kiŋ-\ *noun* (1936)
: a tape with adhesive on one side that has a variety of uses (as to cover a surface when painting an adjacent surface)
mas·och·ism \'ma-sə-ˌki-zəm, 'ma-zə- *also* 'mā-\ *noun* [International Scientific Vocabulary, from Leopold von Sacher-*Masoch* (died 1895) German novelist] (circa 1893)
1 : a sexual perversion characterized by pleasure in being subjected to pain or humiliation especially by a love object — compare SADISM
2 : pleasure in being abused or dominated **:** a taste for suffering
— **mas·och·ist** \-kist\ *noun*
— **mas·och·is·tic** \ˌma-sə-'kis-tik, ˌma-zə- *also* ˌmā-\ *adjective*
— **mas·och·is·ti·cal·ly** \-'kis-ti-k(ə-)lē\ *adverb*
ma·son \'mā-sᵊn\ *noun* [Middle English, from Old French *maçon*, of Germanic origin; akin to Old English *macian* to make] (13th century)
1 : a skilled worker who builds by laying units of substantial material (as stone or brick)
2 *capitalized* **:** FREEMASON
Ma·son·ic \mə-'sä-nik\ *adjective* (1797)
: of, relating to, or characteristic of Freemasons or Freemasonry
Ma·son·ite \'mā-sᵊn-ˌīt\ *trademark*
— used for fiberboard made from steam-exploded wood fiber
ma·son jar \'mā-sᵊn-\ *noun, often M capitalized* [John L. *Mason*, 19th century American inventor] (1888)
: a widemouthed jar used especially for home canning
ma·son·ry \'mā-sᵊn-rē\ *noun, plural* **-ries** (13th century)
1 a : something constructed of materials used by masons **b :** the art, trade, or occupation of a mason **c :** work done by a mason
2 *capitalized* **:** FREEMASONRY
mason wasp *noun* (1792)
: any of various solitary wasps that construct nests of hardened mud
Ma·so·ra *or* **Ma·so·rah** \mə-'sōr-ə, -'sȯr-\ *noun* [New Hebrew *mĕsōrāh*, from Late Hebrew *māsōreth* tradition, from Hebrew, bond] (1613)

: a body of notes on the textual traditions of the Hebrew Old Testament compiled by scribes during the 1st millennium of the Christian era
Mas·o·rete *or* **Mas·so·rete** \'ma-sə-ˌrēt\ *noun* [Middle French *massoreth*, from Late Hebrew *māsōreth*] (1587)
: one of the scribes who compiled the Masora
— **Mas·o·ret·ic** \ˌma-sə-'re-tik\ *adjective*
masque *also* **mask** \'mask\ *noun* [Middle French *masque* — more at MASK] (1514)
1 : MASQUERADE
2 : a short allegorical dramatic entertainment of the 16th and 17th centuries performed by masked actors
masqu·er \'mas-kər\ *variant of* MASKER
¹**mas·quer·ade** \ˌmas-kə-'rād\ *noun* [Middle French, from Old Italian dialect *mascarada*, from Old Italian *maschera* mask] (1587)
1 a : a social gathering of persons wearing masks and often fantastic costumes **b :** a costume for wear at such a gathering
2 : an action or appearance that is mere disguise or outward show
²**masquerade** *intransitive verb* **-ad·ed; -ad·ing** (1692)
1 a : to disguise oneself; *also* **:** to go about disguised **b :** to take part in a masquerade
2 : to assume the appearance of something one is not
— **mas·quer·ad·er** *noun*
¹**mass** \'mas\ *noun* [Middle English, from Old English *mæsse*, modification of (assumed) Vulgar Latin *messa*, literally, dismissal at the end of a religious service, from Late Latin *missa*, from Latin, feminine of *missus*, past participle of *mittere* to send] (before 12th century)
1 *capitalized* **:** the liturgy of the Eucharist especially in accordance with the traditional Latin rite
2 *often capitalized* **:** a celebration of the Eucharist ⟨Sunday *masses* held at three different hours⟩
3 : a musical setting for the ordinary of the Mass
²**mass** *noun* [Middle English *masse*, from Middle French, from Latin *massa*, from Greek *maza*; akin to Greek *massein* to knead — more at MINGLE] (15th century)
1 a : a quantity or aggregate of matter usually of considerable size **b** (1) **:** EXPANSE, BULK (2) **:** massive quality or effect ⟨impressed me with such *mass* and such vividness —F. M. Ford⟩ (3) **:** the principal part or main body ⟨the great *mass* of the continent is buried under an ice cap —Walter Sullivan⟩ (4) **:** AGGREGATE, WHOLE ⟨men in the *mass*⟩ **c :** the property of a body that is a measure of its inertia and that is commonly taken as a measure of the amount of material it contains and causes it to have weight in a gravitational field
2 : a large quantity, amount, or number ⟨a great *mass* of material⟩
3 a : a large body of persons in a compact group **:** a body of persons regarded as an aggregate **b :** the great body of the people as contrasted with the elite — often used in plural ⟨the underprivileged and disadvantaged *masses* —C. A. Buss⟩
synonym see BULK
³**mass** (14th century)
transitive verb
: to form or collect into a mass
intransitive verb
: to assemble in a mass ⟨three thousand students had *massed* in the plaza —A. E. Neville⟩
⁴**mass** *adjective* (1733)
1 a : of or relating to the mass of the people ⟨*mass* market⟩ ⟨*mass* education⟩; *also* **:** being one of or at one with the mass **:** AVERAGE, COMMONPLACE ⟨*mass* man⟩ **b :** participated in by or affecting a large number of individuals ⟨*mass* destruction⟩ ⟨*mass* demonstrations⟩ **c :** having a large-scale character **:** WHOLESALE ⟨*mass* production⟩

2 : viewed as a whole **:** TOTAL ⟨the *mass* effect of a design⟩
mas·sa \'ma-sə\ *noun* [by alteration] (1774) *Southern* **:** MASTER
Mas·sa·chu·set *or* **Mas·sa·chu·sett** \ˌma-sə-'chü-sət, -zət *also* ˌmas-'chü-\ *noun, plural* **Massachusets** *or* **Massachuset** *or* **Massachusetts** *or* **Massachusett** [Massachuset, a locality, literally, at the big hill] (1616)
1 : a member of an American Indian people of Massachusetts
2 : the extinct Algonquian language of the Massachuset people
¹**mas·sa·cre** \'ma-si-kər\ *noun* [Middle French] (circa 1578)
1 : the act or an instance of killing a number of usually helpless or unresisting human beings under circumstances of atrocity or cruelty
2 : a cruel or wanton murder
3 : a wholesale slaughter of animals
4 : an act of complete destruction ⟨the author's *massacre* of traditional federalist presuppositions —R. G. McCloskey⟩
²**massacre** *transitive verb* **mas·sa·cred; mas·sa·cring** \-k(ə-)riŋ\ (1581)
1 : to kill by massacre **:** SLAUGHTER
2 : MANGLE 2 ⟨words were misspelled and syntax *massacred* —Bice Clemow⟩
— **mas·sa·crer** \-kər-ər, -krər\ *noun*
¹**mas·sage** \mə-'säzh, -'säj\ *noun* [French, from *masser* to massage, from Arabic *massa* to stroke] (circa 1860)
: manipulation of tissues (as by rubbing, kneading, or tapping) with the hand or an instrument for therapeutic purposes
²**massage** *transitive verb* **mas·saged; mas·sag·ing** (1887)
1 : to subject to massage
2 a : to treat flatteringly **:** BLANDISH **b :** MANIPULATE 3, DOCTOR 2b ⟨researchers *massaged* the data to support their thesis⟩
— **mas·sag·er** *noun*
massage parlor *noun* (1913)
: an establishment that provides massage treatments; *also* **:** one offering sexual services in addition to or in lieu of massage
mas·sa·sau·ga \ˌma-sə-'sȯ-gə\ *noun* [*Missisauga* River, Ontario, Canada] (1835)
: a small North American rattlesnake (*Sistrurus catenatus*)
mass card *noun* (1948)
: a card notifying the recipient (as a bereaved family) that a mass is to be offered for the repose of the soul of a specified deceased person
mass defect *noun* (circa 1923)
: the difference between the mass of an isotope and its mass number
mass driver *noun* (1977)
: a large electromagnetic catapult designed to hurl material (as from an asteroid) into space
mas·sé \ma-'sā\ *noun* [French, from past participle of *masser* to make a massé shot, from *masse* sledgehammer, from Middle French *mace* mace] (1873)
: a shot in billiards or pool made by hitting the cue ball vertically or nearly vertically on the side to drive it around one ball in order to strike another
mas·se·ter \mə-'sē-tər, ma-\ *noun* [New Latin, from Greek *masētēr*, from *masasthai* to chew — more at MANDIBLE] (1666)
: a large muscle that raises the lower jaw and assists in mastication
— **mas·se·ter·ic** \ˌma-sə-'ter-ik\ *adjective*
mas·seur \ma-'sər, mə-\ *noun* [French, from *masser*] (1876)
: a man who practices massage
mas·seuse \-'sə(r)z, -'süz\ *noun* [French, feminine of *masseur*] (1876)

: a woman who practices massage

mas·sif \ma-'sēf\ *noun* [French, from *massif*, adjective, from Middle French] (1885)
1 : a principal mountain mass
2 : a block of the earth's crust bounded by faults or flexures and displaced as a unit without internal change

mas·sive \'ma-siv\ *adjective* [Middle English *massiffe*, from Middle French *massif*, from *masse* mass] (15th century)
1 : forming or consisting of a large mass: **a** BULKY **b** : WEIGHTY, HEAVY ⟨*massive* walls⟩ ⟨a *massive* volume⟩ **c** : impressively large or ponderous **d** : having no regular form but not necessarily lacking crystalline structure ⟨*massive* sandstone⟩
2 a : large, solid, or heavy in structure ⟨*massive* jaw⟩ **b** : large in scope or degree ⟨the feeling of frustration, of being ineffectual, is *massive* —David Halberstam⟩ **c** (1) : large in comparison to what is typical ⟨*massive* dose of penicillin⟩ (2) : being extensive and severe ⟨*massive* hemorrhage⟩ ⟨*massive* collapse of a lung⟩ (3) : imposing in excellence or grandeur : MONUMENTAL ⟨*massive* simplicity⟩
3 : having mass ⟨a *massive* boson⟩
— **mas·sive·ly** *adverb*
— **mas·sive·ness** *noun*

mass·less \'mas-ləs\ *adjective* (1879)
: having no mass ⟨a *massless* particle⟩

mass–mar·ket \'mas-'mär-kət\ *adjective* (1952)
: sold through such retail outlets as supermarkets and drugstores as well as through bookstores ⟨a *mass-market* paperback⟩; *also* : of, relating to, or publishing mass-market materials

mass medium *noun, plural* **mass media** (1923)
: a medium of communication (as newspapers, radio, or television) that is designed to reach the mass of the people — usually used in plural

mass noun *noun* (1933)
: a noun (as *sand* or *water*) that characteristically denotes in many languages a homogeneous substance or a concept without subdivisions and that in English is preceded in indefinite singular constructions by *some* rather than *a* or *an* — compare COUNT NOUN

mass number *noun* (1923)
: an integer that approximates the mass of an isotope and designates the number of nucleons in the nucleus

mass–pro·duce \,mas-prə-'düs, -'dyüs\ *transitive verb* [back-formation from *mass production*] (1923)
: to produce in quantity usually by machinery
— **mass production** *noun*

mass spectrograph *noun* (1920)
: an instrument used to separate and often to determine the masses of isotopes

mass spectrometry *noun* (1943)
: an instrumental method for identifying the chemical constitution of a substance by means of the separation of gaseous ions according to their differing mass and charge — called also *mass spectroscopy*
— **mass spectrometric** *adjective*
— **mass spectrometer** *noun*

mass spectrum *noun* (1920)
: the spectrum of a stream of gaseous ions separated according to their mass and charge

massy \'ma-sē\ *adjective* (14th century)
: MASSIVE

¹mast \'mast\ *noun* [Middle English, from Old English *mæst*; akin to Old High German *mast* mast, Latin *malus*] (before 12th century)
1 : a long pole or spar rising from the keel or deck of a ship and supporting the yards, booms, and rigging
2 : a slender vertical or nearly vertical structure (as an upright post in various cranes)
3 : a disciplinary proceeding at which the commanding officer of a naval unit hears and

disposes of cases against enlisted men — called also *captain's mast*
— **mast·ed** \'mas-təd\ *adjective*
— **before the mast 1** : forward of the foremast **2** : as a common sailor

²mast *transitive verb* (1627)
: to furnish with a mast

³mast *noun* [Middle English, from Old English *mæst*; akin to Old High German *mast* food, mast, and probably to Old English *mete* food — more at MEAT] (before 12th century)
: nuts (as acorns) accumulated on the forest floor and often serving as food for animals (as hogs)

mas·ta·ba \'mas-tə-bə\ *noun* [Arabic *maṣṭabah* stone bench] (1882)
: an Egyptian tomb of the time of the Memphite dynasties that is oblong in shape with sloping sides and a flat roof

mast cell \'mast-\ *noun* [part translation of German *Mastzelle*, from *Mast* food, mast (from Old High German) + *Zelle* cell] (circa 1890)
: a large cell that occurs especially in connective tissue and has basophilic granules containing substances (as histamine and heparin) which mediate allergic reactions

mas·tec·to·my \ma-'stek-tə-mē\ *noun, plural* **-mies** [Greek *mastos* breast + English *-ectomy*] (circa 1923)
: excision of the breast

¹mas·ter \'mas-tər\ *noun* [Middle English, from Old English *magister* & Old French *maistre*, both from Latin *magister*; akin to Latin *magnus* large — more at MUCH] (before 12th century)
1 a (1) : a male teacher (2) : a person holding an academic degree higher than a bachelor's but lower than a doctor's **b** *often capitalized* : a revered religious leader **c** : a worker or artisan qualified to teach apprentices **d** (1) : an artist, performer, or player of consummate skill (2) : a great figure of the past (as in science or art) whose work serves as a model or ideal
2 a : one having authority over another : RULER, GOVERNOR **b** : one that conquers or masters : VICTOR, SUPERIOR ⟨in this young, obscure challenger the champion found his *master*⟩ **c** : a person licensed to command a merchant ship **d** (1) : one having control (2) : an owner especially of a slave or animal **e** : the employer especially of a servant **f** (1) *dialect* : HUSBAND (2) : the male head of a household
3 a (1) *archaic* : MR. (2) : a youth or boy too young to be called *mister* — used as a title **b** : the eldest son of a Scottish viscount or baron
4 a : a presiding officer in an institution or society (as a college) **b** : any of several officers of court appointed to assist (as by hearing and reporting) a judge
5 a : a master mechanism or device **b** : an original from which copies can be made; *especially* : a master phonograph record or magnetic tape
— **mas·ter·ship** \-,ship\ *noun*

²master *adjective* (12th century)
: being or relating to a master: as **a** : having chief authority : DOMINANT **b** : SKILLED, PROFICIENT ⟨a prosperous *master* builder —*Current Biography*⟩ **c** : PRINCIPAL, PREDOMINANT **d** : SUPERLATIVE — often used in combination ⟨a *master*-liar⟩ **e** : being a device or mechanism that controls the operation of another mechanism or that establishes a standard (as a dimension or weight) **f** : being or relating to a master from which duplicates are made

³master *transitive verb* **mas·tered; mas·ter·ing** \-t(ə-)riŋ\ (13th century)
1 : to become master of : OVERCOME
2 a : to become skilled or proficient in the use of ⟨*master* a foreign language⟩ **b** : to gain a thorough understanding of ⟨had *mastered* every aspect of publishing —*Current Biography*⟩
3 : to produce a master phonograph record or magnetic tape of (as a musical rendition)

master–at–arms *noun, plural* **masters–at–arms** (1748)
: a petty officer charged with maintaining discipline aboard ship

master bedroom *noun* (1925)
: a large or principal bedroom

master chief petty officer *noun* (1958)
: an enlisted man in the navy or coast guard ranking above a senior chief petty officer

master chief petty officer of the coast guard (1966)
: the ranking petty officer in the coast guard serving as adviser to the commandant

master chief petty officer of the navy (1966)
: the ranking petty officer in the navy serving as adviser to the chief of naval operations

master class *noun* (1952)
: a seminar for advanced music students conducted by a master musician

mas·ter·ful \'mas-tər-fəl\ *adjective* (15th century)
1 a : inclined and usually competent to play the master **b** : suggestive of a domineering nature
2 : having or reflecting the power and skill of a master ☆ □
— **mas·ter·ful·ly** \-fə-lē\ *adverb*
— **mas·ter·ful·ness** *noun*

master gunnery sergeant *noun* (1958)
: a noncommissioned officer in the marine corps ranking above a master sergeant

master key *noun* (1576)
: a key designed to open several different locks

mas·ter·ly \'mas-tər-lē\ *adjective* (15th century)
: suitable to or resembling that of a master; *especially* : indicating thorough knowledge or superior skill and power ⟨a *masterly* performance⟩

usage see MASTERFUL

— mas·ter·li·ness *noun*

— masterly *adverb*

¹**mas·ter·mind** \'mas-tər-ˌmīnd, ˌmas-tər-'\ *noun* (1720)
: a person who supplies the directing or creative intelligence for a project

²**mastermind** *transitive verb* (1940)
: to be the mastermind of

master of arts *often M&A capitalized* (15th century)
1 : the recipient of a master's degree that usually signifies that the recipient has passed an integrated course of study in one or more of the humanities and sometimes has completed a thesis involving research or a creative project and that typically requires two years of work beyond a bachelor's degree
2 : the degree making one a master of arts — abbreviation *M.A., A.M.*

master of ceremonies (1662)
1 : a person who determines the forms to be observed on a public occasion
2 : a person who acts as host at a formal event
3 : a person who acts as host for a program of entertainment (as on television)

master of science *often M&S capitalized* (circa 1905)
1 : the recipient of a master's degree that usually signifies that the recipient has passed an integrated course of study in one or more of the sciences and sometimes has completed a thesis involving research and that typically requires two years of work beyond a bachelor's degree
2 : the degree making one a master of science — abbreviation *M.S., M.Sc.*

mas·ter·piece \'mas-tər-ˌpēs\ *noun* (1605)
1 : a work done with extraordinary skill; *especially* : a supreme intellectual or artistic achievement
2 : a piece of work presented to a medieval guild as evidence of qualification for the rank of master

master plan *noun* (circa 1930)
: a plan giving overall guidance

master race *noun* (1937)
: a people held to be racially preeminent and hence fitted to rule or enslave other peoples

master's *noun* (1939)
: a master's degree

master sergeant *noun* (circa 1934)
: a noncommissioned officer ranking in the army above a sergeant first class and below a staff sergeant major, in the air force above a technical sergeant and below a senior master sergeant, and in the marine corps above a gunnery sergeant and below a master gunnery sergeant

mas·ter·sing·er \'mas-tər-ˌsiŋ-ər\ *noun* (1810)
: MEISTERSINGER

mas·ter·stroke \-ˌstrōk\ *noun* (1679)
: a masterly performance or move

mas·ter·work \-ˌwərk\ *noun* (1617)
: MASTERPIECE

mas·tery \'mas-t(ə-)rē\ *noun* [Middle English *maistrie*, from Old French, from *maistre* master] (13th century)
1 a : the authority of a master : DOMINION b : the upper hand in a contest or competition : SUPERIORITY, ASCENDANCY
2 a : possession or display of great skill or technique b : skill or knowledge that makes one master of a subject : COMMAND

mast·head \'mast-ˌhed\ *noun* (1748)
1 : the top of a mast
2 a : the printed matter in a newspaper or periodical that gives the title and pertinent details of ownership, advertising rates, and subscription rates b : the name of a publication (as a newspaper) displayed on the top of the first page

mas·tic \'mas-tik\ *noun* [Middle English *mastik*, from Latin *mastiche*, from Greek *mas-*

tichē, probably back-formation from *mastichan*] (14th century)
1 : an aromatic resinous exudate from mastic trees used chiefly in varnishes
2 : any of various pasty materials used as protective coatings or cements

mas·ti·cate \'mas-tə-ˌkāt\ *verb* **-cat·ed; -cat·ing** [Late Latin *masticatus*, past participle of *masticare*, from *masticare*, from Latin *masticare* to gnash the teeth; akin to Greek *masasthai* to chew — more at MANDIBLE] (1649)
transitive verb
1 : to grind or crush (food) with or as if with the teeth in preparation for swallowing : CHEW
2 : to soften or reduce to pulp by crushing or kneading
intransitive verb
: CHEW
— mas·ti·ca·tion \ˌmas-tə-'kā-shən\ *noun*
— mas·ti·ca·tor \'mas-tə-ˌkā-tər\ *noun*

¹**mas·ti·ca·to·ry** \'mas-ti-kə-ˌtōr-ē, -ˌtȯr-\ *adjective*
1 : used for or adapted to chewing ⟨*masticatory* limbs of an arthropod⟩
2 : of, relating to, or involving the organs of mastication ⟨*masticatory* paralysis⟩

²**masticatory** *noun, plural* **-ries** (circa 1611)
: a substance chewed to increase saliva

mastic tree *noun* (15th century)
: a small southern European evergreen tree (*Pistacia lentiscus*) of the cashew family that yields mastic

mas·tiff \'mas-təf\ *noun* [Middle English *mastif*, modification of Middle French *mastin*, from (assumed) Vulgar Latin *mansuetinus*, from Latin *mansuetus* tame — more at MANSUETUDE] (14th century)
: any of a breed of very large massive powerful smooth-coated dogs that are apricot, fawn, or brindle and are often used as guard dogs

mas·ti·goph·o·ran \ˌmas-tə-'gä-fə-rən\ *noun* [ultimately from Greek *mastig-, mastix* whip + *pherein* to carry — more at BEAR] (circa 1911)
: any of a subphylum (Mastigophora) of protozoans comprising forms with flagella and including many often treated as algae

mastiff

— mastigophoran *adjective*

mas·ti·tis \ma-'stī-təs\ *noun, plural* **-tit·i·des** \-'sti-tə-ˌdēz\ [New Latin, from Greek *mastos* breast] (circa 1842)
: inflammation of the breast or udder usually caused by infection
— mas·tit·ic \-'sti-tik\ *adjective*

mas·to·don \'mas-tə-ˌdän, -dən\ *noun* [New Latin *mastodont-, mastodon*, from Greek *mastos* + *odont-, odon, odous* tooth — more at TOOTH] (1813)
1 : any of numerous extinct mammals (genus *Mastodon* synonym *Mammut*) that differ from the related mammoths and existing elephants chiefly in the form of the molar teeth
2 : one that is unusually large
— mas·to·don·ic \ˌmas-tə-'dä-nik\ *adjective*
— mas·to·dont \'mas-tə-ˌdänt\ *adjective or noun*

¹**mas·toid** \'mas-ˌtȯid\ *adjective* [New Latin *mastoides* resembling a nipple, mastoid, from Greek *mastoeidēs*, from *mastos* breast] (1732)
1 : being the process of the temporal bone behind the ear; *also* : being any of several bony elements that occupy a similar position in the skull of lower vertebrates
2 : of, relating to, or occurring in the region of the mastoid process

²**mastoid** *noun* (1842)
: a mastoid bone or process

mastoid cell *noun* (1800)

: one of the small cavities in the mastoid process that develop after birth and are filled with air

mas·toid·ec·to·my \ˌmas-ˌtȯi-'dek-tə-mē\ *noun, plural* **-mies** [International Scientific Vocabulary] (1898)
: surgical removal of part of the mastoid process of the temporal bone

mas·toid·itis \ˌmas-ˌtȯi-'dī-təs\ *noun* [New Latin] (circa 1890)
: inflammation of the mastoid and especially of the mastoid cells

mas·tur·bate \'mas-tər-ˌbāt\ *verb* **-bat·ed; -bat·ing** [Latin *masturbatus*, past participle of *masturbari*] (1857)
transitive verb
: to practice masturbation on
intransitive verb
: to practice masturbation
— mas·tur·ba·tor \-ˌbā-tər\ *noun*

mas·tur·ba·tion \ˌmas-tər-'bā-shən\ *noun* (1766)
: erotic stimulation especially of one's own genital organs commonly resulting in orgasm and achieved by manual or other bodily contact exclusive of sexual intercourse, by instrumental manipulation, occasionally by sexual fantasies, or by various combinations of these agencies

mas·tur·ba·to·ry \'mas-tər-bə-ˌtōr-ē, -ˌtȯr-\ *adjective* (1864)
1 : of, relating to, or involving masturbation ⟨*masturbatory* fantasies⟩
2 : excessively self-absorbed or self-indulgent ⟨write tedious, *masturbatory* books . . . about themselves for people to read . . . with envy —D. R. Katz⟩

¹**mat** \'mat\ *noun* [Middle English, from Old English *meatte*, from Late Latin *matta*, of Semitic origin; akin to Hebrew *miṭṭāh* bed] (before 12th century)
1 a (1) : a piece of coarse, woven, plaited, or felted fabric used especially as a floor covering or a support (2) : a piece of material placed at a door for wiping soiled shoe soles b : a decorative piece of material used under a small item (as a dish) especially for support or protection c : a large thick pad or cushion used as a surface for wrestling, tumbling, and gymnastics
2 : something made up of densely tangled or adhering strands especially of organic matter ⟨algal *mat*⟩ ⟨a *mat* of unkempt hair⟩
3 : a flat slab usually of reinforced concrete used as the supporting base of a building

²**mat** *verb* **mat·ted; mat·ting** (1549)
transitive verb
1 : to provide with a mat or matting
2 a : to form into a tangled mass b : to pack down so as to form a dense mass
intransitive verb
: to become matted

³**mat** \'mat\ *transitive verb* **mat·ted; mat·ting** (1602)
1 : to make (as a metal, glass, or color) matte
2 : to provide (a picture) with a mat

⁴**mat** *variant of* ²MATTE

⁵**mat** *noun* [French *mat* dull color, unpolished surface, from *mat*, adjective — more at MATTE] (1845)
: a border going around a picture between picture and frame or serving as the frame

⁶**mat** *noun* (1904)
: MATRIX 2a

mat·a·dor \'ma-tə-ˌdȯr\ *noun* [Spanish, from *matar* to kill] (1681)
: a bullfighter who has the principal role and who kills the bull in a bullfight

¹**match** \'mach\ *noun* [Middle English *macche*, from Old English *gemæcca* mate,

equal; akin to Old English *macian* to make — more at MAKE] (before 12th century)
1 a : a person or thing equal or similar to another **b :** one able to cope with another **c :** an exact counterpart
2 : a pair suitably associated ⟨carpet and curtains are a *match*⟩
3 a : a contest between two or more parties ⟨a golf *match*⟩ ⟨a soccer *match*⟩ ⟨a shouting *match*⟩ **b :** a contest (as in tennis or volleyball) completed when one player or side wins a specified number of sets or games
4 a : a marriage union **b :** a prospective partner in marriage

²match (14th century)
transitive verb
1 a : to encounter successfully as an antagonist **b** (1) **:** to set in competition or opposition (2) **:** to provide with a worthy competitor **c :** to set in comparison
2 : to join or give in marriage
3 a (1) **:** to put in a set possessing equal or harmonizing attributes (2) **:** to cause to correspond **:** SUIT **b** (1) **:** to be the counterpart of; *also* **:** to compare favorably with (2) **:** to harmonize with **c :** to provide with a counterpart **d :** to provide funds complementary to
4 : to fit together or make suitable for fitting together
5 a : to flip or toss (coins) and compare exposed faces **b :** to toss coins with
intransitive verb
: to be a counterpart
— **match·able** \'ma-chə-bəl\ *adjective*
— **match·er** *noun*

³match *noun* [Middle English *macche*, from Middle French *meiche*] (1549)
1 : a chemically prepared wick or cord formerly used in firing firearms or powder
2 : a short slender piece of flammable material (as wood) tipped with a combustible mixture that bursts into flame when slightly heated through friction (as by being scratched against a rough surface)

match·board \'mach-,bōrd, -,bȯrd\ *noun* (circa 1858)
: a board with a groove cut along one edge and a tongue along the other so as to fit snugly with the edges of similarly cut boards

match·book \-,bŭk\ *noun* (1944)
: a small folder containing rows of paper matches

match·box \-,bäks\ *noun* (1786)
: a box for matches

match·less \-ləs\ *adjective* (circa 1530)
: having no equal **:** PEERLESS
— **match·less·ly** *adverb*

match·lock \-,läk\ *noun* (1637)
1 : a slow-burning match lowered over a hole in the breech of a musket to ignite the charge
2 : a musket equipped with a matchlock

match·mak·er \-,mā-kər\ *noun* (circa 1639)
: one that arranges a match; *especially* **:** one who tries to bring two unmarried individuals together in an attempt to promote a marriage
— **match·mak·ing** \-kiŋ\ *noun*

match play *noun* (1893)
: golf competition in which the winner is the person or team winning the greater number of holes — compare STROKE PLAY

match point *noun* (1921)
: a situation (as in tennis) in which one player or side will win the match by winning the next point; *also* **:** the point itself

match·stick \'mach-,stik\ *noun* (1791)
1 : a slender piece especially of wood from which a match is made
2 : something resembling a matchstick especially in slenderness

match·up \-,əp\ *noun* (1964)
: ¹MATCH

match·wood \-,wŭd\ *noun* (1838)
: small pieces of wood **:** SPLINTERS

¹mate \'māt\ *transitive verb* **mat·ed; mat·ing** [Middle English, from Middle French *mater*, from Old French *mat*, noun, checkmate, from Arabic *māt* (in *shāh māt*)] (14th century)
: CHECKMATE 2

²mate *noun* (14th century)
: CHECKMATE 1

³mate *noun* [Middle English, probably from Middle Low German *māt*; akin to Old English *gemetta* guest at one's table, *mete* food — more at MEAT] (14th century)
1 a (1) **:** ASSOCIATE, COMPANION (2) *chiefly British* **:** an assistant to a more skilled worker **:** HELPER (3) *chiefly British* **:** FRIEND, BUDDY — often used as a familiar form of address **b** *archaic* **:** MATCH, PEER
2 : a deck officer on a merchant ship ranking below the captain
3 : one of a pair: as **a :** either member of a couple and especially a married couple **b :** either member of a breeding pair of animals **c :** either of two matched objects

⁴mate *verb* **mat·ed; mat·ing** (1509)
transitive verb
1 *archaic* **:** EQUAL, MATCH
2 : to join or fit together **:** COUPLE
3 a : to join together as mates **b :** to provide a mate for
intransitive verb
1 : to become mated ⟨gears that *mate* well⟩
2 : COPULATE

ma·té *or* **ma·te** \'mä-,tā\ *noun* [French & American Spanish; French *maté*, from American Spanish *mate* maté, vessel for drinking it, from Quechua *mati* vessel] (1758)
1 : a tealike beverage drunk especially in South America
2 : a South American shrub or tree (*Ilex paraguariensis*) of the holly family whose leaves and shoots are used in making maté; *also* **:** these leaves and shoots

mate·lot \'mat-,lō, 'ma-tə-\ *noun* [French, from Middle French, from Middle Dutch *mattenoot*, literally, bedmate] (1911)
British **:** SAILOR

ma·te·lote \,ma-t³l-'ōt, mat-'lōt\ *noun* [French, literally, sailor's wife, from *matelot*] (circa 1736)
: a stew made usually of fish in a seasoned wine sauce

ma·ter \'mā-tər\ *noun* [Latin — more at MOTHER] (circa 1859)
chiefly British **:** MOTHER

ma·ter·fa·mil·i·as \,mā-tər-fə-'mi-lē-əs, ,mä-\ *noun* [Latin, from *mater* + *familias*, archaic genitive of *familia* household — more at FAMILY] (1756)
: a woman who is head of a household

¹ma·te·ri·al \mə-'tir-ē-əl\ *adjective* [Middle English *materiel*, from Middle French & Late Latin; Middle French, from Late Latin *materialis*, from Latin *materia* matter — more at MATTER] (14th century)
1 a (1) **:** relating to, derived from, or consisting of matter; *especially* **:** PHYSICAL ⟨the *material* world⟩ (2) **:** BODILY ⟨*material* needs⟩ **b** (1) **:** of or relating to matter rather than form ⟨*material* cause⟩ (2) **:** of or relating to the subject matter of reasoning; *especially* **:** EMPIRICAL ⟨*material* knowledge⟩
2 : having real importance or great consequences ⟨facts *material* to the investigation⟩
3 a : being of a physical or worldly nature **b :** relating to or concerned with physical rather than spiritual or intellectual things ⟨*material* progress⟩ ☆
— **ma·te·ri·al·ly** \-ē-ə-lē\ *adverb*
— **ma·te·ri·al·ness** *noun*

²material *noun* (1556)
1 a (1) **:** the elements, constituents, or substances of which something is composed or can be made (2) **:** matter that has qualities which give it individuality and by which it may be categorized ⟨sticky *material*⟩ ⟨explosive *materials*⟩ **b** (1) **:** something (as data) that may be worked into a more finished form

⟨*material* for a biography⟩ (2) **:** something used for or made the object of study ⟨*material* for the next semester⟩ (3) **:** a performer's repertoire ⟨a comedian's *material*⟩ **c :** MATTER 3b **d :** CLOTH **e :** a person potentially suited to some pursuit ⟨varsity *material*⟩ ⟨leadership *material*⟩
2 a : apparatus necessary for doing or making something ⟨writing *materials*⟩ **b :** MATÉRIEL

ma·te·ri·al·ise *British variant of* MATERIALIZE

ma·te·ri·al·ism \mə-'tir-ē-ə-,li-zəm\ *noun* (1748)
1 a : a theory that physical matter is the only or fundamental reality and that all being and processes and phenomena can be explained as manifestations or results of matter **b :** a doctrine that the only or the highest values or objectives lie in material well-being and in the furtherance of material progress **c :** a doctrine that economic or social change is materially caused — compare HISTORICAL MATERIALISM
2 : a preoccupation with or stress upon material rather than intellectual or spiritual things
— **ma·te·ri·al·ist** \-list\ *noun or adjective*
— **ma·te·ri·al·is·tic** \-,tir-ē-ə-'lis-tik\ *adjective*
— **ma·te·ri·al·is·ti·cal·ly** \-ti-k(ə-)lē\ *adverb*

ma·te·ri·al·i·ty \mə-,tir-ē-'a-lə-tē\ *noun, plural* **-ties** (1570)
1 : the quality or state of being material
2 : something that is material

ma·te·ri·al·i·za·tion \mə-,tir-ē-ə-lə-'zā-shən\ *noun* (1843)
1 : the action of materializing or becoming materialized
2 : something that has been materialized; *especially* **:** APPARITION

ma·te·ri·al·ize \mə-'tir-ē-ə-,līz\ *verb* **-ized; -iz·ing** (1710)
transitive verb
1 a : to make material **:** OBJECTIFY **b :** to cause to appear in bodily form ⟨*materialize* the spirits of the dead⟩
2 : to cause to be materialistic
intransitive verb
1 : to assume bodily form
2 a : to appear especially suddenly **b :** to come into existence
— **ma·te·ri·al·iz·er** *noun*

materials science *noun* (1961)
: the scientific study of the properties and applications of materials of construction or manufacture (as ceramics, metals, polymers, and composites)
— **materials scientist** *noun*

☆ SYNONYMS
Material, physical, corporeal, phenomenal, sensible, objective mean of or belonging to actuality. MATERIAL implies formation out of tangible matter; used in contrast with *spiritual* or *ideal* it may connote the mundane, crass, or grasping ⟨*material* values⟩. PHYSICAL applies to what is perceived directly by the senses and may contrast with *mental, spiritual*, or *imaginary* ⟨the *physical* benefits of exercise⟩. CORPOREAL implies having the tangible qualities of a body such as shape, size, or resistance to force ⟨artists have portrayed angels as *corporeal* beings⟩. PHENOMENAL applies to what is known or perceived through the senses rather than by intuition or rational deduction ⟨scientists concerned with the *phenomenal* world⟩. SENSIBLE stresses the capability of readily or forcibly impressing the senses ⟨the earth's rotation is not *sensible* to us⟩. OBJECTIVE may stress material or independent existence apart from a subject perceiving it ⟨no *objective* evidence of damage⟩. See in addition RELEVANT.

ma·te·ria med·i·ca \mə-'tir-ē-ə-'me-di-kə\ *noun* [New Latin, literally, medical matter] (1699)
1 : substances used in the composition of medical remedies : DRUGS, MEDICINE
2 a : a branch of medical science that deals with the sources, nature, properties, and preparation of drugs **b** : a treatise on materia medica

ma·té·ri·el *or* **ma·te·ri·el** \mə-ˌtir-ē-'el\ *noun* [French *matériel*, from *matériel*, adjective] (1814)
: equipment, apparatus, and supplies used by an organization or institution

ma·ter·nal \mə-'tər-nᵊl\ *adjective* [Middle English, from Middle French *maternel*, from Latin *maternus*, from *mater* mother — more at MOTHER] (15th century)
1 : of, relating to, belonging to, or characteristic of a mother : MOTHERLY
2 a : related through a mother ⟨his *maternal* aunt⟩ **b** : inherited or derived from the female parent ⟨*maternal* genes⟩
— **ma·ter·nal·ly** \-nᵊl-ē\ *adverb*

¹ma·ter·ni·ty \mə-'tər-nə-tē\ *noun, plural* **-ties** (1611)
1 a : the quality or state of being a mother : MOTHERHOOD **b** : the qualities of a mother : MOTHERLINESS
2 : a hospital facility designed for the care of women before and during childbirth and for the care of newborn babies

²maternity *adjective* (1893)
1 : designed for wear during pregnancy ⟨a *maternity* dress⟩
2 : effective for the period close to and including childbirth ⟨*maternity* leave⟩

mat·ey \'mā-tē\ *adjective* (1915)
chiefly British : COMPANIONABLE
— **mat·ey·ness** \-nəs\ *noun, chiefly British*

math \'math\ *noun* (circa 1878)
: MATHEMATICS

math·e·mat·i·cal \ˌmath-'ma-ti-kəl\, ˌma-thə-\ *also* **math·e·mat·ic** \-tik\ *adjective* [Middle English *mathematicalle*, from Latin *mathematicus*, from Greek *mathēmatikos*, from *mathēmat-*, *mathēma* learning, mathematics, from *manthanein* to learn; probably akin to Gothic *mundon* to pay attention] (15th century)
1 : of, relating to, or according with mathematics
2 a : rigorously exact : PRECISE **b** : CERTAIN
3 : possible but highly improbable ⟨only a *mathematical* chance⟩
— **math·e·mat·i·cal·ly** \-ti-k(ə-)lē\ *adverb*

mathematical expectation *noun* (1838)
: EXPECTED VALUE

mathematical induction *noun* (1838)
: INDUCTION 2b

mathematical logic *noun* (1858)
: SYMBOLIC LOGIC

math·e·ma·ti·cian \ˌmath-mə-'ti-shən\, ˌma-thə-\ *noun* (15th century)
: a specialist or expert in mathematics

math·e·mat·ics \ˌmath-'ma-tiks\, ˌma-thə-\ *noun plural but usually singular in construction* (1581)
1 : the science of numbers and their operations, interrelations, combinations, generalizations, and abstractions and of space configurations and their structure, measurement, transformations, and generalizations
2 : a branch of, operation in, or use of mathematics ⟨the *mathematics* of physical chemistry⟩

math·e·ma·ti·za·tion \ˌmath-mə-tə-'zā-shən, ˌma-thə-\ *noun* (1928)
: reduction to mathematical form
— **math·e·ma·tize** \'math-mə-ˌtīz, 'ma-thə-\ *verb*

maths \'maths\ *noun plural* (1911)
chiefly British : MATHEMATICS

mat·in \'ma-tᵊn\ *adjective* [Middle English, from Old French] (14th century)
: of or relating to matins or to early morning

mat·in·al \'ma-tᵊn-əl\ *adjective* (1803)
1 : of or relating to matins
2 : EARLY

mat·i·nee *or* **mat·i·née** \ˌma-tᵊn-'ā\ *noun* [French *matinée*, literally, morning, from Old French, from *matin* morning, from Latin *matutinum*, from neuter of *matutinus* of the morning, from *Matuta*, goddess of morning; akin to Latin *maturus* ripe — more at MATURE] (1858)
: a musical or dramatic performance or social or public event held in the daytime and especially the afternoon

matinee idol *noun* (1902)
: a handsome male performer

mat·ins \'ma-tᵊnz\ *noun plural but singular or plural in construction, often capitalized* [Middle English *matines*, from Old French, from Late Latin *matutinae*, from Latin, feminine plural of *matutinus*] (14th century)
1 : the night office forming with lauds the first of the canonical hours
2 : MORNING PRAYER

matr- *or* **matri-** *or* **matro-** *combining form* [Latin *matr-*, *matri-*, from *matr-*, *mater*]
: mother ⟨*matriarch*⟩ ⟨*matronymic*⟩

ma·tri·arch \'mā-trē-ˌärk\ *noun* (1606)
: a female who rules or dominates a family, group, or state; *specifically* : a mother who is head and ruler of her family and descendants
— **ma·tri·ar·chal** \ˌmā-trē-'är-kəl\ *adjective*

ma·tri·ar·chate \'mā-trē-ˌär-kət, -ˌkāt\ *noun* (1885)
: MATRIARCHY 1

ma·tri·ar·chy \'mā-trē-ˌär-kē\ *noun, plural* **-chies** (1885)
1 : a family, group, or state governed by a matriarch
2 : a system of social organization in which descent and inheritance are traced through the female line

ma·tri·cide \'ma-trə-ˌsīd, 'mā-\ *noun* (1594)
1 [Latin *matricidium*, from *matr-* + *-cidium* -cide] : murder of a mother by her son or daughter
2 [Latin *matricida*, from *matr-* + *-cida* -cide] : one that murders his or her mother
— **ma·tri·cid·al** \ˌma-trə-'sī-dᵊl, ˌmā-\ *adjective*

ma·tric·u·late \mə-'tri-kyə-ˌlāt\ *verb* **-lat·ed; -lat·ing** [Medieval Latin *matriculatus*, past participle of *matriculare*, from Late Latin *matricula* public roll, diminutive of *matric-*, *matrix* list, from Latin, breeding female] (1577)
transitive verb
: to enroll as a member of a body and especially of a college or university
intransitive verb
: to become matriculated
— **ma·tric·u·lant** \-lənt\ *noun*
— **ma·tric·u·la·tion** \-ˌtri-kyə-'lā-shən\ *noun*

ma·tri·lin·eal \ˌma-trə-'li-nē-əl, ˌmā-\ *adjective* (1904)
: relating to, based on, or tracing descent through the maternal line ⟨*matrilineal* society⟩
— **ma·tri·lin·eal·ly** \-nē-ə-lē\ *adverb*

mat·ri·mo·nial \ˌma-trə-'mō-nē-əl, -nyəl\ *adjective* (15th century)
: of or relating to marriage, the married state, or married persons
— **mat·ri·mo·nial·ly** *adverb*

mat·ri·mo·ny \'ma-trə-ˌmō-nē\ *noun* [Middle English, from Middle French *matremoine*, from Latin *matrimonium*, from *matr-*, *mater* mother, matron — more at MOTHER] (14th century)
: the union of man and woman as husband and wife : MARRIAGE

matrimony vine *noun* (circa 1818)
: a shrub or vine (genus *Lycium*) of the nightshade family with often showy flowers and usually red berries

ma·trix \'mā-triks\ *noun, plural* **ma·tri·ces** \'mā-trə-ˌsēz, 'ma-\ *or* **ma·trix·es** \'mā-trik-səz\ [Latin, female animal used for breeding, parent plant, from *matr-*, *mater*] (1555)
1 : something within or from which something else originates, develops, or takes form
2 a : a mold from which a relief surface (as a piece of type) is made **b** : DIE 3a(1) **c** : an engraved or inscribed die or stamp **d** : an electroformed impression of a phonograph record used for mass-producing duplicates of the original
3 a : the natural material (as soil or rock) in which something (as a fossil or crystal) is embedded **b** : material in which something is enclosed or embedded (as for protection or study)
4 a : the intercellular substance in which tissue cells (as of connective tissue) are embedded **b** : the thickened epithelium at the base of a fingernail or toenail from which new nail substance develops
5 a : a rectangular array of mathematical elements (as the coefficients of simultaneous linear equations) that can be combined to form sums and products with similar arrays having an appropriate number of rows and columns **b** : something resembling a mathematical matrix especially in rectangular arrangement of elements into rows and columns **c** : an array of circuit elements (as diodes and transistors) for performing a specific function
6 : a main clause that contains a subordinate clause

ma·tron \'mā-trən\ *noun* [Middle English *matrone*, from Middle French, from Latin *matrona*, from *matr-*, *mater*] (14th century)
1 a : a married woman usually marked by dignified maturity or social distinction **b** : a woman who supervises women or children (as in a school or police station) **c** : the chief officer in a women's organization
2 : a female animal kept for breeding

ma·tron·ly \'mā-trən-lē\ *adjective* (1656)
: having the character of or suitable to a matron

matron of honor (1903)
: a bride's principal married wedding attendant

mat·ro·nym·ic \ˌma-trə-'ni-mik\ *noun* [*matr-* + *-onymic* (as in *patronymic*)] (1794)
: a name derived from that of the mother or a maternal ancestor

¹matte *or* **matt** \'mat\ *variant of* ³MAT

²matte *also* **matt** \'mat\ *adjective* [French *mat*, from Old French, faded, defeated] (circa 1648)
: lacking or deprived of luster or gloss: as **a** : having a usually smooth even surface free from shine or highlights ⟨*matte* metals⟩ ⟨a *matte* finish⟩ **b** : having a rough or granular surface

³matte \'mat\ *noun* [French, from Middle French, crude metal, curdled milk, from feminine of *mat* thick, dull, matte] (1839)
1 : a crude mixture of sulfides formed in smelting sulfide ores of metals (as copper, lead, or nickel)
2 : a motion-picture effect in which part of a scene is blocked out and later replaced by footage containing other material (as a background painting)

¹mat·ter \'ma-tər\ *noun* [Middle English *matere*, from Old French, from Latin *materia* matter, physical substance, from *mater*] (13th century)

\ə\ abut \ᵊ\ kitten \ər\ further \a\ ash \ā\ ace
\ä\ mop, mar \au̇\ out \ch\ chin \e\ bet \ē\ easy
\g\ go \i\ hit \ī\ ice \j\ job \ŋ\ sing \ō\ go
\ȯ\ law \ȯi\ boy \th\ thin \t͟h\ the \ü\ loot \u̇\ foot
\y\ yet \zh\ vision *see also* Guide to Pronunciation

1 a : a subject under consideration **b** : a subject of disagreement or litigation **c** *plural* : the events or circumstances of a particular situation **d** : the subject or substance of a discourse or writing **e** : something of an indicated kind or having to do with an indicated field or situation ⟨this is a serious *matter*⟩ ⟨as a *matter* of policy⟩ ⟨*matters* of faith⟩ **f** : something to be proved in law **g** *obsolete* : sensible or serious material as distinguished from nonsense or drollery **h** (1) *obsolete* : REASON, CAUSE (2) : a source especially of feeling or emotion **i** : PROBLEM, DIFFICULTY
2 a : the substance of which a physical object is composed **b** : material substance that occupies space, has mass, and is composed predominantly of atoms consisting of protons, neutrons, and electrons, that constitutes the observable universe, and that is interconvertible with energy **c** : a material substance of a particular kind or for a particular purpose ⟨vegetable *matter*⟩ **d** (1) : material (as feces or urine) discharged from the living body (2) : material discharged by suppuration : PUS
3 a : the indeterminate subject of reality; *especially* : the element in the universe that undergoes formation and alteration **b** : the formless substratum of all things which exists only potentially and upon which form acts to produce realities
4 : a more or less definite amount or quantity ⟨cooks in a *matter* of minutes⟩
5 : something written or printed
6 : MAIL
7 *Christian Science* : the illusion that the objects perceived by the physical senses have the reality of substance
— **for that matter** : so far as that is concerned
— **no matter** : without regard to : irrespective of ⟨points in the same direction *no matter* how it is tilted⟩
— **the matter** : WRONG ⟨nothing's *the matter* with me⟩
²**matter** *intransitive verb* (1530)
1 : to form or discharge pus : SUPPURATE ⟨*mattering* wound⟩
2 : to be of importance : SIGNIFY
matter of course (1739)
: something that is to be expected as a natural or logical consequence
mat·ter-of-fact \ˌma-tə-rə(v)-'fakt\ *adjective* (1712)
: adhering to the unembellished facts; *also* : being plain, straightforward, or unemotional
— **mat·ter-of-fact·ly** \-'fak(t)-lē\ *adverb*
— **mat·ter-of-fact·ness** \-'fak(t)-nəs\ *noun*
mat·tery \'ma-tə-rē\ *adjective* (14th century)
: producing or containing pus or material resembling pus ⟨eyes all *mattery*⟩
Mat·the·an *or* **Mat·thae·an** \ma-'thē-ən, mə-\ *adjective* [Late Latin *Matthaeus*] (1897)
: of, relating to, or characteristic of the evangelist Matthew or the gospel ascribed to him
Mat·thew \'ma-(ˌ)thyü *also* -(ˌ)thü\ *noun* [French *Mathieu*, from Late Latin *Matthaeus*, from Greek *Matthaios*, from Hebrew *Mattithyāh*]
1 : an apostle traditionally identified as the author of the first Gospel in the New Testament
2 : the first Gospel in the New Testament — see BIBLE table
¹**mat·ting** \'ma-tin\ *noun* (circa 1847)
1 : material for mats
2 : MATS
²**matting** *noun* [from gerund of ⁴*mat*] (1854)
: a dull lusterless surface (as on gilding, metalwork, or satin)
mat·tins *often capitalized, chiefly British variant of* MATINS
mat·tock \'ma-tək\ *noun* [Middle English *mattok*, from Old English *mattuc*] (before 12th century)
: a digging and grubbing tool with features of an adze and an ax or pick

mat·tress \'ma-trəs\ *noun* [Middle English *materas*, from Old French, from Arabic *maṭraḥ* place where something is thrown] (14th century)
1 a : a fabric case filled with resilient material (as cotton, hair, feathers, foam rubber, or an arrangement of coiled springs) used either alone as a bed or on a bedstead **b** : an inflatable airtight sack for use as a mattress
2 : a device (as of interwoven brush and poles) used to protect a shoreline, bank, or streambed from erosion

mattock

mat·u·rate \'ma-chə-ˌrāt\ *verb* **-rat·ed; -rat·ing** (1622)
: MATURE
mat·u·ra·tion \ˌma-chə-'rā-shən\ *noun* (1541)
1 a : the process of becoming mature **b** : the emergence of personal and behavioral characteristics through growth processes **c** : the final stages of differentiation of cells, tissues, or organs
2 a : the entire process by which diploid gonocytes are transformed into haploid gametes that includes both meiosis and physiological and structural changes **b** : SPERMIOGENESIS
— **mat·u·ra·tion·al** \-shnəl, -shə-n°l\ *adjective*
¹**ma·ture** \mə-'túr, -'tyúr *also* -'chúr\ *adjective* **ma·tur·er; -est** [Middle English, from Latin *maturus* ripe; akin to Latin *mane* in the morning, *manus* good] (15th century)
1 : based on slow careful consideration ⟨a *mature* judgment⟩
2 a (1) : having completed natural growth and development : RIPE (2) : having undergone maturation **b** : having attained a final or desired state ⟨*mature* wine⟩ **c** : having achieved a low but stable growth rate ⟨paper is a *mature* industry⟩
3 a : of or relating to a condition of full development **b** : characteristic of or suitable to a mature individual ⟨*mature* outlook⟩
4 : due for payment ⟨a *mature* loan⟩
5 : belonging to the middle portion of a cycle of erosion
— **ma·ture·ly** *adverb*
²**mature** *verb* **ma·tured; ma·tur·ing** (15th century)
transitive verb
: to bring to maturity or completion
intransitive verb
1 : to become fully developed or ripe
2 : to become due
ma·tu·ri·ty \mə-'túr-ə-tē, -'tyúr- *also* -'chúr-\ *noun* (15th century)
1 : the quality or state of being mature; *especially* : full development
2 : termination of the period that an obligation has to run
ma·tu·ti·nal \ˌma-chú-'tī-n°l; mə-'tüt-nəl, -'tyüt-, -'tü-t°n-əl, -'tyü-\ *adjective* [Late Latin *matutinalis*, from Latin *matutinus* — more at MATINEE] (circa 1656)
: of, relating to, or occurring in the morning : EARLY
— **ma·tu·ti·nal·ly** *adverb*
mat·zo *or* **mat·zoh** \'mät-sə *also* -(ˌ)sō\ *noun, plural* **mat·zoth** \-ˌsōt, -ˌsōth, -sōs\ *or* **mat·zos** *or* **mat·zohs** \-səz, -səs *also* -ˌsōz\ [Yiddish *matse*, from Hebrew *maṣṣāh*] (circa 1846)
1 : unleavened bread eaten especially at the Passover
2 : a wafer of matzo
matzo ball *noun* (1952)
: a small ball-shaped dumpling made from matzo meal
maud·lin \'mȯd-lən\ *adjective* [alteration of Mary *Magdalene*; from her depiction as a weeping penitent] (1509)

1 : drunk enough to be emotionally silly
2 : weakly and effusively sentimental ◇
mau·gre \'mȯ-gər\ *preposition* [Middle English, from Middle French *maugré*, from *maugré* displeasure, from *mau, mal* evil + *gré* pleasure] (13th century)
archaic : in spite of
¹**maul** \'mȯl\ *noun* [Middle English *malle* mace, maul, from Old French *mail*, from Latin *malleus*; akin to Old Church Slavonic *mlatŭ* hammer, Latin *molere* to grind — more at MEAL] (13th century)
: a heavy often wooden-headed hammer used especially for driving wedges; *also* : a tool like a sledgehammer with one wedge-shaped end that is used to split wood
²**maul** *transitive verb* (13th century)
1 : BEAT, BRUISE
2 : MANGLE 1
3 : to handle roughly
— **maul·er** *noun*
maul·stick \'mȯl-stik\ *noun* [part translation of Dutch *maalstok*, from obsolete Dutch *malen* to paint + Dutch *stok* stick, stock] (circa 1658)
: a stick used by painters as a rest for the hand while working
mau·mau \'maů-ˌmaů\ *verb* **mau-maued; mau·mau·ing** *often both Ms capitalized* [*Mau Mau*, anti-European secret society in colonial Kenya] (1970)
transitive verb
: to intimidate (as an official) by hostile confrontation or threats
intransitive verb
: to engage in mau-mauing someone
maun \'mȯn, 'män, mən\ *verbal auxiliary* [Middle English *man*, from Old Norse, present of *munu* shall, will; akin to Old English *gemynd* mind — more at MIND] (13th century)
chiefly Scottish : MUST
maun·der \'mȯn-dər, 'män-\ *intransitive verb* **maun·dered; maun·der·ing** \-d(ə-)rin\ [probably imitative] (1621)
1 *dialect British* : GRUMBLE
2 : to wander slowly and idly
3 : to speak indistinctly or disconnectedly
— **maun·der·er** \-dər-ər\ *noun*
Maun·dy Thursday \'mȯn-dē-, 'män-\ *noun* [Middle English *maunde* ceremony of washing the feet of the poor on Maundy Thursday, from Old French *mandé*, from Latin *mandatum* command; from Jesus' words in John 13:34 — more at MANDATE] (15th century)
: the Thursday before Easter observed in commemoration of the institution of the Eucharist
mau·so·le·um \ˌmȯ-sə-'lē-əm, ˌmȯ-zə-\ *noun, plural* **-leums** *or* **-lea** \-'lē-ə\ [Middle English, from Latin, from Greek *mausōleion*, from *Mausōlos* Mausolus (died about 353 B.C.) ruler of Caria] (15th century)

◇ WORD HISTORY

maudlin In the New Testament of the Bible one of the most devoted followers of Jesus is Mary Magdalene, who was so called because she was thought to have come from the Palestinian city of Magdala. The popular pronunciation of *Magdalene* in early Modern English is indicated by spellings such as *Maudlen* and *Mawdlin*, which represent borrowings from medieval French *Madelaine*, the French development of Late Latin *Magdalena*. By the 16th century it had become an artistic tradition in scenes of the crucifixion and burial of Jesus to portray Mary Magdalene as weeping. So identified with weeping did she become that by the 17th century *maudlin* had come to mean "tearful, lachrymose." Later the word was used to describe a tearful show of emotion and especially the overwrought display of emotion brought on by drunkenness.

1 : a large tomb; *especially* **:** a usually stone building with places for entombment of the dead above ground
2 : a large gloomy building or room ◇

mauve \'mōv, 'mȯv\ *noun* [French, mallow, from Latin *malva*] (1859)
1 a : a moderate purple, violet, or lilac color **b :** a strong purple
2 : a dyestuff that produces a mauve color
— **mauve** *adjective*

ma·ven *or* **ma·vin** \'mā-vən\ *noun* [Yiddish *meyvn*, from Late Hebrew *mēbhīn*] (circa 1952)
: one who is experienced or knowledgeable **:** EXPERT; *also* **:** FREAK 4

¹mav·er·ick \'mav-rik, 'ma-və-\ *noun* [Samuel A. *Maverick* (died 1870) American pioneer who did not brand his calves] (1867)
1 : an unbranded range animal; *especially* **:** a motherless calf
2 : an independent individual who does not go along with a group or party ◇

²maverick *adjective* (1886)
: characteristic of, suggestive of, or inclined to be a maverick

ma·vis \'mā-vəs\ *noun* [Middle English, from Middle French *mauvis*] (14th century)
: SONG THRUSH

ma·vour·neen \mə-'vu̇r-‚nēn\ *noun* [Irish *mo mhuirnín*] (1800)
Irish **:** my darling

maw \'mȯ\ *noun* [Middle English, from Old English *maga*; akin to Old High German *mago* stomach, Lithuanian *makas* purse] (before 12th century)
1 : the receptacle into which food is taken by swallowing: **a :** STOMACH **b :** CROP
2 a : the throat, gullet, or jaws especially of a voracious animal **b :** something suggestive of a gaping maw

mawk·ish \'mȯ-kish\ *adjective* [Middle English *mawke* maggot, from Old Norse *mathkr* — more at MAGGOT] (circa 1697)
1 : having an insipid often unpleasant taste
2 : sickly or puerilely sentimental
— **mawk·ish·ly** *adverb*
— **mawk·ish·ness** *noun*

max \'maks\ *noun* (1968)
: MAXIMUM 1, 2
— **to the max :** to the greatest extent possible

maxi \'mak-sē\ *noun, plural* **max·is** [*maxi-*] (1967)
: a long skirt, dress, or coat

maxi- *combining form* [*maximum*]
1 : extra long ⟨*maxiskirt*⟩
2 : extra large ⟨*maxi*-problems⟩

max·il·la \mak-'si-lə\ *noun, plural* **max·il·lae** \-'si-(‚)lē, -‚lī\ *or* **maxillas** [Latin, diminutive of *mala* jaw] (1676)
1 a : JAW 1a **b** (1) **:** an upper jaw especially of humans and other mammals in which the bony elements are closely fused (2) **:** either of the two bones that lie with one on each side of the upper jaw lateral to the premaxilla and that in higher vertebrates bear most of the teeth
2 : one of the first or second pair of mouthparts posterior to the mandibles in insects, myriapods, crustaceans, and closely related arthropods
— **max·il·lary** \'mak-sə-‚ler-ē, *chiefly British* mak-si-lə-rē\ *adjective or noun*

max·il·li·ped \mak-'si-lə-‚ped\ *noun* [International Scientific Vocabulary *maxilli-* (from Latin *maxilla*) + *-ped*] (1846)
: any of the crustacean appendages that comprise the first pair or first three pairs situated next behind the maxillae

max·il·lo·fa·cial \mak-‚si-(‚)lō-'fā-shəl, ‚mak-sə-(‚)lō-\ *adjective* (circa 1923)
: of, relating to, or treating the maxilla and the face ⟨*maxillofacial* surgeons⟩

max·im \'mak-səm\ *noun* [Middle English *maxime*, from Middle French, from Medieval

Latin *maxima*, from Latin, feminine of *maximus*, superlative of *magnus* large — more at MUCH] (1567)
1 : a general truth, fundamental principle, or rule of conduct
2 : a saying of proverbial nature

max·i·mal \'mak-s(ə-)məl\ *adjective* (1882)
1 : being an upper limit **:** HIGHEST
2 : most comprehensive **:** COMPLETE
— **max·i·mal·ly** *adverb*

max·i·mal·ist \-s(ə-)mə-list\ *noun* (1907)
: one who advocates immediate and direct action to secure the whole of a program or set of goals

maxi·min \'mak-sə-‚min\ *noun* [*maximum* + *minimum*] (1951)
: the maximum of a set of minima; *especially* **:** the largest of a set of minimum possible gains each of which occurs in the least advantageous outcome of a strategy followed by a participant in a situation governed by the theory of games — compare MINIMAX

max·i·mise *British variant of* MAXIMIZE

max·i·mize \'mak-sə-‚mīz\ *transitive verb* **-mized; -miz·ing** (1802)
1 : to increase to a maximum
2 : to make the most of
3 : to find a maximum value of
— **max·i·mi·za·tion** \‚mak-sə-mə-'zā-shən\ *noun*
— **max·i·miz·er** \'mak-sə-‚mī-zər\ *noun*

max·i·mum \'mak-s(ə-)məm\ *noun, plural* **max·i·ma** \-sə-mə\ *or* **maximums** \-s(ə-)məmz\ [Latin, neuter of *maximus*] (1740)
1 a : the greatest quantity or value attainable or attained **b :** the period of highest, greatest, or utmost development
2 : an upper limit allowed (as by a legal authority) or allowable (as by the circumstances of a particular case)
3 : the largest of a set of numbers; *specifically* **:** the largest value assumed by a real-valued continuous function defined on a closed interval
— **maximum** *adjective*

maximum likelihood *noun* (1959)
: a statistical method for estimating population parameters (as the mean and variance) from sample data that selects as estimates those parameter values maximizing the probability of obtaining the observed data

ma·xixe \mə-'shēsh, -'shē-shə\ *noun, plural* **ma·xi·xes** \-'shē-shəz\ [Brazilian Portuguese] (1914)
: a ballroom dance of Brazilian origin that resembles the two-step

max·well \'maks-‚wel, -wəl\ *noun* [James Clerk *Maxwell*] (1900)
: the centimeter-gram-second electromagnetic unit of magnetic flux equal to the flux per square centimeter of normal cross section in a region where the magnetic induction is one gauss **:** 10^{-8} weber

¹may \'mā\ *verbal auxiliary, past* **might** \'mīt\; *present singular & plural* **may** [Middle English (1st & 3d singular present indicative), from Old English *mæg*; akin to Old High German *mag* (1st & 3d singular present indicative) have power, am able (infinitive *magan*), and perhaps to Greek *mēchos* means, expedient] (before 12th century)
1 a *archaic* **:** have the ability to **b :** have permission to ⟨you *may* go now⟩ **:** be free to ⟨a rug on which children *may* sprawl —C. E. Silberman⟩ — used nearly interchangeably with *can* **c** — used to indicate possibility or probability ⟨you *may* be right⟩ ⟨things you *may* need⟩; sometimes used interchangeably with *can* ⟨one of those slipups that *may* happen from time to time —Jessica Mitford⟩ ⟨copula *may* optionally be deleted —J. D. McCawley⟩; sometimes used where *might* would be expected ⟨you *may* think from a little distance that the country was solid woods —Robert Frost⟩

2 — used in auxiliary function to express a wish or desire especially in prayer, imprecation, or benediction ⟨long *may* he reign⟩
3 — used in auxiliary function expressing purpose or expectation ⟨I laugh that I *may* not weep⟩ or contingency ⟨she'll do her duty come what *may*⟩ or concession ⟨he *may* be slow but he is thorough⟩ or choice ⟨the angler *may* catch them with a dip net, or he *may* cast a large, bare treble hook —Nelson Bryant⟩
4 : SHALL, MUST — used in law where the sense, purpose, or policy requires this interpretation
usage see CAN

²may \'mā\ *noun* [Middle English, from Old English *mæg* kinsman, kinswoman, maiden] (before 12th century)
archaic **:** MAIDEN

May \'mā\ *noun* [Middle English, from Old French & Latin; Old French *mai*, from Latin *Maius*, from *Maia*, Roman goddess] (12th century)
1 : the 5th month of the Gregorian calendar
2 *often not capitalized* **:** the early vigorous blooming part of human life **:** PRIME
3 : the festivities of May Day

\ə\ abut \ʻə\ kitten \ər\ further \a\ ash \ā\ ace
\ä\ mop, mar \au̇\ out \ch\ chin \e\ bet \ē\ easy
\g\ go \i\ hit \ī\ ice \j\ job \ŋ\ sing \ō\ go
\o̊\ law \o̊i\ boy \th\ thin \t͟h\ the \ü\ loot \u̇\ foot
\y\ yet \zh\ vision *see also* Guide to Pronunciation

4 *not capitalized* **a :** green or flowering branches used for May Day decorations **b :** a plant that yields may: as (1) : HAWTHORN (2) : a spring-flowering spirea

ma·ya \'mä-yə, 'mī-ə\ *noun* [Sanskrit *māyā*] (1788)
: the sense-world of manifold phenomena held in Vedanta to conceal the unity of absolute being; *broadly* : ILLUSION

Ma·ya \'mī-ə\ *noun, plural* **Maya** *or* **Mayas** [Spanish] (1825)
1 a : a Mayan language of the ancient Maya peoples recorded in inscriptions **b :** YUCATEC; *especially* **:** the older form of that language known from documents of the Spanish period **2 :** a member of a group of Indian peoples chiefly of Yucatán, Belize, and Guatemala whose languages are Mayan

Ma·yan \'mī-ən\ *noun* (1900)
1 : a member of the peoples speaking Mayan languages **2 :** an extensive language family of Central America and Mexico
— **Mayan** *adjective*

Mayanist \'mī-ə-nist\ *noun* (1950)
: a specialist in Mayan culture and history

may·ap·ple \'mā-ˌa-pəl\ *noun* [*May*] (circa 1733)
: a North American herb (*Podophyllum peltatum*) of the barberry family with a poisonous rootstock, one or two large-lobed peltate leaves, and a large single white flower followed by a yellow egg-shaped edible fruit; *also* **:** its fruit

¹may·be \'mā-bē *also* 'me-\ *adverb* (15th century)
: PERHAPS

²maybe *noun* (circa 1586)
: UNCERTAINTY

May·day \'mā-ˌdā\ [French *m'aider* help me] (1927)
— an international radio-telephone signal word used as a distress call

May Day \'mā-ˌdā\ *noun* (13th century)
: May 1 celebrated as a springtime festival and in some countries as Labor Day

may·est *or* **mayst** \'mā-əst, 'māst\ *archaic present 2d singular of* MAY

may·flow·er \'mā-ˌflau̇(-ə)r\ *noun* (1594)
: any of various spring-blooming plants; *especially* **:** ARBUTUS 2

may·fly \'mā-flī\ *noun* (circa 1653)
: any of an order (Ephemeroptera) of insects with an aquatic nymph and a short-lived fragile adult having membranous wings and two or three long caudal styles — called also *ephemerid*

mayfly

may·hap \'mā-ˌhap, mā-'\ *adverb* [from the phrase *may hap*] (circa 1531)
: PERHAPS

may·hem \'mā-ˌhem, 'mā-əm\ *noun* [Middle English *mayme*, from Anglo-French *mahaim*, from Old French, loss of a limb, from *maynier* to maim, probably of Germanic origin; akin to Middle High German *meiden* gelding, Old Norse *meitha* to injure] (15th century)
1 a : willful and permanent deprivation of a bodily member resulting in the impairment of a person's fighting ability **b :** willful and permanent crippling, mutilation, or disfigurement of any part of the body **2 :** needless or willful damage or violence

may·ing \'mā-iŋ\ *noun, often capitalized* (14th century)
: the celebrating of May Day

mayn't \'mā-ənt, 'mānt\ (circa 1631)
: may not

mayo \'mā-(ˌ)ō\ *noun* (circa 1960)
: MAYONNAISE

may·on·naise \'mā-ə-ˌnāz, ˌmā-ə-'\ *noun* [French] (1841)
: a dressing made of egg yolks, vegetable oils, and vinegar or lemon juice

may·or \'mā-ər, 'me(-ə)r, *especially before names* (ˌ)mer\ *noun* [Middle English *maire*, from Old French, from Latin *major* greater — more at MAJOR] (14th century)
: an official elected or appointed to act as chief executive or nominal head of a city, town, or borough
— **may·or·al** \'mā-ə-rəl, 'me-ə-; ˌmā-'ȯr-əl\ *adjective*

may·or·al·ty \'mā-ə-rəl-tē, 'me-; 'mer-əl-\ *noun* [Middle English *mairaltee*, from Middle French *mairalté*, from Old French, from *maire*] (14th century)
: the office or term of office of a mayor

may·or·ess \'mā-ə-rəs, 'me-\ *noun* (15th century)
chiefly British
1 : the wife or official hostess of a mayor **2 :** a woman holding the office of mayor
usage see -ESS

may·pole \'mā-ˌpōl\ *noun, often capitalized* (1554)
: a tall flower-wreathed pole forming a center for May Day sports and dances

may·pop \'mā-ˌpäp\ *noun* [alteration of *maracock*, perhaps from Virginia Algonquian] (1851)
: a climbing perennial passionflower (*Passiflora incarnata*) of the southern U.S. with a large ovoid yellow edible but insipid berry; *also* **:** its fruit

May·time \'mā-ˌtīm\ *noun* (14th century)
: the month of May

maz·ard \'ma-zərd\ *noun* [obsolete English *mazard* mazer, alteration of English *mazer*] (1602)
chiefly dialect **:** HEAD, FACE

¹maze \'māz\ *transitive verb* **mazed; maz·ing** [Middle English] (13th century)
1 *chiefly dialect* **:** STUPEFY, DAZE **2 :** BEWILDER, PERPLEX

²maze *noun* (14th century)
1 a : a confusing intricate network of passages **b :** something intricately or confusingly elaborate or complicated ⟨a *maze* of regulations⟩ **2** *chiefly dialect* **:** a state of bewilderment
— **maze·like** \-ˌlīk\ *adjective*

ma·zer \'mā-zər\ *noun* [Middle English, from Middle French *mazere*, of Germanic origin; akin to Old High German *masar* gnarled excrescence on a tree] (14th century)
: a large drinking bowl originally of a hard wood

ma·zur·ka \mə-'zər-kə, -'zu̇r-\ *also* **ma·zour·ka** \-'zu̇r-\ *noun* [Russian, from Polish *mazurek*, from *Mazury* Masuria, region of northeast Poland] (1818)
1 : a Polish folk dance in moderate triple measure **2 :** music for the mazurka or in its rhythm usually in moderate ¾ or ⅜ time

mazy \'mā-zē\ *adjective* (1579)
: resembling a maze

¹maz·zard \'ma-zərd\ *noun* [origin unknown] (1578)
: SWEET CHERRY; *especially* **:** wild or seedling sweet cherry used as a rootstock for grafting

²mazzard *variant of* MAZZARD

mbi·ra \em-'bir-ə\ *noun* [Shona] (circa 1911)
: an African musical instrument that consists of a wooden or gourd resonator and a varying number of tuned metal or wooden strips that vibrate when plucked

MC \ˌem-'sē\ *noun* (1790)
: MASTER OF CEREMONIES

Mc·Car·thy·ism \mə-'kär-thē-ˌi-zəm *also* -'kär-tē-\ *noun* [Joseph R. *McCarthy*] (1950)
: a mid-20th century political attitude characterized chiefly by opposition to elements held to be subversive and by the use of tactics involving personal attacks on individuals by means of widely publicized indiscriminate allegations especially on the basis of unsubstantiated charges
— **Mc·Car·thy·ite** \-ˌīt\ *noun or adjective*

Mc·Coy \mə-'kȯi\ *noun* [alteration of *Mackay* (in the phrase *the real Mackay*), of unknown origin] (1922)
: something that is neither imitation nor substitute — often used in the phrase *the real McCoy*

Mc·In·tosh \'ma-kən-ˌtäsh\ *noun* [John *McIntosh* (flourished 1796) Canadian settler] (1878)
: a juicy bright red eating apple with a thin skin, white flesh, and aromatic slightly tart flavor

M–day \'em-ˌdā\ *noun* [*mobilization day*] (1924)
: a day on which a military mobilization is to begin

me \'mē\ *pronoun, objective case of* I [Middle English, from Old English *mē*; akin to Old High German *mīh* me, Latin *me*, Greek *me*, Sanskrit *mā*] □
mea cul·pa \ˌmā-ə-'ku̇l-pə, ˌmā-ä-, -'ku̇l-(ˌ)pä\ *noun* [Latin, through my fault] (1602)
: a formal acknowledgment of personal fault or error

¹mead \'mēd\ *noun* [Middle English *mede*, from Old English *medu*; akin to Old High German *metu* mead, Greek *methy* wine] (before 12th century)
: a fermented beverage made of water and honey, malt, and yeast

²mead *noun* [Middle English *mede*, from Old English *mǣd*] (before 12th century)
archaic **:** MEADOW

mead·ow \'me-(ˌ)dō\ *noun, often attributive* [Middle English *medwe*, from Old English *mǣdwe*, oblique case form of *mǣd*; akin to Old English *māwan* to mow — more at MOW] (before 12th century)
: land in or predominantly in grass; *especially* **:** a tract of moist low-lying usually level grassland
— **mead·owy** \'me-də-wē\ *adjective*

meadow beauty *noun* (1840)
: any of a genus (*Rhexia* of the family Melastomaceae, the meadow-beauty family) of low perennial American herbs with showy solitary or cymose flowers

meadow fescue *noun* (1794)
: a tall vigorous perennial European fescue grass (*Festuca pratensis*) with broad flat leaves widely cultivated for permanent pasture and hay

meadow grass *noun* (13th century)
: any of various grasses (as of the genus *Poa*) that thrive in the presence of abundant moisture; *especially* **:** KENTUCKY BLUEGRASS

mead·ow·land \'me-dō-ˌland, -də-\ *noun* (1530)
: land that is or is used for meadow

mead·ow·lark \'me-dō-,lärk, -də-\ *noun* (1611)
: any of several American songbirds (genus *Sturnella*) that are streaked brown above and in northernmost forms have a yellow breast marked with a black crescent

meadowlark

meadow mouse *noun* (1801)
: any of various voles (especially genus *Microtus*) that frequent open fields — called also *meadow vole*

meadow mushroom *noun* (1884)
: a common edible brown-spored agaric (*Agaricus campestris*) that occurs in moist open organically rich soil and is often cultivated

meadow nematode *noun* (1946)
: any of numerous plant-parasitic nematode worms (especially genus *Pratylenchus*) that destructively invade the roots of plants

meadow rue *noun* (1668)
: any of a genus (*Thalictrum*) of widely distributed plants of the buttercup family with decompound or compound leaves

meadow saffron *noun* (1578)
: AUTUMN CROCUS

meadow spittlebug *noun* (1942)
: a North American spittlebug (*Philaenus spumarius*) that does severe damage especially to grasses

mead·ow·sweet \'me-dō-,swēt, -də-\ *noun* (1530)
1 : SPIREA 1; *especially* : a North American native or naturalized spirea (as *Spiraea alba* and *S. latifolia*)
2 : any of a genus (*Filipendula*) of herbs closely related to the spireas

mea·ger *or* **mea·gre** \'mē-gər\ *adjective* [Middle English *megre*, from Middle French *maigre*, from Latin *macr-, macer* lean; akin to Old English *mæger* lean, Greek *makros* long] (14th century)
1 : having little flesh : THIN
2 a : lacking desirable qualities (as richness or strength) ⟨leading a *meager* life⟩ **b** : deficient in quality or quantity ⟨a *meager* diet⟩ ☆
— **mea·ger·ly** *adverb*
— **mea·ger·ness** *noun*

¹meal \'mē(ə)l\ *noun* [Middle English *meel* appointed time, meal, from Old English *mæl*; akin to Old High German *māl* time, Latin *metiri* to measure — more at MEASURE] (before 12th century)
1 : an act or the time of eating a portion of food to satisfy appetite
2 : the portion of food eaten at a meal ◆

²meal *noun* [Middle English *mele*, from Old English *melu*; akin to Old High German *melo* meal, Latin *molere* to grind, Greek *mylē* mill] (before 12th century)
1 : the usually coarsely ground and unbolted seeds of a cereal grass or pulse; *especially* : CORNMEAL
2 : a product resembling seed meal especially in particle size or texture

-meal *adverb combining form* [Middle English *-mele*, from Old English *-mǣlum*, from *mǣlum*, dative plural of *mǣl*]
: by a (specified) portion or measure at a time ⟨piece*meal*⟩

mea·lie \'mē-lē\ *noun* [Afrikaans *mielie*] (1855)
South African : INDIAN CORN; *also* : an ear of Indian corn

meals–on–wheels *noun plural but singular in construction* (1961)
: a service that delivers daily hot meals to the homes of elderly or disabled people

meal ticket *noun* (circa 1899)
: one that serves as the ultimate source of one's income ⟨an advanced degree was his *meal ticket*⟩

meal·time \'mē(ə)l-,tīm\ *noun* (12th century)
: the usual time for serving a meal

meal·worm \-,wərm\ *noun* (1658)
: the larva of various beetles (genus *Tenebrio*) that infests and pollutes grain products but is often raised as food for insectivorous animals, for laboratory use, or as fishing bait

mealy \'mē-lē\ *adjective* **meal·i·er; -est** (1533)
1 : soft, dry, and friable
2 : containing meal : FARINACEOUS
3 a : covered with meal or with fine granules **b** : flecked with another color **c** : SPOTTY, UNEVEN **d** : PALLID, BLANCHED ⟨a *mealy* complexion⟩
4 : MEALYMOUTHED

mealy·bug \'mē-lē-,bəg\ *noun* (1824)
: any of a family (Pseudococcidae) of scale insects that have a white powdery covering and are destructive pests especially of fruit trees

mealy·mouthed \'mē-lē-,maúthd, -,maútht\ *adjective* (circa 1572)
: not plain or straightforward : DEVIOUS ⟨a *mealymouthed* politician⟩

¹mean \'mēn\ *verb* **meant** \'ment\; **meaning** \'mē-niŋ\ [Middle English *menen*, from Old English *mǣnan*; akin to Old High German *meinen* to have in mind, Old Church Slavonic *měniti* to mention] (before 12th century)
transitive verb
1 a : to have in the mind as a purpose : INTEND ⟨she *means* to win⟩ — sometimes used interjectionally with *I*, chiefly in informal speech for emphasis ⟨he throws, I *mean*, hard⟩ or to introduce a phrase restating the point of a preceding phrase ⟨we try to answer what we can, but I *mean* we're not God —Bobbie Ann Mason⟩ **b** : to design for or destine to a specified purpose or future ⟨I was meant to teach⟩
2 : to serve or intend to convey, show, or indicate : SIGNIFY ⟨a red sky *means* rain⟩
3 : to have importance to the degree of ⟨health *means* everything⟩
4 : to direct to a particular individual
intransitive verb
: to have an intended purpose ⟨he *means* well⟩
— **mean·er** \'mē-nər\ *noun*
— **mean business** : to be in earnest

²mean *adjective* [Middle English *mene*, from *imene* common, shared, from Old English *gemǣne*; akin to Old High German *gimeini* common, Latin *communis* common, *munus* service, gift, Sanskrit *mayate* he exchanges] (14th century)
1 : lacking distinction or eminence : HUMBLE
2 : lacking in mental discrimination : DULL
3 a : of poor shabby inferior quality or status ⟨*mean* city streets⟩ **b** : worthy of little regard : CONTEMPTIBLE — often used in negative constructions as a term of praise ⟨no *mean* feat⟩
4 : lacking dignity or honor : BASE
5 a : PENURIOUS, STINGY **b** : characterized by petty selfishness or malice **c** : causing trouble or bother : VEXATIOUS **d** : EXCELLENT, EFFECTIVE ⟨plays a *mean* trumpet⟩ ⟨a lean, *mean* athlete⟩
6 : ASHAMED 1b ☆
— **mean·ness** \'mēn-nəs\ *noun*

³mean *adjective* [Middle English *mene*, from Middle French *meien*, from Latin *medianus* — more at MEDIAN] (14th century)
1 : occupying a middle position : intermediate in space, order, time, kind, or degree
2 : occupying a position about midway between extremes; *especially* : being the mean of a set of values : AVERAGE ⟨the *mean* temperature⟩
3 : serving as a means : INTERMEDIARY
synonym see AVERAGE

⁴mean *noun* (14th century)
1 a (1) : something intervening or intermediate (2) : a middle point between extremes **b** : a value that lies within a range of values and is computed according to a prescribed law: as (1) : ARITHMETIC MEAN (2) : EXPECTED VALUE **c** : either of the middle two terms of a proportion
2 *plural but singular or plural in construction* : something useful or helpful to a desired end
3 *plural* : resources available for disposal; *especially* : material resources affording a secure life
— **by all means** : most assuredly : CERTAINLY

☆ SYNONYMS
Meager, scanty, scant, skimpy, spare, sparse mean falling short of what is normal, necessary, or desirable. MEAGER implies the absence of elements, qualities, or numbers necessary to a thing's richness, substance, or potency ⟨a *meager* portion of meat⟩. SCANTY stresses insufficiency in amount, quantity, or extent ⟨supplies too *scanty* to last the winter⟩. SCANT suggests a falling short of what is desired or desirable rather than of what is essential ⟨in January the daylight hours are *scant*⟩. SKIMPY usually suggests niggardliness or penury as the cause of the deficiency ⟨tacky housing developments on *skimpy* lots⟩. SPARE may suggest a slight falling short of adequacy or merely an absence of superfluity ⟨a *spare*, concise style of writing⟩. SPARSE implies a thin scattering of units ⟨a *sparse* population⟩.

Mean, ignoble, abject, sordid mean being below the normal standards of human decency and dignity. MEAN suggests having such repellent characteristics as small-mindedness, ill temper, or cupidity ⟨*mean* and petty satire⟩. IGNOBLE suggests a loss or lack of some essential high quality of mind or spirit ⟨an *ignoble* scramble after material possessions⟩. ABJECT may imply degradation, debasement, or servility ⟨*abject* poverty⟩. SORDID is stronger than all of these in stressing physical or spiritual degradation and abjectness ⟨a *sordid* story of murder and revenge⟩.

◇ WORD HISTORY
meal It may be natural to suppose that the *meal* of "three meals a day" has some relation to the *meal* of "ground meal," since both words pertain to food, but in fact they are unrelated. The *meal* of "ground meal" is descended from Old English *melu*, a word akin to Old High German *malan* "to grind," as well as to Latin *molere* "to grind." Derived from *molere* is Latin *molina* "mill," the ultimate source of the English noun and verb *mill*. The *meal* of "three meals a day," on the other hand, is from Old English *mæl* or *mēl* "measure, appointed time, mealtime." It is akin to Old High German *māl* "time," and much more distantly to Latin *metiri* "to measure." As *mēl* became *meel* in Middle English, the word became more closely associated with food than with time or measurement. The modern senses and spelling were established by the end of the 17th century. A relative of this *meal* can be seen in *piecemeal*, where *-meal* is a suffix having the sense "by a specified portion or measure at a time."

\ə\ **abut** \ˈə\ **kitten** \ər\ **further** \a\ **ash** \ā\ **ace**
\ä\ **mop, mar** \aú\ **out** \ch\ **chin** \e\ **bet** \ē\ **easy**
\g\ **go** \i\ **hit** \ī\ **ice** \j\ **job** \ŋ\ **sing** \ō\ **go**
\ȯ\ **law** \ȯi\ **boy** \th\ **thin** \th\ **the** \ü\ **loot** \ú\ **foot**
\y\ **yet** \zh\ **vision** *see also* Guide to Pronunciation

— **by means of :** through the use of
— **by no means :** in no way **:** not at all

¹me·an·der \mē-'an-dər\ *noun* [Latin *maeander*, from Greek *maiandros*, from *Maiandros* (now *Menderes*), river in Asia Minor] (1576)
1 : a winding path or course; *especially* **:** LABYRINTH
2 : a turn or winding of a stream
— **me·an·drous** \-drəs\ *adjective*

²meander *intransitive verb* **-dered; -der·ing** \-d(ə-)riŋ\ (circa 1612)
1 : to follow a winding or intricate course
2 : to wander aimlessly or casually without urgent destination **:** RAMBLE
synonym see WANDER

mean deviation *noun* (1858)
: the mean of the absolute values of the numerical differences between the numbers of a set (as statistical data) and their mean or median

mean distance *noun* (circa 1889)
: the arithmetical mean of the maximum and minimum distances of an orbiting celestial object from its primary

mean free path *noun* (1879)
: the average distance traversed between collisions by particles (as molecules of a gas or free electrons in metal) in a system of agitated particles

mean·ie *also* **meany** \'mē-nē\ *noun, plural* **meanies** (1910)
: a mean or spiteful person

mean·ing \'mē-niŋ\ *noun* (14th century)
1 a : the thing one intends to convey especially by language **:** PURPORT **b :** the thing that is conveyed especially by language **:** IMPORT
2 : something meant or intended **:** AIM ⟨a mischievous *meaning* was apparent⟩
3 : significant quality; *especially* **:** implication of a hidden or special significance ⟨a glance full of *meaning*⟩
4 a : the logical connotation of a word or phrase **b :** the logical denotation or extension of a word or phrase
— **meaning** *adjective*
— **mean·ing·ly** \-niŋ-lē\ *adverb*

mean·ing·ful \-fəl\ *adjective* (1852)
1 a : having a meaning or purpose **b :** full of meaning **:** SIGNIFICANT ⟨a *meaningful* life⟩
2 : having an assigned function in a language system ⟨*meaningful* propositions⟩
— **mean·ing·ful·ly** \-fə-lē\ *adverb*
— **mean·ing·ful·ness** *noun*

mean·ing·less \'mē-niŋ-ləs\ *adjective* (1797)
1 : having no meaning; *especially* **:** lacking any significance
2 : having no assigned function in a language system
— **mean·ing·less·ly** *adverb*
— **mean·ing·less·ness** *noun*

¹mean·ly \'mēn-lē\ *adverb* (14th century)
obsolete **:** fairly well **:** MODERATELY

²meanly *adverb* (15th century)
: in a mean manner: as **a :** in a lowly manner **:** HUMBLY **b :** in an inferior manner **:** BADLY **c :** in a base or ungenerous manner

mean proportional *noun* (1571)
: GEOMETRIC MEAN; *especially* **:** the square root (as *x*) of the product of two numbers (as *a* and *b*) when expressed as the means of a proportion (as *a/x = x/b*)

mean solar day *noun* (1816)
: the interval between successive transits of a given meridian by the mean sun

mean–spir·it·ed \'mēn-'spir-ə-təd, ,mēn-\ *adjective* (1694)
: exhibiting or characterized by meanness of spirit
— **mean–spir·it·ed·ness** \-nəs\ *noun*

mean square *noun* (1845)
: the mean of the squares of a set of values

mean square deviation *noun* (1948)
1 : VARIANCE 5
2 : STANDARD DEVIATION

means test \'mēnz-\ *noun* (1930)

: an examination into the financial state of a person to determine his eligibility for public assistance
— **means–test·ed** \-,tes-təd\ *adjective*

mean sun *noun* (circa 1890)
: a fictitious sun used for timekeeping that moves uniformly along the celestial equator and maintains a constant rate of apparent motion equal to the average rate of apparent motion of the real sun

¹mean·time \'mēn-,tīm\ *noun* (14th century)
: the intervening time

²meantime *adverb* (1588)
: MEANWHILE

mean time *noun* (circa 1864)
: time that is based on the motion of the mean sun — called also *mean solar time*

mean value theorem *noun* (1902)
1 : a theorem in differential calculus: if a function of one variable is continuous on a closed interval and differentiable on the interval minus its endpoints there is at least one point where the derivative of the function is equal to the slope of the line joining the endpoints of the curve representing the function on the interval
2 : a theorem in integral calculus: if a function of one variable is continuous on a closed interval and differentiable on the interval minus its endpoints, there is at least one point in the interval where the product of the value of the function and the length of the interval is equal to the integral of the function over the interval

¹mean·while \'mēn-,hwīl, -,wīl\ *noun* (14th century)
: MEANTIME

²meanwhile *adverb* (14th century)
1 : during the intervening time
2 : at the same time

mea·sle \'mē-zəl\ *noun* [singular of *measles*] (1863)
: a cysticercus tapeworm larva; *specifically* **:** one found in the muscles of a domesticated mammal

mea·sles \'mē-zəlz\ *noun plural but singular or plural in construction* [Middle English *meseles*, plural of *mesel* measles, spot characteristic of measles; akin to Middle Dutch *masel* spot characteristic of measles] (14th century)
1 a : an acute contagious viral disease marked by an eruption of distinct red circular spots **b :** any of various eruptive diseases (as German measles)
2 [Middle English *mesel* infested with tapeworms, literally, leprous, from Old French, from Medieval Latin *misellus* leper, from Latin, wretch, from *misellus*, diminutive of *miser* miserable] **:** infestation with or disease caused by larval tapeworms in the muscles and tissues

mea·sly \'mēz-lē, 'mē-zə-\ *adjective* **mea·sli·er; -est** (1687)
1 : infected with measles
2 a : containing larval tapeworms **b :** infested with trichinae
3 : contemptibly small

¹mea·sure \'me-zhər, 'mā-\ *noun* [Middle English *mesure*, from Old French, from Latin *mensura*, from *mensus*, past participle of *metiri* to measure; akin to Old English *mæth* measure, Greek *metron*] (13th century)
1 a (1) **:** an adequate or due portion (2) **:** a moderate degree; *also* **:** MODERATION, TEMPERANCE (3) **:** a fixed or suitable limit **:** BOUNDS ⟨rich beyond *measure*⟩ **b :** the dimensions, capacity, or amount of something ascertained by measuring **c :** an estimate of what is to be expected (as of a person or situation) **d** (1) **:** a measured quantity (2) **:** AMOUNT, DEGREE
2 a : an instrument or utensil for measuring **b** (1) **:** a standard or unit of measurement — see WEIGHT table (2) **:** a system of standard units of measure ⟨metric *measure*⟩
3 : the act or process of measuring

4 a (1) **:** MELODY, TUNE (2) **:** DANCE; *especially* **:** a slow and stately dance **b :** rhythmic structure or movement **:** CADENCE: as (1) **:** poetic rhythm measured by temporal quantity or accent; *specifically* **:** METER (2) **:** musical time **c** (1) **:** a grouping of a specified number of musical beats located between two consecutive vertical lines on a staff (2) **:** a metrical unit **:** FOOT
5 : an exact divisor of a number
6 : a basis or standard of comparison ⟨wealth is not a *measure* of happiness⟩
7 : a step planned or taken as a means to an end; *specifically* **:** a proposed legislative act
— **for good measure :** in addition to the minimum required **:** as an extra

²measure *verb* **mea·sured; mea·sur·ing** \'me-zhə-riŋ, 'mā-; 'mezh-riŋ, 'māzh-\ (14th century)
transitive verb
1 a : to choose or control with cautious restraint **:** REGULATE ⟨*measure* his acts⟩ **b :** to regulate by a standard **:** GOVERN
2 : to allot or apportion in measured amounts ⟨*measure* out 3 cups⟩
3 : to lay off by making measurements
4 : to ascertain the measurements of
5 : to estimate or appraise by a criterion ⟨*measures* his skill against his rival⟩
6 *archaic* **:** to travel over **:** TRAVERSE
7 : to serve as a means of measuring ⟨a thermometer *measures* temperature⟩
intransitive verb
1 : to take or make a measurement
2 : to have a specified measurement
— **mea·sur·abil·i·ty** \,me-zhə-rə-'bi-lə-tē, ,mā-; ,mezh-rə-, ,māzh-\ *noun*
— **mea·sur·able** \'me-zhə-rə-bəl, 'mā-; 'mezh-rə-, 'māzh-\ *adjective*
— **mea·sur·ably** \-blē\ *adverb*
— **mea·sur·er** \-zhər-ər\ *noun*

mea·sured \'me-zhərd, 'mā-\ *adjective* (14th century)
1 : marked by due proportion
2 a : marked by rhythm **:** regularly recurrent ⟨a *measured* gait⟩ **b :** METRICAL
3 : DELIBERATE, CALCULATED ⟨a *measured* response⟩
— **mea·sured·ly** *adverb*

mea·sure·less \-zhər-ləs\ *adjective* (14th century)
1 : having no observable limit **:** IMMEASURABLE ⟨the *measureless* universe⟩
2 : very great ⟨had *measureless* energy⟩

mea·sure·ment \'me-zhər-mənt, 'mā-\ *noun* (1751)
1 : the act or process of measuring
2 : a figure, extent, or amount obtained by measuring **:** DIMENSION
3 : MEASURE 2b

measurement ton *noun* (circa 1934)
: TON 1c

measure up *intransitive verb* (1910)
1 : to have necessary or fitting qualifications — often used with *to*
2 : to be the equal (as in ability) — used with *to*

measuring worm *noun* (1843)
: LOOPER 1

meat \'mēt\ *noun* [Middle English *mete*, from Old English; akin to Old High German *maz* food] (before 12th century)
1 a : FOOD; *especially* **:** solid food as distinguished from drink **b :** the edible part of something as distinguished from its covering (as a husk or shell)
2 : animal tissue considered especially as food: **a :** FLESH 2b **b :** FLESH 1a; *specifically* **:** flesh of domesticated animals
3 *archaic* **:** ¹MEAL 1; *especially* **:** DINNER
4 a : the core of something **:** HEART **b :** PITH 2b ⟨a novel with *meat*⟩
5 : favorite pursuit or interest
— **meat·ed** \'mē-təd\ *adjective*
— **meat·less** *adjective*

meat–and–potatoes *adjective* (1949)
1 : of fundamental importance **:** BASIC; *also* **:** concerned with or emphasizing the basic aspects of something
2 : PRACTICAL; *also* **:** EVERYDAY
3 : providing or preferring simple food (as meat and potatoes)

meat and potatoes *noun plural but singular or plural in construction* (1951)
: the most interesting or fundamental part **:** MEAT 4

meat–ax \'mēt-ˌaks\ *noun* (1834)
1 : CLEAVER 1
2 : an extreme or heavy-handed method of cutting or altering something

meat·ball \-ˌbȯl\ *noun* (circa 1838)
: a small ball of chopped or ground meat often mixed with bread crumbs and spices

meat·head \-ˌhed\ *noun* (1945)
: a stupid or bungling person

meat loaf *noun* (1899)
: a dish of ground meat seasoned and baked in the form of a loaf

meat market *noun* (1896)
: a depersonalizing environment in which people are treated as sexual or economic resources

meat·pack·ing \'mēt-ˌpa-kiŋ\ *noun* (1873)
: the wholesale meat industry

me·a·tus \mē-'ā-təs\ *noun, plural* **me·a·tus·es** \-tə-səz\ *or* **me·a·tus** \-'ā-təs, -ˌtüs\ [Late Latin, from Latin, going, passage, from *meatus*, past participle of *meare* to go — more at PERMEATE] (1665)
: a natural body passage

meaty \'mē-tē\ *adjective* **meat·i·er; -est** (circa 1787)
1 a : full of meat **b :** having the character of meat
2 : rich especially in matter for thought **:** SUBSTANTIAL ⟨actors looking for *meaty* roles⟩
— **meat·i·ness** *noun*

mec·a·myl·amine \ˌme-kə-'mi-lə-ˌmēn\ *noun* [from *Mecamylamine*, a trademark] (1955)
: a drug that in the hydrochloride $C_{11}H_{21}N \cdot HCl$ is used orally as a ganglionic blocking agent to effect a rapid lowering of severely elevated blood pressure

mec·ca \'me-kə\ *noun, often capitalized* [*Mecca*, Saudi Arabia, a destination of pilgrims in the Islamic world] (1850)
: a center of activity sought as a goal by people sharing a common interest

mechan- *or* **mechano-** *combining form* [Greek, from *mēchanē* machine — more at MACHINE]
: mechanical ⟨*mechano*receptor⟩

¹**me·chan·ic** \mi-'ka-nik\ *adjective* [Middle English, probably from Middle French *mechanique*, adjective & noun, from Latin *mechanicus*, from Greek *mēchanikos*, from *mēchanē*] (14th century)
1 : of or relating to manual work or skill
2 : MECHANICAL 3a

²**mechanic** *noun* (1562)
1 : a manual worker **:** ARTISAN
2 : MACHINIST; *especially* **:** one who repairs machines

¹**me·chan·i·cal** \mi-'ka-ni-kəl\ *adjective* (15th century)
1 a (1) **:** of or relating to machinery or tools ⟨*mechanical* applications of science⟩ ⟨a *mechanical* genius⟩ ⟨*mechanical* aptitude⟩ (2) **:** produced or operated by a machine or tool ⟨*mechanical* power⟩ ⟨a *mechanical* refrigerator⟩ ⟨a *mechanical* saw⟩ **b :** of or relating to manual operations
2 : of or relating to artisans or machinists ⟨the *mechanical* trades⟩
3 a : done as if by machine **:** seemingly uninfluenced by the mind or emotions **:** AUTOMATIC ⟨her singing was cold and *mechanical*⟩ **b :** of or relating to technicalities or petty matters
4 a : relating to, governed by, or in accordance with the principles of mechanics ⟨*me-*

chanical work⟩ ⟨*mechanical* energy⟩ **b :** relating to the quantitative relations of force and matter ⟨*mechanical* pressure of wind on a tower⟩
5 : caused by, resulting from, or relating to a process that involves a purely physical as opposed to a chemical change ⟨*mechanical* erosion of rock⟩
synonym see SPONTANEOUS
— **me·chan·i·cal·ly** \-ni-k(ə-)lē\ *adverb*

²**mechanical** *noun* (1590)
1 *obsolete* **:** MECHANIC 1
2 : a piece of finished copy consisting typically of type proofs and artwork positioned and mounted for photomechanical reproduction

mechanical advantage *noun* (1894)
: the advantage gained by the use of a mechanism in transmitting force; *specifically* **:** the ratio of the force that performs the useful work of a machine to the force that is applied to the machine

mechanical drawing *noun* (circa 1890)
1 : drawing done with the aid of instruments
2 : a drawing made with instruments

mechanical engineering *noun* (circa 1890)
: a branch of engineering concerned primarily with the industrial application of mechanics and with the production of tools, machinery, and their products

mech·a·ni·cian \ˌme-kə-'ni-shən\ *noun* (1570)
: MECHANIC, MACHINIST

me·chan·ics \mi-'ka-niks\ *noun plural but singular or plural in construction* (1648)
1 : a branch of physical science that deals with energy and forces and their effect on bodies
2 : the practical application of mechanics to the design, construction, or operation of machines or tools
3 : mechanical or functional details or procedure

mech·a·nism \'me-kə-ˌni-zəm\ *noun* (1662)
1 a : a piece of machinery **b :** a process or technique for achieving a result
2 : mechanical operation or action **:** WORKING 2
3 : a doctrine that holds natural processes (as of life) to be mechanically determined and capable of complete explanation by the laws of physics and chemistry
4 : the fundamental physical or chemical processes involved in or responsible for an action, reaction, or other natural phenomenon (as organic evolution)

mech·a·nist \-nist\ *noun* (1606)
1 *archaic* **:** MECHANIC
2 : an adherent of the doctrine of mechanism

mech·a·nis·tic \ˌme-kə-'nis-tik\ *adjective* (1884)
1 : mechanically determined ⟨*mechanistic* universe⟩
2 : of or relating to a mechanism or the doctrine of mechanism
3 : MECHANICAL
— **mech·a·nis·ti·cal·ly** \-ti-k(ə-)lē\ *adverb*

mech·a·nize \'me-kə-ˌnīz\ *transitive verb* **-nized; -niz·ing** (1678)
1 : to make mechanical; *especially* **:** to make automatic or routine
2 a : to equip with machinery especially to replace human or animal labor **b :** to equip with armed and armored motor vehicles **c :** to provide with mechanical power
3 : to produce by or as if by machine
— **mech·a·niz·able** \-ˌnī-zə-bəl\ *adjective*
— **mech·a·ni·za·tion** \ˌme-kə-nə-'zā-shən\ *noun*
— **mech·a·niz·er** \'me-kə-ˌnī-zər\ *noun*

mech·a·no·chem·is·try \ˌme-kə-nō-'ke-mə-strē\ *noun* (1928)
: chemistry that deals with the conversion of chemical energy into mechanical work (as in the contraction of a muscle)

— **mech·a·no·chem·i·cal** \-'ke-mi-kəl\ *adjective*

mech·a·no·re·cep·tor \-ri-'sep-tər\ *noun* (1927)
: a neural end organ (as a tactile receptor) that responds to a mechanical stimulus (as a change in pressure)
— **mech·a·no·re·cep·tion** \-'sep-shən\ *noun*
— **mech·a·no·re·cep·tive** \-'sep-tiv\ *adjective*

Mech·lin \'me-klən\ *noun* [*Mechlin*, Belgium] (1699)
: a delicate bobbin lace used for dresses and millinery

mec·li·zine \'me-klə-ˌzēn\ *noun* [methyl + chlor- + -izine (alteration of *azine*)] (1954)
: a drug $C_{25}H_{27}ClN_2$ used usually in the form of its hydrochloride to treat nausea and vertigo

me·co·ni·um \mi-'kō-nē-əm\ *noun* [Latin, literally, poppy juice, from Greek *mēkōnion*, from *mēkōn* poppy; akin to Old High German *mago* poppy] (1706)
: a dark greenish mass that accumulates in the bowel during fetal life and is discharged shortly after birth

med \'med\ *adjective* (1891)
: MEDICAL ⟨*med* school⟩

me·da·ka \mə-'dä-kə\ *noun* [Japanese] (1933)
: a small Japanese freshwater fish (*Oryzias latipes*) usually silvery brown in the wild but from pale yellow to deep red in aquarium strains

med·al \'me-d°l\ *noun* [Middle French *medaille*, from Old Italian *medaglia* coin worth half a denarius, medal, from (assumed) Vulgar Latin *medalis* half, alteration of Late Latin *medialis* middle, from Latin *medius* — more at MID] (circa 1578)
1 : a small usually metal object bearing a religious emblem or picture
2 : a piece of metal often resembling a coin and having a stamped design that is issued to commemorate a person or event or awarded for excellence or achievement

Medal for Merit (1942)
: a U.S. decoration awarded to civilians for exceptionally meritorious conduct in the performance of outstanding services

med·al·ist *or* **med·al·list** \'me-d°l-ist\ *noun* (circa 1757)
1 : a designer, engraver, or maker of medals
2 : a recipient of a medal as an award

me·dal·lic \mə-'da-lik\ *adjective* (1702)
: of, relating to, or shown on a medal

me·dal·lion \mə-'dal-yən\ *noun* [French *médaillon*, from Italian *medaglione*, augmentative of *medaglia*] (1658)
1 : a large medal
2 : something resembling a large medal; *especially* **:** a tablet or panel in a wall or window bearing a figure in relief, a portrait, or an ornament
3 *also* **me·dail·lon** \mā-dȧ-yōⁿ\ **:** a small round or oval serving (as of meat)

Medal of Freedom (1945)
: a U.S. decoration awarded to civilians for meritorious achievement in any of various fields

Medal of Honor (1898)
: a U.S. military decoration awarded in the name of the Congress for conspicuous intrepidity at the risk of life in action with an enemy

medal play *noun* (1899)
: STROKE PLAY

med·dle \'me-d°l\ *intransitive verb* **med·dled; med·dling** \'med-liŋ, 'me-d°l-iŋ\ [Middle English *medlen*, from Middle French *mesler, medler*, from (assumed) Vulgar Latin

misculare, from Latin *miscēre* to mix — more at MIX] (14th century)
: to interest oneself in what is not one's concern **:** interfere without right or propriety
— **med·dler** \'med-lər, 'me-d⁰l-ər\ *noun*
med·dle·some \'me-d⁰l-səm\ *adjective* (1615)
: given to meddling
synonym see IMPERTINENT
— **med·dle·some·ness** *noun*
Mede \'mēd\ *noun* [Middle English, from Latin *Medus,* from Greek *Mēdos*] (14th century)
: a native or inhabitant of ancient Media in Persia
Me·dea \mə-'dē-ə\ *noun* [Latin, from Greek *Mēdeia*]
: an enchantress noted in Greek mythology for helping Jason gain the Golden Fleece and for repeatedly resorting to murder to gain her ends
med·e·vac \'me-də-,vak, -dē-\ *noun* [*med*ical *evac*uation] (1966)
1 : emergency evacuation of the sick or wounded (as from a combat area)
2 : a helicopter used for medevac
med·fly \'med-,flī\ *noun, often capitalized* (1935)
: MEDITERRANEAN FRUIT FLY
¹me·dia \'mē-dē-ə\ *noun, plural* **me·di·ae** \-dē-,ē\ (1841)
1 [Late Latin, from Latin, feminine of *medius;* from the voiced stops' being regarded as intermediate between the tenues and the aspirates]
: a voiced stop
2 [New Latin, from Latin] **:** the middle coat of the wall of a blood or lymph vessel consisting chiefly of circular muscle fibers
²media *noun, plural* **me·di·as** *often attributive* [plural of *medium*] (1923)
1 : a medium of cultivation, conveyance, or expression; *especially* **:** MEDIUM 2b
2 a *singular or plural in construction* **:** MASS MEDIA **b** *plural* **:** members of the mass media
□
me·di·ad \'mē-dē-,ad\ *adverb* (1878)
: toward the median line or plane of a body or part
media event *noun* (1972)
: a publicity event staged for coverage by the news media
me·dia·gen·ic \,mē-dē-ə-'je-nik\ *adjective* (1971)
: attractive or well-suited to the communications media
me·di·al \'mē-dē-əl\ *adjective* [Late Latin *medialis,* from Latin *medius*] (1570)
1 : MEAN, AVERAGE
2 a : being or occurring in the middle **b :** extending toward the middle
3 : situated between the extremes of initial and final in a word or morpheme
— **medial** *noun*
— **me·di·al·ly** \-ə-lē\ *adverb*
¹me·di·an \'mē-dē-ən\ *noun* (15th century)
1 : a medial part (as a vein or nerve)
2 a : a value in an ordered set of values below and above which there is an equal number of values or which is the arithmetic mean of the two middle values if there is no one middle number **b :** a vertical line that divides the histogram of a frequency distribution into two parts of equal area **c :** a value of a random variable for which all greater values make the distribution function greater than one half and all lesser values make it less than one half
3 a : a line from a vertex of a triangle to the midpoint of the opposite side **b :** a line joining the midpoints of the nonparallel sides of a trapezoid
4 : MEDIAN STRIP
synonym see AVERAGE
²median *adjective* [Middle French or Latin; Middle French, from Latin *medianus,* from *medius* middle — more at MID] (1645)

1 : being in the middle or in an intermediate position **:** MEDIAL
2 : lying in the plane dividing a bilateral animal into right and left halves
3 : relating to or constituting a statistical median
4 : produced without occlusion along the lengthwise middle line of the tongue
— **me·di·an·ly** *adverb*
median strip *noun* (1948)
: a paved or planted strip dividing a highway into lanes according to direction of travel
me·di·ant \'mē-dē-ənt\ *noun* [Italian *mediante,* from Late Latin *mediant-, medians,* present participle of *mediare* to be in the middle] (circa 1741)
: the third tone of a diatonic scale
me·di·as·ti·num \,mē-dē-ə-'stī-nəm\ *noun, plural* **-na** \-nə\ [New Latin, from Medieval Latin, neuter of *mediastinus* medial, from Latin *medius*] (1541)
: the space in the chest between the pleural sacs of the lungs that contains all the viscera of the chest except the lungs and pleurae; *also* **:** this space with its contents
— **me·di·as·ti·nal** \-'stī-n⁰l\ *adjective*
¹me·di·ate \'mē-dē-ət\ *adjective* [Middle English, from Late Latin *mediatus* intermediate, from past participle of *mediare*] (15th century)
1 : occupying a middle position
2 a : acting through an intervening agency **b :** exhibiting indirect causation, connection, or relation
— **me·di·a·cy** \-dē-ə-sē\ *noun*
— **me·di·ate·ly** *adverb*
²me·di·ate \'mē-dē-,āt\ *verb* **-at·ed; -at·ing** [Medieval Latin *mediatus,* past participle of *mediare,* from Late Latin, to be in the middle, from Latin *medius* middle] (1568)
transitive verb
1 a : to effect by action as an intermediary **b :** to bring accord out of by action as an intermediary
2 a : to act as intermediary agent in bringing, effecting, or communicating **:** CONVEY **b :** to transmit as intermediate mechanism or agency
intransitive verb
1 : to interpose between parties in order to reconcile them
2 : to reconcile differences
synonym see INTERPOSE
— **me·di·a·tive** \-,ā-tiv\ *adjective*
— **me·di·a·to·ry** \-ə-,tōr-ē, -ə-,tòr-\ *adjective*
me·di·a·tion \,mē-dē-'ā-shən\ *noun* (14th century)
: the act or process of mediating; *especially* **:** intervention between conflicting parties to promote reconciliation, settlement, or compromise
— **me·di·a·tion·al** \-shnəl, -shə-n⁰l\ *adjective*
me·di·a·tor \'mē-dē-,ā-tər\ *noun* [Middle English, from Late Latin, from *mediare*] (14th century)
1 : one that mediates; *especially* **:** one that mediates between parties at variance
2 : a mediating agent in a physical, chemical, or biological process
me·di·a·trix \-'ā-triks\ *noun* [Middle English, from Late Latin, feminine of *mediator*] (15th century)
: a woman who is a mediator
¹med·ic \'me-dik\ *noun* [Middle English *medike,* from Latin *medica,* from Greek *mēdikē,* from feminine of *mēdikos* of Media, from *Mēdia* Media] (15th century)
: any of a genus (*Medicago*) of leguminous herbs (as alfalfa)
²medic *noun* [Latin *medicus*] (1659)
: one engaged in medical work or study; *especially* **:** CORPSMAN
med·i·ca·ble \'me-di-kə-bəl\ *adjective* (circa 1616)
: CURABLE, REMEDIABLE

med·ic·aid \'me-di-,kād\ *noun, often capitalized* [*medical aid*] (1966)
: a program of medical aid designed for those unable to afford regular medical service and financed by the state and federal governments
med·i·cal \'me-di-kəl\ *adjective* [French or Late Latin; French *médical,* from Late Latin *medicalis,* from Latin *medicus* physician, from *mederi* to remedy, heal; akin to Avestan *vī-mad-* healer, Greek *medesthai* to be mindful of — more at METE] (1646)
1 : of, relating to, or concerned with physicians or the practice of medicine
2 : requiring or devoted to medical treatment
— **med·i·cal·ly** \-k(ə-)lē\ *adverb*
medical examiner *noun* (1877)
: a public officer who conducts autopsies of bodies to find the cause of death
me·di·ca·ment \mi-'di-kə-mənt, 'me-di-kə-\ *noun* [Middle French, from Latin *medicamentum,* from *medicare*] (1541)
: a substance used in therapy
— **me·di·ca·men·tous** \mi-,di-kə-'men-təs, ,me-di-kə-\ *adjective*
medi·care \'me-di-,ker, -,kar\ *noun, often capitalized* [blend of *medical* and *care*] (1955)
: a government program of medical care especially for the aged
med·i·cate \'me-də-,kāt\ *transitive verb* **-cat·ed; -cat·ing** [Latin *medicatus,* past participle of *medicare* to heal, from *medicus*] (circa 1623)
1 : to treat medicinally
2 : to impregnate with a medicinal substance ⟨*medicated* soap⟩
med·i·ca·tion \,me-də-'kā-shən\ *noun* (15th century)
1 : the act or process of medicating
2 : a medicinal substance **:** MEDICAMENT
me·dic·i·na·ble \mi-'dis-nə-bəl, -'di-s⁰n-ə-; in Shakespeare 'med-sə-nə-\ *adjective* (14th century)
: MEDICINAL
me·dic·i·nal \mə-'dis-nəl, -'di-s⁰n-əl; in Shakespeare & Milton ,me-di-'sī-n⁰l & 'med-sə-nəl\ *adjective* (14th century)
1 : tending or used to cure disease or relieve pain
2 : SALUTARY
— **medicinal** *noun*
— **me·dic·i·nal·ly** *adverb*
medicinal leech *noun* (circa 1890)
: a large European freshwater leech (*Hirudo medicinalis*) formerly used by physicians for bleeding patients
med·i·cine \'me-də-sən, *British usually* 'med-sən\ *noun* [Middle English, from Old French, from Latin *medicina,* from feminine of *medicinus* of a physician, from *medicus*] (13th century)
1 a : a substance or preparation used in treating disease **b :** something that affects well-being

2 a : the science and art dealing with the maintenance of health and the prevention, alleviation, or cure of disease **b :** the branch of medicine concerned with the nonsurgical treatment of disease
3 : a substance (as a drug or potion) used to treat something other than disease
4 : an object held in traditional American Indian belief to give control over natural or magical forces; *also* **:** magical power or a magical rite
— **medicine** *transitive verb*
medicine ball *noun* (1895)
: a heavy stuffed leather-covered ball used for conditioning exercises
medicine dropper *noun* (1898)
: DROPPER 2
medicine man *noun* (1801)
: a priestly healer or sorcerer especially among the American Indians **:** SHAMAN
medicine show *noun* (circa 1906)
: a traveling show using entertainers to attract a crowd among which remedies or nostrums are sold
med·i·co \'me-di-ˌkō\ *noun, plural* **-cos** [Italian *medico* or Spanish *médico*, both from Latin *medicus*] (1689)
: a medical practitioner **:** PHYSICIAN; *also* **:** a medical student
med·i·co·le·gal \ˌme-di-kō-'lē-gəl\ *adjective* [New Latin *medicolegalis*, from Latin *medicus* medical + *-o-* + *legalis* legal] (1835)
: of or relating to both medicine and law
¹me·di·e·val *or* **me·di·ae·val** \ˌmē-'dē-vəl, mi-, me-, -dē-'ē-vəl\ *adjective* [New Latin *medium aevum* Middle Ages] (1827)
1 : of, relating to, or characteristic of the Middle Ages
2 : extremely outmoded or antiquated
— **me·di·e·val·ly** *adverb*
²medieval *or* **mediaeval** *noun* (1856)
: a person of the Middle Ages
me·di·e·val·ism \-və-ˌli-zəm\ *noun* (1853)
1 : medieval quality, character, or state
2 : devotion to the institutions, arts, and practices of the Middle Ages
me·di·e·val·ist \-'dēv-list, -'dē-və-, -dē-'ēv-, -dē-'ē-və-\ *noun* (circa 1859)
1 : a specialist in medieval history and culture
2 : a connoisseur or devotee of medieval arts and culture
Medieval Latin *noun* (circa 1889)
: the Latin used especially for liturgical and literary purposes from the 7th to the 15th centuries inclusive
me·di·na \mə-'dē-nə\ *noun* [Arabic *madīna* city] (1906)
: the non-European part of a northern African city
me·di·o·cre \ˌmē-dē-'ō-kər\ *adjective* [Middle English, from Middle French, from Latin *mediocris*, from *medius* middle + Old Latin *ocris* stony mountain; akin to Latin *acer* sharp — more at EDGE] (circa 1586)
: of moderate or low quality, value, ability, or performance **:** ORDINARY, SO-SO
me·di·oc·ri·ty \ˌmē-dē-'ä-krə-tē\ *noun, plural* **-ties** (1531)
1 a : the quality or state of being mediocre **b :** moderate ability or value
2 : a mediocre person
med·i·tate \'me-də-ˌtāt\ *verb* **-tat·ed; -tat·ing** [Latin *meditatus*, past participle of *meditari*, frequentative of *medēri* to remedy — more at MEDICAL] (1560)
intransitive verb
: to engage in contemplation or reflection
transitive verb
1 : to focus one's thoughts on **:** reflect on or ponder over
2 : to plan or project in the mind **:** INTEND, PURPOSE
synonym see PONDER
— **med·i·ta·tor** \-ˌtā-tər\ *noun*
med·i·ta·tion \ˌme-də-'tā-shən\ *noun* (13th century)

1 : a discourse intended to express its author's reflections or to guide others in contemplation
2 : the act or process of meditating
med·i·ta·tive \'me-də-ˌtā-tiv\ *adjective* (circa 1656)
1 : disposed or given to meditation
2 : marked by or conducive to meditation
— **med·i·ta·tive·ly** *adverb*
— **med·i·ta·tive·ness** *noun*
Med·i·ter·ra·nean \ˌme-də-tə-'rā-nē-ən, -nyən\ *adjective* (15th century)
1 a : of, relating to, or characteristic of the Mediterranean Sea **b :** of, relating to, or characteristic of the peoples, lands, or cultures bordering the Mediterranean Sea
2 *not capitalized* [Latin *mediterraneus*, from *medius* middle + *terra* land — more at TERRACE] **:** enclosed or nearly enclosed with land
3 : of or relating to a group or physical type of the Caucasian race characterized by medium or short stature, slender build, dolichocephaly, and dark complexion
Mediterranean flour moth *noun* (1895)
: a small largely gray and black nearly cosmopolitan pyralid moth (*Anagasta kuehniella*) whose larva destroys processed grain products
Mediterranean fruit fly *noun* (1907)
: a small widely distributed dipteran fly (*Ceratitis capitata*) with black-and-white markings whose larva lives and feeds in ripening fruit
¹me·di·um \'mē-dē-əm\ *noun, plural* **medi·ums** *or* **me·dia** \-dē-ə\ [Latin, from neuter of *medius* middle — more at MID] (1593)
1 a : something in a middle position **b :** a middle condition or degree **:** MEAN
2 : a means of effecting or conveying something: as **a** (1) **:** a substance regarded as the means of transmission of a force or effect (2) **:** a surrounding or enveloping substance (3) **:** the tenuous material (as gas and dust) in space that exists outside large agglomerations of matter (as stars) ⟨interstellar *medium*⟩ **b** *plural usually* media (1) **:** a channel or system of communication, information, or entertainment — compare MASS MEDIUM (2) **:** a publication or broadcast that carries advertising (3) **:** a mode of artistic expression or communication (4) **:** something (as a magnetic disk) on which information may be stored **c :** GO-BETWEEN, INTERMEDIARY **d** *plural mediums* **:** an individual held to be a channel of communication between the earthly world and a world of spirits **e :** material or technical means of artistic expression
3 a : a condition or environment in which something may function or flourish **b** *plural media* (1) **:** a nutrient system for the artificial cultivation of cells or organisms and especially bacteria (2) **:** a fluid or solid in which organic structures are placed (as for preservation or mounting) **c :** a liquid with which pigment is mixed by a painter
usage see MEDIA
²medium *adjective* (1711)
: intermediate in quantity, quality, position, size, or degree
medium frequency *noun* (1920)
: a radio frequency between high frequency and low frequency — see RADIO FREQUENCY table
me·di·um·is·tic \ˌmē-dē-ə-'mis-tik\ *adjective* (1868)
: of, relating to, or having the qualities of a spiritualistic medium
medium of exchange (1714)
: something commonly accepted in exchange for goods and services and recognized as representing a standard of value
me·di·um·ship \'mē-dē-əm-ˌship\ *noun* (1868)
: the capacity, function, or profession of a spiritualistic medium
med·lar \'med-lər\ *noun* [Middle English *medeler*, from Middle French *medlier*, from *medle* medlar fruit, from Latin *mespilum*, from Greek *mespilon*] (14th century)

: a small Eurasian tree (*Mespilus germanica*) of the rose family whose fruit resembles a crab apple and is used in preserves; *also* **:** its fruit
¹med·ley \'med-lē\ *noun, plural* **medleys** [Middle English *medle*, from Middle French *medlee*, from feminine of *medlé*, past participle of *medler* to mix — more at MEDDLE] (14th century)
1 *archaic* **:** MELEE
2 : a diverse assortment or mixture; *especially* **:** HODGEPODGE
3 : a musical composition made up of a series of songs or short musical pieces
²medley *adjective* (14th century)
: MIXED, MOTLEY
medley relay *noun* (1949)
: a relay race in swimming in which each member of a team uses a different stroke
me·dul·la \mə-'də-lə\ *noun, plural* **-las** *or* **-lae** \-(ˌ)lē, -ˌlī\ [Middle English, from Latin] (15th century)
1 *plural* **medullae a :** MARROW 1 **b :** MEDULLA OBLONGATA
2 a : the inner or deep part of an animal or plant structure ⟨the adrenal *medulla*⟩ **b :** MYELIN SHEATH
medulla ob·lon·ga·ta \-ˌä-ˌbloŋ-'gä-tə\ *noun, plural* **medulla oblongatas** *or* **medullae ob·lon·ga·tae** \-'gä-tē, -ˌtī\ [New Latin, literally, oblong medulla] (1676)
: the part of the vertebrate brain that is continuous posteriorly with the spinal cord and that contains the centers controlling involuntary vital functions — see BRAIN illustration
med·ul·lary \'me-dᵊl-ˌer-ē, 'me-jə-ˌler-; mə-'dᵊl-ə-rē\ *adjective* (1620)
1 : of or relating to the pith of a plant
2 : of or relating to a medulla and especially the medulla oblongata
medullary ray *noun* (1830)
1 : a primary tissue composed of radiating bands of parenchyma cells extending between the vascular bundles of herbaceous dicotyledonous stems and connecting the pith with the cortex
2 : VASCULAR RAY
medullary sheath *noun* (circa 1846)
: MYELIN SHEATH
med·ul·lat·ed \'me-dᵊl-ˌā-təd, 'me-jə-ˌlā-\ *adjective* (1867)
1 : MYELINATED
2 : having a medulla — used of fibers other than nerve fibers
me·dul·lo·blas·to·ma \mə-ˌdə-lō-ˌblas-'tō-mə\ *noun, plural* **-tomas** *also* **-to·ma·ta** \-'tō-mə-tə\ [New Latin, from *medulla* + *-o-* + *blast-* + *-oma*] (1925)
: a malignant tumor of the central nervous system arising in the cerebellum especially in children
me·du·sa \mi-'dü-sə, -'dyü-, -zə\ *noun*
1 *capitalized* [Latin, from Greek *Medousa*] **:** a mortal Gorgon who is slain when decapitated by Perseus
2 *plural* **me·du·sae** \-ˌsē, -ˌzē, -ˌsī, -ˌzī\ [New Latin, from Latin] **:** JELLYFISH 1a
— **me·du·san** \-sᵊn, -zᵊn\ *adjective or noun*
— **me·du·soid** \-ˌsȯid, -ˌzȯid\ *adjective or noun*
meed \'mēd\ *noun* [Middle English, from Old English *mēd*; akin to Old High German *miata* reward, Greek *misthos*] (before 12th century)
1 *archaic* **:** an earned reward or wage
2 : a fitting return or recompense
meek \'mēk\ *adjective* [Middle English, of Scandinavian origin; akin to Old Norse *mjūkr* gentle; akin to Welsh *mwyth* soft] (13th century)

1 : enduring injury with patience and without resentment **:** MILD
2 : deficient in spirit and courage **:** SUBMISSIVE
3 : not violent or strong **:** MODERATE
— **meek·ly** adverb
— **meek·ness** noun

meer·kat \'mir-ˌkat\ noun [Afrikaans, from Dutch, a kind of monkey, from Middle Dutch meercatte monkey, from meer sea + catte cat] (1801)
: any of several African mongooses; especially **:** a burrowing highly social mammal (Suricata suricatta) of southern Africa that is chiefly grayish with inconspicuous black markings

meer·schaum \'mir-shəm, -ˌshȯm\ noun [German, from Meer sea + Schaum foam] (1784)
1 : a fine light white clayey mineral that is a hydrous magnesium silicate found chiefly in Asia Minor and is used especially for tobacco pipes
2 : a tobacco pipe of meerschaum

¹meet \'mēt\ verb met \'met\; **meet·ing** [Middle English meten, from Old English mētan; akin to Old English gemōt assembly — more at MOOT] (before 12th century)
transitive verb
1 a : to come into the presence of **:** FIND **b :** to come together with especially at a particular time or place ⟨I'll meet you at the station⟩ **c :** to come into contact or conjunction with **:** JOIN **d :** to appear to the perception of
2 : to encounter as antagonist or foe **:** OPPOSE
3 : to enter into conference, argument, or personal dealings with
4 : to conform to especially with exactitude and precision ⟨a concept to meet all requirements⟩
5 : to pay fully **:** SETTLE
6 : to cope with ⟨was able to meet every social situation⟩
7 : to provide for ⟨enough money to meet our needs⟩
8 : to become acquainted with
9 : ENCOUNTER, EXPERIENCE
10 : to receive or greet in an official capacity
intransitive verb
1 a : to come face-to-face **b :** to come together for a common purpose **:** ASSEMBLE **c :** to come together as contestants, opponents, or enemies
2 : to form a junction or confluence ⟨the lines meet in a point⟩
3 : to occur together
— **meet·er** noun
— **meet halfway :** to compromise with
— **meet with :** to be subjected to **:** ENCOUNTER ⟨the proposal met with opposition⟩

²meet noun (circa 1834)
1 : the act of assembling for a hunt or for competitive sports
2 : a competition in which individuals (as athletes) match skills

³meet adjective [Middle English mete, from Old English gemǣte; akin to Old English metan to mete] (14th century)
: precisely adapted to a particular situation, need, or circumstance **:** very proper
synonym see FIT
— **meet·ly** adverb

meet·ing \'mē-tiŋ\ noun (14th century)
1 : an act or process of coming together: as **a :** an assembly for a common purpose (as worship) **b :** a session of horse or dog racing
2 : a permanent organizational unit of the Society of Friends
3 : INTERSECTION, JUNCTION

meet·ing·house \-ˌhau̇s\ noun (1632)
: a building used for public assembly and especially for Protestant worship

meeting of minds (1939)
: AGREEMENT, CONCORD

mef·e·nam·ic acid \ˌme-fə-'na-mik-\ noun [dimethyl- + fen- (by shortening & alteration from phenyl) + aminobenzoic acid] (circa 1964)
: a drug $C_{15}H_{15}NO_2$ used as an anti-inflammatory

mega- or **meg-** combining form [Greek, from megas large — more at MUCH]
1 a : great **:** large ⟨megaspore⟩ **b :** greatly surpassing others of its kind ⟨megahit⟩
2 : million **:** multiplied by one million ⟨megohm⟩ ⟨megacycle⟩

mega·bar \'me-gə-ˌbär\ noun [International Scientific Vocabulary] (1903)
: a unit of pressure equal to one million bars

mega·bit \-ˌbit\ noun (1956)
: one million bits

mega·buck \-ˌbək\ noun (1946)
: one million dollars; also **:** an indeterminately large sum of money — usually used in plural

mega·byte \-ˌbīt\ noun [from the fact that 1,048,576 (2^{20}) is the power of 2 closest to one million] (1970)
: a unit of computer information storage capacity equal to 1,048,576 bytes

mega·city \-ˌsi-tē\ noun (1968)
: MEGALOPOLIS 1

mega·cor·po·ra·tion \ˌme-gə-ˌkȯr-pə-'rā-shən\ noun (1973)
: a huge and powerful corporation

mega·cy·cle \'me-gə-ˌsī-kəl\ noun (1926)
: one million cycles; especially **:** MEGAHERTZ

mega·deal \-ˌdēl\ noun (1981)
: a business deal involving a lot of money

mega·death \-ˌdeth\ noun (1953)
: one million deaths — usually used as a unit in reference to nuclear warfare

mega·dose \-ˌdōs\ noun (1973)
: a large dose (as of a vitamin)

mega·fau·na \-ˌfȯ-nə, -ˌfä-\ noun (1935)
: fauna consisting of individuals large enough to be visible to the naked eye
— **mega·fau·nal** \-nᵊl\ adjective

mega·ga·mete \ˌme-gə-'ga-ˌmēt also -gə-ˈmēt\ noun (1891)
: MACROGAMETE

mega·ga·me·to·phyte \-gə-'mē-tə-ˌfīt\ noun (1933)
: the female gametophyte produced by a megaspore

mega·hertz \'me-gə-ˌhərts, -ˌherts\ noun [International Scientific Vocabulary] (1941)
: a unit of frequency equal to one million hertz — abbreviation MHz

mega·hit \-ˌhit\ noun (1982)
: something (as a motion picture) that is extremely successful

mega·kar·yo·cyte \ˌme-gə-'kar-ē-ō-ˌsīt\ noun (1890)
: a large cell that has a lobulated nucleus, is found especially in the bone marrow, and is the source of blood platelets
— **mega·kar·yo·cyt·ic** \-ˌkar-ē-ō-'si-tik\ adjective

megal- or **megalo-** combining form [New Latin, from Greek, from megal-, megas — more at MUCH]
: large **:** of giant size ⟨megalopolis⟩ **:** grandiose ⟨megalomania⟩

mega·lith \'me-gə-ˌlith\ noun (1853)
: a very large usually rough stone used in prehistoric cultures as a monument or building block
— **mega·lith·ic** \ˌme-gə-'li-thik\ adjective

megalith

meg·a·lo·blast \'me-gə-lō-ˌblast\ noun (1899)
: a large erythroblast that appears in the blood especially in pernicious anemia
— **meg·a·lo·blas·tic** \ˌme-gə-lō-'blas-tik\ adjective

meg·a·lo·ma·nia \ˌme-gə-lō-'mā-nē-ə, -nyə\ noun [New Latin] (circa 1890)
1 : a mania for great or grandiose performance

2 : a delusional mental disorder that is marked by infantile feelings of personal omnipotence and grandeur
— **meg·a·lo·ma·ni·ac** \-'mā-nē-ˌak\ adjective or noun
— **meg·a·lo·ma·ni·a·cal** \-mə-'nī-ə-kəl\ also **meg·a·lo·man·ic** \-'ma-nik\ adjective
— **meg·a·lo·ma·ni·a·cal·ly** \-mə-'nī-ə-k(ə-)lē\ adverb

meg·a·lop·o·lis \ˌme-gə-'lä-pə-ləs\ noun (circa 1828)
1 : a very large city
2 : a thickly populated region centering in a metropolis or embracing several metropolises
— **meg·a·lo·pol·i·tan** \-lō-'pä-lə-t°n\ noun or adjective

-megaly noun combining form [New Latin -megalia, from Greek megal-, megas]
: abnormal enlargement ⟨hepatomegaly⟩

mega·par·sec \ˌme-gə-'pär-ˌsek\ noun [International Scientific Vocabulary] (1933)
: a unit of measure for distances in intergalactic space equal to one million parsecs

¹mega·phone \'me-gə-ˌfōn\ noun (1878)
: a cone-shaped device used to intensify or direct the voice
— **mega·phon·ic** \ˌme-gə-'fä-nik\ adjective

²megaphone (1901)
transitive verb
: to transmit or address through or as if through a megaphone
intransitive verb
: to speak through or as if through a megaphone

mega·proj·ect \-ˌprä-ˌjekt, -jikt also -ˌprō-\ noun (1982)
: a major project or undertaking (as in business or construction)

Me·gar·i·an \mə-'gar-ē-ən, me-\ adjective (1603)
: of or relating to a Socratic school of philosophy founded by Euclid of Megara and noted for its subtle attention to logic
— **Megarian** noun

Me·gar·ic \-'gar-ik\ adjective (1656)
: MEGARIAN
— **Megaric** noun

mega·scop·ic \ˌme-gə-'skä-pik\ adjective [mega- + -scopic (as in microscopic)] (1879)
1 : MACROSCOPIC 1 ⟨megascopic features of leaves⟩
2 : based on or relating to observations made with the unaided eye
— **mega·scop·i·cal·ly** \-pi-k(ə-)lē\ adverb

mega·spo·ran·gi·um \ˌme-gə-spə-'ran-jē-əm\ noun [New Latin] (1886)
: a sporangium that develops only megaspores

mega·spore \'me-gə-ˌspōr, -ˌspȯr\ noun [International Scientific Vocabulary] (1858)
: a spore in heterosporous plants that gives rise to female gametophytes and is generally larger than a microspore
— **mega·spor·ic** \ˌme-gə-'spōr-ik, -'spȯr-\ adjective

mega·spo·ro·gen·e·sis \ˌme-gə-ˌspōr-ə-'je-nə-səs, -ˌspȯr-\ noun [New Latin] (circa 1928)
: the formation and maturation of a megaspore

mega·spo·ro·phyll \-'spōr-ə-ˌfil, -'spȯr-\ noun (circa 1899)
: a sporophyll that develops only megasporangia

mega·star \'me-gə-ˌstär\ noun (1975)
: SUPERSTAR

mega·ton \'me-gə-ˌtən\ noun (1952)
: an explosive force equivalent to that of one million tons of TNT

mega·ton·nage \-ˌtə-nij\ noun (1955)
: the destructive capability expressed in megatons especially of a collection of nuclear weapons

mega·vi·ta·min \ˌme-gə-'vī-tə-mən, British usually -'vi-\ adjective (1970)
: relating to or consisting of very large doses of vitamins ⟨megavitamin therapy⟩

mega·vi·ta·mins \-mənz\ *noun plural* (1974)
: a large quantity of vitamins

mega·watt \'me-gə-ˌwät\ *noun* [International Scientific Vocabulary] (circa 1900)
: one million watts

me·gil·lah \mə-'gi-lə\ *noun* [Yiddish *megile*, from Hebrew *mĕgillāh* scroll, volume (used especially of the Book of Esther, read aloud at the Purim celebration)] (circa 1952)
slang **:** a long involved story or account ⟨the whole *megillah*⟩

me·gilp \mə-'gilp\ *noun* [origin unknown] (1768)
: a gelatinous preparation commonly of linseed oil and mastic varnish that is used by artists as a vehicle for oil colors

meg·ohm \'meg-ˌōm\ *noun* [International Scientific Vocabulary] (circa 1868)
: one million ohms

me·grim \'mē-grəm\ *noun* [Middle English *migreime*, from Middle French *migraine* — more at MIGRAINE] (14th century)
1 a : MIGRAINE **b :** VERTIGO, DIZZINESS
2 a : FANCY, WHIM **b** *plural* **:** low spirits

Mei·ji \'mā-(ˌ)jē\ *noun* [Japanese, literally, enlightened rule] (1873)
: the period of the reign (1868–1912) of Emperor Mutsuhito of Japan

mei·kle \'mē-kəl\ *variant of* MICKLE

mei·ny *noun, plural* **meinies** [Middle English *meynie* — more at MENIAL] (13th century)
1 \'mā-nē\ *archaic* **:** RETINUE, COMPANY
2 \'men-yē\ *chiefly Scottish* **:** MULTITUDE

mei·o·sis \mī-'ō-səs\ *noun* [New Latin, from Greek *meiōsis* diminution, from *meioun* to diminish, from *meiōn* less; akin to Sanskrit *mīyate* he diminishes] (1550)
1 : the presentation of a thing with underemphasis especially in order to achieve a greater effect **:** UNDERSTATEMENT
2 : the cellular process that results in the number of chromosomes in gamete-producing cells being reduced to one half and that involves a reduction division in which one of each pair of homologous chromosomes passes to each daughter cell and a mitotic division — compare MITOSIS
— **mei·ot·ic** \mī-'ä-tik\ *adjective*
— **mei·ot·i·cal·ly** \-ti-k(ə-)lē\ *adverb*

Meis·sen \'mī-sᵊn\ *noun* [*Meissen*, Saxony, Germany] (1863)
: a ceramic ware made at Meissen near Dresden; *especially* **:** a European porcelain developed under the patronage of the king of Saxony about 1715 and used for both ornamental and table wares — called also *Meissen china, Meissen ware*

Mei·ster·sing·er \'mīs-tər-ˌsiŋ-ər, -ˌziŋ-\ *noun, plural* **Meistersinger** *or* **Meister·singers** [German, from Middle High German, from *meister* master + *singer* singer] (1845)
: a member of any of various German guilds formed chiefly in the 15th and 16th centuries by workingmen and craftsmen for the cultivation of poetry and music

mel·a·mine \'me-lə-ˌmēn\ *noun* [German *Melamin*] (circa 1835)
1 : a white crystalline organic base $C_3H_6N_6$ with a high melting point that is used especially in melamine resins
2 : a melamine resin or a plastic made from such a resin

melamine resin *noun* (1939)
: a thermosetting resin made from melamine and an aldehyde and used especially in molded or laminated products, adhesives, and coatings

melan- *or* **melano-** *combining form* [Middle English, from Middle French, from Late Latin, from Greek, from *melan-, melas;* perhaps akin to Lithuanian *mėlynas* blue, Sanskrit *malina* dirty]
1 : black **:** dark ⟨*melanic*⟩ ⟨*melanin*⟩
2 : melanin ⟨*melanophore*⟩

mel·an·cho·lia \ˌme-lən-'kō-lē-ə\ *noun* [New Latin, from Late Latin, melancholy] (circa 1693)
: a mental condition characterized by extreme depression, bodily complaints, and often hallucinations and delusions; *especially* **:** a manic-depressive psychosis
— **mel·an·cho·li·ac** \-lē-ˌak\ *noun*

mel·an·chol·ic \ˌme-lən-'kä-lik\ *adjective* (14th century)
1 : of, relating to, or subject to melancholy **:** DEPRESSED
2 : of or relating to melancholia
3 : tending to depress the spirits **:** SADDENING
— **melancholic** *noun*

¹mel·an·choly \'me-lən-ˌkä-lē\ *noun, plural* **-chol·ies** [Middle English *malencolie*, from Middle French *melancolie*, from Late Latin *melancholia*, from Greek, from *melan-* + *cholē* bile — more at GALL] (14th century)
1 a : an abnormal state attributed to an excess of black bile and characterized by irascibility or depression **b :** BLACK BILE **c :** MELANCHOLIA
2 a : depression of spirits **:** DEJECTION **b :** a pensive mood

²melancholy *adjective* (14th century)
1 a : suggestive or expressive of melancholy ⟨sang in a *melancholy* voice⟩ **b :** causing or tending to cause sadness or depression of mind or spirit **:** DISMAL ⟨a *melancholy* thought⟩
2 a : depressed in spirits **:** DEJECTED, SAD **b :** PENSIVE

Mel·a·ne·sian \ˌme-lə-'nē-zhən, -shən\ *noun* (1849)
1 : a language group consisting of the Austronesian languages of Melanesia
2 : a member of the dominant native group of Melanesia
— **Melanesian** *adjective*

mé·lange \mā-'läⁿzh, -'länj\ *noun* [French, from Middle French, from *mesler, meler* to mix — more at MEDDLE] (1653)
: a mixture often of incongruous elements

¹me·lan·ic \mə-'la-nik\ *adjective* (1826)
1 : MELANOTIC
2 : affected with or characterized by melanism

²melanic *noun* (1952)
: a melanic individual

mel·a·nin \'me-lə-nən\ *noun* (1843)
: a dark brown or black animal or plant pigment

mel·a·nism \'me-lə-ˌni-zəm\ *noun* (1843)
1 : an increased amount of black or nearly black pigmentation (as of skin, feathers, or hair) of an individual or kind of organism
2 : intense human pigmentation of the skin, eyes, and hair
— **mel·a·nis·tic** \ˌme-lə-'nis-tik\ *adjective*

mel·a·nite \'me-lə-ˌnīt\ *noun* [German *Melanit*, from *melan-*] (circa 1807)
: a black andradite garnet
— **mel·a·nit·ic** \ˌme-lə-'ni-tik\ *adjective*

mel·a·nize \'me-lə-ˌnīz\ *transitive verb* **-nized; -niz·ing** (1885)
1 : to convert into or infiltrate with melanin
2 : to make dark or black
— **mel·a·ni·za·tion** \ˌme-lə-nə-'zā-shən\ *noun*

me·la·no·blast \mə-'la-nə-ˌblast, 'me-lə-nō-\ *noun* [International Scientific Vocabulary] (1901)
: a cell that is a precursor of a melanocyte or melanophore

me·la·no·cyte \mə-'la-nə-ˌsīt, 'me-lə-nō-\ *noun* [International Scientific Vocabulary] (circa 1890)
: an epidermal cell that produces melanin

melanocyte–stimulating hormone *noun* (1953)
: either of two vertebrate hormones of the pituitary gland especially of reptiles and amphibians that darken the skin by stimulating melanin dispersion in pigment-containing cells — called also *melanophore-stimulating hormone*

me·la·no·gen·e·sis \mə-ˌla-nə-'je-nə-səs, ˌme-lə-nō-\ *noun* [New Latin] (circa 1928)
: the formation of melanin

mel·a·no·ma \ˌme-lə-'nō-mə\ *noun, plural* **-mas** *also* **-ma·ta** \-mə-tə\ [New Latin] (1830)
: a usually malignant tumor containing dark pigment

me·la·no·phore \mə-'la-nə-ˌfōr, 'me-lə-nə-, -ˌför\ *noun* (1903)
: a melanin-containing cell especially of fishes, amphibians, and reptiles

me·la·no·some \-ˌsōm\ *noun* (1940)
: a melanin-producing granule in a melanocyte

mel·a·not·ic \ˌme-lə-'nä-tik\ *adjective* (1829)
: having or characterized by black pigmentation

mel·a·to·nin \ˌme-lə-'tō-nən\ *noun* [Greek *melas* black + *-tonin* (as in *serotonin*)] (1958)
: a vertebrate hormone of the pineal gland that produces lightening of the skin by causing concentration of melanin in pigment-containing cells

mel·ba toast \'mel-bə-\ *noun* [Nellie *Melba*] (1925)
: very thin crisp toast

Mel·chite *or* **Mel·kite** \'mel-ˌkīt\ *noun* [Medieval Latin *Melchita*, from Middle Greek *Melchitēs*, literally, royalist, from Syriac *malkā* king] (1619)
1 : an Eastern Christian chiefly of Syria and Egypt adhering to Chalcedonian orthodoxy in preference to Monophysitism
2 : a member of a Uniate body derived from the Melchites

¹Mel·chiz·e·dek \mel-'ki-zə-ˌdek\ *noun* [Greek *Melchisedek*, from Hebrew *Malkîṣedheq*]
: a priest-king of Jerusalem who prepared a ritual meal for Abraham and received tithes from him

²Melchizedek *adjective* (1842)
: of or relating to the higher order of the Mormon priesthood

¹meld \'meld\ *verb* [German *melden* to announce, from Old High German *meldōn;* akin to Old English *meldian* to announce, Lithuanian *malda* prayer] (1897)
transitive verb
: to declare or announce (a card or combination of cards) for a score in a card game especially by placing face up on the table
intransitive verb
: to declare a card or combination of cards as a meld

²meld *noun* (1897)
: a card or combination of cards that is or can be melded in a card game

³meld *noun* [blend of *melt* and *weld*] (1936)
: MERGE, BLEND

⁴meld *noun* (1954)
: BLEND, MIXTURE

me·lee *also* **mê·lée** \'mā-ˌlā, mā-'\ *noun* [French *mêlée*, from Old French *meslee*, from *mesler* to mix — more at MEDDLE] (circa 1648)
: a confused struggle; *especially* **:** a hand-to-hand fight among several people

mel·ic \'me-lik\ *adjective* [Latin *melicus*, from Greek *melikos*, from *melos* song — more at MELODY] (1699)
: of or relating to song **:** LYRIC; *especially* **:** of or relating to Greek lyric poetry of the 7th and 6th centuries B.C.

mel·i·lot \'me-lə-ˌlät\ *noun* [Middle English *melilot*, from Old French *melilot*, from Latin *melilotos*, from Greek *melilōtos*, from *meli* honey + *lōtos* clover, lotus — more at MELLIFLUOUS] (14th century)

\ə\ **abut** \ᵊ\ **kitten** \ər\ **further** \a\ **ash** \ā\ **ace**
\ä\ **mop, mar** \au̇\ **out** \ch\ **chin** \e\ **bet** \ē\ **easy**
\g\ **go** \i\ **hit** \ī\ **ice** \j\ **job** \ŋ\ **sing** \ō\ **go**
\ȯ\ **law** \ȯi\ **boy** \th\ **thin** \t̲h̲\ **the** \ü\ **loot** \u̇\ **foot**
\y\ **yet** \zh\ **vision** *see also* Guide to Pronunciation

: SWEET CLOVER; *especially* : a yellow-flowered sweet clover (*Melilotus officinalis*)

me·lio·rate \'mēl-yə-,rāt, 'mē-lē-ə-\ *verb* **-rat·ed; -rat·ing** [Late Latin *melioratus*, past participle of *meliorare*, from Latin *melior* better; akin to Latin *multus* much, Greek *mala* very] (1542)
: AMELIORATE
— **me·lio·ra·tion** \,mēl-yə-'rā-shən, ,mē-lē-ə-\ *noun*
— **me·lio·ra·tive** \'mēl-yə-,rā-tiv, 'mē-lē-ə-\ *adjective*
— **me·lio·ra·tor** \-,rā-tər\ *noun*

me·lio·rism \'mēl-yə-,ri-zəm, 'mē-lē-ə-\ *noun* (1877)
: the belief that the world tends to become better and that humans can aid its betterment
— **me·lio·rist** \-rist\ *adjective or noun*
— **me·lio·ris·tic** \,mēl-yə-'ris-tik, ,mē-lē-ə-\ *adjective*

me·lis·ma \mi-'liz-mə\ *noun, plural* **-ma·ta** \-mə-tə\ [New Latin, from Greek, song, melody, from *melizein* to sing, from *melos* song] (circa 1880)
1 : a group of notes or tones sung on one syllable in plainsong
2 : melodic embellishment or ornamentation
3 : CADENZA
— **mel·is·mat·ic** \,me-ləz-'ma-tik\ *adjective*

mell \'mel\ *verb* [Middle English, from Middle French *mesler*] (14th century)
: MIX

mel·lif·lu·ent \me-'li-flə-wənt\ *adjective* [Late Latin *mellifluent-, mellifluens*, from Latin *mell-, mel* + *fluent-, fluens*, present participle of *fluere*] (1601)
: MELLIFLUOUS
— **mel·lif·lu·ent·ly** *adverb*

mel·lif·lu·ous \me-'li-flə-wəs, mə-\ *adjective* [Middle English *mellyfluous*, from Late Latin *mellifluus*, from Latin *mell-, mel* honey + *fluere* to flow; akin to Gothic *milith* honey, Greek *melit-, meli*] (15th century)
1 : having a smooth rich flow ⟨a *mellifluous* voice⟩
2 : filled with something (as honey) that sweetens ◇
— **mel·lif·lu·ous·ly** *adverb*
— **mel·lif·lu·ous·ness** *noun*

mel·lo·phone \'me-lə-,fōn\ *noun* [¹*mellow* + *-phone*] (1926)
: a valved brass instrument similar in form and range to the French horn

mel·lo·tron \'me-lə-,trän\ *noun* [from *Mellotron*, a trademark] (1967)
: an electronic keyboard instrument programmed to produce the tape-recorded sounds usually of orchestral instruments

¹**mel·low** \'me-(,)lō\ *adjective* [Middle English *melowe*] (15th century)
1 a *of a fruit* : tender and sweet because of ripeness b *of a wine* : well aged and pleasingly mild
2 a : made gentle by age or experience b : rich and full but free from garishness or stridency c : warmed and relaxed by or as if by liquor d : PLEASANT, AGREEABLE e : LAID-BACK
3 *of soil* : having a soft and loamy consistency
— **mel·low·ly** *adverb*
— **mel·low·ness** *noun*

²**mellow** (1572)
transitive verb
: to make mellow
intransitive verb
: to become mellow

me·lo·de·on \mə-'lō-dē-ən\ *noun* [German *Melodion*, from *Melodie* melody, from Old French] (1847)
: a small reed organ in which a suction bellows draws air inward through the reeds

me·lod·ic \mə-'lä-dik\ *adjective* (1823)
: of or relating to melody : MELODIOUS
— **me·lod·i·cal·ly** \-di-k(ə-)lē\ *adverb*

me·lo·di·ous \mə-'lō-dē-əs\ *adjective* (14th century)

1 : having a pleasing melody
2 : of, relating to, or producing melody
— **me·lo·di·ous·ly** *adverb*
— **me·lo·di·ous·ness** *noun*

mel·o·dist \'me-lə-dist\ *noun* (1789)
1 : SINGER
2 : a composer of melodies

mel·o·dize \'me-lə-,dīz\ *verb* **-dized; -diz·ing** (1662)
intransitive verb
: to compose a melody
transitive verb
: to make melodious : set to melody
— **mel·o·diz·er** *noun*

melo·dra·ma \'me-lə-,drä-mə, -,dra-\ *noun* [modification of French *mélodrame*, from Greek *melos* song + French *drame* drama, from Late Latin *drama*] (1809)
1 a : a work (as a movie or play) characterized by extravagant theatricality and by the predominance of plot and physical action over characterization b : the genre of dramatic literature constituted by such works
2 : something resembling a melodrama or having a melodramatic quality
— **melo·dra·ma·tist** \,me-lə-'dra-mə-tist, -'drä-\ *noun*

melo·dra·mat·ic \,me-lə-drə-'ma-tik\ *adjective* (1816)
1 : of, relating to, or characteristic of melodrama
2 : appealing to the emotions : SENSATIONAL
synonym see DRAMATIC
— **melo·dra·mat·i·cal·ly** \-ti-k(ə-)lē\ *adverb*

melo·dra·mat·ics \-tiks\ *noun plural but singular or plural in construction* (1915)
: melodramatic conduct or writing

melo·dra·ma·tise *British variant of* MELODRAMATIZE

melo·dra·ma·tize \,me-lə-'dra-mə-,tīz, -'drä-\ *transitive verb* (1820)
1 : to make melodramatic ⟨*melodramatize* a situation⟩
2 : to make a melodrama of (as a novel)
— **melo·dra·ma·ti·za·tion** \-,dra-mə-tə-'zā-shən, -,drä-\ *noun*

mel·o·dy \'me-lə-dē\ *noun, plural* **-dies** [Middle English *melodie*, from Old French, from Late Latin *melodia*, from Greek *melōidia* chanting, music, from *melos* limb, musical phrase, song (probably akin to Breton *mell* joint) + *aeidein* to sing — more at ODE] (13th century)
1 : a sweet or agreeable succession or arrangement of sounds : TUNEFULNESS
2 : a rhythmic succession of single tones organized as an aesthetic whole

mel·on \'me-lən\ *noun, often attributive* [Middle English, from Middle French, from Late Latin *melon-, melo*, short for Latin *melopepon-, melopepo*, from Greek *mēlopepōn*, from *mēlon* apple + *pepōn*, an edible gourd — more at PUMPKIN] (14th century)
1 : any of various gourds (as a muskmelon or watermelon) usually eaten raw as fruits
2 : something rounded like a melon: as a : the rounded organ in the front of the head of some cetaceans b *plural, slang* : large breasts
3 a : a surplus of profits available for distribution to stockholders b : a financial windfall

mel·pha·lan \'mel-fə-,lan\ *noun* [probably from *methanol* + *phenylalan*ine] (circa 1964)
: an antineoplastic drug $C_{13}H_{18}Cl_2N_2O_2$

Mel·pom·e·ne \mel-'pä-mə-(,)nē\ *noun* [Latin, from Greek *Melpomenē*]
: the Greek Muse of tragedy

¹**melt** \'melt\ *verb* [Middle English, from Old English *meltan*; akin to Old Norse *melta* to digest, Greek *meldein* to melt] (before 12th century)
intransitive verb
1 : to become altered from a solid to a liquid state usually by heat

2 a : DISSOLVE, DISINTEGRATE ⟨the sugar *melted* in the coffee⟩ b : to disappear as if by dissolving ⟨her anger *melted* at his kind words⟩
3 *obsolete* : to become subdued or crushed (as by sorrow)
4 : to become mild, tender, or gentle
5 : to lose outline or distinctness : BLEND
transitive verb
1 : to reduce from a solid to a liquid state usually by heat
2 : to cause to disappear or disperse
3 : to make tender or gentle : SOFTEN
— **melt·abil·i·ty** \,mel-tə-'bi-lə-tē\ *noun*
— **melt·able** \'mel-tə-bəl\ *adjective*
— **melt·er** *noun*

²**melt** *noun* (1854)
1 a : material in the molten state b : the mass melted at a single operation or the quantity melted during a specified period
2 a : the action or process of melting or the period during which it occurs ⟨the spring *melt*⟩ b : the condition of being melted
3 : a sandwich with melted cheese ⟨a tuna *melt*⟩

³**melt** *noun* [Middle English *milte*, from Old English; akin to Old High German *miltzi* spleen] (before 12th century)
: SPLEEN; *especially* : spleen of slaughtered animals for use as feed or food

melt·down \'melt-,daùn\ *noun* (1963)
1 : the accidental melting of the core of a nuclear reactor
2 : a rapid or disastrous decline or collapse

melt·ing \'mel-tiṅ\ *adjective* (1565)
: TENDER, DELICATE ⟨a love song's *melting* lyric⟩
— **melt·ing·ly** *adverb*

melting point *noun* (1823)
: the temperature at which a solid melts

melting pot *noun* (1912)
1 a : a place where racial amalgamation and social and cultural assimilation are going on ⟨long cherished the myth of the public school as the *melting pot* —M. R. Berube⟩ b : the population of such a place
2 : a process of blending that often results in invigoration or novelty

mel·ton \'mel-t°n\ *noun* [*Melton* Mowbray, town in England] (1823)
: a heavy smooth woolen fabric with short nap

melt·wa·ter \'melt-,wò-tər, -,wä-\ *noun* (1923)
: water derived from the melting of ice and snow

mem \'mem\ *noun* [Hebrew *mēm*, literally, water] (circa 1823)
: the 13th letter of the Hebrew alphabet — see ALPHABET table

mem·ber \'mem-bər\ *noun, often attributive* [Middle English *membre*, from Old French, from Latin *membrum*; akin to Gothic *mimz* flesh, Greek *mēros* thigh] (14th century)
1 : a body part or organ: as a : LIMB b : PENIS c : a unit of structure in a plant body
2 : one of the individuals composing a group
3 : a person baptized or enrolled in a church
4 : a constituent part of a whole: as a : a syntactic or rhythmic unit of a sentence : CLAUSE

◇ WORD HISTORY
mellifluous Having a much longer history as a sweetener than cane sugar, honey has since ancient times been a symbol of sweetness. In English we continue to speak of those halcyon days following a wedding as a *honeymoon* and to refer to an eloquent orator as *honey-tongued*. Less obviously, we are using the same metaphor when we speak of a voice as being *mellifluous*. In Latin *mel* meant "honey" and *fluere* meant to "to flow," hence the Late Latin word *mellifluus* literally meant "flowing like honey."

b : one of the propositions of a syllogism **c :** one of the elements of a set or class **d :** either of the equated elements in a mathematical equation
synonym see PART

mem·bered \'mem-bərd\ *adjective* (14th century)
: made up of or divided into members

mem·ber·ship \'mem-bər-ˌship\ *noun* (1647)
1 : the state or status of being a member
2 : the body of members ⟨an organization with a large *membership*⟩
3 : the relation between an element of a set or class and the set or class — compare INCLUSION 3

mem·brane \'mem-ˌbrān\ *noun* [Middle English, from Latin *membrana* skin, parchment, from *membrum*] (15th century)
1 : a thin soft pliable sheet or layer especially of animal or plant origin
2 : a piece of parchment forming part of a roll
— mem·braned \'mem-ˌbrānd\ *adjective*

mem·bra·nous \'mem-brə-nəs\ *adjective* (1597)
1 : of, relating to, or resembling membrane
2 : thin, pliable, and often somewhat transparent ⟨*membranous* leaves⟩
3 : characterized or accompanied by the formation of a usually abnormal membrane or membranous layer ⟨*membranous* croup⟩
— mem·bra·nous·ly *adverb*

membranous labyrinth *noun* (1840)
: the sensory structures of the inner ear

me·men·to \mə-'men-(ˌ)tō, ÷mō-\ *noun, plural* **-tos** *or* **-toes** [Middle English, from Latin, remember, imperative of *meminisse* to remember; akin to Latin *ment-, mens* mind — more at MIND] (1580)
: something that serves to warn or remind; *also* **:** SOUVENIR □

me·men·to mo·ri \mə-'men-tō-'mōr-ē, -'mȯr-ē\ *noun, plural* **memento mori** [Latin, remember that you must die] (1596)
: a reminder of mortality; *especially* **:** DEATH'S HEAD

Mem·non \'mem-ˌnän\ *noun* [Greek *Memnōn*]
: an Ethiopian king slain by Achilles at a late stage of the Trojan War

memo \'me-(ˌ)mō\ *noun, plural* **mem·os** (1889)
: MEMORANDUM

mem·oir \'mem-ˌwär, -ˌwȯr\ *noun* [Middle French *memoire*, from *memoire* memory, from Latin *memoria*] (1567)
1 : an official note or report **:** MEMORANDUM
2 a : a narrative composed from personal experience **b :** AUTOBIOGRAPHY — usually used in plural **c :** BIOGRAPHY
3 a : an account of something noteworthy **:** REPORT **b** *plural* **:** the record of the proceedings of a learned society
— mem·oir·ist \-ist\ *noun*

mem·o·ra·bil·ia \ˌme-mə-rə-'bi-lē-ə, -'bē-lē-ə, -'bil-yə\ *noun plural* [Latin, from neuter plural of *memorabilis*] (circa 1807)
: things that are remarkable and worthy of remembrance; *also* **:** things that stir recollection **:** MEMENTOS

mem·o·ra·bil·i·ty \-'bi-lə-tē\ *noun* (circa 1661)
: the quality or state of being easy to remember or worth remembering

mem·o·ra·ble \'mem-rə-bəl, 'mə-mə-rə-, 'me-mər-\ *adjective* [Middle English, from Latin *memorabilis*, from *memorare* to remind, mention, from *memor* mindful] (15th century)
: worth remembering **:** NOTABLE
— mem·o·ra·ble·ness *noun*
— mem·o·ra·bly \-blē\ *adverb*

mem·o·ran·dum \ˌme-mə-'ran-dəm\ *noun, plural* **-dums** *or* **-da** \-də\ [Middle English, to be remembered, from Latin, neuter of *memorandus*, gerundive of *memorare*] (circa 1543)
1 : an informal record; *also* **:** a written reminder

2 : an informal written note of a transaction or proposed instrument
3 a : an informal diplomatic communication **b :** a usually brief communication written for interoffice circulation **c :** a communication that contains directive, advisory, or informative matter □

¹me·mo·ri·al \mə-'mōr-ē-əl, -'mȯr-\ *adjective* [Middle English, from Latin *memorialis*, from *memoria* memory] (14th century)
1 : serving to preserve remembrance **:** COMMEMORATIVE
2 : of or relating to memory
— me·mo·ri·al·ly \-ə-lē\ *adverb*

²memorial *noun* (14th century)
1 : something that keeps remembrance alive: as **a :** MONUMENT **b :** something (as a speech or ceremony) that commemorates **c :** KEEPSAKE, MEMENTO
2 a : RECORD, MEMOIR ⟨language and literature . . . the *memorials* of another age —J. H. Fisher⟩ **b :** MEMORANDUM, NOTE; *specifically* **:** a legal abstract **c :** a statement of facts addressed to a government and often accompanied by a petition or remonstrance

Memorial Day *noun* (1869)
1 : May 30 formerly observed as a legal holiday in most states of the U.S. in remembrance of war dead
2 : the last Monday in May observed as a legal holiday in most states of the U.S.
3 : CONFEDERATE MEMORIAL DAY

me·mo·ri·al·ise *British variant of* MEMORIALIZE

me·mo·ri·al·ist \mə-'mōr-ē-ə-list, -'mȯr-\ *noun* (1706)
1 : a person who writes or signs a memorial
2 : a person who writes a memoir

me·mo·ri·al·ize \-ˌlīz\ *transitive verb* **-ized; -iz·ing** (1798)
1 : to address or petition by a memorial
2 : COMMEMORATE

memorial park *noun* (circa 1928)
: CEMETERY

me·mo·ri·ter \mə-'mȯr-ə-ˌter, -'mär-\ *adjective* [Latin, adverb, by memory, from *memor*] (circa 1812)
: marked by emphasis on memorization

mem·o·rise *British variant of* MEMORIZE

mem·o·rize \'me-mə-ˌrīz\ *transitive verb* **-rized; -riz·ing** (1838)
: to commit to memory **:** learn by heart
— mem·o·riz·able \ˌme-mə-'rī-zə-bəl\ *adjective*
— mem·o·ri·za·tion \ˌme-mə-rə-'zā-shən, ˌme-mə-(ˌ)rī-, ˌmem-rə-\ *noun*
— mem·o·riz·er *noun*

mem·o·ry \'mem-rē, 'me-mə-\ *noun, plural* **-ries** [Middle English *memorie*, from Middle French, from Latin *memor*ia, from *memor* mindful; akin to Old English *gemimor* well-known, Greek *mermēra* care, Sanskrit *smarati* he remembers] (14th century)
1 a : the power or process of reproducing or recalling what has been learned and retained especially through associative mechanisms **b :** the store of things learned and retained from an organism's activity or experience as evidenced by modification of structure or behavior or by recall and recognition
2 a : commemorative remembrance ⟨erected a statue in *memory* of the hero⟩ **b :** the fact or condition of being remembered ⟨days of recent *memory*⟩
3 a : a particular act of recall or recollection **b :** an image or impression of one that is remembered ⟨fond *memories* of her youth⟩ **c :** the time within which past events can be or are remembered ⟨within the *memory* of living men⟩
4 a : a device or a component of a device in which information especially for a computer can be inserted and stored and from which it may be extracted when wanted **b :** capacity for storing information ⟨four megabytes of *memory*⟩

5 : a capacity for showing effects as the result of past treatment or for returning to a former condition — used especially of a material (as metal or plastic) ☆

memory lane *noun* (1954)
: an imaginary path through the nostalgically remembered past — usually used in such phrases as *a walk down memory lane*

memory trace *noun* (1923)
: ENGRAM

mem·sa·hib \'mem-ˌsä-(ˌ)(h)ib, -ˌsäb\ *noun* [Hindi, from English *ma'am* + Hindi *sahib* sahib] (1857)
: a white foreign woman of high social status living in India; *especially* **:** the wife of a British official

men *plural of* MAN

men- *or* **meno-** *combining form* [New Latin, from Greek *mēn* month — more at MOON]
: menstruation ⟨*meno*rrhagia⟩

¹men·ace \'me-nəs\ *noun* [Middle English, from Middle French, from Latin *minacia*, from *minac-, minax* threatening, from *minari* to threaten — more at MOUNT] (14th century)
1 : a show of intention to inflict harm **:** THREAT

☆ **SYNONYMS**
Memory, remembrance, recollection, reminiscence mean the capacity for or the act of remembering, or the thing remembered. MEMORY applies both to the power of remembering and to what is remembered ⟨gifted with a remarkable *memory*⟩ ⟨that incident was now just a distant *memory*⟩. REMEMBRANCE applies to the act of remembering or the fact of being remembered ⟨any *remembrance* of his deceased wife was painful⟩. RECOLLECTION adds an implication of consciously bringing back to mind often with some effort ⟨after a moment's *recollection* he produced the name⟩. REMINISCENCE suggests the recalling of usually pleasant incidents, experiences, or feelings from a remote past ⟨recorded my grandmother's *reminiscences* of her Iowa girlhood⟩.

□ **USAGE**
memento A fairly rare variant of *memento*, spelled with an *o* as its first vowel, is found just often enough in edited prose ⟨a nostalgic *momento* of an earlier century —Joseph Wechsberg (*New Yorker*)⟩ to have been entered in a few dictionaries. Our first evidence for it is in an 1853 letter written by Chauncey A. Goodrich, professor at Yale, Noah Webster's son-in-law, and first editor in chief of Merriam-Webster dictionaries. It has also been found in the writings of George Eliot and Dylan Thomas. Although our file of evidence keeps growing, *momento* is still infrequently used, and many people think it an error. It is best to use *memento*.

memorandum Although some commentators warn against the use of *memoranda* as a singular and condemn the plural *memorandas*, our evidence indicates that these forms are rarely encountered in print. We have a little evidence of the confusion of forms, including use of *memorandum* as a plural, in speech (as at congressional hearings). As plurals *memoranda* and *memorandums* are about equally frequent.

\ə\ **abut** \ᵊ\ **kitten** \ər\ **further** \a\ **ash** \ā\ **ace**
\ä\ **mop, mar** \aů\ **out** \ch\ **chin** \e\ **bet** \ē\ **easy**
\g\ **go** \i\ **hit** \ī\ **ice** \j\ **job** \ŋ\ **sing** \ō\ **go**
\ȯ\ **law** \ȯi\ **boy** \th\ **thin** \t͟h\ **the** \ü\ **loot** \ů\ **foot**
\y\ **yet** \zh\ **vision** *see also* Guide to Pronunciation

2 a : one that represents a threat : DANGER **b** : a person who causes annoyance

²menace *verb* **men·aced; men·ac·ing** (14th century)
transitive verb
1 : to make a show of intention to harm
2 : to represent or pose a threat to : ENDANGER
intransitive verb
: to act in a threatening manner
— **men·ac·ing·ly** \-nə-siŋ-lē\ *adverb*

me·nad *variant of* MAENAD

men·a·di·one \,me-nə-'dī-,ōn, -dī-'\ *noun* [*methyl* + *na*pthalene + *di-* + ket*one*] (1941)
: a yellow crystalline compound $C_{11}H_8O_2$ with the biological activity of natural vitamin K

mé·nage \mā-'näzh\ *noun* [French, from Old French *mesnage* dwelling, from (assumed) Vulgar Latin *mansionaticum*, from Latin *mansion-, mansio* mansion] (1698)
: a domestic establishment : HOUSEHOLD; *also* : HOUSEKEEPING

mé·nage à trois \-ä-'trwä\ *noun* [French, literally, household for three] (1891)
: an arrangement in which three persons (as a married pair and the lover of one of the pair) share sexual relations especially while living together

me·nag·er·ie \mə-'naj-rē, -'na-jə- *also* -'nazh-rē, -'na-zhə-\ *noun* [French *ménagerie*, from Middle French, management of a household or farm, from *menage*] (1676)
1 a : a place where animals are kept and trained especially for exhibition **b :** a collection of wild or foreign animals kept especially for exhibition
2 : a varied mixture 〈a wonderful *menagerie* of royal hangers-on —V. S. Pritchett〉

men·ar·che \'me-,när-kē\ *noun* [New Latin, from *men-* + Greek *archē* beginning] (1900)
: the beginning of the menstrual function; *especially* : the first menstrual period of an individual
— **men·ar·che·al** \,me-när-'kē-əl\ *adjective*

¹mend \'mend\ *verb* [Middle English, short for *amenden* — more at AMEND] (13th century)
transitive verb
1 : to free from faults or defects: as **a :** to improve in manners or morals : REFORM **b :** to set right : CORRECT **c :** to put into good shape or working order again : patch up : REPAIR **d :** to improve or strengthen (as a relationship) by negotiation or conciliation — used chiefly in the phrase *mend fences* 〈spends the weekend *mending* political fences —E. O. Hauser〉 **e** : to restore to health : CURE
2 : to make amends or atonement for 〈least said, soonest *mended*〉
intransitive verb
1 : to improve morally : REFORM
2 : to become corrected or improved
3 : to improve in health; *also* : HEAL ☆
— **mend·able** \'men-də-bəl\ *adjective*
— **mend·er** *noun*

²mend *noun* (14th century)
1 : an act of mending : REPAIR
2 : a mended place
— **on the mend** : getting better : IMPROVING

men·da·cious \men-'dā-shəs\ *adjective* [Latin *mendac-, mendax* — more at AMEND] (1616)
: given to or characterized by deception or falsehood or divergence from absolute truth 〈*mendacious* tales of his adventures〉
synonym see DISHONEST
— **men·da·cious·ly** *adverb*
— **men·da·cious·ness** *noun*

men·dac·i·ty \men-'da-sə-tē\ *noun, plural* **-ties** (1646)
1 : the quality or state of being mendacious
2 : LIE

Men·de \'men-dē, -dā\ *noun, plural* **Mende** *or* **Mendes** (1732)
1 : a Mande language of southern Sierra Leone and eastern Liberia

2 : a member of a people speaking Mende

men·de·le·vi·um \,men-də-'lē-vē-əm, -'lā-\ *noun* [New Latin, from Dmitry *Mendeleyev*] (1955)
: a radioactive element that is artificially produced — see ELEMENT table

Men·de·lian \men-'dē-lē-ən, -'dēl-yən\ *adjective* (1901)
: of, relating to, or according with Mendel's laws or Mendelism
— **Mendelian** *noun*

Mendelian factor *noun* (1927)
: GENE

Mendelian inheritance *noun* (circa 1923)
: PARTICULATE INHERITANCE

Men·del·ism \'men-dᵊl-,i-zəm\ *noun* (1903)
: the principles or the operations of Mendel's laws; *also* : PARTICULATE INHERITANCE
— **Men·del·ist** \-dᵊl-ist\ *adjective or noun*

Men·del's law \'men-dᵊlz-\ *noun* [Gregor *Mendel*] (1903)
1 : a principle in genetics: hereditary units occur in pairs that separate during gamete formation so that every gamete receives but one member of a pair — called also *law of segregation*
2 : a principle in genetics limited and modified by the subsequent discovery of the phenomenon of linkage: the different pairs of hereditary units are distributed to the gametes independently of each other, the gametes combine at random, and the various combinations of hereditary pairs occur in the zygotes according to the laws of chance — called also *law of independent assortment*
3 : a principle in genetics proved subsequently to be subject to many limitations: because one of each pair of hereditary units dominates the other in expression, characters are inherited alternatively on an all-or-nothing basis — called also *law of dominance*

men·di·can·cy \'men-di-kən(t)-sē\ *noun* (1790)
1 : the condition of being a beggar
2 : the practice of begging

men·di·cant \'men-di-kənt\ *noun* [Middle English, from Latin *mendicant-, mendicans*, present participle of *mendicare* to beg, from *mendicus* beggar — more at AMEND] (14th century)
1 : BEGGAR 1
2 *often capitalized* : a member of a religious order (as the Franciscans) combining monastic life and outside religious activity and originally owning neither personal nor community property : FRIAR
— **mendicant** *adjective*

men·dic·i·ty \men-'di-sə-tē\ *noun* [Middle English *mendicite*, from Middle French *mendicité*, from Latin *mendicitat-, mendicitas*, from *mendicus*] (15th century)
: MENDICANCY

Men·e·la·us \,me-nᵊl-'ā-əs\ *noun* [Latin, from Greek *Menelaos*]
: a king of Sparta, brother of Agamemnon, and husband of the abducted Helen of Troy

men·folk \'men-,fōk\ *or* **men·folks** \-,fōks\ *noun plural* (1802)
1 : men in general
2 : the men of a family or community

men·ha·den \men-'hā-dᵊn, mən-\ *noun, plural* **-den** *also* **-dens** [of Algonquian origin; akin to Narraganset *munnawhatteaûg* menhaden] (1792)
: a marine fish (*Brevoortia tyrannus*) of the herring family abundant along the Atlantic coast of the U.S. where it is used for bait or converted into oil and fertilizer; *also* : any of several congeneric fishes

men·hir \'men-,hir\ *noun* [French, from Breton, from *men* stone + *hir* long] (1840)
: a single upright rude monolith usually of prehistoric origin

¹me·nial \'mē-nē-əl, -nyəl\ *noun* (14th century)

: a person doing menial work; *specifically* : a domestic servant or retainer

²menial *adjective* [Middle English *meynial*, from *meynie* household, retinue, from Old French *mesnie*, from (assumed) Vulgar Latin *mansionata*, from Latin *mansion-, mansio* dwelling — more at MANSION] (15th century)
1 : of or relating to servants : LOWLY
2 a : appropriate to a servant : HUMBLE, SERVILE 〈answered in *menial* tones〉 **b :** lacking interest or dignity 〈a *menial* task〉
— **me·nial·ly** *adverb*

Mé·nière's disease \mən-'yerz-, 'men-yərz-\ *noun* [Prosper *Ménière* (died 1862) French physician] (1876)
: a disorder of the membranous labyrinth of the inner ear that is marked by recurrent attacks of dizziness, tinnitus, and deafness — called also *Ménière's syndrome*

mening- *or* **meningo-** *also* **meningi-** *combining form* [New Latin, from *mening-, meninx*]
1 : meninges 〈*meningo*coccus〉 〈*meningi*tis〉
2 : meninges and 〈*meningo*encephalitis〉

men·in·ge·al \,me-nən-'jē-əl\ *adjective* (1829)
: of, relating to, or affecting the meninges

meninges *plural of* MENINX

me·nin·gi·o·ma \mə-,nin-jē-'ō-mə\ *noun, plural* **-mas** *or* **-ma·ta** \-'ō-mə-tə\ [New Latin] (1922)
: a slow-growing encapsulated tumor arising from the meninges and often causing damage by pressing upon the brain and adjacent parts

men·in·gi·tis \,me-nən-'jī-təs\ *noun, plural* **-git·i·des** \-'ji-tə-,dēz\ [New Latin] (1828)
1 : inflammation of the meninges and especially of the pia mater and the arachnoid
2 : a usually bacterial disease in which inflammation of the meninges occurs
— **men·in·git·ic** \-'ji-tik\ *adjective*

me·nin·go·coc·cus \mə-,niŋ-gə-'kä-kəs, -,nin-jə-\ *noun, plural* **-coc·ci** \-'käk-,sī, -,sē; -'kä-,kī, -,kē\ [New Latin] (circa 1893)
: the bacterium (*Neisseria meningitidis*) that causes cerebrospinal meningitis
— **me·nin·go·coc·cal** \-'kä-kəl\ *also* **me·nin·go·coc·cic** \-'käk-sik, -'kä-kik\ *adjective*

me·nin·go·en·ceph·a·li·tis \-gō-ən-,se-fə-'lī-təs, -jō-\ *noun, plural* **-lit·i·des** \-'li-tə-,dēz\ [New Latin] (circa 1860)
: inflammation of the brain and meninges
— **me·nin·go·en·ceph·a·lit·ic** \-'li-tik\ *adjective*

me·ninx \'mē-niŋ(k)s, 'me-\ *noun, plural* **me·nin·ges** \mə-'nin-(,)jēz\ [New Latin, from Greek *mēning-, mēninx* membrane] (1543)
: any of the three membranes that envelop the brain and spinal cord

me·nis·cus \mə-'nis-kəs\ *noun, plural* **me·nis·ci** \-'ni-,skī, -,skē, -,sī\ *also* **me·nis·cus·es** [New Latin, from Greek *mēniskos*, from diminutive of *mēnē* moon, crescent — more at MOON] (1693)
1 : a concavo-convex lens
2 : a crescent or crescent-shaped body
3 : the curved upper surface of a column of liquid
4 : a fibrous cartilage within a joint especially of the knee

☆ **SYNONYMS**
Mend, repair, patch, rebuild mean to put into good order something that has been injured, damaged, or defective. MEND implies making whole or sound something broken, torn, or injured (*mended* the torn dress). REPAIR applies to the fixing of more extensive damage or dilapidation (*repaired* the back steps). PATCH implies an often temporary fixing of a hole or break with new material (*patch* worn jeans). REBUILD suggests making like new without completely replacing (a *rebuilt* automobile engine).

Men·no·nite \'me-nə-ˌnīt\ *noun* [German *Mennonit,* from *Menno* Simons] (1565)
: a member of any of various Protestant groups derived from the Anabaptist movement in Holland and characterized by congregational autonomy and rejection of military service

meno- — see MEN-

me·no mos·so \ˌmā-nō-'mò(s)-(ˌ)sò\ *adverb* [Italian] (circa 1854)
: less rapid — used as a direction in music

men·o·pause \'me-nə-ˌpòz, 'mē-\ *noun* [French *ménopause,* from *méno-* men- + *pause* stop, pause] (1872)
: the period of natural cessation of menstruation occurring usually between the ages of 45 and 50
— **men·o·paus·al** \ˌme-nə-'pò-zəl, ˌmē-\ *adjective*

me·no·rah \mə-'nòr-ə, -'nòr-\ *noun* [Hebrew *mĕnōrāh* candlestick] (1888)
: a candelabrum with seven or nine candles that is used in Jewish worship

men·or·rha·gia \ˌme-nə-'rā-j(ē-)ə, -'rā-zhə; -'rä-jə, -zhə\ *noun* [New Latin] (circa 1784)
: abnormally profuse menstrual flow

menorah

men·sal \'men(t)-səl\ *adjective* [Middle English, from Late Latin *mensalis,* from Latin *mensa* table] (15th century)
: of, relating to, or done at the table

mensch \'men(t)sh\ *noun* [Yiddish *mentsh* human being, from Middle High German *mensch,* from Old High German *mennisco;* akin to Old English *man* human being, man] (1953)
: a person of integrity and honor

¹mense \'men(t)s\ *noun* [Middle English *menske* honor, from Old Norse *mennska* humanity; akin to Old English *man*] (circa 1500)
chiefly Scottish : PROPRIETY
— **mense·ful** \-fəl\ *adjective*
— **mense·less** \-ləs\ *adjective*

²mense *transitive verb* **mensed; mens·ing** (1540)
chiefly Scottish : to do honor to : GRACE

men·ses \'men-ˌsēz\ *noun plural but singular or plural in construction* [Latin, literally, months, plural of *mensis* month — more at MOON] (1597)
: the menstrual flow

Men·she·vik \'men(t)-shə-ˌvik, -ˌvēk\ *noun, plural* **Mensheviks** *or* **Men·she·vi·ki** \ˌmen(t)-shə-'vi-kē, -'vē-kē\ [Russian *men'shevik,* from *men'she* less; from their forming the minority group of the party] (1907)
: a member of a wing of the Russian Social Democratic party before and during the Russian Revolution believing in the gradual achievement of socialism by parliamentary methods in opposition to the Bolsheviks
— **Men·she·vism** \'men(t)-shə-ˌvi-zəm\ *noun*
— **Men·she·vist** \-vist\ *noun or adjective*

mens rea \'menz-'rē-ə\ *noun* [New Latin, literally, guilty mind] (1861)
: criminal intent

men's room *noun* (1929)
: a room equipped with one or more sinks, toilets, and usually urinals for the use of men and boys

men·stru·al \'men(t)-strü-əl, -strəl\ *adjective* (14th century)
: of or relating to menstruation

men·stru·ate \'men(t)-strü-ˌwāt, 'men-ˌstrāt\ *intransitive verb* **-at·ed; -at·ing** [Late Latin *menstruatus,* past participle of *menstruari,* from Latin *menstrua* menses, from neuter plural of *menstruus* monthly, from *mensis*] (1800)
: to undergo menstruation

men·stru·a·tion \ˌmen(t)-strü-'wā-shən, men-'strä-\ *noun* (circa 1784)
: a discharging of blood, secretions, and tissue debris from the uterus that recurs in nonpregnant breeding-age primate females at approximately monthly intervals and that is considered to represent a readjustment of the uterus to the nonpregnant state following proliferative changes accompanying the preceding ovulation; *also* : PERIOD 6c

men·stru·um \'men(t)-strü-əm, -strəm\ *noun, plural* **-stru·ums** *or* **-strua** \-strü-ə, -strä\ [Medieval Latin, literally, menses, alteration of Latin *menstrua*] (1612)
: a substance that dissolves a solid or holds it in suspension; *also* : SOLVENT

men·su·ra·ble \'men(t)s-rə-bəl, 'men(t)sh-; 'men(t)-sə-rə-, -shə-\ *adjective* [Late Latin *mensurabilis,* from *mensurare* to measure, from Latin *mensura* measure — more at MEASURE] (1604)
1 : capable of being measured : MEASURABLE
2 : MENSURAL 1
— **men·sur·abil·i·ty** \ˌmen(t)s-rə-'bi-lə-tē, ˌmen(t)sh-; ˌmen(t)-sə-rə-, -shə-\ *noun*

men·su·ral \'men(t)s-rəl, 'men(t)sh-; 'men(t)-sə-rəl, -shə-\ *adjective* [Late Latin *mensuralis* measurable, from Latin *mensura*] (1609)
1 : of, relating to, or being polyphonic music originating in the 13th century with each note having a definite and exact time value
2 : of or relating to measure

men·su·ra·tion \ˌmen(t)-sə-'rā-shən, -shə-\ *noun* (1571)
1 : the act of measuring : MEASUREMENT
2 : geometry applied to the computation of lengths, areas, or volumes from given dimensions or angles

mens·wear \'menz-ˌwar, -ˌwer\ *noun* (1908)
: clothing for men

-ment \mənt; *in verbs derived by functional shift (as* ²ORNAMENT) ˌment *also* mənt\ *noun suffix* [Middle English, from Old French, from Latin *-mentum;* akin to Latin *-men,* suffix denoting concrete result, Greek *-mat-, -ma*]
1 a : concrete result, object, or agent of a (specified) action ⟨embank*ment*⟩ ⟨entangle*ment*⟩ b : concrete means or instrument of a (specified) action ⟨entertain*ment*⟩
2 a : action : process ⟨encircle*ment*⟩ ⟨develop*ment*⟩ b : place of a (specified) action ⟨encamp*ment*⟩
3 : state or condition resulting from (a specified action) ⟨involve*ment*⟩

¹men·tal \'men-t°l\ *adjective* [Middle English, from Middle French, from Late Latin *mentalis,* from Latin *ment-, mens* mind — more at MIND] (15th century)
1 a : of or relating to the mind; *specifically* : of or relating to the total emotional and intellectual response of an individual to external reality ⟨*mental* health⟩ b : of or relating to intellectual as contrasted with emotional activity c : of, relating to, or being intellectual as contrasted with overt physical activity d : occurring or experienced in the mind : INNER ⟨*mental* anguish⟩ e : relating to the mind, its activity, or its products as an object of study : IDEOLOGICAL f : relating to spirit or idea as opposed to matter
2 a (1) : of, relating to, or affected by a psychiatric disorder ⟨a *mental* patient⟩ ⟨*mental* illness⟩ (2) : mentally disordered : MAD, CRAZY b : intended for the care or treatment of persons affected by psychiatric disorders ⟨*mental* hospitals⟩
3 : of or relating to telepathic or mind-reading powers
— **men·tal·ly** \-t°l-ē\ *adverb*

²mental *adjective* [Latin *mentum* chin — more at MOUTH] (circa 1727)
: of or relating to the chin : GENIAL

mental age *noun* (1912)
: a measure used in psychological testing that expresses an individual's mental attainment in terms of the number of years it takes an average child to reach the same level

mental deficiency *noun* (1856)
: MENTAL RETARDATION

men·tal·ist \'men-t°l-ist\ *noun* (1930)
: MIND READER

men·tal·is·tic \ˌmen-t°l-'is-tik\ *adjective* (1882)
1 : of or relating to any school of psychology or psychiatry that in contrast to behaviorism values subjective data (as those gained by introspection) in the study and explanation of behavior
2 : of or relating to mental phenomena
— **men·tal·ism** \'men-t°l-ˌi-zəm\ *noun*

men·tal·i·ty \men-'ta-lə-tē\ *noun, plural* **-ties** (1691)
1 : mental power or capacity : INTELLIGENCE
2 : mode or way of thought : OUTLOOK

mental retardation *noun* (1914)
: subaverage intellectual ability that is equivalent to or less than an IQ of 70, is present from birth or infancy, and is manifested especially by abnormal development, by learning difficulties, and by problems in social adjustment

men·ta·tion \men-'tā-shən\ *noun* [Latin *ment-, mens* + English *-ation*] (1850)
: mental activity

men·thol \'men-ˌthòl, -ˌthōl\ *noun* [German, ultimately from Latin *mentha* mint] (1876)
: a crystalline alcohol $C_{10}H_{20}O$ that occurs especially in mint oils and has the odor and cooling properties of peppermint

men·tho·lat·ed \'men(t)-thə-ˌlā-təd\ *adjective* (1922)
: containing or impregnated with menthol ⟨a *mentholated* salve⟩

¹men·tion \'men(t)-shən\ *noun* [Middle English *mencioun,* from Middle French *mention,* from Latin *mention-, mentio;* akin to Latin *meminisse* to remember, *ment-, mens* mind] (14th century)
1 : the act or an instance of citing or calling attention to someone or something especially in a casual or incidental manner
2 : formal citation for outstanding achievement

²mention *transitive verb* **men·tioned; men·tion·ing** \'men(t)-sh(ə-)niŋ\ (1530)
: to make mention of : refer to; *also* : to cite for outstanding achievement
— **men·tion·able** \'men(t)-sh(ə-)nə-bəl\ *adjective*
— **men·tion·er** \-sh(ə-)nər\ *noun*
— **not to mention** : to say nothing of

¹men·tor \'men-ˌtòr, -tər\ *noun* [Latin, from Greek *Mentōr*]
1 *capitalized* : a friend of Odysseus entrusted with the education of Odysseus' son Telemachus
2 a : a trusted counselor or guide b : TUTOR, COACH
— **men·tor·ship** \-ˌship\ *noun*

²mentor *transitive verb* (1983)
: to serve as a mentor for

men·tum \'men-təm\ *noun, plural* **men·ta** \-tə\ [Latin, chin — more at MOUTH] (1826)
: a median plate of the labium of an insect

menu \'men-(ˌ)yü, 'mān-\ *noun, plural* **menus** [French, from *menu* small, detailed, from Old French — more at MINUET] (1837)
1 a : a list of the dishes that may be ordered (as in a restaurant) or that are to be served (as at a banquet) b (1) : a comparable list or assortment of offerings ⟨a *menu* of television programs⟩ (2) : a list shown on the display of a computer from which a user can select the operation the computer is to perform

2 : the dishes available for or served at a meal; *also* : the meal itself ◆

menu–driv·en \-ˌdri-vən\ *adjective* (1977)
: relating to or being a computer program in which options are offered to the user via menus

me·ow \mē-ˈau̇\ *noun* [imitative] (1600)
1 : the cry of a cat
2 : a spiteful or malicious remark
— **meow** *intransitive verb*

me·per·i·dine \mə-ˈper-ə-ˌdēn\ *noun* [*methyl* + pi*peridine*] (1947)
: a synthetic narcotic drug $C_{15}H_{21}NO_2$ used in the form of its hydrochloride as an analgesic, sedative, and antispasmodic

Meph·is·toph·e·les \ˌme-fə-ˈstä-fə-ˌlēz\ *noun* [German]
: a chief devil in the Faust legend
— **Me·phis·to·phe·lian** \ˌmef-ə-stə-ˈfēl-yən, mə-ˌfis-tə-\ *or* **Me·phis·to·phe·lean** *same, or* ˌme-fə-ˌstä-fə-ˈlē-ən\ *adjective*

me·phit·ic \mə-ˈfi-tik\ *adjective* (circa 1623)
: of, relating to, or resembling mephitis : foul-smelling

me·phi·tis \mə-ˈfī-təs\ *noun* [Latin] (circa 1706)
: a noxious, pestilential, or foul exhalation from the earth; *also* : STENCH

mep·ro·bam·ate \ˌme-prō-ˈba-ˌmāt\ *noun* [*methyl* + *propyl* + dicar*bamate*] (1955)
: a bitter carbamate $C_9H_{18}N_2O_4$ used as a tranquilizer

-mer *noun combining form* [International Scientific Vocabulary, from Greek *meros* part — more at MERIT]
: member of a (specified) class ⟨mono*mer*⟩

mer·bro·min \ˌmər-ˈbrō-mən\ *noun* [*mercuric* + *brom-* + fluoresc*ein*] (1945)
: a green crystalline mercurial compound $C_{20}H_8Br_2HgNa_2O_6$ used as a topical antiseptic and germicide in the form of its red solution

Mer·cal·li scale \mer-ˈkä-lē-, (ˌ)mər-\ *noun* [Giuseppe *Mercalli* (died 1914) Italian priest and geologist] (1921)
: a scale of earthquake intensity ranging from I for an earthquake detected only by seismographs to XII for one causing total destruction of all buildings

mer·can·tile \ˈmər-kən-ˌtēl, -ˌtīl\ *adjective* [French, from Italian, from *mercante* merchant, from Latin *mercant-, mercans*, from present participle of *mercari* to trade — more at MARKET] (1642)
1 : of or relating to merchants or trading
2 : of, relating to, or having the characteristics of mercantilism ⟨*mercantile* system⟩

mer·can·til·ism \-ˌtē-ˌli-zəm, -ˌtī-, -tə-\ *noun* (1873)
1 : the theory or practice of mercantile pursuits : COMMERCIALISM
2 : an economic system developing during the decay of feudalism to unify and increase the power and especially the monetary wealth of a nation by a strict governmental regulation of the entire national economy usually through policies designed to secure an accumulation of bullion, a favorable balance of trade, the development of agriculture and manufactures, and the establishment of foreign trading monopolies
— **mer·can·til·ist** \-list\ *noun or adjective*
— **mer·can·til·is·tic** \ˌmər-kən-ˌtē-ˈlis-tik, -ˌtī-, -tə-\ *adjective*

mer·cap·tan \(ˌ)mər-ˈkap-ˌtan\ *noun* [German, from Danish, from Medieval Latin *mercurium captans*, literally, seizing mercury] (1835)
: any of various compounds that contain a thiol functional group : THIOL 1

mer·cap·to·pu·rine \(ˌ)mər-ˌkap-tə-ˈpyu̇r-ˌēn\ *noun* [*mercapta*n + *-o-* + *purine*] (circa 1952)
: an antimetabolite $C_5H_4N_4S$ that interferes especially with the metabolism of purine bases

and the biosynthesis of nucleic acids and that is sometimes useful in the treatment of acute leukemia

Mer·ca·tor \(ˌ)mər-ˈkā-tər\ *adjective* (circa 1876)
: of, relating to, or drawn on the Mercator projection

Mercator projection *noun* [Gerardus *Mercator*] (circa 1881)
: a conformal map projection in the usual case of which the meridians are drawn parallel to each other and the parallels of latitude are straight lines whose distance from each other increases with their distance from the equator

Mercator projection

¹mer·ce·nary \ˈmər-sᵊn-ˌer-ē\ *noun, plural* **-nar·ies** [Middle English, from Latin *mercenarius, mercennarius*, irregular from *merced-, merces* wages — more at MERCY] (14th century)
: one that serves merely for wages; *especially* : a soldier hired into foreign service

²mercenary *adjective* (1532)
1 : serving merely for pay or sordid advantage : VENAL; *also* : GREEDY
2 : hired for service in the army of a foreign country
— **mer·ce·nar·i·ly** \ˌmər-sᵊn-ˈer-ə-lē\ *adverb*
— **mer·ce·nar·i·ness** \ˈmər-sᵊn-ˌer-ē-nəs\ *noun*

mer·cer \ˈmər-sər\ *noun* [Middle English, from Old French *mercier* merchant, from *mers* merchandise, from Latin *merc-, merx*] (13th century)
British : a dealer in usually expensive fabrics

mer·cer·ise *British variant of* MERCERIZE

mer·cer·ize \ˈmər-sə-ˌrīz\ *transitive verb* **-ized; -iz·ing** [John *Mercer* (died 1866) English calico printer] (1859)
: to give (as cotton yarn) luster, strength, and receptiveness to dyes by treatment under tension with caustic soda
— **mer·cer·i·za·tion** \ˌmərs-rə-ˈzā-shən, ˌmər-sə-\ *noun*

mer·cery \ˈmərs-rē, ˈmər-sə-\ *noun, plural* **-cer·ies** (14th century)
British : a mercer's wares, shop, or occupation

¹mer·chan·dise \ˈmər-chən-ˌdīz, -ˌdīs\ *noun* [Middle English *marchaundise*, from Old French *marcheandise*, from *marcheant*] (13th century)
1 *archaic* : the occupation of a merchant : TRADE
2 : the commodities or goods that are bought and sold in business : WARES

²merchandise *also* **mer·chan·dize** \-ˌdīz\ *verb* **-dised** *also* **-dized; -dis·ing** *also* **diz·ing** (14th century)
intransitive verb
archaic : to carry on commerce : TRADE
transitive verb
1 : to buy and sell in business
2 : to promote for or as if for sale ⟨*merchandise* a movie star⟩
— **mer·chan·dis·er** *noun*

mer·chan·dis·ing *also* **mer·chan·diz·ing** \-ˌdī-ziŋ\ *noun* (1932)
: sales promotion as a comprehensive function including market research, development of

new products, coordination of manufacture and marketing, and effective advertising and selling

¹mer·chant \ˈmər-chənt\ *noun* [Middle English *marchant*, from Old French *marcheant*, from (assumed) Vulgar Latin *mercatant-, mercatans*, from present participle of *mercatare* to trade, frequentative of Latin *mercari* — more at MARKET] (13th century)
1 : a buyer and seller of commodities for profit : TRADER
2 : the operator of a retail business : STOREKEEPER
3 : one that is noted for a particular quality or activity : SPECIALIST ⟨a speed *merchant* on the base paths⟩
— **merchant** *adjective*

²merchant (14th century)
intransitive verb
archaic : to deal or trade as a merchant
transitive verb
: to deal or trade in

mer·chant·able \ˈmər-chən-tə-bəl\ *adjective* (15th century)
: of commercially acceptable quality : SALABLE
— **mer·chant·abil·i·ty** \ˌmər-chən-tə-ˈbi-lə-tē\ *noun*

merchant bank *noun* (1930)
chiefly British : a bank that specializes in bankers' acceptances and in underwriting or syndicating equity or bond issues
— **merchant banker** *noun*
— **merchant banking** *noun*

mer·chant·man \ˈmər-chənt-mən\ *noun* (15th century)
1 *archaic* : MERCHANT
2 : a ship used in commerce

merchant marine *noun* (1855)
1 : the privately or publicly owned commercial ships of a nation
2 : the personnel of a merchant marine

merchant ship *noun* (15th century)
: MERCHANTMAN 2

Mer·cian \ˈmər-sh(ē-)ən\ *noun* (1513)
1 : a native or inhabitant of Mercia
2 : the Old English dialect of Mercia
— **Mercian** *adjective*

mer·ci·ful \ˈmər-si-fəl\ *adjective* (14th century)
: full of mercy : COMPASSIONATE; *also* : providing relief
— **mer·ci·ful·ness** \-fəl-nəs\ *noun*

mer·ci·ful·ly \-f(ə-)lē\ *adverb* (14th century)
1 : in a merciful manner
2 : FORTUNATELY 2 ⟨*mercifully* we didn't have to attend the meeting⟩

mer·ci·less \ˈmər-si-ləs\ *adjective* (14th century)
: having or showing no mercy : PITILESS
— **mer·ci·less·ly** *adverb*
— **mer·ci·less·ness** *noun*

mer·cu·rate \ˈmər-kyə-ˌrāt\ *transitive verb* **-rat·ed; -rat·ing** (1923)
: to combine or treat with mercury or a mercury salt
— **mer·cu·ra·tion** \ˌmər-kyə-ˈrā-shən\ *noun*

¹mer·cu·ri·al \(ˌ)mər-ˈkyu̇r-ē-əl\ *adjective* (14th century)

1 : of, relating to, or born under the planet Mercury
2 : having qualities of eloquence, ingenuity, or thievishness attributed to the god Mercury or to the influence of the planet Mercury
3 : characterized by rapid and unpredictable changeableness of mood
4 : of, relating to, containing, or caused by mercury
synonym see INCONSTANT
— **mer·cu·ri·al·ly** \-ē-ə-lē\ *adverb*
— **mer·cu·ri·al·ness** *noun*

²mercurial *noun* (1676)
: a pharmaceutical or chemical containing mercury

mer·cu·ric \(ˌ)mər-ˈkyu̇r-ik\ *adjective* (circa 1828)
: of, relating to, or containing mercury; *especially* **:** containing mercury with a valence of two

mercuric chloride *noun* (1874)
: a heavy crystalline poisonous compound $HgCl_2$ used as a disinfectant and fungicide and in photography

Mer·cu·ro·chrome \(ˌ)mər-ˈkyu̇r-ə-ˌkrōm\ *trademark*
— used for merbromin

mer·cu·rous \(ˌ)mər-ˈkyu̇r-əs, ˈmər-kyə-rəs\ *adjective* (circa 1865)
: of, relating to, or containing mercury; *especially* **:** containing mercury with a valence of one

mercurous chloride *noun* (circa 1885)
: CALOMEL

mer·cu·ry \ˈmər-kyə-rē, -k(ə-)rē\ *noun, plural* **-ries** [Latin *Mercurius,* Roman god and the planet]
1 *a capitalized* **:** a Roman god of commerce, eloquence, travel, cunning, and theft who serves as messenger to the other gods — compare HERMES **b** *often capitalized, archaic* **:** a bearer of messages or news or a conductor of travelers
2 [Middle English *mercurie,* from Medieval Latin *mercurius,* from Latin, the god] **a :** a heavy silver-white poisonous metallic element that is liquid at ordinary temperatures and is used especially in scientific instruments — called also *quicksilver;* see ELEMENT table **b :** the mercury in a thermometer or barometer
3 *capitalized* **:** the planet nearest the sun — see PLANET table

mercury chloride *noun* (circa 1885)
: a chloride of mercury: as **a :** CALOMEL **b :** MERCURIC CHLORIDE

mercury–vapor lamp *noun* (1904)
: an electric lamp in which the discharge takes place through mercury vapor — called also *mercury lamp*

mer·cy \ˈmər-sē\ *noun, plural* **mercies** [Middle English, from Old French *merci,* from Medieval Latin *merced-, merces,* from Latin, price paid, wages, from *merc-, merx* merchandise] (13th century)
1 a : compassion or forbearance shown especially to an offender or to one subject to one's power; *also* **:** lenient or compassionate treatment ⟨begged for *mercy*⟩ **b :** imprisonment rather than death imposed as penalty for first-degree murder
2 a : a blessing that is an act of divine favor or compassion **b :** a fortunate circumstance ⟨it was a *mercy* they found her before she froze⟩
3 : compassionate treatment of those in distress ⟨works of *mercy* among the poor⟩ ☆ ◇
— **mercy** *adjective*
— **at the mercy of :** wholly in the power of **:** with no way to protect oneself against

mercy killing *noun* (1935)
: EUTHANASIA

merde \ˈmerd, ˈmard\ *noun* [French, from Old French, from Latin *merda;* perhaps akin to Lithuanian *smirdėti* to stink] (1920)
: ²CRAP 1a, 2 — sometimes considered vulgar

¹mere \ˈmir\ *noun* [Middle English, from Old English — more at MARINE] (before 12th century)
chiefly British **:** an expanse of standing water **:** LAKE, POOL

²mere *noun* [Middle English, from Old English *mǣre;* akin to Old Norse *landamǣri* borderland] (before 12th century)
: BOUNDARY; *also* **:** LANDMARK

³mere \ˈmir\ *adjective, superlative* **mer·est** [Middle English, from Latin *merus;* akin to Old English *āmerian* to purify and perhaps to Greek *marmairein* to sparkle — more at MORN] (1536)
1 : having no admixture **:** PURE
2 *obsolete* **:** being nothing less than **:** ABSOLUTE
3 : being nothing more than ⟨a *mere* mortal⟩
— **mere·ly** *adverb*

-mere *noun combining form* [French *-mère,* from Greek *meros* part — more at MERIT]
: part **:** segment ⟨met*amere*⟩

me·ren·gue \mə-ˈreŋ-(ˌ)gā\ *noun* [American Spanish *merengue* & Haitian Creole *méringue*] (1936)
: a ballroom dance of Haitian and Dominican origin in which one foot is dragged on every step; *also* **:** the music for a merengue

mer·e·tri·cious \ˌmer-ə-ˈtri-shəs\ *adjective* [Latin *meretricius,* from *meretric-, meretrix* prostitute, from *merēre* to earn — more at MERIT] (circa 1626)
1 : of or relating to a prostitute **:** having the nature of prostitution ⟨*meretricious* relationship⟩
2 a : tawdrily and falsely attractive ⟨the paradise they found was a piece of *meretricious* trash —Carolyn See⟩ **b :** superficially significant **:** PRETENTIOUS ⟨scholarly names to provide fig-leaves of respectability for *meretricious* but stylish books —*Times Literary Supplement*⟩
synonym see GAUDY
— **mer·e·tri·cious·ly** *adverb*
— **mer·e·tri·cious·ness** *noun*

mer·gan·ser \(ˌ)mər-ˈgan(t)-sər\ *noun* [New Latin, from Latin *mergus,* a waterfowl (from *mergere*) + *anser* goose — more at GOOSE] (1752)
: any of various fish-eating diving ducks (especially genus *Mergus*) with a slender bill hooked at the end and serrated along the margins and usually a crested head

merganser

merge \ˈmərj\ *verb* **merged; merg·ing** [Latin *mergere;* akin to Sanskrit *majjati* he dives] (1636)
transitive verb
1 *archaic* **:** to plunge or engulf in something **:** IMMERSE
2 : to cause to combine, unite, or coalesce
3 : to blend gradually by stages that blur distinctions
intransitive verb
1 : to become combined into one
2 : to blend or come together without abrupt change ⟨*merging* traffic⟩
synonym see MIX
— **mer·gence** \ˈmər-jən(t)s\ *noun*

merg·er \ˈmər-jər\ *noun* [*merge* + *-er* (as in *waiver*)] (1728)
1 *law* **:** the absorption of an estate, a contract, or an interest in another, of a minor offense in a greater, or of an obligation into a judgment
2 a : the act or process of merging **b :** absorption by a corporation of one or more others; *also* **:** any of various methods of combining two or more organizations (as business concerns)

me·rid·i·an \mə-ˈri-dē-ən\ *noun* [Middle English, from Middle French *meridien,* from me-

ridien of noon, from Latin *meridianus,* from *meridies* noon, south, irregular from *medius* mid + *dies* day — more at MID, DEITY] (14th century)
1 *archaic* **:** the hour of noon **:** MIDDAY
2 : a great circle of the celestial sphere passing through its poles and the zenith of a given place
3 : a high point
4 a (1) **:** a great circle on the surface of the earth passing through the poles (2) **:** the half of such a circle included between the poles **b :** a representation of such a circle or half circle numbered for longitude on a map or globe — see LONGITUDE illustration
— **meridian** *adjective*

¹me·rid·i·o·nal \mə-ˈri-dē-ə-nᵊl\ *adjective* [Middle English, from Middle French *meridionel,* from Late Latin *meridionalis,* from Latin *meridies*] (14th century)
1 : of, relating to, or situated in the south **:** SOUTHERN
2 : of, relating to, or characteristic of people living in the south especially of France
3 : of, relating to, or situated on or along a meridian
— **me·rid·i·o·nal·ly** \-nᵊl-ē\ *adverb*

²meridional *noun* (1591)
: a native or inhabitant of southern Europe and especially southern France

me·ringue \mə-ˈraŋ\ *noun* [French] (1706)

\ə\ **abut** \ᵊ\ **kitten** \ər\ **further** \a\ **ash** \ā\ **ace**
\ä\ **mop, mar** \au̇\ **out** \ch\ **chin** \e\ **bet** \ē\ **easy**
\g\ **go** \i\ **hit** \ī\ **ice** \j\ **job** \ŋ\ **sing** \ō\ **go**
\ȯ\ **law** \ȯi\ **boy** \th\ **thin** \t̲h̲\ **the** \ü\ **loot** \u̇\ **foot**
\y\ **yet** \zh\ **vision** *see also* Guide to Pronunciation

1 : a dessert topping baked from a mixture of stiffly beaten egg whites and sugar
2 : a shell made of meringue and filled with fruit or ice cream

me·ri·no \mə-'rē-(ˌ)nō\ *noun, plural* **-nos** [Spanish] (1810)
1 : any of a breed of fine-wooled white sheep originating in Spain and producing a heavy fleece of exceptional quality
2 : a soft wool or wool and cotton clothing fabric resembling cashmere
3 : a fine wool and cotton yarn used for hosiery and knitwear
— **merino** *adjective*

-merism *noun combining form* [International Scientific Vocabulary, from Greek *meros* part — more at MERIT]
: possession of (such) an arrangement of or relation among constituent chemical units ⟨tautomerism⟩

mer·i·stem \'mer-ə-ˌstem\ *noun* [Greek *meristos* divided (from *merizein* to divide, from *meros*) + English *-em* (as in *system*)] (1874)
: a formative plant tissue usually made up of small cells capable of dividing indefinitely and giving rise to similar cells or to cells that differentiate to produce the definitive tissues and organs
— **mer·i·ste·mat·ic** \ˌmer-əs-tə-'ma-tik\ *adjective*
— **mer·i·ste·mat·i·cal·ly** \-ti-k(ə-)lē\ *adverb*

me·ris·tic \mə-'ris-tik\ *adjective* [Greek *meristos*] (1894)
1 : SEGMENTAL
2 : involving modification in number or in geometrical relation of body parts ⟨*meristic* variation in flower petals⟩
— **me·ris·ti·cal·ly** \-ti-k(ə-)lē\ *adverb*

¹mer·it \'mer-ət\ *noun* [Middle English, from Middle French *merite*, from Latin *meritum*, from neuter of *meritus*, past participle of *merēre* to deserve, earn; akin to Greek *meiresthai* to receive as one's portion, *meros* part] (14th century)
1 a *obsolete* **:** reward or punishment due **b :** the qualities or actions that constitute the basis of one's deserts **c :** a praiseworthy quality **:** VIRTUE **d :** character or conduct deserving reward, honor, or esteem; *also* **:** ACHIEVEMENT
2 : spiritual credit held to be earned by performance of righteous acts and to ensure future benefits
3 a *plural* **:** the intrinsic nature of a legal case apart from considerations of circumstance, jurisdiction, or procedure **b :** individual significance or justification

²merit (1526)
transitive verb
: to be worthy of or entitled or liable to **:** EARN
intransitive verb
1 *obsolete* **:** to be entitled to reward or honor
2 : DESERVE

mer·i·toc·ra·cy \ˌmer-ə-'tä-krə-sē\ *noun, plural* **-cies** [¹*merit* + *-o-* + *-cracy*] (1958)
1 : a system in which the talented are chosen and moved ahead on the basis of their achievement
2 : leadership selected on the basis of intellectual criteria
— **mer·it·o·crat·ic** \ˌmer-ə-tə-'kra-tik\ *adjective*

mer·it·o·crat \'mer-ə-tə-ˌkrat\ *noun* (1960) *chiefly British* **:** a person who advances through a meritocratic system

mer·i·to·ri·ous \ˌmer-ə-'tōr-ē-əs, -'tòr-\ *adjective* (15th century)
: deserving of honor or esteem
— **mer·i·to·ri·ous·ly** *adverb*
— **mer·i·to·ri·ous·ness** *noun*

merit system *noun* (1879)
: a system by which appointments and promotions in the civil service are based on competence rather than political favoritism

¹merle *also* **merl** \'mər(-)l\ *noun* [Middle English, from Middle French, from Latin

merulus; akin to Old English *ōsle* blackbird, Old High German *amsla*] (15th century)
: BLACKBIRD 1a

²merle *noun* [origin unknown] (1905)
: a bluish or reddish gray mixed with splotches of black that is the color of the coats of some dogs

mer·lin \'mər-lən\ *noun* [Middle English *merlioun*, from Anglo-French *merilun*, from Old French *esmerillon*, augmentative of *esmeril*, of Germanic origin; akin to Old High German *smiril* merlin] (14th century)
: a small compact Holarctic falcon (*Falco columbarius*) which has a broad dark terminal band on the tail and of which the upperparts are slate blue in males and dark brown in females — compare PIGEON HAWK 1

Mer·lin \'mər-lən\ *noun* [Medieval Latin *Merlinus*, from Middle Welsh *Myrddin*]
: a prophet and magician in Arthurian legend

mer·lon \'mər-lən\ *noun* [French, from Italian *merlone*, augmentative of *merlo* battlement, from Medieval Latin *merulus*, from Latin, merle] (circa 1704)
: any of the solid intervals between crenellations of a battlement — see BATTLEMENT illustration

mer·lot \mer-'lō\ *noun, often capitalized* [French] (circa 1941)
: a dry red wine made from a widely grown grape originally used in the Bordeaux region of France for blending

mer·maid \'mər-ˌmād\ *noun* [Middle English *mermayde*, from *mere* sea (from Old English) + *mayde* maid — more at MARINE] (14th century)
: a fabled marine creature with the head and upper body of a woman and the tail of a fish

mer·man \-ˌman, -mən\ *noun* (1601)
: a fabled marine creature with the head and upper body of a man and the tail of a fish

mero- *combining form* [International Scientific Vocabulary, from Greek, from *meros* part — more at MERIT]
: part **:** partial ⟨*meroblastic*⟩

mer·o·blas·tic \ˌmer-ə-'blas-tik\ *adjective* [International Scientific Vocabulary] (1870)
: characterized by incomplete cleavage as a result of the presence of a mass of yolk material — compare HOLOBLASTIC
— **mer·o·blas·ti·cal·ly** \-ti-k(ə-)lē\ *adverb*

mer·o·crine \'mer-ə-krən, -ˌkrīn, -ˌkrēn\ *adjective* [International Scientific Vocabulary, from *mero-* + Greek *krinein* to separate — more at CERTAIN] (circa 1905)
: producing a secretion that is discharged without major damage to the secretory cells; *also* **:** produced by a merocrine gland

mer·o·mor·phic \ˌmer-ə-'mòr-fik\ *adjective* (circa 1890)
: relating to or being a function of a complex variable that is analytic everywhere in a region except for singularities at each of which infinity is the limit and each of which is contained in a neighborhood where the function is analytic except for the singular point itself

mer·o·my·o·sin \ˌmer-ə-'mī-ə-sən\ *noun* (1952)
: either of two structural subunits of myosin that are obtained especially by tryptic digestion

-merous *adjective combining form* [New Latin *-merus*, from Greek *-merēs*, from *meros* — more at MERIT]
: having (such or so many) parts ⟨*dimerous*⟩

Mer·o·vin·gian \ˌmer-ə-'vin-j(ē-)ən\ *adjective* [French *mérovingien*, from Medieval Latin *Merovingi* Merovingians, from *Merovaeus* Merowig (died 458) Frankish founder of the dynasty] (circa 1694)
: of or relating to the first Frankish dynasty reigning from about A.D. 500 to 751
— **Merovingian** *noun*

mer·o·zo·ite \ˌmer-ə-'zō-ˌīt\ *noun* [International Scientific Vocabulary, from *mero-* + *zo-* + *-ite*] (1900)

: a sporozoan trophozoite produced by schizogony that is capable of initiating a new sexual or asexual cycle of development

mer·ri·ment \'mer-i-mənt\ *noun* (1576)
1 : lighthearted gaiety or fun-making **:** HILARITY
2 : a lively celebration or party **:** FESTIVITY

mer·ry \'mer-ē\ *adjective* **mer·ri·er; -est** [Middle English *mery*, from Old English *myrge, merge*; akin to Old High German *murg* short — more at BRIEF] (before 12th century)
1 *archaic* **:** giving pleasure **:** DELIGHTFUL
2 : full of gaiety or high spirits **:** MIRTHFUL
3 : marked by festivity or gaiety
4 : QUICK, BRISK ⟨a *merry* pace⟩ ☆
— **mer·ri·ly** \'mer-ə-lē\ *adverb*
— **mer·ri·ness** \'mer-ē-nəs\ *noun*

mer·ry–an·drew \ˌmer-ē-'an-(ˌ)drü\ *noun, often M&A capitalized* [*merry* + *Andrew*, proper name] (1673)
: a person who clowns publicly

mer·ry–go–round \'mer-ē-gō-ˌraúnd, -gə-\ *noun* (1729)
1 : an amusement park ride with seats often in the form of animals (as horses) revolving about a fixed center
2 : a cycle of activity that is complex, fast-paced, or difficult to break out of ⟨the corporate *merry-go-round*⟩

mer·ry·mak·er \'mer-ē-ˌmā-kər\ *noun* (1827)
: REVELER

mer·ry·mak·ing \-kiŋ\ *noun* (1714)
1 : gay or festive activity **:** CONVIVIALITY
2 : a convivial occasion **:** FESTIVITY

mer·ry·thought \'mer-ē-ˌthòt\ *noun* (1607) *chiefly British* **:** WISHBONE

merry widow *noun, often M&W capitalized* [*The Merry Widow*, operetta (1905) by Franz Lehár] (1964)
: a strapless corset or bustier usually having garters attached

Mer·thi·o·late \(ˌ)mər-'thī-ə-ˌlāt, -lət\ *trademark*
— used for thimerosal

mes- *or* **meso-** *combining form* [Latin, from Greek, from *mesos* — more at MID]
1 : mid **:** in the middle ⟨*meso*carp⟩
2 : intermediate (as in size or type) ⟨*meso*morph⟩ ⟨*meso*n⟩

me·sa \'mā-sə\ *noun* [Spanish, literally, table, from Latin *mensa*] (1759)
: an isolated relatively flat-topped natural elevation usually more extensive than a butte and less extensive than a plateau; *also* **:** a broad terrace with an abrupt slope on one side **:** BENCH

més·al·liance \ˌmā-ˌzal-'yäⁿs, ˌmā-zə-'lī-ən(t)s\ *noun, plural* **mésalliances** \-'yäⁿs(-əz), -'lī-ən(t)-səz\ [French, from *més-* mis- + *alliance*] (1782)
: a marriage with a person of inferior social position

mes·arch \'me-ˌzärk, 'mē-, -ˌsärk\ *adjective* (1891)
: having metaxylem developed both internal and external to the protoxylem

☆ SYNONYMS
Merry, blithe, jocund, jovial, jolly mean showing high spirits or lightheartedness. MERRY suggests cheerful, joyous, uninhibited enjoyment of frolic or festivity (a *merry* group of revelers). BLITHE suggests carefree, innocent, or even heedless gaiety (arrived late in his usual *blithe* way). JOCUND stresses elation and exhilaration of spirits (singing, dancing, and *jocund* feasting). JOVIAL suggests the stimulation of conviviality and good fellowship (dinner put them in a *jovial* mood). JOLLY suggests high spirits expressed in laughing, bantering, and jesting (our *jolly* host enlivened the party).

mes·cal \me-'skal, mə-\ *noun* [American Spanish *mezcal, mescal,* from Nahuatl *mexcalli* mescal liquor] (1702)
1 : a small cactus (*Lophophora williamsii*) with rounded stems covered with jointed tubercles that are used as a stimulant and antispasmodic especially among the Mexican Indians
2 a : a usually colorless Mexican liquor distilled especially from the central leaves of maguey plants **b :** a plant from which mescal is produced; *especially* **:** MAGUEY

mescal button *noun* (1888)
: one of the dried discoid tops of the mescal

mescal 1

Mes·ca·le·ro \ˌmes-kə-'ler-(ˌ)ō\ *noun, plural* **Mescalero** or **Mescaleros** [American Spanish, from *mezcal, mescal* maguey, mescal liquor] (1844)
: a member of an Apache people of Texas and New Mexico

mes·ca·line \'mes-kə-lən, -ˌlēn\ *noun* (1896)
: a hallucinatory crystalline alkaloid $C_{11}H_{17}NO_3$ that is the chief active principle in mescal buttons

mesdames *plural of* MADAM, *or of* MADAME, *or of* MRS.

mesdemoiselles *plural of* MADEMOISELLE

me·seems \mi-'sēmz\ *impersonal verb, past* **me·seemed** \-'sēmd\ (15th century)
archaic **:** it seems to me

me·sem·bry·an·the·mum \mə-ˌzem-brē-'an(t)-thə-məm\ *noun* [New Latin, irregular from Greek *mesēmbria* midday (from *mes-* + *hēmera* day) + *anthemon* flower, from *anthos* — more at ANTHOLOGY] (1753)
: any of a genus (*Mesembryanthemum*) of chiefly southern African fleshy-leaved herbs or subshrubs of the carpetweed family

mes·en·ceph·a·lon \ˌme-ˌzen-'se-fə-ˌlän, ˌmē-, -zᵊn-, -ˌsen-, -sᵊn-, -lən\ *noun* [New Latin] (1846)
: MIDBRAIN
— **mes·en·ce·phal·ic** \-ˌzen(t)-sə-'fa-lik, -zᵊn(t)-, -ˌsen(t)-, -sᵊn(t)-\ *adjective*

mes·en·chy·mal \mə-'zeŋ-kə-məl, -'seŋ-; ˌme-zᵊn-'kī-məl, ˌmē-, -sᵊn-\ *adjective* [International Scientific Vocabulary] (1886)
: of, resembling, or being mesenchyme

mes·en·chyme \'me-zᵊn-ˌkīm, 'mē-, -sᵊn-\ *noun* [German *Mesenchym,* from *mes-* + New Latin *-enchyma*] (1888)
: loosely organized undifferentiated mostly mesodermal cells that give rise to such structures as connective tissues, blood, lymphatics, bone, and cartilage

mes·en·ter·on \(ˌ)me-'zen-tə-ˌrän, ˌmē-, -'sen-, -rən\ *noun, plural* **-tera** \-tə-rə\ [New Latin] (1877)
: the part of the alimentary canal that is developed from the archenteron and is lined with hypoblast

mes·en·tery \'me-zᵊn-ˌter-ē, -sᵊn-\ *noun, plural* **-ter·ies** [Middle English *mesenterie,* from Middle French & Medieval Latin; Middle French *mesentere,* from Medieval Latin *mesenterion,* from Greek, from *mes-* + *enteron* intestine — more at INTER-] (15th century)
1 a : one or more vertebrate membranes that consist of a double fold of the peritoneum and invest the intestines and their appendages and connect them with the dorsal wall of the abdominal cavity **b :** a fold of membrane comparable to a mesentery and supporting a viscus (as the heart) that is not a part of the digestive tract
2 : a support or partition in an invertebrate like the vertebrate mesentery
— **mes·en·ter·ic** \ˌme-zᵊn-'ter-ik, -sᵊn-\ *adjective*

¹mesh \'mesh\ *noun* [Middle English, probably from Middle Dutch *maesche;* akin to Old

High German *masca* mesh, Lithuanian *mazgos* knot] (14th century)
1 : one of the openings between the threads or cords of a net; *also* **:** one of the similar spaces in a network — often used to designate screen size as the number of openings per linear inch
2 a : the fabric of a net **b :** a woven, knit, or knotted material of open texture with evenly spaced holes **c :** an arrangement of interlocking metal links used especially for jewelry
3 a : an interlocking or intertwining arrangement or construction **:** NETWORK **b :** WEB, SNARE — usually used in plural
4 : working contact (as of the teeth of gears) ⟨in *mesh*⟩
— **meshed** \'mesht\ *adjective*

²mesh (circa 1547)
transitive verb
1 a : to catch in the openings of a net **b :** ENMESH, ENTANGLE
2 : to cause to resemble network
3 a : to cause (as gears) to engage **b :** to coordinate closely **:** INTERLOCK
intransitive verb
1 : to become entangled in or as if in meshes
2 : to be in or come into mesh — used especially of gears
3 : to fit or work together properly **:** COORDINATE

me·shuga or **me·shug·ge** also **me·shug·ah** or **me·shug·gah** \mə-'shu̇-gə\ *adjective* [Yiddish *meshuge,* from Hebrew *mĕshuggā'*] (1892)
: CRAZY, FOOLISH

me·shug·gen·er \-'shu̇-gə-nər\ *noun* [Yiddish *meshugener,* from *meshuge*] (1900)
: a foolish or crazy person

mesh·work \'mesh-ˌwərk\ *noun* (1830)
: NETWORK ⟨a vascular *meshwork*⟩

me·si·al \'mē-zē-əl, -sē-\ *adjective* (1803)
1 : MIDDLE, MEDIAN
2 : of, relating to, or being the surface of a tooth that is next to the tooth in front of it or that is closest to the middle of the front of the jaw — compare DISTAL 2
— **me·si·al·ly** \-ə-lē\ *adverb*

¹me·sic \'me-zik, 'mē-, -sik\ *adjective* [*mes-* + *-ic*] (1926)
: characterized by, relating to, or requiring a moderate amount of moisture ⟨a *mesic* habitat⟩ ⟨a *mesic* plant⟩ — compare HYDRIC, XERIC

²mesic *adjective* [*meson* + *-ic*] (1939)
: of or relating to a meson

me·mer·ic \mez-'mer-ik *also* mes-\ *adjective* (1829)
1 : of, relating to, or induced by mesmerism
2 : FASCINATING, IRRESISTIBLE
— **mes·mer·i·cal·ly** \-i-k(ə-)lē\ *adverb*

mes·mer·ise *British variant of* MESMERIZE

mes·mer·ism \'mez-mə-ˌri-zəm *also* 'mes-\ *noun* [F. A. *Mesmer*] (1784)
1 : hypnotic induction held to involve animal magnetism; *broadly* **:** HYPNOTISM
2 : hypnotic appeal
— **mes·mer·ist** \-rist\ *noun*

mes·mer·ize \-mə-ˌrīz\ *transitive verb* **-ized; -iz·ing** (1829)
1 : to subject to mesmerism; *also* **:** HYPNOTIZE
2 : SPELLBIND, FASCINATE ◆
— **mes·mer·iz·er** *noun*

mesne \'mēn\ *adjective* [Anglo-French, alteration of Middle French *meien* — more at MEAN] (1548)
: INTERMEDIATE, INTERVENING — used in law

mesne lord *noun* (1614)
: a feudal lord who holds land as tenant of a superior (as a king) but who is lord to his own tenant

meso- — see MES-

me·so·carp \'me-zə-ˌkärp, 'mē-, -sə-\ *noun* (1849)
: the middle layer of a pericarp — see ENDOCARP illustration

me·so·cy·clone \ˌme-zə-'sī-ˌklōn, ˌmē-, -sə-'sī-\ *noun* (1975)

: a rapidly rotating air mass within a thunderstorm that often gives rise to a tornado

me·so·derm \'me-zə-ˌdərm, 'mē-, -sə-\ *noun* [International Scientific Vocabulary] (1873)
: the middle of the three primary germ layers of an embryo that is the source of many bodily tissues and structures (as bone, muscle, connective tissue, and dermis); *broadly* **:** tissue derived from this germ layer
— **me·so·der·mal** \ˌme-zə-'dər-məl, ˌmē-, -sə-\ *adjective*

me·so·glea or **me·so·gloea** \ˌme-zə-'glē-ə, ˌmē-, -sə-\ *noun* [New Latin, from *mes-* + Late Greek *gloia, glia* glue — more at CLAY] (1886)
: a gelatinous substance between the endoderm and ectoderm of sponges or coelenterates

Me·so·lith·ic \-'li-thik\ *adjective* [International Scientific Vocabulary] (1866)
: of, relating to, or being a transitional period of the Stone Age between the Paleolithic and the Neolithic

me·so·mere \'me-zə-ˌmir, 'mē-, -sə-\ *noun* (circa 1900)
: a blastomere of medium size; *also* **:** an intermediate part of the mesoderm

me·so·morph \'me-zə-ˌmȯrf, 'mē-, -sə-\ *noun* [*mesoderm* + *-morph*] (1940)
: a mesomorphic body or person

me·so·mor·phic \ˌme-zə-'mȯr-fik, ˌmē-, -sə-\ *adjective* [*mesoderm* + *-morphic;* from the predominance in such types of structures developed from the mesoderm] (1940)
1 : of or relating to the component in W. H. Sheldon's classification of body types that measures especially the degree of muscularity and bone development
2 : having a husky muscular body build
— **me·so·mor·phy** \'me-zə-ˌmȯr-fē, -sə-\ *noun*

me·son \'me-ˌzän, 'mā-, 'mē-, -ˌsän\ *noun* [International Scientific Vocabulary *mes-* + *²-on*] (1939)
: any of a group of fundamental particles (as the pion and kaon) made up of a quark and an antiquark that are subject to the strong force

◇ **WORD HISTORY**
mesmerize Franz Anton Mesmer (1734–1815), from whose surname *mesmerize* is derived, was an Austrian physician. A graduate of a traditional medical school in Vienna, Mesmer early on formulated unorthodox medical beliefs. He claimed that a mysterious fluid, which he eventually called "animal magnetism," permeates all matter. Forced to leave Vienna for practicing "magic," Mesmer settled in Paris and soon put his theories of animal magnetism into practice. His therapy basically consisted of having patients sit around a tub of dilute sulfuric acid from which iron bars protruded. As the patients touched the previously "magnetized" bars, the outflowing current of animal magnetism, as well as a tap from Mesmer's magic wand, caused them to become highly agitated. Once the necessary crises had been produced, Mesmer effected the individual cures by having the animal magnetism flow from his body to the patient's. A royal commission's finding that the "cures" were entirely due to the imagination failed to dampen the rage for Mesmer's treatment. What Mesmer had discovered—or rediscovered—was the technique once called "artificial somnambulism" and now known as hypnotism.

and have zero or an integer number of quantum units of spin
— **me·son·ic** \me-'zä-nik, mä-, mē-, -'sä-\ *adjective*
me·so·neph·ros \,me-zə-'ne-frəs, ,mē-, -sə-, -,fräs\ *noun, plural* **-neph·roi** \-,fròi\ [New Latin, from *mes-* + Greek *nephros* kidney — more at NEPHRITIS] (1887)
: either member of the second and midmost of the three paired vertebrate renal organs that functions in adult fishes and amphibians but functions only in the embryo of reptiles, birds, and mammals in which it is replaced by a metanephros in the adult — compare METANEPHROS, PRONEPHROS
— **me·so·neph·ric** \-frik\ *adjective*
me·so·pause \'me-zə-,pòz, 'mē-, -sə-\ *noun* [*mesosphere* + *pause*] (1950)
: the upper boundary of the mesosphere where the temperature of the atmosphere reaches its lowest point
me·so·pe·lag·ic \,me-zə-pə-'la-jik, ,mē-, -sə-\ *adjective* (1947)
: of or relating to oceanic depths from about 600 feet to 3000 feet (200 to 1000 meters)
me·so·phyll \'me-zə-,fil, 'mē-, -sə-\ *noun* [New Latin *mesophyllum*, from *mes-* + Greek *phyllon* leaf — more at BLADE] (1839)
: the parenchyma between the epidermal layers of a foliage leaf
— **me·so·phyl·lic** \,me-zə-'fi-lik, ,mē-, -sə-\ *or* **me·so·phyl·lous** \-ləs\ *adjective*
me·so·phyte \'me-zə-,fīt, 'mē-, -sə-\ *noun* [International Scientific Vocabulary] (1899)
: a plant that grows under medium conditions of moisture
— **me·so·phyt·ic** \,me-zə-'fi-tik, ,mē-, -sə-\ *adjective*
me·so·scale \'me-zə-,skāl, 'mē-, -sə-\ *adjective* (1956)
: of intermediate size; *especially* : of or relating to a meteorological phenomenon approximately 10 to 1000 kilometers in horizontal extent ⟨*mesoscale* cloud pattern⟩
me·so·some \-,sōm\ *noun* (1960)
: an organelle of bacteria that appears as an invagination of the plasma membrane and functions either in DNA replication and cell division or excretion of exoenzymes
me·so·sphere \-,sfir\ *noun* (1950)
: the part of the earth's atmosphere between the stratosphere and the thermosphere in which temperature decreases with altitude to the atmosphere's absolute minimum of about −112°F (−80°C)
— **me·so·spher·ic** \,me-zə-'sfir-ik, ,mē-, -sə-, -'sfer-\ *adjective*
me·so·the·li·o·ma \,me-zə-,thē-lē-'ō-mə, ,mē-, -sə-\ *noun, plural* **-mas** *or* **-ma·ta** \-mə-tə\ [New Latin] (circa 1899)
: a tumor derived from mesothelial tissue (as that lining the peritoneum or pleura)
me·so·the·li·um \-'thē-lē-əm\ *noun, plural* **-lia** \-lē-ə\ [New Latin, from *mes-* + epithelium] (1886)
: epithelium derived from mesoderm that lines the body cavity of a vertebrate embryo and gives rise to epithelia (as of the peritoneum, pericardium, and pleurae), striated muscle, heart muscle, and several minor structures
— **me·so·the·li·al** \-lē-əl\ *adjective*
me·so·tho·rac·ic \-thə-'ra-sik\ *adjective* (1839)
: of or relating to the mesothorax
me·so·tho·rax \-'thòr-,aks, -'thòr-\ *noun* [New Latin] (circa 1826)
: the middle of the three segments of the thorax of an insect — see INSECT illustration
me·so·tro·phic \,me-zə-'trō-fik, ,mē-, -sə-, -'trä-fik\ *adjective* (1940)
of a body of water : having a moderate amount of dissolved nutrients — compare EUTROPHIC, OLIGOTROPHIC
Me·so·zo·ic \-'zō-ik\ *adjective* (1840)
: of, relating to, or being an era of geological history comprising the interval between the

Permian and the Tertiary or the corresponding system of rocks that was marked by the presence of dinosaurs, marine and flying reptiles, ammonites, ferns, and gymnosperms and the appearance of angiosperms, mammals, and birds — see GEOLOGIC TIME table
— **Mesozoic** *noun*
mes·quite \mə-'skēt, me-\ *noun* [American Spanish, from Nahuatl *mizquitl*] (1759)
: any of several spiny leguminous trees or shrubs (genus *Prosopis* and especially *P. glandulosa*) chiefly of the southwestern U.S. that often form extensive thickets and have sweet pods eaten by livestock; *also* : the wood of the mesquite used especially in grilling food
¹mess \'mes\ *noun* [Middle English *mes*, from Middle French, from Late Latin *missus* course at a meal, from *missus*, past participle of *mittere* to put, from Latin, to send — more at SMITE] (14th century)
1 : a quantity of food: **a** *archaic* : food set on a table at one time **b** : a prepared dish of soft food; *also* : a mixture of ingredients cooked or eaten together **c** : enough food of a specified kind for a dish or a meal ⟨picked a *mess* of peas for dinner⟩
2 a : a group of persons who regularly take their meals together; *also* : a meal so taken **b** : a place where meals are regularly served to a group : MESS HALL
3 a : a disordered, untidy, offensive, or unpleasant state or condition ⟨your room is in a *mess*⟩ **b** : one that is disordered, untidy, offensive, or unpleasant usually because of blundering, laxity, or misconduct ⟨[the movie] is a *mess*, as sloppy in concept as it is in execution —Judith Crist⟩ ⟨made a *mess* of his life⟩
²mess (14th century)
transitive verb
1 : to provide with meals at a mess
2 a : to make dirty or untidy : DISARRANGE ⟨warned not to *mess* up your room⟩ **b** : to mix up : BUNGLE ⟨really *messed* up my life⟩
3 : to interfere with ⟨magnetic storms that *mess* up communications —*Time*⟩
4 : to rough up : MANHANDLE ⟨*mess* him up good so he won't double-cross us again⟩
intransitive verb
1 : to take meals with a mess
2 : to make a mess
3 a : PUTTER, TRIFLE ⟨small boys and girls who like to *mess* around with paints⟩ **b** : to handle or play with something especially carelessly ⟨don't *mess* with my camera⟩ — often used with *around* **c** : to take an active interest in something or someone ⟨*messing* around with new video techniques⟩; *also* : INTERFERE, MEDDLE ⟨*messing* in other people's affairs⟩ ⟨you'd better not *mess* with me⟩
4 : to become confused or make an error — usually used with *up* ⟨got another chance and didn't want to *mess* up again⟩
¹mes·sage \'me-sij\ *noun* [Middle English, from Old French, from Medieval Latin *missaticum*, from Latin *missus*, past participle of *mittere*] (14th century)
1 : a communication in writing, in speech, or by signals
2 : a messenger's errand or function
3 : an underlying theme or idea
²message *verb* **mes·saged; mes·sag·ing** (1583)
transitive verb
1 : to send as a message or by messenger
2 : to send a message to
intransitive verb
: to communicate by message
mes·sa·line \,me-sə-'lēn\ *noun* [French] (circa 1890)
: a soft lightweight silk dress fabric with a satin weave
mes·san \'me-s°n\ *noun* [Scottish Gaelic *measan*] (15th century)
chiefly Scottish : LAPDOG 1

mess around *intransitive verb* (circa 1932)
1 : to waste time : DAWDLE, IDLE
2 a : ASSOCIATE ⟨don't *mess around* with admirals much —K. M. Dodson⟩ **b** : FLIRT, PHILANDER ⟨caught him *messing around* with my wife⟩
messeigneurs *plural of* MONSEIGNEUR
mes·sen·ger \'me-s°n-jər\ *noun* [Middle English *messangere*, from Old French *messagier*, from *message*] (14th century)
1 : one who bears a message or does an errand: as **a** *archaic* : FORERUNNER, HERALD **b** : a dispatch bearer in government or military service **c** : an employee who carries messages
2 : a light line used in hauling a heavier line (as between ships)
3 : a substance (as a hormone) that mediates a biological effect
4 : MESSENGER RNA
messenger RNA *noun* (1961)
: an RNA produced by transcription that carries the code for a particular protein from the nuclear DNA to a ribosome in the cytoplasm and acts as a template for the formation of that protein — compare TRANSFER RNA
mess hall *noun* (1862)
: a hall or building (as on an army post) in which mess is served
mes·si·ah \mə-'sī-ə\ *noun* [Hebrew *māshīaḥ* & Aramaic *měshīḥā*, literally, anointed]
1 *capitalized* **a** : the expected king and deliverer of the Jews **b** : JESUS 1
2 : a professed or accepted leader of some hope or cause
— **mes·si·ah·ship** \-,ship\ *noun*
mes·si·an·ic \,me-sē-'a-nik\ *adjective* [probably from French *messianique*, from *messianisme*] (circa 1834)
1 : of or relating to a messiah
2 : marked by idealism and an aggressive crusading spirit ⟨a *messianic* sense of historic mission —Edmond Taylor⟩
mes·si·a·nism \'me-sē-ə-,ni-zəm; mə-'sī-ə-, me-\ *noun* [French *messianisme*, from *messie* messiah + *-anisme* (as in *christianisme* Christianity)] (1876)
1 : belief in a messiah as the savior of mankind
2 : religious devotion to an ideal or cause
Mes·si·as \mə-'sī-əs\ *noun* [Middle English, from Late Latin, from Greek, from Aramaic *měshīḥā*]
: MESSIAH 1
messieurs *plural of* MONSIEUR
mess jacket *noun* (1891)
: a fitted waist-length man's jacket worn especially as part of a dress uniform
mess kit *noun* (circa 1877)
: a compact kit of nested cooking and eating utensils for use by soldiers and campers
mess·mate \'mes-,māt\ *noun* (1746)
: a person with whom one regularly takes mess (as on a ship)
mess over *transitive verb* (1965)
slang : to treat harshly or unfairly : ABUSE
Messrs. \'me-sərz\ *plural of* MR.
⟨*Messrs.* Jones, Brown, and Robinson⟩
mes·suage \'mes-wij\ *noun* [Middle English, from Anglo-French, probably alteration of Old French *mesnage* — more at MÉNAGE] (14th century)
: PREMISE 3b
messy \'me-sē\ *adjective* **mess·i·er; -est** (1843)
1 : marked by confusion, disorder, or dirt : UNTIDY ⟨a *messy* room⟩
2 : lacking neatness or precision : CARELESS, SLOVENLY ⟨*messy* thinking⟩
3 : extremely unpleasant or trying ⟨*messy* lawsuits⟩
— **mess·i·ly** \'me-sə-lē\ *adverb*
— **mess·i·ness** \'me-sē-nəs\ *noun*
mes·ti·za \me-'stē-zə\ *noun* [Spanish, feminine of *mestizo*] (circa 1582)
: a woman who is a mestizo

mes·ti·zo \-(ˌ)zō\ *noun, plural* **-zos** [Spanish, from *mestizo,* adjective, mixed, from Late Latin *mixticius,* from Latin *mixtus,* past participle of *miscēre* to mix — more at MIX] (1582)
: a person of mixed blood; *specifically* : a person of mixed European and American Indian ancestry

mes·tra·nol \'mes-trə-ˌnȯl, -ˌnōl\ *noun* [meth- + *estrogen* + *pregnane* (C₂₁H₃₆) + ¹-*ol*] (1962)
: a synthetic estrogen $C_{21}H_{26}O_2$ used in oral contraceptives

met *past and past participle of* MEET

meta- *or* **met-** *prefix* [New Latin & Medieval Latin, from Latin or Greek; Latin, from Greek, among, with, after, from *meta* among, with, after; akin to Old English *mid, mith* with, Old High German *mit*]
1 a : occurring later than or in succession to : after ⟨*meta*estrus⟩ **b** : situated behind or beyond ⟨*met*encephalon⟩ ⟨*meta*carpus⟩ **c** : later or more highly organized or specialized form of ⟨*meta*xylem⟩
2 : change : transformation
3 [*metaphysics*] : more comprehensive : transcending ⟨*meta*psychology⟩ — used with the name of a discipline to designate a new but related discipline designed to deal critically with the original one ⟨*meta*mathematics⟩
4 a : involving substitution at or characterized by two positions in the benzene ring that are separated by one carbon atom ⟨*meta*-xylene⟩ **b** : derived from by loss of water ⟨*meta*phosphoric acid⟩

met·a·bol·ic \ˌme-tə-'bä-lik\ *adjective* (1845)
: of, relating to, or based on metabolism
— **met·a·bol·i·cal·ly** \-li-k(ə-)lē\ *adverb*

me·tab·o·lism \mə-'ta-bə-ˌli-zəm\ *noun* [International Scientific Vocabulary, from Greek *metabolē* change, from *metaballein* to change, from *meta-* + *ballein* to throw — more at DEVIL] (1872)
1 a : the sum of the processes in the buildup and destruction of protoplasm; *specifically* : the chemical changes in living cells by which energy is provided for vital processes and activities and new material is assimilated **b** : the sum of the processes by which a particular substance is handled in the living body **c** : the sum of the metabolic activities taking place in a particular environment ⟨the *metabolism* of a lake⟩
2 : METAMORPHOSIS 2 — usually used in combination ⟨holo*metabolism*⟩

me·tab·o·lite \-ˌlīt\ *noun* (1884)
1 : a product of metabolism
2 : a substance essential to the metabolism of a particular organism or to a particular metabolic process

me·tab·o·lize \-ˌlīz\ *verb* **-lized; -liz·ing** (1887)
transitive verb
: to subject to metabolism
intransitive verb
: to perform metabolism
— **me·tab·o·liz·able** \mə-ˌta-bə-'lī-zə-bəl\ *adjective*

¹meta·car·pal \ˌme-tə-'kär-pəl\ *adjective* (1739)
: of, relating to, or being the metacarpus or a metacarpal

²metacarpal *noun* (1854)
: a bone of the part of the hand or forefoot between the carpus and the phalanges that typically contains five more or less elongated bones when all the digits are present

meta·car·pus \ˌme-tə-'kär-pəs\ *noun* [New Latin] (1676)
: the part of the hand or forefoot that contains the metacarpals

meta·cen·ter \'me-tə-ˌsen-tər\ *noun* [French *métacentre,* from *méta-* meta- + *centre* center] (1794)
: the point of intersection of the vertical through the center of buoyancy of a floating body with the vertical through the new center of buoyancy when the body is displaced

meta·cen·tric \ˌme-tə-'sen-trik\ *adjective* (1798)
1 : of or relating to a metacenter
2 : having the centromere medially situated so that the two chromosomal arms are of roughly equal length
— **metacentric** *noun*

metacenter: *1* center of gravity, *2* center of buoyancy, *3* new center of buoyancy when floating body is displaced, *4* point of intersection

meta·cer·car·ia \ˌme-tə-(ˌ)sər-'kar-ē-ə, -'ker-\ *noun* [New Latin] (1928)
: a tailless encysted late larva of a digenetic trematode that is usually the form which is infective for the definitive host
— **meta·cer·car·i·al** \-ē-əl\ *adjective*

meta·chro·mat·ic \-krō'ma-tik\ *adjective* (1876)
1 : staining or characterized by staining in a different color or shade from what is typical ⟨*metachromatic* granules in a bacterium⟩
2 : having the capacity to stain different elements of a cell or tissue in different colors or shades ⟨*metachromatic* stains⟩

meta·eth·ics \-'e-thiks\ *noun plural but usually singular in construction* (1949)
: the study of the meanings of ethical terms, the nature of ethical judgments, and the types of ethical arguments
— **meta·eth·i·cal** \-thi-kəl\ *adjective*

meta·fic·tion \-'fik-shən\ *noun* (1978)
: fiction which refers to or takes as its subject fictional writing and its conventions
— **meta·fic·tion·al** \-shnəl, -shə-nᵊl\ *adjective*
— **meta·fic·tion·ist** \-sh(ə-)nist\ *noun*

meta·gal·axy \-'ga-lək-sē\ *noun* [International Scientific Vocabulary] (1930)
: the entire system of galaxies : UNIVERSE
— **meta·ga·lac·tic** \-gə-'lak-tik\ *adjective*

meta·gen·e·sis \-'je-nə-səs\ *noun* [New Latin] (circa 1864)
: alternation of generations in animals; *especially* : regular alteration of a sexual and an asexual generation
— **meta·ge·net·ic** \-jə-'ne-tik\ *adjective*

¹met·al \'me-tᵊl\ *noun, often attributive* [Middle English, from Old French, from Latin *metallum* mine, metal, from Greek *metallon*] (14th century)
1 : any of various opaque, fusible, ductile, and typically lustrous substances that are good conductors of electricity and heat, form cations by loss of electrons, and yield basic oxides and hydroxides; *especially* : one that is a chemical element as distinguished from an alloy
2 a : METTLE 1a **b** : the material or substance out of which a person or thing is made
3 : glass in its molten state
4 a : printing type metal **b** : matter set in metal type
5 : ROAD METAL
6 : HEAVY METAL

²metal *transitive verb* **-aled** *or* **-alled; -al·ing** *or* **-al·ling** (1610)
: to cover or furnish with metal

meta·lan·guage \'me-tə-ˌlaŋ-gwij\ *noun* (1936)
: a language used to talk about language

meta·lin·guis·tic \'me-tə-liŋ-ˌgwis-tik\ *adjective* (1944)
: of or relating to a metalanguage or to metalinguistics

meta·lin·guis·tics \-tiks\ *noun plural but singular in construction* (1949)
: a branch of linguistics that deals with the relation between language and other cultural factors in a society

metall- *or* **metallo-** *combining form* [New Latin, from Latin *metallum*]
: metal ⟨*metallo*phone⟩

¹me·tal·lic \mə-'ta-lik\ *adjective* (15th century)
1 a : of, relating to, or being a metal **b** : made of or containing a metal **c** : having properties of a metal
2 : yielding metal
3 : resembling metal: as **a** : having iridescent and reflective properties ⟨*metallic* blond hair⟩ **b** : having an acrid quality like that of metal ⟨the tea has a *metallic* taste⟩
4 a : having a harsh resonance : GRATING ⟨a *metallic* voice⟩ **b** : having an impersonal or mechanical quality ⟨a *metallic* smile⟩
— **me·tal·li·cal·ly** \-li-k(ə-)lē\ *adverb*

²metallic *noun* (1952)
: a fiber or yarn made of or coated with metal; *also* : a fabric made with this

met·al·lif·er·ous \ˌme-tᵊl-'i-f(ə-)rəs\ *adjective* [Latin *metallifer,* from *metallum* + *-fer* -ferous] (circa 1656)
: yielding or containing metal

met·al·lize *also* **met·al·ize** \'me-tᵊl-ˌīz\ *transitive verb* **met·al·lized** *also* **met·al·ized; met·al·liz·ing** *also* **met·al·iz·ing** (1594)
: to coat, treat, or combine with a metal
— **met·al·li·za·tion** \ˌme-tᵊl-ə-'zā-shən\ *noun*

met·al·log·ra·phy \ˌme-tᵊl-'ä-grə-fē\ *noun* [International Scientific Vocabulary] (circa 1864)
: a study of the structure of metals especially with the microscope
— **met·al·log·ra·pher** \ˌme-tᵊl-'ä-grə-fər\ *noun*
— **me·tal·lo·graph·ic** \mə-ˌta-lə-'gra-fik\ *adjective*
— **me·tal·lo·graph·i·cal·ly** \-'gra-fi-k(ə-)lē\ *adverb*

¹met·al·loid \'me-tᵊl-ˌȯid\ *noun* (1832)
1 : a nonmetal that can combine with a metal to form an alloy
2 : an element intermediate in properties between the typical metals and nonmetals

²metalloid *also* **met·al·loi·dal** \ˌme-tᵊl-'ȯi-dᵊl\ *adjective* (circa 1850)
1 : resembling a metal
2 : of, relating to, or being a metalloid

me·tal·lo·phone \mə-'ta-lə-ˌfōn\ *noun* (circa 1883)
: a percussion musical instrument consisting of a series of metal bars of varying pitch struck with hammers

met·al·lur·gy \'me-tᵊl-ˌər-jē, *especially British* mə-'ta-lər-\ *noun* [New Latin *metallurgia,* from *metall-* + *-urgia* -urgy] (circa 1704)
: the science and technology of metals
— **met·al·lur·gi·cal** \ˌme-tᵊl-'ər-ji-kəl\ *adjective*
— **met·al·lur·gi·cal·ly** \-k(ə-)lē\ *adverb*
— **met·al·lur·gist** \'me-tᵊl-ˌər-jist, *especially British* mə-'ta-lər-\ *noun*

met·al·mark \'me-tᵊl-ˌmärk\ *noun* (circa 1909)
: any of a family (Riodinidae) of small or medium-sized usually brightly colored chiefly tropical butterflies that often have metallic coloration on the wings

met·al·smith \-ˌsmith\ *noun* (14th century)
: a person skilled in metalworking

met·al·ware \-ˌwar, -ˌwer\ *noun* (1896)
: ware made of metal; *especially* : metal utensils for household use

met·al·work \-ˌwərk\ *noun* (circa 1850)
: the product of metalworking; *especially* : a metal object of artistic merit
— **met·al·work·er** \-ˌwər-kər\ *noun*

met·al·work·ing \-ˌwər-kiŋ\ *noun* (1882)
: the act or process of shaping things out of metal

\ə\ **abut** \ᵊ\ **kitten** \ər\ **further** \a\ **ash** \ā\ **ace**
\ä\ **mop, mar** \au̇\ **out** \ch\ **chin** \e\ **bet** \ē\ **easy**
\g\ **go** \i\ **hit** \ī\ **ice** \j\ **job** \ŋ\ **sing** \ō\ **go**
\ȯ\ **law** \ȯi\ **boy** \th\ **thin** \t͟h\ **the** \ü\ **loot** \u̇\ **foot**
\y\ **yet** \zh\ **vision** *see also* Guide to Pronunciation

meta·math·e·mat·ics \'me-tə-ˌmath-'ma-tiks, -ma-thə-\ *noun plural but usually singular in construction* (circa 1890)
: a field of study concerned with the formal structure and properties (as the consistency and completeness of axioms) of mathematical systems
— **meta·math·e·mat·i·cal** \-ti-kəl\ *adjective*

meta·mere \'me-tə-ˌmir\ *noun* [International Scientific Vocabulary] (1877)
: any of a linear series of primitively similar segments into which the body of a higher invertebrate or vertebrate is divisible
— **meta·mer·ic** \ˌme-tə-'mer-ik, -'mir-\ *adjective*
— **meta·mer·i·cal·ly** \-i-k(ə-)lē\ *adverb*

me·tam·er·ism \mə-'ta-mə-ˌri-zəm\ *noun* (1877)
: the condition of having or the stage of evolutionary development characterized by a body made up of metameres

meta·mor·phic \ˌme-tə-'mȯr-fik\ *adjective* (1816)
1 : of or relating to metamorphosis
2 *of a rock* **:** of, relating to, or produced by metamorphism
— **meta·mor·phi·cal·ly** \-fi-k(ə-)lē\ *adverb*

meta·mor·phism \-'mȯr-ˌfi-zəm\ *noun* (1845)
: a change in the constitution of rock; *specifically* **:** a pronounced change effected by pressure, heat, and water that results in a more compact and more highly crystalline condition

meta·mor·phose \-ˌfōz, -ˌfōs\ *verb* **-phosed; -phos·ing** [probably from Middle French *metamorphoser*, from *metamorphose* metamorphosis, from Latin *metamorphosis*] (1576)
transitive verb
1 a : to change into a different physical form especially by supernatural means **b :** to change strikingly the appearance or character of **:** TRANSFORM ⟨you are so *metamorphosed* I can hardly think you my master —Shakespeare⟩
2 : to cause (rock) to undergo metamorphism
intransitive verb
1 : to undergo metamorphosis
2 : to become transformed
synonym see TRANSFORM

meta·mor·pho·sis \ˌme-tə-'mȯr-fə-səs\ *noun, plural* **-pho·ses** \-ˌsēz\ [Latin, from Greek *metamorphōsis*, from *metamorphoun* to transform, from *meta-* + *morphē* form] (1533)
1 a : change of physical form, structure, or substance especially by supernatural means **b :** a striking alteration in appearance, character, or circumstances
2 : a marked and more or less abrupt developmental change in the form or structure of an animal (as a butterfly or a frog) occurring subsequent to birth or hatching

met·anal·y·sis \ˌme-tə-'na-lə-səs\ *noun* (1914)
: a reanalysis of the division between sounds or words resulting in different constituents (as in the development of *an apron* from *a napron*)

meta·neph·ros \-'ne-frəs, -ˌfräs\ *noun, plural* **-roi** \-ˌfrȯi\ [New Latin, from *meta-* + Greek *nephros* kidney — more at NEPHRITIS] (1884)
: either member of the final and most caudal pair of the three successive pairs of vertebrate renal organs that functions as a permanent adult kidney in reptiles, birds, and mammals but is not present at all in lower forms — compare MESONEPHROS, PRONEPHROS
— **meta·neph·ric** \-frik\ *adjective*

meta·phase \'me-tə-ˌfāz\ *noun* [International Scientific Vocabulary] (1887)
: the stage of mitosis and meiosis in which the chromosomes become arranged in the equatorial plane of the spindle

metaphase plate *noun* (1939)
: a section in the equatorial plane of the metaphase spindle having the chromosomes oriented upon it

met·a·phor \'me-tə-ˌfȯr *also* -fər\ *noun* [Middle French or Latin; Middle French *metaphore*, from Latin *metaphora*, from Greek, from *metapherein* to transfer, from *meta-* + *pherein* to bear — more at BEAR] (1533)
1 : a figure of speech in which a word or phrase literally denoting one kind of object or idea is used in place of another to suggest a likeness or analogy between them (as in *drowning in money*); *broadly* **:** figurative language — compare SIMILE
2 : an object, activity, or idea treated as a metaphor **:** SYMBOL 2
— **met·a·phor·ic** \ˌme-tə-'fȯr-ik, -'fär-\ *or* **met·a·phor·i·cal** \-i-kəl\ *adjective*
— **met·a·phor·i·cal·ly** \-i-k(ə-)lē\ *adverb*

meta·phos·phate \ˌme-tə-'fäs-ˌfāt\ *noun* [International Scientific Vocabulary] (1833)
: a salt or ester of a metaphosphoric acid

meta·phos·pho·ric acid \-ˌfäs-'fȯr-ik, -'fär-; -ˌfäs-f(ə-)rik-\ *noun* (1833)
: a glassy solid acid HPO_3 or $(HPO_3)_n$ formed by heating orthophosphoric acid

meta·phrase \'me-tə-ˌfrāz\ *noun* (1640)
: a literal translation

meta·phys·ic \ˌme-tə-'fi-zik\ *noun* [Middle English *metaphesyk*, from Medieval Latin *metaphysica*] (14th century)
1 a : METAPHYSICS **b :** a particular system of metaphysics
2 : the system of principles underlying a particular study or subject **:** PHILOSOPHY 3b
— **metaphysic** *adjective*

meta·phys·i·cal \-'fi-zi-kəl\ *adjective* (15th century)
1 : of or relating to metaphysics
2 a : of or relating to the transcendent or to a reality beyond what is perceptible to the senses **b :** SUPERNATURAL
3 : highly abstract or abstruse; *also* **:** THEORETICAL
4 *often capitalized* **:** of or relating to poetry especially of the early 17th century that is highly intellectual and philosophical and marked by unconventional imagery
— **meta·phys·i·cal·ly** \-k(ə-)lē\ *adverb*

Metaphysical *noun* (1898)
: a metaphysical poet of the 17th century

meta·phy·si·cian \ˌme-tə-fə-'zi-shən\ *noun* (15th century)
: a student of or specialist in metaphysics

meta·phys·ics \-'fi-ziks\ *noun plural but singular in construction* [Medieval Latin *Metaphysica*, title of Aristotle's treatise on the subject, from Greek *(ta) meta (ta) physika*, literally, the (works) after the physical (works); from its position in his collected works] (1569)
1 a (1) **:** a division of philosophy that is concerned with the fundamental nature of reality and being and that includes ontology, cosmology, and often epistemology (2) **:** ONTOLOGY 2 **b :** abstract philosophical studies **:** a study of what is outside objective experience
2 : METAPHYSIC 2

meta·pla·sia \-'plā-zh(ē-)ə\ *noun* [New Latin] (1890)
1 : transformation of one tissue into another
2 : abnormal replacement of cells of one type by cells of another
— **meta·plas·tic** \-'plas-tik\ *adjective*

meta·psy·chol·o·gy \-sī-'kä-lə-jē\ *noun* [International Scientific Vocabulary] (circa 1909)
: speculative psychology concerned with postulating the structure (as the ego and id) and processes (as cathexis) of the mind which usually cannot be demonstrated objectively
— **meta·psy·cho·log·i·cal** \-ˌsī-kə-'lä-ji-kəl\ *adjective*

meta·se·quoia \-si-'kwȯi-ə\ *noun* [New Latin] (1948)
: any of a genus (*Metasequoia*) of fossil and living deciduous coniferous trees of the bald cypress family that have leaves, buds, and branches arranged oppositely and flat leaves resembling needles

meta·so·ma·tism \-'sō-mə-ˌti-zəm\ *noun* (1886)
: metamorphism that involves changes in the chemical composition as well as in the texture of rock
— **meta·so·mat·ic** \-sō-'ma-tik\ *adjective*

meta·sta·ble \-'stā-bəl\ *adjective* [International Scientific Vocabulary] (1897)
: having or characterized by only a slight margin of stability ⟨a *metastable* compound⟩
— **meta·sta·bil·i·ty** \-stə-'bi-lə-tē\ *noun*
— **meta·sta·bly** \-'stā-b(ə-)lē\ *adverb*

me·tas·ta·sis \mə-'tas-tə-səs\ *noun, plural* **-ta·ses** \-ˌsēz\ [New Latin, from Late Latin, transition, from Greek, from *methistanai* to change, from *meta-* + *histanai* to set — more at STAND] (1663)
: change of position, state, or form: as **a :** transfer of a disease-producing agency from the site of disease to another part of the body **b :** a secondary metastatic growth of a malignant tumor
— **met·a·stat·ic** \ˌme-tə-'sta-tik\ *adjective*
— **met·a·stat·i·cal·ly** \-ti-k(ə-)lē\ *adverb*

me·tas·ta·size \mə-'tas-tə-ˌsīz\ *intransitive verb* **-sized; -siz·ing** (1907)
: to spread by or as if by metastasis

¹meta·tar·sal \ˌme-tə-'tär-səl\ *adjective* (1739)
: of, relating to, or being the part of the human foot or of the hind foot in quadrupeds between the tarsus and the phalanges

²metatarsal *noun* (1854)
: a metatarsal bone

meta·tar·sus \ˌme-tə-'tär-səs\ *noun* [New Latin] (1676)
: the metatarsal part of a human foot or of a hind foot in quadrupeds

me·ta·te \mə-'tä-tē\ *noun* [Spanish, from Nahuatl *metatl*] (1834)
: a stone with a concave upper surface used as the lower millstone for grinding grains and especially maize

me·tath·e·sis \mə-'ta-thə-səs\ *noun, plural* **-e·ses** \-ˌsēz\ [Late Latin, from Greek, from *metatithenai* to transpose, from *meta-* + *tithenai* to place — more at DO] (1577)
: a change of place or condition: as **a :** transposition of two phonemes in a word (as in the development of *crud* from *curd* or the pronunciation \'pur-tē\ for *pretty*) **b :** a chemical reaction in which different kinds of molecules exchange parts to form other kinds of molecules
— **met·a·thet·i·cal** \ˌme-tə-'the-ti-kəl\ *or* **met·a·thet·ic** \-tik\ *adjective*
— **met·a·thet·i·cal·ly** \-ti-k(ə-)lē\ *adverb*

meta·tho·rac·ic \ˌme-tə-thə-'ra-sik\ *adjective* (circa 1839)
: of, relating to, or situated in or on the metathorax ⟨*metathoracic* legs⟩

meta·tho·rax \-'thȯr-ˌaks, -'thȯr-\ *noun* [New Latin] (1816)
: the posterior segment of the thorax of an insect — see INSECT illustration

meta·xy·lem \-'zī-ləm, -ˌlem\ *noun* (1902)
: the part of the primary xylem that differentiates after the protoxylem and that is distinguished typically by broader tracheids and vessels with pitted or reticulate walls

meta·zo·al \-'zō-əl\ *adjective* [New Latin *Metazoa*] (1928)
: of or relating to the metazoans

meta·zo·an \-'zō-ən\ *noun* [New Latin *Metazoa*, from *meta-* + *-zoa*] (1884)
: any of a group (*Metazoa*) that comprises all animals having the body composed of cells differentiated into tissues and organs and usually a digestive cavity lined with specialized cells
— **metazoan** *adjective*

¹mete \'mēt\ *transitive verb* **met·ed; met·ing** [Middle English, from Old English *metan;* akin to Old High German *mezzan* to measure, Latin *modus* measure, Greek *medesthai* to be mindful of] (before 12th century)
1 *archaic* : MEASURE
2 : to give out by measure : DOLE — usually used with *out* ⟨*mete* out punishment⟩

²mete *noun* [Middle English, from Anglo-French, from Latin *meta*] (15th century)
: BOUNDARY ⟨*metes* and bounds⟩

me·tem·psy·cho·sis \mə-ˌtem(p)-si-'kō-səs, ˌme-təm-ˌsī-\ *noun* [Late Latin, from Greek *metempsychōsis,* from *metempsychousthai* to undergo metempsychosis, from *meta-* + *empsychos* animate, from *en-* + *psychē* soul — more at PSYCH-] (1591)
: the passing of the soul at death into another body either human or animal

met·en·ceph·a·lon \ˌmet-ˌen-'se-fə-ˌlän, -lən\ *noun* [New Latin] (circa 1871)
: the anterior segment of the developing vertebrate hindbrain or the corresponding part of the adult brain composed of the cerebellum and pons
— **met·en·ce·phal·ic** \-ˌen(t)-sə-'fa-lik\ *adjective*

me·te·or \'mē-tē-ər, -ˌȯr\ *noun* [Middle English, from Middle French *meteore,* from Medieval Latin *meteorum,* from Greek *meteōron,* from neuter of *meteōros* high in air, from *meta-* + *-eōros,* from *aeirein* to lift] (15th century)
1 : an atmospheric phenomenon (as lightning or a snowfall)
2 a : any of the small particles of matter in the solar system that are directly observable only by their incandescence from frictional heating on entry into the atmosphere **b** : the streak of light produced by the passage of a meteor

me·te·or·ic \ˌmē-tē-'ȯr-ik, -'är-\ *adjective* (1789)
1 : of, relating to, or derived from the earth's atmosphere ⟨*meteoric* water⟩
2 a : of or relating to a meteor **b** : resembling a meteor in speed or in sudden and temporary brilliance ⟨a *meteoric* rise to fame⟩
— **me·te·or·i·cal·ly** \-i-k(ə-)lē\ *adverb*

me·te·or·ite \'mē-tē-ə-ˌrīt\ *noun* (1824)
: a meteor that reaches the surface of the earth without being completely vaporized
— **me·te·or·it·ic** \ˌmē-tē-ə-'ri-tik\ *also* **me·te·or·it·i·cal** \-ti-kəl\ *adjective*

me·te·or·it·ics \ˌmē-tē-ə-'ri-tiks\ *noun plural but singular in construction* (circa 1930)
: a science that deals with meteors
— **me·te·or·it·i·cist** \-'ri-tə-sist\ *noun*

me·te·or·oid \'mē-tē-ə-ˌrȯid\ *noun* (1865)
1 : a meteor particle itself without relation to the phenomena it produces when entering the earth's atmosphere
2 : a meteor in orbit around the sun
— **me·te·or·oi·dal** \ˌmē-tē-ə-'rȯi-dᵊl\ *adjective*

me·te·o·rol·o·gy \ˌmē-tē-ə-'rä-lə-jē\ *noun* [French or Greek; French *météorologie,* from Middle French, from Greek *meteōrologia,* from *meteōron* + *-logia* -logy] (1620)
1 : a science that deals with the atmosphere and its phenomena and especially with weather and weather forecasting
2 : the atmospheric phenomena and weather of a region
— **me·te·o·ro·log·ic** \-rə-'lä-jik\ *or* **me·te·o·ro·log·i·cal** \-ji-kəl\ *adjective*
— **me·te·o·ro·log·i·cal·ly** \-ji-k(ə-)lē\ *adverb*
— **me·te·o·rol·o·gist** \-'rä-lə-jist\ *noun*

¹me·ter \'mē-tər\ *noun* [Middle English, from Old English & Middle French; Old English *mēter,* from Latin *metrum,* from Greek *metron* measure, meter; Middle French *metre,* from

Old French, from Latin *metrum* — more at MEASURE] (before 12th century)
1 a : systematically arranged and measured rhythm in verse: (1) : rhythm that continuously repeats a single basic pattern ⟨iambic *meter*⟩ (2) : rhythm characterized by regular recurrence of a systematic arrangement of basic patterns in larger figures ⟨ballad *meter*⟩ **b** : a measure or unit of metrical verse — usually used in combination ⟨penta*meter*⟩; compare FOOT 4 **c** : a fixed metrical pattern : verse form
2 : the basic recurrent rhythmical pattern of note values, accents, and beats per measure in music

²me·ter \'mē-tər\ *noun* [Middle English, from *meten* to mete] (14th century)
: one that measures; *especially* : an official measurer of commodities

³me·ter *noun* [French *mètre,* from Greek *metron* measure] (1797)
: the base unit of length in the International System of Units that is equal to the distance traveled by light in a vacuum in 1/299,792,458 second or to about 39.37 inches — see METRIC SYSTEM table

⁴me·ter *noun* [-*meter*] (1815)
1 : an instrument for measuring and sometimes recording the time or amount of something ⟨a parking *meter*⟩ ⟨a gas *meter*⟩
2 : POSTAGE METER; *also* : a postal marking printed by a postage meter

⁵me·ter *transitive verb* (1884)
1 : to measure by means of a meter
2 : to supply in a measured or regulated amount
3 : to print postal indicia on by means of a postage meter

-me·ter *noun combining form* [French -*mètre,* from Greek *metron* measure]
: instrument or means for measuring ⟨baro*meter*⟩

me·ter–ki·lo·gram–sec·ond *adjective* (circa 1940)
: of, relating to, or being a system of units using the meter, kilogram, and second as its base units — abbreviation *mks*

me·ter maid *noun* (1957)
: a woman assigned by a police or traffic department to write tickets for parking violations

me·ter·stick \'mē-tər-ˌstik\ *noun* (1931)
: a measuring stick one meter long that is marked off in centimeters and usually millimeters

met·es·trus \ˌmet-'es-trəs\ *noun* [New Latin] (1900)
: the period of regression that follows estrus

meth- *or* **metho-** *combining form* [International Scientific Vocabulary, from *methyl*]
: methyl ⟨*meth*acrylic⟩

meth·ac·ry·late \ˌme-'tha-krə-ˌlāt\ *noun* [International Scientific Vocabulary] (1865)
1 : a salt or ester of methacrylic acid
2 : an acrylic resin or plastic made from a derivative of methacrylic acid

meth·acryl·ic acid \ˌme-thə-'kri-lik-\ *noun* [International Scientific Vocabulary] (1865)
: an acid $C_4H_6O_2$ used especially in making acrylic resins or plastics

meth·a·done \'me-thə-ˌdōn\ *also* **meth·a·don** \-ˌdän\ *noun* [*meth*yl + *amino* + *d*iphenyl + *-one*] (1947)
: a synthetic addictive narcotic drug $C_{21}H_{27}NO$ used especially in the form of its hydrochloride for the relief of pain and as a substitute narcotic in the treatment of heroin addiction

meth·am·phet·amine \ˌme-tham-'fe-tə-ˌmēn, -thəm-, -mən\ *noun* (1949)
: an amine $C_{10}H_{15}N$ used medically in the form of its crystalline hydrochloride especially in the treatment of obesity and often used illicitly as a stimulant — called also *methedrine*

meth·a·na·tion \ˌme-thə-'nā-shən\ *noun* (1926)

: the production of methane especially from carbon monoxide and hydrogen

meth·ane \'me-ˌthān, *British usually* 'mē-\ *noun* [International Scientific Vocabulary] (circa 1868)
: a colorless odorless flammable gaseous hydrocarbon CH_4 that is a product of decomposition of organic matter and of the carbonization of coal, is used as a fuel and as a starting material in chemical synthesis, and is the simplest of the alkanes

meth·a·nol \'me-thə-ˌnȯl, -ˌnōl\ *noun* [International Scientific Vocabulary] (1894)
: a light volatile flammable poisonous liquid alcohol CH_3OH used especially as a solvent, antifreeze, or denaturant for ethyl alcohol and in the synthesis of other chemicals

meth·aqua·lone \me-'tha-kwə-ˌlōn\ *noun* [*meth-* + -*a-* (of unknown origin) + *qu*inoline + *az*ole + -*one*] (1961)
: a sedative and hypnotic nonbarbiturate drug $C_{16}H_{14}N_2O$ that is habit-forming — compare QUAALUDE

meth·e·drine \'me-thə-ˌdrēn, -drən\ *noun* [from *Methedrine,* a trademark] (1939)
: METHAMPHETAMINE

me·theg·lin \mə-'the-glən\ *noun* [Welsh *meddyglyn*] (1533)
: ¹MEAD

met·he·mo·glo·bin \ˌmet-'hē-mə-ˌglō-bən\ *noun* [International Scientific Vocabulary] (1870)
: a soluble brown crystalline basic blood pigment that differs from hemoglobin in containing ferric iron and in being unable to combine reversibly with molecular oxygen

met·he·mo·glo·bi·ne·mia \ˌmet-ˌhē-mə-ˌglō-bə-'nē-mē-ə\ *noun* [New Latin] (1888)
: the presence of methemoglobin in the blood

me·the·na·mine \mə-'thē-nə-ˌmēn, -mən\ *noun* [*methene* (methylene) + *amine*] (1926)
: hexamethylenetetramine especially when used as a urinary antiseptic

meth·i·cil·lin \ˌme-thə-'si-lən\ *noun* [*meth-* + peni*cillin*] (1961)
: a semisynthetic penicillin $C_{17}H_{19}N_2O_6NaS$ that is especially effective against penicillinase-producing staphylococci

me·thinks \mi-'thiŋ(k)s\ *impersonal verb, past* **me·thought** \-'thȯt\ [Middle English *me thinketh,* from Old English *mē thincth,* from *mē* (dative of *ic* I) + *thincth* seems, from *thyncan* to seem — more at I, THINK] (before 12th century)
archaic : it seems to me

me·thi·o·nine \mə-'thī-ə-ˌnēn\ *noun* [International Scientific Vocabulary, from *methyl* + *thion-* + -²*ine*] (1928)
: a crystalline sulfur-containing essential amino acid $C_5H_{11}NO_2S$

meth·od \'me-thəd\ *noun* [Middle French or Latin; Middle French *methode,* from Latin *methodus,* from Greek *methodos,* from *meta-* + *hodos* way] (1541)
1 : a procedure or process for attaining an object: as **a** (1) : a systematic procedure, technique, or mode of inquiry employed by or proper to a particular discipline or art (2) : a systematic plan followed in presenting material for instruction **b** (1) : a way, technique, or process of or for doing something (2) : a body of skills or techniques
2 : a discipline that deals with the principles and techniques of scientific inquiry
3 a : orderly arrangement, development, or classification : PLAN **b** : the habitual practice of orderliness and regularity
4 *capitalized* : a dramatic technique by which an actor seeks to gain complete identification

\ə\ abut \ᵊ\ kitten \ər\ further \a\ ash \ā\ ace
\ä\ mop, mar \au̇\ out \ch\ chin \e\ bet \ē\ easy
\g\ go \i\ hit \ī\ ice \j\ job \ŋ\ sing \ō\ go
\ȯ\ law \ȯi\ boy \th\ thin \t͟h\ the \ü\ loot \u̇\ foot
\y\ yet \zh\ vision *see also* Guide to Pronunciation

with the inner personality of the character being portrayed ☆

me·thod·i·cal \mə-'thä-di-kəl\ also **me·thod·ic** \-dik\ adjective (1570)
1 : arranged, characterized by, or performed with method or order ⟨a methodical treatment of the subject⟩
2 : habitually proceeding according to method : SYSTEMATIC ⟨methodical in his daily routine⟩
— **me·thod·i·cal·ly** \-di-k(ə-)lē\ adverb
— **me·thod·i·cal·ness** \-di-kəl-nəs\ noun

meth·od·ise British variant of METHODIZE

meth·od·ism \'me-thə-ˌzəm\ noun (1739)
1 capitalized **a** : the doctrines and practice of Methodists **b** : the Methodist churches
2 : methodical procedure

meth·od·ist \-dist\ noun (1593)
1 : a person devoted to or laying great stress on method
2 capitalized : a member of one of the denominations deriving from the Wesleyan revival in the Church of England, having Arminian doctrine and in the U.S. modified episcopal polity, and stressing personal and social morality
— **methodist** adjective, often capitalized
— **meth·od·is·tic** \ˌme-thə-'dis-tik\ adjective

meth·od·ize \'me-thə-ˌdīz\ transitive verb **-ized; -iz·ing** (1589)
: to reduce to method : SYSTEMATIZE
synonym see ORDER

method of fluxions noun (circa 1719)
: DIFFERENTIAL CALCULUS

meth·od·o·log·i·cal \ˌme-thə-dᵊl-'ä-ji-kəl\ adjective (1849)
: of or relating to method or methodology
— **meth·od·o·log·i·cal·ly** \-k(ə-)lē\ adverb

meth·od·ol·o·gist \-thə-'dä-lə-jist\ noun (1865)
: a student of methodology

meth·od·ol·o·gy \-thə-'dä-lə-jē\ noun, plural **-gies** [New Latin methodologia, from Latin methodus + -logia -logy] (1800)
1 : a body of methods, rules, and postulates employed by a discipline : a particular procedure or set of procedures
2 : the analysis of the principles or procedures of inquiry in a particular field

meth·o·trex·ate \ˌme-thə-'trek-ˌsāt\ noun [meth- + -trexate, of unknown origin] (1955)
: a toxic anticancer drug $C_{20}H_{22}N_8O_5$ that is an analogue of folic acid and an antimetabolite

me·thoxy·chlor \me-'thäk-si-ˌklȯr, -ˌklȯr\ noun [meth- + oxy- + chlor-] (1947)
: a chlorinated hydrocarbon insecticide $C_{16}H_{15}Cl_3O_2$

me·thoxy·flu·rane \me-ˌthäk-sē-'flu̇r-ˌān\ noun [meth- + oxy- + fluor- + ethane] (1962)
: a potent nonexplosive inhalational general anesthetic $C_3H_4Cl_2F_2O$ administered as a vapor

Me·thu·se·lah \mə-'thü-zə-lə, -'thyü-\ -'th(y)üz-lə\ noun [Hebrew Mĕthūšelah]
1 : an ancestor of Noah held to have lived 969 years
2 : an oversize wine bottle holding about 6 liters

meth·yl \'me-thəl\ noun [International Scientific Vocabulary, back-formation from methylene] (circa 1844)
: an alkyl group CH_3 derived from methane by removal of one hydrogen atom
— **me·thyl·ic** \me-'thi-lik\ adjective

methyl acetate noun (1885)
: a flammable fragrant liquid $C_3H_6O_2$ used as a solvent and paint remover and in organic synthesis

methyl alcohol noun (circa 1847)
: METHANOL

me·thyl·amine \ˌme-thə-lə-'mēn, -'la-mən; mə-'thi-lə-ˌmēn\ noun [International Scientific Vocabulary] (circa 1850)
: a flammable explosive gas CH_3NH_2 with a strong ammoniacal odor used especially in organic synthesis (as of dyes and insecticides)

meth·yl·ase \'me-thə-ˌlās, -ˌlāz\ noun (circa 1952)
: an enzyme that catalyzes methylation (as of RNA or DNA)

meth·yl·ate \'me-thə-ˌlāt\ transitive verb **-at·ed; -at·ing** (1861)
: to introduce the methyl group into
— **meth·yl·a·tion** \ˌme-thə-'lā-shən\ noun
— **meth·yl·a·tor** \'me-thə-ˌlā-tər\ noun

methyl bromide noun (circa 1897)
: a poisonous gaseous compound CH_3Br used chiefly as a fumigant against rodents, worms, and insects

meth·yl·cel·lu·lose \ˌme-thəl-'sel-yə-ˌlōs, -ˌlōz\ noun (1921)
: any of various gummy products of cellulose methylation that swell in water and are used especially as emulsifiers, adhesives, thickeners, and bulk laxatives

meth·yl·cho·lan·threne \-kə-'lan-ˌthrēn\ noun [methyl + cholic acid + anthracene] (1937)
: a potent carcinogenic hydrocarbon $C_{21}H_{16}$

meth·yl·do·pa \ˌme-thəl-'dō-pə\ noun (1954)
: a drug $C_{10}H_{13}NO_4$ used to lower blood pressure

meth·y·lene \'me-thə-ˌlēn, -lən\ noun [French méthylène, from Greek methy wine + hylē wood — more at MEAD] (1835)
: a bivalent hydrocarbon group CH_2 derived from methane by removal of two hydrogen atoms

methylene blue noun (circa 1890)
: a basic thiazine dye $C_{16}H_{18}ClN_3S \cdot 3H_2O$ used especially as a biological stain, an antidote in cyanide poisoning, and an oxidation-reduction indicator

methylene chloride noun (1880)
: a nonflammable liquid CH_2Cl_2 used especially as a solvent, paint remover, and aerosol propellant

methyl ethyl ketone noun (1876)
: a flammable liquid compound C_4H_8O similar to acetone and used chiefly as a solvent — abbreviation MEK

methyl isocyanate noun (circa 1894)
: an extremely toxic chemical CH_3NCO used especially in the manufacture of pesticides — abbreviation MIC

meth·yl·mer·cury \ˌme-thəl-'mər-kyə-rē, -'mər-k(ə-)rē\ noun (1919)
: any of various toxic compounds of mercury containing the complex CH_3Hg- that often occur as pollutants which accumulate in living organisms (as fish) especially in higher levels of a food chain

methyl methacrylate noun (1933)
: a volatile flammable liquid $C_5H_8O_2$ that polymerizes readily and is used especially as a monomer for resins

meth·yl·naph·tha·lene \ˌme-thəl-'naf-thə-ˌlēn, -'nap-\ noun (circa 1885)
: either of two isomeric hydrocarbons $C_{11}H_{10}$; especially : an oily liquid used in determining cetane numbers

methyl orange noun (1881)
: an alkaline dye used as a chemical indicator that in dilute solution is yellow when neutral and pink when acid

methyl parathion noun (1957)
: a potent synthetic organophosphate insecticide $C_8H_{10}NO_5PS$ that is more toxic than parathion

meth·yl·phe·ni·date \ˌme-thəl-'fe-nə-ˌdāt, -'fē-\ noun [methyl + phenyl + piperidine + acetate] (1958)
: a mild stimulant $C_{14}H_{19}NO_2$ of the central nervous system used in the form of its hydrochloride to treat narcolepsy and hyperkinetic behavior disorders in children

meth·yl·pred·nis·o·lone \-pred-'ni-sə-ˌlōn\ noun (1957)
: a glucocorticoid $C_{22}H_{30}O_5$ that is a derivative of prednisolone and is used as an anti-inflammatory agent; also : any of several of its salts (as an acetate) used similarly

meth·yl·xan·thine \-'zan-ˌthēn\ noun (1949)
: a methylated xanthine derivative (as caffeine, theobromine, or theophylline)

meth·y·ser·gide \ˌme-thə-'sər-ˌjīd\ noun [methyl + lysergic acid + amide] (1962)
: a serotonin antagonist $C_{21}H_{27}N_3O_2$ used in the form of its maleate especially in the treatment and prevention of migraine headaches

met·i·cal \'me-ti-kəl\ noun, plural **met·i·cais** \-(ˌ)kī\ also **meticals** [Portuguese, from Arabic mithqāl] (1981)
— see MONEY table

me·tic·u·lous \mə-'ti-kyə-ləs\ adjective [Latin meticulosus fearful, irregular from metus fear] (1827)
: marked by extreme or excessive care in the consideration or treatment of details
synonym see CAREFUL
— **me·tic·u·los·i·ty** \-ˌti-kyə-'lä-sə-tē\ noun
— **me·tic·u·lous·ly** \-'ti-kyə-ləs-lē\ adverb
— **me·tic·u·lous·ness** \-nəs\ noun

mé·tier also **me·tier** \'me-ˌtyā, me-'\ noun [French, from (assumed) Vulgar Latin misterium, alteration of Latin ministerium work, ministry] (1792)
1 : VOCATION, TRADE
2 : an area of activity in which one excels : FORTE
synonym see WORK

mé·tis \mā-'tē(s)\ noun, plural **mé·tis** \-'tē(s), -'tēz\ [French, from Late Latin mixticius mixed — more at MESTIZO] (1816)
: one of mixed blood; especially, often capitalized : the offspring of an American Indian and a person of European ancestry

met·o·nym \'me-tə-ˌnim\ noun [back-formation from metonymy] (1862)
: a word used in metonymy

me·ton·y·my \mə-'tä-nə-mē\ noun, plural **-mies** [Latin metonymia, from Greek metōnymia, from meta- + -ōnymon -onym] (1547)
: a figure of speech consisting of the use of the name of one thing for that of another of which it is an attribute or with which it is associated (as "crown" in "lands belonging to the crown")
— **met·o·nym·ic** \ˌme-tə-'ni-mik\ or **met·o·nym·i·cal** \-mi-kəl\ adjective

me-too \'mē-'tü\ adjective (1926)
1 : marked by similarity to or by adoption of successful or persuasive policies or practices used or promoted by someone else
2 : similar or identical to an established product (as a drug) with no significant advantage over it
— **me-too·er** \-ər\ noun
— **me-too·ism** \-ˌi-zəm\ noun

met·o·pe \'me-tə-(ˌ)pē\ noun [Greek metopē, from meta- + opē opening; akin to Greek ōps eye, face — more at EYE] (1563)

☆ **SYNONYMS**
Method, mode, manner, way, fashion, system mean the means taken or procedure followed in achieving an end. METHOD implies an orderly logical effective arrangement usually in steps ⟨effective teaching methods⟩. MODE implies an order or course followed by custom, tradition, or personal preference ⟨the preferred mode of transportation⟩. MANNER is close to MODE but may imply a procedure or method that is individual or distinctive ⟨an odd manner of conducting⟩. WAY is very general and may be used for any of the preceding words ⟨has her own way of doing things⟩. FASHION may suggest a peculiar or characteristic way of doing something ⟨rushing about in his typical fashion⟩. SYSTEM suggests a fully developed or carefully formulated method often emphasizing the idea of rational orderliness ⟨a filing system⟩.

METRIC SYSTEM[1]

LENGTH

Unit	Abbreviation	Number of Meters	Approximate U.S. Equivalent
kilometer	km	1,000	0.62 mile
hectometer	hm	100	328.08 feet
dekameter	dam	10	32.81 feet
meter	m	1	39.37 inches
decimeter	dm	0.1	3.94 inches
centimeter	cm	0.01	0.39 inch
millimeter	mm	0.001	0.039 inch
micrometer	μm	0.000001	0.000039 inch

AREA

Unit	Abbreviation	Number of Square Meters	Approximate U.S. Equivalent
square kilometer	sq km or km^2	1,000,000	0.3861 square miles
hectare	ha	10,000	2.47 acres
are	a	100	119.60 square yards
square centimeter	sq cm or cm^2	0.0001	0.155 square inch

VOLUME

Unit	Abbreviation	Number of Cubic Meters	Approximate U.S. Equivalent
cubic meter	m^3	1	1.307 cubic yards
cubic decimeter	dm^3	0.001	61.023 cubic inches
cubic centimeter	cu cm or cm^3 also cc	0.000001	0.061 cubic inch

CAPACITY

Unit	Abbreviation	Number of Liters	cubic	dry	liquid
kiloliter	kl	1,000	1.31 cubic yards		
hectoliter	hl	100	3.53 cubic feet	2.84 bushels	
dekaliter	dal	10	0.35 cubic foot	1.14 pecks	2.64 gallons
liter	l	1	61.02 cubic inches	0.908 quart	1.057 quarts
cubic decimeter	dm^3	1	61.02 cubic inches	0.908 quart	1.057 quarts
deciliter	dl	0.10	6.1 cubic inches	0.18 pint	0.21 pint
centiliter	cl	0.01	0.61 cubic inch		0.338 fluid ounce
milliliter	ml	0.001	0.061 cubic inch		0.27 fluid dram
microliter	μl	0.000001	0.000061 cubic inch		0.00027 fluid dram

MASS AND WEIGHT

Unit	Abbreviation	Number of Grams	Approximate U.S. Equivalent
metric ton	t	1,000,000	1.102 short tons
kilogram	kg	1,000	2.2046 pounds
hectogram	hg	100	3.527 ounces
dekagram	dag	10	0.353 ounce
gram	g	1	0.035 ounce
decigram	dg	0.10	1.543 grains
centigram	cg	0.01	0.154 grain
milligram	mg	0.001	0.015 grain
microgram	μg	0.000001	0.000015 grain

[1]For metric equivalents of U.S. units, see Weights and Measures table

: the space between two triglyphs of a Doric frieze often adorned with carved work

met·o·pon \'me-tə-ˌpän\ *noun* [*meth*- + hydro- + *morphine* + -*one*] (1941)
: a narcotic drug $C_{18}H_{21}NO_3$ that is derived from morphine and is used in the form of the hydrochloride to relieve pain

me·tre \'mē-tər\ *chiefly British variant of* METER

¹met·ric \'me-trik\ *noun* [Greek *metrikē*, from feminine of *metrikos* in meter, by measure, from *metron* measure — more at MEASURE] (1760)
1 *plural* : a part of prosody that deals with metrical structure
2 : a standard of measurement ⟨no *metric* exists that can be applied directly to happiness —*Scientific Monthly*⟩
3 : a mathematical function that associates with each pair of elements of a set a real nonnegative number with the general properties of distance such that the number is zero only if the two elements are identical, the number is the same regardless of the order in which the two elements are taken, and the number associated with one pair of elements plus that associated with one member of the pair and a third element is equal to or greater than the number associated with the other member of the pair and the third element

²metric *adjective* [French *métrique*, from *mè-tre* meter] (1864)
: of, relating to, or using the metric system ⟨a *metric* study⟩
— **met·ri·cal·ly** \-tri-k(ə-)lē\ *adverb*

-metric *or* **-metrical** *adjective combining form*
1 : of, employing, or obtained by (such) a meter ⟨galvano*metric*⟩
2 : of or relating to (such) an art, process, or science of measuring ⟨geo*metrical*⟩

met·ri·cal \'me-tri-kəl\ *or* **met·ric** \-trik\ *adjective* (15th century)
1 : of, relating to, or composed in meter
2 : of or relating to measurement
— **met·ri·cal·ly** \-tri-k(ə-)lē\ *adverb*

met·ri·ca·tion \ˌme-tri-ˈkā-shən\ *noun* (1965)
: the act or process of metricizing; *specifically* : conversion of an existent system of units into the metric system

met·ri·cize \'me-trə-ˌsīz\ *transitive verb* **-cized; -ciz·ing** (1873)
: to change into or express in the metric system

metric space *noun* (1927)
: a mathematical set for which a metric is defined for any pair of elements

metric system *noun* (1864)
: a decimal system of weights and measures based on the meter and on the kilogram

metric ton *noun* (circa 1890)
— see METRIC SYSTEM table

me·trist \'me-trist, 'mē-\ *noun* (1535)
1 : a maker of verses
2 : one skillful in handling meter
3 : a student of meter or metrics

¹met·ro \'me-(ˌ)trō, *in French context also* mā-'\ *noun, plural* **metros** [French *métro*, short for (*chemin de fer*) *métropolitain* metropolitan railroad] (1904)
: SUBWAY b

²met·ro \'me-(ˌ)trō\ *adjective* (1953)
: METROPOLITAN 2

me·trol·o·gy \me-ˈträ-lə-jē\ *noun* [French *métrologie*, from Greek *metrologia* theory of ratios, from *metron* measure — more at MEASURE] (1816)
1 : the science of weights and measures or of measurement
2 : a system of weights and measures
— **met·ro·log·i·cal** \ˌme-trə-ˈlä-ji-kəl\ *adjective*
— **me·trol·o·gist** \me-ˈträ-lə-jist\ *noun*

met·ro·ni·da·zole \ˌme-trə-ˈnī-də-ˌzōl\ *noun* [*methyl* + *-tron-* (probably alteration of *nitro-*) + *imide* + *azole*] (1962)
: a drug $C_6H_9N_3O_3$ used especially in treating vaginal trichomoniasis

met·ro·nome \ˈme-trə-ˌnōm\ *noun* [Greek *metron* + *-nomos* controlling, from *nomos* law — more at NIMBLE] (1816)
: an instrument designed to mark exact time by a regularly repeated tick

met·ro·nom·ic \ˌme-trə-ˈnä-mik\ *also* **met·ro·nom·i·cal** \-mi-kəl\ *adjective* (1866)
: mechanically regular (as in action or tempo)
— **met·ro·nom·i·cal·ly** \-mi-k(ə-)lē\ *adverb*

me·trop·o·lis \mə-ˈträ-p(ə-)ləs\ *noun* [Middle English, from Late Latin, from Greek *mētropolis,* from *mētr-, mētēr* mother + *polis* city — more at MOTHER, POLICE] (14th century)
1 : the chief or capital city of a country, state, or region
2 : the city or state of origin of a colony (as of ancient Greece)
3 a : a city regarded as a center of a specified activity ⟨a great business *metropolis*⟩ **b :** a large important city ⟨the world's great *metropolises* —P. E. James⟩

¹met·ro·pol·i·tan \ˌme-trə-ˈpä-lə-tᵊn\ *noun* (14th century)
1 : the primate of an ecclesiastical province
2 : one who lives in a metropolis or displays metropolitan manners or customs

²metropolitan *adjective* [Middle English, from Late Latin *metropolitanus* of the see of a metropolitan, from *metropolita,* noun, metropolitan, from Late Greek *mētropolitēs,* from *mētropolis* see of a metropolitan, from Greek, capital] (15th century)
1 : of or constituting a metropolitan or his see
2 : of, relating to, or characteristic of a metropolis and sometimes including its suburbs
3 : of, relating to, or constituting a mother country as distinguished from a colony

me·tror·rha·gia \ˌmē-trə-ˈrā-j(ē-)ə, -ˈrä-zhə; -ˈrä-jə, -zhə\ *noun* [New Latin, from *metro-* womb (from Greek *mētra,* from *mētr-, mētēr* mother) + *-rrhagia* — more at MOTHER] (1879)
: profuse uterine bleeding especially between menstrual periods

-metry *noun combining form* [Middle English *-metrie,* from Middle French, from Latin *-metria,* from Greek, from *metrein* to measure, from *metron* — more at MEASURE]
: art, process, or science of measuring ⟨chronometry⟩ ⟨photometry⟩

met·tle \ˈme-tᵊl\ *noun* [alteration of *metal*] (1581)
1 a : vigor and strength of spirit or temperament ⟨suspected to have more tongue in his head than *mettle* in his bosom —Sir Walter Scott⟩ **b :** staying quality : STAMINA ⟨trucks had proved their *mettle* in army transport —*Pioneer & Pacemaker*⟩
2 : quality of temperament or disposition ⟨gentlemen of brave *mettle* —Shakespeare⟩
synonym see COURAGE
— **met·tled** \-tᵊld\ *adjective*
— **on one's mettle :** aroused to do one's best

met·tle·some \ˈme-tᵊl-səm\ *adjective* (1662)
: full of mettle : SPIRITED

meu·nière \ˌ(ˌ)mə(r)n-ˈyer, ˌmœn-\ *adjective* [French (*à la*) *meunière,* literally, in the manner of a miller's wife] (1903)
: rolled lightly in flour and sautéed in butter ⟨sole *meunière*⟩

Meur·sault \mə(r)-ˈsō, mœ-\ *noun* [French, from *Meursault,* commune in France] (1833)
: a dry white burgundy wine

¹mew \ˈmyü\ *noun* [Middle English, from Old English *mǣw;* akin to Old Norse *mār* gull] (before 12th century)
: GULL; *especially* : the common European gull (*Larus canus*)

²mew *verb* [Middle English *mewen,* of imitative origin] (14th century)
intransitive verb
: to utter a mew or similar sound ⟨gulls *mewed* over the bay⟩
transitive verb
: to utter by mewing : MEOW

³mew *noun* (1596)
: MEOW

⁴mew *noun* [Middle English *mewe,* from Middle French *mue,* from *muer* to molt, from Latin *mutare* to change — more at MUTABLE] (14th century)
1 : an enclosure for trained hawks — usually used in plural
2 : a place for hiding or retirement
3 *plural but singular or plural in construction, chiefly British* **a** (1) **:** stables usually with living quarters built around a court (2) **:** living quarters adapted from such stables **b :** back street : ALLEY

⁵mew *transitive verb* (15th century)
: to shut up : CONFINE — often used with *up*

mewl \ˈmyü(ə)l\ *intransitive verb* [imitative] (1600)
: to cry weakly : WHIMPER

Mex·i·can \ˈmek-si-kən\ *noun* (1604)
1 a : a native or inhabitant of Mexico **b :** a person of Mexican descent **c** *Southwest* **:** a person of mixed Spanish and Indian descent
2 : NAHUATL
— **Mexican** *adjective*

Mexican bean beetle *noun* (1921)
: a spotted ladybug (*Epilachna varivestis*) that feeds on the leaves of beans

Mexican jumping bean *noun* (circa 1929)
: JUMPING BEAN

Mexican Spanish *noun* (1945)
: the Spanish used in Mexico

Mexican standoff *noun* (1891)
: a situation in which no one emerges a clear winner; *also* : DEADLOCK

me·ze \ˈme-ˌzā, ˈmä-(ˌ)zā\ *noun, plural* **mezes** *also* **meze** [New Greek & Turkish; New Greek *mezes,* from Turkish *meze,* perhaps from Arabic dialect *mazza, māzza*] (1926)
: an appetizer in Greek or Middle Eastern cuisine often served with an aperitif

me·ze·re·on \mə-ˈzir-ē-ən\ *noun* [Middle English *mizerion,* from Medieval Latin *mezereon,* from Arabic *māzariyūn,* from Persian] (15th century)
: a small European shrub (*Daphne mezereum* of the family Thymelaeaceae, the mezereon family) with fragrant lilac purple flowers and poisonous emetic leaves, fruit, and bark

me·zu·zah *or* **me·zu·za** \mə-ˈzù-zə\ *noun, plural* **-zahs** *or* **-zas** *or* **-zot** \-ˈzù-ˌzōt\ [Hebrew *mĕzūzāh* doorpost] (1650)
: a small parchment scroll inscribed with Deuteronomy 6:4–9 and 11:13–21 and the name Shaddai and placed in a case fixed to the doorpost by some Jewish families as a sign and reminder of their faith

mez·za·nine \ˈme-zᵊn-ˌēn, ˌme-zᵊn-ˈ\ *noun* [French, from Italian *mezzanino,* from *mezzano* middle, from Latin *medianus* middle, median] (1711)
1 : a low-ceilinged story between two main stories of a building; *especially* : an intermediate story that projects in the form of a balcony
2 a : the lowest balcony in a theater **b :** the first few rows of such a balcony

mez·za vo·ce \ˌmet-sä-ˈvō-(ˌ)chā, ˌmed-zä-\ *adverb or adjective* [Italian, half voice] (1775)
: with medium or half volume — used as a direction in music

mez·zo \ˈmet-(ˌ)sō, ˈmed-(ˌ)zō\ *noun, plural* **mezzos** [Italian, literally, middle, moderate, half, from Latin *medius* — more at MID] (1832)

: MEZZO-SOPRANO

mez·zo for·te \ˌmet-(ˌ)sō-ˈfȯr-ˌtā, ˌmed-(ˌ)zō-, -ˈfȯr-tē\ *adjective or adverb* [Italian] (1811)
: moderately loud — used as a direction in music

mez·zo pia·no \-pē-ˈä-(ˌ)nō\ *adjective or adverb* [Italian] (1811)
: moderately soft — used as a direction in music

mez·zo–re·lie·vo *or* **mez·zo–ri·lie·vo** \-ri-ˈlē-(ˌ)vō, -rēl-ˈyā-(ˌ)vō\ *noun, plural* **-vos** [Italian *mezzorilievo,* from *mezzo* + *rilievo* relief] (1598)
: sculptural relief intermediate between bas-relief and high relief

mez·zo–so·pra·no \-sə-ˈpra-(ˌ)nō, -ˈprä-\ *noun* [Italian *mezzosoprano,* from *mezzo* + *soprano* soprano] (circa 1753)
1 : a woman's voice with a range between that of the soprano and contralto
2 : a singer having a mezzo-soprano voice

mez·zo·tint \ˈmet-sō-ˌtint, ˈmed-zō-\ *noun* [modification of Italian *mezzatinta,* from *mezza* (feminine of *mezzo*) + *tinta* tint] (1738)
1 : a manner of engraving on copper or steel by scraping or burnishing a roughened surface to produce light and shade
2 : an engraving produced by mezzotint

mho \ˈmō\ *noun, plural* **mhos** [backward spelling of *ohm*] (1883)
: a unit of conductance equal to the reciprocal of the ohm : SIEMENS

mi \ˈmē\ *noun* [Medieval Latin, from the syllable sung to this note in a medieval hymn to Saint John the Baptist] (15th century)
: the 3d tone of the diatonic scale in solmization

MIA \ˌem-(ˌ)ī-ˈā\ *noun* [*missing in action*] (1944)
: a member of the armed forces whose whereabouts following a combat mission are unknown and whose death cannot be established beyond reasonable doubt

Mi·ami \mī-ˈa-mē, -mə\ *noun, plural* **Mi·ami** *or* **Mi·am·is** (1722)
: a member of an American Indian people originally of Wisconsin and Indiana

mi·aow \mē-ˈaù\ *variant of* MEOW

mi·as·ma \mī-ˈaz-mə, mē-\ *noun, plural* **-mas** *also* **-ma·ta** \-mə-tə\ [New Latin, from Greek, defilement, from *miainein* to pollute] (1665)
1 : a vaporous exhalation formerly believed to cause disease; *also* : a heavy vaporous emanation or atmosphere ⟨a *miasma* of tobacco smoke⟩
2 : an influence or atmosphere that tends to deplete or corrupt ⟨freed from the *miasma* of poverty —Sir Arthur Bryant⟩; *also* : an atmosphere that obscures : FOG ⟨retreated into an asexual mental *miasma* —*Times Literary Supplement*⟩
— **mi·as·mal** \-məl\ *adjective*
— **mi·as·mat·ic** \ˌmī-əz-ˈma-tik\ *adjective*
— **mi·as·mic** \mī-ˈaz-mik, mē-\ *adjective*
— **mi·as·mi·cal·ly** \-mi-k(ə-)lē\ *adverb*

mi·ca \ˈmī-kə\ *noun* [New Latin, from Latin, grain, crumb; perhaps akin to Greek *mikros* small] (1777)
: any of various colored or transparent mineral silicates crystallizing in monoclinic forms that readily separate into very thin leaves
— **mi·ca·ceous** \mī-ˈkā-shəs\ *adjective*

Mi·cah \ˈmī-kə\ *noun* [Hebrew *Mīkhāh,* short for *Mīkhāyāh*]
1 : a Hebrew prophet of the 8th century B.C.
2 : a prophetic book of canonical Jewish and Christian Scripture — see BIBLE table

Mi·caw·ber \mi-ˈkȯ-bər, -ˈkä-\ *noun* [Wilkins *Micawber,* character in the novel *David Copperfield* (1849–50) by Charles Dickens] (1852)
: one who is poor but lives in optimistic expectation of better fortune
— **Mi·caw·ber·ish** \-bə-rish\ *adjective*

mice *plural of* MOUSE

mi·celle \mī-'sel\ *noun* [New Latin *micella,* from Latin *mica*] (1881)
: a unit of structure built up from polymeric molecules or ions: as **a** : an ordered region in a fiber (as of cellulose or rayon) **b** : a molecular aggregate that constitutes a colloidal particle
— **mi·cel·lar** \-'se-lər\ *adjective*

Mi·chael \'mī-kəl\ *noun* [Hebrew *Mīkhā'ēl*]
: one of the four archangels named in Hebrew tradition

Mi·chae·lis constant \mī-'kā-ləs-, mə-\ *noun* [Leonor *Michaelis* (died 1949) American biochemist] (1949)
: a constant that is a measure of the kinetics of an enzyme reaction and that is equivalent to the concentration of substrate at which the reaction takes place at one half its maximum rate

Mich·ael·mas \'mi-kəl-məs\ *noun* [Middle English *mychelmesse,* from Old English *Michaeles mæsse* Michael's mass] (before 12th century)
: September 29 celebrated as the feast of Saint Michael the Archangel

Michaelmas daisy *noun* (1785)
: a wild aster; *especially* : one blooming about Michaelmas

Mi·che·as \'mī-kē-əs, mī-'\ *noun* [Late Latin *Michaeas,* from Greek *Michaias,* from Hebrew *Mīkhāyāh*]
: MICAH

mick \'mik\ *noun, often capitalized* [*Mick,* nickname for *Michael,* common Irish given name] (1856)
: IRISHMAN — often taken to be offensive

Mick·ey Finn \mi-kē-'fin\ *noun* [probably from the name *Mickey Finn*] (1928)
: a drink of liquor doctored with a purgative or a drug

Mickey Mouse \'mi-kē-'maùs\ *adjective* [*Mickey Mouse,* cartoon character created by Walt Disney] (1936)
1 *often not capitalized* : being or performing insipid or corny popular music
2 : lacking importance : INSIGNIFICANT ⟨*Mickey Mouse* courses, where you don't work too hard —Willie Cager⟩
3 : annoyingly petty ⟨*Mickey Mouse* regulations⟩

mick·le \'mi-kəl\ *adjective* [Middle English *mikel,* from Old English *micel* — more at MUCH] (before 12th century)
chiefly Scottish : GREAT, MUCH
— **mickle** *adverb, chiefly Scottish*

Mic·mac \'mik-,mak\ *noun, plural* **Micmac** *or* **Micmacs** [Micmac *mi'kəmaw*] (1830)
1 : a member of an American Indian people of eastern Canada
2 : the Algonquian language of the Micmac people

micr- *or* **micro-** *combining form* [Middle English *micro-,* from Latin, from Greek *mikr-, mikro-,* from *mikros, smikros* small, short; perhaps akin to Old English *smēalīc* careful, exquisite]
1 a : small : minute ⟨*micro*capsule⟩ **b** : used for or involving minute quantities or variations ⟨*micro*barograph⟩
2 : one millionth part of a (specified) unit ⟨*micro*gram⟩
3 a : using microscopy ⟨*micro*dissection⟩ : used in microscopy **b** : revealed by or having the structure discernible only by microscopic examination ⟨*micro*organism⟩
4 : abnormally small ⟨*micro*cyte⟩
5 : of or relating to a small area ⟨*micro*climate⟩
6 : employed in or connected with microphotographing or microfilming ⟨*micro*copy⟩

¹mi·cro \'mī-(,)krō\ *adjective* [*micr-*] (1923)
1 : very small; *especially* : MICROSCOPIC
2 : involving minute quantities or variations

²micro *noun, plural* **micros** (1971)
1 : MICROCOMPUTER
2 : MICROPROCESSOR

mi·cro·am·pere \,mī-krō-'am-,pir\ *noun* (circa 1890)
: a unit of current equal to one millionth of an ampere

mi·cro·anal·y·sis \-ə-'na-lə-səs\ *noun* (1856)
: chemical analysis on a small or minute scale that usually requires special, very sensitive, or small-scale apparatus
— **mi·cro·an·a·lyst** \-'a-nᵊl-ist\ *noun*
— **mi·cro·an·a·lyt·i·cal** \-'i-ti-kəl\ *also* **mi·cro·an·a·lyt·ic** \-,a-nᵊl-'i-tik\ *adjective*

mi·cro·anat·o·my \-ə-'na-tə-mē\ *noun* (circa 1899)
: HISTOLOGY
— **mi·cro·an·a·tom·i·cal** \-,a-nə-'tä-mi-kəl\ *adjective*

mi·cro·bal·ance \'mī-krō-,ba-lən(t)s\ *noun* (1903)
: a balance designed to measure very small weights

mi·cro·baro·graph \,mī-krō-'bar-ə-,graf\ *noun* [International Scientific Vocabulary] (1904)
: a barograph for recording small and rapid changes

mi·crobe \'mī-,krōb\ *noun* [International Scientific Vocabulary *micr-* + Greek *bios* life — more at QUICK] (1881)
: MICROORGANISM, GERM
— **mi·cro·bi·al** \mī-'krō-bē-əl\ *also* **mi·cro·bic** \-bik\ *adjective*

mi·cro·beam \'mī-krō-,bēm\ *noun* (1950)
: a beam of radiation of small cross section ⟨a focused laser *microbeam*⟩ ⟨a *microbeam* of electrons⟩

mi·cro·bi·ol·o·gy \,mī-krō-bī-'ä-lə-jē\ *noun* [International Scientific Vocabulary] (1888)
: a branch of biology dealing especially with microscopic forms of life
— **mi·cro·bi·o·log·i·cal** \-,bī-ə-'lä-ji-kəl\ *also* **mi·cro·bi·o·log·ic** \-'lä-jik\ *adjective*
— **mi·cro·bi·o·log·i·cal·ly** \-ji-k(ə-)lē\ *adverb*
— **mi·cro·bi·ol·o·gist** \-bī-'ä-lə-jist\ *noun*

mi·cro·brew \'mī-krō-,brü\ *noun* (1987)
: a beer produced by a microbrewery

mi·cro·brew·ery \,mī-krō-'brü-ə-rē, -'brü(-ə)r-ē\ *noun* (1984)
: a small brewery making specialty beer in limited quantities
— **mi·cro·brew·er** \'mī-krō-,brü-ər, -,brü(-ə)r\ *noun*
— **mi·cro·brew·ing** \-,brü-iŋ\ *noun*

mi·cro·burst \'mī-krō-,bərst\ *noun* (1982)
: a violent short-lived localized downdraft that creates extreme wind shears at low altitudes and is usually associated with thunderstorms

mi·cro·bus \-,bəs\ *noun* (1945)
: a station wagon shaped like a bus

mi·cro·cal·o·rim·e·ter \-,ka-lə-'ri-mə-tər\ *noun* (1911)
: an instrument for measuring very small quantities of heat
— **mi·cro·ca·lo·ri·met·ric** \-,ka-lə-rə-'me-trik; -kə-,lòr-ə-, -,lōr-, -,lär-\ *adjective*
— **mi·cro·cal·o·rim·e·try** \-,ka-lə-'ri-mə-trē\ *noun*

mi·cro·cap·sule \'mī-krō-,kap-səl, -(,)sül *also* -,syü(ə)l\ *noun* (1961)
: a tiny capsule containing material (as an adhesive or a medicine) that is released when the capsule is broken, melted, or dissolved

mi·cro·cas·sette \,mī-krō-kə-'set, -ka-\ *noun* (1979)
: a small cassette of magnetic tape that is used especially for dictation

¹mi·cro·ce·phal·ic \-sə-'fa-lik\ *adjective* (circa 1856)
: having a small head; *specifically* : having an abnormally small head

²microcephalic *noun* (circa 1873)
: one that is microcephalic

mi·cro·ceph·a·ly \-'se-fə-lē\ *noun* [New Latin *microcephalia,* from *microcephalus* microcephalic, from *micr-* + Greek *kephalē* head — more at CEPHALIC] (1863)
: a condition of abnormal smallness of the head usually associated with mental defects

mi·cro·chip \'mī-krō-,chip\ *noun* (1969)
: INTEGRATED CIRCUIT

mi·cro·cir·cuit \-,sər-kət\ *noun* (1959)
: a compact electronic circuit : INTEGRATED CIRCUIT
— **mi·cro·cir·cuit·ry** \,mī-krō-'sər-kə-trē\ *noun*

mi·cro·cir·cu·la·tion \,mī-krō-,sər-kyə-'lā-shən\ *noun* (1959)
: blood circulation in the microvascular system; *also* : the microvascular system itself
— **mi·cro·cir·cu·la·to·ry** \-'sər-kyə-lə-,tōr-ē, -,tòr-\ *adjective*

mi·cro·cli·mate \'mī-krō-,klī-mət\ *noun* [International Scientific Vocabulary] (1925)
: the essentially uniform local climate of a usually small site or habitat
— **mi·cro·cli·mat·ic** \,mī-krō-klī-'ma-tik\ *adjective*

mi·cro·cline \'mī-krō-,klīn\ *noun* [German *Mikroklin,* from *mikr-* micr- + Greek *klinein* to lean — more at LEAN] (1849)
: a triclinic mineral of the feldspar group that is like orthoclase in composition

mi·cro·coc·cus \,mī-krō-'kä-kəs\ *noun, plural* **-coc·ci** \-'käk-(,)sī, -(,)sē; -'kä-(,)kī, -(,)kē\ [New Latin] (1870)
: a small spherical bacterium; *especially* : any of a genus (*Micrococcus*) of gram-positive chiefly harmless bacteria that typically occur in irregular clusters
— **mi·cro·coc·cal** \-'kä-kəl\ *adjective*

mi·cro·code \'mī-krə-,kōd\ *noun* (circa 1962)
: the microinstructions especially of a microprocessor

mi·cro·com·put·er \'mī-krō-kəm-,pyü-tər\ *noun* (1971)
1 : a very small computer that uses a microprocessor to handle information
2 : MICROPROCESSOR

mi·cro·copy \'mī-krō-,kä-pē\ *noun* [International Scientific Vocabulary] (1935)
: a photographic copy in which graphic matter is reduced in size (as on microfilm)

mi·cro·cosm \'mī-krə-,kä-zəm\ *noun* [Middle English, from Medieval Latin *microcosmus,* modification of Greek *mikros kosmos*] (15th century)
1 : a little world; *especially* : the human race or human nature seen as an epitome of the world or the universe
2 : a community or other unity that is an epitome of a larger unity
— **mi·cro·cos·mic** \,mī-krə-'käz-mik\ *adjective*
— **mi·cro·cos·mi·cal·ly** \-mi-k(ə-)lē\ *adverb*
— **in microcosm** : in a greatly diminished size, form, or scale

microcosmic salt *noun* (1783)
: a white crystalline salt $NaNH_5PO_4 \cdot 4H_2O$ used as a flux in testing for metallic oxides and salts

mi·cro·cos·mos \'mī-krə-,käz-məs, -,mōs, -,mäs\ *noun* [Middle English *mycrocossmos,* from Medieval Latin *microcosmus*] (13th century)
1 : MICROCOSM
2 : the microscopic or submicroscopic world

mi·cro·crys·tal \'mī-krō-,kris-tᵊl\ *noun* (1886)
: a crystal visible only under the microscope
— **mi·cro·crys·tal·line** \,mī-krō-'kris-tə-lən *also* -,līn *or* -,lēn\ *adjective*
— **mi·cro·crys·tal·lin·i·ty** \-,kris-tə-'li-nə-tē\ *noun*

mi·cro·cul·ture \'mī-krō-,kəl-chər\ *noun* (1892)

1 : a microscopic culture of cells or organisms
2 : the culture of a small group of human beings with limited perspective
— **mi·cro·cul·tur·al** \ˌmī-krō-'kəlch-rəl, -'kəl-chə-\ *adjective*

mi·cro·cu·rie \'mī-krō-ˌkyu̇r-ē, ˌmī-krō-kyu̇-'rē\ *noun* (1911)
: a unit of quantity or of radioactivity equal to one millionth of a curie

mi·cro·cyte \'mī-krə-ˌsīt\ *noun* [International Scientific Vocabulary] (1876)
: a small red blood cell present especially in some anemias
— **mi·cro·cyt·ic** \ˌmī-krə-'si-tik\ *adjective*

mi·cro·den·si·tom·e·ter \'mī-krō-ˌden(t)-sə-'tä-mə-tər\ *noun* (1935)
: a densitometer for measuring the densities of very small areas of a photographic film or plate
— **mi·cro·den·si·to·met·ric** \-sə-tə-'me-trik\ *adjective*
— **mi·cro·den·si·tom·e·try** \-sə-'tä-mə-trē\ *noun*

mi·cro·dis·sec·tion \ˌmī-krō-di-'sek-shən, -dī-\ *noun* (1915)
: dissection under the microscope; *specifically* : dissection of cells and tissues by means of fine needles that are precisely manipulated by levers

mi·cro·dot \'mī-krə-ˌdät, -krō-\ *noun* (1946)
: a photographic reproduction of printed matter reduced to the size of a dot for ease or security of transmittal

mi·cro·earth·quake \ˌmī-krō-'ərth-ˌkwāk\ *noun* (1965)
: an earthquake of low intensity

mi·cro·eco·nom·ics \-ˌe-kə-'nä-miks, -ˌē-kə-\ *noun plural but usually singular in construction* (1947)
: a study of economics in terms of individual areas of activity (as a firm, household, or prices) — compare MACROECONOMICS
— **mi·cro·eco·nom·ic** \-'nä-mik\ *adjective*

mi·cro·elec·trode \ˌmī-krō-i-'lek-ˌtrōd\ *noun* (1917)
: a minute electrode; *especially* : one that is inserted in a living biological cell or tissue in studying its electrical characteristics

mi·cro·elec·tron·ics \-i-ˌlek-'trä-niks\ *noun plural* (1958)
1 *singular in construction* : a branch of electronics that deals with the miniaturization of electronic circuits and components
2 : devices, equipment, or circuits produced using the methods of microelectronics
— **mi·cro·elec·tron·ic** \-nik\ *adjective*
— **mi·cro·elec·tron·i·cal·ly** \-ni-k(ə-)lē\ *adverb*

mi·cro·elec·tro·pho·re·sis \-i-ˌlek-trə-fə-'rē-səs\ *noun* [New Latin] (1936)
: electrophoresis in which the movement of single particles is observed in a microscope; *also* : electrophoresis in which micromethods are used
— **mi·cro·elec·tro·pho·ret·ic** \-'re-tik\ *adjective*
— **mi·cro·elec·tro·pho·ret·i·cal·ly** \-ti-k(ə-)lē\ *adverb*

mi·cro·el·e·ment \-'e-lə-mənt\ *noun* (1936)
: TRACE ELEMENT

mi·cro·en·cap·su·late \-in-'kap-sə-ˌlāt\ *transitive verb* (1963)
: to enclose in a microcapsule ⟨*microencapsulated* aspirin⟩
— **mi·cro·en·cap·su·la·tion** \-in-ˌkap-sə-'lā-shən\ *noun*

mi·cro·en·vi·ron·ment \-in-'vī-rən-mənt, -'vī(-ə)rn-\ *noun* (1938)
: a small or relatively small usually distinctly specialized and effectively isolated habitat (as a forest canopy) or environment (as of a nerve cell)
— **mi·cro·en·vi·ron·men·tal** \-ˌvī-rən-'men-tᵊl\ *adjective*

mi·cro·evo·lu·tion \-ˌe-və-'lü-shən *also* -ˌē-və-\ *noun* (1940)
: comparatively minor evolutionary change involving the accumulation of variations in populations usually below the species level
— **mi·cro·evo·lu·tion·ary** \-shə-ˌner-ē\ *adjective*

mi·cro·far·ad \'mī-krō-ˌfar-ˌad, -ˌfar-əd\ *noun* (1873)
: a unit of capacitance equal to one millionth of a farad

mi·cro·fau·na \ˌmī-krō-'fȯ-nə, -'fä-\ *noun* [New Latin] (1902)
1 : minute animals; *especially* : those invisible to the naked eye ⟨the soil *microfauna*⟩
2 : a small or strictly localized fauna (as of a microenvironment)
— **mi·cro·fau·nal** \-'fȯ-nᵊl, -'fä-\ *adjective*

mi·cro·fi·bril \-'fī-brəl, -'fi-\ *noun* (1938)
: a fine fibril; *especially* : one of the submicroscopic elongated bundles of cellulose of a plant cell wall
— **mi·cro·fi·bril·lar** \-brə-lər\ *adjective*

mi·cro·fiche \'mī-krō-ˌfēsh, -ˌfish\ *noun, plural* **-fiche** *or* **-fiches** \-ˌfē-shəz, -ˌfēsh, -ˌfishəz, -ˌfish\ [French, from *micr-* micr- + *fiche* fiche] (1950)
: a sheet of microfilm containing rows of microimages of pages of printed matter

mi·cro·fil·a·ment \ˌmī-krō-'fi-lə-mənt\ *noun* (1963)
: any of the minute actin-containing protein filaments of eukaryotic cytoplasm that function in maintaining structure and in intracellular movement

mi·cro·fi·lar·ia \-fə-'lar-ē-ə, -'ler-\ *noun* [New Latin] (1878)
: a minute larval filaria
— **mi·cro·fi·lar·i·al** \-ē-əl\ *adjective*

¹mi·cro·film \'mī-krə-ˌfilm\ *noun* [International Scientific Vocabulary] (1927)
: a film bearing a photographic record on a reduced scale of printed or other graphic matter

²microfilm (1937)
transitive verb
: to reproduce on microfilm
intransitive verb
: to make microfilms
— **mi·cro·film·able** \ˌmī-krə-'fil-mə-bəl\ *adjective*
— **mi·cro·film·er** \'mī-krə-ˌfil-mər\ *noun*

mi·cro·flo·ra \ˌmī-krə-'flōr-ə, -'flȯr-\ *noun* [New Latin] (1904)
1 : minute plants; *especially* : those invisible to the naked eye
2 : a small or strictly localized flora (as of a microenvironment)
— **mi·cro·flo·ral** \-əl\ *adjective*

mi·cro·form \'mī-krə-ˌfȯrm\ *noun* (1958)
1 : a process for reproducing printed matter in a much reduced size ⟨documents in *microform*⟩
2 a : matter reproduced by microform **b** : MICROCOPY

mi·cro·fos·sil \ˌmī-krō-'fä-səl\ *noun* (1924)
: a fossil that can be studied only microscopically and that may be either a fragment of a larger organism or an entire minute organism

mi·cro·fun·gus \-'fəŋ-gəs\ *noun* [New Latin] (1874)
: a fungus (as a mold) with a microscopic fruiting body

mi·cro·ga·mete \-'ga-ˌmēt *also* -gə-'mēt\ *noun* [International Scientific Vocabulary] (circa 1891)
: the smaller and usually male gamete of a heterogamous organism

mi·cro·ga·me·to·cyte \-gə-'mē-tə-ˌsīt\ *noun* [International Scientific Vocabulary] (1902)
: a gametocyte producing microgametes

mi·cro·gram \'mī-krə-ˌgram\ *noun* [International Scientific Vocabulary] (circa 1890)
: one millionth of a gram — see METRIC SYSTEM table

mi·cro·graph \-ˌgraf\ *noun* [International Scientific Vocabulary] (1904)
: a graphic reproduction of the image of an object formed by a microscope
— **micrograph** *transitive verb*

mi·cro·graph·ics \ˌmī-krə-'gra-fiks\ *noun plural but singular in construction* (1969)
: the industry concerned with the manufacture and sale of graphic material in microform; *also* : the production of such material
— **mi·cro·graph·ic** \-fik\ *adjective*
— **mi·cro·graph·i·cal·ly** \-fi-k(ə-)lē\ *adverb*

mi·cro·grav·i·ty \-'gra-və-tē\ *noun* (1974)
: a condition in space in which only minuscule forces are experienced : virtual absence of gravity; *broadly* : a condition of weightlessness

mi·cro·groove \'mī-krō-ˌgrüv\ *noun* (1948)
: a narrow continuous V-shaped spiral track that has closely spaced turns and that is used on long-playing records

mi·cro·hab·i·tat \ˌmī-krō-'ha-bə-ˌtat\ *noun* (1933)
: the microenvironment in which an organism lives ⟨decaying wood creates a *microhabitat* for insects⟩

mi·cro·im·age \-'i-mij\ *noun* (1950)
: an image (as on a microfilm) that is greatly reduced in size

mi·cro·inch \-'inch\ *noun* (1941)
: one millionth of an inch

mi·cro·in·jec·tion \ˌmī-krō-in-'jek-shən\ *noun* (1921)
: injection under the microscope; *specifically* : injection into tissues by means of a fine mechanically controlled capillary tube
— **mi·cro·in·ject** \-'jekt\ *transitive verb*

mi·cro·in·struc·tion \-'strək-shən\ *noun* (1959)
: a computer instruction that activates the circuits necessary to perform a single machine operation usually as part of the execution of a machine-language instruction

mi·cro·lep·i·dop·tera \ˌmī-krō-ˌle-pə-'däp-tə-rə\ *noun plural* [New Latin] (1852)
: lepidopterous insects (as tortricids) that belong to families of minute or medium-sized moths
— **mi·cro·lep·i·dop·ter·ous** \-tə-rəs\ *adjective*

mi·cro·li·ter \'mī-krō-ˌlē-tər\ *noun* [International Scientific Vocabulary] (circa 1890)
: a unit of capacity equal to one millionth of a liter — see METRIC SYSTEM table

mi·cro·lith \'mī-krə-ˌlith\ *noun* [International Scientific Vocabulary] (1908)
: a tiny blade tool especially of the Mesolithic usually in a geometric shape (as that of a triangle) and often set in a bone or wooden haft
— **mi·cro·lith·ic** \ˌmī-krə-'li-thik\ *adjective*

mi·cro·man·age \ˌmī-krō-'ma-nij\ *transitive verb* (1979)
: to manage with great or excessive control or attention to details
— **mi·cro·man·age·ment** \-mənt\ *noun*
— **mi·cro·man·ag·er** \-'ma-ni-jər\ *noun*

mi·cro·ma·nip·u·la·tion \ˌmī-krō-mə-ˌni-pyə-'lā-shən\ *noun* (1921)
: the technique or practice of microdissection and microinjection

mi·cro·ma·nip·u·la·tor \-'ni-pyə-ˌlā-tər\ *noun* (1921)
: an instrument for micromanipulation

mi·cro·mere \'mī-krō-ˌmir\ *noun* [International Scientific Vocabulary] (1877)
: a small blastomere — see BLASTULA illustration

mi·cro·me·te·or·ite \ˌmī-krō-'mē-tē-ə-ˌrīt\ *noun* (1949)
1 : a meteorite so small that it can pass through the earth's atmosphere without becoming intensely heated
2 : a very small particle in interplanetary space
— **mi·cro·me·te·or·it·ic** \-ˌmē-tē-ə-'ri-tik\ *adjective*

mi·cro·me·te·or·oid \-'mē-tē-ə-ˌròid\ *noun* (1954)
: MICROMETEORITE 2

mi·cro·me·te·o·rol·o·gy \-ˌmē-tē-ə-ˌ'rä-lə-jē\ *noun* (1930)
: meteorology that deals with small-scale weather systems ranging up to several kilometers in diameter and confined to the lower troposphere
— **mi·cro·me·te·o·ro·log·i·cal** \-ˌmē-tē-ˌòr-ə-'lä-ji-kəl, -ˌär-ə-, -ə-rə-\ *adjective*
— **mi·cro·me·te·o·rol·o·gist** \-ˌmē-tē-ə-'rä-lə-jist\ *noun*

¹mi·crom·e·ter \mī-'krä-mə-tər\ *noun* [French *micromètre*, from *micr-* + *-mètre* -meter] (1670)
1 : an instrument used with a telescope or microscope for measuring minute distances
2 : a caliper for making precise measurements that has a spindle moved by a finely threaded screw

micrometer 2

²mi·cro·me·ter \'mī-krō-ˌmē-tər\ *noun* [International Scientific Vocabulary *micr-* + ³*meter*] (1880)
: a unit of length equal to one millionth of a meter — called also *micron*; see METRIC SYSTEM table

mi·cro·meth·od \'mī-krō-ˌme-thəd\ *noun* (1919)
: a method (as of microanalysis) that requires only very small quantities of material or that involves the use of the microscope

mi·cro·mini \ˌmī-krō-'mi-nē\ *noun* (1966)
: a very short miniskirt

mi·cro·min·i·a·ture \-'mi-nē-ə-ˌchùr, -'mi-ni-ˌchùr, -'min-yə-, -chər, -ˌtyùr, -ˌtùr\ *adjective* (1958)
1 : MICROMINIATURIZED
2 : suitable for use with microminiaturized parts

mi·cro·min·i·a·tur·i·za·tion \-ˌmi-nē-ə-ˌchür-ə-'zā-shən, -ˌmi-ni-ˌchür-, -ˌmin-yə-ˌchür-, -chər-, -ˌtyùr-, -ˌtùr-\ *noun* (1955)
: the process of producing microminiaturized things

mi·cro·min·i·a·tur·ized \-'mi-nē-ə-chə-ˌrīzd, -'mi-ni-chə-, -'min-yə-chə-, -ˌtyù-, -ˌtù-\ *adjective* (1959)
: reduced to or produced in a very small size and especially in a size smaller than one considered miniature

mi·cro·mole \'mī-krə-ˌmōl\ *noun* [International Scientific Vocabulary] (1936)
: one millionth of a mole
— **mi·cro·mo·lar** \ˌmī-krə-'mō-lər\ *adjective*

mi·cro·mor·phol·o·gy \ˌmī-krō-mòr-'fä-lə-jē\ *noun* (1945)
: MICROSTRUCTURE
— **mi·cro·mor·pho·log·i·cal** \-fə-'lä-ji-kəl\ *adjective*

mi·cron \'mī-ˌkrän\ *noun* [New Latin, from Greek *mikron*, neuter of *mikros* small — more at MICR-] (1885)
: ²MICROMETER

Mi·cro·ne·sian \ˌmī-krə-'nē-zhən, -shən\ *noun* (1847)
1 : a native or inhabitant of Micronesia
2 : a group of Austronesian languages spoken in the Micronesian islands
— **Micronesian** *adjective*

mi·cron·ize \'mī-krə-ˌnīz\ *transitive verb* **-ized; -iz·ing** [*micron*] (1940)
: to pulverize especially into particles a few micrometers in diameter

mi·cro·nu·cle·us \ˌmī-krō-'nü-klē-əs, -'nyü-\ *noun* [New Latin] (1892)
: a minute nucleus; *specifically* **:** one that is primarily concerned with reproductive and genetic functions in most ciliated protozoans

mi·cro·nu·tri·ent \-'nü-trē-ənt, -'nyü-\ *noun* (1939)

1 : TRACE ELEMENT
2 : an organic compound (as a vitamin) essential in minute amounts to the growth and health of an animal

mi·cro·or·gan·ism \-'òr-gə-ˌni-zəm\ *noun* [International Scientific Vocabulary] (1880)
: an organism of microscopic or ultramicroscopic size

mi·cro·pa·le·on·tol·o·gy \-ˌpā-lē-ˌän-'tä-lə-jē, -lē-ən-, *especially British* -ˌpa-\ *noun* [International Scientific Vocabulary] (1883)
: the study of microscopic fossils
— **mi·cro·pa·le·on·to·log·i·cal** \-ˌän-t°l-'ä-ji-kəl\ *also* **mi·cro·pa·le·on·to·log·ic** \-jik\ *adjective*
— **mi·cro·pa·le·on·tol·o·gist** \-ˌän-'tä-lə-jist, -ən-\ *noun*

mi·cro·par·ti·cle \-'pär-ti-kəl\ *noun* (1929)
: a very small particle; *especially* **:** one that is microscopic in size

mi·cro·phage \'mī-krə-ˌfāj *also* -ˌfäzh\ *noun* [International Scientific Vocabulary] (1890)
: a small phagocyte

mi·cro·phone \'mī-krə-ˌfōn\ *noun* [International Scientific Vocabulary] (1878)
: an instrument whereby sound waves are caused to generate or modulate an electric current usually for the purpose of transmitting or recording sound (as speech or music)
— **mi·cro·phon·ic** \ˌmī-krə-'fä-nik\ *adjective*

mi·cro·phon·ics \ˌmī-krə-'fä-niks\ *noun plural* (1929)
: noises in a loudspeaker caused by mechanical shock or vibration of the electronic components

mi·cro·pho·to·graph \-'fō-tə-ˌgraf\ *noun* [International Scientific Vocabulary] (1858)
1 : a small photograph that is normally magnified for viewing **:** MICROCOPY
2 : PHOTOMICROGRAPH
— **microphotograph** *transitive verb*
— **mi·cro·pho·tog·ra·pher** \-fə-'tä-grə-fər\ *noun*
— **mi·cro·pho·to·graph·ic** \-ˌfō-tə-'gra-fik\ *adjective*
— **mi·cro·pho·tog·ra·phy** \-fə-'tä-grə-fē\ *noun*

mi·cro·pho·tom·e·ter \-fō-'tä-mə-tər\ *noun* [International Scientific Vocabulary] (1899)
: an instrument for measuring the amount of light transmitted or reflected by small areas or for measuring the relative densities of spectral lines on a photographic film or plate
— **mi·cro·pho·to·met·ric** \-ˌfō-tə-'me-trik\ *adjective*
— **mi·cro·pho·to·met·ri·cal·ly** \-tri-k(ə-)lē\ *adverb*
— **mi·cro·pho·tom·e·try** \-fō-'tä-mə-trē\ *noun*

mi·cro·phyll \'mī-krə-ˌfil\ *noun* [International Scientific Vocabulary] (1935)
1 : a small leaf
2 : a leaf (as of a club moss) with single unbranched veins and no demonstrable gap around the leaf trace
— **mi·cro·phyl·lous** \ˌmī-krə-'fi-ləs\ *adjective*

mi·cro·phys·ics \ˌmī-krō-'fi-ziks\ *noun* (1885)
: the physics of molecules, atoms, and elementary particles
— **mi·cro·phys·i·cal** \-'fi-zi-kəl\ *adjective*
— **mi·cro·phys·i·cal·ly** \-k(ə-)lē\ *adverb*

mi·cro·pi·pette *or* **mi·cro·pi·pet** \-pī-'pet\ *noun* (1918)
1 : a pipette for the measurement of minute volumes
2 : a small and extremely fine-pointed pipette used in making microinjections

mi·cro·plank·ton \-'plan(k)-tən, -ˌtän\ *noun* [International Scientific Vocabulary] (1903)
: microscopic plankton

mi·cro·pore \'mī-krə-ˌpōr, -ˌpòr\ *noun* [International Scientific Vocabulary] (1884)
: a very fine pore

mi·cro·po·ros·i·ty \-pə-'rä-sə-tē, -ˌpò-\ *noun*
— **mi·cro·po·rous** \ˌmī-krə-'pōr-əs, -'pòr-\ *adjective*

mi·cro·prism \'mī-krə-ˌpri-zəm\ *noun* (1966)
: a usually circular area on the focusing screen of a camera that is made up of tiny prisms and causes the image in the viewfinder to blur if the subject is not in focus

mi·cro·probe \-ˌprōb\ *noun* (1944)
: a device for microanalysis that operates by exciting radiation in a minute area of material so that the composition may be determined from the emission spectrum

mi·cro·ces·sor \ˌmī-krō-'prä-ˌse-sər, -'prō-\ *noun* (1970)
: a computer processor contained on an integrated-circuit chip; *also* **:** such a processor with memory and associated circuits

mi·cro·pro·gram \-'prō-ˌgram, -grəm\ *noun* (1953)
: a routine composed of microinstructions used in microprogramming

mi·cro·pro·gram·ming \-ˌgra-min\ *noun* (1953)
: the use of routines stored in memory rather than specialized circuits to control a device (as a computer)

mi·cro·pro·jec·tor \-prə-'jek-tər\ *noun* (1927)
: a projector utilizing a compound microscope for projecting on a screen a greatly enlarged image of a microscopic object
— **mi·cro·pro·jec·tion** \-'jek-shən\ *noun*

mi·cro·pub·lish·ing \-'pə-bli-shin\ *noun* (1966)
: publishing in microform
— **mi·cro·pub·lish·er** \-bli-shər\ *noun*

mi·cro·pul·sa·tion \-ˌpəl-'sā-shən\ *noun* (1949)
: a pulsation having a short period ⟨a *micropulsation* of the earth's magnetic field with a period in the range from a fraction of a second to several hundred seconds⟩

mi·cro·punc·ture \-'pən(k)-chər\ *noun* (1948)
: an extremely small puncture (as of a nephron); *also* **:** an act of making a micropuncture

mi·cro·pyle \'mī-krə-ˌpīl\ *noun* [French, from *micr-* + Greek *pylē* gate] (1821)
1 : a minute opening in the integument of an ovule of a seed plant
2 : a differentiated area of surface in an egg through which a sperm enters
— **mi·cro·py·lar** \ˌmī-krə-'pī-lər\ *adjective*

mi·cro·quake \'mī-krō-ˌkwāk\ *noun* (1967)
: MICROEARTHQUAKE

mi·cro·ra·di·og·ra·phy \ˌmī-krō-ˌrā-dē-'ä-grə-fē\ *noun* (1913)
: radiography in which an X-ray photograph is prepared showing minute internal structure
— **mi·cro·ra·dio·graph** \-'rā-dē-ə-ˌgraf\ *noun*
— **mi·cro·ra·dio·graph·ic** \-ˌrā-dē-ə-'gra-fik\ *adjective*

mi·cro·read·er \'mī-krō-ˌrē-dər\ *noun* (1949)
: an apparatus that gives an enlarged image of a microphotograph especially for reading

mi·cro·re·pro·duc·tion \ˌmī-krō-ˌrē-prə-'dək-shən\ *noun* (1938)
: the reproduction of written or printed matter in microform; *also* **:** an item so reproduced

mi·cro·scale \'mī-krō-ˌskāl\ *noun* (1931)
: a very small scale

mi·cro·scope \'mī-krə-ˌskōp\ *noun* [New Latin *microscopium*, from *micr-* + *-scopium* -scope] (1654)
1 : an optical instrument consisting of a lens or combination of lenses for making enlarged

images of minute objects; *especially* **:** COM-POUND MICROSCOPE
2 : an instrument using radiations other than light or using vibrations for making enlarged images of minute objects ⟨acoustic *microscope*⟩

mi·cro·scop·ic \ˌmī-krə-'skä-pik\ *or* **mi·cro·scop·i·cal** \-pi-kəl\ *adjective* (1732)
1 : resembling a microscope especially in perception
2 a : invisible or indistinguishable without the use of a microscope **b :** very small or fine or precise
3 : of, relating to, or conducted with the microscope or microscopy
— **mi·cro·scop·i·cal·ly** \-pi-k(ə-)lē\ *adverb*

mi·cros·co·py \mī-'kräs-kə-pē\ *noun* (circa 1665)
: the use of or investigation with the microscope
— **mi·cros·co·pist** \-pist\ *noun*

mi·cro·sec·ond \'mī-krō-ˌse-kənd, -kənt\ *noun* [International Scientific Vocabulary] (1906)
: one millionth of a second

mi·cro·seism \'mī-krə-ˌsī-zəm\ *noun* [International Scientific Vocabulary *micr-* + Greek *seismos* earthquake — more at SEISMIC] (1887)
: a feeble rhythmically and persistently recurring earth tremor
— **mi·cro·seis·mic** \ˌmī-krə-'sīz-mik, -'sīs-\ *adjective*
— **mi·cro·seis·mic·i·ty** \-sīz-'mi-sə-tē, -sīs-\ *noun*

mi·cro·some \'mī-krə-ˌsōm\ *noun* [German *Mikrosom*, from *mikr-* micr- + *-som* -some] (1885)
1 : any of various minute cellular structures (as a ribosome)
2 : a particle in a particulate fraction that is obtained by heavy centrifugation of broken cells and consists of various amounts of ribosomes, fragmented endoplasmic reticulum, and mitochondrial cristae
— **mi·cro·som·al** \ˌmī-krə-'sō-məl\ *adjective*

mi·cro·spec·tro·pho·tom·e·ter \ˌmī-krə-ˌspek-trə-fō-'tä-mə-tər\ *noun* (1949)
: a spectrophotometer adapted to the examination of light transmitted by a very small specimen (as a single organic cell)
— **mi·cro·spec·tro·pho·to·met·ric** \-ˌfō-tə-'me-trik\ *adjective*
— **mi·cro·spec·tro·pho·tom·e·try** \-fō-'tä-mə-trē\ *noun*

mi·cro·sphere \'mī-krə-ˌsfir\ *noun* (1894)
: a minute sphere
— **mi·cro·spher·i·cal** \ˌmī-krə-'sfir-i-kəl, -'sfer-\ *adjective*

mi·cro·spo·ran·gi·um \ˌmī-krō-spə-'ran-jē-əm\ *noun* [New Latin] (1881)
: a sporangium that develops only microspores
— **mi·cro·spo·ran·gi·ate** \-jē-ət\ *adjective*

mi·cro·spore \'mī-krə-ˌspōr, -ˌspȯr\ *noun* [International Scientific Vocabulary] (1858)
: any of the spores in heterosporous plants that give rise to male gametophytes and are generally smaller than the megaspore
— **mi·cro·spo·rous** \ˌmī-krə-'spōr-əs, -'spȯr-; mī-'kräs-pə-rəs\ *adjective*

mi·cro·spo·ro·cyte \-'spȯr-ə-ˌsīt, -'spȯr-\ *noun* (1940)
: a microspore mother cell

mi·cro·spo·ro·gen·e·sis \ˌmī-krə-ˌspōr-ə-'je-nə-səs, -ˌspȯr-\ *noun* [New Latin] (1921)
: the formation and maturation of microspores

mi·cro·spo·ro·phyll \-'fil\ *noun* (circa 1890)
: a sporophyll that develops only microsporangia

mi·cro·state \'mī-krō-ˌstāt\ *noun* (1962)
: a nation that is extremely small in area and population

mi·cro·struc·ture \'mī-krō-ˌstrək-chər\ *noun* [International Scientific Vocabulary] (1885)
: the microscopic structure of a material (as a mineral or a biological cell)
— **mi·cro·struc·tur·al** \ˌmī-krō-'strək-chə-rəl, -'strək-shrəl\ *adjective*

mi·cro·sur·gery \ˌmī-krō-'sərj-rē, -'sər-jə-\ *noun* (1926)
: minute dissection or manipulation (as by a micromanipulator or laser beam) of living structures or tissue
— **mi·cro·sur·gi·cal** \-'sər-ji-kəl\ *adjective*

mi·cro·switch \-ˌswich\ *noun* (1940)
: a very small switch that is sensitive to minute motions and is used especially in automatic devices

mi·cro·tech·nique \ˌmī-krō-tek-'nēk\ *also* **mi·cro·tech·nic** \-'tek-nik, -tek-'nēk\ *noun* [International Scientific Vocabulary] (1892)
: any of various methods of handling and preparing material for microscopic observation and study

mi·cro·tome \'mī-krə-ˌtōm\ *noun* [International Scientific Vocabulary] (1856)
: an instrument for cutting sections (as of organic tissues) for microscopic examination

mi·cro·tone \'mī-krə-ˌtōn\ *noun* (1920)
: a musical interval smaller than a halftone
— **mi·cro·ton·al** \ˌmī-krə-'tō-nᵊl\ *adjective*
— **mi·cro·ton·al·i·ty** \-tō-'na-lə-tē\ *noun*
— **mi·cro·ton·al·ly** \-'tō-nᵊl-ē\ *adverb*

mi·cro·tu·bule \ˌmī-krō-'tü-(ˌ)byü(ə)l, -'tyü-\ *noun* (1961)
: any of the minute tubules in eukaryotic cytoplasm that are composed of the protein tubulin and form an important component of the cytoskeleton, mitotic spindle, cilia, and flagella
— **mi·cro·tu·bu·lar** \-byə-lər\ *adjective*

mi·cro·vas·cu·lar \-'vas-kyə-lər\ *adjective* (1959)
: of, relating to, or constituting the part of the circulatory system made up of minute vessels (as venules or capillaries) that average less than 0.3 millimeters in diameter
— **mi·cro·vas·cu·la·ture** \-lə-ˌchu̇r, -ˌtyu̇r, -ˌtu̇r\ *noun*

mi·cro·vil·lus \-'vi-ləs\ *noun* [New Latin] (1953)
: a microscopic projection of a tissue, cell, or cell organelle; *especially* **:** any of the fingerlike outward projections of some cell surfaces
— **mi·cro·vil·lar** \-'vi-lər\ *adjective*
— **mi·cro·vil·lous** \-'vi-ləs\ *adjective*

mi·cro·volt \'mī-krō-ˌvōlt\ *noun* (1868)
: one millionth of a volt

mi·cro·watt \-ˌwät\ *noun* (circa 1909)
: one millionth of a watt

¹mi·cro·wave \-ˌwāv\ *noun, often attributive* (1931)
1 : a comparatively short electromagnetic wave; *especially* **:** one between about 1 millimeter and 1 meter in wavelength
2 : MICROWAVE OVEN

²microwave *transitive verb* (1973)
: to cook or heat in a microwave oven
— **mi·cro·wav·able** *or* **mi·cro·wave·able** \ˌmī-krə-'wā-və-bəl\ *adjective*

microwave oven *noun* (1963)
: an oven in which food is cooked by the heat produced by the absorption of microwave energy by water molecules in the food

mi·cro·world \-ˌwər(-ə)ld\ *noun* (1955)
: a small universe; *specifically* **:** the natural universe observed at the microscopic or submicroscopic level

mic·tu·rate \'mik-chə-ˌrāt, 'mik-tə-\ *intransitive verb* **-rat·ed; -rat·ing** [Latin *micturire* to desire to urinate, from *meiere* to urinate; akin to Old English *mīgan* to urinate, Greek *omeichein*] (1842)
: URINATE
— **mic·tu·ri·tion** \ˌmik-chə-'ri-shən, ˌmik-tə-\ *noun*

¹mid \'mid\ *adjective* [Middle English, from Old English *midde*; akin to Old High German

mitti middle, Latin *medius*, Greek *mesos*] (before 12th century)
1 : being the part in the middle or midst ⟨in *mid* ocean⟩ — often used in combination ⟨*mid*-August⟩
2 : occupying a middle position ⟨the *mid* finger⟩
3 *of a vowel* **:** articulated with the arch of the tongue midway between its highest and its lowest elevation
— **mid** *adverb*

²mid *preposition* (1808)
: AMID

mid·air \'mid-'ar, -'er\ *noun* (1667)
: a point or region in the air not immediately adjacent to the ground ⟨planes collided in *midair*⟩

Mi·das \'mī-dəs\ *noun* [Latin, from Greek]
: a legendary Phrygian king who is given the power of turning everything he touches to gold

Midas touch *noun* (1883)
: an uncanny ability for making money in every venture

mid·brain \'mid-ˌbrān\ *noun* (1875)
: the middle of the three primary divisions of the developing vertebrate brain or the corresponding part of the adult brain — called also *mesencephalon*; see BRAIN illustration

mid·course \-'kōrs, -'kȯrs\ *adjective* (circa 1956)
: being or occurring in the middle part of a course (as of a spacecraft) ⟨a *midcourse* correction⟩

mid·day \'mid-ˌdā, -'dā\ *noun, often attributive* (before 12th century)
: the middle of the day

mid·den \'mi-dᵊn\ *noun* [Middle English *midding*, of Scandinavian origin; akin to Old Norse *myki* dung & Old Norse *dyngja* manure pile — more at DUNG] (14th century)
1 : DUNGHILL
2 a : a refuse heap; *especially* **:** KITCHEN MIDDEN **b :** a small pile (as of seeds, bones, or leaves) gathered by a rodent (as a pack rat)

¹mid·dle \'mi-dᵊl\ *adjective* [Middle English *middel*, from Old English; akin to Old English *midde*] (before 12th century)
1 : equally distant from the extremes **:** MEDIAL, CENTRAL ⟨the *middle* house in the row⟩
2 : being at neither extreme **:** INTERMEDIATE
3 *capitalized* **a :** constituting a division intermediate between those prior and later or upper and lower ⟨*Middle* Paleozoic⟩ **b :** constituting a period of a language or literature intermediate between one called *Old* and one called *New* or *Modern* ⟨*Middle* Dutch⟩
4 *of a verb form or voice* **:** typically asserting that a person or thing both performs and is affected by the action represented

²middle *noun* (before 12th century)
1 : a middle part, point, or position
2 : the central portion of the human body **:** WAIST
3 : the position of being among or in the midst of something
4 : something intermediate between extremes **:** MEAN
5 : the center of an offensive or defensive formation; *especially* **:** the area between the second baseman and the shortstop

middle age *noun* (14th century)
: the period of life from about 40 to about 60
— **mid·dle–aged** \ˌmi-dᵊl-'ājd\ *adjective*
— **mid·dle–ag·er** \-'ā-jər\ *noun*

Middle Ages *noun plural* (1616)
: the period of European history from about A.D. 500 to about 1500

Middle America *noun* (1898)
1 : the region of the western hemisphere including Mexico, Central America, often the West Indies, and sometimes Colombia and Venezuela
2 : the midwestern section of the U.S.

3 : the middle-class segment of the U.S. population; *especially* **:** the traditional or conservative element of the middle class
— **middle–American** *adjective*
— **Middle American** *noun*
mid·dle·brow \'mi-dᵊl-ˌbraů\ *noun* (1925)
: a person who is moderately but not highly cultivated
— **middlebrow** *adjective*
middle C *noun* (1840)
: the note designated by the first ledger line below the treble staff and the first above the bass staff
mid·dle–class \ˌmi-dᵊl-'klas\ *adjective* (1836)
: of or relating to the middle class; *especially*
: characterized by a high material standard of living, sexual morality, and respect for property
— **mid·dle–class·ness** \-nəs\ *noun*
middle class *noun* (1766)
: a class occupying a position between the upper class and the lower class; *especially* **:** a fluid heterogeneous socioeconomic grouping composed principally of business and professional people, bureaucrats, and some farmers and skilled workers sharing common social characteristics and values
middle distance *noun* (1813)
1 : a part of a pictorial representation or scene between the foreground and the background
2 : any footrace distance usually from 800 to 1500 meters or from 880 yards to one mile
Middle Dutch *noun* (circa 1959)
: the Dutch language in use from about 1100 to about 1500 — see INDO-EUROPEAN LANGUAGES table
middle ear *noun* (1852)
: a small membrane-lined cavity that is separated from the outer ear by the eardrum and that transmits sound waves from the eardrum to the partition between the middle and inner ears through a chain of tiny bones
Middle English *noun* (1830)
: the English in use from the 12th to 15th centuries — see INDO-EUROPEAN LANGUAGES table
middle finger *noun* (before 12th century)
: the midmost of the five digits of the hand
Middle French *noun* (1889)
: the French in use from the 14th to 16th centuries — see INDO-EUROPEAN LANGUAGES table
middle game *noun* (1894)
: the middle phase of a board game; *specifically* **:** the part of a chess game after the pieces have been developed when players attempt to gain and exploit positional and material superiority — compare ENDGAME, OPENING
Middle Greek *noun* (1889)
: the Greek language used in the 7th to 15th centuries
middle ground *noun* (1801)
1 : a standpoint midway between extremes
2 : MIDDLE DISTANCE 1
Middle High German *noun* (1889)
: the High German in use from about 1100 to 1500 — see INDO-EUROPEAN LANGUAGES table
Middle Irish *noun* (1952)
: the Irish in use between the 10th and 13th centuries — see INDO-EUROPEAN LANGUAGES table
middle lamella *noun* (circa 1886)
: a layer of pectinaceous intercellular material lying between the walls of adjacent plant cells — see CELL illustration
Middle Low German *noun* (circa 1889)
: the Low German in use from about 1100 to 1500 — see INDO-EUROPEAN LANGUAGES table
mid·dle·man \'mi-dᵊl-ˌman\ *noun* (1795)
: an intermediary between two parties; *especially* **:** a dealer or agent intermediate between the producer of goods and the retailer or consumer
middle management *noun* (circa 1948)
: management personnel intermediate between operational supervisors and policy-making administrators
— **middle manager** *noun*

middle name *noun* (1835)
: a name between one's first name and surname
middle–of–the–road *adjective* (1894)
: standing for or following a course of action midway between extremes; *especially* **:** being neither liberal nor conservative in politics
— **mid·dle–of–the–road·er** \-'rō-dər\ *noun*
— **mid·dle–of–the–road·ism** \-'rō-ˌdi-zəm\ *noun*
middle of the road (1918)
: a course of action or a standpoint midway between extremes
Middle Persian *noun* (1930)
: any of the varieties of Persian in use from about 200 B.C. to about A.D. 1000
mid·dler \'mid-lər, 'mi-dᵊl-ər\ *noun* (1882)
: one belonging to an intermediate group, division, or class: as **a :** a student in the second-year class of a three-year program (as at a seminary or law school) **b :** a student in the second- or third-year class in some private secondary schools having a four-year course **c :** a student in a division in some private schools that corresponds approximately to junior high school
middle school *noun* (1945)
: a school usually including grades 5 to 8 or 6 to 8
— **middle school·er** \-ˌskü-lər\ *noun*
Middle Scots *noun* (circa 1903)
: the Scots language in use between the latter half of the 15th and the early decades of the 17th centuries
middle term *noun* (1685)
: the term of a syllogism that occurs in both premises
mid·dle·weight \'mi-dᵊl-ˌwāt\ *noun* (1889)
: one of average weight; *specifically* **:** a boxer in a weight division having a maximum limit of 160 pounds for professionals and 165 pounds for amateurs — compare LIGHT HEAVYWEIGHT, WELTERWEIGHT
Middle Welsh *noun* (circa 1922)
: the Welsh in use from about 1150 to 1500 — see INDO-EUROPEAN LANGUAGES table
¹mid·dling \'mid-liŋ, -lən\ *noun* (1543)
1 : any of various commodities of intermediate size, quality, or position
2 *plural but singular or plural in construction* **:** a granular product of grain milling; *especially* **:** a wheat milling by-product used in animal feeds
²middling *adjective* (1550)
1 : of middle, medium, or moderate size, degree, or quality
2 : MEDIOCRE, SECOND-RATE
— **middling** *adverb*
— **mid·dling·ly** \-lē\ *adverb*
mid·dor·sal \'mid-'dȯr-səl\ *adjective* (1879)
: of, relating to, or situated in the middle part or median line of the back
mid·dy \'mi-dē\ *noun, plural* **middies** [by shortening & alteration] (1818)
1 : MIDSHIPMAN
2 : a loosely fitting blouse with a sailor collar worn by women and children
mid·field \'mid-ˌfēld, ˌmid-'\ *noun* (15th century)
1 : the middle portion of a field; *especially* **:** the portion of a playing field (as in football) that is midway between goals
2 : the players on a team (as in lacrosse or soccer) that normally play in the midfield
mid·field·er \-ˌfēl-dər, -'fēl\ *noun* (1938)
: a member of a midfield
Mid·gard \'mid-ˌgärd\ *noun* [Old Norse *mithgarthr*]
: the abode of human beings in Norse mythology
midge \'mij\ *noun* [Middle English *migge*, from Old English *mycg*; akin to Old High German *mucka* midge, Greek *myia* fly, Latin *musca*] (before 12th century)
: a tiny dipteran fly (as a chironomid)

midg·et \'mi-jət\ *noun, often attributive* [*midge*] (1865)
1 : a very small person; *specifically* **:** a person of unusually small size who is physically well-proportioned
2 : something (as an animal) much smaller than usual
3 : a front-engine, single-seat, open-wheel racing car smaller and of less engine displacement than standard cars of the type
mid·gut \'mid-ˌgət\ *noun* (1875)
: the middle part of an alimentary canal
midi \'mi-dē\ *noun* [¹*mid* + -*i* (as in *mini*)] (1967)
: a dress, skirt, or coat that usually extends to the mid-calf
Mid·i·an·ite \'mi-dē-ə-ˌnīt\ *noun* [*Midian*, son of Abraham] (1560)
: a member of an ancient northern Arabian people
mid·land \'mid-lənd, -ˌland\ *noun* (1555)
1 : the interior or central region of a country
2 *capitalized* **a :** the dialect of English spoken in the midland counties of England **b :** the dialect of English spoken in an area of the east central U.S. often divided into north Midland extending westward from an area including southern New Jersey; northern Delaware and Maryland; central and southern Pennsylvania; and central Ohio, Indiana, and Illinois and south Midland extending westward and southwestward from an area including the Appalachian regions of Virginia, North Carolina, South Carolina, and Georgia; Tennessee, Kentucky, West Virginia; and southern Ohio, Indiana, and Illinois
— **midland** *adjective, often capitalized*
— **Mid·land·er** \-lən-dər, -ˌlan-\ *noun*
mid·lat·i·tudes \'mid-'la-tə-ˌtüdz, ˌmid-, -ˌtyüdz\ *noun plural* (1925)
: latitudes of the temperate zones or from about 30 to 60 degrees north or south of the equator
— **mid·lat·i·tude** \-ˌtüd, -ˌtyüd\ *adjective*
mid·life \'mid-'līf\ *noun* (1898)
: MIDDLE AGE
midlife crisis *noun* (1965)
: a period of emotional turmoil in middle age characterized especially by a strong desire for change
mid·line \'mid-ˌlīn, -'līn\ *noun* (circa 1859)
: a median line; *especially* **:** the median line or median plane of the body or some part of the body
mid·most \-ˌmōst\ *adjective* (before 12th century)
1 : being in or near the exact middle
2 : most intimate **:** INNERMOST
— **midmost** *adverb or adjective*
mid·night \'mid-ˌnīt\ *noun* (before 12th century)
1 : the middle of the night; *specifically* **:** 12 o'clock at night
2 : deep or extended darkness or gloom
— **midnight** *adjective*
— **mid·night·ly** *adverb or adjective*
midnight blue *noun* (1916)
: a deep blackish blue
midnight sun *noun* (1857)
: the sun above the horizon at midnight in the arctic or antarctic summer
mid·point \'mid-ˌpȯint, -'pȯint\ *noun* (14th century)
: a point at or near the center or middle
mid·rash \'mid-ˌdräsh\ *noun, plural* **mid·rash·im** \mi-'drä-shəm\ [Hebrew *midhrāsh* exposition, explanation] (1613)
1 : a haggadic or halakic exposition of the underlying significance of a Bible text
2 : a collection of midrashim

\ə\ abut \ᵊ\ kitten \ər\ further \a\ ash \ā\ ace
\ä\ mop, mar \aů\ out \ch\ chin \e\ bet \ē\ easy
\g\ go \i\ hit \ī\ ice \j\ job \ŋ\ sing \ō\ go
\ȯ\ law \ȯi\ boy \th\ thin \th̲\ the \ü\ loot \ů\ foot
\y\ yet \zh\ vision *see also* Guide to Pronunciation

3 *capitalized* : the midrashic literature written during the first Christian millennium
— **mid·rash·ic** \mi-'drä-shik\ *adjective, often capitalized*

mid·rib \'mid-,rib\ *noun* (1794)
: the central vein of a leaf

mid·riff \'mi-,drif\ *noun* [Middle English *midrif*, from Old English *midhrif*, from *midde* mid + *hrif* belly; akin to Old High German *href* body, and probably to Latin *corpus* body] (before 12th century)
1 : DIAPHRAGM 1
2 : the mid-region of the human torso
3 a : a section of a woman's garment that covers the midriff **b** : a woman's garment that exposes the midriff

mid–rise \'mid-,rīz, -'rīz\ *adjective* (1967)
: being approximately 5 to 10 stories high ⟨*mid-rise* condominiums⟩

mid·sag·it·tal \'mid-'sa-jə-t°l\ *adjective* (1947)
: median and sagittal

mid·sec·tion \-,sek-shən\ *noun* (1936)
: a section midway between the extremes; *especially* : MIDRIFF 2

mid·ship·man \'mid-,ship-mən, ,mid-'\ *noun* (1685)
: a person in training for a naval commission; *especially* : a student in a naval academy

mid·ships \'mid-,ships\ *adverb* (circa 1828)
: AMIDSHIPS

mid·size \-,sīz\ *also* **mid·sized** \-,sīzd\ *adjective* (1970)
: of intermediate size ⟨*midsize* car⟩

mid·sole \-,sōl\ *noun* (1926)
: a layer (as of leather or rubber) between the insole and the outsole of a shoe

midst \'midst, 'mitst\ *noun* [Middle English *middest*, alteration of *middes*, short for *amiddes* amid] (15th century)
1 : the interior or central part or point : MIDDLE ⟨in the *midst* of the forest⟩
2 : a position of proximity to the members of a group ⟨a traitor in our *midst*⟩
3 : the condition of being surrounded or beset ⟨in the *midst* of his troubles⟩
4 : a period of time about the middle of a continuing act or condition ⟨in the *midst* of a meal⟩
— **midst** *preposition*

mid·stream \'mid-'strēm, -,strēm\ *noun* (1669)
1 : the middle of a stream
2 : an intermediate stage in an act or process ⟨the tone changes in *midstream*⟩

mid·sum·mer \-'sə-mər, -,səm-\ *noun* (before 12th century)
1 : the middle of summer
2 : the summer solstice
— **midsummer** *adjective*

Midsummer Day *noun* (before 12th century)
: June 24 celebrated as the feast of the nativity of John the Baptist

mid·term \'mid-,tərm (*usual for 1b*), -'tərm\ *noun* (1906)
1 a : the middle of an academic term **b** : an examination at midterm
2 : the approximate middle of a term of office

mid·town \'mid-,taun, -'taun\ *noun* (1926)
: a central section of a city; *especially* : one situated between sections conventionally called *downtown* and *uptown*
— **midtown** *adjective*

¹mid·way \'mid-,wā, -'wā\ *adverb* (13th century)
: in the middle of the way or distance : HALFWAY

²mid·way \-,wā\ *noun* [Midway (*Plaisance*), Chicago, site of the amusement section of the Columbian Exposition 1893] (1893)
: an avenue at a fair, carnival, or amusement park for concessions and amusements

mid·week \-,wēk\ *noun* (1707)
: the middle of the week
— **midweek** *adjective or adverb*

— **mid·week·ly** \-,wē-klē, -'wē-\ *adjective or adverb*

¹mid·wife \'mid-,wīf\ *noun* [Middle English *midwif*, from *mid* with (from Old English) + *wif* woman] (14th century)
1 : a person who assists women in childbirth
2 : one that helps to produce or bring forth something

²midwife *transitive verb* **mid·wifed** \-,wīft\ *or* **mid·wived** \-,wīvd\; **mid·wif·ing** \-,wī-fiŋ\ *or* **mid·wiv·ing** \-,wī-viŋ\ (1638)
: to assist in producing, bringing forth, or bringing about

mid·wife·ry \,mid-'wi-f(ə-)rē, -'wī-; 'mid-,wī-\ *noun* (15th century)
1 : the art or act of assisting at childbirth; *also* : OBSTETRICS
2 : the art, act, or process of producing, bringing forth, or bringing about

mid·win·ter \'mid-'win-tər, -,win-\ *noun* (before 12th century)
1 : the winter solstice
2 : the middle of winter
— **midwinter** *adjective*

mid·year \-,yir\ *noun* (1896)
1 a : an examination at the middle of an academic year **b** *plural* : the set of examinations at the middle of an academic year; *also* : the period of such examinations
2 a : the middle or middle portion of a calendar year **b** : the middle of an academic year
— **midyear** *adjective*

mien \'mēn\ *noun* [by shortening & alteration from ¹*demean*] (1513)
1 : air or bearing especially as expressive of attitude or personality : DEMEANOR ⟨of aristocratic *mien*⟩
2 : APPEARANCE, ASPECT ⟨the inherent dangers of government encroachment . . . presented such a distasteful *mien* —H. W. Baldwin⟩
synonym see BEARING

¹miff \'mif\ *noun* [origin unknown] (1623)
1 : a fit of ill humor
2 : a trivial quarrel

²miff *transitive verb* (1811)
: to put into an ill humor : OFFEND

¹might \'mīt\ [Middle English, from Old English *meahte, mihte*; akin to Old High German *mahta, mohta* could] *past of* MAY (before 12th century)
— used in auxiliary function to express permission, liberty, probability, possibility in the past ⟨the president *might* do nothing without the board's consent⟩ or a present condition contrary to fact ⟨if you were older you *might* understand⟩ or less probability or possibility than *may* ⟨*might* get there before it rains⟩ or as a polite alternative to *may* ⟨*might* I ask who is calling⟩ or to *ought* or *should* ⟨you *might* at least apologize⟩

²might *noun* [Middle English, from Old English *miht*; akin to Old High German *maht* might, *magan* to be able — more at MAY] (before 12th century)
1 a : the power, authority, or resources wielded (as by an individual or group) ⟨the *might* of the armed forces⟩ **b** (1) : bodily strength (2) : the power, energy, or intensity of which one is capable ⟨striving with *might* and main⟩
2 *dialect* : a great deal
synonym see POWER

might·i·ly \'mī-t°l-ē\ *adverb* (before 12th century)
1 : in a mighty manner : VIGOROUSLY ⟨applauded *mightily*⟩
2 : very much ⟨depressed me *mightily*⟩

might·i·ness \'mī-tē-nəs\ *noun* (14th century)
: the quality or state of being mighty

mightn't \'mī-t°nt\ (1889)
: might not

¹mighty \'mī-tē\ *adjective* **might·i·er; -est** (before 12th century)
1 : possessing might : POWERFUL
2 : accomplished or characterized by might ⟨a *mighty* thrust⟩

3 : great or imposing in size or extent : EXTRAORDINARY

²mighty *adverb* (14th century)
: EXTREMELY, VERY ⟨a *mighty* handy gadget⟩ □

mi·gnon \mēn-'yōⁿ, min-'yȯn\ *noun* (circa 1919)
: FILET MIGNON

mi·gnon·ette \,min-yə-'net\ *noun* [French *mignonnette*, from obsolete French, feminine of *mignonnet* dainty, from Middle French, from *mignon* darling] (1798)
: any of a genus (*Reseda* of the family Resedaceae, the mignonette family) of herbs; *especially* : a garden annual (*R. odorata*) bearing racemes of fragrant whitish flowers

mi·graine \'mī-,grān, British often 'mē-\ *noun* [French, modification of Late Latin *hemicrania* pain in one side of the head, from Greek *hēmikrania*, from *hēmi-* hemi- + *kranion* cranium] (15th century)
1 : a condition marked by recurrent severe headache often with nausea and vomiting
2 : an episode or attack of migraine
— **mi·grain·ous** \-grā-nəs\ *adjective*

mi·grant \'mī-grənt\ *noun* [Latin *migrant-, migrans*, present participle of *migrare*] (1760)
: one that migrates: as **a** : a person who moves regularly in order to find work especially in harvesting crops **b** : an animal that shifts from one habitat to another
— **migrant** *adjective*

mi·grate \'mī-,grāt, mī-'\ *intransitive verb* **mi·grat·ed; mi·grat·ing** [Latin *migratus*, past participle of *migrare*; perhaps akin to Greek *ameibein* to change] (1697)
1 : to move from one country, place, or locality to another
2 : to pass usually periodically from one region or climate to another for feeding or breeding
3 : to change position in an organism or substance ⟨filarial worms *migrate* within the human body⟩
— **mi·gra·tion** \mī-'grā-shən\ *noun*
— **mi·gra·tion·al** \-shnəl, -shə-n°l\ *adjective*
— **mi·gra·tor** \'mī-,grā-tər, mī-'\ *noun*

mi·gra·to·ry \'mī-grə-,tōr-ē, -,tȯr-\ *adjective* (1753)
1 : of, relating to, or characterized by migration
2 : WANDERING, ROVING

mih·rab \'mē-rəb\ *noun* [Arabic *miḥrāb*] (1816)
: a niche or chamber in a mosque indicating the direction of Mecca

mi·ka·do \mə-'kä-(,)dō\ *noun, plural* **-dos** [Japanese] (1727)
: an emperor of Japan

¹mike \'mīk\ *noun* [by shortening & alteration] (1924)
: MICROPHONE

²mike *transitive verb* **miked; mik·ing** (1939)
: to supply with a microphone

Mike \'mīk\ (1942)

□ USAGE

mighty The use of *mighty* as an intensive usually conveys a folksy down-home feeling ⟨plain and simple fare . . . but *mighty* filling and *mighty* satisfying —*Asheville (N.C.) Citizen-Times*⟩. It is used especially to create a chatty style ⟨turnip greens, corn bread and biscuits. That sounds *mighty* good to me —Julia Child⟩ or to stress a rural atmosphere ⟨a man must be *mighty* serious about his squirrel hunting —Stuart Williams, *Field & Stream*⟩. In a more formal context, *mighty* is used to create additional emphasis by drawing attention to itself ⟨the chairman made sure that there were *mighty* few of them —Mollie Panter-Downes⟩.

— a communications code word for the letter *m*

¹mil \'mil\ *noun* [Latin *mille* thousand] (1721)
1 : THOUSAND ⟨found a salinity of 38.4 per *mil*⟩
2 : a monetary unit formerly used in Cyprus equal to 1/1000 pound
3 : a unit of length equal to ¹⁄₁₀₀₀ inch used especially in measuring thickness (as of plastic films)
4 : a unit of angular measurement equal to ¹⁄₆₄₀₀ of 360 degrees and used especially in artillery

²mil *noun, plural* **military** [short for *million*] (circa 1955)
slang **:** a million dollars

mi·la·dy \mi-'lā-dē, *US also* mī-\ *noun* [French, from English *my lady*] (1839)
1 : an Englishwoman of noble or gentle birth
2 : a woman of fashion

milch \'milk, 'milch, 'milks\ *adjective* [Middle English *milche*, from Old English *-milce;* akin to Old English *melcan* to milk — more at EMULSION] (14th century)
: MILK

mil·chig \'mil-ḵik\ *adjective* [Yiddish *milkhik,* from *milkh* milk, from Middle High German, from Old High German *miluh* — more at MILK] (circa 1928)
: made of or derived from milk or dairy products — compare FLEISHIG, PAREVE

mild \'mī(ə)ld\ *adjective* [Middle English, from Old English *milde;* akin to Greek *malthakos* soft, Latin *mollis* — more at MELT] (before 12th century)
1 : gentle in nature or behavior ⟨has a *mild* disposition⟩
2 a (1) **:** moderate in action or effect ⟨a *mild* cigar⟩ (2) **:** not sharp or bitter ⟨*mild* cheese⟩ ⟨*mild* ale⟩ **b :** not being or involving what is extreme ⟨an analysis under *mild* conditions⟩ ⟨a *mild* slope⟩
3 : not severe **:** TEMPERATE ⟨a *mild* climate⟩ ⟨*mild* symptoms of disease⟩
— **mild·ly** \'mī(ə)l(d)-lē\ *adverb*
— **mild·ness** \'mī(ə)l(d)-nəs\ *noun*

¹mil·dew \'mil-,dü, -,dyü\ *noun* [Middle English, from Old English *meledēaw* honeydew; akin to Old High German *militou* honeydew] (14th century)
1 a : a superficial usually whitish growth produced especially on organic matter or living plants by fungi (as of the families Erysiphaceae and Peronosporaceae) **b :** a fungus producing mildew
2 : a discoloration caused by fungi
— **mil·dewy** \-ē\ *adjective*

²mildew (circa 1552)
transitive verb
: to affect with or as if with mildew
intransitive verb
: to become affected with mildew

mild steel *noun* (1868)
: a low-carbon structural steel that is easily worked

mile \'mī(ə)l\ *noun* [Middle English, from Old English *mīl,* from Latin *milia* miles, from *milia passuum,* literally, thousands of paces, from *milia,* plural of *mille* thousand] (before 12th century)
1 : any of various units of distance: as **a :** a unit equal to 5280 feet — see WEIGHT table **b :** NAUTICAL MILE
2 : a race of a mile
3 : a relatively great distance or interval — used chiefly adverbially in plural ⟨was *miles* too small⟩

mile·age \'mī-lij\ *noun* (1754)
1 : an allowance for traveling expenses at a certain rate per mile
2 : aggregate length or distance in miles: as **a :** the total miles traveled especially in a given period of time **b :** the amount of service that something will yield especially as expressed in terms of miles of travel **c :** the average number of miles a car will travel on a gallon of gasoline that is used as a measure of fuel economy ⟨gets good *mileage*⟩
3 a : USEFULNESS ⟨got a lot of *mileage* left in her⟩ **b :** benefit derived from something ⟨got good political *mileage* from the debates⟩

mile·post \'mī(ə)l-,pōst\ *noun* (1768)
1 : a post indicating the distance in miles from or to a given point; *also* **:** a post placed a mile from a similar post
2 : MILESTONE 2

mil·er \'mī-lər\ *noun* (1889)
1 : one that competes in mile races — often qualified in combination ⟨a quarter-*miler*⟩
2 : one that is a specified number of miles in length — used in combination ⟨a 15-*miler*⟩

mi·les glo·ri·o·sus \'mē-,lās-,glōr-ə-'ō-səs, -,glōr-\ *noun, plural* **mi·li·tes glo·ri·o·si** \'mē-lə-,tās-,glōr-ē-'ō-(,)sē, -,glōr-\ [Latin] (1917)
: a boastful soldier; *especially* **:** a stock character of this type in comedy

mile·stone \'mī(ə)l-,stōn\ *noun* (circa 1746)
1 : a stone serving as a milepost
2 : a significant point in development

milestone 1

mil·foil \'mil-,fȯil\ *noun* [Middle English, from Old French, from Latin *millefolium,* from *mille* + *folium* leaf — more at BLADE] (13th century)
1 : YARROW
2 : WATER MILFOIL

mil·i·ar·ia \,mi-lē-'ar-ē-ə, -'er-\ *noun* [New Latin, from Latin, feminine of *miliarius*] (1807)
: an inflammatory disorder of the skin characterized by redness, eruption, burning or itching, and the release of sweat in abnormal ways (as by the eruption of vesicles) due to blockage of the ducts of the sweat glands; *especially* **:** PRICKLY HEAT
— **mil·i·ar·i·al** \-əl\ *adjective*

mil·i·ary \'mi-lē-,er-ē\ *adjective* [Latin *miliarius* of millet, from *milium* millet — more at MILLET] (1685)
: having or made up of many small projections or lesions ⟨*miliary* tubercles⟩

mi·lieu \mēl-'yə(r), -'yü; 'mēl-,yü, mē-lyœ̄\ *noun, plural* **milieus** *or* **mi·lieux** \-'yə(r)(z), -'yüz; -,yü(z), -lyœ̄(z)\ [French, from Old French, midst, from *mi* middle (from Latin *medius*) + *lieu* place, from Latin *locus* — more at MID, STALL] (1854)
: the physical or social setting in which something occurs or develops **:** ENVIRONMENT
synonym see BACKGROUND

mil·i·tance \'mi-lə-tən(t)s\ *noun* (circa 1947)
: MILITANCY

mil·i·tan·cy \-tən(t)-sē\ *noun* (1648)
: the quality or state of being militant

mil·i·tant \-tənt\ *adjective* (15th century)
1 : engaged in warfare or combat **:** FIGHTING
2 : aggressively active (as in a cause) **:** COMBATIVE ⟨*militant* conservationists⟩ ⟨a *militant* attitude⟩
synonym see AGGRESSIVE
— **militant** *noun*
— **mil·i·tant·ly** *adverb*
— **mil·i·tant·ness** *noun*

mil·i·tar·ia \,mi-lə-'ter-ē-ə\ *noun plural* (1964)
: military objects (as firearms and uniforms) of historical value or interest

mil·i·tari·ly \,mi-lə-'ter-ə-lē\ *adverb* (1660)
1 : in a military manner
2 : from a military standpoint

mil·i·ta·rise *British variant of* MILITARIZE

mil·i·ta·rism \'mi-lə-tə-,ri-zəm\ *noun* (1864)
1 a : predominance of the military class or its ideals **b :** exaltation of military virtues and ideals
2 : a policy of aggressive military preparedness
— **mil·i·ta·rist** \-rist\ *noun or adjective*

— **mil·i·ta·ris·tic** \,mi-lə-tə-'ris-tik\ *adjective*
— **mil·i·ta·ris·ti·cal·ly** \-ti-k(ə-)lē\ *adverb*

mil·i·ta·rize \'mi-lə-tə-,rīz\ *transitive verb* **-rized; -riz·ing** (1880)
1 : to equip with military forces and defenses
2 : to give a military character to
3 : to adapt for military use
— **mil·i·ta·ri·za·tion** \,mi-lə-t(ə-)rə-'zā-shən\ *noun*

¹mil·i·tary \'mi-lə-,ter-ē\ *adjective* [Middle English, from Middle French *militaire,* from Latin *militaris,* from *milit-, miles* soldier] (15th century)
1 a : of or relating to soldiers, arms, or war **b :** of or relating to armed forces; *especially* **:** of or relating to ground or sometimes ground and air forces as opposed to naval forces
2 a : performed or made by armed forces **b :** supported by armed force
3 : of or relating to the army

²military *noun, plural* **military** *also* **mil·i·tar·ies** (1736)
1 : military persons; *especially* **:** army officers
2 : ARMED FORCES

military–industrial complex *noun* (1961)
: an informal alliance of the military and related government departments with defense industries that is held to influence government policy

military police *noun* (1827)
: a branch of an army that exercises guard and police functions

military press *noun* (1939)
: ¹PRESS 9

military science *noun* (circa 1830)
: the principles of military conflict

military time *noun* (1955)
: time measured in hours numbered to twenty-four (as 0100 or 2300) from one midnight to the next

mil·i·tate \'mi-lə-,tāt\ *intransitive verb* **-tat·ed; -tat·ing** [Latin *militatus,* past participle of *militare* to engage in warfare, from *milit-, miles*] (1642)
: to have weight or effect ⟨his boyish appearance *militated* against his getting an early promotion⟩
usage see MITIGATE

mi·li·tia \mə-'li-shə\ *noun* [Latin, military service, from *milit-, miles*] (circa 1660)
1 a : a part of the organized armed forces of a country liable to call only in emergency **b :** a body of citizens organized for military service
2 : the whole body of able-bodied male citizens declared by law as being subject to call to military service

mi·li·tia·man \-mən\ *noun* (1780)
: a member of a militia

mil·i·um \'mi-lē-əm\ *noun, plural* **mil·ia** \-lē-ə\ [New Latin, from Latin, millet — more at MILLET] (1856)
: a small whitish lump in the skin due to retention of keratin in an oil gland duct — called also *whitehead*

¹milk \'milk\ *noun* [Middle English, from Old English *meolc, milc;* akin to Old High German *miluh* milk, Old English *melcan* to milk — more at EMULSION] (before 12th century)
1 a : a fluid secreted by the mammary glands of females for the nourishment of their young; *especially* **:** cow's milk used as a food by humans **b :** LACTATION ⟨cows in *milk*⟩
2 : a liquid resembling milk in appearance: as **a :** the latex of a plant **b :** the juice of a coconut **c :** the contents of an unripe kernel of grain

²milk (before 12th century)
transitive verb

1 a (1) **:** to draw milk from the breasts or udder of (2) *obsolete* **:** SUCKLE 2 **b :** to draw (milk) from the breast or udder **c :** SUCKLE 1 — used of lower mammals
2 : to draw something from as if by milking: as **a :** to induce (a snake) to eject venom **b :** to draw or coerce profit or advantage from illicitly or to an extreme degree **:** EXPLOIT
intransitive verb
: to draw or yield milk
³**milk** *adjective* (14th century)
: giving milk; *specifically* **:** bred or suitable primarily for milk production ⟨*milk* cows⟩
milk–and–water *adjective* (1783)
: WEAK, INSIPID
milk chocolate *noun* (1904)
: chocolate made with milk solids
milk·er \'mil-kər\ *noun* (15th century)
1 : one that milks an animal
2 : one that yields milk
milk fever *noun* (1758)
1 : a febrile disorder following parturition
2 : a disease of fresh cows, sheep, or goats that is caused by excessive drain on the body mineral reserves during the establishment of the milk flow
milk·fish \'milk-ˌfish\ *noun* (circa 1890)
: a large fork-tailed silvery herbivorous food fish (*Chanos chanos*) of warm parts of the Pacific and Indian oceans that is the sole living representative of its family (Chanidae)
milk glass *noun* (1874)
: an opaque and typically milky white glass used especially for novelty and ornamental objects
milk house *noun* (1589)
: a building for the cooling, handling, or bottling of milk
milk leg *noun* (circa 1860)
: a painful swelling of the leg caused by inflammation and clotting in the veins and affecting some postpartum women
milk–liv·ered \'milk-ˌli-vərd\ *adjective* (1605)
archaic **:** COWARDLY, TIMOROUS
milk·maid \-ˌmād\ *noun* (1552)
: DAIRYMAID
milk·man \-ˌman, -mən\ *noun* (1589)
: one who sells or delivers milk and milk products
milk of magnesia (1880)
: a milky white suspension of magnesium hydroxide in water used as an antacid and laxative
milk punch *noun* (1704)
: a mixed drink of alcoholic liquor, milk, and sugar
milk run *noun* [from the resemblance in regularity and uneventfulness to the morning delivery of milk] (1925)
: a short, routine, or uneventful flight
milk shake *noun* (1889)
: a thoroughly shaken or blended drink made of milk, a flavoring syrup, and often ice cream
milk sickness *noun* (1823)
1 : an acute disease characterized by weakness, vomiting, and constipation and caused by eating dairy products or meat from cattle poisoned by various plants
2 : TREMBLE 2
milk snake *noun* (1800)
: a common harmless grayish or tan American colubrid snake (*Lampropeltis triangulum*) having an arrow-shaped occipital marking and brown blotches on the body bordered with black or rings usually of black, red, and yellow; *broadly* **:** KING SNAKE
milk·sop \'milk-ˌsäp\ *noun* [Middle English, literally, bread soaked in milk] (14th century)
: an unmanly man **:** MOLLYCODDLE
milk sugar *noun* (1846)
: LACTOSE
milk tooth *noun* (circa 1752)
: a deciduous tooth of a young mammal; *especially* **:** one of the human dentition including four incisors, two canines, and four molars in each jaw

milk vein *noun* (1844)
: a large subcutaneous vein that extends along the lower side of the abdomen of a cow and returns blood from the udder — see COW illustration
milk vetch *noun* [from the popular belief that it increases the milk yield of goats] (1597)
: any of a genus (*Astragalus*) of leguminous herbs; *especially* **:** an Old World perennial (*A. glycyphyllos*) that has sulfur yellow flowers in dense spikes
milk·weed \'milk-ˌwēd\ *noun* (circa 1598)
: any of various plants that secrete latex; *especially* **:** any of a genus (*Asclepias* of the family Asclepiadaceae, the milkweed family) of erect chiefly perennial herbs with milky juice and umbellate flowers
milkweed bug *noun* (1905)
: a large black red-marked bug (*Oncopeltus fasciatus*) cultured as a research organism
milkweed butterfly *noun* (1880)
: any of a family (Danaidae) or nymphalid subfamily (Danaine) of large butterflies feeding on plants of the milkweed family as larvae; *especially* **:** MONARCH BUTTERFLY
milk·wort \'milk-ˌwərt, -ˌwȯrt\ *noun* (1578)
: any of a genus (*Polygala* of the family Polygalaceae, the milkwort family) of plants typically having showy flowers with three sometimes crested petals united below into a tube and an irregular calyx with two petaloid sepals
milky \'mil-kē\ *adjective* **milk·i·er; -est** (14th century)
1 : resembling milk in color or consistency
2 : MILD, TIMOROUS
3 a : consisting of, containing, or abounding in milk **b :** yielding milk; *specifically* **:** having the characteristics of a good milk producer
— **milk·i·ness** *noun*
milky disease *noun* (circa 1940)
: a destructive bacterial disease of scarab beetle grubs and especially Japanese beetle larvae
Milky Way *noun*
1 : a broad luminous irregular band of light that stretches completely around the celestial sphere and is caused by the light of myriads of faint stars
2 : MILKY WAY GALAXY
word history see GALAXY
Milky Way galaxy *noun*
: the galaxy of which the sun and the solar system are a part and which contains the myriads of stars that comprise the Milky Way
¹**mill** \'mil\ *noun* [Middle English *mille*, from Old English *mylen*, from Late Latin *molina, molinum*, from feminine and neuter of *molinus* of a mill, of a millstone, from Latin *mola* mill, millstone; akin to Latin *molere* to grind — more at MEAL] (before 12th century)
1 : a building provided with machinery for grinding grain into flour
2 a : a machine or apparatus (as a quern) for grinding grain **b :** a machine for crushing or comminuting
3 : a machine that manufactures by the continuous repetition of some simple action
4 : a building or collection of buildings with machinery for manufacturing
5 a : a machine formerly used for stamping coins **b :** a machine for expelling juice from vegetable tissues by pressure or grinding
6 : MILLING MACHINE, MILLING CUTTER
7 a : a slow, laborious, or mechanical process or routine **b :** one that produces or processes people or things mechanically or in large numbers ⟨a diploma *mill*⟩ ⟨a rumor *mill*⟩
8 : a difficult and often educational experience — used in the phrase *through the mill*
9 *slang* **:** the engine of an automobile or boat
²**mill** (1552)
transitive verb
1 : to subject to an operation or process in a mill: as **a :** to grind into flour, meal, or powder **b :** to shape or dress by means of a rotary cutter **c :** to mix and condition (as rubber) by passing between rotating rolls

2 : to give a raised rim or a ridged or corrugated edge to (a coin)
3 : to cut grooves in the metal surface of (as a knob)
intransitive verb
1 : to hit out with the fists
2 : to move in a circle or in an eddying mass; *also* **:** WANDER
3 : to undergo milling
³**mill** *noun* [Latin *mille* thousand] (1786)
: a money of account equal to ¹⁄₁₀ cent
⁴**mill** *variant of* ²MIL
mill·age \'mi-lij\ *noun* (1891)
: a rate (as of taxation) expressed in mills per dollar
mill·dam \'mil-ˌdam\ *noun* (12th century)
: a dam to make a millpond; *also* **:** MILLPOND
mille \'mil\ *noun* [Latin] (1894)
: THOUSAND
mille–feuille \mēl-'fwē\ *noun* [French, from *mille feuilles* a thousand leaves] (1895)
: a dish composed of puff pastry layered with a filling (as salmon or cream)
mil·le·fi·o·ri \ˌmi-lə-fē-'ȯr-ē, -'ȯr-\ *noun* [Italian, from *mille fiori* a thousand flowers] (1849)
: ornamental glass produced by cutting cross sections of fused bundles of glass rods of various colors and sizes
mille·fleur *or* **mille·fleurs** \(ˌ)mēl-'flər, -'flȯr\ *adjective* [French *mille-fleurs*, from *mille fleurs* a thousand flowers] (1908)
: having an allover pattern of small flowers and plants ⟨*millefleur* tapestry⟩
¹**mil·le·nar·i·an** \ˌmi-lə-'ner-ē-ən\ *adjective* (1631)
1 a : of or relating to belief in a millennium **b :** APOCALYPTIC 2
2 : of or relating to 1000 years
²**millenarian** *noun* (circa 1674)
: one that believes in a millennium
mil·le·nar·i·an·ism \-ē-ə-ˌni-zəm\ *noun* (circa 1847)
1 : belief in the millennium of Christian prophecy
2 : belief in a coming ideal society and especially one created by revolutionary action
¹**mil·le·na·ry** \'mi-lə-ˌner-ē, mə-'le-nə-rē\ *noun, plural* **-ries** [Late Latin *millenarium*, from neuter of *millenarius* of a thousand, from Latin *milleni* one thousand each, from *mille*] (1550)
1 a : a group of 1000 units or things **b :** 1000 years **:** MILLENNIUM
2 : MILLENARIAN
²**millenary** *adjective* [Latin *millenarius*] (circa 1641)
1 : relating to or consisting of 1000
2 : suggesting a millennium
mil·len·ni·al \mə-'le-nē-əl\ *adjective* (1664)
: of or relating to a millennium
mil·len·ni·al·ism \-ē-ə-ˌli-zəm\ *noun* (1906)
: MILLENARIANISM
mil·len·ni·al·ist \-list\ *noun* (circa 1841)
: MILLENARIAN
mil·len·ni·um \mə-'le-nē-əm\ *noun, plural* **-nia** \-nē-ə\ *or* **-niums** [New Latin, from Latin *mille* thousand + New Latin *-ennium* (as in *biennium*)] (circa 1638)
1 a : the thousand years mentioned in Revelation 20 during which holiness is to prevail and Christ is to reign on earth **b :** a period of great happiness or human perfection
2 a : a period of 1000 years **b :** a 1000th anniversary or its celebration
mill·er \'mi-lər\ *noun* (14th century)
1 : one that operates a mill; *specifically* **:** one that grinds grain into flour
2 : any of various moths having powdery wings
3 a : MILLING MACHINE **b :** a tool for use in a milling machine
mil·ler·ite \'mi-lə-ˌrīt\ *noun* [German *Millerit*, from William H. *Miller* (died 1880) English mineralogist] (1854)

: sulfide of nickel NiS usually occurring as a mineral in capillary yellow crystals

mill·er's-thumb \,mi-lərz-'thəm\ *noun* (15th century)
: any of several small freshwater spiny-finned sculpins (genus *Cottus*) of Europe and North America

mil·les·i·mal \mə-'le-sə-məl\ *noun* [Latin *millesimus,* adjective, thousandth, from *mille*] (1719)
: the quotient of a unit divided by 1000 **:** one of 1000 equal parts
— **millesimal** *adjective*
— **mil·les·i·mal·ly** \-mə-lē\ *adverb*

mil·let \'mi-lət\ *noun* [Middle English *milet,* from Middle French, diminutive of *mil,* from Latin *milium;* akin to Greek *melinē* millet] (15th century)
1 : any of various small-seeded annual cereal and forage grasses: **a :** a grass (*Panicum miliaceum*) cultivated for its grain which is used for food **b :** any of several grasses related to common millet
2 : the seed of a millet

milli- *combining form* [French, from Latin *milli-* thousand, from *mille*]
: thousandth ⟨*milli*ampere⟩

mil·li·am·pere \,mi-lē-'am,pir\ *noun* [International Scientific Vocabulary] (1885)
: one thousandth of an ampere

mil·liard \'mil-,yärd, 'mi-lē-,ärd\ *noun* [French, from Middle French *miliart,* from *mili-* (from *milion* million)] (1793)
British **:** a thousand millions — see NUMBER table

mil·li·ary \'mi-lē-,er-ē\ *adjective* [Latin *milliarius, miliarius* consisting of a thousand, one mile long, from *mille* thousand, mile] (1644)
: marking the distance of a Roman mile

mil·li·bar \'mi-lə-,bär\ *noun* [International Scientific Vocabulary] (1910)
: a unit of atmospheric pressure equal to ¹⁄₁₀₀₀ bar or 1000 dynes per square centimeter

mil·li·cu·rie \,mi-lə-'kyùr-(,)ē, -kyù-'rē\ *noun* [International Scientific Vocabulary] (1910)
: one thousandth of a curie

mil·li·de·gree \-di-'grē\ *noun* (1942)
: one thousandth of a degree

mil·lieme \mē(l)-'yem\ *noun, plural* **mil·liemes** \-'yem(z)\ [French *millième* thousandth, from Middle French, from *mille* thousand, from Latin] (1902)
: a unit of value of Egypt and Sudan equal to ¹⁄₁₀₀₀ pound

mil·li·gal \'mi-lə-,gal\ *noun* [International Scientific Vocabulary] (1914)
: a unit of acceleration equivalent to ¹⁄₁₀₀₀ gal

mil·li·gram \-,gram\ *noun* [French *milligramme,* from *milli-* + *gramme* gram] (circa 1810)
— see METRIC SYSTEM table

mil·li·hen·ry \-,hen-rē\ *noun* [International Scientific Vocabulary] (1897)
: one thousandth of a henry

mil·li·lam·bert \-,lam-bərt\ *noun* (1916)
: one thousandth of a lambert

mil·li·li·ter \'mi-lə-,lē-tər\ *noun* [French *millilitre,* from *milli-* + *litre* liter] (circa 1810)
— see METRIC SYSTEM table

mil·lime \mə-'lēm\ *noun* [modification of Arabic *mallim,* from French *millième*] (circa 1919)
— see *dinar* at MONEY table

mil·li·me·ter \'mi-lə-,mē-tər\ *noun* [French *millimètre,* from *milli-* + *mètre* meter] (1807)
— see METRIC SYSTEM table

mil·li·mi·cron \,mi-lə-'mī-,krän\ *noun* [International Scientific Vocabulary] (1904)
: NANOMETER

mil·li·mole \'mi-lə-,mōl\ *noun* [International Scientific Vocabulary *milli-* + ⁵*mole*] (circa 1904)
: one thousandth of a mole (as of a substance)
— **mil·li·mo·lar** \-,mō-lər\ *adjective*

mil·li·ner \'mi-lə-nər\ *noun* [irregular from *Milan,* Italy; from the importation of women's finery from Italy in the 16th century] (1530)
: a person who designs, makes, trims, or sells women's hats ◇

mil·li·nery \'mi-lə-,ner-ē\ *noun* (circa 1688)
1 : women's apparel for the head
2 : the business or work of a milliner

mill·ing \'mi-liŋ\ *noun* (1817)
: a corrugated edge on a coin

milling cutter *noun* (1884)
: a rotary tool-steel cutter used in a milling machine for shaping and dressing metal surfaces

milling machine *noun* (1876)
: a machine tool on which work usually of metal secured to a carriage is shaped by rotating milling cutters

mil·lion \'mi(l)-yən\ *noun, plural* **millions** or **million** [Middle English *milioun,* from Middle French *milion,* from Old Italian *milione,* augmentative of *mille* thousand, from Latin] (14th century)
1 — see NUMBER table
2 : a very large number ⟨*millions* of cars on the road⟩
3 : the mass of common people ⟨someone who writes for the *millions* —Bergen Evans⟩
— **million** *adjective*
— **mil·lion·fold** \-,fōld\ *adverb or adjective*
— **mil·lionth** \'mi(l)-yən(t)th\ *adjective or noun*

mil·lion·aire \,mi(l)-yə-'nar, -'ner, 'mi(l)-yə-,\ *noun* [French *millionnaire,* from *million,* from Middle French *milion*] (1826)
: a person whose wealth is estimated at a million or more (as of dollars or pounds)

mil·lion·air·ess \-'ar-əs, -'er-, -,ar-, -,er-\ *noun* (1881)
1 : a woman who is a millionaire
2 : the wife of a millionaire

mil·li·os·mol \,mi-lē-'äz-,mōl, -'äs-\ *noun* (1939)
: one thousandth of an osmol

mil·li·pede \'mi-lə-,pēd\ *noun* [Latin *millepeda,* a small crawling animal, from *mille* thousand + *ped-, pes* foot — more at FOOT] (1601)
: any of a class (Diplopoda) of myriapod arthropods having usually a cylindrical segmented body covered with hard integument, two pairs of legs on most apparent segments, and unlike centipedes no poison fangs

mil·li·ra·di·an \,mi-lə-'rā-dē-ən\ *noun* [International Scientific Vocabulary] (1954)
: one thousandth of a radian

mil·li·rem \'mi-lə-,rem\ *noun* (1947)
: one thousandth of a rem

mil·li·roent·gen \,mi-lə-'rent-gən, -'ränt-, -jən, -shən\ *noun* [International Scientific Vocabulary] (1947)
: one thousandth of a roentgen

mil·li·sec·ond \'mi-lə-,se-kənd, -kənt\ *noun* [International Scientific Vocabulary] (1909)
: one thousandth of a second

mil·li·volt \-,vōlt\ *noun* [International Scientific Vocabulary] (1861)
: one thousandth of a volt

mil·li·watt \-,wät\ *noun* [International Scientific Vocabulary] (circa 1914)
: one thousandth of a watt

mill·pond \'mil-,pänd\ *noun* (14th century)
: a pond created by damming a stream to produce a head of water for operating a mill

mill·race \-,rās\ *noun* (15th century)
: a canal in which water flows to and from a mill wheel; *also* **:** the current that drives the wheel

mill·stone \'mil-,stōn\ *noun* (before 12th century)
1 : either of two circular stones used for grinding (as grain)
2 a : something that grinds or crushes **b :** a heavy burden

mill·stream \-,strēm\ *noun* (before 12th century)

1 : a stream whose flow is utilized to run a mill
2 : MILLRACE

mill wheel *noun* (before 12th century)
: a waterwheel that drives a mill

mill·work \'mil-,wərk\ *noun* (1899)
: woodwork (as doors, sashes, or trim) manufactured at a mill

mill·wright \-,rīt\ *noun* (14th century)
1 : one whose occupation is planning and building mills or setting up their machinery
2 : one who maintains and cares for mechanical equipment (as of a mill or factory)

mi·lo \'mī-(,)lō\ *noun, plural* **milos** [perhaps from Sesotho *maili*] (1882)
: a small usually early and drought-resistant grain sorghum with compact bearded heads of large yellow or whitish seeds

mi·lord \mi-'lòr(d)\ *noun* [French, from English *my lord*] (1596)
: an Englishman of noble or gentle birth

mil·pa \'mil-pə\ *noun* [Mexican Spanish, from Nahuatl *mīlpan*] (1844)
1 a : a small field in Mexico or Central America that is cleared from the forest, cropped for a few seasons, and abandoned for a fresh clearing **b :** a maize field in Mexico or Central America
2 : the maize plant

Milque·toast \'milk-,tōst\ *noun* [Caspar *Milquetoast,* comic strip character created by H. T. Webster (died 1952) American cartoonist] (1935)
: a timid, meek, or unassertive person

mil·reis \mil-'rāsh, -'rās\ *noun, plural* **mil·reis** *same or* -'rāz, -'räzh\ [Portuguese *milréis*] (1589)
1 : a Portuguese unit of value equal before 1911 to 1000 reis
2 : the basic monetary unit of Brazil until 1942
3 : a coin representing one milreis

milt \'milt\ *noun* [probably from Middle Dutch *milte* milt of fish, spleen; akin to Old English *milte* spleen — more at MELT] (15th century)
: the sperm-containing fluid of a male fish

mim \'mim\ *adjective* [imitative of the act of pursing the lips] (1641)
dialect **:** affectedly shy or modest

¹mime \'mīm *also* 'mēm\ *noun* [Latin *mimus,* from Greek *mimos*] (1603)
1 : an ancient dramatic entertainment representing scenes from life usually in a ridiculous manner
2 a : an actor in a mime **b :** one that practices mime
3 : MIMIC 2
4 : PANTOMIME 3a,b

²mime *verb* **mimed; mim·ing** (1616)

◇ WORD HISTORY
milliner The Italian city of Milan was a significant source of luxury goods for 16th century England. Milan bonnets, Milan gloves, Milan ribbons, Milan point lace, Milan jewelry—all represented the best in Renaissance finery. The purveyors of these goods imported from Milan were called—regardless of their actual nationality—*milaners* or *millaners* or, in the variant that survives today, *milliners*. Eventually, *milliner* was extended to all merchants specializing in fancy accessories, the actual origin of the merchandise notwithstanding. For several centuries *milliner* could refer to a purveyor of luxury items of any kind. Apparently, not until the 19th century was *milliner* reserved exclusively for makers or retailers of women's hats.

intransitive verb
: to act a part with mimic gesture and action usually without words
transitive verb
1 : MIMIC
2 : to act out in the manner of a mime
— **mim·er** *noun*
mim·eo·graph \'mi-mē-ə-ˌgraf\ *noun* [from *Mimeograph*, a trademark] (1889)
: a duplicator for making many copies that utilizes a stencil through which ink is pressed
— **mimeograph** *transitive verb*
mi·me·sis \mə-'mē-səs, mī-\ *noun* [Late Latin, from Greek *mimēsis*, from *mimeisthai*] (1550)
: IMITATION, MIMICRY
mi·met·ic \-'me-tik\ *adjective* [Late Latin *mimeticus*, from Greek *mimētikos*, from *mimeisthai* to imitate, from *mimos* mime] (1637)
1 : IMITATIVE
2 : relating to, characterized by, or exhibiting mimicry ⟨*mimetic* coloring of a butterfly⟩
— **mi·met·i·cal·ly** \-ti-k(ə-)lē\ *adverb*
¹mim·ic \'mi-mik\ *noun* (1590)
1 : MIME 2
2 : one that mimics
²mimic *adjective* [Latin *mimicus*, from Greek *mimikos*, from *mimos* mime] (1598)
1 a : IMITATIVE **b** : IMITATION, MOCK ⟨a *mimic* battle⟩
2 : of or relating to mime or mimicry
³mimic *transitive verb* **mim·icked** \-mikt\; **mim·ick·ing** (1687)
1 : to imitate closely : APE
2 : to ridicule by imitation
3 : SIMULATE
4 : to resemble by biological mimicry
synonym see COPY
mim·ic·ry \'mi-mi-krē\ *noun, plural* **-ries** (1687)
1 a : an instance of mimicking **b** : the action, practice, or art of mimicking
2 : a superficial resemblance of one organism to another or to natural objects among which it lives that secures it a selective advantage (as protection from predation)
mi·mo·sa \mə-'mō-sə, mī-, -zə\ *noun* [New Latin, from Latin *mimus* mime] (1751)
1 : any of a genus (*Mimosa*) of leguminous trees, shrubs, and herbs of tropical and warm regions with usually bipinnate often prickly leaves and globular heads of small white or pink flowers
2 : SILK TREE
3 : a mixed drink consisting of champagne and orange juice
mi·na \'mī-nə\ *noun* [Latin, from Greek *mna*, of Semitic origin; akin to Hebrew *māneh* mina] (circa 1580)
: an ancient unit of weight and value equal to ¹⁄₆₀ talent
min·able *or* **mine·able** \'mī-nə-bəl\ *adjective* (circa 1570)
: capable of being mined
min·a·ret \ˌmi-nə-'ret, 'mi-nə-ˌ\ *noun* [French, from Turkish *minare*, from Arabic *manārah* lighthouse] (1682)
: a tall slender tower of a mosque having one or more balconies from which the summons to prayer is cried by the muezzin
mi·na·to·ry \'mi-nə-ˌtōr-ē, 'mī-, -ˌtòr-\ *adjective* [Late Latin *minatorius*, from Latin *minari* to threaten — more at MOUNT] (1532)
: having a menacing quality : THREATENING
min·au·dière \ˌmē-nōd-'yer\ *noun* [French, feminine of *minaudier* affected, coquettish, from *minauder* to mince] (1940)

minaret

: a small decorative case for carrying small articles (as cosmetics or jewelry)
¹mince \'min(t)s\ *verb* **minced; minc·ing** [Middle English, from Middle French *mincer*, from (assumed) Vulgar Latin *minutiare*, from Latin *minutia* smallness — more at MINUTIA] (14th century)
transitive verb
1 a : to cut or chop into very small pieces **b** : to subdivide minutely; *especially* : to damage by cutting up
2 : to utter or pronounce with affectation
3 a *archaic* : MINIMIZE **b** : to restrain (words) within the bounds of decorum
intransitive verb
: to walk with short steps in a prim affected manner
— **minc·er** *noun*
²mince *noun* (1600)
1 : small chopped bits (as of food); *specifically* : MINCEMEAT
2 *British* : HAMBURGER 1a
mince·meat \'min(t)s-ˌmēt\ *noun* (1663)
1 : minced meat
2 : a finely chopped mixture (as of raisins, apples, and spices) sometimes with meat that is often used as pie filling
3 : a state of destruction or annihilation — used in the phrase *make mincemeat of*
minc·ing \'min(t)-sin\ *adjective* (1530)
: affectedly dainty or delicate
— **minc·ing·ly** \-sin-lē\ *adverb*
¹mind \'mīnd\ *noun* [Middle English, from Old English *gemynd*; akin to Old High German *gimunt* memory, Latin *ment-, mens* mind, *monēre* to remind, warn, Greek *menos* spirit, *mnasthai, mimnēskesthai* to remember] (before 12th century)
1 : RECOLLECTION, MEMORY ⟨keep that in *mind*⟩ ⟨time out of *mind*⟩
2 a : the element or complex of elements in an individual that feels, perceives, thinks, wills, and especially to reason **b** : the conscious mental events and capabilities in an organism **c** : the organized conscious and unconscious adaptive mental activity of an organism
3 : INTENTION, DESIRE ⟨I changed my *mind*⟩
4 : the normal or healthy condition of the mental faculties
5 : OPINION, VIEW
6 : DISPOSITION, MOOD
7 a : a person or group embodying mental qualities ⟨the public *mind*⟩ **b** : intellectual ability
8 *capitalized, Christian Science* : GOD 1b
9 : a conscious substratum or factor in the universe
²mind (14th century)
transitive verb
1 *chiefly dialect* : REMIND
2 *chiefly dialect* : REMEMBER
3 : to attend to closely
4 a (1) : to become aware of : NOTICE (2) : to regard with attention : consider important — often used in the imperative with following *you* for emphasis ⟨I'm not against inspiration, *mind* you; I simply refuse to sit and stare at a blank page waiting for it —Dennis Whitcomb⟩ **b** *chiefly dialect* : INTEND, PURPOSE
5 a : to give heed to attentively in order to obey **b** : to follow the orders or instructions of
6 a : to be concerned about **b** : DISLIKE ⟨I don't *mind* going⟩
7 a : to be careful : SEE ⟨*mind* you finish it⟩ **b** : to be cautious about ⟨*mind* the broken rung⟩
8 : to give protective care to : TEND
intransitive verb
1 : to be attentive or wary
2 : to become concerned : CARE
3 : to pay obedient heed or attention
— **mind·er** *noun*
mind-bend·ing \'mīn(d)-ˌben-din\ *adjective* (1965)
: MIND-BLOWING
mind-blow·ing \-ˌblō-in\ *adjective* (1967)
1 : PSYCHEDELIC 1a

2 : MIND-BOGGLING
— **mind-blow·er** \-ˌblō(-ə)r\ *noun*
mind-bog·gling \-ˌbä-g(ə-)lin\ *adjective* (1964)
: mentally or emotionally exciting or overwhelming
— **mind-bog·gling·ly** \-lē\ *adverb*
mind·ed \'mīn-dəd\ *adjective* (15th century)
1 : INCLINED, DISPOSED
2 : having a mind especially of a specified kind or concerned with a specified thing — usually used in combination ⟨narrow-*minded*⟩ ⟨health-*minded*⟩
— **mind·ed·ness** \-dəd-nəs\ *noun*
mind-ex·pand·ing \'mīnd-ik-ˌspan-din\ *adjective* (1963)
: PSYCHEDELIC 1a
mind·ful \'mīn(d)-fəl\ *adjective* (14th century)
1 : bearing in mind : AWARE
2 : inclined to be aware
— **mind·ful·ly** \-fə-lē\ *adverb*
— **mind·ful·ness** *noun*
mind·less \-ləs\ *adjective* (before 12th century)
1 a : marked by a lack of mind or consciousness ⟨a *mindless* sleep⟩ **b** (1) : marked by or displaying no use of the powers of the intellect ⟨*mindless* violence⟩ (2) : requiring little attention or thought; *especially* : not intellectually challenging or stimulating ⟨*mindless* work⟩ ⟨a *mindless* movie⟩
2 : not mindful : HEEDLESS ⟨*mindless* of the consequences⟩
— **mind·less·ly** *adverb*
— **mind·less·ness** *noun*
mind reader *noun* (1887)
: one that professes or is held to be able to perceive another's thought without normal means of communication
— **mind reading** *noun*
mind-set \'mīn(d)-ˌset\ *noun* (1926)
1 : a mental attitude or inclination
2 : a fixed state of mind
mind's eye *noun* (15th century)
: the mental faculty of conceiving imaginary or recollected scenes; *also* : the mental picture so conceived ⟨in the *mind's eye* one sees dinosaurs, mammoths, and sabertoothed tigers —F. P. Brooks Jr.⟩
¹mine \'mīn\ *adjective* [Middle English *min*, from Old English *mīn* — more at MY] (before 12th century)
: MY — used before a word beginning with a vowel or *h* ⟨this treasure in *mine* arms —Shakespeare⟩ or sometimes as a modifier of a preceding noun; archaic except in an elevated style
²mine *pronoun singular or plural in construction* (before 12th century)
: that which belongs to me — used without a following noun as a pronoun equivalent in meaning to the adjective *my*
³mine *noun* [Middle English, from Middle French, from (assumed) Vulgar Latin *mina*, probably of Celtic origin; akin to Welsh *mwyn* ore] (14th century)
1 a : a pit or excavation in the earth from which mineral substances are taken **b** : an ore deposit
2 : a subterranean passage under an enemy position
3 : an encased explosive that is placed in the ground or in water and set to explode when disturbed
4 : a rich source of supply
⁴mine *verb* **mined; min·ing** (14th century)
transitive verb
1 a : to dig under to gain access or cause the collapse of (an enemy position) **b** : UNDERMINE
2 a : to get (as ore) from the earth **b** : to extract from a source ⟨information *mined* from the files⟩
3 : to burrow beneath the surface of ⟨larva that *mines* leaves⟩
4 : to place military mines in, on, or under ⟨*mine* a harbor⟩

5 a : to dig into for ore or metal **b :** to process for obtaining a natural constituent ⟨*mine* the air for nitrogen⟩ **c :** to seek valuable material in
intransitive verb
: to dig a mine
— **min·er** *noun*
mine·field \'mīn-ˌfēld\ *noun* (1886)
1 : an area (as of water or land) set with mines
2 : something resembling a minefield especially in having many dangers or requiring extreme caution
mine·lay·er \-ˌlā-ər, -ˌle(-ə)r\ *noun* (1909)
: a naval vessel for laying underwater mines
¹min·er·al \'min-rəl, 'mi-nə-\ *noun* [Middle English, from Medieval Latin *minerale,* from neuter of *mineralis*] (15th century)
1 : ORE
2 : an inorganic substance (as in the ash of calcined tissue)
3 *obsolete* **:** MINE
4 : something neither animal nor vegetable
5 a : a solid homogeneous crystalline chemical element or compound that results from the inorganic processes of nature; *broadly* **:** any of various naturally occurring homogeneous substances (as stone, coal, salt, sulfur, sand, petroleum, water, or natural gas) obtained usually from the ground **b :** a synthetic substance having the chemical composition and crystalline form and properties of a naturally occurring mineral
6 *plural, British* **:** MINERAL WATER
²mineral *adjective* [Middle English, from Medieval Latin *mineralis,* from *minera* mine, ore, from Old French *miniere,* from *mine*] (15th century)
1 : of or relating to minerals; *also* **:** INORGANIC
2 : impregnated with mineral substances
min·er·al·ise *British variant of* MINERALIZE
min·er·al·ize \'min-rə-ˌlīz, 'mi-nə-\ *transitive verb* **-ized; -iz·ing** (1655)
1 : to transform (a metal) into an ore
2 a : to impregnate or supply with minerals or an inorganic compound **b :** to convert into mineral or inorganic form
3 : PETRIFY
— **min·er·al·iz·able** \ˌmin-rə-'lī-zə-bəl, ˌmi-nə-\ *adjective*
— **min·er·al·i·za·tion** \-rə-lə-'zā-shən\ *noun*
— **min·er·al·iz·er** \'min-rə-ˌlī-zər, 'mi-nə-\ *noun*
mineral kingdom *noun* (circa 1691)
: a basic group of natural objects that includes inorganic objects — compare ANIMAL KINGDOM, PLANT KINGDOM
min·er·al·o·cor·ti·coid \ˌmin-rə-lō-'kȯr-tə-ˌkȯid, ˌmi-nə-\ *noun* (1946)
: a corticosteroid (as aldosterone) that affects chiefly the electrolyte and fluid balance in the body — compare GLUCOCORTICOID
min·er·al·o·gy \ˌmi-nə-'rä-lə-jē, -'ra-\ *noun* [probably from (assumed) New Latin *mineralogia,* irregular from Medieval Latin *minerale* + Latin *-logia* -logy] (1690)
1 : a science dealing with minerals, their crystallography, properties, classification, and the ways of distinguishing them
2 : the minerological characteristics of an area, a rock, or a rock formation
— **min·er·al·og·i·cal** \ˌmi-nə-rə-'lä-ji-kəl, ˌmin-rə-\ *also* **min·er·al·og·ic** \-'lä-jik\ *adjective*
— **min·er·al·og·i·cal·ly** \-'lä-ji-k(ə-)lē\ *adverb*
— **min·er·al·o·gist** \ˌmi-nə-'rä-lə-jist, -'ra-\ *noun*
mineral oil *noun* (1805)
: an oil of mineral origin; *especially* **:** a refined petroleum oil used especially as a laxative
mineral spirits *noun plural but singular or plural in construction* (1927)
: a petroleum distillate that is used especially as a paint or varnish thinner
mineral water *noun* (1562)

: water naturally or artificially infused with mineral salts or gases (as carbon dioxide)
mineral wax *noun* (circa 1864)
: a wax of mineral origin; *especially* **:** OZOKERITE
mineral wool *noun* (circa 1881)
: any of various lightweight vitreous fibrous materials used especially in heat and sound insulation
Mi·ner·va \mə-'nər-və\ *noun* [Latin]
: the Roman goddess of wisdom — compare ATHENA
min·e·stro·ne \ˌmi-nə-'strō-nē, -'strȯn\ *noun* [Italian, augmentative of *minestra,* from *minestrare* to serve, dish up, from Latin *ministrare,* from *minister* servant — more at MINISTER] (1891)
: a rich thick vegetable soup usually with dried beans and pasta (as macaroni or vermicelli)
mine·sweep·er \'mīn-ˌswē-pər\ *noun* (1905)
: a warship designed for removing or neutralizing mines by dragging
— **mine·sweep·ing** \-piŋ\ *noun*
Ming \'miŋ\ *noun* [Chinese (Beijing) *míng* luminous] (1795)
: a Chinese dynasty dated 1368–1644 and marked by restoration of earlier traditions and in the arts by perfection of established techniques
min·gle \'miŋ-gəl\ *verb* **min·gled; min·gling** \-g(ə-)liŋ\ [Middle English *menglen,* frequentative of *mengen* to mix, from Old English *mengan;* akin to Middle High German *mengen* to mix, Greek *massein* to knead] (15th century)
transitive verb
1 : to bring or mix together or with something else usually without fundamental loss of identity **:** INTERMIX
2 *archaic* **:** to prepare by mixing **:** CONCOCT
intransitive verb
1 : to become mingled
2 a : to come into contact **:** ASSOCIATE **b :** to move about (as in a group) ⟨*mingled* with the guests⟩
synonym see MIX
ming tree \'miŋ-\ *noun* [perhaps from *Ming*] (1948)
: a dwarfed evergreen conifer grown as bonsai; *also* **:** an artificial plant resembling this
min·gy \'min-jē\ *adjective* **min·gi·er; -est** [perhaps blend of ¹*mean* and *stingy*] (1912)
: MEAN, STINGY
¹mini \'mi-nē\ *adjective* [*mini-*] (1954)
1 : small in relation to others of the same kind
2 : of short length or duration **:** BRIEF
²mini *noun, plural* **min·is** (1961)
: something small of its kind: as **a :** MINICAR **b :** MINISKIRT **c :** MINICOMPUTER
mini- *combining form* [*miniature*]
: smaller or briefer than usual, normal, or standard ⟨*mini*course⟩ ⟨*mini*bus⟩
¹min·i·a·ture \'mi-nē-ə-ˌchur, 'mi-ni-ˌchur, 'min-yə-, -chər, -ˌchər, -ˌtyur, -ˌtur\ *noun* [Italian *miniatura* art of illuminating a manuscript, from Medieval Latin, from Latin *miniatus,* past participle of *miniare* to color with minium, from *minium* red lead] (circa 1586)
1 a : a copy on a much reduced scale **b :** something small of its kind
2 : a painting in an illuminated book or manuscript
3 : the art of painting miniatures
4 : a very small portrait or other painting (as on ivory or metal) ◇
— **min·i·a·tur·ist** \-ˌchur-ist, -chər-, -ˌtyur-, -ˌtur\ *noun*
— **min·i·a·tur·is·tic** \ˌmi-nē-ə-chə-'ris-tik, ˌmi-ni-, ˌmin-yə-, -ˌtyu-, -ˌtu-\ *adjective*
— **in miniature :** in a greatly diminished size, form, or scale
²miniature *adjective* (1714)
: being or represented on a small scale
synonym see SMALL
miniature golf *noun* (1915)

: a novelty golf game played with a putter on a miniature course usually having tunnels, bridges, sharp corners, and obstacles
miniature pin·scher \-'pin(t)-shər\ *noun* (1929)
: any of a breed of toy dogs that suggest a small Doberman pinscher and are 10 to 12½ inches (25 to 32 centimeters) in height at the withers
miniature schnauzer *noun* (circa 1929)
: any of a breed of schnauzers that are 12 to 14 inches (30 to 36 centimeters) in height at the withers and are classified as terriers

miniature schnauzer

min·i·a·tur·ize \'mi-nē-ə-chə-ˌrīz, 'mi-ni-chə-, 'min-yə-chə-, -ˌtyu-, -ˌtu-\ *transitive verb* **-ized; -iz·ing** (1946)
: to design or construct in small size
— **min·i·a·tur·i·za·tion** \ˌmi-nē-ə-ˌchur-ə-'zā-shən, ˌmi-ni-, ˌmin-yə-, -chər-, -ˌtyur-, -ˌtur-\ *noun*
mini-bike \'mi-nē-ˌbīk\ *noun* (1962)
: a small one-passenger motorcycle with a low frame and raised handlebars
— **mini-bik·er** *noun*
mini-bus \-ˌbəs\ *noun* (1958)
: a small bus or van
Mini-cam \-ˌkam\ *trademark*
— used for a portable television camera
mini-camp \-ˌkamp\ *noun* (1979)
: a special abbreviated training camp for football players held especially in the spring or early summer
mini-car \-ˌkär\ *noun* (1949)
: a very small automobile; *especially* **:** SUBCOMPACT
mini-com·put·er \ˌmi-nē-kəm-'pyü-tər\ *noun* (1968)
: a small computer that is intermediate between a microcomputer and a mainframe in size, speed, and capacity, that can support time-sharing, and that is often dedicated to a single application
mini-course \'mi-nē-ˌkȯrs, -ˌkȯrs\ *noun* (1970)
: a brief course of study usually lasting less than a semester

◇ WORD HISTORY
miniature The Latin name for the red coloring now commonly known as cinnabar or red lead was *minium.* Cinnabar, or *minium,* was used to embellish manuscripts in the era before the printing press. Titles, large initial letters, and decorative drawings were done in red as a contrast to the black ink of the regular text. The Latin verb meaning to color with minium was *miniare.* In early Italian, its meaning was broadened to the point where it simply meant "to decorate a manuscript," and the noun *miniature* was used to refer to any manuscript illustration, regardless of the colors used. Since the illustrations in manuscripts (called illuminations) are small by comparison with most other paintings, the word *miniature,* borrowed into English from Italian *miniatura,* came to mean not only a manuscript illumination but any small portrait or painting, and eventually anything very small.

\ə\ abut \ᵊ\ kitten \ər\ **further** \a\ ash \ā\ ace
\ä\ mop, mar \au̇\ out \ch\ chin \e\ bet \ē\ easy
\g\ go \i\ hit \ī\ ice \j\ job \ŋ\ sing \ō\ go
\ȯ\ law \ȯi\ boy \th\ thin \ṯh\ the \ü\ loot \u̇\ foot
\y\ yet \zh\ vision *see also* Guide to Pronunciation

min·ié ball \'mi-nē-, ,mi-nē-'ā-\ *noun* [Claude Étienne *Minié* (died 1879) French army officer] (1859)
: a rifle bullet with a conical head used in muzzle-loading firearms

min·i·fy \'mi-nə-,fī\ *transitive verb* **-fied; -fy·ing** [Latin *minus* less + English *-ify*] (1676)
: LESSEN

min·i·kin \'mi-ni-kən\ *noun* [obsolete Dutch *minneken* darling, ultimately from Middle Dutch *minne* love, beloved; akin to Old English *gemynd* mind, memory — more at MIND] (1761)
archaic : a small or dainty creature
— **minikin** *adjective*

mini·lab \'mi-nē-,lab\ *noun* (1982)
: a retail outlet offering rapid on-site film development and printing

min·im \'mi-nəm\ *noun* [Latin *minimus* least] (15th century)
1 : HALF NOTE
2 : something very minute
3 — see WEIGHT table
— **minim** *adjective*

min·i·mal \'mi-nə-məl\ *adjective* (1666)
1 : relating to or being a minimum: as **a** : the least possible ⟨a victory won with *minimal* loss of life⟩ **b** : barely adequate ⟨a *minimal* standard of living⟩ **c** : very small or slight ⟨a *minimal* interest in art⟩
2 *often capitalized* : of, relating to, or being minimal art or minimalism
— **min·i·mal·ly** \-mə-lē\ *adverb*

minimal art *noun* (1965)
: abstract art consisting primarily of simple geometric forms executed in an impersonal style

minimal brain dysfunction *noun* (1972)
: ATTENTION DEFICIT DISORDER

min·i·mal·ism \'mi-nə-mə-,li-zəm\ *noun* (1969)
1 : MINIMAL ART
2 : a style or technique (as in music, literature, or design) that is characterized by extreme spareness and simplicity

¹**min·i·mal·ist** \-list\ *noun* (1907)
1 : one who favors restricting the functions and powers of a political organization or the achievement of a set of goals to a minimum
2 a : a minimal artist **b** : an adherent of minimalism

²**minimalist** *adjective* (1967)
: of, relating to, or done in the style of minimalism

minimal pair *noun* (1942)
: two linguistic units that differ in a single distinctive feature or constituent (as voice in the initial consonants of *bat* and *pat*)

mini·max \'mi-ni-,maks\ *noun* [*minimum* + *maximum*] (1918)
: the minimum of a set of maxima; *especially* : the smallest of a set of maximum possible losses each of which occurs in the most unfavorable outcome of a strategy followed by a participant in a situation governed by the theory of games — compare MAXIMIN

mini·mill \'mi-nē-,mil\ *noun* (1969)
: a relatively small-scale steel mill that uses scrap metal as starting material

min·i·mise *British variant of* MINIMIZE

min·i·mize \'mi-nə-,mīz\ *transitive verb* **-mized; -miz·ing** (1802)
1 : to reduce or keep to a minimum
2 : to underestimate intentionally : play down : SOFT-PEDAL ⟨*minimizing* losses in our own forces while maximizing those of the enemy⟩
— **min·i·mi·za·tion** \,mi-nə-mə-'zā-shən\ *noun*
— **min·i·miz·er** \'mi-nə-,mī-zər\ *noun*

min·i·mum \'mi-nə-məm\ *noun, plural* **-i·ma** \-nə-mə\ *or* **-mums** [Latin, neuter of *minimus* smallest; akin to Latin *minor* smaller — more at MINOR] (1674)
1 : the least quantity assignable, admissible, or possible

2 : the least of a set of numbers; *specifically* : the smallest value assumed by a continuous function defined on a closed interval
3 a : the lowest degree or amount of variation (as of temperature) reached or recorded **b** : the lowest speed allowed on a highway
— **minimum** *adjective*

minimum wage *noun* (1860)
1 : LIVING WAGE
2 : the lowest wage paid or permitted to be paid; *specifically* : a wage fixed by legal authority or by contract as the least that may be paid either to employed persons generally or to a particular category of employed persons

min·ing \'mī-nin\ *noun* (1523)
: the process or business of working mines

min·ion \'min-yən\ *noun* [Middle French *mignon*] (1501)
1 : a servile dependent, follower, or underling
2 : one highly favored : IDOL
3 : a subordinate or petty official

mini·park \'mi-nē-,pärk\ *noun* (1967)
: a small city park

mini·school \-,skül\ *noun* (1968)
: an experimental school offering specialized or individual instruction to its students

min·is·cule \'mi-nəs-,kyü(ə)l\ *variant of* MINUSCULE

mini·se·ries \'mi-nē-,sir-(,)ēz\ *noun* (1973)
: a television production of a story presented in sequential episodes

mini·skirt \'mi-nē-,skərt\ *noun* (1965)
: a woman's short skirt with the hemline several inches above the knee
— **mini·skirt·ed** *adjective*

mini·state \-,stāt\ *noun* (1966)
: a small independent nation

¹**min·is·ter** \'mi-nə-stər\ *noun* [Middle English *ministre*, from Old French, from Latin *minister* servant; akin to Latin *minor* smaller] (14th century)
1 : AGENT
2 a : one officiating or assisting the officiant in church worship **b** : a clergyman especially of a Protestant communion
3 a : the superior of one of several religious orders — called also *minister-general* **b** : the assistant to the rector or the bursar of a Jesuit house
4 : a high officer of state entrusted with the management of a division of governmental activities
5 a : a diplomatic representative (as an ambassador) accredited to the court or seat of government of a foreign state **b** : a diplomatic representative ranking below an ambassador

²**minister** *intransitive verb* **-tered; -ter·ing** \-st(ə-)rin\ (14th century)
1 : to perform the functions of a minister of religion
2 : to give aid or service ⟨*minister* to the sick⟩

min·is·te·ri·al \,mi-nə-'stir-ē-əl\ *adjective* (1561)
1 : of, relating to, or characteristic of a minister or the ministry
2 a : being or having the characteristics of an act or duty prescribed by law as part of the duties of an administrative office **b** : relating to or being an act done after ascertaining the existence of a specified state of facts in obedience to a legal order without exercise of personal judgment or discretion
3 : acting or active as an agent : INSTRUMENTAL
— **min·is·te·ri·al·ly** \-ē-ə-lē\ *adverb*

minister plenipotentiary *noun, plural* **ministers plenipotentiary** (1796)
: a diplomatic agent ranking below an ambassador but possessing full power and authority

minister resident *noun, plural* **ministers resident** (1848)
: a diplomatic agent resident at a foreign court or seat of government and ranking below a minister plenipotentiary

¹**min·is·trant** \'mi-nə-strənt\ *adjective* (1667)

archaic : performing service in attendance on someone

²**ministrant** *noun* (1818)
: one that ministers

min·is·tra·tion \,mi-nə-'strā-shən\ *noun* (14th century)
: the act or process of ministering

min·is·try \'mi-nə-strē\ *noun, plural* **-tries** (14th century)
1 : MINISTRATION
2 : the office, duties, or functions of a minister
3 : the body of ministers of religion : CLERGY
4 : AGENCY 2, INSTRUMENTALITY
5 : the period of service or office of a minister or ministry
6 *often capitalized* **a** : the body of ministers governing a nation or state from which a smaller cabinet is sometimes selected **b** : the group of ministers constituting a cabinet
7 a : a government department presided over by a minister **b** : the building in which the business of a ministry is transacted

mini·van \'mi-nē-,van\ *noun* (1960)
: a small van

min·i·ver \'mi-nə-vər\ *noun* [Middle English *meniver*, from Middle French *menu vair* small vair] (13th century)
: a white fur worn originally by medieval nobles and used chiefly for robes of state

mink \'mink\ *noun, plural* **mink** *or* **minks** [Middle English] (15th century)
1 : soft fur or pelt of the mink varying in color from white to dark brown
2 : either of two slender-bodied semiaquatic carnivorous mammals (*Mustela vison* of North America and *M. lutreola* of Eurasia) that resemble the related weasels and have partially webbed feet, a rather short bushy tail, and a soft thick coat

mink 2

min·ke whale \'min-kə-\ *noun* [part translation of Norwegian *minkehval*, from *minke-* (perhaps from *Meincke*, a crewman of Svend Foyn (died 1894) Norwegian whaler) + *hval* whale] (1939)
: a small grayish baleen whale (*Balaenoptera acutorostrata*) with a whitish underside — called also *minke*

min·ne·sing·er \'mi-nə-,sin-ər, -,zin-\ *noun* [German, from Middle High German, from *minne* love + *singer* singer] (1825)
: any of a class of German poets and musicians of the 12th to the 14th centuries

Min·ne·so·ta Multiphasic Personality Inventory \,mi-nə-'sō-tə-,məl-ti-'fā-zik-, -,məl-,tī-\ *noun* [University of *Minnesota*] (1943)
: a test of personal and social adjustment based on a complex scaling of the answers to an elaborate true or false test

min·now \'mi-(,)nō\ *noun, plural* **minnows** *also* **minnow** [Middle English *menawe*; akin to Old English *myne* minnow, Old High German *munewa*, a kind of fish] (15th century)
1 a : a small cyprinid, killifish, or topminnow **b** : any of various small fish that are less than a designated size and are not game fish
2 : a live or artificial minnow used as bait

¹**Mi·no·an** \mə-'nō-ən, mī-\ *adjective* [Latin *minous* of Minos, from Greek *minōios*, from *Minōs* Minos] (1894)
: of or relating to a Bronze Age culture of Crete (3000 B.C.–1100 B.C.)

²**Minoan** *noun* (1902)
: a native or inhabitant of ancient Crete

¹**mi·nor** \'mī-nər\ *adjective* [Latin, smaller, inferior; akin to Old High German *minniro* smaller, Latin *minuere* to lessen] (1526)
1 : inferior in importance, size, or degree : comparatively unimportant
2 : not having reached majority
3 a : having half steps between the second and third, the fifth and sixth, and sometimes the

seventh and eighth degrees ⟨*minor* scale⟩ **b** : based on a minor scale ⟨*minor* key⟩ **c** : less by a semitone than the corresponding major interval ⟨*minor* third⟩ **d** : having a minor third above the root ⟨*minor* triad⟩
4 : not serious or involving risk to life ⟨*minor* illness⟩
5 : of or relating to an academic subject requiring fewer courses than a major

²minor *noun* (1612)
1 : a person who has not attained majority
2 : a minor musical interval, scale, key, or mode
3 a : a minor academic subject **b** : a student taking a specified minor
4 : a determinant or matrix obtained from a given determinant or matrix by eliminating the row and column in which a given element lies
5 *plural* : minor league baseball — used with *the*

³minor *intransitive verb* (1926)
: to take courses in a minor subject

minor axis *noun* (1862)
: the chord of an ellipse passing through the center and perpendicular to the major axis

minor element *noun* (circa 1945)
: TRACE ELEMENT

Mi·nor·ite \ˈmī-nə-ˌrīt\ *noun* [from *Friar Minor* Franciscan] (circa 1587)
: FRANCISCAN

mi·nor·i·ty \mə-ˈnȯr-ə-tē, mī-, -ˈnär-\ *noun*, *plural* **-ties** *often attributive* (1547)
1 a : the period before attainment of majority **b** : the state of being a legal minor
2 : the smaller in number of two groups constituting a whole; *specifically* : a group having less than the number of votes necessary for control
3 a : a part of a population differing from others in some characteristics and often subjected to differential treatment **b** : a member of a minority group ⟨an effort to hire more *minorities*⟩

minority leader *noun* (1949)
: the leader of the minority party in a legislative body

minor league *noun* (1889)
: a league of professional clubs in a sport other than the recognized major leagues

minor order *noun* (1844)
: one of the Roman Catholic or Eastern clerical orders that are lower in rank and less sacred in character than major orders — usually used in plural

minor party *noun* (1949)
: a political party whose electoral strength is so small as to prevent its gaining control of a government except in rare and exceptional circumstances

minor penalty *noun* (1936)
: a two-minute suspension of a player in ice hockey with no substitute allowed

minor planet *noun* (1861)
: ASTEROID

minor premise *noun* (circa 1741)
: the premise of a syllogism that contains the minor term

minor seminary *noun* (circa 1948)
: a Roman Catholic seminary giving all or part of high school and junior college training with emphasis on preparing candidates for a major seminary

minor suit *noun* (1916)
: either of the suits diamonds or clubs having inferior scoring value in bridge

minor term *noun* (1843)
: the term of a syllogism that forms the subject of the conclusion

Mi·nos \ˈmī-nəs\ *noun* [Latin, from Greek *Minōs*]
: a son of Zeus and Europa and king of Crete who for his just rule is made supreme judge in the underworld after his death

Mi·no·taur \ˈmi-nə-ˌtȯr, ˈmī-\ *noun* [Middle English, from Middle French, from Latin *Minotaurus*, from Greek *Minōtauros*, from *Minōs* + *tauros* bull]

: a monster shaped half like a man and half like a bull, confined in the labyrinth built by Daedalus for Minos, and given a periodic tribute of youths and maidens as food until slain by Theseus

mi·nox·i·dil \mə-ˈnäk-sə-ˌdil\ *noun* [perhaps from *a*mino + *oxi-* (alteration of *oxy-*) + *piperidine* + *-yl*] (1972)
: a peripheral vasodilator $C_9H_{15}N_5O$ used orally to treat hypertension and topically in a propylene glycol solution to promote hair regrowth in some forms of baldness

min·ster \ˈmin(t)-stər\ *noun* [Middle English, monastery, church attached to a monastery, from Old English *mynster*, from Late Latin *monasterium* monastery] (before 12th century)
: a large or important church often having cathedral status

min·strel \ˈmin(t)-strəl\ *noun* [Middle English *menestrel*, from Middle French, official, servant, minstrel, from Late Latin *ministerialis* imperial household officer, from Latin *ministerium* service, from *minister* servant — more at MINISTER] (14th century)
1 : one of a class of medieval musical entertainers; *especially* : a singer of verses to the accompaniment of a harp
2 a : MUSICIAN **b** : POET
3 a : any of a troupe of performers typically giving a program of black American melodies, jokes, and impersonations and usually wearing blackface **b** : a performance by a troupe of minstrels

min·strel·sy \-sē\ *noun* [Middle English *minstralcie*, from Middle French *menestralsie*, from *menestrel*] (14th century)
1 : the singing and playing of a minstrel
2 : a body of minstrels
3 : a group of songs or verse

¹mint \ˈmint\ *noun* [Middle English *minte*, from Old English, from Latin *mentha, menta*; akin to Greek *minthē* mint] (before 12th century)
1 : any of a family (Labiatae, the mint family) of aromatic plants with a square stem and a 4-lobed ovary which produces four one-seeded nutlets in fruit; *especially* : any of a genus (*Mentha*) of mints that have white, purple, or pink verticillate flowers with a nearly regular corolla and four equal stamens and that include some used in flavoring and cookery
2 : a confection flavored with mint
— **minty** \ˈmin-tē\ *adjective*

²mint *noun* [Middle English *mynt* coin, money, from Old English *mynet*, from Latin *moneta* mint, coin, from *Moneta*, epithet of Juno; from the fact that the Romans coined money in the temple of Juno Moneta] (15th century)
1 : a place where coins, medals, or tokens are made
2 : a place where something is manufactured
3 : a vast sum or amount

³mint *transitive verb* (1546)
1 : to make (as coins) out of metal : COIN
2 : CREATE, PRODUCE
— **mint·er** *noun*

⁴mint *adjective* (1902)
: unmarred as if fresh from a mint ⟨in *mint* condition⟩

mint·age \ˈmin-tij\ *noun* (circa 1570)
1 : the action or process of minting coins
2 : an impression placed upon a coin
3 : coins produced by minting or in a single period of minting

mint julep *noun* (1809)
: JULEP 2

min·u·end \ˈmin-yə-ˌwend\ *noun* [Latin *minuendum*, neuter of *minuendus*, gerundive of *minuere* to lessen — more at MINOR] (1706)
: a number from which the subtrahend is to be subtracted

min·u·et \ˌmin-yə-ˈwet\ *noun* [French *menuet*, from obsolete French, tiny, from Old French, from *menu* small, from Latin *minutus*] (1673)

1 : a slow graceful dance in ¾ time characterized by forward balancing, bowing, and toe pointing
2 : music for or in the rhythm of a minuet

¹mi·nus \ˈmī-nəs\ *preposition* [Middle English, from Latin *minus*, adverb, less, from neuter of *minor* smaller — more at MINOR] (15th century)
1 : diminished by : LESS ⟨seven *minus* four is three⟩
2 : deprived of : WITHOUT ⟨*minus* his hat⟩

²minus *noun* (1654)
1 : a negative quantity
2 : DEFICIENCY, DEFECT

³minus *adjective* (1800)
1 : algebraically negative ⟨a *minus* quantity⟩
2 : having negative qualities
3 : relating to or being a particular one of the two mating types that are required for successful fertilization in sexual reproduction in some lower plants (as a fungus)
4 : falling low in a specified range ⟨B *minus*⟩

¹mi·nus·cule \ˈmi-nəs-ˌkyü(ə)l *also* mi-ˈnəs-\ *noun* [French, from Latin *minusculus* rather small, diminutive of *minor* smaller] (1705)
1 a : one of several ancient and medieval writing styles developed from cursive and having simplified and small forms **b** : a letter in this style
2 : a lowercase letter

²minuscule *adjective* (circa 1741)
1 : written in or in the size or style of minuscules
2 : very small

minus sign *noun* (1668)
: a sign − used in mathematics to indicate subtraction (as in 8−6=2) or a negative quantity (as in −10°)

¹min·ute \ˈmi-nət\ *noun* [Middle English, from Middle French, from Late Latin *minuta*, from Latin *minutus* small, from past participle of *minuere* to lessen — more at MINOR] (14th century)
1 : a 60th part of an hour of time or of a degree : 60 seconds
2 : the distance one can traverse in a minute
3 : a short space of time : MOMENT
4 a : a brief note (as of summary or recommendation) **b** : MEMORANDUM, DRAFT **c** *plural* : the official record of the proceedings of a meeting

²minute *transitive verb* **min·ut·ed; min·ut·ing** (circa 1648)
: to make notes or a brief summary of

³mi·nute \mī-ˈnüt, mə-, -ˈnyüt\ *adjective* **mi·nut·er; -est** [Latin *minutus*] (circa 1626)
1 : very small : INFINITESIMAL
2 : of small importance : TRIFLING
3 : marked by close attention to details
synonym see SMALL, CIRCUMSTANTIAL
— **mi·nute·ness** *noun*

minute hand *noun* (1726)
: the long hand that marks the minutes on the face of a watch or clock

¹mi·nute·ly \mī-ˈnüt-lē, mə-, -ˈnyüt-\ *adverb* (1599)
1 : into very small pieces
2 : in a minute manner or degree

²min·ute·ly \ˈmi-nət-lē\ *adjective* (1605)
archaic : minute by minute

min·ute·man \ˈmi-nət-ˌman\ *noun* (1774)
: a member of a group of armed men pledged to take the field at a minute's notice during and immediately before the American Revolution

min·ute steak \ˈmi-nət-\ *noun* (1921)
: a small thin steak that can be quickly cooked

\ə\ abut \ᵊ\ kitten \ər\ further \a\ ash \ā\ ace
\ä\ mop, mar \au̇\ out \ch\ chin \e\ bet \ē\ easy
\g\ go \i\ hit \ī\ ice \j\ job \ŋ\ sing \ō\ go
\ȯ\ law \ȯi\ boy \th\ thin \t̲h̲\ the \ü\ loot \u̇\ foot
\y\ yet \zh\ vision *see also* Guide to Pronunciation

mi·nu·tia \mə-'nü-sh(ē-)ə, mī-, -'nyü-\ *noun*, *plural* **-ti·ae** \-shē-ˌē, -ˌī\ [Latin *minutiae* trifles, details, from plural of *minutia* smallness, from *minutus*] (1751)
: a minute or minor detail — usually used in plural

minx \'min(k)s\ *noun* [origin unknown] (1592)
1 : a pert girl
2 *obsolete* : a wanton woman

min·yan \'min-yən\ *noun*, *plural* **-ya·nim** \ˌmin-yə-'nēm\ *or* **-yans** [Hebrew *minyān*, literally, number, count] (1753)
: the quorum of 10 adult Jews required for communal worship

Mio·cene \'mī-ə-ˌsēn\ *adjective* [*mio-* (from Greek *meiōn* less) + *-cene* — more at MEIOSIS] (1831)
: of, relating to, or being an epoch of the Tertiary between the Pliocene and the Oligocene or the corresponding system of rocks — see GEOLOGIC TIME table
— **Miocene** *noun*

mi·o·sis \mī-'ō-səs, mē-\ *noun*, *plural* **mi·o·ses** \-ˌsēz\ [New Latin, from Greek *myein* to be closed (of the eyes) + New Latin *-osis*] (1819)
: excessive smallness or contraction of the pupil of the eye

¹mi·ot·ic \-'ä-tik\ *noun* (1864)
: an agent that causes miosis

²miotic *adjective* (1864)
: relating to or characterized by miosis

mi·que·let \ˌmi-kə-'let, ˌmē-\ *noun* [Spanish *miquelete*] (1827)
: a Spanish or French irregular soldier during the Peninsular War

mir \'mir\ *noun* [Russian] (1877)
: a village community in czarist Russia in which land was owned jointly but cultivated by individual families

mi·ra·bi·le dic·tu \mə-ˌrä-bə-lē-'dik-(ˌ)tü\ [Latin] (1831)
: wonderful to relate

mi·ra·cid·i·um \ˌmir-ə-'si-dē-əm, ˌmī-rə-\ *noun*, *plural* **-cid·ia** \-dē-ə\ [New Latin, from Greek *meirak-*, *meirax* youth, stripling + New Latin *-idium*] (1898)
: the free-swimming ciliated first larva of a digenetic trematode that seeks out and penetrates a suitable snail intermediate host in which it develops into a sporocyst
— **mi·ra·cid·i·al** \-dē-əl\ *adjective*

mir·a·cle \'mir-i-kəl\ *noun* [Middle English, from Old French, from Late Latin *miraculum*, from Latin, a wonder, marvel, from *mirari* to wonder at] (12th century)
1 : an extraordinary event manifesting divine intervention in human affairs
2 : an extremely outstanding or unusual event, thing, or accomplishment
3 *Christian Science* : a divinely natural phenomenon experienced humanly as the fulfillment of spiritual law

miracle drug *noun* (1950)
: a drug usually newly discovered that elicits a dramatic response in a patient's condition — called also *wonder drug*

miracle fruit *noun* (1964)
: a tropical African shrub (*Synsepalum dulcificum*) of the sapodilla family whose fruit contains a glycoprotein that when applied to the tongue causes sour substances to taste sweet; *also* : its fruit

miracle play *noun* (circa 1852)
1 : a medieval drama based on episodes from the life of a saint or martyr
2 : MYSTERY PLAY

mi·rac·u·lous \mə-'ra-kyə-ləs\ *adjective* [Middle English, from Middle French *miraculeux*, from Medieval Latin *miraculosus*, from Latin *miraculum*] (15th century)
1 : of the nature of a miracle : SUPERNATURAL ⟨a *miraculous* event⟩
2 : suggesting a miracle : MARVELOUS ⟨gave proof of a *miraculous* memory *—Time*⟩

3 : working or able to work miracles ⟨*miraculous* power⟩
— **mi·rac·u·lous·ly** *adverb*
— **mi·rac·u·lous·ness** *noun*

mir·a·dor \'mir-ə-ˌdòr, ˌmir-ə-'\ *noun* [Spanish, from Catalan, from *mirar* to look at, from Latin *mirari*] (1797)
: a turret, window, or balcony designed to command an extensive outlook

mi·rage \mə-'räzh\ *noun* [French, from *mirer* to look at, from Latin *mirari*] (1803)
1 : an optical effect that is sometimes seen at sea, in the desert, or over a hot pavement, that may have the appearance of a pool of water or a mirror in which distant objects are seen inverted, and that is caused by the bending or reflection of rays of light by a layer of heated air of varying density
2 : something illusory and unattainable like a mirage

Mi·ran·da \mə-'ran-də\ *adjective* [from *Miranda v. Arizona*, the U.S. Supreme Court ruling establishing such rights] (1972)
: of, relating to, or being the legal rights of an arrested person to have an attorney and to remain silent so as to avoid self-incrimination ⟨*Miranda* warnings⟩

¹mire \'mīr\ *noun* [Middle English, from Old Norse *mȳrr*; akin to Old English *mōs* marsh — more at MOSS] (14th century)
1 : wet spongy earth (as of a bog or marsh)
2 : heavy often deep mud or slush
3 : a troublesome or intractable situation ⟨found themselves in a *mire* of debt⟩
— **miry** \'mīr-ē\ *adjective*

²mire *verb* **mired; mir·ing** (15th century)
transitive verb
1 a : to cause to stick fast in or as if in mire **b** : to hamper or hold back as if by mire : ENTANGLE
2 : to cover or soil with mire
intransitive verb
: to stick or sink in mire

mi·rex \'mī-ˌreks\ *noun* [origin unknown] (1962)
: an organochlorine insecticide $C_{10}Cl_{12}$ used especially against ants

mirk, mirky *variant of* MURK, MURKY

mir·li·ton \ˌmir-lə-'tōⁿ\ *noun* [French] (circa 1909)
: CHAYOTE

¹mir·ror \'mir-ər\ *noun* [Middle English *mirour*, from Old French, from *mirer* to look at, from Latin *mirari* to wonder at] (13th century)
1 : a polished or smooth surface (as of glass) that forms images by reflection
2 a : something that gives a true representation **b** : an exemplary model
— **mir·rored** \-ə(r)d\ *adjective*
— **mir·ror·like** \-ˌlīk\ *adjective*

²mirror *transitive verb* (1593)
: to reflect in or as if in a mirror

mirror image *noun* (1885)
: something that has its parts reversely arranged in comparison with another similar thing or that is reversed with reference to an intervening axis or plane

mirth \'mərth\ *noun* [Middle English, from Old English *myrgth*, from *myrge* merry — more at MERRY] (before 12th century)
: gladness or gaiety as shown by or accompanied with laughter
— **mirth·ful** \-fəl\ *adjective*
— **mirth·ful·ly** \-fə-lē\ *adverb*
— **mirth·ful·ness** *noun*
— **mirth·less** \-ləs\ *adjective*
— **mirth·less·ly** \-lē\ *adverb*

¹MIRV \'mərv\ *noun* [multiple *i*ndependently targeted *r*eentry *v*ehicle] (1967)
: a missile with two or more warheads designed to strike separate enemy targets; *also* : any of the warheads of such a missile

²MIRV *verb* **MIRVed; MIRV·ing** (1969)
transitive verb
: to equip with MIRV warheads

intransitive verb
: to arm one's forces with MIRVs

mis- *prefix* [partly from Middle English, from Old English; partly from Middle English *mes-*, *mis-*, from Old French *mes-*, of Germanic origin; akin to Old English *mis-*; akin to Old English *missan* to miss]
1 a : badly : wrongly ⟨*mis*judge⟩ **b** : unfavorably ⟨*mis*esteem⟩ **c** : in a suspicious manner ⟨*mis*doubt⟩
2 : bad : wrong ⟨*mis*deed⟩
3 : opposite or lack of ⟨*mis*trust⟩
4 : not ⟨*mis*know⟩

mis·act
mis·ad·dress
mis·ad·just
mis·ad·min·is·tra·tion
mis·ad·vise
mis·aim
mis·align
mis·align·ment
mis·al·lo·cate
mis·al·lo·ca·tion
mis·anal·y·sis
mis·ap·pli·ca·tion
mis·ap·ply
mis·ap·prais·al
mis·ar·tic·u·late
mis·as·sem·ble
mis·as·sump·tion
mis·at·trib·ute
mis·at·tri·bu·tion
mis·bal·ance
mis·be·have
mis·be·hav·er
mis·be·hav·ior
mis·bound
mis·but·ton
mis·cal·cu·late
mis·cal·cu·la·tion
mis·cap·tion
mis·cat·a·log
mis·chan·nel
mis·char·ac·ter·i·za·tion
mis·char·ac·ter·ize
mis·charge
mis·choice
mis·ci·ta·tion
mis·clas·si·fi·ca·tion
mis·clas·si·fy
mis·code
mis·com·pre·hen·sion
mis·com·pu·ta·tion
mis·com·pute
mis·con·ceive
mis·con·ceiv·er
mis·con·cep·tion
mis·con·nect
mis·con·nec·tion
mis·con·struc·tion
mis·con·strue
mis·copy
mis·cor·re·la·tion
mis·cre·ate
mis·cre·a·tion
mis·cut
mis·date
mis·deem
mis·de·fine
mis·de·scribe
mis·de·scrip·tion
mis·de·vel·op
mis·di·ag·nose
mis·di·ag·no·sis
mis·dial
mis·dis·tri·bu·tion
mis·di·vi·sion
mis·draw
mis·ed·u·cate
mis·ed·u·ca·tion
mis·em·pha·sis
mis·em·pha·size
mis·em·ploy
mis·em·ploy·ment
mis·es·ti·mate
mis·es·ti·ma·tion
mis·eval·u·ate
mis·eval·u·a·tion
mis·field
mis·file
mis·fo·cus
mis·func·tion
mis·gauge
mis·gov·ern
mis·gov·ern·ment
mis·grade
mis·iden·ti·fi·ca·tion
mis·iden·ti·fy
mis·in·form
mis·in·for·ma·tion
mis·kick
mis·la·bel
mis·learn
mis·lo·cate
mis·lo·ca·tion
mis·man·age
mis·man·age·ment
mis·mark
mis·mar·riage
mis·match
mis·mate
mis·or·der
mis·ori·ent
mis·ori·en·ta·tion
mis·pack·age
mis·per·ceive
mis·per·cep·tion
mis·plan
mis·po·si·tion
mis·print
mis·pro·gram
mis·quo·ta·tion
mis·quote
mis·rec·ol·lec·tion
mis·re·cord
mis·ref·er·ence
mis·reg·is·ter
mis·reg·is·tra·tion
mis·re·late
mis·re·mem·ber
mis·ren·der
mis·re·port
mis·route
mis·set
mis·shape
mis·shap·en
mis·shap·en·ly
mis·sort
mis·strike
mis·throw
mis·time
mis·ti·tle
mis·train
mis·tran·scribe
mis·tran·scrip·tion
mis·trans·late
mis·trans·la·tion
mis·truth
mis·tune
mis·type
mis·uti·li·za·tion
mis·vo·cal·i·za·tion
mis·write

mis·ad·ven·ture \ˌmi-səd-ˈven-chər\ *noun* [Middle English *mesaventure,* from Old French, from *mesavenir* to chance badly, from *mes-* mis- + *avenir* to chance, happen, from Latin *advenire* — more at ADVENTURE] (14th century)
: MISFORTUNE, MISHAP

mis·al·li·ance \ˌmi-sə-ˈlī-ən(t)s\ *noun* [modification of French *mésalliance*] (1738)
1 : an improper alliance
2 a : MÉSALLIANCE **b** : a marriage between persons unsuited to each other

mis·an·thrope \ˈmi-sᵊn-ˌthrōp\ *noun* [Greek *misanthrōpos* hating mankind, from *misein* to hate + *anthrōpos* human being] (1683)
: a person who hates or distrusts mankind

mis·an·throp·ic \ˌmi-sᵊn-ˈthrä-pik\ *adjective* (1762)
1 : of, relating to, or characteristic of a misanthrope
2 : marked by a hatred or contempt for mankind
synonym see CYNICAL
— **mis·an·throp·i·cal·ly** \-pi-k(ə-)lē\ *adverb*

mis·an·thro·py \mi-ˈsan(t)-thrə-pē\ *noun* (circa 1656)
: a hatred or distrust of mankind

mis·ap·pre·hend \(ˌ)mis-ˌa-pri-ˈhend\ *transitive verb* (circa 1629)
: to apprehend wrongly : MISUNDERSTAND
— **mis·ap·pre·hen·sion** \-ˈhen(t)-shən\ *noun*

mis·ap·pro·pri·ate \ˌmi-sə-ˈprō-prē-ˌāt\ *transitive verb* (1857)
: to appropriate wrongly (as by theft or embezzlement)
— **mis·ap·pro·pri·a·tion** \-ˌprō-prē-ˈā-shən\ *noun*

mis·be·come \ˌmis-bi-ˈkəm\ *transitive verb* **-came** \-ˈkām\; **-come; -com·ing** (1530)
: to be inappropriate or unbecoming to

mis·be·got·ten \-bi-ˈgä-tᵊn\ *adjective* (1554)
1 : unlawfully conceived : ILLEGITIMATE ⟨a *misbegotten* child⟩
2 a : having a disreputable or improper origin : ill-conceived ⟨antiquated and *misbegotten* tax laws —R. M. Blough⟩ **b** : CONTEMPTIBLE, DEFORMED ⟨a *misbegotten* scoundrel⟩

mis·be·lief \ˌmis-bə-ˈlēf\ *noun* (13th century)
: erroneous or false belief

mis·be·lieve \-ˈlēv\ *intransitive verb* (14th century)
obsolete : to hold a false or unorthodox belief

mis·be·liev·er \-ˈlē-vər\ *noun* (15th century)
: HERETIC, INFIDEL

mis·brand \ˌmis-ˈbrand\ *transitive verb* (circa 1930)
: to brand falsely or in a misleading way; *specifically* : to label in violation of statutory requirements

mis·call \ˌmis-ˈkȯl\ *transitive verb* (14th century)
: to call by a wrong name : MISNAME

mis·car·riage \ˌmis-ˈkar-ij, ˈmis-ˌ\ *noun* (circa 1652)
1 : corrupt or incompetent management; *especially* : a failure in the administration of justice
2 : spontaneous expulsion of a human fetus before it is viable and especially between the 12th and 28th weeks of gestation

mis·car·ry \ˌmis-ˈkar-ē, ˈmis-ˌkar-ē\ *intransitive verb* (14th century)
1 *obsolete* : to come to harm
2 : to suffer miscarriage of a fetus
3 : to fail to achieve the intended purpose : go wrong or amiss ⟨the plan *miscarried*⟩

mis·cast \ˌmis-ˈkast\ *transitive verb* **-cast; -cast·ing** (1925)
: to cast in an unsuitable role ⟨life had *miscast* her in the role of wife and mother —Edna Ferber⟩

mis·ce·ge·na·tion \(ˌ)mi-ˌse-jə-ˈnā-shən, ˌmi-si-jə-ˈnā-\ *noun* [irregular from Latin *miscēre* to mix + *genus* race — more at MIX, KIN] (1864)
: a mixture of races; *especially* : marriage or cohabitation between a white person and a member of another race
— **mis·ce·ge·na·tion·al** \-shnəl, -shə-nᵊl\ *adjective*

mis·cel·la·nea \ˌmi-sə-ˈlā-nē-ə, -nyə\ *noun plural* [Latin, from neuter plural of *miscellaneus*] (1571)
: a collection of miscellaneous objects or writings

mis·cel·la·neous \ˌmi-sə-ˈlā-nē-əs, -nyəs\ *adjective* [Latin *miscellaneus,* from *miscellus* mixed] (1637)
1 : consisting of diverse things or members : HETEROGENEOUS
2 a : having various traits **b** : dealing with or interested in diverse subjects ⟨as a writer I was too *miscellaneous* —George Santayana⟩
— **mis·cel·la·neous·ly** *adverb*
— **mis·cel·la·neous·ness** *noun*

mis·cel·la·nist \ˈmi-sə-ˌlā-nist, *chiefly British* mi-ˈse-lə-nist\ *noun* (1810)
: a writer of miscellanies

mis·cel·la·ny \-nē\ *noun, plural* **-nies** [probably modification of French *miscellanées,* plural, from Latin *miscellanea*] (1615)
1 a *plural* : separate writings collected in one volume **b** : a collection of writings on various subjects
2 : a mixture of various things

mis·chance \ˌmis-ˈchan(t)s\ *noun* [Middle English *meschaunce,* from Old French *meschance,* from *mes-* mis- + *chance* chance] (14th century)
1 : bad luck
2 : a piece of bad luck : MISHAP
synonym see MISFORTUNE

mis·chief \ˈmis-chəf, ˈmish-\ *noun* [Middle English *meschief,* from Old French, calamity, from *mes-* + *chief* head, end — more at CHIEF] (14th century)
1 : a specific injury or damage attributed to a particular agent
2 : a cause or source of harm, evil, or irritation; *especially* : a person who causes mischief
3 a : action that annoys or irritates **b** : the quality or state of being mischievous : MISCHIEVOUSNESS ⟨had *mischief* in his eyes⟩

mis·chie·vous \ˈmis-chə-vəs, ˈmish-; ÷mis-ˈchē-vē-əs, mish-\ *adjective* (14th century)
1 : HARMFUL, INJURIOUS ⟨*mischievous* gossip⟩
2 a : able or tending to cause annoyance, trouble, or minor injury **b** : irresponsibly playful ⟨*mischievous* behavior⟩ □
— **mis·chie·vous·ly** *adverb*
— **mis·chie·vous·ness** *noun*

misch metal \ˈmish-\ *noun* [German *Mischmetall,* from *mischen* to mix + *Metall* metal] (1916)
: a complex alloy of rare earth metals used especially in tracer bullets and as a flint in lighters

mis·ci·ble \ˈmi-sə-bəl\ *adjective* [Medieval Latin *miscibilis,* from Latin *miscēre* to mix — more at MIX] (1570)
: capable of being mixed; *specifically* : capable of mixing in any ratio without separation of two phases ⟨*miscible* liquids⟩
— **mis·ci·bil·i·ty** \ˌmi-sə-ˈbi-lə-tē\ *noun*

mis·com·mu·ni·ca·tion \ˌmis-kə-ˌmyü-nə-ˈkā-shən\ *noun* (1964)
: failure to communicate clearly

mis·con·duct \-ˈkän-(ˌ)dəkt\ *noun* (1710)
1 : mismanagement especially of governmental or military responsibilities
2 : intentional wrongdoing; *specifically* : deliberate violation of a law or standard especially by a government official : MALFEASANCE
3 a : improper behavior **b** : ADULTERY
— **mis·con·duct** \-kən-ˈdəkt\ *transitive verb*

mis·count \-ˈkaȯnt\ *verb* [Middle English *misconten,* from Middle French *mesconter,* from *mes-* + *conter* to count] (14th century)
intransitive verb
: to make a wrong count
transitive verb
: to count wrongly : MISCALCULATE
— **miscount** \-ˈkaȯnt, ˈmis-ˌ\ *noun*

¹mis·cre·ant \ˈmis-krē-ənt\ *adjective* [Middle English *miscreaunt,* from Middle French *mescreant,* present participle of *mescroire* to disbelieve, from *mes-* + *croire* to believe, from Latin *credere* — more at CREED] (14th century)
1 : UNBELIEVING, HERETICAL
2 : DEPRAVED, VILLAINOUS

²miscreant *noun* (14th century)
1 : INFIDEL, HERETIC
2 : one who behaves criminally or viciously

¹mis·cue \ˌmis-ˈkyü, ˈmis-ˌkyü\ *noun* (1873)
1 : a faulty stroke in billiards in which the cue slips
2 : MISTAKE, SLIP

²miscue *intransitive verb* (1894)
: to make a miscue

mis·deal \ˌmis-ˈdē(ə)l\ *verb* **-dealt** \-ˈdelt\; **-deal·ing** (1850)
intransitive verb
: to deal cards incorrectly
transitive verb
: to deal incorrectly
— **misdeal** *noun*

mis·deed \-ˈdēd\ *noun* (before 12th century)
: a wrong deed : OFFENSE

mis·de·mean·ant \-di-ˈmē-nənt\ *noun* (1819)
: a person convicted of a misdemeanor

mis·de·mean·or \-di-ˈmē-nər\ *noun* (15th century)
1 : a crime less serious than a felony
2 : MISDEED

mis·di·rect \-də-ˈrekt, -(ˌ)dī-\ *transitive verb* (1603)
1 : to give a wrong direction to
2 : to direct wrongly ⟨*misdirected* their energies⟩

mis·di·rec·tion \-ˈrek-shən\ *noun* (1768)
1 a : the act or an instance of misdirecting **b** : the state of being misdirected
2 : a wrong direction

mis·do \ˌmis-ˈdü\ *verb* **-did** \-ˈdid\; **-done** \-ˈdən\; **-do·ing** \-ˈdü-iŋ\; **-does** \-ˈdəz\ (before 12th century)
intransitive verb
obsolete : to act wrongly : transgress the laws of God ⟨the erring soul not wilfully *misdoing* —John Milton⟩
transitive verb
: to do (something) incorrectly or poorly
— **mis·do·er** \-ˈdü-ər\ *noun*

misdoing *noun* (15th century)
: the act or an instance of misbehaving : MISCONDUCT

mis·doubt \ˌmis-ˈdaȯt\ *transitive verb* (circa 1540)
1 : DOUBT
2 : SUSPECT, FEAR
— **misdoubt** *noun*

□ USAGE
mischievous A pronunciation \mis-ˈchē-vē-əs\ and a consequent spelling *mischievious* are of long standing: evidence for the spelling goes back to the 16th century. Our pronunciation files contain modern attestations ranging from dialect speakers to Herbert Hoover. But both the pronunciation and the spelling are still considered nonstandard.

\ə\ **abut** \ᵊ\ **kitten** \ər\ **further** \a\ **ash** \ā\ **ace**
\ä\ **mop, mar** \aȯ\ **out** \ch\ **chin** \e\ **bet** \ē\ **easy**
\g\ **go** \i\ **hit** \ī\ **ice** \j\ **job** \ŋ\ **sing** \ō\ **go**
\ȯ\ **law** \ȯi\ **boy** \th\ **thin** \t͟h\ **the** \ü\ **loot** \u̇\ **foot**
\y\ **yet** \zh\ **vision** *see also* Guide to Pronunciation

mise–en–scène \ˌmē-ˌzäⁿ-'sen, -'sän\ *noun,* plural **mise–en–scènes** \-'sen(z), -'sän(z)\ [French *mise en scène*] (1833)
1 a : the arrangement of actors and scenery on a stage for a theatrical production **b :** stage setting
2 a : the physical setting of an action **:** CONTEXT **b :** ENVIRONMENT, MILIEU
synonym see BACKGROUND

mi·ser \'mī-zər\ *noun* [Latin *miser* miserable] (circa 1560)
: a mean grasping person; *especially* **:** one who is extremely stingy with money

mis·er·a·ble \'mi-zər-bəl, 'miz-rə-, 'mi-zə-rə-\ *adjective* [Middle English, from Middle French, from Latin *miserabilis* wretched, pitiable, from *miserari* to pity, from *miser*] (15th century)
1 : being in a pitiable state of distress or unhappiness (as from want or shame) ⟨*miserable* refugees⟩
2 a : wretchedly inadequate or meager ⟨a *miserable* hovel⟩ **b :** causing extreme discomfort or unhappiness ⟨a *miserable* situation⟩
3 : being likely to discredit or shame ⟨his *miserable* neglect of his wife⟩ ⟨it was *miserable* of you to make fun of him⟩
— **miserable** *noun*
— **mis·er·a·ble·ness** *noun*
— **mis·er·a·bly** \-blē\ *adverb*

mi·se·re·re \ˌmi-zə-'rir-ē, -'rer-; ˌmē-zə-'rā-(ˌ)rā\ *noun* [Middle English, from Latin, be merciful, from *miserere* to be merciful, from *miser* wretched; from the first word of the Psalm] (13th century)
1 *capitalized* **:** the 50th Psalm in the Vulgate
2 : MISERICORD
3 : a vocal complaint or lament

mi·ser·i·cord or **mi·ser·i·corde** \mə-'zer-ə-ˌkȯrd, -'ser-\ *noun* [Medieval Latin *misericordia* seat in church, from Latin, mercy, from *misericord-, misericors* merciful, from *miseri- + cord-, cor* heart — more at HEART] (circa 1515)
: a small projection on the bottom of a hinged church seat that gives support to a standing worshiper when the seat is turned up

mi·ser·ly \'mī-zər-lē\ *adjective* (1593)
: of, relating to, or characteristic of a miser; *especially* **:** marked by grasping meanness and penuriousness
synonym see STINGY
— **mi·ser·li·ness** *noun*

mis·ery \'mi-zə-rē, 'miz-rē\ *noun,* plural **-er·ies** (14th century)
1 : a state of suffering and want that is the result of poverty or affliction
2 : a circumstance, thing, or place that causes suffering or discomfort
3 : a state of great unhappiness and emotional distress
synonym see DISTRESS

mis·es·teem \ˌmi-sə-'stēm\ *transitive verb* (1611)
: to esteem wrongly; *especially* **:** to hold in too little regard

mis·fea·sance \mis-'fē-zⁿ(t)s\ *noun* [Middle French *mesfaisance,* from *mesfaire* to do wrong, from *mes-* mis- + *faire* to make, do, from Latin *facere* — more at DO] (1596)
: TRESPASS; *specifically* **:** the performance of a lawful action in an illegal or improper manner
— **mis·fea·sor** \-'fē-zər, -ˌzȯr\ *noun*

¹mis·fire \mis-'fīr\ *intransitive verb* (1752)
1 : to have the explosive or propulsive charge fail to ignite at the proper time ⟨the engine *misfired*⟩
2 : to fail to fire ⟨the gun *misfired*⟩
3 : to miss an intended effect or objective

²mis·fire \ˌmis-'fīr, 'mis-ˌ\ *noun* (1839)
1 : a failure (as of a cartridge or firearm) to fire
2 : something that misfires

mis·fit \'mis-ˌfit *also* ˌmis-'fit\ *noun* (circa 1823)
1 : something that fits badly

2 : one who is poorly adapted to a situation or environment ⟨social *misfits*⟩

mis·for·tune \mis-'fȯr-chən\ *noun* (15th century)
1 a : an event or conjunction of events that causes an unfortunate or distressing result **:** bad luck ⟨by *misfortune* he fell into bad company⟩ ⟨had the *misfortune* to break his leg⟩ **b :** an unhappy situation ⟨always ready to help people in *misfortune*⟩
2 : a distressing or unfortunate incident or event ⟨*misfortunes* never come singly⟩ ☆

mis·give \mis-'giv\ *verb* **-gave** \-'gāv\; **-giv·en** \-'gi-vən\; **-giv·ing** (1513)
transitive verb
: to suggest doubt or fear to
intransitive verb
: to be fearful or apprehensive

mis·giv·ing \-'gi-viŋ\ *noun* (1601)
: a feeling of doubt or suspicion especially concerning a future event

mis·guid·ance \mis-'gī-dⁿ(t)s\ *noun* (1640)
: MISDIRECTION

mis·guide \-'gīd\ *transitive verb* (14th century)
: to lead astray **:** MISDIRECT ⟨prejudice *misguides* our minds⟩
— **mis·guid·er** *noun*

mis·guid·ed \(ˌ)mis-'gī-dəd\ *adjective* (1659)
: led or prompted by wrong or inappropriate motives or ideals ⟨well-meaning but *misguided* do-gooders⟩
— **mis·guid·ed·ly** \-lē\ *adverb*
— **mis·guid·ed·ness** \-nəs\ *noun*

mis·han·dle \-'han-dⁿl\ *transitive verb* (1530)
1 : to treat roughly **:** MALTREAT
2 : to deal with or manage wrongly or ignorantly

mis·shan·ter \mi-'shän-tər\ *noun* [Middle English *misaunter,* alteration of *mesaventure*] (1742)
chiefly Scottish **:** MISADVENTURE

mis·hap \'mis-ˌhap, mis-'\ *noun* (14th century)
1 : an unfortunate accident
2 : bad luck **:** MISFORTUNE
synonym see MISFORTUNE

mis·hear \ˌmis-'hir\ *verb* **-heard** \-'hərd\; **-hear·ing** \-'hir-iŋ\ (before 12th century)
transitive verb
: to hear wrongly
intransitive verb
: to misunderstand what is heard

mis·hit \ˌmis-'hit\ *transitive verb* **-hit; -hit·ting** (1904)
: to hit in a faulty manner
— **mis·hit** \ˌmis-'hit, 'mis-ˌ\ *noun*

mish·mash \'mish-ˌmash, -ˌmäsh\ *noun* [Middle English & Yiddish; Middle English *mysse masche,* perhaps reduplication of *mash* mash; Yiddish *mish-mash,* perhaps reduplication of *mishn* to mix] (15th century)
: HODGEPODGE, JUMBLE

Mish·nah or **Mish·na** \'mish-nə\ *noun* [Hebrew *mishnāh* instruction, oral law] (1610)
: the collection of mostly halakic Jewish traditions compiled about A.D. 200 and made the basic part of the Talmud
— **Mish·na·ic** \mish-'nā-ik\ *adjective*

mis·im·pres·sion \ˌmi-sim-'pre-shən\ *noun* (1670)
: a mistaken impression

mis·in·ter·pret \ˌmi-sⁿn-'tər-prət, -pət\ *transitive verb* (1547)
1 : to explain wrongly
2 : to understand wrongly
— **mis·in·ter·pre·ta·tion** \-ˌtər-prə-'tā-shən, -pə-\ *noun*

mis·join·der \ˌmis-'jȯin-dər\ *noun* (circa 1847)
: an improper union of parties or of causes of action in a single legal proceeding

mis·judge \ˌmis-'jəj\ (15th century)
intransitive verb
: to be mistaken in judgment
transitive verb
1 : to estimate wrongly

2 : to have an unjust opinion of
— **mis·judg·ment** \-'jəj-mənt\ *noun*

Mi·ski·to \mis-'kē-(ˌ)tō\ *noun,* plural **Miskito** or **Miskitos** (1789)
1 : a member of an American Indian people of the Atlantic coast of Nicaragua and Honduras
2 : the language of the Miskito people

mis·know \ˌmis-'nō\ *transitive verb* **-knew** \-'nü, -'nyü\; **-known** \-'nōn\; **-know·ing** (1535)
: MISUNDERSTAND
— **mis·knowl·edge** \-'nä-lij\ *noun*

mis·lay \ˌmis-'lā\ *transitive verb* **-laid** \-'lād\; **-lay·ing** (1614)
: to put in an unremembered place **:** LOSE

mis·lead \ˌmis-'lēd\ *verb* **-led** \-'led\; **-lead·ing** (before 12th century)
transitive verb
: to lead in a wrong direction or into a mistaken action or belief often by deliberate deceit
intransitive verb
: to lead astray
synonym see DECEIVE
— **mis·lead·er** *noun*
— **mis·lead·ing·ly** \-'lē-diŋ-lē\ *adverb*

mis·leared \-'lird, -'lerd\ *adjective* [¹*mis-* + *lear* to learn] (1560)
chiefly Scottish **:** UNMANNERLY, ILL-BRED

mis·like \-'līk\ *transitive verb* (before 12th century)
1 *archaic* **:** DISPLEASE
2 : DISLIKE
— **mislike** *noun*

mis·name \-'nām\ *transitive verb* (1537)
: to name incorrectly **:** MISCALL

mis·no·mer \ˌmis-'nō-mər\ *noun* [Middle English *misnoumer,* from Middle French *mesnommer* to misname, from *mes-* mis- + *nommer* to name, from Latin *nominare* — more at NOMINATE] (15th century)
1 : the misnaming of a person in a legal instrument
2 a : a use of a wrong name **b :** a wrong name or designation
— **mis·no·mered** \-mərd\ *adjective*

mi·so \'mē-(ˌ)sō\ *noun* [Japanese] (1727)
: a high-protein food paste consisting chiefly of soybeans, salt, and usually fermented grain (as barley or rice) and ranging in taste from very salty to very sweet

mi·sog·a·my \mi-'sä-gə-mē, mī-\ *noun* [Greek *misein* to hate + English *-gamy*] (circa 1656)
: a hatred of marriage
— **mi·sog·a·mist** \-mist\ *noun*

mi·sog·y·ny \mi-'sä-jə-nē\ *noun* [Greek *misogynia,* from *misein* to hate + *gynē* woman — more at QUEEN] (circa 1656)
: a hatred of women
— **mi·sog·y·nic** \ˌmi-sə-'ji-nik, -'gī-\ *adjective*
— **mi·sog·y·nist** \mə-'sä-jə-nist\ *noun or adjective*
— **mi·sog·y·nis·tic** \mə-ˌsä-jə-'nis-tik\ *adjective*

mi·sol·o·gy \mə-'sä-lə-jē\ *noun* [Greek *misologia,* from *misein* + *-logia* -logy] (1833)

☆ **SYNONYMS**
Misfortune, mischance, adversity, mishap mean adverse fortune or an instance of this. MISFORTUNE may apply to either the incident or conjunction of events that is the cause of an unhappy change of fortune or to the ensuing state of distress ⟨never lost hope even in the depths of *misfortune*⟩. MISCHANCE applies especially to a situation involving no more than slight inconvenience or minor annoyance ⟨took the wrong road by *mischance*⟩. ADVERSITY applies to a state of grave or persistent misfortune ⟨had never experienced great *adversity*⟩. MISHAP applies to an often trivial instance of bad luck ⟨the usual *mishaps* of a family vacation⟩.

: a hatred of argument, reasoning, or enlightenment

mis·o·ne·ism \ˌmi-sə-ˈnē-ˌi-zəm\ *noun* [Italian *misoneismo,* from Greek *misein* + *neos* new + Italian *-ismo* -ism — more at NEW] (1886)
: a hatred, fear, or intolerance of innovation or change

mis·place \mis-ˈplās\ *transitive verb* (1594)
1 a : to put in a wrong or inappropriate place ⟨*misplace* a comma⟩ **b :** MISLAY ⟨*misplaced* the keys⟩
2 : to set on a wrong object or eventuality ⟨his trust had been *misplaced*⟩
— **mis·place·ment** \-ˈplās-mənt\ *noun*

mis·play \mis-ˈplā\ *noun* (1867)
: a wrong or unskillful play **:** ERROR
— **mis·play** \mis-ˈplā, ˈmis-ˌ\ *transitive verb*

¹mis·pri·sion \(ˌ)mis-ˈpri-zhən\ *noun* [Middle English, from Middle French *mesprison* error, wrongdoing, from Old French, from *mesprendre* to make a mistake, from *mes-* mis- + *prendre* to take, from Latin *prehendere* to seize — more at GET] (15th century)
1 a : neglect or wrong performance of official duty **b :** concealment of treason or felony by one who is not a participant in the treason or felony **c :** seditious conduct against the government or the courts
2 : MISUNDERSTANDING, MISINTERPRETATION

²misprision *noun* [*misprize*] (1586)
: CONTEMPT, SCORN

mis·prize \mis-ˈprīz\ *transitive verb* [Middle French *mesprisier,* from *mes-* mis- + *prisier* to appraise — more at PRIZE] (14th century)
1 : to hold in contempt **:** DESPISE
2 : UNDERVALUE

mis·pro·nounce \ˌmis-prə-ˈnaun(t)s\ *transitive verb* (1593)
: to pronounce incorrectly or in a way regarded as incorrect

mis·pro·nun·ci·a·tion \-ˌnən(t)-sē-ˈā-shən *also* -ˌnaun(t)-\ *noun* (1530)
: the act or an instance of mispronouncing

mis·read \mis-ˈrēd\ *transitive verb* **-read** \-ˈred\; **-read·ing** \-ˈrē-diŋ\ (1809)
1 : to read incorrectly
2 : to misinterpret in or as if in reading ⟨totally *misread* the lesson of history —Christopher Hollis⟩

mis·reck·on \-ˈre-kən\ *verb* (circa 1525)
: MISCOUNT, MISCALCULATE

mis·rep·re·sent \(ˌ)mis-ˌre-pri-ˈzent\ *transitive verb* (1647)
1 : to give a false or misleading representation of usually with an intent to deceive or be unfair ⟨*misrepresented* the facts⟩
2 : to serve badly or improperly as a representative of
— **mis·rep·re·sen·ta·tion** \(ˌ)mis-ˌre-pri-ˌzen-ˈtā-shən, -zən-\ *noun*
— **mis·rep·re·sen·ta·tive** \-ˈzen-tə-tiv\ *adjective*

¹mis·rule \mis-ˈrül\ *transitive verb* (14th century)
: to rule incompetently **:** MISGOVERN

²misrule *noun* (14th century)
1 : the action of misruling **:** the condition of being misruled
2 : DISORDER, ANARCHY

¹miss \ˈmis\ *verb* [Middle English, from Old English *missan;* akin to Old High German *missan* to miss] (before 12th century)
transitive verb
1 : to fail to hit, reach, or contact
2 : to discover or feel the absence of
3 : to fail to obtain
4 : ESCAPE, AVOID ⟨just *missed* hitting the other car⟩
5 : to leave out **:** OMIT
6 : to fail to comprehend, sense, or experience ⟨*missed* the point of the speech⟩
7 : to fail to perform or attend ⟨had to *miss* school for a week⟩
intransitive verb

1 *archaic* **:** to fail to get, reach, or do something
2 : to fail to hit something
3 a : to be unsuccessful **b :** MISFIRE ⟨the engine *missed*⟩
— **miss·able** \ˈmi-sə-bəl\ *adjective*
— **miss a beat :** to deviate from regular smooth performance ⟨the company changed ownership without *missing a beat*⟩
— **miss out on :** to lose a good opportunity for ⟨*missed out on* a better job⟩
— **miss the boat :** to fail to take advantage of an opportunity

²miss *noun* (12th century)
1 *chiefly dialect* **:** disadvantage or regret resulting from loss ⟨we know the *miss* of you, and even hunger . . . to see you —Samuel Richardson⟩
2 a : a failure to hit **b :** a failure to attain a desired result
3 : MISFIRE

³miss *noun* [short for *mistress*] (circa 1667)
1 *capitalized* **a** — used as a title prefixed to the name of an unmarried woman or girl **b :** used before the name of a place or of a line of activity or before some epithet to form a title for a usually young unmarried female who is representative of the thing indicated ⟨*Miss* America⟩
2 : young lady — used without a name as a conventional term of address to a young woman
3 : a young unmarried woman or girl

mis·sa can·ta·ta \ˌmi-sə-kən-ˈtä-tə\ *noun* [New Latin, sung mass] (circa 1903)
: HIGH MASS

mis·sal \ˈmi-səl\ *noun* [Middle English *messel,* from Middle French & Medieval Latin; Middle French, from Medieval Latin *missale,* from neuter of *missalis* of the mass, from Late Latin *missa* mass — more at MASS] (14th century)
: a book containing all that is said or sung at mass during the entire year

mis·send \ˌmis-ˈsend\ *transitive verb* **-sent** \-ˈsent\; **-send·ing** (15th century)
: to send incorrectly ⟨*missent* mail⟩

mis·sense \ˈmis-ˌsen(t)s\ *noun* [¹*mis-* + *-sense* (as in *nonsense*)] (1961)
: genetic mutation involving alteration of one or more codons so that different amino acids are determined — compare ANTISENSE, NONSENSE

¹mis·sile \ˈmi-səl, *chiefly British* -ˌsīl\ *adjective* [Latin *missilis,* from *mittere* to throw, send] (1611)
1 : capable of being thrown or projected to strike a distant object
2 : adapted for throwing or hurling missiles

²missile *noun* (circa 1656)
: an object (as a weapon) thrown or projected usually so as to strike something at a distance ⟨stones, artillery shells, bullets, and rockets are *missiles*⟩: as **a :** GUIDED MISSILE **b :** BALLISTIC MISSILE

mis·sil·eer \ˌmi-sə-ˈlir\ *noun* (1958)
: MISSILEMAN

mis·sile·man \ˈmi-səl-mən\ *noun* (1951)
: one engaged in designing, building, or operating guided missiles

mis·sile·ry \ˈmi-səl-rē\ *noun* (1880)
: MISSILES; *especially* **:** GUIDED MISSILES

miss·ing \ˈmi-siŋ\ *adjective* (circa 1530)
: ABSENT; *also* **:** LOST ⟨*missing* in action⟩

missing link *noun* (1851)
1 : an absent member needed to complete a series or resolve a problem
2 : a hypothetical intermediate form between humans and their presumed simian progenitors

mis·si·ol·o·gy \ˌmi-sē-ˈä-lə-jē\ *noun* [*missio*n + *-logy*] (1924)
: the study of the church's mission especially with respect to missionary activity

¹mis·sion \ˈmi-shən\ *noun* [New Latin, Medieval Latin, & Latin; New Latin *missio*n-, *missio* religious mission, from Medieval Latin,

task assigned, from Latin, act of sending, from *mittere* to send] (1606)
1 *obsolete* **:** the act or an instance of sending
2 a : a ministry commissioned by a religious organization to propagate its faith or carry on humanitarian work **b :** assignment to or work in a field of missionary enterprise **c** (1) **:** a mission establishment (2) **:** a local church or parish dependent on a larger religious organization for direction or financial support **d** *plural* **:** organized missionary work **e :** a course of sermons and services given to convert the unchurched or quicken Christian faith
3 : a body of persons sent to perform a service or carry on an activity: as **a :** a group sent to a foreign country to conduct diplomatic or political negotiations **b :** a permanent embassy or legation **c :** a team of specialists or cultural leaders sent to a foreign country
4 a : a specific task with which a person or a group is charged **b** (1) **:** a definite military, naval, or aerospace task ⟨a bombing *mission*⟩ ⟨a space *mission*⟩ (2) **:** a flight operation of an aircraft or spacecraft in the performance of a mission ⟨a *mission* to Mars⟩
5 : CALLING, VOCATION

²mission *transitive verb* **mis·sioned; mis·sion·ing** \ˈmi-sh(ə-)niŋ\ (1692)
1 : to send on or entrust with a mission
2 : to carry on a religious mission among or in

³mission *adjective* (1904)
1 : of or relating to a style used in the early Spanish missions of the southwestern U.S. ⟨*mission* architecture⟩
2 : of, relating to, or having the characteristics of a style of plain heavy usually oak furniture originating in the U.S. in the early part of the 20th century

¹mis·sion·ary \ˈmi-shə-ˌner-ē\ *adjective* (1644)
1 : relating to, engaged in, or devoted to missions
2 : characteristic of a missionary

²missionary *noun, plural* **-ar·ies** (circa 1656)
: a person undertaking a mission and especially a religious mission

missionary position *noun* [perhaps from the notion that missionaries insisted that this coital position is the only acceptable one] (1948)
: a coital position in which the female lies on her back with the male on top and with his face opposite hers

mis·sion·er \ˈmi-sh(ə-)nər\ *noun* (1654)
: MISSIONARY

mis·sion·ize \ˈmi-shə-ˌnīz\ *verb* **-ized; -iz·ing** (1826)
intransitive verb
: to carry on missionary work
transitive verb
: to do missionary work among
— **mis·sion·i·za·tion** \ˌmi-shə-nə-ˈzā-shən\ *noun*
— **mis·sion·iz·er** \ˈmi-shə-ˌnī-zər\ *noun*

Mis·sis·sip·pi·an \ˌmi-sə-ˈsi-pē-ən, (ˌ)mis-ˈsi-\ *adjective* [*Mississippi* River] (1835)
1 : of or relating to Mississippi, its people, or the Mississippi River
2 : of, relating to, or being the period of the Paleozoic era in North America following the Devonian and preceding the Pennsylvanian or the corresponding system of rocks — see GEOLOGIC TIME table
— **Mississippian** *noun*

mis·sive \ˈmi-siv\ *noun* [Middle French *lettre missive,* literally, letter intended to be sent] (1501)
: a written communication **:** LETTER

miss·out \ˈmis-ˌaut\ *noun* (1945)

\ə\ **abut** \ᵊ\ **kitten** \ər\ **further** \a\ **ash** \ā\ **ace** \ä\ **mop, mar** \au\ **out** \ch\ **chin** \e\ **bet** \ē\ **easy** \g\ **go** \i\ **hit** \ī\ **ice** \j\ **job** \ŋ\ **sing** \ō\ **go** \o\ **law** \oi\ **boy** \th\ **thin** \th\ **the** \ü\ **loot** \u\ **foot** \y\ **yet** \zh\ **vision** *see also* Guide to Pronunciation

: a throw of dice that loses the main bet
miss out *transitive verb* (1870)
British : to leave out : OMIT
mis·speak \ˌmis-'spēk\ **-spoke** \-'spōk\;
-spo·ken \-'spō-kən\; **-speak·ing** (14th
century)
transitive verb
1 : to speak (as a word) incorrectly
2 : to express (oneself) imperfectly or incor-
rectly ⟨claims now that he *misspoke* himself⟩
intransitive verb
: to speak incorrectly : misspeak oneself
mis·spell \ˌmis-'spel\ *transitive verb* (1655)
: to spell incorrectly
mis·spell·ing \-'spe-liŋ\ *noun* (circa 1696)
: an incorrect spelling
mis·spend \ˌmis-'spend\ *transitive verb*
-spent \-'spent\; **-spend·ing** (14th century)
: to spend wrongly : SQUANDER ⟨a *misspent*
life⟩
mis·state \ˌmis-'stāt\ *transitive verb* (1650)
: to state incorrectly : give a false account of
— **mis·state·ment** \-mənt\ *noun*
mis·step \-'step\ *noun* (circa 1800)
1 : a mistake in judgment or action : BLUNDER
2 : a wrong step
mis·sus *or* **mis·sis** \'mi-səz, -səs, *especially
Southern* -zəz\ *noun* [alteration of *mistress*]
(1790)
1 *dialect* : MISTRESS 1a
2 : WIFE ⟨men spend money on themselves, but
argue over every dime the *missus* wants —W.
A. Lydgate⟩
missy \'mi-sē\ *noun* (1676)
: a young girl : MISS
¹mist \'mist\ *noun* [Middle English, from Old
English; akin to Middle Dutch *mist* mist,
Greek *omichlē*] (before 12th century)
1 : water in the form of particles floating or
falling in the atmosphere at or near the surface
of the earth and approaching the form of rain
2 : something that obscures understanding
⟨*mists* of antiquity⟩
3 : a film before the eyes
4 a : a cloud of small particles or objects sug-
gestive of a mist **b** : a suspension of a finely
divided liquid in a gas **c** : a fine spray
5 : a drink of liquor served over cracked ice
²mist (before 12th century)
intransitive verb
1 : to be or become misty
2 : to become moist or blurred
transitive verb
: to cover or spray with or convert to mist
mis·tak·able \mə-'stā-kə-bəl\ *adjective*
(1646)
: capable of being misunderstood or mistaken
¹mis·take \mə-'stāk\ *verb* **mis·took** \-'stůk\;
mis·tak·en \-'stā-kən\; **mis·tak·ing** [Mid-
dle English, from Old Norse *mistaka* to take
by mistake, from *mis-* + *taka* to take — more
at TAKE] (14th century)
transitive verb
1 : to blunder in the choice of ⟨*mistook* her
way in the dark⟩
2 a : to misunderstand the meaning or inten-
tion of : MISINTERPRET ⟨don't *mistake* me, I
mean exactly what I said⟩ **b** : to make a wrong
judgment of the character or ability of
3 : to identify wrongly : confuse with another
⟨I *mistook* him for his brother⟩
intransitive verb
: to be wrong ⟨you *mistook* when you thought
I laughed at you —Thomas Hardy⟩
— **mis·tak·en·ly** *adverb*
— **mis·tak·er** *noun*
²mistake *noun* (1638)
1 : a misunderstanding of the meaning or im-
plication of something
2 : a wrong action or statement proceeding
from faulty judgment, inadequate knowledge,
or inattention
synonym *see* ERROR
¹mis·ter \'mis-tər, *for 1* ˌmis-tər *or in rapid
speech* (ˌ)mis(t)\ *noun* [alteration of ¹*master*]
(1551)

1 *capitalized* : MR. — used sometimes in writ-
ing instead of *Mr.*
2 : SIR — used without a name as a general-
ized term of direct address of a man who is a
stranger ⟨hey, *mister*, do you want to buy a pa-
per⟩
3 : a man not entitled to a title of rank or an
honorific or professional title ⟨though he was
only a *mister*, he was a greater scholar in his
field than any PhD⟩
4 : HUSBAND
²mist·er \'mis-tər\ *noun* [²*mist* + ²*-er*] (1973)
: a device for spraying a mist
mis·think \ˌmis-'thiŋk\ *verb* **-thought**
\-'thȯt\; **-think·ing** (circa 1530)
intransitive verb
archaic : to think mistakenly or unfavorably
transitive verb
archaic : to think badly or unfavorably of
mis·tle·toe \'mi-səl-ˌtō, *chiefly British* 'mi-
zəl-\ *noun* [Middle English *mistilto*, from Old
English *misteltān*, from *mistel* mistletoe + *tān*
twig; akin to Old High German & Old Saxon
mistil mistletoe and to Old High German *zein*
twig] (before 12th century)
: a European semiparasitic green shrub (*Vis-
cum album* of the family Loranthaceae, the
mistletoe family) with thick leaves, small yel-
lowish flowers, and waxy-white glutinous ber-
ries; *broadly* : any of various plants of the
mistletoe family (as of an American genus
Phoradendron) resembling the true mistletoe
mis·tral \'mis-trəl, mi-'sträl\ *noun* [French,
from Provençal, from *mistral* masterful, from
Late Latin *magistralis* of a teacher — more
at MAGISTRAL] (1604)
: a strong cold dry northerly wind of southern
France
mis·treat \ˌmis-'trēt\ *transitive verb* [Middle
English *mistreten*, probably from Middle
French *mestraitier*, from Old French, from
mes- mis- + *traitier* to treat — more at
TREAT] (15th century)
: to treat badly : ABUSE
— **mis·treat·ment** \-mənt\ *noun*
mis·tress \'mis-trəs\ *noun* [Middle English
maistresse, from Middle French, from Old
French, feminine of *maistre* master — more
at MASTER] (15th century)
1 : a woman who has power, authority, or
ownership: **as a** : the female head of a house-
hold **b** : a woman who employs or supervises
servants **c** : a woman who is in charge of a
school or other establishment **d** : a woman of
the Scottish nobility having a status compara-
ble to that of a master
2 a *chiefly British* : a female teacher or tutor **b**
: a woman who has achieved mastery in some
field
3 : something personified as female that rules,
directs, or dominates ⟨when Rome was *mis-
tress* of the world⟩
4 a : a woman other than his wife with whom
a married man has a continuing sexual rela-
tionship **b** *archaic* : SWEETHEART
5 a — used archaically as a title prefixed to
the name of a married or unmarried woman **b**
chiefly Southern & Midland : MRS. 1a
mistress of ceremonies (1952)
: a woman who presides at a public ceremony
or who acts as hostess of a stage, radio, or
television show
mis·tri·al \'mis-ˌtrī(ə)l\ *noun* (1628)
: a trial that has no legal effect by reason of
some error or serious prejudicial misconduct
in the proceedings
¹mis·trust \ˌmis-'trəst\ *noun* (14th century)
: a lack of confidence : DISTRUST
synonym *see* UNCERTAINTY
— **mis·trust·ful** \-fəl\ *adjective*
— **mis·trust·ful·ly** \-fə-lē\ *adverb*
— **mis·trust·ful·ness** *noun*
²mistrust (14th century)
transitive verb
1 : to have no trust or confidence in : SUSPECT
⟨*mistrusted* his neighbors⟩

2 : to doubt the truth, validity, or effectiveness
of ⟨*mistrusted* his own judgment⟩
3 : SURMISE ⟨your mind *mistrusted* there was
something wrong —Robert Frost⟩
intransitive verb
: to be suspicious
misty \'mis-tē\ *adjective* **mist·i·er; -est** (be-
fore 12th century)
1 a : obscured by mist **b** : consisting of or
marked by mist
2 a : INDISTINCT ⟨a *misty* recollection of the
event⟩ **b** : VAGUE, CONFUSED ⟨avoided the large,
vague, *misty* issues —Reuben Abel⟩
3 : TEARFUL
— **mist·i·ly** \-tə-lē\ *adverb*
— **mist·i·ness** \-tē-nəs\ *noun*
misty–eyed \'mis-tē-ˌīd\ *adjective* (1928)
1 : having tearful eyes
2 : DREAMY, SENTIMENTAL ⟨*misty-eyed* recollec-
tions⟩
mis·un·der·stand \(ˌ)mi-ˌsən-dər-'stand\
transitive verb **-stood** \-'stůd\; **-stand·ing**
(13th century)
1 : to fail to understand
2 : to interpret incorrectly
mis·un·der·stand·ing *noun* (15th century)
1 : a failure to understand : MISINTERPRETA-
TION
2 : QUARREL, DISAGREEMENT
mis·us·age \ˌmis-'yü-sij, ˌmish-, -zij\ *noun*
[Middle French *mesusage,* from *mes-* mis- +
usage usage] (1532)
1 : bad treatment : ABUSE
2 : wrong or improper use (as of words)
¹mis·use \-'yüz\ *transitive verb* [Middle En-
glish, partly from *mis-* + *usen* to use; partly
from Middle French *mesuser* to abuse, from
Old French, from *mes-* + *user* to use] (14th
century)
1 : to use incorrectly : MISAPPLY ⟨*misused* his
talents⟩
2 : ABUSE, MISTREAT ⟨*misused* his servants⟩
— **mis·us·er** *noun*
²mis·use \-'yüs\ *noun* (14th century)
: incorrect or improper use : MISAPPLICATION
¹mite \'mīt\ *noun* [Middle English, from Old
English *mīte;* akin to Middle Dutch *mite* mite,
small copper coin and perhaps to Old High
German *meizan* to cut] (before 12th century)
: any of numerous small acarid arachnids that
often infest animals, plants, and stored foods
and include important disease vectors
²mite *noun* [Middle English, from Middle
French or Middle Dutch; Middle French,
small Flemish copper coin, from Middle
Dutch] (14th century)
1 : a small coin or sum of money
2 a : a very little : BIT **b** : a very small object
or creature
— **a mite** : SOMEWHAT, RATHER ⟨could be
that I am a *mite* prejudiced —John Fischer⟩
¹mi·ter *or* **mi·tre** \'mī-tər\ *noun* [Middle En-
glish *mitre,* from Middle French, from Latin
mitra headband, turban, from Greek] (14th
century)
1 : a liturgical
headdress worn
by bishops and
abbots
2 a : a surface
forming the
beveled end or
edge of a piece
where a joint is

miter 2a: *1* plain, *2* milled,
3 rabbeted

made by cutting two pieces at an angle and fit-
ting them together **b** : MITER JOINT
²miter *or* **mitre** *transitive verb* **mi·tered** *or*
mi·tred; mi·ter·ing *or* **mi·tring** \'mī-tə-
riŋ\ (14th century)
1 : to confer a miter on
2 a : to match or fit together in a miter joint **b**
: to bevel the ends of for making a miter joint
— **mi·ter·er** \'mī-tər-ər\ *noun*
miter box *noun* (1678)
: a device for guiding a handsaw at the proper
angle in making a miter joint in wood

miter joint *noun* (1688)
: a joint made by fastening together usually perpendicularly parts with the ends cut at an angle

miter square *noun* (1678)
: a bevel with an immovable arm at an angle of 45 degrees for striking marking lines; *also*
: a square with an arm adjustable to any angle

Mith·ra·ic \mi-'thrā-ik\ *adjective* [Late Greek *mithraikos* of Mithras, ancient Persian god of light, from Greek *Mithras,* from Old Persian *Mithra*] (1678)
: of or relating to an oriental mystery cult for men flourishing in the late Roman empire
— **Mith·ra·ism** \'mith-rə-,i-zəm, -(,)rā-\ *noun*
— **Mith·ra·ist** \mi-'thrā-ist\ *noun or adjective*

mith·ri·date \'mith-rə-,dāt\ *noun* [Medieval Latin *mithridatum,* from Late Latin *mithridatium,* from Latin, dogtooth violet (used as an antidote), from Greek *mithridation,* from *Mithridatēs* Mithridates VI] (1528)
: an antidote against poison; *especially* : an electuary held to be effective against poison

mi·ti·cide \'mī-tə-,sīd\ *noun* [*mite*] (circa 1946)
: an agent used to kill mites
— **mi·ti·cid·al** \,mī-tə-'sī-d°l\ *adjective*

mit·i·gate \'mi-tə-,gāt\ *transitive verb* **-gat·ed; -gat·ing** [Middle English, from Latin *mitigatus,* past participle of *mitigare* to soften, from *mitis* soft + *-igare* (akin to Latin *agere* to drive); akin to Old Irish *moíth* soft — more at AGENT] (15th century)
1 : to cause to become less harsh or hostile : MOLLIFY ⟨aggressiveness may be *mitigated* or . . . channeled —Ashley Montagu⟩
2 a : to make less severe or painful : ALLEVI-ATE **b** : EXTENUATE □
synonym see RELIEVE
— **mit·i·ga·tion** \,mi-tə-'gā-shən\ *noun*
— **mit·i·ga·tive** \'mi-tə-,gā-tiv\ *adjective*
— **mit·i·ga·tor** \-,gā-tər\ *noun*
— **mit·i·ga·to·ry** \'mi-ti-gə-,tōr-ē, -,tȯr-\ *adjective*

mi·to·chon·dri·on \,mī-tə-'kän-drē-ən\ *noun, plural* **-dria** \-drē-ə\ [New Latin, from Greek *mitos* thread + *chondrion,* diminutive of *chondros* grain] (1901)
: any of various round or long cellular organelles of most eukaryotes that are found outside the nucleus, produce energy for the cell through cellular respiration, and are rich in fats, proteins, and enzymes — see CELL illustration
— **mi·to·chon·dri·al** \-drē-əl\ *adjective*

mi·to·gen \'mī-tə-jən\ *noun* [*mitosis* + *-gen*] (circa 1951)
: a substance that induces mitosis
— **mi·to·gen·ic** \,mī-tə-'je-nik\ *adjective*
— **mi·to·ge·nic·i·ty** \-jə-'ni-sə-tē\ *noun*

mi·to·my·cin \,mī-tə-'mī-s°n\ *noun* [International Scientific Vocabulary *mito-* (probably from New Latin *mitosis*) + *-mycin*] (1956)
: a complex of antibiotic substances which is produced by a Japanese streptomyces (*Streptomyces caespitosus*) and one form of which acts directly on DNA and shows promise as an anticancer agent

mi·to·sis \mī-'tō-səs\ *noun, plural* **-to·ses** \-,sēz\ [New Latin, from Greek *mitos* thread] (1887)
1 : a process that takes place in the nucleus of a dividing cell, involves typically a series of steps consisting of prophase, metaphase, anaphase, and telophase, and results in the formation of two new nuclei each having the same number of chromosomes as the parent nucleus — compare MEIOSIS
2 : cell division in which mitosis occurs
— **mi·tot·ic** \-'tä-tik\ *adjective*
— **mi·tot·i·cal·ly** \-ti-k(ə-)lē\ *adverb*

mi·tral \'mī-trəl\ *adjective* (1610)
1 : resembling a miter

2 : of, relating to, being, or adjoining a mitral valve or orifice

mitral valve *noun* (1705)
: BICUSPID VALVE

mi·tre·wort *also* **mi·ter·wort** \'mī-tər-,wərt, -,wȯrt\ *noun* (circa 1818)
: any of a genus (*Mitella*) of rhizomatous perennial herbs of the saxifrage family that bear a capsule resembling a bishop's miter

mitt \'mit\ *noun* [short for *mitten*] (1765)
1 a : a woman's glove that leaves the fingers uncovered **b** : MITTEN 1 **c** : a baseball catcher's or first baseman's glove made in the style of a mitten
2 *slang* : HAND

mit·ten \'mi-t°n\ *noun* [Middle English *mitain,* from Middle French *mitaine,* from Old French, from *mite* mitten] (14th century)
1 : a covering for the hand and wrist having a separate section for the thumb only
2 : MITT 1a

mit·ti·mus \'mi-tə-məs\ *noun* [Latin, we send, from *mittere* to send] (circa 1591)
: a warrant of commitment to prison

mitz·vah \'mits-və\ *noun, plural* **mitz·voth** \-,vōt, -,vōth, -,vōs\ *or* **mitz·vahs** [Hebrew *miswāh*] (1650)
1 : a commandment of the Jewish law
2 : a meritorious or charitable act

¹mix \'miks\ *verb* [Middle English, back-formation from *mixte* mixed, from Middle French, from Latin *mixtus,* past participle of *miscēre* to mix; akin to Greek *mignynai* to mix] (15th century)
transitive verb
1 a (1) : to combine or blend into one mass (2) : to combine with another **b** : to bring into close association ⟨*mix* business with pleasure⟩
2 a : to form by mixing components ⟨*mix* a drink at the bar⟩ **b** : to produce (a sound recording) by electronically combining or adjusting sounds from more than one source
3 : CONFUSE — often used with *up* ⟨*mixes* things up in his eagerness to speak out —Irving Howe⟩
intransitive verb
1 a : to become mixed **b** : to be capable of mixing
2 : to enter into relations : ASSOCIATE
3 : CROSSBREED
4 : to become involved : PARTICIPATE ⟨decided not to *mix* in politics⟩ ☆
— **mix·able** \'mik-sə-bəl\ *adjective*
— **mix it up** : to engage in a fight, contest, or dispute

²mix *noun* (circa 1586)
1 : an act or process of mixing
2 : a product of mixing: as **a** : a commercially prepared mixture of food ingredients ⟨a cake *mix*⟩ **b** : a combination of different kinds ⟨the right *mix* of jobs, people and amenities —*London Times*⟩
3 : MIXER 2b

mixed \'mikst\ *adjective* [Middle English *mixte*] (15th century)
1 : combining characteristics of more than one kind; *specifically* : combining features of two or more systems of government ⟨a *mixed* constitution⟩
2 : made up of or involving individuals or items of more than one kind: as **a** : made up of or involving persons differing in race, national origin, religion, or class **b** : made up of or involving individuals of both sexes ⟨*mixed* company⟩ ⟨a *mixed* school⟩
3 : including or accompanied by inconsistent, incompatible, or contrary elements ⟨*mixed* emotions⟩ ⟨received *mixed* reviews⟩ ⟨a *mixed* blessing⟩
4 : deriving from two or more races or breeds ⟨a stallion of *mixed* blood⟩

mixed alphabet *noun* (1931)
: an alphabet (as in a cryptographic system) that has been rearranged or disordered systematically or randomly

mixed bag *noun* (1926)

: a miscellaneous collection : ASSORTMENT

mixed bud *noun* (1900)
: a bud that produces a branch and leaves as well as flowers

mixed drink *noun* (1943)
: an alcoholic beverage prepared from two or more ingredients

mixed farming *noun* (1872)
: the growing of food or cash crops, feed crops, and livestock on the same farm

mixed grill *noun* (1913)
: meats (as lamb chop, kidney, and bacon) and vegetables broiled together and served on one plate

mixed marriage *noun* (1829)
: a marriage between persons of different races or religions

mixed–media *adjective* (1962)
: MULTIMEDIA

mixed metaphor *noun* (1800)
: a figure of speech combining inconsistent or incongruous metaphors

mixed nerve *noun* (1878)
: a nerve containing both sensory and motor fibers

mixed number *noun* (1542)
: a number (as $5\frac{2}{3}$) composed of an integer and a fraction

mixed–up \'mikst-'əp\ *adjective* (1862)
: marked by bewilderment, perplexity, or disorder : CONFUSED

mix·er \'mik-sər\ *noun* (circa 1611)
1 : one that mixes: as **a** (1) : one whose work is mixing the ingredients of a product (2) : one who balances and controls the dialogue, music, and sound effects to be recorded for or

☆ SYNONYMS
Mix, mingle, commingle, blend, merge, coalesce, amalgamate, fuse mean to combine into a more or less uniform whole. MIX may or may not imply loss of each element's identity ⟨*mix* the salad greens⟩ ⟨*mix* a drink⟩. MINGLE usually suggests that the elements are still somewhat distinguishable or separately active ⟨fear *mingled* with anticipation in my mind⟩. COMMINGLE implies a closer or more thorough mingling ⟨a sense of duty *commingled* with a fierce pride drove her⟩. BLEND implies that the elements as such disappear in the resulting mixture ⟨*blended* several teas to create a balanced flavor⟩. MERGE suggests a combining in which one or more elements are lost in the whole ⟨in his mind reality and fantasy *merged*⟩. COALESCE implies an affinity in the merging elements and usually a resulting organic unity ⟨telling details that *coalesce* into a striking portrait⟩. AMALGAMATE implies the forming of a close union without complete loss of individual identities ⟨refugees who were readily *amalgamated* into the community⟩. FUSE stresses oneness and indissolubility of the resulting product ⟨a building in which modernism and classicism are *fused*⟩.

□ USAGE
mitigate *Mitigate* is sometimes used as an intransitive (followed by *against*) where *militate* might be expected. Even though Faulkner used it ⟨some intangible and invisible social force that *mitigates* against him —William Faulkner⟩ and one critic thinks it should be called an American idiom, it is usually considered a mistake.

\ə\ **abut** \ᵊ\ **kitten** \ər\ **further** \a\ **ash** \ā\ **ace** \ä\ **mop, mar** \aù\ **out** \ch\ **chin** \e\ **bet** \ē\ **easy** \g\ **go** \i\ **hit** \ī\ **ice** \j\ **job** \ŋ\ **sing** \ō\ **go** \ȯ\ **law** \ȯi\ **boy** \th\ **thin** \t͟h\ **the** \ü\ **loot** \ù\ **foot** \y\ **yet** \zh\ **vision** *see also* Guide to Pronunciation

with a motion picture or television **b** : a container, device, or machine for mixing **c** : a game, stunt, or dance used at a get-together to give members of the group an opportunity to meet one another in a friendly and informal atmosphere
2 : one that mixes with others: as **a** : a person considered in regard to casual sociability ⟨was shy and a poor *mixer*⟩ **b** : a nonalcoholic beverage (as ginger ale) used in a mixed drink
mix·ol·o·gy \mik-'sä-lə-jē\ *noun* (1948)
: the art or skill of preparing mixed drinks
— **mix·ol·o·gist** \-jist\ *noun*
Mix·tec \mēs-'tek, mis-, mēsh-, mish-\ *noun*, *plural* **Mixtec** *or* **Mixtecs** [American Spanish *mixteco*] (1850)
1 : the language of the Mixtec people
2 : a member of an American Indian people of the state of Oaxaca, Mexico
mix·ture \'miks-chər\ *noun* [Middle English, from Middle French, from Old French *mixture*, from Latin *mixtura*, from *mixtus*] (15th century)
1 a : the act, the process, or an instance of mixing **b** (1) : the state of being mixed (2) : the relative proportions of constituents; *especially* : the proportion of fuel to air produced in a carburetor
2 : a product of mixing : COMBINATION: as **a** : a portion of matter consisting of two or more components in varying proportions that retain their own properties **b** : a fabric woven of variously colored threads **c** : a combination of several different kinds
mix–up \'miks-,əp\ *noun* (1841)
1 : a state or instance of confusion
2 : MIXTURE
3 : CONFLICT, FIGHT
¹**miz·zen** *also* **miz·en** \'mi-z³n\ *noun* [Middle English *meson*, from Middle French *misaine* foremast sail, probably ultimately from Latin *medianus* of the middle — more at MEDIAN] (15th century)
1 : a fore-and-aft sail set on the mizzenmast
2 : MIZZENMAST
²**mizzen** *also* **mizen** *adjective* (15th century)
: of or relating to the mizzenmast
miz·zen·mast \-,mast, -məst\ *noun* (15th century)
: the mast aft or next aft of the mainmast in a ship
¹**miz·zle** \'mi-zəl\ *intransitive verb* **miz·zled; miz·zling** \'mi-zə-liŋ, 'miz-liŋ\ [Middle English *misellen;* akin to Flemish *mizzelen* to drizzle, Middle Dutch *mist* fog, mist] (15th century)
: to rain in very fine drops : DRIZZLE
— **mizzle** *noun*
— **miz·zly** \'mi-zə-lē, 'miz-lē\ *adjective*
²**mizzle** *intransitive verb* **miz·zled; miz·zling** \'mi-zə-liŋ, 'miz-liŋ\ [origin unknown] (1781)
chiefly British : to depart suddenly
¹**mne·mon·ic** \ni-'mä-nik\ *adjective* [Greek *mnēmonikos*, from *mnēmōn* mindful, from *mimnēskesthai* to remember — more at MIND] (1753)
1 : assisting or intended to assist memory; *also* : of or relating to mnemonics
2 : of or relating to memory
— **mne·mon·i·cal·ly** \-ni-k(ə-)lē\ *adverb*
²**mnemonic** *noun* (1858)
: a mnemonic device or code
mne·mon·ics \ni-'mä-niks\ *noun plural but singular in construction* (circa 1721)
: a technique of improving the memory
Mne·mos·y·ne \ni-'mä-s³n-ē, -z³n-\ *noun* [Latin, from Greek *Mnēmosynē*]
: the Greek goddess of memory and mother of the Muses by Zeus
-mo *noun suffix* [duodecimo]
— after numerals or their names to indicate the number of leaves made by folding a sheet of paper ⟨sixteen*mo*⟩ ⟨16*mo*⟩
moa \'mō-ə\ *noun* [Maori] (1842)

: any of various usually very large, extinct flightless birds of New Zealand of a ratite family (Dinornithidae) including one (*Dinornis giganteus*) about 12 feet (3.7 meters) in height
Mo·ab·ite \'mō-ə-,bīt\ *noun* [Middle English, from Late Latin *Moabita, Moabites*, from Greek *Mōabitēs*, from *Mōab* Moab, ancient kingdom in Syria] (14th century)
: a member of an ancient Semitic people related to the Hebrews
— **Moabite** *or* **Mo·ab·it·ish** \-,bī-tish\ *adjective*
¹**moan** \'mōn\ *noun* [Middle English *mone*, from (assumed) Old English *mān*] (13th century)
1 : LAMENTATION, COMPLAINT
2 : a low prolonged sound of pain or of grief
²**moan** (14th century)
transitive verb
1 : to bewail audibly : LAMENT
2 : to utter with moans
intransitive verb
1 : LAMENT, COMPLAIN
2 a : to make a moan : GROAN **b** : to emit a sound resembling a moan ⟨the wind *moaned* in the trees⟩
— **moan·er** \'mō-nər\ *noun*
moat \'mōt\ *noun* [Middle English *mote*, probably from Middle French *motte* hill, mound] (14th century)
1 : a deep and wide trench around the rampart of a fortified place (as a castle) that is usually filled with water
2 : a channel resembling a moat (as about a seamount or for confinement of animals in a zoo)

moat 1

— **moat·ed** \'mō-təd\ *adjective*
— **moat·like** \-,līk\ *adjective*
¹**mob** \'mäb\ *noun* [Latin *mobile vulgus* vacillating crowd] (1688)
1 : a large or disorderly crowd; *especially* : one bent on riotous or destructive action
2 : the lower classes of a community : MASSES, RABBLE
3 *chiefly Australian* : a flock, drove, or herd of animals
4 : a criminal set : GANG; *especially, often capitalized* : MAFIA 1
5 *chiefly British* : a group of people : CROWD
synonym see CROWD
— **mob·bish** \'mä-bish\ *adjective*
²**mob** *transitive verb* **mobbed; mob·bing** (1709)
1 : to crowd about and attack or annoy ⟨*mobbed* by autograph hunters⟩ ⟨a crow *mobbed* by songbirds⟩
2 : to crowd into or around ⟨customers *mob* the stores on sale days⟩
mob·cap \'mäb-,kap\ *noun* [*mob* woman's cap + *cap*] (1795)
: a woman's fancy indoor cap made with a high full crown and often tied under the chin
mo·be pearl *or* **mo·bé pearl** \'mō-,bā-, ,mō-'\ *noun, often M capitalized* [origin unknown] (1955)
: MABE
¹**mo·bile** \'mō-bəl, -,bīl *also* -,bēl\ *adjective* [Middle English *mobyll*, from Middle French *mobile*, from Latin *mobilis*, from *movēre* to move] (15th century)
1 : capable of moving or being moved : MOVABLE ⟨a *mobile* missile launcher⟩
2 a : changeable in appearance, mood, or purpose ⟨*mobile* face⟩ **b** : ADAPTABLE, VERSATILE
3 : MIGRATORY

4 a : characterized by the mixing of social groups **b** : having the opportunity for or undergoing a shift in status within the hierarchical social levels of a society ⟨socially *mobile* workers⟩
5 : marked by the use of vehicles for transportation ⟨*mobile* warfare⟩
6 : of or relating to a mobile
— **mo·bil·i·ty** \mō-'bi-lə-tē\ *noun*
²**mo·bile** \'mō-,bēl\ *noun* (1936)
: a construction or sculpture frequently of wire and sheet metal shapes with parts that can be set in motion by air currents; *also* : a similar structure (as of paper or plastic) suspended so that it moves in a current of air
-mobile *combining form* [auto*mobile*]
1 : motorized vehicle ⟨snow*mobile*⟩
2 : automotive vehicle bringing services to the public ⟨blood*mobile*⟩ ⟨book*mobile*⟩
mobile home *noun* (1949)
: a dwelling structure built on a steel chassis and fitted with wheels that is intended to be hauled to a usually permanent site — compare MOTOR HOME
mo·bi·lise *chiefly British variant of* MOBILIZE
mo·bi·li·za·tion \,mō-bə-lə-'zā-shən\ *noun* (1799)
1 : the act of mobilizing
2 : the state of being mobilized
mo·bi·lize \'mō-bə-,līz\ *verb* **-lized; -liz·ing** (1838)
transitive verb
1 a : to put into movement or circulation ⟨*mobilize* financial assets⟩ **b** : to release (something stored in the organism) for bodily use
2 a : to assemble and make ready for war duty **b** : to marshal (as resources) for action ⟨*mobilize* support for a proposal⟩
intransitive verb
: to undergo mobilization
Mö·bi·us strip \'mē-bē-əs-, 'mə(r)-, 'mō-\ *noun* [August F. *Möbius* (died 1868) German mathematician] (1904)
: a one-sided surface that is constructed from a rectangle by holding one end fixed, rotating the opposite end through 180 degrees, and joining it to the first end

Möbius strip

mo·bled \'mä-bəld\ *adjective* [past participle of *moble* to muffle, probably frequentative of *mob* to muffle, of unknown origin] (1603)
: being wrapped or muffled in or as if in a hood
mob·oc·ra·cy \mä-'bä-krə-sē\ *noun* (1754)
1 : rule by the mob
2 : the mob as a ruling class
— **mob·o·crat** \'mä-bə-,krat\ *noun*
— **mob·o·crat·ic** \,mä-bə-'kra-tik\ *adjective*
mob·ster \'mäb-stər\ *noun* (1917)
: a member of a criminal gang
moc \'mäk\ *noun* (1948)
: MOCCASIN 1
moc·ca·sin \'mä-kə-sən\ *noun* [Virginia Algonquian *mockasin*] (circa 1612)
1 a : a soft leather heelless shoe or boot with the sole brought up the sides of the foot and over the toes where it is joined with a puckered seam to a U-shaped piece lying on top of the foot **b** : a regular shoe having a seam on the forepart of the vamp imitating the seam of a moccasin
2 a : WATER MOCCASIN **b** : a snake (as of the genus *Natrix*) resembling a water moccasin
moccasin flower *noun* (1680)
: any of several lady's slippers (genus *Cypripedium*); *especially* : a once common woodland orchid (*C. acaule*) of eastern North America with pink or white moccasin-shaped flowers
mo·cha \'mō-kə\ *noun* [*Mocha*, Yemen] (1773)

1 a (1) **:** a superior Arabian coffee consisting of small green or yellowish beans (2) **:** a coffee of superior quality **b :** a flavoring made of a strong coffee infusion or of a mixture of cocoa or chocolate with coffee
2 : a pliable suede-finished glove leather from African sheepskins
3 : a dark chocolate-brown color

¹**mock** \'mäk, 'mȯk\ verb [Middle English, from Middle French *mocquer*] (15th century)
transitive verb
1 : to treat with contempt or ridicule **:** DERIDE
2 : to disappoint the hopes of
3 : DEFY, CHALLENGE
4 a : to imitate (as a mannerism) closely **:** MIMIC **b :** to mimic in sport or derision
intransitive verb
: JEER, SCOFF
synonym see RIDICULE, COPY
— **mock·er** noun
— **mock·ing·ly** \'mä-kiŋ-lē, 'mȯ-\ adverb

²**mock** noun (15th century)
1 : an act of ridicule or derision **:** JEER
2 : one that is an object of derision or scorn
3 : MOCKERY
4 a : an act of imitation **b :** something made as an imitation

³**mock** adjective (1548)
: of, relating to, or having the character of an imitation **:** SIMULATED, FEIGNED ⟨the *mock* solemnity of the parody⟩

⁴**mock** adverb (circa 1619)
: in an insincere or counterfeit manner — usually used in combination ⟨*mock*-serious⟩

mock·ery \'mä-k(ə-)rē, 'mȯ-\ noun, plural **-er·ies** (15th century)
1 : insulting or contemptuous action or speech **:** DERISION
2 : a subject of laughter, derision, or sport
3 a : a counterfeit appearance **:** IMITATION **b :** an insincere, contemptible, or impertinent imitation ⟨makes a *mockery* of justice⟩
4 : something ridiculously or impudently unsuitable

¹**mock–he·ro·ic** \ˌmäk-hi-'rō-ik, ˌmȯk-\ adjective (circa 1712)
: ridiculing or burlesquing heroic style, character, or action ⟨a *mock-heroic* poem⟩
— **mock–he·ro·ical·ly** \-i-k(ə-)lē\ adverb

²**mock–heroic** noun (1728)
: a mock-heroic composition — called also *mock-epic*

mock·ing·bird \'mä-kiŋ-ˌbərd, 'mȯ-\ noun (1676)
: a common grayish bird (*Mimus polyglottos*) especially of the southern U.S. that is remarkable for its exact imitations of the notes of other birds

mock orange noun (1731)
1 : any of a genus (*Philadelphus*) of ornamental shrubs of the saxifrage family of which several are widely grown for their showy white flowers — called also *philadelphus, syringa*
2 : any of several usually shrubby plants considered to resemble the orange

mock turtle soup noun (1783)
: a soup made of meat (as calf's head or veal), wine, and spices in imitation of green turtle soup

mock–up \'mäk-ˌəp, 'mȯk-\ noun (1920)
: a full-sized structural model built accurately to scale chiefly for study, testing, or display

¹**mod** \'mäd\ noun [probably from ²*mod*] (1960)
: one who wears mod clothes

²**mod** adjective [short for *modern*] (1964)
1 : of, relating to, or being the characteristic style of 1960s British youth culture
2 : HIP, TRENDY

mod·acryl·ic fiber \ˌmä-də-'kri-lik-\ noun [*modified acrylic*] (1960)
: any of various synthetic textile fibers that are long-chain polymers composed of 35 to 85 percent by weight of acrylonitrile units

mod·al \'mō-dᵊl\ adjective [Medieval Latin *modalis*, from Latin *modus*] (1569)
1 : of or relating to modality in logic
2 : containing provisions as to the mode of procedure or the manner of taking effect — used of a contract or legacy
3 : of or relating to a musical mode
4 : of or relating to structure as opposed to substance
5 : of, relating to, or constituting a grammatical form or category characteristically indicating predication of an action or state in some manner other than as a simple fact
6 : of or relating to a statistical mode
— **mod·al·ly** \-dᵊl-ē\ adverb

modal auxiliary noun (circa 1904)
: an auxiliary verb (as *can, must, might, may*) that is characteristically used with a verb of predication and expresses a modal modification and that in English differs formally from other verbs in lacking *-s* and *-ing* forms

mo·dal·i·ty \mō-'da-lə-tē\ noun, plural **-ties** (circa 1617)
1 a : the quality or state of being modal **b :** a modal quality or attribute **:** FORM
2 : the classification of logical propositions according to their asserting or denying the possibility, impossibility, contingency, or necessity of their content
3 : one of the main avenues of sensation (as vision)
4 : a usually physical therapeutic agency

mod con \ˌmäd-'kän\ noun [from *mod. con.*, abbreviation for *modern convenience*] (1934) *chiefly British* **:** a modern convenience — usually used in plural

¹**mode** \'mōd\ noun [Middle English *moede*, from Latin *modus* measure, manner, musical mode — more at METE] (14th century)
1 a : an arrangement of the eight diatonic notes or tones of an octave according to one of several fixed schemes of their intervals **b :** a rhythmical scheme (as in 13th and 14th century music)
2 : ²MOOD 2
3 [Late Latin *modus*, from Latin] **a :** ²MOOD 1 **b :** the modal form of the assertion or denial of a logical proposition
4 a : a particular form or variety of something **b :** a form or manner of expression **:** STYLE
5 : a possible, customary, or preferred way of doing something ⟨explained in the usual solemn *mode*⟩
6 a : a manifestation, form, or arrangement of being; *specifically* **:** a particular form or manifestation of an underlying substance **b :** a particular functioning arrangement or condition **:** STATUS ⟨a spacecraft in reentry *mode*⟩ ⟨a computer operating in parallel *mode*⟩
7 a : the most frequent value of a set of data **b :** a value of a random variable for which a function of probabilities defined on it achieves a relative maximum
8 : any of various stationary vibration patterns of which an elastic body or oscillatory system is capable ⟨the vibration *mode* of an airplane propeller blade⟩ ⟨the vibrational *modes* of a molecule⟩
synonym see METHOD

²**mode** noun [French, from Latin *modus*] (circa 1645)
: a prevailing fashion or style (as of dress or behavior)
synonym see FASHION

¹**mod·el** \'mä-dᵊl\ noun [Middle French *modelle*, from Old Italian *modello*, from (assumed) Vulgar Latin *modellus*, from Latin *modulus* small measure, from *modus*] (1575)
1 *obsolete* **:** a set of plans for a building
2 *dialect British* **:** COPY, IMAGE
3 : structural design ⟨a home on the *model* of an old farmhouse⟩
4 : a usually miniature representation of something; *also* **:** a pattern of something to be made
5 : an example for imitation or emulation

6 : a person or thing that serves as a pattern for an artist; *especially* **:** one who poses for an artist
7 : ARCHETYPE
8 : an organism whose appearance a mimic imitates
9 : one who is employed to display clothes or other merchandise **:** MANNEQUIN
10 a : a type or design of clothing **b :** a type or design of product (as a car)
11 : a description or analogy used to help visualize something (as an atom) that cannot be directly observed
12 : a system of postulates, data, and inferences presented as a mathematical description of an entity or state of affairs
13 : VERSION ☆

²**model** verb **mod·eled** or **mod·elled; mod·el·ing** or **mod·el·ling** \'mäd-liŋ, 'mä-dᵊl-iŋ\ (1625)
transitive verb
1 : to plan or form after a pattern **:** SHAPE
2 *archaic* **:** to make into an organization (as an army, government, or parish)
3 a : to shape or fashion in a plastic material **b :** to produce a representation or simulation of ⟨using a computer to *model* a problem⟩
4 : to construct or fashion in imitation of a particular model ⟨*modeled* its constitution on that of the U.S.⟩
5 : to display by wearing, using, or posing with ⟨*modeled* gowns⟩
intransitive verb
1 : to design or imitate forms **:** make a pattern ⟨enjoys *modeling* in clay⟩
2 : to work or act as a fashion model
— **mod·el·er** \'mäd-lər, 'mä-dᵊl-ər\ noun

³**model** adjective (1844)
1 : serving as or capable of serving as a pattern ⟨a *model* student⟩
2 : being a usually miniature representation of something ⟨a *model* airplane⟩

mo·dem \'mō-ˌdəm, -ˌdem\ noun [*modulator + demodulator*] (circa 1952)
: a device that converts signals produced by one type of device (as a computer) to a form compatible with another (as a telephone)

¹**mod·er·ate** \'mä-d(ə-)rət\ adjective [Middle English, from Latin *moderatus*, from past participle of *moderare* to moderate; akin to Latin *modus* measure] (15th century)
1 a : avoiding extremes of behavior or expression **:** observing reasonable limits ⟨a *moderate* drinker⟩ **b :** CALM, TEMPERATE
2 a : tending toward the mean or average amount or dimension **b :** having average or less than average quality **:** MEDIOCRE

\ə\ **abut** \ᵊ\ **kitten** \ər\ **further** \a\ **ash** \ā\ **ace** \ä\ **mop, mar** \aú\ **out** \ch\ **chin** \e\ **bet** \ē\ **easy** \g\ **go** \i\ **hit** \ī\ **ice** \j\ **job** \ŋ\ **sing** \ō\ **go** \ȯ\ **law** \ȯi\ **boy** \th\ **thin** \t͟h\ **the** \ü\ **loot** \ú\ **foot** \y\ **yet** \zh\ **vision** *see also* Guide to Pronunciation

3 : professing or characterized by political or social beliefs that are not extreme
4 : limited in scope or effect
5 : not expensive **:** reasonable or low in price
6 *of a color* **:** of medium lightness and medium chroma
— **mod·er·ate·ly** *adverb*
— **mod·er·ate·ness** *noun*

²**mod·er·ate** \'mä-də-ˌrāt\ *verb* **-at·ed; -at·ing** (15th century)
transitive verb
1 : to lessen the intensity or extremeness of ⟨the sun *moderated* the chill⟩
2 : to preside over or act as chairman of
intransitive verb
1 : to act as a moderator
2 : to become less violent, severe, or intense
— **mod·er·a·tion** \ˌmä-də-'rā-shən\ *noun*

³**mod·er·ate** \'mä-d(ə-)rət\ *noun* (1794)
: one who holds moderate views or who belongs to a group favoring a moderate course or program

moderate breeze *noun* (circa 1881)
: wind having a speed of 13 to 18 miles (21 to 29 kilometers) per hour — see BEAUFORT SCALE table

moderate gale *noun* (1704)
: wind having a speed of 32 to 38 miles (51 to 61 kilometers) per hour — see BEAUFORT SCALE table

mo·der·a·to \ˌmä-də-'rä-(ˌ)tō\ *adverb or adjective* [Italian, from Latin *moderatus*] (circa 1724)
: MODERATE — used as a direction in music to indicate tempo

mod·er·a·tor \'mä-də-ˌrā-tər\ *noun* (circa 1560)
1 : one who arbitrates **:** MEDIATOR
2 : one who presides over an assembly, meeting, or discussion: as **a :** the presiding officer of a Presbyterian governing body **b :** the nonpartisan presiding officer of a town meeting **c :** the chairman of a discussion group
3 : a substance (as graphite) used for slowing down neutrons in a nuclear reactor
— **mod·er·a·tor·ship** \-ˌship\ *noun*

¹**mod·ern** \'mä-dərn, ÷'mä-d(ə-)rən\ *adjective* [Late Latin *modernus*, from Latin *modo* just now, from *modus* measure — more at METE] (1585)
1 a : of, relating to, or characteristic of the present or the immediate past **:** CONTEMPORARY **b :** of, relating to, or characteristic of a period extending from a relevant remote past to the present time
2 : involving recent techniques, methods, or ideas **:** UP-TO-DATE
3 *capitalized* **:** of, relating to, or having the characteristics of the present or most recent period of development of a language
4 : of or relating to modernism **:** MODERNIST
— **mo·der·ni·ty** \mə-'dər-nə-tē, mä- *also* -'der-\ *noun*
— **mod·ern·ly** \'mä-dərn-lē\ *adverb*
— **mod·ern·ness** \-dərn-nəs\ *noun*

²**modern** *noun* (1585)
1 a : a person of modern times or views **b :** an adherent of modernism **:** MODERNIST
2 : a style of printing type distinguished by regularity of shape, precise curves, straight hairline serifs, and heavy downstrokes

mo·derne \mō-'dern, mə-\ *noun, often capitalized* [French, modern] (1955)
: ART DECO

Modern Hebrew *noun* (1949)
: NEW HEBREW

mod·ern·i·sa·tion, mod·ern·ise *British variant of* MODERNIZATION, MODERNIZE

mod·ern·ism \'mä-dər-ˌni-zəm\ *noun* (1737)
1 : a practice, usage, or expression peculiar to modern times
2 *often capitalized* **:** a tendency in theology to accommodate traditional religious teaching to contemporary thought and especially to devalue supernatural elements

3 : modern artistic or literary philosophy and practice; *especially* **:** a self-conscious break with the past and a search for new forms of expression
— **mod·ern·ist** \-nist\ *noun or adjective*
— **mod·ern·is·tic** \ˌmä-dər-'nis-tik\ *adjective*

mod·ern·i·za·tion \ˌmä-dər-nə-'zā-shən\ *noun* (1770)
1 : the act of modernizing **:** the state of being modernized
2 : something modernized **:** a modernized version

mod·ern·ize \'mä-dər-ˌnīz\ *verb* **-ized; -iz·ing** (1748)
transitive verb
: to make modern (as in taste, style, or usage)
intransitive verb
: to adopt modern ways
— **mod·ern·iz·er** *noun*

modern pentathlon *noun* (circa 1912)
: a composite contest in which all contestants compete in a 300-meter freestyle swim, a 4000-meter cross-country run, a 5000-meter 30-jump equestrian steeplechase, épée fencing, and target shooting at 25 meters

mod·est \'mä-dəst\ *adjective* [Latin *modestus* moderate; akin to Latin *modus* measure] (1565)
1 a : placing a moderate estimate on one's abilities or worth **b :** neither bold nor self-assertive **:** tending toward diffidence
2 : arising from or characteristic of a modest nature
3 : observing the proprieties of dress and behavior **:** DECENT
4 a : limited in size, amount, or scope **b :** UNPRETENTIOUS ⟨a *modest* cottage⟩
synonym see SHY, CHASTE
— **mod·est·ly** *adverb*

mod·es·ty \'mä-də-stē\ *noun* (1531)
1 : freedom from conceit or vanity
2 : propriety in dress, speech, or conduct

mo·di·cum \'mä-di-kəm *also* 'mō-\ *noun* [Middle English, from Latin, neuter of *modicus* moderate, from *modus* measure] (15th century)
: a small portion **:** a limited quantity

mod·i·fi·ca·tion \ˌmä-də-fə-'kā-shən\ *noun* (1603)
1 : the limiting of a statement **:** QUALIFICATION
2 : ¹MODE 6a
3 a : the making of a limited change in something; *also* **:** the result of such a change **b :** a change in an organism caused by environmental factors
4 : a limitation or qualification of the meaning of a word by another word, by an affix, or by internal change

mod·i·fi·er \'mä-də-ˌfī(-ə)r\ *noun* (1583)
1 : one that modifies
2 : a word or phrase that makes specific the meaning of another word or phrase
3 : a gene that modifies the effect of another

mod·i·fy \'mä-də-ˌfī\ *verb* **-fied; -fy·ing** [Middle English *modifien*, from Middle French *modifier*, from Latin *modificare* to measure, moderate, from *modus*] (14th century)
transitive verb
1 : to make less extreme **:** MODERATE
2 a : to limit or restrict the meaning of especially in a grammatical construction **b :** to change (a vowel) by umlaut
3 a : to make minor changes in **b :** to make basic or fundamental changes in often to give a new orientation to or to serve a new end ⟨the wing of a bird is an arm *modified* for flying⟩
intransitive verb
: to undergo change
synonym see CHANGE
— **mod·i·fi·abil·i·ty** \ˌmä-də-ˌfī-ə-'bi-lə-tē\ *noun*
— **mod·i·fi·able** \'mä-də-ˌfī-ə-bəl\ *adjective*

mo·dil·lion \mō-'dil-yən\ *noun* [Italian *modiglione*] (1563)

: an ornamental block or bracket under the corona of the cornice (as in the Corinthian order)

mod·ish \'mō-dish\ *adjective* (1660)
: FASHIONABLE, STYLISH ⟨a *modish* hat⟩ ⟨a *modish* writer⟩
— **mod·ish·ly** *adverb*
— **mod·ish·ness** *noun*

mo·diste \mō-'dēst\ *noun* [French, from *mode* style, mode] (circa 1840)
: one who makes and sells fashionable dresses and hats for women

Mo·dred \'mō-dred\ *noun*
: a knight of the Round Table and nephew of King Arthur

mod·u·la·bil·i·ty \ˌmä-jə-lə-'bi-lə-tē\ *noun* (1928)
: the capability of being modulated

mod·u·lar \'mä-jə-lər\ *adjective* (1798)
1 : of, relating to, or based on a module or a modulus
2 : constructed with standardized units or dimensions for flexibility and variety in use
— **mod·u·lar·i·ty** \ˌmä-jə-'lar-ə-tē\ *noun*
— **mod·u·lar·ly** \'mä-jə-lər-lē\ *adverb*

modular arithmetic *noun* (1959)
: arithmetic that deals with whole numbers where the numbers are replaced by their remainders after division by a fixed number ⟨in a *modular arithmetic* with modulus 5, 3 multiplied by 4 is 2⟩

mod·u·lar·ized \'mä-jə-lə-ˌrīzd\ *adjective* (1959)
1 : containing or consisting of modules
2 : produced in the form of modules

mod·u·late \'mä-jə-ˌlāt\ *verb* **-lat·ed; -lat·ing** [Latin *modulatus*, past participle of *modulari* to play, sing, from *modulus* small measure, rhythm, diminutive of *modus* measure — more at METE] (1615)
transitive verb
1 : to tune to a key or pitch
2 : to adjust to or keep in proper measure or proportion **:** TEMPER
3 : to vary the amplitude, frequency, or phase of (a carrier wave or a light wave) for the transmission of intelligence (as by radio); *also* **:** to vary the velocity of electrons in an electron beam
intransitive verb
1 : to play or sing with modulation
2 : to pass from one musical key into another by means of intermediary chords or notes that have some relation to both keys
3 : to pass gradually from one state to another
— **mod·u·la·tor** \-ˌlā-tər\ *noun*
— **mod·u·la·to·ry** \-lə-ˌtōr-ē, -ˌtȯr-\ *adjective*

mod·u·la·tion \ˌmä-jə-'lā-shən\ *noun* (1531)
1 : a regulating according to measure or proportion **:** TEMPERING
2 : an inflection of the tone or pitch of the voice; *specifically* **:** the use of stress or pitch to convey meaning
3 : a change from one musical key to another by modulating
4 : the process of modulating a carrier or signal (as in radio); *also* **:** the result of this process

mod·ule \'mä-(ˌ)jü(ə)l\ *noun* [Latin *modulus*] (circa 1628)
1 : a standard or unit of measurement
2 : the size of some one part taken as a unit of measure by which the proportions of an architectural composition are regulated
3 a : any in a series of standardized units for use together: as (1) **:** a unit of furniture or architecture (2) **:** an educational unit which covers a single subject or topic **b :** a usually packaged functional assembly of electronic components for use with other such assemblies
4 : an independently-operable unit that is a part of the total structure of a space vehicle
5 a : a subset of an additive group that is also a group under addition **b :** a mathematical set that is a commutative group under addition and that is closed under multiplication which

is distributive from the left or right or both by elements of a ring and for which $a(bx) = (ab)x$ or $(xb)a = x(ba)$ or both where a and b are elements of the ring and x belongs to the set

mod·u·lo \'mä-jə-ˌlō\ *preposition* [New Latin, ablative of *modulus*] (1897)
: with respect to a modulus of ⟨19 and 54 are congruent *modulo* 7⟩

mod·u·lus \'mä-jə-ləs\ *noun, plural* **-li** \-ˌlī, -ˌlē\ [New Latin, from Latin, small measure] (1753)
1 a : the factor by which a logarithm of a number to one base is multiplied to obtain the logarithm of the number to a new base **b** : ABSOLUTE VALUE 2 **c** (1) : the number (as a positive integer) or other mathematical entity (as a polynomial) in a congruence that divides the difference of the two congruent members without leaving a remainder — compare RESIDUE b (2) : the number of different numbers used in a system of modular arithmetic
2 : a constant or coefficient that expresses usually numerically the degree to which a body or substance possesses a particular property (as elasticity)

mo·dus ope·ran·di \ˌmō-dəs-ˌä-pə-'ran-dē, -ˌdī\ *noun, plural* **mo·di operandi** \'mō-ˌdē-, 'mō-ˌdī-\ [New Latin] (1654)
: a method of procedure

mo·dus vi·ven·di \ˌmō-dəs-vi-'ven-dē, -ˌdī\ *noun, plural* **mo·di vivendi** \'mō-ˌdē-, 'mō-ˌdī-\ [New Latin, manner of living] (circa 1879)
1 : a feasible arrangement or practical compromise; *especially* : one that bypasses difficulties
2 : a manner of living : a way of life

Mogen David *variant of* MAGEN DAVID

mog·gy *also* **mog·gie** \'mä-gē\ *noun, plural* **mog·gies** [probably from *Moggy*, from *Mog*, nickname from the name *Margaret*] (circa 1911)
British : CAT

¹mo·gul \'mō-(ˌ)gəl\ *noun* [Persian *Mughul*, from Mongolian *mongγol* Mongol] (1588)
1 *or* **mo·ghul** *capitalized* : an Indian Muslim of or descended from one of several conquering groups of Mongol, Turkish, and Persian origin; *especially* : GREAT MOGUL
2 : a great personage : MAGNATE
— **mogul** *adjective*, often capitalized

²mo·gul \'mō-gul\ *noun* [German dialect; akin to German dialect (Viennese) *mugl* small hill] (1959)
: a bump in a ski run

mo·hair \'mō-ˌhar, -ˌher\ *noun* [modification of obsolete Italian *mocaiarro*, from Arabic *mukhayyar*, literally, choice] (1619)
: a fabric or yarn made wholly or in part of the long silky hair of the Angora goat; *also* : this hair

Mo·ham·med·an *variant of* MUHAMMADAN

Mo·hawk \'mō-ˌhòk\ *noun, plural* **Mohawk** *or* **Mohawks** [of Algonquian origin; akin to Narraganset *or* Massachuset *Mohowawog* Mohawk, literally, cannibal] (1634)
1 : a member of an American Indian people of the Mohawk River valley, New York
2 : the Iroquoian language of the Mohawk people
3 : a hairstyle with a narrow center strip of upright hair and the sides shaved ◇

Mo·he·gan \mō-'hē-gən, mə-\ *or* **Mo·hi·can** \-'hē-kən\ *noun, plural* **Mohegan** *or* **Mohegans** *or* **Mohican** *or* **Mohicans** (1660)
: a member of an American Indian people of southeastern Connecticut

Mo·hi·can \mō-'hē-kən, mə-\ *variant of* MAHICAN

Mo·ho \'mō-ˌhō\ *noun* [short for *Mohorovicic discontinuity*, from Andrija *Mohorovičić* (died 1936) Yugoslavian geologist] (1952)
: the boundary layer between the earth's crust and mantle whose depth varies from about 3

miles (5 kilometers) beneath the ocean floor to about 25 miles (40 kilometers) beneath the continents

Mo·hock \'mō-ˌhäk\ *noun* [alteration of *Mohawk*] (circa 1712)
: one of a gang of aristocratic ruffians who assaulted and otherwise maltreated people in London streets in the early 18th century
— **Mo·hock·ism** \-ˌhä-ˌki-zəm\ *noun*

Mo·ho·ro·vi·cic discontinuity \ˌmō-hə-'rō-və-ˌchich-\ *noun* (1936)
: MOHO

Mohs' scale \'mōz-, 'mōs-, 'mō-səz-\ *noun* [Friedrich *Mohs* (died 1839) German mineralogist] (1879)
: a scale of hardness for minerals that ranges from a value of 1 for talc to 10 for diamond

mo·hur \'mō-(ə)r, mə-'hùr\ *noun* [Hindi *muhr* gold coin, seal, from Persian, from Middle Persian; akin to Sanskrit *mudrā* seal] (1690)
: a former gold coin of India and Persia equal to 15 rupees

moi·e·ty \'mòi-ə-tē\ *noun, plural* **-ties** [Middle English *moite*, from Middle French *moité*, from Late Latin *medietat-, medietas*, from Latin *medius* middle — more at MID] (15th century)
1 a : one of two equal parts : HALF **b** : one of two approximately equal parts
2 : one of the portions into which something is divided : COMPONENT, PART
3 : one of two basic complementary tribal subdivisions

¹moil \'mòi(ə)l\ *verb* [Middle English *moillen*, from Middle French *moillier*, from (assumed) Vulgar Latin *molliare*, from Latin *mollis* soft — more at MOLLIFY] (15th century)
transitive verb
chiefly dialect : to make wet or dirty
intransitive verb
1 : to work hard : DRUDGE
2 : to be in continuous agitation : CHURN, SWIRL
— **moil·er** *noun*

²moil *noun* (1612)
1 : hard work : DRUDGERY
2 : CONFUSION, TURMOIL

moil·ing \'mòi-liŋ\ *adjective* (1603)
1 a : requiring hard work **b** : INDUSTRIOUS ⟨*moiling* workers⟩
2 : violently agitated : TURBULENT
— **moil·ing·ly** \-lē\ *adverb*

Moi·rai \'mòi-ˌrī\ *noun plural* [Greek, from plural of *moira* lot, fate; akin to Greek *meros* part — more at MERIT]
: FATE 4

moire \mòi-(ə)r, 'mòr, 'mwär\ *noun* [French, from English *mohair*] (1660)
archaic : a watered mohair

moi·ré \mò-'rā, mwä-\ *or* **moire** \same or 'mòi(-ə)r, 'mòr, 'mwär\ *noun* [French *moiré*, from *moiré* like moire, from *moire*] (1818)
1 a : an irregular wavy finish on a fabric **b** : a ripple pattern on a surface
2 : a fabric having a wavy watered appearance
3 : an independent usually shimmering pattern seen when two geometrically regular patterns (as two sets of parallel lines or two halftone screens) are superimposed especially at an acute angle
— **moiré** *or* **moire** *adjective*

moist \'mòist\ *adjective* [Middle English *moiste*, from Middle French, perhaps from (assumed) Vulgar Latin *muscidus*, alteration of Latin *mucidus* slimy, from *mucus* nasal mucus] (14th century)
1 : slightly or moderately wet : DAMP
2 : TEARFUL
3 : characterized by high humidity
synonym see WET
— **moist·ly** *adverb*
— **moist·ness** \'mòis(t)-nəs\ *noun*

moist·en \'mòi-sⁿn\ *verb* **moist·ened**; **moist·en·ing** \'mòis-niŋ, 'mòi-sⁿn-iŋ\ (1580)
transitive verb
: to make moist

intransitive verb
: to become moist
— **moist·en·er** \'mòis-nər, 'mòi-sⁿn-ər\ *noun*

mois·ture \'mòis-chər, 'mòish-\ *noun* [Middle English, modification of Middle French *moistour*, from *moiste*] (14th century)
: liquid diffused or condensed in relatively small quantity

mois·tur·ise *British variant of* MOISTURIZE

mois·tur·ize \-chə-ˌrīz\ *transitive verb* **-ized**; **-iz·ing** (1945)
: to add moisture to ⟨*moisturize* the air⟩
— **mois·tur·iz·er** *noun*

mo·jo \'mō-(ˌ)jō\ *noun, plural* **mojoes** *or* **mojos** [probably of African origin; akin to Fulani *moco'o* medicine man] (1926)
: a magic spell, hex, or charm; *broadly* : magical power

moke \'mōk\ *noun* [origin unknown] (1848)
1 *slang British* : DONKEY
2 *slang Australian* : ¹NAG

mol·al \'mō-ləl\ *adjective* [⁵mole] (1905)
: of, relating to, or containing a mole of solute per 1000 grams of solvent
— **mo·lal·i·ty** \mō-'la-lə-tē\ *noun*

¹mo·lar \'mō-lər\ *noun* [Middle English *molares*, plural, from Latin *molaris*, from *molaris* of a mill, from *mola* millstone — more at MILL] (14th century)
: a tooth with a rounded or flattened surface adapted for grinding; *specifically* : one of the cheek teeth in mammals behind the incisors and canines — see TOOTH illustration

²molar *adjective* (1626)
1 : pulverizing by friction : GRINDING
2 : of, relating to, or located near the molar teeth

³molar *adjective* [⁵mole] (1902)
1 : of or relating to a mole of a substance ⟨the *molar* volume of a gas⟩
2 : containing one mole of solute in one liter of solution
— **mo·lar·i·ty** \mō-'lar-ə-tē\ *noun*

mo·las·ses \mə-'la-səz\ *noun* [modification of Portuguese *melaço*, from Late Latin *mellaceum* grape juice, from Latin *mell-, mel* honey — more at MELLIFLUOUS] (1582)
1 : the thick dark to light brown syrup that is separated from raw sugar in sugar manufacture

\ə\ **abut** \ᵊ\ **kitten** \ər\ **further** \a\ **ash** \ā\ **ace** \ä\ **mop, mar** \aù\ **out** \ch\ **chin** \e\ **bet** \ē\ **easy** \g\ **go** \i\ **hit** \ī\ **ice** \j\ **job** \ŋ\ **sing** \ō\ **go** \ò\ **law** \òi\ **boy** \th\ **thin** \t͟h\ **the** \ü\ **loot** \ù\ **foot** \y\ **yet** \zh\ **vision** *see also* Guide to Pronunciation

2 : a syrup made from boiling down sweet vegetable or fruit juice ⟨citrus *molasses*⟩

¹mold \'mōld\ *noun* [Middle English, from Old English *molde;* akin to Old High German *molta* soil, Latin *molere* to grind — more at MEAL] (before 12th century)
1 : crumbling soft friable earth suited to plant growth **:** SOIL; *especially* **:** soil rich in humus — compare LEAF MOLD
2 *dialect British* **a :** the surface of the earth **:** GROUND **b :** the earth of the burying ground
3 *archaic* **:** earth that is the substance of the human body ⟨be merciful great Duke to men of *mold* —Shakespeare⟩

²mold *noun* [Middle English, modification of Old French *modle,* from Latin *modulus,* diminutive of *modus* measure — more at METE] (13th century)
1 : distinctive nature or character **:** TYPE
2 : the frame on or around which an object is constructed
3 a : a cavity in which a substance is shaped: as (1) **:** a matrix for casting metal (2) **:** a form in which food is given a decorative shape **b :** a molded object
4 : MOLDING
5 a *obsolete* **:** an example to be followed **b :** PROTOTYPE **c :** a fixed pattern **:** DESIGN

³mold *transitive verb* (14th century)
1 *archaic* **:** to knead (dough) into a desired consistency or shape
2 : to give shape to ⟨the wind *molds* the waves⟩
3 : to form in a mold ⟨*mold* candles⟩
4 : to determine or influence the quality or nature of ⟨*mold* public opinion⟩
5 : to fit the contours of
6 : to ornament with molding or carving ⟨*molded* picture frames⟩
— **mold·able** \'mōl-də-bəl\ *adjective*
— **mold·er** *noun*

⁴mold *noun* [Middle English *mowlde,* perhaps alteration of *mowle,* from *moulen* to grow moldy, of Scandinavian origin; akin to Old Norse *mygla* to grow moldy] (14th century)
1 : a superficial often woolly growth produced especially on damp or decaying organic matter or on living organisms
2 : a fungus (as of the order Mucorales) that produces mold

⁵mold *intransitive verb* (1530)
: to become moldy

mold·board \'mōl(d)-ˌbōrd, -ˌbord\ *noun* (1508)
1 : a curved iron plate attached above a plowshare to lift and turn the soil
2 : the flat or curved blade (as of a bulldozer) that pushes material to one side as the machine advances

mold·er \'mōl-dər\ *intransitive verb* **mold·ered; mold·er·ing** \-d(ə-)riŋ\ [frequentative of ⁵*mold*] (1531)
: to crumble into particles **:** DISINTEGRATE, DECAY

mold·ing \'mōl-diŋ\ *noun* (14th century)
1 a : the art or occupation of a molder **b :** an object produced by molding
2 a : a decorative recessed or relieved surface **b :** a decorative plane or curved strip used for ornamentation or finishing

molding 2a: *1* fillet and fascia, *2* torus, *3* reeding, *4* cavetto, *5* scotia, *6* congé, *7* beak

moldy \'mōl-dē\ *adjective* **mold·i·er; -est** (14th century)
1 : of, resembling, or covered with a mold-producing fungus
2 a : being old and moldering **:** CRUMBLING **b :** ANTIQUATED, FUSTY ⟨*moldy* tradition⟩
— **mold·i·ness** *noun*

¹mole \'mōl\ *noun* [Middle English, from Old English *māl;* akin to Old High German *meil* spot] (14th century)
: a pigmented spot, mark, or small permanent protuberance on the human body; *especially* **:** NEVUS

²mole *noun* [Middle English; akin to Middle Low German *mol*] (14th century)
1 : any of numerous burrowing insectivores (especially family Talpidae) with tiny eyes, concealed ears, and soft fur
2 : one who works in the dark
3 : a machine for tunneling
4 : a spy (as a double agent) who establishes a cover long before beginning espionage

³mole *noun* [Middle English, from Latin *mola* mole, literally, mill, millstone — more at MILL] (15th century)
: an abnormal mass in the uterus especially when containing fetal tissues

⁴mole *noun* [Middle French, from Old Italian *molo,* from Late Greek *mōlos,* from Latin *moles,* literally, mass, exertion; akin to Greek *mōlos* exertion] (circa 1548)
1 : a massive work formed of masonry and large stones or earth laid in the sea as a pier or breakwater
2 : the harbor formed by a mole

⁵mole *also* **mol** \'mōl\ *noun* [German *Mol,* short for *Molekulargewicht* molecular weight, from *molekular* molecular + *Gewicht* weight] (1902)
: the base unit of amount of pure substance in the International System of Units that contains the same number of elementary entities as there are atoms in exactly 12 grams of the isotope carbon 12

⁶mo·le \'mō-lā\ *noun* [Mexican Spanish, from Nahuatl *mōlli* sauce] (1927)
: a spicy sauce made with chilies and usually chocolate and served with meat

mo·lec·u·lar \mə-'le-kyə-lər\ *adjective* (1823)
1 : of, relating to, or produced by molecules ⟨*molecular* oxygen⟩
2 : of or relating to simple or elementary organization
— **mo·lec·u·lar·ly** \-lē\ *adverb*

molecular biology *noun* (1938)
: a branch of biology dealing with the ultimate physicochemical organization of living matter and especially with the molecular basis of inheritance and protein synthesis
— **molecular biologist** *noun*

molecular formula *noun* (circa 1903)
: a chemical formula that is based on both analysis and molecular weight and gives the total number of atoms of each element in a molecule — compare STRUCTURAL FORMULA

molecular mass *noun* (1970)
: the mass of a molecule that is equal to the sum of the masses of all the atoms contained in the molecule

molecular orbital *noun* (1932)
: a solution of the Schrödinger equation that describes the probable location of an electron relative to the nuclei in a molecule and so indicates the nature of any bond in which the electron is involved

molecular sieve *noun* (1926)
: a crystalline substance (as a zeolite) characterized by uniformly sized pores of molecular dimension that can adsorb small molecules and is used especially in separations

molecular weight *noun* (1880)
: the average mass of a molecule of a compound compared to ¹/₁₂ the mass of carbon 12 and calculated as the sum of the atomic weights of the constituent atoms

mol·e·cule \'mä-li-ˌkyü(ə)l\ *noun* [French *molécule,* from New Latin *molecula,* diminutive of Latin *moles* mass] (1794)
1 : the smallest particle of a substance that retains all the properties of the substance and is composed of one or more atoms
2 : a tiny bit **:** PARTICLE

mole·hill \'mōl-ˌhil\ *noun* (15th century)
: a little mound or ridge of earth pushed up by a mole

mole·skin \-ˌskin\ *noun* (1668)
1 : the skin of the mole used as fur
2 a : a heavy durable cotton fabric with a short thick velvety nap on one side **b :** a garment made of moleskin — usually used in plural

mo·lest \mə-'lest\ *transitive verb* [Middle English, from Middle French *molester,* from Latin *molestare,* from *molestus* burdensome, annoying; akin to Latin *moles* mass] (14th century)
1 : to annoy, disturb, or persecute especially with hostile intent or injurious effect
2 : to make annoying sexual advances to; *especially* **:** to force physical and usually sexual contact on
— **mo·les·ta·tion** \ˌmō-ˌles-'tā-shən, ˌmä-, -ləs-\ *noun*
— **mo·lest·er** \mə-'les-tər\ *noun*

mo·line \mə-'lēn, -'līn\ *adjective* [(assumed) Anglo-French *moliné,* from Old French *molin* mill, from Late Latin *molinum* — more at MILL] (1562)
of a heraldic cross **:** having the end of each arm forked and recurved — see CROSS illustration

moll \'mäl, 'mȯl\ *noun* [probably from *Moll,* nickname for *Mary*] (1604)
1 : PROSTITUTE
2 a : DOLL 2 **b :** a gangster's girlfriend

mol·li·fy \'mä-lə-ˌfī\ *verb* **-fied; -fy·ing** [Middle English *mollifien,* from Middle French *mollifier,* from Late Latin *mollificare,* from Latin *mollis* soft; akin to Greek *amaldynein* to soften, Sanskrit *mrdu* soft, and probably to Greek *malakos* soft, *amblys* dull, Old English *meltan* to melt] (15th century)
transitive verb
1 : to soothe in temper or disposition **:** APPEASE ⟨*mollified* the staff with a raise⟩
2 : to reduce the rigidity of **:** SOFTEN
3 : to reduce in intensity **:** ASSUAGE, TEMPER
intransitive verb
archaic **:** SOFTEN, RELENT
synonym see PACIFY
— **mol·li·fi·ca·tion** \ˌmä-lə-fə-'kā-shən\ *noun*

mol·lus·ci·cide \mə-'ləs-kə-ˌsīd, -'lə-sə-\ *noun* [New Latin *Mollusca* + English *-i-* + *-cide*] (circa 1947)
: an agent for destroying mollusks (as snails)
— **mol·lus·ci·cid·al** \-ˌləs-kə-'sī-dᵊl, -ˌlə-sə-\ *adjective*

mol·lusk *or* **mol·lusc** \'mä-ləsk\ *noun* [French *mollusque,* from New Latin *Mollusca,* from Latin, neuter plural of *molluscus* thinshelled (of a nut), from *mollis*] (1783)
: any of a large phylum (Mollusca) of invertebrate animals (as snails, clams, or squids) with a soft unsegmented body usually enclosed in a calcareous shell; *broadly* **:** SHELLFISH
— **mol·lus·can** *also* **mol·lus·kan** \mə-'ləs-kən, mä-\ *adjective*

mol·ly *also* **mol·lie** \'mä-lē\ *noun, plural* **mollies** [by shortening from New Latin *Mollienisia,* former genus name, from Comte François N. *Mollien* (died 1850) French statesman] (circa 1933)
: any of several brightly colored live-bearers (genus *Poecilia* of the family Poeciliidae) highly valued as aquarium fishes

¹mol·ly·cod·dle \'mä-lē-ˌkä-dᵊl\ *noun* [*Molly,* nickname for *Mary*] (1833)
: a pampered or effeminate man or boy

²mollycoddle *transitive verb* **-cod·dled; -cod·dling** \-ˌkäd-liŋ, -ˌkä-dᵊl-iŋ\ (1864)
: to surround with an excessive or absurd degree of indulgence and attention
synonym see INDULGE
— **mol·ly·cod·dler** \-ˌkäd-lər, -ˌkä-dᵊl-ər\ *noun*

Mo·loch \'mä-lək, 'mō-ˌläk\ *noun* [Late Latin, from Greek, from Hebrew *Mōlekh*]

: a Semitic god to whom children were sacrificed

Mo·lo·tov cocktail \'mä-lə-ˌtȯf-, 'mȯ-, 'mō-, -ˌtȯv-\ *noun* [Vyacheslav M. *Molotov*] (1939)
: a crude bomb made of a bottle filled with a flammable liquid (as gasoline) and usually fitted with a wick (as a saturated rag) that is ignited just before the bottle is hurled

¹**molt** \'mōlt\ *verb* [alteration of Middle English *mouten*, from Old English *-mūtian* to change, from Latin *mutare* — more at MUTABLE] (1591)
intransitive verb
: to shed hair, feathers, shell, horns, or an outer layer periodically
transitive verb
: to cast off (an outer covering) periodically; *specifically* : to throw off (the old cuticle) — used of arthropods
— **molt·er** *noun*

²**molt** *noun* (1815)
: the act or process of molting; *specifically* : ECDYSIS

mol·ten \'mōl-t°n\ *adjective* [Middle English, from past participle of *melten* to melt] (14th century)
1 *obsolete* : made by melting and casting
2 : fused or liquefied by heat : MELTED ⟨*molten* lava⟩
3 : having warmth or brilliance : GLOWING ⟨the *molten* sunlight of warm skies —T. B. Costain⟩

mol·to \'mōl-(ˌ)tō, 'mȯl-\ *adverb* [Italian, from Latin *multum*, from neuter of *multus* much] (circa 1801)
: MUCH, VERY — used in music directions ⟨*molto* vivace⟩

mo·ly \'mō-lē\ *noun* [Latin, from Greek *mōly*]
: a mythical herb with a black root, white blossoms, and magical powers

mo·lyb·date \mə-'lib-ˌdāt\ *noun* (1794)
: a salt of molybdenum containing the group MoO_4 or Mo_2O_7

mo·lyb·de·nite \mə-'lib-də-ˌnīt\ *noun* [New Latin *molybdena*] (1796)
: a blue usually foliated mineral consisting of molybdenum disulfide that is a source of molybdenum

mo·lyb·de·num \-nəm\ *noun* [New Latin, from *molybdena*, a lead ore, molybdenite, molybdenum, from Latin *molybdaena* galena, from Greek *molybdaina*, from *molybdos* lead] (1816)
: a metallic element that resembles chromium and tungsten in many properties, is used especially in strengthening and hardening steel, and is a trace element in plant and animal metabolism — see ELEMENT table

molybdenum disulfide *noun* (circa 1931)
: a compound MoS_2 used especially as a lubricant in grease

mom \'mäm, 'məm\ *noun* [short for *momma*] (circa 1894)
: MOTHER

mom–and–pop \'mäm-ən(d)-'päp\ *adjective* (1951)
: being a small owner-operated business

mome \'mōm\ *noun* [origin unknown] (1553)
archaic : BLOCKHEAD, FOOL

mo·ment \'mō-mənt\ *noun* [Middle English, from Middle French, from Latin *momentum* movement, particle sufficient to turn the scales, moment, from *movēre* to move] (14th century)
1 a : a minute portion or point of time : INSTANT **b** : a comparatively brief period of time
2 a : present time ⟨at the *moment* she is working on a novel⟩ **b** : a time of excellence or conspicuousness ⟨he has his *moments*⟩
3 : importance in influence or effect ⟨a matter of great *moment*⟩
4 *obsolete* : a cause or motive of action
5 : a stage in historical or logical development

6 a : tendency or measure of tendency to produce motion especially about a point or axis **b** : the product of quantity (as a force) and the distance to a particular axis or point
7 a : the mean of the *n*th powers of the deviations of the observed values in a set of statistical data from a fixed value **b** : the expected value of a power of the deviation of a random variable from a fixed value
synonym see IMPORTANCE

mo·men·tar·i·ly \ˌmō-mən-'ter-ə-lē\ *adverb* (circa 1666)
1 : for a moment
2 *archaic* : INSTANTLY
3 : at any moment : in a moment □

mo·men·tary \'mō-mən-ˌter-ē\ *adjective* (15th century)
1 a : continuing only a moment : FLEETING **b** : having a very brief life
2 : operative or recurring at every moment
synonym see TRANSIENT
— **mo·men·tar·i·ness** *noun*

mo·ment·ly \'mō-mənt-lē\ *adverb* (1676)
1 : from moment to moment
2 : at any moment
3 : for a moment
usage see MOMENTARILY

mo·men·to *variant of* MEMENTO
usage see MEMENTO

moment of inertia (1830)
: a measure of the resistance of a body to angular acceleration about a given axis that is equal to the sum of the products of each element of mass in the body and the square of the element's distance from the axis

moment of truth (1932)
1 : the final sword thrust in a bullfight
2 : a moment of crisis on whose outcome much or everything depends

mo·men·tous \mō-'men-təs, mə-\ *adjective* (1652)
: IMPORTANT, CONSEQUENTIAL
— **mo·men·tous·ly** *adverb*
— **mo·men·tous·ness** *noun*

mo·men·tum \mō-'men-təm, mə-\ *noun, plural* **mo·men·ta** \-'men-tə\ *or* **momentums** [New Latin, from Latin, movement] (1610)
1 : a property of a moving body that the body has by virtue of its mass and motion and that is equal to the product of the body's mass and velocity; *broadly* : a property of a moving body that determines the length of time required to bring it to rest when under the action of a constant force or moment
2 : strength or force gained by motion or through the development of events : IMPETUS ⟨the campaign gained *momentum*⟩

mom·ma \'mä-mə, 'mə-mə\ *variant of* MAMA

mom·my \'mä-mē, 'mə-mē\ *noun, plural* **mom·mies** [alteration of *mammy*] (1899)
: MOTHER

mommy track *noun* (1989)
: a career path that allows a mother flexible or reduced work hours but tends to slow or block advancement

Mo·mus \'mō-məs\ *noun* [Latin, from Greek *Mōmos*]
: the Greek god of censure and mockery

mon \'män\ *dialect chiefly British variant of* MAN

Mon \'mōn\ *noun, plural* **Mon** *or* **Mons** (1798)
1 : a member of the dominant native people of Pegu division, Myanmar (Burma)
2 : the Mon-Khmer language of the Mon people

mon- *or* **mono-** *combining form* [Middle English, from Middle French & Latin; Middle French, from Latin, from Greek, from *monos* alone, single — more at MONK]
1 : one : single : alone ⟨*mono*plane⟩ ⟨*mono*drama⟩
2 a : containing one (usually specified) atom, radical, or group ⟨*mono*hydroxy⟩ **b** : monomolecular ⟨*mono*layer⟩

mon·a·chal \'mä-ni-kəl\ *adjective* [Middle French or Late Latin; Middle French, from Late Latin *monachalis*, from *monachus* monk — more at MONK] (1587)
: MONASTIC
— **mon·a·chism** \'mä-nə-ˌki-zəm\ *noun*

mo·nad \'mō-ˌnad\ *noun* [Late Latin *monad-, monas*, from Greek, from *monos*] (1615)
1 a : UNIT, ONE **b** : ATOM 1 **c** : an elementary individual substance which reflects the order of the world and from which material properties are derived
2 : a flagellated protozoan (as of the genus *Monas*)
— **mo·nad·ic** \mō-'na-dik, mə-\ *adjective*
— **mo·nad·ism** \'mō-ˌna-ˌdi-zəm\ *noun*

mon·adel·phous \ˌmä-nə-'del-fəs\ *adjective* (1806)
of stamens : united by the filaments into one group usually forming a tube around the gynoecium

mo·nad·nock \mə-'nad-ˌnäk\ *noun* [Mount *Monadnock*, N.H.] (1893)
: INSELBERG

mon·an·dry \'mä-ˌnan-drē\ *noun, plural* **-dries** [*mon-* + *-andry* (as in *polyandry*)] (1855)
: a marriage form or custom in which a woman has only one husband at a time

mon·arch \'mä-nərk, -ˌnärk\ *noun* [Late Latin *monarcha*, from Greek *monarchos*, from *mon-* + *-archos* -arch] (15th century)
1 : a person who reigns over a kingdom or empire: as **a** : a sovereign ruler **b** : a constitutional king or queen
2 : one that holds preeminent position or power
3 : MONARCH BUTTERFLY
— **mo·nar·chal** \mə-'när-kəl, mä-\ *or* **mo·nar·chi·al** \-kē-əl\ *adjective*

□ **USAGE**
momentarily The question about what sense *momentarily* can properly be used in originated in 1926, when an English commentator opined that *momentarily* should be restricted in meaning to "for a moment" (its most common use) and *momently* to "from moment to moment." The first problem with this decree was that both words were already being used in both senses. A second problem, one the commentator could not have foreseen, was that *momentarily* would become the usual word and *momently* would recede sharply in use. Later commentators shifted their objection to the sense of *momentarily* meaning "at any moment"; this sense was assigned to *momently*. Now *momently* has indeed been so used ⟨an embittered man . . . *momently* expecting death from heart disease —*Time* (1950)⟩. But *momentarily* had already had the same meaning for some time ⟨during the early part of the morning, I *momentarily* expected his coming —Charlotte Brontë (1847)⟩ ⟨additional arrests were expected *momentarily* —*Sun* (Baltimore) (1928)⟩, and its use continues ⟨was expecting to be drafted *momentarily* —Robert A. Caro (1989)⟩. We have no very recent use of *momently* in this meaning, but it is still used occasionally in the sense "from moment to moment," indicating a continuing process over time ⟨the stink grew *momently* more revolting —Mervyn Peake⟩. The critics remain at odds, some disapproving *momentarily* in sense 3, others approving. Our evidence clearly shows that it is standard.

\ə\ **abut** \ᵊ\ **kitten** \ər\ **further** \a\ **ash** \ā\ **ace** \ä\ **mop, mar** \au̇\ **out** \ch\ **chin** \e\ **bet** \ē\ **easy** \g\ **go** \i\ **hit** \ī\ **ice** \j\ **job** \ŋ\ **sing** \ō\ **go** \ȯ\ **law** \ȯi\ **boy** \th\ **thin** \t̲h̲\ **the** \ü\ **loot** \u̇\ **foot** \y\ **yet** \zh\ **vision** *see also* Guide to Pronunciation

monarch butterfly *noun* (1890)
: a large migratory American butterfly (*Danaus plexippus*) that has orange-brown wings with black veins and borders and a larva that feeds on milkweed

monarch butterfly

Mo·nar·chi·an \mə-'när-kē-ən, mä-\ *noun* (1765)
: an adherent of one of two anti-Trinitarian groups of the 2d and 3d centuries A.D. teaching that God is one person as well as one being
— **Mo·nar·chi·an·ism** \-kē-ə-,ni-zəm\ *noun*

mo·nar·chi·cal \mə-'när-ki-kəl, mä-\ *also* **mo·nar·chic** \-kik\ *adjective* (1576)
: of, relating to, suggestive of, or characteristic of a monarch or monarchy
— **mo·nar·chi·cal·ly** \-ki-k(ə-)lē\ *adverb*

mon·ar·chism \'mä-nər-,ki-zəm, -,när-\ *noun* (1838)
: monarchical government or principles
— **mon·ar·chist** \-kist\ *noun or adjective*

mon·ar·chy \'mä-nər-kē *also* -,när-\ *noun, plural* **-chies** (14th century)
1 : undivided rule or absolute sovereignty by a single person
2 : a nation or state having a monarchical government
3 : a government having an hereditary chief of state with life tenure and powers varying from nominal to absolute

mo·nar·da \mə-'när-də\ *noun* [New Latin, from Nicolás *Monardes* (died 1588) Spanish botanist] (1712)
: any of a genus (*Monarda*) of coarse North American mints with a tubular many-nerved calyx and whorls of showy flowers

mon·as·tery \'mä-nə-,ster-ē\ *noun, plural* **-ter·ies** [Middle English *monasterie*, from Late Latin *monasterium*, from Late Greek *monastērion*, from Greek, hermit's cell, from *monazein* to live alone, from *monos* single — more at MONK] (15th century)
: a house for persons under religious vows; *especially* : an establishment for monks

mo·nas·tic \mə-'nas-tik\ *adjective* (circa 1563)
1 : of or relating to monasteries or to monks or nuns
2 : resembling (as in seclusion or ascetic simplicity) life in a monastery
— **monastic** *noun*
— **mo·nas·ti·cal·ly** \-ti-k(ə-)lē\ *adverb*
— **mo·nas·ti·cism** \-tə-,si-zəm\ *noun*

mon·atom·ic \,mä-nə-'tä-mik\ *adjective* (1848)
: consisting of one atom; *especially* : having but one atom in the molecule

mon·au·ral \(,)mä-'nȯr-əl\ *adjective* (1931)
: MONOPHONIC 2
— **mon·au·ral·ly** \-ə-lē\ *adverb*

mon·a·zite \'mä-nə-,zīt\ *noun* [German *Monazit*, from Greek *monazein*] (1836)
: a mineral that is a yellow, red, or brown phosphate of cerium and other rare earth elements and thorium and is found often in sand and gravel deposits

Mon·day \'mən-dē, -(,)dā\ *noun* [Middle English, from Old English *mōnandæg*; akin to Old High German *mānatag* Monday; akin to Old English *mōna* moon and to Old English *dæg* day] (before 12th century)
: the second day of the week
— **Mon·days** \-dēz\ *adverb*

Monday–morning quarterback *noun* [from a fan's usually critical rehashing of the weekend football game strategy] (1941)
: one who second-guesses

— **Monday–morning quarterbacking** *noun*

mon·e·cious *variant of* MONOECIOUS

mo·ner·an \mō-'nir-ən, mə-\ *noun* [New Latin *Monera*, kingdom comprising prokaryotes, ultimately from Greek *monērēs* single] (1869)
: PROKARYOTE
— **moneran** *adjective*

M1 rifle \'em-'wən-\ *noun* (1938)
: a .30 caliber gas-operated clip-fed semiautomatic rifle used by U.S. troops in World War II

mon·es·trous \(,)mä-'nes-trəs\ *adjective* (1900)
: experiencing estrus once each year or breeding season

mon·e·tar·ism \'mä-nə-tə-,ri-zəm *also* 'mən-\ *noun* (1969)
: a theory in economics that stable economic growth can be assured only by control of the rate of increase of the money supply to match the capacity for growth of real productivity
— **mon·e·tar·ist** \-rist\ *noun or adjective*

mon·e·tary \'mä-nə-,ter-ē *also* 'mə-\ *adjective* [Late Latin *monetarius* of a mint, of money, from Latin *moneta*] (circa 1812)
: of or relating to money or to the mechanisms by which it is supplied to and circulates in the economy
— **mon·e·tar·i·ly** \,mä-nə-'ter-ə-lē *also* ,mə-\ *adverb*

monetary aggregate *noun* (1979)
: one of the formal categories of money (as cash and demand deposits or bank credits) in a national economy that is used as a measure in predictions of economic growth

monetary unit *noun* (circa 1864)
: the standard unit of value of a currency

mon·e·tize \'mä-nə-,tīz *also* 'mə-\ *transitive verb* **-tized; -tiz·ing** [Latin *moneta*] (circa 1879)
1 : to coin into money; *also* : to establish as legal tender
2 : to purchase (public or private debt) and thereby free for other uses moneys that would have been devoted to debt service
— **mon·e·ti·za·tion** \,mä-nə-tə-'zā-shən *also* ,mə-\ *noun*

¹**mon·ey** \'mə-nē\ *noun, plural* **moneys** *or* **mon·ies** \'mə-nēz\ *often attributive* [Middle English *moneye*, from Middle French *moneie*, from Latin *moneta* mint, money — more at MINT] (14th century)
1 : something generally accepted as a medium of exchange, a measure of value, or a means of payment: as **a** : officially coined or stamped metal currency **b** : MONEY OF ACCOUNT **c** : PAPER MONEY
2 a : wealth reckoned in terms of money **b** : an amount of money **c** *plural* : sums of money : FUNDS
3 : a form or denomination of coin or paper money
4 a : the first, second, and third place winners (as in a horse or dog race) — usually used in the phrases *in the money* or *out of the money* **b** : prize money ⟨his horse took third *money*⟩
5 a : persons or interests possessing or controlling great wealth **b** : a position of wealth ⟨born into *money*⟩ ◊
— **for one's money** : according to one's preference or opinion
— **on the money** : exactly right or accurate

²**money** *adjective* (1935)
: involving or reliable in a crucial situation ⟨a *money* player⟩ ⟨a *money* pitch⟩

mon·ey–back \-'bak\ *adjective* (1922)
: providing that the consumer is entitled to a refund if the purchased product is unsatisfactory ⟨a *money-back* guarantee⟩

mon·ey·bags \'mə-nē-,bagz\ *noun plural but singular or plural in construction* (1596)
1 : WEALTH
2 : a wealthy person

money changer *noun* (15th century)
1 : one whose business is the exchanging of kinds or denominations of currency
2 : a device for holding and dispensing sorted change

mon·eyed *also* **mon·ied** \'mə-nēd\ *adjective* (15th century)
1 : having money : WEALTHY
2 : consisting in or derived from money

mon·ey·er \'mə-nē-ər\ *noun* [Middle English, from Old French *monier*, from Late Latin *monetarius* master of a mint, coiner, from *monetarius* of a mint — more at MONETARY] (15th century)
: an authorized coiner of money : MINTER

mon·ey–grub·ber \'mə-nē-,grə-bər\ *noun* (1840)
: a person bent on accumulating money
— **mon·ey–grub·bing** \-biŋ\ *adjective or noun*

mon·ey·lend·er \-,len-dər\ *noun* (circa 1780)
: one whose business is lending money; *specifically* : PAWNBROKER

mon·ey·mak·er \-,mā-kər\ *noun* (1834)
1 : one that accumulates wealth
2 : one that produces profit
— **mon·ey·mak·ing** \-kiŋ\ *adjective or noun*

mon·ey·man \-,man\ *noun* (circa 1585)
: FINANCIER

money market *noun* (1950)
: the trade in short-term negotiable instruments (as certificates of deposit or U.S. Treasury securities)

money of account (1691)
: a denominator of value or basis of exchange which is used in keeping accounts and for which there may or may not be an equivalent coin or denomination of paper money

money order *noun* (1802)
: an order issued by a post office, bank, or telegraph office for payment of a specified sum of money usually at any branch of the organization

mon·ey–spin·ner \'mə-nē-,spi-nər\ *noun* (1859)
chiefly British : MONEYMAKER
— **mon·ey–spin·ning** \-niŋ\ *adjective or noun, chiefly British*

mon·ey·wort \-,wərt, -,wȯrt\ *noun* (1578)
: a trailing perennial herb (*Lysimachia nummularia*) of the primrose family with rounded opposite leaves and solitary yellow flowers in their axils

¹**mon·ger** \'məŋ-gər, 'mäŋ-\ *noun* [Middle English *mongere*, from Old English *mangere*, from Latin *mangon-, mango*, of Greek origin; akin to Greek *manganon* charm, philter] (before 12th century)
1 : BROKER, DEALER — usually used in combination ⟨ale*monger*⟩

◇ WORD HISTORY
money One of the epithets of the goddess Juno, the wife of Jupiter in ancient Roman myth, was *Moneta*. When the Romans established a mint at the temple of Juno Moneta, this epithet became a generic Latin term for a place where money was made as well as for money itself. The English words *mint* and *money* are both ultimately borrowings from Latin *moneta*. The considerable difference between the two words may be accounted for by the widely different routes by which each came into English. *Mint*, continuing Old English *mynet*, as well as the German word *Münze* "coin" (continuing Old High German *munizza*), goes back to a prehistoric West Germanic borrowing from Latin *moneta*. *Money*, on the other hand, was borrowed from medieval French in the Middle English period as *moneye*; Old French *moneie*, in turn, is a Romance descendant of Latin *moneta*.

MONEY

NAME	SYMBOL	SUBDIVISION	COUNTRY
afghani	Af	100 puls	Afghanistan
baht or tical	B	100 satang	Thailand
balboa		100 centesimos	Panama
birr		100 cents	Ethiopia
bolivar	B	100 centimos	Venezuela
boliviano	$b	100 centavos	Bolivia
cedi	₵	100 pesewas	Ghana
colón	C or ₵	100 centimos	Costa Rica
colón	₵	100 centavos	El Salvador
cordoba	C$	100 centavos	Nicaragua
dalasi		100 bututs	Gambia
deutsche mark	DM	100 pfennig	Germany
dinar	DA	100 centimes	Algeria
dinar	BD	1000 fils	Bahrain
dinar	ID	1000 fils	Iraq
dinar	JD	1000 fils	Jordan
dinar	KD	1000 fils	Kuwait
dinar	LD	1000 dirhams	Libya
dinar	D	1000 millimes	Tunisia
dinar[1]	£	1000 fils	Yemen
dinar		100 paras	Yugoslavia
dirham	DH	100 centimes	Morocco
dirham		100 fils	United Arab Emirates
dobra	Db	100 centimos	Sao Tome and Principe
dollar	EC$[2] or $	100 cents	Antigua and Barbuda, Dominica, Grenada, St. Kitts-Nevis, St. Lucia, St. Vincent and the Grenadines
dollar	$A or $	100 cents	Australia
dollar	$ or B$	100 cents	Bahamas
dollar	$ or Bds$	100 cents	Barbados
dollar	$	100 cents	Belize
dollar	$	100 cents	Bermuda
dollar	B$	100 sen or cents	Brunei
dollar	$	100 cents	Canada
dollar or yuan	NT$	100 cents	China (Taiwan)
dollar	$ or F$	100 cents	Fiji
dollar	$ or G$	100 cents	Guyana
dollar	$ or HK$	100 cents	Hong Kong
dollar	$ or J$	100 cents	Jamaica
dollar	L$	100 cents	Liberia
dollar	NZ$	100 cents	New Zealand
dollar	$ or S$	100 cents	Singapore
dollar	$ or TT$	100 cents	Trinidad and Tobago
dollar	$	100 cents	United States
dollar	$ or Z$	100 cents	Zimbabwe
dollar—see RINGGIT, below			
dong		100 xu	Vietnam
drachma	Dr	100 lepta	Greece
escudo		100 centavos	Cape Verde
escudo	$ or Esc	100 centavos	Portugal
florin—see GULDEN, below			
forint	Ft	100 filler	Hungary
franc	BF or F or FR	100 centimes	Belgium
franc	Fr or FR or F or CFA[3]	100 centimes	Benin, Burkina Faso, Cameroon, Central African Republic, Chad, Congo, Equitorial Guinea, Gabon, Ivory Coast, Mali, Niger, Senegal, Togo
franc	F or FBu	100 centimes	Burundi
franc	Fr or F	100 centimes	Djibouti
franc	Fr or F	100 centimes	France
franc	GF	100 centimes	Guinea
franc	F or Flux	100 centimes	Luxembourg
franc	FMG	100 centimes	Madagascar
franc	FR or RF	100 centimes	Rwanda
franc	Fr or FR	100 centimes or rappen	Switzerland
gourde	G	100 centimes	Haiti
guarani	G or ₲	100 centimos	Paraguay
gulden or guilder or florin	f or Fl or G	100 cents	Netherlands
gulden or guilder or florin	Sf	100 cents	Suriname
kina	K	100 toea	Papua New Guinea
kip	K	100 at	Laos
koruna	Kčs	100 haleru	Czech Republic
koruna	Kčs	100 haleru	Slovakia
krona	KR	100 aurar (singular eyrir)	Iceland
krona	SKr or KR	100 ore	Sweden
krone	DKr	100 ore	Denmark
krone	KR or Nkr	100 ore	Norway
kwacha	K	100 tambala	Malawi
kwacha	K	100 ngwee	Zambia

NAME	SYMBOL	SUBDIVISION	COUNTRY
kwanza		100 lwei	Angola
kyat	K	100 pyas	Myanmar
lat			Latvia
lek		100 qindarka	Albania
lempira	L	100 centavos	Honduras
leone	Le	100 cents	Sierra Leone
leu		100 bani (singular ban)	Romania
lev		100 stotinki	Bulgaria
lilangeni (plural emalangeni)	E	100 cents	Swaziland
lira	L or Lit	100 centesimi[4]	Italy
lira or pound	£ or £M or Lm	100 cents	Malta
lira	TL	100 kurus	Turkey
livre—see POUND, below			
loti (plural maloti)		100 licente or lisente (singular sente)	Lesotho
mark—see DEUTSCHE MARK, above			
markka	Fmk	100 pennia	Finland
metical		100 centavos	Mozambique
naira	₦	100 kobo	Nigeria
ngultrum	Nu	100 chetrums	Bhutan
ouguiya		5 khoums	Mauritania
pa'anga	T$	100 seniti	Tonga
pataca		100 avos	Macao
peseta	PTA	100 centimos[4]	Spain
peso			Argentina
peso		100 centavos	Chile
peso		100 centavos	Colombia
peso		100 centavos	Cuba
peso	RD$	100 centavos	Dominican Republic
peso		100 centavos	Guinea-Bissau
peso	$	100 centavos	Mexico
peso or piso	P	100 sentimos or centavos	Philippines
peso	$	100 centesimos	Uruguay
pound	£	100 cents	Cyprus
pound	£E	100 piastres	Egypt
pound	£	100 pence (singular penny)	Ireland
pound or livre	L	100 piastres	Lebanon
pound	£S	100 piastres	Sudan
pound		100 piastres	Syria
pound	£	100 pence (singular penny)	United Kingdom
pound—see LIRA, above			
pula	P	100 thebe	Botswana
quetzal	Q	100 centavos	Guatemala
rand	R	100 cents	South Africa
real		100 centavos	Brazil
rial	R or Rl	100 dinars	Iran
rial	RO	1000 baiza	Oman
rial[1] also riyal	YR or R	100 fils	Yemen
rial—see RIYAL, below			
riel		100 sen	Cambodia
ringgit or dollar	$ or M$	100 sen	Malaysia
riyal	QR	100 dirhams	Qatar
riyal also rial		100 halala	Saudi Arabia
riyal—see RIAL, above			
ruble		100 kopecks	Russia
rufiyaa	Rf	100 laari	Maldives
rupee	Re (plural Rs)	100 paise	India
rupee	Re (plural Rs)	100 cents	Mauritius
rupee	Re (plural Rs)	100 paisa	Nepal
rupee	Re (plural Rs)	100 paisa	Pakistan
rupee	SR	100 cents	Seychelles
rupee	Re (plural Rs)	100 cents	Sri Lanka
rupiah	Rp	100 sen	Indonesia
schilling	S or Sch	100 groschen	Austria
shekel or sheqel	IS	100 agorot	Israel
shilling	S or KSh	100 cents	Kenya
shilling		100 cents	Somalia
shilling	TSh	100 cents	Tanzania
shilling		100 cents	Uganda
sol		100 centavos	Peru
sucre		100 centavos	Ecuador
taka	Tk	100 paisa or poisha	Bangladesh
tala	$	100 sene	Western Samoa
tical—see BAHT, above			
tugrik		100 mongo	Mongolia
vatu			Vanuatu
won		100 chon	North Korea
won		100 chon	South Korea
yen	¥	100 sen	Japan
yuan		100 fen	China (mainland)
yuan—see DOLLAR, above			
zaire	Z	100 makuta (singular likuta)	Zaire
zloty	Zl	100 groszy	Poland

[1]The currencies of the formerly separate countries of Southern Yemen and the Yemen Arab Republic are both legal in unified Yemen.

[2]Dollars issued by the Eastern Caribbean Central Bank, established to promote economic cooperation among the member nations.

[3]Francs issued by the African Financial Community (Communauté Financière Africaine), established to promote economic cooperation among the member nations.

[4]Now a subdivision in name only.

2 : a person who attempts to stir up or spread something that is usually petty or discreditable — usually used in combination ⟨war*monger*⟩

²monger *transitive verb* **mon·gered; mon·ger·ing** \-g(ə-)riŋ\ (circa 1864)
: PEDDLE

mon·go \ˈmäŋ-(ˌ)gō\ *noun, plural* **mongo** [Mongolian *möngö*] (1935)
— see *tugrik* at MONEY table

Mon·gol \ˈmäŋ-gəl; ˈmän-ˌgōl, ˈmäŋ-\ *noun* [Mongolian *mongyol*] (1698)
1 : a member of any of a group of traditionally pastoral peoples of Mongolia
2 : MONGOLIAN 1
3 : a person of Mongoloid racial stock
4 *often not capitalized* **:** one affected with Down's syndrome
— Mongol *adjective*

¹Mon·go·lian \män-ˈgōl-yən, mäŋ-, -ˈgō-lē-ən\ *adjective* (1706)
1 : of, relating to, or constituting Mongolia, the Mongolian People's Republic, the Mongols, or Mongolian
2 : MONGOLOID 2

²Mongolian *noun* (1846)
1 a : the language of the Mongol people **b :** a family of Altaic languages that includes the languages of the Mongols and the Kalmucks
2 a : MONGOL 1 **b :** a person of Mongoloid racial stock **c :** a native or inhabitant of Mongolia

Mongolian gerbil *noun* (1948)
: a gerbil (*Meriones unguiculatus*) of Mongolia and northern China that has an external resemblance to a rat, has a high capacity for temperature regulation, and is used as an experimental laboratory animal

Mon·gol·ic \män-ˈgä-lik, mäŋ-\ *adjective* (1834)
: MONGOLOID 1

mon·gol·ism \ˈmäŋ-gə-ˌli-zəm\ *noun* (1900)
: DOWN'S SYNDROME

Mon·gol·oid \ˈmäŋ-gə-ˌlȯid\ *adjective* (1868)
1 : of, constituting, or characteristic of a major racial stock native to Asia as classified according to physical features (as the presence of an epicanthic fold) that includes peoples of northern and eastern Asia, Malaysians, Eskimos, and often American Indians
2 *often not capitalized* **:** of, relating to, or affected with Down's syndrome
— Mongoloid *noun*

mon·goose \ˈmän-ˌgüs, ˈmäŋ-\ *noun, plural* **mon·goos·es** *also* **mon·geese** \-ˌgēs\ [Hindi & Marathi *māgūs*, from Prakrit *maṁgūsa*] (1698)
: any of the viverrid mammals that comprise two subfamilies (Herpestinae and Galidiinae) often grouped in a separate family (Herpestidae), that include agile ferret-

mongoose

sized mammals sometimes with bands or stripes, and that feed on small animals and fruits

mon·grel \ˈmäŋ-grəl, ˈməŋ-\ *noun* [Middle English, probably from *mong* mixture, short for *ymong*, from Old English *gemong* crowd — more at AMONG] (15th century)
1 : an individual resulting from the interbreeding of diverse breeds or strains; *especially* **:** one of unknown ancestry
2 : a cross between types of persons or things
— mongrel *adjective*
— mon·grel·i·za·tion \ˌmäŋ-grə-lə-ˈzā-shən, ˌməŋ-\ *noun*
— mon·grel·ize \ˈmäŋ-grə-ˌlīz, ˈməŋ-\ *transitive verb*

monies *plural of* MONEY

mon·i·ker *also* **mon·ick·er** \ˈmä-ni-kər\ *noun* [probably from Shelta (language of Irish itinerants) *mŭnnik*, modification of Irish *ainm*] (1851)
: NAME, NICKNAME

mo·ni·li·a·sis \ˌmō-nə-ˈlī-ə-səs, ˌmä-\ *noun, plural* **-a·ses** \-ˌsēz\ [New Latin, from *Monilia*, genus of fungi, from Latin *monile* necklace] (1920)
: CANDIDIASIS

mo·nil·i·form \mə-ˈni-lə-ˌfȯrm\ *adjective* [Latin *monile* necklace — more at MANE] (circa 1803)
: jointed or constricted at regular intervals so as to resemble a string of beads ⟨a *moniliform* root⟩ ⟨*moniliform* insect antennae⟩

mon·ish \ˈmä-nish\ *transitive verb* [Middle English *monesen*, alteration of *monesten*, from Old French *monester*, from (assumed) Vulgar Latin *monestare*, from Latin *monēre* to warn] (14th century)
: WARN

mo·nism \ˈmō-ˌni-zəm, ˈmä-\ *noun* [German *Monismus*, from *mon-* + *-ismus* -ism] (1862)
1 a : a view that there is only one kind of ultimate substance **b :** the view that reality is one unitary organic whole with no independent parts
2 : MONOGENESIS
3 : a viewpoint or theory that reduces all phenomena to one principle
— mo·nist \ˈmō-nist, ˈmä-\ *noun*
— mo·nis·tic \mō-ˈnis-tik, mä-\ *adjective*

mo·ni·tion \mō-ˈni-shən, mə-\ *noun* [Middle English *monicioun*, from Middle French *monition*, from Latin *monition-, monitio*, from *monēre*] (14th century)
1 : WARNING, CAUTION
2 : an intimation of danger

¹mon·i·tor \ˈmä-nə-tər\ *noun* [Latin, one that warns, overseer, from *monēre* to warn — more at MIND] (1546)
1 a : a student appointed to assist a teacher **b :** one that warns or instructs **c :** one that monitors or is used in monitoring: as (1) **:** a cathode-ray tube used for display (as of television pictures or computer information) (2) **:** a device for observing a biological condition or function ⟨a heart *monitor*⟩
2 : any of various large tropical Old World lizards (genus *Varanus* of the family Varanidae) closely related to the iguanas
3 [*Monitor*, first ship of the type] **a :** a heavily armored warship formerly used in coastal operations having a very low freeboard and one or more revolving gun turrets **b :** a small modern warship with shallow draft for coastal bombardment
4 : a raised central portion of a roof having low windows or louvers for providing light and air
— mon·i·to·ri·al \ˌmä-nə-ˈtōr-ē-əl, -ˈtȯr-\ *adjective*
— mon·i·tor·ship \ˈmä-nə-tər-ˌship\ *noun*

²monitor *transitive verb* **mon·i·tored; mon·i·tor·ing** \ˈmä-nə-t(ə-)riŋ\ (1924)
: to watch, keep track of, or check usually for a special purpose

¹mon·i·to·ry \ˈmä-nə-ˌtōr-ē, -ˌtȯr-\ *adjective* [Middle English, from Latin *monitorius*, from *monēre*] (15th century)
: giving admonition **:** WARNING

²monitory *noun, plural* **-ries** (15th century)
: a letter containing an admonition or warning

¹monk \ˈməŋk\ *noun* [Middle English, from Old English *munuc*, from Late Latin *monachus*, from Late Greek *monachos*, from Greek, adjective, single, from *monos* single, alone] (before 12th century)
: a man who is a member of a religious order and lives in a monastery; *also* **:** FRIAR

²monk *noun* (1843)
: MONKEY

monk·ery \ˈməŋ-kə-rē\ *noun, plural* **-er·ies** (1536)
1 : monastic life or practice **:** MONASTICISM

2 : a monastic house **:** MONASTERY

¹mon·key \ˈməŋ-kē\ *noun, plural* **monkeys** [probably of Low German origin; akin to *Moneke*, name of an ape, probably of Romance origin; akin to Old Spanish *mona* monkey] (circa 1530)
1 : a nonhuman primate mammal with the exception usually of the lemurs and tarsiers; *especially* **:** any of the smaller longer-tailed primates as contrasted with the apes
2 a : a person resembling a monkey **b :** a ludicrous figure **:** DUPE
3 : any of various machines, implements, or vessels; *especially* **:** the falling weight of a pile driver
4 : a desperate desire for or addiction to drugs — often used in the phrase *monkey on one's back; broadly* **:** a persistent or annoying encumbrance or problem

²monkey *verb* **mon·keyed; mon·key·ing** (1859)
transitive verb
: MIMIC, MOCK
intransitive verb
1 : to act in a grotesque or mischievous manner
2 a : FOOL, TRIFLE — often used with *around*
b : TAMPER — usually used with *with*

monkey bars *noun plural* (1955)
: a three-dimensional framework of horizontal and vertical bars from which children can hang and swing

monkey business *noun* (1883)
: SHENANIGAN 2

monkey jacket *noun* (1830)
: MESS JACKET

mon·key·pod \ˈməŋ-kē-ˌpäd\ *noun* (1888)
1 : an ornamental tropical leguminous tree (*Samanea saman* synonym *Pithecolobium saman*) that has bipinnate leaves, globose clusters of flowers with crimson stamens, sweet-pulp pods eaten by cattle, and wood used in carving — called also *rain tree*
2 : the wood of a monkeypod

monkey puzzle *noun* (1866)
: a tall araucaria (*Araucaria araucana*) that is native to Chile and western Argentina but widely grown elsewhere — called also *monkey puzzle tree*

mon·key·shine \ˈməŋ-kē-ˌshīn\ *noun* (circa 1832)
: PRANK — usually used in plural

monkey wrench *noun* (circa 1858)
1 : a wrench with one fixed and one adjustable jaw at right angles to a straight handle
2 : something that disrupts ⟨threw a *monkey wrench* into the peace negotiations⟩

monk·fish \ˈməŋk-ˌfish\ *noun* (1666)
: either of two goosefishes (*Lophius americanus* of America and *L. piscatorius* of Europe) used for food

Mon–Khmer \ˌmōn-kə-ˈmer\ *noun* (1887)
: a language family containing Mon, Khmer, and a number of other languages of southeast Asia

monk·hood \ˈməŋk-ˌhud\ *noun* (before 12th century)
1 : the character, condition, or profession of a monk **:** MONASTICISM
2 : monks as a class

monk·ish \ˈməŋ-kish\ *adjective* (1546)
1 : of, relating to, or resembling a monk; *also* **:** resembling that of a monk
2 : inclined to disciplinary self-denial

monk's cloth *noun* (circa 1847)
: a coarse heavy fabric in basket weave made originally of worsted and used for monk's habits but now chiefly of cotton or linen and used for draperies

monk seal *noun* (1841)
: any of a genus (*Monachus*) of hair seals of Hawaii, the Mediterranean Sea, and formerly the Caribbean Sea

monks·hood \ˈməŋ(k)s-ˌhud\ *noun* (1578)
: any of a genus (*Aconitum*) of usually bluish flowered poisonous herbs of the buttercup

family; *especially* **:** a poisonous Eurasian herb (*A. napellus*) often cultivated for its showy terminal racemes of white or purplish flowers — compare WOLFSBANE

¹mo·no \'mä-(,)nō\ *noun, plural* **mon·os** [²*mono*] (1959)
: monophonic reproduction

²mono *adjective* (1961)
: MONOPHONIC 2

³mono *noun* (1962)
: INFECTIOUS MONONUCLEOSIS

mono- — see MON-

mono·ac·id \,mä-nō-'a-səd\ *noun* (1863)
: an acid having only one acid hydrogen atom

mono·ac·id·ic \-ə-'si-dik\ *adjective* (circa 1929)
: able to react with one molecule of a monobasic acid to form a salt or ester — used especially of bases

mono·amine \,mä-nō-ə-'mēn\ *noun* [International Scientific Vocabulary] (1951)
: an amine RNH₂ that has one organic substituent attached to the nitrogen atom; *especially* **:** one (as serotonin) that is functionally important in neural transmission

monoamine oxidase *noun* (1951)
: an enzyme that deaminates monoamines oxidatively and that functions in the nervous system by breaking down monoamine neurotransmitters oxidatively

mono·am·in·er·gic \,mä-nō-,a-mə-'nər-jik\ *adjective* (1966)
: liberating or involving monoamines (as serotonin or norepinephrine) in neural transmission ⟨*monoaminergic* neurons⟩ ⟨*monoaminergic* mechanisms⟩

mono·ba·sic \,mä-nə-'bā-sik\ *adjective* [International Scientific Vocabulary] (1842)
of an acid **:** having only one replaceable hydrogen atom

mono·car·box·yl·ic \-,kär-(,)bäk-'si-lik\ *adjective* (circa 1909)
: containing one carboxyl group ⟨acetic acid is a *monocarboxylic* acid⟩

mono·car·pic \-'kär-pik\ *adjective* [probably from (assumed) New Latin *monocarpicus*, from New Latin *mon-* + *-carpicus* -carpic] (1849)
: bearing fruit but once and then dying

mono·cha·si·um \-'kä-zē-əm, -zhē-\ *noun, plural* **-sia** \-zē-ə, -zhē-\ [New Latin, from *mon-* + *-chasium* (as in *dichasium*)] (circa 1890)
: a cymose inflorescence that produces only one main axis
— **mono·cha·sial** \-zē-əl, -zhē-\ *adjective*

mono·chord \'mä-nə-,kòrd\ *noun* [Middle English *monocorde*, from Middle French, from Medieval Latin *monochordum*, from Greek *monochordon*, from *mon-* + *chordē* string — more at YARN] (15th century)
: an instrument of ancient origin for measuring and demonstrating the mathematical relations of musical tones and that consists of a single string stretched over a sound box and a movable bridge set on a graduated scale

mono·chro·mat \'mä-nə-krō-,mat, ,mä-nə-'\ *noun* [*mon-* + Greek *chrōmat-, chrōma*] (1902)
: a completely color-blind individual

mono·chro·mat·ic \,mä-nə-krō-'ma-tik\ *adjective* [Latin *monochromatos*, from Greek *monochrōmatos*, from *mon-* + *chrōmat-, chrōma* color] (1822)
1 a : having or consisting of one color or hue **b :** MONOCHROME 2
2 : consisting of radiation of a single wavelength or of a very small range of wavelengths
3 : of, relating to, or exhibiting monochromatism
— **mono·chro·mat·i·cal·ly** \-ti-k(ə-)lē\ *adverb*
— **mono·chro·ma·tic·i·ty** \-,krō-mə-'ti-sə-tē\ *noun*

mono·chro·ma·tism \-'krō-mə-,ti-zəm\ *noun* (circa 1930)
: complete color blindness in which all colors appear as shades of gray

mono·chro·ma·tor \,mä-nə-'krō-,mā-tər\ *noun* [*monochromat*ic + *illuminat*or] (1909)
: a device for isolating a narrow portion of a spectrum

¹mono·chrome \'mä-nə-,krōm\ *noun* [Medieval Latin *monochroma*, from Latin, feminine of *monochromos* of one color, from Greek *monochrōmos*, from *mon-* + *-chrōmos* -chrome] (1662)
: a painting, drawing, or photograph in a single hue
— **mono·chro·mic** \,mä-nə-'krō-mik\ *adjective*
— **mono·chrom·ist** \'mä-nə-,krō-mist\ *noun*

²monochrome *adjective* (1849)
1 : of, relating to, or made with a single color or hue
2 : involving or producing visual images in a single color or in varying tones of a single color or (as gray) ⟨*monochrome* film⟩ ⟨*monochrome* television monitor⟩

mon·o·cle \'mä-ni-kəl\ *noun* [French, from Late Latin *monoculus* having one eye, from Latin *mon-* + *oculus* eye — more at EYE] (circa 1858)
: an eyeglass for one eye
— **mon·o·cled** \-kəld\ *adjective*

mono·cline \'mä-nə-,klīn\ *noun* (1879)
: an oblique geologic fold

mono·clin·ic \,mä-nə-'kli-nik\ *adjective* [International Scientific Vocabulary] (circa 1864)
: having one oblique intersection of the crystallographic axes

monocle

monoclinic system *noun* (1869)
: a crystal system characterized by three unequal axes with one oblique intersection

mono·clo·nal \,mä-nə-'klō-nᵊl\ *adjective* (1914)
: produced by, being, or composed of cells derived from a single cell ⟨*monoclonal* antibodies⟩ ⟨a *monoclonal* tumor⟩
— **monoclonal** *noun*

mono·coque \,mä-nə-,kōk, -,käk\ *noun* [French, from *mon-* + *coque* shell, probably from Latin *coccum* kermes — more at COCOON] (1913)
1 : a type of construction (as of a fuselage) in which the outer skin carries all or a major part of the stresses
2 : a type of vehicle construction (as of an automobile) in which the body is integral with the chassis

mono·cot \-,kät\ *noun* (1890)
: MONOCOTYLEDON

mono·cot·y·le·don \,mä-nə-,kä-tᵊl-'ē-dᵊn\ *noun* [ultimately from New Latin *mon-* + *cotyledon* cotyledon] (circa 1727)
: any of a class or subclass (Liliopsida or Monocotyledoneae) of chiefly herbaceous seedplants having an embryo with a single cotyledon, usually parallel-veined leaves, and floral organs arranged in cycles of three — compare DICOTYLEDON
— **mono·cot·y·le·don·ous** \-dᵊn-əs\ *adjective*

mo·noc·ra·cy \mä-'nä-krə-sē, mə-\ *noun* (1651)
: government by a single person
— **mono·crat** \'mä-nə-,krat\ *noun*
— **mono·crat·ic** \,mä-nə-'kra-tik\ *adjective*

mono·crys·tal \'mä-nə-,kris-tᵊl\ *noun* (1926)
: a single crystal
— **monocrystal** *adjective*
— **mono·crys·tal·line** \,mä-nə-'kris-tə-lən *also* -,līn, -,lēn\ *adjective*

¹mon·oc·u·lar \mä-'nä-kyə-lər, mə-\ *adjective* [Late Latin *monoculus* having one eye] (1640)
1 : of, involving, or affecting a single eye

2 : suitable for use with only one eye
— **mon·oc·u·lar·ly** *adverb*

²monocular *noun* (1936)
: a monocular device

mono·cul·ture \'mä-nə-,kəl-chər\ *noun* (1915)
1 : the cultivation or growth of a single crop or organism especially on agricultural or forest land
2 : a crop or a population of a single kind of organism grown on land in monoculture
— **mono·cul·tur·al** \,mä-nə-'kəlch-rəl, -'kəl-chə-\ *adjective*

mono·cy·clic \,mä-nə-'sī-klik, -'si-\ *adjective* [International Scientific Vocabulary] (1910)
: containing one ring in the molecular structure

mono·cyte \'mä-nə-,sīt\ *noun* [International Scientific Vocabulary] (circa 1913)
: a large white blood cell with finely granulated chromatin dispersed throughout the nucleus that is formed in the bone marrow, enters the blood, and migrates into the connective tissue where it differentiates into a macrophage
— **mono·cyt·ic** \,mä-nə-'si-tik\ *adjective*

mono·dis·perse \,mä-nō-dis-'pərs\ *adjective* [*mon-* + *disperse*, adjective, from *disperse*, verb] (1925)
: characterized by particles of uniform size in a dispersed phase

mon·o·dist \'mä-nə-dist\ *noun* (1751)
: a writer, singer, or composer of monody

mono·dra·ma \'mä-nə-,drä-mə, -,dra-\ *noun* (1793)
: a drama acted or designed to be acted by a single person
— **mono·dra·mat·ic** \,mä-nə-drə-'ma-tik\ *adjective*

mon·o·dy \'mä-nə-dē\ *noun, plural* **-dies** [Medieval Latin *monodia*, from Greek *monōidia*, from *monōidos* singing alone, from *mon-* + *aeidein* to sing — more at ODE] (circa 1623)
1 : an ode sung by one voice (as in a Greek tragedy)
2 : an elegy or dirge performed by one person
3 a : a monophonic vocal piece **b :** the monophonic style of 17th century opera
— **mo·nod·ic** \mə-'nä-dik\ *or* **mo·nod·i·cal** \-di-kəl\ *adjective*
— **mo·nod·i·cal·ly** \-di-k(ə-)lē\ *adverb*

mon·oe·cious \mə-'nē-shəs, mä-\ *adjective* [ultimately from Greek *mon-* + *oikos* house — more at VICINITY] (1753)
1 : having pistillate and staminate flowers on the same plant
2 : having male and female sex organs in the same individual **:** HERMAPHRODITIC

mon·oe·cism \-'nē-,si-zəm\ *noun* (1875)
: the condition of being monoecious

mono·es·ter \,mä-nō-,es-tər\ *noun* (1927)
: an ester (as of a dibasic acid) that contains only one ester group

mono·fil·a·ment \,mä-nə-'fi-lə-mənt\ *noun* (1940)
: a single untwisted synthetic filament (as of nylon)

mo·nog·a·mist \mə-'nä-gə-mist\ *noun* (1651)
: one who practices or upholds monogamy

mo·nog·a·my \-mē\ *noun* [French *monogamie*, from Late Latin *monogamia*, from Greek, from *monogamos* monogamous, from *mon-* + *gamos* marriage, from *gamein* to marry] (1612)
1 *archaic* **:** the practice of marrying only once during a lifetime
2 : the state or custom of being married to one person at a time

3 : the condition or practice of having a single mate during a period of time ⟨*monogamy* is common among birds⟩
— **mo·nog·a·mous** \mə-'nä-gə-məs\ *also* **mono·gam·ic** \ˌmä-nə-'ga-mik\ *adjective*
— **mo·nog·a·mous·ly** *adverb*

mono·gas·tric \ˌmä-nə-'gas-trik\ *adjective* (1814)
: having a stomach with only a single compartment ⟨swine, chicks, and human beings are *monogastric*⟩

mono·ge·ne·an \-'jē-nē-ən\ *noun* [New Latin *Monogenea*, group name] (1899)
: a monogenetic trematode
— **monogenean** *adjective*

mono·gen·e·sis \-'je-nə-səs\ *noun* [New Latin] (circa 1859)
: origin of diverse individuals or kinds (as of language) by descent from a single ancestral individual or kind

mono·ge·net·ic \-jə-'ne-tik\ *adjective* (1873)
1 : relating to or involving monogenesis
2 : of, relating to, or being any of a subclass (Monogenea) of trematode worms that ordinarily live as ectoparasites on a single host (as a fish or amphibian) throughout their entire life cycle

mono·gen·ic \-'je-nik\ *adjective* [International Scientific Vocabulary] (1939)
: of, relating to, or controlled by a single gene and especially by either of an allelic pair
— **mono·gen·i·cal·ly** \-ni-k(ə-)lē\ *adverb*

mono·germ \'mä-nə-ˌjərm\ *adjective* [mon- + *germinate*] (1950)
: producing or being a fruit that gives rise to a single plant ⟨a *monogerm* sugar beet⟩

mono·glot \-ˌglät\ *adjective* [mono- + -glot (as in *polyglot*)] (1830)
: MONOLINGUAL
— **monoglot** *noun*

mono·glyc·er·ide \ˌmä-nə-'gli-sə-ˌrīd\ *noun* (1860)
: any of various esters of glycerol in which only one of the three hydroxyl groups is esterified and which are often used as emulsifiers

¹mono·gram \'mä-nə-ˌgram\ *noun* [Late Latin *monogramma*, from Greek *mon-* + *gramma* letter — more at GRAM] (circa 1696)
: a sign of identity usually formed of the combined initials of a name
— **mono·gram·mat·ic** \ˌmä-nə-grə-'ma-tik\ *adjective*

²monogram *transitive verb* **-grammed; -gram·ming** (1868)
: to mark with a monogram
— **mono·gram·mer** \-ˌgra-mər\ *noun*

¹mono·graph \'mä-nə-ˌgraf\ *noun* (1821)
: a learned treatise on a small area of learning; *also* **:** a written account of a single thing
— **mono·graph·ic** \ˌmä-nə-'gra-fik\ *adjective*

²monograph *transitive verb* (1876)
: to write a monograph on

mo·nog·y·nous \mə-'nä-jə-nəs, mä-\ *adjective* (circa 1890)
: of, relating to, or living in monogyny

mo·nog·y·ny \-nē\ *noun* [International Scientific Vocabulary] (1876)
: the state or custom of having only one wife at a time

mono·hull \'mä-nə-ˌhəl\ *noun* (1967)
: a vessel (as a sailboat) with a single hull — compare MULTIHULL

mono·hy·brid \ˌmä-nō-'hī-brəd\ *noun* (1903)
: an individual or strain heterozygous for one specified gene
— **monohybrid** *adjective*

mono·hy·dric \-'hī-drik\ *adjective* (1880)
: MONOHYDROXY

mono·hy·droxy \-(ˌ)hī-'dräk-sē\ *adjective* [International Scientific Vocabulary *monohydroxy-*, from mon- + hydroxy-] (circa 1934)
: containing one hydroxyl group in the molecule

mono·lay·er \'mä-nō-ˌlā-ər, -ˌle(-ə)r\ *noun* (1926)

: a single continuous layer or film that is one cell or molecule in thickness

mono·lin·gual \ˌmä-nə-'liŋ-gwəl, ˌmō-, -'liŋ-gyə-wəl\ *adjective* (1926)
: knowing or using only one language
— **monolingual** *noun*

mono·lith \'mä-nᵊl-ˌith\ *noun* [French *monolithe*, from *monolithe* consisting of a single stone, from Latin *monolithus*, from Greek *monolithos*, from mon- + *lithos* stone] (1848)
1 : a single great stone often in the form of an obelisk or column
2 : a massive structure
3 : an organized whole that acts as a single unified powerful or influential force

mono·lith·ic \ˌmä-nᵊl-'i-thik\ *adjective* (1825)
1 a : of, relating to, or resembling a monolith **:** HUGE, MASSIVE **b** (1) **:** formed from a single crystal ⟨a *monolithic* silicon chip⟩ (2) **:** produced in or on a monolithic chip ⟨a *monolithic* circuit⟩
2 a : cast as a single piece ⟨a *monolithic* concrete wall⟩ **b :** formed or composed of material without joints or seams ⟨a *monolithic* floor covering⟩ ⟨a *monolithic* furnace lining⟩ **c :** consisting of or constituting a single unit
3 a : constituting a massive undifferentiated and often rigid whole ⟨a *monolithic* society⟩ **b :** exhibiting or characterized by often rigidly fixed uniformity ⟨*monolithic* party unity⟩
— **mono·lith·i·cal·ly** \-thi-k(ə-)lē\ *adverb*

mono·logue *also* **mono·log** \'mä-nᵊl-ˌȯg, -ˌäg\ *noun* [Middle French *monologue*, from mon- + *-logue*] (1549)
1 a : SOLILOQUY **2 b :** a dramatic sketch performed by one actor **c :** the routine of a stand-up comic
2 : a literary composition written in the form of a soliloquy
3 : a long speech monopolizing conversation
— **mono·logu·ist** \-ˌȯ-gist, -ˌä-\ *or* **mo·nol·o·gist** \same *or* mə-'nä-lə-jist, -gist\ *noun*

mono·ma·nia \ˌmä-nə-'mā-nē-ə, -nyə\ *noun* [New Latin] (1823)
1 : mental illness especially when limited in expression to one idea or area of thought
2 : excessive concentration on a single object or idea
— **mono·ma·ni·ac** \-nē-ˌak\ *noun or adjective*
— **mono·ma·ni·a·cal** \-mə-'nī-ə-kəl\ *adjective*
— **mono·ma·ni·a·cal·ly** \-k(ə-)lē\ *adverb*

mono·mer \'mä-nə-mər\ *noun* [International Scientific Vocabulary] (1914)
: a chemical compound that can undergo polymerization
— **mo·no·mer·ic** \ˌmä-nə-'mer-ik, ˌmō-\ *adjective*

mono·me·tal·lic \ˌmä-nō-mə-'ta-lik\ *adjective* (1877)
1 : of or relating to monometallism
2 : consisting of or employing one metal

mono·met·al·lism \-'me-tᵊl-ˌi-zəm\ *noun* [International Scientific Vocabulary mon- + -metallism (as in *bimetallism*)] (1879)
: the adoption of one metal only in a currency
— **mono·met·al·list** \-tᵊl-ist\ *noun*

mo·nom·e·ter \mə-'nä-mə-tər, mä-\ *noun* [Late Latin, from Greek *monometros*, from mon- + *metron* measure — more at MEASURE] (circa 1846)
: a line of verse consisting of a single metrical foot or dipody

mo·no·mi·al \mä-'nō-mē-əl, mə-\ *noun* [blend of mon- and -nomial (as in *binomial*)] (circa 1706)
1 : a mathematical expression consisting of a single term
2 : a taxonomic name consisting of a single word or term
— **monomial** *adjective*

mono·mo·lec·u·lar \ˌmä-nə-mə-'le-kyə-lər\ *adjective* (1917)

: being only one molecule thick ⟨a *monomolecular* film⟩
— **mono·mo·lec·u·lar·ly** *adverb*

mono·mor·phe·mic \-mȯr-'fē-mik\ *adjective* (1936)
: consisting of only one morpheme ⟨the word *talk* is *monomorphemic* but *talked* is not⟩

mono·mor·phic \-'mȯr-fik\ *adjective* (circa 1879)
: having but a single form, structural pattern, or genotype ⟨a *monomorphic* species of insect⟩
— **mono·mor·phism** \-ˌfi-zəm\ *noun*

mono·nu·cle·ar \-'nü-klē-ər, -'nyü-, ÷-kyə-lər\ *adjective* [International Scientific Vocabulary] (1886)
: having only one nucleus ⟨a *mononuclear* cell⟩
— **mononuclear** *noun*

mono·nu·cle·at·ed \-'nü-klē-ˌā-təd, -'nyü-\ *also* **mono·nu·cle·ate** \-klē-ət, -ˌāt\ *adjective* (1890)
: MONONUCLEAR

mono·nu·cle·o·sis \-ˌnü-klē-'ō-səs, -ˌnyü-\ *noun* [New Latin, from International Scientific Vocabulary *mononuclear* + New Latin *-osis*] (1920)
: an abnormal increase of mononuclear white blood cells in the blood; *specifically* **:** INFECTIOUS MONONUCLEOSIS

mono·nu·cle·o·tide \-'nü-klē-ə-ˌtīd, -'nyü-\ *noun* (1908)
: a nucleotide that is derived from one molecule each of a nitrogenous base, a sugar, and a phosphoric acid

mo·noph·a·gous \mə-'nä-fə-gəs, mä-\ *adjective* (circa 1868)
: feeding on or utilizing a single kind of food; *especially* **:** feeding on a single kind of plant or animal
— **mo·noph·a·gy** \-fə-jē\ *noun*

mono·pho·nic \ˌmä-nə-'fä-nik, -'fō-\ *adjective* (circa 1864)
1 : having a single unaccompanied melodic line
2 : of or relating to sound transmission, recording, or reproduction involving a single transmission path
— **mono·pho·ni·cal·ly** \-ni-k(ə-)lē\ *adverb*

mo·noph·o·ny \mə-'nä-fə-nē, mä-\ *noun* (circa 1890)
: monophonic music

mon·oph·thong \'mä-nə(f)-ˌthȯŋ\ *noun* [Late Greek *monophthongos* single vowel, from Greek mon- + *phthongos* sound] (1616)
: a vowel sound that throughout its duration has a single constant articulatory position
— **mon·oph·thon·gal** \ˌmä-nə(f)-'thȯŋ-(g)əl\ *adjective*

mono·phy·let·ic \ˌmä-nō-fī-'le-tik\ *adjective* [International Scientific Vocabulary] (1874)
: of or relating to a single stock; *specifically* **:** developed from a single common ancestral form
— **mono·phy·ly** \'mä-nə-ˌfī-lē\ *noun*

Mo·noph·y·site \mə-'nä-fə-ˌsīt\ *noun* [Medieval Latin *Monophysita*, from Middle Greek *Monophysitēs*, from Greek mon- + *physis* nature — more at PHYSICS] (1698)
: one holding the doctrine that Christ's nature remains altogether divine and not human even though he has taken on an earthly and human body with its cycle of birth, life, and death
— **Monophysite** *or* **Mo·noph·y·sit·ic** \-ˌnä-fə-'si-tik\ *adjective*
— **Mo·noph·y·sit·ism** \-'nä-fə-ˌsī-ˌti-zəm\ *noun*

mono·plane \'mä-nə-ˌplān\ *noun* (1907)
: an airplane with only one main supporting surface

¹mono·ploid \'mä-nə-ˌplȯid\ *adjective* (1928)
1 : HAPLOID
2 : having or being the basic haploid number of chromosomes in a polyploid series of organisms

²monoploid *noun* [International Scientific Vocabulary] (1944)
: a monoploid individual or organism

mono·po·di·al \ˌmä-nə-ˈpō-dē-əl\ *adjective* [New Latin *monopodium* main axis, from *mon-* + *-podium*] (1876)
: having or involving the formation of offshoots from a main axis
— **mono·po·di·al·ly** \-dē-ə-lē\ *adverb*

mono·pole \ˈmä-nə-ˌpōl\ *noun* (1937)
1 : a single positive or negative electrical charge; *also* : a hypothetical north or south magnetic pole existing alone
2 : a radio antenna consisting of a single often straight element

mo·nop·o·lise *British variant of* MONOPOLIZE

mo·nop·o·list \mə-ˈnä-pə-list\ *noun* (1601)
: one who monopolizes
— **mo·nop·o·lis·tic** \-ˌnä-pə-ˈlis-tik\ *adjective*
— **mo·nop·o·lis·ti·cal·ly** \-ti-k(ə-)lē\ *adverb*

mo·nop·o·lize \mə-ˈnä-pə-ˌlīz\ *transitive verb* **-lized; -liz·ing** (1611)
: to get a monopoly of : assume complete possession or control of ⟨*monopolize* a conversation⟩
— **mo·nop·o·li·za·tion** \-ˌnä-pə-lə-ˈzā-shən\ *noun*
— **mo·nop·o·liz·er** \-ˈnä-pə-ˌlī-zər\ *noun*

mo·nop·o·ly \mə-ˈnä-p(ə-)lē\ *noun, plural* **-lies** [Latin *monopolium*, from Greek *monopōlion*, from *mon-* + *pōlein* to sell] (1534)
1 : exclusive ownership through legal privilege, command of supply, or concerted action
2 : exclusive possession or control
3 : a commodity controlled by one party
4 : one that has a monopoly

mono·pro·pel·lant \ˌmä-nō-prə-ˈpe-lənt\ *noun* (circa 1945)
: a rocket propellant containing both the fuel and the oxidizer in a single substance

mo·nop·so·ny \mə-ˈnäp-sə-nē\ *noun, plural* **-nies** [*mon-* + *-opsony* (as in *oligopsony*)] (1933)
: an oligopsony limited to one buyer
— **mo·nop·so·nis·tic** \-ˌnäp-sə-ˈnis-tik\ *adjective*

mono·rail \ˈmä-nə-ˌrāl\ *noun* (1897)
: a single rail serving as a track for a wheeled vehicle; *also* : a vehicle traveling on such a track

monorail

mon·or·chid \mä-ˈnȯr-kəd\ *noun* [irregular from Greek *mon-orchis*, from *mon-* + *orchis* testicle — more at ORCHIS] (1874)
: an individual who has only one testis or only one descended into the scrotum
— **monorchid** *adjective*
— **mon·or·chi·dism** \-kə-ˌdi-zəm\ *noun*

mono·rhyme \ˈmä-nə-ˌrīm\ *noun* (1731)
: a strophe or poem in which all the lines have the same end rhyme
— **mono·rhymed** \-ˌrīmd\ *adjective*

mono·sac·cha·ride \ˌmä-nə-ˈsa-kə-ˌrīd\ *noun* [International Scientific Vocabulary] (1896)
: a sugar not decomposable to simpler sugars by hydrolysis

mono·so·di·um glu·ta·mate \ˌmä-nə-ˌsō-dē-əm-ˈglü-tə-ˌmāt\ *noun* (1929)
: a crystalline salt $C_5H_8O_4NaN$ used to enhance the flavor of food — abbreviation *MSG*

mono·some \ˈmä-nə-ˌsōm\ *noun* (circa 1909)
1 : a chromosome lacking a synaptic mate; *especially* : an unpaired X chromosome
2 : a single ribosome

mono·so·mic \ˌmä-nə-ˈsō-mik\ *adjective* (1926)
: having one less than the diploid number of chromosomes
— **monosomic** *noun*

mono·so·my \ˈmä-nə-ˌsō-mē\ *noun*

mono·spe·cif·ic \ˌmä-nō-spə-ˈsi-fik\ *adjective* (1947)
: specific for a single antigen or receptor site on an antigen
— **mono·spec·i·fic·i·ty** \-ˌspe-sə-ˈfi-sə-tē\ *noun*

mono·stele \ˈmä-nə-ˌstēl, ˌmä-nə-ˈstē-lē\ *noun* (circa 1900)
: PROTOSTELE
— **mono·ste·lic** \ˌmä-nə-ˈstē-lik\ *adjective*
— **mono·ste·ly** \ˈmä-nə-ˌstē-lē\ *noun*

mono·syl·lab·ic \ˌmä-nə-sə-ˈla-bik\ *adjective* [probably from French *monosyllabique*, from *monosyllabe*] (1768)
1 : consisting of one syllable or of monosyllables
2 : using or speaking only monosyllables
3 : conspicuously brief in answering or commenting : TERSE
— **mono·syl·lab·i·cal·ly** \-bi-k(ə-)lē\ *adverb*
— **mono·syl·la·bic·i·ty** \-ˌsi-lə-ˈbi-sə-tē\ *noun*

mono·syl·la·ble \ˈmä-nə-ˌsi-lə-bəl, ˌmä-nə-ˈ\ *noun* [modification of Middle French or Late Latin; Middle French *monosyllabe*, from Late Latin *monosyllabon*, from Greek, from neuter of *monosyllabos* having one syllable, from *mon-* + *syllabē* syllable] (1533)
: a word of one syllable

mono·syn·ap·tic \ˌmä-nō-sə-ˈnap-tik\ *adjective* (1942)
: having or involving a single neural synapse
— **mono·syn·ap·ti·cal·ly** \-ti-k(ə-)lē\ *adverb*

mono·ter·pene \ˌmä-nə-ˈtər-ˌpēn\ *noun* (circa 1959)
: any of a class of terpenes $C_{10}H_{16}$ containing two isoprene units per molecule; *also* : a derivative of a monoterpene

mono·the·ism \ˈmä-nə-(ˌ)thē-ˌi-zəm\ *noun* (1660)
: the doctrine or belief that there is but one God
— **mono·the·ist** \-ˌthē-ist\ *noun*
— **mono·the·is·tic** \ˌmä-nə-thē-ˈis-tik\ *also* **mono·the·is·ti·cal** \-ti-kəl\ *adjective*
— **mono·the·is·ti·cal·ly** \-ti-k(ə-)lē\ *adverb*

¹mono·tone \ˈmä-nə-ˌtōn\ *noun* [Greek *monotonos* monotonous] (1644)
1 : a succession of syllables, words, or sentences in one unvaried key or pitch
2 : a single unvaried musical tone
3 : a tedious sameness or reiteration
4 : a person unable to produce or to distinguish between musical intervals

²monotone *adjective* (1769)
1 : MONOTONIC 2
2 : having a uniform color

mono·ton·ic \ˌmä-nə-ˈtä-nik\ *adjective* (1797)
1 : characterized by the use of or uttered in a monotone
2 : having the property either of never increasing or of never decreasing as the values of the independent variable or the subscripts of the terms increase ⟨*monotonic* functions⟩ ⟨a *monotonic* sequence⟩
— **mono·ton·i·cal·ly** \-ni-k(ə-)lē\ *adverb*
— **mono·to·nic·i·ty** \ˌmä-nə-tō-ˈni-sə-tē\ *noun*

mo·not·o·nous \mə-ˈnä-tᵊn-əs, -ˈnät-nəs\ *adjective* [Greek *monotonos*, from *mon-* + *tonos* tone] (1778)
1 : uttered or sounded in one unvarying tone
: marked by a sameness of pitch and intensity
2 : tediously uniform or unvarying
— **mo·not·o·nous·ly** *adverb*
— **mo·not·o·nous·ness** *noun*

mo·not·o·ny \mə-ˈnä-tᵊn-ē, -ˈnät-nē\ *noun* (1706)
1 : tedious sameness
2 : sameness of tone or sound

mono·treme \ˈmä-nə-ˌtrēm\ *noun* [New Latin *Monotremata*, from Greek *mon-* + *trēmat-, trēma* hole — more at TREMATODE] (1835)
: any of an order (Monotremata) of egg-laying mammals comprising the platypuses and echidnas

mono·type \ˈmä-nə-ˌtīp\ *noun* (1882)
: an impression on paper of a design painted usually with the finger or a brush on a surface (as glass)

Monotype *trademark*
— used for a keyboard typesetting machine that casts and sets type in separate characters

mono·typ·ic \ˌmä-nə-ˈti-pik\ *adjective* [*mon-* + *type* + *-ic*] (circa 1859)
: including a single representative — used especially of a genus with only one species

mono·un·sat·u·rat·ed \ˌmä-nō-ˌən-ˈsa-chə-ˌrā-təd\ *adjective* (circa 1939)
: containing one double or triple bond per molecule — used especially of an oil or fatty acid; compare POLYUNSATURATED
— **mono·un·sat·u·rate** \-ˈsa-chə-rət\ *noun*

mono·va·lent \ˌmä-nə-ˈvā-lənt\ *adjective* [International Scientific Vocabulary] (1869)
1 : having a valence of one
2 : containing antibodies specific for or antigens of a single strain of a microorganism ⟨a *monovalent* vaccine⟩

mon·ovu·lar \(ˌ)mä-ˈnäv-yə-lər, -ˈnōv-\ *adjective* (1929)
: MONOZYGOTIC

mon·ox·ide \mə-ˈnäk-ˌsīd\ *noun* [International Scientific Vocabulary] (1869)
: an oxide containing one atom of oxygen in a molecule

mono·zy·got·ic \ˌmä-nə-zī-ˈgä-tik\ *adjective* (1916)
: derived from a single egg ⟨*monozygotic* twins⟩

Mon·roe Doctrine \mən-ˈrō- *also* ˈmən- *or* ˈmän-\ *noun* [James *Monroe*] (1853)
: a statement of U.S. foreign policy expressing opposition to extension of European control or influence in the western hemisphere

mon·sei·gneur \ˌmōⁿ-ˌsān-ˈyər\ *noun, plural* **mes·sei·gneurs** \ˌmā-ˌsān-ˈyər(z)\ [French, literally, my lord] (1602)
: a French dignitary (as a prince or prelate) — used as a title preceding a title of office or rank

mon·sieur \məs-ˈyə(r), məsh-; mə-ˈsir\ *noun, plural* **mes·sieurs** \məs-ˈyə(r)(z), məsh-, mäs-; mə-ˈsir(z)\ [Middle French, literally, my lord] (1512)
: a Frenchman of high rank or station — used as a title equivalent to *Mister* and prefixed to the name of a Frenchman

mon·si·gnor \män-ˈsē-nyər, mən-\ *noun, plural* **monsignors** *or* **mon·si·gno·ri** \ˌmän-ˌsēn-ˈyȯr-ē, -ˈyȯr-\ [Italian *monsignore*, from French *monseigneur*] (1641)
: a Roman Catholic prelate having a dignity or titular distinction (as of domestic prelate or protonotary apostolic) usually conferred by the pope — used as a title prefixed to the surname or to the given name and surname
— **mon·si·gno·ri·al** \ˌmän-ˌsēn-ˈyȯr-ē-əl, -ˈyȯr-\ *adjective*

mon·soon \män-ˈsün, ˈmän-ˌ\ *noun* [obsolete Dutch *monssoen*, from Portuguese *monção*, from Arabic *mawsim* time, season] (1584)
1 : a periodic wind especially in the Indian Ocean and southern Asia
2 : the season of the southwest monsoon in India and adjacent areas that is characterized by very heavy rainfall
3 : rainfall that is associated with the monsoon
— **mon·soon·al** \-ˈsü-nᵊl, -ˌsü-\ *adjective*

\ə\ abut \ᵊ\ kitten \ər\ further \a\ ash \ā\ ace
\ä\ mop, mar \au̇\ out \ch\ chin \e\ bet \ē\ easy
\g\ go \i\ hit \ī\ ice \j\ job \ŋ\ sing \ō\ go
\ȯ\ law \ȯi\ boy \th\ thin \th̠\ the \ü\ loot \u̇\ foot
\y\ yet \zh\ vision *see also* Guide to Pronunciation

mons pu·bis \'mänz-'pyü-bəs\ *noun, plural* **mon·tes pubis** \-'män-tēz-\ [New Latin, pubic eminence] (circa 1903)
: a rounded eminence of fatty tissue upon the pubic symphysis especially of the human female

¹**mon·ster** \'män(t)-stər\ *noun* [Middle English *monstre*, from Middle French, from Latin *monstrum* omen, monster, from *monēre* to warn — more at MIND] (14th century)
1 a : an animal or plant of abnormal form or structure **b :** one who deviates from normal or acceptable behavior or character
2 : a threatening force
3 a : an animal of strange or terrifying shape **b :** one unusually large for its kind
4 : something monstrous; *especially* : a person of unnatural or extreme ugliness, deformity, wickedness, or cruelty
5 : one that is highly successful

²**monster** *adjective* (1837)
: enormous or impressive in size, extent, or numbers

mon·strance \'män(t)-strən(t)s\ *noun* [Middle English *monstrans*, from Middle French *monstrance*, from Medieval Latin *monstrantia*, from Latin *monstrant-*, *monstrans*, present participle of *monstrare* to show, from *monstrum*] (15th century)
: a vessel in which the consecrated Host is exposed for the adoration of the faithful

mon·stros·i·ty \män-'strä-sə-tē\ *noun, plural* **-ties** (15th century)
1 a : a malformation of a plant or animal **b :** something deviating from the normal : FREAK
2 : the quality or state of being monstrous
3 a : an object of great and often frightening size, force, or complexity **b :** an excessively bad or shocking example

monstrance

mon·strous \'män(t)-strəs\ *adjective* (15th century)
1 *obsolete* : STRANGE, UNNATURAL
2 : having extraordinary often overwhelming size : GIGANTIC
3 a : having the qualities or appearance of a monster **b :** teeming with monsters
4 a : extraordinarily ugly or vicious : HORRIBLE **b :** shockingly wrong or ridiculous
5 : deviating greatly from the natural form or character : ABNORMAL
6 : very great — used as an intensive ☆
— **mon·strous·ly** *adverb*
— **mon·strous·ness** *noun*

mons ve·ne·ris \'mänz-'ve-nə-rəs\ *noun, plural* **mon·tes veneris** \'män-,tēz-\ [New Latin, literally, eminence of Venus or of venery] (1621)
: the mons pubis of the human female

mon·ta·dale \'män-tə-,dāl\ *noun* [*Montana* state + *dale*] (1949)
: any of an American breed of white-faced hornless sheep noted for heavy fleece and good meat conformation

¹**mon·tage** \män-'täzh, mōⁿ(n)-, -'tàzh\ *noun* [French, from *monter* to mount] (1929)
1 : the production of a rapid succession of images in a motion picture to illustrate an association of ideas
2 a : a literary, musical, or artistic composite of juxtaposed more or less heterogeneous elements **b :** a composite picture made by combining several separate pictures
3 : a heterogeneous mixture : JUMBLE ⟨a *montage* of emotions⟩

²**montage** *transitive verb* **mon·taged; mon·tag·ing** (1944)
: to combine into or depict in a montage

mon·ta·gnard \,mōⁿ-,tän-'yär(d)\ *noun, often capitalized* [French, mountaineer, from *montagne* mountain, from Old French *montaigne*] (1842)

: a member of any of various peoples inhabiting the highlands of central and southern Vietnam
— **montagnard** *adjective, often capitalized*

Mon·ta·gue \'män-tə-,gyü\ *noun*
: the family of Romeo in Shakespeare's *Romeo and Juliet*

mon·tane \,män-'tān, 'män-,\ *adjective* [Latin *montanus* of a mountain — more at MOUNTAIN] (1863)
1 : of, relating to, growing in, or being the biogeographic zone of relatively moist cool upland slopes below timberline dominated by large coniferous trees
2 : of, relating to, or made up of montane plants or animals

Mon·ta·nist \'män-tⁿn-ist\ *noun* [*Montanus*, 2d century A.D. Phrygian schismatic] (1577)
: an adherent of a Christian sect arising in the late second century and stressing apocalyptic expectations, the continuing prophetic gifts of the Spirit, and strict ascetic discipline
— **Mon·ta·nism** \-tⁿn-,i-zəm\ *noun*

mon·tan wax \'män-tⁿn-\ *noun* [Latin *montanus* of a mountain] (1908)
: a hard brittle mineral wax obtained usually from lignites by extraction and used especially in polishes, carbon paper, and insulating compositions

mon·te \'män-tē\ *noun* [Spanish, bank, mountain, heap, from Italian, from Latin *mont-*, *mons* mountain] (1824)
1 : a card game in which players select any two of four cards turned face up in a layout and bet that one of them will be matched before the other as cards are dealt one at a time from the pack — called also *monte bank*
2 : THREE-CARD MONTE

Mon·te Car·lo \,män-ti-'kär-(,)lō\ *adjective* [*Monte Carlo*, Monaco, famous for its gambling casino] (1949)
: of, relating to, or involving the use of random sampling techniques and often the use of computer simulation to obtain approximate solutions to mathematical or physical problems especially in terms of a range of values each of which has a calculated probability of being the solution ⟨*Monte Carlo* calculations⟩

mon·teith \män-'tēth\ *noun* [*Monteith*, 17th century Scottish eccentric who wore a cloak with a scalloped hem] (1683)
: a large silver punch bowl with scalloped rim

Mon·te·rey cypress \,män-tə-,rā-\ *noun* [*Monterey*, California] (1873)
: a California cypress (*Cupressus macrocarpa*) that is endemic to the Monterey and Carmel seacoast and is often planted for ornament or in a windbreak

Monterey Jack *noun* (circa 1947)
: a semisoft whole-milk cheese with high moisture content

Monterey pine *noun* (1834)
: a pine (*Pinus radiata*) native to coastal California that is widely grown especially in the southern hemisphere for its wood

mon·te·ro \män-'ter-(,)ō\ *noun, plural* **-ros** [Spanish, hunter, from *monte* mountain] (1622)
: a round hunter's cap with ear flaps

Mon·te·zu·ma's revenge \,män-tə-'zü-məz-\ *noun* [*Montezuma* II] (1962)
: diarrhea contracted in Mexico especially by tourists

month \'mən(t)th\ *noun, plural* **months** \'mən(t)s, 'mən(t)ths\ [Middle English, from Old English *mōnath;* akin to Old High German *mānōd* month, Old English *mōna* moon] (before 12th century)
1 : a measure of time corresponding nearly to the period of the moon's revolution and amounting to approximately 4 weeks or 30 days or ¹⁄₁₂ of a year
2 *plural* : an indefinite usually extended period of time ⟨he has been gone for *months*⟩
3 : one ninth of the typical duration of human pregnancy ⟨she was in her eighth *month*⟩

month·long \'mən(t)th-'lȯṅ\ *adjective* (1843)
: lasting a month

¹**month·ly** \-lē\ *adverb* (circa 1534)
: once a month : by the month

²**monthly** *adjective* (1572)
1 a : of or relating to a month **b :** payable or reckoned by the month
2 : lasting a month
3 : occurring or appearing every month

³**monthly** *noun, plural* **monthlies** (1833)
1 : a monthly periodical
2 *plural* : a menstrual period

Monthly Meeting *noun* (circa 1772)
: a district unit of an organization of Friends

month's mind *noun* (15th century)
: a Roman Catholic requiem mass held a month after a person's death

Mont·mo·ren·cy \,mänt-mə-'ren(t)-sē\ *noun* [French, from *Montmorency*, France] (1924)
: a cherry that is grown commercially for its bright red sour fruit; *also* : the fruit

mont·mo·ril·lon·ite \,mänt-mə-'ri-lə-,nīt, -'rē-ə-,nīt\ *noun* [French, from *Montmorillon*, commune in western France] (1854)
: a soft clayey mineral that is a hydrous aluminum silicate with considerable capacity for exchanging part of the aluminum for magnesium and bases
— **mont·mo·ril·lon·it·ic** \-,ri-lə-'ni-tik, -,rē-ə-'ni-\ *adjective*

Mon·tra·chet \,mōⁿ-trä-'she\ *noun* [French, from *Montrachet*, vineyard in Burgundy, France] (1833)
: a dry white burgundy wine

mon·u·ment \'män-yə-mənt\ *noun* [Middle English, from Latin *monumentum*, literally, memorial, from *monēre* to remind — more at MIND] (13th century)
1 *obsolete* : a burial vault : SEPULCHRE
2 : a written legal document or record : TREATISE
3 a (1) : a lasting evidence, reminder, or example of someone or something notable or great (2) : a distinguished person **b :** a memorial stone or a building erected in remembrance of a person or event
4 *archaic* : an identifying mark : EVIDENCE; *also* : PORTENT, SIGN
5 *obsolete* : a carved statue : EFFIGY
6 : a boundary or position marker (as a stone)
7 : NATIONAL MONUMENT
8 : a written tribute

mon·u·men·tal \,män-yə-'men-tᵊl\ *adjective* (1604)
1 : of or relating to a monument
2 : serving as or resembling a monument : MASSIVE; *also* : highly significant : OUTSTANDING
3 : very great
— **mon·u·men·tal·i·ty** \-mən-'ta-lə-tē, -,men-\ *noun*
— **mon·u·men·tal·ly** \-tᵊl-ē\ *adverb*

MONTHS OF THE PRINCIPAL CALENDARS

GREGORIAN[1]

Name	Days
January	
begins 10 days after the winter solstice	31
February	28
in leap years	29
March	31
April	30
May	31
June	30
July	31
August	31
September	30
October	31
November	30
December	31

JEWISH

Name	Days
Tishri	
in year 5753 began Sept. 28, 1992	30
Heshvan	29 *or* 30
Kislev	29 *or* 30
Tebet	29
Shebat	30
Adar[2]	29 *or* 30
Nisan[3]	30
Iyar	29
Sivan	30
Tammuz	29
Ab	30
Elul	29

ISLAMIC

Name	Days
Muharram[4]	
in A.H. 1413 began July 2, 1992	30
Safar	29
Rabi I	30
Rabi II	29
Jumada I	30
Jumada II	29
Rajab	30
Sha'ban	29
Ramadan	30
Shawwal	29
Dhu'l-Qa'dah	30
Dhu'l-Hijja	29
in leap years	30

[1] The equinoxes occur about March 21 and September 23, the solstices about June 22 and December 22.

[2] In leap years an intercalary month of 30 days takes the place of Adar, and is sometimes called Adar I. Adar then becomes the 29-day Veadar or Adar Sheni (sometimes called Adar II), and retains the usual festivals and holidays of Adar.

[3] The first month of the ecclesiastical year; anciently called Abib.

[4] Retrogresses through the seasons; the Islamic year is lunar and each month begins at the approximate new moon; the year 1 A.H. began on Friday, July 16, A.D. 622.

mon·u·men·tal·ize \-'men-t°l-,īz\ *transitive verb* **-ized; -iz·ing** (1857)
: to record or memorialize lastingly by a monument

mon·u·ron \'män-yə-,rän\ *noun* [mon- + urea + [1]-on] (circa 1957)
: a persistent herbicide $C_9H_{11}ClN_2O$ used especially to control broad-leaved weeds

mon·zo·nite \män-'zō-,nīt, 'män-zə-\ *noun*

[French, from Mount *Monzoni,* Italy] (1895)
: a granular igneous rock composed of plagioclase and orthoclase in about equal quantities together with augite and a little biotite

moo \'mü\ *intransitive verb* [imitative] (1549)
: to make the throat noise of a cow
— **moo** *noun*

mooch \'müch\ *verb* [probably from French dialect *muchier* to hide, lurk] (1851)
intransitive verb
1 : to wander aimlessly **:** AMBLE; *also* **:** SNEAK
2 : SPONGE, CADGE
transitive verb
1 : to take surreptitiously **:** STEAL
2 : BEG, CADGE
— **mooch·er** *noun*

[1]**mood** \'müd\ *noun* [Middle English, from Old English *mōd;* akin to Old High German *muot* mood] (before 12th century)
1 : a conscious state of mind or predominant emotion **:** FEELING; *also* **:** the expression of mood especially in art or literature
2 *archaic* **:** a fit of anger **:** RAGE
3 a : a prevailing attitude **:** DISPOSITION **b :** a receptive state of mind predisposing to action **c :** a distinctive atmosphere or context **:** AURA

[2]**mood** *noun* [alteration of [1]*mode*] (1569)
1 : the form of a syllogism as determined by the quantity and quality of its constituent propositions
2 : distinction of form or a particular set of inflectional forms of a verb to express whether the action or state it denotes is conceived as fact or in some other manner (as command, possibility, or wish)
3 : MODE 1b

moody \'mü-dē\ *adjective* **mood·i·er; -est** (1593)
1 : subject to depression **:** GLOOMY
2 : subject to moods **:** TEMPERAMENTAL
3 : expressive of a mood
— **mood·i·ly** \'mü-d°l-ē\ *adverb*
— **mood·i·ness** \'mü-dē-nəs\ *noun*

moo·la *or* **moo·lah** \'mü-(,)lä, -lə\ *noun* [origin unknown] (1939)
slang **:** MONEY

[1]**moon** \'mün\ *noun* [Middle English *mone,* from Old English *mōna;* akin to Old High German *māno* moon, Latin *mensis* month, Greek *mēn* month, *mēnē* moon] (before 12th century)
1 a *often capitalized* **:** the earth's natural satellite that shines by the sun's reflected light, revolves about the earth from west to east in about 29½ days with reference to the sun or about 27⅓ days with reference to the stars, and has a diameter of 2160 miles (3475 kilometers), a mean distance from the earth of about 238,900 miles (384,400 kilometers), and a mass about one eighteenth that of the earth — usually used with *the* **b :** one complete moon cycle consisting of four phases **c :** SATELLITE 2; *specifically* **:** a natural satellite of a planet
2 : an indefinite usually extended period of time ⟨a labor of many *moons*⟩
3 : MOONLIGHT
4 : something that resembles a moon: as **a :** a highly translucent spot on old porcelain **b :** LUNULE **c** *slang* **:** naked buttocks
5 : something impossible or inaccessible ⟨reach for the *moon*⟩
— **moon·like** \-,līk\ *adjective*
— **over the moon :** very pleased **:** in high spirits

[2]**moon** (1836)
transitive verb
1 : to spend in idle reverie **:** DREAM — used with *away*
2 *slang* **:** to expose one's naked buttocks to
intransitive verb
: to spend time in idle reverie **:** behave abstractedly

moon·beam \'mün-,bēm\ *noun* (1590)
: a ray of light from the moon

moon blindness *noun* (circa 1720)
: a recurrent inflammation of the eye of the horse

moon·calf \'mün-,kaf, -,kȧf\ *noun* (1614)
: a foolish or absentminded person **:** SIMPLETON

moon·dust \-,dəst\ *noun* (circa 1959)
: fine dry particles of the moon's soil

moon·eye \-,ī\ *noun* (1842)
: any of a genus (*Hiodon*) of silvery North American freshwater fishes that resemble shad

moon–eyed \-'īd\ *adjective* (1699)
: having the eyes wide open

moon·faced \-,fāst\ *adjective* (1855)
: having a round face

moon·fish \-,fish\ *noun,* plural **moonfish** *or* **moon·fish·es** (1646)
: any of various compressed often short deep-bodied silvery or yellowish marine fishes: as **a :** OPAH **b :** PLATY

moon·flow·er \-,flaù(-ə)r\ *noun* (circa 1909)
: a tropical American morning glory (*Calonyction aculeatum* synonym *Ipomoea alba*) with fragrant flowers; *also* **:** any of several related plants

Moon·ie \'mü-nē\ *noun* [Sun Myung *Moon* (born 1920) Korean evangelist] (1974)
: a member of the Unification Church founded by Sun Myung Moon

moon·ish \'mü-nish\ *adjective* (15th century)
: influenced by the moon; *also* **:** CAPRICIOUS
— **moon·ish·ly** *adverb*

moon·less \'mün-ləs\ *adjective* (1508)
: lacking the light of the moon

moon·let \-lət\ *noun* (1832)
: a small natural or artificial satellite

[1]**moon·light** \-,līt\ *noun* (14th century)
: the light of the moon

[2]**moonlight** *intransitive verb* **moon·light·ed; moon·light·ing** [back-formation from *moonlight*] (1957)
: to hold a second job in addition to a regular one
— **moon·light·er** *noun*

moon·lit \-,lit\ *adjective* (circa 1827)
: lighted by the moon

moon·quake \-,kwāk\ *noun* (1946)
: a seismic event on the moon

moon·rise \-,rīz\ *noun* (1728)
1 : the rising of the moon above the horizon
2 : the time of the moon's rising

moon·scape \-,skāp\ *noun* (1916)
: the surface of the moon as seen or as depicted; *also* **:** a landscape resembling this surface
word history SEE LANDSCAPE

moon·seed \-,sēd\ *noun* (1739)
: a twining plant (*Menispermum canadense* of the family Menispermaceae, the moonseed family) of eastern North America that has crescent-shaped seeds and black fruits

moon·set \-,set\ *noun* (1845)
1 : the descent of the moon below the horizon
2 : the time of the moon's setting

moon shell *noun* (1936)
: any of a cosmopolitan family (Naticidae) of carnivorous marine snails having smooth globose shells

moon shell

moon·shine \'mün-,shīn\ *noun* (15th century)
1 : MOONLIGHT
2 : empty talk **:** NONSENSE

\ə\ **abut** \°\ **kitten** \ər\ **further** \a\ **ash** \ā\ **ace**
\ä\ **mop, mar** \aù\ **out** \ch\ **chin** \e\ **bet** \ē\ **easy**
\g\ **go** \i\ **hit** \ī\ **ice** \j\ **job** \ŋ\ **sing** \ō\ **go**
\ȯ\ **law** \ȯi\ **boy** \th\ **thin** \th\ **the** \ü\ **loot** \ù\ **foot**
\y\ **yet** \zh\ **vision** *see also* Guide to Pronunciation

3 : intoxicating liquor; *especially* : illegally distilled corn whiskey

moon·shin·er \-,shī-nər\ *noun* (1860)
: a maker or seller of illicit whiskey

moon shot *noun* (1958)
: a spacecraft mission to the moon

moon·stone \-,stōn\ *noun* (1632)
: a transparent or translucent feldspar of pearly or opaline luster used as a gem

moon·struck \-,strək\ *adjective* (1674)
: affected by or as if by the moon: as **a** : mentally unbalanced **b** : romantically sentimental **c** : lost in fantasy or reverie

moon·ward \-wərd\ *adverb* (1855)
: toward the moon

moony \'mü-nē\ *adjective* (circa 1586)
1 : of or relating to the moon
2 a : crescent-shaped **b** : resembling the full moon : ROUND
3 : MOONLIT
4 : DREAMY, MOONSTRUCK

¹moor \'mu̇r\ *noun* [Middle English *mor*, from Old English *mōr*; akin to Old High German *muor* moor] (before 12th century)
1 *chiefly British* : an expanse of open rolling infertile land
2 : a boggy area; *especially* : one that is peaty and dominated by grasses and sedges

²moor *verb* [Middle English *moren*; akin to Middle Dutch *meren, maren* to tie, moor] (15th century)
transitive verb
: to make fast with or as if with cables, lines, or anchors
intransitive verb
1 : to secure a boat by mooring : ANCHOR
2 : to be made fast

Moor \'mu̇r\ *noun* [Middle English *More*, from Middle French, from Latin *Maurus* inhabitant of Mauretania] (14th century)
1 : one of the Arab and Berber conquerors of Spain
2 : BERBER
— **Moor·ish** \-ish\ *adjective*

moor·age \'mu̇r-ij\ *noun* (1648)
1 : an act of mooring
2 : a place to moor

moor·hen \'mu̇r-,hen\ *noun* (14th century)
: the common gallinule (*Gallinula chloropus*) of the New World, Eurasia, and Africa

moor·ing \-iŋ\ *noun* (15th century)
1 : an act of making fast a boat or aircraft with lines or anchors
2 a : a place where or an object to which something (as a craft) can be moored **b** : a device (as a line or chain) by which an object is secured in place
3 : an established practice or stabilizing influence : ANCHORAGE 2 — usually used in plural

moor·land \-lənd, -,land\ *noun* (before 12th century)
: land consisting of moors : a stretch of moor

moose \'müs\ *noun, plural* **moose** [of Algonquian origin; akin to Massachuset *moos* moose] (1603)
1 : a ruminant mammal (*Alces alces*) with humped shoulders, long legs, and broadly palmated antlers that is the largest existing member of the deer family and inhabits forested areas of Canada, the northern U.S., Europe, and Asia

moose 1

2 *capitalized* [Loyal Order of *Moose*] : a member of a major benevolent and fraternal order

¹moot \'müt\ *noun* [Middle English, from Old English *mōt, gemōt*; akin to Middle High German *muoze* meeting] (before 12th century)
1 : a deliberative assembly primarily for the administration of justice; *especially* : one held by the freemen of an Anglo-Saxon community
2 *obsolete* : ARGUMENT, DISCUSSION

²moot *transitive verb* (before 12th century)
1 *archaic* : to discuss from a legal standpoint : ARGUE
2 a : to bring up for discussion : BROACH **b** : DEBATE

³moot *adjective* (circa 1587)
1 a : open to question : DEBATABLE **b** : subjected to discussion : DISPUTED
2 : deprived of practical significance : made abstract or purely academic

moot court *noun* (1788)
: a mock court in which law students argue hypothetical cases for practice

¹mop \'mäp\ *noun* [Middle English *mappe*] (15th century)
1 : an implement made of absorbent material fastened to a handle and used especially for cleaning floors
2 : something that resembles a mop; *especially* : a thick mass of hair

²mop *verb* **mopped; mop·ping** (1709)
transitive verb
: to use a mop on: as **a** : to clean or clear away by mopping ⟨*mop* the floors⟩ — often used with *up* ⟨*mop* up the spillage⟩ **b** : to wipe as if with a mop ⟨*mopped* his brow with a handkerchief⟩
intransitive verb
: to clean a surface (as a floor) with a mop
— **mop·per** *noun*

mop·board \'mäp-,bōrd, -,bȯrd\ *noun* (1853)
: BASEBOARD

¹mope \'mōp\ *intransitive verb* **moped; mop·ing** [probably from obsolete *mop, mope* fool] (1568)
1 *archaic* : to act in a dazed or stupid manner
2 : to give oneself up to brooding : become listless or dejected
3 : to move slowly or aimlessly : DAWDLE
— **mop·er** *noun*
— **mop·ey** \'mō-pē\ *adjective*

²mope *noun* (1693)
1 : one that mopes
2 *plural* : BLUES 1

mo·ped \'mō-,ped\ *noun* [Swedish, from *motor* motor + *pedal* pedal] (1955)
: a lightweight low-powered motorbike that can be pedaled

mop·pet \'mä-pət\ *noun* [obsolete English *mop* fool, child] (1601)
1 *archaic* : BABY, DARLING
2 : CHILD

mop-up \'mäp-,əp\ *noun* (1900)
: a concluding action

mop up (circa 1811)
transitive verb
1 *British* : to consume eagerly
2 : to gather as if by absorbing : GARNER ⟨*mopped up* all the awards⟩
3 : to overcome decisively : TROUNCE
4 : to clear (an area) of remaining pockets of resistance in the wake of a military offensive
intransitive verb
: to complete a project or transaction

mo·quette \mō-'ket\ *noun* [French] (1762)
: a carpet or upholstery fabric having a velvety pile

mor \'mȯr\ *noun* [Danish, literally, humus] (1931)
: forest humus that forms a layer of largely organic matter abruptly distinct from the mineral soil beneath

mo·ra \'mȯr-ə, 'mȯr-\ *noun, plural* **mo·rae** \'mȯr-(,)ē, 'mȯr-, -,ī\ *or* **mo·ras** [Latin, delay; akin to Old Irish *maraid* it lasts] (1832)
: the minimal unit of measure in quantitative verse equivalent to the time of an average short syllable

mo·raine \mə-'rān\ *noun* [French, from French dialect (Savoy) *morêna*] (1789)
: an accumulation of earth and stones carried and finally deposited by a glacier
— **mo·rain·al** \-'rā-nᵊl\ *adjective*
— **mo·rain·ic** \-'rā-nik\ *adjective*

¹mor·al \'mȯr-əl, 'mär-\ *adjective* [Middle English, from Middle French, from Latin *moralis*, from *mor-, mos* custom] (14th century)
1 a : of or relating to principles of right and wrong in behavior : ETHICAL ⟨*moral* judgments⟩ **b** : expressing or teaching a conception of right behavior ⟨a *moral* poem⟩ **c** : conforming to a standard of right behavior **d** : sanctioned by or operative on one's conscience or ethical judgment ⟨a *moral* obligation⟩ **e** : capable of right and wrong action ⟨a *moral* agent⟩
2 : probable though not proved : VIRTUAL ⟨a *moral* certainty⟩
3 : having the effects of such on the mind, confidence, or will ⟨a *moral* victory⟩ ⟨*moral* support⟩ ☆
— **mor·al·ly** \-ə-lē\ *adverb*

²mor·al \'mȯr-əl, 'mär-; *3 is* mə-'ral\ *noun* (15th century)
1 a : the moral significance or practical lesson (as of a story) **b** : a passage pointing out usually in conclusion the lesson to be drawn from a story
2 *plural* **a** : moral practices or teachings : modes of conduct **b** : ETHICS
3 : MORALE

mo·rale \mə-'ral\ *noun* [in sense 1, from French, from feminine of *moral*, adjective; in other senses, modification of French *moral* morale, from *moral*, adjective] (1752)
1 : moral principles, teachings, or conduct
2 a : the mental and emotional condition (as of enthusiasm, confidence, or loyalty) of an individual or group with regard to the function or tasks at hand **b** : a sense of common purpose with respect to a group : ESPRIT DE CORPS
3 : the level of individual psychological well-being based on such factors as a sense of purpose and confidence in the future

moral hazard *noun* (circa 1917)
: the possibility of loss to an insurance company arising from the character or circumstances of the insured

mor·al·ise *British variant of* MORALIZE

mor·al·ism \'mȯr-ə-,li-zəm, 'mär-\ *noun* (1828)
1 a : the habit or practice of moralizing **b** : a conventional moral attitude or saying
2 : an often exaggerated emphasis on morality (as in politics)

mor·al·ist \-list\ *noun* (1621)
1 : one who leads a moral life
2 : a philosopher or writer concerned with moral principles and problems

3 : one concerned with regulating the morals of others

mor·al·is·tic \ˌmȯr-ə-'lis-tik, ˌmär-\ *adjective* (1865)
1 : characterized by or expressive of a concern with morality
2 : characterized by or expressive of a narrow and conventional moral attitude
— **mor·al·is·ti·cal·ly** \-ti-k(ə-)lē\ *adverb*

mo·ral·i·ty \mə-'ra-lə-tē, mȯ-\ *noun, plural* **-ties** (14th century)
1 a : a moral discourse, statement, or lesson **b** : a literary or other imaginative work teaching a moral lesson
2 a : a doctrine or system of moral conduct **b** *plural* : particular moral principles or rules of conduct
3 : conformity to ideals of right human conduct
4 : moral conduct : VIRTUE

morality play *noun* (1929)
1 : an allegorical play popular especially in the 15th and 16th centuries in which the characters personify abstract qualities or concepts (as virtues, vices, or death)
2 : something which involves a direct conflict between right and wrong or good and evil and from which a moral lesson may be drawn

mor·al·ize \'mȯr-ə-ˌlīz, 'mär-\ *verb* **-ized; -iz·ing** (15th century)
transitive verb
1 : to explain or interpret morally
2 a : to give a moral quality or direction to **b** : to improve the morals of
intransitive verb
: to make moral reflections
— **mor·al·i·za·tion** \ˌmȯr-ə-lə-'zā-shən, ˌmär-\ *noun*
— **mor·al·iz·er** \'mȯr-ə-ˌlī-zər, 'mär-\ *noun*

moral philosophy *noun* (1606)
: ETHICS; *also* : the study of human conduct and values

mo·rass \mə-'ras, mȯ-\ *noun* [Dutch *moeras*, modification of Old French *maresc*, of Germanic origin; akin to Old English *mersc* marsh — more at MARSH] (1655)
1 : MARSH, SWAMP
2 : something that traps, confuses, or impedes ⟨a *morass* of troubles⟩
— **mo·rassy** \-'ra-sē\ *adjective*

mor·a·to·ri·um \ˌmȯr-ə-'tōr-ē-əm, ˌmär-, -'tȯr-\ *noun, plural* **-riums** *or* **-ria** \-ē-ə\ [New Latin, from Late Latin, neuter of *moratorius* dilatory, from Latin *morari* to delay, from *mora* delay] (1875)
1 a : a legally authorized period of delay in the performance of a legal obligation or the payment of a debt **b** : a waiting period set by an authority
2 : a suspension of activity

Mo·ra·vi·an \mə-'rā-vē-ən\ *noun* (1555)
1 a : a native or inhabitant of Moravia **b** : the group of Czech dialects spoken in Moravia
2 : a member of a Protestant denomination arising from a 15th century religious reform movement in Bohemia and Moravia
— **Moravian** *adjective*

mo·ray eel \mə-'rā, 'mȯr-(ˌ)ā-\ *noun* [Portuguese *moréia*, from Latin *muraena*, from Greek *myraina*] (1926)
: any of numerous often brightly colored eels (family Muraenidae) that have sharp teeth capable of inflicting a severe bite, that occur in warm seas, and that include a chiefly Mediterranean eel (*Muraena helena*) sometimes used for food — called also **moray**

mor·bid \'mȯr-bəd\ *adjective* [Latin *morbidus* diseased, from *morbus* disease] (1656)
1 a : of, relating to, or characteristic of disease ⟨*morbid* anatomy⟩ **b** : affected with or induced by disease ⟨a *morbid* condition⟩ **c** : productive of disease ⟨*morbid* substances⟩
2 : abnormally susceptible to or characterized by gloomy or unwholesome feelings
3 : GRISLY, GRUESOME ⟨*morbid* details⟩ ⟨*morbid* curiosity⟩

— **mor·bid·ly** *adverb*
— **mor·bid·ness** *noun*

mor·bid·i·ty \mȯr-'bi-də-tē\ *noun* (circa 1721)
1 : the quality or state of being morbid
2 : the relative incidence of disease

mor·ceau \mȯr-'sō\ *noun, plural* **mor·ceaux** \-'sō(z)\ [French, from Old French *morsel* morsel] (1751)
: a short literary or musical piece

mor·dan·cy \'mȯr-d°n(t)-sē\ *noun* (circa 1656)
1 : a biting and caustic quality of style : INCISIVENESS
2 : a sharply critical or bitter quality of thought or feeling : HARSHNESS

¹**mor·dant** \'mȯr-d°nt\ *adjective* [Middle English, from Middle French, present participle of *mordre* to bite, from Latin *mordēre*; perhaps akin to Sanskrit *mṛdnāti* he presses, rubs] (15th century)
1 : biting and caustic in thought, manner, or style : INCISIVE ⟨a *mordant* wit⟩
2 : acting as a mordant
3 : BURNING, PUNGENT
synonym see CAUSTIC
— **mor·dant·ly** *adverb*

²**mordant** *noun* (1791)
1 : a chemical that fixes a dye in or on a substance by combining with the dye to form an insoluble compound
2 : a corroding substance used in etching

³**mordant** *transitive verb* (1836)
: to treat with a mordant

Mor·de·cai \'mȯr-di-ˌkī\ *noun* [Hebrew *Mordĕkhai*]
: a relative of Esther who gives advice on saving the Jews from the destruction planned by Haman

mor·dent \'mȯr-d°nt, mȯr-'dent\ *noun* [Italian *mordente*, from Latin *mordent-, mordens*, present participle of *mordēre*] (1806)
: a musical ornament made by a quick alternation of a principal tone with the tone immediately below it

¹**more** \'mȯr, 'mȯr\ *adjective* [Middle English, from Old English *māra*; akin to Old English *mā*, adverb, more, Old High German *mēr*, Old Irish *mó* more] (before 12th century)
1 : GREATER ⟨something *more* than she expected⟩
2 : ADDITIONAL, FURTHER ⟨*more* guests arrived⟩

²**more** *adverb* (before 12th century)
1 a : in addition ⟨a couple of times *more*⟩ **b** : MOREOVER
2 : to a greater or higher degree — often used with an adjective or adverb to form the comparative ⟨*more* evenly matched⟩

³**more** *noun* (before 12th century)
1 : a greater quantity, number, or amount ⟨liked the idea better the *more* I thought about it⟩
2 : something additional : an additional amount
3 *obsolete* : persons of higher rank

⁴**more** *pronoun, singular or plural in construction* (13th century)
: additional persons or things or a greater amount ⟨*more* were found as the search continued⟩ ⟨*more* was spilled⟩

more and more *adverb* (13th century)
: to a progressively increasing extent

mo·reen \mə-'rēn, mȯ-\ *noun* [probably irregular from *moire*] (circa 1691)
: a strong fabric of wool, wool and cotton, or cotton with a plain glossy or moiré finish

mo·rel \mə-'rel, mȯ-\ *noun* [French *morille*, probably from (assumed) Vulgar Latin *mauricula*, from *maurus* brown, from Latin *Maurus* inhabitant of Mauretania] (1672)
: any of several edible fungi (genus *Morchella*, especially *M. esculenta*) having a cap with a highly pitted surface

mo·rel·lo \mə-'re-(ˌ)lō\ *noun, plural* **-los** [probably modification of Flemish *amarelle*,

marelle, from Medieval Latin *amarellum*, a sour cherry, from Latin *amarus* bitter, sour] (1598)
: a cultivated sour cherry (as the Montmorency) having a dark-colored skin and juice

more or less *adverb* (13th century)
1 : to a varying or undetermined extent or degree : SOMEWHAT ⟨they were *more or less* willing to help⟩
2 : with small variations : APPROXIMATELY ⟨contains 16 acres *more or less*⟩

more·over \mȯr-'ō-vər, mȯr-, 'mȯr-, 'mȯr-\ *adverb* (14th century)
: in addition to what has been said : BESIDES

mo·res \'mȯr-ˌāz, 'mȯr- *also* -(ˌ)ēz\ *noun plural* [Latin, plural of *mor-, mos* custom] (circa 1899)
1 : the fixed morally binding customs of a particular group
2 : moral attitudes
3 : HABITS, MANNERS ▢

¹**mo·resque** \mȯ-'resk, mə-\ *adjective, often capitalized* [French, from Spanish *morisco*, from *moro* Moor, from Latin *Maurus*] (circa 1611)
: having the characteristics of Moorish art or architecture

²**moresque** *noun, often capitalized* (circa 1752)
: an ornament or decorative motif in Moorish style

mor·gan \'mȯr-gən\ *noun* [Thomas Hunt *Morgan*] (1919)
1 : a unit of inferred distance between genes on a chromosome that is used in constructing genetic maps and is equal to the distance for which the frequency of crossing over between specific pairs of genes is 100 percent
2 : CENTIMORGAN

Mor·gan \'mȯr-gən\ *noun* [Justin *Morgan* (died 1798) American teacher] (1841)
: any of an American breed of light strong horses originated in Vermont from the progeny of one prepotent stallion of uncertain ancestry

mor·ga·nat·ic \ˌmȯr-gə-'na-tik\ *adjective* [New Latin *matrimonium ad morganaticam*, literally, marriage with morning gift] (circa 1741)
: of, relating to, or being a marriage between a member of a royal or noble family and a person of inferior rank in which the rank of the

\ə\ abut \ᵊ\ kitten \ər\ further \a\ ash \ā\ ace
\ä\ mop, mar \au̇\ out \ch\ chin \e\ bet \ē\ easy
\g\ go \i\ hit \ī\ ice \j\ job \ŋ\ sing \ō\ go
\ȯ\ law \ȯi\ boy \th\ thin \t͟h\ the \ü\ loot \u̇\ foot
\y\ yet \zh\ vision *see also* Guide to Pronunciation

inferior partner remains unchanged and the children of the marriage do not succeed to the titles, fiefs, or entailed property of the parent of higher rank

— **mor·ga·nat·i·cal·ly** \-ti-k(ə-)lē\ adverb

mor·gan·ite \'mȯr-gə-ˌnīt\ noun [J. P. Morgan (died 1913)] (1911)
: a rose-colored gem variety of beryl

Morgan le Fay \-lə-'fā\ noun [Old French Morgain la fee Morgan the fairy]
: a sorceress and sister of King Arthur

mor·gen \'mȯr-gə(n)\ noun, plural **morgen** [Dutch, literally, morning] (1626)
: a Dutch and southern African unit of land area equal to 2.116 acres (0.856 hectare)

morgue \'mȯrg\ noun [French] (1821)
1 : a place where the bodies of persons found dead are kept until identified and claimed by relatives or are released for burial
2 : a collection of reference works and files of reference material in a newspaper or news periodical office

mor·i·bund \'mȯr-ə-(ˌ)bənd, 'mär-\ adjective [Latin moribundus, from mori to die — more at MURDER] (circa 1721)
1 : being in the state of dying : approaching death
2 : being in a state of inactivity or obsolescence

— **mor·i·bun·di·ty** \ˌmȯr-ə-'bən-də-tē, ˌmär-\ noun

¹mo·ri·on \'mȯr-ē-ˌän, 'mȯr-\ noun [Middle French] (1563)
: a high-crested helmet with no visor

²morion noun [modification of Latin mormorion] (1748)
: a nearly black variety of smoky quartz

Mo·ris·co \mə-'ris-(ˌ)kō, mȯ-\ noun, plural **-cos** or **-coes** [Spanish, from morisco, adjective, from moro Moor] (1629)
: MOOR; especially : a Spanish Moor
— **Morisco** adjective

Mor·mon \'mȯr-mən\ noun
1 : the ancient redactor and compiler of the Book of Mormon presented as divine revelation by Joseph Smith
2 : LATTER-DAY SAINT; especially : a member of the Church of Jesus Christ of Latter-day Saints
— **Mor·mon·ism** \-mə-ˌni-zəm\ noun

Mormon cricket noun (1896)
: a large dark wingless katydid (Anabrus simplex) that resembles a cricket and is found in the arid parts of the western U.S. where it is occasionally an abundant pest of crops

morn \'mȯrn\ noun [Middle English, from Old English morgen; akin to Old High German morgan morning and perhaps to Greek marmairein to sparkle] (before 12th century)
1 : DAWN
2 : MORNING

Mor·nay sauce \mȯr-'nā-\ noun [Philippe de Mornay] (circa 1924)
: a cheese-flavored cream sauce

morn·ing \'mȯr-niŋ\ noun [Middle English, from morn + -ing (as in evening)] (13th century)
1 a : DAWN **b** : the time from sunrise to noon **c** : the time from midnight to noon
2 : a period of first development : BEGINNING

morn·ing–after pill \ˌmȯr-niŋ-'af-tər-\ noun [from its being taken after rather than before intercourse] (1966)
: an oral drug that interferes with pregnancy by blocking implantation of a fertilized egg in the human uterus

morning glory noun (1814)
: any of various usually twining plants (genus Ipomoea of the family Convolvulaceae, the morning-glory family) with showy trumpet-shaped flowers; broadly : a plant of the morning-glory family including herbs, shrubs, or trees with alternate leaves and regular pentamerous flowers

morning line noun (circa 1935)

: a bookmaker's list of entries for a race meet and the probable odds on each that is printed or posted before the betting begins

Morning Prayer noun (1552)
: a service of liturgical prayer used for regular morning worship in churches of the Anglican communion

morn·ings \'mȯr-niŋz\ adverb (1652)
: in the morning repeatedly : on any morning

morning sickness noun (1879)
: nausea and vomiting that occur on rising in the morning especially during the earlier months of pregnancy

morning star noun (1535)
: a bright planet (as Venus) seen in the eastern sky before or at sunrise

Mo·ro \'mȯr-(ˌ)ō, 'mȯr-\ noun, plural **Moros** [Spanish, literally, Moor, from Latin Maurus] (1886)
1 : a member of any of several Muslim peoples of the southern Philippines
2 : any of the Austronesian languages of the Moro peoples

mo·roc·co \mə-'rä-(ˌ)kō\ noun [Morocco, Africa] (1634)
: a fine leather from goatskin tanned with sumac

mo·ron \'mȯr-ˌän, 'mȯr-\ noun [irregular from Greek mōros foolish, stupid] (1910)
1 : a mentally retarded person who has a potential mental age of between 8 and 12 years and is capable of doing routine work under supervision
2 : a very stupid person
— **mo·ron·ic** \mə-'rä-nik, mȯ-\ adjective
— **mo·ron·i·cal·ly** \-ni-k(ə-)lē\ adverb
— **mo·ron·ism** \'mȯr-ˌä-ˌni-zəm, 'mȯr-\ noun
— **mo·ron·i·ty** \mə-'rä-nə-tē, mȯ-\ noun

mo·rose \mə-'rōs, mȯ-\ adjective [Latin morosus, literally, capricious, from mor-, mos will] (1565)
1 : having a sullen and gloomy disposition
2 : marked by or expressive of gloom
synonym see SULLEN
— **mo·rose·ly** adverb
— **mo·rose·ness** noun
— **mo·ros·i·ty** \-'rä-sə-tē\ noun

morph \'mȯrf\ noun [back-formation from morpheme] (1947)
1 a : ALLOMORPH **b** : a distinctive collocation of phones (as a portmanteau form) that serves as the realization of more than one morpheme in a context (as the French du for the sequence of de and le)
2 a : a local population of a species that consists of interbreeding organisms and is distinguishable from other populations by morphology or behavior though capable of interbreeding with them **b** : a phenotypic variant of a species

morph- or **morpho-** combining form [German, from Greek, from morphē]
1 : form ⟨morphogenesis⟩
2 : morpheme ⟨morphophonemics⟩

-morph noun combining form [International Scientific Vocabulary, from -morphous]
: one having (such) a form ⟨isomorph⟩

mor·phac·tin \mȯr-'fak-tən\ noun [probably from morph- + active + ¹-in] (1966)
: any of several synthetic fluorine-containing compounds that tend to produce morphological changes and suppress growth in plants

mor·phal·lax·is \ˌmȯr-fə-'lak-səs\ noun, plural **-lax·es** \-ˌsēz\ [New Latin, from morph- + Greek allaxis exchange, from allassein to change, exchange, from allos other — more at ELSE] (1901)
: regeneration of a part or organism from a fragment by reorganization without cell proliferation

mor·pheme \'mȯr-ˌfēm\ noun [French morphème, from Greek morphē form] (1926)
: a distinctive collocation of phonemes (as the free form pin or the bound form -s of pins) that contains no smaller meaningful parts

— **mor·phe·mic** \mȯr-'fē-mik\ adjective
— **mor·phe·mi·cal·ly** \-mi-k(ə-)lē\ adverb

mor·phe·mics \mȯr-'fē-miks\ noun plural but singular in construction (1947)
1 : a branch of linguistic analysis that consists of the study of morphemes
2 : the structure of a language in terms of morphemes

Mor·pheus \'mȯr-fē-əs, -ˌfyüs, -ˌfüs\ noun [Latin, from Greek]
: the Greek god of dreams

mor·phia \'mȯr-fē-ə\ noun [New Latin, from Morpheus] (1818)
: MORPHINE

-morphic adjective combining form [probably from French -morphique, from Greek morphē]
: having (such) a form ⟨endomorphic⟩

mor·phine \'mȯr-ˌfēn\ noun [French, from Morpheus] (1828)
: a bitter crystalline addictive narcotic base $C_{17}H_{19}NO_3$ that is the principal alkaloid of opium and is used in the form of a soluble salt (as a hydrochloride or a sulfate) as an analgesic and sedative ◇

mor·phin·ism \'mȯr-ˌfē-ˌni-zəm, -fə-\ noun (1882)
: a disordered condition of health produced by habitual use of morphine

-morphism noun combining form [Late Latin -morphus -morphous, from Greek -morphos]
: quality or state of having (such) a form ⟨heteromorphism⟩

mor·pho \'mȯr-(ˌ)fō\ noun, plural **morphos** [New Latin, from Greek Morphō, epithet of Aphrodite] (1853)
: any of a genus (Morpho of the family Morphoidae) of large showy tropical American butterflies that typically have a brilliant blue metallic luster on the upper surface of the wings

mor·pho·gen \'mȯr-fə-jən, -ˌjen\ noun (1950)
: a diffusible chemical substance that exerts control over morphogenesis especially by forming a gradient in concentration

mor·pho·gen·e·sis \ˌmȯr-fə-'je-nə-səs\ noun [New Latin] (circa 1890)
: the formation and differentiation of tissues and organs — compare ORGANOGENESIS

mor·pho·ge·net·ic \-jə-'ne-tik\ adjective (1884)
: relating to or concerned with the development of normal organic form ⟨morphogenetic movements of early embryonic cells⟩
— **mor·pho·ge·net·i·cal·ly** \-ti-k(ə-)lē\ adverb

mor·pho·gen·ic \-'je-nik\ adjective (circa 1890)
: MORPHOGENETIC

mor·phol·o·gy \mȯr-'fä-lə-jē\ noun [German Morphologie, from morph- + -logie -logy] (1830)

◇ WORD HISTORY
morphine The word morphine is based on classical mythology. Hypnos, the Greek god of sleep, was usually conceived as perpetually reclining on a couch, surrounded by his numerous sons, the Dreams. Prominent among the sons was Morpheus, who, when called upon by the chief gods to intervene in mortal affairs, had the power to make human forms appear to dreamers. (Greek Morpheus is appropriately a derivative of morphē "form, shape.") The drug morphine was first isolated in 1806 by the German pharmacologist Friedrich Wilhelm Adam Sertürner (1783–1841). Sertürner named this derivative of opium morphium, after the god of dreams, for the deep sleep it induces in addition to relieving pain. English borrowed the French version of this name, morphine, without change.

1 a : a branch of biology that deals with the form and structure of animals and plants **b :** the form and structure of an organism or any of its parts
2 a : a study and description of word formation (as inflection, derivation, and compounding) in language **b :** the system of word-forming elements and processes in a language
3 a : a study of structure or form **b :** STRUCTURE, FORM
4 : the external structure of rocks in relation to the development of erosional forms or topographic features
— **mor·pho·log·i·cal** \ˌmȯr-fə-ˈlä-ji-kəl\ *also* **mor·pho·log·ic** \-ˈlä-jik\ *adjective*
— **mor·pho·log·i·cal·ly** \-k(ə-)lē\ *adverb*
— **mor·phol·o·gist** \mȯr-ˈfä-lə-jist\ *noun*

mor·phom·e·try \mȯr-ˈfä-mə-trē\ *noun* (circa 1856)
: measurement of external form
— **mor·pho·met·ric** \ˌmȯr-fə-ˈme-trik\ *adjective*
— **mor·pho·met·ri·cal·ly** \-tri-k(ə-)lē\ *adverb*

mor·pho·pho·ne·mics \ˌmȯr-fō-fə-ˈnē-miks\ *noun plural but singular in construction* (1939)
1 : a study of the phonemic differences between allomorphs of the same morpheme
2 : the distribution of allomorphs in one morpheme
3 : the structure of a language in terms of morphophonemics

-morphous *adjective combining form* [Greek *-morphos,* from *morphē*]
: having (such) a form ⟨isomorphous⟩

-morphy *noun combining form* [International Scientific Vocabulary, from *-morphous*]
: quality or state of having (such) a form ⟨endomorphy⟩

mor·ris \ˈmȯr-əs, ˈmär-\ *noun* [Middle English *moreys daunce,* from *moreys* Moorish (from *More* Moor) + *daunce* dance] (1512)
: a vigorous English dance traditionally performed by men wearing costumes and bells

morris chair *noun* [William *Morris*] (1900)
: an easy chair with adjustable back and removable cushions

mor·row \ˈmär-(ˌ)ō, ˈmȯr-\ *noun* [Middle English *morn, morwen* morn] (13th century)
1 *archaic* : MORNING
2 : the next day
3 : the time immediately after a specified event

Morse code \ˈmȯrs-\ *noun* [Samuel F. B. *Morse*] (1867)
: either of two codes consisting of variously spaced dots and dashes or long and short sounds used for transmitting messages by audible or visual signals

morris chair

¹mor·sel \ˈmȯr-səl\ *noun* [Middle English, from Old French, diminutive of *mors* bite, from Latin *morsus,* from *mordēre* to bite — more at MORDANT] (14th century)
1 : a small piece of food : BITE
2 : a small quantity : FRAGMENT
3 a : a tasty dish **b :** something delectable and pleasing
4 : a negligible person

²morsel *transitive verb* **-seled** *or* **-selled; -sel·ing** *or* **-sel·ling** (1598)
: to divide into or distribute in small pieces

¹mort \ˈmȯrt\ *noun* [probably alteration of Middle English *mot* horn note, from Middle French, word, horn note — more at MOT] (circa 1500)
1 : a note sounded on a hunting horn when a deer is killed
2 : KILLING 1

INTERNATIONAL MORSE CODE

a	· —	á	· — — · —
b	— · · ·	ä	· — · —
c	— · — ·	é	· · — · ·
d	— · ·	ñ	— — · — —
e	·	ö	— — — ·
f	· · — ·	ü	· · — —
g	— — ·	1	· — — — —
h	· · · ·	2	· · — — —
i	· ·	3	· · · — —
j	· — — —	4	· · · · —
k	— · —	5	· · · · ·
l	· — · ·	6	— · · · ·
m	— —	7	— — · · ·
n	— ·	8	— — — · ·
o	— — —	9	— — — — ·
p	· — — ·	0	— — — — —
q	— — · —	,	— — · · — — (comma)
r	· — ·	.	· — · — · —
s	· · ·	?	· · — — · ·
t	—	;	— · — · — ·
u	· · —	:	— — — · · ·
v	· · · —	'	· — — — — · (apostrophe)
w	· — —	-	— · · · · — (hyphen)
x	— · · —	/	— · · — ·
y	— · — —	(	— · — — · (left parenthesis)
z	— — · ·	)	— · — — · — (right parenthesis)

²mort *noun* [perhaps back-formation from ¹*mortal*] (1694)
: a great quantity or number

mor·ta·del·la \ˌmȯr-tə-ˈde-lə\ *noun* [Italian, from Latin *murtatum* sausage seasoned with myrtle berries, from *murtus* myrtle] (1613)
: a large smoked sausage made of beef, pork, and pork fat and seasoned with pepper and garlic

¹mor·tal \ˈmȯr-tᵊl\ *adjective* [Middle English, from Middle French, from Latin *mortalis,* from *mort-, mors* death — more at MURDER] (14th century)
1 : causing or having caused death : FATAL ⟨a *mortal* injury⟩
2 a : subject to death ⟨*mortal* man⟩ **b :** POSSIBLE, CONCEIVABLE ⟨have done every *mortal* thing⟩ **c :** DEADLY 3 ⟨waited three *mortal* hours⟩
3 : marked by unrelenting hostility : IMPLACABLE ⟨a *mortal* enemy⟩
4 : marked by great intensity or severity : EXTREME ⟨*mortal* fear⟩ ⟨a *mortal* shame⟩
5 : HUMAN ⟨*mortal* limitations⟩
6 : of, relating to, or connected with death ⟨*mortal* agony⟩
synonym see DEADLY

²mortal *adverb* (15th century)
chiefly dialect : MORTALLY

³mortal *noun* (1567)
: a human being

mor·tal·i·ty \mȯr-ˈta-lə-tē\ *noun* (14th century)
1 : the quality or state of being mortal
2 : the death of large numbers (as of people or animals)
3 *archaic* : DEATH
4 : the human race
5 a : the number of deaths in a given time or place **b :** the proportion of deaths to population **c :** the number lost or the rate of loss or failure

mortality table *noun* (1880)
: an actuarial table based on mortality statistics over a number of years

mor·tal·ly \ˈmȯr-tᵊl-ē\ *adverb* (14th century)
1 : in a deadly or fatal manner : to death ⟨*mortally* wounded⟩
2 : to an extreme degree : INTENSELY ⟨*mortally* afraid⟩

mortal mind *noun* (1875)
Christian Science : a belief that life, substance, and intelligence are in and of matter : ILLUSION

mortal sin *noun* (15th century)
: a sin (as murder) that is deliberately committed and is of such serious consequence according to Thomist theology that it deprives the soul of sanctifying grace — compare VENIAL SIN

¹mor·tar \ˈmȯr-tər\ *noun* [Middle English *morter,* from Old English *mortere* & Middle French *mortier,* from Latin *mortarium*] (before 12th century)
1 : a strong vessel in which material is pounded or rubbed with a pestle
2 [Middle French *mortier*] **a :** a muzzle-loading cannon having a tube short in relation to its caliber that is used to throw projectiles with low muzzle velocities at high angles **b :** any of several similar firing devices

²mortar *noun* [Middle English, from Old French *mortier,* from Latin *mortarium*] (14th century)
: a plastic building material (as a mixture of cement, lime, or gypsum plaster with sand and water) that hardens and is used in masonry or plastering
— **mor·tar·less** *adjective*

³mortar *transitive verb* (14th century)
: to plaster or make fast with mortar

mor·tar·board \ˈmȯr-tər-ˌbȯrd, -ˌbȯrd\ *noun* (1854)
1 a : HAWK 2 **b :** a board or platform about three feet (one meter) square for holding mortar
2 : an academic cap consisting of a closely fitting headpiece with a broad flat projecting square top

mortarboard 2

¹mort·gage \ˈmȯr-gij\ *noun* [Middle English *morgage,* from Middle French, from Old French, from *mort* dead (from Latin *mortuus*) + *gage* gage — more at MURDER] (15th century)
1 : a conveyance of or lien against property that is defeated upon payment or performance according to stipulated terms
2 a : the instrument evidencing the mortgage **b :** the state of the property so mortgaged **c :** the interest of the mortgagee in such property

²mortgage *transitive verb* **mort·gaged; mort·gag·ing** (15th century)
1 : to grant or convey by a mortgage
2 : to subject to a claim or obligation : PLEDGE

mort·gag·ee \ˌmȯr-gi-ˈjē\ *noun* (1584)
: a person to whom property is mortgaged

mort·gag·or \ˌmȯr-gi-ˈjȯr\ *also* **mort·gag·er** \ˈmȯr-gi-jər\ *noun* (1584)
: a person who mortgages property

mor·ti·cian \mȯr-ˈti-shən\ *noun* [Latin *mort-, mors* death] (1895)
: UNDERTAKER 2

mor·ti·fi·ca·tion \ˌmȯr-tə-fə-ˈkā-shən\ *noun* (14th century)
1 : the subjection and denial of bodily passions and appetites by abstinence or self-inflicted pain or discomfort
2 : NECROSIS, GANGRENE
3 a : a sense of humiliation and shame caused by something that wounds one's pride or self-respect **b :** the cause of such humiliation

mor·ti·fy \ˈmȯr-tə-ˌfī\ *verb* **-fied; -fy·ing** [Middle English *mortifien,* from Middle French *mortifier,* from Late Latin *mortificare,* from Latin *mort-, mors*] (14th century)
transitive verb

1 *obsolete* **:** to destroy the strength, vitality, or functioning of
2 : to subdue or deaden (as the body or bodily appetites) especially by abstinence or self-inflicted pain or discomfort
3 : to subject to severe and vexing embarrassment — SHAME
intransitive verb
1 : to practice mortification
2 : to become necrotic or gangrenous

¹**mor·tise** *also* **mor·tice** \'mȯr-təs\ *noun* [Middle English *mortays*, from Middle French *mortaise*] (15th century)
: a hole, groove, or slot into or through which some other part of an arrangement of parts fits or passes; *especially* **:** a cavity cut into a piece of material (as timber) to receive a tenon — see DOVETAIL illustration

²**mortise** *also* **mortice** *transitive verb* **mor·tised** *also* **mor·ticed; mor·tis·ing** *also* **mor·tic·ing** (15th century)
1 : to join or fasten securely; *specifically* **:** to join or fasten by a tenon and mortise
2 : to cut or make a mortise in

mort·main \'mȯrt-ˌmān\ *noun* [Middle English *morte-mayne*, from Middle French *mortemain*, from Old French, from *morte* (feminine of *mort* dead) + *main* hand, from Latin *manus* — more at MANUAL] (15th century)
1 a : an inalienable possession of lands or buildings by an ecclesiastical or other corporation **b :** the condition of property or other gifts left to a corporation in perpetuity especially for religious, charitable, or public purposes
2 : the influence of the past regarded as controlling the present

¹**mor·tu·ary** \'mȯr-chə-ˌwer-ē\ *adjective* [Latin *mortuarius* of the dead, from *mortuus* dead] (1514)
1 : of or relating to the burial of the dead
2 : of, relating to, or characteristic of death

²**mortuary** *noun, plural* **-ar·ies** (1865)
: a place in which dead bodies are kept until burial; *especially* **:** FUNERAL HOME

mor·u·la \'mȯr-(y)ə-lə, 'mär-\ *noun, plural* **-lae** \-ˌlē, -ˌlī\ [New Latin, from Latin *morum* mulberry, from Greek *moron*] (1874)
: a globular solid mass of blastomeres formed by cleavage of a zygote that typically precedes the blastula
— **mor·u·lar** \-lər\ *adjective*
— **mor·u·la·tion** \ˌmȯr-(y)ə-'lā-shən, ˌmär-\ *noun*

¹**mo·sa·ic** \mō-'zā-ik\ *noun* [Middle English *musycke*, from Middle French *mosaique*, from Old Italian *mosaico*, from Medieval Latin *musaicum*, alteration of Late Latin *musivum*, from Latin *museum, musaeum*] (15th century)
1 : a surface decoration made by inlaying small pieces of variously colored material to form pictures or patterns; *also* **:** the process of making it
2 : a picture or design made in mosaic
3 : something resembling a mosaic ⟨a *mosaic* of visions and daydreams and memories —Lawrence Shainberg⟩
4 : an organism or one of its parts composed of cells of more than one genotype **:** CHIMERA 3
5 : a virus disease of plants characterized by diffuse light and dark green or yellow and green mottling of the foliage
6 : a composite map made of photographs taken by an aircraft or spacecraft
7 : the part of a television camera tube consisting of many minute photoelectric particles that convert light to an electric charge
— **mo·sa·ic·like** \-'zā-ik-ˌlīk\ *adjective*

²**mosaic** *adjective* (1585)
1 : of, relating to, produced by, or resembling a mosaic
2 : exhibiting mosaicism
3 : DETERMINATE 5
— **mo·sa·i·cal·ly** \-'zā-ə-k(ə-)lē\ *adverb*

³**mosaic** *transitive verb* **-icked; -ick·ing** (1839)
1 : to decorate with mosaics
2 : to form into a mosaic

Mo·sa·ic \mō-'zā-ik\ *adjective* [New Latin *Mosaicus*, from *Moses* Moses] (1662)
: of or relating to Moses or the institutions or writings attributed to him

mo·sa·i·cism \mō-'zā-ə-ˌsi-zəm\ *noun* (1926)
: the condition of possessing cells of two or more different genetic constitutions

mo·sa·i·cist \-sist\ *noun* (1847)
1 a : a designer of mosaics **b :** a worker who makes mosaics
2 : a dealer in mosaics

mo·sa·saur \'mō-zə-ˌsȯr\ *noun* [New Latin *Mosasaurus*, from Latin *Mosa* the river Meuse + Greek *sauros* lizard] (1841)
: any of a family (Mosasauridae) of very large extinct marine fish-eating lizards of the Upper Cretaceous with limbs modified into paddles that are related to the recent monitor lizards

Mo·selle \mō-'zel\ *noun* [German *Moselwein*, from *Mosel* Moselle, river in Germany + German *wein* wine] (1693)
: a white wine from the Moselle valley

Mo·ses \'mō-zəz *also* -zəs\ *noun* [Latin, from Greek *Mōsēs*, from Hebrew *Mōsheh*]
: a Hebrew prophet who led the Israelites out of Egyptian slavery and at Mount Sinai delivered to them the Law establishing God's covenant with them

mo·sey \'mō-zē\ *intransitive verb* **mo·seyed; mo·sey·ing** [origin unknown] (1829)
1 : to hurry away
2 : to move in a leisurely or aimless manner **:** SAUNTER ⟨*moseyed* around the general store, testing the cheese straight off the round —Eric Sevareid⟩

mo·shav \mō-'shäv\ *noun, plural* **mo·sha·vim** \ˌmō-shə-'vēm\ [New Hebrew *mōshābh*, from Hebrew, dwelling] (1931)
: a cooperative settlement of small individual farms in Israel — compare KIBBUTZ

Mos·lem \'mäz-ləm *also* 'mäs-\ *variant of* MUSLIM

Mo·so·tho \mō-'sō-(ˌ)tō, -'sü-(ˌ)tü\ *noun, plural* **Ba·so·tho** \bä-\ (1952)
: a member of the Basotho people

mosque \'mäsk\ *noun* [Middle French *mosquee*, from Old Italian *moschea*, from Old Spanish *mezquita*, from Arabic *masjid* temple, from *sajada* to prostrate oneself, worship] (1711)
: a building used for public worship by Muslims

mos·qui·to \mə-'skē-(ˌ)tō\ *noun, plural* **-toes** *also* **-tos** [Spanish, diminutive of *mosca* fly, from Latin *musca* — more at MIDGE] (circa 1583)
: any of a family (Culicidae) of dipteran flies with females that have a set of slender organs in the proboscis adapted to puncture the skin of animals and to suck their blood and that are in some cases vectors of serious diseases
— **mos·qui·to·ey** \-'skē-tə-wē\ *adjective*

mosquito fish *noun* (1928)
: either of two North American live-bearers (*Gambusia affinis* and *Heterandria formosa* of the family Poeciliidae) used especially to exterminate mosquito larvae

mosquito hawk *noun* (1737)
: DRAGONFLY

mosquito net *noun* (1745)
: a net or screen for keeping out mosquitoes

¹**moss** \'mȯs\ *noun* [Middle English *mos*; akin to Old High German *mos* moss, Latin *muscus*] (before 12th century)
1 *chiefly Scottish* **:** BOG, SWAMP; *especially* **:** a peat bog
2 a : any of a class (Musci) of bryophytic plants having a small leafy often tufted stem bearing sex organs at its tip; *also* **:** a clump or sward of these plants **b :** any of various plants resembling moss in appearance or habit of growth
3 : a mossy covering

— **moss·like** \-ˌlīk\ *adjective*

²**moss** *transitive verb* (15th century)
: to cover or overgrow with moss

moss agate *noun* (1798)
: an agate mineral containing brown, black, or green mosslike or dendritic markings

moss animal *noun* (1881)
: BRYOZOAN

moss·back \'mȯs-ˌbak\ *noun* (1872)
1 : a large sluggish fish (as a largemouth bass)
2 : an extremely old-fashioned or reactionary person **:** FOGY
— **moss·backed** \-ˌbakt\ *adjective*

moss green *noun* (1884)
: a variable color averaging a moderate yellow-green

moss–grown \'mȯs-ˌgrōn\ *adjective* (14th century)
1 : overgrown with moss
2 : ANTIQUATED

moss pink *noun* (circa 1856)
: a low-growing perennial phlox (*Phlox subulata*) widely cultivated for its abundant usually pink or white flowers

moss rose *noun* (1776)
: an old-fashioned garden rose (*Rosa centifolia mucosa*) that has a glandular mossy calyx and flower stalk

moss–troop·er \'mȯs-ˌtrü-pər\ *noun* (1645)
1 : one of a class of 17th century raiders in the marshy border country between England and Scotland
2 : PIRATE
— **moss–troop·ing** \-piŋ\ *adjective*

mossy \'mȯ-sē\ *adjective* **moss·i·er; -est** (15th century)
1 : resembling moss
2 : covered with moss or something like moss
3 : ANTIQUATED ⟨the *mossy* precepts of the . . . prescriptive grammarians —Thomas Pyles⟩

mossy zinc *noun* (1910)
: a granulated form of zinc made by pouring melted zinc into water

¹**most** \'mōst\ *adjective* [Middle English, from Old English *mǣst*; akin to Old High German *meist* most, Old English *māra* more — more at MORE] (before 12th century)
1 : greatest in quantity, extent, or degree ⟨the *most* ability⟩
2 : the majority of ⟨*most* people⟩

²**most** *adverb* (before 12th century)
1 : to the greatest or highest degree — often used with an adjective or adverb to form the superlative ⟨the *most* challenging job he ever had⟩
2 : to a very great degree ⟨was *most* persuasive⟩

³**most** *noun* (12th century)
: the greatest amount ⟨it's the *most* I can do⟩
— **at most** *or* **at the most :** as an extreme limit ⟨took him an hour *at most*⟩

⁴**most** *pronoun, singular or plural in construction* (13th century)
: the greatest number or part ⟨*most* become discouraged and quit⟩

⁵**most** *adverb* [by shortening] (circa 1584)
: ALMOST ⟨we'll be crossing the river *most* any time now —Hamilton Basso⟩ □

-most *adjective suffix* [Middle English, alteration of -*mest* (as in *formest* foremost)]
: most ⟨inner*most*⟩ **:** most toward ⟨head*most*⟩

most·ly \'mōst-lē\ *adverb* (1594)
: for the greatest part **:** MAINLY

Most Reverend (15th century)
— used as a title for an archbishop or a Roman Catholic bishop

mot \'mō\ *noun, plural* **mots** \'mō(z)\ [French, word, saying, from Late Latin *muttum* grunt — more at MOTTO] (1631)
: a pithy or witty saying

¹mote \'mōt\ *verbal auxiliary* [Middle English, from Old English *mōtan* to be allowed to — more at MUST] (before 12th century)
archaic **:** MAY, MIGHT

²mote \'mōt\ *noun* [Middle English *mot*, from Old English; akin to Middle Dutch & Frisian *mot* sand] (before 12th century)
: a small particle **:** SPECK

mo·tel \mō-'tel\ *noun* [blend of *motor* and *hotel*] (1925)
: an establishment which provides lodging and parking and in which the rooms are usually accessible from an outdoor parking area

mo·tet \mō-'tet\ *noun* [Middle English, from Middle French, diminutive of *mot*] (14th century)
: a polyphonic choral composition on a sacred text usually without instrumental accompaniment

moth \'mȯth\ *noun, plural* **moths** \'mȯthz, 'mȯths\ [Middle English *mothe*, from Old English *moththe*; akin to Middle High German *motte* moth] (before 12th century)
1 : CLOTHES MOTH
2 : any of various usually nocturnal lepidopteran insects with antennae that are often feathery, with a stouter body, duller coloring, and proportionally smaller wings than the butterflies, and with larvae that are plant-eating caterpillars
— **moth·like** \-,līk\ *adjective*
— **mothy** \'mȯ-thē\ *adjective*

¹moth·ball \'mȯth-,bȯl\ *noun* (1906)
1 : a ball made formerly of camphor but now often of naphthalene and used to keep moths from clothing
2 *plural* **:** a condition of protective storage ⟨put the ships in *mothballs* after the war⟩; *also* **:** a state of having been rejected for further use or dismissed from further consideration ⟨put that idea in *mothballs*⟩

²mothball *transitive verb* (1943)
1 : to deactivate (as a ship) and prevent deterioration chiefly by dehumidification
2 : to withdraw from use or service and keep in reserve

moth bean *noun* [probably by folk etymology from Marathi *maṭh* moth bean] (1884)
: a bean (*Phaseolus aconitifolius*) that is cultivated especially in India for its cylindrical pods and small yellowish brown seeds

moth–eat·en \'mȯth-,ē-t³n\ *adjective* (14th century)
1 : eaten into by moth larvae ⟨*moth-eaten* clothes⟩
2 a : DILAPIDATED **b :** ANTIQUATED, OUTMODED

¹moth·er \'mə-thər\ *noun* [Middle English *moder*, from Old English *mōdor*; akin to Old High German *muoter* mother, Latin *mater*, Greek *mētēr*, Sanskrit *mātṛ*] (before 12th century)
1 a : a female parent **b** (1) **:** a woman in authority; *specifically* **:** the superior of a religious community of women (2) **:** an old or elderly woman
2 : SOURCE, ORIGIN ⟨necessity is the *mother* of invention⟩
3 : maternal tenderness or affection
4 [short for *motherfucker*] **:** one that is particularly impressive or contemptible — sometimes considered vulgar
— **moth·er·hood** \-,hu̇d\ *noun*
— **moth·er·less** \-ləs\ *adjective*
— **moth·er·less·ness** *noun*

²mother *adjective* (13th century)
1 a : of, relating to, or being a mother **b** : bearing the relation of a mother
2 : derived from or as if from one's mother

3 : acting as or providing parental stock — used without reference to sex

³mother *transitive verb* **moth·ered; moth·er·ing** \-thə-riŋ, -thriŋ\ (1548)
1 a : to give birth to **b :** to give rise to **:** PRODUCE
2 : to care for or protect like a mother

⁴mother *noun* [archaic *mother* dregs, lees; akin to Middle Dutch *moeder* dregs] (circa 1828)
: MOTHER OF VINEGAR

moth·er·board \-,bōrd, -,bȯrd\ *noun* (1972)
: the main circuit board especially of a microcomputer

Mother Car·ey's chicken \-'kar-ēz-, -'ker-\ *noun* [origin unknown] (1767)
: STORM PETREL

mother cell *noun* (1845)
: a cell that gives rise to other cells usually of a different sort

mother country *noun* (1587)
1 : the country from which the people of a colony or former colony derive their origin
2 : the country of one's parents or ancestors; *also* **:** FATHERLAND
3 : a country that is the origin of something

moth·er·fuck·er \'mə-thər-,fə-kər\ *noun* (1959)
: one that is formidable, contemptible, or offensive — usually considered obscene; usually used as a generalized term of abuse
— **moth·er·fuck·ing** \-kiŋ\ *adjective*

Mother Goose *noun*
: the legendary author of a collection of nursery rhymes first published in London about 1760

mother hen *noun* (1954)
: a person who assumes an overly protective maternal attitude

moth·er·house \-,hau̇s\ *noun* (1661)
1 : the convent in which the superior of a religious community resides
2 : the original convent of a religious community

Mother Hub·bard \-'hə-bərd\ *noun* [probably from *Mother Hubbard*, character in a nursery rhyme] (1884)
: a loose usually shapeless dress

moth·er·in·law \'mə-thər-ən-,lȯ, 'mȧth-rən-, 'mə-thərn-\ *noun, plural* **moth·ers–in–law** \'mə-thər-zən-\ (14th century)
1 : the mother of one's spouse
2 *archaic* **:** STEPMOTHER

moth·er·land \'mə-thər-,land\ *noun* (1711)
1 : a country regarded as a place of origin (as of an idea or a movement)
2 : MOTHER COUNTRY 2

mother lode *noun* (1874)
1 : the principal vein or lode of a region
2 : a principal source or supply

moth·er·ly \-lē\ *adjective* (before 12th century)
1 : of, relating to, or characteristic of a mother ⟨*motherly* advice⟩
2 : resembling a mother **:** MATERNAL
— **moth·er·li·ness** *noun*

moth·er·na·ked \,mə-thər-'nā-kəd, *especially Southern* -'ne-kəd\ *adjective* (14th century)
: stark naked

Mother Nature *noun* (1601)
: nature personified as a woman considered as the source and guiding force of creation

moth·er·of·pearl \,mə-thə-rə(v)-'pər(-ə)l\ *noun* (circa 1510)
: the hard pearly iridescent substance forming the inner layer of a mollusk shell

mother of vinegar (1601)
: a slimy membrane composed of yeast and bacterial cells that develops on the surface of alcoholic liquids undergoing acetous fermentation and is added to wine or cider to produce vinegar — called also *mother*

Mother's Day *noun* (1908)
: the 2d Sunday in May appointed for the honoring of mothers

mother tongue *noun* (14th century)
1 : one's native language
2 : a language from which another language derives

mother wit *noun* (15th century)
: natural wit or intelligence

¹moth·proof \'mȯth-,prüf\ *adjective* (1893)
: impervious to penetration by moths ⟨*mothproof* wool⟩

²mothproof *transitive verb* (1925)
: to make mothproof
— **moth·proof·er** *noun*

mo·tif \mō-'tēf\ *noun* [French, motive, motif, from Middle French — more at MOTIVE] (1848)
1 : a usually recurring salient thematic element (as in the arts); *especially* **:** a dominant idea or central theme
2 : a single or repeated design or color
— **mo·tif·ic** \-'tē-fik, -'ti-\ *adjective*

¹mo·tile \'mō-t³l, -,tīl\ *adjective* [Latin *motus*, past participle of *movēre*] (circa 1859)
: exhibiting or capable of movement
— **mo·til·i·ty** \mō-'ti-lə-tē\ *noun*

²motile *noun* (1886)
: a person whose prevailing mental imagery takes the form of inner feelings of action

¹mo·tion \'mō-shən\ *noun* [Middle English *mocioun*, from Middle French *motion*, from Latin *motion-, motio* movement, from *movēre* to move] (14th century)
1 a : an act, process, or instance of changing place **:** MOVEMENT **b :** an active or functioning state or condition ⟨set the divorce proceedings in *motion*⟩
2 : an impulse or inclination of the mind or will
3 a : a proposal for action; *especially* **:** a formal proposal made in a deliberative assembly **b :** an application made to a court or judge to obtain an order, ruling, or direction
4 *obsolete* **a :** a puppet show **b :** PUPPET
5 : MECHANISM
6 a : an act or instance of moving the body or its parts **:** GESTURE **b** *plural* **:** ACTIVITIES, MOVEMENTS
7 : melodic change of pitch
— **mo·tion·al** \'mō-shnəl, -shə-n³l\ *adjective*
— **mo·tion·less** \'mō-shən-ləs\ *adjective*
— **mo·tion·less·ly** *adverb*
— **mo·tion·less·ness** *noun*
— **in motion** *of an offensive football player* **:** running parallel to the line of scrimmage before the snap

²motion *verb* **mo·tioned; mo·tion·ing** \'mō-sh(ə-)niŋ\ (1747)
intransitive verb
: to signal by a movement or gesture ⟨the pitcher *motioned* to the catcher⟩
transitive verb
: to direct by a motion ⟨*motioned* me to the seat⟩

motion picture *noun* (1896)
1 : a series of pictures projected on a screen in rapid succession with objects shown in successive positions slightly changed so as to produce the optical effect of a continuous picture in which the objects move
2 : a representation (as of a story) by means of motion pictures **:** MOVIE

motion sickness *noun* (1942)
: sickness induced by motion (as in travel by air, car, or ship) and characterized by nausea

mo·ti·vate \'mō-tə-,vāt\ *transitive verb* **-vat·ed; -vat·ing** (1885)
: to provide with a motive **:** IMPEL ⟨questions that excite and *motivate* youth⟩
— **mo·ti·va·tive** \-,vā-tiv\ *adjective*
— **mo·ti·va·tor** \-,vā-tər\ *noun*

\ə\ abut \'ə\ kitten \ər\ further \a\ ash \ā\ ace
\ä\ mop, mar \au̇\ out \ch\ chin \e\ bet \ē\ easy
\g\ go \i\ hit \ī\ ice \j\ job \ŋ\ sing \ō\ go
\ȯ\ law \ȯi\ boy \th\ thin \th\ the \ü\ loot \u̇\ foot
\y\ yet \zh\ vision *see also* Guide to Pronunciation

mo·ti·va·tion \ˌmō-tə-'vā-shən\ noun (1873)
1 a : the act or process of motivating **b :** the condition of being motivated
2 : a motivating force, stimulus, or influence **:** INCENTIVE, DRIVE
— **mo·ti·va·tion·al** \-shnəl, -shə-nᵊl\ adjective
— **mo·ti·va·tion·al·ly** adverb

¹mo·tive \'mō-tiv, 2 is also mō-'tēv\ noun [Middle English, from Middle French motif, from motif, adjective, moving, from Medieval Latin motivus, from Latin motus, past participle of movēre to move] (15th century)
1 : something (as a need or desire) that causes a person to act
2 : a recurrent phrase or figure that is developed through the course of a musical composition
3 : MOTIF ☆
— **mo·tive·less** \-ləs\ adjective
— **mo·tive·less·ly** adverb
— **mo·ti·vic** \-'tē-vik\ adjective

²mo·tive \'mō-tiv\ adjective [Middle French or Medieval Latin; Middle French motif, from Medieval Latin motivus] (1502)
1 : moving or tending to move to action
2 : of or relating to motion or the causing of motion ⟨motive energy⟩

³mo·tive \'mō-tiv\ transitive verb **mo·tived; mo·tiv·ing** (circa 1650)
: MOTIVATE

motive power noun (1889)
1 : an agency (as water or steam) used to impart motion especially to machinery
2 : something (as a locomotive or a motor) that provides motive power to a system

mo·tiv·i·ty \mō-'ti-və-tē\ noun (circa 1687)
: the power of moving or producing motion

mot juste \mō-zhɶst\ noun, plural **mots justes** \same\ [French] (1912)
: the exactly right word or phrasing

¹mot·ley \'mät-lē\ adjective [Middle English, perhaps from mot mote, speck] (14th century)
1 : variegated in color ⟨a motley coat⟩
2 : composed of diverse often incongruous elements ⟨a motley crowd⟩

²motley noun [Middle English, probably from ¹motley] (14th century)
1 : a woolen fabric of mixed colors made in England between the 14th and 17th centuries
2 : a garment made of motley; especially **:** the characteristic dress of the professional fool
3 : JESTER, FOOL
4 : a mixture especially of incongruous elements

mot·mot \'mät-ˌmät\ noun [New Latin momot, motmot] (1837)
: any of a family (Momotidae) of long-tailed mostly green nonpasserine birds of Central and South American tropical forests

mo·to·cross \'mō-tō-ˌkrós\ noun [French, from moto motorcycle (short for motocyclette) + cross-country, from English] (1951)
: a closed-course motorcycle race over natural or simulated rough terrain (as with steep inclines, hairpin turns, and mud); also **:** the sport of engaging in motocross races

mo·to·neu·ron \ˌmō-tə-'nü-ˌrän, -'nyü-; -'nür-ˌän, -'nyür-\ noun [motor + neuron] (1908)
: a neuron that passes from the central nervous system or a ganglion toward a muscle and conducts an impulse that causes movement — called also motor neuron
— **mo·to·neu·ro·nal** \-'nür-ə-nᵊl, -'nyür-; -nù-'rō-nᵊl, -nyù-\ adjective

¹mo·tor \'mō-tər\ noun [Latin, from movēre to move] (1586)
1 : one that imparts motion; specifically **:** PRIME MOVER
2 : any of various power units that develop energy or impart motion: as **a :** a small compact engine **b :** INTERNAL COMBUSTION ENGINE; especially **:** a gasoline engine **c :** a rotating machine that transforms electrical energy into mechanical energy

3 : MOTOR VEHICLE; especially **:** AUTOMOBILE
— **mo·tor·dom** \-dəm\ noun
— **mo·tor·less** \-ləs\ adjective

²motor adjective (1840)
1 a : causing or imparting motion **b :** of, relating to, or being a motoneuron or a nerve containing motoneurons ⟨motor fiber⟩ **c :** of, relating to, concerned with, or involving muscular movement ⟨motor areas of the brain⟩
2 a : equipped with or driven by a motor **b :** of, relating to, or involving an automobile **c :** designed for motor vehicles or motorists

³motor (1896)
intransitive verb
1 : to travel by automobile **:** DRIVE
2 : to move or proceed at a vigorous steady pace ⟨motored down the field for a touchdown⟩
transitive verb
: to transport by automobile

mo·tor·bike \'mō-tər-ˌbīk\ noun (1903)
: a small usually lightweight motorcycle
— **motorbike** intransitive verb

mo·tor·boat \-ˌbōt\ noun (1902)
: a boat propelled usually by an internal combustion engine
— **mo·tor·boat·er** \-ˌbō-tər\ noun
— **mo·tor·boat·ing** \-tiŋ\ noun

motor bus noun (1901)
: BUS 1a — called also motor coach

mo·tor·cade \'mō-tər-ˌkād\ noun (1913)
: a procession of motor vehicles
— **motorcade** intransitive verb

mo·tor·car \-ˌkär\ noun (circa 1890)
1 : AUTOMOBILE
2 usually **motor car :** a railroad car containing motors for propulsion

motor court noun (1936)
: MOTEL

mo·tor·cy·cle \'mō-tər-ˌsī-kəl\ noun [motor bicycle] (1896)
: a 2-wheeled automotive vehicle having one or two saddles
— **motorcycle** intransitive verb
— **mo·tor·cy·clist** \-k(ə-)list\ noun

motor home noun (1965)
: a large motor vehicle equipped as living quarters — compare MOBILE HOME

mo·tor·ic \mō-'tór-ik, -'tär-\ adjective (1930)
: MOTOR 1c
— **mo·tor·i·cal·ly** \-i-k(ə-)lē\ adverb

motor inn noun (1951)
: MOTEL; especially **:** a large multistory motel — called also motor hotel

mo·tor·ise British variant of MOTORIZE

mo·tor·ist \'mō-tə-rist\ noun (1896)
: a person who travels by automobile

mo·tor·ize \'mō-tə-ˌrīz\ transitive verb **-ized; -iz·ing** (circa 1913)
1 : to equip with a motor
2 : to equip with automobiles
— **mo·tor·i·za·tion** \ˌmō-tə-rə-'zā-shən\ noun

motor lodge noun (1949)
: MOTEL

mo·tor·man \'mō-tər-mən\ noun (1890)
: an operator of a motor-driven vehicle (as a streetcar or subway train)

mo·tor·mouth \-ˌmauth\ noun (1971)
: a person who talks excessively

motor pool noun (1942)
: a group of motor vehicles centrally controlled (as by a governmental agency) and dispatched for use as needed

motor sailer noun (1923)
: a motorboat with sailing equipment

motor scooter noun (1919)
: a low 2- or 3-wheeled automotive vehicle resembling a child's scooter and having a seat so that the rider does not straddle the engine

motor ship noun (1915)
: a seagoing ship propelled by an internal combustion engine

motor torpedo boat noun (1940)
: PT BOAT

mo·tor·truck \'mō-tər-ˌtrək\ noun (1930)

: an automotive truck used especially for transporting freight

motor unit noun (1925)
: a motoneuron together with the muscle fibers on which it acts

motor vehicle noun (1890)
: an automotive vehicle not operated on rails; especially **:** one with rubber tires for use on highways

mo·tor·way \'mō-tər-ˌwā\ noun (1903)
chiefly British **:** SUPERHIGHWAY

motte \'mät\ noun [Middle English mote, from Old French mote, motte] (13th century)
: MOUND, HILL; especially **:** a hill serving as a site for a Norman castle in Britain

motte and bailey noun (1900)
: a medieval Norman castle consisting of two connecting ditched stockaded mounds with the higher mound surmounted by the keep and the lower one containing barracks and other buildings

¹mot·tle \'mä-tᵊl\ noun [probably back-formation from motley] (1676)
1 : a colored spot
2 a : a surface having colored spots or blotches **b :** the arrangement of such spots or blotches on a surface
3 : MOSAIC 5
— **mot·tled** \-tᵊld\ adjective

²mottle transitive verb **mot·tled; mot·tling** \'mät-liŋ, 'mä-tᵊl-iŋ\ (1676)
: to mark with spots or blotches of different color or shades of color as if stained
— **mot·tler** \'mät-lər, 'mä-tᵊl-ər\ noun

mottled enamel noun (1928)
: spotted tooth enamel caused by drinking water containing excessive fluorides during the time the teeth are calcifying

mot·to \'mä-(ˌ)tō\ noun, plural **mottoes** also **mottos** [Italian, from Late Latin muttum grunt, from Latin muttire to mutter] (1588)
1 : a sentence, phrase, or word inscribed on something as appropriate to or indicative of its character or use
2 : a short expression of a guiding principle

moue \'mü\ noun [French, from Middle French — more at MOW] (1850)
: a little grimace **:** POUT

mou·flon also **mouf·flon** \mü-'flōⁿ\ noun [French mouflon, from Italian dialect muvrone, from Late Latin mufron-, mufro] (1774)
: either of two wild sheep (Ovis orientalis and O. musimon) of the mountains of Sardinia, Corsica and western Asia that have large curling horns in the males and are sometimes included in a single species

mouflon

mou·jik \mü-'zhēk, -'zhik\ *variant of* MUZHIK

mou·lage \mü-'läzh\ *noun* [French, molding, from Middle French, from *mouler* to mold, from Old French *modle* mold — more at MOLD] (1902)
1 : an impression or cast made for use especially as evidence in a criminal investigation
2 : the taking of an impression for use as evidence in a criminal investigation

mould \'mōld\ *variant of* MOLD

mould·ing \'mōl-diŋ\ *variant of* MOLDING

moult \'mōlt\ *variant of* MOLT

¹mound \'maund\ *transitive verb* [origin unknown] (1515)
1 *archaic* : to enclose or fortify with a fence or a ridge of earth
2 : to form into a mound

²mound *noun, often attributive* [origin unknown] (1551)
1 *archaic* : HEDGE, FENCE
2 a (1) : an artificial bank or hill of earth or stones; *especially* : one constructed over a burial or ceremonial site (2) : the slightly elevated ground on which a baseball pitcher stands **b** : a rounded hill or natural formation
3 a : HEAP, PILE ⟨*mounds* of work⟩ **b** : a small rounded mass ⟨a *mound* of mashed potatoes⟩

Mound Builder *noun* (1838)
: a member of a prehistoric American Indian people whose extensive earthworks are found from the Great Lakes down the Mississippi valley to the Gulf of Mexico

¹mount \'maunt\ *noun* [Middle English, from Old English *munt* & Old French *mont*, both from Latin *mont-, mons*; akin to Welsh *mynydd* mountain, Latin *minari* to project, threaten] (before 12th century)
1 : a high hill — used especially before an identifying name ⟨*Mount* Everest⟩
2 *archaic* : EARTHWORK 1
3 : MOUND 2a(1)

²mount *verb* [Middle English, from Middle French *monter*, from (assumed) Vulgar Latin *montare*, from Latin *mont-, mons*] (14th century)
intransitive verb
1 : RISE, ASCEND
2 : to increase in amount or extent ⟨expenses began to *mount*⟩
3 : to get up on something above the level of the ground; *especially* : to seat oneself (as on a horse) for riding
transitive verb
1 a : to go up : CLIMB **b** (1) : to seat or place oneself on (2) : COVER 6a
2 a : to lift up : RAISE **b** (1) : to put or have (as artillery) in position (2) : to have as equipment **c** (1) : to organize and equip ⟨an attacking force⟩ ⟨*mount* an army⟩ (2) : to launch and carry out (as an assault or a campaign)
3 : to set on something that elevates
4 a : to cause to get on a means of conveyance **b** : to furnish with animals for riding
5 : to post or set up for defense or observation ⟨*mounted* some guards⟩
6 a : to attach to a support **b** : to arrange or assemble for use or display
7 a : to prepare (as a specimen) for examination or display **b** : to prepare and supply with materials needed for performance or execution ⟨*mount* an opera⟩
— **mount·able** \'maun-tə-bəl\ *adjective*
— **mount·er** *noun*

³mount *noun* (15th century)
1 : an act or instance of mounting; *specifically* : an opportunity to ride a horse in a race
2 : FRAME, SUPPORT: as **a** : the material (as cardboard) on which a picture is mounted **b** : a jewelry setting **c** (1) : an undercarriage or part on which a device (as a motor or an artillery piece) rests in service (2) : an attachment for an accessory **d** : a hinge, card, or acetate envelope for mounting a stamp **e** : a glass slide with its accessories on which objects are placed for examination with a microscope

3 : a means of conveyance; *especially* : SADDLE HORSE

moun·tain \'maun-tⁿn\ *noun, often attributive* [Middle English, from Old French *montaigne*, from (assumed) Vulgar Latin *montanea*, from feminine of *montaneus* of a mountain, alteration of Latin *montanus*, from *mont-, mons*] (13th century)
1 a : a landmass that projects conspicuously above its surroundings and is higher than a hill **b** : an elongated ridge
2 a : a great mass **b** : a vast number or quantity

mountain ash *noun* (1597)
: any of various trees or shrubs (genus *Sorbus*) of the rose family with pinnate leaves and red or orange-red fruits

mountain bike *noun* (1984)
: an all-terrain bicycle with wide knobby tires, straight handlebars, and typically 18 or 21 gears
— **mountain biker** *noun*
— **mountain biking** *noun*

mountain bluebird *noun* (1860)
: a bluebird (*Sialia currucoides*) of western North America having a blue-breasted rather than red-breasted male

mountain cranberry *noun* (1848)
: a low evergreen shrub (*Vaccinium vitis-idaea minus*) of north temperate uplands with red edible berries — called also *lingonberry*

mountain dew *noun* (1827)
: MOONSHINE 3

moun·tain·eer \,maun-tⁿn-'ir\ *noun* (1610)
1 : a native or inhabitant of a mountainous region
2 : a person who climbs mountains for sport

moun·tain·eer·ing *noun* (1803)
: the sport or technique of scaling mountains

mountain goat *noun* (1833)
: a ruminant mammal (*Oreamnos americanus*) of mountainous northwestern North America that has a thick white coat and slightly curved horns and resembles a goat

mountain goat

mountain gorilla *noun* (1939)
: a gorilla (*Gorilla gorilla beringei*) inhabiting the Virunga mountain range

mountain laurel *noun* (1759)
: a North American evergreen shrub or small tree (*Kalmia latifolia*) of the heath family with glossy leaves and umbels of rose-colored or white flowers

mountain lion *noun* (1859)
: COUGAR

mountain mahogany *noun* (1810)
: any of a genus (*Cercocarpus*) of western North American evergreen shrubs or small trees of the rose family

mountain man *noun* (1839)
: an American frontiersman (as a trapper) at home in the wilderness

moun·tain·ous \'maun-tⁿn-əs, 'maunt-nəs\ *adjective* (14th century)
1 : containing many mountains
2 : resembling a mountain : HUGE
— **moun·tain·ous·ly** *adverb*
— **moun·tain·ous·ness** *noun*

mountain sheep *noun* (1802)
: any of various wild sheep (as bighorn, argali, or Dall sheep) inhabiting high mountains

mountain sickness *noun* (1848)
: altitude sickness experienced especially above 10,000 feet (3000 meters) and caused by insufficient oxygen in the air

moun·tain·side \'maun-tⁿn-,sīd\ *noun* (14th century)
: the side of a mountain

mountain time *noun, often M capitalized* (1883)

: the time of the 7th time zone west of Greenwich that includes the Rocky mountain states of the U.S. — see TIME ZONE illustration

moun·tain·top \'maun-tⁿn-,täp\ *noun* (1593)
: the summit of a mountain

moun·tainy \'maun-tⁿn-ē, 'maunt-nē\ *adjective* (1613)
1 : MOUNTAINOUS
2 : of, relating to, or living in mountains

¹moun·te·bank \'maun-ti-,baŋk\ *noun* [Italian *montimbanco*, from *montare* to mount (from—assumed—Vulgar Latin) + *in* in, on (from Latin) + *banco, banca* bench — more at BANK] (1577)
1 : a person who sells quack medicines from a platform
2 : a boastful unscrupulous pretender : CHARLATAN
— **moun·te·bank·ery** \-,baŋ-k(ə-)rē\ *noun*

²mountebank (1607)
transitive verb
obsolete : to beguile or transform by trickery ⟨I'll *mountebank* their loves —Shakespeare⟩
intransitive verb
: to play the mountebank

Mount·ie \'maun-tē\ *noun* [*mount*ed policeman] (1914)
: a member of the Royal Canadian Mounted Police

mount·ing \'maun-tiŋ\ *noun* (1563)
: ³MOUNT 2

mourn \'mōrn, 'mȯrn\ *verb* [Middle English, from Old English *murnan*; akin to Old High German *mornēn* to mourn, Greek *mermēra* care — more at MEMORY] (before 12th century)
intransitive verb
1 : to feel or express grief or sorrow
2 : to show the customary signs of grief for a death; *especially* : to wear mourning
3 : to murmur mournfully — used especially of doves
transitive verb
1 : to feel or express grief or sorrow for
2 : to utter mournfully
— **mourn·er** *noun*
— **mourn·ing·ly** \'mōr-niŋ-lē, 'mȯr-\ *adverb*

mourn·ful \'mōrn-fəl, 'mȯrn-\ *adjective* (15th century)
1 : expressing sorrow : SORROWFUL
2 : full of sorrow : SAD
3 : causing sorrow or melancholy : GLOOMY
— **mourn·ful·ly** \-fə-lē\ *adverb*
— **mourn·ful·ness** *noun*

mourn·ing \'mōr-niŋ, 'mȯr-\ *noun* (13th century)
1 : the act of sorrowing
2 a : an outward sign (as black clothes or an armband) of grief for a person's death **b** : a period of time during which signs of grief are shown

mourning cloak *noun* (1898)
: a blackish brown nymphalid butterfly (*Nymphalis antiopa*) with a broad yellow border on the wings found in temperate parts of Europe, Asia, and North America

mourning dove *noun* (1833)
: a wild American dove (*Zenaida macroura*) with a pointed tail and a plaintive coo

¹mouse \'maus\ *noun, plural* **mice** \'mīs\ [Middle English, from Old English *mūs*; akin to Old High German *mūs* mouse, Latin *mus*, Greek *mys* mouse, muscle] (before 12th century)
1 : any of numerous small rodents (as of the genus *Mus*) with pointed snout, rather small ears, elongated body, and slender tail
2 : a timid person

3 : a dark-colored swelling caused by a blow; *specifically* : BLACK EYE
4 : a small mobile manual device that controls movement of the cursor and selection of functions on a computer display

²mouse \'maůz\ *verb* **moused; mous·ing** (13th century)
intransitive verb
1 : to hunt for mice
2 : to search or move stealthily or slowly
transitive verb
1 *obsolete* **a :** BITE, GNAW **b :** to toy with roughly
2 : to search for carefully — usually used with *out*

mouse–ear \'maůs-,ir\ *noun* (13th century)
1 : a Eurasian hawkweed (*Hieracium pilosella*) that has soft hairy leaves and has been introduced into North America
2 : any of several plants other than mouse-ear that have soft hairy leaves

mouse–ear chickweed *noun* (1731)
: any of several hairy chickweeds (genus *Cerastium* and especially *C. vulgatum*)

mous·er \'maů-sər, *US also & chiefly British* -zər\ *noun* (15th century)
: a catcher of mice and rats; *especially* : a cat proficient at mousing

¹mouse·trap \'maůs-,trap\ *noun* (15th century)
1 : a trap for mice
2 : a stratagem that lures one to defeat or destruction
3 : TRAP 2b

²mousetrap *transitive verb* (circa 1864)
: to snare in or as if in a mousetrap

Mous·que·taire \,mü-skə-'tar, -'ter\ *noun* [French — more at MUSKETEER] (1705)
: a French musketeer; *especially* : one of the royal musketeers of the 17th and 18th centuries conspicuous for their daring and their dandified dress

mous·sa·ka \,mü-sə-'kä\ *noun* [New Greek *mousakas*, from Turkish *musakka*] (1931)
: a Middle Eastern dish of ground meat (as lamb or beef) and sliced eggplant often topped with a seasoned sauce

¹mousse \'müs\ *noun* [French, literally, froth, moss, of Germanic origin; akin to Old High German *mos* moss — more at MOSS] (1892)
1 : a light spongy food usually containing cream or gelatin
2 : a molded chilled dessert made with sweetened and flavored whipped cream or egg whites and gelatin 〈chocolate *mousse*〉
3 : a foamy preparation used in styling hair

²mousse *transitive verb* **moussed; mous·ing** (1984)
: to style (hair) with mousse

mous·se·line \,mü-sə-'lēn, ,müs-'lēn\ *noun* [French, literally, muslin — more at MUSLIN] (1696)
1 : a fine sheer fabric (as of rayon) that resembles muslin
2 a : a sauce (as hollandaise) to which whipped cream or beaten egg whites have been added **b :** MOUSSE 1 〈salmon *mousseline*〉

mousseline de soie \-də-'swä\ *noun, plural* **mousselines de soie** *same*\ [French, literally, silk muslin] (1850)
: a silk muslin having a crisp finish

mous·tache *variant of* MUSTACHE
mous·ta·chio *variant of* MUSTACHIO
Mous·te·ri·an \mü-'stir-ē-ən\ *adjective* [French *moustérien*, from *Le Moustier*, cave in Dordogne, France] (1890)
: of or relating to a Middle Paleolithic culture that is characterized by well-made flake tools often considered the work of Neanderthal man

mousy *or* **mous·ey** \'maů-sē, -zē\ *adjective* **mous·i·er; -est** (1853)
: of, relating to, or resembling a mouse: as **a** : QUIET, STEALTHY **b :** TIMID, RETIRING **c :** grayish brown
— **mous·i·ly** \-sə-lē, -zə-\ *adverb*
— **mous·i·ness** \-sē-nəs, -zē-\ *noun*

¹mouth \'maůth\ *noun, plural* **mouths** \'maůthz *also* 'maůz, 'maůths; *in synecdochic compounds like "blabbermouths" ths more frequently* 'ths] *often attributive* [Middle English, from Old English *mūth*; akin to Old High German *mund* mouth and perhaps to Latin *mentum* chin] (before 12th century)
1 a : the natural opening through which food passes into the body of an animal and which in vertebrates is typically bounded externally by the lips and internally by the pharynx and encloses the tongue, gums, and teeth **b :** GRIMACE 〈made a *mouth*〉 **c :** an individual requiring food 〈had too many *mouths* to feed〉
2 a : VOICE, SPEECH 〈finally gave *mouth* to her feelings〉 **b :** MOUTHPIECE 3a **c** (1) : a tendency to excessive talk (2) : saucy or disrespectful language : IMPUDENCE
3 : something that resembles a mouth especially in affording entrance or exit: as **a** : the place where a stream enters a larger body of water **b :** the surface opening of an underground cavity **c :** the opening of a container **d :** an opening in the side of an organ flue pipe
— **mouth–like** \'maůth-,līk\ *adjective*
— **down in the mouth :** DEJECTED, SULKY

²mouth \'maůth *also* 'maůth\ *verb* (14th century)
transitive verb
1 a : SPEAK, PRONOUNCE **b :** to utter bombastically : DECLAIM **c :** to repeat without comprehension or sincerity 〈always *mouthing* platitudes〉 **d :** to form soundlessly with the lips 〈the librarian *mouthed* the word "quiet"〉 **e :** to utter indistinctly : MUMBLE 〈*mouthed* his words〉
2 : to take into the mouth; *especially* : EAT
intransitive verb
1 a : to talk pompously : RANT — often used with *off* **b :** to talk insolently or impudently — usually used with *off*
2 : to move the mouth especially so as to make faces
— **mouth·er** *noun*

mouth·breed·er \'maůth-,brē-dər\ *noun* (1927)
: any of several fishes that carry their eggs and young in the mouth; *especially* : a North African cichlid fish (*Haplochromis multicolor*) often kept in aquariums

mouthed \'maůthd, 'maůtht\ *adjective* (14th century)
: having a mouth especially of a specified kind — often used in combination 〈a soft-*mouthed* fish〉

mouth·ful \'maůth-,fúl\ *noun* (15th century)
1 a : as much as a mouth will hold **b :** the quantity usually taken into the mouth at one time
2 : a small quantity
3 a : a very long word or phrase **b :** a comment or a statement rich in meaning or substance

mouth hook *noun* (1937)
: one of a pair of hooked larval mouthparts of some dipteran flies that function as jaws

mouth organ *noun* (1866)
: HARMONICA 2

mouth·part \'maůth-,pärt\ *noun* (1799)
: a structure or appendage near the mouth (as of an insect) especially when adapted for use in gathering or eating food

mouth·piece \-,pēs\ *noun* (1683)
1 : something placed at or forming a mouth
2 : a part (as of an instrument) that goes in the mouth or to which the mouth is applied
3 a : one that expresses or interprets another's views : SPOKESMAN **b** *slang* : a criminal lawyer

mouth–to–mouth *adjective* (1941)
: of, relating to, or being a method of artificial respiration in which the rescuer's mouth is placed tightly over the victim's mouth in order to force air into the victim's lungs by blowing forcefully enough every few seconds to inflate them

mouth·wash \'maůth-,wósh, -,wäsh\ *noun* (1840)
: a usually antiseptic liquid preparation for cleaning the mouth and teeth or freshening the breath

mouth·wa·ter·ing \-,wó-tə-riŋ, -,wä-\ *adjective* (1900)
: arousing the appetite : tantalizingly delicious or appealing 〈a *mouthwatering* aroma〉
— **mouth·wa·ter·ing·ly** \-lē\ *adverb*

mouthy \'maů-thē, -thē\ *adjective* **mouth·i·er; -est** (1589)
1 : excessively talkative : GARRULOUS
2 : marked by bombast or back talk

mou·ton \'mü-,tän, mü-'\ *noun* [French, sheep, sheepskin, from Middle French, ram — more at MUTTON] (1944)
: processed sheepskin that has been sheared and dyed to resemble beaver or seal

¹mov·able *or* **move·able** \'mü-və-bəl\ *adjective* (14th century)
1 : capable of being moved
2 : changing date from year to year 〈movable holidays〉
— **mov·abil·i·ty** \,mü-və-'bi-lə-tē\ *noun*
— **mov·able·ness** \'mü-və-bəl-nəs\ *noun*
— **mov·ably** \-blē\ *adverb*

²movable *or* **moveable** *noun* (15th century)
: something (as an article of furniture) that can be removed or displaced

¹move \'müv\ *verb* **moved; mov·ing** [Middle English, from Middle French *movoir*, from Latin *movēre*; probably akin to Sanskrit *mīvati* he moves, pushes] (13th century)
intransitive verb
1 a (1) : to go or pass to another place or in a certain direction with a continuous motion 〈*moved* into the shade〉 (2) : to proceed toward a certain state or condition 〈*moving* up the executive ladder〉 (3) : to become transferred during play 〈checkers *move* along diagonally adjacent squares〉 (4) : to keep pace 〈*moving* with the times〉 **b :** to start away from some point or place : DEPART **c :** to change one's residence or location
2 : to carry on one's life or activities in a specified environment 〈*moves* in the best circles〉
3 : to change position or posture : STIR 〈told him to be quiet and not to *move*〉
4 : to take action : ACT
5 a : to begin operating or functioning or working in a usual way **b :** to show marked activity 〈after a brief lull things really began to *move*〉 **c :** to move a piece (as in chess or checkers) during one's turn
6 : to make a formal request, application, or appeal
7 : to change hands by being sold or rented 〈goods that were *moving* slowly〉
8 *of the bowels* : EVACUATE
transitive verb
1 a (1) : to change the place or position of (2) : to dislodge or displace from a fixed position : BUDGE **b :** to transfer (as a piece in chess) from one position to another
2 a (1) : to cause to go or pass from one place to another with a continuous motion 〈*moved* the flag slowly up and down〉 (2) : to cause to advance **b :** to cause to operate or function : ACTUATE 〈this button *moves* the whole machine〉 **c :** to put into activity or rouse up from inactivity
3 : to cause to change position or posture
4 : to prompt or rouse to the doing of something : PERSUADE 〈the report *moved* the faculty to take action〉
5 a : to stir the emotions, feelings, or passions of 〈was deeply *moved* by such kindness〉 **b :** to affect in such a way as to lead to an indicated show of emotion 〈the story *moved* her to tears〉
6 a *obsolete* : BEG **b :** to make a formal application to
7 : to propose formally in a deliberative assembly 〈*moved* adjournment〉
8 : to cause (the bowels) to void

9 : to cause to change hands through sale or rent ☆

²**move** *noun* (1656)
1 a : the act of moving a piece (as in chess) **b :** the turn of a player to move
2 a : a step taken so as to gain an objective **:** MANEUVER ⟨a *move* to end the dispute⟩ **b :** the action of moving from a motionless position **c :** a change of residence or location **d :** an agile or deceptive action especially in sports
— **on the move 1 :** in a state of moving about from place to place ⟨a salesman is constantly *on the move*⟩ **2 :** in a state of moving ahead or making progress ⟨said that civilization is always *on the move*⟩

move in *intransitive verb* (1898)
: to occupy a dwelling or place of work
— **move in on :** to make advances or aggressive movements toward

move·less \'müv-ləs\ *adjective* (1578)
: being without movement **:** FIXED, IMMOBILE
— **move·less·ly** *adverb*
— **move·less·ness** *noun*

move·ment \'müv-mənt\ *noun* (14th century)
1 a (1) **:** the act or process of moving; *especially* **:** change of place or position or posture (2) **:** a particular instance or manner of moving **b** (1) **:** a tactical or strategic shifting of a military unit **:** MANEUVER (2) **:** the advance of a military unit **c :** ACTION, ACTIVITY — usually used in plural
2 a : TENDENCY, TREND ⟨detected a *movement* toward fairer pricing⟩ **b :** a series of organized activities working toward an objective; *also* **:** an organized effort to promote or attain an end ⟨the civil rights *movement*⟩
3 : the moving parts of a mechanism that transmit a definite motion
4 a : MOTION 7 **b :** the rhythmic character or quality of a musical composition **c :** a distinct structural unit or division having its own key, rhythmic structure, and themes and forming part of an extended musical composition **d :** particular rhythmic flow of language **:** CADENCE
5 a : the quality (as in a painting or sculpture) of representing or suggesting motion **b :** the vibrant quality in literature that comes from elements that constantly hold a reader's interest ⟨as a quickly moving action-filled plot⟩
6 a : an act of voiding the bowels **b :** matter expelled from the bowels at one passage

mov·er \'mü-vər\ *noun* (14th century)
: one that moves or sets something in motion; *especially* **:** one whose business or occupation is the moving of household goods from one residence to another

mover and shaker *noun, plural* **movers and shakers** (1951)
: a person who is active or influential in some field of endeavor

mov·ie \'mü-vē\ *noun* [*moving picture*] (1912)
1 : MOTION PICTURE
2 *plural* **:** a showing of a motion picture
3 *plural* **:** the motion-picture medium or industry

mov·ie·dom \'mü-vē-dəm\ *noun* (1916)
: FILMDOM

mov·ie·go·er \-,gō(-ə)r\ *noun* (1923)
: FILMGOER
— **mov·ie·going** \-,gō-iŋ, -,gȯ(-)iŋ\ *noun*

mov·ie·mak·er \-,mā-kər\ *noun* (1915)
: one who makes movies
— **mov·ie·mak·ing** \-,mā-kiŋ\ *noun*

mov·ing *adjective* (14th century)
1 a : marked by or capable of movement **b :** of or relating to a change of residence ⟨*moving* expenses⟩ **c :** used for transferring furnishings from one residence to another ⟨a *moving* van⟩ **d :** involving a motor vehicle that is in motion ⟨a *moving* violation⟩
2 a : producing or transferring motion or action **b :** stirring deeply in a way that evokes a strong emotional response ⟨a *moving* story of a faithful dog⟩ ☆
— **mov·ing·ly** \'mü-viŋ-lē\ *adverb*

moving picture *noun* (1896)
: MOTION PICTURE

Mov·i·ola \,mü-vē-'ō-lə\ *trademark*
— used for a device for editing motion-picture film and synchronizing the sound

¹**mow** \'maů\ *noun* [Middle English, heap, stack, from Old English *mūga;* akin to Old Norse *mūgi* heap] (before 12th century)
1 : a piled-up stack (as of hay or fodder); *also* **:** a pile of hay or grain in a barn
2 : the part of a barn where hay or straw is stored

²**mow** \'mō\ *verb* **mowed; mowed** *or* **mown** \'mōn\; **mow·ing** [Middle English, from Old English *māwan;* akin to Old High German *māen* to mow, Latin *metere* to reap, mow, Greek *aman*] (before 12th century)
transitive verb
1 a : to cut down with a scythe or sickle or machine **b :** to cut the standing herbage (as grass) of
2 a (1) **:** to kill or destroy in great numbers or mercilessly ⟨machine guns *mowed* down the enemy⟩ (2) **:** to cause to fall **:** KNOCK DOWN **b :** to overcome swiftly and decisively **:** ROUT ⟨*mowed* down the opposing team⟩
intransitive verb
: to cut down standing herbage (as grass)
— **mow·er** \'mō(-ə)r\ *noun*

³**mow** \'maů, 'mō\ *noun* [Middle English *mowe,* from Middle French *moue,* of Germanic origin; akin to Middle Dutch *mouwe* protruding lip] (14th century)
: GRIMACE

⁴**mow** \'maů, 'mō\ *intransitive verb* (15th century)
: to make grimaces

mox·ie \'mäk-sē\ *noun* [from *Moxie,* a trademark for a soft drink] (1930)
1 : ENERGY, PEP
2 : COURAGE, DETERMINATION
3 : KNOW-HOW, EXPERTISE

moyen–âge \mwȧ-ye-näzh\ *adjective* [French *moyen âge* Middle Ages] (1849)
: of or relating to medieval times

moz·za·rel·la \,mät-sə-'re-lə\ *noun* [Italian, diminutive of *mozza,* a kind of cheese, from *mozzare* to cut off, from *mozzo* cut off, docked, from (assumed) Vulgar Latin *mutius,* alteration of Latin *mutilus*] (1911)
: a moist white unsalted unripened cheese of mild flavor and a smooth rubbery texture

moz·zet·ta \mōt-'se-tə\ *noun* [Italian, probably from *mozzo* cut off] (1774)
: a short cape with a small ornamental hood worn over the rochet by Roman Catholic prelates

M phase *noun* [*mitosis*] (1945)
: the period in the cell cycle during which cell division takes place — compare G₁ PHASE, G₂ PHASE, S PHASE

Mr. \'mis-tər, *in rapid speech especially in sense* 2 \(,)mis(t)\ *noun, plural* **Messrs.** \'me-sərz\ [*Mr.* from Middle English, abbreviation of *maister* master; *Messrs.* abbreviation of *Messieurs,* from French, plural of *Monsieur*] (15th century)
1 — used as a conventional title of courtesy except when usage requires the substitution of a title of rank or an honorific or professional title before a man's surname ⟨spoke to *Mr.* Doe⟩
2 — used in direct address as a conventional title of respect before a man's title of office ⟨may I ask one more question, *Mr.* President⟩
3 — used before the name of a place (as a country or city) or of a profession or activity (as a sport) or before some epithet (as *clever*) to form a title applied to a male viewed or recognized as representative of the thing indicated ⟨*Mr.* Baseball⟩

Mr. Charlie \-'chär-lē\ *noun* [*Charlie,* from *Charles,* proper name] (circa 1941)
: a white man **:** white people — usually used disparagingly

mri·dan·ga \mri-'dän-gə, ,mər-i-\ *or* **mri·dan·gam** \-gəm\ *noun* [Sanskrit *mṛdaṅga*] (1921)
: a drum of India that is shaped like an elongated barrel and has tuned heads of different diameters

Mrs. \'mi-səz, -səs, *especially Southern* 'mi-zəz, -zəs, *or in rapid speech in sense* 1 \(,)miz, *or before given names* \(,)mis\ *noun, plural* **Mes·dames** \mā-'däm, -'dam\ [*Mrs.* abbreviation of *mistress; Mesdames* from French, plural of *Madame*] (1615)
1 a — used as a conventional title of courtesy except when usage requires the substitution of a title of rank or an honorific or professional title before a married woman's surname ⟨spoke to *Mrs.* Doe⟩ **b** — used before the name of a place (as a country or city) or of a profession or activity (as a sport) or before some epithet (as *clever*) to form a title applied to a married woman viewed or recognized as representative of the thing indicated ⟨*Mrs.* Golf⟩
2 : WIFE ⟨took the *Mrs.* to dinner⟩

Mrs. Grun·dy \-'grən-dē\ *noun* [from a character alluded to in Thomas Morton's *Speed the Plough* (1798)] (1813)
: one marked by prudish conventionality in personal conduct

Ms. \'miz\ *noun, plural* **Mss.** *or* **Mses.** \'mi-zəz\ [probably blend of *Miss* and *Mrs.*] (1949)
— used instead of *Miss* or *Mrs.* (as when the marital status of a woman is unknown or irrelevant) ⟨*Ms.* Mary Smith⟩

M16 \,em-(,)sik-'stēn\ *noun* [model *16*] (1968)
: a .223 caliber (5.56 mm.) gas-operated magazine-fed rifle for semiautomatic or automatic operation used by U.S. troops since the mid 1960s — called also *M16 rifle*

mu \'myü, 'mü\ *noun* [Greek *my*] (1823)
: the 12th letter of the Greek alphabet — see ALPHABET table

☆ **SYNONYMS**
Move, actuate, drive, impel mean to set or keep in motion. MOVE is very general and implies no more than the fact of changing position ⟨*moved* the furniture⟩. ACTUATE stresses transmission of power so as to work or set in motion ⟨turbines *actuated* by waterpower⟩. DRIVE implies imparting forward and continuous motion and often stresses the effect rather than the impetus ⟨a ship *driven* aground by hurricane winds⟩. IMPEL is usually figurative and suggests a great motivating impetus ⟨a candidate *impelled* by ambition⟩.

Moving, impressive, poignant, affecting, touching, pathetic mean having the power to produce deep emotion. MOVING may apply to any strong emotional effect including thrilling, agitating, saddening, or calling forth pity or sympathy ⟨a *moving* appeal for contributions⟩. IMPRESSIVE implies compelling attention, admiration, wonder, or conviction ⟨an *impressive* list of achievements⟩. POIGNANT applies to what keenly or sharply affects one's sensitivities ⟨a *poignant* documentary on the homeless⟩. AFFECTING is close to MOVING but most often suggests pathos ⟨an *affecting* deathbed reunion⟩. TOUCHING implies arousing tenderness or compassion ⟨the *touching* innocence in a child's eyes⟩. PATHETIC implies moving to pity or sometimes contempt ⟨*pathetic* attempts to justify misconduct⟩.

\ə\ **abut** \ᵊ\ **kitten** \ər\ **further** \a\ **ash** \ā\ **ace**
\ä\ **mop, mar** \aů\ **out** \ch\ **chin** \e\ **bet** \ē\ **easy**
\g\ **go** \i\ **hit** \ī\ **ice** \j\ **job** \ŋ\ **sing** \ō\ **go**
\ȯ\ **law** \ȯi\ **boy** \th\ **thin** \t̲h̲\ **the** \ü\ **loot** \ů\ **foot**
\y\ **yet** \zh\ **vision** *see also* Guide to Pronunciation

muc- *or* **muci-** *or* **muco-** *combining form* [Latin *muc-*, from *mucus*]
1 : mucus ⟨*muco*protein⟩
2 : mucous and ⟨*muco*cutaneous⟩

¹**much** \'məch\ *adjective* **more** \'mōr, 'mȯr\; **most** \'mōst\ [Middle English *muche* large, much, from *michel, muchel,* from Old English *micel, mycel;* akin to Old High German *mihhil* great, large, Latin *magnus,* Greek *megas,* Sanskrit *mahat*] (13th century)
1 : great in quantity, amount, extent, or degree ⟨there is *much* truth in what you say⟩ ⟨taken too *much* time⟩
2 *obsolete* : many in number
3 : more than is expected or acceptable : more than enough ⟨eighty bedrooms, a bit *much* for a family of seven —Peter Dragadze⟩
— **too much 1** : WONDERFUL, EXCITING **2** : TERRIBLE, AWFUL

²**much** *adverb* **more; most** (13th century)
1 a (1) : to a great degree or extent : CONSIDERABLY ⟨*much* happier⟩ (2) : VERY **b** (1) : FREQUENTLY, OFTEN (2) : by or for a long time ⟨didn't get to work *much* before noon⟩ **c** : by far ⟨was *much* the brightest student⟩
2 : NEARLY, APPROXIMATELY ⟨looks *much* the way his father did⟩
— **as much** : the same in quantity

³**much** *noun* (13th century)
1 : a great quantity, amount, extent, or degree ⟨gave away *much*⟩
2 : something considerable or impressive ⟨was not *much* to look at⟩

mu·cha·cho \mü-'chä-(ˌ)chō\ *noun, plural* **-chos** [Spanish, probably from *mocho* cropped, shorn] (1591)
1 *chiefly Southwest* : a male servant
2 *chiefly Southwest* : a young man

much as *conjunction* (circa 1699)
: however much : even though

much less *conjunction* (1710)
: to say nothing of — used especially in negative contexts to add to one item another denoting something less likely ⟨can hardly grow, *much less* ripen, till the stock is in the earth —Jonathan Swift⟩ ⟨he is never going to get out of the eighth grade, *much less* ever make it to college —Thomas Meehan⟩

much·ness \'məch-nəs\ *noun* (14th century)
: the quality or state of being great : GREATNESS
— **much of a muchness** : very much the same

mu·ci·lage \'myü-s(ə-)lij\ *noun* [Middle English *muscilage,* from Late Latin *mucilago* mucus, musty juice, from Latin *mucus*] (15th century)
1 : a gelatinous substance of various plants (as legumes or seaweeds) that contains protein and polysaccharides and is similar to plant gums
2 : an aqueous usually viscid solution (as of a gum) used especially as an adhesive

mu·ci·lag·i·nous \ˌmyü-sə-'la-jə-nəs\ *adjective* [Middle English *muscilaginous,* from Late Latin *mucilaginosus,* from *mucilagin-, mucilago*] (15th century)
1 : STICKY, VISCID
2 : of, relating to, full of, or secreting mucilage
— **mu·ci·lag·i·nous·ly** *adverb*

mu·cin \'myü-sᵊn\ *noun* [International Scientific Vocabulary *muc-*] (1846)
: any of various mucoproteins that occur especially in secretions of mucous membranes
— **mu·cin·ous** \-sᵊn-əs, 'myüs-nəs\ *adjective*

¹**muck** \'mək\ *noun* [Middle English *muk,* perhaps from Old English *-moc;* akin to Old Norse *myki* dung] (13th century)
1 : soft moist farmyard manure
2 : slimy dirt or filth
3 : defamatory remarks or writings
4 a (1) : dark highly organic soil (2) : MIRE, MUD **b** : something resembling muck : GUNK

5 : material removed in the process of excavating or mining
— **mucky** \'mə-kē\ *adjective*

²**muck** (14th century)
transitive verb
1 a : to clean up; *especially* : to clear of manure or filth — usually used with *out* **b** : to clear of muck
2 : to dress (as soil) with muck
3 : to dirty with or as if with muck : SOIL
intransitive verb
1 : to move or load muck (as in a mine)
2 : to engage in aimless activity — usually used with *about* or *around*
— **muck·er** *noun*

muck–a–muck \'mə-kə-ˌmək\ *or* **muck·ety–muck** \'mə-kə-tē-\ *noun* (1912)
: HIGH-MUCK-A-MUCK

muck·luck *variant of* MUKLUK

muck·rake \'mək-ˌrāk\ *intransitive verb* [obsolete *muckrake,* noun, rake for dung] (1910)
: to search out and publicly expose real or apparent misconduct of a prominent individual or business ◇
— **muck·rak·er** *noun*

muck up *transitive verb* (1896)
: to make a mess of : BUNGLE, SPOIL

mu·co·cu·ta·ne·ous \ˌmyü-kō-kyü-'tā-nē-əs\ *adjective* (1898)
: made up of or involving both typical skin and mucous membrane

¹**mu·coid** \'myü-ˌkȯid\ *adjective* [International Scientific Vocabulary *muc-*] (1849)
: resembling mucus

²**mucoid** *noun* [International Scientific Vocabulary] (1900)
: MUCOPROTEIN

mu·co·lyt·ic \ˌmyü-kə-'li-tik\ *adjective* (circa 1923)
: hydrolyzing mucopolysaccharides : tending to break down or lower the viscosity of mucin-containing body secretions or components ⟨*mucolytic* enzymes⟩

mu·co·pep·tide \ˌmyü-kō-'pep-ˌtīd\ *noun* (1959)
: PEPTIDOGLYCAN

mu·co·poly·sac·cha·ride \'myü-kō-ˌpä-li-'sa-kə-ˌrīd\ *noun* [International Scientific Vocabulary] (1938)
: GLYCOSAMINOGLYCAN

mu·co·pro·tein \ˌmyü-kə-'prō-ˌtēn also -'prō-tē-ən\ *noun* (1925)
: any of various complex conjugated proteins (as mucins) that contain polysaccharides and occur in body fluids and tissues

mu·co·sa \myü-'kō-zə\ *noun, plural* **-sae** \-(ˌ)zē, -ˌzī\ *or* **-sas** [New Latin, from Latin, feminine of *mucosus* mucous] (1880)
: MUCOUS MEMBRANE
— **mu·co·sal** \-zəl\ *adjective*

mu·cous \'myü-kəs\ *adjective* [Latin *mucosus,* from *mucus*] (1646)
1 : of, relating to, or resembling mucus
2 : secreting or containing mucus
3 : covered with or as if with mucus : SLIMY

mucous membrane *noun* (1812)
: a membrane rich in mucous glands; *specifically* : one that lines body passages and cavities which communicate directly or indirectly with the exterior

mu·cro \'myü-ˌkrō\ *noun, plural* **mu·cro·nes** \myü-'krō-(ˌ)nēz\ [New Latin *mucron-, mucro,* from Latin, point, edge] (1646)
: an abrupt sharp terminal point or tip or process (as of a leaf)
— **mu·cro·nate** \'myü-krə-ˌnāt\ *adjective*

mu·cus \'myü-kəs\ *noun* [Latin, nasal mucus; akin to Greek *myxa* mucus] (1661)
: a viscid slippery secretion that is usually rich in mucins and is produced by mucous membranes which it moistens and protects

¹**mud** \'məd\ *noun* [Middle English *mudde,* probably from Middle Low German] (14th century)

1 : a slimy sticky mixture of solid material with a liquid and especially water; *especially* : soft wet earth
2 : abusive and malicious remarks or charges ⟨political campaigners slinging *mud* at each other⟩
3 : ANATHEMA 1b — usually used in the phrase *one's name is mud*

²**mud** *transitive verb* **mud·ded; mud·ding** (1593)
1 : to make muddy or turbid
2 : to treat or plaster with mud

mud dauber *noun* (1856)
: any of various wasps (especially family Sphecidae) that construct mud cells in which the female places an egg with spiders or insects paralyzed by a sting to serve as food for the larva

¹**mud·dle** \'mə-dᵊl\ *verb* **mud·dled; mud·dling** \'məd-liŋ, 'mə-dᵊl-iŋ\ [probably from obsolete Dutch *moddelen,* from Middle Dutch, from *modde* mud; akin to Middle Low German *mudde*] (1676)
transitive verb
1 : to make turbid or muddy
2 : to befog or stupefy especially with liquor
3 : to mix confusedly
4 : to make a mess of : BUNGLE
intransitive verb
: to think or act in a confused aimless way
— **mud·dler** \'məd-lər, 'mə-dᵊl-ər\ *noun*

²**muddle** *noun* (circa 1818)
1 : a state of especially mental confusion
2 : a confused mess
— **mud·dly** \'məd-lē, 'mə-dᵊl-ē\ *adjective*

mud·dle·head·ed \ˌmə-dᵊl-'he-dəd\ *adjective* (1759)
1 : mentally confused
2 : INEPT, BUNGLING
— **mud·dle·head·ed·ly** *adverb*
— **mud·dle·head·ed·ness** *noun*

muddle through *intransitive verb* (circa 1864)
: to achieve a degree of success without much planning or effort

¹**mud·dy** \'mə-dē\ *adjective* **mud·di·er; -est** (15th century)
1 : morally impure : BASE
2 a : full of or covered with mud **b** : characteristic or suggestive of mud ⟨a *muddy* flavor⟩ ⟨*muddy* colors⟩ **c** : turbid with sediment
3 a : lacking in clarity or brightness : CLOUDY, DULL ⟨a *muddy* recording⟩ ⟨eyes *muddy* with sleep⟩ **b** : obscure in meaning : MUDDLED, CONFUSED ⟨*muddy* thinking⟩ ⟨a *muddy* style⟩

◇ WORD HISTORY
muckrake John Bunyan's religious allegory *The Pilgrim's Progress* (1678) includes a character identified as "a man . . . with a Muckrake in his hand," who busies himself so much with raking the muck—that is, with attending to worldly things—that his gaze is always downward and he never sees a celestial crown held above him. The metaphor inspired some occasional uses of *muckrake* in the 19th century, most notably in political circles, but the word received its greatest boost when it was used by Theodore Roosevelt in an April 1906 speech criticizing the excesses of journalists who had achieved popularity by exposing the corruption of public figures and institutions. Roosevelt said, "The men with the muckrakes are often indispensable to the well-being of society; but only if they know when to stop raking the muck." The term *muckraker* quickly became established in popular use as a name for reform writers such as Lincoln Steffens, Ida M. Tarbell, Edwin Markham, and Upton Sinclair. Although originally meant to be pejorative, the word was adopted by the writers themselves, and it acquired connotations of courageous honesty and social conscience.

— **mud·di·ly** \'mə-dᵊl-ē\ *adverb*

— **mud·di·ness** \'mə-dē-nəs\ *noun*

²**muddy** *transitive verb* **mud·died; mud·dy·ing** (1601)
1 : to soil or stain with or as if with mud
2 : to make turbid
3 : to make cloudy or dull
4 : CONFUSE

Mu·de·jar \mü-'the-,här, -,kär\ *noun, plural* **-ja·res** \-'the-hä-,räs, -kä-\ [Spanish *mudéjar*, from Arabic *mudajjan*, literally, allowed to remain] (1893)
: a Muslim living under a Christian king especially during the 8th to 11th centuries
— **Mudejar** *adjective*

mud·flat \'məd-,flat\ *noun* (1813)
: a level tract lying at little depth below the surface of water or alternately covered and left bare by the tide

mud·flow \-,flō\ *noun* (circa 1900)
: a moving mass of soil made fluid by rain or melting snow

mud·guard \-,gärd\ *noun* (1886)
1 a : FENDER d **b** : SPLASH GUARD
2 : a strip of material applied to a shoe upper just above the sole for protection against dampness or as an ornament

mud puppy *noun* (1882)
: a large American salamander (*Necturus maculosus*) that has external gills and is gray to rusty brown usually with bluish black spots

mud puppy

mu·dra \mə-'drä\ *noun* [Sanskrit *mudrā*] (1811)
: one of the symbolic hand gestures used in religious ceremonies and dances of India

mud·room \'məd-,rüm, -,rům\ *noun* (circa 1950)
: a room in a house designed especially for the shedding of dirty or wet footwear and clothing and located typically off the kitchen or in the basement

mud·sill \-,sil\ *noun* (1685)
1 : a supporting sill (as of a building or bridge) resting directly on a base and especially the earth
2 : a person of the lowest social level

mud·skip·per \-,ski-pər\ *noun* (1860)
: any of several Asian and Polynesian gobies (genera *Periophthalmus* and *Boleophthalmus*) that are able to skip about actively over wet mud and sand

mud·sling·er \-,sliŋ-ər\ *noun* (circa 1890)
: one that uses offensive epithets and invective especially against a political opponent
— **mud·sling·ing** \-,sliŋ-iŋ\ *noun*

mud·stone \-,stōn\ *noun* (circa 1736)
: an indurated shale produced by the consolidation of mud

mud turtle *noun* (1785)
: any of a genus (*Kinosternon*) of bottom-dwelling freshwater turtles with two transverse hinges on the plastron

Muen·ster \'mən(t)-stər, 'mün(t)-, 'mùn(t)-, 'min(t)-\ *noun* [*Münster, Munster*, France] (1902)
: a semisoft cheese that may be bland or sharp in flavor

mues·li \'myüs-lē, 'myüz-\ *noun* [German dialect (Swiss) *Müsli*, diminutive of German *Mus* soft food, mush, from Old High German *muos*; akin to Old English *mōs* food and probably to Old English *mete* food — more at MEAT] (1939)
: a breakfast cereal of Swiss origin consisting of rolled oats, nuts, and fruit

mu·ez·zin \mü-'e-zᵊn, myü-; 'mwe-zᵊn\ *noun* [Arabic *mu'adhdhin*] (1585)
: a Muslim crier who calls the hour of daily prayers

¹**muff** \'məf\ *noun* [Dutch *mof*, from Middle French *moufle* mitten, from Medieval Latin *muffula*] (1599)
1 : a warm tubular covering for the hands
2 : a cluster of feathers on the side of the face of some domestic fowls

²**muff** *verb* [probably from ¹*muff*] (1827)
transitive verb
1 : to handle awkwardly : BUNGLE
2 : to fail to hold (a ball) when attempting a catch
intransitive verb
1 : to act or do something stupidly or clumsily
2 : to muff a ball — compare FUMBLE

muff 1

³**muff** *noun* (1871)
1 : a bungling performance
2 : a failure to hold a ball in attempting a catch

muf·fin \'mə-fən\ *noun* [probably from Low German *muffen*, plural of *muffe* cake] (1703)
: a quick bread made of batter containing egg and baked in a muffin pan

muf·fle \'mə-fəl\ *transitive verb* **muf·fled; muf·fling** \'mə-f(ə-)liŋ\ [Middle English *muflen*] (15th century)
1 : to wrap up so as to conceal or protect : ENVELOP
2 *obsolete* : BLINDFOLD
3 a : to wrap or pad with something to dull the sound ⟨*muffle* the oarlocks⟩ **b** : to deaden the sound of
4 : KEEP DOWN, SUPPRESS

muf·fler \'mə-flər\ *noun* (circa 1536)
1 a : a scarf worn around the neck **b** : something that hides or disguises
2 : a device to deaden noise; *especially* : one forming part of the exhaust system of an automotive vehicle
— **muf·flered** *adjective*

¹**muf·ti** \'məf-tē, 'mùf-\ *noun* [Arabic *muftī*] (1586)
: a professional jurist who interprets Muslim law

²**muf·ti** \'məf-tē\ *noun* [probably from ¹*mufti*] (1816)
: ordinary dress as distinguished from that denoting an occupation or station ⟨a priest in *mufti*⟩; *especially* : civilian clothes when worn by a person in the armed forces

¹**mug** \'məg\ *noun* [origin unknown] (1664)
1 : a cylindrical drinking cup
2 a : the face or mouth of a person **b** : GRIMACE **c** : MUG SHOT
3 a *chiefly British* (1) : FOOL, BLOCKHEAD (2) : a person easily deceived **b** : PUNK, THUG
— **mug·ful** *noun*

²**mug** *verb* **mugged; mug·ging** (1855)
intransitive verb
: to pose or make faces especially to attract attention or for a camera
transitive verb
: PHOTOGRAPH

³**mug** *transitive verb* **mugged; mug·ging** [probably from earlier *mug* to strike in the face, perhaps from ¹*mug*] (circa 1864)
: to assault usually with intent to rob
— **mug·gee** \,mə-'gē\ *noun*

¹**mug·ger** \'mə-gər\ *noun* [Hindi *magar*, from Sanskrit *makara* water monster] (1844)
: a common usually harmless freshwater crocodile (*Crocodylus palustris*) of southeastern Asia

²**mugger** *noun* [³*mug*] (1863)
: one who attacks with intent to rob

³**mugger** *noun* [²*mug*] (1892)
: one that grimaces especially before an audience

mug·gy \'mə-gē\ *adjective* **mug·gi·er; -est** [English dialect *mug* drizzle] (1746)
: being warm, damp, and close
— **mug·gi·ness** \'mə-gē-nəs\ *noun*

Mu·ghal *variant of* MOGUL

mu·gho pine \'mü-(,)gō-, 'myü-\ *noun* [probably from French *mugho* mugho pine, from Italian *mugo*] (circa 1756)
: a shrubby spreading pine (*Pinus mugo mughus*) widely cultivated as an ornamental — called also *mugo pine*

mug's game \'məgz-\ *noun* (1910)
: a profitless or futile activity

mug shot *noun* (1950)
: a photograph of usually a person's head and especially face; *specifically* : a police photograph of a suspect's face or profile

mug up (circa 1860)
intransitive verb
British : to study intensively (as for an examination)
transitive verb
: to work up by study

mug·wump \'məg-,wəmp\ *noun* [obsolete slang *mugwump* kingpin, from Massachuset *mugquomp, muggumquomp* war leader] (1884)
1 : a bolter from the Republican party in 1884
2 : an independent in politics ◇

Mu·ham·mad·an \mō-'ha-mə-dən, -'hä- *also* mü-\ *adjective* (1681)
: of or relating to Muhammad or Islam
— **Muhammadan** *noun*
— **Mu·ham·mad·an·ism** \-də-,ni-zəm\ *noun*

Muhammadan calendar *noun* (circa 1889)
: ISLAMIC CALENDAR

Muhammadan era *noun* (circa 1889)
: ISLAMIC ERA

Mu·har·ram \mü-'har-əm\ *noun* [Arabic *Muḥarram*] (circa 1615)
1 : the 1st month of the Islamic year — see MONTH table
2 : a Muslim festival held during Muharram

mu·ja·hid·een *or* **mu·ja·hed·in** *also* **mu·ja·hed·een** \mü-,jä-hi-'dēn, mü-, -jä-\ *noun plural* [Arabic *mujāhidīn*, plural of *mujāhid*, literally, person who wages jihad] (1922)
: Islamic guerrilla fighters especially in the Middle East

mu·jik \mü-'zhēk, -'zhik\ *variant of* MUZHIK

muk·luk \'mək-,lək\ *noun* [Yupik *maklak* bearded seal] (1868)

\ə\ abut \ᵊ\ kitten \ər\ further \a\ ash \ā\ ace
\ä\ mop, mar \au̇\ out \ch\ chin \e\ bet \ē\ easy
\g\ go \i\ hit \ī\ ice \j\ job \ŋ\ sing \ō\ go
\ȯ\ law \ȯi\ boy \th\ thin \t̲h̲\ the \ü\ loot \u̇\ foot
\y\ yet \zh\ vision *see also* Guide to Pronunciation

1 : a sealskin or reindeer-skin boot worn by Eskimos

2 : a boot often of duck with a soft leather sole and worn over several pairs of socks

muk·tuk \'mək-ˌtək\ *noun* [Inuit *maktak*] (1835)

: whale skin used for food

mu·lat·to \mə-'la-(ˌ)tō, mù-, myù-, -'lä-\ *noun*, *plural* **-toes** *or* **-tos** [Spanish *mulato*, from *mulo* mule, from Latin *mulus*] (1593)

1 : the first-generation offspring of a black person and a white person

2 : a person of mixed white and black ancestry

mul·ber·ry \'məl-ˌber-ē, -b(ə-)rē\ *noun* [Middle English *murberie*, *mulberie*, from Middle French *moure* mulberry (from Latin *morum*, from Greek *moron*) + Middle English *berie* berry] (14th century)

1 : any of a genus (*Morus* of the family Moraceae, the mulberry family) of trees with an edible usually purple multiple fruit that is an aggregate of juicy one-seeded drupes; *also* : the fruit

2 : a dark purple or purplish black

mulch \'məlch\ *noun* [perhaps irregular from English dialect *melch* soft, mild] (1657)

: a protective covering (as of sawdust, compost, or paper) spread or left on the ground to reduce evaporation, maintain even soil temperature, prevent erosion, control weeds, enrich the soil, or keep fruit (as strawberries) clean

— **mulch** *transitive verb*

¹**mulct** \'məlkt\ *noun* [Latin *multa*, *mulcta*] (1598)

: FINE, PENALTY

²**mulct** *transitive verb* (1611)

1 : to punish by a fine

2 a : to defraud especially of money : SWINDLE b : to obtain by fraud, duress, or theft

¹**mule** \'myü(ə)l\ *noun* [Middle English, from Old French *mul*, from Latin *mulus*] (13th century)

1 a : a hybrid between a horse and a donkey; *especially* : the offspring of a male donkey and a mare b : a self-sterile plant whether hybrid or not c : a usually sterile hybrid

2 : a very stubborn person

3 : a machine for simultaneously drawing and twisting fiber into yarn or thread and winding it into cops

4 *slang* : a person who smuggles or delivers illicit drugs

²**mule** *noun* [Middle French, a kind of slipper, from Latin *mulleus* shoe worn by magistrates] (1562)

: a shoe or slipper without quarter or heel strap — compare SCUFF

mule deer *noun* (1805)

: a long-eared deer (*Odocoileus hemionus*) of western North America that is larger and more heavily built than the common whitetail

mule skinner *noun* (1870)

: MULETEER

mu·le·ta \mü-'lā-tə, myü-\ *noun* [Spanish, crutch, muleta, diminutive of *mula* she-mule, from Latin, feminine of *mulus* mule] (1838)

mule deer

: a small cloth attached to a short tapered stick and used by a matador in place of the large cape during the final stage of a bullfight

mu·le·teer \ˌmyü-lə-'tir\ *noun* [French *muletier*, from *mulet*, from Old French, diminutive of *mul* mule] (1538)

: one who drives mules

mu·ley \'myü-lē, 'mü-, 'mù-\ *adjective* [of Celtic origin; akin to Irish & Scottish Gaelic *maol* bald, hornless, Welsh *moel*] (1840)

: POLLED, HORNLESS; *especially* : naturally hornless

mu·li·eb·ri·ty \ˌmyü-lē-'e-brə-tē\ *noun* [Late Latin *muliebritat-*, *muliebritas*, from Latin *muliebris* of a woman, from *mulier* woman] (1592)

: FEMININITY

mul·ish \'myü-lish\ *adjective* [¹*mule*] (1751)

: unreasonably and inflexibly obstinate

synonym see OBSTINATE

— **mul·ish·ly** *adverb*

— **mul·ish·ness** *noun*

¹**mull** \'məl\ *verb* [Middle English, from *mul*, *mol* dust, probably from Middle Dutch; akin to Old English *melu* meal — more at MEAL] (15th century)

transitive verb

1 : to grind or mix thoroughly : PULVERIZE

2 : to consider at length : PONDER — often used with *over*

intransitive verb

: MEDITATE, PONDER

²**mull** *transitive verb* [origin unknown] (1618)

: to heat, sweeten, and flavor (as wine or cider) with spices

³**mull** *noun* [by shortening & alteration from *mulmul* muslin, from Hindi *malmal*] (1798)

: a soft fine sheer fabric of cotton, silk, or rayon

⁴**mull** *noun* [German, from Danish *muld*, from Old Norse *mold* dust, soil; akin to Old High German *molta* dust, soil — more at MOLD] (1928)

1 : friable forest humus that forms a layer of mixed organic matter and mineral soil and merges gradually into the mineral soil beneath

2 : a finely powdered solid especially in a suspension

mul·lah \'mə-lə, 'mù-\ *noun* [Turkish *molla* & Persian & Hindi *mulla*, from Arabic *mawlā*] (1613)

: an educated Muslim trained in traditional religious law and doctrine and usually holding an official post

— **mul·lah·ism** \-lə-ˌi-zəm\ *noun*

mul·lein *also* **mul·len** \'mə-lən\ *noun* [Middle English *moleyne*, from Anglo-French *moleine*] (14th century)

: any of a genus (*Verbascum*) of usually woolly-leaved Eurasian herbs of the snapdragon family including some that are naturalized in North America

mullein pink *noun* (circa 1850)

: an Old World herb (*Lychnis coronaria*) of the pink family cultivated chiefly for its woolly herbage and crimson flowers

mull·er \'mə-lər\ *noun* [alteration of Middle English *molour*, probably from *mullen* to grind] (1612)

: a stone or piece of wood, metal, or glass used as a pestle for pounding or grinding

Mül·le·ri·an \myü-'lir-ē-ən, mi-, ˌmə-\ *adjective* [Fritz *Müller* (died 1897) German zoologist] (1899)

: of, relating to, or being mimicry that exists between two or more inedible or dangerous species (as of butterflies) and that is considered in evolutionary theory to be a mechanism reducing loss to predation by simplification of the recognition process

mul·let \'mə-lət\ *noun*, *plural* **mullet** *or* **mullets** [Middle English *molet*, from Middle French *mulet*, from Latin *mullus* red mullet, from Greek *myllos*] (14th century)

: any of a family (Mugilidae) of valuable chiefly marine food fishes with an elongate rather stout body

mul·li·gan \'mə-li-gən\ *noun* [probably from the name *Mulligan*] (circa 1949)

: a free shot sometimes given a golfer in informal play when the previous shot was poorly played

mulligan stew *noun* [probably from the name *Mulligan*] (1904)

: a stew made from whatever ingredients are available

mul·li·ga·taw·ny \ˌmə-li-gə-'tò-nē, -'tä-\ *noun* [Tamil *milakutanni*, from *milaku* pepper + *tanni* water] (1784)

: a rich soup usually of chicken stock seasoned with curry

mul·lion \'məl-yən\ *noun* [probably alteration of *monial* mullion] (1567)

: a slender vertical member that forms a division between units of a window, door, or screen or is used decoratively

— **mullion** *transitive verb*

mull·ite \'mə-ˌlīt\ *noun* [*Mull*, island of the Inner Hebrides] (1924)

: a mineral that is an orthorhombic silicate of aluminum which is resistant to corrosion and heat and is used as a refractory

multi- *combining form* [Middle English, from Middle French or Latin; Middle French, from Latin, from *multus* much, many — more at MELIORATE]

1 a : many : multiple : much ⟨*multi*valent⟩ b : more than two ⟨*multi*lateral⟩ c : more than one ⟨*multi*parous⟩

2 : many times over ⟨*multi*millionaire⟩

mul·ti·age	mul·ti·fre·quen·cy
mul·ti·agen·cy	mul·ti·func·tion
mul·ti·armed	mul·ti·func·tion·al
mul·ti·at·om	mul·ti·gen·er·a·tion·al
mul·ti·au·thor	
mul·ti·ax·i·al	mul·ti·gen·ic
mul·ti·band	mul·ti·grade
mul·ti·bank	mul·ti·grain
mul·ti·bar·rel	mul·ti·grid
mul·ti·bar·reled	mul·ti·group
mul·ti·bil·lion	mul·ti·hand·i·capped
mul·ti·bil·lion·aire	mul·ti·head·ed
mul·ti·blad·ed	mul·ti·hos·pi·tal
mul·ti·branched	mul·ti·hued
mul·ti·build·ing	mul·ti–in·dus·try
mul·ti·cam·pus	mul·ti–in·sti·tu·tion·al
mul·ti·car	
mul·ti·car·bon	mul·ti·lane
mul·ti·caus·al	mul·ti·lev·el
mul·ti·cell	mul·ti·lev·eled
mul·ti·celled	mul·ti·line
mul·ti·cel·lu·lar	mul·ti·lobed
mul·ti·cel·lu·lar·i·ty	mul·ti·manned
mul·ti·cen·ter	mul·ti·mega·ton
mul·ti·chain	mul·ti·mega·watt
mul·ti·cham·bered	mul·ti·mem·ber
mul·ti·chan·nel	mul·ti·me·tal·lic
mul·ti·char·ac·ter	mul·ti·mil·len·ni·al
mul·ti·city	mul·ti·mil·lion
mul·ti·cli·ent	mul·ti·mil·lion·aire
mul·ti·coat·ed	mul·ti·mode
mul·ti·col·or	mul·ti·mo·lec·u·lar
mul·ti·col·ored	mul·ti·na·tion
mul·ti·col·umn	mul·ti·nu·cle·ar
mul·ti·com·po·nent	mul·ti·nu·cle·ate
mul·ti·con·duc·tor	mul·ti·nu·cle·at·ed
mul·ti·copy	mul·ti·or·gas·mic
mul·ti·coun·ty	mul·ti·page
mul·ti·course	mul·ti·paned
mul·ti·cu·rie	mul·ti·pa·ram·e·ter
mul·ti·cur·ren·cy	mul·ti·part
mul·ti·di·a·lec·tal	mul·ti·par·ti·cle
mul·ti·di·men·sion·al	mul·ti·par·ty
mul·ti·di·men·sion·al·i·ty	mul·ti·path
	mul·ti·phase
mul·ti·di·rec·tion·al	mul·ti·phasic
mul·ti·dis·ci·plin·ary	mul·ti·pho·ton
mul·ti·dis·ci·pline	mul·ti·pic·ture
mul·ti·di·vi·sion·al	mul·ti·piece
mul·ti·do·main	mul·ti·pi·on
mul·ti·drug	mul·ti·pis·ton
mul·ti·elec·trode	mul·ti·plant
mul·ti·el·e·ment	mul·ti·play·er
mul·ti·em·ploy·er	mul·ti·pole
mul·ti·en·gine	mul·ti·pow·er
mul·ti·eth·nic	mul·ti·prob·lem
mul·ti·fac·et·ed	mul·ti·prod·uct
mul·ti·fam·i·ly	mul·ti·pur·pose
mul·ti·fil·a·ment	mul·ti·range
mul·ti·flash	mul·ti·re·gion·al
mul·ti·fo·cal	mul·ti·re·li·gious

mul·ti·room
mul·ti·screen
mul·ti·ser·vice
mul·ti·sid·ed
mul·ti·site
mul·ti·size
mul·ti·skilled
mul·ti·source
mul·ti·spe·cies
mul·ti·speed
mul·ti·sport
mul·ti·stemmed
mul·ti·step
mul·ti·sto·ried
mul·ti·sto·ry
mul·ti·strand·ed
mul·ti·syl·lab·ic
mul·ti·sys·tem

mul·ti·tal·ent·ed
mul·ti·ter·mi·nal
mul·ti·tiered
mul·ti·ton
mul·ti·tone
mul·ti·tow·ered
mul·ti·track
mul·ti·tril·lion
mul·ti·union
mul·ti·unit
mul·ti·use
mul·ti·vi·ta·min
mul·ti·vol·ume
mul·ti·wall
mul·ti·war·head
mul·ti·wave·length
mul·ti·year

mul·ti·cul·tur·al \ˌməl-tē-ˈkəlch-rəl, -ˌtī-, -ˈkəl-chə-\ *adjective* (1941)
: of, relating to, reflecting, or adapted to diverse cultures ⟨a *multicultural* society⟩ ⟨*multicultural* education⟩ ⟨a *multicultural* menu⟩
— **mul·ti·cul·tur·al·ism** \-rə-ˌli-zəm\ *noun*

mul·ti·en·zyme \-ˈen-ˌzīm\ *adjective* (1961)
: composed of or involving two or more enzymes that function in a biosynthetic pathway ⟨*multienzyme* complex⟩

mul·ti·fac·to·ri·al \-fak-ˈtōr-ē-əl, -ˈtȯr-\ *adjective* (1920)
1 : having characters or a mode of inheritance dependent on a number of genes at different loci
2 *or* **mul·ti·fac·tor** \-ˈfak-tər\ : having, involving, or produced by a variety of elements or causes
— **mul·ti·fac·to·ri·al·ly** \-fak-ˈtōr-ē-ə-lē, -ˈtȯr-\ *adverb*

mul·ti·far·i·ous \ˌməl-tə-ˈfar-ē-əs, -ˈfer-\ *adjective* [Medieval Latin *multifarius*, from Latin *multifariam* in many places] (1593)
: having or occurring in great variety : DIVERSE
— **mul·ti·far·i·ous·ness** *noun*

mul·ti·flo·ra rose \ˌməl-tə-ˈflōr-ə-, -ˈflȯr-\ *noun* [New Latin *multiflora*, specific epithet, literally, having many flowers] (1829)
: a vigorous thorny rose (*Rosa multiflora*) with clusters of small flowers

mul·ti·fold \ˈməl-ti-ˌfōld\ *adjective* (1806)
: MANY, NUMEROUS

mul·ti·form \ˈməl-ti-ˌfȯrm\ *adjective* [French *multiforme*, from Latin *multiformis*, from *multi-* + *-formis* -form] (1603)
: having many forms or appearances
— **mul·ti·for·mi·ty** \ˌməl-ti-ˈfȯr-mə-tē\ *noun*

mul·ti·germ \ˌməl-ti-ˈjərm, -ˌtī-\ *adjective* [probably from *multi-* + *germ*inate] (1950)
: producing or being a fruit cluster capable of giving rise to several plants ⟨a *multigerm* variety of sugar beet⟩

mul·ti·hull \ˈməl-ti-ˌhəl, -ˌtī-\ *noun* (1960)
: a vessel (as a catamaran or trimaran) with multiple side-by-side hulls — compare MONOHULL

mul·ti·lat·er·al \ˌməl-ti-ˈla-t(ə-)rəl, -ˌtī-\ *adjective* (1696)
1 : having many sides
2 : involving or participated in by more than two nations or parties ⟨*multilateral* agreements⟩
— **mul·ti·lat·er·al·ism** \-ˈla-t(ə-)rə-ˌli-zəm\ *noun*
— **mul·ti·lat·er·al·ist** \-list\ *noun*
— **mul·ti·lat·er·al·ly** *adverb*

mul·ti·lay·ered \-ˈlā-ərd, -ˈle-(ə)rd\ *or* **mul·ti·lay·er** \-ˈlā-ər, -ˈle(-ə)r\ *adjective* (1923)
: having or involving several distinct layers, strata, or levels

mul·ti·lin·gual \-ˈliŋ-gwəl, -ˈliŋ-gyə-wəl\ *adjective* (1838)
1 : of, containing, or expressed in several languages ⟨a *multilingual* sign⟩ ⟨*multilingual* dictionaries⟩

2 : using or able to use several languages ⟨*multilingual* translators⟩
— **mul·ti·lin·gual·ism** \-gwə-ˌli-zəm, -gyə-wə-\ *noun*
— **mul·ti·lin·gual·ly** \-gwə-lē, -gyə-wə-lē\ *adverb*

mul·ti·me·dia \-ˈmē-dē-ə\ *adjective* (1962)
: using, involving, or encompassing several media ⟨a *multimedia* approach to learning⟩
— **multimedia** *noun*

mul·ti·mod·al \-ˈmō-dᵊl\ *adjective* (1902)
: having or involving several modes, modalities, or maxima ⟨*multimodal* distributions⟩ ⟨*multimodal* responses⟩

mul·ti·na·tion·al \-ˈnash-nəl, -ˈna-shə-nᵊl\ *adjective* (1926)
1 : of or relating to more than two nationalities ⟨a *multinational* society⟩
2 a : of, relating to, or involving more than two nations ⟨a *multinational* alliance⟩ **b** : having divisions in more than two countries ⟨a *multinational* corporation⟩
— **multinational** *noun*

mul·ti·no·mi·al \-ˈnō-mē-əl\ *noun* [*multi-* + *-nomial* (as in *binomial*)] (1674)
: a mathematical expression that consists of the sum of several terms : POLYNOMIAL
— **multinomial** *adjective*

mul·tip·a·rous \ˌməl-ˈti-pə-rəs\ *adjective* [New Latin *multiparus*, from *multi-* + Latin *-parus* -parous] (1646)
1 : producing many or more than one at a birth
2 : having experienced one or more previous parturitions

mul·ti·par·tite \ˌməl-ti-ˈpär-ˌtīt\ *adjective* [Latin *multipartitus*, from *multi-* + *partitus*, past participle of *partire* to divide, from *part-*, *pars* part] (circa 1721)
1 : divided into several or many parts
2 : having numerous members or signatories ⟨a *multipartite* treaty⟩

¹mul·ti·ple \ˈməl-tə-pəl\ *adjective* [French, from Latin *multiplex*, from *multi-* + *-plex* -fold — more at -FOLD] (1647)
1 : consisting of, including, or involving more than one ⟨*multiple* births⟩
2 : MANY, MANIFOLD ⟨*multiple* achievements⟩
3 : shared by many ⟨*multiple* ownership⟩
4 : having numerous aspects or functions : VARIOUS
5 : being a group of terminals which make a circuit available at a number of points
6 : formed by coalescence of the ripening ovaries of several flowers ⟨a *multiple* fruit⟩

²multiple *noun* (1685)
1 a : the product of a quantity by an integer ⟨35 is a *multiple* of 7⟩ **b** : something in units of more than one or two
2 : PARALLEL 4b
3 *chiefly British* : CHAIN STORE

multiple allele *noun* (1938)
: an allele of a genetic locus having more than two allelic forms within a population

multiple–choice *adjective* (1926)
1 : having several answers from which one is to be chosen ⟨a *multiple-choice* question⟩
2 : composed of multiple-choice questions ⟨a *multiple-choice* test⟩

multiple factor *noun* (1915)
: one of a group of nonallelic genes that according to the multiple-factor hypothesis control various quantitative hereditary characters

multiple myeloma *noun* (1897)
: a disease of bone marrow that is characterized by the presence of numerous myelomas in various bones of the body

multiple personality *noun* (1901)
: an hysterical neurosis in which the personality becomes dissociated into two or more distinct but complex and socially and behaviorally integrated parts each of which becomes dominant and controls behavior from time to time to the exclusion of the others — compare SCHIZOPHRENIA, SPLIT PERSONALITY

multiple regression *noun* (1924)

: regression in which one variable is estimated by the use of more than one other variable

multiple sclerosis *noun* (1885)
: a demyelinating disease marked by patches of hardened tissue in the brain or the spinal cord and associated especially with partial or complete paralysis and jerking muscle tremor

multiple star *noun* (1850)
: several stars in close proximity that appear to form a single system

multiple store *noun* (1929)
chiefly British : CHAIN STORE

mul·ti·plet \ˈməl-tə-plət\ *noun* (1922)
1 : a spectrum line having several components
2 : a group of elementary particles that are different in charge but similar in other properties (as mass)

multiple–valued *adjective* (1882)
: having at least one and sometimes more of the values of the range associated with each value of the domain ⟨a *multiple-valued* function⟩ — compare SINGLE-VALUED

¹mul·ti·plex \ˈməl-tə-ˌpleks\ *adjective* [Latin] (1557)
1 : MANY, MULTIPLE
2 : being or relating to a system of transmitting several messages or signals simultaneously on the same circuit or channel

²multiplex (1907)
transitive verb
: to send (messages or signals) by a multiplex system
intransitive verb
: to multiplex messages or signals
— **mul·ti·plex·er** *also* **mul·ti·plex·or** \-ˌplek-sər\ *noun*

³multiplex *noun* (1985)
: a complex that houses several movie theaters

mul·ti·pli·cand \ˌməl-tə-plə-ˈkand\ *noun* [Latin *multiplicandus*, gerundive of *multiplicare*] (1594)
: the number that is to be multiplied by another

mul·ti·pli·ca·tion \ˌməl-tə-plə-ˈkā-shən\ *noun* [Middle English *multiplicacioun*, from Middle French *multiplication*, from Latin *multiplication-*, *multiplicatio*, from *multiplicare* to multiply] (14th century)
1 : the act or process of multiplying : the state of being multiplied
2 a : a mathematical operation that at its simplest is an abbreviated process of adding an integer to itself a specified number of times and that is extended to other numbers in accordance with laws that are valid for integers **b** : any of various mathematical operations that are analogous in some way to multiplication of the real numbers but are defined for other or larger sets of elements (as complex numbers, vectors, matrices, or functions)

multiplication sign *noun* (1907)
: a symbol used to indicate multiplication: **a** : TIMES SIGN **b** : DOT 2b

mul·ti·pli·ca·tive \ˌməl-tə-ˈpli-kə-tiv, ˈməl-tə-plə-ˌkā-tiv\ *adjective* (1653)
1 : tending or having the power to multiply
2 : of, relating to, or associated with a mathematical operation of multiplication ⟨the *multiplicative* property of 0 requires that $a \cdot 0 = 0$ and $0 \cdot a = 0$⟩
— **mul·ti·pli·ca·tive·ly** *adverb*

multiplicative identity *noun* (1958)
: an identity element (as 1 in the group of rational numbers without 0) that in a given mathematical system leaves unchanged any element by which it is multiplied

multiplicative inverse *noun* (1958)
: an element of a mathematical set that when multiplied by a given element yields the identity element — called also *reciprocal*

\ə\ abut \ᵊ\ kitten \ər\ further \a\ ash \ā\ ace \ä\ mop, mar \aů\ out \ch\ chin \e\ bet \ē\ easy \g\ go \i\ hit \ī\ ice \j\ job \ŋ\ sing \ō\ go \ȯ\ law \ȯi\ boy \th\ thin \t͟h\ the \ü\ loot \ů\ foot \y\ yet \zh\ vision *see also* Guide to Pronunciation

mul·ti·plic·i·ty \ˌməl-tə-'pli-sə-tē\ *noun, plural* **-ties** [Middle English, from Middle French *multiplicité*, from Late Latin *multiplicitat-, multiplicitas*, from Latin *multiplic-, multiplex*] (15th century)
1 a : the quality or state of being multiple or various **b :** the number of components in a system (as a multiplet or a group of energy levels)
2 : a great number
3 : the number of times a root of an equation or zero of a function occurs when there is more than one root or zero ⟨the *multiplicity* of $x = 2$ for the equation $(x - 2)^3 = 0$ is 3⟩

mul·ti·pli·er \'məl-tə-ˌplī-(ə)r\ *noun* (15th century)
: one that multiplies: as **a :** a number by which another number is multiplied **b :** an instrument or device for multiplying or intensifying some effect **c :** a machine, mechanism, or circuit that multiplies figures

¹mul·ti·ply \'məl-tə-ˌplī\ *verb* **-plied; -ply·ing** [Middle English *multiplien*, from Old French *multiplier*, from Latin *multiplicare*, from *multiplic-, multiplex* multiple] (13th century)
transitive verb
1 : to increase in number especially greatly or in multiples **: AUGMENT**
2 a : to find the product of by multiplication ⟨*multiply* 7 and 8⟩ **b :** to use as a multiplicand in multiplication with another number ⟨*multiply* 7 by 8⟩
intransitive verb
1 a : to become greater in number **: SPREAD b : BREED, PROPAGATE**
2 : to perform multiplication
synonym see INCREASE

²mul·ti·ply \-plē\ *adverb* (1881)
: in a multiple manner **:** in several ways ⟨*multiply* handicapped children⟩

mul·ti–ply \ˌməl-ti-'plī, -ˌtī-\ *adjective* (1926)
: composed of several plies

mul·ti·po·lar \-'pō-lər\ *adjective* [International Scientific Vocabulary] (1859)
1 : having several poles ⟨a *multipolar* generator⟩ ⟨*multipolar* mitoses⟩
2 : having several dendrites ⟨*multipolar* nerve cells⟩
3 : characterized by more than two centers of power or interest ⟨a *multipolar* world⟩
— **mul·ti·po·lar·i·ty** \-pō-'lar-ə-tē\ *noun*

mul·ti·po·ten·tial \-pə-'ten(t)-shəl\ *adjective* (1913)
: having the potential of becoming any of several mature cell types ⟨*multipotential* stem cell⟩

mul·ti·pro·cess·ing \-'prä-ˌse-siŋ, -'prō-, -sə-siŋ\ *noun* (1961)
: the processing of several computer programs at the same time especially by a computer system with two or more processors sharing a single memory
— **mul·ti·pro·ces·sor** \-sər\ *noun*

mul·ti·pro·gram·ming \-'prō-ˌgra-miŋ, -grə-\ *noun* (1959)
: the technique of utilizing several interleaved programs concurrently in a single computer system

mul·ti·pronged \-'prȯŋd\ *adjective* (1957)
1 : having several prongs ⟨*multipronged* fishing spears⟩
2 : having several distinct aspects or elements ⟨a *multipronged* attack on the problem⟩

mul·ti·ra·cial \-'rā-shəl\ *adjective* (1923)
: composed of, involving, or representing various races
— **mul·ti·ra·cial·ism** \-shə-ˌli-zəm\ *noun*

mul·ti·sense \'məl-ti-ˌsen(t)s\ *adjective* (1957)
: having several meanings ⟨*multisense* words⟩

mul·ti·sen·so·ry \ˌməl-ti-'sen(t)-sə-rē, -'sen(t)s-rē\ *adjective* (1949)
: relating to or involving several physiological senses ⟨*multisensory* teaching methods⟩ ⟨*multisensory* experience⟩

mul·ti·spec·tral \-'spek-trəl\ *adjective* (1965)
: of or relating to two or more ranges of frequencies or wavelengths in the electromagnetic spectrum

mul·ti·stage \'məl-ti-ˌstāj, -ˌtī-\ *adjective* (1904)
1 : having successive operating stages; *especially* **:** having propulsion units that operate in turn ⟨*multistage* rockets⟩
2 : conducted by or occurring in stages ⟨a *multistage* investigation⟩

mul·ti·state \-ˌstāt\ *adjective* (1944)
1 : having divisions in several states ⟨*multistate* enterprises⟩
2 : of, relating to, or involving several states ⟨a *multistate* attack on environmental pollution⟩

mul·ti·task·ing \-ˌtas-kiŋ\ *noun, often attributive* (1966)
: the concurrent performance of several jobs by a computer

mul·ti·tude \'məl-tə-ˌtüd, -ˌtyüd\ *noun* [Middle English, from Middle French or Latin; Middle French, from Latin *multitudin-, multitudo*, from *multus* much — more at MELIORATE] (14th century)
1 : the state of being many
2 : a great number **: HOST**
3 : a great number of people
4 : POPULACE, PUBLIC

mul·ti·tu·di·nous \ˌməl-tə-'tüd-nəs, -'tyüd-; -'tü-d°n-əs, -'tyü-\ *adjective* (1604)
1 : including a multitude of individuals **: POPULOUS** ⟨the *multitudinous* city⟩
2 : existing in a great multitude ⟨*multitudinous* opportunities⟩
3 : existing in or consisting of innumerable elements or aspects ⟨*multitudinous* applause⟩
— **mul·ti·tu·di·nous·ly** *adverb*
— **mul·ti·tu·di·nous·ness** *noun*

mul·ti·us·er \ˌməl-tī-'yü-zər, -tē-, -ti-\ *adjective* (1964)
: able to be used by more than one person simultaneously

mul·tiv·a·lence \ˌməl-'ti-və-lən(t)s\ *noun* (circa 1881)
: the quality or state of having many values, meanings, or appeals

mul·tiv·a·lent \ˌməl-ti-'vā-lənt, -ˌtī-, *especially in sense 3* ˌməl-'ti-və-\ *adjective* [International Scientific Vocabulary] (1874)
1 : POLYVALENT
2 : represented more than twice in the somatic chromosome number ⟨*multivalent* chromosomes⟩
3 : having many values, meanings, or appeals
— **multivalent** *noun*

mul·ti·var·i·able \ˌməl-ti-'ver-ē-ə-bəl, -ˌtī-, -'var-\ *adjective* (1963)
: MULTIVARIATE

mul·ti·var·i·ate \-'ver-ē-ət, -ˌāt\ *adjective* [*multi-* + *variable* + *³-ate*] (1951)
: having or involving a number of independent mathematical or statistical variables ⟨*multivariate* calculus⟩ ⟨*multivariate* data analysis⟩

mul·ti·ver·si·ty \-'vər-sə-tē, -ˌstē\ *noun, plural* **-ties** [*multi-* + *-versity* (as in *university*)] (1963)
: a very large university with many component schools, colleges, or divisions and widely diverse functions

mul·ti·vol·tine \-'vȯl-ˌtēn, -'vȯl-\ *adjective* [*multi-* + *-voltine* having a given number of broods (from French, from Italian *volta* time, turn) — more at VOLT] (1874)
: having several broods in a season ⟨*multivoltine* insects⟩

mul·ture \'məl-chər, *Scottish usually* 'mü-tər\ *noun* [Middle English *multyr*, from Middle French *molture*, literally, grinding, from (assumed) Vulgar Latin *molitura*, from Latin *molitus*, past participle of *molere* to grind — more at MEAL] (14th century)
chiefly Scottish **:** a fee for grinding grain at a mill

¹mum \'məm\ *adjective* [probably imitative of a sound made with closed lips] (14th century)
: SILENT ⟨keep *mum*⟩

²mum *intransitive verb* **mummed; mum·ming** [Middle English *mommen*, from Middle French *momer* to go masked] (1530)
1 : to perform in a pantomime
2 : to go about merrymaking in disguise during festivals

³mum *noun* [German *Mumme*] (1640)
: a strong ale or beer

⁴mum *chiefly British variant of* MOM

⁵mum *noun* (1917)
: CHRYSANTHEMUM

mum·ble \'məm-bəl\ *verb* **mum·bled; mum·bling** \-b(ə-)liŋ\ [Middle English *momelen*, of imitative origin] (14th century)
intransitive verb
: to utter words in a low confused indistinct manner **: MUTTER**
transitive verb
1 : to utter with a low inarticulate voice
2 : to chew or bite with or as if with toothless gums
— **mumble** *noun*
— **mum·bler** \-b(ə-)lər\ *noun*
— **mum·bly** \-b(ə-)lē\ *adjective*

mum·ble·ty–peg \'məm-bəl-(tē-)ˌpeg, -blē-ˌpeg\ *also* **mum·ble–the–peg** \-bəl-(thə-)ˌpeg, -blē-ˌpeg\ *or* **mumble peg** \-ˌpeg, -blē-\ *noun* [from the phrase *mumble the peg;* from the loser's originally having to pull out with his teeth a peg driven into the ground] (1627)
: a game in which the players try to flip a knife from various positions so that the blade will stick into the ground

mum·bo jum·bo \ˌməm-bō-'jəm-(ˌ)bō\ *noun* [*Mumbo Jumbo*, a masked figure among Mandingo peoples of western Africa] (1738)
1 : an object of superstitious homage and fear
2 a : a complicated often ritualistic observance with elaborate trappings **b :** complicated activity usually intended to obscure and confuse
3 : unnecessarily involved and incomprehensible language **: GIBBERISH**

mum·mer \'mə-mər\ *noun* [Middle French *momeur*, from *momer* to go masked] (1502)
1 : a performer in a pantomime; *broadly* **: ACTOR**
2 : one who goes merrymaking in disguise during festivals

mum·mery \'mə-mə-rē\ *noun, plural* **-mer·ies** (circa 1530)
1 : a performance by mummers
2 : a ridiculous, hypocritical, or pretentious ceremony or performance

mum·mi·chog \'mə-mi-ˌchȯg, -ˌchäg\ *noun* [Narraganset *moamitteaúg*] (1787)
: a common American killifish (*Fundulus heteroclitus* of the family Cyprinodontidae)

mum·mi·fy \'mə-mi-ˌfī\ *verb* **-fied; -fy·ing** (1628)
transitive verb
1 : to embalm and dry as or as if a mummy
2 a : to make into or like a mummy **b :** to cause to dry up and shrivel
intransitive verb
: to dry up and shrivel like a mummy
— **mum·mi·fi·ca·tion** \ˌmə-mi-fə-'kā-shən\ *noun*

¹mum·my \'mə-mē\ *noun, plural* **mummies** [Middle English *mummie* powdered parts of a mummified body used as a drug, from Middle French *momie*, from Medieval Latin *mumia* mummy, powdered mummy, from Arabic *mūmiyah* bitumen, mummy, from Persian *mūm* wax] (1615)
1 a : a body embalmed or treated for burial with preservatives in the manner of the ancient

Egyptians **b** : a body unusually well preserved **2** : one resembling a mummy

²mummy *chiefly British variant of* MOMMY

mumps \'məmps\ *noun plural but singular or plural in construction* [from plural of obsolete *mump* grimace] (1598)

: an acute contagious virus disease marked by fever and by swelling especially of the parotid gland

munch \'mənch\ *verb* [Middle English *monchen*, probably of imitative origin] (14th century)
transitive verb
: to eat with a chewing action ⟨many a mouthful is *munched* in private —Washington Irving⟩; *also* : to snack on ⟨drank coffee and *munched* homemade cookies —Lady Bird Johnson⟩
intransitive verb
: to eat or chew something; *also* : SNACK — usually used with *on*
— **munch·er** *noun*

Mun·chau·sen syndrome \'mən-,chau-zən-, ,mən-'chau-\ *noun* [Baron K. F. H. von *Münchausen* (died 1797) German soldier and proverbial teller of exaggerated tales] (1951)
: a condition characterized by the feigning of the symptoms of a disease or injury in order to undergo diagnostic tests, hospitalization, or medical or surgical treatment — called also *Munchausen's syndrome*

munch·ies \'mən-chēz\ *noun plural* (circa 1971)
1 : hunger pangs
2 : light snack foods

munch·kin \'mənch-,kin\ *noun* [the *Munchkins*, diminutive creatures in *The Wonderful Wizard of Oz* (1900) by L. Frank Baum] (1972)
: a person who is notably small and often endearing

Mun·da \'mùn-də\ *noun* (1901)
: a branch of the Austroasiatic language family spoken by tribal peoples of central and eastern India

mun·dane \,mən-'dān, 'mən-,\ *adjective* [Middle English *mondeyne*, from Middle French *mondain*, from Late Latin *mundanus*, from Latin *mundus* world] (15th century)
1 : of, relating to, or characteristic of the world
2 : characterized by the practical, transitory, and ordinary : COMMONPLACE ⟨the *mundane* concerns of day-to-day life⟩
synonym see EARTHLY
— **mun·dane·ly** *adverb*
— **mun·dane·ness** \-'dān-nəs, -,dān-\ *noun*
— **mun·dan·i·ty** \,mən-'dā-nə-tē\ *noun*

mun·dun·gus \,mən-'dəŋ-gəs\ *noun* [modification of Spanish *mondongo* tripe] (1641)
archaic : foul-smelling tobacco

mung bean \'məŋ-\ *noun* [Hindi *mũg*, from Sanskrit *mudga*] (1910)
: an erect bushy annual bean (*Phaseolus aureus*) that is widely cultivated in warm regions for its edible usually green or yellow seeds, for forage, and as the chief source of bean sprouts; *also* : the seed of the mung bean

mun·go \'məŋ-(,)gō\ *noun, plural* **mungos** [origin unknown] (1857)
: reclaimed wool of poor quality and very short staple

mu·ni \'myü-nē\ *noun* (1973)
: MUNICIPAL

¹mu·nic·i·pal \myù-'ni-s(ə-)pəl *also* myə-, mə-, -'ni-sə-bəl, ÷,myü-nə-'si-pəl\ *adjective* [Latin *municipalis* of a municipality, from *municip-, municeps* inhabitant of a municipality, from *munus* duty, service + *capere* to take — more at MEAN, HEAVE] (circa 1540)
1 : of or relating to the internal affairs of a major political unit (as a nation)

2 a : of, relating to, or characteristic of a municipality **b** : having local self-government
3 : restricted to one locality

²municipal *noun* (1925)
: a security issued by a state or local government or by an authority set up by such a government — usually used in plural

municipal court *noun* (1828)
1 : a court that sits in some cities and larger towns and that usually has civil and criminal jurisdiction over cases arising within the municipality
2 : POLICE COURT

mu·nic·i·pal·i·ty \myù-,ni-sə-'pa-lə-tē\ *noun, plural* **-ties** (1790)
1 : a primarily urban political unit having corporate status and usually powers of self-government
2 : the governing body of a municipality

mu·nic·i·pal·ize \myù-'ni-sə-pə-,līz\ *transitive verb* **-ized; -iz·ing** (1880)
: to bring under municipal ownership or supervision
— **mu·nic·i·pal·i·za·tion** \-,ni-s(ə-)pə-lə-'zā-shən\ *noun*

mu·nic·i·pal·ly \myù-'ni-sə-p(ə-)lē\ *adverb* (circa 1842)
: by or in terms of a municipality

mu·nif·i·cent \myù-'ni-fə-sənt\ *adjective* [back-formation from *munificence*, from Latin *munificentia*, from *munificus* generous, from *munus* service, gift — more at MEAN] (1583)
1 : very liberal in giving or bestowing : LAVISH
2 : characterized by great liberality or generosity
synonym see LIBERAL
— **mu·nif·i·cence** \-sən(t)s\ *noun*
— **mu·nif·i·cent·ly** *adverb*

mu·ni·ment \'myü-nə-mənt\ *noun* [Middle English, from Anglo-French, from Middle French, defense, from Latin *munimentum*, from *munire* to fortify] (15th century)
1 : the evidence (as documents) that enables one to defend the title to an estate or a claim to rights and privileges — usually used in plural
2 *archaic* : a means of defense

mu·ni·tion \myù-'ni-shən\ *noun* [Middle French, from Latin *munition-, munitio*, from *munire* to fortify, from *moenia* walls; akin to Latin *murus* wall and perhaps to Sanskrit *minoti* he builds, fastens] (1508)
1 *archaic* : RAMPART, DEFENSE
2 : ARMAMENT, AMMUNITION
— **munition** *transitive verb*

Mun·ster *variant of* MUENSTER

mun·tin \'mən-t³n\ *noun* [alteration of *montant* vertical dividing bar, from French, from present participle of *monter* to rise — more at MOUNT] (1774)
: a strip separating panes of glass in a sash

munt·jac \'mən(t)-,jak, 'mən-,chak\ *noun* [Sundanese (Austronesian language of western Java) *mənyčak*] (circa 1798)
: any of a genus (*Muntiacus*) of small deer of southeastern Asia and the East Indies — called also *barking deer*

mu·on \'myü-,än\ *noun* [contraction of earlier *mu-meson*, from *mu*] (1952)
: an unstable lepton that is common in the cosmic radiation near the earth's surface, has a mass about 207 times the mass of the electron, and exists in negative and positive forms
— **mu·on·ic** \myü-'ä-nik\ *adjective*

muntjac

mu·on·i·um \myü-'ō-nē-əm, -'ä-\ *noun* [New Latin] (1957)
: a short-lived quasi-atom consisting of an electron and a positive muon

¹mu·ral \'myùr-əl\ *adjective* [Latin *muralis*, from *murus* wall — more at MUNITION] (1586)
1 : of, relating to, or resembling a wall
2 : applied to and made integral with a wall or ceiling surface

²mural *noun* (1916)
: a mural work of art (as a painting)
— **mu·ral·ist** \-ə-list\ *noun*

mu·ram·ic acid \myù-'ra-mik-\ *noun* [Latin *murus* wall + English + glucos*amine* + ¹-*ic*] (1957)
: an amino sugar $C_9H_{17}NO_7$ that is a lactic acid derivative of glucosamine and is found especially in bacterial cell walls and in blue-green algae

¹mur·der \'mər-dər\ *noun* [partly from Middle English *murther*, from Old English *morthor*; partly from Middle English *murdre*, from Old French, of Germanic origin; akin to Old English *morthor*; akin to Old High German *mord* murder, Latin *mort-, mors* death, *mori* to die, *mortuus* dead, Greek *brotos* mortal] (before 12th century)
1 : the crime of unlawfully killing a person especially with malice aforethought
2 a : something very difficult or dangerous ⟨the traffic was *murder*⟩ **b** : something outrageous or blameworthy ⟨getting away with *murder*⟩

²murder *verb* **mur·dered; mur·der·ing** \'mər-d(ə-)riŋ\ (13th century)
transitive verb
1 : to kill (a human being) unlawfully and with premeditated malice
2 : to slaughter wantonly : SLAY
3 a : to put an end to **b** : TEASE, TORMENT **c** : MUTILATE, MANGLE ⟨*murders* French⟩ **d** : to defeat badly
intransitive verb
: to commit murder
synonym see KILL

mur·der·ee \,mər-də-'rē\ *noun* (1920)
: an actual or potential victim of a murder

mur·der·er \'mər-dər-ər\ *noun* (14th century)
: one who murders; *especially* : one who commits the crime of murder

mur·der·ess \'mər-də-rəs\ *noun* (14th century)
: a woman who murders

mur·der·ous \'mər-d(ə-)rəs\ *adjective* (1535)
1 a : having the purpose or capability of murder **b** : characterized by or causing murder or bloodshed
2 : having the ability or power to overwhelm : DEVASTATING ⟨*murderous* heat⟩
— **mur·der·ous·ly** *adverb*
— **mur·der·ous·ness** *noun*

mu·rein \'myùr-ē-ən, 'myùr-,ēn\ *noun* [*muram*ic acid + -*ein*, alteration of ²-*ine*] (1964)
: PEPTIDOGLYCAN

mu·rex \'myùr-,eks\ *noun, plural* **mu·ri·ces** \'myùr-ə-,sēz\ *or* **mu·rex·es** [New Latin, from Latin, mollusk yielding a purple dye; akin to Greek *myak-, myax* mussel] (1589)
: any of a genus (*Murex*) of marine gastropod mollusks having a rough and often spinose shell, abounding in tropical seas, and yielding a purple dye

mu·ri·ate \'myùr-ē-,āt\ *noun* [French, back-formation from (*acide*) *muriatique* muriatic acid] (1790)
: CHLORIDE

\ə\ abut \ᵊ\ kitten \ər\ further \a\ ash \ā\ ace
\ä\ mop, mar \au̇\ out \ch\ chin \e\ bet \ē\ easy
\g\ go \i\ hit \ī\ ice \j\ job \ŋ\ sing \ō\ go
\ȯ\ law \ȯi\ boy \th\ thin \t͟h\ the \ü\ loot \u̇\ foot
\y\ yet \zh\ vision *see also* Guide to Pronunciation

mu·ri·at·ic acid \ˌmyu̇r-ē-'a-tik-\ *noun* [French *muriatique*, from Latin *muriaticus* pickled in brine, from *muria* brine] (1790) : HYDROCHLORIC ACID

mu·rid \'myu̇r-əd\ *adjective* [ultimately from Latin *mur-, mus* mouse — more at MOUSE] (circa 1909) : of or relating to a family (Muridae) comprising the typical mice and rats — **murid** *noun*

mu·rine \'myu̇r-ˌīn\ *adjective* [ultimately from Latin *mur-, mus*] (1607) : of or relating to a murid genus (*Mus*) or its subfamily (Murinae) which includes the common household rats and mice; *also* : of, relating to, or involving these rodents and especially the house mouse — **murine** *noun*

murine typhus *noun* (1933) : a mild febrile disease that is marked by headache and rash, is caused by a rickettsia (*Rickettsia mooseri*), is widespread in nature in rodents, and is transmitted to humans by a flea

murk \'mərk\ *noun* [Middle English *mirke*, from Old English *mirce*; akin to Old Norse *myrkr* darkness] (before 12th century) : GLOOM, DARKNESS; *also* : FOG — **murk** *adjective, archaic*

murky \'mər-kē\ *adjective* **murk·i·er; -est** (14th century) **1** : characterized by a heavy dimness or obscurity caused by or like that caused by overhanging fog or smoke **2** : characterized by thickness and heaviness of air : FOGGY, MISTY **3** : darkly vague or obscure ⟨*murky* official rhetoric⟩ — **murk·i·ly** \-kə-lē\ *adverb* — **murk·i·ness** \-kē-nəs\ *noun*

¹mur·mur \'mər-mər\ *noun* [Middle English *murmure*, from Middle French, from Latin *murmur* murmur, roar, of imitative origin] (14th century) **1** : a half-suppressed or muttered complaint : GRUMBLING **2 a** : a low indistinct but often continuous sound **b** : a soft or gentle utterance **3** : an atypical sound of the heart indicating a functional or structural abnormality

²murmur (14th century) *intransitive verb* **1** : to make a murmur ⟨the breeze *murmured* in the pines⟩ **2** : COMPLAIN, GRUMBLE *transitive verb* : to say in a murmur — **mur·mur·er** *noun*

mur·mur·ous \'mər-mə-rəs, 'mərm-rəs\ *adjective* (1582) : filled with or characterized by murmurs : low and indistinct — **mur·mur·ous·ly** *adverb*

Mur·phy \'mər-fē\ *noun* [Miss *Murphy*, nonexistent prostitute used to lure victims] (1959) : any of various confidence games; *especially* : one in which the victim believes he is paying for sex

Murphy bed *noun* [William L. *Murphy* (died 1959) American inventor] (1925) : a bed that may be folded or swung into a closet

Murphy's Law *noun* [Edward A. *Murphy* (born 1917) American engineer] (1958) : an observation: anything that can go wrong will go wrong

mur·rain \'mər-ən, 'mə-rən\ *noun* [Middle English *moreyne*, from Middle French *morine*, from *morir* to die, from Latin *mori* — more at MURDER] (14th century) : a pestilence or plague especially affecting domestic animals

murre \'mər\ *noun* [origin unknown] (1602) : any of a genus (*Uria*) of seabirds; *especially* : a common bird (*U. aalge*) of northern seas

mur·rey \'mər-ē, 'mə-rē\ *noun* [Middle English, from Middle French *moré*, from Medieval Latin *moratum*, from neuter of *moratus* mulberry colored, from Latin *morum* mulberry — more at MULBERRY] (15th century) : a purplish black : MULBERRY

mur·ther \'mər-thər\ *chiefly dialect variant of* MURDER

mus·ca·det \ˌməs-kə-'dā, -'de\ *noun, often capitalized* [French, from Provençal, muscadet grape, from *musc* musk] (circa 1899) : a dry white wine from the Loire valley of France

mus·ca·dine \'məs-kə-ˌdīn\ *noun* [probably alteration of *muscatel*] (circa 1785) : a grape (*Vitis rotundifolia*) of the southern U.S. with musky fruits borne in small clusters; *also* : the fruit

mus·cae vo·li·tan·tes \'məs-ˌkē-ˌvä-lə-'tan-ˌtēz, 'mə-ˌsē-\ *noun plural* [New Latin, literally, flying flies] (1797) : spots before the eyes due to cells and cell fragments in the vitreous humor and lens

mus·ca·rine \'məs-kə-ˌrēn\ *noun* [German *Muskarin*, from New Latin (*Amanita*) *muscaria* fly agaric] (1872) : a toxic ammonium base $[C_9H_{20}NO_2]^+$ that is biochemically related to acetylcholine, is found especially in fly agaric, and acts directly on smooth muscle

mus·ca·rin·ic \ˌməs-kə-'ri-nik\ *adjective* (1936) : relating to, resembling, producing, or mediating the parasympathetic effects (as a slowed heart rate and increased activity of smooth muscle) produced by muscarine ⟨*muscarinic* receptors⟩ — compare NICOTINIC

mus·cat \'məs-ˌkat, -kət\ *noun* [Middle French, from Old Provençal, from *muscat* musky, from *musc* musk, from Late Latin *muscus* — more at MUSK] (1548) **1** : MUSCATEL **2** : any of several cultivated grapes used in making wine and raisins

mus·ca·tel \ˌməs-kə-'tel\ *noun* [Middle English *muskadelle*, from Middle French *muscadel*, from Old Provençal, from *muscadel* resembling musk, from *muscat*] (15th century) **1** : a sweet fortified wine from muscat grapes **2** : a raisin from muscat grapes

¹mus·cle \'mə-səl\ *noun, often attributive* [Middle English, from Middle French, from Latin *musculus*, from diminutive of *mus* mouse — more at MOUSE] (14th century) **1 a** : a body tissue consisting of long cells that contract when stimulated and produce motion **b** : an organ that is essentially a mass of muscle tissue attached at either end to a fixed point and that by contracting moves or checks the movement of a body part **2 a** : muscular strength : BRAWN **b** : effective strength : POWER ⟨political *muscle*⟩ ◇

²muscle *verb* **mus·cled; mus·cling** \'mə-s(ə-)liŋ\ (1913) *transitive verb* : to move or force by or as if by muscular effort ⟨*muscled* him out of office⟩ *intransitive verb* : to make one's way by brute strength or by force

mus·cle-bound \'mə-səl-ˌbau̇nd\ *adjective* (1879) **1** : having some of the muscles tense and enlarged and of impaired elasticity sometimes as a result of excessive exercise **2** : lacking in flexibility : RIGID

muscle car \-ˌkär\ *noun* (1969) : any of a group of American-made 2-door sports coupes with powerful engines designed for high-performance driving

mus·cled \'mə-səld\ *adjective* (1644) : having muscles especially of a specified kind — often used in combination ⟨hard-*muscled* arms⟩

muscle spindle *noun* (1894) : a sensory end organ in a muscle that is sensitive to stretch in the muscle, consists of small striated muscle fibers richly supplied with nerve fibers, and is enclosed in a connective tissue sheath — called also *stretch receptor*

mus·co·vite \'məs-kə-ˌvīt\ *noun* [Medieval Latin or New Latin *Muscovia, Moscovia* Moscow] (1535) **1** *capitalized* **a** : a native or resident of the ancient principality of Moscow or of the city of Moscow **b** : RUSSIAN **2** [*muscovy (glass)*] : a mineral that is a colorless to pale brown potassium mica — **Muscovite** *adjective*

Mus·co·vy duck \'məs-ˌkō-vē-\ *noun* [*Muscovy*, principality of Moscow, Russia] (1657) : a large dark crested duck (*Cairina moschata*) of Central and South America that is widely kept in domestication

muscul- *or* **musculo-** *combining form* [Late Latin *muscul-*, from Latin *musculus*] **1** : muscle ⟨*muscular*⟩ **2** : muscular and ⟨*musculo*skeletal⟩

mus·cu·lar \'məs-kyə-lər\ *adjective* (1681) **1 a** : of, relating to, or constituting muscle **b** : of, relating to, or performed by the muscles **2** : having well-developed musculature **3 a** : of or relating to physical strength : BRAWNY **b** : having strength of expression or character : VIGOROUS ⟨*muscular* prose⟩ — **mus·cu·lar·i·ty** \ˌməs-kyə-'lar-ə-tē\ *noun* — **mus·cu·lar·ly** \'məs-kyə-lər-lē\ *adverb*

muscular dystrophy *noun* (1886) : any of a group of hereditary diseases characterized by progressive wasting of muscles

mus·cu·la·ture \'məs-kyə-lə-ˌchu̇r, -chər, -ˌtyu̇r, -ˌtu̇r\ *noun* [French, from Latin *musculus*] (1875) : the muscles of all or a part of the animal body

mus·cu·lo·skel·e·tal \ˌməs-kyə-lō-'ske-lə-t°l\ *adjective* (circa 1944) : of, relating to, or involving both musculature and skeleton

¹muse \'myüz\ *verb* **mused; mus·ing** [Middle English, from Middle French *muser* to gape, idle, muse, from *muse* mouth of an animal, from Medieval Latin *musus*] (14th century) *intransitive verb* **1** : to become absorbed in thought; *especially* : to turn something over in the mind meditatively and often inconclusively **2** *archaic* : WONDER, MARVEL

◇ WORD HISTORY

muscle The rippling muscles of a bodybuilder may not conjure in most people's imagination the image of a small rodent, but in a number of older Indo-European languages the word for "muscle" was identical with or a derivative of the word for "mouse." Hence Greek *mys* and Old English *mūs* mean both "mouse" and "muscle." Latin *musculus* (from which, via medieval French, comes English *muscle*) and Russian *myshtsa*, both words meaning "muscle," are derivatives of words meaning "mouse," respectively, *mus* and *mysh'*. (In some English dialects and in Scots, *mouse* continued to be applied to certain fleshy cuts of meat at least into the 19th century.) The usual explanation for this usage is that the lump of a contracting muscle in the upper arm or leg—perhaps more in the eyes of a child than an adult—has some resemblance to the furtive movement of a mouse. Alternatively, however, both the "mouse" and "muscle" senses of the word may reflect derivation from an Indo-European verbal base meaning "move," from which Latin *movēre* "to move" also descends.

transitive verb
: to think or say reflectively
synonym see PONDER
— **mus·er** *noun*
²**muse** *noun* (15th century)
: a state of deep thought or dreamy abstraction
³**muse** *noun* [Middle English, from Middle French, from Latin *Musa*, from Greek *Mousa*] (14th century)
1 *capitalized* **:** any of the nine sister goddesses in Greek mythology presiding over song and poetry and the arts and sciences
2 : a source of inspiration; *especially* **:** a guiding genius
3 : POET
mu·se·ol·o·gy \,myü-zē-'ä-lə-jē\ *noun* [*museum* + *-logy*] (1885)
: the science or profession of museum organization and management
— **mu·seo·log·i·cal** \-ə-'lä-ji-kəl\ *adjective*
— **mu·se·ol·o·gist** \-'ä-lə-jist\ *noun*
mu·sette \myü-'zet\ *noun* [Middle English, from Middle French, diminutive of *muse* bagpipe, from *muser* to muse, play the bagpipe] (14th century)
1 : a bellows-blown bagpipe popular in France in the 17th and 18th centuries
2 : a small knapsack; *also* **:** a similar bag with one shoulder strap — called also *musette bag*
mu·se·um \myü-'zē-əm\ *noun* [Latin *Museum* place for learned occupation, from Greek *Mouseion*, from neuter of *Mouseios* of the Muses, from *Mousa*] (1672)
: an institution devoted to the procurement, care, study, and display of objects of lasting interest or value; *also* **:** a place where objects are exhibited
museum piece *noun* (1901)
1 : something preserved in or suitable for a museum
2 : one that is out-of-date **:** a thing of the past
¹**mush** \'məsh, *especially 3 also* 'mùsh\ *noun* [probably alteration of *mash*] (1671)
1 : a thick porridge made with cornmeal boiled in water or milk
2 : something soft and spongy or shapeless
3 a : weak sentimentality **:** DRIVEL **b :** mawkish amorousness
²**mush** (circa 1781)
transitive verb
chiefly dialect **:** to reduce to a crumbly mass
intransitive verb
of an airplane **:** to fly in a partly or nearly stalled condition
— **mush·er** *noun*
³**mush** *intransitive verb* [probably from French *marchons*, 1st plural imperative of *marcher* to move, march, from Middle French *marchier* — more at MARCH] (1897)
: to travel especially over snow with a sled drawn by dogs — often used as a command to a dog team
— **mush·er** *noun*
⁴**mush** *noun* (1902)
: a trip especially across snow with a dog team
¹**mush·room** \'məsh-,rüm, -,rùm; *chiefly Northern & Midland* -,rün; *dialect* 'mə-shə-,rüm, -,rùm, -,rün\ *noun* [alteration of Middle English *musseroun*, from Middle French *mousseron*, from Late Latin *mussirion-, mussirio*] (1533)
1 a : an enlarged complex aboveground fleshy fruiting body of a fungus (as a basidiomycete) that consists typically of a stem bearing a pileus; *especially* **:** one that is edible **b :** FUNGUS
2 : UPSTART
3 : something resembling a mushroom
²**mushroom** *intransitive verb* (1894)
1 : to collect wild mushrooms
2 a : to well up and spread out laterally from a central source **b :** to become enlarged or extended **:** GROW

3 : to spring up suddenly or multiply rapidly
mushroom cloud *noun* (circa 1909)
: a mushroom-shaped cloud; *specifically* **:** one caused by the explosion of a nuclear weapon
mushy \'mə-shē, *especially 2 also* 'mù-\ *adjective* **mush·i·er; -est** (1839)
1 a : having the consistency of mush **:** SOFT **b :** lacking in definition or precision
2 : excessively tender or emotional; *especially* **:** mawkishly amorous
— **mush·i·ly** \'mə-shə-lē, 'mù-\ *adverb*
— **mush·i·ness** \'mə-shē-nəs, 'mù-\ *noun*
mu·sic \'myü-zik\ *noun, often attributive* [Middle English *musik*, from Old French *musique*, from Latin *musica*, from Greek *mousikē* any art presided over by the Muses, especially music, from feminine of *mousikos* of the Muses, from *Mousa* Muse] (13th century)
1 a : the science or art of ordering tones or sounds in succession, in combination, and in temporal relationships to produce a composition having unity and continuity **b :** vocal, instrumental, or mechanical sounds having rhythm, melody, or harmony
2 a : an agreeable sound **:** EUPHONY ⟨her voice was *music* to my ears⟩ **b :** musical quality ⟨the *music* of verse⟩
3 : a musical accompaniment ⟨a play set to *music*⟩
4 : the score of a musical composition set down on paper
5 : a distinctive type or category of music ⟨there is a *music* for everybody —Eric Salzman⟩
¹**mu·si·cal** \'myü-zi-kəl\ *adjective* [Middle English, from Middle French, from Medieval Latin *musicalis*, from *musica*] (15th century)
1 a : of or relating to music **b :** having the pleasing harmonious qualities of music **:** MELODIOUS
2 : having an interest in or talent for music
3 : set to or accompanied by music
4 : of or relating to musicians or music lovers
— **mu·si·cal·ly** \-k(ə-)lē\ *adverb*
²**musical** *noun* (1823)
1 *archaic* **:** MUSICALE
2 : a film or theatrical production typically of a sentimental or humorous nature that consists of musical numbers and dialogue based on a unifying plot
musical box *noun* (1829)
chiefly British **:** MUSIC BOX
musical chairs *noun plural but singular in construction* (1877)
: a game in which players march to music around a row of chairs numbering one less than the players and scramble for seats when the music stops; *also* **:** a situation or series of events suggesting the game of musical chairs (as in rapid change or confusing activity)
musical comedy *noun* (1765)
: MUSICAL 2
mu·si·cale \,myü-zi-'kal\ *noun* [French *soirée musicale*, literally, musical evening] (1872)
: a social entertainment with music as the leading feature
mu·si·cal·ise *British variant of* MUSICALIZE
mu·si·cal·i·ty \,myü-zi-'ka-lə-tē\ *noun* (1853)
1 : sensitivity to, knowledge of, or talent for music
2 : the quality or state of being musical **:** MELODIOUSNESS
mu·si·cal·ize \'myü-zi-kə-,līz\ *transitive verb* **-ized; -iz·ing** (1919)
: to set to music
— **mu·si·cal·i·za·tion** \,myü-zi-kə-lə-'zā-shən\ *noun*
musical saw *noun* (1927)
: a handsaw made to produce melody by bending the blade while sounding it with a hammer or violin bow
music box *noun* (1844)
: a container enclosing an apparatus that reproduces music mechanically when activated by a clockwork

music drama *noun* (1877)
: an opera in which the action is not interrupted by formal song divisions (as recitatives or arias) and the music is determined solely by dramatic appropriateness
music hall *noun* (1842)
: a vaudeville theater; *also* **:** VAUDEVILLE
mu·si·cian \myü-'zi-shən\ *noun* (14th century)
: a composer, conductor, or performer of music; *especially* **:** INSTRUMENTALIST
— **mu·si·cian·ly** \-lē\ *adjective*
— **mu·si·cian·ship** \-,ship\ *noun*
music of the spheres (1609)
: an ethereal harmony thought by the Pythagoreans to be produced by the vibration of the celestial spheres
mu·si·col·o·gy \,myü-zi-'kä-lə-jē\ *noun* [Italian *musicologia*, from Latin *musica* music + *-logia* -logy] (1909)
: a study of music as a branch of knowledge or field of research as distinct from composition or performance
— **mu·si·co·log·i·cal** \-kə-'lä-ji-kəl\ *adjective*
— **mu·si·col·o·gist** \-'kä-lə-jist\ *noun*
¹**mus·ing** \'myü-ziŋ\ *noun* (14th century)
: MEDITATION
²**musing** *adjective* (15th century)
: thoughtfully abstracted **:** MEDITATIVE
— **mus·ing·ly** \-lē\ *adverb*
mu·sique con·crète \myü-'zēk-kōⁿ-'kret, mē-\ *noun* [French, literally, concrete music] (1952)
: a recorded montage of natural sounds often electronically modified and presented as a musical composition
musk \'məsk\ *noun* [Middle English *muske*, from Middle French *musc*, from Late Latin *muscus*, from Late Greek *moschos*, from (assumed) Middle Persian *mušk-*, from Sanskrit *muṣka* testicle, from diminutive of *mūṣ* mouse; akin to Old English *mūs* mouse] (14th century)
1 a : a substance with a penetrating persistent odor obtained from a sac beneath the abdominal skin of the male musk deer and used as a perfume fixative; *also* **:** a similar substance from another animal or a synthetic substitute **b :** the odor of musk; *also* **:** an odor resembling musk especially in heaviness or persistence
2 : any of various plants with musky odors; *especially* **:** MUSK PLANT
musk deer *noun* (1681)
: any of a genus (*Moschus*) of small heavy-limbed hornless deer of central Asian uplands with tusked musk-producing males
mus·keg \'məs-,keg, -,kāg\ *noun* [Cree *maskeʾk*] (1806)
1 : BOG; *especially* **:** a sphagnum bog of northern North America often with tussocks
2 : a usually thick deposit of partially decayed vegetable matter of wet boreal regions
mus·kel·lunge \'məs-kə-,lənj\ *noun, plural* **muskellunge** [alteration of Canadian French *maskinongé*, from Ojibwa *maʾskinoʾšeʾ*] (1789)
: a large North American pike (*Esox masquinongy*) that has dark markings, may weigh over 60 pounds (27 kilograms), and is a valuable sport fish
mus·ket \'məs-kət\ *noun* [Middle French *mousquet*, from Old Italian *moschetto* small artillery piece, sparrow hawk, from diminutive of *mosca* fly, from Latin *musca* — more at MIDGE] (circa 1587)

\ə\ **abut** \ᵊ\ **kitten** \ər\ **further** \a\ **ash** \ā\ **ace**
\ä\ **mop, mar** \aù\ **out** \ch\ **chin** \e\ **bet** \ē\ **easy**
\g\ **go** \i\ **hit** \ī\ **ice** \j\ **job** \ŋ\ **sing** \ō\ **go**
\ò\ **law** \òi\ **boy** \th\ **thin** \th\ **the** \ü\ **loot** \ù\ **foot**
\y\ **yet** \zh\ **vision** *see also* Guide to Pronunciation

: a heavy large-caliber muzzle-loading usually smoothbore shoulder gun carried by infantry ◆

mus·ke·teer \ˌməs-kə-'tir\ noun [modification of Middle French mousquetaire, from mousquet] (1590)
1 : a soldier armed with a musket
2 [from the musketeers' friendship in the novel Les Trois Mousquetaires (1844) by Alexandre Dumas] : a good friend : BUDDY

mus·ket·ry \'məs-kə-trē\ noun (1646)
1 : MUSKETS
2 : MUSKETEERS
3 a : musket fire **b** : the art or science of using small arms especially in battle

mus·kie or **mus·ky** \'məs-kē\ noun, plural **muskies** (1894)
: MUSKELLUNGE

musk·mel·on \'məsk-ˌme-lən\ noun (1573)
: a usually sweet musky-odored edible melon that is the fruit of a trailing or climbing Asian herbaceous vine (Cucumis melo): as **a** : any of various melons of small or moderate size with netted skin that include most of the muskmelons cultivated in North America **b** : CANTALOUPE 1 **c** : WINTER MELON

Mus·ko·ge·an or **Mus·kho·ge·an** \(ˌ)məs-'kō-gē-ən\ noun (1891)
: a language family of southeastern U.S. that includes Muskogee

Mus·ko·gee \mə-'skō-gē\ noun, plural **Muskogee** or **Muskogees** (1775)
1 : a member of an American Indian people of Georgia and eastern Alabama constituting the nucleus of the Creek confederacy
2 : the language of the Muskogees and of some of the Seminoles

musk ox noun (1744)
: a heavyset shaggy-coated wild ox (Ovibos moschatus) now confined to Greenland and the barren northern lands of North America

musk ox

musk plant noun (1852)
: a yellow-flowered North American herb (Mimulus moschatus) of the snapdragon family that has hairy foliage and sometimes a musky odor

musk·rat \'məs-ˌkrat\ noun, plural **muskrat** or **muskrats** [probably by folk etymology from a word of Algonquian origin; akin to Massachuset musquash muskrat] (1607)
: an aquatic rodent (Ondatra zibethica) of the U.S. and Canada with a long scaly laterally compressed tail, webbed hind feet, and dark glossy brown fur; also : its fur or pelt

musk rose noun (1577)
: a rose (Rosa moschata) of the Mediterranean region with white flowers having a musky odor

musk thistle noun (1731)
: a Eurasian thistle (Carduus nutans) that has nodding musky flower heads and is naturalized in eastern North America

musk turtle noun (1868)
: any of various small American freshwater turtles (genera Sternotherus and Kinosternon) that have musk glands; especially : a dark turtle (S. odoratus) having a strong musky odor

musky \'məs-kē\ adjective **musk·i·er; -est** (1613)
: having an odor of or resembling musk
— **musk·i·ness** noun

Mus·lim \'məz-ləm, 'mus-, 'muz-\ noun [Arabic muslim, literally, one who surrenders (to God)] (1615)
1 : an adherent of Islam
2 : BLACK MUSLIM
— **Muslim** adjective

Muslim era noun (1948)
: ISLAMIC ERA

mus·lin \'məz-lən\ noun [French mousseline, from Italian mussolina, from Arabic mawṣilī of Mosul, from al-Mawṣil Mosul, Iraq] (1609)
: a plain-woven sheer to coarse cotton fabric

mus·quash \'məs-ˌkwäsh, -ˌkwȯsh\ noun [Massachuset] (1633)
: MUSKRAT

¹muss \'məs\ noun [origin unknown] (1591)
1 obsolete **a** : a game in which players scramble for small objects thrown to the ground **b** : SCRAMBLE
2 slang : a confused conflict : ROW
3 : a state of disorder : MESS

²muss transitive verb (1837)
: to make untidy : DISARRANGE

mus·sel \'mə-səl\ noun [Middle English muscle, from Old English muscelle, from (assumed) Vulgar Latin muscula, from Latin musculus muscle, mussel] (before 12th century)
1 : a marine bivalve mollusk (especially genus Mytilus) usually having a dark elongated shell
2 : a freshwater bivalve mollusk (as of Unio, Anodonta, or related genera) that is especially abundant in rivers of the central U.S. and has a shell with a lustrous nacreous lining

Mus·sul·man also **Mus·sal·man** \'mə-səl-mən\ noun, plural **Mus·sul·men** \-mən\ or **Mussulmans** [Turkish müslüman & Persian musulmān, modification of Arabic muslim] (circa 1583)
: MUSLIM

mussy \'mə-sē\ adjective **muss·i·er; -est** (circa 1859)
: characterized by clutter or muss : MESSY
— **muss·i·ly** \'mə-sə-lē\ adverb
— **muss·i·ness** \'mə-sē-nəs\ noun

¹must \'məs(t), 'məst\ verb, present & past all persons **must** [Middle English moste, from Old English mōste, past indicative & subjunctive of mōtan to be allowed to, have to; akin to Old High German muozan to be allowed to, have to]
verbal auxiliary
(before 12th century)
1 a : be commanded or requested to ⟨you must stop⟩ **b** : be urged to : ought by all means to ⟨you must read that book⟩
2 : be compelled by physical necessity to ⟨man must eat to live⟩ : be required by immediate or future need or purpose to ⟨we must hurry to catch the bus⟩
3 a : be obliged to : be compelled by social considerations to ⟨I must say you're looking well⟩ **b** : be required by law, custom, or moral conscience to ⟨we must obey the rules⟩ **c** : be determined to ⟨if you must go at least wait for me⟩ **d** : be unreasonably or perversely compelled to ⟨why must you be so stubborn⟩
4 : be logically inferred or supposed to ⟨it must be time⟩
5 : be compelled by fate or by natural law to ⟨what must be will be⟩
6 : was or were presumably certain to : was or were bound to ⟨if he really was there I must have seen him⟩
7 dialect : MAY, SHALL — used chiefly in questions
intransitive verb
archaic : to be obliged to go ⟨I must to Coventry —Shakespeare⟩

²must \'məst\ noun (1616)
1 : an imperative need or duty : REQUIREMENT
2 : an indispensable item : ESSENTIAL ⟨exercise is a must⟩

³must noun [Middle English, from Old English, from Latin mustum] (before 12th century)
: the expressed juice of fruit and especially grapes before and during fermentation; also : the pulp and skins of the crushed grapes

⁴must noun [Middle English (Scots) moist, from Middle French must, alteration of musc musk] (15th century)
1 : MUSK
2 : MOLD, MUSTINESS

mus·tache \'məs-ˌtash, (ˌ)mə-'stash\ noun [Middle French moustache, from Old Italian mustaccio, from Middle Greek moustaki, diminutive of Greek mystak-, mystax upper lip, mustache] (1585)
1 : the hair growing on the human upper lip; especially : such hair grown and often trimmed in a particular style
2 : hair or bristles about the mouth of a mammal
— **mus·tached** adjective

mus·ta·chio \(ˌ)mə-'sta-shē-ˌō, -'stä-, -shō\ noun, plural **-chios** [Spanish & Italian; Spanish mostacho, from Italian mustaccio, from Old Italian] (1588)
: MUSTACHE; especially : a large mustache
— **mus·ta·chioed** \-shē-ˌōd, -shōd\ adjective

mus·tang \'məs-ˌtaŋ\ noun [Mexican Spanish mestengo, from Spanish, stray, from mesteño strayed, from mesta annual roundup of cattle that disposed of strays, from Medieval Latin (animalia) mixta mixed animals] (1808)
1 : the small hardy naturalized horse of the western plains directly descended from horses brought in by the Spaniards; also : BRONC
2 slang : a commissioned officer (as in the U.S. Navy) who has risen from the ranks

mus·tard \'məs-tərd\ noun [Middle English, from Old French mostarde, from moust must, from Latin mustum] (13th century)
1 a : a pungent yellow powder of the seeds of any of several common mustards (Brassica hirta, B. nigra, or B. juncea) used as a condiment or in medicine as a stimulant and diuretic, an emetic, or a counterirritant **b** slang : ZEST
2 : any of several herbs (genus Brassica of the family Cruciferae, the mustard family) with lobed leaves, yellow flowers, and linear beaked pods
3 : a dark to moderate yellow
— **mus·tardy** \-tər-dē\ adjective

mustard gas noun (1917)
: an irritant vesicant oily liquid $C_4H_8Cl_2S$ used especially as a chemical weapon

mustard plaster noun (1810)
: a counterirritant and rubefacient plaster containing powdered mustard

¹mus·ter \'məs-tər\ noun [Middle English mustre, from Middle French mostre, monstre, from monstrer] (14th century)
1 : a representative specimen : SAMPLE
2 a : an act of assembling; specifically : formal military inspection **b** : critical examination **c** : an assembled group : COLLECTION **d** : INVENTORY

²muster verb **mus·tered; mus·ter·ing** \-t(ə-)riŋ\ [Middle English mustren to show,

muster, from Middle French *monstrer,* from Latin *monstrare* to show, from *monstrum* evil omen, monster — more at MONSTER] (15th century)
transitive verb
1 a : to cause to gather **:** CONVENE **b :** to enroll formally — usually used with *in* or *into* ⟨was *mustered* into the army⟩ **c :** to call the roll of **2 a :** to bring together **:** COLLECT **b :** to call forth **:** ROUSE
3 : to amount to **:** COMPRISE
intransitive verb
: to come together **:** CONGREGATE
synonym see SUMMON
muster out *transitive verb* (1834)
: to discharge from service
muster roll *noun* (1605)
: INVENTORY, ROSTER; *specifically* **:** a register of the officers and men in a military unit or ship's company
musth *also* **must** \'məst\ *noun* [Hindi *mast* intoxicated, from Persian] (1878)
: a periodic state of the bull elephant characterized especially by aggressive behavior and usually connected with the rutting season
mustn't \'mə-sᵊnt\ (1741)
: must not
must–see \'məst-'sē\ *noun* (1946)
: something (as a film) that must or should be seen
— **must–see** *adjective*
musty \'məs-tē\ *adjective* **must·i·er; -est** (1530)
1 a : impaired by damp or mildew **:** MOLDY **b :** tasting of mold **c :** smelling of damp and decay **:** FUSTY
2 a : TRITE, STALE **b** (1) **:** ANTIQUATED (2) **:** SUPERANNUATED
synonym see MALODOROUS
— **must·i·ly** \'məs-tə-lē\ *adverb*
— **must·i·ness** \-tē-nəs\ *noun*
mu·ta·ble \'myü-tə-bəl\ *adjective* [Middle English, from Latin *mutabilis,* from *mutare* to change; akin to Old English *mīthan* to conceal, Sanskrit *mināti* he exchanges, deceives] (14th century)
1 : prone to change **:** INCONSTANT
2 a : capable of change or of being changed **b :** capable of or liable to mutation
— **mu·ta·bil·i·ty** \,myü-tə-'bi-lə-tē\ *noun*
— **mu·ta·bly** \'myü-tə-blē\ *adverb*
mu·ta·gen \'myü-tə-jən\ *noun* [International Scientific Vocabulary *mutation* + *-gen*] (1933)
: an agent (as mustard gas or various radiations) that tends to increase the frequency or extent of mutation
— **mu·ta·gen·ic** \,myü-tə-'je-nik\ *adjective*
— **mu·ta·gen·i·cal·ly** \-ni-k(ə-)lē\ *adverb*
mu·ta·gen·e·sis \,myü-tə-'je-nə-səs\ *noun* [New Latin] (1948)
: the occurrence or induction of mutation
mu·ta·ge·nic·i·ty \-jə-'ni-sə-tē\ *noun* (1956)
: the capacity to induce mutations
mu·tant \'myü-tᵊnt\ *adjective* [Latin *mutant-, mutans,* present participle of *mutare*] (1903)
: of, relating to, or produced by mutation
— **mutant** *noun*
mu·tase \'myü-,tās, -,tāz\ *noun* [International Scientific Vocabulary *mut-* (from Latin *mutare*) + *-ase*] (1938)
: any of various enzymes that catalyze molecular rearrangements and especially those involving the transfer of phosphate from one hydroxyl group to another in the same molecule
mu·tate \'myü-,tāt, myü-'\ *verb* **mu·tat·ed; mu·tat·ing** [Latin *mutatus,* past participle of *mutare*] (1818)
intransitive verb
: to undergo mutation
transitive verb
: to cause to undergo mutation
— **mu·ta·tive** \'myü-,tā-tiv, -tə-tiv\ *adjective*
mu·ta·tion \myü-'tā-shən\ *noun* (14th century)

1 : a significant and basic alteration **:** CHANGE
2 : UMLAUT
3 a : a relatively permanent change in hereditary material involving either a physical change in chromosome relations or a biochemical change in the codons that make up genes; *also* **:** the process of producing a mutation **b :** an individual strain or trait resulting from mutation
— **mu·ta·tion·al** \-shnəl, -shə-nᵊl\ *adjective*
— **mu·ta·tion·al·ly** *adverb*
mu·ta·tis mu·tan·dis \m(y)ü-'tä-təs-m(y)ü-'tän-dəs, -'tä-təs-, -'tan-\ *adverb* [Middle English, from Medieval Latin] (15th century)
1 : with the necessary changes having been made
2 : with the respective differences having been considered
mutch·kin \'məch-kən\ *noun* [Middle English (Scots) *muchekyn*] (15th century)
: a Scottish unit of liquid capacity equal to 0.90 pint (0.42 liter)
¹mute \'myüt\ *adjective* **mut·er; mut·est** [alteration of Middle English *muet,* from Middle French, from Old French *mu,* from Latin *mutus,* probably from *mu,* representation of a muttered sound] (1513)
1 : unable to speak **:** DUMB
2 : characterized by absence of speech: as **a :** felt or experienced but not expressed ⟨touched her hand in *mute* sympathy⟩ **b :** refusing to plead directly or stand trial ⟨the prisoner stands *mute*⟩
3 : remaining silent, undiscovered, or unrecognized
4 a : contributing nothing to the pronunciation of a word ⟨the *b* in *plumb* is *mute*⟩ **b :** contributing to the pronunciation of a word but not representing the nucleus of a syllable ⟨the *e* in *mate* is *mute*⟩
— **mute·ly** *adverb*
— **mute·ness** *noun*
²mute *noun* (1530)
1 : STOP 9
2 : a person who cannot or does not speak
3 : a device attached to a musical instrument to reduce, soften, or muffle its tone
³mute *transitive verb* **mut·ed; mut·ing** (1883)
1 : to muffle, reduce, or eliminate the sound of
2 : to tone down **:** SOFTEN, SUBDUE ⟨*mute* a color⟩
⁴mute *intransitive verb* **mut·ed; mut·ing** [Middle English, from Middle French *meutir,* short for *esmeutir,* from Old French *esmeltir,* of Germanic origin; akin to Middle Dutch *smelten* to melt, defecate (used of birds)] (15th century)
of a bird **:** to evacuate the cloaca
mut·ed \'myü-təd\ *adjective* (1861)
1 : provided with or produced or modified by the use of a mute
2 a : being mute **:** SILENT **b :** toned down **:** LOW-KEY, SUBDUED
— **mut·ed·ly** *adverb*
mute swan *noun* (1785)
: a common white swan (*Cygnus olor*) that produces no loud notes, is native to Europe and western Asia, and has been introduced into parts of the U.S.
mu·ti·late \'myü-tᵊl-,āt\ *transitive verb* **-lat·ed; -lat·ing** [Latin *mutilatus,* past participle of *mutilare,* from *mutilus* truncated, maimed] (1534)
1 : to cut up or alter radically so as to make imperfect ⟨the child *mutilated* the book with his scissors⟩
2 : to cut off or permanently destroy a limb or essential part of **:** CRIPPLE
synonym see MAIM
— **mu·ti·la·tion** \,myü-tᵊl-'ā-shən\ *noun*
— **mu·ti·la·tor** \'myü-tᵊl-,ā-tər\ *noun*
mu·tine \'myü-tᵊn\ *intransitive verb* **mu·tined; mu·tin·ing** [Middle French (*se*) *mutiner*] (1555)

obsolete **:** REBEL, MUTINY
mu·ti·neer \,myü-tᵊn-'ir\ *noun* (1610)
: one that mutinies
mu·ti·nous \'myü-tᵊn-əs, 'myüt-nəs\ *adjective* (1578)
1 a : disposed to or in a state of mutiny **:** REBELLIOUS **b :** TURBULENT, UNRULY
2 : of, relating to, or constituting mutiny
— **mu·ti·nous·ly** *adverb*
— **mu·ti·nous·ness** *noun*
mu·ti·ny \'myü-tᵊn-ē, 'myüt-nē\ *noun, plural* **-nies** [*mutine* to rebel, from Middle French (*se*) *mutiner,* from *mutin* mutinous, from *meute* revolt, from (assumed) Vulgar Latin *movita,* from feminine of *movitus,* alteration of Latin *motus,* past participle of *movēre* to move] (1567)
1 *obsolete* **:** TUMULT, STRIFE
2 : forcible or passive resistance to lawful authority; *especially* **:** concerted revolt (as of a naval crew) against discipline or a superior officer
synonym see REBELLION
— **mutiny** *intransitive verb*
mut·ism \'myü-,ti-zəm\ *noun* [French *mutisme,* from Latin *mutus* mute] (1824)
: the condition of being mute
mutt \'mət\ *noun* [short for *muttonhead* dull-witted person] (1901)
1 : a stupid or insignificant person **:** FOOL
2 : a mongrel dog **:** CUR
mut·ter \'mə-tər\ *verb* [Middle English *muteren,* of imitative origin] (14th century)
intransitive verb
1 : to utter sounds or words indistinctly or with a low voice and with the lips partly closed
2 : to murmur complainingly or angrily **:** GRUMBLE
transitive verb
: to utter especially in a low or imperfectly articulated manner
— **mutter** *noun*
— **mut·ter·er** \-tər-ər\ *noun*
mut·ton \'mə-tᵊn\ *noun* [Middle English *motoun,* from Old French *moton* ram, wether, of Celtic origin; akin to Old Irish *molt* wether] (13th century)
: the flesh of a mature sheep used for food
— **mut·tony** \'mə-tᵊn-ē, 'mət-nē\ *adjective*
mut·ton–chops \'mə-tᵊn-,chäps\ *noun plural* (1865)
: side-whiskers that are narrow at the temple and broad and round by the lower jaws — called also *muttonchop whiskers*
mut·ton·fish \-,fish\ *noun* [from its flavor] (1735)
: a common snapper (*Lutjanus analis*) of the warmer parts of the western Atlantic that is usually olive green and sometimes nearly white or tinged with rosy red and that is a commercially important food and sport fish — called also *mutton snapper*
mu·tu·al \'myü-chə-wəl, -chəl; 'myüch-wəl\ *adjective* [Middle English, from Middle French *mutuel,* from Latin *mutuus* lent, borrowed, mutual, from *mutare* to change — more at MUTABLE] (15th century)
1 a : directed by each toward the other or the others ⟨*mutual* affection⟩ **b :** having the same feelings one for the other ⟨they had long been *mutual* enemies⟩ **c :** shared in common ⟨enjoying their *mutual* hobby⟩ **d :** JOINT
2 : characterized by intimacy
3 : of or relating to a plan whereby the members of an organization share in the profits and expenses; *specifically* **:** of, relating to, or taking the form of an insurance method in which

the policyholders constitute the members of the insuring company

— **mu·tu·al·ly** *adverb*

mutual fund *noun* (1934)
: an open-end investment company that invests money of its shareholders in a usually diversified group of securities of other corporations

mu·tu·al·ism \'myü-chə-wə-,li-zəm, 'myü-chə-,li-, 'myüch-wə-,li-\ *noun* (1849)
1 : the doctrine or practice of mutual dependence as the condition of individual and social welfare
2 : mutually beneficial association between different kinds of organisms
— **mu·tu·al·ist** \-list\ *noun*
— **mu·tu·al·is·tic** \,myü-chə-wə-'lis-tik, ,myü-chə-'lis-, ,myüch-wə-'lis-\ *adjective*

mu·tu·al·i·ty \,myü-chə-'wa-lə-tē\ *noun* (circa 1586)
1 : the quality or state of being mutual
2 : a sharing of sentiments

mu·tu·al·ize \'myü-chə-wə-,līz, 'myü-chə-,līz, 'myüch-wə-,līz\ *transitive verb* **-ized; -iz·ing** (1812)
: to make mutual
— **mu·tu·al·i·za·tion** \,myü-chə-wə-lə-'zā-shən, ,myü-chə-lə-, ,myüch-wə-lə-\ *noun*

mutually exclusive *adjective* (1874)
: being related such that each excludes or precludes the other ⟨*mutually exclusive* events⟩; *also* : INCOMPATIBLE ⟨their outlooks were not *mutually exclusive*⟩

mutuel *noun* (1908)
: PARI-MUTUEL

muu·muu \'mü-,mü\ *noun* [Hawaiian *mu'umu'u*, from *mu'umu'u* cut off] (1923)
: a loose often long dress having bright colors and patterns and adapted from the dresses originally distributed by missionaries to the native women of Hawaii

Mu·zak \'myü-,zak\ *trademark*
— used for recorded background music transmitted by wire to the loudspeaker of a subscriber (as an office)

mu·zhik \mü-'zhēk, -'zhik\ *noun* [Russian] (1568)
: a Russian peasant

¹muz·zle \'mə-zəl\ *noun* [Middle English *musell*, from Middle French *musel*, from diminutive of *muse* mouth of an animal, from Medieval Latin *musus*] (15th century)
1 : the projecting jaws and nose of an animal : SNOUT
2 a : a fastening or covering for the mouth of an animal used to prevent eating or biting **b** : something (as censorship) that restrains normal expression

muzzle 2a

3 : the open end of an implement; *especially* : the discharging end of a weapon

²muzzle *transitive verb* **muz·zled; muz·zling** \'məz-liŋ, 'mə-zə-\ (15th century)
1 : to fit with a muzzle
2 : to restrain from expression : GAG
— **muz·zler** \-lər\ *noun*

muz·zy \'mə-zē\ *adjective* **muz·zi·er; -est** [perhaps blend of *muddled* and *fuzzy*] (circa 1728)
1 a : deficient in brightness : DULL, GLOOMY ⟨a *muzzy* day⟩ **b** : lacking in clarity and precision ⟨his conclusions can be *muzzy* and naive —*Times Literary Supplement*⟩
2 : muddled or confused in mind
— **muz·zi·ly** \'mə-zə-lē\ *adverb*
— **muz·zi·ness** \'mə-zē-nəs\ *noun*

MX \,em-'eks\ *noun* [missile, experimental] (1976)
: a mobile ICBM having up to 10 independently targeted nuclear warheads

my \'mī, mə\ *adjective* [Middle English, from Old English *mīn*, from *mīn*, suppletive genitive of *ic* I; akin to Old English *mē* me] (12th century)
1 : of or relating to me or myself especially as possessor, agent, or object of an action ⟨*my* car⟩ ⟨*my* promise⟩ ⟨*my* injuries⟩
2 — used interjectionally to express surprise and sometimes reduplicated ⟨*my* oh *my*⟩; used also interjectionally with names of various parts of the body to express doubt or disapproval ⟨*my* foot⟩

my- *or* **myo-** *combining form* [New Latin, from Greek, from *mys* mouse, muscle — more at MOUSE]
: muscle ⟨*myo*globin⟩ : muscle and ⟨*myo*neural⟩

my·al·gia \mī-'al-j(ē-)ə\ *noun* [New Latin] (1860)
: pain in one or more muscles
— **my·al·gic** \-jik\ *adjective*

my·as·the·nia \,mī-əs-'thē-nē-ə\ *noun* [New Latin] (circa 1856)
: muscular debility
— **my·as·then·ic** \-'the-nik\ *adjective or noun*

myasthenia gra·vis \-'gra-vəs, -'grä-\ *noun* [New Latin, literally, grave myasthenia] (1900)
: a disease characterized by progressive weakness and exhaustibility of voluntary muscles without atrophy or sensory disturbance and caused by an autoimmune attack on acetylcholine receptors at the neuromuscular junction

myc- *or* **myco-** *combining form* [New Latin, from Greek *mykēt-, mykēs* fungus; akin to Greek *myxa* nasal mucus]
: fungus ⟨*myco*logy⟩ ⟨*myco*sis⟩

my·ce·li·um \mī-'sē-lē-əm\ *noun, plural* **-lia** \-lē-ə\ [New Latin, from *myc-* + Greek *hēlos* nail, wart, callus] (1836)
: the mass of interwoven filamentous hyphae that forms especially the vegetative portion of the thallus of a fungus and is often submerged in another body (as of soil or organic matter or the tissues of a host); *also* : a similar mass of filaments formed by some bacteria (as streptomyces)
— **my·ce·li·al** \-əl\ *adjective*

My·ce·nae·an \,mī-sə-'nē-ən\ *also* **My·ce·ni·an** \mī-'sē-nē-ən\ *adjective* (1598)
1 : of, relating to, or characteristic of Mycenae, its people, or the period (1400 to 1100 B.C.) of Mycenae's political ascendancy
2 : characteristic of the Bronze Age Mycenaean culture of the eastern Mediterranean area
— **Mycenaean** *noun*

my·ce·to·ma \,mī-sə-'tō-mə\ *noun, plural* **-mas** *or* **-ma·ta** \-mə-tə\ [New Latin, from Greek *mykēt-, mykēs*] (1874)
: a condition marked by invasion of the deep subcutaneous tissues with fungi or actinomycetes; *also* : a tumorous mass occurring in such a condition
— **my·ce·to·ma·tous** \-mə-təs\ *adjective*

my·ce·toph·a·gous \,mī-sə-'tä-fə-gəs\ *adjective* [Greek *mykēt-, mykēs* + English *-phagous*] (circa 1890)
: feeding on fungi

my·ce·to·zo·an \mī-,sē-tə-'zō-ən\ *noun* [New Latin *Mycetozoa*, order of protozoans, from Greek *mykēt-, mykēs* + New Latin *-zoa*] (1881)
: SLIME MOLD
— **mycetozoan** *adjective*

-mycin *noun combining form* [streptomycin]
: substance obtained from a fungus-like bacterium ⟨erythro*mycin*⟩

my·co·bac·te·ri·um \,mī-kō-bak-'tir-ē-əm\ *noun* [New Latin] (1909)
: any of a genus (*Mycobacterium*) of nonmotile aerobic acid-fast bacteria that include numerous saprophytes and the pathogens causing tuberculosis and leprosy
— **my·co·bac·te·ri·al** \-ē-əl\ *adjective*

my·co·flo·ra \,mī-kə-'flōr-ə, -'flor-\ *noun* [New Latin] (1945)
: the fungi characteristic of a region or special environment

my·col·o·gy \mī-'kä-lə-jē\ *noun* [New Latin *mycologia*, from *myc-* + Latin *-logia* -logy] (1836)
1 : a branch of biology dealing with fungi
2 : fungal life
— **my·co·log·i·cal** \,mī-kə-'lä-ji-kəl\ *adjective*
— **my·co·log·i·cal·ly** \,mī-kə-'lä-ji-k(ə-)lē\ *adverb*
— **my·col·o·gist** \mī-'kä-lə-jist\ *noun*

my·coph·a·gist \mī-'kä-fə-jist\ *noun* [*mycophagy*, from *myc-* + *-phagy*] (1861)
: one that eats fungi (as mushrooms)
— **my·coph·a·gy** \-jē\ *noun*

my·coph·a·gous \-gəs\ *adjective* (circa 1909)
: feeding on fungi

my·co·phile \'mī-kō-,fīl\ *noun* (1953)
: a person whose hobby is hunting wild edible mushrooms

my·co·plas·ma \,mī-kō-'plaz-mə\ *noun, plural* **-mas** *or* **-ma·ta** \-mə-tə\ [New Latin] (1955)
: any of a genus (*Mycoplasma*) of minute pleomorphic gram-negative chiefly nonmotile microorganisms without cell walls that are intermediate in some respects between viruses and bacteria and are mostly parasitic usually in mammals — called also *pleuropneumonia-like organism*
— **my·co·plas·mal** \-məl\ *adjective*

mycoplasma–like organism *noun* (1968)
: any of a group of prokaryotic organisms that resemble mycoplasmas, cause disease in plants, are transmitted by insect vectors, and have proved extremely difficult to grow in artificial media

my·cor·rhi·za \,mī-kə-'rī-zə\ *noun, plural* **-zae** \-,zē\ *or* **-zas** [New Latin, from *myc-* + Greek *rhiza* root — more at ROOT] (1895)
: the symbiotic association of the mycelium of a fungus with the roots of a seed plant
— **my·cor·rhi·zal** \-zəl\ *adjective*

my·co·sis \mī-'kō-səs\ *noun, plural* **my·co·ses** \-,sēz\ [New Latin] (1876)
: infection with or disease caused by a fungus
— **my·cot·ic** \-'kä-tik\ *adjective*

my·co·tox·in \,mī-kə-'täk-sən\ *noun* (1962)
: a toxic substance produced by a fungus and especially a mold

my·dri·a·sis \mə-'drī-ə-səs\ *noun* [Latin, from Greek] (circa 1775)
: a long-continued or excessive dilatation of the pupil of the eye
— **myd·ri·at·ic** \,mi-drē-'a-tik\ *adjective or noun*

myel- *or* **myelo-** *combining form* [New Latin, from Greek, from *myelos*, probably from *myōn* cluster of muscles, from *mys* mouse, muscle — more at MOUSE]
: marrow : spinal cord ⟨*myel*encephalon⟩

my·e·len·ceph·a·lon \,mī-ə-len-'se-fə-,län, -lən\ *noun* [New Latin] (1871)
: the posterior part of the developing vertebrate hindbrain or the corresponding part of the adult brain composed of the medulla oblongata
— **my·e·len·ce·phal·ic** \-,len(t)-sə-'fa-lik\ *adjective*

my·e·lin \'mī-ə-lən\ *noun* [International Scientific Vocabulary] (1873)
: a soft white somewhat fatty material that forms a thick myelin sheath about the protoplasmic core of a myelinated nerve fiber
— **my·e·lin·ic** \,mī-ə-'li-nik\ *adjective*
— **my·e·lin·at·ed** \'mī-ə-lə-,nā-təd\ *adjective* (1899)

: having a myelin sheath ⟨*myelinated* nerve fibers⟩

myelin sheath *noun* (1896)
: a layer of myelin surrounding some nerve fibers — called also *medullary sheath*

my·e·li·tis \ˌmī-ə-'lī-təs\ *noun, plural* **-lit·i·des** \-'li-tə-ˌdēz\ [New Latin] (1835)
: inflammation of the spinal cord or of the bone marrow

my·e·lo·blast \'mī-ə-lə-ˌblast\ *noun* [International Scientific Vocabulary] (circa 1904)
: a large mononuclear nongranular bone-marrow cell; *especially* : one that is a precursor of a myelocyte
— **my·e·lo·blas·tic** \ˌmī-ə-lə-'blas-tik\ *adjective*

my·e·lo·cyte \'mī-ə-lə-ˌsīt\ *noun* [International Scientific Vocabulary] (1891)
: a bone-marrow cell; *especially* : a motile cell with cytoplasmic granules that gives rise to the granulocytes of the blood and occurs abnormally in the circulating blood
— **my·e·lo·cyt·ic** \ˌmī-ə-lə-'si-tik\ *adjective*

my·e·lo·fi·bro·sis \ˌmī-ə-lō-fī-'brō-səs\ *noun* [New Latin] (1947)
: an anemic condition in which bone marrow becomes fibrotic and the liver and spleen usually exhibit a development of blood-cell precursors
— **my·e·lo·fi·brot·ic** \-'brä-tik\ *adjective*

my·e·log·e·nous \ˌmī-ə-'lä-jə-nəs\ *adjective* [International Scientific Vocabulary] (1876)
: of, relating to, originating in, or produced by the bone marrow ⟨*myelogenous* sarcoma⟩

myelogenous leukemia *noun* (1904)
: leukemia characterized by proliferation of myeloid tissue (as of the bone marrow and spleen) and an abnormal increase in the number of granulocytes, myelocytes, and myeloblasts in the circulating blood — called also *myelocytic leukemia, myeloid leukemia*

my·e·loid \'mī-ə-ˌlȯid\ *adjective* [International Scientific Vocabulary] (1857)
: of, relating to, or resembling bone marrow

my·e·lo·ma \ˌmī-ə-'lō-mə\ *noun* [New Latin] (circa 1857)
: a primary tumor of the bone marrow
— **my·e·lo·ma·tous** \-mə-təs\ *adjective*

my·e·lop·a·thy \-'lä-pə-thē\ *noun* [International Scientific Vocabulary] (circa 1891)
: a disease or disorder of the spinal cord or bone marrow
— **my·e·lo·path·ic** \ˌmī-ə-lō-'pa-thik\ *adjective*

my·e·lo·pro·lif·er·a·tive \'mī-ə-lō-prə-'lif(ə-)rə-tiv, -fə-ˌrā-\ *adjective* (1951)
: of, relating to, or being a disorder (as leukemia) marked by excessive proliferation of bone marrow elements and especially blood cell precursors

my·ia·sis \mī-'ī-ə-səs, mē-\ *noun, plural* **my·ia·ses** \-ˌsēz\ [New Latin, from Greek *myia* fly — more at MIDGE] (1837)
: infestation with fly maggots

My·lar \'mī-ˌlär\ *trademark*
— used for a polyester film

my·nah *or* **my·na** \'mī-nə\ *noun* [Hindi *mainā* hill mynah from Sanskrit *madana*, a kind of bird] (1769)
: any of various Asian starlings (especially genera *Acridotheres, Gracula,* and *Sturnus*); *especially* : a dark brown slightly crested bird (*A. tristis*) of southeastern Asia with a white tail tip and wing markings and bright yellow bill and feet — compare HILL MYNAH

myn·heer \mīn-'her\ *noun* [Dutch *mijnheer,* from *mijn* my + *heer* master, sir] (1652)
: a male Netherlander — used as a title equivalent to *Mr.*

myo- — see MY-

myo·blast \'mī-ə-ˌblast\ *noun* [International Scientific Vocabulary] (1884)
: an undifferentiated cell capable of giving rise to muscle cells

myo·car·di·tis \ˌmī-ə-(ˌ)kär-'dī-təs\ *noun* [New Latin] (1866)
: inflammation of the myocardium

myo·car·di·um \ˌmī-ə-'kär-dē-əm\ *noun* [New Latin, from *myo-* + Greek *kardia* heart — more at HEART] (1879)
: the middle muscular layer of the heart wall
— **myo·car·di·al** \-dē-əl\ *adjective*

myo·clo·nus \ˌmī-ə-'klä-nəs\ *noun* [New Latin] (1883)
: irregular involuntary contraction of a muscle usually resulting from functional disorder of controlling motoneurons; *also* : a condition characterized by myoclonus
— **myo·clon·ic** \ˌmī-ə-'klä-nik\ *adjective*

myo·elec·tric \ˌmī-ō-i-'lek-trik\ *also* **myo·elec·tri·cal** \-tri-kəl\ *adjective* (circa 1919)
: of, relating to, or utilizing electricity generated by muscle

myo·fi·bril \ˌmī-ə-'fī-brəl, -'fi-\ *noun* [New Latin *myofibrilla,* from *my-* + *fibrilla* fibril] (1898)
: any of the longitudinal parallel contractile elements of a muscle cell that are composed of myosin and actin
— **myo·fi·bril·lar** \-brə-lər\ *adjective*

myo·fil·a·ment \-'fi-lə-mənt\ *noun* (1949)
: one of the individual filaments of actin or myosin that make up a myofibril

myo·gen·ic \-'je-nik\ *adjective* [International Scientific Vocabulary] (1904)
: taking place or functioning in ordered rhythmic fashion because of the inherent properties of cardiac muscle rather than specific neural stimuli ⟨a *myogenic* heartbeat⟩

myo·glo·bin \-'glō-bən, 'mī-ə-,\ *noun* [International Scientific Vocabulary] (1925)
: a red iron-containing protein pigment in muscles that is similar to hemoglobin

myo·ino·si·tol \ˌmī-ō-i-'nō-sə-ˌtȯl, -ˌtōl\ *noun* (1951)
: a biologically active inositol that is a component of the vitamin B complex and a lipotropic agent

my·ol·o·gy \mī-'ä-lə-jē\ *noun* [French or New Latin; French *myologie,* from New Latin *myologia,* from *my-* + Latin *-logia* -logy] (1649)
: a scientific study of muscles

my·o·ma \mī-'ō-mə\ *noun, plural* **-mas** *or* **-ma·ta** \-mə-tə\ [New Latin] (1875)
: a tumor consisting of muscle tissue
— **my·o·ma·tous** \-mə-təs\ *adjective*

myo·neu·ral \ˌmī-ə-'nùr-əl, -'nyùr-\ *adjective* (1905)
: of, relating to, or connecting muscles and nerves ⟨*myoneural* junctions⟩

my·op·a·thy \mī-'ä-pə-thē\ *noun* [International Scientific Vocabulary] (circa 1849)
: a disorder of muscle tissue or muscles
— **myo·path·ic** \ˌmī-ə-'pa-thik\ *adjective*

my·ope \'mī-ˌōp\ *noun* [French, from Late Latin *myops* myopic, from Greek *myōps,* from *myein* to be closed + *ōps* eye, face — more at EYE] (1728)
: a myopic person

my·o·pia \mī-'ō-pē-ə\ *noun* [New Latin, from Greek *myōpia,* from *myōp-, myōps*] (circa 1752)
1 : a condition in which the visual images come to a focus in front of the retina of the eye resulting especially in defective vision of distant objects
2 : a lack of foresight or discernment : a narrow view of something
— **my·o·pic** \-'ō-pik, -'ä-\ *adjective*
— **my·o·pi·cal·ly** \-pi-k(ə-)lē\ *adverb*

my·o·sin \'mī-ə-sən\ *noun* [International Scientific Vocabulary *my-* + ²*-ose* + ¹*-in*] (1942)
: a fibrous globulin of muscle that can split ATP and that reacts with actin to form actomyosin

my·o·sis, my·ot·ic *variant of* MIOSIS, MIOTIC

myo·si·tis \ˌmī-ə-'sī-təs\ *noun* [New Latin, irregular from Greek *mys* muscle, mouse] (circa 1819)
: muscle soreness

myo·tome \'mī-ə-ˌtōm\ *noun* [International Scientific Vocabulary] (1894)
: the portion of an embryonic somite from which skeletal musculature is produced

myo·to·nia \ˌmī-ə-'tō-nē-ə\ *noun* [New Latin] (circa 1896)
: tonic spasm of one or more muscles; *also* : a condition characterized by such spasms
— **myo·ton·ic** \-'tä-nik\ *adjective*

¹**myr·i·ad** \'mir-ē-əd\ *noun* [Greek *myriad-, myrias,* from *myrioi* countless, ten thousand] (1555)
1 : ten thousand
2 : a great number ⟨a *myriad* of ideas⟩

²**myriad** *adjective* (1791)
1 : INNUMERABLE ⟨those *myriad* problems⟩
2 : having innumerable aspects or elements ⟨the *myriad* activity of the new land —Meridel Le Sueur⟩

myr·ia·pod *also* **myr·io·pod** \'mir-ē-ə-ˌpäd\ *noun* [ultimately from Greek *myrioi* + *pod-, pous* foot — more at FOOT] (1826)
: any of a group (Myriapoda) of arthropods having the body made up of numerous similar segments nearly all of which bear true jointed legs and including the millipedes and centipedes
— **myriapod** *also* **myriopod** *adjective*

my·ris·tic acid \mə-'ris-tik-, mī-\ *noun* [International Scientific Vocabulary, from New Latin *Myristica,* genus of trees] (1848)
: a crystalline fatty acid $C_{14}H_{28}O_2$ occurring especially in the form of glycerides in most fats

myrmeco- *combining form* [Greek *myrmēko-,* from *myrmēk-, myrmēx* — more at PISMIRE]
: ant ⟨*myrmeco*philous⟩

myr·me·col·o·gy \ˌmər-mə-'kä-lə-jē\ *noun* [International Scientific Vocabulary] (circa 1902)
: the scientific study of ants
— **myr·me·co·log·i·cal** \-kə-'lä-ji-kəl\ *adjective*
— **myr·me·col·o·gist** \-'kä-lə-jist\ *noun*

myr·me·co·phile \'mər-mi-kə-ˌfīl\ *noun* [International Scientific Vocabulary] (1898)
: an organism that habitually shares an ant nest

myr·me·coph·i·lous \ˌmər-mə-'kä-fə-ləs\ *adjective* (1866)
: fond of, associated with, or benefited by ants

myr·mi·don \'mər-mə-ˌdän, -dən\ *noun* [Middle English *Mirmydon,* Latin *Myrmidon-, Myrmido,* from Greek *Myrmidōn*] (15th century)
1 *capitalized* : a member of a legendary Thessalian people who accompanied their king Achilles in the Trojan War
2 : a loyal follower; *especially* : a subordinate who executes orders unquestioningly or unscrupulously

my·rob·a·lan \mī-'rä-bə-lən, mə-\ *noun* [Middle French *mirobolan,* from Latin *myrobalanus,* from Greek *myrobalanos,* from *myron* unguent + *balanos* acorn — more at GLAND] (circa 1530)
: the dried astringent fruit of an East Indian tree (genus *Terminalia* of the family Combretaceae) used chiefly in tanning and in inks

myrrh \'mər\ *noun* [Middle English *myrre,* from Old English, from Latin *myrrha,* from Greek, of Semitic origin; akin to Arabic *murr* myrrh] (before 12th century)
: a yellowish brown to reddish brown aromatic gum resin with a bitter slightly pungent taste obtained from a tree (especially *Commiphora*

\ə\ **abut** \ə\ **kitten** \ər\ **further** \a\ **ash** \ā\ **ace**
\ä\ **mop, mar** \aù\ **out** \ch\ **chin** \e\ **bet** \ē\ **easy**
\g\ **go** \i\ **hit** \ī\ **ice** \j\ **job** \ŋ\ **sing** \ō\ **go**
\ò\ **law** \òi\ **boy** \th\ **thin** \th\ **the** \ü\ **loot** \ù\ **foot**
\y\ **yet** \zh\ **vision** *see also* Guide to Pronunciation

abyssinica of the family Burseraceae) of eastern Africa and Arabia; *also* : a mixture of myrrh and labdanum

myr·tle \'mər-tʰl\ *noun, often attributive* [Middle English *mirtille*, from Middle French, from Medieval Latin *myrtillus*, from Latin *myrtus*, from Greek *myrtos*] (1562) **1 a** : a common evergreen bushy shrub (*Myrtus communis*) of southern Europe with oval to lance-shaped shiny leaves, fragrant white or rosy flowers, and black berries **b** : any of a family (Myrtaceae, the myrtle family) of chiefly tropical shrubs or trees to which the common myrtle belongs **2 a** : ¹PERIWINKLE 1a **b** : CALIFORNIA LAUREL

my·self \mī-'self, mə-, *Southern also* -'sef\ *pronoun* (before 12th century) **1** : that identical one that is I — used reflexively ⟨I'm going to get *myself* a new suit⟩, for emphasis ⟨I *myself* will go⟩, or in absolute constructions ⟨*myself* a tourist, I nevertheless avoided other tourists⟩ **2** : my normal, healthy, or sane condition ⟨didn't feel *myself* yesterday⟩ □

myrtle 1a

mys·ta·gogue \'mis-tə-ˌgäg\ *noun* [Latin *mystagogus*, from Greek *mystagōgos*, from *mystēs* initiate (perhaps akin to Greek *myein* to be closed) + *agein* to lead — more at AGENT] (circa 1550) **1** : one who initiates another into a mystery cult **2** : one who understands or teaches mystical doctrines — **mys·ta·go·gy** \-ˌgä-jē, -ˌgō-\ *noun*

mys·te·ri·ous \mis-'tir-ē-əs\ *adjective* (1600) **1 a** : of, relating to, or constituting mystery ⟨the *mysterious* ways of God⟩ **b** : exciting wonder, curiosity, or surprise while baffling efforts to comprehend or identify : MYSTIFYING ⟨heard a *mysterious* noise⟩ ⟨a *mysterious* stranger⟩ **2** : stirred by or attracted to the inexplicable — **mys·te·ri·ous·ly** *adverb* — **mys·te·ri·ous·ness** *noun*

¹mys·tery \'mis-t(ə-)rē\ *noun, plural* **-ter·ies** [Middle English *mysterie*, from Latin *mysterium*, from Greek *mystērion*, from *mystēs* initiate] (14th century) **1 a** : a religious truth that one can know only by revelation and cannot fully understand **b** (1) : any of the 15 events (as the Nativity, the Crucifixion, or the Assumption) serving as a subject for meditation during the saying of the rosary (2) *capitalized* : a Christian sacrament; *specifically* : EUCHARIST **c** (1) : a secret religious rite believed (as in Eleusinian and Mithraic cults) to impart enduring bliss to the initiate (2) : a cult devoted to such rites **2 a** : something not understood or beyond understanding : ENIGMA **b** *obsolete* : a private secret **c** : the secret or specialized practices or ritual peculiar to an occupation or a body of people ⟨the *mysteries* of the tailor's craft⟩ **d** : a piece of fiction dealing usually with the solution of a mysterious crime **3** : profound, inexplicable, or secretive quality or character ⟨the *mystery* of her smile⟩ ☆

²mystery *noun, plural* **-ter·ies** [Middle English, from Late Latin *misterium, mysterium*, alteration of *ministerium* service, occupation, from *minister* servant — more at MINISTER] (14th century) **1** *archaic* : TRADE, CRAFT **2** *archaic* : a body of persons engaged in a particular trade, business, or profession : GUILD **3** : MYSTERY PLAY

mystery play *noun* [²*mystery*] (1852) : a medieval drama based on scriptural incidents (as the creation of the world, the Flood,

or the life, death, and resurrection of Christ) — compare MIRACLE PLAY

¹mys·tic \'mis-tik\ *adjective* [Middle English *mistik*, from Latin *mysticus* of mysteries, from Greek *mystikos*, from *mystēs* initiate] (14th century) **1** : MYSTICAL 1a **2** : of or relating to mysteries or esoteric rites : OCCULT **3** : of or relating to mysticism or mystics **4 a** : MYSTERIOUS **b** : OBSCURE, ENIGMATIC **c** : inducing a feeling of awe or wonder **d** : having magical properties

²mystic *noun* (1679) **1** : a follower of a mystical way of life **2** : an advocate of a theory of mysticism

mys·ti·cal \'mis-ti-kəl\ *adjective* (15th century) **1 a** : having a spiritual meaning or reality that is neither apparent to the senses nor obvious to the intelligence ⟨the *mystical* food of the sacrament⟩ **b** : involving or having the nature of an individual's direct subjective communion with God or ultimate reality ⟨the *mystical* experience of the Inner Light⟩ **2** : MYSTERIOUS, UNINTELLIGIBLE **3** : MYSTIC 2, 3 — **mys·ti·cal·ly** \-k(ə-)lē\ *adverb*

mys·ti·cism \'mis-tə-ˌsi-zəm\ *noun* (1736) **1** : the experience of mystical union or direct communion with ultimate reality reported by mystics **2** : the belief that direct knowledge of God, spiritual truth, or ultimate reality can be attained through subjective experience (as intuition or insight) **3 a** : vague speculation : a belief without sound basis **b** : a theory postulating the possibility of direct and intuitive acquisition of ineffable knowledge or power

mys·ti·fi·ca·tion \ˌmis-tə-fə-'kā-shən\ *noun* (1815) **1** : an act or instance of mystifying **2** : the quality or state of being mystified **3** : something designed to mystify

mys·ti·fy \'mis-tə-ˌfī\ *transitive verb* **-fied; -fy·ing** [French *mistifier*, from *mystère* mystery, from Latin *mysterium*] (circa 1734) **1** : to perplex the mind of : BEWILDER **2** : to make mysterious or obscure ⟨*mystify* an interpretation of a prophecy⟩ — **mys·ti·fi·er** \-ˌfī(-ə)r\ *noun* — **mys·ti·fy·ing·ly** \-ˌfī-iŋ-lē\ *adverb*

mys·tique \mi-'stēk\ *noun* [French, from *mystique,* adjective, mystic, from Latin *mysticus*] (1891) **1** : an air or attitude of mystery and reverence developing around something or someone **2** : the special esoteric skill essential in a calling or activity

myth \'mith\ *noun* [Greek *mythos*] (1830) **1 a** : a usually traditional story of ostensibly historical events that serves to unfold part of the world view of a people or explain a practice, belief, or natural phenomenon **b** : PARABLE, ALLEGORY **2 a** : a popular belief or tradition that has grown up around something or someone; *especially* : one embodying the ideals and institutions of a society or segment of society ⟨seduced by the American *myth* of individualism —Orde Coombs⟩ **b** : an unfounded or false notion **3** : a person or thing having only an imaginary or unverifiable existence **4** : the whole body of myths

myth·i·cal \'mith-i-kəl\ *or* **myth·ic** \-ik\ *adjective* (1669) **1** : based on or described in a myth especially as contrasted with history **2** *usually mythical* : existing only in the imagination : FICTITIOUS, IMAGINARY ⟨sportswriters picked a *mythical* all-star team⟩

3 *usually mythic* : having qualities suitable to myth : LEGENDARY ⟨the twilight of a *mythic* professional career —Clayton Riley⟩ *synonym* see FICTITIOUS — **myth·i·cal·ly** \-thi-k(ə-)lē\ *adverb*

myth·i·cize \'mi-thə-ˌsīz\ *transitive verb* **-cized; -ciz·ing** (1840) **1** : to turn into or envelop in myth **2** : to treat as myth — **myth·i·ciz·er** *noun*

myth·mak·er \'mith-ˌmā-kər\ *noun* (1871) : a creator of myths or of mythical situations or lore — **myth·mak·ing** \-kiŋ\ *noun*

my·thog·ra·phy \mi-'thä-grə-fē\ *noun* [Greek *mythographia*, from *mythos* + *-graphia* -graphy] (1851) **1** : the representation of mythical subjects in art **2** : a critical compilation of myths — **my·thog·ra·pher** \-fər\ *noun*

myth·o·log·i·cal \ˌmi-thə-'lä-ji-kəl\ *also* **myth·o·log·ic** \-jik\ *adjective* (1614) **1** : of or relating to mythology or myths : dealt with in mythology **2** : lacking factual basis or historical validity : MYTHICAL, FABULOUS — **myth·o·log·i·cal·ly** \-ji-k(ə-)lē\ *adverb*

my·thol·o·gize \mi-'thä-lə-ˌjīz\ *verb* **-gized; -giz·ing** (1603) *transitive verb* **1** *obsolete* : to explain the mythological significance of **2** : to build a myth around : MYTHICIZE *intransitive verb* **1** : to relate, classify, and explain myths **2** : to create or perpetuate myths

☆ **SYNONYMS**
Mystery, problem, enigma, riddle, puzzle mean something which baffles or perplexes. MYSTERY applies to what cannot be fully understood by human reason or less strictly to whatever resists or defies explanation ⟨the *mystery* of the stone monoliths⟩. PROBLEM applies to any question or difficulty calling for a solution or causing concern ⟨the *problems* created by high technology⟩. ENIGMA applies to utterance or behavior that is very difficult to interpret ⟨his suicide was an *enigma* his family never understood⟩. RIDDLE suggests an enigma or problem involving paradox or apparent contradiction ⟨the *riddle* of the reclusive pop star⟩. PUZZLE applies to an enigma or problem that challenges ingenuity for its solution ⟨the mechanisms of heredity were long a *puzzle* for scientists⟩.

□ **USAGE**
myself *Myself* is often used where *I* or *me* might be expected: as subject ⟨to wonder what *myself* will say —Emily Dickinson⟩ ⟨others and *myself* continued to press for the legislation⟩, after *as, than,* or *like* ⟨an aversion to paying such people as *myself* to tutor⟩ ⟨was enough to make a better man than *myself* quail⟩ ⟨old-timers like *myself*⟩, and as object ⟨now here you see *myself* with the diver⟩ ⟨for my wife and *myself* it was a happy time⟩. Such uses almost always occur when the speaker or writer is referring to himself or herself as an object of discourse rather than as a participant in discourse. The other reflexive personal pronouns are similarly but less frequently used in the same circumstances. Critics have frowned on these uses since around the turn of the century, probably unaware that they serve a definite purpose. Users themselves are as unaware as the critics—they simply follow their instincts. These uses are standard.

— **my·thol·o·giz·er** *noun*

my·thol·o·gy \mi-'thä-lə-jē\ *noun, plural* **-gies** [French or Late Latin; French *mythologie*, from Late Latin *mythologia* interpretation of myths, from Greek, legend, myth, from *mythologein* to relate myths, from *mythos* + *logos* speech — more at LEGEND] (1603)
1 : an allegorical narrative
2 : a body of myths: as **a** : the myths dealing with the gods, demigods, and legendary heroes of a particular people **b** : MYTHOS 2 ⟨cold war *mythology*⟩
3 : a branch of knowledge that deals with myth
4 : a popular belief or assumption that has grown up around someone or something ⟨defective *mythologies* that ignore masculine depth of feeling —Robert Bly⟩
— **my·thol·o·ger** \-jər\ *noun*
— **my·thol·o·gist** \-jist\ *noun*

mytho·ma·nia \,mi-thə-'mā-nē-ə, -nyə\ *noun* [New Latin, from Greek *mythos* + Late Latin *mania* mania] (circa 1909)
: an excessive or abnormal propensity for lying and exaggerating
— **mytho·ma·ni·ac** \-nē-,ak\ *noun or adjective*

mytho·poe·ia \,mi-thə-'pē-ə\ *noun* [Late Latin, from Greek *mythopoiia*, from *mythopoiein* to make a myth, from *mythos* + *poiein* to make — more at POET] (1846)
: a creating of myth : a giving rise to myths
— **mytho·poe·ic** \-'pē-ik\ *also* **mytho·po·et·ic** \-pō-'e-tik\ *or* **mytho·po·et·i·cal** \-ti-kəl\ *adjective*

my·thos \'mi-,thōs, -,thäs\ *noun, plural* **my·thoi** \-,thói\ [Greek] (1753)
1 a : MYTH 1a **b** : MYTHOLOGY 2a
2 : a pattern of beliefs expressing often symbolically the characteristic or prevalent attitudes in a group or culture
3 : THEME, PLOT

mythy \'mi-thē\ *adjective* (1931)
: resembling, concerned with, or of a subject for myth ⟨a *mythy* theme⟩

my word *interjection* (1841)
— used to express surprise or astonishment

myx·ede·ma \,mik-sə-'dē-mə\ *noun* [New Latin, from Greek *myxa* lamp wick, nasal mucus + New Latin *edema* edema — more at MUCUS] (1877)
: severe hypothyroidism characterized by firm inelastic edema, dry skin and hair, and loss of mental and physical vigor

— **myx·ede·ma·tous** \-'de-mə-təs, -'dē-\ *adjective*

myx·o·ma \mik-'sō-mə\ *noun, plural* **-mas** *or* **-ma·ta** \-mə-tə\ [New Latin, from Greek *myxa*] (1870)
: a soft tumor made up of gelatinous connective tissue like that of the umbilical cord
— **myx·o·ma·tous** \-mə-təs\ *adjective*

myx·o·ma·to·sis \mik-,sō-mə-'tō-səs\ *noun* [New Latin, from *myxomat-, myxoma*] (1927)
: a condition characterized by the presence of myxomas in the body; *specifically* : a severe virus disease of rabbits that is caused by a poxvirus transmitted by mosquitoes and that has been used in the biological control of rabbits in plague areas

myxo·my·cete \,mik-sō-'mī-,sēt, ,mik-sō-(,)mī-'\ *noun* [ultimately from Greek *myxa* + *mykēt-, mykēs* fungus — more at MYC-] (1877)
: SLIME MOLD

myxo·vi·rus \'mik-sə-,vī-rəs\ *noun* [New Latin, from Greek *myxa* + New Latin *virus* virus; from its affinity for certain mucins] (1955)
: any of a group of rather large RNA-containing viruses that includes the influenza viruses
— **myxo·vi·ral** \,mik-sə-'vī-rəl\ *adjective*

N *is the fourteenth letter of the English alphabet. It came through the Latin by way of Etruscan from the Greek* nu, *which was borrowed from Phoenician* nun. *It represents either of two nasal consonant sounds: one, the* n *in* new, *is called an alveolar* n, *and is usually formed in English by bringing the tip of the tongue against the gums behind the upper front teeth; the other, called a velar* n, *occurs before* k *or* g *in such words as* sink *and* sing, *and is produced by pressing the back of the tongue against the velum (or rear roof of the mouth).* N *sometimes forms the nucleus of a syllable without a vowel, as in* hidden *and* listen. *It is silent in some words after* m, *as in* hymn. *Small* n *is believed to have evolved from an early Greek form of* nu *similar to the Roman capital* N *except that its cross-stroke slanted from the lower left to the upper right. Eventually this cross-stroke rose higher along the left side of the letter while the angle it formed on the right side rounded to a single curved line.*

n \'en\ *noun, plural* **n's** *or* **ns** \'enz\ *often capitalized, often attributive* (before 12th century) **1 a :** the 14th letter of the English alphabet **b :** a graphic representation of this letter **c :** a speech counterpart of orthographic *n* **2 :** a graphic device for reproducing the letter *n* **3 a :** one designated *n* especially as the 14th in order or class **b :** an indefinite number; *especially* : a constant integer or a variable taking on integral values **4 :** something shaped like the letter N **5 :** the haploid or gametic number of chromosomes **6 :** EN 2

-n — see -EN

'n \ən, °n\ *conjunction* [by shortening] **:** THAN

'n' *also* **'n** \ən, °n\ *conjunction* **:** AND ⟨fish *'n'* chips⟩

naan *variant of* NAN

nab \'nab\ *transitive verb* **nabbed; nab·bing** [perhaps alteration of English dialect *nap*] (1686) **1 :** to catch or seize in arrest **:** APPREHEND **2 :** to seize suddenly

nabe \'nāb\ *noun* [by shortening & alteration from *neighborhood*] (1935) **:** a neighborhood theater — usually used in plural with *the*

na·bob \'nā-ˌbäb\ *noun* [Urdu *nawwāb*, from Arabic *nuwwāb*, plural of *nā'ib* governor] (1612) **1 :** a provincial governor of the Mogul empire in India **2 :** a person of great wealth or prominence

Na·both \'nā-ˌbäth\ *noun* [Hebrew *Nābhōth*] **:** the owner of a vineyard coveted and seized by Ahab king of Israel

na·celle \nə-'sel\ *noun* [French, literally, small boat, from Late Latin *navicella*, diminutive of Latin *navis* ship — more at NAVE] (1904) **:** a streamlined enclosure (as for an engine) on an aircraft

na·cho \'nä-(ˌ)chō\ *noun, plural* **nachos** [American Spanish, perhaps from Spanish *nacho* flat-nosed] (1969) **:** a tortilla chip topped with melted cheese and often additional savory toppings (as hot peppers or refried beans)

na·cre \'nā-kər\ *noun* [Middle French, from Old Italian *naccara* drum, nacre, from Arabic *naqqārah* drum] (1718) **:** MOTHER-OF-PEARL
— **na·cre·ous** \-krē-əs, -k(ə-)rəs\ *adjective*

NAD \ˌen-(ˌ)ā-'dē\ *noun* [nicotinamide *a*denine *d*inucleotide] (circa 1962) **:** a coenzyme $C_{21}H_{27}N_7O_{14}P_2$ of numerous dehydrogenases that occurs in most cells and plays an important role in all phases of intermediary metabolism as an oxidizing agent or when in the reduced form as a reducing agent for various metabolites — called also *nicotinamide adenine dinucleotide, diphosphopyridine nucleotide, DPN*

na·da \'nä-də\ *noun* [Spanish, from Latin (*res*) *nata* situation, circumstance, literally, a thing come into being] (1914) **:** NOTHING

Na–dene *also* **Na–dé·né** \nä-'dā-(ˌ)nä, -'de-, -nē\ *noun, often D capitalized* [*na-* (from Haida *na* to dwell & Tlingit *na* people) + *Déné*] (1915) **:** a hypothetically related group of American Indian languages that includes the Athabascan family, Tlingit, and Haida

NADH \ˌen-(ˌ)ā-(ˌ)dē-'āch\ *noun* [NAD + H, symbol for hydrogen] (1965) **:** the reduced form of NAD

na·dir \'nā-ˌdir, 'nā-dər\ *noun* [Middle English, from Middle French, from Arabic *nazīr* opposite] (15th century) **1 :** the point of the celestial sphere that is directly opposite the zenith and vertically downward from the observer **2 :** the lowest point

NADP \ˌen-(ˌ)ā-(ˌ)dē-'pē\ *noun* [*n*icotinamide *a*denine *d*inucleotide *p*hosphate] (circa 1962) **:** a coenzyme $C_{21}H_{28}N_7O_{17}P_3$ of numerous dehydrogenases (as that acting on glucose-6-phosphate) that occurs especially in red blood cells and plays a role in intermediary metabolism similar to NAD but acting often on different metabolites — called also *nicotinamide adenine dinucleotide phosphate, TPN, triphosphopyridine nucleotide*

NADPH \ˌen-(ˌ)ā-(ˌ)dē-(ˌ)pē-'āch\ *noun* [NADP + H, symbol for hydrogen] (circa 1966) **:** the reduced form of NADP

¹nag \'nag\ *noun* [Middle English *nagge*; akin to Dutch *negge* small horse] (15th century) **:** HORSE; *especially* : one that is old or in poor condition

²nag *verb* **nagged; nag·ging** [probably of Scandinavian origin; akin to Old Norse *gnaga* to gnaw; akin to Old English *gnagan* to gnaw] (circa 1828) *intransitive verb* **1 :** to find fault incessantly **:** COMPLAIN **2 :** to be a persistent source of annoyance or distraction *transitive verb* **1 :** to irritate by constant scolding or urging **2 :** BADGER, WORRY
— **nag·ger** *noun*
— **nagging** *adjective*
— **nag·ging·ly** \'na-giŋ-lē\ *adverb*

³nag *noun* (1925) **:** one who nags habitually

na·ga·na \nə-'gä-nə\ *noun* [Zulu *unakane, ulunakane*] (1895) **:** trypanosomiasis (especially when caused by *Trypanosoma brucei*) of domestic animals

nah \'na, 'nä, 'nȧ\ *variant of* NO

Na·huatl \'nä-ˌwä-t°l\ *noun* [Spanish *náhuatl*, from Nahuatl *Nāhuatl*] (1822) **:** a group of closely related Uto-Aztecan languages that includes the speech of several peoples (as the Aztecs) of central and southern Mexico and Central America
— **Na·huat·lan** \nä-'wät-lən\ *adjective or noun*

Na·hum \'nā-əm, -həm\ *noun* [Hebrew *Naḥūm*] **1 :** a Hebrew prophet of the 7th century B.C. **2 :** a prophetic book of canonical Jewish and Christian Scripture — see BIBLE table

na·iad \'nā-əd, 'nī-, -ˌad\ *noun, plural* **na·iads** *or* **na·ia·des** \-ə-ˌdēz\ [Middle English, from Middle French or Latin; Middle French *naïade*, from Latin *naiad-, naias*, from Greek, from *nan* to flow — more at NOURISH] (14th century) **1 :** any of the nymphs in classical mythology living in and giving life to lakes, rivers, springs, and fountains **2 :** any of the aquatic young of a mayfly, dragonfly, damselfly, or stone fly — compare NYMPH 3 **3 :** any of a genus (*Najas* of the family Najadaceae) of submerged aquatic plants

¹na·ïf *or* **na·if** \nä-'ēf\ *adjective* [French] (1598) **:** NAIVE

²naïf *or* **naif** *noun* (1893) **:** a naive person

¹nail \'nā(ə)l\ *noun* [Middle English, from Old English *nægl*; akin to Old High German *nagal* nail, fingernail, Latin *unguis* fingernail, toenail, claw, Greek *onyx*] (before 12th century) **1 a :** a horny sheath protecting the upper end of each finger and toe of humans and most other primates **b :** a structure (as a claw) that terminates a digit and corresponds to a nail **2 :** a slender usually pointed and headed fastener designed to be pounded in

²nail *transitive verb* (before 12th century) **1 :** to fasten with or as if with a nail **2 :** to fix in steady attention ⟨*nailed* his eye on the crack⟩ **3 a :** CATCH, TRAP **b :** to detect and expose usually so as to discredit **4 a :** STRIKE, HIT **b :** to put out (a runner) in baseball **5 :** to perform or complete perfectly or impressively ⟨*nailed* a jump shot⟩
— **nail·er** *noun*

nail–bit·er \'nā(ə)l-ˌbī-tər\ *noun* (1971) **:** something (as a close contest) that induces tension or anxiety ⟨lost a tough, 14-inning *nail-biter* —Steve Pate⟩

nail·brush \-ˌbrəsh\ *noun* (1802) **:** a small firm-bristled brush for cleaning the hands and especially the fingernails

nail down *transitive verb* (1615) **1 :** to gain or win decisively ⟨*nail down* his consent⟩ **2 :** to settle or establish clearly and unmistakably

nail file *noun* (1875) **:** a small narrow instrument (as of metal or cardboard) with a rough or emery surface that is used for shaping fingernails

nain·sook \'nān-ˌsu̇k\ *noun* [Hindi *nainsukh*, from *nain* eye + *sukh* delight] (1790) **:** a soft lightweight muslin

nai·ra \'nī-rə\ *noun* [alteration of *Nigeria*] (1972) — see MONEY table

na·ive *or* **na·ïve** \nä-'ēv\ *adjective* **na·iv·er; -est** [French *naïve*, feminine of *naïf*, from Old French, inborn, natural, from Latin *nativus*] (1654) **1 :** marked by unaffected simplicity **:** ARTLESS, INGENUOUS

2 a : deficient in worldly wisdom or informed judgment; *especially* : CREDULOUS **b :** not previously subjected to experimentation or a particular experimental situation ⟨made the test with *naive* rats⟩; *also* : not having previously used a particular drug (as marijuana)
3 : SELF-TAUGHT, PRIMITIVE
synonym see NATURAL
— **na·ive·ly** *or* **na·ïve·ly** *adverb*
— **na·ive·ness** *noun*

na·ive·té *also* **na·ive·te** *or* **na·ive·té** \(ˌ)nä-ˌēv-ˈtā, -ˌē-və-; nä-ˈēv-ˌtā, -ˈē-və-\ *noun* [French *naïveté*, from Old French, inborn character, from *naif*] (1673)
1 : a naive remark or action
2 : the quality or state of being naive

na·ive·ty *also* **na·ive·ty** \nä-ˈē-və-tē, -ˈēv-tē\ *noun, plural* **-ties** (1708)
chiefly British : NAÏVETÉ

na·ked \ˈnā-kəd, *especially Southern* ˈne-kəd\ *adjective* [Middle English, from Old English *nacod*; akin to Old High German *nackot* naked, Latin *nudus*, Greek *gymnos*] (before 12th century)
1 : not covered by clothing : NUDE
2 : devoid of customary or natural covering : BARE: as **a :** not enclosed in a sheath or scabbard **b :** not provided with a shade **c** *of a plant or one of its parts* : lacking pubescence or enveloping or subtending parts **d :** lacking foliage or vegetation **e** *of an animal or one of its parts* : lacking an external covering (as of hair, feathers, or shell)
3 a : scantily supplied or furnished **b :** lacking embellishment : UNADORNED
4 : UNARMED, DEFENSELESS
5 : lacking confirmation or support
6 : devoid of concealment or disguise
7 : unaided by any optical device or instrument ⟨visible to the *naked* eye⟩
8 : not backed by the writer's ownership of the commodity contract or security
synonym see BARE
— **na·ked·ly** *adverb*
— **na·ked·ness** *noun*

na·led \ˈnā-ˌled\ *noun* [origin unknown] (circa 1962)
: a short-lived insecticide $C_4H_7Br_2Cl_2O_4P$ of relatively low toxicity to warm-blooded animals that is used especially to control crop pests and mosquitoes

na·li·dix·ic acid \ˌnā-lə-ˈdik-sik-\ *noun* [perhaps from *naphthyridine* ($C_8H_6N_2$ — from *naphth-* + *pyridine*) + carb*oxylic acid*] (1964)
: an antibacterial agent $C_{12}H_{12}N_2O_3$ that is used especially in the treatment of genitourinary infections

na·lor·phine \na-ˈlȯr-ˌfēn\ *noun* [*N-allyl* + *morphine*] (circa 1953)
: a white crystalline compound $C_{19}H_{21}NO_3$ that is derived from morphine and is used in the form of its hydrochloride as a respiratory stimulant to counteract poisoning by morphine and similar narcotic drugs

nal·ox·one \na-ˈläk-ˌsōn\ *noun* [*N-allyl* + hydr*oxy-* + *-one*] (1964)
: a potent antagonist $C_{19}H_{21}NO_4$ of narcotic drugs and especially morphine that is administered especially as the hydrochloride

nal·trex·one \nal-ˈtrek-ˌsōn\ *noun* [*N-allyl* + *trex-* (as in *methotrexate*) + *-one*] (1973)
: a narcotic antagonist $C_{20}H_{23}NO_4$

nam·by–pam·by \ˌnam-bē-ˈpam-bē\ *adjective* [*Namby Pamby*, nickname given to Ambrose Philips] (1745)
1 : lacking in character or substance : INSIPID
2 : WEAK, INDECISIVE ◆
— **namby–pamby** *noun*

¹name \ˈnām\ *noun* [Middle English, from Old English *nama*; akin to Old High German *namo* name, Latin *nomen*, Greek *onoma*, *onyma*] (before 12th century)
1 a : a word or phrase that constitutes the distinctive designation of a person or thing **b :** a word or symbol used in logic to designate an entity

2 : a descriptive often disparaging epithet ⟨called him *names*⟩
3 a : REPUTATION ⟨gave the town a bad *name*⟩ **b :** an illustrious record : FAME ⟨made a *name* for himself in golf⟩ **c :** a person or thing with a reputation
4 : FAMILY, CLAN
5 : appearance as opposed to reality ⟨a friend in *name* only⟩
6 : one referred to by a name ⟨praise his holy *name*⟩
— **in the name of 1 :** by authority of ⟨open *in the name of* the law⟩ **2 :** for the reason of : using the excuse of ⟨called for reforms *in the name of* progress⟩

²name *transitive verb* **named; nam·ing** (before 12th century)
1 : to give a name to : CALL
2 a : to mention or identify by name **b :** to accuse by name
3 : to nominate for office : APPOINT
4 : to decide on : CHOOSE ⟨*name* the day for the wedding⟩
5 : to mention explicitly : SPECIFY ⟨unwilling to *name* a price⟩
— **nam·er** *noun*

³name *adjective* (1598)
1 : of, relating to, or bearing a name ⟨*name* tags⟩
2 : appearing in the name of a literary or theatrical production
3 a : having an established reputation **b :** featuring celebrities

name·able *also* **nam·able** \ˈnā-mə-bəl\ *adjective* (1780)
1 : worthy of being named : MEMORABLE
2 : capable of being named : IDENTIFIABLE

name–call·ing \ˈnām-ˌkȯ-liŋ\ *noun* (1853)
: the use of offensive names especially to win an argument or to induce rejection or condemnation (as of a person or project) without objective consideration of the facts

name day *noun* (1721)
: the church feast day of the saint after whom one is named

name–drop·ping \-ˌdrä-piŋ\ *noun* (1950)
: the practice of seeking to impress others by studied but apparently casual mention of prominent persons as associates
— **name–drop·per** \-pər\ *noun*

name·less \ˈnām-ləs\ *adjective* (14th century)
1 : OBSCURE, UNDISTINGUISHED
2 : not known by name : ANONYMOUS
3 : having no legal right to a name : ILLEGITIMATE
4 : not having been given a name : UNNAMED
5 : not marked with a name ⟨a *nameless* grave⟩
6 a : incapable of precise description : INDEFINABLE **b :** too repulsive or distressing to describe
— **name·less·ly** *adverb*
— **name·less·ness** *noun*

name·ly \ˈnām-lē\ *adverb* (14th century)
: that is to say : TO WIT

name of the game *noun* (1966)
1 : the essential quality or matter ⟨patience is the *name of the game* in coastal duck hunting —Dick Beals⟩
2 : the fundamental goal of an activity

name·plate \-ˌplāt\ *noun* (circa 1859)
: something (as a plate or plaque) bearing a name (as of a resident or manufacturer)

name·sake \-ˌsāk\ *noun* [probably from *name's sake*] (1646)
: one that has the same name as another; *especially* : one who is named after another or for whom another is named

nan \ˈnän, ˈnan\ *noun* [Hindi & Persian; Hindi *nān*, from Persian] (1948)
: a round flat leavened bread especially of the Indian subcontinent

nana \ˈna-nə\ *noun* [probably of baby-talk origin] (circa 1844)
: GRANDMOTHER

nance \ˈnan(t)s\ *noun* [short for *nancy*, from the name *Nancy*] (1920)
1 : an effeminate male — often used disparagingly
2 : HOMOSEXUAL — often used disparagingly

NAND \ˈnand\ *noun* [*not AND*] (1958)
: a computer logic circuit that produces an output which is the inverse of that of an AND circuit

nan·di·na \nan-ˈdī-nə, -ˈdē-\ *noun* [New Latin, from Japanese *nanten*] (circa 1890)
: a widely cultivated Asian evergreen shrub (*Nandina domestica*) of the barberry family

nan·keen \nan-ˈkēn\ *noun* [*Nanking* (Nanjing), China] (1755)
1 : a durable brownish yellow cotton fabric originally loomed by hand in China
2 *plural* : trousers made of nankeen

Nan·kin \ˈnan-kin, ˈnän-\ *or* **Nan·king** \-ˈkiŋ\ *noun* [*Nanking* (Nanjing), China] (1781)
: Chinese porcelain decorated in blue on a white ground

nan·no·plank·ton \ˌna-nō-ˈplaŋ(k)-tən, -ˌtän\ *noun* [New Latin, from Greek *nanos*, *nannos* dwarf + New Latin *plankton* plankton] (1912)
: the smallest plankton that consists of those organisms (as bacteria) passing through nets of very fine mesh silk cloth

nan·ny *also* **nan·nie** \ˈna-nē\ *noun, plural* **nannies** [probably of baby-talk origin] (1795)
: a child's nurse : NURSEMAID

nanny goat *noun* [*Nanny*, nickname for *Anne*] (1788)
: a female domestic goat

nano- *combining form* [International Scientific Vocabulary, from Greek *nanos* dwarf]
: one billionth (10^{-9}) part of ⟨*nano*second⟩

nano·gram \ˈna-nə-ˌgram\ *noun* [International Scientific Vocabulary] (1951)
: one billionth of a gram

nano·me·ter \ˈna-nə-ˌmē-tər\ *noun* [International Scientific Vocabulary] (1963)
: one billionth of a meter

nano·sec·ond \-ˌse-kənd, -kənt\ *noun* [International Scientific Vocabulary] (1959)
: one billionth of a second

nano·tech·nol·o·gy \ˌna-nō-tek-ˈnä-lə-jē\ *noun* (1987)
: the art of manipulating materials on an atomic or molecular scale especially to build microscopic devices (as robots)

nano·tes·la \ˈna-nō-ˌtes-lə\ *noun* (1968)
: a unit of magnetic flux density equal to 10^{-9} tesla

Nan·tua sauce \nän(n)-ˈtwä-\ *noun* [*Nantua*, France] (circa 1961)

\ə\ **abut** \ᵊ\ **kitten** \ər\ **further** \a\ **ash** \ā\ **ace**
\ä\ **mop, mar** \au̇\ **out** \ch\ **chin** \e\ **bet** \ē\ **easy**
\g\ **go** \i\ **hit** \ī\ **ice** \j\ **job** \ŋ\ **sing** \ō\ **go**
\ȯ\ **law** \ȯi\ **boy** \th\ **thin** \t̲h̲\ **the** \ü\ **loot** \u̇\ **foot**
\y\ **yet** \zh\ **vision** *see also* Guide to Pronunciation

: a cream sauce flavored with shellfish (as lobster)

Na·o·mi \nā-'ō-mē\ *noun* [Hebrew *Nā'ŏmī*]
: the mother-in-law of the Old Testament heroine Ruth

¹**nap** \'nap\ *intransitive verb* **napped; napping** [Middle English *nappen,* from Old English *hnappian;* akin to Old High German *hnaffezen* to doze] (before 12th century)
1 : to sleep briefly especially during the day : DOZE
2 : to be off guard

²**nap** *noun* (14th century)
: a short sleep especially during the day : SNOOZE

³**nap** *noun* [Middle English *noppe,* from Middle Dutch, flock of wool, nap] (15th century)
: a hairy or downy surface (as on a fabric)
— **nap·less** \-ləs\ *adjective*
— **napped** \'napt\ *adjective*

⁴**nap** *transitive verb* **napped; nap·ping** (1620)
: to raise a nap on (fabric or leather)

⁵**nap** *noun* [from to go *nap* (to make all the points in the card game Napoleon)] (1895)
British : a pick or recommendation as a good bet to win a contest (as a horse race); *also*
: one named in a nap

⁶**nap** *transitive verb* **napped; nap·ping** (1927)
British : to pick or single out in a nap

napa cabbage \'na-pə-\ *noun* [perhaps from Japanese dialect *nappa* greens] (1980)
: CHINESE CABBAGE b

napa leather *noun* [*Napa,* California] (1897)
: a glove leather made by tawing sheepskins with a soap-and-oil mixture; *also* : a similarly soft leather

¹**na·palm** \'nā-,päm, -,pälm *also* 'na- *also* nə-'pä(l)m\ *noun* [*naphthene* + *palm*itate] (1942)
1 : a thickener consisting of a mixture of aluminum soaps used in jelling gasoline (as for incendiary bombs)
2 : fuel jelled with napalm

²**napalm** *transitive verb* (1950)
: to assault with napalm

nape \'nāp, 'nap\ *noun* [Middle English] (14th century)
: the back of the neck

na·pery \'nā-p(ə-)rē\ *noun* [Middle English, from Middle French *naperie,* from *nappe, nape* tablecloth — more at NAPKIN] (14th century)
: household linen; *especially* : TABLE LINEN

Naph·ta·li \'naf-tə-,lī\ *noun* [Hebrew *Naphtālī*]
: a son of Jacob and the traditional eponymous ancestor of one of the tribes of Israel

naph·tha \'naf-thə, ÷'nap-\ *noun* [Latin, from Greek, of Iranian origin; akin to Persian *neft* naphtha] (1572)
1 : any of various volatile often flammable liquid hydrocarbon mixtures used chiefly as solvents and diluents
2 : PETROLEUM

naph·tha·lene \-,lēn\ *noun* [alteration of earlier *naphthaline,* irregular from *naphtha*] (1821)
: a crystalline aromatic hydrocarbon $C_{10}H_8$ usually obtained by distillation of coal tar and used especially in organic synthesis

naph·thene \'naf-,thēn, ÷'nap-\ *noun* (1884)
: CYCLOPARAFFIN
— **naph·then·ic** \,naf-'thē-nik, ÷,nap-, -'the-\ *adjective*

naph·thol \'naf-,thȯl, ÷'nap-, -,thōl\ *noun* [International Scientific Vocabulary] (1849)
1 : either of two isomeric derivatives $C_{10}H_8O$ of naphthalene used as antiseptics and in the manufacture of dyes
2 : any of various hydroxy derivatives of naphthalene that resemble the simpler phenols

naph·thyl·amine \naf-'thi-lə-,mēn, ÷nap-\ *noun* [International Scientific Vocabulary] (1857)

: either of two isomeric crystalline bases $C_{10}H_9N$ used especially as dye intermediates

na·pi·er grass \'nā-pē-ər-\ *noun* [*Napier,* town in South Africa] (1914)
: a tall stout African perennial grass (*Pennisetum purpureum*) that resembles sugarcane and is widely grown for forage — called also *elephant grass*

Na·pier·ian logarithm \nə-'pir-ē-ən-, nā-\ *noun* [John *Napier*] (1816)
: NATURAL LOGARITHM

Na·pi·er's bones \'nā-pē-ərz-\ *noun* (circa 1658)
: a set of graduated rods (as of wood or bone) invented by John Napier and used for multiplication and division based on the principles of logarithms

na·pi·form \'nā-pə-,fȯrm\ *adjective* [Latin *napus* turnip (perhaps from Greek *napy, sinapy* mustard) + International Scientific Vocabulary *-iform*] (circa 1846)
: globular at the top and tapering off abruptly — used especially of roots

nap·kin \'nap-kən\ *noun* [Middle English *nappekin,* from *nappe* tablecloth, from Middle French, from Latin *mappa* napkin] (14th century)
1 : a piece of material (as cloth or paper) used at table to wipe the lips or fingers and protect the clothes
2 : a small cloth or towel: as **a** *dialect British* : HANDKERCHIEF **b** *chiefly Scottish* : KERCHIEF **c** *chiefly British* : DIAPER 3
3 : SANITARY NAPKIN

na·po·leon \nə-'pōl-yən, -'pō-lē-ən\ *noun* [French *napoléon,* from *Napoléon* Napoleon I] (1814)
1 : a former French 20-franc gold coin
2 : an oblong pastry with a filling of cream, custard, or jelly
3 *capitalized* : one like Napoleon I (as in ambition)

nappe \'nap\ *noun* [French, tablecloth, sheet, nappe — more at NAPKIN] (1904)
1 : SHEET 6
2 : a large mass thrust over other rocks
3 : one of the two sheets that lie on opposite sides of the vertex and together make up a cone

¹**nap·py** \'na-pē\ *noun* [obsolete *nappy,* adjective, foaming] (1700)
chiefly Scottish : LIQUOR; *specifically* : ALE

²**nappy** *noun, plural* **nappies** [English dialect *nap* bowl, from Middle English, from Old English *hnæpp* bowl; akin to Old High German *hnapf* bowl] (1864)
: a rimless shallow open serving dish

³**nappy** *noun, plural* **nappies** [*nap*kin + ⁴*-y*] (1927)
chiefly British : DIAPER 3

⁴**nappy** *adjective* **nap·pi·er; -est** [³*nap*] (1928)
: KINKY 1

na·prap·a·thy \nə-'pra-pə-thē\ *noun* [Czech *naprava* correction + English *-pathy*] (1909)
: a system of treatment by manipulation of connective tissue and adjoining structures (as ligaments, joints, and muscles) and by dietary measures that is held to facilitate the recuperative and regenerative processes of the body

narc \'närk\ *noun* [short for *narcotics agent*] (1967)
slang : a person (as a government agent) who investigates narcotics violations

nar·cis·sism \'när-sə-,si-zəm\ *noun* [German *Narzissismus,* from *Narziss* Narcissus, from Latin *Narcissus*] (1822)
1 : EGOISM, EGOCENTRISM
2 : love of or sexual desire for one's own body ◆
— **nar·cis·sist** \'när-sə-sist\ *noun or adjective*
— **nar·cis·sis·tic** \,när-sə-'sis-tik\ *adjective*

nar·cis·sus \när-'si-səs\ *noun* [Latin, from Greek *Narkissos*]

1 *capitalized* : a beautiful youth in Greek mythology who pines away for love of his own reflection and is then turned into the narcissus flower
2 *plural* **nar·cis·si** \-'si-,sī, -(,)sē\ *or* **nar·cis·sus·es** *or* **narcissus** [New Latin, genus name, from Latin, narcissus, from Greek *narkissos*] : DAFFODIL; *especially* : one whose flowers have a short corona and are usually borne separately

nar·co \'när-(,)kō\ *noun, plural* **narcos** (1955)
slang : NARC

nar·co·lep·sy \'när-kə-,lep-sē\ *noun, plural* **-sies** [International Scientific Vocabulary, from Greek *narkē*] (1880)
: a condition characterized by brief attacks of deep sleep
— **nar·co·lep·tic** \,när-kə-'lep-tik\ *adjective*

nar·co·lep·tic \,när-kə-'lep-tik\ *noun* (1928)
: a person who is subject to attacks of narcolepsy

nar·co·sis \när-'kō-səs\ *noun, plural* **-co·ses** \-,sēz\ [New Latin, from Greek *narkōsis,* action of benumbing, from *narkoun*] (circa 1693)
: a state of stupor, unconsciousness, or arrested activity produced by the influence of narcotics or other chemicals

¹**nar·cot·ic** \när-'kä-tik\ *noun* [Middle English *narkotik,* from Middle French *narcotique,* from *narcotique,* adjective, from Medieval Latin *narcoticus,* from Greek *narkōtikos,* from *narkoun* to benumb, from *narkē* numbness — more at SNARE] (14th century)
1 a : a drug (as opium) that in moderate doses dulls the senses, relieves pain, and induces profound sleep but in excessive doses causes stupor, coma, or convulsions **b** : a drug (as marijuana or LSD) subject to restriction similar to that of addictive narcotics whether physiologically addictive and narcotic or not
2 : something that soothes, relieves, or lulls

²**narcotic** *adjective* (1526)
1 a : having the properties of or yielding a narcotic **b** : inducing mental lethargy : SOPORIFEROUS
2 : of, induced by, or concerned with narcotics
3 : of, involving, or intended for narcotic addicts
— **nar·cot·i·cal·ly** \-ti-k(ə-)lē\ *adverb*

nar·co·tize \'när-kə-,tīz\ *verb* **-tized; -tiz·ing** [International Scientific Vocabulary] (1526)

◇ WORD HISTORY

narcissism The term *narcissism* represents the result of modern science finding a psychological truth in an ancient myth. In Greek mythology Narcissus was a youth so strikingly beautiful that he attracted many would-be lovers, both male and female. He spurned the attentions of all of them. Finally, Nemesis, the goddess of retribution, in response to the prayer of one rejected lover, contrived that Narcissus should catch sight of his own reflection in a pool on Mount Helicon. Narcissus became so entranced with his own beauty that he could not bear to tear himself away. He lay beside the pool day after day until he wasted away and finally expired. By an act of the gods his body was metamorphosed into the flower now known as the narcissus. Modern psychologists were reminded of the myth of Narcissus as they studied individuals morbidly interested in themselves or sexually attracted to their own bodies. In 1899 a German psychologist coined the term *Narzissismus* to describe this form of self-love. In 1905 Havelock Ellis, in his *Studies in the Psychology of Sex,* accepted this coinage and used *narcissism* as the English equivalent.

transitive verb
1 a : to treat with or subject to a narcotic **b** : to put into a state of narcosis
2 : to soothe to unconsciousness or unawareness
intransitive verb
: to act as a narcotizing agent
nard \\'närd\\ *noun* [Middle English *narde,* from Old English, from Latin *nardus,* from Greek *nardos,* of Semitic origin; akin to Hebrew *nērd* nard] (before 12th century)
: SPIKENARD 1b
na·res \\'nar-(,)ēz, 'ner-\\ *noun plural* [Middle English, from Latin, plural of *naris;* akin to Latin *nasus* nose — more at NOSE] (14th century)
: the pair of openings of the nose or nasal cavity of a vertebrate
nar·ghi·le \\'när-gə-lē\\ *or* **nar·gi·leh** \\-,le\\ *noun* [Persian *nārgīla,* from *nārgīl* coconut, of Indo-Aryan origin; akin to Sanskrit *nārikela* coconut; from the original material used in making its bowl] (1758)
: a water pipe that originated in the Near East
¹**nark** \\'närk\\ *noun* [perhaps from Romany *nak* nose] (circa 1860)
British **:** STOOL PIGEON
²**nark** *variant of* NARC
³**nark** *transitive verb* [origin unknown] (1888)
British **:** IRRITATE, ANNOY
Nar·ra·gan·set *or* **Nar·ra·gan·sett** \\,nar-ə-'gan(t)-sət\\ *noun, plural* **Narraganset** *or* **Narragansets** *or* **Narragansett** *or* **Narragansetts** (1622)
1 : a member of an American Indian people of Rhode Island
2 : the Algonquian language of the Narraganset people
nar·rate \\'nar-,āt, na-'rāt\\ *transitive verb* **nar·rat·ed; nar·rat·ing** [Latin *narratus,* past participle of *narrare,* from Latin *gnarus* knowing; akin to Latin *gnoscere, noscere* to know — more at KNOW] (1656)
: to tell (as a story) in detail; *also* **:** to provide spoken commentary for (as a movie or television show)
— **nar·ra·tor** \\'nar-,ā-tər; na-'rā-, nə-; 'nar-ə-\\ *noun*
nar·ra·tion \\na-'rā-shən, nə-\\ *noun* (15th century)
1 : the act or process or an instance of narrating
2 : STORY, NARRATIVE
— **nar·ra·tion·al** \\-shnəl, -shə-n²l\\ *adjective*
nar·ra·tive \\'nar-ə-tiv\\ *noun* (1566)
1 : something that is narrated **:** STORY
2 : the art or practice of narration
3 : the representation in art of an event or story; *also* **:** an example of such a representation
— **narrative** *adjective*
— **nar·ra·tive·ly** *adverb*
nar·ra·tol·o·gy \\,nar-ə-'tä-lə-jē\\ *noun* (1976)
: the study of structure in narratives
— **nar·ra·to·log·i·cal** \\-tə-'lä-ji-kəl\\ *adjective*
— **nar·ra·tol·o·gist** \\-'tä-lə-jist\\ *noun*
¹**nar·row** \\'nar-(,)ō\\ *adjective* [Middle English *narowe,* from Old English *nearu;* akin to Old High German *narwa* scar] (before 12th century)
1 a : of slender width **b :** of less than standard width **c** *of a textile* **:** woven in widths less than 18 inches (46 centimeters)
2 : limited in size or scope
3 a : illiberal in views or disposition **:** PREJUDICED **b** *chiefly dialect* **:** STINGY, NIGGARDLY
4 a : barely sufficient **:** CLOSE **b :** barely successful
5 : minutely precise **:** METICULOUS
6 *of a ration* **:** relatively rich in protein as compared with carbohydrate and fat
7 : TENSE 3
— **nar·row·ly** *adverb*
— **nar·row·ness** *noun*
²**narrow** (before 12th century)

transitive verb
1 : to decrease the breadth or extent of **:** CONTRACT — often used with *down*
2 : to decrease the scope or sphere of **:** LIMIT — often used with *down*
intransitive verb
: to lessen in width or extent **:** CONTRACT — often used with *down*
³**narrow** *noun* (13th century)
: a narrow part or passage; *specifically* **:** a strait connecting two bodies of water — usually used in plural but singular or plural in construction
nar·row·band \\'nar-ō-,band, 'nar-ə-\\ *adjective* (1950)
: operating at, responsive to, or including a narrow range of frequencies
narrow boat *noun* (1949)
British **:** a barge with a beam of less than seven feet (2.1 meters)
nar·row·cast·ing \\'nar-ō-,kas-tiŋ, 'nar-ə-\\ *noun* (1928)
: radio or television transmission aimed at a narrowly defined area or audience (as paying subscribers or night workers)
nar·row–mind·ed \\,nar-ō-'mīn-dəd, ,nar-ə-\\ *adjective* (1625)
: lacking in tolerance or breadth of vision **:** PETTY
— **nar·row–mind·ed·ly** *adverb*
— **nar·row–mind·ed·ness** *noun*
nar·thex \\'när-,theks\\ *noun* [Late Greek *narthēx,* from Greek, giant fennel, cane, casket] (circa 1673)
1 : the portico of an ancient church
2 : a vestibule leading to the nave of a church
nar·whal \\'när-,wäl, -,hwäl, -,wəl\\ *also* **nar·whale** \\-,wäl, -,hwäl\\ *noun* [Norwegian & Danish *narhval* & Swedish *narval,* probably modification of Icelandic *nárhvalur,* from Old Norse *nāhvalr,* from *nār* corpse + *hvalr* whale; from its color] (1646)
: an arctic cetacean (*Monodon monoceros*) about 20 feet (6 meters) long with the male having a long twisted ivory tusk

narwhal

nary \\'nar-ē, 'ner-\\ *adjective* [alteration of *ne'er a*] (1746)
: not any ⟨*nary* a person wanted to go⟩
¹**na·sal** \\'nā-zəl\\ *noun* [Middle English, from Middle French, from Old French, from *nes* nose, from Latin *nasus* — more at NOSE] (14th century)
1 : the nosepiece of a helmet
2 : a nasal part
3 : a nasal consonant
²**nasal** *adjective* (1656)
1 : of or relating to the nose
2 a : uttered with the soft palate lowered and with passage of air through the nose (as with \\m\\, \\n\\, \\ŋ\\, \\ō^m\\, or \\a^m\\) **b :** characterized by resonance produced through the nose
3 *of a musical tone* **:** SHARP, PENETRATING
— **na·sal·i·ty** \\nā-'za-lə-tē\\ *noun*
— **na·sal·ly** \\'nā-zə-lē, 'nāz-lē\\ *adverb*
na·sal·ize \\'nā-zə-,līz\\ *verb* **-ized; -iz·ing** (1817)
transitive verb
: to make nasal or pronounce as a nasal sound
— **na·sal·i·za·tion** \\,nā-zə-lə-'zā-shən\\ *noun*
na·scence \\'nā-s²n(t)s, 'nā-\\ *noun* (1570)
: NASCENCY
na·scen·cy \\-s²n(t)-sē\\ *noun, plural* **-cies** (1682)

: BIRTH, ORIGIN
na·scent \\'na-s²nt, 'nā-\\ *adjective* [Latin *nascent-, nascens,* present participle of *nasci* to be born] (circa 1624)
: coming or having recently come into existence
naso- *combining form* [Latin *nasus* nose]
1 : nose and ⟨*naso*pharynx⟩
2 : nasal ⟨*naso*gastric⟩
na·so·gas·tric \\,nā-zō-'gas-trik\\ *adjective* (1942)
: being or performed by intubation of the stomach through the nasal passages ⟨*nasogastric* tube⟩ ⟨*nasogastric* suction⟩
na·so·pha·ryn·geal \\-fə-'rin-j(ē-)əl, -,far-ən-'jē-əl\\ *adjective* (1872)
: of, relating to, or affecting the nose and pharynx or the nasopharynx
na·so·phar·ynx \\-'far-iŋ(k)s\\ *noun* [New Latin] (1877)
: the upper part of the pharynx continuous with the nasal passages
nas·tic \\'nas-tik\\ *adjective* [Greek *nastos* close-pressed, from *nassein* to press] (1908)
: of, relating to, or constituting a movement of a plant part caused by disproportionate growth or increase of turgor in one surface
nas·tur·tium \\nə-'stər-shəm, na-\\ *noun* [Latin, a cress] (1704)
: any of a genus (*Tropaeolum* of the family Tropaeolaceae, the nasturtium family) of herbs of Central and South America with showy spurred flowers and pungent seeds; *especially* **:** either of two widely cultivated ornamentals (*T. majus* and *T. minus*)

nasturtium

nas·ty \\'nas-tē\\ *adjective* **nas·ti·er; -est** [Middle English] (14th century)
1 a : disgustingly filthy **b** : physically repugnant
2 : INDECENT, OBSCENE
3 : MEAN, TAWDRY
4 a : extremely hazardous or harmful ⟨had a *nasty* climb to reach the summit⟩ **b :** causing severe pain or suffering ⟨a *nasty* wound⟩ **c :** sharply unpleasant **:** DISAGREEABLE ⟨*nasty* weather⟩
5 a : difficult to understand or deal with **:** VEXATIOUS ⟨a *nasty* problem⟩ **b :** psychologically unsettling **:** TRYING ⟨a *nasty* fear that she was lost⟩
6 : lacking in courtesy or sportsmanship ⟨a *nasty* trick⟩
synonym see DIRTY
— **nas·ti·ly** \\-tə-lē\\ *adverb*
— **nas·ti·ness** \\-tē-nəs\\ *noun*
— **nasty** *noun*
na·tal \\'nā-t²l\\ *adjective* [Middle English, from Latin *natalis,* from *natus,* past participle of *nasci* to be born — more at NATION] (15th century)
1 : NATIVE
2 : of, relating to, or present at birth; *especially* **:** associated with one's birth ⟨a *natal* star⟩
na·tal·i·ty \\nā-'ta-lə-tē, nə-\\ *noun, plural* **-ties** (1888)
: BIRTHRATE
na·tant \\'nā-t²nt\\ *adjective* [Middle English *natand,* from Latin *natant-, natans,* present participle of *natare* to swim; akin to Latin *nare* to swim; akin to Greek *nein, nēchein* to swim, Sanskrit *snāti* he bathes] (15th century)
: swimming or floating in water ⟨*natant* decapods⟩
na·ta·tion \\nā-'tā-shən, na-\\ *noun* (1542)
: the action or art of swimming

\\ə\\ abut	\\³\\ kitten	\\ər\\ further \\a\\ ash \\ā\\ ace
\\ä\\ mop, mar	\\au̇\\ out	\\ch\\ chin \\e\\ bet \\ē\\ easy
\\g\\ go	\\i\\ hit	\\ī\\ ice \\j\\ job \\ŋ\\ sing \\ō\\ go
\\o̊\\ law	\\o̊i\\ boy	\\th\\ thin \\t̲h̲\\ the \\ü\\ loot \\u̇\\ foot
\\y\\ yet	\\zh\\ vision	*see also* Guide to Pronunciation

na·ta·to·ri·al \ˌnā-tə-ˈtōr-ē-əl, ˌna-, -ˈtȯr-\ *or* **na·ta·to·ry** \ˈnā-tə-ˌtōr-ē, ˈna-, -ˌtȯr-\ *adjective* (1816)
1 : of or relating to swimming
2 : adapted to or characterized by swimming ⟨a *natatorial* leg of an aquatic insect⟩
na·ta·to·ri·um \ˌnā-tə-ˈtōr-ē-əm, ˌna-, -ˈtȯr-\ *noun* [Late Latin, from Latin *natare*] (circa 1890)
: an indoor swimming pool
natch \ˈnach\ *adverb* [by shortening & alteration from *naturally*] (circa 1945)
slang **:** of course **:** NATURALLY
Natch·ez \ˈna-chiz\ *noun, plural* **Natchez** (1845)
1 : a member of an American Indian people of southwestern Mississippi
2 : the language of the Natchez people
na·tes \ˈnā-ˌtēz\ *noun plural* [Latin, plural of *natis* buttock] (circa 1706)
: BUTTOCKS
nathe·less \ˈnāth-ləs\ *or* **nath·less** \ˈnath-\ *adverb* [Middle English, from Old English *nā thē læs* not the less] (before 12th century)
archaic **:** NEVERTHELESS, NOTWITHSTANDING
na·tion \ˈnā-shən\ *noun* [Middle English *nacioun*, from Middle French *nation*, from Latin *nation-*, *natio* birth, race, nation, from *nasci* to be born; akin to Latin *gignere* to beget — more at KIN] (14th century)
1 a (1) **:** NATIONALITY 5a (2) **:** a politically organized nationality (3) **:** a non-Jewish nationality ⟨why do the *nations* conspire —Psalms 2:1 (Revised Standard Version)⟩ **b :** a community of people composed of one or more nationalities and possessing a more or less defined territory and government **c :** a territorial division containing a body of people of one or more nationalities and usually characterized by relatively large size and independent status
2 *archaic* **:** GROUP, AGGREGATION
3 : a tribe or federation of tribes (as of American Indians)
¹na·tion·al \ˈnash-nəl, ˈna-shə-nᵊl\ *adjective* (1597)
1 : of or relating to a nation
2 : NATIONALIST
3 : comprising or characteristic of a nationality
4 : belonging to or maintained by the federal government
5 : of, relating to, or being a coalition government formed by most or all major political parties usually in a crisis
— **na·tion·al·ly** *adverb*
²national *noun* (1887)
1 : one that owes allegiance to or is under the protection of a nation without regard to the more formal status of citizen or subject
2 : a competition that is national in scope — usually used in plural
synonym see CITIZEN
national bank *noun* (1790)
1 : CENTRAL BANK
2 : a bank operating under federal charter and supervision
national forest *noun* (circa 1905)
: a usually forested area of considerable extent that is preserved by government decree from private exploitation and is harvested only under supervision
National Guard *noun* (1847)
1 : a militia force recruited by each state of the U.S., equipped by the federal government, and jointly maintained subject to the call of either
2 *often not capitalized* **:** a military establishment serving as a national constabulary and defense force
national income *noun* (1878)
: the aggregate of earnings from a nation's current production including compensation of employees, interest, rental income, and profits of business after taxes
na·tion·al·ise *chiefly British variant of* NATIONALIZE

na·tion·al·ism \ˈnash-nə-ˌli-zəm, ˈna-shə-nᵊl-ˌi-zəm\ *noun* (1844)
: loyalty and devotion to a nation; *especially* **:** a sense of national consciousness exalting one nation above all others and placing primary emphasis on promotion of its culture and interests as opposed to those of other nations or supranational groups
¹na·tion·al·ist \-list, -ist\ *noun* (1715)
1 : an advocate of or believer in nationalism
2 *capitalized* **:** a member of a political party or group advocating national independence or strong national government
²nationalist *adjective* (1889)
1 : of, relating to, or advocating nationalism
2 *capitalized* **:** of, relating to, or being a political group advocating or associated with nationalism
na·tion·al·is·tic \ˌnash-nə-ˈlis-tik, ˌna-shə-nᵊl-ˈis-tik\ *adjective* (1866)
1 : of, favoring, or characterized by nationalism ⟨*nationalistic* election speeches⟩
2 : NATIONAL 1
— **na·tion·al·is·ti·cal·ly** \-ti-k(ə-)lē\ *adverb*
na·tion·al·i·ty \ˌnash-nə-ˈna-lə-tē, ˌnash-ˈna-\ *noun, plural* **-ties** (1691)
1 : national character
2 : NATIONALISM
3 a : national status; *specifically* **:** a legal relationship involving allegiance on the part of an individual and usually protection on the part of the state **b :** membership in a particular nation
4 : political independence or existence as a separate nation
5 a : a people having a common origin, tradition, and language and capable of forming or actually constituting a nation-state **b :** an ethnic group constituting one element of a larger unit (as a nation)
na·tion·al·ize \ˈnash-nə-ˌlīz, ˈna-shə-nᵊl-ˌīz\ *transitive verb* **-ized; -iz·ing** (1800)
1 : to give a national character to
2 : to invest control or ownership of in the national government
— **na·tion·al·i·za·tion** \ˌnash-nə-lə-ˈzā-shən, ˌna-shə-nᵊl-ə-\ *noun*
— **na·tion·al·iz·er** \ˈnash-nə-ˌlī-zər, ˈna-shə-nᵊl-ˌī-zər\ *noun*
national monument *noun* (1916)
: a place of historic, scenic, or scientific interest set aside for preservation usually by presidential proclamation
national park *noun* (1868)
: an area of special scenic, historical, or scientific importance set aside and maintained by a national government and in the U.S. by an act of Congress
national seashore *noun* (1962)
: a recreational area adjacent to a seacoast and maintained by the federal government
national socialism *noun, often N&S capitalized* (1931)
: NAZISM
— **national socialist** *adjective, often N&S capitalized*
na·tion·hood \ˈnā-shən-ˌhu̇d\ *noun* (1850)
: NATIONALITY 1, 3a, 4
na·tion–state \ˈnā-shən-ˈstāt, -ˌstāt\ *noun* (1918)
: a form of political organization under which a relatively homogeneous people inhabits a sovereign state; *especially* **:** a state containing one as opposed to several nationalities
¹na·tion·wide \ˌnā-shən-ˈwīd\ *adjective* (1912)
: extending throughout a nation
²nationwide *adverb* (1926)
: throughout the nation
¹na·tive \ˈnā-tiv\ *adjective* [Middle English *natif*, from Middle French, from Latin *nativus*, from *natus*, past participle of *nasci* to be born — more at NATION] (14th century)
1 : INBORN, INNATE ⟨*native* talents⟩

2 : belonging to a particular place by birth ⟨*native* to Wisconsin⟩
3 *archaic* **:** closely related
4 : belonging to or associated with one by birth
5 : NATURAL, NORMAL
6 a : grown, produced, or originating in a particular place or in the vicinity **:** LOCAL **b :** living or growing naturally in a particular region **:** INDIGENOUS
7 : SIMPLE, UNAFFECTED
8 a : constituting the original substance or source **b :** found in nature especially in an unadulterated form ⟨mining *native* silver⟩
9 *chiefly Australian* **:** having a usually superficial resemblance to a specified English plant or animal ☆
— **na·tive·ly** *adverb*
— **na·tive·ness** *noun*
²native *noun* (1535)
1 : one born or reared in a particular place
2 a : an original or indigenous inhabitant **b :** something indigenous to a particular locality
3 : a local resident; *especially* **:** a person who has always lived in a place as distinguished from a visitor or temporary resident
Native American *noun* (1925)
: AMERICAN INDIAN
— **Native American** *adjective*
na·tiv·ism \ˈnā-ti-ˌvi-zəm\ *noun* (1844)
1 : a policy of favoring native inhabitants as opposed to immigrants
2 : the revival or perpetuation of an indigenous culture especially in opposition to acculturation
— **na·tiv·ist** \-vist\ *noun or adjective*
— **na·tiv·is·tic** \ˌnā-ti-ˈvis-tik\ *adjective*
na·tiv·i·ty \nə-ˈti-və-tē, nā-\ *noun, plural* **-ties** [Middle English *nativite*, from Middle French *nativité*, from Medieval Latin *nativitat-*, *nativitas*, from Late Latin, birth, from Latin *nativus*] (14th century)
1 : the process or circumstances of being born **:** BIRTH; *especially, capitalized* **:** the birth of Jesus
2 : a horoscope at or of the time of one's birth
3 : the place of origin
na·tri·ure·sis \ˌnā-trē-yu̇-ˈrē-səs\ *noun* [New Latin, from *natrium* sodium (from International Scientific Vocabulary *natron*) + *uresis* urination, from Greek *ourēsis*, from *ourein* to urinate — more at URINE] (1957)
: excessive loss of sodium in the urine
— **na·tri·uret·ic** \-ˈre-tik\ *adjective or noun*
na·tro·lite \ˈnā-trə-ˌlīt\ *noun* [German *Natrolith*, from *Natron* (from French) + *-lith* -lite] (circa 1805)
: a hydrous silicate of sodium and aluminum that is related to zeolite
na·tron \ˈnā-ˌträn, -trən\ *noun* [French, from Spanish *natrón*, from Arabic *naṭrūn*, from Greek *nitron*] (1684)
: a hydrous native sodium carbonate used in ancient times in embalming, in ceramic pastes, and as a cleansing agent
¹nat·ter \ˈna-tər\ *intransitive verb* [probably imitative] (1942)
: CHATTER 2
²natter *noun* (1943)

☆ **SYNONYMS**
Native, indigenous, endemic, aboriginal mean belonging to a locality. NATIVE implies birth or origin in a place or region and may suggest compatibility with it ⟨*native* tribal customs⟩. INDIGENOUS applies to species or races and adds to NATIVE the implication of not having been introduced from elsewhere ⟨maize is *indigenous* to America⟩. ENDEMIC implies being peculiar to a region ⟨edelweiss is *endemic* in the Alps⟩. ABORIGINAL implies having no known race preceding in occupancy of the region ⟨the *aboriginal* peoples of Australia⟩.

chiefly British **:** idle talk or conversation **:** CHAT

nat·ty \'na-tē\ *adjective* **nat·ti·er; -est** [perhaps alteration of earlier *netty,* from obsolete *net* neat, clean] (1557)
: trimly neat and tidy **:** SMART
— **nat·ti·ly** \'na-t°l-ē\ *adverb*
— **nat·ti·ness** \'na-tē-nəs\ *noun*

¹**nat·u·ral** \'na-chə-rəl, 'nach-rəl\ *adjective* [Middle English, from Middle French, from Latin *naturalis* of nature, from *natura* nature] (14th century)
1 : based on an inherent sense of right and wrong 〈*natural* justice〉
2 a : being in accordance with or determined by nature **b :** having or constituting a classification based on features existing in nature
3 a (1) : begotten as distinguished from adopted; *also* **:** LEGITIMATE **(2) :** being a relation by actual consanguinity as distinguished from adoption 〈*natural* parents〉 **b :** ILLEGITIMATE 〈a *natural* child〉
4 : having an essential relation with someone or something **:** following from the nature of the one in question 〈his guilt is a *natural* deduction from the evidence〉
5 : implanted or being as if implanted by nature **:** seemingly inborn 〈a *natural* talent for art〉
6 : of or relating to nature as an object of study and research
7 : having a specified character by nature 〈a *natural* athlete〉
8 a : occurring in conformity with the ordinary course of nature **:** not marvelous or supernatural 〈*natural* causes〉 **b :** formulated by human reason alone rather than revelation 〈*natural* religion〉 〈*natural* rights〉 **c :** having a normal or usual character 〈events followed their *natural* course〉
9 : possessing or exhibiting the higher qualities (as kindliness and affection) of human nature 〈a noble . . . brother . . . ever most kind and *natural* —Shakespeare〉
10 a : growing without human care; *also* **:** not cultivated 〈*natural* prairie unbroken by the plow〉 **b :** existing in or produced by nature **:** not artificial 〈*natural* turf〉 〈*natural* curiosities〉 **c :** relating to or being natural food
11 a : being in a state of nature without spiritual enlightenment **:** UNREGENERATE 〈*natural* man〉 **b :** living in or as if in a state of nature untouched by the influences of civilization and society
12 a : having a physical or real existence as contrasted with one that is spiritual, intellectual, or fictitious 〈a corporation is a legal but not a *natural* person〉 **b :** of, relating to, or operating in the physical as opposed to the spiritual world 〈*natural* laws describe phenomena of the physical universe〉
13 a : closely resembling an original **:** true to nature **b :** marked by easy simplicity and freedom from artificiality, affectation, or constraint **c :** having a form or appearance found in nature
14 a : having neither flats nor sharps 〈the *natural* scale of C major〉 **b :** being neither sharp nor flat **c :** having the pitch modified by the natural sign
15 : of an off-white or beige color ☆
— **nat·u·ral·ness** \-nəs\ *noun*

²**natural** *noun* (1533)
1 : one born without the usual powers of reason and understanding
2 a : a sign ♮ placed on any degree of the musical staff to nullify the effect of a preceding sharp or flat **b :** a note or tone affected by the natural sign
3 : a result or combination that immediately wins the stake in a game; *specifically* **:** a throw of 7 or 11 on the first cast in craps
4 a : one having natural skills, talents, or abilities **b :** something that is likely to become an immediate success **c :** one that is obviously suitable for a specific purpose

5 : AFRO

natural childbirth *noun* (1933)
: a system of managing childbirth in which the mother receives preparatory education in order to remain conscious during and assist in delivery with minimal or no use of drugs or anesthetics

natural family planning *noun* (1975)
: a method of birth control that involves abstention from sexual intercourse during the period of ovulation which is determined through observation and measurement of bodily symptoms

natural food *noun* (1917)
: food that has undergone minimal processing and contains no preservatives or artificial additives

natural gas *noun* (1825)
1 : gas issuing from the earth's crust through natural openings or bored wells; *especially* **:** a combustible mixture of methane and higher hydrocarbons used chiefly as a fuel and raw material
2 : gas manufactured from organic matter (as coal)

natural history *noun* (1567)
1 : a treatise on some aspect of nature
2 : the natural development of something (as an organism or disease) over a period of time
3 : the study of natural objects especially in the field from an amateur or popular point of view

nat·u·ral·ise *British variant of* NATURALIZE

nat·u·ral·ism \'na-chə-rə-,li-zəm, 'nach-rə-\ *noun* (circa 1641)
1 : action, inclination, or thought based only on natural desires and instincts
2 : a theory denying that an event or object has a supernatural significance; *specifically* **:** the doctrine that scientific laws are adequate to account for all phenomena
3 : realism in art or literature; *specifically* **:** a theory in literature emphasizing scientific observation of life without idealization or the avoidance of the ugly

nat·u·ral·ist \-list\ *noun* (1587)
1 : one that advocates or practices naturalism
2 : a student of natural history; *especially* **:** a field biologist

nat·u·ral·is·tic \,na-chə-rə-'lis-tik, ,nach-rə-\ *also* **nat·u·ral·ist** \'na-chə-rə-list, 'nach-rə-\ *adjective* (1838)
: of, characterized by, or according with naturalism
— **nat·u·ral·is·ti·cal·ly** \,na-chə-rə-'lis-ti-k(ə-)lē, ,nach-rə-\ *adverb*

nat·u·ral·ize \'na-chə-rə-,līz, 'nach-rə-\ *verb* **-ized; -iz·ing** (1593)
transitive verb
1 : to introduce into common use or into the vernacular
2 : to bring into conformity with nature
3 : to confer the rights of a national on; *especially* **:** to admit to citizenship
4 : to cause (as a plant) to become established as if native
intransitive verb
: to become established as if native
— **nat·u·ral·i·za·tion** \,na-chə-rə-lə-'zā-shən, ,nach-rə-\ *noun*

natural killer cell *noun* (1975)
: a large granular lymphocyte capable of killing a tumor or microbial cell without prior exposure to the target cell and without having it presented with or marked by a histocompatibility antigen

natural law *noun* (15th century)
: a body of law or a specific principle held to be derived from nature and binding upon human society in the absence of or in addition to positive law

natural logarithm *noun* (1816)
: a logarithm with *e* as a base

nat·u·ral·ly \'na-chər-ə-lē, 'nach-rə-, 'na-chər-\ *adverb* (14th century)

1 : by nature **:** by natural character or ability 〈*naturally* timid〉
2 : according to the usual course of things **:** as might be expected 〈we *naturally* dislike being hurt〉
3 a : without artificial aid 〈hair that curls *naturally*〉 **b :** without affectation 〈speak *naturally*〉
4 : with truth to nature **:** REALISTICALLY

natural number *noun* (1763)
: the number 1 or any number (as 3, 12, 432) obtained by adding 1 to it one or more times **:** a positive integer

natural philosophy *noun* (14th century)
: NATURAL SCIENCE; *especially* **:** PHYSICAL SCIENCE
— **natural philosopher** *noun*

natural resource *noun* (1870)
1 *plural* **:** industrial materials and capacities (as mineral deposits and waterpower) supplied by nature
2 : RESOURCE 1b

natural science *noun* (14th century)
: any of the sciences (as physics, chemistry, or biology) that deal with matter, energy, and their interrelations and transformations or with objectively measurable phenomena
— **natural scientist** *noun*

natural selection *noun* (1857)
: a natural process that results in the survival and reproductive success of individuals or groups best adjusted to their environment and that leads to the perpetuation of genetic qualities best suited to that particular environment

natural theology *noun* (1677)
: theology deriving its knowledge of God from the study of nature independent of special revelation

na·ture \'nā-chər\ *noun* [Middle English, from Middle French, from Latin *natura,* from *natus,* past participle of *nasci* to be born — more at NATION] (14th century)
1 a : the inherent character or basic constitution of a person or thing **:** ESSENCE **b :** DISPOSITION, TEMPERAMENT
2 a : a creative and controlling force in the universe **b :** an inner force or the sum of such forces in an individual
3 : a kind or class usually distinguished by fundamental or essential characteristics 〈documents of a confidential *nature*〉 〈acts of a ceremonial *nature*〉
4 : the physical constitution or drives of an organism; *especially* **:** an excretory organ or function — used in phrases like *the call of nature*
5 : a spontaneous attitude (as of generosity)

☆ **SYNONYMS**
Natural, ingenuous, naive, unsophisticated, artless mean free from pretension or calculation. NATURAL implies lacking artificiality and self-consciousness and having a spontaneousness suggesting the natural rather than the man-made world 〈her unaffected, *natural* manner〉. INGENUOUS implies inability to disguise or conceal one's feelings or intentions 〈the *ingenuous* enthusiasm of children〉. NAIVE suggests lack of worldly wisdom often connoting credulousness and unchecked innocence 〈politically *naive*〉. UNSOPHISTICATED implies a lack of experience and training necessary for social ease and adroitness 〈*unsophisticated* adolescents〉. ARTLESS suggests a naturalness resulting from unawareness of the effect one is producing on others 〈*artless* charm〉. See in addition REGULAR.

\ə\ abut \°\ kitten \ər\ **further** \a\ ash \ā\ ace
\ä\ mop, mar \au̇\ out \ch\ chin \e\ bet \ē\ easy
\g\ go \i\ hit \ī\ ice \j\ job \ŋ\ sing \ō\ go
\ȯ\ law \ȯi\ boy \th\ thin \th\ the \ü\ loot \u̇\ foot
\y\ yet \zh\ vision *see also* Guide to Pronunciation

6 : the external world in its entirety
7 a : humankind's original or natural condition **b :** a simplified mode of life resembling this condition
8 : the genetically controlled qualities of an organism
9 : natural scenery
synonym see TYPE
na·tur·ism \'nā-chə-,ri-zəm\ *noun* (1847)
1 : NATURALISM 1, 2
2 : the worship of the forces of nature
3 : NUDISM
— **na·tur·ist** \-rist\ *noun*
na·tu·rop·a·thy \,nā-chə-'rä-pə-thē\ *noun* (1901)
: a system of treatment of disease that avoids drugs and surgery and emphasizes the use of natural agents (as air, water, and sunshine) and physical means (as manipulation and electrical treatment)
— **na·tu·ro·path** \'nā-chər-ə-,path, 'na-\ *noun*
— **na·tu·ro·path·ic** \,nā-chər-ə-'pa-thik, ,na-; ,nā-,tyùr-ə-, -'tùr-\ *adjective*
Nau·ga·hyde \'nò-gə-,hïd, 'nä-\ *trademark*
— used for vinyl-coated fabrics
¹**naught** \'nòt, 'nät\ *pronoun* [Middle English *nought*, from Old English *nāwiht*, from *nā* no + *wiht* creature, thing — more at NO, WIGHT] (before 12th century)
: NOTHING ⟨efforts came to *naught*⟩
word history see NAUGHTY
²**naught** *noun* (before 12th century)
1 : NOTHINGNESS, NONEXISTENCE
2 : the arithmetical symbol 0 : ZERO, CIPHER
naugh·ty \'nò-tē, 'nä-\ *adjective* **naugh·ti·er; -est** [Middle English *noughti*, from *nought*] (14th century)
1 a *archaic* **:** vicious in moral character : WICKED **b :** guilty of disobedience or misbehavior
2 : lacking in taste or propriety ◇
— **naugh·ti·ly** \-tᵊl-ē\ *adverb*
— **naugh·ti·ness** \'nò-tē-nəs, 'nä-\ *noun*
nau·ma·chia \nò-'mā-kē-ə, -'ma-\ *noun, plural* **-chi·ae** \-kē-,ē, -kē-,ï\ *or* **-chi·as** [Latin, from Greek, naval battle, from *naus* ship + *machesthai* to fight — more at NAVE] (1596)
1 : an ancient Roman spectacle representing a naval battle
2 : a place for naumachiae
nau·pli·us \'nò-plē-əs\ *noun, plural* **-plii** \-plē-,ï, -,ē\ [New Latin, from Latin, a shellfish, from Greek *nauplios*] (1836)
: a crustacean larva in usually the first stage after leaving the egg and with three pairs of appendages, a median eye, and little or no segmentation
nau·sea \'nò-zē-ə, -sē-ə; 'nò-zhə, -shə\ *noun* [Latin, seasickness, nausea, from Greek *nautia, nausia*, from *nautēs* sailor] (1569)
1 : a stomach distress with distaste for food and an urge to vomit
2 : extreme disgust ◇
— **nau·se·ant** \-zhē-ənt, -shē-, -zē-, -sē-\ *noun or adjective*
nau·se·ate \'nò-zhē-,āt, -shē-, -zē-, -sē-\ *verb* **-at·ed; -at·ing** (1640)
intransitive verb
1 : to become affected with nausea
2 : to feel disgust
transitive verb
: to affect with nausea or disgust
nauseating *adjective* (1645)
: causing nausea or especially disgust
usage see NAUSEOUS
— **nau·se·at·ing·ly** *adverb*
nau·seous \'nò-shəs, 'nò-zē-əs\ *adjective* (1612)
1 : causing nausea or disgust : NAUSEATING
2 : affected with nausea or disgust □
— **nau·seous·ly** *adverb*
— **nau·seous·ness** *noun*
nautch \'nòch\ *noun* [Hindi *nāc*, from Sanskrit *nṛtya*, from *nṛtyati* he dances] (1809)

: an entertainment in India consisting chiefly of dancing by professional dancing girls
nau·ti·cal \'nò-ti-kəl, 'nä-\ *adjective* [Latin *nauticus*, from Greek *nautikos*, from *nautēs* sailor, from *naus* ship — more at NAVE] (1552)
: of, relating to, or associated with seamen, navigation, or ships
— **nau·ti·cal·ly** \-k(ə-)lē\ *adverb*
nautical mile *noun* (1834)
: any of various units of distance used for sea and air navigation based on the length of a minute of arc of a great circle of the earth and differing because the earth is not a perfect sphere: as **a :** a British unit equal to 6080 feet (1853.2 meters) **b :** an international unit equal to 6076.115 feet (1852 meters) used officially in the U.S. since July 1, 1959
nau·ti·loid \'nò-tᵊl-,òid, 'nä-\ *noun* (circa 1847)
: any of a subclass (Nautiloidea) of shell-bearing cephalopods that were abundant in the Ordovician and especially the Silurian but are represented in the recent fauna only by the nautiluses
— **nautiloid** *adjective*
nau·ti·lus \'nò-tᵊl-əs, 'nä-\ *noun, plural* **-lus·es** *or* **-li** \-tᵊl-,ī, -,ē\ [New Latin, from Latin, paper nautilus, from Greek *nautilos*, literally, sailor, from *naus* ship] (1601)
1 : any of a genus (*Nautilus*) of cephalopod mollusks of the South Pacific and Indian Oceans with a spiral chambered shell that is pearly on the inside — called also *chambered nautilus*

nautilus

2 : PAPER NAUTILUS
nav·aid \'na-,vād\ *noun* [*nav*igation *aid*] (1956)
: a device or system (as a radar beacon) that provides a navigator with navigational data
Na·va·jo *also* **Na·va·ho** \'na-və-,hō, 'nä-\ *noun, plural* **-jo** *or* **-jos** *also* **-ho** *or* **-hos** [Spanish (*Apache de*) *Navajó*, literally, Apache of Navajó, from *Navajó*, area occupied by Navajos, probably from Tewa (Pueblo Indian language of northern New Mexico) *navahu·*, literally, arroyo with planted fields] (1780)
1 : a member of an American Indian people of northern New Mexico and Arizona
2 : the language of the Navajo people
na·val \'nā-vəl\ *adjective* [Middle English, from Latin *navalis*, from *navis* ship] (15th century)
1 *obsolete* **:** of or relating to ships or shipping
2 a : of or relating to a navy **b :** consisting of or involving warships
naval architect *noun* (circa 1885)
: one who designs ships
naval stores *noun plural* [from their former use in the construction and maintenance of wooden sailing vessels] (1678)
: products (as turpentine, pitch, and rosin) obtained from resinous conifers and especially pines
¹**nave** \'nāv\ *noun* [Middle English, from Old English *nafu*; akin to Old English *nafela* navel] (before 12th century)
: the hub of a wheel
²**nave** *noun* [Medieval Latin *navis*, from Latin, ship; akin to Old English *nōwend* sailor, Greek *naus* ship, Sanskrit *nau*] (1673)
: the main part of the interior of a church; *especially* **:** the long narrow central hall in a cruciform church that rises higher than the aisles flanking it to form a clerestory
na·vel \'nā-vəl\ *noun* [Middle English, from Old English *nafela*; akin to Old High German *nabalo* navel, Latin *umbilicus*, Greek *ompha-los*] (before 12th century)

1 : a depression in the middle of the abdomen that marks the point of former attachment of the umbilical cord or yolk stalk
2 : the central point : MIDDLE
navel orange *noun* (1888)
: a seedless orange having a pit at the apex where the fruit encloses a small secondary fruit — called also *navel*
¹**na·vic·u·lar** \nə-'vi-kyə-lər\ *adjective* [Middle English *naviculare*, from Latin *navicula* boat, diminutive of *navis*] (15th century)
1 : shaped like a boat ⟨a *navicular* bone⟩
2 : of, relating to, or involving a navicular bone ⟨*navicular* disease⟩
²**navicular** *noun* [New Latin (*os*) *naviculare* navicular bone] (1816)
: a navicular bone; *especially* **:** one situated on the big-toe side of the tarsus

□ USAGE
nauseous Those who insist that *nauseous* can properly be used only in sense 1 and that in sense 2 it is an error for *nauseated* are mistaken. Current evidence shows these facts: *nauseous* is most frequently used to mean physically affected with nausea, usually after a linking verb such as *feel* or *become;* figurative use is quite a bit less frequent. Use of *nauseous* in sense 1 is much more often figurative than literal, and this use appears to be losing ground to *nauseating. Nauseated,* while not rare, is less common than *nauseous* in sense 2.

◇ WORD HISTORY
naughty The word *wight* "person, creature" is a more or less deliberate archaism in 20th century English, but a fragment of *wight* survives buried in a few much more familiar words. In Old English, *wiht,* the predecessor of *wight,* meant "thing" as well as "creature" and entered into indefinite pronouns such as *āwiht, ōwiht* "anything" and *nāwiht, nōwiht* "nothing." The latter shrank in Middle English to *naught* and *nought,* which by the end of the Middle English period had merged in pronunciation and become, in effect, spelling variants. A distinctive development of *nought* was its use as an adverb meaning "not at all, absolutely not." Reduced under weak stress to *not,* in Middle English it competed with and eventually ousted the older negative *ne* to become the ordinary negative adverb of Modern English. In a completely different direction, Old English *nāwiht, nōwiht* "nothing" came to be used adjectivally to mean "good for nothing, valueless." Then as *naught, nought* in Middle English they developed the meaning "bad, wicked." *Naught* was extended by the adjective suffix *-i* in late Middle English to give Modern English *naughty,* though the word now typically refers only to very mild wickedness, such as the pranks of misbehaving children or the improprieties of adults.

nausea The ancient Greeks were a seafaring people, so shipboard motion sickness was hardly unknown to them. In fact, the Greek word for it, *nausia* (or *neutia*) was a derivative of *naus,* meaning "ship." Since the dominant symptom of seasickness, as we call it, is an upset stomach and the concomitant urge to vomit, *nausia* became synonymous with similar stomach distress of any origin. The word was borrowed into Latin as *nausea* and from Latin into English. Ever since, many a landlubber has been in the throes of nausea without ever having gone near the ocean.

nav·i·ga·ble \'na-vi-gə-bəl\ *adjective* (15th century)
1 : deep enough and wide enough to afford passage to ships
2 : capable of being steered
— **nav·i·ga·bil·i·ty** \ˌna-vi-gə-'bi-lə-tē\ *noun*
— **nav·i·ga·bly** \'na-vi-gə-blē\ *adverb*
nav·i·gate \'na-və-ˌgāt\ *verb* **-gat·ed; -gat·ing** [Latin *navigatus,* past participle of *navigare,* from *navis* ship + *-igare* (from *agere* to drive) — more at AGENT] (1588)
intransitive verb
1 : to travel by water : SAIL
2 : to steer a course through a medium; *specifically* : to operate an airplane
3 : GET AROUND, MOVE
transitive verb
1 a : to sail over, on, or through **b** : to make one's way over or through : TRAVERSE
2 a : to steer or manage (a boat) in sailing **b** : to operate or control the course of (as an airplane)
nav·i·ga·tion \ˌna-və-'gā-shən\ *noun* (1547)
1 : the act or practice of navigating
2 : the science of getting ships, aircraft, or spacecraft from place to place; *especially* : the method of determining position, course, and distance traveled
3 : ship traffic or commerce
— **nav·i·ga·tion·al** \-shnəl, -shə-nᵊl\ *adjective*
— **nav·i·ga·tion·al·ly** *adverb*
nav·i·ga·tor \'na-və-ˌgā-tər\ *noun* (1590)
: one that navigates or is qualified to navigate
nav·vy \'na-vē\ *noun, plural* **navvies** [by shortening & alteration from *navigator* construction worker on a canal] (circa 1834)
chiefly British : an unskilled laborer
na·vy \'nā-vē\ *noun, plural* **navies** [Middle English *navie,* from Middle French, from Latin *navigia* ships, from *navigare*] (14th century)
1 : a group of ships : FLEET
2 : a nation's ships of war and of logistic support
3 *often capitalized* : the complete naval establishment of a nation including yards, stations, ships, and personnel
4 : a dark grayish purplish blue
navy bean *noun* (1856)
: a white-seeded kidney bean grown especially for its nutritious seeds
Navy Cross *noun* (1919)
: a U.S. Navy decoration awarded for extraordinary heroism in operations against an armed enemy
navy yard *noun* (1771)
: a yard where naval vessels are built or repaired
na·wab \nə-'wäb\ *noun* [Urdu *nawwāb*] (1758)
: NABOB
¹**nay** \'nā\ *adverb* [Middle English, from Old Norse *nei,* from *ne* not + *ei* ever — more at NO, AYE] (13th century)
: NO
²**nay** *noun* (14th century)
1 : DENIAL, REFUSAL
2 a : a negative reply or vote **b** : one who votes no
³**nay** *conjunction* (1560)
: not merely this but also : not only so but ⟨the letter made him happy, *nay,* ecstatic⟩
nay·say·er \'nā-ˌsā-ər, -ˌse-(ə)r\ *noun* (1721)
: one who denies, refuses, opposes, or is skeptical or cynical about something
— **nay–say·ing** \-ˌsā-iŋ\ *noun*
Naz·a·rene \ˌna-zə-'rēn\ *noun* [Middle English *Nazarene,* from Late Latin *Nazarenus,* from Greek *Nazarēnos,* from *Nazareth* Nazareth, Palestine] (13th century)
1 : a native or resident of Nazareth
2 a : CHRISTIAN 1a **b** : a member of the Church of the Nazarene that is a Protestant denomination deriving from the merging of three holi-

ness groups, stressing sanctification, and following Methodist polity
Na·zi \'nät-sē, 'nat-\ *noun* [German, by shortening & alteration from *Nationalsozialist,* from *national* national + *Sozialist* socialist] (1930)
1 : a member of a German fascist party controlling Germany from 1933 to 1945 under Adolf Hitler
2 *often not capitalized* : one who resembles a German Nazi
— **nazi** *adjective, often capitalized*
— **na·zi·fi·ca·tion** \ˌnät-si-fə-'kā-shən, ˌnat-\ *noun, often capitalized*
— **na·zi·fy** \'nät-si-ˌfī, 'nat-\ *transitive verb, often capitalized*
Naz·i·rite *or* **Naz·a·rite** \'na-zə-ˌrīt\ *noun* [Late Latin *nazaraeus,* from Greek *naziraios, nazaraios,* from Hebrew *nāzīr,* literally, consecrated] (1560)
: a Jew of biblical times consecrated to God by a vow to avoid drinking wine, cutting the hair, and being defiled by the presence of a corpse
— **Naz·i·rit·ism** \-ˌrī-ˌti-zəm\ *noun*
Na·zism \'nät-ˌsi-zəm, 'nat-\ *or* **Na·zi·ism** \-sē-ˌi-zəm\ *noun* [*Nazi* + *-ism*] (1934)
: the body of political and economic doctrines held and put into effect by the National Socialist German Workers' party in the Third German Reich including the totalitarian principle of government, state control of all industry, predominance of groups assumed to be racially superior, and supremacy of the führer
NCO \ˌen-(ˌ)sē-'ō\ *noun* (circa 1810)
: NONCOMMISSIONED OFFICER
NC–17 \ˌen-'sē-ˌse-vən-'tēn\ *certification mark*
— used to certify that a motion picture is of such a nature that no one under the age of 17 can be admitted; compare G, PG, PG-13, R
-nd *symbol*
— used after the figure 2 to indicate the ordinal number *second* ⟨2nd⟩ ⟨72nd⟩
né \'nā\ *adjective* [French, literally, born — more at NÉE] (1905)
1 — used to indicate the original, former, or legal name of a man ⟨Robert Roe, *né* John Doe⟩
2 : originally or formerly called
ne- *or* **neo-** *combining form* [Greek, from *neos* new — more at NEW]
1 a : new : recent ⟨*Neo*gene⟩ **b** : new and different period or form of ⟨*Neo*platonism⟩ : in a new and different form or manner ⟨*Neo*platonic⟩ **c** : New World ⟨*Neo*tropical⟩ **d** : new and abnormal ⟨*neo*plasm⟩
2 : new chemical compound isomeric with or otherwise related to (such) a compound ⟨*neo*stigmine⟩
Ne·an·der·thal \nē-'an-dər-ˌtȯl, -ˌthȯl; nā-'än-dər-ˌtäl\ *adjective* (1861)
1 *also* **Ne·an·der·tal** \-ˌtȯl, -ˌtäl\ : being, relating to, or resembling Neanderthal man
2 : suggesting a caveman in appearance, mentality, or behavior
— **Neanderthal** *noun*
Neanderthal man *noun* [*Neanderthal,* valley in western Germany] (1863)
: a Middle Paleolithic hominid (*Homo sapiens neanderthalensis*) known from skeletal remains in Europe, northern Africa, and western Asia
— **Ne·an·der·thal·oid** \-ˌtȯ-ˌlȯid, -ˌthȯ-, -ˌtä-\ *adjective or noun*
¹**neap** \'nēp\ *adjective* [Middle English *neep,* from Old English *nēp* being at the stage of neap tide] (before 12th century)
: of, relating to, or constituting a neap tide
²**neap** *noun* (1584)
: NEAP TIDE
Ne·a·pol·i·tan \ˌnē-ə-'pä-lə-tᵊn\ *noun* [Middle English, from Latin *neapolitanus* of Naples, from Greek *neapolitēs* citizen of Naples, from *Neapolis* Naples] (15th century)
: a native or inhabitant of Naples, Italy
— **Neapolitan** *adjective*
Neapolitan ice cream *noun* (1895)

: a brick of from two to four layers of ice cream of different flavors
neap tide *noun* (circa 1548)
: a tide of minimum range occurring at the first and the third quarters of the moon
¹**near** \'nir\ *adverb* [Middle English *ner,* partly from *ner* nearer, from Old English *nēar,* comparative of *nēah* nigh; partly from Old Norse *nær* nearer, comparative of *nā-* nigh — more at NIGH] (13th century)
1 : at, within, or to a short distance or time
2 : ALMOST, NEARLY ⟨*near* dead⟩
3 : in a close or intimate manner : CLOSELY ⟨*near* related⟩
4 *archaic* : in a frugal manner
²**near** *preposition* (13th century)
: close to
³**near** *adjective* (14th century)
1 a : not far distant in time, place, or degree ⟨in the *near* future⟩ **b** : almost happening : narrowly missed or avoided ⟨a *near* win in the primary⟩ ⟨a *near* midair collision⟩ **c** : nearly not happening ⟨a *near* escape⟩
2 : closely related or intimately associated
3 a : being the closer of two ⟨the *near* side⟩ **b** : being the left-hand one of a pair ⟨the *near* wheel of a cart⟩
4 : DIRECT, SHORT ⟨the *nearest* road⟩
5 : STINGY, CLOSEFISTED
6 a : closely resembling the standard or typical ⟨a *near* desert⟩ **b** : approximating the genuine ⟨*near* silk⟩
— **near·ness** *noun*
⁴**near** *verb* (1513)
: APPROACH
near beer *noun* (1909)
: any of various malt liquors considered nonalcoholic because they contain less than a specified percentage of alcohol
near·by \nir-'bī, 'nir-ˌ\ *adverb or adjective* (14th century)
: close at hand
Ne·arc·tic \ˌnē-'ärk-tik, -'är-tik\ *adjective* (1858)
: of, relating to, or being the biogeographic subregion that includes Greenland and North America north of tropical Mexico
near gale *noun* (circa 1975)
: MODERATE GALE — see BEAUFORT SCALE table
near–in·fra·red \ˌnir-ˌin-frə-'red, -(ˌ)frä-\ *adjective* (1950)
: of or relating to the shorter wavelengths of radiation in the infrared spectrum and especially to those between 0.7 and 2.5 micrometers
near·ly \'nir-lē\ *adverb* (1561)
1 : in a close manner or relationship ⟨*nearly* related⟩
2 a : almost but not quite ⟨*nearly* identical⟩ ⟨*nearly* a year later⟩ **b** : to the least extent ⟨not *nearly* as good as we expected⟩
near miss *noun* (1940)
1 a : a miss (as with a bomb) close enough to cause damage **b** : something that falls just short of success
2 a : a near collision (as between aircraft) **b** : CLOSE CALL
near money *noun* (1942)
: assets (as savings accounts or government bonds) quickly and easily converted to cash
near point *noun* (1876)
: the point nearest the eye at which an object is accurately focused on the retina at full accommodation
near·shore \'nir-ˌshȯr, -ˌshȯr, 'nir-ˌ\ *adjective* (1896)
: extending outward an indefinite but usually short distance from shore ⟨*nearshore* sediments⟩

\ə\ **abut** \ᵊ\ **kitten** \ər\ **further** \a\ **ash** \ā\ **ace**
\ä\ **mop, mar** \au̇\ **out** \ch\ **chin** \e\ **bet** \ē\ **easy**
\g\ **go** \i\ **hit** \ī\ **ice** \j\ **job** \ŋ\ **sing** \ō\ **go**
\ȯ\ **law** \ȯi\ **boy** \th\ **thin** \t͟h\ **the** \ü\ **loot** \u̇\ **foot**
\y\ **yet** \zh\ **vision** *see also* Guide to Pronunciation

near·side \-ˌsīd\ *adjective* (circa 1840)
British : LEFT-HAND 1
— **nearside** *noun*

near·sight·ed \-ˌsī-təd\ *adjective* (1686)
: able to see near things more clearly than distant ones : MYOPIC
— **near·sight·ed·ly** *adverb*
— **near·sight·ed·ness** *noun*

near–ul·tra·vi·o·let \ˌnir-ˌəl-trə-'vī-(ə-)lət\ *adjective* (1951)
: of, relating to, or being the longest wavelengths of radiation especially between 300 and 400 nanometers

¹neat \'nēt\ *noun, plural* **neat** *or* **neats** [Middle English *neet,* from Old English *nēat;* akin to Old High German *nōz* head of cattle, Old English *nēotan* to make use of, Lithuanian *nauda* use] (before 12th century)
: the common domestic bovine (*Bos taurus*)

²neat *adjective* [Middle French *net,* from Latin *nitidus* bright, neat, from *nitēre* to shine; probably akin to Middle Irish *níam* luster] (1542)
1 : free from dirt and disorder : habitually clean and orderly
2 a : free from admixture or dilution : STRAIGHT ⟨*neat* brandy⟩ **b** : free from irregularity : SMOOTH ⟨*neat* silk⟩
3 : marked by tasteful simplicity ⟨a *neat* outfit⟩
4 a : PRECISE, SYSTEMATIC **b** : marked by skill or ingenuity : ADROIT
5 : NET ⟨*neat* profit⟩
6 : FINE, ADMIRABLE
— **neat·ly** *adverb*
— **neat·ness** *noun*

³neat *adverb* (1649)
: without admixture or dilution : STRAIGHT

neat·en \'nē-t²n\ *transitive verb* **neat·ened; neat·en·ing** \'nēt-niŋ, 'nē-t²n-iŋ\ (1898)
1 : to set in order : make neat
2 : to finish (as a piece of sewing) carefully

neath \'nēth\ *preposition* (1787)
dialect : BENEATH

neat·herd \'nēt-ˌhərd\ *noun* (14th century)
: HERDSMAN

neat's–foot oil \'nēts-ˌfut-\ *noun* (1787)
: a pale yellow fatty oil made especially from the bones of cattle and used chiefly as a leather dressing

neb \'neb\ *noun* [Middle English, from Old English; akin to Old Norse *nef* beak] (before 12th century)
1 a : the beak of a bird or tortoise : BILL **b** *chiefly dialect* : a person's mouth **c** : NOSE 1, SNOUT
2 : NIB, TIP

neb·bish \'ne-bish\ *noun* [Yiddish *nebekh* poor, unfortunate, from Czech *nebohý*] (1951)
: a timid, meek, or ineffectual person
— **neb·bishy** \-bi-shē\ *adjective*

ne·ben·kern \'nā-bən-ˌkərn, -ˌkern\ *noun* [German, literally, subsidiary nucleus] (1898)
: a 2-stranded helical structure of the proximal tail region of a spermatozoon that is derived from mitochondria

neb·u·la \'ne-byə-lə\ *noun, plural* **-lae** \-ˌlē, -ˌlī\ *also* **-las** [New Latin, from Latin, mist, cloud; akin to Old High German *nebul* fog, Greek *nephelē, nephos* cloud] (circa 1738)
1 : any of numerous clouds of gas or dust in interstellar space
2 : GALAXY; *especially* : a galaxy other than the Milky Way galaxy — not used technically
— **neb·u·lar** \-lər\ *adjective*

nebular hypothesis *noun* (1837)
: a hypothesis in astronomy: the solar system has evolved from a hot gaseous nebula

neb·u·lize \'ne-byə-ˌlīz\ *transitive verb* **-lized; -liz·ing** [Latin *nebula*] (1872)
: to reduce to a fine spray
— **neb·u·li·za·tion** \ˌne-byə-lə-'zā-shən\ *noun*
— **neb·u·liz·er** \'ne-byə-ˌlī-zər\ *noun*

neb·u·los·i·ty \ˌne-byə-'lä-sə-tē\ *noun, plural* **-ties** (1761)

1 : the quality or state of being nebulous
2 : nebulous matter; *also* : NEBULA 1

neb·u·lous \'ne-byə-ləs\ *adjective* [Latin *nebulosus* misty, from *nebula*] (1784)
1 : of, relating to, or resembling a nebula : NEBULAR
2 : INDISTINCT, VAGUE
— **neb·u·lous·ly** *adverb*
— **neb·u·lous·ness** *noun*

nec·es·sar·i·ly \ˌne-sə-'ser-ə-lē\ *adverb* (15th century)
1 : of necessity : UNAVOIDABLY
2 : as a logical result or consequence

¹nec·es·sary \'ne-sə-ˌser-ē\ *adjective* [Middle English *necessarie,* from Latin *necessarius,* from *necesse* necessary, probably from *ne-* not + *cedere* to withdraw — more at NO] (14th century)
1 a : of an inevitable nature : INESCAPABLE **b** (1) : logically unavoidable (2) : that cannot be denied without contradiction **c** : determined or produced by the previous condition of things **d** : COMPULSORY
2 : absolutely needed : REQUIRED

²necessary *noun, plural* **-sar·ies** (14th century)
: an indispensable item : ESSENTIAL

necessary condition *noun* (1817)
1 : a proposition whose falsity assures the falsity of another
2 : a state of affairs that must prevail if another is to occur : PREREQUISITE

ne·ces·si·tar·i·an·ism \ni-ˌse-sə-'ter-ē-ə-ˌni-zəm\ *noun* (1854)
: the theory that results follow by invariable sequence from causes
— **ne·ces·si·tar·i·an** \-'ter-ē-ən\ *adjective or noun*

ne·ces·si·tate \ni-'se-sə-ˌtāt\ *transitive verb* **-tat·ed; -tat·ing** (1628)
1 : to make necessary : REQUIRE
2 : FORCE, COMPEL
— **ne·ces·si·ta·tion** \-ˌse-sə-'tā-shən\ *noun*

ne·ces·si·tous \ni-'se-sə-təs\ *adjective* (1611)
1 : NEEDY, IMPOVERISHED
2 : URGENT, PRESSING
3 : NECESSARY
— **ne·ces·si·tous·ly** *adverb*
— **ne·ces·si·tous·ness** *noun*

ne·ces·si·ty \ni-'se-sə-tē, -'ses-tē\ *noun, plural* **-ties** [Middle English *necessite,* from Middle French *necessité,* from Latin *necessitat-, necessitas,* from *necesse*] (14th century)
1 : the quality or state of being necessary
2 a : pressure of circumstance **b** : physical or moral compulsion **c** : impossibility of a contrary order or condition
3 : the quality or state of being in need; *especially* : POVERTY
4 a : something that is necessary : REQUIREMENT **b** : an urgent need or desire
— **of necessity** : in such a way that it cannot be otherwise; *also* : as a necessary consequence

¹neck \'nek\ *noun* [Middle English *nekke,* from Old English *hnecca;* akin to Old High German *hnac* nape] (before 12th century)
1 a (1) : the part of an animal that connects the head with the body (2) : the siphon of a bivalve mollusk (as a clam) **b** : the part of a garment that covers or is next to the neck
2 : a relatively narrow part suggestive of a neck: as **a** (1) : the constricted end of a bottle (2) : the slender proximal end of a fruit **b** : CERVIX 2 **c** : the part of a stringed musical instrument extending from the body and supporting the fingerboard and strings **d** : a narrow stretch of land **e** : STRAIT 1b **f** : the part of a tooth between the crown and the root — see TOOTH illustration **g** : a column of solidified magma of a volcanic pipe or laccolith
3 : a narrow margin ⟨won by a *neck*⟩
4 : REGION, PART ⟨my *neck* of the woods⟩

²neck (1842)
transitive verb
1 : to kiss and caress amorously
2 : to reduce in diameter
intransitive verb
1 : to engage in amorous kissing and caressing
2 : to become constricted : NARROW

neck and neck *adverb or adjective* (1799)
: very close (as in a race)

necked \'nekt\ *adjective* (14th century)
: having a neck especially of a specified kind — often used in combination ⟨long-*necked*⟩

neck·er·chief \'ne-kər-chəf, -(ˌ)chif, -ˌchēf\ *noun, plural* **-chiefs** *also* **-chieves** *see* HANDKERCHIEF *plural*\ [Middle English *nekkerchef,* from *nekke* + *kerchef* kerchief] (14th century)
: a kerchief for the neck

neck·ing \'ne-kiŋ\ *noun* (1804)
1 : a narrow molding near the top of a column or pilaster
2 : the act or practice of kissing and caressing amorously

neck·lace \'ne-kləs\ *noun* (circa 1590)
: an ornament worn around the neck

neck·line \'nek-ˌlīn\ *noun* (1904)
: the line of the neck opening of a garment

neck–rein \-ˌrān\ (1940)
intransitive verb
of a saddle horse : to respond to the pressure of a rein on one side of the neck by turning in the opposite direction
transitive verb
: to direct (a horse) by pressures of the rein on the neck

neck·tie \-ˌtī\ *noun* (1838)
: a narrow length of material worn about the neck and tied in front; *especially* : FOUR-IN-HAND

neck·wear \-ˌwar, -ˌwer\ *noun* (circa 1879)
: articles of clothing (as ties and scarves) worn about the neck

necr- *or* **necro-** *combining form* [Late Latin, from Greek *nekr-, nekro-,* from *nekros* dead body — more at NOXIOUS]
1 : those that are dead ⟨*necro*philia⟩
2 : one that is dead ⟨*necro*psy⟩

ne·crol·o·gy \nə-'krä-lə-jē, ne-\ *noun, plural* **-gies** [New Latin *necrologium,* from *necr-* + *-logium* (as in Medieval Latin *eulogium* eulogy)] (1799)
1 : OBITUARY
2 : a list of the recently dead
— **nec·ro·log·i·cal** \ˌne-krə-'lä-ji-kəl\ *adjective*
— **ne·crol·o·gist** \nə-'krä-lə-jist, ne-\ *noun*

nec·ro·man·cy \'ne-krə-ˌman(t)-sē\ *noun* [alteration of Middle English *nigromancie,* from Middle French, from Medieval Latin *nigromantia,* by folk etymology from Late Latin *necromantia,* from Late Greek *nekromanteia,* from Greek *nekr-* + *-manteia* -mancy] (1522)
1 : conjuration of the spirits of the dead for purposes of magically revealing the future or influencing the course of events
2 : MAGIC, SORCERY
— **nec·ro·man·cer** \-sər\ *noun*
— **nec·ro·man·tic** \ˌne-krə-'man-tik\ *adjective*
— **nec·ro·man·ti·cal·ly** \-ti-k(ə-)lē\ *adverb*

ne·croph·a·gous \nə-'krä-fə-gəs, ne-\ *adjective* (1835)
: feeding on corpses or carrion ⟨*necrophagous* insects⟩

nec·ro·phil·ia \ˌne-krə-'fi-lē-ə\ *noun* [New Latin] (1892)
: obsession with and usually erotic interest in or stimulation by corpses
— **nec·ro·phil·i·ac** \-'fi-lē-ˌak\ *adjective or noun*
— **nec·ro·phil·ic** \-'fi-lik\ *adjective*

ne·croph·i·lism \nə-'krä-fə-ˌli-zəm, ne-\ *noun* (1864)
: NECROPHILIA

nec·rop·o·lis \nə-'krä-pə-ləs, ne-\ *noun, plural* **-lis·es** *or* **-les** \-,lēz\ *or* **-leis** \-,lās\ *or* **-li** \-,lī, -,lē\ [Late Latin, city of the dead, from Greek *nekropolis,* from *nekr-* + *-polis* -polis] (1819)
: CEMETERY; *especially* : a large elaborate cemetery of an ancient city

¹**nec·rop·sy** \'ne-,kräp-sē\ *noun, plural* **-sies** (1856)
: AUTOPSY 1

²**necropsy** *transitive verb* **-sied; -sy·ing** (1927)
: to perform an autopsy on

ne·cro·sis \nə-'krō-səs, ne-\ *noun, plural* **ne·cro·ses** \-,sēz\ [Late Latin, from Greek *nekrōsis,* from *nekroun* to make dead, from *nekros* dead body] (1665)
: usually localized death of living tissue
— **ne·crot·ic** \-'krä-tik\ *adjective*

nec·ro·tiz·ing \'ne-krə-,tī-ziŋ\ *adjective* [Greek *nekrōtikos* necrotic, from *nekroun*] (1899)
: causing, associated with, or undergoing necrosis ⟨*necrotizing* infections⟩ ⟨*necrotizing* tissue⟩

nec·tar \'nek-tər\ *noun* [Latin, from Greek *nektar*]
1 a : the drink of the Greek and Roman gods **b** : something delicious to drink **c** : a beverage of fruit juice and pulp ⟨apricot *nectar*⟩
2 : a sweet liquid that is secreted by the nectaries of a plant and is the chief raw material of honey
— **nec·tar·ous** \-t(ə-)rəs\ *adjective*

nec·tar·ine \,nek-tə-'rēn\ *noun* [obsolete *nectarine,* adjective, like nectar] (1611)
: a peach with a smooth-skinned fruit that is a frequent somatic mutation of the normal peach; *also* : its fruit

nec·tary \'nek-t(ə-)rē\ *noun, plural* **-tar·ies** [New Latin *nectarium,* irregular from Latin *nectar* + *-arium* -ary] (1759)
: a plant gland that secretes nectar

née *or* **nee** \'nā\ *adjective* [French *née,* feminine of *né,* literally, born, past participle of *naître* to be born, from Latin *nasci* — more at NATION] (1758)
1 — used to identify a woman by her maiden family name
2 : originally or formerly called ⟨the Brewers *née* Pilots who also are in their third year —Fred Ciampa⟩

¹**need** \'nēd\ *noun* [Middle English *ned,* from Old English *nīed, nēd;* akin to Old High German *nōt* distress, need, Old Prussian *nautin* need] (before 12th century)
1 : necessary duty : OBLIGATION
2 a : a lack of something requisite, desirable, or useful **b** : a physiological or psychological requirement for the well-being of an organism **3** : a condition requiring supply or relief **4** : lack of the means of subsistence : POVERTY

²**need** *verb* **need·ed; need·ing; needs** *or (auxiliary)* **need** (before 12th century)
intransitive verb
1 : to be needful or necessary
2 : to be in want
transitive verb
: to be in need of : REQUIRE
verbal auxiliary
: be under necessity or obligation to ⟨you *need* not answer⟩ □

¹**need·ful** \'nēd-fəl\ *adjective* (12th century)
1 : being in need
2 : NECESSARY, REQUISITE
— **need·ful·ly** \-fə-lē\ *adverb*
— **need·ful·ness** *noun*

²**needful** *noun* (1709)
1 : something needed or requisite
2 : MONEY

¹**nee·dle** \'nē-d³l\ *noun* [Middle English *nedle,* from Old English *nǣdl;* akin to Old High German *nādala* needle, *nājan* to sew, Latin *nēre* to spin, Greek *nēn*] (before 12th century)
1 a : a small slender usually steel instrument that has an eye for thread or surgical sutures at one end and that is used for sewing **b** : any of various devices for carrying thread and making stitches (as in crocheting or knitting) **c** (1) : a slender hollow instrument for introducing material into or removing material from the body parenterally (2) : any of various slender hollow devices used to introduce matter (as air) into or remove it from an object (as a ball)
2 a : a slender bar of magnetized steel that when allowed to turn freely (as in a compass) indicates the direction of a magnetic field (as of the earth) **b** : a slender usually sharp-pointed indicator on a dial
3 a : a slender pointed object resembling a needle: as (1) : a pointed crystal (2) : a sharp rock (3) : OBELISK **b** : a needle-shaped leaf (as of a conifer) **c** : a slender rod (as of jewel or steel) with a rounded tip used in a phonograph to transmit vibrations from a record : STYLUS **d** : a slender pointed rod controlling a fine inlet or outlet (as in a valve)
4 : a teasing or gibing remark
— **nee·dle·like** \'nē-d³l-,(l)īk\ *adjective*

²**needle** *verb* **nee·dled; nee·dling** \'nēd-liŋ, 'nē-d³l-iŋ\ (circa 1715)
transitive verb
1 : to sew or pierce with or as if with a needle
2 a : TEASE, TORMENT **b** : to incite to action by repeated gibes ⟨*needled* the boy into a fight⟩
intransitive verb
: SEW, EMBROIDER
— **nee·dler** \'nēd-lər, 'nē-d³l-ər\ *noun*

nee·dle·fish \'nē-d³l-,fish\ *noun* (1601)
1 : any of a family (Belonidae) of elongate green and silvery chiefly marine bony fishes with long slender jaws
2 : PIPEFISH

needlefish 1

nee·dle·point \-,point\ *noun* (1865)
1 : lace worked with a needle over a paper pattern
2 : embroidery done on canvas usually in simple even stitches across counted threads
— **needlepoint** *adjective*

need·less \'nēd-ləs\ *adjective* (14th century)
: not needed : UNNECESSARY ⟨*needless* waste⟩ ⟨*needless* to say⟩
— **need·less·ly** *adverb*
— **need·less·ness** *noun*

nee·dle·wom·an \'nē-d³l-,wu̇-mən\ *noun* (1535)
: a woman who does needlework; *especially* : SEAMSTRESS

nee·dle·work \-,wərk\ *noun* (14th century)
1 : work done with a needle; *especially* : work (as embroidery) other than plain sewing
2 : the occupation of one who does needlework
— **nee·dle·work·er** \-,wər-kər\ *noun*

needn't \'nē-d³nt\ (1865)
: need not

needs \'nēdz\ *adverb* [Middle English *nedes,* from Old English *nēdes,* from genitive of *nēd* need] (before 12th century)
: of necessity : NECESSARILY ⟨must *needs* be recognized⟩

needy \'nē-dē\ *adjective* **need·i·er; -est** (12th century)
: being in want : POVERTY-STRICKEN ⟨*needy* families⟩
— **need·i·ness** *noun*

neem \'nēm\ *noun* [Hindi *nīm,* from Sanskrit *nimba*] (1813)
: a large East Indian tree (*Azadirachta indica* of the family Meliaceae) whose trunk exudes a tenacious gum and has a bitter bark used as a tonic and whose fruit and seeds yield a medicinal aromatic oil

neep \'nēp\ *noun* [Middle English *nepe,* from Old English *nǣp,* from Latin *napus* — more at NAPIFORM] (before 12th century)
chiefly Scottish : TURNIP

ne'er \'nar, 'ner\ *adverb* (13th century)
: NEVER

ne'er–do–well \-dü-,wel\ *noun* (1736)
: an idle worthless person
— **ne'er–do–well** *adjective*

ne·far·i·ous \ni-'far-ē-əs, -'fer-\ *adjective* [Latin *nefarius,* from *nefas* crime, from *ne-* not + *fas* right, divine law; perhaps akin to Greek *themis* law, *tithenai* to place — more at DO] (circa 1609)
: flagrantly wicked or impious : EVIL
synonym see VICIOUS
— **ne·far·i·ous·ly** *adverb*

ne·gate \ni-'gāt\ *transitive verb* **ne·gat·ed; ne·gat·ing** [Latin *negatus,* past participle of *negare* to say no, deny, from *neg-* no, not (akin to *ne-* not) — more at NO] (circa 1623)
1 : to deny the existence or truth of
2 : to cause to be ineffective or invalid
synonym see NULLIFY
— **ne·gate** *noun*
— **ne·ga·tor** \-'gā-tər\ *noun*

ne·ga·tion \ni-'gā-shən\ *noun* (15th century)
1 a : the action or logical operation of negating or making negative **b** : a negative statement, judgment, or doctrine; *especially* : a logical proposition formed by asserting the falsity of a given proposition
2 a : something that is the absence of something actual : NONENTITY **b** : something considered the opposite of something regarded as positive
— **ne·ga·tion·al** \-shnəl, -shə-n³l\ *adjective*

¹**neg·a·tive** \'ne-gə-tiv\ *adjective* (15th century)
1 a : marked by denial, prohibition, or refusal ⟨received a *negative* answer⟩; *also* : marked by absence, withholding, or removal of something positive ⟨the *negative* motivation of shame —Garrett Hardin⟩ **b** (1) : denying a predicate of a subject or a part of a subject ⟨"no A is B" is a *negative* proposition⟩ (2) : denoting the absence or the contradictory of something ⟨*nontoxic* is a *negative* term⟩ (3) : expressing negation ⟨*negative* particles such as *no* and *not*⟩ **c** : ADVERSE, UNFAVORABLE ⟨the reviews were mostly *negative*⟩
2 a : lacking positive qualities; *especially* : DISAGREEABLE **b** : marked by features of hostility, withdrawal, or pessimism that hinder or oppose constructive treatment or development ⟨a *negative* outlook⟩ ⟨*negative* criticism⟩

□ USAGE
need Those who live in western Pennsylvania, central Ohio, Tennessee, or southeastern Colorado—somewhere in the area known as Midland to linguistic geographers—may have heard a curious idiom in which *need* is followed directly by a past participle, as in "the house needs painted," where the more widely used version would be "the house needs painting" or "the house needs to be painted." The idiom appears to be limited to the Midland area and, as far as we know now, is used almost exclusively in speech. A few people have told us that they have seen it in newspapers, but we have no printed evidence. One dictionary edited in England mentions the construction but says only that it is "widely disliked," which does not tell us much about possible dialectal restrictions. We do know that the construction exists in Scottish English, and it may be that the construction came from Scotland to this country. But 19th century use is only conjectural, so we cannot be sure.

3 a (1) : less than zero and opposite in sign to a positive number that when added to the given number yields zero ⟨−2 is a *negative* number⟩ (2) : having more outgo than income : constituting a loss ⟨*negative* cash flow⟩ ⟨*negative* worth⟩ **b** : extending or generated in a direction opposite to an arbitrarily chosen regular direction or position ⟨*negative* angle⟩ **4 a** : being, relating to, or charged with electricity of which the electron is the elementary unit **b** : having more electrons than protons ⟨a *negative* ion⟩ **c** (1) : having lower electric potential and constituting the part toward which the current flows from the external circuit ⟨the *negative* pole⟩ (2) : being the electron-emitting electrode of an electron tube **5 a** : not affirming the presence of the organism or condition in question ⟨a *negative* TB test⟩ **b** : directed or moving away from a source of stimulation ⟨*negative* tropism⟩ **c** : less than the pressure of the atmosphere ⟨*negative* pressure⟩ **6** : having the light and dark parts in approximately inverse order to those of the original photographic subject **7** *of a lens* : diverging light rays and forming a virtual inverted image
— **neg·a·tive·ly** *adverb*
— **neg·a·tive·ness** *noun*
— **neg·a·tiv·i·ty** \ˌne-gə-ˈti-və-tē\ *noun*

²**negative** *noun* (1571) **1 a** : a reply that indicates the withholding of assent : REFUSAL (2) *archaic* : a right of veto (3) *obsolete* : an adverse vote : VETO **b** : a proposition which denies or contradicts another; *especially* : the one of a pair of propositions in which negation is expressed **2 a** : something that is the opposite or negation of something else **b** : DRAWBACK, LIABILITY **3 a** : an expression (as the word *no*) of negation or denial **b** : a negative number **4** : the side that upholds the contradictory proposition in a debate **5** : a negative photographic image on transparent material used for printing positive pictures; *also* : the material that carries such an image **6** : a reverse impression taken from a piece of sculpture or ceramics

³**negative** *transitive verb* **-tived; -tiv·ing** (1706) **1 a** : to refuse assent to **b** : to reject by or as if by a vote **2** : to demonstrate the falsity of **3** : to deny the truth, reality, or validity of **4** : NEUTRALIZE, COUNTERACT

negative feedback *noun* (1934) : feedback that tends to stabilize a process by reducing its rate or output when its effects are too great

negative income tax *noun* (1966) : a system of federal subsidy payments to families with incomes below a stipulated level

negative transfer *noun* (1921) : the impeding of learning or performance in a situation by the carry-over of learned responses from another situation

neg·a·tiv·ism \ˈne-gə-ti-ˌvi-zəm\ *noun* (1824) **1** : an attitude of mind marked by skepticism especially about nearly everything affirmed by others **2** : a tendency to refuse to do, to do the opposite of, or to do something at variance with what is asked
— **neg·a·tiv·ist** \-vist\ *noun or adjective*
— **neg·a·tiv·is·tic** \ˌne-gə-ti-ˈvis-tik\ *adjective*

¹**ne·glect** \ni-ˈglekt\ *transitive verb* [Latin *neglectus*, past participle of *neglegere, neclegere*, from *nec-* not (akin to *ne-* not) + *legere* to gather — more at NO, LEGEND] (1529) **1** : to give little attention or respect to : DISREGARD **2** : to leave undone or unattended to especially through carelessness ☆
— **ne·glect·er** *noun*

²**neglect** *noun* (1588) **1** : an act or instance of neglecting something **2** : the condition of being neglected

ne·glect·ful \ni-ˈglek(t)-fəl\ *adjective* (1644) : given to neglecting : CARELESS, HEEDLESS
synonym see NEGLIGENT
— **ne·glect·ful·ly** \-fə-lē\ *adverb*
— **ne·glect·ful·ness** *noun*

neg·li·gee *also* **neg·li·gé** \ˌne-glə-ˈzhā, ˈne-glə-ˌ\ *noun* [French *négligé*, from past participle of *négliger* to neglect, from Latin *neglegere*] (1756) **1** : a woman's long flowing usually sheer dressing gown **2** : carelessly informal or incomplete attire

neg·li·gence \ˈne-gli-jən(t)s\ *noun* (14th century) **1 a** : the quality or state of being negligent **b** : failure to exercise the care that a prudent person usually exercises **2** : an act or instance of being negligent

neg·li·gent \-jənt\ *adjective* [Middle English, from Middle French & Latin; Middle French, from Latin *neglegent-, neglegens*, present participle of *neglegere*] (14th century) **1** : marked by or given to neglect especially habitually or culpably : not taking prudent care **2** : marked by a carelessly easy manner ☆
— **neg·li·gent·ly** *adverb*

neg·li·gi·ble \ˈne-gli-jə-bəl\ *adjective* [Latin *neglegere, negligere*] (1829) : so small or unimportant or of so little consequence as to warrant little or no attention : TRIFLING
— **neg·li·gi·bil·i·ty** \ˌne-gli-jə-ˈbi-lə-tē\ *noun*
— **neg·li·gi·bly** \ˈne-gli-jə-blē\ *adverb*

ne·go·tia·ble \ni-ˈgō-sh(ē-)ə-bəl\ *adjective* (1758) : capable of being negotiated: as **a** : transferable from one person to another by being delivered with or without endorsement so that the title passes to the transferee ⟨*negotiable* securities⟩ **b** : capable of being traversed, dealt with, or accomplished ⟨a difficult but *negotiable* road⟩ ⟨*negotiable* demands⟩ **c** : open to discussion or dispute
— **ne·go·tia·bil·i·ty** \-ˌgō-sh(ē-)ə-ˈbi-lə-tē\ *noun*

ne·go·ti·ant \-ˈgō-sh(ē-)ənt\ *noun* (circa 1611) : one that negotiates

ne·go·ti·ate \ni-ˈgō-shē-ˌāt, ÷-sē-\ *verb* **-at·ed; -at·ing** [Latin *negotiatus*, past participle of *negotiari* to carry on business, from *negotium* business, from *neg-* not + *otium* leisure — more at NEGATE] (1599) *intransitive verb* : to confer with another so as to arrive at the settlement of some matter *transitive verb* **1 a** : to deal with (some matter or affair that requires ability for its successful handling) : MANAGE **b** : to arrange for or bring about through conference, discussion, and compromise ⟨*negotiate* a treaty⟩ **2 a** : to transfer (as a bill of exchange) to another by delivery or endorsement **b** : to convert into cash or the equivalent value ⟨*negotiate* a check⟩ **3 a** : to successfully travel along or over ⟨*negotiate* a turn⟩ **b** : COMPLETE, ACCOMPLISH ⟨*negotiate* the trip in two hours⟩
— **ne·go·ti·a·tor** \-ˌā-tər\ *noun*
— **ne·go·ti·a·to·ry** \-sh(ē-)ə-ˌtōr-ē, ÷-sē-, -ˌtȯr-\ *adjective*

ne·go·ti·a·tion \ni-ˌgō-shē-ˈā-shən, ÷-sē-\ *noun* (15th century) : the action or process of negotiating or being negotiated — often used in plural

Ne·gress \ˈnē-grəs\ *noun* (1786) : a black woman or girl — sometimes taken to be offensive

Ne·gril·lo \ni-ˈgri-(ˌ)lō, -ˈgrē-(ˌ)yō\ *noun, plural* **-los** *or* **-loes** [Spanish, diminutive of *negro*] (1853) : a member of a people (as Pygmies) belonging to a group of dark-skinned peoples of small stature that live in Africa

Ne·gri·to \nə-ˈgrē-(ˌ)tō\ *noun, plural* **-tos** *or* **-toes** [Spanish, diminutive of *negro*] (1812) : a member of a people (as the Andamanese) belonging to a group of dark-skinned peoples of small stature that live in Oceania and the southeastern part of Asia

ne·gri·tude \ˈne-grə-ˌtüd, ˈnē-, -ˌtyüd\ *noun* [French *négritude*, from *nègre* Negro + *-i-* + *-tude*] (1950) **1** : a consciousness of and pride in the cultural and physical aspects of the African heritage **2** : the state or condition of being black

Ne·gro \ˈnē-(ˌ)grō\ *noun, plural* **Negroes** [Spanish or Portuguese, from *negro* black, from Latin *nigr-, niger*] (1555) **1** : a member of the black race distinguished from members of other races by usually inherited physical and physiological characteristics without regard to language or culture; *especially* : a member of a people belonging to the African branch of the black race — sometimes taken to be offensive **2** : a person of Negro descent — sometimes taken to be offensive
— **Negro** *adjective*
— **Ne·gro·ness** \-grō-nəs\ *noun*

ne·groid \ˈnē-ˌgrȯid\ *adjective, often capitalized* (1859) : of, resembling, related to, or characteristic of the Negro race
— **negroid** *noun, often capitalized*

ne·gro·phobe \ˈnē-grə-ˌfōb\ *noun, often capitalized* (1900) : one who strongly dislikes or fears black people
— **ne·gro·pho·bia** \ˌnē-grə-ˈfō-bē-ə\ *noun, often capitalized*

☆ **SYNONYMS**

Neglect, disregard, ignore, overlook, slight, forget mean to pass over without giving due attention. NEGLECT implies giving insufficient attention to something that has a claim to one's attention ⟨habitually *neglected* his studies⟩. DISREGARD suggests voluntary inattention ⟨*disregarded* the wishes of other members⟩. IGNORE implies a failure to regard something obvious ⟨*ignored* the snide remark⟩. OVERLOOK suggests disregarding or ignoring through haste or lack of care ⟨in my rush I *overlooked* a key example⟩. SLIGHT implies contemptuous or disdainful disregarding or omitting ⟨*slighted* several major authors in her survey⟩. FORGET may suggest either a willful ignoring or a failure to impress something on one's mind ⟨*forget* what others say and listen to me⟩.

Negligent, neglectful, lax, slack, remiss mean culpably careless or indicative of such carelessness. NEGLIGENT implies inattention to one's duty or business ⟨*negligent* about writing a note of thanks⟩. NEGLECTFUL adds a more disapproving implication of laziness or deliberate inattention ⟨a society callously *neglectful* of the poor⟩. LAX implies a blameworthy lack of strictness, severity, or precision ⟨a reporter *lax* about accurate quotation⟩. SLACK implies want of due or necessary diligence or care ⟨*slack* workmanship and slipshod construction⟩. REMISS implies blameworthy carelessness shown in slackness, forgetfulness, or neglect ⟨had been *remiss* in her familial duties⟩.

¹ne·gus \'nē-gəs, ni-'güs\ *noun* [Amharic *nəgus*, from Ge'ez *něgŭša nagašt* king of kings] (1594)
: KING — used as a title of the sovereign of Ethiopia

²ne·gus \'nē-gəs\ *noun* [Francis *Negus* (died 1732) English colonel] (1743)
: a beverage of wine, hot water, sugar, lemon juice, and spices

Ne·he·mi·ah \,nē-(h)ə-'mī-ə\ *noun* [Hebrew *Něḥemyāh*]
1 : a Jewish leader of the 5th century B.C. who supervised the rebuilding of the Jerusalem city walls and instituted religious reforms in the city
2 : a narrative and historical book of canonical Jewish and Christian Scripture — see BIBLE table

Ne·he·mi·as \-'mī-əs\ *noun* [Late Latin, from Hebrew *Něḥemyāh*]
: NEHEMIAH

neigh \'nā\ *intransitive verb* [Middle English *neyen*, from Old English *hnǣgan;* akin to Middle High German *něgen* to neigh] (before 12th century)
: to make the prolonged cry of a horse
— **neigh** *noun*

¹neigh·bor \'nā-bər\ *noun* [Middle English, from Old English *nēahgebūr* (akin to Old High German *nāhgibūr*); akin to Old English *nēah* near and Old English *gebūr* dweller — more at NIGH, BOOR] (before 12th century)
1 : one living or located near another
2 : FELLOWMAN

²neighbor *adjective* (1530)
: being immediately adjoining or relatively near

³neighbor *verb* **neigh·bored; neigh·bor·ing** \-b(ə-)riŋ\ (circa 1586)
transitive verb
: to adjoin immediately or lie relatively near to
intransitive verb
1 : to live or be located as a neighbor
2 : to associate in a neighborly way

neigh·bor·hood \'nā-bər-,hu̇d\ *noun* (15th century)
1 : neighborly relationship
2 : the quality or state of being neighbors **:** PROXIMITY
3 a : a place or region near **:** VICINITY **b :** an approximate amount, extent, or degree ⟨cost in the *neighborhood* of $10⟩
4 a : the people living near one another **b :** a section lived in by neighbors and usually having distinguishing characteristics
5 : the set of all points belonging to a given set whose distances from a given point are less than a given positive number; *broadly* **:** a set that contains a neighborhood

neigh·bor·ly \-lē\ *adjective* (1558)
: of, relating to, or characteristic of congenial neighbors; *especially* **:** FRIENDLY
synonym see AMICABLE
— **neigh·bor·li·ness** *noun*

neigh·bour \-bər\ *chiefly British variant of* NEIGHBOR

¹nei·ther \'nē-ṯhər *also* 'nī-\ *conjunction* [Middle English, alteration (influenced by *either*) of *nauther, nother,* from Old English *nāhwæther, nōther,* from *nā, nō* not + *hwæther* which of two, whether] (12th century)
1 : not either ⟨*neither* black nor white⟩
2 : also not ⟨*neither* did I⟩ □

²neither *pronoun* (13th century)
: not the one or the other of two or more □

³neither *adjective* (14th century)
: not either ⟨*neither* hand⟩

⁴neither *adverb* (1551)
1 *chiefly dialect* **:** EITHER ⟨are not to be understood *neither* —Earl of Chesterfield⟩
2 : similarly not **:** also not ⟨just as the serf was not permitted to leave the land, so *neither* was his offspring —G. P. Coulton⟩

nek·ton \'nek-tən, -,tän\ *noun* [German *Nekton,* from Greek *nēkton,* neuter of *nēktos*

swimming, from *nēchein* to swim — more at NATANT] (1893)
: free-swimming aquatic animals essentially independent of wave and current action
— **nek·ton·ic** \nek-'tä-nik\ *adjective*

nel·son \'nel-sən\ *noun* [probably from the name *Nelson*] (1889) ·
: a wrestling hold marked by the application of leverage against an opponent's arm, neck, and head — compare FULL NELSON, HALF NELSON

nemat- *or* **nemato-** *combining form* [New Latin, from Greek *nēmat-, nēma,* from *nēn* to spin — more at NEEDLE]
1 : thread ⟨*nemat*ocyst⟩
2 : nematode ⟨*nemat*ology⟩

ne·mat·ic \ni-'ma-tik\ *adjective* [International Scientific Vocabulary *nemat-* + *¹-ic*] (1923)
: of, relating to, or being the phase of a liquid crystal characterized by arrangement of the long axes of the molecules in parallel lines but not layers — compare CHOLESTERIC, SMECTIC

nem·a·to·cide *or* **nem·a·ti·cide** \'ne-mə-tə-,sīd, ni-'ma-tə-\ *noun* (1898)
: a substance or preparation used to destroy nematodes
— **nem·a·to·ci·dal** *also* **nem·a·ti·ci·dal** \,ne-mə-tə-'sī-d°l, ni-,ma-tə-\ *adjective*

nem·a·to·cyst \-,sist\ *noun* [International Scientific Vocabulary] (1875)
: one of the stinging organelles of coelenterates used in catching prey

nem·a·tode \'ne-mə-,tōd\ *noun* [ultimately from Greek *nēmat-, nēma*] (1865)
: any of a phylum (Nematoda or Nemata) of elongated cylindrical worms parasitic in animals or plants or free-living in soil or water

nem·a·tol·o·gy \,ne-mə-'tä-lə-jē\ *noun* (circa 1916)
: a branch of zoology that deals with nematodes
— **nem·a·tol·og·i·cal** \,ne-mə-t°l-'ä-ji-kəl\ *adjective*
— **nem·a·tol·o·gist** \,ne-mə-'tä-lə-jist\ *noun*

Nem·bu·tal \'nem-byə-,to̝l\ *trademark*
— used for the sodium salt of pentobarbital

ne·mer·te·an \ni-'mər-tē-ən\ *noun* [ultimately from Greek *Nēmertēs* Nemertes, one of the Nereids] (1861)
: any of a phylum (Nemertea synonym Rhynchocoela) of often vividly colored marine worms most of which burrow in the mud or sand along seacoasts — called also *ribbon worm*
— **nem·er·tine** \'ne-mər-,tīn\ *adjective or noun*

nem·e·sis \'ne-mə-səs\ *noun* [Latin, from Greek]
1 *capitalized* **:** the Greek goddess of retributive justice
2 *plural* **-e·ses** \-,sēz\ **a :** one that inflicts retribution or vengeance **b :** a formidable and usually victorious rival or opponent
3 *plural* **-eses :** an act or effect of retribution **b :** BANE 2

ne·moph·i·la \ni-'mä-fə-lə\ *noun* [New Latin, from Greek *nemos* wooded pasture + *philos* loving] (1838)
: any of a genus (*Nemophila*) of American annual herbs of the waterleaf family cultivated for their showy blue or white sometimes spotted flowers

ne·ne \'nā-(,)nā\ *noun* [Hawaiian *nēnē*] (1902)
: an endangered goose (*Branta sandvicensis* synonym *Nesochen sandvicensis*) of the Hawaiian Islands that usually inhabits waterless uplands and feeds on berries and vegetation

nene

neo- — see NE-

neo·clas·sic \,nē-ō-'kla-sik\ *or* **neo·clas·si·cal** \-si-kəl\ *adjective* (1877)
: of, relating to, or constituting a revival or adaptation of the classical especially in literature, music, art, or architecture
— **neo·clas·si·cism** \-'kla-sə-,si-zəm\ *noun*
— **neo·clas·si·cist** \-sist\ *noun or adjective*

neo·co·lo·nial·ism \,nē-ō-kə-'lōn-yə-,li-zəm, -'lō-nē-ə-,li-\ *noun* (1961)
: the economic and political policies by which a great power indirectly maintains or extends its influence over other areas or people
— **neo·co·lo·nial** \-'lōn-yəl, -'lō-nē-əl\ *adjective*
— **neo·co·lo·nial·ist** \-yə-list, -ə-list\ *noun or adjective*

neo·con·ser·va·tive \-kən-'sər-və-tiv\ *noun* (1955)
: a former liberal espousing political conservatism
— **neo·con·ser·va·tism** \-və-,ti-zəm\ *noun*
— **neoconservative** *adjective*

neo·cor·tex \,nē-ō-'kȯr-,teks\ *noun* [New Latin; from its being the cortex of the phylogenetically most recently developed part of the brain] (1909)
: the dorsal region of the cerebral cortex that is unique to mammals

neo·cor·ti·cal \-'kȯr-ti-kəl\ *adjective* (1909)
: of or relating to the neocortex

neo–Dar·win·ian \-där-'wi-nē-ən\ *adjective, often N capitalized* (1895)
: of or relating to neo-Darwinism

neo–Dar·win·ism \-'där-wə-,ni-zəm\ *noun, often N capitalized* (circa 1900)
: a theory of evolution that is a synthesis of Darwin's theory in terms of natural selection and modern population genetics
— **neo–Dar·win·ist** \-'där-wə-nist\ *noun, often N capitalized*

neo·dym·i·um \,nē-ō-'di-mē-əm\ *noun* [New Latin, from *ne-* + *-dymium* (from *didymium*)] (1885)
: a yellow metallic element of the rare-earth group that is used in magnets and lasers — see ELEMENT table

neo–Ex·pres·sion·ism \-ik-'spre-shə-,ni-zəm\ *noun, often N capitalized* (1961)
: a revival of expressionism in art characterized by intense colors, dramatic usually figural forms, and emotive subject matter
— **neo–Ex·pres·sion·ist** \-nist\ *noun or adjective, often N capitalized*

\ə\ abut \ᵊ\ kitten \ər\ further \a\ ash \ā\ ace
\ä\ mop, mar \au̇\ out \ch\ chin \e\ bet \ē\ easy
\g\ go \i\ hit \ī\ ice \j\ job \ŋ\ sing \ō\ go
\ȯ\ law \ȯi\ boy \th\ thin \ṯh\ the \ü\ loot \u̇\ foot
\y\ yet \zh\ vision *see also* Guide to Pronunciation

neo·Freud·ian \-'fròi-dē-ən\ adjective, often N capitalized (1945)
: of or relating to a school of psychoanalysis that differs from Freudian orthodoxy in emphasizing the importance of social and cultural factors in the development of an individual's personality
— **neo·Freudian** noun, often N capitalized
Neo·gene \'nē-ə-,jēn\ adjective [International Scientific Vocabulary ne- + -gene (from Greek -genēs born) — more at -GEN] (1878)
: of, relating to, or being the later portion of the Tertiary including the Miocene and Pliocene or the corresponding system of rocks
— **Neogene** noun
neo·Goth·ic \,nē-ō-'gä-thik\ adjective (1892)
: of, relating to, or constituting a revival or adaptation of the Gothic especially in literature or architecture
neo·im·pres·sion·ism \,nē-ō-im-'pre-shə-,ni-zəm\ noun, often N&I capitalized [French néo-impressionisme, from né- ne- + impressionisme impressionism] (1892)
: a late 19th century French art theory and practice characterized by an attempt to make impressionism more precise in form and the use of a pointillist painting technique
— **neo·im·pres·sion·ist** \-'pre-sh(ə-)nist\ adjective or noun, often N&I capitalized
Neo·Lat·in \-'la-tᵊn\ noun [International Scientific Vocabulary] (1850)
1 : NEW LATIN
2 : ROMANCE 5
neo·lib·er·al \-'li-b(ə-)rəl\ noun (1945)
: a liberal who de-emphasizes traditional liberal doctrines in order to seek progress by more pragmatic methods
— **neoliberal** adjective
— **neo·lib·er·al·ism** \-b(ə-)rə-,li-zəm\ noun
neo·lith \'nē-ə-,lith\ noun [back-formation from neolithic] (1882)
: a Neolithic stone implement
neo·lith·ic \,nē-ə-'li-thik\ adjective (1865)
1 capitalized : of or relating to the latest period of the Stone Age characterized by polished stone implements
2 : belonging to an earlier age and now outmoded
ne·ol·o·gism \nē-'ä-lə-,ji-zəm\ noun [French néologisme, from ne- + log- + -isme -ism] (1800)
1 : a new word, usage, or expression
2 : a meaningless word coined by a psychotic
— **ne·ol·o·gis·tic** \-,ä-lə-'jis-tik\ adjective
neo·Mal·thu·sian \,nē-ō-mal-'thü-zhən, -mòl-, -'thyü-\ adjective (1896)
: advocating control of population growth (as by contraception)
— **neo·Malthusian** noun
— **neo·Mal·thu·sian·ism** \-zhə-,ni-zəm\ noun
neo·my·cin \,nē-ə-'mī-sᵊn\ noun (1949)
: a broad-spectrum highly toxic antibiotic or mixture of antibiotics produced by a streptomyces (Streptomyces fradiae) and used medically especially to treat local infections
¹ne·on \'nē-,än\ noun [Greek, neuter of neos new — more at NEW] (1898)
1 : a colorless odorless mostly inert gaseous element that is found in minute amounts in air and is used in electric lamps — see ELEMENT table
2 a : a discharge lamp in which the gas contains a large proportion of neon **b :** a sign composed of such lamps **c :** the illumination provided by such lamps or signs
— **ne·oned** \-,änd\ adjective
²neon adjective (1904)
1 : of, relating to, or using neon
2 : extremely bright : FLUORESCENT ⟨neon yellow⟩
neo·na·tal \,nē-ō-'nā-tᵊl\ adjective (1902)
: of, relating to, or affecting the newborn and especially the human infant during the first month after birth ⟨neonatal mortality⟩

— **neo·na·tal·ly** \-tᵊl-ē\ adverb
ne·o·nate \'nē-ə-,nāt\ noun [New Latin neonatus, from ne- + Latin natus, past participle of nasci to be born — more at NATION] (1932)
: a newborn child; especially : a child less than a month old
neo·na·tol·o·gy \,nē-ə-nā-'tä-lə-jē\ noun (1960)
: a branch of medicine concerned with the care, development, and diseases of newborn infants
— **neo·na·tol·o·gist** \-jist\ noun
neo·Na·zi \,nē-ō-'nät-sē, -'nat-\ noun (1938)
: a member of a group espousing the programs and policies of Hitler's Nazis
— **neo·Nazi** adjective
— **neo·Na·zism** \-'nät-,si-zəm, -'nat-\ noun
neo·or·tho·dox \,nē-ō-'òr-thə-,däks\ adjective (1946)
: of or relating to a 20th century movement in Protestant theology characterized by a reaction against liberalism and emphasis on various scripturally based Reformation doctrines
— **neo·or·tho·doxy** \-,däk-sē\ noun
neo·phil·ia \,nē-ə-'fi-lē-ə\ noun (circa 1947)
: love of or enthusiasm for what is new or novel
— **neo·phil·i·ac** \-lē-,ak\ noun
neo·phyte \'nē-ə-,fīt\ noun [Middle English, from Late Latin neophytus, from Greek neophytos, from neophytos newly planted, newly converted, from ne- + phyein to bring forth — more at BE] (14th century)
1 : a new convert : PROSELYTE
2 : NOVICE 1
3 : TYRO, BEGINNER
neo·pla·sia \,nē-ə-'plā-zh(ē-)ə\ noun [New Latin] (1890)
1 : the formation of tumors
2 : a tumorous condition
neo·plasm \'nē-ə-,pla-zəm\ noun [International Scientific Vocabulary] (1864)
: a new growth of tissue serving no physiological function : TUMOR
neo·plas·tic \,nē-ə-'plas-tik\ adjective [International Scientific Vocabulary] (circa 1890)
1 : of, relating to, or constituting a neoplasm or neoplasia
2 : of or relating to neoplasticism
neo·plas·ti·cism \-tə-,si-zəm\ noun [French néo-plasticisme, from ne- + plastique plastic + -isme -ism] (1933)
: DE STIJL
— **neo·plas·ti·cist** \-sist\ noun
Neo·pla·to·nism \,nē-ō-'plā-tᵊn-,i-zəm\ noun (1845)
1 : Platonism modified in later antiquity to accord with Aristotelian, post-Aristotelian, and oriental conceptions that conceives of the world as an emanation from an ultimate indivisible being with whom the soul is capable of being reunited in trance or ecstasy
2 : a doctrine similar to ancient Neoplatonism
— **Neo·pla·ton·ic** \-plə-'tä-nik, -plä-\ adjective
— **Neo·pla·to·nist** \-'plä-tᵊn-ist\ noun
neo·prene \'nē-ə-,prēn\ noun [ne- + chloroprene] (1937)
: a synthetic rubber made by the polymerization of chloroprene, characterized by superior resistance (as to oils), and used especially for special-purpose clothing (as gloves and wet suits)
neo·re·al·ism \,nē-ō-'rē-ə-,li-zəm, -'ri-ə-\ noun (1950)
: a movement especially in Italian filmmaking characterized by the simple direct depiction of lower-class life
— **neo·re·al·ist** \-list\ adjective or noun
— **neo·re·al·is·tic** \-,rē-ə-'lis-tik, -,ri-ə-\ adjective
Neo·ri·can \,nē-ō-'rē-kən\ noun [American Spanish neorriqueño Puerto Rican living in

New York City, blend of Spanish neoyorquino New Yorker and puertorriqueño Puerto Rican] (1970)
: a Puerto Rican who lives on the U.S. mainland or has lived there but has returned to Puerto Rico
neo·scho·las·ti·cism \,nē-ō-skə-'las-tə-,si-zəm\ noun (circa 1909)
: a movement among Catholic scholars aiming to restate medieval Scholasticism in a manner suited to present intellectual needs
neo·stig·mine \,nē-ə-'stig-,mēn\ noun [ne- + -stigmine (as in physostigmine)] (1941)
: a cholinergic drug used in the form of its bromide $C_{12}H_{19}BrN_2O_2$ or a methyl sulfate derivative $C_{13}H_{22}N_2O_6S$ especially in the treatment of some ophthalmic conditions and in the diagnosis and treatment of myasthenia gravis
ne·o·te·ny \nē-'ä-tᵊn-ē\ noun [New Latin neotenia, from ne- + Greek teinein to stretch — more at THIN] (1901)
1 : retention of some larval or immature characters in adulthood
2 : attainment of sexual maturity during the larval stage
— **ne·o·ten·ic** \,nē-ə-'te-nik\ adjective
ne·o·ter·ic \,nē-ə-'ter-ik\ adjective [Late Latin neotericus, from Late Greek neōterikos, from Greek, youthful, from neōterios, comparative of neos new, young — more at NEW] (1596)
: recent in origin : MODERN
Neo·trop·i·cal \,nē-ō-'trä-pi-kəl\ also **Neo·trop·ic** \-pik\ adjective [International Scientific Vocabulary] (1858)
: of, relating to, or constituting the biogeographic region that extends south, east, and west from the central plateau of Mexico
neo·trop·ics \-'trä-piks\ noun plural (1923)
: the Neotropical region
neo·type \'nē-ə-,tīp\ noun (1905)
: a type specimen that is selected subsequent to the description of a species to replace a preexisting type that has been lost or destroyed
Ne·pali \nə-'pò-lē, -'pä-, -'pa-\ noun, plural **Nepali** also **Ne·pal·is** [Hindi naipālī of Nepal, from Sanskrit naipālīya, from Nepāla Nepal] (circa 1885)
1 : a native or inhabitant of Nepal
2 : an Indo-Aryan language spoken in Nepal
— **Nepali** adjective
ne·pen·the \nə-'pen(t)-thē\ noun [Latin nepenthes, from Greek nēpenthes, neuter of nēpenthēs banishing pain and sorrow, from nē- not + penthos grief, sorrow; akin to Greek pathos suffering — more at NO, PATHOS] (1580)
1 : a potion used by the ancients to induce forgetfulness of pain or sorrow
2 : something capable of causing oblivion of grief or suffering
— **ne·pen·the·an** \-thē-ən\ adjective
neph·e·line \'ne-fə-,lēn\ also **neph·e·lite** \-,līt\ noun [French néphéline, from Greek nephelē cloud — more at NEBULA] (circa 1814)
: a hexagonal mineral that is a usually glassy crystalline silicate of sodium, potassium, and aluminum common in igneous rocks
— **neph·e·lin·ic** \,ne-fə-'li-nik\ adjective
neph·e·lin·ite \'ne-fə-lə-,nīt\ noun [International Scientific Vocabulary] (circa 1863)
: a silica-deficient igneous rock having nepheline as the predominant mineral
— **neph·e·lin·it·ic** \,ne-fə-lə-'ni-tik\ adjective
neph·e·lom·e·ter \,ne-fə-'lä-mə-tər\ noun [Greek nephelē cloud + International Scientific Vocabulary -meter] (1884)
1 : an instrument for measuring the extent or degree of cloudiness
2 : an instrument for determining the concentration or particle size of suspensions by means of transmitted or reflected light
— **neph·e·lo·met·ric** \,ne-fə-lō-'me-trik\ adjective

— **neph·e·lo·met·ri·cal·ly** \-tri-k(ə-)lē\ *adverb*

— **neph·e·lom·e·try** \-'lä-mə-trē\ *noun*

neph·ew \'ne-(ˌ)fyü, *chiefly British* -(ˌ)vyü\ *noun* [Middle English *nevew*, from Old French *neveu*, from Latin *nepot-, nepos* grandson, nephew; akin to Old English *nefa* grandson, nephew, Sanskrit *napāt* grandson] (14th century)
1 a : a son of one's brother or sister or of one's brother-in-law or sister-in-law **b :** an illegitimate son of an ecclesiastic
2 *obsolete* **:** a lineal descendant; *especially* **:** GRANDSON

nepho·scope \'ne-fə-ˌskōp\ *noun* [Greek *nephos* cloud + International Scientific Vocabulary *-scope* — more at NEBULA] (1881)
: an instrument for observing the direction and velocity of clouds

nephr- *or* **nephro-** *combining form* [New Latin, from Greek, from *nephros* — more at NEPHRITIS]
: kidney ⟨*nephric*⟩ ⟨*nephrology*⟩

ne·phrec·to·my \ni-'frek-tə-mē\ *noun, plural* **-mies** [International Scientific Vocabulary] (1880)
: the surgical removal of a kidney
— **ne·phrec·to·mize** \-ˌmīz\ *transitive verb*

neph·ric \'ne-frik\ *adjective* (1887)
: RENAL

ne·phrid·i·um \ni-'fri-dē-əm\ *noun, plural* **-ia** \-dē-ə\ [New Latin] (1877)
: a tubular glandular excretory organ characteristic of various invertebrates
— **ne·phrid·i·al** \-dē-əl\ *adjective*

neph·rite \'ne-ˌfrīt\ *noun* [German *Nephrit*, from Greek *nephros*; from its formerly being worn as a remedy for kidney diseases] (1794)
: a compact tremolite or actinolite that is the commoner and less valuable kind of jade and that varies in color from white to dark green or black

ne·phrit·ic \ni-'fri-tik\ *adjective* (1580)
1 : RENAL
2 : of, relating to, or affected with nephritis

ne·phri·tis \ni-'frī-təs\ *noun, plural* **ne·phrit·i·des** \-'fri-tə-ˌdēz\ [Late Latin, from Greek, from *nephros* kidney; probably akin to Middle English *nere* kidney] (1580)
: acute or chronic inflammation of the kidney caused by infection, degenerative process, or vascular disease

ne·phrol·o·gy \ni-'frä-lə-jē\ *noun* (circa 1842)
: a branch of medicine concerned with the kidneys
— **ne·phrol·o·gist** \-jist\ *noun*

neph·ron \'ne-ˌfrän\ *noun* [German, from Greek *nephros*] (1932)
: a single excretory unit of the vertebrate kidney

ne·phrop·a·thy \ni-'frä-pə-thē\ *noun, plural* **-thies** [International Scientific Vocabulary] (circa 1900)
: an abnormal state of the kidney; *especially* **:** one associated with or secondary to some other pathological process
— **neph·ro·path·ic** \ˌne-frə-'pa-thik\ *adjective*

ne·phro·sis \ni-'frō-səs\ *noun* [New Latin] (1916)
: a noninflammatory disease of the kidneys chiefly affecting function of the nephrons; *also* **:** NEPHROTIC SYNDROME
— **ne·phrot·ic** \-'frä-tik\ *adjective or noun*

neph·ro·stome \'ne-frə-ˌstōm\ *noun* [New Latin *nephrostoma*, from *nephr-* + *stoma* stoma] (1888)
: the ciliated funnel-shaped coelomic opening of a typical nephridium

nephrotic syndrome *noun* (1939)
: an abnormal condition that is marked by deficiency of albumin in the blood and its excretion in the urine due to altered permeability of the glomerular basement membranes

neph·ro·tox·ic \ˌne-frə-'täk-sik\ *adjective* (1902)
: poisonous to the kidney ⟨*nephrotoxic* drugs⟩; *also* **:** resulting from or marked by poisoning of the kidney ⟨*nephrotoxic* effects⟩
— **neph·ro·tox·ic·i·ty** \-täk-'si-sə-tē\ *noun*

ne plus ul·tra \ˌnā-ˌplu̇s-'əl-trə, ˌnē-\ *noun* [New Latin, (go) no more beyond] (1638)
1 : the highest point capable of being attained **:** ACME
2 : the most profound degree of a quality or state

nep·o·tism \'ne-pə-ˌti-zəm\ *noun* [French *népotisme*, from Italian *nepotismo*, from *nepote* nephew, from Latin *nepot-, nepos* grandson, nephew — more at NEPHEW] (1670)
: favoritism (as in appointment to a job) based on kinship
— **nep·o·tis·tic** \ˌne-pə-'tis-tik\ *adjective*

Nep·tune \'nep-ˌtün, -ˌtyün\ *noun* [Latin *Neptunus*]
1 a : the Roman god of the sea — compare POSEIDON **b :** OCEAN
2 : the planet 8th in order from the sun — see PLANET table
— **Nep·tu·ni·an** \nep-'tü-nē-ən, -'tyü-\ *adjective*

nep·tu·ni·um \nep-'tü-nē-əm, -'tyü-\ *noun* [New Latin, from International Scientific Vocabulary *Neptune*] (1941)
: a radioactive metallic element that is chemically similar to uranium and is obtained in nuclear reactors as a by-product in the production of plutonium — see ELEMENT table

nerd \'nərd\ *noun* [perhaps from *nerd*, a creature in the children's book *If I Ran the Zoo* (1950) by Dr. Seuss (Theodor Geisel)] (1951)
: an unstylish, unattractive, or socially inept person; *especially* **:** one slavishly devoted to intellectual or academic pursuits ⟨computer *nerds*⟩ ◇
— **nerd·ish** \'nər-dish\ *adjective*
— **nerdy** \-dē\ *adjective*

ne·re·id \'nir-ē-əd\ *noun* [New Latin *Nereidae*, from *Nereis*, a genus, from Latin, Nereid] (1840)
: any of a family (Nereidae) of polychaete worms; *especially* **:** any of a genus (*Nereis*) of usually large often dimorphic and greenish mostly marine worms
— **nereid** *adjective*

Ne·re·id \'nir-ē-əd\ *noun* [Latin *Nereid-, Nereis*, from Greek *Nēreid-, Nēreis*, from *Nēreus* Nereus] (1680)
: any of the sea nymphs fathered by Nereus

Ne·re·us \'nir-ē-əs\ *noun* [Latin, from Greek *Nēreus*]
: a sea-god in Greek mythology

ne·rit·ic \nə-'ri-tik\ *adjective* [International Scientific Vocabulary, perhaps from New Latin *Nerita*, genus of marine snails] (1891)
: of, relating to, inhabiting, or constituting the belt or region of shallow water adjoining the seacoast

ne·rol \'ner-ˌȯl, 'nir-\ *noun* [International Scientific Vocabulary *ner-* (from *neroli* oil) + *-ol*] (1869)
: a liquid alcohol $C_{10}H_{18}O$ that has a rose scent and is used in perfumery

ner·o·li oil \'ner-ə-lē\ *noun* [French *néroli*, from Italian *neroli*, from Anna Maria de La Trémoille, princess of *Nerola* (flourished 1670)] (1849)
: a fragrant pale yellow essential oil obtained from orange flowers and used especially in cologne and as a flavoring

nerts \'nərts\ *noun plural* [alteration of *nuts*] (circa 1932)
slang **:** NONSENSE, NUTS — often used interjectionally

ner·va·tion \ˌnər-'vā-shən\ *noun* (1849)
: an arrangement or system of nerves; *also* **:** VENATION

¹nerve \'nərv\ *noun* [Latin *nervus* sinew, nerve; akin to Greek *neuron* sinew, nerve, *nēn* to spin — more at NEEDLE] (14th century)
1 : SINEW, TENDON ⟨strain every *nerve*⟩
2 : any of the filamentous bands of nervous tissue that connect parts of the nervous system with the other organs, conduct nervous impulses, and are made up of axons and dendrites together with protective and supportive structures
3 a : power of endurance or control **:** FORTITUDE, STRENGTH **b :** ASSURANCE, BOLDNESS; *also* **:** presumptuous audacity **:** GALL
4 a : a sore or sensitive point **b** *plural* **:** nervous disorganization or collapse **:** NERVOUSNESS
5 : VEIN 3
6 : the sensitive pulp of a tooth
synonym see TEMERITY

²nerve *transitive verb* **nerved; nerv·ing** (circa 1749)
: to give strength or courage to **:** supply with physical or moral force

nerve cell *noun* (1858)
: NEURON; *also* **:** CELL BODY

nerve center *noun* (1868)
1 : CENTER 2c
2 : a source of leadership, organization, control, or energy ⟨the financial *nerve center* of the nation⟩

nerve cord *noun* (1877)
1 : the pair of closely united ventral longitudinal nerves with their segmental ganglia that is characteristic of many elongate invertebrates (as earthworms)
2 : the dorsal tubular cord of nervous tissue above the notochord of a chordate that comprises or develops into the central nervous system

nerved \'nərvd\ *adjective* (1800)
1 a : VEINED ⟨a *nerved* wing⟩ **b :** having veins or nerves especially of a specified kind or number — used in combination ⟨fan-*nerved* leaves⟩
2 : showing courage or strength

nerve ending *noun* (circa 1890)
: a structure forming the distal end of a nerve axon

nerve fiber *noun* (circa 1847)
: any of the processes (as axons or dendrites) of a neuron

nerve gas *noun* (1940)

◇ WORD HISTORY
nerd The word *nerd* was first noted in an article on teenage slang that appeared in the October 8, 1951, issue of *Newsweek:* "In Detroit, someone who would once be called a drip or a square is now, regrettably, a nerd, or, in a less severe case, a scurve." No one knows if Detroit was actually the birthplace of *nerd*, but the word went on to a remarkably successful career in American English. It provided a label for a new character in postwar America: the student wholly devoted to intellectual interests and unable or unwilling to mix with the masses of young people for whom higher education was a less intensely serious matter. While the collegiate *nerd* was supplanted by *dweeb, dork, wonk,* and newer words, *nerd* expanded into adult realms, and the word became an only slightly derogatory epithet for a narrowly focused specialist, especially in the common collocation *computer nerd*. The origin of *nerd* remains unclear; the children's author Theodore Geisel ("Dr. Seuss") used *nerd* for an imaginary creature in *If I Ran the Zoo* (1950), but his coinage may be unrelated to the appearance of the word in 1951 Detroit.

: an organophosphate chemical weapon that interferes with normal nerve transmission and induces intense bronchial spasm with resulting inhibition of respiration

nerve growth factor *noun* (1962)
: a protein that promotes development of the sensory and sympathetic nervous systems and is required for maintenance of sympathetic neurons

nerve impulse *noun* (1900)
: the progressive physicochemical change in the membrane of a nerve fiber that follows stimulation and serves to transmit a record of sensation from a receptor or an instruction to act to an effector — called also *nervous impulse*

nerve·less \ˈnərv-ləs\ *adjective* (1742)
1 : lacking strength or courage : FEEBLE
2 : exhibiting control or balance : POISED, COOL
— **nerve·less·ly** *adverb*
— **nerve·less·ness** *noun*

nerve net *noun* (1904)
: a network of nerve cells apparently continuous with one another and conducting impulses in all directions; *also* : a primitive nervous system (as in a jellyfish) consisting of such a network

nerve–rack·ing *or* **nerve–wrack·ing** \ˈnərv-ˌra-kin\ *adjective* (1812)
: extremely trying on the nerves (a *nerve‑racking* ordeal)

nerve trunk *noun* (1851)
: a bundle of nerve fibers enclosed in a connective tissue sheath

ner·vos·i·ty \ˌnər-ˈvä-sə-tē\ *noun* (1787)
: the quality or state of being nervous

ner·vous \ˈnər-vəs\ *adjective* (14th century)
1 *archaic* : SINEWY, STRONG
2 : marked by strength of thought, feeling, or style : SPIRITED (a vibrant tight-packed *nervous* style of writing)
3 : of, relating to, or composed of neurons
4 a : of or relating to the nerves; *also* : originating in or affected by the nerves (*nervous* energy) b : easily excited or irritated : JUMPY c : TIMID, APPREHENSIVE (a *nervous* smile)
5 a : tending to produce nervousness or agitation : UNEASY (a *nervous* situation) b : appearing or acting unsteady, erratic, or irregular — used of inanimate things
synonym see VIGOROUS
— **ner·vous·ly** *adverb*
— **ner·vous·ness** *noun*

nervous breakdown *noun* (1905)
: an attack of mental or emotional disorder especially when of sufficient severity to require hospitalization

nervous Nel·lie *or* **nervous Nel·ly** \-ˈne-lē\ *noun, plural* **nervous Nellies** *often 1st N capitalized* [from the name *Nellie*] (1926)
: a timid or worrisome person

nervous system *noun* (1740)
: the bodily system that in vertebrates is made up of the brain and spinal cord, nerves, ganglia, and parts of the receptor organs and that receives and interprets stimuli and transmits impulses to the effector organs — compare CENTRAL NERVOUS SYSTEM; AUTONOMIC NERVOUS SYSTEM, PERIPHERAL NERVOUS SYSTEM

ner·vure \ˈnər-vyər\ *noun* [French, from *nerf* sinew, from Latin *nervus*] (1816)
: VEIN 3

nervy \ˈnər-vē\ *adjective* **nerv·i·er; -est** (1607)
1 *archaic* : SINEWY, STRONG
2 a : showing calm courage : BOLD b : marked by effrontery or presumption : BRASH
3 : EXCITABLE, NERVOUS
— **nerv·i·ly** \-və-lē\ *adverb*
— **nerv·i·ness** \-vē-nəs\ *noun*

ne·science \ˈne-sh(ē-)ən(t)s, ˈnē-, -sē-ən(t)s\ *noun* [Late Latin *nescientia*, from Latin *nescient-, nesciens*, present participle of *nescire* not to know, from *ne-* not + *scire* to know — more at NO, SCIENCE] (1612)
: lack of knowledge or awareness : IGNORANCE

— **ne·scient** \-sh(ē-)ənt, -sē-ənt\ *adjective*

ness \ˈnes\ *noun* [Middle English *nasse*, from Old English *næss;* akin to Old English *nasu* nose — more at NOSE] (before 12th century)
: CAPE, PROMONTORY

-ness \nəs\ *noun suffix* [Middle English *-nes*, from Old English; akin to Old High German *-nissa* -ness]
: state : condition : quality : degree (good*ness*)

Nes·sel·rode \ˈne-səl-ˌrōd\ *noun* [Count Karl R. *Nesselrode* (died 1862) Russian statesman] (1845)
: a mixture of candied fruits, nuts, and maraschino used in puddings, pies, and ice cream

Nes·sus \ˈne-səs\ *noun* [Latin, from Greek *Nessos*]
: a centaur slain by Hercules for trying to carry away Hercules' wife but avenged by means of a poisoned garment that causes Hercules to die in torment

¹nest \ˈnest\ *noun* [Middle English, from Old English; akin to Old High German *nest* nest, Latin *nidus*] (before 12th century)
1 a : a bed or receptacle prepared by an animal and especially a bird for its eggs and young b : a place or specially modified structure serving as an abode of animals and especially of their immature stages (an ants' *nest*)
c : a receptacle resembling a bird's nest
2 a : a place of rest, retreat, or lodging : HOME (grown children who have left the *nest*) b : DEN, HANGOUT
3 : the occupants or frequenters of a nest
4 a : a group of similar things : AGGREGATION (a *nest* of giant mountains —Helen MacInnes) b : HOTBED 2 (a *nest* of rebellion)
5 : a group of objects made to fit close together or one within another
6 : an emplaced group of weapons

²nest (13th century)
intransitive verb
1 : to build or occupy a nest : settle in or as if in a nest
2 : to fit compactly together or within one another : EMBED
transitive verb
1 : to form a nest for
2 : to pack compactly together
3 : to form a hierarchy, series, or sequence of with each member, element, or set contained in or containing the next (*nested* subroutines in a computer program)

nest egg *noun* (14th century)
1 : a natural or artificial egg left in a nest to induce a fowl to continue to lay there
2 : a fund of money accumulated as a reserve

nest·er \ˈnes-tər\ *noun* (1880)
1 *West* : a homesteader or squatter who takes up land on open range for a farm
2 : one that nests

nes·tle \ˈne-səl\ *verb* **nes·tled; nes·tling** \-s(ə-)liŋ\ [Middle English, from Old English *nestlian*, from *nest*] (before 12th century)
intransitive verb
1 *archaic* : NEST 1
2 : to settle snugly or comfortably
3 : to lie in an inconspicuous or sheltered manner
transitive verb
1 : to settle, shelter, or house in or as if in a nest (the children were *nestled* all snug in their beds —Clement Moore)
2 : to press closely and affectionately (*nestles* a kitten in her arms)
— **nes·tler** \-s(ə-)lər\ *noun*

nest·ling \ˈnest-liŋ\ *noun* (14th century)
: a young bird that has not abandoned the nest

Nes·tor \ˈnes-tər, -ˌtȯr\ *noun* [Latin, from Greek *Nestōr*]
1 : a king of Pylos who serves in his old age as a counselor to the Greeks at Troy
2 *often not capitalized* : one who is a patriarch or leader in a field

Nes·to·ri·an \ne-ˈstōr-ē-ən, -ˈstȯr-\ *adjective* (1565)

1 : of or relating to the doctrine ascribed to Nestorius and ecclesiastically condemned in 431 that divine and human persons remained separate in the incarnate Christ
2 : of or relating to a church separating from Byzantine Christianity after 431, centering in Persia, and surviving chiefly in Asia Minor
— **Nestorian** *noun*
— **Nes·to·ri·an·ism** \-ə-ˌni-zəm\ *noun*

¹net \ˈnet\ *noun* [Middle English *nett*, from Old English; akin to Old High German *nezzi* net] (before 12th century)
1 a : an open-meshed fabric twisted, knotted, or woven together at regular intervals b : something made of net: as (1) : a device for catching fish, birds, or insects (2) : a fabric barricade which divides a court in half (as in tennis or volleyball) and over which a ball or shuttlecock must be hit to be in play (3) : the fabric that encloses the sides and back of the goal in various games (as soccer or hockey)
2 : an entrapping device or situation (caught in the *net* of suspicious circumstances)
3 : something resembling a net in reticulation (as of lines, fibers, or figures)
4 a : a group of communications stations operating under unified control b : NETWORK 4
— **net·less** \-ləs\ *adjective*
— **net·like** \-ˌlīk\ *adjective*
— **net·ty** \ˈne-tē\ *adjective*

²net *transitive verb* **net·ted; net·ting** (1593)
1 : to cover or enclose with or as if with a net
2 : to catch in or as if in a net
3 : to cover with or as if with a network
4 a : to hit (a ball) into the net for the loss of a point in a racket game b : to hit (a ball or puck) into the goal for a score (as in hockey or soccer)
— **net·ter** *noun*

³net *adjective* [Middle English, clean, bright, from Middle French — more at NEAT] (15th century)
1 : free from all charges or deductions: as a : remaining after the deduction of all charges, outlay, or loss (*net* earnings) (*net* worth) — compare GROSS b : excluding all tare (*net* weight)
2 : excluding all nonessential considerations : BASIC, FINAL (the *net* result) (*net* effect)

⁴net *transitive verb* **net·ted; net·ting** (1758)
1 a : to receive by way of profit : CLEAR b : to produce by way of profit : YIELD
2 : to get possession of : GAIN

⁵net *noun* (circa 1904)
1 : a net amount, profit, weight, or price
2 : the score of a golfer in a handicap match after deducting his handicap from his gross
3 : ESSENCE, GIST

neth·er \ˈne-thər\ *adjective* [Middle English, from Old English *nithera*, from *nither* down; akin to Old High German *nidar* down, Sanskrit *ni*] (before 12th century)
1 : situated down or below : LOWER (the *nether* side)
2 : situated or believed to be situated beneath the earth's surface (the *nether* regions)

neth·er·most \-ˌmōst\ *adjective* (14th century)
: farthest down : LOWEST

neth·er·world \-ˌwərld\ *noun* (1638)
1 : the world of the dead
2 : UNDERWORLD 4 (the *netherworld* of deceit, subversion, and espionage —R. M. Nixon)

net·mind·er \ˈnet-ˌmīn-dər\ *noun* (1937)
: GOALKEEPER

net·su·ke \ˈnets-(ˌ)kā, -kē, -ke *also* ˈnet-sü-\ *noun, plural* **netsuke** *or* **netsukes** [Japanese] (1876)
: a small and often intricately carved toggle (as of wood, ivory, or metal) used to fasten a small container to a kimono sash

nett *British variant of* NET

net·ting \ˈne-tiŋ\ *noun* (1567)
1 : NETWORK 1

2 : the act or process of making a net or network

3 : the act, process, or right of fishing with a net

¹net·tle \'ne-t⁰l\ *noun* [Middle English, from Old English *netel;* akin to Old High German *nazza* nettle, Greek *adikē*] (before 12th century)

1 : any of a genus (*Urtica* of the family Urticaceae, the nettle family) of chiefly coarse herbs armed with stinging hairs

2 : any of various prickly or stinging plants other than the true nettles (genus *Urtica*)

²nettle *transitive verb* **net·tled; net·tling** \'net-liŋ, 'ne-t⁰l-iŋ\ (15th century)

1 : to strike or sting with or as if with nettles

2 : to arouse to sharp but transitory annoyance or anger

synonym see IRRITATE

nettle rash *noun* (1740)
: URTICARIA

net·tle·some \'ne-t⁰l-səm\ *adjective* (1766)
: causing vexation : IRRITATING

net–veined \'net-,vānd\ *adjective* (1861)
: having veins arranged in a fine network ⟨a *net-veined* leaf⟩ — compare PARALLEL-VEINED; see VENATION illustration
— **net venation** *noun*

net–winged \-,wiŋd\ *adjective* (circa 1890)
: having wings with a fine network of veins

¹net·work \'net-,wərk\ *noun* (1560)

1 : a fabric or structure of cords or wires that cross at regular intervals and are knotted or secured at the crossings

2 : a system of lines or channels resembling a network

3 a : an interconnected or interrelated chain, group, or system ⟨a *network* of hotels⟩ **b :** a system of computers, terminals, and databases connected by communications lines

4 a : a group of radio or television stations linked by wire or radio relay **b :** a radio or television company that produces programs for broadcast over such a network

²network (1887)
transitive verb

1 : to cover with or as if with a network ⟨a continent . . . so *networked* with navigable rivers and canals —*Lamp*⟩

2 *chiefly British* **:** to distribute for broadcast on a television network; *also* **:** BROADCAST 3

3 : to join (as computers) in a network
intransitive verb
: to engage in networking

net·work·ing *noun* (1966)

1 : the exchange of information or services among individuals, groups, or institutions

2 : the establishment or use of a computer network

Neuf·châ·tel \,nü-shä-'tel, ,nyü-, ,nə(r)-\ *noun* [French, from *Neufchâtel,* France] (circa 1865)
: a soft unripened cheese similar to cream cheese but containing less fat and more moisture

neume \'nüm, 'nyüm\ *noun* [Middle English, from Medieval Latin *pneuma, neuma,* from Greek *pneuma* breath — more at PNEUMATIC] (14th century)
: any of various symbols used in the notation of Gregorian chant
— **neu·mat·ic** \nù-'ma-tik, nyù-\ *adjective*

neur- *or* **neuro-** *combining form* [New Latin, from Greek, nerve, sinew, from *neuron* — more at NERVE]

1 : nerve ⟨*neural*⟩ ⟨*neuro*logy⟩

2 : neural : neural and ⟨*neuro*muscular⟩

neu·ral \'nùr-əl, 'nyùr-\ *adjective* (circa 1847)

1 : of, relating to, or affecting a nerve or the nervous system

2 : situated in the region of or on the same side of the body as the brain and spinal cord : DORSAL
— **neu·ral·ly** \-ə-lē\ *adverb*

neural arch *noun* (circa 1860)

: the cartilaginous or bony arch enclosing the spinal cord on the dorsal side of a vertebra

neural crest *noun* (circa 1885)
: the ridge of one of the folds forming the neural tube that gives rise to the spinal ganglia and various structures of the autonomic nervous system

neu·ral·gia \nù-'ral-jə, nyù-\ *noun* [New Latin] (circa 1834)
: acute paroxysmal pain radiating along the course of one or more nerves usually without demonstrable changes in the nerve structure
— **neu·ral·gic** \-jik\ *adjective*

neural net *noun* (1949)
: a computer architecture in which a number of processors are interconnected in a manner suggestive of the connections between neurons in a human brain and which is able to learn by a process of trial and error — called also *neural network*

neural plate *noun* (1888)
: a thickened plate of ectoderm along the dorsal midline of the early vertebrate embryo that gives rise to the neural tube and crests

neural tube *noun* (1888)
: the hollow longitudinal dorsal tube formed by infolding and subsequent fusion of the opposite ectodermal folds in the vertebrate embryo that gives rise to the brain and spinal cord

neur·amin·i·dase \,nùr-ə-'mi-nə-,dās, ,nyùr-, -,dāz\ *noun* [*neuramin*ic acid, an amino acid + *-ide* + *-ase*] (1956)
: a glycosidase that splits mucoproteins by breaking a glucoside link and occurs especially in influenza viruses as an antigen

neur·as·the·nia \,nùr-əs-'thē-nē-ə, ,nyùr-\ *noun* [New Latin] (1856)
: an emotional and psychic disorder that is characterized especially by easy fatigability and often by lack of motivation, feelings of inadequacy, and psychosomatic symptoms
— **neur·as·then·ic** \-'the-nik, -'thē-\ *adjective or noun*
— **neur·as·then·i·cal·ly** \-ni-k(ə-)lē\ *adverb*

neu·ri·lem·ma \,nùr-ə-'le-mə, ,nyùr-\ *noun* [New Latin, from *neur-* + Greek *eilēma* covering, coil, from *eilein* to wind; akin to Greek *eilyein* to wrap — more at VOLUBLE] (1852)
: the plasma membrane surrounding a Schwann cell of a myelinated nerve fiber and separating layers of myelin
— **neu·ri·lem·mal** \-'le-məl\ *adjective*

neu·ri·tis \nù-'rī-təs, nyù-\ *noun, plural* **-rit·i·des** \-'ri-tə-,dēz\ *or* **-ri·tis·es** [New Latin] (1840)
: an inflammatory or degenerative lesion of a nerve marked especially by pain, sensory disturbances, and impaired or lost reflexes
— **neu·rit·ic** \-'ri-tik\ *adjective or noun*

neu·ro·ac·tive \,nùr-ō-'ak-tiv, ,nyùr-\ *adjective* (1961)
: stimulating neural tissue

neu·ro·anat·o·my \-ə-'na-tə-mē\ *noun* (circa 1899)
: the anatomy of nervous tissue and the nervous system
— **neu·ro·an·a·tom·i·cal** \-,a-nə-'tä-mi-kəl\ *also* **neu·ro·an·a·tom·ic** \-mik\ *adjective*
— **neu·ro·anat·o·mist** \-ə-'na-tə-mist\ *noun*

neu·ro·bi·ol·o·gy \-bī-'ä-lə-jē\ *noun* (1906)
: a branch of the life sciences that deals with the anatomy, physiology, and pathology of the nervous system
— **neu·ro·bi·o·log·i·cal** \-,bī-ə-'lä-ji-kəl\ *adjective*
— **neu·ro·bi·ol·o·gist** \-bī-'ä-lə-jist\ *noun*

neu·ro·blas·to·ma \-blas-'tō-mə\ *noun, plural* **-mas** *or* **-ma·ta** \-mə-tə\ [New Latin, from International Scientific Vocabulary *neuroblast* embryonic ganglion cell, from *neur-* + *-blast* -blast] (1910)

: a malignant tumor formed of embryonic ganglion cells

neu·ro·chem·is·try \-'ke-mə-strē\ *noun* (1924)

1 : the study of the chemical makeup and activities of nervous tissue

2 : chemical processes and phenomena related to the nervous system
— **neu·ro·chem·i·cal** \-'ke-mi-kəl\ *adjective or noun*
— **neu·ro·chem·ist** \-'ke-mist\ *noun*

neu·ro·de·gen·er·a·tive \-di-'je-nə-rə-tiv, -'jen-rə-; -'je-nə-,rā-; -dē-\ *adjective* (1907)
: relating to or characterized by degeneration of nervous tissue

neu·ro·en·do·crine \-'en-də-krən, -,krīn, -,krēn\ *adjective* (1922)

1 : of, relating to, or being a hormonal substance that influences the activity of nerves

2 : of, relating to, or functioning in neurosecretion

neu·ro·en·do·cri·nol·o·gy \-,en-də-kri-'nä-lə-jē, -,(,)krī-\ *noun* (1922)
: a branch of the life sciences dealing with neurosecretion and the physiological interaction between the central nervous system and the endocrine system
— **neu·ro·en·do·cri·no·log·i·cal** \-,krin⁰l-'ä-ji-kəl, -,krī-, -,krē-\ *adjective*
— **neu·ro·en·do·cri·nol·o·gist** \-kri-'nä-lə-jist, -,(,)krī-\ *noun*

neu·ro·fi·bril \-'fī-brəl, -'fi-\ *noun* [New Latin *neurofibrilla,* from *neur-* + *fibrilla* fibril] (1898)
: a fine proteinaceous fibril that is found in cytoplasm (as of a neuron or a paramecium) and is capable of conducting excitation
— **neu·ro·fi·bril·lary** \-brə-,ler-ē\ *adjective*

neu·ro·fi·bro·ma \-fī-'brō-mə\ *noun* (1892)
: a fibroma composed of nervous and connective tissue and produced by proliferation of Schwann cells

neu·ro·fi·bro·ma·to·sis \-(,)fī-,brō-mə-'tō-səs\ *noun* [New Latin, from *neurofibromat-, neurofibroma*] (1896)
: a disorder inherited as an autosomal dominant and characterized especially by brown spots on the skin, neurofibromas of peripheral nerves, and deformities of subcutaneous tissue and bone

neu·ro·gen·ic \,nùr-ə-'je-nik, ,nyùr-\ *adjective* (1901)

1 : originating in or controlled by nervous tissue ⟨*neurogenic* heartbeat⟩

2 : induced or modified by nervous factors; *especially* **:** disordered because of abnormally altered neural relations
— **neu·ro·gen·i·cal·ly** \-ni-k(ə-)lē\ *adverb*

neu·ro·glia \nù-'rō-glē-ə, nyù-, -'rä-; ,n(y)ùr-ə-'glē-ə, -'glī-\ *noun* [New Latin, from *neur-* + Middle Greek *glia* glue — more at CLAY] (1873)
: supporting tissue intermingled with the essential elements of nervous tissue especially in the brain, spinal cord, and ganglia
— **neu·ro·gli·al** \-əl\ *adjective*

neu·ro·hor·mon·al \,nùr-ō-hȯr-'mō-n⁰l, ,nyùr-\ *adjective* (circa 1935)

1 : involving both neural and hormonal mechanisms

2 : of, relating to, or being a neurohormone

neu·ro·hor·mone \-'hȯr-,mōn\ *noun* [International Scientific Vocabulary] (1935)
: a hormone (as acetylcholine or norepinephrine) produced by or acting on nervous tissue

neu·ro·hu·mor \-'hyü-mər, -'yü-\ *noun* (1932)
: NEUROHORMONE; *especially* **:** NEUROTRANSMITTER
— **neu·ro·hu·mor·al** \-mə-rəl\ *adjective*

\ə\ **abut** \⁰\ **kitten** \ər\ **further** \a\ **ash** \ā\ **ace**
\ä\ **mop, mar** \aù\ **out** \ch\ **chin** \e\ **bet** \ē\ **easy**
\g\ **go** \i\ **hit** \ī\ **ice** \j\ **job** \ŋ\ **sing** \ō\ **go**
\ȯ\ **law** \ȯi\ **boy** \th\ **thin** \t͟h\ **the** \ü\ **loot** \ù\ **foot**
\y\ **yet** \zh\ **vision** *see also* Guide to Pronunciation

neu·ro·hy·poph·y·sis \-hī-'pä-fə-səs\ *noun* [New Latin] (1912)
: the portion of the pituitary gland that is composed of the infundibulum and posterior lobe and is concerned with the secretion of various hormones — **neu·ro·hy·po·phy·se·al** *or* **neu·ro·hy·po·phy·si·al** \-(,)hī-,pä-fə-'sē-əl, -,hī-pə-fə-, -'zē-, -,hī-pə-'fi-zē-\ *adjective*

neu·ro·lep·tic \,nur-ə-'lep-tik, ,nyur-\ *noun* [French *neuroleptique*, from *neur-* + *-leptique* affecting, from Greek *lēptikos* seizing, from *lambanein* to take, seize — more at LATCH] (1958)
: any of the powerful tranquilizers (as the phenothiazines) used especially to treat psychosis and believed to act by blocking dopamine nervous receptors — called also *antipsychotic* — **neuroleptic** *adjective*

neu·rol·o·gist \nu-'rä-lə-jist, nyu-\ *noun* (1832)
: one specializing in neurology; *especially* : a physician skilled in the diagnosis and treatment of disease of the nervous system

neu·rol·o·gy \-jē\ *noun* [New Latin *neurologia*, from *neur-* + *-logia* -logy] (circa 1681)
: the scientific study of the nervous system especially in respect to its structure, functions, and abnormalities — **neu·ro·log·i·cal** \,nur-ə-'lä-ji-kəl, ,nyur-\ *or* **neu·ro·log·ic** \-jik\ *adjective* — **neu·ro·log·i·cal·ly** \-ji-k(ə-)lē\ *adverb*

neu·ro·ma \nu-'rō-mə, nyu-\ *noun, plural* **-mas** *or* **-ma·ta** \-mə-tə\ [New Latin] (circa 1847)
: a tumor or mass growing from a nerve and usually consisting of nerve fibers

neu·ro·mus·cu·lar \,nur-ō-'məs-kyə-lər, ,nyur-\ *adjective* [International Scientific Vocabulary] (1864)
: of or relating to nerves and muscles; *especially* : jointly involving nervous and muscular elements ⟨a *neuromuscular* junction⟩

neu·ron \'nu-,rän, 'nyu-; 'nur-,än, 'nyur-\ *also* **neu·rone** \-,rōn, -,ōn\ *noun* [New Latin *neuron*, from Greek, nerve, sinew — more at NERVE] (1891)
: a grayish or reddish granular cell with specialized processes that is the fundamental functional unit of nervous tissue — **neu·ro·nal** \'nur-ən-ᵊl, 'nyur-; nu-'rō-nᵊl, nyu-\ *also* **neu·ron·ic** \nu-'rä-nik, nyu-\ *adjective*

neu·ro·pa·thol·o·gy \,nur-ō-pə-'thä-lə-jē, ,nyur-, -pa-\ *noun* [International Scientific Vocabulary] (1853)
: pathology of the nervous system — **neu·ro·path·o·log·ic** \-,pa-thə-'lä-jik\ *or* **neu·ro·path·o·log·i·cal** \-ji-kəl\ *adjective* — **neu·ro·pa·thol·o·gist** \-pə-'thä-lə-jist, -pa-\ *noun*

neu·rop·a·thy \nu-'rä-pə-thē, nyu-\ *noun, plural* **-thies** [International Scientific Vocabulary] (1857)
: an abnormal and usually degenerative state of the nervous system or nerves; *also* : a systemic condition that stems from a neuropathy — **neu·ro·path·ic** \,nur-ə-'pa-thik, ,nyur-\ *adjective* — **neu·ro·path·i·cal·ly** \-thi-k(ə-)lē\ *adverb*

neu·ro·pep·tide \,nur-ə-'pep-,tīd, ,nyur-\ *noun* (1975)
: an endogenous peptide that influences neural activity or functioning

neu·ro·phar·ma·col·o·gy \,nur-ō-,fär-mə-'kä-lə-jē, ,nyur-\ *noun* (1950)
1 : a branch of medical science dealing with the action of drugs on and in the nervous system
2 : the properties and reactions of a drug on and in the nervous system — **neu·ro·phar·ma·co·log·i·cal** \-kə-'lä-ji-kəl\ *also* **neu·ro·phar·ma·co·log·ic** \-jik\ *adjective* — **neu·ro·phar·ma·col·o·gist** \-'kä-lə-jist\ *noun*

neu·ro·phys·i·ol·o·gy \-,fi-zē-'ä-lə-jē\ *noun* (1868)
: physiology of the nervous system — **neu·ro·phys·i·o·log·i·cal** \-ə-'lä-ji-kəl\ *also* **neu·ro·phys·i·o·log·ic** \-jik\ *adjective* — **neu·ro·phys·i·o·log·i·cal·ly** \-ji-k(ə-)lē\ *adverb* — **neu·ro·phys·i·ol·o·gist** \-'ä-lə-jist\ *noun*

neu·ro·psy·chi·a·try \-sə-'kī-ə-trē, -sī-\ *noun* (1918)
: a branch of medicine concerned with both neurology and psychiatry — **neu·ro·psy·chi·at·ric** \-,sī-kē-'a-trik\ *adjective* — **neu·ro·psy·chi·at·ri·cal·ly** \-tri-k(ə-)lē\ *adverb* — **neu·ro·psy·chi·a·trist** \-sə-'kī-ə-trist, -sī-\ *noun*

neu·ro·psy·chol·o·gy \-sī-'kä-lə-jē\ *noun* (circa 1893)
: a science concerned with the integration of psychological observations on behavior and the mind with neurological observations on the brain and nervous system — **neu·ro·psy·cho·log·i·cal** \-,sī-kə-'lä-ji-kəl\ *adjective* — **neu·ro·psy·chol·o·gist** \-sī-'kä-lə-jist\ *noun*

neu·rop·ter·an \nu-'räp-tə-rən, nyu-\ *noun* [ultimately from Greek *neur-* + *pteron* wing — more at FEATHER] (circa 1842)
: any of an order (Neuroptera) of usually net-winged insects that include the lacewings and ant lions — **neuropteran** *adjective* — **neu·rop·ter·ous** \-rəs\ *adjective*

neu·ro·ra·di·ol·o·gy \,nur-ō-,rā-dē-'ä-lə-jē, ,nyur-\ *noun* (1938)
: radiology of the nervous system — **neu·ro·ra·dio·log·i·cal** \-ə-'lä-ji-kəl\ *adjective* — **neu·ro·ra·di·ol·o·gist** \-'ä-lə-jist\ *noun*

neu·ro·sci·ence \-'sī-ən(t)s\ *noun* (1963)
: a branch (as neurophysiology) of the life sciences that deals with the anatomy, physiology, biochemistry, or molecular biology of nerves and nervous tissue and especially with their relation to behavior and learning — **neu·ro·sci·en·tif·ic** \-,sī-ən-'ti-fik\ *adjective* — **neu·ro·sci·en·tist** \-'sī-ən-tist\ *noun*

neu·ro·se·cre·tion \-si-'krē-shən\ *noun* (1941)
1 : the process of producing a secretion by nerve cells
2 : a secretion produced by neurosecretion — **neu·ro·se·cre·to·ry** \-'krē-tə-rē\ *adjective*

neu·ro·sen·so·ry \-'sen(t)-sə-rē, -'sen(t)s-rē\ *adjective* (1929)
: of or relating to afferent nerves

neu·ro·sis \nu-'rō-səs, nyu-\ *noun, plural* **-ro·ses** \-,sēz\ [New Latin] (circa 1784)
: a mental and emotional disorder that affects only part of the personality, is accompanied by a less distorted perception of reality than in a psychosis, does not result in disturbance of the use of language, and is accompanied by various physical, physiological, and mental disturbances (as visceral symptoms, anxieties, or phobias)

neu·ros·po·ra \nu-'räs-p(ə-)rə, nyu-\ *noun* [New Latin, from *neur-* + *spora* spore] (1928)
: any of a genus (*Neurospora* of the family Sordariaceae) of ascomycetous fungi which are used extensively in genetic research and have black perithecia and persistent asci and some of which have salmon-pink or orange spore masses and are severe pests in bakeries

neu·ro·sur·gery \-'sər-jə-rē, -'sərj-rē\ *noun* (1904)
: surgery of nervous structures (as nerves, the brain, or the spinal cord) — **neu·ro·sur·geon** \-'sər-jən\ *noun* — **neu·ro·sur·gi·cal** \-'sər-ji-kəl\ *adjective*

¹neu·rot·ic \nu-'rä-tik\ *adjective* (1873)
: of, relating to, constituting, or affected with neurosis — **neu·rot·i·cal·ly** \-ti-k(ə-)lē\ *adverb*

²neurotic *noun* (1896)
1 : one affected with a neurosis
2 : an emotionally unstable individual

neu·rot·i·cism \nu-'rä-tə-,si-zəm, nyu-\ *noun* (1900)
: a neurotic character, condition, or trait

neu·ro·tox·ic \,nur-ō-'täk-sik, ,nyur-\ *adjective* (circa 1903)
: toxic to the nerves or nervous tissue — **neu·ro·tox·ic·i·ty** \-,täk-'si-sə-tē\ *noun*

neu·ro·tox·in \-'täk-sən\ *noun* [International Scientific Vocabulary] (1902)
: a poisonous complex especially of protein that acts on the nervous system

neu·ro·trans·mis·sion \-tran(t)s-'mi-shən, -tranz-\ *noun* (1961)
: the transmission of nerve impulses across a synapse

neu·ro·trans·mit·ter \-tran(t)s-'mi-tər, -tranz-\ *noun* (1961)
: a substance (as norepinephrine or acetylcholine) that transmits nerve impulses across a synapse

neu·ro·trop·ic \-'trä-pik\ *adjective* [International Scientific Vocabulary] (1903)
: having an affinity for or localizing selectively in nerve tissue ⟨a *neurotropic* virus⟩

neu·ru·la \'nur-ə-lə, 'nyur-, -yə-lə\ *noun, plural* **-lae** \-,lē\ *or* **-las** [New Latin, from *neur-* + Latin *-ula* -ule] (circa 1890)
: an early vertebrate embryo which follows the gastrula and in which nervous tissue begins to differentiate and the basic pattern of the vertebrate begins to emerge — **neu·ru·la·tion** \,nur-ə-'lā-shən, ,nyur-, -yə-\ *noun*

neus·ton \'nu-,stän, 'nyu-\ *noun* [German, from Greek, neuter of *neustos* swimming, from *nein* to swim — more at NATANT] (1928)
: minute organisms that float in the surface film of water

¹neu·ter \'nu-tər, 'nyu-\ *adjective* [Middle English *neutre*, from Middle French & Latin; Middle French *neutre*, from Latin *neuter*, literally, neither, from *ne-* not + *uter* which of two — more at NO, WHETHER] (14th century)
1 a : of, relating to, or constituting the gender that ordinarily includes most words or grammatical forms referring to things classed as neither masculine nor feminine **b** : neither active nor passive : INTRANSITIVE
2 : taking no side : NEUTRAL
3 : lacking or having imperfectly developed or nonfunctional generative organs ⟨the worker bee is *neuter*⟩

²neuter *noun* (15th century)
1 a : a noun, pronoun, adjective, or inflectional form or class of the neuter gender **b** : the neuter gender
2 : one that is neutral
3 a : WORKER 2 **b** : a spayed or castrated animal

³neuter *transitive verb* (1903)
: CASTRATE, ALTER

¹neu·tral \'nu-trəl, 'nyu-\ *noun* (15th century)
1 : one that is neutral
2 : a neutral color
3 : a position of disengagement (as of gears)

²neutral *adjective* [Middle French, from (assumed) Medieval Latin *neutralis*, from Latin, of neuter gender, from *neutr-, neuter*] (1549)
1 : not engaged on either side; *specifically* : not aligned with a political or ideological grouping ⟨a *neutral* nation⟩
2 : of or relating to a neutral state or power ⟨*neutral* territory⟩

3 a : not decided or pronounced as to characteristics **:** INDIFFERENT **b** (1) **:** ACHROMATIC (2) **:** nearly achromatic **c** (1) **:** NEUTER 3 (2) **:** lacking stamens or pistils **d :** neither acid nor basic **e :** not electrically charged
4 : produced with the tongue in the position it has when at rest ⟨the *neutral* vowels of \ə-'bəv\ *above*⟩
— **neu·tral·ly** \-trə-lē\ *adverb*
— **neu·tral·ness** *noun*
neu·tral·ise *British variant of* NEUTRALIZE
neu·tral·ism \'nü-trə-,li-zəm, 'nyü-\ *noun* (1579)
1 : NEUTRALITY
2 : a policy or the advocacy of neutrality especially in international affairs
— **neu·tral·ist** \-list\ *noun*
— **neu·tral·is·tic** \,nü-trə-'lis-tik, ,nyü-\ *adjective*
neu·tral·i·ty \nü-'tra-lə-tē, nyü-\ *noun* (15th century)
: the quality or state of being neutral; *especially* **:** refusal to take part in a war between other powers
neu·tral·i·za·tion \,nü-trə-lə-'zā-shən, ,nyü-\ *noun* (1808)
1 : an act or process of neutralizing
2 : the quality or state of being neutralized
neu·tral·ize \'nü-trə-,līz, 'nyü-\ *verb* **-ized; -iz·ing** (1759)
transitive verb
1 : to make chemically neutral
2 a : to counteract the activity or effect of **:** make ineffective ⟨propaganda that is difficult to *neutralize*⟩ **b :** KILL, DESTROY
3 : to make electrically inert by combining equal positive and negative quantities
4 : to invest (as a territory or a nation) with conventional or obligatory neutrality conferring inviolability during a war
5 : to make neutral by blending with the complementary color
6 : to give (as a pair of phonemes) a nondistinctive form or pronunciation ⟨\t\ and \d\ are *neutralized* when pronounced as flaps⟩
intransitive verb
: to undergo neutralization
— **neu·tral·iz·er** *noun*
neutral red *noun* (1890)
: a basic dye used chiefly as a biological stain and acid-base indicator
neutral spirits *noun plural but singular or plural in construction* (1919)
: ethyl alcohol of 190 or higher proof used especially for blending other alcoholic liquors
neu·tri·no \nü-'trē-(,)nō, nyü-\ *noun, plural* **-nos** [Italian, from *neutro* neutral, neuter, from Latin *neutr-, neuter*] (1934)
: an uncharged elementary particle that is believed to be massless or to have a very small mass, that has any of three forms, and that interacts only rarely with other particles
— **neu·tri·no·less** \-ləs\ *adjective*
neu·tron \'nü-,trän, 'nyü-\ *noun* [probably from *neutral*] (1932)
: an uncharged elementary particle that has a mass nearly equal to that of the proton and is present in all known atomic nuclei except the hydrogen nucleus
— **neu·tron·ic** \nü-'trä-nik, nyü-\ *adjective*
neutron activation analysis *noun* (1951)
: an analytical method used to determine the chemical elements comprising a material by bombarding it with neutrons to produce radioactive atoms whose radiations are indicative of the elements present — called also *neutron activation*
neutron bomb *noun* (1959)
: a nuclear bomb designed to produce lethal neutrons but less blast and fire damage than other nuclear bombs
neutron star *noun* (1934)
: a hypothetical dense celestial object that consists primarily of closely packed neutrons and that results from the collapse of a much larger stellar body

¹neu·tro·phil \'nü-trə-,fil, 'nyü-\ *or* **neu·tro·phil·ic** \,nü-trə-'fi-lik, ,nyü-\ *adjective* [International Scientific Vocabulary *neutro-* (from Latin *neutr-, neuter* neither) + *-phil*] (circa 1890)
: staining to the same degree with acid or basic dyes ⟨*neutrophil* granulocytes⟩
²neutrophil *noun* (1897)
: a granulocyte that is the chief phagocytic white blood cell of the blood
né·vé \nā-'vā\ *noun* [French dialect (Swiss), from (assumed) Vulgar Latin *nivatum*, from Latin *niv-, nix* snow — more at SNOW] (1843)
: the partially compacted granular snow that forms the surface part of the upper end of a glacier; *broadly* **:** a field of granular snow
nev·er \'ne-vər\ *adverb* [Middle English, from Old English *nǣfre*, from *ne* not + *ǣfre* ever — more at NO] (before 12th century)
1 : not ever **:** at no time ⟨*never* saw her before⟩
2 : not in any degree **:** not under any condition ⟨*never* the wiser for his experience⟩
never mind *conjunction* (1954)
: MUCH LESS, LET ALONE — used especially in negative contexts to add to one term another denoting something less likely ⟨with this knee I can hardly walk, *never mind* run⟩
nev·er·more \,ne-vər-'mōr, -'mȯr\ *adverb* (12th century)
: never again
nev·er–nev·er land \,ne-vər-'ne-vər-\ *noun* (1907)
: an ideal or imaginary place
nev·er·the·less \,ne-vər-thə-'les\ *adverb* (14th century)
: in spite of that **:** HOWEVER ⟨her childish but *nevertheless* real delight —Richard Corbin⟩
ne·vus \'nē-vəs\ *noun, plural* **ne·vi** \-,vī\ [New Latin, from Latin *naevus*] (circa 1836)
: a congenital pigmented area on the skin **:** BIRTHMARK
¹new \'nü, *chiefly British* 'nyü, *in place names usually* (,)nü *or* nə *or* (,)ni\ *adjective* [Middle English, from Old English *nīwe*; akin to Old High German *niuwi* new, Latin *novus*, Greek *neos*] (before 12th century)
1 : having existed or having been made but a short time **:** RECENT, MODERN
2 a (1) **:** having been seen, used, or known for a short time **:** NOVEL ⟨rice was a *new* crop for the area⟩ (2) **:** UNFAMILIAR ⟨visit *new* places⟩ **b :** being other than the former or old ⟨a steady flow of *new* money⟩
3 : having been in a relationship or condition but a short time ⟨*new* to the job⟩
4 a : beginning as the resumption or repetition of a previous act or thing ⟨a *new* day⟩ ⟨the *new* edition⟩ **b :** made or become fresh ⟨awoke a *new* person⟩
5 : different from one of the same category that has existed previously ⟨*new* realism⟩
6 : of dissimilar origin and usually of superior quality ⟨introducing *new* blood⟩
7 *capitalized* **:** MODERN 3; *especially* **:** having been in use after medieval times ☆
— **new·ish** \'nü-ish, 'nyü-\ *adjective*
— **new·ness** *noun*
²new *adverb* (before 12th century)
: NEWLY, RECENTLY — usually used in combination
New Age *adjective* (1956)
1 : of, relating to, or being a late 20th century social movement drawing on ancient concepts especially from Eastern and American Indian traditions and incorporating such themes as holism, concern for nature, spirituality, and metaphysics
2 : of, relating to, or being a soft soothing form of instrumental music often used to promote relaxation
¹new·born \-,bȯrn\ *adjective* (14th century)
1 : recently born
2 : born anew
²newborn *noun, plural* **newborn** *or* **newborns** (1879)
: a newborn individual

New·burg *or* **New·burgh** \'nü-,bərg, 'nyü-\ *adjective* [origin unknown] (1902)
: served with a sauce made of cream, butter, sherry, and egg yolks ⟨lobster *Newburg*⟩ ⟨shrimp *Newburg*⟩
New·cas·tle disease \'nü-,ka-səl-, 'nyü-; n(y)ü-'\ *noun* [*Newcastle* upon Tyne, England] (1927)
: a destructive virus disease of birds and especially domestic fowl that involves respiratory and nervous symptoms
new·com·er \'nü-,kə-mər, 'nyü-\ *noun* (15th century)
1 : one recently arrived
2 : BEGINNER
New Criticism *noun* (1941)
: an analytic literary criticism that is marked by concentration on the language, imagery, and emotional or intellectual tensions in literary works
— **New Critic** *noun*
— **New Critical** *adjective*
New Deal *noun* [from the supposed resemblance to the situation of freshness and equality of opportunity afforded by a fresh deal in a card game] (1932)
: the legislative and administrative program of President F. D. Roosevelt designed to promote economic recovery and social reform during the 1930s; *also* **:** the period of this program
— **New Dealer** *noun*
— **New Deal·ish** \-'dē-lish\ *adjective*
— **New Deal·ism** \-'dē(ə)-,li-zəm\ *noun*
new drug *noun* (circa 1951)
: a drug that has not been declared safe and effective by qualified experts under the conditions prescribed, recommended, or suggested in the label and that may be a new chemical formula or an established drug prescribed for use in a new way
new economics *noun plural but usually singular in construction* (1928)
: an economic concept that is a logical extension of Keynesianism and that holds that appropriate fiscal and monetary maneuvering can maintain healthy economic growth and prosperity indefinitely
new·el \'nü-əl, 'nyü-\ *noun* [Middle English *nowell*, from Middle French *nouel* stone of a fruit, from Late Latin *nucalis* like a nut, from Latin *nuc-, nux* nut — more at NUT] (14th century)
1 : an upright post about which the steps of a circular staircase wind
2 : a post at the foot of a straight stairway or one at a landing
New English Bible *noun* (1957)
: a translation of the Bible by a British interdenominational committee first published in its entirety in 1970
new·fan·gled \'nü-'faŋ-gəld\ *adjective* [Middle English, from *newefangel*, from *new* + (assumed) Old English *-fangol*, from Old English

\ə\ abut \ᵊ\ kitten \ər\ further \a\ ash \ā\ ace
\ä\ mop, mar \au̇\ out \ch\ chin \e\ bet \ē\ easy
\g\ go \i\ hit \ī\ ice \j\ job \ŋ\ sing \ō\ go
\ȯ\ law \ȯi\ boy \th\ thin \th̶\ the \ü\ loot \u̇\ foot
\y\ yet \zh\ vision *see also* Guide to Pronunciation

fōn (past participle *fangen*) to take, seize — more at PACT] (14th century)
1 : attracted to novelty
2 : of the newest style or kind ⟨had many *newfangled* gadgets in the kitchen⟩
— **new·fan·gled·ness** *noun*

new–fash·ioned \-'fa-shənd\ *adjective* (1592)
1 : made in a new fashion or form
2 : UP-TO-DATE

new·found \-'faund\ *adjective* (15th century)
: newly found ⟨a *newfound* friend⟩

New·found·land \'nü-fən(d)-lənd, 'nyü-, -,land; n(y)ü-'faund-lənd\ *noun* [*Newfoundland*, Canada] (1773)
: any of a breed of very large heavy highly intelligent, black, black and white, or bronze dogs developed in Newfoundland

Newfoundland

New·gate \'nü-,gāt, 'nyü-, -gət\ *noun* (14th century)
: a London prison razed in 1902

New Greek *noun* (circa 1958)
: Greek as used by the Greeks since the end of the medieval period

New Hebrew *noun* (circa 1959)
: the Hebrew language in use in present-day Israel

new·ie \'nü-ē, 'nyü-\ *noun* (circa 1945)
: something new

New Jer·sey tea \nü-'jər-zē-, nyü-\ *noun* [*New Jersey*, state of U.S.; from the use of its leaves as a substitute for tea during the American Revolution] (1759)
: a low deciduous shrub (*Ceanothus americanus*) of the buckthorn family that is found in the eastern U.S. and has dull green leaves and small white flowers borne in large terminal panicles

New Je·ru·sa·lem \-jə-'rü-s(ə-)ləm, -zə-ləm; -'rüz-ləm\ *noun* [from the phrase "the holy city, *New Jerusalem*" (Revelation 21:2)] (1535)
1 : the final abode of souls redeemed by Christ
2 : an ideal earthly community

New Journalism *noun* (1967)
: journalism that features the author's subjective responses to people and events and that often includes fictional elements meant to illuminate and dramatize those responses

New Latin *noun* (circa 1889)
: Latin as used since the end of the medieval period especially in scientific description and classification

New Left *noun* (1960)
: a political movement originating especially among students in the 1960s, favoring confrontational tactics, often breaking with traditional leftist ideologies, and associated especially with antiwar, antinuclear, feminist, and ecological issues
— **new leftist** *noun, often N&L capitalized*

new·ly \'nü-lē, 'nyü-\ *adverb* (before 12th century)
1 : LATELY, RECENTLY ⟨a *newly* married couple⟩
2 : ANEW, AFRESH

new·ly·wed \-,wed\ *noun* (1918)
: a person recently married

new·mar·ket \'nü-,mär-kət, 'nyü-\ *noun* [*Newmarket*, England] (1837)
: a long close-fitting coat worn in the 19th century

new math *noun* (1964)
: basic mathematics taught with emphasis on abstraction and the principles of set theory — called also *new mathematics*

new moon *noun* (before 12th century)
1 : the moon's phase when it is in conjunction with the sun so that its dark side is toward the earth; *also* **:** the thin crescent moon seen shortly after sunset for a few days after the actual occurrence of the new moon phase
2 : the first day of each Jewish month marked by a special liturgy

New Right *noun* (1966)
: a political movement made up especially of Protestants, opposed especially to secular humanism, and concerned with issues especially of church and state, patriotism, laissez-faire economics, pornography, and abortion

news \'nüz, 'nyüz\ *noun plural but singular in construction, often attributive* (15th century)
1 a : a report of recent events **b :** previously unknown information ⟨I've got *news* for you⟩
2 a : material reported in a newspaper or news periodical or on a newscast **b :** matter that is newsworthy
3 : NEWSCAST □
— **news·less** \-ləs\ *adjective*

news agency *noun* (1873)
: an organization that supplies news to subscribing newspapers, periodicals, and newscasters

news·agent \'nüz-,ā-jənt, 'nyüz-\ *noun* (1851)
chiefly British **:** NEWSDEALER

news·boy \-,boi\ *noun* (1764)
: one who delivers or sells newspapers

news·break \-,brāk\ *noun* (1944)
: a newsworthy event

news·cast \-,kast\ *noun* [*news* + broad*cast*] (circa 1939)
: a radio or television broadcast of news
— **news·cast·er** \-,kas-tər\ *noun*

news conference *noun* (1946)
: PRESS CONFERENCE

news·deal·er \-,dē-lər\ *noun* (1861)
: a dealer in newspapers, magazines, and often paperback books

news·hound \-,haund\ *noun* (1918)
: an aggressive journalist

news·let·ter \-,le-tər\ *noun* (1903)
: a small publication (as a leaflet or newspaper) containing news of interest chiefly to a special group

news·mag·a·zine \-,ma-gə-,zēn, -'zēn\ *noun* (1923)
1 : a usually weekly magazine devoted chiefly to summarizing and analyzing news
2 : MAGAZINE 4c

news·man \-mən, -,man\ *noun* (1596)
: one who gathers, reports, or comments on the news **:** REPORTER, CORRESPONDENT

news·mon·ger \-,mən-gər, -,mäŋ-\ *noun* (1592)
: one who is active in gathering and repeating news; *especially* **:** GOSSIP

¹news·pa·per \'nüz-,pā-pər, 'nyüz-, -n(y)üs-\ *noun* (1670)
1 : a paper that is printed and distributed usually daily or weekly and that contains news, articles of opinion, features, and advertising
2 : an organization that publishes a newspaper
3 : the paper of a newspaper **:** NEWSPRINT

²newspaper *intransitive verb* (1943)
: to do newspaper work

news·pa·per·man \-,man\ *noun* (1806)
: one who owns or is employed by a newspaper

news·pa·per·wom·an \-,wu-mən\ *noun* (1881)
: a woman who owns or is employed by a newspaper

new·speak \'nü-,spēk, 'nyü-\ *noun, often capitalized* [*Newspeak*, a language "designed to diminish the range of thought," in the novel *1984* (1949) by George Orwell] (1950)
: propagandistic language marked by euphemism, circumlocution, and the inversion of customary meanings **:** DOUBLE-TALK 2

news·peo·ple \'nüz-,pē-pəl, 'nyüz-\ *noun plural* (1972)
: REPORTERS

news·per·son \-,pər-s°n\ *noun* (1973)
: REPORTER

news·print \-,print\ *noun* (1909)
: paper made chiefly from groundwood pulp and used mostly for newspapers

news·read·er \-,rē-dər\ *noun* (1925)
chiefly British **:** one who broadcasts the news

news·reel \-,rēl\ *noun* (1916)
: a short movie dealing with current events

news·room \-,rüm, -,rum\ *noun* (1929)
1 : a place (as an office) where news is prepared for publication or broadcast
2 : NEWSSTAND

news·stand \-,stand\ *noun* (1872)
: a place (as an outdoor stall) where newspapers and periodicals are sold

New Style *adjective* (1615)
: using or according to the Gregorian calendar

news·week·ly \-,wē-klē\ *noun* (1947)
: a weekly newspaper or newsmagazine

news·wom·an \-,wu-mən\ *noun* (1928)
: a woman who is a reporter

news·wor·thy \-,wər-thē\ *adjective* (1932)
: sufficiently interesting to the general public to warrant reporting (as in a newspaper)
— **news·wor·thi·ness** \-thē-nəs\ *noun*

news·writ·ing \-,rī-tiŋ\ *noun* (1916)
: JOURNALISM 1a

newsy \'nü-zē, 'nyü-\ *adjective* **news·i·er; -est** (1832)
1 : containing or filled with news ⟨*newsy* letters⟩
2 : NEWSWORTHY
— **news·i·ness** *noun*

newt \'nüt, 'nyüt\ *noun* [Middle English, alteration (resulting from misdivision of *an ewte*) of *ewte* — more at EFT] (15th century)
: any of various small semiaquatic salamanders (as of the genus *Triturus*)

newt

New Testament *noun* (14th century)
: the second part of the Christian Bible comprising the canonical Gospels and Epistles and also the book of Acts and book of Revelation
— see BIBLE table

new·ton \'nü-t°n, 'nyü-\ *noun* [Sir Isaac *Newton*] (1904)
: the unit of force in the meter-kilogram-second system equal to the force required to impart an acceleration of one meter per second per second to a mass of one kilogram

new town *noun* (1918)
: an urban development comprising a small to medium-sized city with a broad range of housing and planned industrial, commercial, and recreational facilities

new wave *noun, often N&W capitalized* (1960)
1 : a cinematic movement that is characterized by improvisation, abstraction, and subjective

□ USAGE

news The habit of sounding a \y\ in *news* is British, but it is also practiced by some Americans who insist that the more common American pronunciation \nüz\ is incorrect. This opinion rests on the belief that the *ew* should be sounded \yü\, as in *few, hew,* and *pew.* At work in the usual American pronunciation of *news* is a type of dissimilation in which the sound \y\, formed with the tongue tip near the roof of the mouth, is lost when it follows a similarly formed sound such as \d,j,l,n,r,s,t,z,ch,sh,zh\. Even in modern British speech the pronunciation of words like *lewd, sewer,* and *suit* generally lacks a \y\ before the \ü\, showing that such dissimilation is not mere American carelessness. Similarly, the absence of \y\ in the American pronunciation of words like *dew, duty, astute,* and *presume* is standard and acceptable, not uncultivated.

symbolism and that often makes use of experimental photographic techniques
2 : a new movement in a particular field
3 : rock music characterized by cohesive ensemble playing and usually lyrics which express anger and social discontent
4 : DERNIER CRI; *especially* **:** fashion that is strikingly outrageous
— **new–wave** \'nü-ˌwāv, 'nyü-, -ˌwāv\ *adjective*
— **new wav·er** \-ˈwā-vər\ *noun*
New World *noun* (1555)
: WESTERN HEMISPHERE; *especially* **:** the continental landmass of North and South America
New Year *noun* (13th century)
1 : the calendar year about to start or recently started
2 a : NEW YEAR'S DAY **b :** the first days of a calendar year
3 : ROSH HASHANAH
New Year's Day *noun* (13th century)
: the first day of the calendar year observed as a legal holiday in many countries
¹next \'nekst\ *adjective* [Middle English, from Old English *nīehst*, superlative of *nēah* nigh — more at NIGH] (before 12th century)
1 : immediately adjacent (as in place, rank, or time)
2 : any other considered hypothetically ⟨knew it as well as the *next* man⟩
²next *preposition* (before 12th century)
: nearest or adjacent to
³next *adverb* (14th century)
1 : in the time, place, or order nearest or immediately succeeding ⟨*next* we drove home⟩ ⟨the *next* closest school⟩
2 : on the first occasion to come ⟨when *next* we meet⟩
next–door \'neks(t)-ˈdōr, -ˈdȯr\ *adjective* (1749)
: located or living in the next building, house, apartment, or room; *broadly* **:** NEARBY, ADJACENT
next door *adverb* (1579)
: in or to the next building, house, apartment, or room ⟨lives *next door*⟩; *broadly* **:** in or at an adjacent place
— **next door to :** NEXT TO
next friend *noun* (1579)
: a person admitted to or appointed by a court to act for the benefit of a person (as an infant) lacking full legal capacity
next of kin (1766)
: one or more persons in the nearest degree of relationship to another person
¹next to *preposition* (1633)
1 : immediately following or adjacent to
2 : in comparison to ⟨*next to* you I'm wealthy⟩
²next to *adverb* (1667)
: very nearly **:** ALMOST ⟨it was *next to* impossible to see in the fog⟩
nex·us \'nek-səs\ *noun, plural* **nex·us·es** \-sə-səz\ *or* **nex·us** \-səs, -ˌsüs\ [Latin, from *nectere* to bind] (1663)
1 : CONNECTION, LINK; *also* **:** a causal link
2 : a connected group or series
3 : CENTER, FOCUS
Nez Percé *or* **Nez Perce** \'nez-ˈpərs, 'nes-ˈpers, ÷ˈnā-per-ˈsā\ *noun, plural* **Nez Percé** *or* **Nez Per·cés** *same or* -ˈpər-ˌsəz, -ˈper-, ÷-per-ˈsā(z)\ *or* **Nez Perce** *or* **Nez Per·ces** *same or* -ˈpər-səz, -ˈper-\ [French, literally, pierced nose] (1812)
1 : a member of an American Indian people of Idaho, Washington, and Oregon
2 : the language of the Nez Percé people
ngul·trum \eŋ-ˈgúl-trəm, en-\ *noun* [Tibetan] (1973)
— see MONEY table
ngwee \eŋ-ˈgwē, en-\ *noun, plural* **ngwee** [Bemba, literally, bright] (1966)
— see *kwacha* at MONEY table
ni·a·cin \'nī-ə-sən\ *noun* [nicotinic acid + ¹-in] (1942)
: NICOTINIC ACID; *also* **:** NICOTINAMIDE

ni·a·cin·amide \ˌnī-ə-'si-nə-ˌmīd\ *noun* (1942)
: NICOTINAMIDE
Ni·ag·a·ra \nī-'a-g(ə-)rə\ *noun* [*Niagara* Falls] (1841)
: an overwhelming flood **:** TORRENT ⟨a *Niagara* of protests⟩
ni·al·amide \nī-'a-lə-ˌmīd\ *noun* [*nicotinic* acid + *amyl* + *amide*] (1959)
: a synthetic antidepressant drug $C_{16}H_{18}N_4O_2$ that is an inhibitor of monoamine oxidase
nib \'nib\ *noun* [probably alteration of *neb*] (1585)
1 : BILL, BEAK
2 a : the sharpened point of a quill pen **b :** PEN POINT; *also* **:** each of the two divisions of a pen point
3 : a small pointed or projecting part
¹nib·ble \'ni-bəl\ *verb* **nib·bled; nib·bling** \-b(ə-)liŋ\ [origin unknown] (circa 1512)
transitive verb
1 a : to bite gently **b :** to eat or chew in small bits
2 : to take away bit by bit ⟨waves *nibbling* the shore⟩
intransitive verb
1 : to take gentle, small, or cautious bites; *also* **:** SNACK
2 : to deal with something as if by nibbling
— **nib·bler** \-b(ə-)lər\ *noun*
²nibble *noun* (1658)
1 : an act of nibbling
2 : a very small quantity or portion (as of food); *also* **:** SNACK
3 : a tentative expression of interest
Ni·be·lung \'nē-bə-ˌlúŋ\ *noun, plural* **-lungs** *also* **-lung·en** \-ˌlúŋ-ən\ [German] (1861)
1 : a member of a race of dwarfs in Germanic legend
2 : any of the followers of Siegfried
3 : any of the Burgundian kings in the medieval German *Nibelungenlied*
nibs \'nibz\ *noun plural but singular in construction* [origin unknown] (circa 1821)
: an important or self-important person — usually used in the phrases *his nibs* or *her nibs* as if a title of honor
ni·cad \'nī-ˌkad\ *noun* [¹*nickel* + *cad*mium] (1965)
: a rechargeable dry cell that has a nickel cathode and a cadmium anode
nic·co·lite \'ni-kə-ˌlīt\ *noun* [New Latin *niccolum* nickel, probably from Swedish *nickel*] (1868)
: a pale copper-red usually massive mineral of metallic luster that is essentially a nickel arsenide
nice \'nīs\ *adjective* **nic·er; nic·est** [Middle English, foolish, wanton, from Old French, from Latin *nescius* ignorant, from *nescire* not to know — more at NESCIENCE] (14th century)
1 *obsolete* **a :** WANTON, DISSOLUTE **b :** COY, RETICENT
2 a : showing fastidious or finicky tastes **:** PARTICULAR **b :** exacting in requirements or standards **:** PUNCTILIOUS
3 : possessing, marked by, or demanding great or excessive precision and delicacy
4 *obsolete* **:** TRIVIAL
5 a : PLEASING, AGREEABLE ⟨a *nice* time⟩ ⟨a *nice* person⟩ **b :** well-executed ⟨*nice* shot⟩ **c :** APPROPRIATE, FITTING
6 a : socially acceptable **:** WELL-BRED **b :** VIRTUOUS, RESPECTABLE
7 : POLITE, KIND ⟨that's *nice* of you to say⟩ ◊
synonym see CORRECT
— **nice** *adverb*
— **nice·ly** *adverb*
— **nice·ness** *noun*
Ni·cene \'nī-ˌsēn, nī-'\ *adjective* [Middle English, from Late Latin *nicaenus*, from Latin *Nicaea* Nicaea, from Greek *Nikaia*] (14th century)
1 : of or relating to Nicaea or the Nicaeans

2 : of or relating to the ecumenical church council held in Nicaea in A.D. 325 or to the Nicene Creed
Nicene Creed *noun* (circa 1569)
: a Christian creed expanded from a creed issued by the first Nicene Council, beginning "I believe in one God," and used in liturgical worship
nice–nel·ly \'nīs-ˈne-lē\ *adjective, often 2d N capitalized* [from the name *Nelly*] (1925)
1 : marked by euphemism
2 : PRUDISH
— **nice nelly** *noun, often 2d N capitalized*
— **nice–nel·ly·ism** \-ˌi-zəm\ *noun, often 2d N capitalized*
nice·ty \'nī-sə-tē, -stē\ *noun, plural* **-ties** [Middle English *nicete*, from Middle French *niceté* foolishness, from *nice*, adjective] (14th century)
1 : the quality or state of being nice
2 : an elegant, delicate, or civilized feature ⟨enjoy the *niceties* of life⟩
3 : a fine point or distinction **:** SUBTLETY ⟨the *niceties* of table manners⟩
4 : careful attention to details **:** delicate exactness **:** PRECISION
5 : delicacy of taste or feeling **:** FASTIDIOUSNESS
¹niche \'nich, ÷'nēsh\ *noun* [French, from Middle French, from *nicher* to nest, from (assumed) Vulgar Latin *nidicare*, from Latin *nidus* nest — more at NEST] (1611)
1 a : a recess in a wall especially for a statue **b :** something that resembles a niche
2 a : a place, employment, status, or activity for which a person or thing is best fitted **b :** a habitat supplying the factors necessary for the existence of an organism or species **c :** the ecological role of an organism in a community especially in regard to food consumption **d :** a specialized market

niche 1a

²niche *transitive verb* **niched; nich·ing** (1752)
: to place in or as if in a niche
Ni·chrome \'nī-ˌkrōm\ *trademark*

◇ WORD HISTORY
nice This bland-looking, workaday word has undergone a remarkable semantic evolution over the course of its history. *Nice* was borrowed from Old French, in which it meant "foolish, simpleminded." (French had in turn borrowed the word at an early date from the Latin adjective *nescius* "ignorant, not knowing," a derivative of the verb *nescire* "to not know.") In Middle English, from the original sense "foolish, frivolous," the word developed an extraordinarily diverse range of meanings, from "fainthearted, cowardly" to "fastidious, scrupulous" to "lascivious." Of these only the "fastidious" sense has survived into the 19th and 20th centuries, in phrases like "a nice distinction." Not until the 18th century did *nice* come to be employed in the now common meaning "pleasing, agreeable"; in the 1864 revision of Noah Webster's *American Dictionary of the English Language*, this usage was still considered both improper and a peculiarity of the British, the American equivalent being *fine*. Succeeding Merriam-Webster dictionaries labeled the sense as colloquial until the 1934 publication of *Webster's New International Dictionary, Second Edition*.

— used for an alloy of nickel, chromium, and iron that is commonly used in the heating elements of electrical appliances

¹nick \'nik\ *noun* [Middle English *nyke,* probably alteration of *nocke* nock] (15th century)
1 a : a small notch or groove **b :** a break in one strand of two-stranded DNA caused by a missing phosphodiester bond **c :** a small cut incurred in shaving
2 : a final critical moment ⟨in the *nick* of time⟩
3 *slang British* **:** PRISON; *also* **:** POLICE STATION
4 *British* **:** CONDITION ⟨in good *nick*⟩
²nick (1523)
transitive verb
1 : to jot down **:** RECORD
2 a : to make a nick in **:** NOTCH, CHIP **b :** to cut into or wound slightly ⟨a bullet *nicked* his leg⟩
3 : to cut short ⟨cold weather, which *nicked* steel and automobile output —*Time*⟩
4 : to catch at the right point or time
5 : CHEAT, OVERCHARGE
6 a *slang British* **:** ARREST **b** *slang British* **:** STEAL
intransitive verb
1 : to make petty attacks **:** SNIPE
2 : to complement one another genetically and produce superior offspring
nick·el *also* **nick·le** \'ni-kəl\ *noun* [probably from Swedish *nickel,* from German *Kupfernickel* niccolite, probably from *Kupfer* copper + *Nickel* goblin; from the deceptive copper color of niccolite] (1755)
1 : a silver-white hard malleable ductile metallic element capable of a high polish and resistant to corrosion that is used chiefly in alloys and as a catalyst — see ELEMENT table
2 a (1) **:** the U.S. 5-cent piece regularly containing 25 percent nickel and 75 percent copper (2) **:** the Canadian 5-cent piece **b :** five cents
3 : a pass defense in football that employs five defensive backs
¹nick·el–and–dime \,ni-kəl-ən-'dīm\ *adjective* (1950)
1 : involving or offering only a small amount of money
2 : SMALL-TIME
²nickel–and–dime *transitive verb* **nick·eled–and–dimed** \,ni-kəld-ən-'dīmd\ *or* **nick·el–and–dimed** \-ən-'dīmd\; **nick·el·ing–and–dim·ing** \-'dī-miŋ\ *or* **nickel–and–diming** (1961)
: to impair, weaken, or defeat gradually (as through a series of small incursions or excessive attention to detail)
nick·el·if·er·ous \,ni-kə-'li-f(ə-)rəs\ *adjective* (1821)
: containing nickel
nick·el·ode·on \,ni-kə-'lō-dē-ən\ *noun* [probably from *nickel* + *-odeon* (as in *melodeon* music hall)] (1907)
1 : an early movie theater to which admission usually cost five cents
2 : JUKEBOX
nickel silver *noun* (1860)
: GERMAN SILVER
¹nick·er \'ni-kər\ *intransitive verb* **nick·ered; nick·er·ing** \-k(ə-)riŋ\ [perhaps alteration of *neigh*] (1641)
: NEIGH, WHINNY
— **nicker** *noun*
²nicker *noun* [perhaps from *nicker* one that nicks] (1910)
slang British **:** ¹POUND 2a
nick·nack *variant of* KNICKKNACK
¹nick·name \'nik-,nām\ *noun* [Middle English *nekename* additional name, alteration (resulting from misdivision of *an ekename*) of *ekename,* from *eke* eke, also + *name* name] (15th century)
1 : a usually descriptive name given instead of or in addition to the one belonging to a person, place, or thing
2 : a familiar form of a proper name (as of a person or a city) ◆
²nickname *transitive verb* (1536)

1 : MISNAME, MISCALL
2 : to give a nickname to
— **nick·nam·er** *noun*
ni·co·ti·a·na \ni-,kō-shē-'a-nə, -'ä-nə, -'ā-nə\ *noun* [New Latin, from *herba nicotiana,* literally, Nicot's herb, from Jean *Nicot* (died 1600) French diplomat and scholar] (1600)
: any of several tobaccos (as *Nicotiana alata*) grown for their showy flowers
nic·o·tin·amide \,ni-kə-'tē-nə-,mīd, -'ti-\ *noun* [International Scientific Vocabulary] (1895)
: a compound $C_6H_6N_2O$ of the vitamin B complex found especially as a constituent of coenzymes and used similarly to nicotinic acid
nicotinamide adenine dinucleotide *noun* (1961)
: NAD
nicotinamide adenine dinucleotide phosphate *noun* (1962)
: NADP
nic·o·tine \'ni-kə-,tēn\ *noun* [French, from New Latin *nicotiana*] (1819)
: a poisonous alkaloid $C_{10}H_{14}N_2$ that is the chief active principle of tobacco and is used as an insecticide
nic·o·tin·ic \,ni-kə-'tē-nik, -'ti-\ *adjective* [International Scientific Vocabulary] (1873)
: relating to, resembling, producing, or mediating the effects produced by nicotine on nerve fibers at autonomic ganglia and at the neuromuscular junctions of voluntary muscle which increases activity in small doses and inhibits it in larger doses ⟨*nicotinic* receptors⟩ — compare MUSCARINIC
nicotinic acid *noun* (1873)
: an acid $C_6H_5NO_2$ of the vitamin B complex found widely in animals and plants and used especially against pellagra — called also *niacin*
nic·ti·tate \'nik-tə-,tāt\ *intransitive verb* **-tated; -tat·ing** [alteration of *nictate* to wink, from Latin *nictatus,* past participle of *nictare* — more at CONNIVE] (circa 1834)
: WINK
nictitating membrane *noun* (1713)
: a thin membrane found in many vertebrates at the inner angle or beneath the lower lid of the eye and capable of extending across the eyeball
ni·dic·o·lous \nī-'di-kə-ləs\ *adjective* [Latin *nidus* nest + English *-colous* — more at NEST] (circa 1902)
1 : reared for a time in a nest
2 : sharing the nest of another kind of animal
ni·di·fi·ca·tion \,ni-də-fə-'kā-shən, ,nī-\ *noun* [Medieval Latin *nidification-, nidificatio,* from Latin *nidificare* to build a nest, from *nidus* nest] (1658)
: the act, process, or technique of building a nest
ni·dif·u·gous \nī-'di-fyə-gəs\ *adjective* [Latin *nidus* nest + *fugere* to flee — more at FUGITIVE] (1896)
: leaving the nest soon after hatching
ni·dus \'nī-dəs\ *noun, plural* **ni·di** \'nī-,dī\ *or* **ni·dus·es** [New Latin, from Latin] (1742)
1 : a nest or breeding place; *especially* **:** a place or substance in an animal or plant where bacteria or other organisms lodge and multiply
2 : a place where something originates, develops, or is located
niece \'nēs\ *noun* [Middle English *nece* granddaughter, niece, from Old French *niece,* from Late Latin *neptia,* from Latin *neptis;* akin to Latin *nepot-, nepos* grandson, nephew — more at NEPHEW] (14th century)
1 : a daughter of one's brother, sister, brother-in-law, or sister-in-law
2 : an illegitimate daughter of an ecclesiastic
¹ni·el·lo \nē-'e-(,)lō\ *noun, plural* **ni·el·li** \-(,)lē\ *or* **niellos** [Italian, from Medieval Latin *nigellum,* from neuter of Latin *nigellus* blackish, diminutive of *niger* black] (1816)
1 : any of several black enamel-like alloys usually of sulfur with silver, copper, and lead

2 : the art or process of decorating metal with incised designs filled with niello
3 : a piece of metal or an object decorated with niello
²niello *transitive verb* (1866)
: to inlay or ornament with niello
ni·fed·i·pine \nə-'fe-də-,pēn, -pən\ *noun* [probably *nitr-* + *-fe-* (from *phenyl*) + *-dipine* (by alteration & shortening from *pyridine*)] (1974)
: a calcium channel blocker $C_{17}H_{18}N_2O_6$ that is a coronary vasodilator used especially in the treatment of angina pectoris
Nifl·heim \'ni-vəl-,hām\ *noun* [Old Norse *Niflheimr*]
: the abode of the dead in Norse mythology
¹nif·ty \'nif-tē\ *adjective* **nif·ti·er; -est** [origin unknown] (1865)
: very good **:** very attractive **:** FINE ⟨*nifty* clothes⟩
— **nif·ti·ly** \'nif-tə-lē\ *adverb*
²nifty *noun, plural* **nifties** (1923)
: something that is nifty; *especially* **:** a clever or neatly turned phrase or joke
Ni·ger–Con·go \,nī-jər-'kän-(,)gō\ *noun* [*Niger* (river) + *Congo* (river)] (circa 1950)
: a language family that includes the Mande and Kwa branches and that is spoken by most of the indigenous peoples of west, central, and south Africa
¹nig·gard \'ni-gərd\ *noun* [Middle English, of Scandinavian origin; akin to Old Norse *hnøggr* niggardly; akin to Old English *hnēaw* niggardly] (14th century)
: a meanly covetous and stingy person **:** MISER
— **niggard** *adjective*
²niggard (circa 1600)
intransitive verb
obsolete **:** to act niggardly
transitive verb
obsolete **:** to treat in a niggardly manner
nig·gard·ly \-lē\ *adjective* (1571)
1 : grudgingly mean about spending or granting **:** BEGRUDGING
2 : provided in meanly limited supply
synonym see STINGY
— **nig·gard·li·ness** *noun*
— **niggardly** *adverb*
nig·ger \'ni-gər\ *noun* [alteration of earlier *neger,* from Middle French *negre,* from Spanish or Portuguese *negro,* from *negro* black, from Latin *niger*] (1700)
1 : a black person — usually taken to be offensive
2 : a member of any dark-skinned race — usually taken to be offensive
3 : a member of a socially disadvantaged class of persons ⟨it's time for somebody to lead all of America's *niggers* . . . all the people who feel left out of the political process —Ron Dellums⟩ □
¹nig·gle \'ni-gəl\ *verb* **nig·gled; nig·gling**

◇ **WORD HISTORY**

nickname The earliest sense of *nickname* is a descriptive name given to a person, or even a place, in addition to the proper name, while today it can also refer to a shortened or familiar form of a proper name. In Middle English the word expressed the first of these senses very explicitly. The noun *eke,* meaning "addition or extension," was combined with *name,* and thus an *ekename* was an additional name. By the 15th century *an ekename,* by misperception of the boundary between article and noun, was taken to be *a nekename,* and both *ekename* and *nekename* begin to appear in writing. The latter, in the modern form *nickname,* eventually superseded the former. The noun *eke* involved in the history of *nickname* is related both to the verb *eke,* as in "to eke out a living," and to the once common but now archaic adverb *eke* "too, also."

\-g(ə-)liŋ\ [origin unknown] (circa 1616)
intransitive verb
1 a : TRIFLE **b :** to spend too much effort on minor details
2 : to find fault constantly in a petty way **:** CARP ⟨she haggles, she *niggles,* she wears out our patience —Virginia Woolf⟩
3 : GNAW
transitive verb
: to give stingily or in tiny portions
— **nig·gler** \-g(ə-)lər\ *noun*
²**niggle** *noun* (1886)
chiefly British **:** a trifling doubt, objection, or complaint
nig·gling \'ni-g(ə-)liŋ\ *adjective* (1599)
: PETTY; *also* **:** bothersome or persistent especially in a petty or tiresome way ⟨*niggling* injuries⟩
— **niggling** *noun*
— **nig·gling·ly** \-lē\ *adverb*
¹**nigh** \'nī\ *adverb* [Middle English, from Old English *nēah;* akin to Old High German *nāh,* adverb, nigh, preposition, nigh, after, Old Norse *nā-* nigh] (before 12th century)
1 : near in place, time, or relationship — often used with *on, onto,* or *unto*
2 : NEARLY, ALMOST
²**nigh** *adjective* (before 12th century)
1 : CLOSE, NEAR
2 *chiefly dialect* **:** DIRECT, SHORT
3 : being on the left side ⟨the *nigh* horse⟩
³**nigh** *preposition* (before 12th century)
: NEAR
⁴**nigh** (13th century)
transitive verb
: to draw or come near to **:** APPROACH
intransitive verb
: to draw near
¹**night** \'nīt\ *noun* [Middle English, from Old English *niht;* akin to Old High German *naht* night, Latin *noct-, nox,* Greek *nykt-, nyx*] (before 12th century)
1 : the time from dusk to dawn when no sunlight is visible
2 a : an evening or night taken as an occasion or point of time ⟨the opening *night*⟩ **b :** an evening set aside for a particular purpose
3 a : the quality or state of being dark **b :** a condition or period felt to resemble the darkness of night: as (1) **:** a period of dreary inactivity or affliction (2) **:** absence of moral values **c :** the beginning of darkness **:** NIGHTFALL
— **night·less** \-ləs\ *adjective*
²**night** *adjective* (before 12th century)
1 : of, relating to, or associated with the night ⟨*night* air⟩
2 : intended for use at night ⟨a *night* lamp⟩
3 a : existing, occurring, or functioning at night ⟨*night* baseball⟩ ⟨a *night* nurse⟩ **b :** active or functioning best at night ⟨*night* people⟩
night and day *adverb* (before 12th century)
: all the time **:** CONTINUALLY
night blindness *noun* (1754)
: reduced visual capacity in faint light (as at night)
— **night–blind** \'nīt-,blīnd\ *adjective*
night–blooming cereus *noun* (1832)
: any of several night-blooming cacti; *especially* **:** a slender sprawling or climbing cactus (*Selenicereus grandiflorus*) often cultivated for its large showy fragrant white flowers
night-cap \'nīt-,kap\ *noun* (14th century)
1 : a cloth cap worn with nightclothes
2 : a usually alcoholic drink taken at the end of the day
3 : the final race or contest of a day's sports; *especially* **:** the second game of a baseball doubleheader
night-clothes \-,klō(th)z\ *noun plural* (1602)
: garments for wear in bed
¹**night-club** \-,kləb\ *noun* (1894)
: a place of entertainment open at night usually serving food and liquor, having a floor

show, and providing music and space for dancing
²**nightclub** *intransitive verb* (1936)
: to patronize nightclubs
— **night·club·ber** *noun*
night court *noun* (1934)
: a criminal court in a large city that sits at night (as for the summary disposition of criminal charges and the granting of bail)
night crawler *noun* (1924)
: EARTHWORM; *especially* **:** a large earthworm found on the soil surface at night
night-dress \'nīt-,dres\ *noun* (circa 1714)
1 : NIGHTGOWN
2 : NIGHTCLOTHES
night-fall \'nīt-,fȯl\ *noun* (1700)
: the close of the day **:** DUSK
night-glow \-,glō\ *noun* (1951)
: airglow seen during the night
night-gown \-,gaȯn\ *noun* (14th century)
1 *archaic* **:** DRESSING GOWN
2 : a loose garment for wear in bed
night-hawk \-,hȯk\ *noun* (1611)
1 a : any of a genus (*Chordeiles*) of American nightjars related to the whippoorwill **b :** a common European nightjar (*Caprimulgus europaeus*)
2 : a person who habitually is active late at night

nighthawk 1a

night heron *noun* (1784)
: any of various widely distributed nocturnal or crepuscular herons (especially genus *Nycticorax*)
night-ie \'nī-tē\ *or* **nighty** *noun, plural* **night-ies** [*night*gown + *-ie*] (1871)
: a nightgown for a woman or child
night-in-gale \'nī-t°n-,gāl, -tiŋ-\ *noun* [Middle English, alteration of Old English *nihtegale,* from *niht* + *galan* to sing — more at YELL] (13th century)
: any of several Old World thrushes (genus *Erithacus* and especially *E. megarhynchos*) noted for the sweet usually nocturnal song of the male; *also* **:** any of various other birds that sing at night

nightingale

night-jar \'nīt-,jär\ *noun* [from its harsh sound] (1630)
: any of a family (Caprimulgidae) of medium-sized long-winged crepuscular or nocturnal birds (as the whippoorwills and nighthawks) having a short bill, short legs, and soft mottled plumage and feeding on insects which they catch on the wing — called also *goatsucker*
night latch *noun* (1854)
: a door lock having a spring bolt operated from the outside by a key and from the inside by a knob
night letter *noun* (1910)
: a telegram sent at night at a reduced rate for delivery the following morning
night-life \'nīt-,līf\ *noun* (1852)
: the activity of or entertainment provided for pleasure-seekers at night (as in nightclubs); *also* **:** establishments providing nightlife
night-light \-,līt\ *noun* (1839)
: a light kept burning throughout the night
¹**night-long** \-,lȯŋ\ *adjective* (1850)
: lasting the whole night ⟨*nightlong* festivities⟩
²**night-long** \-'lȯŋ\ *adverb* (1870)
: through the whole night
¹**night-ly** \-lē\ *adjective* (before 12th century)
1 : happening, done, or used by night or every night

2 : of or relating to the night or every night
²**nightly** *adverb* (15th century)
: every night; *also* **:** at or by night
night-mare \'nīt-,mar, -,mer\ *noun* [Middle English, from ¹*night* + ¹*mare*] (14th century)
1 : an evil spirit formerly thought to oppress people during sleep
2 : a frightening dream that usually awakens the sleeper
3 : something (as an experience, situation, or object) having the monstrous character of a nightmare or producing a feeling of anxiety or terror
— **nightmare** *adjective*
— **night·mar·ish** \-,mar-ish, -,mer-\ *adjective*
— **night·mar·ish·ly** *adverb*
night owl *noun* (circa 1846)
: a person who keeps late hours at night
night rail \-,rāl\ *noun* [*night* + *rail,* a woman's loose garment] (1554)
archaic **:** NIGHTGOWN
night raven *noun* (before 12th century)
: a bird that cries at night
night rider *noun* (1877)
: a member of a secret band who ride masked at night doing acts of violence for the purpose of punishing or terrorizing
nights \'nīts\ *adverb* (before 12th century)
: in the nighttime repeatedly **:** on any night ⟨works *nights*⟩
night-scope \'nīt-,skōp\ *noun* (1972)
: an optical device usually using infrared radiation that enables a person to see objects in the dark better
night-shade \-,shād\ *noun* (before 12th century)
1 : any of a genus (*Solanum* of the family Solanaceae, the nightshade family) of herbs, shrubs, and trees having alternate leaves, cymose flowers, and fruits that are berries and including some poisonous weeds, various ornamentals, and important crop plants (as the potato and eggplant)
2 : BELLADONNA 1
night-shirt \-,shərt\ *noun* (1857)
: a nightgown resembling a shirt
night-side \-,sīd\ *noun* (1848)

◇ WORD HISTORY
nightmare During the Middle Ages there was a widespread belief in an evil spirit that visits and lies on people as they sleep. Known as a *mare* in Old English, this evil spirit, or incubus, became known in Middle English as a *nightmare* after the time of its supposed visitation. It was not until the 16th century that the word *nightmare* came to refer to a frightening dream. Again, evil spirits were involved, for they were credited with causing such dreams. *Mare* in the sense of "a female horse," is an entirely different, unrelated word, though it too is from Old English.

\ə\ **abut** \ᵊ\ **kitten** \ər\ **further** \a\ **ash** \ā\ **ace**
\ä\ **mop, mar** \aȯ\ **out** \ch\ **chin** \e\ **bet** \ē\ **easy**
\g\ **go** \i\ **hit** \ī\ **ice** \j\ **job** \ŋ\ **sing** \ō\ **go**
\ȯ\ **law** \ȯi\ **boy** \th\ **thin** \th̲\ **the** \ü\ **loot** \u̇\ **foot**
\y\ **yet** \zh\ **vision** *see also* Guide to Pronunciation

: the side of a celestial body (as the earth, the moon, or a planet) not in daylight

night soil *noun* (circa 1774)
: human excrement used especially for fertilizing the soil

night·spot \'nīt-ˌspät\ *noun* (1936)
: NIGHTCLUB

night·stand \-ˌstand\ *noun* (1892)
: NIGHT TABLE

night·stick \-ˌstik\ *noun* (1887)
: a police officer's club

night table *noun* (1788)
: a small bedside table or stand

night·time \-ˌtīm\ *noun, often attributive* (14th century)
: the time from dusk to dawn

night·walk·er \-ˌwȯ-kər\ *noun* (15th century)
1 : a person who roams about at night especially with criminal intent
2 : PROSTITUTE, STREETWALKER

ni·hil·ism \'nī-(h)ə-ˌli-zəm, 'nē-\ *noun* [German *Nihilismus*, from Latin *nihil* nothing — more at NIL] (circa 1817)
1 a : a viewpoint that traditional values and beliefs are unfounded and that existence is senseless and useless **b** : a doctrine that denies any objective ground of truth and especially of moral truths
2 a (1) : a doctrine or belief that conditions in the social organization are so bad as to make destruction desirable for its own sake independent of any constructive program or possibility (2) *capitalized* : the program of a 19th century Russian party advocating revolutionary reform and using terrorism and assassination **b** : TERRORISM
— **ni·hil·ist** \-list\ *noun or adjective*
— **ni·hil·is·tic** \ˌnī-(h)ə-'lis-tik, ˌnē-\ *adjective*

-nik *noun suffix* [Yiddish, from Polish & Ukrainian]
: one connected with or characterized by being ⟨beat*nik*⟩

Ni·ke \'nī-kē\ *noun* [Greek *Nīkē*]
: the Greek goddess of victory

nil \'nil\ *noun* [Latin, nothing, contraction of *nihil*, from Old Latin *nihilum*, from *ne-* not + *hilum* trifle — more at NO] (1833)
: NOTHING, ZERO
— **nil** *adjective*

nile green *noun, often N capitalized* [*Nile* River, Africa] (1871)
: a pale yellow green

Nile perch *noun* (1926)
: a large predaceous food fish (*Lates niloticus*) of the rivers and lakes of northern and central Africa that may exceed 200 pounds (91 kilograms) in weight

nill \'nil\ *verb* [Middle English *nilen*, from Old English *nyllan*, from *ne* not + *wyllan* to wish — more at NO, WILL] (before 12th century)
intransitive verb
archaic : to be unwilling : will not ⟨will you *nill* you, I will marry you —Shakespeare⟩
transitive verb
archaic : REFUSE

Ni·lot·ic \nī-'lä-tik\ *adjective* [Latin *Niloticus*, from Greek *Neilōtēs*, from *Neilos* Nile] (1653)
1 : of or relating to the Nile or the peoples of the Nile basin
2 : of, relating to, or being the languages of the Nilotic people

nil·po·tent \'nil-ˌpō-t³nt\ *adjective* [Latin *nil* nothing + *potent-, potens* having power — more at POTENT] (1870)
: equal to zero when raised to some power ⟨*nilpotent* matrices⟩

¹nim \'nim\ *verb* **nimmed; nim·ming** [earlier *nim* to take, from Middle English *nimen*, from Old English *niman*] (12th century)
transitive verb
archaic : STEAL, FILCH
intransitive verb
archaic : THIEVE

²nim *noun* [probably from ¹*nim*] (1901)

: any of various games in which counters are laid out in one or more piles and each player in turn draws one or more counters with the object of taking the last counter, forcing the opponent to take it, or taking the most or fewest counters

nim·ble \'nim-bəl\ *adjective* **nim·bler** \-b(ə-)lər\; **nim·blest** \-b(ə-)ləst\ [Middle English *nimel*, from Old English *numol* holding much, from *niman* to take; akin to Old High German *neman* to take, Greek *nemein* to distribute, manage, *nomos* pasture, *nomos* usage, custom, law] (14th century)
1 : quick and light in motion : AGILE ⟨*nimble* fingers⟩
2 a : marked by quick, alert, clever conception, comprehension, or resourcefulness ⟨a *nimble* mind⟩ **b** : RESPONSIVE, SENSITIVE ⟨a *nimble* listener⟩
— **nim·ble·ness** \-bəl-nəs\ *noun*
— **nim·bly** \-blē\ *adverb*

nim·bo·stra·tus \ˌnim-bō-'strā-təs, -'stra-\ *noun* [New Latin, from Latin *nimbus* + New Latin *stratus* stratus] (circa 1909)
: a low dark gray rainy cloud layer — see CLOUD illustration

nim·bus \'nim-bəs\ *noun, plural* **nim·bi** \-ˌbī, -ˌbē\ *or* **nim·bus·es** [Latin, rainstorm, cloud; probably akin to Latin *nebula* cloud — more at NEBULA] (1616)
1 a : a luminous vapor, cloud, or atmosphere about a god or goddess when on earth **b** : a cloud or atmosphere (as of romance) about a person or thing
2 : an indication (as a circle) of radiant light or glory about the head of a drawn or sculptured divinity, saint, or sovereign
3 a : a rain cloud **b** : THUNDERHEAD; *also* : CUMULUS 2

nimbus 2

ni·mi·e·ty \ni-'mī-ə-tē\ *noun, plural* **-ties** [Late Latin *nimietas*, from Latin *nimius* too much, adjective, from *nimis*, adverb] (circa 1564)
: EXCESS, REDUNDANCY

nim·i·ny–pim·i·ny \ˌni-mə-nē-'pi-mə-nē\ *adjective* [probably alteration of *namby-pamby*] (1786)
: affectedly refined : FINICKY

Nim·rod \'nim-ˌräd\ *noun* [Hebrew *Nimrōdh*]
1 : a descendant of Ham represented in Genesis as a mighty hunter and a king of Shinar
2 *not capitalized* : HUNTER

nin·com·poop \'nin-kəm-ˌpüp, 'niŋ-\ *noun* [origin unknown] (1676)
: FOOL, SIMPLETON
— **nin·com·poop·ery** \-ˌpü-pə-rē\ *noun*

nine \'nīn\ *noun* [Middle English, from *nyne*, adjective, from Old English *nigon;* akin to Old High German *niun* nine, Latin *novem*, Greek *ennea*] (before 12th century)
1 — see NUMBER table
2 : the ninth in a set or series ⟨wears a *nine*⟩
3 : something having nine units or members: as **a** *capitalized* : the nine Muses **b** : a baseball team **c** : the first or last nine holes of an 18-hole golf course
— **nine** *adjective*
— **nine** *pronoun, plural in construction*
— **to the nines 1** : to perfection **2** : in a highly elaborate or showy manner ⟨dressed *to the nines*⟩

nine days' wonder *noun* (1594)
: something or someone that creates a short-lived sensation — called also *nine day wonder*

nine·fold \'nīn-ˌfōld, -'fōld\ *adjective* (before 12th century)
1 : being nine times as great or as many
2 : having nine units or members
— **nine·fold** \-'fōld\ *adverb*

nine·pin \-ˌpin\ *noun* (1580)

1 *plural but singular in construction* : a bowling game resembling tenpins played without the headpin
2 : a pin used in ninepins

nine·teen \nīn-'tēn, 'nīn-ˌ\ *noun* [Middle English *nynetene*, adjective, from Old English *nigontene*, from *nigon* + *-tīene* (akin to Old English *tīen* ten) — more at TEN] (before 12th century)
— see NUMBER table
— **nineteen** *adjective*
— **nineteen** *pronoun, plural in construction*
— **nine·teenth** \-'tēn(t)th, -ˌtēn(t)th\ *adjective or noun*

nine·ty \'nīn-tē\ *noun, plural* **nineties** [Middle English *ninety*, adjective, from Old English *nigontig*, short for *hundnigontig*, from *hundnigontig*, noun, group of 90, from *hund-*, literally, hundred + *nigon* nine + *-tig* group of 10; akin to Old English *tīen* ten] (before 12th century)
1 — see NUMBER table
2 *plural* : the numbers 90 to 99; *specifically* : the years 90 to 99 in a lifetime or century
— **nine·ti·eth** \-tē-əth\ *adjective or noun*
— **ninety** *adjective*
— **ninety** *pronoun, plural in construction*

nin·hy·drin \nin-'hī-drən\ *noun* [from *Ninhydrin*, a trademark] (1913)
: a poisonous crystalline oxidizing agent $C_9H_6O_4$ used especially as an analytical reagent

nin·ja \'nin-jə, -ˌ(ˌ)jä\ *noun, plural* **ninja** *also* **ninjas** [Japanese, from *nin-* persevere + *-ja* person] (1975)
: a person trained in ancient Japanese martial arts and employed especially for espionage and assassinations

nin·ny \'ni-nē\ *noun, plural* **ninnies** [perhaps by shortening & alteration from *an innocent*] (1593)
: FOOL, SIMPLETON

nin·ny·ham·mer \'ni-nē-ˌha-mər\ *noun* (1592)
: NINNY

ni·non \'nē-ˌnän\ *noun* [probably from French *Ninon*, nickname for *Anne*] (1911)
: a smooth sheer fabric

ninth \'nīn(t)th\ *noun, plural* **ninths** \'nīn(t)s, 'nīn(t)ths\ (13th century)
1 — see NUMBER table
2 a : a musical interval embracing an octave and a second **b** : the tone at this interval **c** : a chord containing a ninth
— **ninth** *adjective or adverb*

ninth cranial nerve *noun* (circa 1961)
: GLOSSOPHARYNGEAL NERVE

ni·o·bate \'nī-ə-ˌbāt\ *noun* [New Latin *niobium* + English ¹*-ate*] (1845)
: a salt containing an anionic grouping of niobium and oxygen

Ni·o·be \'nī-ə-bē\ *noun* [Latin, from Greek *Niobē*]
: a daughter of Tantalus and wife of Amphion who while weeping for her slain children is turned into a stone from which her tears continue to flow

ni·o·bi·um \nī-'ō-bē-əm\ *noun* [New Latin, from Latin *Niobe;* from its occurrence in tantalite] (1845)
: a lustrous light gray ductile metallic element that resembles tantalum chemically and is used in alloys — see ELEMENT table

¹nip \'nip\ *verb* **nipped; nip·ping** [Middle English *nippen;* akin to Old Norse *hnippa* to prod] (14th century)
transitive verb
1 a : to catch hold of and squeeze tightly between two surfaces, edges, or points : PINCH, BITE ⟨the dog *nipped* his ankle⟩ **b** : to pinch in (as a garment) ⟨a dress *nipped* at the waist⟩
2 a : to sever by or as if by pinching sharply **b** : to destroy the growth, progress, or fulfillment of ⟨*nipped* in the bud⟩
3 : to injure or make numb with cold : CHILL

4 : SNATCH, STEAL
5 : to defeat by a small margin
intransitive verb
1 : to move briskly, nimbly, or quickly
2 *chiefly British* **:** to make a quick trip
²**nip** *noun* (1549)
1 : something that nips: as **a** *archaic* **:** a sharp
biting comment **b :** a sharp stinging cold ⟨a
nip in the air⟩ **c :** a biting or pungent flavor
: TANG ⟨cheese with a *nip*⟩
2 : the act of nipping **:** PINCH, BITE
3 : the region of a squeezing or crushing de-
vice (as a calender) where the rolls or jaws are
closest together
4 : a small portion
³**nip** *noun* [probably from *nipperkin*, a liquor
container] (circa 1796)
: a small quantity of liquor **:** SIP; *also* **:** a very
small bottle of liquor
⁴**nip** *intransitive verb* **nipped; nip·ping**
(1887)
: to take liquor in nips **:** TIPPLE
ni·pa \'nē-pə\ *noun* [probably from Italian,
from Malay *nipah* nipa palm] (1779)
: thatch made of leaves of the nipa palm
nip and tuck \ˌnip-ən(d)-'tək\ *adjective or ad-
verb* (1832)
: being so close that the lead or advantage
shifts rapidly from one opponent to another
nipa palm *noun* (1882)
: a semiaquatic creeping palm
(*Nipa fruticans*) found chiefly
from India to Melanesia
nip·per \'ni-pər\ *noun* (1541)
1 : any of various devices (as
pincers) for nipping — usu-
ally used in plural
2 a *chiefly British* **:** a boy
employed as a helper (as of a
carter or hawker) **b :** CHILD;
especially **:** a small boy
nip·ping \'ni-piŋ\ *adjective*
(1547)
: SHARP, CHILLING
— **nip·ping·ly** \-lē\ *adverb*
nip·ple \'ni-pəl\ *noun* [earlier
neble, nible, probably dimin-
utive of *neb, nib*] (1530)

nipa palm

1 : the protuberance of a mammary gland
upon which in the female the lactiferous ducts
open and from which milk is drawn
2 a : an artificial teat through which a bottle-
fed infant nurses **b :** a device with an orifice
through which the discharge of a liquid can be
regulated
3 a : a protuberance resembling or suggesting
the nipple of a breast **b :** a small projection
through which oil or grease is injected into
machinery
4 : a pipe coupling consisting of a short piece
of threaded tubing
— **nip·pled** \-pəld\ *adjective*
Nip·pon·ese \ˌni-pə-'nēz, -'nēs\ *adjective*
[*Nippon,* Japan] (1859)
: JAPANESE
— **Nipponese** *noun*
nip·py \'ni-pē\ *adjective* **nip·pi·er; -est**
(1575)
1 : marked by a tendency to nip ⟨a *nippy* dog⟩
2 : brisk, quick, or nimble in movement
: SNAPPY
3 : PUNGENT, SHARP
4 : CHILLY, CHILLING ⟨a *nippy* day⟩
— **nip·pi·ly** \'ni-pə-lē\ *adverb*
— **nip·pi·ness** \'ni-pē-nəs\ *noun*
nip–up \'nip-ˌəp\ *noun* (1938)
: a spring from a supine position to a standing
position
nir·va·na \nir-'vä-nə, (ˌ)nər-\ *noun, often capi-
talized* [Sanskrit *nirvāṇa,* literally, act of extin-
guishing, from *nis-* out + *vāti* it blows —
more at WIND] (1801)
1 : the final beatitude that transcends suffer-
ing, karma, and samsara and is sought espe-
cially in Buddhism through the extinction of
desire and individual consciousness

2 a : a place or state of oblivion to care, pain,
or external reality; *also* **:** BLISS, HEAVEN **b :** a
goal hoped for but apparently unattainable
: DREAM
— **nir·van·ic** \-'vä-nik, -'va-\ *adjective*
Ni·san \'ni-sᵊn, nē-'sän\ *noun* [Hebrew *Nīsān*]
(14th century)
: the 7th month of the civil year or the 1st
month of the ecclesiastical year in the Jewish
calendar — see MONTH table
ni·sei \nē-'sā, 'nē-ˌ\ *noun, plural* **nisei** *often
capitalized* [Japanese, literally, second genera-
tion, from *ni* second + *sei* generation] (1929)
: a son or daughter of Japanese immigrants
who is born and educated in America and es-
pecially in the U.S.
ni·si \'nī-ˌsī\ *adjective* [Latin, unless, from *ne-
not + si* if] (1836)
: taking effect at a specified time unless previ-
ously modified or avoided by cause shown,
further proceedings, or a condition fulfilled ⟨a
decree *nisi*⟩
Nis·sen hut \'ni-sᵊn-\ *noun* [Peter N. *Nissen*
(died 1930) British mining engineer] (1932)
: a prefabricated shelter with a semicircular
arching roof of corrugated iron sheeting and a
concrete floor
ni·sus \'nī-səs\ *noun, plural* **ni·sus** \-səs,
-ˌsüs\ [Latin, from *niti* to lean, rely, strive;
akin to Latin *nictare* to wink — more at CON-
NIVE] (1699)
: a mental or physical effort to attain an end
: a perfective urge or endeavor
¹**nit** \'nit\ *noun* [Middle English *nite,* from Old
English *hnitu;* akin to Old High German *hniz*
nit, Greek *konid-, konis*] (before 12th century)
: the egg of a louse or other parasitic insect;
also **:** the insect itself when young
²**nit** *noun* (circa 1941)
chiefly British **:** NITWIT
nite *variant of* NIGHT
ni·ter \'nī-tər\ *noun* [Middle English *nitre* na-
tron, from Middle French, from Latin *nitrum,*
from Greek *nitron,* from Egyptian *ntry*] (1684)
1 : POTASSIUM NITRATE
2 *archaic* **:** CHILE SALTPETER
nit·ery *also* **nit·er·ie** \'nī-tə-rē\ *noun, plural*
nit·er·ies [*nite* + *-ery* (as in *eatery*); *niterie*
from *nite* + French *-erie -ery*] (circa 1934)
: NIGHTCLUB
nit·id \'ni-təd\ *adjective* [Latin *nitidus* —
more at NEAT] (circa 1656)
: BRIGHT, LUSTROUS
ni·ti·nol \'nī-tᵊn-ˌȯl, -ˌōl\ *noun* [nickel + *ti*tani-
um + *-nol* (from *N*aval *O*rdnance *L*aboratory,
where it was created)] (1968)
: a nonmagnetic alloy of titanium and nickel
that after being deformed returns to its original
shape upon being reheated
nit·pick \'nit-ˌpik\ *verb* [back-formation from
nit-picking] (1966)
intransitive verb
: to engage in nit-picking
transitive verb
: to criticize by nit-picking
— **nitpick** *noun*
— **nit·pick·er** *noun*
— **nit·picky** \-ˌpi-kē\ *adjective*
nit–pick·ing \'nit-ˌpi-kiŋ\ *noun* [¹*nit*] (1956)
: minute and usually unjustified criticism
nitr– *or* **nitro–** *combining form* [*niter*]
1 : nitrogen ⟨*nitr*ide⟩
2 *usually* **nitro–** **:** containing the univalent
group NO₂ composed of one nitrogen and two
oxygen atoms ⟨*nitro*benzene⟩
ni·trate \'nī-ˌtrāt, -trət\ *noun* [French, from *ni-
trique*] (1794)
1 : a salt or ester of nitric acid
2 : sodium nitrate or potassium nitrate used as
a fertilizer
nitrate of soda (1843)
: sodium nitrate used as a fertilizer
ni·tra·tion \nī-'trā-shən\ *noun* (1887)
: the process of adding a nitro group to an or-
ganic compound
— **ni·trate** \'nī-ˌtrāt\ *transitive verb*

— **ni·tra·tor** \-ˌtrā-tər\ *noun*
ni·tre *chiefly British variant of* NITER
ni·tric acid \'nī-trik-\ *noun* [French *nitrique,*
from *nitre* niter, from Middle French] (1794)
: a corrosive liquid inorganic acid HNO₃ used
especially as an oxidizing agent, in nitrations,
and in making organic compounds (as fertiliz-
ers, explosives, and dyes)
nitric oxide *noun* (1807)
: a colorless poisonous gas NO formed by ox-
idation of nitrogen or ammonia
¹**ni·tride** \'nī-ˌtrīd\ *noun* [International Scien-
tific Vocabulary] (1850)
: a binary compound of nitrogen with a more
electropositive element
²**nitride** *transitive verb* **ni·trid·ed; ni·trid·
ing** (1928)
: to case-harden (as steel) by causing the sur-
face to absorb nitrogen
ni·tri·fi·ca·tion \ˌnī-trə-fə-'kā-shən\ *noun*
(1827)
: the oxidation (as by bacteria) of ammonium
salts to nitrites and the further oxidation of ni-
trites to nitrates
ni·tri·fi·er \'nī-trə-ˌfī(-ə)r\ *noun* (1903)
: any of the nitrifying bacteria
ni·tri·fy·ing \'nī-trə-ˌfī-iŋ\ *adjective* [French
nitrifier to convert into nitrite, from *nitr-*]
(1827)
: active in or relating to nitrification ⟨*nitrifying*
organisms⟩ ⟨*nitrifying* activities⟩
nitrifying bacteria *noun plural* (1925)
: bacteria of a family (Nitrobacteraceae) com-
prising gram-negative bacteria commonly
found in the soil and obtaining energy through
the process of nitrification
ni·trile \'nī-trəl, -ˌtrīl\ *noun* [International Sci-
entific Vocabulary *nitr-* + *-il, -ile* (from Latin
-ilis ¹*-ile*)] (1848)
: an organic cyanide containing the group CN
which on hydrolysis yields an acid with elimi-
nation of ammonia
ni·trite \'nī-ˌtrīt\ *noun* (1800)
: a salt or ester of nitrous acid
¹**ni·tro** \'nī-(ˌ)trō\ *adjective* [*nitr-*] (1892)
: containing or being the univalent group NO₂
united through nitrogen
²**nitro** *noun, plural* **nitros** (1903)
: any of various nitrated products; *specifically*
: NITROGLYCERIN
ni·tro·ben·zene \ˌnī-trō-'ben-ˌzēn, -ben-'\
noun [International Scientific Vocabulary]
(1868)
: a poisonous yellow insoluble oil C₆H₅NO₂
with an almond odor that is used especially as
a solvent, as a mild oxidizing agent, and in
making aniline
ni·tro·cel·lu·lose \-'sel-yə-ˌlōs, -ˌlōz\ *noun*
[International Scientific Vocabulary] (1882)
: any of several nitric-acid esters of cellulose
used especially for making explosives, plas-
tics, and varnishes
ni·tro·fu·ran \ˌnī-trō-'fyu̇r-ˌan, -fyu̇-'ran\ *noun*
(1930)
: any of several nitro derivatives of furan used
as bacteria-inhibiting agents
ni·tro·gen \'nī-trə-jən\ *noun, often attributive*
[French *nitrogène,* from *nitre* niter + *-gène*
-gen] (1794)
: a colorless tasteless odorless element that as
a diatomic gas is relatively inert and consti-
tutes 78 percent of the atmosphere by volume
and that occurs as a constituent of all living
tissues — see ELEMENT table
— **ni·trog·e·nous** \nī-'trä-jə-nəs\ *adjective*
ni·tro·ge·nase \nī-'trä-jə-ˌnās, 'nī-trə-jə-
ˌnāz\ *noun* (1934)
: an enzyme of various nitrogen-fixing bacte-
ria that catalyzes the reduction of molecular
nitrogen to ammonia

\ə\ **abut** \ᵊ\ **kitten** \ər\ **further** \a\ **ash** \ā\ **ace**
\ä\ **mop, mar** \au̇\ **out** \ch\ **chin** \e\ **bet** \ē\ **easy**
\g\ **go** \i\ **hit** \ī\ **ice** \j\ **job** \ŋ\ **sing** \ō\ **go**
\ȯ\ **law** \ȯi\ **boy** \th\ **thin** \t̲h̲\ **the** \ü\ **loot** \u̇\ **foot**
\y\ **yet** \zh\ **vision** *see also* Guide to Pronunciation

nitrogen balance noun (1944)
: the difference between nitrogen intake and nitrogen loss in the body or the soil

nitrogen cycle noun (1908)
: a continuous series of natural processes by which nitrogen passes successively from air to soil to organisms and back to air or soil involving principally nitrogen fixation, nitrification, decay, and denitrification

nitrogen dioxide noun (1885)
: a toxic reddish brown gas NO_2 that is a strong oxidizing agent, is produced by combustion (as of fossil fuels), and is an atmospheric pollutant

nitrogen fixation noun (1895)
: the metabolic assimilation of atmospheric nitrogen into ammonia by soil microorganisms and especially rhizobia

nitrogen–fixer noun (1912)
: any of various soil microorganisms that are involved in nitrogen fixation

nitrogen–fixing adjective (1899)
: capable of nitrogen fixation ⟨nitrogen-fixing bacteria⟩

nitrogen mustard noun (1943)
: any of various toxic blistering compounds analogous to mustard gas but containing nitrogen instead of sulfur

nitrogen narcosis noun (1937)
: a state of euphoria and exhilaration that occurs when nitrogen in normal air enters the bloodstream at approximately seven times atmospheric pressure (as in deep-water diving) — called also rapture of the deep

nitrogen oxide noun (circa 1934)
: any of several oxides of nitrogen most of which are produced in combustion and are considered to be atmospheric pollutants: as **a** : NITRIC OXIDE **b** : NITROGEN DIOXIDE **c** : NITROUS OXIDE

nitrogen tetroxide noun (1885)
: a colorless toxic gas N_2O_4 that is a dimer of nitrogen dioxide and that in liquid form is used as an oxidizer in rocket engines

ni·tro·glyc·er·in or **ni·tro·glyc·er·ine** \ˌnī-trə-ˈglis-rən, -ˈgli-sə-\ noun [International Scientific Vocabulary] (1857)
: a heavy oily explosive poisonous liquid $C_3H_5N_3O_9$ used chiefly in making dynamites and in medicine as a vasodilator

ni·tro·meth·ane \ˌnī-trō-ˈme-ˌthān, British usually -ˈmē-\ noun (1872)
: a liquid nitroparaffin CH_3NO_2 that is used as an industrial solvent, in chemical synthesis, and as a fuel for rockets and high-performance engines

ni·tro·par·af·fin \-ˈpar-ə-fən\ noun [International Scientific Vocabulary] (1892)
: any of various nitro derivatives of alkanes

nitros- or **nitroso-** combining form [New Latin nitrosus nitrous]
: containing the group NO ⟨nitrosamine⟩

ni·tro·sa·mine \nī-ˈtrō-sə-ˌmēn\ noun (1878)
: any of various organic compounds which are characterized by the grouping NNO and some of which are powerful carcinogens

ni·trous \ˈnī-trəs\ adjective [New Latin nitrosus, from Latin, full of natron, from nitrum natron — more at NITER] (1601)
archaic : of, relating to, or containing niter

nitrous acid noun (1676)
: an unstable acid HNO_2 known only in solution or in the form of its salts

nitrous oxide noun (1800)
: a colorless gas N_2O that when inhaled produces loss of sensibility to pain preceded by exhilaration and sometimes laughter and is used especially as an anesthetic in dentistry and that is an atmospheric pollutant produced by combustion and a suspected contributor to greenhouse warming — called also laughing gas

nit·ty–grit·ty \ˈni-tē-ˌgri-tē, ˌni-tē-ˈ\ noun [origin unknown] (1963)

: what is essential and basic : specific practical details ⟨get down to the nitty-gritty of the problem⟩
— **nitty–gritty** adjective

nit·wit \ˈnit-ˌwit\ noun [probably from German dialect nit not + English wit] (circa 1922)
: a scatterbrained or stupid person

¹nix \ˈniks\ noun [German nichts nothing] (1789)
: NOTHING

²nix transitive verb (circa 1934)
: VETO, REJECT ⟨the court nixed the merger⟩

³nix adverb (circa 1909)
: NO — used to express disagreement or the withholding of permission; often used with on ⟨they said nix on our plan⟩

⁴nix noun [German, from Old High German nihhus; akin to Old English nicor water monster and perhaps to Greek nizein to wash] (1833)
: a water sprite of Germanic folklore

¹nix·ie \ˈnik-sē\ noun [German Nixe female nix, from Old High German nichessa, feminine of nihhus nix] (1816)
: ⁴NIX

²nix·ie also **nixy** \ˈnik-sē\ noun, plural **nix·ies** [¹nix + -ie] (circa 1890)
: a piece of mail that is undeliverable because illegibly or incorrectly addressed

Nix·ie \ˈnik-sē\ trademark
— used for an electronic indicator tube

ni·zam \ni-ˈzäm, ˈnī-ˌzam, nī-ˈ\ noun [Hindi nizām order, governor, from Arabic niẓām] (1768)
: one of a line of sovereigns of Hyderabad, India, reigning from 1713 to 1950
— **ni·zam·ate** \ni-ˈzä-ˌmāt, nī-ˈza-\ noun

¹no \ˈnō\ adverb [Middle English, from Old English nā, from ne not + ā always; akin to Old Norse & Old High German ne not, Latin ne-, Greek nē- — more at AYE] (before 12th century)
1 a chiefly Scottish : NOT **b** — used as a function word to express the negative of an alternative choice or possibility ⟨shall we go out to dinner or no⟩
2 : in no respect or degree — used in comparisons
3 : not so — used to express negation, dissent, denial, or refusal ⟨no, I'm not going⟩
4 — used with a following adjective to imply a meaning expressed by the opposite positive statement ⟨in no uncertain terms⟩
5 — used as a function word to emphasize a following negative or to introduce a more emphatic, explicit, or comprehensive statement
6 — used as an interjection to express surprise, doubt, or incredulity
7 — used in combination with a verb to form a compound adjective ⟨no-bake pie⟩

²no adjective (12th century)
1 a : not any ⟨no parking⟩ ⟨no disputing the decision⟩ **b** : hardly any : very little ⟨finished in no time⟩
2 : not a : quite other than a ⟨he's no expert⟩
3 — used in combination with a noun to form a compound adjective ⟨a no-nonsense realist⟩

³no \ˈnō\ noun, plural **noes** or **nos** \ˈnōz\ (1588)
1 : an act or instance of refusing or denying by the use of the word no : DENIAL
2 a : a negative vote or decision **b** plural : persons voting in the negative

No or **Noh** \ˈnō\ noun, plural **No** or **Noh** [Japanese nō, literally, talent] (1871)
: classic Japanese dance-drama having a heroic theme, a chorus, and highly stylized action, costuming, and scenery

no–account adjective (1845)
: of no account : TRIFLING ⟨her no-account relatives⟩

No·a·chi·an \nō-ˈā-kē-ən\ adjective [Hebrew Nōaḥ Noah] (1678)
1 : of or relating to the patriarch Noah or his time
2 : ANCIENT, ANTIQUATED

No·ah \ˈnō-ə\ noun [Hebrew Nōaḥ]

: an Old Testament patriarch who built the ark in which he, his family, and living creatures of every kind survived the Flood

¹nob \ˈnäb\ noun [probably alteration of knob] (circa 1700)
1 : HEAD 1
2 : a jack of the same suit as the starter in cribbage that scores one point for the holder — usually used in the phrases his nob or his nobs

²nob noun [perhaps from ¹nob] (1703)
chiefly British : one in a superior position in life

nob·ble \ˈnä-bəl\ transitive verb **nob·bled; nob·bling** \-b(ə-)liŋ\ [perhaps irregular frequentative of nab] (1847)
1 British : to incapacitate (a racehorse) especially by drugging
2 slang British **a** : to win over to one's side **b** : STEAL **c** : SWINDLE, CHEAT **d** : to get hold of : CATCH
— **nob·bler** \-b(ə-)lər\ noun

nob·by \ˈnä-bē\ adjective **nob·bi·er; -est** (1788)
: CHIC, SMART

No·bel·ist \nō-ˈbe-list\ noun (1938)
: a winner of a Nobel prize

no·bel·i·um \nō-ˈbe-lē-əm\ noun [New Latin, from Alfred B. Nobel] (1957)
: a radioactive element produced artificially — see ELEMENT table

No·bel prize \nō-ˈbel-, ˈnō-ˌbel-\ noun (1900)
: any of various annual prizes (as in peace, literature, medicine) established by the will of Alfred Nobel for the encouragement of persons who work for the interests of humanity

no·bil·i·ty \nō-ˈbi-lə-tē\ noun [Middle English nobilite, from Middle French nobilité, from Latin nobilitat-, nobilitas, from nobilis] (14th century)
1 : the quality or state of being noble in character, quality, or rank
2 : the body of persons forming the noble class in a country or state : ARISTOCRACY

¹no·ble \ˈnō-bəl\ adjective **no·bler** \-b(ə-)lər\; **no·blest** \-b(ə-)ləst\ [Middle English, from Old French, from Latin nobilis well-known, noble, from noscere to come to know — more at KNOW] (13th century)
1 a : possessing outstanding qualities : ILLUSTRIOUS **b** : FAMOUS, NOTABLE
2 : of high birth or exalted rank : ARISTOCRATIC
3 a : possessing very high or excellent qualities or properties ⟨noble wine⟩ **b** : very good or excellent
4 : grand or impressive especially in appearance ⟨noble edifice⟩
5 : possessing, characterized by, or arising from superiority of mind or character or of ideals or morals : LOFTY ⟨a noble ambition⟩
6 : chemically inert or inactive especially toward oxygen ⟨a noble metal such as platinum⟩ — compare BASE 6a
synonym see MORAL
— **no·ble·ness** \-bəl-nəs\ noun
— **no·bly** \-blē also -bə-lē\ adverb

²noble noun (14th century)
1 : a person of noble rank or birth
2 : an old English gold coin equivalent to 6s 8d

noble gas noun (1902)
: any of a group of rare gases that include helium, neon, argon, krypton, xenon, and sometimes radon and that exhibit great stability and extremely low reaction rates — called also inert gas

no·ble·man \ˈnō-bəl-mən\ noun (14th century)
: a man of noble rank : PEER

noble savage noun (1672)
: a mythic conception of people belonging to non-European cultures as having innate natural simplicity and virtue uncorrupted by European civilization; also : a person exemplifying this conception

no·blesse \nō-'bles\ *noun* [Middle English, from Old French *noblesce*, from *noble*] (13th century)
1 : noble birth or condition
2 : the members especially of the French nobility

no·blesse oblige \nō-'bles-ə-'blēzh\ *noun* [French, literally, nobility obligates] (1837)
: the obligation of honorable, generous, and responsible behavior associated with high rank or birth

no·ble·wom·an \'nō-bəl-,wu̇-mən\ *noun* (13th century)
: a woman of noble rank : PEERESS

¹**no·body** \'nō-bə-dē, -,bä-dē\ *pronoun* (14th century)
: no person : not anybody □

²**nobody** *noun, plural* **no·bod·ies** (1581)
: a person of no influence or consequence

no-brain·er \'nō-'brā-nər\ *noun* (1973)
: something that requires a minimum of thought

no·cent \'nō-sᵊnt\ *adjective* [Middle English, from Latin *nocent-, nocens*, from present participle of *nocēre* to harm, hurt — more at NOXIOUS] (15th century)
: HARMFUL

no·ci·cep·tive \,nō-si-'sep-tiv\ *adjective* [Latin *nocēre* + English *-i-* + re*ceptive*] (1904)
1 *of a stimulus* : PAINFUL, INJURIOUS
2 : of, induced by, or responding to a nociceptive stimulus — used especially of receptors or protective reflexes

¹**nock** \'näk\ *noun* [Middle English *nocke* notched tip on the end of a bow; akin to Middle Dutch *nocke* summit] (14th century)
1 : one of the notches cut in either of two tips of horn fastened on the ends of a bow or in the bow itself for holding the string
2 a : the part of an arrow having a notch for the bowstring **b** : the notch itself

²**nock** *transitive verb* (14th century)
1 : to make a nock in (a bow or arrow)
2 : to fit (an arrow) against the bowstring

no contest *noun* (1952)
: NOLO CONTENDERE

noct·am·bu·list \näk-'tam-byə-list\ *noun* [Latin *noct-, nox* night + *-ambulist* (as in *somnambulist*) — more at NIGHT] (circa 1731)
: SLEEPWALKER

noc·ti·lu·cent cloud \,näk-tə-'lü-sᵊnt-\ *noun* [*noctilucent* ultimately from Latin *noct-* + *lucent-, lucens* lucent] (1910)
: a luminous thin usually colored cloud seen especially at twilight at a height of about 50 miles (80 kilometers)

noc·tu·id \'näk-chə-wəd, 'näk-tə-\ *noun* [New Latin *Noctuidae*, from *Noctua*, genus of moths, from Latin, the little owl (*Athene noctua*); akin to Latin *nox* night] (1894)
: any of a large family (Noctuidae) of medium-sized often dull-colored moths with larvae (as cutworms and armyworms) that are often destructive agricultural pests
— **noctuid** *adjective*

noc·turn \'näk-,tərn\ *noun* [Middle English *nocturne*, from Middle French, from Medieval Latin *nocturna*, from Latin, feminine of *nocturnus*] (14th century)
: a principal division of the office of matins

noc·tur·nal \näk-'tər-nᵊl\ *adjective* [Middle English, from Middle French or Late Latin; Middle French, from Late Latin *nocturnalis*, from Latin *nocturnus* of night, nocturnal, from *noct-, nox* night] (15th century)
1 : of, relating to, or occurring in the night ⟨a *nocturnal* journey⟩
2 : active at night ⟨a *nocturnal* predator⟩
— **noc·tur·nal·ly** \-nᵊl-ē\ *adverb*

noc·turne \'näk-,tərn\ *noun* [French, adjective, nocturnal, from Latin *nocturnus*] (1862)
: a work of art dealing with evening or night; *especially* : a dreamy pensive composition for the piano — compare AUBADE 3

noc·u·ous \'nä-kyə-wəs\ *adjective* [Latin *nocuus*, from *nocēre* to harm — more at NOXIOUS] (1635)
: HARMFUL
— **noc·u·ous·ly** *adverb*

¹**nod** \'näd\ *verb* **nod·ded; nod·ding** [Middle English *nodden*; perhaps akin to Old High German *hnotōn* to shake] (14th century)
intransitive verb
1 : to make a quick downward motion of the head whether deliberately (as in expressing assent, salutation, or command) or involuntarily (as from drowsiness)
2 : to incline or sway from the vertical as though ready to fall
3 : to bend or sway the upper part gently downward or forward : bob gently
4 : to make a slip or error in a moment of abstraction
transitive verb
1 : to incline (as the head) downward or forward
2 : to bring, invite, or send by a nod ⟨*nodded* them into the room⟩
3 : to signify by a nod ⟨*nodded* their approval⟩
— **nod·der** *noun*

²**nod** *noun* (circa 1541)
1 : the act or an instance of nodding ⟨gave a *nod* of greeting⟩
2 : an indication especially of approval or recognition ⟨received the party's *nod* as candidate for governor⟩

nod·al \'nō-dᵊl\ *adjective* (1831)
: being, relating to, or located at or near a node
— **no·dal·i·ty** \nō-'da-lə-tē\ *noun*
— **nod·al·ly** \'nō-dᵊl-ē\ *adverb*

nodding *adjective* (1590)
1 : bending downward or forward : PENDULOUS, DROOPING ⟨a plant with *nodding* flowers⟩
2 : SLIGHT, SUPERFICIAL ⟨a *nodding* acquaintance⟩

nod·dle \'nä-dᵊl\ *noun* [Middle English *nodle* back of the head or neck] (1579)
: HEAD, PATE

nod·dy \'nä-dē\ *noun, plural* **noddies** [probably short for obsolete *noddypoll*, alteration of *hoddypoll* fumbling inept person] (circa 1530)
1 : a stupid person
2 : any of several stout-bodied terns (especially genus *Anous*) of warm seas

node \'nōd\ *noun* [Middle English, from Latin *nodus* knot, node; akin to Middle Irish *naidm* bond] (15th century)
1 a : a pathological swelling or enlargement (as of a rheumatic joint) **b** : a discrete mass of one kind of tissue enclosed in tissue of a different kind
2 : an entangling complication (as in a drama) : PREDICAMENT
3 : either of the two points where the orbit of a planet or comet intersects the ecliptic; *also* : either of the points at which the orbit of an earth satellite crosses the plane of the equator
4 a : a point, line, or surface of a vibrating body or system that is free or relatively free from vibratory motion **b** : a point at which a wave has an amplitude of zero
5 a : a point at which subsidiary parts originate or center **b** : a point on a stem at which a leaf or leaves are inserted **c** : a point at which a curve intersects itself in such a manner that the branches have different tangents **d** : VERTEX 1b

node of Ran·vier \-'rän-vē-,ā\ [Louis A. *Ranvier* (died 1922) French histologist] (circa 1885)
: a constriction in the myelin sheath of a myelinated nerve fiber

nod off *intransitive verb* (1914)
: to fall asleep

no·dose \'nō-,dōs\ *adjective* [Latin *nodosus*, from *nodus*] (circa 1721)
: having numerous or conspicuous protuberances
— **no·dos·i·ty** \nō-'dä-sə-tē\ *noun*

nod·u·lar \'nä-jə-lər\ *adjective* (1794)
: of, relating to, characterized by, or occurring in the form of nodules ⟨*nodular* lesions⟩

nod·u·la·tion \,nä-jə-'lā-shən\ *noun* (1872)
1 : the process of forming nodules and especially root nodules containing symbiotic bacteria
2 : NODULE

nod·ule \'nä-(,)jü(ə)l\ *noun* [Middle English, from Latin *nodulus*, diminutive of *nodus*] (15th century)
: a small mass of rounded or irregular shape: as **a** : a small rounded lump of a mineral or mineral aggregate **b** : a swelling on a leguminous root that contains symbiotic bacteria **c** : a small abnormal knobby bodily protuberance (as a tumorous growth or a calcification near an arthritic joint)

no·dus \'nō-dəs\ *noun, plural* **no·di** \'nō-,dī, -,dē\ [Latin, knot, node] (circa 1738)
: COMPLICATION, DIFFICULTY

no·el \nō-'el\ *noun* [French *noël* Christmas, carol, from Latin *natalis* birthday, from *natalis* natal] (1811)
1 : a Christmas carol
2 *capitalized* : CHRISTMAS

noes *plural of* NO

no·et·ic \nō-'e-tik\ *adjective* [Greek *noētikos* intellectual, from *noein* to think, from *nous* mind] (1653)
: of, relating to, or based on the intellect

no-fault *adjective* (1967)
1 : of, relating to, or being a motor vehicle insurance plan under which someone involved in an accident is compensated usually up to a stipulated limit for actual losses (as for property damage, medical bills, and lost wages) by that person's own insurance company regardless of who is responsible for the accident
2 : of, relating to, or being a divorce law under which neither party is held responsible for the breakup of the marriage
3 : characterized by the absence of a prevailing sense of individual responsibility (as for behavior) ⟨a *no-fault* society⟩

no-frills \'nō-'frilz\ *adjective* (1960)
: offering or providing only the essentials : not fancy, elaborate, or luxurious

nog \'näg\ *noun* [origin unknown] (1693)
1 : a strong ale formerly brewed in Norfolk, England
2 [by shortening] : EGGNOG

nog·gin \'nä-gən\ *noun* [origin unknown] (1630)
1 : a small mug or cup
2 : a small quantity (as a gill) of drink
3 : a person's head

□ **USAGE**
nobody The indefinite pronouns *nobody* and *no one* share with other indefinite pronouns the characteristic of taking a singular verb and, more often than not, a plural pronoun in reference. The use of the plural pronoun—*they, their, them*—has traditionally been disapproved by those who insist that agreement in number is more important than avoidance of gender-specific third-person singular pronouns. But the use of the plural pronouns has long been established ⟨*nobody* was in their right place —Jane Austen (1814)⟩ and increasing resistance to generic *he* may be easing their acceptance. Usage is still mixed ⟨*nobody* attains reality for my mother until he eats —Flannery O'Connor⟩ ⟨*nobody* naturally likes a mind quicker than their own —F. Scott Fitzgerald⟩.

\ə\ **abut** \ᵊ\ **kitten** \ər\ **further** \a\ **ash** \ā\ **ace**
\ä\ **mop, mar** \au̇\ **out** \ch\ **chin** \e\ **bet** \ē\ **easy**
\g\ **go** \i\ **hit** \ī\ **ice** \j\ **job** \ŋ\ **sing** \ō\ **go**
\ȯ\ **law** \ȯi\ **boy** \th\ **thin** \t̲h\ **the** \ü\ **loot** \u̇\ **foot**
\y\ **yet** \zh\ **vision** *see also* Guide to Pronunciation

nog·ging \'nä-gən, -giŋ\ *noun* [*nog* wooden block the size of a brick] (1825)
: rough brick masonry used to fill in the open spaces of a wooden frame

¹**no–good** \'nō-ˌgu̇d\ *adjective* (1908)
: having no worth, virtue, use, or chance of success

²**no–good** \'nō-ˌgu̇d\ *noun* (1924)
: a no-good person or thing

Noh *variant of* NO

no–hit *adjective* (1916)
: of, relating to, or being a baseball game or a part of a game in which a pitcher allows the opposition no base hits

no–hit·ter \ˌnō-'hi-tər\ *noun* (1947)
: a no-hit game in baseball

no–holds–barred \ˌnō-ˌhōl(d)z-'bärd\ *adjective* (1942)
: free of restrictions or hampering conventions ⟨a *no-holds-barred* contest⟩

no–hop·er \'nō-ˌhō-pər\ *noun* (circa 1943)
chiefly British : one that has no chance of success

no·how \'nō-ˌhau̇\ *adverb* (1775)
1 : in no manner or way : not at all ⟨was *no-how* equal to the task⟩
2 *dialect* : ANYHOW

noil \'nȯi(ə)l\ *noun* [origin unknown] (circa 1624)
: short fiber removed during the combing of a textile fiber and often separately spun into yarn

noir \'nwär\ *noun, often attributive* [short for *film noir*] (1980)
1 : crime fiction featuring hard-boiled cynical characters and bleak sleazy settings
2 : FILM NOIR
— **noir·ish** \-ish\ *adjective*

¹**noise** \'nȯiz\ *noun* [Middle English, from Old French, strife, quarrel, noise, from Latin *nausea* nausea] (13th century)
1 : loud, confused, or senseless shouting or outcry
2 a : SOUND; *especially* : one that lacks agreeable musical quality or is noticeably unpleasant **b** : any sound that is undesired or interferes with one's hearing of something **c** : an unwanted signal or a disturbance (as static or a variation of voltage) in an electronic device or instrument (as radio or television); *broadly* : a disturbance interfering with the operation of a usually mechanical device or system **d** : electromagnetic radiation (as light or radio waves) that is composed of several frequencies and that involves random changes in frequency or amplitude **e** : irrelevant or meaningless data or output occurring along with desired information
3 : common talk : RUMOR; *especially* : SLANDER
4 : something that attracts attention ⟨the play . . . will make little *noise* in the world —Brendan Gill⟩
5 : something spoken or uttered
— **noise·less** \-ləs\ *adjective*
— **noise·less·ly** *adverb*

²**noise** *verb* **noised; nois·ing** (14th century)
intransitive verb
1 : to talk much or loudly
2 : to make a noise
transitive verb
: to spread by rumor or report — usually used with *about* or *abroad* ⟨the scandal was quickly *noised* about⟩

noise·mak·er \'nȯiz-ˌmā-kər\ *noun* (1574)
: one that makes noise; *especially* : a device (as a horn or rattle) used to make noise at parties
— **noise·mak·ing** \-kiŋ\ *noun or adjective*

noise pollution *noun* (1966)
: annoying or harmful noise (as of automobiles or jet airplanes) in an environment

noi·sette \nwä-'zet, nwä-\ *noun* [French, diminutive of *nois* choice cut of meat, literally, nut, from Old French, from Latin *nux* — more at NUT] (1891)

: a small piece of lean meat

noi·some \'nȯi-səm\ *adjective* [Middle English *noysome,* from *noy* annoyance, from Old French *enui, anoi* — more at ENNUI] (14th century)
1 : NOXIOUS, HARMFUL
2 a : offensive to the senses and especially to the sense of smell **b** : highly obnoxious or objectionable
synonym see MALODOROUS
— **noi·some·ly** *adverb*
— **noi·some·ness** *noun*

noisy \'nȯi-zē\ *adjective* **nois·i·er; -est** (1693)
1 : making noise
2 : full of or characterized by noise or clamor
3 : noticeably showy, gaudy, or bright : CONSPICUOUS
— **nois·i·ly** \'nȯi-zə-lē\ *adverb*
— **nois·i·ness** \-zē-nəs\ *noun*

no·li me tan·ge·re \nō-lē-(ˌ)mē-'tan-jə-rē, -ˌlī-, -(ˌ)mā-\ *noun* [Latin, do not touch me; from Jesus' words to Mary Magdalene (John 20:17)] (1591)
: a warning against touching or interference

nol·le pro·se·qui \ˌnä-lē-'prä-sə-ˌkwī\ *noun* [Latin, to be unwilling to pursue] (1681)
: an entry on the record of a legal action denoting that the prosecutor or plaintiff will proceed no further in an action or suit either as a whole or as to some count or as to one or more of several defendants

no·lo \'nō-(ˌ)lō\ *noun* (1914)
: NOLO CONTENDERE

no–load \'nō-ˌlōd\ *adjective* (1963)
: charging no sales commission ⟨a *no-load* mutual fund⟩
— **no–load** \'nō-ˌlōd\ *noun*

no·lo con·ten·de·re \ˌnō-(ˌ)lō-kən-'ten-də-rē\ *noun* [Latin, I do not wish to contend] (1872)
: a plea in a criminal prosecution that without admitting guilt subjects the defendant to conviction but does not preclude denying the truth of the charges in a collateral proceeding

nol–pros \'näl-'präs\ *transitive verb* **nol–prossed; nol–pros·sing** [*nol*le *pros*equi] (circa 1878)
: to discontinue by entering a nolle prosequi

no·ma \'nō-mə\ *noun* [New Latin, from Greek *nomē,* from *nemein* to spread (of an ulcer), literally, to graze, pasture — more at NIMBLE] (1834)
: a spreading invasive gangrene chiefly of the lining of the cheek and lips that is usually fatal and occurs most often in persons severely debilitated by disease or profound nutritional deficiency

no·mad \'nō-ˌmad, *British also* 'nä-\ *noun* [Latin *nomad-, nomas* member of a wandering pastoral people, from Greek, from *nemein*] (1579)
1 : a member of a people who have no fixed residence but move from place to place usually seasonally and within a well-defined territory
2 : an individual who roams about aimlessly
— **nomad** *adjective*
— **no·mad·ism** \'nō-ˌma-ˌdi-zəm\ *noun*

no·mad·ic \nō-'ma-dik\ *adjective* (circa 1818)
1 : of, relating to, or characteristic of nomads ⟨a *nomadic* tribe⟩
2 : roaming about from place to place aimlessly, frequently, or without a fixed pattern of movement

no–man's–land \'nō-ˌmanz-ˌland\ *noun* (14th century)
1 a : an area of unowned, unclaimed, or uninhabited land **b** : an unoccupied area between opposing armies
2 : an anomalous, ambiguous, or indefinite area especially of operation, application, or jurisdiction ⟨the *no-man's-land* between art and science⟩

nom·bril \'näm-brəl\ *noun* [Middle French, literally, navel, ultimately from Latin *umbilicus*] (1562)
: the center point of the lower half of an armorial escutcheon

nom de guerre \ˌnäm-di-'ger\ *noun, plural* **noms de guerre** \ˌnäm(z)-di-\ [French, literally, war name] (1679)
: PSEUDONYM

nom de plume \ˌnäm-di-'plüm\ *noun, plural* **noms de plume** \ˌnäm(z)-di-\ [French, pen name; probably coined in English] (1823)
: PSEUDONYM, PEN NAME

nome \'nōm\ *noun* [Greek *nomos* pasture, district — more at NIMBLE] (circa 1727)
: a province of ancient Egypt

no·men \'nō-mən\ *noun, plural* **no·mi·na** \'nä-mə-nə, 'nō-\ [Latin *nomin-, nomen* name — more at NAME] (circa 1890)
: the second of the three usual names of an ancient Roman male

no·men·cla·tor \'nō-mən-ˌklā-tər\ *noun* [Latin, slave whose duty was to announce the names of persons met during a political campaign, from *nomen* + *calare* to call — more at LOW] (1585)
1 : a book containing collections or lists of words
2 *archaic* : one who announces the names of guests or of persons generally
3 : one who gives names to or invents names for things

no·men·cla·to·ri·al \ˌnō-mən-klə-'tōr-ē-əl, -'tȯr-\ *adjective* (1885)
: relating to or connected with nomenclature

no·men·cla·ture \'nō-mən-ˌklā-chər *also* nō-'men-klə-, -ˌchu̇r, -'men-, -chər, -ˌtyu̇r, -ˌtu̇r\ *noun* [Latin *nomenclatura* assigning of names, from *nomen* + *calatus,* past participle of *calare*] (1610)
1 : NAME, DESIGNATION
2 : the act or process or an instance of naming
3 a : a system or set of terms or symbols especially in a particular science, discipline, or art **b** : an international system of standardized New Latin names used in biology for kinds and groups of kinds of animals and plants
— **no·men·cla·tur·al** \ˌnō-mən-'klach-rəl, -'klā-chə-\ *adjective*

no·men con·ser·van·dum \'nō-mən-ˌkän(t)-sər-'van-dəm\ *noun, plural* **no·mi·na con·ser·van·da** \'nä-mə-nə-ˌkän(t)-sər-'van-də, 'nō-\ [New Latin, name to be kept] (circa 1925)
: a biological taxonomic name that is preserved by special sanction in exception to the usual rules

nomen du·bi·um \-'dü-bē-əm, -'dyü-\ *noun, plural* **nomina du·bia** \-bē-ə\ [New Latin, doubtful name] (1937)
: a taxonomic name that cannot be assigned with certainty to any taxonomic group because the description is insufficient for identification and the original specimens no longer exist

nomen nu·dum \-'nü-dəm, -'nyü-\ *noun, plural* **nomina nu·da** \-də\ [New Latin, bare name] (1900)
: a proposed taxonomic name that is invalid because the group designated is not described or illustrated sufficiently for recognition, that has no nomenclatural status, and that consequently can be used as though never previously proposed

¹**nom·i·nal** \'nä-mə-nᵊl, 'näm-nəl\ *adjective* [Middle English *nominalle,* from Medieval Latin *nominalis,* from Latin, of a name, from *nomin-, nomen* name — more at NAME] (15th century)
1 : of, relating to, or being a noun or a word or expression taking a noun construction
2 a : of, relating to, or constituting a name **b** : bearing the name of a person
3 a : existing or being something in name or form only ⟨*nominal* head of his party⟩ **b** : of, being, or relating to a designated or theoretical

size that may vary from the actual **:** APPROXI-
MATE **c :** TRIFLING, INSIGNIFICANT
4 *of a rate of interest* **a :** equal to the annual
rate of simple interest that would obtain if in-
terest were not compounded when in fact it is
compounded and paid for periods of less than
a year **b :** equal to the percentage by which a
repaid loan exceeds the principal borrowed
with no adjustment made for inflation
5 : being according to plan **:** SATISFACTORY
⟨everything was *nominal* during the spacecraft
launch⟩
— **nom·i·nal·ly** *adverb*
²**nominal** *noun* (1904)
: a word or word group functioning as a noun
nom·i·nal·ism \'nä-mə-nᵊl-,i-zəm, 'näm-nə-
,li-zəm\ *noun* (1844)
1 : a theory that there are no universal essenc-
es in reality and that the mind can frame no
single concept or image corresponding to any
universal or general term
2 : the theory that only individuals and no ab-
stract entities (as essences, classes, or proposi-
tions) exist — compare ESSENTIALISM, REAL-
ISM
— **nom·i·nal·ist** \-ist, -list\ *noun*
— **nominalist** *or* **nom·i·nal·is·tic** \,nä-
mə-nᵊl-'is-tik, ,näm-nə-'lis-\ *adjective*
nominal value *noun* (circa 1901)
: PAR 1b
nominal wages *noun plural* (1898)
: wages measured in money as distinct from
actual purchasing power
nom·i·nate \'nä-mə-,nāt\ *transitive verb* **-nat-
ed; -nat·ing** [Latin *nominatus*, past partici-
ple of *nominare*, from *nomin-, nomen* name
— more at NAME] (1545)
1 : DESIGNATE, NAME
2 a : to appoint or propose for appointment to
an office or place **b :** to propose as a candidate
for election to office **c :** to propose for an hon-
or ⟨*nominate* her for player of the year⟩
3 : to enter (a horse) in a race
— **nom·i·na·tor** \-,nā-tər\ *noun*
nom·i·na·tion \,nä-mə-'nā-shən\ *noun* (15th
century)
1 : the act, process, or an instance of nominat-
ing
2 : the state of being nominated
nom·i·na·tive \'näm-nə-tiv, 'nä-mə-; *2 & 3
are also* 'nä-mə-,nā-\ *adjective* [Middle En-
glish *nominatyf*, from Middle French or Latin;
Middle French *nominatif*, from Latin (*casus*)
nominativus nominative case, from *nominare;*
from the traditional use of the nominative
form in naming a noun] (14th century)
1 a : marking typically the subject of a verb
especially in languages that have relatively
full inflection ⟨*nominative* case⟩ **b :** of or relat-
ing to the nominative case ⟨a *nominative* end-
ing⟩
2 : nominated or appointed by nomination
3 : bearing a person's name
— **nominative** *noun*
nom·i·nee \,nä-mə-'nē\ *noun* [*nominate*]
(1688)
: a person who has been nominated
no·mo·gram \'nä-mə-,gram, 'nō-\ *noun*
[Greek *nomos* law + International Scientific
Vocabulary *-gram* — more at NIMBLE] (1908)
: a graphic representation that consists of sev-
eral lines marked off to scale and arranged in
such a way that by using a straightedge to
connect known values on two lines an un-
known value can be read at the point of inter-
section with another line
no·mo·graph \-,graf\ *noun* (circa 1909)
: NOMOGRAM
— **no·mo·graph·ic** \,nä-mə-'gra-fik, ,nō-\
adjective
— **no·mog·ra·phy** \nō-'mä-grə-fē\ *noun*
no·mo·log·i·cal \,nä-mə-'lä-ji-kəl, ,nō-\ *ad-
jective* [*nomology* science of physical and log-
ical laws, from Greek *nomos* + English *-logy*]
(1845)

: relating to or expressing basic physical laws
or rules of reasoning ⟨*nomological* universals⟩
no·mo·thet·ic \-'the-tik\ *adjective* [Greek *no-
mothetikos* of legislation, from *nomothetēs*
lawgiver, from *nomos* law + *-thetēs* one who
establishes, from *tithenai* to put — more at
DO] (1658)
: relating to, involving, or dealing with ab-
stract, general, or universal statements or laws
-nomy *noun combining form* [Middle English
-nomie, from Old French, from Latin *-nomia*,
from Greek, from *nomos*]
: system of laws governing or sum of knowl-
edge regarding a (specified) field ⟨agro*nomy*⟩
non- \(')nän *also* ,nən *or* 'nən *before* '-*stressed
syllable,* ,nän *also* ,nən *before* ,-*stressed or un-
stressed syllable; the variant with* ə *is also to
be understood at pronounced entries, though
not shown*\ *prefix* [Middle English, from Mid-
dle French, from Latin *non* not, from Old Latin
noenum, from *ne-* not + *oinom*, neuter of *oi-
nos* one — more at NO, ONE]
1 : not **:** other than **:** reverse of **:** absence of
2 : of little or no consequence **:** unimportant
: worthless ⟨*nonissues*⟩ ⟨*nonsystem*⟩
3 : lacking the usual especially positive char-
acteristics of the thing specified ⟨*noncelebra-
tion*⟩ ⟨*nonart*⟩

non·abra·sive	non·ar·chi·tect	non·broad·cast	non·com·mu·ta·tiv·
non·ab·sorb·able	non·ar·chi·tec·ture	non·build·ing	i·ty
non·ab·sor·bent	non·ar·gu·ment	non·burn·able	non·com·pa·ra·bil·
non·ab·sorp·tive	non·aris·to·crat·ic	non·buy·ing	i·ty
non·ab·stract	non·ar·o·mat·ic	non·cab·i·net	non·com·pa·ra·ble
non·ac·a·dem·ic	non·art	non·cak·ing	non·com·pat·i·ble
non·ac·cep·tance	non·art·ist	non·call·able	non·com·pe·ti·tion
non·ac·count·able	non·ar·tis·tic	non·cam·pus	non·com·pet·i·tive
non·ac·cred·it·ed	non·as·cet·ic	non·can·cel·able	non·com·pet·i·tor
non·ac·cru·al	non·as·pi·rin	non·can·cer·ous	non·com·ple·men·
non·achieve·ment	non·as·ser·tive	non·can·ni·bal·is·tic	ta·ry
non·ac·id	non·as·so·ci·at·ed	non·cap·i·tal	non·com·plex
non·acid·ic	non·as·tro·nom·i·cal	non·cap·i·tal·ist	non·com·pli·ance
non·ac·quis·i·tive	non·ath·lete	non·car·cin·o·gen	non·com·pli·cat·ed
non·act·ing	non·ath·let·ic	non·car·ci·no·gen·ic	non·com·ply·ing
non·ac·tion	non·atom·ic	non·car·di·ac	non·com·pos·er
non·ac·ti·vat·ed	non·at·tached	non·ca·reer	non·com·pound
non·ac·tor	non·at·tach·ment	non·car·ri·er	non·com·pre·hen·
non·adap·tive	non·at·ten·dance	non·cash	sion
non·ad·dict	non·at·tend·er	non·ca·su·al	non·com·press·ible
non·ad·dic·tive	non·au·di·to·ry	non–Cath·o·lic	non·com·put·er
non·adi·a·bat·ic	non·au·thor	non·caus·al	non·com·put·er·ized
non·adi·a·bat·ic	non·au·thor·i·tar·i·an	non·cel·e·bra·tion	non·con·cep·tu·al
non·ad·ja·cent	non·au·to·mat·ed	non·ce·leb·ri·ty	non·con·cern
non·ad·mir·er	non·au·to·mat·ic	non·cel·lu·lar	non·con·clu·sion
non·ad·mis·sion	non·au·to·mo·tive	non·cel·lu·los·ic	non·con·cur·rent
non·aes·thet·ic	non·avail·abil·i·ty	non·cen·tral	non·con·dens·able
non·af·fil·i·at·ed	non·bac·te·ri·al	non·cer·tif·i·cat·ed	non·con·di·tioned
non·af·flu·ent	non·bar·bi·tu·rate	non·cer·ti·fied	non·con·duct·ing
non–Af·ri·can	non·ba·sic	non·char·ac·ter	non·con·duc·tion
non·ag·gres·sion	non·bear·ing	non·char·is·mat·ic	non·con·duc·tive
non·ag·gres·sive	non·be·hav·ior·al	non·chau·vin·ist	non·con·fer·ence
non·ag·ri·cul·tur·al	non·be·ing	non·chem·i·cal	non·con·fi·dence
non·al·co·hol·ic	non·be·lief	non–Chris·tian	non·con·fi·den·tial
non·al·ler·gen·ic	non·be·liev·er	non·chro·no·log·i·	non·con·flict·ing
non·al·ler·gic	non·bel·lig·er·en·cy	cal	non·con·fron·ta·tion
non·al·pha·bet·ic	non·bel·lig·er·ent	non·church	non·con·fron·ta·
non·alu·mi·num	non·bet·ting	non·church·go·er	tion·al
non·am·big·u·ous	non·bib·lio·graph·ic	non·cir·cu·lar	non·con·gru·ent
non–Amer·i·can	non·bi·na·ry	non·cir·cu·lat·ing	non·con·ju·gat·ed
non·an·a·lyt·ic	non·bind·ing	non·cit·i·zen	non·con·nec·tion
non·an·a·tom·ic	non·bio·de·grad·able	non·clan·des·tine	non·con·scious
non·an·i·mal	non·bio·graph·i·cal	non·class	non·con·sec·u·tive
non·an·swer	non·bi·o·log·i·cal	non·clas·si·cal	non·con·sen·su·al
non·an·tag·o·nis·tic	non·bi·o·log·i·cal·ly	non·clas·si·fied	non·con·ser·va·tion
non·an·thro·po·log·i·	non·bi·ol·o·gist	non·class·room	non·con·ser·va·tive
cal	non·bit·ing	non·cler·i·cal	non·con·sol·i·dat·ed
non·an·thro·pol·o·	non·black	non·cling	non·con·stant
gist	non·body	non·clin·i·cal	non·con·sti·tu·
non·an·ti·bi·ot·ic	non·bond·ed	non·clog·ging	tion·al
non·an·ti·gen·ic	non·bo·ta·nist	non·co·er·cive	non·con·struc·tion
non·ap·pear·ance	non·brand	non·cog·ni·tive	non·con·struc·tive
non·aquat·ic	non·break·able	non·co·her·ent	non·con·sum·er
non·aque·ous	non·breath·ing	non·co·in·ci·dence	non·con·sum·ing
non·ar·a·ble	non·breed·er	non·co·i·tal	non·con·sump·tion
non·ar·bi·trar·i·ness	non·breed·ing	non·cok·ing	non·con·sump·tive
non·ar·bi·trary		non·co·la	non·con·tact
		non·col·lec·tor	non·con·ta·gious
		non·col·lege	non·con·tem·po·rary
		non·col·le·giate	non·con·tig·u·ous
		non·col·lin·ear	non·con·tin·gent
		non·col·or	non·con·tin·u·ous
		non·col·ored	non·con·tract
		non·col·or·fast	non·con·trac·tu·al
		non·com·bat	non·con·tra·dic·tion
		non·com·bat·ive	non·con·tra·dic·to·ry
		non·com·bus·ti·ble	non·con·trib·u·to·ry
		non·com·mer·cial	non·con·trol·la·ble
		non·com·mit·ment	non·con·trolled
		non·com·mit·ted	non·con·trol·ling
		non·com·mu·ni·cat·	non·con·tro·ver·sial
		ing	non·con·ven·tion·al
		non·com·mu·ni·ca·	non·con·vert·ible
		tion	non·co·pla·nar
		non·com·mu·ni·ca·	non·cor·po·rate
		tive	non·cor·re·la·tion
		non·com·mu·nist	non·cor·rod·ible
		non·com·mu·ni·ty	non·cor·rod·ing
		non·com·mu·ta·tive	non·cor·ro·sive
			non·coun·try

non·coun·ty
non·cov·er·age
non·cre·a·tive
non·cre·a·tiv·i·ty
non·cre·den·tialed
non·crime
non·crim·i·nal
non·cri·sis
non·crit·i·cal
non·crush·able
non·crys·tal·line
non·cu·li·nary
non·cul·ti·vat·ed
non·cul·ti·va·tion
non·cul·tur·al
non·cu·mu·la·tive
non·cur·rent
non·cus·tom·er
non·cy·clic
non·cy·cli·cal
non·dance
non·danc·er
non–Dar·win·i·an
non·de·cep·tive
non·de·ci·sion
non·de·creas·ing
non·de·duc·tive
non·de·fer·ra·ble
non·de·form·ing
non·de·gen·er·ate
non·de·grad·able
non·de·gree
non·del·e·gate
non·de·lib·er·ate
non·de·lin·quent
non·de·liv·ery
non·de·mand·ing
non·dem·o·crat·ic
non·de·nom·i·na·tion·al
non·de·nom·i·na·tion·al·ism
non·de·part·men·tal
non·de·pen·dent
non·de·plet·able
non·de·plet·ing
non·de·po·si·tion
non·de·pressed
non·de·riv·a·tive
non·de·scrip·tive
non·de·sert
non·de·tach·able
non·de·ter·min·is·tic
non·de·vel·op·ment
non·de·vi·ant
non·di·a·bet·ic
non·di·a·lyz·able
non·di·dac·tic
non·dif·fus·ible
non·di·men·sion·al
non·dip·lo·mat·ic
non·di·rect·ed
non·di·rec·tion·al
non·dis·abled
non·dis·clo·sure
non·dis·count
non·dis·cre·tion·ary
non·dis·crim·i·na·tion
non·dis·crim·i·na·to·ry
non·dis·cur·sive
non·dis·per·sive
non·dis·rup·tive
non·di·ver·si·fied
non·doc·tor
non·doc·tri·naire
non·doc·u·men·ta·ry
non·dog·mat·ic
non·dol·lar
non·do·mes·tic
non·dom·i·nant
non·dra·mat·ic
non·driv·er
non·drug
non·du·ra·ble

non·earn·ing
non·ec·cle·si·as·ti·cal
non·econ·o·mist
non·ed·i·ble
non·ed·i·to·ri·al
non·ed·u·ca·tion
non·ed·u·ca·tion·al
non·ef·fec·tive
non·elas·tic
non·elect·ed
non·elec·tion
non·elec·tive
non·elec·tric
non·elec·tri·cal
non·elec·tron·ic
non·el·e·men·ta·ry
non·elite
non·emer·gen·cy
non·emo·tion·al
non·em·phat·ic
non·em·pir·i·cal
non·em·ploy·ee
non·em·ploy·ment
non·emp·ty
non·en·cap·su·lat·ed
non·end·ing
non·en·er·gy
non·en·force·abil·i·ty
non·en·force·ment
non·en·gage·ment
non·en·gi·neer·ing
non·en·ter·tain·ment
non·en·zy·mat·ic
non·en·zy·mic
non·equi·lib·ri·um
non·equiv·a·lence
non·equiv·a·lent
non·erot·ic
non·es·tab·lished
non·es·tab·lish·ment
non·es·ter·i·fied
non·eth·i·cal
non·eth·nic
non–Eu·ro·pe·an
non·eval·u·a·tive
non·ev·i·dence
non·ex·clu·sive
non·ex·ec·u·tive
non·ex·empt
non·ex·is·ten·tial
non·ex·ot·ic
non·ex·pend·able
non·ex·per·i·men·tal
non·ex·pert
non·ex·plan·a·to·ry
non·ex·ploi·ta·tion
non·ex·ploit·a·tive
non·ex·ploit·ive
non·ex·plo·sive
non·ex·posed
non·ex·tant
non·fact
non·fac·tor
non·fac·tu·al
non·fac·ul·ty
non·fad·ing
non·fa·mil·ial
non·fam·i·ly
non·fan
non·farm
non·farm·er
non·fa·tal
non·fat·ten·ing
non·fat·ty
non·fed·er·al
non·fed·er·at·ed
non·fem·i·nist
non·fil·a·men·tous
non·fil·ter·able
non·fi·nal
non·fi·nan·cial
non·fi·nite
non·fis·sion·able
non·flu·o·res·cent
non·fly·ing

non·food
non·for·feit·able
non·for·fei·ture
non·for·mal
non·fos·sil
non·frat·er·ni·za·tion
non·freez·ing
non·friv·o·lous
non·fro·zen
non·fuel
non·ful·fill·ment
non·func·tion·al
non·func·tion·ing
non·game
non·gas·eous
non·gay
non·ge·net·ic
non·gen·i·tal
non·geo·met·ri·cal
non·ghet·to
non·glam·or·ous
non·glare
non·golf·er
non·gov·ern·ment
non·gov·ern·men·tal
non·grad·ed
non·grad·u·ate
non·gram·mat·i·cal
non·gran·u·lar
non·grav·i·ta·tion·al
non·greasy
non·gre·gar·i·ous
non·grow·ing
non·growth
non·guest
non·ha·lo·ge·nat·ed
non·hand·i·capped
non·hap·pen·ing
non·har·dy
non·har·mon·ic
non·haz·ard·ous
non·heme
non·he·mo·lyt·ic
non·he·red·i·tary
non·hi·er·ar·chi·cal
non–His·pan·ic
non·his·tor·i·cal
non·home
non·ho·mo·ge·neous
non·ho·mol·o·gous
non·hor·mon·al
non·hos·pi·tal
non·hos·pi·tal·ized
non·hos·tile
non·hous·ing
non·hu·man
non·hunt·er
non·hunt·ing
non·hy·gro·scop·ic
non·hys·ter·i·cal
non·ide·al
non·iden·ti·ty
non·ideo·log·i·cal
non·im·age
non·im·i·ta·tive
non·im·mi·grant
non·im·mune
non·im·pact
non·im·pli·ca·tion
non·im·por·ta·tion
non·in·clu·sion
non·in·creas·ing
non·in·cum·bent
non·in·de·pen·dence
non–In·di·an
non·in·dig·e·nous
non·in·di·vid·u·al
non–In·do–Eu·ro·pe·an
non·in·dus·tri·al
non·in·dus·tri·al·ized
non·in·dus·try
non·in·fect·ed
non·in·fec·tious
non·in·fec·tive

non·in·fest·ed
non·in·flam·ma·ble
non·in·flam·ma·to·ry
non·in·fla·tion·ary
non·in·flec·tion·al
non·in·flu·ence
non·in·for·ma·tion
non·ini·tial
non·in·ju·ry
non·in·sect
non·in·sec·ti·cid·al
non·in·stall·ment
non·in·sti·tu·tion·al
non·in·sti·tu·tion·al·ized
non·in·struc·tion·al
non·in·stru·men·tal
non·in·sur·ance
non·in·sured
non·in·te·gral
non·in·te·grat·ed
non·in·tel·lec·tu·al
non·in·ter·act·ing
non·in·ter·ac·tive
non·in·ter·change·able
non·in·ter·course
non·in·ter·est
non·in·ter·fer·ence
non·in·ter·sect·ing
non·in·tim·i·dat·ing
non·in·tox·i·cant
non·in·tox·i·cat·ing
non·in·tru·sive
non·in·tu·i·tive
non·ion·iz·ing
non·ir·ra·di·at·ed
non·ir·ri·gat·ed
non·ir·ri·tant
non·ir·ri·tat·ing
non·is·sue
non–Jap·a·nese
non–Jew
non–Jew·ish
non·join·er
non·ju·di·cial
non·ju·ry
non·jus·ti·cia·ble
non·ko·sher
non·la·bor
non·land·own·er
non·lan·guage
non·law·yer
non·lead·ed
non·league
non·le·gal
non·le·gume
non·le·gu·mi·nous
non·le·thal
non·lex·i·cal
non·li·brar·i·an
non·li·brary
non·life
non·lin·e·al
non·lin·e·ar
non·lin·e·ar·i·ty
non·lin·guis·tic
non·liq·uid
non·lit·er·al
non·lit·er·ary
non·liv·ing
non·lo·cal
non·log·i·cal
non·lu·mi·nous
non·mag·net·ic
non·main·stream
non·ma·jor
non·ma·lig·nant
non·mal·lea·ble
non·man·age·ment
non·man·a·ge·ri·al
non·man·u·al
non·man·u·fac·tur·ing
non·mar·i·tal

non·mar·ket
non–Marx·ist
non·ma·te·ri·al
non·ma·te·ri·al·is·tic
non·math·e·mat·i·cal
non·math·e·ma·ti·cian
non·ma·tric·u·lat·ed
non·mean·ing·ful
non·mea·sur·able
non·meat
non·me·chan·i·cal
non·mech·a·nis·tic
non·med·i·cal
non·meet·ing
non·mem·ber
non·mem·ber·ship
non·men·tal
non·mer·cu·ri·al
non·meta·mer·ic
non·met·a·phor·i·cal
non·met·ric
non·met·ri·cal
non·met·ro
non·met·ro·pol·i·tan
non·mi·cro·bi·al
non·mi·grant
non·mi·gra·to·ry
non·mil·i·tant
non·mil·i·tary
non·mi·met·ic
non·mi·nor·i·ty
non·mo·bile
non·mo·lec·u·lar
non·mon·e·tar·ist
non·mon·e·tary
non·mon·ey
non·mo·nog·a·mous
non·mo·tile
non·mo·til·i·ty
non·mo·tor·ized
non·mov·ing
non·mu·nic·i·pal
non·mu·sic
non·mu·si·cal
non·mu·si·cian
non·mu·tant
non·my·e·lin·at·ed
non·mys·ti·cal
non·nar·ra·tive
non·na·tion·al
non·na·tive
non·nat·u·ral
non·ne·ces·si·ty
non·neg·li·gent
non·ne·go·tia·ble
non·net·work
non·news
non·ni·trog·e·nous
non·nor·ma·tive
non·nov·el
non·nu·cle·at·ed
non·nu·mer·i·cal
non·nu·tri·tious
non·nu·tri·tive
non·ob·scene
non·ob·ser·vance
non·ob·ser·vant
non·ob·vi·ous
non·oc·cu·pa·tion·al
non·oc·cur·rence
non·of·fi·cial
non·ohm·ic
non·oily
non·op·er·at·ic
non·op·er·at·ing
non·op·er·a·tion·al
non·op·er·a·tive
non·op·ti·mal
non·or·gan·ic
non·or·tho·dox
non·over·lap·ping
non·own·er
non·ox·i·diz·ing
non·paid

non·par·al·lel
non·par·a·sit·ic
non·par·tic·i·pant
non·par·tic·i·pat·ing
non·par·tic·i·pa·tion
non·par·tic·i·pa·to·ry
non·par·ty
non·pas·sive
non·past
non·pay·ing
non·pay·ment
non·per·for·mance
non·per·form·er
non·per·ish·able
non·per·mis·sive
non·per·son·al
non·pe·tro·leum
non·phi·los·o·pher
non·phil·o·soph·i·cal
non·pho·ne·mic
non·pho·net·ic
non·phos·phate
non·pho·to·graph·ic
non·phys·i·cal
non·phy·si·cian
non·pla·nar
non·plas·tic
non·play
non·play·ing
non·po·et·ic
non·poi·son·ous
non·po·lar·iz·able
non·po·lice
non·po·lit·i·cal
non·po·lit·i·cal·ly
non·pol·i·ti·cian
non·pol·lut·ing
non·poor
non·po·rous
non·pos·ses·sion
non·prac·ti·cal
non·prac·tic·ing
non·preg·nant
non·print
non·prob·lem
non·pro·duc·ing
non·pro·fes·sion·al
non·pro·fes·sion·al·ly
non·pro·fes·so·ri·al
non·pro·gram
non·pro·gram·mer
non·pro·gres·sive
non·pro·pri·etary
non·psy·chi·at·ric
non·psy·chi·a·trist
non·psy·cho·log·i·cal
non·psy·chot·ic
non·pub·lic
non·pu·ni·tive
non·pur·po·sive
non·quan·ti·fi·able
non·quan·ti·ta·tive
non·ra·cial
non·ra·cial·ly
non·ra·dio·ac·tive
non·rail·road
non·ran·dom
non·ran·dom·ness
non·rat·ed
non·ra·tio·nal
non·re·ac·tive
non·re·ac·tor
non·re·al·is·tic
non·re·ap·point·ment
non·re·ceipt
non·re·cip·ro·cal
non·rec·og·ni·tion
non·re·cy·cla·ble
non·re·duc·ing
non·re·dun·dant
non·re·fill·able
non·re·flect·ing

non·reg·u·lat·ed
non·reg·u·la·tion
non·rel·a·tive
non·rel·e·vant
non·re·li·gious
non·re·new·able
non·re·new·al
non·re·pay·able
non·rep·re·sen·ta·tive
non·re·pro·duc·tive
non·res·i·den·tial
non·res·o·nant
non·re·spon·dent
non·re·spond·er
non·re·sponse
non·re·spon·sive
non·re·strict·ed
non·re·trac·tile
non·ret·ro·ac·tive
non·re·us·able
non·re·vers·ible
non·rev·o·lu·tion·ary
non·ri·ot·er
non·ri·ot·ing
non·ro·tat·ing
non·rou·tine
non·roy·al
non·rub·ber
non·rul·ing
non·ru·mi·nant
non–Rus·sian
non·sal·able
non·sa·line
non·sa·pon·i·fi·able
non·schiz·o·phren·ic
non·school
non·sci·en·tif·ic
non·sci·en·tist
non·sea·son·al
non·sec·re·tory
non·se·cure
non·sed·i·ment·able
non·seg·re·gat·ed
non·seg·re·ga·tion
non·se·lect·ed
non·se·lec·tive
non–self–gov·ern·ing
non·sen·sa·tion·al
non·sen·si·tive
non·sen·su·ous
non·sen·tence
non·sep·tate
non·se·quen·tial
non·se·ri·ous
non·sex·ist
non·sex·u·al
non·shrink
non·shrink·able
non·sign·er
non·si·mul·ta·neous
non·sink·able
non·skat·er
non·skel·e·tal
non·ski·er
non·smok·er
non·smok·ing
non·so·cial·ist
non·so·lar
non·so·lu·tion
non·spa·tial
non·speak·er
non·speak·ing
non·spe·cial·ist
non·spe·cif·ic
non·spe·cif·i·cal·ly
non·spec·tac·u·lar
non·spec·u·la·tive
non·speech
non·spher·i·cal
non·sta·tion·ary
non·sta·tis·ti·cal
non·steady
non·sto·ry
non·stra·te·gic

non·struc·tur·al
non·struc·tured
non·stu·dent
non·style
non·sub·ject
non·sub·jec·tive
non·sub·si·dized
non·suc·cess
non·sug·ar
non·su·per·im·pos·able
non·su·per·vi·so·ry
non·sur·gi·cal
non·swim·mer
non·sym·bol·ic
non·sym·met·ric
non·sym·met·ri·cal
non·syn·chro·nous
non·sys·tem·at·ic
non·sys·tem·ic
non·tar·iff
non·tax·able
non·teach·ing
non·tech·ni·cal
non·tem·po·ral
non·ten·ured
non·ter·mi·nal
non·the·at·ri·cal
non·the·ist
non·the·is·tic
non·theo·log·i·cal
non·the·o·ret·i·cal
non·ther·a·peu·tic
non·think·ing
non·threat·en·ing
non·tid·al
non·to·bac·co
non·ton·al
non·to·tal·i·tar·i·an
non·tox·ic
non·tra·di·tion·al
non·trans·fer·able
non·treat·ment
non·triv·i·al
non·trop·i·cal
non·tur·bu·lent
non·typ·i·cal
non·unan·i·mous
non·uni·form
non·uni·for·mi·ty
non·union·ized
non·unique
non·unique·ness
non·uni·ver·sal
non·uni·ver·si·ty
non·ur·ban
non·ur·gent
non·util·i·tar·i·an
non·util·i·ty
non·uto·pi·an
non·val·id
non·va·lid·i·ty
non·vas·cu·lar
non·veg·e·tar·i·an
non·ven·om·ous
non·vet·er·an
non·vi·a·ble
non·view·er
non·vi·ral
non·vir·gin
non·vis·cous
non·vi·su·al
non·vo·cal
non·vo·ca·tion·al
non·vol·ca·nic
non·vol·un·tary
non·vot·er
non·vot·ing
non·war
non·win·ning
non·woody
non·work
non·work·er
non·work·ing
non·writ·er
non·yel·low·ing

non·ad·di·tive \ˈnän-ˈa-də-tiv\ *adjective* (1926)
1 : not having a numerical value equal to the sum of values for the component parts
2 : of, relating to, or being a genic effect that is not additive
— **non·ad·di·tiv·i·ty** \ˌnän-ˌa-də-ˈti-və-tē\ *noun*

non·age \ˈnä-nij, ˈnō-\ *noun* [Middle English, from Middle French, from *non-* + *age* age] (15th century)
1 : MINORITY 1
2 a : a period of youth **b :** lack of maturity

no·na·ge·nar·i·an \ˌnō-nə-jə-ˈner-ē-ən, ˌnä-\ *noun* [Latin *nonagenarius* containing ninety, from *nonageni* ninety each, from *nonaginta* ninety, from *nona-* (akin to *novem* nine) + *-ginta* (akin to *viginti* twenty) — more at NINE, VIGESIMAL] (1804)
: a person whose age is in the nineties
— **nonagenarian** *adjective*

no·na·gon \ˈnō-nə-ˌgän\ *noun* [Latin *nonus* ninth + English *-gon* — more at NOON] (circa 1639)
: a polygon of nine angles and nine sides

non·aligned \ˌnän-ə-ˈlīnd\ *adjective* (1960)
: not allied with other nations and especially with either the Communist or the non-Communist blocs
— **non·align·ment** \-mənt\ *noun*

non·al·le·lic \ˌnän-ə-ˈlē-lik, -ˈle-\ *adjective* (1945)
: not behaving as alleles toward one another ⟨*nonallelic* genes⟩

non–A, non–B hepatitis \ˈnän-ˈā-ˈnän-ˈbē-\ *noun* (1976)
: hepatitis clinically and immunologically similar to hepatitis A and hepatitis B but caused by different viruses

non·bank \ˈnän-ˈbaŋk\ *noun, often attributive* (1939)
: a business that is not an officially established bank but offers many similar services
— **non·bank·ing** \-ˈbaŋ-kiŋ\ *adjective*

non·bond·ing \-ˈbän-diŋ\ *adjective* (1952)
: being or occupied by electrons especially of an atom's valence shell that are not involved in a chemical bond ⟨a *nonbonding* atomic orbital⟩

¹non·book \-ˈbûk\ *adjective* (1949)
: being something other than a book; *especially* **:** being a library holding (as a microfilm) that is not a book

²non·book \-ˈbûk\ *noun* (1960)
: a book of little literary merit which is often a compilation (as of pictures, press clippings, or speeches)

non·busi·ness \-ˈbiz-nəs, -nəz\ *adjective* (1927)
: not related to business; *especially* **:** not related to one's primary business

non·ca·lo·ric \ˌnän-kə-ˈlȯr-ik, -ˈlōr-\ *adjective* (1950)
: free from or very low in calories

non·can·di·date \ˈnän-ˈkan-də-ˌdāt, -ˈka-nə-, -dət\ *noun* (1944)
: a person who is not a candidate; *especially* **:** one who has refused to be a candidate for a particular political office
— **non·can·di·da·cy** \-də-sē\ *noun*

¹nonce \ˈnän(t)s\ *noun* [Middle English *nanes*, alteration (from misdivision of *then anes* in such phrases as *to then anes* for the one purpose) of *anes* one purpose, irregular from *an*, *on* one — more at ONE] (13th century)
1 : the one, particular, or present occasion, purpose, or use (for the *nonce*)
2 : the time being

²nonce *adjective* (1884)
: occurring, used, or made only once or for a special occasion ⟨a *nonce* word⟩

non·cha·lance \ˌnän-shə-ˈlän(t)s; ˈnän-shə-ˌlän(t)s, -lən(t)s\ *noun* (1678)
: the quality or state of being nonchalant

non·cha·lant \-ˈlänt, -ˌlänt, -lənt\ *adjective* [French, from Old French, from present participle

ciple of *nonchaloir* to disregard, from *non-* + *chaloir* to concern, from Latin *calēre* to be warm — more at LEE] (circa 1734)
: having an air of easy unconcern or indifference
synonym see COOL
— **non·cha·lant·ly** *adverb*

non·chro·mo·som·al \ˌnän-ˌkrō-mə-ˈsō-məl\ *adjective* (1960)
1 : not situated on a chromosome
2 : not involving chromosomes

non·com \ˈnän-ˌkäm\ *noun* (1883)
: NONCOMMISSIONED OFFICER

non·com·bat·ant \ˌnän-kəm-ˈba-tᵊnt *also* ˈnän-ˈkäm-bə-tənt\ *noun* (1811)
: one that does not engage in combat: as **a :** a member (as a chaplain) of the armed forces whose duties do not include fighting **b :** CIVILIAN
— **noncombatant** *adjective*

non·com·mis·sioned officer \ˌnän-kə-ˈmishənd-\ *noun* (1703)
: a subordinate officer (as a sergeant) in the army, air force, or marine corps appointed from among enlisted personnel

non·com·mit·tal \-kə-ˈmi-tᵊl\ *adjective* (1829)
1 : giving no clear indication of attitude or feeling
2 : having no clear or distinctive character
— **non·com·mit·tal·ly** \-tᵊl-ē\ *adverb*

non com·pos men·tis \ˌnän-ˈkäm-pəs-ˈmentəs, ˌnōn-\ *adjective* [Latin, literally, not having mastery of one's mind] (1607)
: not of sound mind

non·con·cur \ˌnän-kən-ˈkər\ *intransitive verb* (circa 1847)
: to refuse or fail to concur
— **non·con·cur·rence** \-ˈkər-ən(t)s, -ˈkə-rən(t)s\ *noun*

non·con·duc·tor \-kən-ˈdək-tər\ *noun* (1751)
: a substance that conducts heat, electricity, or sound only in very small degree

non·con·form \-kən-ˈfȯrm\ *intransitive verb* [back-formation from *nonconformist*] (1681)
: to fail to conform
— **non·con·form·er** *noun*

non·con·for·mance \-ˈfȯr-mən(t)s\ *noun* (1843)
: failure to conform

non·con·form·ism \-ˈfȯr-ˌmi-zəm\ *noun* (1844)
: NONCONFORMITY

non·con·form·ist \-ˈfȯr-mist\ *noun* (1619)
1 *often capitalized* **:** a person who does not conform to an established church; *especially* **:** one who does not conform to the Church of England
2 : a person who does not conform to a generally accepted pattern of thought or action
— **nonconformist** *adjective, often capitalized*

non·con·for·mi·ty \-ˈfȯr-mə-tē\ *noun* (1618)
1 a : failure or refusal to conform to an established church **b** *often capitalized* **:** the movement or principles of English Protestant dissent **c** *often capitalized* **:** the body of English Nonconformists
2 : refusal to conform to an established or conventional creed, rule, or practice
3 : absence of agreement or correspondence

non·co·op·er·a·tion \ˌnän-kō-ˌä-pə-ˈrā-shən\ *noun* (1795)
: failure or refusal to cooperate; *specifically* **:** refusal through civil disobedience of a people to cooperate with the government of a country
— **non·co·op·er·a·tion·ist** \-sh(ə-)nist\ *noun*
— **non·co·op·er·a·tor** \-ˈä-pə-ˌrā-tər\ *noun*

\ə\ abut \ᵊ\ kitten \ər\ further \a\ ash \ā\ ace
\ä\ mop, mar \au̇\ out \ch\ chin \e\ bet \ē\ easy
\g\ go \i\ hit \ī\ ice \j\ job \ŋ\ sing \ō\ go
\ȯ\ law \ȯi\ boy \th\ thin \t͟h\ the \ü\ loot \u̇\ foot
\y\ yet \zh\ vision *see also* Guide to Pronunciation

non·co·op·er·a·tive \-'ä-p(ə-)rə-tiv, -pə-,rā-\ *adjective* (1922)
: of, relating to, or characterized by noncooperation

non·cred·it \'nän-'kre-dət\ *adjective* (1965)
: not offering credit toward a degree ⟨*noncredit* courses⟩

non·cross·over \-'kró-,sō-vər\ *adjective* (1919)
: having or being chromosomes that have not participated in genetic crossing-over ⟨*noncrossover* offspring⟩

non·cus·to·di·al \-kə-'stō-dē-əl\ *adjective* (1973)
: of or being a parent who does not have legal custody of a child

non·dairy \-'der-ē, -'dar-; 'nän-,\ *adjective* (1968)
: containing no milk or milk products ⟨*nondairy* whipped topping⟩

non·de·duct·ible \,nän-di-'dək-tə-bəl\ *adjective* (1943)
: not deductible; *especially* : not deductible for income tax purposes
— **non·de·duct·ibil·i·ty** \-,dək-tə-'bi-lə-tē\ *noun*

non·de·fense \,nän-di-'fen(t)s\ *adjective* (1961)
: not used or intended for or associated with the military ⟨*nondefense* spending⟩

non·de·script \,nän-di-'skript\ *adjective* [*non-* + Latin *descriptus*, past participle of *describere* to describe] (circa 1807)
1 : belonging or appearing to belong to no particular class or kind : not easily described
2 : lacking distinctive or interesting qualities : DULL, DRAB
— **nondescript** *noun*

non·de·struc·tive \-di-'strək-tiv\ *adjective* (1926)
: not destructive; *specifically* : not causing destruction of material being investigated or treated ⟨*nondestructive* testing of metal⟩
— **non·de·struc·tive·ly** *adverb*
— **non·de·struc·tive·ness** *noun*

non·dia·paus·ing \,nän-,dī-ə-'pó-ziŋ\ *adjective* (1963)
1 : not having a diapause
2 : not being in a state of diapause

non·di·rec·tive \,nän-də-'rek-tiv, -(,)dī-\ *adjective* (1931)
: of, relating to, or being psychotherapy, counseling, or interviewing in which the counselor refrains from interpretation or explanation but encourages the client (as by repeating phrases) to talk freely

non·dis·junc·tion \,nän-dis-'jəŋ(k)-shən\ *noun* [International Scientific Vocabulary] (1913)
: failure of homologous chromosomes or sister chromatids to separate subsequent to metaphase in meiosis or mitosis so that one daughter cell has both and the other neither of the chromosomes
— **non·dis·junc·tion·al** \-shnəl, -shə-nᵊl\ *adjective*

non·dis·tinc·tive \-di-'stiŋ(k)-tiv\ *adjective* (1916)
of a speech sound : having no signaling value

non·di·vid·ing \,nän-də-'vī-diŋ\ *adjective* (1945)
: not undergoing cell division

non·dor·mant \'nän-'dòr-mənt\ *adjective* (1940)
1 : being in such a condition that germination is possible ⟨*nondormant* seeds⟩
2 : being in active vegetative growth ⟨*nondormant* plants⟩

non·drink·er \-'driŋ-kər\ *noun* (1899)
: a person who abstains from alcoholic beverages
— **non·drink·ing** \-kiŋ\ *adjective*

non·dry·ing oil \'nän-'drī-iŋ-\ *noun* (1905)
: a highly saturated oil (as olive oil) that is unable to solidify when exposed in a thin film to air

¹none \'nən\ *pronoun, singular or plural in construction* [Middle English, from Old English *nān*, from *ne* not + *ān* one — more at NO, ONE] (before 12th century)
1 : not any
2 : not one : NOBODY
3 : not any such thing or person
4 : no part : NOTHING □

²none *adjective* (before 12th century)
archaic : not any : NO

³none *adverb* (1651)
1 : by no means : not at all ⟨*none* too soon to begin⟩
2 : in no way : to no extent ⟨*none* the worse for wear⟩

⁴none \'nōn\ *noun, often capitalized* [Late Latin *nona*, from Latin, 9th hour of the day from sunrise — more at NOON] (1845)
: the fifth of the canonical hours
word history see NOON

non·eco·nom·ic \,nän-,e-kə-'nä-mik, -,ē-kə-\ *adjective* (1920)
: not economic; *especially* : having no economic importance or implication

non·elec·tro·lyte \,nän-ə-'lek-trə-,līt\ *noun* (1891)
: a substance that does not readily ionize when dissolved or melted and is a poor conductor of electricity

non·en·ti·ty \-'en-tə-tē, -'e-nə-\ *noun* (circa 1600)
1 : something that does not exist or exists only in the imagination
2 : NONEXISTENCE
3 : a person of little consequence or significance

nones \'nōnz\ *noun plural but singular or plural in construction* [Middle English *nonys*, from Latin *nonae*, from feminine plural of *nonus* ninth] (14th century)
1 : the ninth day before the ides according to ancient Roman reckoning
2 *often capitalized* : ⁴NONE
word history see NOON

non·es·sen·tial \,nän-i-'sen(t)-shəl\ *adjective* (1751)
1 : not essential
2 : synthesized by the body in sufficient quantity to satisfy dietary needs ⟨*nonessential* amino acids⟩
— **nonessential** *noun*

none·such \'nən-,səch\ *noun* (1590)
: a person or thing without an equal
— **nonesuch** *adjective*

no·net \nō-'net\ *noun* [Italian *nonetto*, from *nono* ninth, from Latin *nonus* — more at NOON] (1865)
: a combination of nine instruments or voices; *also* : a musical composition for such a combination

none·the·less \,nən-thə-'les\ *adverb* (1847)
: NEVERTHELESS

non–eu·clid·e·an \,nän-yü-'kli-dē-ən\ *adjective, often E capitalized* (circa 1864)
: not assuming or in accordance with all the postulates of Euclid's *Elements* ⟨*non-euclidean* geometry⟩

non·event \'nän-i-,vent, ,nän-i-'\ *noun* (1962)
1 a : an expected event that fails to take place or to satisfy expectations **b** : an often highly publicized event of little intrinsic interest or significance
2 : an occurrence that is officially ignored

non·ex·is·tence \,nän-ig-'zis-tən(t)s\ *noun* (1646)
: absence of existence : the negation of being
— **non·ex·is·tent** \-tənt\ *adjective*

non·fat \'nän-'fat\ *adjective* (1926)
: lacking fat solids : having fat solids removed ⟨*nonfat* milk⟩

non·fea·sance \'nän-'fē-zᵊn(t)s\ *noun* [*non-* + obsolete English *feasance* doing, execution] (1596)
: failure to act; *especially* : failure to do what ought to be done

non·fer·rous \-'fer-əs\ *adjective* (1887)

1 : not containing, including, or relating to iron
2 : of or relating to metals other than iron

non·fic·tion \-'fik-shən\ *noun* (1909)
: literature that is not fictional
— **non·fic·tion·al** \,nän-'fik-shnəl, -shə-nᵊl\ *adjective*

non·fig·u·ra·tive \'nän-'fi-gyə-rə-tiv, -'fi-gə-\ *adjective* (1927)
: NONOBJECTIVE 2

non·flam·ma·ble \-'fla-mə-bəl\ *adjective* (1915)
: not flammable; *specifically* : not easily ignited and not burning rapidly if ignited
— **non·flam·ma·bil·i·ty** \,nän-,fla-mə-'bi-lə-tē\ *noun*

non·flow·er·ing \'nän-'flaù(-ə)r-iŋ\ *adjective* (circa 1934)
: producing no flowers; *specifically* : lacking a flowering stage in the life cycle

non·flu·en·cy \-'flü-ən(t)-sē\ *noun, plural -cies* (circa 1945)
1 : lack of fluency
2 : an instance of nonfluency

non·gon·o·coc·cal \,nän-,gä-nə-'kä-kəl\ *adjective* (1961)
: not caused by a gonococcus ⟨*nongonococcal* urethritis⟩

non gra·ta \,nän-'gra-tə, -'grä-\ *adjective* [*persona non grata*] (1925)
: not approved : UNWELCOME

non·green \'nän-'grēn\ *adjective* (1897)
: not green; *specifically* : containing no chlorophyll ⟨*nongreen* saprophytes⟩

non·he·ro \'nän-'hē-(,)rō, -'hir-(,)ō\ *noun* (1940)
: ANTI-HERO

non·his·tone \-'his-,tōn\ *adjective* (circa 1966)
: relating to or being any of the eukaryotic proteins (as DNA polymerase) that bind to nuclear DNA but are not histones

non–Hodg·kin's lymphoma \'nän-'häj-kənz-\ *noun* (1976)
: any of the numerous malignant lymphomas (as Burkitt's lymphoma) that are not classified as Hodgkin's disease

□ **USAGE**
none As the entry here indicates, this pronoun takes either a singular or a plural verb. Yet many people are convinced that *none* is singular only. We know about these people because they write to newspaper editors and to broadcasters, and a small number of them write usage books. The idea that *none* must be singular is rooted in etymology: *nān*, its Old English equivalent, was formed from a negative particle *ne-* "not" and *ān* "one." The first person we know of who combined knowledge of the etymology with disapproval of the plural verb was Charles Coote, an Englishman who published a grammar in 1788. He was apparently not so familiar with the grammar of Old English, where *nān* was both singular and plural. King Alfred the Great, in fact, used *nān* as a plural as far back as A.D. 888. Many of Coote's contemporaries knew that *none* was both singular and plural, and most writers on usage to this day know it, but the notion of its unalterable singularity has become part of the folklore of English usage. Here are a few examples of both constructions ⟨but *none* of these things move me —Acts 20:24 (Authorized Version)⟩ ⟨all agree in one judgment, and *none* ever varies his opinion —Samuel Johnson⟩ ⟨*none* are wretched but by their own fault —Samuel Johnson⟩ ⟨she has seed from four different people, but *none* of it comes up —Jane Austen⟩. A recent commentator thinks that where either construction can be chosen, the singular is a bit more emphatic, but either number can be an effective choice in context.

non·iden·ti·cal \ˌnän-(ˌ)ī-'den-ti-kəl, -ə-'den-\ *adjective* (1890)
1 : DIFFERENT
2 : FRATERNAL 2

no·nil·lion \nō-'nil-yən\ *noun, often attributive* [French, from Latin *nonus* ninth + French *-illion* (as in *million*) — more at NOON] (1690)
— see NUMBER table

non·in·duc·tive \ˌnän-in-'dək-tiv\ *adjective* (1896)
: not inductive; *especially* : having negligible inductance

non·in·ter·ven·tion \-ˌin-tər-'ven(t)-shən\ *noun* (1831)
: the state or policy of not intervening ⟨*nonintervention* in the affairs of other countries⟩
— **non·in·ter·ven·tion·ist** \-'ven(t)-sh(ə-)nist\ *noun or adjective*

non·in·va·sive \-in-'vā-siv, -ziv\ *adjective* (1971)
: not involving penetration (as by surgery or hypodermic needle) of the skin of the intact organism ⟨*noninvasive* diagnostic techniques⟩

non·in·volve·ment \-in-'välv-mənt, -'vȯlv- *also* -'väv-, -'vȯv-\ *noun* (1936)
: absence of involvement or emotional attachment
— **non·in·volved** \-'vä(l)vd, -'vȯ(l)vd\ *adjective*

non·ion·ic \-(ˌ)ī-'ä-nik\ *adjective* (1929)
: not ionic; *especially* : not dependent on a surface-active anion for effect ⟨*nonionic* surfactants⟩

non·join·der \ˌnän-'jȯin-dər\ *noun* (1833)
: failure to include a necessary party to a suit at law

non·judg·men·tal \ˌnän-ˌjəj-'men-tᵊl\ *adjective* (1952)
: avoiding judgments based on one's personal and especially moral standards

non·jur·ing \ˌnän-'jur-iŋ\ *adjective* [*non-* + Latin *jurare* to swear — more at JURY] (1691)
: not swearing allegiance — used especially of a member of a party in Great Britain that would not swear allegiance to William and Mary or to their successors

non·ju·ror \-'jur-ər, -'jur-ˌȯr\ *noun* (1691)
: a person refusing to take an oath especially of allegiance, supremacy, or abjuration; *specifically* : one of the beneficed clergy in England and Scotland refusing to take an oath of allegiance to William and Mary or to their successors after the revolution of 1688

non·lit·er·ate \-'li-t(ə-)rət\ *adjective* (1947)
1 : not literate
2 : having no written language
— **nonliterate** *noun*

non·met·al \-'me-tᵊl\ *noun* (circa 1864)
: a chemical element (as boron, carbon, or nitrogen) that lacks the characteristics of a metal

non·me·tal·lic \ˌnän-mə-'ta-lik\ *adjective* (1815)
1 : not metallic
2 : of, relating to, or being a nonmetal

non·mor·al \ˌnän-'mȯr-əl, -'mär-\ *adjective* (circa 1866)
: not falling into or existing in the sphere of morals or ethics

non·neg·a·tive \-'ne-gə-tiv\ *adjective* (1885)
: not negative: as **a** : being either positive or zero **b** : taking on nonnegative values ⟨a *nonnegative* function⟩

non·nu·cle·ar \-'nü-klē-ər, -'nyü-, ÷-kyə-lər\ *adjective* (1953)
1 : not nuclear: as **a** : being a weapon whose destructive power is not derived from a nuclear reaction **b** : not operated by, using, or produced by nuclear energy **c** : not using or involving nuclear weapons
2 : not having nuclear weapons ⟨a *nonnuclear* country⟩

no–no \'nō-ˌnō\ *noun, plural* **no–no's** *or* **no-nos** (circa 1942)
: something unacceptable or forbidden

non·ob·jec·tive \ˌnän-əb-'jek-tiv\ *adjective* (1905)
1 : not objective
2 : representing or intended to represent no natural or actual object, figure, or scene ⟨*nonobjective* art⟩
— **non·ob·jec·tiv·ism** \-ti-ˌvi-zəm\ *noun*
— **non·ob·jec·tiv·ist** \-vist\ *noun*
— **non·ob·jec·tiv·i·ty** \-ˌäb-ˌjek-'ti-və-tē, -əb-\ *noun*

non ob·stan·te \ˌnän-əb-'stan-tē, ˌnōn-\ *preposition* [Middle English, from Medieval Latin] (15th century)
: NOTWITHSTANDING

non–oil \ˌnän-'ȯi(ə)l\ *adjective* (1979)
1 : not relating to, containing, or derived from oil
2 : being a net importer of petroleum or petroleum products ⟨*non-oil* nations⟩

no–nonsense *adjective* (1928)
: tolerating no nonsense : SERIOUS, BUSINESSLIKE

non·or·gas·mic \ˌnän-ȯr-'gaz-mik\ *adjective* (1973)
: not capable of experiencing orgasm

no·nox·y·nol–9 \nä-'näk-si-ˌnȯl-'nīn, nə-, -ˌnȯl-\ *noun* [*nonyl* (the radical C_9H_{19}) + *oxy-* + *phenol* + *9* (from the fact that the compounds it contains have an average of nine ethylene oxide groups per molecule)] (1980)
: a spermicide used in contraceptive products

non·para·met·ric \-ˌpar-ə-'me-trik\ *adjective* (1942)
: not involving the estimation of parameters of a statistical function ⟨*nonparametric* statistical tests⟩

¹non·pa·reil \ˌnän-pə-'rel\ *adjective* [Middle English *nonparaille*, from Middle French *nonpareil*, from *non-* + *pareil* equal, from (assumed) Vulgar Latin *pariculus*, from Latin *par* equal] (15th century)
: having no equal

²nonpareil *noun* (1593)
1 : an individual of unequaled excellence : PARAGON
2 a : a small flat disk of chocolate covered with white sugar pellets **b** : sugar in small pellets of various colors

non·par·ti·san \ˌnän-'pär-tə-zən, -sən\ *adjective* (1885)
: not partisan; *especially* : free from party affiliation, bias, or designation ⟨*nonpartisan* ballot⟩ ⟨a *nonpartisan* board⟩
— **non·par·ti·san·ship** \-ˌship\ *noun*

non·pas·ser·ine \-'pa-sə-ˌrīn\ *adjective* (circa 1909)
: not passerine; *especially* : of or relating to an order (Coraciiformes) of arboreal birds including the rollers, kingfishers, and hornbills

non·patho·gen·ic \ˌnän-ˌpa-thə-'je-nik\ *adjective* (1884)
: not capable of inducing disease — compare AVIRULENT

non·peak \'nän-ˌpēk\ *adjective* (circa 1914)
: OFF-PEAK

non·per·form·ing \ˌnän-pə(r)-'fȯr-miŋ\ *adjective* (1979)
: not bringing in the expected return ⟨*nonperforming* loans⟩ ⟨*nonperforming* assets⟩

non·per·sis·tent \-pər-'sis-tənt, -'zis-\ *adjective* (1900)
: not persistent: as **a** : decomposed rapidly by environmental action ⟨*nonpersistent* insecticides⟩ **b** : capable of being transmitted by a vector for only a relatively short time ⟨*nonpersistent* viruses⟩

non·per·son \'nän-ˌpər-sᵊn\ *noun* (circa 1909)
: a person who is regarded as nonexistent: as **a** : UNPERSON **b** : one having no social or legal status

non pla·cet \'nän-'plā-sət, 'nōn-\ *noun* [Latin, it does not please] (1589)
: a negative vote

¹non·plus \ˌnän-'pləs\ *noun* [Latin *non plus* no more] (1582)
: a state of bafflement or perplexity : QUANDARY

²nonplus *transitive verb* **-plussed** *also* **-plused** \-'pləst\; **-plus·sing** *also* **-plus·ing** \-'plə-siŋ\ (1591)
: to cause to be at a loss as to what to say, think, or do : PERPLEX
synonym see PUZZLE

non·point \'nän-'pȯint\ *adjective* (1977)
: not occurring at a single well-defined site; *specifically* : being pollution that cannot be traced to a single location

non·po·lar \ˌnän-'pō-lər\ *adjective* (1892)
: not polar; *especially* : consisting of molecules not having a dipole ⟨a *nonpolar* solvent⟩

non pos·su·mus \ˌnän-'pä-sə-məs, 'nōn-\ *noun* [Latin, we cannot] (1883)
: a statement expressing inability to do something

non·pre·scrip·tion \ˌnän-pri-'skrip-shən\ *adjective* (1958)
: capable of being bought without a doctor's prescription ⟨*nonprescription* drugs⟩

non·pro·duc·tive \-prə-'dək-tiv\ *adjective* (1901)
: not productive: as **a** : failing to produce or yield : UNPRODUCTIVE ⟨a *nonproductive* oil well⟩ **b** : not directly concerned with production ⟨the *nonproductive* labor of clerks and inspectors⟩ **c** *of a cough* : DRY
— **non·pro·duc·tive·ness** *noun*

non·prof·it \'nän-'prä-fət\ *adjective* (1903)
: not conducted or maintained for the purpose of making a profit ⟨a *nonprofit* organization⟩
— **nonprofit** *noun*

non·pro·lif·er·a·tion \ˌnän-prə-ˌli-fə-'rā-shən\ *adjective* (1964)
: providing for the stoppage of proliferation (as of nuclear arms) ⟨*nonproliferation* treaty⟩
— **nonproliferation** *noun*

non·pros \ˌnän-'präs\ *transitive verb* **non-prossed; non·pros·sing** [*non prosequitur*] (1755)
: to enter a non prosequitur against

non pro·se·qui·tur \ˌnän-prə-'se-kwə-tər, ˌnōn-\ *noun* [Late Latin, he does not prosecute] (1768)
: a judgment entered against the plaintiff in a suit in which that party does not appear to prosecute

non·pro·tein \'nän-'prō-ˌtēn, -'prō-tē-ən\ *adjective* (1926)
: not being or derived from protein ⟨the *nonprotein* part of an enzyme⟩ ⟨*nonprotein* nitrogen⟩

non·read·er \-'rē-dər\ *noun* (1924)
1 : one who does not or cannot read
2 : a child who is very slow in learning to read
— **non·read·ing** \-diŋ\ *adjective*

non·re·com·bi·nant \ˌnän-(ˌ)rē-'käm-bə-nənt\ *adjective* (1962)
: not exhibiting the results of genetic recombination
— **nonrecombinant** *noun*

non·re·course \ˌnän-'rē-ˌkȯrs, -ˌkȯrs, -ri-\ *adjective* (1926)
: being or based on an agreement in which the lender has no right of recourse to the borrower's assets beyond stated limits ⟨a *nonrecourse* note⟩ ⟨a *nonrecourse* loan⟩

non·re·cur·rent \ˌnän-ri-'kər-ənt, -'kə-rənt\ *adjective* (circa 1864)
: not recurring

non·re·cur·ring \-ri-'kər-iŋ, -'kə-riŋ\ *adjective* (circa 1864)
: NONRECURRENT; *specifically* : unlikely to happen again — used of financial transactions that affect a profit and loss statement abnormally

non·re·fund·able \-ri-'fən-də-bəl\ *adjective* (1963)
: not subject to refunding or being refunded ⟨a *nonrefundable* bond⟩ ⟨a *nonrefundable* fee⟩

non·rel·a·tiv·is·tic \-ˌre-lə-ti-'vis-tik\ *adjective* (1930)
1 : not based on or involving the theory of relativity ⟨*nonrelativistic* equations⟩ ⟨*nonrelativistic* kinematics⟩
2 : of, relating to, or being a body moving at less than a relativistic velocity
— **non·rel·a·tiv·is·ti·cal·ly** \-'vis-ti-k(ə-)lē\ *adverb*

non·rep·re·sen·ta·tion·al \-ˌre-pri-ˌzen-'tā-shnəl, -zən-, -shə-nᵊl\ *adjective* (1923)
: NONOBJECTIVE 2
— **non·rep·re·sen·ta·tion·al·ism** \-shnə-ˌli-zəm, -shə-nᵊl-ˌi-zəm\ *noun*

non·res·i·dence \ˈnän-ˈre-zə-dən(t)s, -ˈrez-dən(t)s, -ˌden(t)s\ *noun* (1585)
: the state or fact of being nonresident

non·res·i·den·cy \-ˈre-zə-dən(t)-sē, -ˈrez-dən(t)-, -ˌden(t)-\ *noun* (1584)
: NONRESIDENCE

non·res·i·dent \-ˈre-zə-dənt, -ˈrez-dənt, -ˌdent\ *adjective* (1540)
: not residing in a particular place
— **nonresident** *noun*

non·re·sis·tance \ˌnän-ri-'zis-tən(t)s\ *noun* (1643)
: the principles or practice of passive submission to constituted authority even when unjust or oppressive; *also* : the principle or practice of not resisting violence by force

non·re·sis·tant \-tənt\ *adjective* (1702)
: not resistant; *specifically* : susceptible to the effects of a deleterious agent (as an insecticide, a pathogen, or an extreme environmental condition)
— **nonresistant** *noun*

non·re·stric·tive \-ri-'strik-tiv\ *adjective* (1916)
: not restrictive; *specifically* : not limiting the reference of a modified word or phrase

nonrestrictive clause *noun* (1916)
: a descriptive clause that is not essential to the definiteness of the meaning of the word it modifies (as *who is retired* in "my father, who is retired, does volunteer work")

non·re·turn·able \-ri-'tər-nə-bəl\ *adjective* (1903)
: not returnable; *specifically* : not returnable to a dealer in exchange for a deposit ⟨*nonreturnable* bottles⟩
— **nonreturnable** *noun*

non·rig·id \ˈnän-ˈri-jəd\ *adjective* (1909)
: not rigid; *especially* : maintaining form by pressure of contained gas ⟨a *nonrigid* airship⟩

non·sched·uled \-ˈske-(ˌ)jü(ə)ld, -jəld\ *adjective* (1947)
: licensed to transport by air without a regular schedule ⟨*nonscheduled* airlines⟩

¹non·sci·ence \-ˈsī-ən(t)s\ *noun* (1855)
: something (as a discipline) that is not a science

²nonscience *adjective* (1944)
: of or relating to fields other than science

non·se·cre·tor \ˌnän-si-ˈkrē-tər\ *noun* (1944)
: an individual of blood group A, B, or AB who does not secrete the antigens characteristic of these blood groups in bodily fluids (as saliva)

non·sec·tar·i·an \-(ˌ)sek-ˈter-ē-ən\ *adjective* (1831)
: not having a sectarian character : not affiliated with or restricted to a particular religious group

non·self \ˈnän-ˈself, *Southern also* -ˈsef\ *noun* (1963)
: material that is foreign to the body of an organism

¹non·sense \ˈnän-ˌsen(t)s, ˈnän(t)-sən(t)s\ *noun* (1614)
1 a : words or language having no meaning or conveying no intelligible ideas **b** (1) : language, conduct, or an idea that is absurd or

contrary to good sense (2) : an instance of absurd action
2 a : things of no importance or value : TRIFLES **b** : affected or impudent conduct ⟨took no *nonsense* from subordinates⟩
3 : genetic information consisting of one or more codons that do not code for any amino acid and usually cause termination of the molecular chain in protein synthesis — compare ANTISENSE, MISSENSE
— **non·sen·si·cal** \ˌnän-'sen(t)-si-kəl\ *adjective*
— **non·sen·si·cal·ly** \-k(ə-)lē\ *adverb*
— **non·sen·si·cal·ness** \-kəl-nəs\ *noun*

²nonsense *adjective* (1778)
1 : consisting of an arbitrary grouping of speech sounds or symbols ⟨'shróg-ˌthī-əmpth' is a *nonsense* word⟩ ⟨a *nonsense* syllable⟩
2 : consisting of one or more codons that are genetic nonsense

nonsense verse *noun* (1799)
: humorous or whimsical verse that features absurd characters and actions and often contains evocative but meaningless nonce words

non se·qui·tur \ˈnän-ˈse-kwə-tər *also* -ˌtür\ *noun* [Latin, it does not follow] (1540)
1 : an inference that does not follow from the premises; *specifically* : a fallacy resulting from a simple conversion of a universal affirmative proposition or from the transposition of a condition and its consequent
2 : a statement (as a response) that does not follow logically from anything previously said

non·sig·nif·i·cant \ˌnän-sig-'ni-fi-kənt\ *adjective* (1902)
: not significant: as **a** : INSIGNIFICANT **b** : MEANINGLESS **c** : having or yielding a value lying within limits between which variation is attributed to chance ⟨a *nonsignificant* statistical test⟩
— **non·sig·nif·i·cant·ly** *adverb*

non·sked \ˈnän-ˈsked\ *noun* [by shortening & alteration from *nonscheduled*] (1949)
: a nonscheduled transport plane or airline

non·skid \-ˈskid\ *adjective* (1904)
: designed or equipped to prevent skidding

non·slip \-ˈslip\ *adjective* (1903)
: designed to reduce or prevent slipping

non·so·cial \-ˈsō-shəl\ *adjective* (1902)
: not socially oriented : lacking a social component

non·sport·ing \-ˈspōr-tiŋ, -ˈspór-\ *adjective* (1852)
: lacking the qualities characteristic of a hunting dog

non·stan·dard \-ˈstan-dərd\ *adjective* (1923)
1 : not standard
2 : not conforming in pronunciation, grammatical construction, idiom, or word choice to the usage generally characteristic of educated native speakers of a language — compare SUBSTANDARD

non·start·er \-ˈstär-tər\ *noun* (1902)
1 : one that does not start
2 : someone or something that is not productive or effective ⟨his son has been, in politics a *nonstarter* —Anthony Lejeune⟩

non·ste·roi·dal \ˌnän-stə-ˈrói-dᵊl\ *also* **non·ste·roid** \ˈnän-ˈstir-ˌóid, -ˈster-\ *adjective* (1964)
: of, relating to, or being a compound and especially a drug that is not a steroid
— **nonsteroid** *noun*

non·stick \ˈnän-ˈstik\ *adjective* [³*stick*] (1958)
: allowing of easy removal of cooked food particles ⟨a *nonstick* coating in a frying pan⟩

non·stop \-ˈstäp\ *adjective* (1902)
: done, made, or held without a stop : not easing or letting up
— **nonstop** *adverb*

non·such \ˈnən-ˌsəch *also* ˈnän-\ *variant of* NONESUCH

non·suit \ˈnän-ˈsüt\ *noun* [Middle English, from Anglo-French *nounsuyte*, from *noun-* non- + Old French *siute* following, pursuit — more at SUIT] (14th century)

: a judgment against a plaintiff for failure to prosecute a case or inability to establish a prima facie case
— **nonsuit** *transitive verb*

non·sup·port \ˌnän-sə-ˈpōrt, -ˈpórt\ *noun* (1909)
: failure to support; *specifically* : failure (as of a parent) to honor a statutory or contractual obligation to provide maintenance

non·syl·lab·ic \-sə-ˈla-bik\ *adjective* (circa 1909)
: not constituting a syllable or the nucleus of a syllable ⟨the second vowel of a falling diphthong is *nonsyllabic* (as \i\ in \ói\)⟩

non·sys·tem \ˈnän-ˈsis-təm\ *noun* (1964)
: a system that lacks effective organization

non·tar·get \-ˈtär-gət\ *adjective* (1945)
: not being the intended object of action by a particular agent ⟨effect of insecticides on *nontarget* organisms⟩

non·ter·mi·nat·ing \-ˈtər-mə-ˌnā-tiŋ\ *adjective* (circa 1908)
: not terminating or ending; *especially* : being a decimal for which there is no place to the right of the decimal point such that all places farther to the right contain the entry 0 ⟨1/3 gives the *nonterminating* decimal .33333 . . .⟩

non·ther·mal \-ˈthər-məl\ *adjective* (circa 1964)
: not produced by heat; *specifically* : of, relating to, or being radiation having a spectrum that is not the spectrum of a blackbody

non·ti·tle \-ˈtī-tᵊl\ *adjective* (1968)
: of, relating to, or being an athletic contest in which a title is not at stake

non trop·po \ˈnän-ˈtró-(ˌ)pō, ˈnōn-\ *adverb or adjective* [Italian, literally, not too much] (circa 1854)
: without excess — used to qualify a direction in music

non–U \ˈnän-ˈyü\ *adjective* (1954)
: not characteristic of the upper classes

non·union \-ˈyün-yən\ *adjective* (1863)
1 : not belonging to or connected with a trade union ⟨*nonunion* carpenters⟩
2 : not recognizing or favoring trade unions or their members
3 : not produced or worked on by members of a trade union ⟨*nonunion* lettuce⟩

non·use \ˈnän-ˈyüs\ *noun* (1542)
1 : failure to use ⟨*nonuse* of available material⟩
2 : the fact or condition of not being used

non·us·er \-ˈyü-zər\ *noun* (1926)
: one who does not make use of something (as an available public facility or a harmful drug)

non·van·ish·ing \-ˈva-ni-shiŋ\ *adjective* (1907)
: not zero or becoming zero

non·vec·tor \-ˈvek-tər\ *noun* (1956)
: an organism (as an insect) that does not transmit a particular pathogen (as a virus)

non·ver·bal \-ˈvər-bəl\ *adjective* (1924)
: not verbal: as **a** : being other than verbal ⟨*nonverbal* factors⟩ **b** : involving minimal use of language ⟨*nonverbal* tests⟩ **c** : ranking low in verbal skill
— **non·ver·bal·ly** \-bə-lē\ *adverb*

non·vin·tage \-ˈvin-tij\ *adjective* (1924)
: undated and usually blended to approximate a standard ⟨a *nonvintage* wine⟩

non·vi·o·lence \-ˈvī-ə-lən(t)s\ *noun* (1920)
1 : abstention from violence as a matter of principle; *also* : the principle of such abstention
2 a : the quality or state of being nonviolent : avoidance of violence **b** : nonviolent demonstrations for the purpose of securing political ends ⟨studied the history and techniques of *nonviolence*⟩

non·vi·o·lent \-lənt\ *adjective* (1920)
: abstaining or free from violence
— **non·vi·o·lent·ly** *adverb*

non·vol·a·tile \ˈnän-ˈvä-lə-tᵊl\ *adjective* (1866)

: not volatile: as **a** : not vaporizing readily ⟨a *nonvolatile* solvent⟩ **b** *of a computer memory* : retaining data when power is shut off

non–West·ern \-'wes-tərn\ *adjective* (1902)
1 : not being part of the western tradition ⟨*non-Western* countries⟩
2 : of or relating to non-Western societies ⟨*non-Western* values⟩

non·white \-'hwīt, -'wīt\ *noun* (1927)
: a person whose features and especially whose skin color are distinctively different from those of peoples of northwestern Europe; *especially* : one who has African ancestors of the black race
— **nonwhite** *adjective*

non·word \-'wərd\ *noun* (1961)
: a word that has no meaning, is not known to exist, or is disapproved

non·wo·ven \-'wō-vən\ *adjective* (1945)
1 : made of fibers held together by interlocking or bonding (as by chemical or thermal means) : not woven, knitted, or felted ⟨*nonwoven* fabric⟩
2 : made of nonwoven fabric ⟨a *nonwoven* dress⟩
— **nonwoven** *noun*

non·ze·ro \-'zē-(,)rō, -'zir-(,)ō\ *adjective* (1905)
1 : being, having, or involving a value other than zero
2 : having phonetic content ⟨*nonzero* affixes⟩

¹noo·dle \'nü-d°l\ *noun* [perhaps alteration of *noddle*] (1753)
1 : a stupid person : SIMPLETON
2 : HEAD, NOGGIN

²noodle *noun* [German *Nudel*] (1779)
: a food paste made with egg and shaped typically in ribbon form

³noodle *intransitive verb* **noo·dled; noo·dling** \'nüd-liŋ, 'nü-d°l-iŋ\ [imitative] (circa 1937)
: to improvise on an instrument in an informal or desultory manner

nook \'nùk\ *noun* [Middle English *noke, nok*] (14th century)
1 *chiefly Scottish* : a right-angled corner
2 a : an interior angle formed by two meeting walls : RECESS **b** : a secluded or sheltered place or part ⟨searched every *nook* and cranny⟩

nooky \'nù-kē\ *noun* [perhaps from *nook* + ⁴-y] (1928)
1 : SEXUAL INTERCOURSE — often considered vulgar
2 : the female partner in sexual intercourse — often considered vulgar

noon \'nün\ *noun* [Middle English, from Old English *nōn* ninth hour from sunrise, from Latin *nona*, from feminine of *nonus* ninth; akin to Latin *novem* nine — more at NINE] (13th century)
1 : MIDDAY; *specifically* : 12 o'clock at midday
2 *archaic* : MIDNIGHT — used chiefly in the phrase *noon of night*
3 : the highest point ◇

noon·day \-,dā\ *noun* (1535)
: MIDDAY

no one *pronoun* (before 12th century)
: no person : NOBODY
usage see NOBODY

noon·ing \'nü-niŋ, -nən\ *noun* (circa 1652)
1 *chiefly dialect* : a meal eaten at noon
2 *chiefly dialect* : a period at noon for eating or resting

noon·tide \'nün-,tīd\ *noun* (12th century)
1 : NOONTIME
2 : the culminating point

noon·time \-,tīm\ *noun* (14th century)
: the time of noon : MIDDAY

¹noose \'nüs, *British also* 'nüz\ *noun* [Middle English *nose*, perhaps of Provençal origin; akin to Provençal *nous* knot, from Latin *nodus* — more at NODE] (15th century)
1 : a loop with a running knot that binds closer the more it is drawn
2 : something that snares like a noose

²noose *transitive verb* **noosed; noos·ing** (1600)
1 : to secure by a noose
2 : to make a noose in or of

noo·sphere \'nō-ə-,sfir\ *noun* [International Scientific Vocabulary *noo*- mind (from Greek *noos, nous*) + *sphere* sphere] (1945)
: the sphere of human consciousness and mental activity especially in regard to its influence on the biosphere and in relation to evolution

Noot·ka \'nüt-kə\ *noun, plural* **Nootka** *or* **Nootkas** (1841)
1 : a member of a Wakashan people inhabiting the West Coast of Vancouver Island
2 : the language of the Nootka people

no·pal \nō-'päl, -'pal; 'nō-pəl\ *noun* [Spanish, from Nahuatl *nohpalli*] (1730)
: any of a genus (*Nopalea*) of cacti of Mexico and Central America that differ from the prickly pears in having erect petals and scarlet flowers with the stamens much longer than the petals; *broadly* : PRICKLY PEAR

no-par *or* **no-par–value** *adjective* (1922)
: having no nominal value ⟨*no-par* stocks⟩

nope \'nōp, or with glottal stop instead of p\ *adverb* [by alteration] (1888)
: NO

¹nor \nər, 'nòr, *Southern also* 'när\ *conjunction* [Middle English, contraction of *nother* neither, nor, from *nother*, pronoun & adjective, neither — more at NEITHER] (14th century)
1 — used as a function word to introduce the second or last member or the second and each following member of a series of items each of which is negated ⟨neither here *nor* there⟩ ⟨not done by you *nor* me *nor* anyone⟩
2 — used as a function word to introduce and negate a following clause or phrase
3 *chiefly British* : NEITHER

²nor *conjunction* [Middle English, perhaps from ¹*nor*] (15th century)
dialect : THAN

nor- *combining form* [*normal*]
: homologue containing one less methyl group ⟨*nor*epinephrine⟩

NOR \'nòr\ *noun* [*not OR*] (1957)
: a computer logic circuit that produces an output that is the inverse of that of an OR circuit

nor·adren·a·line *also* **nor·adren·a·lin** \,nòr-ə-'dre-n°l-ən\ *noun* (1932)
: NOREPINEPHRINE

nor·ad·ren·er·gic \,nòr-,a-drə-'nər-jik\ *adjective* [*noradren*aline + *-ergic*] (1963)
: liberating, activated by, or involving norepinephrine in the transmission of nerve impulses ⟨*noradrenergic* nerve endings⟩ ⟨*noradrenergic* nerve fibers⟩

¹Nor·dic \'nòr-dik\ *adjective* [French *nordique*, from *nord* north, from Old English *north*] (1898)
1 : of or relating to the Germanic peoples of northern Europe and especially of Scandinavia
2 : of or relating to a group or physical type of the Caucasian race characterized by tall stature, long head, light skin and hair, and blue eyes
3 a : of or relating to competitive ski events involving cross-country racing, ski jumping, or biathlon — compare ALPINE **b** : of, relating to, or being cross-country skiing

²Nordic *noun* (1901)
1 : a native of northern Europe
2 : a person of Nordic physical type
3 : a member of the peoples of Scandinavia

nor·epi·neph·rine \'nòr-,e-pə-'ne-frən\ *noun* (1945)
: a catecholamine $C_8H_{11}NO_3$ that is the chemical means of transmission across synapses in postganglionic neurons of the sympathetic nervous system and in some parts of the central nervous system, is a vasopressor hormone of the adrenal medulla, and is a precursor of epinephrine in its major biosynthetic pathway

nor·eth·in·drone \,nò-'re-thən-,drōn\ *noun* [*nor-* + *ethinyl* + *hydr-* + *-one* (as in *progesterone*)] (1958)
: a synthetic progestational hormone $C_{20}H_{26}O_2$ used in oral contraceptives often in the form of its acetate

Nor·folk jacket \'nòr-fək-, -,fòk-\ *noun* [*Norfolk*, England] (1866)
: a loose-fitting belted single-breasted jacket with box pleats

Norfolk terrier *noun* (1964)
: any of a breed of dogs developed in England and resembling the Norwich terrier but having folded-over ears

no·ri \'nō-rē, 'nòr-ē\ *noun* [Japanese] (1892)
: dried laver seaweed pressed into thin sheets and used especially as a seasoning or as a wrapper for sushi

nor·land \'nòr-lənd\ *noun* (circa 1578)
chiefly dialect : NORTHLAND

norm \'nòrm\ *noun* [Latin *norma*, literally, carpenter's square] (1674)
1 : an authoritative standard : MODEL
2 : a principle of right action binding upon the members of a group and serving to guide, control, or regulate proper and acceptable behavior
3 : AVERAGE: as **a** : a set standard of development or achievement usually derived from the average or median achievement of a large group **b** : a pattern or trait taken to be typical in the behavior of a social group **c** : a widespread practice, procedure, or custom : RULE ⟨standing ovations became the *norm*⟩
4 a : a real-valued nonnegative function defined on a vector space and satisfying the conditions that the function is zero if and only if the vector is zero, the function of the product of a scalar and a vector is equal to the product of the absolute value of the scalar and the function of the vector, and the function of the sum of two vectors is less than or equal to the sum of the functions of the two vectors; *specifically* : the square root of the sum of the squares of the absolute values of the elements of a matrix or of the components of a vector **b** : the greatest distance between two successive points of a set of points that partition an interval into smaller intervals
synonym see AVERAGE

¹nor·mal \'nòr-məl\ *adjective* [Latin *normalis*, from *norma*] (circa 1696)
1 : PERPENDICULAR; *especially* : perpendicular to a tangent at a point of tangency

◇ WORD HISTORY

noon *Noon* has not always indicated that time of day at which the sun is most nearly overhead. According to the Roman method of reckoning time, the hours of the day were counted from sunrise to sunset, so that *nona*, short for *nona hora* "ninth hour," denoted the ninth hour of daylight, about 3 P.M. in modern reckoning. *Nona* was borrowed into Old English as *nōn*, which denoted either the ninth hour of the day or the liturgical office of nones that was read at this time. In early Middle English, however, *non* or *none* (later *noon*) was applied to a meal eaten before nones was read, perhaps originally an afternoon snack. If this was the case, however, the meaning seems soon to have shifted to the major midday meal, and then to midday itself, a sense that Modern English *noon* has retained. The word *none* or *nones* was later borrowed from Latin to refer specifically to the liturgical office.

\ə\ abut \°\ kitten \ər\ further \a\ ash \ā\ ace
\ä\ mop, mar \au̇\ out \ch\ chin \e\ bet \ē\ easy
\g\ go \i\ hit \ī\ ice \j\ job \ŋ\ sing \ō\ go
\ȯ\ law \ȯi\ boy \th\ thin \t̲h̲\ the \ü\ loot \u̇\ foot
\y\ yet \zh\ vision *see also* Guide to Pronunciation

2 a : according with, constituting, or not deviating from a norm, rule, or principle **b :** conforming to a type, standard, or regular pattern **3 :** occurring naturally ⟨*normal* immunity⟩ **4 a :** of, relating to, or characterized by average intelligence or development **b :** free from mental disorder **:** SANE **5 a** *of a solution* **:** having a concentration of one gram equivalent of solute per liter **b :** containing neither basic hydroxyl nor acid hydrogen ⟨*normal* silver phosphate⟩ **c :** not associated ⟨*normal* molecules⟩ **d :** having a straight-chain structure ⟨*normal* pentane⟩ ⟨*normal* butyl alcohol⟩ **6** *of a subgroup* **:** having the property that every coset produced by operating on the left by a given element is equal to the coset produced by operating on the right by the same element **7 :** relating to, involving, or being a normal curve or normal distribution ⟨*normal* approximation to the binomial distribution⟩ **8** *of a matrix* **:** having the property of commutativity under multiplication by the transpose of the matrix each of whose elements is a conjugate complex number with respect to the corresponding element of the given matrix ◇
synonym see REGULAR
— **nor·mal·i·ty** \nȯr-'ma-lə-tē\ *noun*
— **nor·mal·ly** \'nȯr-mə-lē\ *adverb*
²normal *noun* (circa 1738)
1 a : a normal line **b :** the portion of a normal line to a plane curve between the curve and the x-axis
2 : one that is normal
3 : a form or state regarded as the norm **:** STANDARD
normal curve *noun* (1894)
: the symmetrical bell-shaped curve of a normal distribution
nor·mal·cy \'nȯr-məl-sē\ *noun* (1857)
: the state or fact of being normal
normal distribution *noun* (1897)
: a probability density function that approximates the distribution of many random variables (as the proportion of outcomes of a particular sort in a large number of independent repetitions of an experiment in which the probabilities remain constant from trial to trial) and that has the form

$$f(x) = \frac{1}{\sigma\sqrt{2\pi}}\, e^{-\frac{1}{2}\left(\frac{x-\mu}{\sigma}\right)^2}$$

where μ is the mean and σ is the standard deviation — compare NORMAL CURVE
nor·mal·ise *British variant of* NORMALIZE
nor·mal·ize \'nȯr-mə-ˌlīz\ *transitive verb* **-ized; -iz·ing** (1865)
1 : to make conform to or reduce to a norm or standard
2 : to make normal (as by a transformation of variables)
3 : to bring or restore (as relations between countries) to a normal condition
— **nor·mal·iz·able** \-ˌlī-zə-bəl\ *adjective*
— **nor·mal·i·za·tion** \ˌnȯr-mə-lə-'zā-shən\ *noun*
nor·mal·iz·er \'nȯr-mə-ˌlī-zər\ *noun* (1926)
1 : one that normalizes
2 a : a subgroup consisting of those elements of a group for which the group operation with regard to a given element is commutative **b :** the set of elements of a group for which the group operation with regard to every element of a given subgroup is commutative
normal school *noun* [translation of French *école normale;* from the fact that the first French school so named was intended to serve as a model] (1839)
: a usually 2-year school for training chiefly elementary teachers
Nor·man \'nȯr-mən\ *noun* [Middle English, from Old French *Normant,* from Old Norse *Northmann-, Northmathr* Norseman, from *northr* north + *mann-, mathr* man; akin to Old

English *north* north and to Old English *man* man] (13th century)
1 : a native or inhabitant of Normandy: **a :** one of the Scandinavian conquerors of Normandy in the 10th century **b :** one of the Norman-French conquerors of England in 1066
2 : NORMAN-FRENCH
— **Norman** *adjective*
Norman architecture *noun* (1797)
: a Romanesque style first appearing in and near Normandy about A.D. 950; *also* : architecture resembling or imitating this style
nor·mande \nȯr-'mand\ *adjective* [French, from feminine of *normand* Norman, from *Normandy,* France] (circa 1929)
: prepared with any of several foods traditionally associated with Normandy (as cream, apples, cider, or calvados) ⟨veal *normande*⟩
Norman–French *noun* (1605)
1 : the French language of the medieval Normans
2 : the modern dialect of Normandy
nor·ma·tive \'nȯr-mə-tiv\ *adjective* [French *normatif,* from *norme* norm, from Latin *norma*] (1878)
1 : of, relating to, or determining norms or standards ⟨*normative* tests⟩
2 : conforming to or based on norms ⟨*normative* behavior⟩ ⟨*normative* judgments⟩
3 : prescribing norms ⟨*normative* rules of ethics⟩ ⟨*normative* grammar⟩
— **nor·ma·tive·ly** *adverb*
— **nor·ma·tive·ness** *noun*
normed \'nȯrmd\ *adjective* (1935)
: being a mathematical entity upon which a norm is defined ⟨a *normed* vector space⟩
nor·mo·ten·sive \ˌnȯr-mō-'ten(t)-siv\ *adjective* [*normal* + *-o-* + *-tensive* (as in *hypotensive*)] (circa 1941)
: having blood pressure typical of the group to which one belongs
— **normotensive** *noun*
nor·mo·ther·mia \-'thər-mē-ə\ *noun* [New Latin, from *normal*is normal + *-o-* + *-thermia* -thermy] (1960)
: normal body temperature
— **nor·mo·ther·mic** \-mik\ *adjective*
Norn \'nȯrn\ *noun* [Old Norse]
: any of the three Norse goddesses of fate
¹Norse \'nȯrs\ *noun, plural* **Norse** [probably from obsolete Dutch *noorsch,* adjective, Norwegian, Scandinavian, alteration of obsolete Dutch *noordsch* northern, from Dutch *noord* north; akin to Old English *north* north] (circa 1688)
1 a : NORWEGIAN 2 **b :** any of the western Scandinavian dialects or languages **c :** the Scandinavian group of Germanic languages
2 *plural* **a :** SCANDINAVIANS **b :** NORWEGIANS
²Norse *adjective* (1768)
1 : of or relating to ancient Scandinavia or the language of its inhabitants
2 : NORWEGIAN
Norse·man \'nȯrs-mən\ *noun* (1817)
: any of the ancient Scandinavians
¹north \'nȯrth\ *adverb* [Middle English, from Old English; akin to Old High German *nord* north and perhaps to Greek *nerteros* lower, infernal] (before 12th century)
: to, toward, or in the north
²north *adjective* (before 12th century)
1 : situated toward or at the north ⟨the *north* entrance⟩
2 : coming from the north ⟨a *north* wind⟩
³north *noun* (13th century)
1 a : the direction of the north terrestrial pole **:** the direction to the left of one facing east **b :** the compass point directly opposite to south
2 *capitalized* **a :** regions or countries lying to the north of a specified or implied point of orientation **b :** the industrially and economically developed nations of the world — compare SOUTH
3 *often capitalized* **a :** the one of four positions at 90-degree intervals that lies to the

north or at the top of a diagram **b :** a person occupying this position in the course of a specified activity (as the game of bridge)
north·bound \'nȯrth-ˌbau̇nd\ *adjective* (1903)
: traveling or headed north
north by east (1725)
: a compass point that is one point east of due north **:** N11°15′E
north by west (circa 1771)
: a compass point that is one point west of due north **:** N11°15′W
¹north·east \nȯr-'thēst, *nautical* nȯ-'rēst\ *adverb* (before 12th century)
: to, toward, or in the northeast
²northeast *adjective* (before 12th century)
1 : coming from the northeast ⟨a *northeast* wind⟩
2 : situated toward or at the northeast ⟨the *northeast* corner⟩
³northeast *noun* (12th century)
1 a : the general direction between north and east **b :** the point midway between the north and east compass points
2 *capitalized* **:** regions or countries lying to the northeast of a specified or implied point of orientation
northeast by east (circa 1771)
: a compass point that is one point east of due northeast **:** N56°15′E
northeast by north (circa 1771)
: a compass point that is one point north of due northeast **:** N33°45′E
north·east·er \nȯr-'thē-stər, nȯ-'rē-\ *noun* (1774)
1 : a strong northeast wind
2 : a storm with northeast winds
north·east·er·ly \nȯr-'thē-stər-lē\ *adverb or adjective* (1739)
1 : from the northeast
2 : toward the northeast
north·east·ern \-stərn\ *adjective* (14th century)
1 *often capitalized* **:** of, relating to, or characteristic of a region conventionally designated Northeast
2 : lying toward or coming from the northeast
— **north·east·ern·most** \-stərn-ˌmōst\ *adjective*
North·east·ern·er \-stə(r)-nər\ *noun* (1961)
: a native or inhabitant of a northeastern region (as of the U.S.)
¹north·east·ward \nȯr-'thēs-twərd, nȯ-'rēs-\ *adverb or adjective* (1553)
: toward the northeast
— **north·east·wards** \-twərdz\ *adverb*
²northeastward *noun* (1892)
: NORTHEAST
north·er \'nȯr-thər\ *noun* (1820)
1 : a strong north wind
2 : a storm with north winds
¹north·er·ly \-lē\ *adjective or adverb* [³*north* + *-erly* (as in *easterly*)] (1551)

◇ WORD HISTORY
normal In Latin *norma* was the word for a carpenter's square, the tool which ensures that a carpenter can regularly reproduce corners and edges that are straight and that form right angles. *Norma* also had the extended sense "standard" or "pattern." Similarly, *normalis,* the Latin adjective formed from *norma,* had the literal meaning "forming a right angle" and by the Late Latin period the extended sense "according to rule." It is from this extended sense that we derive most of the English senses of *normal.* Incidentally, *normal school,* as a name for a college devoted to teacher training, is a translation of the French term *école normale.* The term derives from the fact that the first school named *école normale* was intended to serve as a standard or model for other teaching schools.

1 : situated toward or belonging to the north ⟨the *northerly* border⟩
2 : coming from the north ⟨a *northerly* wind⟩
²northerly *noun, plural* **-lies** (1955)
: a wind from the north
¹north·ern \'nȯr-<u>th</u>ə(r)n\ *adjective* [Middle English *northerne,* from Old English; akin to Old High German *nordrōni* northern, Old English *north* north] (before 12th century)
1 *capitalized* **a** : of, relating to, or characteristic of a region conventionally designated North **b** : of, relating to, or constituting the northern dialect
2 a : lying toward the north **b** : coming from the north ⟨a *northern* storm⟩
— **north·ern·most** \-ˌmōst\ *adjective*
²northern *noun* (1950)
1 *capitalized* : the dialect of English spoken in the part of the U.S. north of a line running northwest through central New Jersey, below the northern tier of counties in Pennsylvania, through northern Ohio, Indiana, and Illinois, across central Iowa, and through the northwest corner of South Dakota
2 : ³PIKE 1a
northern corn rootworm *noun* (1952)
: a corn rootworm (*Diabrotica barberi* synonym *D. longicornis*) often destructive to Indian corn in the northern parts of the central and eastern U.S.
Northern Cross *noun*
: a cross formed by six stars in Cygnus
North·ern·er \'nȯr-<u>th</u>ə(r)-nər\ *noun* (1599)
: a native or inhabitant of the North; *especially* : a native or resident of the northern part of the U.S.
northern harrier *noun* (1980)
: a widely distributed brown or grayish hawk (*Circus cyaneus*) that inhabits open and marshy regions and has a conspicuous white patch on the rump — called also *marsh hawk*

northern harrier

northern hemisphere *noun, often N&H capitalized* (circa 1771)
: the half of the earth that lies north of the equator
northern lights *noun plural* (14th century)
: AURORA BOREALIS
northern oriole *noun* (1974)
: an American oriole (*Icterus galbula*) that is characterized by the black and orange plumage of the male and that includes the Baltimore oriole of the eastern U.S. and a more western form (*I. g. bullockii*) with a black and orange head
northern pike *noun* (1856)
: ³PIKE 1a
northern white cedar *noun* (1926)
: an arborvitae (*Thuja occidentalis*) of eastern North America that has branchlets in horizontal planes; *also* : its wood — called also *white cedar*
North Germanic *noun* (circa 1930)
: a subdivision of the Germanic languages including Icelandic, Norwegian, Swedish, and Danish — see INDO-EUROPEAN LANGUAGES table
north·ing \'nȯr-thiŋ, -thiŋ\ *noun* (1669)
1 : difference in latitude to the north from the last preceding point of reckoning
2 : northerly progress
north·land \'nȯrth-ˌland, -lənd\ *noun, often capitalized* (before 12th century)
: land in the north : the north of a country
North·man \'nȯrth-mən\ *noun* (before 12th century)
: NORSEMAN
north–north·east \'nȯrth-ˌnȯr-'thēst, -ˌnȯ-'rēst\ *noun* (14th century)

: a compass point that is two points east of due north : N22°30′E
north–north·west \'nȯrth-ˌnȯr(th)-'west\ *noun* (14th century)
: a compass point that is two points west of due north : N22°30′W
north pole *noun* (14th century)
1 a *often N&P capitalized* : the northernmost point of the earth; *broadly* : the corresponding point of a celestial body (as a planet) **b** : the zenith of the heavens as viewed from the north terrestrial pole
2 *of a magnet* : the pole that points toward the north when the magnet is freely suspended
north–seeking pole *noun* (circa 1920)
: NORTH POLE 2
North Star *noun*
: the star of the northern hemisphere toward which the axis of the earth points — called also *polestar*
¹North·um·bri·an \nȯr-'thəm-brē-ən\ *adjective* (1622)
1 : of, relating to, or characteristic of ancient Northumbria, its people, or its language
2 : of, relating to, or characteristic of Northumberland, its people, or its language
²Northumbrian *noun* (1752)
1 : a native or inhabitant of ancient Northumbria
2 : a native or inhabitant of Northumberland
3 a : the Old English dialect of Northumbria **b** : the Modern English dialect of Northumberland
¹north·ward \'nȯrth-wərd\ *adverb or adjective* (before 12th century)
: toward the north
— **north·wards** \-wərdz\ *adverb*
²northward *noun* (14th century)
: northward direction or part ⟨sail to the *northward*⟩
¹north·west \nȯrth-'west, *nautical* nȯr-'west\ *adverb* (before 12th century)
: to, toward, or in the northwest
²northwest *adjective* (before 12th century)
1 : coming from the northwest ⟨a *northwest* wind⟩
2 : situated toward or at the northwest ⟨the *northwest* corner⟩
³northwest *noun* (12th century)
1 a : the general direction between north and west **b** : the point midway between the north and west compass points
2 *capitalized* : regions or countries lying to the northwest of a specified or implied point of orientation
northwest by north (circa 1771)
: a compass point that is one point north of due northwest : N33°45′W
northwest by west (circa 1771)
: a compass point that is one point west of due northwest : N56°15′W
north·west·er \nȯr(th)-'wes-tər\ *noun* (1737)
: a strong northwest wind
north·west·er·ly \-lē\ *adverb or adjective* (circa 1611)
1 : from the northwest
2 : toward the northwest
north·west·ern \-'wes-tərn\ *adjective* (1612)
1 *often capitalized* : of, relating to, or characteristic of a region conventionally designated Northwest
2 : lying toward or coming from the northwest
— **north·west·ern·most** \-ˌmōst\ *adjective*
North·west·ern·er \-'wes-tə(r)-nər\ *noun* (1955)
: a native or inhabitant of the Northwest and especially of the northwestern part of the U.S.
¹north·west·ward \-'wes-twərd\ *adverb or adjective* (14th century)
: toward the northwest
— **north·west·wards** \-twərdz\ *adverb*
²northwestward *noun* (1796)
: NORTHWEST

nor·trip·ty·line \nȯr-'trip-tə-ˌlēn\ *noun* [*nor-* + *-tript-* (perhaps from *tri*cyclic + he*pta*-) + *-yl* + ²*-ine*] (1964)
: a tricyclic antidepressant $C_{19}H_{21}N$
Nor·way maple \'nȯr-ˌwā-\ *noun* (1797)
: a European maple (*Acer platanoides*) with dark green or often reddish or red veined leaves that is much planted for shade in the U.S.
Norway rat *noun* (circa 1759)
: BROWN RAT
Norway spruce *noun* (1797)
: a widely cultivated spruce (*Picea abies*) that is native to northern Europe and has a pyramidal shape, spreading branches and pendulous branchlets, dark foliage, and long pendulous cones
Nor·we·gian \nȯr-'wē-jən\ *noun* [Medieval Latin *Norwegia* Norway] (1605)
1 a : a native or inhabitant of Norway **b** : a person of Norwegian descent
2 : the Germanic language of the Norwegian people
— **Norwegian** *adjective*
Norwegian elkhound *noun* (1930)
: any of a Norwegian breed of short-bodied medium-sized dogs with erect ears and a very heavy coat of gray hairs with black tips
Nor·wich terrier \'nȯr-(ˌ)wich-, *British* 'när-ich- *or* 'när-ij-\ *noun* [*Norwich*, England] (1931)
: any of an English breed of small active low-set terriers that have a long straight wiry coat and erect ears

Norwegian elkhound

¹nose \'nōz\ *noun* [Middle English, from Old English *nosu;* akin to Old High German *nasa* nose, Latin *nasus*] (before 12th century)
1 a : the part of the face that bears the nostrils and covers the anterior part of the nasal cavity; *broadly* : this part together with the nasal cavity **b** : the anterior part of the head at the top or end of the muzzle : SNOUT, PROBOSCIS
2 a : the sense of smell : OLFACTION **b** : AROMA, BOUQUET
3 : the vertebrate olfactory organ
4 a : the forward end or projection of something **b** : the projecting or working end of a tool
5 : the stem of a boat or its protective metal covering
6 a : the nose as a symbol of prying or meddling curiosity or interference **b** : a knack for discovery or understanding ⟨a keen *nose* for absurdity⟩
— **on the nose 1 a** : at or to a target point ⟨the bombs landed right *on the nose*⟩ **b** (1) : on target : ACCURATE (2) : ACCURATELY **2** : to win — used of horse or dog racing bets
²nose *verb* **nosed; nos·ing** (circa 1587)
transitive verb
1 : to detect by or as if by smell : SCENT
2 a : to push or move with the nose **b** : to move (as a vehicle) ahead slowly or cautiously ⟨*nosed* my car into the parking space⟩
3 : to touch or rub with the nose : NUZZLE
intransitive verb
1 : to use the nose in examining, smelling, or showing affection
2 : to search impertinently : PRY
3 : to move ahead slowly or cautiously ⟨the boat *nosed* around the bend⟩

\ə\ abut \ᵊ\ kitten \ər\ further \a\ ash \ā\ ace
\ä\ mop, mar \au̇\ out \ch\ chin \e\ bet \ē\ easy
\g\ go \i\ hit \ī\ ice \j\ job \ŋ\ sing \ō\ go
\ȯ\ law \ȯi\ boy \th\ thin \<u>th</u>\ the \ü\ loot \u̇\ foot
\y\ yet \zh\ vision *see also* Guide to Pronunciation

nose·band \'nōz-ˌband\ *noun* (1611)
: the part of a headstall that passes over a horse's nose

nose·bleed \-ˌblēd\ *noun* (1848)
: an attack of bleeding from the nose

nose cone *noun* (1949)
: a protective cone constituting the forward end of an aerospace vehicle

nosed \'nōzd\ *adjective* (1505)
: having a nose especially of a specified kind — usually used in combination ⟨snub-*nosed*⟩

nose·dive \'nōz-ˌdīv\ *noun* (1912)
1 : a downward nose-first plunge of a flying object (as an airplane)
2 : a sudden extreme drop ⟨stock prices took a *nosedive*⟩
— **nose–dive** *intransitive verb*

no–see–um \nō-'sē-əm\ *noun* [from the words (as supposedly spoken by American Indians) *no see um* you don't see them] (1848)
: BITING MIDGE

nose·gay \'nōz-ˌgā\ *noun* [Middle English, from *nose* nose + *gay* ornament, literally, something gay, from *gay*] (15th century)
: a small bunch of flowers : POSY

nose·guard \-ˌgärd\ *noun* (1950)
: a defensive lineman in football who plays opposite the offensive center

nose job *noun* (1963)
: RHINOPLASTY

nose out *transitive verb* (circa 1630)
1 : to discover often by prying
2 : to defeat by a narrow margin

nose·piece \-ˌpēs\ *noun* (1611)
1 : a piece of armor for protecting the nose
2 : the end piece of a microscope body to which an objective is attached
3 : the bridge of a pair of eyeglasses

nose tackle *noun* (1977)
: NOSEGUARD

nose·wheel \-ˌhwēl, -ˌwēl\ *noun* (1934)
: a landing-gear wheel under the nose of an airplane

nos·ey par·ker \'nō-zē-'pär-kər\ *noun, often N&P capitalized* [probably from the name *Parker*] (1907)
chiefly British : BUSYBODY

¹nosh \'näsh\ *noun* (1952)
: a light meal : SNACK

²nosh *verb* [Yiddish *nashn*, from Middle High German *naschen* to eat on the sly] (1956)
intransitive verb
: to eat a snack
transitive verb
: CHEW, MUNCH
— **nosh·er** *noun*

no–show \'nō-ˌshō, -'shō\ *noun* (1941)
1 : a person who reserves space (as on an airplane) but neither uses nor cancels the reservation
2 : a person who buys a ticket (as to a sporting event) but does not attend; *broadly* : a person who is expected but who does not show up
3 : failure to show up

nos·ing \'nō-ziŋ\ *noun* (circa 1775)
: the usually rounded edge of a stair tread that projects over the riser; *also* : a similar rounded projection

nos·o·co·mi·al \ˌnä-sə-'kō-mē-əl\ *adjective* [Late Latin *nosocomium* hospital, from Late Greek *nosokomeion*, from Greek *nosokomos* one who tends the sick, from *nosos* disease + *-komos*; akin to Greek *kamnein* to suffer, toil, Sanskrit *śamyati* he tires] (circa 1843)
: originating or taking place in a hospital ⟨*nosocomial* infection⟩

no·sol·o·gy \nō-'sä-lə-jē, -'zä-\ *noun* [probably from New Latin *nosologia*, from Greek *nosos* disease + New Latin *-logia* -logy] (circa 1721)
1 : a classification or list of diseases
2 : a branch of medical science that deals with classification of diseases
— **no·so·log·i·cal** \ˌnō-sə-'lä-ji-kəl\ *or* **no·so·log·ic** \-jik\ *adjective*
— **no·so·log·i·cal·ly** \-ji-k(ə-)lē\ *adverb*

nos·tal·gia \nä-'stal-jə, nə- *also* nò-, nō-; nə-'stäl-\ *noun* [New Latin, from Greek *nostos* return home + New Latin *-algia;* akin to Greek *neisthai* to return, Old English ge*nesan* to survive, Sanskrit *nasate* he approaches] (1770)
1 : the state of being homesick : HOMESICKNESS
2 : a wistful or excessively sentimental yearning for return to or of some past period or irrecoverable condition; *also* : something that evokes nostalgia
— **nos·tal·gic** \-jik\ *adjective or noun*
— **nos·tal·gi·cal·ly** \-ji-k(ə-)lē\ *adverb*

nos·tal·gist \-jist\ *noun* (1953)
: a person given to nostalgia for the past

nos·toc \'näs-ˌtäk\ *noun* [New Latin] (1650)
: any of a genus (*Nostoc*) of blue-green algae that fix nitrogen

nos·tril \'näs-trəl\ *noun* [Middle English *nosethirl*, from Old English *nosthyrl*, from *nosu* nose + *thyrel* hole; akin to Old English *thurh* through] (before 12th century)
1 : either of the external nares; *broadly* : either of the nares with the adjoining passage on the same side of the septum
2 : either fleshy lateral wall of the nose

word history see THRILL

nos·trum \'näs-trəm\ *noun* [Latin, neuter of *noster* our, ours, from *nos* we — more at US] (1602)
1 : a medicine of secret composition recommended by its preparer but usually without scientific proof of its effectiveness
2 : a usually questionable remedy or scheme : PANACEA

nosy *or* **nos·ey** \'nō-zē\ *adjective* **nos·i·er; -est** [¹*nose*] (1882)
: of prying or inquisitive disposition or quality : INTRUSIVE
— **nos·i·ly** \'nō-zə-lē\ *adverb*
— **nos·i·ness** \-zē-nəs\ *noun*

not \'nät\ *adverb* [Middle English, alteration of *nought*, from *nought*, pronoun — more at NAUGHT] (13th century)
1 — used as a function word to make negative a group of words or a word
2 — used as a function word to stand for the negative of a preceding group of words ⟨is sometimes hard to see and sometimes *not*⟩

NOT \'nät\ *noun* [*not*] (1947)
: a logical operator that produces a statement that is the inverse of an input statement

nota *plural of* NOTUM

no·ta be·ne \ˌnō-tə-'bē-nē, -'be-\ [Latin, mark well] (circa 1721)
— used to call attention to something important

no·ta·bil·i·ty \ˌnō-tə-'bi-lə-tē\ *noun, plural* **-ties** (1832)
: a notable or prominent person

¹no·ta·ble \'nō-tə-bəl, *for 2 also* 'nä-\ *adjective* (14th century)
1 a : worthy of note : REMARKABLE **b** : DISTINGUISHED, PROMINENT
2 *archaic* : efficient or capable in performance of housewifely duties
— **no·ta·ble·ness** *noun*

²notable \'nō-tə-bəl\ *noun* (1815)
1 : a person of note : NOTABILITY
2 *plural, often capitalized* : a group of persons summoned especially in monarchical France to act as a deliberative body

no·ta·bly \'nō-tə-blē\ *adverb* (14th century)
1 : in a notable manner : to a high degree ⟨was *notably* impressed⟩
2 : ESPECIALLY, PARTICULARLY ⟨other powers, *notably* Britain and the United States —C. A. Fisher⟩

no·tar·i·al \nō-'ter-ē-əl\ *adjective* (15th century)
1 : of, relating to, or characteristic of a notary public
2 : done or executed by a notary public
— **no·tar·i·al·ly** \-ə-lē\ *adverb*

no·ta·ri·za·tion \ˌnō-tə-rə-'zā-shən\ *noun* (1940)

1 : the act, process, or an instance of notarizing
2 : the notarial certificate appended to a document

no·ta·rize \'nō-tə-ˌrīz\ *transitive verb* **-rized; -riz·ing** (1926)
: to acknowledge or attest as a notary public

no·ta·ry public \'nō-tə-rē-\ *noun, plural* **notaries public** *or* **notary publics** [Middle English *notary* clerk, notary public, from Latin *notarius* clerk, secretary, from *notarius* of shorthand, from *nota* note, shorthand character] (15th century)
: a public officer who attests or certifies writings (as a deed) to make them authentic and takes affidavits, depositions, and protests of negotiable paper — called also *notary*

no·tate \'nō-ˌtāt\ *transitive verb* **no·tat·ed; no·tat·ing** [back-formation from *notation*] (1903)
: to put into notation

no·ta·tion \nō-'tā-shən\ *noun* [Latin *notation-, notatio,* from *notare* to note] (1584)
1 : ANNOTATION, NOTE
2 a : the act, process, method, or an instance of representing by a system or set of marks, signs, figures, or characters **b** : a system of characters, symbols, or abbreviated expressions used in an art or science or in mathematics or logic to express technical facts or quantities
— **no·ta·tion·al** \-shnəl, -shə-nᵊl\ *adjective*

¹notch \'näch\ *noun* [perhaps alteration (from misdivision of *an otch*) of (assumed) *otch*, from Middle French *oche*] (1577)
1 a : a V-shaped indentation **b** : a slit made to serve as a record **c** : a rounded indentation cut into the pages of a book on the edge opposite the spine
2 : a deep close pass : GAP
3 : DEGREE, STEP
— **notched** \'nächt\ *adjective*

²notch *transitive verb* (1600)
1 : to cut or make a notch in
2 a : to mark or record by a notch **b** : SCORE, ACHIEVE — sometimes used with *up*

notch·back \'näch-ˌbak\ *noun* (1965)
: an automobile with a trunk whose lid forms a distinct deck; *also* : the back of such an automobile

¹note \'nōt\ *transitive verb* **not·ed; not·ing** [Middle English, from Old French *noter,* from Latin *notare* to mark, note, from *nota*] (13th century)
1 a : to notice or observe with care **b** : to record or preserve in writing
2 a : to make special mention of : REMARK **b** : INDICATE, SHOW
— **not·er** *noun*

²note *noun* [Middle English, from Old French, from Latin *nota* mark, character, written note] (13th century)
1 a (1) *obsolete* : MELODY, SONG (2) : TONE 2a (3) : CALL, SOUND; *especially* : the musical call of a bird **b** : a written symbol used to indicate duration and pitch of a tone by its shape and position on the staff
2 a : a characteristic feature (as of odor or flavor) **b** : something (as an emotion or disposition) like a note in tone or resonance ⟨a *note* of sadness⟩ ⟨end on a high *note*⟩
3 a (1) : MEMORANDUM (2) : a condensed or informal record **b** (1) : a brief comment or explanation (2) : a printed comment or reference

♩	whole
♩	half
♩	quarter
♩	eighth
♩	sixteenth
♩	thirty-second
♩	sixty-fourth

note 1b

set apart from the text **c** (1) **:** a written promise to pay a debt (2) **:** a piece of paper money **d** (1) **:** a short informal letter (2) **:** a formal diplomatic communication **e :** a scholarly or technical essay shorter than an article and restricted in scope **f :** a sheet of notepaper
4 a : DISTINCTION, REPUTATION ⟨a figure of international *note*⟩ **b :** OBSERVATION, NOTICE ⟨took full *note* of the proceedings⟩ **c :** KNOWLEDGE, INFORMATION
synonym see SIGN
note·book \'nōt-ˌbůk\ *noun* (1579)
1 : a book for notes or memoranda
2 : a small portable microcomputer about the size of an ordinary loose-leaf binder
note·case \-ˌkās\ *noun* (1838)
British **:** WALLET 2a
not·ed \'nō-təd\ *adjective* (14th century)
: well-known by reputation **:** EMINENT, CELEBRATED
synonym see FAMOUS
— **not·ed·ly** *adverb*
— **not·ed·ness** *noun*
note·less \'nōt-ləs\ *adjective* (circa 1616)
: not noticed **:** UNDISTINGUISHED
note of hand (circa 1738)
: PROMISSORY NOTE
note·pad \'nōt-ˌpad\ *noun* (1922)
: PAD 4
note·pa·per \-ˌpā-pər\ *noun* (1849)
: writing paper suitable for notes
note·wor·thy \-ˌwər-thē\ *adjective* (1552)
: worthy of or attracting attention especially because of some special excellence
— **note·wor·thi·ly** \-ˌthə-lē\ *adverb*
— **note·wor·thi·ness** \-thē-nəs\ *noun*
not-for–profit *adjective* (circa 1973)
: NONPROFIT
noth·er *or* **'noth·er** \'nə-thər\ *adjective* [alteration (from misdivision of *another*) of *other*, adjective] (1956)
: OTHER — used especially in the phrase *a whole nother;* used chiefly in speech or informal prose
¹noth·ing \'nə-thiŋ\ *pronoun* [Middle English, from Old English *nān thing, nāthing,* from *nān* no + *thing* thing — more at NONE] (before 12th century)
1 : not any thing **:** no thing ⟨leaves *nothing* to the imagination⟩
2 : no part
3 : one of no interest, value, or consequence ⟨they mean *nothing* to me⟩
— **nothing doing :** by no means **:** definitely no
— **nothing for it :** no alternative ⟨*nothing for it* but to start over⟩
²nothing *adverb* (12th century)
: not at all **:** in no degree
— **nothing like :** not nearly ⟨it's *nothing like* thorough enough⟩
³nothing *noun* (1535)
1 a : something that does not exist **b :** the absence of all magnitude or quantity; *also* **:** ZERO 1a **c :** NOTHINGNESS 3b
2 : someone or something of no or slight value or size
⁴nothing *adjective* (1611)
: of no account **:** WORTHLESS
noth·ing·ness \-nəs\ *noun* (circa 1631)
1 : the quality or state of being nothing: as **a :** NONEXISTENCE **b :** utter insignificance **c :** DEATH
2 : something insignificant or valueless
3 a : VOID, EMPTINESS **b :** a metaphysical entity opposed to and devoid of being and regarded by some existentialists as the ground of anxiety
¹no·tice \'nō-təs\ *noun* [Middle English, from Middle French, acquaintance, from Latin *notitia* knowledge, acquaintance, from *notus* known, from past participle of *noscere* to come to know — more at KNOW] (15th century)

1 a (1) **:** warning or intimation of something **:** ANNOUNCEMENT (2) **:** notification by one of the parties to an agreement or relation of intention of terminating it at a specified time (3) **:** the condition of being warned or notified — usually used in the phrase *on notice* **b :** INFORMATION, INTELLIGENCE
2 a : ATTENTION, HEED **b :** polite or favorable attention **:** CIVILITY
3 : a written or printed announcement
4 : a short critical account or examination
²notice *transitive verb* **no·ticed; no·tic·ing** (15th century)
1 : to give notice of
2 a : to comment upon **b :** REVIEW
3 a : to treat with attention or civility **b :** to take notice of **:** MARK
4 : to give a formal notice to
— **no·tic·er** *noun*
no·tice·able \'nō-tə-sə-bəl\ *adjective* (1796)
1 : worthy of notice
2 : capable of being noticed ☆
— **no·tice·ably** \-blē\ *adverb*
notice board *noun* (1854)
chiefly British **:** a board bearing a notice or on which notices may be posted; *especially* **:** BULLETIN BOARD
no·ti·fi·able \'nō-tə-ˌfī-ə-bəl, ˌnō-tə-'\ *adjective* (1889)
: required by law to be reported to official health authorities ⟨a *notifiable* disease⟩
no·ti·fi·ca·tion \ˌnō-tə-fə-'kā-shən\ *noun* (14th century)
1 : the act or an instance of notifying
2 : a written or printed matter that gives notice
no·ti·fy \'nō-tə-ˌfī\ *transitive verb* **-fied; -fy·ing** [Middle English *notifien,* from Middle French *notifier* to make known, from Late Latin *notificare,* from Latin *notus* known] (14th century)
1 *obsolete* **:** to point out
2 : to give notice of or report the occurrence of ⟨he *notified* his intention to sue⟩
3 : to give formal notice to ⟨*notify* a family of the death of a relation⟩
synonym see INFORM
— **no·ti·fi·er** \-ˌfī(-ə)r\ *noun*
no–till \'nō-'til\ *noun* (1968)
: NO-TILLAGE
no–till·age \-'ti-lij\ *noun* (1968)
: a system of farming that consists of planting a narrow slit trench without tillage and with the use of herbicides to suppress weeds
no·tion \'nō-shən\ *noun* [Latin *notion-, notio,* from *noscere*] (1537)
1 a (1) **:** an individual's conception or impression of something known, experienced, or imagined (2) **:** an inclusive general concept (3) **:** a theory or belief held by a person or group **b :** a personal inclination **:** WHIM
2 *obsolete* **:** MIND, INTELLECT
3 *plural* **:** small useful items **:** SUNDRIES
synonym see IDEA
no·tion·al \'nō-shnəl, -shə-nᵊl\ *adjective* (1597)
1 : THEORETICAL, SPECULATIVE
2 : existing in the mind only **:** IMAGINARY
3 : given to foolish or fanciful moods or ideas
4 a : of, relating to, or being a notion or idea **:** CONCEPTUAL **b** (1) **:** presenting an idea of a thing, action, or quality ⟨*has* is *notional* in *he has luck,* relational in *he has gone*⟩ (2) **:** of or representing what exists or occurs in the world of things as distinguished from syntactic categories
— **no·tion·al·i·ty** \ˌnō-shə-'na-lə-tē\ *noun*
— **no·tion·al·ly** \'nō-shnə-lē, -shə-nᵊl-ē\ *adverb*
no·to·chord \'nō-tə-ˌkòrd\ *noun* [Greek *nōton, nōtos* back + Latin *chorda* cord — more at CORD] (1848)
: a longitudinal flexible rod of cells that in the lowest chordates (as a lancelet or a lamprey) and in the embryos of the higher vertebrates forms the supporting axis of the body

— **no·to·chord·al** \ˌnō-tə-'kòr-dᵊl\ *adjective*
no·to·ri·e·ty \ˌnō-tə-'rī-ə-tē\ *noun, plural* **-ties** [Middle French or Medieval Latin; Middle French *notorieté,* from Medieval Latin *notorietat-, notorietas,* from *notorius*] (circa 1650)
1 : the quality or state of being notorious
2 : a notorious person
no·to·ri·ous \nō-'tōr-ē-əs, nə-, -'tòr-\ *adjective* [Medieval Latin *notorius,* from Late Latin *notorium* information, indictment, from Latin *noscere* to come to know — more at KNOW] (1534)
: generally known and talked of; *especially* **:** widely and unfavorably known
synonym see FAMOUS
no·to·ri·ous·ly \-lē\ *adverb* (1512)
1 : in a notorious manner
2 : as is notorious **:** as is very well known
no–trump *adjective* (1899)
: being a bid, contract, or hand suitable to play without any suit being trumps
— **no–trump** *noun*
no·tum \'nō-təm\ *noun, plural* **no·ta** \'nō-tə\ [New Latin, from Greek *nōton* back] (1877)
: the dorsal surface of a thoracic segment of an insect
¹not·with·stand·ing \ˌnät-with-'stan-diŋ, -with-\ *preposition* [Middle English *notwithstonding,* from *not* + *withstonding,* present participle of *withstonden* to withstand] (14th century)
: DESPITE ⟨*notwithstanding* their lack of experience, they were an immediate success⟩ — often used after its object ⟨the motion passed, our objection *notwithstanding*⟩
²notwithstanding *adverb* (15th century)
: NEVERTHELESS, HOWEVER
³notwithstanding *conjunction* (15th century)
: ALTHOUGH
nou·gat \'nü-gət, *especially British* -ˌgä\ *noun* [French, from Provençal, from Old Provençal *nogat,* from *noga* nut, from (assumed) Vulgar Latin *nuca,* from Latin *nuc-, nux* — more at NUT] (1827)
: a confection of nuts or fruit pieces in a sugar paste
nought \'nòt, 'nät\ *variant of* NAUGHT
word history see NAUGHTY

nou·me·non \\'nü-mə-ˌnän\\ *noun, plural* **-na** \\-nə, -ˌnä\\ [German, from Greek *nooumenon* that which is apprehended by thought, from neuter of present passive participle of *noein* to think, conceive, from *nous* mind] (1796)
: a posited object or event as it appears in itself independent of perception by the senses
— **nou·men·al** \\-mə-nᵊl\\ *adjective*

noun \\'naůn\\ *noun* [Middle English *nowne*, from Anglo-French *noun* name, noun, from Old French *nom*, from Latin *nomen* — more at NAME] (14th century)
: any member of a class of words that typically can be combined with determiners to serve as the subject of a verb, can be interpreted as singular or plural, can be replaced with a pronoun, and refer to an entity, quality, state, action, or concept

noun phrase *noun, often N&P capitalized* (1923)
: a phrase formed by a noun and all its modifiers and determiners; *broadly* : any syntactic element (as a clause, clitic, pronoun, or zero element) with a noun's function (as the subject of a verb or the object of a verb or preposition) — abbreviation NP

nour·ish \\'nər-ish, 'nə-rish\\ *transitive verb* [Middle English *nurishen*, from Old French *noriss-*, stem of *norrir*, from Latin *nutrire* to suckle, nourish; akin to Greek *nan* to flow, *noteros* damp, Sanskrit *snauti* it drips] (14th century)
1 : NURTURE, REAR
2 : to promote the growth of ⟨no occasions to exercise the feelings nor *nourish* passion —L. O. Coxe⟩
3 a : to furnish or sustain with nutriment : FEED **b** : MAINTAIN, SUPPORT ⟨their profits . . . *nourish* other criminal activities —Beverly Smith⟩
— **nour·ish·er** *noun*

nour·ish·ing *adjective* (14th century)
: giving nourishment : NUTRITIOUS

nour·ish·ment \\'nər-ish-mənt, 'nə-rish-\\ *noun* (15th century)
1 a : FOOD, NUTRIMENT **b** : SUSTENANCE 3 ⟨books for intellectual *nourishment*⟩
2 : the act of nourishing : the state of being nourished

nous *noun* [Greek *noos, nous* mind] (1678)
1 \\'nüs *also* 'naůs\\ : MIND, REASON: as **a** : an intelligent purposive principle of the world **b** : the divine reason regarded in Neoplatonism as the first emanation of God
2 \\'naůs\\ *chiefly British* : COMMON SENSE, ALERTNESS

nou·veau \\nü-'vō\\ *adjective* [French, from Middle French *novel*] (1828)
: newly arrived or developed

nou·veau riche \\ˌnü-ˌvō-'rēsh\\ *noun, plural* **nou·veaux riches** *same*\\ [French, literally, new rich] (1813)
: a person newly rich : PARVENU

nou·velle \\nü-'vel\\ *adjective* [*nouvelle* cuisine] (1976)
: of or relating to nouvelle cuisine ⟨a *nouvelle* restaurant⟩

nouvelle cuisine *noun* [French, literally, new cuisine] (1975)
: a form of French cuisine that uses little flour or fat and stresses light sauces and the use of fresh seasonal produce; *also* : any national cuisine that stresses lightness and freshness in preparation ⟨American *nouvelle cuisine*⟩

nouvelle vague \\-'väg, -'våg\\ *noun* [French] (1959)
: NEW WAVE 1, 2

no·va \\'nō-və\\ *noun, plural* **novas** *or* **no·vae** \\-(ˌ)vē, -ˌvī\\ [New Latin, feminine of Latin *novus* new] (1927)
: a star that suddenly increases its light output tremendously and then fades away to its former obscurity in a few months or years
— **no·va·like** \\-və-ˌlīk\\ *adjective*

no·vac·u·lite \\nō-'va-kyə-ˌlīt\\ *noun* [Latin *novacula* razor] (1796)
: a very hard fine-grained siliceous rock used for whetstones and possibly of sedimentary origin

no·va·tion \\nō-'vā-shən\\ *noun* [Late Latin *novation-, novatio* renewal, legal novation, from Latin *novare* to make new, from *novus*] (1682)
: the substitution of a new legal obligation for an old one

¹nov·el \\'nä-vəl\\ *adjective* [Middle English, from Middle French, new, from Latin *novellus*, from diminutive of *novus* new — more at NEW] (15th century)
1 : new and not resembling something formerly known or used
2 : original or striking especially in conception or style ⟨a *novel* scheme to collect money⟩
synonym see NEW

²novel *noun* [Italian *novella*] (1639)
1 : an invented prose narrative that is usually long and complex and deals especially with human experience through a usually connected sequence of events
2 : the literary genre consisting of novels ◇
— **nov·el·is·tic** \\ˌnä-və-'lis-tik\\ *adjective*
— **nov·el·is·ti·cal·ly** \\-ti-k(ə-)lē\\ *adverb*

nov·el·ette \\ˌnä-və-'let\\ *noun* (1814)
: NOVELLA 2

nov·el·ett·ish \\-'le-tish\\ *adjective* (1904)
: of, relating to, or characteristic of a novelette; *especially* : SENTIMENTAL

nov·el·ist \\'näv-list, 'nä-və-\\ *noun* (1728)
: a writer of novels

nov·el·ize \\'nä-və-ˌlīz\\ *transitive verb* **-ized; -iz·ing** (1828)
: to convert into the form of a novel ⟨*novelize* a play⟩
— **nov·el·iza·tion** \\ˌnä-və-lə-'zā-shən\\ *noun*

no·vel·la \\nō-'ve-lə\\ *noun, plural* **novellas** *or* **no·vel·le** \\-'ve-lē\\ [Italian, from feminine of *novello* new, from Latin *novellus*] (1898)
1 *plural* **novelle** : a story with a compact and pointed plot
2 *plural usually* **novellas** : a work of fiction intermediate in length and complexity between a short story and a novel

nov·el·ty \\'nä-vəl-tē\\ *noun, plural* **-ties** [Middle English *novelte*, from Middle French *noveleté*, from *novel*] (14th century)
1 : something new or unusual
2 : the quality or state of being novel : NEWNESS
3 : a small manufactured article intended mainly for personal or household adornment — usually used in plural

¹No·vem·ber \\nō-'vem-bər, nə-\\ *noun* [Middle English *Novembre*, from Old French, from Latin *November*, ninth month of the early Roman calendar, from *novem* nine — more at NINE] (13th century)
: the 11th month of the Gregorian calendar

²November (1956)
— a communications code word for the letter *n*

no·vem·de·cil·lion \\ˌnō-ˌvem-di-'sil-yən\\ *noun, often attributive* [Latin *novemdecim* nineteen (from *novem* + *decem* ten) + English *-illion* (as in *million*) — more at TEN] (circa 1934)
— see NUMBER table

no·ve·na \\nō-'vē-nə\\ *noun* [Medieval Latin, from Latin, feminine of *novenus* nine each, from *novem*] (1853)
: a Roman Catholic period of prayer lasting nine consecutive days

nov·ice \\'nä-vəs\\ *noun* [Middle English, from Middle French, from Medieval Latin *novicius*, from Latin, newly imported, from *novus* — more at NEW] (14th century)
1 : a person admitted to probationary membership in a religious community
2 : BEGINNER, TYRO

no·vi·ti·ate \\nō-'vi-shət, nə-\\ *noun* [French *noviciat*, from Medieval Latin *noviciatus*, from *novicius*] (1600)
1 : the period or state of being a novice
2 : a house where novices are trained
3 : NOVICE

no·vo·bi·o·cin \\ˌnō-və-'bī-ə-sən\\ *noun* [*novo-* (perhaps modification of Latin *niveus* snowy, specific epithet of the bacterium *Streptococcus niveus*) + *bi-* + *-mycin*] (1956)
: a weak dibasic acid $C_{31}H_{36}N_2O_{11}$ that is highly toxic to humans and is used as an antimicrobial drug in some serious cases of staphylococcic and urinary tract infection

No·vo·cain \\'nō-və-ˌkān\\ *trademark*
— used for a preparation containing the hydrochloride of procaine

no·vo·caine \\-ˌkān\\ *noun* [International Scientific Vocabulary *novo-* (from Latin *novus* new) + *cocaine*] (1910)
: PROCAINE; *also* : its hydrochloride

¹now \\'naů\\ *adverb* [Middle English, from Old English *nū*; akin to Old High German *nū* now, Latin *nunc*, Greek *nyn*] (before 12th century)
1 a : at the present time or moment **b** : in the time immediately before the present ⟨thought of them just *now*⟩ **c** : in the time immediately to follow : FORTHWITH ⟨come in *now*⟩
2 — used with the sense of present time weakened or lost to express command, request, or admonition ⟨*now* hear this⟩ ⟨*now* you be sure to write⟩
3 — used with the sense of present time weakened or lost to introduce an important point or indicate a transition (as of ideas)
4 : SOMETIMES ⟨*now* one and *now* another⟩
5 : under the present circumstances
6 : at the time referred to ⟨*now* the trouble began⟩

²now *conjunction* (before 12th century)
: in view of the fact that : SINCE — often followed by *that* ⟨*now* that we are here⟩

³now *noun* (12th century)
: the present time or moment ⟨been ill up to *now*⟩

⁴now *adjective* (14th century)
1 : of or relating to the present time : EXISTING ⟨the *now* president⟩
2 a : excitingly new ⟨*now* clothes⟩ **b** : constantly aware of what is new ⟨*now* people⟩ ⟨the *now* generation⟩

NOW account \\'naů-\\ *noun* [negotiable order of withdrawal] (1974)
: a savings account on which checks may be drawn

now·a·days \\'naů-(ə-)ˌdāz\\ *adverb* [Middle English *now a dayes*, from *¹now* + *a dayes* during the day] (14th century)
: at the present time

now and then *adverb* (15th century)

◇ WORD HISTORY

novel Italian *novella*, meaning literally "item of news," came to be applied in the 13th century to the short tales or fables that were becoming a popular literary form. Simple in plot and character development, these tales typically dealt with humorous, political, or amorous events, especially in a satiric way. Since similar tales were also becoming popular in England, English borrowed the word as *novel* in the 17th century. As the novel developed, however, the notion of brevity was abandoned and the narratives became considerably longer. During the 18th century the novel matured as a literary form, presenting psychologically developed characters in an extended, complex plot. At the end of the 19th century, English again borrowed the Italian word *novella*, this time intact to refer specifically to the medieval Italian stories of authors such as Boccaccio, and later to refer to a work of fiction intermediate in length between a short story and a novel.

: from time to time : OCCASIONALLY ⟨*now and then* we go off to the country⟩

no·way *adverb* (13th century)

1 \'nō-,wā\ *or* **no·ways** \-,wāz\ : NOWISE

2 *usually* **no way** \-'wā\ : NO — used emphatically

¹no·where \'nō-,hwer, -,hwar, -hwər *or without* h\ *adverb* (before 12th century)

1 : not in or at any place

2 : to no place

²nowhere *noun* (1831)

1 : a nonexistent place

2 : an unknown, distant, or obscure place or state ⟨rose to fame out of *nowhere*⟩

— miles from nowhere : in an extremely remote place

nowhere near *adverb* (15th century)

: not nearly

no·wheres \'nō-,hwerz, -,hwarz, -hwərz *or without* h\ *adverb* (circa 1866)

chiefly dialect : NOWHERE

no·whith·er \'nō-,hwi-thər, -,wi-thər; ,nō-'\ *adverb* (before 12th century)

: to or toward no place

no–win \'nō-'win, -,win\ *adjective* (1962)

: not likely to give victory, success, or satisfaction : that cannot be won ⟨a *no-win* situation⟩ ⟨a *no-win* war⟩

no·wise \'nō-,wīz\ *adverb* (14th century)

: not at all

now·ness \'naù-nəs\ *noun* (1674)

: the quality or state of existing or occurring in or belonging to the present time

nowt \'naùt *also* 'nōt\ *dialect English variant of* NOUGHT

nox·ious \'näk-shəs\ *adjective* [Middle English *noxius*, from Latin, from *noxa* harm; akin to Latin *nocēre* to harm, *nec-, nex* violent death, Greek *nekros* dead body] (15th century)

1 a : physically harmful or destructive to living beings ⟨*noxious* wastes that poison our streams⟩ **b** : constituting a harmful influence on mind or behavior : morally corrupting ⟨*noxious* doctrines⟩

2 : DISTASTEFUL, OBNOXIOUS

synonym see PERNICIOUS

— nox·ious·ly *adverb*

— nox·ious·ness *noun*

noz·zle \'nä-zəl\ *noun* [diminutive of *nose*] (1683)

1 a : a projecting vent of something **b** : a short tube with a taper or constriction used (as on a hose) to speed up or direct a flow of fluid **c** : a part in a rocket engine that accelerates the exhaust gases from the combustion chamber to a high velocity

2 *slang* : NOSE

NSAID \'en-,sed *also* -,säd\ *noun* [*nonsteroidal anti-inflammatory drug*] (1985)

: a nonsteroidal anti-inflammatory drug (as ibuprofen)

-n't *verb combining form*

: not (isn*'t*)

nth \'en(t)th\ *adjective* [*n* (indefinite number) + *-th*] (1852)

1 : numbered with an unspecified or indefinitely large ordinal number ⟨for the *nth* time⟩

2 : EXTREME, UTMOST ⟨to the *nth* degree⟩

n–type \'en-,tīp\ *adjective* [*negative* + *type*] (1946)

: relating to or being a semiconductor in which charge is carried by electrons — compare P-TYPE

nu \'nü, 'nyü\ *noun* [Greek *ny*, of Semitic origin; akin to Hebrew *nūn* nun] (circa 1823)

: the 13th letter of the Greek alphabet — see ALPHABET table

nu·ance \'nü-,än(t)s, 'nyü-, -,äⁿs; nü-', nyü-'\ *noun* [French, from Middle French, shade of color, from *nuer* to make shades of color, from *nue* cloud, from Latin *nubes;* perhaps akin to Welsh *nudd* mist] (1781)

1 : a subtle distinction or variation

2 : a subtle quality : NICETY

3 : sensibility to, awareness of, or ability to express delicate shadings (as of meaning, feeling, or value)

— nu·anced \-,än(t)st, -'än(t)st\ *adjective*

nub \'nəb\ *noun* [alteration of English dialect *knub*, probably from Low German *knubbe*] (1727)

1 : KNOB, LUMP

2 : NUBBIN

3 : GIST, POINT

nub·bin \'nə-bən\ *noun* [perhaps diminutive of *nub*] (1692)

1 : something (as an ear of Indian corn) that is small for its kind, stunted, undeveloped, or imperfect

2 : a small usually projecting part or bit

3 : NUB 3

nub·ble \'nə-bəl\ *noun* [diminutive of *nub*] (1818)

: a small knob or lump

— nub·bly \-b(ə-)lē\ *adjective*

nub·by \'nə-bē\ *adjective* **nub·bi·er; -est** [*nub* + ¹*-y*] (circa 1876)

1 : having or being like nubbles

2 : having nubs ⟨a *nubby* knit fabric⟩

Nu·bi·an \'nü-bē-ən, 'nyü-\ *noun* (15th century)

1 a : a native or inhabitant of Nubia **b** : a member of one of the group of dark-skinned peoples that formed a powerful empire between Egypt and Ethiopia from the 6th to the 14th centuries

2 : any of several languages spoken in central and northern Sudan

— Nubian *adjective*

nu·bile \'nü-,bīl, 'nyü-, -bəl\ *adjective* [French, from Latin *nubilis*, from *nubere* to marry — more at NUPTIAL] (circa 1642)

1 : of marriageable condition or age

2 : sexually attractive — used of a young woman

— nu·bil·i·ty \nü-'bi-lə-tē, nyü-\ *noun*

nu·cel·lus \nü-'se-ləs, nyü-\ *noun, plural* **nu·cel·li** \-'se-,lī\ [New Latin, from Latin *nucella* small nut, from *nuc-, nux* nut — more at NUT] (1882)

: the central and chief part of a plant ovule that encloses the female gametophyte

— nu·cel·lar \-'se-lər\ *adjective*

nu·chal \'nü-kəl, 'nyü-\ *adjective* [Medieval Latin *nucha* nape, from Arabic *nukhāʿ* spinal marrow] (1835)

: of, relating to, or lying in the region of the nape

nucle- *or* **nucleo-** *combining form* [French *nuclé-, nucléo-*, from New Latin *nucleus*]

1 : nucleus ⟨*nucleo*plasm⟩

2 : nucleic acid ⟨*nucleo*protein⟩

nu·cle·ar \'nü-klē-ər, 'nyü-, ÷-kyə-lər\ *adjective* (1846)

1 : of, relating to, or constituting a nucleus

2 a : of or relating to the atomic nucleus ⟨*nuclear* reaction⟩ ⟨*nuclear* physics⟩ **b** : used in or produced by a nuclear reaction (as fission) ⟨*nuclear* fuel⟩ ⟨*nuclear* waste⟩ ⟨*nuclear* energy⟩ **c** (1) : being a weapon whose destructive power derives from an uncontrolled nuclear reaction (2) : of, produced by, or involving nuclear weapons ⟨the *nuclear* age⟩ ⟨*nuclear* war⟩ (3) : armed with nuclear weapons ⟨*nuclear* powers⟩ **d** : of, relating to, or powered by nuclear energy ⟨a *nuclear* submarine⟩ ⟨the *nuclear* debate⟩ □

nuclear family *noun* (1947)

: a family group that consists only of father, mother, and children

nuclear magnetic resonance *noun* (1942)

: the magnetic resonance of an atomic nucleus

nuclear medicine *noun* (1952)

: a branch of medicine dealing with the use of radioactive materials in the diagnosis and treatment of disease

nuclear membrane *noun* (1888)

: a double membrane enclosing a cell nucleus and having its outer part continuous with the endoplasmic reticulum — see CELL illustration

nuclear–powered *adjective* (1948)

: powered by nuclear energy

nuclear resonance *noun* (1940)

: the resonance absorption of a gamma ray by a nucleus identical to the nucleus that emitted the gamma ray

nuclear sap *noun* (1877)

: the clear homogeneous ground substance of a cell nucleus — called also *karyolymph*

nuclear winter *noun* (1983)

: the chilling of climate that is hypothesized to be a consequence of nuclear war and to result from the prolonged blockage of sunlight by high-altitude dust clouds produced by nuclear explosions

nu·cle·ase \'nü-klē-,ās, 'nyü-, -,āz\ *noun* (1902)

: any of various enzymes that promote hydrolysis of nucleic acids

nu·cle·ate \'nü-klē-,āt, 'nyü-\ *verb* **-at·ed; -at·ing** [Late Latin *nucleatus*, past participle of *nucleare* to become stony, from Latin *nucleus*] (circa 1864)

transitive verb

1 : to form into a nucleus : CLUSTER

2 : to act as a nucleus for

3 : to supply nuclei to

intransitive verb

1 : to form a nucleus

2 : to act as a nucleus

3 : to begin to form

— nu·cle·ation \,nü-klē-'ā-shən, ,nyü-\ *noun*

— nu·cle·a·tor \'nü-klē-,ā-tər, 'nyü-\ *noun*

nu·cle·at·ed \'nü-klē-,ā-təd, 'nyü-\ *or* **nu·cle·ate** \-klē-ət\ *adjective* [Latin *nucleatus*, from *nucleus* kernel] (1845)

1 : having a nucleus or nuclei ⟨*nucleated* cells⟩

2 *usually* **nucleate** : originating or occurring at nuclei ⟨*nucleate* boiling⟩

nu·cle·ic acid \nü-'klē-ik-, -'klā-, nyü-\ *noun* [from their occurrence in cell nuclei] (1892)

: any of various acids (as DNA or RNA) that are composed of nucleotide chains

nu·cle·in \'nü-klē-ən, 'nyü-\ *noun* (1878)

1 : NUCLEOPROTEIN

2 : NUCLEIC ACID

nu·cle·o·cap·sid \,nü-klē-ō-'kap-səd, ,nyü-\ *noun* (1963)

: the nucleic acid and surrounding protein coat in a virus

nu·cle·oid \'nü-klē-,óid, 'nyü-\ *noun* (1938)

: the DNA-containing area of a prokaryotic cell (as a bacterium)

nu·cle·o·lus \nü-'klē-ə-ləs, nyü-\ *noun, plural* **-li** \-,lī\ [New Latin, from Latin, diminutive of *nucleus*] (1845)

: a spherical body of the nucleus of most eukaryotes that becomes enlarged during protein synthesis, is associated with a nucleolus organizer, and contains the DNA templates for ribosomal RNA — see CELL illustration

□ USAGE

nuclear Though disapproved of by many, pronunciations ending in \-kyə-lər\ have been found in widespread use among educated speakers including scientists, lawyers, professors, congressmen, U.S. cabinet members, and at least one U.S. president and one vice president. While most common in the U.S., these pronunciations have also been heard from British and Canadian speakers.

\ə\ abut \ᵊ\ kitten \ər\ further \a\ ash \ā\ ace
\ä\ mop, mar \aù\ out \ch\ chin \e\ bet \ē\ easy
\g\ go \i\ hit \ī\ ice \j\ job \ŋ\ sing \ō\ go
\ò\ law \òi\ boy \th\ thin \th\ the \ü\ loot \ù\ foot
\y\ yet \zh\ vision *see also* Guide to Pronunciation

— **nu·cle·o·lar** \-lər\ *adjective*

nucleolus organizer *noun* (1939)
: the specific part of a chromosome with which its nucleolus is associated especially during its reorganization after nuclear division — called also *nucleolar organizer*

nu·cle·on \'nü-klē-,än, 'nyü-\ *noun* [International Scientific Vocabulary] (1923)
1 : a nuclear particle: **a** : PROTON **b** : NEUTRON
2 : a hypothetical single entity with one-half unit of isospin that can manifest itself as either a proton or a neutron
— **nu·cle·on·ic** \,nü-klē-'ä-nik, ,nyü-\ *adjective*

nu·cle·on·ics \,nü-klē-'ä-niks, ,nyü-\ *noun plural but singular or plural in construction* (1937)
: a branch of physical science that deals with nucleons or with all phenomena of the atomic nucleus

nu·cle·o·phile \'nü-klē-ə-,fīl, 'nyü-\ *noun* (1943)
: a nucleophilic substance (as an electron-donating reagent)

nu·cle·o·phil·ic \,nü-klē-ə-'fi-lik, ,nyü-\ *adjective* (1933)
1 *of an atom, ion, or molecule* : having an affinity for atomic nuclei : being an electron donor
2 : involving a nucleophilic species ⟨a *nucleophilic* reaction⟩ — compare ELECTROPHILIC
— **nu·cleo·phil·i·cal·ly** \-li-k(ə-)lē\ *adverb*
— **nu·cle·o·phi·lic·i·ty** \-klē-ō-fi-'li-sə-tē\ *noun*

nu·cle·o·plasm \'nü-klē-ə-,pla-zəm, 'nyü-\ *noun* [International Scientific Vocabulary] (1888)
: the protoplasm of a nucleus; *especially* : NUCLEAR SAP
— **nu·cle·o·plas·mic** \-klē-ə-'plaz-mik\ *adjective*

nu·cle·o·pro·tein \,nü-klē-ō-'prō-,tēn, ,nyü-, -'prō-tē-ən\ *noun* [International Scientific Vocabulary] (1907)
: a compound that consists of a protein (as a histone) conjugated with a nucleic acid (as a DNA) and that is the principal constituent of the hereditary material in chromosomes

nu·cle·o·side \'nü-klē-ə-,sīd, 'nyü-\ *noun* [International Scientific Vocabulary *nucle-* + [2]*-ose* + *-ide*] (1911)
: a compound (as guanosine or adenosine) that consists of a purine or pyrimidine base combined with deoxyribose or ribose and is found especially in DNA or RNA

nu·cle·o·some \-,sōm\ *noun* (1962)
: any of the repeating globular subunits of chromatin that consist of a complex of DNA and histone
— **nu·cle·o·so·mal** \,nü-klē-ə-'sō-məl, ,nyü-\ *adjective*

nu·cle·o·syn·the·sis \,nü-klē-ō-'sin(t)-thə-səs, ,nyü-\ *noun* [New Latin] (1960)
: the production of a chemical element from simpler nuclei (as of hydrogen) especially in a star
— **nu·cle·o·syn·thet·ic** \-sin-'the-tik\ *adjective*

nu·cle·o·tid·ase \,nü-klē-ə-'tī-,dās, ,nyü-, -,dāz\ *noun* (1911)
: a phosphatase that promotes hydrolysis of a nucleotide (as into a nucleoside and phosphoric acid)

nu·cle·o·tide \'nü-klē-ə-,tīd, 'nyü-\ *noun* [International Scientific Vocabulary, irregular from *nucle-* + *-ide*] (1908)
: any of several compounds that consist of a ribose or deoxyribose sugar joined to a purine or pyrimidine base and to a phosphate group and that are the basic structural units of nucleic acids (as RNA and DNA) — compare NUCLEOSIDE

nu·cle·us \'nü-klē-əs, 'nyü-\ *noun, plural* **nu·clei** \-klē-,ī\ *also* **nu·cle·us·es** [New Latin, from Latin, kernel, diminutive of *nuc-, nux* nut — more at NUT] (1704)
1 : the small brighter and denser portion of a galaxy or of the head of a comet
2 : a central point, group, or mass about which gathering, concentration, or accretion takes place: as **a** : a cellular organelle of eukaryotes that is essential to cell functions (as reproduction and protein synthesis), is composed of nuclear sap and a nucleoprotein-rich network from which chromosomes and nucleoli arise, and is enclosed in a definite membrane — see CELL illustration **b** : a mass of gray matter or group of nerve cells in the central nervous system **c** : a characteristic and stable complex of atoms or groups in a molecule; *especially* : RING ⟨the naphthalene *nucleus*⟩ **d** : the positively charged central portion of an atom that comprises nearly all of the atomic mass and that consists of protons and neutrons except in hydrogen which consists of one proton only
3 : the peak of sonority in the utterance of a syllable

nu·clide \'nü-,klīd, 'nyü-\ *noun* [*nucleus* + Greek *eidos* form, species — more at IDOL] (1947)
: a species of atom characterized by the constitution of its nucleus and hence by the number of protons, the number of neutrons, and the energy content
— **nu·clid·ic** \nü-'kli-dik, nyü-\ *adjective*

[1]**nude** \'nüd, 'nyüd\ *adjective* **nud·er; nud·est** [Latin *nudus* naked — more at NAKED] (1531)
1 : lacking something essential especially to legal validity ⟨a *nude* contract⟩
2 a : devoid of a natural or conventional covering; *especially* : not covered by clothing or a drape **b** (1) : of the color of a white person's flesh (2) : giving the appearance of nudity ⟨a *nude* dress⟩ **c** : featuring nudes ⟨a *nude* movie⟩ **d** : frequented by naked people ⟨a *nude* beach⟩
synonym see BARE
— **nude** *adverb*
— **nude·ly** *adverb*
— **nude·ness** *noun*
— **nu·di·ty** \'nü-də-tē, 'nyü-\ *noun*

[2]**nude** *noun* (1708)
1 a : a representation of a nude human figure **b** : a nude person
2 : the condition of being nude ⟨in the *nude*⟩

nudge \'nəj\ *verb* **nudged; nudg·ing** [origin unknown] (1675)
transitive verb
1 : to touch or push gently; *especially* : to seek the attention of by a push of the elbow
2 : to prod lightly : urge into action
3 : APPROACH ⟨its circulation is *nudging* the four million mark —Bennett Cerf⟩
intransitive verb
: to give a nudge
— **nudge** *noun*
— **nudg·er** *noun*

nu·di·branch \'nü-də-,braŋk, 'nyü-\ *noun, plural* **-branchs** [New Latin *Nudibranchia*, from Latin *nudus* + Greek *branchia* gills] (1847)
: any of an order (Nudibranchia) of marine gastropod mollusks without a shell in the adult state and without true gills
— **nudibranch** *adjective*

nud·ism \'nü-,di-zəm, 'nyü-\ *noun* (1929)
: the practice of going nude especially in sexually mixed groups and during periods of time spent at specially secluded places
— **nud·ist** \'nü-dist, 'nyü-\ *adjective or noun*

nud·nick *or* **nud·nik** \'nůd-nik\ *noun* [Yiddish *nudnik*, from *nudyen* to bore, from Polish *nudzić*, from *nuda* boredom] (1947)
: a person who is a bore or nuisance

nu·ga·to·ry \'nü-gə-,tōr-ē, 'nyü-, -,tór-\ *adjective* [Latin *nugatorius*, from *nugari* to trifle, from *nugae* trifles] (1603)
1 : of little or no consequence : TRIFLING, INCONSEQUENTIAL

2 : having no force : INOPERATIVE
synonym see VAIN

nug·get \'nə-gət\ *noun* [origin unknown] (1852)
1 : a solid lump; *especially* : a native lump of precious metal
2 : TIDBIT 2 ⟨*nuggets* of wisdom⟩
3 : a small usually rounded piece of food ⟨chicken *nuggets*⟩

nui·sance \'nü-s[ə]n(t)s, 'nyü-\ *noun* [Middle English *nusaunce*, from Anglo-French, from Old French *nuire* to harm, from Latin *nocēre* — more at NOXIOUS] (15th century)
1 : HARM, INJURY
2 : one that is annoying, unpleasant, or obnoxious : PEST

nuisance tax *noun* (1924)
: an excise tax collected in small amounts on a wide range of commodities directly from the consumer

[1]**nuke** \'nük, 'nyük\ *noun* [by shortening & alteration from *nuclear*] (1959)
1 : a nuclear weapon
2 : a nuclear-powered electric generating station

[2]**nuke** *transitive verb* **nuked; nuk·ing** (1967)
1 : to attack or destroy with or as if with nuclear bombs
2 : MICROWAVE

[1]**null** \'nəl\ *adjective* [Middle French *nul*, literally, not any, from Latin *nullus*, from *ne-* not + *ullus* any; akin to Latin *unus* one — more at NO, ONE] (circa 1567)
1 : having no legal or binding force : INVALID
2 : amounting to nothing : NIL
3 : having no value : INSIGNIFICANT
4 a : having no elements ⟨*null* set⟩ **b** : having zero as a limit ⟨*null* sequence⟩ **c** *of a matrix* : having all elements equal to zero
5 a : indicating usually by a zero reading on a scale when a given quantity (as current or voltage) is zero or when two quantities are equal — used of an instrument **b** : being or relating to a method of measurement in which an unknown quantity (as of electric current) is compared with a known quantity of the same kind and found equal by a null detector
6 : of, being, or relating to zero
7 : ZERO 1c

[2]**null** *noun* (1605)
1 : ZERO 3a(1)
2 a : a condition of a radio receiver when minimum or zero signal is received **b** : a minimum or zero value of an electric current or of a radio signal

[3]**null** *transitive verb* (1643)
: to make null

nul·lah \'nə-lə\ *noun* [Hindi *nālā*] (1776)
: GULLY, RAVINE

null and void *adjective* (1669)
: having no force, binding power, or validity

null hypothesis *noun* (1935)
: a statistical hypothesis to be tested and accepted or rejected in favor of an alternative; *specifically* : the hypothesis that an observed difference (as between the means of two samples) is due to chance alone and not due to a systematic cause

nul·li·fi·ca·tion \,nə-lə-fə-'kā-shən\ *noun* (1798)
1 : the act of nullifying : the state of being nullified
2 : the action of a state impeding or attempting to prevent the operation and enforcement within its territory of a law of the U.S.
— **nul·li·fi·ca·tion·ist** \-sh(ə-)nist\ *noun*

nul·li·fi·er \'nə-lə-,fī(-ə)r\ *noun* (1832)
: one that nullifies; *specifically* : one maintaining the right of nullification against the U.S. government

nul·li·fy \'nə-lə-,fī\ *transitive verb* **-fied; -fy·ing** [Late Latin *nullificare*, from Latin *nullus*] (1535)
1 : to make null; *especially* : to make legally null and void

2 : to make of no value or consequence ☆

nul·lip·a·rous \nə-'li-pə-rəs\ *adjective* [New Latin *nullipara* one who has never borne an offspring, from Latin *nullus* not any + -*para* -para] (1859)
: of, relating to, or being a female that has not borne offspring

nul·li·ty \'nə-lə-tē\ *noun, plural* **-ties** (1570)
1 a : the quality or state of being null; *especially* **:** legal invalidity **b** (1) **:** NOTHINGNESS; *also* **:** INSIGNIFICANCE (2) **:** a mere nothing **:** NONENTITY
2 : one that is null; *specifically* **:** an act void of legal effect
3 : the number of elements in a basis of a null-space

null-space \'nəl-,spās\ *noun* (1884)
: a subspace of a vector space consisting of vectors that under a given linear transformation are mapped onto zero

numb \'nəm\ *adjective* [Middle English *nomen*, from past participle of *nimen* to take — more at NIM] (14th century)
1 : devoid of sensation especially as a result of cold or anesthesia
2 : devoid of emotion **:** INDIFFERENT
— **numb** *transitive verb*
— **numb·ing·ly** \'nə-miŋ-lē\ *adverb*
— **numb·ly** \'nəm-lē\ *adverb*
— **numb·ness** *noun*

¹num·ber \'nəm-bər\ *noun* [Middle English *nombre*, from Old French, from Latin *numerus*] (14th century)
1 a (1) **:** a sum of units **:** TOTAL (2) **:** COMPLEMENT 1b (3) **:** an indefinite usually large total ⟨a *number* of members were absent⟩ ⟨the *number* of elderly is rising⟩ (4) *plural* **:** a numerous group **:** MANY (5) **:** a numerical preponderance **b** (1) **:** the characteristic of an individual by which it is treated as a unit or of a collection by which it is treated in terms of units (2) **:** an ascertainable total ⟨bugs beyond *number*⟩ **c** (1) **:** a unit belonging to an abstract mathematical system and subject to specified laws of succession, addition, and multiplication; *especially* **:** NATURAL NUMBER (2) **:** an element (as π) of any of many mathematical systems obtained by extension of or analogy with the natural number system (3) *plural* **:** ARITHMETIC
2 : a distinction of word form to denote reference to one or more than one; *also* **:** a form or group of forms so distinguished
3 *plural* **a** (1) **:** metrical structure **:** METER (2) **:** metrical lines **:** VERSES **b** *archaic* **:** musical sounds **:** NOTES
4 a : a word, symbol, letter, or combination of symbols representing a number **b :** a numeral or combination of numerals or other symbols used to identify or designate ⟨dialed the wrong *number*⟩ **c :** a member of a sequence or collection designated by especially consecutive numbers (as an issue of a periodical) (2) **:** a position in a numbered sequence **d :** a group of one kind ⟨not of their *number*⟩
5 : one singled out from a group **:** INDIVIDUAL: as **a :** GIRL, WOMAN ⟨met an attractive *number* at the dance⟩ **b** (1) **:** a musical, theatrical, or literary selection or production (2) **:** ROUTINE, ACT **c :** an item of merchandise and especially clothing
6 : insight into a person's ability or character ⟨had my *number*⟩
7 *plural but singular or plural in construction* **a :** a form of lottery in which an individual wagers on the appearance of a certain combination of digits (as in regularly published numbers) — called also *numbers game* **b :** ²POLICY 2a
8 *plural* **a :** figures representing amounts of money usually in dollars spent, earned, or involved **b** (1) **:** STATISTICS 2; *especially* **:** individual statistics (as of an athlete) (2) **:** RATING 3c
9 : a person represented by a number or considered without regard to individuality ⟨at the university I was just a *number*⟩
usage see AMOUNT
— **by the numbers 1 :** in unison to a specific count or cadence **2 :** in a systematic, routine, or mechanical manner
▶The Table of Numbers is on page 1254

²number *verb* **num·bered; num·ber·ing** \-b(ə-)riŋ\ (14th century)
transitive verb
1 : COUNT, ENUMERATE
2 : to claim as part of a total **:** INCLUDE
3 : to restrict to a definite number ⟨your days are *numbered*⟩
4 : to assign a number to
5 : to amount to in number **:** TOTAL ⟨the crew *numbers* 100⟩
intransitive verb
1 : to reach a total number
2 : to call off numbers in sequence □
— **num·ber·able** \-b(ə-)rə-bəl\ *adjective*
— **num·ber·er** \-bər-ər\ *noun*

number cruncher *noun* (1966)
1 : a computer that performs fast numerical calculations especially on large amounts of data
2 : a person concerned with complex numerical data (as statistics)
— **number crunching** *noun*

num·ber·less \'nəm-bər-ləs\ *adjective* (1573)
: INNUMERABLE, COUNTLESS

number line *noun* (1960)
: a line of infinite extent whose points correspond to the real numbers according to their distance in a positive or negative direction from a point arbitrarily taken as zero

¹number one *noun* (circa 1705)
1 : one's own interests or welfare **:** ONESELF ⟨looking out for *number* one⟩ — often written *No. 1*
2 : one that is first in rank, importance, or influence — often written *No. 1*

²number one *adjective* (1839)
1 : first in rank, importance, or influence **:** FOREMOST ⟨cancer is the country's *number* one killer⟩ — often written *No. 1*
2 : of highest or of high quality

Num·bers \'nəm-bərz\ *noun plural but singular in construction*
: the mainly narrative fourth book of canonical Jewish and Christian Scripture — see BIBLE table

number theory *noun* (1912)
: the study of the properties of integers
— **number theoretic** *adjective*
— **number theorist** *noun*

numb·skull \'nəm-,skəl\ *variant of* NUMSKULL

nu·men \'nü-mən, 'nyü-\ *noun, plural* **nu·mi·na** \-mə-nə\ [Latin, nod, divine will, numen; akin to Latin *nutare* to nod, Greek *neuein*] (1628)
: a spiritual force or influence often identified with a natural object, phenomenon, or place

nu·mer·a·ble \'nüm-rə-bəl, 'nü-mə-; 'nyüm-, 'nyü-mə-\ *adjective* [Latin *numerabilis*, from *numerare* to count] (1570)
: capable of being counted

¹nu·mer·al \'nüm-rəl, 'nü-mə-; 'nyüm-, 'nyü-mə-\ *adjective* [Middle English, from Middle French, from Late Latin *numeralis*, from Latin *numerus*] (14th century)
1 : of, relating to, or expressing numbers
2 : consisting of numbers or numerals
— **nu·mer·al·ly** *adverb*

²numeral *noun* (1686)
1 : a conventional symbol that represents a number
2 *plural* **:** numbers that designate by year a school or college class and that are awarded for distinction in an extracurricular activity

¹nu·mer·ate \'nü-mə-,rāt, 'nü-mə-; 'nyüm-, 'nyü-mə-\ *transitive verb* **-at·ed; -at·ing** [Latin *numeratus*, past participle of *numerare* to count, from *numerus*] (circa 1721)
: ENUMERATE

²nu·mer·ate \'nüm-rət, 'nü-mə-; 'nyüm-, 'nyü-mə-\ *adjective* [Latin *numerus* number +

English -*ate* (as in *literate*)] (1959)
: marked by the capacity for quantitative thought and expression
— **nu·mer·a·cy** \'n(y)üm-rə-sē, 'n(y)ü-mə-\ *noun*

nu·mer·a·tion \,nü-mə-'rā-shən, ,nyü-\ *noun* (15th century)
1 a : the act or process or an instance of counting or numbering; *also* **:** a system of counting or numbering **b :** an act or instance of designating by a number
2 : the art of reading in words numbers expressed by numerals

nu·mer·a·tor \'nü-mə-,rā-tər, 'nyü-\ *noun* (1575)
1 : the part of a fraction that is above the line and signifies the number of parts of the denominator taken
2 : one that numbers

¹nu·mer·ic \nü-'mer-ik, nyü-\ *adjective* (circa 1828)
: NUMERICAL; *especially* **:** denoting a number or a system of numbers ⟨*numeric* code⟩ ⟨a *numeric* sign⟩

²nu·mer·ic *noun* (1879)
: NUMBER, NUMERAL

nu·mer·i·cal \nü-'mer-i-kəl, nyü-\ *adjective* [Latin *numerus*] (1628)
1 : of or relating to numbers ⟨the *numerical* superiority of the enemy⟩
2 : expressed in or involving numbers or a number system ⟨*numerical* standing in a class⟩ ⟨a *numerical* code⟩
— **nu·mer·i·cal·ly** \-k(ə-)lē\ *adverb*

☆ SYNONYMS

Nullify, negate, annul, abrogate, invalidate mean to deprive of effective or continued existence. NULLIFY implies counteracting completely the force, effectiveness, or value of something ⟨a penalty *nullified* the touchdown⟩. NEGATE implies the destruction or canceling out of each of two things by the other ⟨the arguments *negate* each other⟩. ANNUL suggests making ineffective or nonexistent often by legal or official action ⟨the treaty *annuls* all previous agreements⟩. ABROGATE is like ANNUL but more definitely implies a legal or official purposeful act ⟨a law to *abrogate* trading privileges⟩. INVALIDATE implies making something powerless or unacceptable by declaration of its logical or moral or legal unsoundness ⟨the court *invalidated* the statute⟩.

□ USAGE

number There is a rule of thumb well-known in the newspaper business that *a number* takes a plural verb and *the number* a singular verb. Our files show that this rule is generally observed, even outside the newspaper business ⟨a *number* of celebrated modern manuscripts are available in published form —*New Yorker*⟩ ⟨the total *number* of emigrés is now estimated rather elastically —Barbara Tuchman⟩. When an adjective like *growing* or *increasing* is added, however, *a number* often takes a singular verb ⟨an increasing *number* of Ministers now believes the Government could be forced to go to the country —Ian Aitken⟩. We find some examples ⟨a large *number* of men was visible —Tom Clancy⟩ where the plural idea is belied by a singular verb; perhaps such instances are the result of uncritical copyediting. In this case, the rule of thumb is a good rule to follow.

TABLE OF NUMBERS

CARDINAL NUMBERS[1]				ORDINAL NUMBERS[4]		
NAME[2]	SYMBOL			NAME[5]	SYMBOL[6]	
	Hindu-Arabic	*Roman*[3]				
zero *or* naught *or* cipher	0			first	1st	
one	1	I		second	2d *or* 2nd	
two	2	II		third	3d *or* 3rd	
three	3	III		fourth	4th	
four	4	IV		fifth	5th	
five	5	V		sixth	6th	
six	6	VI		seventh	7th	
seven	7	VII		eighth	8th	
eight	8	VIII		ninth	9th	
nine	9	IX		tenth	10th	
ten	10	X		eleventh	11th	
eleven	11	XI		twelfth	12th	
twelve	12	XII		thirteenth	13th	
thirteen	13	XIII		fourteenth	14th	
fourteen	14	XIV		fifteenth	15th	
fifteen	15	XV		sixteenth	16th	
sixteen	16	XVI		seventeenth	17th	
seventeen	17	XVII		eighteenth	18th	
eighteen	18	XVIII		nineteenth	19th	
nineteen	19	XIX		twentieth	20th	
twenty	20	XX		twenty-first	21st	
twenty-one	21	XXI		twenty-second	22d *or* 22nd	
twenty-two	22	XXII		twenty-third	23d *or* 23rd	
twenty-three	23	XXIII		twenty-fourth	24th	
twenty-four	24	XXIV		twenty-fifth	25th	
twenty-five	25	XXV		twenty-sixth	26th	
twenty-six	26	XXVI		twenty-seventh	27th	
twenty-seven	27	XXVII		twenty-eighth	28th	
twenty-eight	28	XXVIII		twenty-ninth	29th	
twenty-nine	29	XXIX		thirtieth	30th	
thirty	30	XXX		thirty-first	31st	
thirty-one	31	XXXI		thirty-second *etc*	32d *or* 32nd	
thirty-two *etc*	32	XXXII		fortieth	40th	
forty	40	XL		forty-first	41st	
forty-one *etc*	41	XLI		forty-second *etc*	42d *or* 42nd	
fifty	50	L		fiftieth	50th	
sixty	60	LX		sixtieth	60th	
seventy	70	LXX		seventieth	70th	
eighty	80	LXXX		eightieth	80th	
ninety	90	XC		ninetieth	90th	
one hundred	100	C		hundredth *or* one hundredth	100th	
on hundred and one *or* one hundred one	101	CI		hundred and first *or* one hundred and first	101st	
one hundred and two *etc*	102	CII		hundred and seconds *etc*	102d *or* 102nd	
two hundred	200	CC		two hundredth	200th	
three hundred	300	CCC		three hundredth	300th	
four hundred	400	CD		four hundredth	400th	
five hundred	500	D		five hundredth	500th	
six hundred	600	DC		six hundredth	600th	
seven hundred	700	DCC		seven hundredth	700th	
eight hundred	800	DCCC		eight hundredth	800th	
nine hundred	900	CM		nine hundredth	900th	
one thousand *or* ten hundred *etc*	1,000	M		thousandth *or* one thousandth	1,000th	
two thousand *etc*	2,000	MM		two thousandth *etc*	2,000th	
five thousand	5,000	V̄		ten thousandth	10,000th	
ten thousand	10,000	X̄		hundred thousandth *or* one hundred thousandth	100,000th	
one hundred thousand	100,000	C̄		millionth *or* one millionth	1,000,000th	
one million	1,000,000	M̄				

[1]The cardinal numbers are used in simple counting or in answer to "how many?" The words for these numbers may be used as nouns (he counted to *twelve*), as pronouns (*twelve* were found), or as adjectives (*twelve* boys).

[2]In formal contexts the numbers one to one hundred and in less formal contexts the numbers one to nine are commonly written out, while larger numbers are given in numerals. In nearly all contexts a number occurring at the beginning of a sentence is usually written out. Except in very formal contexts numerals are invariably used for dates. Hindu-Arabic numbers from 1,000 to 9,999 are often written without commas or spaces (1000, 9999). Year numbers are always written without commas (1783).

[3]The Roman numerals are written either in capitals or in lowercase letters.

[4]The ordinal numbers are used to show the order of succession in which such items as names, objects, and periods of time are considered (the *twelfth* month; the *fourth* row of seats; the *18th* century).

[5]Each of the terms for the ordinal numbers excepting *first* and *second* is used in designating one of a number of parts into which a whole may be divided (a *fourth*; a *sixth*; a *tenth*) and as the denominator in fractions designating the number of such parts constituting a certain portion of a whole (*one fourth*; *three fifths*). When used as nouns the fractions are usually written as two words, although they are regularly hyphenated as adjectives (a *two-thirds* majority). When fractions are written in numerals, the cardinal symbols are used (¼, ⅗, ⅚).

[6]The Hindu-Arabic symbols for the cardinal numbers may be read as ordinals in certain contexts (January 1 = January first; 2 Samuel = Second Samuel). The Roman numerals are sometimes read as ordinals (Henry IV = Henry the Fourth); sometimes they are written with the ordinal suffixes (XIXth Dynasty).

DENOMINATIONS ABOVE ONE MILLION

American system[1]				British system[1]			
NAME	VALUE IN POWERS OF TEN	NUMBER OF ZEROS[2]	NUMBER OF GROUPS OF THREE 0'S AFTER 1,000	NAME	VALUE IN POWERS OF TEN	NUMBER OF ZEROS[2]	POWERS OF 1,000,000
billion	10^9	9	2	milliard	10^9	9	—
trillion	10^{12}	12	3	billion	10^{12}	12	2
quadrillion	10^{15}	15	4	trillion	10^{18}	18	3
quintillion	10^{18}	18	5	quadrillion	10^{24}	24	4
sextillion	10^{21}	21	6	quintillion	10^{30}	30	5
septillion	10^{24}	24	7	sextillion	10^{36}	36	6
octillion	10^{27}	27	8	septillion	10^{42}	42	7
nonillion	10^{30}	30	9	octillion	10^{48}	48	8
decillion	10^{33}	33	10	nonillion	10^{54}	54	9
undecillion	10^{36}	36	11	decillion	10^{60}	60	10
duodecillion	10^{39}	39	12	undecillion	10^{66}	66	11
tredecillion	10^{42}	42	13	duodecillion	10^{72}	72	12
quattuordecillion	10^{45}	45	14	tredecillion	10^{78}	78	13
quindecillion	10^{48}	48	15	quattuordecillion	10^{84}	84	14
sexdecillion	10^{51}	51	16	quindecillion	10^{90}	90	15
septendecillion	10^{54}	54	17	sexdecillion	10^{96}	96	16
octodecillion	10^{57}	57	18	septendecillion	10^{102}	102	17
novemdecillion	10^{60}	60	19	octodecillion	10^{108}	108	18
vigintillion	10^{63}	63	20	novemdecillion	10^{114}	114	19
centillion	10^{303}	303	100	vigintillion	10^{120}	120	20
				centillion	10^{600}	600	100

[1]The American system of numeration for denominations above one million was modeled on the French system but more recently the French system has been changed to correspond to the German and British systems. In the American system each of the denominations above 1,000 millions (the American *billion*) is 1,000 times the preceding one (one trillion = 1,000 billions; one quadrillion = 1,000 trillions). In the British system the first denomination above 1,000 millions (the British *milliard*) is 1,000 times the preceding one, but each of the denominations above 1,000 milliards (the British *billion*) is 1,000,000 times the preceding one (one trillion = 1,000,000 billions; one quadrillion = 1,000,000 trillions).

[2]For convenience in reading large numerals, the thousands, millions, etc., are usually separated by commas (21,530; 1,155,465) or especially in technical contexts by spaces (1 155 465). Serial numbers (as a social security number) are often written with hyphens (042-24-4705).

numerical analysis *noun* (1946)
: the study of quantitative approximations to the solutions of mathematical problems including consideration of the errors and bounds to the errors involved

numerical taxonomy *noun* (1963)
: taxonomy in which many quantitatively measured characters are given equal weight in the determination of taxa and the construction of diagrams indicating systematic relationships
— **numerical taxonomic** *adjective*
— **numerical taxonomist** *noun*

nu·mer·ol·o·gy \ˌnü-mə-ˈrä-lə-jē, ˌnyü-\ *noun* [Latin *numerus* + English *-o-* + *-logy*] (1911)
: the study of the occult significance of numbers
— **nu·mer·o·log·i·cal** \-mə-rə-ˈlä-ji-kəl\ *adjective*
— **nu·mer·ol·o·gist** \-mə-ˈrä-lə-jist\ *noun*

nu·me·ro uno \ˌnü-mə-rō-ˈü-(ˌ)nō, ˌnyü-\ *noun or adjective* [Italian *numero uno* or Spanish *número uno*] (1968)
: NUMBER ONE

nu·mer·ous \ˈnüm-rəs, ˈnü-mə-; ˈnyüm-, ˈnyü-mə-\ *adjective* [Middle English, from Middle French *numereux*, from Latin *numerosus*, from *numerus*] (15th century)
: consisting of great numbers of units or individuals ⟨born into a *numerous* family⟩; *also*
: MANY ⟨received *numerous* complaints⟩
— **nu·mer·ous·ly** *adverb*
— **nu·mer·ous·ness** *noun*

nu·mi·nous \ˈnü-mə-nəs, ˈnyü-\ *adjective* [Latin *numin-, numen* numen] (1647)
1 : SUPERNATURAL, MYSTERIOUS
2 : filled with a sense of the presence of divinity : HOLY
3 : appealing to the higher emotions or to the aesthetic sense : SPIRITUAL
— **nu·mi·nous·ness** \-nəs\ *noun*

nu·mis·mat·ic \ˌnü-məz-ˈma-tik, -məs-, ˌnyü-\ *adjective* [French *numismatique*, from Latin *nomismat-, nomisma* coin, from Greek, current coin, from *nomizein* to use, from *nomos* custom, law — more at NIMBLE] (1792)
1 : of or relating to numismatics
2 : of or relating to currency : MONETARY
— **nu·mis·mat·i·cal·ly** \-ti-k(ə-)lē\ *adverb*

nu·mis·mat·ics \-tiks\ *noun plural but singular in construction* (circa 1828)
: the study or collection of coins, tokens, and paper money and sometimes related objects (as medals)
— **nu·mis·ma·tist** \nü-ˈmiz-mə-tist, nyü-\ *noun*

num·mu·lar \ˈnəm-yə-lər\ *adjective* [French *nummulaire*, from Latin *nummulus*, diminutive of *nummus* coin, probably from Greek *nomismos* customary, from *nomos*] (1846)
: characterized by circular or oval lesions or drops ⟨*nummular* dermatitis⟩

num·mu·lit·ic limestone \ˌnəm-yə-ˈli-tik-\ *noun* [New Latin *Nummulites*, genus of foraminifers, from Latin *nummulus*] (1833)
: the most widely distributed and distinctive formation of the Eocene in Europe, Asia, and northern Africa

num·skull \ˈnəm-ˌskəl\ *noun* [*numb* + *skull*] (1717)
1 : a thick or muddled head
2 : a dull or stupid person : DUNCE

¹nun \ˈnən\ *noun* [Middle English, from Old English *nunne*, from Late Latin *nonna*] (before 12th century)
: a woman belonging to a religious order; *especially* : one under solemn vows of poverty, chastity, and obedience
— **nun·like** \-ˌlīk\ *adjective*

²nun \ˈnün\ *noun* [Hebrew *nūn*] (circa 1823)
: the 14th letter of the Hebrew alphabet — see ALPHABET table

nun·a·tak \ˈnə-nə-ˌtak\ *noun* [Inuit (Greenland) *nunataq*] (1877)
: a hill or mountain completely surrounded by glacial ice

Nunc Di·mit·tis \ˌnəŋk-də-ˈmi-təs, ˌnùnk-\ *noun* [Latin, now lettest thou depart; from the first words of the canticle] (1552)
: the prayer of Simeon in Luke 2:29–32 used as a canticle

nun·cha·ku \ˈnən-ˌchək, ˌnən-ˈchä-kü\ *noun* [Japanese dialect (Okinawa)] (1970)
: a weapon that consists of two hardwood sticks joined at their ends by a short length of rawhide, cord, or chain

nun·ci·a·ture \ˈnən(t)-sē-ə-ˌchùr, ˈnùn(t)-, -chər, -ˌtyùr, -ˌtùr\ *noun* [Italian *nunciatura*, from *nuncio*] (1652)
1 : a papal diplomatic mission headed by a nuncio
2 : the office or period of office of a nuncio

nun·cio \ˈnən(t)-sē-ˌō, ˈnùn(t)-\ *noun, plural* **-ci·os** [Italian, from Latin *nuntius* messenger, message] (1528)
: a papal legate of the highest rank permanently accredited to a civil government

nun·cle \ˈnəŋ-kəl\ *noun* [by alteration (from misdivision of *an uncle*)] (circa 1589)
chiefly dialect : UNCLE

nun·cu·pa·tive \ˈnən-kyù-ˌpā-tiv, ˈnəŋ-; ˌnən-ˈkyù-pə-\ *adjective* [Medieval Latin *nuncupativus*, from Late Latin, so-called, from Latin *nuncupatus*, past participle of *nuncupare* to name, probably ultimately from *nomen* name + *capere* to take — more at NAME, HEAVE] (1546)
: not written : ORAL ⟨a *nuncupative* will⟩

nun·nery \ˈnən-rē, ˈnə-nə-\ *noun, plural* **-ner·ies** (14th century)
: a convent of nuns

Nu·pe \ˈnü-(ˌ)pā\ *noun, plural* **Nupe** or **Nupes** (1883)
1 : the language of the Nupe people
2 : a member of a people of west central Nigeria

¹nup·tial \ˈnəp-shəl, -chəl, ÷-shə-wəl, ÷-chə-wəl\ *adjective* [Latin *nuptialis*, from *nuptiae*, plural, wedding, from *nubere* to marry; perhaps akin to Greek *nymphē* bride, nymph] (15th century)
1 : of or relating to marriage or the marriage ceremony
2 : characteristic of or occurring in the breeding season ⟨*nuptial* flight⟩

²nuptial *noun* (circa 1555)
: MARRIAGE, WEDDING — usually used in plural

nup·tial·i·ty \ˌnəp-shē-ˈa-lə-tē, -chē-\ *noun, plural* **-ties** (1899)
: the marriage rate

Nur·i·stani \ˌnùr-ə-ˈstä-nē, ˌnyùr-\ *noun* [*Nuristan*, Afghanistan] (1957)
: KAFIRI

¹nurse \ˈnərs\ *noun* [Middle English, from Old French *nurice*, from Late Latin *nutricia*, from Latin, feminine of *nutricius* nourishing — more at NUTRITIOUS] (13th century)
1 a : a woman who suckles an infant not her own : WET NURSE **b** : a woman who takes care of a young child : DRY NURSE
2 : one that looks after, fosters, or advises
3 : a person who is skilled or trained in caring for the sick or infirm especially under the supervision of a physician
4 a : a member of an insect society that belongs to the worker caste and cares for the young **b** : a female mammal used to suckle the young of another

²nurse *verb* **nursed; nurs·ing** [Middle English *nurshen* to suckle, nourish, contraction of *nurishen*] (14th century)
transitive verb
1 a : to nourish at the breast : SUCKLE **b** : to take nourishment from the breast of
2 : REAR, EDUCATE
3 a : to promote the development or progress of **b** : to manage with care or economy ⟨*nursed* the business through hard times⟩ **c** : to take charge of and watch over
4 a : to care for and wait on (as a sick person) **b** : to attempt to cure by care and treatment

5 : to hold in one's memory or consideration ⟨*nurse* a grievance⟩
6 a : to use, handle, or operate carefully so as to conserve energy or avoid injury or pain ⟨*nurse* a sprained ankle⟩ **b** : to use sparingly **c** : to consume slowly or over a long period ⟨*nurse* a cup of coffee⟩
intransitive verb
1 a : to feed an offspring from the breast **b** : to feed at the breast : SUCK
2 : to act or serve as a nurse
— **nurs·er** *noun*

nurse·maid \ˈnərs-ˌmād\ *noun* (1657)
: a girl or woman who is regularly employed to look after children

nurse–mid·wife \-ˈmid-ˌwīf\ *noun* (1952)
: a registered nurse with additional training as a midwife who delivers infants and provides antepartum and postpartum care
— **nurse–mid·wife·ry** \-ˌmid-ˈwi-f(ə-)rē, -ˈwī-; -ˈmid-ˌwī-\ *noun*

nurse–prac·ti·tion·er \-prak-ˈti-sh(ə-)nər\ *noun* (1969)
: a registered nurse who is qualified through advanced training to assume some of the duties and responsibilities formerly assumed only by a physician

nurs·ery \ˈnərs-rē, ˈnər-sə-\ *noun, plural* **-er·ies** (14th century)
1 *obsolete* : attentive care : FOSTERAGE
2 a : a child's bedroom **b** : a place where children are temporarily cared for in their parents' absence **c** : DAY NURSERY
3 a : something that fosters, develops, or promotes **b** : a place in which persons are trained or educated
4 : an area where plants are grown for transplanting, for use as stocks for budding and grafting, or for sale
5 : a place where young animals grow or are cared for

nurs·ery·man \-mən\ *noun* (1672)
: one whose occupation is the cultivation of plants (as trees and shrubs) especially for sale

nursery rhyme *noun* (1832)
: a short rhyme for children that often tells a story

nursery school *noun* (1835)
: a school for children usually under five years

nurse's aide *noun* (1943)
: a worker who assists trained nurses in a hospital by performing unspecialized services (as giving baths)

nurse shark *noun* [alteration of Middle English *nusse*] (1851)
: any of various sharks of a widely distributed family (Orectolobidae); *especially* : a shark (*Ginglymostoma cirratum*) of the warmer parts of the Atlantic Ocean

nurs·ing *noun* (1860)
1 : the profession of a nurse ⟨schools of *nursing*⟩
2 : the duties of a nurse ⟨proper *nursing* is difficult work⟩

nursing home *noun* (1896)
: a privately operated establishment providing maintenance and personal or nursing care for persons (as the aged or the chronically ill) who are unable to care for themselves properly

nurs·ling \ˈnərs-liŋ\ *noun* (1557)
1 : one that is solicitously cared for
2 : a nursing child

nur·tur·ance \ˈnər-chə-rən(t)s\ *noun* (circa 1938)
: affectionate care and attention
— **nur·tur·ant** \-rənt\ *adjective*

¹**nur·ture** \'nər-chər\ *noun* [Middle English, from Middle French *norriture*, from Late Latin *nutritura* act of nursing, from Latin *nutritus*, past participle of *nutrire* to suckle, nourish — more at NOURISH] (14th century)
1 : TRAINING, UPBRINGING
2 : something that nourishes : FOOD
3 : the sum of the influences modifying the expression of the genetic potentialities of an organism

²**nurture** *transitive verb* **nur·tured; nur·tur·ing** \'nərch-riṅ, 'nər-chə-\ (15th century)
1 : to supply with nourishment
2 : EDUCATE
3 : to further the development of : FOSTER
— **nur·tur·er** \'nər-chər-ər\ *noun*

¹**nut** \'nət\ *noun* [Middle English *nute, note,* from Old English *hnutu;* akin to Old High German *nuz* nut and perhaps to Latin *nux* nut] (before 12th century)
1 a (1) : a hard-shelled dry fruit or seed with a separable rind or shell and interior kernel (2) : the kernel of a nut **b** : a dry indehiscent one-seeded fruit with a woody pericarp
2 a : a hard problem or undertaking **b** : CORE, HEART
3 : a perforated block usually of metal that has an internal screw thread and is used on a bolt or screw for tightening or holding something
4 : the ridge in a stringed instrument (as a violin) over which the strings pass on the upper end of the fingerboard
5 : a small lump (as of butter)
6 a : a foolish, eccentric, or crazy person **b** : ENTHUSIAST ⟨a movie *nut*⟩
7 *plural* : NONSENSE — often used interjectionally
8 *slang* : a person's head
9 : TESTIS — usually considered vulgar
10 : the amount of money that must be earned in order to break even
11 : EN 1
— **nut·like** \-,līk\ *adjective*

²**nut** *intransitive verb* **nut·ted; nut·ting** (1604)
: to gather or seek nuts

nu·tate \'nü-,tāt, 'nyü-\ *intransitive verb* **nu·tat·ed; nu·tat·ing** (1880)
: to exhibit or undergo nutation

nu·ta·tion \nü-'tā-shən, nyü-\ *noun* [Latin *nutation-, nutatio,* from *nutare* to nod, rock — more at NUMEN] (1612)
1 *archaic* : the act of nodding the head
2 : oscillatory movement of the axis of a rotating body (as the earth) : WOBBLE
3 : a spontaneous usually spiral movement of a growing plant part
— **nu·ta·tion·al** \-shnəl, -shə-n°l\ *adjective*

nut–brown \'nət-'braün\ *adjective* (14th century)
: of the color of a brown nut

nut·case \-,kās\ *noun* (1959)
: NUT 6a

nut·crack·er \-,kra-kər\ *noun* (circa 1548)
: an implement for cracking nuts

nut·gall \-,gȯl\ *noun* (15th century)
: a gall that resembles a nut; *especially* : a gall produced on oak

nut grass *noun* (1775)
: a perennial sedge (*Cyperus rotundus*) of wide distribution that has slender rootstocks bearing small edible tubers resembling nuts; *also* : a related sedge (*C. esculentus*)

nut·hatch \'nət-,hach\ *noun* [Middle English *notehache,* from *note* nut + *-hache;* akin to Old English to*haccian* to hack — more at HACK] (14th century)
: any of various small tree-climbing chiefly insectivorous birds (family Sittidae and

nuthatch

especially genus *Sitta*) that have a compact body, a narrow bill, a short tail, and sometimes a black cap

nut·house \'nət-,haüs\ *noun* (1900)
slang : an insane asylum

nut·let \'nət-lət\ *noun* (1856)
1 a : a small nut **b** : a small fruit similar to a nut
2 : the stone of a drupelet

nut·meg \'nət-,meg, -,mäg\ *noun* [Middle English *notemigge, notemuge,* ultimately from Old Provençal *noz muscada,* from *noz* nut (from Latin *nuc-, nux*) + *muscada,* feminine of *muscat* musky — more at MUSCAT] (15th century)
: an aromatic seed that is used as a spice and is produced by an evergreen tree (*Myristica fragrans* of the family Myristicaceae, the nutmeg family) native to the Moluccas; *also* : a tree yielding nutmeg

nut·pick \'nət-,pik\ *noun* (circa 1889)
: a small sharp-pointed implement for extracting the kernels from nuts

nu·tria \'nü-trē-ə, 'nyü-\ *noun* [American Spanish, from Spanish, otter, modification of Latin *lutra;* probably akin to Old English *oter* otter] (1820)
1 : the durable usually light brown fur of a nutria
2 : a large South American semiaquatic rodent (*Myocastor coypus*) with webbed hind feet that has been introduced into parts of Europe, Asia, and North America

¹**nu·tri·ent** \'nü-trē-ənt, 'nyü-\ *adjective* [Latin *nutrient-, nutriens,* present participle of *nutrire* to nourish — more at NOURISH] (1650)
: furnishing nourishment

²**nutrient** *noun* (circa 1828)
: a nutritive substance or ingredient

nu·tri·ment \'nü-trə-mənt, 'nyü-\ *noun* [Middle English, from Latin *nutrimentum,* from *nutrire*] (15th century)
: something that nourishes or promotes growth and repairs the natural wastage of organic life

nu·tri·tion \nü-'tri-shən, nyü-\ *noun* [Middle English *nutricioun,* from Middle French *nutrition,* from Late Latin *nutrition-, nutritio,* from Latin *nutrire*] (15th century)
: the act or process of nourishing or being nourished; *specifically* : the sum of the processes by which an animal or plant takes in and utilizes food substances
— **nu·tri·tion·al** \-'trish-nəl, -'tri-shə-n°l\ *adjective*
— **nu·tri·tion·al·ly** *adverb*

nu·tri·tion·ist \-'tri-sh(ə-)nist\ *noun* (1926)
: a specialist in the study of nutrition

nu·tri·tious \nü-'tri-shəs, nyü-\ *adjective* [Latin *nutricius,* from *nutric-, nutrix* nurse, from *nutrire* to nourish — more at NOURISH] (1665)
: NOURISHING
— **nu·tri·tious·ly** *adverb*
— **nu·tri·tious·ness** *noun*

nu·tri·tive \'nü-trə-tiv, 'nyü-\ *adjective* (14th century)
1 : of or relating to nutrition
2 : NOURISHING
— **nu·tri·tive·ly** *adverb*

nutritive ratio *noun* (1897)
: the ratio of digestible protein to other nutrients in a foodstuff or ration

nuts \'nəts\ *adjective* (1785)
1 : ENTHUSIASTIC, KEEN ⟨everyone seems *nuts* about it —Lois Long⟩
2 : INSANE, CRAZY ⟨said that it was a novel and all the people who said otherwise were *nuts* —Flannery O'Connor⟩ ◆

nuts and bolts *noun* (1967)
1 : the working parts or elements
2 : the practical workings of a machine or enterprise as opposed to theoretical considerations or speculative possibilities
— **nuts–and–bolts** *adjective*

nut·sedge \'nət-,sej\ *noun* (circa 1909)
: NUT GRASS

nut·shell \'nət-,shel\ *noun* (13th century)
1 : the hard external covering in which the kernel of a nut is enclosed
2 : something of small size, amount, or scope
— **in a nutshell** : in a very brief statement

nut·ter \'nə-tər\ *noun* (1958)
slang British : NUT 6a

nut·ty \'nə-tē\ *adjective* **nut·ti·er; -est** (15th century)
1 : having or producing nuts
2 : having a flavor like that of nuts
3 : ECCENTRIC, SILLY; *also* : mentally unbalanced
— **nut·ti·ly** \-tə-lē\ *adverb*
— **nut·ti·ness** *noun*

nux vom·i·ca \'nəks-'vä-mi-kə\ *noun, plural* **nux vomica** [New Latin, literally, emetic nut] (14th century)
1 : the poisonous seed of an Asian tree (*Strychnos nux-vomica* of the family Loganiaceae) that contains several alkaloids and especially strychnine and brucine; *also* : the tree yielding nux vomica
2 : a drug containing nux vomica

nuz·zle \'nə-zəl\ *verb* **nuz·zled; nuz·zling** \'nəz-liṅ, 'nə-zə-\ [Middle English *noselen* to bring the nose toward the ground, from *nose*] (1530)
intransitive verb
1 : to work with or as if with the nose; *especially* : to root, rub, or snuff something
2 : to lie close or snug : NESTLE
transitive verb
1 : to root, rub, or touch with or as if with the nose : NUDGE
2 : to rub or push gently (as one's face) against something ⟨*nuzzled* her face into the pillow⟩

ny·a·la \nē-'ä-lə\ *noun, plural* **nyalas** or **nyala** [of Bantu origin; akin to Venda *dzi-nyálà* nyala buck] (1894)
: an antelope (*Tragelaphus angasi*) of southeastern Africa with vertical white stripes on the sides of the body and with shaggy black hair along the male underside; *also* : a related antelope (*T. buxtoni*) of Ethiopia

nyc·ta·lo·pia \,nik-tə-'lō-pē-ə\ *noun* [New Latin, from

nyala

Latin *nyctalops* suffering from night blindness, from Greek *nyktalops*, from *nykt-*, *nyx* night + *alaos* blind + *ōp-*, *ōps* eye — more at NIGHT, EYE] (1684)
: NIGHT BLINDNESS

ny·lon \'nī-,län\ *noun* [coined word] (1938)
1 : any of numerous strong tough elastic synthetic polyamide materials that are fashioned into fibers, filaments, bristles, or sheets and used especially in textiles and plastics
2 *plural* : stockings made of nylon

nymph \'nim(p)f\ *noun* [Middle English *nimphe*, from Middle French, from Latin *nympha* bride, nymph, from Greek *nymphē* — more at NUPTIAL] (14th century)
1 : any of the minor divinities of nature in classical mythology represented as beautiful maidens dwelling in the mountains, forests, trees, and waters
2 : GIRL
3 : any of various immature insects; *especially* : a larva of an insect (as a grasshopper, true bug, or mayfly) with incomplete metamorphosis that differs from the imago especially in size and in its incompletely developed wings and genitalia — compare NAIAD 2
— **nymph·al** \'nim(p)-fəl\ *adjective*

nym·pha·lid \nim-'fa-ləd, 'nim-fə-ləd\ *noun* [New Latin *Nymphalidae*, ultimately from Latin *nympha* nymph] (1897)
: any of a family (Nymphalidae) of butterflies (as a mourning cloak or fritillary) with the first pair of legs reduced in size in both sexes and useless for walking
— **nymphalid** *adjective*

nym·phet *also* **nym·phette** \nim-'fet, 'nim(p)-fət\ *noun* (1955)
: a sexually precocious girl barely in her teens

nym·pho \'nim(p)-(,)fō\ *noun, plural* **nym·phos** [short for *nymphomaniac*] (circa 1910)
: a person affected by nymphomania : NYMPHOMANIAC

nym·pho·lep·sy \'nim(p)-fə-,lep-sē\ *noun* [*nympholept*, from Greek *nympholēptos* frenzied, literally, caught by nymphs, from *nymphē* + *lambanein* to seize — more at LATCH] (1775)
1 : a demoniac enthusiasm held by the ancients to seize one bewitched by a nymph
2 : a frenzy of emotion
— **nym·pho·lept** \-,lept\ *noun*
— **nym·pho·lep·tic** \,nim(p)-fə-'lep-tik\ *adjective*

nym·pho·ma·nia \,nim(p)-fə-'mā-nē-ə, -nyə\ *noun* [New Latin, from *nymphae* inner lips of the vulva (from Latin, plural of *nympha*) + Late Latin *mania* mania] (1775)
: excessive sexual desire by a female
— **nym·pho·ma·ni·ac** \-nē-,ak\ *noun or adjective*
— **nym·pho·ma·ni·a·cal** \-mə-'nī-ə-kəl\ *adjective*

Ny·norsk \nü-'nȯrsk, nyü-, nē-\ *noun* [Norwegian, literally, new Norwegian] (1931)
: a literary form of Norwegian based on the spoken dialects of Norway — compare BOKMÅL

nys·tag·mus \nis-'tag-məs\ *noun* [New Latin, from Greek *nystagmos* drowsiness, from *nystazein* to doze; probably akin to Lithuanian *snusti* to doze] (1822)
: a rapid involuntary oscillation of the eyeballs (as from dizziness)
— **nys·tag·mic** \-mik\ *adjective*

nys·ta·tin \'nis-tə-tən\ *noun* [*New York State* (where it was developed) + ¹-*in*] (1952)
: an antibiotic that is derived from a soil actinomycete (*Streptomyces noursei*) and is used especially in the treatment of candidiasis

O *is the fifteenth letter of the English alphabet. It comes through Latin, via Etruscan, from Greek. The Greeks in turn took the letter from Phoenician, where it represented a consonant sound called* 'ayin, *sounding like an* h *pronounced harshly and with the vocal cords vibrating (rather like the sound one might make, for example, while being throttled). The Greeks, not having this consonant sound, assigned the letter-symbol to the short and long* o *vowel sounds. They later reassigned these two sounds to the separate letter-symbols* omicron *and* omega, *but the Romans continued to use one symbol for both.* O *stands for various sounds in English, the chief of which are its long sound, as in* bone, *its short sound, as in* nod, *and the sounds heard in the words* orb, son, do, *and* wolf. *With other vowels and with itself it forms several digraphs (*œa, œe, œi, œo, œu, *and* œy*), some representing simple vowels and others representing diphthongs. Small* o *developed by a simple reduction in the size of the capital form.*

o \'ō\ *noun, plural* **o's** *or* **os** \'ōz\ *often capitalized, often attributive* (before 12th century)
1 a : the 15th letter of the English alphabet **b :** a graphic representation of this letter **c :** a speech counterpart of orthographic *o*
2 : a graphic device for reproducing the letter *o*
3 : one designated *o* especially as the 15th in order or class
4 : something shaped like the letter O; *especially :* ZERO

O \'ō\ *variant of* OH

o- *or* **oo-** *combining form* [Greek ōi-, ōio-, from ōion — more at EGG]
: egg ⟨*oo*logy⟩; *specifically :* ovum ⟨*oo*gonium⟩

-o- [Middle English, from Old French, from Latin, from Greek, thematic vowel of many nouns and adjectives in combination]
— used as a connective vowel originally to join word elements of Greek origin and now also to join word elements of Latin or other origin ⟨speed*o*meter⟩ ⟨elastom*o*er⟩

¹-o *noun suffix* [perhaps from ¹*oh*]
: one that is, has the qualities of, or is associated with ⟨buck*o*⟩

²-o *interjection suffix* [probably from ¹*oh*]
— in interjections formed from other parts of speech ⟨cheeri*o*⟩ ⟨right*o*⟩

o' *also* **o** \ə, ō\ *preposition* [Middle English *o*, *o-*, contraction of *on* & *of*] (13th century)
1 *chiefly dialect :* ON
2 : OF ⟨one o'clock⟩

oaf \'ōf\ *noun, plural* **oafs** [of Scandinavian origin; akin to Old Norse *alfr* elf — more at ELF] (1625)
1 : a stupid person **:** BOOB
2 : a big clumsy slow-witted person
— **oaf·ish** \'ō-fish\ *adjective*
— **oaf·ish·ly** *adverb*
— **oaf·ish·ness** *noun*

oak \'ōk\ *noun, plural* **oaks** *or* **oak** *often attributive* [Middle English *ook*, from Old English *āc*; akin to Old High German *eih* oak and perhaps to Greek *aigilōps*, a kind of oak] (before 12th century)
1 a : any of a genus (*Quercus*) of trees or shrubs of the beech family that produce acorns; *also :* any of various plants related to or resembling the oaks **b :** the tough hard durable wood of an oak tree
2 : the leaves of an oak used as decoration
— **oak·en** \'ō-kən\ *adjective*

oak apple *noun* (15th century)
: a large round gall produced on oak leaves and twigs by a gall wasp (especially *Amphibolips confluenta* or *Andricus quercuscalifornicus*)

oak–leaf cluster *noun* (1918)

: a bronze or silver cluster of oak leaves and acorns added to various military decorations to signify a second or subsequent award of the basic decoration

oak·moss \'ōk-ˌmȯs\ *noun* (1921)
: any of several lichens (as *Evernia prunastri*) that grow on oak trees and yield a resin used in perfumery

oa·kum \'ō-kəm\ *noun* [Middle English *okum*, from Old English *ācumba* tow, from *ā-* (separative & perfective prefix) + *-cumba* (akin to Old English *camb* comb) — more at ABIDE] (15th century)
: loosely twisted hemp or jute fiber impregnated with tar or a tar derivative and used in caulking seams and packing joints

oak wilt *noun* (1942)
: a destructive disease of oak trees that is caused by a fungus (*Ceratocystis fagacearum*) and is characterized by wilting, discoloration, and defoliation

¹oar \'ōr, 'ȯr\ *noun* [Middle English *oor*, from Old English *ār*; akin to Old Norse *ār* oar] (before 12th century)
1 : a long pole with a broad blade at one end used for propelling or steering a boat
2 : OARSMAN
— **oared** \'ōrd, 'ȯrd\ *adjective*

²oar (1610)
transitive verb
: to propel with or as if with oars **:** ROW
intransitive verb
: to progress by or as if by using oars

oar·fish \'ōr-ˌfish, 'ȯr-\ *noun* (1860)
: any of several sea fishes (genus *Regalecus* and especially *R. glesne*) with narrow soft bodies from 20 to 30 feet (6 to 9 meters) long, a red dorsal fin running the entire length of the body, and red-tipped anterior rays rising above the head

oar·lock \-ˌläk\ *noun* (before 12th century)
: a usually U-shaped device for holding an oar in place

oars·man \'ōrz-mən, 'ȯrz-\ *noun* (1701)
: one who rows especially in a racing crew
— **oars·man·ship** \-ˌship\ *noun*

oars·wom·an \-ˌwu̇-mən\ *noun* (1882)
: a woman who rows especially in a racing crew

oa·sis \ō-'ā-səs\ *noun, plural* **oa·ses** \-ˌsēz\ [Late Latin, from Greek] (1613)
1 : a fertile or green area in an arid region (as a desert)
2 : something that provides refuge, relief, or pleasant contrast

oast \'ōst\ *noun* [Middle English *ost*, from Old English *āst*; akin to Middle Dutch *eest* kiln, Latin *aestus* heat, *aestas* summer — more at EDIFY] (before 12th century)

: a usually conical kiln used for drying hops, malt, or tobacco — called also *oast·house* \-ˌhau̇s\

oat \'ōt\ *noun, often attributive* [Middle English *ote*, from Old English *āte*] (before 12th century)
1 a : any of several grasses (genus *Avena*); *especially :* a widely cultivated cereal grass (*A. sativa*) **b :** a crop or plot of the oat; *also :* oat seed — usually used in plural but singular or plural in construction
2 *archaic :* a reed instrument made of an oat straw

oat·cake \'ōt-ˌkāk\ *noun* (14th century)
: a thin flat oatmeal cake

oat–cell \-ˌsel\ *adjective* (1903)
: of, relating to, or being a highly malignant form of cancer especially of the lungs that is characterized by rapid proliferation of small anaplastic cells ⟨*oat-cell* carcinomas⟩

oat 1a

oat·en \'ō-t°n\ *adjective* (14th century)
: of or relating to oats, oat straw, or oatmeal

oat·er \'ō-tər\ *noun* (1946)
: WESTERN 2

oat grass *noun* (1578)
: WILD OAT 1a; *broadly :* one of several grasses resembling the oat

oath \'ōth\ *noun, plural* **oaths** \'ōthz, 'ōths\ [Middle English *ooth*, from Old English *āth*; akin to Old High German *eid* oath, Middle Irish *oeth*] (before 12th century)
1 a (1) **:** a solemn usually formal calling upon God or a god to witness to the truth of what one says or to witness that one sincerely intends to do what one says (2) **:** a solemn attestation of the truth or inviolability of one's words **b :** something (as a promise) corroborated by an oath
2 : an irreverent or careless use of a sacred name; *broadly :* SWEARWORD

oat·meal \'ōt-ˌmēl, 'ōt-ˌmē(ə)l\ *noun* (14th century)
1 a : meal made from oats **b :** rolled oats
2 : porridge made from ground or rolled oats

ob- *prefix* [New Latin, from Latin, in the way, against, toward, from *ob* in the way of, on account of; akin to Old Church Slavonic *o*, *ob* on, around]
: inversely ⟨*ob*ovate⟩

Oba·di·ah \ˌō-bə-'dī-ə\ *noun* [Hebrew 'Ōbhadhyāh]
1 : a Hebrew prophet
2 : a prophetic book of canonical Jewish and Christian Scripture — see BIBLE table

¹ob·bli·ga·to \ˌä-blə-'gä-(ˌ)tō\ *adjective* [Italian, obligatory, from past participle of *obbligare* to oblige, from Latin *obligare* — more at OBLIGE] (1794)
: not to be omitted **:** OBLIGATORY — used as a direction in music; compare AD LIBITUM

²obbligato *noun, plural* **-tos** *also* **-ti** \-'gä-tē\ (1845)
1 : an elaborate especially melodic part accompanying a solo or principal melody and usually played by a single instrument ⟨a song with violin *obbligato*⟩
2 : ACCOMPANIMENT 2b; *especially :* an attendant background sound

ob·cor·date \ˌäb-'kȯr-ˌdāt\ *adjective* (1775)
: heart-shaped with the notch apical ⟨*obcordate* leaf⟩

ob·du·ra·cy \'äb-də-rə-sē, -dyə-; äb-'du̇r-ə-, əb-, -'dyu̇r-\ *noun, plural* **-cies** (1597)
: the quality or state of being obdurate

ob·du·rate \'äb-də-rət, -dyə-; äb-'du̇r-ət, əb-, -'dyu̇r-\ *adjective* [Middle English, from Latin *obduratus*, past participle of *obdurare* to harden, from *ob-* against + *durus* hard — more at DURING] (15th century)
1 a : stubbornly persistent in wrongdoing **b :** hardened in feelings

2 : resistant to persuasion or softening influences

synonym see INFLEXIBLE
— **ob·du·rate·ly** adverb
— **ob·du·rate·ness** noun

obe·ah \'ō-bē-ə\ also **obi** \'ō-bē\ noun, often capitalized [of African origin; akin to Twi ɔ-bayifó sorcerer, Ibo díbìà folk healer] (1760)
: a system of belief among blacks chiefly of the British West Indies, the Guianas, and the southeastern U.S. that is characterized by the use of sorcery and magic ritual

obe·di·ence \ō-'bē-dē-ən(t)s, ə-\ noun (13th century)
1 a : an act or instance of obeying **b :** the quality or state of being obedient
2 : a sphere of jurisdiction; especially **:** an ecclesiastical or sometimes secular dominion

obe·di·ent \-ənt\ adjective [Middle English, from Old French, from Latin oboedient-, oboediens, from present participle of oboedire to obey] (13th century)
: submissive to the restraint or command of authority : willing to obey ☆
— **obe·di·ent·ly** adverb

obei·sance \ō-'bē-s°n(t)s, ə-, -'bā-\ noun [Middle English obeisaunce obedience, obeisance, from Middle French obeissance, from obeissant, present participle of obeir to obey] (14th century)
1 : a movement of the body made in token of respect or submission : BOW
2 : DEFERENCE, HOMAGE
— **obei·sant** \-s°nt\ adjective
— **obei·sant·ly** adverb

obe·lia \ō-'bēl-yə\ noun [New Latin] (1868)
: any of a genus (Obelia) of small colonial marine hydroids with colonies branched like trees

obe·lisk \'ä-bə-ˌlisk also 'ō-\ noun [Middle French obelisque, from Latin obeliscus, from Greek obeliskos, from diminutive of obelos] (1569)
1 : an upright 4-sided usually monolithic pillar that gradually tapers as it rises and terminates in a pyramid
2 a : OBELUS **b :** DAGGER 2b

obe·lize \-ˌlīz\ transitive verb **-lized; -liz·ing** (circa 1656)
: to designate or annotate with an obelus

obe·lus \-ləs\ noun, plural **ob·e·li** \-ˌlī, -ˌlē\ [Middle English, from Late Latin, from Greek obelos spit, pointed pillar, obelus] (14th century)
1 : a symbol − or ÷ used in ancient manuscripts to mark a questionable passage
2 : the symbol ÷

Ober·on \'ō-bə-ˌrän, -rən\ noun [French, from Old French Auberon]
: the king of the fairies in medieval folklore

obese \ō-'bēs\ adjective [Latin obesus, from ob- against + esus, past participle of edere to eat — more at OB-, EAT] (1651)
: excessively fat

obe·si·ty \ō-'bē-sə-tē\ noun (1611)
: a condition characterized by excessive bodily fat

obey \ō-'bā, ə-\ verb **obeyed; obey·ing** [Middle English obeien, from Old French obeir, from Latin oboedire, from ob- toward + -oedire (akin to audire to hear) — more at OB-, AUDIBLE] (14th century)
transitive verb
1 : to follow the commands or guidance of
2 : to conform to or comply with ⟨obey an order⟩ ⟨falling objects obey the laws of physics⟩
intransitive verb
: to behave obediently
— **obey·er** noun

ob·fus·cate \'äb-fə-ˌskāt; äb-'fəs-ˌkāt, əb-\ transitive verb **-cat·ed; -cat·ing** [Late Latin obfuscatus, past participle of obfuscare, from Latin ob- in the way + fuscus dark brown — more at OB-, DUSK] (1577)
1 a : DARKEN **b :** to make obscure
2 : CONFUSE
— **ob·fus·ca·tion** \ˌäb-(ˌ)fəs-'kā-shən\ noun
— **ob·fus·ca·to·ry** \äb-'fəs-kə-ˌtōr-ē, əb-, -ˌtȯr-\ adjective

obi \'ō-bē\ noun [Japanese] (1876)
: a broad sash worn especially with a Japanese kimono

Obie \'ō-bē\ noun [O.B., abbreviation for off Broadway] (1965)
: an award presented annually by a professional organization for notable achievement in plays performed off-Broadway

obit \ō-'bit, 'ō-bət, especially British 'ä-bit\ noun [Middle English, from Middle French obit, from Latin obitus death, from obire to go to meet, die, from ob- in the way + ire to go — more at ISSUE] (15th century)
: OBITUARY

obi·ter dic·tum \ˌō-bə-tər-'dik-təm, ˌä-\ noun, plural **obiter dic·ta** \-tə\ [Late Latin, literally, something said in passing] (1812)
1 : an incidental and collateral opinion that is uttered by a judge but is not binding
2 : an incidental remark or observation

obit·u·ary \ə-'bi-chə-ˌwer-ē, ō-, -'bi-chə-rē\ noun, plural **-ar·ies** [Medieval Latin obituarium, from Latin obitus death] (1738)
: a notice of a person's death usually with a short biographical account
— **obit·u·ar·ist** \-'bi-chə-ˌwər-ist, -'bi-chə-rist\ noun
— **obituary** adjective

¹ob·ject \'äb-jikt, -(ˌ)jekt\ noun [Middle English, from Medieval Latin objectum, from Latin, neuter of objectus, past participle of obicere to throw in the way, present, hinder, from ob- in the way + jacere to throw — more at OB-, JET] (14th century)
1 a : something material that may be perceived by the senses ⟨I see an object in the distance⟩ **b :** something that when viewed stirs a particular emotion (as pity) ⟨look to the tragic loading of this bed . . . the object poisons sight; let it be hid —Shakespeare⟩
2 : something mental or physical toward which thought, feeling, or action is directed ⟨an object for study⟩ ⟨the object of my affection⟩ ⟨delicately carved art objects⟩
3 a : the goal or end of an effort or activity **:** PURPOSE, OBJECTIVE ⟨their object is to investigate the matter thoroughly⟩ **b :** a cause for attention or concern ⟨money is no object⟩
4 : a thing that forms an element of or constitutes the subject matter of an investigation or science
5 a : a noun or noun equivalent (as a pronoun, gerund, or clause) denoting the goal or result of the action of a verb **b :** a noun or noun equivalent in a prepositional phrase
synonym see INTENTION
— **ob·ject·less** \-ləs\ adjective
— **ob·ject·less·ness** noun

²ob·ject \əb-'jekt\ verb [Middle English, from Latin objectus, past participle of obicere to throw in the way, object] (15th century)
transitive verb
: to put forth in opposition or as an objection ⟨objected that the statement was misleading⟩
intransitive verb
1 : to oppose something firmly and usually with words or arguments
2 : to feel distaste for something
— **ob·jec·tor** \-'jek-tər\ noun

ob·ject ball \'äb-jik(t)-, -(ˌ)jek(t)-\ noun (1856)
: the ball first struck by the cue ball in pool or billiards; also **:** a ball hit by the cue ball

ob·jec·ti·fy \əb-'jek-tə-ˌfī\ transitive verb **-fied; -fy·ing** (circa 1837)
1 : to treat as an object or cause to have objective reality
2 : to give expression to (as an abstract notion, feeling, or ideal) in a form that can be experienced by others ⟨it is the essence of the fairy tale to objectify differing facets of the child's emotional experience —John Updike⟩
— **ob·jec·ti·fi·ca·tion** \-ˌjek-tə-fə-'kā-shən\ noun

ob·jec·tion \əb-'jek-shən\ noun (14th century)
1 : an act of objecting
2 a : a reason or argument presented in opposition **b :** a feeling or expression of disapproval

ob·jec·tion·able \-sh(ə-)nə-bəl\ adjective (1781)
: UNDESIRABLE, OFFENSIVE
— **ob·jec·tion·able·ness** noun
— **ob·jec·tion·ably** \-blē\ adverb

¹ob·jec·tive \əb-'jek-tiv, äb-\ adjective (1620)
1 a : relating to or existing as an object of thought without consideration of independent existence — used chiefly in medieval philosophy **b :** of, relating to, or being an object, phenomenon, or condition in the realm of sensible experience independent of individual thought and perceptible by all observers **:** having reality independent of the mind ⟨objective reality⟩ ⟨our reveries . . . are significantly and repeatedly shaped by our transactions with the objective world —Marvin Reznikoff⟩ — compare SUBJECTIVE 3a **c** of a symptom of disease **:** perceptible to persons other than the affected individual — compare SUBJECTIVE 4c **d :** involving or deriving from sense perception or experience with actual objects, conditions, or phenomena ⟨objective awareness⟩ ⟨objective data⟩
2 : relating to, characteristic of, or constituting the case of words that follow prepositions or transitive verbs
3 a : expressing or dealing with facts or conditions as perceived without distortion by personal feelings, prejudices, or interpretations ⟨objective art⟩ ⟨an objective history of the war⟩ ⟨an objective judgment⟩ **b** of a test **:** limited to choices of fixed alternatives and reducing subjective factors to a minimum
synonym see MATERIAL, FAIR
— **ob·jec·tive·ly** adverb
— **ob·jec·tive·ness** noun
— **ob·jec·tiv·i·ty** \ˌäb-ˌjek-'ti-və-tē, əb-\ noun

²objective noun (1835)
1 : a lens or system of lenses that forms an image of an object
2 a : something toward which effort is directed **:** an aim, goal, or end of action **b :** a strategic position to be attained or a purpose to be achieved by a military operation
synonym see INTENTION

☆ SYNONYMS
Obedient, docile, tractable, amenable mean submissive to the will of another. OBEDIENT implies compliance with the demands or requests of one in authority ⟨obedient to the government⟩. DOCILE implies a predisposition to submit readily to control or guidance ⟨a docile child⟩. TRACTABLE suggests having a character that permits easy handling or managing ⟨tractable beasts of burden⟩. AMENABLE suggests a willingness to yield or to cooperate either because of a desire to be agreeable or because of a natural open-mindedness ⟨amenable to new ideas⟩.

\ə\ **abut** \ᵊ\ **kitten** \ər\ **further** \a\ **ash** \ā\ **ace** \ä\ **mop, mar** \au̇\ **out** \ch\ **chin** \e\ **bet** \ē\ **easy** \g\ **go** \i\ **hit** \ī\ **ice** \j\ **job** \ŋ\ **sing** \ō\ **go** \ȯ\ **law** \ȯi\ **boy** \th\ **thin** \t͟h\ **the** \ü\ **loot** \u̇\ **foot** \y\ **yet** \zh\ **vision** see also Guide to Pronunciation

objective complement *noun* (1870)
: a noun, adjective, or pronoun used in the predicate as complement to a verb and as qualifier of its direct object (as *chairman* in "we elected him chairman")

objective correlative *noun* (1919)
: something (as a situation or chain of events) that symbolizes or objectifies a particular emotion and that may be used in creative writing to evoke a desired emotional response in the reader

ob·jec·tiv·ism \əb-'jek-ti-,vi-zəm, äb-\ *noun* (1854)
1 : any of various theories asserting the validity of objective phenomena over subjective experience; *especially* : REALISM 2a
2 : an ethical theory that moral good is objectively real or that moral precepts are objectively valid
3 : a 20th century movement in poetry growing out of imagism and putting stress on form
— **ob·jec·tiv·ist** \-vist\ *adjective or noun*
— **ob·jec·tiv·is·tic** \-,jek-ti-'vis-tik\ *adjective*

object language \'äb-jikt-, -(,)jekt-\ *noun* (1935)
: TARGET LANGUAGE

object lesson \'äb-jikt-, -(,)jekt-\ *noun* (1831)
: something that serves as a practical example of a principle or abstract idea

ob·jet d'art \,ōb-,zhä-'där\ *noun, plural* **objets d'art** *same*\ [French, literally, art object] (1865)
1 : an article of some artistic value
2 : CURIO — called also *objet*

ob·jet trou·vé \'ōb-,zhä-trü-'vā\ *noun, plural* **objets trouvés** *same*\ [French, literally, found object] (1937)
: a natural object (as a piece of driftwood) found by chance and held to have aesthetic value especially through the working of natural forces on it; *also* : an artifact not originally intended as art but held to have aesthetic value especially when displayed as a work of art

ob·jur·ga·tion \,äb-jər-'gā-shən\ *noun* [Middle English *objurgacyon*, from Middle French or Latin; Middle French *objurgation*, from Latin *objurgation-, objurgatio*, from *objurgare* to scold, blame, from *ob-* against + *jurgare* to quarrel, literally, to take to law, from *jur-, jus* law + *-igare* (from *agere* to lead) — more at OB-, JUST, AGENT] (15th century)
: a harsh rebuke
— **ob·jur·gate** \'äb-jər-,gāt\ *transitive verb*
— **ob·jur·ga·to·ry** \əb-'jər-gə-,tōr-ē, -,tȯr-\ *adjective*

ob·lan·ceo·late \(,)äb-'lan(t)-sē-ə-,lāt\ *adjective* (1850)
: inversely lanceolate ⟨an *oblanceolate* leaf⟩
— see LEAF illustration

ob·last \'ä-,blast, 'ö-bləst\ *noun, plural* **oblasts** *also* **ob·las·ti** \-,blas-tē, -bləs-\ [Russian *oblast'*] (circa 1886)
: a political subdivision of Imperial Russia or of a republic in the U.S.S.R.

¹ob·late \ä-'blāt, 'ä-,\ *adjective* [probably from New Latin *oblatus*, from *ob-* + *-latus* (as in *prolatus* prolate)] (1705)
: flattened or depressed at the poles ⟨an *oblate* spheroid⟩
— **ob·late·ness** *noun*

²ob·late \'ä-,blāt\ *noun* [Medieval Latin *oblatus*, literally, one offered up, from Latin, past participle of *offerre* — more at OFFER] (1864)
1 : a layman living in a monastery under a modified rule and without vows
2 : a member of one of several Roman Catholic communities of men or women

ob·la·tion \ə-'blā-shən, ō-\ *noun* [Middle English *oblacioun*, from Middle French *oblation*, from Late Latin *oblation-, oblatio*, from Latin *offerre*] (15th century)
1 : the act of making a religious offering; *specifically, capitalized* : the act of offering the eucharistic elements to God

2 : something offered in worship or devotion
: a holy gift offered usually at an altar or shrine

¹ob·li·gate \'ä-blə-,gāt\ *transitive verb* **-gat·ed; -gat·ing** [Latin *obligatus*, past participle of *obligare*] (1533)
1 : to bind legally or morally : CONSTRAIN
2 : to commit (as funds) to meet an obligation

²ob·li·gate \'ä-bli-gət, -blə-,gāt\ *adjective* (1887)
1 : restricted to one particularly characteristic mode of life ⟨an *obligate* parasite⟩
2 : biologically essential for survival ⟨*obligate* mutualism⟩
— **ob·li·gate·ly** *adverb*

ob·li·ga·tion \,ä-blə-'gā-shən\ *noun* (14th century)
1 : the action of obligating oneself to a course of action (as by a promise or vow)
2 a : something (as a formal contract, a promise, or the demands of conscience or custom) that obligates one to a course of action **b** : a debt security (as a mortgage or corporate bond) **c** : a commitment (as by a government) to pay a particular sum of money; *also* : an amount owed under such an obligation ⟨unable to meet its *obligations*, the company went into bankruptcy⟩
3 a : a condition or feeling of being obligated **b** : a debt of gratitude
4 : something one is bound to do : DUTY, RESPONSIBILITY

oblig·a·to·ry \ə-'bli-gə-,tōr-ē, ä-, -,tȯr- *also* 'ä-bli-gə-\ *adjective* (15th century)
1 : binding in law or conscience
2 : relating to or enforcing an obligation ⟨a writ *obligatory*⟩
3 : MANDATORY, REQUIRED ⟨*obligatory* military service⟩; *also* : so commonplace as to be a convention, fashion, or cliché ⟨the *obligatory* death scene in opera⟩
4 : OBLIGATE 1
— **oblig·a·to·ri·ly** \ə-,bli-gə-'tōr-ə-lē, ä-, -'tȯr- *also* ,ä-bli-gə-\ *adverb*

oblige \ə-'blīj\ *verb* **obliged; oblig·ing** [Middle English, from Old French *obliger*, from Latin *obligare*, literally, to bind to, from *ob-* toward + *ligare* to bind — more at LIGATURE] (14th century)
transitive verb
1 : to constrain by physical, moral, or legal force or by the exigencies of circumstance ⟨*obliged* to find a job⟩
2 a : to put in one's debt by a favor or service ⟨we are much *obliged* for your help⟩ **b** : to do a favor for ⟨always ready to *oblige* a friend⟩
intransitive verb
: to do something as or as if a favor
synonym see FORCE
— **oblig·er** *noun*

ob·li·gee \,ä-blə-'jē\ *noun* (1574)
: one to whom another is obligated (as by a contract); *specifically* : one who is protected by a surety bond

oblig·ing \ə-'blī-jiŋ\ *adjective* (1632)
: willing to do favors : ACCOMMODATING
synonym see AMIABLE
— **oblig·ing·ly** \-jiŋ-lē\ *adverb*
— **oblig·ing·ness** *noun*

ob·li·gor \,ä-blə-'gȯr, -'jȯr\ *noun* (1541)
: one who is bound by a legal obligation

¹oblique \ō-'blēk, ə-, -'blīk; *military usually* ī\ *adjective* [Middle English *oblike*, from Latin *obliquus*] (15th century)
1 a : neither perpendicular nor parallel : INCLINED **b** : having the axis not perpendicular to the base ⟨an *oblique* cone⟩ **c** : having no right angle ⟨an *oblique* triangle⟩
2 a : not straightforward : INDIRECT; *also* : OBSCURE **b** : DEVIOUS, UNDERHANDED
3 : situated obliquely and having one end not inserted on bone ⟨*oblique* muscles⟩
4 : taken from an airplane with the camera directed horizontally or diagonally downward ⟨an *oblique* photograph⟩
— **oblique·ly** *adverb*

— **oblique·ness** *noun*

²oblique *noun* (circa 1608)
1 : something (as a line) that is oblique
2 : any of several oblique muscles; *especially* : any of the thin flat muscles forming the middle and outer layers of the lateral walls of the abdomen

³oblique *adverb* (1667)
: at a 45 degree angle ⟨to the right *oblique*, march⟩

oblique angle *noun* (1695)
: an acute or obtuse angle

oblique case *noun* (1530)
: a grammatical case other than the nominative or vocative

obliq·ui·ty \ō-'bli-kwə-tē, ə-\ *noun, plural* **-ties** (15th century)
1 : deviation from moral rectitude or sound thinking
2 a : deviation from parallelism or perpendicularity; *also* : the amount of such deviation **b** : the angle between the planes of the earth's equator and orbit having a value of about 23°27' ⟨*obliquity* of the ecliptic⟩
3 a : indirectness or deliberate obscurity of speech or conduct **b** : an obscure or confusing statement

oblit·er·ate \ə-'bli-tə-,rāt, ō-\ *transitive verb* **-at·ed; -at·ing** [Latin *oblitteratus*, past participle of *oblitterare*, from *ob-* ob- + *littera* letter] (1609)
1 : to make undecipherable or imperceptible by obscuring or wearing away
2 a : to remove utterly from recognition or memory **b** : to remove from existence : destroy utterly all trace, indication, or significance of **c** : to cause to disappear (as a bodily part or a scar) or collapse (as a duct conveying body fluid) : REMOVE 4 ⟨a blood vessel *obliterated* by inflammation⟩
3 : CANCEL 4
— **oblit·er·a·tion** \-,bli-tə-'rā-shən\ *noun*
— **oblit·er·a·tor** \-'bli-tə-,rā-tər\ *noun*

oblit·er·a·tive \ə-'bli-tə-,rā-tiv, ō-, -rə-tiv\ *adjective* (circa 1812)
: inducing or characterized by obliteration: as **a** : causing or accompanied by closure or collapse of a lumen ⟨*obliterative* arterial disease⟩ **b** : tending to make inconspicuous ⟨*obliterative* behavior⟩

obliv·i·on \ə-'bli-vē-ən, ō-, ä-\ *noun* [Middle English, from Middle French, from Latin *oblivion-, oblivio*, from *oblivisci* to forget, perhaps from *ob-* in the way + *levis* smooth — more at OB-, LEVIGATE] (14th century)
1 : the fact or condition of forgetting or having forgotten; *especially* : the condition of being oblivious
2 : the condition or state of being forgotten or unknown

obliv·i·ous \-vē-əs\ *adjective* (15th century)
1 : lacking remembrance, memory, or mindful attention
2 : lacking active conscious knowledge or awareness — usually used with *of* or *to*
— **obliv·i·ous·ly** *adverb*
— **obliv·i·ous·ness** *noun*

ob·long \'ä-,blȯŋ\ *adjective* [Middle English, from Latin *oblongus*, from *ob-* toward + *longus* long — more at LONG] (15th century)
: deviating from a square, circular, or spherical form by elongation in one dimension ⟨an *oblong* piece of paper⟩ ⟨an *oblong* melon⟩
— **oblong** *noun*

ob·lo·quy \'ä-blə-kwē\ *noun, plural* **-quies** [Middle English, from Late Latin *obloquium*, from *obloqui* to speak against, from *ob-* against + *loqui* to speak] (15th century)
1 : a strongly condemnatory utterance : abusive language
2 : the condition of one that is discredited : bad repute
synonym see ABUSE

ob·nox·ious \äb-'näk-shəs, əb-\ *adjective* [Latin *obnoxius,* from *ob* in the way of, exposed to + *noxa* harm — more at NOXIOUS] (1597) **1** *archaic* **:** exposed to something unpleasant or harmful — used with *to* **2** *archaic* **:** deserving of censure **3** **:** odiously or disgustingly objectionable **:** highly offensive — **ob·nox·ious·ly** *adverb* — **ob·nox·ious·ness** *noun*

ob·nu·bi·late \äb-'nü-bə-ˌlāt, -'nyü-\ *transitive verb* **-lat·ed; -lat·ing** [Latin *obnubilatus,* past participle of *obnubilare,* from *ob-* in the way + *nubilare* to be cloudy, from *nubilus* cloudy, from *nubes* cloud — more at OB-, NUANCE] (1583) **:** BECLOUD, OBSCURE — **ob·nu·bi·la·tion** \-ˌnü-bə-'lā-shən, -ˌnyü-\ *noun*

oboe \'ō-(ˌ)bō\ *noun* [Italian, from French *hautbois* — more at HAUTBOIS] (1794) **:** a double-reed woodwind instrument having a conical tube, a brilliant penetrating tone, and a usual range from B flat below middle C upward for over 2½ octaves — **obo·ist** \'ō-(ˌ)bō-ist\ *noun*

obol \'ä-bəl, 'ō-\ *noun* [Latin *obolus,* from Greek *obolos, obelos,* literally, spit] (1579) **:** an ancient Greek coin or weight equal to ⅙ drachma

oboe

ob·ovate \(ˌ)äb-'ō-ˌvāt\ *adjective* (1785) **:** ovate with the narrower end basal ⟨*obovate* leaves⟩ — see LEAF illustration

ob·ovoid \-ˌvȯid\ *adjective* (1819) **:** ovoid with the broad end toward the apex ⟨an *obovoid* fruit⟩

ob·scene \äb-'sēn, əb-\ *adjective* [Middle French, from Latin *obscenus, obscaenus*] (1593) **1** **:** disgusting to the senses **:** REPULSIVE **2 a :** abhorrent to morality or virtue; *specifically* **:** designed to incite to lust or depravity **b :** containing or being language regarded as taboo in polite usage ⟨*obscene* lyrics⟩ **c :** repulsive by reason of crass disregard of moral or ethical principles ⟨an *obscene* misuse of power⟩ **d :** so excessive as to be offensive ⟨*obscene* wealth⟩ ⟨*obscene* waste⟩ *synonym* see COARSE — **ob·scene·ly** *adverb*

ob·scen·i·ty \-'se-nə-tē *also* -'sē-\ *noun, plural* **-ties** (1589) **1** **:** the quality or state of being obscene **2** **:** something (as an utterance or act) that is obscene

ob·scur·ant \äb-'skyür-ənt, əb-\ *or* **ob·scu·ran·tic** \ˌäb-skyə-'ran-tik\ *adjective* (1878) **:** tending to make obscure — **obscurant** *noun*

ob·scu·ran·tism \äb-'skyür-ən-ˌti-zəm, əb-; ˌäb-skyü-'ran-\ *noun* (1834) **1** **:** opposition to the spread of knowledge **:** a policy of withholding knowledge from the general public **2 a :** a style (as in literature or art) characterized by deliberate vagueness or abstruseness **b :** an act or instance of obscurantism — **ob·scu·ran·tist** \-ən-tist, -'ran-tist\ *noun or adjective*

¹ob·scure \äb-'skyür, əb-\ *adjective* [Middle English, from Middle French *obscur,* from Latin *obscurus*] (15th century) **1 a :** DARK, DIM **b :** shrouded in or hidden by darkness **c :** not clearly seen or easily distinguished **:** FAINT **2** **:** not readily understood or clearly expressed; *also* **:** MYSTERIOUS

3 **:** relatively unknown: as **a :** REMOTE, SECLUDED **b :** not prominent or famous ⟨an *obscure* poet⟩ **4** **:** constituting the unstressed vowel \ə\ or having unstressed \ə\ as its value ☆ — **ob·scure·ly** *adverb* — **ob·scure·ness** *noun*

²obscure *transitive verb* **ob·scured; ob·scur·ing** (15th century) **1** **:** to make dark, dim, or indistinct **2** **:** to conceal or hide by or as if by covering **3** **:** to reduce (a vowel) to the value \ə\ — **ob·scu·ra·tion** \ˌäb-skyü-'rā-shən\ *noun*

³obscure *noun* (1667) **:** OBSCURITY

ob·scu·ri·ty \äb-'skyür-ə-tē, əb-\ *noun, plural* **-ties** (14th century) **1** **:** one that is obscure **2** **:** the quality or state of being obscure

ob·se·qui·ous \əb-'sē-kwē-əs, äb-\ *adjective* [Middle English, compliant, from Latin *obsequiosus,* from *obsequium* compliance, from *obsequi* to comply, from *ob-* toward + *sequi* to follow — more at OB-, SUE] (15th century) **:** marked by or exhibiting a fawning attentiveness *synonym* see SUBSERVIENT — **ob·se·qui·ous·ly** *adverb* — **ob·se·qui·ous·ness** *noun*

ob·se·quy \'äb-sə-kwē\ *noun, plural* **-quies** [Middle English *obsequie,* from Middle French, from Medieval Latin *obsequiae* (plural), alteration of Latin *exsequiae,* from *exsequi* to follow out, execute — more at EXECUTION] (15th century) **:** a funeral or burial rite — usually used in plural

ob·serv·able \əb-'zər-və-bəl\ *adjective* (1609) **1** **:** NOTEWORTHY **2** **:** capable of being observed **:** DISCERNIBLE — **ob·serv·abil·i·ty** \-ˌzər-və-'bi-lə-tē\ *noun* — **observable** *noun* — **ob·serv·ably** \-'zər-və-blē\ *adverb*

ob·ser·vance \əb-'zər-vən(t)s\ *noun* (13th century) **1 a :** a customary practice, rite, or ceremony ⟨Sabbath *observances*⟩ **b :** a rule governing members of a religious order **2** **:** an act or instance of following a custom, rule, or law ⟨*observance* of the speed limits⟩ **3** **:** an act or instance of watching

¹ob·ser·vant \-vənt\ *adjective* (1602) **1 a :** paying strict attention **:** WATCHFUL ⟨an *observant* spectator⟩ **b :** KEEN, PERCEPTIVE **2** **:** careful in observing (as rites, laws, or customs) **:** MINDFUL ⟨pious and religiously *observant* families —Sidney Hook⟩ ⟨always *observant* of the amenities⟩ — **ob·ser·vant·ly** *adverb*

²observant *noun* (1605) *obsolete* **:** an assiduous or obsequious servant or attendant

ob·ser·va·tion \ˌäb-sər-'vā-shən, -zər-\ *noun* [Middle French, from Latin *observation-, observatio,* from *observare*] (1535) **1** **:** an act or instance of observing a custom, rule, or law **:** OBSERVANCE **2 a :** an act of recognizing and noting a fact or occurrence often involving measurement with instruments ⟨weather *observations*⟩ **b :** a record or description so obtained **3** **:** a judgment on or inference from what one has observed; *broadly* **:** REMARK, STATEMENT **4** *obsolete* **:** attentive care **:** HEED **5** **:** the condition of one that is observed ⟨under *observation* at the hospital⟩ — **ob·ser·va·tion·al** \-shnəl, -shə-nᵊl\ *adjective* — **ob·ser·va·tion·al·ly** *adverb*

ob·ser·va·to·ry \əb-'zər-və-ˌtōr-ē, -ˌtȯr-\ *noun, plural* **-ries** [probably from New Latin *observatorium,* from Latin *observare*] (1676) **1** **:** a building or place given over to or equipped for observation of natural phenome-

na (as in astronomy); *also* **:** an institution whose primary purpose is making such observations **2** **:** a situation or structure commanding a wide view

ob·serve \əb-'zərv\ *verb* **ob·served; ob·serv·ing** [Middle English, from Middle French *observer,* from Latin *observare* to guard, watch, observe, from *ob-* in the way, toward + *servare* to keep — more at CONSERVE] (14th century) *transitive verb* **1** **:** to conform one's action or practice to (as a law, rite, or condition) **:** comply with **2** **:** to inspect or take note of as an augury, omen, or presage **3** **:** to celebrate or solemnize (as a ceremony or festival) in a customary or accepted way **4 a :** to watch carefully especially with attention to details or behavior for the purpose of arriving at a judgment **b :** to make a scientific observation on or of **5** **:** to come to realize or know especially through consideration of noted facts **6** **:** to utter as a remark *intransitive verb* **1 a :** to take notice **b :** to make observations **:** WATCH **2** **:** REMARK, COMMENT *synonym* see KEEP — **ob·serv·ing·ly** \-'zər-viŋ-lē\ *adverb*

ob·serv·er \əb-'zər-vər\ *noun* (circa 1550) **:** one that observes: as **a :** a representative sent to observe but not participate officially in an activity (as a meeting or war) **b :** an expert analyst and commentator in a particular field ⟨political *observers*⟩

ob·sess \əb-'ses, äb-\ *verb* [Latin *obsessus,* past participle of *obsidēre* to frequent, besiege, from *ob-* against + *sedēre* to sit — more at OB-, SIT] (1531) *transitive verb* **:** to haunt or excessively preoccupy the mind of ⟨was *obsessed* with the idea⟩ *intransitive verb* **:** to engage in obsessive thinking **:** become obsessed with an idea

ob·ses·sion \äb-'se-shən, əb-\ *noun* (1680) **1** **:** a persistent disturbing preoccupation with an often unreasonable idea or feeling; *broadly* **:** compelling motivation ⟨an *obsession* with profits⟩ **2** **:** something that causes an obsession — **ob·ses·sion·al** \-'sesh-nəl, -'se-shə-nᵊl\ *adjective*

\ə\ abut \ᵊ\ kitten \ər\ further \a\ ash \ā\ ace \ä\ mop, mar \au̇\ out \ch\ chin \e\ bet \ē\ easy \g\ go \i\ hit \ī\ ice \j\ job \ŋ\ sing \ō\ go \ȯ\ law \ȯi\ boy \th\ thin \tẖ\ the \ü\ loot \u̇\ foot \y\ yet \zh\ vision *see also* Guide to Pronunciation

— **ob·ses·sion·al·ly** *adverb*

ob·ses·sive \äb-'se-siv, əb-\ *adjective* (1901)
1 a : tending to cause obsession **b** : excessive often to an unreasonable degree
2 : of, relating to, or characterized by obsession : deriving from obsession
— **obsessive** *noun*
— **ob·ses·sive·ly** *adverb*
— **ob·ses·sive·ness** *noun*

obsessive–compulsive *adjective* (1927)
: relating to or characterized by recurring obsessions and compulsions especially as symptoms of a neurotic state
— **obsessive–compulsive** *noun*

ob·sid·i·an \əb-'si-dē-ən\ *noun* [New Latin *obsidianus*, from Latin *obsidianus lapis*, false manuscript reading for *obsianus lapis*, literally, stone of Obsius, from *Obsius*, its supposed discoverer] (1796)
: a dark natural glass formed by the cooling of molten lava

ob·so·lesce \ˌäb-sə-'les\ *verb* **-lesced; -lesc·ing** [Latin *obsolescere*] (1873)
intransitive verb
: to be or become obsolescent
transitive verb
: to make obsolescent

ob·so·les·cence \-'le-sᵊn(t)s\ *noun* (circa 1841)
: the process of becoming obsolete or the condition of being nearly obsolete ⟨the gradual *obsolescence* of machinery⟩ ⟨reduced to *obsolescence*⟩

ob·so·les·cent \-sᵊnt\ *adjective* (1755)
: going out of use : becoming obsolete
— **ob·so·les·cent·ly** *adverb*

¹**ob·so·lete** \ˌäb-sə-'lēt, 'äb-sə-ˌ\ *adjective* [Latin *obsoletus*, from past participle of *obsolescere* to grow old, become disused, perhaps from *ob-* toward + *solēre* to be accustomed] (1579)
1 a : no longer in use or no longer useful **b** : of a kind or style no longer current : OLD-FASHIONED
2 *of a plant or animal part* : indistinct or imperfect as compared with a corresponding part in related organisms : VESTIGIAL
synonym see OLD
— **ob·so·lete·ly** *adverb*
— **ob·so·lete·ness** *noun*

²**obsolete** *transitive verb* **-let·ed; -let·ing** (1640)
: to make obsolete

ob·sta·cle \'äb-sti-kəl, -ˌsti-\ *noun* [Middle English, from Middle French, from Latin *obstaculum*, from *obstare* to stand in front of, from *ob-* in the way + *stare* to stand — more at OB-, STAND] (14th century)
: something that impedes progress or achievement

obstacle course *noun* (1943)
: a military training course filled with obstacles (as hurdles, fences, walls, and ditches) that must be negotiated; *broadly* : a series of obstacles that must be overcome

ob·stet·ric \əb-'ste-trik, äb-\ *or* **ob·stet·ri·cal** \-tri-kəl\ *adjective* [modification of Latin *obstetricius*, from *obstetric-, obstetrix* midwife, from *obstare*] (1742)
: of, relating to, or associated with childbirth or obstetrics
— **ob·stet·ri·cal·ly** \-tri-k(ə-)lē\ *adverb*

ob·ste·tri·cian \ˌäb-stə-'tri-shən\ *noun* (circa 1828)
: a physician specializing in obstetrics

ob·stet·rics \əb-'ste-triks, äb-\ *noun plural but singular or plural in construction* (circa 1819)
: a branch of medical science that deals with birth and with its antecedents and sequels

ob·sti·na·cy \'äb-stə-nə-sē\ *noun, plural* **-cies** (14th century)
1 a : the quality or state of being obstinate : STUBBORNNESS **b** : the quality or state of being difficult to remedy, relieve, or subdue ⟨the *obstinacy* of tuberculosis⟩

2 : an instance of being obstinate

ob·sti·nate \'äb-stə-nət\ *adjective* [Middle English, from Latin *obstinatus*, past participle of *obstinare* to be resolved, from *ob-* in the way + *-stinare* (akin to *stare* to stand)] (14th century)
1 : perversely adhering to an opinion, purpose, or course in spite of reason, arguments, or persuasion
2 : not easily subdued, remedied, or removed ⟨*obstinate* fever⟩ ☆
— **ob·sti·nate·ly** *adverb*
— **ob·sti·nate·ness** *noun*

ob·strep·er·ous \əb-'stre-p(ə-)rəs, äb-\ *adjective* [Latin *obstreperus*, from *obstrepere* to clamor against, from *ob-* against + *strepere* to make a noise] (circa 1600)
1 : marked by unruly or aggressive noisiness : CLAMOROUS ⟨*obstreperous* merriment⟩
2 : stubbornly resistant to control : UNRULY
synonym see VOCIFEROUS
— **ob·strep·er·ous·ly** *adverb*
— **ob·strep·er·ous·ness** *noun*

ob·struct \əb-'strəkt, äb-\ *transitive verb* [Latin *obstructus*, past participle of *obstruere*, from *ob-* in the way + *struere* to build, heap up — more at OB-, STREW] (1590)
1 : to block or close up by an obstacle
2 : to hinder from passage, action, or operation : IMPEDE
3 : to cut off from sight ⟨a wall *obstructs* the view⟩
synonym see HINDER
— **ob·struc·tive** \-'strək-tiv\ *adjective or noun*
— **ob·struc·tive·ness** *noun*
— **ob·struc·tor** \-tər\ *noun*

ob·struc·tion \əb-'strək-shən, äb-\ *noun* (1533)
1 a : an act of obstructing **b** : the state of being obstructed; *especially* : a condition of being clogged or blocked
2 : something that obstructs

ob·struc·tion·ism \-shə-ˌni-zəm\ *noun* (1879)
: deliberate interference with the progress or business especially of a legislative body
— **ob·struc·tion·ist** \-sh(ə-)nist\ *noun or adjective*
— **ob·struc·tion·is·tic** \-ˌstrək-shə-'nis-tik\ *adjective*

ob·tain \əb-'tān, äb-\ *verb* [Middle English *obteinen*, from Middle French & Latin; Middle French *obtenir*, from Latin *obtinēre* to hold on to, possess, obtain, from *ob-* in the way + *tenēre* to hold — more at THIN] (15th century)
transitive verb
: to gain or attain usually by planned action or effort
intransitive verb
1 *archaic* : SUCCEED
2 : to be generally recognized or established : PREVAIL
— **ob·tain·abil·i·ty** \-ˌtā-nə-'bi-lə-tē\ *noun*
— **ob·tain·able** \-'tā-nə-bəl\ *adjective*
— **ob·tain·er** *noun*
— **ob·tain·ment** \-'tān-mənt\ *noun*

ob·tect \əb-'tekt, äb-\ *also* **ob·tect·ed** \-'tek-təd\ *adjective* [Latin *obtectus*, past participle of *obtegere* to cover over, from *ob-* in the way + *tegere* to cover — more at THATCH] (circa 1902)
: enclosed in or characterized by enclosure in a firm chitinous case or covering ⟨an *obtect* pupa⟩

ob·trude \əb-'trüd, äb-\ *verb* **ob·trud·ed; ob·trud·ing** [Latin *obtrudere* to thrust at, from *ob-* in the way + *trudere* to thrust — more at OB-, THREAT] (circa 1609)
transitive verb
1 : to thrust out : EXTRUDE
2 : to force or impose (as oneself or one's ideas) without warrant or request
intransitive verb
: to become unduly prominent or interfering : INTRUDE

— **ob·trud·er** *noun*

ob·tru·sion \-'trü-zhən\ *noun* [Late Latin *obtrusion-, obtrusio*, from Latin *obtrudere*] (1579)
1 : an act of obtruding
2 : something that is obtruded

ob·tru·sive \-'trü-siv, -ziv\ *adjective* (1667)
1 a : forward in manner or conduct ⟨*obtrusive* behavior⟩ **b** : undesirably prominent
2 : thrust out : PROTRUDING
synonym see IMPERTINENT
— **ob·tru·sive·ly** *adverb*
— **ob·tru·sive·ness** *noun*

ob·tund \äb-'tənd\ *transitive verb* [Middle English, from Latin *obtundere*] (14th century)
: to reduce the edge or violence of : DULL ⟨*obtunded* reflexes⟩

ob·tu·ra·tion \ˌäb-tyə-'rā-shən, -tə-\ *noun* [Latin *obturation-, obturatio*, from *obturare* to obstruct] (1610)
: OBSTRUCTION, CLOSURE
— **ob·tu·rate** \'äb-tyə-ˌrāt, -tə-\ *transitive verb*

ob·tu·ra·tor \'äb-tyə-ˌrā-tər, -tə-\ *noun* [New Latin, from Latin *obturare*] (circa 1741)
: one that closes: as **a** : one (as a prosthetic device) that closes or blocks up an opening (as a fissure in the palate) **b** : a hooded swelling of the placenta that fits over the nucellus in some plants

ob·tuse \äb-'tüs, əb-, -'tyüs\ *adjective* **ob·tus·er; -est** [Middle English, from Latin *obtusus* blunt, dull, from past participle of *obtundere* to beat against, blunt, from *ob-* against + *tundere* to beat — more at OB-, CONTUSION] (15th century)
1 a : not pointed or acute : BLUNT **b** (1) *of an angle* : exceeding 90 degrees but less than 180 degrees (2) : having an obtuse angle ⟨an *obtuse* triangle⟩ — see TRIANGLE illustration **c** *of a leaf* : rounded at the free end
2 a : lacking sharpness or quickness of sensibility or intellect : INSENSITIVE, STUPID **b** : difficult to comprehend : not clear or precise in thought or expression
synonym see DULL
— **ob·tuse·ly** *adverb*
— **ob·tuse·ness** *noun*

¹**ob·verse** \äb-'vərs, əb-, 'äb-ˌ\ *adjective* [Latin *obversus*, from past participle of *obvertere* to turn toward, from *ob-* toward + *vertere* to turn — more at OB-, WORTH] (circa 1656)
1 : facing the observer or opponent
2 : having the base narrower than the top ⟨an *obverse* leaf⟩
3 : constituting the obverse of something : OPPOSITE
— **ob·verse·ly** *adverb*

²**ob·verse** \'äb-ˌvərs, äb-'\ *noun* (1658)
1 : the side of a coin or currency note bearing the chief device and lettering; *broadly* : a front or principal surface
2 : a counterpart having the opposite orientation or force ⟨their rise was merely the *obverse* of the Empire's fall —A. J. Toynbee⟩; *also* : OPPOSITE 1 ⟨joy and its *obverse*, sorrow⟩

☆ **SYNONYMS**
Obstinate, dogged, stubborn, pertinacious, mulish mean fixed and unyielding in course or purpose. OBSTINATE implies usually an unreasonable persistence ⟨an *obstinate* proponent of conspiracy theories⟩. DOGGED suggests an admirable often tenacious and unwavering persistence ⟨pursued the story with *dogged* perseverance⟩. STUBBORN implies sturdiness in resisting change which may or may not be admirable ⟨a person too *stubborn* to admit error⟩. PERTINACIOUS suggests an annoying or irksome persistence ⟨a *pertinacious* salesclerk refusing to take no for an answer⟩. MULISH implies a thoroughly unreasonable obstinacy ⟨a *mulish* determination to have his own way⟩.

3 : a proposition inferred immediately from another by denying the opposite of what the given proposition affirms (the *obverse* of "all *A* is *B*" is "no *A* is not *B*")

ob·vi·ate \'äb-vē-,āt\ *transitive verb* **-at·ed; -at·ing** [Late Latin *obviatus*, past participle of *obviare* to meet, withstand, from Latin *ob-viam*] (1598)
: to anticipate and prevent (as a situation) or make unnecessary (as an action)
— **ob·vi·a·tion** \,äb-vē-'ā-shən\ *noun*

ob·vi·ous \'äb-vē-əs\ *adjective* [Latin *obvius*, from *obviam* in the way, from *ob* in the way of + *viam*, accusative of *via* way — more at OB-, VIA] (1603)
1 *archaic* **:** being in the way or in front
2 : easily discovered, seen, or understood
synonym see EVIDENT
— **ob·vi·ous·ness** *noun*

ob·vi·ous·ly \-lē\ *adverb* (1638)
1 : in an obvious manner (showed his anger *obviously*)
2 : as is plainly evident (*obviously*, something is wrong)

oca \'ō-kə\ *noun* [Spanish, from Quechua *oqa*] (1604)
: either of two South American wood sorrels (*Oxalis crenata* and *O. tuberosa*) cultivated for their edible tubers; *also* **:** the tuber of an oca

oc·a·ri·na \,ä-kə-'rē-nə\ *noun* [Italian, from Italian dialect, diminutive of *oca* goose, from Late Latin *auca*, from Latin *avis* bird — more at AVIARY] (1877)
: a simple wind instrument typically having an oval body with finger holes and a projecting mouthpiece

ocarina

Oc·cam's ra·zor \'ä-kəmz-\ *noun* [William of *Occam*] (circa 1837)
: a scientific and philosophic rule that entities should not be multiplied unnecessarily which is interpreted as requiring that the simplest of competing theories be preferred to the more complex or that explanations of unknown phenomena be sought first in terms of known quantities

¹oc·ca·sion \ə-'kā-zhən\ *noun* [Middle English, from Middle French or Latin; Middle French, from Latin *occasion-, occasio*, from *occidere* to fall, fall down, from *ob-* toward + *cadere* to fall — more at OB-, CHANCE] (14th century)
1 : a favorable opportunity or circumstance (did not have *occasion* to talk with them)
2 a : a state of affairs that provides a ground or reason (the *occasion* of the discord was their mutual intolerance) **b :** an occurrence or condition that brings something about; *especially* **:** the immediate inciting circumstance as distinguished from the fundamental cause (his insulting remark was the *occasion* of a bitter quarrel)
3 a : HAPPENING, INCIDENT **b :** a time at which something happens **:** INSTANCE
4 a : a need arising from a particular circumstance **b** *archaic* **:** a personal want or need — usually used in plural
5 *plural* **:** AFFAIRS, BUSINESS
6 : a special event or ceremony **:** CELEBRATION
— **on occasion :** from time to time

²occasion *transitive verb* **-sioned; -sion·ing** \-'kāzh-niŋ, -'kā-zhə-\ (15th century)
: BRING ABOUT, CAUSE

oc·ca·sion·al \-'kāzh-nəl, -'kā-zhə-nᵊl\ *adjective* (circa 1631)
1 a : of or relating to a particular occasion (a budget able to meet *occasional* demands as well as regular ones) **b :** created for a particular occasion (*occasional* verse)

2 : acting as the occasion or contributing cause of something
3 : encountered, occurring, appearing, or taken at irregular or infrequent intervals (*occasional* visitors) (an *occasional* vacation)
4 : acting in a specified capacity from time to time (an *occasional* lecturer)
5 : designed or constructed to be used as the occasion demands (*occasional* furniture)

oc·ca·sion·al·ly \-'kāzh-nə-lē, -'kā-zhə-nᵊl-ē\ *adverb* (1630)
: on occasion **:** NOW AND THEN

Oc·ci·dent \'äk-sə-dənt, -,dent\ *noun* [Middle English, from Middle French, from Latin *occident-, occidens*, from present participle of *occidere* to fall, set (of the sun)] (14th century)
: WEST 2a

oc·ci·den·tal \,äk-sə-'den-tᵊl\ *adjective, often capitalized* (14th century)
1 : of, relating to, or situated in the Occident **:** WESTERN
2 : of or relating to Occidentals
— **oc·ci·den·tal·ly** *adverb*

Occidental *noun* (1857)
: a member of one of the occidental peoples; *especially* **:** a person of European ancestry

Oc·ci·den·tal·ism \,äk-sə-'den-tᵊl-,i-zəm\ *noun* (1839)
: the characteristic features of occidental peoples or culture

oc·ci·den·tal·ize \-tᵊl-,īz\ *transitive verb* **-ized; -iz·ing** *often capitalized* (1870)
: to make occidental (as in culture)

oc·cip·i·tal \äk-'si-pə-tᵊl\ *adjective* (1541)
: of, relating to, or located within or near the occiput or the occipital bone
— **occipital** *noun*
— **oc·cip·i·tal·ly** *adverb*

occipital bone *noun* (1679)
: a compound bone that forms the posterior part of the skull and bears a condyle by which the skull articulates with the atlas

occipital condyle *noun* (circa 1860)
: an articular surface on the occipital bone by which the skull articulates with the atlas

occipital lobe *noun* (circa 1890)
: the posterior lobe of each cerebral hemisphere that bears the visual areas and has the form of a 3-sided pyramid

oc·ci·put \'äk-sə-(,)pət\ *noun, plural* **oc·ciputs** *or* **oc·cip·i·ta** \äk-'si-pə-tə\ [Middle English, from Latin *occipit-, occiput*, from *ob-* against + *capit-, caput* head — more at OB-, HEAD] (14th century)
: the back part of the head or skull

Oc·ci·tan \'äk-sə-,tan\ *noun* [French, from Medieval Latin *occitanus*, from Old Provençal *oc* yes (contrasted with Old French *oïl* yes) + Medieval Latin *-itanus* (perhaps as in *aquitanus* of Aquitaine)] (1958)
: PROVENÇAL 2
— **Occitan** *adjective*

oc·clude \ə-'klüd, ä-\ *verb* **oc·clud·ed; oc·clud·ing** [Latin *occludere*, from *ob-* in the way + *claudere* to shut, close — more at CLOSE] (1597)
transitive verb
1 : to close up or block off **:** OBSTRUCT (a thrombus *occluding* a coronary artery); *also* **:** CONCEAL
2 : SORB
intransitive verb
1 : to come into contact with cusps of the opposing teeth fitting together (his teeth do not *occlude* properly)
2 : to become occluded

occluded front *noun* (circa 1938)
: OCCLUSION 2

oc·clu·sal \ə-'klü-səl, ä-, -zəl\ *adjective* (1897)
: of or relating to the grinding or biting surface of a tooth or to occlusion of the teeth

oc·clu·sion \ə-'klü-zhən\ *noun* [Latin *occludere*] (1645)
1 : the act of occluding **:** the state of being occluded: as **a :** the complete obstruction of the breath passage in the articulation of a speech sound **b :** the bringing of the opposing surfaces of the teeth of the two jaws into contact; *also* **:** the relation between the surfaces when in contact **c :** the inclusion or sorption of gas trapped during solidification of a material
2 : the front formed by a cold front overtaking a warm front and lifting the warm air above the earth's surface

oc·clu·sive \-siv, -ziv\ *adjective* [Latin *occlusus*, past participle of *occludere*] (1888)
1 : serving to occlude
2 : characterized by occlusion

¹oc·cult \ə-'kəlt, ä-\ *transitive verb* [Latin *occultare*, frequentative of *occulere*] (1500)
: to shut off from view or exposure **:** COVER, ECLIPSE
— **oc·cult·er** *noun*

²oc·cult \ə-'kəlt, ä-; 'ä-,kəlt\ *adjective* [Latin *occultus*, from past participle of *occulere* to cover up, from *ob-* in the way + *-culere* (akin to *celare* to conceal) — more at OB-, HELL] (1567)
1 : not revealed **:** SECRET
2 : not easily apprehended or understood **:** ABSTRUSE, MYSTERIOUS
3 : hidden from view **:** CONCEALED
4 : of or relating to the occult
5 : not manifest or detectable by clinical methods alone (*occult* carcinoma); *also* **:** not present in macroscopic amounts (*occult* blood in a stool)
— **oc·cult·ly** *adverb*

³occult \same as ²\ *noun* (1923)
: matters regarded as involving the action or influence of supernatural or supernormal powers or some secret knowledge of them — used with *the*

oc·cul·ta·tion \,ä-(,)kəl-'tā-shən\ *noun* (15th century)
1 : the state of being hidden from view or lost to notice
2 : the interruption of the light from a celestial body or of the signals from a spacecraft by the intervention of a celestial body; *especially* **:** an eclipse of a star or planet by the moon

oc·cult·ism \ə-'kəl-,ti-zəm, ä-; 'ä-,kəl-\ *noun* (1881)
: occult theory or practice **:** belief in or study of the action or influence of supernatural or supernormal powers
— **oc·cult·ist** \-tist\ *noun*

oc·cu·pan·cy \'ä-kyə-pən(t)-sē\ *noun, plural* **-cies** (1596)
1 : the fact or condition of holding, possessing, or residing in or on something (*occupancy* of the estate)
2 : the act or fact of taking or having possession (as of unowned land) to acquire ownership
3 : the fact or condition of being occupied (*occupancy* by more than 400 persons is unlawful)
4 : the use to which a property is put (industrial *occupancy*)
5 : a building or part of a building intended to be occupied (as by a tenant) (multiple *occupancy* buildings)

oc·cu·pant \-pənt\ *noun* (1596)
1 : one who occupies a particular place; *especially* **:** RESIDENT
2 : one who acquires title by occupancy

oc·cu·pa·tion \,ä-kyə-'pā-shən\ *noun* [Middle English *occupacioun*, from Middle French *occupation*, from Latin *occupation-, occupatio*, from *occupare*] (14th century)

1 a : an activity in which one engages ⟨in the first three grades learning to read is perhaps the major *occupation* of the pupil —J. B. Conant⟩ **b :** the principal business of one's life **: VOCATION**

2 a : the possession, use, or settlement of land **: OCCUPANCY b :** the holding of an office or position

3 a : the act or process of taking possession of a place or area **: SEIZURE b :** the holding and control of an area by a foreign military force **c :** the military force occupying a country or the policies carried out by it

synonym see WORK

— **oc·cu·pa·tion·al** \-shnəl, -shə-nᵊl\ *adjective*

— **oc·cu·pa·tion·al·ly** *adverb*

occupational therapy *noun* (1915)

: therapy by means of activity; *especially* **:** creative activity prescribed for its effect in promoting recovery or rehabilitation

— **occupational therapist** *noun*

oc·cu·py \'ä-kyə-ˌpī\ *transitive verb* **-pied; -py·ing** [Middle English *occupien* to take possession of, occupy, modification of Middle French *occuper*, from Latin *occupare*, from *ob-* toward + *-cupare* (akin to *capere* to seize) — more at OB-, HEAVE] (14th century)

1 : to engage the attention or energies of

2 a : to take up (a place or extent in space) ⟨this chair is *occupied*⟩ ⟨the fireplace will *occupy* this corner of the room⟩ **b :** to take or fill (an extent in time) ⟨the hobby *occupies* all of my free time⟩

3 a : to take or hold possession or control of ⟨enemy troops *occupied* the ridge⟩ **b :** to fill or perform the functions of (an office or position)

4 : to reside in as an owner or tenant

— **oc·cu·pi·er** \-ˌpī(-ə)r\ *noun*

oc·cur \ə-'kər\ *intransitive verb* **oc·curred; oc·cur·ring** \-'kər-iŋ, -'kə-riŋ\ [Latin *occurrere*, from *ob-* in the way + *currere* to run — more at OB-, CAR] (1534)

1 : to be found or met with **:** APPEAR

2 : to come into existence **:** HAPPEN

3 : to come to mind

oc·cur·rence \ə-'kər-ən(t)s, -'kə-rən(t)s\ *noun* (1539)

1 : something that occurs ⟨a startling *occurrence*⟩

2 : the action or instance of occurring ⟨the repeated *occurrence* of petty theft in the locker room⟩ ☆

¹oc·cur·rent \ə-'kər-ənt, -'kə-rənt\ *adjective* [Middle English, from Middle French, from Latin *occurrent-, occurrens,* present participle of *occurrere*] (15th century)

1 : occurring at a particular time or place **:** CURRENT

2 : INCIDENTAL

²occurrent *noun* (1535)

: something that occurs as distinguished from something that continues to exist

ocean \'ō-shən\ *noun, often attributive* [Middle English *ocean,* from Latin *oceanus,* from Greek *Ōkeanos,* a river thought of as encircling the earth, ocean] (14th century)

1 a : the whole body of salt water that covers nearly three fourths of the surface of the globe **b :** any of the large bodies of water (as the Atlantic Ocean) into which the great ocean is divided

2 : a very large or unlimited space or quantity

ocean·ar·i·um \ˌō-shə-'nar-ē-əm, -'ner-\ *noun, plural* **-iums** *or* **-ia** \-ē-ə\ (1938)

: a large marine aquarium

ocean·front \'ō-shən-ˌfrənt\ *noun* (1919)

: a shore area on the ocean

ocean·go·ing \-ˌgō-iŋ\ *adjective* (1885)

: of, relating to, or designed for travel on the ocean

oce·an·ic \ˌō-shē-'a-nik\ *adjective* (1656)

1 a : of or relating to the ocean **b :** occurring in or frequenting the ocean and especially the open sea as distinguished from littoral or neritic waters

2 : VAST, GREAT

Oce·anid \ō-'sē-ə-nəd\ *noun* [Greek *ōkeanid-, ōkeanis,* from *Ōkeanos* Oceanus]

: any of the ocean nymphs that are daughters of Oceanus and Tethys in Greek mythology

ocean·og·ra·phy \ˌō-shə-'nä-grə-fē\ *noun* [International Scientific Vocabulary] (1859)

: a science that deals with the oceans and includes the delimitation of their extent and depth, the physics and chemistry of their waters, marine biology, and the exploitation of their resources

— **ocean·og·ra·pher** \-fər\ *noun*

— **ocean·o·graph·ic** \-nə-'gra-fik\ *also* **ocean·o·graph·i·cal** \-fi-kəl\ *adjective*

— **ocean·o·graph·i·cal·ly** \-fi-k(ə-)lē\ *adverb*

ocean·ol·o·gy \ˌō-shə-'nä-lə-jē\ *noun* (circa 1864)

: OCEANOGRAPHY; *specifically* **:** the science of marine resources and technology

— **ocean·ol·o·gist** \-'nä-lə-jist\ *noun*

ocean perch *noun* (1943)

: any of several marine scorpaenid food fishes (genus *Sebastes*) **a :** REDFISH a; *also* **:** a related food fish (*S. fasciatus*) **b :** one (*S. alutus*) abundant in the northeastern Pacific from Japan to the Bering Sea to southern California

ocean sunfish *noun* (1629)

: a large bony fish (*Mola mola* of the order Tetraodontiformes) having high dorsal and anal fins and a body nearly oval in outline and attaining a length of 10 feet (3 meters) and a weight in excess of 2 tons (1.8 metric tons)

Oce·anus \ō-'sē-ə-nəs\ *noun* [Latin, from Greek *Ōkeanos*]

: a Titan who rules over a great river encircling the earth in Greek mythology

ocel·lus \ō-'se-ləs\ *noun, plural* **ocel·li** \-'se-ˌlī, -(ˌ)lē\ [New Latin, from Latin, diminutive of *oculus* eye — more at EYE] (1819)

1 : a minute simple eye or eyespot of an invertebrate

2 : an eyelike colored spot (as on a peacock feather or the wings of some butterflies)

— **ocel·lar** \ō-'se-lər\ *adjective*

oce·lot \'ä-sə-ˌlät, 'ō-\ *noun* [French, from Nahuatl *ōcēlōtl* jaguar] (1774)

: a medium-sized American wildcat (*Felis pardalis*) that ranges from Texas to northern Argentina and has a tawny yellow or grayish coat dotted and striped with black

ocelot

ocher *or* **ochre** \'ō-kər\ *noun* [Middle English *oker,* from Middle French *ocre,* from Latin *ochra,* from Greek *ōchra,* from feminine of *ōchros* yellow] (14th century)

1 : an earthy usually red or yellow and often impure iron ore used as a pigment

2 : the color of ocher; *especially* **:** the color of yellow ocher

— **ocher·ous** \'ō-k(ə-)rəs\ *or* **ochre·ous** \'ō-k(ə-)rəs, -krē-əs\ *adjective*

och·loc·ra·cy \ä-'klä-krə-sē\ *noun* [Greek & Middle French; Middle French *ochlocratie,* from Greek *ochlokratia,* from *ochlos* mob + *-kratia* -cracy] (1584)

: government by the mob **:** mob rule

— **och·lo·crat** \'ä-klə-ˌkrat\ *noun*

— **och·lo·crat·ic** \ˌä-klə-'kra-tik\ *or* **och·lo·crat·i·cal** \-ti-kəl\ *adjective*

-ock *noun suffix* [Middle English *-oc,* from Old English]

: small one ⟨hill*ock*⟩

Ock·ham's razor \'ä-kəmz-\ *variant of* OCCAM'S RAZOR

o'·clock \ə-'kläk, ō-\ *adverb* [contraction of *of the clock*] (circa 1601)

1 : according to the clock ⟨the time is three *o'clock*⟩

2 : — used for indicating position or direction as if on a clock dial that is oriented vertically or horizontally ⟨an airplane approaching at six *o'clock*⟩

oco·ti·llo \ˌō-kə-'tē-(ˌ)yō\ *noun, plural* **-llos** [Mexican Spanish] (1856)

: a thorny scarlet-flowered candlewood (*Fouquieria splendens* of the family Fouquieriaceae) of the southwestern U.S. and Mexico

ocotillo

octa- *or* **octo-** *also* **oct-** *combining form* [Greek *okta-, oktō-, okt-* (from *oktō*) & Latin *octo-, oct-,* from *octo* — more at EIGHT]

: eight ⟨*octa*ne⟩ ⟨*octo*roon⟩

oc·ta·gon \'äk-tə-ˌgän\ *noun* [Latin *octagonum,* from Greek *oktagōnon,* from *okta-* + *-gōnon* -gon] (1639)

: a polygon of eight angles and eight sides

— **oc·tag·o·nal** \äk-'ta-gə-nᵊl\ *adjective*

— **oc·tag·o·nal·ly** \-nᵊl-ē\ *adverb*

oc·ta·he·dral \ˌäk-tə-'hē-drəl\ *adjective* (1758)

1 : having eight plane faces

2 : of, relating to, or formed in octahedrons

— **oc·ta·he·dral·ly** \-drə-lē\ *adverb*

oc·ta·he·dron \-drən\ *noun, plural* **-drons** *or* **-dra** \-drə\ [Greek *oktaedron,* from *okta-* + *-edron* -hedron] (1570)

: a solid bounded by eight plane faces

oc·tal \'äk-tᵊl\ *adjective* (1948)

: of, relating to, or being a number system with a base of eight

oc·tam·e·ter \äk-'ta-mə-tər\ *noun* [Late Latin, having eight feet, from Late Greek *oktametros,* from *okta-* + *metron* measure — more at MEASURE] (1889)

: a line of verse consisting of eight metrical feet

oc·tane \'äk-ˌtān\ *noun* [International Scientific Vocabulary] (circa 1872)

1 : any of several isomeric liquid alkanes C_8H_{18}

2 : OCTANE NUMBER

octane number *noun* (1931)

: a number that is used to measure the antiknock properties of a liquid motor fuel (as gasoline) with a higher number indicating a

smaller likelihood of knocking — called also *octane rating*; compare CETANE NUMBER

oc·tant \'äk-tənt\ *noun* [Latin *octant-, octans* eighth of a circle, from *octo*] (1731)
1 : an instrument for observing altitudes of a celestial body from a moving ship or aircraft
2 : any of the eight parts into which a space is divided by three coordinate planes

oc·ta·pep·tide \,äk-tə-'pep-,tīd\ *noun* (1961)
: a protein fragment or molecule (as oxytocin or vasopressin) that consists of eight amino acids linked in a polypeptide chain

oc·tave \'äk-tiv, -təv, -,tāv\ *noun* [Middle English, from Medieval Latin *octava*, from Latin, feminine of *octavus* eighth, from *octo* eight — more at EIGHT] (14th century)
1 : an 8-day period of observances beginning with a festival day
2 a : a stanza of eight lines : OTTAVA RIMA **b** : the first eight lines of an Italian sonnet
3 a : a musical interval embracing eight diatonic degrees **b** : a tone or note at this interval **c** : the harmonic combination of two tones an octave apart **d** : the whole series of notes, tones, or digitals comprised within this interval and forming the unit of the modern scale **e** : an organ stop giving tones an octave above those corresponding to the digitals
4 : the interval between two frequencies (as in an electromagnetic spectrum) having a ratio of 2 to 1
5 : a group of eight

oc·ta·vo \äk-'tā-(,)vō, -'tä-\ *noun, plural* **-vos** [Latin, ablative of *octavus* eighth] (1582)
: the size of a piece of paper cut eighth from a sheet; *also* : a book, a page, or paper of this size

oc·tet \äk-'tet\ *noun* (1879)
1 : a group or set of eight: as **a** : OCTAVE 2b **b** : the performers of an octet
2 : a musical composition for eight instruments or voices

oc·til·lion \äk-'til-yən\ *noun* [French, from Middle French, from *oct-* octa- + *-illion* (as in *million*)] (1690)
— see NUMBER table

Oc·to·ber \äk-'tō-bər\ *noun* [Middle English *Octobre*, from Old English & Old French; Old English *October*, from Latin, 8th month of the early Roman calendar, from *octo*; Old French, from Latin *October*] (before 12th century)
: the 10th month of the Gregorian calendar

oc·to·de·cil·lion \,äk-tō-di-'sil-yən\ *noun* [Latin *octodecim* eighteen + English *-illion* (as in *million*)] (1939)
— see NUMBER table

oc·to·ge·nar·i·an \,äk-tə-jə-'ner-ē-ən\ *noun* [Latin *octogenarius* containing eighty, from *octogeni* eighty each, from *octoginta* eighty, from *octo* eight + *-ginta* (akin to *viginti* twenty) — more at VIGESIMAL] (1815)
: a person whose age is in the eighties
— **octogenarian** *adjective*

oc·to·ploid \'äk-tə-,plòid\ *adjective* [International Scientific Vocabulary] (1925)
: having a chromosome number eight times the basic haploid chromosome number
— **octoploid** *noun*

oc·to·pod \'äk-tə-,päd\ *noun* [ultimately from Greek *oktōpod-, oktōpous* scorpion, from *oktō-* octa- + *pod-, pous* foot — more at FOOT] (circa 1836)
: any of an order (Octopoda) of cephalopod mollusks (as an octopus or argonaut) that have eight arms bearing sessile suckers
— **octopod** *adjective*

oc·to·pus \'äk-tə-pəs, -,pús\ *noun, plural* **-pus·es** *or* **-pi** \-,pī\ [New Latin *Octopod-, Octopus*, from Greek *oktōpous*] (1758)
1 : any of a genus (*Octopus*) of cephalopod mollusks that have eight

octopus 1

muscular arms equipped with two rows of suckers; *broadly* : any octopod excepting the paper nautilus
2 : something that resembles an octopus especially in having many centrally directed branches

oc·to·roon \,äk-tə-'rün\ *noun* [*octa-* + *-roon* (as in *quadroon*)] (1861)
: a person of one-eighth black ancestry

oc·to·syl·lab·ic \,äk-tə-sə-'la-bik\ *adjective* [Late Latin *octosyllabus*, from Greek *oktasyllabos*, from *okta-* octa- + *syllabē* syllable] (circa 1771)
1 : consisting of eight syllables
2 : composed of verses of eight syllables
— **octosyllabic** *noun*

oc·to·syl·la·ble \'äk-tə-,si-lə-bəl, ,äk-tə-'\ *noun* (circa 1846)
: a word or line of eight syllables

oc·to·thorp \'äk-tə-,thórp, -tō-\ *noun* [*octo-* + *thorp*, of unknown origin; from the eight points on its circumference] (1971)
: the symbol #

¹oc·u·lar \'ä-kyə-lər\ *adjective* [Late Latin *ocularis* of eyes, from Latin *oculus* eye] (circa 1575)
1 a : done or perceived by the eye ⟨*ocular* inspection⟩ **b** : based on what has been seen ⟨*ocular* testimony⟩
2 a : of or relating to the eye ⟨*ocular* muscles⟩
b : resembling an eye in form or function

²ocular *noun* (1835)
: EYEPIECE

oc·u·lar·ist \'ä-kyə-lə-rist\ *noun* (1866)
: a person who makes and fits artificial eyes

oc·u·list \'ä-kyə-list\ *noun* [French *oculiste*, from Latin *oculus*] (1615)
1 : OPHTHALMOLOGIST
2 : OPTOMETRIST

oc·u·lo·mo·tor \,ä-kyə-lə-'mō-tər\ *adjective* [Latin *ocul*us eye + English *-o-* + *motor*] (circa 1890)
1 : moving or tending to move the eyeball
2 : of or relating to the oculomotor nerve

oculomotor nerve *noun* (1881)
: either of the pair of chiefly motor nerves that comprise the 3d pair of cranial nerves, arise from the midbrain, and supply four muscles of the eye

oc·u·lus \'ä-kyə-ləs\ *noun, plural* **oc·u·li** \-,lī, -,lē\ [Latin, literally, eye — more at EYE] (1848)
1 : a circular or oval window
2 : a circular opening at the top of a dome

od *or* **odd** \'äd\ *interjection, often capitalized* [euphemism for *God*] (1695)
archaic — used as a mild oath

¹OD \,ō-'dē\ *noun* [*overdose*] (circa 1960)
1 : an overdose of a narcotic
2 : one who has taken an OD

²OD *intransitive verb* **OD'd** *or* **ODed; OD'·ing; OD's** (1966)
1 : to become ill or die of an OD
2 : to have or experience too much of something — used with *on* ⟨*OD* on television⟩

oda·lisque \'ō-d³l-,isk\ *noun* [French, from Turkish *odalık*, from *oda* room] (circa 1681)
1 : a female slave
2 : a concubine in a harem

odd \'äd\ *adjective* [Middle English *odde*, from Old Norse *oddi* point of land, triangle, odd number; akin to Old English *ord* point of a weapon] (14th century)
1 a : being without a corresponding mate ⟨an *odd* shoe⟩ **b** (1) : left over after others are paired or grouped (2) : separated from a set or series
2 a : somewhat more than the indicated approximate quantity, extent, or degree — usually used in combination ⟨300-*odd* pages⟩ **b** (1) : left over as a remainder ⟨had a few *odd* dollars for entertainment after paying his bills⟩ (2) : constituting a small amount ⟨had some *odd* change in her pocket⟩

3 a : being any of the integers (as −3, −1, +1, and +3) that are not exactly divisible by two **b** : marked by an odd number of units **c** : being a function such that $f(-x) = -f(x)$ where the sign is reversed but the absolute value remains the same if the sign of the independent variable is reversed
4 a : not regular, expected, or planned ⟨worked at *odd* jobs⟩ **b** : encountered or experienced from time to time : OCCASIONAL
5 : having an out-of-the-way location : REMOTE
6 : differing markedly from the usual or ordinary or accepted : PECULIAR ◇
synonym see STRANGE
— **odd·ness** *noun*

odd·ball \'äd-,bòl\ *noun* (1948)
: one that is eccentric
— **oddball** *adjective*

Odd Fellow *noun* [Independent Order of *Odd Fellows*] (1795)
: a member of a major benevolent and fraternal order

odd·i·ty \'ä-də-tē\ *noun, plural* **-ties** (1713)
1 : an odd person, thing, event, or trait
2 : the quality or state of being odd

odd lot *noun* (1897)
: a number or quantity other than the usual unit in transactions; *especially* : a quantity of less than 100 shares of stock

odd·ly \'äd-lē\ *adverb* (1610)
1 : in an odd manner
2 : it is odd that ⟨was quite happy, *oddly* enough⟩

odd man out *noun* (1923)
: a person who differs from the other members of a group

odd·ment \'äd-mənt\ *noun* (1796)
1 a : something left over : REMNANT **b** *plural* : ODDS AND ENDS
2 : something odd : ODDITY

odd permutation *noun* (1929)
: a permutation that is produced by the successive application of an odd number of interchanges of pairs of elements

odd–pin·nate \'äd-'pi-,nāt\ *adjective* (circa 1890)
: having leaflets on each side of the petiole and having a single leaflet at the tip of the petiole
— **odd–pin·nate·ly** *adverb*

odds \'ädz\ *noun plural but singular or plural in construction* (circa 1520)
1 a *archaic* : INEQUALITIES **b** *obsolete* : degree of unlikeness

◇ WORD HISTORY

odd Old Norse *oddi* originally meant "point of land." From the roughly triangular shape of a point of land, *oddi* was generalized to mean "triangle." A point of land can be seen as the apex of a triangle, with the other two angles forming a pair and the apex the unpaired angle, so *oddi* was extended to mean "odd number," the item of a threesome left over after the other two items are paired off. During the time when Scandinavians dominated northern and central England in the Middle Ages, *oddi* was presumably borrowed into English, though it is first recorded only in 14th century Middle English as the adjective *odde* "without a corresponding mate." Already in Middle English, *odde* could mean "unconforming, irregular," though in reference to people it usually meant "outstanding, illustrious." The modern sense "peculiar, eccentric" did not become widely used before the 17th century.

\ə\ abut \ᵊ\ kitten \ər\ further \a\ ash \ā\ ace
\ä\ mop, mar \aủ\ out \ch\ chin \e\ bet \ē\ easy
\g\ go \i\ hit \ī\ ice \j\ job \ŋ\ sing \ō\ go
\ȯ\ law \ȯi\ boy \th\ thin \th\ the \ü\ loot \ủ\ foot
\y\ yet \zh\ vision see also Guide to Pronunciation

2 a : an amount by which one thing exceeds or falls short of another ⟨won the election by considerable *odds*⟩ **b** (1) : a difference favoring one of two opposed things ⟨overwhelming *odds*⟩ (2) : a difference in terms of advantage or disadvantage ⟨what's the *odds*, if thinking so makes them happy —Flora Thompson⟩ **c** (1) : the probability that one thing is so or will happen rather than another : CHANCES ⟨the *odds* are against it⟩ (2) : the ratio of the probability of one event to that of an alternative event

3 : DISAGREEMENT, VARIANCE — usually used with *at* ⟨faculty and administration often are at *odds* on everything —W. E. Brock (born 1930)⟩

4 a : special favor : PARTIALITY **b** : an allowance granted by one making a bet to one accepting the bet and designed to equalize the chances favoring one of the bettors **c** : the ratio between the amount to be paid off for a winning bet and the amount of the bet

— **by all odds** : in every way : without question ⟨*by all odds* the best book of the year⟩

odds and ends *noun plural* (circa 1746)
1 a : miscellaneous articles **b** : miscellaneous small matters (as of business) to be attended to **2** : miscellaneous remnants or leftovers ⟨*odds and ends* of food⟩

odds-maker \'ädz-ˌmā-kər\ *noun* (circa 1949)
: one who figures odds

odds-on \'ädz-'ón, -'än\ *adjective* (1890)
1 : having or viewed as having a better than even chance to win ⟨the *odds-on* favorite⟩ **2** : not involving much risk : pretty sure ⟨an *odds-on* bet⟩

odd trick *noun* (1897)
: each trick in excess of six won by declarer's side at bridge — compare BOOK 9

ode \'ōd\ *noun* [Middle French or Late Latin; Middle French, from Late Latin, from Greek *ōidē*, literally, song, from *aeidein, aidein* to sing; akin to Greek *audē* voice] (1588)
: a lyric poem usually marked by exaltation of feeling and style, varying length of line, and complexity of stanza forms
— **od-ist** \-ist\ *noun*

-ode *noun combining form* [Greek *-odos*, from *hodos*]
1 : way : path ⟨electr*ode*⟩ **2** : electrode ⟨di*ode*⟩

ode-um \ō-'dē-əm, 'ō-dē-\ *noun, plural* **odea** \-ə\ [Latin & Greek; Latin, from Greek *ōideion,* from *ōidē* song] (1616)
1 : a small roofed theater of ancient Greece and Rome used chiefly for competitions in music and poetry **2** : a theater or concert hall

od-ic \'ō-dik\ *adjective* (1863)
: of, relating to, or forming an ode

Odin \'ō-dᵊn\ *noun* [Danish, from Old Norse *Ōthinn*]
: the supreme god and creator in Norse mythology

odi-ous \'ō-dē-əs\ *adjective* [Middle English, from Middle French *odieus,* from Latin *odiosus,* from *odium*] (14th century)
: exciting or deserving hatred or repugnance ⟨*odious* associates⟩ ⟨an *odious* business⟩
— **odi-ous-ly** *adverb*
— **odi-ous-ness** *noun*

odi-um \'ō-dē-əm\ *noun* [Latin, hatred, from *odisse* to hate; akin to Old English *atol* terrible, Greek *odyssasthai* to be angry] (1602)
1 : the state or fact of being subjected to hatred and contempt as a result of a despicable act or blameworthy circumstance **2** : hatred and condemnation accompanied by loathing or contempt : DETESTATION **3** : disrepute or infamy attached to something : OPPROBRIUM

odom-e-ter \ō-'dä-mə-tər\ *noun* [French *odomètre,* from Greek *hodometron,* from *hodos* way, road + *metron* measure — more at MEASURE] (1791)
: an instrument for measuring the distance traveled (as by a vehicle)

odo-nate \'ō-dᵊn-ˌāt, ō-'dä-(ˌ)nāt\ *noun* [irregular from Greek *odous, odōn* tooth] (1947)
: any of an order (Odonata) of predaceous insects comprising the dragonflies and damselflies
— **odonate** *adjective*

odont- *or* **odonto-** *combining form* [French, from Greek, *odont-, odous* — more at TOOTH]
: tooth ⟨*odonto*blast⟩

-odont *adjective combining form* [Greek *odont-, odous* tooth]
: having teeth of a (specified) nature ⟨acro*dont*⟩

-odontia *noun combining form* [New Latin, from Greek *odont-, odous*]
: form, condition, or mode of treatment of the teeth ⟨ortho*dontia*⟩

odon-to-blast \ō-'dän-tə-ˌblast\ *noun* [International Scientific Vocabulary] (1878)
: any of the elongated radially arranged cells on the surface of the dental pulp that secrete dentin
— **odon-to-blas-tic** \-ˌdän-tə-'blas-tik\ *adjective*

odon-to-glos-sum \ō-ˌdän-tə-'glä-səm\ *noun* [New Latin, from Greek *odont-* + *glōssa* tongue — more at GLOSS] (1880)
: any of a genus (*Odontoglossum*) of widely cultivated tropical American orchids

odon-toid process \ō-'dän-ˌtóid-\ *noun* (circa 1819)
: a toothlike process projecting from the anterior end of the centrum of the axis vertebra on which the atlas vertebra rotates

odor \'ō-dər\ *noun* [Middle English *odour,* from Middle French, from Latin *odor;* akin to Latin *olēre* to smell, Greek *ozein* to smell, *osmē* smell, odor] (13th century)
1 a : a quality of something that stimulates the olfactory organ : SCENT **b** : a sensation resulting from adequate stimulation of the olfactory organ : SMELL
2 a : a characteristic or predominant quality : FLAVOR ⟨the *odor* of sanctity⟩ **b** : REPUTE, ESTIMATION ⟨in bad *odor*⟩
3 *archaic* : something that emits a sweet or pleasing scent : PERFUME
synonym see SMELL
— **odored** \'ō-dərd\ *adjective*
— **odor-less** \-dər-ləs\ *adjective*

odor-ant \'ō-də-rənt\ *noun* (1935)
: an odorous substance; *especially* : one added to a dangerous odorless substance to warn of its presence

odor-if-er-ous \ˌō-də-'ri-f(ə-)rəs\ *adjective* (15th century)
1 : yielding an odor : ODOROUS **2** : morally offensive
— **odor-if-er-ous-ly** *adverb*
— **odor-if-er-ous-ness** *noun*

odor-ize \'ō-də-ˌrīz\ *transitive verb* **-ized; -iz-ing** (1884)
: to make odorous : SCENT

odor-ous \'ō-də-rəs\ *adjective* (15th century)
: having an odor : as **a** : FRAGRANT **b** : MALODOROUS ☆
— **odor-ous-ly** *adverb*
— **odor-ous-ness** *noun*

odour *chiefly British variant of* ODOR

Odys-se-an \ō-'di-sē-ən ("*Odysseus*"), ˌä-də-'sē-ən ("*journey*")\ *adjective* (circa 1711)
: of, relating to, or characteristic of Odysseus or his journey

Odys-seus \ō-'di-sē-əs, -'dis-yəs, -'di-shəs, -'di-ˌshüs\ *noun* [Greek]
: a king of Ithaca and Greek leader in the Trojan War who after the war wanders 10 years before reaching home

od-ys-sey \'ä-də-sē\ *noun, plural* **-seys** [the *Odyssey,* epic poem attributed to Homer recounting the long wanderings of Odysseus] (1889)
1 : a long wandering or voyage usually marked by many changes of fortune **2** : an intellectual or spiritual wandering or quest

oe-cu-men-i-cal \especially British ˌē-\ *variant of* ECUMENICAL

oe-de-ma *chiefly British variant of* EDEMA

oe-di-pal \'e-də-pəl, 'ē-\ *adjective, often capitalized* (1939)
: of, relating to, or resulting from the Oedipus complex
— **oe-di-pal-ly** \-pə-lē\ *adverb, often capitalized*

¹Oe-di-pus \-pəs\ *noun* [Latin, from Greek *Oidipous*]
: the son of Laius and Jocasta who in fulfillment of an oracle unknowingly kills his father and marries his mother

²Oedipus *adjective* (1910)
: OEDIPAL

Oedipus complex *noun* (1910)
: the positive libidinal feelings of a child toward the parent of the opposite sex and hostile or jealous feelings toward the parent of the same sex that may be a source of adult personality disorder when unresolved

oeil-de-boeuf \ˌə(r)-də-'bəf, ˌói-\ *noun, plural* **oeils-de-boeuf** \same\ [French *œil-de-bœuf,* literally, ox's eye] (1849)
: OCULUS 1

oeil-lade \ˌə(r)-'yäd, œ-yàd\ *noun* [Middle French *œillade,* from *oeil* eye, from Latin *oculus* — more at EYE] (1592)
: a glance of the eye; *especially* : OGLE

OEM \ˌō-(ˌ)ē-'em\ *noun* [original equipment manufacturer] (1968)
: one that produces complex equipment (as a computer system) from components usually bought from other manufacturers

oe-nol-o-gy *variant of* ENOLOGY

Oe-no-ne \ē-'nō-nē\ *noun* [Latin, from Greek *Oinōnē*]
: a nymph who is abandoned by her husband Paris for Helen of Troy

oe-no-phile \'ē-nə-ˌfīl\ *noun* [French *œno-phile,* from *œno-* (from Greek *oinos* wine) + *-phile* -phile — more at WINE] (1930)
: a lover or connoisseur of wine

¹o'er \'ōr, 'ór\ *adverb* (1592)
: OVER

²o'er *preposition* (1593)
: OVER

oer-sted \'ər-stəd\ *noun* [Hans Christian Oersted] (1930)
: the unit of magnetic field strength in the centimeter-gram-second system

oe-soph-a-gus *chiefly British variant of* ESOPHAGUS

oestr- *or* **oestro-** *chiefly British variant of* ESTR-

oeu-vre \œvrᵊ\ *noun, plural* **oeuvres** \same\ [French *œuvre,* literally, work, from Latin *opera* — more at OPERA] (1875)
: a substantial body of work constituting the lifework of a writer, an artist, or a composer

☆ SYNONYMS
Odorous, fragrant, redolent, aromatic mean emitting and diffusing scent. ODOROUS applies to whatever has a strong distinctive smell whether pleasant or unpleasant ⟨*odorous* cheeses should be tightly wrapped⟩. FRAGRANT applies to things (as flowers or spices) with sweet or agreeable odors ⟨a *fragrant* rose⟩. REDOLENT applies usually to a place or thing impregnated with odors ⟨the kitchen was *redolent* of garlic and tomatoes⟩. AROMATIC applies to things emitting pungent often fresh odors ⟨an *aromatic* blend of tobaccos⟩.

¹of \əv, *before consonants also* ə; 'əv, 'äv\ *preposition* [Middle English, off, of, from Old English, adverb & preposition; akin to Old High German *aba* off, away, Latin *about* from, away, Greek *apo*] (before 12th century)
1 — used as a function word to indicate a point of reckoning ⟨north *of* the lake⟩
2 a — used as a function word to indicate origin or derivation ⟨a man *of* noble birth⟩ **b** — used as a function word to indicate the cause, motive, or reason ⟨died *of* flu⟩ **c :** BY ⟨plays *of* Shakespeare⟩ **d :** on the part of ⟨very kind *of* you⟩
3 — used as a function word to indicate the component material, parts, or elements or the contents ⟨throne *of* gold⟩ ⟨cup *of* water⟩
4 a — used as a function word to indicate the whole that includes the part denoted by the preceding word ⟨most *of* the army⟩ **b** — used as a function word to indicate a whole or quantity from which a part is removed or expended ⟨gave *of* his time⟩
5 a : relating to **:** ABOUT ⟨stories *of* her travels⟩ **b :** in respect to ⟨slow *of* speech⟩
6 a — used as a function word to indicate belonging or a possessive relationship ⟨king *of* England⟩ **b** — used as a function word to indicate relationship between a result determined by a function or operation and a basic entity (as an independent variable) ⟨a function *of* x⟩ ⟨the product *of* two numbers⟩
7 — used as a function word to indicate something from which a person or thing is delivered ⟨eased *of* her pain⟩ or with respect to which someone or something is made destitute ⟨robbed *of* all their belongings⟩
8 a — used as a function word to indicate a particular example belonging to the class denoted by the preceding noun ⟨the city *of* Rome⟩ **b** — used as a function word to indicate apposition ⟨that fool *of* a husband⟩
9 a — used as a function word to indicate the object of an action denoted or implied by the preceding noun ⟨love *of* nature⟩ **b** — used as a function word to indicate the application of a verb ⟨cheats him *of* a dollar⟩ or of an adjective ⟨fond *of* candy⟩
10 — used as a function word to indicate a characteristic or distinctive quality or possession ⟨a woman *of* courage⟩
11 a — used as a function word to indicate the position in time of an action or occurrence ⟨died *of* a Monday⟩ **b :** BEFORE ⟨quarter *of* ten⟩
12 *archaic* **:** ON ⟨a plague *of* all cowards —Shakespeare⟩
²of \əv, *before consonants also* ə\ *verbal auxiliary* [by alteration] (1837)
nonstandard **:** HAVE — used in place of the contraction '*ve* often in representations of uneducated speech ⟨I could *of* beat them easy —Ring Lardner⟩
ofay \'ō-,fā, ō-'\ *noun* [origin unknown] (1925)
: a white person — usually used disparagingly ◇
¹off \'ȯf\ *adverb* [Middle English *of*, from Old English — more at OF] (before 12th century)
1 a (1) **:** from a place or position ⟨march *off*⟩; *specifically* **:** away from land ⟨ship stood *off* to sea⟩ (2) **:** at a distance in space or time ⟨stood 10 paces *off*⟩ ⟨a long way *off*⟩ **b :** from a course **:** ASIDE ⟨turned *off* into a bypath⟩; *specifically* **:** away from the wind **c :** into an unconscious state ⟨dozed *off*⟩
2 a : so as to be separated from support ⟨rolled to the edge of the table and *off*⟩ or close contact ⟨blew the lid *off*⟩ ⟨the handle came *off*⟩ **b :** so as to be divided ⟨surface marked *off* into squares⟩
3 a : to a state of discontinuance or suspension ⟨shut *off* an engine⟩ **b** — used as an intensifier ⟨drink *off* a glass⟩ ⟨finish it *off*⟩
4 : in absence from or suspension of regular work or service ⟨take time *off* for lunch⟩
5 : OFFSTAGE

²off *preposition* (before 12th century)
1 a — used as a function word to indicate physical separation or distance from a position of rest, attachment, or union ⟨take it *off* the table⟩ ⟨a path *off* the main walk⟩ ⟨a shop just *off* the main street⟩ **b :** to seaward of ⟨two miles *off* shore⟩
2 — used as a function word to indicate the object of an action ⟨borrowed a dollar *off* him⟩ ⟨dined *off* oysters⟩
3 a — used as a function word to indicate the suspension of an occupation or activity ⟨*off* duty⟩ ⟨*off* liquor⟩ **b :** below the usual standard or level of ⟨*off* his game⟩
³off *adjective* (1666)
1 a : more removed or distant ⟨the *off* side of the building⟩ **b :** SEAWARD **c :** RIGHT
2 a : started on the way ⟨*off* on a spree⟩ **b :** not taking place or staying in effect ⟨the deal was *off*⟩ **c :** not operating or not placed so as to permit operation
3 a : not corresponding to fact **:** INCORRECT ⟨*off* in his reckoning⟩ **b :** POOR, SUBNORMAL **c :** not entirely sane **:** ECCENTRIC **d :** REMOTE, SLIGHT ⟨an *off* chance⟩
4 a : spent off duty ⟨reading on his *off* days⟩ **b :** SLACK ⟨*off* season⟩
5 a : OFF-COLOR **b :** INFERIOR ⟨*off* grade of oil⟩; *also* **:** affected with putrefaction **c :** DOWN ⟨stocks were *off*⟩
6 : CIRCUMSTANCED ⟨worse *off*⟩
⁴off (1717)
intransitive verb
: to go away **:** DEPART — used chiefly as an imperative ⟨*off*, or I'll shoot⟩
transitive verb
slang **:** KILL, MURDER
of·fal \'ȯ-fəl, 'ä-\ *noun* [Middle English, from *of* off + *fall*] (14th century)
1 : the waste or by-product of a process: as **a :** trimmings of a hide **b :** the by-products of milling used especially for stock feeds **c :** the viscera and trimmings of a butchered animal removed in dressing
2 : RUBBISH
off and on *adverb* (1535)
: with periodic cessation **:** INTERMITTENTLY ⟨rained *off and on* all day⟩
¹off·beat \'ȯf-,bēt\ *noun* (circa 1928)
: the unaccented beat of a musical measure
²off·beat \-'bēt\ *adjective* (1938)
: ECCENTRIC, UNCONVENTIONAL
off Broadway *noun, often* O *capitalized* [from its usually being produced in smaller theaters outside of the Broadway theatrical district] (1954)
: a part of the New York professional theater stressing fundamental and artistic values and formerly engaging in experimentation
— **off–Broadway** *adjective or adverb, often* O *capitalized*
off·cast \'ȯf-,kast\ *adjective* (1571)
: cast off **:** DISCARDED
— **offcast** *noun*
off–col·or \'ȯf-'kə-lər\ *or* **off–col·ored** \-lərd\ *adjective* (1860)
1 a : not having the right or standard color **b :** being out of sorts
2 a : of doubtful propriety **:** DUBIOUS **b :** verging on the indecent
off·cut \'ȯf-,kət\ *noun* (circa 1664)
chiefly British **:** something that is cut off (as a waste piece of lumber)
of·fend \ə-'fend\ *verb* [Middle English, from Middle French *offendre*, from Latin *offendere* to strike against, offend, from *ob*- against + *-fendere* to strike — more at OB-, DEFEND] (14th century)
intransitive verb
1 a : to transgress the moral or divine law **:** SIN ⟨if it be a sin to covet honor, I am the most *offending* soul alive —Shakespeare⟩ **b :** to violate a law or rule **:** do wrong ⟨*offend* against the law⟩

2 a : to cause difficulty, discomfort, or injury ⟨took off his shoe and removed the *offending* pebble⟩ **b :** to cause dislike, anger, or vexation ⟨thoughtless words that *offend* needlessly⟩
transitive verb
1 a : VIOLATE, TRANSGRESS **b :** to cause pain to **:** HURT
2 *obsolete* **:** to cause to sin or fall
3 : to cause to feel vexation or resentment usually by violation of what is proper or fitting ⟨was *offended* by their language⟩ ☆
— **of·fend·er** *noun*
of·fense *or* **of·fence** \ə-'fen(t)s, *especially for 3* 'ä-,fen(t)s, 'ȯ-\ *noun* [Middle English, from Middle French, from Latin *offensa*, from feminine of *offensus*, past participle of *offendere*] (14th century)
1 a *obsolete* **:** an act of stumbling **b** *archaic* **:** a cause or occasion of sin **:** STUMBLING BLOCK
2 : something that outrages the moral or physical senses
3 a : the act of attacking **:** ASSAULT **b :** the means or method of attacking or of attempting to score **c :** the offensive team or members of a team playing offensive positions **d :** scoring ability
4 a : the act of displeasing or affronting **b :** the state of being insulted or morally outraged ⟨takes *offense* at the slightest criticism⟩

☆ **SYNONYMS**
Offend, outrage, affront, insult mean to cause hurt feelings or deep resentment. OFFEND need not imply an intentional hurting but it may indicate merely a violation of the victim's sense of what is proper or fitting ⟨hoped that my remarks had not *offended* her⟩. OUTRAGE implies offending beyond endurance and calling forth extreme feelings ⟨*outraged* by their accusations⟩. AFFRONT implies treating with deliberate rudeness or contemptuous indifference to courtesy ⟨deeply *affronted* by his callousness⟩. INSULT suggests deliberately causing humiliation, hurt pride, or shame ⟨managed to *insult* every guest at the party⟩.

◇ **WORD HISTORY**
ofay *Ofay* is a derogatory word for a white person, now perhaps obsolescent, recorded in urban African-American speech since the 1920s. Soon after it first saw print, theories about the word's origin proliferated. Probably the most common is that *ofay* is a Pig Latin permutation of *foe*. However, if a word meaning "enemy" were to be so disguised, the rather literary word *foe* is an unlikely choice, and this explanation is most likely an after-the-fact guess that suits popular notions of what the underlying meaning of the word *should* be. More serious have been attempts to find an African source for *ofay;* the word sounds as if it could come from any of a number of West African languages, but none of the suggestions thus far put forward is entirely compelling. There is also the absence of any documentation for *ofay* before it appeared in a New York City newspaper, the *Inter-State Tattler*, in March, 1925, and shortly thereafter in essays by the Harlem Renaissance authors Rudolph Fisher and George S. Schuyler published in the magazine *American Mercury*. Perhaps we should look no further than 1920s Harlem, culturally creative in many respects, for this piece of linguistic creativity.

\ə\ abut \'ə\ kitten \ər\ further \a\ ash \ā\ ace \ä\ mop, mar \aú\ out \ch\ chin \e\ bet \ē\ easy \g\ go \i\ hit \ī\ ice \j\ job \ŋ\ sing \ō\ go \ȯ\ law \ȯi\ boy \th\ thin \t͟h\ the \ü\ loot \ú\ foot \y\ yet \zh\ vision　*see also* Guide to Pronunciation

5 a : a breach of a moral or social code **:** SIN, MISDEED **b :** an infraction of law; *especially* **:** MISDEMEANOR ☆☆
— **of·fense·less** \-ləs\ *adjective*

¹**of·fen·sive** \ə-'fen(t)-siv, *especially for 1* 'ä-,fen(t)-, 'ò-\ *adjective* (circa 1548)
1 a : making attack **:** AGGRESSIVE **b :** of, relating to, or designed for attack ⟨*offensive* weapons⟩ **c :** of or relating to an attempt to score in a game or contest; *also* **:** of or relating to a team in possession of the ball or puck
2 : giving painful or unpleasant sensations **:** NAUSEOUS, OBNOXIOUS ⟨*offensive* odor of garbage⟩
3 : causing displeasure or resentment
— **of·fen·sive·ly** *adverb*
— **of·fen·sive·ness** *noun*

²**offensive** *noun* (1720)
1 : the act of an attacking party
2 : ATTACK

¹**of·fer** \'ò-fər, 'ä-\ *verb* **of·fered; of·fer·ing** \-f(ə-)riŋ\ [Middle English, in sense 1, from Old English *offrian*, from Late Latin *offerre*, from Latin, to present, tender, from *ob-* toward + *ferre* to carry; in other senses, from Old French *offrir*, from Latin *offerre* — more at BEAR] (before 12th century)
transitive verb
1 a : to present as an act of worship or devotion **:** SACRIFICE **b :** to utter (as a prayer) in devotion
2 a : to present for acceptance or rejection **:** TENDER ⟨was *offered* a job⟩ **b :** to present in order to satisfy a requirement ⟨candidates for degrees may *offer* French as one of their foreign languages⟩
3 a : PROPOSE, SUGGEST ⟨*offer* a solution to a problem⟩ **b :** to declare one's readiness or willingness ⟨*offered* to help me⟩
4 a : to try or begin to exert **:** PUT UP ⟨*offered* stubborn resistance⟩ **b :** THREATEN ⟨*offered* to strike him with his cane⟩
5 : to make available **:** AFFORD; *especially* **:** to place (merchandise) on sale
6 : to present in performance or exhibition
7 : to propose as payment **:** BID
intransitive verb
1 : to present something as an act of worship or devotion **:** SACRIFICE
2 *archaic* **:** to make an attempt
3 : to present itself
4 : to make a proposal (as of marriage)

²**offer** *noun* (15th century)
1 a : a presenting of something for acceptance ⟨considering job *offers* from several firms⟩ ⟨an *offer* of marriage⟩ **b :** an undertaking to do an act or give something on condition that the party to whom the proposal is made do some specified act or make a return promise
2 *obsolete* **:** OFFERING
3 : a price named by one proposing to buy **:** BID
4 a : ATTEMPT, TRY **b :** an action or movement indicating a purpose or intention
— **on offer** *chiefly British* **:** being offered especially for sale

of·fer·ing \'ò-f(ə-)riŋ, 'ä-\ *noun* (before 12th century)
1 a : the act of one who offers **b :** something offered; *especially* **:** a sacrifice ceremonially offered as a part of worship **c :** a contribution to the support of a church
2 : something offered for sale or patronage ⟨latest *offerings* of the leading novelists⟩
3 : a course of instruction or study

of·fer·to·ry \'ò-fə(r)-,tōr-ē, 'ä-, -,tòr-\ *noun, plural* **-ries** [Medieval Latin *offertorium*, from Late Latin *offerre*] (1539)
1 *often capitalized* **a :** the eucharistic offering of bread and wine to God before they are consecrated at Communion **b :** a verse from a Psalm said or sung at the beginning of the offertory
2 a : the period of collection and presentation of the offerings of the congregation at public worship **b :** a musical composition played or sung during an offertory

¹**off·hand** \'òf-'hand, -,hand\ *adverb* (1694)
: without premeditation or preparation **:** EXTEMPORE ⟨couldn't give the figures *offhand*⟩

²**offhand** *adjective* (1708)
1 : CASUAL, INFORMAL ⟨a relaxed, *offhand* manner⟩
2 : done or made offhand ⟨*offhand* excuses⟩

off·hand·ed \-'han-dəd, -,han-\ *adjective* (1835)
: OFFHAND
— **off·hand·ed·ly** *adverb*
— **off·hand·ed·ness** *noun*

off–hour \'òf-,aù(-ə)r\ *noun* (1932)
1 : a period of time other than a rush hour
2 : a period of time other than regular business hours

of·fice \'ä-fəs, 'ò-\ *noun* [Middle English, from Middle French, from Latin *officium* service, duty, office, from *opus* work + *facere* to make, do — more at OPERATE, DO] (13th century)
1 a : a special duty, charge, or position conferred by an exercise of governmental authority and for a public purpose **:** a position of authority to exercise a public function and to receive whatever emoluments may belong to it **b :** a position of responsibility or some degree of executive authority
2 [Middle English, from Old French, from Late Latin *officium*, from Latin] **:** a prescribed form or service of worship; *specifically, capitalized* **:** DIVINE OFFICE
3 : a religious or social ceremonial observance **:** RITE
4 a : something that one ought to do or must do **:** an assigned or customary duty, task, or role **b :** the proper or customary action of something **:** FUNCTION **c :** something done for another **:** SERVICE
5 : a place where a particular kind of business is transacted or a service is supplied: as **a :** a place in which the functions of a public officer are performed **b :** the directing headquarters of an enterprise or organization **c :** the place in which a professional person conducts business
6 *plural, chiefly British* **:** the apartments, attached buildings, or outhouses in which the activities attached to the service of a house are carried on
7 a : a major administrative unit in some governments ⟨British Foreign *Office*⟩ **b :** a subdivision of some government departments ⟨Patent *Office*⟩
synonym see FUNCTION

office boy *noun* (1846)
: a boy or man employed for odd jobs in a business office

of·fice-hold·er \-,hōl-dər\ *noun* (1818)
: one holding a public office

¹**of·fi·cer** \'ä-fə-sər, 'ò-\ *noun* [Middle English, from Middle French *officier*, from Medieval Latin *officiarius*, from Latin *officium*] (14th century)
1 a *obsolete* **:** AGENT **b :** one charged with police duties
2 : one who holds an office of trust, authority, or command ⟨the *officers* of the bank⟩
3 a : one who holds a position of authority or command in the armed forces; *specifically* **:** COMMISSIONED OFFICER **b :** the master or any of the mates of a merchant or passenger ship

²**officer** *transitive verb* (1670)
1 : to furnish with officers
2 : to command or direct as an officer

officer of arms (circa 1500)
: any of the officers (as king of arms, herald, or pursuivant) of a monarch or government responsible for devising and granting armorial bearings

¹**of·fi·cial** \ə-'fi-shəl *also* ō-\ *noun* (14th century)
1 : one who holds or is invested with an office **:** OFFICER ⟨government *officials*⟩
2 : one who administers the rules of a game or sport especially as a referee or umpire

²**official** *adjective* (circa 1604)
1 : of or relating to an office, position, or trust ⟨*official* duties⟩
2 : holding an office
3 a : AUTHORITATIVE, AUTHORIZED ⟨*official* statement⟩ **b :** prescribed or recognized as authorized ⟨an *official* language⟩ **c :** described by the U.S. Pharmacopeia or the National Formulary
4 : befitting or characteristic of a person in office ⟨extended an *official* greeting⟩
— **of·fi·cial·ly** \-'fi-sh(ə-)lē\ *adverb*

of·fi·cial·dom \-'fi-shəl-dəm\ *noun* (1863)
: officials as a class

of·fi·cial·ese \-,fi-shə-'lēz, -'lēs\ *noun* (1884)
: the characteristic language of official statements **:** wordy, pompous, or obscure language

of·fi·cial·ism \-'fi-shə-,li-zəm\ *noun* (1857)
: lack of flexibility and initiative combined with excessive adherence to regulations in the behavior of usually government officials

of·fi·ci·ant \ə-'fi-shē-ənt\ *noun* (1844)
: one (as a priest) that officiates at a religious rite

¹**of·fi·ci·ary** \ə-'fi-shē-,er-ē, ō-, ä-\ *noun, plural* **-ar·ies** [Medieval Latin *officiarius*] (1611)
1 : OFFICER, OFFICIAL
2 : a body of officers or officials

²**officiary** *adjective* (1612)
: connected with, derived from, or having a title or rank by virtue of holding an office ⟨*officiary* earl⟩

of·fi·ci·ate \ə-'fi-shē-,āt\ *verb* **-at·ed; -at·ing** (1631)
transitive verb
1 : to carry out (an official duty or function)
2 : to serve as a leader or celebrant of (a ceremony)
3 : to administer the rules of (a game or sport) especially as a referee or umpire
intransitive verb
1 : to perform a ceremony, function, or duty ⟨*officiate* at a wedding⟩
2 : to act in an official capacity **:** act as an official (as at a sports contest)
— **of·fi·ci·a·tion** \-,fi-shē-'ā-shən\ *noun*

☆ **SYNONYMS**
Offense, resentment, umbrage, pique, dudgeon, huff mean an emotional response to or an emotional state resulting from a slight or indignity. OFFENSE implies hurt displeasure (takes deep *offense* at racial slurs). RESENTMENT suggests a longer lasting indignation or smoldering ill will ⟨harbored a lifelong *resentment* of his brother⟩. UMBRAGE may suggest hurt pride, resentment, or suspicion of another's motives ⟨took *umbrage* at the offer of advice⟩. PIQUE applies to a transient feeling of wounded vanity ⟨in a *pique* I foolishly declined the invitation⟩. DUDGEON suggests an angry fit of indignation ⟨stormed out of the meeting in high *dudgeon*⟩. HUFF implies a peevish short-lived spell of anger usually at a petty cause ⟨in a *huff* he slammed the door⟩.

Offense, sin, vice, crime, scandal mean a transgression of law. OFFENSE applies to the infraction of any law, rule, or code ⟨at that school no *offense* went unpunished⟩. SIN implies an offense against moral or religious law ⟨the *sin* of blasphemy⟩. VICE applies to a habit or practice that degrades or corrupts ⟨regarded gambling as a *vice*⟩. CRIME implies a serious offense punishable by the law of the state ⟨the *crime* of murder⟩. SCANDAL applies to an offense that outrages the public conscience ⟨a career ruined by a sex *scandal*⟩.

of·fi·ci·nal \ə-'fi-sᵊn-əl, ȯ-, ä-; ˌȯ-fə-'sī-nᵊl, ˌä-\ *adjective* [Medieval Latin *officinalis* of a storeroom, from *officina* storeroom, from Latin, workshop, from *opific-, opifex* workman, from *opus* work + *facere* to do] (circa 1720)
: MEDICINAL ⟨a monograph on *officinal* flora⟩

of·fi·cious \ə-'fi-shəs\ *adjective* [Latin *officiosus,* from *officium* service, office] (1565)
1 *archaic* **a** : KIND, OBLIGING **b** : DUTIFUL
2 : volunteering one's services where they are neither asked nor needed : MEDDLESOME
3 : INFORMAL, UNOFFICIAL
synonym see IMPERTINENT
— **of·fi·cious·ly** *adverb*
— **of·fi·cious·ness** *noun*

off·ing \'ȯ-fiŋ, 'ä-\ *noun* [¹*off*] (1627)
1 : the part of the deep sea seen from the shore
2 : the near or foreseeable future ⟨in the *offing*⟩

off·ish \'ȯ-fish\ *adjective* [¹*off*] (1831)
: STANDOFFISH
— **off·ish·ness** *noun*

off–key \'ȯf-'kē\ *adjective or adverb* (1927)
1 : varying in pitch from the proper tone of a melody
2 : IRREGULAR, ANOMALOUS

off–kil·ter \-'kil-tər\ *adjective* (circa 1944)
: not in perfect balance : a bit askew

off–lim·its \'ȯf-'li-məts\ *adjective* (1945)
: not to be entered or patronized by a designated class (as military personnel); *also* : not to be interfered with, considered, or spoken of ⟨the subject of sex was *off-limits* in her family⟩

off–line \-'līn\ *adjective* (1950)
: not connected to or served by a system and especially a computer or telecommunications system; *also* : done independently of a system ⟨*off-line* computer storage⟩
— **off–line** *adverb*

off–load \(ˌ)ȯf-'lōd, 'ȯf-\ *verb* (1850)
: UNLOAD

off of *preposition* (1593)
: OFF ☐

off–off–Broadway *noun, often both Os capitalized* [from its relation to off Broadway being analogous to the relation of off Broadway to Broadway] (1965)
: an avant-garde theatrical movement in New York
— **off–off–Broadway** *adjective or adverb, often both Os capitalized*

off–peak \'ȯf-'pēk\ *adjective* (1920)
: not being in the period of maximum use or business : not peak ⟨telephone rates during *off-peak* hours⟩

off–price \'ȯf-'prīs\ *adjective* (1952)
: of, relating to, selling, or being discounted merchandise ⟨an *off-price* store⟩ ⟨*off-price* apparel⟩

off·print \'ȯf-ˌprint\ *noun* (1885)
: a separately printed excerpt (as a magazine article)
— **offprint** *transitive verb*

off–put·ting \-ˌpu̇-tiŋ\ *adjective* (1828)
: that puts one off : REPELLENT, DISCONCERTING
— **off–put·ting·ly** \-lē\ *adverb*

off–ramp \-ˌramp\ *noun* (1954)
: a ramp by which one leaves a limited-access highway

off–road \'ȯf-'rōd\ *adjective* (1968)
: of, relating to, done with, or being a vehicle designed especially to operate away from public roads

off·scour·ing \-ˌskau̇(-ə)r-iŋ\ *noun* (1526)
1 : someone rejected by society : OUTCAST
2 : something that is scoured off : REFUSE

off·screen \'ȯf-'skrēn\ *adverb or adjective* (1935)
1 : out of sight of the motion picture or television viewer
2 : in private life

off–sea·son \'ȯf-ˌsē-zᵊn\ *noun* (1848)
: a time of suspended or reduced activity; *especially* : the time during which an athlete is not training or competing

¹off·set \'ȯf-ˌset\ *noun* (circa 1555)
1 a *archaic* : OUTSET, START **b** : CESSATION
2 a (1) : a short prostrate lateral shoot arising from the base of a plant (2) : a small bulb arising from the base of another bulb **b** : a lateral or collateral branch (as of a family or race) : OFFSHOOT **c** : a spur from a range of hills
3 a : a horizontal ledge on the face of a wall formed by a diminution of its thickness above **b** : DISPLACEMENT **c** : an abrupt change in the dimension or profile of an object or the part set off by such change
4 : something that sets off to advantage or embellishes something else : FOIL
5 : an abrupt bend in an object by which one part is turned aside out of line
6 : something that serves to counterbalance or to compensate for something else; *especially* : either of two balancing ledger items
7 a : unintentional transfer of ink (as from a freshly printed sheet) **b** : a printing process in which an inked impression from a plate is first made on a rubber-blanketed cylinder and then transferred to the paper being printed
— **offset** *adjective or adverb*

²off·set \'ȯf-ˌset, *verb transitive senses are also* ȯf-'\ *verb* **-set; -set·ting** (1792)
transitive verb
1 a : to place over against something : BALANCE ⟨credits *offset* debits⟩ **b** : to serve as a counterbalance for : COMPENSATE ⟨his speed *offset* his opponent's greater weight⟩
2 : to form an offset in ⟨*offset* a wall⟩
intransitive verb
: to become marked by offset

off·shoot \'ȯf-ˌshüt\ *noun* (1710)
1 a : a collateral or derived branch, descendant, or member : OUTGROWTH **b** : a lateral branch (as of a mountain range)
2 : a branch of a main stem especially of a plant

¹off·shore \'ȯf-'shōr, -'shȯr\ *adverb* (1720)
1 : from the shore : SEAWARD; *also* : at a distance from the shore
2 : outside the country : ABROAD

²off·shore \'ȯf-ˌ\ *adjective* (1845)
1 : coming or moving away from the shore toward the water ⟨an *offshore* breeze⟩
2 a : situated off the shore but within waters under a country's control ⟨*offshore* fisheries⟩ **b** : distant from the shore — compare INSHORE
3 : situated or operating in a foreign country ⟨*offshore* mutual funds⟩ ⟨*offshore* banking⟩

³off·shore \'ȯf-ˌ\ *preposition* (1965)
: off the shore of

off·side \'ȯf-'sīd\ *adverb or adjective* (1867)
: illegally in advance of the ball or puck

off–site \-'sīt\ *adjective or adverb* (1946)
: not located or occurring at the site of a particular activity

off–speed \-'spēd\ *adjective* (1965)
: being slower than usual or expected ⟨throwing *off-speed* pitches⟩

off·spring \'ȯf-ˌspriŋ\ *noun, plural* **offspring** *also* **offsprings** [Middle English *ofspring,* from Old English, from *of* off + *springan* to spring] (before 12th century)
1 a : the progeny of an animal or plant : YOUNG **b** : CHILD
2 a : PRODUCT, RESULT ⟨scholarly manuscripts —the labored *offsprings* of PhDs —Donna Martin⟩ **b** : OFFSHOOT 1a

off·stage \'ȯf-'stāj, -ˌstāj\ *adverb or adjective* (1921)
1 : on a part of the stage not visible to the audience
2 : in private life ⟨known *offstage* as a kindly person⟩
3 : behind the scenes : out of the public view ⟨much of the important work of the conference was done *offstage*⟩

off–the–books *adjective* (1980)
: not reported or recorded ⟨*off-the-books* transactions⟩ ⟨*off-the-books* covert operations⟩
— **off the books** *adverb*

off–the–cuff *adjective* (1938)

: not prepared in advance : SPONTANEOUS, INFORMAL ⟨*off-the-cuff* remarks⟩
— **off–the–cuff** *adverb*

off–the–peg *adjective* (1959)
chiefly British : READY-MADE 1

off–the–rack *adjective* (1965)
: READY-MADE 1 ⟨*off-the-rack* suits⟩

off–the–record *adjective* (1933)
: given or made in confidence and not for publication ⟨*off-the-record* comments⟩

off–the–shelf *adjective* (1950)
: available as a stock item : not specially designed or custom-made ⟨made of *off-the-shelf* components⟩

off–the–wall *adjective* (circa 1966)
: highly unusual : BIZARRE ⟨an *off-the-wall* sense of humor⟩

off·track \'ȯf-'trak\ *adverb or adjective* (1944)
: away from a racetrack ⟨betting *offtrack*⟩ ⟨*offtrack* bookies⟩

off–white \'ȯf-'hwīt, -'wīt\ *noun* (1927)
: a yellowish or grayish white

off year *noun* (1873)
1 : a year in which no major election is held
2 : a year of diminished activity or production ⟨an *off year* for auto sales⟩

oft \'ȯft\ *adverb* [Middle English, from Old English; akin to Old High German *ofto* often] (before 12th century)
: OFTEN

of·ten \'ȯ-fən, ÷'ȯf-tən\ *adverb* [Middle English, alteration of *oft*] (14th century)
: many times : FREQUENTLY

of·ten·times \-ˌtīmz\ *or* **oft·times** \'ȯf(t)-ˌtīmz\ *adverb* (14th century)
: OFTEN, REPEATEDLY

ogee *also* **OG** \'ō-ˌjē\ *noun* [obsolete English *ogee* ogive; from the use of such moldings in ogives] (1677)
1 : a molding with an S-shaped profile
2 : a pointed arch having on each side a reversed curve near the apex — see ARCH illustration

ogham *or* **ogam** \'ä-gəm, 'ō-; 'ō(-ə)m\ *noun* [Irish *ogham,* from Middle Irish *ogom, ogum*] (1729)
: the alphabetic system of 5th and 6th century Irish in which an alphabet of 20 letters is represented by notches for vowels and lines for consonants and which is known principally from inscriptions cut on the edges of rough standing tombstones
— **ogham·ic** \ä-'gä-mik, ō-; 'ō-(ə-)mik\ *adjective*
— **ogham·ist** \'ä-gə-mist, 'ō-; 'ō-(ə-)mist\ *noun*

ogi·val \ō-'jī-vəl\ *adjective* (1841)
: of, relating to, or having the form of an ogive or an ogee

ogive \'ō-ˌjīv\ *noun* [Middle English *oggif* stone comprising an arch, from Middle French *augive* diagonal arch] (1611)
1 a : a diagonal arch or rib across a Gothic vault **b** : a pointed arch
2 : a graph of a distribution function or a cumulative frequency distribution
3 : OGEE 1

¹ogle \'ō-gəl *also* 'ä-\ *verb* **ogled; ogling** \-g(ə-)liŋ\ [probably from Low German *oegeln,* from *oog* eye; akin to Old High German *ouga* eye — more at EYE] (1682)

☐ USAGE
off of The *of* is often criticized as superfluous, a comment that is irrelevant because *off of* is an idiom. It is much more common in speech than in edited writing and is more common in American English than in British.

intransitive verb
: to glance with amorous invitation or challenge
transitive verb
1 : to eye amorously or provocatively
2 : to look at especially with greedy or interested attention
— **ogler** \-g(ə-)lər\ *noun*

²ogle *noun* (1711)
: an amorous or coquettish glance

ogre \'ō-gər\ *noun* [French, probably ultimately from Latin *Orcus,* god of the underworld] (1713)
1 : a hideous giant of fairy tales and folklore that feeds on human beings : MONSTER
2 : a dreaded person or object
— **ogre·ish** \'ō-g(ə-)rish\ *adjective*

ogress \'ō-g(ə-)rəs\ *noun* (1713)
: a female ogre

¹oh \(')ō\ *interjection* [Middle English *o*] (13th century)
1 — used to express an emotion (as surprise or desire) or in response to physical stimuli
2 — used in direct address ⟨*oh,* waiter! Will you come here, please?⟩
3 — used to express acknowledgment or understanding of a statement
4 — used to introduce an example or approximation

²oh \'ō\ *noun* [*o;* from the similarity of the symbol for zero (0) to the letter *O*] (1936)
: ZERO

ohia \ō-'hē-ə\ *noun* [Hawaiian *'ōhi'a*] (1824)
: LEHUA

ohia lehua *noun* [Hawaiian *'ōhi'a-lehua*] (1888)
: LEHUA

ohm \'ōm\ *noun* [Georg Simon *Ohm*] (1867)
: the practical meter-kilogram-second unit of electric resistance equal to the resistance of a circuit in which a potential difference of one volt produces a current of one ampere
— **ohm·ic** \'ō-mik\ *adjective*
— **ohm·i·cal·ly** \-mi-k(ə-)lē\ *adverb*

ohm·me·ter \'ō(m)-,mē-tər\ *noun* [International Scientific Vocabulary] (circa 1890)
: an instrument for indicating resistance in ohms directly

Ohm's law \'ōmz-\ *noun* (1863)
: a law in electricity: the strength of a direct current is directly proportional to the potential difference and inversely proportional to the resistance of the circuit

-oic *adjective suffix* [French *-oïque* (as in *acide caproïque* caproic acid)]
: containing carboxyl or a derivative ⟨benz*oic* acid⟩

¹-oid *noun suffix*
: something resembling a (specified) object or having a (specified) quality ⟨glob*oid*⟩

²-oid *adjective suffix* [Middle French & Latin; Middle French *-oïde,* from Latin *-oïdes,* from Greek *-oeidēs,* from *-o-* + *eidos* appearance, form — more at WISE]
: resembling : having the form or appearance of ⟨petal*oid*⟩

oid·i·um \ō-'i-dē-əm\ *noun, plural* **-ia** \-dē-ə\ [New Latin, from *o-* + *-idium*] (1857)
1 a : any of a genus (*Oidium* of the family Moniliaceae) of imperfect fungi many of which are now considered to be conidial stages of various powdery mildews **b** : one of the small conidia borne in chains by various fungi (as an oidium) — called also *arthrospore*
2 : a powdery mildew caused by an oidium especially in the grape

¹oil \'ói(ə)l\ *noun, often attributive* [Middle English *oile,* from Old French, from Latin *oleum* olive oil, from Greek *elaion,* from *elaia* olive] (13th century)
1 a : any of numerous unctuous combustible substances that are liquid or can be liquefied easily on warming, are soluble in ether but not in water, and leave a greasy stain on paper or cloth **b** (1) : PETROLEUM (2) : the petroleum industry

2 : a substance (as a cosmetic preparation) of oily consistency ⟨bath *oil*⟩
3 a : an oil color used by an artist **b** : a painting done in oil colors
4 : unctuous or flattering speech

²oil (15th century)
transitive verb
: to smear, rub over, furnish, or lubricate with oil
intransitive verb
: to take on fuel oil
— **oil the hand** *or* **oil the palm** : BRIBE, TIP

oil beetle *noun* (1658)
: any of various blister beetles (genus *Meloe* or a related genus) that emit a yellowish liquid from the leg joints when disturbed

oil-bird \'ói(ə)l-,bərd\ *noun* (circa 1890)
: a nocturnal bird (*Steatornis caripensis*) of northern South America and Trinidad that is related to the nightjars, feeds chiefly on the fatty fruits of various palms, and has fatty young from which oil is extracted for use instead of butter — called also *guacharo*

oil cake *noun* (1743)
: the solid residue after extracting the oil from seeds (as of cotton)

oil·can \'ói(ə)l-,kan\ *noun* (1839)
: a can for oil; *especially* : a spouted can designed to release oil drop by drop (as for lubricating machinery)

oil·cloth \-,klóth\ *noun* (1796)
: cloth treated with oil or paint and used for table and shelf coverings

oil color *noun* (1539)
1 : a pigment used for oil paint
2 : OIL PAINT

oiled \'ói(ə)ld\ *adjective* (1535)
1 : lubricated, treated, or covered with or as if with oil ⟨*oiled* paper⟩
2 *slang* : DRUNK 1a

oil·er \'ói-lər\ *noun* (circa 1846)
1 : one (as a workman) that oils something
2 : a receptacle or device for applying oil
3 *plural* : OILSKIN 3
4 : an auxiliary naval vessel used for refueling at sea

oil field *noun* (1894)
: a region rich in petroleum deposits; *especially* : one that has been brought into production

oil gland *noun* (circa 1836)
: a gland (as of the skin) that produces an oily secretion; *specifically* : UROPYGIAL GLAND

oil·man \'ói(ə)l-mən, -,man\ *noun* (1865)
1 : an oil company executive
2 : an oil field worker

oil of vitriol (1580)
: concentrated sulfuric acid

oil of wintergreen (1866)
: the methyl ester of salicylic acid that is used as a flavoring and as a counterirritant

oil paint *noun* (1790)
: paint in which a drying oil is the vehicle

oil painting *noun* (1782)
1 : the act or art of painting in oil colors **b** : a picture painted in oils
2 : painting that uses pigments originally ground in oil

oil palm *noun* (circa 1864)
: an African pinnate-leaved palm (*Elaeis guineensis*) cultivated for its clustered fruit whose flesh and seeds yield oil

oil pan *noun* (1908)
: the lower section of the crankcase used as a lubricating-oil reservoir on an internal combustion engine

oil patch *noun* (circa 1952)
1 : OIL FIELD
2 : the petroleum industry

oil·seed \'ói(ə)l-,sēd\ *noun* (1562)
: a seed or crop (as flaxseed) grown mainly for oil

oil shale *noun* (1873)
: a rock (as shale) from which oil can be recovered by distillation

oil·skin \'ói(ə)l-,skin\ *noun* (1812)

1 : an oiled waterproof cloth used for coverings and garments
2 : an oilskin raincoat
3 *plural* : an oilskin suit of coat and trousers

oil slick *noun* (1889)
: a film of oil floating on water

oil·stone \'ói(ə)l-,stōn\ *noun* (1585)
: a whetstone for use with oil

oil well *noun* (1847)
: a well from which petroleum is obtained

oily \'ói-lē\ *adjective* **oil·i·er; -est** (14th century)
1 : of, relating to, or consisting of oil
2 a : covered or impregnated with oil ⟨*oily* rags⟩ **b** : relatively high in naturally secreted oils ⟨*oily* skin⟩ ⟨*oily* hair⟩
3 : excessively smooth or suave in manner
— **oil·i·ly** \'ói-lə-lē\ *adverb*
— **oil·i·ness** \-lē-nəs\ *noun*

oink \'óiŋk\ *noun* [imitative] (1941)
: the natural noise of a hog
— **oink** *intransitive verb*

oint·ment \'óint-mənt\ *noun* [Middle English, alteration of *oignement,* from Old French, ultimately from Latin *unguentum,* from *unguere* to anoint; akin to Old High German *ancho* butter, Sanskrit *anakti* he salves] (14th century)
: a salve or unguent for application to the skin

oi·ti·ci·ca \,ói-tə-'sē-kə\ *noun* [Portuguese, from Tupi] (1901)
: any of several South American trees; *especially* : a Brazilian tree (*Licania rigida*) with seeds that yield a drying oil similar to tung oil

Ojib·wa *or* **Ojib·way** \ō-'jib-(,)wä\ *noun, plural* **Ojibwa** *or* **Ojibwas** *or* **Ojibway** *or* **Ojibways** [Ojibwa *očipwe',* an Ojibwa band] (1700)
1 : a member of an American Indian people of the region around Lake Superior and westward
2 : an Algonquian language of the Ojibwa people

¹OK *or* **okay** \ō-'kā, in assenting or agreeing also '\ō-,kā\ *adverb or adjective* [abbreviation of *oll korrect,* facetious alteration of *all correct*] (1839)
: ALL RIGHT ◇

²OK *or* **okay** \ō-'kā\ *noun* (1841)
: APPROVAL, ENDORSEMENT

³OK *or* **okay** \ō-'kā\ *transitive verb* **OK'd** *or* **okayed; OK'·ing** *or* **okay·ing** (1888)
: APPROVE, AUTHORIZE

oka *variant of* OCA

◇ WORD HISTORY
OK *OK,* one of the most successful of all Americanisms, has long been the subject of etymological claims and counterclaims. According to the most plausible account, it arose in the late 1830s from a journalistic fad for reducing phrases to abbreviations. At the height of the fad it became fashionable to alter some of the abbreviations on the basis of pseudo-uneducated misspellings, so that *A.R.* for *all right* was transformed to *O.W.* on the basis of *oll wright,* and *N.G.* for *no go* to *K.G.* Hence *OK,* when it appeared in the Boston *Morning Post* on March 23, 1839—the earliest printed occurrence that anyone has yet found—is glossed as *oll korrect,* presumably a deliberate misspelling of *all correct. OK* might well have passed into oblivion with such other initialisms, but in the 1840 American presidential campaign it became associated with the Democratic O.K. Club, in which *O.K.* stood for *Old Kinderhook,* after Kinderhook, New York, the birthplace of the Democrats' candidate, Martin Van Buren. Humorous expansions of *OK,* including *oll korrect,* were bandied back and forth by both Democrats and Whigs. By 1841 *OK* had gone beyond the political arena to become an interjectional equivalent for "All right!"

oka·pi \ō-'kä-pē\ *noun* [Mvu'ba (language of northeast Zaire)] (1900)
: an ungulate mammal (*Okapia johnstoni*) of Zaire that is closely related to the giraffe but has a relatively short neck, a coat typically of solid reddish chestnut on the trunk, yellowish white on the cheeks, and purplish black and cream rings on the upper parts of the legs

okapi

okey-doke \ō-kē-'dōk\ *or* **okey-dokey** \-'dō-kē\ *adverb* [reduplication of *OK*] (circa 1932)
— used to express assent

Okie \'ō-kē\ *noun* [*Ok*lahoma + *-ie*] (1938)
: a migrant agricultural worker; *especially* : one from Oklahoma in the 1930s — sometimes used disparagingly

okra \'ō-krə, *Southern also* -krē\ *noun* [of African origin; akin to Ibo *ókùrù* okra] (1679)
1 : a tall annual (*Abelmoschus esculentus*) of the mallow family that is cultivated for its mucilaginous green pods used especially in soups or stews; *also* : the pods of this plant
2 : ¹GUMBO 1

¹-ol *noun suffix* [International Scientific Vocabulary, from *alcohol*]
: chemical compound (as an alcohol or phenol) containing hydroxyl ⟨glycer*ol*⟩ ⟨cres*ol*⟩

²-ol — see -OLE

³-ol *noun combining form* [International Scientific Vocabulary, from Latin *oleum* oil — more at OIL]
: hydrocarbon chemically related to benzene ⟨xyl*ol*⟩

¹old \'ōld; *for sense 9 usually* 'ōl\ *adjective* [Middle English, from Old English *eald*; akin to Old High German *alt* old, Latin *alere* to nourish, *alescere* to grow, *altus* high, deep] (before 12th century)
1 a : dating from the remote past : ANCIENT ⟨*old* traditions⟩ **b** : persisting from an earlier time ⟨an *old* ailment⟩ ⟨they brought up the same *old* argument⟩ **c** : of long standing ⟨an *old* friend⟩
2 a : distinguished from an object of the same kind by being of an earlier date ⟨many still used the *old* name⟩ **b** *capitalized* : belonging to an early period in the development of a language or literature ⟨*Old* Persian⟩
3 : having existed for a specified period of time ⟨a girl three years *old*⟩
4 : of, relating to, or originating in a past era ⟨*old* chronicles record the event⟩
5 a : advanced in years or age ⟨an *old* man⟩ **b** : showing the characteristics of age ⟨looked *old* at 20⟩
6 : EXPERIENCED ⟨an *old* trooper speaking of the last war⟩
7 : FORMER ⟨his *old* students⟩
8 a : showing the effects of time or use : WORN, AGED ⟨*old* shoes⟩ **b** : well advanced toward reduction by running water to the lowest level possible — used of topographic features **c** : no longer in use : DISCARDED ⟨*old* rags⟩ **d** : of a grayish or dusty color ⟨*old* mauve⟩ **e** : TIRESOME ⟨gets *old* fast⟩
9 a : long familiar ⟨same *old* story⟩ ⟨good *old* Joe⟩ **b** — used as an intensive ⟨a high *old* time⟩ **c** — used to express an attitude of affection or amusement ⟨a big *old* dog⟩ ⟨flex the *old* biceps⟩ ⟨any *old* time⟩ ☆

²old *noun* (13th century)
1 : one of a specified age — usually used in combination ⟨a 3-year-*old*⟩
2 : old or earlier time — used in the phrase *of old* ⟨mighty men of *old*⟩

old boy *noun* (1868)
1 *often O&B capitalized, British* : an alumnus especially of a boys' school

2 : a man who is a member of a long-standing and usually influential clique especially in a professional, business, or social sphere

Old Bulgarian *noun* (1861)
: OLD CHURCH SLAVONIC

Old Catholic *noun* (1871)
: a member of one of various hierarchical and liturgical churches separating from the Roman Catholic Church at various times since the 18th century

Old Christmas *noun* (1863)
chiefly Midland : EPIPHANY 1

Old Church Slavonic *noun* (circa 1929)
: the Slavic language used in the liturgical and Biblical translations of Cyril and Methodius as attested in manuscripts of the 10th and 11th centuries — called also *Old Church Slavic*; see INDO-EUROPEAN LANGUAGES table

old country *noun, often O&C capitalized* (1782)
: an emigrant's country of origin; *especially* : one in Europe — usually used with *the*

old·en \'ōl-dən\ *adjective* (14th century)
: of or relating to a bygone era

Old English *noun* (13th century)
1 a : the language of the English people from the time of the earliest documents in the 7th century to about 1100 — see INDO-EUROPEAN LANGUAGES table **b** : English of any period before Modern English
2 : BLACK LETTER

Old English sheepdog *noun* (1891)
: any of a breed of tailless dogs developed in England and having a profuse bluegray and white coat

Old English sheepdog

old·fan·gled \'ōl(d)-'faŋ-gəld\ *adjective* [*old* + *-fangled* (as in *newfangled*)] (1842)
: OLD-FASHIONED

¹old–fash·ioned \-'fa-shənd\ *adjective* (1596)
1 a : of, relating to, or characteristic of a past era ⟨wears an *old-fashioned* black bow tie —Green Peyton⟩ **b** : adhering to customs of a past era
2 : OUTMODED
— **old–fash·ioned·ly** \-shən(d)-lē\ *adverb*
— **old–fash·ioned·ness** \-nəs\ *noun*

²old–fashioned *noun* (1901)
: a cocktail usually made with whiskey, bitters, sugar, a twist of lemon peel, and a small amount of water or soda

Old French *noun* (1708)
: the French language from the 9th to the 16th century; *especially* : French from the 9th to the 13th century — see INDO-EUROPEAN LANGUAGES table

Old Glory *noun* (1862)
: the flag of the U.S.

old gold *noun* (1879)
: a dark yellow

old guard *noun, often O&G capitalized* (1850)
1 : a group of established prestige and influence
2 : the conservative members of an organization (as a political party)

old hand *noun* (circa 1785)
: HAND 10e

old hat *adjective* (1911)
1 : OLD-FASHIONED
2 : lacking in freshness : TRITE

Old High German *noun* (circa 1884)
: High German exemplified in documents prior to the 12th century — see INDO-EUROPEAN LANGUAGES table

old·ie \'ōl-dē\ *noun* (1874)
: one that is old; *especially* : a popular song of an earlier day

Old Ionic *noun* (circa 1889)
: the Greek dialect of the Homeric epics

Old Iranian *noun* (1939)
: any Iranian language in use in the period B.C.

Old Irish *noun* (circa 1884)
: the Irish in use from the 7th century to about 950 — see INDO-EUROPEAN LANGUAGES table

old·ish \'ōl-dish\ *adjective* (circa 1669)
: somewhat old or elderly

old lady *noun* (1836)
1 : WIFE
2 : MOTHER
3 : GIRLFRIEND; *especially* : one with whom a man cohabits

Old Latin *noun* (circa 1889)
: Latin used in the early inscriptions and in literature prior to the classical period

old–line \'ōl(d)-'līn\ *adjective* (1856)
1 a : having a reputation or authority based on length or proven quality of service ⟨an *old-line* firm⟩ **b** : of established prestige and influence ⟨*old-line* families⟩
2 : adhering to traditional policies or practices : CONSERVATIVE

old maid *noun* (circa 1530)
1 : SPINSTER 3
2 : a prim fussy person ⟨he was a real *old maid* about burning rubbish —R. C. Ruark⟩
3 : a simple card game in which cards are matched in pairs and the player holding the unmatched card at the end loses
— **old–maid·ish** \'ōl(d)-'mā-dish\ *adjective*
— **old–maid·ish·ness** \-nəs\ *noun*

old man *noun* (1768)
1 a : HUSBAND **b** : FATHER
2 *capitalized* : one in authority; *especially* : COMMANDING OFFICER
3 : BOYFRIEND; *especially* : one with whom a woman cohabits

old–man's beard \'ōl(d)-'manz-\ *noun* (1742)
1 : any of several clematises (especially *Clematis vitalba*) having plumose styles
2 : a greenish gray pendulous lichen (*Usnea barbata*) growing on trees

old master *noun* (1824)
: a work of art by an established master and especially by any of the distinguished painters of the 16th, 17th, or early 18th century; *also* : such an artist

Old Nick \'ōl(d)-'nik\ *noun* (1668)
— used as a name of the devil

☆ **SYNONYMS**
Old, ancient, venerable, antique, antiquated, archaic, obsolete mean having come into existence or use in the more or less distant past. OLD may apply to either actual or merely relative length of existence ⟨*old* houses⟩ ⟨an *old* sweater of mine⟩. ANCIENT applies to occurrence, existence, or use in or survival from the distant past ⟨*ancient* accounts of dragons⟩. VENERABLE stresses the impressiveness and dignity of great age ⟨the family's *venerable* patriarch⟩. ANTIQUE applies to what has come down from a former or ancient time ⟨collected *antique* Chippendale furniture⟩. ANTIQUATED implies being discredited or outmoded or otherwise inappropriate to the present time ⟨*antiquated* teaching methods⟩. ARCHAIC implies having the character or characteristics of a much earlier time ⟨the play used *archaic* language to convey a sense of period⟩. OBSOLETE may apply to something regarded as no longer acceptable or useful even though it is still in existence ⟨a computer that makes earlier models *obsolete*⟩.

\ə\ **abut** \ᵊ\ **kitten** \ər\ **further** \a\ **ash** \ā\ **ace**
\ä\ **mop, mar** \au̇\ **out** \ch\ **chin** \e\ **bet** \ē\ **easy**
\g\ **go** \i\ **hit** \ī\ **ice** \j\ **job** \ŋ\ **sing** \ō\ **go**
\ȯ\ **law** \ȯi\ **boy** \th\ **thin** \t͟h\ **the** \ü\ **loot** \u̇\ **foot**
\y\ **yet** \zh\ **vision** *see also* Guide to Pronunciation

Old Norse *noun* (1844)
: the North Germanic language of the Scandinavian peoples prior to about 1350 — see INDO-EUROPEAN LANGUAGES table

Old North French *noun* (circa 1930)
: the northern dialects of Old French including especially those of Normandy and Picardy

Old Persian *noun* (circa 1909)
: an ancient Iranian language known from cuneiform inscriptions from the 5th and 6th centuries B.C. — see INDO-EUROPEAN LANGUAGES table

Old Prussian *noun* (1872)
: a Baltic language used in East Prussia until the 17th century — see INDO-EUROPEAN LANGUAGES table

old rose *noun* (1893)
: a variable color averaging a grayish red

Old Saxon *noun* (1841)
: the language of the Saxons of northwest Germany until about the 12th century — see INDO-EUROPEAN LANGUAGES table

old school *noun* (1749)
: adherents of traditional policies and practices

old school tie *noun* (1932)
1 a : an attitude of conservatism, aplomb, and upper-class solidarity associated with English public school graduates **b** : a necktie displaying the colors of an English public school
2 : clannishness among members of an established clique

old-shoe \'ōl(d)-'shü\ *adjective* (1944)
: characterized by familiarity or freedom from restraint : COMFORTABLE, UNPRETENTIOUS

old sledge *noun* (1830)
: SEVEN-UP

old-squaw \'ōl(d)-'skwo\ *noun* (1838)
: a common sea duck (*Clangula hyemalis*) of the more northern parts of the northern hemisphere

old-ster \'ōl(d)-stər\ *noun* (1848)
: an old or elderly person

old style *noun* (1617)
1 *O&S capitalized* : a style of reckoning time used before the adoption of the Gregorian calendar
2 : a style of type distinguished by graceful irregularity among individual letters, bracketed serifs, and but slight contrast between light and heavy strokes

Old Style *adjective* (1678)
: using or according to the Julian calendar

Old Swedish *noun* (circa 1909)
: the Swedish language as exemplified in documents prior to about 1350

Old Testament *noun* (14th century)
: the first part of the Christian Bible containing the books of the Jewish canon of Scripture — see BIBLE table

old-time \'ōl(d)-'tīm\ *adjective* (1824)
1 : of, relating to, or characteristic of an earlier period ⟨*old-time* songs⟩
2 : of long standing ⟨*old-time* residents⟩

old-tim-er \-'tī-mər, -,tī-mər\ *noun* (1879)
1 a : VETERAN **b** : OLDSTER
2 : something that is old-fashioned : ANTIQUE

old-timey \'ōl(d)-'tī-mē\ *adjective* (1850)
: of a kind or style prevalent in or reminiscent of an earlier time ⟨*old-timey* music⟩

Old Welsh *noun* (1882)
: the Welsh language exemplified in documents prior to about 1150 — see INDO-EUROPEAN LANGUAGES table

old-wife \'ōl(d)-,wīf\ *noun* (1588)
1 : any of several marine fishes (as an alewife, menhaden, or triggerfish)
2 : OLD-SQUAW

old wives' tale *noun* (1656)
: an often traditional belief that is not based on fact : SUPERSTITION

old-world \'ōl(d)-'wər(-ə)ld\ *adjective* (1712)
: of, relating to, or characteristic of the Old World; *especially* : having the charm or picturesque qualities of the Old World ⟨narrow *old-world* streets⟩

Old World *noun* (circa 1596)
: the eastern hemisphere exclusive of Australia; *specifically* : Europe

ole \'ōl\ *adjective* [by alteration] (1844)
: OLD

ole- *or* **oleo-** *combining form* [French olé-, oléo-, from Latin ole-, from oleum — more at OIL]
: oil ⟨*oleo*graph⟩

-ole *also* **-ol** *noun combining form* [International Scientific Vocabulary, from Latin oleum]
1 : chemical compound containing a 5-membered usually heterocyclic ring ⟨pyrr*ole*⟩
2 : chemical compound not containing hydroxyl ⟨eucalypt*ol*⟩ — especially in names of ethers ⟨safr*ole*⟩

olé \ō-'lā\ *noun* [Spanish] (1922)
: ²BRAVO

ole-ag-i-nous \,ō-lē-'a-jə-nəs\ *adjective* [Middle English, from Middle French oleagineux, from Latin oleagineus of an olive tree, from olea olive tree, from Greek elaia] (15th century)
1 : resembling or having the properties of oil : OILY; *also* : containing or producing oil
2 : marked by an offensively ingratiating manner or quality
— **ole-ag-i-nous-ly** *adverb*
— **ole-ag-i-nous-ness** *noun*

ole-an-der \'ō-lē-,an-dər, ,ō-lē-'\ *noun* [Medieval Latin, alteration of arodandrum, lorandrum, perhaps alteration of Latin rhododendron — more at RHODODENDRON] (1548)
: a poisonous evergreen shrub (*Nerium oleander*) of the dogbane family with fragrant white to red flowers

ole-an-do-my-cin \,ō-lē-,an-də-'mī-s°n\ *noun* [oleandrose, a sugar derived from oleandrin (a glycoside contained in oleander leaves) + -o- + -mycin] (1956)
: an antibiotic $C_{35}H_{61}NO_{12}$ produced by a streptomyces (*Streptomyces antibioticus*)

ole-as-ter \'ō-lē-,as-tər, ,ō-lē-'\ *noun* [Middle English, from Latin, from olea] (14th century)
: any of several plants (genus *Elaeagnus* of the family Elaeagnaceae, the oleaster family) having alternate leaves and perfect flowers with four stamens; *especially* : RUSSIAN OLIVE

ole-ate \'ō-lē-,āt\ *noun* (circa 1823)
: a salt or ester of oleic acid

olec-ra-non \ō-'le-krə-,nän\ *noun* [New Latin, from Greek ōlekranon, from ōlenē elbow + kranion skull — more at ELL, CRANIUM] (circa 1741)
: the process of the ulna projecting behind the elbow joint

ole-fin \'ō-lə-fən\ *noun* [International Scientific Vocabulary, from French (gaz) oléfiant ethylene, from Latin oleum] (1860)
1 : ALKENE
2 : a synthetic fiber (as polypropylene) derived from an alkene
— **ole-fin-ic** \,ō-lə-'fi-nik\ *adjective*

oleic acid *noun* (1819)
: a monounsaturated fatty acid $C_{18}H_{34}O_2$ found in natural fats and oils

ole-in \'ō-lē-ən\ *noun* [French oléine, from Latin oleum] (1838)
1 : an ester of glycerol and oleic acid
2 : the liquid portion of a fat

oleo \'ō-lē-,ō\ *noun* [short for oleomargarine] (1884)
: MARGARINE

oleo-graph \'ō-lē-ə-,graf\ *noun* [International Scientific Vocabulary] (1873)
: a chromolithograph printed on cloth to imitate an oil painting

oleo-mar-ga-rine \,ō-lē-ō-'mär-jə-rən, -,rēn; -'märj-rən\ *noun* [French oléomargarine, from olé- + margarine margarine] (1873)
: MARGARINE

oleo-res-in \,ō-lē-ō-'re-z°n\ *noun* [International Scientific Vocabulary] (circa 1846)
1 : a natural plant product (as copaiba) containing chiefly essential oil and resin; *especially* : TURPENTINE 1b
2 : a preparation consisting essentially of oil holding resin in solution
— **oleo-res-in-ous** \-'re-z°n-əs, -'rez-nəs\ *adjective*

ole-um \'ō-lē-əm\ *noun* [Latin, olive oil — more at OIL] (circa 1823)
1 *plural* **olea** \-lē-ə\ : OIL
2 *plural* **oleums** : a heavy oily strongly corrosive solution of sulfur trioxide in anhydrous sulfuric acid

O level *noun* (1949)
1 : the lowest of three levels of standardized British examinations in a secondary school subject; *also* : successful completion of an O-level examination in a particular subject — called also *Ordinary level*; compare A LEVEL, S LEVEL
2 a : the level of education required to pass an O-level examination **b** : a course leading to an O-level examination

ol-fac-tion \äl-'fak-shən, ōl-\ *noun* (circa 1846)
1 : the sense of smell
2 : the act or process of smelling

ol-fac-tom-e-ter \,äl-,fak-'tä-mə-tər, ,ōl-\ *noun* (1889)
: an instrument for measuring the sensitivity of the sense of smell

ol-fac-to-ry \äl-'fak-t(ə-)rē, ōl-\ *adjective* [Latin olfactorius, from olfacere to smell, from olēre to smell + facere to do — more at ODOR, DO] (circa 1658)
: of, relating to, or connected with the sense of smell

olfactory bulb *noun* (circa 1860)
: a bulbous anterior projection of the olfactory lobe that is the place of termination of the olfactory nerves and is especially well developed in lower vertebrates (as fishes)

olfactory lobe *noun* (circa 1860)
: an anterior projection of each cerebral hemisphere that is continuous anteriorly with the olfactory nerve

olfactory nerve *noun* (1670)
: either of the pair of nerves that are the first cranial nerves and that arise in the olfactory neurosensory cells of the nasal mucous membrane and pass to the anterior part of the cerebrum

olig- *or* **oligo-** *combining form* [Medieval Latin, from Greek, from oligos; perhaps akin to Armenian atkat scant]
: few ⟨*oligo*phagous⟩

ol-i-garch \'ä-lə-,gärk, 'ō-\ *noun* [Greek oligarchēs, from olig- + -archēs -arch] (circa 1610)
: a member or supporter of an oligarchy

ol-i-gar-chic \,ä-lə-'gär-kik, ,ō-\ *or* **ol-i-gar-chi-cal** \-ki-kəl\ *adjective* (1586)
: of, relating to, or based on an oligarchy

ol-i-gar-chy \'ä-lə-,gär-kē, 'ō-\ *noun, plural* **-chies** (1542)
1 : government by the few
2 : a government in which a small group exercises control especially for corrupt and selfish purposes; *also* : a group exercising such control
3 : an organization under oligarchic control

Ol-i-go-cene \'ä-li-gō-,sēn, 'ō-, ə-'li-gə-\ *adjective* [International Scientific Vocabulary] (circa 1859)
: of, relating to, or being an epoch of the Tertiary between the Eocene and Miocene or the corresponding system of rocks — see GEOLOGIC TIME table
— **Oligocene** *noun*

ol-i-go-chaete \-,kēt\ *noun* [New Latin Oligochaeta, ultimately from Greek olig- + chaitē long hair] (1896)

: any of a class or order (Oligochaeta) of hermaphroditic terrestrial or aquatic annelids (as an earthworm) that lack a specialized head
— **oligochaete** *adjective*

ol·i·go·clase \'ä-li-gō-,klās, 'ō-, -,klāz; ə-'li-gə-\ *noun* [German *Oligoklas*, from *olig-* olig- + Greek *klasis* breaking, from *klan* to break — more at CLAST] (1832)
: a mineral of the plagioclase series

ol·i·go·den·dro·cyte \'ä-li-gō-'den-drə-,sīt, 'ō-; ə-,li-gə-\ *noun* [International Scientific Vocabulary, from *olig-* + *dendr-* + *-cyte*] (1932)
: a neuroglial cell resembling an astrocyte but smaller with few and slender processes having few branches

ol·i·go·den·drog·lia \-den-'drä-glē-ə, -'drò\ *noun* [New Latin, from *oligodendro*cyte + *-glia* (form of neuroglia)] (1924)
: neuroglia made up of oligodendrocytes that is held to function in myelin formation in the central nervous system
— **ol·i·go·den·drog·li·al** \-glē-əl\ *adjective*

olig·o·mer \ə-'li-gə-mər\ *noun* (1952)
: a polymer or polymer intermediate containing relatively few structural units
— **olig·o·mer·ic** \-,li-gə-'mer-ik\ *adjective*
— **olig·o·mer·i·za·tion** \-mə-rə-'zā-shən\ *noun*

ol·i·go·nu·cle·o·tide \-'nü-klē-ə-,tīd, -'nyü-\ *noun* (1942)
: a chain of usually up to 20 nucleotides

ol·i·goph·a·gous \,ä-lə-'gä-fə-gəs, ,ō-\ *adjective* (1920)
: eating only a few specific kinds of food
— **ol·i·goph·a·gy** \-'gä-fə-jē\ *noun*

ol·i·gop·o·ly \-'gä-pə-lē\ *noun* [*olig-* + *-poly* (as in *monopoly*)] (1895)
: a market situation in which each of a few producers affects but does not control the market
— **ol·i·gop·o·lis·tic** \-,gä-pə-'lis-tik\ *adjective*

ol·i·gop·so·ny \-'gäp-sə-nē\ *noun* [*olig-* + Greek *opsōnia* purchase of victuals, from *opsōnein* to purchase victuals, from *opson* food + *ōneisthai* to buy — more at VENAL] (1942)
: a market situation in which each of a few buyers exerts a disproportionate influence on the market
— **ol·i·gop·so·nis·tic** \-,gäp-sə-'nis-tik\ *adjective*

ol·i·go·sac·cha·ride \,ä-li-gō-'sa-kə-,rīd, ,ō-; ə-'li-gə-\ *noun* [International Scientific Vocabulary] (1930)
: a saccharide (as a disaccharide) that contains a known small number of monosaccharide units

ol·i·go·tro·phic \-'trō-fik\ *adjective* [International Scientific Vocabulary] (1928)
: deficient in plant nutrients ⟨*oligotrophic* boggy acid soils⟩; *especially* : having abundant dissolved oxygen ⟨an *oligotrophic* body of water⟩ — compare EUTROPHIC, MESOTROPHIC

olio \'ō-lē-,ō\ *noun, plural* **oli·os** [modification of Spanish *olla*] (circa 1643)
1 : OLLA PODRIDA 1
2 a : a miscellaneous mixture : HODGEPODGE **b** : a miscellaneous collection (as of literary or musical selections)

ol·i·va·ceous \,ä-lə-'vā-shəs\ *adjective* (1776)
: OLIVE 1

¹ol·ive \'ä-liv, -ləv\ *noun* [Middle English, from Old French, from Latin *oliva*, from Greek *elaia*] (13th century)
1 a : a Mediterranean evergreen tree (*Olea europaea* of the family Oleaceae, the olive family) cultivated for its drupaceous fruit that is an important food and source of oil; *also* : the fruit **b** : any of various shrubs and trees resembling the olive
2 : any of several colors resembling that of the unripe fruit of the olive tree that are yellowish green

3 : an oval eminence on each ventrolateral aspect of the medulla oblongata

²olive *adjective* (1657)
1 : of the color olive or olive green
2 : approaching olive in color or complexion

olive branch *noun* (14th century)
1 : a branch of the olive tree especially when used as a symbol of peace
2 : an offer or gesture of conciliation or goodwill

olive drab *noun* (1897)
1 : a grayish olive
2 a : a wool or cotton fabric of an olive drab color **b** : a uniform of this fabric

olive green *noun* (circa 1757)
: a greenish olive

oliv·en·ite \ō-'li-və-,nīt\ *noun* [German *Olivenit*, from *oliven-*, *olive* (mineral)] (1820)
: a mineral that is a basic arsenate of copper

Ol·i·ver \'ä-lə-vər\ *noun* [French *Olivier*]
: the close friend of Roland in the Charlemagne legends

ol·iv·ine \'ä-lə-,vēn\ *noun* [German *Olivin*, from Latin *oliva*] (1794)
: a usually greenish mineral that is a complex silicate of magnesium and iron used especially in refractories — compare PERIDOT
— **ol·iv·in·ic** \-'vi-nik\ *or* **ol·iv·in·it·ic** \-və-'ni-tik\ *adjective*

ol·la \'ä-lə, 'ò-lə\ *noun* [Spanish, from Latin *olla, aulla* pot; akin to Sanskrit *ukhā* pot and probably to Gothic *auhns* oven] (1622)
: a large bulging widemouthed earthenware vessel sometimes with looped handles used (as by Pueblo Indians) for storage, cooking, or as a container for water

olla

ol·la po·dri·da \-pə-'drē-də\ *noun, plural* **olla podridas** \-'drē-dəz\ *also* **ollas podridas** [Spanish, literally, rotten pot] (1599)
1 : a rich highly seasoned stew of meat and vegetables usually including sausage and chick-peas that is slowly simmered and is a traditional Spanish and Latin-American dish
2 : HODGEPODGE

olo·li·u·qui \,ō-,lō-lē-'ü-kē\ *noun* [Spanish *ololiuque*, from Nahuatl *ololiuhqui*, literally, something rolled into a ball] (1915)
: a woody stemmed Mexican vine (*Rivea corymbosa*) of the morning glory family having small fleshy fruits with single seeds that are used especially by the Indians for medicinal, narcotic, and religious purposes

olo·ro·so \,ō-lə-'rō-(,)sō\ *noun, plural* **-sos** [Spanish, from *oloroso* fragrant, from *olor* odor, from Latin, from *olēre* to smell — more at ODOR] (1876)
: a dry full-bodied Spanish sherry

olym·pi·ad \ə-'lim-pē-,ad, ō-\ *noun, often capitalized* [Middle English, from Middle French *Olympiade*, from Latin *Olympiad-, Olympias*, from Greek, from *Olympia*, site of ancient Olympic Games] (14th century)
1 : one of the 4-year intervals between Olympic Games by which time was reckoned in ancient Greece
2 : a quadrennial celebration of the modern Olympic Games

¹Olym·pi·an \-pē-ən\ *adjective* (15th century)
1 : of or relating to Mount Olympus in Thessaly
2 : befitting or characteristic of an Olympian; *especially* : LOFTY ⟨his . . . formula of glib simplicity and *Olympian* arrogance —Richard Pollak⟩

²Olympian *adjective* (1593)
1 : of or relating to the ancient Greek region of Olympia

2 : of, relating to, or constituting the Olympic Games

³Olympian *noun* (1606)
: a participant in Olympic Games

⁴Olympian *noun* (1843)
1 : one of the ancient Greek deities dwelling on Olympus
2 : a being of lofty detachment or superior attainments

Olympian Games *noun plural* (1593)
: OLYMPIC GAMES 1

Olym·pia oyster \ə-'lim-pē-ə-, ō-\ *noun* [*Olympia*, Washington] (1908)
: a small flavorful native oyster (*Ostrea lurida*) of the Puget Sound area of the Pacific coast of North America — called also *Olympia*

Olym·pic \ə-'lim-pik, ō-\ *adjective* (1590)
1 : ¹OLYMPIAN
2 : of or relating to the Olympic Games

Olympic Games *noun plural* (circa 1610)
1 : an ancient Panhellenic festival held every fourth year and made up of contests of sports, music, and literature with the victor's prize a crown of wild olive
2 : a modified revival of the ancient Olympic Games consisting of international athletic contests that are held at separate winter and summer gatherings at four year intervals — called also *Olympics*

Olym·pus \ə-'lim-pəs, ō-\ *noun* [Latin, from Greek *Olympos*] (1580)
: a mountain in Thessaly that in Greek mythology is the abode of the gods

om \'ōm\ *noun* [Sanskrit] (1788)
: a mantra consisting of the sound \'ōm\ and used in contemplation of ultimate reality

-oma *noun suffix, plural* **-omas** *or* **-omata** [Latin *omat-, -oma*, from Greek *-ōmat-, -ōma*, from *-ō-* (stem vowel of causative verbs in *-oun*) + *-mat-, -ma*, suffix denoting result — more at -MENT]
: tumor ⟨aden*oma*⟩ ⟨fibr*oma*⟩

Oma·ha \'ō-mə-,hò, -,hä\ *noun, plural* **Omaha** *or* **Omahas** (1804)
: a member of an American Indian people of northeastern Nebraska

oma·sum \ō-'mā-səm\ *noun, plural* **oma·sa** \-sə\ [New Latin, from Latin, tripe of a bullock] (circa 1706)
: the third chamber of the ruminant stomach that is situated between the reticulum and the abomasum — compare RUMEN

om·bre \'äm-bər; 'äm-brē, 'əm-, -,brä\ *noun* [French or Spanish; French *hombre*, from Spanish, literally, man — more at HOMBRE] (circa 1661)
: an old three-handed card game popular in Europe especially in the 17th and 18th centuries

om·bré \'äm-,brā\ *adjective* [French, past participle of *ombrer* to shade, from Italian *ombrare*, from *ombra* shade, from Latin *umbra* — more at UMBRAGE] (circa 1896)
: having colors or tones that shade into each other — used especially of fabrics in which the color is graduated from light to dark
— **ombré** *noun*

om·buds·man \'äm-,bùdz-mən, 'òm-, -bədz-, -,man; äm-'bùdz-, òm-\ *noun, plural* **-men** \-mən\ [Swedish, literally, representative, from Old Norse *umbothsmathr*, from *umboth* commission + *mathr* man] (1959)
1 : a government official (as in Sweden or New Zealand) appointed to receive and investigate complaints made by individuals against abuses or capricious acts of public officials

\ə\ **abut** \ə\ **kitten** \ər\ **further** \a\ **ash** \ā\ **ace** \ä\ **mop, mar** \aù\ **out** \ch\ **chin** \e\ **bet** \ē\ **easy** \g\ **go** \i\ **hit** \ī\ **ice** \j\ **job** \ŋ\ **sing** \ō\ **go** \ò\ **law** \òi\ **boy** \th\ **thin** \t͟h\ **the** \ü\ **loot** \ù\ **foot** \y\ **yet** \zh\ **vision** *see also* Guide to Pronunciation

2 : one that investigates reported complaints (as from students or consumers), reports findings, and helps to achieve equitable settlements ◇
— **om·buds·man·ship** \-,ship\ *noun*

-ome *noun suffix* [New Latin *-oma*, from Latin, *-oma*]
: mass ⟨phyll*ome*⟩

ome·ga \ō-'mā-gə, -'mē-, -'me-\ *noun* [Middle English, from Middle French, from Greek *ō mega*, literally, large o] (15th century)
1 : the 24th and last letter of the Greek alphabet — see ALPHABET table
2 : LAST, ENDING
3 a : a negatively charged elementary particle that has a mass 3270 times the mass of an electron — called also *omega minus* **b :** a very short-lived unstable meson with mass 1532 times the mass of an electron — called also *omega meson*

ome·ga–3 \-'thrē\ *adjective* (1980)
: being or composed of polyunsaturated fatty acids that have the final double bond in the hydrocarbon chain between the third and fourth carbon atoms from one end of the molecule and that are found especially in fish, fish oils, vegetable oils, and green leafy vegetables

om·e·lette *or* **om·e·let** \'äm-lət, 'ä-mə-\ *noun* [French *omelette*, alteration of Middle French *alumelle*, literally, knife blade, modification of Latin *lamella*, diminutive of *lamina* thin plate] (circa 1611)
: beaten eggs cooked without stirring until set and served folded in half ◇

omen \'ō-mən\ *noun* [Latin *omin-, omen*] (1582)
: an occurrence or phenomenon believed to portend a future event **:** AUGURY

omen·tum \ō-'men-təm\ *noun, plural* **-ta** \-tə\ *or* **-tums** [Latin; perhaps akin to Latin *indu-ere* to put on, *exuere* to take off — more at EXUVIAE] (1547)
: a fold of peritoneum connecting or supporting abdominal structures (as the viscera); *also*
: a fold of peritoneum free at one end
— **omen·tal** \-'men-t°l\ *adjective*

omer \'ō-mər\ *noun* [Hebrew *'ōmer*] (circa 1608)
1 : an ancient Hebrew unit of dry capacity equal to 1/10 ephah
2 a *often capitalized* **:** the sheaf of barley traditionally offered in Jewish Temple worship on the second day of the Passover **b** *capitalized* **:** a 7-week liturgical period of expectancy between the second day of the Passover and Shabuoth

omi·cron \'ä-mə-,krän, 'ō-, *British* ō-'mī-(,)krän\ *noun* [Middle English, from Middle French, from Greek *o mikron*, literally, small o] (15th century)
: the 15th letter of the Greek alphabet — see ALPHABET table

om·i·nous \'ä-mə-nəs\ *adjective* (1587)
: being or exhibiting an omen **:** PORTENTOUS; *especially* **:** foreboding or foreshowing evil **:** INAUSPICIOUS ☆
— **om·i·nous·ly** *adverb*
— **om·i·nous·ness** *noun*

omis·si·ble \ō-'mi-sə-bəl\ *adjective* (1816)
: that may be omitted

omis·sion \ō-'mi-shən, ə-\ *noun* [Middle English *omissioun*, from Late Latin *omission-, omissio*, from Latin *omittere*] (14th century)
1 a : something neglected or left undone **b :** apathy toward or neglect of duty
2 : the act of omitting **:** the state of being omitted

omit \ō-'mit, ə-\ *transitive verb* **omit·ted; omit·ting** [Middle English *omitten*, from Latin *omittere*, from *ob-* toward + *mittere* to let go, send — more at OB-] (15th century)
1 : to leave out or leave unmentioned
2 : to fail to perform or make use of **:** FORBEAR
3 *obsolete* **:** DISREGARD
4 *obsolete* **:** GIVE UP

om·ma·tid·i·um \,ä-mə-'ti-dē-əm\ *noun, plural* **-tid·ia** \-dē-ə\ [New Latin, from Greek *ommat-, omma* eye; akin to Greek *ōps* eye — more at EYE] (1884)
: one of the elements corresponding to a small simple eye that make up the compound eye of an arthropod
— **om·ma·tid·i·al** \-dē-əl\ *adjective*

omni- *combining form* [Latin, from *omnis*]
: all **:** universally ⟨*omni*directional⟩

¹**om·ni·bus** \'äm-ni-(,)bəs\ *noun* [French, from Latin, for all, dative plural of *omnis*] (1829)
1 : a usually automotive public vehicle designed to carry a large number of passengers **:** BUS
2 : a book containing reprints of a number of works

²**omnibus** *adjective* (1842)
1 : of, relating to, or providing for many things at once
2 : containing or including many items

om·ni·com·pe·tent \,äm-ni-'käm-pə-tənt\ *adjective* (1827)
: able to handle any situation; *especially* **:** having the authority or legal capacity to act in all matters
— **om·ni·com·pe·tence** \-tən(t)s\ *noun*

om·ni·di·rec·tion·al \,äm-ni-də-'rek-shnəl, -,nī-, -(,)dī-, -shə-n°l\ *adjective* (1927)
: being in or involving all directions; *especially* **:** receiving or sending radio waves equally well in all directions ⟨*omni*directional antenna⟩

om·ni·far·i·ous \,äm-nə-'far-ē-əs, -'fer-\ *adjective* [Late Latin *omnifarius*, from Latin *omni-* + *-farius* (as in *multifarius* diverse) — more at MULTIFARIOUS] (1653)
: of all varieties, forms, or kinds

om·nif·i·cent \äm-'ni-fə-sənt\ *adjective* [Latin *omni-* + English *-ficent* (as in *magnificent*)] (1677)
: unlimited in creative power

om·nip·o·tence \äm-'ni-pə-tən(t)s\ *noun* (15th century)
1 : the quality or state of being omnipotent
2 : an agency or force of unlimited power

¹**om·nip·o·tent** \-tənt\ *adjective* [Middle English, from Middle French, from Latin *omnipotent-, omnipotens*, from *omni-* + *potent-, potens* potent] (14th century)
1 *often capitalized* **:** ALMIGHTY 1
2 : having virtually unlimited authority or influence
3 *obsolete* **:** ARRANT
— **om·nip·o·tent·ly** *adverb*

²**omnipotent** *noun* (1600)
1 : one who is omnipotent
2 *capitalized* **:** GOD 1

om·ni·pres·ence \,äm-ni-'pre-z°n(t)s\ *noun* (1601)
: the quality or state of being omnipresent **:** UBIQUITY

om·ni·pres·ent \-z°nt\ *adjective* (1609)
: present in all places at all times

om·ni·range \'äm-ni-,rānj\ *noun* (1946)
: a system of radio navigation in which any bearing relative to a special radio transmitter on the ground may be chosen and flown by an airplane pilot — called also *omnidirectional range*

om·ni·science \äm-'ni-shən(t)s\ *noun* [Medieval Latin *omniscientia*, from Latin *omni-* + *scientia* knowledge — more at SCIENCE] (1612)
: the quality or state of being omniscient

om·ni·scient \-shənt\ *adjective* [New Latin *omniscient-, omnisciens*, back-formation from Medieval Latin *omniscientia*] (1604)
1 : having infinite awareness, understanding, and insight
2 : possessed of universal or complete knowledge
— **om·ni·scient·ly** *adverb*

om·ni·um–gath·er·um \,äm-nē-əm-'ga-thə-rəm\ *noun, plural* **omnium–gatherums**

[Latin *omnium* (genitive plural of *omnis*) + English *gather* + Latin *-um*, noun ending] (1530)
: a miscellaneous collection (as of things or persons)

om·ni·vore \'äm-ni-,vōr, -,vȯr\ *noun* [New Latin *omnivora*, neuter plural of *omnivorus*, from Latin] (1890)

☆ **SYNONYMS**

Ominous, portentous, fateful mean having a menacing or threatening aspect. OMINOUS implies having a menacing, alarming character foreshadowing evil or disaster ⟨*ominous* rumblings from a once-dormant volcano⟩. PORTENTOUS suggests being frighteningly big or impressive but now seldom definitely connotes forwarning of calamity ⟨an eerie and *portentous* stillness⟩. FATEFUL suggests being of momentous or decisive importance ⟨the *fateful* conference that led to war⟩.

◇ **WORD HISTORY**

ombudsman For a word that became current in late 20th century America, *ombudsman* has deep roots: it can be traced back to the Old Norse word *umbothsmathr*. Compounded from *umboth* "commission," and *mathr* "man," *umbothsmathr* had the meaning "commissary" or "manager." The word evolved into Modern Swedish *ombudsman*, acquiring the generic sense of "representative" or "commissioner." In 1809 the Swedish government established the office of *justitieombudsmannen*, or justice commissioner, who was empowered to investigate and redress the complaints of private citizens regarding abuse and maladministration on the part of public officials and bureaucrats. This functionary established a reputation as the one person to whom the victim of bureaucratic abuse could resort when other channels had failed. The concept of an ombudsman later spread to Finland, Denmark, and Norway. In 1962 New Zealand decided to appoint a comparably empowered official and to confer upon him the title of *ombudsman*. The establishment of the office of ombudsman in New Zealand inspired other parts of the English-speaking world to create their own officials with similar powers under this name.

omelette Although the word *omelette* bears little resemblance to the Latin word *lamina*, the shape of an omelette does resemble a thin plate, which is what *lamina*, the ultimate source of *omelette*, means. The Romans used the noun *lamella*, the diminutive form of *lamina*, to mean "thin metal plate." This diminutive became in Old French *lemele* "blade of a knife." By a process somewhat similar to that which produced our *apron* from an earlier *napron*, la *lemele* "the blade" was misinterpreted as *l'alemele*, which accounts for the appearance of the initial vowel. In Middle French the word *ale-melle* became *alumelle* and then was altered to *alumette*, by substitution of the suffix *-ette* for *-elle*. It also acquired the additional meaning "dish made with beaten eggs," since such a dish resembled a thin plate or blade. In turn, *alumette* was altered to *amelette* by transposition of the *l* and *m* sounds (a process called metathesis). It finally changed again (influenced by southern dialect words for "egg" descended from Old Provençal *ou*) to *omelette*. The word, now often written *omelet*, has been in English since the 17th century, when an omelette was described as "a pancake of egges."

: one that is omnivorous

om·niv·o·rous \äm-'niv-rəs, -'ni-və-\ *adjective* [Latin *omnivorus*, from *omni-* + *-vorus* *-vorous*] (circa 1656)
1 : feeding on both animal and vegetable substances
2 : avidly taking in everything as if devouring or consuming
— **om·niv·o·rous·ly** *adverb*

om·pha·los \'äm(p)-fə-ˌläs, -ləs\ *noun* [Greek, navel — more at NAVEL] (1855)
: a central point : HUB 2, FOCAL POINT

om·pha·lo·skep·sis \ˌäm(p)-fə-lō-'skep-səs\ *noun* [New Latin, from Greek *omphalos* + *skepsis* examination — more at SPY] (1925)
: contemplation of one's navel as an aid to meditation; *also* : INERTIA 2

¹on \'òn, 'än\ *preposition* [Middle English *an*, *on*, preposition & adverb, from Old English; akin to Old High German *ana* on, Greek *ana* up, on] (before 12th century)
1 a — used as a function word to indicate position in contact with and supported by the top surface of ⟨the book is lying *on* the table⟩ **b** — used as a function word to indicate position in or in contact with an outer surface ⟨the fly landed *on* the ceiling⟩ ⟨I have a cut *on* my finger⟩ ⟨paint *on* the wall⟩ **c** — used as a function word to indicate position in close proximity with ⟨a village *on* the sea⟩ ⟨stay *on* your opponent⟩ **d** — used as a function word to indicate direction or location with respect to something ⟨*on* the south⟩ ⟨the garden is *on* the side of the house⟩
2 a — used as a function word to indicate a source of attachment or support ⟨*on* a string⟩ ⟨stand *on* one foot⟩ ⟨hang it *on* a nail⟩ **b** — used as a function word to indicate a source of dependence ⟨you can rely *on* me⟩ ⟨feeds *on* insects⟩ ⟨lives *on* a pension⟩ **c** — used as a function word to indicate means of conveyance ⟨*on* the bus⟩ or presence within the confines or in possession of ⟨had a knife *on* him⟩
3 — used as a function word to indicate a time frame during which something takes place ⟨a parade *on* Sunday⟩ or an instant, action, or occurrence when something begins or is done ⟨*on* cue⟩ ⟨*on* arriving home, I found your letter⟩ ⟨news *on* the hour⟩ ⟨cash *on* delivery⟩
4 *archaic* : OF
5 a — used as a function word to indicate manner of doing something; often used with *the* ⟨*on* the sly⟩ ⟨keep everything *on* the up-and-up⟩ **b** — used as a function word to indicate means or agency ⟨cut myself *on* a knife⟩ ⟨talk *on* the telephone⟩ **c** — used as a function word to indicate a medium of expression; used originally to refer to physical position ⟨best show *on* television⟩
6 a (1) — used as a function word to indicate active involvement in a condition or status ⟨*on* fire⟩ ⟨*on* the increase⟩ ⟨*on* the lookout⟩ (2) : regularly using or showing the effects of using ⟨*on* drugs⟩ **b** — used as a function word to indicate involvement with the activity, work, or function of ⟨*on* tour⟩ ⟨*on* the jury⟩ ⟨*on* duty⟩ **c** — used as a function word to indicate position or status in proper relationship with a standard or objective ⟨*on* schedule⟩
7 a — used as a function word to indicate reason, ground, or basis ⟨as for an action, opinion, or computation⟩ ⟨I have it *on* good authority⟩ ⟨*on* one condition⟩ ⟨the interest will be 10 cents *on* the dollar⟩ **b** — used as a function word to indicate the cause or source ⟨profited *on* the sale of stock⟩ **c** — used as a function word to indicate the focus of obligation or responsibility ⟨drinks are *on* the house⟩ ⟨put the blame *on* my actions⟩
8 a — used as a function word to indicate the object of collision, opposition, or hostile action ⟨bumped my head *on* a limb⟩ ⟨an attack *on* religion⟩ ⟨pulled a gun *on* me⟩ **b** — used as a function word to indicate the object with respect to some disadvantage, handicap, or

detriment ⟨has three inches in height *on* me⟩ ⟨a 3-game lead *on* the second-place team⟩ ⟨the joke's *on* me⟩
9 a — used as a function word to indicate destination or the focus of some action, movement, or directed effort ⟨crept up *on* him⟩ ⟨feast your eyes *on* this⟩ ⟨working *on* my skiing⟩ ⟨made a payment *on* the loan⟩ **b** — used as a function word to indicate the focus of feelings, determination, or will ⟨have pity *on* me⟩ ⟨keen *on* sports⟩ ⟨a curse *on* you⟩ **c** — used as a function word to indicate the object with respect to some misfortune or disadvantageous event ⟨the crops died *on* them⟩ **d** — used as a function word to indicate the subject of study, discussion, or consideration ⟨a book *on* insects⟩ ⟨reflect *on* that a moment⟩ ⟨agree *on* price⟩
10 — used as a function word to indicate reduplication or succession in a series ⟨loss *on* loss⟩

²on *adverb* (before 12th century)
1 a : in or into a position of contact with an upper surface especially so as to be positioned for use or operation ⟨put the plates *on*⟩ **b** : in or into a position of being attached to or covering a surface; *especially* : in or into the condition of being worn ⟨put his new shoes *on*⟩
2 a : forward or at a more advanced point in space or time ⟨went *on* home⟩ ⟨later *on*⟩ **b** : in continuance or succession ⟨rambled *on*⟩ ⟨and so *on*⟩
3 : into operation or a position permitting operation ⟨switched the light *on*⟩

³on *adjective* (circa 1541)
1 : engaged in an activity or function ⟨as in a dramatic role⟩
2 a (1) : being in operation ⟨the radio is *on*⟩ (2) : placed so as to permit operation ⟨the switch is *on*⟩ **b** : taking place ⟨the game is *on*⟩
3 : aware of something — usually used with *to* ⟨my boss was *on* to me⟩
4 : INTENDED, PLANNED ⟨has nothing *on* for tonight⟩
5 *British* : talking or harping incessantly — used with *about*
6 *chiefly British* : regarded as possible or feasible — usually used in negative constructions
7 a : engaged in or as if in a performance ⟨the comedian was always *on*⟩ **b** : being at a high level of performance

¹-on *noun suffix* [International Scientific Vocabulary, alteration of *-one*]
: chemical compound not a ketone or other oxo compound ⟨parathi*on*⟩

²-on *noun suffix* [from *-on* (in *ion*)]
1 : subatomic particle ⟨nucle*on*⟩
2 a : unit : quantum ⟨phot*on*⟩ ⟨magnet*on*⟩ **b** : basic hereditary component ⟨cistr*on*⟩ ⟨oper-*on*⟩

³-on *noun suffix* [New Latin, from *-on* (in *argon*)]
: noble gas ⟨rad*on*⟩

on–again, off–again *adjective* (1948)
: existing briefly and then disappearing in an intermittent unpredictable way ⟨*on-again, off-again* fads⟩

on·a·ger \'ä-ni-jər\ *noun* [Middle English, wild ass, from Latin, from Greek *onagros*, from *onos* ass + *agros* field — more at ACRE] (14th century)
1 : an Asian wild ass (*Equus hemionus onager* synonym *E. onager*) that usually has a broad dorsal stripe and is related to the kiang
2 [Late Latin, from Latin] : a heavy catapult used in ancient and medieval times

on and off *adverb* (1855)
: OFF AND ON

onager 2

— **on–and–off** *adjective*

onan·ism \'ō-nə-ˌni-zəm\ *noun* [probably from New Latin *onanismus*, from *Onan*, son of Judah (Genesis 38:9)] (circa 1741)
1 : MASTURBATION
2 : COITUS INTERRUPTUS
3 : SELF-GRATIFICATION
— **onan·is·tic** \ˌō-nə-'nis-tik\ *adjective*

on·board \'òn-'bōrd, 'än-, -'bórd\ *adjective* (1960)
: carried within or occurring aboard a vehicle (as a satellite or spacecraft) ⟨an *onboard* computer⟩

¹once \'wən(t)s\ *adverb* [Middle English *ones*, from genitive of *on* one] (12th century)
1 : one time and no more
2 : at any one time : under any circumstances : EVER
3 : at some indefinite time in the past : FORMERLY
4 : by one degree of relationship
— **once and for all 1** : with finality : DEFINITIVELY **2** : for the last time

²once *noun* (13th century)
: one single time : one time at least
— **at once 1** : at the same time : SIMULTANEOUSLY **2** : IMMEDIATELY **3** : ²BOTH

³once *adjective* (1691)
: that once was : FORMER

⁴once *conjunction* (1761)
: at the moment when : AS SOON AS

once-over \ˌwən(t)s-'ō-vər, 'wən(t)s-ˌ\ *noun* (1914)
: a swift examination or survey; *especially* : a swift comprehensive appraising glance

once that *conjunction* (1874)
: ONCE

on·cho·cer·ci·a·sis \ˌäŋ-kō-ˌsər-'kī-ə-səs\ *noun, plural* **-a·ses** \-ˌsēz\ [New Latin, from *Onchocerca*, genus of worms] (1911)
: infestation with or disease caused by filarial worms (genus *Onchocerca*); *especially* : a human disease caused by a worm (*O. volvulus*) that is native to Africa but now present in parts of tropical America and is transmitted by several blackflies

on·cid·i·um \än-'si-dē-əm, äŋ-'ki-\ *noun* [New Latin, from Greek *onkos* barbed hook — more at ANGLE] (circa 1868)
: any of a genus (*Oncidium*) of showy tropical American chiefly epiphytic orchids

onco- *combining form* [New Latin, from Greek *onkos* bulk, mass; akin to Greek *enenkein* to carry — more at ENOUGH]
: tumor ⟨*onco*logy⟩

on·co·gene \'äŋ-kō-ˌjēn\ *noun* (1969)
: a gene having the potential to cause a normal cell to become cancerous

on·co·gen·e·sis \ˌäŋ-kō-'je-nə-səs\ *noun* [New Latin] (circa 1932)
: the induction or formation of tumors

on·co·gen·ic \-'je-nik\ *adjective* (1936)
1 : relating to tumor formation
2 : tending to cause tumors
— **on·co·ge·nic·i·ty** \-jə-'ni-sə-tē\ *noun* (1944)
: the capacity to induce or form tumors

on·col·o·gy \än-'kä-lə-jē, äŋ-\ *noun* (circa 1857)
: the study of tumors
— **on·co·log·i·cal** \ˌäŋ-kə-'lä-ji-kəl\ *also* **on·co·log·ic** \-jik\ *adjective*
— **on·col·o·gist** \än-'kä-lə-jist, äŋ-\ *noun*

on·com·ing \'òn-ˌkə-miŋ, 'än-\ *adjective* (1844)
1 a : coming nearer in time or space ⟨the *on-coming* year⟩ ⟨an *oncoming* car⟩ **b** : FUTURE ⟨looked forward to his *oncoming* visit⟩
2 : EMERGENT, RISING ⟨the *oncoming* generation⟩

on·cor·na·vi·rus \ˌäŋ-ˌkȯr-nə-ˈvī-rəs\ *noun* [*onco-* + RNA + *virus*] (1970)
: any of a group of RNA-containing viruses that produce tumors

¹one \ˈwən\ *adjective* [Middle English *on, an,* from Old English *ān;* akin to Old High German *ein* one, Latin *unus* (Old Latin *oinos*), Sanskrit *eka*] (before 12th century)
1 : being a single unit or thing ⟨*one* day at a time⟩
2 a : being one in particular ⟨early *one* morning⟩ **b** : being preeminently what is indicated ⟨*one* fine person⟩
3 a : being the same in kind or quality ⟨both of *one* species⟩ **b** (1) : constituting a unified entity of two or more components ⟨the combined elements form *one* substance⟩ (2) : being in agreement or union ⟨am *one* with you on this⟩
4 a : SOME 1 ⟨will see you again *one* day⟩ **b** : being a certain individual specified by name ⟨*one* John Doe made a speech⟩
5 : ONLY 2 ⟨the *one* person she wanted to marry⟩

²one *noun* (before 12th century)
1 — see NUMBER table
2 : the number denoting unity
3 a : the first in a set or series — often used with an attributive noun ⟨day *one*⟩ **b** : an article of clothing of a size designated *one* ⟨wears a *one*⟩
4 : a single person or thing ⟨has the *one* but needs the other⟩
5 : a one-dollar bill
— at one : at harmony : in a state of agreement
— for one : as one example ⟨I *for one* disagree⟩

³one *pronoun* (13th century)
1 : a certain indefinitely indicated person or thing ⟨saw *one* of his friends⟩
2 a : an individual of a vaguely indicated group : anyone at all ⟨*one* never knows⟩ **b** : used as a third person substitute for a first person pronoun ⟨I'd like to read more but *one* doesn't have the time⟩
3 : a single instance of a specified action ⟨felt like belting him *one* —John Casey⟩ □

-one *noun suffix* [International Scientific Vocabulary, alteration of *-ene*]
: ketone or related or analogous compound or class of compounds ⟨lact*one*⟩ ⟨quin*one*⟩

one another *pronoun* (1526)
: EACH OTHER
usage see EACH OTHER

one–armed bandit \ˈwən-ˈärm(d)-\ *also* **one–arm bandit** *noun* (1934)
: SLOT MACHINE 2

one–bag·ger \-ˈba-gər\ *noun* (1952)
: SINGLE 2

one–di·men·sion·al *adjective* (1883)
1 : having one dimension
2 : lacking depth : SUPERFICIAL ⟨*one-dimensional* characters⟩
— one–di·men·sion·al·i·ty *noun*

one·fold \ˈwən-ˌfōld, -ˈfōld\ *adjective* (before 12th century)
: constituting a single undivided whole

one–hand·ed \-ˈhan-dəd\ *adjective* (15th century)
1 : having or using only one hand ⟨could beat him up *one-handed*⟩
2 a : designed for or requiring the use of only one hand **b** : effected by the use of only one hand

one–horse \-ˈhȯrs\ *adjective* (1750)
1 : drawn or operated by one horse
2 : SMALL, SMALL-TIME ⟨a *one-horse* town⟩

Onei·da \ō-ˈnī-də\ *noun, plural* **Oneida** *or* **Oneidas** [Oneida *oneˀyóteˀ,* literally, standing rock] (1666)
1 : a member of an American Indian people originally of New York
2 : the Iroquoian language of the Oneida people

onei·ric \ō-ˈnī-rik\ *adjective* [Greek *oneiros* dream; akin to Armenian *anurǰ* dream] (1859)
1 : of or relating to dreams : DREAMY
— onei·ri·cal·ly \-ri-k(ə-)lē\ *adverb*

onei·ro·man·cy \ō-ˈnī-rə-ˌman(t)-sē\ *noun* [Greek *oneiros* + English *-mancy*] (1652)
: divination by means of dreams

one–line octave *noun* (1931)
: the musical octave that begins on middle C
— see PITCH illustration

one–lin·er \ˌwən-ˈlī-nər\ *noun* (1967)
: a very succinct joke or witticism

one–man *adjective* (1842)
: of or relating to just one individual: as **a** : consisting of only one individual ⟨a *one-man* committee⟩ **b** : done, presented, or produced by only one individual ⟨a *one-man* stage play⟩ (2) : featuring the work of a single artist (as a painter) ⟨a *one-man* show of oils⟩ **c** : designed for or limited to one individual

one·ness \ˈwən-nəs\ *noun* (1594)
: the quality or state or fact of being one: as **a** : SINGLENESS **b** : INTEGRITY, WHOLENESS **c** : HARMONY **d** : SAMENESS, IDENTITY **e** : UNITY, UNION

one–night·er \ˌwən-ˈnī-tər\ *noun* (circa 1937)
: ONE-NIGHT STAND

one–night stand *noun* (1880)
1 : a performance (as of a play or concert) given (as by a traveling group of actors or musicians) only once in each of a series of localities
2 a : a locality used for one-night stands **b** : a stopover for a one-night stand
3 : a sexual encounter limited to a single occasion; *also* : a partner in such an encounter

one–note \ˈwən-ˌnōt\ *adjective* (1973)
: unvarying in tone or emphasis : MONOTONOUS

one–off \ˌwən-ˈȯf\ *adjective* (1934)
British : limited to a single time, occasion, or instance : ONE-SHOT, UNIQUE
— one–off *noun*

one–on–one \ˌwən-ȯn-ˈwən, ˌwən-än-\ *adjective or adverb* (1967)
1 : playing directly against a single opposing player
2 : involving a direct encounter between one person and another

one–piece *adjective* (1880)
: consisting of or made in a single undivided piece ⟨a *one-piece* bathing suit⟩
— one–piec·er \ˈwən-ˌpē-sər\ *noun*

oner·ous \ˈä-nə-rəs, ˈō-\ *adjective* [Middle English, from Middle French *onereus,* from Latin *onerosus,* from *oner-, onus* burden; akin to Sanskrit *anas* cart] (14th century)
1 : involving, imposing, or constituting a burden : TROUBLESOME ⟨an *onerous* task⟩
2 : having legal obligations that outweigh the advantages ⟨*onerous* contract⟩ ☆
— oner·ous·ly *adverb*
— oner·ous·ness *noun*

one·self \(ˌ)wən-ˈself, *Southern also* -ˈsef\ *also* **one's self** \(ˌ)wən-, ˌwənz-\ *pronoun* (1548)
1 : a person's self : one's own self — used reflexively as object of a preposition or verb or for emphasis in various constructions
2 : one's normal, healthy, or sane condition or self
— be oneself : to conduct oneself in a usual or fitting manner

one–shot \ˈwən-ˌshät\ *adjective* (1927)
1 : that is complete or effective through being done or used or applied only once ⟨there is no easy *one-shot* answer to the problem⟩
2 : that is not followed by something else of the same kind ⟨a *one-shot* tax cut⟩
— one–shot *noun*

one–sid·ed \ˈwən-ˈsī-dəd\ *adjective* (1813)
1 a (1) : having one side prominent : LOPSIDED (2) : having or occurring on one side only **b** : limited to one side : PARTIAL ⟨a *one-sided* interpretation⟩
2 : UNILATERAL ⟨a *one-sided* decision⟩
— one–sid·ed·ly *adverb*
— one–sid·ed·ness *noun*

ones place *noun* (1976)
: UNITS PLACE

one–step \ˈwən-ˌstep\ *noun* (1911)
1 : a ballroom dance in ¾ time marked by quick walking steps backward and forward
2 : music used for the one-step
— one–step *intransitive verb*

one–stop \-ˈstäp\ *adjective* (1934)
: being or relating to a business that provides a complete range of goods or services of a particular kind

one–tailed \ˈwən-ˈtāl(d)\ *also* **one–tail** \-ˈtāl\ *adjective* (1947)
: being a statistical test for which the critical region consists of all values of the test statistic greater than a given value or less than a given value but not both — compare TWO-TAILED

¹one·time \ˈwən-ˌtīm\ *adjective* (1840)
1 : FORMER, SOMETIME ⟨a *onetime* actor⟩
2 : occurring only once : ONE-SHOT

²onetime *adverb* (1886)
: FORMERLY

one–to–one \ˌwən-tə-ˈwən, -də-\ *adjective* (1873)
1 : pairing each element of a set uniquely with an element of another set
2 : ONE-ON-ONE 2

one–track *adjective* (1926)
: marked by often narrowly restricted attention to or absorption in just one thing ⟨a *one-track* mind⟩

one–two \ˈwən-ˈtü, -ˌtü\ *noun* (1809)
1 : a combination of two quick blows in rapid succession in boxing; *especially* : a left jab followed at once by a hard blow with the right hand
2 *or* **one–two punch** : a combination of two forces acting against something

one–up \ˌwən-ˈəp, ˈwən-\ *transitive verb* [back-formation from *one-upmanship*] (1963)
: to practice one-upmanship on

one up *adjective* (1919)

☆ **SYNONYMS**
Onerous, burdensome, oppressive, exacting mean imposing hardship. ONEROUS stresses being laborious and heavy especially because distasteful ⟨the *onerous* task of cleaning up the mess⟩. BURDENSOME suggests causing mental as well as physical strain ⟨*burdensome* responsibilities⟩. OPPRESSIVE implies extreme harshness or severity in what is imposed ⟨the *oppressive* tyranny of a police state⟩. EXACTING implies rigor or sternness rather than tyranny or injustice in the demands made or in the one demanding ⟨an *exacting* employer⟩.

□ **USAGE**
one Sense 2a is usually a sign of a formal style. A formal style excludes the participation of the reader or hearer; thus *one* is used where a less formal style might address the reader directly ⟨for the consequences of such choices, *one* has only oneself to thank —Walker Gibson⟩. This generic *one* has never been common in informal use in either British or American English, and people who start sentences with *one* often shift to another pronoun more natural to casual discourse ⟨when *one* is learning the river, he is not allowed to do or think about anything else —Mark Twain⟩. Use of *one* to replace a first-person pronoun—sense 2b—has occasionally been criticized. It is more common in British English than in American ⟨I'm watching this pretty carefully and I hope that the issue will come up in the Lords and *one* may be able to speak about it —Donald Coggan, Archbishop of Canterbury⟩. See in addition YOU.

: being in a position of advantage — usually used with *on*

one–up·man·ship \,wən-'əp-mən-,ship\ *also* **one–ups·man·ship** \-'əps-mən-\ *noun* (1952)
: the art or practice of outdoing or keeping one jump ahead of a friend or competitor ⟨engaged in a round of verbal *one-upmanship*⟩
word history see GAMESMANSHIP

one–way *adjective* (1824)
1 : that moves in or allows movement in only one direction ⟨*one-way* street⟩
2 : ONE-SIDED, UNILATERAL ⟨a *one-way* conversation⟩
3 : that functions in only one of two or more ways

on·go·ing \'ȯn-,gō-iŋ, 'än-, -,gó(-)iŋ\ *adjective* (1877)
1 a : being actually in process **b** : CONTINUING
2 : continuously moving forward : GROWING
— **on·go·ing·ness** \-nəs\ *noun*

on·ion \'ən-yən\ *noun* [Middle English, from Middle French *oignon*, from Latin *union-, unio*] (14th century)
1 : a widely cultivated Asian herb (*Allium cepa*) of the lily family with pungent edible bulbs; *also* : its bulb
2 : any of various plants of the same genus as the onion
— **on·iony** \-yə-nē\ *adjective*

onion dome *noun* (1941)
: a dome (as of a church) having the general shape of an onion
— **onion–domed** *adjective*

onion ring *noun* (1946)
: a ring of sliced onion coated with batter or crumbs and fried

on·ion·skin \-,skin\ *noun* (1879)
: a thin strong translucent paper of very light weight

oni·um \'ō-nē-əm\ *adjective* [-onium] (1905)
: being or characterized by a usually complex cation

-onium *noun suffix* [New Latin, from *ammonium*]
: an ion having a positive charge ⟨hydr*onium*⟩
— compare -IUM 1b

on–line *adjective or adverb* (1950)
: connected to, served by, or available through a system and especially a computer or telecommunications system ⟨an *on-line* database⟩; *also* : done while connected to a system ⟨*online* computer storage⟩

on·look·er \'ȯn-,lu̇-kər, 'än-\ *noun* (1606)
: one that looks on; *especially* : a passive spectator
— **on·look·ing** \-kiŋ\ *adjective*

¹on·ly \'ōn-lē\ *adjective* [Middle English, from Old English *ānlīc*, from *ān* one — more at ONE] (before 12th century)
1 : unquestionably the best : PEERLESS
2 : alone in its class or kind : SOLE ⟨an *only* child⟩

²only *adverb* (14th century)
1 a : as a single fact or instance and nothing more or different : MERELY ⟨has *only* lost one election —George Orwell⟩ **b** : SOLELY, EXCLUSIVELY ⟨known *only* to him⟩
2 : at the very least ⟨it was *only* too true⟩
3 a : in the final outcome ⟨will *only* make you sick⟩ **b** : with nevertheless the final result ⟨won the battles, *only* to lose the war⟩
4 a : as recently as ⟨*only* last week⟩ **b** : in the immediate past ⟨*only* just talked to her⟩ □

³only *conjunction* (14th century)
1 a : with the restriction that : BUT ⟨you may go, *only* come back early⟩ **b** : and yet : HOWEVER ⟨they look very nice, *only* we can't use them⟩
2 : were it not that : EXCEPT ⟨I'd introduce you to her, *only* you'd win her —Jack London⟩

on·o·mas·tic \,ä-nə-'mas-tik\ *adjective* [Greek *onomastikos*, from *onomazein* to name, from *onoma* name — more at NAME] (1716)
: of, relating to, or consisting of a name or names

— **on·o·mas·ti·cal·ly** \-ti-k(ə-)lē\ *adverb*

on·o·mas·tics \-tiks\ *noun plural but singular or plural in construction* (1930)
1 a : the science or study of the origins and forms of words especially as used in a specialized field **b** : the science or study of the origin and forms of proper names of persons or places
2 : the system underlying the formation and use of words especially for proper names or of words used in a specialized field

on·o·ma·tol·o·gy \,ä-nə-mə-'tä-lə-jē\ *noun* [French *onomatologie*, from Greek *onomat-, onoma* name + French *-logie* -logy] (circa 1847)
: ONOMASTICS
— **on·o·ma·tol·o·gist** \-jist\ *noun*

on·o·mato·poe·ia \,ä-nə-,mä-tə-'pē-ə, -,ma-\ *noun* [Late Latin, from Greek *onomatopoiia*, from *onomat-, onoma* name + *poiein* to make — more at POET] (circa 1577)
1 : the naming of a thing or action by a vocal imitation of the sound associated with it (as *buzz, hiss*)
2 : the use of words whose sound suggests the sense
— **on·o·mato·poe·ic** \-'pē-ik\ *or* **on·o·mato·po·et·ic** \-pō-'e-tik\ *adjective*
— **on·o·mato·poe·i·cal·ly** \-'pē-ə-k(ə-)lē\ *or* **on·o·mato·po·et·i·cal·ly** \-pō-'e-ti-k(ə-)lē\ *adverb*

On·on·da·ga \,ä-nə(n)-'dò-gə, -'dā-, -'dä-\ *noun, plural* **-ga** *or* **-gas** [Onondaga *onóʔtàʔke*, the chief Onondaga town] (1684)
1 : a member of an American Indian people of New York and Canada
2 : the Iroquoian language of the Onondaga people

on–ramp \'ȯn-,ramp, 'än-\ *noun* (1958)
: a ramp by which one enters a limited-access highway

on·rush \-,rəsh\ *noun* (1844)
1 : a rushing forward or onward
2 : ONSET
— **on·rush·ing** \-,rə-shiŋ\ *adjective*

on–screen \'ȯn-'skrēn, 'än-\ *adverb or adjective* (1955)
: in a motion picture or a television program

on·set \-,set\ *noun* (1535)
1 : ATTACK, ASSAULT ⟨withstand the *onset* of the army⟩
2 : BEGINNING, COMMENCEMENT ⟨the *onset* of winter⟩

on·shore \'ȯn-,shȯr, 'än-, -,shȯr\ *adjective* (1875)
1 : coming or moving from the water toward or onto the shore ⟨an *onshore* wind⟩
2 a : situated on or near the shore as distinguished from being in deep or open water **b** : situated on land
3 : DOMESTIC 2 ⟨*onshore* markets⟩
— **on·shore** \'ȯn-', 'än-'\ *adverb*

on–side \-'sīd\ *adverb or adjective* (1871)
: not offside : in a position legally to play or receive the ball or puck

onside kick *noun* (1926)
: a kickoff in football in which the ball travels just far enough to be legally recoverable by the kicking team

on–site \-'sīt\ *adjective or adverb* (1946)
: carried out or located at the place connected with a particular activity ⟨*on-site* training in construction skills⟩

on·slaught \'än-,slȯt, 'ȯn-\ *noun* [modification of Dutch *aanslag* act of striking; akin to Old English *an* on and to Old English *slēan* to strike — more at SLAY] (circa 1625)
: an especially fierce attack; *also* : something resembling such an attack ⟨an *onslaught* of technological changes⟩

on·stage \'ȯn-'stāj, 'än-, -,stāj\ *adverb or adjective* (1925)
: on a part of the stage visible to the audience

on·stream \'ȯn-'strēm, 'än-\ *adverb or adjective* (1930)
: in or into production ⟨plants scheduled to come *onstream*⟩

ont- *or* **onto-** *combining form* [New Latin, from Late Greek, from Greek *ont-, ōn*, present participle of *einai* to be — more at IS]
1 : being : existence ⟨*ont*ology⟩
2 : organism ⟨*onto*geny⟩

-ont *noun combining form* [Greek *ont-, ōn*, present participle]
: cell : organism ⟨dipl*ont*⟩

on–the–job *adjective* (1946)
: of, relating to, or being something (as training or experience) learned, gained, or done while working at a job and often under supervision

on·tic \'än-tik\ *adjective* (1942)
: of, relating to, or having real being
— **on·ti·cal·ly** \-ti-k(ə-)lē\ *adverb*

¹on·to \'ȯn-(,)tü, 'än-\ *preposition* (1581)
1 : to a position on
2 : in or into a state of awareness about ⟨put me *onto* your methods⟩
3 — used as a function word to indicate a set each element of which is the image of at least one element of another set ⟨a function mapping the set *S* onto the set *T*⟩

²onto *adjective* (1942)
: mapping elements in such a way that every element in one set is the image of at least one element in another set ⟨a function that is one-to-one and *onto*⟩

on·to·gen·e·sis \,än-tə-'je-nə-səs\ *noun* [New Latin] (1875)
: ONTOGENY

on·to·ge·net·ic \-jə-'ne-tik\ *adjective* [International Scientific Vocabulary] (1878)
1 : of, relating to, or appearing in the course of ontogeny
2 : based on visible morphological characters
— **on·to·ge·net·i·cal·ly** \-ti-k(ə-)lē\ *adverb*

on·tog·e·ny \än-'tä-jə-nē\ *noun* [International Scientific Vocabulary] (1872)
: the development or course of development especially of an individual organism

on·to·log·i·cal \,än-t²l-'ä-ji-kəl\ *adjective* (1782)
1 : of or relating to ontology
2 : relating to or based upon being or existence
— **on·to·log·i·cal·ly** \-k(ə-)lē\ *adverb*

ontological argument *noun* (1877)
: an argument for the existence of God based upon the meaning of the term *God*

on·tol·o·gy \än-'tä-lə-jē\ *noun* [New Latin *ontologia*, from *ont-* + *-logia* -logy] (circa 1721)
1 : a branch of metaphysics concerned with the nature and relations of being
2 : a particular theory about the nature of being or the kinds of existents

\ə\ **abut** \ᵊ\ **kitten** \ər\ **further** \a\ **ash** \ā\ **ace**
\ä\ **mop, mar** \au̇\ **out** \ch\ **chin** \e\ **bet** \ē\ **easy**
\g\ **go** \i\ **hit** \ī\ **ice** \j\ **job** \ŋ\ **sing** \ō\ **go**
\ȯ\ **law** \ȯi\ **boy** \th\ **thin** \t̲h̲\ **the** \ü\ **loot** \u̇\ **foot**
\y\ **yet** \zh\ **vision** *see also* Guide to Pronunciation

— **on·tol·o·gist** \-jist\ *noun*

onus \'ō-nəs\ *noun* (circa 1640)
1 [Latin — more at ONEROUS] **a** : BURDEN **b** : a disagreeable necessity : OBLIGATION **c** : BLAME **d** : STIGMA
2 [New Latin *onus (probandi)*, literally, burden of proving] : BURDEN OF PROOF

¹on·ward \'ȯn-wərd, 'än-\ *also* **on·wards** \-wərdz\ *adverb* (1532)
: toward or at a point lying ahead in space or time : FORWARD

²onward *adjective* (1674)
: directed or moving onward : FORWARD

on·y·choph·o·ran \ˌä-ni-'kä-fə-rən\ *noun* [New Latin *Onychophora*, group name, from Greek *onych-, onyx* claw + *-phoros* -phore] (circa 1890)
: PERIPATUS
— **onychophoran** *adjective*

-onym *noun combining form* [Middle English, from Latin *-onymum*, from Greek *-ōnymon*, from *onyma* — more at NAME]
: name : word ⟨ant*onym*⟩

on·yx \'ä-niks\ *noun* [Middle English *onix*, from Middle French & Latin; Middle French, from Latin *onych-, onyx*, from Greek, literally, claw, nail — more at NAIL] (14th century)
: a translucent chalcedony in parallel layers of different colors

oo- — see O-

oo·cyst \'ō-ə-ˌsist\ *noun* [International Scientific Vocabulary] (1875)
: ZYGOTE; *specifically* : a sporozoan zygote undergoing sporogenous development

oo·cyte \'ō-ə-ˌsīt\ *noun* [International Scientific Vocabulary] (1895)
: an egg before maturation : a female gametocyte

oo·dles \'ü-dᵊlz\ *noun plural but singular or plural in construction* [origin unknown] (1869)
: a great quantity : LOT

oog·a·mous \ō-'ä-gə-məs\ *adjective* (1888)
: having or involving a small motile male gamete and a large immobile female gamete
— **oog·a·my** \-mē\ *noun*

oo·gen·e·sis \ˌō-ə-'je-nə-səs\ *noun* [New Latin] (circa 1879)
: formation and maturation of the egg
— **oo·ge·net·ic** \-jə-'ne-tik\ *adjective*

oo·go·ni·um \ˌō-ə-'gō-nē-əm\ *noun, plural* **-nia** \-nē-ə\ [New Latin] (1867)
1 : a female sexual organ in various algae and fungi that corresponds to the archegonium of ferns and mosses
2 : a descendant of a primordial germ cell that gives rise to oocytes
— **oo·go·ni·al** \-nē-əl\ *adjective*

¹ooh \'ü\ *interjection* (1939)
— used to express amazement, joy, or surprise

²ooh *intransitive verb* (1951)
: to exclaim in amazement, joy, or surprise ⟨*oohing* and aahing over the new automobiles⟩
— **ooh** *noun*

oo·lite \'ō-ə-ˌlīt\ *noun* [probably from French *oolithe*, from *oo-* o- + *-lithe* -lite] (1785)
: a rock consisting of small round grains usually of calcium carbonate cemented together
— **oo·lit·ic** \ˌō-ə-'li-tik\ *adjective*

ool·o·gist \ō-'ä-lə-jist\ *noun* (1863)
1 : a person specializing in the study of birds' eggs
2 : a collector of birds' eggs
— **ool·o·gy** \-jē\ *noun*

oo·long \'ü-ˌlȯn\ *noun* [Chinese (Beijing) *wūlóng*, literally, black dragon] (1850)
: tea made from leaves that have been partially fermented before firing

oom·pah \ˈüm-(ˌ)pä, 'ùm-\ *also* **oom·pah-pah** \ˌüm-(ˌ)pä-'pä, ˌùm-\ *noun* [imitative] (1877)
: a repeated rhythmic bass accompaniment especially in a band
— **oompah** *verb*

oomph \'ùm(p)f\ *noun* [imitative of a sound made under exertion] (1936)
1 : personal charm or magnetism : GLAMOUR
2 : SEX APPEAL
3 : PUNCH, VITALITY

oo·pho·rec·to·my \ˌō-ə-fə-'rek-tə-mē\ *noun, plural* **-mies** [New Latin *oophoron* ovary (from *o-* + Greek *-phoron*, neuter of *-phoros* -phore) + English *-ectomy*] (1872)
: OVARIECTOMY

oops \'(w)ù(ə)ps\ *interjection* (1933)
— used typically to express mild apology, surprise, or dismay

Oort cloud \'ȯrt-, 'ȯrt-\ *noun* [Jan Oort (died 1992) Dutch astronomer] (1968)
: a spherical shell of small frozen bodies believed to surround the sun far beyond the orbit of Pluto and from which some are dislodged when perturbed (as by a passing star) to fall toward the sun as comets

oo·spore \'ō-ə-ˌspōr, -ˌspȯr\ *noun* [International Scientific Vocabulary]
: ZYGOTE; *especially* : a spore produced by heterogamous fertilization that yields a sporophyte

oo·the·ca \ˌō-ə-'thē-kə\ *noun, plural* **oo·the·cae** \-'thē-(ˌ)kē, -(ˌ)sē\ [New Latin] (circa 1856)
: a firm-walled and distinctive egg case (as of a cockroach)
— **oo·the·cal** \-'thē-kəl\ *adjective*

oo·tid \'ō-ə-ˌtid\ *noun* [irregular from *o-* + *-id*] (1904)
: an egg cell after meiosis

¹ooze \'üz\ *noun* [Middle English *wose*, from Old English *wāse* mire; akin to Old Norse *veisa* stagnant water] (before 12th century)
1 : a soft deposit (as of mud, slime, or shells) on the bottom of a body of water
2 : a piece of soft wet plastic ground

²ooze *verb* **oozed; ooz·ing** [Middle English *wosen*, from *wose* sap] (14th century)
intransitive verb
1 : to pass or flow slowly through or as if through small openings or interstices
2 : to move slowly or imperceptibly ⟨the crowd began to *ooze* forward —Bruce Marshall⟩
3 a : to exude moisture **b** : to exude something often in a faintly repellent manner ⟨*ooze* with sympathy⟩
transitive verb
1 : to emit slowly
2 : EXUDE 2 ⟨*ooze* confidence⟩

³ooze *noun* [Middle English *wose* sap, juice, from Old English *wōs*; akin to Old High German *waso* damp] (circa 1581)
1 : a decoction of vegetable material used for tanning leather
2 : the act of oozing
3 : something that oozes

oozy \'ü-zē\ *adjective* **ooz·i·er; -est** (14th century)
1 : containing or composed of ooze : resembling ooze
2 : exuding moisture : SLIMY

op \'äp\ *noun* (1964)
: OPTICAL ART

opac·i·ty \ō-'pa-sə-tē\ *noun, plural* **-ties** [French *opacité* shadiness, from Latin *opacitat-, opacitas*, from *opacus* shaded, dark] (circa 1611)
1 : the quality or state of a body that makes it impervious to the rays of light; *broadly* : the relative capacity of matter to obstruct the transmission of radiant energy
2 a : obscurity of sense : UNINTELLIGIBLENESS **b** : the quality or state of being mentally obtuse : DULLNESS
3 : an opaque spot in a normally transparent structure (as the lens of the eye)

opah \'ō-pə, -ˌpä\ *noun* [perhaps from Ibo *úbà*] (1750)
: a large elliptical marine bony fish (*Lampris guttatus* of the family Lampridae) with brilliant colors

opal \'ō-pəl\ *noun* [Latin *opalus*, from Greek *opallios*, from Sanskrit *upala* stone, jewel] (1591)
: a mineral that is a hydrated amorphous silica softer and less dense than quartz and typically with definite and often marked iridescent play of colors

opal·es·cent \ˌō-pə-'le-sᵊnt\ *adjective* (circa 1813)
: reflecting an iridescent light
— **opal·es·cence** \-sᵊn(t)s\ *noun*
— **opal·es·cent·ly** \-sᵊnt-lē\ *adverb*

opal·ine \'ō-pə-ˌlīn, -ˌlēn\ *adjective* (1784)
: resembling opal

opaque \ō-'pāk\ *adjective* [Latin *opacus*] (1641)
1 : exhibiting opacity : blocking the passage of radiant energy and especially light
2 a : hard to understand or explain ⟨*opaque* prose⟩ **b** : OBTUSE, THICKHEADED
— **opaque** *noun*
— **opaque·ly** *adverb*
— **opaque·ness** *noun*

opaque projector *noun* (1951)
: a projector using reflected light for projecting an image of an opaque object or matter on an opaque support (as a photograph)

op art \'äp-\ *noun* (1964)
: OPTICAL ART
— **op artist** *noun*

ope \'ōp\ *verb* **oped; op·ing** (15th century)
archaic : OPEN

op–ed \'äp-'ed\ *noun, often O&E capitalized, often attributive* [short for *opposite editorial*] (1970)
: a page of special features usually opposite the editorial page of a newspaper

¹open \'ō-pən, -pᵊm\ *adjective* **open·er** \'ōp-nər, 'ō-pə-\; **open·est** \'ōp-nəst, 'ō-pə-\ [Middle English, from Old English; akin to Old High German *offan* open, Old English *ūp* up] (before 12th century)
1 : having no enclosing or confining barrier : accessible on all or nearly all sides ⟨cattle grazing on an *open* range⟩
2 a (1) : being in a position or adjustment to permit passage : not shut or locked ⟨an *open* door⟩ (2) : having a barrier (as a door) so adjusted as to allow passage ⟨the house was *open*⟩ **b** : having the lips parted ⟨stood there with his mouth wide *open*⟩ **c** : not buttoned or zipped ⟨an *open* shirt⟩
3 a : completely free from concealment : exposed to general view or knowledge ⟨their hostilities eventually erupted with *open* war⟩ **b** : exposed or vulnerable to attack or question : SUBJECT ⟨*open* to doubt⟩
4 a : not covered with a top, roof, or lid ⟨an *open* car⟩ ⟨her eyes were *open*⟩ **b** : having no protective covering ⟨*open* wiring⟩ ⟨an *open* wound⟩
5 : not restricted to a particular group or category of participants ⟨*open* to the public⟩ ⟨*open* housing⟩: as **a** : enterable by both amateur and professional contestants ⟨an *open* tournament⟩ **b** : enterable by a registered voter regardless of political affiliation ⟨an *open* primary⟩
6 : fit to be traveled over : presenting no obstacle to passage or view ⟨the *open* road⟩ ⟨*open* country⟩
7 : having the parts or surfaces laid out in an expanded position : spread out : UNFOLDED ⟨an *open* book⟩
8 a : LOW 13 (2) : formed with the tongue in a lower position ⟨Italian has an *open* and a close *e*⟩ **b** (1) : having clarity and resonance unimpaired by undue tension or constriction of the throat ⟨an *open* vocal tone⟩ (2) *of a tone* : produced by an open string or on a wind instrument by the lip without the use of slides, valves, or keys
9 a : available to follow or make use of ⟨the only course *open* to us⟩ **b** : not taken up with duties or engagements ⟨keep an hour *open* on Friday⟩ **c** : not finally decided : subject to further consideration ⟨the salary is *open*⟩ ⟨an

open question⟩ **d :** available for a qualified applicant **:** VACANT ⟨the job is still *open*⟩ **e :** remaining available for use or filling until canceled ⟨an *open* order for more items⟩ **f :** available for future purchase ⟨these items are in *open* stock⟩
10 a : characterized by ready accessibility and usually generous attitude: as (1) **:** generous in giving (2) **:** willing to hear and consider or to accept and deal with **:** RESPONSIVE (3) **:** free from reserve or pretense **:** FRANK **b :** accessible to the influx of new factors (as foreign goods) ⟨an *open* market⟩
11 a : having openings, interruptions, or spaces: as (1) **:** being porous and friable ⟨*open* soil⟩ (2) **:** sparsely distributed **:** SCATTERED ⟨*open* population⟩ (3) *of a compound* **:** having components separated by a space in writing or printing ⟨as *opaque projector*⟩ **b :** not made up of a continuous closed circuit of channels ⟨the insect circulatory system is *open*⟩
12 a *of an organ pipe* **:** not stopped at the top **b** *of a string on a musical instrument* **:** not stopped by the finger
13 : being in operation ⟨an *open* microphone⟩; *especially* **:** ready for business, patronage, or use ⟨the store is *open* from 9 to 5⟩ ⟨the new highway will be *open* next week⟩
14 a (1) **:** characterized by lack of effective regulation of various commercial enterprises ⟨an *open* town⟩ (2) **:** not repressed by legal controls ⟨*open* gambling⟩ **b :** free from checking or hampering restraints ⟨an *open* economy⟩ **c :** relatively unguarded by opponents ⟨passed to an *open* teammate⟩
15 : having been opened by a first ante, bet, or bid ⟨the bidding is *open*⟩
16 *of punctuation* **:** characterized by sparing use especially of the comma
17 a : containing none of its endpoints ⟨an *open* interval⟩ **b :** being a set or composed of sets each point of which has a neighborhood all of whose points are contained in the set ⟨the interior of a sphere is an *open* set⟩
18 a : being an incomplete electrical circuit **b :** not allowing the flow of electricity ⟨an *open* switch⟩
synonym see FRANK, LIABLE
— **open** *adverb*
— **open·ly** \'ō-pən-lē\ *adverb*
— **open·ness** \-pə(n)-nəs\ *noun*

²**open** *verb* **opened** \'ō-pənd, 'ō-p³md\; **open·ing** \'ōp-niŋ, 'ō-pə-\ (before 12th century)
transitive verb
1 a : to move (as a door) from a closed position **b :** to make available for entry or passage by turning back (as a barrier) or removing (as a cover or an obstruction)
2 a : to make available for or active in a regular function ⟨*open* a new store⟩ **b :** to make accessible for a particular purpose ⟨*opened* new land for settlement⟩ ⟨*open* the way for changes⟩ **c :** to initiate access to (a computer file) prior to use
3 a : to disclose or expose to view **:** REVEAL **b :** to make more discerning or responsive **:** ENLIGHTEN ⟨must *open* our minds to the problems⟩ **c :** to bring into view or come in sight of by changing position
4 a : to make an opening in ⟨*opened* the boil⟩ **b :** to loosen and make less compact ⟨*open* the soil⟩
5 : to spread out **:** UNFOLD ⟨*opened* the book⟩
6 a : to enter upon **:** BEGIN ⟨*opened* the meeting⟩ **b :** to commence action in a card game by making (a first bid), putting a first bet in (the pot), or playing (a card or suit) as first lead
7 : to restore or recall (as an order) from a finally determined state to a state in which the parties are free to prosecute or oppose
intransitive verb
1 : to become open ⟨the office *opened* early⟩
2 a : to spread out **:** EXPAND ⟨the wound *opened* under the strain⟩ **b :** to become disclosed ⟨a beautiful vista *opened* before us⟩

3 : to become enlightened or responsive
4 : to give access ⟨the rooms *open* onto a hall⟩
5 : SPEAK OUT 2 ⟨finally he *opened* freely on the subject⟩
6 a : to begin a course or activity ⟨the play *opens* on Tuesday⟩ **b :** to make a bet, bid, or lead in commencing a round or hand of a card game
— **open·abil·i·ty** \,ōp-nə-'bi-lə-tē, ,ō-pə-\ *noun*
— **open·able** \'ōp-nə-bəl, 'ō-pə-\ *adjective*

³**open** *noun* (13th century)
1 : OPENING
2 : open and unobstructed space: as **a :** OPEN AIR **b :** open water
3 : an open contest, competition, or tournament
4 : a public or unconcealed state or position

open admission *noun* (1969)
: OPEN ENROLLMENT 2

open–air *adjective* (1830)
: OUTDOOR

open air *noun* (15th century)
: the space where air is unconfined; *especially* **:** OUTDOORS

open–and–shut *adjective* (1841)
1 : perfectly simple **:** OBVIOUS
2 : easily settled ⟨an *open-and-shut* case⟩

open bar *noun* (1973)
: a bar (as at a wedding reception) at which drinks are served free — compare CASH BAR

open·cast \'ō-pən-,kast\ *adjective* (circa 1890)
chiefly British **:** worked from a surface open to the air ⟨an *opencast* mine⟩ ⟨*opencast* mining⟩

open chain *noun* (1884)
: an arrangement of atoms represented in a structural formula by a chain whose ends are not joined so as to form a ring

open city *noun* (1914)
: a city that is not occupied or defended by military forces and that is not allowed to be bombed under international law

open dating *noun* (1971)
: the marking of perishable food products with a clearly readable date indicating when the food was packaged or the last date on which it should be sold or used

open door *noun* (1526)
1 : a recognized right of admittance **:** freedom of access
2 : a policy giving opportunity for commercial relations with a country to all nations on equal terms
— **open–door** *adjective*

open–end *adjective* (1917)
: organized to allow for contingencies: as **a :** permitting additional debt to be incurred under the original indenture subject to specified conditions ⟨an *open-end* mortgage⟩ **b :** having a fluctuating capitalization of shares that are issued or redeemed at the current net asset value or at a figure in fixed ratio to this ⟨an *open-end* investment company⟩ — compare CLOSED-END

open–end·ed \,ō-pən-'en-dəd\ *adjective* (1825)
: not rigorously fixed: as **a :** adaptable to the developing needs of a situation **b :** permitting or designed to permit spontaneous and unguided responses
— **open–end·ed·ness** *noun*

open enrollment *noun* (1964)
1 : the voluntary enrollment of a student in a public school other than the one assigned on the basis of residence
2 : enrollment on demand as a student in an institution of higher learning irrespective of formal qualifications

open·er \'ōp-nər, 'ō-pə-\ *noun* (15th century)
: one that opens ⟨a bottle *opener*⟩: as **a** *plural* **:** cards of sufficient value for a player to open the betting in a poker game **b :** the first item, contest, or event of a series
— **for openers :** to begin with

open–eyed \,ō-pən-'īd\ *adjective* (1601)

1 : having the eyes open
2 : carefully observant **:** DISCERNING

open–hand·ed \-'han-dəd\ *adjective* (1593)
: GENEROUS, MUNIFICENT
— **open–hand·ed·ly** *adverb*
— **open–hand·ed·ness** *noun*

open–heart *adjective* (1960)
: of, relating to, or performed on a heart temporarily relieved of circulatory function and surgically opened for inspection and treatment ⟨*open-heart* surgery⟩

open–heart·ed \,ō-pən-'här-təd\ *adjective* (1611)
1 : candidly straightforward **:** FRANK
2 : responsive to emotional appeal
— **open–heart·ed·ly** *adverb*
— **open–heart·ed·ness** *noun*

open–hearth *adjective* (1885)
: of, relating to, involving, or produced in the open-hearth process ⟨*open-hearth* steel⟩

open–hearth process *noun* (1882)
: a process of making steel from pig iron in a furnace of the regenerative reverberatory type

open house *noun* (15th century)
1 : ready and usually informal hospitality or entertainment for all comers
2 : a house or apartment open for inspection especially by prospective buyers or tenants

open·ing \'ōp-niŋ, 'ō-pə-\ *noun* (13th century)
1 a : an act or instance of making or becoming open **b :** an act or instance of beginning **:** COMMENCEMENT; *especially* **:** a formal and usually public event by which something new is put officially into operation
2 : something that is open: as **a** (1) **:** BREACH, APERTURE (2) **:** an open width **:** SPAN **b :** an area without trees or with scattered usually mature trees that occurs as a break in a forest **c :** two pages that face one another in a book
3 : something that constitutes a beginning: as **a :** a planned series of moves made at the beginning of a game of chess or checkers — compare ENDGAME, MIDDLE GAME **b :** a first performance
4 a : OCCASION, CHANCE **b :** an opportunity for employment

open letter *noun* (1878)
: a published letter of protest or appeal usually addressed to an individual but intended for the general public

open loop *noun* (1947)
: a control system for an operation or process in which there is no self-correcting action as there is in a closed loop

open marriage *noun* (1971)
: a marriage in which the partners agree to let each other have sexual partners outside the marriage

open–mind·ed \,ō-pən-'mīn-dəd\ *adjective* (1828)
: receptive to arguments or ideas
— **open–mind·ed·ly** *adverb*
— **open–mind·ed·ness** *noun*

open–mouthed \,ō-pən-'maůthd, -'maůtht\ *adjective* (15th century)
1 : CLAMOROUS, VOCIFEROUS
2 : having the mouth wide open
3 : struck with amazement or wonder
— **open–mouth·ed·ly** \-'maů-thəd-lē, -thəd-\ *adverb*
— **open–mouth·ed·ness** \-'maů-thəd-nəs, -thəd-\ *noun*

open–pol·li·nat·ed \,ō-pən-'pä-lə-,nā-təd\ *adjective* (1925)
: pollinated by natural agencies without human intervention

open season *noun* (circa 1890)
1 : a period when it is legal to kill or catch game or fish protected at other times by law

2 : a time during which someone or something is the object of sustained attack or criticism

open secret *noun* (1828)
: a supposedly secret but generally known matter

open sentence *noun* (1937)
: a statement (as in mathematics) that contains at least one blank or unknown and that becomes true or false when the blank is filled or a quantity is substituted for the unknown

open ses·a·me \-'se-sə-mē\ *noun* [from *open sesame,* the magical command used by Ali Baba to open the door of the robbers' den in *Ali Baba and the Forty Thieves*] (circa 1837)
: something that unfailingly brings about a desired end

open shop *noun* (1903)
: an establishment in which eligibility for employment and retention on the payroll are not determined by membership or nonmembership in a labor union though there may be an agreement by which a union is recognized as sole bargaining agent

open sight *noun* (1591)
: a firearm rear sight having an open notch

open stance *noun* (1948)
: a stance (as in golf) in which the forward foot is farther from the line of play than the back foot — compare CLOSED STANCE

open syllable *noun* (1891)
: a syllable ended by a vowel or diphthong

open up (1582)
transitive verb
1 : to make available
2 : to make plain or visible **:** DISCLOSE
3 : to open by cutting into
intransitive verb
1 : to spread out or come into view ⟨the road *opens up* ahead⟩
2 : to commence firing
3 : to become communicative ⟨tried to get the patient to *open up*⟩

open·work \'ō-pən-,wərk\ *noun, often attributive* (1598)
: work constructed so as to show openings through its substance **:** work that is perforated or pierced ⟨wrought-iron *openwork*⟩
— **open–worked** \-,wərkt\ *adjective*

¹**opera** *plural of* OPUS

²**op·era** \'ä-p(ə-)rə, *Southern also* 'ä-prē\ *noun* [Italian, work, opera, from Latin, work, pains; akin to Latin *oper-, opus* — more at OPERATE] (1644)
1 : a drama set to music and made up of vocal pieces with orchestral accompaniment and orchestral overtures and interludes; *specifically* **:** GRAND OPERA
2 : the score of a musical drama
3 : the performance of an opera; *also* **:** a house where operas are performed

op·er·a·ble \'ä-p(ə-)rə-bəl\ *adjective* (1646)
1 : fit, possible, or desirable to use **:** PRACTICABLE
2 : likely to result in a favorable outcome upon surgical treatment ⟨an *operable* cancer⟩
— **op·er·a·bil·i·ty** \,ä-p(ə-)rə-'bi-lə-tē\ *noun*
— **op·er·a·bly** \'ä-p(ə-)rə-blē\ *adverb*

op·éra bouffe \'ō-pä-rä-'büf, 'ä-p(ə-)rə-\ *noun* [French, from Italian *opera buffa*] (1870)
: satirical comic opera

opera buf·fa \-'bü-fə\ *noun* [Italian, literally, comic opera] (1802)
: an 18th century farcical comic opera with dialogue in recitative

opéra co·mique \-kä-'mēk, -kō-\ *noun* [French, literally, comic opera] (1744)
: an opera characterized by spoken dialogue interspersed between the arias and ensemble numbers — compare GRAND OPERA

opera glass *noun* (1738)
: a small low-power binocular without prisms for use at the opera or theater — often used in plural

op·era·go·er \'ä-p(ə)rə-,gō(-ə)r\ *noun* (1850)
: a person who frequently goes to operas
— **op·era·go·ing** \-,gō-iŋ, -,gó(-)iŋ\ *noun*

opera hat *noun* (1810)
: a man's collapsible top hat

opera glass

opera house *noun* (1720)
: a theater devoted principally to the performance of operas; *broadly* **:** THEATER

op·er·and \,ä-pə-'rand\ *noun* [Latin *operandum,* neuter of gerundive of *operari*] (1886)
: something (as a quantity or data) that is operated on (as in a mathematical operation); *also* **:** the address in a computer instruction of data to be operated on

¹**op·er·ant** \'ä-pə-rənt\ *adjective* (15th century)
1 : functioning or tending to produce effects **:** EFFECTIVE ⟨an *operant* conscience⟩
2 : of or relating to the observable or measurable
3 : of, relating to, or being an operant or operant conditioning ⟨*operant* behavior⟩
— **op·er·ant·ly** *adverb*

²**operant** *noun* (1937)
: behavior (as bar pressing by a rat to obtain food) that operates on the environment to produce rewarding and reinforcing effects

operant conditioning *noun* (1941)
: conditioning in which the desired behavior or increasingly closer approximations to it are followed by a rewarding or reinforcing stimulus — compare CLASSICAL CONDITIONING

opera se·ria \-'ser-ē-ə, -'sir-\ *noun* [Italian, literally, serious opera] (circa 1854)
: an 18th century opera with a heroic or legendary subject

op·er·ate \'ä-pə-,rāt, 'ä-,prāt\ *verb* **-at·ed; -at·ing** [Latin *operatus,* past participle of *operari* to work, from *oper-, opus* work; akin to Old English *efnan* to perform, Sanskrit *apas* work] (1588)
intransitive verb
1 : to perform a function **:** exert power or influence ⟨factors *operating* against our success⟩
2 : to produce an appropriate effect ⟨the drug *operated* quickly⟩
3 a : to perform an operation or a series of operations **b :** to perform surgery **c :** to carry on a military or naval action or mission
4 : to follow a course of conduct that is often irregular ⟨crooked gamblers *operating* in the club⟩
transitive verb
1 : BRING ABOUT, EFFECT
2 a : to cause to function **:** WORK **b :** to put or keep in operation
3 : to perform an operation on; *especially* **:** to perform surgery on

op·er·at·ic \,ä-pə-'ra-tik\ *adjective* (1749)
1 : of or relating to opera
2 : grand, dramatic, or romantic in style or effect
— **op·er·at·i·cal·ly** \-ti-k(ə-)lē\ *adverb*

operating *adjective* (1808)
: of, relating to, or used for or in operations ⟨*operating* expenses⟩ ⟨a hospital *operating* room⟩

operating system *noun* (1961)
: software that controls the operation of a computer and directs the processing of programs (as by assigning storage space in memory and controlling input and output functions)

op·er·a·tion \,ä-pə-'rā-shən\ *noun* [Middle English *operacioun,* from Middle French *operation,* from Latin *operation-, operatio,* from *operari*] (14th century)
1 : performance of a practical work or of something involving the practical application of principles or processes

2 a : an exertion of power or influence ⟨the *operation* of a drug⟩ **b :** the quality or state of being functional or operative ⟨the plant is now in *operation*⟩ **c :** a method or manner of functioning ⟨a machine of very simple *operation*⟩
3 : EFFICACY, POTENCY — archaic except in legal usage
4 : a procedure carried out on a living body usually with instruments especially for the repair of damage or the restoration of health
5 : any of various mathematical or logical processes (as addition) of deriving one entity from others according to a rule
6 a : a usually military action, mission, or maneuver including its planning and execution **b** *plural* **:** the office on the flight line of an airfield where pilots file clearance for flights and where flying from the field is controlled **c** *plural* **:** the agency of an organization charged with carrying on the principal planning and operating functions of a headquarters and its subordinate units
7 : a business transaction especially when speculative
8 : a single step performed by a computer in the execution of a program

op·er·a·tion·al \-shnəl, -shə-nºl\ *adjective* (circa 1909)
1 : of or relating to operation or to an operation ⟨the *operational* gap between planning and production⟩
2 : of, relating to, or based on operations
3 a : of, engaged in, or connected with execution of military or naval operations in campaign or battle **b :** ready for or in condition to undertake a destined function
— **op·er·a·tion·al·ly** *adverb*

op·er·a·tion·al·ism \-shnə-,li-zəm, -shə-nºl-,i-zəm\ *noun* (1931)
: a view that the concepts or terms used in nonanalytic scientific statements must be definable in terms of identifiable and repeatable operations
— **op·er·a·tion·al·ist** \-list, -ist\ *noun*
— **op·er·a·tion·al·is·tic** \-,rā-shnə-'lis-tik, -shə-nºl-'is-tik\ *adjective*

op·er·a·tion·ism \,ä-pə-'rā-shə-,ni-zəm\ *noun* (1935)
: OPERATIONALISM
— **op·er·a·tion·ist** \-sh(ə-)nist\ *noun*

operations research *noun* (1945)
: the application of scientific and especially mathematical methods to the study and analysis of problems involving complex systems — called also *operational research*

¹**op·er·a·tive** \'ä-p(ə-)rə-tiv, 'ä-pə-,rā-\ *adjective* (15th century)
1 : producing an appropriate effect **:** EFFICACIOUS
2 : exerting force or influence **:** OPERATING
3 a : having to do with physical operations (as of machines) **b :** WORKING ⟨an *operative* craftsman⟩
4 : based on or consisting of an operation ⟨*operative* dentistry⟩
— **op·er·a·tive·ly** *adverb*
— **op·er·a·tive·ness** *noun*

²**operative** *noun* (circa 1810)
1 : OPERATOR: as **a :** ARTISAN, MECHANIC **b :** a secret agent **c :** PRIVATE DETECTIVE

op·er·a·tor \'ä-pə-,rā-tər, 'ä-,prā-\ *noun* (1611)
1 : one that operates: as **a :** one that operates a machine or device **b :** one that operates a business **c :** one that performs surgical operations **d :** one that deals in stocks or commodities
2 a : MOUNTEBANK, FRAUD **b :** a shrewd and skillful person who knows how to circumvent restrictions or difficulties
3 a : something and especially a symbol that denotes or performs a mathematical or logical operation **b :** a mathematical function
4 : a binding site in a DNA chain at which a genetic repressor binds to inhibit the initiation of transcription of messenger RNA by one or more nearby structural genes — called also *operator gene;* compare OPERON

— **op·er·a·tor·less** *adjective*
¹oper·cu·lar \ō-ˈpər-kyə-lər\ *adjective* (1830)
: of, relating to, or constituting an operculum
²opercular *noun* (circa 1890)
: an opercular part (as a bone or scale)
oper·cu·late \ō-ˈpər-kyə-lət\ *also* **oper·cu·lat·ed** \-ˌlā-təd\ *adjective* (circa 1775)
: having an operculum
oper·cu·lum \ō-ˈpər-kyə-ləm\ *noun, plural* **-la** \-lə\ *also* **-lums** [New Latin, from Latin, cover, from *operire* to shut, cover] (1752)
1 : a body process or part that suggests a lid: as **a** : a horny or shelly plate on the posterior dorsal surface of the foot in many gastropod mollusks that closes the shell when the animal is retracted **b** : the covering of the gills of a fish — see FISH illustration
2 : a lid or covering flap (as of a moss capsule or a pyxidium in a seed plant)
op·er·et·ta \ˌä-pə-ˈre-tə\ *noun* [Italian, diminutive of *opera*] (1770)
: a usually romantic comic opera that includes songs and dancing
— **op·er·et·tist** \-ˈre-tist\ *noun*
op·er·on \ˈä-pə-ˌrän\ *noun* [French *opéron*, from *opérer* to bring about, effect (from Latin *operari*) + *-on* ²-on] (1961)
: a group of closely linked genes that produces a single messenger RNA molecule in transcription and that consists of structural genes and regulating elements (as an operator and promoter)
op·er·ose \ˈä-pə-ˌrōs\ *adjective* [Latin *operosus*, from *oper-, opus* work — more at OPERATE] (1678)
: TEDIOUS, WEARISOME
— **op·er·ose·ly** *adverb*
— **op·er·ose·ness** *noun*
Ophe·lia \ō-ˈfēl-yə\ *noun*
: the daughter of Polonius in Shakespeare's *Hamlet*
ophid·i·an \ō-ˈfi-dē-ən\ *adjective* [ultimately from Greek *ophis*] (1883)
: of, relating to, or resembling snakes
— **ophidian** *noun*
Ophir \ˈō-fər\ *noun* [Hebrew *Ōphīr*]
: a biblical land of uncertain location but reputedly rich in gold
ophit·ic \ä-ˈfi-tik, ō-\ *adjective* [*ophite* serpentine (stone), from Latin *ophites*, from Greek *ophitēs* (*lithos*), from *ophitēs* snakelike, from *ophis* snake; akin to Sanskrit *ahi* snake and probably to Latin *anguis* snake, *anguilla* eel, Greek *enchelys* eel, *echidna* viper, *echinos* hedgehog, Old English *igil*] (1875)
: having or being a rock fabric in which lath-shaped plagioclase crystals are enclosed in later formed augite
ophi·u·roid \ˌō-fē-ˈyùr-ˌòid, ˌä-\ *noun* [New Latin *Ophiuroidea*, group name, from *Ophiura*, genus name, from Greek *ophis* + *oura* tail — more at ASS] (circa 1879)
: BRITTLE STAR
— **ophiuroid** *adjective*
ophthalm- *or* **ophthalmo-** *combining form* [Greek, from *ophthalmos*]
: eye ⟨*ophthalmology*⟩
oph·thal·mia \äf-ˈthal-mē-ə, äp-\ *noun* [Middle English *obtalmia*, from Late Latin *ophthalmia*, from Greek, from *ophthalmos* eye; akin to Greek *ōps* eye — more at EYE] (14th century)
: inflammation of the conjunctiva or the eyeball
oph·thal·mic \-mik\ *adjective* (circa 1741)
1 : of, relating to, or situated near the eye
2 : supplying or draining the eye or structures in the region of the eye ⟨*ophthalmic* artery⟩
oph·thal·mol·o·gist \ˌäf-thə(l)-ˈmä-lə-jist, ˌäp-, -ˌthal-\ *noun* (1834)
: a physician that specializes in ophthalmology
— compare OPTICIAN, OPTOMETRIST
oph·thal·mol·o·gy \-ˈmä-lə-jē\ *noun* (circa 1842)
: a branch of medical science dealing with the structure, functions, and diseases of the eye

— **oph·thal·mo·log·ic** \-mə-ˈlä-jik\ *or* **oph·thal·mo·log·i·cal** \-ji-kəl\ *adjective*
— **oph·thal·mo·log·i·cal·ly** \-ji-k(ə-)lē\ *adverb*
oph·thal·mo·scope \äf-ˈthal-mə-ˌskōp, äp-\ *noun* [International Scientific Vocabulary] (circa 1857)
: an instrument for use in viewing the interior of the eye and especially the retina
— **oph·thal·mo·scop·ic** \(ˌ)äf-ˌthal-mə-ˈskä-pik, (ˌ)äp-\ *adjective*
— **oph·thal·mos·co·py** \ˌäf-thəl-ˈmäs-kə-pē, ˌäp-, -ˌthal-\ *noun*
-opia *noun combining form* [New Latin, from Greek *-ōpia*, from *ōps*]
1 : condition of having (such) vision ⟨diplo*pia*⟩
2 : condition of having (such) a visual defect ⟨hyper*opia*⟩
¹opi·ate \ˈō-pē-ət, -ˌāt\ *noun* (15th century)
1 : a preparation or derivative of opium; *broadly* : a narcotic or opioid peptide
2 : something that induces rest or inaction or quiets uneasiness
²opiate *adjective* (1543)
1 a : containing or mixed with opium **b** : of, relating to, binding, or being an opiate ⟨*opiate* receptors⟩
2 a : inducing sleep : NARCOTIC **b** : causing dullness or inaction
opine \ō-ˈpīn\ *verb* **opined; opin·ing** [Middle English, from Middle French *opiner*, from Latin *opinari* to have an opinion] (15th century)
intransitive verb
: to express opinions
transitive verb
: to state as an opinion
opin·ion \ə-ˈpin-yən\ *noun* [Middle English, from Middle French, from Latin *opinion-, opinio*, from *opinari*] (14th century)
1 a : a view, judgment, or appraisal formed in the mind about a particular matter **b** : APPROVAL, ESTEEM
2 a : belief stronger than impression and less strong than positive knowledge **b** : a generally held view
3 a : a formal expression of judgment or advice by an expert **b** : the formal expression (as by a judge, court, or referee) of the legal reasons and principles upon which a legal decision is based ☆
— **opin·ioned** \-yənd\ *adjective*
opin·ion·at·ed \-yə-ˌnā-təd\ *adjective* (1601)
: unduly adhering to one's own opinion or to preconceived notions
— **opin·ion·at·ed·ly** *adverb*
— **opin·ion·at·ed·ness** *noun*
opin·ion·a·tive \-ˌnā-tiv\ *adjective* (1536)
1 : of, relating to, or consisting of opinion : DOCTRINAL
2 : OPINIONATED
— **opin·ion·a·tive·ly** *adverb*
— **opin·ion·a·tive·ness** *noun*
opi·oid \ˈō-pē-ˌòid\ *adjective* (1957)
1 : possessing some properties characteristic of opiate narcotics but not derived from opium
2 : of, involving, or induced by an opioid substance or an opioid peptide
opioid peptide *noun* (1976)
: any of a group of endogenous neural polypeptides (as an endorphin or enkephalin) that bind especially to opiate receptors and mimic some of the pharmacological properties of opiate drugs — called also *opioid*
opis·tho·branch \ə-ˈpis-thə-ˌbraŋk\ *noun, plural* **-branchs** [New Latin *Opisthobranchia*, from Greek *opisthen* behind (akin to Greek *epi* on) + *branchia* gills — more at EPI-] (circa 1856)
: any of a subclass (Opisthobranchia) of marine gastropod mollusks that have the gills when present posterior to the heart and often lack a shell
— **opisthobranch** *adjective*

opi·um \ˈō-pē-əm\ *noun* [Middle English, from Latin, from Greek *opion*, from diminutive of *opos* sap] (14th century)
1 : a bitter brownish addictive narcotic drug that consists of the dried juice of the opium poppy
2 : something having an effect like that of opium
opium poppy *noun* (1863)
: an annual Eurasian poppy (*Papaver somniferum*) cultivated since antiquity as the source of opium, for its edible oily seeds, or for its showy flowers
opos·sum \ə-ˈpä-səm\ *noun, plural* **opos·sums** *also* **opossum** [Virginia Algonquian, literally, white animal] (1610)
1 : any of a family (Didelphidae) of American marsupials that usually have a pointed snout and prehensile tail; *especially* : a common omnivorous largely nocturnal and arboreal mammal (*Didelphis virginiana*) of North America having grayish to blackish fur with white on the cheeks

opossum 1

2 : any of several Australian phalangers
¹op·po·nent \ə-ˈpō-nənt\ *noun* [Latin *opponent-, opponens*, present participle of *opponere*] (1588)
1 : one that takes an opposite position (as in a debate, contest, or conflict)
2 : a muscle that opposes or counteracts and limits the action of another
²opponent *adjective* (1647)
1 : ANTAGONISTIC, OPPOSING
2 : situated in front
op·por·tune \ˌä-pər-ˈtün, -ˈtyün\ *adjective* [Middle English, from Middle French *opportun*, from Latin *opportunus*, from *ob-* toward + *portus* port, harbor — more at OB-, FORD] (15th century)
1 : suitable or convenient for a particular occurrence ⟨an *opportune* moment⟩
2 : occurring at an appropriate time ⟨an *opportune* offer of assistance⟩
— **op·por·tune·ly** *adverb*
— **op·por·tune·ness** \-ˈt(y)ün-nəs\ *noun*
op·por·tun·ism \-ˈtü-ˌni-zəm, -ˈtyü-\ *noun* (1870)
: the art, policy, or practice of taking advantage of opportunities or circumstances often with little regard for principles or consequences

☆ SYNONYMS
Opinion, view, belief, conviction, persuasion, sentiment mean a judgment one holds as true. OPINION implies a conclusion thought out yet open to dispute ⟨each expert seemed to have a different *opinion*⟩. VIEW suggests a subjective opinion ⟨very assertive in stating his *views*⟩. BELIEF implies often deliberate acceptance and intellectual assent ⟨a firm *belief* in her party's platform⟩. CONVICTION applies to a firmly and seriously held belief ⟨the *conviction* that animal life is as sacred as human⟩. PERSUASION suggests a belief grounded on assurance (as by evidence) of its truth ⟨was of the *persuasion* that everything changes⟩. SENTIMENT suggests a settled opinion reflective of one's feelings ⟨her feminist *sentiments* are well-known⟩.

\ə\ **abut** \ᵊ\ **kitten** \ər\ **further** \a\ **ash** \ā\ **ace**
\ä\ **mop, mar** \au̇\ **out** \ch\ **chin** \e\ **bet** \ē\ **easy**
\g\ **go** \i\ **hit** \ī\ **ice** \j\ **job** \ŋ\ **sing** \ō\ **go**
\ȯ\ **law** \ȯi\ **boy** \th\ **thin** \th\ **the** \ü\ **loot** \u̇\ **foot**
\y\ **yet** \zh\ **vision** *see also* Guide to Pronunciation

— **op·por·tun·ist** \-'tü-nist, -'tyü-\ *noun or adjective*

op·por·tu·nis·tic \-tü-'nis-tik, -tyü-\ *adjective* (1892)
: taking advantage of opportunities as they arise: as **a** : exploiting opportunities with little regard to principle or consequences ⟨a politician considered *opportunistic*⟩ **b** : feeding on whatever food is available ⟨*opportunistic* feeders⟩ **c** : being or caused by a usually harmless microorganism that can become pathogenic when the host's resistance is impaired ⟨*opportunistic* infections⟩
— **op·por·tu·nis·ti·cal·ly** \-ti-k(ə-)lē\ *adverb*

op·por·tu·ni·ty \ˌä-pər-'tü-nə-tē, -'tyü-\ *noun, plural* **-ties** (14th century)
1 : a favorable juncture of circumstances ⟨the halt provided an *opportunity* for rest and refreshment⟩
2 : a good chance for advancement or progress

opportunity cost *noun* (1911)
: the cost of making an investment that is the difference between the return on one investment and the return on an alternative

op·pos·able \ə-'pō-zə-bəl\ *adjective* (1667)
1 : capable of being opposed or resisted
2 : capable of being placed against one or more of the remaining digits of a hand or foot ⟨the *opposable* human thumb⟩
— **op·pos·abil·i·ty** \-ˌpō-zə-'bi-lə-tē\ *noun*

op·pose \ə-'pōz\ *transitive verb* **op·posed; op·pos·ing** [French *opposer*, from Latin *opponere* (perfect indicative *opposui*), from *ob-* against + *ponere* to place — more at OB-, POSITION] (1579)
1 : to place opposite or against something
2 : to place over against something so as to provide resistance, counterbalance, or contrast
3 : to offer resistance to ☆
— **op·pos·er** *noun*

op·posed \-'pōzd\ *adjective* (1596)
: set or placed in opposition : CONTRARY ⟨with politicians, as *opposed* to soap, you cannot return what you have bought —Felix G. Rohatyn⟩

op·pose·less \ə-'pōz-ləs\ *adjective* (1605)
archaic : IRRESISTIBLE

¹op·po·site \'ä-pə-zət, 'äp-sət\ *adjective* [Middle English, from Middle French, from Latin *oppositus*, past participle of *opponere*] (14th century)
1 a : set over against something that is at the other end or side of an intervening line or space ⟨*opposite* interior angles⟩ ⟨*opposite* ends of a diameter⟩ **b** : situated in pairs on an axis with each member being separated from the other by half the circumference of the axis ⟨*opposite* leaves⟩ — compare ALTERNATE
2 a : occupying an opposing and often antagonistic position ⟨*opposite* sides of the question⟩ **b** : diametrically different (as in nature or character) ⟨*opposite* meanings⟩
3 : contrary to one another or to a thing specified : REVERSE ⟨gave them *opposite* directions⟩
4 : being the other of a pair that are corresponding or complementary in position, function, or nature ⟨members of the *opposite* sex⟩
5 : of, relating to, or being the side of a baseball field that is near the first base line for a right-handed batter and near the third base line for a left-handed batter ☆
— **op·po·site·ly** *adverb*
— **op·po·site·ness** *noun*

²opposite *noun* (15th century)
1 : something that is opposed to some other often specified thing
2 : ANTONYM
3 : ADDITIVE INVERSE; *especially* : the additive inverse of a real number

³opposite *adverb* (1667)
: on or to an opposite side

⁴opposite *preposition* (1758)
1 : across from and usually facing on the same level with ⟨sat *opposite* each other⟩

2 : in a role complementary to ⟨played *opposite* the leading man in the comedy⟩

opposite number *noun* (1906)
: a member of a system or class who holds relatively the same position as a particular member in a corresponding system or class : COUNTERPART

op·po·si·tion \ˌä-pə-'zi-shən\ *noun* (14th century)
1 : a configuration in which one celestial body is opposite another in the sky or in which the elongation is near or equal to 180 degrees
2 : the relation between two propositions having the same subject and predicate but differing in quantity or quality or both
3 : an act of setting opposite or over against : the condition of being so set
4 : hostile or contrary action or condition
5 a : something that opposes; *specifically* : a body of persons opposing something **b** *often capitalized* : a political party opposing and prepared to replace the party in power
— **op·po·si·tion·al** \-'zish-nəl, -'zi-shə-nᵊl\ *adjective*

op·po·si·tion·ist \-'zi-sh(ə-)nist\ *noun* (1773)
: a member of an opposition
— **oppositionist** *adjective*

op·press \ə-'pres\ *transitive verb* [Middle English, from Middle French *oppresser*, from Latin *oppressus*, past participle of *opprimere*, from *ob-* against + *premere* to press — more at OB-, PRESS] (14th century)
1 a *archaic* : SUPPRESS **b** : to crush or burden by abuse of power or authority
2 : to burden spiritually or mentally : weigh heavily upon
synonym see WRONG
— **op·pres·sor** \-'pre-sər\ *noun*

op·pres·sion \ə-'pre-shən\ *noun* (14th century)
1 a : unjust or cruel exercise of authority or power **b** : something that oppresses especially in being an unjust or excessive exercise of power
2 : a sense of being weighed down in body or mind : DEPRESSION

op·pres·sive \ə-'pre-siv\ *adjective* (circa 1677)
1 : unreasonably burdensome or severe ⟨*oppressive* legislation⟩
2 : TYRANNICAL
3 : overwhelming or depressing to the spirit or senses ⟨an *oppressive* climate⟩
synonym see ONEROUS
— **op·pres·sive·ly** *adverb*
— **op·pres·sive·ness** *noun*

op·pro·bri·ous \ə-'prō-brē-əs\ *adjective* (14th century)
1 : expressive of opprobrium : SCURRILOUS ⟨*opprobrious* language⟩
2 : deserving of opprobrium : INFAMOUS
— **op·pro·bri·ous·ly** *adverb*
— **op·pro·bri·ous·ness** *noun*

op·pro·bri·um \-brē-əm\ *noun* [Latin, from *opprobrium* to reproach, from *ob* in the way of + *probrum* reproach; akin to Latin *pro* forward and to Latin *ferre* to carry, bring — more at OB-, FOR, BEAR] (1656)
1 : something that brings disgrace
2 a : public disgrace or ill fame that follows from conduct considered grossly wrong or vicious **b** : CONTEMPT, REPROACH

op·pugn \ə-'pyün, ä-\ *transitive verb* [Middle English, from Latin *oppugnare*, from *ob-* against + *pugnare* to fight — more at OB-, PUNGENT] (15th century)
1 : to fight against
2 : to call in question
— **op·pugn·er** *noun*

Ops \'äps\ *noun* [Latin]
: the Roman goddess of abundance and the wife of Saturn

op·sin \'äp-sən\ *noun* [probably from *rhodopsin*] (1951)
: any of various colorless proteins that in combination with retinal or a related prosthetic

group form a visual pigment (as rhodopsin) in a reaction which is reversed by light

-opsis *noun combining form, plural* **-opses** *or* **-opsides** [New Latin, from Greek, from *opsis* appearance, vision]
: structure resembling a (specified) thing ⟨cary*opsis*⟩

op·son·ic \äp-'sä-nik\ *adjective* (1903)
: of, relating to, or involving opsonin

op·so·nin \'äp-sə-nən\ *noun* [Latin *opsonare* to buy provisions, cater (from Greek *opsōnein*) + English ¹-*in* — more at OLIGOPSONY] (1903)
: an antibody of blood serum that makes foreign cells more susceptible to the action of the phagocytes

-opsy *noun combining form* [Greek *-opsia*, from *opsis*]
: examination ⟨necr*opsy*⟩

opt \'äpt\ *intransitive verb* [French *opter*, from Latin *optare*] (1877)
: to make a choice; *especially* : to decide in favor of something ⟨*opted* for a tax increase —Tom Wicker⟩

op·ta·tive \'äp-tə-tiv\ *adjective* (15th century)
1 a : of, relating to, or constituting a verbal mood that is expressive of wish or desire **b** : of, relating to, or constituting a sentence that is expressive of wish or hope
2 : expressing desire or wish
— **optative** *noun*
— **op·ta·tive·ly** *adverb*

¹op·tic \'äp-tik\ *adjective* [Middle English, from Middle French *optique*, from Medieval Latin *opticus*, from Greek *optikos*, from *opsesthai* to be going to see; akin to Greek *opsis* appearance, *ōps* eye — more at EYE] (14th century)
: of or relating to vision or the eye

²optic *noun* (1600)
1 : EYE
2 a : any of the elements (as lenses, mirrors, or light guides) of an optical instrument or system — usually used in plural **b** : an optical instrument

op·ti·cal \'äp-ti-kəl\ *adjective* (1570)
1 : of or relating to the science of optics
2 a : of or relating to vision : VISUAL **b** : VISIBLE 1 ⟨*optical* wavelength⟩ **c** : of, relating to, or being objects that emit light in the visible

range of frequencies ⟨an *optical* galaxy⟩ **d**
: using the properties of light to aid vision ⟨an
optical instrument⟩
3 a : of, relating to, or utilizing light especial-
ly instead of other forms of energy ⟨*optical*
microscopy⟩ **b :** involving the use of light-
sensitive devices to acquire information for a
computer ⟨*optical* character recognition⟩
4 : of or relating to optical art
— **op·ti·cal·ly** \-k(ə-)lē\ *adverb*
optical activity *noun* (1877)
: ability of a chemical substance to rotate the
plane of vibration of polarized light to the
right or left
optical art *noun* (1964)
: nonobjective art characterized by the use of
straight or curved lines or geometric patterns
often for an illusory effect (as of motion)
optical bench *noun* (1883)
: an apparatus that is fitted for the convenient
location and adjustment of light sources and
optical devices and that is used for the obser-
vation and measurement of optical phenomena
optical disk *noun* (1980)
: a disk with a plastic coating on which infor-
mation (as music or visual images) is recorded
digitally (as in the form of tiny pits) and
which is read by using a laser
optical fiber *noun* (1962)
: a single fiber-optic strand
optical glass *noun* (1840)
: flint or crown glass of well-defined charac-
teristics used especially for making lenses
optical illusion *noun* (1794)
: ILLUSION 2a(1)
optically active *adjective* (1885)
: capable of rotating the plane of polarization
of light to the right or left — used of com-
pounds, molecules, or atoms
optical rotation *noun* (1895)
: the angle through which the plane of vibra-
tion of polarized light that traverses an optical-
ly active substance is rotated
optic axis *noun* (1664)
: a line in a doubly refracting medium that is
parallel to the direction in which all compo-
nents of plane-polarized light travel with the
same speed
optic chiasma *noun* (1872)
: the X-shaped partial decussation on the un-
dersurface of the hypothalamus through which
the optic nerves are continuous with the brain
— called also *optic chiasm*
optic cup *noun* (circa 1885)
: the optic vesicle after invaginating to form a
2-layered cup from which the retina and pig-
mented layer of the eye will develop —
called also *eyecup*
optic disk *noun* (circa 1890)
: BLIND SPOT 1a
op·ti·cian \äp-'ti-shən\ *noun* (1687)
1 : a maker or dealer in optical items and
instruments
2 : a person who reads prescriptions for visual
correction, orders lenses, and dispenses spec-
tacles and contact lenses — compare OPH-
THALMOLOGIST, OPTOMETRIST
optic lobe *noun* (1854)
: either of two prominences of the midbrain
concerned with vision
optic nerve *noun* (1615)
: either of the pair of nerves that comprise the
2d pair of cranial nerves, arise from the ven-
tral part of the diencephalon, supply the retina,
and conduct visual stimuli to the brain — see
EYE illustration
op·tics \'äp-tiks\ *noun plural but singular in
construction* (1579)
: a science that deals with the genesis and
propagation of light, the changes that it under-
goes and produces, and other phenomena
closely associated with it
optic vesicle *noun* (circa 1885)
: an evagination of each lateral wall of the em-
bryonic vertebrate forebrain from which the
nervous structures of the eye develop

op·ti·mal \'äp-tə-məl\ *adjective* (1890)
: most desirable or satisfactory **:** OPTIMUM
— **op·ti·mal·i·ty** \,äp-tə-'ma-lə-tē\ *noun*
— **op·ti·mal·ly** \-mə-lē\ *adverb*
op·ti·mi·sa·tion, op·ti·mise *British variant
of* OPTIMIZATION, OPTIMIZE
op·ti·mism \'äp-tə-,mi-zəm\ *noun* [French *op-
timisme,* from Latin *optimum,* noun, best, from
neuter of *optimus* best; akin to Latin *ops* pow-
er — more at OPULENT] (1759)
1 : a doctrine that this world is the best possi-
ble world
2 : an inclination to put the most favorable
construction upon actions and events or to an-
ticipate the best possible outcome
— **op·ti·mist** \-mist\ *noun*
— **op·ti·mis·tic** \,äp-tə-'mis-tik\ *adjective*
— **op·ti·mis·ti·cal·ly** \-ti-k(ə-)lē\ *adverb*
Op·ti·mist \'äp-tə-mist\ *noun* [*Optimist
(Club)*] (1911)
: a member of a major international service
club
op·ti·mi·za·tion \,äp-tə-mə-'zā-shən\ *noun*
(1857)
: an act, process, or methodology of making
something (as a design, system, or decision) as
fully perfect, functional, or effective as possi-
ble; *specifically* **:** the mathematical procedures
(as finding the maximum of a function) in-
volved in this
op·ti·mize \'äp-tə-,mīz\ *transitive verb*
-mized; -miz·ing (1857)
: to make as perfect, effective, or functional as
possible
— **op·ti·miz·er** \-,mī-zər\ *noun*
op·ti·mum \'äp-tə-məm\ *noun, plural* **-ma**
\-mə\ *also* **-mums** [Latin] (1879)
1 : the amount or degree of something that is
most favorable to some end; *especially* **:** the
most favorable condition for the growth and
reproduction of an organism
2 : greatest degree attained or attainable under
implied or specified conditions
— **optimum** *adjective*
¹**op·tion** \'äp-shən\ *noun* [French, from Latin
option-, optio free choice; akin to Latin *optare*
to choose] (circa 1604)
1 : an act of choosing
2 a : the power or right to choose **:** freedom of
choice **b :** a privilege of demanding fulfill-
ment of a contract on any day within a speci-
fied time **c :** a contract conveying a right to
buy or sell designated securities, commodities,
or property interest at a specified price during
a stipulated period; *also* **:** the right conveyed
by an option **d :** a right of an insured person to
choose the form in which payments due on a
policy shall be made or applied
3 : something that may be chosen: as **a :** an
alternative course of action ⟨didn't have many
options open⟩ **b :** an item that is offered in ad-
dition to or in place of standard equipment
4 : an offensive football play in which a back
may choose whether to pass or run with the
ball — called also *option play*
synonym *see* CHOICE
²**option** *transitive verb* (1926)
: to grant or take an option on
op·tion·al \'äp-shnəl, -shə-nʲl\ *adjective*
(1792)
: involving an option **:** not compulsory
— **op·tion·al·i·ty** \,äp-shə-'na-lə-tē\ *noun*
— **op·tion·al·ly** *adverb*
opto- *combining form* [Greek *optos,* verbal of
opsesthai — more at OPTIC]
1 : vision ⟨*opto*metry⟩
2 : optic and ⟨*opto*electronics⟩
op·to·elec·tron·ics \,äp-(,)tō-i-lek-'trä-niks,
-ē-lek-\ *noun plural but singular in construc-
tion* (1959)
: a branch of electronics that deals with elec-
tronic devices for emitting, modulating, trans-
mitting, and sensing light
— **op·to·elec·tron·ic** \-nik\ *adjective*
op·to·ki·net·ic \,äp-tō-kə-'ne-tik, -kī-\ *adjec-
tive* (1925)

: of, relating to, or involving movements of
the eyes
op·tom·e·trist \äp-'tä-mə-trist\ *noun* (1903)
: a specialist licensed to practice optometry
— compare OPHTHALMOLOGIST, OPTICIAN
op·tom·e·try \-trē\ *noun* [International Scien-
tific Vocabulary] (1886)
: the art or profession of examining the eye for
defects and faults of refraction and prescribing
correctional lenses or exercises
— **op·to·met·ric** \,äp-tə-'me-trik\ *adjective*
opt out *intransitive verb* (1951)
: to choose not to participate in something —
often used with *of* ⟨*opted out* of the project⟩
op·u·lence \'ä-pyə-lən(t)s\ *noun* (circa 1510)
1 : WEALTH, AFFLUENCE
2 : ABUNDANCE, PROFUSION
op·u·lent \-lənt\ *adjective* [Latin *opulentus,*
from *ops* power, help; akin to Latin *opus*
work] (1601)
: exhibiting or characterized by opulence: as **a**
: having a large estate or property **:** WEALTHY
⟨hoping to marry an *opulent* widow⟩ **b :** amply
or plentifully provided or fashioned often to
the point of ostentation ⟨living in *opulent* com-
fort⟩
synonym *see* RICH
— **op·u·lent·ly** *adverb*
opun·tia \ō-'pən(t)-sh(ē-)ə\ *noun* [Latin, a
plant, from feminine of *opuntius* of Opus,
from *Opunt-, Opus* Opus, ancient city in
Greece] (1601)
: any of a large genus (*Opuntia*) of cacti with
usually yellow flowers and flat or terete joints
usually studded with tubercles bearing spines
or prickly hairs — compare CHOLLA, PRICKLY
PEAR
opus \'ō-pəs\ *noun, plural* **op·era** \'ō-pə-rə,
'ä-\ *also* **opus·es** \'ō-pə-səz\ [Latin *oper-,
opus* — more at OPERATE] (1809)
: WORK; *especially* **:** a musical composition or
set of compositions usually numbered in the
order of its issue
opus·cule \ō-'pəs-(,)kyü(ə)l\ *noun* [French,
from Latin *opusculum,* diminutive of *opus*]
(circa 1656)
: a small or petty work **:** OPUSCULUM
opus·cu·lum \ō-'pəs-kyə-ləm\ *noun, plural*
-la \-lə\ [Latin] (1654)
: a minor work (as of literature) — usually
used in plural
¹**or** \ər, 'ȯr, *Southern also* 'är\ *conjunction*
[Middle English, alteration of *other,* alteration
of Old English *oththe;* akin to Old High Ger-
man *eddo* or] (13th century)
1 — used as a function word to indicate an
alternative ⟨coffee *or* tea⟩ ⟨sink *or* swim⟩, the
equivalent or substitutive character of two
words or phrases ⟨lessen *or* abate⟩, or approx-
imation or uncertainty ⟨in five *or* six days⟩
2 *archaic* **:** EITHER
3 *archaic* **:** WHETHER
4 — used in logic as a sentential connective
that forms a complex sentence which is true
when at least one of its constituent sentences
is true; compare DISJUNCTION
²**or** *preposition* [Middle English, from *or,* ad-
verb, early, before, from Old Norse *ār;* akin to
Old English *ǣr* early — more at ERE] (13th
century)
archaic **:** BEFORE
³**or** *conjunction* (13th century)
archaic **:** BEFORE
⁴**or** *noun* [Middle English, from Middle
French, gold, from Latin *aurum* — more at
AUREUS] (15th century)
: the heraldic color gold or yellow
OR \'ȯr\ *noun* [¹*or*] (1947)
: a logical operator that requires either of two
inputs to be present or conditions to be met for

an output to be made or a statement to be executed ⟨*OR* gate in a computer⟩

¹-or *noun suffix* [Middle English, from Old French *-eur, -eor* & Latin *-or*; Old French *-eur*, from Latin *-or*; Old French *-eor*, from Latin *-ator*, from *-a-*, verb stem + *-tor*, agent suffix; akin to Greek *-tōr*, agent suffix, Sanskrit *-tā*]
: one that does a (specified) thing ⟨grant*or*⟩

²-or *noun suffix* [Middle English, from Old French *-eur*, from Latin *-or*]
: condition : activity ⟨demean*or*⟩

ora *plural of* OS

or·ache *or* **or·ach** \'ór-ich, 'är-\ *noun* [Middle English *orage, arage*, from Middle French *arrache*, from (assumed) Vulgar Latin *atrapic-, atrapex*, from Greek *atraphaxys*] (13th century)
: any of various herbs (genus *Atriplex*) of the goosefoot family that include some (as *A. hortensis*) used as potherbs

or·a·cle \'ór-ə-kəl, 'är-\ *noun* [Middle English, from Middle French, from Latin *oraculum*, from *orare* to speak — more at ORATION] (15th century)
1 a : a person (as a priestess of ancient Greece) through whom a deity is believed to speak **b** : a shrine in which a deity reveals hidden knowledge or the divine purpose through such a person **c** : an answer or decision given by an oracle
2 a : a person giving wise or authoritative decisions or opinions **b** : an authoritative or wise expression or answer

orac·u·lar \ò-'ra-kyə-lər, ə-\ *adjective* [Latin *oraculum*] (1678)
1 : of, relating to, or being an oracle
2 : resembling an oracle (as in solemnity of delivery)
synonym see DICTATORIAL
— **orac·u·lar·i·ty** \-,ra-kyə-'lar-ə-tē\ *noun*
— **orac·u·lar·ly** \-'ra-kyə-lər-lē\ *adverb*

¹oral \'ór-əl, 'ór-, 'är-\ *adjective* [Latin *or-, os* mouth; akin to Old Norse *ōss* mouth of a river, Sanskrit *ās* mouth] (1628)
1 a : uttered by the mouth or in words : SPOKEN **b** : using speech or the lips especially in teaching the deaf
2 a : of, given through, or involving the mouth **b** : being on or relating to the same surface as the mouth
3 a : of, relating to, or characterized by the first stage of psychosexual development in psychoanalytic theory during which libidinal gratification is derived from intake (as of food), by sucking, and later by biting **b** : of, relating to, or characterized by personality traits of passive dependency and aggressiveness
usage see VERBAL
— **oral·i·ty** \ò-'ra-lə-tē, ō-\ *noun*
— **oral·ly** \'ór-ə-lē, 'ór-, 'är-\ *adverb*

²oral *noun* (1876)
: an oral examination — usually used in plural

oral history *noun* (1955)
1 : tape-recorded historical information obtained in interviews concerning personal experiences and recollections; *also* : the study of such information
2 : a written work based on oral history
— **oral historian** *noun*

oral·ism \'ór-ə-,li-zəm, 'ór-, 'är-\ *noun* (1883)
: advocacy or use of the oral method of teaching the deaf
— **oral·ist** \-list\ *noun*

orang \ə-'raŋ\ *noun* [by shortening] (1778)
: ORANGUTAN

¹or·ange \'är-inj, 'är-(ə)nj; *chiefly Northern & Midland* 'ór-inj, 'ór-(ə)nj\ *noun* [Middle English, from Middle French, from Old Provençal *auranja*, from Arabic *nāranj*, from Persian *nārang*, from Sanskrit *nāraṅga* orange tree] (14th century)
1 a : a globose berry with a yellowish to reddish orange rind and a sweet edible pulp **b** : any of various rather small evergreen trees (genus *Citrus*) with ovate unifoliolate leaves, hard yellow wood, fragrant white flowers, and fruits that are oranges
2 : any of several trees or fruits resembling the orange
3 : any of a group of colors that lie midway between red and yellow in hue

²orange *adjective* (1542)
1 : of or relating to the orange
2 : of the color orange

Orange *adjective* (1795)
: of, relating to, or sympathizing with Orangemen
— **Or·ange·ism** \'är-in-,ji-zəm, 'är(ə)-n-, 'ór-in-, 'ór(ə)n-\ *noun*

or·ange·ade \,är-in-'jād, ,är(-ə)n-, ,ór-in-, ,ór(-ə)n-\ *noun* [French, from *orange* + *-ade*] (1706)
: a beverage of sweetened orange juice mixed with water

orange chromide *noun* [*chromide*, ultimately from Greek *chromis*, a sea fish] (1933)
: a brilliant orange or yellow red-spotted fish (*Etroplus maculatus*) often kept in tropical aquariums

orange hawkweed *noun* (circa 1900)
: a European hawkweed (*Hieracium aurantiacum*) that has flower heads with bright orange-red rays and is a troublesome weed especially in northeastern North America

Or·ange·man \'är-inj-mən, 'är-(ə)nj-, 'ór-inj-, 'ór(ə)nj-\ *noun* [William III of England, prince of *Orange*] (1796)
1 : a member of a secret society organized in the north of Ireland in 1795 to defend the British sovereign and to support the Protestant religion
2 : a Protestant Irishman especially of Ulster

orange peel *noun* (circa 1909)
: a rough surface (as on porcelain) like that of an orange

orange pekoe *noun* (circa 1877)
: tea made from the smallest and youngest leaves of the shoot

or·ange·ry *also* **or·ange·rie** \'är-inj-rē, 'är(-ə)nj-, 'ór-inj-, 'ór(-ə)nj-\ *noun, plural* **-ries** (1664)
: a protected place and especially a greenhouse for raising oranges in cool climates

or·ange·wood \'är-inj-,wùd, 'är(-ə)nj-, 'ór-inj-, 'ór(-ə)nj-\ *noun* (1884)
: the wood of the orange tree used especially in turnery and carving

or·ang·ish \'är-in-jish, 'är-(ə)n-, 'ór-in-, 'ór(-ə)n-\ *adjective* (1967)
: somewhat orange

orang·u·tan \ə-'raŋ-ə-,taŋ, -'raŋ-gə-, -,tan\ *noun* [Bazaar Malay (Malay-based pidgin), from Malay *orang* man + *hutan* forest] (1691)
: a largely herbivorous arboreal anthropoid ape (*Pongo pygmaeus*) of Borneo and Sumatra that is about two thirds as large as the gorilla and has brown skin, long sparse reddish brown hair, and very long arms ◇

or·angy *or* **or·ang·ey** \'är-in-jē, 'är(-ə)n-, 'ór-in-, 'ór(-ə)n-\ *adjective* (1778)
: resembling or suggestive of an orange (as in flavor or color)

orangutan

orate \ò-'rāt, ō-; 'ór-,āt, 'ór-\ *intransitive verb* **orat·ed; orat·ing** [back-formation from *oration*] (circa 1600)
: to speak in an elevated and often pompous manner

ora·tion \ə-'rā-shən, ò-\ *noun* [Latin *oration-, oratio* speech, oration, from *orare* to plead, speak, pray; akin to Hittite *ariya-* to consult an oracle and perhaps to Greek *ara* prayer] (1502)
: an elaborate discourse delivered in a formal and dignified manner

or·a·tor \'ór-ə-tər, 'är-\ *noun* (15th century)
1 : one who delivers an oration
2 : one distinguished for skill and power as a public speaker

Or·a·to·ri·an \,ór-ə-'tór-ē-ən, ,är-, -'tòr-\ *noun* (circa 1656)
: a member of the Congregation of the Oratory of Saint Philip Neri founded in Rome in 1575 and comprising independent communities of secular priests under obedience but without vows
— **Oratorian** *adjective*

or·a·tor·i·cal \,ór-ə-'tór-i-kəl, ,är-ə-'tär-\ *adjective* (1589)
: of, relating to, or characteristic of an orator or oratory
— **or·a·tor·i·cal·ly** \-k(ə-)lē\ *adverb*

or·a·to·rio \,ór-ə-'tór-ē-,ō, ,är-, -'tòr-\ *noun, plural* **-rios** [Italian, from the *Oratorio di San Filippo Neri* (Oratory of Saint Philip Neri) in Rome] (circa 1738)
: a lengthy choral work usually of a religious nature consisting chiefly of recitatives, arias, and choruses without action or scenery

¹or·a·to·ry \'ór-ə-,tór-ē, 'är-, -,tòr-\ *noun, plural* **-ries** [Middle English *oratorie*, from Late Latin *oratorium*, from *orare*] (14th century)
1 : a place of prayer; *especially* : a private or institutional chapel
2 *capitalized* : an Oratorian congregation, house, or church

²oratory *noun* [Latin *oratoria*, from feminine of *oratorius* oratorical, from *orare*] (1593)
1 : the art of speaking in public eloquently or effectively
2 a : public speaking that employs oratory **b** : public speaking that is characterized by the use of stock phrases and that appeals chiefly to the emotions

¹orb \'órb\ *noun* [Middle English, from Middle French *orbe*, from Latin *orbis* circle, disk, orb] (14th century)
1 : any of the concentric spheres in old astronomy surrounding the earth and carrying the celestial bodies in their revolutions
2 *archaic* : something circular : CIRCLE, ORBIT
3 : a spherical body; *especially* : a spherical celestial object
4 : EYE

◇ WORD HISTORY

orangutan The orangutan, native to Borneo and Sumatra, has been known in western Europe since the 17th century. The name for the animal, similar in most European languages to the English word, is borrowed from two Malay words, *orang* "man, person," and *hutan* "forest," but the Malay word for "orangutan" is *mawas*, and the precise origin of the compound *orangutan* is not known. Presumably Europeans borrowed it from Bazaar Malay, a group of restructured forms of Malay used as common languages by the many non-Malay speakers of the Indonesian archipelago. Queried by Europeans about the name of the animal and not knowing the actual Malay word, inhabitants of the islands perhaps responded by making up *orangutan* on the spot, the sense "forest man" fitting well enough as a descriptive epithet. There has been a tendency ever since *orangutan* was borrowed to rhyme the second and last syllables (as if \raŋ\ and \taŋ\) and in some European languages including English a *g* is sometimes added to the last syllable.

5 : a sphere surmounted by a cross symbolizing kingly power and justice
²orb (1600)
transitive verb
1 : to form into a disk or circle
2 *archaic* **:** ENCIRCLE, SURROUND, ENCLOSE
intransitive verb
archaic **:** to move in an orbit
or·bic·u·lar \òr-'bi-kyə-lər\ *adjective* [Middle English *orbiculer*, from Middle French or Late Latin; Middle French *orbiculaire*, from Late Latin *orbicularis*, from Latin *orbiculus*, diminutive of *orbis*] (15th century)
: SPHERICAL, CIRCULAR
— **or·bic·u·lar·ly** \-'bi-kyə-lər-lē\ *adverb*
or·bic·u·late \òr-'bi-kyə-lət\ *adjective* (circa 1760)
: circular or nearly circular in outline ⟨an *orbiculate* leaf⟩ — see LEAF illustration
¹or·bit \'òr-bət\ *noun* [Middle English, from Medieval Latin *orbita*, from Latin, rut, track, probably from *orbis*] (15th century)
: the bony socket of the eye
— **or·bit·al** \'òr-bə-'t°l\ *adjective*
²orbit *noun* [Latin *orbita* path, rut, orbit] (1696)
1 a : a path described by one body in its revolution about another (as by the earth about the sun or by an electron about an atomic nucleus); *also* **:** one complete revolution of a body describing such a path **b :** a circular path
2 : a range or sphere of activity or influence
synonym see RANGE
— **or·bit·al** \-'t°l\ *adjective*
³orbit (1943)
transitive verb
1 : to revolve in an orbit around **:** CIRCLE
2 : to send up and make revolve in an orbit ⟨*orbit* a satellite⟩
intransitive verb
: to travel in circles
or·bit·al \'òr-bə-t°l\ *noun* [*orbital,* adjective] (1932)
: a subdivision of a nuclear shell containing zero, one, or two electrons
or·bit·er \-bə-tər\ *noun* (1951)
: one that orbits: as **a :** a spacecraft designed to orbit a celestial body without landing on its surface **b :** SPACE SHUTTLE
orb weaver *noun* (1889)
: any of a family (Araneidae) of North American spiders that have eight similar eyes and typically spin a large elaborate web
or·ca \'òr-kə\ *noun* [New Latin *Orca,* genus name, from Latin, a whale, probably modification of Greek *oryg-, oryx* — more at ORYX] (1866)
: KILLER WHALE
Or·ca·di·an \òr-'kā-dē-ən\ *noun* [Latin *Orcades* Orkney Islands] (1661)
: a native or inhabitant of the Orkney Islands
— **Orcadian** *adjective*
or·chard \'òr-chərd\ *noun* [Middle English, from Old English *ortgeard,* from *ort-* (from Latin *hortus* garden) + *geard* yard — more at YARD] (before 12th century)
: a planting of fruit trees, nut trees, or sugar maples; *also* **:** the trees of such a planting
orchard grass *noun* (1765)
: a widely grown tall stout hay and pasture grass (*Dactylis glomerata*) that grows in tufts and has loose open panicles
or·chard·ist \'òr-chər-dist\ *noun* (1794)
: an owner or supervisor of orchards
or·ches·tra \'òr-kəs-trə, -,kes-\ *noun* [Latin, from Greek *orchēstra,* from *orcheisthai* to dance; perhaps akin to Sanskrit *r̥gháyati* he trembles, he rages] (1606)
1 a : the circular space used by the chorus in front of the proscenium in an ancient Greek theater **b :** a corresponding semicircular space in a Roman theater used for seating important persons
2 a : the space in front of the stage in a modern theater that is used by an orchestra **b :** the forward section of seats on the main floor of a

theater **c :** the main floor of a theater
3 : a group of musicians including especially string players organized to perform ensemble music — compare BAND
or·ches·tral \òr-'kes-trəl\ *adjective* (circa 1811)
1 : of, relating to, or composed for an orchestra
2 : suggestive of an orchestra or its musical qualities
— **or·ches·tral·ly** \-trə-lē\ *adverb*
or·ches·trate \'òr-kə-,strāt\ *transitive verb* **-trat·ed; -trat·ing** (1880)
1 a : to compose or arrange (music) for an orchestra **b :** to provide with orchestration ⟨*orchestrate* a ballet⟩
2 : to arrange or combine so as to achieve a desired or maximum effect ⟨*orchestrated* preparations for the banquet⟩
— **or·ches·tra·tor** *also* **or·ches·trat·er** \-,strā-tər\ *noun*
or·ches·tra·tion \,òr-kə-'strā-shən\ *noun* (circa 1859)
1 : the arrangement of a musical composition for performance by an orchestra; *also* **:** orchestral treatment of a musical composition
2 : harmonious organization ⟨develop a world community through *orchestration* of cultural diversities —L. K. Frank⟩
— **or·ches·tra·tion·al** \-shnəl, -shə-n°l\ *adjective*
or·chid \'òr-kəd\ *noun* [irregular from New Latin *Orchis*] (1845)
1 : any of a large family (Orchidaceae, the orchid family) of perennial epiphytic or terrestrial monocotyledonous plants that usually have showy 3-petaled flowers with the middle petal enlarged into a lip and differing from the others in shape and color
2 : a light purple
— **or·chid·like** \-,līk\ *adjective*

orchid 1

or·chi·da·ceous \,òr-kə-'dā-shəs\ *adjective* [New Latin *Orchidaceae,* family name, from *Orchis*] (1838)
1 : of, relating to, or resembling the orchids
2 : SHOWY, OSTENTATIOUS
or·chis \'òr-kəs\ *noun* [New Latin, from Latin, orchid, from Greek, testicle, orchid; akin to Middle Irish *uirgge* testicle] (1562)
: ORCHID; *especially* **:** any of a genus (*Orchis*) with fleshy roots and a spurred lip
or·dain \òr-'dān\ *verb* [Middle English *ordeinen,* from Old French *ordener,* from Late Latin *ordinare,* from *ordin-, ordo* order] (14th century)
transitive verb
1 : to invest officially (as by the laying on of hands) with ministerial or priestly authority
2 a : to establish or order by appointment, decree, or law **:** ENACT **b :** DESTINE, FOREORDAIN
intransitive verb
: to issue an order
— **or·dain·er** *noun*
— **or·dain·ment** \-'dān-mənt\ *noun*
or·deal \òr-'dē(-ə)l, 'òr-,\ *noun* [Middle English *ordal,* from Old English *ordāl;* akin to Old High German *urteil* judgment, Old English *dāl* division — more at DEAL] (before 12th century)
1 : a primitive means used to determine guilt or innocence by submitting the accused to dangerous or painful tests believed to be under supernatural control ⟨*ordeal* by fire⟩
2 : a severe trial or experience
¹or·der \'òr-dər\ *verb* **or·dered; or·der·ing** \'òr-d(ə-)riŋ\ [Middle English, from *ordre,* noun] (13th century)
transitive verb

1 : to put in order **:** ARRANGE
2 a : to give an order to **:** COMMAND **b :** DESTINE, ORDAIN **c :** to command to go or come to a specified place **d :** to give an order for ⟨*order* a meal⟩
intransitive verb
1 : to bring about order **:** REGULATE
2 a : to issue orders **:** COMMAND **b :** to give or place an order ☆
— **or·der·able** \-ə-bəl\ *adjective*
— **or·der·er** \-dər-ər\ *noun*
²order *noun* [Middle English, from Middle French *ordre,* from Medieval Latin & Latin; Medieval Latin *ordin-, ordo* ecclesiastical order, from Latin, arrangement, group, class; akin to Latin *ordiri* to lay the warp, begin] (14th century)
1 a : a group of people united in a formal way: as (1) **:** a fraternal society ⟨the Masonic *Order*⟩ (2) **:** a community under a religious rule; *especially* **:** one requiring members to take solemn vows **b :** a badge or medal of such a society; *also* **:** a military decoration
2 a : any of the several grades of the Christian ministry **b** *plural* **:** the office of a person in the Christian ministry **c** *plural* **:** ORDINATION
3 a : a rank, class, or special group in a community or society **b :** a class of persons or things grouped according to quality, value, or natural characteristics: as (1) **:** a category of taxonomic classification ranking above the family and below the class (2) **:** the broadest category in soil classification
4 (1) **:** RANK, LEVEL ⟨a statesman of the first *order*⟩ (2) **:** CATEGORY, CLASS ⟨in emergencies of this *order* —R. B. Westerfield⟩ **b** (1) **:** the arrangement or sequence of objects or of events in time ⟨listed the items in *order* of importance⟩ (2) **:** a sequential arrangement of mathematical elements **c :** DEGREE 12a, b **d** (1) **:** the number of times differentiation is applied

order 8b: *1* Corinthian, *2* Doric, *3* Ionic

\ə\ abut \°\ kitten \ər\ further \a\ ash \ā\ ace
\ä\ mop, mar \au̇\ out \ch\ chin \e\ bet \ē\ easy
\g\ go \i\ hit \ī\ ice \j\ job \ŋ\ sing \ō\ go
\o̊\ law \o̊i\ boy \th\ thin \t͟h\ the \ü\ loot \u̇\ foot
\y\ yet \zh\ vision *see also* Guide to Pronunciation

successively ⟨derivatives of higher *order*⟩ (2) *of a differential equation* **:** the order of the derivative of highest order **e :** the number of columns or rows or columns and rows in a magic square, determinant, or matrix ⟨the *order* of a matrix with 2 rows and 3 columns is 2 by 3⟩ **f :** the number of elements in a finite mathematical group
5 a (1) **:** a sociopolitical system ⟨was opposed to changes in the established *order*⟩ (2) **:** a particular sphere or aspect of a sociopolitical system ⟨the present economic *order*⟩ **b :** a regular or harmonious arrangement ⟨the *order* of nature⟩
6 a : a prescribed form of a religious service **:** RITE **b :** the customary mode of procedure especially in debate ⟨point of *order*⟩
7 a : the state of peace, freedom from confused or unruly behavior, and respect for law or proper authority ⟨promised to restore law and *order*⟩ **b :** a specific rule, regulation, or authoritative direction **:** COMMAND
8 a : a style of building **b :** a type of column and entablature forming the unit of a style
9 a : state or condition especially with regard to functioning or repair ⟨things were in terrible *order*⟩ **b :** a proper, orderly, or functioning condition ⟨their passports were in *order*⟩ ⟨the phone is out of *order*⟩
10 a : a written direction to pay money to someone **b :** a commission to purchase, sell, or supply goods or to perform work **c :** goods or items bought or sold **d :** an assigned or requested undertaking ⟨landing men on the moon was a large *order*⟩
11 : ORDER OF THE DAY ⟨flat roofs were the *order* in the small villages⟩
 — **or·der·less** \-ləs\ *adjective*
 — **in order :** APPROPRIATE, DESIRABLE ⟨an apology is *in order*⟩
 — **in order to :** for the purpose of
 — **on order :** in the process of being ordered
 — **on the order of 1 :** after the fashion of **:** LIKE ⟨much *on the order of* Great Lakes bulk carriers —*Ships and the Sea*⟩ **2 :** ABOUT, APPROXIMATELY ⟨spent *on the order of* two million dollars⟩
 — **to order :** according to the specifications of an order ⟨shoes made *to order*⟩

order arms *noun* [from the command *order arms*!] (1844)
1 : a position in the manual of arms in which the rifle is held vertically beside the right leg with the butt resting on the ground
2 : a command to return the rifle to order arms from present arms or to drop the hand from a hand salute

or·dered \'òr-dərd\ *adjective* (1579)
: characterized by order: as **a :** marked by regularity or discipline ⟨led an *ordered* life⟩ **b :** marked by regular or harmonious arrangement or disposition ⟨an *ordered* landscape⟩ ⟨the *ordered* crystal structure⟩ **c :** having elements arranged or identified according to a rule: as (1) **:** having the property that every pair of different elements is related by a transitive relationship that is not symmetric (2) **:** having elements labeled by ordinal numbers ⟨an *ordered* triple has a first, second, and third element⟩

or·der·li·ness \'òrd-ər-lē-nəs\ *noun* (1571)
: the quality or state of being orderly

¹or·der·ly \-lē\ *adjective* (circa 1577)
1 a (1) **:** arranged or disposed in some order or pattern **:** REGULAR ⟨*orderly* rows of houses⟩ (2) **:** not marked by disorder **:** TIDY ⟨keeps an *orderly* desk⟩ **b :** governed by law **:** REGULATED ⟨an *orderly* universe⟩ **c :** METHODICAL ⟨an *orderly* mind⟩
2 : well behaved **:** PEACEFUL ⟨an *orderly* crowd⟩
 — **orderly** *adverb*

²orderly *noun, plural* **-lies** (1781)

1 : a soldier assigned to perform various services (as carrying messages) for a superior officer
2 : a hospital attendant who does routine or heavy work (as cleaning, carrying supplies, or moving patients)

order of business [*order of business* (predetermined sequence of matters to be dealt with by an assembly)] (circa 1890)
: a matter which must be dealt with **:** TASK ⟨the discipline problem was the first *order of business* at the meeting of the school board⟩

order of magnitude (1875)
: a range of magnitude extending from some value to ten times that value

order of the day (1698)
1 : the business or tasks appointed for an assembly for a given day
2 : the characteristic or dominant feature or activity ⟨growth and change are the *order of the day* in every field —Ruth G. Strickland⟩

¹or·di·nal \'òrd-nəl, 'òr-d°n-°l\ *noun* (14th century)
1 *capitalized* [Middle English, from Medieval Latin *ordinale*, from Late Latin, neuter of *ordinalis*] **:** a book of rites for the ordination of deacons, priests, and bishops
2 [Late Latin *ordinalis*, from *ordinalis*, *adjective*] **:** ORDINAL NUMBER

²ordinal *adjective* [Late Latin *ordinalis*, from Latin *ordin-*, *ordo*] (1599)
1 : of a specified order or rank in a series
2 : of or relating to a taxonomic order

ordinal number *noun* (1607)
1 : a number designating the place (as first, second, or third) occupied by an item in an ordered sequence — see NUMBER table
2 : a number assigned to an ordered set that designates both the order of its elements and its cardinal number

or·di·nance \'òrd-nən(t)s, 'òr-d°n-ən(t)s\ *noun* [Middle English, from Middle French & Medieval Latin; Middle French *ordenance*, literally, act of arranging, from Medieval Latin *ordinantia*, from Latin *ordinant-*, *ordinans*, present participle of *ordinare* to put in order — more at ORDAIN] (14th century)
1 a : an authoritative decree or direction **:** ORDER **b :** a law set forth by a governmental authority; *specifically* **:** a municipal regulation
2 : something ordained or decreed by fate or a deity
3 : a prescribed usage, practice, or ceremony
synonym see LAW

or·di·nand \'òr-d°n-'and\ *noun* [Late Latin *ordinandus*, gerundive of *ordinare* to ordain] (circa 1842)
: a candidate for ordination

¹or·di·nary \'òr-d°n-,er-ē\ *noun, plural* **-nar·ies** [Middle English *ordinarie*, from Anglo-French & Medieval Latin; Anglo-French, from Medieval Latin *ordinarius*, from Latin *ordinarius*, *adjective*] (14th century)
1 a (1) **:** a prelate exercising original jurisdiction over a specified territory or group (2) **:** a clergyman appointed formerly in England to attend condemned criminals **b :** a judge of probate in some states of the U.S.
2 *often capitalized* **:** the parts of the Mass that do not vary from day to day
3 : the regular or customary condition or course of things — usually used in the phrase *out of the ordinary*
4 a *British* **:** a meal served to all comers at a fixed price **b** *chiefly British* **:** a tavern or eating house serving regular meals
5 : a common heraldic charge (as the bend) of simple form

²ordinary *adjective* [Middle English *ordinarie*, from Latin *ordinarius*, from *ordin-*, *ordo* order] (15th century)
1 : of a kind to be expected in the normal order of events **:** ROUTINE, USUAL
2 : having or constituting immediate or original jurisdiction; *also* **:** belonging to such jurisdiction

3 a : of common quality, rank, or ability **b :** deficient in quality **:** POOR, INFERIOR
synonym see COMMON
 — **or·di·nar·i·ly** \,òr-d°n-'er-ə-lē\ *adverb*
 — **or·di·nar·i·ness** \'òrd-°n-,er-ē-nəs\ *noun*

ordinary–language philosophy *noun* (1957)
: a trend in philosophical analysis that seeks to resolve philosophical perplexity by revealing sources of puzzlement in the misunderstanding of ordinary language

Ordinary level *noun* (1947)
: O LEVEL

ordinary seaman *noun* (1702)
: a seaman of some experience but not as skilled as an able seaman

ordinary share *noun* (1891)
British **:** a share of common stock

or·di·nate \'òrd-nət, 'òr-d°n-ət, -d°n-,āt\ *noun* [New Latin (*linea*) *ordinate* (*applicata*), literally, line applied in an orderly manner] (1676)
: the Cartesian coordinate obtained by measuring parallel to the y-axis — compare ABSCISSA

or·di·na·tion \,òr-d°n-'ā-shən\ *noun* (14th century)
: the act or an instance of ordaining **:** the state of being ordained

ord·nance \'òrd-nən(t)s\ *noun* [Middle English *ordinaunce*, from Middle French *ordenance*, literally, act of arranging] (14th century)
1 a : military supplies including weapons, ammunition, combat vehicles, and maintenance tools and equipment **b :** a service of the army charged with the procuring, distributing, and safekeeping of ordnance
2 : CANNON, ARTILLERY

or·do \'òr-(,)dō\ *noun, plural* **ordos** *or* **or·di·nes** \'òr-d°n-,ēz\ [Medieval Latin, from Latin, order] (1849)
: a list of offices and feasts of the Roman Catholic Church for each day of the year

or·don·nance \,òr-d°n-'äⁿs\ *noun* [French, alteration of Middle French *ordenance*] (1644)
: disposition of the parts (as of a literary composition) with regard to one another and the whole **:** ARRANGEMENT

Or·do·vi·cian \,òr-də-'vi-shən\ *adjective* [Latin *Ordovices*, ancient people in northern Wales] (1879)
: of, relating to, or being the period between the Cambrian and the Silurian or the corresponding system of rocks — see GEOLOGIC TIME table
 — **Ordovician** *noun*

or·dure \'òr-jər\ *noun* [Middle English, from Middle French, from *ord* filthy, from Latin *horridus* horrid] (14th century)
1 : EXCREMENT
2 : something that is morally degrading

¹ore \'ōr, 'òr\ *noun, often attributive* [Middle English *or, oor*, partly from Old English *ōra* ore; partly from Old English *ār* brass; akin to Old High German *ēr* bronze, Latin *aes* copper, bronze] (before 12th century)
1 : a mineral containing a valuable constituent (as metal) for which it is mined and worked
2 : a source from which valuable matter is extracted

²ore \'ər-ə\ *noun, plural* **ore** [Swedish *öre* & Danish & Norwegian *øre*] (1716)
 — see *krona, krone* at MONEY table

ore·ad \'ōr-ē-,ad, 'òr-, -ē-əd\ *noun* [Middle English *oreades*, plural, from Latin *oread-*, *oreas*, from Greek *oriad-*, *oreias*, from *oreios* of a mountain, from *oros* mountain — more at ORIENT] (14th century)
: any of the nymphs of mountains and hills in Greek mythology

ore dressing *noun* (1862)
: mechanical preparation (as by crushing) and concentration (as by flotation) of ore

oreg·a·no \ə-'re-gə-ˌnō\ *noun* [American Spanish *orégano,* from Spanish, wild marjoram, from Latin *origanum* — more at ORIGANUM] (1771)
1 : a bushy perennial mint (*Origanum vulgare*) that is used as a seasoning and a source of aromatic oil — called also *origanum, wild marjoram*
2 : any of several plants (genera *Lippia* and *Coleus*) other than oregano of the vervain or mint families

Or·e·gon grape \'òr-i-gən-, -ˌär-, -ˌgän-\ *noun* [*Oregon,* state of the U.S.] (1869)
: an evergreen shrub (*Mahonia aquifolium*) of the barberry family that has yellow flowers, bears edible bluish black berries, and is native to western North America

Or·eo \'òr-ē-(ˌ)ō, 'òr-, 'är-\ *noun* [from *Oreo,* trademark for a chocolate cookie with a white cream filling] (1969)
: a black person who adopts the characteristic mentality and behavior of white middle-class society — usually used disparagingly

Oregon grape

Ores·tes \ə-'res-(ˌ)tēz, ò-\ *noun* [Latin, from Greek *Orestēs*]
: the son of Agamemnon and Clytemnestra who with his sister Electra avenges his father by killing his mother and her lover Aegisthus

or·gan \'òr-gən\ *noun* [Middle English, partly from Old English *organa,* from Latin *organum,* from Greek *organon,* literally, tool, instrument; partly from Old French *organe,* from Latin *organum;* akin to Greek *ergon* work — more at WORK] (before 12th century)
1 a *archaic* **:** any of various musical instruments; *especially* **:** WIND INSTRUMENT **b** (1) **:** a wind instrument consisting of sets of pipes made to sound by compressed air and controlled by keyboards and producing a variety of musical effects — called also *pipe organ* (2) **:** REED ORGAN (3) **:** an instrument in which the sound and resources of the pipe organ are approximated by means of electronic devices (4) **:** any of various similar cruder instruments
2 a : a differentiated structure (as a heart, kidney, leaf, or stem) consisting of cells and tissues and performing some specific function in an organism **b :** bodily parts performing a function or cooperating in an activity ⟨the eyes and related structures that make up the visual *organs*⟩
3 : a subordinate group or organization that performs specialized functions ⟨the various *organs* of government⟩
4 : PERIODICAL

organ- *or* **organo-** *combining form* [Middle English, from Medieval Latin, from Latin *organum*]
1 : organ ⟨*organo*genesis⟩
2 : organic ⟨*organo*mercurial⟩

or·gan·dy *also* **or·gan·die** \'òr-gən-dē\ *noun, plural* **-dies** [French *organdi*] (1835)
: a very fine transparent muslin with a stiff finish

or·gan·elle \ˌòr-gə-'nel\ *noun* [New Latin *organella,* from Latin *organum*] (1920)
: a specialized cellular part (as a mitochondrion, lysosome, or ribosome) that is analogous to an organ

or·gan–grind·er \'òr-gən-ˌgrīn-dər\ *noun* (circa 1807)
: one that cranks a hand organ; *especially* **:** a street musician who operates a barrel organ

¹or·gan·ic \òr-'ga-nik\ *adjective* (1517)
1 *archaic* **:** INSTRUMENTAL
2 a : of, relating to, or arising in a bodily organ **b :** affecting the structure of the organism

3 a (1) **:** of, relating to, or derived from living organisms (2) **:** of, relating to, yielding, or involving the use of food produced with the use of feed or fertilizer of plant or animal origin without employment of chemically formulated fertilizers, growth stimulants, antibiotics, or pesticides ⟨*organic* farming⟩ ⟨*organic* produce⟩ **b** (1) **:** of, relating to, or containing carbon compounds (2) **:** relating to, being, or dealt with by a branch of chemistry concerned with the carbon compounds of living beings and most other carbon compounds
4 a : forming an integral element of a whole **:** FUNDAMENTAL ⟨incidental music rather than *organic* parts of the action —Francis Fergusson⟩ **b :** having systematic coordination of parts **:** ORGANIZED ⟨an *organic* whole⟩ **c :** having the characteristics of an organism **:** developing in the manner of a living plant or animal ⟨society is *organic*⟩
5 : of, relating to, or constituting the law by which a government or organization exists
— **or·gan·i·cal·ly** \-ni-k(ə-)lē\ *adverb*
— **or·gan·ic·i·ty** \ˌòr-gə-'ni-sə-tē\ *noun*

²organic *noun* (1942)
: an organic substance: as **a :** a fertilizer of plant or animal origin **b :** a pesticide whose active component is an organic compound or a mixture of organic compounds

or·gan·i·cism \òr-'ga-nə-ˌsi-zəm\ *noun* [International Scientific Vocabulary] (1883)
1 a : the explanation of life and living processes in terms of the levels of organization of living systems rather than in terms of the properties of their smallest components **b :** VITALISM
2 : any of various theories that attribute to society or the universe as a whole an existence or characteristics analogous to those of a biological organism
— **or·gan·i·cist** \-sist\ *noun or adjective*

or·ga·ni·sa·tion, or·ga·nis·er *British variant of* ORGANIZATION, ORGANIZE, ORGANIZER

or·gan·ism \'òr-gə-ˌni-zəm\ *noun* (circa 1774)
1 : a complex structure of interdependent and subordinate elements whose relations and properties are largely determined by their function in the whole
2 : an individual constituted to carry on the activities of life by means of organs separate in function but mutually dependent **:** a living being
— **or·gan·is·mic** \ˌòr-gə-'niz-mik\ *also* **or·gan·is·mal** \-məl\ *adjective*
— **or·gan·is·mi·cal·ly** \-mi-k(ə-)lē\ *adverb*

or·gan·ist \'òr-gə-nist\ *noun* (1591)
: a person who plays the organ

¹or·ga·ni·za·tion \ˌòr-gə-nə-'zā-shən, ˌòrg-nə-\ *noun* (15th century)
1 a : the act or process of organizing or of being organized **b :** the condition or manner of being organized
2 a : ASSOCIATION, SOCIETY ⟨charitable *organizations*⟩ **b :** an administrative and functional structure (as a business or a political party); *also* **:** the personnel of such a structure

²organization *adjective* (1949)
: characterized by complete conformity to the standards and requirements of an organization ⟨an *organization* man⟩

or·ga·ni·za·tion·al \-shnəl, -shə-nᵊl\ *adjective* (1881)
1 : of or relating to an organization **:** involving organization ⟨the *organizational* state of a crystal⟩
2 : ORGANIZATION
— **or·ga·ni·za·tion·al·ly** *adverb*

or·ga·nize \'òr-gə-ˌnīz\ *verb* **-nized; -niz·ing** (15th century)
transitive verb
1 : to cause to develop an organic structure
2 : to form into a coherent unity or functioning whole **:** INTEGRATE ⟨trying to *organize* her thoughts⟩

3 a : to set up an administrative structure for **b :** to persuade to associate in an organization; *especially* **:** UNIONIZE
4 : to arrange by systematic planning and united effort
intransitive verb
1 : to undergo physical or organic organization
2 : to arrange elements into a whole of interdependent parts
3 : to form an organization; *specifically* **:** to form or persuade workers to join a union
synonym see ORDER
— **or·gan·iz·able** \ˌòr-gə-'nī-zə-bəl\ *adjective*

organized *adjective* (1817)
1 : having a formal organization to coordinate and carry out activities ⟨*organized* baseball⟩ ⟨*organized* crime⟩
2 : affiliated by membership in an organization (as a union) ⟨*organized* steelworkers⟩

or·ga·niz·er \'òr-gə-ˌnī-zər\ *noun* (1849)
1 : one that organizes
2 : a region of a developing embryo or a substance produced by such a region that is capable of inducing a specific type of development in undifferentiated tissue — called also *inductor*

or·gan·o·chlo·rine \ˌòr-gə-nō-'klòr-ˌēn, òr-ˌga-nə-, -'klòr-, -ən\ *adjective* (1961)
: of, relating to, or belonging to the chlorinated hydrocarbon pesticides (as aldrin, DDT, or dieldrin)
— **organochlorine** *noun*

organ of Cor·ti \-'kòr-tē\ [Alfonso *Corti* (died 1876) Italian anatomist] (1882)
: a complex epithelial structure in the cochlea that rests on the internal surface of the basilar membrane and in mammals is the chief part of the ear by which sound is directly perceived

or·gan·o·gen·e·sis \ˌòr-gə-nō-'je-nə-səs, òr-ˌga-nə-\ *noun* [New Latin] (circa 1860)
: the origin and development of bodily organs
— compare MORPHOGENESIS
— **or·gan·o·ge·net·ic** \-jə-'ne-tik\ *adjective*

or·gan·o·lep·tic \ˌòr-gə-nō-'lep-tik, òr-ˌga-nə-\ *adjective* [French *organoleptique,* from *organ-* + Greek *lēptikos* disposed to take, from *lambanein* to take — more at LATCH] (1852)
1 : being, affecting, or relating to qualities (as taste, color, odor, and feel) of a substance (as a food or drug) that stimulate the sense organs
2 : involving use of the sense organs ⟨*organoleptic* evaluation of foods⟩
— **or·gan·o·lep·ti·cal·ly** \-ti-k(ə-)lē\ *adverb*

or·ga·nol·o·gy \ˌòr-gə-'nä-lə-jē\ *noun* [International Scientific Vocabulary] (circa 1842)
: the study of the organs of plants and animals

or·gan·o·mer·cu·ri·al \ˌòr-gə-nō-(ˌ)mər-'kyúr-ē-əl, òr-ˌga-nə-\ *noun* (1938)
: an organic compound or a pharmaceutical preparation containing mercury

or·gan·o·me·tal·lic \-mə-'ta-lik\ *adjective* [International Scientific Vocabulary] (1852)
: of, relating to, or being an organic compound that usually contains a metal or metalloid bonded directly to carbon
— **organometallic** *noun*

or·ga·non \'òr-gə-ˌnän\ *noun* [Greek, literally, tool — more at ORGAN] (1610)
: an instrument for acquiring knowledge; *specifically* **:** a body of principles of scientific or philosophic investigation

or·gan·o·phos·phate \ˌòr-gə-nō-'fäs-ˌfāt, òr-ˌga-nō-\ *noun* (1949)
: an organophosphorus compound (as a pesticide)
— **organophosphate** *adjective*

or·gan·o·phos·pho·rus \-'fäs-f(ə-)rəs\ *also*
or·gan·o·phos·pho·rous \-fäs-'fōr-əs,
-'fȯr-\ *adjective* (1950)
: of, relating to, or being a phosphorus-containing organic compound and especially a pesticide (as malathion) that acts by inhibiting cholinesterase
— **organophosphorus** *noun*

organ–pipe cactus *noun* (1908)
: any of several tall upright cacti (as *Lemaireocereus thurberi* or *L. marginatus*) of the southwestern U.S. and adjacent Mexico that usually branch at the base to form several upright stems

or·ga·num \'ȯr-gə-nəm\ *noun* [Medieval Latin, from Latin, organ] (1614)
1 : ORGANON
2 : early polyphony of the late Middle Ages that consists of one or more voice parts accompanying the cantus firmus in parallel motion usually at a fourth, fifth, or octave above or below; *also* : a composition in this style

or·gan·za \ȯr-'gan-zə\ *noun* [probably alteration of *Lorganza*, a trademark] (1820)
: a sheer dress fabric (as of silk or nylon) resembling organdy

or·gan·zine \'ȯr-gən-ˌzēn\ *noun* [French or Italian; French *organsin*, from Italian *organzino*] (1699)
: a raw silk yarn used for warp threads in fine fabrics

or·gasm \'ȯr-ˌga-zəm\ *noun* [New Latin *orgasmus*, from Greek *orgasmos*, from *organ* to grow ripe, be lustful; probably akin to Sanskrit *ūrjā* sap, strength] (circa 1763)
: intense or paroxysmal excitement; *especially*
: the climax of sexual excitement that is usually accompanied by the ejaculation of semen in the male and vaginal contractions in the female
— **or·gas·mic** \ȯr-'gaz-mik\ *also* **or·gas·tic** \-'gas-tik\ *adjective*

or·geat \'ȯr-ˌzhä(t)\ *noun* [French, from Middle French, from *orge* barley, from Latin *hordeum*; akin to Old High German *gersta* barley] (1754)
: a sweet almond-flavored nonalcoholic syrup used as a cocktail ingredient or food flavoring

or·gi·as·tic \ˌȯr-jē-'as-tik\ *adjective* [Greek *orgiastikos*, from *orgiazein* to celebrate orgies, from *orgia*] (1698)
1 : of, relating to, or marked by orgies
2 : characterized by unrestrained emotion
: FRENZIED
— **or·gi·as·ti·cal·ly** \-ti-k(ə-)lē\ *adverb*

or·gone \'ȯr-ˌgōn\ *noun* [probably from *orgasm* + *-one* (as in *hormone*)] (1942)
: a vital energy held to pervade nature and be a factor in health in the theories of Wilhelm Reich

or·gu·lous \'ȯr-gyə-ləs, -gə-\ *adjective* [Middle English, from Old French *orgueilleus*, from *orgueil* pride, of Germanic origin; akin to Old High German *urguol* distinguished] (13th century)
: PROUD

or·gy \'ȯr-jē\ *noun, plural* **orgies** [Middle French *orgie*, from Latin *orgia*, plural, from Greek; akin to Greek *ergon* work — more at WORK] (circa 1561)
1 : secret ceremonial rites held in honor of an ancient Greek or Roman deity and usually characterized by ecstatic singing and dancing
2 a : drunken revelry **b** : a sexual encounter involving many people; *also* : an excessive sexual indulgence
3 : something that resembles an orgy in lack of control or moderation ⟨an *orgy* of destruction⟩

-oria *plural of* -ORIUM

-orial *adjective suffix* [Middle English, from Latin *-orius* -ory + Middle English *-al*]
: of, belonging to, or connected with ⟨combinat*orial*⟩

orib·a·tid \ȯ-'ri-bə-təd, ˌȯr-ə-'ba-təd\ *noun*
[New Latin *Oribatidae* (coextensive with *Ori-*

batoidea), from *Oribata*, genus name, from Greek *oribatēs* walking the mountains, from *oros* mountain + *-batēs* from *bainein* to go — more at ORIENT, COME] (1875)
: any of a superfamily (Oribatoidea) of small oval eyeless nonparasitic mites having a heavily sclerotized integument with a leathery appearance
— **oribatid** *adjective*

ori·el \'ȯr-ē-əl, 'ȯr-\ *noun* [Middle English, porch, oriel, from Middle French *oriol* porch] (14th century)
: a large bay window projecting from a wall and supported by a corbel or bracket

¹**ori·ent** \'ȯr-ē-ənt, 'ȯr-, -ē-ˌent\ *noun* [Middle English, from Middle French, from Latin *orient-, oriens,* from present participle of *oriri* to rise; akin to Sanskrit *ṛṇoti* he moves, arises, Greek *ornynai* to rouse, *oros* mountain] (14th century)
1 *archaic* : EAST 1b
2 *capitalized* : EAST 2
3 a : a pearl of great luster **b** : the luster of a pearl ◇

²**orient** *adjective* (15th century)
1 *archaic* : ORIENTAL 1
2 a : LUSTROUS, SPARKLING ⟨*orient* gems⟩ **b** *archaic* : RADIANT, GLOWING
3 *archaic* : rising in the sky

³**ori·ent** \'ȯr-ē-ˌent, 'ȯr-\ *transitive verb* [French *orienter*, from Middle French, from *orient*] (circa 1741)
1 a : to cause to face or point toward the east; *specifically* : to build (a church or temple) with the longitudinal axis pointing eastward and the chief altar at the eastern end **b** : to set or arrange in any determinate position especially in relation to the points of the compass **c** : to ascertain the bearings of
2 a : to set right by adjusting to facts or principles **b** : to acquaint with the existing situation or environment
3 : to direct (as a book or film) toward the interests of a particular group
4 : to cause the axes of the molecules of to assume the same direction
usage see ORIENTATE

ori·en·tal \ˌȯr-ē-'en-tᵊl, 'ȯr-\ *adjective* (14th century)
1 *often capitalized* : of, relating to, or situated in the Orient
2 a : of superior grade, luster, or value **b** : being corundum or sapphire but simulating another gem in color
3 *often capitalized* : of, relating to, or having the characteristics of Orientals
4 *capitalized* : of, relating to, or constituting the biogeographic region that includes Asia south and southeast of the Himalayas and the Malay Archipelago west of Wallace's line
— **ori·en·tal·ly** \-tᵊl-ē\ *adverb*

Oriental *noun* (15th century)
: a member of one of the indigenous peoples of the Orient

oriental fruit moth *noun* (1921)
: a small nearly cosmopolitan moth (*Grapholita molesta*) probably of Japanese origin whose larva is injurious to the twigs and fruit of orchard trees and especially the peach — called also *oriental peach moth*

Ori·en·ta·lia \ˌȯr-ē-ən-'tāl-yə, ˌȯr-, -ˌen-, -'tā-lē-ə\ *noun plural* [New Latin] (1903)
: materials concerning or characteristic of the Orient

ori·en·tal·ism \ˌȯr-ē-'en-tᵊl-ˌi-zəm\ *noun, often capitalized* (1769)
1 : a trait, custom, or habit of expression characteristic of oriental peoples
2 : scholarship or learning in oriental subjects
— **ori·en·tal·ist** \-tᵊl-ist\ *noun, often capitalized*

ori·en·tal·ize \-tᵊl-ˌīz\ *verb* **-ized; -iz·ing** (1823)
transitive verb
often capitalized : to make oriental

intransitive verb
often capitalized : to become oriental

Oriental poppy *noun* (1731)
: an Asian perennial poppy (*Papaver orientale*) that is commonly cultivated for its large showy flowers

Oriental rug *noun* (1881)
: a handwoven or hand-knotted one-piece rug or carpet made in the Orient — called also *Oriental carpet*

ori·en·tate \'ȯr-ē-ən-ˌtāt, 'ȯr-, -ˌen-\ *verb* **-tat·ed; -tat·ing** (1849)
transitive verb
: ORIENT
intransitive verb
: to face or turn to the east □

ori·en·ta·tion \ˌȯr-ē-ən-'tā-shən, ˌȯr-, -ˌen-\ *noun* (1839)
1 a : the act or process of orienting or of being oriented **b** : the state of being oriented; *broadly* : ARRANGEMENT, ALIGNMENT
2 : a usually general or lasting direction of thought, inclination, or interest
3 : change of position by organs, organelles, or organisms in response to external stimulus
— **ori·en·ta·tion·al** \-shnəl, -shə-nᵊl\ *adjective*
— **ori·en·ta·tion·al·ly** *adverb*

ori·ent·ed \'ȯr-ē-ˌen-təd, 'ȯr-\ *adjective* (1944)
: intellectually, emotionally, or functionally directed ⟨humanistically *oriented* scholars⟩

ori·en·teer \ˌȯr-ē-ən-'tir, ˌȯr-, -ˌen-\ *noun* [back-formation from *orienteering*] (1965)
: one who engages in orienteering

ori·en·teer·ing \ˌȯr-ē-ən-'tir-iŋ, ˌȯr-, -ˌen-\ *noun* [modification of Swedish *orientering*, from *orientera* to orient] (1948)
: a cross-country race in which each participant uses a map and compass to navigate between checkpoints along an unfamiliar course

□ **USAGE**
orientate This back-formation from *orientation* had been in use for about a century when it was first criticized as a needlessly long variant of *orient*. A surprisingly large number of handbooks and other commentators have subsequently disparaged *orientate*. Since the whole controversy boils down to three letters and one syllable, one might think the matter too trivial to have drawn so much attention. Both *orient* and *orientate* are standard, but *orientate* is more common in British English (where the conservatives tend to be clerically *orientated* —*Times Literary Supplement*) ⟨more emotionally or culturally *orientated* toward Europe —Duke of Edinburgh⟩. *Orient* is the usual choice in American English.

◇ **WORD HISTORY**
orient As the ancient Romans did not have magnetic compasses, they depended upon the position of the rising sun to determine their daytime bearings. The direction from which the sun rose was called *oriens*, deriving from the present participle of the verb *oriri*, meaning "to rise." The word *oriens* also came to be used for the part of the world in the direction from which the sun rose, the East. After *oriens* was borrowed into English as *Orient*, it became the name for all the lands to the east of Europe, and especially eastern Asia. With the spread of Christianity across Europe it became customary to build churches with their longitudinal axes pointing eastward toward Jerusalem. This practice gave rise to the use of *orient* as a verb meaning "to cause to face or point toward the east." This sense served as the basis for development of the verb's other senses in English.

or·i·fice \'òr-ə-fəs, 'är-\ *noun* [Middle English, from Middle French, from Late Latin *orificium*, from Latin *or-, os* mouth + *facere* to make, do — more at ORAL, DO] (15th century) : an opening (as a vent, mouth, or hole) through which something may pass
— **or·i·fi·cial** \ˌòr-ə-'fi-shəl, ˌär-\ *adjective*

ori·flamme \'òr-ə-ˌflam, 'är-\ *noun* [Middle English *oriflamble*, the banner of Saint Denis, from Middle French, from Medieval Latin *aurea flamma*, literally, golden flame] (1600) : a banner, symbol, or ideal inspiring devotion or courage

ori·ga·mi \ˌòr-ə-'gä-mē\ *noun* [Japanese, from *ori* fold + *kami* paper] (1956) : the Japanese art or process of folding squares of paper into representational shapes

orig·a·num \ə-'ri-gə-nəm\ *noun* [Middle English, from Latin, from Latin, wild marjoram, from Greek *origanon*] (14th century) : any of several aromatic mints (especially genus *Origanum*) used as seasonings; *especially* : OREGANO 1

or·i·gin \'òr-ə-jən, 'är-\ *noun* [Middle English *origine*, probably from Middle French, from Latin *origin-, origo*, from *oriri* to rise — more at ORIENT] (15th century)
1 : ANCESTRY, PARENTAGE
2 a : rise, beginning, or derivation from a source **b** : the point at which something begins or rises or from which it derives ⟨the *origin* of the custom is forgotten⟩; *also* : something that creates, causes, or gives rise to another ⟨this spring is the *origin* of the brook⟩
3 : the more fixed, central, or larger attachment of a muscle
4 : the intersection of coordinate axes ✩

¹orig·i·nal \ə-'rij-ə-nᵊl, -'rij-nəl\ *noun* (14th century)
1 *archaic* : the source or cause from which something arises; *specifically* : ORIGINATOR
2 a : that from which a copy, reproduction, or translation is made **b** : a work composed first-hand
3 a : a person of fresh initiative or inventive capacity **b** : a unique or eccentric person

²original *adjective* (14th century)
1 : of, relating to, or constituting an origin or beginning ⟨INITIAL ⟨the *original* part of the house⟩
2 a : not secondary, derivative, or imitative **b** : being the first instance or source from which a copy, reproduction, or translation is or can be made
3 : independent and creative in thought or action : INVENTIVE
synonym see NEW

orig·i·nal·i·ty \ə-ˌri-jə-'na-lə-tē\ *noun* (1742)
1 : the quality or state of being original
2 : freshness of aspect, design, or style
3 : the power of independent thought or constructive imagination

orig·i·nal·ly \ə-'rij-ə-nᵊl-ē; -'rij-nə-lē, -'ri-jən-\ *adverb* (14th century)
1 *archaic* : by origin or derivation : INHERENTLY
2 : in the beginning : in the first place : INITIALLY
3 : in a fresh or original manner

original sin *noun* (14th century) : the state of sin that according to Christian theology characterizes all human beings as a result of Adam's fall

orig·i·nate \ə-'ri-jə-ˌnāt\ *verb* **-nat·ed; -nat·ing** (1667)
transitive verb : to give rise to : INITIATE
intransitive verb : to take or have origin : BEGIN
synonym see SPRING
— **orig·i·na·tion** \-ˌri-jə-'nā-shən\ *noun*
— **orig·i·na·tor** \-'ri-jə-ˌnā-tər\ *noun*

orig·i·na·tive \ə-'ri-jə-ˌnā-tiv, -nə-\ *adjective* (1827) : having ability to originate : CREATIVE
— **orig·i·na·tive·ly** *adverb*

O–ring \'ō-ˌriŋ\ *noun* (1946) : a ring (as of synthetic rubber) used as a gasket

ori·ole \'òr-ē-ˌōl, 'òr-, -ē-əl\ *noun* [French *oriol*, from Latin *aureolus*, diminutive of *aureus* golden — more at AUREUS] (1776)
1 : any of various usually brightly colored Old World passerine birds (family Oriolidae and especially genus *Oriolus*)
2 : any of various New World passerine birds (family Icteridae and especially genus *Icterus*) of which the males are usually black and yellow or black and orange

oriole 2

Ori·on \ə-'rī-ən, ò-\ *noun* [Latin, from Greek *Ōriōn*]
1 : a giant hunter slain by Artemis in Greek mythology
2 [Latin (genitive *Orionis*)] : a constellation on the equator east of Taurus represented on charts by the figure of a hunter with belt and sword

or·is·mol·o·gy \ˌòr-əz-'mä-lə-jē, ˌär-\ *noun* [Greek *horismos* definition (from *horizein* to define) + English *-logy* — more at HORIZON] (1816) : the science of defining technical terms
— **or·is·mo·log·i·cal** \ˌòr-əz-mə-'lä-ji-kəl, ˌär-; ò-ˌriz-\ *adjective*

or·i·son \'òr-ə-sən, 'är-, -zən\ *noun* [Middle English, from Old French, from Late Latin *oration-, oratio*, from Latin, oration] (13th century) : PRAYER

-ori·um *noun suffix, plural* **-oriums** *or* **-oria** [Latin, from neuter of *-orius -ory*] : ¹-ORY ⟨haustorium⟩

Ori·ya \ò-'rē-ə\ *noun* (1801) : the Indo-Aryan language of Orissa, India

Or·lean·ist \'òr-lē-ə-nist, òr-'lē-(ə-)nist\ *noun* (1834) : a supporter of the Orleans family in its claim to the throne of France by descent from a younger brother of Louis XIV

Or·lon \'òr-ˌlän\ *trademark*
— used for an acrylic fiber

or·lop deck \'òr-ˌläp-\ *noun* [Middle English *overlop* deck of a single decker, from Middle Low German *overlōp*, literally, something that overleaps] (1758) : the lowest deck in a ship having four or more decks

Or·mazd \'òr-(ˌ)məzd, -ˌmazd\ *noun* [Persian *Urmazd*, from Middle Persian, from Avestan *Ahuramazdāh-*] (1603) : AHURA MAZDA

or·mo·lu \'òr-mə-ˌlü\ *noun, often attributive* [French *or moulu*, literally, ground gold] (1765) : golden or gilded brass or bronze used for decorative purposes (as in mounts for furniture)

¹or·na·ment \'òr-nə-mənt\ *noun* [Middle English, from Old French *ornement*, from Latin *ornamentum*, from *ornare*] (13th century)
1 *archaic* : a useful accessory
2 a : something that lends grace or beauty **b** : a manner or quality that adorns
3 : one whose virtues or graces add luster to a place or society
4 : the act of adorning or being adorned
5 : an embellishing note not belonging to the essential harmony or melody — called also *embellishment, fioritura*

²or·na·ment \-ˌment\ *transitive verb* (1720) : to provide with ornament : EMBELLISH
synonym see ADORN

¹or·na·men·tal \ˌòr-nə-'men-tᵊl\ *adjective* (1646) : of, relating to, or serving as ornament; *specifically* : grown as an ornamental
— **or·na·men·tal·ly** \-tᵊl-ē\ *adverb*

²ornamental *noun* (1650) : a decorative object; *especially* : a plant cultivated for its beauty rather than for use

or·na·men·ta·tion \ˌòr-nə-mən-'tā-shən, -ˌmen-\ *noun* (1851)
1 : something that ornaments : EMBELLISHMENT
2 : the act or process of ornamenting : the state of being ornamented

or·nate \òr-'nāt\ *adjective* [Middle English *ornat*, from Latin *ornatus*, past participle of *ornare* to furnish, embellish; akin to Latin *ordo* order — more at ORDER] (15th century)
1 : marked by elaborate rhetoric or florid style
2 : elaborately or excessively decorated
— **or·nate·ly** *adverb*
— **or·nate·ness** *noun*

or·nery \'òr-nə-rē, 'är-; 'òrn-rē, 'ärn-\ *adjective*
or·neri·er; -est [alteration of *ordinary*] (1816) : having an irritable disposition : CANTANKEROUS ◇
— **or·neri·ness** *noun*

ornith- *or* **ornitho-** *combining form* [Latin, from Greek, from *ornith-, ornis* — more at ERNE] : bird ⟨ornithology⟩

☆ **SYNONYMS**
Origin, source, inception, root mean the point at which something begins its course or existence. ORIGIN applies to the things or persons from which something is ultimately derived and often to the causes operating before the thing itself comes into being ⟨an investigation into the *origin* of baseball⟩. SOURCE applies more often to the point where something springs into being ⟨the *source* of the Nile⟩ ⟨the *source* of recurrent trouble⟩. INCEPTION stresses the beginning of something without implying causes ⟨the business has been a success since its *inception*⟩. ROOT suggests a first, ultimate, or fundamental source often not easily discerned ⟨the real *root* of the violence⟩.

◇ **WORD HISTORY**
ornery The word *ornery* was originally a vernacular, nonstandard pronunciation of *ordinary*, produced by loss of the syllable coming just after the initial primary stress—a common process in polysyllabic English words. The first hint of such a pronunciation is a three-syllable phonetic spelling of *ordinary* in *The English-School Reformed*, a guide to English spelling and pronunciation by one R. Brown published in 1700. It is not until the 19th century that the spelling *ornery* actually appears, in both British and American writing, presumably at the point that its meaning had shifted far enough from the "commonplace" sense of *ordinary* that its link with this spelling was forgotten and *ornery* was perceived as a distinct word. At first *ornery* is attested in the senses "of poor quality" or "unpleasant," though it soon is found with the meaning "cantankerous" that it usually has today. Spellings such as *o'n'ry* recorded in the 20th century show further phonetic loss: dropping of the first \r\ and deletion of the syllable following the primary stress.

\ə\ abut \ᵊ\ kitten \ər\ further \a\ ash \ā\ ace
\ä\ mop, mar \au̇\ out \ch\ chin \e\ bet \ē\ easy
\g\ go \i\ hit \ī\ ice \j\ job \ŋ\ sing \ō\ go
\ȯ\ law \ȯi\ boy \th\ thin \t͟h\ the \ü\ loot \u̇\ foot
\y\ yet \zh\ vision *see also* Guide to Pronunciation

or·nith·ic \ȯr-'ni-thik\ *adjective* [Greek *ornithikos,* from *ornith-, ornis*] (1854)
: of, relating to, or characteristic of birds

or·ni·thine \'ȯr-nə-ˌthēn\ *noun* [International Scientific Vocabulary *ornith*uric acid (a compound of which ornithine is a component, found in the urine of birds) + ²*-ine*] (1881)
: a crystalline amino acid $C_5H_{12}N_2O_2$ that functions especially in urea production as a carrier by undergoing conversion to citrulline and then arginine in reaction with ammonia and carbon dioxide followed by recovery along with urea by enzymatic hydrolysis of arginine

or·nith·is·chi·an \ˌȯr-nə-'this-kē-ən\ *noun* [New Latin *Ornithischia,* from *ornith-* + *ischium*] (1933)
: any of an order (Ornithischia) of herbivorous dinosaurs (as a stegosaurus) that have the pubis of the pelvis rotated backward to a position parallel and close to the ischium — compare SAURISCHIAN
— **ornithischian** *adjective*

or·ni·thol·o·gy \ˌȯr-nə-'thä-lə-jē\ *noun, plural* **-gies** [New Latin *ornithologia,* from *ornith-* + *-logia* -logy] (1678)
1 : a branch of zoology dealing with birds
2 : a treatise on ornithology
— **or·ni·tho·log·i·cal** \-thə-'lä-ji-kəl\ *also* **or·ni·tho·log·ic** \-jik\ *adjective*
— **or·ni·tho·log·i·cal·ly** \-ji-k(ə-)lē\ *adverb*
— **or·ni·thol·o·gist** \-'thä-lə-jist\ *noun*

or·nith·o·pod \ȯr-'ni-thə-ˌpäd, 'ȯr-ni-thə-\ *noun* [ultimately from Greek *ornith-* + *pod-, pous* foot — more at FOOT] (circa 1890)
: any of a suborder (Ornithopoda) of bipedal ornithischian dinosaurs (as a hadrosaur) with digitigrade walking limbs usually having only three functional toes

or·ni·thop·ter \'ȯr-nə-ˌthäp-tər\ *noun* [International Scientific Vocabulary *ornith-* + *-pter* (as in *helicopter*)] (1908)
: an aircraft designed to derive its chief support and propulsion from flapping wings

or·ni·tho·sis \ˌȯr-nə-'thō-səs\ *noun, plural* **-tho·ses** \-ˌsēz\ [New Latin] (1939)
: PSITTACOSIS

¹**oro-** *combining form* [Greek *oros* — more at ORIENT]
: mountain ⟨*oro*graphy⟩

²**oro-** *combining form* [Latin *or-, os* — more at ORAL]
: mouth ⟨*oro*pharynx⟩

oro·gen·e·sis \ˌȯr-ə-'je-nə-səs, ˌȯr-\ *noun* [New Latin] (1886)
: OROGENY
— **oro·ge·net·ic** \-jə-'ne-tik\ *adjective*

orog·e·ny \ò-'rä-jə-nē\ *noun* [International Scientific Vocabulary] (1890)
: the process of mountain formation especially by folding of the earth's crust
— **oro·gen·ic** \ˌȯr-ə-'je-nik, ˌȯr-\ *adjective*

oro·graph·ic \ˌȯr-ə-'gra-fik, ˌȯr-\ *also* **oro·graph·i·cal** \-fi-kəl\ *adjective* (circa 1803)
: of or relating to mountains; *especially* : associated with or induced by the presence of mountains ⟨*oro*graphic rainfall⟩

orog·ra·phy \ò-'rä-grə-fē\ *noun* [International Scientific Vocabulary] (circa 1846)
: a branch of physical geography that deals with mountains

Oro·mo \ò-'rō-(ˌ)mō, ō-\ *noun, plural* **Oromos** *or* **Oromo** (1893)
1 : a member of a Cushitic-speaking people of southern Ethiopia and adjacent parts of Kenya
2 : the Cushitic language of the Oromo

oro·pha·ryn·geal \ˌȯr-ə-ˌfar-ən-'jē-əl, ˌȯr-, -fə-'rin-j(ē-)əl\ *adjective* (1885)
1 : of or relating to the oropharynx
2 : of or relating to the mouth and pharynx

oro·phar·ynx \-'far-iŋ(k)s\ *noun* (1887)

: the part of the pharynx that is below the soft palate and above the epiglottis and is continuous with the mouth

oro·tund \'ȯr-ə-ˌtənd, 'är-, 'ȯr-\ *adjective* [modification of Latin *ore rotundo,* literally, with round mouth] (circa 1799)
1 : marked by fullness, strength, and clarity of sound : SONOROUS
2 : POMPOUS, BOMBASTIC
— **oro·tun·di·ty** \ˌȯr-ə-'tən-də-tē, ˌär-, ˌȯr-\ *noun*

¹**or·phan** \'ȯr-fən\ *noun* [Middle English, from Late Latin *orphanus,* from Greek *orphanos;* akin to Old High German *erbi* inheritance, Latin *orbus* orphaned] (15th century)
1 : a child deprived by death of one or usually both parents
2 : a young animal that has lost its mother
3 : one deprived of some protection or advantage ⟨*orphans* of the storm⟩
— **orphan** *adjective*
— **or·phan·hood** \-ˌhùd\ *noun*

²**orphan** *transitive verb* **or·phaned; or·phan·ing** \'ȯr-fə-niŋ, 'ȯrf-niŋ\ (1814)
: to cause to become an orphan

or·phan·age \'ȯr-fə-nij, 'ȯrf-nij\ *noun* (circa 1580)
1 : the state of being an orphan
2 : an institution for the care of orphans

orphan drug *noun* (1981)
: a drug that is not developed or marketed because its extremely limited use makes it unprofitable

orphan's court *noun* (1713)
: a probate court which in some states has jurisdiction over the affairs of minors and the administration of estates

Or·pheus \'ȯr-ˌfyüs, -fē-əs\ *noun* [Latin, from Greek]
: a poet and musician in Greek mythology who almost rescues his wife Eurydice from Hades by charming Pluto and Persephone with his lyre

or·phic \'ȯr-fik\ *adjective* (1678)
1 *capitalized* : of or relating to Orpheus or the rites or doctrines ascribed to him
2 : MYSTIC, ORACULAR
3 : FASCINATING, ENTRANCING
— **or·phi·cal·ly** \-fi-k(ə-)lē\ *adverb*

Or·phism \'ȯr-ˌfi-zəm\ *noun* [*Orpheus,* its reputed founder] (1880)
: a mystic Greek religion offering initiates purification of the soul from innate evil and release from the cycle of reincarnation

or·phrey \'ȯr-frē\ *noun, plural* **orphreys** [Middle English *orfrey,* from Middle French *orfreis,* from Medieval Latin *aurifrigium,* from Latin *aurum* gold + *Phrygius* Phrygian — more at AUREUS] (13th century)
1 **a** : elaborate embroidery **b** : a piece of such embroidery
2 : an ornamental border or band especially on an ecclesiastical vestment

or·pi·ment \'ȯr-pə-mənt\ *noun* [Middle English, from Middle French, from Latin *auripigmentum,* from *aurum* + *pigmentum* pigment] (14th century)
: native orange to lemon-yellow arsenic trisulfide

or·pine \'ȯr-pən\ *noun* [Middle English *orpin,* from Middle French, from *orpiment*] (14th century)
: an herb (*Sedum telephium* of the family Crassulaceae, the orpine family) that has fleshy leaves and pink or purple flowers and was formerly used in folk medicine; *broadly* : SEDUM

Or·ping·ton \'ȯr-piŋ-tən\ *noun* [*Orpington,* England] (1897)
: any of an English breed of large deep-chested domestic fowls

or·rery \'ȯr-ər-ē, 'är-\ *noun, plural* **or·rer·ies** [Charles Boyle (died 1731) 4th Earl of *Orrery*] (1713)

: an apparatus showing the relative positions and motions of bodies in the solar system by balls moved by a clockwork

orrery

or·ris \'ȯr-əs, 'är-\ *noun* [probably alteration of Middle English *ireos,* from Medieval Latin, alteration of Latin *iris* iris] (1545)
: ORRISROOT

or·ris·root \-ˌrüt, -ˌrùt\ *noun* (1598)
: the fragrant rootstock of any of three European irises (*Iris florentina, I. germanica,* and *I. pallida*) used especially in perfumery

ort \'ȯrt\ *noun* [Middle English, from Middle Low German *orte*] (15th century)
: a morsel left at a meal : SCRAP

orth- *or* **ortho-** *combining form* [Middle English, from Middle French, straight, right, true, from Latin, from Greek, from *orthos;* akin to Sanskrit *ūrdhva* high, upright]
1 : straight : upright : vertical ⟨*ortho*grade⟩
2 : perpendicular ⟨*orthor*hombic⟩
3 : correct : corrective ⟨*ortho*dontia⟩
4 **a** : hydrated or hydroxylated to the highest degree ⟨*ortho*phosphoric acid⟩ **b** : involving substitution at or characterized by or having the relationship of two neighboring positions in the benzene ring ⟨*ortho*-xylene⟩

or·thi·con \'ȯr-thi-ˌkän\ *noun* [International Scientific Vocabulary *orth-* + *icono*scope] (1939)
: a camera tube similar to but more sensitive than an iconoscope in which the charges are scanned by a low-velocity beam

or·tho \'ȯr-(ˌ)thō\ *adjective* (1904)
: ORTHOCHROMATIC

or·tho·cen·ter \'ȯr-thə-ˌsen-tər\ *noun* [International Scientific Vocabulary] (1869)
: the common intersection of the three altitudes of a triangle or their extensions or of the several altitudes of a polyhedron provided these latter exist and meet in a point

or·tho·chro·mat·ic \ˌȯr-thə-krō-'ma-tik\ *adjective* [International Scientific Vocabulary] (1887)
1 : of, relating to, or producing tone values of light and shade in a photograph that correspond to the tones in nature
2 : sensitive to all colors except red

or·tho·clase \'ȯr-thə-ˌklās, -ˌklāz\ *noun* [German *Orthoklas,* from *orth-* + Greek *klasis* breaking, from *klan* to break — more at CLAST] (1849)
: a mineral consisting of a monoclinic form of feldspar

or·tho·don·tia \ˌȯr-thə-'dän(t)-sh(ē-)ə\ *noun* [New Latin] (circa 1849)
: ORTHODONTICS

or·tho·don·tics \-'dän-tiks\ *noun plural but singular in construction* (1909)
: a branch of dentistry dealing with irregularities of the teeth and their correction (as by means of braces)
— **or·tho·don·tic** \-tik\ *adjective*
— **or·tho·don·ti·cal·ly** \-ti-k(ə-)lē\ *adverb*
— **or·tho·don·tist** \-'dän-tist\ *noun*

¹**or·tho·dox** \'ȯr-thə-ˌdäks\ *adjective* [Middle English *orthodoxe,* from Middle French or Late Latin; Middle French *orthodoxe,* from Late Latin *orthodoxus,* from Late Greek *orthodoxos,* from Greek *orth-* + *doxa* opinion — more at DOXOLOGY] (15th century)
1 **a** : conforming to established doctrine especially in religion **b** : CONVENTIONAL
2 *capitalized* : of, relating to, or constituting any of various conservative religious or political groups: as **a** : EASTERN ORTHODOX **b** : of or relating to Orthodox Judaism
— **or·tho·dox·ly** *adverb*

²orthodox *noun, plural* **orthodox** *also* **or·tho·dox·es** (1587)
1 : one that is orthodox
2 *capitalized* : a member of an Eastern Orthodox church

Orthodox Judaism *noun* (1904)
: Judaism that adheres to the Torah and Talmud as interpreted in an authoritative rabbinic law code and applies their principles and regulations to modern living — compare CONSERVATIVE JUDAISM, REFORM JUDAISM

or·tho·doxy \'òr-thə-ˌdäk-sē\ *noun, plural* **-dox·ies** (1630)
1 : the quality or state of being orthodox
2 : an orthodox belief or practice
3 *capitalized* **a** : Eastern Orthodox Christianity **b** : ORTHODOX JUDAISM

or·tho·epy \'òr-thə-ˌwe-pē, òr-'thō-ə-pē\ *noun* [New Latin *orthoepia*, from Greek *orthoepeia*, from *orth-* + *epos* word — more at VOICE] (1668)
1 : the customary pronunciation of a language
2 : the study of the pronunciation of a language
— **or·tho·ep·ic** \ˌòr-thə-'we-pik\ *adjective*
— **or·tho·ep·i·cal·ly** \-pi-k(ə-)lē\ *adverb*
— **or·tho·epist** \'òr-thə-ˌwe-pist, òr-'thō-ə-pist\ *noun*

or·tho·gen·e·sis \ˌòr-thə-'je-nə-səs\ *noun* [New Latin] (1895)
: variation of organisms in successive generations that in some evolutionary theories takes place in some predestined direction and results in progressive evolutionary trends independent of external factors
— **or·tho·ge·net·ic** \-jə-'ne-tik\ *adjective*
— **or·tho·ge·net·i·cal·ly** \-ti-k(ə-)lē\ *adverb*

or·thog·o·nal \òr-'thä-gə-nᵊl\ *adjective* [Middle French, from Latin *orthogonius*, from Greek *orthogōnios*, from *orth-* + *gōnia* angle — more at -GON] (1612)
1 a : intersecting or lying at right angles **b** : having perpendicular slopes or tangents at the point of intersection ⟨*orthogonal* curves⟩
2 : having a sum of products or an integral that is zero or sometimes one under specified conditions: as **a** *of real-valued functions* : having the integral of the product of each pair of functions over a specific interval equal to zero **b** *of vectors* : having the scalar product equal to zero **c** *of a square matrix* : having the sum of products of corresponding elements in any two rows or any two columns equal to one if the rows or columns are the same and equal to zero otherwise : having a transpose with which the product equals the identity matrix
3 *of a linear transformation* : having a matrix that is orthogonal : preserving length and distance
4 : composed of mutually orthogonal elements ⟨an *orthogonal* basis of a vector space⟩
5 : statistically independent
— **or·thog·o·nal·i·ty** \-ˌthä-gə-'na-lə-tē\ *noun*
— **or·thog·o·nal·ly** \-'thä-gə-nᵊl-ē\ *adverb*

or·thog·o·nal·ize \òr-'thä-gə-nᵊl-ˌīz\ *transitive verb* **-ized; -iz·ing** (1930)
: to make orthogonal
— **or·thog·o·nal·i·za·tion** \-ˌthä-gə-nᵊl-ə-'zā-shən\ *noun*

or·tho·grade \'òr-thə-ˌgrād\ *adjective* (1902)
: walking with the body upright or vertical

or·tho·graph·ic \ˌòr-thə-'gra-fik\ *also* **or·tho·graph·i·cal** \-fi-kəl\ *adjective* (1706)
1 : of, relating to, being, or prepared by orthographic projection ⟨an *orthographic* map⟩
2 a : of or relating to orthography **b** : correct in spelling
— **or·tho·graph·i·cal·ly** \-fi-k(ə-)lē\ *adverb*

orthographic projection *noun* (1668)
1 : projection of a single view of an object (as a view of the front) onto a drawing surface in which the lines of projection are perpendicular to the drawing surface

2 : the representation of related views of an object as if they were all in the same plane and projected by orthographic projection

object *A* with top view, front view, and right view in orthographic projection

or·thog·ra·phy \òr-'thä-grə-fē\ *noun* [Middle English *ortografie*, from Middle French, from Latin *orthographia*, from Greek, from *orth-* + *graphein* to write — more at CARVE] (15th century)
1 a : the art of writing words with the proper letters according to standard usage **b** : the representation of the sounds of a language by written or printed symbols
2 : a part of language study that deals with letters and spelling

or·tho·mo·lec·u·lar \ˌòr-thə-mə-'le-kyə-lər\ *adjective* (1968)
: relating to, based on, using, or being a theory according to which disease and especially mental illness may be cured by restoring the optimum amounts of substances normally present in the body ⟨*orthomolecular* therapy⟩ ⟨an *orthomolecular* psychiatrist⟩

or·tho·nor·mal \ˌòr-thə-'nòr-məl\ *adjective* (1932)
1 *of real-valued functions* : orthogonal with the integral of the square of each function over a specified interval equal to one
2 : being or composed of orthogonal elements of unit length ⟨*orthonormal* basis of a vector space⟩

or·tho·pe·dic *also* **or·tho·pae·dic** \ˌòr-thə-'pē-dik\ *adjective* [French *orthopédique*, from *orthopédie* orthopedics, from *orth-* + Greek *paid-, pais* child — more at FEW] (1840)
1 : of, relating to, or employed in orthopedics
2 : marked by deformities or crippling
— **or·tho·pe·di·cal·ly** \-'pē-di-k(ə-)lē\ *adverb*

or·tho·pe·dics *also* **or·tho·pae·dics** \-'pē-diks\ *noun plural but singular or plural in construction* (circa 1853)
: a branch of medicine concerned with the correction or prevention of skeletal deformities
— **or·tho·pe·dist** \-'pē-dist\ *noun*

or·tho·phos·phate \ˌòr-thə-'fäs-ˌfāt\ *noun* (1859)
: a salt or ester of orthophosphoric acid

or·tho·phos·pho·ric acid \ˌòr-thə-ˌfäs-'fòr-ik-, -'fär-; -ˌfäs-f(ə-)rik-\ *noun* [International Scientific Vocabulary] (1885)
: PHOSPHORIC ACID 1

or·tho·psy·chi·a·try \-sə-'kī-ə-trē, -(ˌ)sī-\ *noun* (circa 1927)
: prophylactic psychiatry concerned especially with incipient psychiatric and mental disorders in youth
— **or·tho·psy·chi·at·ric** \-ˌsī-kē-'a-trik\ *adjective*
— **or·tho·psy·chi·a·trist** \-sə-'kī-ə-trist, -(ˌ)sī-\ *noun*

or·thop·tera \òr-'thäp-tə-rə\ *noun plural* [New Latin, order name, from *orth-* + Greek *pteron* wing — more at FEATHER] (1828)
: insects that are orthopterans

or·thop·ter·an \òr-'thäp-tə-rən\ *noun* [New Latin *Orthoptera*] (circa 1842)
: any of an order (Orthoptera) of insects (as crickets, grasshoppers, and sometimes mantises) that are characterized by biting mouthparts, two pairs of wings or none, and an incomplete metamorphosis
— **orthopteran** *adjective*
— **or·thop·ter·ist** \-rist\ *noun*
— **or·thop·ter·oid** \-ˌròid\ *noun or adjective*

or·tho·rhom·bic \ˌòr-thə-'räm-bik\ *adjective* [International Scientific Vocabulary] (circa 1859)
: of, relating to, or constituting a system of crystallization characterized by three unequal axes at right angles to each other

or·tho·scop·ic \ˌòr-thə-'skä-pik\ *adjective* [International Scientific Vocabulary *orth-* + *-scopic* (as in *microscopic*)] (1853)
: giving an image in correct and normal proportions

or·tho·sis \òr-'thō-səs\ *noun, plural* **or·tho·ses** \-ˌsēz\ [New Latin, from Greek *orthōsis* straightening, from *orthoun* to straighten, from *orthos*] (1958)
: ORTHOTIC

or·tho·stat·ic \ˌòr-thə-'sta-tik\ *adjective* (1902)
: of, relating to, or caused by erect posture ⟨*orthostatic* hypotension⟩

or·thot·ic \òr-'thä-tik\ *noun* [New Latin *orthosis*] (1955)
: a support or brace for weak or ineffective joints or muscles

or·thot·ics \-tiks\ *noun plural but singular in construction* (1957)
: a branch of mechanical and medical science that deals with the support and bracing of weak or ineffective joints or muscles
— **or·thot·ic** \-tik\ *adjective*
— **or·tho·tist** \òr-'thä-tist, 'òr-thə-tist\ *noun*

or·thot·ro·pous \òr-'thä-trə-pəs\ *adjective* [International Scientific Vocabulary] (1830)
: having the ovule straight so that the chalaza, hilum, and micropyle are in the same axial line

or·to·lan \'òr-tᵊl-ən\ *noun* [French or Italian; French, from Italian *ortolano*, literally, gardener, from Latin *hortulanus*, from *hortulus*, diminutive of *hortus* garden — more at YARD] (1656)
: an Old World bunting (*Emberiza hortulana*) having a greenish gray head and breast, streaky brown back and wings, and a yellow throat

Or·vie·to \òr-'vyā-(ˌ)tō\ *noun* [*Orvieto*, city in central Italy] (1846)
: a usually dry Italian white wine

¹-ory *noun suffix* [Middle English *-orie*, from Latin *-orium*, from neuter of *-orius*, adjective suffix]
1 : place of or for ⟨observat*ory*⟩
2 : something that serves for ⟨cremat*ory*⟩

²-ory *adjective suffix* [Middle English *-orie*, from Middle French & Latin; Middle French, from Latin *-orius*]
1 : of, relating to, or characterized by ⟨gusta*tory*⟩
2 : serving for, producing, or maintaining ⟨justifica*tory*⟩

oryx \'òr-iks, 'òr-, 'är-\ *noun, plural* **oryx** *or* **oryx·es** [New Latin, from Latin, a gazelle, from Greek, pickax, antelope, kind of whale, from *oryssein* to dig; akin to Latin *runcare* to grub up, weed, Sanskrit *luñcati* he plucks] (1535)
: any of a small genus (*Oryx*) of large heavily-built African and Arabian antelopes that have a light-colored coat with dark conspicuous markings especially on the face

oryx

or·zo \'òrd-(ˌ)zō\ *noun* [Italian, literally, barley, from Latin *hordeum* — more at ORGEAT] (circa 1929)
: rice-shaped pasta

¹os \'äs\ *noun, plural* **os·sa** \'ä-sə\ [Latin *oss-, os* — more at OSSEOUS] (15th century)
: BONE

²os \'ōs\ *noun, plural* **ora** \'ōr-ə, 'ȯr-ə\ [Latin *or-, os* — more at ORAL] (1737)
: MOUTH, ORIFICE

Osage \ō-'säj, 'ō-,\ *noun, plural* **Osag·es** or **Osage** (1698)
1 : a member of an American Indian people originally of Missouri
2 : the Siouan language of the Osage people

Osage orange *noun* (1817)
: an ornamental usually thorny American tree (*Maclura pomifera*) of the mulberry family with shiny ovate leaves and hard bright orange wood; *also* **:** its yellowish globose fruit

Os·can \'äs-kən\ *noun* [Latin *Oscus*] (1753)
1 : a member of a people of ancient Italy occupying Campania
2 : the language of the Oscan people — see INDO-EUROPEAN LANGUAGES table

¹Os·car \'äs-kər\ *trademark*
— used especially for any of a number of golden statuettes awarded annually by a professional organization for notable achievement in motion pictures

²Oscar (1952)
— a communications code word for the letter *o*

os·cil·late \'ä-sə-,lāt\ *intransitive verb* **-lated; -lat·ing** [Latin *oscillatus,* past participle of *oscillare* to swing, from *oscillum* swing] (1726)
1 a : to swing backward and forward like a pendulum **b :** to move or travel back and forth between two points
2 : to vary between opposing beliefs, feelings, or theories
3 : to vary above and below a mean value
synonym see SWING
— **os·cil·la·to·ry** \'ä-sə-lə-,tōr-ē, -,tȯr-\ *adjective*

os·cil·la·tion \,ä-sə-'lā-shən\ *noun* (1658)
1 : the action or state of oscillating
2 : VARIATION, FLUCTUATION
3 : a flow of electricity changing periodically from a maximum to a minimum; *especially* **:** a flow periodically changing direction
4 : a single swing (as of an oscillating body) from one extreme limit to the other
— **os·cil·la·tion·al** \-shnəl, -shə-nᵊl\ *adjective*

os·cil·la·tor \'ä-sə-,lā-tər\ *noun* (1835)
1 : one that oscillates
2 : a device for producing alternating current; *especially* **:** a radio-frequency or audio-frequency generator

oscillo- *combining form* [International Scientific Vocabulary, from Latin *oscillare*]
: wave **:** oscillation ⟨*oscillo*scope⟩

os·cil·lo·gram \ä-'si-lə-,gram, ə-\ *noun* [International Scientific Vocabulary] (1903)
: a record made by an oscillograph or oscilloscope

os·cil·lo·graph \-,graf\ *noun* [International Scientific Vocabulary] (1893)
: an instrument for recording alternating current wave forms or other electrical oscillations
— **os·cil·lo·graph·ic** \ä-,si-lə-'gra-fik, ,ä-sə-lə-\ *adjective*
— **os·cil·lo·graph·i·cal·ly** \-fi-k(ə-)lē\ *adverb*
— **os·cil·log·ra·phy** \,ä-sə-'lä-grə-fē\ *noun*

os·cil·lo·scope \ä-'si-lə-,skōp, ə-\ *noun* [International Scientific Vocabulary] (1906)
: an instrument in which the variations in a fluctuating electrical quantity appear temporarily as a visible wave form on the fluorescent screen of a cathode-ray tube
— **os·cil·lo·scop·ic** \ä-,si-lə-'skä-pik, ,ä-sə-lə-\ *adjective*

os·cine \'ä-,sīn\ *adjective* [New Latin *Oscines,* suborder name, from Latin, plural of *oscin-, oscen* songbird, bird giving omens by its cry, from *obs-, ob-* in front of, in the way + *canere* to sing — more at OB-, CHANT] (1883)
: of or relating to a large suborder (Oscines) of passerine birds (as larks, shrikes, finches, orioles, and crows) characterized by a vocal apparatus highly specialized for singing
— **oscine** *noun*

Os·co-Um·bri·an \,äs-kō-'əm-brē-ən\ *noun* [Latin *Oscus* + English *Umbrian*] (1894)
: a subdivision of the Italic branch of the Indo-European language family containing Oscan and Umbrian

os·cu·late \'äs-kyə-,lāt\ *transitive verb* **-lated; -lat·ing** [Latin *osculatus,* past participle of *osculari,* from *osculum* kiss, from diminutive of *os* mouth — more at ORAL] (circa 1656)
: KISS

os·cu·la·tion \,äs-kyə-'lā-shən\ *noun* (circa 1658)
: the act of kissing; *also* **:** KISS
— **os·cu·la·to·ry** \'äs-kyə-lə-,tōr-ē, -,tȯr-\ *adjective*

os·cu·lum \'äs-kyə-ləm\ *noun* [New Latin, from Latin, diminutive of *os* mouth] (1887)
: an excurrent opening of a sponge

¹-ose *adjective suffix* [Middle English, from Latin *-osus*]
: full of **:** having **:** possessing the qualities of ⟨cym*ose*⟩

²-ose *noun suffix* [French, from *glucose*]
1 : carbohydrate ⟨amyl*ose*⟩; *especially* **:** sugar ⟨pent*ose*⟩
2 : primary hydrolysis product ⟨prote*ose*⟩

Osee \'ō-,zē, ō-'zā-ə\ *noun* [Late Latin, from Hebrew *Hōshēa'*]
: HOSEA

osier \'ō-zhər\ *noun* [Middle English, from Middle French, from Medieval Latin *auseria* osier bed] (14th century)
1 : any of various willows (especially *Salix viminalis*) whose pliable twigs are used for furniture and basketry
2 : a willow rod used in basketry
3 : any of several American dogwoods

Osi·ris \ō-'sī-rəs\ *noun* [Latin, from Greek, from Egyptian *Ws'r*]
: the Egyptian god of the underworld and husband and brother of Isis

-osis *noun suffix, plural* **-oses** or **-osises** [Middle English, from Latin, from Greek *-ōsis,* from *-ō-* (stem of causative verbs in *-oun*) + *-sis*]
1 a : action **:** process **:** condition ⟨hypn*osis*⟩ **b :** abnormal or diseased condition ⟨leuk*osis*⟩
2 : increase **:** formation ⟨leukocyt*osis*⟩

Os·man·li \äz-'man-lē\ *noun* [Turkish *osmanlı,* from *Osman,* founder of the Ottoman Empire] (1813)
1 : OTTOMAN 1
2 : TURKISH

os·me·te·ri·um \,äz-mə-'tir-ē-əm\ *noun, plural* **-ria** \-ē-ə\ [New Latin, irregular from Greek *osmē* odor] (1816)
: a protrusible forked glandular process that emits a disagreeable odor, is borne on the first thoracic segment of the larvae of many swallowtails and related butterflies, and is a defensive organ

osmic acid *noun* (1842)
: OSMIUM TETROXIDE

os·mi·rid·i·um \,äz-mə-'ri-dē-əm\ *noun* [Greek *osmē* + New Latin *iridium*] (1880)
: IRIDOSMINE

os·mi·um \'äz-mē-əm\ *noun* [New Latin, from Greek *osmē* odor] (1804)
: a hard brittle blue-gray or blue-black polyvalent metallic element of the platinum group with a high melting point that is the heaviest metal known and is used especially as a catalyst and in hard alloys — see ELEMENT table

osmium tetroxide *noun* (1876)
: a crystalline compound OsO_4 that is an oxide of osmium, has a poisonous irritating vapor, and is used as a catalyst, oxidizing agent, and biological fixative and stain

os·mol or **os·mole** \'äz-,mōl, 'äs-\ *noun* [blend of *osmosis* and *mol* (⁵*mole*)] (1942)
: a standard unit of osmotic pressure based on a one molal concentration of an ion in a solution

os·mo·lal·i·ty \,äz-mō-'la-lə-tē, ,äs-\ *noun, plural* **-ties** [*osmol* + *-al* + *-ity*] (circa 1944)
: the concentration of an osmotic solution especially when measured in osmols or milliosmols per 1000 grams of solvent
— **os·mo·lal** \äz-mō-ləl, äs-\ *adjective*

os·mo·lar·i·ty \,äz-mō-'lar-ə-tē, ,äs-\ *noun, plural* **-ties** [*osmol* + *-ar* + *-ity*] (1948)
: the concentration of an osmotic solution especially when measured in osmols or milliosmols per liter of solution
— **os·mo·lar** \äz-'mō-lər, äs-\ *adjective*

os·mom·e·ter \äz-'mä-mə-tər, äs-\ *noun* [*osmosis* + *-meter*] (1854)
: an apparatus for measuring osmotic pressure
— **os·mo·met·ric** \,äz-mə-'me-trik, ,äs-\ *adjective*
— **os·mom·e·try** \äz-'mä-mə-trē\ *noun*

os·mo·reg·u·la·tion \'äz-mō-,re-gyə-'lā-shən, ,äs-\ *noun* [*osmosis* + *regulation*] (1927)
: regulation of osmotic pressure especially in the body of a living organism

os·mo·reg·u·la·to·ry \-'re-gyə-lə-,tōr-ē, -,tȯr-\ *adjective* (circa 1911)
: of, relating to, or concerned with the maintenance of constant osmotic pressure

os·mo·sis \äz-'mō-səs, äs-\ *noun* [New Latin, short for *endosmosis*] (1867)
1 : movement of a solvent through a semipermeable membrane (as of a living cell) into a solution of higher solute concentration that tends to equalize the concentrations of solute on the two sides of the membrane
2 : a process of absorption or diffusion suggestive of the flow of osmotic action; *especially* **:** a usually effortless often unconscious assimilation ⟨learned a number of languages by *osmosis* —Roger Kimball⟩

os·mot·ic \-'mä-tik\ *adjective* (1854)
: of, relating to, or having the properties of osmosis
— **os·mot·i·cal·ly** \-ti-k(ə-)lē\ *adverb*

osmotic pressure *noun* (1888)
: the pressure produced by or associated with osmosis and dependent on molar concentration and absolute temperature: as **a :** the maximum pressure that develops in a solution separated from a solvent by a membrane permeable only to the solvent **b :** the pressure that must be applied to a solution to just prevent osmosis

osmotic shock *noun* (1950)
: a rapid change in the osmotic pressure (as by transfer to a medium of different concentration) affecting a living system

os·mun·da \äz-'mən-də\ *noun* [New Latin, from Medieval Latin, from Old French *osmonde*] (1789)
: any of a genus (*Osmunda*) of rather large ferns (as the cinnamon fern) with pinnate or bipinnate fronds and fibrous creeping rhizomes

os·prey \'äs-prē, -,prā\ *noun, plural* **ospreys** [Middle English *ospray,* from (assumed) Middle French *osfraie,* from Latin *ossifraga,* a bird of prey] (15th century)
1 : a large fish-eating hawk (*Pandion haliaetus*) that is a dark brown color above and mostly pure white below
2 : a feather trimming used for millinery

osprey 1

ossa *plural of* OS

os·se·in \'ä-sē-ən\ *noun* [International Scientific Vocabulary, from Latin *oss-, os*] (1857)
: the collagen of bones

os·se·ous \\'ä-sē-əs\\ *adjective* [Latin *osseus,* from *oss-, os* bone; akin to Greek *osteon* bone, Sanskrit *asthi*] (1682)
: BONY 1

Os·sete \\'ä-,sēt\\ *also* **Os·set** \\'ä-,sət, -,set\\ *noun* [Russian *osetin,* from *Osetiya* Ossetia, from Georgian *Oseti,* from *osi* Ossete] (1814)
: a member of a people of the central Caucasus
— **Os·se·tian** \\ä-'sē-shən\\ *adjective or noun*

Os·set·ic \\ä-'se-tik\\ *noun* (circa 1890)
: the Iranian language of the Ossetes

Os·si·an·ic \\,ä-sē-'a-nik, -shē-\\ *adjective* (1808)
: of, relating to, or resembling the legendary Irish bard Ossian, the poems ascribed to him, or the rhythmic prose style used by James Macpherson in the poems he claimed to have translated from Ossian

os·si·cle \\'ä-si-kəl\\ *noun* [Latin *ossiculum,* diminutive of *oss-, os*] (1578)
: a small bone or bony structure (as the malleus, incus, or stapes)
— **os·sic·u·lar** \\ä-'si-kyə-lər\\ *adjective*

os·si·fi·ca·tion \\,ä-sə-fə-'kā-shən\\ *noun* (1697)
1 a : the natural process of bone formation **b :** the hardening (as of muscular tissue) into a bony substance
2 : a mass or particle of ossified tissue
3 : a tendency toward or state of being molded into a rigid, conventional, sterile, or unimaginative condition

os·si·frage \\'ä-sə-frij, -,frāj\\ *noun* [Latin *ossifraga,* a bird of prey, from feminine of *ossifragus* bone-breaking, from *oss-, os* + *frangere* to break — more at BREAK] (1601)
: LAMMERGEIER

os·si·fy \\'ä-sə-,fī\\ *verb* **-fied; -fy·ing** [Latin *oss-, os* + English *-ify*] (1713)
intransitive verb
1 : to change into bone
2 : to become hardened or conventional and opposed to change
transitive verb
1 : to change (as cartilage) into bone
2 : to make rigidly conventional and opposed to change

os·so bu·co *also* **os·so buc·co** \\,ō-sō-'bü-(,)kō, ,ȯ-sō-\\ *noun* [Italian *ossobuco* veal shank, literally, pierced bone] (1935)
: braised veal shanks

os·su·ary \\'ä-shə-,wer-ē, -syə-, -sə-\\ *noun,* plural **-ar·ies** [Late Latin *ossuarium,* from Latin, neuter of *ossuarius* of bones, from Old Latin *ossua,* plural of *oss-, os*] (1658)
: a depository for the bones of the dead

oste- *or* **osteo-** *combining form* [New Latin, from Greek, from *osteon* — more at OSSEOUS]
: bone 〈*oste*al〉 〈*osteo*myelitis〉

os·te·al \\'äs-tē-əl\\ *adjective* [International Scientific Vocabulary] (1877)
: of, relating to, or resembling bone; *also* : affecting or involving bone or the skeleton

os·te·i·tis \\,äs-tē-'ī-təs\\ *noun* [New Latin] (circa 1847)
: inflammation of bone

os·ten·si·ble \\ä-'sten(t)-sə-bəl, ə-\\ *adjective* [French, from Latin *ostensus,* past participle of *ostendere* to show, from *obs-, ob-* in the way + *tendere* to stretch — more at OB-, THIN] (circa 1771)
1 : intended for display : open to view
2 : being such in appearance : plausible rather than demonstrably true or real 〈the *ostensible* purpose for the trip〉
synonym see APPARENT

os·ten·si·bly \\-blē\\ *adverb* (1765)
1 : in an ostensible manner
2 : to all outward appearances

os·ten·sive \\ä-'sten(t)-siv\\ *adjective* (1782)
1 : OSTENSIBLE 2

2 : of, relating to, or constituting definition by exemplifying the thing or quality being defined
— **os·ten·sive·ly** *adverb*

os·ten·so·ri·um \\,äs-tən-'sōr-ē-əm, -,ten-, -'sȯr-\\ *noun,* plural **-ria** \\-ē-ə\\ [Medieval Latin, from Latin *ostendere*] (circa 1772)
: MONSTRANCE

os·ten·ta·tion \\,äs-tən-'tā-shən\\ *noun* [Middle English *ostentacion,* from Middle French *ostentation,* from Latin *ostentation-, ostentatio,* from *ostentare* to display, frequentative of *ostendere*] (15th century)
1 : excessive display : PRETENTIOUSNESS
2 *archaic* : an act of displaying

os·ten·ta·tious \\-shəs\\ *adjective* (1673)
: marked by or fond of conspicuous or vainglorious and sometimes pretentious display
synonym see SHOWY
— **os·ten·ta·tious·ly** *adverb*
— **os·ten·ta·tious·ness** *noun*

os·te·o·ar·thri·tis \\,äs-tē-ō-är-'thrī-təs\\ *noun* [New Latin] (1878)
: arthritis marked by degeneration of the cartilage and bone of joints
— **os·te·o·ar·thrit·ic** \\-'thri-tik\\ *adjective*

os·te·o·blast \\'äs-tē-ə-,blast\\ *noun* [International Scientific Vocabulary] (1875)
: a bone-forming cell
— **os·te·o·blas·tic** \\,äs-tē-ə-'blas-tik\\ *adjective*

os·te·o·clast \\'äs-tē-ə-,klast\\ *noun* [International Scientific Vocabulary *oste-* + Greek *klastos* broken — more at CLAST] (1872)
: any of the large multinucleate cells closely associated with areas of bone resorption
— **os·te·o·clas·tic** \\,äs-tē-ə-'klas-tik\\ *adjective*

os·te·o·cyte \\'äs-tē-ə-,sīt\\ *noun* (1942)
: a cell that is characteristic of adult bone and is isolated in a lacuna of the bone substance

os·te·o·gen·e·sis \\,äs-tē-ə-'je-nə-səs\\ *noun* [New Latin] (1830)
: development and formation of bone

osteogenesis im·per·fec·ta \\-,im-(,)pər-'fek-tə\\ *noun* [New Latin, imperfect osteogenesis] (circa 1901)
: a hereditary disease marked especially by extreme brittleness of the long bones

os·te·o·gen·ic \\,äs-tē-ə-'je-nik\\ *adjective* (1867)
1 : producing bone
2 : originating in bone

osteogenic sarcoma *noun* (circa 1923)
: OSTEOSARCOMA

¹os·te·oid \\'äs-tē-,ȯid\\ *adjective* [International Scientific Vocabulary] (1840)
: resembling bone

²osteoid *noun* (1934)
: uncalcified bone matrix

os·te·ol·o·gy \\,äs-tē-'ä-lə-jē\\ *noun* [New Latin *osteologia,* from Greek, description of bones, from *oste-* + *-logia* -logy] (1670)
1 : a branch of anatomy dealing with the bones
2 : the bony structure of an organism
— **os·te·o·log·i·cal** \\-tē-ə-'lä-ji-kəl\\ *adjective*
— **os·te·ol·o·gist** \\-tē-'ä-lə-jist\\ *noun*

os·te·o·ma \\,äs-tē-'ō-mə\\ *noun,* plural **-mas** *or* **-ma·ta** \\-mə-tə\\ [New Latin] (circa 1849)
: a benign tumor composed of bone tissue

os·te·o·ma·la·cia \\,äs-tē-ō-mə-'lā-sh(ē-)ə\\ *noun* [New Latin, from *oste-* + Greek *malakia* softness, from *malakos* soft — more at MOLLIFY] (circa 1834)
: a disease of adults that is characterized by softening of the bones and is analogous to rickets in the immature

os·te·o·my·e·li·tis \\-,mī-ə-'lī-təs\\ *noun* [New Latin] (1854)
: an infectious inflammatory disease of bone often of bacterial origin that is marked by local death and separation of tissue

os·te·o·path \\'äs-tē-ə-,path\\ *noun* (1897)
: a practitioner of osteopathy

os·te·op·a·thy \\,äs-tē-'ä-pə-thē\\ *noun* [New Latin *osteopathia,* from *oste-* + Latin *-pathia* -pathy] (1899)
: a system of medical practice based on a theory that diseases are due chiefly to loss of structural integrity which can be restored by manipulation of the parts supplemented by therapeutic measures (as use of medicine or surgery)
— **os·te·o·path·ic** \\,äs-tē-ə-'pa-thik\\ *adjective*
— **os·te·o·path·i·cal·ly** \\-thi-k(ə-)lē\\ *adverb*

os·te·o·plas·ty \\'äs-tē-ə-,plas-tē\\ *noun* (circa 1860)
: plastic surgery on bone; *especially* : replacement of lost bone tissue or reconstruction of defective bony parts
— **os·te·o·plas·tic** \\,äs-tē-ə-'plas-tik\\ *adjective*

os·te·o·po·ro·sis \\,äs-tē-ō-pə-'rō-səs\\ *noun,* plural **-ro·ses** \\-,sēz\\ [New Latin, from *oste-* + *porosis* rarefaction, from *porus* pore + *-osis*] (1846)
: a condition that affects especially older women and is characterized by decrease in bone mass with decreased density and enlargement of bone spaces producing porosity and fragility
— **os·te·o·po·rot·ic** \\-'rä-tik\\ *adjective*

os·te·o·sar·co·ma \\-sär-'kō-mə\\ *noun,* plural **-mas** *or* **-ma·ta** \\-mə-tə\\ [New Latin] (circa 1826)
: a sarcoma derived from bone or containing bone tissue

os·ti·na·to \\,äs-tə-'nä-(,)tō, ,ȯs-\\ *noun,* plural **-tos** *also* **-ti** \\-tē\\ [Italian, obstinate, from Latin *obstinatus*] (circa 1876)
: a musical figure repeated persistently at the same pitch throughout a composition — compare IMITATION, SEQUENCE

os·ti·ole \\'äs-tē-,ōl\\ *noun* [New Latin *ostiolum,* from Latin, diminutive of *ostium*] (circa 1857)
: a small bodily aperture, orifice, or pore

os·ti·um \\'äs-tē-əm\\ *noun,* plural **os·tia** \\-tē-ə\\ [New Latin, from Latin, door, mouth of a river; akin to Latin *os* mouth — more at ORAL] (1828)
: a mouthlike opening in a bodily organ

os·tler *variant of* HOSTLER

ost·mark \\'ȯst-,märk, 'ȯst-\\ *noun* [German, literally, East mark] (1948)
: the former East German mark

os·to·my \\'äs-tə-mē\\ *noun,* plural **-mies** [*colostomy*] (1957)
: an operation (as a colostomy) to create an artificial passage for bodily elimination

-ostosis *noun combining form,* plural **-ostoses** *or* **-ostosises** [New Latin, from Greek *-ostōsis,* from *osteon* bone — more at OSSEOUS]
: ossification of a (specified) part or to a (specified) degree 〈hyper*ostosis*〉

os·tra·cise *British variant of* OSTRACIZE

os·tra·cism \\'äs-trə-,si-zəm\\ *noun* (1588)
1 : a method of temporary banishment by popular vote without trial or special accusation practiced in ancient Greece
2 : exclusion by general consent from common privileges or social acceptance

os·tra·cize \\-,sīz\\ *transitive verb* **-cized; -ciz·ing** [Greek *ostrakizein* to banish by voting with potsherds, from *ostrakon* shell, potsherd — more at OYSTER] (1649)
1 : to exile by ostracism

\\ə\\ abut \\ᵊ\\ kitten \\ər\\ further \\a\\ ash \\ā\\ ace
\\ä\\ mop, mar \\aú\\ out \\ch\\ chin \\e\\ bet \\ē\\ easy
\\g\\ go \\i\\ hit \\ī\\ ice \\j\\ job \\ŋ\\ sing \\ō\\ go
\\ȯ\\ law \\ȯi\\ boy \\th\\ thin \\th\\ the \\ü\\ loot \\ú\\ foot
\\y\\ yet \\zh\\ vision *see also* Guide to Pronunciation

2 : to exclude from a group by common consent ◇

os·tra·cod \'äs-trə-ˌkäd\ *also* **os·tra·code** \-ˌkōd\ *noun* [ultimately from Greek *ostrakon*] (1865)
: any of a subclass (Ostracoda) of very small active mostly freshwater crustaceans that have the body enclosed in a bivalve carapace, the body segmentation obscured, the abdomen rudimentary, and only seven pairs of appendages

os·tra·co·derm \'äs-trə-kō-ˌdərm, äs-'tra-kə-\ *noun* [ultimately from Greek *ostrakon* + *derma* skin — more at DERM-] (1891)
: any of the early fossil jawless fishes of the Lower Paleozoic usually having a bony covering of plates or scales

os·tra·con \'äs-trə-ˌkän\ *noun, plural* **-tra·ca** \-trə-kə\ [Greek *ostrakon* potsherd, shell — more at OYSTER] (1883)
: a fragment (as of pottery) containing an inscription — usually used in plural

os·trich \'äs-trich, 'ȯs- *also* -trij\ *noun* [Middle English, from Old French *ostrusce*, from (assumed) Vulgar Latin *avis struthio*, from Latin *avis* bird + Late Latin *struthio* ostrich — more at STRUTHIOUS] (13th century)
1 a : a swift-footed 2-toed flightless ratite bird (*Struthio camelus*) of Africa that is the largest of existing birds and often weighs 300 pounds (140 kilograms) **b :** RHEA **c :** leather made from ostrich skin
2 [from the belief that the ostrich when pursued hides its head in the sand and believes itself to be unseen] **:** one who attempts to avoid danger or difficulty by refusing to face it
— **os·trich·like** \-ˌlīk\ *adjective*

Os·tro·goth \'äs-trə-ˌgäth\ *noun* [Middle English, from Late Latin *Ostrogothi*, plural] (14th century)
: a member of the eastern division of the Goths
— **Os·tro·goth·ic** \ˌäs-trə-'gä-thik\ *adjective*

Os·we·go tea \ä-'swē-gō-\ *noun* [*Oswego* River, N. Y.] (1752)
: a North American mint (*Monarda didyma*) with showy scarlet irregular flowers

ot- *or* **oto-** *combining form* [Greek *ōt-, ōto-,* from *ōt-, ous* — more at EAR]
: ear ⟨*otitis*⟩ **:** ear and ⟨*oto*laryngology⟩

Othel·lo \ə-'the-(ˌ)lō, ō-\ *noun*
: a Moor in the military service of Venice, husband of Desdemona, and protagonist of Shakespeare's tragedy *Othello*

¹oth·er \'ə-thər\ *adjective* [Middle English, from Old English *ōther;* akin to Old High German *andar* other, Sanskrit *antara*] (before 12th century)
1 a : being the one (as of two or more) remaining or not included ⟨held on with one hand and waved with the *other* one⟩ **b :** being the one or ones distinct from that or those first mentioned or implied ⟨taller than the *other* boys⟩ **c :** SECOND ⟨every *other* day⟩
2 : not the same **:** DIFFERENT ⟨any *other* color would have been better⟩ ⟨something *other* than it seems to be⟩
3 : ADDITIONAL ⟨sold in the U.S. and 14 *other* countries⟩
4 a : recently past ⟨the *other* evening⟩ **b :** FORMER ⟨in *other* times⟩

²other *noun* (before 12th century)
1 a : one that remains of two or more **b :** a thing opposite to or excluded by something else ⟨went from one side to the *other*⟩
2 : a different or additional one ⟨the *others* came later⟩

³other *pronoun, sometimes plural in construction* (before 12th century)
1 *obsolete* **a :** one of two that remains **b :** each preceding one
2 : a different or additional one ⟨something or *other*⟩

⁴other *adverb* (13th century)
: OTHERWISE — used with *than* ⟨was unable to see them *other* than by going to their home⟩

oth·er–di·rect·ed \ˌə-thər-də-'rek-təd, -dī-\ *adjective* (1950)
: directed in thought and action primarily by external norms rather than by one's own scale of values
— **oth·er–di·rect·ed·ness** *noun*

oth·er·guess \'ə-thər-ˌges\ *adjective* [alteration of English dialect *othergates*] (1632)
archaic **:** DIFFERENT

oth·er·ness \'ə-thər-nəs\ *noun* (1587)
1 : the quality or state of being other or different
2 : something that is other or different

other than *preposition* (1679)
: with the exception of **:** EXCEPT FOR, BESIDES ⟨*other than* that, nothing happened⟩

oth·er·where \-ˌhwer, -ˌhwar, -ˌwer, -ˌwar\ *adverb* (14th century)
: ELSEWHERE

oth·er·while \-ˌhwīl, -ˌwīl\ *also* **oth·er·whiles** \-ˌhwīlz, -ˌwīlz\ *adverb* (13th century)
chiefly dialect **:** at another time

¹oth·er·wise \-ˌwīz\ *pronoun* [Middle English, from Old English (*on*) *ōthre wīsan* in another manner] (before 12th century)
: something or anything else **:** something to the contrary ⟨do very little to enforce competition—and have never intended *otherwise* —Milton Viorst⟩

²otherwise *adverb* (13th century)
1 : in a different way or manner ⟨glossed over or *otherwise* handled —*Playboy*⟩
2 : in different circumstances ⟨might *otherwise* have left⟩
3 : in other respects ⟨an *otherwise* flimsy farce —*Current Biography*⟩
4 : if not ⟨do what I tell you, *otherwise* you'll be sorry⟩
5 : NOT — paired with an adjective, adverb, noun, or verb to indicate its contrary or to suggest an indefinite alternative ⟨people whose deeds, admirable or *otherwise* —John Fischer⟩ ⟨almost thirty thousand women, Irish and *otherwise* —J. M. Burns⟩ ⟨his opinion as to the success or *otherwise* of it —*Australian Dictionary of Biography*⟩

³otherwise *adjective* (14th century)
: DIFFERENT ⟨if conditions were *otherwise*⟩

other woman *noun* (1855)
: a woman with whom a married man has an affair — usually used with *the*

oth·er·world \'ə-thər-ˌwərld\ *noun* (13th century)
: a world beyond death or beyond present reality

oth·er·world·ly \ˌə-thər-'wərl(d)-lē\ *adjective* (1879)
1 a : of, relating to, or resembling that of a world other than the actual world **b :** devoted to preparing for a world to come
2 : devoted to intellectual or imaginative pursuits
— **oth·er·world·li·ness** *noun*

¹-otic *adjective suffix* [Greek *-ōtikos,* from *-ōtos,* ending of verbals, from *-o-* (stem of causative verbs in *-oun*) + *-tos,* suffix forming verbals — more at -ED]
: of, relating to, or characterized by a (specified) action, process, or condition ⟨symbi*otic*⟩

²-otic *adjective combining form* [Greek *ōtikos* of the ear, from *ōt-, ous* ear]
: having (such) a relationship to the ear ⟨di*chotic*⟩

oti·ose \'ō-shē-ˌōs, 'ō-tē-\ *adjective* [Latin *otiosus,* from *otium* leisure] (1794)
1 : producing no useful result **:** FUTILE
2 : being at leisure **:** IDLE
3 : lacking use or effect **:** FUNCTIONLESS
synonym see VAIN
— **oti·ose·ly** *adverb*
— **oti·ose·ness** *noun*
— **oti·os·i·ty** \ˌō-shē-'ä-sə-tē, ˌō-tē-\ *noun*

oti·tis \ō-'tī-təs\ *noun* [New Latin] (circa 1799)
: inflammation of the ear

otitis me·dia \-'mē-dē-ə\ *noun* [New Latin] (1874)
: inflammation of the middle ear marked by pain, fever, dizziness, and abnormalities of hearing

oto·cyst \'ō-tə-ˌsist\ *noun* [International Scientific Vocabulary; from its probable auditory function] (1877)
: a fluid-containing organ of many invertebrates that contains an otolith **:** STATOCYST
— **oto·cys·tic** \ˌō-tə-'sis-tik\ *adjective*

oto·lar·yn·gol·o·gy \ˌō-tō-ˌlar-ən-'gä-lə-jē\ *noun* (1897)
: a medical specialty concerned especially with the ear, nose, and throat
— **oto·lar·yn·go·log·i·cal** \-gə-'lä-ji-kəl\ *adjective*
— **oto·lar·yn·gol·o·gist** \-'gä-lə-jist\ *noun*

oto·lith \'ō-t²l-ˌith\ *noun* [French *otolithe,* from *ot-* + *-lithe* -lith] (circa 1836)
: a calcareous concretion in the inner ear of a vertebrate or in the otocyst of an invertebrate
— **oto·lith·ic** \ˌō-t²l-'i-thik\ *adjective*

oto·rhi·no·lar·yn·gol·o·gy \ˌō-tō-ˌrī-nō-ˌlar-ən-'gä-lə-jē\ *noun* (circa 1900)
: OTOLARYNGOLOGY
— **oto·rhi·no·lar·yn·go·log·i·cal** \-gə-'lä-ji-kəl\ *adjective*
— **oto·rhi·no·lar·yn·gol·o·gist** \-'gä-lə-jist\ *noun*

oto·scle·ro·sis \ˌō-tō-sklə-'rō-səs\ *noun* [New Latin] (1901)
: growth of spongy bone in the inner ear that causes progressively increasing deafness

oto·tox·ic \ˌō-tə-'täk-sik\ *adjective* (1951)
: producing, involving, or being adverse effects on organs or nerves involved in hearing or balance
— **oto·tox·ic·i·ty** \-täk-'si-sə-tē\ *noun*

ot·ta·va \ō-'tä-və\ *adverb or adjective* [Italian, octave, from Medieval Latin *octava*] (1848)
: at an octave higher or lower than written — used as a direction in music

ottava ri·ma \-'rē-mə\ *noun, plural* **ottava rimas** [Italian, literally, eighth rhyme] (1820)
: a stanza of eight lines of heroic verse with a rhyme scheme of *abababcc*

Ot·ta·wa \'ä-tə-wə, -ˌwä, -ˌwȯ\ *noun, plural* **-was** *or* **-wa** (1687)
: a member of an American Indian people of Michigan and southern Ontario

ot·ter \'ä-tər\ *noun, plural* **otters** *also* **otter** [Middle English *oter,* from Old English *otor;* akin to Old High German *ottar* otter, Greek *hydōr* water — more at WATER] (before 12th century)
1 : any of various largely aquatic carnivorous mammals (as genus *Lutra* or *Enhydra*) that are

◇ **WORD HISTORY**

ostracize The Greek word *osteon* "bone" and its relatives *ostreon* "oyster" and *ostrakon* are names for hard, brittle objects. *Ostrakon* could refer to a seashell, an earthen vessel, or the broken fragment of such a vessel. Such potsherds served ancient Athenians as ballots in a particular kind of popular vote. Once a year the male citizens could gather in the agora or marketplace of Athens to decide who, if anyone, should be banished temporarily for the good of the city. Each voter wrote a name on his *ostrakon.* If at least six thousand votes were cast and if a majority of them named one man, then that man was banished. The verb to describe this banishment, and the source of English *ostracize,* was *ostrakizein,* a derivative of *ostrakos.* When the word *ostracism* first appeared in English in the 16th century, it was used only in historical reference to the ancient Athenian custom. Nonhistorical use began early in the 17th century, and nowadays *ostracism* refers more generally to exclusion from a social group by common consent.

related to the weasels and minks and usually have webbed and clawed feet and dark brown fur

2 : the fur or pelt of an otter

otter 1

ot·ter hound *noun* [from its use in hunting otters] (1607)
: any of a British breed of large hounds that have a wiry water-resistant coat and a keen scent

ot·to \'ä-(ˌ)tō\ *variant of* ATTAR

ot·to·man \'ä-tə-mən\ *noun* (1605)
1 *capitalized* **a :** a member of a Turkish dynasty founded by Osman I that ruled the Ottoman Empire **b :** a citizen or functionary of the Ottoman Empire
2 [French *ottomane*, from feminine of *ottoman*, adjective] **a :** an upholstered often overstuffed seat or couch usually without a back **b :** an overstuffed footstool
3 : a heavy clothing fabric characterized by pronounced crosswise ribs

Ot·to·man \'ä-tə-mən\ *adjective* [French, adjective & noun, probably from Italian *ottomano*, from Arabic *'othmānī*, from *'Othmān* Osman I, founder of the Ottoman Empire] (1603)
: of or relating to the Ottoman Empire, its rulers, or its citizens or functionaries

oua·bain \wä-'bā-ən, 'wä-ˌbān\ *noun* [International Scientific Vocabulary, from French *ouabaïo*, an African tree, from Somali *waabayyo* arrow poison] (1893)
: a poisonous glycoside $C_{29}H_{44}O_{12}$ obtained from several African shrubs or trees (genera *Strophanthus* and *Acokanthera*) of the dogbane family and used medically like digitalis and in Africa as an arrow poison

ou·bli·ette \ˌü-blē-'et\ *noun* [French, from Middle French, from *oublier* to forget, from (assumed) Vulgar Latin *oblitare*, frequentative of Latin *oblivisci* to forget — more at OBLIVION] (1819)
: a dungeon with an opening only at the top

¹ouch \'aùch\ *noun* [Middle English, alteration (from misdivision of *a nouche*) of *nouche*, from Middle French, of Germanic origin; akin to Old High German *nusca* clasp] (14th century)
1 *obsolete :* CLASP, BROOCH
2 a : a setting for a precious stone **b :** JEWEL, ORNAMENT; *especially :* a buckle or brooch set with precious stones

²ouch *interjection* [origin unknown] (1838)
— used especially to express sudden pain

oud \'üd\ *noun* [Arabic *'ūd*, literally, wood] (1738)
: a musical instrument of the lute family used in southwest Asia and northern Africa

¹ought \'ot\ *verbal auxiliary* [Middle English *oughte* (1st & 3d singular present indicative), from *oughte*, 1st & 3d singular past indicative & subjunctive of *owen* to own, owe — more at OWE] (12th century)
— used to express obligation ⟨*ought* to pay our debts⟩, advisability ⟨*ought* to take care of yourself⟩, natural expectation ⟨*ought* to be here by now⟩, or logical consequence ⟨the result *ought* to be infinity⟩

²ought \'ò(k)t\ *transitive verb* [Middle English *oughte*, 1st & 3d singular past indicative of *owen*] (13th century)
1 *chiefly Scottish :* POSSESS
2 *chiefly Scottish :* OWE

³ought \'ot\ *noun* (1678)
: moral obligation : DUTY

⁴ought \'ot, 'ät\ *variant of* AUGHT

oughtn't \'o-t²nt\ (1884)
: ought not

ou·gui·ya \ü-'gwē-ə, -'gē-ə\ *noun, plural* **ou·gui·ya** [Arabic dialect *ūgīyah*, from Arabic *ūqīyah*, literally, ounce] (1973)

— see MONEY table

Oui·ja \'wē-jə, -jē\ *trademark*
— used for a board with the alphabet and other signs on it that is used with a planchette to seek spiritualistic or telepathic messages

¹ounce \'aún(t)s\ *noun* [Middle English, from Middle French *unce*, from Latin *uncia* 12th part, ounce, from *unus* one — more at ONE] (14th century)
1 a : a unit of weight equal to ¹⁄₁₂ troy pound — see WEIGHT table **b :** a unit of weight equal to ¹⁄₁₆ avoirdupois pound **c :** a small amount ⟨an *ounce* of common sense⟩
2 : FLUIDOUNCE

²ounce *noun* [Middle English *once* lynx, from Middle French, alteration (by misdivision, as if *l'once* the ounce) of *lonce*, from (assumed) Vulgar Latin *lyncea*, from Latin *lync-, lynx*] (1774)
: SNOW LEOPARD

our \är, 'aú(-ə)r\ *adjective* [Middle English *oure*, from Old English *ūre*; akin to Old High German *unsēr* our, Old English *ūs* us] (before 12th century)
: of or relating to us or ourselves or ourself especially as possessors or possessor, agents or agent, or objects or object of an action ⟨*our* throne⟩ ⟨*our* actions⟩ ⟨*our* being chosen⟩

Our Father *noun* [from the opening words] (1882)
: LORD'S PRAYER

ours \'aú(-ə)rz, ärz\ *pronoun, singular or plural in construction* (14th century)
: that which belongs to us — used without a following noun as a pronoun equivalent in meaning to the adjective *our*

our·self \är-'self, aú(-ə)r-\ *pronoun* (14th century)
: MYSELF — used to refer to the single-person subject when *we* is used instead of *I* (as by a sovereign) ⟨will keep *ourself* till supper time alone —Shakespeare⟩

our·selves \-'selvz\ *pronoun plural* (15th century)
1 : those identical ones that are we — compare WE 1; used reflexively ⟨we're doing it solely for *ourselves*⟩, for emphasis ⟨we *ourselves* will never go⟩, or in absolute constructions ⟨*ourselves* no longer young, we can sympathize with those who are old⟩
2 : our normal, healthy, or sane condition ⟨just not *ourselves* today⟩

-ous *adjective suffix* [Middle English, from Old French *-ous, -eus, -eux*, from Latin *-osus*]
1 : full of : abounding in : having : possessing the qualities of ⟨clamor*ous*⟩ ⟨poison*ous*⟩
2 : having a valence lower than in compounds or ions named with an adjective ending in *-ic* ⟨mercur*ous*⟩

ou·sel \'ü-zəl\ *variant of* OUZEL

Ou·shak \ü-'shäk\ *noun, often attributive* [from *Oushak, Ushak* (Uşak), town in Turkey] (1901)
: a heavy wool Oriental rug characterized especially by bright primary colors and an elaborate medallion pattern

oust \'aúst\ *transitive verb* [Middle English, from Anglo-French *ouster*, from Old French *oster*, from Late Latin *obstare* to ward off, from Latin, to stand in the way, from *ob-* in the way + *stare* to stand — more at OB-, STAND] (15th century)
1 a : to remove from or dispossess of property or position by legal action, by force, or by the compulsion of necessity **b :** to take away (as a right or authority) : BAR, REMOVE
2 : to take the place of : SUPPLANT
synonym see EJECT

oust·er \'aús-tər\ *noun* [Anglo-French, to oust] (1531)
1 a : a wrongful dispossession **b :** a judgment removing an officer or depriving a corporation of a franchise
2 : EXPULSION

¹out \'aút\ *adverb* [Middle English, from Old English *ūt*; akin to Old High German *ūz* out,

Greek *hysteros* later, Sanskrit *ud* up, out] (before 12th century)
1 a (1) **:** in a direction away from the inside or center ⟨went *out* into the garden⟩ (2) **:** OUTSIDE ⟨it's raining *out*⟩ **b :** from among others **c :** away from the shore **d :** away from home or work ⟨*out* to lunch⟩ **e :** away from a particular place
2 a : so as to be missing or displaced from the usual or proper place ⟨left a word *out*⟩ ⟨threw his shoulder *out*⟩ **b :** into the possession or control of another ⟨lend *out* money⟩ **c :** into a state of loss or defeat ⟨was voted *out*⟩ **d :** into a state of vexation ⟨they do not mark me, and that brings me *out* —Shakespeare⟩ **e :** into groups or shares ⟨sorted *out* her notes⟩ ⟨parceled *out* the farm⟩
3 a : to the point of depletion, extinction, or exhaustion ⟨the food ran *out*⟩ ⟨turn the light *out*⟩ ⟨all tuckered *out*⟩ **b :** to completion or satisfaction ⟨hear me *out*⟩ ⟨work the problem *out*⟩ **c :** to the full or a great extent or degree ⟨all decked *out*⟩ ⟨stretched *out* on the floor⟩
4 a : in or into the open ⟨the sun came *out*⟩ **b :** OUT LOUD ⟨cried *out*⟩ **c :** in or into public circulation ⟨the evening paper isn't *out* yet⟩ ⟨hand *out* pamphlets⟩ ⟨the library book is still *out*⟩
5 a : at an end ⟨before the day is *out*⟩ **b :** in or into an insensible or unconscious state ⟨she was *out* cold⟩ **c :** in or into a useless state ⟨landed the plane with one engine *out*⟩ **d :** so as to put a player or side out or to be put out in baseball
6 — used on a two-way radio circuit to indicate that a message is complete and no reply is expected

²out (before 12th century)
transitive verb
: EJECT, OUST
intransitive verb
: to become publicly known ⟨the truth will *out*⟩

³out *preposition* (13th century)
— used as a function word to indicate an outward movement ⟨ran *out* the door⟩ ⟨looked *out* the window⟩

⁴out *adjective* (13th century)
1 a : situated outside : EXTERNAL **b :** OUT-OF-BOUNDS

\ə\ abut \ᵊ\ kitten \ər\ further \a\ ash \ā\ ace
\ä\ mop, mar \aú\ out \ch\ chin \e\ bet \ē\ easy
\g\ go \i\ hit \ī\ ice \j\ job \ŋ\ sing \ō\ go
\ò\ law \òi\ boy \th\ thin \t͟h\ the \ü\ loot \ù\ foot
\y\ yet \zh\ vision *see also* Guide to Pronunciation

2 : situated at a distance **:** OUTLYING ⟨the *out* islands⟩

3 : not being in power

4 : ABSENT

5 : put out while at bat or baserunning in baseball

6 : directed outward or serving to direct something outward ⟨the *out* basket⟩

7 : not being in vogue or fashion

8 : not to be considered **:** out of the question

9 : DETERMINED 1 ⟨was *out* to get revenge⟩

⁵**out** *noun* (1717)

1 : OUTSIDE

2 : one who is out of office or power or on the outside ⟨a matter of *outs* versus ins⟩

3 a : an act or instance of putting a player out or of being put out in baseball **b :** a player that is put out

4 : a way of escaping from an embarrassing or difficult situation

— on the outs : on unfriendly terms **:** at variance

out- *prefix* [¹*out*]

: in a manner that exceeds or surpasses and sometimes overpowers or defeats ⟨*out*maneuver⟩

out·achieve	out·or·ga·nize
out·act	out·pass
out·bar·gain	out·per·form
out·bid	out·pitch
out·bitch	out·play
out·bluff	out·plot
out·box	out·pol·i·tick
out·brag	out·poll
out·brawl	out·pop·u·late
out·bulk	out·pow·er
out·buy	out·pray
out·catch	out·preach
out·charge	out·price
out·climb	out·pro·duce
out·coach	out·prom·ise
out·com·pete	out·punch
out·dance	out·rate
out·daz·zle	out·re·bound
out·de·bate	out·re·pro·duce
out·de·liv·er	out·ri·val
out·de·sign	out·roar
out·drag	out·row
out·dress	out·rush
out·drink	out·sail
out·drive	out·scheme
out·du·el	out·scoop
out·earn	out·score
out·eat	out·shout
out·fight	out·sing
out·fig·ure	out·sit
out·fish	out·skate
out·fly	out·soar
out·fum·ble	out·spar·kle
out·gain	out·speed
out·glit·ter	out·sprint
out·gross	out·stride
out·hit	out·swear
out·ho·mer	out·swim
out·hunt	out·talk
out·hus·tle	out·think
out·in·trigue	out·throw
out·jump	out·trade
out·kick	out·vie
out·kill	out·vote
out·last	out·wait
out·leap	out·walk
out·learn	out·watch
out·man	out·wres·tle
out·ma·neu·ver	out·write
out·ma·nip·u·late	out·yell
out·march	out·yield
out·mus·cle	

out·age \'aù-tij\ *noun* (1899)

1 : a quantity or bulk of something lost in transportation or storage

2 a : a failure or interruption in use or functioning **b :** a period of interruption especially of electric current

out–and–out \ˌaù̇t-ᵊn(d)-ˈaù̇t\ *adjective* (1813)

: being such completely at all times, in every way, or from every point of view ⟨an *out-and-out* fraud⟩

out–and–out·er \-ˈaù̇-tər\ *noun* (circa 1812)

: one who goes to extremes

out·back \'aù̇t-ˌbak, -ˌbak\ *noun* (1893)

: isolated rural country especially of Australia

out·bal·ance \ˌaù̇t-ˈba-lən(t)s\ *transitive verb* (1644)

: OUTWEIGH

¹**out·board** \'aù̇t-ˌbōrd, -ˌbȯrd\ *adjective* (circa 1823)

1 : situated outboard

2 : having, using, or limited to the use of an outboard motor

²**outboard** *adverb* (circa 1848)

1 : outside a ship's bulwarks **:** in a lateral direction from the hull

2 : in a position closer or closest to either of the wingtips of an airplane or to the sides of an automobile

³**outboard** *noun* (1935)

1 : OUTBOARD MOTOR

2 : a boat with an outboard motor

outboard motor *noun* (1909)

: a small internal combustion engine with propeller integrally attached for mounting at the stern of a small boat

out·bound \'aù̇t-ˌbaù̇nd\ *adjective* (1598)

: outward bound ⟨*outbound* traffic⟩

out·brave \ˌaù̇t-ˈbrāv\ *transitive verb* (1589)

1 : to face or resist defiantly

2 : to exceed in courage

out·break \'aù̇t-ˌbrāk\ *noun* (1602)

1 a : a sudden or violent increase in activity or currency ⟨the *outbreak* of war⟩ **b :** a sudden rise in the incidence of a disease ⟨an *outbreak* of measles⟩ **c :** a sudden increase in numbers of a harmful organism and especially an insect within a particular area ⟨an *outbreak* of locusts⟩

2 : INSURRECTION, REVOLT

out·breed *transitive verb* **-bred** \-ˌbred, -ˈbred\; **-breed·ing** (circa 1909)

1 \'aù̇t-ˌbrēd\ **:** to subject to outbreeding

2 \ˌaù̇t-ˈ\ **:** to breed faster than

out·breed·ing \'aù̇t-ˌbrē-diŋ\ *noun* (1901)

: the interbreeding of individuals or stocks that are relatively unrelated

out·build·ing \'aù̇t-ˌbil-diŋ\ *noun* (1626)

: a building (as a stable or a woodshed) separate from but accessory to a main house

out·burst \-ˌbərst\ *noun* (1657)

1 : a violent expression of feeling ⟨an *outburst* of anger⟩

2 : a surge of activity or growth ⟨new *outbursts* of creative power —C. E. Montague⟩

3 : ERUPTION ⟨volcanic *outbursts*⟩

out·bye *or* **out·by** \ü̇t-ˈbī\ *adverb* [Middle English (Scots) *out-by*, from *out* + *by*] (15th century)

chiefly Scottish **:** a short distance away; *also* **:** OUTDOORS

out·cast \'aù̇t-ˌkast\ *noun* (14th century)

1 : one that is cast out or refused acceptance (as by society) **:** PARIAH

2 [Scots *cast out* to quarrel] *Scottish* **:** QUARREL

— outcast *adjective*

out·caste \-ˌkast\ *noun* (1876)

1 : a Hindu who has been ejected from his caste for violation of its customs or rules

2 : one who has no caste

out·class \ˌaù̇t-ˈklas\ *transitive verb* (1870)

: to excel or surpass so decisively as to be or appear to be of a higher class

out·come \'aù̇t-ˌkəm\ *noun* (1788)

: something that follows as a result or consequence

¹**out·crop** \'aù̇t-ˌkräp\ *noun* (1805)

1 : a coming out of bedrock or of an unconsolidated deposit to the surface of the ground

2 : the part of a rock formation that appears at the surface of the ground

²**out·crop** \'aù̇t-ˌkräp, ˌaù̇t-ˈ\ *intransitive verb* (circa 1847)

1 : to project from the surrounding soil ⟨ledges *outcropping* from the eroded slope⟩

2 : to come to the surface **:** APPEAR

out·crop·ping \'aù̇t-ˌkrä-piŋ\ *noun* (1872)

: OUTCROP

¹**out·cross** \'aù̇t-ˌkrȯs\ *noun* (1890)

1 : a cross between relatively unrelated individuals

2 : the progeny of an outcross

²**outcross** *transitive verb* (1918)

: to cross with a relatively unrelated individual or strain

out·cry \'aù̇t-ˌkrī\ *noun* (14th century)

1 a : a loud cry **:** CLAMOR **b :** a vehement protest

2 : AUCTION

out·dat·ed \ˌaù̇t-ˈdā-təd\ *adjective* (1616)

: no longer current **:** OUTMODED

— out·dat·ed·ly *adverb*

— out·dat·ed·ness *noun*

out·dis·tance \ˌaù̇t-ˈdis-tən(t)s\ *transitive verb* (1857)

: to go far ahead of (as in a race) **:** OUTSTRIP

out·do \-ˈdü\ *transitive verb* **-did** \-ˈdid\; **-done** \-ˈdən\; **-do·ing** \-ˈdü-iŋ\; **-does** \-ˈdəz\

1 : to go beyond in action or performance

2 : DEFEAT, OVERCOME

synonym see EXCEED

out·door \'aù̇t-ˌdōr, -ˌdȯr; 'aù̇t-ˈ\ *also* **out·doors** \-ˌdōrz, -ˌdȯrz; 'aù̇t-ˈ\ *adjective* [*out (of) door, out (of) doors*] (1748)

1 : of or relating to the outdoors

2 a : performed outdoors ⟨*outdoor* sports⟩ **b :** OUTDOORSY ⟨an *outdoor* couple⟩

3 : not enclosed **:** having no roof ⟨an *outdoor* restaurant⟩

¹**out·doors** \ˌaù̇t-ˈdōrz, -ˈdȯrz; 'aù̇t-ˈ\ *adverb* (1817)

: outside a building **:** in or into the open air

²**outdoors** *noun plural but singular in construction* (1844)

1 : a place or location away from the confines of a building

2 : the world away from human habitations

out·doors·man \-mən\ *noun* (1918)

: one who spends much time in the outdoors or in outdoor activities

— out·doors·man·ship \-ˌship\ *noun*

out·doorsy \ˌaù̇t-ˈdōr-zē, -ˈdȯr-\ *adjective* (1936)

1 : relating to, characteristic of, or appropriate for the outdoors ⟨*outdoorsy* clothing⟩

2 : fond of outdoor activities ⟨sounded rugged and *outdoorsy* —*N.Y. Times*⟩

out·draw \ˌaù̇t-ˈdrȯ\ *transitive verb* **-drew** \-ˈdrü\; **-drawn** \-ˈdrȯn\; **-draw·ing** (circa 1909)

1 : to attract a larger audience or following than

2 : to draw a handgun more quickly than

out·er \'aù̇-tər\ *adjective* [Middle English, from ⁴*out* + ¹*-er*] (13th century)

1 : existing independent of mind **:** OBJECTIVE

2 a : situated farther out ⟨the *outer* limits⟩ **b :** being away from a center **c :** situated or belonging on the outside ⟨the *outer* covering⟩

out·er·coat \'aù̇-tər-ˌkōt\ *noun* (1948)

: COAT 1a

outer ear *noun* (1935)

: the outer visible portion of the ear that collects and directs sound waves toward the eardrum by way of a canal which extends inward through the temporal bone

out·er·most \'aù̇-tər-ˌmōst\ *adjective* (14th century)

: farthest out

outer planet *noun* (1941)

: any of the planets Jupiter, Saturn, Uranus, Neptune, and Pluto whose orbits lie beyond the asteroid belt

outer space *noun* (1901)

: space immediately outside the earth's atmosphere; *broadly* **:** interplanetary or interstellar space

out·er·wear \'aù̇-tər-ˌwar, -ˌwer\ *noun* (1921)

: clothing for outdoor wear

out·face \aút-'fās\ *transitive verb* (circa 1529)
1 : to cause to waver or submit by or as if by staring
2 : to confront unflinchingly **: DEFY**

out·fall \'aút-ˌfól\ *noun* (1629)
: the outlet of a body of water (as a river or lake); *especially* : the mouth of a drain or sewer

out·field \-ˌfēld\ *noun* (1868)
1 : the part of a baseball field beyond the infield and between the foul lines
2 : the baseball defensive positions comprising right field, center field, and left field; *also* : the players who occupy these positions
— **out·field·er** \-ˌfēl-dər\ *noun*

¹out·fit \'aút-ˌfit\ *noun* (circa 1769)
1 : the act of fitting out or equipping (as for a voyage or expedition)
2 a : the tools or equipment for the practice of a trade **b :** wearing apparel with accessories usually for a special occasion or activity **c :** physical, mental, or moral endowments or resources
3 : a group that works as a team **: ORGANIZATION**; *especially* : a military unit

²outfit *verb* **out·fit·ted; out·fit·ting** (1847)
transitive verb
1 : to furnish with an outfit
2 : SUPPLY 〈*outfitting* every family with shoes —*American Guide Series: Vermont*〉
intransitive verb
: to acquire an outfit
synonym see FURNISH

out·fit·ter \-ˌfi-tər\ *noun* (1846)
: one that outfits: as **a : HABERDASHER b :** a business providing equipment, supplies, and often trained guides (as for hunting trips); *also* : a guide working for such an outfitter

out·flank \aút-'flaŋk\ *transitive verb* (1765)
1 : to get around the flank of (an opposing force)
2 : GET AROUND, CIRCUMVENT

¹out·flow \'aút-ˌflō, ˌaút-'\ *intransitive verb* (circa 1580)
: to flow out

²out·flow \'aút-ˌflō\ *noun* (circa 1864)
1 : a flowing out 〈the *outflow* of dollars〉
2 : something that flows out 〈*outflow* of a sewage treatment plant〉

out·foot \ˌaút-'fút\ *transitive verb* (1737)
: to outdo in speed **: OUTSTRIP**

out·fox \-'fäks\ *transitive verb* (1924)
: OUTSMART

out–front \-'frənt\ *adjective* (1968)
: FRANK, OPEN

out·gas \'aút-ˌgas, ˌaút-'\ (1925)
transitive verb
1 : to remove occluded gases from usually by heating; *broadly* : to remove gases from
2 : to remove (gases) from a material or a space
intransitive verb
: to lose gases

out·gen·er·al \ˌaút-'jen-rəl, -'je-nə-\ *transitive verb* (1767)
: to surpass in generalship **: OUTMANEUVER**

¹out·giv·ing \'aút-ˌgi-viŋ\ *noun* (1663)
: something that is given out; *especially* : a public statement or utterance

²outgiving *adjective* (1942)
: socially responsive and demonstrative

¹out·go \ˌaút-'gō\ *transitive verb* (1530)
: to go beyond **: OUTDO**

²out·go \'aút-ˌgō\ *noun, plural* **outgoes** (circa 1640)
1 : something that goes out; *specifically* **: EXPENDITURE**
2 a : the act of going out **b : DEPARTURE**
3 : OUTLET 1a

out·go·ing \'aút-ˌgō-iŋ, -ˌgó(-)iŋ\ *adjective* (1633)
1 a : going away **: DEPARTING** 〈an *outgoing* ship〉 **b :** retiring or withdrawing from a place or position 〈the *outgoing* president〉 **c :** directed to an intended recipient 〈*outgoing* mail〉

2 : openly friendly and responsive **: EXTROVERTED**
— **out·go·ing·ness** *noun*

out·go·ings \-ˌgō-iŋz, -ˌgó(-)iŋz\ *noun plural* (1765)
British **:** costs incurred **: EXPENSES**

out–group \'aút-ˌgrüp\ *noun* (circa 1907)
: a group that is distinct from one's own and so usually an object of hostility or dislike — compare IN-GROUP 1

out·grow \ˌaút-'grō\ *transitive verb* **-grew** \-'grü\; **-grown** \-'grōn\; **-grow·ing** (1594)
1 : to grow or increase faster than 〈mankind is *outgrowing* food supplies —R. C. Murphy〉
2 : to grow too large or too mature for 〈*outgrew* his best suit〉 〈the need to *outgrow* the habit of war —Norman Cousins〉

out·growth \'aút-ˌgrōth\ *noun* (1837)
1 : a process or product of growing out 〈an *outgrowth* of hair〉
2 : CONSEQUENCE, BY-PRODUCT 〈crime is often an *outgrowth* of poverty〉

out·guess \ˌaút-'ges\ *transitive verb* (1911)
: to anticipate the expectations, intentions, or actions of **: OUTWIT**

out·gun \-'gən\ *transitive verb* (1691)
: to surpass in firepower; *broadly* **: OUTDO**

out·haul \'aút-ˌhól\ *noun* (1840)
: a rope used to haul a sail taut along a spar

out–Her·od \ˌaút-'her-əd\ *transitive verb* [*out-* + *Herod* the Great, depicted in medieval mystery plays as a blustering tyrant] (1602)
: to exceed in violence or extravagance — usually used in the phrase *out-Herod Herod*

out·house \'aút-ˌhaús\ *noun* (14th century)
: OUTBUILDING; *especially* **: PRIVY 1a**

out·ing \'aú-tiŋ\ *noun* (1821)
1 : a brief usually outdoor pleasure trip
2 : an athletic competition or race; *also* : an appearance therein
3 : a usually public presentation or appearance (as in a particular role) 〈her first *outing* as a novelist〉
4 : the public disclosure of the covert homosexuality of a prominent person by homosexual activists

outing flannel *noun* (1890)
: a flannelette sometimes having an admixture of wool

out·land \'aút-ˌland, -lənd\ *noun* (before 12th century)
1 : a foreign land
2 *plural* **:** the outlying regions of a country **: PROVINCES**
— **outland** *adjective*

out·land·er \-ˌlan-dər, -lən-\ *noun* (1598)
: a person who belongs to another region, culture, or group **: FOREIGNER, STRANGER**

out·land·ish \ˌaút-'lan-dish\ *adjective* (before 12th century)
1 : of or relating to another country **: FOREIGN**
2 a : strikingly out of the ordinary **: BIZARRE** 〈an *outlandish* costume〉 **b :** exceeding proper or reasonable limits or standards
3 : remote from civilization
synonym see STRANGE
— **out·land·ish·ly** *adverb*
— **out·land·ish·ness** *noun*

¹out·law \'aút-ˌló\ *noun* [Middle English *outlawe*, from Old English *ūtlaga*, from Old Norse *ūtlagi*, from *ūt* out (akin to Old English *ūt* out) + *lag-, lǫg* law — more at OUT, LAW] (before 12th century)
1 : a person excluded from the benefit or protection of the law
2 a : a lawless person or a fugitive from the law **b :** a person or organization under a ban or restriction **c :** one that is unconventional or rebellious
3 : an animal (as a horse) that is wild and unmanageable
— **outlaw** *adjective*

²outlaw *transitive verb* (before 12th century)
1 a : to deprive of the benefit and protection of law : declare to be an outlaw **b :** to make illegal 〈*outlawed* dueling〉

2 : to place under a ban or restriction
3 : to remove from legal jurisdiction or enforcement
— **out·law·ry** \'aút-ˌlòr-ē\ *noun*

¹out·lay \'aút-ˌlā, ˌaút-'\ *transitive verb* **-laid** \-ˌlād, -'lād\; **-lay·ing** (1555)
: to lay out (money) **: EXPEND**

²out·lay \'aút-ˌlā\ *noun* (1798)
1 : the act of expending
2 : EXPENDITURE, PAYMENT 〈*outlays* for national defense〉

out·let \'aút-ˌlet, -lət\ *noun* [Middle English *ut-lete*, from *ut* out + *-lete* watercourse, from Old English *gelæt*, from *lætan* to let] (13th century)
1 a : a place or opening through which something is let out **: EXIT, VENT b :** a means of release or satisfaction for an emotion or impulse 〈sexual *outlets*〉 **c :** a medium of expression or publication
2 : a stream flowing out of a lake or pond
3 a : a market for a commodity **b :** an agency (as a store or dealer) through which a product is marketed 〈retail *outlets*〉
4 : a receptacle for the plug of an electrical device

outlet pass *noun* (circa 1975)
: a pass made in basketball by the player taking a defensive rebound to a teammate to start a fast break

out·li·er \-ˌlī(-ə)r\ *noun* (1676)
1 : a person whose residence and place of business are at a distance
2 : something (as a geological feature) that is situated away from or classed differently from a main or related body

¹out·line \'aút-ˌlīn\ *noun* (1662)
1 a : a line that marks the outer limits of an object or figure **: BOUNDARY b : SHAPE**
2 a : a style of drawing in which contours are marked without shading **b :** a sketch in outline
3 a : a condensed treatment of a particular subject 〈an *outline* of world history〉 **b :** a summary of a written work **: SYNOPSIS**
4 : a preliminary account of a project **: PLAN**
5 : a fishing line set out overnight **: TROTLINE**
☆

²outline *transitive verb* (circa 1790)
1 : to draw the outline of
2 : to indicate the principal features or different parts of 〈*outlined* their responsibilities〉

out·live \ˌaút-'liv\ *transitive verb* (15th century)
1 : to live beyond or longer than 〈*outlived* most of his friends〉 〈*outlive* its usefulness〉
2 : to survive the effects of 〈universities . . . *outlive* many political and social changes —J. B. Conant〉

out·look \'aút-ˌlúk\ *noun* (1667)

☆ **SYNONYMS**
Outline, contour, profile, silhouette mean the line that bounds and gives form to something. OUTLINE applies to a line marking the outer limits or edges of a body or mass 〈traced the *outline* of his hand〉. CONTOUR stresses the quality of an outline or a bounding surface as being smooth, jagged, curving, or sharply angled 〈a car with flowing *contours*〉. PROFILE suggests a varied and sharply defined outline against a lighter background 〈a portrait of her face in *profile*〉. SILHOUETTE suggests a shape especially of a head or figure with all detail blacked out in shadow leaving only the outline clearly defined 〈photograph in *silhouette* against a bright sky〉.

\ə\ **abut** \ᵊ\ **kitten** \ər\ **further** \a\ **ash** \ā\ **ace**
\ä\ **mop, mar** \aú\ **out** \ch\ **chin** \e\ **bet** \ē\ **easy**
\g\ **go** \i\ **hit** \ī\ **ice** \j\ **job** \ŋ\ **sing** \ō\ **go**
\ò\ **law** \òi\ **boy** \th\ **thin** \t͟h\ **the** \ü\ **loot** \ú\ **foot**
\y\ **yet** \zh\ **vision** *see also* Guide to Pronunciation

1 a : a place offering a view **b :** a view from a particular place
2 : POINT OF VIEW ⟨a positive *outlook* on life⟩
3 : the act of looking out
4 : the prospect for the future ⟨the *outlook* for steel demand in the U.S. —*Wall Street Journal*⟩
synonym see PROSPECT

out loud *adverb* (1821)
: loudly enough to be heard **:** ALOUD

out·ly·ing \ˈaut-ˌlī-iŋ\ *adjective* (circa 1690)
: remote from a center or main body ⟨*outlying* areas⟩

out·match \aut-ˈmach\ *transitive verb* (1603)
: to prove superior to **:** OUTDO

out–mi·grant \ˈaut-ˌmī-grənt\ *noun* (1945)
: one that out-migrates

out–mi·grate \-ˌgrāt\ *intransitive verb* (1953)
: to leave one region or community in order to settle in another especially as part of a large-scale and continuing movement of population
— compare IN-MIGRATE
— **out–mi·gra·tion** \ˌaut-mī-ˈgrā-shən\ *noun*

out·mode \ˌaut-ˈmōd\ *transitive verb* **out·mod·ed; out·mod·ing** [*out* (*of*) *mode*] (1906)
: to make unfashionable or obsolete

out·mod·ed \-ˈmō-dəd\ *adjective* (1903)
1 : not being in style
2 : no longer acceptable, current, or usable ⟨*outmoded* customs⟩

out·most \ˈaut-ˌmōst\ *adjective* (12th century)
: farthest out **:** OUTERMOST

out·num·ber \ˌaut-ˈnəm-bər\ *transitive verb* (1670)
: to exceed in number

out of *preposition* (before 12th century)
1 a (1) — used as a function word to indicate direction or movement from within to the outside of ⟨walked *out of* the room⟩ (2) — used as a function word to indicate a change in quality, state, or form ⟨woke up *out of* a deep sleep⟩ **b** (1) — used as a function word to indicate a position or situation beyond the range, limits, or sphere of ⟨*out of* control⟩ (2) — used as a function word to indicate a position or state away from the usual or expected ⟨*out of* practice⟩
2 — used as a function word to indicate origin, source, or cause ⟨a remarkable colt *out of* an ordinary mare⟩ ⟨built *out of* old lumber⟩ ⟨came *out of* fear⟩
3 — used as a function word to indicate exclusion from or deprivation of ⟨cheated him *out of* his savings⟩ ⟨*out of* breath⟩
4 — used as a function word to indicate choice or selection from a group ⟨one *out of* four survived⟩
— **out of it 1 :** not part of a group, activity, or fashion **2 :** in a dazed or confused state

out–of–body *adjective* (1970)
: relating to or involving a feeling of separation from one's body and of being able to view oneself and others from an external perspective ⟨an *out-of-body* experience⟩

out–of–bounds \ˌaut-ə(v)-ˈbaun(d)z\ *adverb or adjective* (1857)
: outside the prescribed boundaries or limits

out–of–date \-ˈdāt\ *adjective* (1628)
: OUTMODED, OBSOLETE

out–of–door \-ˈdōr, -ˈdȯr\ *or* **out–of–doors** \-ˈdōrz, -ˈdȯrz\ *adjective* (1800)
: OUTDOOR

out–of–doors *noun plural but singular in construction* (1819)
: OUTDOORS

out–of–pock·et \-ˈpä-kət\ *adjective* (1885)
: requiring an outlay of cash ⟨*out-of-pocket* expenses⟩

out–of–sight \ˌau-də-ˈsīt\ *adjective* (1893)
slang **:** WONDERFUL

out–of–the–way \ˌaut-ə(v)-thə-ˈwā\ *adjective* (1704)
1 : UNUSUAL ⟨*out-of-the-way* information⟩

2 : being off the beaten track ⟨an *out-of-the-way* restaurant⟩

out·pace \aut-ˈpās\ *transitive verb* (1611)
1 : to surpass in speed
2 : OUTDO

out·pa·tient \ˈaut-ˌpā-shənt\ *noun* (1715)
: a patient who is not hospitalized overnight but who visits a hospital, clinic, or associated facility for diagnosis or treatment — compare INPATIENT

out·place·ment \ˌaut-ˈplās-mənt, ˈaut-ˌ\ *noun* (1970)
: the process of easing unwanted or unneeded executives out of a company by providing company-paid assistance in finding them new jobs

out·point \ˌaut-ˈpóint\ *transitive verb* (1883)
1 : to sail closer to the wind than
2 : to win more points than (as in a boxing match)

out·port \ˈaut-ˌpōrt, -ˌpȯrt\ *noun* (1642)
1 *chiefly British* **:** a port other than the main port of a country
2 : a small fishing village especially in Newfoundland

out·post \ˈaut-ˌpōst\ *noun* (1757)
1 a : a security detachment dispatched by a main body of troops to protect it from enemy surprise **b :** a military base established by treaty or agreement in another country
2 a : an outlying or frontier settlement **b :** an outlying branch or position of a main organization or group

¹out·pour \ˌaut-ˈpōr, -ˈpȯr, ˈaut-ˌ\ *transitive verb* (1671)
: to pour out

²out·pour \ˈaut-ˌpōr, -ˌpȯr\ *noun* (1864)
: OUTPOURING

out·pour·ing \ˈaut-ˌpōr-iŋ, -ˌpȯr-\ *noun* (15th century)
1 : the act of pouring out
2 : something that pours out or is poured out **:** OUTFLOW

out·pull \ˌaut-ˈpul\ *transitive verb* (1926)
: OUTDRAW 1

¹out·put \ˈaut-ˌput\ *noun* (circa 1858)
1 : something produced: as **a :** mineral, agricultural, or industrial production ⟨steel *output*⟩ **b :** mental or artistic production ⟨literary *output*⟩ **c :** the amount produced by a person in a given time **d :** power or energy produced or delivered by a machine or system (as for storage or for conversion in kind or in characteristics) ⟨solar X-ray *output*⟩ **e :** the information produced by a computer
2 : the act, process, or an instance of producing
3 : the terminal for the output on an electrical device

²output *transitive verb* **out·put·ted** *or* **out·put; out·put·ting** (1858)
: to produce as output

out·race \ˌaut-ˈrās\ *transitive verb* (1657)
: OUTPACE

¹out·rage \ˈaut-ˌrāj\ *noun* [Middle English, from Middle French, excess, outrage, from *outre* beyond, in excess, from Latin *ultra* — more at ULTRA-] (14th century)
1 : an act of violence or brutality
2 a : INJURY, INSULT ⟨do no *outrages* on silly women or poor passengers —Shakespeare⟩ **b :** an act that violates accepted standards of behavior or taste ⟨an *outrage* alike against decency and dignity —John Buchan⟩
3 : the anger and resentment aroused by injury or insult ◇

²outrage *transitive verb* **out·raged; out·rag·ing** (1590)
1 a : RAPE **b :** to violate the standards or principles of ⟨he has *outraged* respectability past endurance —John Braine⟩
2 : to arouse anger or resentment in usually by some grave offense
synonym see OFFEND

out·ra·geous \(ˌ)aut-ˈrā-jəs\ *adjective* (14th century)

1 a : exceeding the limits of what is usual **b :** not conventional or matter-of-fact **:** FANTASTIC
2 : VIOLENT, UNRESTRAINED
3 a : going beyond all standards of what is right or decent ⟨an *outrageous* disregard of human rights⟩ **b :** deficient in propriety or good taste ⟨*outrageous* language⟩ ⟨*outrageous* manners⟩
— **out·ra·geous·ly** *adverb*
— **out·ra·geous·ness** *noun*

ou·trance \ü-ˈträⁿs\ *noun* [Middle English, from Middle French, from *outrer* to pass beyond, carry to excess, from *outre*] (15th century)
: the last extremity

out·range \ˌaut-ˈrānj\ *transitive verb* (1858)
: to surpass in range

out·rank \-ˈraŋk\ *transitive verb* (1842)
1 : to rank higher than
2 : to exceed in importance

ou·tré \ü-ˈtrā\ *adjective* [French, from past participle of *outrer* to carry to excess] (1722)
: violating convention or propriety **:** BIZARRE
word history see OUTRAGE

¹out·reach \ˌaut-ˈrēch\ (circa 1568) *transitive verb*
1 a : to surpass in reach **b :** EXCEED ⟨the demand *outreaches* the supply⟩
2 : to get the better of by trickery
intransitive verb
1 : to go too far
2 : to reach out

²out·reach \ˈaut-ˌrēch\ *noun* (1870)
1 : the act of reaching out
2 : the extent or limit of reach ⟨the *outreach* of the Ohio floods —Clifton Johnson⟩
3 : the extending of services or assistance beyond current or usual limits ⟨an *outreach* program⟩; *also* **:** the extent of such services or assistance

¹out·ride \ˌaut-ˈrīd\ *transitive verb* **-rode** \-ˈrōd\; **-rid·den** \-ˈri-dᵊn\; **-rid·ing** \-ˈrī-diŋ\ (1530)
1 : to ride better, faster, or farther than **:** OUTSTRIP
2 : to ride out (a storm)

²out·ride \ˈaut-ˌrīd\ *noun* (1880)
: an unstressed syllable or group of syllables added to a foot in sprung rhythm but not counted in the scansion

out·rid·er \-ˌrī-dər\ *noun* (1530)
1 : a mounted attendant
2 : one who escorts or clears the way for a vehicle or person
3 : FORERUNNER, HARBINGER

out·rig·ger \ˈaut-ˌri-gər\ *noun* (1748)
1 a : a projecting spar with a shaped log at the end attached to a canoe to prevent upsetting **b :** a spar or projecting beam run out from a ship's side to help secure the masts or from a mast to extend a rope or sail **c :** a projecting support for an oarlock; *also* **:** a boat equipped with these supports
2 : a projecting member run out from a main structure to provide additional stability or to

◇ WORD HISTORY

outrage Given the meaning of *outrage*, the assumption might be that the word is a compound of *out* and *rage*. Actually, such is not the case at all. The word's ultimate source is Latin *ultra* "beyond." *Ultra* developed into medieval French *outre*. To the adverb *outre* was appended the suffix *-age* to produce the noun *outrage*. Originally meaning "excess," *outrage* also developed the meaning "an act of violence or brutality." It was this sense that was borrowed into Middle English in the 14th century. In the 18th century English went back to a derivative of French *outre* once again, this time borrowing *outré* "bizarre," the past participle of the verb *outrer* "to carry to excess."

support something; *especially* **:** a projecting frame to support the elevator or tailplanes of an airplane or the rotor of a helicopter

¹out·right \ˌau̇t-ˈrīt\ *adverb* (14th century)
1 *archaic* **:** straight ahead **:** DIRECTLY
2 : in entirety **:** COMPLETELY ⟨rejected the proposal *outright*⟩
3 : without restraint or reservation ⟨laughed *outright*⟩
4 : on the spot **:** INSTANTANEOUSLY ⟨was killed *outright*⟩
5 : without lien or encumbrance ⟨purchased the property *outright* for cash⟩

²out·right \ˈau̇t-ˌrīt\ *adjective* (1532)
1 a : being completely or exactly what is stated ⟨an *outright* lie⟩ **b :** given without reservation ⟨*outright* grants for research⟩ **c :** made without encumbrance or lien ⟨*outright* sale⟩
2 *archaic* **:** proceeding directly onward
— **out·right·ly** *adverb*

out·run \ˌau̇t-ˈrən\ *transitive verb* **-ran** \-ˈran\; **-run; -run·ning** (1526)
1 : to run faster than
2 : EXCEED, SURPASS ⟨his ambitions *outrun* his abilities⟩

out·sell \-ˈsel\ *transitive verb* **-sold** \-ˈsōld\; **-sell·ing** (1609)
1 *archaic* **:** to exceed in value
2 : to exceed in number of items sold
3 : to surpass in selling or salesmanship

out·set \ˈau̇t-ˌset\ *noun* (1759)
: BEGINNING, START

out·shine \ˌau̇t-ˈshīn\ *verb* **-shone** \-ˈshōn, *especially British* -ˈshän\ *or* **-shined; -shin·ing** (1596)
transitive verb
1 a : to shine brighter than **b :** to excel in splendor or showiness
2 : OUTDO, SURPASS ⟨*outshone* most of the other films in quality —Kathleen Karr⟩
intransitive verb
: to shine out

out·shoot \ˌau̇t-ˈshüt\ *transitive verb* **-shot** \-ˈshät\; **-shoot·ing** (1530)
1 : to surpass in shooting or making shots
2 : to shoot or go beyond

¹out·side \ˌau̇t-ˈsīd, ˈau̇t-ˌ\ *noun* (1505)
1 a : a place or region beyond an enclosure or boundary: as **(1) :** the world beyond the confines of an institution (as a prison) **(2)** *often capitalized, Alaska* **:** the world beyond the territory or state of Alaska; *especially* **:** the 48 contiguous states **b :** the area farthest from a specified point of reference: as **(1) :** the side of home plate farthest from the batter **(2) :** the part of a playing area toward the sidelines **(3) :** the part of a playing area away from the goal
2 : an outer side or surface
3 : an outer manifestation **:** APPEARANCE
4 : the extreme limit of a guess **:** MAXIMUM ⟨the crowd numbered 10,000 at the *outside*⟩

²outside *adjective* (1634)
1 a : of, relating to, or being on or toward the outer side or surface ⟨the *outside* edge⟩ **b :** of, relating to, or being on or toward the outer side of a curve or turn **c :** of, relating to, or being on or near the outside ⟨an *outside* pitch⟩
2 a : situated or performed outside a particular place **b :** connected with or giving access to the outside ⟨*outside* telephone line⟩
3 : MAXIMUM
4 a : not included or originating in a particular group or organization ⟨blamed the riot on *outside* agitators⟩ **b :** not belonging to one's regular occupation or duties ⟨*outside* interests⟩
5 : barely possible **:** REMOTE ⟨an *outside* chance⟩
6 : made or done from the outside ⟨borrowed a basketball and practiced his *outside* shot⟩

³outside *adverb* (1813)
1 : on or to the outside
2 : OUTDOORS

⁴outside *preposition* (1826)
1 — used as a function word to indicate movement to or position on the outer side of

2 : beyond the limits of ⟨*outside* the scope of this report⟩ ⟨*outside* the law⟩
3 : EXCEPT

outside of *preposition* (circa 1840)
1 : OUTSIDE
2 : ASIDE FROM

out·sid·er \ˌau̇t-ˈsī-dər, ˈau̇t-ˌ\ *noun* (1800)
1 : a person who does not belong to a particular group
2 *chiefly British* **:** a contender not expected to win
— **out·sid·er·ness** *noun*

out·sight \ˈau̇t-ˌsīt\ *noun* (1605)
: the power or act of perceiving external things ⟨the clear-eyed insight and *outsight* of the born writer —*New Yorker*⟩

¹out·size \ˈau̇t-ˌsīz\ *noun* (1845)
: an unusual size; *especially* **:** a size larger than the standard

²outsize *also* **out·sized** \-ˌsīzd\ *adjective* (1880)
1 : unusually large or heavy
2 : exaggerated or extravagant in size or degree

out·skirt \ˈau̇t-ˌskərt\ *noun* (1596)
: a part remote from the center **:** BORDER — usually used in plural ⟨on the *outskirts* of town⟩

out·slick \ˌau̇t-ˈslik\ *transitive verb* (1926)
: to get the better of especially by trickery or cunning

out·smart \ˌau̇t-ˈsmärt\ *transitive verb* (1924)
: to get the better of; *especially* **:** OUTWIT

out·sole \ˈau̇t-ˌsōl\ *noun* (1884)
: the outside sole of a boot or shoe

out·sourc·ing \-ˌsȯr-siŋ, -ˌsȯr-\ *noun* (1982)
: the practice of subcontracting manufacturing work to outside and especially foreign or non-union companies

out·speak \ˌau̇t-ˈspēk\ *transitive verb* **-spoke** \-ˈspōk\; **-spo·ken** \-ˈspō-kən\; **-speak·ing** (1603)
1 : to excel in speaking
2 : to declare openly or boldly

out·spend \-ˈspend\ *transitive verb* (1586)
1 : to exceed the limits of in spending ⟨*outspends* his income⟩
2 : to spend more than ⟨*outspent* the other candidates⟩

out·spent \-ˈspent\ *adjective* (1652)
: completely worn out **:** EXHAUSTED ⟨spurred him, like an *outspent* horse, to death —P. B. Shelley⟩

out·spo·ken \ˌau̇t-ˈspō-kən\ *adjective* (circa 1808)
1 : direct and open in speech or expression **:** FRANK ⟨*outspoken* in his criticism —*Current Biography*⟩
2 : spoken or expressed without reserve ⟨his *outspoken* advocacy of gun control⟩
— **out·spo·ken·ly** *adverb*
— **out·spo·ken·ness** \-kən-nəs\ *noun*

out·spread \ˌau̇t-ˈspred\ *transitive verb* **-spread; -spread·ing** (14th century)
: to spread out

out·stand \ˌau̇t-ˈstand\ *verb* **-stood; -stand·ing** (1571)
transitive verb
: to endure beyond ⟨I have *outstood* my time —Shakespeare⟩
intransitive verb
: STAND OUT

out·stand·ing \ˌau̇t-ˈstan-diŋ, ˈau̇t-ˌ\ *adjective* (1611)
1 : standing out **:** PROJECTING
2 a : UNPAID ⟨left several bills *outstanding*⟩ **b :** continuing to exist **:** UNRESOLVED ⟨a long *outstanding* problem in astronomy⟩ **c** *of securities* **:** publicly issued and sold
3 a : standing out from a group **:** CONSPICUOUS **b :** marked by eminence and distinction
synonym see NOTICEABLE
— **out·stand·ing·ly** \-diŋ-lē\ *adverb*

out·stare \ˌau̇t-ˈstar, -ˈster\ *transitive verb* (1596)
: OUTFACE 1

out·sta·tion \ˈau̇t-ˌstā-shən\ *noun* (1844)
: a remote or outlying station

out·stay \ˌau̇t-ˈstā\ *transitive verb* (1600)
1 : OVERSTAY 1 ⟨*outstayed* their welcome⟩
2 : to surpass in staying power ⟨*outstayed* his competitors⟩

out·stretch \ˌau̇t-ˈstrech\ *transitive verb* (15th century)
: to stretch out **:** EXTEND

out·strip \ˌau̇t-ˈstrip\ *transitive verb* [*out-* + obsolete *strip* to move fast] (1580)
1 : to go faster or farther than
2 : to get ahead of **:** leave behind ⟨has civilization *outstripped* the ability of its users to use it? —Margaret Mead⟩
synonym see EXCEED

out·take \ˈau̇t-ˌtāk\ *noun* (1902)
1 : a passage outward **:** FLUE, VENT
2 : something that is taken out: as **a :** a take that is not used in an edited version of a film or video tape **b :** a recorded musical selection not included in a record album

out·turn \ˈau̇t-ˌtərn\ *noun* (1800)
: a quantity produced **:** OUTPUT

¹out·ward \ˈau̇t-wərd\ *adjective* (before 12th century)
1 : moving, directed, or turned toward the outside or away from a center ⟨an *outward* flow⟩
2 : situated on the outside **:** EXTERIOR
3 : of or relating to the body or to appearances rather than to the mind or the inner life ⟨*outward* beauty⟩
4 : EXTERNAL

²outward *or* **out·wards** \-wərdz\ *adverb* (before 12th century)
1 : toward the outside
2 *obsolete* **:** on the outside **:** EXTERNALLY

³outward *noun* (1606)
: external form, appearance, or reality

out·ward–bound \ˌau̇t-wərd-ˈbau̇nd\ *adjective* (1602)
: bound in an outward direction or to foreign parts ⟨an *outward-bound* ship⟩

out·ward·ly \ˈau̇t-wərd-lē\ *adverb* (14th century)
1 a : on the outside **:** EXTERNALLY **b :** toward the outside
2 : in outward state, behavior, or appearance ⟨was *outwardly* friendly⟩

out·ward·ness \-nəs\ *noun* (1580)
1 : the quality or state of being external
2 : concern with or responsiveness to outward things

out·wash \ˈau̇t-ˌwȯsh, -ˌwäsh\ *noun* (1894)
: detritus chiefly consisting of gravel and sand carried by running water from the melting ice of a glacier and laid down in stratified deposits

out·wear \ˌau̇t-ˈwar, -ˈwer\ *transitive verb* **-wore** \-ˈwȯr, -ˈwōr\; **-worn** \-ˈwōrn, -ˈwȯrn\; **-wear·ing** (circa 1541)
1 : WEAR OUT, EXHAUST
2 : to last longer than ⟨a fabric that *outwears* others⟩

out·weigh \-ˈwā\ *transitive verb* (1597)
: to exceed in weight, value, or importance ⟨the advantages *outweigh* the disadvantages⟩

out·wit \ˌau̇t-ˈwit\ *transitive verb* **-wit·ted; -wit·ting** (1652)
1 : to get the better of by superior cleverness **:** OUTSMART
2 *archaic* **:** to surpass in wisdom

¹out·work \ˌau̇t-ˈwərk\ *transitive verb* (13th century)
1 : WORK OUT, COMPLETE
2 : to work harder, faster, or better than

²out·work \ˈau̇t-ˌwərk\ *noun* (circa 1615)
: a minor defensive position constructed outside a fortified area

out·work·er \-ˌwər-kər\ *noun* (1813)

\ə\ abut \ˈə, ˌə\ kitten \ər\ further \a\ ash \ā\ ace \ä\ mop, mar \au̇\ out \ch\ chin \e\ bet \ē\ easy \g\ go \i\ hit \ī\ ice \j\ job \ŋ\ sing \ō\ go \ȯ\ law \ȯi\ boy \th\ thin \t̲h̲\ the \ü\ loot \u̇\ foot \y\ yet \zh\ vision *see also* Guide to Pronunciation

chiefly British **:** a person who works at home for a business firm

out·worn \ˌaùt-ˈwōrn, -ˈwòrn\ *adjective* (1565)
: no longer useful or acceptable **:** OUTMODED ⟨an *outworn* social system⟩

out–year \ˈaùt-ˌyir\ *noun* (1981)
: the year beyond a current fiscal year — usually used in plural except when attributive

ou·zel \ˈü-zəl\ *noun* [Middle English *ousel,* from Old English *ōsle* — more at MERLE] (before 12th century)
1 : BLACKBIRD 1a; *also* **:** a related bird (*Turdus torquatus*)
2 : DIPPER 1

ou·zo \ˈü-(ˌ)zō, -(ˌ)zò\ *noun* [New Greek] (1898)
: a colorless anise-flavored unsweetened Greek liqueur

ov- *or* **ovi-** *or* **ovo-** *combining form* [Latin *ov-, ovi-,* from *ovum* — more at EGG]
: egg ⟨*ovicide*⟩ **:** ovum ⟨*oviduct*⟩

ova *plural of* OVUM

¹oval \ˈō-vəl\ *noun* (1570)
1 : an oval figure or object
2 : a racetrack in the shape of an oval or a rectangle having rounded corners

²oval *adjective* [Medieval Latin *ovalis,* from Late Latin, of an egg, from Latin *ovum*] (1577)
: having the shape of an egg; *also* **:** broadly elliptical
　— **oval·i·ty** \ō-ˈva-lə-tē\ *noun*
　— **oval·ly** \-və-lē\ *adverb*
　— **oval·ness** *noun*

ov·al·bu·min \ä-val-ˈbyü-mən, ˌō-\ *noun* (circa 1836)
1 : the principal albumin of white of egg; *especially* **:** the crystalline part of egg albumins
2 : dried whites of eggs

Oval Office *noun* [from the *Oval Office,* the U.S. president's office in the west wing of the White House] (1962)
: the seat of the executive department of the U.S. government

oval window *noun* (1683)
: FENESTRA 1a

Ovam·bo \ō-ˈvam-(ˌ)bō, -ˈväm-\ *noun, plural* **Ovambo** *or* **Ovambos** (1853)
1 : a member of a Bantu people of northern Namibia
2 : the Bantu language of the Ovambo people

ovar·i·an \ō-ˈvar-ē-ən, -ˈver-\ *also* **ovar·i·al** \-ē-əl\ *adjective* (circa 1834)
: of, relating to, or involving an ovary

ovari·ec·to·my \ō-ˌvar-ē-ˈek-tə-mē, -ˌver-\ *noun, plural* **-mies** (1889)
: the surgical removal of an ovary
　— **ovari·ec·to·mized** \-ˌmīzd\ *adjective*

ovar·i·ole \ō-ˈvar-ē-ˌōl, -ˈver-\ *noun* [(assumed) New Latin *ovariolum,* diminutive of *ovarium*] (1877)
: one of the tubes of which the ovaries of most insects are composed

ovar·i·ot·o·my \ō-ˌvar-ē-ˈä-tə-mē, -ˌver-\ *noun, plural* **-mies** (1844)
1 : surgical incision of an ovary
2 : OVARIECTOMY

ova·ry \ˈō-və-rē, ˈōv-rē\ *noun, plural* **-ries** [New Latin *ovarium,* from Latin *ovum* egg] (1658)
1 : one of the typically paired essential female reproductive organs that produce eggs and in vertebrates female sex hormones
2 : the enlarged rounded usually basal portion of the pistil or gynoecium of an angiospermous plant that bears the ovules and consists of one or more carpels — see FLOWER illustration

ovate \ˈō-ˌvāt\ *adjective* (1760)
1 : shaped like an egg
2 : having an outline like a longitudinal section of an egg with the basal end broader ⟨*ovate* leaves⟩ — see LEAF illustration

ova·tion \ō-ˈvā-shən\ *noun* [Latin *ovation-, ovatio,* from *ovare* to exult; akin to Greek *euoi,* interjection used in bacchic revels] (1533)
1 : a ceremony attending the entering of Rome by a general who had won a victory of less importance than that for which a triumph was granted
2 : an expression or demonstration of popular acclaim especially by enthusiastic applause ⟨received a standing *ovation*⟩

ov·en \ˈə-vən\ *noun* [Middle English, from Old English *ofen;* akin to Old High German *ofan* oven and perhaps to Greek *ipnos* oven] (before 12th century)
: a chamber used for baking, heating, or drying

ov·en·bird \-ˌbərd\ *noun* [from the shape of its nest] (circa 1825)
1 : any of various South American small brown passerine birds (genus *Furnarius*)
2 : an American warbler (*Seiurus aurocapillus*) that builds a domeshaped nest on the ground

ovenbird 2

ov·en·proof \-ˌprüf\ *adjective* (circa 1940)
: capable of withstanding the temperature range of a kitchen oven ⟨*ovenproof* dishes⟩

¹over \ˈō-vər\ *adverb* [Middle English, adverb & preposition, from Old English *ofer;* akin to Old High German *ubar* (preposition) above, beyond, over, Latin *super,* Greek *hyper*] (before 12th century)
1 a : across a barrier or intervening space; *especially* **:** across the goal line in football **b :** forward beyond an edge or brink and often down ⟨wandered too near the cliff and fell *over*⟩ **c :** across the brim ⟨soup boiled *over*⟩ **d :** so as to bring the underside up ⟨turned his cards *over*⟩ **e :** from a vertical to a prone or inclined position ⟨knocked the lamp *over*⟩ **f :** from one person or side to another ⟨hand it *over*⟩ **g :** ACROSS ⟨got his point *over*⟩ **h :** to one's home ⟨invite some friends *over*⟩ **i :** on the other side of an intervening space ⟨the next town *over*⟩ **j :** to agreement or concord ⟨won them *over*⟩
2 a (1) **:** beyond some quantity, limit, or norm often by a specified amount or to a specified degree ⟨show ran a minute *over*⟩ (2) **:** in an excessive manner **b :** INORDINATELY **b :** till a later time (as the next day) **:** OVERNIGHT ⟨stay *over*⟩ ⟨sleep *over*⟩
3 a : ABOVE **b :** so as to cover the whole surface ⟨windows boarded *over*⟩
4 — used on a two-way radio circuit to indicate that a message is complete and a reply is expected
5 a : THROUGH ⟨read it *over*⟩; *also* **:** in an intensive or comprehensive manner **b :** once more ⟨do it *over*⟩

²over *preposition* (before 12th century)
1 — used as a function word to indicate motion or situation in a position higher than or above another ⟨towered *over* his mother⟩ ⟨flew *over* the lake⟩ ⟨rode *over* the old Roman road⟩
2 a — used as a function word to indicate the possession of authority, power, or jurisdiction in regard to some thing or person ⟨respected those *over* him⟩ **b** — used as a function word to indicate superiority, advantage, or preference ⟨a big lead *over* the others⟩ **c** — used as a function word to indicate one that is overcome, circumvented, or disregarded ⟨passed *over* the governor's veto⟩
3 a : more than ⟨cost *over* $5⟩ **b :** ABOVE 4

4 a — used as a function word to indicate position upon or movement down upon ⟨laid a blanket *over* the child⟩ ⟨hit him *over* the head⟩
b (1) **:** all through or throughout ⟨showed me *over* the house⟩ ⟨went *over* his notes⟩ (2) — used as a function word connecting one mathematical set and another whose elements are coefficients or values of parameters used to form elements of the first set ⟨polynomials *over* the field of real numbers⟩ **c** — used as a function word to indicate a particular medium or channel of communication ⟨*over* the radio⟩
5 — used as a function word to indicate position on or motion to the other side or beyond ⟨lives *over* the way⟩ ⟨fell *over* the edge⟩
6 a : THROUGHOUT, DURING ⟨*over* the past 25 years⟩ **b :** until the end of ⟨stay *over* Sunday⟩
7 a — used as a function word to indicate an object of solicitude, interest, consideration, or reference ⟨the Lord watches *over* his own⟩ **b** — used as a function word to indicate the object of an expressed or implied occupation, activity, or concern ⟨trouble *over* money⟩ ⟨met with advisers *over* lunch⟩ □

³over *adjective* (before 12th century)
1 a : UPPER, HIGHER **b :** OUTER, COVERING **c :** EXCESSIVE ⟨*over* imagination⟩
2 a : not used up **:** REMAINING ⟨something *over* to provide for unusual requirements —J. A. Todd⟩ **b :** having or showing an excess or surplus
3 : being at an end ⟨the day is *over*⟩
4 : fried on both sides ⟨ordered two eggs *over*⟩
　— **over easy :** fried on one side then turned and fried lightly on the other side ⟨eggs *over easy*⟩

⁴over *transitive verb* **overed; over·ing** \ˈō-və-riŋ, ˈōv-riŋ\ (1837)
: to leap over

over- *prefix*
1 : so as to exceed or surpass ⟨*over*achieve⟩
2 : EXCESSIVE ⟨*over*stimulation⟩
3 : to an excessive degree ⟨*over*thin⟩

over·ab·stract	over·anx·ious
over·abun·dance	over·ap·pli·ca·tion
over·abun·dant	over·arous·al
over·ac·cen·tu·ate	over·ar·range
over·ad·just·ment	over·ar·tic·u·late
over·ad·ver·tise	over·as·sert
over·ag·gres·sive	over·as·ser·tion
over·alert	over·as·ser·tive
over·am·bi·tious	over·as·sess·ment
over·am·bi·tious·ness	over·at·ten·tion
over·am·pli·fied	over·bake
over·anal·y·sis	over·beat
over·an·a·lyt·i·cal	over·be·jew·eled
over·an·a·lyze	over·bill
over·anx·i·ety	over·bleach
	over·boil

over·bold
over·bor·row
over·breath·ing
over·brief
over·bright
over·broad
over·browse
over·bru·tal
over·burn
over·busy
over·care·ful
over·cau·tion
over·cau·tious
over·cen·tral·i·za·tion
over·cen·tral·ize
over·chill
over·civ·i·lized
over·claim
over·clas·si·fi·ca·tion
over·clas·si·fy
over·clean
over·clear
over·coach
over·com·mer·cial·i·za·tion
over·com·mer·cial·ize
over·com·mu·ni·cate
over·com·mu·ni·ca·tion
over·com·plex
over·com·pli·ance
over·com·pli·cate
over·com·pli·cat·ed
over·com·press
over·con·cen·tra·tion
over·con·cern
over·con·cerned
over·con·fi·dence
over·con·fi·dent
over·con·fi·dent·ly
over·con·sci·en·tious
over·con·scious
over·con·ser·va·tive
over·con·struct
over·con·sume
over·con·sump·tion
over·con·trol
over·cook
over·cool
over·cor·rect
over·count
over·cred·u·lous
over·crit·i·cal
over·cul·ti·va·tion
over·cure
over·dec·o·rate
over·dec·o·ra·tion
over·de·mand·ing
over·de·pen·dence
over·de·pen·dent
over·de·sign
over·dif·fer·en·ti·a·tion
over·di·rect
over·dis·count
over·di·ver·si·ty
over·doc·u·ment
over·dra·mat·ic
over·dra·ma·tize
over·drink
over·dry
over·ea·ger
over·ea·ger·ness
over·ear·nest
over·ed·it
over·ed·u·cate
over·ed·u·cat·ed
over·ed·u·ca·tion
over·elab·o·rate
over·elab·o·ra·tion
over·em·bel·lish

over·emote
over·emo·tion·al
over·em·pha·sis
over·em·pha·size
over·em·phat·ic
over·en·am·ored
over·en·cour·age
over·en·er·get·ic
over·en·gi·neer
over·en·rolled
over·en·ter·tained
over·en·thu·si·asm
over·en·thu·si·as·tic
over·equipped
over·es·ti·mate
over·es·ti·ma·tion
over·eval·u·a·tion
over·ex·ag·ger·ate
over·ex·ag·ger·a·tion
over·ex·cite
over·ex·cit·ed
over·ex·er·cise
over·ex·ert
over·ex·er·tion
over·ex·pand
over·ex·pan·sion
over·ex·pec·ta·tion
over·ex·plain
over·ex·plic·it
over·ex·ploit
over·ex·ploi·ta·tion
over·ex·trac·tion
over·ex·trap·o·la·tion
over·ex·trav·a·gant
over·ex·u·ber·ant
over·fac·ile
over·fa·mil·iar
over·fa·mil·iar·i·ty
over·fas·tid·i·ous
over·fat
over·fa·vor
over·fer·til·i·za·tion
over·fer·til·ize
over·fo·cus
over·fond
over·ful·fill
over·fund
over·fussy
over·gen·er·al·i·za·tion
over·gen·er·al·ize
over·gen·er·os·i·ty
over·gen·er·ous
over·gen·er·ous·ly
over·glam·or·ize
over·gov·ern
over·han·dle
over·har·vest
over·hasty
over·ho·mog·e·nize
over·hunt
over·hunt·ing
over·hype
over·ide·al·ize
over·iden·ti·fi·ca·tion
over·iden·ti·fy
over·imag·i·na·tive
over·im·press
over·in·debt·ed·ness
over·in·dulge
over·in·dul·gence
over·in·dul·gent
over·in·dus·tri·al·ize
over·in·flate
over·in·flat·ed
over·in·fla·tion
over·in·form
over·in·formed
over·in·ge·nious
over·in·ge·nu·ity
over·in·sis·tent
over·in·tel·lec·tu·al·i·za·tion
over·in·tel·lec·tu·al·ize

over·in·tense
over·in·ten·si·ty
over·in·ter·pre·ta·tion
over·in·vest·ment
over·la·bor
over·la·bored
over·lad·en
over·large
over·lav·ish
over·lend
over·length
over·length·en
over·light
over·lit·er·al
over·lit·er·ary
over·load
over·long
over·loud
over·lush
over·man·age
over·man·nered
over·ma·ture
over·ma·tu·ri·ty
over·med·i·cate
over·med·i·ca·tion
over·mighty
over·milk
over·mine
over·mix
over·mod·est
over·mod·est·ly
over·mus·cled
over·nice
over·nour·ish
over·nu·tri·tion
over·ob·vi·ous
over·op·er·ate
over·opin·ion·at·ed
over·op·ti·mism
over·op·ti·mist
over·op·ti·mis·tic
over·op·ti·mis·ti·cal·ly
over·or·ches·trate
over·or·ga·nize
over·or·ga·nized
over·or·na·ment
over·pack·age
over·pay
over·pay·ment
over·ped·al
over·peo·ple
over·plan
over·plant
over·plot
over·po·tent
over·praise
over·pre·cise
over·pre·scribe
over·pre·scrip·tion
over·priv·i·leged
over·prize
over·pro·cess
over·pro·duce
over·pro·duc·tion
over·pro·gram
over·prom·ise
over·pro·mote
over·pro·tect
over·pro·tec·tion
over·pro·tec·tive
over·pro·tec·tive·ness
over·pump

over·achiev·er \ˌō-və-rə-ˈchē-vər\ *noun* (1952)
: one who achieves success over and above the standard or expected level especially at an early age
— **over·achieve** \-ˈchēv\ *intransitive verb*
— **over·achieve·ment** \-mənt\ *noun*
over·act \ˌō-vər-ˈakt\ (1611)
intransitive verb

over·rate
over·re·act
over·re·ac·tion
over·re·fined
over·re·fine·ment
over·reg·u·late
over·reg·u·la·tion
over·re·li·ance
over·re·port
over·re·spond
over·rich
over·rig·id
over·salt
over·san·guine
over·sat·u·rate
over·sat·u·ra·tion
over·sauce
over·scru·pu·lous
over·se·cre·tion
over·sen·si·tive
over·sen·si·tive·ness
over·sen·si·tiv·i·ty
over·se·ri·ous
over·se·ri·ous·ly
over·ser·vice
over·sim·plis·tic
over·smoke
over·so·lic·i·tous
over·so·phis·ti·cat·ed
over·spe·cial·i·za·tion
over·spe·cial·ize
over·spec·u·late
over·spec·u·la·tion
over·sta·bil·i·ty
over·staff
over·stim·u·late
over·stim·u·la·tion
over·stock
over·strain
over·stress
over·stretch
over·struc·tured
over·sub·tle
over·suds
over·sup·ply
over·sus·pi·cious
over·sweet
over·sweet·en
over·sweet·ness
over·swing
over·talk
over·talk·a·tive
over·tax
over·tax·a·tion
over·thin
over·think
over·tight·en
over·tip
over·tired
over·train
over·treat
over·treat·ment
over·use
over·uti·li·za·tion
over·uti·lize
over·vi·o·lent
over·viv·id
over·wa·ter
over·wea·ry
over·wind
over·with·hold
over·zeal·ous
over·zeal·ous·ness

1 : to act more than is necessary
2 : to overact a part
transitive verb
: to exaggerate in acting
— **over·ac·tion** \-ˈak-shən\ *noun*
over·ac·tive \-ˈak-tiv\ *adjective* (1854)
: excessively or abnormally active
— **over·ac·tiv·i·ty** \-ak-ˈti-və-tē\ *noun*
over against *preposition* (1517)
1 : as opposed to **2** : in contrast with
¹over·age \ˌō-vər-ˈāj\ *also* **over·aged** \-ˈājd\ *adjective* [²over + age] (15th century)
1 : too old to be useful
2 : older than is normal for one's position, function, or grade
²over·age \ˈō-və-rij, ˈōv-rij\ *noun* [³over + -age] (1909)
: SURPLUS, EXCESS
¹over·all \ˌō-vər-ˈol\ *adverb* (13th century)
1 : ALL OVER 1 ⟨the pattern used *overall*⟩
2 : from one end to the other ⟨600 feet long *overall*⟩
3 a : in view of all the circumstances or conditions ⟨*overall*, the sale was a success⟩ **b** : as a whole : GENERALLY ⟨doesn't do as well *overall*⟩ **c** : with everyone or everything taken into account ⟨was third *overall* in earnings⟩ ⟨got 31 miles to the gallon *overall*⟩
²over·all \ˈō-vər-ˌol\ *noun* (1815)
1 *plural* **a** *archaic* : loose protective trousers worn over regular clothes **b** : trousers of strong material usually with a bib and shoulder straps
2 *chiefly British* : a loose-fitting protective smock worn over regular clothing
³over·all \ˈō-vər-ˈol, ˈō-vər-ˌ\ *adjective* (1894)
1 : including everything
2 : viewed as a whole : GENERAL
over·alled \ˈō-vər-ˌold\ *adjective* (1908)
: wearing overalls
over and above *preposition* (15th century)
: in addition to : BESIDES
over and over *adverb* (15th century)
: REPEATEDLY
over·arch·ing \ˌō-vər-ˈär-chiŋ\ *adjective* (1720)
1 : forming an arch overhead
2 : dominating or embracing all else ⟨*overarching* goals⟩
over·arm \ˈō-vər-ˌärm\ *adjective* (1864)
1 : OVERHAND
2 *of a swimming stroke* : made with the arm lifted out of the water and stretched forward over the shoulder to begin the stroke
over·awe \ˌō-vər-ˈo\ *transitive verb* (1579)
: to restrain or subdue by awe
¹over·bal·ance \ˌō-vər-ˈba-lən(t)s\ *transitive verb* (1608)
1 : OUTWEIGH
2 : to cause to lose balance
²over·bal·ance \ˈō-vər-ˌ\ *noun* (1659)
: something more than an equivalent
over·bear \ˌō-vər-ˈbar, -ˈber\ *transitive verb* **-bore** \-ˈbōr, -ˈbor\; **-borne** \-ˈbōrn, -ˈborn\ *also* **-born** \-ˈborn\; **-bear·ing** (1535)
1 : to bring down by superior weight or force : OVERWHELM
2 a : to domineer over **b** : to surpass in importance or cogency : OUTWEIGH
overbearing *adjective* (circa 1677)
1 a : tending to overwhelm : OVERPOWERING **b** : decisively important : DOMINANT
2 : harshly and haughtily arrogant
synonym see PROUD
— **over·bear·ing·ly** \-iŋ-lē\ *adverb*
over·bid \ˌō-vər-ˈbid\ *verb* **-bid; -bid·ding** (circa 1616)
intransitive verb
1 : to bid in excess of value

2 a : to bid more than the scoring capacity of a hand at cards **b** *British* **:** to make a higher bid than the preceding one
transitive verb
: to bid beyond or in excess of; *especially* **:** to bid more than the value of (one's hand at cards)
— **over·bid** \'ō-vər-ˌbid\ *noun*

over·bite \'ō-vər-ˌbīt\ *noun* (1887)
: the projection of the upper anterior teeth over the lower in the normal occlusal position of the jaws

over·blouse \-ˌblaůs, -ˌblaůz\ *noun* (1921)
: a usually fitted or belted blouse worn untucked

¹**over·blown** \ˌō-vər-'blōn\ *adjective* [³*blow*] (1616)
: past the prime of bloom ⟨*overblown* roses⟩

²**overblown** *adjective* [¹*blow*] (1864)
1 : excessively large in girth **:** PORTLY
2 : INFLATED ⟨*overblown* claims⟩ ⟨*overblown* rhetoric⟩; *also* **:** PRETENTIOUS

over·board \'ō-vər-ˌbōrd, -ˌbȯrd\ *adverb* (before 12th century)
1 : over the side of a ship or boat into the water
2 : to extremes of enthusiasm
3 : into discard **:** ASIDE

over·book \ˌō-vər-'bůk\ (1903)
transitive verb
: to issue reservations for (as an airplane flight) in excess of the space available
intransitive verb
: to issue reservations in excess of the space available

over·bought \-'bȯt\ *adjective* (1929)
: not likely to show an immediate rise in price because of prior heavy buying and accompanying price rises ⟨an *overbought* market⟩

over·build \-'bild\ *verb* **-built** \-'bilt\; **-building** (1601)
transitive verb
: to build beyond the actual demand of
intransitive verb
: to build houses or commercial developments in excess of demand

¹**over·bur·den** \-'bər-d²n\ *transitive verb* (1532)
: to place an excessive burden on

²**over·bur·den** \'ō-vər-ˌbər-d²n\ *noun* (1855)
: material overlying a deposit of useful geological materials or bedrock

over·buy \ˌō-vər-'bī\ *verb* **-bought** \-'bȯt\; **-buy·ing** (1745)
transitive verb
: to buy in excess of needs or demand
intransitive verb
: to make purchases beyond one's needs or in excess of one's ability to pay

over·call \-'kȯl\ (circa 1903)
transitive verb
: to make a higher bid than (the previous bid or bidder) in a card game
intransitive verb
: to bid over an opponent's bid in bridge when one's partner has not bid or doubled
— **over·call** \'ō-vər-ˌkȯl\ *noun*

over·ca·pac·i·ty \ˌō-vər-kə-'pa-sə-tē, -'pas-tē\ *noun* (1928)
: excessive capacity for production or services in relation to demand

over·cap·i·tal·ize \-'ka-pə-t²l-ˌīz, -'kap-t²l-\ *transitive verb* (1890)
1 : to put a nominal value on the capital of (a corporation) higher than actual cost or fair market value
2 : to capitalize beyond what the business or the profit-making prospects warrant
— **over·cap·i·tal·i·za·tion** \-ˌka-pə-t²l-ə-'zā-shən, -ˌkap-t²l-\ *noun*

¹**over·cast** *transitive verb* **-cast; -cast·ing** (14th century)
1 \ˌō-vər-'kast, 'ō-vər-ˌ\ **:** DARKEN, OVERSHADOW

2 \'ō-vər-ˌ\ **:** to sew (raw edges of a seam) with long slanting widely spaced stitches to prevent raveling

²**over·cast** \'ō-vər-ˌkast, ˌō-vər-'\ *adjective* (1536)
: clouded over ⟨an *overcast* day⟩

³**over·cast** \'ō-vər-ˌkast\ *noun* (1686)
: COVERING; *especially* **:** a covering of clouds over the sky

over·cast·ing \'ō-vər-ˌkas-tiŋ\ *noun* (1885)
: the act of stitching raw edges of fabric to prevent raveling; *also* **:** the stitching so done

overcast stitch *noun* (1891)
: a small close embroidery stitch sometimes done over a foundation thread and used to form outlines

over·charge \ˌō-vər-'chärj\ (14th century)
transitive verb
1 : to charge too much or too fully
2 : to fill too full
3 : EXAGGERATE, OVERDRAW
intransitive verb
: to make an excessive charge
— **over·charge** \'ō-vər-ˌ\ *noun*

over·cloud \ˌō-vər-'klaůd\ *transitive verb* (1592)
: to overspread with or as if with clouds

over·coat \'ō-vər-ˌkōt\ *noun* (1802)
1 : a warm coat worn over indoor clothing
2 : a protective coating (as of paint)

over·come \ˌō-vər-'kəm\ *verb* **-came** \-'kām\; **-come; -com·ing** [Middle English, from Old English *ofercuman*, from *ofer* over + *cuman* to come] (before 12th century)
transitive verb
1 : to get the better of **:** SURMOUNT ⟨*overcome* difficulties⟩
2 : OVERWHELM
intransitive verb
: to gain the superiority **:** WIN
synonym see CONQUER
— **over·com·er** *noun*

over·com·mit \-kə-'mit\ *transitive verb* (1951)
: to commit excessively: as **a :** to obligate (as oneself) beyond the ability for fulfillment **b :** to allocate (resources) in excess of the capacity for replenishment
— **over·com·mit·ment** \-mənt\ *noun*

over·com·pen·sa·tion \-ˌkäm-pən-'sā-shən, -ˌpen-\ *noun* (1912)
: excessive compensation; *specifically* **:** excessive reaction to a feeling of inferiority, guilt, or inadequacy leading to an exaggerated attempt to overcome the feeling
— **over·com·pen·sate** \-'käm-pən-ˌsāt\ *verb*
— **over·com·pen·sa·to·ry** \-kəm-'pen(t)-sə-ˌtōr-ē, -ˌtȯr-\ *adjective*

over·crowd \ˌō-vər-'kraůd\ (1766)
transitive verb
: to cause to be too crowded
intransitive verb
: to crowd together too much

over·cut \-'kət\ *transitive verb* (1906)
: to cut excessively; *specifically* **:** to cut timber from (a forest) in excess of annual growth or an allotted annual amount

over·de·ter·mined \-di-'tər-mənd\ *adjective* (1915)
1 : excessively determined
2 : having more than one determining psychological factor

over·de·vel·op \-di-'ve-ləp\ *transitive verb* (1869)
: to develop excessively; *especially* **:** to subject (exposed photographic material) to a developing solution for excessive time or at excessive temperature, agitation, or concentration
— **over·de·vel·op·ment** \-mənt\ *noun*

over·do \ˌō-vər-'dü\ *verb* **-did** \-'did\; **-done** \-'dən\; **-do·ing** \-'dü-iŋ\; **-does** \-'dəz\ (before 12th century)
transitive verb
1 a : to do in excess **b :** to use to excess **c :** EXAGGERATE
2 : to cook too long
3 : EXHAUST
intransitive verb
: to go to extremes

over·dog \'ō-vər-ˌdȯg\ *noun* [³*over* + under*dog*] (1938)
: one that is dominant or victorious

over·dom·i·nance \ˌō-vər-'dä-mə-nən(t)s, -'däm-nən(t)s\ *noun* (1947)
: the condition wherein a heterozygote produces a phenotype more extreme or better adapted than that of the homozygote
— **over·dom·i·nant** \-nənt\ *adjective*

¹**over·dose** \'ō-vər-ˌdōs\ *noun* (1700)
1 : too great a dose (as of a therapeutic agent); *also* **:** a lethal or toxic amount (as of a drug)
2 : an excessive quantity or amount ⟨an *overdose* of sports⟩
— **over·dos·age** \ˌō-vər-'dō-sij\ *noun*

²**over·dose** \ˌō-vər-'dōs\ (1727)
transitive verb
: to give an overdose or too many doses to
intransitive verb
: to take or experience an overdose — usually used with *on*

over·draft \'ō-vər-ˌdraft\ *noun* (1878)
1 : an act of overdrawing at a bank **:** the state of being overdrawn; *also* **:** the sum overdrawn
2 : LINE OF CREDIT

over·draw \ˌō-vər-'drȯ\ *verb* **-drew** \-'drü\; **-drawn** \-'drȯn\; **-draw·ing** (1734)
transitive verb
1 : to draw checks on (a bank account) for more than the balance ⟨the account was *overdrawn*⟩
2 : EXAGGERATE, OVERSTATE
intransitive verb
: to make an overdraft

over·drawn *adjective* (1866)
: having an overdrawn account

¹**over·dress** \ˌō-vər-'dres\ (1706)
transitive verb
: to dress or adorn to excess
intransitive verb
: to dress oneself to excess

²**over·dress** \'ō-vər-ˌdres\ *noun* (1812)
: a dress worn over another

over·drive \'ō-vər-ˌdrīv\ *noun* (1926)
1 : an automotive transmission gear that transmits to the drive shaft a speed greater than engine speed
2 : a state of heightened activity ⟨going into rhetorical *overdrive*⟩

¹**over·dub** \'ō-vər-ˌdəb\ *noun* (circa 1965)
1 : the act or an instance of overdubbing
2 : recorded sound that is overdubbed ⟨vocal *overdubs*⟩

²**over·dub** \ˌō-vər-'dəb\ *transitive verb* (1967)
: to transfer (recorded sound) onto a recording that bears sound recorded earlier in order to produce a combined effect

over·due \-'dü, -'dyü\ *adjective* (1845)
1 a : unpaid when due **b :** delayed beyond an appointed time
2 : too great **:** EXCESSIVE
3 : more than ready

over·eat \ˌō-vər-'ēt\ *intransitive verb* **over·ate** \-'āt\; **over·eat·en** \-'ē-t²n\; **over·eat·ing** (1599)
: to eat to excess
— **over·eat·er** \ˌō-vər-'ē-tər, 'ō-vər-ˌ\ *noun*

over·ex·pose \ˌō-vər-ik-'spōz\ *transitive verb* (1869)
: to expose excessively; *especially* **:** to expose (as film) to excessive radiation (as light)
— **over·ex·po·sure** \-'spō-zhər\ *noun*

over·ex·tend \ˌō-vər-ik-'stend\ *transitive verb* (1937)

overcast stitch

: to extend or expand beyond a safe or reasonable point; *especially* **:** to commit (oneself) financially beyond what can be paid
— **over·ex·ten·sion** \-'sten(t)-shən\ *noun*

over·fa·tigue \ˌō-vər-fə-'tēg\ *noun* (1727)
: excessive fatigue especially when carried beyond the recuperative capacity of the individual
— **over·fa·tigued** \-'tēgd\ *adjective*

over·feed \ˌō-vər-'fēd\ *verb* **-fed** \-'fed\; **-feed·ing** (1608)
transitive verb
: to feed to excess
intransitive verb
: to eat to excess

over·fill \-'fil\ (13th century)
transitive verb
: to fill to overflowing
intransitive verb
: to become full to overflowing

over·fish \-'fish\ *transitive verb* (1867)
: to fish to the detriment of (a fishing ground) or to the depletion of (a kind of organism)

over·flight \'ō-vər-ˌflīt\ *noun* (1950)
: a passage over an area in an airplane

¹over·flow \ˌō-vər-'flō\ (before 12th century)
transitive verb
1 : to cover with or as if with water **:** INUNDATE
2 : to flow over the brim of
3 : to cause to overflow
intransitive verb
1 : to flow over bounds
2 : to fill a space to capacity and spread beyond its limits ⟨the crowd *overflowed* into the street⟩

²over·flow \'ō-vər-ˌflō\ *noun* (1589)
1 : a flowing over **:** INUNDATION
2 : something that flows over **:** SURPLUS
3 : an outlet or receptacle for surplus liquid

over·fly \ˌō-vər-'flī\ *transitive verb* **-flew** \-'flü\; **-flown** \-'flōn\; **-fly·ing** (14th century)
: to fly over; *especially* **:** to pass over in an airplane or spacecraft

over·gar·ment \'ō-vər-ˌgär-mənt\ *noun* (15th century)
: an outer garment

over·glaze \-ˌglāz\ *adjective* (1879)
: applied or suitable for applying on top of a fired glaze ⟨*overglaze* enamels⟩
— **overglaze** *noun*

over·graze \ˌō-vər-'grāz\ *transitive verb* (1919)
: to allow animals to graze (as a pasture) to the point of damaging vegetational cover

over·grow \ˌō-vər-'grō\ *verb* **-grew** \-'grü\; **-grown** \-'grōn\; **-grow·ing** (14th century)
transitive verb
1 : to grow over so as to cover with herbage
2 : to grow beyond or rise above **:** OUTGROW
intransitive verb
1 : to grow excessively
2 : to become grown over
— **over·growth** \'ō-vər-ˌgrōth\ *noun*

overgrown *adjective* (1604)
: grown abnormally or excessively large ⟨dismissed him as an *overgrown* adolescent⟩

¹over·hand \'ō-vər-ˌhand\ *adjective* (1656)
: made with the hand brought forward and down from above shoulder level
— **overhand** *adverb*
— **over·hand·ed** \ˌō-vər-'han-dəd\ *adverb or adjective*

²overhand *transitive verb* (1871)
: to sew with short vertical stitches

³overhand *noun* (circa 1934)
: an overhand stroke (as in handball)

overhand knot *noun* (1840)
: a small knot often used to prevent the end of a cord from fraying — see KNOT illustration

¹over·hang \'ō-vər-ˌhaŋ, ˌō-vər-'\ *verb* **-hung** \-ˌhəŋ, -'həŋ\; **-hang·ing** (1592)
transitive verb
1 : to project over
2 : to impend over **:** THREATEN

intransitive verb
: to project so as to be over something

²over·hang \'ō-vər-ˌhaŋ\ *noun* (1864)
1 : the part of the bow or stern of a ship that projects over the water above the waterline
2 : something that overhangs; *also* **:** the extent of the overhanging
3 : a projection of the roof or upper story of a building beyond the wall of the lower part
4 : an excess supply of a commodity that cannot be readily converted, sold, or disposed of ⟨dollar *overhang*⟩ ⟨inventory *overhang*⟩

over·haul \ˌō-vər-'hȯl\ *transitive verb* (1705)
1 a : to examine thoroughly **b** (1) **:** REPAIR (2) **:** to renovate, revise, or renew thoroughly
2 : to haul or drag over
3 : OVERTAKE
— **over·haul** \'ō-vər-ˌhȯl\ *noun*

¹over·head \ˌō-vər-'hed\ *adverb* (15th century)
: above one's head **:** ALOFT

²over·head \'ō-vər-ˌhed\ *adjective* (1874)
1 a : operating, lying, or coming from above **b :** having the driving part above the part driven ⟨valves operated by an *overhead* camshaft⟩
2 : of or relating to overhead ⟨*overhead* costs⟩

³over·head \'ō-vər-ˌhed\ *noun* (1914)
1 : business expenses (as rent, insurance, or heating) not chargeable to a particular part of the work or product
2 : CEILING; *especially* **:** the ceiling of a ship's compartment
3 : a stroke in a racket game made above head height **:** SMASH

overhead projector *noun* (1951)
: a projector for projecting onto a vertical screen magnified images of graphic material on a horizontal transparency illuminated from below — called also *overhead*

over·hear \ˌō-vər-'hir\ *verb* **-heard** \-'hərd\; **-hear·ing** \-'hir-iŋ\ (1549)
transitive verb
: to hear without the speaker's knowledge or intention
intransitive verb
: to overhear something

over·heat \-'hēt\ (14th century)
transitive verb
1 : to heat to excess
2 : to stimulate or agitate unduly
intransitive verb
: to become heated beyond a safe or desirable point

over·heat·ed \-'hē-təd\ *adjective* (1953)
: PERFERVID

over·is·sue \ˌō-vər-'i-(ˌ)shü\ *noun* (1803)
: an issue exceeding the limit of capital, credit, or authority
— **over·is·su·ance** \-'i-shə-wən(t)s\ *noun*
— **overissue** *transitive verb*

over·joyed \-'jȯid\ *adjective* (1594)
: feeling great joy

¹over·kill \ˌō-vər-'kil\ *transitive verb* (1957)
: to obliterate (a target) with more nuclear force than required

²over·kill \'ō-vər-ˌkil\ *noun* (1958)
1 : a destructive capacity greatly exceeding that required for a given target
2 : an excess of something (as a quantity or an action) beyond what is required or suitable for a particular purpose ⟨a propaganda *overkill*⟩ ⟨an *overkill* in weaponry⟩
3 : killing in excess of what is intended or required

¹over·land \'ō-vər-ˌland, -lənd\ *adverb* (12th century)
: by, on, or across land

²overland *adjective* (1800)
: going or accomplished over the land instead of by sea ⟨*overland* emigrants⟩ ⟨an *overland* route⟩

over·lap \ˌō-vər-'lap\ (1726)
transitive verb
1 : to extend over or past and cover a part of
2 : to have something in common with
intransitive verb

1 : to occupy the same area in part **:** lap over
2 : to have something in common
— **over·lap** \'ō-vər-ˌlap\ *noun*

¹over·lay \ˌō-vər-'lā\ *transitive verb* **-laid** \-'lād\; **-lay·ing** (14th century)
1 a : to lay or spread over or across **:** SUPERIMPOSE **b :** to prepare an overlay for
2 : OVERLIE 2

²over·lay \'ō-vər-ˌlā\ *noun* (1794)
: a covering either permanent or temporary: as
a : an ornamental veneer **b :** a decorative and contrasting design or article placed on top of a plain one **c :** a transparent sheet containing graphic matter to be superimposed on another sheet

over·leaf \'ō-vər-ˌlēf, -'lēf\ *adverb* (1843)
: on the other side of a leaf (as of a book)

over·leap \ˌō-vər-'lēp\ *transitive verb* **-leaped** *or* **-leapt** \-'lēpt *also* -'lept\; **-leap·ing** \-'lē-piŋ\ (before 12th century)
1 : to leap over or across
2 : to defeat (oneself) by going too far

over·learn \-'lərn\ *transitive verb* (1874)
: to continue to study or practice after attaining proficiency

over·lie \-'lī\ *transitive verb* **-lay** \-'lā\; **-lain** \-'lān\; **-ly·ing** \-'lī-iŋ\ (13th century)
1 : to lie over or upon
2 : to cause the death of by lying upon

¹over·look \-'lůk\ *transitive verb* (14th century)
1 : to look over **:** INSPECT
2 a : to look down upon from above **b :** to rise above or afford a view of
3 a : to look past **:** MISS **b :** IGNORE 1 **c :** EXCUSE 2
4 : SUPERINTEND, OVERSEE
5 : to look on with the evil eye **:** BEWITCH
synonym see NEGLECT

²over·look \'ō-vər-ˌlůk\ *noun* (1861)
: a place from which one may look down on a scene ⟨plenty of *overlooks* and trails —Thelma H. Bell⟩

over·lord \'ō-vər-ˌlȯrd\ *noun* (13th century)
1 : a lord over other lords **:** a lord paramount
2 a : an absolute or supreme ruler **b :** one having great power or authority ⟨a corporate *overlord*⟩
— **over·lord·ship** \-ˌship, ˌō-vər-'\ *noun*

over·ly \'ō-vər-lē\ *adverb* (1821)
: to an excessive degree

¹over·man \-mən, -ˌman\ *noun* (13th century)
1 : a man in authority over others; *specifically* **:** FOREMAN
2 \-ˌman\ [translation of German *Übermensch*] **:** SUPERMAN 1

²over·man \ˌō-vər-'man\ *transitive verb* (circa 1637)
: to have or get too many personnel for the needs of ⟨*overman* a ship⟩

over·man·tel \'ō-vər-ˌman-t°l\ *noun* (1882)
: an ornamental structure (as a painting) above a mantelpiece
— **overmantel** *adjective*

over·mas·ter \ˌō-vər-'mas-tər\ *transitive verb* (14th century)
: OVERPOWER, SUBDUE

over·mas·ter·ing \-'mas-tə-riŋ\ *adjective* (1645)
: DOMINANT ⟨*overmastering* behavior⟩ ⟨the *overmastering* question⟩

over·match \-'mach\ *transitive verb* (14th century)
1 : to be more than a match for **:** DEFEAT
2 : to match with a superior opponent

¹over·much \-'məch\ *adjective* (13th century)
: too much

²overmuch *adverb* (14th century)
: in too great a degree

³over·much \'ō-vər-,məch, ,ō-vər-'\ *noun* (14th century)
: too great an amount

¹over·night \,ō-vər-'nīt\ *adverb* (14th century)
1 a : on the evening before **b :** during the night ⟨stayed away *overnight*⟩
2 : very quickly or suddenly ⟨became famous *overnight*⟩

²overnight *adjective* (1824)
1 : of, lasting, or staying the night
2 : SUDDEN, RAPID ⟨an *overnight* sensation⟩

³overnight \'ō-vər-,nīt, ,ō-vər-'\ *intransitive verb* (1891)
: to stay overnight

⁴over·night \'ō-vər-,nīt\ *noun* (1959)
: an overnight stay

overnight bag *noun* (1925)
: a suitcase of a size to carry clothing and personal articles for an overnight trip — called also *overnight case*

over·night·er \,ō-vər-'nī-tər\ *noun* (1949)
: OVERNIGHT BAG

¹over·pass \,ō-vər-'pas\ *transitive verb* (14th century)
1 : to pass across, over, or beyond : CROSS; *also* : SURPASS
2 : TRANSGRESS
3 : DISREGARD, IGNORE

²over·pass \'ō-vər-,pas\ *noun* (1929)
: a crossing of two highways or of a highway and pedestrian path or railroad at different levels where clearance to traffic on the lower level is obtained by elevating the higher level; *also* : the upper level of such a crossing

over·per·suade \,ō-vər-pər-'swād\ *transitive verb* (1624)
: to persuade to act contrary to one's conviction or preference
— **over·per·sua·sion** \-'swā-zhən\ *noun*

over·plaid \'ō-vər-,plad\ *noun* (1926)
: a textile design consisting of a plaid pattern superimposed on another plaid or on a textured ground; *also* : a fabric with such a design
— **over·plaid·ed** *adjective*

over·play \,ō-vər-'plā\ (1819)
transitive verb
1 a : to present (as a dramatic role) extravagantly : EXAGGERATE **b :** to place too much emphasis on
2 : to rely too much on the strength of — usually used in the phrase *overplay one's hand*
3 : to strike a golf ball beyond (a putting green)
intransitive verb
: to exaggerate a part or effect

over·plus \'ō-vər-,pləs\ *noun* [Middle English, part translation of Middle French *surplus*] (14th century)
: SURPLUS

over·pop·u·late \,ō-vər-'päp-yə-,lāt\ (1868)
transitive verb
: to furnish or provide with more than the environment or market will bear
intransitive verb
: to become overly populous

over·pop·u·la·tion \,ō-vər-,pä-pyə-'lā-shən\ *noun* (1823)
: the condition of having a population so dense as to cause environmental deterioration, an impaired quality of life, or a population crash

over·pow·er \,ō-vər-'pau̇(-ə)r\ *transitive verb* (1593)
1 : to overcome by superior force : SUBDUE
2 : to affect with overwhelming intensity ⟨the stench *overpowered* us⟩
3 : to provide with more power than is needed or desirable ⟨a dangerously *overpowered* car⟩
— **over·pow·er·ing·ly** \-'pau̇(-ə)r-iŋ-lē\ *adverb*

over·pres·sure \'ō-vər-,pre-shər\ *noun* (1644)
: pressure significantly above what is usual or normal

over·price \,ō-vər-'prīs\ *transitive verb* (1605)
: to price too high

¹over·print \,ō-vər-'print\ *transitive verb* (1863)
: to print over with something additional

²over·print \'ō-vər-,\ *noun* (1876)
: something added by or as if by overprinting; *especially* : a printed marking added to a postage or revenue stamp especially to alter the original or to commemorate a special event

over·proof \,ō-vər-'prüf\ *adjective* (1807)
: containing more alcohol than proof spirit

over·pro·por·tion \-prə-'pōr-shən, -'pȯr-\ *transitive verb* (1642)
: to make disproportionately large
— **overproportion** *noun*
— **over·pro·por·tion·ate** \-sh(ə-)nət\ *adjective*
— **over·pro·por·tion·ate·ly** *adverb*

over·qual·i·fied \-'kwä-lə-,fīd\ *adjective* (1954)
: having more education, training, or experience than a job calls for

over·reach \,ō-və(r)-'rēch\ (14th century)
transitive verb
1 : to reach above or beyond : OVERTOP
2 : to defeat (oneself) by seeking to do or gain too much
3 : to get the better of especially in dealing and bargaining and typically by unscrupulous or crafty methods
intransitive verb
1 *of a horse* : to strike the forefoot with the front part of the hind foot
2 a : to go to excess **b :** EXAGGERATE
3 : to overreach oneself
— **over·reach** \'ō-və(r)-,rēch, ,ō-və(r)-'\ *noun*
— **over·reach·er** \-,rē-chər, -'rē-chər\ *noun*

over·rep·re·sent·ed \'ō-və(r)-,re-pri-'zen-təd\ *adjective* (1900)
: represented excessively; *especially* : having representatives in a proportion higher than the average
— **over·rep·re·sen·ta·tion** \-,re-pri-,zen-'tā-shən, -zən-\ *noun*

¹over·ride \-'rīd\ *transitive verb* **-rode** \-'rōd\; **-rid·den** \-'ri-d²n\; **-rid·ing** \-'rī-diŋ\ (before 12th century)
1 : to ride over or across : TRAMPLE
2 : to ride (as a horse) too much or too hard
3 a : to prevail over : DOMINATE **b :** to set aside : ANNUL ⟨*override* a veto⟩ **c :** to neutralize the action of (as an automatic control)
4 : to extend or pass over; *especially* : OVERLAP

²over·ride \'ō-və(r)-,rīd\ *noun* (1931)
1 : a commission paid to managerial personnel on sales made by subordinates
2 : ROYALTY 5a
3 : a device or system used to override a control
4 : an act or an instance of overriding

over·ripe \,ō-və(r)-'rīp\ *adjective* (1671)
1 : passed beyond maturity or ripeness toward decay
2 a : DECADENT **b :** lacking originality or vigor
— **over–ripe·ness** \-nəs\ *noun*

over·rule \-'rül\ *transitive verb* (1576)
1 : to rule over : GOVERN
2 : to prevail over : OVERCOME
3 a : to rule against **b :** to set aside : REVERSE

¹over·run \-'rən\ *transitive verb* **-ran** \-'ran\; **-run; -run·ning** (before 12th century)
1 a (1) **:** to defeat decisively and occupy the positions of (2) **:** to invade and occupy or ravage **b :** to spread or swarm over : INFEST
2 a : to run or go beyond or past ⟨the plane *overran* the runway⟩ **b :** EXCEED **c :** to readjust (set type) by shifting letters or words from one line into another
3 : to flow over

²over·run \'ō-və(r)-,rən\ *noun* (1898)
1 : an act or instance of overrunning; *especially* : an exceeding of the costs estimated in a contract for development and manufacture of new equipment

2 : the amount by which something overruns
3 : a run in excess of the quantity ordered by a customer

over·scale \'ō-vər-,skāl\ *or* **over·scaled** \-,skāld\ *adjective* (1953)
: OVERSIZE ⟨an *overscale* coat⟩ ⟨an *overscale* sofa⟩

over·sea \,o-vər-'sē, 'ō-vər-,\ *adjective or adverb* (12th century)
chiefly British : OVERSEAS

¹over·seas \,ō-vər-'sēz\ *adverb* (1533)
: beyond or across the sea ⟨lived *overseas* for a time⟩

²over·seas \'ō-vər-,sēz\ *adjective* (1892)
1 : of or relating to movement, transport, or communication over the sea ⟨an *overseas* liner⟩
2 : situated, originating in, or relating to lands beyond the sea ⟨*overseas* installations⟩ ⟨*overseas* immigrants⟩

over·see \,ō-vər-'sē\ *transitive verb* **-saw** \-'sȯ\; **-seen** \-'sēn\; **-see·ing** (before 12th century)
1 : SURVEY, WATCH
2 a : INSPECT, EXAMINE **b :** SUPERVISE

over·seer \'ō-və(r)-,sir, -,sē-ər, ,ō-və(r)-'\ *noun* (1523)
: SUPERVISOR, SUPERINTENDENT

over·sell \,ō-vər-'sel\ *transitive verb* **-sold** \-'sōld\; **-sell·ing** (circa 1879)
1 a : to sell too much or too many to **b :** to sell too much or too many of
2 : to make excessive claims for
— **over·sell** \'ō-vər-,sel\ *noun*

over·set \-'set\ *transitive verb* **-set; -set·ting** (1583)
1 a : to disturb mentally or physically : UPSET **b :** to turn or tip over : OVERTURN
2 : to set too much type matter for
— **over·set** \'ō-vər-,set\ *noun*

over·sexed \,ō-vər-'sekst\ *adjective* (1898)
: exhibiting an excessive sexual drive or interest

over·shad·ow \-'sha-(,)dō\ *transitive verb* (before 12th century)
1 : to cast a shadow over
2 : to exceed in importance : OUTWEIGH

over·shirt \'ō-vər-,shərt\ *noun* (1805)
: a shirt usually worn over another shirt without being tucked in

over·shoe \-,shü\ *noun* (1823)
: an outer shoe; *especially* : GALOSH

over·shoot \,ō-vər-'shüt\ *transitive verb* **-shot** \-'shät\; **-shoot·ing** (14th century)
1 : to pass swiftly beyond
2 : to shoot or pass over or beyond so as to miss
3 : to excel in shooting
— **over·shoot** \'ō-vər-,shüt\ *noun*

¹over·shot \'ō-vər-,shät\ *adjective* (circa 1535)
1 : actuated by the weight of water passing over and flowing from above ⟨an *overshot* waterwheel⟩
2 a : having the upper jaw extending beyond the lower **b :** projecting beyond the lower jaw

²overshot *noun* (1945)
: a pattern or weave featuring filling threads which pass two or more warp yarns before reentering the fabric

over·sight \'ō-vər-,sīt\ *noun* (15th century)
1 a : watchful and responsible care **b :** regulatory supervision ⟨congressional *oversight*⟩
2 : an inadvertent omission or error

over·sim·ple \,ō-vər-'sim-pəl\ *adjective* (15th century)
: too simple : not thoroughgoing or exhaustive ⟨*oversimple* theories⟩
— **over·sim·ply** \-plē\ *adverb*

over·sim·pli·fy \-'sim-plə-,fī\ (1923)
transitive verb
: to simplify to such an extent as to bring about distortion, misunderstanding, or error
intransitive verb
: to engage in undue or extreme simplification

— over·sim·pli·fi·ca·tion \-ˌsim-plə-fə-'kā-shən\ *noun*

over·size \ˌō-vər-'sīz\ *or* **over·sized** \-'sīzd\ *adjective* (1853)
: being of more than standard or ordinary size ⟨*oversize* pillows⟩ ⟨an *oversize* shirt⟩

over·skirt \'ō-vər-ˌskərt\ *noun* (1870)
: a skirt worn over another skirt

over·slaugh \ō-vər-'slȯ\ *transitive verb* [Dutch *overslaan* to pass over, omit, from Middle Dutch *overslaun*, from *over*- over- + *slaen* to strike] (1846)
: to pass over for appointment or promotion in favor of another

over·sleep \ˌō-vər-'slēp\ *verb* **-slept** \-'slept\; **-sleep·ing** (14th century)
intransitive verb
: to sleep beyond the time for waking
transitive verb
: to allow (oneself) to oversleep

over·slip \ˌō-vər-'slip\ *transitive verb* (15th century)
obsolete : ESCAPE

over·sold \ˌō-vər-'sōld\ *adjective* (1926)
: likely to show a rise in price because of prior heavy selling and accompanying decline in price ⟨an *oversold* stock⟩

over·soul \'ō-vər-ˌsōl\ *noun* (circa 1844)
: the absolute reality and basis of all existences conceived as a spiritual being in which the ideal nature imperfectly manifested in human beings is perfectly realized

over·spend \ˌō-vər-'spend\ *verb* **-spent** \-'spent\; **-spend·ing** (circa 1618)
transitive verb
1 : to spend or use to excess : EXHAUST
2 : to exceed in expenditure
intransitive verb
: to spend beyond one's means
— over·spend·er *noun*

over·spill \'ō-vər-ˌspil\ *noun* (1884)
1 : the act or an instance of spilling over
2 *chiefly British* : the movement of excess urban population into less crowded areas

over·spread \ˌō-vər-'spred\ *transitive verb* **-spread; -spread·ing** (before 12th century)
: to spread over or above
— over·spread \'ō-vər-ˌspred\ *noun*

over·state \-'stāt\ *transitive verb* (1803)
: to state in too strong terms : EXAGGERATE
— over·state·ment \-mənt\ *noun*

over·stay \-'stā\ *transitive verb* (1646)
: to stay beyond the time or the limits of

over·steer \'ō-vər-ˌstir\ *noun* (1951)
: the tendency of an automobile to steer into a sharper turn than the driver intends sometimes with a thrusting of the rear to the outside; *also* : the action or an instance of oversteer

over·step \ˌō-vər-'step\ *transitive verb* (before 12th century)
: EXCEED, TRANSGRESS

over·sto·ry \'ō-vər-ˌstōr-ē, -ˌstȯr-\ *noun* (1925)
1 : the layer of foliage in a forest canopy
2 : the trees contributing to an overstory

over·strew \ˌō-vər-'strü\ *transitive verb* **-strewed; -strewed** *or* **-strewn** \-'strün\; **-strew·ing** (circa 1570)
1 : to strew or scatter about
2 : to cover here and there

over·stride \-'strīd\ *transitive verb* **-strode** \-'strōd\; **-strid·den** \-'stri-dᵊn\; **-strid·ing** \-'strī-diŋ\ (13th century)
1 a : to stride over, across, or beyond b : BESTRIDE
2 : to stride faster than or beyond

over·strung \-'strəŋ\ *adjective* (1810)
: too highly strung : too sensitive

over·stuff \-'stəf\ *transitive verb* (1904)
1 : to stuff too full
2 : to cover (as a chair or sofa) completely and deeply with upholstery

over·sub·scribe \-səb-'skrīb\ *transitive verb* (1891)
: to subscribe for more of than is available

— over·sub·scrip·tion \-'skrip-shən\ *noun*

overt \ō-'vərt, 'ō-(ˌ)vərt\ *adjective* [Middle English, from Middle French *ouvert, overt*, from past participle of *ouvrir* to open, from (assumed) Vulgar Latin *operire*, alteration of Latin *aperire*] (14th century)
: open to view : MANIFEST
— overt·ly *adverb*
— overt·ness *noun*

over·take \ˌō-vər-'tāk\ *transitive verb* **-took** \-'tuk\; **-tak·en** \-'tā-kən\; **-tak·ing** [Middle English, from ¹*over* + *taken* to take] (13th century)
1 a : to catch up with b : to catch up with and pass by
2 : to come upon suddenly

over–the–counter *adjective* (1921)
1 : not traded or effected on an organized securities exchange ⟨*over-the-counter* transactions⟩ ⟨*over-the-counter* securities⟩
2 : sold lawfully without prescription ⟨*over-the-counter* drugs⟩

over–the–hill *adjective* (1946)
1 : past one's prime
2 : advanced in age

over–the–top *adjective* (1985)
: extremely or excessively flamboyant or outrageous ⟨an *over-the-top* performance⟩

over–the–transom *adjective* (circa 1952)
: offered without prior arrangement especially for publication : UNSOLICITED ⟨an *over-the-transom* manuscript⟩

over·throw \ˌō-vər-'thrō\ *transitive verb* **-threw** \-'thrü\; **-thrown** \-'thrōn\; **-throw·ing** (14th century)
1 : OVERTURN, UPSET
2 : to cause the downfall of : BRING DOWN, DEFEAT
3 : to throw a ball over or past (as a base or a receiver)
— over·throw \'ō-vər-ˌthrō\ *noun*

over·time \'ō-vər-ˌtīm\ *noun* (1536)
1 : time in excess of a set limit: as a : working time in excess of a standard day or week b : an extra period of play in a contest
2 : the wage paid for overtime
— overtime *adverb*

over·tone \-ˌtōn\ *noun* (1867)
1 a : one of the higher tones produced simultaneously with the fundamental and that with the fundamental comprise a complex musical tone : HARMONIC 1a b : HARMONIC 2
2 : the color of the light reflected (as by a paint)
3 : a secondary effect, quality, or meaning : SUGGESTION 3, CONNOTATION

over·top \ˌō-vər-'täp\ *transitive verb* (circa 1594)
1 : to rise above the top of
2 : to be superior to
3 : SURPASS

over·trade \-'trād\ *intransitive verb* (1734)
: to trade beyond one's capital

over·trick \'ō-vər-ˌtrik\ *noun* (1903)
: a card trick won in excess of the number bid

over·trump \ˌō-vər-'trəmp\ (1746)
transitive verb
: to trump with a higher trump card than the highest previously played on the same trick
intransitive verb
: to play a higher trump card than the highest previously played on the same trick

¹over·ture \'ō-və(r)-ˌchu̇r, -chər, -ˌtyu̇r, -ˌtu̇r\ *noun* [Middle English, literally, opening, from Middle French, from (assumed) Vulgar Latin *opertura*, alteration of Latin *apertura* — more at APERTURE] (15th century)
1 a : an initiative toward agreement or action : PROPOSAL b : something introductory : PRELUDE
2 a : the orchestral introduction to a musical dramatic work b : an orchestral concert piece written especially as a single movement in sonata form

²overture *transitive verb* **-tured; -tur·ing** (circa 1650)
1 : to put forward as an overture
2 : to make or present an overture to

¹over·turn \ˌō-vər-'tərn\ (13th century)
transitive verb
1 : to cause to turn over : UPSET
2 : INVALIDATE, DESTROY
intransitive verb
: UPSET, TURN OVER

²over·turn \'ō-vər-ˌtərn\ *noun* (circa 1592)
1 : the act of overturning : the state of being overturned
2 : the sinking of surface water and rise of bottom water in a lake or sea that results from changes in temperature that commonly occur in spring and fall

over·val·ue \ˌō-vər-'val-(ˌ)yü\ *transitive verb* (1597)
: to assign an excessive or fictitious value to
— over·valu·a·tion \-ˌval-yə-'wā-shən\ *noun*

over·view \'ō-vər-ˌvyü\ *noun* (1588)
: a general survey : SUMMARY

over·volt·age \ˌō-vər-'vōl-tij\ *noun* (1907)
1 : the excess potential required for the discharge of an ion at an electrode over and above the equilibrium potential of the electrode
2 : voltage in excess of the normal operating voltage of a device or circuit

over·wear \-'war, -'wer\ *transitive verb* **-wore** \-'wȯr, -'wȯr\; **-worn** \-'wȯrn, -'wȯrn\; **-wear·ing** (1578)
: WEAR OUT, EXHAUST

over·ween·ing \-'wē-niŋ\ *adjective* [Middle English *overwening*, present participle of *overwenen* to be arrogant, from *over* + *wenen* to ween] (14th century)
1 : ARROGANT, PRESUMPTUOUS
2 : IMMODERATE, EXAGGERATED
— over·ween·ing·ly *adverb*

over·weigh \-'wā\ *transitive verb* (13th century)
1 : to exceed in weight
2 : OPPRESS 2

¹over·weight \'ō-vər-ˌwāt, 2 is usually ˌō-vər-'\ *noun* (1552)
1 : weight over and above what is required or allowed
2 : excessive or burdensome weight

²over·weight \ˌō-vər-'wāt\ *transitive verb* (1603)
1 : to give too much weight or consideration to
2 : to weight excessively

³over·weight \ˌō-vər-'wāt\ *adjective* (1638)
: exceeding expected, normal, or proper weight; *especially* : exceeding the bodily weight normal for one's age, height, and build

over·whelm \ˌō-vər-'hwelm, -'welm\ *transitive verb* [Middle English, from ¹*over* + *whelmen* to turn over, cover up] (14th century)
1 : OVERTURN, OVERTHROW
2 a : to cover over completely : SUBMERGE b : to overcome by superior force or numbers c : to overpower in thought or feeling

over·whelm·ing *adjective* (1742)
: tending or serving to overwhelm ⟨an *overwhelming* majority⟩; *also* : EXTREME, GREAT ⟨*overwhelming* indifference⟩
— over·whelm·ing·ly *adverb*

¹over·win·ter \ˌō-vər-'win-tər\ *intransitive verb* (before 12th century)
: to survive the winter

²overwinter *adjective* (1900)
: occurring during the period spanning the winter

over with *adjective* (1915)
: being at an end : FINISHED, COMPLETED

\ə\ abut \ᵊ\ kitten \ər\ further \a\ ash \ā\ ace
\ä\ mop, mar \au̇\ out \ch\ chin \e\ bet \ē\ easy
\g\ go \i\ hit \ī\ ice \j\ job \ŋ\ sing \ō\ go
\ȯ\ law \ȯi\ boy \th\ thin \th\ the \ü\ loot \u̇\ foot
\y\ yet \zh\ vision *see also* Guide to Pronunciation

over·work \ˌō-vər-'wərk\ (1818)
transitive verb
1 : to cause to work too hard, too long, or to exhaustion
2 : to decorate all over
3 a : to work too much on **:** OVERDO **b :** to make excessive use of
intransitive verb
: to work too much or too long **:** OVERDO
— **overwork** *noun*

over·write \ˌō-və(r)-'rīt\ *verb* **-wrote** \-'rōt\; **-writ·ten** \-'ri-tᵊn\; **-writ·ing** \-'rī-tiŋ\ (1699)
transitive verb
1 : to write over the surface of
2 : to write in inflated or overly elaborate style
intransitive verb
: to write too much or in an overly elaborate style

over·wrought \-'rȯt\ *adjective* [past participle of *overwork*] (1670)
1 : extremely excited **:** AGITATED
2 : elaborated to excess **:** OVERDONE

ovi- *or* **ovo-**
— see OV-

ovi·cide \'ō-və-ˌsīd\ *noun* [International Scientific Vocabulary] (1913)
: an agent that kills eggs; *especially* **:** an insecticide effective against the egg stage
— **ovi·cid·al** \ˌō-və-'sī-dᵊl\ *adjective*

ovi·duct \'ō-və-ˌdəkt\ *noun* [New Latin *oviductus*, from *ov-* + *ductus* duct] (1672)
: a tube that serves exclusively or especially for the passage of eggs from an ovary
— **ovi·duc·tal** \ˌō-və-'dək-tᵊl\ *adjective*

ovine \'ō-ˌvīn\ *adjective* [Late Latin *ovinus*, from Latin *ovis* sheep — more at EWE] (circa 1828)
: of, relating to, or resembling sheep
— **ovine** *noun*

ovip·a·rous \ō-'vi-p(ə-)rəs\ *adjective* [Latin *oviparus*, from *ov-* + *-parus* -parous] (1646)
: producing eggs that develop and hatch outside the maternal body; *also* **:** involving the production of such eggs

ovi·pos·it \'ō-və-ˌpä-zət, ˌō-və-'\ *intransitive verb* [probably back-formation from *ovipositor*] (1816)
: to lay eggs — used especially of insects
— **ovi·po·si·tion** \ˌō-və-pə-'zi-shən\ *noun*
— **ovi·po·si·tion·al** \-'zish-nəl, -'zi-shə-nᵊl\ *adjective*

ovi·pos·i·tor \'ō-və-ˌpä-zə-tər, ˌō-və-'\ *noun* [New Latin, from Latin *ov-* + *positor* one that places, from *ponere* to place — more at POSITION] (1816)
: a specialized organ (as of an insect) for depositing eggs — see INSECT illustration

ovoid \'ō-ˌvȯid\ *also* **ovoi·dal** \ō-'vȯi-dᵊl\ *adjective* [French *ovoïde*, from Latin *ovum* egg — more at EGG] (circa 1828)
: resembling an egg in shape **:** OVATE
— **ovoid** *noun*

ovo·lo \'ō-və-ˌlō\ *noun, plural* **-los** [Italian, diminutive of *uovo, ovo* egg, from Latin *ovum*] (1663)
: a rounded convex molding

Ovon·ics \ō-'vä-niks\ *noun plural but usually singular in construction* [Stanford R. *Ov*shinsky (born 1923) American inventor + electron*ics*] (1968)
: a branch of electronics that deals with applications of the change from an electrically nonconducting state to a semiconducting state shown by glasses of special composition upon application of a certain minimum voltage
— **ovon·ic** \-nik\ *adjective*

ovo·tes·tis \ˌō-vō-'tes-təs\ *noun* [New Latin] (1877)
: a hermaphrodite gonad (as in some scale insects)

ovo·vi·vip·a·rous \ˌō-vō-ˌvī-'vi-p(ə-)rəs\ *adjective* (1801)
: producing eggs that develop within the maternal body (as of various fishes or reptiles)

and hatch within or immediately after extrusion from the parent
— **ovo·vi·vip·a·rous·ly** *adverb*
— **ovo·vi·vip·a·rous·ness** *noun*

ovu·late \'äv-yə-ˌlāt, 'ōv-, -lət\ *adjective* (1861)
: bearing an ovule

ovu·la·tion \ˌäv-yə-'lā-shən, ˌōv-\ *noun* (1848)
: the discharge of a mature ovum from the ovary
— **ovu·late** \'äv-yə-ˌlāt, 'ōv-\ *verb*

ovu·la·to·ry \'äv-yə-lə-ˌtȯr-ē, 'ōv-, -ˌtȯr-\ *adjective* (1931)
: of, relating to, or involving ovulation

ovule \'äv-(ˌ)yü(ə)l, 'ōv-\ *noun* [New Latin *ovulum*, diminutive of Latin *ovum*] (1830)
1 : an outgrowth of the ovary of a seed plant that is a megasporangium and encloses an embryo sac within a nucellus
2 : a small egg; *especially* **:** one in an early stage of growth

ovum \'ō-vəm\ *noun, plural* **ova** \-və\ [New Latin, from Latin, egg — more at EGG] (circa 1706)
: a female gamete **:** MACROGAMETE

ow \'au̇, 'ü\ *interjection* [from *ow*, interjection expressing surprise, from Middle English] (circa 1911)
— used especially to express sudden pain

owe \'ō\ *verb* **owed; ow·ing** [Middle English, to possess, own, owe, from Old English *āgan*; akin to Old High German *eigun* (1st & 3d plural present indicative) possess, Sanskrit *īśe* he possesses] (before 12th century)
transitive verb
1 a *archaic* **:** POSSESS, OWN **b :** to have or bear (an emotion or attitude) to someone or something ⟨*owes* the boss a grudge⟩
2 a (1) **:** to be under obligation to pay or repay in return for something received **:** be indebted in the sum of ⟨*owes* me $5⟩ (2) **:** to be under obligation to render (as duty or service) ⟨I *owe* you a favor⟩ **b :** to be indebted to ⟨*owes* the grocer for supplies⟩
3 : to be indebted for ⟨*owed* his wealth to his father⟩ ⟨*owes* much to good luck⟩
intransitive verb
1 : to be in debt ⟨*owes* for his house⟩
2 : to be attributable ⟨an idea that *owes* to Greek philosophy⟩

owing *adjective* (15th century)
: due to be paid ⟨has bills *owing*⟩

owing to *preposition* (1695)
: BECAUSE OF ⟨delayed *owing to* a crash⟩

owl \'au̇(ə)l\ *noun* [Middle English *owle*, from Old English *ūle*; akin to Old High German *uwila* owl] (before 12th century)
: any of an order (Strigiformes) of chiefly nocturnal birds of prey with a large head and eyes, short hooked bill, strong talons, and soft fluffy often mottled brown plumage

owl·et \'au̇-lət\ *noun* (1542)
: a small or young owl

owl·ish \'au̇-lish\ *adjective* (1611)
: resembling or suggesting an owl
— **owl·ish·ly** *adverb*
— **owl·ish·ness** *noun*

¹own \'ōn\ *adjective* [Middle English *owen*, from Old English *āgen*; akin to Old High German *eigan* own, Old Norse *eiginn*, Old English *āgan* to possess — more at OWE] (before 12th century)
1 : belonging to oneself or itself — usually used following a possessive case or possessive adjective ⟨cooked my *own* dinner⟩
2 : — used to express immediate or direct kinship ⟨an *own* son⟩ ⟨an *own* sister⟩

²own (before 12th century)
transitive verb
1 a : to have or hold as property **:** POSSESS **b :** to have power over **:** CONTROL ⟨wanted to *own* his own life⟩
2 : to acknowledge to be true, valid, or as claimed **:** ADMIT ⟨*own* a debt⟩

intransitive verb
: to acknowledge something to be true, valid, or as claimed — used with *to* or *up*
synonym see ACKNOWLEDGE
— **own·er** \'ō-nər\ *noun*

³own *pronoun, singular or plural in construction* (before 12th century)
: one or ones belonging to oneself — used after a possessive and without a following noun ⟨gave out books so that each of us had our *own*⟩ ⟨a room of your *own*⟩
— **on one's own :** for or by oneself **:** independently of assistance or control

own·er·ship \'ō-nər-ˌship\ *noun* (1583)
1 : the state, relation, or fact of being an owner
2 : a group or organization of owners

ox \'äks\ *noun, plural* **ox·en** \'äk-sən\ *also* **ox** [Middle English, from Old English *oxa*; akin to Old High German *ohso* ox, Sanskrit *ukṣā* bull, and perhaps to Sanskrit *ukṣati* he moistens, Greek *hygros* wet — more at HUMOR] (before 12th century)
1 : a domestic bovine mammal (*Bos taurus*); *broadly* **:** a bovine mammal
2 : an adult castrated male domestic ox

ox- *or* **oxo-** *combining form* [French, from *oxygène*]
: oxygen ⟨*oxa*cillin⟩

ox·a·cil·lin \ˌäk-sə-'si-lən\ *noun* [*ox-* + *azole* + *penicillin*] (1962)
: a semisynthetic penicillin that is especially effective in the control of infections caused by penicillin-resistant staphylococci

ox·a·late \'äk-sə-ˌlāt\ *noun* (1791)
: a salt or ester of oxalic acid

ox·al·ic acid \(ˌ)äk-'sa-lik-\ *noun* [French (*acide*) *oxalique*, from Latin *oxalis*] (1791)
: a poisonous strong acid (COOH)₂ or $H_2C_2O_4$ that occurs in various plants as oxalates and is used especially as a bleaching or cleaning agent and as a chemical intermediate

ox·al·is \äk-'sa-ləs\ *noun* [New Latin, genus name, from Latin, wood sorrel, from Greek, from *oxys* sharp — more at OXYGEN] (circa 1706)
: WOOD SORREL

ox·a·lo·ac·e·tate \ˌäk-sə-lō-'a-sə-ˌtāt\ *also* **ox·al·ac·e·tate** \ˌäk-sə-'la-\ *noun* (1891)
: a salt or ester of oxaloacetic acid

ox·a·lo·ace·tic acid \ˌäk-sə-lō-ə-'sē-tik-\ *also* **ox·al·ace·tic acid** \ˌäk-sə-lə-'sē-tik-\ *noun* [*oxalic* + *acetic acid*] (1896)
: a crystalline acid $C_4H_4O_5$ that is formed by reversible oxidation of malic acid (as in carbohydrate metabolism via the Krebs cycle) and in reversible transamination reactions (as from aspartic acid)

ox·a·lo·suc·cin·ic acid \'äk-sə-lō-sək-ˌsi-nik-, äk-ˌsa-lō-\ *noun* [*oxalic* + *succinic acid*] (1925)
: a tricarboxylic acid $C_6H_6O_7$ that is formed as an intermediate in the Krebs cycle

ox·az·e·pam \äk-'sa-zə-ˌpam\ *noun* [hydr*oxy-* + di*azepam*] (1964)
: a tranquilizing drug $C_{15}H_{11}ClN_2O_2$

ox·blood \'äks-ˌbləd\ *noun* (1705)
: a moderate reddish brown

ox·bow \'äks-ˌbō\ *noun* (14th century)
1 : a U-shaped frame forming a collar about an ox's neck and supporting the yoke
2 : something (as a bend in a river) resembling an oxbow

oxbow 1

— **oxbow** *adjective*

Ox·bridge \'äks-ˌbrij\ *adjective* [*Ox*ford + Cam*bridge*] (1960)
: of, relating to, or characteristic of Oxford and Cambridge Universities — compare PLATEGLASS, REDBRICK 2

ox·cart \-ˌkärt\ *noun* (1749)
: a cart drawn by oxen

ox·eye \-ˌī\ *noun* (15th century)

: any of several composite plants (as of the genera *Chrysanthemum* or *Heliopsis*) having heads with both disk and ray flowers; *especially* : DAISY 1b

oxeye daisy *noun* (circa 1763)
: DAISY 1b

ox·ford \'äks-fərd\ *noun* [*Oxford,* England] (circa 1890)
1 : a low shoe laced or tied over the instep
2 : a soft durable cotton or synthetic fabric made in plain or basket weaves — called also *oxford cloth*

Oxford down *noun, often D capitalized* [*Oxfordshire,* England] (1859)
: any of a Down breed of large hornless sheep developed by crossing Cotswolds and Hampshires — called also *Oxford*

Oxford movement *noun* (1841)
: a High Church movement within the Church of England begun at Oxford in 1833

ox·heart \'äks-,härt\ *noun* (1870)
: any of various large sweet cherries

ox·i·dant \'äk-sə-dənt\ *noun* (1884)
: OXIDIZING AGENT
— **oxidant** *adjective*

ox·i·dase \'äk-sə-,dās, -,dāz\ *noun* [International Scientific Vocabulary] (1896)
: any of various enzymes that catalyze oxidations; *especially* : one able to react directly with molecular oxygen
— **ox·i·da·sic** \,äk-sə-'dā-sik, -zik\ *adjective*

ox·i·da·tion \,äk-sə-'dā-shən\ *noun* [French, from *oxider, oxyder* to oxidize, from *oxide*] (1791)
1 : the act or process of oxidizing
2 : the state or result of being oxidized
— **ox·i·da·tive** \'äk-sə-,dā-tiv\ *adjective*
— **ox·i·da·tive·ly** *adverb*

oxidation number *noun* (1926)
: a positive or negative number that represents the effective charge of an atom or element and that indicates the extent or possibility of its oxidation (the usual *oxidation number* of sodium is +1 and of oxygen −2) — called also *oxidation state*

oxidation–reduction *noun* (1909)
: a chemical reaction in which one or more electrons are transferred from one atom or molecule to another

oxidative phosphorylation *noun* (1954)
: the synthesis of ATP by phosphorylation of ADP for which energy is obtained by electron transport and which takes place in the mitochondria during aerobic respiration

ox·ide \'äk-,sīd\ *noun* [French *oxide, oxyde,* from *ox-* (from *oxygène* oxygen) + *-ide* (from *acide* acid)] (1790)
: a binary compound of oxygen with a more electropositive element or group
— **ox·id·ic** \äk-'si-dik\ *adjective*

ox·i·dize \'äk-sə-,dīz\ *verb* **-dized; -diz·ing** (1806)
transitive verb
1 : to combine with oxygen
2 : to dehydrogenate especially by the action of oxygen
3 : to change (a compound) by increasing the proportion of the electronegative part or change (an element or ion) from a lower to a higher positive valence : remove one or more electrons from (an atom, ion, or molecule)
intransitive verb
: to become oxidized
— **ox·i·diz·able** \,äk-sə-'dī-zə-bəl\ *adjective*

ox·i·diz·er \-,dī-zər\ *noun* (1875)
: OXIDIZING AGENT; *especially* : one used to support the combustion of a rocket propellant

oxidizing agent *noun* (1903)
: a substance that oxidizes something especially chemically (as by accepting electrons)

ox·i·do·re·duc·tase \'äk-sə-dō-ri-'dək-,tās, -,tāz\ *noun* [*oxid*ation + *-o-* + *reduct*ion + *-ase*] (1922)

: an enzyme that catalyzes an oxidation-reduction reaction

ox·ime \'äk-,sēm\ *noun* [International Scientific Vocabulary *ox-* + *-ime* (from *imide*)] (circa 1890)
: any of various compounds obtained chiefly by the action of hydroxylamine on aldehydes and ketones and characterized by the bivalent grouping C=NOH

ox·lip \'äk-,slip\ *noun* [(assumed) Middle English *oxeslippe,* from Old English *oxanslyppe,* literally, ox dung, from *oxa* ox + *slypa, slyppe* paste — more at SLIP] (before 12th century)
: a Eurasian primula (*Primula elatior*) having usually yellow flowers

oxo \'äk-,(,)sō\ *adjective* [*ox-*] (circa 1926)
: containing oxygen

oxo- — see OX-

Ox·o·ni·an \äk-'sō-nē-ən\ *noun* [Medieval Latin *Oxonia* (Oxford)] (circa 1540)
: a student or graduate of Oxford University
— **Oxonian** *adjective*

ox·tail \'äks-,tāl\ *noun* (15th century)
: the tail of a beef animal; *especially* : the skinned tail used for food (as in soup)

ox·ter \'äk-stər\ *noun* [Middle English (Scots), alteration of Old English *ōxta;* akin to Old English *eax* axis, axle — more at AXIS] (15th century)
1 *chiefly Scottish & Irish* : ARMPIT 1
2 *chiefly Scottish & Irish* : ARM

ox·tongue \'äks-,təŋ\ *noun* (14th century)
: a European hawkweed (*Picris echioides*) that has yellow flowers and is now naturalized in the eastern U.S.

oxy \'äk-sē\ *adjective* [French, from *oxygène* oxygen] (1910)
: containing oxygen or additional oxygen — often used in combination (*oxy*hemoglobin)

oxy·acet·y·lene \,äk-sē-ə-'se-t^əl-ən, -t^əl-,ēn\ *adjective* [International Scientific Vocabulary] (1909)
: of, relating to, or utilizing a mixture of oxygen and acetylene (an *oxyacetylene* torch)

oxy·ac·id \'äk-sē-,a-səd\ *noun* (circa 1841)
: an acid (as sulfuric acid) that contains oxygen — called also *oxygen acid*

ox·y·gen \'äk-si-jən\ *noun, often attributive* [French *oxygène,* from Greek *oxys,* adjective, acidic, literally, sharp + French *-gène* -gen; akin to Latin *acer* sharp — more at EDGE] (1790)
: a colorless tasteless odorless gaseous element that constitutes 21 percent of the atmosphere and is found in water, in most rocks and minerals, and in numerous organic compounds, that is capable of combining with all elements except the inert gases, that is active in physiological processes, and that is involved especially in combustion — see ELEMENT table
— **ox·y·gen·ic** \,äk-si-'je-nik\ *adjective*
— **ox·y·gen·less** \'äk-si-jən-ləs\ *adjective*

ox·y·gen·ate \'äk-si-jə-,nāt, äk-'si-jə-\ *transitive verb* **-at·ed; -at·ing** (1790)
: to impregnate, combine, or supply (as blood) with oxygen
— **ox·y·gen·a·tion** \,äk-si-jə-'nā-shən, äk-,si-jə-\ *noun*

ox·y·gen·a·tor \'äk-si-jə-,nā-tər, äk-'si-jə-\ *noun* (circa 1864)
: one that oxygenates; *specifically* : an apparatus that oxygenates the blood extracorporeally (as during open-heart surgery)

oxygen cycle *noun* (1935)
: the cycle whereby atmospheric oxygen is converted to carbon dioxide in animal respiration and regenerated by green plants in photosynthesis

oxygen debt *noun* (1923)
: a cumulative deficit of oxygen available for oxidative metabolism that develops during periods of intense bodily activity and must be made good when the body returns to rest

oxygen demand *noun* (1950)
: BIOCHEMICAL OXYGEN DEMAND

oxygen mask *noun* (1920)
: a device worn over the nose and mouth (as by pilots at high altitudes) through which oxygen is supplied from a storage tank

oxygen tent *noun* (1925)
: a canopy which can be placed over a bedridden person and within which a flow of oxygen can be maintained

oxy·he·mo·glo·bin \,äk-si-'hē-mə-,glō-bən\ *noun* [International Scientific Vocabulary] (1873)
: hemoglobin loosely combined with oxygen that it releases to the tissues

oxy·hy·dro·gen \-'hī-drə-jən\ *adjective* (1827)
: of, relating to, or utilizing a mixture of oxygen and hydrogen (*oxyhydrogen* torch)

ox·y·mo·ron \,äk-si-'mȯr-,än, -'mȯr-\ *noun, plural* **-mo·ra** \-'mȯr-ə, -'mȯr-\ [Late Greek *oxymōron,* from neuter of *oxymōros* pointedly foolish, from Greek *oxys* sharp, keen + *mōros* foolish] (1657)
: a combination of contradictory or incongruous words (as *cruel kindness*)
— **ox·y·mo·ron·ic** \-mə-'rä-nik, -mȯ-\ *adjective*
— **ox·y·mo·ron·i·cal·ly** \-ni-k(ə-)lē\ *adverb*

oxy·phen·bu·ta·zone \,äk-sē-,fen-'byü-tə-,zōn\ *noun* [*oxy* + *phenyl*butazone] (1961)
: a phenylbutazone derivative $C_{19}H_{20}N_2O_3$ used for its anti-inflammatory, analgesic, and antipyretic effects

oxy·phil·ic \,äk-si-'fi-lik\ *adjective* [Greek *oxys* acidic + English *-phil* — more at OXYGEN] (1901)
: ACIDOPHILIC

oxy·tet·ra·cy·cline \-,te-trə-'sī-,klēn\ *noun* (1953)
: a yellow crystalline broad-spectrum antibiotic $C_{22}H_{24}N_2O_9$ produced by a soil actinomycete (*Streptomyces rimosus*)

oxy·to·cic \,äk-si-'tō-sik\ *adjective* [International Scientific Vocabulary, from Greek *oxys* sharp, quick + *tokos* childbirth, from *tiktein* to bear — more at THANE] (1873)
: hastening parturition; *also* : inducing contraction of uterine smooth muscle
— **oxytocic** *noun*

oxy·to·cin \-'tō-s^ən\ *noun* [International Scientific Vocabulary, from *oxytocic*] (1928)
: a pituitary octapeptide hormone $C_{43}H_{66}N_{12}O_{12}S_2$ that stimulates especially the contraction of uterine muscle and the secretion of milk

oxy·uri·a·sis \,äk-si-yu̇-'rī-ə-səs\ *noun* [New Latin, from *Oxyuris,* genus of worms] (circa 1909)
: infestation with or disease caused by pinworms (family Oxyuridae)

oy·er and ter·mi·ner \,ȯi-ər-ən(d)-'tər-mə-nər\ *noun* [Middle English, part translation of Anglo-French *oyer et terminer,* literally, to hear and determine] (15th century)
1 : a commission authorizing a British judge to hear and determine a criminal case at the assizes
2 : a high criminal court in some U.S. states

¹oyez \ō-'yez, -'yā, -'yes, 'ō-,\ *verb imperative* [Middle English, from Anglo-French, hear ye, imperative plural of *oir* to hear, from Latin *audire* — more at AUDIBLE] (15th century)
— used by a court or public crier to gain attention before a proclamation

²oyez *noun, plural* **oyes·ses** \-'ye-səz, -,ye-səz\ (15th century)
: a cry of oyez

oys·ter \'òis-tər\ *noun, often attributive* [Middle English *oistre*, from Middle French, from Latin *ostrea*, from Greek *ostreon;* akin to Greek *ostrakon* shell, *osteon* bone — more at OSSEOUS] (13th century)
1 a : any of various marine bivalve mollusks (family Ostreidae) that have a rough irregular shell closed by a single adductor muscle and include commercially important shellfish **b :** any of various mollusks resembling or related to the oysters
2 : something that is or can be readily made to serve one's personal ends ⟨the world was her *oyster*⟩
3 : a small mass of muscle contained in a concavity of the pelvic bone on each side of the back of a fowl
4 : an extremely taciturn person
5 : a grayish-white color
oyster bed *noun* (1591)
: a place where oysters grow or are cultivated
oys·ter·catch·er \-ˌka-chər, -ˌke-\ *noun* (1731)
: any of a genus (*Haematopus*) of wading birds that have stout legs, a heavy wedge-shaped bill, and often black-and-white plumage
oyster crab *noun* (1756)
: a tiny crab (*Pinnotheres ostreum*) that lives as a commensal in the gill cavity of the oyster
oyster cracker *noun* (1873)
: a small salted usually round cracker
oyster drill *noun* (1925)
: DRILL 4a

oys·ter·ing \'òis-t(ə-)riŋ\ *noun* (1662)
: the act or business of taking oysters for the market or for food
oys·ter·man \'òis-tər-mən\ *noun* (1552)
: one who gathers, opens, breeds, or sells oysters
oyster mushroom *noun* (1875)
: an edible mushroom (*Pleurotus ostreatus*) that grows especially on deciduous trees and dead wood
oyster plant *noun* (1821)
: SALSIFY
oysters Rocke·fel·ler \-ˈrä-ki-ˌfe-lər\ *noun plural* [probably from John D. *Rockefeller* (died 1937)] (1939)
: a dish of oysters on the half shell cooked with various savory toppings typically including chopped spinach and a seasoned sauce
ozo·ke·rite \ˌō-zō-ˈkir-ˌīt\ *also* **ozo·ce·rite** \-ˈsir-\ *noun* [German *Ozokerit*, from Greek *ozein* to smell + *kēros* wax — more at CERUMEN] (circa 1837)
: a waxy mineral mixture of hydrocarbons that is colorless or white when pure and often of unpleasant odor and is used especially in making candles and in electrotyping
ozon·a·tion \ˌō-(ˌ)zō-ˈnā-shən\ *noun* (1854)
: the treatment or combination of a substance or compound with ozone
— ozon·ate \'ō-(ˌ)zō-ˌnāt, -zə-\ *transitive verb*
ozone \'ō-ˌzōn\ *noun* [German *Ozon*, from Greek *ozōn*, present participle of *ozein* to smell — more at ODOR] (circa 1840)

1 : a triatomic very reactive form of oxygen that is a bluish irritating gas of pungent odor, that is formed naturally in the atmosphere by a photochemical reaction and is a major air pollutant in the lower atmosphere but a beneficial component of the upper atmosphere, and that is used for oxidizing, bleaching, disinfecting, and deodorizing
2 : pure and refreshing air
— ozo·nic \ō-ˈzō-nik, -ˈzä-\ *adjective*
ozone hole *noun* (1986)
: an area of the ozone layer (as near the south pole) that is seasonally depleted of ozone
ozone layer *noun* (1929)
: an atmospheric layer at heights of about 20 to 30 miles (32 to 48 kilometers) that is normally characterized by high ozone content which blocks most solar ultraviolet radiation from entry into the lower atmosphere
ozon·ide \'ō-(ˌ)zō-ˌnīd\ *noun* (1867)
: a compound of ozone; *specifically* **:** a compound formed by the addition of ozone to the double or triple bond of an unsaturated organic compound
ozon·ize \-ˌnīz\ *transitive verb* **-ized; -iz·ing** (1850)
: to treat, impregnate, or combine with ozone
— ozon·i·za·tion \ˌō-(ˌ)zō-nə-ˈzā-shən\ *noun*
— ozon·iz·er \'ō-(ˌ)zō-ˌnī-zər\ *noun*
ozo·no·sphere \ō-ˈzō-nə-ˌsfir\ *noun* (1933)
: OZONE LAYER

P *is the sixteenth letter of the English alphabet. It comes through Latin, via Etruscan, from Greek* pi, *which in turn was borrowed from Phoenician* pê, *representing the sound which it has ever since retained, that of a voiceless bilabial stop (the* p *in English* pet*). P is sometimes silent in English, especially in the combinations* pn, ps, *and* pt *found at the beginning of certain words from Greek (for example,* pneumatic, *p*sychic, *and* ptomaine*). With* h *it unites to form the independent digraph* ph, *which represents the Greek* phi *and has the value of* f *in words from that language (such as* ph*rase and gra*ph*ic). In related foreign words, English* p *corresponds to German* pf *or* f *and rarely to* b *in other Indo-European languages; compare, for example, English* p*low with German P*flug *("plow") and English dee*p *with German tie*f *and Lithuanian du*bus *(both meaning "deep"). Small* p *was formed by reducing the size of the capital and placing the letter lower on the line.*

p \'pē\ *noun, plural* **p's** *or* **ps** \'pēz\ *often capitalized, often attributive* (before 12th century)
1 a : the 16th letter of the English alphabet **b :** a graphic representation of this letter **c :** a speech counterpart of orthographic *p*
2 : a graphic device for reproducing the letter *p*
3 : one designated *p* especially as the 16th in order or class
4 [abbreviation for *pass*] **a :** a grade rating a student's work as passing **b :** one graded or rated with a P
5 : something shaped like the letter P

pa \'pä, 'pȯ\ *noun* [short for *papa*] (1811)
: FATHER

PA \(ˌ)pē-'ā\ *noun* (1970)
: PHYSICIAN'S ASSISTANT

pa·an·ga \pä-'äŋ-gə, -'äŋ-ə\ *noun* [Tongan, literally, seed from a species of vine] (1966)
— see MONEY table

PABA \'pa-bə, 'pä-; ˌpē-(ˌ)ā-'bē-(ˌ)ā\ *noun* [*para-*aminobenzoic *a*cid] (1943)
: PARA-AMINOBENZOIC ACID

pab·lum \'pa-bləm\ *noun* [from *Pablum,* a trademark for an infant cereal] (1948)
: PABULUM 3

pab·u·lum \'pa-byə-ləm\ *noun* [Latin, food, fodder; akin to Latin *pascere* to feed — more at FOOD] (1733)
1 : FOOD; *especially* **:** a suspension or solution of nutrients in a state suitable for absorption
2 : intellectual sustenance
3 : something (as writing or speech) that is insipid, simplistic, or bland

pa·ca \'pä-kə, 'pa-\ *noun* [Portuguese & Spanish, from Tupi *páka*] (1657)
: either of two large chiefly Central and South American rodents that constitute a genus (*Agouti* synonym *Cuniculus*) and typically have a white-spotted brownish coat

paca

¹pace \'pās\ *noun*
[Middle English *pas,* from Old French, step, from Latin *passus,* from *pandere* to spread — more at FATHOM] (14th century)
1 a : rate of movement; *especially* **:** an established rate of locomotion **b :** rate of progress; *specifically* **:** parallel rate of growth or development ⟨supplies kept *pace* with demand⟩ **c :** an example to be emulated; *specifically* **:** first place in a competition ⟨three strokes off the *pace* —*Time*⟩ **d** (1) **:** rate of performance or delivery **:** TEMPO; *especially* **:** SPEED ⟨serves

with great *pace*⟩ ⟨a *pace* bowler in cricket⟩ (2) **:** rhythmic animation **:** FLUENCY ⟨writes with color, with zest, and with *pace* —Amy Loveman⟩
2 : a manner of walking **:** TREAD
3 a : STEP 2a(1) **b :** any of various units of distance based on the length of a human step
4 a *plural* **:** an exhibition or test of skills or capacities ⟨the trainer put the tiger through its *paces*⟩ **b :** GAIT; *especially* **:** a fast 2-beat gait (as of the horse) in which the legs move in lateral pairs and support the animal alternately on the right and left legs

²pace *verb* **paced; pac·ing** (1513)
intransitive verb
1 a : to walk with often slow or measured tread **b :** to move along **:** PROCEED
2 : to go at a pace — used especially of a horse
transitive verb
1 a : to measure by pacing — often used with *off* ⟨*paced* off a 10-yard penalty⟩ **b :** to cover at a walk ⟨could hear him *pacing* the floor⟩
2 : to cover (a course) by pacing — used of a horse
3 a : to set or regulate the pace of ⟨taught them how to *pace* their solos for . . . impact —Richard Goldstein⟩; *also* **:** to establish a moderate or steady pace for (oneself) **b** (1) **:** to go before **:** PRECEDE (2) **:** to set an example for **:** LEAD **c :** to keep pace with

³pa·ce \'pā-(ˌ)sē; 'pä-(ˌ)chā, -(ˌ)kā\ *preposition* [Latin, ablative of *pac-, pax* peace, permission — more at PACT] (1863)
: contrary to the opinion of — usually used as an expression of deference to someone's contrary opinion; usually italic ⟨easiness is a virtue in grammar, *pace* old-fashioned grammarians —Philip Howard⟩

pace car *noun* (1965)
: an automobile that leads the field of competitors through a pace lap but does not participate in the race

pace lap *noun* (1971)
: a lap of an auto racecourse by the entire field of competitors before the start of a race to allow the engines to warm up and to permit a flying start

pace·mak·er \'pās-ˌmā-kər\ *noun* (1884)
1 a : one that sets the pace for another **b :** one that takes the lead or sets an example
2 a : a body part (as the sinoatrial node of the heart) that serves to establish and maintain a rhythmic activity **b :** an electrical device for stimulating or steadying the heartbeat or reestablishing the rhythm of an arrested heart
— pace·mak·ing \-kiŋ\ *noun*

pac·er \'pā-sər\ *noun* (circa 1661)
1 : one that paces; *specifically* **:** a horse whose predominant gait is the pace

2 : PACEMAKER
pace·set·ter \'pās-ˌse-tər\ *noun* (1895)
: PACEMAKER 1
— pace·set·ting \-tiŋ\ *adjective*

pa·chi·si \pə-'chē-zē\ *noun* [Hindi *pacīsī,* from *pacīs* twenty-five] (1867)
: an ancient board game played with dice and counters on a cruciform board in which players attempt to be the first to reach the home square

pa·chu·co \pə-'chü-(ˌ)kō\ *noun, plural* **-cos** [American Spanish] (1943)
: a young Mexican-American having a taste for flashy clothes and a special jargon and usually belonging to a neighborhood gang

pachy·derm \'pa-ki-ˌdərm\ *noun* [French *pachyderme,* from Greek *pachydermos* thick-skinned, from *pachys* thick + *derma* skin; akin to Sanskrit *bahu* dense, much — more at DERM-] (1838)
: any of various nonruminant hoofed mammals (as an elephant, a rhinoceros, or a pig) most of which have a thick skin

pachy·der·ma·tous \ˌpa-ki-'dər-mə-təs\ *adjective* [ultimately from Greek *pachys* + *dermat-, derma* skin] (1823)
1 : of or relating to the pachyderms
2 a : THICK, THICKENED ⟨*pachydermatous* skin⟩ **b :** CALLOUS, INSENSITIVE

pach·y·san·dra \ˌpa-ki-'san-drə\ *noun* [New Latin, irregular from Greek *pachys* + New Latin *-andrus* -androus] (1813)
: any of a genus (*Pachysandra*) of shrubby evergreen plants of the box family often used as a ground cover

pachy·tene \'pa-ki-ˌtēn\ *noun* [International Scientific Vocabulary *pachy-* (from Greek *pachys*) + *-tene*] (1912)
: the stage of meiotic prophase that immediately follows the zygotene and that is characterized by paired chromosomes thickened and visibly divided into chromatids and by the occurrence of crossing-over
— pachytene *adjective*

pa·cif·ic \pə-'si-fik\ *adjective* [Middle English *pacifique,* from Latin *pacificus,* from *pac-, pax* peace + *-i- + -ficus* -fic — more at PACT] (circa 1548)
1 a : tending to lessen conflict **:** CONCILIATORY **b :** rejecting the use of force as an instrument of policy
2 a : having a soothing appearance or effect ⟨mild *pacific* breezes⟩ **b :** mild of temper **:** PEACEABLE
3 *capitalized* **:** of, relating to, bordering on, or situated near the Pacific Ocean
— pa·cif·i·cal·ly \-fi-k(ə-)lē\ *adverb*

pac·i·fi·ca·tion \ˌpa-sə-fə-'kā-shən\ *noun* (15th century)
1 a : the act or process of pacifying **:** the state of being pacified **b :** the act of forcibly suppressing or eliminating a population considered to be hostile
2 : a treaty of peace

pa·cif·i·ca·tor \pə-'si-fə-ˌkā-tər\ *noun* (1539)
: PACIFIER 1

pa·cif·i·cism \pə-'si-fə-ˌsi-zəm\ *noun* (1910)
: PACIFISM
— pa·cif·i·cist \-sist\ *noun*

Pacific salmon *noun* (1888)
: any of several anadromous salmonid fishes (genus *Oncorhynchus*) chiefly of the northern Pacific including the sockeye, coho, chum salmon, and chinook salmon

Pacific time \pə-'si-fik-\ *noun* [*Pacific* Ocean] (1883)
: the time of the 8th time zone west of Greenwich that includes the Pacific coastal region of the U.S. — see TIME ZONE illustration

pac·i·fi·er \'pa-sə-ˌfī(-ə)r\ *noun* (1533)

\ə\ abut \ˀ\ kitten \ər\ further \a\ ash \ā\ ace
\ä\ mop, mar \aů\ out \ch\ chin \e\ bet \ē\ easy
\g\ go \i\ hit \ī\ ice \j\ job \ŋ\ sing \ō\ go
\ȯ\ law \ȯi\ boy \th\ thin \ṯh\ the \ü\ loot \ů\ foot
\y\ yet \zh\ vision *see also* Guide to Pronunciation

1 : one that pacifies
2 : a usually nipple-shaped device for babies to suck or bite on

pac·i·fism \'pa-sə-,fi-zəm\ *noun* [French *pacifisme*, from *pacifique* pacific] (1902)
1 : opposition to war or violence as a means of settling disputes; *specifically* **:** refusal to bear arms on moral or religious grounds
2 : an attitude or policy of nonresistance
— **pac·i·fist** \-fist\ *noun*

pac·i·fist \'pa-sə-fist\ *or* **pac·i·fis·tic** \,pa-sə-'fis-tik\ *adjective* (1908)
1 : of, relating to, or characteristic of pacifism or pacifists
2 : strongly and actively opposed to conflict and especially war
— **pac·i·fis·ti·cal·ly** \,pa-sə-'fis-ti-k(ə-)lē\ *adverb*

pac·i·fy \'pa-sə-,fī\ *transitive verb* **-fied; -fy·ing** [Middle English *pacifien*, from Latin *pacificare*, from *pac-, pax* peace] (15th century)
1 a : to allay the anger or agitation of **:** SOOTHE ⟨*pacify* a crying child⟩ **b :** APPEASE, PROPITIATE
2 a : to restore to a tranquil state **:** SETTLE ⟨made an attempt to *pacify* the commotion⟩ **b :** to reduce to a submissive state **:** SUBDUE ⟨forces moved in to *pacify* the country⟩ ☆
— **pac·i·fi·able** \,pa-sə-'fī-ə-bəl\ *adjective*

Pa·cin·i·an corpuscle \pə-'si-nē-ən-\ *noun* [Filippo *Pacini* (died 1883) Italian anatomist] (circa 1860)
: an oval capsule that terminates some sensory nerve fibers especially in the skin of the hands and feet

¹pack \'pak\ *noun, often attributive* [Middle English, of Low German or Dutch origin; akin to Middle Low German & Middle Dutch *pak* pack] (13th century)
1 a : a bundle arranged for convenience in carrying especially on the back **b :** a group or pile of related objects **c** (1) **:** a number of individual components packaged as a unit ⟨a *pack* of cigarettes⟩ (2) **:** CONTAINER (3) **:** a compact unitized assembly to perform a specific function (4) **:** a stack of magnetic disks in a container for use as a storage device
2 a : the contents of a bundle **b :** a large amount or number **:** HEAP ⟨a *pack* of lies⟩ **c :** a full set of playing cards
3 a : an act or instance of packing **b :** a method of packing
4 a : a set of persons with a common interest **:** CLIQUE **b :** an organized troop (as of Cub Scouts)
5 a (1) **:** a group of domesticated animals trained to hunt or run together (2) **:** a group of often predatory animals of the same kind ⟨a wolf *pack*⟩ (3) **:** a large group of individuals massed together (as in a race) **b :** WOLF PACK
6 : a concentrated or compacted mass (as of snow or ice)
7 : wet absorbent material for therapeutic application to the body
8 a : a cosmetic paste for the face **b :** an application or treatment of oils or creams for conditioning the scalp and hair
9 : material used in packing

²pack (14th century)
transitive verb
1 a : to make into a compact bundle **b :** to fill completely ⟨fans *packed* the stadium⟩ **c :** to fill with packing ⟨*pack* a joint in a pipe⟩ **d :** to load with a pack ⟨*pack* a mule⟩ **e :** to put in a protective container ⟨goods *packed* for shipment⟩
2 a : to crowd together **b :** to increase the density of **:** COMPRESS
3 a : to cause or command to go without ceremony ⟨*packed* him off to school⟩ **b :** to bring to an end ⟨GIVE UP — used with *up* or *in* ⟨might *pack* up the assignment⟩ used especially in the phrase *pack it in*
4 : to gather into tight formation **:** make a pack of (as hounds)
5 : to cover or surround with a pack

6 a : to transport on foot or on the back of an animal ⟨*pack* a canoe overland⟩ **b :** to wear or carry as equipment ⟨*pack* a gun⟩ **c :** to be supplied or equipped with **:** POSSESS ⟨a storm *packing* hurricane winds⟩ **d :** to cause or be capable of making (an impact) ⟨a book that *packs* a man-sized punch —C. J. Rolo⟩
intransitive verb
1 a : to go away without ceremony **:** DEPART ⟨simply *packed* up and left⟩ **b :** QUIT, STOP — used with *up* or *in* ⟨why don't you *pack* in, before you kill yourself —Millard Lampell⟩
2 a : to stow goods and equipment for transportation **b :** to be suitable for packing ⟨a knit dress *packs* well⟩
3 a : to assemble in a group **:** CONGREGATE **b :** to crowd together
4 : to become built up or compacted in a layer or mass ⟨the ore *packed* into a stony mass⟩
5 a : to carry goods or equipment **b :** to travel with one's baggage ⟨*pack* by horse⟩
— **pack·abil·i·ty** \,pa-kə-'bi-lə-tē\ *noun*
— **pack·able** \'pa-kə-bəl\ *adjective*

³pack *transitive verb* [obsolete *pack* to make a secret agreement] (1587)
1 : to influence the composition of (as a political agency) so as to bring about a desired result ⟨*pack* a jury⟩
2 *archaic* **:** to arrange (the cards in a pack) so as to cheat

⁴pack *adjective* [perhaps from obsolete *pack* to make a secret agreement] (1701)
chiefly Scottish **:** INTIMATE

¹pack·age \'pa-kij\ *noun* (1611)
1 *archaic* **:** the act or process of packing
2 a : a small or moderate-sized pack **:** PARCEL **b :** a commodity or a unit of a product uniformly wrapped or sealed **c :** a preassembled unit
3 : a covering wrapper or container
4 : something that suggests a package: as **a :** PACKAGE DEAL **b :** a radio or television series offered for sale at a lump sum **c :** contract benefits gained through collective bargaining **d :** a ready-made computer program or collection of related software **e :** a travel arrangement contract that offers for a fixed price transportation, accommodations, and often sightseeing and entertainment **f :** a collection of related items; *especially* **:** one to be considered or acted on together ⟨presented his tax *package* to the nation⟩

²package *transitive verb* **pack·aged; pack·ag·ing** (1921)
1 a : to make into a package; *especially* **:** to produce as an entertainment package **b :** to present (as a product) in such a way as to heighten its appeal to the public
2 : to enclose in a package or covering
— **pack·ag·er** *noun*

package deal *noun* (circa 1948)
1 : an offer or agreement involving a number of related items or one making acceptance of one item dependent on the acceptance of another
2 : the items offered in a package deal

package store *noun* (circa 1918)
: a store that sells bottled or canned alcoholic beverages for consumption off the premises

pack animal *noun* (1847)
: an animal used for carrying packs

pack·board \'pak-,bōrd, -,bȯrd\ *noun* (1939)
: a usually canvas-covered light wood or metal frame with shoulder straps used for carrying goods and equipment

packed \'pakt\ *adjective* (1777)
1 a : COMPRESSED ⟨hard-*packed* snow⟩ **b :** that is crowded or stuffed — often used in combination ⟨an action-*packed* story⟩
2 : filled to capacity ⟨played to a *packed* house⟩

pack·er \'pa-kər\ *noun* (14th century)
1 : one that packs: as **a :** one engaged in processing food (as meat) and distributing it to re-

tailers **b :** an automotive vehicle with a closed body and a compressing device (as for compacting rubbish) in the rear
2 : PORTER 1
3 : one that conveys goods by means of a pack

pack·et \'pa-kət\ *noun* [Middle English, from Middle French *pacquet*, of Germanic origin; akin to Middle Dutch *pak* pack] (15th century)
1 a : a small bundle or parcel **b :** a small thin package **c** *British* (1) **:** PAY ENVELOPE (2) **:** SALARY, PAYCHECK **d** *chiefly British* **:** a considerable amount ⟨that trip will cost you a *packet*⟩
2 a : a number of letters dispatched at one time **b :** a small group, cluster, or mass
3 : a passenger boat usually carrying mail and cargo
4 *British* **:** a pack of cigarettes
5 : a short fixed-length section of data that is transmitted as a unit in an electronic communications network

pack·horse \'pak-,hȯrs\ *noun* (circa 1500)
: a horse used as a pack animal

pack ice *noun* (1850)
: sea ice formed into a mass by the crushing together of pans, floes, and brash

pack·ing \'pa-kiŋ\ *noun* (14th century)
1 a : the action or process of packing something; *also* **:** a method of packing **b :** the processing of food and especially meat for future sale
2 : material (as a covering or stuffing) used to protect packed goods (as for shipping); *also* **:** material used for making airtight or watertight ⟨*packing* for a faucet⟩

pack·ing·house \-,haùs\ *noun* (1834)
: an establishment for slaughtering livestock and processing and packing meat, meat products, and by-products; *also* **:** for processing and packing other foodstuffs — called also *packing plant*

pack·man \'pak-mən\ *noun* (circa 1625)
: PEDDLER

pack rat *noun* (1885)
1 : WOOD RAT; *especially* **:** a bushy-tailed rodent (*Neotoma cinerea*) of the Rocky Mountain area that has well-developed cheek pouches and hoards food and miscellaneous objects
2 : one who collects or hoards especially unneeded items

pack·sack \'pak-,sak\ *noun* (1851)
: a case (as of canvas) held on the back by shoulder straps and used to carry gear when traveling on foot

pack·sad·dle \-,sa-dᵊl\ *noun* (14th century)
: a saddle designed to support loads on the backs of pack animals

pack·thread \-,thred\ *noun* (14th century)
: strong thread or small twine used for sewing or tying packs or parcels

pact \'pakt\ *noun* [Middle English, from Middle French, from Latin *pactum*, from neuter of *pactus*, past participle of *pacisci* to agree, contract; akin to Old English *fōn* to seize, Latin

pax peace, *pangere* to fix, fasten, Greek *pēg-nynai*) (15th century)
: ⁴COMPACT; *especially* : an international treaty

¹**pad** \'pad\ *verb* **pad·ded; pad·ding** [perhaps from Middle Dutch *paden* to follow a path, from *pad* path] (1553)
transitive verb
: to traverse on foot
intransitive verb
: to go on foot : WALK; *especially* : to walk with or as if with padded feet ⟨the dog *padded* along beside him⟩ ⟨*padding* around in bedroom slippers⟩

²**pad** *noun* [Middle Dutch *pad*] (1567)
1 *dialect British* : PATH
2 : a horse that moves along at an easy pace
3 *archaic* : FOOTPAD

³**pad** *noun* [origin unknown] (1570)
1 a : a thin flat mat or cushion: as (1) : a piece of soft stuffed material used as or under a saddle (2) : padding used to shape an article of clothing (3) : a guard worn to shield body parts against impact (4) : a piece of usually folded absorbent material (as gauze) used as a surgical dressing or protective covering (5) : frictional material that presses against the disks in a disk brake **b** : a piece of material saturated with ink for inking the surface of a rubber stamp
2 a : the foot of an animal **b** : the cushioned thickening of the underside of the toes of an animal
3 : a floating leaf of a water plant
4 : a collection of sheets of paper glued together at one end
5 a (1) : a section of an airstrip used for warm-ups or turnarounds (2) : an area used for helicopter takeoffs and landings **b** : LAUNCHPAD **c** : a horizontal concrete surface (as for parking a mobile home)
6 a : BED **b** : living quarters

⁴**pad** *transitive verb* **pad·ded; pad·ding** (1827)
1 a : to furnish with a pad or padding **b** : MUTE, MUFFLE
2 : to expand or increase especially with needless, misleading, or fraudulent matter ⟨*pad* an expense account⟩ — often used with *out* ⟨they *pad* out their bibliographies —J. P. Kenyon⟩

⁵**pad** *noun* [imitative] (1594)
: a soft muffled or slapping sound

pad·ding \'pa-diŋ\ *noun* (1828)
: material with which something is padded

¹**pad·dle** \'pa-dᵊl\ *intransitive verb* **pad·dled; pad·dling** \'pad-liŋ, 'pa-dᵊl-iŋ\ [origin unknown] (1530)
1 : to move the hands or feet about in shallow water
2 *archaic* : to use the hands or fingers in toying or caressing
3 : TODDLE
— **pad·dler** \'pad-lər, 'pa-dᵊl-ər\ *noun*

²**paddle** *noun* [Middle English *padell* spade-shaped tool for cleaning a plow] (1624)
1 a : a usually wooden implement that has a long handle and a broad flattened blade and that is used to propel and steer a small craft (as a canoe) **b** : an implement often with a short handle and a broad flat blade that is used for stirring, mixing, or hitting; *especially* : one used to hit a ball in any of various games (as table tennis)
2 a : any of the broad boards at the circumference of a paddle wheel or waterwheel **b** : any of the broad blades attached to a shaft (as in an ice cream machine) and used for stirring
3 : a computer input device with a dial used to control linear movement of a cursor on a computer display

³**paddle** *verb* **pad·dled; pad·dling** \'pad-liŋ, 'pa-dᵊl-iŋ\ (1677)
intransitive verb
: to go on or through water by or as if by means of a paddle or paddle wheel
transitive verb

1 a : to propel by a paddle **b** : to transport in a paddled craft ⟨*paddled* us to shore in his canoe⟩
2 a : to beat or stir with or as if with a paddle (as in washing or dyeing) **b** : to punish by or as if by beating with a paddle
— **pad·dler** \'pad-lər, 'pa-dᵊl-ər\ *noun*

pad·dle·ball \'pa-dᵊl-,bȯl\ *noun* (1935)
: a game like handball played by hitting the ball with a paddle; *also* : the ball used in this game

pad·dle·board \-,bōrd, -,bȯrd\ *noun* (1938)
: a long narrow buoyant board used for riding the surf or in rescuing swimmers

pad·dle·boat \-,bōt\ *noun* (1874)
: a boat propelled by a paddle wheel

pad·dle·fish \-,fish\ *noun* (1807)
: any of a family (Polyodontidae) of ganoid fishes; *especially* : a large fish (*Polyodon spathula*) of the Mississippi valley that has a long paddle-shaped snout

paddlefish

paddle tennis *noun* (1925)
: a game like tennis that is played with a paddle and rubber ball on a small court

paddle wheel *noun* (1685)
: a wheel with paddles around its circumference used to propel a boat

paddle wheeler *noun* (1924)
: a steamer propelled by a paddle wheel

pad·dock \'pa-dək, -dik\ *noun* [alteration of Middle English *parrok*, from Old English *pearroc*, from Medieval Latin *parricus*] (1622)
1 a : a usually enclosed area used especially for pasturing or exercising animals; *especially* : an enclosure where racehorses are saddled and paraded before a race **b** *Australian & New Zealand* : an often enclosed field
2 : an area at an automobile racecourse where racing cars are parked

pad·dy *also* **padi** \'pa-dē\ *noun, plural* **pad·dies** *also* **pad·is** [Malay *padi*] (1623)
1 : RICE; *especially* : threshed unmilled rice
2 : wet land in which rice is grown

Pad·dy \'pa-dē\ *noun, plural* **Paddies** [from *Paddy*, Hiberno-English nickname for *Patrick*] (1780)
: IRISHMAN — often taken to be offensive

pad·dy wagon \'pa-dē-\ *noun* [probably from *Paddy*] (1930)
: an enclosed motortruck used by police to carry prisoners — called also *Black Maria, patrol wagon*

pad·lock \'pad-,läk\ *noun* [Middle English *padlok*, from *pad-* (of unknown origin) + *lok* lock] (15th century)
: a removable lock with a shackle that can be passed through a staple or link and then secured
— **padlock** *transitive verb*

pa·dre \'pä-(,)drā, -drē\ *noun* [Spanish or Italian or Portuguese, literally, father, from Latin *pater* — more at FATHER] (1584)
1 : a Christian clergyman; *especially* : PRIEST
2 : a military chaplain

pa·dro·ne \pə-'drō-nē\ *noun, plural* **-nes** *or* **-ni** \-nē\ [Italian, protector, owner, from Latin *patronus* patron] (1670)
1 a : MASTER **b** : an Italian innkeeper
2 : one that secures employment especially for Italian immigrants

pad·u·a·soy \'pa-jə-wə-,sȯi, 'paj-wə-\ *noun* [alteration of earlier *poudesoy*, from French *pou-de-soie*] (1663)
: a corded silk fabric; *also* : a garment made of it

pae·an \'pē-ən\ *noun* [Latin, hymn of thanksgiving especially addressed to Apollo, from

Greek *paian, paiōn,* from *Paian, Paiōn,* epithet of Apollo in the hymn] (1589)
: a joyous song or hymn of praise, tribute, thanksgiving, or triumph; *broadly* : ENCOMIUM, TRIBUTE

paed- *or* **paedo-** — see PED-

pae·di·at·ric, pae·di·a·tri·cian, pae·di·at·rics *chiefly British variant of* PEDIATRIC, PEDIATRICIAN, PEDIATRICS

pae·do·gen·e·sis \,pē-dō-'je-nə-səs\ *noun* [New Latin] (circa 1871)
: reproduction by young or larval animals : NEOTENY
— **pae·do·ge·net·ic** \-jə-'ne-tik\ *or* **pae·do·gen·ic** \-'je-nik\ *adjective*
— **pae·do·ge·net·i·cal·ly** \-jə-'ne-ti-k(ə-)lē\ *adverb*

pae·do·mor·phic \,pē-də-'mȯr-fik\ *adjective* (1891)
: of, relating to, or involving paedomorphosis or paedomorphism

pae·do·mor·phism \-'mȯr-,fi-zəm\ *noun* (circa 1891)
: retention in the adult of infantile or juvenile characters

pae·do·mor·pho·sis \-'mȯr-fə-səs\ *noun* [New Latin, from *paed-* + Greek *morphōsis* formation, from *morphoun* to form, from *morphē* form] (1922)
: phylogenetic change that involves retention of juvenile characters by the adult

pa·el·la \pä-'e-lə, -'ā-; -'äl-yə, -'ā-yə\ *noun* [Catalan, literally, pot, pan, from Middle French *paelle*, from Latin *patella* small pan — more at PATELLA] (circa 1892)
: a saffron-flavored dish containing rice, meat, seafood, and vegetables

pae·on \'pē-ən, -,än\ *noun* [Latin, from Greek *paiōn,* from *paian, paiōn* paean] (1603)
: a metrical foot of four syllables with one long and three short syllables (as in classical prosody) or with one stressed and three unstressed syllables (as in English prosody)

pa·gan \'pā-gən\ *noun* [Middle English, from Late Latin *paganus,* from Latin, country dweller, from *pagus* country district; akin to Latin *pangere* to fix — more at PACT] (14th century)
1 : HEATHEN 1; *especially* : a follower of a polytheistic religion (as in ancient Rome)
2 : one who has little or no religion and who delights in sensual pleasures and material goods : an irreligious or hedonistic person
— **pagan** *adjective*
— **pa·gan·ish** \-gə-nish\ *adjective*

pa·gan·ism \'pā-gə-,ni-zəm\ *noun* (15th century)
1 a : pagan beliefs or practices **b** : a pagan religion
2 : the quality or state of being a pagan

pa·gan·ize \-,nīz\ *verb* **-ized; -iz·ing** (1615)
transitive verb
: to make pagan
intransitive verb
: to become pagan
— **pa·gan·iz·er** *noun*

¹**page** \'pāj\ *noun* [Middle English, from Middle French, from Old French] (14th century)
1 a (1) : a youth being trained for the medieval rank of knight and in the personal service of a knight (2) : a youth attendant on a person of rank especially in the medieval period **b** : a boy serving as an honorary attendant at a formal function (as a wedding)
2 : one employed to deliver messages, assist patrons, serve as a guide, or attend to similar duties
3 : an act or instance of paging ⟨a *page* came over the loudspeaker⟩

\ə\ abut \ᵊ\ kitten \ər\ further \a\ ash \ā\ ace
\ä\ mop, mar \au̇\ out \ch\ chin \e\ bet \ē\ easy
\g\ go \i\ hit \ī\ ice \j\ job \ŋ\ sing \ō\ go
\ȯ\ law \ȯi\ boy \th\ thin \th\ the \ü\ loot \u̇\ foot
\y\ yet \zh\ vision *see also* Guide to Pronunciation

²page *transitive verb* **paged; pag·ing** (15th century)
1 : to wait on or serve in the capacity of a page
2 : to summon by repeatedly calling out the name of

³page *noun* [Middle French, from Latin *pagina*; akin to Latin *pangere* to fix, fasten — more at PACT] (1589)
1 a : one of the leaves of a publication or manuscript; *also* : a single side of one of these leaves **b** : the material printed or written on a page
2 a : a written record **b** : a noteworthy event or period 〈one of the brightest *pages* of my life〉
3 : a sizable subdivision of computer memory; *also* : a block of information that fills a page and can be transferred as a unit between the internal and external storage of a computer

⁴page *verb* **paged; pag·ing** (1628)
transitive verb
: to number or mark the pages of
intransitive verb
: to turn the pages (as of a book or magazine) especially in a steady or haphazard manner — usually used with *through*

pag·eant \'pa-jənt\ *noun* [Middle English *pagyn, padgeant,* literally, scene of a play, from Medieval Latin *pagina,* perhaps from Latin, page] (14th century)
1 a : a mere show : PRETENSE **b** : an ostentatious display
2 : SHOW, EXHIBITION; *especially* : an elaborate colorful exhibition or spectacle often with music that consists of a series of tableaux, of a loosely unified drama, or of a procession usually with floats
3 : PAGEANTRY 1

pag·eant·ry \'pa-jən-trē\ *noun* (1608)
1 : pageants and the presentation of pageants
2 : colorful, rich, or splendid display : SPECTACLE
3 : mere show : empty display

page boy *noun* (1874)
1 : a boy serving as a page
2 *usually* **pageboy** : an often shoulder-length hairdo with the ends of the hair turned under in a smooth roll

pag·er \'pā-jər\ *noun* (1901)
: one that pages; *especially* : BEEPER

Pag·et's disease \'pa-jəts-\ *noun* [Sir James Paget (died 1899) English surgeon] (1889)
1 : an eczematous inflammatory precancerous condition especially of the nipple and areola
2 : a chronic disease in which the bones become enlarged, weak, and deformed

page–turn·er \'pāj-ˌtər-nər\ *noun* (1972)
: an engrossing book or story

pag·i·nate \'pa-jə-ˌnāt\ *transitive verb* **-nat·ed; -nat·ing** [Latin *pagina* page] (1884)
: ⁴PAGE

pag·i·na·tion \ˌpa-jə-'nā-shən\ *noun* (1841)
1 : the action of paging : the condition of being paged
2 a : the numbers or marks used to indicate the sequence of pages (as of a book) **b** : the number and arrangement of pages or an indication of these

pa·go·da \pə-'gō-də\ *noun* [Portuguese *pagode* oriental idol, temple] (1588)
: a Far Eastern tower usually with roofs curving upward at the division of each of several stories and erected as a temple or memorial

Pah·la·vi \'pa-lə-(ˌ)vē, 'pä-\ *noun* [Persian *pahlawī,* from *Pahlav* Parthia, from Old Persian *Parthava*] (1773)
1 : the Iranian language of Sassanian Persia — see INDO-EUROPEAN LANGUAGES table
2 : a script used for writing Pahlavi

pagoda

¹paid \'pād\ *past and past participle of* PAY
²paid *adjective* (1817)
1 : marked by the receipt of pay 〈*paid* vacation time〉
2 : being or having been paid or paid for 〈a *paid* official〉 〈a *paid* political announcement〉

pail \'pā(ə)l\ *noun* [Middle English *payle, paille*] (14th century)
1 : a usually cylindrical container with a handle : BUCKET
2 : the quantity that a pail contains
— **pail·ful** \-ˌfül\ *noun*

pail·lard \pī-'yär, pā-'yär\ *noun* [French *paillarde,* from *Paillard,* late 19th century French restaurateur] (1972)
: a piece of beef or veal usually pounded thin and grilled

pail·lette \pī-'yet, pā-'yet, pə-'let\ *noun* [French, from *paille* straw — more at PALLET] (circa 1890)
1 : a small shiny object (as a spangle) applied in clusters as a decorative trimming (as on women's clothing)
2 : a trimming made of paillettes

¹pain \'pān\ *noun* [Middle English, from Old French *peine,* from Latin *poena,* from Greek *poinē* payment, penalty; akin to Greek *tinein* to pay, *tinesthai* to punish, Avestan *kaēnā* revenge, Sanskrit *cayate* he revenges] (14th century)
1 : PUNISHMENT
2 a : usually localized physical suffering associated with bodily disorder (as a disease or an injury); *also* : a basic bodily sensation induced by a noxious stimulus, received by naked nerve endings, characterized by physical discomfort (as pricking, throbbing, or aching), and typically leading to evasive action **b** : acute mental or emotional distress or suffering : GRIEF
3 *plural* : the throes of childbirth
4 *plural* : trouble, care, or effort taken for the accomplishment of something 〈was at *pains* to reassure us〉
5 : one that irks or annoys or is otherwise troublesome — often used in such phrases as *pain in the neck*
— **pain·less** \-ləs\ *adjective*
— **pain·less·ly** *adverb*
— **pain·less·ness** *noun*
— **on pain of** *or* **under pain of** : subject to penalty or punishment of 〈ordered not to leave the country *on pain of* death〉

²pain (14th century)
transitive verb
1 : to make suffer or cause distress to : HURT
2 *archaic* : to put (oneself) to trouble or exertion
intransitive verb
1 *archaic* : SUFFER
2 : to give or have a sensation of pain

pained \'pānd\ *adjective* (14th century)
1 : feeling pain : HURT
2 : expressing or involving pain 〈a *pained* expression〉 〈with *pained* surprise〉

pain·ful \'pān-fəl\ *adjective* **pain·ful·ler** \-fə-lər\; **pain·ful·lest** (14th century)
1 a : feeling or giving pain **b** : IRKSOME, ANNOYING
2 : requiring effort or exertion 〈a long *painful* trip〉
3 *archaic* : CAREFUL, DILIGENT
— **pain·ful·ly** \-f(ə-)lē\ *adverb*
— **pain·ful·ness** \-fəl-nəs\ *noun*

pain·kill·er \-ˌki-lər\ *noun* (1853)
: something (as a drug) that relieves pain
— **pain·kill·ing** \-liŋ\ *adjective*

¹pains·tak·ing \'pān-ˌstā-kiŋ\ *noun* (1538)
: the action of taking pains : diligent care and effort

²painstaking *adjective* (1696)
: taking pains : expending, showing, or involving diligent care and effort
— **pains·tak·ing·ly** \-kiŋ-lē\ *adverb*

¹paint \'pānt\ *verb* [Middle English, from Old French *peint,* past participle of *peindre,* from

Latin *pingere* to tattoo, embroider, paint; akin to Old English *fāh* variegated, Greek *poikilos* variegated, *pikros* sharp, bitter] (13th century)
transitive verb
1 a (1) : to apply color, pigment, or paint to (2) : to color with a cosmetic **b** (1) : to apply with a movement resembling that used in painting (2) : to treat with a liquid by brushing or swabbing 〈*paint* the wound with iodine〉
2 a (1) : to produce in lines and colors on a surface by applying pigments (2) : to depict by such lines and colors **b** : to decorate, adorn, or variegate by applying lines and colors **c** : to produce or evoke as if by painting 〈*paints* glowing pictures of the farm〉
3 : to touch up or cover over by or as if by painting
4 : to depict as having specified or implied characteristics 〈*paints* them whiter than the evidence justifies —Oliver La Farge〉
intransitive verb
1 : to practice the art of painting
2 : to use cosmetics

²paint *noun* (1602)
1 : the action of painting : something produced by painting
2 : MAKEUP; *especially* : a cosmetic to add color
3 a (1) : a mixture of a pigment and a suitable liquid to form a closely adherent coating when spread on a surface in a thin coat (2) : the pigment used in this mixture especially when in the form of a cake 〈a box of *paints*〉 **b** : an applied coating of paint
4 : PINTO
5 : FREE THROW LANE

paint·brush \'pānt-ˌbrəsh\ *noun* (1827)
1 : a brush for applying paint
2 a : INDIAN PAINTBRUSH 1 **b** : ORANGE HAWKWEED

painted bunting *noun* (circa 1811)
: a brightly colored finch (*Passerina ciris*) that is found from the southern U.S. to Panama

painted cup *noun* (1787)
: INDIAN PAINTBRUSH 1

painted lady *noun* (1753)
1 : a migratory nymphalid butterfly (*Vanessa cardui*) with wings mottled in brown, orange, black, and white
2 : PROSTITUTE 1a

painted trillium *noun* (1855)
: a trillium (*Trillium undulatum*) of northeastern North America that has a solitary flower with white petals streaked with purple

painted turtle *noun* (1876)
: a North American turtle (*Chrysemys picta*) having a greenish to black carapace with yellow, red, or olive bordered scutes and a yellow plastron

¹paint·er \'pān-tər\ *noun* (14th century)
: one that paints: as **a** : an artist who paints **b** : one who applies paint especially as an occupation

²paint·er \'pān-tər\ *noun* [Middle English *paynter,* probably from Middle French *pendoir, pentoir* clothesline, from *pendre* to hang — more at PENDANT] (14th century)
: a line used for securing or towing a boat

³paint·er *noun* [alteration of *panther*] (circa 1764)
: COUGAR

paint·er·ly \'pān-tər-lē\ *adjective* (1586)
: of, relating to, or typical of a painter : ARTISTIC
— **paint·er·li·ness** *noun*

painter's colic *noun* (circa 1834)
: intestinal colic associated with obstinate constipation due to chronic lead poisoning

paint·ing \'pān-tiŋ\ *noun* (13th century)
1 : a product of painting; *especially* : a work produced through the art of painting
2 : the art or occupation of painting

paint·work \'pānt-ˌwərk\ *noun* (1888)
chiefly British
1 : work with paint
2 : PAINT 3b

¹pair \'par, 'per\ *noun, plural* **pairs** *or* **pair** [Middle English *paire*, from Old French, from Latin *paria* equal things, from neuter plural of *par* equal] (14th century)
1 a (1) : two corresponding things designed for use together ⟨a *pair* of shoes⟩ (2) : two corresponding bodily parts or members ⟨a *pair* of hands⟩ **b** : something made up of two corresponding pieces ⟨a *pair* of trousers⟩ **2 a** : two similar or associated things: as (1) : two mated animals (2) : a couple in love, engaged, or married ⟨were a devoted *pair*⟩ (3) : two playing cards of the same value or denomination and especially of the same rank (4) : two horses harnessed side by side (5) : two members of a deliberative body that agree not to vote on a specific issue during a time agreed on; *also* : an agreement not to vote made by the two members **b** : a partnership especially of two players in a contest against another partnership **3** *chiefly dialect* : a set or series of small objects (as beads)
²pair (1606)
transitive verb
1 a : to make a pair of — often used with *off* or *up* ⟨*paired* off the animals⟩ **b** : to cause to be a member of a pair **c** : to arrange a voting pair between
2 : to arrange in pairs
intransitive verb
1 : to constitute a member of a pair ⟨a sock that didn't *pair*⟩
2 a : to become associated with another — often used with *off* or *up* ⟨*paired* up with an old friend⟩ **b** : to become grouped or separated into pairs — often used with *off* ⟨*paired* off for the next dance⟩
pair–bond \-,bänd\ *noun* (1940)
: a monogamous relationship
— **pair–bond·ing** *noun*
paired–associate learning *noun* (1966)
: the learning of syllables, digits, or words in pairs (as in the study of a foreign language) so that one member of the pair evokes recall of the other
pair of compasses (1563)
: COMPASS 3c
pair of virginals (1542)
: VIRGINAL
pair production *noun* (1934)
: the transformation of a quantum of radiant energy simultaneously into an electron and a positron when the quantum interacts with the intense electric field near a nucleus
pai·sa \pī-'sä\ *noun* [ultimately from Hindi *paisā*, a quarter-anna coin] (1956)
1 *plural* **paisa** — see *rupee, taka* at MONEY table
2 *plural* **pai·se** \-'sā\ — see *rupee* at MONEY table
pais·ley \'pāz-lē\ *adjective, often capitalized* [*Paisley,* Scotland] (1824)
1 : made typically of soft wool and woven or printed with colorful curved abstract figures
2 : marked by designs, patterns, or figures typically used in paisley fabrics ⟨a *paisley* print⟩
— **paisley** *noun*
Pai·ute \'pī-,yüt\ *noun* (1827)
1 : a member of an American Indian people originally of Utah, Arizona, Nevada, and California
2 : either of the two Uto-Aztecan languages of the Paiute people
pa·ja·ma \pə-'jä-mə, -'ja-\ *noun* [Hindi *pājāma*, from Persian *pā* leg + *jāma* garment] (1883)
: PAJAMAS
— **pa·ja·maed** \-məd\ *adjective*
pa·ja·mas \-məz\ *noun plural* [plural of *pajama*] (1800)
1 : loose lightweight trousers formerly much worn in the Near East
2 : a loose usually two-piece lightweight suit designed especially for sleeping or lounging

pak choi \'päk-'chȯi, 'pak-\ *variant of* BOK CHOY
pa·ke·ha \'pä-kə-,hä, 'pä-kē-ə\ *noun, plural* **pakeha** *or* **pakehas** *often capitalized* [Maori] (1832)
chiefly New Zealand : a person who is not of Maori descent; *especially* : a white person
Paki \'pa-kē, 'pä-\ *noun* [short for *Pakistani*] (1964)
chiefly British : a Pakistani immigrant — usually used disparagingly
¹pal \'pal\ *noun* [Romany *phral, phal* brother, friend, from Sanskrit *bhrātr* brother; akin to Old English *brōthor* brother] (circa 1682)
: a close friend
— **pal·ship** \-,ship\ *noun*
²pal *intransitive verb* **palled; pal·ling** (1879)
: to be or become pals : associate as pals ⟨they've *palled* around for years⟩
¹pal·ace \'pa-ləs\ *noun* [Middle English *palais*, from Old French, from Latin *palatium*, from *Palatium,* the Palatine Hill in Rome where the emperors' residences were built] (13th century)
1 a : the official residence of a chief of state (as a monarch or a president) **b** *chiefly British* : the official residence of an archbishop or bishop
2 a : a large stately house **b** : a large public building **c** : a highly decorated place for public amusement or refreshment ⟨a movie *palace*⟩ ◇
²palace *adjective* (14th century)
1 : of or relating to a palace
2 : of, relating to, or involving the intimates of a chief executive ⟨a *palace* revolution⟩ ⟨*palace* politics⟩
3 : LUXURIOUS, DELUXE
pal·a·din \'pa-lə-dən\ *noun* [French, from Italian *paladino,* from Medieval Latin *palatinus* courtier, from Late Latin, imperial official — more at PALATINE] (1592)
1 : a trusted military leader (as for a medieval prince)
2 : a leading champion of a cause
palae- *or* **palaeo-** *chiefly British variant of* PALE-
pa·laes·tra \pə-'les-trə\ *noun, plural* **-trae** \-(,)trē\ [Middle English *palestre* arena, from Latin *palaestra* place for wrestling, from Greek *palaistra,* from *palaiein* to wrestle] (1580)
1 : a school in ancient Greece or Rome for sports (as wrestling)
2 : GYMNASIUM
pa·lan·quin \,pa-lən-'kēn, -'kwin, -'kin, 'pa-lən-,; pə-'laŋ-kwən\ *noun* [Portuguese *palanquim,* from Malay or Javanese *pelangki,* of Indo-Aryan origin; akin to Bengali *pālaṅka* bed] (1588)
: a conveyance formerly used especially in eastern Asia usually for one person that consists of an enclosed litter borne on the shoulders of men by means of poles
pal·at·able \'pa-lə-tə-bəl\ *adjective* (1669)
1 : agreeable to the palate or taste
2 : agreeable or acceptable to the mind ☆
— **pal·at·abil·i·ty** \,pa-lə-tə-'bi-lə-tē\ *noun*
— **pal·at·able·ness** *noun*
— **pal·at·ably** \,pa-lə-tə-blē\ *adverb*
pal·a·tal \'pa-lə-t³l\ *adjective* (1728)
1 : formed with some part of the tongue near or touching the hard palate posterior to the teethridge ⟨the \sh\ and \y\ in English and the \k\ of *ich* \ik\ in German are examples of *palatal* consonants⟩ **b** *of a vowel* : FRONT 2
2 : of, relating to, forming, or affecting the palate
— **palatal** *noun*
— **pal·a·tal·ly** \-t³l-ē\ *adverb*
pal·a·tal·i·za·tion \,pa-lə-t³l-ə-'zā-shən\ *noun* (1863)
1 : the quality or state of being palatalized
2 : an act or instance of palatalizing an utterance (in rapid speech the \t\ in *got* undergoes *palatalization* before *you* to yield \'gächə\)

pal·a·tal·ize \'pa-lə-t³l-,īz\ *transitive verb* **-ized; -iz·ing** (1867)
: to pronounce as or change into a palatal sound
pal·ate \'pa-lət\ *noun* [Middle English, from Latin *palatum*] (14th century)
1 : the roof of the mouth separating the mouth from the nasal cavity
2 a : a usually intellectual taste or liking **b** : the sense of taste
pa·la·tial \pə-'lā-shəl\ *adjective* [Latin *palatium* palace] (1754)
1 : of, relating to, or being a palace
2 : suitable to a palace : MAGNIFICENT
— **pa·la·tial·ly** \-shə-lē\ *adverb*
— **pa·la·tial·ness** *noun*
pa·lat·i·nate \pə-'la-t³n-ət\ *noun* (circa 1580)
: the territory of a palatine
¹pal·a·tine \'pa-lə-,tīn\ *adjective* [Middle English, from Latin *palatinus* imperial, from *palatium*] (15th century)
1 a : possessing royal privileges **b** : of or relating to a palatine or a palatinate
2 a : of or relating to a palace especially of a Roman or Holy Roman emperor **b** : PALATIAL
²palatine \-,tīn, *3 is also* -,tēn\ *noun* [Late Latin *palatinus* imperial official, from Latin *palatinus,* adjective] (1591)

\ə\ abut \ᵊ\ kitten \ər\ further \a\ ash \ā\ ace
\ä\ mop, mar \au̇\ out \ch\ chin \e\ bet \ē\ easy
\g\ go \i\ hit \ī\ ice \j\ job \ŋ\ sing
\ō\ law \ȯi\ boy \th\ thin \t͟h\ the \ü\ loot \u̇\ foot
\y\ yet \zh\ vision *see also* Guide to Pronunciation

1 a : a feudal lord having sovereign power within his domains **b :** a high officer of an imperial palace
2 *capitalized* **:** a native or inhabitant of the Palatinate
3 [French, from Elisabeth Charlotte of Bavaria (died 1722) Princess *Palatine*] **:** a fur cape or stole covering the head and shoulders
³**pal·a·tine** \-ˌtīn\ *adjective* [French *palatin*, from Latin *palatum* palate] (circa 1656)
: of, relating to, or lying near the palate
⁴**pal·a·tine** \-ˌtīn\ *noun* (1854)
: either of a pair of bones that are situated behind and between the maxillae and in humans are of extremely irregular form
¹**pa·la·ver** \pə-ˈla-vər, -ˈlä-\ *noun* [Portuguese *palavra* word, speech, from Late Latin *parabola* parable, speech] (1735)
1 a : a long parley usually between persons of different cultures or levels of sophistication **b :** CONFERENCE, DISCUSSION
2 a : idle talk **b :** misleading or beguiling speech
²**palaver** *verb* **pa·lav·ered; pa·lav·er·ing** \pə-ˈla-və-riŋ, -ˈlä-; -ˈlav-riŋ, -ˈläv-\ (1773)
intransitive verb
1 : to talk profusely or idly
2 : PARLEY
transitive verb
: to use palaver to **:** CAJOLE
pa·laz·zo \pə-ˈlät-(ˌ)sō\ *noun, plural* **pa·laz·zi** \-(ˌ)sē\ [Italian, from Latin *palatium* palace] (circa 1666)
: a large imposing building (as a museum or a place of residence) especially in Italy
¹**pale** \ˈpā(ə)l\ *noun* [Middle English, from Middle French *pal* stake, from Latin *palus* — more at POLE] (12th century)
1 *archaic* **:** PALISADE, PALING
2 a : one of the stakes of a palisade **b :** PICKET
3 a : a space or field having bounds **:** ENCLOSURE **b :** a territory or district within certain bounds or under a particular jurisdiction
4 : an area or the limits within which one is privileged or protected (as from censure) ⟨conduct that was beyond the *pale*⟩
5 : a perpendicular stripe on a heraldic shield
²**pale** *transitive verb* **paled; pal·ing** (14th century)
: to enclose with pales **:** FENCE
³**pale** *adjective* **pal·er; pal·est** [Middle English, from Middle French, from Latin *pallidus*, from *pallēre* to be pale — more at FALLOW] (14th century)
1 : deficient in color or intensity of color **:** PALLID ⟨a *pale* complexion⟩
2 : not bright or brilliant **:** DIM ⟨a *pale* sun shining through the fog⟩
3 : FEEBLE, FAINT ⟨a *pale* imitation⟩
4 : deficient in chroma ⟨a *pale* pink⟩
— **pale·ly** \ˈpā(ə)l-lē\ *adverb*
— **pale·ness** \-nəs\ *noun*
— **pal·ish** \ˈpā-lish\ *adjective*
⁴**pale** *verb* **paled; pal·ing** (14th century)
intransitive verb
: to become pale
transitive verb
: to make pale
pale- *or* **paleo-** *combining form* [Greek *palai-, palaio-* ancient, from *palaios*, from *palai* long ago; probably akin to Greek *tēle* far off, Sanskrit *carama* last]
1 : involving or dealing with ancient forms or conditions ⟨*paleo*botany⟩
2 : early **:** primitive **:** archaic ⟨*Paleo*lithic⟩
pa·lea \ˈpā-lē-ə\ *noun, plural* **pa·le·ae** \-lē-ˌē\ [New Latin, from Latin, chaff — more at PALLET] (1753)
1 : one of the chaffy scales on the receptacle of many composite plants
2 : the upper bract that with the lemma encloses the flower in grasses
— **pa·le·al** \-lē-əl\ *adjective*
Pa·le·arc·tic \ˌpā-lē-ˈärk-tik, -ˈär-tik\ *adjective* (1858)

: of, relating to, or being a biogeographic region or subregion that includes Europe, Asia north of the Himalayas, northern Arabia, and Africa north of the Sahara
pale dry *adjective* (1953)
: dry and light colored ⟨*pale dry* ginger ale⟩
pale·face \ˈpā(ə)l-ˌfās\ *noun* (1822)
: a white person
pa·leo·an·thro·pol·o·gy \ˌpā-lē-ō-ˌan(t)-thrə-ˈpä-lə-jē, *especially British* ˌpa-\ *noun* (1916)
: a branch of anthropology dealing with fossil hominids
— **pa·leo·an·thro·po·log·i·cal** \-pə-ˈlä-ji-kəl\ *adjective*
— **pa·leo·an·thro·pol·o·gist** \-ˈpä-lə-jist\ *noun*
pa·leo·bi·ol·o·gy \-bī-ˈä-lə-jē\ *noun* (1893)
: a branch of paleontology concerned with the biology of fossil organisms
— **pa·leo·bi·o·log·i·cal** \-bī-ə-ˈlä-ji-kəl\ *also* **pa·leo·bi·o·log·ic** \-ˈlä-jik\ *adjective*
— **pa·leo·bi·ol·o·gist** \-bī-ˈä-lə-jist\ *noun*
pa·leo·bot·a·ny \-ˈbä-tᵊn-ē, -ˈbät-nē\ *noun* [International Scientific Vocabulary] (1872)
: a branch of botany dealing with fossil plants
— **pa·leo·bo·tan·i·cal** \-bə-ˈta-ni-kəl\ *or* **pa·leo·bo·tan·ic** \-ˈta-nik\ *adjective*
— **pa·leo·bo·tan·i·cal·ly** \-ni-k(ə-)lē\ *adverb*
— **pa·leo·bot·a·nist** \-ˈbä-tᵊn-ist, -ˈbät-nist\ *noun*
Pa·leo·cene \ˈpā-lē-ə-ˌsēn, *especially British* ˈpa-\ *adjective* [International Scientific Vocabulary] (1877)
: of, relating to, or being the earliest epoch of the Tertiary or the corresponding system of rocks — see GEOLOGIC TIME table
— **Paleocene** *noun*
pa·leo·cli·ma·tol·o·gy \ˌpā-lē-ō-ˌklī-mə-ˈtä-lə-jē, *especially British* ˌpa-\ *noun* [International Scientific Vocabulary] (circa 1909)
: a science dealing with the climate of past ages
— **pa·leo·cli·ma·tol·o·gist** \-jist\ *noun*
pa·leo·ecol·o·gy \-i-ˈkä-lə-jē, -e-ˈkä-\ *noun* (1898)
: a branch of ecology that is concerned with the characteristics of ancient environments and with their relationships to ancient plants and animals
— **pa·leo·eco·log·i·cal** \-ˌē-kə-ə-ˈlä-ji-kəl, -ˌe-kə-\ *also* **pa·leo·eco·log·ic** \-jik\ *adjective*
— **pa·leo·ecol·o·gist** \-i-ˈkä-lə-jist, -e-ˈkä-\ *noun*
Pa·leo·gene \ˈpā-lē-ə-ˌjēn, *especially British* ˈpa-\ *adjective* [German *Paläogen*, from *palä-* pale- + *-gen* (from Greek *-genēs* born) — more at -GEN] (1882)
: of, relating to, or being the earlier part of the Tertiary including the Paleocene, Eocene, and Oligocene or the corresponding system of rocks
— **Paleogene** *noun*
pa·leo·ge·og·ra·phy \ˌpā-lē-ō-jē-ˈä-grə-fē, *especially British* ˌpa-\ *noun* [International Scientific Vocabulary] (1881)
: the geography of ancient times or of a particular past geological epoch
— **pa·leo·geo·graph·ic** \-ˌjē-ə-ˈgra-fik\ *or* **pa·leo·geo·graph·i·cal** \-fi-kəl\ *adjective*
— **pa·leo·geo·graph·i·cal·ly** \-fi-k(ə-)lē\ *adverb*
pa·leo·graph·ic \-ə-ˈgra-fik\ *or* **pa·leo·graph·i·cal** \-fi-kəl\ *adjective* (circa 1842)
: relating to writings of former times
— **pa·leo·graph·i·cal·ly** \-fi-k(ə-)lē\ *adverb*
pa·le·og·ra·phy \ˌpā-lē-ˈä-grə-fē, *especially British* ˌpa-\ *noun* [New Latin *palaeographia*, from Greek *palai-* pale- + *-graphia* -graphy] (circa 1818)
1 : the study of ancient writings and inscriptions

2 a : an ancient manner of writing **b :** ancient writings
— **pa·le·og·ra·pher** \-fər\ *noun*
Pa·leo-In·di·an \ˌpā-lē-ō-ˈin-dē-ən, *especially British* ˌpa-\ *noun* (1940)
: one of the early American hunting people of Asian origin extant in the late Pleistocene
— **Paleo–Indian** *adjective*
Pa·leo·lith·ic \ˌpā-lē-ə-ˈli-thik, *especially British* ˌpa-\ *adjective* [International Scientific Vocabulary] (1865)
: of or relating to the earliest period of the Stone Age characterized by rough or chipped stone implements
pa·leo·mag·ne·tism \ˌpā-lē-ō-ˈmag-nə-ˌti-zəm, *especially British* ˌpa-\ *noun* (1854)
1 : the intensity and direction of residual magnetization in ancient rocks
2 : a science that deals with paleomagnetism
— **pa·leo·mag·net·ic** \-mag-ˈne-tik\ *adjective*
— **pa·leo·mag·net·i·cal·ly** \-ti-k(ə-)lē\ *adverb*
— **pa·leo·mag·ne·tist** \-ˈmag-nə-tist\ *noun*
pa·le·on·tol·o·gy \ˌpā-lē-ˌän-ˈtä-lə-jē, -ən-, *especially British* ˌpa-\ *noun* [French *paléontologie*, from *palé-* pale- + Greek *onta* existing things (from neuter plural of *ont-, ōn*, present participle of *einai* to be) + French *-logie* -logy — more at IS] (1838)
: a science dealing with the life of past geological periods as known from fossil remains
— **pa·le·on·to·log·i·cal** \-ˌän-tᵊl-ˈä-ji-kəl\ *or* **pa·le·on·to·log·ic** \-jik\ *adjective*
— **pa·le·on·tol·o·gist** \-ˌän-ˈtä-lə-jist, -ən-\ *noun*
pa·leo·pa·thol·o·gy \ˌpā-lē-ō-pə-ˈthä-lə-jē, -pa-ˈthä-, *especially British* ˌpa-lē-\ *noun* (1893)
: a branch of pathology concerned with diseases of former times as evidenced especially in fossil or other remains
— **pa·leo·patho·log·i·cal** \-ˌpa-thə-ˈlä-ji-kəl\ *adjective*
— **pa·leo·pa·thol·o·gist** \-pə-ˈthä-lə-jist, -pa-\ *noun*
Pa·leo·zo·ic \ˌpā-lē-ə-ˈzō-ik, *especially British* ˌpa-\ *adjective* (1838)
: of, relating to, originating in, or being an era of geological history that extends from the beginning of the Cambrian to the close of the Permian and is marked by the culmination of nearly all classes of invertebrates except the insects and in the later epochs by the appearance of terrestrial plants, amphibians, and reptiles; *also* **:** relating to the corresponding system of rocks — see GEOLOGIC TIME table
— **Paleozoic** *noun*
pa·leo·zo·ol·o·gy \-zō-ˈä-lə-jē, -zə-ˈwä-\ *noun* [International Scientific Vocabulary] (1857)
: a branch of paleontology dealing with ancient and fossil animals
— **pa·leo·zoo·log·i·cal** \-ˌzō-ə-ˈlä-ji-kəl\ *adjective*
— **pa·leo·zo·ol·o·gist** \-jist\ *noun*
pal·et \ˈpā-lət, ˈpā-lət\ *noun* [*pale* palea + ¹*-et*] (circa 1880)
: PALEA
pal·ette \ˈpa-lət\ *noun* [French, from Middle French, diminutive of *pale* spade, from Latin *pala*; probably akin to Latin *pangere* to fix — more at PACT] (1622)
1 : a thin oval or rectangular board or tablet that a painter holds and mixes pigments on
2 a : the set of colors put on the palette (**b** 1)
: a particular range, quality, or use of color (2)
: a comparable range, quality, or use of available elements especially in another art (as music)
palette knife *noun* (1759)
: a knife with usually a flexible steel blade and no cutting edge used to mix colors or to apply colors (as to a painting)

pal·frey \'pȯl-frē\ *noun, plural* **palfreys** [Middle English, from Old French *palefrei*, from Medieval Latin *palafredus*, from Late Latin *paraveredus* post-horse for secondary roads, from Greek *para-* beside, subsidiary + Late Latin *veredus* post-horse, from a Gaulish word akin to Welsh *gorwydd* horse; akin to Old Irish *réidid* he rides — more at PARA-, RIDE] (13th century)
archaic : a saddle horse other than a warhorse; *especially* : a lady's light easy-gaited horse

Pa·li \'pä-lē\ *noun* [Sanskrit *pāli* row, series of Buddhist sacred texts] (1800)
: an Indo-Aryan language used as the liturgical and scholarly language of Theravada Buddhism — see INDO-EUROPEAN LANGUAGES table

pal·i·mo·ny \'pa-lə-ˌmō-nē\ *noun* [blend of *pal* and *alimony*] (1979)
: a court-ordered allowance paid by one member of a couple formerly living together out of wedlock to the other

pa·limp·sest \'pa-ləm(p)-ˌsest, pə-'lim(p)-\ *noun* [Latin *palimpsestus*, from Greek *palimpsēstos* scraped again, from *palin* + *psēn* to rub, scrape; akin to Sanskrit *psāti*, *babhasti* he chews] (1825)
1 : writing material (as a parchment or tablet) used one or more times after earlier writing has been erased
2 : something having usually diverse layers or aspects apparent beneath the surface

pal·in·drome \'pa-lən-ˌdrōm\ *noun* [Greek *palindromos* running back again, from *palin* back, again + *dramein* to run; akin to Greek *polos* axis, pole — more at POLE, DROMEDARY] (circa 1629)
: a word, verse, or sentence (as "Able was I ere I saw Elba") or a number (as 1881) that reads the same backward or forward
— **pal·in·drom·ic** \ˌpa-lən-'drō-mik, -'drä-\ *adjective*
— **pal·in·drom·ist** \'pa-lən-ˌdrō-mist\ *noun*

pal·ing \'pā-liŋ\ *noun* (15th century)
1 : a fence of pales or pickets
2 : wood for making pales
3 : a pale or picket for a fence

pal·in·gen·e·sis \ˌpa-lən-'je-nə-səs\ *noun* [New Latin, from Greek *palin* again + Latin *genesis* genesis] (1818)
: METEMPSYCHOSIS

pal·in·ge·net·ic \-jə-'ne-tik\ *adjective* (1833)
: of or relating to palingenesis

pal·in·ode \'pa-lə-ˌnōd\ *noun* [Greek *palinōidia*, from *palin* + *aeidein* to sing — more at ODE] (1599)
1 : an ode or song recanting or retracting something in an earlier poem
2 : a formal retraction

¹pal·i·sade \ˌpa-lə-'sād\ *noun* [French *palissade*, ultimately from Latin *palus* stake — more at POLE] (1600)
1 a : a fence of stakes especially for defense **b** : a long strong stake pointed at the top and set close with others as a defense
2 : a line of bold cliffs

²palisade *transitive verb* **-sad·ed; -sad·ing** (1632)
: to fortify with palisades

palisade cell *noun* (1875)
: a cell of the palisade layer

palisade layer *noun* (1914)
: a layer of columnar cells rich in chloroplasts found beneath the upper epidermis of foliage leaves — called also *palisade mesophyll*, *palisade parenchyma*, *palisade tissue*; compare SPONGY PARENCHYMA

¹pall \'pȯl\ *verb* [Middle English, short for *appallen* to become pale — more at APPALL] (14th century)
intransitive verb
1 : to lose strength or effectiveness
2 : to lose in interest or attraction ⟨his humor began to *pall* on us⟩
3 : to become tired of something
transitive verb

1 : to cause to become insipid
2 : to deprive of pleasure in something by satiating
synonym see SATIATE

²pall *noun* [Middle English, cloak, mantle, from Old English *pæll*, from Latin *pallium*] (14th century)
1 : PALLIUM 1a
2 a : a square of linen usually stiffened with cardboard that is used to cover the chalice **b** (1) : a heavy cloth draped over a coffin (2) : a coffin especially when holding a body
3 : something that covers or conceals; *especially* : an overspreading element that produces an effect of gloom ⟨a *pall* of thick black smoke⟩

³pall *transitive verb* (15th century)
: to cover with a pall : DRAPE

Pal·la·di·an \pə-'lā-dē-ən, -'lä-\ *adjective* (1731)
: of or relating to a revived classical style in architecture based on the works of Andrea Palladio
— **Pal·la·di·an·ism** \-ə-ˌni-zəm\ *noun*

¹pal·la·di·um \pə-'lā-dē-əm\ *noun* [Middle English, from Latin, from Greek *palladion*, from *Pallad-, Pallas*]
1 *capitalized* : a statue of Pallas whose preservation was believed to ensure the safety of Troy
2 *plural* **pal·la·dia** \-dē-ə\ : SAFEGUARD

²palladium *noun* [New Latin, from *Pallad-, Pallas*, an asteroid] (1803)
: a silver-white ductile malleable metallic element of the platinum group that is used especially in electrical contacts, as a catalyst, and in alloys — see ELEMENT table
— **pal·la·dous** \pə-'lā-dəs\ *adjective*

Pal·las \'pa-ləs\ *noun* [Latin *Pallad-, Pallas*, from Greek]
: ATHENA

pall·bear·er \'pȯl-ˌbar-ər, -ˌber-\ *noun* [²pall] (1707)
: a person who helps to carry the coffin at a funeral; *also* : a member of the escort or honor guard of the coffin who does not actually help to carry it

¹pal·let \'pa-lət\ *noun* [Middle English *pailet*, from (assumed) Middle French *paillet*, from *paille* straw, from Latin *palea* chaff, straw; akin to Sanskrit *palāva* chaff] (14th century)
1 : a straw-filled tick or mattress
2 : a small, hard, or temporary bed

²pallet *noun* [Middle English *palette*, literally, small shovel, from Middle French — more at PALETTE] (1558)
1 : a wooden flat-bladed instrument
2 : a lever or surface in a timepiece that receives an impulse from the escapement wheel and imparts motion to a balance or pendulum
3 : a portable platform for handling, storing, or moving materials and packages (as in warehouses, factories, or vehicles)

pal·let·ise *British variant of* PALLETIZE

pal·let·ize \'pa-lə-ˌtīz\ *transitive verb* **-ized; -iz·ing** (1944)
: to place on, transport, or store by means of pallets
— **pal·let·i·za·tion** \ˌpa-lə-tə-'zā-shən\ *noun*
— **pal·let·iz·er** \'pa-lə-ˌtī-zər\ *noun*

pal·lette \pa-'let\ *noun* [alteration of *palette*] (1834)
: one of the plates at the armpits of a suit of armor — see ARMOR illustration

pal·li·al \'pa-lē-əl\ *adjective* [New Latin *pallium*] (1836)
1 : of, relating to, or produced by a mantle of a mollusk
2 : of or relating to the cerebral cortex

pal·liasse \pal-'yas\ *noun* [modification of French *paillasse*, from *paille* straw] (1763)
: a thin straw mattress used as a pallet

pal·li·ate \'pa-lē-ˌāt\ *transitive verb* **-at·ed; -at·ing** [Middle English, from Late Latin *pal-*

liatus, past participle of *palliare* to cloak, conceal, from Latin *pallium* cloak] (15th century)
1 : to reduce the violence of (a disease) : ABATE
2 : to cover by excuses and apologies
3 : to moderate the intensity of ⟨trying to *palliate* the boredom⟩
— **pal·li·a·tion** \ˌpa-lē-'ā-shən\ *noun*
— **pal·li·a·tor** \'pa-lē-ˌā-tər\ *noun*

¹pal·li·a·tive \'pa-lē-ˌā-tiv, 'pal-yə-\ *adjective* (15th century)
: serving to palliate ⟨*palliative* surgery⟩
— **pal·lia·tive·ly** *adverb*

²palliative *noun* (1724)
: something that palliates

pal·lid \'pa-ləd\ *adjective* [Latin *pallidus* — more at PALE] (1590)
1 : deficient in color : WAN ⟨a *pallid* countenance⟩
2 : lacking sparkle or liveliness : DULL ⟨a *pallid* entertainment⟩
— **pal·lid·ly** *adverb*
— **pal·lid·ness** *noun*

pal·li·um \'pa-lē-əm\ *noun, plural* **-lia** \-lē-ə\ *or* **-li·ums** [Middle English, from Latin] (12th century)
1 a : a white woolen band with pendants in front and back worn over the chasuble by a pope or archbishop as a symbol of full episcopal authority **b** : a draped rectangular cloth worn as a cloak by men of ancient Greece and Rome
2 [New Latin, from Latin, cloak] **a** : CEREBRAL CORTEX **b** : the mantle of a mollusk, brachiopod, or bird

pall-mall \ˌpel-'mel, ˌpal-'mal, US often ˌpȯl-'mȯl\ *noun* [Middle French *pallemaille*, from Italian *pallamaglio*, from *palla* ball (of Germanic origin; akin to Old High German *balla* ball) + *maglio* mallet, from Latin *malleus* — more at BALL, MAUL] (1598)
: a 17th century game in which each player attempts to drive a wooden ball with a mallet down an alley and through a raised ring in as few strokes as possible; *also* : the alley in which it is played

pal·lor \'pa-lər\ *noun* [Middle English, from Latin, from *pallēre* to be pale — more at FALLOW] (15th century)
: deficiency of color especially of the face : PALENESS

pal·ly \'pa-lē\ *adjective* (1895)
: sharing the relationship of pals : INTIMATE

¹palm \'päm, 'pälm, 'pȯm, 'pȯlm, New England also 'päm\ *noun* [Middle English, from Old English, from Latin *palma* palm of the hand, palm tree; from the resemblance of the tree's leaves to the outstretched hand; akin to Greek *palamē* palm of the hand, Old English *folm*, Old Irish *lám* hand] (before 12th century)
1 : any of a family (Palmae, the palm family) of mostly tropical or subtropical monocotyledonous trees, shrubs, or vines with usually a simple stem and a terminal crown of large pinnate or fan-shaped leaves
2 : a leaf of the palm as a symbol of victory or rejoicing; *also* : a branch (as of laurel) similarly used
3 : a symbol of triumph; *also* : VICTORY, TRIUMPH
4 : an addition to a military decoration in the form of a palm frond especially to indicate a second award of the basic decoration
— **palm·like** \-ˌlīk\ *adjective*

²palm *noun* [Middle English *paume*, from Middle French, from Latin *palma*] (14th century)
1 : the somewhat concave part of the human hand between the bases of the fingers and the

\ə\ abut \ᵊ\ kitten \ər\ further \a\ ash \ā\ ace
\ä\ mop, mar \au̇\ out \ch\ chin \e\ bet \ē\ easy
\g\ go \i\ hit \ī\ ice \j\ job \ŋ\ sing \ō\ go
\ȯ\ law \ȯi\ boy \th\ thin \th\ the \ü\ loot \u̇\ foot
\y\ yet \zh\ vision *see also* Guide to Pronunciation

wrist or the corresponding part of the forefoot of a lower mammal
2 : a flat expanded part especially at the end of a base or stalk (as of an anchor)
3 [Latin *palmus*, from *palma*] : a unit of length based on the breadth or length of the hand
4 : something (as a part of a glove) that covers the palm of the hand
5 : an act of palming (as of cards)
³**palm** *transitive verb* (1673)
1 a : to conceal in or with the hand ⟨*palm* a card⟩ **b** : to pick up stealthily
2 : to impose by fraud ⟨a second imposter to be *palmed* upon you —Sir Walter Scott⟩
3 : to touch with the palm: as **a** : to stroke with the palm or hand **b** : to shake hands with **c** : to allow (in a basketball) to come to rest momentarily in the hand while dribbling thus committing a violation
pal·mar \'pal-mər, 'pä-, 'päl-, 'pȯ-, 'pȯl-\ *adjective* (1656)
: of, relating to, or involving the palm of the hand
pal·ma·ry \'pal-mə-rē, 'pä-, 'päl-, 'pȯ-, 'pȯl-\ *adjective* [Latin *palmarius* deserving the palm, from *palma*] (1657)
: OUTSTANDING, BEST
pal·mate \'pal-ˌmāt, 'pä-, 'päl-, 'pȯ-, 'pȯl-\ *also* **pal·mat·ed** \-ˌmā-təd\ *adjective* (circa 1760)
: resembling a hand with the fingers spread: as **a** : having lobes radiating from a common point ⟨a *palmate* leaf⟩ — see LEAF illustration **b** : having the distal portion broad, flat, and lobed ⟨a *palmate* antler⟩
— **pal·mate·ly** *adverb*
— **pal·ma·tion** \-'mā-shən, pä-, 'päl-, 'pȯ-, 'pȯl-\ *noun*
palmed \'pämd, 'pälmd, 'pȯmd, 'pȯlmd, *New England also* 'pȧmd\ *adjective* (15th century)
: having a palm of a specified kind — used in combination ⟨leather-*palmed* gloves⟩
palm·er \'pä-mər, 'päl-, 'pȯ-, 'pȯl-\ *noun* (13th century)
: a person wearing two crossed palm leaves as a sign of a pilgrimage made to the Holy Land
palm·er·worm \-ˌwərm\ *noun* (1560)
: a caterpillar that suddenly appears in great numbers devouring herbage
pal·mette \ˌpal-'met\ *noun* [French, from *palme* palm, from Latin *palma*] (1850)
: a decorative motif suggestive of a palm
pal·met·to \pal-'me-(ˌ)tō *also* pä-, päl-, pȯ-, pȯl-\ *noun, plural* **-tos** *or* **-toes** [modification of Spanish *palmito*, from *palma* palm, from Latin] (circa 1746)
1 : any of several usually low-growing fan-leaved palms; *especially* : CABBAGE PALMETTO
2 : strips of the leaf blade of a palmetto used in weaving
palm·ist \'pä-mist, 'päl-, 'pȯ-, 'pȯl-\ *noun* [probably back-formation from *palmistry*] (1886)
: one who practices palmistry
palm·ist·ry \'pä-mə-strē, 'päl-, 'pȯ-, 'pȯl-\ *noun* [Middle English *pawmestry*, probably from *paume* palm + *maistrie* mastery] (15th century)
: the art or practice of reading a person's character or future from the lines on the palms
pal·mi·tate \'pal-mə-ˌtāt, pä-, 'päl-, 'pȯ-, 'pȯl-\ *noun* (1873)
: a salt or ester of palmitic acid
pal·mit·ic acid \(ˌ)pal-'mi-tik-, (ˌ)pä-, (ˌ)päl-, (ˌ)pȯ-, (ˌ)pȯl-\ *noun* [International Scientific Vocabulary, from *palmitin*] (1857)
: a waxy crystalline saturated fatty acid $C_{16}H_{32}O_2$ occurring free or in the form of es-

ters (as glycerides) in most fats and fatty oils and in several essential oils and waxes
pal·mi·tin \'pal-mə-tən, 'pä-, 'päl-, 'pȯ-, 'pȯl-\ *noun* [French *palmitine*, probably from *palmite* pith of the palm tree, from Spanish *palmito*] (1857)
: an ester of glycerol and palmitic acid; *especially* : a solid ester found in animal fats
palm off *transitive verb* (1822)
1 : to dispose of usually by trickery or guile
2 : PASS OFF 2
palm oil *noun* (1705)
: an edible fat obtained from the flesh of the fruit of several palms and used especially in soap and lubricating greases
Palm Sunday *noun* [from the palm branches strewn in Christ's way] (before 12th century)
: the Sunday before Easter celebrated in commemoration of Christ's triumphal entry into Jerusalem
palmy \'pä-mē, 'päl-, 'pȯ-, 'pȯl- *New England also* 'pȧ-mē\ *adjective* **palm·i·er; -est** (1602)
1 : marked by prosperity : FLOURISHING
2 : abounding in or bearing palms
pal·my·ra \pal-'mī-rə\ *noun* [Portuguese *palmeira*, from *palma* palm, from Latin] (1698)
: a tall fan-leaved palm (*Borassus flabellifer*) of India cultivated for its hard resistant wood, fiber, and sugar-rich sap — called also *palmyra palm*
pal·o·mi·no \ˌpa-lə-'mē-(ˌ)nō\ *noun, plural* **-nos** [American Spanish, from Spanish, like a dove, from Latin *palumbinus*, from *palumbes* ringdove; akin to Greek *peleia* dove, Latin *pallēre* to be pale — more at FALLOW] (1914)
: a horse that is pale cream to gold in color and has a flaxen or white mane and tail
pa·loo·ka \pə-'lü-kə\ *noun* [origin unknown] (1925)
1 : an inexperienced or incompetent boxer
2 : OAF, LOUT
pal·o·ver·de \ˌpa-lō-'ver-(ˌ)dā, ˌpä-, -'vər-\ *noun* [Mexican Spanish, literally, green tree] (1854)
1 : any of several small spiny leguminous trees or shrubs (genus *Cercidium*) that have greenish branches and are found chiefly in dry regions of the southwestern U.S. and Mexico
2 : JERUSALEM THORN
palp \'palp\ *noun* [New Latin *palpus*] (1842)
: PALPUS
pal·pa·ble \'pal-pə-bəl\ *adjective* [Middle English, from Late Latin *palpabilis*, from Latin *palpare* to stroke, caress — more at FEEL] (14th century)
1 : capable of being touched or felt : TANGIBLE
2 : easily perceptible : NOTICEABLE
3 : easily perceptible by the mind : MANIFEST
synonym see PERCEPTIBLE
— **pal·pa·bil·i·ty** \ˌpal-pə-'bi-lə-tē\ *noun*
— **pal·pa·bly** \'pal-pə-blē\ *adverb*
pal·pate \'pal-ˌpāt\ *transitive verb* **pal·pat·ed; pal·pat·ing** [probably back-formation from *palpation*, from Latin *palpation-, palpatio*, from *palpare*] (circa 1852)
: to examine by touch especially medically
— **pal·pa·tion** \pal-'pā-shən\ *noun*
pal·pe·bral \pal-'pē-brəl\ *adjective* [Late Latin *palpebralis*, from Latin *palpebra* eyelid; akin to Latin *palpare*] (1840)
: of, relating to, or located on or near the eyelids
pal·pi·tant \'pal-pə-tənt\ *adjective* (1837)
: marked by trembling or throbbing
pal·pi·tate \'pal-pə-ˌtāt\ *intransitive verb* **-tat·ed; -tat·ing** [Latin *palpitatus*, past participle of *palpitare*, frequentative of *palpare* to stroke] (circa 1623)
: to beat rapidly and strongly : THROB
— **pal·pi·ta·tion** \ˌpal-pə-'tā-shən\ *noun*
pal·pus \'pal-pəs\ *noun, plural* **pal·pi** \-ˌpī, -(ˌ)pē\ [New Latin, from Latin, caress, soft palm of the hand, from *palpare*] (1813)

: a segmented usually tactile or gustatory process on an arthropod mouthpart — see INSECT illustration
pals·grave \'pȯlz-ˌgrāv\ *noun* [Dutch *paltsgrave*] (1539)
: COUNT PALATINE 1a
pal·sied \'pȯl-zēd\ *adjective* (1550)
: affected with or as if with palsy
¹**pal·sy** \'pȯl-zē\ *noun, plural* **palsies** [Middle English *parlesie*, from Middle French *paralisie*, from Latin *paralysis*] (14th century)
1 : PARALYSIS
2 : a condition marked by uncontrollable tremor of the body or a part
²**palsy** *transitive verb* **pal·sied; pal·sy·ing** (1615)
: to affect with or as if with palsy
³**palsy** \'pal-zē\ *adjective* (1951)
: PALSY-WALSY
palsy–walsy \ˌpal-zē-'wal-zē\ *adjective* [reduplication of *palsy*] (1943)
slang : being or appearing to be very intimate
pal·ter \'pȯl-tər\ *intransitive verb* **pal·tered; pal·ter·ing** \-t(ə-)riŋ\ [origin unknown] (1601)
1 : to act insincerely or deceitfully : EQUIVOCATE
2 : HAGGLE, CHAFFER
synonym see LIE
— **pal·ter·er** \-tər-ər\ *noun*
pal·try \'pȯl-trē\ *adjective* **pal·tri·er; -est** [obsolete *paltry* trash, from dialect *palt, pelt* piece of coarse cloth, trash; akin to Middle Low German *palte* rag] (1570)
1 : INFERIOR, TRASHY
2 : MEAN, DESPICABLE
3 : TRIVIAL
4 : MEAGER, MEASLY ⟨made a *paltry* donation⟩
— **pal·tri·ness** *noun*
pa·lu·dal \pə-'lü-dᵊl, 'pal-yə-dᵊl\ *adjective* [Latin *palud-, palus* marsh; akin to Sanskrit *palvala* pond] (circa 1820)
: of or relating to marshes or fens : MARSHY
paly \'pā-lē\ *adjective* (1560)
archaic : somewhat pale : PALLID
pal·y·nol·o·gy \ˌpa-lə-'nä-lə-jē\ *noun* [Greek *palynein* to sprinkle, from *palē* fine meal] (1944)
: a branch of science dealing with pollen and spores
— **pal·y·no·log·i·cal** \-nə-'lä-ji-kəl\ *also* **pal·y·no·log·ic** \-jik\ *adjective*
— **pal·y·no·log·i·cal·ly** \-ji-k(ə-)lē\ *adverb*
— **pal·y·nol·o·gist** \-'nä-lə-jist\ *noun*
pam·pa \'pam-pə, 'päm-\ *noun, plural* **pam·pas** \-pəz, -pəs\ [American Spanish, from Quechua] (1704)
: an extensive generally grass-covered plain of temperate South America east of the Andes : PRAIRIE
pam·pas grass \-pəz-, -pəs-\ *noun* (circa 1851)
: a South American grass (*Cortaderia selloana*) often grown for ornament that has showy white panicles borne on tall stems
pam·pe·an \'pam-pē-ən, 'päm-, pam-', päm-'\ *adjective* (1839)
: of or relating to the pampas of South America or their Indian inhabitants
pam·per \'pam-pər\ *transitive verb* **pam·pered; pam·per·ing** \-p(ə-)riŋ\ [Middle English, probably of Dutch origin; akin to Flemish *pamperen* to pamper] (14th century)
1 *archaic* : to cram with rich food : GLUT
2 a : to treat with extreme or excessive care and attention ⟨*pampered* their guests⟩ **b** : GRATIFY, HUMOR ⟨enabled him to *pamper* his wanderlust —*New Yorker*⟩
synonym see INDULGE
— **pam·per·er** \-pər-ər\ *noun*
pam·pe·ro \pam-'per-(ˌ)ō, päm-\ *noun, plural* **-ros** [American Spanish, from *pampa*] (1818)
: a strong cold wind from the west or southwest that sweeps over the pampas

palmetto 1

pam·phlet \'pam(p)-flət\ *noun* [Middle English *pamflet* unbound booklet, from *Pamphilus seu De Amore* Pamphilus or On Love, popular Latin love poem of the 12th century] (14th century)
: an unbound printed publication with no cover or with a paper cover ◆
¹pam·phle·teer \,pam(p)-flə-'tir\ *noun* (1642)
: a writer of pamphlets attacking something or urging a cause
²pamphleteer *intransitive verb* (1698)
1 : to write and publish pamphlets
2 : to engage in partisan arguments indirectly in writings
¹pan \'pan\ *noun* [Middle English *panne*, from Old English (akin to Old High German *phanna* pan), from Latin *patina*, from Greek *patanē*] (before 12th century)
1 a : a usually broad, shallow, and open container for domestic use (as for warming, baking, or frying) **b** : any of various similar usually metal receptacles: as (1) : the hollow part of the lock in a firelock or flintlock gun that receives the priming (2) : either of the receptacles in a pair of scales (3) : a round shallow metal container for separating metal (as gold) from waste by washing
2 a (1) : a natural basin or depression in land (2) : a similar artificial basin (as for evaporating brine) **b** : a drifting fragment of the flat thin ice that forms in bays or along the shore
3 : HARDPAN 1
4 *slang* : FACE
5 : a harsh criticism
²pan *verb* **panned; pan·ning** (1839)
transitive verb
1 a : to wash in a pan for the purpose of separating heavy particles **b** : to separate (as gold) by panning **c** : to place in a pan
2 : to criticize severely ⟨the show was *panned*⟩
intransitive verb
1 : to wash material (as earth or gravel) in a pan in search of metal (as gold)
2 : to yield precious metal in the process of panning — usually used with *out*
³pan \'pän\ *noun* [Hindi *pān*, from Sanskrit *parṇa* wing, leaf — more at FERN] (1616)
1 : a betel leaf
2 : a masticatory of betel nut, mineral lime, and pan
⁴pan \'pan\ *noun* [short for *panorama*] (circa 1922)
1 : the process of panning a motion-picture or video camera
2 : a shot in which the camera is panned
⁵pan \'pan\ *verb* **panned; pan·ning** (1930)
transitive verb
: to rotate (as a motion-picture camera) so as to keep an object in the picture or secure a panoramic effect
intransitive verb
1 : to pan a motion-picture or video camera
2 *of a camera* : to undergo panning
Pan \'pan\ *noun* [Latin, from Greek]
: a Greek god of pastures, flocks, and shepherds usually represented as having the legs, horns, and ears of a goat
pan- *combining form* [Greek, from *pan*, neuter of *pant-*, *pas* all, every; akin to Tocharian B *pont-* all]
1 : all : completely ⟨*panchromatic*⟩
2 a : involving all of a (specified) group ⟨*Pan-American*⟩ **b** : advocating or involving the union of a (specified) group ⟨*Pan-Slavism*⟩
3 : whole : general ⟨*panleukopenia*⟩
pan·a·cea \,pa-nə-'sē-ə\ *noun* [Latin, from Greek *panakeia*, from *panakēs* all-healing, from *pan-* + *akos* remedy] (1548)
: a remedy for all ills or difficulties : CURE-ALL
— **pan·a·ce·an** \-'sē-ən\ *adjective*
pa·nache \pə-'nash, -'näsh\ *noun* [Middle French *pennache*, from Old Italian *pennacchio*, from Late Latin *pinnaculum* small wing — more at PINNACLE] (1553)

1 : an ornamental tuft (as of feathers) especially on a helmet
2 : dash or flamboyance in style and action : VERVE ◆
pa·na·da \pə-'nä-də\ *noun* [Spanish, from *pan* bread, from Latin *panis* — more at FOOD] (circa 1598)
: a paste of flour or bread crumbs and water or stock used as a base for sauce or a binder for forcemeat or stuffing
pan·a·ma \'pa-nə-,mä, -,mȯ\ *noun, often capitalized* [American Spanish *panamá*, from Panama, Central America] (1848)
: a lightweight hat of natural-colored straw hand-plaited of narrow strips from the young leaves of the jipijapa; *also* : a machine-made imitation of this
Panama Red *noun* (1967)
: marijuana of a reddish tint that is of Panamanian origin and is held to be very potent
Pan–Amer·i·can \,pa-nə-'mer-ə-kən\ *adjective* (1889)
: of, relating to, or involving the independent republics of North and South America
Pan–Amer·i·can·ism \-kə-,ni-zəm\ *noun* (1901)
: a movement for greater cooperation among the Pan-American nations
pan·a·tela \,pa-nə-'te-lə\ *noun* [American Spanish, from *panatela* a long thin biscuit, ultimately from Latin *panis* bread] (1847)
: a long slender straight-sided cigar
¹pan·cake \'pan-,kāk\ *noun* (14th century)
: a flat cake of thin batter and cooked (as on a griddle) on both sides
²pancake *verb* **pan·caked; pan·cak·ing** (1911)
intransitive verb
: to make a pancake landing
transitive verb
: to cause to pancake
Pan–Cake \'pan-,kāk\ *trademark*
— used for a cosmetic in semimoist cake form
pancake landing *noun* (1928)
: a landing in which the airplane is stalled usually unintentionally above the landing surface causing it to drop abruptly in an approximately horizontal position with little forward motion
pan·cet·ta \(,)pan-'che-tə\ *noun* [Italian, from diminutive of *pancia* belly, paunch, from Latin *pantic-*, *pantex*] (1974)
: unsmoked bacon used especially in Italian cuisine
pan·chax \'pan-,kaks\ *noun* [New Latin] (1961)
: any of various small brilliantly colored Old World killifishes (genus *Aplocheilus*) often kept in the tropical aquarium
Pan·chen Lama \'pän-chən-\ *noun* [*Panchen* from Chinese (Beijing) *bānchán*] (1794)
: the lama who is the chief spiritual adviser of the Dalai Lama
pan·chro·mat·ic \,pan-krō-'ma-tik\ *adjective* [International Scientific Vocabulary] (1903)
: sensitive to light of all colors in the visible spectrum ⟨*panchromatic* film⟩
pan·cra·ti·um \pan-'krā-shē-əm\ *noun* [Latin, from Greek *pankration*, from *pan-* + *kratos* strength — more at HARD] (1603)
: an ancient Greek athletic contest involving both boxing and wrestling
pan·cre·as \'pan-krē-əs, 'pan-\ *noun* [New Latin, from Greek *pankreas* sweetbread, from *pan-* + *kreas* flesh, meat — more at RAW] (1578)
: a large lobulated gland of vertebrates that secretes digestive enzymes and the hormones insulin and glucagon
— **pan·cre·at·ic** \,pan-krē-'a-tik, ,pan-\ *adjective*
pancreat- *combining form* [New Latin, from Greek *pankreat-*, *pancreas*]
: pancreas ⟨*pancreatic*⟩

pan·cre·a·tec·to·my \,pan-krē-ə-'tek-tə-mē, ,pan-\ *noun* (circa 1900)
: surgical removal of all or part of the pancreas
— **pan·cre·a·tec·to·mized** \-,mīzd\ *adjective*
pancreatic duct *noun* (circa 1860)
: a duct leading from the pancreas and opening into the duodenum
pancreatic juice *noun* (circa 1666)
: a clear alkaline secretion of pancreatic enzymes (as trypsin and lipase) that flows into the duodenum and acts on food already acted on by the gastric juice and saliva
pan·cre·a·tin \'pan-krē-ə-tən; 'paŋ-krē-, 'pan-\ *noun* (circa 1860)
: a mixture of enzymes from the pancreatic juice; *also* : a preparation containing such a mixture
pan·cre·a·ti·tis \,paŋ-krē-ə-'tī-təs, ,pan-\ *noun, plural* **-tit·i·des** \-'ti-tə-,dēz\ [New Latin] (circa 1842)
: inflammation of the pancreas
pan·cre·o·zy·min \-krē-ō-'zī-mən\ *noun* [*pancreas* + *-o-* + *zym-* + *¹-in*] (1943)
: CHOLECYSTOKININ
pan·cy·to·pe·nia \,pan-,sī-tə-'pē-nē-ə\ *noun* [New Latin, from *pan-* + *cyt-* + *-penia*] (circa 1941)

◆ WORD HISTORY

pamphlet *Pamphilus, seu De Amore* ("Pamphilus, or About Love"), written in the late 12th century by an author now unknown, was a Latin poem describing a series of amusing amorous adventures. In its day *Pamphilus* enjoyed widespread popularity among those literate in Latin, especially university students. In the late Middle Ages, short compilations of popular classical authors were often given French diminutives based on the vernacular form of the author's name. Hence *Esopet* was a familiar title for the works of *Esope* (Aesop) and *Avionet* for Avianus (a Roman fabulist of around 400 A.D.). Similarly, *Pamphilus* became *Pamphilet* in Old French. Borrowed into Anglo-Latin as *panfletus* or *pamfletus* and into later Middle English as *pamfilet* or *pamflet*, the word denoted any short written work. In the 17th century *pamphlet* became associated particularly with polemics on controversial social, political, or religious issues, and it was borrowed back into French in the sense "diatribe."

panache *Pinnaculum*, a derivative of Latin *pinna* ("feather," "wing," or "battlement"), was a Late Latin word meaning "small wing" or "gable." The Italian outcome of *pinnaculum* was *pennachio*, which alluded to a plume of feathers decorating a warrior's helmet. This word was borrowed into 16th century French as *pennache* and later altered to *panache*. The figurative sense of French *panache* developed from the verve and swagger associated with anyone bold enough to wear such a distinctive mark as a colorful plume both in battle and among the ranks of polite society. This meaning of the French word apparently first appeared in English at the end of the 19th century in translations of Edmond Rostand's popular play *Cyrano de Bergerac*—Cyrano himself being the perfect example of panache. Another more straightforward development from Late Latin *pinnaculum* is English *pinnacle*.

: an abnormal reduction in the number of erythrocytes, white blood cells, and blood platelets in the blood; *also* : a disorder (as aplastic anemia) characterized by such a reduction

pan·da \'pan-də\ *noun* [French, perhaps from a language of the southeast Himalayas] (1835)
1 : a long-tailed largely herbivorous mammal (*Ailurus fulgens*) that is related to and resembles the American raccoon, has long rusty or chestnut fur, and is found from the Himalayas to China
2 : GIANT PANDA

A panda 1, B giant panda

panda car *noun* [from its black and white coloration] (1967)
British : a police patrol car
pan·da·nus \pan-'dā-nəs, -'da-\ *noun, plural* **-ni** \-nī\ [New Latin, genus name, from Malay *pandan* screw pine] (1830)
: SCREW PINE; *also* : a fiber made from screw-pine leaves and used for woven products (as mats)
Pan·da·rus \'pan-də-rəs\ *noun* [Latin, from Greek *Pandaros*]
: a Lycian archer in the Trojan War who in medieval legend procures Cressida for Troilus
pan·dect \'pan-ˌdekt\ *noun* [Late Latin *Pandectae*, the Pandects, digest of Roman civil law (6th century A.D.), from Latin, plural of *pandectes* encyclopedic work, from Greek *pandektēs* all-receiving, from *pan-* + *dechesthai* to receive; akin to Greek *dokein* to seem, seem good — more at DECENT] (1533)
1 : a complete code of the laws of a country or system of law
2 : a treatise covering an entire subject
¹pan·dem·ic \pan-'de-mik\ *adjective* [Late Latin *pandemus*, from Greek *pandēmos* of all the people, from *pan-* + *dēmos* people — more at DEMAGOGUE] (1666)
: occurring over a wide geographic area and affecting an exceptionally high proportion of the population ⟨*pandemic* malaria⟩
²pandemic *noun* (circa 1853)
: a pandemic outbreak of a disease
Pan·de·mo·ni·um \ˌpan-də-'mō-nē-əm\ *noun* [New Latin, from Greek *pan-* + *daimōn* evil spirit — more at DEMON]
1 : the capital of Hell in Milton's *Paradise Lost*
2 : the infernal regions : HELL
3 *not capitalized* : a wild uproar : TUMULT
¹pan·der \'pan-dər\ *noun* [Middle English *Pandare* Pandarus, from Latin *Pandarus*] (1530)
1 a : a go-between in love intrigues **b :** PIMP
2 : someone who caters to or exploits the weaknesses of others ◊
²pander *intransitive verb* **pan·dered; pan·der·ing** \-d(ə-)riŋ\ (1602)

: to act as a pander; *especially* : to provide gratification for others' desires ⟨films that *pander* to the basest emotions⟩
— pan·der·er \-dər-ər\ *noun*
pan·dit \'pan-dət, 'pən-\ *noun* [Hindi *paṇḍit*, from Sanskrit *paṇḍita*] (circa 1828)
: a wise or learned man in India — often used as an honorary title
pan·do·ra \pan-'dōr-ə, -'dȯr-\ *noun* [Italian, from Late Latin *pandura* 3-stringed lute, from Greek *pandoura*] (1597)
: BANDORE
Pan·do·ra's box \pan-'dōr-əz-, -'dȯr-\ *noun* [from the box, sent by the gods to Pandora, which she was forbidden to open and which loosed a swarm of evils upon mankind when she opened it out of curiosity] (1579)
: a prolific source of troubles
pan·dow·dy \pan-'daù-dē\ *noun, plural* **-dies** [origin unknown] (1805)
: a deep-dish spiced apple dessert sweetened with sugar, molasses, or maple syrup and covered with a rich crust
pan·dy \'pan-dē\ *transitive verb* **pan·died; pan·dy·ing** [probably from Latin *pande*, imperative singular of *pandere* to spread out (the hand); command of the schoolmaster to the boy — more at FATHOM] (1863)
British **:** to punish (a schoolboy) with a blow on the palm of the hand especially with a ferule
pane \'pān\ *noun* [Middle English *pan, pane* strip of cloth, pane, from Middle French *pan*, from Latin *pannus* cloth, rag — more at VANE] (14th century)
: a piece, section, or side of something: as **a :** a framed sheet of glass in a window or door **b :** one of the sections into which a sheet of postage stamps is cut for distribution
— paned \'pānd\ *adjective*
pan·e·gyr·ic \ˌpa-nə-'jir-ik, -'jī-rik\ *noun* [Latin *panegyricus*, from Greek *panēgyrikos*, from *panēgyrikos* of or for a festival assembly, from *panēgyris* festival assembly, from *pan-* + *agyris* assembly; akin to Greek *ageirein* to gather] (1603)
: a eulogistic oration or writing; *also* : formal or elaborate praise
synonym see ENCOMIUM
— pan·e·gyr·i·cal \-'jir-i-kəl, -'jī-ri-\ *adjective*
— pan·e·gyr·i·cal·ly \-k(ə-)lē\ *adverb*
pan·e·gy·rist \ˌpa-nə-'jir-ist, -'jī-rist\ *noun* (1605)
: EULOGIST
¹pan·el \'pa-nᵊl\ *noun* [Middle English, piece of cloth, slip of parchment, jury schedule, from Middle French, piece of cloth, piece, from (assumed) Vulgar Latin *pannellus*, diminutive of Latin *pannus*] (14th century)
1 a (1) **:** a schedule containing names of persons summoned as jurors (2) **:** the group of persons so summoned (3) **:** JURY 1 **b** (1) **:** a group of persons selected for some service (as investigation or arbitration) ⟨a *panel* of experts⟩ (2) **:** a group of persons who discuss before an audience a topic of public interest; *also* **:** PANEL DISCUSSION (3) **:** a group of entertainers or guests engaged as players in a quiz or guessing game on a radio or television program
2 : a separate or distinct part of a surface: as **a :** a fence section **:** HURDLE **b** (1) **:** a thin usually rectangular board set in a frame (as in a door) (2) **:** a usually sunken or raised section of a surface set off by a margin (3) **:** a flat usually rectangular piece of construction material (as plywood or precast masonry) made to form part of a surface **c :** a vertical section of fabric (as a gore) **d :** COMIC STRIP; *also* **:** a frame of a comic strip **e :** any of several units of construction of an airplane wing surface
3 : a thin flat piece of wood on which a picture is painted; *also* **:** a painting on such a surface

4 a : a section of a switchboard **b :** a flat often insulating support (as for computer hardware or parts of an electrical device) usually with control handles on one face **c :** a usually vertical mount for controls or dials (as of instruments of measurement)
²panel *transitive verb* **-eled** *or* **-elled; -el·ing** *or* **-el·ling** (15th century)
: to furnish or decorate with panels ⟨*paneled* the living room⟩
panel discussion *noun* (circa 1938)
: a formal discussion by a panel
pan·el·ing *also* **pan·el·ling** *noun* (1824)
: panels joined in a continuous surface; *especially* **:** decorative wood panels so joined
pan·el·ist \'pa-nᵊl-ist\ *noun* (1951)
: a member of a discussion or advisory panel or of a radio or television panel
panel truck *noun* (1937)
: a small motortruck with a fully enclosed body
pan·e·te·la *variant of* PANATELA
pan·et·to·ne \ˌpä-nə-'tō-nē, ˌpa-\ *noun* [Italian, from *panetto* small loaf, diminutive of *pane* bread, from Latin *panis* — more at FOOD] (1922)
: a usually yeast-leavened bread containing raisins and candied fruit
pan·fish \'pan-ˌfish\ *noun* (1805)
: a small food fish (as a sunfish) usually taken with hook and line and not available on the market
pan·fry \'pan-ˌfrī, pan-'frī\ *transitive verb* (circa 1929)
: to cook in a frying pan with a small amount of fat
pan·ful \'pan-ˌfùl\ *noun* (circa 1864)
: as much or as many as a pan will hold
¹pang \'paŋ\ *noun* [origin unknown] (15th century)
1 : a brief piercing spasm of pain
2 : a sharp attack of mental anguish ⟨*pangs* of remorse⟩ ⟨a *pang* of jealousy struck me —Graham Greene⟩
²pang *transitive verb* (1502)
: to cause to have pangs : TORMENT
pan·ga \'päŋ-gə\ *noun* [Swahili] (1925)
: MACHETE
pan·gen·e·sis \ˌpan-'je-nə-səs\ *noun* [New Latin] (1868)
: a disproven hypothetical mechanism of heredity in which the cells throw off particles that collect in the reproductive products or in buds so that the egg or bud contains particles from all parts of the parent
— pan·ge·net·ic \-jə-'ne-tik\ *adjective*
Pan·gloss·ian \pan-'glä-sē-ən, paŋ-, -'glȯ-\ *adjective* [*Pangloss*, optimistic tutor in Voltaire's *Candide* (1759)] (1831)

: marked by the view that all is for the best in this best of possible worlds : excessively optimistic

pan·go·la grass \pan-'gō-lə-, paṇ-\ *noun* [alteration of *Pongola grass,* from the *Pongola River,* South Africa] (1948)
: a rapid-growing perennial grass (*Digitaria decumbens*) of southern Africa that has been introduced into the southern U.S. as a pasture grass

pan·go·lin \'paṇ-gə-lən, 'pan-\ *noun* [Malay dialect *pĕngguling*] (1774)
: any of a family (Manidae) of Asian and African edentate mammals having the body covered with large imbricated horny scales

pangolin

¹pan·han·dle \'pan-ˌhan-dᵊl\ *noun* (1856)
: a narrow projection of a larger territory (as a state) ⟨the Texas *panhandle*⟩

²panhandle *verb* **pan·han·dled; pan·han·dling** \-ˌhan(d)-liṇ, -ˌhan-dᵊl-iṇ\ [back-formation from *panhandler,* probably from *panhandle,* noun; from the extended forearm] (1903)
intransitive verb
: to stop people on the street and ask for food or money : BEG
transitive verb
1 : to accost on the street and beg from
2 : to get by panhandling
— **pan·han·dler** \-ˌhan(d)-lər, -ˌhan-dᵊl-ər\ *noun*

Pan·hel·len·ic \ˌpan-hə-'le-nik\ *adjective* (1847)
1 : of or relating to all Greece or all the Greeks
2 : of or relating to the Greek-letter sororities or fraternities in American colleges and universities or to an association representing them

pan·hu·man \ˌpan-'hyü-mən, -'yü-\ *adjective* (circa 1909)
: of or relating to all humanity ⟨the *panhuman* problem of evil —R. K. Merton⟩

¹pan·ic \'pa-nik\ *adjective* [French *panique,* from Greek *panikos,* literally, of Pan, from *Pan*] (1603)
1 : of, relating to, or resembling the mental or emotional state believed induced by the god Pan ⟨*panic* fear⟩
2 : of, relating to, or arising from a panic ⟨a wave of *panic* buying⟩
3 : of or relating to the god Pan

²panic *noun* (1708)
1 : a sudden overpowering fright; *especially* : a sudden unreasoning terror often accompanied by mass flight
2 : a sudden widespread fright concerning financial affairs that results in a depression of values caused by extreme measures for protection of property (as securities)
3 *slang* : one that is very funny ◇
synonym see FEAR
— **pan·icky** \'pa-ni-kē\ *adjective*

³panic *verb* **pan·icked** \-nikt\; **pan·ick·ing** (1827)
transitive verb
1 : to affect with panic
2 : to produce demonstrative appreciation on the part of ⟨*panic* an audience with a gag⟩
intransitive verb
: to be affected with panic

panic button *noun* (circa 1950)
: something setting off a precipitous emergency response ⟨there was no pushing of *panic* buttons at the White House, no rushing of troops —J. C. Harsch⟩

pan·ic grass \'pa-nik-\ *noun* [Middle English *panik,* from Middle French or Latin; Middle French *panic* foxtail millet, from Latin *panicum,* from *panus* stalk of a panicle] (1597)

: any of various grasses (*Panicum* and related genera) including some important forage and cereal grasses

pan·i·cle \'pa-ni-kəl\ *noun* [Latin *panicula,* diminutive of *panus*] (1597)
1 : a compound racemose inflorescence — see INFLORESCENCE illustration
2 : a pyramidal loosely branched flower cluster
— **pan·i·cled** \-kəld\ *adjective*
— **pa·nic·u·late** \'pa-ni-kyə-lət, pə-\ *adjective*

pan·ic-strick·en \'pa-nik-ˌstri-kən\ *adjective* (1804)
: overcome with panic

pan·i·cum \'pa-ni-kəm\ *noun* [New Latin, from Latin, foxtail millet] (circa 1864)
: any of a large and widely distributed genus (*Panicum*) of grasses that have a very diverse habit and 1- to 2-flowered spikelets arranged in a panicle

Pan·ja·bi \ˌpən-'jä-bē, -'ja-\ *noun* [Hindi *pañjābī,* from *pañjāb* of Punjab] (1854)
1 : an Indo-Aryan language of the Punjab
2 : PUNJABI 2

pan·jan·drum \pan-'jan-drəm\ *noun, plural* **-drums** *also* **-dra** \-drə\ [Grand *Panjandrum,* burlesque title of an imaginary personage in some nonsense lines by Samuel Foote] (1755)
: a powerful personage or pretentious official

pan·leu·ko·pe·nia \ˌpan-ˌlü-kə-'pē-nē-ə\ *noun* [New Latin] (1940)
: an acute usually fatal viral epizootic disease especially of cats characterized by fever, diarrhea and dehydration, and extensive destruction of white blood cells

pan·mic·tic \ˌpan-'mik-tik\ *adjective* [*pan-* + Greek *miktos,* verbal of *mignynai* to mix] (1943)
: of, relating to, or exhibiting panmixia

pan·mix·ia \-'mik-sē-ə\ *noun* [New Latin, from *pan-* + Greek *mixis* act of mingling, mating, from *mignynai* to mix — more at MIX] (circa 1889)
: random mating within a breeding population

panne \'pan\ *noun* [French, from Old French *penne, panne* fur used for lining, from Latin *pinna* feather, wing — more at PEN] (circa 1794)
1 : a silk or rayon velvet with lustrous pile flattened in one direction — called also *panne velvet*
2 : a heavy silk or rayon satin with high luster and waxy smoothness

pan·nier *also* **pan·ier** \'pan-yər, 'pa-nē-ər\ *noun* [Middle English *panier,* from Middle French, from Latin *panarium,* from *panis* bread — more at FOOD] (13th century)
1 : a large container: as **a** : a basket often carried on the back of an animal or the shoulders of a person **b** : one of a pair of packs or baskets hung over the rear wheel of a vehicle (as a bicycle)
2 a : one of a pair of hoops formerly used to expand women's skirts at the sides **b** : an overskirt draped at the sides of a skirt for an effect of fullness

pannier 2b

pan·ni·kin \'pa-ni-kən\ *noun* [¹*pan* + *-nikin* (as in *cannikin*)] (1823)
British : a small pan or cup

pa·no·cha \pə-'nō-chə\ *or* **pa·no·che** \-chē\ *variant of* PENUCHE

pan·o·plied \'pa-nə-plēd\ *adjective* (1832)
: dressed in or having a panoply

pan·op·tic \pa-'näp-tik\ *adjective* [Greek *panoptēs* all-seeing, from *pan-* + *opsesthai* to be going to see — more at OPTIC] (1826)
: being or presenting a comprehensive or panoramic view

pan·o·ply \'pa-nə-plē\ *noun, plural* **-plies** [Greek *panoplia,* from *pan-* + *hopla* arms, ar-

mor, plural of *hoplon* tool, weapon — more at HOPLITE] (1632)
1 a : a full suit of armor **b** : ceremonial attire
2 : something forming a protective covering
3 a : a magnificent or impressive array ⟨the full *panoply* of a military funeral⟩ **b** : a display of all appropriate appurtenances ⟨has the *panoply* of science fiction . . . but it is not true science fiction —Isaac Asimov⟩

pan·o·rama \ˌpa-nə-'ra-mə, -'rä-\ *noun* [*pan-* + Greek *horama* sight, from *horan* to see — more at WARY] (1796)
1 a : CYCLORAMA 1 **b** : a picture exhibited a part at a time by being unrolled before the spectator
2 a : an unobstructed or complete view of an area in every direction **b** : a comprehensive presentation of a subject ⟨a *panorama* of American history⟩ **c** : RANGE
3 : a mental picture of a series of images or events
— **pan·o·ram·ic** \-'ra-mik\ *adjective*
— **pan·o·ram·i·cal·ly** \-mi-k(ə-)lē\ *adverb*

pan out *intransitive verb* [²*pan*] (circa 1868)
: TURN OUT; *especially* : SUCCEED ⟨the signs revealed that the experiment wasn't *panning out* —Ronald Reagan⟩

pan·pipe \'pan-ˌpīp\ *noun* [*Pan,* its traditional inventor] (1820)
: a primitive wind instrument consisting of a series of short vertical pipes of graduated length bound together with the mouthpieces in an even row — often used in plural

panpipe

pan·sex·u·al \ˌpan-'sek-sh(ə-)wəl, -shəl\ *adjective* (1926)
: exhibiting or implying many forms of sexual expression
— **pan·sex·u·al·i·ty** \ˌpan-ˌsek-shə-'wa-lə-tē\ *noun*

Pan–Slav·ism \ˌpan-'slä-ˌvi-zəm, -'sla-\ *noun* (1850)
: a political and cultural movement originally emphasizing the cultural ties between the Slavic peoples but later associated with Russian expansionism
— **Pan–Slav·ic** \-'slä-vik, -'slä-\ *adjective*
— **Pan–Slav·ist** \-'slä-vist, -'sla-\ *noun*

¹pan·sy \'pan-zē\ *noun, plural* **pansies** [Middle English *pensee,* from Middle French *pensée,* from *pensée* thought, from feminine of *pensé,* past participle of *penser* to think, from Latin *pensare* to ponder — more at PENSIVE] (15th century)
1 : a garden plant (*Viola wittrockiana*) derived chiefly from the wild pansy (*Viola tricolor*) of Europe by hybridizing the latter with other wild violets; *also* : its flower

\ə\ abut \ᵊ\ kitten \ər\ further \a\ ash \ā\ ace
\ä\ mop, mar \aů\ out \ch\ chin \e\ bet \ē\ easy
\g\ go \i\ hit \ī\ ice \j\ job \ṇ\ sing \ō\ go
\ȯ\ law \ȯi\ boy \th\ thin \t͟h\ the \ü\ loot \ů\ foot
\y\ yet \zh\ vision *see also* Guide to Pronunciation

2 a : an effeminate man or boy — usually used disparagingly **b :** a male homosexual — usually used disparagingly

²**pansy** *adjective* (1929)
: EFFEMINATE 1; *also* : HOMOSEXUAL — usually used disparagingly

¹**pant** \'pant\ *verb* [Middle English, modification of Middle French *pantaisier,* from (assumed) Vulgar Latin *phantasiare* to have hallucinations, from Greek *phantasioun,* from *phantasia* appearance, imagination — more at FANCY] (14th century)
intransitive verb
1 a : to breathe quickly, spasmodically, or in a labored manner **b :** to run panting 〈*panting* along beside the bicycle〉 **c :** to move with or make a throbbing or puffing sound
2 : to long eagerly : YEARN
3 : THROB, PULSATE
transitive verb
: to utter with panting : GASP

²**pant** *noun* (1513)
1 a : a panting breath **b :** the visible movement of the chest accompanying such a breath
2 : a throbbing or puffing sound

³**pant** *noun* [short for *pantaloons*] (1840)
1 : an outer garment covering each leg separately and usually extending from the waist to the ankle — usually used in plural
2 *plural, chiefly British* **:** men's underpants
3 *plural* **:** PANTIE
word history see PANTALOON
— with one's pants down : in an embarrassing position (as of being unprepared to act)

⁴**pant** *adjective* (1899)
: of or relating to pants 〈a *pant* leg〉

pant- *or* **panto-** *combining form* [Middle French, from Latin, from Greek, from *pant-, pas* — more at PAN-]
: all 〈*pant*isocracy〉

Pan·ta·gru·el \,pan-tə-'grü-əl; pan-'ta-grə-wəl, -,wel\ *noun* [French]
: the huge son of Gargantua in Rabelais's *Pantagruel*
— Pan·ta·gru·el·ian \,pan-tə-grü-'e-lē-ən, (,)pan-,ta-grə-'we-\ *adjective*
— Pan·ta·gru·el·ism \,pan-tə-'grü-ə-,li-zəm; pan-'ta-grə-wə-,li-zəm, -,we-\ *noun*
— Pan·ta·gru·el·ist \-list\ *noun*

pan·ta·lets *or* **pan·ta·lettes** \,pan-tə-'lets\ *noun plural* [*pantaloons*] (1834)
: long drawers with a ruffle at the bottom of each leg worn especially by women and children in the first half of the 19th century

pan·ta·loon \,pan-tə-'lün\ *noun* [Middle French & Old Italian; Middle French *Pantalon,* from Old Italian *Pantaleone, Pantalone,* from Old Italian *Pantaleone, Pantalone*] (circa 1590)
1 a *or* **pan·ta·lo·ne** \-tə-'lō-nē\ *capitalized*
: a character in the commedia dell'arte that is usually a skinny old dotard who wears spectacles, slippers, and a tight-fitting combination of trousers and stockings **b :** a buffoon in pantomimes
2 *plural* **a :** wide breeches worn especially in England during the reign of Charles II **b :** close-fitting trousers usually having straps passing under the instep and worn especially in the 19th century
3 : loose-fitting usually shorter than ankle-length trousers ◇

pant·dress \'pant-,dres\ *noun* (1964)
: a dress having a divided skirt

pan·tech·ni·con \pan-'tek-ni-kən\ *noun* [short for *pantechnicon van,* from *pantechnicon* storage warehouse] (1891)
British : ³VAN 1

pan·the·ism \'pan(t)-thē-,i-zəm\ *noun* [French *panthéisme,* from *panthéiste* pantheist, from English *pantheist,* from *pan-* + Greek *theos* god] (1732)
1 : a doctrine that equates God with the forces and laws of the universe
2 : the worship of all gods of different creeds, cults, or peoples indifferently; *also* : toleration

of worship of all gods (as at certain periods of the Roman empire)
— pan·the·ist \-thē-ist\ *noun*
— pan·the·is·tic \,pan(t)-thē-'is-tik\ *also* **pan·the·is·ti·cal** \-ti-kəl\ *adjective*
— pan·the·is·ti·cal·ly \-ti-k(ə-)lē\ *adverb*

pan·the·on \'pan(t)-thē-,än, -ən\ *noun* [Middle English *Panteon,* a temple at Rome, from Latin *Pantheon,* from Greek *pantheion* temple of all the gods, from neuter of *pantheios* of all gods, from *pan-* + *theos* god] (14th century)
1 : a temple dedicated to all the gods
2 : a building serving as the burial place of or containing memorials to the famous dead of a nation
3 : the gods of a people; *especially* : the officially recognized gods
4 : a group of illustrious persons

pan·ther \'pan(t)-thər\ *noun, plural* **panthers** *also* **panther** [Middle English *pantere,* from Old French, from Latin *panthera,* from Greek *panthēr*] (13th century)
1 : LEOPARD; *as* **a :** a leopard of a hypothetical exceptionally large fierce variety **b :** a leopard of the black color phase
2 : COUGAR
3 : JAGUAR

pant·ie *or* **panty** \'pan-tē\ *noun, plural* **panties** [³*pant*] (1908)
: a woman's or child's undergarment covering the lower trunk and made with closed crotch — usually used in plural
word history see PANTALOON

pantie girdle *noun* (1941)
: a woman's girdle having a sewed-in or detachable crotch and made with or without garters and bones

pan·tile \'pan-,tīl\ *noun* [¹*pan*] (1640)
1 : a roofing tile whose cross section is an ogee curve
2 : a roofing tile of which the cross section is an arc of a circle and which is laid with alternate convex and concave surfaces uppermost
— pan·tiled \-,tīld\ *adjective*

pant·i·soc·ra·cy \,pan-tə-'sä-krə-sē, ,pan-,tī-\ *noun, plural* **-cies** [*pant-* + *isocracy* equal rule, from Greek *isokratia,* from *is-* + *-kratia* -cracy] (1794)
: a utopian community in which all rule equally
— pant·i·so·crat·ic \,pan-,tī-sə-'kra-tik\ *or* **pant·i·so·crat·i·cal** \-'kra-ti-kəl\ *adjective*
— pant·i·soc·ra·tist \,pan-tə-'sä-krə-tist, ,pan-,tī-\ *noun*

pan·to \'pan-(,)tō\ *noun, plural* **pantos** (1852)
British : PANTOMIME 2c

pan·to·fle \pan-'tō-fəl, -'tä-, -'tü-; 'pan-tə-fəl\ *noun* [Middle English *pantufle,* from Middle French *pantoufle*] (15th century)
: SLIPPER

pan·to·graph \'pan-tə-,graf\ *noun* [French *pantographe,* from *pant-* + *-graphe* -graph] (1723)
1 : an instrument for copying (as a map) on a predetermined scale consisting of four light rigid bars jointed in parallelogram form; *also* : any of various extensible devices of similar construction (as for use as brackets or gates)

pantograph 1

2 : an electrical trolley carried by a collapsible and adjustable frame
— pan·to·graph·ic \,pan-tə-'gra-fik\ *adjective*

¹**pan·to·mime** \'pan-tə-,mīm\ *noun* [Latin *pantomimus,* from *pant-* + *mimus* mime] (1589)
1 : PANTOMIMIST
2 a : an ancient Roman dramatic performance featuring a solo dancer and a narrative chorus

b : any of various dramatic or dancing performances in which a story is told by expressive bodily or facial movements of the performers **c :** a British theatrical entertainment of the Christmas season based on a nursery tale and featuring topical songs, tableaux, and dances
3 a : conveyance of a story by bodily or facial movements especially in drama or dance **b :** the art or genre of conveying a story by bodily movements only
— pan·to·mim·ic \,pan-tə-'mi-mik\ *adjective*

²**pantomime** *verb* **-mimed; -mim·ing** (1768)
intransitive verb
: to engage in pantomime
transitive verb
: to represent by pantomime

pan·to·mim·ist \'pan-tə-,mī-mist, -,mi-\ *noun* (1838)
1 : an actor or dancer in pantomimes
2 : a composer of pantomimes

pan·to·the·nate \,pan-tə-'the-,nāt, pan-'tä-thə-,nāt\ *noun* (circa 1934)
: a salt or ester of pantothenic acid

pan·to·then·ic acid \,pan-tə-'the-nik-, -'thē-\ *noun* [Greek *pantothen* from all sides, from *pant-, pas* all — more at PAN-] (1933)
: a viscous oily acid $C_9H_{17}NO_5$ of the vitamin B complex found in all living tissues

pan·trop·i·cal \,pan-'trä-pi-kəl\ *also* **pan·trop·ic** \-'pik\ *adjective* (1936)
: occurring or distributed throughout the tropical regions of the earth

pan·try \'pan-trē\ *noun, plural* **pantries** [Middle English *panetrie,* from Middle French *paneterie,* from Old French, from *panetier* servant in charge of the pantry, from *pan* bread, from Latin *panis* — more at FOOD] (14th century)
1 : a room or closet used for storing (as provisions) or from which food is brought to the table
2 : a room (as in a hotel or hospital) for preparation of foods on order

pan·try·man \-mən\ *noun* (circa 1567)
: a man in charge of or working in a pantry (as in a hotel or hospital)

pants suit *noun* (1964)
: PANTSUIT

pant·suit \'pant-,süt\ *noun* (1964)
: a woman's ensemble consisting usually of a long jacket and tailored pants of the same material
— pant·suit·ed *adjective*

panty hose *noun* (1963)

◇ WORD HISTORY
pantaloon A stock figure in the commedia dell'arte, a form of Italian comic theater popular throughout Europe from about the 16th to the mid-18th century, was Pantalone, an avaricious, lecherous, and scheming old man who often ended up being duped and humiliated. His costume consisted of a soft brimless hat; a pleated black cassock; slippers; and a vest, breeches, and stockings that were conspicuously red and tight-fitting. In later representations of the character, the breeches and stockings were replaced by long trousers. When trousers of a similar style became popular during the Restoration in England, they became known as *pantaloons,* Pantaloon being an anglicization of *Pantalone.* Even as fashions changed over the years, *pantaloons* remained the name for various types of trousers. The clipped form *pants,* an Americanism first current around 1840, became a standard word for the garment, serving as the basis for new formations (denoting new garments), such as *underpants* and *panties.*

: a one-piece undergarment for women that consists of hosiery made with a panty-style top — usually plural in construction

panty raid *noun* (circa 1952)
: a raid on a women's dormitory by college men usually to obtain panties as trophies

panty·waist \'pan-tē-ˌwāst\ *noun* (circa 1936)
: SISSY
— **pantywaist** *adjective*

Pan·urge \'pa-ˌnərj, pa-'nürzh\ *noun* [French]
: a witty rascal and companion of Pantagruel in Rabelais's *Pantagruel*

pan·zer \'pan-zər, 'pän(t)-sər\ *noun* [German *Panzer* tank, armor, coat of mail, from Middle High German *panzier*, from Old French *pan-cière*, from *pance*, *panche* belly — more at PAUNCH] (circa 1939)
: TANK 3; *specifically* : a German tank of World War II

panzer division *noun* (circa 1939)
: a German armored division

¹**pap** \'pap\ *noun* [Middle English *pappe*; of imitative origin] (13th century)
1 *chiefly dialect* : NIPPLE, TEAT
2 : something shaped like a nipple

²**pap** *noun* [Middle English] (15th century)
1 : a soft food for infants or invalids
2 : political patronage
3 : something lacking solid value or substance

pa·pa \'pä-pə, *chiefly British* pə-'pä, -'pä\ *noun* [French (baby talk)] (1681)
: FATHER

Pa·pa \pə-'pä, 'pä-pə\ (1952)
— a communications code word for the letter *p*

pa·pa·cy \'pā-pə-sē\ *noun, plural* **-cies** [Middle English *papacie*, from Medieval Latin *papatia*, from Late Latin *papa* pope — more at POPE] (14th century)
1 : the office of pope
2 : a succession or line of popes
3 : the term of a pope's reign
4 *capitalized* : the system of government of the Roman Catholic Church of which the pope is the supreme head

Pa·pa·go \'pä-pə-ˌgō, 'pä-\ *noun, plural* **Papago** *or* **Papagos** (1839)
1 : a member of an American Indian people of southwestern Arizona and northwestern Mexico
2 : the Uto-Aztecan language of the Papago people

pa·pa·in \pə-'pä-ən, -'pī-ən\ *noun* [International Scientific Vocabulary, from *papaya*] (circa 1890)
: a protease in the juice of unripe papaya that is used especially as a tenderizer for meat and in medicine

pa·pal \'pā-pəl\ *adjective* [Middle English, from Middle French, from Medieval Latin *papalis*, from Late Latin *papa*] (14th century)
: of or relating to a pope or to the Roman Catholic Church; *also* : resembling a pope or that of a pope
— **pa·pal·ly** \-pə-lē\ *adverb*

papal cross *noun* (circa 1889)
: a figure of a cross having a long upright shaft and three crossbars with the longest at or somewhat above its middle and the two other successively shorter crossbars above the longest one — see CROSS illustration

papal infallibility *noun* (1870)
: the Roman Catholic doctrine that the pope cannot err when speaking ex cathedra in defining a doctrine of Christian faith or morals

Pa·pa·ni·co·laou smear \ˌpä-pə-'nē-kə-ˌlaü-, ˌpa-pə-'ni-\ *noun* [George N. Papanicolaou (died 1962) American medical scientist] (1950)
: PAP SMEAR

Papanicolaou test *noun* (1946)
: PAP SMEAR

pa·pa·raz·zo \ˌpä-pə-'rät-(ˌ)sō\ *noun, plural* **-raz·zi** \-(ˌ)sē\ [Italian] (1966)
: a free-lance photographer who aggressively pursues celebrities for the purpose of taking candid photographs

pa·pav·er·ine \pə-'pa-və-ˌrēn, -'pav-rən, -'pa-və-\ *noun* [International Scientific Vocabulary, from Latin *papaver* poppy] (1857)
: a crystalline alkaloid $C_{20}H_{21}NO_4$ that is found in opium and is used chiefly as an antispasmodic for its ability to relax smooth muscle

pa·paw *noun* [probably modification of Spanish *papaya*] (1624)
1 \'pä-ˌpo\ : PAPAYA
2 \'pä-(ˌ)po, 'po-\ : a North American tree (*Asimina triloba*) of the custard-apple family with purple flowers and an edible fruit; *also* : its fruit

pa·pa·ya \pə-'pī-ə\ *noun* [Spanish, of American Indian origin; akin to Arawak *papáia*] (1598)
: a tropical American tree (*Carica papaya* of the family Caricaceae, the papaya family) with an oblong to globose yellow edible fruit; *also* : its fruit

¹**pa·per** \'pā-pər\ *noun* [Middle English *papir*, from Middle French *papier*, from Latin *papyrus* papyrus, paper, from Greek *papyros* papyrus] (14th century)
1 a (1) : a felted sheet of usually vegetable fibers laid down on a fine screen from a water suspension (2) : a similar sheet of other material (as plastic) b : a piece of paper
2 a : a piece of paper containing a written or printed statement : DOCUMENT ⟨pedigree *papers*⟩ b : a piece of paper containing writing or print c : a formal written composition often designed for publication and often intended to be read aloud ⟨presented a scholarly *paper* at the meeting⟩ d : a piece of written schoolwork
3 : a paper container or wrapper
4 : NEWSPAPER
5 : the negotiable notes or instruments of commerce
6 : WALLPAPER
7 : TICKETS; *especially* : free passes
8 : PAPERBACK
— **on paper** 1 : in writing ⟨wants these promises *on paper*⟩ 2 : in theory ⟨the plan looks good *on paper*⟩ 3 : figured at face value ⟨*on paper* the stock was worth nearly a million dollars⟩

²**paper** *verb* **pa·pered; pa·per·ing** \'pā-p(ə-)riŋ\ (1594)
transitive verb
1 *archaic* : to put down or describe in writing
2 : to fold or enclose in paper
3 : to cover or line with paper; *especially* : to apply wallpaper to
4 : to fill by giving out free passes ⟨*paper* the theater for opening night⟩
5 : to cover (an area) with advertising bills, circulars, or posters
intransitive verb
: to hang wallpaper
— **pa·per·er** \-pər-ər\ *noun*

³**paper** *adjective* (1594)
1 a : made of paper, paperboard, or papier-mâché ⟨a *paper* bag⟩ b : PAPERY
2 : of or relating to clerical work or written communication
3 : existing only in theory : NOMINAL ⟨a *paper* blockade⟩
4 : admitted by free passes ⟨a *paper* audience⟩
5 : finished with a crisp smooth surface similar to that of paper ⟨*paper* taffeta⟩

pa·per·back \'pā-pər-ˌbak\ *noun* (1899)
: a book with a flexible paper binding
— **paperback** *also* **pa·per·backed** \-ˌbakt\ *adjective*

paper birch *noun* (1810)
: a North American birch (*Betula papyrifera*) with peeling white bark and toothed ovate leaves

pa·per·board \'pā-pər-ˌbōrd, -ˌbord\ *noun* (1549)

: a material made from cellulose fiber (as wood pulp) like paper but usually thicker

pa·per·bound \-ˌbaund\ *noun* (1950)
: PAPERBACK
— **paperbound** *adjective*

pa·per·boy \-ˌboi\ *noun* (1876)
: a boy who delivers newspapers : NEWSBOY

paper chromatography *noun* (1948)
: chromatography that uses paper strips or sheets as the adsorbent stationary phase through which a solution flows and that is used especially to separate amino acids

paper clip *noun* (1919)
: a length of wire bent into flat loops that is used to hold papers together

paper cutter *noun* (circa 1828)
1 : PAPER KNIFE
2 : a machine or device for cutting or trimming sheets of paper to required dimensions

pa·per·hang·er \'pā-pər-ˌhaŋ-ər\ *noun* (1796)
1 : one that applies wallpaper
2 *slang* : one who passes worthless checks

pa·per·hang·ing \-ˌhaŋ-iŋ\ *noun* (1873)
: the act of applying wallpaper

paper knife *noun* (circa 1807)
1 : a knife for slitting envelopes or uncut pages
2 : the knife of a paper cutter

pa·per·less \'pā-pər-ləs\ *adjective* (1969)
: recording or relaying information by electronic media rather than on paper ⟨*paperless* offices⟩

pa·per·mak·er \'pā-pər-ˌmā-kər\ *noun* (circa 1580)
: one that makes paper
— **pa·per·mak·ing** \-kiŋ\ *noun*

paper money *noun* (1691)
1 : money consisting of government notes and banknotes
2 : BANK MONEY

paper mulberry *noun* (1777)
: an Asian tree (*Broussonetia papyrifera*) of the mulberry family that is widely grown as a shade tree

paper nautilus *noun* (1835)
: a pelagic cephalopod (genus *Argonauta*) of which the female has a delicate papery shell

paper nautilus

paper over *transitive verb* (1955)
1 : to gloss over, explain away, or patch up (as major differences or disparities) especially in order to maintain a semblance of unity or agreement
2 : HIDE, CONCEAL

paper profit *noun* (1893)
: a profit that can be realized only by selling something (as a security) that has appreciated in market value

paper–thin *adjective* (1928)
: extremely thin ⟨*paper-thin* partitions⟩

paper tiger *noun* (1850)
: one that is outwardly powerful or dangerous but inwardly weak or ineffectual

paper trail *noun* (1965)
: documents (as financial records or published materials) from which a person's actions may be traced or opinions learned

pa·per–train \'pā-pər-ˌtrān\ *transitive verb* (1971)
: to train (as a dog) to defecate and urinate on paper indoors

pa·per·weight \-ˌwāt\ *noun* (circa 1858)

: a usually small heavy object used to hold down loose papers (as on a desk)

pa·per·work \-,wərk\ *noun* (1889)
: routine clerical or record-keeping work often incidental to a more important task

pa·pery \'pā-p(ə-)rē\ *adjective* (1627)
: resembling paper in thinness or consistency ⟨*papery* leaves⟩ ⟨*papery* silk⟩
— **pa·per·i·ness** *noun*

pa·pe·terie \'pa-pə-trē, ,pa-pə-'\ *noun* [French] (circa 1847)
: packaged fancy stationery

¹**Pa·phi·an** \'pā-fē-ən\ *noun* [Latin *paphius*, from Greek *paphios*, from *Paphos*, ancient city of Cyprus that was the center of worship of Aphrodite] (1598)
1 *often not capitalized* : PROSTITUTE
2 : a native or inhabitant of Paphos

²**Paphian** *adjective* (1605)
1 : of or relating to illicit love : WANTON
2 : of or relating to Paphos or its people

Pa·pia·men·to \,pä-pyə-'men-(,)tō\ *also* **Pa·pia·men·tu** \-(,)tü\ *noun* [Spanish, from Papiamento *papya* talk + -*mentu* -ment] (1923)
: a Spanish-based creole language of Netherlands Antilles

pa·pier col·lé \,pä-,pyā-(,)ko-'lā, ,pa-\ *noun, plural* **papiers collés** \-,pyā-(,)ko-'lā(z)\ [French, glued paper] (1935)
: COLLAGE

¹**pa·pier-mâ·ché** \,pā-pər-mə-'shā, ,pa-,pyā-mə-, -(,)ma-\ *noun* [French, literally, chewed paper] (1753)
: a light strong molding material of wastepaper pulped with glue and other additives

²**papier-mâché** *adjective* (1753)
1 : formed of papier-mâché
2 : UNREAL, ARTIFICIAL

pa·pil·i·o·na·ceous \pə-,pi·lē-ə-'nā-shəs\ *adjective* [Latin *papilion-, papilio* butterfly — more at PAVILION] (1668)
: having a corolla (as in the bean or pea) with usually five petals that include a large standard enclosing two lateral wings and a lower carina

pa·pil·la \pə-'pi·lə\ *noun, plural* **pa·pil·lae** \-'pi,(,)lē, -,lī\ [Latin, nipple, from diminutive of *papula* pimple; akin to Lithuanian *papas* nipple] (1713)
: a small projecting body part similar to a nipple in form: **a** : a vascular process of connective tissue extending into and nourishing the root of a hair, feather, or developing tooth **b** : any of the vascular protuberances of the dermal layer of the skin extending into the epidermal layer and often containing tactile corpuscles **c** : any of the small protuberances on the upper surface of the tongue
— **pap·il·lary** \'pa-pə-,ler-ē, *especially British* pə-'pi-lə-rē\ *adjective*
— **pap·il·late** \'pa-pə-,lāt, pə-'pi-lət\ *adjective*
— **pap·il·lose** \'pa-pə-,lōs, pə-'pi-,lōs\ *adjective*

pap·il·lo·ma \,pa-pə-'lō-mə\ *noun, plural* **-mas** *or* **-ma·ta** \-mə-tə\ [New Latin] (1866)
1 : a benign tumor (as a wart) due to overgrowth of epithelial tissue on papillae of vascular connective tissue (as of the skin)
2 : an epithelial tumor caused by a virus
— **pap·il·lo·ma·tous** \-'lō-mə-təs\ *adjective*

pap·il·lo·ma·vi·rus \-,vī-rəs\ *noun* [New Latin] (1960)
: any of a group of papovaviruses that cause papillomas

pa·pil·lon \,pä-pē-'yⁿ, ,pa-\ *noun* [French, literally, butterfly, from Latin *papilion-, papilio*] (1907)
: any of a breed of small slender toy spaniels having large erect heavily fringed ears

pa·pil·lote \,pä-pē-'yōt, ,pa-\ *noun* [French, from *papillon* butterfly] (1818)
: a greased usually paper wrapper in which food (as meat or fish) is cooked

pa·pist \'pā-pist\ *noun, often capitalized* [Middle French or New Latin; Middle French *papiste*, from *pape* pope; New Latin *papista*, from Late Latin *papa* pope] (1534)
: ROMAN CATHOLIC — usually used disparagingly
— **papist** *adjective*

pa·pist·ry \'pā-pə-strē\ *noun* (1535)
: the Roman Catholic religion — usually used disparagingly

pa·poose \pa-'püs, pə-\ *noun* [Narraganset *papoòs*] (1634)
: a young child of American Indian parents

pa·po·va·vi·rus \pə-'pō-və-,vī-rəs\ *noun* [*pa*pilloma + *po*lyoma + *va*cuolating + *virus*] (1962)
: any of a group of viruses that have a capsid composed of 72 subunits and that are associated with or responsible for various neoplasms (as some warts) of mammals

pap·pose \'pa-,pōs\ *adjective* (1691)
: having or being a pappus

pap·pus \'pa-pəs\ *noun, plural* **pap·pi** \'pa-,pī, -,pē\ [Latin, from Greek *pappos*] (circa 1704)
: an appendage or tuft of appendages that crowns the ovary or fruit in various seed plants and functions in dispersal of the fruit

pap·py \'pa-pē\ *noun* (1763)
chiefly Southern & Midland : PAPA

pa·pri·ka \pa-'prē-kə, pə-\ *noun* [Hungarian, from Serbo-Croatian, from *papar* ground pepper, ultimately from Latin *piper* — more at PEPPER] (circa 1896)
: a usually mild red condiment consisting of the dried finely ground pods of various cultivated sweet peppers; *also* : a sweet pepper used for making paprika

Pap smear \'pap-\ *noun* [George N. *Papanicolaou* (died 1962) American medical scientist] (1952)
: a method for the early detection of uterine cancer that involves the staining of exfoliated cells using a special technique which differentiates diseased tissue — called also *Papanicolaou smear, Papanicolaou test, Pap test*

Pap·u·an \'pa-pyə-wən, -pə-\ *noun* (1814)
1 : a native or inhabitant of Papua
2 : a member of any of the native peoples of New Guinea and adjacent areas of Melanesia
3 : any of a heterogeneous group of languages spoken in New Guinea, New Britain, and the Solomon islands
— **Papuan** *adjective*

pap·u·lar \'pa-pyə-lər\ *adjective* (circa 1820)
: consisting of or characterized by papules

pap·ule \'pa-(,)pyü(ə)l\ *noun* [Latin *papula*] (1864)
: a small solid usually conical elevation of the skin

pap·y·rol·o·gy \,pa-pə-'rä-lə-jē\ *noun* [International Scientific Vocabulary] (1898)
: the study of papyrus manuscripts
— **pap·y·rol·o·gist** \-jist\ *noun*

pa·py·rus \pə-'pī-rəs\ *noun, plural* **pa·py·ri** \-'pī-(,)rē, -,rī\ *or* **pa·py·rus·es** [Middle English, from Latin — more at PAPER] (14th century)
1 : a tall sedge (*Cyperus papyrus*) of the Nile valley
2 : the pith of the papyrus plant especially when cut in strips and pressed into a material to write on
3 a : a writing on papyrus **b** : a written scroll made of papyrus

¹**par** \'pär\ *noun* [Latin, one that is equal, from *par* equal] (1622)
1 a : the established value of the monetary unit of one country expressed in terms of the monetary unit of another country using the same metal as the

papyrus 1

standard of value **b** : the face amount of an instrument of value (as a check or note): as (1) : the monetary value assigned to each share of stock in the charter of a corporation (2) : the principal of a bond
2 : common level : EQUALITY — usually used with *on* ⟨judged the recording to be on a *par* with previous ones⟩
3 a : an amount taken as an average or norm **b** : an accepted standard; *specifically* : a usual standard of physical condition or health
4 : the score standard for each hole of a golf course; *also* : a score equal to par
— **par** *adjective*
— **par for the course** : not unusual : NORMAL

²**par** *transitive verb* **parred; par·ring** (1950)
: to score par on (a hole)

pa·ra \'pär-ə\ *noun, plural* **paras** *or* **para** [Turkish, from Persian *pārah*, literally, piece] (1687)
1 a : any of several monetary units of the Turkish Empire **b** : a coin representing one para
2 [Serbo-Croatian, from Turkish] — see *dinar* at MONEY table

¹**para-** *or* **par-** *prefix* [Middle English, from Middle French, from Latin, from Greek, from *para*; akin to Greek *pro* before — more at FOR]
1 : beside : alongside of : beyond : aside from ⟨*para*thyroid⟩ ⟨*par*enteral⟩
2 a : closely related to ⟨*par*aldehyde⟩ **b** : involving substitution at or characterized by two opposite positions in the benzene ring that are separated by two carbon atoms ⟨*para*dichlorobenzene⟩
3 a : faulty : abnormal ⟨*par*esthesia⟩ **b** : associated in a subsidiary or accessory capacity ⟨*para*medical⟩ **c** : closely resembling : almost ⟨*para*typhoid⟩

²**para-** *combining form* [*parachute*]
: parachute ⟨*para*trooper⟩

-para *noun combining form, plural* **-paras** *or* **-parae** [Latin, from *parere* to give birth to — more at PARE]
: woman delivered of (so many) children ⟨primi*para*⟩

para·ami·no·ben·zo·ic acid \,par-ə-ə-,mē-,nō-,ben-'zō-ik-, ,par-ə-,a-mə-(,)nō-\ *noun* [International Scientific Vocabulary] (1906)
: a colorless para-substituted aminobenzoic acid that is a growth factor of the vitamin B complex — called also *PABA*

para·ami·no·sal·i·cyl·ic acid \-,sa-lə-'si-lik-\ *noun* (1946)
: the white crystalline para-substituted isomer of aminosalicylic acid that is made synthetically and is used in the treatment of tuberculosis

para·bi·o·sis \,par-ə-(,)bī-'ō-səs, -bē-\ *noun* [New Latin] (1903)
1 : reversible suspension of obvious vital activities
2 : anatomical and physiological union of two organisms
— **para·bi·ot·ic** \-'ä-tik\ *adjective*
— **para·bi·ot·i·cal·ly** \-ti-k(ə-)lē\ *adverb*

par·a·ble \'par-ə-bəl\ *noun* [Middle English, from Middle French, from Late Latin *parabola*, from Greek *parabolē* comparison, from *paraballein* to compare, from *para-* + *ballein* to throw — more at DEVIL] (14th century)
: EXAMPLE; *specifically* : a usually short fictitious story that illustrates a moral attitude or a religious principle

pa·rab·o·la \pə-'ra-bə-lə\ *noun* [New Latin, from Greek *parabolē*, literally, comparison] (1579)
1 : a plane curve generated by a point moving so that its distance from a fixed point is equal to its distance from a fixed line : the intersection of a right circular cone with a plane parallel to an element of the cone
2 : something bowl-shaped (as an antenna or microphone reflector)

par·a·bol·ic \ˌpar-ə-'bä-lik\ *adjective* [in sense 1, from Late Latin *parabola* parable; in sense 2, from New Latin *parabola*] (1669)
1 : expressed by or being a parable : ALLEGORICAL
2 : of, having the form of, or relating to a parabola 〈motion in a *parabolic* curve〉
— **par·a·bol·i·cal·ly** \-li-k(ə-)lē\ *adverb*

pa·rab·o·loid \pə-'ra-bə-ˌlȯid\ *noun* (circa 1702)
: a surface all of whose intersections by planes are either parabolas and ellipses or parabolas and hyperbolas
— **pa·rab·o·loi·dal** \-ˌra-bə-'lȯi-dᵊl\ *adjective*

¹par·a·chute \'par-ə-ˌshüt\ *noun* [French, from *para-* (as in *parasol*) + *chute* fall — more at CHUTE] (1785)
1 : a device for slowing the descent of a person or object through the air that consists of a usually hemispherical fabric canopy beneath which the person or object is suspended
2 : PATAGIUM
3 : a device or structure suggestive of a parachute in form, use, or operation
— **para·chut·ic** \ˌpar-ə-'shü-tik\ *adjective*

²parachute *verb* **-chut·ed; -chut·ing** (1809)
transitive verb
: to convey by means of a parachute
intransitive verb
: to descend by means of a parachute

para·chut·ist \'par-ə-ˌshü-tist\ *noun* (1888)
: one that parachutes: as **a** : PARATROOPER **b** : a person who parachutes as a sport

Par·a·clete \'par-ə-ˌklēt\ *noun* [Middle English *Paraclyte*, from Late Latin *Paracletus*, *Paraclitus*, from Greek *Paraklētos*, literally, advocate, intercessor, from *parakalein* to invoke, from *para-* + *kalein* to call — more at LOW] (15th century)
: HOLY SPIRIT

¹pa·rade \pə-'rād\ *noun* [French, from Middle French, from *parer* to prepare — more at PARE] (circa 1656)
1 : a pompous show : EXHIBITION
2 a : the ceremonial formation of a body of troops before a superior officer **b** : a place where troops assemble regularly for parade
3 a : an informal procession **b** : a public procession **c** : a showy array or succession 〈a *parade* of tycoons' castles —Gail Sheehy〉
4 a : a place for strolling **b** : those who promenade

²parade *verb* **pa·rad·ed; pa·rad·ing** (1686)
transitive verb
1 : to cause to maneuver or march : MARSHAL
2 : PROMENADE
3 : to exhibit ostentatiously
intransitive verb
1 : to march in or as if in a procession
2 : PROMENADE
3 a : SHOW OFF **b** : MASQUERADE 〈myths which *parade* as modern science —M. R. Cohen〉
synonym see SHOW
— **pa·rad·er** *noun*

para·di·chlo·ro·ben·zene \ˌpar-ə-ˌdī-ˌklȯr-ə-'ben-ˌzēn, -ˌklȯr-, -ˌben-'\ *noun* [International Scientific Vocabulary] (1876)
: a white crystalline compound $C_6H_4Cl_2$ made by chlorinating benzene and used chiefly as a fumigant against clothes moths

par·a·did·dle \'par-ə-ˌdi-dᵊl\ *noun* [origin unknown] (1927)
: a quick succession of drumbeats slower than a roll and alternating left- and right-hand strokes in a typical L-R-L-L, R-L-R-R pattern

par·a·digm \'par-ə-ˌdīm *also* -ˌdim\ *noun* [Late Latin *paradigma*, from Greek *para-*

deigma, from *paradeiknynai* to show side by side, from *para-* + *deiknynai* to show — more at DICTION] (15th century)
1 : EXAMPLE, PATTERN; *especially* : an outstandingly clear or typical example or archetype
2 : an example of a conjugation or declension showing a word in all its inflectional forms
3 : a philosophical and theoretical framework of a scientific school or discipline within which theories, laws, and generalizations and the experiments performed in support of them are formulated
— **par·a·dig·mat·ic** \ˌpar-ə-dig-'ma-tik\ *adjective*
— **par·a·dig·mat·i·cal·ly** \-ti-k(ə-)lē\ *adverb*

par·a·di·sa·ic \ˌpar-ə-ˌdī-'sā-ik, -'zā-\ *adjective* [*paradise* + *-aic* (as in *Hebraic*)] (1754)
: PARADISIACAL
— **par·a·di·sa·i·cal** \-'sā-ə-kəl, -'zā-\ *adjective*
— **par·a·di·sa·i·cal·ly** \-ə-k(ə-)lē\ *adverb*

par·a·dis·al \ˌpar-ə-'dī-səl, -zəl\ *adjective* (1560)
: PARADISIACAL

par·a·dise \'par-ə-ˌdīs, -ˌdīz\ *noun* [Middle English *paradis*, from Old French, from Late Latin *paradisus*, from Greek *paradeisos*, literally, enclosed park, of Iranian origin; akin to Avestan *pairi-daēza* enclosure; akin to Greek *peri* around and to Greek *teichos* wall — more at PERI-, DOUGH] (12th century)
1 a : EDEN **2 b** : an intermediate place or state where the righteous departed await resurrection and judgment **c** : HEAVEN
2 : a place or state of bliss, felicity, or delight
— **par·a·dis·i·al** \ˌpar-ə-'dī-sē-əl, -zē-\ *also*
— **par·a·dis·i·cal** \-si-kəl, -zi-\ *adjective*

par·a·di·si·a·cal \ˌpar-ə-də-'sī-ə-kəl, -ˌdī-, -'zī-\ *or* **par·a·dis·i·ac** \-'dī-zē-ˌak, -sē-\ *adjective* [Late Latin *paradisiacus*, from *paradisus*] (1649)
: of, relating to, or resembling paradise
— **par·a·di·si·a·cal·ly** \-də-'sī-ə-k(ə-)lē, -ˌdī-, -'zī-\ *adverb*

pa·ra·dor \ˌpä-rä-'thȯr\ *noun* [Spanish, inn, from *parar* to stop, lodge for the night, from Latin *parare* to prepare — more at PARE] (1845)
: a usually government-operated hostelry found especially in Spain

par·a·dox \'par-ə-ˌdäks\ *noun* [Latin *paradoxum*, from Greek *paradoxon*, from neuter of *paradoxos* contrary to expectation, from *para-* + *dokein* to think, seem — more at DECENT] (1540)
1 : a tenet contrary to received opinion
2 a : a statement that is seemingly contradictory or opposed to common sense and yet is perhaps true **b** : a self-contradictory statement that at first seems true **c** : an argument that apparently derives self-contradictory conclusions by valid deduction from acceptable premises
3 : something or someone with seemingly contradictory qualities or phases

par·a·dox·i·cal \ˌpar-ə-'däk-si-kəl\ *adjective* (1581)
1 a : of the nature of a paradox **b** : inclined to paradoxes
2 : not being the normal or usual kind 〈*paradoxical* pulse〉
— **par·a·dox·i·cal·i·ty** \-ˌdäk-si-'ka-lə-tē\ *noun*
— **par·a·dox·i·cal·ly** \-'däk-si-k(ə-)lē\ *adverb*
— **par·a·dox·i·cal·ness** \-kəl-nəs\ *noun*

paradoxical sleep *noun* (1964)
: REM SLEEP

par·aes·the·sia *variant of* PARESTHESIA

par·af·fin \'par-ə-fən\ *noun* [German, from Latin *parum* too little (akin to Greek *pauros* little, *paid-, pais* child) + *affinis* bordering on — more at FEW, AFFINITY] (1838)
1 a : a waxy crystalline flammable substance obtained especially from distillates of wood,

coal, petroleum, or shale oil that is a complex mixture of hydrocarbons and is used chiefly in coating and sealing, in candles, in rubber compounding, and in pharmaceuticals and cosmetics **b** : any of various mixtures of similar hydrocarbons including mixtures that are semisolid or oily
2 : ALKANE
3 *chiefly British* : KEROSENE
— **par·af·fin·ic** \ˌpar-ə-'fi-nik\ *adjective*

para·for·mal·de·hyde \ˌpar-ə-fȯr-'mal-də-ˌhīd, -fər-\ *noun* (1894)
: a white powder $(CH_2O)_x$ that consists of a polymer of formaldehyde and is used especially as a fungicide

para·gen·e·sis \ˌpar-ə-'je-nə-səs\ *noun* [New Latin] (1853)
: the formation of minerals in contact in such a manner as to affect one another's development
— **para·ge·net·ic** \-jə-'ne-tik\ *adjective*
— **para·ge·net·i·cal·ly** \-ti-k(ə-)lē\ *adverb*

¹par·a·gon \'par-ə-ˌgän, -gən\ *noun* [Middle French, from Old Italian *paragone*, literally, touchstone, from *paragonare* to test on a touchstone, from Greek *parakonan* to sharpen, from *para-* + *akonē* whetstone, from *akē* point; akin to Greek *akmē* point — more at EDGE] (circa 1548)
: a model of excellence or perfection

²paragon *transitive verb* (circa 1586)
1 : to compare with : PARALLEL
2 : to put in rivalry : MATCH
3 *obsolete* : SURPASS

¹par·a·graph \'par-ə-ˌgraf\ *noun* [Middle French & Medieval Latin; Middle French *paragraphe*, from Medieval Latin *paragraphus* sign marking a paragraph, from Greek *paragraphos* line used to mark change of persons in a dialogue, from *paragraphein* to write alongside, from *para-* + *graphein* to write — more at CARVE] (1525)
1 a : a subdivision of a written composition that consists of one or more sentences, deals with one point or gives the words of one speaker, and begins on a new usually indented line **b** : a short composition or note that is complete in one paragraph
2 : a character (as ¶) used to indicate the beginning of a paragraph and as a reference mark
— **par·a·graph·ic** \ˌpar-ə-'gra-fik\ *adjective*

²paragraph (1764)
transitive verb
1 : to write paragraphs about
2 : to divide into paragraphs
intransitive verb
: to write paragraphs

par·a·graph·er \'par-ə-ˌgra-fər\ *noun* (1822)
: a writer of paragraphs especially for the editorial page of a newspaper

para·in·flu·en·za virus \ˌpar-ə-ˌin-flü-'en-zə-\ *noun* (1959)
: any of several paramyxoviruses that are associated with or responsible for some respiratory infections especially in children — called also *parainfluenza*

para·jour·nal·ism \ˌpar-ə-'jər-nᵊl-ˌi-zəm\ *noun* (1965)
: journalism that is heavily colored by the opinions of the reporter

par·a·keet \'par-ə-ˌkēt\ *noun* [Spanish & Middle French; Spanish *periquito*, from Middle French *perroquet* parrot] (1581)
: any of numerous usually small slender parrots with a long graduated tail

para·lan·guage \'par-ə-ˌlaŋ-gwij\ *noun* (circa 1958)

parabola 1:
F fixed point;
CD fixed line;
x moving point;
AB axis;
xy distance from
x to *CD*;
pp′ parabola

\ə\ abut \ᵊ\ kitten \ər\ further \a\ ash \ā\ ace
\ä\ mop, mar \aù\ out \ch\ chin \e\ bet \ē\ easy
\g\ go \i\ hit \ī\ ice \j\ job \ŋ\ sing \ō\ go
\ȯ\ law \ȯi\ boy \th\ thin \th\ the \ü\ loot \ù\ foot
\y\ yet \zh\ vision *see also* Guide to Pronunciation

: optional vocal effects (as tone of voice) that accompany and that may communicate meaning

par·al·de·hyde \pa-'ral-də-ˌhīd, pə-\ *noun* (1857)
: a colorless liquid polymeric modification $C_6H_{12}O_3$ of acetaldehyde used as a hypnotic

para·le·gal \ˌpar-ə-'lē-gəl\ *adjective* (1971)
: of, relating to, or being a paraprofessional who assists a lawyer
— **para·le·gal** \ˌpar-ə-ˌlē-gəl\ *noun*

para·lin·guis·tics \ˌpar-ə-liŋ-'gwis-tiks\ *noun* (circa 1958)
: the study of paralanguage
— **para·lin·guis·tic** \-tik\ *adjective*

Par·a·li·pom·e·non \ˌpar-ə-lə-'pä-mə-ˌnän, -lī-\ *noun* [Late Latin, from Greek *Paraleipomenōn*, genitive of *Paraleipomena*, literally, things left out, from neuter plural of passive present participle of *paraleipein* to leave out, from *para-* + *leipein* to leave; from its forming a supplement to Samuel and Kings — more at LOAN]
: CHRONICLES

par·al·lac·tic \ˌpar-ə-'lak-tik\ *adjective* [New Latin *parallacticus*, from Greek *parallaktikos*, from *parallaxis*] (1630)
: of, relating to, or due to parallax

par·al·lax \'par-ə-ˌlaks\ *noun* [Middle French *parallaxe*, from Greek *parallaxis*, from *parallassein* to change, from *para-* + *allassein* to change, from *allos* other] (1580)
: the apparent displacement or the difference in apparent direction of an object as seen from two different points not on a straight line with the object; *especially* : the angular difference in direction of a celestial body as measured from two points on the earth's orbit

¹**par·al·lel** \'par-ə-ˌlel, -ləl\ *adjective* [Latin *parallelus*, from Greek *parallēlos*, from *para* beside + *allēlōn* of one another, from *allos* . . . *allos* one . . . another, from *allos* other — more at ELSE] (1549)
1 a : extending in the same direction, everywhere equidistant, and not meeting ⟨*parallel* rows of trees⟩ **b** : everywhere equally distant ⟨concentric spheres are *parallel*⟩
2 a : having parallel sides ⟨a *parallel* reamer⟩ **b** : being or relating to an electrical circuit having a number of conductors in parallel **c** : arranged in parallel ⟨a *parallel* processor⟩ **d** : relating to or being a connection in a computer system in which the bits of a byte are transmitted over separate channels at the same time — compare SERIAL
3 a : similar, analogous, or interdependent in tendency or development **b** : readily compared : COMPANION **c** : having identical syntactical elements in corresponding positions; *also* : being such an element **d** (1) : having the same tonic — used of major and minor keys and scales (2) : keeping the same distance apart in musical pitch
4 : performed while keeping one's skis parallel ⟨*parallel* turns⟩
synonym see SIMILAR

²**parallel** *noun* (1551)
1 a : a parallel line, curve, or surface **b** : one of the imaginary circles on the surface of the earth paralleling the equator and marking the latitude; *also* : the corresponding line on a globe or map — see LATITUDE illustration **c** : a character ‖ used in printing especially as a reference mark
2 a : something equal or similar in all essential particulars : COUNTERPART **b** : SIMILARITY, ANALOGUE
3 : a comparison to show resemblance : a tracing of similarity
4 a : the state of being physically parallel : PARALLELISM **b** : an arrangement of electrical devices in a circuit in which the same potential difference is applied to two or more resistances with each resistance being on a different branch of the circuit — compare SERIES **c** : an arrangement or state that permits several

operations or tasks to be performed simultaneously rather than consecutively

³**parallel** *transitive verb* (1598)
1 : to indicate analogy of : COMPARE
2 a : to show something equal to : MATCH **b** : to correspond to
3 : to place so as to be parallel in direction with something
4 : to extend, run, or move in a direction parallel to

⁴**parallel** *adverb* (1787)
: in a parallel manner

parallel bars *noun plural* (1868)
1 : a pair of wooden bars supported horizontally above the floor at the same height or at different heights usually by a common base and used in gymnastics
2 : an event in gymnastics competition in which even or uneven parallel bars are used

par·al·lel·e·pi·ped \ˌpar-ə-ˌle-lə-'pī-pəd *also* -ˌle-'le-pə-ˌped\ *noun* [Greek *parallēlepipedon*, from *parallēlos* + *epipedon* plane surface, from neuter of *epipedos* flat, from *epi-* epi- + *pedon* ground; akin to Latin *ped-*, *pes* foot — more at FOOT] (1570)
: a 6-faced polyhedron all of whose faces are parallelograms lying in pairs of parallel planes

par·al·lel·ism \'par-ə-ˌle-ˌli-zəm, -lə-ˌli-\ *noun* (1610)
1 : the quality or state of being parallel
2 : RESEMBLANCE, CORRESPONDENCE
3 : repeated syntactical similarities introduced for rhetorical effect
4 : a theory that mind and matter accompany one another but are not causally related
5 : the development of similar new characters by two or more related organisms in response to similarity of environment — called also *parallel evolution*

par·al·lel·o·gram \ˌpar-ə-'le-lə-ˌgram\ *noun* [Late Latin or Greek; Late Latin *parallelogrammum*, from Greek *parallēlogrammon*, from neuter of *parallēlogrammos* bounded by parallel lines, from *parallēlos* + *grammē* line, from *graphein* to write — more at CARVE] (1570)
: a quadrilateral with opposite sides parallel and equal

par·al·lel–veined \ˌpar-ə-ˌlel-'vānd, -ləl-\ *adjective* (1861)
of a leaf : having veins arranged nearly parallel to one another — compare NET-VEINED

pa·ral·o·gism \pə-'ra-lə-ˌji-zəm\ *noun* [Middle French *paralogisme*, from Late Latin *paralogismus*, from Greek *paralogismos*, from *paralogos* unreasonable, from *para-* + *logos* speech, reason — more at LEGEND] (1565)
: a fallacious argument

par·a·lyse *British variant of* PARALYZE

pa·ral·y·sis \pə-'ra-lə-səs\ *noun, plural* **-y·ses** \-ˌsēz\ [Latin, from Greek, from *paralyein* to loosen, disable, from *para-* + *lyein* to loosen — more at LOSE] (1525)
1 : complete or partial loss of function especially when involving the motion or sensation in a part of the body
2 : loss of the ability to move
3 : a state of powerlessness or incapacity to act

paralysis agi·tans \-'a-jə-ˌtanz\ *noun* [New Latin, literally, shaking palsy] (1817)
: PARKINSON'S DISEASE

¹**par·a·lyt·ic** \ˌpar-ə-'li-tik\ *adjective* [Middle English *paralytyk*, from Middle French *paralitike*, from Latin *paralyticus*, from Greek *paralytikos*, from *paralyein*] (14th century)
1 : affected with or characterized by paralysis
2 : of, relating to, or resembling paralysis
— **par·a·lyt·i·cal·ly** \-ti-k(ə-)lē\ *adverb*

²**paralytic** *noun* (14th century)
: one affected with paralysis

par·a·lyze \'par-ə-ˌlīz\ *transitive verb* **-lyzed; -lyz·ing** [French *paralyser*, back-formation from *paralysie* paralysis, from Latin *paralysis*] (1804)
1 : to affect with paralysis

2 : to make powerless or ineffective
3 : UNNERVE
4 : STUN, STUPEFY
5 : to bring to an end : PREVENT, DESTROY
— **par·a·ly·za·tion** \ˌpar-ə-lə-'zā-shən\ *noun*
— **par·a·lyz·er** \'par-ə-ˌlī-zər\ *noun*
— **par·a·lyz·ing·ly** \-ˌlī-ziŋ-lē\ *adverb*

para·mag·net \'par-ə-ˌmag-nət\ *noun* [backformation from *paramagnetic*] (circa 1900)
: a paramagnetic substance

para·mag·net·ic \ˌpar-ə-mag-'ne-tik\ *adjective* [International Scientific Vocabulary] (circa 1850)
: being or relating to a magnetizable substance (as aluminum) that has small but positive susceptibility which varies little with magnetizing force
— **para·mag·net·i·cal·ly** \-ti-k(ə-)lē\ *adverb*
— **para·mag·ne·tism** \-'mag-nə-ˌti-zəm\ *noun*

par·a·me·cium \ˌpar-ə-'mē-sh(ē-)əm, -sē-əm\ *noun, plural* **-cia** \-sh(ē-)ə, -sē-ə\ *also* **-ci·ums** [New Latin, from Greek *paramēkēs* oblong, from *para-* + *mēkos* length; akin to Greek *makros* long — more at MEAGER] (1752)
: any of a genus (*Paramecium*) of ciliate protozoans that have an elongate body rounded at the anterior end and an oblique funnel-shaped buccal groove bearing the mouth at the extremity

para·med·ic \ˌpar-ə-'me-dik\ *also* **para·med·i·cal** \-di-kəl\ *noun* (1967)
1 : a person who works in a health field in an auxiliary capacity to a physician (as by giving injections and taking X rays)
2 : a specially trained medical technician licensed to provide a wide range of emergency services (as defibrillation and the intravenous administration of drugs) before or during transportation to a hospital — compare EMT

para·med·i·cal \ˌpar-ə-'me-di-kəl\ *also* **para·med·ic** \-dik\ *adjective* (1921)
: concerned with supplementing the work of highly trained medical professionals ⟨*paramedical* aides and technicians⟩

par·a·ment \'par-ə-mənt\ *noun* [Middle English, from Medieval Latin *paramentum*, from *parare* to adorn, from Latin, to prepare — more at PARE] (15th century)
: an ornamental ecclesiastical hanging or vestment

pa·ram·e·ter \pə-'ram-ə-tər\ *noun* [New Latin, from *para-* + Greek *metron* measure — more at MEASURE] (1656)
1 a : an arbitrary constant whose value characterizes a member of a system (as a family of curves); *also* : a quantity (as a mean or variance) that describes a statistical population **b** : an independent variable used to express the coordinates of a variable point and functions of them — compare PARAMETRIC EQUATION
2 : any of a set of physical properties whose values determine the characteristics or behavior of something ⟨*parameters* of the atmosphere such as temperature, pressure, and density⟩
3 : something represented by a parameter : a characteristic element; *broadly* : CHARACTERISTIC, ELEMENT, FACTOR ⟨political dissent as a *parameter* of modern life⟩
4 : LIMIT, BOUNDARY — usually used in plural ⟨the *parameters* of science fiction⟩
— **par·a·met·ric** \ˌpar-ə-'me-trik\ *adjective*
— **par·a·met·ri·cal·ly** \-tri-k(ə-)lē\ *adverb*

pa·ram·e·ter·ize \pə-'ra-mə-tə-ˌrīz, -mə-ˌtrīz\ *or* **pa·ram·e·trize** \-'ra-mə-ˌtrīz\ *transitive verb* **-ter·ized** *or* **-trized; -ter·iz·ing** *or* **-triz·ing** (1940)
: to express in terms of parameters
— **pa·ram·e·ter·i·za·tion** \-ˌra-mə-tə-rə-'zā-shən, -mə-trə-\ *or* **pa·ram·e·tri·za·tion** \-mə-trə-\ *noun*

parametric equation *noun* (1909)

: any of a set of equations that express the coordinates of the points of a curve as functions of one parameter or that express the coordinates of the points of a surface as functions of two parameters

para·mil·i·tary \,par-ə-'mi-lə-,ter-ē\ adjective (1935)
: of, relating to, being, or characteristic of a force formed on a military pattern especially as a potential auxiliary military force ⟨a *paramilitary* border patrol⟩ ⟨*paramilitary* training⟩

par·am·ne·sia \,par-,am-'nē-zhə, -əm-\ noun [New Latin, from *para-* + *-mnesia* (as in *amnesia*)] (1888)
: a disorder of memory; *especially* : DÉJÀ VU 1

¹**par·a·mount** \'par-ə-,maunt\ adjective [Anglo-French *paramont*, from Old French *par* by (from Latin *per*) + *amont* above, from *a* to (from Latin *ad*) + *mont* mountain — more at FOR, AT, MOUNT] (1579)
: superior to all others : SUPREME
synonym see DOMINANT
— **par·a·mount·cy** \-,maun(t)-sē\ noun
— **par·a·mount·ly** \-,maunt-lē\ adverb

²**paramount** noun (1616)
: a supreme ruler

par·amour \'par-ə-,mur\ noun [Middle English, from *par amour* by way of love, from Middle French] (14th century)
: an illicit lover

par·am·y·lum \,pa-'ra-mə-ləm\ noun [New Latin, from *para-* + Latin *amylum* starch — more at AMYL-] (1897)
: a reserve carbohydrate that is found in various protozoans and algae and resembles starch

para·myxo·vi·rus \,par-ə-'mik-sə-,vī-rəs\ noun [New Latin] (1962)
: any of a group of RNA-containing viruses (as the mumps, measles, and parainfluenza viruses)

pa·rang \'pär-aŋ\ noun [Malay] (1839)
: a short sword, cleaver, or machete common in Malaysia and Indonesia

para·noia \,par-ə-'noi-ə\ noun [New Latin, from Greek, madness, from *paranous* demented, from *para-* + *nous* mind] (circa 1811)
1 : a psychosis characterized by systematized delusions of persecution or grandeur usually without hallucinations
2 : a tendency on the part of an individual or group toward excessive or irrational suspiciousness and distrustfulness of others
— **para·noi·ac** \-'noi-,ak, -'noi-ik\ also **para·noic** \-'noi(-i)k, -'nō-ik\ adjective or noun
— **para·noi·cal·ly** \-'noi(-i)-k(ə-)lē, -'nō-i-k(ə-)lē\ adverb

para·noid \'par-ə-,noid\ also **para·noi·dal** \,par-ə-'noi-dᵊl\ adjective (1904)
1 : characterized by or resembling paranoia
2 : characterized by suspiciousness, persecutory trends, or megalomania
3 : extremely fearful
— **paranoid** noun

paranoid schizophrenia noun (1940)
: schizophrenia characterized especially by persecutory or grandiose delusions or hallucinations or by delusional jealousy

para·nor·mal \,par-ə-'nor-məl, 'par-ə-,\ adjective (circa 1920)
: not scientifically explainable : SUPERNATURAL
— **paranormal** noun
— **para·nor·mal·i·ty** \,par-ə-,nor-'ma-lə-tē\ noun
— **para·nor·mal·ly** \-'nor-mə-lē\ adverb

para·nymph \'par-ə-,nim(p)f\ noun [Late Latin *paranymphus*, from Greek *paranymphos*, from *para-* + *nymphē* bride — more at NUPTIAL] (1600)
1 : a friend going with a bridegroom to fetch home the bride in ancient Greece; *also* : the bridesmaid conducting the bride to the bridegroom
2 a : BEST MAN b : BRIDESMAID

par·a·pet \'par-ə-pət, -,pet\ noun [Italian *parapetto*, from *parare* to shield (from Latin, to prepare) + *petto* chest, from Latin *pectus* — more at PARE, PECTORAL] (1590)
1 : a wall, rampart, or elevation of earth or stone to protect soldiers : BREASTWORK
2 : a low wall or railing to protect the edge of a platform, roof, or bridge — called also *parapet wall*
— **par·a·pet·ed** \-,pe-təd\ adjective

pa·raph \'par-əf, pə-'raf\ noun [Middle French, from Latin *paragraphus* paragraph] (1584)
: a flourish at the end of a signature

par·a·pher·na·lia \,par-ə-fə(r)-'nāl-yə\ noun plural but singular or plural in construction [Medieval Latin, ultimately from Greek *parapherna* bride's property beyond her dowry, from *para-* + *phernē* dowry, from *pherein* to bear — more at BEAR] (1651)
1 : the separate real or personal property of a married woman that she can dispose of by will and sometimes according to common law during her life
2 : personal belongings
3 a : articles of equipment : FURNISHINGS b : accessory items : APPURTENANCES

¹**para·phrase** \'par-ə-,frāz\ noun [Middle French, from Latin *paraphrasis*, from Greek, from *paraphrazein* to paraphrase, from *para-* + *phrazein* to point out] (1548)
1 : a restatement of a text, passage, or work giving the meaning in another form
2 : the use or process of paraphrasing in studying or teaching composition

²**paraphrase** verb **-phrased; -phras·ing** (1596)
intransitive verb
: to make a paraphrase
transitive verb
: to make a paraphrase of
— **para·phras·able** \,par-ə-'frā-zə-bəl\ adjective
— **para·phras·er** noun

para·phras·tic \,par-ə-'fras-tik\ adjective [French *paraphrastique*, from Greek *paraphrastikos*, from *paraphrazein*] (circa 1623)
: having the nature of or being a paraphrase
— **para·phras·ti·cal·ly** \-ti-k(ə-)lē\ adverb

pa·raph·y·sis \pə-'ra-fə-səs\ noun, plural **-y·ses** \-,sēz\ [New Latin, from Greek, sucker, offshoot, from *paraphyein* to produce at the side, from *para-* + *phyein* to bring forth — more at BE] (1857)
: one of the slender sterile filaments borne among the sporogenous or gametogenous organs in cryptogamic plants

para·ple·gia \,par-ə-'plē-j(ē-)ə\ noun [New Latin, from Greek *paraplēgiē* hemiplegia, from *para-* + *-plēgia* -plegia] (circa 1657)
: paralysis of the lower half of the body with involvement of both legs
— **para·ple·gic** \-jik\ adjective or noun

para·po·di·um \-'pō-dē-əm\ noun, plural **-dia** \-dē-ə\ [New Latin] (1877)
1 : either of a pair of fleshy lateral processes borne by most segments of a polychaete worm
2 : a lateral expansion on each side of the foot usually forming a broad swimming organ in some gastropods
— **para·po·di·al** \-dē-əl\ adjective

para·pro·fes·sion·al \-prə-'fesh-nəl, -'fe-shə-nᵊl\ noun (1965)
: a trained aide who assists a professional person (as a teacher or doctor)
— **paraprofessional** adjective

para·psy·chol·o·gy \,par-ə-(,)sī-'kä-lə-jē\ noun [International Scientific Vocabulary] (1925)
: a field of study concerned with the investigation of evidence for paranormal psychological phenomena (as telepathy, clairvoyance, and psychokinesis)
— **para·psy·cho·log·i·cal** \-,sī-kə-'lä-ji-kəl\ adjective
— **para·psy·chol·o·gist** \-(,)sī-'kä-lə-jist\ noun

para·quat \'par-ə-,kwät\ noun [*para-* + *qua*ternary] (circa 1961)
: a highly toxic contact herbicide containing a salt of a cation $[C_{12}H_{14}N_2]^{2+}$

para·ros·an·i·line \,par-ə-,rō-'za-nᵊl-ən\ noun [International Scientific Vocabulary] (circa 1879)
: a white crystalline base $C_{19}H_{19}N_3O$ that is the parent compound of many dyes; *also* : its red chloride used especially as a biological stain

Pa·ra rubber \'par-ə-, pə-'rä-\ noun [*Pará*, Brazil] (1857)
: native rubber from South American rubber trees (genus *Hevea* and especially *H. brasiliensis*)

Para rubber tree noun (1930)
: a South American rubber tree (*Hevea brasiliensis*)

para·sail·ing \'par-ə-,sā-liŋ\ noun (1967)
: the recreational sport of soaring in a parachute while being towed usually by a motorboat

par·a·sang \'par-ə-,saŋ\ noun [Latin *parasanga*, from Greek *parasangēs*, of Iranian origin; akin to Persian *farsung* parasang] (1594)
: any of various Persian units of distance; *especially* : an ancient unit of about four miles (six kilometers)

para·sex·u·al \-'sek-sh(ə-)wəl, -shəl\ adjective (1954)
: relating to or being reproduction that results in recombination of genes from different individuals but does not involve meiosis and formation of a zygote by fertilization as in sexual reproduction ⟨the *parasexual* cycle in some fungi⟩
— **para·sex·u·al·i·ty** \-,sek-shə-'wa-lə-tē\ noun

pa·ra·shah \'pär-ə-,shä\ noun [Hebrew *pārāshāh*, literally, explanation] (1624)
: a passage in Jewish Scripture dealing with a single topic; *specifically* : a section of the Torah assigned for weekly reading in synagogue worship

par·a·site \'par-ə-,sīt\ noun [Middle French, from Latin *parasitus*, from Greek *parasitos*, from *para-* + *sitos* grain, food] (1539)
1 : a person who exploits the hospitality of the rich and earns welcome by flattery
2 : an organism living in, with, or on another organism in parasitism
3 : something that resembles a biological parasite in dependence on something else for existence or support without making a useful or adequate return ☆

☆ SYNONYMS
Parasite, sycophant, toady, leech, sponge mean a usually obsequious flatterer or self-seeker. PARASITE applies to one who clings to a person of wealth, power, or influence or is useless to society ⟨a jet-setter with an entourage of *parasites*⟩. SYCOPHANT adds to this a strong suggestion of fawning, flattery, or adulation ⟨a powerful prince surrounded by *sycophants*⟩. TOADY emphasizes the servility and snobbery of the self-seeker ⟨cultivated leaders of society and became their *toady*⟩. LEECH stresses persistence in clinging to or bleeding another for one's own advantage ⟨a *leech* living off his family and friends⟩. SPONGE stresses the parasitic laziness, dependence, and opportunism of the cadger ⟨a shiftless *sponge*, always looking for a handout⟩.

\ə\ abut \ᵊ\ kitten \ər\ further \a\ ash \ā\ ace \ä\ mop, mar \au\ out \ch\ chin \e\ bet \ē\ easy \g\ go \i\ hit \ī\ ice \j\ job \ŋ\ sing \ō\ go \o\ law \oi\ boy \th\ thin \t͟h\ the \ü\ loot \u̇\ foot \y\ yet \zh\ vision *see also* Guide to Pronunciation

— **par·a·sit·ic** \par-ə-'si-tik\ *also* **par·a·sit·i·cal** \-ti-kəl\ *adjective*

— **par·a·sit·i·cal·ly** \-ti-k(ə-)lē\ *adverb*

par·a·sit·i·cid·al \par-ə-,si-tə-'sī-dᵊl\ *adjective* (1892)
: destructive to parasites

— **par·a·sit·i·cide** \-'si-tə-,sīd\ *noun*

par·a·sit·ise *British variant of* PARASITIZE

par·a·sit·ism \'par-ə-sə-,ti-zəm, -,sī-\ *noun* (1611)
1 : the behavior of a parasite
2 : an intimate association between organisms of two or more kinds; *especially* : one in which a parasite obtains benefits from a host which it usually injures
3 : PARASITOSIS

par·a·sit·ize \-sə-,tīz, -,sī-\ *transitive verb* **-ized; -iz·ing** (1890)
: to infest or live on or with as a parasite

— **par·a·sit·i·za·tion** \,par-ə-sə-tə-'zā-shən, -,sī-\ *noun*

par·a·sit·oid \'par-ə-sə-,tóid, -,sī-\ *noun* (1922)
: an insect and especially a wasp that completes its larval development within the body of another insect eventually killing it and is free-living as an adult

— **parasitoid** *adjective*

par·a·si·tol·o·gy \,par-ə-sə-'tä-lə-jē, -,sī-\ *noun* [Latin *parasitus* + International Scientific Vocabulary *-logy*] (1882)
: a branch of biology dealing with parasites and parasitism especially among animals

— **par·a·si·to·log·i·cal** \-,si-tᵊl-'ä-ji-kəl, -,sī-\ *also* **par·a·si·to·log·ic** \-jik\ *adjective*

— **par·a·si·to·log·i·cal·ly** \-ji-k(ə-)lē\ *adverb*

— **par·a·si·tol·o·gist** \-sə-'tä-lə-jist, -,sī-\ *noun*

par·a·sit·o·sis \-sə-'tō-səs, -,sī-\ *noun, plural* **-o·ses** \-,sēz\ [New Latin] (circa 1899)
: infestation with or disease caused by parasites

par·a·sol \'par-ə-,sȯl, -,säl\ *noun* [French, from Old Italian *parasole*, from *parare* to shield + *sole* sun, from Latin *sol* — more at PARAPET, SOLAR] (1660)
: a lightweight umbrella used as a sunshade especially by women

¹para·sym·pa·thet·ic \,par-ə-,sim-pə-'the-tik\ *adjective* [International Scientific Vocabulary] (1905)
: of, relating to, being, or acting on the parasympathetic nervous system

²parasympathetic *noun* (1925)
1 : a parasympathetic nerve
2 : PARASYMPATHETIC NERVOUS SYSTEM

parasympathetic nervous system *noun* (circa 1934)
: the part of the autonomic nervous system that contains chiefly cholinergic fibers, that tends to induce secretion, to increase the tone and contractility of smooth muscle, and to slow heart rate, and that consists of a cranial and a sacral part — compare SYMPATHETIC NERVOUS SYSTEM

para·sym·pa·tho·mi·met·ic \,par-ə-'sim-pə-(,)thō-mī-'me-tik, -mə-\ *adjective* [International Scientific Vocabulary] (1942)
: simulating parasympathetic nervous action in physiological effect

para·syn·the·sis \,par-ə-'sin(t)-thə-səs\ *noun* [New Latin] (1862)
: the formation of words by adding a derivative ending and prefixing a particle (as in *denationalize*)

— **para·syn·thet·ic** \-sin-'the-tik\ *adjective*

para·tac·tic \,par-ə-'tak-tik\ *also* **para·tac·ti·cal** \-ti-kəl\ *adjective* (1871)
: of or relating to parataxis

— **para·tac·ti·cal·ly** \-ti-k(ə-)lē\ *adverb*

para·tax·is \,par-ə-'tak-səs\ *noun* [New Latin, from Greek, act of placing side by side, from *paratassein* to place side by side, from *para-* + *tassein* to arrange] (circa 1842)

: the placing of clauses or phrases one after another without coordinating or subordinating connectives

para·thi·on \,par-ə-'thī-ən, -,än\ *noun* [*para-* + *thiophosphate* + *¹-on*] (1947)
: an extremely toxic insecticide $C_{10}H_{14}NO_5PS$

par·a·thor·mone \,par-ə-'thȯr-,mōn\ *noun* [from *Parathormone*, a trademark] (1925)
: PARATHYROID HORMONE

¹para·thy·roid \-'thī-,rȯid\ *noun* (1897)
: PARATHYROID GLAND

²parathyroid *adjective* [International Scientific Vocabulary] (1902)
: of, relating to, or produced by the parathyroid glands

para·thy·roid·ec·to·my \-,rȯi-'dek-tə-mē\ *noun, plural* **-mies** (1903)
: partial or complete excision of the parathyroid glands

— **para·thy·roid·ec·to·mized** \-,mīzd\ *adjective*

parathyroid gland *noun* [International Scientific Vocabulary] (circa 1903)
: any of usually four small endocrine glands that are adjacent to or embedded in the thyroid gland and produce parathyroid hormone

parathyroid hormone *noun* (1953)
: a hormone of the parathyroid gland that regulates the metabolism of calcium and phosphorus in the body

para·troop·er \'par-ə-,trü-pər\ *noun* (1927)
: a member of the paratroops

para·troops \-,trüps\ *noun plural* [²*para-*] (1940)
: troops trained and equipped to parachute from an airplane

— **para·troop** \-,trüp\ *adjective*

¹para·ty·phoid \,par-ə-'tī-,fȯid, -(,)tī-'\ *adjective* [International Scientific Vocabulary] (1902)
1 : resembling typhoid fever
2 : of or relating to paratyphoid or its causative organisms ⟨*paratyphoid* infection⟩

²paratyphoid *noun* (1903)
: a salmonellosis that resembles typhoid fever and is commonly contracted by eating contaminated food — called also *paratyphoid fever*

para·vane \'par-ə-,vān\ *noun* [probably from French *para-* warding off (as in *parachute*) + English *vane*] (1919)
: a torpedo-shaped protective device with serrate teeth in its forward end used underwater by a ship in mined areas to sever the moorings of mines

par·boil \'pär-,bȯil\ *transitive verb* [Middle English, from *parboilen* to boil thoroughly, from Middle French *parboillir*, from Late Latin *perbullire*, from Latin *per-* thoroughly (from *per* through) + *bullire* to boil, from *bulla* bubble — more at FOR] (14th century)
: to boil briefly as a preliminary or incomplete cooking procedure

par·buck·le \'pär-,bə-kəl\ *noun* [origin unknown] (1626)
: a purchase for hoisting or lowering a cylindrical object by making fast the middle of a long rope aloft and looping both ends around the object which rests in the loops and rolls in them as the ends are hauled up or paid

parbuckle

out; *also* : a single line made fast at one end and passed around an object that is used similarly

— **parbuckle** *transitive verb*

Par·cae \'pär-,kī, -,sē\ *noun plural* [Latin]
: FATE 4

¹par·cel \'pär-səl\ *noun* [Middle English, from Middle French, from (assumed) Vulgar Latin

particella, from Latin *particula* small part — more at PARTICLE] (14th century)
1 a : FRAGMENT, PORTION **b** : a volume of a fluid (as air) considered as a single entity within a greater volume of the same fluid
2 : a tract or plot of land
3 : a company, collection, or group of persons, animals, or things : LOT ⟨the whole story was a *parcel* of lies⟩
4 a : a wrapped bundle : PACKAGE **b** : a unit of salable merchandise

²parcel *adverb* (15th century)
archaic : PARTLY

³parcel *adjective* (15th century)
: PART-TIME, PARTIAL

⁴parcel *transitive verb* **-celed** *or* **-celled; -cel·ing** *or* **-cel·ling** \'pär-s(ə-)liŋ\ (15th century)
1 : to divide into parts : DISTRIBUTE — often used with *out*
2 : to make up into a parcel : WRAP
3 : to cover (as a rope) with strips of canvas or tape

parcel post *noun* (1837)
1 : a mail service handling parcels
2 : packages handled by parcel post

par·ce·nary \'pär-sᵊn-,er-ē\ *noun* [Anglo-French *parcenarie*, from Old French *parçonerie*, from *parçon* portion, from Latin *partition-, partitio* partition] (1544)
: COPARCENARY 1

par·ce·ner \'pärs-nər, 'pär-sᵊn-ər\ *noun* [Anglo-French, from Old French *parçonier*, from *parçon*] (1574)
: COPARCENER

parch \'pärch\ *verb* [Middle English] (14th century)
transitive verb
1 : to toast under dry heat
2 : to shrivel with heat
3 : to dry or shrivel with cold
intransitive verb
: to become dry or scorched

parched \'pärcht\ *adjective* (circa 1552)
: deprived of natural moisture; *also* : THIRSTY

Par·chee·si \pär-'chē-zē, pər-, *especially British* -sē\ *trademark*
— used for a board game adapted from pachisi

parch·ment \'pärch-mənt\ *noun* [Middle English *parchemin*, from Middle French, modification of Latin *pergamena*, from Greek *pergamēnē*, from feminine of *Pergamēnos* of Pergamum, from *Pergamon* Pergamum] (14th century)
1 : the skin of a sheep or goat prepared for writing on
2 : strong, tough, and often somewhat translucent paper made to resemble parchment
3 : a parchment manuscript; *also* : an academic diploma

¹pard \'pärd\ *noun* [Middle English *parde*, from Middle French, from Latin *pardus*, from Greek *pardos*] (14th century)
: LEOPARD

²pard *noun* [short for *pardner*] (1850)
chiefly dialect : PARTNER, CHUM

par·die *or* **par·di** *or* **par·dy** \pər-'dē, pär-\ *interjection* [Middle English *pardee*, from Old French *par Dé* by God] (14th century)
archaic — used as a mild oath

pard·ner \'pärd-nər\ *noun* [alteration of *partner*] (1795)
chiefly dialect : PARTNER, CHUM

¹par·don \'pär-dᵊn\ *noun* [Middle English, from Middle French, from *pardoner*] (14th century)
1 : INDULGENCE 1
2 : the excusing of an offense without exacting a penalty
3 a : a release from the legal penalties of an offense **b** : an official warrant of remission of penalty
4 : excuse or forgiveness for a fault, offense, or discourtesy ⟨I beg your *pardon*⟩

²pardon transitive verb **par·doned; par·don·ing** \'pärd-niŋ, 'pär-d°n-iŋ\ [Middle English, from Middle French pardoner, from Late Latin perdonare to grant freely, from Latin per- thoroughly + donare to give — more at PARBOIL, DONATION] (15th century)
1 a : to absolve from the consequences of a fault or crime **b** : to allow (an offense) to pass without punishment : FORGIVE **c** : to relieve of a penalty improperly assessed
2 : TOLERATE
synonym see EXCUSE
par·don·able \'pärd-nə-bəl, 'pär-d°n-ə-bəl\ adjective (15th century)
: admitting of being pardoned : EXCUSABLE ⟨pardonable offenses⟩
— **par·don·able·ness** noun
— **par·don·ably** \-blē\ adverb
par·don·er \'pärd-nər, 'pär-d°n-ər\ noun (14th century)
1 : a medieval preacher delegated to raise money for religious works by soliciting offerings and granting indulgences
2 : one that pardons
pare \'par, 'per\ transitive verb **pared; par·ing** [Middle English, from Middle French parer to prepare, trim, from Latin parare to prepare, acquire; akin to Latin parere to give birth to, produce, Lithuanian perėti to hatch] (14th century)
1 : to trim off an outside, excess, or irregular part of ⟨pare apples⟩ ⟨paring his nails⟩
2 : to diminish or reduce by or as if by paring ⟨pare expenses⟩ ⟨the novel was pared down to 200 pages⟩
— **par·er** noun
par·e·gor·ic \,par-ə-'gòr-ik, -'gōr-, -'gär-\ noun [French parégorique mitigating pain, from Late Latin paregoricus, from Greek parēgorikos, from parēgorein to talk over, soothe, from para- + agora assembly, from ageirein to gather] (circa 1847)
: camphorated tincture of opium used especially to relieve pain
pa·ren·chy·ma \pə-'reŋ-kə-mə\ noun [New Latin, from Greek, visceral flesh, from parenchein to pour in beside, from para- + en- en- + chein to pour — more at FOUND] (1651)
1 : a tissue of higher plants that consists of thin-walled living photosynthetic or storage cells capable of division even when mature and that makes up much of the substance of leaves and roots, the pulp of fruits, and parts of stems and supporting structures
2 : the essential and distinctive tissue of an organ or an abnormal growth as distinguished from its supportive framework
— **par·en·chy·ma·tous** \,par-ən-'kī-mə-təs, -'ki-\ or **pa·ren·chy·mal** \pə-'reŋ-kə-məl, ,par-ən-'kī-\ adjective
¹par·ent \'par-ənt, 'per-\ noun [Middle English, from Middle French, from Latin parent-, parens; akin to Latin parere to give birth to] (15th century)
1 a : one that begets or brings forth offspring **b** : a person who brings up and cares for another
2 a : an animal or plant that is regarded in relation to its offspring **b** : the material or source from which something is derived **c** : a group from which another arises and to which it usually remains subsidiary ⟨a parent company⟩
— **parent** adjective
— **pa·ren·tal** \pə-'ren-t°l\ adjective
— **pa·ren·tal·ly** \-t°l-ē\ adverb
— **par·ent·less** \'par-ənt-ləs, 'per-\ adjective
²parent transitive verb (1663)
: to be or act as the parent of : ORIGINATE, PRODUCE
par·ent·age \'par-ən-tij, 'per-\ noun [Middle English, from Middle French, from parent] (15th century)

1 a : descent from parents or ancestors : LINEAGE ⟨a person of noble parentage⟩ **b** : DERIVATION, ORIGIN ⟨a tradition of uncertain parentage⟩
2 : PARENTHOOD
par·en·ter·al \pa-'ren-tə-rəl\ adjective [International Scientific Vocabulary para- + enteral] (circa 1910)
: situated or occurring outside the intestine; especially : introduced otherwise than by way of the intestines
— **par·en·ter·al·ly** \-rə-lē\ adverb
pa·ren·the·sis \pə-'ren(t)-thə-səs\ noun, plural **-the·ses** \-,sēz\ [Late Latin, from Greek, literally, act of inserting, from parentithenai to insert, from para- + en- en- + tithenai to place — more at DO] (circa 1550)
1 a : an amplifying or explanatory word, phrase, or sentence inserted in a passage from which it is usually set off by punctuation **b** : a remark or passage that departs from the theme of a discourse : DIGRESSION
2 : INTERLUDE, INTERVAL
3 : one or both of the curved marks () used in writing and printing to enclose a parenthetical expression or to group a symbolic unit in a logical or mathematical expression
— **par·en·thet·i·cal** \,par-ən-'the-ti-kəl\ also **par·en·thet·ic** \-tik\ adjective
— **par·en·thet·i·cal·ly** \-ti-k(ə-)lē\ adverb
pa·ren·the·size \pə-'ren(t)-thə-,sīz\ transitive verb **-sized; -siz·ing** (1837)
: to make a parenthesis of : enclose within parentheses
par·ent·hood \'par-ənt-,hùd, 'per-\ noun (1856)
: the state of being a parent; specifically : the position, function, or standing of a parent
par·ent·ing \'par-ən-tiŋ, 'per-\ noun (1958)
1 : the raising of a child by its parents
2 : the act or process of becoming a parent
3 : the act of caring for someone in the manner of a parent
parent–teacher association noun, often **P&TA capitalized** (1915)
: an organization of local groups of teachers and the parents of their pupils that works for the improvement of the schools and the benefit of the pupils
pa·re·sis \pə-'rē-səs, 'par-ə-\ noun, plural **pa·re·ses** \-,sēz\ [New Latin, from Greek, from parienai to let fall, from para- + hienai to let go, send — more at JET] (1693)
1 : slight or partial paralysis
2 : GENERAL PARESIS
— **pa·ret·ic** \pə-'re-tik\ adjective or noun
par·es·the·sia \,par-əs-'thē-zhə\ noun [New Latin, from para- + -esthesia (as in anesthesia)] (circa 1860)
: a sensation of pricking, tingling, or creeping on the skin that has no objective cause
— **par·es·thet·ic** \-'the-tik\ adjective
pa·reu or **pa·reo** \'pär-ā-(,)ü\ noun [Tahitian] (1860)
: a wraparound skirt usually made from a rectangular piece of printed cloth and worn by men and women throughout Polynesia
pa·reve \'pär-(ə-)və\ adjective [Yiddish parev] (1941)
: made without milk, meat, or their derivatives ⟨pareve margarine⟩ — compare FLEISHIG, MILCHIG
par ex·cel·lence \'pär-ek-sə-'lä°s\ adjective [French, literally, by excellence] (1695)
: being the best of a kind : PREEMINENT ⟨a salesman par excellence⟩
par·fait \pär-'fā\ noun [French, literally, something perfect, from parfait perfect, from Latin perfectus] (1894)
1 : a flavored custard containing whipped cream and syrup frozen without stirring
2 : a cold dessert made of layers of fruit, syrup, ice cream, and whipped cream
parfait glass noun (circa 1951)
: a tall narrow glass with a short stem

par·fleche \'pär-,flesh\ noun [Canadian French parflèche, from French parer to ward off + flèche arrow] (1827)
1 : a raw hide soaked in lye to remove the hair and dried
2 : an article (as a bag or case) made of parfleche
par·fo·cal \,pär-'fō-kəl\ adjective [Latin par equal + English focal] (1886)
: being or having lenses or lens sets (as eyepieces) with the corresponding focal points all in the same plane
— **par·fo·cal·i·ty** \,pär-fō-'ka-lə-tē\ noun
— **par·fo·cal·ize** \,pär-'fō-kə-,līz\ transitive verb
parge \'pärj\ transitive verb **parged; parg·ing** (1701)
: PARGET
¹par·get \'pär-jət\ transitive verb **-get·ed** or **-get·ted; -get·ing** or **-get·ting** [Middle English pargetten, from Middle French parjeter to throw on top of, from par- thoroughly (from Latin per-) + jeter to throw — more at JET] (14th century)
: to coat with plaster; especially : to apply ornamental or waterproofing plaster to
²parget noun (14th century)
1 : plaster, whitewash, or roughcast for coating a wall
2 : plasterwork especially in raised ornamental figures on walls
par·gy·line \'pär-jə-,lēn\ noun [propargyl (an alcohol) + ²-ine] (1961)
: a monoamine oxidase inhibitor $C_{11}H_{13}N$ that is used in the hydrochloride especially as an antihypertensive agent
parhelic circle noun (1890)
: a luminous circle or halo parallel to the horizon at the altitude of the sun — called also parhelic ring
par·he·lion \pär-'hēl-yən\ noun, plural **-lia** \-lē-ə\ [Latin parelion, from Greek parēlion, from para- + hēlios sun — more at SOLAR] (1647)
: any of several bright spots often tinged with color that often appear on the parhelic circle
— **par·he·lic** \-'hē-lik\ adjective
pa·ri·ah \pə-'rī-ə\ noun [Tamil paraiyan, literally, drummer] (1613)
1 : a member of a low caste of southern India
2 : OUTCAST 1
par·i·an \'par-ē-ən, 'per-\ noun [Parian, adjective; from its suitability for making statuettes] (1850)
: a porcelain composed essentially of kaolin and feldspar and usually used unglazed in ornamental articles
Par·i·an \'par-ē-ən, 'per-\ adjective (1611)
: of or relating to the island of Paros noted for its marble used extensively for sculpture in ancient times
Parian ware noun (1894)
1 : PARIAN
2 : articles made of parian
¹pa·ri·e·tal \pə-'rī-ə-t°l\ adjective [Middle French, from New Latin pariet-, paries wall of a cavity or hollow organ, from Latin, wall] (15th century)
1 a : of or relating to the walls of a part or cavity **b** : of, relating to, or forming the upper posterior wall of the head
2 : attached to the main wall rather than the axis or a cross wall of a plant ovary — used of an ovule or a placenta
3 : of or relating to college living or its regulation; especially : of or relating to parietals
²parietal noun (15th century)
1 : a parietal part (as a bone, scale, or plate)

2 *plural* **:** the regulations governing the visiting privileges of members of the opposite sex in campus dormitories

pa·ri·e·tal bone *noun* (15th century)
: either of a pair of bones of the roof of the skull between the frontal bones and the occipital bones

parietal cell *noun* (1875)
: any of the large oval cells of the gastric mucous membrane that secrete hydrochloric acid

parietal lobe *noun* (circa 1889)
: the middle division of each cerebral hemisphere that contains an area concerned with bodily sensations

pari–mu·tu·el \ˌpar-i-ˈmyü-chə-wəl, -chəl; -ˈmyüch-wəl\ *noun* [French *pari mutuel*, literally, mutual stake] (1888)
1 : a betting pool in which those who bet on competitors finishing in the first three places share the total amount bet minus a percentage for the management
2 : a machine for registering the bets and computing the payoffs in pari-mutuel betting

par·ing \ˈpar-iŋ, ˈper-\ *noun* (14th century)
1 : the act of cutting away an edge or surface
2 : something pared off ⟨apple *parings*⟩

paring knife *noun* (1591)
: a small short-bladed knife (as for paring fruit)

pa·ri pas·su \ˈpar-i-ˈpa-(ˌ)sü\ *adverb or adjective* [Latin, with equal step] (1567)
: at an equal rate or pace

Par·is \ˈpar-əs\ *noun* [Latin, from Greek]
: a son of Priam whose abduction of Helen leads to the Trojan War

Par·is green \ˈpar-əs-\ *noun* [*Paris,* France] (1868)
1 : a very poisonous copper-based bright green powder that is used as an insecticide and pigment
2 : a brilliant yellowish green

par·ish \ˈpar-ish\ *noun* [Middle English *parisshe,* from Middle French *paroche,* from Late Latin *parochia,* from Late Greek *paroikia,* from *paroikos* Christian, from Greek, stranger, from *para-* + *oikos* house — more at VICINITY] (14th century)
1 a (1) **:** the ecclesiastical unit of area committed to one pastor (2) **:** the residents of such an area **b** *British* **:** a subdivision of a county often coinciding with an original ecclesiastical parish and constituting the unit of local government
2 : a local church community composed of the members or constituents of a Protestant church
3 : a civil division of the state of Louisiana corresponding to a county in other states

pa·rish·ion·er \pə-ˈri-sh(ə-)nər\ *noun* [Middle English *parisshoner,* probably modification of Middle French *parrochien,* from *parroche*] (15th century)
: a member or inhabitant of a parish

¹par·i·ty \ˈpar-ə-tē\ *noun, plural* **-ties** [Latin *paritas,* from *par* equal] (circa 1609)
1 : the quality or state of being equal or equivalent
2 a : equivalence of a commodity price expressed in one currency to its price expressed in another **b :** equality of purchasing power established by law between different kinds of money at a given ratio
3 : an equivalence between farmers' current purchasing power and their purchasing power at a selected base period maintained by government support of agricultural commodity prices
4 a : the property of an integer with respect to being odd or even ⟨3 and 7 have the same *parity*⟩ **b** (1) **:** the state of being odd or even used as the basis of a method of detecting errors in binary-coded data (2) **:** PARITY BIT
5 : the property of oddness or evenness of a quantum mechanical function
6 : the symmetry of behavior in an interaction of a physical entity (as a subatomic particle) with that of its mirror image

²par·i·ty *noun* [*-parous*] (1878)
: the state or fact of having borne offspring; *also* **:** the number of children previously borne

parity bit *noun* (1957)
: a bit added to an array of bits (as on magnetic tape) to provide parity

¹park \ˈpärk\ *noun* [Middle English, from Old French *parc* enclosure, from Medieval Latin *parricus*] (13th century)
1 a : an enclosed piece of ground stocked with game and held by royal prescription or grant **b :** a tract of land that often includes lawns, woodland, and pasture attached to a country house and is used as a game preserve and for recreation
2 a : a piece of ground in or near a city or town kept for ornament and recreation **b :** an area maintained in its natural state as a public property
3 a *West* **:** a level valley between mountain ranges **b :** an open space and especially a grassland that is often all or partly surrounded by woodland and is suitable for cultivation or grazing
4 a : a space occupied by military animals, vehicles, or materials **b :** PARKING LOT
5 : an enclosed arena or stadium used especially for ball games
6 : an area designed for a specified industrial, commercial, or residential use ⟨amusement *park*⟩ ⟨industrial *park*⟩ ⟨mobile home *park*⟩
— **park·like** \ˈpärk-ˌlīk\ *adjective*

²park (1526)
transitive verb
1 : to enclose in a park
2 a (1) **:** to bring (a vehicle) to a stop and keep standing at the edge of a public way (2) **:** to leave temporarily on a public way or in a parking lot or garage **b :** to land and leave (as an airplane) **c :** to establish (as a satellite) in orbit
3 a : to set and leave temporarily ⟨*parked* his hat on the chair⟩ **b :** to place, settle, or establish especially for a considerable time ⟨kids *parked* in front of the TV⟩ ⟨*parked* her money in a savings account⟩
4 : to assemble (as equipment or stores) in a military dump or park
intransitive verb
: to park a vehicle
— **park·er** *noun*

par·ka \ˈpär-kə\ *noun* [Aleut, from Russian dialect, ultimately from Nenets (Samoyedic language of northern Russia)] (1780)
1 : a hooded fur pullover garment for arctic wear
2 : a usually lined fabric outerwear pullover or jacket

parking lot *noun* (1924)
: an area used for the parking of motor vehicles

parking meter *noun* (1936)
: a coin-operated device which registers the purchase of parking time for a motor vehicle

par·kin·so·nian \ˌpär-kən-ˈsō-nē-ən, -nyən\ *adjective* (1906)
1 : of or similar to that of parkinsonism
2 : affected with parkinsonism and especially Parkinson's disease

par·kin·son·ism \ˈpär-kən-sə-ˌni-zəm\ *noun* (circa 1923)
1 : PARKINSON'S DISEASE
2 : a nervous disorder that resembles Parkinson's disease

Par·kin·son's disease \ˈpär-kən-sənz-\ *noun* [James *Parkinson* (died 1824) English physician] (1877)
: a chronic progressive nervous disease chiefly of later life that is linked to decreased dopamine production in the substantia nigra and is marked by tremor and weakness of resting muscles and by a shuffling gait — called also *paralysis agitans, Parkinson's, Parkinson's syndrome*

Parkinson's Law *noun* [C. Northcote *Parkinson* (born 1909) English historian] (1955)

1 : an observation in office organization: the number of subordinates increases at a fixed rate regardless of the amount of work produced
2 : an observation in office organization: work expands so as to fill the time available for its completion

park·land \ˈpärk-ˌland\ *noun* (1907)
: land with clumps of trees and shrubs in cultivated condition used as or suitable for use as a park

park·way \ˈpärk-ˌwā\ *noun* (1887)
: a broad landscaped thoroughfare

par·lance \ˈpär-lən(t)s\ *noun* [Middle French, from Old French, from *parler*] (circa 1580)
1 : SPEECH; *especially* **:** formal debate or parley
2 : manner or mode of speech **:** IDIOM

par·lan·do \pär-ˈlän-(ˌ)dō\ *or* **par·lan·te** \-(ˌ)tā\ *adjective* [*parlando* from Italian, verbal of *parlare* to speak, from Medieval Latin *parabolare; parlante* from Italian, present participle of *parlare*] (circa 1854)
: delivered or performed in a style suggestive of speech — used as a direction in music

¹par·lay \ˈpär-ˌlā, -lē\ *transitive verb* [French *paroli,* noun, parlay, from Italian dialect, plural of *parolo,* perhaps from *paro* equal, from Latin *par*] (1828)
1 : to bet in a parlay
2 a : to exploit successfully **b :** to increase or otherwise transform into something of much greater value

²parlay *noun* (1904)
: a series of two or more bets so set up in advance that the original stake plus its winnings are risked on the successive wagers; *broadly* **:** the fresh risking of an original stake together with its winnings

parle \ˈpär(-ə)l\ *intransitive verb* **parled; parl·ing** [Middle English, to parley, from Middle French *parler*] (14th century)
archaic **:** PARLEY
— **parle** *noun, archaic*

¹par·ley \ˈpär-lē\ *noun, plural* **parleys** [Middle English *parlai* speech, probably from Middle French *parlee,* from feminine of *parlé,* past participle of *parler* to speak, from Medieval Latin *parabolare,* from Late Latin *parabola* speech, parable — more at PARABLE] (1581)
1 a : a conference for discussion of points in dispute **b :** a conference with an enemy
2 : DISCUSSION

²par·ley *intransitive verb* **par·leyed; par·ley·ing** (1591)
: to speak with another **:** CONFER; *specifically* **:** to discuss terms with an enemy

par·lia·ment \ˈpär-lə-mənt *also* ˈpärl-yə-\ *noun* [Middle English, from Old French *parlement,* from *parler*] (13th century)
1 : a formal conference for the discussion of public affairs; *specifically* **:** a council of state in early medieval England
2 a : an assemblage of the nobility, clergy, and commons called together by the British sovereign as the supreme legislative body in the United Kingdom **b :** a similar assemblage in another nation or state
3 a : the supreme legislative body of a usually major political unit that is a continuing institution comprising a series of individual assemblages **b :** the British House of Commons
4 : one of several principal courts of justice existing in France before the revolution of 1789

par·lia·men·tar·i·an \ˌpär-lə-ˌmen-ˈter-ē-ən, -mən- *also* ˌpärl-yə-\ *noun* (1644)
1 *often capitalized* **:** an adherent of the parliament in opposition to the king during the English Civil War
2 : an expert in the rules and usages of a deliberative assembly (as a parliament)
3 : a member of a parliament

par·lia·men·ta·ry \-ˈmen-t(ə-)rē\ *adjective* (1616)

1 a : of or relating to a parliament **b :** enacted, done, or ratified by a parliament
2 : of or adhering to the parliament as opposed to the king during the English Civil War
3 : of, based on, or having the characteristics of parliamentary government
4 : of or relating to members of a parliament
5 : of or according to parliamentary law ⟨*parliamentary* procedure⟩

parliamentary government *noun* (1858)
: a system of government having the real executive power vested in a cabinet composed of members of the legislature who are individually and collectively responsible to the legislature

parliamentary law *noun* (1893)
: the rules and precedents governing the proceedings of deliberative assemblies and other organizations

¹par·lor \'pär-lər\ *noun* [Middle English *parlour*, from Old French, from *parler*] (13th century)
1 : a room used primarily for conversation or the reception of guests: as **a :** a room in a private dwelling for the entertainment of guests **b :** a conference chamber or private reception room **c :** a room in an inn, hotel, or club for conversation or semiprivate uses
2 : any of various business places ⟨a funeral *parlor*⟩ ⟨a beauty *parlor*⟩ ◆

²parlor *adjective* (1552)
1 : used in or suitable for a parlor ⟨*parlor* furniture⟩
2 a : fostered or advocated in comfortable seclusion without consequent action or application to affairs ⟨*parlor* bolshevism⟩ **b :** given to or characterized by fostering or advocating something (as a doctrine) in such a manner ⟨*parlor* socialist⟩

parlor car *noun* (1868)
: an extra-fare railroad passenger car for day travel equipped with individual chairs

parlor game *noun* (1872)
: a game suitable for playing indoors

parlor grand *noun* (1856)
: a grand piano intermediate in length between a concert grand and a baby grand

par·lour \'pär-lər\ *chiefly British variant of* PARLOR

par·lous \'pär-ləs\ *adjective* [Middle English, alteration of *perilous*] (14th century)
1 *obsolete* **:** dangerously shrewd or cunning
2 : full of danger or risk **:** HAZARDOUS
— **par·lous·ly** *adverb*

Par·me·san \'pär-mə-ˌzän, -ˌzhän, -ˌzən, -ˌzan\ *noun* [*Parmesan* of Parma, from Middle French *parmesan*, from Old Italian *parmigiano*] (1538)
: a very hard dry sharply flavored cheese that is sold grated or in wedges

par·mi·gia·na \ˌpär-mi-'jä-nə, -'zhän; 'pär-mi-ˌzhän, -ˌzän\ *or* **par·mi·gia·no** \-'jä-(ˌ)nō\ *adjective* [Italian *parmigiana*, feminine of *parmigiano* of Parma, from *Parma*] (1943)
: made or covered with Parmesan cheese ⟨veal *parmigiana*⟩

Par·nas·si·an \pär-'na-sē-ən\ *adjective* (circa 1644)
1 [Latin *parnassius* of Parnassus, from Greek *parnasios*, from *Parnasos* Parnassus, mountain in Greece sacred to Apollo and the Muses] **:** of or relating to poetry
2 [French *parnassien*, from *Parnasse* Parnassus; from *Le Parnasse contemporain* (1866), an anthology of poetry] **:** of or relating to a school of French poets of the second half of the 19th century emphasizing metrical form rather than emotion
— **Parnassian** *noun*

pa·ro·chi·al \pə-'rō-kē-əl\ *adjective* [Middle English *parochiall*, from Middle French *parochial*, from Late Latin *parochialis*, from *parochia* parish — more at PARISH] (14th century)
1 : of or relating to a church parish
2 : of or relating to a parish as a unit of local government

3 : confined or restricted as if within the borders of a parish **:** limited in range or scope (as to a narrow area or region) **:** PROVINCIAL, NARROW
— **pa·ro·chi·al·ly** \-kē-ə-lē\ *adverb*

pa·ro·chi·al·ism \-kē-ə-ˌli-zəm\ *noun* (1847)
: the quality or state of being parochial; *especially* **:** selfish pettiness or narrowness (as of interests, opinions, or views)

parochial school *noun* (1755)
: a private school maintained by a religious body usually for elementary and secondary instruction

par·o·dist \'par-ə-dist\ *noun* (1742)
: a writer of parodies

¹par·o·dy \'par-ə-dē\ *noun, plural* **-dies** [Latin *parodia*, from Greek *parōidia*, from *para-* + *aidein* to sing — more at ODE] (1598)
1 : a literary or musical work in which the style of an author or work is closely imitated for comic effect or in ridicule
2 : a feeble or ridiculous imitation
synonym *see* CARICATURE
— **pa·rod·ic** \pə-'rä-dik, pa-\ *adjective*
— **par·o·dis·tic** \ˌpar-ə-'dis-tik\ *adjective*

²parody *transitive verb* **-died; -dy·ing** (circa 1745)
1 : to compose a parody on ⟨*parody* a poem⟩
2 : to imitate in the manner of a parody

par·ol \'par-əl\ *noun* [Middle French *parole*] (1590)
: WORD OF MOUTH
— **parol** *adjective*

¹pa·role \pə-'rōl\ *noun* [French, speech, parole, from Middle French, from Late Latin *parabola* speech — more at PARABLE] (circa 1616)
1 : a promise made with or confirmed by a pledge of one's honor; *especially* **:** the promise of a prisoner of war to fulfill stated conditions in consideration of his release
2 : a watchword given only to officers of the guard and of the day
3 : a conditional release of a prisoner serving an indeterminate or unexpired sentence
4 a : language viewed as a specific individual usage **:** PERFORMANCE **b :** a linguistic act — compare LANGUE
— **parole** *adjective*

²parole *transitive verb* **pa·roled; pa·rol·ing** (1790)
: to release (a prisoner) on parole

pa·rol·ee \pə-ˌrō-'lē, -'rō-(ˌ); ˌpar-ə-'lē\ *noun* (1903)
: one released on parole

par·o·no·ma·sia \ˌpar-ə-nō-'mā-zh(ē-)ə, ˌpar-ˌä-nə-'mā-\ *noun* [Latin, from Greek, from *paronomazein* to call with a slight change of name, from *para-* + *onoma* name — more at NAME] (1577)
: a play on words **:** PUN
— **par·o·no·mas·tic** \-'mas-tik\ *adjective*

par·o·nym \'par-ə-ˌnim\ *noun* [Late Latin *paronymon*, from Greek *parōnymon*, neuter of *parōnymos*] (circa 1846)
: a paronymous word

par·on·y·mous \pə-'rä-nə-məs, pa-\ *adjective* [Greek *parōnymos*, from *para-* + *-ōnymos* (as in *homōnymos* homonymous)] (circa 1661)
1 : CONJUGATE 4
2 a : formed from a word in another language **b :** having a form similar to that of a cognate foreign word

pa·rot·id \pə-'rä-təd\ *adjective* [New Latin *parotid-, parotis* parotid gland, from Latin, tumor near the ear, from Greek *parōtid-, parōtis*, from *para-* + *ōt-, ous* ear — more at EAR] (1687)
: of or relating to the parotid gland

parotid gland *noun* (circa 1771)
: either of a pair of large serous salivary glands situated below and in front of the ear

par·o·ti·tis \ˌpar-ō-'tī-təs\ *noun* (1822)
: inflammation of the parotid glands; *also*
: MUMPS

par·ous \'par-əs, 'per-\ *adjective* [*-parous*] (circa 1889)
: having produced offspring

-parous *adjective combining form* [Latin *-parus*, from *parere* to give birth to, produce — more at PARE]
: giving birth to **:** producing ⟨multi*parous*⟩

Par·ou·sia \pär-ü-'sē-ə, pə-'rü-zē-ə\ *noun* [Greek, literally, presence, from *paront-, parōn*, present participle of *pareinai* to be present, from *para-* + *einai* to be — more at IS] (1875)
: SECOND COMING

par·ox·ysm \'par-ək-ˌsi-zəm *also* pə-'räk-\ *noun* [French & Medieval Latin; French *paroxysme*, from Medieval Latin *paroxysmus*, from Greek *paroxysmos*, from *paroxynein* to stimulate, from *para-* + *oxynein* to provoke, from *oxys* sharp — more at OXYGEN] (15th century)
1 : a fit, attack, or sudden increase or recurrence of symptoms (as of a disease) **:** CONVULSION ⟨a *paroxysm* of coughing⟩
2 : a sudden violent emotion or action **:** OUTBURST ⟨a *paroxysm* of rage⟩
— **par·ox·ys·mal** \ˌpar-ək-'siz-məl *also* pə-ˌräk-\ *adjective*

¹par·quet \'pär-ˌkā\ *transitive verb* **par·queted** \-'kād\; **par·quet·ing** \-'kā-iŋ\ (1678)
1 : to furnish with a floor of parquet
2 : to make of parquetry

²par·quet \'pär-ˌkā, pär-\ *noun* [French, from Middle French, small enclosure, from *parc* park] (1816)
1 a : a patterned wood surface (as flooring or paneling); *especially* **:** one made of parquetry
b : PARQUETRY
2 : the main floor of a theater; *specifically* **:** the part from the front of the stage to the parquet circle

parquet circle *noun* (1854)
: the part of the main floor of a theater that is beneath the galleries

par·que·try \'pär-kə-trē\ *noun, plural* **-tries** (circa 1842)

◇ **WORD HISTORY**

parlor Within some medieval religious orders a rule of silence was enforced, and the members of a community belonging to the order could speak with each other or outsiders only in a special room. In 12th century Old French this room was called the *parleure*, a derivative of the verb *parler* "to speak." The Old French word was borrowed at an early date into Middle English as *parlure* or *parlour*. In both French and English the sense of the word was extended to rooms such as a chamber for private conversation off the main hall of a manor house, or a room in a municipal building used for conferences. In England the *parlour* in an ordinary middle-class home developed into the best-furnished room in the house, often facing the street, where a family received guests; the word eventually became virtually synonymous with *drawing room* or *living room*. A late 19th century development originally unique to the U.S. was the use of *parlor* with a preceding attributive noun to denote a well-appointed commercial establishment. Though the *Oxford English Dictionary* labeled such usages as "commercial cant," no stigma is attached to *ice cream parlor, beauty parlor,* or *funeral parlor* in 20th century American English.

: work in the form of usually geometrically patterned wood laid or inlaid especially for floors

parr \'pär\ *noun, plural* **parr** *also* **parrs** [origin unknown] (circa 1722)
: a young salmon actively feeding in freshwater

par·ra·keet *variant of* PARAKEET

par·rel *or* **par·ral** \'par-əl\ *noun* [Middle English *perell*, from alteration of *parail* apparel, short for *apparail*, from Middle French *apareil*, from *apareillier* to prepare — more at APPAREL] (15th century)
: a rope loop or sliding collar by which a yard or spar is held to a mast in such a way that it may be hoisted or lowered

par·ri·cid·al \ˌpar-ə-'sī-dᵊl\ *adjective* (1627)
: of, relating to, or guilty of parricide

par·ri·cide \'par-ə-ˌsīd\ *noun* (1554)
1 [Latin *parricida* killer of a close relative, from *parri-* (perhaps akin to Greek *pēos* kinsman by marriage) + *-cida* -cide] : one that murders his or her father, mother, or a close relative
2 [Latin *parricidium* murder of a close relative, from *parri-* + *-cidium* -cidium] : the act of a parricide

¹par·rot \'par-ət\ *noun* [probably irregular from Middle French *perroquet*] (circa 1525)
1 : any of numerous widely distributed tropical zygodactyl birds (order Psittaciformes and especially family Psittacidae) that have a distinctive stout curved hooked bill, are often crested and brightly variegated, and include some excellent mimics
2 : a person who sedulously echoes another's words
— **parrot** *adjective*

²parrot *transitive verb* (1596)
: to repeat by rote

parrot fever *noun* (1930)
: PSITTACOSIS

parrot fish *noun* (1712)
: any of a family (Scaridae) of usually brightly colored chiefly tropical marine fishes that have the teeth in each jaw fused into a cutting plate like a beak

par·ry \'par-ē\ *verb* **par·ried**; **par·ry·ing** [probably from French *parez*, imperative of *parer* to parry, from Old Provençal *parar*, from Latin *parare* to prepare — more at PARE] (1672)
intransitive verb
1 : to ward off a weapon or blow
2 : to evade or turn aside something
transitive verb
1 : to ward off (as a blow)
2 : to evade especially by an adroit answer ⟨*parry* an embarrassing question⟩
— **parry** *noun*

¹parse \'pärs, *chiefly British* 'pärz\ *verb* **parsed**; **pars·ing** [Latin *pars orationis* part of speech] (1553)
transitive verb
1 a : to resolve (as a sentence) into component parts of speech and describe them grammatically **b** : to describe grammatically by stating the part of speech and explaining the inflection and syntactical relationships
2 : to examine in a minute way : analyze critically ⟨*parses* appellate court opinions⟩
intransitive verb
1 : to give a grammatical description of a word or a group of words
2 : to admit of being parsed

²parse *noun* (1963)
: a product or an instance of parsing

par·sec \'pär-ˌsek\ *noun* [*par*allax + *sec*ond] (1913)
: a unit of measure for interstellar space equal to the distance to an object having a parallax of one second or to 3.26 light-years

pars·er \'pär-sər\ *noun* (circa 1864)
: one that parses; *specifically* : a computer program that breaks down text into recognized strings of characters for further analysis

Par·si *also* **Par·see** \'pär-(ˌ)sē\ *noun* [Persian *pārsī*, from *Pārs* Persia] (1615)
1 : a Zoroastrian descended from Persian refugees settled principally at Bombay
2 : the Iranian dialect of the Parsi religious literature
— **Par·si·ism** \-ˌi-zəm\ *noun*

par·si·mo·ni·ous \ˌpär-sə-'mō-nē-əs\ *adjective* (1598)
: exhibiting or marked by parsimony; *especially* : frugal to the point of stinginess
synonym *see* STINGY
— **par·si·mo·ni·ous·ly** *adverb*

par·si·mo·ny \'pär-sə-ˌmō-nē\ *noun* [Middle English *parcimony*, from Latin *parsimonia*, from *parsus*, past participle of *parcere* to spare] (15th century)
1 a : the quality of being careful with money or resources : THRIFT **b** : the quality or state of being stingy
2 : economy in the use of means to an end; *especially* : economy of explanation in conformity with Occam's razor

pars·ley \'pär-slē\ *noun* [Middle English *persely*, from Old English *petersilie*, from (assumed) Vulgar Latin *petrosilium*, alteration of Latin *petroselinum*, from Greek *petroselinon*, from *petros* stone + *selinon* celery] (before 12th century)
: a European biennial herb (*Petroselinum crispum*) of the carrot family that is widely cultivated for its leaves which are used as a culinary herb or garnish

pars·leyed *also* **pars·lied** \-slēd\ *adjective* (1952)
: garnished or flavored with parsley ⟨*parsleyed* potatoes⟩

pars·nip \'pär-snəp\ *noun* [Middle English *pasnepe*, modification of Middle French *pasnaie*, from Latin *pastinaca*, from *pastinum* 2-pronged dibble] (14th century)
: a Eurasian biennial herb (*Pastinaca sativa*) of the carrot family with large pinnate leaves and yellow flowers that is cultivated for its long tapered edible root; *also* : the root

par·son \'pär-sᵊn\ *noun* [Middle English *persone*, from Old French, from Medieval Latin *persona*, literally, person, from Latin] (13th century)
1 : RECTOR
2 : CLERGYMAN; *especially* : a Protestant pastor
word history *see* PERSON

par·son·age \'pär-s(ə-)nij, 'pär-sᵊn-ij\ *noun* (15th century)
: the house provided by a church for its pastor

Par·sons ta·ble \'pär-sᵊnz-\ *noun* [*Parsons* School of Design, New York City] (1967)
: a usually rectangular table having straight legs that are flush with the edge of the top

¹part \'pärt\ *noun* [Middle English, from Old French & Old English, from Latin *part-*, *pars*; perhaps akin to Latin *parare* to prepare — more at PARE] (before 12th century)
1 a (1) : one of the often indefinite or unequal subdivisions into which something is or is regarded as divided and which together constitute the whole (2) : an essential portion or integral element **b** : one of several or many equal units of which something is composed or into which it is divisible : an amount equal to another amount ⟨mix one *part* of the powder with three *parts* of water⟩ **c** (1) : an exact divisor of a quantity : ALIQUOT (2) : PARTIAL FRACTION **d** : one of the constituent elements of a plant or animal body: as (1) : ORGAN, MEMBER (2) *plural* : PRIVATE PARTS **e** : a division of a literary work **f** (1) : a vocal or instrumental line or melody in concerted music or in harmony (2) : a particular voice or instrument in concerted music; *also* : the score for it **g** : a constituent member of a machine or other apparatus; *also* : a spare part

2 : something falling to one in a division or apportionment : SHARE
3 : one's share or allotted task (as in an action) ⟨one must do one's *part*⟩
4 : one of the opposing sides in a conflict or dispute
5 : a general area of indefinite boundaries — usually used in plural ⟨you're not from around these *parts*⟩ ⟨took off for *parts* unknown⟩
6 : a function or course of action performed
7 a : an actor's lines in a play **b** : the role of a character in a play
8 : a constituent of character or capacity : TALENT ⟨a man of many *parts*⟩
9 : the line where the hair is parted ☆
— **for the most part** : in general : on the whole ⟨*for the most part* the crowd was orderly⟩
— **in part** : in some degree : PARTIALLY
— **on the part of** : with regard to the one specified

²part *verb* [Middle English, from Old French *partir*, from Latin *partire* to divide, from *part-*, *pars*] (13th century)
intransitive verb
1 a : to separate from or take leave of someone **b** : to take leave of one another
2 : to become separated into parts
3 a : to go away : DEPART **b** : DIE
4 : to become separated, detached, or broken
5 : to relinquish possession or control ⟨hated to *part* with that money⟩
transitive verb
1 a : to divide into parts **b** : to separate by combing on each side of a line **c** : to break or suffer the breaking of (as a rope or anchor chain)
2 : to divide into shares and distribute : APPORTION
3 a : to remove from contact or association ⟨if aught but death *part* thee and me —Ruth 1:17 (Authorized Version)⟩ **b** : to keep separate ⟨the narrow channel that *parts* England from France⟩ **c** : to hold (as brawlers) apart **d** : to separate by a process of extraction, elimination, or secretion
4 a *archaic* : LEAVE, QUIT **b** *dialect British* : RELINQUISH, GIVE UP
synonym *see* SEPARATE

³part *adverb* (1513)
: PARTLY

⁴part *adjective* (1818)
: PARTIAL 1

par·take \pär-'tāk, pər-\ *verb* **-took** \-'tůk\; **-tak·en** \-'tā-kən\; **-tak·ing** [back-formation from *partaker*, alteration of *part taker*] (circa 1585)
intransitive verb
1 : to take part in or experience something along with others ⟨*partake* in the revelry⟩ ⟨*partake* of the good life⟩

parsnip

☆ **SYNONYMS**

Part, portion, piece, member, division, section, segment, fragment mean something less than the whole. PART is a general term appropriate when indefiniteness is required ⟨they ran only *part* of the way⟩. PORTION implies an assigned or allotted part ⟨cut the pie into six *portions*⟩. PIECE applies to a separate or detached part of a whole ⟨a puzzle with 500 *pieces*⟩. MEMBER suggests one of the functional units composing a body ⟨a structural *member*⟩. DIVISION applies to a large or diversified part ⟨the manufacturing *division* of the company⟩. SECTION applies to a relatively small or uniform part ⟨the entertainment *section* of the newspaper⟩. SEGMENT applies to a part separated or marked out by or as if by natural lines of cleavage ⟨the retired *segment* of the population⟩. FRAGMENT applies to a part produced by or as if by breaking off or shattering ⟨only a *fragment* of the play still exists⟩.

2 : to have a portion (as of food or drink)
3 : to possess or share a certain nature or attribute ⟨the experience *partakes* of a mystical quality⟩
transitive verb
: to take part in
synonym see SHARE
— **par·tak·er** *noun*

part and parcel *noun* (15th century)
: an essential or integral component ⟨stress was *part and parcel* of the job⟩

part·ed \'pär-təd\ *adjective* (1590)
1 a : divided into parts **b :** cleft so that the divisions reach nearly but not quite to the base — usually used in combination ⟨a 3-*parted* corolla⟩
2 *archaic* **:** DEAD

par·terre \pär-'ter\ *noun* [French, from Middle French, from *par terre* on the ground] (circa 1639)
1 : an ornamental garden with paths between the beds
2 : the part of the main floor of a theater that is behind the orchestra; *especially* **:** PARQUET CIRCLE

par·the·no·car·py \'pär-thə-nō-,kär-pē\ *noun* [International Scientific Vocabulary, from Greek *parthenos* virgin + *karpos* fruit — more at HARVEST] (1911)
: the production of fruits without fertilization ⟨bananas set fruit by *parthenocarpy* and without pollination⟩
— **par·the·no·car·pic** \,pär-thə-nō-'kär-pik\ *adjective*

par·the·no·gen·e·sis \,pär-thə-nō-'je-nə-səs\ *noun* [New Latin, from Greek *parthenos* + Latin *genesis* genesis] (1849)
: reproduction by development of an unfertilized usually female gamete that occurs especially among lower plants and invertebrate animals

par·the·no·ge·net·ic \-jə-'ne-tik\ *adjective* (1872)
: of, characterized by, or produced by parthenogenesis
— **par·the·no·ge·net·i·cal·ly** \-ti-k(ə-)lē\ *adverb*

Par·the·non \'pär-thə-,nän\ *noun* [Latin, from Greek *Parthenōn*] (circa 1841)
: a Doric temple of Athena built on the acropolis at Athens in the 5th century B.C.

Par·thi·an \'pär-thē-ən\ *adjective* (1579)
1 : of, relating to, or characteristic of ancient Parthia or its people
2 : relating to, being, or having the effect of a shot fired while in real or feigned retreat
— **Parthian** *noun*

¹par·tial \'pär-shəl\ *adjective* [Middle English *parcial*, from Middle French *partial*, from Medieval Latin *partialis*, from Late Latin, of a part, from Latin *part-*, *pars* part] (14th century)
1 : of or relating to a part rather than the whole **:** not general or total ⟨a *partial* solution⟩
2 : inclined to favor one party more than the other **:** BIASED
3 : markedly fond of someone or something — used with *to* ⟨*partial* to pizza⟩

²partial *noun* (1880)
: OVERTONE 1a

partial denture *noun* (1860)
: a usually removable artificial replacement of one or more teeth

partial derivative *noun* (1889)
: the derivative of a function of several variables with respect to one of them and with the remaining variables treated as constants

partial differential equation *noun* (1889)
: a differential equation containing at least one partial derivative

partial differentiation *noun* (circa 1890)
: the process of finding a partial derivative

partial fraction *noun* (1816)
: one of the simpler fractions into the sum of which the quotient of two polynomials may be decomposed

par·tial·i·ty \,pär-shē-'a-lə-tē, pär-'sha-lə-tē\ *noun, plural* **-ties** (15th century)
1 : the quality or state of being partial **:** BIAS
2 : a special taste or liking

par·tial·ly \'pär-sh(ə-)lē\ *adverb* (15th century)
1 *archaic* **:** in a biased manner **:** with partiality
2 : to some extent **:** in some degree

partially ordered *adjective* (1941)
: having some or all elements connected by a relation that is reflexive, transitive, and antisymmetric

partial pressure *noun* (1857)
: the pressure exerted by a (specified) component in a mixture of gases

partial product *noun* (circa 1924)
: a product obtained by multiplying a multiplicand by one digit of a multiplier having more than one digit

par·ti·ble \'pär-tə-bəl\ *adjective* (14th century)
: capable of being parted **:** DIVISIBLE ⟨a *partible* inheritance⟩
— **par·ti·bil·i·ty** \,pär-tə-'bi-lə-tē\ *noun*

par·tic·i·pant \pär-'ti-sə-pənt, pər-\ *noun* (1562)
: one that participates
— **participant** *adjective*

par·tic·i·pate \pär-'ti-sə-,pāt, pər-\ *verb* **-pat·ed; -pat·ing** [Latin *participatus*, past participle of *participare*, from *particip-*, *particeps* participant, from *part-*, *pars* part + *capere* to take — more at HEAVE] (1531)
transitive verb
archaic **:** PARTAKE
intransitive verb
1 : to possess some of the attributes of a person, thing, or quality
2 a : to take part ⟨always tried to *participate* in class discussions⟩ **b :** to have a part or share in something
synonym see SHARE
— **par·tic·i·pa·tor** \-,pā-tər\ *noun*

par·tic·i·pa·tion \(,)pär-,ti-sə-'pā-shən, pər-\ *noun* (14th century)
1 : the act of participating
2 : the state of being related to a larger whole

par·tic·i·pa·tion·al \-'pā-shnəl, -'pā-shə-n°l\ *adjective* (1959)
: PARTICIPATORY

par·tic·i·pa·tive \pär-'ti-sə-pə-tiv, pər-, -,pā-tiv\ *adjective* (1951)
: relating to or involving participation; *especially* **:** of, relating to, or being a style of management in which subordinates participate in decision making

par·tic·i·pa·to·ry \pär-'ti-sə-pə-,tōr-ē, pər-, -,tȯr-\ *adjective* (1881)
: characterized by or involving participation; *especially* **:** providing the opportunity for individual participation ⟨*participatory* democracy⟩

par·tic·ip·i·al \,pär-tə-'si-pē-əl\ *adjective* [Latin *participialis*, from *participium*] (1591)
: of, relating to, or formed with or from a participle
— **par·tic·ip·i·al·ly** \-pē-ə-lē\ *adverb*

par·ti·ci·ple \'pär-tə-,si-pəl\ *noun* [Middle English, from Middle French, modification of Latin *participium*, from *particip-*, *particeps*] (14th century)
: a word having the characteristics of both verb and adjective; *especially* **:** an English verbal form that has the function of an adjective and at the same time shows such verbal features as tense and voice and capacity to take an object

par·ti·cle \'pär-ti-kəl\ *noun* [Middle English, from Latin *particula*, from diminutive of *part-*, *pars*] (14th century)
1 a : a minute quantity or fragment **b :** a relatively small or the smallest discrete portion or amount of something
2 *archaic* **:** a clause or article of a composition or document
3 : any of the basic units of matter and energy (as a molecule, atom, proton, electron, or photon)

4 : a unit of speech expressing some general aspect of meaning or some connective or limiting relation and including the articles, most prepositions and conjunctions, and some interjections and adverbs ⟨the *particle up* has a perfective meaning in phrases such as *beat up* and *cut up*⟩
5 : a small eucharistic wafer distributed to a Roman Catholic layman at Communion

particle accelerator *noun* (1946)
: ACCELERATOR d

par·ti·cle-board \-,bȯrd, -,bȯrd\ *noun* (circa 1957)
: a composition board made of very small pieces of wood bonded together

particle physics *noun* (1946)
: a branch of physics dealing with the constitution, properties, and interactions of elementary particles especially as revealed in experiments using particle accelerators — called also *high-energy physics*
— **particle physicist** *noun*

par·ti–col·or \'pär-tē-,kə-lər\ *or* **par·ti–col·ored** \-lərd\ *adjective* [obsolete English *party* parti-color, from Middle English *parti*, from Middle French, striped, from past participle of *partir* to divide] (1535)
: showing different colors or tints; *especially* **:** having a predominant color broken by patches of one or more other colors ⟨*parti-color* setters⟩
— **parti–color** *noun*

¹par·tic·u·lar \pə(r)-'ti-kyə-lər, -k(ə-)lər\ *adjective* [Middle English *particuler*, from Middle French, from Late Latin *particularis*, from Latin *particula* small part] (14th century)
1 : of, relating to, or being a single person or thing ⟨the *particular* person I had in mind⟩
2 *obsolete* **:** PARTIAL
3 : of, relating to, or concerned with details ⟨gave us a very *particular* account of the trip⟩
4 a : distinctive among other examples or cases of the same general category **:** notably unusual ⟨suffered from measles of *particular* severity⟩ **b :** being one unit or element among others ⟨*particular* incidents in a story⟩
5 a : denoting an individual member or subclass in logic **b :** affirming or denying a predicate to a part of the subject — used of a proposition in logic ⟨"some men are wise" is a *particular* affirmative⟩
6 a : concerned over or attentive to details **:** METICULOUS ⟨a very *particular* gardener⟩ **b :** nice in taste **:** FASTIDIOUS **c :** hard to please **:** EXACTING
synonym see CIRCUMSTANTIAL, SPECIAL

²particular *noun* (15th century)
1 *archaic* **:** a separate part of a whole
2 a : an individual fact, point, circumstance, or detail **b :** a specific item or detail of information or news ⟨bill of *particulars*⟩
3 a : an individual or a specific subclass (as in logic) falling under some general concept or term **b :** a particular proposition in logic
synonym see ITEM
— **in particular :** in distinction from others **:** SPECIFICALLY

par·tic·u·lar·ise British variant of PARTICULARIZE

par·tic·u·lar·ism \pə(r)-'ti-k(yə)lə-,ri-zəm *also* pär-\ *noun* (1824)
1 : exclusive or special devotion to a particular interest
2 : a political theory that each political group has a right to promote its own interests and especially independence without regard to the interests of larger groups
3 : a tendency to explain complex social phenomena in terms of a single causative factor

\ə\ abut \ᵊ\ kitten \ər\ further \a\ ash \ā\ ace
\ä\ mop, mar \au̇\ out \ch\ chin \e\ bet \ē\ easy
\g\ go \i\ hit \ī\ ice \j\ job \ŋ\ sing \ō\ go
\ȯ\ law \ȯi\ boy \th\ thin \t͟h\ the \ü\ loot \u̇\ foot
\y\ yet \zh\ vision *see also* Guide to Pronunciation

— **par·tic·u·lar·ist** \-rist\ *noun or adjective*

— **par·tic·u·lar·is·tic** \-,ti-k(yə-)lə-'ris-tik\ *adjective*

par·tic·u·lar·i·ty \pə(r)-,ti-kyə-'lar-ə-tē *also* (,)pär-\ *noun, plural* **-ties** (1528)
1 a : a minute detail **:** PARTICULAR **b :** an individual characteristic **:** PECULIARITY; *also* **:** SINGULARITY
2 : the quality or state of being particular as distinguished from universal
3 a : attentiveness to detail **:** EXACTNESS **b :** the quality or state of being fastidious in behavior or expression

par·tic·u·lar·i·za·tion \-,ti-k(yə-)lə-rə-'zā-shən\ *noun* (1657)
: the act of particularizing **:** the condition of being particularized

par·tic·u·lar·ize \pə(r)-'ti-k(yə-)lə-,rīz *also* pär-\ *verb* **-ized; -iz·ing** (1593)
transitive verb
: to state in detail **:** SPECIFY
intransitive verb
: to go into details

par·tic·u·lar·ly \pə(r)-'ti-kyə-(lər-)lē, -kyə-lə-lē; pə(r)-'ti-k(ə-)lē; *also* pär-\ *adverb* (14th century)
1 : in a particular manner **:** in detail
2 : to an unusual degree
3 : in particular **:** SPECIFICALLY

¹**par·tic·u·late** \pär-'ti-kyə-lət *also* -,lāt\ *adjective* [Latin *particula*] (1871)
: of or relating to minute separate particles

²**particulate** *noun* (1942)
: a particulate substance

particulate inheritance *noun* (1889)
: inheritance of characters specifically transmitted by genes in accord with Mendel's laws

¹**part·ing** \'pär-tiŋ\ *noun* (15th century)
: a place or point where a division or separation occurs
— **parting of the ways 1 :** a point of separation or divergence **2 :** a place or time at which a choice must be made

²**parting** *adjective* (circa 1577)
: given, taken, or performed at parting ⟨a *parting* kiss⟩

par·ti pris \'pär-,tē-'prē\ *noun, plural* **partis pris** \-,tē-'prē(z)\ [French, literally, side taken] (1860)
: a preconceived opinion **:** PREJUDICE
— **parti pris** *adjective*

¹**par·ti·san** *also* **par·ti·zan** \'pär-tə-zən, -sən, -,zan, *chiefly British* ,pär-tə-'zan\ *noun* [Middle French *partisan*, from Old Italian *partigiano*, from *parte* part, party, from Latin *part-, pars* part] (1555)
1 : a firm adherent to a party, faction, cause, or person; *especially* **:** one exhibiting blind, prejudiced, and unreasoning allegiance
2 a : a member of a body of detached light troops making forays and harassing an enemy **b :** a member of a guerrilla band operating within enemy lines
synonym see FOLLOWER
— **partisan** *adjective*
— **par·ti·san·ly** \-lē\ *adverb*
— **par·ti·san·ship** \-,ship\ *noun*

²**par·ti·san** *or* **par·ti·zan** \'pär-tə-zən, -sən\ *noun* [Middle French *partisane*, from Old Italian *partigiana*, feminine of *partigiano*] (1556)
: a weapon of the 16th and 17th centuries with long shaft and broad blade

par·ti·ta \pär-'tē-tə\ *noun* [Italian, from *partire* to divide, from Latin — more at PART] (1880)
1 : VARIATION 4
2 : SUITE 2b(1)

par·tite \'pär-,tīt\ *adjective* [Latin *partitus*, from past participle of *partire*] (circa 1570)
1 : divided into a usually specified number of parts
2 : PARTED 1b ⟨a *partite* leaf⟩

¹**par·ti·tion** \pär-'ti-shən, pər-\ *noun* (15th century)
1 : the action of parting **:** the state of being parted **:** DIVISION

2 : something that divides; *especially* **:** an interior dividing wall
3 : one of the parts or sections of a whole

²**partition** *transitive verb* (1741)
1 a : to divide into parts or shares **b :** to divide (as a country) into two or more territorial units having separate political status
2 : to separate or divide by a partition (as a wall) — often used with *off*
— **par·ti·tion·er** \-'ti-sh(ə-)nər\ *noun*

par·ti·tion·ist \-'ti-sh(ə-)nist\ *noun* (circa 1900)
: an advocate of political partition

par·ti·tive \'pär-tə-tiv\ *adjective* (14th century)
1 : serving to part or divide into parts
2 a : of, relating to, or denoting a part ⟨a *partitive* construction⟩ **b :** serving to indicate the whole of which a part is specified ⟨*partitive* genitive⟩
— **par·ti·tive·ly** *adverb*

part·let \'pärt-lət\ *noun* [Middle English (Scots) *patelet*, from Middle French *patelette*, from diminutive of *patte* paw] (1519)
: a 16th century chemisette with a band or collar

part·ly \'pärt-lē\ *adverb* (1523)
: in some measure or degree **:** PARTIALLY

¹**part·ner** \'pärt-nər *also* 'pärd-\ *noun* [Middle English *partener*, alteration of *parcener*, from Anglo-French, coparcener — more at PARCENER] (14th century)
1 *archaic* **:** one that shares **:** PARTAKER
2 a : one associated with another especially in an action **:** ASSOCIATE, COLLEAGUE **b :** either of two persons who dance together **c :** one of two or more persons who play together in a game against an opposing side **d :** either of two people living together; *especially* **:** SPOUSE
3 : a member of a partnership; *also* **:** such membership
4 : one of the heavy timbers that strengthen a ship's deck to support a mast — usually used in plural
— **part·ner·less** \-ləs\ *adjective*

²**partner** (1611)
transitive verb
1 : to join or associate with another as partner
2 : to provide with a partner
intransitive verb
: to act as a partner

partners desk *noun* (1946)
: a large desk with an open kneehole which allows use of the desk by two people seated opposite each other

part·ner·ship \-,ship\ *noun* (1576)
1 : the state of being a partner **:** PARTICIPATION
2 a : a legal relation existing between two or more persons contractually associated as joint principals in a business **b :** the persons joined together in a partnership
3 : a relationship resembling a legal partnership and usually involving close cooperation between parties having specified and joint rights and responsibilities

part of speech (1509)
: a traditional class of words distinguished according to the kind of idea denoted and the function performed in a sentence

par·ton \'pär-,tän\ *noun* [*particle* + ²*-on*] (1969)
: a hypothetical particle (as a quark or gluon) that is held to be a constituent of hadrons

par·tridge \'pär-trij, *dialect* 'pa-trij\ *noun, plural* **partridge** *or* **par·tridg·es** [Middle English *partrich*, modification of Old French *perdris*, modification of Latin *perdic-, perdix*, from Greek *perdik-, perdix*] (14th century)
1 : any of various typically medium-sized stout-bodied Old World gallinaceous game birds (*Perdix, Alectoris*, and related genera) with variegated plumage
2 : any of numerous gallinaceous birds (as the American ruffed grouse or bobwhite) somewhat like the Old World partridges in size, habits, or value as game

par·tridge·ber·ry \-,ber-ē\ *noun* (1714)
: an American trailing evergreen plant (*Mitchella repens*) of the madder family with insipid scarlet berries; *also* **:** its fruit

partridge 1

part–song \'pärt-,soŋ\ *noun* (1850)
: a usually unaccompanied song consisting of two or more voice parts with one part carrying the melody

part–time \'pärt-'tīm\ *adjective* (1891)
: involving or working less than customary or standard hours ⟨a *part-time* job⟩ ⟨*part-time* students⟩
— **part–time** *adverb*
— **part–tim·er** \-,tī-mər, -'tī-\ *noun*

¹**par·tu·ri·ent** \pär-'tùr-ē-ənt, -'tyùr-\ *adjective* [Latin *parturient-, parturiens*, present participle of *parturire* to be in labor, from *parere* to give birth to — more at PARE] (1592)
1 : bringing forth or about to bring forth young
2 : of or relating to parturition

²**parturient** *noun* (1947)
: a parturient individual

par·tu·ri·tion \,pär-chə-'ri-shən, ,pär-tyù-, ,pär-tə-\ *noun* [Late Latin *parturition-, parturitio*, from Latin *parturire*] (1646)
: the action or process of giving birth to offspring

part·way \'pärt-'wā\ *adverb* (1859)
1 : to some extent **:** PARTIALLY, PARTLY
2 : at a point in the way or distance ⟨*partway* through the trip they met some friends⟩

¹**par·ty** \'pär-tē\ *noun, plural* **parties** [Middle English *partie* part, party, from Old French, from *partir* to divide — more at PART] (14th century)
1 : a person or group taking one side of a question, dispute, or contest
2 : a group of persons organized for the purpose of directing the policies of a government
3 : a person or group participating in an action or affair ⟨mountain-climbing *party*⟩ ⟨a *party* to the transaction⟩
4 : a particular individual **:** PERSON ⟨an old *party* approaching 80⟩
5 : a detail of soldiers
6 : a social gathering; *also* **:** the entertainment provided for it
— **party** *adjective*

²**party** *intransitive verb* **par·tied; par·ty·ing** (1919)
: to attend or give parties; *broadly* **:** REVEL 1
— **par·ty·er** \-tē-ər\ *noun*

party line *noun* (1834)
1 : the policy or practice of a political party
2 : a single telephone circuit connecting two or more subscribers with the exchange — called also *party wire*
3 : the principles or policies of an individual or organization; *also* **:** the explanation or interpretation usually put forth ⟨the *party line* that her mother was a saint —Leslie Bennetts⟩
— **par·ty–lin·er** \,pär-tē-'lī-nər\ *noun*

party poop·er \-'pü-pər\ *noun* [³*poop* + *-er*] (1954)
: one who refuses to join in the fun of a party; *broadly* **:** one who refuses to go along with everyone else

party wall *noun* (circa 1798)
: a wall which divides two adjoining properties and in which each of the owners shares the rights

pa·rure \pə-'rùr\ *noun* [French, literally, adornment, from Old French *pareure*, from *parer* to prepare, adorn — more at PARE] (1818)
: a matched set of ornaments (as jewelry)

par value *noun* (1807)
: PAR 1b(1)

par·ve \'pär-və\ *variant of* PAREVE

par·ve·nu \'pär-və-ˌnü, -ˌnyü\ *noun, plural* **-nus** \-ˌn(y)üz\ [French, from past participle of *parvenir* to arrive, from Latin *pervenire*, from *per* through + *venire* to come — more at FOR, COME] (1802)
: one that has recently or suddenly risen to an unaccustomed position of wealth or power and has not yet gained the prestige, dignity, or manner associated with it
— **parvenu** *adjective*

par·ve·nue \-ˌnü, -ˌnyü\ *noun* [French, from *parvenue*, feminine of *parvenum*, past participle] (1826)
: a woman who is a parvenu
— **parvenue** *adjective*

par·vis *also* **par·vise** \'pär-vəs\ *noun* [Middle English *parvis*, from Middle French, modification of Late Latin *paradisus* enclosed park — more at PARADISE] (14th century)
1 : a court or enclosed space before a building (as a church)
2 : a single portico or colonnade before a church

par·vo \'pär-ˌvō\ *noun* (1980)
: PARVOVIRUS 2

par·vo·vi·rus \'pär-vō-ˌvī-rəs\ *noun* [New Latin, from Latin *parvus* small (akin to Greek *pauros* small, *paid-, pais* child) + New Latin *-o-* + *virus* — more at FEW] (1965)
1 : any of a group of small single-stranded DNA viruses pathogenic for vertebrates
2 : a highly contagious febrile disease of dogs that is caused by a parvovirus and marked by loss of appetite, lethargy, often bloody diarrhea and vomiting, and sometimes death

pas \'pä\ *noun, plural* **pas** \'pä(z)\ [French, from Latin *passus* step — more at PACE] (1707)
1 : the right of precedence
2 : a dance step or combination of steps

pas·cal \pas-'kal, päs-'käl\ *noun* [Blaise *Pascal*] (1956)
1 : a unit of pressure in the meter-kilogram-second system equivalent to one newton per square meter
2 *usually P capitalized or all capitals* : a structured computer programming language developed from Algol and designed to process both numerical and textual data

Pas·cal's triangle \pas-'kalz-, päs-'kälz-\ *noun* (1886)
: a system of numbers triangularly arranged in rows that consist of the coefficients in the expansion of $(a + b)^n$ for $n = 0, 1, 2, 3, \ldots$

Pasch \'pask\ *also* **Pas·cha** \'päs-kə\ *noun* [Middle English *pasche* Passover, Easter, from Old French, from Late Latin *pascha*, from Late Greek, from Greek, Passover, from Hebrew *pesaḥ*] (12th century)
1 : EASTER
2 : PASSOVER
— **pas·chal** \'pas-kəl\ *adjective*

paschal full moon *noun* (1892)
: the 14th day of a lunar month occurring on or next after March 21 according to a fixed set of ecclesiastical calendar rules and without regard to the real moon

Paschal Lamb *noun* (15th century)
: AGNUS DEI 2

pas de bour·rée \ˌpä-də-bù-'rā\ *noun, plural* **pas de bourrée** *same*\ *or* **pas de bour·rées** \-'rä(z)\ [French, literally, bourrée step] (1897)
: a walking or running ballet step usually executed on the points of the toes

pas de chat \-'sha\ *noun, plural* **pas de chat** *same*\ [French, literally, cat's step] (1914)
: a forward leap in ballet

pas de deux \-'də(r), -'dü\ *noun, plural* **pas de deux** \-'dər(z), -'də(z), -'dü(z)\ [French, literally, step for two] (circa 1762)
1 : a dance or figure for two performers

2 : an intricate relationship or activity involving two parties or things

pas de qua·tre \-'kat, -'ka-trə, -'kätrᵊ\ *noun, plural* **pas de quatre** *same*\ [French, literally, step for four] (1884)
: a dance or figure for four performers

pas de trois \-'trwä, -'twä\ *noun, plural* **pas de trois** \-'trwä(z), -'twä(z)\ [French, literally, step for three] (circa 1762)
: a dance or figure for three performers

pa·se \'pä-ˌsä\ *noun* [Spanish, literally, feint, from *pase* let him pass, from *pasar* to pass, from (assumed) Vulgar Latin *passare*] (1937)
: a movement of a cape by a matador in drawing a bull and taking his charge

pa·seo \pä-'sā-(ˌ)ō, pä-'sā\ *noun, plural* **pa·se·os** [Spanish, from *pasear* to take a stroll, from *paso* passage, step, from Latin *passus*] (1832)
1 a : a leisurely stroll : PROMENADE b : a public walk or boulevard
2 : a formal entrance march of bullfighters into an arena

¹**pash** \'pash\ *transitive verb* [Middle English *passhen*] (14th century)
dialect English : SMASH

²**pash** *noun* [origin unknown] (1611)
dialect English : HEAD

pa·sha \'pä-shə, 'pa-; pə-'shä, -'shò\ *noun* [Turkish *paşa*] (1646)
: a man of high rank or office (as in Turkey or northern Africa)

Pash·to \'pəsh-(ˌ)tō\ *noun* [Pashto *pašto*] (1784)
: the Iranian language of the Pashtuns

Pash·tun \ˌpəsh-'tün\ *noun, plural* **Pashtuns** *or* **Pashtun** (1815)
: a member of a people of eastern and southern Afghanistan and adjacent parts of Pakistan

Pa·siph·a·ë \pə-'si-fə-ˌē\ *noun* [Latin, from Greek *Pasiphaē*]
: the wife of Minos and mother of the Minotaur by a white bull

pasque·flow·er \'pask-ˌflaù-(-ə)r\ *noun* [modification of Middle French *passefleur*, from *passer* to pass (from Old French) + *fleur* flower, from Latin *flor-, flos* — more at BLOW] (1597)
: any of several low perennial herbs (genus *Anemone*) of the buttercup family with palmately compound leaves and large usually white or purple early spring flowers

pas·qui·nade \ˌpas-kwə-'nād\ *noun* [Middle French, from Italian *pasquinata*, from *Pasquino*, name given to a statue in Rome on which lampoons were posted] (1658)
1 : a lampoon posted in a public place
2 : satirical writing : SATIRE
— **pasquinade** *transitive verb*

¹**pass** \'pas\ *verb* [Middle English, from Old French *passer*, from (assumed) Vulgar Latin *passare*, from Latin *passus* step — more at PACE] (13th century)
intransitive verb
1 : MOVE, PROCEED, GO
2 a : to go away : DEPART b : DIE — often used with *on*
3 a : to move in a path so as to approach and continue beyond something : move past; *especially* : to move past another vehicle going in the same direction b : to run the normal course — used of time or a period of time ⟨the hours pass quickly⟩
4 a : to go or make one's way through ⟨allow no one to *pass*⟩ b : to go uncensured, unchallenged, or seemingly unnoticed ⟨let the remark *pass*⟩
5 : to go from one quality, state, or form to another ⟨*passes* from a liquid to a gaseous state⟩
6 a : to sit in inquest or judgment b (1) : to render a decision, verdict, or opinion ⟨the court *passed* on the legality of wiretapping⟩ (2) : to become legally rendered ⟨judgment *passed* for the plaintiff⟩
7 : to go from the control, ownership, or possession of one person or group to that of an-

other ⟨the throne *passed* to the king's son⟩ ⟨title *passes* to the buyer upon payment in full⟩
8 a : HAPPEN, OCCUR b : to take place or be exchanged as or in a social, personal, or business interaction ⟨words *passed*⟩
9 a : to become approved by a legislature or body empowered to sanction or reject ⟨the proposal *passed*⟩ b : to undergo an inspection, test, or course of study successfully
10 a : to serve as a medium of exchange b : to be accepted or regarded ⟨drivel that *passes* for literature⟩ c : to identify oneself or be identified as something one isn't ⟨tried to *pass* as an adult⟩ ⟨Mom could *pass* as my sister⟩
11 a *obsolete* : to make a pass in fencing b : to throw or hit a ball or puck to a teammate — often used with *off*
12 a : to decline to bid, double, or redouble in a card game b : to withdraw from the current poker pot
transitive verb
1 : to go beyond: as a : SURPASS, EXCEED ⟨*passes* all expectations⟩ b : to advance or develop beyond c : to go past (one moving in the same direction)
2 : to omit a regularly scheduled declaration and payment of (a dividend)
3 a : to go across, over, or through : CROSS b : to live through (as an experience or peril) : UNDERGO c : to go through (as a test) successfully
4 a : to secure the approval of ⟨the bill *passed* the Senate⟩ b : to cause or permit to win approval or legal or official sanction ⟨*pass* a law⟩ c : to give approval or a passing grade to ⟨*pass* the students⟩
5 a : to let (as time or a period of time) go by especially while involved in a leisure activity ⟨I'll read to *pass* the time⟩ b : to let go unnoticed : OVERLOOK, DISREGARD
6 a : PLEDGE b : to transfer the right to or property in ⟨*pass* title to a house⟩
7 a : to put in circulation ⟨*pass* bad checks⟩ b (1) : to transfer or transmit from one to another (2) : to relay or communicate (as information) to another c : to cause or enable to go : TRANSPORT d : to throw or hit (a ball or puck) especially to a teammate
8 a : to pronounce (as a sentence or opinion) especially judicially b : UTTER ⟨*passed* a cutting remark⟩
9 a : to cause or permit to go past or through a barrier b : to move or cause to move in a particular manner or direction ⟨*passed* my hand over my face⟩ ⟨*pass* the rope through the loop⟩ c : to cause to march or go by in order ⟨*pass* the troops in review⟩
10 : to emit or discharge from a bodily part and especially the bowels
11 a : to give a base on balls to b : to hit a ball past (an opponent) in a game (as tennis)
— **pass·er** *noun*
— **pass muster** : to gain approval or acceptance
— **pass the buck** : to shift a responsibility to someone else
— **pass the hat** : to take up a collection for money
— **pass the time of day** : to exchange greetings or engage in pleasant conversation

²**pass** *noun* [Middle English, from Middle French *pas*, from Latin *passus*] (14th century)
1 : a means (as an opening, road, or channel) by which a barrier may be passed or access to a place may be gained; *especially* : a low place in a mountain range
2 : a position to be held usually against odds

³**pass** *noun* [¹*pass*] (1523)
1 : REALIZATION ⟨brought his dream to *pass*⟩
2 : the act or an instance of passing : PASSAGE

3 : a usually distressing or bad state of affairs ⟨what has brought you to such a *pass*?⟩
4 a : a written permission to move about freely in a place or to leave or enter it **b :** a written leave of absence from a military post or station for a brief period **c :** a permit or ticket allowing free transportation or free admission
5 *archaic* **:** a thrust or lunge in fencing
6 a : a transference of objects by sleight of hand or other deceptive means **b :** a moving of the hands over or along something
7 *archaic* **:** an ingenious sally (as of wit)
8 : the passing of an examination or course of study; *also* **:** the mark or certification of such passing
9 : a single complete mechanical operation; *also* **:** a single complete cycle of operations (as for processing, manufacturing, or printing)
10 a (1) **:** a transfer of a ball or a puck from one player to another on the same team (2) **:** a ball or puck so transferred **b :** PASSING SHOT
11 : BASE ON BALLS
12 : an election not to bid, bet, or draw an additional card in a card game
13 : a throw of dice in the game of craps that wins the bet for the shooter — compare ³CRAP 2, MISSOUT
14 : a single passage or movement (as of an airplane) over a place or toward a target
15 a : EFFORT, TRY **b :** a sexually inviting gesture or approach
16 : PASE

pass·able \'pa-sə-bəl\ *adjective* (15th century)
1 a : capable of being passed, crossed, or traveled on ⟨*passable* roads⟩ **b :** capable of being freely circulated
2 : good enough **:** ADEQUATE
— **pass·ably** \-blē\ *adverb*

pas·sa·ca·glia \ˌpä-sə-'käl-yə, ˌpa-sə-'kal-yə\ *noun* [modification of Spanish *pasacalle*, from *pasar* to pass + *calle* street, from Latin *callis* path — more at PASE] (1659)
1 a : an old Italian or Spanish dance tune **b :** an instrumental musical composition consisting of variations usually on a ground bass in moderately slow triple time
2 : an old dance performed to a passacaglia

pas·sa·do \pə-'sä-(ˌ)dō\ *noun, plural* **-dos** *or* **-does** [modification of French *passade* (from Italian *passata*) or Italian *passata*, from *passare* to pass, from (assumed) Vulgar Latin] (1588)
archaic **:** a thrust in fencing with one foot advanced

¹pas·sage \'pa-sij\ *noun* (13th century)
1 a : a way of exit or entrance **:** a road, path, channel, or course by which something passes **b :** a corridor or lobby giving access to the different rooms or parts of a building or apartment
2 a : the action or process of passing from one place, condition, or stage to another **b :** DEATH 1 **c :** a continuous movement or flow ⟨the *passage* of time⟩
3 a (1) **:** a specific act of traveling or passing especially by sea or air (2) **:** a privilege of conveyance as a passenger **:** ACCOMMODATIONS **:** the passing of a legislative measure or law **:** ENACTMENT
4 : a right, liberty, or permission to pass
5 a : something that happens or is done **:** INCIDENT **b :** something that takes place between two persons mutually
6 a : a usually brief portion of a written work or speech that is relevant to a point under discussion or noteworthy for content or style **b :** a phrase or short section of a musical composition **c :** a detail of a work of art (as a painting)
7 : the act or action of passing something or undergoing a passing
8 : incubation of a pathogen (as a virus) in culture, a living organism, or a developing egg
²passage *verb* **pas·saged; pas·sag·ing** (1824)
intransitive verb

: to go past or across **:** CROSS
transitive verb
: to subject to passage ⟨*passaged* a virus⟩
pas·sage·way \-ˌwā\ *noun* (1649)
: a way that allows passage
pas·sage·work \-ˌwərk\ *noun* (1865)
: a section of a musical composition characteristically unimportant thematically and consisting especially of ornamental figures
pas·sant \'pa-sᵊnt\ *adjective* [Middle English *passaunt*, from Middle French *passant*, from present participle of *passer* to pass] (15th century)
: walking with the farther forepaw raised — used of a heraldic animal
pass away *intransitive verb* (13th century)
1 : to go out of existence
2 : DIE 1
pass·band \'pas-ˌband\ *noun* (1922)
: a band of frequencies (as in a radio circuit or a light filter) that is transmitted with maximum efficiency
pass·book \-ˌbůk\ *noun* (1828)
: BANKBOOK
pass degree *noun* (1868)
: a bachelor's degree without honors that is taken at a British university
pas·sé \pa-'sā\ *adjective* [French, from past participle of *passer*] (1775)
1 : past one's prime
2 a : OUTMODED **b :** behind the times
passed ball *noun* (1861)
: a baseball pitch not hit by the batter that passes the catcher when it should have been caught and allows a base runner to advance — compare WILD PITCH
passed pawn *noun* (1797)
: a chess pawn that has no enemy pawn in front of it on its own or an adjacent file
pas·sel \'pa-səl\ *noun* [alteration of *parcel*] (1835)
: a large number or amount ◇
passe·men·terie \pas-'men-t(ə-)rē\ *noun* [French, from *passement* ornamental braid, from *passer*] (1794)
: a fancy edging or trimming made of braid, cord, gimp, beading, or metallic thread
pas·sen·ger \'pa-sᵊn-jər\ *noun, often attributive* [Middle English *passager*, from Middle French, from *passager*, adjective, passing, from *passage* act of passing, from *passer*] (14th century)
1 : WAYFARER
2 : a traveler in a public or private conveyance
passenger pigeon *noun* (1802)
: an extinct but formerly abundant North American migratory pigeon (*Ectopistes migratorius*)
passe–par·tout \ˌpas-pər-'tü, -ˌpär-\ *noun* [French, from *passe partout* pass everywhere] (1675)
1 : MASTER KEY
2 a : ⁵MAT **b :** a method of framing in which a picture, a mat, a glass, and a back (as of cardboard) are held together by strips of paper or cloth pasted over the edges
3 : a strong paper gummed on one side and used especially for mounting pictures
pass·er·by \ˌpa-sər-'bī, 'pa-sər-,\ *noun, plural* **pass·ers·by** \-sərz-\ (1568)
: one who passes by
pas·ser·ine \'pa-sə-ˌrīn\ *adjective* [Latin *passerinus* of sparrows, from *passer* sparrow] (1776)
: of or relating to the largest order (Passeriformes) of birds which includes more than half of all living birds and consists chiefly of altricial songbirds of perching habits — compare OSCINE
— **passerine** *noun*
pas seul \pä-'səl, -'sər(-ə)l\ *noun* [French, literally, solo step] (1813)
: a solo dance or dance figure
pass–fail \'pas-'fā(ə)l\ *adjective* (1959)

: being a system of grading whereby the grades "pass" and "fail" replace the traditional letter grades
— **pass–fail** *noun*
pas·si·ble \'pa-sə-bəl\ *adjective* [Middle English, from Middle French, from Late Latin *passibilis*, from Latin *passus*, past participle of *pati* to suffer — more at PATIENT] (14th century)
: capable of feeling or suffering
pas·sim \'pa-səm; 'pa-ˌsim, 'pä-\ *adverb* [Latin, from *passus* scattered, from past participle of *pandere* to spread — more at FATHOM] (1803)
: HERE AND THERE
¹pass·ing \'pa-siŋ\ *noun* (14th century)
: the act of one that passes or causes to pass; *especially* **:** DEATH 1
— **in passing :** by the way **:** INCIDENTALLY
²passing *adjective* (14th century)
1 : going by or past ⟨a *passing* pedestrian⟩
2 : having a brief duration ⟨a *passing* whim⟩
3 *obsolete* **:** SURPASSING
4 : SUPERFICIAL ⟨a *passing* acquaintance⟩ ⟨a *passing* resemblance⟩
5 a : of, relating to, or used in or for the act or process of passing ⟨*passing* lanes⟩ **b :** given on satisfactory completion of an examination or course of study ⟨a *passing* grade⟩
³passing *adverb* (14th century)
: to a surpassing degree **:** EXCEEDINGLY ⟨*passing* strange⟩
passing note *noun* (1730)
: a nonharmonic tone interposed between essential harmonic tones of adjacent chords — called also *passing tone*
passing shot *noun* (circa 1949)
: a stroke (as in tennis) that drives the ball to one side and beyond the reach of an opponent
pas·sion \'pa-shən\ *noun* [Middle English, from Old French, from Late Latin *passion-, passio* suffering, being acted upon, from Latin *pati* to suffer — more at PATIENT] (13th century)
1 *often capitalized* **a :** the sufferings of Christ between the night of the Last Supper and his death **b :** an oratorio based on a gospel narrative of the Passion
2 *obsolete* **:** SUFFERING
3 : the state or capacity of being acted on by external agents or forces
4 a (1) **:** EMOTION ⟨his ruling *passion* is greed⟩ (2) *plural* **:** the emotions as distinguished from reason **b :** intense, driving, or overmastering feeling or conviction **c :** an outbreak of anger

5 a : ardent affection **:** LOVE **b :** a strong liking or desire for or devotion to some activity, object, or concept **c :** sexual desire **d :** an object of desire or deep interest ☆
— **pas·sion·less** \-ləs\ *adjective*

pas·sion·al \'pa-shə-nᵊl, 'pash-nəl\ *adjective* (15th century)
: of, relating to, or marked by passion

pas·sion·ate \'pa-sh(ə-)nət\ *adjective* (15th century)
1 a : easily aroused to anger **b :** filled with anger **:** ANGRY
2 a : capable of, affected by, or expressing intense feeling **b :** ENTHUSIASTIC, ARDENT
3 : swayed by or affected with sexual desire
synonym see IMPASSIONED
— **pas·sion·ate·ly** *adverb*
— **pas·sion·ate·ness** *noun*

pas·sion·flow·er \'pa-shən-ˌflaȯ(-ə)r\ *noun* [from the fancied resemblance of parts of the flower to the instruments of Christ's crucifixion] (1633)
: any of a genus (*Passiflora* of the family Passifloraceae, the passionflower family) of chiefly tropical woody tendriled climbing vines or erect herbs with usually showy flowers and pulpy often edible berries

passionflower

passion fruit *noun* (1752)
: the edible fruit of a passionflower

Pas·sion·ist \'pa-sh(ə-)nist\ *noun* [Italian *passionista*, from *passione* passion, from Late Latin *passion-, passio*] (1832)
: a member of a Roman Catholic mendicant order founded by Saint Paul of the Cross in Italy in 1720 and devoted chiefly to missionary work and retreats

passion play *noun, often 1st P capitalized* (1870)
: a dramatic representation of the scenes connected with the passion and crucifixion of Christ

Passion Sunday *noun* (14th century)
: the fifth Sunday in Lent

Pas·sion·tide \'pa-shən-ˌtīd\ *noun* (1847)
: the last two weeks of Lent

Passion Week *noun* (15th century)
1 : HOLY WEEK
2 : the week between Passion Sunday and Palm Sunday

pas·siv·ate \'pa-si-ˌvāt\ *transitive verb* **-at·ed; -at·ing** (1913)
1 : to make inactive or less reactive ⟨*passivate* the surface of steel by chemical treatment⟩
2 : to protect (as a solid-state device) against contamination by coating or surface treatment
— **pas·siv·ation** \ˌpa-si-'vā-shən\ *noun*

¹pas·sive \'pa-siv\ *adjective* [Middle English, from Latin *passivus*, from *passus*, past participle] (14th century)
1 a (1) : acted upon by an external agency **(2) :** receptive to outside impressions or influences **b (1) :** asserting that the grammatical subject of a verb is subjected to or affected by the action represented by that verb **(2) :** containing or yielding a passive verb form **c (1) :** lacking in energy or will **:** LETHARGIC **(2) :** tending not to take an active or dominant part **d :** induced by an outside agency ⟨*passive* exercise of a paralyzed leg⟩
2 a : not active or operating **:** INERT **b :** of, relating to, or making direct use of the sun's heat usually without the intervention of mechanical devices ⟨*passive* technique⟩ ⟨*passive* solar house⟩ **c :** LATENT **d (1) :** of, relating to, or characterized by a state of chemical inactivity; *especially* **:** resistant to corrosion **(2) :** not involving expenditure of chemical energy

⟨*passive* transport across a cell membrane⟩ **e** *of an electronic element* **:** exhibiting no gain or control **f :** operating solely by means of the power of an input signal ⟨a *passive* communication satellite that reflects television signals⟩ **g :** relating to the detection of an object through its emission of energy
3 a : receiving or enduring without resistance **:** SUBMISSIVE **b :** existing or occurring without being active, open, or direct ⟨*passive* support⟩
4 : of, relating to, or being business activity in which the investor does not have immediate control over income
synonym see INACTIVE
— **pas·sive·ly** *adverb*
— **pas·sive·ness** *noun*
— **pas·siv·i·ty** \pa-'si-və-tē\ *noun*

²passive *noun* (1530)
1 : a passive verb form
2 : the passive voice of a language □

passive immunity *noun* (1895)
: immunity acquired by transfer of antibodies (as by injection of serum from an individual with active immunity)
— **passive immunization** *noun*

passive resistance *noun* (1819)
: resistance especially to a government or an occupying power characterized mainly by noncooperation

passive restraint *noun* (1970)
: a restraint (as a self-locking seat belt) that acts automatically to protect an automobile rider during a crash

passive smoking *noun* (1971)
: the involuntary inhalation of tobacco smoke (as from another's cigarette) especially by a nonsmoker

passive transfer *noun* (1935)
: a local transfer of skin sensitivity from an allergic to a normal person by injection of serum from the former that is used especially for identifying specific allergens when a high degree of allergic sensitivity is suspected

pas·siv·ism \'pa-si-ˌvi-zəm\ *noun* (1872)
: a passive attitude, behavior, or way of life
— **pas·siv·ist** \-vist\ *noun*

pass·key \'pas-ˌkē\ *noun* (circa 1817)
1 : MASTER KEY
2 : SKELETON KEY

pass off *transitive verb* (1799)
1 : to make public or offer for sale with intent to deceive
2 : to give a false identity or character to

pass out (1899)
intransitive verb
1 : DIE 1
2 : to lose consciousness
transitive verb
: to reject (a deal in bridge) as unplayable because everyone has passed on the first round of bidding

Pass·over \'pas-ˌō-vər\ *noun* [from the exemption of the Israelites from the slaughter of the firstborn in Egypt (Exodus 12:23–27)] (1530)
: a Jewish holiday beginning on the 14th of Nisan and commemorating the Hebrews' liberation from slavery in Egypt

pass over *transitive verb* (14th century)
1 : to ignore in passing
2 : to pay no attention to the claims of **:** DISREGARD

pass·port \'pas-ˌpȯrt, -ˌpȯrt\ *noun* [Middle English (Scots) *pasport*, from Middle French *passeport*, from *passer* to pass + *port* port, from Latin *portus* — more at FORD] (15th century)
1 a : a formal document issued by an authorized official of a country to one of its citizens that is usually necessary for exit from and re-entry into the country, that allows the citizen to travel in a foreign country in accordance with visa requirements, and that requests pro-

tection for the citizen while abroad **b :** a license issued by a country permitting a foreign citizen to pass or take goods through its territory **:** SAFE-CONDUCT **c :** a document of identification required by law to be carried by persons residing or traveling within a country

\ə\ **abut** \ᵊ\ **kitten** \ər\ **further** \a\ **ash** \ā\ **ace**
\ä\ **mop, mar** \aȯ\ **out** \ch\ **chin** \e\ **bet** \ē\ **easy**
\g\ **go** \i\ **hit** \ī\ **ice** \j\ **job** \ŋ\ **sing** \ō\ **go**
\ȯ\ **law** \ȯi\ **boy** \th\ **thin** \th\ **the** \ü\ **loot** \u̇\ **foot**
\y\ **yet** \zh\ **vision** *see also* Guide to Pronunciation

2 a : a permission or authorization to go somewhere **b :** something that secures admission, acceptance, or attainment ⟨education as a *passport* to success⟩

pass–through *noun* (1951)
1 : the act, action, or process of offsetting increased costs by raising prices
2 : an opening in a wall between two rooms through which something (as dishes) may be passed

pass up *transitive verb* (1896)
: to let go by without accepting or taking advantage of ⟨*pass up* a chance for promotion⟩; *also* **:** DECLINE, REJECT

pass·word \'pas-ˌwərd\ *noun* (circa 1817)
1 : something that enables one to pass or gain admission: as **a :** a spoken word or phrase required to pass by a guard **b :** a sequence of characters required for access to a computer system
2 : WATCHWORD

¹past \'past\ *adjective* [Middle English, from past participle of *passen* to pass] (14th century)
1 a : AGO ⟨12 years *past*⟩ **b :** just gone or elapsed ⟨for the *past* few months⟩
2 : having existed or taken place in a period before the present **:** BYGONE
3 : of, relating to, or constituting a verb tense that is expressive of elapsed time and that in English is usually formed by internal vowel change (as in *sang*) or by the addition of a suffix (as in *laughed*)
4 : having served as a specified officer in an organization ⟨*past* president⟩

²past *preposition* (14th century)
1 a : beyond the age for or of ⟨*past* playing with dolls⟩ **b :** AFTER ⟨half *past* two⟩
2 a : at the farther side of **:** BEYOND **b :** in a course or direction going close to and then beyond ⟨drove *past* the house⟩
3 *obsolete* **:** more than
4 : beyond the capacity, range, or sphere of ⟨*past* belief⟩

³past *noun* (1590)
1 a : time gone by **b :** something that happened or was done in the past ⟨regret the *past*⟩
2 a : the past tense of a language **b :** a verb form in the past tense
3 : a past life, history, or course of action; *especially* **:** one that is kept secret
— **past·less** \'pas(t)-ləs\ *adjective*

⁴past *adverb* (1784)
: so as to reach and go beyond a point near at hand

pas·ta \'päs-tə *also* 'pas-\ *noun* [Italian, from Late Latin] (1874)
1 : paste in processed form (as spaghetti) or in the form of fresh dough (as ravioli)
2 : a dish of cooked pasta

¹paste \'pāst\ *noun* [Middle English, from Middle French, from Late Latin *pasta* dough, paste] (14th century)
1 a : a dough that contains a considerable proportion of fat and is used for pastry crust or fancy rolls **b :** a confection made by evaporating fruit with sugar or by flavoring a gelatin, starch, or gum arabic preparation **c :** a smooth food product made by evaporation or grinding ⟨tomato *paste*⟩ ⟨almond *paste*⟩ **d :** a shaped dough (as spaghetti or ravioli) prepared from semolina, farina, or wheat flour
2 : a soft plastic mixture or composition: as **a :** a preparation usually of flour or starch and water used as an adhesive or a vehicle for mordant or color **b :** clay or a clay mixture used in making pottery or porcelain
3 : a brilliant glass of high lead content used for the manufacture of artificial gems

²paste *transitive verb* **past·ed; past·ing** (1561)
1 : to cause to adhere by or as if by paste **:** STICK
2 : to cover with something pasted on

³paste *transitive verb* **past·ed; past·ing** [alteration of *baste*] (1846)
1 : to strike hard at
2 : to beat or defeat soundly

¹paste·board \'pās(t)-ˌbȯrd, -ˌbȯrd\ *noun* (1562)
1 : a solid paperboard with a paper facing; *broadly* **:** PAPERBOARD
2 : TICKET

²pasteboard *adjective* (1599)
1 : made of pasteboard
2 : SHAM, UNSUBSTANTIAL ⟨prefabricated plots and *pasteboard* heroes —Peter Andrews⟩

paste·down \-ˌdau̇n\ *noun* (circa 1888)
: the outer leaf of an endpaper that is pasted down to the inside of the front or back cover of a book

¹pas·tel \pa-'stel\ *noun* [French, from Italian *pastello*, from Late Latin *pastellus* woad, from diminutive of *pasta*] (1662)
1 : a paste made of powdered pigment ranging from pale to deep colors and used for making crayons; *also* **:** a crayon made of such paste
2 a : a drawing in pastel **b :** the process or art of drawing with pastels
3 : a light literary sketch
4 : any of various pale or light colors

²pastel *adjective* (1884)
1 a : of or relating to a pastel **b :** made with pastels
2 : pale and light in color
3 : lacking in body or vigor

pas·tel·ist *or* **pas·tel·list** \-'ste-list\ *noun* (1881)
: an artist who works with pastels

pas·tern \'pas-tərn\ *noun* [Middle French *pasturon*, from *pasture* tether attached to a horse's foot, alteration of (assumed) Old French *pastoire*, from Medieval Latin *pastoria*, from Latin, feminine of *pastorius* of a herdsman, from *pastor* herdsman — more at PASTOR] (circa 1530)
1 : a part of the foot of an equine extending from the fetlock to the top of the hoof — see HORSE illustration
2 : a part of the leg of an animal other than an equine that corresponds to the pastern

paste·up \'pāst-ˌəp\ *noun* (circa 1930)
: MECHANICAL; *also* **:** the process of making mechanicals

pas·teur·ise *British variant of* PASTEURIZE

pas·teur·i·za·tion \ˌpas-chə-rə-'zā-shən, ˌpas-tyə-, -tə-\ *noun* (1886)
1 : partial sterilization of a substance and especially a liquid (as milk) at a temperature and for a period of exposure that destroys objectionable organisms without major chemical alteration of the substance
2 : partial sterilization of perishable food products (as fruit or fish) with radiation (as gamma rays)

pas·teur·ize \'pas-chə-ˌrīz, 'pas-tyə-, -tə-\ *transitive verb* **-ized; -iz·ing** [Louis *Pasteur*] (1881)
: to subject to pasteurization
— **pas·teur·iz·er** *noun*

Pasteur treatment *noun* (1926)
: a method of aborting rabies by stimulating production of antibodies through successive inoculations with attenuated virus of gradually increasing strength

pas·tic·cio \pa-'stē-ch(ē-,)ō, pä-\ *noun, plural* **-ci** \-(ˌ)chē\ *or* **-cios** [Italian, literally, pasty, from (assumed) Vulgar Latin *pasticium*, from Late Latin *pasta*] (1752)
: PASTICHE

pas·tiche \pas-'tēsh, päs-\ *noun* [French, from Italian *pasticcio*] (1878)
1 : a literary, artistic, musical, or architectural work that imitates the style of previous work; *also* **:** such stylistic imitation
2 a : a musical, literary, or artistic composition made up of selections from different works **:** POTPOURRI **b :** HODGEPODGE
— **pas·ti·cheur** \ˌpas-tē-'shər, ˌpäs-\ *noun*

past·ies \'pās-tēz\ *noun plural* [²*paste*] (circa 1954)

: small round coverings for a woman's nipples worn especially by a stripteaser

pas·tille \pas-'tē(ə)l\ *also* **pas·til** \'pas-t°l\ *noun* [French *pastille*, from Latin *pastillus* small loaf, lozenge; akin to Latin *panis* bread — more at FOOD] (1658)
1 : a small mass of aromatic paste for fumigating or scenting the air of a room
2 : an aromatic or medicated lozenge **:** TROCHE

pas·time \'pas-ˌtīm\ *noun* (15th century)
: something that amuses and serves to make time pass agreeably **:** DIVERSION

pas·ti·na \ˌpäs-tē-nə\ *noun* [Italian, diminutive of *pasta* pasta] (circa 1948)
: very small bits of pasta used in soup or broth

pas·tis \päs-'tēs\ *noun* [French, from French dialect (Marseilles), literally, jumble, kind of pastry, from Provençal, from Old Provençal *pastitz* cake, from (assumed) Vulgar Latin *pasticium*] (1926)
: a French liqueur flavored with aniseed

past master *noun* (1762)
1 : one who has held the office of worshipful master in a lodge of Freemasons or of master in a guild, club, or society
2 [alteration of *passed master*] **:** one who is expert **:** ADEPT

past·ness \'pas(t)-nəs\ *noun* (1829)
1 : the quality or state of being past
2 : the subjective quality of something being remembered rather than immediately experienced

¹pas·tor \'pas-tər\ *noun* [Middle English *pastour*, from Middle French, from Latin *pastor* herdsman, from *pascere* to feed — more at FOOD] (14th century)
: a spiritual overseer; *especially* **:** a clergyman serving a local church or parish
— **pas·tor·ship** \-ˌship\ *noun*

²pastor *transitive verb* **pas·tored; pas·tor·ing** \-t(ə-)riŋ\ (1623)
: to serve as pastor of (as a church)

³pas·tor \päs-'tȯr\ *noun* [Spanish, from Latin] (1849)
chiefly Southwest **:** HERDSMAN

¹pas·to·ral \'pas-t(ə-)rəl\ *adjective* [Middle English, from Latin *pastoralis*, from *pastor* herdsman] (15th century)
1 a (1) **:** of, relating to, or composed of shepherds or herdsmen (2) **:** devoted to or based on livestock raising **b :** of or relating to the countryside **:** not urban **c :** portraying or expressive of the life of shepherds or country people especially in an idealized and conventionalized manner ⟨*pastoral* poetry⟩ **d :** pleasingly peaceful and innocent **:** IDYLLIC
2 a : of or relating to spiritual care or guidance especially of a congregation **b :** of or relating to the pastor of a church
— **pas·to·ral·ly** \-t(ə-)rə-lē\ *adverb*
— **pas·to·ral·ness** *noun*

²pastoral \'pas-t(ə-)rəl; *1d is often* ˌpas-tə-'räl, -'räl\ *noun* (1584)
1 a : a literary work (as a poem or play) dealing with shepherds or rural life in a usually artificial manner and typically drawing a contrast between the innocence and serenity of the simple life and the misery and corruption of city and especially court life **b :** pastoral poetry or drama **c :** a rural picture or scene **d :** PASTORALE 1b
2 : CROSIER 1
3 : a letter of a pastor to his charge: as **a :** a letter addressed by a bishop to his diocese **b :** a letter of the house of bishops of the Protestant Episcopal Church to be read in each parish

pas·to·rale \ˌpas-tə-'räl, -'ral *also* -'rä-lē\ *noun* [Italian, from *pastorale* of herdsmen, from Latin *pastoralis*] (1724)
1 a : an opera of the 16th or 17th centuries having a pastoral plot **b :** an instrumental or vocal composition having a pastoral theme
2 : PASTORAL 1a

Pastoral Epistle *noun* (1836)
: one of three New Testament letters including two addressed to Timothy and one to Titus that give advice on matters of church government and discipline

pas·to·ral·ism \'pas-t(ə-)rə-,li-zəm\ *noun* (1854)
1 : the quality or style characteristic of pastoral writing
2 a : livestock raising **b** : social organization based on livestock raising as the primary economic activity
— **pas·to·ral·ist** \-list\ *noun or adjective*

pas·tor·ate \'pas-t(ə-)rət\ *noun* (1795)
1 : the office, state, jurisdiction, or tenure of office of a pastor
2 : a body of pastors

past participle *noun* (1798)
: a participle that typically expresses completed action, that is traditionally one of the principal parts of the verb, and that is traditionally used in English in the formation of perfect tenses in the active voice and of all tenses in the passive voice

past perfect *adjective* (1889)
: of, relating to, or constituting a verb tense that is traditionally formed in English with *had* and denotes an action or state as completed at or before a past time spoken of
— **past perfect** *noun*

pas·tra·mi *also* **pas·tromi** \pə-'strä-mē\ *noun* [Yiddish *pastrame*, from Romanian *pastramă* pressed and cured meat] (1936)
: a highly seasoned smoked beef prepared especially from shoulder cuts

pas·try \'pās-trē\ *noun, plural* **pastries** [¹*paste*] (circa 1538)
1 a : PASTE 1a **b** : sweet baked goods made of dough having a high fat content
2 : a piece of pastry

past tense *noun* (1813)
: a verb tense expressing action or state in or as if in the past: **a** : a verb tense expressive of elapsed time (as *wrote* in "on arriving I wrote a letter") **b** : a verb tense expressing action or state in progress or continuance or habitually done or customarily occurring at a past time (as *was writing* in "I was writing while he dictated" or *loved* in "their sons loved fishing")

pas·tur·age \'pas-chə-rij\ *noun* (circa 1533)
: PASTURE

¹pas·ture \'pas-chər\ *noun* [Middle English, from Middle French, from Late Latin *pastura*, from Latin *pastus*, past participle of *pascere* to feed — more at FOOD] (14th century)
1 : plants (as grass) grown for the feeding especially of grazing animals
2 : land or a plot of land used for grazing
3 : the feeding of livestock : GRAZING

²pasture *verb* **pas·tured; pas·tur·ing** (14th century)
intransitive verb
: GRAZE, BROWSE
transitive verb
1 : to feed (as cattle) on pasture
2 : to use as pasture

pas·ture·land \'pas-chər-,land\ *noun* (1591)
: PASTURE 2

¹pas·ty \'pas-tē\ *noun, plural* **pasties** [Middle English *pastee*, from Middle French *pasté*, from *paste* dough, paste] (13th century)
1 : ²PIE 1, 2; *especially* : a meat pie
2 : TURNOVER 5

²pasty \'pās-tē\ *adjective* **past·i·er; -est** (1659)
: resembling paste; *especially* : pallid and unhealthy in appearance
— **past·i·ness** \-nəs\ *noun*

PA system \,pē-'ā-\ *noun* (circa 1936)
: PUBLIC-ADDRESS SYSTEM

¹pat \'pat\ *noun* [Middle English *patte*, probably of imitative origin] (15th century)
1 : a light blow especially with the hand or a flat instrument
2 : a light tapping often rhythmical sound

3 : something (as butter) shaped into a small flat usually square individual portion
— **pat on the back** : an expression of approval

²pat *adverb* (1578)
: in a pat manner : APTLY, PERFECTLY

³pat *verb* **pat·ted; pat·ting** (1591)
transitive verb
1 : to strike lightly with a flat instrument
2 : to flatten, smooth, or put into place or shape with light blows
3 : to tap or stroke gently with the hand to soothe, caress, or show approval
intransitive verb
: to strike or beat gently

⁴pat *adjective* (1646)
1 a : exactly suited to the purpose or occasion : APT **b** : suspiciously appropriate : CONTRIVED
2 : learned, mastered, or memorized exactly
3 : FIRM, UNYIELDING
4 : reduced to a simple or mechanical form : STANDARD, TRITE

pa·ta·ca \pə-'tä-kə\ *noun* [Portuguese] (1830)
— see MONEY table

pat–a–cake \'pa-də-,kāk, 'pat-ə-\ *variant of* PATTY-CAKE

pa·ta·gi·um \pə-'tā-jē-əm\ *noun, plural* **-gia** \-jē-ə\ [New Latin, from Latin, gold edging on a tunic] (1826)
1 : the fold of skin connecting the forelimbs and hind limbs of some tetrapods (as flying squirrels)
2 : the fold of skin in front of the main segments of a bird's wing

¹patch \'pach\ *noun* [Middle English *pacche*] (14th century)
1 : a piece of material used to mend or cover a hole or a weak spot
2 : a tiny piece of black silk or court plaster worn on the face or neck especially by women to hide a blemish or to heighten beauty
3 a : a piece of material (as adhesive plaster) used medically usually to cover a wound or repair a defect **b** : a shield worn over the socket of an injured or missing eye
4 a : a small piece : SCRAP **b** : a part or area distinct from that about it ⟨cabbage *patch*⟩ **c** : a period of time : SPELL ⟨was going through a rough *patch*⟩
5 : a piece of cloth sewed on a garment as an ornament or insignia; *especially* : SHOULDER PATCH
6 : a temporary connection in a communication system (as a telephone hookup)
7 : a minor usually temporary correction or modification in a computer program

²patch *transitive verb* (15th century)
1 : to mend, cover, or fill up a hole or weak spot in
2 : to provide with a patch
3 a : to make of patches or fragments **b** : to mend or put together especially in hasty or shabby fashion — usually used with *up* **c** : to make a patch in (a computer program)
4 : to connect (as circuits) by a patch cord
synonym see MEND

³patch *noun* [perhaps by folk etymology from Italian dialect *paccio*] (1549)
: FOOL, DOLT

patch·board \'pach-,bōrd, -,bórd\ *noun* (1934)
: a switchboard in which circuits are interconnected by patch cords

patch cord *noun* (1926)
: a wire with a plug at each end that is used to connect electrical devices

patch·ou·li *also* **patch·ou·ly** \'pa-chə-lē, pə-'chü-lē\ *noun* [Tamil *paccuḷi*] (1845)
: a heavy perfume made from a fragrant essential oil from an East Indian shrubby mint (*Pogostemon cablin*); *also* : the plant itself

patch pocket *noun* (1895)
: a flat pocket applied to the outside of a garment

patch test *noun* (1933)

: a test for determining allergic sensitivity that is made by applying to the unbroken skin small pads soaked with the allergen to be tested

patch·work \'pach-,wərk\ *noun, often attributive* (1692)
1 : something composed of miscellaneous or incongruous parts : HODGEPODGE
2 : pieces of cloth of various colors and shapes sewn together to form a covering

patchwork quilt *noun* (1840)
1 : a quilt made of patchwork
2 : PATCHWORK 1

patchwork 2

patchy \'pa-chē\ *adjective* **patch·i·er; -est** (1798)
1 : marked by, consisting of, or diversified with patches
2 : irregular in appearance, makeup, or quality
— **patch·i·ly** \'pa-chə-lē\ *adverb*
— **patch·i·ness** \'pa-chē-nəs\ *noun*

pate \'pāt\ *noun* [Middle English] (14th century)
1 : HEAD
2 : the crown of the head
3 : BRAIN — used chiefly disparagingly
— **pat·ed** \'pā-təd\ *adjective*

pâte \'pät\ *noun* [French, literally, paste, from Old French *paste*] (1863)
: PASTE 2b

pâ·té *also* **pate** \pä-'tā, pa-\ *noun* [French, from Middle French *pasté* — more at PASTY] (1706)
1 : a meat or fish pie or patty
2 : a spread of finely chopped or pureed seasoned meat ⟨chicken liver *pâté*⟩

pâ·té de foie gras \(,)pä-,tā-də-,fwä-'grä, (,)pa-,tā-\ *noun, plural* **pâ·tés de foie gras** \-,tā(z)-\ [French, literally, pâté of fat liver] (1827)
: a pâté of fat goose liver and usually truffles sometimes with added fat pork

pa·tel·la \pə-'te-lə\ *noun, plural* **-lae** \-'te-(,)lē, -,lī\ *or* **-las** [Latin, from diminutive of *patina* shallow dish] (1693)
: a thick flat triangular movable bone that forms the anterior point of the knee and protects the front of the joint — called also *kneecap*
— **pa·tel·lar** \-'te-lər\ *adjective*

pa·tel·li·form \pə-'te-lə-,fórm\ *adjective* [New Latin *Patella*, genus including the limpet, from Latin, small shallow dish] (1819)
1 : resembling a limpet or limpet shell
2 : disk-shaped with a narrow rim

pat·en \'pa-tᵊn\ *noun* [Middle English, from Middle French *patene*, from Medieval Latin & Latin; Medieval Latin *patina*, from Latin, shallow dish, from Greek *patanē*] (14th century)
1 : a plate usually made of precious metal and used to carry the bread at the Eucharist
2 a : PLATE **b** : something (as a metal disk) resembling a plate

pa·ten·cy \'pa-tᵊn(t)-sē, 'pā-\ *noun* (1656)
: the quality or state of being patent

¹pat·ent \/1–3 are 'pa-tᵊnt, chiefly British 'pā-; 4 'pā-; 5 'pā-, pa-; 6–7 'pa-, 'pā-, British usually 'pā-\ *adjective* [Middle English, from Middle French, from Latin *patent-, patens*, from present participle of *patēre* to be open — more at FATHOM] (14th century)
1 a : open to public inspection — used chiefly in the phrase *letters patent* **b** (1) : secured by letters patent or by a patent to the exclusive

control and possession of a particular individual or party (2) **:** protected by a patent **:** made under a patent ⟨*patent* locks⟩ **c :** protected by a trademark or a trade name so as to establish proprietary rights analogous to those conveyed by letters patent or a patent **:** PROPRIETARY ⟨*patent* drugs⟩
2 : of, relating to, or concerned with the granting of patents especially for inventions ⟨a *patent* lawyer⟩
3 : making exclusive or proprietary claims or pretensions
4 : affording free passage **:** UNOBSTRUCTED ⟨a *patent* opening⟩
5 : PATULOUS, SPREADING ⟨a *patent* calyx⟩
6 *archaic* **:** ACCESSIBLE, EXPOSED
7 : readily visible or intelligible **:** OBVIOUS
synonym see EVIDENT
— **pat·ent·ly** *adverb*

²pat·ent \'pa-tᵊnt, *British also* 'pā-\ *noun* (14th century)
1 : an official document conferring a right or privilege **:** LETTERS PATENT
2 a : a writing securing to an inventor for a term of years the exclusive right to make, use, or sell an invention **b :** the monopoly or right so granted **c :** a patented invention
3 : PRIVILEGE, LICENSE
4 : an instrument making a conveyance of public lands; *also* **:** the land so conveyed
5 : PATENT LEATHER

³pat·ent *transitive verb* (1675)
1 : to obtain or grant a patent right to
2 : to grant a privilege, right, or license to by patent
3 : to obtain or secure by patent; *especially* **:** to secure by letters patent exclusive right to make, use, or sell
— **pat·ent·abil·i·ty** \,pa-tᵊn-tə-'bi-lə-tē, *British also* ,pā-\ *noun*
— **pat·ent·able** \'pa-tᵊn-tə-bəl, *British also* 'pā-\ *adjective*

pat·ent·ed \'pa-tᵊn-təd, *British also* 'pā-\ *adjective* (1951)
: originated by or peculiar to one person or group **:** INDIVIDUALIZED

pat·en·tee \,pa-tᵊn-'tē, *British also* ,pā-\ *noun* (15th century)
: one to whom a grant is made or a privilege secured by patent

pat·ent flour \'pa-tᵊn(t)-, *British also* 'pā-\ *noun* (1886)
: a high-grade wheat flour that consists solely of endosperm

pat·ent leather \'pa-tᵊn(t)-, *British usually* 'pā-\ *noun* (1829)
: a leather with a hard smooth glossy surface

patent medicine *noun* (1770)
: a packaged nonprescription drug which is protected by a trademark and whose contents are incompletely disclosed; *also* **:** any drug that is a proprietary

patent office *noun* (1696)
: a government office for examining claims to patents and granting patents

pat·en·tor \'pa-tᵊn-tər, ,pa-tᵊn-'tòr, *British also* 'pā-, ,pā-\ *noun* (circa 1890)
: one that grants a patent

patent right *noun* (1805)
: a right granted by letters patent; *especially* **:** the exclusive right to an invention

pa·ter *noun* (14th century)
1 \'pä-,ter\ *often capitalized* **:** PATERNOSTER
2 \'pā-tər\ [Latin] *chiefly British* **:** FATHER

pa·ter·fa·mil·i·as \,pa-tər-fə-'mi-lē-əs, ,pä-, ,pā-\ *noun, plural* **pa·tres·fa·mil·i·as** \,pā-, ,trēz-, ,pä-,träs-\ [Middle English, from Latin, from *pater* father + *familias*, archaic genitive of *familia* household — more at FATHER, FAMILY] (15th century)
1 : the male head of a household
2 : the father of a family

pa·ter·nal \pə-'tər-nᵊl\ *adjective* [Middle English, from Late Latin *paternalis*, from Latin *paternus* paternal, from *pater*] (15th century)

1 a : of or relating to a father **b :** like that of a father ⟨*paternal* benevolence⟩
2 : received or inherited from one's male parent
3 : related through one's father ⟨*paternal* grandfather⟩
— **pa·ter·nal·ly** \-nᵊl-ē\ *adverb*

pa·ter·nal·ism \pə-'tər-nᵊl-i-zəm\ *noun* (1881)
1 : a system under which an authority undertakes to supply needs or regulate conduct of those under its control in matters affecting them as individuals as well as in their relations to authority and to each other
2 : a policy or practice based on or characteristic of paternalism
— **pa·ter·nal·ist** \-nᵊl-ist\ *noun or adjective*
— **pa·ter·nal·is·tic** \-,tər-nᵊl-'is-tik\ *adjective*
— **pa·ter·nal·is·ti·cal·ly** \-ti-k(ə-)lē\ *adverb*

pa·ter·ni·ty \pə-'tər-nə-tē\ *noun* (1582)
1 : the quality or state of being a father
2 : origin or descent from a father

paternity test *noun* (1926)
: a test especially of DNA or genetic traits to determine whether a given man could be the biological father of a given child

pa·ter·nos·ter \,pä-tər-'näs-tər, 'pa-tər-,, 'pä-,ter-', -'näs-,ter\ *noun* [Middle English, from Old English, from Medieval Latin, from Latin *pater noster* our father, from the opening words] (before 12th century)
1 *often capitalized* **:** LORD'S PRAYER
2 : a word formula repeated as a prayer or magical charm

path \'path, 'path\ *noun, plural* **paths** \'pathz, 'paths, 'pathz, 'paths\ [Middle English, from Old English *pæth;* akin to Old High German *pfad* path] (before 12th century)
1 : a trodden way
2 : a track specially constructed for a particular use
3 a : COURSE, ROUTE **b :** a way of life, conduct, or thought
4 a : the continuous series of positions or configurations that can be assumed in any motion or process of change by a moving or varying system **b :** a sequence of arcs in a network that can be traced continuously without retracing any arc
5 : PATHWAY 2

path- or **patho-** *combining form* [New Latin, from Greek, from *pathos*, literally, suffering — more at PATHOS]
: pathological state **:** disease ⟨*patho*gen⟩

-path *noun combining form* [German, back-formation from *-pathie* -pathy]
1 : practitioner of a (specified) system of medicine that emphasizes one aspect of disease or its treatment ⟨naturo*path*⟩
2 [International Scientific Vocabulary, from Greek *-pathēs*, adjective, suffering, from *pathos*] **a :** one suffering from a disorder (of such a part or system) ⟨psycho*path*⟩ **b :** one perceiving ⟨tele*path*⟩

Pa·than \pə-'tän, pä-\ *noun* [Hindi *Paṭhān*, from Pashto (eastern dialect) *Pakhtana*, plural of *Pakhtun*] (1638)
: PASHTUN

path·break·ing \'path-,brā-kiŋ\ *adjective* (1914)
: TRAILBLAZING

pa·thet·ic \pə-'the-tik\ *adjective* [Middle French or Late Latin; Middle French *pathetique*, from Late Latin *patheticus*, from Greek *pathētikos* capable of feeling, pathetic, from *paschein* (aorist *pathein*) to experience, suffer — more at PATHOS] (1598)
1 : having a capacity to move one to either compassionate or contemptuous pity
2 : marked by sorrow or melancholy **:** SAD
synonym see MOVING
— **pa·thet·i·cal** \-ti-kəl\ *adjective*
— **pa·thet·i·cal·ly** \-ti-k(ə-)lē\ *adverb*

pathetic fallacy *noun* (1856)
: the ascription of human traits or feelings to inanimate nature (as in *cruel sea*)

path·find·er \'path-,fīn-dər, 'path-\ *noun* (1840)
: one that discovers a way; *especially* **:** one that explores untraversed regions to mark out a new route
— **path·find·ing** \-diŋ\ *noun or adjective*

path·less \-ləs\ *adjective* (1591)
: UNTRODDEN, TRACKLESS
— **path·less·ness** *noun*

patho·bi·ol·o·gy \,pa-thō-bī-'ä-lə-jē\ *noun* (circa 1909)
: PATHOLOGY

path·o·gen \'pa-thə-jən\ *noun* [International Scientific Vocabulary] (1880)
: a specific causative agent (as a bacterium or virus) of disease

path·o·gen·e·sis \,pa-thə-'je-nə-səs\ *noun* [New Latin] (1876)
: the origination and development of a disease

path·o·ge·net·ic \-jə-'ne-tik\ *adjective* [International Scientific Vocabulary] (1838)
1 : of or relating to pathogenesis
2 : PATHOGENIC 2

path·o·gen·ic \-'je-nik\ *adjective* [International Scientific Vocabulary] (1852)
1 : PATHOGENETIC 1
2 : causing or capable of causing disease
— **path·o·ge·nic·i·ty** \-jə-'ni-sə-tē\ *noun*

pa·tho·gno·mon·ic \,pa-thə(g)-nō-'mä-nik\ *adjective* [Greek *pathognōmonikos*, from *path-* + *gnōmonikos* fit to judge, from *gnōmōn* interpreter; akin to Greek *gignōskein* to know — more at KNOW] (1625)
: distinctively characteristic of a particular disease

path·o·log·i·cal \,pa-thə-'lä-ji-kəl\ *also* **path·o·log·ic** \-jik\ *adjective* (1688)
1 : of or relating to pathology
2 : altered or caused by disease
— **path·o·log·i·cal·ly** \-ji-k(ə-)lē\ *adverb*

pa·thol·o·gist \pə-'thä-lə-jist, pa-\ *noun* (1650)
: a specialist in pathology; *specifically* **:** one who interprets and diagnoses the changes caused by disease in tissues and body fluids

pa·thol·o·gy \-jē\ *noun, plural* **-gies** [New Latin *pathologia* & Middle French *pathologie*, from Greek *pathologia* study of the emotions, from *path-* + *-logia* -logy] (1611)
1 : the study of the essential nature of diseases and especially of the structural and functional changes produced by them
2 : something abnormal: **a :** the structural and functional deviations from the normal that constitute disease or characterize a particular disease **b :** deviation from propriety or from an assumed normal state of something nonliving or nonmaterial

path·o·phys·i·ol·o·gy \'pa-thō-,fi-zē-'ä-lə-jē\ *noun* (1947)
: the physiology of abnormal states; *specifically* **:** the functional changes that accompany a particular syndrome or disease
— **path·o·phys·i·o·log·i·cal** \-zē-ə-'lä-ji-kəl\ *also* **path·o·phys·i·o·log·ic** \-jik\ *adjective*

pa·thos \'pā-,thäs, -,thòs, -,thōs *also* 'pa-\ *noun* [Greek, suffering, experience, emotion, from *paschein* (aorist *pathein*) to experience, suffer; perhaps akin to Lithuanian *kęsti* to suffer] (1591)
1 : an element in experience or in artistic representation evoking pity or compassion
2 : an emotion of sympathetic pity

path·way \'path-,wā, 'path-\ *noun* (15th century)
1 : PATH, COURSE
2 : a line of communication over interconnecting neurons extending from one organ or center to another
3 : the sequence of enzyme catalyzed reactions by which an energy-yielding substance is utilized by protoplasm ⟨metabolic *pathways*⟩

-pathy *noun combining form* [Latin *-pathia*, from Greek *-patheia*, from *-pathēs* suffering, from *pathos*]
1 : feeling : suffering ⟨em*pathy*⟩ : perception ⟨tele*pathy*⟩
2 : disorder of (such) a part or kind ⟨neuro*pathy*⟩
3 : system of medicine based on (such) a factor ⟨osteo*pathy*⟩

pa·tience \ˈpā-shən(t)s\ *noun* (13th century)
1 : the capacity, habit, or fact of being patient
2 *chiefly British* : SOLITAIRE 2

¹pa·tient \ˈpā-shənt\ *adjective* [Middle English *pacient*, from Middle French, from Latin *patient-*, *patiens*, from present participle of *pati* to suffer; perhaps akin to Greek *pēma* suffering] (14th century)
1 : bearing pains or trials calmly or without complaint
2 : manifesting forbearance under provocation or strain
3 : not hasty or impetuous
4 : steadfast despite opposition, difficulty, or adversity
5 a : able or willing to bear — used with *of* **b** : SUSCEPTIBLE, ADMITTING ⟨*patient* of one interpretation⟩
— **pa·tient·ly** *adverb*

²patient *noun* (14th century)
1 a : an individual awaiting or under medical care and treatment **b** : the recipient of any of various personal services
2 : one that is acted upon

pa·ti·na \pə-ˈtē-nə, ˈpa-tə-nə\ *noun, plural* **pa·ti·nas** \-nəz\ *or* **pa·ti·nae** \-ˌnē, -ˌnī\ [Italian, from Latin, shallow dish — more at PATEN] (1748)
1 a : a usually green film formed naturally on copper and bronze by long exposure or artificially (as by acids) and often valued aesthetically for its color **b** : a surface appearance of something grown beautiful especially with age or use
2 : an appearance or aura that is derived from association, habit, or established character
3 : a superficial covering or exterior

pat·i·nate \ˈpa-tə-ˌnāt\ *verb* **-nat·ed; -nat·ing** (1880)
transitive verb
: to give a patina to
intransitive verb
: to take on a patina — usually used in the past participle ⟨*patinated* bronze⟩
— **pat·i·na·tion** \ˌpa-tə-ˈnā-shən\ *noun*

¹pa·tine \pa-ˈtēn\ *noun* [French, from Italian *patina*] (1883)
: PATINA

²patine *transitive verb* **pa·tined; pa·tin·ing** (1896)
: to cover with a patina

pa·tio \ˈpa-tē-ˌō *also* ˈpä-\ *noun, plural* **pa·ti·os** [Spanish] (1828)
1 : COURTYARD; *especially* : an inner court open to the sky
2 : a recreation area that adjoins a dwelling, is often paved, and is adapted especially to outdoor dining

pa·tis·se·rie *or* **pâ·tis·se·rie** \pə-ˈti-sə-rē, pä-\ *noun* [French *pâtisserie*, from Middle French *pastiserie*, from *pasticier* to make pastry, from (assumed) Old French *pastitz* cake, from (assumed) Vulgar Latin *pasticium*, from Late Latin *pasta* dough] (1784)
1 : PASTRY
2 : a pastry shop

pâ·tis·sier *or* **pa·tis·sier** \pä-tis-ˈyā\ *noun* [French *pâtissier*, from Old French *pasticier*, from (assumed) Old French *pastitz* cake] (circa 1905)
: a pastry chef

pa·tois \ˈpa-ˌtwä, ˈpä-\ *noun, plural* **pa·tois** \-ˌtwäz\ [French] (1643)
1 a : a dialect other than the standard or literary dialect **b** : uneducated or provincial speech
2 : the characteristic special language of an occupational or social group : JARGON

patr- *or* **patri-** *or* **patro-** *combining form* [*patr-*, *patri-* from Latin, from *patr-*, *pater*; *patr-*, *patro-* from Greek, from *patr-*, *patēr* — more at FATHER]
: father ⟨*patri*stic⟩

pa·tri·arch \ˈpā-trē-ˌärk\ *noun* [Middle English *patriarche*, from Old French, from Late Latin *patriarcha*, from Greek *patriarchēs*, from *patria* lineage (from *patr-*, *patēr* father) + *-archēs* -arch — more at FATHER] (13th century)
1 a : one of the scriptural fathers of the human race or of the Hebrew people **b** : a man who is father or founder **c** (1) : the oldest member or representative of a group (2) : a venerable old man **d** : a man who is head of a patriarchy
2 a : any of the bishops of the ancient or Eastern Orthodox sees of Constantinople, Alexandria, Antioch, and Jerusalem or the ancient and Western see of Rome with authority over other bishops **b** : the head of any of various Eastern churches **c** : a Roman Catholic bishop next in rank to the pope with purely titular or with metropolitan jurisdiction
3 : a Mormon of the Melchizedek priesthood empowered to perform the ordinances of the church and pronounce blessings within a stake or prescribed jurisdiction

pa·tri·ar·chal \ˌpā-trē-ˈär-kəl\ *adjective* (15th century)
: of, relating to, or being a patriarch or patriarchy

patriarchal cross *noun* (circa 1727)
: a chiefly heraldic cross denoting a cardinal's or archbishop's rank and having two crossbars of which the lower is the longer and intersects the upright above or at its center — see CROSS illustration

pa·tri·ar·ch·ate \ˈpā-trē-ˌär-kət, -ˌkāt\ *noun* (1617)
1 a : the office, jurisdiction, or time in office of a patriarch **b** : the residence or headquarters of a patriarch
2 : PATRIARCHY

pa·tri·ar·chy \-ˌär-kē\ *noun, plural* **-chies** (1632)
1 : social organization marked by the supremacy of the father in the clan or family, the legal dependence of wives and children, and the reckoning of descent and inheritance in the male line; *broadly* : control by men of a disproportionately large share of power
2 : a society or institution organized according to the principles or practices of patriarchy

pa·tri·cian \pə-ˈtri-shən\ *noun* [Middle English *patricion*, from Middle French *patricien*, from Latin *patricius*, from *patres* senators, from plural of *pater* father — more at FATHER] (15th century)
1 : a member of one of the original citizen families of ancient Rome
2 a : a person of high birth : ARISTOCRAT **b** : a person of breeding and cultivation
— **patrician** *adjective*

pa·tri·ci·ate \-ˈtri-shē-ət, -ˌāt\ *noun* (circa 1656)
1 : the position or dignity of a patrician
2 : a patrician class

pat·ri·cide \ˈpa-trə-ˌsīd\ *noun* (1593)
1 [Latin *patricida*, from *patr-* + *-cida* -cide]
: one who murders his or her own father
2 [Late Latin *patricidium*, from Latin *patr-* + *-cidium* -cide] : the murder of one's own father
— **pat·ri·cid·al** \ˌpa-trə-ˈsī-dᵊl\ *adjective*

pat·ri·lin·eal \ˌpa-trə-ˈli-nē-əl\ *adjective* (1904)
: relating to, based on, or tracing descent through the paternal line ⟨*patrilineal* society⟩

pat·ri·mo·ny \ˈpa-trə-ˌmō-nē\ *noun* [Middle English *patrimonie*, from Middle French, from Latin *patrimonium*, from *patr-*, *pater* father] (14th century)
1 a : an estate inherited from one's father or ancestor **b** : anything derived from one's father or ancestors : HERITAGE

2 : an estate or endowment belonging by ancient right to a church
— **pat·ri·mo·ni·al** \ˌpa-trə-ˈmō-nē-əl\ *adjective*

pa·tri·ot \ˈpā-trē-ət, -ˌät, *chiefly British* ˈpa-trē-ət\ *noun* [Middle French *patriote* compatriot, from Late Latin *patriota*, from Greek *patriōtēs*, from *patria* lineage, from *patr-*, *patēr* father] (1605)
: one who loves his or her country and supports its authority and interests

pa·tri·ot·ic \ˌpā-trē-ˈä-tik, *chiefly British* ˌpa-\ *adjective* (1757)
1 : inspired by patriotism
2 : befitting or characteristic of a patriot
— **pa·tri·ot·i·cal·ly** \-ti-k(ə-)lē\ *adverb*

pa·tri·ot·ism \ˈpā-trē-ə-ˌti-zəm, *chiefly British* ˈpa-\ *noun* (circa 1726)
: love for or devotion to one's country

Patriots' Day *noun* (1897)
: the third Monday in April observed as a legal holiday in Maine and Massachusetts in commemoration of the battles of Lexington and Concord in 1775

pa·tris·tic \pə-ˈtris-tik\ *adjective* (circa 1828)
: of or relating to the church fathers or their writings
— **pa·tris·ti·cal** \-ti-kəl\ *adjective*

pa·tris·tics \-tiks\ *noun plural but singular in construction* (1847)
: the study of the writings and background of the church fathers

Pa·tro·clus \pə-ˈtrō-kləs, -ˈträ-\ *noun* [Latin, from Greek *Patroklos*]
: a Greek hero and friend of Achilles slain by Hector at Troy

¹pa·trol \pə-ˈtrōl\ *noun* (1664)
1 a : the action of traversing a district or beat or of going the rounds along a chain of guards for observation or the maintenance of security **b** : the person performing such an action **c** : a unit of persons or vehicles employed for reconnaissance, security, or combat
2 : a subdivision of a Boy Scout troop or Girl Scout troop

²patrol *verb* **pa·trolled; pa·trol·ling** [French *patrouiller*, from Middle French, to tramp around in the mud, from *patte* paw — more at PATTEN] (1691)
intransitive verb
: to carry out a patrol
transitive verb
: to carry out a patrol of
— **pa·trol·ler** *noun*

pa·trol·man \pə-ˈtrōl-mən\ *noun* (1867)
: one who patrols; *especially* : a police officer assigned to a beat

patrol wagon *noun* (1887)
: PADDY WAGON

pa·tron \ˈpā-trən, *for 6 also* pə-ˈtrōⁿ\ *noun* [Middle English, from Middle French, from Medieval Latin & Latin; Medieval Latin *patronus* patron saint, patron of a benefice, pattern, from Latin, defender, from *patr-*, *pater*] (14th century)
1 a : a person chosen, named, or honored as a special guardian, protector, or supporter **b** : a wealthy or influential supporter of an artist or writer **c** : a social or financial sponsor of a social function (as a ball or concert)
2 : one that uses wealth or influence to help an individual, an institution, or a cause
3 : one who buys the goods or uses the services offered especially by an establishment
4 : the holder of the right of presentation to an English ecclesiastical benefice
5 : a master in ancient times who freed his slave but retained some rights over him

\ə\ abut \ᵊ\ kitten \ər\ further \a\ ash \ā\ ace
\ä\ mop, mar \au̇\ out \ch\ chin \e\ bet \ē\ easy
\g\ go \i\ hit \ī\ ice \j\ job \ŋ\ sing \ō\ go
\ȯ\ law \ȯi\ boy \th\ thin \t̷h\ the \ü\ loot \u̇\ foot
\y\ yet \zh\ vision *see also* Guide to Pronunciation

6 [French, from Middle French] : the proprietor of an establishment (as an inn) especially in France
7 : the chief male officer in some fraternal lodges having both men and women members
— **pa·tron·al** \'pā-trə-nᵊl; *British* pə-'trōnᵊl, pa-\ *adjective*
pa·tron·age \'pa-trə-nij, 'pā-\ *noun* (14th century)
1 : ADVOWSON
2 : the support or influence of a patron
3 : kindness done with an air of superiority
4 : business or activity provided by patrons ⟨the new branch library is expected to have a heavy *patronage*⟩
5 a : the power to make appointments to government jobs especially for political advantage **b** : the distribution of jobs on the basis of patronage **c** : jobs distributed by patronage
pa·tron·ess \'pā-trə-nəs\ *noun* (15th century) : a woman who is a patron
pa·tron·ise *British variant of* PATRONIZE
pa·tron·ize \'pā-trə-ˌnīz, 'pa-\ *transitive verb* **-ized; -iz·ing** (1589)
1 : to act as patron of : provide aid or support for
2 : to adopt an air of condescension toward : treat haughtily or coolly
3 : to be a frequent or regular customer or client of
— **pa·tron·i·za·tion** \ˌpā-trə-nə-'zā-shən, pa-\ *noun*
— **pa·tron·iz·ing·ly** \'pā-trə-ˌnī-ziŋ-lē, 'pa-\ *adverb*
patron saint *noun* (1717)
1 : a saint to whose protection and intercession a person, a society, a church, or a place is dedicated
2 : an original leader or prime exemplar
pat·ro·nym·ic \ˌpa-trə-'ni-mik\ *noun* [Late Latin *patronymicum*, from neuter of *patronymicus*, from Greek *patrōnymikos*, from *patronymia* patronymic, from *patr-* + *onyma* name — more at NAME] (1612) : a name derived from that of the father or a paternal ancestor usually by the addition of an affix
— **patronymic** *adjective*
pa·troon \pə-'trün\ *noun* [French *patron* & Spanish *patrón*, from Medieval Latin *patronus*, from Latin, patron] (1743)
1 *archaic* : the captain or officer commanding a ship
2 [Dutch, from French *patron*] : the proprietor of a manorial estate especially in New York originally granted under Dutch rule but in some cases existing until the mid-19th century
pat·sy \'pat-sē\ *noun, plural* **pat·sies** [perhaps from Italian *pazzo* fool] (1903) : a person who is easily manipulated or victimized : SUCKER
pat·ten \'pa-tᵊn\ *noun* [Middle English *patin*, from Middle French, from *patte* paw, hoof, from (assumed) Vulgar Latin *patta*, of imitative origin] (14th century) : a clog, sandal, or overshoe often with a wooden sole or metal device to elevate the foot and increase the wearer's height or aid in walking in mud
¹pat·ter \'pa-tər\ *verb* [Middle English *patren*, from *paternoster*] (14th century)
transitive verb : to say or speak in a rapid or mechanical manner
intransitive verb
1 : to recite prayers (as paternosters) rapidly or mechanically
2 : to talk glibly and volubly
3 : to speak or sing rapid-fire words in a theatrical performance
— **pat·ter·er** \-tər-ər\ *noun*
²patter *noun* (1758)
1 : a specialized lingo : CANT; *especially* : the jargon of criminals (as thieves)
2 : the spiel of a street hawker or of a circus barker

3 : empty chattering talk
4 a (1) : the rapid-fire talk of a comedian (2) : the talk with which an entertainer accompanies a routine **b** : the words of a comic song or of a rapidly spoken usually humorous monologue introduced into such a song
³patter *verb* [frequentative of ³*pat*] (1611)
intransitive verb
1 : to strike or pat rapidly and repeatedly
2 : to run with quick light-sounding steps
transitive verb : to cause to patter
⁴patter *noun* (1844) : a quick succession of light sounds or pats
¹pat·tern \'pa-tərn\ *noun* [Middle English *patron*, from Middle French, from Medieval Latin *patronus*] (14th century)
1 : a form or model proposed for imitation : EXEMPLAR
2 : something designed or used as a model for making things ⟨a dressmaker's *pattern*⟩
3 : a model for making a mold into which molten metal is poured to form a casting
4 : an artistic, musical, literary, or mechanical design or form
5 : a natural or chance configuration ⟨frost *pattern*⟩ ⟨the *pattern* of events⟩
6 : a length of fabric sufficient for an article (as of clothing)
7 a : the distribution of shrapnel, bombs on a target, or shot from a shotgun **b** : the grouping made on a target by bullets
8 : a reliable sample of traits, acts, tendencies, or other observable characteristics of a person, group, or institution ⟨behavior *pattern*⟩ ⟨spending *pattern*⟩
9 a : the flight path prescribed for an airplane that is coming in for a landing **b** : a prescribed route to be followed by a pass receiver in football
10 : TEST PATTERN
11 : a discernible coherent system based on the intended interrelationship of component parts ⟨foreign policy *patterns*⟩
12 : frequent or widespread incidence ⟨a *pattern* of dissent⟩
synonym see MODEL
— **pat·terned** \-tərnd\ *adjective*
— **pat·tern·less** *adjective*
²pattern (circa 1586)
transitive verb
1 *dialect chiefly English* **a** : MATCH **b** : IMITATE
2 : to make, adapt, or fashion according to a pattern
3 : to furnish, adorn, or mark with a design
intransitive verb : to form a pattern
pat·tern·ing \'pa-tər-niŋ\ *noun* (1862)
1 : decoration, composition, or configuration according to a pattern
2 : physiotherapy that is designed to improve malfunctioning nervous control by means of feedback from muscular activity imposed by an outside source or induced by other muscles
pat·ty *also* **pat·tie** \'pa-tē\ *noun, plural* **pat·ties** [French *pâté* pâté] (1710)
1 : a little pie
2 a : a small flat cake of chopped food ⟨a hamburger *patty*⟩ **b** : a small flat candy ⟨a peppermint *patty*⟩
3 : PATTY SHELL
pat·ty-cake \-ˌkāk\ *noun* [alteration of *pat-a-cake*, from the opening words of the rhyme] (1889) : a game in which two participants (as mother and child) clap their hands together to the rhythm of an accompanying nursery rhyme
pat·ty-pan \-ˌpan\ *noun* [*pattypan* pan for baking patties] (1900) : a summer squash having a scalloped edge — called also *cymling*
patty shell *noun* (1909) : a shell of puff pastry made to hold a creamed meat, fish, or vegetable filling

pat·u·lous \'pa-chə-ləs\ *adjective* [Latin *patulus*, from *patēre* to be open — more at FATHOM] (1616) : spreading widely from a center ⟨a tree with *patulous* branches⟩
pat·zer \'pät-sər, 'pat-\ *noun* [probably from German *Patzer* bungler, from *patzen* to blunder] (1959) : an inept chess player
pau·ci·ty \'pȯ-sə-tē\ *noun* [Middle English *paucite*, from Middle French or Latin; Middle French *paucité*, from Latin *paucitat-, paucitas*, from *paucus* little — more at FEW] (15th century)
1 : smallness of number : FEWNESS
2 : smallness of quantity : DEARTH
Paul \'pȯl\ *noun* [Latin *Paulus*, from Greek *Paulos*] : an early Christian apostle and missionary and author of several New Testament epistles
Paul Bun·yan \-'bən-yən\ *noun* : a giant lumberjack of American folklore
Pau·li exclusion principle \'pau̇-lē-\ *noun* [Wolfgang *Pauli*] (1926) : EXCLUSION PRINCIPLE — called also *Pauli principle*
Pau·line \'pȯ-ˌlīn\ *adjective* (1817) : of or relating to the apostle Paul, his epistles, or the doctrine or theology implicit in his epistles
Paul·ist \'pȯ-list\ *noun* (circa 1883) : a member of the Roman Catholic Congregation of the Missionary Priests of Saint Paul the Apostle founded by I. T. Hecker in the U.S. in 1858
pau·low·nia \pȯ-'lō-nē-ə\ *noun* [New Latin, from Anna *Pavlovna* (died 1865) Russian princess] (1843) : any of a genus (*Paulownia*) of Chinese trees of the snapdragon family; *especially* : one (*P. tomentosa*) widely cultivated for its panicles of fragrant violet flowers
paunch \'pȯnch, 'pänch\ *noun* [Middle English, from Middle French *panche*, from Latin *pantic-, pantex*] (14th century)
1 a : the belly and its contents **b** : POTBELLY
2 : RUMEN
paunchy \'pȯn-chē, 'pän-\ *adjective* **paunchi·er; -est** (1598) : having a potbelly
— **paunch·i·ness** *noun*
pau·per \'pȯ-pər\ *noun* [Latin, poor — more at POOR] (1516)
1 : a person destitute of means except such as are derived from charity; *specifically* : one who receives aid from funds designated for the poor
2 : a very poor person
— **pau·per·ism** \-pə-ˌri-zəm\ *noun*
pau·per·ize \'pȯ-pə-ˌrīz\ *transitive verb* **-ized; -iz·ing** (1834) : to reduce to poverty
pau·piette \pō-'pyet\ *noun* [French *paupiette*, from Italian *polpetta* meat croquette, diminutive of *polpa* pulp, flesh, from Latin *pulpa*] (1889) : a thin slice of meat or fish wrapped around a forcemeat filling
¹pause \'pȯz\ *noun* [Middle English, from Latin *pausa*, from Greek *pausis*, from *pauein* to stop] (15th century)
1 : a temporary stop
2 a : a break in a verse **b** : a brief suspension of the voice to indicate the limits and relations of sentences and their parts
3 : temporary inaction especially as caused by uncertainty : HESITATION
4 a : the sign denoting a fermata **b** : a mark (as a period or comma) used in writing or printing to indicate or correspond to a pause of voice
5 : a reason or cause for pausing (as to reconsider) ⟨a thought that should give one *pause*⟩
²pause *verb* **paused; paus·ing** (15th century)
intransitive verb

1 : to stop temporarily
2 : to linger for a time
transitive verb
: to cause to pause **:** STOP
pa·vane \pə-'vän, -'van\ *also* **pa·van** *same or* 'pa-vən\ *noun* [Middle French *pavane*, from Italian *pavana*, from feminine of *pavano* of Padua, from *Pava* (Tuscan *Padova*) Padua] (1535)
1 : a stately court dance by couples that was introduced from southern Europe into England in the 16th century
2 : music for the pavane; *also* **:** music having the slow duple rhythm of a pavane
pave \'pāv\ *transitive verb* **paved; pav·ing** [Middle English, from Middle French *paver*, from Latin *pavire* to strike, pound; perhaps akin to Greek *paiein* to strike] (14th century)
1 : to lay or cover with material (as asphalt or concrete) that forms a firm level surface for travel
2 : to cover firmly and solidly as if with paving material
3 : to serve as a covering or pavement of
— **pav·er** *noun*
— **pave the way :** to prepare a smooth easy way **:** facilitate development
pa·vé \pa-'vā\ *also* **pa·véed** *or* **pa·véd** \pa-'vād\ *or* **pa·ve** \pa-'vā\ *adjective* [*pavé* from French, from past participle of *paver* to pave] (1903)
of jewels **:** set as close together as possible to conceal a metal base
pave·ment \'pāv-mənt\ *noun* [Middle English, from Old French, from Latin *pavimentum*, from *pavire*] (13th century)
1 : a paved surface: as **a :** the artificially covered surface of a public thoroughfare **b** *chiefly British* **:** SIDEWALK
2 : the material with which something is paved
3 : something that suggests a pavement (as in flatness, hardness, and extent of surface)
pav·id \'pa-vəd\ *adjective* [Latin *pavidus*, from *pavēre* to be frightened; akin to Latin *pavire*] (circa 1656)
: TIMID
¹pa·vil·ion \pə-'vil-yən\ *noun* [Middle English *pavilon*, from Old French *paveillon*, from Latin *papilion-, papilio* butterfly; perhaps akin to Old High German *fīfaltra* butterfly] (13th century)
1 a : a large often sumptuous tent **b :** something resembling a canopy or tent ⟨tree ferns spread their delicate *pavilions* —Blanche E. Baughan⟩
2 a : a part of a building projecting from the rest **b :** one of several detached or semidetached units into which a building is sometimes divided
3 a : a light sometimes ornamental structure in a garden, park, or place of recreation that is used for entertainment or shelter **b :** a temporary structure erected at an exposition by an individual exhibitor
4 : the lower faceted part of a brilliant below the girdle
²pavilion *transitive verb* (14th century)
: to furnish or cover with or put in a pavilion
pav·ing \'pā-viŋ\ *noun* (15th century)
: PAVEMENT
pav·ior *or* **pav·iour** \'pāv-yər\ *noun* [Middle English *pavier*, from *paven* to pave] (15th century)
British **:** one that paves
pav·lo·va \'pav-lə-və, pav-'lō-\ *noun, often capitalized* [Anna *Pavlova*] (1926)
: a dessert of Australian and New Zealand origin consisting of a meringue shell topped with whipped cream and usually fruit
Pav·lov·i·an \pav-'lȯ-vē-ən, -'lō-; -'lȯ-fē-\ *adjective* (1926)
1 : of or relating to Ivan Pavlov or to his work and theories ⟨*Pavlovian* conditioning⟩

2 : being or expressing a conditioned or predictable reaction **:** AUTOMATIC ⟨the candidates gave *Pavlovian* answers⟩
¹paw \'pȯ\ *noun* [Middle English, from Middle French *poue*] (14th century)
1 : the foot of a quadruped (as a lion or dog) that has claws; *broadly* **:** the foot of an animal
2 : a human hand especially when large or clumsy
²paw (15th century)
transitive verb
1 : to touch or strike at with a paw
2 : to feel or touch clumsily, rudely, or sexually
3 : to scrape or beat with or as if with a hoof
4 : to flail at or grab for wildly
intransitive verb
1 : to beat or scrape something with or as if with a hoof
2 : to touch or strike with a paw
3 : to feel or touch someone or something clumsily, rudely, or sexually
4 : to flail or grab wildly
paw·ky \'pȯ-kē\ *adjective* [obsolete English dialect *pawk* trick] (1676)
chiefly British **:** artfully shrewd **:** CANNY
pawl \'pȯl\ *noun* [perhaps modification of Dutch *pal* pawl] (1626)
: a pivoted tongue or sliding bolt on one part of a machine that is adapted to fall into notches or interdental spaces on another part (as a ratchet wheel) so as to permit motion in only one direction — see RATCHET WHEEL illustration
¹pawn \'pȯn, 'pän\ *noun* [Middle English *pown*, from Middle French *poon*, from Medieval Latin *pedon-, pedo* foot soldier, from Late Latin, one with broad feet, from Latin *ped-, pes* foot — more at FOOT] (14th century)
1 : one of the chessmen of least value having the power to move only forward ordinarily one square at a time, to capture only diagonally forward, and to be promoted to any piece except a king upon reaching the eighth rank
2 : one that can be used to further the purposes of another
²pawn *noun* [Middle English *paun*, modification of Middle French *pan*] (15th century)
1 a : something delivered to or deposited with another as security for a loan **b :** HOSTAGE
2 : the state of being pledged
3 : something used as a pledge **:** GUARANTY
4 : the act of pawning
³pawn *transitive verb* (1570)
: to deposit in pledge or as security
— **pawn·er** \'pȯ-nər, 'pä-\ *or* **paw·nor** *same or* pȯ-'nȯr, pä-\ *noun*
pawn·bro·ker \'pȯn-ˌbrō-kər, 'pän-\ *noun* (1687)
: one who lends money on the security of personal property pledged in his keeping
— **pawn·bro·king** \-kiŋ\ *noun*
Paw·nee \pȯ-'nē, pä-\ *noun, plural* **Pawnee** *or* **Pawnees** (1770)
: a member of an American Indian people originally of Kansas and Nebraska
pawn off *transitive verb* (1832)
: to get rid of or pass off usually by deception **:** PALM OFF
pawn·shop \'pȯn-ˌshäp, 'pän-\ *noun* (1849)
: a pawnbroker's shop
paw·paw *variant of* PAPAW
pax \'paks, 'päks\ *noun* [Middle English, from Medieval Latin, from Latin, peace — more at PEACE] (14th century)
1 : a tablet decorated with a sacred figure (as of Christ) and sometimes ceremonially kissed by participants at mass
2 : the kiss of peace in the Mass
3 : PEACE; *especially, capitalized* **:** a period of general stability in international affairs under the influence of a dominant military power — usually used in combination with a latinized name ⟨*Pax* Americana⟩
¹pay \'pā\ *verb* **paid** \'pād\ *also in sense 7* **payed; pay·ing** [Middle English, from Old

French *paier*, from Latin *pacare* to pacify, from *pac-, pax* peace] (13th century)
transitive verb
1 a : to make due return to for services rendered or property delivered **b :** to engage for money **:** HIRE ⟨you couldn't *pay* me to do that⟩
2 a : to give in return for goods or service ⟨*pay* wages⟩ **b :** to discharge indebtedness for **:** SETTLE ⟨*pay* a bill⟩ **c :** to make a disposal or transfer of (money)
3 : to give or forfeit in expiation or retribution ⟨*pay* the penalty⟩
4 a : to make compensation for **b :** to requite according to what is deserved ⟨*pay* them back⟩
5 : to give, offer, or make freely or as fitting ⟨*pay* attention⟩ ⟨*pay* your respects⟩
6 a : to return value or profit to ⟨it *pays* you to stay open⟩ **b :** to bring in as a return ⟨an investment *paying* five percent⟩
7 : to slacken (as a rope) and allow to run out — used with *out*
intransitive verb
1 : to discharge a debt or obligation
2 : to be worth the expense or effort ⟨crime doesn't *pay*⟩
3 : to suffer the consequences of an act ☆ ◇
— **pay one's dues 1 :** to earn a right or position through experience, suffering, or hard work **2** *also* **pay dues :** PAY *intransitive verb* 3

\ə\ **abut** \ˀ\ **kitten** \ər\ **further** \a\ **ash** \ā\ **ace**
\ä\ **mop, mar** \au̇\ **out** \ch\ **chin** \e\ **bet** \ē\ **easy**
\g\ **go** \i\ **hit** \ī\ **ice** \j\ **job** \ŋ\ **sing** \ō\ **go**
\ȯ\ **law** \ȯi\ **boy** \th\ **thin** \th̲\ **the** \ü\ **loot** \u̇\ **foot**
\y\ **yet** \zh\ **vision** *see also* Guide to Pronunciation

— **pay one's way** *or* **pay one's own way** : to pay one's share of expenses
— **pay the piper** : to bear the cost of something
— **pay through the nose** : to pay exorbitantly or dearly

²**pay** *noun* (14th century)
1 : something paid for a purpose and especially as a salary or wage : REMUNERATION
2 a : the act or fact of paying or being paid **b** : the status of being paid by an employer : EMPLOY
3 : a person viewed with respect to reliability or promptness in paying debts or bills
4 a : ore or a natural situation that yields metal and especially gold in profitable amounts **b** : an oil-yielding stratum or zone
synonym see WAGE

³**pay** *adjective* (1856)
1 : containing or leading to something precious or valuable
2 : equipped with a coin slot for receiving a fee for use ⟨*pay* telephone⟩
3 : requiring payment

⁴**pay** *transitive verb* **payed** *also* **paid**; **paying** [obsolete French *peier*, from Latin *picare*, from *pic-*, *pix* pitch — more at PITCH] (1627) : to coat with a waterproof composition

pay·able \'pā-ə-bəl\ *adjective* (14th century)
1 : that may, can, or must be paid
2 : PROFITABLE

pay–as–you–go *adjective* (1840)
: of or relating to a system or policy of paying bills when due or of paying for goods and services when purchased

pay·back \'pā-ˌbak\ *noun* (1955)
1 : a return on an investment equal to the original capital outlay; *also* : the period of time elapsed before an investment is recouped
2 : REQUITAL

pay–cable *noun* (1975)
: pay-TV utilizing a cable television system

pay·check \'pā-ˌchek\ *noun* (1899)
1 : a check in payment of wages or salary
2 : WAGES, SALARY

pay·day \-ˌdā\ *noun* (1529)
: a regular day on which wages are paid

pay dirt *noun* (1856)
1 : earth or ore that yields a profit to a miner
2 : a useful or remunerative discovery or object

pay·ee \(ˌ)pā-'ē\ *noun* (1758)
: one to whom money is or is to be paid

pay envelope *noun* (1901)
: an envelope containing one's wages; *also* : WAGES

pay·er \'pā-ər\ *also* **pay·or** \'pā-ər, (ˌ)pā-'òr\ *noun* (14th century)
: one that pays; *especially* : the person by whom a bill or note has been or should be paid

pay·load \'pā-ˌlōd\ *noun* (circa 1922)
1 : the load carried by a vehicle exclusive of what is necessary for its operation; *especially* : the load carried by an aircraft or spacecraft consisting of things (as passengers or instruments) necessary to the purpose of the flight
2 : the weight of a payload

pay·mas·ter \-ˌmas-tər\ *noun* (1550)
: an officer or agent whose duty it is to pay salaries or wages

pay·ment \'pā-mənt\ *noun* (14th century)
1 : the act of paying
2 : something that is paid : PAY
3 : REQUITAL

pay·nim \'pā-nəm\ *noun* [Middle English *painim*, from Old French *paienime* heathendom, from Late Latin *paganismus*, from *paganus* pagan] (13th century)
archaic : PAGAN; *especially* : MUSLIM

¹**pay–off** \'pā-ˌòf\ *noun* (1905)
1 a : PROFIT, REWARD **b** : RETRIBUTION
2 : the act or occasion of receiving money or material gain especially as compensation or as a bribe

3 : the climax of an incident or enterprise; *specifically* : the denouement of a narrative
4 : a decisive fact or factor resolving a situation or bringing about a definitive conclusion

²**payoff** *adjective* (1934)
: yielding results in the final test : DECISIVE

pay off (1710)
transitive verb
1 a : to give all due wages to; *especially* : to pay in full and discharge (an employee) **b** : to pay (a debt or a creditor) in full **c** : BRIBE
2 : to inflict retribution on
3 : to allow (a thread or rope) to run off a spool or drum
intransitive verb
: to yield returns

pay·o·la \pā-'ō-lə\ *noun* [¹*pay* + *-ola* (as in *Pianola*, trademark for a player piano)] (1938)
: undercover or indirect payment (as to a disc jockey) for a commercial favor (as for promoting a particular record)

pay·out \'pā-ˌaut\ *noun* (1943)
: the act of paying out : PAYOFF

pay–per–view *noun* (1980)
: a cable television service by which customers can order access to a single program for a fee

pay phone *noun* (1936)
: a usually coin-operated public telephone

pay·roll \'pā-ˌrōl\ *noun* (1740)
1 : a paymaster's or employer's list of those entitled to pay and of the amounts due to each
2 : the sum necessary for distribution to those on a payroll; *also* : the money to be distributed

pay station *noun* (1919)
: PAY PHONE

pay–TV *noun* (circa 1956)
: a service providing noncommercial television programming (as recent movies and entertainment specials) by means of a scrambled signal to subscribers who are provided with a decoder — called also *pay television;* compare PAY-CABLE, SUBSCRIPTION TV

pay up (15th century)
intransitive verb
: to pay what is due
transitive verb
: to pay in full

PBB \ˌpē-(ˌ)bē-'bē\ *noun* (circa 1975)
: POLYBROMINATED BIPHENYL

PBX \ˌpē-(ˌ)bē-'eks\ *noun* [*private branch exchange*] (circa 1961)
: a private telephone switchboard

PC \ˌpē-'sē\ *noun, plural* **PCs** *or* **PC's** (1978)
: PERSONAL COMPUTER

PCB \ˌpē-(ˌ)sē-'bē\ *noun* (1966)
: POLYCHLORINATED BIPHENYL

PCP \ˌpē-(ˌ)sē-'pē\ *noun* [*phenyl* + *cycl-* + *piperidine*] (circa 1970)
: PHENCYCLIDINE

PDQ \ˌpē-(ˌ)dē-'kyü\ *adverb, often not capitalized* [abbreviation of *pretty damned quick*] (1875)
: IMMEDIATELY

pe \'pā\ *noun* [Hebrew *pē*] (1823)
: the 17th letter of the Hebrew alphabet — see ALPHABET table

pea \'pē\ *noun, plural* **peas** *also* **pease** \'pēz\ *often attributive* [back-formation from Middle English *pease* (taken as a plural), from Old English *pise*, from Latin *pisa*, plural of *pisum*, from Greek *pison*] (1611)
1 a : a variable annual leguminous Eurasian vine (*Pisum sativum*) that is cultivated especially for its rounded smooth or wrinkled edible protein-rich seeds **b** : the seed of the pea **c** *plural* : the immature pods of the pea with their included seeds
2 : any of various leguminous plants related to or resembling the pea — usually used in combination with a qualifying term ⟨chickpea⟩ ⟨black-eyed *pea*⟩; *also* : the seed of such a plant
3 : something resembling a pea (as in size or shape)
word history see SHERRY

pea aphid *noun* (1925)
: a widely distributed aphid (*Acyrthosiphon pisum*) that is a serious pest on legumes (as alfalfa, pea, and clover)

pea bean *noun* (circa 1887)
: any of various kidney beans cultivated for their small white seeds which are used dried (as for baking)

¹**peace** \'pēs\ *noun* [Middle English *pees*, from Old French *pais*, from Latin *pac-*, *pax*; akin to Latin *pacisci* to agree — more at PACT] (12th century)
1 : a state of tranquillity or quiet: as **a** : freedom from civil disturbance **b** : a state of security or order within a community provided for by law or custom ⟨a breach of the *peace*⟩
2 : freedom from disquieting or oppressive thoughts or emotions
3 : harmony in personal relations
4 a : a state or period of mutual concord between governments **b** : a pact or agreement to end hostilities between those who have been at war or in a state of enmity
5 — used interjectionally to ask for silence or calm or as a greeting or farewell
— **at peace** : in a state of concord or tranquillity

²**peace** *intransitive verb* (14th century)
obsolete : to be, become, or keep silent or quiet

peace·able \'pē-sə-bəl\ *adjective* (14th century)
1 a : disposed to peace : not contentious or quarrelsome **b** : quietly behaved
2 : marked by freedom from strife or disorder
— **peace·able·ness** *noun*
— **peace·ably** \-blē\ *adverb*

peace corps *noun* (1960)
: a body of trained personnel sent as volunteers especially to assist underdeveloped nations

peace·ful \'pēs-fəl\ *adjective* (14th century)
1 : PEACEABLE 1
2 : untroubled by conflict, agitation, or commotion : QUIET, TRANQUIL
3 : of or relating to a state or time of peace
4 : devoid of violence or force
synonym see CALM
— **peace·ful·ly** \-fə-lē\ *adverb*
— **peace·ful·ness** *noun*

peace·keep·ing \'pēs-ˌkē-piŋ\ *noun* (1945)
: the preserving of peace; *especially* : international enforcement and supervision of a truce between hostile states or communities
— **peace·keep·er** \-pər\ *noun*

peace·mak·er \-ˌmā-kər\ *noun* (15th century)
: one who makes peace especially by reconciling parties at variance
— **peace·mak·ing** \-kiŋ\ *noun or adjective*

peace·nik \-ˌnik\ *noun* (1965)
: an opponent of the Vietnam War; *broadly* : PACIFIST

peace offering *noun* (circa 1530)
: a gift or service for the purpose of procuring peace or reconciliation

peace officer *noun* (1714)
: a civil officer (as a police officer) whose duty it is to preserve the public peace

peace pipe *noun* (1760)
: CALUMET

peace sign *noun* (1969)
1 : a sign made by holding the palm outward and forming a V with the index and middle fingers and used to indicate the desire for peace
2 : PEACE SYMBOL

peace symbol *noun* (1970)
: the symbol ⊕ used to signify peace

peace·time \'pēs-ˌtīm\ *noun* (1551)
: a time when a nation is not at war

¹**peach** \'pēch\ *noun* [Middle English *peche*, from Middle French (the fruit), from Late Latin *persica*, from Latin (*malum*) *persicum*, literally, Persian fruit] (14th century)
1 a : a low spreading freely branching Chi-

nese tree (*Prunus persica*) of the rose family that is widely cultivated in temperate areas and has lanceolate leaves, sessile usually pink flowers borne on the naked twigs in early spring, and a fruit which is a single-seeded drupe with a hard endocarp, a pulpy white or yellow mesocarp, and a thin downy epicarp **b** : the edible fruit of the peach
2 : a moderate yellowish pink
3 : one resembling a peach (as in sweetness, beauty, or excellence) ◇

²**peach** *verb* [Middle English *pechen,* short for *apechen* to accuse, from (assumed) Anglo-French *apecher,* from Late Latin *impedicare* to entangle — more at IMPEACH] (1570)
transitive verb
: to inform against : BETRAY
intransitive verb
: to turn informer : BLAB

peach leaf curl *noun* (1888)
: leaf curl of the peach that is caused by a fungus (*Taphrina deformans*)

peach tree borer *noun* (1850)
: a blue-black orange-marked clearwing moth (*Synanthedon exitiosa* synonym *Sanninoidea exitiosa*) whose white brown-headed larva bores in the wood of stone fruit trees (as the peach)

peachy \'pē-chē\ *adjective* **peach·i·er; -est** (1599)
1 : resembling a peach
2 : unusually fine : DANDY

¹**pea·cock** \'pē-ˌkäk\ *noun* [Middle English *pecok,* from *pe-* (from Old English *pēa* peafowl, from Latin *pavon-, pavo* peacock) + *cok* cock] (14th century)
1 : a male peafowl distinguished by a crest of upright plumules and by greatly elongated loosely webbed upper tail coverts which are mostly tipped with ocellated spots and can be erected and spread at will in a fan shimmering with iridescent color; *broadly* : PEAFOWL
2 : one making a proud display of himself : SHOW-OFF
— **pea·cock·ish** \-ˌkä-kish\ *adjective*
— **pea·cocky** \-kē\ *adjective*

²**peacock** (1586)
intransitive verb
: SHOW OFF

peacock blue *noun* (1881)
: a moderate greenish blue

peacock flower *noun* (1884)
: ROYAL POINCIANA

pea·fowl \'pē-ˌfaȯl\ *noun* [*pea-* (as in *peacock*) + *fowl*] (1804)
: either of two very large terrestrial pheasants (*Pavo cristatus* and *P. muticus*) of southeastern Asia and the East Indies often reared as ornamental fowls

pea green *noun* (1752)
: a moderate yellow-green

pea·hen \'pē-ˌhen\ *noun* [Middle English *pehenne,* from *pe-* + *henne* hen] (15th century)
: a female peafowl

peafowl: *A* female; *B* male

pea jacket \'pē-\ *noun* [by folk etymology from Dutch *pijjekker,* from *pij,* a kind of cloth + *jekker* jacket] (1721)
: a heavy woolen double-breasted jacket originally worn by sailors — called also *pea·coat* \'pē-ˌkōt\

¹**peak** \'pēk\ *noun* [perhaps alteration of *pike*] (1530)
1 : a pointed or projecting part of a garment; *especially* : the visor of a cap or hat
2 : PROMONTORY
3 : a sharp or pointed end

4 a (1) : the top of a hill or mountain ending in a point (2) : a prominent mountain usually having a well-defined summit **b** : something resembling a mountain peak
5 a : the upper aftermost corner of a fore-and-aft sail **b** : the narrow part of a ship's bow or stern or the part of the hold in it
6 a : the highest level or greatest degree **b** : a high point in a course of development especially as represented on a graph
7 : a point formed by the hair on the forehead
synonym see SUMMIT

²**peak** (1577)
intransitive verb
: to reach a maximum (as of capacity, value, or activity) — often used with *out*
transitive verb
: to cause to come to a peak, point, or maximum

³**peak** *adjective* (1903)
: being at or reaching the maximum

⁴**peak** *intransitive verb* [origin unknown] (1605)
1 : to grow thin or sickly
2 : to dwindle away

⁵**peak** *transitive verb* [from *apeak* held vertically] (1626)
1 : to set (as a gaff) nearer the perpendicular
2 : to hold (oars) with blades well raised

¹**peaked** \'pēkt *also* 'pē-kəd\ *adjective* (15th century)
: having a peak : POINTED
— **peaked·ness** \'pēk(t)-nəs, 'pē-kəd-nəs\ *noun*

²**peak·ed** \'pē-kəd *also* 'pi-kəd\ *adjective* (1835)
: being pale and wan or emaciated : SICKLY

peaky \'pē-kē\ *adjective* (1821)
: ²PEAKED

¹**peal** \'pē(ə)l\ *noun* [Middle English, appeal, summons to church, short for *appel* appeal, from *appelen* to appeal] (14th century)
1 a : the loud ringing of bells **b** : a complete set of changes on a given number of bells **c** : a set of bells tuned to the tones of the major scale for change ringing
2 : a loud sound or succession of sounds ⟨*peals* of laughter⟩

²**peal** (1632)
intransitive verb
: to give out peals
transitive verb
: to utter or give forth loudly

pea·like \'pē-ˌlīk\ *adjective* (1774)
1 : resembling a garden pea especially in size, firmness, and shape ⟨a *pealike* lump under the skin⟩
2 *of a flower* : being showy and papilionaceous

¹**pea·nut** \'pē-(ˌ)nət\ *noun* (1802)
1 : a low-branching widely cultivated leguminous annual herb (*Arachis hypogaea*) with showy yellow flowers having a peduncle which elongates and bends into the soil where the ovary ripens into a pod containing one to three oily edible seeds; *also* : its seed or seed-containing pod
2 : an insignificant or tiny person
3 *plural* : a trifling amount

²**peanut** *adjective* (1836)
: INSIGNIFICANT, PETTY ⟨*peanut* politics⟩

peanut oil *noun* (1882)
: a colorless to yellow fatty nondrying oil that is obtained from peanuts and is used chiefly as a salad oil, in margarine, in soap, and as a vehicle in pharmaceutical preparations and cosmetics

pear \'par, 'per\ *noun* [Middle English *pere,* from Old English *peru,* from (assumed) Vulgar Latin *pira,* from Latin, plural of *pirum*] (before 12th century)
1 : a fleshy pome fruit that is borne by a tree (genus *Pyrus,* especially *P. communis*) of the rose family and is usually larger at the apical end
2 : a tree bearing pears

¹**pearl** \'pər(-ə)l\ *noun* [Middle English *perle,* from Middle French, probably from (assumed) Vulgar Latin *pernula,* diminutive of Latin *perna* upper leg, kind of sea mussel; akin to Old English *fiersn* heel, Greek *pternē*] (14th century)
1 a : a dense variously colored and usually lustrous concretion formed of concentric layers of nacre as an abnormal growth within the shell of some mollusks and used as a gem **b** : MOTHER-OF-PEARL
2 : one that is very choice or precious
3 : something resembling a pearl intrinsically or physically
4 : a nearly neutral slightly bluish medium gray

²**pearl** (14th century)
transitive verb
1 : to set or adorn with pearls
2 : to sprinkle or bead with pearly drops
3 : to form into small round grains
4 : to give a pearly color or luster to
intransitive verb
1 : to form drops or beads like pearls
2 : to fish or search for pearls
— **pearl·er** \'pər-lər\ *noun*

³**pearl** *adjective* (1610)
1 a : of, relating to, or resembling pearl **b** : made of or adorned with pearls
2 : having medium-sized grains

⁴**pearl** *noun or transitive verb* [alteration of *purl*] (1824)
British : PICOT

pearl·es·cent \ˌpər-'le-sᵊnt\ *adjective* (1936)
: having a pearly luster ⟨a *pearlescent* lacquer⟩
— **pearl·es·cence** \-sᵊn(t)s\ *noun*

pearl essence *noun* (circa 1909)
: a translucent substance that occurs in the silvery scales of various fish (as herring) and is used in making artificial pearls, lacquers, and plastics

pearl gray *noun* (1796)
1 : a yellowish to light gray
2 : a pale blue

Pearl Harbor *noun* [*Pearl Harbor,* Oahu, Hawaii, American naval station attacked without warning by the Japanese on December 7, 1941] (1942)
: a sneak attack often with devastating effect

pearl·ite \'pər(-ə)-ˌlīt\ *noun* [French *perlite,* from *perle* pearl] (1888)
: the lamellar mixture of ferrite and cementite in slowly cooled iron-carbon alloys occurring normally as a principal constituent of both steel and cast iron
— **pearl·it·ic** \ˌpər-'li-tik\ *adjective*

pearl·ized \'pər(-ə)-ˌlīzd\ *adjective* (1937)
: given a pearlescent surface or finish

pearl millet *noun* (circa 1890)

◇ WORD HISTORY

peach When the peach, which is native to China, was introduced to the classical world in the first century A.D., it was known in Greek as *mēlon Persikon* and in Latin as *malum Persicum*. Both names literally meant "Persian apple." The fruit may not have reached the Mediterranean directly from Persia, and its attribution to that country in the name simply reflects a general sense that it was eastern in origin. The Latin *malum Persicum* was shortened to *persicum*, which was superseded in Late Latin by the feminine form *persica*. *Persica* developed into Old French *pesche*. In a Middle French form this word provided later Middle English with *peche*, the antecedent of Modern English *peach*.

: a tall cereal grass (*Pennisetum glaucum* synonym *P. americanum*) that has large leaves and dense round spikes and is widely grown for its seeds and for forage

pearl onion *noun* (circa 1890)
: a very small usually pickled onion used especially in appetizers and as a garnish

pearly \'pər-lē\ *adjective* **pearl·i·er; -est** (15th century)
1 : resembling, containing, or adorned with pearls or mother-of-pearl
2 : highly precious

pearly everlasting *noun* (1857)
: an everlasting (*Anaphalis margaritacea*) that has herbage covered with white woolly hairs and corymbose heads with white scarious involucres

pearly nautilus *noun* (1822)
: NAUTILUS 1

pear psylla *noun* (1904)
: a yellowish or greenish jumping plant louse (*Psylla pyricola*) that is often destructive to the pear

pear–shaped \'par-ˌshāpt, 'per-\ *adjective* (1758)
1 : having an oval shape markedly tapering at one end
2 *of a vocal tone* : free from harshness, thinness, or nasality

peart \'pirt\ *adjective* [alteration of *pert*] (1578)
chiefly Southern & Midland : being in good spirits : LIVELY
— **peart·ly** *adverb*

peas·ant \'pe-zᵊnt\ *noun* [Middle English *paissaunt*, from Middle French *paisant*, from Old French, from *paîs* country, from Late Latin *pagensis* inhabitant of a district, from Latin *pagus* district] (15th century)
1 : a member of a European class of persons tilling the soil as small landowners or as laborers; *also* : a member of a similar class elsewhere
2 : a usually uneducated person of low social status

peas·ant·ry \-zᵊn-trē\ *noun* (circa 1553)
1 : PEASANTS
2 : the position, rank, or behavior of a peasant

pease·cod *or* **peas·cod** \'pēz-ˌkäd\ *noun* [Middle English *pesecod*, from *pese* + *cod* bag, husk — more at CODPIECE] (14th century)
: a pea pod

pea·shoot·er \'pē-ˌshü-tər\ *noun* (1803)
: a toy blowgun that uses peas for projectiles

pea soup *noun* (1711)
1 : a thick purée made of dried peas
2 : a thick fog

¹**peat** \'pēt\ *noun, often attributive* [Middle English *pete*, from Medieval Latin *peta*] (14th century)
1 : TURF 2b
2 : partially carbonized vegetable tissue formed by partial decomposition in water of various plants (as mosses of the genus *Sphagnum*)
— **peaty** \'pē-tē\ *adjective*

²**peat** *noun* [origin unknown] (1599)
: a bold lively woman

peat moss *noun* (1880)
: SPHAGNUM

pea·vey *or* **pea·vy** \'pē-vē\ *noun, plural* **peaveys** *or* **peavies** [probably from the name *Peavey*] (1870)
: a lumberman's lever that has a pivoting hooked arm and metal spike at one end — called also *cant dog*; compare CANT HOOK

¹**peb·ble** \'pe-bəl\ *noun* [Middle English *pobble*, from Old English *papolstān*, from *papol-* (of unknown origin) + *stān* stone] (14th century)
1 : a small usually rounded stone especially when worn by the action of water

peavey

2 : transparent and colorless quartz : ROCK CRYSTAL
3 : an irregular, crinkled, or grainy surface
— **peb·bly** \-b(ə-)lē\ *adjective*

²**pebble** *transitive verb* **peb·bled; peb·bling** \-b(ə-)liŋ\ (1605)
1 : to pelt with pebbles
2 : to pave or cover with pebbles or something resembling pebbles
3 : to grain (as leather) so as to produce a rough and irregularly indented surface

pec \'pek\ *noun* (1966)
: PECTORAL MUSCLE

pe·can \pi-'kän, -'kan; 'pē-ˌkan\ *noun* [American French *pacane*, of Algonquian origin; akin to Ojibwa *paka'n*, a hard-shelled nut] (1712)
1 : a large hickory (*Carya illinoensis*) that has roughish bark and hard but brittle wood and is widely grown in the warmer parts of the U.S. and in Mexico for its edible nut
2 : the wood of the pecan tree
3 : the smooth oblong thin-shelled nut of the pecan tree

pec·ca·dil·lo \ˌpe-kə-'di-(ˌ)lō\ *noun, plural* **-loes** *or* **-los** [Spanish *pecadillo*, diminutive of *pecado* sin, from Latin *peccatum*, from neuter of *peccatus*, past participle of *peccare*] (1591)
: a slight offense

pec·cant \'pe-kənt\ *adjective* [Latin *peccant-, peccans*, present participle of *peccare* to stumble, sin] (circa 1604)
1 : guilty of a moral offense : SINNING
2 : violating a principle or rule : FAULTY
— **pec·cant·ly** *adverb*

pec·ca·ry \'pe-kə-rē\ *noun, plural* **-ries** [perhaps modification of Carib *baquira*] (1613)
: any of several largely nocturnal gregarious American mammals resembling the related pigs: as **a** : a grizzled animal (*Tayassu tajacu*) with an indistinct white collar **b** : a blackish animal (*Tayassu pecari*) with a whitish mouth region

pec·ca·vi \pe-'kä-(ˌ)wē, -(ˌ)vē; -'kā-ˌvī\ *noun* [Latin, I have sinned, from *peccare*] (1553)
: an acknowledgment of sin

¹**peck** \'pek\ *noun* [Middle English *pek*, from Middle French] (13th century)
1 — see WEIGHT table
2 : a large quantity or number

²**peck** *verb* [Middle English, perhaps from Middle Low German *pekken*] (14th century)
transitive verb
1 a : to strike or pierce especially repeatedly with the bill or a pointed tool **b** : to make by pecking ⟨*peck* a hole⟩
2 : to pick up with the bill
intransitive verb
1 a : to strike, pierce, or pick up something with or as if with the bill **b** : CARP, NAG
2 : to eat reluctantly and in small bites ⟨*peck* at food⟩

³**peck** *noun* (circa 1591)
1 : an impression or hole made by pecking
2 : a quick sharp stroke

peck·er \'pe-kər\ *noun* (1587)
1 : one that pecks
2 *chiefly British* : COURAGE
3 : PENIS — often considered vulgar

peck·er·wood \'pe-kər-ˌwùd\ *noun* [probably inversion of *woodpecker*] (1904)
: a rural white Southerner — often used disparagingly

pecking order *also* **peck order** *noun* (1928)
1 : the basic pattern of social organization within a flock of poultry in which each bird pecks another lower in the scale without fear of retaliation and submits to pecking by one of higher rank; *broadly* : a dominance hierarchy in a group of social animals
2 : a social hierarchy

peck·ish \'pe-kish\ *adjective* [²*peck*] (1785)
1 *chiefly British* : HUNGRY
2 : CROTCHETY

Peck·sniff·ian \pek-'sni-fē-ən\ *adjective* [Seth *Pecksniff*, character in *Martin Chuzzlewit* (1843–44) by Charles Dickens] (1851)
: unctuously hypocritical : PHARISAICAL

pecky \'pe-kē\ *adjective* [³*peck*] (1848)
1 : marked by lenticular or finger-shaped pockets of decay caused by fungi ⟨*pecky* cypress⟩
2 : containing discolored or shriveled grains ⟨*pecky* rice⟩

pec·o·ri·no \ˌpe-kə-'rē-(ˌ)nō\ *noun, often capitalized* [Italian, from *pecorino* of sheep, from *pecora* sheep, ewe, from Latin, domestic animals, from plural of *pecus* cattle — more at FEE] (1912)
: any of various cheeses of Italian origin made from sheep's milk

pec·ten \'pek-tən\ *noun, plural* **pectens** [New Latin *pectin-, pecten*, from Latin, comb, scallop] (1682)
1 : SCALLOP 1a
2 *plural usually* **pec·ti·nes** \-tə-ˌnēz\ : a body part that resembles a comb; *especially* : a folded vascular pigmented membrane projecting into the vitreous humor in the eye of a bird or reptile

pec·tic \'pek-tik\ *adjective* [French *pectique*, from Greek *pēktikos* coagulating, from *pēgnynai* to fix, coagulate — more at PACT] (1831)
: of, relating to, or derived from pectin

pectic acid *noun* (1831)
: any of various water-insoluble substances formed by hydrolyzing the methyl ester groups of pectins

pec·tin \'pek-tən\ *noun* [French *pectine*, from *pectique*] (1838)
: any of various water-soluble substances that bind adjacent cell walls in plant tissues and yield a gel which is the basis of fruit jellies; *also* : a commercial product rich in pectins

pec·ti·na·ceous \ˌpek-tə-'nā-shəs\ *adjective* (circa 1844)
: of, relating to, or containing pectin

pec·ti·nate \'pek-tə-ˌnāt\ *adjective* [Latin *pectinatus*, from *pectin-, pecten* comb; akin to Greek *kten-, kteis* comb] (1793)
: having narrow parallel projections or divisions suggestive of the teeth of a comb ⟨*pectinate* antennae⟩
— **pec·ti·na·tion** \ˌpek-tə-'nā-shən\ *noun*

pec·tin·es·ter·ase \ˌpek-tə-'nes-tə-ˌrās, -ˌrāz\ *noun* (1945)
: an enzyme that catalyzes the hydrolysis of pectins into pectic acids and methanol

¹**pec·to·ral** \'pek-t(ə-)rəl\ *noun* (15th century)
: something worn on the breast

²**pectoral** *adjective* [Middle English or Latin; Middle French, from Latin *pectoralis*, from *pector-, pectus* breast; akin to Tocharian A *pässäm* breasts, Old Irish *ucht* breast] (1578)
1 : of, situated in or on, or worn on the chest
2 : coming from the breast or heart as the seat of emotion

pectoral cross *noun* (circa 1735)
: a cross worn on the breast especially by a prelate

pectoral fin *noun* (1769)
: either of the fins of a fish that correspond to the forelimbs of a quadruped

pectoral girdle *noun* (circa 1890)
: the bony or cartilaginous arch that supports the forelimbs of a vertebrate

pectoral muscle *noun* (1615)
: any of the muscles which connect the ventral walls of the chest with the bones of the upper arm and shoulder and of which there are two on each side of the human body

pec·u·late \'pe-kyə-ˌlāt\ *transitive verb* **-lat·ed; -lat·ing** [Latin *peculatus*, past participle of *peculari*, from *peculium*] (1802)
: EMBEZZLE
— **pec·u·la·tion** \ˌpe-kyə-'lā-shən\ *noun*
— **pec·u·la·tor** \'pe-kyə-ˌlā-tər\ *noun*

¹pe·cu·liar \pi-'kyül-yər\ *adjective* [Middle English *peculier*, from Latin *peculiaris* of private property, special, from *peculium* private property, from *pecu* cattle; akin to Latin *pecus* cattle — more at FEE] (15th century)
1 : characteristic of only one person, group, or thing : DISTINCTIVE
2 : different from the usual or normal: **a** : SPECIAL, PARTICULAR **b** : ODD, CURIOUS **c** : ECCENTRIC, QUEER ◆
synonym see CHARACTERISTIC, STRANGE
— **pe·cu·liar·ly** *adverb*

²peculiar *noun* (1562)
: something exempt from ordinary jurisdiction; *especially* : a church or parish exempt from the jurisdiction of the ordinary in whose territory it lies

pe·cu·liar·i·ty \pi-,kyül-'yar-ə-tē, -,kyü-lē-'ar-\ *noun, plural* **-ties** (1646)
1 : the quality or state of being peculiar
2 : a distinguishing characteristic
3 : ODDITY, QUIRK

pe·cu·ni·ary \pi-'kyü-nē-,er-ē\ *adjective* [Latin *pecuniarius*, from *pecunia* money — more at FEE] (1502)
1 : consisting of or measured in money
2 : of or relating to money : MONETARY
word history see PECULIAR
— **pe·cu·ni·ar·i·ly** \-,kyü-nē-'er-ə-lē\ *adverb*

ped \'ped\ *noun* [Greek *pedon* ground; akin to Latin *ped-, pes* foot — more at FOOT] (1951)
: a natural soil aggregate

ped- *or* **pedo-** *or* **paed-** *or* **paedo-** *combining form* [Greek *paid-, paido-*, from *paid-, pais* child, boy — more at FEW]
: child ⟨*ped*iatric⟩ : childhood ⟨*paedo*genesis⟩

-ped *or* **-pede** *noun combining form* [Latin *ped-, pes*]
: foot ⟨maxilli*ped*⟩

ped·a·gog·i·cal \,pe-də-'gä-ji-kəl, -'gō-\ *also* **ped·a·gog·ic** \-jik\ *adjective* (1619)
: of, relating to, or befitting a teacher or education
— **ped·a·gog·i·cal·ly** \-ji-k(ə-)lē\ *adverb*

ped·a·gog·ics \-jiks\ *noun plural but singular in construction* (circa 1859)
: PEDAGOGY

ped·a·gogue *also* **ped·a·gog** \'pe-də-,gäg\ *noun* [Middle English *pedagoge*, from Middle French, from Latin *paedagogus*, from Greek *paidagōgos*, slave who escorted children to school, from *paid-* ped- + *agōgos* leader, from *agein* to lead — more at AGENT] (14th century)
: TEACHER, SCHOOLMASTER; *especially* : a dull, formal, or pedantic teacher

ped·a·go·gy \'pe-də-,gō-jē *also* -,gä-, *especially British* -,gä-gē\ *noun* (1583)
: the art, science, or profession of teaching; *especially* : EDUCATION 2

¹ped·al \'pe-dᵊl\ *noun* [Middle French *pedale*, from Italian, from Latin *pedalis*, adjective] (1611)
1 : a lever pressed by the foot in the playing of a musical instrument (as an organ or piano)
2 : a foot lever or treadle by which a part is activated in a mechanism

²ped·al *adjective* [Latin *pedalis*, from *ped-, pes*] (1625)
1 \'pe-dᵊl *also* 'pē-\ : of or relating to the foot
2 \'pe-\ : of, relating to, or involving a pedal

³ped·al \'pe-dᵊl\ *verb* **ped·aled** *also* **ped·alled; ped·al·ing** *also* **ped·al·ling** \'pe-dᵊl-iŋ, 'ped-liŋ\ (1888)
intransitive verb
1 : to ride a bicycle
2 : to use or work a pedal
transitive verb
: to work the pedals of

pedal bone *noun* (1881)
: COFFIN BONE

pe·dal·fer \pə-'dal-fər, -,fer\ *noun* [Greek *pedon* ground + English *al*umen + Latin *ferrum* iron] (1928)
: a soil that lacks a hardened layer of accumulated carbonates

ped·al–note \'pe-dᵊl-,nōt\ *noun* [from the playing of the lowest notes on the organ by means of pedals] (circa 1828)
1 : PEDAL POINT
2 : one of the lowest tones that can be sounded on a brass instrument being an octave below the normal usable range and representing the fundamental of the harmonic series

ped·alo \'pe-də-(,)lō\ *noun, plural* **-los** [French *pédalo*, from *pédale* pedal + *-o* (perhaps as in *meccano* children's construction set)] (1945)
chiefly British : a small recreational paddleboat powered by pedals

pedal point *noun* (1852)
: a single tone usually the tonic or dominant that is normally sustained in the bass and sounds against changing harmonies in the other parts

pedal pushers *noun plural* (1944)
: women's and girls' calf-length trousers

pedal steel *noun* (1969)
: a box-shaped musical instrument with legs that has usually 10 strings which can be altered in pitch by the use of pedals and which are plucked while being pressed with a movable steel bar — called also *pedal steel guitar*

ped·ant \'pe-dᵊnt\ *noun* [Middle French, from Italian *pedante*] (1588)
1 *obsolete* : a male schoolteacher
2 a : one who makes a show of knowledge **b** : one who is unimaginative or who unduly emphasizes minutiae in the presentation or use of knowledge **c** : a formalist or precisionist in teaching

pe·dan·tic \pi-'dan-tik\ *adjective* (circa 1600)
1 : of, relating to, or being a pedant
2 : narrowly, stodgily, and often ostentatiously learned
3 : UNIMAGINATIVE, PEDESTRIAN
— **pe·dan·ti·cal·ly** \-'dan-ti-k(ə-)lē\ *adverb*

ped·ant·ry \'pe-dᵊn-trē\ *noun, plural* **-ries** (1612)
1 : pedantic presentation or application of knowledge or learning
2 : an instance of pedantry

ped·dle \'pe-dᵊl\ *verb* **ped·dled; ped·dling** \'ped-liŋ, 'pe-dᵊl-iŋ\ [back-formation from *peddler*, from Middle English *pedlere*] (1532)
intransitive verb
1 : to travel about with wares for sale; *broadly* : SELL
2 : to be busy with trifles : PIDDLE
transitive verb
1 : to sell or offer for sale from place to place : HAWK; *broadly* : SELL
2 : to deal out or seek to disseminate

ped·dler *also* **ped·lar** \'ped-lər\ *noun* (14th century)
: one who peddles: as **a** : one who offers merchandise (as fresh produce) for sale along the street or from door to door **b** : one who deals in or promotes something intangible (as a personal asset or an idea) ⟨influence *peddlers*⟩

ped·er·ast \'pe-də-,rast\ *noun* [Greek *paiderastēs*, literally, lover of boys, from *paid-* ped- + *erastēs* lover, from *erasthai* to love — more at EROS] (circa 1736)
: one that practices anal intercourse especially with a boy
— **ped·er·as·tic** \,pe-də-'ras-tik\ *adjective*
— **ped·er·as·ty** \'pe-də-,ras-tē\ *noun*

¹ped·es·tal \'pe-dəs-tᵊl\ *noun* [Middle French *piedestal*, from Old Italian *piedestallo*, from *pie di stallo* foot of a stall] (1563)
1 a : the support or foot of a late classic or neoclassic column — see COLUMN illustration **b** : the base of an upright structure
2 : BASE, FOUNDATION
3 : a position of esteem

²pedestal *transitive verb* **-taled** *or* **-talled; -tal·ing** *or* **-tal·ling** (1648)
: to place on or furnish with a pedestal

¹pe·des·tri·an \pə-'des-trē-ən\ *adjective* [Latin *pedestr-, pedester*, literally, going on foot, from *ped-, pes* foot — more at FOOT] (1716)
1 : COMMONPLACE, UNIMAGINATIVE
2 a : going or performed on foot **b** : of, relating to, or designed for walking ⟨a *pedestrian* mall⟩

²pedestrian *noun* (1793)
: a person going on foot : WALKER

pe·des·tri·an·ism \-ə-,ni-zəm\ *noun* (1809)
1 a : the practice of walking **b** : fondness for walking for exercise or recreation
2 : the quality or state of being unimaginative or commonplace

pe·di·at·ric \,pē-dē-'a-trik\ *adjective* (1880)
: of or relating to pediatrics

pe·di·a·tri·cian \,pē-dē-ə-'tri-shən\ *or* **pe·di·a·trist** \,pē-dē-'a-trist, pē-'dī-ə-\ *noun* (circa 1903)
: a specialist in pediatrics

pe·di·at·rics \,pē-dē-'a-triks\ *noun plural but singular or plural in construction* (1884)
: a branch of medicine dealing with the development, care, and diseases of children

pedi·cab \'pe-di-,kab\ *noun* [Latin *ped-, pes* + English *cab*] (1945)
: a tricycle with a 2-seat passenger compartment covered by a usually folding top and a separate seat for a driver who pedals

ped·i·cel \'pe-də-,sel\ *noun* [New Latin *pedicellus*, diminutive of Latin *pediculus*] (1676)
: a slender basal part of an organism or one of its parts: as **a** : a plant stalk that supports a fruiting or spore-bearing organ **b** : a narrow basal attachment (as of the abdomen of an ant) of an animal organ or part
— **ped·i·cel·late** \,pe-də-'se-lət\ *adjective*

ped·i·cle \'pe-di-kəl\ *noun* [Latin *pediculus*, from diminutive of *ped-, pes*] (1626)
1 : PEDICEL b
2 : the part of a skin or tissue graft left attached to the original site during the preliminary stages of union
— **ped·i·cled** \-kəld\ *adjective*

pe·dic·u·late \pi-'di-kyə-lət\ *adjective* [ultimately from Latin *pediculus* little foot, pedicel] (circa 1890)

◇ WORD HISTORY
peculiar The Latin words *pecunia* "property, wealth, money" and *peculium* "property managed by a person incapable of legal ownership, such as a slave or minor" have traditionally been explained as derivatives of *pecu* "flock" or "herd" and its plural *pecua* "farm animals, livestock." The assumption has been that wealth was measured by the Italic and Indo-European ancestors of the Romans in terms of cattle. This assumption is probably incorrect: although *pecunia* and *peculium* are certainly derivatives of *pecu*, the ancient sense of this word was more likely "movable property (that is, property other than land)" rather than "livestock." The latter is a specific application of the word that arose only subsequently, livestock being one major form of movable wealth. The relation between English *pecuniary* and Latin *pecunia* can be seen easily enough, but the relation of English *peculiar* to Latin *peculium* is less straightforward. The Latin derivative adjective *peculiaris* meant originally "pertaining to the property of a slave or minor" and by extension "one's own, personal, private," and hence "special, particular." The meanings "strange" and "eccentric" of English *peculiar* have developed since the word was borrowed from Latin.

pediculate : of or relating to an order (Lophiiformes synonym Pediculati) of marine bony fishes with pectoral fins at the end of an armlike process and part of the dorsal fin modified into a lure

— **pediculate** noun

pe·dic·u·lo·sis \pi-ˌdi-kyə-'lō-səs\ noun [New Latin, from Latin pediculus louse, diminutive of pedis louse] (circa 1890)
: infestation with lice

pe·dic·u·lous \pi-'di-kyə-ləs\ adjective [Latin pediculosus, from pediculus] (circa 1550)
: infested with lice : LOUSY

ped·i·cure \'pe-di-ˌkyu̇r\ noun [French pédicure, from Latin ped-, pes foot + curare to take care, from cura care] (circa 1842)
1 : one who practices chiropody
2 a : care of the feet, toes, and nails **b** : a single treatment of these parts

— **ped·i·cur·ist** \-ˌkyu̇r-ist\ noun

ped·i·gree \'pe-də-ˌgrē\ noun [Middle English pedegru, from Middle French pie de grue crane's foot; from the shape made by the lines of a genealogical chart] (15th century)
1 : a register recording a line of ancestors
2 a : an ancestral line : LINEAGE **b** : the origin and the history of something
3 a : a distinguished ancestry **b** : the recorded purity of breed of an individual or strain

— **ped·i·greed** \-ˌgrēd\ or **pedigree** adjective

ped·i·ment \'pe-də-mənt\ noun [alteration of obsolete English periment, probably alteration of English pyramid] (1592)
1 : a triangular space that forms the gable of a low-pitched roof and that is usually filled with relief sculpture in classical architecture; also : a similar form used as a decoration
2 : a broad gently sloping bedrock surface with low relief that is situated at the base of a steeper slope and is usually thinly covered with alluvial gravel and sand

— **ped·i·men·tal** \ˌpe-də-'men-t°l\ adjective

— **ped·i·ment·ed** \'pe-də-ˌmen-təd\ adjective

ped·i·palp \'pe-də-ˌpalp\ noun [New Latin pedipalpus, from ped-, pes foot + palpus palpus] (1826)
: either of the second pair of appendages of an arachnid (as a spider) that are borne near the mouth and are often modified for a special (as sensory) function

pedo- — see PED-

ped·o·cal \'pe-də-ˌkal\ noun [Greek pedon earth + Latin calc-, calx lime — more at PED, CHALK] (1928)
: a soil that includes a definite hardened layer of accumulated carbonates

— **ped·o·cal·ic** \ˌpe-də-'ka-lik\ adjective

¹pe·do·gen·e·sis \ˌpe-də-'je-nə-səs\ variant of PAEDOGENESIS

²ped·o·gen·e·sis \ˌpe-də-'je-nə-səs\ noun [New Latin, from Greek pedon + Latin genesis] (1936)
: the formation and development of soil

— **ped·o·gen·ic** \-'je-nik\ also **ped·o·ge·net·ic** \-jə-'ne-tik\ adjective

pe·dol·o·gy \pi-'dä-lə-jē, pe-\ noun [Greek pedon + International Scientific Vocabulary -logy] (1912)
: SOIL SCIENCE

— **ped·o·log·i·cal** \ˌpe-d°l-'ä-ji-kəl\ also **ped·o·log·ic** \-jik\ adjective

— **ped·o·log·ist** \pi-'dä-lə-jist, pe-\ noun

pe·dom·e·ter \pi-'dä-mə-tər\ noun [French pédomètre, from Latin ped-, pes foot + French -mètre -meter — more at FOOT] (1723)
: an instrument usually in watch form that records the distance a person covers on foot by responding to the body motion at each step

pe·do·phile \'pe-də-ˌfīl\ noun (1951)
: one affected with pedophilia

pe·do·phil·ia \ˌpe-də-'fi-lē-ə\ noun [New Latin] (1906)
: sexual perversion in which children are the preferred sexual object

— **pe·do·phil·i·ac** \-'fi-lē-ˌak\ or **pe·do·phil·ic** \-'fi-lik\ adjective

pe·dun·cle \'pē-ˌdəŋ-kəl, pi-\ noun [New Latin pedunculus, diminutive of Latin ped-, pes] (circa 1753)
1 : a stalk bearing a flower or flower cluster or a fructification
2 : a narrow part by which some larger part or the whole body of an organism is attached : STALK, PEDICEL
3 : a narrow stalk by which a tumor or polyp is attached

— **pe·dun·cled** \-kəld\ adjective

— **pe·dun·cu·lar** \pi-'dəŋ-kyə-lər\ adjective

pe·dun·cu·lat·ed \pi-'dəŋ-kyə-ˌlā-təd\ also **pe·dun·cu·late** \-lət\ adjective [New Latin pedunculus] (1752)
: having, growing on, or being attached by a peduncle ⟨a pedunculated tumor⟩

¹pee \'pē\ noun (1612)
1 : the letter p
2 plural **pee** British : PENNY

²pee intransitive verb **peed; pee·ing** [euphemism from the initial letter of piss] (circa 1880)
: URINATE — sometimes considered vulgar

³pee noun (1946)
1 : URINE — sometimes considered vulgar
2 : an act of urination — sometimes considered vulgar

¹peek \'pēk\ intransitive verb [Middle English piken] (14th century)
1 a : to look furtively **b** : to peer through a crack or hole or from a place of concealment — often used with in or out
2 : to take a brief look : GLANCE

²peek noun (1843)
1 : a surreptitious look
2 : a brief look : GLANCE

¹peek·a·boo \'pē-kə-ˌbü\ noun [¹peek + ¹boo] (1599)
: a game for amusing a baby by repeatedly hiding one's face or body and popping back into view exclaiming "Peekaboo!"

²peekaboo adjective (1895)
1 : trimmed with eyelet embroidery ⟨a peekaboo blouse⟩
2 : made of a sheer or transparent fabric
3 : offering only limited display or disclosure especially of a teasing sort ⟨peekaboo publicity⟩

¹peel \'pē(ə)l\ verb [Middle English pelen, from Middle French peler, from Latin pilare to remove the hair from, from pilus hair] (13th century)
transitive verb
1 : to strip off an outer layer of ⟨peel an orange⟩
2 : to remove by stripping ⟨peel the label off the can⟩
intransitive verb
1 a : to come off in sheets or scales **b** : to lose an outer layer (as of skin) ⟨his face is peeling⟩
2 : to take off one's clothes
3 : to break away from a group or formation — often used with off

— **peel·able** \'pē-lə-bəl\ adjective

²peel noun (14th century)
1 : the skin or rind of a fruit
2 : a thin layer of organic material that is embedded in a film of collodion and stripped from the surface of an object (as a plant fossil) for microscopic study

³peel noun [Middle English pele, from Middle French, from Latin pala] (14th century)
: a usually long-handled spade-shaped instrument that is used chiefly by bakers for getting something (as bread or pies) into or out of the oven

⁴peel noun [Middle English pel stockade, stake, from Anglo-French, stockade & Middle French, stake, from Latin palus stake — more at POLE] (1726)
: a medieval small massive fortified tower along the Scottish-English border — called also peel tower

¹peel·er \'pē-lər\ noun (1597)
1 : one that peels
2 : a crab that is about to shed its shell
3 : a log of wood (as Douglas fir) suitable for cutting into rotary veneer — called also peeler log

²peeler noun [Sir Robert Peel] (1817)
British : POLICE OFFICER

peel·ing \'pē-liŋ\ noun (1597)
: a peeled-off piece or strip

peel off intransitive verb (1941)
1 : to veer away from an airplane formation especially for diving or landing
2 : DEPART, LEAVE

¹peen \'pēn\ transitive verb (1513)
: to draw, bend, or flatten by or as if by hammering with a peen

²peen noun [probably of Scandinavian origin; akin to Norwegian penn peen] (1683)
: a usually hemispherical or wedge-shaped end of the head of a hammer that is opposite the face and is used especially for bending, shaping, or cutting the material struck

¹peep \'pēp\ intransitive verb [Middle English pepen, of imitative origin] (15th century)
1 : to utter a feeble shrill sound as of a bird newly hatched : CHEEP
2 : to utter the slightest sound

²peep noun (15th century)
1 : a feeble shrill sound : CHEEP
2 : a slight utterance especially of complaint or protest ⟨don't let me hear another peep out of you⟩
3 : any of several small sandpipers

³peep verb [Middle English pepen, perhaps alteration of piken to peek] (15th century)
intransitive verb
1 a : to peer through or as if through a crevice
b : to look cautiously or slyly
2 : to begin to emerge from or as if from concealment : show slightly
transitive verb
: to put forth or cause to protrude slightly

⁴peep noun (1530)
1 : a first glimpse or faint appearance ⟨at the peep of dawn⟩
2 a : a brief look : GLANCE **b** : a furtive look

¹peep·er \'pē-pər\ noun (1591)
1 : one that makes a peeping sound
2 : any of various tree frogs that peep shrilly; especially : SPRING PEEPER

²peeper noun (1652)
1 : one that peeps; specifically : VOYEUR
2 : EYE

peep·hole \'pēp-ˌhōl\ noun (1681)
: a hole or crevice to peep through

Peeping Tom \-'täm\ noun [Peeping Tom, legendary citizen of Coventry who watched Lady Godiva riding naked] (circa 1796)
: a pruriently prying person : VOYEUR

— **Peeping Tom·ism** \-'tä-ˌmi-zəm\ noun

peep show noun (1851)
: an entertainment (as a film) or object (as a small picture) that is viewed through a small opening or a magnifying glass and is usually sexually explicit

peep sight noun (1881)
: a rear sight for a gun having an adjustable metal piece pierced with a small hole to peep through in aiming

¹peer \'pir\ noun [Middle English, from Middle French per, from per, adjective, equal, from Latin par] (13th century)
1 : one that is of equal standing with another : EQUAL; especially : one belonging to the same societal group especially based on age, grade, or status
2 archaic : COMPANION
3 a : a member of one of the five ranks (as duke, marquess, earl, viscount, or baron) of the British peerage **b** : NOBLE 1

— **peer** adjective

²peer transitive verb (14th century)

archaic **:** RIVAL, MATCH

³peer *intransitive verb* [perhaps by shortening & alteration from *appear*] (1591)
1 : to look narrowly or curiously; *especially* **:** to look searchingly at something difficult to discern
2 : to come slightly into view **:** emerge partly

peer·age \'pir-ij\ *noun* (15th century)
1 : the body of peers
2 : the rank or dignity of a peer
3 : a book containing a list of peers with their genealogy, history, and titles

peer·ess \'pir-əs\ *noun* (1689)
1 : the wife or widow of a peer
2 : a woman who holds in her own right the rank of a peer

peer·less \'pir-ləs\ *adjective* (14th century)
: MATCHLESS, INCOMPARABLE

¹peeve \'pēv\ *transitive verb* **peeved; peev·ing** [back-formation from *peevish*] (1908)
: to make peevish or resentful **:** ANNOY
synonym see IRRITATE

²peeve *noun* (1911)
1 : a feeling or mood of resentment
2 : a particular grievance or source of aggravation

pee·vish \'pē-vish\ *adjective* [Middle English *pevish* spiteful] (circa 1530)
1 : querulous in temperament or mood **:** FRETFUL
2 : perversely obstinate
3 : marked by ill temper
— **pee·vish·ly** *adverb*
— **pee·vish·ness** *noun*

pee·wee \'pē-(,)wē\ *noun* [imitative] (1806)
1 : PEWEE
2 : one that is diminutive or small; *especially* **:** a small child
— **peewee** *adjective*

pee·wit \'pē-,wit, 'pyü-ət\ *noun* [imitative] (circa 1529)
: any of several birds; *especially* **:** LAPWING

¹peg \'peg\ *noun* [Middle English *pegge*, probably from Middle Dutch] (15th century)
1 a : a small usually cylindrical pointed or tapered piece (as of wood) used to pin down or fasten things or to fit into or close holes **:** PIN, PLUG **b** *British* **:** CLOTHESPIN **c :** a predetermined level at which something (as a price) is fixed
2 a : a projecting piece used as a support or boundary marker **b :** something (as a fact or opinion) used as a support, pretext, or reason
3 a : one of the movable wooden pegs set in the head of a stringed instrument (as a violin) that are turned to regulate the pitch of the strings — see VIOLIN illustration **b :** a step or degree especially in estimation
4 : a pointed prong or claw for catching or tearing
5 *British* **:** DRINK ⟨poured himself out a stiff peg —Dorothy Sayers⟩
6 : something (as a leg) resembling a peg
7 : THROW; *especially* **:** a hard throw in baseball made in an attempt to put out a base runner

²peg *verb* **pegged; peg·ging** (1543)
transitive verb
1 a : to put a peg into **b** *British* **:** to pin (laundry) on a clothesline
2 : to attach or fix as if with a peg: as **a :** to pin down **b :** RESTRICT **b :** to fix or hold (as prices or wage increases) at a predetermined level or rate **c :** to place in a definite category **:** IDENTIFY
3 : to mark by pegs
4 : THROW
intransitive verb
1 : to work steadily and diligently — often used with *away*
2 : to move along vigorously or hastily **:** HUSTLE

³peg \'peg\ *or* **pegged** \'pegd\ *adjective* (1681)
: wide at the top and narrow at the bottom ⟨*peg* pants⟩

Peg·a·sus \'pe-gə-səs\ *noun* [Latin (genitive *Pegasi*), from Greek *Pēgasos*]
1 : a winged horse that causes the stream Hippocrene to spring from Mount Helicon with a blow of his hoof
2 : poetic inspiration
3 : a northern constellation near the vernal equinoctial point

Peg–Board \'peg-,bȯrd, -,bȯrd\ *trademark*
— used for material (as fiberboard) with regularly spaced perforations into which hooks may be inserted for the storage or display of articles

peg leg *noun* [³*peg*] (1769)
: an artificial leg; *especially* **:** one fitted at the knee

peg·ma·tite \'peg-mə-,tīt\ *noun* [French, from Greek *pēgmat-, pēgma* something fastened together, from *pēgnynai* to fasten together — more at PACT] (circa 1828)
: a coarse variety of granite occurring in dikes or veins
— **peg·ma·tit·ic** \,peg-mə-'ti-tik\ *adjective*

peg-top \'peg-,täp\ *or* **peg–topped** \-'täpt\ *adjective* (1858)
: PEG

peg top *noun* (1788)
1 : ¹PEG **:** a pear-shaped top that is made to spin on the sharp metal peg in its base by the unwinding of a string wound round its center
2 *plural* \-,täps\ **:** peg trousers

pei·gnoir \pān-'wär, pen-\ *noun* [French, literally, garment worn while combing the hair, from Middle French, from *peigner* to comb the hair, from Latin *pectinare*, from *pectin-, pecten* comb — more at PECTINATE] (1835)
: a woman's loose negligee or dressing gown

pein *variant of* PEEN

¹pe·jo·ra·tive \pi-'jȯr-ə-tiv, -'jär- *also* 'pe-jə-rə-tiv *or* 'pē- *or* -,rā- *or* 'pej-rə- *or* 'pēj-\ *noun* (1882)
: a pejorative word or phrase

²pejorative *adjective* [Late Latin *pejoratus*, past participle of *pejorare* to make or become worse, from Latin *pejor* worse; akin to Sanskrit *padyate* he falls, Latin *ped-, pes* foot — more at FOOT] (1888)
: having negative connotations; *especially* **:** tending to disparage or belittle **:** DEPRECIATORY
— **pe·jo·ra·tive·ly** *adverb*

peke \'pēk\ *noun, often capitalized* (1915)
: PEKINGESE 2

Pe·kin \pi-'kin, 'pē-,\ *noun* [*Pekin, Peking* (Beijing), China] (1885)
: any of a breed of large white ducks of Chinese origin used for meat production

Pe·king duck \'pē-,kiŋ-\ *noun* (1955)
: a Chinese dish consisting of roasted duck meat and strips of crispy duck skin topped with scallions and sauce and wrapped in thin pancakes

Pe·king·ese *or* **Pe·kin·ese** \,pē-kə-'nēz, -'nēs; -kiŋ-'ēz, -'ēs\ *noun, plural* **Pekingese** *or* **Pekinese** (1849)
1 a : the Chinese dialect of Beijing **b :** a native or resident of Beijing
2 : any of a Chinese breed of small short-legged dogs with a broad flat face and a profuse long soft coat

Pekingese 2

Peking man *noun* (1926)
: an extinct Pleistocene hominid that is known from skeletal and cultural remains in cave deposits at Cho-k'ou-tien, China and is now classified with the pithecanthropines

pe·koe \'pē-(,)kō *also* 'pe-\ *noun* [Chinese (Xiamen) *pek-ho*] (1712)

: a tea made from young leaves that are slightly larger than those of orange pekoe

pel·age \'pe-lij\ *noun* [French, from Middle French, from *poil* hair, from Latin *pilus*] (circa 1828)
: the hairy covering of a mammal

¹Pe·la·gian \pə-'lā-j(ē-)ən\ *noun* (15th century)
: one agreeing with Pelagius in denying original sin and consequently in holding that mankind has perfect freedom to do either right or wrong

²Pelagian *adjective* (15th century)
: of or relating to Pelagians or Pelagianism

Pe·la·gian·ism \-j(ē-)ə-,ni-zəm\ *noun* (1583)
: the teaching of Pelagius or Pelagians

pe·lag·ic \pə-'la-jik\ *adjective* [Latin *pelagicus*, from Greek *pelagikos*, from *pelagos* sea — more at PLAGAL] (circa 1656)
: of, relating to, or living or occurring in the open sea **:** OCEANIC ⟨*pelagic* sediment⟩ ⟨*pelagic* birds⟩

pel·ar·go·ni·um \,pe-lär-'gō-nē-əm, -lər-\ *noun* [New Latin, from Greek *pelargos* stork (akin to Greek *pelios* livid, *polios* gray) + New Latin *-nium* (as in *Geranium*) — more at FALLOW] (circa 1819)
: any of a genus (*Pelargonium*) of southern African herbs (as a garden geranium) of the geranium family with showy flowers of various shades of red, pink, or white distinguished by a spurred calyx and irregular corolla

Pe·las·gian \pə-'laz-j(ē-)ən, -'laz-gē-ən\ *noun* [Greek *pelasgios*, adjective, Pelasgian, from *Pelasgoi* Pelasgians] (15th century)
: a member of an ancient people mentioned by classical writers as early inhabitants of Greece and the eastern islands of the Mediterranean
— **Pelasgian** *adjective*
— **Pe·las·gic** \-jik, -gik\ *adjective*

pe·lec·y·pod \pə-'le-sə-,päd\ *noun* [New Latin *Pelecypoda*, group name, from Greek *pelekys* ax (akin to Sanskrit *paraśu* ax) + *pod-, pous* foot — more at FOOT] (circa 1890)
: LAMELLIBRANCH

pel·er·ine \,pe-lə-'rēn, 'pe-lə-rən\ *noun* [obsolete French, neckerchief, from French *pèlerine*, feminine of *pèlerin* pilgrim, from Late Latin *pelegrinus* — more at PILGRIM] (1744)
: a woman's narrow cape made of fabric or fur and usually with long ends hanging down in front

Pe·leus \'pēl-,yüs, 'pē-lē-əs\ *noun* [Latin, from Greek *Pēleus*]
: a son of Aeacus who becomes by the goddess Thetis the father of Achilles

pelf \'pelf\ *noun* [Middle English, from Middle French *pelfre* booty] (14th century)
: MONEY, RICHES

pel·i·can \'pe-li-kən\ *noun* [Middle English, from Old English *pellican*, from Late Latin *pelecanus*, from Greek *pelekan*] (before 12th century)
: any of a genus (*Pelecanus*) of large web-footed fish-eating birds with a very large bill and distensible gular pouch

pe·lisse \pə-'lēs, pe-\ *noun* [French, from Late Latin *pellicia*, from feminine of *pellicius* made of skin, from Latin *pellis* skin — more at FELL] (1717)
1 : a long cloak or coat made of fur or lined or trimmed with fur
2 : a woman's loose lightweight cloak with wide collar and fur trimming

pel·la·gra \pə-'la-grə, -'lä-, -'lā-\ *noun* [Italian, from *pelle* skin (from Latin *pellis*) + *-agra* (as in *podagra*, from Latin)] (circa 1811)
: a disease marked by dermatitis, gastrointestinal disorders, and central nervous symptoms and associated with a diet deficient in niacin

— **pel·la·grous** \-grəs\ *adjective*

pel·la·grin \-grən\ *noun* [irregular from *pellagra*] (1865)
: a person who is affected with pellagra

¹**pel·let** \'pe-lət\ *noun* [Middle English *pelote*, from Middle French, from (assumed) Vulgar Latin *pilota*, diminutive of Latin *pila* ball] (14th century)
1 : a usually small rounded, spherical, or cylindrical body (as of food or medicine)
2 : any of various projectiles fired from a weapon (as an air rifle)
— **pel·let·al** \-lə-t°l\ *adjective*

²**pellet** *transitive verb* (1597)
1 : PELLETIZE
2 : to strike with pellets

pellet gun *noun* (1952)
: AIR GUN 1

pel·let·ise *British variant of* PELLETIZE

pel·let·ize \'pe-lə-ˌtīz\ *transitive verb* **-ized; -iz·ing** (1942)
: to form or compact into pellets ⟨*pelletize* ore⟩
— **pel·let·i·za·tion** \ˌpe-lə-tə-'zā-shən\ *noun*
— **pel·let·iz·er** \'pe-lə-ˌtī-zər\ *noun*

pel·li·cle \'pe-li-kəl\ *noun* [Middle French *pellicule*, from Medieval Latin *pellicula*, from Latin, diminutive of *pellis*] (1541)
: a thin skin or film: as **a** : an outer membrane of some protozoans (as euglenoids or paramecia) **b** : a film that reflects a part of the light falling upon it and transmits the rest and that is used for dividing a beam of light (as in a photographic device)

¹**pel·li·to·ry** \'pe-lə-ˌtōr-ē, -ˌtòr-\ *noun, plural* **-ries** [Middle English *peletre*, from Middle French *piretre*, from Latin *pyrethrum* — more at PYRETHRUM] (1533)
: a southern European composite plant (*Anacyclus pyrethrum*) resembling yarrow — called also *pellitory-of-Spain*

²**pellitory** *noun* [Middle English *paritorie*, from Middle French *paritaire*, from Late Latin *parietaria*, from feminine of *parietarius* of a wall, from Latin *pariet-, paries* wall] (1548)
: any of a genus (*Parietaria*) of herbs of the nettle family with alternate leaves and inconspicuous flowers — called also *pellitory-of-the-wall*

pell–mell \ˌpel-'mel\ *adverb* [Middle French *pelemele*] (1596)
1 : in mingled confusion or disorder
2 : in confused haste
— **pell–mell** *adjective or noun*

pel·lu·cid \pə-'lü-səd\ *adjective* [Latin *pellucidus*, from *per* through + *lucidus* lucid — more at FOR] (1619)
1 : admitting maximum passage of light without diffusion or distortion
2 : reflecting light evenly from all surfaces
3 : easy to understand
— **pel·lu·cid·ly** \pə-'lü-səd-lē\ *adverb*

pel·met \'pel-mət\ *noun* [probably modification of French *palmette* palmette] (1821)
: a short valance or small cornice for concealing curtain fixtures

Pe·lops \'pē-ˌläps, 'pe-\ *noun* [Latin, from Greek]
: a son of Tantalus served by his father to the gods for food but later restored to life by them

pe·lo·rus \pə-'lōr-əs, -'lòr-\ *noun* [origin unknown] (1854)
: a navigational instrument resembling a mariner's compass without magnetic needles and having two sight vanes by which bearings are taken

pe·lo·ta \pə-'lō-tə\ *noun* [Spanish, from Old French *pelote* little ball — more at PELLET] (1844)
1 : a court game related to jai alai
2 : the ball used in jai alai

¹**pelt** \'pelt\ *noun* [Middle English, perhaps back-formation from *peltry*] (15th century)
1 : a usually undressed skin with its hair, wool, or fur
2 : a skin stripped of hair or wool for tanning

²**pelt** *transitive verb* (1596)
: to strip off the skin or pelt of (an animal)

³**pelt** *verb* [Middle English] (15th century)
transitive verb
1 a : to strike with a succession of blows or missiles ⟨*pelted* him with stones⟩ **b** : to assail vigorously or persistently ⟨*pelted* her with accusations⟩
2 : HURL, THROW ⟨*pelted* snowballs at them⟩
3 : to beat or dash repeatedly against ⟨hailstones *pelting* the roof⟩
intransitive verb
1 : to deliver a succession of blows or missiles
2 : to beat incessantly
3 : to move rapidly and vigorously : HURRY
— **pelt·er** *noun*

⁴**pelt** *noun* (1513)
: BLOW, WHACK

pel·tate \'pel-ˌtāt\ *adjective* [Latin *pelta* small shield, from Greek *peltē*] (circa 1760)
: shaped like a shield; *specifically* : having the stem or support attached to the lower surface instead of at the base or margin — see LEAF illustration

pelt·ing \'pel-tiŋ\ *adjective* [probably from English dialect *pelt* piece of trash] (1540)
archaic : PALTRY, INSIGNIFICANT

pelt·ry \'pel-trē\ *noun, plural* **peltries** [Middle English, from Anglo-French *pelterie*] (15th century)
: PELTS, FURS; *especially* : raw undressed skins — often used in plural

pel·vic \'pel-vik\ *adjective* (1830)
: of, relating to, or located in or near the pelvis
— **pelvic** *noun*

pelvic fin *noun* (circa 1909)
: one of the paired fins of a fish that are homologous with the hind limbs of a quadruped

pelvic girdle *noun* (1883)
: a bony or cartilaginous arch that supports the hind limbs of a vertebrate

pelvic inflammatory disease *noun* (1974)
: inflammation of the female reproductive tract and especially the fallopian tubes that is caused especially by sexually transmitted disease, occurs more often in women using IUDs, and is a leading cause of female sterility

pel·vis \'pel-vəs\ *noun, plural* **pel·vis·es** \-və-səz\ *or* **pel·ves** \-ˌvēz\ [New Latin, from Latin, basin; perhaps akin to Old English & Old Norse *full* cup] (1615)
1 : a basin-shaped structure in the skeleton of many vertebrates that is formed by the pelvic girdle and adjoining bones of the spine
2 : the cavity of the pelvis
3 : the funnel-shaped cavity of the kidney into which urine is discharged

pel·y·co·saur \'pe-li-kə-ˌsòr\ *noun* [ultimately from Greek *pelyc-, pelyx* bowl + *sauros* lizard] (1904)
: any of an order (Pelycosauria) of primitive Permian quadruped reptiles that resemble mammals and that have extreme development of the dorsal vertebral processes

Pem·broke table \'pem-ˌbrōk-, -ˌbrük-\ *noun* [*Pembroke*, Wales] (1778)
: a small 4-legged table originating in the Georgian period and having two drop leaves and a drawer

Pembroke Welsh corgi *noun* (1938)
: any of a breed of Welsh corgis with pointed ears, straight forelegs, and a short tail — called also *Pembroke*; see WELSH CORGI illustration

pem·mi·can *also* **pem·i·can** \'pe-mi-kən\ *noun* [Cree *pimihka'n*] (1791)
: a concentrated food used by North American Indians and consisting of lean meat dried, pounded fine, and mixed with melted fat; *also* : a similar preparation (as of dried beef, flour, molasses, suet) used for emergency rations

pem·o·line \'pe-mə-ˌlēn\ *noun* [origin unknown] (1961)
: a synthetic organic drug $C_9H_8N_2O_2$ that is a mild stimulant of the central nervous system

pem·phi·gus \'pem(p)-fi-gəs, pem-'fī-\ *noun* [New Latin, from Greek *pemphig-, pemphix* pustule] (circa 1779)
: a disease characterized by large blisters on skin and mucous membranes and often by itching or burning

¹**pen** \'pen\ *transitive verb* **penned; pen·ning** [Middle English *pennen*, from Old English *-pennian*] (13th century)
: to shut in or as if in a pen

²**pen** *noun* [Middle English, perhaps from *pennen*] (14th century)
1 a : a small enclosure for animals **b** : the animals in a pen ⟨a *pen* of sheep⟩
2 : a small place of confinement or storage
3 : a protected dock or slip for a submarine
4 : BULL PEN 2

³**pen** *noun* [Middle English *penne*, from Middle French, feather, pen, from Latin *penna*, *pinna* feather; akin to Greek *pteron* wing — more at FEATHER] (14th century)
1 : an implement for writing or drawing with ink or a similar fluid: as **a** : QUILL **b** : PEN POINT **c** : a penholder containing a pen point **d** : FOUNTAIN PEN **e** : BALLPOINT
2 a : a writing pen regarded as a means of expression ⟨enlisted the *pens* of the best writers —F. H. Chase⟩ **b** : WRITER
3 : the internal horny feather-shaped shell of a squid

⁴**pen** *transitive verb* **penned; pen·ning** (15th century)
: WRITE, INDITE ⟨*pen* a letter⟩

⁵**pen** *noun* [origin unknown] (1550)
: a female swan

⁶**pen** *noun* (1884)
: PENITENTIARY

pe·nal \'pē-n°l\ *adjective* [Middle English, from Middle French, from Latin *poenalis*, from *poena* punishment — more at PAIN] (15th century)
1 : of, relating to, or involving punishment, penalties, or punitive institutions
2 : liable to punishment ⟨a *penal* offense⟩
3 : used as a place of confinement and punishment ⟨a *penal* colony⟩
— **pe·nal·ly** \-n°l-ē\ *adverb*

penal code *noun* (1845)
: a code of laws concerning crimes and offenses and their punishment

pe·nal·ise *British variant of* PENALIZE

pe·nal·ize \'pē-n°l-ˌīz, 'pe-\ *transitive verb* **-ized; -iz·ing** (1868)
1 : to inflict a penalty on
2 : to put at a serious disadvantage
— **pe·nal·i·za·tion** \-n°l-ə-'zā-shən\ *noun*

pen·al·ty \'pe-n°l-tē\ *noun, plural* **-ties** [Medieval Latin *poenalitas*, from Latin *poenalis*] (15th century)
1 : the suffering in person, rights, or property that is annexed by law or judicial decision to the commission of a crime or public offense
2 : the suffering or the sum to be forfeited to which a person agrees to be subjected in case of nonfulfillment of stipulations
3 a : disadvantage, loss, or hardship due to some action **b** : a disadvantage (as loss of yardage, time, or possession of the ball or an addition to or subtraction from the score) imposed on a team or competitor for violation of the rules of a sport
4 : points scored in bridge by the side that defeats the opposing contract — usually used in plural
— **penalty** *adjective*

penalty box *noun* (1931)
: an area alongside an ice hockey rink to which penalized players are confined for the duration of their penalty

penalty kick *noun* (1889)
1 : a free kick in rugby
2 : a free kick at the goal in soccer made from a point 12 yards in front of the goal and allowed for certain violations within a designated area around the goal

penalty shot *noun* (circa 1948)
: an unhindered shot at the goal in ice hockey awarded to an individual for certain violations by an opponent

¹pen·ance \'pe-nən(t)s\ *noun* [Middle English, from Old French, from Medieval Latin *poenitentia* penitence] (14th century)
1 : an act of self-abasement, mortification, or devotion performed to show sorrow or repentance for sin
2 : a sacramental rite that is practiced in Roman, Eastern, and some Anglican churches and that consists of private confession, absolution, and a penance directed by the confessor
3 : something (as a hardship or penalty) resembling an act of penance (as in compensating for an offense)

²penance *transitive verb* **pen·anced; pen·anc·ing** (1600)
: to impose penance on

Pe·na·tes \pə-'nā-tēz, -'nä-\ *noun plural* [Latin, from *penus* food, provisions]
: the Roman gods of the household worshiped in close connection with Vesta and with the Lares

pence \'pen(t)s\ *plural of* PENNY

pen·cel *or* **pen·cil** \'pen(t)-səl\ *noun* [Middle English *pencel*, modification of Old French *penoncel*] (13th century)
: PENNONCEL

pen·chant \'pen-chənt, *especially British* 'päⁿ-shäⁿ\ *noun* [French, from present participle of *pencher* to incline, from (assumed) Vulgar Latin *pendicare*, from Latin *pendere* to weigh] (1672)
: a strong and continued inclination; *broadly* : LIKING
synonym see LEANING

¹pen·cil \'pen(t)-səl\ *noun* [Middle English *pensel*, from Middle French *pincel*, from (assumed) Vulgar Latin *penicellus*, alteration of Latin *penicillus*, diminutive of *peniculus* brush, from diminutive of *penis* tail, penis] (14th century)
1 : an artist's brush
2 : an artist's individual skill or style
3 a : an implement for writing, drawing, or marking consisting of or containing a slender cylinder or strip of a solid marking substance **b** : a small medicated or cosmetic roll or stick for local applications
4 : a set of geometric objects each pair of which has a common property ⟨the lines in a plane through a point comprise a *pencil* of lines⟩
5 : something (as a beam of radiation) long and thin like a pencil

²pencil *transitive verb* **-ciled** *or* **-cilled; -cil·ing** *or* **-cil·ling** \-s(ə-)liŋ\ (circa 1532)
: to paint, draw, write, or mark with a pencil

pen·cil·ing *or* **pen·cil·ling** *noun* (1706)
: the work of the pencil or brush; *also* : a product of this

pencil pusher *noun* (1881)
: a person who does predominantly paperwork

pen·dant *also* **pen·dent** \'pen-dənt; *3 & 4 are also* 'pe-nənt, *5 is also* päⁿ-däⁿ\ *noun* [Middle English *pendaunt*, from Middle French *pendant*, from present participle of *pendre* to hang, from (assumed) Vulgar Latin *pendere*, from Latin *pendēre* to weigh, estimate, pay, *pondus* weight] (14th century)
1 : something suspended: as **a** : an ornament (as on a necklace) allowed to hang free **b** : an electrical fixture suspended from the ceiling
2 : a hanging ornament of roofs or ceilings much used in the later styles of Gothic architecture
3 : a length of line usually used as a connector on a boat or ship; *especially* : a short rope hanging from a spar and having at its free end a block or spliced thimble
4 *chiefly British* : PENNANT 1a
5 a : COMPANION PIECE **b** : something secondary or supplementary

pen·den·cy \'pen-dən-sē\ *noun* (1637)
: the state of being pending

pen·dent *or* **pen·dant** \'pen-dənt\ *adjective* [Middle English *pendaunt*] (14th century)
1 : jutting or leaning over : OVERHANGING ⟨a *pendent* cliff⟩
2 : supported from above : SUSPENDED ⟨icicles *pendent* from the eaves⟩
3 : remaining undetermined : PENDING

pen·den·tive \pen-'den-tiv\ *noun* [French *pendentif*, from Latin *pendent-, pendens*, present participle of *pendēre*] (circa 1741)
: one of the concave triangular members that supports a dome over a square space

1 pendentive

¹pend·ing \'pen-diŋ\ *preposition* [French *pendant*, from present participle of *pendre*] (1642)
1 : DURING
2 : while awaiting

²pending *adjective* (1797)
1 : not yet decided : being in continuance
2 : IMMINENT, IMPENDING

pen·du·lar \'pen-jə-lər, 'pen-dyə-, -də-\ *adjective* (1878)
: being or resembling the movement of a pendulum

pen·du·lous \-ləs\ *adjective* [Latin *pendulus*, from *pendēre* to hang] (circa 1605)
1 *archaic* : poised without visible support
2 a : suspended so as to swing freely ⟨branches hung with *pendulous* vines⟩ **b** : inclined or hanging downward ⟨*pendulous* jowls⟩
3 : marked by vacillation, indecision, or uncertainty
— **pen·du·lous·ness** *noun*

pen·du·lum \-ləm\ *noun* [New Latin, from Latin, neuter of *pendulus*] (1660)
1 : a body suspended from a fixed point so as to swing freely to and fro under the action of gravity and commonly used to regulate movements (as of clockwork)
2 : something (as a state of affairs) that alternates between opposites

Pe·nel·o·pe \pə-'ne-lə-pē\ *noun* [Latin, from Greek *Pēnelopē*]
: the wife of Odysseus who waits faithfully for him during his 20 years' absence

pe·ne·plain *also* **pe·ne·plane** \'pē-ni-,plān, 'pe-\ *noun* [Latin *paene, pene* almost + English *plain* or *plane*] (1889)
: a land surface of considerable area and slight relief shaped by erosion

pen·e·tra·ble \'pe-nə-trə-bəl\ *adjective* (1538)
: capable of being penetrated
— **pen·e·tra·bil·i·ty** \,pe-nə-trə-'bi-lə-tē\ *noun*

pen·e·tra·lia \,pe-nə-'trā-lē-ə\ *noun plural* [Latin, neuter plural of *penetralis* inner, from *penetrare* to penetrate] (1668)
: the innermost or most private parts

pen·e·trance \'pe-nə-trən(t)s\ *noun* [International Scientific Vocabulary, from Latin *penetrare*] (1934)
: the proportion of individuals of a particular genotype that express its phenotypic effect in a given environment

¹pen·e·trant \-trənt\ *adjective* (1543)
: PENETRATING

²penetrant *noun* (circa 1734)
: one that penetrates or is capable of penetrating

pen·e·trate \'pe-nə-,trāt\ *verb* **-trat·ed; -trat·ing** [Latin *penetratus*, past participle of *penetrare*, from *penitus* deep within, far; akin to Latin *penus* provisions] (circa 1530)
transitive verb
1 a : to pass into or through **b** : to enter by overcoming resistance : PIERCE **c** : to gain entrance to

2 a : to see into or through **b** : to discover the inner contents or meaning of
3 : to affect profoundly with feeling
4 : to diffuse through or into
intransitive verb
1 a : to pass, extend, pierce, or diffuse into or through something **b** : to pierce something with the eye or mind
2 : to affect deeply the senses or feelings
synonym see ENTER

pen·e·trat·ing *adjective* (1593)
1 : having the power of entering, piercing, or pervading ⟨a *penetrating* shriek⟩
2 : ACUTE, DISCERNING ⟨*penetrating* insights into life⟩
— **pen·e·trat·ing·ly** \-,trā-tiŋ-lē\ *adverb*

pen·e·tra·tion \,pe-nə-'trā-shən\ *noun* (1605)
1 a : the power to penetrate; *especially* : the ability to discern deeply and acutely **b** : the depth to which something penetrates **c** : the extent to which a commercial product or agency is familiar or sells in a market
2 : the act or process of penetrating: as **a** : the act of entering a country so that actual establishment of influence is accomplished **b** : an attack that penetrates the enemy's front or territory
synonym see DISCERNMENT

pen·e·tra·tive \'pe-nə-,trā-tiv\ *adjective* (15th century)
1 : tending to penetrate : PIERCING
2 : ACUTE ⟨*penetrative* observations⟩
3 : IMPRESSIVE ⟨a *penetrative* speaker⟩

pen·e·trom·e·ter \,pe-nə-'trä-mə-tər\ *noun* [Latin *penetrare* + International Scientific Vocabulary *-meter*] (1905)
: an instrument for measuring firmness or consistency (as of soil)

pen·gö \'pen-,gə(r), -,gȫ\ *noun, plural* **pengö** *or* **pengös** [Hungarian *pengő*, literally, jingling] (1925)
: the basic monetary unit of Hungary from 1925 to 1946

pen·guin \'pen-gwən, 'pen-\ *noun* [obsolete English *penguin* great auk, perhaps from Welsh *pen gwyn* white head (applied to the bird in winter plumage)] (1588)
: any of various erect short-legged flightless aquatic birds (family Spheniscidae) of the southern hemisphere

pen·hold·er \'pen-,hōl-dər\ *noun* (1815)
: a holder or handle for a pen point

-penia *combining form* [New Latin, from Greek *penia*]
: deficiency ⟨leuko*penia*⟩

pen·i·cil·la·mine \,pe-nə-'si-lə-,mēn\ *noun* [*penicillin* + *amine*] (1943)
: an amino acid $C_5H_{11}NO_2S$ that is obtained from penicillins and is used especially in the treatment of poisoning by metals (as copper or lead) and of cystinuria

pen·i·cil·late \,pe-nə-'si-lət, -,lāt\ *adjective* [Latin *penicillus* brush — more at PENCIL] (1819)
: furnished with a tuft of fine filaments ⟨a *penicillate* stigma⟩

pen·i·cil·lin \,pe-nə-'si-lən\ *noun* [New Latin *Penicillium*] (1929)
1 : any of several relatively nontoxic antibiotic acids of the general constitution $C_9H_{11}N_2O_4SR$ that are produced by molds (genus *Penicillium* and especially *P. notatum* or *P. chrysogenum*) or synthetically and are used especially against cocci; *also* : a mixture of such acids
2 : a salt or ester of a penicillin or a mixture of such salts or esters

pen·i·cil·lin·ase \-'si-lə-,nās, -,nāz\ *noun* (1940)

: an enzyme found especially in staphylococcal bacteria that inactivates the penicillins by hydrolyzing them

pen·i·cil·li·um \-'si-lē-əm\ *noun, plural* **-lia** \-lē-ə\ [New Latin, from Latin *penicillus*] (1867)
: any of a genus (*Penicillium* of the family Moniliaceae) of fungi (as a blue mold) that are found chiefly on moist nonliving organic matter

pe·nile \'pē-,nīl\ *adjective* (circa 1861)
: of, relating to, or affecting the penis

pen·in·su·la \pə-'nin(t)-s(ə-)lə, -shə-lə\ *noun* [Latin *paeninsula*, from *paene* almost + *insula* island] (1538)
: a portion of land nearly surrounded by water and connected with a larger body by an isthmus; *also* : a piece of land jutting out into the water whether with or without a well-defined isthmus
— **pen·in·su·lar** \-s(ə-)lər, -shə-lər\ *adjective*

pe·nis \'pē-nəs\ *noun, plural* **pe·nes** \'pē-(,)nēz\ *or* **pe·nis·es** [Latin, penis, tail; akin to Old High German *faselt* penis, Greek *peos*] (1676)
: a male organ of copulation that in male mammals including humans usually functions as the channel by which urine leaves the body

penis envy *noun* (1924)
: the supposed coveting of the penis by a young human female which is held in Freudian psychoanalytic theory to lead to feelings of inferiority and defensive or compensatory behavior

pen·i·tence \'pe-nə-ten(t)s\ *noun* [Middle English, from Old French, from Medieval Latin *poenitentia*, alteration of Latin *paenitentia* regret, from *paenitent-, paenitens*, present participle] (13th century)
: the quality or state of being penitent : sorrow for sins or faults ☆

¹pen·i·tent \-tənt\ *adjective* [Middle English, from Middle French, from Latin *paenitent-, paenitens*, from present participle of *paenitēre* to cause regret, feel regret, perhaps from *paene* almost] (14th century)
: feeling or expressing humble or regretful pain or sorrow for sins or offenses : REPENTANT
— **pen·i·tent·ly** *adverb*

²penitent *noun* (14th century)
1 : a person who repents of sin
2 : a person under church censure but admitted to penance or reconciliation especially under the direction of a confessor

pen·i·ten·tial \,pe-nə-'ten(t)-shəl\ *adjective* (1508)
: of or relating to penitence or penance
— **pen·i·ten·tial·ly** \-'ten(t)-sh(ə-)lē\ *adverb*

¹pen·i·ten·tia·ry \,pe-nə-'ten(t)-sh(ə-)rē\ *noun, plural* **-ries** [Middle English *penitenciary*, from Medieval Latin *poenitentiarius*, from *poenitentia*] (15th century)
1 a : an officer in some Roman Catholic dioceses vested with power from the bishop to deal with cases of a nature normally handled only by the bishop **b** *capitalized* : a cardinal presiding over a tribunal of the Roman curia concerned with dispensations and indulgences
2 : a public institution in which offenders against the law are confined for detention or punishment; *specifically* : a state or federal prison in the U.S.

²pen·i·ten·tia·ry \,pe-nə-'ten(t)-sh(ə-)rē, *l* also -'ten(t)-shē-,er-ē\ *adjective* (1577)
1 : PENITENTIAL
2 : of, relating to, or incurring confinement in a penitentiary

pen·knife \'pen-,nīf\ *noun* [Middle English; from its original use for mending quill pens] (15th century)
: a small pocketknife usually with only one blade

pen·light *also* **pen·lite** \-,līt\ *noun* (1945)

: a small flashlight resembling a fountain pen in size or shape

pen·man \-mən\ *noun* (1539)
1 a : CALLIGRAPHER **b** : COPYIST. SCRIBE **c** : a person with a specified quality or kind of handwriting ⟨a poor *penman*⟩
2 : AUTHOR

pen·man·ship \-,ship\ *noun* (1695)
1 : the art or practice of writing with the pen
2 : quality or style of handwriting

pen name *noun* (circa 1864)
: an author's pseudonym

pen·nant \'pe-nənt\ *noun* [alteration of *pendant*] (1698)
1 a : any of various nautical flags tapering usually to a point or swallowtail and used for identification or signaling **b** : a flag or banner longer in the fly than in the hoist; *especially* : one that tapers to a point
2 : a flag emblematic of championship (as in a professional baseball league); *also* : the championship itself

pen·nate \'pe-,nāt\ *adjective* [irregular from New Latin *Pennales*] (1938)
: of, relating to, or being diatoms of an order (Pennales) usually characterized by a raphe or a structure resembling a raphe and by ornamentation of the valves that is bilaterally symmetrical

pen·ne \'pe(n)-(,)nā\ *noun, plural* **penne** [Italian, plural of *penna*, literally, quill, feather, pen, from Latin *pinna* feather & *penna* wing — more at PEN] (1974)
: short thick diagonally cut tubular pasta

pen·ni \'pe-nē\ *noun, plural* **pen·nia** \-nē-ə\ *also* **penni** *or* **pen·nis** \-nēz\ [Finnish] (circa 1893)
— see *markka* at MONEY table

pen·ni·less \'pe-ni-ləs, 'pe-nºl-əs\ *adjective* (14th century)
: destitute of money

pen·non \'pe-nən\ *noun* [Middle English, from Middle French *penon*, from *penne* quill, wing feather — more at PEN] (14th century)
1 a : a long usually triangular or swallow-tailed streamer typically attached to the head of a lance as an ensign **b** : PENNANT 1a
2 : WING, PINION

pen·non·cel *or* **pen·on·cel** \'pe-nən-,sel\ *noun* [Middle English *penoncell*, from Middle French *penoncel*, diminutive of *penon*] (14th century)
: a small pennon used in late medieval or Renaissance times

Penn·syl·va·nia Dutch \,pen(t)-səl-'vā-nyə-, -nē-ə-\ *noun* (circa 1824)
1 : a people living mostly in eastern Pennsylvania whose characteristic cultural traditions go back to the German migrations of the 18th century
2 : a dialect of High German spoken in parts of Pennsylvania and Maryland
— **Pennsylvania Dutchman** *noun*

Pennsylvania German *noun* (1869)
: PENNSYLVANIA DUTCH

Penn·syl·va·nian \-'vā-nyən, -nē-ən\ *adjective* (1698)
1 : of or relating to Pennsylvania or its people
2 : of, relating to, or being the period of the Paleozoic era in North America between the Mississippian and Permian or the corresponding system of rocks — see GEOLOGIC TIME table
— **Pennsylvanian** *noun*

pen·ny \'pe-nē\ *noun, plural* **pennies** \-nēz\ *or* **pence** \'pen(t)s\ *often attributive* [Middle English, from Old English *penning, penig*; akin to Old High German *pfenning*, a coin] (before 12th century)
1 a : a monetary unit of the United Kingdom formerly equal to ¹⁄₂₄₀ pound but now equal to ¹⁄₁₀₀ pound **b** : a similar monetary unit of any of various other countries in or formerly in the Commonwealth — see *pound* at MONEY table
c : a coin representing one penny

2 : DENARIUS
3 *plural* **pennies** : CENT
4 : a trivial amount
5 : a piece or sum of money ⟨that will cost a pretty *penny*⟩

-penny *adjective combining form* [*penny*; perhaps from the original price per hundred]
: being a (designated) nail size ⟨an eight*penny* nail⟩

pen·ny–an·te \'pe-nē-'an-tē\ *adjective* (1868)
: SMALL-TIME, TWO-BIT

penny ante *noun* (1855)
: poker played for very low stakes

penny arcade *noun* (1908)
: an amusement center having coin-operated devices for entertainment

pen·ny·cress \'pe-nē-,kres\ *noun* (1713)
: a Eurasian herb (*Thlaspi arvense*) with round flat pods that is widely naturalized in the New World

penny dreadful *noun* (circa 1873)
: a novel of violent adventure or crime

pen·ny–pinch·ing \-,pin-chiŋ\ *noun* (1935)
: FRUGALITY, PARSIMONY
— **pen·ny–pinch·er** \-chər\ *noun*
— **penny–pinching** *adjective*

pen·ny·roy·al \,pen-ē-'ròi-(ə)l, 'pe-ni-,rīl\ *noun* [probably by folk etymology from Middle French *poullieul*, modification of Latin *pulegium* fleabane, pennyroyal] (1530)
1 : a European perennial mint (*Mentha pulegium*) with small aromatic leaves
2 : an aromatic North American mint (*Hedeoma pulegioides*) that has blue or violet flowers borne in axillary tufts and yields an oil used in folk medicine or to drive away mosquitoes

penny stock *noun* (circa 1920)
: a usually unlisted highly speculative stock selling for a dollar or less

pen·ny·weight \'pe-nē-,wāt\ *noun* (14th century)
— see WEIGHT table

pen·ny·whistle \-,hwi-səl, -,wi-\ *noun* (1818)
1 : a small fipple flute
2 : a toy whistle

pen·ny–wise \-,wīz\ *adjective* [from the phrase *penny-wise and pound-foolish*] (1607)
: wise or prudent only in dealing with small sums or matters

pen·ny·wort \-,wərt, -,wòrt\ *noun* (14th century)
: any of several usually round-leaved plants (as of the genus *Hydrocotyle* of the carrot family)

pen·ny·worth \'pe-nē-,wərth, *British often* 'pe-nərth\ *noun, plural* **pennyworth** *or* **pennyworths** (before 12th century)
1 : a penny's worth
2 : value for the money spent : BARGAIN
3 : a small quantity : MODICUM

Pe·nob·scot \pə-'näb-,skät, -,skət\ *noun, plural* **-scot** *or* **-scots** (1624)

: a member of an American Indian people of the Penobscot river valley and Penobscot Bay region of Maine

pe·no·che \pə-'nō-chē\ *variant of* PENUCHE

pe·nol·o·gy \pi-'nä-lə-jē\ *noun* [Greek *poinē* penalty + English *-logy* — more at PAIN] (1838)
: a branch of criminology dealing with prison management and the treatment of offenders
— **pe·no·log·i·cal** \ˌpē-nə-'lä-ji-kəl\ *adjective*
— **pe·nol·o·gist** \pi-'nä-lə-jist\ *noun*

pen pal *noun* (1938)
: a friend made and kept through correspondence

pen point *noun* (circa 1864)
: a small thin convex metal device that tapers to a split point, fits into a holder, and is used for writing or drawing

pen pusher *noun* (circa 1905)
: PENCIL PUSHER

¹pen·sion \'pen(t)-shən\ *noun* [Middle English, from Middle French, from Latin *pension-, pensio,* from *pendere* to pay — more at PENDANT] (14th century)
1 \'pen(t)-shən\ : a fixed sum paid regularly to a person: **a** *archaic* : WAGE **b** : a gratuity granted (as by a government) as a favor or reward **c** : one paid under given conditions to a person following retirement from service or to surviving dependents
2 \päⁿs-yōⁿ\ [French, from Middle French] **a** : accommodations especially at a continental European hotel or boardinghouse : ROOM AND BOARD **b** *also* **pen·sio·ne** \pen(t)-'syō-(ˌ)nā\ [*pensione,* from Italian] : a hotel or boardinghouse especially in continental Europe
— **pen·sion·less** \'pen(t)-shən-ləs\ *adjective*

²pension *transitive verb* **pen·sioned; pen·sion·ing** \'pen(t)-sh(ə-)niŋ\ (1702)
1 : to grant or pay a pension to
2 : to dismiss or retire from service with a pension ⟨*pensioned* off his faithful old servant⟩

pen·sion·able \'pen(t)-sh(ə-)nə-bəl\ *adjective* (1882)
chiefly British : of, relating to, qualified for, or qualifying for a pension ⟨*pensionable* employees⟩ ⟨a *pensionable* post⟩

pen·sion·ary \'pen(t)-shə-ˌner-ē\ *noun, plural* **-ar·ies** (1536)
: PENSIONER; *especially* : HIRELING
— **pensionary** *adjective*

pen·sion·er \'pen(t)-sh(ə-)nər\ *noun* (15th century)
1 : a person who receives or lives on a pension
2 *obsolete* **a** : GENTLEMAN-AT-ARMS **b** : RETAINER **c** : MERCENARY, HIRELING

pen·sive \'pen(t)-siv\ *adjective* [Middle English *pensif,* from Middle French, from *penser* to think, from Latin *pensare* to ponder, frequentative of *pendere* to weigh — more at PENDANT] (14th century)
1 : musingly or dreamily thoughtful
2 : suggestive of sad thoughtfulness
— **pen·sive·ly** *adverb*
— **pen·sive·ness** *noun*

pen·ste·mon \pen-'stē-mən, 'pen(t)-stə-\ *noun* [New Latin, from *penta-* + Greek *stēmōn* warp, thread — more at STAMEN] (1760)
: any of a genus (*Penstemon*) of chiefly American herbs of the snapdragon family with showy tubular flowers

pen·stock \'pen-ˌstäk\ *noun* (circa 1607)
1 : a sluice or gate for controlling a flow (as of water)
2 : a conduit or pipe for conducting water

pent \'pent\ *adjective* [probably from past participle of obsolete English *pend* to confine] (1550)
: shut up : CONFINED, REPRESSED ⟨a *pent* crowd⟩ ⟨*pent*-up feelings⟩

penta- *or* **pent-** *combining form* [Middle English, from Greek, from *pente* — more at FIVE]

1 : five ⟨*penta*hedron⟩
2 : containing five atoms or groups ⟨*pent*ane⟩

pen·ta·chlo·ro·phe·nol \ˌpen-tə-ˌklōr-ə-'fē-ˌnōl, -ˌklȯr-, -fi-\ *noun* (1879)
: a crystalline compound C_6Cl_5OH used especially as a wood preservative and fungicide and a disinfectant

pen·ta·cle \'pen-ti-kəl\ *noun* [(assumed) Medieval Latin *pentaculum,* probably from Greek *pente*] (1594)
: PENTAGRAM

pen·tad \'pen-ˌtad\ *noun* [Greek *pentad-, pentas,* from *pente*] (1653)
: a group of five

pen·ta·gon \'pen-tə-ˌgän\ *noun* [Greek *pentagōnon,* from neuter of *pentagōnos* pentagonal, from *penta-* + *gōnia* angle — more at -GON] (1571)
: a polygon of five angles and five sides

Pentagon *noun* [the *Pentagon* building, headquarters of the Department of Defense] (1941)
: the U.S. military leadership

pen·tag·o·nal \pen-'ta-gə-nᵊl\ *noun* (1571)
1 : having five sides and five angles
2 : having a pentagon as a cross section or as a base ⟨a *pentagonal* pyramid⟩
— **pen·tag·o·nal·ly** \-nᵊl-ē\ *adverb*

Pen·ta·gon·ese \ˌpen-tə-gä-'nēz, -'nēs\ *noun* (1951)
: military jargon

pen·ta·gram \'pen-tə-ˌgram\ *noun* [Greek *pentagrammon,* from *penta-* + *-grammon* (akin to *gramma* letter) — more at GRAM] (1833)
: a figure of a 5-pointed star usually made with alternate points connected by a continuous line and used as a magic or occult symbol; *also* : a similar 6-pointed star (as Solomon's seal)

pen·ta·he·dron \ˌpen-tə-'hē-drən\ *noun* [New Latin] (circa 1775)
: a solid bounded by five faces
— **pen·ta·he·dral** \-drəl\ *adjective*

pen·tam·er·ous \pen-'ta-mə-rəs\ *adjective* [New Latin *pentamerus,* from *penta-* (from Greek) + *-merus* -merous] (1826)
: divided into or consisting of five parts; *specifically* : having each floral whorl consisting of five or a multiple of five members

pen·tam·e·ter \pen-'ta-mə-tər\ *noun* [Latin, from Greek *pentametros* having five metrical feet, from *penta-* + *metron* measure — more at MEASURE] (1589)
: a line of verse consisting of five metrical feet

pent·am·i·dine \pen-'ta-mə-ˌdēn, -dən\ *noun* (1941)
: a drug $C_{19}H_{24}N_4O_2$ used especially to treat protozoal infections (as leishmaniasis) and to prevent AIDS-related pneumonia

pen·tane \'pen-ˌtān\ *noun* [International Scientific Vocabulary] (1877)
: any of three isomeric alkanes C_5H_{12} that occur especially in petroleum

pen·tan·gle \'pent-ˌaŋ-gəl, 'pen-ˌtaŋ-\ *noun* (14th century)
: PENTAGRAM

pen·ta·pep·tide \ˌpen-tə-'pep-ˌtīd\ *noun* (1907)
: a polypeptide that contains five amino acid residues

pen·ta·ploid \'pen-tə-ˌplȯid\ *adjective* (1921)
: having or being a chromosome number that is five times the basic number
— **pentaploid** *noun*
— **pen·ta·ploi·dy** \-ˌplȯi-dē\ *noun*

pen·tar·chy \'pen-ˌtär-kē\ *noun* [Greek *pentarchia,* from *penta-* + *-archia* -archy] (1587)
: a group of five countries or districts each under its own ruler or government

Pen·ta·teuch \'pen-tə-ˌtük, -ˌtyük\ *noun* [Middle English *Penteteuke,* from Late Latin *Pentateuchus,* from Greek *Pentateuchos,* from *penta-* + *teuchos* tool, vessel, book, from *teuchein* to make — more at DOUGHTY] (15th century)

: the first five books of Jewish and Christian Scriptures

pen·tath·lete \pen-'tath-ˌlēt\ *noun* (1828)
: an athlete participating in a pentathlon

pen·tath·lon \pen-'tath-lən, -ˌlän\ *noun* [Greek, from *penta-* + *athlon* contest] (1603)
: an athletic contest involving participation by each contestant in five different events; *especially* : MODERN PENTATHLON

pen·ta·ton·ic \ˌpen-tə-'tä-nik\ *adjective* (1864)
: consisting of five tones; *specifically* : being or relating to a scale in which the tones are arranged like a major scale with the fourth and seventh tones omitted

pen·ta·va·lent \ˌpen-tə-'vā-lənt\ *adjective* (1871)
: having a valence of five

pen·taz·o·cine \pen-'ta-zə-ˌsēn\ *noun* [probably from *penta-* + *az-* + *octa-* + *²-ine*] (1963)
: an analgesic drug $C_{19}H_{27}NO$ that is less addictive than morphine

Pen·te·cost \'pen-ti-ˌkȯst, -ˌkäst\ *noun* [Middle English, from Old English *pentecosten,* from Late Latin *pentecoste,* from Greek *pentēkostē,* literally, fiftieth day, from *pentēkostos* fiftieth, from *pentēkonta* fifty, from *penta-* + *-konta* (akin to Latin *viginti* twenty) — more at VIGESIMAL] (before 12th century)
1 : SHABUOTH
2 : a Christian feast on the seventh Sunday after Easter commemorating the descent of the Holy Spirit on the apostles — called also *Whitsunday*

¹Pen·te·cos·tal \ˌpen-ti-'käs-tᵊl, -'kȯs-\ *adjective* (1663)
1 : of, relating to, or suggesting Pentecost
2 : of, relating to, or constituting any of various Christian religious bodies that emphasize individual experiences of grace, spiritual gifts (as glossolalia and faith healing), expressive worship, and evangelism
— **Pen·te·cos·tal·ism** \-tə-ˌli-zəm\ *noun*
— **Pen·te·cos·tal·ist** \-tə-list\ *noun or adjective*

²Pentecostal *noun* (1904)
: a member of a Pentecostal religious body

pent·house \'pent-ˌhau̇s\ *noun* [alteration of Middle English *pentis,* from Middle French *apentiz,* from *apent,* past participle of *apendre, appendre* to attach, hang against — more at APPEND] (1530)
1 a : a shed or roof attached to and sloping from a wall or building **b** : a smaller structure joined to a building : ANNEX
2 : a structure or dwelling built on the roof of a building

pent·land·ite \'pent-lən-ˌdīt\ *noun* [French, from Joseph *Pentland* (died 1873) Irish scientist] (circa 1858)
: a bronzy yellow mineral that is an isometric nickel iron sulfide and the principal ore of nickel

pen·to·bar·bi·tal \ˌpen-tə-'bär-bə-ˌtȯl\ *noun* [*penta-* + *-o-* + *barbital*]
: a granular barbiturate $C_{11}H_{18}N_2O_3$ used especially in the form of its sodium or calcium salt as a sedative, hypnotic, and antispasmodic

pen·to·bar·bi·tone \-ˌtōn\ *noun* [*penta-* + *-o-* + *barbitone*] (1938)
British : PENTOBARBITAL

pen·to·san \'pen-tə-ˌsan\ *noun* [International Scientific Vocabulary] (1892)
: any of various polysaccharides that yield only pentoses on hydrolysis and occur widely in plants

pen·tose \'pen-ˌtōs, -ˌtōz\ *noun* [International Scientific Vocabulary] (1890)
: a monosaccharide $C_5H_{10}O_5$ (as ribose) that contains five carbon atoms in the molecule

Pen·to·thal \'pen-tə-,thȯl\ *trademark*
— used for thiopental

pent·ox·ide \pent-'äk-,sīd\ *noun* [International Scientific Vocabulary] (circa 1872)
: an oxide containing five atoms of oxygen in the molecule

pent·ste·mon *variant of* PENSTEMON

pen·tyl·ene·tet·ra·zol \,pen-t⁹l-,ēn-'te-trə-,zȯl, -,zōl\ *noun* [penta- + meth*ylene* + *tetra-zole* (CH₂N₄)] (1949)
: an analeptic drug $C_6H_{10}N_4$

pe·nu·che \pə-'nü-chē\ *noun* [Mexican Spanish *panocha* raw sugar, from Spanish, ear of maize, ultimately from Latin *panicula* panicle — more at PANICLE] (1871)
: fudge made usually of brown sugar, butter, cream or milk, and nuts

pe·nult \'pē-,nəlt, pi-'\ *noun* [Latin *paenultima* penult, from feminine of *paenultimus* almost last, from *paene* almost + *ultimus* last — more at ULTIMATE] (1537)
: the next to the last member of a series; *especially* : the next to the last syllable of a word

pen·ul·ti·ma \pi-'nəl-tə-mə\ *noun* [Latin] (1589)
: PENULT

pen·ul·ti·mate \pi-'nəl-tə-mət\ *adjective* (1677)
1 : next to the last ⟨the *penultimate* chapter of a book⟩
2 : of or relating to a penult ⟨a *penultimate* accent⟩
— **pen·ul·ti·mate·ly** *adverb*

pen·um·bra \pə-'nəm-brə\ *noun, plural* **-brae** \-(,)brē, -,brī\ *or* **-bras** [New Latin, from Latin *paene* almost + *umbra* shadow — more at UMBRAGE] (1666)
1 a : a space of partial illumination (as in an eclipse) between the perfect shadow on all sides and the full light **b** : a shaded region surrounding the dark central portion of a sunspot
2 : a surrounding or adjoining region in which something exists in a lesser degree : FRINGE
3 : a body of rights held to be guaranteed by implication in a civil constitution
— **pen·um·bral** \-brəl\ *adjective*

pe·nu·ri·ous \pə-'nur-ē-əs, -'nyur-\ *adjective* (1590)
1 : marked by or suffering from penury
2 : given to or marked by extreme stinting frugality
synonym see STINGY
— **pe·nu·ri·ous·ly** *adverb*
— **pe·nu·ri·ous·ness** *noun*

pen·u·ry \'pen-yə-rē\ *noun* [Middle English, from Latin *penuria, paenuria* want; perhaps akin to Latin *paene* almost] (14th century)
1 : a cramping and oppressive lack of resources (as money); *especially* : severe poverty
2 : extreme and often niggardly frugality
synonym see POVERTY

pe·on \'pē-,än, -ən *also* pā-'ōn *for 2, British also* 'pyün *for 1\, noun, plural* **peons** *or* **pe·o·nes** \pā-'ō-nēz\ [Portuguese *peão* & French *pion*, from Medieval Latin *pedon-, pedo* foot soldier — more at PAWN] (1609)
1 : any of various workers in India, Sri Lanka, or Malaysia: as **a** : INFANTRYMAN **b** : ORDERLY
2 [Spanish *peón*, from Latin *pedon-, pedo*] : a member of the landless laboring class in Spanish America
3 *plural* **peons a** : a person held in compulsory servitude to a master for the working out of an indebtedness **b** : DRUDGE, MENIAL

pe·on·age \'pē-ə-nij\ *noun* (1844)
1 a : the use of laborers bound in servitude because of debt **b** : a system of convict labor by which convicts are leased to contractors
2 : the condition of a peon

pe·o·ny \'pē-ə-nē\ *noun, plural* **-nies** [Middle English *piony*, from Middle French *pioine*, from Latin *paeonia*, from Greek *paiōnia*, from *Paiōn* Paeon, physician of the gods] (14th century)
: any of a genus (*Paeonia* of the family Paeoniaceae) of chiefly Eurasian plants with large often double flowers

¹peo·ple \'pē-pəl\ *noun, plural* **people** [Middle English *peple*, from Old French *peuple*, from Latin *populus*] (13th century)
1 *plural* : human beings making up a group or assembly or linked by a common interest
2 *plural* : HUMAN BEINGS, PERSONS — often used in compounds instead of *persons* ⟨sales-*people*⟩
3 *plural* : the members of a family or kinship
4 *plural* : the mass of a community as distinguished from a special class ⟨disputes between the *people* and the nobles⟩ — often used by Communists to distinguish Communists from other people
5 *plural* **peoples** : a body of persons that are united by a common culture, tradition, or sense of kinship, that typically have common language, institutions, and beliefs, and that often constitute a politically organized group
6 : lower animals usually of a specified kind or situation
7 : the body of enfranchised citizens of a state
— **peo·ple·less** \-pə(l)-ləs\ *adjective*

²people *transitive verb* **peo·pled; peo·pling** \-p(ə-)liŋ\ [Middle French *peupler*, from Old French, from *peuple*] (15th century)
1 : to supply or fill with people
2 : to dwell in : INHABIT

peo·ple·hood \'pē-pəl-,hud\ *noun* (circa 1899)
1 : the quality or state of constituting a people
2 : the awareness of the underlying unity that makes the individual a part of a people

people mover *noun* (1968)
: any of various rapid-transit systems (as of moving sidewalks or automated driverless cars) for shuttling people

¹pep \'pep\ *noun* [short for *pepper*] (1912)
: brisk energy or initiative and high spirits

²pep *transitive verb* **pepped; pep·ping** (1925)
: to inject pep into ⟨*pep* him up⟩

pep·er·o·mia \,pe-pə-'rō-mē-ə\ *noun* [New Latin, from Greek *peperi* pepper + *homoios* like, similar — more at HOMEO-] (1882)
: any of a genus (*Peperomia*) of fleshy tropical herbs of the pepper family often cultivated for their showy foliage

pep·los \'pe-pləs, -,pläs\ *also* **pep·lus** \-pləs\ *noun* [Latin *peplus*, from Greek *peplos*] (1776)
: a garment worn like a shawl by women of ancient Greece

pep·lum \-pləm\ *noun* [Latin, from Greek *peplon* peplos] (1866)
: a short section attached to the waistline of a blouse, jacket, or dress
— **pep·lumed** \-pləmd\ *adjective*

peplum

pe·po \'pē-(,)pō\ *noun, plural* **pepos** [Latin, a melon — more at PUMPKIN] (circa 1859)
: an indehiscent fleshy 1-celled or falsely 3-celled many-seeded berry (as a pumpkin, squash, melon, or cucumber) that has a hard rind and is the characteristic fruit of the gourd family

¹pep·per \'pe-pər\ *noun* [Middle English *peper*, from Old English *pipor*, from Latin *piper*, from Greek *peperi*] (before 12th century)
1 a : either of two pungent products from the fruit of an East Indian plant that are used as a condiment, carminative, or stimulant: (1) : BLACK PEPPER (2) : WHITE PEPPER **b** : any of a genus (*Piper* of the family Piperaceae, the pepper family) of tropical mostly jointed climbing shrubs with aromatic leaves; *especially* : a woody vine (*P. nigrum*) with spicate flowers that is widely cultivated in the tropics for its red berries from which black pepper and white pepper are prepared

2 a : any of several products similar to pepper that are obtained from close relatives of the pepper plant **b** : any of various pungent condiments obtained from plants of other genera than that of the pepper
3 a : CAPSICUM 1; *especially* : a New World capsicum (*Capsicum annuum*) whose fruits are hot peppers or sweet peppers **b** : the fruit of a pepper that is usually red or yellow when ripe
— **pepper** *adjective*

²pepper *transitive verb* **pep·pered; pep·per·ing** \'pe-p(ə-)riŋ\ (1538)
1 a : to sprinkle, season, or cover with or as if with pepper **b** : to shower with or as if with shot or other missiles
2 : to hit with rapid repeated blows
3 : to sprinkle as if with pepper ⟨*peppered* the report with statistics⟩
— **pep·per·er** \-pər-ər\ *noun*

pep·per–and–salt \,pe-pər(-ə)n(d)-'sȯlt\ *adjective* (1774)
: SALT-AND-PEPPER

pep·per·box \'pe-pər-,bäks\ *noun* (1546)
1 : a small usually cylindrical box or bottle with a perforated top used for sprinkling ground pepper on food
2 : a pistol of the late 18th century with five or six revolving barrels

pep·per·corn \-,kȯrn\ *noun* (before 12th century)
: a dried berry of the black pepper

peppered moth *noun* (circa 1832)
: a European geometrid moth (*Biston betularia*) that typically has white wings with small black specks but also occurs as a solid black form especially in areas where the air is heavily polluted by industry

pep·per·grass \'pe-pər-,gras\ *noun* (15th century)
: any of a genus (*Lepidium*) of cresses; *especially* : GARDEN CRESS

pepper mill *noun* (circa 1858)
: a hand mill for grinding peppercorns

pep·per·mint \-,mint, -mənt, *in rapid speech* 'pep-mənt *or* -⁹m-ənt\ *noun* (1696)
1 a : a pungent and aromatic mint (*Mentha piperita*) with dark green lanceolate leaves and whorls of small pink flowers in spikes **b** : any of several mints (as *M. arvensis*) that are related to the peppermint
2 : candy flavored with peppermint
— **pep·per·minty** \'pe-pər-,min-tē\ *adjective*

pep·per·o·ni \,pe-pə-'rō-nē\ *noun* [Italian *peperoni* cayenne peppers, plural of *peperone*, augmentative of *pepe* pepper, from Latin *piper* — more at PEPPER] (1921)
: a highly seasoned beef and pork sausage

pepper pot *noun* (1679)
1 *British* : PEPPERBOX 1
2 a : a highly seasoned West Indian stew of vegetables and meat or fish **b** : a thick soup of tripe, meat, dumplings, and vegetables highly seasoned especially with crushed peppercorns — called also *Philadelphia pepper pot*

pepper shaker *noun* (1895)
: a container with a perforated top for sprinkling pepper

pep·per·tree \'pe-pər-,trē\ *noun* (circa 1692)
: a Peruvian evergreen tree (*Schinus molle*) of the cashew family grown as a shade tree in mild regions

pep·pery \'pe-p(ə-)rē\ *adjective* (1699)
1 : of, relating to, or having the qualities of pepper : HOT, PUNGENT ⟨a *peppery* taste⟩
2 : having a hot temper : TOUCHY ⟨a *peppery* boss⟩
3 : FIERY, STINGING ⟨a *peppery* satire⟩
— **pep·per·i·ness** \-nəs\ *noun*

pep pill *noun* (1937)
: any of various stimulant drugs in pill or tablet form

pep·py \'pe-pē\ *adjective* **pep·pi·er; -est** (circa 1918)
: full of pep

— **pep·pi·ness** *noun*

pep·sin \'pep-sən\ *noun* [German, from Greek *pepsis* digestion, from *pessein*] (circa 1844)
1 : a protease of the stomach that breaks down most proteins to polypeptides
2 : a preparation containing pepsin that is obtained from the stomach especially of the hog and is used especially as a digestive

pep·sin·o·gen \pep-'si-nə-jən\ *noun* [International Scientific Vocabulary] (1878)
: a granular zymogen of the gastric glands that is readily converted into pepsin in a slightly acid medium

pep talk *noun* (1925)
: a usually brief, intense, and emotional talk designed to influence or encourage an audience

pep·tic \'pep-tik\ *adjective* [Latin *pepticus*, from Greek *peptikos*, from *peptos* cooked, from *peptein, pessein* to cook, digest — more at COOK] (1651)
1 : relating to or promoting digestion : DIGESTIVE
2 : of, relating to, producing, or caused by pepsin ⟨*peptic* digestion⟩
3 : connected with or resulting from the action of digestive juices ⟨a *peptic* ulcer⟩

pep·ti·dase \'pep-tə-ˌdās, -ˌdāz\ *noun* (1918)
: an enzyme that hydrolyzes simple peptides or their derivatives

pep·tide \'pep-ˌtīd\ *noun* [International Scientific Vocabulary, from *peptone*] (1906)
: any of various amides that are derived from two or more amino acids by combination of the amino group of one acid with the carboxyl group of another and are usually obtained by partial hydrolysis of proteins
— **pep·tid·ic** \pep-'ti-dik\ *adjective*

peptide bond *noun* (1935)
: the chemical bond between carbon and nitrogen in a peptide linkage

peptide linkage *noun* (1925)
: the bivalent group CONH that unites the amino acid residues in a peptide

pep·ti·do·gly·can \ˌpep-tə-dō-'glī-ˌkan\ *noun* (1966)
: a polymer that is composed of polysaccharide and peptide chains and is found especially in bacterial cell walls — called also *mucopeptide, murein*

pep·tone \'pep-ˌtōn\ *noun* [German *Pepton*, from Greek, neuter of *peptos* cooked] (1860)
: any of various water-soluble products of partial hydrolysis of proteins

Pe·quot \'pē-ˌkwät\ *noun* [Narraganset *Pequttôog*] (1631)
: a member of an American Indian people of what is now eastern Connecticut

¹per \'pər\ *preposition* [Latin, through, by means of, by — more at FOR] (14th century)
1 : by the means or agency of : THROUGH ⟨*per* bearer⟩
2 : with respect to every member of a specified group : for each
3 : according to — often used with *as* ⟨*per* instructions⟩ ⟨as *per* usual⟩ □

²per *adverb* (1899)
: for each : APIECE ⟨a bargain at $3.50 *per*⟩

per- *prefix* [Latin, through, throughout, thoroughly, detrimental to, from *per*]
1 : throughout : thoroughly ⟨*per*use⟩
2 a : containing the largest possible or a relatively large proportion of a (specified) chemical element ⟨*per*chloroethylene⟩ **b** : containing an element in its highest or a high oxidation state ⟨*per*chloric acid⟩

¹per·ad·ven·ture \'pər-əd-ˌven-chər, 'per-; ˌpər-əd-', ˌper-\ *adverb* [Middle English *per aventure*, from Old French, by chance] (14th century)
archaic : PERHAPS, POSSIBLY

²peradventure *noun* (1627)
1 : DOUBT ⟨a fact established beyond *peradventure*⟩

2 : CHANCE 4a ⟨beyond *peradventure* of doubt⟩

per·am·bu·late \pə-'ram-byə-ˌlāt\ *verb* **-lat·ed; -lat·ing** [Latin *perambulatus*, past participle of *perambulare*, from *per-* through + *ambulare* to walk] (1568)
transitive verb
1 : to travel over or through especially on foot : TRAVERSE
2 : to make an official inspection of (a boundary) on foot
intransitive verb
: STROLL
— **per·am·bu·la·tion** \-ˌram-byə-'lā-shən\ *noun*
— **per·am·bu·la·to·ry** \-'ram-byə-lə-ˌtōr-ē, -ˌtòr-\ *adjective*

per·am·bu·la·tor \pə-'ram-byə-ˌlā-tər, *for 2 also* 'pram-\ *noun* (1611)
1 : one that perambulates
2 *chiefly British* : a baby carriage

per an·num \(ˌ)pər-'a-nəm\ *adverb* [Medieval Latin] (1536)
: in or for each year

per·bo·rate \(ˌ)pər-'bōr-ˌāt, -'bòr-\ *noun* [International Scientific Vocabulary] (1881)
: a salt that is a compound of a borate with hydrogen peroxide

per·cale \(ˌ)pər-'kā(ə)l, 'pər-; (ˌ)pər-'kal\ *noun* [Persian *pargālah*] (1840)
: a fine closely woven cotton cloth variously finished for clothing, sheeting, and industrial uses

per·ca·line \ˌpər-kə-'lēn\ *noun* [French, from *percale*] (circa 1858)
: a lightweight cotton fabric; *especially* : a glossy fabric used for bookbindings

per cap·i·ta \(ˌ)pər-'ka-pə-tə\ *adverb or adjective* [Medieval Latin, by heads] (1682)
1 : equally to each individual
2 : per unit of population : by or for each person ⟨the highest income *per capita* of any state in the union⟩

per·ceive \pər-'sēv\ *transitive verb* **per·ceived; per·ceiv·ing** [Middle English, from Middle French *perceivre*, from Latin *percipere*, from *per-* thoroughly + *capere* to take — more at HEAVE] (14th century)
1 a : to attain awareness or understanding of **b** : to regard as being such ⟨*perceived* threats⟩ ⟨was *perceived* as a loser⟩
2 : to become aware of through the senses; *especially* : SEE, OBSERVE
— **per·ceiv·able** \-'sē-və-bəl\ *adjective*
— **per·ceiv·ably** \-blē\ *adverb*
— **per·ceiv·er** *noun*

¹per·cent \pər-'sent\ *adverb* [earlier *per cent*, from *per* + Latin *centum* hundred — more at HUNDRED] (1568)
: in the hundred : of each hundred

²percent *noun, plural* **percent** *or* **per·cents** (1667)
1 *plural* **percent a** : one part in a hundred **b** : PERCENTAGE ⟨a large *percent* of his income⟩
2 *percents plural, British* : securities bearing a specified rate of interest

³percent *adjective* (1888)
1 : reckoned on the basis of a whole divided into one hundred parts
2 : paying interest at a specified percent

per·cent·age \pər-'sen-tij\ *noun* (circa 1789)
1 a : a part of a whole expressed in hundredths **b** : the result obtained by multiplying a number by a percent
2 a : a share of winnings or profits **b** : ADVANTAGE, PROFIT ⟨no *percentage* in going around looking like an old sack of laundry —Wallace Stegner⟩
3 : an indeterminate part : PROPORTION
4 a : PROBABILITY **b** : favorable odds

per·cen·tile \pər-'sen-ˌtīl\ *noun* (1885)
: a value on a scale of one hundred that indicates the percent of a distribution that is equal to or below it ⟨a score in the 95th *percentile*⟩

per cen·tum \pər-'sen-təm\ *noun* [*per* + Latin *centum*] (circa 1565)
: PERCENT

per·cept \'pər-ˌsept\ *noun* [back-formation from *perception*] (1837)
: an impression of an object obtained by use of the senses : SENSE-DATUM

per·cep·ti·ble \pər-'sep-tə-bəl\ *adjective* (1603)
: capable of being perceived especially by the senses ⟨a *perceptible* change in her tone⟩ ⟨the light became increasingly *perceptible*⟩ ☆
— **per·cep·ti·bil·i·ty** \-ˌsep-tə-'bi-lə-tē\ *noun*
— **per·cep·ti·bly** \-blē\ *adverb*

per·cep·tion \pər-'sep-shən\ *noun* [Latin *perception-, perceptio* act of perceiving, from *percipere*] (14th century)
1 a : a result of perceiving : OBSERVATION **b** : a mental image : CONCEPT
2 *obsolete* : CONSCIOUSNESS
3 a : awareness of the elements of environment through physical sensation ⟨color *perception*⟩ **b** : physical sensation interpreted in the light of experience
4 a : quick, acute, and intuitive cognition : APPRECIATION **b** : a capacity for comprehension
synonym see DISCERNMENT
— **per·cep·tion·al** \-shnəl, -shə-nᵊl\ *adjective*

per·cep·tive \pər-'sep-tiv\ *adjective* (1656)
1 : responsive to sensory stimuli : DISCERNING ⟨a *perceptive* eye⟩
2 a : capable of or exhibiting keen perception : OBSERVANT ⟨a *perceptive* scholar⟩ **b** : characterized by sympathetic understanding or insight
— **per·cep·tive·ly** *adverb*
— **per·cep·tive·ness** *noun*
— **per·cep·tiv·i·ty** \(ˌ)pər-ˌsep-'ti-və-tē\ *noun*

☆ SYNONYMS

Perceptible, sensible, palpable, tangible, appreciable, ponderable mean apprehensible as real or existent. PERCEPTIBLE applies to what can be discerned by the senses often to a minimal extent ⟨a *perceptible* difference in sound to a careful listener⟩. SENSIBLE applies to whatever is clearly apprehended through the senses or impresses itself strongly on the mind ⟨an abrupt, *sensible* drop in temperature⟩. PALPABLE applies either to what has physical substance or to what is obvious and unmistakable ⟨the tension in the air was almost *palpable*⟩. TANGIBLE suggests what is capable of being handled or grasped both physically and mentally ⟨no *tangible* evidence of UFOs⟩. APPRECIABLE applies to what is distinctly discernible by the senses or definitely measurable ⟨an *appreciable* increase in income⟩. PONDERABLE suggests having definitely measurable weight or importance ⟨exerted a *ponderable* influence on world events⟩.

□ USAGE

per *Per* occurs most frequently in business contexts; its use outside such contexts is often criticized but is quite widespread, especially in sense 2. Its most common and natural nonbusiness uses always involve figures, usually in relation to price ⟨$150 *per* performance⟩, automobiles ⟨32 miles *per* gallon⟩ ⟨55 miles *per* hour⟩, or sports ⟨averages 15 points and 9 rebounds *per* game⟩.

\ə\ abut \ᵊ\ kitten \ər\ **further** \a\ ash \ā\ ace
\ä\ mop, mar \aù\ out \ch\ chin \e\ bet \ē\ easy
\g\ go \i\ hit \ī\ ice \j\ job \ŋ\ sing \ō\ go
\ò\ law \òi\ boy \th\ thin \th̲\ the \ü\ loot \ù\ foot
\y\ yet \zh\ vision *see also* Guide to Pronunciation

per·cep·tu·al \(ˌ)pər-'sep-chə-wəl, -chəl, -shwəl\ *adjective* [*percept* + *-ual* (as in *conceptual*)] (1878)
: of, relating to, or involving perception especially in relation to immediate sensory experience
— **per·cep·tu·al·ly** *adverb*

Per·ce·val \'pər-sə-vəl\ *noun* [Old French]
: a knight of King Arthur who wins a sight of the Holy Grail

¹perch \'pərch\ *noun* [Middle English *perche*, from Middle French, from Latin *pertica* pole] (14th century)
1 : a bar or peg on which something is hung
2 a : a roost for a bird **b** : a resting place or vantage point : SEAT **c** : a prominent position ⟨his new *perch* as president⟩
3 *chiefly British* : ROD 2

²perch (14th century)
intransitive verb
: to alight, settle, or rest on a perch, a height, or a precarious spot
transitive verb
: to place on a perch, a height, or a precarious spot

³perch *noun, plural* **perch** *or* **perch·es** [Middle English *perche*, from Middle French, from Latin *perca*, from Greek *perkē*; akin to Old High German *faro* colored, Latin *porcus*, a spiny fish] (14th century)
1 a : a small European freshwater bony fish (*Perca fluviatilis* of the family Percidae, the perch family) **b** : YELLOW PERCH
2 : any of numerous bony fishes (as of the families Percidae, Centrarchidae, and Serranidae)

per·chance \pər-'chan(t)s\ *adverb* [Middle English *per chance*, from Middle French, by chance] (14th century)
: PERHAPS, POSSIBLY

Per·che·ron \'pər-chə-ˌrän, -shə-\ *noun* [French] (1875)
: any of a breed of powerful rugged draft horses that originated in the Perche region of France

Percheron

per·chlo·rate \(ˌ)pər-'klōr-ˌāt, -'klȯr-, -ət\ *noun* [International Scientific Vocabulary] (1826)
: a salt or ester of perchloric acid

per·chlo·ric acid \(ˌ)pər-'klōr-ik-, -'klȯr-\ *noun* (1818)
: a fuming corrosive strong acid $HClO_4$ that is the most highly oxidized acid of chlorine and a powerful oxidizing agent when heated

per·chlo·ro·eth·y·lene \(ˌ)pər-ˌklȯr-ō-'e-thə-ˌlēn, -ˌklȯr-\ *noun* (1873)
: a colorless nonflammable liquid C_2Cl_4 used often as a solvent in dry cleaning and for removal of grease from metals

per·cip·i·ence \pər-'si-pē-ən(t)s\ *noun* (circa 1774)
: PERCEPTION 4

¹per·cip·i·ent \-ənt\ *noun* [Latin *percipient-, percipiens*, present participle of *percipere* to perceive] (1662)
1 : one that perceives
2 : a person on whose mind a telepathic impulse or message is held to fall

²percipient *adjective* (1692)
: capable of or characterized by perception : DISCERNING
— **per·cip·i·ent·ly** *adverb*

per·co·late \'pər-kə-ˌlāt, ÷-kyə-\ *verb* **-lat·ed; -lat·ing** [Latin *percolatus*, past participle of *percolare*, from *per-* through + *colare* to sieve — more at PER-, COLANDER] (1626)
transitive verb
1 a : to cause (a solvent) to pass through a permeable substance (as a powdered drug) es-

pecially for extracting a soluble constituent **b** : to prepare (coffee) in a percolator
2 : to be diffused through : PENETRATE
intransitive verb
1 : to ooze or trickle through a permeable substance : SEEP
2 a : to become percolated **b** : to become lively or effervescent
3 : to spread gradually ⟨allow the sunlight to *percolate* into our rooms —Norman Douglas⟩
4 : SIMMER 2a
— **per·co·la·tion** \ˌpər-kə-'lā-shən\ *noun*

per·co·la·tor \'pər-kə-ˌlā-tər, ÷-kyə-\ *noun* (circa 1842)
: one that percolates; *specifically* : a coffeepot in which boiling water rising through a tube is repeatedly deflected downward through a perforated basket containing ground coffee beans to extract their essence

per con·tra \(ˌ)pər-'kän-trə\ *adverb* [Italian, by the opposite side (of the ledger)] (1554)
1 a : on the contrary **b** : by way of contrast
2 : as an offset

per cu·ri·am decision \(ˌ)pər-'kyùr-ē-ˌäm-, -'kùr-\ *noun* [Medieval Latin *per curiam*, literally, by the court] (1927)
: a very brief usually unanimous decision of a court rendered without elaborate discussion

per·cuss \pər-'kəs\ *transitive verb* [Latin *percussus*, past participle of *percutere*] (1560)
: to tap sharply; *especially* : to practice percussion on

per·cus·sion \pər-'kə-shən\ *noun* [Middle English, from Latin *percussion-, percussio*, from *percutere* to beat, from *per-* thoroughly + *quatere* to shake] (15th century)
1 : the act of percussing: as **a** : the striking of a percussion cap so as to set off the charge in a firearm **b** : the beating or striking of a musical instrument **c** : the act or technique of tapping the surface of a body part to learn the condition of the parts beneath by the resultant sound
2 : the striking of sound on the ear
3 : percussion instruments that form a section of a band or orchestra
— **percussion** *adjective*

percussion cap *noun* (1823)
: CAP 5

percussion instrument *noun* (1872)
: a musical instrument (as a drum, xylophone, or maraca) sounded by striking, shaking, or scraping

per·cus·sion·ist \pər-'kə-sh(ə-)nist\ *noun* (1939)
: one skilled in the playing of percussion instruments

per·cus·sive \pər-'kə-siv\ *adjective* (1793)
1 : of or relating to percussion; *especially* : operative or operated by striking
2 : having powerful impact
— **per·cus·sive·ly** *adverb*
— **per·cus·sive·ness** *noun*

per·cu·ta·ne·ous \ˌpər-kyù-'tā-nē-əs\ *adjective* (1887)
: effected or performed through the skin
— **per·cu·ta·ne·ous·ly** *adverb*

per·die \(ˌ)pər-'dē, per-\ *variant of* PARDIE

¹per di·em \(ˌ)pər-'dē-əm, -'dī-\ *adverb* [Medieval Latin] (1520)
: by the day : for each day

²per diem *adjective* (1809)
1 : based on use or service by the day : DAILY
2 : paid by the day

³per diem *noun, plural* **per diems** (1812)
1 : a daily allowance
2 : a daily fee

per·di·tion \pər-'di-shən\ *noun* [Middle English *perdicion*, from Late Latin *perdition-, perditio*, from Latin *perdere* to destroy, from *per-* through + *dare* to give — more at PER-, DATE] (14th century)
1 a *archaic* : utter destruction **b** *obsolete*

: LOSS
2 a : eternal damnation **b** : HELL

¹per·du *or* **per·due** \'pər-(ˌ)dü, -(ˌ)dyü; (ˌ)pər-'\ *noun* [French *sentinelle perdue*, literally, lost sentinel] (1605)
obsolete : a soldier assigned to extremely hazardous duty

²per·du *or* **per·due** \per-'dü\ *adjective* [French *perdu*, masculine, & *perdue*, feminine, from past participle of *perdre* to lose, from Latin *perdere*] (1624)
: remaining out of sight

per·du·ra·ble \(ˌ)pər-'dùr-ə-bəl, -'dyùr-; 'pər-jə-rə-\ *adjective* [Middle English, from Middle French, from Late Latin *perdurabilis*, from Latin *perdurare* to endure, from *per-* throughout + *durare* to last — more at DURING] (14th century)
: very durable
— **per·du·ra·bil·i·ty** \(ˌ)pər-ˌdùr-ə-'bil-ət-ē, -ˌdyùr-; ˌpər-jə-rə-\ *noun*
— **per·du·ra·bly** \(ˌ)pər-'dùr-ə-blē, -'dyùr-; 'pər-jə-rə-\ *adverb*

per·dure \(ˌ)pər-'dùr, -'dyùr\ *intransitive verb* **per·dured; per·dur·ing** [Middle English, from Latin *perdurare*] (15th century)
: to continue to exist : LAST

per·e·gri·nate \'per-ə-grə-ˌnāt\ *verb* **-nat·ed; -nat·ing** (1593)
intransitive verb
: to travel especially on foot : WALK
transitive verb
: to walk or travel over : TRAVERSE
— **per·e·gri·na·tion** \ˌper-ə-grə-'nā-shən\ *noun*

¹per·e·grine \'per-ə-grən, -ˌgrēn\ *adjective* [Middle English, from Medieval Latin *peregrinus*, from Latin, foreign — more at PILGRIM] (14th century)
: having a tendency to wander

²peregrine *noun* (1555)
: a swift nearly cosmopolitan falcon (*Falco peregrinus*) that is much used in falconry — called also *peregrine falcon*
word history
see PILGRIM

pe·rei·on \pə-'rī-ˌän\ *or* **pe·re·on** \-'rē-\ *noun* [New Latin, from Greek *peraiōn*, present participle of *peraioun* to transport, from *peraios* situated beyond, from *pera* beyond; akin to Greek *poros* passage — more at FARE] (1855)
: the thorax or the seven metameres comprising the thorax of some crustaceans (as a decapod)

pe·reio·pod \pə-'rī-ə-ˌpäd\ *or* **pe·reo·pod** \-'rē-\ *noun* [New Latin *perion* + English *-pod*] (1893)
: an appendage of the pereion

pe·remp·to·ry \pə-'rem(p)-t(ə-)rē\ *adjective* [Late Latin & Latin; Late Latin *peremptorius*, from Latin, destructive, from *perimere* to take entirely, destroy, from *per-* thoroughly + *emere* to take — more at REDEEM] (15th century)
1 a : putting an end to or precluding a right of action, debate, or delay ⟨a *peremptory* mandamus⟩ **b** : admitting of no contradiction ⟨a *peremptory* conclusion based on absolute evidence⟩
2 : expressive of urgency or command ⟨a *peremptory* call⟩
3 a : characterized by often imperious or arrogant self-assurance ⟨how insolent of late he is become, how proud, how *peremptory* —Shakespeare⟩ **b** : indicative of a peremptory attitude

peregrine

or nature **:** HAUGHTY ⟨a *peremptory* tone⟩ ⟨*peremptory* disregard of an objection⟩
synonym see MASTERFUL
— **pe·remp·to·ri·ly** \-'rem(p)-t(ə-)rə-lē; -,rem(p)-'tȯr-ə-lē, -'tȯr-\ *adverb*
— **pe·remp·to·ri·ness** \-'rem(p)-t(ə-)rē-nəs\ *noun*
peremptory challenge *noun* (circa 1531)
: a challenge (as of a juror) made as of right without assigning any cause
per·en·nate \'per-ə-,nāt, pə-'re-,nāt\ *intransitive verb* **-nat·ed; -nat·ing** [Latin *perennatus*, past participle of *perennare*, from *perennis*] (circa 1623)
: to live over from season to season ⟨a *perennating* rhizome⟩
— **per·en·na·tion** \,per-ə-'nā-shən\ *noun*
pe·ren·ni·al \pə-'re-nē-əl\ *adjective* [Latin *perennis*, from *per-* throughout + *annus* year — more at PER-, ANNUAL] (1644)
1 : present at all seasons of the year
2 : persisting for several years usually with new herbaceous growth from a perennating part ⟨*perennial* asters⟩
3 a : PERSISTENT, ENDURING ⟨*perennial* traditions⟩ **b :** continuing without interruption **:** CONSTANT, PERPETUAL ⟨the *perennial* quest for certainty⟩ ⟨a *perennial* student⟩ **c :** regularly repeated or renewed **:** RECURRENT ⟨death is a *perennial* literary theme⟩
synonym see CONTINUAL
— **perennial** *noun*
— **pe·ren·ni·al·ly** \-nē-ə-lē\ *adverb*
per·e·stroi·ka \,per-ə-'strȯi-kə\ *noun* [Russian *perestroĭka*, literally, restructuring] (1986)
: the policy of economic and governmental reform instituted by Mikhail Gorbachev in the Soviet Union during the mid-1980s
¹per·fect \'pər-fikt\ *adjective* [Middle English *parfit*, from Old French, from Latin *perfectus*, from past participle of *perficere* to carry out, perfect, from *per-* thoroughly + *facere* to make, do — more at DO] (14th century)
1 a : being entirely without fault or defect **:** FLAWLESS ⟨a *perfect* diamond⟩ **b :** satisfying all requirements **:** ACCURATE **c :** corresponding to an ideal standard or abstract concept ⟨a *perfect* gentleman⟩ **d :** faithfully reproducing the original; *specifically* **:** LETTER-PERFECT **e :** legally valid
2 : EXPERT, PROFICIENT ⟨practice makes *perfect*⟩
3 a : PURE, TOTAL **b :** lacking in no essential detail **:** COMPLETE **c** *obsolete* **:** SANE **d :** ABSOLUTE, UNEQUIVOCAL ⟨enjoys *perfect* happiness⟩ **e :** of an extreme kind **:** UNMITIGATED ⟨a *perfect* brat⟩ ⟨an act of *perfect* foolishness⟩
4 *obsolete* **:** MATURE
5 : of, relating to, or constituting a verb form or verbal that expresses an action or state completed at the time of speaking or at a time spoken of
6 *obsolete* **a :** CERTAIN, SURE **b :** CONTENTED, SATISFIED
7 *of a musical interval* **:** belonging to the consonances unison, fourth, fifth, and octave which retain their character when inverted and when raised or lowered by a half step become augmented or diminished
8 a : sexually mature and fully differentiated ⟨a *perfect* insect⟩ **b :** having both stamens and pistils in the same flower ⟨a *perfect* flower⟩ ☆
☐
— **per·fect·ness** \-fik(t)-nəs\ *noun*
²per·fect \pər-'fekt *also* 'pər-fikt\ *transitive verb* (14th century)
1 : to bring to final form
2 : to make perfect **:** IMPROVE, REFINE
— **per·fect·er** *noun*
³per·fect \'pər-fikt\ *noun* (1841)
: the perfect tense of a language; *also* **:** a verb form in the perfect tense
per·fec·ta \pər-'fek-tə\ *noun* [American Spanish *quiniela perfecta* perfect quiniela] (1967)
: a bet in which the bettor picks the first and

second place finishers in order — compare QUINIELA, TRIFECTA
perfect binding *noun* (1926)
: a book binding in which a layer of adhesive holds the pages and cover together
— **per·fect–bound** \'pər-fik(t)-'baund\ *adjective*
perfect game *noun* (circa 1949)
: a baseball game in which a pitcher allows no hits, no runs, and no opposing batter to reach first base
per·fect·ible \pər-'fek-tə-bəl *also* 'pər-fik-\ *adjective* (1635)
: capable of improvement or perfection
— **per·fect·ibil·i·ty** \pər-,fek-tə-'bi-lə-tē *also* ,pər-fik-\ *noun*
per·fec·tion \pər-'fek-shən\ *noun* [Middle English *perfeccioun*, from Old French *perfection*, from Latin *perfection-, perfectio*, from *perficere*] (13th century)
1 : the quality or state of being perfect: as **a :** freedom from fault or defect **:** FLAWLESSNESS **b :** MATURITY **c :** the quality or state of being saintly
2 a : an exemplification of supreme excellence **b :** an unsurpassable degree of accuracy or excellence
3 : the act or process of perfecting
per·fec·tion·ism \-shə-,ni-zəm\ *noun* (circa 1846)
1 a : the doctrine that the perfection of moral character constitutes a person's highest good **b :** the theological doctrine that a state of freedom from sin is attainable on earth
2 : a disposition to regard anything short of perfection as unacceptable
— **per·fec·tion·ist** \-sh(ə-)nist\ *noun or adjective*
— **per·fec·tion·is·tic** \-,fek-shə-'nis-tik\ *adjective*
per·fec·tive \pər-'fek-tiv *also* 'pər-fik-\ *adjective* (1596)
1 *archaic* **a :** tending to make perfect **b :** becoming better
2 : expressing action as complete or as implying the notion of completion, conclusion, or result ⟨*perfective* verb⟩
— **perfective** *noun*
— **per·fec·tive·ly** *adverb*
— **per·fec·tive·ness** *noun*
— **per·fec·tiv·i·ty** \pər-,fek-'ti-və-tē *also* ,pər-fik-\ *noun*
per·fect·ly \'pər-fik(t)-lē\ *adverb* (14th century)
1 : in a perfect manner
2 : to a complete or adequate extent **:** QUITE ⟨was *perfectly* happy until now⟩
perfect number *noun* (14th century)
: an integer (as 6 or 28) the sum of whose integral factors including 1 but excluding itself is equal to itself
per·fec·to \pər-'fek-(,)tō\ *noun, plural* **-tos** [Spanish, perfect, from Latin *perfectus*] (1894)
: a cigar that is thick in the middle and tapers at each end
perfect participle *noun* (1862)
: PAST PARTICIPLE
perfect pitch *noun* (1949)
: ABSOLUTE PITCH 2
perfect square *noun* (1856)
: an integer (as 9 or 36) whose square root is an integer
per·fer·vid \(,)pər-'fər-vəd, 'pər-\ *adjective* [New Latin *perfervidus*, from Latin *per-* thoroughly + *fervidus* fervid] (1856)
: marked by overwrought or exaggerated emotion **:** excessively fervent
synonym see IMPASSIONED
per·fid·i·ous \(,)pər-'fi-dē-əs\ *adjective* (1598)
: of, relating to, or characterized by perfidy
synonym see FAITHLESS
— **per·fid·i·ous·ly** *adverb*
— **per·fid·i·ous·ness** *noun*
per·fi·dy \'pər-fə-dē\ *noun, plural* **-dies** [Latin

perfidia, from *perfidus* faithless, from *per-* detrimental to + *fides* faith — more at PER-, FAITH] (1592)
1 : the quality or state of being faithless or disloyal **:** TREACHERY
2 : an act or an instance of disloyalty
per·fo·li·ate \,pər-'fō-lē-ət, 'pər-\ *adjective* [New Latin *perfoliata*, an herb having leaves pierced by the stem, from Latin *per* through + *foliata*, feminine of *foliatus* foliate] (1687)
: having the basal part naturally united around the stem ⟨a *perfoliate* leaf of a honeysuckle⟩

☆ SYNONYMS
Perfect, whole, entire, intact mean not lacking or faulty in any particular. PERFECT implies the soundness and the excellence of every part, element, or quality of a thing frequently as an unattainable or theoretical state ⟨a *perfect* set of teeth⟩. WHOLE suggests a completeness or perfection that can be sought, gained, or regained ⟨felt like a *whole* person again after vacation⟩. ENTIRE implies perfection deriving from integrity, soundness, or completeness of a thing ⟨the *entire* Beethoven corpus⟩. INTACT implies retention of perfection of a thing in its natural or original state ⟨the boat survived the storm *intact*⟩.

☐ USAGE
perfect Can something be more perfect than something else? Can something be the most perfect of its kind? Writers and speakers of English have long thought so ⟨our sight is the most *perfect* and most delightful of all our senses —Joseph Addison (1712)⟩ ⟨some of their years were much more *perfect* than others —Benjamin Franklin (1752)⟩ ⟨the most *perfect* model of Roman discipline —Edward Gibbon (1776)⟩ ⟨the most *perfect* and precious . . . of antiquity —Thomas Jefferson (1776)⟩ ⟨in order to form a more *perfect* union —*U.S. Constitution* (1787)⟩. *Perfect* had been used in the comparative and superlative since the 14th century and, as the examples show, was common in the 18th century. Yet toward the end of the 18th century some grammarians decided that such use must be wrong in spite of its considerable literary authority. What is perfect is perfect, they said; the word does not admit of comparison. The argument claims to be based on logic. But did logicians agree ⟨man and the more *perfect* animals —John Stuart Mill (*A System of Logic*)⟩? The upshot of all this is that we have now inherited two traditions: a 200-year-old tradition of insisting that *perfect* cannot be compared and a 600-year-old tradition of using *perfect* in the comparative and superlative ⟨I was feeling more *perfect* with every Rainbow [trout] —Norman MacLean⟩ ⟨he felt . . . that circular motion was the most *perfect* —Stephen W. Hawking⟩. Resolution of this conflict lies in the fact that few things in reality are perfect, and when most people use *more perfect* or *most perfect* they are suggesting an approach to perfection. In other words, *more perfect* is equivalent to *more nearly perfect*. Sometimes writers find an excess of perfection ⟨it was perhaps too *perfect* in its unity —W. B. Yeats⟩ ⟨he is too *perfect* to believe —Lady Bird Johnson⟩. All of these uses are perfectly standard, but those who are diffident about *more perfect* can write, as some authors do, *more nearly perfect*.

per·fo·rate \'pər-fə-ˌrāt\ *verb* **-rat·ed; -rat·ing** [Latin *perforatus*, past participle of *perforare* to bore through, from *per-* through + *forare* to bore — more at BORE] (1538)
transitive verb
1 : to make a hole through ⟨an ulcer *perforates* the duodenal wall⟩; *especially* **:** to make a line of holes in to facilitate separation
2 : to pass through or into by or as if by making a hole
intransitive verb
: to penetrate a surface
— **per·fo·rate** \'pər-f(ə-)rət, -fə-ˌrāt\ *adjective*
— **per·fo·ra·tor** \-fə-ˌrā-tər\ *noun*
per·fo·rat·ed \-fə-ˌrā-təd\ *adjective* (1597)
1 : having a hole or perforations; *especially* **:** having a specified number of perforations in 20 millimeters ⟨the stamps are *perforated* 10⟩
2 : characterized by perforation ⟨a *perforated* ulcer⟩
per·fo·ra·tion \ˌpər-fə-ˈrā-shən\ *noun* (15th century)
1 : the act or process of perforating
2 a : a hole or pattern made by or as if by piercing or boring **b :** one of the series of holes between rows of postage stamps in a sheet that serve as an aid in separation
per·force \pər-ˈfōrs, -ˈfȯrs\ *adverb* [Middle English *par force*, from Middle French, by force] (14th century)
1 *obsolete* **:** by physical coercion
2 : by force of circumstances
per·form \pə(r)-ˈfȯrm\ *verb* [Middle English, from Anglo-French *performer*, alteration of Old French *perfournir*, from *per-* thoroughly (from Latin) + *fournir* to complete — more at FURNISH] (14th century)
transitive verb
1 : to adhere to the terms of **:** FULFILL ⟨*perform* a contract⟩
2 : CARRY OUT, DO
3 a : to do in a formal manner or according to prescribed ritual **b :** to give a rendition of **:** PRESENT
intransitive verb
1 : to carry out an action or pattern of behavior **:** ACT, FUNCTION
2 : to give a performance **:** PLAY ☆
— **per·form·abil·i·ty** \-ˌfȯr-mə-ˈbi-lə-tē\ *noun*
— **per·form·able** \-ˈfȯr-mə-bəl\ *adjective*
— **per·form·er** \-ˈfȯr-mər\ *noun*
per·for·mance \pə(r)-ˈfȯr-mən(t)s\ *noun* (15th century)
1 a : the execution of an action **b :** something accomplished **:** DEED, FEAT
2 : the fulfillment of a claim, promise, or request **:** IMPLEMENTATION
3 a : the action of representing a character in a play **b :** a public presentation or exhibition ⟨a benefit *performance*⟩
4 a : the ability to perform **:** EFFICIENCY **b :** the manner in which a mechanism performs ⟨engine *performance*⟩
5 : the manner of reacting to stimuli **:** BEHAVIOR
6 : the linguistic behavior of an individual **:** PAROLE; *also* **:** the ability to speak a certain language — compare COMPETENCE 3
performance art *noun* (1971)
: a nontraditional art form that consists of or features a performance by the artist
— **performance artist** *noun*
per·for·ma·tive \-ˈfȯr-mə-tiv\ *adjective* (1955)
: being or relating to an expression that serves to effect a transaction or that constitutes the performance of the specified act by virtue of its utterance ⟨*performative* verbs such as *promise* and *congratulate*⟩ — compare CONSTATIVE

— **performative** *noun*
per·for·ma·to·ry \-mə-ˌtōr-ē, -ˌtȯr-\ *adjective* (1949)
: PERFORMATIVE; *also* **:** of or relating to performance
performing *adjective* (1889)
: of, relating to, or constituting an art (as drama) that involves public performance ⟨the *performing* arts⟩
¹per·fume \'pər-ˌfyüm, (ˌ)pər-ˈ\ *noun* [Middle French *perfum*, probably from Old Provençal, from *perfumar* to perfume, from *per-* thoroughly (from Latin) + *fumar* to smoke, from Latin *fumare*, from *fumus* smoke — more at FUME] (1533)
1 : the scent of something sweet-smelling
2 : a substance that emits a pleasant odor; *especially* **:** a fluid preparation of natural essences (as from plants or animals) or synthetics and a fixative used for scenting
synonym see FRAGRANCE
²per·fume \(ˌ)pər-ˈfyüm, ˈpər-ˌ\ *transitive verb* **per·fumed; per·fum·ing** (1538)
: to fill or imbue with an odor
per·fum·er \pə(r)-ˈfyü-mər, ˈpər-ˌ\ *noun* (circa 1580)
: one that makes or sells perfumes
per·fum·ery \pə(r)-ˈfyü-mə-rē, -ˈfyüm-rē\ *noun, plural* **-er·ies** (1800)
1 a : the art or process of making perfume **b :** the products made by a perfumer
2 : an establishment where perfumes are made
per·func·to·ry \pər-ˈfəŋ(k)-t(ə-)rē\ *adjective* [Late Latin *perfunctorius*, from Latin *perfungi* to accomplish, get through with, from *per-* through + *fungi* to perform — more at PER-, FUNCTION] (1593)
1 : characterized by routine or superficiality **:** MECHANICAL ⟨a *perfunctory* smile⟩
2 : lacking in interest or enthusiasm
— **per·func·to·ri·ly** \-t(ə-)rə-lē\ *adverb*
— **per·func·to·ri·ness** \-t(ə-)rē-nəs\ *noun*
per·fus·ate \(ˌ)pər-ˈfyü-ˌzāt, -zət\ *noun* (1915)
: a fluid (as a solution pumped through the heart) that is perfused
per·fuse \(ˌ)pər-ˈfyüz\ *transitive verb* **perfused; per·fus·ing** [Middle English, from Latin *perfusus*, past participle of *perfundere* to pour over, from *per-* through + *fundere* to pour — more at FOUND] (15th century)
1 : SUFFUSE
2 a : to cause to flow or spread **:** DIFFUSE **b :** to force a fluid through (an organ or tissue) especially by way of the blood vessels
— **per·fu·sion** \-ˈfyü-zhən\ *noun*
per·fu·sion·ist \(ˌ)pər-ˈfyü-zhə-nist\ *noun* (1964)
: a certified medical technician responsible for extracorporeal oxygenation of the blood during open-heart surgery and for the operation and maintenance of equipment (as a heart-lung machine) controlling it
per·go·la \'pər-gə-lə, pər-ˈgō-\ *noun* [Italian, from Latin *pergula*] (1675)
1 : ARBOR, TRELLIS
2 : a structure usually consisting of parallel colonnades supporting an open roof of girders and cross rafters
¹per·haps \pər-ˈhaps, ˈpraps\ *adverb* [*per* + *hap*] (1528)
: possibly but not certainly **:** MAYBE
²perhaps *noun* (1534)
: something open to doubt or conjecture
pe·ri \'pir-ē\ *noun* [Persian *perī* fairy, genius, from Middle Persian *parīk*; akin to Avestan *pairikā* sorceress] (circa 1780)
1 : a supernatural being in Persian folklore descended from fallen angels and excluded from paradise until penance is accomplished
2 : a beautiful and graceful girl
peri- *prefix* [Latin, from Greek, around, in excess, from *peri*; akin to Greek *peran* to pass through — more at FARE]

1 : all around **:** about ⟨*periscope*⟩
2 : near ⟨*perihelion*⟩
3 : enclosing **:** surrounding ⟨*perineurium*⟩
peri·anth \'per-ē-ˌan(t)th\ *noun* [New Latin *perianthium*, from *peri-* + Greek *anthos* flower — more at ANTHOLOGY] (1828)
: the floral structure comprised of the calyx and corolla especially when the two whorls are fused — see FLOWER illustration
peri·apt \'per-ē-ˌapt\ *noun* [Middle French or Greek; Middle French *periapte*, from Greek *periapton*, from *periaptein* to fasten around (oneself), from *peri-* + *haptein* to fasten] (1584)
: AMULET
peri·car·di·al \ˌper-ə-ˈkär-dē-əl\ *adjective* (1654)
: of, relating to, or affecting the pericardium; *also* **:** situated around the heart
peri·car·di·tis \-ˌkär-ˈdī-təs\ *noun* [New Latin] (circa 1799)
: inflammation of the pericardium
peri·car·di·um \-ˈkär-dē-əm\ *noun, plural* **-dia** \-dē-ə\ [Middle English, from Medieval Latin, from Greek *perikardion*, neuter of *perikardios* around the heart, from *peri-* + *kardia* heart — more at HEART] (15th century)
1 : the conical sac of serous membrane that encloses the heart and the roots of the great blood vessels of vertebrates
2 : a cavity or space that contains the heart of an invertebrate and in arthropods is a part of the hemocoel
peri·carp \'per-ə-ˌkärp\ *noun* [New Latin *pericarpium*, from Greek *perikarpion* pod, from *peri-* + *-karpion* -carp] (1759)
: the ripened and variously modified walls of a plant ovary — see ENDOCARP illustration
peri·chon·dri·um \ˌper-ə-ˈkän-drē-əm\ *noun, plural* **-dria** \-drē-ə\ [New Latin, from *peri-* + Greek *chondros* grain, cartilage] (1741)
: the membrane of fibrous connective tissue that invests cartilage except at joints
— **peri·chon·dral** \-drəl\ *adjective*
pe·ric·o·pe \pə-ˈri-kə-pē\ *noun* [Late Latin, from Greek *perikopē* section, from *peri-* + *kopē* act of cutting, from *koptein* to cut — more at CAPON] (1658)
: a selection from a book; *specifically* **:** LECTION 1
peri·cra·ni·um \ˌper-ə-ˈkrā-nē-əm\ *noun, plural* **-nia** \-nē-ə\ [Middle English *pericraneum*, from Medieval Latin, from Greek *perikranion*, neuter of *perikranios* around the skull, from *peri-* + *kranion* skull — more at CRANIUM] (15th century)

☆ **SYNONYMS**
Perform, execute, discharge, accomplish, achieve, effect, fulfill mean to carry out or into effect. PERFORM implies action that follows established patterns or procedures or fulfills agreed-upon requirements and often connotes special skill ⟨*performed* gymnastics⟩. EXECUTE stresses the carrying out of what exists in plan or in intent ⟨*executed* the hit-and-run⟩. DISCHARGE implies execution and completion of appointed duties or tasks ⟨*discharged* his duties⟩. ACCOMPLISH stresses the successful completion of a process rather than the means of carrying it out ⟨*accomplished* everything they set out to do⟩. ACHIEVE adds to ACCOMPLISH the implication of conquered difficulties ⟨*achieve* greatness⟩. EFFECT adds to ACHIEVE an emphasis on the inherent force in the agent capable of surmounting obstacles ⟨*effected* sweeping reforms⟩. FULFILL implies a complete realization of ends or possibilities ⟨*fulfilled* their ambitions⟩.

: the external periosteum of the skull
— **peri·cra·ni·al** \-nē-əl\ *adjective*

peri·cy·cle \'per-ə-ˌsī-kəl\ *noun* [French *péricycle*, from Greek *perikyklos* spherical, from *peri-* + *kyklos* circle — more at WHEEL] (circa 1892)
: a thin layer of parenchymatous or sclerenchymatous cells that surrounds the stele in most vascular plants
— **peri·cy·clic** \ˌper-ə-'sī-klik, -'si-\ *adjective*

peri·derm \'per-ə-ˌdərm\ *noun* [New Latin *peridermis*, from *peri-* + *-dermis*] (1849)
: an outer layer of tissue; *especially* : a cortical protective layer of many roots and stems that typically consists of phellem, phellogen, and phelloderm

pe·rid·i·um \pə-'ri-dē-əm\ *noun, plural* **pe·rid·ia** \-dē-ə\ [New Latin, from Greek *pēridion*, diminutive of *pēra* leather bag] (circa 1823)
: the outer envelope of the sporophore of many fungi

per·i·dot \'per-ə-ˌdät, -ˌdō(t)\ *noun* [French *péridot*, from Old French *peritot*] (circa 1706)
: a deep yellowish green transparent olivine used as a gem
— **peri·do·tic** \ˌper-ə-'dä-tik, -'dō-\ *adjective*

pe·ri·do·tite \pə-'ri-də-ˌtīt\ *noun* [French *péridotite*, from *péridot*] (1878)
: any of a group of granitoid igneous rocks composed of ferromagnesian minerals and especially olivine
— **pe·ri·do·tit·ic** \pə-ˌri-də-'ti-tik\ *adjective*

peri·gee \'per-ə-(ˌ)jē\ *noun* [Middle French, from New Latin *perigeum*, from Greek *perigeion*, from neuter of *perigeios* near the earth, from *peri-* + *gē* earth] (1594)
: the point in the orbit of an object (as a satellite) orbiting the earth that is nearest to the center of the earth; *also* : the point nearest a planet or a satellite (as the moon) reached by an object orbiting it — compare APOGEE
— **peri·ge·an** \ˌper-ə-'jē-ən\ *adjective*

pe·rig·y·nous \pə-'ri-jə-nəs\ *adjective* [New Latin *perigynus*, from *peri-* + *-gynus* -gynous] (1807)
: borne on a ring or cup of the receptacle surrounding a pistil 〈*perigynous* petals〉; *also* : having perigynous stamens and petals 〈*perigynous* flowers〉
— **pe·rig·y·ny** \-nē\ *noun*

peri·he·lion \ˌper-ə-'hēl-yən\ *noun, plural* **-he·lia** \-'hēl-yə\ [New Latin, from *peri-* + Greek *hēlios* sun — more at SOLAR] (1666)
: the point in the path of a celestial body (as a planet) that is nearest to the sun — compare APHELION
— **peri·he·lial** \-'hēl-yəl\ *adjective*

peri·kar·y·on \ˌper-ə-'kar-ē-ˌän, -ən\ *noun, plural* **-kar·ya** \-ē-ə\ [New Latin, from *peri-* + Greek *karyon* nut, kernel — more at CAREEN] (1897)
: CELL BODY
— **peri·kar·y·al** \-ē-əl\ *adjective*

¹per·il \'per-əl\ *noun* [Middle English, from Old French, from Latin *periculum* — more at FEAR] (13th century)
1 : exposure to the risk of being injured, destroyed, or lost : DANGER 〈fire put the city in *peril*〉
2 : something that imperils : RISK 〈lessen the *perils* of the streets〉

²peril *transitive verb* **-iled** *also* **-illed; -il·ing** *also* **-il·ling** (1567)
: to expose to danger

pe·ril·la \pə-'ri-lə\ *noun* [New Latin] (1900)
: any of a genus (*Perilla*) of Asian mints that have a bilabiate fruiting calyx and rugose nutlets

perilla oil *noun* (1917)
: a light yellow drying oil that is obtained from seeds of perillas

per·il·ous \'per-ə-ləs\ *adjective* (14th century)
: full of or involving peril : HAZARDOUS
synonym see DANGEROUS
— **per·il·ous·ly** *adverb*
— **per·il·ous·ness** *noun*

peri·lune \'per-ə-ˌlün\ *noun* [*peri-* + Latin *luna* moon — more at LUNAR] (1960)
: the point in the path of a body orbiting the moon that is nearest to the center of the moon — compare APOLUNE

peri·lymph \-ˌlim(p)f\ *noun* [International Scientific Vocabulary] (circa 1839)
: the fluid between the membranous and bony labyrinths of the ear

pe·rim·e·ter \pə-'ri-mə-tər\ *noun* [Middle English *perimetre*, from Latin *perimetros*, from Greek, from *peri-* + *metron* measure — more at MEASURE] (15th century)
1 a : the boundary of a closed plane figure **b** : the length of a perimeter
2 : a line or strip bounding or protecting an area
3 : outer limits — often used in plural

peri·my·si·um \ˌper-ə-'mi-zhē-əm, -zē-\ *noun, plural* **-sia** \-zhē-ə, -zē\ [New Latin, irregular from *peri-* + Greek *mys* mouse, muscle — more at MOUSE] (circa 1842)
: the connective-tissue sheath that surrounds a muscle and forms sheaths for the bundles of muscle fibers

peri·na·tal \-'nā-tᵊl\ *adjective* (1952)
: occurring in, concerned with, or being in the period around the time of birth 〈*perinatal* mortality〉 〈*perinatal* care〉
— **peri·na·tal·ly** \-tᵊl-(l)ē\ *adverb*

per·i·ne·um \ˌper-ə-'nē-əm\ *noun, plural* **-nea** \-'nē-ə\ [Middle English, from Late Latin *perinaion*, from Greek, from *peri-* + *inan* to empty out; perhaps akin to Sanskrit *iṣṇāti* he sets in motion] (15th century)
: an area of tissue that marks externally the approximate boundary of the outlet of the pelvis and gives passage to the urinogenital ducts and rectum; *also* : the area between the anus and the posterior part of the external genitalia
— **per·i·ne·al** \-'nē-əl\ *adjective*

peri·neu·ri·um \ˌper-ə-'nur-ē-əm, -'nyur-\ *noun, plural* **-ria** \-ē-ə\ [New Latin, from *peri-* + Greek *neuron* nerve — more at NERVE] (circa 1842)
: the connective-tissue sheath that surrounds a bundle of nerve fibers

¹pe·ri·od \'pir-ē-əd\ *noun* [Middle English *pariode*, from Middle French *periode*, from Medieval Latin, Latin, & Greek; Medieval Latin *periodus* period of time, punctuation mark, from Latin & Greek; Latin, rhetorical period, from Greek *periodos* circuit, period of time, rhetorical period, from *peri-* + *hodos* way] (circa 1530)
1 : the completion of a cycle, a series of events, or a single action : CONCLUSION
2 a (1) : an utterance from one full stop to another : SENTENCE (2) : a well-proportioned sentence of several clauses (3) : PERIODIC SENTENCE **b** : a musical structure or melodic section usually composed of two or more contrasting or complementary phrases and ending with a cadence
3 a : the full pause with which the utterance of a sentence closes **b** : END, STOP
4 *obsolete* : GOAL, PURPOSE
5 a : a point . used to mark the end (as of a declarative sentence or an abbreviation) — often used interjectionally to emphasize that no more need be said 〈I don't remember — *period*〉 **b** : a rhythmical unit in Greek verse composed of a series of two or more cola
6 a : a portion of time determined by some recurring phenomenon **b** (1) : the interval of time required for a cyclic motion or phenomenon to complete a cycle and begin to repeat it-

self (2) : a number *k* that does not change the value of a periodic function *f* when added to the independent variable; *especially* : the smallest such number **c** : a single cyclic occurrence of menstruation
7 a : a chronological division : STAGE **b** : a division of geologic time longer than an epoch and included in an era **c** : a stage of culture having a definable place in time and space
8 a : one of the divisions of the academic day **b** : one of the divisions of the playing time of a game ☆

²period *adjective* (1905)
: of, relating to, or representing a particular historical period 〈*period* furniture〉 〈*period* costumes〉

pe·ri·od·ic \ˌpir-ē-'ä-dik\ *adjective* (1642)
1 : occurring or recurring at regular intervals
2 a : consisting of or containing a series of repeated stages, processes, or digits : CYCLIC 〈*periodic* decimals〉 〈a *periodic* vibration〉 **b** : being a function any value of which recurs at regular intervals
3 : expressed in or characterized by periodic sentences

per·iod·ic acid \ˌpər-(ˌ)ī-'ä-dik-\ *noun* [International Scientific Vocabulary *per-* + *iodic*] (1836)
: any of the strongly oxidizing acids (as H_5IO_6 or HIO_4) that are the most highly oxidized acids of iodine

¹pe·ri·od·i·cal \ˌpir-ē-'ä-di-kəl\ *adjective* (1601)
1 : PERIODIC 1
2 a : published with a fixed interval between the issues or numbers **b** : published in, characteristic of, or connected with a periodical

²periodical *noun* (1798)
: a periodical publication

periodical cicada *noun* (1890)
: SEVENTEEN-YEAR LOCUST

pe·ri·od·i·cal·ly \ˌpir-ē-'ä-di-k(ə-)lē\ *adverb* (1646)
1 : at regular intervals of time
2 : from time to time : FREQUENTLY

pe·ri·od·ic·i·ty \ˌpir-ē-ə-'di-sə-tē\ *noun* (1833)
: the quality, state, or fact of being regularly recurrent or having periods

periodic law *noun* (1872)
: a law in chemistry: the elements when arranged in the order of their atomic numbers show a periodic variation of atomic structure and of most of their properties

periodic sentence *noun* (circa 1928)
: a usually complex sentence that has no subordinate or trailing elements following its principal clause (as in "yesterday while I was walking down the street, I saw him")

☆ **SYNONYMS**
Period, epoch, era, age mean a division of time. PERIOD may designate an extent of time of any length 〈*periods* of economic prosperity〉. EPOCH applies to a period begun or set off by some significant or striking quality, change, or series of events 〈the steam engine marked a new *epoch* in industry〉. ERA suggests a period of history marked by a new or distinct order of things 〈the *era* of global communications〉. AGE is used frequently of a fairly definite period dominated by a prominent figure or feature 〈the *age* of Samuel Johnson〉.

\ə\ **abut** \ᵊ\ **kitten** \ər\ **further** \a\ **ash** \ā\ **ace** \ä\ **mop, mar** \au̇\ **out** \ch\ **chin** \e\ **bet** \ē\ **easy** \g\ **go** \i\ **hit** \ī\ **ice** \j\ **job** \ŋ\ **sing** \ō\ **go** \ȯ\ **law** \ȯi\ **boy** \th\ **thin** \t͟h\ **the** \ü\ **loot** \u̇\ **foot** \y\ **yet** \zh\ **vision** *see also* Guide to Pronunciation

PERIODIC TABLE

This is a common long form of the table. Roman numerals and letters heading the vertical columns indicate the groups (there are differences of opinion regarding the letter designations, those given here being probably the most generally used). The horizontal rows represent the periods, with two series removed from the two very long periods and represented below the main table. Atomic numbers are given above the symbols for the elements. Compare ELEMENT table.

IA¹	IIA²	IIIB	IVB	VB	VIB	VIIB	VIII			IB	IIB	IIIA	IVA	VA	VIA	VIIA³	Zero⁴
1 H																1 H	2 He
3 Li	4 Be											5 B	6 C	7 N	8 O	9 F	10 Ne
11 Na	12 Mg											13 Al	14 Si	15 P	16 S	17 Cl	18 Ar
19 K	20 Ca	21 Sc	22 Ti	23 V	24 Cr	25 Mn	26 Fe	27 Co	28 Ni	29 Cu	30 Zn	31 Ga	32 Ge	33 As	34 Se	35 Br	36 Kr
37 Rb	38 Sr	39 Y	40 Zr	41 Nb	42 Mo	43 Tc	44 Ru	45 Rh	46 Pd	47 Ag	48 Cd	49 In	50 Sn	51 Sb	52 Te	53 I	54 Xe
55 Cs	56 Ba	57 *La	72 Hf	73 Ta	74 W	75 Re	76 Os	77 Ir	78 Pt	79 Au	80 Hg	81 Tl	82 Pb	83 Bi	84 Po	85 At	86 Rn
87 Fr	88 Ra	89 #Ac	104 Unq	105 Unp	106 Unh												

*LANTHANIDE SERIES	58 Ce	59 Pr	60 Nd	61 Pm	62 Sm	63 Eu	64 Gd	65 Tb	66 Dy	67 Ho	68 Er	69 Tm	70 Yb	71 Lu
#ACTINIDE SERIES	90 Th	91 Pa	92 U	93 Np	94 Pu	95 Am	96 Cm	97 Bk	98 Cf	99 Es	100 Fm	101 Md	102 No	103 Lr

¹ Group IA (excluding hydrogen) comprises the alkali metals.
² Group IIA comprises the alkaline-earth metals.
³ Group VIIA (excluding hydrogen) comprises the halogens.
⁴ Group Zero comprises the noble gases.

periodic table *noun* (1895)
: an arrangement of chemical elements based on the periodic law

pe·ri·od·i·za·tion \,pir-ē-ə-də-'zā-shən\ *noun* (1938)
: division (as of history) into periods

peri·odon·tal \,per-ē-ō-'dän-t°l\ *adjective* (1854)
1 : investing or surrounding a tooth
2 : of or affecting periodontal tissues or regions ⟨*periodontal* diseases⟩
— **peri·odon·tal·ly** \-t°l-ē\ *adverb*

periodontal membrane *noun* (circa 1903)
: the fibrous connective-tissue layer covering the cementum of a tooth and holding it in place in the jawbone

peri·odon·tics \-'dän-tiks\ *noun plural but singular or plural in construction* [New Latin *periodontium* periodontal tissue, from *peri-* + Greek *odont-, odous, odōn* tooth — more at TOOTH] (circa 1944)
: a branch of dentistry that deals with diseases of the supporting and investing structures of the teeth including the gums, cementum, periodontal membranes, and alveolar bone
— **peri·odon·tist** \-'dän-tist\ *noun*

peri·odon·tol·o·gy \-,dän-'tä-lə-jē\ *noun* (1914)
: PERIODONTICS

period piece *noun* (1940)
: a piece (as of fiction, art, furniture, or music) whose special value lies in its evocation of an historical period

peri·onych·i·um \,per-ē-ō-'ni-kē-əm\ *noun, plural* **-ia** \-kē-ə\ [New Latin, from *peri-* + Greek *onych-, onyx* nail — more at NAIL] (circa 1879)
: the tissue bordering the root and sides of a fingernail or toenail

peri·os·te·al \,per-ē-'äs-tē-əl\ *adjective* (1830)
1 : situated around or produced external to bone
2 : of, relating to, or involving the periosteum

peri·os·te·um \-tē-əm\ *noun, plural* **-tea** \-tē-ə\ [New Latin, from Late Latin *periosteon,* from Greek, neuter of *periosteos* around the bone, from *peri-* + *osteon* bone — more at OSSEOUS] (1597)
: the membrane of connective tissue that closely invests all bones except at the articular surfaces

peri·os·ti·tis \-,äs-'tī-təs\ *noun* [New Latin] (1843)
: inflammation of the periosteum

¹peri·pa·tet·ic \,per-ə-pə-'te-tik\ *noun* (15th century)
1 *capitalized* : a follower of Aristotle or adherent of Aristotelianism
2 : PEDESTRIAN, ITINERANT
3 *plural* : movement or journeys hither and thither

²peripatetic *adjective* [Middle French & Latin; Middle French *peripatetique,* from Latin *peripateticus,* from Greek *peripatētikos,* from *peripatein* to walk up and down, discourse while pacing (as did Aristotle), from *peri-* + *patein* to tread; akin to Sanskrit *patha* path — more at FIND] (1566)
1 : ARISTOTELIAN
2 a : of, relating to, or given to walking **b** : moving or traveling from place to place : ITINERANT
— **peri·pa·tet·i·cal·ly** \-ti-k(ə-)lē\ *adverb*
— **Peri·pa·tet·i·cism** \-'te-tə-,si-zəm\ *noun*

pe·rip·a·tus \pə-'ri-pə-təs\ *noun* [New Latin, genus name, from Greek *peripatos* act of

walking about, from *peri-* + *patein* to tread] (circa 1931)
: any of a class or phylum (Onychophora) of primitive tropical wormlike invertebrates that appear intermediate between annelid worms and arthropods

peri·pe·teia \,per-ə-pə-'tē-ə, -'tī-\ *noun* [Greek, from *peripiptein* to fall around, change suddenly, from *peri-* + *piptein* to fall — more at FEATHER] (1591)
: a sudden or unexpected reversal of circumstances or situation especially in a literary work

pe·rip·e·ty \pə-'ri-pə-tē\ *noun, plural* **-ties** (1753)
: PERIPETEIA

¹pe·riph·er·al \pə-'ri-f(ə-)rəl\ *adjective* (1808)
1 : of, relating to, involving, or forming a periphery or surface part
2 : of, relating to, or being part of the peripheral nervous system ⟨*peripheral* nerves⟩
3 : of, relating to, or being the outer part of the field of vision ⟨good *peripheral* vision⟩
4 : AUXILIARY, SUPPLEMENTARY ⟨*peripheral* equipment⟩; *also* : of or relating to computer peripherals
— **pe·riph·er·al·ly** *adverb*

²peripheral *noun* (1966)
: a device connected to a computer to provide communication (as input and output) or auxiliary functions (as additional storage)

peripheral nervous system *noun* (1935)
: the part of the nervous system that is outside the central nervous system and comprises the cranial nerves excepting the optic nerve, the spinal nerves, and the autonomic nervous system

pe·riph·ery \pə-'ri-f(ə-)rē\ *noun, plural* **-er·ies** [Middle French *peripherie,* from Late

Latin *peripheria,* from Greek *periphereia,* from *peripherein* to carry around, from *peri-* + *pherein* to carry — more at BEAR (1571)
1 : the perimeter of a circle or other closed curve; *also* : the perimeter of a polygon
2 : the external boundary or surface of a body
3 a : the outward bounds of something as distinguished from its internal regions or center : CONFINES **b** : an area lying beyond the strict limits of a thing
pe·riph·ra·sis \pə-'ri-frə-səs\ *noun, plural* **-ra·ses** \-ˌsēz\ [Latin, from Greek, from *periphrazein* to express periphrastically, from *peri-* + *phrazein* to point out] (1533)
1 : use of a longer phrasing in place of a possible shorter form of expression
2 : an instance of periphrasis
peri·phras·tic \ˌper-ə-'fras-tik\ *adjective* (1805)
1 : of, relating to, or characterized by periphrasis
2 : formed by the use of function words or auxiliaries instead of by inflection ⟨*more fair* is a *periphrastic* comparative⟩
— **peri·phras·ti·cal·ly** \-ti-k(ə-)lē\ *adverb*
pe·riph·y·ton \pə-'ri-fə-ˌtän\ *noun* [New Latin, from Greek *periphytos* (verbal of *periphyein* to grow around, from *peri-* + *phyein* to bring forth, grow) + *-on* (as in *plankton*) — more at BE] (1945)
: organisms (as some algae) that live attached to underwater surfaces
— **peri·phyt·ic** \ˌper-ə-'fi-tik\ *adjective*
peri·plast \'per-ə-ˌplast\ *noun* (1853)
: PLASMA MEMBRANE; *also* : a proteinaceous subcellular layer below the plasma membrane especially of a euglena
pe·rique \pə-'rēk\ *noun* [Louisiana French *périque*] (1882)
: an aromatic fermented Louisiana tobacco used in smoking mixtures
peri·sarc \'per-ə-ˌsärk\ *noun* [International Scientific Vocabulary *peri-* + Greek *sark-, sarx* flesh — more at SARCASM] (circa 1871)
: the outer usually chitinous integument of a hydroid
peri·scope \-ˌskōp\ *noun* [International Scientific Vocabulary] (1879)
: a tubular optical instrument containing lenses and mirrors by which an observer obtains an otherwise obstructed field of view
peri·scop·ic \ˌper-ə-'skä-pik\ *adjective* (1804)
1 : providing a view all around or on all sides ⟨*periscopic* lens⟩
2 : of or relating to a periscope
per·ish \'per-ish\ *verb* [Middle English *perisshen,* from Old French *periss-,* stem of *perir,* from Latin *perire,* from *per-* detrimentally + *ire* to go — more at PER-, ISSUE] (13th century)
intransitive verb
1 : to become destroyed or ruined : DIE ⟨recollection of a past already long since *perished* —Philip Sherrard⟩ ⟨guard against your mistakes or your attempts ⟨*perish* the thought⟩ to cheat —C. B. Davis⟩
2 *chiefly British* : DETERIORATE, SPOIL
transitive verb
1 *chiefly British* : to cause to die : DESTROY
2 : WEAKEN, BENUMB
per·ish·able \'per-i-shə-bəl\ *adjective* (circa 1611)
: liable to perish : liable to spoil or decay ⟨such *perishable* products as fruit, vegetables, butter, and eggs⟩
— **per·ish·abil·i·ty** \ˌper-i-shə-'bi-lə-tē\ *noun*
— **perishable** *noun*
pe·ris·so·dac·tyl \pə-'ri-sə-ˌdak-t°l\ *noun*

[New Latin *Perissodactyla,* from Greek *perissos* excessive, odd in number + *daktylos* finger, toe] (1849)
: any of an order (Perissodactyla) of nonruminant ungulate mammals (as a horse, a tapir, or a rhinoceros) that usually have an odd number of toes, molar teeth with transverse ridges on the grinding surface, and the posterior premolars resembling true molars
— **perissodactyl** *adjective*
peri·stal·sis \ˌper-ə-'stòl-səs, -'stäl-, -'stal-\ *noun, plural* **-stal·ses** \-ˌsēz\ [New Latin, from Greek *peristaltikos* peristaltic] (1859)
: successive waves of involuntary contraction passing along the walls of a hollow muscular structure (as the esophagus or intestine) and forcing the contents onward
peri·stal·tic \-tik\ *adjective* [Greek *peristaltikos,* from *peristellein* to wrap around, from *peri-* + *stellein* to place] (1655)
1 : of, relating to, resulting from, or being peristalsis
2 : having an action suggestive of peristalsis
peristaltic pump *noun* (1962)
: a pump in which fluid is forced along by waves of contraction produced mechanically on flexible tubing
peri·stome \'per-ə-ˌstōm\ *noun* [New Latin *peristoma,* from *peri-* + Greek *stoma* mouth — more at STOMACH] (circa 1796)
1 : the fringe of teeth surrounding the orifice of a moss capsule
2 : the region around the mouth in various invertebrates
— **peri·sto·mi·al** \ˌper-ə-'stō-mē-əl\ *adjective*
peri·style \'per-ə-ˌstīl\ *noun* [French *péristyle,* from Latin *peristylum,* from Greek *peristylon,* from neuter of *peristylos* surrounded by a colonnade, from *peri-* + *stylos* pillar — more at STEER] (1612)
1 : a colonnade surrounding a building or court
2 : an open space enclosed by a colonnade
peri·the·ci·um \ˌper-ə-'thē-shē-əm, -sē-\ *noun, plural* **-cia** \-shē-ə, -sē-\ [New Latin, from *peri-* + Greek *thēkion,* diminutive of *thēkē* case — more at TICK] (circa 1832)
: a spherical, cylindrical, or flask-shaped hollow fruiting body in various ascomycetous fungi that contains the asci and usually opens by a terminal pore
— **peri·the·cial** \-'thē-sh(ē-)əl, -sē-əl\ *adjective*
peri·to·ne·um \ˌper-ə-t°n-'ē-əm\ *noun, plural* **-ne·ums** \-'ē-əmz\ *or* **-nea** \-'ē-ə\ [Middle English, from Late Latin, from Greek *peritonaion,* neuter of *peritonaios* stretched around, from *peri-* + *teinein* to stretch — more at THIN] (15th century)
: the smooth transparent serous membrane that lines the cavity of the abdomen of a mammal and is folded inward over the abdominal and pelvic viscera
— **peri·to·ne·al** \-'ē-əl\ *adjective*
— **peri·to·ne·al·ly** \-ə-lē\ *adverb*
peri·to·ni·tis \ˌper-ə-t°n-'ī-təs\ *noun* [New Latin] (1776)
: inflammation of the peritoneum
pe·rit·ri·chous \pə-'ri-tri-kəs\ *adjective* [*peri-* + Greek *trich-, thrix* hair] (1877)
1 : having flagella uniformly distributed over the body ⟨*peritrichous* bacteria⟩
2 : having a spiral line of modified cilia around the oral disk ⟨*peritrichous* protozoa⟩
— **pe·rit·ri·chous·ly** *adverb*
peri·wig \'per-i-ˌwig\ *noun* [modification of Middle French *perruque* — more at PERUKE] (1529)
: PERUKE
— **peri·wigged** \-ˌwigd\ *adjective*
¹per·i·win·kle \'per-i-ˌwin-kəl\ *noun* [Middle English *perwinke,* from Old English *perwince,* from (assumed) Vulgar Latin *pervinca,* short for Latin *vincapervinca*] (before 12th century)
1 : any of several trailing or woody evergreen

herbs of the dogbane family: as **a** : a European creeper (*Vinca minor*) widely cultivated as a ground cover and for its blue or white flowers — called also *myrtle* **b** : a commonly cultivated subshrub (*Catharanthus roseus* synonym *Vinca rosea*) of the Old World tropics that is the source of several antineoplastic drugs — called also *Madagascar periwinkle*
2 : a light purplish blue — called also *periwinkle blue*
²periwinkle *noun* [(assumed) Middle English, alteration of Old English *pīnewincle,* from Latin *pina,* a kind of mussel (from Greek) + Old English *-wincle* (akin to Danish *vincle* snail shell)] (circa 1530)
: any of various gastropod mollusks: as **a** : any of a genus (*Littorina*) of edible littoral marine snails; *also* : any of various similar or related marine snails **b** : any of several North American freshwater snails

²periwinkle a

per·jure \'pər-jər\ *transitive verb* **per·jured; per·jur·ing** \'pər-jə-riŋ, 'pərj-riŋ\ [Middle French *perjurer,* from Latin *perjurare,* from *per-* detrimentally, for the worse + *jurare* to swear — more at PER-, JURY] (1535)
1 : to make a perjurer of (oneself)
2 *obsolete* : to cause to commit perjury
per·jur·er \'pər-jər-ər\ *noun* (15th century)
: a person guilty of perjury
per·ju·ri·ous \(ˌ)pər-'jùr-ē-əs\ *adjective* (1602)
: marked by perjury ⟨*perjurious* testimony⟩
— **per·ju·ri·ous·ly** *adverb*
per·ju·ry \'pər-jə-rē, 'pərj-rē\ *noun* (14th century)
: the voluntary violation of an oath or vow either by swearing to what is untrue or by omission to do what has been promised under oath : false swearing
¹perk \'pərk\ *verb* [Middle English] (14th century)
intransitive verb
1 a : to thrust up the head, stretch out the neck, or carry the body in a bold or insolent manner **b** : to stick up or out jauntily
2 : to gain in vigor or cheerfulness especially after a period of weakness or depression — usually used with *up* ⟨he's *perked* up noticeably⟩
transitive verb
1 : to make smart or spruce in appearance : FRESHEN, IMPROVE
2 : to thrust up quickly or impudently
²perk *intransitive verb* (1656)
: PERCOLATE
³perk *noun* (1824)
: PERQUISITE — usually used in plural
perky \'pər-kē\ *adjective* **perk·i·er; -est** (1855)
1 : briskly self-assured : COCKY
2 : JAUNTY ⟨a *perky* . . . waltz —*New Yorker*⟩
— **perk·i·ly** \-kə-lē\ *adverb*
— **perk·i·ness** \-kē-nəs\ *noun*
per·lite \'pər-ˌlīt\ *noun* [French, from *perle* pearl] (1833)
: volcanic glass that has a concentric shelly structure, appears as if composed of concretions, is usually grayish and sometimes spherulitic, and when expanded by heat forms a lightweight aggregate used especially in concrete and plaster and as a medium for potting plants
— **per·lit·ic** \ˌpər-'li-tik\ *adjective*
¹perm \'pərm\ *noun* (1927)
: PERMANENT
²perm *transitive verb* (1928)
: to give (hair) a permanent wave

\ə\ abut \ᵊ\ kitten \ər\ further \a\ ash \ā\ ace
\ä\ mop, mar \aù\ out \ch\ chin \e\ bet \ē\ easy
\g\ go \i\ hit \ī\ ice \j\ job \ŋ\ sing \ō\ go
\ò\ law \òi\ boy \th\ thin \th\ the \ü\ loot \ù\ foot
\y\ yet \zh\ vision *see also* Guide to Pronunciation

per·ma·frost \'pər-mə-ˌfrȯst\ *noun* [*permanent* + *frost*] (1943)
: a permanently frozen layer at variable depth below the surface in frigid regions of a planet (as earth)

per·ma·nence \'pər-mə-nən(t)s, 'pərm-nən(t)s\ *noun* (15th century)
: the quality or state of being permanent : DURABILITY

per·ma·nen·cy \-nən(t)-sē\ *noun, plural* **-cies** (1555)
1 : PERMANENCE
2 : something permanent

¹**per·ma·nent** \-nənt\ *adjective* [Middle English, from Middle French, from Latin *permanent-, permanens*, present participle of *permanēre* to endure, from *per-* throughout + *manēre* to remain — more at PER-, MANSION] (15th century)
: continuing or enduring without fundamental or marked change : STABLE
synonym see LASTING
— **per·ma·nent·ly** *adverb*
— **per·ma·nent·ness** *noun*

²**permanent** *noun* (1925)
: a long-lasting hair wave or straightening produced by mechanical and chemical means — called also *permanent wave*

permanent magnet *noun* (1828)
: a magnet that retains its magnetism after removal of the magnetizing force

permanent press *noun* (1964)
1 : the process of treating a fabric with a chemical (as a resin) and heat for setting the shape and for aiding wrinkle resistance
2 : material treated by permanent press
3 : the condition of material treated by permanent press
— **permanent–press** *adjective*

permanent tissue *noun* (circa 1928)
: plant tissue that has completed its growth and differentiation and is usually incapable of meristematic activity

permanent tooth *noun* (1836)
: any of the second set of teeth of a mammal that follow the milk teeth, typically persist into old age, and in humans are 32 in number

per·man·ga·nate \(ˌ)pər-'maŋ-gə-ˌnāt\ *noun* (1841)
1 : a salt containing the anion MnO₄⁻; *especially* : POTASSIUM PERMANGANATE
2 : the anion MnO_4^- of a permanganate

per·me·abil·i·ty \ˌpər-mē-ə-'bi-lə-tē\ *noun* (1759)
1 : the quality or state of being permeable
2 : the property of a magnetizable substance that determines the degree in which it modifies the magnetic flux in the region occupied by it in a magnetic field

per·me·able \'pər-mē-ə-bəl\ *adjective* (15th century)
: capable of being permeated : PENETRABLE; *especially* : having pores or openings that permit liquids or gases to pass through ⟨a *permeable* membrane⟩ ⟨*permeable* limestone⟩

per·me·ase \'pər-mē-ˌās, -ˌāz\ *noun* [International Scientific Vocabulary *perme-* (from *permeate*) + *-ase*] (1957)
: a substance that catalyzes the transport of another substance across a cell membrane

per·me·ate \'pər-mē-ˌāt\ *verb* **-at·ed; -at·ing** [Latin *permeatus*, past participle of *permeare*, from *per-* through + *meare* to go, pass; akin to Middle Welsh *mynet* to go, Czech *míjet* to pass] (1656)
intransitive verb
: to diffuse through or penetrate something
transitive verb
1 : to spread or diffuse through ⟨a room *permeated* with tobacco smoke⟩
2 : to pass through the pores or interstices of
— **per·me·ative** \-ˌā-tiv\ *adjective*

per·me·ation \ˌpər-mē-'ā-shən\ *noun* (circa 1623)
1 : the quality or state of being permeated
2 : the action or process of permeating

per men·sem \(ˌ)pər-'men(t)-səm\ *adverb* [Medieval Latin] (1647)
: by the month

per·meth·rin \(ˌ)pər-'me-thrən\ *noun* [*per-* + *methyl* + *pyrethrin*] (1976)
: a synthetic pyrethrin $C_{21}H_{20}Cl_2O_3$ used especially as an insecticide

Perm·ian \'pər-mē-ən, 'per-\ *adjective* [*Perm*, former province in eastern Russia] (1841)
: of, relating to, or being the last period of the Paleozoic era or the corresponding system of rocks — see GEOLOGIC TIME table
— **Permian** *noun*

per mill \(ˌ)pər-'mil\ *adverb* [*per* + Latin *mille* thousand] (1902)
: per thousand
— **per·mil·lage** \(ˌ)pər-'mi-lij\ *noun*

per·mis·si·ble \pər-'mi-sə-bəl\ *adjective* [Middle English, from Medieval Latin *permissibilis*, from Latin *permissus*, past participle of *permittere*] (15th century)
: that may be permitted : ALLOWABLE
— **per·mis·si·bil·i·ty** \-ˌmi-sə-'bi-lə-tē\ *noun*
— **per·mis·si·ble·ness** \-'mi-sə-bəl-nəs\ *noun*
— **per·mis·si·bly** \-blē\ *adverb*

per·mis·sion \pər-'mi-shən\ *noun* [Middle English, from Middle French, from Latin *permission-, permissio*, from *permittere*] (15th century)
1 : the act of permitting
2 : formal consent : AUTHORIZATION

per·mis·sive \pər-'mi-siv\ *adjective* [Middle English *permyssyf*, from Middle French *permissif*, from Latin *permissus*] (15th century)
1 *archaic* : granted on sufferance : TOLERATED
2 a : granting or tending to grant permission : TOLERANT **b** : deficient in firmness or control : INDULGENT, LAX
3 : allowing discretion : OPTIONAL ⟨reduced the *permissive* retirement age from 65 to 62⟩
— **per·mis·sive·ly** *adverb*
— **per·mis·sive·ness** *noun*

¹**per·mit** \pər-'mit\ *verb* **per·mit·ted; per·mit·ting** [Middle English *permitten*, from Latin *permittere* to let through, permit, from *per-* through + *mittere* to let go, send] (15th century)
transitive verb
1 : to consent to expressly or formally ⟨*permit* access to records⟩
2 : to give leave : AUTHORIZE
3 : to make possible
intransitive verb
: to give an opportunity ⟨if time *permits*⟩
— **per·mit·tee** \pər-ˌmi(t)-'tē, ˌpər-mi(t)-\ *noun*
— **per·mit·ter** *noun*

²**per·mit** \'pər-ˌmit, pər-'\ *noun* (1682)
1 : a written warrant or license granted by one having authority ⟨a gun *permit*⟩
2 : PERMISSION

³**permit** *noun* [perhaps by folk etymology from Spanish *palometa*, a kind of pompano, from diminutive of *paloma* dove, from Latin *palumba, palumbes* — more at PALOMINO] (circa 1945)
: either of two pompanos (*Trachinotus falcatus* and *T. goodei*) that are important game fishes of temperate to tropical waters of the western Atlantic

per·mit·tiv·i·ty \ˌpər-ˌmi-'ti-və-tē, -mə-\ *noun* [¹*permit* + *-ivity* (as in *selectivity*)] (1887)
: the ability of a dielectric to store electrical potential energy under the influence of an electric field measured by the ratio of the capacitance of a condenser with the material as dielectric to its capacitance with vacuum as dielectric — called also *dielectric constant*

per·mu·ta·tion \ˌpər-myù-'tā-shən\ *noun* [Middle English *permutacioun* exchange, transformation, from Middle French *permutation*, from Latin *permutation-, permutatio*, from *permutare*] (14th century)
1 : often major or fundamental change (as in

character or condition) based primarily on rearrangement of existent elements ⟨land-owners and peasants . . . in the *permutations* of their tortured interdependence —P. E. Mosley⟩
2 a : the act or process of changing the lineal order of an ordered set of objects **b** : an ordered arrangement of a set of objects
— **per·mu·ta·tion·al** \-shnəl, -shə-nᵊl\ *adjective*

permutation group *noun* (1904)
: a group whose elements are permutations and in which the product of two permutations is a permutation whose effect is the same as the successive application of the first two

per·mute \pər-'myüt\ *transitive verb* **per·mut·ed; per·mut·ing** [Middle English, to exchange, from Middle French or Latin; Middle French *permuter*, from Latin *permutare*, from *per-* + *mutare* to change — more at MUTABLE] (1878)
: to change the order or arrangement of; *especially* : to arrange in all possible ways
— **per·mut·able** \-'myü-tə-bəl\ *adjective*

per·ni·cious \pər-'ni-shəs\ *adjective* [Middle English, from Middle French *pernicieus*, from Latin *perniciosus*, from *pernicies* destruction, from *per-* + *nec-, nex* violent death — more at NOXIOUS] (15th century)
1 : highly injurious or destructive : DEADLY
2 *archaic* : WICKED ☆
— **per·ni·cious·ly** *adverb*
— **per·ni·cious·ness** *noun*

pernicious anemia *noun* (1874)
: a severe megaloblastic anemia marked by a progressive decrease in the number of red blood cells and by pallor, weakness, and gastrointestinal and nervous disturbances and associated with malabsorption of vitamin B_{12} due to the absence of intrinsic factor

per·nick·e·ty \pər-'ni-kə-tē\ *adjective* [origin unknown] (circa 1818)
: PERSNICKETY

Per·nod \per-'nō, ˌpər-\ *trademark*
— used for a French liqueur

pe·ro·ne·al \ˌper-ō-'nē-əl, pə-'rō-nē-\ *adjective* [New Latin *peroneus*, from *perone* fibula, from Greek *peronē*, literally, pin, from *peirein* to pierce — more at DIAPIR] (1831)
: of, relating to, or located near the fibula

per·oral \(ˌ)pər-'ōr-əl, per-, -'ȯr-, -'är-\ *adjective* [International Scientific Vocabulary] (1908)
: occurring through or by way of the mouth
— **per·oral·ly** \-ə-lē\ *adverb*

per·o·rate \'per-ə-ˌrāt *also* 'pər-\ *intransitive verb* **-rat·ed; -rat·ing** [Latin *peroratus*, past participle of *perorare* to declaim at length, wind up an oration, from *per-* through + *orare* to speak — more at PER-, ORATION] (1603)
1 : to deliver a long or grandiloquent oration
2 : to make a peroration

per·o·ra·tion \ˌper-ə-'rā-shən *also* ˌpər-\ *noun* [Middle English *peroracyon*, from Latin *peroration-, peroratio*, from *perorare*] (15th century)

☆ **SYNONYMS**
Pernicious, baneful, noxious, deleterious, detrimental mean exceedingly harmful. PERNICIOUS implies irreparable harm done through evil or insidious corrupting or undermining ⟨the claim that pornography has a *pernicious* effect on society⟩. BANEFUL implies injury through poisoning or destroying ⟨the *baneful* notion that discipline destroys creativity⟩. NOXIOUS applies to what is both offensive and injurious to the health of a body or mind ⟨*noxious* chemical fumes⟩. DELETERIOUS applies to what has an often unsuspected harmful effect ⟨a diet found to have *deleterious* effects⟩. DETRIMENTAL implies obvious harmfulness to something specified ⟨the *detrimental* effects of excessive drinking⟩.

1 : the concluding part of a discourse and especially an oration
2 : a highly rhetorical speech
— **per·o·ra·tion·al** \,per-ə-'rā-shnəl, ,pər-, -shə-nᵊl\ *adjective*
pe·rov·skite \pə-'räv-,skīt, -'räf-\ *noun* [German *Perowskit*, from Count L. A. *Perovskiĭ* (died 1856) Russian statesman] (1840)
: a yellow, brown, or grayish black mineral sometimes containing rare earth elements
per·ox·i·dase \pə-'räk-sə-,dās, -,dāz\ *noun* (1900)
: an enzyme that catalyzes the oxidation of various substances by peroxides
¹per·ox·ide \pə-'räk-,sīd\ *noun* [International Scientific Vocabulary] (1804)
: an oxide containing a high proportion of oxygen; *especially* **:** a compound (as hydrogen peroxide) in which oxygen is visualized as joined to oxygen
— **per·ox·id·ic** \-,räk-'si-dik\ *adjective*
²peroxide *transitive verb* **-id·ed; -id·ing** (1906)
: to treat with a peroxide; *especially* **:** to bleach (hair) with hydrogen peroxide
³peroxide *adjective* (1920)
: having or being bleached hair ⟨a *peroxide* blonde⟩
per·ox·i·some \pə-'räk-sə-,sōm\ *noun* [*peroxide* + ³*-some*] (1965)
: a cytoplasmic cell organelle containing enzymes (as catalase) which act in oxidative reactions and especially in the production and decomposition of hydrogen peroxide
— **per·ox·i·som·al** \-,räk-sə-'sō-məl\ *adjective*
peroxy- *combining form* [International Scientific Vocabulary *per-* + *oxy*]
: containing the bivalent group O—O ⟨*peroxy*-acetyl nitrate⟩
per·oxy·ace·tyl nitrate \pə-,räk-sē-ə-'sē-tᵊl-; -'as-ə-tᵊl-, -,tēl-\ *noun* (1963)
: a toxic compound $C_2H_3O_5N$ found especially in smog
per·pend \(,)pər-'pend\ *verb* [Middle English, from Latin *perpendere*, from *per-* thoroughly + *pendere* to weigh — more at PER-, PENDANT] (15th century)
transitive verb
: to reflect on carefully **:** PONDER
intransitive verb
: to be attentive **:** REFLECT
¹per·pen·dic·u·lar \,pər-pən-'di-kyə-lər\ *adjective* [Middle English *perpendiculer*, from Middle French, from Latin *perpendicularis*, from *perpendiculum* plumb line, from *per-* + *pendēre* to hang — more at PENDANT] (14th century)
1 a : standing at right angles to the plane of the horizon **:** exactly upright **b :** being at right angles to a given line or plane
2 : extremely steep **:** PRECIPITOUS
3 *often capitalized* **:** of or relating to a medieval English Gothic style of architecture in which vertical lines predominate
4 : relating to, uniting, or consisting of individuals of dissimilar type or on different levels
synonym see VERTICAL
— **per·pen·dic·u·lar·i·ty** \-,di-kyə-'lar-ə-tē\ *noun*
— **per·pen·dic·u·lar·ly** \-'di-kyə-lər-lē\ *adverb*
²perpendicular *noun* (1571)
: a line at right angles to a line or plane (as of the horizon)
per·pe·trate \'pər-pə-,trāt\ *transitive verb* **-trat·ed; -trat·ing** [Latin *perpetratus*, past participle of *perpetrare*, from *per-* through + *patrare* to accomplish, from *pater* father — more at FATHER] (1537)
: to bring about or carry out (as a crime or deception) **:** COMMIT
— **per·pe·tra·tion** \,pər-pə-'trā-shən\ *noun*
— **per·pe·tra·tor** \'pər-pə-,trā-tər\ *noun*
per·pet·u·al \pər-'pe-chə-wəl, -chəl; -'pech-wəl\ *adjective* [Middle English *perpetuel*,

from Middle French, from Latin *perpetuus* uninterrupted, from *per-* through + *petere* to go to — more at FEATHER] (14th century)
1 a : continuing forever **:** EVERLASTING **b** (1) **:** valid for all time (2) **:** holding (as an office) for life or for an unlimited time
2 : occurring continually **:** indefinitely long-continued
3 : blooming continuously through the season
synonym see CONTINUAL
— **per·pet·u·al·ly** *adverb*
perpetual calendar *noun* (1895)
: a table for finding the day of the week for any one of a wide range of dates
perpetual check *noun* (circa 1909)
: an endless succession of checks to which an opponent's king may be subjected to force a draw in chess
per·pet·u·ate \pər-'pe-chə-,wāt\ *transitive verb* **-at·ed; -at·ing** [Latin *perpetuatus*, past participle of *perpetuare*, from *perpetuus*] (1530)
: to make perpetual or cause to last indefinitely ⟨*perpetuate* the species⟩
— **per·pet·u·a·tion** \-,pe-chə-'wā-shən\ *noun*
— **per·pet·u·a·tor** \-'pe-chə-,wā-tər\ *noun*
per·pe·tu·i·ty \,pər-pə-'tü-ə-tē, -'tyü-\ *noun, plural* **-ties** [Middle English *perpetuite*, from Middle French *perpetuité*, from Latin *perpetuitat-*, *perpetuitas*, from *perpetuus*] (15th century)
1 : ETERNITY 2
2 : the quality or state of being perpetual ⟨bequeathed to them in *perpetuity*⟩
3 a : the condition of an estate limited so that it will not take effect or vest within the period fixed by law **b :** an estate so limited
4 : an annuity payable forever
per·phe·na·zine \(,)pər-'fē-nə-,zēn, -'fe-\ *noun* [blend of *piperazine* and *phen-*] (1957)
: a tranquilizing drug $C_{21}H_{26}ClN_3OS$ that is used to control tension, anxiety, and agitation especially in psychotic conditions
per·plex \pər-'pleks\ *transitive verb* [obsolete *perplex*, adjective, involved, perplexed, from Latin *perplexus*, from *per-* thoroughly + *plexus* involved, from past participle of *plectere* to braid, twine — more at PER-, PLY] (1593)
1 : to make unable to grasp something clearly or to think logically and decisively about something ⟨her attitude *perplexes* me⟩ ⟨a *perplexing* problem⟩
2 : to make intricate or involved **:** COMPLICATE
synonym see PUZZLE
per·plexed \-'plekst\ *adjective* (15th century)
1 : filled with uncertainty **:** PUZZLED
2 : full of difficulty
— **per·plexed·ly** \-'plek-səd-lē, -'plekst-lē\ *adverb*
per·plex·i·ty \pər-'plek-sə-tē\ *noun, plural* **-ties** [Middle English *perplexite*, from Middle French *perplexité*, from Late Latin *perplexitat-*, *perplexitas*, from Latin *perplexus*] (14th century)
1 : the state of being perplexed
2 : something that perplexes
3 : ENTANGLEMENT
per·qui·site \'pər-kwə-zət\ *noun* [Middle English, property acquired by means other than inheritance, from Medieval Latin *perquisitum*, from neuter of *perquisitus*, past participle of *perquirere* to purchase, acquire, from Latin, to search for thoroughly, from *per-* thoroughly + *quaerere* to seek] (15th century)
1 : a privilege, gain, or profit incidental to regular salary or wages; *especially* **:** one expected or promised
2 : GRATUITY, TIP
3 : something held or claimed as an exclusive right or possession ⟨concepts . . . not the *perquisites* of any particular groups —Gilbert Ryle⟩
per·ron \'per-ən, pe-rōⁿ\ *noun* [French, from Old French, from *perre*, *pierre* rock, stone, from Latin *petra*, from Greek] (1723)

: an outdoor stairway leading up to a building entrance; *also* **:** a platform at its top
per·ry \'per-ē\ *noun* [Middle English *peirrie*, from Middle French *peré*, from (assumed) Vulgar Latin *piratum*, from Latin *pirum* pear] (14th century)
: fermented pear juice often made sparkling
perse \'pərs\ *adjective* [Middle English *pers*, from Middle French, from Medieval Latin *persus*] (15th century)
: of a dark grayish blue resembling indigo
per se \(,)pər-'sā *also* per-'sä *or* (,)pər-'sē\ *adverb* [Latin] (1572)
: by, of, or in itself or oneself or themselves **:** as such **:** INTRINSICALLY
per second per second *adverb* (1922)
: per second every second — used of acceleration
per·se·cute \'pər-si-,kyüt\ *transitive verb* **-cut·ed; -cut·ing** [Middle English, from Middle French *persecuter*, back-formation from *persecuteur* persecutor, from Late Latin *persecutor*, from *persequi* to persecute, from Latin, to pursue, from *per-* through + *sequi* to follow — more at SUE] (15th century)
1 : to harass in a manner designed to injure, grieve, or afflict; *specifically* **:** to cause to suffer because of belief
2 : to annoy with persistent or urgent approaches (as attacks, pleas, or importunities) **:** PESTER
synonym see WRONG
— **per·se·cu·tee** \,pər-si-,kyü-'tē\ *noun*
— **per·se·cu·tive** \'pər-si-,kyü-tiv\ *adjective*
— **per·se·cu·tor** \-,kyü-tər\ *noun*
— **per·se·cu·to·ry** \-,kyü-,tōr-ē, -,tor-; -,kyü-tə-rē\ *adjective*
per·se·cu·tion \,pər-si-'kyü-shən\ *noun* (14th century)
1 : the act or practice of persecuting especially those who differ in origin, religion, or social outlook
2 : the condition of being persecuted, harassed, or annoyed
Per·se·id \'pər-sē-əd\ *noun* [Latin *Perseus*; from their appearing to radiate from a point in Perseus]
: any of a group of meteors that appear annually about August 11
Per·seph·o·ne \pər-'se-fə-nē\ *noun* [Latin, from Greek *Persephonē*]
: a daughter of Zeus and Demeter abducted by Pluto to reign with him over the underworld
Per·seus \'pər-,süs, -sē-əs\ *noun* [Latin, from Greek]
1 : a son of Zeus and Danaë and slayer of Medusa
2 [Latin (genitive *Persei*), from Greek] **:** a northern constellation between Taurus and Cassiopeia
per·se·ver·ance \,pər-sə-'vir-ən(t)s\ *noun* (14th century)
: the action or condition or an instance of persevering **:** STEADFASTNESS
per·sev·er·a·tion \pər-,se-və-'rā-shən\ *noun* [Latin *perseveration-*, *perseveratio*, from *perseverare*] (1910)
: continuation of something (as repetition of a word) usually to an exceptional degree or beyond a desired point
— **per·sev·er·ate** \-'se-və-,rāt\ *intransitive verb*
per·se·vere \,pər-sə-'vir\ *intransitive verb* **-vered; -ver·ing** [Middle English, from Middle French *perseverer*, from Latin *perseverare*, from *per-* through + *severus* severe] (14th century)
: to persist in a state, enterprise, or undertak-

\ə\ abut \ᵊ\ kitten \ər\ further \a\ ash \ā\ ace
\ä\ mop, mar \au̇\ out \ch\ chin \e\ bet \ē\ easy
\g\ go \i\ hit \ī\ ice \j\ job \ŋ\ sing \ō\ go
\ȯ\ law \ȯi\ boy \th\ thin \t͟h\ the \ü\ loot \u̇\ foot
\y\ yet \zh\ vision *see also* Guide to Pronunciation

ing in spite of counterinfluences, opposition, or discouragement
— **per·se·ver·ing·ly** *adverb*
Per·sian \'pər-zhən, *especially British* -shən\ *noun* (14th century)
1 : one of the people of Persia: as **a :** one of the ancient Iranians who under Cyrus and his successors founded an empire in southwest Asia **b :** a member of one of the peoples forming the modern Iranian nationality
2 a : any of several Iranian languages dominant in Persia at different periods **b :** the modern language of Iran and western Afghanistan — see INDO-EUROPEAN LANGUAGES table
3 : a thin soft silk formerly used especially for linings
4 : PERSIAN CAT
— **Persian** *adjective*
Persian cat *noun* (1824)
: any of a breed of stocky round-headed domestic cats that have a long silky coat and thick ruff

Persian cat

Persian lamb *noun* (1889)
1 : a pelt that is obtained from karakul lambs older than those yielding broadtail and that is characterized by very silky tightly curled fur
2 : the young of the karakul sheep that furnishes skins used in furriery
per·si·flage \'pər-si-ˌfläzh, 'per-\ *noun* [French, from *persifler* to banter, from *per-* thoroughly + *siffler* to whistle, hiss, boo, ultimately from Latin *sibilare*] (1757)
: frivolous bantering talk : light raillery
per·sim·mon \pər-'si-mən\ *noun* [Virginia Algonquian *pessemmin*] (1612)

Persian lamb 2

1 : any of a genus (*Diospyros*) of trees of the ebony family with hard fine wood, oblong leaves, and small bell-shaped flowers; *especially* : an American tree (*D. virginiana*) or a Japanese tree (*D. kaki*)
2 : the usually orange several-seeded globular berry of a persimmon that is edible when fully ripe but usually extremely astringent when unripe
per·sist \pər-'sist, -'zist\ *intransitive verb* [Middle French *persister*, from Latin *persistere*, from *per-* + *sistere* to take a stand, stand firm; akin to Latin *stare* to stand — more at STAND] (1538)
1 : to go on resolutely or stubbornly in spite of opposition, importunity, or warning
2 *obsolete* **:** to remain unchanged or fixed in a specified character, condition, or position
3 : to be insistent in the repetition or pressing of an utterance (as a question or an opinion)
4 : to continue to exist especially past a usual, expected, or normal time
synonym see CONTINUE
— **per·sist·er** *noun*
per·sis·tence \pər-'sis-tən(t)s, -'zis-\ *noun* (1546)
1 : the action or fact of persisting
2 : the quality or state of being persistent; *especially* : PERSEVERANCE
per·sis·ten·cy \-tən(t)-sē\ *noun* (1597)
: PERSISTENCE 2
per·sis·tent \-tənt\ *adjective* [Latin *persistent-, persistens*, present participle of *persistere*] (1826)
1 : existing for a long or longer than usual time or continuously: as **a :** retained beyond the usual period (a *persistent* leaf) **b :** continuing without change in function or structure (*persistent* gills) **c :** effective in the open for an appreciable time usually through slow vola-

tilizing (mustard gas is *persistent*) **d :** degraded only slowly by the environment (*persistent* pesticides) **e :** remaining infective for a relatively long time in a vector after an initial period of incubation (*persistent* viruses)
2 a : continuing or inclined to persist in a course **b :** continuing to exist in spite of interference or treatment (a *persistent* cough)
— **per·sis·tent·ly** *adverb*
per·snick·e·ty \pər-'sni-kə-tē\ *adjective* [alteration of *pernickety*] (circa 1905)
1 a : fussy about small details : FASTIDIOUS (a *persnickety* teacher) **b :** having the characteristics of a snob
2 : requiring great precision (a *persnickety* job)
— **per·snick·e·ti·ness** \-nəs\ *noun*
per·son \'pər-sᵊn\ *noun* [Middle English, from Old French *persone*, from Latin *persona* actor's mask, character in a play, person, probably from Etruscan *phersu* mask, from Greek *prosōpa*, plural of *prosōpon* face, mask — more at PROSOPOPOEIA] (13th century)
1 : HUMAN, INDIVIDUAL — sometimes used in combination especially by those who prefer to avoid *man* in compounds applicable to both sexes (chair*person*) (spokes*person*)
2 : a character or part in or as if in a play
3 a : one of the three modes of being in the Trinitarian Godhead as understood by Christians **b :** the unitary personality of Christ that unites the divine and human natures
4 a *archaic* **:** bodily appearance **b :** the body of a human being; *also* : the body and clothing (unlawful search of the *person*)
5 : the personality of a human being : SELF
6 : one (as a human being, a partnership, or a corporation) that is recognized by law as the subject of rights and duties
7 : reference of a segment of discourse to the speaker, to one spoken to, or to one spoken of as indicated by means of certain pronouns or in many languages by verb inflection ◇
— **per·son·hood** \-ˌhůd\ *noun*
— **in person :** in one's bodily presence
per·so·na \pər-'sō-nə, -ˌnä\ *noun, plural* **per·so·nae** \-(ˌ)nē, -ˌnī\ *or* **personas** [Latin] (1909)
1 : a character assumed by an author in a written work
2 a *plural* **personas** [New Latin, from Latin] **:** an individual's social facade or front that especially in the analytic psychology of C. G. Jung reflects the role in life the individual is playing — compare ANIMA **b :** the personality that a person (as an actor or politician) projects in public : IMAGE
3 *plural* **personae :** a character in a fictional presentation (as a novel or play) — usually used in plural (comic *personae*)
per·son·able \'pərs-nə-bəl, 'pər-sᵊn-ə-bəl\ *adjective* (15th century)
: pleasant or amiable in person : ATTRACTIVE
— **per·son·able·ness** *noun*
per·son·age \'pərs-nij, 'pər-sᵊn-ij\ *noun* (15th century)
1 : a person of rank, note, or distinction; *especially* : one distinguished for presence and personal power
2 : a human individual : PERSON
3 : a dramatic, fictional, or historical character; *also* : IMPERSONATION
per·so·na gra·ta \pər-ˌsō-nə-'gra-tə, -'grä-\ *adjective* [New Latin, acceptable person] (1882)
: personally acceptable or welcome
¹per·son·al \'pərs-nəl, 'pər-sᵊn-əl\ *adjective* [Middle English, from Middle French, from Late Latin *personalis*, from Latin *persona*] (14th century)
1 : of, relating to, or affecting a person : PRIVATE, INDIVIDUAL (*personal* ambition)
2 a : done in person without the intervention of another; *also* : proceeding from a single person **b :** carried on between individuals directly (a *personal* interview)

3 : relating to the person or body
4 : relating to an individual or an individual's character, conduct, motives, or private affairs often in an offensive manner (a *personal* insult)
5 a : being rational and self-conscious (*personal*, responsive government is still possible —John Fischer) **b :** having the qualities of a person rather than a thing or abstraction (a *personal* devil)
6 : of, relating to, or constituting personal property (a *personal* estate)
7 : denoting grammatical person
²personal *noun* (1861)
1 : a short newspaper paragraph relating to the activities of a person or a group or to personal matters
2 : a short personal communication in a special column of the classified ads section of a newspaper or periodical
3 : PERSONAL FOUL
personal computer *noun* (1977)
: MICROCOMPUTER 1
personal effects *noun plural* (1843)
: privately owned items (as clothing and jewelry) normally worn or carried on the person
personal equation *noun* (1845)
: variation (as in observation) occasioned by the personal peculiarities of an individual; *also* : a correction or allowance made for such variation
personal foul *noun* (circa 1829)
: a foul in a game (as basketball) involving usually physical contact with or deliberate roughing of an opponent — compare TECHNICAL FOUL
per·son·al·ise *British variant of* PERSONALIZE
per·son·al·ism \'pərs-nə-ˌli-zəm, 'pər-sᵊn-ə-\ *noun* (circa 1846)
: a doctrine emphasizing the significance, uniqueness, and inviolability of personality
— **per·son·al·ist** \-list\ *noun or adjective*
— **per·son·al·is·tic** \ˌpərs-nə-'lis-tik, ˌpər-sᵊn-ə-\ *adjective*
per·son·al·i·ty \ˌpər-sᵊn-'a-lə-tē, ˌpər-'sna-\ *noun, plural* **-ties** [Middle English *personalite*, from Late Latin *personalitat-, personalitas*, from *personalis*] (15th century)
1 a : the quality or state of being a person **b :** personal existence
2 a : the condition or fact of relating to a particular person; *specifically* : the condition of referring directly to or being aimed disparagingly or hostilely at an individual **b :** an offensively personal remark (angrily resorted to *personalities*)

3 : the complex of characteristics that distinguishes an individual or a nation or group; *especially* **:** the totality of an individual's behavioral and emotional characteristics
4 a : distinction or excellence of personal and social traits; *also* **:** a person having such quality **b :** a person of importance, prominence, renown, or notoriety ⟨a TV *personality*⟩
synonym see DISPOSITION

personality inventory *noun* (1932)
: any of several tests that attempt to characterize the personality of an individual by objective scoring of replies to a large number of questions concerning his or her own behavior — compare MINNESOTA MULTIPHASIC PERSONALITY INVENTORY

personality test *noun* (1914)
: any of several tests that consist of standardized tasks designed to determine various aspects of the personality or the emotional status of the individual examined

per·son·al·ize \'pərs-nə-ˌlīz, 'pər-sᵊn-ə-\ *transitive verb* **-ized; -iz·ing** (circa 1741)
1 : PERSONIFY
2 : to make personal or individual; *specifically* **:** to mark as the property of a particular person ⟨*personalized* stationery⟩
— **per·son·al·i·za·tion** \ˌpərs-nə-lə-'zā-shən, ˌpər-sᵊn-ə-\ *noun*

per·son·al·ly \'pərs-nə-lē, 'pər-sᵊn-ə-\ *adverb* (14th century)
1 : in person ⟨attend to the matter *personally*⟩
2 : as a person **:** in personality ⟨*personally* attractive but not very trustworthy⟩
3 : for oneself **:** as far as oneself is concerned

personal pronoun *noun* (1668)
: a pronoun (as *I*, *you*, or *they*) that expresses a distinction of person

personal property *noun* (1838)
: property other than real property consisting of things temporary or movable **:** CHATTELS

personal tax *noun* (circa 1935)
: DIRECT TAX

per·son·al·ty \'pərs-nəl-tē, 'pər-sᵊn-əl-\ *noun*, *plural* **-ties** [Middle English, from Anglo-French *personalté*, from Late Latin *personalitat-*, *personalitas* personality] (15th century)
: PERSONAL PROPERTY

per·so·na non gra·ta \pər-'sō-nə-ˌnän-'grä-tə, -'grä-\ *adjective* [New Latin, unacceptable person] (1904)
: personally unacceptable or unwelcome

per·son·ate \'pər-sᵊn-ˌāt\ *transitive verb* **-at·ed; -at·ing** (1591)
1 a : IMPERSONATE, REPRESENT **b :** to assume without authority and with fraudulent intent (some character or capacity)
2 : to invest with personality or personal characteristics ⟨*personating* their gods ridiculous, and themselves past shame —John Milton⟩
— **per·son·a·tion** \ˌpər-sᵊn-'ā-shən\ *noun*
— **per·son·a·tive** \'pər-sᵊn-ˌā-tiv\ *adjective*
— **per·son·a·tor** \-ˌāt-ər\ *noun*

per·son–hour \'pər-sᵊn-ˌau̇(-ə)r\ *noun* (1975)
: a unit of one hour's work by one person

per·son·i·fi·ca·tion \pər-ˌsä-nə-fə-'kā-shən\ *noun* (circa 1755)
1 : attribution of personal qualities; *especially* **:** representation of a thing or abstraction as a person or by the human form
2 : a divinity or imaginary being representing a thing or abstraction
3 : EMBODIMENT, INCARNATION

per·son·i·fy \pər-'sä-nə-ˌfī\ *transitive verb* **-fied; -fy·ing** (circa 1741)
1 : to conceive of or represent as a person or as having human qualities or powers
2 : to be the embodiment or personification of **:** INCARNATE ⟨a teacher who *personified* patience⟩
— **per·son·i·fi·er** \-ˌfī(-ə)r\ *noun*

per·son·nel \ˌpər-sᵊn-'el\ *noun* [French, from German *Personale, Personal*, from Medieval Latin *personale*, from Late Latin, neuter of *personalis* personal] (1837)

1 a : a body of persons usually employed (as in a factory, office, or organization) **b per·sonnel** *plural* **:** PERSONS
2 : a division of an organization concerned with personnel

¹**per·spec·tive** \pər-'spek-tiv\ *noun* [Middle English *perspectyf*, from Medieval Latin *perspectivum*, from neuter of *perspectivus* of sight, optical, from Latin *perspectus*, past participle of *perspicere* to look through, see clearly, from *per-* through + *specere* to look — more at PER-, SPY] (14th century)
archaic **:** an optical glass (as a telescope)

²**perspective** *noun* [Middle French, probably modification of Old Italian *prospettiva*, from *prospetto* view, prospect, from Latin *prospectus* — more at PROSPECT] (1563)
1 a : the technique or process of representing on a plane or curved surface the spatial relation of objects as they might appear to the eye; *specifically* **:** representation in a drawing or painting of parallel lines as converging in order to give the illusion of depth and distance **b :** a picture in perspective
2 a : the interrelation in which a subject or its parts are mentally viewed ⟨places the issues in proper *perspective*⟩; *also* **:** POINT OF VIEW **b :** the capacity to view things in their true relations or relative importance ⟨urge you to maintain your *perspective* and to view your own task in a larger framework —W. J. Cohen⟩
3 a : a visible scene; *especially* **:** one giving a distinctive impression of distance **:** VISTA **b :** a mental view or prospect ⟨to gain a broader *perspective* on the international scene —*Current Biography*⟩
4 : the appearance to the eye of objects in respect to their relative distance and positions
— **per·spec·tiv·al** \pər-'spek-ti-vəl, ˌpər-(ˌ)spek-'tī-vəl\ *adjective*

³**perspective** *adjective* [Middle English, optical, from Medieval Latin *perspectivus*] (1570)
1 *obsolete* **:** aiding the vision ⟨his eyes should be like unto the wrong end of a *perspective* glass —Alexander Pope⟩
2 : of, relating to, employing, or seen in perspective ⟨*perspective* drawing⟩
— **per·spec·tive·ly** *adverb*

Per·spex \'pər-ˌspeks\ *trademark*
— used for an acrylic plastic consisting essentially of polymethyl methacrylate

per·spi·ca·cious \ˌpər-spə-'kā-shəs\ *adjective* [Latin *perspicac-, perspicax*, from *per-spicere*] (1640)
: of acute mental vision or discernment **:** KEEN
synonym see SHREWD
— **per·spi·ca·cious·ly** *adverb*
— **per·spi·ca·cious·ness** *noun*
— **per·spi·cac·i·ty** \-'ka-sə-tē\ *noun*

per·spic·u·ous \pər-'spi-kyə-wəs\ *adjective* [Latin *perspicuus* transparent, perspicuous, from *perspicere*] (1586)
: plain to the understanding especially because of clarity and precision of presentation ⟨a *perspicuous* argument⟩
synonym see CLEAR
— **per·spic·u·ity** \ˌpər-spə-'kyü-ə-tē\ *noun*
— **per·spic·u·ous·ly** \pər-'spi-kyə-wəs-lē\ *adverb*
— **per·spic·u·ous·ness** *noun*

per·spi·ra·tion \ˌpər-spə-'rā-shən\ *noun* (1626)
1 : the action or process of perspiring
2 : a saline fluid secreted by the sweat glands **:** SWEAT

per·spi·ra·to·ry \pər-'spī-rə-ˌtōr-ē, 'pər-sp(ə-)rə-, -ˌtòr-\ *adjective* (1725)
: of, relating to, secreting, or inducing perspiration

per·spire \pər-'spīr\ *intransitive verb* **perspired; per·spir·ing** [French *perspirer*, from Middle French, from Latin *per-* through + *spirare* to blow, breathe — more at PER-] (circa 1682)
: to emit matter through the skin; *specifically*

: to secrete and emit perspiration

per·suad·able \pər-'swā-də-bəl\ *adjective* (circa 1598)
: capable of being persuaded

per·suade \pər-'swād\ *transitive verb* **per·suad·ed; per·suad·ing** [Latin *persuadēre*, from *per-* thoroughly + *suadēre* to advise, urge — more at SWEET] (15th century)
1 : to move by argument, entreaty, or expostulation to a belief, position, or course of action
2 : to plead with **:** URGE
— **per·suad·er** *noun*

per·sua·si·ble \-'swā-zə-bəl, -'swā-sə-\ *adjective* [Middle French, from Latin *persuasibilis* persuasive, from *persuasus*, past participle of *persuadēre*] (1502)
: PERSUADABLE

per·sua·sion \pər-'swā-zhən\ *noun* [Middle English *persuasioun*, from Middle French or Latin; Middle French *persuasion*, from Latin *persuasion-, persuasio*, from *persuadēre*] (14th century)
1 a : the act or process or an instance of persuading **b :** a persuading argument **c :** the ability to persuade **:** PERSUASIVENESS
2 : the condition of being persuaded
3 a : an opinion held with complete assurance **b :** a system of religious beliefs; *also* **:** a group adhering to a particular system of beliefs
4 : KIND, SORT
synonym see OPINION

per·sua·sive \-'swā-siv, -ziv\ *adjective* (15th century)
: tending to persuade
— **per·sua·sive·ly** *adverb*
— **per·sua·sive·ness** *noun*

pert \'pərt\ *adjective* [Middle English, open, bold, pert, modification of Old French *apert*, from Latin *apertus* open, from past participle of *aperire* to open] (14th century)
1 a : saucily free and forward **:** flippantly cocky and assured **b :** being trim and chic **:** JAUNTY ⟨a *pert* little hat⟩ **c :** piquantly stimulating ⟨is a *pert* notion⟩
2 : LIVELY, VIVACIOUS
— **pert·ly** *adverb*
— **pert·ness** *noun*

per·tain \pər-'tān\ *intransitive verb* [Middle English *perteinen*, from Middle French *partenir*, from Latin *pertinēre* to reach to, belong, from *per-* through + *tenēre* to hold — more at THIN] (14th century)
1 a (1) **:** to belong as a part, member, accessory, or product (2) **:** to belong as an attribute, feature, or function ⟨the destruction and havoc *pertaining* to war⟩ (3) **:** to belong as a duty or right ⟨responsibilities that *pertain* to fatherhood⟩ **b :** to be appropriate to something ⟨the criteria . . . will be different from those that *pertain* elsewhere —J. B. Conant⟩
2 : to have reference ⟨books *pertaining* to birds⟩

per·ti·na·cious \ˌpər-tᵊn-'ā-shəs\ *adjective* [Latin *pertinac-, pertinax*, from *per-* thoroughly + *tenac-, tenax* tenacious, from *tenēre*] (1626)
1 a : adhering resolutely to an opinion, purpose, or design **b :** perversely persistent
2 : stubbornly unyielding or tenacious
synonym see OBSTINATE
— **per·ti·na·cious·ly** *adverb*
— **per·ti·na·cious·ness** *noun*
— **per·ti·nac·i·ty** \-'a-sə-tē\ *noun*

per·ti·nence \'pər-tᵊn-ən(t)s, 'pərt-nən(t)s\ *noun* (1659)
: the quality or state of being pertinent **:** RELEVANCE

per·ti·nen·cy \-tᵊn-ən(t)-sē, -nən(t)-sē\ *noun* (1598)
: PERTINENCE

\ə\ abut \ᵊ\ kitten \ər\ further \a\ ash \ā\ ace \ä\ mop, mar \au̇\ out \ch\ chin \e\ bet \ē\ easy \g\ go \i\ hit \ī\ ice \j\ job \ŋ\ sing \ō\ go \ȯ\ law \ȯi\ boy \th\ thin \th\ the \ü\ loot \u̇\ foot \y\ yet \zh\ vision *see also* Guide to Pronunciation

per·ti·nent \'pər-t°n-ənt, 'pərt-nənt\ *adjective* [Middle English, from Middle French, from Latin *pertinent-, pertinens,* present participle of *pertinēre*] (14th century)
: having a clear decisive relevance to the matter in hand
synonym see RELEVANT
— **per·ti·nent·ly** *adverb*
per·turb \pər-'tərb\ *transitive verb* [Middle English, from Middle French *perturber,* from Latin *perturbare* to throw into confusion, from *per-* + *turbare* to disturb — more at TURBID] (14th century)
1 : to disturb greatly in mind : DISQUIET
2 : to throw into confusion : DISORDER
3 : to cause to experience a perturbation
synonym see DISCOMPOSE
— **per·turb·able** \-'tər-bə-bəl\ *adjective*
per·tur·ba·tion \,pər-tər-'bā-shən, ,pər-,tər-\ *noun* (14th century)
1 : the action of perturbing : the state of being perturbed
2 : a disturbance of motion, course, arrangement, or state of equilibrium; *especially* : a disturbance of the regular and usually elliptical course of motion of a celestial body that is produced by some force additional to that which causes its regular motion
— **per·tur·ba·tion·al** \-shnəl, -shə-n°l\ *adjective*
per·tus·sis \pər-'tə-səs\ *noun* [New Latin, from Latin *per-* thoroughly + *tussis* cough] (circa 1799)
: WHOOPING COUGH
pe·ruke \pə-'rük\ *noun* [Middle French *perruque,* from Old Italian *parrucca, perrucca* hair, wig] (circa 1573)
: WIG; *specifically* : one of a type popular from the 17th to the early 19th century
— **pe·ruked** \-'rükt\ *adjective*
pe·ruse \pə-'rüz\ *transitive verb* **pe·rused; pe·rus·ing** [Middle English, to use up, deal with in sequence, from Latin *per-* thoroughly + Middle English *usen* to use] (1532)
1 a : to examine or consider with attention and in detail : STUDY **b** : to look over or through in a casual or cursory manner
2 : READ; *especially* : to read over in an attentive or leisurely manner □
— **pe·rus·al** \-'rü-zəl\ *noun*
— **pe·rus·er** *noun*

peruke

per·vade \pər-'vād\ *transitive verb* **per·vad·ed; per·vad·ing** [Latin *pervadere* to go through, pervade, from *per-* through + *vadere* to go — more at PER-, WADE] (1659)
: to become diffused throughout every part of
per·va·sion \pər-'vā-zhən\ *noun* (1661)
: the action of pervading or condition of being pervaded
per·va·sive \pər-'vā-siv, -ziv\ *adjective* (circa 1750)
: that pervades or tends to pervade ⟨a *pervasive* odor⟩
— **per·va·sive·ly** *adverb*
— **per·va·sive·ness** *noun*
per·verse \(,)pər-'vərs, 'pər-,\ *adjective* [Middle English, from Latin *perversus,* from past participle of *pervertere*] (14th century)
1 a : turned away from what is right or good : CORRUPT **b** : IMPROPER, INCORRECT **c** : contrary to the evidence or the direction of the judge on a point of law ⟨*perverse* verdict⟩
2 a : obstinate in opposing what is right, reasonable, or accepted : WRONGHEADED **b** : arising from or indicative of stubbornness or obstinacy
3 : marked by peevishness or petulance : CRANKY

synonym see CONTRARY
— **per·verse·ly** *adverb*
— **per·verse·ness** *noun*
— **per·ver·si·ty** \-'vər-sə-tē, -stē\ *noun*
per·ver·sion \pər-'vər-zhən, -shən\ *noun* (14th century)
1 : the action of perverting : the condition of being perverted
2 : a perverted form; *especially* : an aberrant sexual practice especially when habitual and preferred to normal coitus
per·ver·sive \-'vər-siv, -ziv\ *adjective* (1817)
1 : that perverts or tends to pervert
2 : arising from or indicative of perversion
¹per·vert \pər-'vərt\ *transitive verb* [Middle English, from Middle French *pervertir,* from Latin *pervertere* to overturn, corrupt, pervert, from *per-* thoroughly + *vertere* to turn — more at PER-, WORTH] (14th century)
1 a : to cause to turn aside or away from what is good or true or morally right : CORRUPT **b** : to cause to turn aside or away from what is generally done or accepted : MISDIRECT
2 a : to divert to a wrong end or purpose : MISUSE **b** : to twist the meaning or sense of : MISINTERPRET
synonym see DEBASE
— **per·vert·er** *noun*
²per·vert \'pər-,vərt\ *noun* (circa 1661)
: one that has been perverted; *specifically* : one given to some form of sexual perversion
per·vert·ed \pər-'vər-təd\ *adjective* (14th century)
1 : CORRUPT
2 : marked by perversion
— **per·vert·ed·ly** *adverb*
— **per·vert·ed·ness** *noun*
per·vi·ous \'pər-vē-əs\ *adjective* [Latin *pervius,* from *per-* through + *via* way — more at PER-, WAY] (circa 1614)
1 : ACCESSIBLE ⟨*pervious* to reason⟩
2 : PERMEABLE ⟨*pervious* soil⟩
— **per·vi·ous·ness** *noun*
Pe·sach \'pā-,säk\ *noun* [Hebrew *pesaḥ*] (1613)
: PASSOVER
pe·se·ta \pə-'sā-tə\ *noun* [Spanish, from diminutive of *peso*] (1811)
— see MONEY table
pe·se·wa \pə-'sā-wə\ *noun* [Twi *pésewa,* literally, penny, penny's worth of gold dust] (1965)
— see *cedi* at MONEY table
pes·ky \'pes-kē\ *adjective* **pes·ki·er; -est** [probably irregular from *pest* + -y] (1775)
: TROUBLESOME, VEXATIOUS ⟨*pesky* issues⟩
pe·so \'pā-(,)sō, 'pe-\ *noun, plural* **pesos** [Spanish, literally, weight, from Latin *pensum* — more at POISE] (1555)
1 : an old silver coin of Spain and Spanish America equal to eight reals
2 — see MONEY table
pes·sa·ry \'pe-sə-rē\ *noun, plural* **-ries** [Middle English *pessarie,* from Late Latin *pessarium,* from *pessus, pessum* pessary, from Greek *pessos* oval stone for playing checkers, pessary] (14th century)
1 : a vaginal suppository
2 : a device worn in the vagina to support the uterus, remedy a malposition, or prevent conception
pes·si·mism \'pe-sə-,mi-zəm *also* 'pe-zə-\ *noun* [French *pessimisme,* from Latin *pessimus* worst — more at PEJORATIVE] (1815)
1 : an inclination to emphasize adverse aspects, conditions, and possibilities or to expect the worst possible outcome
2 a : the doctrine that reality is essentially evil **b** : the doctrine that evil overbalances happiness in life
— **pes·si·mist** \-mist\ *noun*
pes·si·mis·tic \,pe-sə-'mis-tik *also* ,pe-zə-\ *adjective* (1868)
: of, relating to, or characterized by pessimism : GLOOMY
synonym see CYNICAL

— **pes·si·mis·ti·cal·ly** \-ti-k(ə-)lē\ *adverb*
pest \'pest\ *noun* [Middle French *peste,* from Latin *pestis*] (1553)
1 : an epidemic disease associated with high mortality; *specifically* : PLAGUE
2 : something resembling a pest in destructiveness; *especially* : a plant or animal detrimental to humans or human concerns (as agriculture or livestock production)
3 : one that pesters or annoys : NUISANCE ◇
— **pesty** \'pes-tē\ *adjective*
pes·ter \'pes-tər\ *transitive verb* **pes·tered; pes·ter·ing** \-t(ə-)riŋ\ [modification of Middle French *empestrer* to hobble, embarrass, from (assumed) Vulgar Latin *impastoriare,* from Latin *in-* + Medieval Latin *pastoria* hobble — more at PASTERN] (1533)
1 *obsolete* : OVERCROWD
2 : to harass with petty irritations : ANNOY
synonym see WORRY
pest·hole \'pest-,hōl\ *noun* (1903)
: a place liable to epidemic disease
pest·house \-,haús\ *noun* (1611)
: a shelter or hospital for those infected with a pestilential or contagious disease
pes·ti·cide \'pes-tə-,sīd\ *noun* (circa 1925)
: an agent used to destroy pests

□ **USAGE**

peruse *Peruse* is a word with a literary flavor. It has been used in sense 2 since the time of Shakespeare and Marlowe, and it has been a useful alternative to the monosyllabic *read* for poets. It was probably a more ordinary word in the past than it is now, although it still has considerable use. About 1906 a writer on usage decided that *peruse* could mean only "to read with care and attention," for what reason we do not know. In time this opinion was echoed by a number of commentators, right down to the present. *Peruse* actually has been used in the "careful and attentive" sense, but writers almost always signal that meaning by a modifier ⟨have you with heed *perused* what I have written to you? —Shakespeare⟩ ⟨the lady in blue velvet, who so attentively *peruses* her book —Washington Irving⟩ ⟨each paragraph was carefully *perused* —Fred Allen⟩. And it has also been used, usually with a qualifier, to suggest casual or leisurely reading ⟨advertisements are now so numerous that they are very negligently *perused* —Samuel Johnson⟩ ⟨mirrors are gazed into, letters dreamily *perused* —Simon Schama⟩. But most of the time it simply means "to read" or "to read over or through" ⟨a magazine that the civilized reader may *peruse* without damage to his stomach —H. L. Mencken⟩ ⟨a dozen men, most of them huddled in dark suits at separate tables, *perusing* newspapers —A. N. Wilson⟩ ⟨these are what the bulk of the population *peruses* —Anthony Burgess⟩.

◇ **WORD HISTORY**

pest In contemporary usage a *pest* may be no more than a nuisance. Originally, however, the word meant something far more serious. In the 16th century when English borrowed *peste,* it was the French word for "plague." Although it could be used of any epidemic disease resulting in many deaths, the word customarily referred specifically to bubonic plague. The word *pest* had not been in English for very long before it was being used indiscriminately of anything destructive or troublesome. While French *peste* has retained all of its original force, the English word can be applied to persons or things that are only mildly irritating. *Pest* is now naturally associated with the verb *pester,* which is etymologically unrelated to it.

pes·tif·er·ous \pes-'ti-f(ə-)rəs\ *adjective* [Middle English, from Latin *pestifer* pestilential, noxious, from *pestis* + *-fer* -ferous] (15th century)
1 : dangerous to society : PERNICIOUS
2 a : carrying or propagating infection : PESTILENTIAL **b** : infected with a pestilential disease
3 : TROUBLESOME, ANNOYING
— **pes·tif·er·ous·ly** *adverb*
— **pes·tif·er·ous·ness** *noun*

pes·ti·lence \'pes-tə-lən(t)s\ *noun* (14th century)
1 : a contagious or infectious epidemic disease that is virulent and devastating; *especially* : BUBONIC PLAGUE
2 : something that is destructive or pernicious ⟨I'll pour this *pestilence* into his ear —Shakespeare⟩

pes·ti·lent \-lənt\ *adjective* [Middle English, from Latin *pestilent-, pestilens* pestilential, from *pestis*] (14th century)
1 : destructive of life : DEADLY
2 : injuring or endangering society : PERNICIOUS
3 : causing displeasure or annoyance
4 : INFECTIOUS, CONTAGIOUS ⟨*pestilent* disease⟩
— **pes·ti·lent·ly** *adverb*

pes·ti·len·tial \,pes-tə-'len(t)-shəl\ *adjective* (14th century)
1 a : causing or tending to cause pestilence : DEADLY **b** : of or relating to pestilence
2 : morally harmful : PERNICIOUS
3 : giving rise to vexation or annoyance : IRRITATING
— **pes·ti·len·tial·ly** \-'len(t)-sh(ə-)lē\ *adverb*

¹pes·tle \'pe-səl, 'pes-t°l\ *noun* [Middle English *pestel*, from Middle French, from Latin *pistillum*, from *pinsere* to pound, crush; akin to Greek *ptissein* to crush, Sanskrit *pinaṣṭi* he pounds] (14th century)
1 : a usually club-shaped implement for pounding or grinding substances in a mortar
2 : any of various devices for pounding, stamping, or pressing

pestle 1 (with mortar)

²pestle *verb* **pes·tled; pes·tling** \'pe-s(ə-)liŋ, 'pes-t°l-iŋ\ (15th century)
transitive verb
archaic : to beat, pound, or pulverize with or as if with a pestle
intransitive verb
: to work with a pestle : use a pestle

pes·to \'pes-(,)tō\ *noun* [Italian, from *pesto*, adjective, pounded, from *pestare* to pound, from Late Latin *pistare*, frequentative of Latin *pinsere*] (1937)
: a sauce made especially of fresh basil, garlic, oil, pine nuts, and grated cheese

¹pet \'pet\ *noun* [perhaps back-formation from Middle English *pety* small — more at PETTY] (1508)
1 a : a pampered and usually spoiled child **b** : a person who is treated with unusual kindness or consideration : DARLING
2 : a domesticated animal kept for pleasure rather than utility

²pet *adjective* (1584)
1 : kept or treated as a pet
2 : expressing fondness or endearment ⟨a *pet* name⟩
3 : FAVORITE ⟨a *pet* project⟩

³pet *verb* **pet·ted; pet·ting** (1629)
transitive verb
1 a : to treat as a pet **b** : to stroke in a gentle or loving manner
2 : to treat with unusual kindness and consideration : PAMPER
intransitive verb
: to engage in amorous embracing, caressing, and kissing : NECK
— **pet·ter** *noun*

⁴pet *noun* [origin unknown] (1590)
: a fit of peevishness, sulkiness, or anger

⁵pet *intransitive verb* **pet·ted; pet·ting** (1629)
: to take offense : SULK

peta- *combining form* [International Scientific Vocabulary, modification of Greek *penta*-]
: quadrillion ⟨*peta*-electron volts⟩

pet·al \'pe-t°l\ *noun* [New Latin *petalum*, from Greek *petalon*; akin to Greek *petannynai* to spread out — more at FATHOM] (circa 1726)
: one of the modified often brightly colored leaves of the corolla of a flower — see FLOWER illustration
— **pet·aled** *or* **pet·alled** \-t°ld\ *adjective*
— **pet·al·like** \-t°l-,(l)īk\ *adjective*

pet·al·oid \'pe-t°l-,óid\ *adjective* (1730)
1 : resembling a flower petal
2 : consisting of petaloid elements

pet·al·ous \'pe-t°l-əs\ *adjective* (circa 1736)
1 : having petals
2 : having (such or so many) petals — used in combination ⟨poly*petalous*⟩

pe·tard \pə-'tär(d)\ *noun* [Middle French, from *peter* to break wind, from *pet* expulsion of intestinal gas, from Latin *peditum*, from neuter of *peditus*, past participle of *pedere* to break wind; akin to Greek *bdein* to break wind] (1598)
1 : a case containing an explosive to break down a door or gate or breach a wall
2 : a firework that explodes with a loud report

pet·a·sos *or* **pet·a·sus** \'pe-tə-səs\ *noun* [Latin & Greek; Latin *petasos*, from Greek *petasos*; akin to Greek *petannynai* to spread out] (1599)
: a broad-brimmed low-crowned hat worn by ancient Greeks and Romans; *especially* : the winged hat of Hermes

pet·cock \'pet-,käk\ *noun* [*pet*- (perhaps from *petty*) + *cock*] (circa 1864)
: a small cock, faucet, or valve for releasing a gas (as air) or draining

pe·te·chia \pə-'tē-kē-ə\ *noun, plural* **-chi·ae** \-kē-,ī\ [New Latin, from Italian *petecchia*, ultimately from Latin *impetigo*] (circa 1796)
: a minute reddish or purplish spot containing blood that appears in skin or mucous membrane especially in some infectious diseases (as typhoid fever)
— **pe·te·chi·al** \-kē-əl\ *adjective*

¹pe·ter \'pē-tər\ *intransitive verb* [origin unknown] (1846)
1 : to diminish gradually and come to an end : GIVE OUT — usually used with *out* ⟨novelists whose creative impetus seems largely to have petered out —*Times Literary Supplement*⟩
2 : to become exhausted — usually used with *out*

²peter *noun* [from the name *Peter*] (circa 1902)
: PENIS — often considered vulgar

Pe·ter \'pē-tər\ *noun* [Late Latin *Petrus*, from Greek *Petros*, from *petra* rock]
1 : a fisherman of Galilee and one of the twelve apostles
2 : either of two hortatory letters written to early Christians and included as books of the New Testament — see BIBLE table

Peter Pan \-'pan\ *noun*
1 : a boy in Sir James Barrie's play *Peter Pan* who lives without growing older in a never-never land
2 : an adult who doesn't want to grow up : one who hangs on to adolescent interests and attitudes

Peter Pan collar *noun* (1908)
: a usually small flat close-fitting collar with rounded ends that meet at the top in front

Peter Principle *noun* [Laurence J. *Peter* (born 1919) American (Canadian-born) educator] (1968)
: an observation: in a hierarchy employees tend to rise to the level of their incompetence

Peter's pence *noun plural but singular in construction* [Middle English; from the tradi-tion that Saint Peter founded the papal see] (13th century)
1 : an annual tribute of a penny formerly paid by each householder in England to the papal see
2 : a voluntary annual contribution made by Roman Catholics to the pope

Peter Pan collar

pet·i·o·lar \,pe-tē-'ō-lər\ *adjective* (1760)
: of, relating to, or proceeding from a petiole

pet·i·o·late \'pe-tē-ə-,lāt, ,pe-tē-'ō-lət\ *adjective* (circa 1753)
: having a stalk or petiole

pet·i·ole \'pe-tē-,ōl\ *noun* [New Latin *petiolus*, from Latin *petiolus, peciolus* small foot, fruit stalk, probably alteration of (assumed) Latin *pediciolus*, diminutive of *pediculus*, diminutive of *ped-, pes* foot — more at FOOT] (1753)
1 : a slender stem that supports the blade of a foliage leaf
2 : PEDUNCLE; *specifically* : a slender abdominal segment joining the rest of the abdomen to the thorax in some insects
— **pet·i·oled** \-,ōld\ *adjective*

pet·i·o·lule \'pe-tē-ō-,lül, ,pe-tē-'ōl-(,)yü(ə)l\ *noun* [New Latin *petiolulus*, diminutive of *petiolus*] (1832)
: a stalk of a leaflet of a compound leaf

pet·it \'pe-tē\ *adjective* [Middle English, small, minor, from Middle French, small] (14th century)
: PETTY 1 — used chiefly in legal compounds

pe·tit bourgeois \pə-,tē-, ,pe-tē-\ *noun* [French, literally, small bourgeois] (1853)
1 : a member of the petite bourgeoisie
2 : PETITE BOURGEOISIE
— **petit bourgeois** *adjective*

¹pe·tite \pə-'tēt\ *adjective* [French, feminine of *petit*] (1784)
: having a small trim figure — usually used of a woman
— **pe·tite·ness** *noun*

²petite *noun* (circa 1929)
: a clothing size for short women

petite bourgeoisie *noun* [French, literally, small bourgeoisie] (1916)
: the lower middle class including especially small shopkeepers and artisans

pe·tit four \,pe-tē-'fōr, pə-,tē-, -'fór; -'fûr\ *noun, plural* **petits fours** *or* **petit fours** \-'fōrz, -'fórz, -'fûr(z)\ [French, literally, small oven] (1884)
: a small cake cut from pound or sponge cake and frosted

¹pe·ti·tion \pə-'ti-shən\ *noun* [Middle English, from Middle French, from Latin *petition-, petitio*, from *petere* to seek, request — more at FEATHER] (14th century)
1 : an earnest request : ENTREATY
2 a : a formal written request made to an official person or organized body (as a court) **b** : a document embodying such a formal written request
3 : something asked or requested
— **pe·ti·tion·ary** \-'ti-shə-,ner-ē\ *adjective*

²petition *verb* **pe·ti·tioned; pe·ti·tion·ing** \-'ti-sh(ə-)niŋ\ (1607)
transitive verb
: to make a request to : SOLICIT
intransitive verb
: to make a request; *especially* : to make a formal written request
— **pe·ti·tion·er** \-sh(ə-)nər\ *noun*

pe·ti·tio prin·ci·pii \pə-'tē-tē-,ō-(,)prin-'ki-pē-,ē\ *noun* [Medieval Latin, literally, postulation of the beginning, begging the question] (1531)
: a logical fallacy in which a premise is assumed to be true without warrant or in which what is to be proved is implicitly taken for granted

pet·it jury \'pe-tē-\ *noun* (15th century)
: a jury of 12 persons impaneled to try and to decide finally upon the facts at issue in causes for trial in a court

petit larceny *noun* (1587)
: larceny involving property of a value below a legally established minimum

pe·tit–maî·tre \pə-,tē-'mātrᵊ\ *noun, plural* **petits–maîtres** *same*\ [French, literally, small master] (1711)
: DANDY, FOP

pe·tit mal \'pe-tē-,mal, -,mäl\ *noun* [French, literally, small illness] (1874)
: epilepsy characterized by mild convulsive seizure with transient clouding of consciousness — compare GRAND MAL

pet·it point \'pe-tē-,póint\ *noun* [French, literally, small point] (1882)
: TENT STITCH; *also* : embroidery made with this stitch

pet peeve *noun* (circa 1919)
: a frequent subject of complaint

petr- *or* **petri-** *or* **petro-** *combining form* [New Latin, from Greek *petr-, petro-,* from *petros* stone & *petra* rock]
1 : stone : rock ⟨petrology⟩
2 : petroleum ⟨petrodollar⟩

pe·tra·le sole \pə-'trä-lē-\ *noun* [*petrale* probably from Italian dialect, a flatfish] (1953)
: a flounder (*Eopsetta jordani*) chiefly of the Pacific waters of North America that is an important food fish — called also *petrale*

Pe·trar·chan sonnet \pi-'trär-kən-, ,pē-, (,)pe-\ *noun* [*Petrarch* (Francesco Petrarca)] (circa 1909)
: ITALIAN SONNET

pe·trel \'pe-trəl, 'pē-\ *noun* [alteration of earlier *pitteral*] (1676)
: any of numerous seabirds (especially families Procellariidae and Hydrobatidae); *especially* : one of the smaller long-winged birds that fly far from land — compare STORM PETREL

pe·tri dish \'pē-trē-\ *noun* [Julius R. *Petri* (died 1921) German bacteriologist] (1892)
: a small shallow dish of thin glass or plastic with a loose cover used especially for cultures in bacteriology

pet·ri·fac·tion \,pe-trə-'fak-shən\ *noun* (15th century)
1 : the process of petrifying
2 : something petrified
3 : the quality or state of being petrified

pet·ri·fi·ca·tion \,pe-trə-fə-'kā-shən\ *noun* (circa 1611)
: PETRIFACTION

pet·ri·fy \'pe-trə-,fī\ *verb* **-fied; -fy·ing** [Middle French *petrifier,* from *petr-* + *-ifier* -ify] (1594)
transitive verb
1 : to convert (organic matter) into stone or a substance of stony hardness by the infiltration of water and the deposition of dissolved mineral matter
2 : to make rigid or inert like stone: **a** : to make lifeless or inactive : DEADEN ⟨slogans are apt to *petrify* a man's thinking —*Saturday Review*⟩ **b** : to confound with fear, amazement, or awe ⟨a novel about an airline pilot that will *petrify* you —Martin Levin⟩
intransitive verb
: to become stone or of stony hardness or rigidity

Pe·trine \'pē-,trīn\ *adjective* [Late Latin *Petrus* Peter] (1846)
1 : of, relating to, or characteristic of the apostle Peter or the doctrines associated with his name

2 : of, relating to, or characteristic of Peter the Great or his reign

pet·ro·chem·i·cal \,pe-trō-'ke-mi-kəl\ *noun* (1942)
: a chemical isolated or derived from petroleum or natural gas
— **pet·ro·chem·is·try** \-'ke-mə-strē\ *noun*

pet·ro·dol·lar \'pe-trō-,dä-lər\ *noun* (1974)
: a dollar's worth of foreign exchange obtained by a petroleum-exporting country through sales abroad — usually used in plural

pet·ro·gen·e·sis \,pe-trō-'je-nə-səs\ *noun* [New Latin] (1901)
: the origin or formation of rocks
— **pet·ro·ge·net·ic** \-jə-'ne-tik\ *adjective*

pet·ro·glyph \'pe-trə-,glif\ *noun* [French *pétroglyphe,* from *pétr-* petr- + *-glyphe* (as in *hiéroglyphe* hieroglyph)] (1870)
: a carving or inscription on a rock

pe·trog·ra·phy \pə-'trä-grə-fē, pe-\ *noun* [New Latin *petrographia,* from *petr-* + Latin *-graphia* -graphy] (1651)
: the description and systematic classification of rocks
— **pe·trog·ra·pher** \-fər\ *noun*
— **pet·ro·graph·ic** \,pe-trə-'gra-fik\ *or* **pet·ro·graph·i·cal** \-fi-kəl\ *adjective*
— **pet·ro·graph·i·cal·ly** \-fi-k(ə-)lē\ *adverb*

pet·rol \'pe-trəl, -,träl\ *noun* [French *essence de pétrole,* literally, essence of petroleum] (1895)
chiefly British : GASOLINE

pet·ro·la·tum \,pe-trə-'lā-təm, -'lä-\ *noun* [New Latin, from Medieval Latin *petroleum*] (1887)
: PETROLEUM JELLY

pe·tro·leum \pə-'trō-lē-əm, -'trōl-yəm\ *noun* [Middle English, from Medieval Latin, from Latin *petr-* + *oleum* oil — more at OIL] (15th century)
: an oily flammable bituminous liquid that may vary from almost colorless to black, occurs in many places in the upper strata of the earth, is a complex mixture of hydrocarbons with small amounts of other substances, and is prepared for use as gasoline, naphtha, or other products by various refining processes

petroleum jelly *noun* (1897)
: a neutral unctuous odorless tasteless substance obtained from petroleum and used especially in ointments and dressings

pe·trol·o·gy \pə-'trä-lə-jē, pe-\ *noun* [International Scientific Vocabulary] (1811)
: a science that deals with the origin, history, occurrence, structure, chemical composition, and classification of rocks
— **pet·ro·log·ic** \,pe-trə-'lä-jik\ *or* **pet·ro·log·i·cal** \-ji-kəl\ *adjective*
— **pet·ro·log·i·cal·ly** \-ji-k(ə-)lē\ *adverb*
— **pe·trol·o·gist** \pə-'trä-lə-jist, pe-\ *noun*

pet·ro·nel \'pe-trə-nəl\ *noun* [perhaps modification of Middle French *poitrinal, petrinal,* from *poitrinal* of the chest, from *poitrine* chest, derivative of Latin *pector-, pectus* — more at PECTORAL] (circa 1577)
: a portable firearm resembling a carbine of large caliber

pe·tro·sal \pə-'trō-səl\ *adjective* [New Latin *petrosa* petrous portion of the temporal bone, from Latin, feminine of *petrosus*] (1741)
: of, relating to, or situated in the region of the petrous portion of the temporal bone or capsule of the inner ear

pe·trous \'pe-trəs, 'pē-\ *adjective* [Middle English, from Middle French *petreux,* from Latin *petrosus,* from *petra* rock, from Greek] (14th century)
: of, relating to, or constituting the exceptionally hard and dense portion of the human temporal bone that contains the internal auditory organs

¹pet·ti·coat \'pe-tē-,kōt\ *noun* [Middle English *petycote* short tunic, petticoat, from *pety* small + *cote* coat] (15th century)
1 : a skirt worn by women, girls, or young children: as **a** : an outer skirt formerly worn by women and small children **b** : a fancy skirt made to show below a draped-up overskirt **c** : an underskirt usually a little shorter than outer clothing and often made with a ruffled, pleated, or lace edge **d** *archaic* : the skirt of a woman's riding habit
2 a : a garment characteristic or typical of women **b** : WOMAN
3 : something (as a valance) resembling a petticoat
— **pet·ti·coat·ed** \-,kō-təd\ *adjective*

²petticoat *adjective* (1660)
: of, relating to, or exercised by women : FEMALE

pet·ti·fog·ger \'pe-tē-,fò-gər, -,fä-\ *noun* [probably from *petty* + obsolete English *fogger* pettifogger] (1576)
1 : a lawyer whose methods are petty, underhanded, or disreputable : SHYSTER
2 : one given to quibbling over trifles
— **pet·ti·fog·ging** \-gin\ *adjective or noun*
— **pet·ti·fog·gery** \-g(ə-)rē\ *noun*

petting zoo *noun* (1968)
: a collection of farm animals or gentle exotic animals for children to pet and feed

pet·tish \'pe-tish\ *adjective* [probably from ⁴*pet*] (circa 1591)
: FRETFUL, PEEVISH
— **pet·tish·ly** *adverb*
— **pet·tish·ness** *noun*

pet·ti·toes \'pe-tē-,tōz\ *noun plural* [plural of obsolete *pettytoe* offal] (1555)
1 : the feet of a pig used as food
2 : TOES, FEET

pet·ty \'pe-tē\ *adjective* **pet·ti·er; -est** [Middle English *pety* small, minor, alteration of *petit*] (14th century)
1 : having secondary rank or importance : MINOR, SUBORDINATE
2 : having little or no importance or significance
3 : marked by or reflective of narrow interests and sympathies : SMALL-MINDED
— **pet·ti·ly** \'pe-tᵊl-ē\ *adverb*
— **pet·ti·ness** \'pe-tē-nəs\ *noun*

petty cash *noun* (1834)
: cash kept on hand for payment of minor items

petty larceny *noun* (1818)
: PETIT LARCENY

petty officer *noun* (1760)
: a subordinate officer in the navy or coast guard appointed from among the enlisted men — compare NONCOMMISSIONED OFFICER

petty officer first class *noun* (1942)
: an enlisted man in the navy or coast guard ranking above a petty officer second class and below a chief petty officer

petty officer second class *noun* (1942)
: an enlisted man in the navy or coast guard ranking above a petty officer third class and below a petty officer first class

petty officer third class *noun* (1942)
: an enlisted man in the navy or coast guard ranking above a seaman and below a petty officer second class

pet·u·lance \'pe-chə-lən(t)s\ *noun* (1610)
: the quality or state of being petulant : PEEVISHNESS

pet·u·lan·cy \-lən(t)-sē\ *noun* (1559)
archaic : PETULANCE

pet·u·lant \-lənt\ *adjective* [Latin or Middle French; Middle French, from Latin *petulant-, petulans;* akin to Latin *petere* to go to, attack, seek — more at FEATHER] (1605)
1 : insolent or rude in speech or behavior
2 : characterized by temporary or capricious ill humor : PEEVISH
— **pet·u·lant·ly** *adverb*

pe·tu·nia \pi-'tün-yə, -'tyün-\ *noun* [New Latin, from obsolete French *petun* tobacco, from Tupi *petima*] (1825)
: any of a genus (*Petunia*) of tropical American herbs of the nightshade family with flowers having funnel-shaped corollas

petunia

pew \'pyü\ *noun* [Middle English *pewe*, from Middle French *puie* balustrade, from Latin *podia*, plural of *podium* parapet, podium, from Greek *podion* base, diminutive of *pod-, pous* foot — more at FOOT] (14th century)
1 : a compartment in the auditorium of a church providing seats for several persons
2 : one of the benches with backs and sometimes doors fixed in rows in a church
pe·wee \'pē-(,)wē\ *noun* [imitative] (1796)
: any of various small olivaceous flycatchers (genus *Contopus*)
pew·hold·er \'pyü-,hōl-dər\ *noun* (1845)
: a renter or owner of a pew
pe·wit *variant of* PEEWIT
pew·ter \'pyü-tər\ *noun* [Middle English, from Middle French *peutre*, from (assumed) Vulgar Latin *peltrum*] (14th century)
1 : any of various alloys having tin as chief component; *especially* : a dull alloy with lead formerly used for domestic utensils
2 : utensils of pewter
3 : a bluish gray
— **pewter** *adjective*
pew·ter·er \'pyü-tər-ər\ *noun* (14th century)
: one that makes pewter utensils
pey·o·te \pā-'ō-tē\ *also* **pey·otl** \-'ō-t³l\ *noun* [Mexican Spanish *peyote*, from Nahuatl *peyotl*] (1849)
1 : a stimulant drug derived from mescal buttons
2 : any of several American cacti (genus *Lophophora*); *especially* : MESCAL
pfen·nig \'fe-nig, -nik, German '(p)fe-nik\ *noun, plural* **pfennig** *also* **pfen·nigs** \'fe-nigz, -niks\ *or* **pfen·ni·ge** \'(p)fe-ni-gə, -ni-yə\ [German, from Old High German *pfenning* — more at PENNY] (1547)
— see *deutsche mark* at MONEY table
PG \'pē-'jē\ *certification mark*
— used to certify that a motion picture is of such a nature that all ages may be allowed admission but parental guidance is suggested; compare G, NC-17, PG-13, R
PG-13 \-,thər(t)-'tēn\ *certification mark*
— used to certify that a motion picture is of such a nature that persons of all ages may be admitted but parental guidance is suggested especially for children under 13; compare G, NC-17, PG, R
pH \'pē-'āch\ *noun* [German, from *Potenz* power + *H* (symbol for hydrogen)] (1909)
: a measure of acidity and alkalinity of a solution that is a number on a scale on which a value of 7 represents neutrality and lower numbers indicate increasing acidity and higher numbers increasing alkalinity and on which each unit of change represents a tenfold change in acidity or alkalinity and that is the negative logarithm of the effective hydrogen-ion concentration or hydrogen-ion activity in gram equivalents per liter of the solution; *also* : the condition represented by a pH number
Phae·dra \'fē-drə\ *noun* [Latin, from Greek *Phaidra*]
: a daughter of Minos who marries Theseus and falls in love with her stepson Hippolytus
Pha·ë·thon \'fā-ə-t³n, -,tən, -,thän\ *noun* [Latin, from Greek *Phaethōn*]
: a son of Helios who drives his father's sun-chariot through the sky but loses control and is struck down by a thunderbolt of Zeus
pha·eton \'fā-ə-t³n\ *noun* [*Phaëthon*] (1742)

1 : any of various light four-wheeled horse-drawn vehicles
2 : TOURING CAR
phage \'fāj *also* 'fäzh\ *noun* [by shortening] (1926)
: BACTERIOPHAGE
-phage *noun combining form* [Greek *-phagos* one that eats, from *-phagos* -phagous]
: virus or cell that destroys cells 〈bacterio-*phage*〉 〈micro*phage*〉
-phagia *noun combining form* [New Latin, from Greek]
: -PHAGY 〈dys*phagia*〉
phago·cyte \'fa-gə-,sīt\ *noun* [International Scientific Vocabulary, from Greek *phagein* + New Latin *-cyta* -cyte) (circa 1884)
: a cell (as a white blood cell) that engulfs and consumes foreign material (as microorganisms) and debris
— **phago·cyt·ic** \,fa-gə-'si-tik\ *adjective*
phago·cy·tize \'fa-gə-sə-,tīz, -,sī-\ *transitive verb* **-tized; -tiz·ing** (1913)
: PHAGOCYTOSE
phago·cy·tose \-sə-,tōs, -sī-, -,tōz\ *transitive verb* **-tosed; -tos·ing** [back-formation from *phagocytosis*] (1912)
: to consume by phagocytosis
phago·cy·to·sis \,fa-gə-sə-'tō-səs, -sī-\ *noun, plural* **-to·ses** \-,sēz\ [New Latin] (1889)
: the engulfing and usually the destruction of particulate matter by phagocytes
— **phago·cy·tot·ic** \-'tä-tik\ *adjective*
-phagous *adjective combining form* [Greek *-phagos*, from *phagein* to eat — more at BAKSHEESH]
: eating 〈sapro*phagous*〉
-phagy *noun combining form, plural* **-phagies** [Greek *-phagia*, from *phagein*]
: eating of a (specified) type or substance 〈geo*phagy*〉
pha·lange \'fā-,lanj, fə-', fā-'\ *noun* [French, from Greek *phalang-, phalanx*] (circa 1860)
: PHALANX 2
pha·lan·ge·al \,fā-lən-'jē-əl, ,fa-; fə-'lan-jē-, fā-\ *adjective* (1831)
: of or relating to a phalanx or the phalanges
pha·lan·ger \fə-'lan-jər, fā-\ *noun* [New Latin, from Greek *phalang-, phalanx*] (circa 1774)
: any of various small to medium-sized marsupial mammals (family Phalangeridae) of the Australian region that are chiefly arboreal and nocturnal and usually densely furred
phal·an·stery \'fa-lən-,ster-ē\ *noun, plural* **-ster·ies** [French *phalanstère* dwelling of a Fourierist community, from Latin *phalang-, phalanx* + French *-stère* (as in *monastère* monastery)] (1846)
1 a : a Fourierist cooperative community **b** : a self-contained structure housing such a community
2 : something resembling a Fourierist phalanstery
pha·lanx \'fā-,laŋ(k)s, British usually 'fa-\ *noun, plural* **pha·lanx·es** *or* **pha·lan·ges** \fə-'lan-(,)jēz, fā-, fā-,, British usually fā-\ [Latin *phalang-, phalanx*, from Greek, battle line, digital bone, literally, log — more at BALK] (1553)
1 : a body of heavily armed infantry in ancient Greece formed in close deep ranks and files; *broadly* : a body of troops in close array
2 *plural* **phalanges** : one of the digital bones of the hand or foot of a vertebrate
3 *plural usually* **phalanxes** **a** : a massed arrangement of persons, animals, or things **b** : an organized body of persons
phal·a·rope \'fa-lə-,rōp\ *noun, plural* **-ropes** *also* **-rope** [French, from New Latin *phalaropod-, phalaropus*, from Greek *phalaris* coot + *pod-, pous* foot; akin to Greek *phalios* having a white spot — more at BALD, FOOT] (circa 1776)
: any of a genus (*Phalaropus*) of small shore-birds that are related to sandpipers but have lobate toes and are good swimmers

phal·lic \'fa-lik\ *adjective* (1789)
1 : of or relating to phallicism 〈a *phallic* cult〉
2 : of, relating to, or resembling a phallus
3 : relating to or being the stage of psychosexual development in psychoanalytic theory during which a child becomes interested in his or her own sexual organs
— **phal·li·cal·ly** \-li-k(ə-)lē\ *adverb*
phal·li·cism \'fa-lə-,si-zəm\ *noun* (1884)
: the worship of the generative principle as symbolized by the phallus
phal·lo·cen·tric \,fa-lə-'sen-trik\ *adjective* (1927)
: centered on or emphasizing the masculine point of view
phal·lus \'fa-ləs\ *noun, plural* **phal·li** \'fa-,lī, -,lē\ *or* **phal·lus·es** [Latin, from Greek *phallos* penis, representation of the penis; probably akin to Latin *flare* to blow — more at BLOW] (circa 1613)
1 : a symbol or representation of the penis
2 : PENIS
-phane *noun combining form* [Greek *phanēs* appearing, from *phainein* to show — more at FANCY]
: substance having a (specified) form, quality, or appearance 〈hydro*phane*〉
phan·er·o·gam \'fa-nə-rə-,gam, fə-'ner-ə-\ *noun* [French *phanérogame*, ultimately from Greek *phaneros* visible (from *phainein*) + *gamos* marriage] (1861)
: a seed plant or flowering plant : SPERMATOPHYTE
phan·er·o·phyte \'fa-nə-rə-,fīt, fə-'ner-ə-\ *noun* [Greek *phaneros* + International Scientific Vocabulary *-phyte*] (1913)
: a perennial plant that bears its perennating buds well above the surface of the ground
Phan·er·o·zo·ic \,fa-nə-rə-'zō-ik\ *adjective* [Greek *phaneros* + English ²-*zoic*] (1930)
: of, relating to, or being an eon of geologic history that comprises the Paleozoic, Mesozoic, and Cenozoic or the corresponding system of rocks — see GEOLOGIC TIME table
— **Phanerozoic** *noun*
phan·tasm \'fan-,ta-zəm\ *noun* [Middle English *fantasme*, from Old French, from Latin *phantasma*, from Greek, from *phantazein* to present to the mind — more at FANCY] (13th century)
1 : a product of fantasy: as **a** : delusive appearance : ILLUSION **b** : GHOST, SPECTER **c** : a figment of the imagination
2 : a mental representation of a real object
— **phan·tas·mal** \fan-'taz-məl\ *adjective*
— **phan·tas·mic** \-mik\ *adjective*
phan·tas·ma \fan-'taz-mə\ *noun, plural* **-ma·ta** \-mə-tə\ [Latin] (1598)
: PHANTASM 1
phan·tas·ma·go·ria \(,)fan-,taz-mə-'gòr-ē-ə, -'gòr-\ *noun* [French *phantasmagorie*, from *phantasme* phantasm (from Old French *fantasme*) + *-agorie* (perhaps from Greek *agora* assembly) — more at AGORA] (circa 1802)
1 : an exhibition or display of optical effects and illusions
2 a : a constantly shifting complex succession of things seen or imagined **b** : a scene that constantly changes
3 : a bizarre or fantastic combination, collection, or assemblage
— **phan·tas·ma·gor·ic** \-'gòr-ik, -'gòr-, -'gär-\ *or* **phan·tas·ma·gor·i·cal** \-i-kəl\ *adjective*
phantasy *variant of* FANTASY
¹phan·tom \'fan-təm\ *noun* [Middle English *fantosme, fantome*, from Middle French *fantosme*, modification of Latin *phantasma*] (14th century)

1 a : something (as a specter) apparent to sense but with no substantial existence **:** APPARITION **b :** something elusive or visionary **:** WILL-O'-THE-WISP **c :** an object of continual dread or abhorrence **:** BUGBEAR ⟨the *phantom* of disease and want⟩
2 : something existing in appearance only
3 : a representation of something abstract, ideal, or incorporeal ⟨she was a *phantom* of delight —William Wordsworth⟩
— **phan·tom·like** \-ˌlīk\ *adverb or adjective*

²**phantom** *adjective* (15th century)
1 : of the nature of, suggesting, or being a phantom **:** ILLUSORY
2 : FICTITIOUS, DUMMY ⟨*phantom* voters⟩

pha·raoh \'fer-(ˌ)ō, 'far-(ˌ)ō, 'fā-(ˌ)rō\ *noun, often capitalized* [Middle English *pharao*, from Old English *pharao*, from Late Latin *pharaon-, pharao*, from Greek *pharaō*, from Hebrew *par'ōh*, from Egyptian *pr-'',*] (before 12th century)
1 : a ruler of ancient Egypt
2 : TYRANT

pharaoh ant *noun* (circa 1947)
: a little red ant (*Monomorium pharaonis*) that is a common household pest

phar·a·on·ic \ˌfer-ā-'ä-nik, ˌfar-\ *adjective, often capitalized* [French *pharaonique*, from *pharaon* pharaoh, from Late Latin *Pharaon-, Pharao*] (circa 1828)
1 : of, relating to, or characteristic of a pharaoh or the pharaohs
2 : enormous in size or magnitude ⟨*pharaonic* construction projects⟩

phar·i·sa·ic \ˌfar-ə-'sā-ik\ *adjective* [Late Latin *pharisaicus*, from Late Greek *pharisaikos*, from Greek *pharisaios* Pharisee] (1618)
1 : PHARISAICAL
2 *capitalized* **:** of or relating to the Pharisees

phar·i·sa·ical \-'sā-ə-kəl\ *adjective* (1531)
: marked by hypocritical censorious self-righteousness
— **phar·i·sa·ical·ly** \-k(ə-)lē\ *adverb*
— **phar·i·sa·ical·ness** \-kəl-nəs\ *noun*

phar·i·sa·ism \'far-ə-(ˌ)sā-ˌi-zəm\ *noun* [New Latin *pharisaismus*, from Greek *pharisaios*] (1610)
1 *capitalized* **:** the doctrines or practices of the Pharisees
2 *often capitalized* **:** pharisaical character, spirit, or attitude **:** HYPOCRISY

phar·i·see \'far-ə-(ˌ)sē\ *noun* [Middle English *pharise*, from Old English *farise*, from Late Latin *pharisaios*, from Greek *pharisaios*, from Aramaic *pĕrīshayyā*, plural of *pĕrīshā*, literally, separated] (before 12th century)
1 *capitalized* **:** a member of a Jewish sect of the intertestamental period noted for strict observance of rites and ceremonies of the written law and for insistence on the validity of their own oral traditions concerning the law
2 : a pharisaical person

¹**phar·ma·ceu·ti·cal** \ˌfär-mə-'sü-ti-kəl\ *adjective* [Late Latin *pharmaceuticus*, from Greek *pharmakeutikos*, from *pharmakeuein* to administer drugs — more at PHARMACY] (1648)
: of, relating to, or engaged in pharmacy or the manufacture and sale of pharmaceuticals ⟨a *pharmaceutical* company⟩
— **phar·ma·ceu·ti·cal·ly** \-ti-k(ə-)lē\ *adverb*

²**pharmaceutical** *noun* (1881)
: a medicinal drug

phar·ma·cist \'fär-mə-sist\ *noun* (1834)
: a person licensed to engage in pharmacy

pharmaco- *combining form* [Greek *pharmako-*, from *pharmakon*]
: medicine **:** drug ⟨*pharmacology*⟩

phar·ma·co·dy·nam·ics \ˌfär-mə-kō-dī-'na-miks, -də-\ *noun plural but singular in construction* (circa 1842)
: a branch of pharmacology dealing with the reactions between drugs and living systems

— **phar·ma·co·dy·nam·ic** \-mik\ *adjective*
— **phar·ma·co·dy·nam·i·cal·ly** \-mi-k(ə-)lē\ *adverb*

phar·ma·cog·no·sy \ˌfär-mə-'käg-nə-sē\ *noun* [International Scientific Vocabulary, from Greek *pharmakon* + *-gnōsia* knowledge, from *gnōsis* — more at GNOSIS] (circa 1885)
: descriptive pharmacology dealing with crude drugs and simples
— **phar·ma·cog·nos·tic** \-ˌkäg-'näs-tik\ *or* **phar·ma·cog·nos·ti·cal** \-ti-kəl\ *adjective*

phar·ma·co·ki·net·ics \-kō-kə-'ne-tiks, -kō-kī-\ *noun plural but singular in construction* (1960)
1 : the study of the bodily absorption, distribution, metabolism, and excretion of drugs
2 : the characteristic interactions of a drug and the body in terms of its absorption, distribution, metabolism, and excretion
— **phar·ma·co·ki·net·ic** \-tik\ *adjective*

phar·ma·col·o·gy \ˌfär-mə-'kä-lə-jē\ *noun* (circa 1721)
1 : the science of drugs including materia medica, toxicology, and therapeutics
2 : the properties and reactions of drugs especially with relation to their therapeutic value
— **phar·ma·co·log·i·cal** \-kə-'lä-ji-kəl\ *also* **phar·ma·co·log·ic** \-jik\ *adjective*
— **phar·ma·co·log·i·cal·ly** \-ji-k(ə-)lē\ *adverb*
— **phar·ma·col·o·gist** \-'kä-lə-jist\ *noun*

phar·ma·co·poe·ia *also* **phar·ma·co·pe·ia** \-kə-'pē-ə\ *noun* [New Latin, from Late Greek *pharmakopoiia* preparation of drugs, from Greek *pharmako-* + *poiein* to make — more at POET] (1621)
1 : a book describing drugs, chemicals, and medicinal preparations; *especially* **:** one issued by an officially recognized authority and serving as a standard
2 : a collection or stock of drugs
— **phar·ma·co·poe·ial** *also* **phar·ma·co·pe·ial** \-əl\ *adjective*

phar·ma·co·ther·a·py \ˌfär-mə-kō-'ther-ə-pē\ *noun* (circa 1909)
: the treatment of disease and especially mental illness with drugs

phar·ma·cy \'fär-mə-sē\ *noun, plural* **-cies** [Late Latin *pharmacia* administration of drugs, from Greek *pharmakeia*, from *pharmakeuein* to administer drugs, from *pharmakon* magic charm, poison, drug] (1651)
1 : the art, practice, or profession of preparing, preserving, compounding, and dispensing medical drugs
2 a : a place where medicines are compounded or dispensed **b :** DRUGSTORE
3 : PHARMACOPOEIA 2

pha·ryn·geal \ˌfar-ən-'jē-əl, fə-'rin-j(ē-)əl\ *adjective* [New Latin *pharyngeus*, from *pharyng-, pharynx*] (1828)
: relating to or located or produced in the region of the pharynx

phar·yn·gi·tis \ˌfar-ən-'jī-təs\ *noun, plural* **-git·i·des** \-'ji-tə-ˌdēz\ (circa 1844)
: inflammation of the pharynx

phar·ynx \'far-iŋ(k)s\ *noun, plural* **pha·ryn·ges** \fə-'rin-(ˌ)jēz\ *also* **phar·ynx·es** [New Latin *pharyng-, pharynx*, from Greek, throat, pharynx; akin to Old Norse *barki* throat and probably to Latin *ferire* to strike — more at BORE] (circa 1693)
1 : the part of the vertebrate alimentary canal between the cavity of the mouth and the esophagus
2 : a differentiated part of the alimentary canal in some invertebrates that may be thickened and muscular, eversible and toothed, or adapted as a suctorial organ

¹**phase** \'fāz\ *noun* [New Latin *phasis*, from Greek, appearance of a star, phase of the moon, from *phainein* to show (middle voice, to appear) — more at FANCY] (1812)

1 : a particular appearance or state in a regularly recurring cycle of changes ⟨*phases* of the moon⟩
2 a : a distinguishable part in a course, development, or cycle ⟨the early *phases* of her career⟩ **b :** an aspect or part (as of a problem) under consideration
3 : the point or stage in a period of uniform circular motion, harmonic motion, or the periodic changes of any magnitude varying according to a simple harmonic law to which the rotation, oscillation, or variation has advanced considered in its relation to a standard position or assumed instant of starting
4 : a homogeneous, physically distinct, and mechanically separable portion of matter present in a nonhomogeneous physicochemical system
5 : an individual or subgroup distinguishably different in appearance or behavior from the norm of the group to which it belongs; *also* **:** the distinguishing peculiarity
— **pha·sic** \'fā-zik\ *adjective*
— **in phase :** in a synchronized or correlated manner
— **out of phase :** in an unsynchronized manner **:** not in correlation

²**phase** *transitive verb* **phased; phas·ing** (1904)
1 : to adjust so as to be in a synchronized condition
2 : to conduct or carry out by planned phases
3 : to introduce in stages — often used with *in* ⟨*phase* in new models⟩

phase–contrast *adjective* (1934)
: of or employing the phase-contrast microscope

phase–contrast microscope *noun* (1947)
: a microscope that translates differences in phase of the light transmitted through or reflected by the object into differences of intensity in the image — called also *phase microscope*

phase·down \'fāz-ˌdaůn\ *noun* (1964)
: a gradual reduction (as in operations)

phase modulation *noun* (1930)
: modulation of the phase of a radio carrier wave by voice or other signal

phase-out \'fā-ˌzaůt\ *noun* (1958)
: a gradual stopping of operations or production **:** a closing down by phases

phase out (1940)
transitive verb
: to discontinue the practice, production, or use of by phases ⟨*phase out* the old machinery⟩
intransitive verb
: to stop production or operation by phases

-phasia *noun combining form* [New Latin, from Greek, speech, from *phasis* utterance, from *phanai* to speak, say — more at BAN]
: speech disorder of a (specified) type ⟨dysphasia⟩

phas·mid \'faz-məd\ *noun* [New Latin *Phasmida*, group name, from *Phasma*, type genus, from Greek, apparition, from *phainein* to show — more at FANCY] (1872)
: any of an order (Phasmatodea synonym Phasmida) of large cylindrical or sometimes flattened chiefly tropical insects (as a walking stick) with long strong legs, strictly phytophagous habits, and slight metamorphosis
— **phasmid** *adjective*

phat·ic \'fa-tik\ *adjective* [Greek *phatos*, verbal of *phanai* to speak] (1923)
: of, relating to, or being speech used for social or emotive purposes rather than for communicating information
— **phat·i·cal·ly** \-ti-k(ə-)lē\ *adverb*

pheas·ant \'fe-zªnt\ *noun, plural* **pheasant** *or* **pheasants** [Middle English *fesaunt*, from Anglo-French, from Old French *fesan*, from Latin *phasianus*, from Greek *phasianos*, from *phasianos* of the Phasis River, from *Phasis*, river in Colchis] (13th century)

1 : any of numerous large often long-tailed and brightly colored Old World gallinaceous birds (*Phasianus* and related genera of the family Phasianidae) including many raised as ornamental or game birds
2 : any of various birds resembling a pheasant

phel·lem \'fe-ˌlem\ *noun* [Greek *phellos* cork + English *-em* (as in *phloem*)] (1887)
: a layer of usually suberized cells produced outwardly by a phellogen

phel·lo·derm \'fe-lə-ˌdərm\ *noun* [Greek *phellos* + International Scientific Vocabulary *-derm*] (1875)
: a layer of parenchyma produced inwardly by a phellogen

phel·lo·gen \'fe-lə-jən\ *noun* [Greek *phellos* + International Scientific Vocabulary *-gen*] (1875)
.: a secondary meristem that initiates phellem and phelloderm in the periderm of a stem — called also *cork cambium*

phen- *or* **pheno-** *combining form* [obsolete *phene* benzene, from French *phène*, from Greek *phainein* to show; from its occurrence in illuminating gas — more at FANCY]
1 : related to or derived from benzene ⟨*phe*nol⟩
2 : containing phenyl ⟨*pheno*barbital⟩

phe·na·caine \'fē-nə-ˌkān\ *noun* [probably from *phene*tidine + *acet-* + *-caine*] (1907)
: a crystalline base $C_{18}H_{22}N_2O_2$ or its hydrochloride used as a local anesthetic

phen·ac·e·tin \fi-'na-sə-tən\ *noun* [International Scientific Vocabulary] (1887)
: a white crystalline compound $C_{10}H_{13}NO_2$ formerly used to ease pain or fever but withdrawn because of its serious side effects — called also *acetophenetidin*

phen·a·kite \'fe-nə-ˌkīt, 'fē-\ *or* **phen·a·cite** \-ˌsīt\ *noun* [German *Phenakit*, from Greek *phenak-, phenax* deceiver; from its being easily mistaken for quartz] (circa 1834)
: a glassy mineral that consists of a beryllium silicate and occurs in rhombohedral crystals

phen·an·threne \fə-'nan-ˌthrēn\ *noun* [International Scientific Vocabulary *phen-* + *an*thracene] (1882)
: a crystalline aromatic hydrocarbon $C_{14}H_{10}$ of coal tar isomeric with anthracene

phen·a·zine \'fe-nə-ˌzēn\ *noun* [International Scientific Vocabulary] (circa 1900)
: a yellowish crystalline base $C_{12}H_8N_2$ used especially in organic synthesis

phen·cy·cli·dine \(ˌ)fen-'si-klə-ˌdēn, -'sī-, -dən\ *noun* [*phen-* + *cycl-* + *-idine*] (1959)
: a piperidine derivative $C_{17}H_{25}N$ used especially as a veterinary anesthetic and sometimes illicitly as a psychedelic drug — called also *angel dust, PCP*

phe·net·ic \fi-'ne-tik\ *adjective* [*phen*otype + *-etic* (as in *genetic*)] (1960)
: of or relating to taxonomic analysis that emphasizes the overall similarities of characteristics among biological taxa without regard to phylogenetic relationships

phe·net·ics \-tiks\ *noun plural but singular in construction* (circa 1960)
: a system of biological classification based on phenetic methods
— **phe·net·i·cist** \-'ne-tə-sist\ *noun*

phen·met·ra·zine \(ˌ)fen-'me-trə-ˌzēn\ *noun* [*phen*yl + *methyl* + *tetra-* + *azine*] (1956)
: a sympathomimetic stimulant $C_{11}H_{15}NO$ used in the form of its hydrochloride as an appetite suppressant

phe·no·bar·bi·tal \ˌfē-nō-'bär-bə-ˌtol\ *noun* (1918)
: a crystalline barbiturate $C_{12}H_{12}N_2O_3$ used as a hypnotic and sedative

phe·no·bar·bi·tone \-bə-ˌtōn\ *noun* (circa 1932)
chiefly British : PHENOBARBITAL

phe·no·copy \'fē-nə-ˌkä-pē\ *noun* [International Scientific Vocabulary *phenotype* + *copy*] (1937)
: a phenotypic variation that is caused by unusual environmental conditions and resembles the normal expression of a genotype other than its own

phe·no·cryst \-ˌkrist\ *noun* [French *phénocryste*, from Greek *phainein* to show + *krystallos* crystal — more at FANCY] (circa 1893)
: one of the prominent embedded crystals of a porphyry
— **phe·no·crys·tic** \ˌfē-nə-'kris-tik\ *adjective*

phe·nol \'fē-ˌnol, -, -ˌnol, fi-'\ *noun* [International Scientific Vocabulary *phen-* + *³-ol*] (circa 1852)
1 : a corrosive poisonous crystalline acidic compound C_6H_5OH present in coal tar and wood tar that in dilute solution is used as a disinfectant
2 : any of various acidic compounds analogous to phenol and regarded as hydroxyl derivatives of aromatic hydrocarbons

phe·no·late \'fē-nºl-ˌāt\ *noun* (1885)
: PHENOXIDE

phe·no·lat·ed \'fē-nºl-ˌā-təd\ *adjective* (1923)
: treated, mixed, or impregnated with phenol

¹phe·no·lic \fi-'nō-lik, -'nä-\ *adjective* (1872)
1 a : of, relating to, or having the characteristics of a phenol **b** : containing or derived from a phenol
2 : of, relating to, or being a phenolic

²phenolic *noun* (1924)
: a usually thermosetting resin or plastic made by condensation of a phenol with an aldehyde and used especially for molding and insulating and in coatings and adhesives — called also *phenolic resin*

phe·nol·o·gy \fi-'nä-lə-jē\ *noun* [*phenomena* + *-logy*] (circa 1884)
1 : a branch of science dealing with the relations between climate and periodic biological phenomena (as bird migration or plant flowering)
2 : periodic biological phenomena (as of a kind of organism) that are correlated with climatic conditions
— **phe·no·log·i·cal** \ˌfē-nºl-'ä-ji-kəl\ *adjective*
— **phe·no·log·i·cal·ly** \-k(ə-)lē\ *adverb*

phe·nol·phtha·lein \ˌfē-nºl-'tha-lē-ən, -'tha-ˌlēn, -'thä-\ *noun* [International Scientific Vocabulary] (circa 1875)
: a white or yellowish white crystalline compound $C_{20}H_{14}O_4$ used in analysis as an indicator because its solution is brilliant red in alkalies and is decolorized by acids and in medicine as a laxative

phenol red *noun* (1916)
: a red crystalline compound $C_{19}H_{14}O_5S$ used especially as an acid-base indicator

phe·nom \'fē-ˌnäm, fi-'näm\ *noun* (circa 1890)
: PHENOMENON; *especially* : a person of phenomenal ability or promise

phe·nom·e·na \fi-'nä-mə-nə, -ˌnä\ *noun, plural* **-nas** (1576)
nonstandard : PHENOMENON ☐

phe·nom·e·nal \fi-'nä-mə-nºl\ *adjective* (1825)
: relating to or being a phenomenon: as **a** : known through the senses rather than through thought or intuition **b** : concerned with phenomena rather than with hypotheses **c** : EXTRAORDINARY, REMARKABLE
synonym see MATERIAL
— **phe·nom·e·nal·ly** \-nºl-ē\ *adverb*

phe·nom·e·nal·ism \-nºl-ˌi-zəm\ *noun* (circa 1865)
1 : a theory that limits knowledge to phenomena only
2 : a theory that all knowledge is of phenomena and that what is construed to be perception of material objects is simply perception of sense-data
— **phe·nom·e·nal·ist** \-ist\ *noun or adjective*
— **phe·nom·e·nal·is·tic** \-ˌnä-mə-nºl-'is-tik\ *adjective*

— **phe·nom·e·nal·is·ti·cal·ly** \-ti-k(ə-)lē\ *adverb*

phe·nom·e·no·log·i·cal \fi-ˌnä-mə-nºl-'ä-ji-kəl\ *adjective* (circa 1858)
1 : of or relating to phenomenology
2 : PHENOMENAL
3 : of or relating to phenomenalism
— **phe·nom·e·no·log·i·cal·ly** \-k(ə-)lē\ *adverb*

phe·nom·e·nol·o·gy \fi-ˌnä-mə-'nä-lə-jē\ *noun, plural* **-gies** [German *Phänomenologie*, from *Phänomenon* phenomenon + *-logie* -logy] (circa 1797)
1 : the study of the development of human consciousness and self-awareness as a preface to philosophy or a part of philosophy
2 a (1) : a philosophical movement that describes the formal structure of the objects of awareness and of awareness itself in abstraction from any claims concerning existence (2) : the typological classification of a class of phenomena ⟨the *phenomenology* of religion⟩ **b** : an analysis produced by phenomenological investigation
— **phe·nom·e·nol·o·gist** \-jist\ *noun*

phe·nom·e·non \fi-'nä-mə-ˌnän, -nən\ *noun, plural* **-na** \-nə, -ˌnä\ *or* **-nons** [Late Latin *phaenomenon*, from Greek *phainomenon*, from neuter of *phainomenos*, present participle of *phainesthai* to appear, middle voice of *phainein* to show — more at FANCY] (1605)
1 *plural* **phenomena** : an observable fact or event
2 *plural* **phenomena a** : an object or aspect known through the senses rather than by thought or intuition **b** : a temporal or spatiotemporal object of sensory experience as distinguished from a noumenon **c** : a fact or event of scientific interest susceptible of scientific description and explanation
3 a : a rare or significant fact or event **b** *plural* **phenomenons** : an exceptional, unusual, or abnormal person, thing, or occurrence
usage see PHENOMENA

phe·no·thi·a·zine \ˌfē-nō-'thī-ə-ˌzēn\ *noun* [International Scientific Vocabulary] (1894)
1 : a greenish yellow crystalline compound $C_{12}H_9NS$ used as an anthelmintic and insecticide especially in veterinary practice
2 : any of various phenothiazine derivatives (as chlorpromazine) that are used as tranquilizing agents especially in the treatment of schizophrenia

phe·no·type \'fē-nə-ˌtīp\ *noun* [German *Phänotypus*, from Greek *phainein* to show + *typos* type] (circa 1911)
: the visible properties of an organism that are produced by the interaction of the genotype and the environment
— **phe·no·typ·ic** \ˌfē-nə-'ti-pik\ *also* **phe·no·typ·i·cal** \-pi-kəl\ *adjective*
— **phe·no·typ·i·cal·ly** \-pi-k(ə-)lē\ *adverb*

\ə\ abut \ᵊ\ kitten \ər\ further \a\ ash \ā\ ace
\ä\ mop, mar \aú\ out \ch\ chin \e\ bet \ē\ easy
\g\ go \i\ hit \ī\ ice \j\ job \ŋ\ sing \ō\ go
\ó\ law \ói\ boy \th\ thin \t͟h\ the \ü\ loot \ú\ foot
\y\ yet \zh\ vision *see also* Guide to Pronunciation

phen·ox·ide \fi-'näk-ˌsīd\ *noun* (1888)
: a salt of a phenol especially in its capacity as a weak acid

phen·tol·amine \fen-'tä-lə-ˌmēn, -mən\ *noun* [*phen-* + *tol*uidine + *amine*] (1952)
: an adrenergic blocking agent $C_{17}H_{19}N_3O$ that is used especially in the diagnosis and treatment of hypertension due to pheochromocytoma

phe·nyl \'fe-nᵊl, 'fē-\ *noun* [International Scientific Vocabulary] (circa 1850)
: a univalent group C_6H_5 that is an aryl group derived from benzene by removal of one hydrogen atom — often used in combination
— **phe·nyl·ic** \fi-'ni-lik\ *adjective*

phe·nyl·al·a·nine \ˌfe-nᵊl-'a-lə-ˌnēn, ˌfē-\ *noun* [International Scientific Vocabulary] (1883)
: an essential amino acid $C_9H_{11}NO_2$ that is converted in the normal body to tyrosine

phen·yl·bu·ta·zone \ˌfe-nᵊl-'byü-tə-ˌzōn\ *noun* [*phenyl* + *butyr*ic acid + *pyr*az*alone* ($C_3H_4N_2O$)] (1952)
: a drug $C_{19}H_{20}N_2O_2$ that is used for its analgesic and anti-inflammatory properties especially in the treatment of arthritis, gout, and bursitis

phen·yl·eph·rine \-'e-ˌfrēn, -frən\ *noun* [*phenyl* + *epi*n*ephrine*] (1947)
: a sympathomimetic agent $C_9H_{13}NO_2$ that is used in the form of the hydrochloride as a vasoconstrictor, a mydriatic, and by injection to raise the blood pressure

phen·yl·eth·yl·amine \ˌfe-nᵊl-ˌe-thəl-'a-ˌmēn, ˌfē-\ *noun* (1939)
: a neurotransmitter $C_8H_{11}N$ that is an amine resembling amphetamine in structure and pharmacological properties; *also* : any of its derivatives

phe·nyl·ke·ton·uria \ˌfe-nᵊl-ˌkē-t°n-'ür-ē-ə, ˌfē-, -'yur-\ *noun* [New Latin, from International Scientific Vocabulary *phenyl* + *ketone* + New Latin *-uria*] (1935)
: an inherited human metabolic disease that is characterized by inability to oxidize a metabolic product of phenylalanine and by severe mental deficiency — abbreviation *PKU*
— **phe·nyl·ke·ton·uric** \-'ür-ik, -'yur-\ *noun or adjective*

phen·yl·pro·pa·nol·amine \ˌfe-nᵊl-ˌprō-pə-'nȯ-lə-ˌmēn, ˌfē-, -ˌnō-; -nȯ-'la-ˌmēn\ *noun* [*phenyl* + *propane* + *¹-ol* + *amine*] (1947)
: a sympathomimetic drug $C_9H_{13}NO$ used in the form of its hydrochloride especially as a nasal and bronchial decongestant and as an appetite suppressant

phen·yl·thio·car·ba·mide \ˌfe-nᵊl-ˌthī-ō-'kär-bə-ˌmīd, ˌfē-\ *noun* (1879)
: a crystalline compound $C_7H_8N_2S$ that is extremely bitter or tasteless depending on the presence or absence of a single dominant gene in the taster — called also *phenylthiourea, PTC*

phen·yl·thio·urea \-ˌthī-ō-yù-'rē-ə\ *noun* (1896)
: PHENYLTHIOCARBAMIDE

phe·nyt·o·in \fə-'ni-tə-wən\ *noun* [di*phenyl*hydan*toin*] (1941)
: a crystalline anticonvulsant compound $C_{15}H_{12}N_2O_2$ used in the form of its sodium salt in the treatment of epilepsy — called also *diphenylhydantoin*

pheo·chro·mo·cy·to·ma \ˌfē-ə-ˌkrō-mə-sə-'tō-mə, -sī-\ *noun, plural* **-mas** *or* **-ma·ta** \-mə-tə\ [New Latin, from International Scientific Vocabulary *pheochromocyte* chromaffin cell + New Latin *-oma*] (circa 1929)
: a tumor that is derived from chromaffin cells and is usually associated with paroxysmal or sustained hypertension

pher·o·mone \'fer-ə-ˌmōn\ *noun* [International Scientific Vocabulary *phero-* (from Greek *pherein* to carry) + *-mone* (as in *hormone*) — more at BEAR] (1959)
: a chemical substance that is produced by an animal and serves especially as a stimulus to other individuals of the same species for one or more behavioral responses
— **pher·o·mon·al** \ˌfer-ə-'mō-nᵊl\ *adjective*

phew *a voiceless bilabial fricative usually followed by a voiceless* (y)ü *or* ē̄ *sound; often read as* 'f(y)ü\ *interjection* (1604)
1 — used to express relief or fatigue
2 — used to express disgust at or as if at an unpleasant odor

phi \'fī\ *noun* [Middle Greek, from Greek *phei*] (circa 1899)
: the 21st letter of the Greek alphabet — see ALPHABET table

phi·al \'fī-(ə)l\ *noun* [Middle English, from Latin *phiala*, from Greek *phialē*] (14th century)
: VIAL

Phi Be·ta Kap·pa \ˌfī-ˌbā-tə-'ka-pə\ *noun* [*Phi Beta Kappa* (*Society*), from *phi* + *beta* + *kappa*, initials of the society's Greek motto *philosophia biou kybernētēs* philosophy the guide of life] (1912)
: a person winning high scholastic distinction in an American college or university and being elected to membership in a national honor society founded in 1776

phil- *or* **philo-** *combining form* [Middle English, from Old French, from Latin, from Greek, from *philos* dear, friendly]
: loving : having an affinity for ⟨*philo*progenitive⟩

¹-phil *or* **-phile** *noun combining form* [French *-phile*, from Greek *-philos* -philous]
: lover : one having an affinity for or a strong attraction to ⟨acido*phil*⟩ ⟨Slavo*phile*⟩

²-phil *or* **-phile** *adjective combining form* [New Latin *-philus*, from Latin, from Greek *-philos*]
: loving : having a fondness or affinity for ⟨Franco*phile*⟩

Phil·a·del·phia lawyer \ˌfi-lə-'del-fyə-, -fē-ə-\ *noun* [*Philadelphia*, Pa.] (1788)
: a lawyer knowledgeable in even the most minute aspects of the law

Philadelphia pepper pot *noun* (1929)
: PEPPER POT 2b

phil·a·del·phus \ˌfi-lə-'del-fəs\ *noun* [New Latin, from Greek *philadelphos* brotherly, from *phil-* + *adelphos* brother — more at -ADELPHOUS] (1950)
: MOCK ORANGE 1

phi·lan·der \fə-'lan-dər\ *intransitive verb* **-dered; -der·ing** \-d(ə-)riŋ\ [from obsolete *philander* lover, philanderer, probably from the name *Philander*] (1737)
1 : to make love to someone with whom marriage is impossible (as because of an existing marriage) or with no intention of proposing marriage
2 : to have many love affairs
— **phi·lan·der·er** \-dər-ər\ *noun*

phil·an·throp·ic \ˌfi-lən-'thrä-pik\ *also* **phil·an·throp·i·cal** \-pi-kəl\ *adjective* (1789)
1 : of, relating to, or characterized by philanthropy : HUMANITARIAN
2 : dispensing or receiving aid from funds set aside for humanitarian purposes
— **phil·an·throp·i·cal·ly** \-pi-k(ə-)lē\ *adverb*

phi·lan·thro·pist \fə-'lan(t)-thrə-pist\ *noun* (circa 1736)
: one who practices philanthropy

phi·lan·thro·poid \-ˌpȯid\ *noun* [blend of *philanthropist* and *anthropoid*] (1945)
: a person who works for a philanthropic organization

phi·lan·thro·py \-pē\ *noun, plural* **-pies** [Late Latin *philanthropia*, from Greek *philanthrōpia*, from *philanthrōpos* loving people, from *phil-* + *anthrōpos* human being] (circa 1623)
1 : goodwill to fellowmen; *especially* : active effort to promote human welfare
2 a : a philanthropic act or gift **b** : an organization distributing or supported by philanthropic funds

phi·lat·e·list \fə-'la-t°l-ist\ *noun* (circa 1865)
: a specialist in philately : one who collects or studies stamps

phi·lat·e·ly \fə-'la-t°l-ē\ *noun* [French *philatélie*, from *phil-* + Greek *ateleia* tax exemption, from *atelēs* free from tax, from *a-* + *telos* tax; perhaps akin to Greek *tlēnai* to bear; from the fact that a stamped letter frees the recipient from paying the mailing charges — more at TOLERATE] (circa 1865)
: the collection and study of postage and imprinted stamps : stamp collecting
— **phil·a·tel·ic** \ˌfi-lə-'te-lik\ *adjective*
— **phil·a·tel·i·cal·ly** \-li-k(ə-)lē\ *adverb*

Phi·le·mon \fə-'lē-mən, fī-\ *noun* [Greek *Philēmōn*]
1 : a friend and probable convert of the apostle Paul
2 : a letter written by Saint Paul to a Christian living in the area of Colossae and included as a book in the New Testament — see BIBLE table
3 : a poor aged Phrygian in Greek mythology who with his wife Baucis treats a disguised Zeus hospitably and is rewarded by him with a splendid temple

phil·har·mon·ic \ˌfi-lər-'mä-nik, -(ˌ)lär-; ˌfil-(ˌ)här-\ *noun* [French *philharmonique*, literally, loving harmony, from Italian *filarmonico*, from *fil-* phil- + *armonia* harmony, from Latin *harmonia*] (1843)
: SYMPHONY ORCHESTRA

phil·hel·lene \(ˌ)fil-'he-ˌlēn\ *or* **phil·hel·len·ic** \ˌfil-hə-'le-nik\ *adjective* [Greek *philellēn*, from *phil-* + *Hellēn* Hellene] (circa 1825)
: admiring Greece or the Greeks
— **philhellene** *noun*
— **phil·hel·le·nism** \(ˌ)fil-'he-lə-ˌni-zəm\ *noun*
— **phil·hel·le·nist** \-nist\ *noun*

-philia *noun combining form* [New Latin, from Greek *philia* friendship, from *philos* dear]
1 : friendly feeling toward ⟨Franco*philia*⟩
2 : tendency toward ⟨hemo*philia*⟩
3 : abnormal appetite or liking for ⟨necro*philia*⟩

-philiac *noun combining form* [New Latin *-philia* + Greek *-akos*, adjective suffix]
1 : one having a tendency toward ⟨hemo*philiac*⟩
2 : one having an abnormal appetite or liking for ⟨copro*philiac*⟩

-philic *adjective combining form* [Greek *-philos* -philous]
: having an affinity for : loving ⟨acido*philic*⟩

Phi·lip·pi·ans \fə-'li-pē-ənz\ *noun plural but singular in construction* [short for *Epistle to the Philippians*]
: a hortatory letter written by Saint Paul to the Christians of Philippi and included as a book in the New Testament — see BIBLE table

phi·lip·pic \fə-'li-pik\ *noun* [Middle French *philippique*, from Latin & Greek; Latin *philippica, orationes philippicae*, speeches of Cicero against Mark Antony, translation of Greek *philippikoi logoi*, speeches of Demosthenes against Philip II of Macedon, literally, speeches relating to Philip] (1592)
: a discourse or declamation full of bitter condemnation : TIRADE

Phil·ip·pine mahogany \'fi-lə-ˌpēn-\ *noun* [*Philippine* Islands] (circa 1924)
: any of several Philippine dipterocarp timber trees (genera *Shorea, Parashorea*, and *Pentacme*) with wood resembling that of the true mahoganies; *also* : its wood

phi·lis·tia \fə-'lis-tē-ə\ *noun plural, often capitalized* [*Philistia*, ancient country of southwest Palestine] (1857)
: the class or world of cultural philistines

Phi·lis·tine \'fi-lə-ˌstēn; fə-'lis-tən, -ˌtēn; 'fi-lə-stən\ *noun* (14th century)
1 : a native or inhabitant of ancient Philistia

2 *often not capitalized* **a :** a person who is guided by materialism and is usually disdainful of intellectual or artistic values **b :** one uninformed in a special area of knowledge ◇
— **philistine** *adjective, often capitalized*
— **phi·lis·tin·ism** \-lə-,stē-,ni-zəm; -'lis-tə-, -,tē-, -lə-stə-\ *noun, often capitalized*

Phil·lips \'fi-ləps\ *adjective* [from *Phillips*, a trademark, from Henry M. *Phillips* 20th century American engineer] (1935)
: of, relating to, or being a screw having a head with a cross slot or the corresponding screwdriver

phil·lu·men·ist \fi-'lü-mə-nist\ *noun* [*phil-* + Latin *lumen* light — more at LUMINARY] (1943)
: one who collects matchbooks or matchbox labels

Phi·loc·te·tes \fi-'läk-tə-,tēz, ,fi-läk-'tē-tēz\ *noun* [Greek *Philoktētēs*]
: a Greek archer who uses the bow of Hercules to slay Paris at Troy

phil·o·den·dron \,fi-lə-'den-drən\ *noun, plural* **-drons** *or* **-dra** \-drə\ [New Latin, from Greek, neuter of *philodendros* loving trees, from *phil-* + *dendron* tree — more at DENDR-] (1877)
: any of various aroid plants (as of the genus *Philodendron*) that are cultivated for their showy foliage

phi·lol·o·gy \fə-'lä-lə-jē *also* fī-\ *noun* [French *philologie*, from Latin *philologia* love of learning and literature, from Greek, from *philologos* fond of learning and literature, from *phil-* + *logos* word, speech — more at LEGEND] (1612)
1 : the study of literature and of disciplines relevant to literature or to language as used in literature
2 a : LINGUISTICS; *especially* **:** historical and comparative linguistics **b :** the study of human speech especially as the vehicle of literature and as a field of study that sheds light on cultural history
— **phil·o·log·i·cal** \,fi-lə-'lä-ji-kəl\ *adjective*
— **phil·o·log·i·cal·ly** \-k(ə-)lē\ *adverb*
— **phi·lol·o·gist** \fə-'lä-lə-jist *also* fī-\ *noun*

Phil·o·mel \'fi-lə-,mel\ *noun* [Latin *Philomela* Philomela, nightingale] (1579)
: NIGHTINGALE

Phil·o·me·la \,fi-lə-'mē-lə\ *noun* [Latin, from Greek *Philomēlē*]
: an Athenian princess in Greek mythology raped and deprived of her tongue by her brother-in-law Tereus, avenged by the killing of his son, and changed into a nightingale while fleeing from him

phil·o·pro·gen·i·tive \,fi-lə-prō-'je-nə-tiv\ *adjective* [*phil-* + Latin *progenitus*, past participle of *progignere* to beget — more at PROGENITOR] (1865)
1 : tending to produce offspring **:** PROLIFIC
2 : of, relating to, or characterized by love of offspring
— **phil·o·pro·gen·i·tive·ness** *noun*

phi·lo·sophe \,fē-lə-'zòf\ *noun* [French, literally, philosopher] (1779)
: one of the deistic or materialistic writers and thinkers of the 18th century French Enlightenment

phi·los·o·pher \fə-'lä-s(ə-)fər\ *noun* [Middle English, modification of Middle French *philosophe*, from Latin *philosophus*, from Greek *philosophos*, from *phil-* + *sophia* wisdom, from *sophos* wise] (14th century)
1 a : a person who seeks wisdom or enlightenment **:** SCHOLAR, THINKER **b :** a student of philosophy
2 a : a person whose philosophical perspective makes meeting trouble with equanimity easier **b :** an expounder of a theory in a particular area of experience **c :** one who philosophizes

philosophers' stone *noun* (14th century)

: an imaginary stone, substance, or chemical preparation believed to have the power of transmuting baser metals into gold and sought by alchemists — called also *philosopher's stone*

phil·o·soph·i·cal \,fi-lə-'sä-fi-kəl\ *also* -'zä-\ *or* **phil·o·soph·ic** \-fik\ *adjective* (14th century)
1 a : of or relating to philosophers or philosophy **b :** based on philosophy
2 : characterized by the attitude of a philosopher; *specifically* **:** calm or unflinching in face of trouble, defeat, or loss
— **phil·o·soph·i·cal·ly** \-fi-k(ə-)lē\ *adverb*

philosophical analysis *noun* (1936)
: ANALYTIC PHILOSOPHY

phi·los·o·phise *British variant of* PHILOSOPHIZE

phi·los·o·phize \fə-'lä-sə-,fīz\ *verb* **-phized; -phiz·ing** (1594)
intransitive verb
1 : to reason in the manner of a philosopher
2 : to expound a moralizing and often superficial philosophy
transitive verb
: to consider from or bring into conformity with a philosophical point of view
— **phi·los·o·phiz·er** *noun*

phi·los·o·phy \fə-'lä-s(ə-)fē\ *noun, plural* **-phies** [Middle English *philosophie*, from Old French, from Latin *philosophia*, from Greek, from *philosophos* philosopher] (14th century)
1 a (1) **:** all learning exclusive of technical precepts and practical arts (2) **:** the sciences and liberal arts exclusive of medicine, law, and theology ⟨a doctor of *philosophy*⟩ (3) **:** the 4-year college course of a major seminary **b** (1) *archaic* **:** PHYSICAL SCIENCE (2) **:** ETHICS **c :** a discipline comprising as its core logic, aesthetics, ethics, metaphysics, and epistemology
2 a : pursuit of wisdom **b :** a search for a general understanding of values and reality by chiefly speculative rather than observational means **c :** an analysis of the grounds of and concepts expressing fundamental beliefs
3 a : a system of philosophical concepts **b :** a theory underlying or regarding a sphere of activity or thought ⟨the *philosophy* of war⟩ ⟨*philosophy* of science⟩
4 a : the most general beliefs, concepts, and attitudes of an individual or group **b :** calmness of temper and judgment befitting a philosopher

philosophy of life (1853)
1 : an overall vision of or attitude toward life and the purpose of life
2 [translation of German *Lebensphilosophie*] **:** any of various philosophies that emphasize human life or life in general

-philous *adjective combining form* [Greek *-philos*, from *philos* dear, friendly]
: loving **:** having an affinity for ⟨hygro*philous*⟩

phil·ter *or* **phil·tre** \'fil-tər\ *noun* [Middle French *philtre*, from Latin *philtrum*, from Greek *philtron*; akin to Greek *philos* dear] (circa 1587)
1 : a potion, drug, or charm held to have the power to arouse sexual passion
2 : a potion credited with magical power

phi phenomenon \'fī-\ *noun* (circa 1928)
: apparent motion resulting from an orderly sequence of stimuli (as lights flashed in rapid succession a short distance apart on a sign) without any actual motion being presented to the eye

phiz \'fiz\ *noun* [by shortening & alteration from *physiognomy*] (1688)
: FACE

phleb- *or* **phlebo-** *combining form* [Middle English *fleb-*, from Middle French, from Late Latin *phlebo-*, from Greek *phleb-*, *phlebo-*, from *phleb-*, *phleps*; perhaps akin to Greek *phlyein*, *phlyzein* to boil over — more at FLUID]
: vein ⟨*phleb*itis⟩

phle·bi·tis \fli-'bī-təs\ *noun* [New Latin] (circa 1834)
: inflammation of a vein

phle·bo·gram \'flē-bə-,gram\ *noun* [International Scientific Vocabulary] (1885)
: a figure of a vein or a record of its movements

phle·bog·ra·phy \fli-'bä-grə-fē\ *noun* [International Scientific Vocabulary] (1937)
: the process of making phlebograms
— **phle·bo·graph·ic** \,flē-bə-'gra-fik\ *adjective*

phle·bol·o·gy \fli-'bä-lə-jē\ *noun* [International Scientific Vocabulary] (1893)
: a branch of medicine concerned with the veins

phle·bo·to·mus fever \fli-'bä-tə-məs-\ *noun* [New Latin *Phlebotomus*, genus of sand flies] (circa 1923)
: SANDFLY FEVER

phle·bot·o·my \fli-'bä-tə-mē\ *noun, plural* **-mies** [Middle English *fleobotomie*, from Middle French *flebotomie*, from Late Latin *phlebotomia*, from Greek, from *phleb-* + *-tomia* -tomy] (14th century)
: the letting of blood for transfusion, diagnosis, or experiment, and especially formerly in the treatment of disease — called also *venesection*
— **phle·bot·o·mist** \-mist\ *noun*

Phleg·e·thon \'fle-gə-,thän\ *noun* [Latin, from Greek *Phlegethōn*]
: a river of fire in Hades

phlegm \'flem\ *noun* [Middle English *fleume*, from Middle French, from Late Latin *phlegmat-*, *phlegma*, from Greek, flame, inflammation, phlegm, from *phlegein* to burn — more at BLACK] (13th century)
1 : the one of the four humors in early physiology that was considered to be cold and moist and to cause sluggishness
2 : viscid mucus secreted in abnormal quantity in the respiratory passages
3 a : dull or apathetic coldness or indifference
b : intrepid coolness or calm fortitude

◇ **WORD HISTORY**

Philistine In the Bible the *Philistines* are the perennial rivals and enemies of the neighboring Israelites. Biblical accounts portray the Philistines as a crude and warlike race. A figurative sense of *philistine* entered the English language as a result of a dispute between the townspeople and the university students in the German town of Jena in 1687. A bloody confrontation prompted a local clergyman to address the issue in a sermon to the townspeople on the value of education. For this sermon he chose his text from Judges 16:9 (Authorized Version): "The Philistines be upon these" *Philister*, the German word for *Philistine*, soon caught on with the students as an epithet first for the town militia and then for townsmen in general. Spreading more widely in German university slang, *Philister* came to be used for an outsider—someone who was not a member of the university community. Familiar with this usage, the English Victorian social and cultural critics Thomas Carlyle and Matthew Arnold, among others, used *Philistine* as an epithet for a materialist in various writings including Carlyle's *Sartor Resartus* (1831) and Arnold's *Culture and Anarchy* (1869). Since then, *philistine* has become widely used of any person who is indifferent or hostile to the arts and smugly accepts conventional values.

— **phleg·my** \'fle-mē\ *adjective*

phleg·mat·ic \fleg-'ma-tik\ *adjective* (14th century)
1 : resembling, consisting of, or producing the humor phlegm
2 : having or showing a slow and stolid temperament
synonym see IMPASSIVE
— **phleg·mat·i·cal·ly** \-ti-k(ə-)lē\ *adverb*

phlo·em \'flō-,em\ *noun* [German, from Greek *phloios, phloos* bark; perhaps akin to Greek *phlein* to teem, abound, *phlyein, phlyzein* to boil over — more at FLUID] (1875)
: a complex tissue in the vascular system of higher plants that consists mainly of sieve tubes and elongated parenchyma cells usually with fibers and that functions in translocation and in support and storage — compare XYLEM

phloem necrosis *noun* (1923)
: a pathological state in a plant characterized by brown discoloration and disintegration of the phloem; *especially* : a fatal disease of the American elm caused by a mycoplasma-like organism transmitted by a leafhopper (*Scaphoideus luteolus*)

phloem ray *noun* (1875)
: a vascular ray or part of a vascular ray that is located in phloem — compare XYLEM RAY

phlo·gis·tic \flō-'jis-tik\ *adjective* (1733)
1 [New Latin *phlogiston*] : of or relating to phlogiston
2 [Greek *phlogistos*] : of or relating to inflammations and fevers

phlo·gis·ton \-tən\ *noun* [New Latin, from Greek, neuter of *phlogistos* inflammable, from *phlogizein* to set on fire, from *phlog-, phlox* flame, from *phlegein*] (1733)
: the hypothetical principle of fire regarded formerly as a material substance

phlog·o·pite \'flä-gə-,pīt\ *noun* [German *Phlogopit*, from Greek *phlogōpos* fiery-looking, from *phlog-, phlox* + *ōps* face — more at EYE] (1850)
: a usually brown to red form of mica

phlox \'fläks\ *noun, plural* **phlox** *or* **phlox·es** [New Latin, from Latin, a flower, from Greek, flame, wallflower] (circa 1706)
: any of a genus (*Phlox* of the family Polemoniaceae, the phlox family) of American annual or perennial herbs that have red, purple, white, or variegated flowers, a salverform corolla with the stamens on its tube, and a 3-valved capsular fruit

phlox

-phobe *noun combining form* [Greek *-phobos* fearing]
: one fearing or averse to (something specified) ⟨Francophobe⟩

pho·bia \'fō-bē-ə\ *noun* [-*phobia*] (1786)
: an exaggerated usually inexplicable and illogical fear of a particular object, class of objects, or situation

-phobia *noun combining form* [New Latin, from Late Latin, from Greek, from *-phobos* fearing, from *phobos* fear, flight, from *phebesthai* to flee; akin to Lithuanian *bėgti* to flee, Old Church Slavonic *bězati*]
1 : exaggerated fear of ⟨acrophobia⟩
2 : intolerance or aversion to ⟨photophobia⟩

pho·bic \'fō-bik\ *adjective* (1897)
: of, relating to, affected with, or constituting phobia
— **phobic** *noun*

-phobic *adjective combining form* [French *-phobique*, from Late Latin *-phobicus*, from Greek *-phobikos*, from *-phobia*]
1 a : having an intolerance or aversion for ⟨photophobic⟩ ⟨Anglophobic⟩ **b** : exhibiting a phobia for ⟨claustrophobic⟩
2 : lacking affinity for ⟨hydrophobic⟩

phoe·be \'fē-(,)bē\ *noun* [imitative] (1700)
: any of a genus (*Sayornis*) of American flycatchers; *especially* : one (*S. phoebe*) of the eastern U.S. that has a slight crest and is plain grayish brown above and yellowish white below

Phoe·be \'fē-bē\ *noun* [Latin, from Greek *Phoibē*, from *phoibē*, feminine of *phoibos*]
: ARTEMIS

Phoe·bus \'fē-bəs\ *noun* [Latin, from Greek *Phoibos*, from *phoibos* radiant]
1 : APOLLO
2 *not capitalized* : SUN

Phoe·ni·cian \fi-'nē-shən, -'ni-\ *noun* (14th century)
1 : a native or inhabitant of ancient Phoenicia
2 : the Semitic language of ancient Phoenicia
— **Phoenician** *adjective*

phoe·nix \'fē-niks\ *noun* [Middle English *fenix*, from Old English, from Latin *phoenix*, from Greek *phoinix*] (before 12th century)
: a legendary bird which according to one account lived 500 years, burned itself to ashes on a pyre, and rose alive from the ashes to live another period; *also* : a person or thing likened to the phoenix
— **phoe·nix·like** \-,līk\ *adjective*

phon \'fän\ *noun* [International Scientific Vocabulary, from Greek *phōne* voice, sound] (1932)
: the unit of loudness on a scale beginning at zero for the faintest audible sound and corresponding to the decibel scale of sound intensity with the number of phons of a given sound being equal to the decibels of a pure 1000-cycle tone judged by the average listener to be equal in loudness to the given sound

phon- *or* **phono-** *combining form* [Latin, from Greek *phōn-, phōno-*, from *phōne* — more at BAN]
: sound : voice : speech ⟨phonate⟩ ⟨phonograph⟩

pho·nate \'fō-,nāt\ *intransitive verb* **pho·nat·ed; pho·nat·ing** (1876)
: to produce vocal sounds and especially speech
— **pho·na·tion** \fō-'nā-shən\ *noun*

¹**phone** \'fōn\ *noun* [Greek *phōnē*] (circa 1866)
: a speech sound considered as a physical event without regard to its place in the sound system of a language

²**phone** *noun* [by shortening] (1884)
1 : TELEPHONE
2 : EARPHONE

³**phone** *verb* **phoned; phon·ing** (1889)
: TELEPHONE

¹**-phone** *noun combining form* [Greek *-phōnos* sounding, from *phōnē*]
1 : sound ⟨homophone⟩ — often in names of musical instruments and sound-transmitting devices ⟨radiophone⟩ ⟨xylophone⟩
2 : speaker of (a specified language) ⟨Francophone⟩

²**-phone** *adjective combining form* [French, from Greek *-phōnos*]
: of or relating to a population that speaks (a specified language) ⟨Francophone⟩

phone-in \'fōn-,in\ *noun* (1968)
: a call-in show (as on radio)

pho·ne·mat·ic \,fō-nē-'ma-tik\ *adjective* (1936)
: PHONEMIC

pho·neme \'fō-,nēm\ *noun* [French *phonème*, from Greek *phōnēmat-, phōnēma* speech sound, utterance, from *phōnein* to sound] (circa 1916)
: any of the abstract units of the phonetic system of a language that correspond to a set of similar speech sounds (as the velar \k\ of *cool* and the palatal \k\ of *keel*) which are perceived to be a single distinctive sound in the language

pho·ne·mic \fə-'nē-mik, fō-\ *adjective* (circa 1931)
1 : of, relating to, or having the characteristics of a phoneme

2 a : constituting members of different phonemes (as \n\ and \m\ in English) **b** : DISTINCTIVE 2
— **pho·ne·mi·cal·ly** \-mi-k(ə-)lē\ *adverb*

pho·ne·mics \-miks\ *noun plural but singular in construction* (1936)
1 : a branch of linguistic analysis that consists of the study of phonemes
2 : the structure of a language in terms of phonemes
— **pho·ne·mi·cist** \-mə-sist\ *noun*

pho·net·ic \fə-'ne-tik\ *adjective* [New Latin *phoneticus*, from Greek *phōnētikos*, from *phōnein* to sound with the voice, from *phōne* voice] (1826)
1 a : of or relating to spoken language or speech sounds **b** : of or relating to the science of phonetics
2 : representing the sounds and other phenomena of speech: as **a** : constituting an alteration of ordinary spelling that better represents the spoken language, that employs only characters of the regular alphabet, and that is used in a context of conventional spelling **b** : representing speech sounds by means of symbols that have one value only **c** : employing for speech sounds more than the minimum number of symbols necessary to represent the significant differences in a speaker's speech
— **pho·net·i·cal·ly** \-ti-k(ə-)lē\ *adverb*

phonetic alphabet *noun* (1848)
1 : a set of symbols (as IPA) used for phonetic transcription
2 : any of various systems of identifying letters of the alphabet by means of code words in voice communication

pho·ne·ti·cian \,fō-nə-'ti-shən *also* ,fä-\ *noun* (1848)
: a specialist in phonetics

pho·net·ics \fə-'ne-tiks\ *noun plural but singular in construction* (1836)
1 : the system of speech sounds of a language or group of languages
2 a : the study and systematic classification of the sounds made in spoken utterance **b** : the practical application of this science to language study

pho·nic \'fä-nik *also* 'fō-\ *adjective* (1823)
1 : of, relating to, or producing sound : ACOUSTIC
2 a : of or relating to the sounds of speech **b** : of or relating to phonics
— **pho·ni·cal·ly** \-ni-k(ə-)lē\ *adverb*

pho·nics \'fä-niks, *1 is also* 'fō-\ *noun plural but singular in construction* (circa 1684)
1 : the science of sound : ACOUSTICS
2 : a method of teaching beginners to read and pronounce words by learning the phonetic value of letters, letter groups, and especially syllables

pho·no \'fō-(,)nō\ *noun, plural* **phonos** (1909)
: PHONOGRAPH

pho·no·car·dio·gram \,fō-nə-'kär-dē-ə-,gram\ *noun* [International Scientific Vocabulary] (1912)
: a graphic record of heart sounds made by means of a microphone, amplifier, and galvanometer

pho·no·car·di·og·ra·phy \-,kär-dē-'ä-grə-fē\ *noun* (1916)
: the process of producing a phonocardiogram
— **pho·no·car·dio·graph** \-'kär-dē-ə-,graf\ *noun*
— **pho·no·car·dio·graph·ic** \-,kär-dē-ə-'gra-fik\ *adjective*

pho·no·gram \'fō-nə-,gram\ *noun* [International Scientific Vocabulary] (1860)
1 : a character or symbol used to represent a word, syllable, or phoneme
2 : a succession of orthographic letters that occurs with the same phonetic value in several words (as the *ight* of *bright, fight,* and *flight*)
— **pho·no·gram·mic** *or* **pho·no·gram·ic** \,fō-nə-'gra-mik\ *adjective*

— **pho·no·gram·mi·cal·ly** or **pho·no·gram·i·cal·ly** \-mi-k(ə-)lē\ *adverb*

pho·no·graph \'fō-nə-,graf\ *noun* (1877)
: an instrument for reproducing sounds by means of the vibration of a stylus or needle following a spiral groove on a revolving disc or cylinder

pho·nog·ra·pher \fə-'nä-grə-fər, fō-\ *noun* (1845)
: a specialist in phonography

pho·no·graph·ic \,fō-nə-'gra-fik, *1 is also* ,fä-\ *adjective* (1828)
1 : of or relating to phonography
2 : of or relating to a phonograph
— **pho·no·graph·i·cal·ly** \-fi-k(ə-)lē\ *adverb*

pho·nog·ra·phy \fə-'nä-grə-fē, fō-\ *noun* (1701)
1 : spelling based on pronunciation
2 : a system of shorthand writing based on sound

pho·no·lite \'fō-nᵊl-,īt\ *noun* [French, from German *Phonolith*, from *phon-* + *-lith;* from its ringing sound when struck] (circa 1828)
: a gray or green volcanic rock consisting essentially of orthoclase and nepheline

pho·nol·o·gy \fə-'nä-lə-jē, fō-\ *noun* (1799)
1 : the science of speech sounds including especially the history and theory of sound changes in a language or in two or more related languages
2 : the phonetics and phonemics of a language at a particular time
— **pho·no·log·i·cal** \,fō-nᵊl-'ä-ji-kəl *also* ,fä-\ *also* **pho·no·log·ic** \-jik\ *adjective*
— **pho·no·log·i·cal·ly** \-ji-k(ə-)lē\ *adverb*
— **pho·nol·o·gist** \fə-'nä-lə-jist, fō-\ *noun*

pho·non \'fō-,nän\ *noun* [phon- + ²-on] (1932)
: a quantum of vibrational energy (as in a crystal)

pho·no·tac·tics \,fo-nə-'tak-tiks\ *noun plural but singular in construction* (1956)
: the area of phonology concerned with the analysis and description of the permitted sound sequences of a language
— **pho·no·tac·tic** \-tik\ *adjective*

¹pho·ny or **pho·ney** \'fō-nē\ *adjective* **pho·ni·er; -est** [perhaps alteration of *fawney* gilded brass ring used in the fawney rig, a confidence game, from Irish *fáinne* ring, from Old Irish *ánne* — more at ANUS] (1900)
: not genuine or real: as **a** (1) : intended to deceive or mislead (2) : intended to defraud : COUNTERFEIT ⟨a *phony* $10 bill⟩ ⟨a *phony* check⟩ **b** : arousing suspicion : probably dishonest ⟨something *phony* about the story⟩ **c** : having no genuine existence : FICTITIOUS ⟨*phony* publicity stories⟩ **d** : FALSE, SHAM ⟨a *phony* name⟩ ⟨*phony* pearls⟩ **e** : making a false show: as (1) : HYPOCRITICAL (2) : SPECIOUS ⟨has a *phony* poetic elegance —*New Republic*⟩
— **pho·ni·ly** \'fō-ni-lē\ *adverb*
— **pho·ni·ness** \'fō-nē-nəs\ *noun*

²phony or **phoney** *noun, plural* **pho·nies** (1902)
: one that is phony

³phony or **phoney** *transitive verb* **pho·nied** or **pho·neyed; pho·ny·ing** or **pho·ney·ing** (circa 1942)
: COUNTERFEIT, FAKE — often used with *up* ⟨a paper *phonied* up on the spur of the moment —William Faulkner⟩

-phony *also* **-phonia** *noun combining form* [Middle English *-phonie*, from Old French *-phonie*, from Latin *-phonia*, from Greek *-phōnia*, from *-phōnos* sounding — more at -PHONE]
1 : sound ⟨tele*phony*⟩
2 *usually* **-phonia** : speech disorder of a (specified) type ⟨dys*phonia*⟩

phoo·ey \'fü-ē\ *interjection* (1929)
— used to express repudiation or disgust

pho·rate \'fōr-,āt, 'for-\ *noun* [phos*phor*us + thio*ate* (salt of a thio acid)] (1959)
: a very toxic organophosphate systemic insecticide $C_7H_{17}O_2PS_3$ that is used especially in seed treatments

-phore *noun combining form* [New Latin *-phorus*, from Greek *-phoros*, from *-phoros* (adjective combining form) carrying, from *pherein* to carry — more at BEAR]
: carrier ⟨gameto*phore*⟩

-phoresis *noun combining form, plural* **-phoreses** [New Latin, from Greek *phorēsis* act of carrying, from *phorein* to carry, wear, frequentative of *pherein*]
: transmission ⟨electro*phoresis*⟩

phos·gene \'fäz-,jēn\ *noun* [Greek *phōs* light + *-genēs* born, produced — more at FANCY, -GEN; from its originally having been obtained by the action of sunlight] (1812)
: a colorless gas $COCl_2$ of unpleasant odor that is a severe respiratory irritant

phosph- or **phospho-** *combining form* [*phosphorus*]
1 : phosphorus ⟨*phosph*ide⟩
2 : phosphate ⟨*phospho*fructokinase⟩

phos·pha·tase \'fäs-fə-,tās, -,tāz\ *noun* (1912)
: an enzyme that accelerates the hydrolysis and synthesis of organic esters of phosphoric acid and the transfer of phosphate groups to other compounds: **a** : ALKALINE PHOSPHATASE **b** : ACID PHOSPHATASE

phos·phate \'fäs-,fāt\ *noun* [French, from *acide phosphorique* phosphoric acid] (1795)
1 a (1) : a salt or ester of a phosphoric acid (2) : the trivalent anion PO_4^{3-} derived from phosphoric acid H_3PO_4 **b** : an organic compound of phosphoric acid in which the acid group is bound to nitrogen or a carboxyl group in a way that permits useful energy to be released (as in metabolism)
2 : an effervescent drink of carbonated water with a small amount of phosphoric acid flavored with fruit syrup
3 : a phosphatic material used for fertilizers

phosphate rock *noun* (1870)
: a rock that consists largely of calcium phosphate usually together with other minerals (as calcium carbonate), is used in making fertilizers, and is a source of phosphorous compounds

phos·phat·ic \fäs-'fa-tik, -'fä-\ *adjective* (1843)
: of, relating to, or containing phosphoric acid or phosphates ⟨*phosphatic* fertilizers⟩

phos·pha·tide \'fäs-fə-,tīd\ *noun* [International Scientific Vocabulary] (1884)
: PHOSPHOLIPID
— **phos·pha·tid·ic** \,fäs-fə-'ti-dik\ *adjective*

phos·pha·ti·dyl \,fäs-fə-'tī-dᵊl, fäs-'fa-tə-dᵊl\ *noun* (1941)
: any of several univalent groups $(RCOO)_2C_3H_5OPO(OH)$ that are derived from phosphatidic acids

phos·pha·ti·dyl·cho·line \,fäs-fə-,tī-dᵊl-'kō-,lēn, (,)fäs-,fa-tə-dᵊl-\ *noun* (1954)
: LECITHIN

phos·pha·ti·dyl·eth·a·nol·amine \-,e-thə-'nä-lə-,mēn, -'nō-\ *noun* (1942)
: any of a group of phospholipids that occur especially in blood plasma and the white matter of the central nervous system — called also *cephalin*

phos·pha·tize \'fäs-fə-,tīz\ *transitive verb* **-tized; -tiz·ing** (1883)
1 : to change to a phosphate or phosphates
2 : to treat with phosphoric acid or a phosphate
— **phos·pha·ti·za·tion** \,fäs-fə-tə-'zā-shən, -,fā-\ *noun*

phos·pha·tu·ria \,fäs-fə-'tùr-ē-ə, -'tyùr-\ *noun* [New Latin, from International Scientific Vocabulary *phosphate* + New Latin *-uria*] (1876)
: the excessive discharge of phosphates in the urine

phos·phene \'fäs-,fēn\ *noun* [International Scientific Vocabulary *phos-* + Greek *phainein* to show — more at FANCY] (circa 1860)
: a luminous impression due to excitation of the retina

phos·phide \-,fīd\ *noun* [International Scientific Vocabulary] (1849)
: a binary compound of phosphorus with a more electropositive element or group

phos·phine \-,fēn\ *noun* [International Scientific Vocabulary] (1873)
1 : a colorless poisonous flammable gas PH_3 that is a weaker base than ammonia and that is used especially to fumigate stored grain
2 : any of various derivatives of phosphine analogous to amines but weaker as bases

phos·phite \-,fīt\ *noun* (1799)
: a salt or ester of phosphorous acid

phos·pho·cre·a·tine \,fäs-(,)fō-'krē-ə-,tēn\ *noun* [International Scientific Vocabulary] (1927)
: a compound $C_4H_{10}N_3O_5P$ of creatine and phosphoric acid that is found especially in vertebrate muscle where it is an energy source for muscle contraction

phos·pho·di·es·ter·ase \-dī-'es-tə-,rās, -,rāz\ *noun* (1936)
: a phosphatase (as from snake venom) that acts on diesters (as some nucleotides) to hydrolyze only one of the two ester groups

phos·pho·enol·pyr·uvate \,fäs-,fō-ə-,nòl-pī-'rü-,vāt, -,nōl-, -,pīr-'yü-\ *noun* (1956)
: a salt or ester of phosphoenolpyruvic acid

phos·pho·enol·pyr·uvic acid \-pī-'rü-vik-, -,pīr-'yü-vik-\ *noun* (1959)
: the phosphate $H_2C=C(OPO_3H_2)COOH$ of the enol form of pyruvic acid that is formed as an intermediate in carbohydrate metabolism

phos·pho·fruc·to·ki·nase \,fäs-(,)fō-,frək-tō-'kī-,nās, -,frük-, -,frük-, -,nāz\ *noun* [phosph- + *fructo*se + *kinase*] (1947)
: an enzyme that functions in carbohydrate metabolism and especially in glycolysis by catalyzing the transfer of a second phosphate (as from ATP) to fructose

phos·pho·glu·co·mu·tase \-,glü-kō-'myü-,tās, -,tāz\ *noun* (1938)
: an enzyme that is found in all plant and animal cells and that catalyzes the reversible isomerization of glucose-1-phosphate to glucose-6-phosphate

phos·pho·glyc·er·al·de·hyde \-,gli-sə-'ral-də-,hīd\ *noun* (1941)
: a phosphate of glyceraldehyde $C_3H_5O_3$-(H_2PO_3) that is formed especially in anaerobic metabolism of carbohydrates by the splitting of a diphosphate of fructose

phos·pho·glyc·er·ate \,fäs-fō-'gli-sə-,rāt\ *noun* (1901)
: a salt or ester of phosphoglyceric acid

phos·pho·gly·cer·ic acid \-gli-'ser-ik-\ *noun* (1857)
: either of two isomeric phosphates $HOOCC_2H_3(OH)OPO_3H_2$ of glyceric acid that are formed as intermediates in photosynthesis and in carbohydrate metabolism

phos·pho·ki·nase \,fäs-fō-'kī-,nās, -,nāz\ *noun* (1946)
: KINASE

phos·pho·li·pase \-'lī-,pās, -,pāz\ *noun* (1945)
: any of several enzymes that hydrolyze lecithins or phosphatidylethanolamines — called also *lecithinase*

phos·pho·lip·id \-'li-pəd\ *noun* (1928)
: any of numerous lipids (as lecithins and phosphatidylethanolamines) in which phosphoric acid as well as a fatty acid is esterified to glycerol and which are found in all living cells and in the bilayers of plasma membranes

phos·pho·mono·es·ter·ase \-,mä-nō-'es-tə-,rās, -,rāz\ *noun* (1933)
: a phosphatase that acts on monoesters

phos·pho·ni·um \fäs-'fō-nē-əm\ *noun* [New Latin] (1871)

: a univalent cation PH_4^+ analogous to ammonium and derived from phosphine; *also* : an organic derivative of phosphonium (as $(C_2H_5)_4P^+$)

phos·pho·pro·tein \ˌfäs-fō-ˈprō-ˌtēn, -ˈprō-tē-ən\ *noun* (circa 1908)
: any of various proteins (as casein) that contain combined phosphoric acid

phos·phor \ˈfäs-fər, -ˌfȯr\ *also* **phos·phore** \-ˌfȯr, -ˌfȯr, -fər\ *noun* [Latin *phosphorus,* from Greek *phōsphoros,* literally, light bringer, from *phōsphoros* light-bearing, from *phōs* light + *pherein* to carry, bring — more at FANCY, BEAR] (1705)
: a phosphorescent substance; *specifically* : a substance that emits light when excited by radiation

phosphor bronze *noun* (1875)
: a bronze of great hardness, elasticity, and toughness that contains a small amount of phosphorus

phos·pho·resce \ˌfäs-fə-ˈres\ *intransitive verb* **-resced; -resc·ing** [probably back-formation from *phosphorescent*] (1794)
: to exhibit phosphorescence

phos·pho·res·cence \-ˈre-sᵊn(t)s\ *noun* (1796)
1 : luminescence that is caused by the absorption of radiation at one wavelength followed by delayed reradiation at a different wavelength and that continues for a noticeable time after the incident radiation stops — compare FLUORESCENCE
2 : an enduring luminescence without sensible heat

phos·pho·res·cent \-sᵊnt\ *adjective* (1766)
: exhibiting phosphorescence
— **phos·pho·res·cent·ly** *adverb*

phos·pho·ric \fäs-ˈfȯr-ik, -ˈfär-; ˈfäs-f(ə-)rik\ *adjective* (1800)
: of, relating to, or containing phosphorus especially with a valence higher than in phosphorous compounds

phosphoric acid *noun* (1791)
1 : a syrupy or deliquescent tribasic acid H_3PO_4 used especially in preparing phosphates (as for fertilizers), in rust-proofing metals, and especially formerly as a flavoring in soft drinks — called also *orthophosphoric acid*
2 : a compound (as pyrophosphoric acid or metaphosphoric acid) consisting of phosphate groups linked directly to each other by oxygen

phos·pho·rite \ˈfäs-fə-ˌrīt\ *noun* (1796)
1 : a fibrous concretionary apatite
2 : PHOSPHATE ROCK
— **phos·pho·rit·ic** \ˌfäs-fə-ˈri-tik\ *adjective*

phos·pho·rol·y·sis \ˌfäs-fə-ˈrä-lə-səs\ *noun* [New Latin] (1937)
: a reversible reaction analogous to hydrolysis in which phosphoric acid functions in a manner similar to that of water with the formation of a phosphate (as glucose-1-phosphate in the breakdown of liver glycogen)
— **phos·pho·ro·lyt·ic** \-rō-ˈli-tik\ *adjective*

phos·pho·rous \ˈfäs-f(ə-)rəs; fäs-ˈfōr-əs, -ˈfȯr-\ *adjective* (1815)
: of, relating to, or containing phosphorus especially with a valence lower than in phosphoric compounds

phosphorous acid *noun* (1794)
: a deliquescent crystalline acid H_3PO_3 used especially as a reducing agent and in making phosphites

phos·pho·rus \ˈfäs-f(ə-)rəs\ *noun, often attributive* [New Latin, from Greek *phōsphoros* light-bearing — more at PHOSPHOR] (1645)
1 : a phosphorescent substance or body; *especially* : one that shines or glows in the dark
2 : a nonmetallic element of the nitrogen family that occurs widely especially as phosphates — see ELEMENT table

phos·pho·ryl \ˈfäs-fə-ˌril\ *noun* [International Scientific Vocabulary] (1871)
: a usually trivalent group PO

phos·phor·y·lase \fäs-ˈfȯr-ə-ˌlās, -ˌlāz\ *noun* (1939)
: any of the enzymes that catalyze phosphorolysis with the formation of organic phosphates

phos·phor·y·late \-ˌlāt\ *transitive verb* **-lat·ed; -lat·ing** (1937)
: to cause (an organic compound) to take up or combine with phosphoric acid or a phosphorus-containing group
— **phos·phor·y·la·tive** \-ˌlā-tiv\ *adjective*

phos·phor·y·la·tion \ˌfäs-ˌfȯr-ə-ˈlā-shən\ *noun* (1925)
: the process of phosphorylating a chemical compound either by reaction with inorganic phosphate or by transfer of phosphate from another organic phosphate; *especially* : the enzymatic conversion of carbohydrates into their phosphoric esters in metabolic processes

phot- *or* **photo-** *combining form* [Greek *phōt-, phōto-,* from *phōt-, phōs* — more at FANCY]
1 : light : radiant energy ⟨*photon*⟩ ⟨*photo*graphy⟩
2 : photograph : photographic ⟨*photo*engraving⟩
3 : photoelectric ⟨*photo*cell⟩

pho·tic \ˈfō-tik\ *adjective* (1843)
1 : of, relating to, or involving light especially in relation to organisms
2 : penetrated by light especially of the sun ⟨the *photic* zone of the ocean⟩
— **pho·ti·cal·ly** \ˈfō-ti-k(ə-)lē\ *adverb*

¹pho·to \ˈfō-(ˌ)tō\ *noun, plural* **photos** (1860)
: PHOTOGRAPH

²photo *verb* (1868)
: PHOTOGRAPH

³photo *adjective* (1889)
: PHOTOGRAPHIC 1

pho·to·au·to·troph \ˌfō-tō-ˈȯ-tə-ˌtrōf\ *noun* (1949)
: a photoautotrophic organism

pho·to·au·to·tro·phic \-ˌȯ-tə-ˈtrō-fik\ *adjective* (1943)
: autotrophic and utilizing energy from light ⟨green plants are *photoautotrophic*⟩
— **pho·to·au·to·tro·phi·cal·ly** \-fi-k(ə-)lē\ *adverb*

pho·to·bi·ol·o·gy \ˌfō-tō-(ˌ)bī-ˈä-lə-jē\ *noun* [International Scientific Vocabulary] (1935)
: a branch of biology that deals with the effects on living beings of radiant energy (as light)
— **pho·to·bi·o·log·i·cal** \-ˌbī-ə-ˈlä-ji-kəl\ *also* **pho·to·bi·o·log·ic** \-ˈlä-jik\ *adjective*
— **pho·to·bi·ol·o·gist** \-(ˌ)bī-ˈä-lə-jist\ *noun*

pho·to·cath·ode \-ˈka-ˌthōd\ *noun* [International Scientific Vocabulary] (1930)
: a cathode that emits electrons when exposed to radiant energy and especially light

pho·to·cell \ˈfō-tə-ˌsel\ *noun* [International Scientific Vocabulary] (1891)
: PHOTOELECTRIC CELL

pho·to·chem·i·cal \ˌfō-tō-ˈke-mi-kəl\ *adjective* (1859)
1 : of, relating to, or resulting from the chemical action of radiant energy and especially light ⟨*photochemical* smog⟩
2 : of or relating to photochemistry ⟨*photochemical* studies⟩
— **pho·to·chem·i·cal·ly** \-k(ə-)lē\ *adverb*

pho·to·chem·is·try \-ˈke-mə-strē\ *noun* (1867)
1 : a branch of chemistry that deals with the effect of radiant energy in producing chemical changes
2 a : photochemical properties ⟨the *photochemistry* of gases⟩ **b** : photochemical processes ⟨*photochemistry* of vision⟩
— **pho·to·chem·ist** \-ˈke-mist\ *noun*

pho·to·chro·mic \ˌfō-tō-ˈkrō-mik\ *adjective* [*phot-* + *chrom-* + *-ic*] (1953)
1 : capable of changing color on exposure to radiant energy (as light) ⟨*photochromic* glass⟩

2 : of, relating to, or utilizing the change of color shown by a photochromic substance ⟨a *photochromic* process⟩
— **pho·to·chro·mism** \-ˌmi-zəm\ *noun*

pho·to·co·ag·u·la·tion \-kō-ˌa-gyə-ˈlā-shən\ *noun* (1961)
: a surgical process of coagulating tissue by means of a precisely oriented high-energy light source (as a laser)

pho·to·com·pose \ˌfō-tō-kəm-ˈpōz\ *transitive verb* (1929)
: to set (as reading matter) by photocomposition
— **pho·to·com·pos·er** *noun*

pho·to·com·po·si·tion \-ˌkäm-pə-ˈzi-shən\ *noun* (1929)
: composition of text directly on film or photosensitive paper for reproduction

pho·to·con·duc·tive \-kən-ˈdək-tiv\ *adjective* (1929)
: having, involving, or operating by photoconductivity

pho·to·con·duc·tiv·i·ty \-ˌkän-ˌdək-ˈti-və-tē, -kən-\ *noun* (1929)
: electrical conductivity that is affected by exposure to electromagnetic radiation (as light)

¹pho·to·copy \ˈfō-tə-ˌkä-pē\ *noun* [International Scientific Vocabulary] (circa 1909)
: a photographic reproduction of graphic matter

²photocopy (1944)
transitive verb
: to make a photocopy of
intransitive verb
: to make a photocopy
— **pho·to·cop·i·er** *noun*

pho·to·cur·rent \ˈfō-tō-ˌkər-ənt, -ˌkə-rənt\ *noun* (1913)
: a stream of electrons produced by photoelectric or photovoltaic effects

pho·to·de·com·po·si·tion \-ˌdē-ˌkäm-pə-ˈzi-shən\ *noun* (1888)
: chemical breaking down (as of a pesticide) by means of radiant energy

pho·to·de·grad·able \-di-ˈgrā-də-bəl\ *adjective* (1971)
: chemically degradable by the action of light ⟨*photodegradable* plastics⟩

pho·to·de·tec·tor \-di-ˈtek-tər\ *noun* (1947)
: any of various devices for detecting and measuring the intensity of radiant energy through photoelectric action

pho·to·di·ode \-ˈdī-ˌōd\ *noun* (1945)
: a photoelectric semiconductor device for detecting and often measuring radiant energy (as light)

pho·to·dis·in·te·gra·tion \-di-ˌsin-tə-ˈgrā-shən\ *noun* (1935)
: disintegration of the nucleus of an atom caused by absorption of radiant energy (as light)
— **pho·to·dis·in·te·grate** \-ˈsin-tə-ˌgrāt\ *transitive verb*

pho·to·dis·so·ci·a·tion \-di-ˌsō-sē-ˈā-shən, -shē-\ *noun* (1925)
: dissociation of the molecules of a substance (as water) caused by absorption of radiant energy
— **pho·to·dis·so·ci·ate** \-ˈsō-sē-ˌāt, -shē-\ *verb*

pho·to·du·pli·ca·tion \-ˌdü-plə-ˈkā-shən, -ˌdyü-\ *noun* (1941)
: the process of making photocopies
— **pho·to·du·pli·cate** \-ˈdü-plə-ˌkāt, -ˈdyü-\ *verb*
— **pho·to·du·pli·cate** \-pli-kət\ *noun*

pho·to·dy·nam·ic \-(ˌ)dī-ˈna-mik\ *adjective* [International Scientific Vocabulary] (1909)
: of, relating to, or having the property of intensifying or inducing a toxic reaction to light (as in the destruction of cancer cells stained with a light-sensitive dye) in a living system
— **pho·to·dy·nam·i·cal·ly** \-mi-k(ə-)lē\ *adverb*

pho·to·elec·tric \ˌfō-tō-i-'lek-trik\ *adjective* [International Scientific Vocabulary] (circa 1879)
: involving, relating to, or utilizing any of various electrical effects due to the interaction of radiation (as light) with matter
— **pho·to·elec·tri·cal·ly** \-tri-k(ə-)lē\ *adverb*

photoelectric cell *noun* (1891)
: an electronic device whose electrical properties are modified by the action of light

photoelectric effect *noun* (1892)
: the emission of free electrons from a metal surface when light strikes it

pho·to·elec·tron \ˌfō-tō-i-'lek-ˌträn\ *noun* [International Scientific Vocabulary] (1912)
: an electron released in photoemission
— **pho·to·elec·tron·ic** \-ˌlek-'trä-nik\ *adjective*

pho·to·emis·sion \-i-'mi-shən\ *noun* (1916)
: the release of electrons from a usually solid material (as a metal) by means of energy supplied by incidence of radiation and especially light
— **pho·to·emis·sive** \-'mi-siv\ *adjective*

pho·to·en·grave \-in-'grāv\ *transitive verb* [back-formation from *photoengraving*] (1892)
: to make a photoengraving of
— **pho·to·en·grav·er** *noun*

pho·to·en·grav·ing *noun* (1872)
1 : a photomechanical process for making linecuts and halftone cuts by photographing an image on a metal plate and then etching
2 a : a plate made by photoengraving **b** : a print made from such a plate

pho·to·es·say \'fō-tō-ˌe-ˌsā\ *noun* (1944)
: a group of photographs (as in a book or magazine) arranged to explore a theme or tell a story

pho·to·ex·ci·ta·tion \ˌfō-tō-ˌek-ˌsī-'tā-shən, -ˌek-sə-\ *noun* (1918)
: the process of exciting the atoms or molecules of a substance by the absorption of radiant energy
— **pho·to·ex·cit·ed** \-ik-'sī-təd, -ek-\ *adjective*

photo finish *noun* (1936)
1 : a race in which contestants are so close that a photograph of them as they cross the finish line has to be examined to determine the winner
2 : a close contest

pho·to·fin·ish·er \ˌfō-tō-'fi-ni-shər\ *noun* (circa 1934)
: one who develops and prints photographic film commercially
— **pho·to·fin·ish·ing** \-shiŋ\ *noun*

pho·to·flash \'fō-tō-ˌflash\ *noun* (1930)
: FLASH 6f

pho·to·flood \-ˌfləd\ *noun* (1933)
: an electric lamp that provides intense sustained illumination for taking photographs

pho·to·flu·o·rog·ra·phy \-flü-'rä-grə-fē, -flȯ-, -flō-\ *noun* (1941)
: the photography of the image produced on a fluorescent screen by X rays

pho·tog \fə-'täg\ *noun* [short for *photographer*] (circa 1906)
: one who takes photographs : PHOTOGRAPHER

pho·to·gen·ic \ˌfō-tə-'je-nik, -'jē-\ *adjective* (1839)
1 : produced or precipitated by light ⟨*photogenic* dermatitis⟩
2 : producing or generating light : PHOSPHORESCENT ⟨*photogenic* bacteria⟩
3 : suitable for being photographed ⟨a *photogenic* smile⟩
— **pho·to·gen·i·cal·ly** \-ni-k(ə-)lē\ *adverb*

pho·to·ge·ol·o·gy \ˌfō-tō-jē-'ä-lə-jē\ *noun* (1941)
: a branch of geology concerned with the identification and study of geological features through the study of aerial or orbital photographs
— **pho·to·geo·log·ic** \-ˌjē-ə-'lä-jik\ *also* **pho·to·geo·log·i·cal** \-ji-kəl\ *adjective*

pho·to·ge·ol·o·gist \-'ä-lə-jist\ *noun*

pho·to·gram \'fō-tə-ˌgram\ *noun* [International Scientific Vocabulary] (1859)
: a shadowlike photograph made by placing objects between light-sensitive paper and a light source

pho·to·gram·me·try \ˌfō-tə-'gra-mə-trē\ *noun* [International Scientific Vocabulary *photogram* photograph (from *phot-* + *-gram*) + *-metry*] (1875)
: the science of making reliable measurements by the use of photographs and especially aerial photographs (as in surveying)
— **pho·to·gram·met·ric** \-grə-'me-trik\ *adjective*
— **pho·to·gram·me·trist** \-'gra-mə-trist\ *noun*

¹pho·to·graph \'fō-tə-ˌgraf\ *noun* (1839)
: a picture or likeness obtained by photography

²photograph (1839)
transitive verb
: to take a photograph of
intransitive verb
1 : to take a photograph
2 : to appear as an image in a photograph ⟨an actress who *photographs* well⟩

pho·tog·ra·pher \fə-'tä-grə-fər\ *noun* (1847)
: one who practices photography; *especially*
: one who makes a business of taking photographs

pho·to·graph·ic \ˌfō-tə-'gra-fik\ *adjective* (1839)
1 : relating to, obtained by, or used in photography
2 : representing nature and human beings with the exactness of a photograph
3 : capable of retaining vivid impressions ⟨a *photographic* mind⟩
— **pho·to·graph·i·cal·ly** \-fi-k(ə-)lē\ *adverb*

pho·tog·ra·phy \fə-'tä-grə-fē\ *noun* (1839)
: the art or process of producing images on a sensitized surface (as a film) by the action of radiant energy and especially light

pho·to·gra·vure \ˌfō-tə-grə-'vyu̇r\ *noun* [French, from *phot-* + *gravure*] (1879)
: a process for printing from an intaglio plate prepared by photographic methods

pho·to·in·duced \ˌfō-tō-in-'düst, -'dyüst\ *adjective* (1947)
: induced by the action of light
— **pho·to·in·duc·tion** \-'dək-shən\ *noun*
— **pho·to·in·duc·tive** \-'dək-tiv\ *adjective*

pho·to·in·ter·pre·ta·tion \-in-ˌtər-prə-'tā-shən, -pə-\ *noun* (1923)
: the science of identifying and describing objects in photographs
— **pho·to·in·ter·pret·er** \-in-'tər-prə-tər, -pə-\ *noun*

pho·to·ion·i·za·tion \-ˌī-ə-nə-'zā-shən\ *noun* (1914)
: ionization (as in the ionosphere) of a molecule or atom caused by absorption of radiant energy
— **pho·to·ion·ize** \-'ī-ə-ˌnīz\ *transitive verb*

pho·to·jour·nal·ism \ˌfō-tō-'jər-nᵊl-ˌi-zəm\ *noun* (1938)
: journalism in which written copy is subordinate to pictorial usually photographic presentation of news stories or in which a high proportion of pictorial presentation is used
— **pho·to·jour·nal·ist** \-nᵊl-ist\ *noun*
— **pho·to·jour·nal·is·tic** \-ˌjər-nᵊl-'is-tik\ *adjective*

pho·to·ki·ne·sis \-kə-'nē-səs, -kī-\ *noun* [New Latin] (1905)
: motion or activity induced by light
— **pho·to·ki·net·ic** \-'ne-tik\ *adjective*

pho·to·li·thog·ra·phy \-li-'thä-grə-fē\ *noun* [International Scientific Vocabulary] (1856)
1 : lithography in which photographically prepared plates are used
2 : a process involving the photographic transfer of a pattern to a surface for etching (as in producing an integrated circuit)
— **pho·to·lith·o·graph** \-'li-thə-ˌgraf\ *noun or transitive verb*
— **pho·to·lith·o·graph·ic** \-ˌli-thə-'gra-fik\ *adjective*
— **pho·to·lith·o·graph·i·cal·ly** \-fi-k(ə-)lē\ *adverb*

pho·tol·y·sis \fō-'tä-lə-səs\ *noun* [New Latin] (1911)
: chemical decomposition by the action of radiant energy
— **pho·to·lyt·ic** \ˌfō-tᵊl-'i-tik\ *adjective*
— **pho·to·lyt·i·cal·ly** \-ti-k(ə-)lē\ *adverb*

pho·to·lyze \'fō-tᵊl-ˌīz\ *transitive verb* **-lyzed; -lyz·ing** (1936)
: to cause to undergo photolysis
— **pho·to·lyz·able** \-ˌī-zə-bəl\ *adjective*

pho·to·map \'fō-tō-ˌmap\ *noun* (1939)
: a photograph which is taken vertically from above (as from an airplane) and upon which a grid and data pertinent to maps have been added
— **photomap** *verb*

pho·to·mask \-ˌmask\ *noun* (1965)
: MASK 2d

pho·to·me·chan·i·cal \ˌfō-tō-mi-'ka-ni-kəl\ *adjective* [International Scientific Vocabulary] (circa 1889)
: relating to or involving any of various processes for producing printed matter from a photographically prepared surface
— **pho·to·me·chan·i·cal·ly** \-ni-k(ə-)lē\ *adverb*

pho·tom·e·ter \fō-'tä-mə-tər\ *noun* [New Latin *photometrum*, from *phot-* + *-metrum* -meter] (1778)
: an instrument for measuring luminous intensity, luminous flux, illumination, or brightness

pho·to·met·ric \ˌfō-tə-'me-trik\ *adjective* (circa 1828)
: of or relating to photometry or the photometer
— **pho·to·met·ri·cal·ly** \-tri-k(ə-)lē\ *adverb*

pho·tom·e·try \fō-'tä-mə-trē\ *noun* [New Latin *photometria*, from *phot-* + *-metria* -metry] (1824)
: a branch of science that deals with measurement of the intensity of light; *also* : the practice of using a photometer

pho·to·mi·cro·graph \ˌfō-tə-'mī-krə-ˌgraf\ *noun* (1858)
: a photograph of a microscope image
— **pho·to·mi·cro·graph·ic** \-ˌmī-krə-'gra-fik\ *adjective*
— **pho·to·mi·crog·ra·phy** \-mī-'krä-grə-fē\ *noun*

pho·to·mon·tage \-män-'täzh, -mōⁿ(n)-, -'täzh\ *noun* [International Scientific Vocabulary] (1931)
: montage using photographic images; *also* : a picture made by photomontage

pho·to·mor·pho·gen·e·sis \ˌfō-tə-ˌmȯr-fə-'je-nə-səs\ *noun* [New Latin] (1959)
: plant morphogenesis controlled by radiant energy (as light)
— **pho·to·mor·pho·gen·ic** \-'je-nik\ *adjective*

pho·to·mo·sa·ic \-mō-'zā-ik\ *noun* (1942)
: a photographic mosaic; *especially* : one composed of aerial or orbital photographs

pho·to·mul·ti·pli·er tube \ˌfō-tō-'məl-tə-ˌplī(-ə)r-\ *noun* (1941)
: a vacuum tube that detects light especially from dim sources through the use of photoemission and successive instances of secondary emission to produce enough electrons to generate a useful current — called also *photomultiplier*

pho·to·mu·ral \-'myu̇r-əl\ *noun* (1927)

: an enlarged photograph usually several yards long used on walls especially as decoration

pho·ton \'fō-ˌtän [*phot-* + ²*-on*] (1916)
1 : a unit of intensity of light at the retina equal to the illumination received per square millimeter of a pupillary area from a surface having a brightness of one candle per square meter
2 : a quantum of electromagnetic radiation
— **pho·ton·ic** \fō-'tä-nik\ *adjective*

pho·to·neg·a·tive \ˌfō-tō-'ne-gə-tiv\ *adjective* (1914)
: exhibiting negative phototropism or phototaxis

pho·ton·ics \fō-'tä-niks\ *noun plural but singular in construction* (1952)
: a branch of physics that deals with the properties and applications of photons especially as a medium for transmitting information

pho·to·nu·cle·ar \ˌfō-tō-'nü-klē-ər, -'nyü-, ÷-kyə-lər\ *adjective* (1941)
: relating to or caused by the incidence of radiant energy (as gamma rays) on atomic nuclei

pho·to–off·set \-'öf-ˌset\ *noun* (1926)
: offset printing from photolithographic plates

photo opportunity *noun* (1972)
: a situation or event that lends itself to and is often arranged expressly for the taking of pictures that favorably publicize the individuals photographed

pho·to·ox·i·da·tion \-ˌäk-sə-'dā-shən\ *noun* (1888)
: oxidation under the influence of radiant energy (as light)
— **pho·to·ox·i·da·tive** \-'äk-sə-ˌdā-tiv\ *adjective*
— **pho·to·ox·i·dize** \-'äk-sə-ˌdīz\ *verb*

pho·to·pe·ri·od \-'pir-ē-əd\ *noun* (1920)
: a recurring cycle of light and dark periods of constant length; *also* : PHOTOPHASE 2
— **pho·to·pe·ri·od·ic** \-ˌpir-ē-'ä-dik\ *adjective*
— **pho·to·pe·ri·od·i·cal·ly** \-di-k(ə-)lē\ *adverb*

pho·to·pe·ri·od·ism \-'pir-ē-ə-ˌdi-zəm\ *noun* (circa 1911)
: a plant or animal's response or capacity to respond to photoperiod

pho·to·phase \'fō-tə-ˌfāz\ *noun* (1944)
1 : LIGHT REACTION
2 : the light period of a photoperiodic cycle of light and dark

pho·to·pho·bia \ˌfō-tə-'fō-bē-ə\ *noun* [New Latin] (circa 1799)
: intolerance to light; *especially* : painful sensitiveness to strong light

pho·to·pho·bic \-'fō-bik\ *adjective* (1858)
1 a : shunning or avoiding light **b** : growing best under reduced illumination
2 : of or relating to photophobia

pho·to·phore \'fō-tə-ˌfōr, -ˌfȯr\ *noun* [International Scientific Vocabulary] (1898)
: a light-emitting organ; *especially* : one of the luminous spots on various marine mostly deep-sea fishes

pho·to·phos·phor·y·la·tion \'fō-tō-ˌfäs-ˌfōr-ə-'lā-shən\ *noun* (1956)
: the synthesis of ATP from ADP and phosphate that occurs in a plant using radiant energy absorbed during photosynthesis

phot·opic \fōt-'ō-pik, -'ä-pik\ *adjective* [New Latin *photopia*, from *phot-* + *-opia*] (1915)
: relating to or being vision in bright light with light-adapted eyes that is mediated by the cones of the retina

pho·to·play \'fō-tō-ˌplā\ *noun* (1910)
: MOTION PICTURE 2

pho·to·po·la·rim·e·ter \ˌfō-tō-ˌpō-lə-'ri-mə-tər\ *noun* (circa 1890)
: an instrument used to measure the intensity and polarization of reflected light (as from clouds enveloping a planet)

pho·to·poly·mer \ˌfō-tō-'pä-lə-mər\ *noun* (1932)
: a photosensitive plastic used especially in the manufacture of printing plates

pho·to·pos·i·tive \-'pä-zə-tiv, -'päz-tiv\ *adjective* (1914)
: exhibiting positive phototropism or phototaxis

pho·to·prod·uct \-'prä-(ˌ)dəkt\ *noun* (1926)
: a product of a photochemical reaction

pho·to·pro·duc·tion \-prə-'dək-shən\ *noun* (1949)
: the production of elementary particles (as mesons) as a result of the action of photons on atomic nuclei

pho·to·re·ac·tion \-rē-'ak-shən\ *noun* (1909)
: a photochemical reaction

pho·to·re·ac·ti·va·tion \-rē-ˌak-tə-'vā-shən\ *noun* (1949)
: repair of DNA (as of a bacterium) especially by a light-dependent enzymatic reaction after damage by ultraviolet irradiation
— **pho·to·re·ac·ti·vat·ing** \-'ak-tə-ˌvā-tiŋ\ *adjective*

photo–realism *noun* (1961)
: realism in painting characterized by extremely meticulous depiction of detail
— **photo–realist** *noun or adjective*

pho·to·re·cep·tion \-ri-'sep-shən\ *noun* (1902)
: perception of waves in the range of visible light; *specifically* : VISION
— **pho·to·re·cep·tive** \-'sep-tiv\ *adjective*

pho·to·re·cep·tor \-'sep-tər\ *noun* (1906)
: a receptor for light stimuli

pho·to·re·con·nais·sance \-ri-'kä-nə-zən(t)s *also* -sən(t)s\ *noun* (1940)
: reconnaissance in which aerial photographs are taken

pho·to·re·duc·tion \-ri-'dək-shən\ *noun* (1888)
: chemical reduction under the influence of radiant energy (as light) : photochemical reduction
— **pho·to·re·duce** \-ri-'düs, -'dyüs\ *transitive verb*

pho·to·re·pro·duc·tion \-ˌrē-prə-'dək-shən\ *noun* (1939)
: reproduction by photographic means; *also* : PHOTOCOPY

pho·to·re·sist \'fō-tō-ri-ˌzist, ˌfō-tō-ri-'\ *noun* (1953)
: a photosensitive resin that loses its resistance to chemical etching when exposed to radiation and is used especially in the transference of a circuit pattern to a semiconductor chip during the production of an integrated circuit

pho·to·res·pi·ra·tion \ˌfō-tō-ˌres-pə-'rā-shən\ *noun* (1945)
: oxidation involving production of carbon dioxide during photosynthesis

pho·to·sen·si·tive \-'sen(t)-s(ə-)tiv\ *adjective* (1886)
: sensitive or sensitized to the action of radiant energy
— **pho·to·sen·si·tiv·i·ty** \-ˌsen(t)-sə-'ti-və-tē\ *noun*

pho·to·sen·si·ti·za·tion \-ˌsen(t)-s(ə-)tə-'zā-shən\ *noun* (circa 1923)
1 : the process of photosensitizing
2 : the condition of being photosensitized; *especially* : the development of an abnormal capacity to react to sunlight typically by edematous swelling and dermatitis

pho·to·sen·si·tize \-'sen(t)-sə-ˌtīz\ *transitive verb* (circa 1923)
: to make sensitive to the influence of radiant energy and especially light
— **pho·to·sen·si·tiz·er** *noun*

pho·to·set \'fō-tō-ˌset\ *transitive verb* **-set; -set·ting** (1957)
: PHOTOCOMPOSE
— **pho·to·set·ter** *noun*

pho·to·sphere \'fō-tə-ˌsfir\ *noun* (1664)
1 : a sphere of light or radiance
2 : the luminous surface layer of the sun or a star
— **pho·to·spher·ic** \ˌfō-tə-'sfir-ik, -'sfer-\ *adjective*

pho·to·stat \'fō-tə-ˌstat\ *transitive verb* (1914)
: to copy by a Photostat device

Photostat *trademark*
— used for a device for making a photographic copy of graphic matter

pho·to·stat·ic \ˌfō-tə-'sta-tik\ *adjective* (1919)
: of, made by, or using a Photostat device ⟨a *photostatic* copy⟩ ⟨a *photostatic* process⟩

pho·to·syn·thate \ˌfō-tō-'sin-ˌthāt\ *noun* [*photosynthesis* + ¹*-ate*] (1913)
: a product of photosynthesis

pho·to·syn·the·sis \-'sin(t)-thə-səs\ *noun* [New Latin] (1898)
: synthesis of chemical compounds with the aid of radiant energy and especially light; *especially* : formation of carbohydrates from carbon dioxide and a source of hydrogen (as water) in the chlorophyll-containing tissues of plants exposed to light
— **pho·to·syn·the·size** \-ˌsīz\ *intransitive verb*
— **pho·to·syn·thet·ic** \-sin-'the-tik\ *adjective*
— **pho·to·syn·thet·i·cal·ly** \-ti-k(ə-)lē\ *adverb*

pho·to·sys·tem \'fō-tō-ˌsis-təm\ *noun* (1964)
: either of two photochemical reactions occurring in chloroplasts: **a** : one that proceeds best in long wavelength light — called also *photosystem I* **b** : one that proceeds best in short wavelength light — called also *photosystem II*

pho·to·tac·tic \ˌfō-tō-'tak-tik\ *adjective* [International Scientific Vocabulary] (1882)
: of, relating to, or exhibiting phototaxis
— **pho·to·tac·ti·cal·ly** \-ti-kə-lē\ *adverb*

pho·to·tax·is \-'tak-səs\ *noun* [New Latin] (circa 1890)
: a taxis in which light is the directive factor

pho·to·te·leg·ra·phy \-tə-'le-grə-fē\ *noun* [International Scientific Vocabulary] (1886)
: FACSIMILE 2

pho·to·tox·ic \-'täk-sik\ *adjective* (1942)
1 : rendering the skin susceptible to damage (as sunburn or blisters) upon exposure to light and especially ultraviolet light
2 : induced by a phototoxic substance
— **pho·to·tox·ic·i·ty** \-ˌtäk-'si-sə-tē\ *noun*

pho·to·tro·pic \ˌfō-tə-'trō-pik, -'trä-\ *adjective* (circa 1890)
: of, relating to, or capable of phototropism
— **pho·to·tro·pi·cal·ly** \-pi-k(ə-)lē\ *adverb*

pho·tot·ro·pism \fō-'tä-trə-ˌpi-zəm\ *noun* [International Scientific Vocabulary] (1899)
: a tropism in which light is the orienting stimulus

pho·to·tube \'fō-tō-ˌtüb, -ˌtyüb\ *noun* (1930)
: an electron tube having a photoemissive cathode whose released electrons are drawn to the anode by reason of its positive potential

pho·to·type·set·ting \ˌfō-tō-'tīp-ˌse-tiŋ\ *noun* (1931)
: PHOTOCOMPOSITION; *especially* : photocomposition done on a keyboard or tape-operated composing machine
— **pho·to·type·set·ter** *noun*

pho·to·vol·ta·ic \-väl-'tā-ik, -vōl-\ *adjective* [International Scientific Vocabulary] (circa 1890)
: of, relating to, or utilizing the generation of a voltage when radiant energy falls on the boundary between dissimilar substances (as two different semiconductors)
— **photovoltaic** *noun*

phrag·mo·plast \'frag-mō-ˌplast\ *noun* [International Scientific Vocabulary *phragmo-* (from Greek *phragmos* fence, from *phrassein* to enclose) + *-plast*] (1912)
: the enlarged barrel-shaped spindle that is characteristic of the later stages of plant mitosis and within which the cell plate forms

phras·al \'frā-zəl\ *adjective* (1871)

: of, relating to, or consisting of a phrase 〈*phrasal* prepositions〉

— **phras·al·ly** \-zə-lē\ *adverb*

¹**phrase** \'frāz\ *noun* [Latin *phrasis*, from Greek, from *phrazein* to point out, explain, tell] (1530)

1 : a characteristic manner or style of expression : DICTION

2 a : a brief expression; *especially* : CATCHWORD **b** : WORD

3 : a short musical thought typically two to four measures long closing with a cadence

4 : a word or group of words forming a syntactic constituent with a single grammatical function 〈an adverbial *phrase*〉

5 : a series of dance movements comprising a section of a pattern

²**phrase** *transitive verb* **phrased; phrasing** (1570)

1 a : to express in words or in appropriate or telling terms **b** : to designate by a descriptive word or phrase

2 : to divide into melodic phrases

phrase book *noun* (1594)

: a book containing idiomatic expressions of a foreign language and their translation

phrase-mak·er \'frāz-,mā-kər\ *noun* (1822)

1 : one who coins impressive phrases

2 : one given to making fine-sounding but often hollow and meaningless phrases

— **phrase-mak·ing** \-kiŋ\ *noun*

phrase-mon·ger \-,məŋ-gər, -,mäŋ-\ *noun* (1815)

: PHRASEMAKER 2

— **phrase-mon·ger·ing** \-g(ə-)riŋ\ *noun*

phra·se·o·log·i·cal \,frā-zē-ə-'lä-ji-kəl\ *adjective* (1664)

1 a : expressed in formal often sententious phrases **b** : marked by frequently insincere use of such phrases

2 : of or relating to phraseology

phra·se·ol·o·gist \,frā-zē-'ä-lə-jist, frā-'zä-\ *noun* (1713)

: one who uses sententious or insincere phrases

phra·se·ol·o·gy \-jē\ *noun, plural* **-gies** [New Latin *phraseologia*, irregular from Greek *phrasis* + *-logia* -logy] (1664)

1 : a manner of organizing words and phrases into longer elements : STYLE

2 : choice of words

phras·ing \'frā-ziŋ\ *noun* (1611)

1 : style of expression : PHRASEOLOGY

2 : the act, method, or result of grouping notes into musical phrases

phra·try \'frā-trē\ *noun, plural* **phratries** [Greek *phratria*, from *phratēr* member of the same clan, member of a phratry — more at BROTHER] (1833)

1 : a kinship group forming a subdivision of a Greek phyle

2 : a tribal subdivision; *specifically* : an exogamous group typically comprising several totemic clans

phre·at·ic \frē-'a-tik\ *adjective* [Greek *phreat-, phrear* well; akin to Armenian *albiwr* spring, Old High German *brunno* — more at BURN] (circa 1890)

1 : of, relating to, or being groundwater

2 : of, relating to, or being an explosion caused by steam derived from groundwater

phre·at·o·phyte \frē-'a-tə-,fīt\ *noun* [Greek *phreat-, phrear* well + English *-o-* + *-phyte*] (1920)

: a deep-rooted plant that obtains its water from the water table or the layer of soil just above it

— **phre·at·o·phyt·ic** \-,a-tə-'fi-tik\ *adjective*

phre·net·ic *variant of* FRENETIC

-phrenia *noun combining form* [New Latin, from Greek *phren-, phrēn* diaphragm, mind]

: disordered condition of mental functions 〈hebe*phrenia*〉

phren·ic \'fre-nik\ *adjective* [New Latin *phrenicus*, from Greek *phren-, phrēn*] (1704)

1 : of or relating to the diaphragm

2 : of or relating to the mind

phre·nol·o·gy \fri-'nä-lə-jē\ *noun* [Greek *phren-, phrēn*] (1805)

: the study of the conformation of the skull based on the belief that it is indicative of mental faculties and character

— **phre·no·log·i·cal** \,fre-nᵒl-'ä-ji-kəl, ,frē-\ *adjective*

— **phre·nol·o·gist** \fri-'nä-lə-jist\ *noun*

phren·sy *variant of* FRENZY

Phry·gian \'fri-j(ē-)ən\ *noun* (15th century)

1 : a native or inhabitant of ancient Phrygia

2 : the extinct Indo-European language of the Phrygians — see INDO-EUROPEAN LANGUAGES table

— **Phrygian** *adjective*

phthal·ic acid \'tha-lik-\ *noun* [International Scientific Vocabulary, short for obsolete *naphthalic acid*, from *naphthalene*] (1857)

: any of three isomeric acids $C_8H_6O_4$ obtained by oxidation of various benzene derivatives

phthalic anhydride *noun* (1855)

: a crystalline cyclic acid anhydride $C_8H_4O_3$ used especially in making alkyd resins

phtha·lo·cy·a·nine \,tha-lō-'sī-ə-,nēn, ,thä-\ *noun* [International Scientific Vocabulary *phthalic acid* + *-o-* + *cyanine*] (1933)

: a bright greenish blue crystalline compound $C_{32}H_{18}N_8$; *also* : any of several metal derivatives that are brilliant fast blue to green dyes or pigments

phthis·ic \'ti-zik\ *noun* [Middle English *tisike*, from Middle French *tisique*, from *tisique* tubercular, from Latin *phthisicus*, from Greek *phthisikos*, from *phthisis*] (14th century)

: PHTHISIS

— **phthisic** *or* **phthis·i·cal** \-zi-kəl\ *adjective*

phthi·sis \'thī-səs, 'tī-, 'fthī- *or with* i *for* ī\ *noun, plural* **phthi·ses** \-,sēz\ [Latin, from Greek, from *phthinein* to waste away; akin to Sanskrit *kṣiṇoti* he destroys] (1526)

: a progressively wasting or consumptive condition; *especially* : pulmonary tuberculosis

phyco- *combining form* [Greek *phykos* seaweed]

: algae 〈*phyco*logy〉

phy·co·cy·a·nin \,fī-kō-'sī-ə-nən\ *noun* [International Scientific Vocabulary *phyco-* + *cyan-* + ¹*-in*] (1875)

: any of various bluish green protein pigments in the cells of blue-green algae

phy·co·er·y·thrin \-'er-i-thrən\ *noun* [International Scientific Vocabulary *phyco-* + *erythr-* + ¹*-in*] (circa 1868)

: any of the red protein pigments in the cells of red algae

phy·col·o·gy \fī-'kä-lə-jē\ *noun* (circa 1847)

: ALGOLOGY

— **phy·co·log·i·cal** \,fī-kə-'lä-ji-kəl\ *adjective*

— **phy·col·o·gist** \fī-'kä-lə-jist\ *noun*

phy·co·my·cete \,fī-kō-'mī-,sēt, -,mī-'sēt\ *noun* [ultimately from Greek *phykos* + *mykēt-, mykēs* fungus — more at MYC-] (circa 1900)

: any of a large class (Phycomycetes) of lower fungi that are in many respects similar to algae and are now often assigned to subdivisions (Mastigomycotina and Zygomycotina)

— **phy·co·my·ce·tous** \-,mī-'sē-təs\ *adjective*

phyl- *or* **phylo-** *combining form* [Latin, from Greek, from *phylē, phylon*; akin to Greek *phyein* to bring forth — more at BE]

: tribe : race : phylum 〈*phylo*geny〉

phy·lac·tery \fə-'lak-t(ə-)rē\ *noun, plural* **-ter·ies** [Middle English *philaterie*, from Medieval Latin *philaterium*, alteration of Late Latin *phylacterium*, from Greek *phylaktērion* amulet, phylactery, from *phylassein* to guard, from *phylak-, phylax* guard] (14th century)

1 : either of two small square leather boxes containing slips inscribed with scriptural passages and traditionally worn on the left arm

and on the head by Jewish men during morning weekday prayers

2 : AMULET

phy·le \'fī-(,)lē\ *noun, plural* **phy·lae** \-,lē\ [Greek *phylē* tribe, phyle] (1863)

: the largest political subdivision among the ancient Athenians

phylactery 1

phy·let·ic \fī-'le-tik\ *adjective* [International Scientific Vocabulary *phyl-* + *-etic* (as in *genetic*)] (1881)

: of or relating to evolutionary change in a single line of descent without branching

— **phy·let·i·cal·ly** \-ti-k(ə-)lē\ *adverb*

phyll- *or* **phyllo-** *combining form* [New Latin, from Greek, from *phyllon* — more at BLADE]

: leaf 〈*phyllo*me〉

-phyll *noun combining form* [New Latin *-phyllum*, from Greek *phyllon* leaf]

: leaf 〈sporo*phyll*〉

phyl·la·ry \'fi-lə-rē\ *noun, plural* **-ries** [New Latin *phyllarium*, from Greek *phyllarion*, diminutive of *phyllon* leaf] (1857)

: one of the involucral bracts subtending the flower head of a composite plant

phyl·lo \'fe-(,)lō, 'fī-\ *noun* [New Greek, sheet of pastry dough, literally, leaf, from Greek *phyllon*] (circa 1950)

: extremely thin pastry dough that is layered to produce a flaky pastry

phyl·lo·clade \'fi-lə-,klād\ *noun* [New Latin *phyllocladium*, from *phyll-* + Greek *klados* branch — more at HOLT] (1858)

: a flattened stem or branch (as a joint of a cactus) that functions as a leaf

phyl·lode \'fi-,lōd\ *noun* [New Latin *phyllodium*, from Greek *phyllōdēs* like a leaf, from *phyllon* leaf] (1848)

: a flat expanded petiole that replaces the blade of a foliage leaf, fulfills the same functions, and is analogous to a cladophyll

phyl·lo·di·um \fi-'lō-dē-əm\ *noun, plural* **-dia** \-dē-ə\ [New Latin] (circa 1847)

: PHYLLODE

phyl·lome \'fi-,lōm\ *noun* [International Scientific Vocabulary] (1875)

: a plant part that is a leaf or is phylogenetically derived from a leaf

phyl·lo·tac·tic \,fi-lə-'tak-tik\ *adjective* (1857)

: of or relating to phyllotaxis

phyl·lo·tax·is \,fi-lə-'tak-səs\ *also* **phyl·lo·taxy** \'fi-lə-,tak-sē\ *noun* [New Latin *phyllotaxis*, from *phyll-* + *-taxis*] (1857)

1 : the arrangement of leaves on a stem and in relation to one another

2 : the study of phyllotaxis and of the laws that govern it

-phyllous *adjective combining form* [New Latin *-phyllus*, from Greek *-phyllos*, from *phyllon* leaf — more at BLADE]

: having (such or so many) leaves, leaflets, or leaflike parts 〈hetero*phyllous*〉

phyl·lox·e·ra \,fi-,läk-'sir-ə, fə-'läk-sə-rə\ *noun* [New Latin, from *phyll-* + Greek *xēros* dry] (1868)

: any of various plant lice (especially genus *Phylloxera*) that differ from aphids especially in wing structure and in being continuously oviparous

phy·lo·ge·net·ic \,fī-lō-jə-'ne-tik\ *adjective* [International Scientific Vocabulary, from New

Latin *phylogenesis* phylogeny, from *phyl-* + *genesis*] (1877)
1 : of or relating to phylogeny
2 : based on natural evolutionary relationships
3 : acquired in the course of phylogenetic development : RACIAL
— **phy·lo·ge·net·i·cal·ly** \-ti-k(ə-)lē\ *adverb*

phy·log·e·ny \fī-'lä-jə-nē\ *noun, plural* **-nies** [International Scientific Vocabulary] (1872)
1 : the evolutionary history of a kind of organism
2 : the evolution of a genetically related group of organisms as distinguished from the development of the individual organism
3 : the history or course of the development of something (as a word or custom)

phy·lum \'fī-ləm\ *noun, plural* **phy·la** \-lə\ [New Latin, from Greek *phylon* tribe, race — more at PHYL-] (1876)
1 a : a direct line of descent within a group **b** : a group that constitutes or has the unity of a phylum; *especially* : one of the usually primary divisions of the animal kingdom
2 : a group of languages related more remotely than those of a family or stock

phys ed \'fiz-'ed\ *noun* (1955)
: PHYSICAL EDUCATION

physi- *or* **physio-** *combining form* [Latin, from Greek, from *physis* — more at PHYSICS]
1 : nature ⟨*physiography*⟩
2 : physical ⟨*physiotherapy*⟩

phys·iat·rist \,fi-zē-'a-trist\ *noun* [*physiatrics* physical medicine, from Greek *physis* + International Scientific Vocabulary *-iatrics*] (circa 1947)
: a physician who specializes in physical medicine

¹**phys·ic** \'fi-zik\ *noun* [Middle English *physik* natural science, art of medicine, from Old French *fisique*, from Latin *physica*, singular, natural science, from Greek *physikē*, from feminine of *physikos* — more at PHYSICS] (14th century)
1 a : the art or practice of healing disease **b** : the practice or profession of medicine
2 : a medicinal agent or preparation; *especially* : PURGATIVE
3 *archaic* : NATURAL SCIENCE

²**physic** *transitive verb* **phys·icked; phys·ick·ing** (14th century)
1 : to treat with or administer medicine to; *especially* : PURGE
2 : HEAL, CURE

¹**phys·i·cal** \'fi-zi-kəl\ *adjective* [Middle English *phisicale* medical, from Medieval Latin *physicalis*, from Latin *physica*] (1597)
1 a : having material existence : perceptible especially through the senses and subject to the laws of nature ⟨everything *physical* is measurable by weight, motion, and resistance —Thomas De Quincey⟩ **b** : of or relating to material things
2 a : of or relating to natural science **b** (1) : of or relating to physics (2) : characterized or produced by the forces and operations of physics
3 a : of or relating to the body **b** : concerned or preoccupied with the body and its needs : CARNAL **c** : characterized by especially rugged and forceful physical activity : ROUGH ⟨a *physical* hockey game⟩ ⟨a *physical* player⟩
synonym see MATERIAL
— **phys·i·cal·ly** \-k(ə-)lē\ *adverb*
— **phys·i·cal·ness** \-kəl-nəs\ *noun*

²**physical** *noun* (1934)
: PHYSICAL EXAMINATION

physical anthropology *noun* (1873)
: anthropology concerned with the comparative study of human evolution, variation, and classification especially through measurement and observation — compare CULTURAL ANTHROPOLOGY
— **physical anthropologist** *noun*

physical education *noun* (1830)

: instruction in the development and care of the body ranging from simple calisthenic exercises to a course of study providing training in hygiene, gymnastics, and the performance and management of athletic games

physical examination *noun* (1884)
: an examination of the bodily functions and condition of an individual

physical geography *noun* (1808)
: geography that deals with the exterior physical features and changes of the earth

phys·i·cal·ism \'fi-zi-kə-,li-zəm\ *noun* (circa 1931)
: a thesis that the descriptive terms of scientific language are reducible to terms which refer to spatiotemporal things or events or to their properties
— **phys·i·cal·ist** \-list\ *noun*
— **phys·i·cal·is·tic** \,fi-zi-kə-'lis-tik\ *adjective*

phys·i·cal·i·ty \,fi-zə-'ka-lə-tē\ *noun, plural* **-ties** (1660)
1 : intensely physical orientation : predominance of the physical usually at the expense of the mental, spiritual, or social
2 : a physical aspect or quality

physical medicine *noun* (1939)
: a branch of medicine concerned with the diagnosis and treatment of disease and disability by physical means (as radiation, heat, and electricity) — compare PHYSICAL THERAPY

physical science *noun* (1802)
: any of the natural sciences (as physics, chemistry, and astronomy) that deal primarily with nonliving materials
— **physical scientist** *noun*

physical therapy *noun* (1922)
: the treatment of disease by physical and mechanical means (as massage, regulated exercise, water, light, heat, and electricity)
— **physical therapist** *noun*

phy·si·cian \fə-'zi-shən\ *noun* [Middle English *fisicien*, from Old French, from *fisique* medicine] (13th century)
1 : a person skilled in the art of healing; *specifically* : a doctor of medicine
2 : one exerting a remedial or salutary influence

physician's assistant *noun* (1970)
: a person certified to provide basic medical services usually under the supervision of a licensed physician — called also *PA, physician assistant*

phys·i·cist \'fi-zə-sist, 'fiz-sist\ *noun* (1840)
1 : a specialist in physics
2 *archaic* : a person skilled in natural science

phys·i·co·chem·i·cal \,fi-zi-kō-'ke-mi-kəl\ *adjective* (1664)
1 : being physical and chemical
2 : of or relating to chemistry that deals with the physicochemical properties of substances
— **phys·i·co·chem·i·cal·ly** \-k(ə-)lē\ *adverb*

phys·ics \'fi-ziks\ *noun plural but singular or plural in construction* [Latin *physica*, plural, natural science, from Greek *physika*, from neuter plural of *physikos* of nature, from *physis* growth, nature, from *phyein* to bring forth — more at BE] (1715)
1 : a science that deals with matter and energy and their interactions
2 a : the physical processes and phenomena of a particular system **b** : the physical properties and composition of something

Phys·io·crat \'fi-zē-ə-,krat\ *noun* [French *physiocrate*, from *physi-* physi- + *-crate* -crat] (1798)
: a member of a school of political economists founded in 18th century France and characterized chiefly by a belief that government policy should not interfere with the operation of natural economic laws and that land is the source of all wealth
— **phys·io·crat·ic** \,fi-zē-ə-'kra-tik\ *adjective, often capitalized*

phys·i·og·nom·ic \,fi-zē-ə(g)-'nä-mik\ *also* **phys·i·og·nom·i·cal** \-mi-kəl\ *adjective* (1588)
: of, relating to, or characteristic of physiognomy or the physiognomy
— **phys·i·og·nom·i·cal·ly** \-mi-k(ə-)lē\ *adverb*

phys·i·og·no·my \,fi-zē-'ä(g)-nə-mē\ *noun, plural* **-mies** [Middle English *phisonomie*, from Middle French, from Late Latin *physiognomonia, physiognomia*, from Greek *physiognomonia*, from *physiognōmōn* judging character by the features, from *physis* nature, physique, appearance + *gnōmōn* interpreter — more at GNOMON] (14th century)
1 : the art of discovering temperament and character from outward appearance
2 : the facial features held to show qualities of mind or character by their configuration or expression
3 : external aspect; *also* : inner character or quality revealed outwardly

phys·i·og·ra·phy \,fi-zē-'ä-grə-fē\ *noun* [probably from French *physiographie*, from *physi-* + *-graphie* -graphy] (circa 1828)
: PHYSICAL GEOGRAPHY
— **phys·i·og·ra·pher** \-fər\ *noun*
— **phys·io·graph·ic** \,fi-zē-ō-'gra-fik\ *also* **phys·io·graph·i·cal** \-fi-kəl\ *adjective*

phys·i·o·log·i·cal \,fi-zē-ə-'lä-ji-kəl\ *or* **phys·i·o·log·ic** \-jik\ *adjective* (1814)
1 : of or relating to physiology
2 : characteristic of or appropriate to an organism's healthy or normal functioning
3 : differing in, involving, or affecting physiological factors ⟨a *physiological* strain of bacteria⟩
— **phys·i·o·log·i·cal·ly** \-ji-k(ə-)lē\ *adverb*

physiological psychology *noun* (1888)
: a branch of psychology that deals with the effects of normal and pathological physiological processes on mental life — called also *psychophysiology*

physiological saline *noun* (1896)
: a solution of a salt or salts that is essentially isotonic with tissue fluids or blood

phys·i·ol·o·gy \,fi-zē-'ä-lə-jē\ *noun* [Latin *physiologia* natural science, from Greek, from *physi-* + *-logia* -logy] (1597)
1 : a branch of biology that deals with the functions and activities of life or of living matter (as organs, tissues, or cells) and of the physical and chemical phenomena involved — compare ANATOMY
2 : the organic processes and phenomena of an organism or any of its parts or of a particular bodily process
— **phys·i·ol·o·gist** \-jist\ *noun*

phys·io·pa·thol·o·gy \'fi-zē-ō-pə-'thä-lə-jē, -pa-\ *noun* (circa 1889)
: a branch of biology or medicine that combines physiology and pathology especially in the study of altered bodily function in disease
— **phys·io·path·o·log·ic** \-,pa-thə-'lä-jik\ *or* **phys·io·path·o·log·i·cal** \-ji-kəl\ *adjective*

phys·io·ther·a·py \,fi-zē-ō-'ther-ə-pē\ *noun* [New Latin *physiotherapia*, from *physi-* + *therapia* therapy] (circa 1903)
: PHYSICAL THERAPY
— **phys·io·ther·a·pist** \-pist\ *noun*

phy·sique \fə-'zēk\ *noun* [French, from *physique* physical, bodily, from Latin *physicus* of nature, from Greek *physikos*] (1813)
: the form or structure of a person's body : bodily makeup

phy·so·stig·mine \,fī-sə-'stig-,mēn\ *noun* [International Scientific Vocabulary, from New Latin *Physostigma*, genus of vines that bear the Calabar bean] (1864)
: a crystalline tasteless alkaloid $C_{15}H_{21}N_3O_2$ from the Calabar bean that is used in medicine especially in the form of its salicylate for its anticholinesterase activity

phyt- *or* **phyto-** *combining form* [New Latin, from Greek, from *phyton*, from *phyein* to bring forth — more at BE]
: plant ⟨*phyto*phagous⟩

phy·tane \'fī-ˌtān\ *noun* (1907)
: an isoprenoid hydrocarbon $C_{20}H_{42}$ that is found especially associated with fossilized plant remains from the Precambrian and later eras

-phyte *noun combining form* [International Scientific Vocabulary, from Greek *phyton* plant]
: plant having a (specified) characteristic or habitat ⟨xero*phyte*⟩

-phytic *adjective combining form* [International Scientific Vocabulary, from Greek *phyton* plant]
: like a plant ⟨holo*phytic*⟩

phy·to·alex·in \ˌfī-tō-ə-'lek-sən\ *noun* [International Scientific Vocabulary *phyt-* + *alexin* substance combating infection, from Greek *alexein* to ward off, protect; akin to Sanskrit *rakṣati* he protects] (1949)
: a chemical substance produced by a plant to combat infection by a pathogen (as a fungus)

phy·to·chem·i·cal \-'ke-mi-kəl\ *adjective* (circa 1858)
: of, relating to, or being phytochemistry
— **phy·to·chem·i·cal·ly** \-mi-k(ə-)lē\ *adverb*

phy·to·chem·is·try \-'ke-mə-strē\ *noun* (1837)
: the chemistry of plants, plant processes, and plant products
— **phy·to·chem·ist** \-'ke-mist\ *noun*

phy·to·chrome \'fī-tə-ˌkrōm\ *noun* (circa 1893)
: a chromoprotein that is present in traces in many plants and that plays a significant role in initiating floral and developmental processes when activated by red or near-infrared radiation

phy·to·fla·gel·late \ˌfī-tō-'fla-jə-lət, -ˌlāt; -flə-'jə-\ *noun* (1935)
: any of various organisms (as dinoflagellates) that are considered a subclass (Phytomastigophora synonym Phytomastigina) usually of algae by botanists and of protozoans by zoologists and that have many characteristics in common with typical algae

phy·to·ge·og·ra·phy \ˌfī-tō-jē-'ä-grə-fē\ *noun* [International Scientific Vocabulary] (1847)
: the biogeography of plants
— **phy·to·ge·og·ra·pher** \-fər\ *noun*
— **phy·to·geo·graph·i·cal** \-ˌjē-ə-'gra-fi-kəl\ *or* **phy·to·geo·graph·ic** \-fik\ *adjective*
— **phy·to·geo·graph·i·cal·ly** \-fi-k(ə-)lē\ *adverb*

phy·to·he·mag·glu·ti·nin \-ˌhē-mə-'glü-tᵊn-ən\ *noun* (1949)
: a proteinaceous hemagglutinin of plant origin used especially to induce mitosis (as in lymphocytes)

phy·to·hor·mone \-'hȯr-ˌmōn\ *noun* [International Scientific Vocabulary] (1933)
: PLANT HORMONE

phy·ton \'fī-ˌtän\ *noun* [New Latin, from Greek, plant] (1848)
1 : a structural unit of a plant consisting of a leaf and its associated portion of stem
2 : the smallest part of a stem, root, or leaf that when severed may grow into a new plant
— **phy·ton·ic** \fī-'tä-nik\ *adjective*

phy·to·path·o·gen \ˌfī-tō-'pa-thə-jən\ *noun* (circa 1930)
: an organism parasitic on a plant host
— **phy·to·path·o·gen·ic** \-ˌpa-thə-'je-nik\ *adjective*

phy·to·pa·thol·o·gy \-pə-'thä-lə-jē, -pa-\ *noun* [International Scientific Vocabulary] (circa 1859)
: plant pathology
— **phy·to·path·o·log·i·cal** \-ˌpa-thə-'lä-ji-kəl\ *adjective*

phy·toph·a·gous \fī-'tä-fə-gəs\ *adjective* (1826)
: feeding on plants ⟨a *phytophagous* insect⟩

phy·to·plank·ter \ˌfī-tō-'plaŋ(k)-tər\ *noun* (1944)
: a planktonic plant

phy·to·plank·ton \-'plaŋ(k)-tən, -ˌtän\ *noun* [International Scientific Vocabulary] (1897)
: planktonic plant life
— **phy·to·plank·ton·ic** \-plaŋ(k)-'tä-nik\ *adjective*

phy·to·so·ci·ol·o·gy \-ˌsō-sē-'ä-lə-jē, -shē-\ *noun* (circa 1928)
: a branch of ecology concerned especially with the structure, composition, and interrelationships of plant communities
— **phy·to·so·cio·log·i·cal** \-sē-ə-'lä-ji-kəl\ *adjective*

phy·tos·ter·ol \fī-'täs-tə-ˌrȯl, -ˌrōl\ *noun* [International Scientific Vocabulary] (1898)
: any of various sterols derived from plants — compare ZOOSTEROL

phy·to·tox·ic \ˌfī-tə-'täk-sik\ *adjective* (1926)
: poisonous to plants
— **phy·to·tox·ic·i·ty** \-ˌtäk-'si-sə-tē\ *noun*

¹pi *also* **pie** \'pī\ *noun, plural* **pies** [origin unknown] (circa 1659)
1 : type that is spilled or mixed
2 : a pi character or matrix

²pi *also* **pie** *verb* **pied; pi·ing** *or* **pie·ing** (1870)
transitive verb
: to spill or throw (type or type matter) into disorder
intransitive verb
: to become pied

³pi *adjective* (circa 1940)
1 : not intended to appear in final printing ⟨*pi* lines⟩
2 : capable of being inserted only by hand ⟨*pi* characters⟩

⁴pi *noun, plural* **pis** \'pīz\ [Middle Greek, from Greek *pei*, of Semitic origin; akin to Hebrew *pē* pe] (1823)
1 : the 16th letter of the Greek alphabet — see ALPHABET table
2 a : the symbol π denoting the ratio of the circumference of a circle to its diameter **b** : the ratio itself : a transcendental number having a value to eight decimal places of 3.14159265

pi·al \'pī-əl, 'pē-\ *adjective* (1889)
: of or relating to the pia mater

pia ma·ter \ˌpī-ə-'mā-tər, ˌpē-ə-'mä-\ *noun* [Middle English, from Medieval Latin, from Latin, tender mother] (14th century)
: the thin vascular membrane that invests the brain and spinal cord internal to the arachnoid and dura mater

pi·a·nism \'pē-ə-ˌni-zəm\ *noun* (1844)
1 : the art or technique of piano playing
2 : the composition or adaptation of music for the piano

¹pi·a·nis·si·mo \ˌpē-ə-'ni-sə-ˌmō\ *adverb or adjective* [Italian, from *piano* softly] (1724)
: very softly — used as a direction in music

²pianissimo *noun, plural* **-mi** \-(ˌ)mē\ *or* **-mos** (1883)
: a passage played, sung, or spoken very softly

pi·a·nist \pē-'a-nist, 'pē-ə-\ *noun* (circa 1828)
: one who plays the piano; *especially* : a skilled or professional performer on the piano

pi·a·nis·tic \ˌpē-ə-'nis-tik\ *adjective* (1881)
1 : of, relating to, or characteristic of the piano
2 : skilled in or well adapted to piano playing
— **pi·a·nis·ti·cal·ly** \-ti-k(ə-)lē\ *adverb*

¹pi·a·no \pē-'ä-(ˌ)nō\ *adverb or adjective* [Italian, from Late Latin *planus* smooth, from Latin, level — more at FLOOR] (1683)
: at a soft volume : SOFT — used as a direction in music

²pi·a·no \pē-'a-(ˌ)nō *also* -'ä-\ *noun, plural* **pi·anos** [Italian, short for *pianoforte*, from *gravicembalo col piano e forte*, literally, harpsi-

chord with soft and loud; from the fact that its tones could be varied in loudness] (1803)
: a musical instrument having steel wire strings that sound when struck by felt-covered hammers operated from a keyboard ◇

piano accordion *noun* (1860)
: an accordion with a keyboard for the right hand resembling and corresponding to the middle register of a piano keyboard

pi·ano·forte \pē-'a-nə-ˌfȯrt, -'ä-, ˌfȯrt, -ˌfȯr-tē; -ˌa-nə-'fȯr-tē, -ˌä-\ *noun* [Italian] (1767)
1 : FORTEPIANO
2 : PIANO
word history see PIANO

piano hinge *noun* (1926)
: a hinge that has a thin pin joint and extends along the full length of the part to be moved

pi·as·sa·va \ˌpē-ə-'sä-və\ *noun* [Portuguese *piassaba*, from Tupi *piasawa*] (1835)
1 : any of several stiff coarse fibers obtained from palms and used especially in cordage or brushes
2 : a palm yielding piassava; *especially* : either of two Brazilian palms (*Attalia funifera* and *Leopoldinia piassaba*)

pi·as·tre *also* **pi·as·ter** \pē-'as-tər, -'äs-\ *noun* [French *piastre*, from Italian *piastra* thin metal plate, coin, from Latin *emplastra*, *emplastrum* plaster] (1592)
1 : PIECE OF EIGHT
2 — see *pound* at MONEY table

pi·az·za \pē-'a-zə, -'ä-, *1 is usually* -'at-sə, -'ät-sə, -'ät-\ *noun, plural* **piazzas** *or* **pi·az·ze** \-'at-(ˌ)sā, -'ät-\ [Italian, from Latin *platea* broad street — more at PLACE] (1563)
1 *plural* **piazze** : an open square especially in an Italian town
2 a : an arcaded and roofed gallery **b** *dialect* : VERANDA, PORCH

pi·broch \'pē-ˌbräk, -ˌbräḵ\ *noun* [Scottish Gaelic *piobaireachd* pipe music] (1719)
: a set of martial or mournful variations for the Scottish Highland bagpipe

¹pic \'pik\ *noun, plural* **pics** *or* **pix** \'piks\ [short for *picture*] (1884)
1 : PHOTOGRAPH
2 : MOTION PICTURE

²pic \'pik, 'pēk\ *noun* [Spanish *pica*, from *picar* to prick] (1926)
: the picador's lance

¹pi·ca \'pī-kə\ *noun* [New Latin, from Latin, magpie — more at PIE] (1563)
: an abnormal desire to eat substances (as chalk or ashes) not normally eaten

◇ WORD HISTORY

piano A harpsichord is played by means of a mechanism that plucks the strings, so it is not possible to achieve fine gradations of loudness. Feeling the need to overcome this drawback, Bartolomeo Cristofori (1655–1731), a Florentine instrument maker, invented a mechanism or action by means of which the strings of the instrument are struck by felt-covered hammers. This device allows the player to produce notes with varying degrees of loudness. In the first published notice of Cristofori's invention in 1711, it was called in Italian *gravicembalo col piano e forte*, "harpsichord with soft and loud." In English the terms *pianoforte* and *fortepiano* were used interchangeably in the 18th century. Eventually, both were largely replaced by *piano*, first attested in 1803, though scholars and performers continue to use *fortepiano* for 18th and early 19th century forms of the instrument.

\ə\ abut \ᵊ\ kitten \ər\ further \a\ ash \ā\ ace
\ä\ mop, mar \au̇\ out \ch\ chin \e\ bet \ē\ easy
\g\ go \i\ hit \ī\ ice \j\ job \ŋ\ sing \ō\ go
\ȯ\ law \ȯi\ boy \th\ thin \th\ the \ü\ loot \u̇\ foot
\y\ yet \zh\ vision *see also* Guide to Pronunciation

²**pica** *noun* [probably from Medieval Latin, collection of church rules] (1588)
1 : 12-point type
2 : a unit of about ⅙ inch used in measuring typographic material
3 : a typewriter type providing 10 characters to the linear inch and six lines to the vertical inch

pic·a·dor \'pi-kə-ˌdȯr, ˌpi-kə-'\ *noun, plural* **picadors** \-ˌdȯrz, -'dȯrz\ *or* **pic·a·do·res** \ˌpi-kə-'dȯr-ēz, -'dȯr-\ [Spanish, from *picar* to prick, from (assumed) Vulgar Latin *piccare* — more at PIKE] (1797)
: a horseman in a bullfight who jabs the bull with a lance to weaken its neck and shoulder muscles

pi·ca·ra \'pē-kä-ˌrä\ *noun* [Spanish *pícara*, feminine of *pícaro*] (circa 1930)
: a woman who is a rogue

¹**pi·ca·resque** \ˌpi-kə-'resk, ˌpē-\ *adjective* [Spanish *picaresco*, from *pícaro*] (1810)
: of or relating to rogues or rascals; *also* : of, relating to, suggesting, or being a type of fiction dealing with the episodic adventures of a usually roguish protagonist ⟨a *picaresque* novel⟩

²**picaresque** *noun* (1895)
: one that is picaresque

pi·ca·ro \'pē-kä-ˌrō\ *noun, plural* **-ros** [Spanish *pícaro*] (1623)
: ROGUE, BOHEMIAN

¹**pic·a·roon** *or* **pick·a·roon** \ˌpi-kə-'rün\ *noun* [Spanish *picarón*, augmentative of *pícaro*] (1624)
1 : PIRATE
2 : PICARO

²**picaroon** *intransitive verb* (1675)
: to act as a pirate

¹**pic·a·yune** \ˌpi-kē-'yün\ *noun* [Provençal *picaioun*, a small coin, from *picaio* money, from *pica* to jingle, of imitative origin] (1804)
1 a : a Spanish half real piece formerly current in the South **b** : HALF DIME
2 : something trivial

²**picayune** *adjective* (1836)
: of little value : PALTRY; *also* : PETTY, SMALL-MINDED
— **pic·a·yun·ish** \-'yü-nish\ *adjective*

pic·ca·lil·li \ˌpi-kə-'li-lē\ *noun* [probably alteration of *pickle*] (1845)
: a relish of chopped vegetables and spices

¹**pic·co·lo** \'pi-kə-ˌlō\ *adjective* [Italian, small] (circa 1854)
: smaller than ordinary size ⟨a *piccolo* banjo⟩

²**piccolo** *noun, plural* **-los** [Italian, short for *piccolo flauto* small flute] (1856)
: a small shrill flute whose range is an octave higher than that of an ordinary flute
— **pic·co·lo·ist** \-ˌlō-ist\ *noun*

pice \'pīs\ *noun, plural* **pice** [Hindi *paisā*] (1615)
: PAISA

pi·ce·ous \'pī-sē-əs\ *adjective* [Latin *piceus*, from *pic-, pix* pitch — more at PITCH] (1826)
: of, relating to, or resembling pitch; *especially* : glossy brownish black in color ⟨an insect with a *piceous* abdomen⟩

¹**pick** \'pik\ *verb* [Middle English *piken*, partly from (assumed) Old English *pīcian* (akin to Middle Dutch *picken* to prick); partly from Middle French *piquer* to prick — more at PIKE] (14th century)
transitive verb
1 : to pierce, penetrate, or break up with a pointed instrument ⟨*picked* the hard clay⟩
2 a : to remove bit by bit ⟨*pick* meat from bones⟩ **b** : to remove covering or adhering matter from ⟨*pick* the bones⟩
3 a : to gather by plucking ⟨*pick* apples⟩ **b** : CHOOSE, SELECT ⟨tried to *pick* the shortest route⟩ ⟨she *picked* out the most expensive dress⟩ **c** : to make (one's way) slowly and carefully ⟨*picked* his way through the rubble⟩
4 a : PILFER, ROB ⟨*pick* pockets⟩ **b** : to obtain useful information from by questioning — used in such phrases as *pick the brains of*
5 : PROVOKE ⟨*pick* a quarrel⟩
6 a : to dig into : PROBE ⟨*pick* his teeth⟩ **b** : to pluck (as a guitar) with a pick or with the fingers **c** : to loosen or pull apart with a sharp point ⟨*pick* wool⟩
7 : to unlock with a device (as a wire) other than the key ⟨*pick* a lock⟩
intransitive verb
1 : to use or work with a pick
2 : to gather or harvest something by plucking
3 : PILFER — used in the phrase *picking and stealing*
4 : to eat sparingly or mincingly ⟨*picking* listlessly at his dinner⟩
— **pick and choose** : to select with care and deliberation
— **pick at** : to criticize repeatedly especially for minor faults : NAG
— **pick on** : to single out for criticism, teasing, or bullying ⟨*picked on* smaller boys⟩; *also* : to single out for a particular purpose or for special attention

²**pick** *noun* (15th century)
1 : a blow or stroke with a pointed instrument
2 a : the act or privilege of choosing or selecting : CHOICE ⟨take your *pick*⟩ **b** : the best or choicest one ⟨the *pick* of the herd⟩
3 : the portion of a crop gathered at one time ⟨the first *pick* of peaches⟩
4 : a screen in basketball

³**pick** *noun* [Middle English *pik*] (14th century)
1 : a heavy wooden-handled iron or steel tool pointed at one or both ends — compare MATTOCK
2 a : TOOTHPICK **b** : PICKLOCK **c** : a small thin piece (as of plastic or metal) used to pluck the strings of a stringed instrument
3 : one of the points on the forepart of the blade of a skate used in figure skating
4 : a comb with long widely spaced teeth used to give height to a hair style

pick 2c

⁴**pick** *transitive verb* [Middle English *pykken* to pitch (a tent); akin to Middle English *pichen* to pitch] (1523)
1 *chiefly dialect* : to throw or thrust with effort : HURL
2 : to throw (a shuttle) across the loom

⁵**pick** *noun* (1627)
1 *dialect English* **a** : the act of pitching or throwing **b** : something thrown
2 a : a throw of the shuttle **b** : a filling thread

pick·a·back \'pi-gē-ˌbak, 'pi-kə-\ *variant of* PIGGYBACK

pick–and–roll \'pik-ən(d)-'rōl\ *noun* (circa 1961)
: a basketball play in which a player sets a screen and then cuts toward the basket for a pass

pick–and–shovel *adjective* (1895)
: done with or as if with a pick and shovel : LABORIOUS

pick·a·nin·ny *or* **pic·a·nin·ny** \'pi-kə-ˌni-nē, ˌpi-kə-'\ *noun, plural* **-nies** [probably ultimately from Portuguese *pequenino*, diminutive of *pequeno* small] (1653)
: a black child — often taken to be offensive

pick·ax \'pik-ˌaks\ *noun* [Middle English *pecaxe*, alteration of *pikois*, from Old French *picois*, from *pic* pick, from Latin *picus* woodpecker — more at PIE] (15th century)

¹**pick·ed** \'pi-kəd\ *adjective* [Middle English, from ³*pick*] (14th century)
chiefly dialect : POINTED, PEAKED

²**picked** \'pikt\ *adjective* [¹*pick*] (circa 1548)
: CHOICE, PRIME

pick·eer \pi-'kir\ *intransitive verb* [probably modification of French *picorer* to maraud, perhaps from Middle French *pecore* sheep, from Old Italian *pecora* — more at PECORINO] (circa 1645)
archaic : to skirmish in advance of an army; *also* : SCOUT, RECONNOITER

pick·er \'pi-kər\ *noun* (14th century)
: one that picks: as **a** : a worker who picks something (as crops) **b** : a tool, implement, or machine used in picking something **c** : a musician who picks a stringed instrument (as a banjo)

pick·er·el \'pi-k(ə-)rəl\ *noun, plural* **-el** *or* **-els** [Middle English *pikerel*, diminutive of *pike*] (13th century)
1 *dialect chiefly British* : a young or small pike **b** : either of two fishes resembling but smaller than the related northern pike: (1) : CHAIN PICKEREL (2) : one (*Esox americanus*) having green or red fins and a black bar below and slanting away from the eye
2 : WALLEYE 3

pick·er·el·weed \-ˌwēd\ *noun* (1836)
: an American shallow-water monocotyledonous plant (*Pontederia cordata* of the family Pontederiaceae) with large leaves and a spike of blue flowers

¹**pick·et** \'pi-kət\ *noun* [French *piquet*, from Middle French, from *piquer* to prick — more at PIKE] (circa 1702)
1 : a pointed or sharpened stake, post, or pale
2 a : a detached body of soldiers serving to guard an army from surprise **b** : a detachment kept ready in camp for such duty **c** : SENTRY
3 : a person posted by a labor organization at a place of work affected by a strike; *also* : a person posted for a demonstration or protest

²**picket** (1745)
transitive verb
1 : to enclose, fence, or fortify with pickets
2 a : to guard with a picket **b** : to post as a picket
3 : TETHER
4 a : to post pickets at **b** : to walk or stand in front of as a picket
intransitive verb
: to serve as a picket
— **pick·et·er** *noun*

pick·et·boat \'pi-kət-ˌbōt\ *noun* (1866)
: a craft used (as by the coast guard) for harbor patrol

picket line *noun* (1856)
1 : a position held by a line of military pickets
2 : a line of people picketing a business, organization, or institution

pick·ings \'pi-kiŋz, -kənz\ *noun plural* (1642)
: something that is picked or picked up: as **a** : gleanable or eatable fragments : SCRAPS **b** : yield or return for effort expended

¹**pick·le** \'pi-kəl\ *noun* [Middle English *pekille*] (15th century)
1 : a solution or bath for preserving or cleaning: as **a** : a brine or vinegar solution in which foods are preserved **b** : any of various baths used in industrial cleaning or processing
2 : a difficult situation : PLIGHT ⟨could see no way out of the *pickle* I was in —R. L. Stevenson⟩
3 : an article of food that has been preserved in brine or in vinegar; *specifically* : a cucumber that has been so preserved
4 *British* : a mischievous or troublesome person

²**pickle** *transitive verb* **pick·led; pick·ling** \-k(ə-)liŋ\ (1570)
1 : to treat, preserve, or clean in or with a pickle
2 : to give a light finish to (as furniture) by bleaching or painting and wiping

³**pickle** *noun* [perhaps from Scots *pickle* to trifle, pilfer] (1552)
1 *Scottish* : GRAIN, KERNEL
2 *Scottish* : a small quantity

pickled *adjective* (circa 1552)

piccolo (illustration caption, lower left)

1 : preserved in or cured with pickle ⟨*pickled* herring⟩
2 : DRUNK 1a ⟨gets thoroughly *pickled* before dinner —*New Yorker*⟩
pick·lock \'pik-ˌläk\ *noun* (1553)
1 : BURGLAR
2 : a tool for picking locks
pick–me–up \'pik-mē-ˌəp\ *noun* (1867)
: something that stimulates or restores **:** TONIC, BRACER
pick·off \'pik-ˌôf\ *noun* (1939)
: a baseball play in which a base runner is picked off
pick off *transitive verb* (1810)
1 : to shoot or bring down especially one by one
2 : to put out (a base runner who is off base) with a quick throw (as from the pitcher or catcher)
3 : INTERCEPT ⟨*picked off* a pass⟩
pick out *transitive verb* (1540)
1 : DISCERN, MAKE OUT
2 : to play the notes of by ear or one by one ⟨*picking out* tunes on the piano⟩
pick over *transitive verb* (1839)
: to examine in order to select the best or remove the unwanted
pick·pock·et \'pik-ˌpä-kət\ *noun* (1591)
: a thief who picks pockets
pick·proof \-ˌprüf\ *adjective* (1933)
: designed to prevent picking ⟨a *pickproof* lock⟩
pick·thank \-ˌthaŋk\ *noun* [from *pick a thank* to seek someone's favor] (15th century)
archaic **:** SYCOPHANT
¹**pick·up** \'pik-ˌəp\ *noun* (1848)
1 : one that is picked up: as **a :** a hitchhiker who is given a ride **b :** a temporary chance acquaintance
2 : the act or process of picking up: as **a :** a revival of business activity **b :** ACCELERATION
3 : the conversion of mechanical movements into electrical impulses in the reproduction of sound; *also* **:** a device (as on a phonograph) for making such conversion
4 a (1) **:** the reception of sound or an image into a radio or television transmitting apparatus for conversion into electrical signals (2) **:** interference (as with such reception) from an adjacent electrical circuit or system **b :** a device (as a microphone or a television camera) for converting sound or the image of a scene into electrical signals **c :** the place where a broadcast originates **d :** the electrical system for connecting a broadcasting station a program produced outside the studio
5 : a light truck having an enclosed cab and an open body with low sides and tailgate — called also *pickup truck*
²**pickup** *adjective* (1909)
: utilizing or comprising local or available personnel especially without formal organization ⟨a *pickup* basketball game⟩
pick up (14th century)
transitive verb
1 a : to take hold of and lift up **b :** to gather together **:** COLLECT ⟨*picked up* all the pieces⟩ **c :** to clean up **:** TIDY
2 : to take (passengers or freight) into a vehicle
3 a : to acquire casually or by chance ⟨*picked up* a valuable antique at an auction⟩ **b :** to acquire by study or experience **:** LEARN ⟨*picking up* a great deal of knowledge in the process —Robert Schleicher⟩ **c :** to obtain especially by payment **:** BUY ⟨*picked up* some groceries⟩ **d :** to acquire (a player) especially from another team through a trade or by financial recompense **e :** to accept for the purpose of paying ⟨offered to *pick up* the tab⟩ **f :** to come down with **:** CATCH ⟨*picked up* a cold⟩ **g :** GAIN ⟨*picked up* a few yards on the last play⟩
4 a : to enter informally into conversation or companionship with (a previously unknown person) ⟨had a brief affair with a girl he *picked*

up in a bar⟩ **b :** to take into custody ⟨the police *picked up* the fugitive⟩
5 a : to catch sight of **:** PERCEIVE ⟨*picked up* the harbor lights⟩ **b :** to come to and follow ⟨*picked up* the outlaw's trail⟩ **c :** to bring within range of sight or hearing ⟨*pick up* distant radio signals⟩ **d :** UNDERSTAND, CATCH ⟨didn't *pick up* the hint⟩
6 a : REVIVE **b :** INCREASE
7 : to resume after a break **:** CONTINUE ⟨*pick up* the discussion tomorrow⟩
8 : to assume responsibility for guarding (an opponent) in an athletic contest
intransitive verb
1 : to recover speed, vigor, or activity **:** IMPROVE ⟨after the strike, business *picked up*⟩
2 : to put things in order ⟨was always *picking up* after her⟩
3 : to pack up one's belongings ⟨couldn't just *pick up* and leave⟩
— pick up on 1 a : UNDERSTAND, APPRECIATE **b :** to become aware of **:** NOTICE **2 :** to adopt as one's own **:** TAKE UP
Pick·wick·ian \(ˌ)pik-'wi-kē-ən\ *adjective* [Samuel *Pickwick*, character in the novel *Pickwick Papers* (1836–37) by Charles Dickens] (1836)
1 : marked by simplicity and generosity
2 : intended or taken in a sense other than the obvious or literal one
picky \'pi-kē\ *adjective* **pick·i·er; -est** (1917)
: FUSSY, CHOOSY ⟨a *picky* eater⟩
pi·clo·ram \'pi-klə-ˌram, 'pī-\ *noun* [*picoline* + *chlor-* + *amine*] (1965)
: a systemic herbicide $C_6H_3Cl_3N_2O_2$ that breaks down only very slowly in the soil
¹**pic·nic** \'pik-(ˌ)nik\ *noun, often attributive* [German or French; German *Picknick*, from French *pique-nique*] (1748)
1 : an excursion or outing with food usually provided by members of the group and eaten in the open; *also* **:** the food provided for a picnic
2 a : a pleasant or amusingly carefree experience ⟨I don't expect being married to be a *picnic* —Josephine Pinckney⟩ **b :** an easy task or feat
3 : a shoulder of pork with much of the butt removed
— pic·nick·y \-(ˌ)ni-kē\ *adjective*
²**picnic** *intransitive verb* **pic·nicked; pic·nick·ing** (1842)
: to go on a picnic **:** eat in picnic fashion
— pic·nick·er *noun*
pico- *combining form* [International Scientific Vocabulary, probably from Spanish *pico* small amount, literally, peak, beak]
1 : one trillionth (10^{-12}) part of ⟨*pico*gram⟩
2 : very small ⟨*pico*narvirus⟩
pi·co·far·ad \ˌpē-kō-'far-ˌad, -əd\ *noun* [International Scientific Vocabulary] (circa 1926)
: one trillionth of a farad
pi·co·gram \'pē-kō-ˌgram, -kə-\ *noun* [International Scientific Vocabulary] (1951)
: one trillionth of a gram
pic·o·line \'pi-kə-ˌlēn, 'pī-\ *noun* [Latin *pic-, pix* pitch + International Scientific Vocabulary ¹*-ol* + ²*-ine* — more at PITCH] (1853)
: any of the three liquid pyridine bases C_6H_7N used chiefly as solvents and in organic synthesis
pi·co·mole \'pē-kō-ˌmōl, -kə-\ *noun* (1968)
: one trillionth of a mole
pi·cor·na·vi·rus \(ˌ)pē-ˌkôr-nə-'vī-rəs\ *noun* [*pico-* + *RNA* + *virus*] (1962)
: any of a group of small RNA-containing viruses that includes the enteroviruses and rhinoviruses
pi·co·sec·ond \ˌpē-kō-'se-kənd, -kənt\ *noun* [International Scientific Vocabulary] (circa 1962)
: one trillionth of a second

¹**pi·cot** \'pē-(ˌ)kō, pē-'\ *noun* [French, literally, small point, from Middle French, from *pic* prick, from *piquer* to prick — more at PIKE] (circa 1882)
: one of a series of small ornamental loops forming an edging on ribbon or lace
²**picot** *transitive verb* (1926)
: to finish with picots
pic·o·tee \ˌpi-kə-'tē\ *noun* [French *picoté* pointed, from *picoter* to mark with points, from *picot*] (1727)
: a flower (as some carnations or tulips) having one basic color with a margin of another color
picr- *or* **picro-** *combining form* [French, from Greek *pikr-, pikro-*, from *pikros* — more at PAINT]
: bitter ⟨*picr*ic acid⟩
pic·ric acid \'pi-krik-\ *noun* [International Scientific Vocabulary] (1852)
: a toxic explosive yellow crystalline strong acid $C_6H_3N_3O_7$ used especially in high explosives and as a dye
pic·ro·tox·in \ˌpi-krō-'täk-sən\ *noun* [International Scientific Vocabulary] (1815)
: a poisonous bitter crystalline stimulant and convulsive drug $C_{30}H_{34}O_{13}$ used intravenously as an antidote for barbiturate poisoning
Pict \'pikt\ *noun* [Middle English *Pictes*, plural, Picts, from Old English *Pihtas*, from Late Latin *Picti*] (before 12th century)
: a member of a people of the north of Scotland who are first noted in historical records in the late 3d century and who became amalgamated with the Scots in the mid-8th century
— Pict·ish \'pik-tish\ *adjective or noun*
pic·to·gram \'pik-tə-ˌgram\ *noun* [International Scientific Vocabulary *picto-* (from Latin *pictus*) + *-gram*] (1910)
: PICTOGRAPH
pic·to·graph \-ˌgraf\ *noun* [Latin *pictus* + English *-o-* + *-graph*] (1851)
1 : an ancient or prehistoric drawing or painting on a rock wall
2 : one of the symbols belonging to a pictorial graphic system
3 : a diagram representing statistical data by pictorial forms
— pic·to·graph·ic \ˌpik-tə-'gra-fik\ *adjective*
pic·tog·ra·phy \pik-'tä-grə-fē\ *noun* (1851)
: use of pictographs **:** PICTURE WRITING 1
¹**pic·to·ri·al** \pik-'tôr-ē-əl, -'tôr-\ *adjective* [Late Latin *pictorius*, from Latin *pictor* painter] (1646)
1 : of or relating to a painter, a painting, or the painting or drawing of pictures ⟨*pictorial* perspective⟩
2 a : of, relating to, or consisting of pictures ⟨*pictorial* records⟩ **b :** illustrated by pictures ⟨*pictorial* weekly⟩ **c :** consisting of or displaying the characteristics of pictographs **d :** suggesting or conveying visual images ⟨*pictorial* poetry⟩
— pic·to·ri·al·ly \-ē-ə-lē\ *adverb*
— pic·to·ri·al·ness *noun*
²**pictorial** *noun* (1844)
: a periodical having much pictorial matter
pic·to·ri·al·ism \-ē-ə-ˌli-zəm\ *noun* (1869)
1 : the use or creation of pictures or visual images
2 : a movement or technique in photography emphasizing artificial often romanticized pictorial qualities
— pic·to·ri·al·ist \-list\ *adjective or noun*
pic·to·ri·al·ize \pik-'tôr-ē-ə-ˌlīz, -'tôr-\ *transitive verb* **-ized; -iz·ing** (1870)
: to represent by a picture or illustrate with pictures

\ə\ abut \'ᵊ\ kitten \ər\ **further** \a\ **ash** \ā\ **ace**
\ä\ mop, mar \aù\ **out** \ch\ **chin** \e\ **bet** \ē\ **easy**
\g\ **go** \i\ **hit** \ī\ **ice** \j\ **job** \ŋ\ **sing**
\ō\ **law** \ói\ **boy** \th\ **thin** \t͟h\ **the** \ü\ **loot** \ù\ **foot**
\y\ **yet** \zh\ **vision** *see also* Guide to Pronunciation

— pic·to·ri·al·i·za·tion \-ˌtōr-ē-ə-lə-'zā-shən, -ˌtȯr-\ *noun*

¹pic·ture \'pik-chər\ *noun* [Middle English, from Latin *pictura,* from *pictus,* past participle of *pingere* to paint — more at PAINT] (15th century)
1 : a design or representation made by various means (as painting, drawing, or photography)
2 a : a description so vivid or graphic as to suggest a mental image or give an accurate idea of something ⟨the book gives a detailed *picture* of what is happening⟩ **b** : a mental image
3 : IMAGE, COPY ⟨the *picture* of his father⟩ ⟨the very *picture* of health⟩
4 a : a transitory visible image or reproduction **b** : MOTION PICTURE **c** *plural* : MOVIES
5 : TABLEAU 1, 2 ⟨stage *pictures*⟩
6 : SITUATION ⟨took a hard look at his financial *picture*⟩

²picture *transitive verb* **pic·tured; pic·tur·ing** \'pik-chə-riŋ, 'pik-shriŋ\ (15th century)
1 : to paint or draw a representation, image, or visual conception of : DEPICT; *also* : ILLUSTRATE
2 : to describe graphically in words
3 : to form a mental image of : IMAGINE

picture–book *adjective* (1922)
: suitable for or suggestive of a picture book: as **a** : PICTURESQUE **b** : PICTURE-PERFECT

picture book *noun* (1847)
: a book that consists wholly or chiefly of pictures

picture hat *noun* (1887)
: a woman's dressy hat with a broad brim

picture–perfect *adjective* (1981)
: completely flawless : PERFECT ⟨made a *picture-perfect* landing⟩

pic·ture–phone \'pik-chər-ˌfōn\ *noun* (1956)
: VIDEOPHONE

picture–postcard *adjective* (1907)
: PICTURESQUE, PICTURE-BOOK ⟨a *picture-postcard* village⟩

picture puzzle *noun* (1898)
: JIGSAW PUZZLE

pic·tur·esque \ˌpik-chə-'resk\ *adjective* [French & Italian; French *pittoresque,* from Italian *pittoresco,* from *pittore* painter, from Latin *pictor,* from *pingere*] (1703)
1 a : resembling a picture : suggesting a painted scene **b** : charming or quaint in appearance
2 : evoking mental images : VIVID
synonym see GRAPHIC
— pic·tur·esque·ly *adverb*
— pic·tur·esque·ness *noun*

picture tube *noun* (1937)
: a cathode-ray tube on which the picture appears in a television receiver

picture window *noun* (1938)
: an outsize usually single-paned window designed to frame an exterior view

picture writing *noun* (1741)
1 : the recording of events or expression of messages by pictures representing actions or facts
2 : the record or message represented by picture writing

pic·tur·ize \'pik-chə-ˌrīz\ *transitive verb* **-ized; -iz·ing** (circa 1846)
: to make a picture of : present in pictures; *especially* : to make into a motion picture
— pic·tur·i·za·tion \ˌpik-chə-rə-'zā-shən\ *noun*

pid·dle \'pi-dᵊl\ *intransitive verb* **pid·dled; pid·dling** \'pid-liŋ, 'pi-dᵊl-iŋ\ [origin unknown] (1545)
1 : DAWDLE, PUTTER
2 : URINATE

pid·dling \'pid-lən, -liŋ; 'pi-dᵊl-ən, -iŋ\ *adjective* (1559)
: TRIVIAL, PALTRY

pid·dock \'pi-dək, -dik\ *noun* [origin unknown] (1851)
: a bivalve mollusk (genus *Pholas* or family Pholadidae) that bores holes in wood, clay, and rocks

pid·gin \'pi-jən\ *noun* [*pidgin English*] (1876)
: a simplified speech used for communication between people with different languages ◇
— pid·gin·i·za·tion \ˌpi-jə-nə-'zā-shən\ *noun*
— pid·gin·ize \'pi-jə-ˌnīz\ *transitive verb*

pidgin English *noun, often P capitalized* [Chinese Pidgin English *pidgin* business] (1859)
: an English-based pidgin; *especially* : one originally used in parts of the Orient

¹pie \'pī\ *noun* [Middle English, from Old French, from Latin *pica;* akin to Latin *picus* woodpecker, Old High German *speh*] (13th century)
: MAGPIE

²pie *noun* [Middle English] (14th century)
1 : a meat dish baked with biscuit or pastry crust — compare POTPIE
2 : a dessert consisting of a filling (as of fruit or custard) in a pastry shell or topped with pastry or both
3 a : AFFAIR, BUSINESS ⟨she wanted her finger . . . in every possible social *pie* —Mary Deasy⟩ **b** : a whole regarded as divisible into shares ⟨giving the less fortunate . . . a larger share of the economic *pie* —R. M. Hutchins⟩

³pie *variant of* PI

¹pie·bald \'pī-ˌbȯld\ *adjective* (1594)
1 : of different colors; *especially* : spotted or blotched with black and white
2 : composed of incongruous parts

²piebald *noun* (1765)
: a piebald animal (as a horse)

¹piece \'pēs\ *noun* [Middle English, from Old French, from (assumed) Vulgar Latin *pettia,* of Gaulish origin; akin to Welsh *peth* thing] (13th century)
1 : a part of a whole: as **a** : FRAGMENT ⟨*pieces* of broken glass⟩ **b** : any of the individual members comprising a unit — often used in combination ⟨a five-*piece* band⟩ ⟨a three-*piece* suit⟩
2 : an object or individual regarded as a unit of a kind or class ⟨a *piece* of fruit⟩
3 : a short distance ⟨down the road a *piece*⟩
4 : a standard quantity (as of length, weight, or size) in which something is made or sold
5 : a literary, journalistic, artistic, dramatic, or musical composition
6 : FIREARM
7 : COIN; *also* : TOKEN
8 : a man used in playing a board game; *specifically* : a chessman of superior rank
9 : OPINION, VIEW ⟨spoke his *piece*⟩
10 a : an act of copulation — usually considered vulgar **b** : the female partner in sexual intercourse — usually considered vulgar
synonym see PART
— of a piece : ALIKE, CONSISTENT
— piece of one's mind : a severe scolding : TONGUE-LASHING
— piece of the action : a share in activity or profit
— to pieces 1 : without reserve or restraint : COMPLETELY **2** : into fragments; *also* : into component parts **3** : out of control ⟨went *to pieces* from shock⟩

²piece *transitive verb* **pieced; piec·ing** (15th century)
1 : to repair, renew, or complete by adding pieces : PATCH
2 : to join into a whole — often used with *together* ⟨his new book . . . has been *pieced* together from talks —Merle Miller⟩
— piec·er *noun*

piece by piece *adverb* (1560)
: by degrees : PIECEMEAL

pièce de ré·sis·tance \pē-ˌes-də-rə-ˌzē-'stän(t)s, -rā-, -'stäⁿs\ *noun, plural* **pièces de ré·sis·tance** *same*\ [French, literally, piece of resistance] (1839)
1 : the chief dish of a meal
2 : an outstanding item or event : SHOWPIECE

piece–dye \'pēs-ˌdī\ *transitive verb* (1920)
: to dye after weaving or knitting

piece goods *noun plural* (1665)
: cloth fabrics sold from the bolt at retail in lengths specified by the customer — called also *yard goods*

¹piece·meal \'pēs-ˌmēl, -'mē(ə)l\ *adverb* (14th century)
1 : one piece at a time : GRADUALLY
2 : in pieces or fragments : APART

²piecemeal *adjective* (1600)
: done, made, or accomplished piece by piece or in a fragmentary way ⟨*piecemeal* reforms in the system⟩

piece of cake (1936)
: something easily done : CINCH, BREEZE

piece of eight (1610)
: an old Spanish peso of eight reals

piece of work (1928)
: a complicated, difficult, or eccentric person

piece·wise \'pēs-ˌwīz\ *adverb* (1674)
: with respect to a number of discrete intervals, sets, or pieces ⟨*piecewise* continuous functions⟩

piece·work \-ˌwərk\ *noun* (1549)
: work done by the piece and paid for at a set rate per unit
— piece·work·er \-ˌwər-kər\ *noun*

pie chart *noun* (1922)
: a circular chart cut by radii into segments illustrating relative magnitudes or frequencies — called also *circle graph*

pie·crust \'pī-ˌkrəst\ *noun* (1582)
: the pastry shell of a pie

¹pied \'pīd\ *adjective* (14th century)
: of two or more colors in blotches; *also* : wearing or having a parti-colored coat ⟨a *pied* horse⟩

²pied *past and past participle of* PI *or of* PIE

pied–à–terre \pē-ˌād-ə-'ter, -ˌād-ä-; ˌpyā-dä-\ *noun, plural* **pieds–à–terre** *same*\ [French, literally, foot to the ground] (1829)
: a temporary or second lodging

pied·mont \'pēd-ˌmänt\ *adjective* [*Piedmont,* region of Italy] (1855)
: lying or formed at the base of mountains
— piedmont *noun*

pied piper *noun, often both Ps capitalized* [the *Pied Piper,* hero of a German folktale who charmed the rats of Hameln, Germany, into a river] (1925)
1 : one that offers strong but delusive enticement

◇ WORD HISTORY
pidgin *Pidgin,* alluding to a makeshift language used between people with no language in common, comes from *Pidgin English,* the name for a particular pidgin based on English that was formerly used along the China coast in commercial transactions between Chinese and foreigners. (Linguists usually call it *Chinese Pidgin English* to distinguish it from other pidgins based on English.) The origin of *pidgin* in *Pidgin English* is mysterious. In Chinese Pidgin English the word *pidgin* means "business, affair, occupation," so that *pidgin English* presumably meant simply "business English," the language used to carry on trade. Consequently, *pidgin* has been explained with little phonetic plausibility as a Chinese mispronunciation of *business* or, alternatively, of Portuguese *ocupação* "occupation." Another theory is that *pidgin* meant originally "pidgin language" and ultimately draws its origin from the *Pidians,* supposedly an American Indian group of Guiana with whom inhabitants of a short-lived English colony were in contact in 1605–06. But while the phonetic shift from *Pidian* to *pidgin* is unobjectionable, the shift of sense and the transfer from Guiana to China two centuries later are entirely hypothetical; moreover, *Pidian* in the sole text where the word is found may actually be a misprint for *Indian.*

2 : a leader who makes irresponsible promises
3 : a charismatic person who attracts followers

pie–eyed \'pī-,īd\ *adjective* (1904)
: INTOXICATED

pie–faced \-,fāst\ *adjective* (circa 1912)
: having a round, smooth, or blank face

pieing *present participle of* PI *or of* PIE

pie in the sky (1911)
: an unrealistic enterprise or prospect of prosperity
— **pie–in–the–sky** *adjective*

pie·plant \'pī-,plant\ *noun* (circa 1847)
: garden rhubarb

pier \'pir\ *noun* [Middle English *per,* from Old English, from Medieval Latin *pera*] (12th century)
1 : an intermediate support for the adjacent ends of two bridge spans
2 : a structure (as a breakwater) extending into navigable water for use as a landing place or promenade or to protect or form a harbor
3 : a vertical structural support: as **a** : the wall between two openings **b** : PILLAR, PILASTER **c** : a vertical member that supports the end of an arch or lintel **d** : an auxiliary mass of masonry used to stiffen a wall
4 : a structural mount (as for a telescope) usually of stonework, concrete, or steel

pierce \'pirs\ *verb* **pierced; pierc·ing** [Middle English *percen,* from Old French *percer,* from (assumed) Vulgar Latin *pertusiare,* from Latin *pertusus,* past participle of *pertundere* to perforate, from *per-* through + *tundere* to beat — more at PER-, CONTUSION] (14th century)
transitive verb
1 a : to run into or through as a pointed weapon does : STAB **b** : to enter or thrust into sharply or painfully
2 : to make a hole through : PERFORATE
3 : to force or make a way into or through
4 : to penetrate with the eye or mind : DISCERN
5 : to penetrate so as to move or touch the emotions of
intransitive verb
: to force a way into or through something
synonym see ENTER

pierced *adjective* (14th century)
1 : having holes; *especially* : decorated with perforations
2 : having the earlobe punctured for an earring ⟨*pierced* ears⟩
3 : designed for pierced ears ⟨*pierced* earrings⟩

piercing *adjective* (14th century)
: PENETRATING: as **a** : LOUD, SHRILL ⟨*piercing* cries⟩ **b** : PERCEPTIVE ⟨*piercing* eyes⟩ **c** : penetratingly cold : BITING ⟨a *piercing* wind⟩ **d** : CUTTING, INCISIVE ⟨*piercing* sarcasm⟩
— **pierc·ing·ly** \'pir-siŋ-lē\ *adverb*

pier glass *noun* (1703)
: a large high mirror; *especially* : one designed to occupy the wall space between windows — called also *pier mirror*

Pi·eri·an \pī-'ir-ē-ən, -'er-\ *adjective* (1591)
1 : of or relating to the region of Pieria in ancient Macedonia or to the Muses who were once worshiped there
2 : of or relating to learning or poetry

pie·ro·gi *also* **pi·ro·gi** \pə-'rō-gē, pi-\ *noun, plural* **-gi** *also* **-gies** [Polish, plural of *pieróg* dumpling, pierogi] (1927)
: a case of dough filled with a savory filling (as of meat, cheese, or vegetables) and cooked by boiling and then panfrying

Pier·rot \'pē-ə-,rō\ *noun* [French, diminutive of *Pierre* Peter] (circa 1770)
: a stock comic character of old French pantomime usually having a whitened face and wearing loose white clothes

pier table *noun* (1803)
: a table to be placed under a pier glass

pies *plural of* PI *or of* PIE

pie safe *noun* (1951)
: a cupboard whose doors have decoratively pierced tin panels for ventilation

pie·tà \,pē-(,)ā-'tä, pyā-\ *noun, often capitalized* [Italian, literally, pity, from Latin *pietat-, pietas*] (1644)
: a representation of the Virgin Mary mourning over the dead body of Christ

pi·e·tism \'pī-ə-,ti-zəm\ *noun* (1697)
1 *capitalized* : a 17th century religious movement originating in Germany in reaction to formalism and intellectualism and stressing Bible study and personal religious experience
2 a : emphasis on devotional experience and practices **b** : affectation of devotion
— **pi·e·tist** \'pī-ə-tist\ *adjective or noun, often capitalized*

pi·e·tis·tic \,pī-ə-'tis-tik\ *adjective* (1830)
1 : of or relating to Pietism
2 a : of or relating to religious devotion or devout persons **b** : marked by overly sentimental or emotional devotion to religion : RELIGIOSE
— **pi·e·tis·ti·cal·ly** \-ti-k(ə-)lē\ *adverb*

pi·e·ty \'pī-ə-tē\ *noun, plural* **pi·e·ties** [French *piété* piety, pity, from Latin *pietat-, pietas,* from *pius* dutiful, pious] (1565)
1 : the quality or state of being pious: as **a** : fidelity to natural obligations (as to parents) **b** : dutifulness in religion : DEVOUTNESS
2 : an act inspired by piety
3 : a conventional belief or standard : ORTHODOXY
synonym see FIDELITY

piezo- *combining form* [Greek *piezein* to press; perhaps akin to Sanskrit *pīḍayati* he squeezes] : pressure ⟨*piezo*meter⟩

pi·e·zo·elec·tric \pē-,ā-(,)zō-ə-'lek-trik, pē-,āt-(,)sō-\ *adjective* [International Scientific Vocabulary] (1883)
: of, relating to, marked by, or functioning by means of piezoelectricity
— **pi·e·zo·elec·tri·cal·ly** \-tri-k(ə-)lē\ *adverb*

pi·e·zo·elec·tric·i·ty \-,lek-'tri-s(ə-)tē\ *noun* [International Scientific Vocabulary] (1883)
: electricity or electric polarity due to pressure especially in a crystalline substance (as quartz)

pi·e·zom·e·ter \,pē-ə-'zä-mə-tər, pē-,āt-'sä-\ *noun* (1820)
: an instrument for measuring pressure or compressibility; *especially* : one for measuring the change of pressure of a material subjected to hydrostatic pressure
— **pi·e·zo·met·ric** \pē-,ā-zə-'me-trik, pē-,āt-sə-\ *adjective*

¹pif·fle \'pi-fəl\ *intransitive verb* **pif·fled; pif·fling** \-f(ə-)liŋ\ [perhaps blend of *piddle* and *trifle*] (circa 1878)
: to talk or act in a trivial, inept, or ineffective way

²piffle *noun* (1890)
: trivial nonsense ⟨pseudo-scientific *piffle*⟩

pif·fling \'pi-flən, -f(ə-)liŋ\ *adjective* (1894)
: of little worth or importance : TRIVIAL

¹pig \'pig\ *noun, often attributive* [Middle English *pigge*] (13th century)
1 : a young swine not yet sexually mature; *broadly* : a wild or domestic swine
2 a : PORK **b** : the dressed carcass of a young swine weighing less than 130 pounds (60 kilograms) **c** : PIGSKIN
3 a : one that resembles a pig ⟨an unkempt . . . person is a *pig* —S. S. Hall⟩ **b** : an animal related to or resembling the pig
4 : a crude casting of metal (as iron)
5 *slang* : an immoral woman
6 *slang* : POLICE OFFICER — usually used disparagingly
— **pig·like** \-,līk\ *adjective*

²pig *verb* **pigged; pig·ging** (15th century)
intransitive verb
1 : FARROW
2 : to live like a pig ⟨*pig* it⟩
transitive verb
: FARROW

pig-boat \'pig-,bōt\ *noun* (1921)
: SUBMARINE

¹pi·geon \'pi-jən\ *noun* [Middle English, from Middle French *pijon,* from Late Latin *pipion-,*

pipio young bird, from Latin *pipire* to chirp] (14th century)
1 : any of a widely distributed family (Columbidae, order Columbiformes) of birds with a stout body, rather short legs, and smooth and compact plumage; *especially* : a member of any of numerous varieties of the rock dove that exist in domestication and in the feral state in cities and towns throughout most of the world
2 : a young woman
3 : an easy mark : DUPE
4 : CLAY PIGEON

²pigeon *noun* [alteration of *pidgin*] (1938)
: an object of special concern : BUSINESS

pigeon breast *noun* (1842)
: a deformity of the chest marked by sharp projection of the sternum

pigeon hawk *noun* (circa 1728)
1 : a falcon of the North American population of the merlin
2 : SHARP-SHINNED HAWK

¹pi·geon·hole \'pi-jən-,hōl\ *noun* (1577)
1 : a hole or small recess for pigeons to nest
2 : a small open compartment (as in a desk or cabinet) for keeping letters or documents
3 : a neat category which usually fails to reflect actual complexities

²pigeonhole *transitive verb* (1840)
1 a : to place in or as if in the pigeonhole of a desk **b** : to lay aside : SHELVE ⟨his reports continued to be *pigeonholed* and his advice not taken —Walter Mills⟩
2 : to assign to a category : CLASSIFY
— **pi·geon·hol·er** \-,hō-lər\ *noun*

pi·geon·ite \'pi-jə-,nīt\ *noun* [*Pigeon* Point, northeast Minn. + ¹-*ite*] (1900)
: a monoclinic mineral of the pyroxene group

pi·geon–liv·ered \'pi-jən-,li-vərd\ *adjective* (1602)
: GENTLE, MILD

pigeon pea *noun* (1725)
: a leguminous woody herb (*Cajanus cajan*) that has trifoliate leaves, yellow flowers, and somewhat flat pods and is much cultivated especially in the tropics; *also* : its small highly nutritious seed

pi·geon–toed \'pi-jən-,tōd\ *adjective* (1801)
: having the toes turned in

pi·geon–wing \-,win\ *noun* (circa 1808)
: a fancy dance step executed by jumping and striking the legs together

pig·fish \'pig-,fish\ *noun* (1860)
: a saltwater grunt (*Orthopristis chrysopterus*) that is a food fish found from Long Island southward

pig·gery \'pi-gə-rē\ *noun, plural* **-ger·ies** (1781)
1 : a place where swine are kept
2 : swinish behavior

pig·gin \'pi-gən\ *noun* [Middle English *pygyn*] (15th century)
: a small wooden pail with one stave extended upward as a handle

pig·gish \'pi-gish\ *adjective* (1792)
1 : of, relating to, or suggestive of a pig ⟨a *piggish* snort⟩
2 : having qualities (as greediness or stubbornness) associated with a pig
— **pig·gish·ly** *adverb*
— **pig·gish·ness** *noun*

pig·gy \'pi-gē\ *adjective* **pig·gi·er; -est** (circa 1845)
: PIGGISH

¹pig·gy·back \'pi-gē-,bak\ *adverb* [alteration of earlier *a pick pack,* of unknown origin] (1565)
1 : up on the back and shoulders
2 : on or as if on the back of another; *especially* : on a railroad flatcar

²piggyback *noun* (circa 1590)
1 : the act of carrying piggyback
2 : the movement of loaded truck trailers on railroad flatcars
³piggyback *adjective* (1823)
1 : marked by being up on the shoulders and back (a child needs hugging, tussling, and *piggyback* rides —Benjamin Spock)
2 : carried or transported piggyback: as **a** : of or relating to the hauling of truck trailers on railroad flatcars **b** : of, relating to, or being a radio or television commercial that is presented in addition to other commercials during one commercial break **c** : being or relating to something carried into space as an extra load by a vehicle (as a spacecraft)
⁴piggyback (1952)
transitive verb
1 : to carry up on the shoulders and back
2 : to haul (as a truck trailer) by railroad car
3 : to set up or cause to function in conjunction with something larger or more important
intransitive verb
1 : to haul truck trailers on railroad cars
2 : to function or be carried on or as if on the back of another
piggy bank *noun* (1941)
: a coin bank often in the shape of a pig
pig·head·ed \ˈpig-ˌhe-dəd\ *adjective* (1620)
: willfully or perversely unyielding : OBSTINATE
 — **pig·head·ed·ly** *adverb*
 — **pig·head·ed·ness** *noun*
pig in a poke (1562)
: something offered in such a way as to obscure its real nature or worth (unwilling to buy a *pig in a poke*)
pig iron *noun* (1665)
: crude iron that is the direct product of the blast furnace and is refined to produce steel, wrought iron, or ingot iron
pig latin *noun, often L capitalized* (1931)
: a jargon that is made by systematic alteration of English (as *ipskay the ointjay* for *skip the joint*)
pig·let \ˈpi-glət\ *noun* (1883)
: a small usually young swine
¹pig·ment \ˈpig-mənt\ *noun* [Latin *pigmentum*, from *pingere* to paint — more at PAINT] (14th century)
1 : a substance that imparts black or white or a color to other materials; *especially* : a powdered substance that is mixed with a liquid in which it is relatively insoluble and used especially to impart color to coating materials (as paints) or to inks, plastics, and rubber
2 : a coloring matter in animals and plants especially in a cell or tissue; *also* : any of various related colorless substances
 — **pig·men·tary** \-mən-ˌter-ē\ *adjective*
²pig·ment \-ˌment, -mənt\ *transitive verb* (1900)
: to color with or as if with pigment
pig·men·ta·tion \ˌpig-mən-ˈtā-shən, -ˌmen-\ *noun* (1866)
: coloration with or deposition of pigment; *especially* : an excessive deposition of bodily pigment
pig·my *variant of* PYGMY
pi·gno·li \pēn-ˈyō-lē\ *or* **pi·gno·lia** \-lē-ə\ *noun* [*pignoli* from Italian, plural of *pignolo*, *pinolo*, from *pigna*, *pina* pine cone, from Latin *pinea*; *pignolia* perhaps modification of *pignoli* — more at PINEAL] (1898)
: PINE NUT
pig·nut \ˈpig-ˌnət\ *noun* (1666)
1 : any of several bitter-flavored hickory nuts
2 : a hickory (as *Carya glabra* and *C. cordiformis*) bearing pignuts
pig out *intransitive verb* (1978)
slang : to eat greedily : GORGE
 — **pig-out** \ˈpig-ˌaut\ *noun*
pig·pen \-ˌpen\ *noun* (1803)
1 : a pen for pigs
2 : a dirty slovenly place
pig·skin \-ˌskin\ *noun* (1855)

1 : the skin of a swine or leather made of it
2 a : a jockey's saddle **b** : FOOTBALL 2a
pig·stick \-ˌstik\ *intransitive verb* (1891)
: to hunt the wild boar on horseback with a spear
 — **pig·stick·er** *noun*
pig·sty \ˈpig-ˌstī\ *noun* (circa 1591)
: PIGPEN
pig·tail \-ˌtāl\ *noun* (1688)
1 : tobacco in small twisted strands or rolls
2 : a tight braid of hair
pig·tailed \-ˌtāld\ *adjective* (1754)
: wearing a pigtail (*pigtailed* little girls)
pig·weed \-ˌwēd\ *noun* (circa 1801)
: any of various strongly growing weedy plants especially of the goosefoot or amaranth families
piing *present participle of* PI *or of* PIE
pi·ka \ˈpē-kə, ˈpī-\ *noun* [perhaps from Evenki (Tungusic language of Siberia)] (1827)
: any of various short-eared small lagomorph mammals (family Ochotonidae) of rocky uplands of Asia and western North America with relatively short hind legs

pika

pi·ka·ke \ˈpē-kä-ˌkā\ *noun* [Hawaiian *pīkake*, literally, peacock, from English] (1938)
: an Asian vine (*Jasminum sambac*) cultivated for its profuse fragrant white flowers
¹pike \ˈpīk\ *noun* [Middle English, from Old English *pīc* pickax] (13th century)
1 : PIKESTAFF 1
2 : a sharp point or spike; *also* : the tip of a spear
 — **piked** \ˈpīkt\ *adjective*
²pike *noun* [Middle English, perhaps of Scandinavian origin; akin to Norwegian dialect *pīk* pointed mountain] (13th century)
dialect English : a mountain or hill having a peaked summit — used especially in place names
³pike *noun, plural* **pike** *or* **pikes** [Middle English, from *¹pike*] (14th century)
1 a : a large elongate long-snouted freshwater bony fish (*Esox lucius*) valued for food and sport and widely distributed in cooler parts of the northern hemisphere — called also *northern, northern pike* **b** : any of various fishes (family Esocidae) related to the pike: as (1) : MUSKELLUNGE (2) : PICKEREL
2 : any of various fishes resembling the pike in appearance or habits
⁴pike *noun* [Middle French *pique*, from *piquer* to prick, from (assumed) Vulgar Latin *piccare*, perhaps from Latin *picus* woodpecker — more at PIE] (circa 1511)
: a heavy spear with a very long shaft used by infantry especially in Europe from the Middle Ages to the 18th century
⁵pike *transitive verb* **piked**; **pik·ing** (1798)
: to pierce, kill, or wound with a pike
⁶pike *intransitive verb* **piked**; **pik·ing** [Middle English *pyken* (reflexive)] (1526)
1 : to leave abruptly (get lonely and sore, and *pike* out —Sinclair Lewis)
2 : to make one's way (*pike* along)
⁷pike *noun* (1812)
1 : TURNPIKE
2 : a railroad or railroad line or system
 — **down the pike 1** : in the course of events (the greatest boxer to come *down the pike* in years) **2** : in the future (today's advances only hint at what's *down the pike*)
⁸pike *noun* [perhaps from *³pike*] (1928)
: a body position (as in diving) in which the hips are bent, the knees are straight, the head is pressed forward, and the hands touch the toes or clasp the legs behind or just above the knees

pike·man \ˈpīk-mən\ *noun* (1566)
: a soldier armed with a pike
pike perch *noun* (1842)
: a fish (as the walleye) of the perch group that resembles the pike
pik·er \ˈpī-kər\ *noun* [*pike* to play cautiously, of unknown origin] (1872)
1 : one who gambles or speculates with small amounts of money
2 : one who does things in a small way; *also* : TIGHTWAD, CHEAPSKATE
pike·staff \ˈpīk-ˌstaf\ *noun* (14th century)
1 : a spiked staff for use on slippery ground
2 : the staff of a foot soldier's pike
pi·ki \ˈpē-kē\ *noun* [Hopi *píki*] (circa 1889)
: bread made especially from blue cornmeal and baked in thin sheets by the Indians of the southwestern U.S.
pi·laf *or* **pi·laff** \pi-ˈläf, -ˈlòf; ˈpē-ˌ\ *or* **pi·lau** *also* **pi·law** \pi-ˈlō, -ˈlò, ˈpē-ˌ; ˈpə-r-ˌ, ˌpē-, -ˌ)lō\ *noun* [Turkish & Persian; Turkish *pilav*, from Persian *pilāv*] (1612)
: a dish made of seasoned rice and often meat
pi·las·ter \pi-ˈlas-tər, ˈpī-ˌlas-\ *noun* [Middle French *pilastre*, from Italian *pilastro*] (1575)
: an upright architectural member that is rectangular in plan and is structurally a pier but architecturally treated as a column and that usually projects a third of its width or less from the wall
pil·chard \ˈpil-chərd\ *noun* [origin unknown] (circa 1530)
1 : a fish (*Sardina pilchardus*) of the herring family resembling the herring and occurring in great schools along the coasts of Europe
2 : any of several sardines related to the European pilchard

1 pilaster

¹pile \ˈpī(ə)l\ *noun* [Middle English, dart, stake, from Old English *pīl*, from Latin *pilum* javelin] (12th century)
1 : a long slender column usually of timber, steel, or reinforced concrete driven into the ground to carry a vertical load
2 : a wedge-shaped heraldic charge usually placed vertically with the broad end up
3 a : a target-shooting arrowhead without cutting edges **b** [Latin *pilum*] : an ancient Roman foot soldier's heavy javelin
²pile *transitive verb* **piled**; **pil·ing** (15th century)
: to drive piles into
³pile *verb* **piled**; **pil·ing** [Middle English, from *⁴pile*] (14th century)
transitive verb
1 : to lay or place in a pile : STACK
2 a : to heap in abundance : LOAD (*piled* potatoes on his plate) **b** : to collect little by little into a mass — usually used with *up*
intransitive verb
1 : to form a pile or accumulation — usually used with *up*
2 : to move or press forward in or as if in a mass : CROWD (*piled* into a car)
⁴pile *noun* [Middle English, from Middle French, from Latin *pila* pillar] (15th century)
1 a (1) : a quantity of things heaped together (2) : a heap of wood for burning a corpse or a sacrifice **b** : any great number or quantity : LOT
2 : a large building or group of buildings
3 : a great amount of money : FORTUNE
4 : REACTOR 3b
⁵pile *noun* [Middle English, from Latin *pilus* hair] (15th century)
1 : a coat or surface of usually short close fine furry hairs

2 : a velvety surface produced by an extra set of filling yarns that form raised loops which are cut and sheared
— **pile·less** \'pī(ə)l-ləs\ *adjective*
⁶**pile** *noun* [Middle English, from Latin *pila* ball] (15th century)
1 : a single hemorrhoid
2 *plural* : HEMORRHOIDS
pi·le·at·ed \'pī-lē-ˌā-təd, 'pi-\ *adjective* (circa 1728)
: having a crest covering the pileum
pileated woodpecker *noun* (1782)
: a large red-crested North American woodpecker (*Dryocopus pileatus*) that is black with white on the face, neck, and undersides of the wings
piled \'pī(ə)ld\ *adjective* (15th century)
: having a pile ⟨a deep-*piled* rug⟩
pile driver *noun* (1772)
: a machine for driving down piles with a drop hammer or a steam or air hammer
pi·le·um \'pī-lē-əm\ *noun, plural* **pi·lea** \-lē-ə\ [New Latin, from Latin *pileus, pileum* felt cap; akin to Greek *pilos* felt] (1874)
: the top of the head of a bird from the bill to the nape
pile-up \'pī(ə)l-ˌəp\ *noun* (circa 1929)
1 : a collision involving usually several motor vehicles
2 a : a jammed tangled mass or pile (as of motor vehicles or people) resulting from collision or accumulation **b** : ACCUMULATION
pi·le·us \'pī-lē-əs\ *noun, plural* **pi·lei** \-lē-ˌī\ [New Latin, from Latin] (1760)
1 : the convex, concave, or flattened spore-bearing structure of some basidiomycetes that is attached superiorly to the stem and typically is expanded with gills or pores on the underside — called also *cap*
2 [Latin] : a pointed or close-fitting cap worn by ancient Romans
pile-wort \'pī(ə)l-ˌwərt, -ˌwȯrt\ *noun* [Middle English *pyle wort*; from its use in treating piles] (15th century)
: LESSER CELANDINE
pil·fer \'pil-fər\ *verb* **pil·fered; pil·fer·ing** \-f(ə-)riŋ\ [Middle French *pelfrer*, from *pelfre* booty] (circa 1548)
intransitive verb
: STEAL; *especially* : to steal stealthily in small amounts and often again and again
transitive verb
: STEAL; *especially* : to steal in small quantities
synonym *see* STEAL
— **pil·fer·able** \-f(ə-)rə-bəl\ *adjective*
— **pil·fer·age** \-f(ə-)rij\ *noun*
— **pil·fer·er** \-fər-ər\ *noun*
— **pil·fer·proof** \-ˌprüf\ *adjective*
pil·gar·lic \pil-'gär-lik\ *noun* [*pilled garlic*] (circa 1529)
1 a : a bald head **b** : a bald-headed man
2 : a man looked upon with humorous contempt or mock pity
pil·grim \'pil-grəm\ *noun* [Middle English, from Old French *peligrin*, from Late Latin *pelegrinus,* alteration of Latin *peregrinus* foreigner, from *peregri* abroad, from *per-* through + *agr-, ager* land — more at FOR, ACRE] (13th century)
1 : one who journeys in foreign lands : WAYFARER
2 : one who travels to a shrine or holy place as a devotee
3 *capitalized* : one of the English colonists settling at Plymouth in 1620 ◇
¹**pil·grim·age** \'pil-grə-mij\ *noun* (14th century)
1 : a journey of a pilgrim; *especially* : one to a shrine or a sacred place
2 : the course of life on earth
²**pilgrimage** *intransitive verb* **-aged; -ag·ing** (14th century)
: to go on a pilgrimage
pilgrim bottle *noun* (1874)
: COSTREL

pil·ing \'pī-liŋ\ *noun* (15th century)
: a structure of piles; *also* : PILES
Pi·li·pi·no \ˌpi-lə-'pē-(ˌ)nō, ˌpē-\ *noun* [Tagalog, literally, Philippine, from Spanish *Filipino*] (1936)
: the Tagalog-based official language of the Republic of the Philippines
¹**pill** \'pil\ *verb* [Middle English *pilen, pillen,* partly from Old English *pilian* to peel, partly from Middle French *piller* to plunder] (12th century)
intransitive verb
dialect chiefly English : to come off in flakes or scales : PEEL
transitive verb
1 *archaic* : to subject to depredation or extortion
2 *dialect* : to peel or strip off
²**pill** *noun* [Middle English *pylle,* from Middle Dutch *pille,* ultimately from Latin *pilula,* from diminutive of *pila* ball] (14th century)
1 a : medicine in a small rounded mass to be swallowed whole **b** *often capitalized* : an oral contraceptive — usually used with *the*
2 : something repugnant or unpleasant that must be accepted or endured
3 : something resembling a pill in size or shape
4 : a disagreeable or tiresome person
³**pill** (1736)
transitive verb
1 : to dose with pills
2 : BLACKBALL
intransitive verb
: to become rough with or mat into little balls ⟨brushed woolens often *pill*⟩
¹**pil·lage** \'pi-lij\ *noun* [Middle English, from Middle French, from *piller* to plunder, abuse] (14th century)
1 : the act of looting or plundering especially in war
2 : something taken as booty
²**pillage** *verb* **pil·laged; pil·lag·ing** (circa 1592)
transitive verb
: to plunder ruthlessly : LOOT
intransitive verb
: to take booty
synonym *see* RAVAGE
— **pil·lag·er** *noun*
¹**pil·lar** \'pi-lər\ *noun* [Middle English *piler,* from Old French, from Medieval Latin *pilare,* from Latin *pila*] (13th century)
1 a : a firm upright support for a superstructure : POST **b** : a usually ornamental column or shaft; *especially* : one standing alone for a monument
2 : a chief supporter : PROP
3 : a solid mass of coal, rock, or ore left standing to support a mine roof
4 : a body part that resembles a column
— **pil·lar·less** *adjective*
— **from pillar to post** : from one place or one predicament to another
²**pillar** *transitive verb* (1607)
: to provide or strengthen with or as if with pillars
pil·lar-box \'pi-lər-ˌbäks\ *noun* (1858)
British : a pillar-shaped mailbox
pill·box \'pil-ˌbäks\ *noun* (1730)
1 : a box for pills; *especially* : a shallow round box of pasteboard
2 : a small low concrete emplacement for machine guns and antitank weapons
3 : a small round hat without a brim; *specifically* : a woman's shallow hat with a flat crown and straight sides
pill bug *noun* [²*pill*; from its rolling into a ball when disturbed] (1843)
: WOOD LOUSE
¹**pil·lion** \'pil-yən\ *noun* [Scottish Gaelic or Irish; Scottish Gaelic *pillean,* diminutive of *peall* covering, couch; Irish *pillín,* diminutive of *peall* covering, couch] (1503)

1 a : a light saddle for women consisting chiefly of a cushion **b** : a pad or cushion put on behind a man's saddle chiefly for a woman to ride on
2 *chiefly British* : a motorcycle or bicycle saddle for a passenger
²**pillion** *adverb* (1926)
chiefly British : on or as if on a pillion ⟨ride *pillion*⟩
¹**pil·lo·ry** \'pi-lə-rē, 'pil-rē\ *noun, plural* **-ries** [Middle English, from Old French *pilori*] (13th century)
1 : a device formerly used for publicly punishing offenders consisting of a wooden frame with holes in which the head and hands can be locked
2 : a means for exposing one to public scorn or ridicule

pillory 1

²**pillory** *transitive verb* **-ried; -ry·ing** (circa 1600)
1 : to set in a pillory as punishment
2 : to expose to public contempt, ridicule, or scorn
¹**pil·low** \'pi-(ˌ)lō\ *noun* [Middle English *pilwe,* from Old English *pyle* (akin to Old High German *pfuliwi*), from Latin *pulvinus*] (before 12th century)
1 a : a support for the head of a reclining person; *especially* : one consisting of a cloth bag filled with feathers, down, sponge rubber, or plastic fiber **b** : something resembling a pillow especially in form
2 : a cushion or pad tightly stuffed and used as a support for the design and tools in making lace with a bobbin
— **pil·lowy** \'pi-lə-wē\ *adjective*
²**pillow** (1629)
transitive verb
1 : to rest or lay on or as if on a pillow
2 : to serve as a pillow for

\ə\ abut \ᵊ\ kitten \ər\ further \a\ ash \ā\ ace
\ä\ mop, mar \au̇\ out \ch\ chin \e\ bet \ē\ easy
\g\ go \i\ hit \ī\ ice \j\ job \ŋ\ sing \ō\ go
\ȯ\ law \ȯi\ boy \th\ thin \t̲h̲\ the \ü\ loot \u̇\ foot
\y\ yet \zh\ vision *see also* Guide to Pronunciation

intransitive verb
: to lay or rest one's head on or as if on a pillow

pillow block *noun* (1844)
: a block or standard to support a journal (as of a shaft) : BEARING

pil·low·case \'pi-lə-ˌkās, -lō-\ *noun* (1724)
: a removable covering for a pillow

pillow lace *noun* [from its being worked over a pillow on which the pattern is marked] (circa 1858)
: lace made with a bobbin

pillow slip *noun* (circa 1828)
: PILLOWCASE

pillow talk *noun* (1939)
: intimate conversation between lovers in bed

pi·lo·car·pine \ˌpī-lə-ˈkär-ˌpēn\ *noun* [International Scientific Vocabulary, from New Latin *Pilocarpus jaborandi*, species of tropical shrubs] (1875)
: a miotic alkaloid $C_{11}H_{16}N_2O_2$ that is obtained from jaborandi and used especially in the treatment of glaucoma

pi·lose \'pī-ˌlōs\ *adjective* [Latin *pilosus*, from *pilus* hair] (1753)
: covered with usually soft hair
— **pi·los·i·ty** \pī-ˈlä-sə-tē\ *noun*

¹**pi·lot** \'pī-lət\ *noun* [Middle French *pilote*, from Italian *pilota*, alteration of *pedota*, from (assumed) Middle Greek *pēdōtēs*, from Greek *pēda* steering oars, plural of *pēdon* oar; probably akin to Greek *pod-*, *pous* foot — more at FOOT] (1530)
1 a : one employed to steer a ship : HELMSMAN **b :** a person who is qualified and usually licensed to conduct a ship into and out of a port or in specified waters **c :** a person who flies or is qualified to fly an aircraft or spacecraft
2 : GUIDE, LEADER
3 : COWCATCHER
4 : a piece that guides a tool or machine part
5 : a television show produced and filmed or taped as a sample of a proposed series
6 : PILOT LIGHT 2
— **pi·lot·less** \-ləs\ *adjective*

²**pilot** *transitive verb* (1649)
1 : to act as a guide to : lead or conduct over a usually difficult course
2 a : to set and conn the course of ⟨*pilot* a ship⟩ **b :** to act as pilot of ⟨*pilot* a plane⟩
synonym see GUIDE

³**pilot** *adjective* (1802)
: serving as a guiding or tracing device, an activating or auxiliary unit, or a trial apparatus or operation ⟨a *pilot* study⟩

pi·lot·age \'pī-lə-tij\ *noun* (circa 1618)
1 : the action or business of piloting
2 : the compensation paid to a licensed ship's pilot

pilot biscuit *noun* (1836)
: HARDTACK — called also *pilot bread*

pilot engine *noun* (1838)
: a locomotive going in advance of a train to make sure that the way is clear

pilot fish *noun* (1634)
: a pelagic carangid fish (*Naucrates ductor*) that has dark stripes and often swims in company with a shark

pi·lot·house \'pī-lət-ˌhaús\ *noun* (1846)
: a deckhouse for a ship's helmsman containing the steering wheel, compass, and navigating equipment

pilot light *noun* (circa 1890)
1 : an indicator light showing where a switch or circuit breaker is located or whether a motor is in operation or power is on — called also *pilot lamp*
2 : a small permanent flame used to ignite gas at a burner

pilot officer *noun* (1919)
: a commissioned officer in the British air force who ranks with a second lieutenant in the army

pilot whale *noun* (1867)
: BLACKFISH 2

pil·sner *or* **pil·sen·er** \'pils-nər, 'pilz-, 'pil-zə-\ *noun* [German, literally, of Pilsen (Plzeň), city in the Czech Republic] (1877)
1 : a light beer with a strong flavor of hops
2 : a tall slender footed glass for beer

Pilt·down man \'pilt-ˌdaún-\ *noun* [Piltdown, East Sussex, England] (circa 1918)
: a supposedly very early hominid erroneously reconstructed from a combination of human and animal skeletal remains the latter of which were later found to have been planted by a hoaxer

pil·u·lar \'pil-yə-lər\ *adjective* (1802)
: of, relating to, or resembling a pill

pil·ule \'pil-(ˌ)yü(ə)l\ *noun* [Middle French, from Latin *pilula* pill — more at PILL] (1543)
: a little pill

pi·lus \'pī-ləs\ *noun, plural* **pi·li** \-ˌlī\ [Latin] (circa 1890)
: a hair or a structure (as of a bacterium) resembling a hair

Pi·ma \'pē-mə\ *noun, plural* **Pimas** *or* **Pima** (1850)
1 : a member of an American Indian people of southern Arizona and northern Mexico
2 : the Uto-Aztecan language of the Pima people
— **Pi·man** \-mən\ *adjective*

pi·ma cotton \'pē-mə, 'pi-\ *noun* [Pima County, Arizona] (1925)
: a cotton that produces fiber of exceptional strength and firmness and that was developed in the southwestern U.S. by selection and breeding of Egyptian cottons

pi·men·to \pə-ˈmen-(ˌ)tō\ *noun, plural* **-tos** *or* **-to** [Spanish *pimienta* allspice, pepper, from Late Latin *pigmenta*, plural of *pigmentum* plant juice, from Latin, pigment] (1660)
1 : ALLSPICE
2 : PIMIENTO

pimento cheese *noun* (1916)
: a Neufchâtel, process, cream, or occasionally cheddar cheese to which ground pimientos have been added

pi·me·son \'pī-ˈme-ˌzän, -ˈmā-, -ˈmē-, -ˌsän\ *noun* [⁴*pi*] (1948)
: PION

pi·mien·to \pə-ˈmen-(ˌ)tō, pəm-ˈyen-\ *noun, plural* **-tos** [Spanish from *pimienta*] (1845)
1 : any of various bluntly conical thick-fleshed sweet peppers of European origin that have a distinctive mild sweet flavor and are used especially as a garnish, as a stuffing for olives, and as a source of paprika
2 : a plant that bears pimientos

¹**pimp** \'pimp\ *noun* [origin unknown] (1600)
: a man who solicits clients for a prostitute

²**pimp** *intransitive verb* (1636)
: to work as a pimp

pim·per·nel \'pim-pər-ˌnel, -pər-nəl\ *noun* [Middle English *pimpernele*, from Middle French *pimprenelle*, from Late Latin *pimpinella*, a medicinal herb] (14th century)
: any of a genus (*Anagallis*) of herbs of the primrose family; *especially* : SCARLET PIMPERNEL

pimp·ing \'pim-pən, -piŋ\ *adjective* [origin unknown] (1687)
1 : PETTY, INSIGNIFICANT
2 *chiefly dialect* : PUNY, SICKLY

pim·ple \'pim-pəl\ *noun* [Middle English *pinple*] (14th century)
1 : a small inflamed elevation of the skin : PAPULE; *especially* : PUSTULE
2 : a swelling or protuberance like a pimple
— **pim·pled** \-pəld\ *adjective*
— **pim·ply** \-p(ə-)lē\ *adjective*

pimp·mo·bile \'pimp-mō-ˌbēl, -mə-\ *noun* (1971)
: an ostentatious luxury car of a kind characteristically used by a pimp

¹**pin** \'pin\ *noun* [Middle English, from Old English *pinn* (akin to Old High German *pfinn* peg), perhaps from Latin *pinna* quill, feather — more at PEN] (before 12th century)

1 a : a piece of solid material (as wood or metal) used especially for fastening separate articles together or as a support by which one article may be suspended from another **b** *obsolete* : the center peg of a target; *also* : the center itself **c :** something that resembles a pin especially in slender elongated form (an electrical connector *pin*) **d** (1) : one of the wooden pieces constituting the target in various games (as bowling) (2) : the peg at which a quoit is pitched (3) : the staff of the flag marking a hole on a golf course **e :** a peg for regulating the tension of the strings of a musical instrument **f :** the part of a key stem that enters a lock **g** (1) : THOLE 1 (2) : a belaying pin
2 a (1) : a small pointed piece of wire with a head used especially for fastening cloth : something of small value : TRIFLE **b :** an ornament or emblem fastened to clothing with a pin **c** (1) : BOBBY PIN (2) : HAIRPIN (3) : SAFETY PIN
3 : LEG — usually used in plural ⟨wobbly on his *pins*⟩
4 : a fall in wrestling

²**pin** *transitive verb* **pinned; pin·ning** (14th century)
1 a : to fasten, join, or secure with a pin **b :** to hold fast or immobile **c :** to present (a young woman) with a fraternity pin as a pledge of affection
2 a : ATTACH, HANG ⟨*pinned* his hopes on a miracle⟩ **b :** to assign the blame or responsibility for ⟨*pin* the robbery on a night watchman⟩ **c :** to define or determine clearly or precisely — usually used with *down* ⟨it is hard to *pin* down exactly when things changed —Katharine Whittemore⟩
3 a : to make (a chess opponent's piece) unable to move without exposing the king to check or a valuable piece to capture **b** *of a wrestler* : to secure a fall over (an opponent)

³**pin** *adjective* (1523)
1 : of or relating to a pin
2 *of leather* : having a grain suggesting the heads of pins

pi·ña cloth \'pēn-yə-\ *noun* [Spanish *piña* pineapple, pinecone, from Latin *pinea* pinecone — more at PINEAL] (circa 1858)
: a lustrous transparent cloth of Philippine origin that is woven of silky pineapple fibers

pi·ña co·la·da \'pēn-yə-kō-ˈlä-də, 'pē-nə-\ *noun* [Spanish, literally, strained pineapple] (1923)
: a tall drink made of rum, cream of coconut, and pineapple juice mixed with ice

pin·a·fore \'pi-nə-ˌfōr, -ˌför\ *noun* [²*pin* + *afore*] (1782)
: a sleeveless usually low-necked garment fastened in the back and worn as an apron or dress
— **pin·a·fored** \-ˌfōrd, -ˌförd\ *adjective*

pi·ña·ta *or* **pi·na·ta** \pēn-ˈyä-tə\ *noun* [Spanish *piñata*, literally, pot, from Italian *pignatta*, probably from *pigna* pinecone — more at PIGNOLI] (1887)
: a decorated vessel (as a pottery jar) filled with candies, fruits, and gifts and hung from the ceiling to be broken with sticks by blindfolded persons as part of especially Latin-American festivities (as at Christmas or for a birthday party)

pin·ball machine \'pin-ˌbȯl-\ *noun* (1936)
: an amusement device in which a ball propelled by a plunger scores points as it rolls down a slanting surface among pins and targets — called also *pinball game*

piñata

pin·bone \'pin-ˌbōn\ *noun* (1640)
: the hipbone especially of a quadruped — see COW illustration

pince–nez \paⁿs-'nā, pan(t)s-\ *noun, plural*
pince–nez \-'nā(z)\ [French, from *pincer* to pinch + *nez* nose, from Latin *nasus* — more at NOSE] (1876)
: eyeglasses clipped to the nose by a spring

pince-nez

pin·cer \'pin(t)-sər, *especially for 1 US often* 'pin-chər\ *noun* [Middle English *pinceour,* from (assumed) Anglo-French *pinceour,* from Middle French *pincier* to pinch, from (assumed) Vulgar Latin *pinctiare, punctiare,* from Latin *punctum* puncture — more at POINT] (14th century)
1 *plural but singular or plural in construction*
a : an instrument having two short handles and two grasping jaws working on a pivot and used for gripping things **b** : a claw (as of a lobster) resembling a pair of pincers : CHELA
2 : one part of a double envelopment in which two military forces converge on opposite sides of an enemy position
— **pin·cer·like** \-,līk\ *adjective*

¹**pinch** \'pinch\ *verb* [Middle English, from (assumed) Old North French *pinchier,* from (assumed) Vulgar Latin *pinctiare*] (14th century)
transitive verb
1 a : to squeeze between the finger and thumb or between the jaws of an instrument **b** : to prune the tip of (a plant or shoot) usually to induce branching **c** : to squeeze or compress painfully **d** : to cause physical or mental pain to **e** (1) : to cause to appear thin or shrunken (2) : to cause to shrivel or wither
2 a : to subject to strict economy or want : STRAITEN **b** : to confine or limit narrowly : CONSTRICT
3 a : STEAL **b** : ARREST
4 : to sail too close to the wind
intransitive verb
1 : COMPRESS, SQUEEZE
2 : to be miserly or closefisted
3 : to press painfully
4 : NARROW, TAPER ⟨the road *pinched* down to a trail —Cecelia Holland⟩
— **pinch pennies** : to practice strict economy

²**pinch** *noun* (15th century)
1 a : a critical juncture : EMERGENCY **b** (1) : PRESSURE, STRESS (2) : HARDSHIP, PRIVATION **c** : DEFICIT
2 a : an act of pinching : SQUEEZE **b** : as much as may be taken between the finger and thumb ⟨a *pinch* of snuff⟩ **c** : a very small amount
3 : a marked thinning of a vein or bed
4 a : THEFT **b** : a police raid; *also* : ARREST
synonym see JUNCTURE

³**pinch** *adjective* (1916)
1 : SUBSTITUTE ⟨*pinch* runner⟩
2 : hit by a pinch hitter ⟨*pinch* homer⟩

pinch bar *noun* (1837)
: a bar similar in form and use to a crowbar and sometimes having an end adapted for pulling spikes or inserting under a heavy wheel that is to be rolled

pinch·beck \'pinch-,bek\ *noun* [Christopher *Pinchbeck* (died 1732) English watchmaker] (1734)
1 : an alloy of copper and zinc used especially to imitate gold in jewelry
2 : something counterfeit or spurious
— **pinchbeck** *adjective*

pinch·er \'pin-chər\ *noun* (15th century)
1 : one that pinches
2 *plural* : PINCERS

pinch–hit \'pinch-'hit, ,pinch-\ *intransitive verb* [back-formation from *pinch hitter*] (1915)
1 : to act or serve in place of another

2 : to bat in the place of another player especially when a hit is particularly needed

pinch hit *noun* (1927)
: a hit made by a pinch hitter

pinch hitter *noun* (1912)
: one that pinch-hits

pinch-pen·ny \'pinch-,pe-nē\ *adjective* (1582)
: STINGY, NIGGARDLY

pin curl *noun* (1896)
: a curl made usually by dampening a strand of hair with water or lotion, coiling it, and securing it by a hairpin or clip

pin·cush·ion \'pin-,ku̇-shən\ *noun* (1632)
: a small cushion in which pins may be stuck ready for use

¹**Pin·dar·ic** \pin-'dar-ik\ *adjective* (1640)
1 : of or relating to the poet Pindar
2 : written in the manner or style characteristic of Pindar

²**Pindaric** *noun* (1685)
1 : a Pindaric ode
2 *plural* : loose irregular verses similar to those used in Pindaric odes

pin·dling \'pin(d)-lən, -liŋ; 'pin-d°l-ən, -iŋ\ *adjective* [perhaps alteration of *spindling*] (1861)
dialect : PUNY, FRAIL

¹**pine** \'pīn\ *noun, often attributive* [Middle English, from Old English *pīn,* from Latin *pinus;* probably akin to Greek *pitys* pine] (before 12th century)
1 : any of a genus (*Pinus* of the family Pinaceae, the pine family) of coniferous evergreen trees that have slender elongated needles and include some valuable timber trees and ornamentals
2 : the straight-grained white or yellow usually durable and resinous wood of a pine varying from extreme softness in the white pine to hardness in the longleaf pine
3 : any of various Australian coniferous trees (as of the genera *Callitris* or *Araucaria*)
4 : PINEAPPLE
5 : BENCH 1c
— **pin·ey** *also* **piny** \'pī-nē\ *adjective*

²**pine** *intransitive verb* **pined; pin·ing** [Middle English, from Old English *pīnian* to suffer, from (assumed) Old English *pīn* punishment, from Latin *poena* — more at PAIN] (14th century)
1 : to lose vigor, health, or flesh (as through grief) : LANGUISH
2 : to yearn intensely and persistently especially for something unattainable ⟨they still *pined* for their lost wealth⟩
synonym see LONG

pi·ne·al \'pī-nē-əl, pī-\ *adjective* [French *pinéal,* from Middle French, from Latin *pinea* pinecone, from feminine of *pineus* of pine, from *pinus*] (1681)
: of, relating to, or being the pineal gland

pi·ne·al·ec·to·my \,pī-nē-ə-'lek-tə-mē, pī-,nē-\ *noun* (1915)
: surgical removal of the pineal gland
— **pi·ne·al·ec·to·mize** \-tə-,mīz\ *transitive verb*

pineal gland *noun* (1712)
: a small usually conical appendage of the brain of all craniate vertebrates that functions primarily as an endocrine organ and that in a few reptiles has the essential structure of an eye — called also *pineal, pineal body, pineal organ*

pine·ap·ple \'pī-,na-pəl\ *noun* (1664)
1 a : a tropical monocotyledonous plant (*Ananas comosus* of the family Bromeliaceae, the pineapple family) that has rigid spiny-margined recurved leaves and a short stalk with a dense oblong head of small abortive flowers **b** : the large edible multiple fruit of the pineapple that consists of the sweet succulent fleshy inflorescence
2 : a hand grenade

pineapple guava *noun* (circa 1924)
: FEIJOA

pine·cone \'pīn-,kōn\ *noun* (1695)
: a cone of a pine tree

pine–drops \'pīn-,dräps\ *noun plural but singular or plural in construction* (1857)
1 : a purplish brown leafless saprophytic plant (*Pterospora andromedea*) of the wintergreen family with racemose drooping white flowers
2 : BEECHDROPS

pine·land \'pīn-,land, -lənd\ *noun* (circa 1658)
: land naturally dominated by pine forests

pi·nene \'pī-,nēn\ *noun* [International Scientific Vocabulary, from Latin *pinus*] (1885)
: either of two liquid isomeric unsaturated bicyclic terpene hydrocarbons $C_{10}H_{16}$ of which one is a major constituent of wood turpentine

pine nut *noun* (before 12th century)
: the edible seed of any of several pines — compare PIÑON

pi·nery \'pī-nə-rē, 'pīn-rē\ *noun, plural* **-er·ies** (1758)
1 : a hothouse or area where pineapples are grown
2 : a grove or forest of pine

pine–sap \'pīn-,sap\ *noun* (1840)
: any of several yellowish or reddish parasitic or saprophytic herbs (genus *Monotropa*) of the wintergreen family resembling the Indian pipe

pine siskin *noun* (1887)
: a North American finch (*Carduelis pinus*) with streaked plumage

pine snake *noun* (1791)
1 : a large constricting snake (*Pituophis melanoleucus*) of the eastern U.S. that is typically white and black and is found especially in coastal regions from New Jersey southward
2 : any of various snakes related to the pine snake

pine tar *noun* (1880)
: tar obtained by destructive distillation of the wood of the pine tree and used especially in roofing and soaps and in the treatment of skin diseases

pi·ne·tum \pī-'nē-təm\ *noun, plural* **pi·ne·ta** \-'nē-tə\ [Latin, from *pinus*] (1842)
: a plantation of pine trees; *especially* : a scientific collection of living coniferous trees

pine·wood \'pīn-,wu̇d\ *noun* (1673)
1 : a wood of pines — often used in plural but singular or plural in construction
2 : the wood of the pine tree

piney woods *noun plural* (1800)
: woodland of the southern U.S. in which pines are the dominant tree

pin·feath·er \'pin-,fe-thər\ *noun* (circa 1775)
: a feather not fully developed; *especially* : a feather just emerging through the skin

pin·fish \-,fish\ *noun* (1878)
: a small compressed dark green grunt (*Lagodon rhomboides*) that has sharp dorsal spines and is found along the Atlantic coast

pin·fold \-,fōld\ *noun* [Middle English, from Old English *pundfald,* from *pund-* enclosure + *fald* fold] (13th century)
1 : ²POUND 1a
2 : a place of restraint

ping \'piŋ\ *noun* [imitative] (1835)
1 : a sharp sound like that of a striking bullet
2 : KNOCK 2b
— **ping** *intransitive verb*

ping·er \'piŋ-ər\ *noun* (1957)
: a device for producing pulses of sound (as for marking an underwater site or detecting an underwater object)

pin·go \'piŋ-(,)gō\ *noun, plural* **pingos** [Inuit *pinguq*] (1938)
: a low hill or mound forced up by hydrostatic pressure in an area underlain by permafrost

ping–pong \'piŋ-,päŋ, -,pȯŋ\ *verb* (1952)
: SHIFT, BOUNCE

Ping–Pong \'piŋ-,päŋ, -,pȯŋ\ *trademark*
— used for table tennis

pin·head \'pin-,hed\ *noun* (1593)

1 : the head of a pin
2 : something very small or insignificant
3 : a very dull or stupid person — **FOOL**
pin·head·ed \-ˌhe-dəd\ *adjective* (1901)
: lacking intelligence or understanding **: DULL, STUPID**
— **pin·head·ed·ness** *noun*
pin·hole \-ˌhōl\ *noun* (1676)
: a small hole made by, for, or as if by a pin
¹pin·ion \'pin-yən\ *noun* [Middle English, from Middle French *pignon*, from (assumed) Vulgar Latin *pinnion-, pinnio*, from Latin *pinna* feather — more at **PEN**] (15th century)
1 : the terminal section of a bird's wing including the carpus, metacarpus, and phalanges; *broadly* **: WING**
2 : FEATHER, QUILL; *also* **: FLIGHT FEATHERS**
— **pin·ioned** \-yənd\ *adjective*
²pinion *transitive verb* (1558)
1 a : to disable or restrain by binding the arms
b : to bind fast **: SHACKLE**
2 : to restrain (a bird) from flight especially by cutting off the pinion of one wing
³pinion *noun* [French *pignon*, from Middle French *peignon*, from *peigne* comb, from Latin *pecten* — more at **PECTINATE**] (1659)
1 : a gear with a small number of teeth designed to mesh with a larger wheel or rack
2 : the smaller of a pair or the smallest of a train of gear wheels
¹pink \'pink\ *noun* [Middle English, from Middle Dutch *pinke*] (15th century)
: a ship with a narrow overhanging stern — called also *pinkie*
²pink *noun* [origin unknown] (1573)
1 : any of a genus (*Dianthus* of the family Caryophyllaceae, the pink family) of herbs having a cylindrical many-veined calyx with bracts at its base
2 a : the very embodiment **: PARAGON b** (1) **:** one dressed in the height of fashion (2) **: ELITE c :** highest degree possible **: HEIGHT** 〈keep their house in the *pink* of repair —Rebecca West〉
— **in the pink :** in the best of health or condition
³pink *noun* (1678)
1 : any of a group of colors bluish red to red in hue, of medium to high lightness, and of low to moderate saturation
2 a : the scarlet color of a fox hunter's coat; *also* **:** a fox hunter's coat of this color **b :** pink-colored clothing **c** *plural* **:** light-colored trousers formerly worn by army officers
3 : PINKO
⁴pink *adjective* (1720)
1 : of the color pink
2 : holding moderately radical and usually socialistic political or economic views
3 : emotionally moved **: EXCITED** — often used as an intensive 〈tickled *pink*〉
— **pink·ness** *noun*
⁵pink *transitive verb* [Middle English, to thrust] (1503)
1 a : to perforate in an ornamental pattern **b :** to cut a saw-toothed edge on
2 a : PIERCE, STAB b : to wound by irony, criticism, or ridicule
pink bollworm *noun* (1906)
: a small dark brown moth (*Pectinophora gossypiella*) whose pinkish larva bores into the flowers and bolls of cotton and is a destructive pest in most cotton-growing regions
pink–collar *adjective* (1977)
: of, relating to, or constituting a class of employees in occupations (as nursing and clerical jobs) traditionally held by women
pink elephants *noun plural* (1940)
: hallucinations arising especially from heavy drinking or use of narcotics 〈began to see *pink elephants*〉
pink·eye \'pink-ˌī\ *noun* (1855)
: an acute highly contagious conjunctivitis of humans and various domestic animals

¹pin·kie \'pin-kē\ *noun* [probably from Dutch *pinkje* small pink, diminutive of *pink*, from Middle Dutch *pinke*] (1840)
: ¹PINK
²pinkie *or* **pin·ky** \'pin-kē\ *noun, plural* **pin·kies** [probably from Dutch *pinkje*, diminutive of *pink* little finger] (circa 1808)
: LITTLE FINGER
pinking shears *noun plural* (circa 1939)
: shears with a saw-toothed inner edge on the blades for making a zigzag cut
pink·ish \'pin-kish\ *adjective* (1784)
: somewhat pink; *especially* **:** tending to be pink in politics
— **pink·ish·ness** *noun*
pink lady *noun* (1936)
: a cocktail consisting of gin, brandy, lemon juice, grenadine, and white of egg shaken with ice and strained
pink·ly \'pin-klē\ *adverb* (1836)
: in a pink manner **:** with a pink hue
pin·ko \'pin-ˌkō\ *noun, plural* **pink·os** *also* **pink·oes** (1936)
: a person who holds advanced liberal or moderately radical political or economic views
pink·root \'pink-ˌrüt, -ˌrut\ *noun* (1763)
: any of several plants (genus *Spigelia*) related to the nux vomica and used as anthelmintics; *especially* **:** an American woodland herb (*S. marilandica*) sometimes cultivated for its showy red and yellow flowers
pink salmon *noun* (1905)
: a small spotted Pacific salmon (*Oncorhynchus gorbuscha*) native to the northern Pacific Ocean and adjacent rivers
pink slip *noun* (1915)
: a notice from an employer that a recipient's employment is being terminated
— **pink–slip** *transitive verb*
pin money *noun* (1697)
1 a : money given by a man to his wife for her own use **b :** money set aside for the purchase of incidentals
2 : a trivial amount of money 〈worked for *pin money*〉
pin·na \'pi-nə\ *noun, plural* **pin·nae** \'pi-ˌnē, -ˌnī\ *or* **pinnas** [New Latin, from Latin, feather, wing — more at **PEN**] (1785)
1 : a leaflet or primary division of a pinnate leaf or frond
2 a : a projecting body part (as a feather, wing, or fin) **b :** the largely cartilaginous projecting portion of the external ear — see **EAR** illustration
pin·nace \'pi-nəs\ *noun* [Middle French *pinace*, probably from Old Spanish *pinaza*, from *pino* pine, from Latin *pinus*] (1538)
1 : a light sailing ship; *especially* **:** one used as a tender
2 : any of various ship's boats
¹pin·na·cle \'pi-ni-kəl\ *noun* [Middle English *pinacle*, from Middle French, from Late Latin *pinnaculum* small wing, gable, from Latin *pinna* wing, battlement] (14th century)
1 : an upright architectural member generally ending in a small spire and used especially in Gothic construction to give weight especially to a buttress
2 : a structure or formation suggesting a pinnacle; *specifically* **:** a lofty peak
3 : the highest point of development or achievement **: ACME**
synonym see **SUMMIT**
²pinnacle *transitive verb* **-cled; -cling** \-k(ə-)lin\ (14th century)
1 : to surmount with a pinnacle
2 : to raise or rear on a pinnacle
pin·nate \'pi-ˌnāt\ *adjective* [New Latin *pinnatus*, from Latin, feathered, from *pinna* feather, wing, fin] (circa 1727)

: resembling a feather especially in having similar parts arranged on opposite sides of an axis like the barbs on the rachis of a feather 〈*pinnate* leaf〉 — see **LEAF** illustration
— **pin·nate·ly** *adverb*
pin·nat·i·fid \pə-'na-tə-fəd, -ˌfid\ *adjective* [New Latin *pinnatifidus*, from *pinnatus* + Latin *-fidus* -fid] (circa 1753)
: cleft in a pinnate manner 〈a *pinnatifid* leaf〉
pin·ner \'pi-nər\ *noun* (1652)
1 : a woman's cap with long lappets worn in the 17th and 18th centuries
2 : one that pins
pin·ni·ped \'pi-nə-ˌped\ *noun* [ultimately from Latin *pinna* + *ped-, pes* foot — more at **FOOT**] (circa 1842)
: any of a suborder (Pinnipedia) of aquatic carnivorous mammals (as a seal or walrus) with all four limbs modified into flippers
— **pinniped** *adjective*
pin·nule \'pin-(ˌ)yü(ə)l\ *noun* [New Latin *pinnula*, from Latin, diminutive of *pinna*] (1748)
1 : any of the secondary branches of a plumose organ especially of a crinoid
2 : one of the ultimate divisions of a twice pinnate leaf
pin·ny \'pi-nē\ *noun, plural* **pinnies** [by shortening & alteration] (1851)
chiefly British **: PINAFORE**
pin oak *noun* (1813)
: a pyramidally-crowned oak (*Quercus palustris*) of wet regions of the eastern U.S. that has deeply cleft toothed leaves and rather small nearly hemispherical acorns
pi·noch·le \'pē-ˌnə-kəl\ *noun* [modification of German dialect *Binokel*, a game resembling bezique, from French dialect *binocle*] (1864)
: a card game played with a 48-card pack containing two each of A, K, Q, J, 10, 9 in each suit with the object to score points by melding certain combinations of cards or by winning tricks that contain scoring cards; *also* **:** the meld of queen of spades and jack of diamonds scoring 40 points in this game
pi·no·cy·to·sis \ˌpi-nə-sə-'tō-səs, ˌpī-, -ˌsī-\ *noun, plural* **-to·ses** \-ˌsēz\ [New Latin, from Greek *pinein* to drink + New Latin *cyt-* + *-osis* — more at **POTABLE**] (1895)
: the uptake of fluid by a cell by invagination and pinching off of the plasma membrane
pi·no·cy·tot·ic \-'tä-tik\ *or* **pi·no·cyt·ic** \ˌpi-nō-'sī-tik, ˌpī-\ *adjective* (1959)
: of, relating to, or being pinocytosis
— **pi·no·cy·tot·i·cal·ly** \-ti-k(ə-)lē\ *adverb*
pi·no·le \pi-'nō-lē\ *noun* [American Spanish, from Nahuatl *pinolli*] (1842)
1 : a finely ground flour made from parched corn
2 : any of various flours resembling pinole and ground from the seeds of other plants
pi·ñon *or* **pin·yon** \'pin-ˌyōn, -ˌyän, -yən; pin-'yōn\ *noun, plural* **pi·ñons** *or* **pin·yons** *or* **pi·ño·nes** \pin-'yō-nēz\ [American Spanish *piñón*, from Spanish, pine nut, from *piña* pinecone, from Latin *pinea* — more at **PINEAL**] (1831)
: any of various low-growing pines (as *Pinus quadrifolia, P. cembroides, P. edulis,* and *P. monophylla*) of western North America with edible seeds; *also* **:** the edible seed of a piñon
pi·not noir \'pē-(ˌ)nō-'nwär, pē-'nō-\ *noun, often P&N capitalized* [French, literally, black Pinot (a grape variety)] (1941)
: a dry red wine produced from the same grape as French burgundy
¹pin·point \'pin-ˌpoint\ *noun* (1849)
1 : something that is extremely small or insignificant
2 : the point of a pin
3 : an extremely small or sharp point
²pinpoint *adjective* (1899)
1 : extremely fine or precise
2 : located, fixed, or directed with extreme precision 〈*pinpoint* targets〉
3 : small as a pinpoint
³pinpoint *transitive verb* (1917)

1 pinnacle 1

1 : to locate or aim with great precision or accuracy
2 a : to fix, determine, or identify with precision **b** : to cause to stand out conspicuously : HIGHLIGHT

¹**pin·prick** \'pin-,prik\ noun (1862)
1 : a small puncture made by or as if by a pin
2 : a petty irritation or annoyance

²**pinprick** (1899)
transitive verb
: to administer pinpricks to
intransitive verb
: to administer pinpricks

pins and needles noun plural (1813)
: a pricking tingling sensation in a limb growing numb or recovering from numbness
— **on pins and needles** : in a nervous or jumpy state of anticipation

pin·set·ter \'pin-,se-tər\ noun (1916)
: an employee or a mechanical device that spots pins in a bowling alley

pin·spot·ter \-,spä-tər\ noun (1946)
: PINSETTER

pin·stripe \-,strīp\ noun, often attributive (1897)
: a very thin stripe especially on a fabric; also
: a suit with such stripes — often used in plural
— **pin–striped** \-,strīpt\ adjective

pint \'pīnt\ noun [Middle English pinte, from Middle French, from Medieval Latin pincta, probably from (assumed) Vulgar Latin feminine of pinctus, past participle of Latin pingere to paint — more at PAINT] (14th century)
1 — see WEIGHT table
2 : a pint pot or vessel

¹**pin·ta** \'pin-tə, -,tä\ noun [American Spanish, from Spanish, spot, mark, from (assumed) Vulgar Latin pincta] (1825)
: a chronic skin disease that is endemic in tropical America, that occurs successively as an initial papule, a generalized eruption, and a patchy loss of pigment, and that is caused by a spirochete (Treponema careteum) morphologically indistinguishable from the causative agent of syphilis

²**pinta** \'pīn-tə\ noun [pint + -a (as in cuppa)] (1959)
British : a pint of milk

pin·ta·ble \'pin-,tā-bəl\ noun (1936)
British : PINBALL MACHINE

pin·tail \'pin-,tāl\ noun, plural **pintail** or **pintails** (1768)
: a bird having elongated central tail feathers; especially : a slender duck (Anas acuta) of the northern hemisphere with the male having a brown head, a white breast with a white line continuing up the side of the neck, and chiefly gray upperparts

pin·tle \'pin-t³l\ noun [Middle English pintel, literally, penis, from Old English; akin to Middle Low German pint penis, Old English pinn pin] (15th century)
: a usually upright pivot pin on which another part turns

¹**pin·to** \'pin-(,)tō\ noun, plural **pintos** also **pintoes** [American Spanish, from pinto spotted, from obsolete Spanish, from (assumed) Vulgar Latin pinctus] (1860)
: a horse or pony marked with patches of white and another color — compare PIEBALD, SKEWBALD

²**pinto** adjective (1865)
: PIED, MOTTLED

pinto

pinto bean noun (1916)
: a mottled kidney bean that is grown chiefly in the southwestern U.S. for food and for stock feed

pint–size \'pīnt-,sīz\ or **pint–sized** \-,sīzd\ adjective (1936)
: SMALL

¹**pin·up** \'pin-,əp\ noun (1943)
: something fastened to a wall: as **a** : a photograph or poster of a person considered to have glamorous qualities **b** : something (as a lamp) designed for wall attachment

²**pinup** adjective (1941)
1 : of or relating to pinups ⟨male pinup calendars⟩
2 : designed for hanging on a wall ⟨a pinup lamp⟩

pinup girl noun (1941)
: a girl or woman whose glamorous qualities make her a suitable subject for a pinup

pin·wale \'pin-,wāl\ adjective (1949)
of a fabric : made with narrow wales

pin·weed \-,wēd\ noun (1814)
: any of a genus (Lechea) of herbs of the rockrose family with slender stems, many small leaves, and tiny flowers

¹**pin·wheel** \-,hwēl, -,wēl\ noun (1869)
1 : a fireworks device in the form of a revolving wheel of colored fire
2 : a toy consisting of lightweight vanes that revolve at the end of a stick
3 : something (as a galaxy) shaped like a pinwheel

²**pinwheel** intransitive verb (circa 1934)
: to move like a pinwheel

pin·worm \-,wərm\ noun (circa 1864)
1 : any of numerous small nematode worms (family Oxyuridae) that infest the intestines and especially the cecum of various vertebrates; especially : a worm (Enterobius vermicularis) parasitic in humans
2 : any of several rather slender insect larvae that burrow in plant tissue

pinx·ter flower \'piŋ(k)-stər-\ noun [Dutch pinkster Whitsuntide] (1857)
: a deciduous pink-flowered azalea (Rhododendron periclymenoides synonym R. nudiflorum) that is native to rich moist woodlands of eastern North America

pin·yin \'pin-'yin\ noun, often capitalized [Chinese (Beijing) pīnyīn to spell phonetically, from pīn to arrange + yīn sound, pronunciation] (1963)
: a system for romanizing Chinese ideograms in which tones are indicated by diacritics and unaspirated consonants are transcribed as voiced — compare WADE-GILES

pi·on \'pī-,än\ noun [contraction of pi-meson] (1950)
: any of four mesons that consist of combinations of two up or down quarks, that may be positive, negative, or neutral, that have a mass about 270 times that of the electron, and that are subject to the strong force
— **pi·on·ic** \pī-'ä-nik\ adjective

¹**pi·o·neer** \,pī-ə-'nir\ noun [Middle French pionier, from Old French peonier foot soldier, from peon foot soldier, from Medieval Latin pedon-, pedo — more at PAWN] (1523)
1 : a member of a military unit usually of construction engineers
2 a : a person or group that originates or helps open up a new line of thought or activity or a new method or technical development **b** : one of the first to settle in a territory
3 : a plant or animal capable of establishing itself in a bare, barren, or open area and initiating an ecological cycle ◇

²**pioneer** (1780)
intransitive verb
: to act as a pioneer ⟨pioneered in the development of airplanes⟩
transitive verb
1 : to open or prepare for others to follow; also : SETTLE
2 : to originate or take part in the development of

³**pioneer** adjective (1840)
1 : ORIGINAL, EARLIEST
2 : relating to or being a pioneer; especially : of, relating to, or characteristic of early settlers or their time

pi·ous \'pī-əs\ adjective [Middle English, from Latin pius] (15th century)
1 a : marked by or showing reverence for deity and devotion to divine worship **b** : marked by conspicuous religiosity ⟨a hypocrite—a thing all pious words and uncharitable deeds —Charles Reade⟩
2 : sacred or devotional as distinct from the profane or secular : RELIGIOUS ⟨a pious opinion⟩
3 : showing loyal reverence for a person or thing : DUTIFUL
4 a : marked by sham or hypocrisy **b** : marked by self-conscious virtue : VIRTUOUS
5 : deserving commendation : WORTHY ⟨a pious effort⟩
— **pi·ous·ly** adverb
— **pi·ous·ness** noun

¹**pip** \'pip\ noun [Middle English pippe, from Middle Dutch (akin to Old High German pfiffiz), from (assumed) Vulgar Latin pipita, alteration of Latin pituita phlegm, pip; perhaps akin to Greek pitys pine — more at PINE] (15th century)
1 a : a disorder of a bird marked by formation of a scale or crust on the tongue **b** : the scale or crust of this disorder
2 a : any of various human ailments; especially : a slight nonspecific disorder **b** chiefly British : a feeling of irritation or annoyance

²**pip** verb **pipped**; **pip·ping** [imitative] (1598)
intransitive verb
1 : ¹PEEP 1
2 : to break through the shell of the egg ⟨the chick pipped⟩
transitive verb
: to break open (the shell of an egg) in hatching

³**pip** noun [origin unknown] (1604)
1 a : one of the dots used on dice and dominoes to indicate numerical value **b** : SPOT 2c
2 a : SPOT, SPECK **b** : ¹SPIKE 6a; also : BLIP
3 : an individual rootstock of the lily of the valley
4 : a diamond-shaped insignia of rank worn by a second lieutenant, lieutenant, or captain in the British army

⁴**pip** noun [short for pippin] (1797)
1 : a small fruit seed; especially : one of several-seeded fleshy fruit
2 : one extraordinary of its kind

◇ WORD HISTORY

pioneer Daniel Boone and the other pioneers who opened up the American West are heroic figures to many, but the origins of the word pioneer are somewhat less than grand. Medieval French pēonier or pīonier, a derivative of peon "foot soldier," also originally meant "foot soldier," but later appeared in the sense "digger, excavator" and by the 14th century designated a solider who dug earthworks and prepared fortifications in advance of the troops who would occupy them. The word was borrowed by English in the latter sense as pioner in the 16th century, and with the modern spelling pioneer continues to refer to troops who build fortifications, roads, and bridges, though in the 20th century American army engineer has replaced it. In the figurative sense "forerunner" or "initiator," however, the English word has gone beyond its French source. Its specific application to a frontiersman first appeared in American English in the early 19th century, in the title of The Pioneers, a novel by James Fenimore Cooper published in 1823.

\ə\ abut \ᵊ\ kitten \ər\ further \a\ ash \ā\ ace
\ä\ mop, mar \au̇\ out \ch\ chin \e\ bet \ē\ easy
\g\ go \i\ hit \ī\ ice \j\ job \ŋ\ sing \ō\ go
\ȯ\ law \ȯi\ boy \th\ thin \t͟h\ the \ü\ loot \u̇\ foot
\y\ yet \zh\ vision see also Guide to Pronunciation

⁵pip *transitive verb* **pipped; pip·ping** [probably from *pip* to blackball, from ³*pip* or ⁴*pip*] (1880)
British **:** to beat by a narrow margin
⁶pip *noun* [imitative] (1907)
chiefly British **:** a short high-pitched tone
pip·age *or* **pipe·age** \'pī-pij\ *noun* (1612)
1 a : transportation by means of pipes **b :** the charge for such transportation
2 : material for pipelines **:** PIPING
pi·pal \'pē-(,)pəl\ *noun* [Hindi *pīpal*, from Sanskrit *pippala*] (1788)
: a large long-lived fig (*Ficus religiosa*) of India
¹pipe \'pīp\ *noun* [Middle English, from Old English *pīpa* (akin to Old High German *pfīfa* pipe), from (assumed) Vulgar Latin *pipa* pipe, from Latin *pipare* to peep, of imitative origin] (before 12th century)
1 a : a tubular wind instrument; *specifically* **:** a small fipple flute held in and played by the left hand **b :** one of the tubes of a pipe organ: (1) **:** FLUE PIPE (2) **:** REED PIPE **c :** BAGPIPE — usually used in plural **d** (1) **:** VOICE, VOCAL CORD — usually used in plural (2) **:** PIPING 1
2 : a long tube or hollow body for conducting a liquid, gas, or finely divided solid or for structural purposes
3 a : a tubular or cylindrical object, part, or passage **b :** a roughly cylindrical and vertical geological formation **c :** the eruptive channel opening into the crater of a volcano
4 a : a large cask of varying capacity used especially for wine and oil **b :** any of various units of liquid capacity based on the size of a pipe; *especially* **:** a unit equal to 2 hogsheads
5 : a device for smoking usually consisting of a tube having a bowl at one end and a mouthpiece at the other
6 : SNAP 2c, CINCH
— **pipe·ful** \-,fúl\ *noun*
— **pipe·less** \'pī-pləs\ *adjective*
— **pipe·like** \'pīp-,līk\ *adjective*
²pipe *verb* **piped; pip·ing** (before 12th century)
intransitive verb
1 a : to play on a pipe **b :** to convey orders by signals on a boatswain's pipe
2 a : to speak in a high or shrill voice **b :** to emit a shrill sound
transitive verb
1 a : to play (a tune) on a pipe **b :** to utter in the shrill tone of a pipe
2 a : to lead or cause to go with pipe music **b** (1) **:** to call or direct by the boatswain's pipe (2) **:** to receive aboard or attend the departure of by sounding a boatswain's pipe
3 : to trim with piping
4 : to furnish or equip with pipes
5 : to convey by or as if by pipes; *especially* **:** to transmit by wire or coaxial cable
6 : NOTICE
pipe clay *noun* (1777)
: highly plastic grayish white clay used especially in making tobacco pipes and for whitening leather
pipe cleaner *noun* (1870)
: something used to clean the inside of a pipe; *specifically* **:** a piece of flexible wire in which tufted fabric is twisted and which is used to clean the stem of a tobacco pipe
pipe cutter *noun* (circa 1890)
: a tool or machine for cutting pipe; *especially* **:** a hand tool comprising a grasping device and one or more sharp-edged wheels that cut into the pipe as the tool is rotated
pipe down *intransitive verb* [²*pipe*] (1850)
: to stop talking or making noise
pipe dream *noun* [from the fantasies brought about by the smoking of opium] (1896)

pipe cutter

: an illusory or fantastic plan, hope, or story
pipe·fish \'pīp-,fish\ *noun* (1769)
: any of various fishes (family Syngnathidae) that are related to the sea horses and have a tube-shaped snout and a long slender body covered with bony plates
pipe fitter *noun* (circa 1883)
: a worker who installs and repairs piping
pipe fitting *noun* (circa 1890)
1 : a piece (as a coupling or elbow) used to connect pipes or as accessory to a pipe
2 : the work of a pipe fitter
pipe·line \'pīp-,līn\ *noun* (1860)
1 : a line of pipe with pumps, valves, and control devices for conveying liquids, gases, or finely divided solids
2 : a direct channel for information
3 : the processes through which supplies pass from or as if from source to user
— **in the pipeline :** undergoing preparation, production, or completion **:** in the works
pipe of peace (1705)
: CALUMET
pipe organ *noun* (1885)
: ORGAN 1b(1)
pip·er \'pī-pər\ *noun* (before 12th century)
: one that plays on a pipe
pi·per·a·zine \pi-'per-ə-,zēn, pī-\ *noun* [International Scientific Vocabulary *piper*idine + *azine*] (1889)
: a crystalline heterocyclic base $C_4H_{10}N_2$ used especially as an anthelmintic
pi·per·i·dine \pi-'per-ə-,dēn, pī-\ *noun* [International Scientific Vocabulary *piper*ine + -*idine*] (1854)
: a liquid heterocyclic base $C_5H_{11}N$ that has a peppery ammoniacal odor and is obtained usually by hydrolysis of piperine
pip·er·ine \'pi-pə-,rēn\ *noun* [probably from French *pipérine*, from Latin *piper* pepper] (1820)
: a white crystalline alkaloid $C_{17}H_{19}NO_3$ that is the chief active constituent of pepper
pi·per·o·nal \pī-'per-ə-,nal\ *noun* [International Scientific Vocabulary *piper*ine + -*one* + ³-*al*] (1869)
: a crystalline aldehyde $C_8H_6O_3$ with an odor of heliotrope
pi·per·o·nyl bu·tox·ide \pī-'per-ə-,nil-byü-'täk-,sīd, -nᵊl-\ *noun* [*pipero*nal + -*yl* + *buty*l + *oxide*] (1945)
: an insecticide $C_{19}H_{30}O_5$; *especially* **:** an oily liquid containing this compound that is used chiefly as a synergist (as for pyrethrum insecticides)
pipe·stone \'pīp-,stōn\ *noun* (circa 1805)
: a pink or mottled pink-and-white argillaceous stone used especially by American Indians to make carved objects (as tobacco pipes)
pipe stop *noun* (circa 1909)
: an organ stop composed of flue pipes
pi·pette *or* **pi·pet** \pī-'pet\ *noun* [French *pipette*, diminutive of *pipe* pipe, cask, from (assumed) Vulgar Latin *pipa*, *pippa* pipe] (1839)
: a small piece of apparatus which typically consists of a narrow tube into which fluid is drawn by suction (as for dispensing or measurement) and retained by closing the upper end
— **pipette** *also* **pipet** *verb*
pipe up *intransitive verb* (1889)
: SPEAK UP
pipe wrench *noun* (circa 1875)
: a wrench for gripping and turning a cylindrical object (as a pipe) usually by use of two serrated jaws so designed as to grip the pipe when turning in one direction only
¹pip·ing \'pī-piŋ\ *noun* (13th century)
1 a : a sound, note, or call like that of a pipe **b :** the music of a pipe
2 : a quantity or system of pipes
3 : trimming stitched in seams or along edges (as of clothing, slipcovers, or curtains)
²piping *adjective* (15th century)
1 : SHRILL ⟨a *piping* voice⟩

2 : TRANQUIL ⟨*piping* times of peace —Shakespeare⟩
piping hot *adjective* (14th century)
: very hot
pip·it \'pi-pət\ *noun* [imitative] (1768)
: any of various small singing birds (family Motacillidae and especially genus *Anthus*) resembling the lark
pip·kin \'pip-kən\ *noun* [perhaps from *pipe*] (1565)
: a small earthenware or metal pot usually with a horizontal handle
pip·pin \'pi-pən\ *noun* [Middle English *pepin*, from Middle French] (15th century)
1 : any of numerous apples that have usually yellow or greenish yellow skins strongly flushed with red and are used especially for cooking
2 : a highly admired or very admirable person or thing
pip–pip \,pi(p)-'pip\ *interjection* [probably from *pip-pip*, imitating the sound of a horn] (1907)
British — used to express farewell
pip·sis·se·wa \pip-'si-sə-,wò\ *noun* [perhaps from Eastern Abenaki *kpi-psk^wáhsawe*, literally, flower of the woods] (1789)
: any of a genus (*Chimaphila* and especially *C. umbellata*) of evergreen herbs of the wintergreen family with astringent leaves used as a tonic and diuretic
pip–squeak \'pip-,skwēk\ *noun* (1910)
: one that is small or insignificant
pi·quance \'pē-kən(t)s, -kwən(t)s\ *noun* (1883)
: PIQUANCY
pi·quan·cy \'pē-kən(t)-sē, 'pi-kwən(t)-\ *noun* (1664)
: the quality or state of being piquant
pi·quant \'pē-kənt, -,känt; 'pi-kwənt\ *adjective* [Middle French, from present participle of *piquer*] (1630)
1 : agreeably stimulating to the palate; *especially* **:** SPICY
2 : engagingly provocative; *also* **:** having a lively arch charm
synonym see PUNGENT
— **pi·quant·ly** *adverb*
— **pi·quant·ness** *noun*
¹pique \'pēk\ *noun* (1592)
: a transient feeling of wounded vanity **:** RESENTMENT ⟨a fit of *pique*⟩
synonym see OFFENSE
²pique *transitive verb* **piqued; piqu·ing** [French *piquer*, literally, to prick — more at PIKE] (1669)
1 : to arouse anger or resentment in **:** IRRITATE ⟨what *piques* linguistic conservatives —T. H. Middleton⟩
2 a : to excite or arouse by a provocation, challenge, or rebuff ⟨sly remarks to *pique* their curiosity⟩ **b :** PRIDE ⟨he *piques* himself on his skill as a cook⟩
synonym see PROVOKE
pi·qué *or* **pi·que** \pi-'kā, 'pē-,\ *noun* [French *piqué*, from past participle of *piquer* to prick, quilt] (1852)
1 : a durable ribbed clothing fabric of cotton, rayon, or silk
2 : decoration of a tortoiseshell or ivory object with inlaid fragments of gold or silver
pi·quet \pi-'kā, -'ket\ *noun* [French] (1646)
: a two-handed card game played with 32 cards
pi·ra·cy \'pī-rə-sē\ *noun, plural* **-cies** [Medieval Latin *piratia*, from Late Greek *peirateia*, from Greek *peiratēs* pirate] (1537)
1 : an act of robbery on the high seas; *also* **:** an act resembling such robbery
2 : robbery on the high seas
3 : the unauthorized use of another's production, invention, or conception especially in infringement of a copyright
pi·ra·gua \pə-'rä-gwə, -'rä-\ *noun* [Spanish] (1609)
1 : DUGOUT 1

2 : a 2-masted flat-bottomed boat

pi·ra·nha \pə-ˈrä-nə, -ˈrän-yə, -ˈran-\ *noun* [Portuguese, from Tupi *pirāya*, from *pira* fish + *āya* tooth] (1869)
: any of various usually small South American characin fishes (genus *Serrasalmo*) having very sharp teeth and including some that may attack and inflict dangerous wounds upon humans and large animals — called also *caribe*

pi·ra·ru·cu \pi-ˌrär-ə-ˈkü\ *noun* [Portuguese, from Tupi *pirauruku*, from *pira* fish + *uruku* annatto] (1840)
: a very large edible bony fish (*Arapaima gigas* of the family Osteoglossidae) of the rivers of northern South America

¹pi·rate \ˈpī-rət\ *noun* [Middle English, from Middle French or Latin; Middle French, from Latin *pirata*, from Greek *peiratēs*, from *peiran* to attempt — more at FEAR] (14th century)
: one who commits or practices piracy
— **pi·rat·i·cal** \pə-ˈra-ti-kəl, pī-\ *adjective*
— **pi·rat·i·cal·ly** \-k(ə-)lē\ *adverb*

²pirate *verb* **pi·rat·ed; pi·rat·ing** (1574)
transitive verb
1 : to commit piracy on
2 : to take or appropriate by piracy: as **a** : to reproduce without authorization especially in infringement of copyright **b** : to lure away from another employer by offers of betterment
intransitive verb
: to commit or practice piracy

pirn \ˈpərn, *2 is also* ˈpirn\ *noun* [Middle English] (15th century)
1 : QUILL 1a(1)
2 *chiefly Scottish* : a device resembling a reel

pi·ro·gi *variant of* PIEROGI

pi·rogue \ˈpē-ˌrōg\ *noun* [French, from Spanish *piragua*, from Carib *piraua*] (1666)
1 : DUGOUT 1
2 : a boat like a canoe

piro·plasm \ˈpir-ə-ˌpla-zəm\ *or* **piro·plas·ma** \ˌpir-ə-ˈplaz-mə\ *noun, plural* **piro·plasms** *or* **piro·plas·ma·ta** \ˌpir-ə-ˈplaz-mə-tə\ [New Latin *Piroplasma*, genus of piroplasms] (1901)
: BABESIA

pi·rosh·ki *or* **pi·rozh·ki** \pi-ˈrōsh-kē, -ˈrōsh-ˈkē\ *noun plural* [Russian *pirozhki*, plural of *pirozhok*, diminutive of *pirog* pastry] (1912)
: small pastries with meat, cheese, or vegetable filling

pir·ou·ette \ˌpir-ə-ˈwet\ *noun* [French, literally, teetotum] (1706)
: a rapid whirling about of the body; *especially* : a full turn on the toe or ball of one foot in ballet
— **pirouette** *intransitive verb*

pis *plural of* PI

pis al·ler \pē-za-ˈlā\ *noun, plural* **pis al·lers** \-ˈlā(z)\ [French, literally, to go worst] (1676)
: a last resource or device : EXPEDIENT

pis·ca·to·ri·al \ˌpis-kə-ˈtōr-ē-əl, -ˈtȯr-\ *adjective* (1828)
: PISCATORY

pis·ca·to·ry \ˈpis-kə-ˌtōr-ē, -ˌtȯr-\ *adjective* [Latin *piscatorius*, from *piscari* to fish, from *piscis*] (1633)
: of, relating to, or dependent on fish or fishing

Pi·sce·an \ˈpī-sē-ən, ˈpi-sē-, ˈpis-kē-\ *noun* (1925)
: PISCES 2b

Pi·sces \ˈpī-(ˌ)sēz *also* ˈpi-ˌsēz *or* ˈpis-ˌkās\ *noun plural but singular in construction* [Middle English, from Latin (genitive *Piscium*), from plural of *piscis* fish — more at FISH]
1 : a zodiacal constellation directly south of Andromeda
2 a : the 12th sign of the zodiac in astrology — see ZODIAC table **b** : one born under this sign

pi·sci·cul·ture \ˈpī-sə-ˌkəl-chər, ˈpi-sə-, ˈpis-kə-\ *noun* [probably from French, from Latin *piscis* + French *culture* culture] (1859)
: fish culture

pi·sci·na \pə-ˈsē-nə, -ˈsī-\ *noun* [Medieval Latin, from Latin, fishpond, from *piscis*] (1793)
: a basin with a drain near the altar of a church for disposing of water from liturgical ablutions

pi·scine \ˈpī-ˌsēn, ˈpi-ˌsīn, ˈpis-ˌkīn\ *adjective* [Latin *piscinus*, from *piscis*] (1799)
: of, relating to, or characteristic of fish

pi·sciv·o·rous \pə-ˈsi-və-rəs, pī-\ *adjective* [Latin *piscis* + English *-vorous*] (1668)
: feeding on fishes

pish \ˈpish\ *interjection* (1592)
— used to express disdain or contempt

¹pi·si·form \ˈpī-sə-ˌfȯrm\ *adjective* [Latin *pisum* pea + English *-iform* — more at PEA] (1767)
: resembling a pea in size or shape

²pisiform *noun* (circa 1771)
: a bone on the ulnar side of the carpus in most mammals

pis·mire \ˈpis-ˌmīr, ˈpiz-\ *noun* [Middle English *pissemire*, from *pisse* urine + *mire* ant, of Scandinavian origin; akin to Old Norse *maurr* ant; akin to Latin *formica* ant, Greek *myrmēx*] (14th century)
: ANT

pis·mo clam \ˈpiz-(ˌ)mō-\ *noun, often P capitalized* [*Pismo* Beach, Calif.] (1913)
: a thick-shelled clam (*Tivela stultorum*) of the southwest coast of North America used extensively for food

pi·so \ˈpē-(ˌ)sō\ *noun* [probably from Tagalog, from Spanish *peso*] (circa 1975)
: the peso of the Philippines

pi·so·lite \ˈpī-sə-ˌlīt\ *noun* [New Latin *pisolithus*, from Greek *pisos* pea + *-lithos* -lith] (1708)
: a limestone composed of pisiform concretions
— **pi·so·lit·ic** \ˌpī-sə-ˈli-tik\ *adjective*

¹piss \ˈpis\ *verb* [Middle English, from Old French *pissier*, from (assumed) Vulgar Latin *pissiare*, of imitative origin] (14th century)
intransitive verb
: URINATE — sometimes considered vulgar
transitive verb
: to urinate in or on — sometimes considered vulgar

²piss *noun* (14th century)
1 : URINE — sometimes considered vulgar
2 : an act of urinating — often used with *take*; sometimes considered vulgar

piss·ant \ˈpis-ˌant\ *noun, often attributive* [*pissant* ant, from *¹piss + ant*] (circa 1946)
: one that is insignificant — used as a generalized term of abuse; sometimes considered vulgar

piss away *transitive verb* (1949)
: to fritter away : SQUANDER — sometimes considered vulgar

pissed \ˈpist\ *adjective* (1929)
1 *chiefly British* : DRUNK 1a — sometimes considered vulgar
2 : ANGRY, IRRITATED — often used with *off*; sometimes considered vulgar

piss off (1953)
intransitive verb
British : to leave immediately : SCRAM — usually used as a command; sometimes considered vulgar
transitive verb
: ANGER, IRRITATE — sometimes considered vulgar

pis·soir \pi-ˈswär\ *noun* [French, from Middle French, from *pisser* to urinate, from Old French *pissier*] (1919)
: a public urinal usually located on the street in some European countries

pis·ta·chio \pə-ˈsta-sh(ē-)ō, -ˈstä-\ *noun, plural* **-chios** [Italian *pistacchio*, from Latin *pistacium* pistachio nut, from Greek *pistakion*, from *pistakē* pistachio tree, of Iranian origin; akin to Persian *pistah* pistachio tree] (1598)
: a small Asian tree (*Pistacia vera*) of the cashew family whose drupaceous fruit contains a greenish edible seed; *also* : its seed

pis·ta·reen \ˌpis-tə-ˈrēn\ *noun* [probably modification of Spanish *peseta* peseta] (1744)
: an old Spanish silver piece circulating at a debased rate

piste \ˈpēst\ *noun* [French, from Middle French, from Old Italian *pista*, from *pistare* to trample down, pound — more at PISTON] (circa 1741)
: TRAIL; *especially* : a downhill ski trail

pis·til \ˈpis-t²l\ *noun* [New Latin *pistillum*, from Latin, pestle — more at PESTLE] (1749)
: a single carpel or group of fused carpels usually differentiated into an ovary, style, and stigma — see FLOWER illustration

pis·til·late \ˈpis-tə-ˌlāt\ *adjective* (circa 1828)
: having pistils; *specifically* : having pistils but no stamens

pis·tol \ˈpis-t²l\ *noun* [Middle French *pistole*, from German, from Middle High German *pischulle*, from Czech *píšt'ala*, literally, pipe, fife; akin to Czech *píšt'ět* to squeak] (circa 1570)
: a handgun whose chamber is integral with the barrel; *broadly* : HANDGUN
— **pistol** *transitive verb*

pis·tole \pis-ˈtōl\ *noun* [Middle French] (1592)
: an old gold 2-escudo piece of Spain; *also* : any of several old gold coins of Europe of approximately the same value

pis·tol·eer \ˌpis-tə-ˈlir\ *noun* (1832)
: one who is armed with a pistol

pistol grip *noun* (1874)
1 : a grip of a shotgun or rifle shaped like a pistol stock
2 : a handle shaped like a pistol stock

pistol–whip *transitive verb* (circa 1942)
: to beat with a pistol

pis·ton \ˈpis-tən\ *noun* [French, from Italian *pistone*, from *pistare* to pound, from Old Italian, from Medieval Latin, from Latin *pistus*, past participle of *pinsere* to crush — more at PESTLE] (1704)
1 : a sliding piece moved by or moving against fluid pressure which usually consists of a short cylinder fitting within a cylindrical vessel along which it moves back and forth
2 a : a sliding valve moving in a cylinder in a brass instrument which when depressed by a finger knob serves to lower the instrument's pitch **b** : a button on an organ console to bring in a previously selected registration

piston pin *noun* (1897)
: WRIST PIN

piston ring *noun* (1867)
: a springy split metal ring for sealing the gap between a piston and the cylinder wall

piston rod *noun* (1786)
: CONNECTING ROD

¹pit \ˈpit\ *noun* [Middle English, from Old English *pytt* (akin to Old High German *pfuzzi* well), from Latin *puteus* well, pit] (before 12th century)
1 a (1) : a hole, shaft, or cavity in the ground (2) : MINE (3) : a scooped-out place used for burning something (as charcoal) **b** : an area often sunken or depressed below the adjacent floor area: as (1) : an enclosure in which animals are made to fight each other (2) : a space at the front of a theater for the orchestra (3) : an area in a securities or commodities exchange in which members trade (as stocks)
2 a : HELL — used with *the* **b** : a place or situation of futility, misery, or degradation **c** *plural* : WORST (it's the *pits*)
3 : a hollow or indentation especially in the surface of an organism: as **a** : a natural hollow in the surface of the body **b** : one of the indented scars left in the skin by a pustular disease : POCKMARK **c** : a minute depression in the secondary wall of a plant cell functioning

\ə\ **abut** \²\ **kitten** \ər\ **further** \a\ **ash** \ā\ **ace**
\ä\ **mop, mar** \au̇\ **out** \ch\ **chin** \e\ **bet** \ē\ **easy**
\g\ **go** \i\ **hit** \ī\ **ice** \j\ **job** \ŋ\ **sing** \ō\ **go**
\ȯ\ **law** \ȯi\ **boy** \th\ **thin** \th\ **the** \ü\ **loot** \u̇\ **foot**
\y\ **yet** \zh\ **vision** *see also* Guide to Pronunciation

in the intercellular movement of water and dissolved material
4 : any of the areas alongside an auto race-course used for refueling and repairing the cars during a race — often used in plural with *the*

²**pit** *verb* **pit·ted; pit·ting** (15th century)
transitive verb
1 a : to place, cast, bury, or store in a pit **b :** to make pits in; *especially* **:** to scar or mark with pits
2 a : to set (as gamecocks) into or as if into a pit to fight **b :** to set into opposition or rivalry — usually used with *against*
intransitive verb
1 : to become marked with pits; *especially* **:** to preserve for a time an indentation made by pressure
2 : to make a pit stop

³**pit** *noun* [Dutch, from Middle Dutch — more at PITH] (1841)
: the stone of a drupaceous fruit

⁴**pit** *transitive verb* **pit·ted; pit·ting** (1913)
: to remove the pit from (a fruit)

¹**pi·ta** \'pē-tə\ *noun* [Spanish & Portuguese] (1698)
1 : any of several fiber-yielding plants (as an agave)
2 : the fiber of a pita; *also* **:** any of several fibers from other sources

²**pita** *noun* [New Greek] (1951)
: a thin flat bread that can be separated easily into two layers to form a pocket — called also *pita bread*

pit–a–pat \,pit-i-'pat\ *noun* [imitative] (1582)
: PITTER-PATTER
— **pit–a–pat** *adverb or adjective*
— **pit–a–pat** *intransitive verb*

pit boss *noun* (1949)
: a person who supervises the gaming tables in a casino

pit bull *noun* (1930)
: a dog (as an American Staffordshire terrier) of any of several breeds or a real or apparent hybrid with one or more of these breeds that was developed and is now often trained for fighting and is noted for strength and stamina

pit bull terrier *noun* (1945)
1 : PIT BULL
2 : AMERICAN PIT BULL TERRIER

¹**pitch** \'pich\ *noun* [Middle English *pich*, from Old English *pic*, from Latin *pic-, pix*; akin to Greek *pissa* pitch, Old Church Slavonic *pĭcĭlŭ*] (before 12th century)
1 : a black or dark viscous substance obtained as a residue in the distillation of organic materials and especially tars
2 : any of various bituminous substances
3 : resin obtained from various conifers and often used medicinally
4 : any of various artificial mixtures resembling resinous or bituminous pitches

²**pitch** *transitive verb* (before 12th century)
: to cover, smear, or treat with or as if with pitch

³**pitch** *verb* [Middle English *pichen*] (13th century)
transitive verb
1 : to erect and fix firmly in place ⟨*pitch* a tent⟩
2 : to throw usually with a particular objective or toward a particular point ⟨*pitch* hay onto a wagon⟩: as **a :** to throw (a baseball) to a batter **b :** to toss (as coins) so as to fall at or near a mark ⟨*pitch* pennies⟩ **c :** to put aside or discard by or as if by throwing ⟨*pitched* the trash into the bin⟩ ⟨decided to *pitch* the whole idea⟩
3 : to present or advertise for sale especially in a high-pressure way
4 a (1) **:** to cause to be at a particular level or of a particular quality (2) **:** to set in a particular musical key **b :** to cause to be set at a particular angle **:** SLOPE
5 : to utter glibly and insincerely
6 a : to use as a starting pitcher **b :** to play as pitcher

7 : to hit (a golf ball) in a high arc with backspin so that it rolls very little after striking the green
intransitive verb
1 a : to fall precipitately or headlong **b** (1) *of a ship* **:** to have the bow alternately plunge precipitately and rise abruptly (2) *of an aircraft, missile, or spacecraft* **:** to turn about a lateral axis so that the forward end rises or falls in relation to the after end **c :** BUCK 1
2 : ENCAMP
3 : to hit upon or happen upon something ⟨*pitch* upon the perfect gift⟩
4 : to incline downward **:** SLOPE
5 a : to throw a ball to a batter **b :** to play ball as a pitcher **c :** to pitch a golf ball
6 : to make a sales pitch
synonym see THROW
— **pitch into 1 :** ATTACK, ASSAIL **2 :** to set to work on energetically

⁴**pitch** *noun* (1542)
1 a : SLOPE;
also **:** degree of slope **:** RAKE **b** **:** the distance between any of various things: as (1) **:** distance between one point on a gear tooth and the corresponding point on the next tooth (2) **:** distance from any point on the thread of a screw to the corresponding point on an adjacent thread measured parallel to the axis **c :** the theoretical distance a propeller would advance longitudinally in one revolution **d :** the number of teeth or threads per inch **e :** a unit of width of type based on the number of times a letter can be set in a linear inch
2 : the action or a manner of pitching; *especially* **:** an up-and-down movement — compare YAW
3 *archaic* **:** TOP, ZENITH
4 a : the relative level, intensity, or extent of some quality or state ⟨tensions rose to a feverish *pitch*⟩ **b** (1) **:** the property of a sound and especially a musical tone that is determined by the frequency of the waves producing it **:** highness or lowness of sound (2) **:** a standard frequency for tuning instruments **c** (1) **:** the difference in the relative vibration frequency of the human voice that contributes to the total meaning of speech (2) **:** a definite relative pitch that is a significant phenomenon in speech
5 : a steep place **:** DECLIVITY
6 *chiefly British* **a :** an outdoor site (as for camping or doing business) **b :** PLAYING FIELD 1
7 : an all-fours game in which the first card led is a trump
8 a : an often high-pressure sales presentation **b :** ADVERTISEMENT
9 a : the delivery of a baseball by a pitcher to a batter **b :** a baseball so thrown **c :** PITCHOUT 2
— **pitched** \'picht\ *adjective*

pitch–black \'pich-'blak\ *adjective* (1599)
: extremely dark or black

pitch-blende \'pich-,blend\ *noun* [part translation of German *Pechblende*, from *Pech* pitch + *Blende* blende] (1770)
: a brown to black mineral that consists of massive uraninite, has a distinctive luster, contains radium, and is the chief ore-mineral source of uranium

pitch–dark \'pich-'därk\ *adjective* (1827)
: extremely dark **:** PITCH-BLACK

pitched battle *noun* (1607)

: an intensely fought battle in which the opposing forces are locked in close combat

¹**pitch·er** \'pi-chər\ *noun* [Middle English *picher*, from Old French *pichier*, from Medieval Latin *bicarius* goblet] (13th century)
1 : a container for holding and pouring liquids that usually has a lip or spout and a handle
2 : a modified leaf of a pitcher plant in which the hollowed petiole and base of the blade form an elongated receptacle
— **pitch·er·ful** \-,fúl\ *noun*

²**pitcher** *noun* (circa 1722)
: one that pitches; *specifically* **:** the player that pitches in a game of baseball

pitcher plant *noun* (1819)
: a plant (especially family Sarraceniaceae, the pitcher-plant family) with leaves modified into pitchers in which insects are trapped and digested by means of liquids secreted by the leaves

pitch-fork \'pich-,fórk\ *noun* (13th century)
: a long-handled fork that has two or three long somewhat curved prongs and is used especially in pitching hay
— **pitchfork** *transitive verb*

pitch in *intransitive verb* (1843)
1 : to begin to work
2 : to contribute to a common endeavor

pitch-man \'pich-mən\ *noun* (circa 1926)
: one who makes a sales pitch: as **a :** one who sells merchandise on the streets or from a concession **b :** one who does radio or TV commercials

pitch-out \'pich-,aút\ *noun* (1912)
1 : a pitch in baseball deliberately out of reach of the batter to enable the catcher to put out a base runner especially with a throw
2 : a lateral pass in football between two backs behind the line of scrimmage
— **pitch out** *intransitive verb*

pitch pine *noun* (1676)
1 : any of several pines that yield pitch; *especially* **:** a 3-leaved pine (*Pinus rigida*) of eastern North America
2 : the wood of a pitch pine

pitch pipe *noun* (1711)
: a small reed pipe or flue pipe producing one or more tones to establish the pitch in singing or in tuning an instrument

pitch-pole \'pich-,pōl\ *verb* [pitchpole somersault, from ³*pitch* + *pole, poll* head] (1851)
intransitive verb
: to turn end over end ⟨the catamaran *pitchpoled*⟩
transitive verb
: to cause to turn end over end

pitch-wom-an \-,wú-mən\ *noun* (1957)
: a woman who makes a sales pitch

pitchy \'pi-chē\ *adjective* (15th century)
1 a : full of pitch **:** TARRY **b :** of, relating to, or having the qualities of pitch
2 : PITCH-BLACK

pit·e·ous \'pi-tē-əs\ *adjective* (14th century)
: of a kind to move to pity or compassion
— **pit·e·ous·ly** *adverb*
— **pit·e·ous·ness** *noun*

pit·fall \'pit-,fól\ *noun* (14th century)
1 : TRAP, SNARE; *specifically* **:** a pit flimsily covered or camouflaged and used to capture and hold animals or men
2 : a hidden or not easily recognized danger or difficulty

¹**pith** \'pith\ *noun* [Middle English, from Old English *pitha;* akin to Middle Dutch & Middle Low German *pit* pith, pit] (before 12th century)
1 a : a usually continuous central strand of spongy tissue in the stems of most vascular plants that probably functions chiefly in storage **b :** any of various loose spongy plant tissues that resemble true pith **c :** the soft or spongy interior of a part of the body
2 a : the essential part **:** CORE **b :** substantial quality (as of meaning)
3 : IMPORTANCE

²**pith** *transitive verb* (1805)

four-line octave
three-line octave
two-line octave
one-line octave
Middle C
small octave
great octave
contraoctave
subcontraoctave

staff notation of pitch 4b(1)

1 a : to kill (as cattle) by piercing or severing the spinal cord **b :** to destroy the spinal cord or central nervous system of (as a frog) usually by passing a wire or needle up and down the vertebral canal
2 : to remove the pith from (a plant stem)
pit·head \'pit-ˌhed\ *noun* (1839)
chiefly British **:** the top of a mining pit or coal shaft; *also* **:** the immediately adjacent ground and buildings
pith·e·can·thro·pine \ˌpi-thi-'kan(t)-thrə-ˌpīn\ *noun* (1925)
: any of a group of Pleistocene hominids (as Java man, Peking man, and Heidelberg man) that have a smaller cranial capacity than modern humans (*Homo sapiens*) but a greater cranial capacity than the australopithecines, prominent eyebrow ridges, a receding forehead, constriction of the skull behind the eye sockets, and relatively large canine and incisor teeth and that were formerly considered to comprise a genus (*Pithecanthropus*) but are now grouped in a single species (*Homo erectus*)
— **pithecanthropine** *adjective*
pith·e·can·thro·pus \-'kan(t)-thrə-pəs, -ˌkan-'thrō-\ *noun, plural* **-pi** \-ˌpī, -ˌpē\ [New Latin, from Greek *pithēkos* ape + *anthrōpos* human being] (1895)
: PITHECANTHROPINE
pith helmet *noun* (1889)
: TOPEE
pith ray *noun* (1902)
: MEDULLARY RAY
pithy \'pi-thē\ *adjective* **pith·i·er; -est** (1562)
1 : consisting of or abounding in pith
2 : having substance and point **:** tersely cogent
synonym see CONCISE
— **pith·i·ly** \'pi-thə-lē\ *adverb*
— **pith·i·ness** \'pi-thē-nəs\ *noun*
piti·able \'pi-tē-ə-bəl\ *adjective* (15th century)
1 : deserving or exciting pity **:** LAMENTABLE
2 : of a kind to evoke mingled pity and contempt especially because of inadequacy ⟨a *pitiable* excuse⟩
synonym see CONTEMPTIBLE
— **piti·able·ness** *noun*
— **piti·ably** \-blē\ *adverb*
piti·er \'pi-tē-ər\ *noun* (1601)
: one that pities
piti·ful \'pi-ti-fəl\ *adjective* (14th century)
1 *archaic* **:** full of pity **:** COMPASSIONATE
2 a : deserving or arousing pity or commiseration **b :** exciting pitying contempt (as by meanness or inadequacy)
— **piti·ful·ly** \-f(ə-)lē\ *adverb*
— **piti·ful·ness** \-fəl-nəs\ *noun*
piti·less \'pi-ti-ləs, 'pi-tᵊl-əs\ *adjective* (15th century)
: devoid of pity **:** MERCILESS
— **piti·less·ly** *adverb*
— **piti·less·ness** *noun*
pit·man \'pit-mən\ *noun* (1703)
1 *plural* **pit·men** \-mən\ **:** one who works in or near a pit (as in a coal mine)
2 *plural* **pitmans :** CONNECTING ROD
pi·ton \'pē-ˌtän\ *noun* [French] (1893)
: a spike, wedge, or peg that is driven into a rock or ice surface as a support (as for a mountain climber)
pi·tot–stat·ic tube \ˌpē-ˌtō-'sta-tik-\ *noun, often P capitalized* (1926)
: a device that consists of a pitot tube and a static tube and that measures pressures in such a way that the relative speed of a fluid can be determined
pi·tot tube \'pē-ˌtō-\ *noun, often P capitalized* [French (*tube de*) *Pitot*, from Henri *Pitot* (died 1771) French physicist] (circa 1859)
1 : a device that consists of a tube having a short right-angled bend which is placed vertically in a moving body of fluid with the mouth of the bent part directed upstream and that is used with a manometer to measure the velocity of fluid flow
2 : PITOT-STATIC TUBE

pit saw *noun* (1679)
: a handsaw worked by two persons one of whom stands on or above the log being sawed into planks and the other below it usually in a pit
pit stop *noun* (1932)
1 : a stop at the pits during an automobile race
2 a : a stop (as during a trip) for fuel, food, or rest or for use of a rest room **b** (1) **:** a place where a pit stop can be made (2) **:** an establishment providing food or drink
pit·tance \'pi-tᵊn(t)s\ *noun* [Middle English *pitance*, from Old French, piety, pity, from Medieval Latin *pietantia*, from *pietant-, pietans*, present participle of *pietari* to be charitable, from Latin *pietas* piety — more at PITY] (14th century)
: a small portion, amount, or allowance; *also* **:** a meager wage or remuneration
pit·ted \'pi-təd\ *adjective* (before 12th century)
: marked with pits
pit·ter–pat·ter \'pi-tər-ˌpa-tər, 'pi-tē-ˌ\ *noun* [reduplication of ⁴*patter*] (15th century)
: a rapid succession of light sounds or beats
: PATTER
— **pitter–patter** \ˌpi-tər-', ˌpi-tē-'\ *adverb or adjective*
— **pitter–patter** *same as adverb*\ *intransitive verb*
pit·ting *noun* (1665)
1 : an arrangement of pits
2 : the action or process of forming pits
3 : the bringing of gamecocks together to fight
pit·tos·po·rum \pə-'täs-pə-rəm\ *noun* [New Latin, from Greek *pitta, pissa* pitch + *spora* seed — more at PITCH, SPORE] (1789)
: any of various Old World shrubs or trees (genus *Pittosporum* of the family Pittosporaceae) planted especially as ornamentals in warm regions
¹pi·tu·i·tary \pə-'tü-ə-ˌter-ē, -'tyü-\ *adjective* [Latin *pituita* phlegm; from the former belief that the pituitary gland secreted phlegm — more at PIP] (1615)
1 : of or relating to the pituitary gland
2 : caused or characterized by secretory disturbances of the pituitary gland ⟨a *pituitary* dwarf⟩
²pituitary *noun, plural* **-tar·ies** (1845)
: PITUITARY GLAND
pituitary gland *noun* (1825)
: a small oval endocrine organ that is attached to the infundibulum of the brain, consists of an epithelial anterior lobe joined by an intermediate part to a posterior lobe of nervous origin, and produces various internal secretions directly or indirectly impinging on most basic body functions — called also *hypophysis, pituitary body*; see BRAIN illustration
pit viper *noun* (circa 1885)
: any of various mostly New World venomous snakes (subfamily Crotalinae of the family Viperidae) with a sensory pit on each side of the head and hollow perforated fangs
¹pity \'pi-tē\ *noun, plural* **pit·ies** [Middle English *pite*, from Old French *pité*, from Latin *pietat-, pietas* piety, pity, from *pius* pious] (13th century)
1 a : sympathetic sorrow for one suffering, distressed, or unhappy **b :** capacity to feel pity
2 : something to be regretted ⟨it's a *pity* you can't go⟩ ☆
²pity *verb* **pit·ied; pity·ing** (15th century)
transitive verb
: to feel pity for
intransitive verb
: to feel pity
pity·ing *adjective* (1589)
: expressing or feeling pity
— **pity·ing·ly** \-iŋ-lē\ *adverb*
pit·y·ri·a·sis \ˌpi-ti-'rī-ə-səs\ *noun* [New Latin, from Greek, from *pityron* scurf] (circa 1693)
: a condition of humans or domestic animals marked by dry scaling or scurfy patches of skin

più \'pyü, pē-'ü\ *adverb* [Italian, from Latin *plus*] (1724)
: MORE — used to qualify an adverb or adjective used as a direction in music
Pi·ute *variant of* PAIUTE
¹piv·ot \'pi-vət\ *noun* [French] (1611)
1 : a shaft or pin on which something turns
2 a : a person, thing, or factor having a major or central role, function, or effect **b :** a key player or position; *specifically* **:** an offensive position of a basketball player standing usually with back to the basket to relay passes, shoot, or provide a screen for teammates
3 : the action of pivoting
²pivot *adjective* (1796)
1 : turning on or as if on a pivot
2 : PIVOTAL
³pivot (1841)
intransitive verb
: to turn on or as if on a pivot
transitive verb
1 : to provide with, mount on, or attach by a pivot
2 : to cause to pivot
— **pivot·able** \-və-tə-bəl\ *adjective*
piv·ot·al \'pi-və-tᵊl\ *adjective* (1844)
1 : of, relating to, or constituting a pivot
2 : vitally important **:** CRUCIAL
— **piv·ot·al·ly** \-tᵊl-ē\ *adverb*
piv·ot·man \'pi-vət-ˌman\ *noun* (circa 1814)
: one who plays the pivot; *specifically* **:** a center on a basketball team
pivot tooth *noun* (1842)
: an artificial crown attached to the root of a tooth by a usually metallic pin — called also *pivot crown*
pix *plural of* PIC
pix·el \'pik-səl, -ˌsel\ *noun* [*pix* + *element*] (1969)
1 : any of the small discrete elements that together constitute an image (as on a television screen)
2 : any of the detecting elements of a charge-coupled device used as an optical sensor
¹pix·ie *or* **pixy** \'pik-sē\ *noun, plural* **pix·ies** [origin unknown] (1746)
: FAIRY; *specifically* **:** a cheerful mischievous sprite
— **pix·ie·ish** \-sē-ish\ *adjective*
²pixie *or* **pixy** *adjective* (1943)
: playfully mischievous
— **pixi·ness** *noun*
pix·i·lat·ed *or* **pix·il·lat·ed** \'pik-sə-ˌlā-təd\ *adjective* [irregular from *pixie*] (1848)

☆ **SYNONYMS**
Pity, compassion, commiseration, condolence, sympathy mean the act or capacity for sharing the painful feelings of another. PITY implies tender or sometimes slightly contemptuous sorrow for one in misery or distress (felt *pity* for the captives). COMPASSION implies pity coupled with an urgent desire to aid or to spare (treats the homeless with great *compassion*). COMMISERATION suggests pity expressed outwardly in exclamations, tears, or words of comfort (murmurs of *commiseration* filled the loser's headquarters). CONDOLENCE applies chiefly to formal expression of grief to one who has suffered loss (expressed their *condolences* to the widow). SYMPATHY often suggests a tender concern but can also imply a power to enter into another's emotional experience of any sort (went to my best friend for *sympathy*) (in *sympathy* with her desire to locate her natural parents).

\ə\ **abut** \ᵊ\ **kitten** \ər\ **further** \a\ **ash** \ā\ **ace**
\ä\ **mop, mar** \au̇\ **out** \ch\ **chin** \e\ **bet** \ē\ **easy**
\g\ **go** \i\ **hit** \ī\ **ice** \j\ **job** \ŋ\ **sing** \ō\ **go**
\ȯ\ **law** \ȯi\ **boy** \th\ **thin** \th̲\ **the** \ü\ **loot** \u̇\ **foot**
\y\ **yet** \zh\ **vision** *see also* Guide to Pronunciation

1 : somewhat unbalanced mentally; *also* **:** BE-MUSED
2 : WHIMSICAL
— **pix·i·la·tion** \ˌpik-sə-'lā-shən\ *noun*
piz·za \'pēt-sə\ *noun* [Italian, perhaps of Germanic origin; akin to Old High German *bizzo*, *pizzo* bite, bit, *bīzan* to bite — more at BITE] (1935)
: an open pie made typically of flattened bread dough spread with a savory mixture usually including tomatoes and cheese and often other toppings and baked — called also *pizza pie*
— **pizza·like** \-ˌlīk\ *adjective*
piz·zazz *or* **pi·zazz** \pə-'zaz\ *noun* [origin unknown] (1937)
: the quality of being exciting or attractive: as **a :** GLAMOUR **b :** VITALITY
— **piz·zazzy** *or* **pi·zazzy** \-'za-zē\ *adjective*
piz·ze·ria \ˌpēt-sə-'rē-ə\ *noun* [Italian, from *pizza*] (1943)
: an establishment where pizzas are made or sold
¹piz·zi·ca·to \ˌpit-si-'kä-(ˌ)tō\ *noun, plural* **-ca·ti** \-'kä-(ˌ)tē\ (1845)
: a note or passage played by plucking strings
²pizzicato *adverb or adjective* [Italian, past participle of *pizzicare* to pluck] (circa 1854)
: by means of plucking instead of bowing — used as a direction in music; compare ARCO
piz·zle \'pi-zəl\ *noun* [probably from Flemish *pezel*; akin to Low German *pesel* pizzle] (1523)
1 : the penis of an animal
2 : a whip made of a bull's pizzle
pj's \'pē-ˌjäz\ *noun plural* [*pa*jamas] (1951)
: PAJAMAS
PK \ˌpē-'kā\ *noun* (1943)
: PSYCHOKINESIS
pla·ca·ble \'pla-kə-bəl, 'plā-\ *adjective* (1586)
: easily placated **:** TOLERANT, TRACTABLE
— **pla·ca·bil·i·ty** \ˌpla-kə-'bi-lə-tē, ˌplā-\ *noun*
— **pla·ca·bly** \'pla-kə-blē, 'plā-\ *adverb*
¹plac·ard \'pla-kərd, -ˌkärd\ *noun* [Middle English *placquart* formal document, from Middle French, from *plaquier* to plate — more at PLAQUE] (1560)
1 : a notice posted in a public place **:** POSTER
2 : a small card or metal plaque
²plac·ard \-ˌkärd, -kərd\ *transitive verb* (1813)
1 a : to cover with or as if with posters **b :** to post in a public place
2 : to announce by or as if by posting
pla·cate \'plā-ˌkāt, 'pla-\ *transitive verb* **pla·cat·ed; pla·cat·ing** [Latin *placatus*, past participle of *placare* — more at PLEASE] (1678)
: to soothe or mollify especially by concessions **:** APPEASE
synonym see PACIFY
— **pla·cat·er** *noun*
— **pla·cat·ing·ly** \-ˌkā-tiŋ-lē\ *adverb*
— **pla·ca·tion** \plā-'kā-shən, pla-\ *noun*
— **pla·ca·tive** \'plā-ˌkā-tiv, 'pla-\ *adjective*
— **pla·ca·to·ry** \'plā-kə-ˌtōr-ē, 'pla-, -ˌtȯr-\ *adjective*
¹place \'plās\ *noun* [Middle English, from Old French, open space, from Latin *platea* broad street, from Greek *plateia* (*hodos*), from feminine of *platys* broad, flat; akin to Sanskrit *pr̥thu* broad, Latin *planta* sole of the foot] (13th century)
1 a : physical environment **:** SPACE **b :** a way for admission or transit **c :** physical surroundings **:** ATMOSPHERE
2 a : an indefinite region or expanse ⟨all over the *place*⟩ **b :** a building or locality used for a special purpose ⟨a *place* of learning⟩ ⟨a fine eating *place*⟩ **c** *archaic* **:** the three-dimensional compass of a material object
3 a : a particular region, center of population, or location ⟨a nice *place* to visit⟩ **b :** a building, part of a building, or area occupied as a home ⟨our summer *place*⟩
4 : a particular part of a surface or body **:** SPOT

5 : relative position in a scale or series: as **a :** position in a social scale ⟨kept them in their *place*⟩ **b :** a step in a sequence ⟨in the first *place*, it's none of your business⟩ **c :** a position at the conclusion of a competition ⟨finished in last *place*⟩
6 a : a proper or designated niche ⟨the *place* of education in society⟩ **b :** an appropriate moment or point ⟨this is not the *place* to discuss compensation —Robert Moses⟩
7 a : an available seat or accommodation ⟨needs a *place* to stay⟩ **b :** an empty or vacated position ⟨new ones will take their *place*⟩
8 : the position of a figure in relation to others of a row or series; *especially* **:** the position of a digit within a numeral
9 a : remunerative employment **:** JOB **b :** prestige accorded to one of high rank **:** STATUS ⟨an endless quest for preferment and *place* —*Time*⟩
10 : a public square **:** PLAZA
11 : a small street or court
12 : second place at the finish (as of a horse race)
— **in place 1 :** in an original or proper position **2 :** in the same spot without forward or backward movement ⟨run *in place*⟩
²place *verb* **placed; plac·ing** (15th century)
transitive verb
1 a : to put in or as if in a particular place or position **:** SET **b :** to present for consideration ⟨a question *placed* before the group⟩ **c :** to put in a particular state ⟨*place* a performer under contract⟩ **d :** to direct to a desired spot **e :** to cause (the voice) to produce free and well resonated singing or speaking tones
2 a : to assign to a position in a series or category **:** RANK **b :** ESTIMATE ⟨*placed* the value of the estate too high⟩ **c :** to identify by connecting with an associated context ⟨couldn't quite *place* her face⟩ ⟨police *placed* them at the crime scene⟩
3 : to distribute in an orderly manner **:** ARRANGE
4 : to appoint to a position
5 : to find a place (as a home or employment) for
6 a : to give (an order) to a supplier **b :** to give an order for ⟨*place* a bet⟩ **c :** to try to establish a connection for ⟨*place* a telephone call⟩
intransitive verb
: to earn a given spot in a competition; *specifically* **:** to come in second (as in a horse race)
— **place·able** \'plā-sə-bəl\ *adjective*
pla·ce·bo *noun, plural* **-bos** (13th century)
1 \plä-'chā-(ˌ)bō\ [Middle English, from Latin, I shall please, from *placēre* to please — more at PLEASE] **:** the Roman Catholic vespers for the dead
2 \plə-'sē-\ [Latin, I shall please] **a** (1) **:** a medication prescribed more for the mental relief of the patient than for its actual effect on a disorder (2) **:** an inert or innocuous substance used especially in controlled experiments testing the efficacy of another substance (as a drug) **b :** something tending to soothe
placebo effect *noun* (1950)
: improvement in the condition of a sick person that occurs in response to treatment but cannot be considered due to the specific treatment used
place·hold·er \'plās-ˌhōl-dər\ *noun* (1958)
: a symbol in a mathematical or logical expression that may be replaced by the name of any element of a set
¹place·kick \'plās-ˌkik\ *noun* (1856)
: the kicking of a ball (as a football) placed or held in a stationary position on the ground
²placekick *transitive verb* (1856)
1 : to kick (a ball) from a stationary position
2 : to score by means of a placekick
— **place·kick·er** *noun*
place·less \-ləs\ *adjective* (14th century)
: lacking a fixed location

— **place·less·ly** *adverb*
place·man \-mən\ *noun* (1741)
: a political appointee to a public office especially in 18th century Britain
place mat *noun* (1928)
: a small often rectangular table mat on which a place setting is laid
place·ment \'plās-mənt\ *noun* (1844)
1 : an act or instance of placing: as **a :** an accurately hit ball (as in tennis) that an opponent cannot return **b :** the assignment of a person to a suitable place (as a job or a class in school)
2 : PLACEKICK
placement test *noun* (1928)
: a test usually given to a student entering an educational institution to determine specific knowledge or proficiency in various subjects for the purpose of assignment to appropriate courses or classes
place–name \'plās-ˌnām\ *noun* (1868)
: the name of a geographical locality
pla·cen·ta \plə-'sen-tə\ *noun, plural* **-centas** *or* **-cen·tae** \-'sen-(ˌ)tē\ [New Latin, from Latin, flat cake, from Greek *plakoenta*, accusative of *plakoeis*, from *plak-, plax* flat surface — more at FLUKE] (1691)
1 : the vascular organ in mammals except monotremes and marsupials that unites the fetus to the maternal uterus and mediates its metabolic exchanges through a more or less intimate association of uterine mucosal with chorionic and usually allantoic tissues; *also* **:** an analogous organ in another animal
2 : a sporangium-bearing surface; *especially* **:** the part of the carpel bearing ovules
— **pla·cen·tal** \-'sen-t²l\ *adjective or noun*
pla·cen·ta·tion \ˌpla-s²n-'tā-shən, plə-ˌsen-\ *noun* (1760)
1 : the arrangement of placentas and ovules in a plant ovary
2 a : the development of the placenta and attachment of the fetus to the uterus during pregnancy **b :** the morphological type of a placenta
¹plac·er \'plā-sər\ *noun* (1579)
: one that places: as **a :** one that deposits or arranges **b :** one of the winners in a competition
²plac·er \'pla-sər\ *noun* [Spanish, from Catalan, submarine plain, from *plaza* place, from Latin *platea* broad street — more at PLACE] (1848)
: an alluvial, marine, or glacial deposit containing particles of valuable mineral and especially of gold
place setting *noun* (1944)
: a table service for one person
place value *noun* (1911)
: the value of the place of a digit in a numeral
plac·id \'pla-səd\ *adjective* [Latin *placidus*, from *placēre* to please — more at PLEASE] (1626)
1 : serenely free of interruption or disturbance ⟨*placid* skies⟩ ⟨a *placid* disposition⟩
2 : COMPLACENT
synonym see CALM
— **pla·cid·i·ty** \pla-'si-də-tē, plə-\ *noun*
— **plac·id·ly** \'pla-səd-lē\ *adverb*
— **plac·id·ness** *noun*
plack·et \'pla-kət\ *noun* [origin unknown] (1605)
1 a : a slit in a garment (as a skirt) often forming the closure **b** *archaic* **:** a pocket especially in a woman's skirt
2 *archaic* **a :** PETTICOAT **b :** WOMAN
plac·oid \'pla-ˌkȯid\ *adjective* [Greek *plak-, plax* flat surface] (1842)
: of, relating to, or being a scale of dermal origin with an enamel-tipped spine characteristic of the elasmobranchs
pla·gal \'plā-gəl\ *adjective* [Medieval Latin *plagalis*, ultimately from Greek *plagios* oblique, sideways, from *plagos* side; akin to Latin *plaga* net, region, Greek *pelagos* sea] (1597)
1 *of a church mode* **:** having the keynote on the 4th scale step — compare AUTHENTIC 4a

2 *of a cadence* **:** progressing from the subdominant chord to the tonic — compare AUTHENTIC 4b

plage \ˈpläzh\ *noun* [French, beach, luminous surface, from Italian *piaggia* beach, from Late Latin *plagia*, from Greek *plagios* oblique] (1888)
1 : the beach of a seaside resort
2 : a bright region on the sun caused by the light emitted by clouds of calcium or hydrogen and often associated with a sunspot

pla·gia·rise *British variant of* PLAGIARIZE

pla·gia·rism \ˈplā-jə-ˌri-zəm *also* -jē-ə-\ *noun* (1621)
1 : an act or instance of plagiarizing
2 : something plagiarized ◇
— **pla·gia·rist** \-rist\ *noun*
— **pla·gia·ris·tic** \ˌplā-jə-ˈris-tik *also* -jē-ə-\ *adjective*

pla·gia·rize \ˈplā-jə-ˌrīz *also* -jē-ə-\ *verb* **-rized; -riz·ing** [*plagiary*] (1716)
transitive verb
: to steal and pass off (the ideas or words of another) as one's own **:** use (a created production) without crediting the source
intransitive verb
: to commit literary theft **:** present as new and original an idea or product derived from an existing source
— **pla·gia·riz·er** *noun*

pla·gia·ry \ˈplā-jē-ˌer-ē, -jə-rē\ *noun, plural* **-ries** [Latin *plagiarus*, literally, kidnapper, from *plagium* netting of game, kidnapping, from *plaga* net, trap] (1601)
1 *archaic* **:** one that plagiarizes
2 : PLAGIARISM

pla·gio·clase \ˈplā-j(ē-)ə-ˌklās, ˈplā-, -ˌklāz\ *noun* [Greek *plagios* oblique + *klasis* breaking, from *klan* to break — more at CLAST] (circa 1868)
: a triclinic feldspar; *especially* **:** one having calcium or sodium in its composition

pla·gio·tro·pic \ˌplā-j(ē-)ə-ˈtrō-pik, ˌplā-ˈträ-\ *adjective* [Greek *plagios* + International Scientific Vocabulary *-tropic*] (1882)
: having the longer axis inclined away from the vertical

¹plague \ˈplāg\ *noun* [Middle English *plage*, from Middle French, from Late Latin *plaga*, from Latin, blow; akin to Latin *plangere* to strike — more at PLAINT] (14th century)
1 a : a disastrous evil or affliction **:** CALAMITY **b :** a destructively numerous influx ⟨a *plague* of locusts⟩
2 a : an epidemic disease causing a high rate of mortality **:** PESTILENCE **b :** a virulent contagious febrile disease that is caused by a bacterium (*Yersinia pestis*) and that occurs in bubonic, pneumonic, and septicemic forms — called also *black death*
3 a : a cause of irritation **:** NUISANCE **b :** a sudden unwelcome outbreak ⟨a *plague* of burglaries⟩

²plague *transitive verb* **plagued; plagu·ing** (15th century)
1 : to smite, infest, or afflict with or as if with disease, calamity, or natural evil
2 a : to cause worry or distress to **:** HAMPER, BURDEN **b :** to disturb or annoy persistently
synonym see WORRY
— **plagu·er** *noun*

plagu·ey *or* **plaguy** \ˈplā-gē, ˈple-\ *adjective* (1615)
: causing irritation or annoyance **:** TROUBLESOME
— **plaguey** *adverb*
— **plagu·i·ly** \-gə-lē\ *adverb*

plaice \ˈplās\ *noun, plural* **plaice** [Middle English *plaice*, from Middle French *plaïs*, from Late Latin *platessa*] (13th century)
: any of various flatfishes; *especially* **:** a large European flounder (*Pleuronectes platessa*) with red spots

plaid \ˈplad\ *noun* [Scottish Gaelic *plaide*] (1512)

1 : a rectangular length of tartan worn over the left shoulder as part of the Scottish national costume
2 a : a twilled woolen fabric with a tartan pattern **b :** a fabric with a pattern of tartan or an imitation of tartan
3 a : TARTAN 1 **b :** a pattern of unevenly spaced repeated stripes crossing at right angles
— **plaid** *adjective*
— **plaid·ed** \ˈpla-dəd\ *adjective*

¹plain \ˈplān\ *intransitive verb* [Middle English, from Old French *plaindre*, from Latin *plangere* to lament — more at PLAINT] (14th century)
archaic **:** COMPLAIN

²plain *noun* [Middle English, from Old French, from Latin *planum*, from neuter of *planus* flat, plain — more at FLOOR] (14th century)
1 a : an extensive area of level or rolling treeless country **b :** a broad unbroken expanse
2 : something free from artifice, ornament, or extraneous matter

³plain *adjective* (14th century)
1 *archaic* **:** EVEN, LEVEL
2 : lacking ornament **:** UNDECORATED
3 : free of extraneous matter **:** PURE
4 : free of impediments to view **:** UNOBSTRUCTED
5 a (1) **:** evident to the mind or senses **:** OBVIOUS ⟨it's perfectly *plain* that they will resist⟩ (2) **:** CLEAR ⟨let me make my meaning *plain*⟩ **b :** marked by outspoken candor **:** free from duplicity or subtlety **:** BLUNT ⟨*plain* talk⟩
6 a : belonging to the great mass of humans **b :** lacking special distinction or affectation **:** ORDINARY
7 : characterized by simplicity **:** not complicated ⟨*plain* home-cooked meals⟩
8 : lacking beauty or ugliness
synonym see COMMON, EVIDENT, FRANK
— **plain·ly** *adverb*
— **plain·ness** \ˈplān-nəs\ *noun*

⁴plain *adverb* (14th century)
: in a plain manner ⟨saw them clearly and told you *plain* —American Documentation⟩

⁵plain *adverb* [partly from Middle English *plein* entire, complete, from Middle French, full, from Latin *plenus*; partly from ⁴*plain* — more at FULL] (1535)
: ABSOLUTELY ⟨it *plain* galled me to pay fancy prices —F. R. Buckley⟩

plain·chant \ˈplān-ˌchant\ *noun* [French *plain-chant*, literally, plain song] (circa 1741)
: PLAINSONG

plain·clothes \ˈplān-ˈklō(th)z\ *adjective* (1866)
: dressed in civilian clothes while on duty — used especially of a police officer

plain·clothes·man \ˈplān-ˈklō(th)z-mən, -ˌman\ *noun* (1899)
: a plainclothes police officer

plain–Jane \ˈplān-ˈjān\ *adjective* [from the name *Jane*] (1912)
: not fancy or glamorous **:** ORDINARY

plain–laid \ˈplān-ˈlād\ *adjective* (1881)
of a rope **:** consisting of three strands laid right-handed

Plain People *noun* (1904)
: members of any of various Protestant groups (as Mennonites) especially in the U.S. who wear distinctively plain clothes and adhere to a simple and traditional style of life excluding many conveniences of modern technology

Plains \ˈplānz\ *adjective* (1844)
: of or relating to North American Indians of the Great Plains or to their culture

plain sailing *noun* (1756)
: easy progress over an unobstructed course

plains·man \ˈplānz-mən\ *noun* [Great *Plains* + *man*] (1870)
: an inhabitant of the plains

plain·song \ˈplān-ˌsȯŋ\ *noun* (1513)
: a monophonic rhythmically free liturgical chant of any of various Christian rites; *especially* **:** GREGORIAN CHANT

plain·spo·ken \-ˈspō-kən\ *adjective* (1678)
: CANDID, FRANK
— **plain·spo·ken·ness** \-kən-nəs\ *noun*

plaint \ˈplānt\ *noun* [Middle English, from Middle French, from Latin *planctus*, from *plangere* to strike, beat one's breast, lament; akin to Old High German *fluokhōn* to curse, Greek *plēssein* to strike] (13th century)
1 : LAMENTATION, WAIL
2 : PROTEST, COMPLAINT

plain·text \ˈplān-ˌtekst\ *noun* (1918)
: the intelligible form of an encrypted text or of its elements — compare CIPHERTEXT

plaint·ful \ˈplānt-fəl\ *adjective* (14th century)
: MOURNFUL

plain·tiff \ˈplān-təf\ *noun* [Middle English *plaintif*, from Middle French, from *plaintif*, adjective] (14th century)
: a person who brings a legal action — compare DEFENDANT

plain·tive \ˈplān-tiv\ *adjective* [Middle English *plaintif* grieving, from Middle French, from *plaint*] (1579)
: expressive of suffering or woe **:** MELANCHOLY
— **plain·tive·ly** *adverb*
— **plain·tive·ness** *noun*

plain–vanilla *adjective* (1975)
: lacking special features or qualities **:** BASIC

plain weave *noun* (1888)
: a weave in which the threads interlace alternately

plain–woven *adjective* (1925)
: made in plain weave

plais·ter \ˈplas-tər, ˈpläs-\ *variant of* PLASTER

¹plait \ˈplāt, ˈplat\ *noun* [Middle English *pleit*, from Middle French, from (assumed) Vulgar Latin *plicitum*, from neuter of Latin *plicitus*, past participle of *plicare* to fold — more at PLY] (14th century)
1 : PLEAT
2 : a braid of material (as hair or straw); *specifically* **:** PIGTAIL

²plait *transitive verb* (14th century)
1 : PLEAT 1
2 a : to interweave the strands or locks of **:** BRAID **b :** to make by plaiting
— **plait·er** *noun*

plait·ing *noun* (15th century)
: the interlacing of strands **:** BRAIDING

¹plan \ˈplan\ *noun* [French, plane, foundation, ground plan; partly from Latin *planum* level ground, from neuter of *planus* level; partly from French *planter* to plant, fix in place, from Late Latin *plantare* — more at FLOOR, PLANT] (1706)
1 : a drawing or diagram drawn on a plane: as **a :** a top or horizontal view of an object **b :** a large-scale map of a small area
2 a : a method for achieving an end **b :** an often customary method of doing something

◇ WORD HISTORY
plagiarism The Latin noun *plaga* denoted a hunting net or snare used for capturing game. The netting of such animals was termed *plagium*. By extension, this word was also used for the crime of kidnapping children or freemen and selling them as slaves. The kidnapper was called by the derivative noun *plagiarius*. We know that by the time of the poet Martial, who died about A.D. 103, *plagiarius* was also being used to refer to a literary thief or plagiarist. When Latin *plagiarius* was borrowed into English as *plagiary* in the 17th century, both the original and literary senses were carried over. Only the literary sense of *plagiary* appears in the English derivatives *plagiarism* and *plagiarize*.

\ə\ abut \ᵊ\ kitten \ər\ further \a\ ash \ā\ ace
\ä\ mop, mar \au̇\ out \ch\ chin \e\ bet \ē\ easy
\g\ go \i\ hit \ī\ ice \j\ job \ŋ\ sing \ō\ go
\ȯ\ law \ȯi\ boy \th\ thin \t̷h\ the \ü\ loot \u̇\ foot
\y\ yet \zh\ vision *see also* Guide to Pronunciation

PLANETS

NAME	SYMBOL	MEAN DISTANCE FROM THE SUN		PERIOD OF REVOLUTION IN DAYS OR YEARS	EQUATORIAL DIAMETER IN MILES
		astronomical units	million miles		
Mercury	☿	0.387	36.0	87.97 days	3,032
Venus	♀	0.723	67.2	224.70 days	7,523
Earth	⊕	1.000	92.9	365.26 days	7,928
Mars	♂	1.524	141.5	686.98 days	4,218
Jupiter	♃	5.203	483.4	11.86 years	88,900
Saturn	♄	9.522	884.6	29.46 years	74,900
Uranus	♅	19.201	1783.8	84.01 years	31,800
Neptune	♆	30.074	2793.9	164.79 years	30,800
Pluto	♇	39.725	3690.5	247.69 years	1,400

: PROCEDURE **c :** a detailed formulation of a program of action **d :** GOAL, AIM
3 : an orderly arrangement of parts of an overall design or objective
4 : a detailed program (as for payment or the provision of some service) ⟨pension *plan*⟩ ☆
— **plan·less** \-ləs\ *adjective*
— **plan·less·ly** *adverb*
— **plan·less·ness** *noun*
²**plan** *verb* **planned; plan·ning** (1728)
transitive verb
1 : to arrange the parts of **:** DESIGN
2 : to devise or project the realization or achievement of ⟨*plan* a program⟩
3 : to have in mind **:** INTEND
intransitive verb
: to make plans
— **plan·ner** *noun*
plan- or **plano-** *combining form* [Latin *planus*]
1 : flat ⟨*plano*sol⟩
2 : flat and ⟨*plano*-concave⟩
pla·nar \'plā-nər, -,när\ *adjective* (1850)
1 : of, relating to, or lying in a plane
2 : two-dimensional in quality
— **pla·nar·i·ty** \plā-'nar-ə-tē\ *noun*
pla·nar·ia \plə-'nar-ē-ə, -'ner-\ *noun* [New Latin, from feminine of Late Latin *planarius* lying on a plane, from Latin *planum* plane] (circa 1909)
: PLANARIAN; *especially* **:** any of a genus (*Planaria*) of 2-eyed planarian worms
pla·nar·i·an \-ē-ən\ *noun* [New Latin *Planaria*] (circa 1858)
: any of various dark-colored freshwater triclad flatworms (family Planariidae) with two eyespots and a triangular head; *broadly* **:** TRICLAD
pla·na·tion \plā-'nā-shən\ *noun* (1877)
: the condition or process of becoming flattened
plan·chet \'plan-chət\ *noun* [diminutive of *planch* flat plate, from Middle French *planche*] (1611)
1 : a metal disk to be stamped as a coin
2 : a small metal or plastic disk
plan·chette \plan-'shet\ *noun* [French, from diminutive of *planche* plank, from Latin *planca*] (1860)
: a small triangular or heart-shaped board supported on casters at two points and a vertical pencil at a third and believed to produce automatic writing when lightly touched by the fingers; *also* **:** a similar board without a pencil
Planck's constant \'pläŋ(k)s-, 'plaŋ(k)s-\ *noun* [Max K.E.L. *Planck*] (1910)
: a constant that gives the unvarying ratio of the energy of a quantum of radiation to its frequency and that has an approximate value of 6.626×10^{-34} J·S — symbol *h*
¹**plane** \'plān\ *verb* **planed; plan·ing** [Middle English, from Middle French *planer*, from Late Latin *planus* level — more at FLOOR] (14th century)
transitive verb
1 a : to make smooth or even **:** LEVEL **b :** to make smooth or even by use of a plane

2 : to remove by planing — often used with *away* or *off*
intransitive verb
1 : to work with a plane
2 : to do the work of a plane
— **plan·er** *noun*
²**plane** *noun* [Middle English, from Middle French, from Latin *platanus*, from Greek *platanos*; probably akin to Greek *platys* broad — more at PLACE] (14th century)
: any of a genus (*Platanus* of the family Platanaceae, the plane-tree family) of trees with large palmately lobed leaves and flowers in globose heads — called also *buttonwood, plane tree, sycamore*
³**plane** *noun* [Middle English, from Middle French, from Late Latin *plana*, from *planare*] (14th century)
: a tool for smoothing or shaping a wood surface
⁴**plane** *noun* [Latin *planum*, from neuter of *planus* level] (1604)
1 a : a surface of such nature that a straight line joining two of its points lies wholly in the surface **b :** a flat or level surface
2 : a level of existence, consciousness, or development ⟨on the intellectual *plane*⟩
3 a : one of the main supporting surfaces of an airplane **b** [by shortening] **:** AIRPLANE
⁵**plane** *adjective* [Latin *planus*] (1704)
1 : having no elevations or depressions **:** FLAT
2 a : of, relating to, or dealing with geometric planes **b :** lying in a plane ⟨a *plane* curve⟩
synonym see LEVEL
⁶**plane** *intransitive verb* **planed; plan·ing** [Middle English, from Middle French *planer*, from *plain* level, plain] (15th century)
1 a : to fly while keeping the wings motionless **b :** to skim across the surface of the water
2 : to travel by airplane
plane angle *noun* (1570)
: an angle that for a given dihedral angle is formed by two intersecting lines each of which lies on a face of the dihedral angle and is perpendicular to the edge of the face
plane geometry *noun* (1747)
: a branch of elementary geometry that deals with plane figures
plane·load \'plān-,lōd\ *noun* (1941)
: a load that fills an airplane
plane of polarization (1831)
: the plane in which the magnetic-vibration component of plane-polarized electromagnetic radiation lies
plane–polarized *adjective* (circa 1853)
: vibrating in a single plane ⟨*plane-polarized* light waves⟩
pla·ner tree \'plā-nər-\ *noun* [J. J. *Planer* (died 1789) German botanist] (circa 1810)
: a small-leaved North American tree (*Planera aquatica*) of the elm family with an oval ribbed fruit
plan·et \'pla-nət\ *noun* [Middle English *plan-*

ete, from Old French, from Late Latin *planeta*, modification of Greek *planēt-, planēs,* literally, wanderer, from *planasthai* to wander — more at FLOOR] (13th century)
1 a : any of the seven celestial bodies sun, moon, Venus, Jupiter, Mars, Mercury, and Saturn that in ancient belief have motions of their own among the fixed stars **b** (1) **:** any of the large bodies that revolve around the sun in the solar system (2) **:** a similar body associated with another star **c :** EARTH — usually used with *the*
2 : a celestial body held to influence the fate of human beings
3 : a person or thing of great importance **:** LUMINARY ◇
— **plan·et·like** \-,līk\ *adjective*
plane table *noun* (1607)
: an instrument consisting essentially of a drawing board on a tripod with a ruler pointed at the object observed and used for plotting the lines of a survey directly from observation
plan·e·tar·i·um \,pla-nə-'ter-ē-əm\ *noun, plural* **-i·ums** *or* **-ia** \-ē-ə\ (1860)
1 : a model or representation of the solar system
2 a : an optical device for projecting various celestial images and effects **b :** a building or room housing such a projector
plan·e·tary \'pla-nə-,ter-ē\ *adjective* (1607)
1 a : of, relating to, being, or resembling a planet **b :** ERRATIC, WANDERING **c :** having a motion like that of a planet ⟨*planetary* electrons⟩ **d :** IMMENSE ⟨the scope of this project has reached *planetary* proportions⟩

☆ **SYNONYMS**
Plan, design, plot, scheme, project
mean a method devised for making or doing something or achieving an end. PLAN always implies mental formulation and sometimes graphic representation ⟨*plans* for a house⟩. DESIGN often suggests a particular pattern and some degree of achieved order or harmony ⟨a *design* for a new dress⟩. PLOT implies a laying out in clearly distinguished sections with attention to their relations and proportions ⟨the *plot* of the play⟩. SCHEME stresses calculation of the end in view and may apply to a plan motivated by craftiness and self-interest ⟨a *scheme* to defraud the government⟩. PROJECT often stresses imaginative scope and vision ⟨a *project* to develop the waterfront⟩.

◇ **WORD HISTORY**
planet In scanning the nighttime sky, ancient astronomers observed that while the vast majority of stars maintained fixed relative positions, there were five heavenly bodies that looked like bright stars but quite obviously changed their position in relation to each other and to the fixed stars. These five—Mercury, Venus, Mars, Jupiter, and Saturn—were called by the Greeks *planētes asteres* "wandering stars," or simply *planētes* "wanderers." The corresponding Latin expression was *stellae errantes* or *erraticae,* which also means "wandering stars." By the second century A.D. the borrowed Greek words *planētes* and *planētai* (the latter from a different noun derivative of the verb *planasthai* "to wander") were also appearing in Latin as *planetes* and *planetae* respectively; *planetae,* the singular of which was *planeta,* became the usual word in Late and Medieval Latin. Through medieval French, Middle English borrowed this word in the 14th century, which ultimately became *planet* in Modern English. Of course, we now know that the planets "wander" because they revolve around the sun, as does the earth.

³plane

2 a : of, relating to, or belonging to the earth **:** TERRESTRIAL **b :** GLOBAL, WORLDWIDE **3 :** having or consisting of an epicyclic train of gear wheels

planetary nebula *noun* (1785)
: a usually compact luminous ring-shaped nebula that is composed of matter which has been ejected from a hot star at its center

planetary science *noun* (1969)
: PLANETOLOGY
 — **planetary scientist** *noun*

plan·e·tes·i·mal \ˌpla-nə-ˈte-sə-məl, -zə-məl\ *noun* [*planet* + *-esimal* (as in *infinitesimal*)] (1903)
: any of numerous small solid celestial bodies that may have existed at an early stage of the development of the solar system

planetesimal hypothesis *noun* (1904)
: a hypothesis in astronomy: the planets have evolved by aggregation from planetesimals

plan·et·oid \ˈpla-nə-ˌtȯid\ *noun* (1803)
: a small body resembling a planet; *especially* **:** ASTEROID
 — **plan·et·oi·dal** \ˌpla-nə-ˈtȯi-dᵊl\ *adjective*

plan·et·ol·o·gy \ˌpla-nə-ˈtä-lə-jē\ *noun, plural* **-gies** (1907)
: a branch of astronomy that deals with the condensed matter of the solar system and especially with the planets and their moons
 — **plan·et·o·log·i·cal** \ˌpla-nə-tᵊl-ˈä-ji-kəl\ *adjective*
 — **plan·et·ol·o·gist** \ˌpla-nə-ˈtä-lə-jist\ *noun*

plan·et–strick·en \ˈpla-nət-ˌstri-kən\ *or* **plan·et–struck** \-ˌstrək\ *adjective* (1599)
1 *archaic* **:** affected by the influence of a planet
2 *archaic* **:** PANIC-STRICKEN

planet wheel *noun* (1827)
: a gear wheel that revolves around the wheel with which it meshes in an epicyclic train

plan·et·wide \ˈpla-nət-ˈwīd\ *adjective* (1969)
: extending throughout or involving an entire planet

plan·form \ˈplan-ˌfȯrm\ *noun* (1908)
: the contour of an object (as an airplane) or mass as viewed from above

plan·gen·cy \ˈplan-jən(t)-sē\ *noun* (1858)
: the quality or state of being plangent

plan·gent \-jənt\ *adjective* [Latin *plangent-, plangens,* present participle of *plangere* to strike, lament — more at PLAINT] (1858)
1 : having a loud reverberating sound
2 : having an expressive and especially plaintive quality
 — **plan·gent·ly** *adverb*

pla·nim·e·ter \plā-ˈni-mə-tər, plə-\ *noun* [French *planimètre,* from Latin *planum* plane + French *-mètre* -meter] (circa 1858)
: an instrument for measuring the area of a plane figure by tracing its boundary line

pla·ni·met·ric \ˌplā-nə-ˈme-trik\ *adjective* (circa 1828)
1 : of, relating to, or made by means of a planimeter ⟨*planimetric* measurements⟩
2 *of a map* **:** having no indications of relief
 — **pla·ni·met·ri·cal·ly** \-tri-k(ə-)lē\ *adverb*

plan·ish \ˈpla-nish\ *transitive verb* [Middle English *planysshen,* from Middle French *planiss-,* stem of *planir* to make smooth, from *plan* level, from Latin *planus* — more at FLOOR] (14th century)
: to smooth, toughen, and finish (metal) by hammering lightly
 — **plan·ish·er** *noun*

pla·ni·sphere \ˈplā-nə-ˌsfir\ *noun* [alteration of Middle English *planisperie,* from Medieval Latin *planisphaerium,* from Latin *planum* plane + *sphaera* sphere] (1571)
: a representation of the circles of the sphere on a plane; *especially* **:** a polar projection of the celestial sphere and the stars on a plane with adjustable circles or other appendages for showing celestial phenomena for any given time

pla·ni·spher·ic \ˌplā-nə-ˈsfir-ik, -ˈsfer-\ *adjective*

¹plank \ˈplaŋk\ *noun* [Middle English, from Old North French *planke,* from Latin *planca*] (13th century)
1 a : a heavy thick board; *especially* **:** one 2 to 4 inches (5 to 10 centimeters) thick and at least 8 inches (20 centimeters) wide **b :** an object made of a plank or planking **c :** PLANKING
2 a : an article in the platform of a political party **b :** a principal item of a policy or program

²plank *transitive verb* (15th century)
1 : to cover, build, or floor with planks
2 : SET DOWN 1, 2 — usually used with *down*
3 : to cook and serve on a board ⟨*planked* salmon⟩ ⟨*planked* steak⟩

plank·ing *noun* (15th century)
1 : the act or process of covering or fitting with planks
2 : a quantity of planks

plank·ter \ˈplaŋ(k)-tər\ *noun* [Greek *planktēr* wanderer, from *plazesthai*] (1935)
: a planktonic organism

plank·ton \ˈplaŋ(k)-tən, -ˌtän\ *noun* [German, from Greek, neuter of *planktos* drifting, from *plazesthai* to wander, drift, middle voice of *plazein* to drive astray; akin to Latin *plangere* to strike — more at PLAINT] (1891)
: the passively floating or weakly swimming usually minute animal and plant life of a body of water
 — **plank·ton·ic** \plaŋ(k)-ˈtä-nik\ *adjective*

Planned Parenthood *service mark*
 — used for research and dissemination of information on contraception

plan·ning *noun* (1748)
: the act or process of making or carrying out plans; *specifically* **:** the establishment of goals, policies, and procedures for a social or economic unit ⟨*city planning*⟩ ⟨*business planning*⟩

plano- — see PLAN-

pla·no–con·cave \ˌplā-nō-(ˌ)kän-ˈkāv, -ˈkän-,\ *adjective* (1693)
: flat on one side and concave on the other

pla·no–con·vex \-(ˌ)kän-ˈveks, -ˈkän-,, -kən-ˈ\ *adjective* (1665)
: flat on one side and convex on the other

pla·nog·ra·phy \plā-ˈnä-grə-fē, plə-\ *noun* (circa 1909)
: a process (as lithography) for printing from a plane surface
 — **pla·no·graph·ic** \ˌplā-nə-ˈgra-fik\ *adjective*

pla·no·sol \ˈplā-nə-ˌsäl, -ˌsȯl\ *noun* [*plan-* + Latin *solum* ground, soil] (1938)
: any of an intrazonal group of soils that have a strongly leached upper layer over a compacted clay or silt and occur on smooth flat uplands

plan position indicator *noun* (1932)
: a radarscope having a sweep synchronized with a usually rotating antenna so that the radar return can be used to find range and bearing

¹plant \ˈplant\ *verb* [Middle English, from Old English *plantian,* from Late Latin *plantare* to plant, fix in place, from Latin, to plant, from *planta* plant] (before 12th century)
transitive verb
1 a : to put or set in the ground for growth ⟨*plant* seeds⟩ **b :** to set or sow with seeds or plants **c :** IMPLANT
2 a : ESTABLISH, INSTITUTE **b :** COLONIZE, SETTLE **c :** to place (animals) in a new locality **d :** to stock with animals
3 a : to place in or on the ground **b :** to place firmly or forcibly ⟨*planted* a hard blow on his chin⟩
4 a : CONCEAL **b :** to covertly place for discovery, publication, or dissemination
intransitive verb
: to plant something
 — **plant·able** \ˈplan-tə-bəl\ *adjective*

²plant *noun* [Middle English *plante,* from Old English, from Latin *planta*] (before 12th century)
1 a : a young tree, vine, shrub, or herb planted or suitable for planting **b :** any of a kingdom (Plantae) of living things typically lacking locomotive movement or obvious nervous or sensory organs and possessing cellulose cell walls
2 a : the land, buildings, machinery, apparatus, and fixtures employed in carrying on a trade or an industrial business **b :** a factory or workshop for the manufacture of a particular product **c :** the total facilities available for production or service **d :** the buildings and other physical equipment of an institution
3 : an act of planting
4 : something or someone planted
 — **plant-like** \-ˌlīk\ *adjective*

Plan·tag·e·net \plan-ˈta-jə-nət, -ˈtaj-nət\ *adjective* [*Plantagenet,* nickname of the family adopted as surname] (1868)
: of or relating to a royal house ruling England from 1154 to 1485
 — **Plantagenet** *noun*

¹plan·tain \ˈplan-tᵊn\ *noun* [Middle English, from Old French, from Latin *plantagin-, plantago,* from *planta* sole of the foot; from its broad leaves — more at PLACE] (13th century)
: any of a genus (*Plantago* of the family Plantaginaceae, the plantain family) of short-stemmed elliptic-leaved herbs with spikes of minute greenish flowers

²plantain *noun* [Spanish *plántano, plátano* plane tree, banana tree, from Medieval Latin *plantanus* plane tree, alteration of Latin *platanus* — more at PLANE] (1555)
1 : a banana plant (*Musa paradisiaca*)
2 : the angular greenish starchy fruit of the plantain that is a staple food in the tropics when cooked

plantain lily *noun* (1882)
: any of a genus (*Hosta*) of perennial plants of the lily family with densely growing basal leaves and racemose white or violet flowers — called also *hosta, funkia*

plan·tar \ˈplan-tər, -ˌtär\ *adjective* [Latin *plantaris,* from *planta* sole — more at PLACE] (circa 1706)
: of or relating to the sole of the foot ⟨*plantar* wart⟩

plan·ta·tion \plan-ˈtā-shən\ *noun* (1569)
1 : a usually large group of plants and especially trees under cultivation
2 : a settlement in a new country or region ⟨Plymouth *Plantation*⟩
3 a : a place that is planted or under cultivation **b :** an agricultural estate usually worked by resident labor

plant·er \ˈplan-tər\ *noun* (14th century)
1 : one that cultivates plants: as **a** (1) **:** FARMER (2) **:** one who owns or operates a plantation **b :** a planting machine or implement
2 : one who settles or founds a place and especially a new colony
3 : a container in which ornamental plants are grown

planter's punch *noun* (1924)
: a punch of rum, lime or lemon juice, sugar, water, and sometimes bitters

plant food *noun* (1869)
1 : FOOD 1b
2 : FERTILIZER

plant hormone *noun* (1935)
: an organic substance other than a nutrient that in minute amounts modifies a plant physiological process; *especially* **:** one produced by a plant and active elsewhere than at the site of production

plan·ti·grade \'plan-tə-ˌgrād\ *adjective* [French, from Latin *planta* sole + French -*grade*] (1831)
: walking on the sole with the heel touching the ground ⟨humans are *plantigrade*⟩
— **plantigrade** *noun*

plant·ing *noun* (1632)
: an area where plants are grown for commercial or decorative purposes; *also* : the plants cultivated in such an area

plant kingdom *noun* (1884)
: a basic group of natural objects that includes all living and extinct plants — compare ANIMAL KINGDOM, MINERAL KINGDOM

plant·let \'plant-lət\ *noun* (1816)
: a small or young plant

plant louse *noun* (1805)
: APHID; *also* : any of various small insects (as a jumping plant louse) of similar habits

plan·to·cra·cy \plan-'tä-krə-sē\ *noun* [*planter* + -*o*- + -*cracy*] (circa 1846)
1 : a ruling class made up of planters
2 : government by planters

plants·man \'plants-mən, -ˌman\ *noun* (1881)
: a person skilled with plants : an expert gardener or horticulturist

plan·u·la \'plan-yə-lə\ *noun, plural* -**lae** \-ˌlē, -ˌlī\ [New Latin, from Latin *planus* level, flat — more at FLOOR] (1870)
: the very young usually flattened oval or oblong free-swimming ciliated larva of a coelenterate

plaque \'plak\ *noun* [French, from Middle French, metal sheet, from *plaquier* to plate, from Middle Dutch *placken* to piece, patch; akin to Middle Dutch *placke* piece, Middle High German *placke* patch] (1848)
1 a : an ornamental brooch; *especially* : the badge of an honorary order b : a flat thin piece (as of metal) used for decoration c : a commemorative or identifying inscribed tablet
2 a : a localized abnormal patch on a body part or surface b : a film of mucus that harbors bacteria on a tooth c : an atherosclerotic lesion d : a histopathologic lesion of brain tissue that is characteristic of Alzheimer's disease and consists of a cluster of degenerating nerve endings and dendrites around a core of amyloid
3 : a clear area in a bacterial culture produced by destruction of cells by a virus

¹plash \'plash\ *noun* [probably imitative] (1513)
: SPLASH

²plash (1542)
intransitive verb
: to cause a splashing or spattering effect
transitive verb
: to break the surface of (water) : SPLASH

-plasia *or* **-plasy** *noun combining form* [New Latin *-plasia*, from Greek *plasis* molding, from *plassein*]
: development : formation ⟨hyper*plasia*⟩ ⟨homo*plasy*⟩

plasm \'pla-zəm\ *noun* [Late Latin *plasma* something molded] (1747)
: PLASMA

plasm- *or* **plasmo-** *combining form* [French, from New Latin *plasma*]
: plasma ⟨*plasmo*dium⟩ ⟨*plasmo*lysis⟩

-plasm *noun combining form* [German *-plasma*, from New Latin *plasma*]
: formative or formed material (as of a cell or tissue) ⟨endo*plasm*⟩

plas·ma \'plaz-mə\ *noun* [German, from Late Latin, something molded, from Greek, from *plassein* to mold — more at PLASTER] (1772)
1 : a green faintly translucent quartz
2 [New Latin, from Late Latin] a : the fluid part of blood, lymph, or milk as distinguished from suspended material b : the juice that can be expressed from muscle
3 : PROTOPLASM
4 : a collection of charged particles (as in the atmospheres of stars or in a metal) containing about equal numbers of positive ions and elec-

trons and exhibiting some properties of a gas but differing from a gas in being a good conductor of electricity and in being affected by a magnetic field
— **plas·mat·ic** \plaz-'ma-tik\ *adjective*

plasma cell *noun* (1888)
: a lymphocyte that is a mature antibody-secreting B cell

plas·ma·gel \'plaz-mə-ˌjel\ *noun* (1923)
: gelated cytoplasm; *especially* : the outer firm zone of a pseudopodium

plas·ma·gene \-ˌjēn\ *noun* [International Scientific Vocabulary] (1939)
: an extranuclear determiner of hereditary characteristics with a capacity for replication similar to that of a nuclear gene

plasma jet *noun* (1957)
: a stream of very hot ionized plasma; *also* : a device for producing such a stream

plas·ma·lem·ma \ˌplaz-mə-'le-mə\ *noun* [New Latin, from *plasma* + Greek *lemma* husk — more at LEMMA] (1923)
: PLASMA MEMBRANE

plasma membrane *noun* (1900)
: a semipermeable limiting layer of cell protoplasm — called also *cell membrane;* see CELL illustration

plas·ma·phe·re·sis \ˌplaz-mə-fə-'rē-səs, -'fer-ə-səs\ *noun* [New Latin, from *plasm-* + Greek *aphairesis* taking off — more at APHAERESIS] (1914)
: a process for obtaining blood plasma without depleting the donor or patient of other blood constituents (as red blood cells) by separating out the plasma from the whole blood and returning the rest to the donor's or patient's circulatory system

plas·ma·sol \'plaz-mə-ˌsäl, -ˌsȯl, -ˌsōl\ *noun* (1923)
: cytoplasm in the form of a sol especially in a pseudopodium or amoeboid cell

plasma torch *noun* (1959)
: a device that heats a gas by electrical means to form a plasma for high-temperature operations (as melting metal)

plas·mid \'plaz-məd\ *noun* [*plasma* + ²-*id*] (1952)
: an extrachromosomal ring of DNA especially of bacteria that replicates autonomously

plas·min \-mən\ *noun* (circa 1866)
: a proteolytic enzyme that dissolves the fibrin of blood clots

plas·min·o·gen \plaz-'mi-nə-jən\ *noun* (1945)
: the precursor of plasmin that is found in blood plasma and serum

plas·mo·des·ma \ˌplaz-mə-'dez-mə\ *also* **plas·mo·desm** \'plaz-mə-ˌde-zəm\ *noun, plural* -**des·ma·ta** \-'dez-mə-tə\ *or* -**desmas** \-'dez-məz\ [New Latin *plasmodesma*, from *plasma* + Greek *desmat-, desma* bond, from *dein* to bind — more at DIADEM] (1905)
: one of the cytoplasmic strands that pass through openings in some plant cell walls and provide living bridges between cells

plas·mo·di·um \plaz-'mō-dē-əm\ *noun, plural* -**dia** \-dē-ə\ [New Latin, from *plasm-* + -*odium* thing resembling, from Greek -*ōdēs* like] (1875)
1 a : a motile multinucleate mass of protoplasm resulting from fusion of uninucleate amoeboid cells; *also* : an organism (as a stage of a slime mold) that consists of such a structure b : SYNCYTIUM 1
2 : an individual malaria parasite

plas·mog·a·my \plaz-'mä-gə-mē\ *noun* [International Scientific Vocabulary] (1912)
: fusion of the cytoplasm of two or more cells as distinguished from fusion of nuclei

plas·mol·y·sis \plaz-'mä-lə-səs\ *noun* [New Latin] (1883)
: shrinking of the cytoplasm away from the wall of a living cell due to outward osmotic flow of water
— **plas·mo·lyt·ic** \ˌplaz-mə-'li-tik\ *adjective*

plas·mo·lyze \'plaz-mə-ˌlīz\ *verb* -**lyzed; -lyz·ing** (1888)
transitive verb
: to subject to plasmolysis
intransitive verb
: to undergo plasmolysis

-plast *noun combining form* [Middle French -*plaste* thing molded, from Late Latin -*plastus*, from Greek -*plastos*, from *plastos* molded, from *plassein*]
: organized particle or granule : cell ⟨chromo*plast*⟩

¹plas·ter \'plas-tər\ *noun* [Middle English, from Old English, from Latin *emplastrum*, from Greek *emplastron*, from *emplassein* to plaster on, from *en*- + *plassein* to mold, plaster; perhaps akin to Latin *planus* level, flat — more at FLOOR] (before 12th century)
1 : a medicated or protective dressing that consists of a film (as of cloth or plastic) spread with a usually medicated substance (adhesive *plaster*); *broadly* : something applied to heal and soothe
2 : a pasty composition (as of lime, water, and sand) that hardens on drying and is used for coating walls, ceilings, and partitions
— **plas·tery** \-t(ə-)rē\ *adjective*

²plaster *verb* **plas·tered; plas·ter·ing** \-t(ə-)riŋ\ (14th century)
transitive verb
1 : to overlay or cover with plaster : COAT
2 : to apply a plaster to
3 a : to cover over or conceal as if with a coat of plaster b : to apply as a coating or incrustation c : to smooth down with a sticky or shiny substance ⟨*plastered* his hair down⟩
4 : to fasten or apply tightly to another surface
5 : to treat with plaster of paris
6 : to affix to or place on especially conspicuously or in quantity
7 : to inflict heavy damage or loss on especially by a concentrated or unremitting attack
intransitive verb
: to apply plaster
— **plas·ter·er** \-tər-ər\ *noun*

plas·ter·board \'plas-tər-ˌbȯrd, -ˌbȯrd\ *noun* (1897)
: a board made of several plies of fiberboard, paper, or felt usually bonded to a hardened gypsum plaster core and used especially as wallboard

plaster cast *noun* (1825)
1 : a sculptor's model in plaster of paris
2 : a rigid dressing of gauze impregnated with plaster of paris

plas·tered \'plas-tərd\ *adjective* (1902)
: DRUNK, INTOXICATED

plastering *noun* (15th century)
1 : a coating of or as if of plaster
2 : a decisive defeat

plaster of par·is \-'par-əs\ *often 2d P capitalized* [*Paris*, France] (15th century)
: a white powdery slightly hydrated calcium sulfate $CaSO_4 \cdot \frac{1}{2} H_2O$ or $2CaSO_4 \cdot H_2O$ made by calcining gypsum and used chiefly for casts and molds in the form of a quick-setting paste with water

plaster saint *noun* (1890)
: a person without human failings

plas·ter·work \'plas-tər-ˌwərk\ *noun* (1600)
: plastering often ornate in design used to finish architectural constructions

¹plas·tic \'plas-tik\ *adjective* [Latin *plasticus* of molding, from Greek *plastikos*, from *plassein* to mold, form] (1632)
1 : FORMATIVE, CREATIVE ⟨*plastic* forces in nature⟩
2 a : capable of being molded or modeled ⟨*plastic* clay⟩ b : capable of adapting to varying conditions : PLIABLE ⟨ecologically *plastic* animals⟩
3 : SCULPTURAL
4 : made or consisting of a plastic
5 : capable of being deformed continuously and permanently in any direction without rupture

6 : of, relating to, or involving plastic surgery
7 : having a quality suggestive of mass-produced plastic goods; *especially* **:** ARTIFICIAL 4 ⟨*plastic* smiles⟩ ☆
²**plastic** *noun* (1905)
1 : a plastic substance; *specifically* **:** any of numerous organic synthetic or processed materials that are mostly thermoplastic or thermosetting polymers of high molecular weight and that can be made into objects, films, or filaments
2 : credit cards used for payment
— **plas·ticky** \ˈplas-ti-kē\ *adjective*
-plastic *adjective combining form* [Greek *-plastikos,* from *plassein*]
1 : developing **:** forming ⟨thrombo*plastic*⟩
2 : of or relating to (something designated by a term ending in *-plasm, -plast, -plasty,* or *-plasy*) ⟨homo*plastic*⟩ ⟨neo*plastic*⟩
plas·ti·cal·ly \ˈplas-ti-k(ə-)lē\ *adverb* (1835)
1 : in a plastic manner
2 : with respect to plastic qualities
plastic art *noun* (circa 1907)
1 : art (as sculpture or bas-relief) characterized by modeling **:** three-dimensional art
2 : visual art (as painting, sculpture, or film) especially as distinguished from art that is written (as poetry or music) — often used in plural
plastic foam *noun* (1943)
: EXPANDED PLASTIC
plas·ti·cine *also* **plas·ti·cene** \ˈplas-tə-ˌsēn\ *noun* [from *Plasticine,* a trademark] (1897)
: a plastic paste used for models and sculptures
plas·tic·i·ty \pla-ˈsti-sə-tē\ *noun* (circa 1783)
1 : the quality or state of being plastic; *especially* **:** capacity for being molded or altered
2 : the ability to retain a shape attained by pressure deformation
3 : the capacity of organisms with the same genotype to vary in developmental pattern, in phenotype, or in behavior according to varying environmental conditions
plas·ti·cize \ˈplas-tə-ˌsīz\ *transitive verb* **-cized; -ciz·ing** (1919)
1 : to make plastic
2 : to treat with a plastic ⟨a *plasticized* mattress cover⟩
— **plas·ti·ci·za·tion** \ˌplas-tə-sə-ˈzā-shən\ *noun*
plas·ti·ciz·er \ˈplas-tə-ˌsī-zər\ *noun* (1925)
: one that plasticizes; *specifically* **:** a chemical added especially to rubbers and resins to impart flexibility, workability, or stretchability
plastic surgeon *noun* (1946)
: a specialist in plastic surgery
plastic surgery *noun* (1842)
: surgery concerned with the repair, restoration, or improvement of lost, injured, defective, or misshapen body parts
plas·tid \ˈplas-təd\ *noun* [German, from Greek *plastos* molded] (1885)
: any of various cytoplasmic organelles (as an amyloplast or chloroplast) of photosynthetic cells that serve in many cases as centers of special metabolic activities
— **plas·tid·i·al** \pla-ˈsti-dē-əl\ *adjective*
plas·ti·sol \ˈplas-tə-ˌsäl, -ˌsȯl\ *noun* [*plastic* + ⁴*sol*] (1946)
: a substance consisting of a mixture of a resin and a plasticizer that can be molded, cast, or made into a continuous film by application of heat
plas·to·cy·a·nin \ˌplas-tō-ˈsī-ə-nən\ *noun* [Greek *plastos* + English *cyan-* + ¹*-in*] (1961)
: a copper-containing protein that acts as an intermediary in photosynthetic electron transport
plas·to·qui·none \ˌplas-(ˌ)tō-kwi-ˈnōn, -ˈkwi-ˌ\ *noun* [Greek *plastos* + English *quinone*] (1958)
: a plant substance that is related to vitamin K and plays a role in photosynthetic phosphorylation

plas·tral \ˈplas-trəl\ *adjective* (1889)
: of or relating to a plastron
plas·tron \ˈplas-trən\ *noun* [Middle French, from Old Italian *piastrone,* augmentative of *piastra* thin metal plate — more at PIASTRE] (circa 1507)
1 a : a metal breastplate formerly worn under the hauberk **b :** a quilted pad worn in fencing practice to protect the chest, waist, and the side on which the weapon is held
2 : the ventral part of the shell of a tortoise or turtle consisting typically of nine symmetrically placed bones overlaid by horny plates
3 a : a trimming like a bib for a woman's dress **b :** DICKEY 1a
4 : a thin film of air held by water-repellent hairs of some aquatic insects
-plasty *noun combining form* [French *-plastie,* from Late Greek *-plastia* molding, from Greek *-plastēs* molder, from *plassein*]
: plastic surgery ⟨osteo*plasty*⟩
-plasy — see -PLASIA
¹**plat** \ˈplat\ *transitive verb* **plat·ted; plat·ting** [Middle English, alteration of *plaiten*] (14th century)
: PLAIT
²**plat** *noun* (1535)
: PLAIT
³**plat** *noun* [probably alteration of *plot*] (15th century)
1 : a small piece of ground (as a lot or quadrat) **:** PLOT
2 : a plan, map, or chart of a piece of land with actual or proposed features (as lots); *also* **:** the land represented
⁴**plat** *transitive verb* **plat·ted; plat·ting** (1751)
: to make a plat of
plat·an \ˈpla-tᵊn\ *noun* [Middle English, from Latin *platanus* — more at PLANE] (14th century)
: ²PLANE
plat du jour \ˌplä-də-ˈzhu̇r, ˌpla-\ *noun, plural* **plats du jour** *same*\ [French, literally, plate of the day] (1906)
: a dish that is featured by a restaurant on a particular day
¹**plate** \ˈplāt\ *noun* [Middle English, from Old French, from *plate,* feminine of *plat* flat, from (assumed) Vulgar Latin *plattus,* probably from Greek *platys* broad, flat — more at PLACE] (14th century)
1 a : a smooth flat thin piece of material **b** (1) **:** forged, rolled, or cast metal in sheets usually thicker than ¼ inch (6 millimeters) (2) **:** a very thin layer of metal deposited on a surface of base metal by plating **c :** one of the broad metal pieces used in armor; *also* **:** armor of such plates **d** (1) **:** a lamina or plaque (as of bone or horn) that forms part of an animal body; *especially* **:** SCUTE (2) **:** the thin under portion of the forequarter of beef; *especially* **:** the fatty back part — see BEEF illustration **e :** HOME PLATE **f :** any of the large movable segments into which the earth's crust is divided according to the theory of plate tectonics
2 [Middle English; partly from Old French *plate* plate, piece of silver; partly from Old Spanish *plata* silver, from (assumed) Vulgar Latin *platta* metal plate, from feminine of *plattus* flat] **a** *obsolete* **:** a silver coin **b :** precious metal; *especially* **:** silver bullion
3 [Middle English, from Middle French *plat* dish, plate, from *plat* flat] **a :** domestic hollowware made of or plated with gold, silver, or base metals **b :** a shallow usually circular vessel from which food is eaten or served **c** (1) **:** a quantity to fill a plate **:** PLATEFUL (2) **:** a main course served on a plate (3) **:** food and service supplied to one person ⟨a dinner at $10 a *plate*⟩ **d** (1) **:** a prize given to the winner in a contest (2) *British* **:** a horse race in which the contestants compete for a prize of fixed value rather than stakes **e :** a dish or pouch passed in taking collections **f :** a flat glass dish used chiefly for culturing microorganisms

4 a : a prepared surface from which printing is done **b :** a sheet of material (as glass) coated with a light-sensitive photographic emulsion **c** (1) **:** the usually flat or grid-formed anode of an electron tube at which electrons collect (2) **:** a metallic grid with its interstices filled with active material that forms one of the structural units of a battery **d :** LICENSE PLATE
5 : a horizontal structural member that provides bearing and anchorage especially for the trusses of a roof or the rafters
6 : the part of a denture that fits to the mouth; *broadly* **:** DENTURE
7 : a full-page illustration often on different paper from the text pages
8 : a schedule of matters to deal with ⟨have a lot on my *plate* now⟩
— **plate·ful** \-ˌfu̇l\ *noun*
— **plate·like** \-ˌlīk\ *adjective*
²**plate** *transitive verb* **plat·ed; plat·ing** (14th century)
1 : to cover or equip with plate: as **a :** to provide with armor plate **b :** to cover with an adherent layer mechanically, chemically, or electrically; *also* **:** to deposit (as a layer) on a surface
2 : to make a printing surface from or for
3 : to fix or secure with a plate
4 : to cause (as a runner) to score in baseball
¹**pla·teau** \pla-ˈtō, ˈpla-ˌ\ *noun, plural* **pla·teaus** *or* **pla·teaux** \-ˈtōz, -ˌtōz\ [French, from Middle French, platter, from *plat* flat] (1796)
1 a : a usually extensive land area having a relatively level surface raised sharply above adjacent land or at least one side **:** TABLELAND **b :** a similar undersea feature
2 a : a region of little or no change in a graphic representation **b :** a relatively stable level, period, or condition
3 : a level of attainment or achievement ⟨the 500-point *plateau*⟩
²**plateau** *intransitive verb* (1939)
: to reach a level, period, or condition of stability
plate·glass \ˈplāt-ˈglas, -ˌglas\ *adjective, often capitalized* (1968)
: of, relating to, or being the British universities founded in the latter half of the twentieth century — compare OXBRIDGE, REDBRICK
plate glass *noun* (circa 1741)
: rolled, ground, and polished sheet glass
plate·let \ˈplāt-lət\ *noun* (1895)
: a minute flattened body (as of ice or a mineral); *especially* **:** BLOOD PLATELET
plate·mak·er \ˈplāt-ˌmā-kər\ *noun* (1904)

☆ **SYNONYMS**
Plastic, pliable, pliant, ductile, malleable, adaptable mean susceptible of being modified in form or nature. PLASTIC applies to substances soft enough to be molded yet capable of hardening into the desired fixed form ⟨*plastic* materials allow the sculptor greater freedom⟩. PLIABLE suggests something easily bent, folded, twisted, or manipulated ⟨*pliable* rubber tubing⟩. PLIANT may stress flexibility and sometimes connote springiness ⟨an athletic shoe with a *pliant* sole⟩. DUCTILE applies to what can be drawn out or extended with ease ⟨*ductile* metals such as copper⟩. MALLEABLE applies to what may be pressed or beaten into shape ⟨the *malleable* properties of gold enhance its value⟩. ADAPTABLE implies the capability of being easily modified to suit other conditions, needs, or uses ⟨computer hardware that is *adaptable*⟩.

\ə\ abut \ᵊ\ kitten \ər\ further \a\ ash \ā\ ace \ä\ mop, mar \au̇\ out \ch\ chin \e\ bet \ē\ easy \g\ go \i\ hit \ī\ ice \j\ job \ŋ\ sing \ō\ go \ȯ\ law \ȯi\ boy \th\ thin \t͟h\ the \ü\ loot \u̇\ foot \y\ yet \zh\ vision *see also* Guide to Pronunciation

: a machine for making printing plates and especially offset printing plates
— **plate·mak·ing** \-kiŋ\ *noun*

plat·en \'pla-tᵊn\ *noun* [Middle French *plateine*, from *plate*] (1541)
1 : a flat plate; *especially* : one that exerts or receives pressure (as in a printing press)
2 : the roller of a typewriter or printer

plat·er \'plā-tər\ *noun* (1777)
1 : one that plates
2 a : a horse that runs chiefly in plate races **b** : a racehorse that competes in the lowest grade of races

plate rail *noun* (1902)
: a rail or narrow shelf along the upper part of a wall for holding plates or ornaments

plat·er·esque \ˌpla-tə-'resk\ *adjective, often capitalized* [Spanish *plateresco*, from *platero* silversmith, from *plata* silver] (circa 1864)
: of, relating to, or being a 16th century Spanish architectural style characterized by elaborate ornamentation suggestive of silver plate

plate tectonics *noun plural but singular in construction* (1969)
: a theory in geology: the lithosphere of the earth is divided into a small number of plates which float on and travel independently over the mantle and much of the earth's seismic activity occurs at the boundaries of these plates — compare CONTINENTAL DRIFT

plat·form \'plat-ˌfȯrm\ *noun, often attributive* [Middle French *plate-forme* diagram, map, literally, flat form] (1535)
1 : PLAN, DESIGN
2 : a declaration of the principles on which a group of persons stands; *especially* : a declaration of principles and policies adopted by a political party or a candidate
3 a (1) : a usually raised horizontal flat surface; *especially* : a raised flooring (as for speakers or performers) (2) : a device or structure incorporating or providing a platform; *especially* : such a structure on legs used for offshore drilling (as for oil) **b** : a place or opportunity for public discussion
4 a : a usually thick layer (as of cork) between the inner sole and outer sole of a shoe **b** : a shoe having such a sole
5 : a vehicle (as a satellite or aircraft) used for a particular activity or purpose or to carry a usually specified kind of equipment

platform balance *noun* (1811)
: a balance having a platform on which objects are weighed — called also *platform scale*

platform rocker *noun* (1944)
: a chair that rocks on a stable platform

platform tennis *noun* (1955)
: a variation of paddle tennis that is played on a platform enclosed by a wire fence

pla·ti·na \pla-'tē-nə\ *noun* [Spanish] (1750)
: PLATINUM

plat·ing \'plā-tiŋ\ *noun* (1831)
1 : the act or process of plating
2 a : a coating of metal plates **b** : a thin coating of metal

plat·i·nize \'pla-tᵊn-ˌīz\ *transitive verb* **-nized; -niz·ing** (1825)
: to cover, treat, or combine with platinum or a compound of platinum

plat·i·no·cy·a·nide \ˌpla-tᵊn-ō-'sī-ə-ˌnīd\ *noun* (1845)
: a fluorescent complex salt formed by the union of a compound of platinum and cyanide with another cyanide

plat·i·num \'plat-nəm, 'pla-tᵊn-əm\ *noun, often attributive* [New Latin, from Spanish *platina*, from diminutive of *plata* silver — more at PLATE] (1812)
1 : a heavy precious grayish white noncorroding ductile malleable metallic element that fuses with difficulty and is used especially in chemical ware and apparatus, as a catalyst, and in dental and jewelry alloys — see ELEMENT table
2 : a moderate gray

platinum blonde *noun* (1931)

1 : a person whose hair is of a pale silvery blonde color
2 : the color of the hair of a platinum blonde

plat·i·tude \'pla-tə-ˌtüd, -ˌtyüd\ *noun* [French, from *plat* flat, dull] (1812)
1 : the quality or state of being dull or insipid
2 : a banal, trite, or stale remark

plat·i·tu·di·nal \ˌpla-tə-'tüd-nəl, -'tyüd-; -'tü-dᵊn-əl, -'tyü-\ *adjective* (1870)
: PLATITUDINOUS

plat·i·tu·di·nar·i·an \-ˌtü-dᵊn-'er-ē-ən, -ˌtyü-\ *noun* (1855)
: one given to the use of platitudes

plat·i·tu·di·nize \-'tü-dᵊn-ˌīz, -'tyü-\ *intransitive verb* **-nized; -niz·ing** [*platitudinous*] (1885)
: to utter platitudes

plat·i·tu·di·nous \-'tüd-nəs, -'tyüd-; -'tü-dᵊn-əs, -'tyü-\ *adjective* [*platitude* + *-inous* (as in *multitudinous*)] (1862)
: having the characteristics of a platitude : full of platitudes ⟨*platitudinous* remarks⟩
— **plat·i·tu·di·nous·ly** *adverb*

pla·ton·ic \plə-'tä-nik, plā-\ *adjective* [Latin *platonicus*, from Greek *platōnikos*, from *Platōn* Plato] (1533)
1 *capitalized* : of, relating to, or characteristic of Plato or Platonism
2 a : relating to or based on platonic love; *also* : experiencing or professing platonic love **b** : of, relating to, or being a relationship marked by the absence of romance or sex
3 : NOMINAL, THEORETICAL
— **pla·ton·i·cal·ly** \-ni-k(ə-)lē\ *adverb*

platonic love *noun, often P capitalized* (1631)
1 : love conceived by Plato as ascending from passion for the individual to contemplation of the universal and ideal
2 : a close relationship between two persons in which sexual desire is nonexistent or has been suppressed or sublimated

Pla·to·nism \'plā-tᵊn-ˌi-zəm\ *noun* (circa 1570)
1 a : the philosophy of Plato stressing especially that actual things are copies of transcendent ideas and that these ideas are the objects of true knowledge apprehended by reminiscence **b** : NEOPLATONISM
2 : PLATONIC LOVE
— **Pla·to·nist** \-tᵊn-ist\ *noun*
— **Pla·to·nis·tic** \ˌplā-tᵊn-'is-tik\ *adjective*

Pla·to·nize \'plā-tᵊn-ˌīz\ *verb* **-nized; -niz·ing** (1608)
intransitive verb
: to adopt, imitate, or conform to Platonic opinions
transitive verb
: to explain in accordance with or adapt to Platonic doctrines; *especially* : IDEALIZE

¹pla·toon \plə-'tün, pla-\ *noun* [French *peloton* small detachment, literally, ball, from Middle French *pelote* little ball — more at PELLET] (1637)
1 : a subdivision of a company-size military unit normally consisting of two or more squads or sections
2 : a group of persons sharing a common characteristic or activity ⟨a *platoon* of waiters⟩; *especially* : a group of football players who are trained for either offense or defense and are sent into or withdrawn from the game as a body

²platoon (1963)
transitive verb
: to play (one player) alternately with another player in the same position (as on a baseball team)
intransitive verb
1 : to alternate with another player at the same position
2 : to use alternate players at the same position

platoon sergeant *noun* (1915)

: a noncommissioned officer in the army ranking above a staff sergeant and below a first sergeant

Platt·deutsch \'plat-ˌdȯich, 'plät-\ *noun* [German, from Dutch *Platduitsch*, literally, Low German, from *plat* flat, low + *duitsch* German] (1677)
: the Low German speech of northern Germany comprising several dialects

plat·ter \'pla-tər\ *noun* [Middle English *plater*, from Anglo-French, from Middle French *plat* plate] (13th century)
1 a : a large plate used especially for serving meat **b** : PLATE 3c(2)
2 : a phonograph record
— **plat·ter·ful** \-ˌfu̇l\ *noun*
— **on a platter** : without effort : very easily ⟨can have the presidency *on a platter* —Jonathan Daniels⟩

¹platy \'plā-tē\ *adjective* (1533)
: resembling a plate; *also* : consisting of plates or flaky layers — used chiefly of soil or mineral formations

²platy \'pla-tē\ *noun, plural* **platy** *or* **plat·ys** *or* **plat·ies** [New Latin *Platypoecilus*, former genus name of the fish] (1931)
: either of two live-bearers (*Xiphophorus maculatus* and *X. variatus* of the family Poeciliidae) that are popular aquarium fishes and are noted for variability and brilliant color — called also *platyfish* \-ˌfish\

platy·hel·minth \ˌpla-ti-'hel-ˌmin(t)th\ *noun* [ultimately from Greek *platys* broad, flat + *helminth-, helmis* helminth] (circa 1890)
: any of a phylum (Platyhelminthes) of soft-bodied usually much flattened acoelomate worms (as the planarians, flukes, and tapeworms) — called also *flatworm*
— **platy·hel·min·thic** \-hel-'min(t)-thik, -'min-tik\ *adjective*

platy·pus \'pla-ti-pəs, -ˌpu̇s\ *noun, plural* **platy·pus·es** *also* **platy·pi** \-ˌpī, -ˌpē\ [New Latin, from Greek *platypous* flat-footed, from *platys* broad, flat + *pous* foot — more at PLACE, FOOT] (1799)
: a small carnivorous aquatic oviparous mammal (*Ornithorhynchus anatinus*) of eastern Australia and Tasmania that has a fleshy bill resembling that of a duck, dense fur, webbed feet, and a broad flattened tail

platypus

plat·yr·rhine \'pla-ti-ˌrīn\ *adjective* (1857)
1 [New Latin *Platyrrhina*, from Greek *platyrrhin-, platyrrhis* broad-nosed, from *platys* + *rhin-, rhis* nose] : of, relating to, or being any of a division (Platyrrhina) of monkeys all of which are New World monkeys and are characterized by a broad nasal septum, usually 36 teeth, and often a prehensile tail
2 [Greek *platyrrhin-, platyrrhis*] : having a short broad nose
— **platyrrhine** *noun*

plau·dit \'plȯ-dət\ *noun* [Latin *plaudite* applaud, plural imperative of *plaudere* to applaud] (1624)
1 : an act or round of applause
2 : enthusiastic approval — usually used in plural ⟨received the *plaudits* of the critics⟩

plau·si·bil·i·ty \ˌplȯ-zə-'bi-lə-tē\ *noun, plural* **-ties** (1649)
1 : the quality or state of being plausible
2 : something plausible

plau·si·ble \'plȯ-zə-bəl\ *adjective* [Latin *plausibilis* worthy of applause, from *plausus*, past participle of *plaudere*] (1565)
1 : superficially fair, reasonable, or valuable but often specious ⟨a *plausible* pretext⟩

2 : superficially pleasing or persuasive ⟨a swindler . . . , then a quack, then a smooth, *plausible* gentleman —R. W. Emerson⟩
3 : appearing worthy of belief ⟨the argument was both powerful and *plausible*⟩
— **plau·si·ble·ness** *noun*
— **plau·si·bly** \-blē\ *adverb*
plau·sive \'plȯ-ziv, -siv\ *adjective* [Latin *plausus,* past participle] (1600)
1 : manifesting praise or approval
2 *obsolete* **:** PLEASING
3 *archaic* **:** SPECIOUS
¹play \'plā\ *noun* [Middle English, from Old English *plega;* akin to Old English *plegan* to play, Middle Dutch *pleyen*] (before 12th century)
1 a : SWORDPLAY **b** *archaic* **:** GAME, SPORT **c :** the conduct, course, or action of a game **d :** a particular act or maneuver in a game: as (1) **:** the action during an attempt to advance the ball in football (2) **:** the action in which a player is put out in baseball **e :** the action in which cards are played after bidding in a card game **f :** the moving of a piece in a board game (as chess) **g :** one's turn in a game ⟨it's your *play*⟩
2 a *obsolete* **:** SEXUAL INTERCOURSE **b :** amorous flirtation **:** DALLIANCE
3 a : recreational activity; *especially* **:** the spontaneous activity of children **b :** absence of serious or harmful intent **:** JEST ⟨said it in *play*⟩ **c :** the act or an instance of playing on words or speech sounds **d :** GAMING, GAMBLING
4 a (1) **:** an act, way, or manner of proceeding **:** MANEUVER ⟨that was a *play* to get your fingerprints —Erle Stanley Gardner⟩ (2) **:** DEAL, VENTURE **b** (1) **:** OPERATION, ACTIVITY ⟨other motives surely come into *play* —M. R. Cohen⟩ (2) **:** brisk, fitful, or light movement ⟨the gem presented a dazzling *play* of colors⟩ (3) **:** free or unimpeded motion (as of a part of a machine); *also* **:** the length or measure of such motion (4) **:** scope or opportunity for action
5 : emphasis or publicity especially in the news media ⟨wished the country received a better *play* in the American press —Hugh Mac-Lennan⟩
6 : a move or series of moves calculated to arouse friendly feelings — usually used with *make* ⟨made a big *play* for the girl —Will Herman⟩
7 a : the stage representation of an action or story **b :** a dramatic composition **:** DRAMA
synonym see FUN
— **in play :** in condition or position to be legitimately played
— **out of play :** not in play
²play (before 12th century)
intransitive verb
1 a : to engage in sport or recreation **:** FROLIC **b :** to have sexual relations; *especially* **:** to have promiscuous or illicit sexual relations — usually used in the phrase *play around* **c** (1) **:** to move aimlessly about **:** TRIFLE (2) **:** to toy or fiddle around with something ⟨*played* with her food⟩ (3) **:** to deal or behave frivolously or mockingly **:** JEST (4) **:** to deal in a light, speculative, or sportive manner (5) **:** to make use of double meaning or of the similarity of sound of two words for stylistic or humorous effect
2 a : to take advantage ⟨*playing* on fears⟩ **b** (1) **:** FLUTTER, FRISK (2) **:** to move or operate in a lively, irregular, or intermittent manner **c :** to move or function freely within prescribed limits **d :** to produce a stream ⟨hoses *playing* on a fire⟩
3 a (1) **:** to perform music ⟨*play* on a violin⟩ (2) **:** to sound in performance ⟨the organ is *playing*⟩ (3) **:** to emit sounds ⟨the radio is *playing*⟩ (4) **:** to reproduce recorded sounds ⟨a record is *playing*⟩ **b** (1) **:** to act in a dramatic production (2) **:** SHOW, RUN ⟨what's *playing* at the theater⟩ **c :** to be suitable for dramatic performance **d :** to act with special consideration so as to gain favor, approval, or sympathy ⟨might *play* to popular prejudices to serve his

political ends —V. L. Parrington⟩ — often used in the phrase *play up to*
4 a : to engage or take part in a game **b :** to perform in a position in a specified manner ⟨the outfielders were *playing* deep⟩ **c :** to perform an action during one's turn in a game **d :** GAMBLE **e** (1) **:** to behave or conduct oneself in a specified way ⟨*play* safe⟩ (2) **:** to feign a specified state or quality ⟨*play* dead⟩ (3) **:** to take part in or assent to some activity **:** COOPERATE ⟨*play* along with his scheme⟩ (4) **:** to act so as to prove advantageous to another — usually used in the phrase *play into the hands of*
5 : to gain approval **:** GO OVER ⟨her idea did not *play* well⟩
transitive verb
1 a (1) **:** to engage in or occupy oneself with ⟨*play* baseball⟩ (2) **:** to engage in (an activity) as a game (3) **:** to deal with, handle, or manage (4) **:** EXPLOIT, MANIPULATE **b :** to pretend to engage in the activities of ⟨*play* war⟩ ⟨children *playing* house⟩ **c** (1) **:** to amount to by one's efforts ⟨*played* an important role in their success⟩ (2) **:** to perform or execute for amusement or to deceive or mock ⟨*play* a trick⟩ (3) **:** WREAK ⟨*play* havoc⟩
2 a (1) **:** to put on a performance of (a play) (2) **:** to act in the character or part of (3) **:** to act or perform in ⟨*played* leading theaters⟩ **b :** to perform or act the part of ⟨*play* the fool⟩
3 a (1) **:** to contend against in or as if in a game (2) **:** to use as a contestant in a game ⟨the coach did not *play* him⟩ (3) **:** to perform the duties associated with (a certain position) ⟨*played* quarterback⟩ (4) **:** to guard or move into position to defend against (an opponent) in a specified manner **b** (1) **:** to wager in a game **:** STAKE (2) **:** to make wagers on ⟨*play* the races⟩ (3) **:** to speculate on or in ⟨*play* the stock market⟩ (4) **:** to operate on the basis of ⟨*play* a hunch⟩ **c :** to put into action in a game; *especially* **:** to remove (a playing card) from one's hand and place usually faceup on a table in one's turn either as part of a scoring combination or as one's contribution to a trick **d :** to catch or pick up (a batted ball) **:** FIELD ⟨*played* the ball bare-handed⟩ **e :** to direct the course of (as a ball) **:** HIT ⟨*played* a wedge shot to the green⟩; *also* **:** to cause (a ball or puck) to rebound ⟨*played* the ball off the backboard⟩
4 a : to perform (music) on an instrument ⟨*play* a waltz⟩ **b :** to perform music on ⟨*play* the violin⟩ **c :** to perform music of (a certain composer) **d** (1) **:** to cause (as a radio or phonograph) to emit sounds (2) **:** to cause the recorded sound or image of (as a record or a magnetic tape) to be reproduced
5 a : WIELD, PLY **b :** to discharge, fire, or set off with continuous effect ⟨*played* the hose on the burning building⟩ **c :** to cause to move or operate lightly and irregularly or intermittently **d :** to keep (a hooked fish) in action
— **play·abil·i·ty** \ˌplā-ə-'bi-lə-tē\ *noun*
— **play·able** \'plā-ə-bəl\ *adjective*
— **play ball :** COOPERATE
— **play both ends against the middle :** to set opposing interests against each other to one's own ultimate profit
— **play by ear :** to deal with something without previous planning or instructions
— **play games :** to try to hide the truth from someone by deceptive means
— **play one's cards :** to act with the means available to one
— **play possum :** to pretend to be asleep or dead
— **play second fiddle :** to take a subordinate position
— **play the field :** to date or have romantic connections with more than one person
— **play the game :** to act according to a code or set of standards
— **play with fire :** to do something risky or dangerous
— **play with oneself :** MASTURBATE

pla·ya \'plī-ə\ *noun* [Spanish, literally, beach, from Late Latin *plagia* — more at PLAGE] (1854)
: the flat-floored bottom of an undrained desert basin that becomes at times a shallow lake
play·act \'plā-ˌakt\ *verb* [back-formation from *playacting*] (1901)
transitive verb
: ACT OUT 1a
intransitive verb
1 a : to take part in theatrical performances especially as a professional **b :** to make believe
2 : to engage in theatrical or insincere behavior
— **play·act·ing** *noun*
play–action pass *noun* (1964)
: a pass play in football in which the quarterback fakes a handoff before passing the ball — called also *play-action*
play·back \'plā-ˌbak\ *noun* (1929)
: an act or instance of reproducing recorded sound or pictures often immediately after recording
play back *transitive verb* (1949)
: to perform a playback of (a usually recently recorded disc or tape)
play·bill \'plā-ˌbil\ *noun* (1616)
: a bill advertising a play and usually announcing the cast
Playbill *trademark*
— used for a theater program
play·book \-ˌbu̇k\ *noun* (1535)
1 : one or more plays in book form
2 : a notebook containing diagrammed football plays
play·boy \-ˌbȯi\ *noun* (1907)
: a man who lives a life devoted chiefly to the pursuit of pleasure
play–by–play \ˌplā-ˌbī-'plā, ˌplā-ˌbī-'\ *adjective* (1931)
1 : being or giving a running commentary on a sports event
2 : relating each event as it occurs
— **play–by–play** *noun*
play down *transitive verb* (1930)
: to attach little importance to **:** MINIMIZE
played out *adjective* (circa 1859)
1 : worn out or used up
2 : tired out **:** SPENT
play·er \'plā-ər\ *noun* (14th century)
: one that plays: as **a :** a person who plays a game **b :** MUSICIAN **c :** ACTOR **d :** a device that reproduces recorded material (as video images or music) from a usually specified medium **e :** one actively involved especially in a competitive field or process **:** PARTICIPANT
player piano *noun* (1907)
: a piano containing a mechanism by which it plays automatically
play·fel·low \'plā-ˌfe-(ˌ)lō\ *noun* (1513)
: PLAYMATE
play·field \-ˌfēld\ *noun* (1883)
: a playground for outdoor athletics
play·ful \'plā-fəl\ *adjective* (13th century)
1 : full of play **:** FROLICSOME, SPORTIVE ⟨a *playful* kitten⟩
2 : HUMOROUS, JOCULAR
— **play·ful·ly** \-fə-lē\ *adverb*
— **play·ful·ness** *noun*
play·girl \-ˌgər(-ə)l\ *noun* (1938)
: a woman who lives a life devoted chiefly to the pursuit of pleasure
play·go·er \-ˌgō-(ə)r\ *noun* (1822)
: a person who frequently attends plays
play·ground \-ˌgrau̇nd\ *noun* (1794)
1 : a piece of land used for and usually equipped with facilities for recreation especially by children

\ə\ **abut** \ᵊ\ **kitten** \ər\ **further** \a\ **ash** \ā\ **ace** \ä\ **mop, mar** \au̇\ **out** \ch\ **chin** \e\ **bet** \ē\ **easy** \g\ **go** \i\ **hit** \ī\ **ice** \j\ **job** \ŋ\ **sing** \ō\ **go** \ȯ\ **law** \ȯi\ **boy** \th\ **thin** \t͟h\ **the** \ü\ **loot** \u̇\ **foot** \y\ **yet** \zh\ **vision** *see also* Guide to Pronunciation

2 : an area known or suited for activity of a specified sort ⟨a vacation *playground*⟩

play·house \-,haùs\ *noun* (before 12th century)
1 : THEATER
2 : a small house for children to play in

playing card *noun* (1543)
: one of a set of 24 to 78 thin rectangular pieces of paperboard or plastic marked on one side to show its rank and suit and used in playing any of numerous games

playing field *noun* (circa 1584)
1 : a field for various games; *especially* **:** the part of a field officially marked off for play
2 : a set of conditions for competition (as in business) — usually used in such phrases as *a level playing field*

play·land \'plā-,land\ *noun* (1918)
: PLAYGROUND

play·let \-lət\ *noun* (1884)
: a short play

play·list \-,list\ *noun* (1972)
: a list of recordings to be played on the air by a radio station

play·mak·er \-,mā-kər\ *noun* (circa 1942)
: a player who leads the offense for a team (as in basketball or hockey)
— **play·mak·ing** \-kiŋ\ *noun or adjective*

play·mate \-,māt\ *noun* (1642)
: a companion in play

play–off \'plā-,óf\ *noun* (1895)
1 : a final contest or series of contests to determine the winner between contestants or teams that have tied
2 : a series of contests played after the end of the regular season to determine a championship

play off *transitive verb* (1807)
1 a : to set in opposition for one's own gain **b :** to set in contrast
2 : to complete the playing of (an interrupted contest)
3 : to break (a tie) by a play-off

play out (1596)
transitive verb
1 a : to perform to the end ⟨*play out* a role⟩ **b :** USE UP, FINISH
2 : UNREEL, UNFOLD ⟨*played out* a length of line —Gordon Webber⟩
intransitive verb
: to become spent or exhausted

play·pen \'plā-,pen\ *noun* (1931)
: a portable usually collapsible enclosure in which a baby or young child may play

play·room \-,rüm, -,rùm\ *noun* (1819)
: RUMPUS ROOM

play·suit \-,süt\ *noun* (1908)
: a sports and play outfit for women or children that consists usually of a blouse and shorts

play therapy *noun* (1939)
: psychotherapy in which a child is encouraged to reveal feelings and conflicts in play rather than by verbalization

play·thing \'plā-,thiŋ\ *noun* (1675)
: TOY

play·time \-,tīm\ *noun* (1661)
: a time for play or diversion

play up *transitive verb* (1909)
: EMPHASIZE; *also* **:** EXAGGERATE, OVEREMPHASIZE

play·wear \'plā-,war, -,wer\ *noun* (1964)
: informal clothing worn for leisure activities

play·wright \'plā-,rīt\ *noun* [¹*play* + obsolete *wright* maker — more at WRIGHT] (1687)
: a person who writes plays

play·writ·ing *also* **play·wright·ing** \-,rī-tiŋ\ *noun* (1809)
: the writing of plays

pla·za \'pla-zə, 'plä-\ *noun* [Spanish, from Latin *platea* broad street — more at PLACE] (1683)
1 a : a public square in a city or town **b :** an open area usually located near urban buildings and often featuring walkways, trees and shrubs, places to sit, and sometimes shops

2 : a place on a thoroughfare (as a turnpike) at which all traffic must temporarily stop (as to pay tolls)
3 : an area adjacent to an expressway which has service facilities (as a restaurant, service station, and rest rooms)
5 : SHOPPING CENTER

plea \'plē\ *noun* [Middle English *plaid, plai,* from Old French *plait, plaid,* from Medieval Latin *placitum,* from Latin, decision, decree, from neuter of *placitus,* past participle of *placēre* to please, be decided — more at PLEASE] (13th century)
1 : a legal suit or action
2 : an allegation made by a party in support of a cause: as **a :** an allegation of fact — compare DEMURRER **b** (1) **:** a defendant's answer to a plaintiff's declaration in common-law practice (2) **:** an accused person's answer to a charge or indictment in criminal practice **c :** a plea of guilty to an indictment
3 : something offered by way of excuse or justification ⟨left early with the *plea* of a headache⟩
4 : an earnest entreaty **:** APPEAL ⟨their *plea* for understanding must be answered⟩
synonym see APOLOGY

plea bargaining *noun* (1964)
: the negotiation of an agreement between a prosecutor and a defendant whereby the defendant is permitted to plead guilty to a reduced charge
— **plea–bargain** *intransitive verb*
— **plea bargain** *noun*

pleach \'plēch, 'plāch\ *transitive verb* [Middle English *plechen,* from Old North French *plechier,* from (assumed) Vulgar Latin *plactiare,* alteration of *plectere* to braid — more at PLY] (14th century)
: INTERLACE, PLAIT

plead \'plēd\ *verb* **plead·ed** \'plē-dəd\ *or* **pled** *also* **plead** \'pled\; **plead·ing** [Middle English *plaiden* to institute a lawsuit, from Middle French *plaidier,* from *plaid* plea] (13th century)
intransitive verb
1 : to argue a case or cause in a court of law
2 a : to make an allegation in an action or other legal proceeding; *especially* **:** to answer the previous pleading of the other party by denying facts therein stated or by alleging new facts **b :** to conduct pleadings
3 : to make a plea of a specified nature ⟨*plead* not guilty⟩
4 a : to argue for or against a claim **b :** to entreat or appeal earnestly
transitive verb
1 : to maintain (as a case or cause) in a court of law or other tribunal
2 : to allege in or by way of a legal plea
3 : to offer as a plea usually in defense, apology, or excuse
— **plead·able** \'plē-də-bəl\ *adjective*
— **plead·er** *noun*
— **plead·ing·ly** \'plē-diŋ-lē\ *adverb*

pleading *noun* (14th century)
1 : advocacy of a cause in a court of law
2 a : one of the formal usually written allegations and counter allegations made alternately by the parties in a legal action or proceeding **b :** the action or process performed by the parties in presenting such formal allegations until a single point at issue is produced **c :** the introduction of one of these allegations and especially the first one **d :** the body of rules according to which these allegations are framed
3 : the act or an instance of making a plea
4 : a sincere entreaty

pleas·ance \'ple-z°n(t)s\ *noun* (14th century)
1 : a feeling of pleasure **:** DELIGHT
2 : a pleasant retreat or recreation place usually attached to a mansion

pleas·ant \'ple-z°nt\ *adjective* [Middle English *plesaunt,* from Middle French *plaisant,* from present participle of *plaisir*] (14th century)

1 : having qualities that tend to give pleasure **:** AGREEABLE ⟨a *pleasant* day⟩
2 : having or characterized by pleasing manners, behavior, or appearance
— **pleas·ant·ly** *adverb*
— **pleas·ant·ness** *noun*

pleas·ant·ry \-z°n-trē\ *noun, plural* **-ries** (1655)
1 : an agreeable playfulness in conversation **:** BANTER
2 : a humorous act or remark **:** JEST
3 : a polite social remark ⟨exchanged *pleasantries*⟩

¹**please** \'plēz\ *verb* **pleased; pleas·ing** [Middle English *plesen,* from Middle French *plaisir,* from Latin *placēre;* akin to Latin *placare* to placate and perhaps to Greek *plak-, plax* flat surface — more at FLUKE] (14th century)
intransitive verb
1 : to afford or give pleasure or satisfaction
2 : LIKE, WISH ⟨do as you *please*⟩
3 *archaic* **:** to have the kindness ⟨will you *please* to enter the carriage —Charles Dickens⟩
transitive verb
1 : to give pleasure to **:** GRATIFY
2 : to be the will or pleasure of ⟨may it *please* your Majesty⟩
— **pleas·er** \'plē-zər\ *noun*

²**please** *adverb* (1667)
1 — used as a function word to express politeness or emphasis in a request ⟨*please* come in⟩
2 — used as a function word to express polite affirmation ⟨have some tea? *Please*⟩

pleas·ing \'plē-ziŋ\ *adjective* (14th century)
: giving pleasure **:** AGREEABLE ⟨the sun's *pleasing* warmth⟩
— **pleas·ing·ly** \-lē\ *adverb*
— **pleas·ing·ness** *noun*

plea·sur·able \'plezh-rə-bəl, 'plāzh-; 'ple-zhə-, 'plā-\ *adjective* (1579)
: PLEASANT, GRATIFYING
— **plea·sur·abil·i·ty** \,plezh-rə-'bi-lə-tē, ,plāzh-; ,ple-zhə-, ,plā-\ *noun*
— **plea·sur·able·ness** \'plezh-rə-bəl-nəs, 'plāzh-; 'ple-zhə-, 'plā-\ *noun*
— **plea·sur·ably** \-blē\ *adverb*

¹**plea·sure** \'ple-zhər, 'plā-\ *noun* [Middle English *plesure,* alteration of *plesir,* from Middle French *plaisir,* from *plaisir* to please] (14th century)
1 : DESIRE, INCLINATION ⟨wait upon his *pleasure* —Shakespeare⟩
2 : a state of gratification
3 a : sensual gratification **b :** frivolous amusement
4 : a source of delight or joy

²**pleasure** *verb* **plea·sured; plea·sur·ing** \'plezh-riŋ, 'plāzh-; 'ple-zhə-, 'plā-\ (1537)
transitive verb
1 : to give pleasure to **:** GRATIFY
2 : to give sexual pleasure to
intransitive verb
1 : to take pleasure **:** DELIGHT
2 : to seek pleasure

pleasure dome *noun* (1797)
: a place of pleasurable entertainment or recreation **:** RESORT

plea·sure·less \'ple-zhər-ləs, 'plā-\ *adjective* (1814)
: giving no pleasure

pleasure principle *noun* (1912)
: a tendency for individual behavior to be directed toward immediate satisfaction of instinctual drives and immediate relief from pain or discomfort

¹**pleat** \'plēt\ *transitive verb* [Middle English *pleten,* from *pleit, plete* plait] (14th century)
1 : FOLD; *especially* **:** to arrange in pleats ⟨*pleat* a skirt⟩
2 : PLAIT 2
— **pleat·er** *noun*

²**pleat** *noun* [Middle English *plete*] (15th century)

: a fold in cloth made by doubling material over on itself; *also* : something resembling such a fold

— **pleat·less** \-ləs\ *adjective*

pleb \'pleb\ *noun* (1865)
: PLEBEIAN

plebe \'plēb\ *noun* [obsolete *plebe* common people, from French *plèbe,* from Latin *plebs*] (1833)
: a freshman at a military or naval academy

¹**ple·be·ian** \pli-'bē-ən\ *noun* [Latin *plebeius* of the common people, from *plebs* common people] (1533)
1 : a member of the Roman plebs
2 : one of the common people

— **ple·be·ian·ism** \-ə-,ni-zəm\ *noun*

²**plebeian** *adjective* (1566)
1 : of or relating to plebeians
2 : crude or coarse in manner or style : COMMON

— **ple·be·ian·ly** *adverb*

pleb·i·scite \'ple-bə-,sīt, -sət *also* -,sēt\ *noun* [Latin *plebis scitum* law voted by the comitia, literally, decree of the common people] (1860)
: a vote by which the people of an entire country or district express an opinion for or against a proposal especially on a choice of government or ruler

— **ple·bi·sci·ta·ry** \ple-'bi-sə-,ter-ē, pli-; ,ple-bə-'sī-tə-rē\ *adjective*

plebs \'plebz, 'pleps\ *noun, plural* **ple·bes** \'plē-(,)bēz, 'plā-,bās\ [Latin] (1647)
1 : the general populace
2 : the common people of ancient Rome

ple·cop·ter·an \pli-'käp-tə-rən\ *noun* [New Latin *Plecoptera,* group name, from Greek *plekein* to braid + *pteron* wing — more at PLY, FEATHER] (circa 1890)
: STONE FLY

— **plecopteran** *adjective*

plec·trum \'plek-trəm\ *noun, plural* **plec·tra** \-trə\ *or* **plectrums** [Latin, from Greek *plēktron,* from *plēssein* to strike — more at PLAINT] (1626)
: ³PICK 2c

¹**pledge** \'plej\ *noun* [Middle English, security, from Middle French *plege,* from Late Latin *plebium,* from (assumed) Late Latin *plebere* to pledge, probably of Germanic origin; akin to Old High German *pflegan* to take care of — more at PLIGHT] (14th century)
1 a : a bailment of a chattel as security for a debt or other obligation without involving transfer of title **b** : the chattel so delivered **c** : the contract incidental to such a bailment
2 a : the state of being held as a security or guaranty **b** : something given as security for the performance of an act
3 : a token, sign, or earnest of something else
4 : a gage of battle
5 : TOAST 3
6 a : a binding promise or agreement to do or forbear **b** (1) : a promise to join a fraternity, sorority, or secret society (2) : a person who has so promised

²**pledge** *transitive verb* **pledged; pledging** (15th century)
1 : to make a pledge of; *especially* : PAWN
2 : to drink to the health of
3 : to bind by a pledge
4 : to promise the performance of by a pledge

— **pledg·er** \'ple-jər\ *or* **pled·gor** \'ple-jər, ple-'jȯr\ *noun*

pledg·ee \ple-'jē\ *noun* (1766)
: one to whom a pledge is given

pled·get \'ple-jət\ *noun* [origin unknown] (circa 1540)
: a compress or pad used to apply medication to or absorb discharges (as from a wound)

-plegia *noun combining form* [New Latin, from Greek *-plēgia,* from *plēssein* to strike — more at PLAINT]
: paralysis ⟨di*plegia*⟩

ple·iad \'plē-əd, 'plā-, -,ad, *chiefly British* 'plī-\ *noun* [French *Pléiade,* group of seven 16th century French poets, from Middle French,

group of seven tragic poets of ancient Alexandria, from Greek *Pleiad-, Pleias,* from singular of *Pleiades*] (circa 1839)
: a group of usually seven illustrious or brilliant persons or things

Pleiad *noun*
: any of the Pleiades

Ple·ia·des \'plē-ə-,dēz, 'plā-, *chiefly British* 'plī-\ *noun plural* [Latin, from Greek]
1 : the seven daughters of Atlas turned into a group of stars in Greek mythology
2 : a conspicuous cluster of stars in the constellation Taurus that includes six stars in the form of a very small dipper

plein air \,plān-'ar, -'er; ple-'nar, -'ner\ *adjective* [French, open air] (1894)
1 : of or relating to painting in outdoor daylight
2 : of or relating to a branch of impressionism that attempts to represent outdoor light and air

— **plein-air·ism** \plā-'nar-,i-zəm, ple-, -'ner-\ *noun*

— **plein-air·ist** \-ist\ *noun*

pleio- *or* **pleo-** *or* **plio-** *combining form* [Greek *pleiōn, pleōn* — more at PLUS]
: more ⟨*pleio*tropic⟩ ⟨*pleo*morphic⟩ ⟨*Plio*cene⟩

pleio·tro·pic \,plī-ə-'trō-pik, -'trä-\ *adjective* (1938)
: producing more than one genic effect; *specifically* : having multiple phenotypic expressions ⟨a *pleiotropic* gene⟩

— **plei·ot·ro·py** \plī-'ä-trə-pē\ *noun*

Pleis·to·cene \'plīs-tə-,sēn\ *adjective* [Greek *pleistos* most + International Scientific Vocabulary *-cene;* akin to Greek *pleiōn* more] (1839)
: of, relating to, or being the earlier epoch of the Quaternary or the corresponding system of rocks — see GEOLOGIC TIME table

— **Pleistocene** *noun*

ple·na·ry \'plē-nə-rē, 'ple-\ *adjective* [Middle English, from Late Latin *plenarius,* from Latin *plenus* full — more at FULL] (15th century)
1 : complete in every respect : ABSOLUTE, UNQUALIFIED ⟨*plenary* power⟩
2 : fully attended or constituted by all entitled to be present ⟨a *plenary* session⟩
synonym see FULL

plenary indulgence *noun* (1675)
: a remission of the entire temporal punishment for sin

ple·nip·o·tent \pli-'ni-pə-tənt\ *adjective* [Late Latin *plenipotent-, plenipotens,* from Latin *plenus + potent-, potens* powerful — more at POTENT] (1658)
: PLENIPOTENTIARY

¹**plen·i·po·ten·tia·ry** \,ple-nə-pə-'ten(t)-sh(ə-)rē, -shē-,er-ē\ *adjective* [Medieval Latin *plenipotentiarius,* adjective & noun, from Late Latin *plenipotent-, plenipotens*] (circa 1645)
1 : invested with full power
2 : of or relating to a plenipotentiary

²**plenipotentiary** *noun, plural* **-ries** (circa 1656)
: a person and especially a diplomatic agent invested with full power to transact business

plen·ish \'ple-nish\ *transitive verb* [Middle English (Scots) *plenyssen* to fill up, from Middle French *pleniss-,* stem of *plenir,* from *plen* full, from Latin *plenus*] (1513)
chiefly British : EQUIP

plen·i·tude \'ple-nə-,tüd, -,tyüd\ *noun* [Middle English *plenitude,* from Middle French or Latin; Middle French, from Latin *plenitudo,* from *plenus*] (15th century)
1 : the quality or state of being full : COMPLETENESS
2 : a great sufficiency : ABUNDANCE

plen·i·tu·di·nous \,ple-nə-'tüd-nəs, -'tyüd-; -'tü-d³n-əs, -'tyü-\ *adjective* [Latin *plenitudin-, plenitudo*] (1895)
: characterized by plenitude

plen·te·ous \'plen-tē-əs\ *adjective* [Middle English *plentevous, plenteous,* from Middle French *plentiveus,* from *plentif* abundant, from *plenté* plenty] (14th century)

1 : FRUITFUL, PRODUCTIVE ⟨a *plenteous* harvest —J. G. Frazer⟩ — usually used with *in* or *of* ⟨the seasons had been *plenteous* in corn —George Eliot⟩
2 : constituting or existing in plenty ⟨*plenteous* grace with thee is found —Charles Wesley⟩

— **plen·te·ous·ly** *adverb*

— **plen·te·ous·ness** *noun*

plen·ti·ful \'plen-ti-fəl\ *adjective* (15th century)
1 : containing or yielding plenty ⟨a *plentiful* land⟩
2 : characterized by, constituting, or existing in plenty ☆

— **plen·ti·ful·ly** \-fə-lē\ *adverb*

— **plen·ti·ful·ness** *noun*

plen·ti·tude \'plen-tə-,tüd, -,tyüd\ *noun* [by alteration (influenced by *plenty*)] (1615)
: PLENITUDE

¹**plen·ty** \'plen-tē\ *noun* [Middle English *plente,* from Old French *plenté,* from Late Latin *plenitat-, plenitas,* from Latin, fullness, from *plenus* full — more at FULL] (13th century)
1 a : a full or more than adequate amount or supply ⟨had *plenty* of time to finish the job⟩ **b** : a large number or amount ⟨in *plenty* of trouble⟩
2 : the quality or state of being copious : PLENTIFULNESS

²**plenty** *adjective* (14th century)
1 : plentiful in amount, number, or supply ⟨if reasons were as *plenty* as blackberries —Shakespeare⟩
2 : AMPLE ⟨*plenty* work to be done —*Time*⟩ □

³**plenty** *adverb* (1842)
: more than sufficiently : to a considerable degree ⟨the nights were *plenty* cold —F. B. Gipson⟩ □

☆ **SYNONYMS**

Plentiful, ample, abundant, copious mean more than sufficient without being excessive. PLENTIFUL implies a great or rich supply ⟨peaches are *plentiful* this summer⟩. AMPLE implies a generous sufficiency to satisfy a particular requirement ⟨*ample* food to last the winter⟩. ABUNDANT suggests an even greater or richer supply than does PLENTIFUL ⟨streams *abundant* with fish⟩. COPIOUS stresses largeness of supply rather than fullness or richness ⟨*copious* examples of bureaucratic waste⟩.

□ **USAGE**

²**plenty** Many commentators object to the use of adjective sense 2 in writing; it appears to be limited chiefly to spoken English. Sense 1 is literary but is no longer in common use.

³**plenty** Many handbooks advise avoiding the adverb *plenty* in writing; "use *very, quite,* or a more precise word," they advise. Actually *plenty* is often a more precise word than its recommended replacements; *very, fully,* or *quite* will not work as well in these typical quotations ⟨it's already *plenty* hot for us in the kitchen without some dolt opening the oven —C. H. Bridges⟩ ⟨may not be rising quite as rapidly as other health costs, but it is going up *plenty* fast —*Changing Times*⟩. It is not used in more formal writing.

ple·num \'ple-nəm, 'plē-\ *noun, plural* **-nums** *or* **-na** \-nə\ [New Latin, from Latin, neuter of *plenus*] (1678)
1 a : a space or all space every part of which is full of matter **b** (1) **:** a condition in which the pressure of the air in an enclosed space is greater than that of the outside atmosphere (2) **:** an enclosed space in which such a condition exists
2 : a general assembly of all members especially of a legislative body
3 : the quality or state of being full

ple·och·ro·ism \plē-'ä-krə-,wi-zəm\ *noun* [International Scientific Vocabulary *pleochroic*, from *pleio-* + Greek *chrōs* skin, color] (1857)
: the property of a crystal showing different colors when viewed by light that vibrates parallel to different axes
— **pleo·chro·ic** \,plē-ə-'krō-ik\ *adjective*

pleo·mor·phic \,plē-ə-'mȯr-fik\ *adjective* (1886)
: able to assume different forms **:** POLYMORPHIC ⟨*pleomorphic* bacteria⟩ ⟨a *pleomorphic* sarcoma⟩
— **pleo·mor·phism** \-,fi-zəm\ *noun*

ple·o·nasm \'plē-ə-,na-zəm\ *noun* [Late Latin *pleonasmus*, from Greek *pleonasmos*, from *pleonazein* to be excessive, from *pleiōn, pleōn* more — more at PLUS] (1610)
1 : the use of more words than those necessary to denote mere sense (as in *the man he said*) **:** REDUNDANCY
2 : an instance or example of pleonasm
— **ple·o·nas·tic** \,plē-ə-'nas-tik\ *adjective*
— **ple·o·nas·ti·cal·ly** \-ti-k(ə-)lē\ *adverb*

ple·o·pod \'plē-ə-,päd\ *noun* [Greek *plein* to sail + English *-o-* + *-pod*; from its use in swimming — more at FLOW] (circa 1890)
: an abdominal limb of a crustacean

ple·ro·cer·coid \,plir-ō-'sər-,kȯid\ *noun* [Greek *plērēs* full + *kerkos* tail — more at FULL] (1906)
: the solid elongate infective larva of some tapeworms usually occurring in the muscles of fishes

ple·si·o·saur \'plē-sē-ə-,sȯr, -zē-\ *noun* [ultimately from Greek *plēsios* close (akin to Greek *pelas* near) + *sauros* lizard] (1839)
: any of a suborder (Plesiosauria) of Mesozoic marine reptiles with dorsoventrally flattened bodies and limbs modified into paddles

pleth·o·ra \'ple-thə-rə\ *noun* [Medieval Latin, from Greek *plēthōra*, literally, fullness, from *plēthein* to be full — more at FULL] (1541)
1 : a bodily condition characterized by an excess of blood and marked by turgescence and a florid complexion
2 : EXCESS, SUPERFLUITY; *also* **:** PROFUSION, ABUNDANCE
— **ple·tho·ric** \plə-'thȯr-ik, ple-, -'thär-; 'ple-thə-rik\ *adjective*

ple·thys·mo·gram \ple-'thiz-mə-,gram, plə-\ *noun* (1894)
: a tracing made by a plethysmograph

ple·thys·mo·graph \-,graf\ *noun* [International Scientific Vocabulary, from Greek *plēthysmos* increase, from *plēthynein* to increase, from *plēthys* mass, quantity, from *plēthein*] (1872)
: an instrument for determining and registering variations in the size of an organ or limb resulting from changes in the amount of blood present or passing through it
— **ple·thys·mo·graph·ic** \-,thiz-mə-'gra-fik\ *adjective*
— **ple·thys·mo·graph·i·cal·ly** \-fi-k(ə-)lē\ *adverb*
— **pleth·ys·mog·ra·phy** \,ple-thiz-'mä-grə-fē\ *noun*

pleu·ra \'plur-ə\ *noun, plural* **pleu·rae** \'plur-,ē, -,ī\ *or* **pleuras** [Middle English, from Medieval Latin, from Greek, rib, side] (15th century)
: the delicate serous membrane that lines each half of the thorax of mammals and is folded back over the surface of the lung of the same side
— **pleu·ral** \'plur-əl\ *adjective*

pleu·ri·sy \'plur-ə-sē\ *noun* [Middle English *pluresie*, from Middle French *pleuresie*, from Late Latin *pleurisis*, alteration of Latin *pleuritis*, from Greek, from *pleura* side] (14th century)
: inflammation of the pleura usually with fever, painful and difficult respiration, cough, and exudation of fluid or fibrinous material into the pleural cavity
— **pleu·rit·ic** \plu-'ri-tik\ *adjective*

pleu·ro·pneu·mo·nia \,plur-ō-nu-'mō-nyə, -ō-nyü-\ *noun* [New Latin] (1725)
1 : combined inflammation of the pleura and lungs
2 : an acute febrile and often fatal respiratory disorder of cattle, goats, sheep, and related animals caused by a mycoplasma (*Mycoplasma mycoides*)

pleuropneumonia–like organism *noun* (1935)
: MYCOPLASMA

pleus·ton \'plü-stən, -,stän\ *noun* [International Scientific Vocabulary *pleus-* (irregular from Greek *plein* to sail, float) + *-on* (as in *plankton*)] (1943)
: organisms living in the thin surface layer existing at the air-water interface of a body of fresh water
— **pleus·ton·ic** \plü-'stä-nik\ *adjective*

-plex *noun combining form* [partly from Latin *-plex* (as in *duplex*); partly from *complex*]
1 : a figure of a given power ⟨googol*plex*⟩
2 : a building divided into an often specified number of spaces (as apartments or movie theaters) ⟨four*plex*⟩ ⟨multi*plex*⟩

plex·i·form \'plek-sə-,fȯrm\ *adjective* [New Latin *plex*us + English *-iform*] (circa 1828)
: of, relating to, or having the form or characteristics of a plexus

Plex·i·glas \'plek-si-,glas\ *trademark*
— used for acrylic plastic sheets and molding powders

plex·us \'plek-səs\ *noun, plural* **plex·us·es** \-sə-səz\ [New Latin, from Latin *plectere* to braid — more at PLY] (1682)
1 : a network of anastomosing or interlacing blood vessels or nerves
2 : an interwoven combination of parts or elements in a structure or system

pli·able \'plī-ə-bəl\ *adjective* [Middle English, from Middle French, from *plier* to bend, fold — more at PLY] (14th century)
1 a : supple enough to bend freely or repeatedly without breaking **b :** yielding readily to others **:** COMPLAISANT
2 : adjustable to varying conditions
synonym see PLASTIC
— **pli·abil·i·ty** \,plī-ə-'bi-lə-tē\ *noun*
— **pli·able·ness** \'plī-ə-bəl-nəs\ *noun*
— **pli·ably** \-blē\ *adverb*

pli·an·cy \'plī-ən(t)-sē\ *noun* (1699)
: the quality or state of being pliant

pli·ant \'plī-ənt\ *adjective* (14th century)
1 : PLIABLE 1a
2 : easily influenced **:** YIELDING
3 : suitable for varied uses
synonym see PLASTIC
— **pli·ant·ly** *adverb*
— **pli·ant·ness** *noun*

pli·ca \'plī-kə\ *noun, plural* **pli·cae** \-,kē, -,sē\ [Medieval Latin, from Latin *plicare* to fold — more at PLY] (circa 1706)
: a fold or folded part; *especially* **:** a groove or fold of skin

pli·cate \'plī-,kāt\ *adjective* [Latin *plicatus*, past participle of *plicare*] (1760)
1 : folded lengthwise like a fan ⟨a *plicate* leaf⟩
2 : having the surface thrown up into or marked with parallel ridges ⟨*plicate* wing cases⟩

pli·ca·tion \plī-'kā-shən\ *noun* (14th century)

1 : the act or process of folding **:** the state of being folded
2 : FOLD

plié \plē-'ā\ *noun* [French, from past participle of *plier* to bend] (1892)
: a bending of the knees outward by a ballet dancer with the back held straight

pli·ers \'plī-(ə)rz\ *noun plural but singular or plural in construction* [²*ply*] (circa 1569)
: a small pincers for holding small objects or for bending and cutting wire

¹plight \'plīt\ *transitive verb* [Middle English, from Old English *plihtan* to endanger, from *pliht* danger; akin to Old English *plēon* to expose to danger, Old High German *pflegan* to take care of] (13th century)
: to put or give in pledge **:** ENGAGE ⟨*plight* one's troth⟩
— **plight·er** *noun*

²plight *noun* (13th century)
: a solemnly given pledge **:** ENGAGEMENT

³plight *noun* [Middle English *plit* condition, from Anglo-French, from (assumed) Vulgar Latin *plicitum* fold — more at PLAIT] (13th century)
: an unfortunate, difficult, or precarious situation

plim·soll \'plim(p)-səl, 'plim-,sȯl\ *noun* [probably from the supposed resemblance of the upper edge of the shoe's mudguard to the Plimsoll mark on a ship] (1907)
British **:** SNEAKER 2

Plimsoll mark *noun* [Samuel *Plimsoll* (died 1898) English shipping reformer] (1884)
: a load line or a set of load-line markings on an oceangoing cargo ship — called also *Plimsoll line*

Plimsoll mark: *TF* tropical freshwater mark; *F* freshwater mark; *T* tropical load line; *S* summer load line; *W* winter load line; *WNA* winter load line, North Atlantic

¹plink \'plink\ *verb* [imitative] (1941) *intransitive verb*
1 : to make a tinkling sound
2 : to shoot at random targets in an informal and noncompetitive manner
transitive verb
1 : to cause to make a tinkling sound
2 : to shoot at especially in a casual manner
— **plink·er** *noun*

²plink *noun* (1954)
: a tinkling metallic sound

plinth \'plin(t)th\ *noun* [Latin *plinthus*, from Greek *plinthos*] (1601)
1 a : the lowest member of a base **:** SUBBASE **b :** a block upon which the moldings of an architrave or trim are stopped at the bottom
2 : a usually square block serving as a base; *broadly* **:** any of various bases or lower parts — see BASE illustration
3 : a course of stones forming a continuous foundation or base course

plio- — see PLEIO-

Pli·o·cene \'plī-ə-,sēn\ *adjective* (1831)
: of, relating to, or being the latest epoch of the Tertiary or the corresponding system of rocks — see GEOLOGIC TIME table
— **Pliocene** *noun*

Plio·film \'plī-ə-,film\ *trademark*
— used for a glossy membrane made of rubber hydrochloride and used especially for packaging

plique-à-jour \,plēk-(,)ä-'zhür\ *noun* [French, literally, braid letting in daylight] (1878)
: a style of enameling in which usually transparent enamels are fused into the openings of a metal filigree to produce an effect suggestive of stained glass

plis·kie *or* **plis·ky** \'plis-kē\ *noun, plural* **pliskies** [origin unknown] (1706)
chiefly Scottish **:** PRACTICAL JOKE, TRICK

plis·sé *or* **plis·se** \pli-'sā\ *noun* [French *plissé*, from past participle of *plisser* to pleat, from Middle French, from *pli* fold, from *plier* to fold — more at PLY] (1873)
1 : a textile finish of permanently puckered designs formed by treating with a sodium hydroxide solution
2 : a fabric with a plissé finish

plod \'pläd\ *verb* **plod·ded; plod·ding** [origin unknown] (1562)
intransitive verb
1 : to work laboriously and monotonously : DRUDGE
2 a : to walk heavily or slowly : TRUDGE **b** : to proceed slowly or tediously ⟨the movie just *plods* along⟩
transitive verb
: to tread slowly or heavily along or over
— **plod** *noun*
— **plod·der** *noun*
— **plod·ding·ly** \'plä-diŋ-lē\ *adverb*

-ploid *adjective combining form* [International Scientific Vocabulary, from *diploid* & *haploid*]
: having or being a chromosome number that bears (such) a relationship to or is (so many) times the basic chromosome number of a given group ⟨polyploid⟩

ploi·dy \'ploi-dē\ *noun* [from such words as *diploidy, hexaploidy*] (1939)
: degree of repetition of the basic number of chromosomes

PL/1 \,pē-(,)el-'wən\ *noun* [programming *language* (version) *1*] (1965)
: a general-purpose language for programming a computer

¹plonk \'pläŋk, 'ploŋk\ *variant of* PLUNK

²plonk *noun* [short for earlier *plink-plonk*, perhaps modification of French *vin blanc* white wine] (1930)
chiefly British : cheap or inferior wine

plop \'pläp\ *verb* **plopped; plop·ping** [imitative] (1821)
intransitive verb
1 : to fall, drop, or move suddenly with a sound like that of something dropping into water
2 : to allow the body to drop heavily ⟨*plopped* into a chair⟩
transitive verb
: to set, drop, or throw heavily
— **plop** *noun*

plo·sion \'plō-zhən\ *noun* (1899)
: EXPLOSION 3

plo·sive \'plō-siv\ *noun* [short for *explosive*] (1899)
: STOP 9
— **plosive** *adjective*

¹plot \'plät\ *noun* [Middle English, from Old English] (before 12th century)
1 a : a small area of planted ground ⟨a vegetable *plot*⟩ **b** : a small piece of land in a cemetery **c** : a measured piece of land : LOT
2 : GROUND PLAN, PLAT
3 : the plan or main story of a literary work
4 : a secret plan for accomplishing a usually evil or unlawful end : INTRIGUE
5 : a graphic representation (as a chart) ☆
— **plot·less** \-ləs\ *adjective*
— **plot·less·ness** *noun*

²plot *verb* **plot·ted; plot·ting** (1588)
transitive verb
1 a : to make a plot, map, or plan of **b** : to mark or note on or as if on a map or chart
2 : to lay out in plots
3 a : to locate (a point) by means of coordinates **b** : to locate (a curve) by plotted points **c** : to represent (an equation) by means of a curve so constructed
4 : to plan or contrive especially secretly
5 : to invent or devise the plot of (a literary work)
intransitive verb
1 : to form a plot : SCHEME
2 : to be located by means of coordinates ⟨the data *plot* at a single point⟩

Plo·ti·nism \plō-'tī-,ni-zəm, 'plō-t³n-,i-zəm\ *noun* (circa 1890)
: the Neoplatonic ideas of the philosopher Plotinus
— **Plo·ti·nist** \-'tī-nist, -t³n-ist\ *noun*

plot·line \'plät-,līn\ *noun* (1952)
: PLOT 3

plot·tage \'plä-tij\ *noun* (1936)
: the area included in a plot of land

plot·ter \'plä-tər\ *noun* (1588)
: one that plots: as **a** : a person who schemes or conspires **b** : a contriver of a literary plot **c** : a device for plotting; *specifically* : an instrument that graphs computer output

plot·ty \'plä-tē\ *adjective* **plot·ti·er; -est** (1897)
: marked by intricacy of plot or intrigue

plough·man's lunch \'plaů-mənz-\ *noun* (1970)
: a cold lunch served especially in an English pub typically including bread, cheese, and pickled onions

plo·ver \'plə-vər, 'plō-\ *noun, plural* **plover** *or* **plovers** [Middle English, from Middle French, from (assumed) Vulgar Latin *pluviarius*, from Latin *pluvia* rain — more at PLUVIAL] (14th century)
1 : any of a family (Charadriidae) of shore-inhabiting birds that differ from the sandpipers in having a short hard-tipped bill and usually a stouter more compact build
2 : any of various birds (as a turnstone or sandpiper) related to the plovers

¹plow *or* **plough** \'plaů\ *noun* [Middle English, from Old English *plōh* hide of land; akin to Old High German *pfluog* plow] (12th century)
1 : an implement used to cut, lift, and turn over soil especially in preparing a seedbed
2 : any of various devices (as a snowplow) operating like a plow

²plow *or* **plough** (15th century)
transitive verb
1 a : to turn, break up, or work with a plow **b** : to make (as a furrow) with a plow
2 : to cut into, open, or make furrows or ridges in with or as if with a plow
3 : to cleave the surface of or move through (water) ⟨whales *plowing* the ocean⟩
4 : to clear away snow from with a snowplow ⟨*plow* the street⟩
intransitive verb
1 a : to use a plow **b** : to bear or admit of plowing
2 a : to move in a way resembling that of a plow ⟨the car *plowed* into a fence⟩ **b** : to proceed steadily and laboriously ⟨had to *plow* through a stack of letters⟩
— **plow·able** \-ə-bəl\ *adjective*
— **plow·er** \'plaů(-ə)r\ *noun*

plow back *transitive verb* (1930)
: to reinvest (profits) in a business
— **plow·back** \'plaů-,bak\ *noun*

plow·boy \'plaů-,boi\ *noun* (1596)
1 : a boy who leads the team drawing a plow
2 : a country youth

plow·man \-mən, -,man\ *noun* (13th century)
1 : a man who guides a plow
2 : a farm laborer

plow·share \'plaů-,sher, -,shar\ *noun* [Middle English *ploughshare*, from *plough* plow + *schare* plowshare — more at SHARE] (14th century)
: a part of a plow that cuts the furrow

plow under *transitive verb* (1900)
: to cause to disappear : BURY, OVERWHELM

ploy \'ploi\ *noun* [probably from *employ*] (1722)
1 : ESCAPADE, FROLIC
2 a : a tactic intended to embarrass or frustrate an opponent **b** : a devised or contrived move : STRATAGEM ⟨a *ploy* to get her to open the door —Robert B. Parker⟩

¹pluck \'plək\ *verb* [Middle English, from Old English *pluccian*; akin to Middle High German *pflücken* to pluck] (before 12th century)

transitive verb
1 : to pull or pick off or out
2 a : to remove something (as hairs) from by or as if by plucking ⟨*pluck* one's eyebrows⟩ **b** : ROB, FLEECE
3 : to move, remove, or separate forcibly or abruptly ⟨*plucked* the child from the middle of the street⟩
4 a : to pick, pull, or grasp at **b** : to play by sounding the strings with the fingers or a pick
intransitive verb
: to make a sharp pull or twitch
— **pluck·er** *noun*

²pluck *noun* (15th century)
1 : an act or instance of plucking or pulling
2 : the heart, liver, lungs, and windpipe of a slaughtered animal especially as an item of food
3 : courageous readiness to fight or continue against odds : dogged resolution

plucky \'plə-kē\ *adjective* **pluck·i·er; -est** (1842)
: SPIRITED, BRAVE
— **pluck·i·ly** \'plə-kə-lē\ *adverb*
— **pluck·i·ness** \'plə-kē-nəs\ *noun*

¹plug \'pləg\ *noun* [Dutch, from Middle Dutch *plugge*; akin to Middle High German *pfloc* plug] (1627)
1 a : a piece used to fill a hole : STOPPER **b** : an obtruding or obstructing mass of material resembling a stopper
2 : a flat compressed cake of tobacco
3 : a small core or segment removed from a larger object
4 : something inferior; *especially* : an inferior often aged or unsound horse; *also* : a quiet steady cold-blooded horse usually of light or moderate weight
5 a : HYDRANT, FIREPLUG **b** : SPARK PLUG
6 : an artificial angling lure used primarily for casting and made with one or more sets of gang hooks
7 : any of various devices resembling or functioning like a plug: as **a** : a male fitting for making an electrical connection to a live circuit by insertion in a receptacle (as an outlet) **b** : a device for connecting electric wires to a jack
8 : a piece of favorable publicity or a favorable mention usually incorporated in general matter

²plug *verb* **plugged; plug·ging** (1630)
transitive verb
1 : to stop, make tight, or secure by inserting a plug
2 : to hit with a bullet : SHOOT
3 : to advertise or publicize insistently
intransitive verb

\ə\ abut \³\ kitten \ər\ further \a\ ash \ā\ ace
\ä\ mop, mar \aů\ out \ch\ chin \e\ bet \ē\ easy
\g\ go \i\ hit \ī\ ice \j\ job \ŋ\ sing
\ō\ law \oi\ boy \th\ thin \t̲h̲\ the \ü\ loot \ů\ foot
\y\ yet \zh\ vision *see also* Guide to Pronunciation

1 : to become plugged — usually used with *up*

2 : to work doggedly and persistently ⟨*plugged* away at her homework⟩

3 : to fire shots

— **plug·ger** *noun*

— **plug into** *vt* : to connect or become connected to by or as if by means of a plug ⟨the city was *plugged into* the new highway system⟩

plugged \'pləgd\ *adjective* (1694)

1 *of a coin* : altered by the insertion of a plug of base metal

2 : closed by or as if by a plug : OBSTRUCTED

plug hat *noun* (1863)

: a man's stiff hat (as a bowler or top hat)

plug-in \'pləg-,in\ *adjective* (1922)

: designed to be connected to an electric circuit by plugging in ⟨a *plug-in* toy⟩

— **plug–in** *noun*

plug in (1903)

intransitive verb

: to establish an electric circuit by inserting a plug

transitive verb

: to attach or connect to a service outlet

plug·o·la \(,)plə-'gō-lə\ *noun* [*plug* + *-ola* (as in *payola*)] (1959)

: incidental advertising on radio or television that is not purchased like regular advertising

plug-ug·ly \'pləg-,əg-lē\ *noun* (1856)

: THUG, TOUGH; *especially* : one hired to intimidate

plum \'pləm\ *noun, often attributive* [Middle English, from Old English *plūme*, modification of Latin *prunum* plum, from Greek *proumnon*] (before 12th century)

1 a : any of numerous trees and shrubs (genus *Prunus*) with globular or oval smooth-skinned fruits that are drupes with oblong seeds **b** : the edible fruit of a plum

2 : any of various trees with edible fruits resembling plums; *also* : the fruit

3 a : a raisin when used in desserts **b** : SUGARPLUM

4 : something superior or very desirable; *especially* : something desirable given in return for a favor

5 : a dark reddish purple

— **plum·like** \-,līk\ *adjective*

plum·age \'plü-mij\ *noun* [Middle English, from Middle French, from Old French, from *plume* feather — more at PLUME] (14th century)

: the feathers of a bird

— **plum·aged** \-mijd\ *adjective*

¹**plumb** \'pləm\ *noun* [Middle English, from (assumed) Old French *plomb* lead, from Latin *plumbum*] (14th century)

: a lead weight attached to a line and used to indicate a vertical direction

— **out of plumb** *or* **off plumb** : out of vertical or true

²**plumb** *adverb* (15th century)

1 : straight down or up : VERTICALLY

2 *chiefly dialect* : to a complete degree : ABSOLUTELY ⟨'you're *plumb* crazy,' she remarked, with easy candor —*Harper's Weekly*⟩

3 : in a direct manner : EXACTLY; *also* : without interval of time : IMMEDIATELY

³**plumb** (15th century)

transitive verb

1 : to weight with lead

2 a : to measure the depth of with a plumb **b** : to examine minutely and critically ⟨*plumbing* the book's complexities⟩

3 : to adjust or test by a plumb line

4 : to seal with lead

5 [back-formation from *plumber*] : to supply with or install as plumbing

intransitive verb

: to work as a plumber

⁴**plumb** *adjective* (15th century)

1 : exactly vertical or true

2 : THOROUGH, COMPLETE

synonym see VERTICAL

plum·ba·go \,pləm-'bā-(,)gō\ *noun, plural* **-gos** [Latin *plumbagin-, plumbago* galena, from *plumbum*] (1747)

1 [New Latin, from Latin] : any of a genus (*Plumbago* of the family Plumbaginaceae, the plumbago family) of woody chiefly tropical plants with alternate leaves and spikes of showy flowers

2 : GRAPHITE 1

plumb bob *noun* (circa 1840)

: the metal bob of a plumb line

plumb·er \'plə-mər\ *noun* [Middle English, from Middle French *plommier, plombier*, from Latin *plumbarius*, from *plumbum*] (15th century)

1 : a dealer or worker in lead

2 : one who installs, repairs, and maintains piping, fittings, and fixtures involved in the distribution and use of water in a building

plumber's helper *noun* (1952)

: PLUNGER d — called also *plumber's friend*

plumber's snake *noun* (1938)

: a long flexible rod or cable usually of steel that is used to free clogged pipes

plumb·ing \'plə-miŋ\ *noun* (1666)

1 : the act of using a plumb

2 : a plumber's occupation or trade

3 a : the apparatus (as pipes and fixtures) concerned in the distribution and use of water in a building **b** : an internal system that resembles plumbing; *especially* : one consisting of conduits or channels for conveying fluids

plumb·ism \'pləm-,bi-zəm\ *noun* [Latin *plumbum* lead] (1876)

: lead poisoning especially when chronic

plumb line *noun* (15th century)

1 : a line (as of cord) that has at one end a weight (as a plumb bob) and is used especially to determine verticality

2 : a line directed to the center of gravity of the earth : a vertical line

¹**plume** \'plüm\ *noun* [Middle English, from Middle French, from Latin *pluma* small soft feather — more at FLEECE] (14th century)

1 : a feather of a bird: as **a** : a large conspicuous or showy feather **b** : CONTOUR FEATHER **c** : PLUMAGE **d** : a cluster of distinctive feathers

2 a : material (as a feather, cluster of feathers, or a tuft of hair) worn as an ornament **b** : a token of honor or prowess : PRIZE

3 : something resembling a feather (as in shape, appearance, or lightness): as **a** : a plumose appendage of a plant **b** : an elongated and usually open and mobile column or band (as of smoke, exhaust gases, or blowing snow) **c** : an animal structure having a main shaft bearing many hairs or filamentous parts; *especially* : a full bushy tail

²**plume** *transitive verb* **plumed; plum·ing** (15th century)

1 a : to provide or deck with feathers **b** : to array showily

2 : to indulge (oneself) in pride with an obvious or vain display of self-satisfaction

3 *of a bird* **a** : to preen and arrange the feathers of (itself) **b** : to preen and arrange (feathers)

plumed \'plümd\ *adjective* (15th century)

: provided or adorned with or as if with a plume — often used in combination ⟨a white-*plumed* egret⟩

plume·let \'plüm-lət\ *noun* (circa 1847)

: a small tuft or plume

plu·me·ria \plü-'mir-ē-ə\ *noun* [New Latin, genus name, from Charles *Plumier* (died 1704) French botanist] (1753)

: FRANGIPANI

¹**plum·met** \'plə-mət\ *noun* [Middle English *plomet*, from Middle French *plombet* ball of lead, from *plomb* lead, from (assumed) Old French — more at PLUMB] (14th century)

: PLUMB; *also* : PLUMB LINE

²**plummet** *intransitive verb* (1937)

1 : to fall perpendicularly ⟨birds *plummeted* down⟩

2 : to drop sharply and abruptly ⟨prices *plummeted*⟩

plum·my \'plə-mē\ *adjective* **plum·mi·er; -est** (1759)

1 a : full of plums ⟨a rich *plummy* cake⟩ **b** : CHOICE, DESIRABLE ⟨got a *plummy* role in the movie⟩

2 a : having a plum color **b** : rich and mellow often to the point of affectation ⟨a *plummy* singing voice⟩

plu·mose \'plü-,mōs\ *adjective* (circa 1727)

1 : having feathers or plumes : FEATHERED

2 : FEATHERY

¹**plump** \'pləmp\ *verb* [Middle English] (14th century)

intransitive verb

1 : to drop, sink, or come in contact suddenly or heavily ⟨*plumped* down in the chair⟩

2 : to favor or decide in favor of someone or something strongly or emphatically — used with *for*

transitive verb

1 : to drop, cast, or place suddenly or heavily

2 : to give support and favorable publicity to

²**plump** *noun* (15th century)

: a sudden plunge, fall, or blow; *also* : the sound made by a plump

³**plump** *adverb* (1594)

1 : with a sudden or heavy drop

2 a : straight down **b** : straight ahead

3 : without qualification : DIRECTLY

⁴**plump** *noun* [Middle English *plumpe*] (15th century)

chiefly dialect : GROUP, FLOCK ⟨a *plump* of ducks rose at the same time —H. D. Thoreau⟩

⁵**plump** *verb* [⁶*plump*] (1533)

transitive verb

: to make plump

intransitive verb

: to become plump

⁶**plump** *adjective* [Middle English, dull, blunt, from Middle Dutch *plomp*] (1569)

1 : having a full rounded usually pleasing form ⟨a *plump* woman⟩

2 : AMPLE, ABUNDANT

— **plump·ish** \'pləm-pish\ *adjective*

plump·en \'pləm-pən\ *verb* (1687)

: ⁵PLUMP

¹**plump·er** \'pləm-pər\ *noun* [⁵*plump*] (1690)

: an object carried in the mouth to fill out the cheeks

²**plumper** *noun* [¹*plump*] (circa 1785)

chiefly British : a vote for only one candidate when two or more are to be elected to the same office

¹**plump·ly** \'pləm-plē\ *adverb* (1611)

: in a plump way ⟨a *plumply* pretty girl⟩

²**plumply** *adverb* [³*plump*] (1786)

: in a wholehearted manner and without hesitation or circumlocution : FORTHRIGHTLY

¹**plump·ness** \'pləmp-nəs\ *noun* (1545)

: the quality or state of being plump

²**plumpness** *noun* (1780)

: freedom from hesitation or circumlocution

plum pudding *noun* (1711)

: a rich boiled or steamed pudding containing fruits and spices

plum tomato *noun* (circa 1900)

: a small oblong tomato

plu·mule \'plü-(,)myü(ə)l\ *noun* [New Latin *plumula*, from Latin, diminutive of *pluma* small soft feather — more at FLEECE] (circa 1741)

1 : the primary bud of a plant embryo usually situated at the apex of the hypocotyl and consisting of leaves and an epicotyl

2 : a down feather

plumy \'plü-mē\ *adjective* **plum·i·er; -est** (1582)

1 : DOWNY

2 : having or resembling plumes

plumule of morning glory seedling:
1 hypocotyl
2 plumule
3 cotyledons

¹plun·der \'plən-dər\ *verb* **plun·dered; plun·der·ing** \-d(ə-)riŋ\ [German *plündern*] (1632)
transitive verb
1 a : to take the goods of by force (as in war) **:** PILLAGE, SACK ⟨invaders *plundered* the town⟩ **b :** to take by force or wrongfully **:** STEAL, LOOT
2 : to make extensive use of as if by plundering **:** use or use up wrongfully ⟨*plunder* the land⟩
intransitive verb
: to commit robbery or looting
— **plun·der·er** \-dər-ər\ *noun*

²plunder *noun* (1643)
1 : an act of plundering **:** PILLAGING
2 : something taken by force, theft, or fraud **:** LOOT
3 *chiefly dialect* **:** personal or household effects
synonym see SPOIL

plun·der·ous \-d(ə-)rəs\ *adjective* (1845)
: given to plundering

¹plunge \'plənj\ *verb* **plunged; plung·ing** [Middle English, from Middle French *plonger*, from (assumed) Vulgar Latin *plumbicare*, from Latin *plumbum* lead] (14th century)
transitive verb
1 : to cause to penetrate or enter quickly and forcibly into something
2 : to cause to enter a state or course of action usually suddenly, unexpectedly, or violently
intransitive verb
1 : to thrust or cast oneself into or as if into water
2 a : to become pitched or thrown headlong or violently forward and downward; *also* **:** to move oneself in such a manner **b :** to act with reckless haste **:** enter suddenly or unexpectedly **c :** to bet or gamble heavily and recklessly
3 : to descend or dip suddenly

²plunge *noun* (15th century)
: an act or instance of plunging **:** DIVE; *also* **:** SWIM

plung·er \'plən-jər\ *noun* (1611)
: one that plunges: as **a :** DIVER **b :** a reckless gambler or speculator **c** (1) **:** a sliding reciprocating piece driven by or against fluid pressure; *especially* **:** PISTON (2) **:** a piece with a motion more or less like that of a ram or piston **d :** a rubber suction cup on a handle used to free plumbing traps and waste outlets of obstructions

plunk \'pləŋk\ *verb* [imitative] (1805)
transitive verb
1 : to pluck or hit so as to produce a quick, hollow, metallic, or harsh sound
2 : to set down suddenly **:** PLUMP
intransitive verb
1 : to make a plunking sound
2 : to drop abruptly **:** DIVE
3 : to come out in favor of someone or something — used with *for*
— **plunk** *noun*
— **plunk·er** *noun*

plunk down (1891)
intransitive verb
: to drop abruptly **:** settle into position
transitive verb
1 a : to put down usually firmly or abruptly ⟨*plunked* the money *down* on the counter⟩ **b :** to settle (oneself) into position ⟨*plunked* himself *down* on the bench⟩
2 : to pay out

plu·per·fect \ˌplü-'pər-fikt\ *adjective* [Middle English *pluperfyth*, modification of Late Latin *plusquamperfectus*, literally, more than perfect] (15th century)
1 : PAST PERFECT
2 : utterly perfect or complete
— **pluperfect** *noun*

plu·ral \'plur-əl\ *adjective* [Middle English, from Middle French & Latin; Middle French *plurel*, from Latin *pluralis*, from *plur-, plus* more — more at PLUS] (14th century)
1 : of, relating to, or constituting a class of grammatical forms usually used to denote more than one or in some languages more than two ⟨*genetics* is *plural* in form but takes a singular *verb*⟩
2 : relating to, consisting of, or containing more than one or more than one kind or class ⟨a *plural* society⟩
— **plural** *noun*
— **plu·ral·ly** \-ə-lē\ *adverb*

plu·ral·ism \'plur-ə-ˌli-zəm\ *noun* (1818)
1 : the holding of two or more offices or positions (as benefices) at the same time
2 : the quality or state of being plural
3 a : a theory that there are more than one or more than two kinds of ultimate reality **b :** a theory that reality is composed of a plurality of entities
4 a : a state of society in which members of diverse ethnic, racial, religious, or social groups maintain an autonomous participation in and development of their traditional culture or special interest within the confines of a common civilization **b :** a concept, doctrine, or policy advocating this state
— **plu·ral·ist** \-list\ *adjective or noun*
— **plu·ral·is·tic** \ˌplur-ə-'lis-tik\ *adjective*
— **plu·ral·is·ti·cal·ly** \-ti-k(ə-)lē\ *adverb*

plu·ral·i·ty \plu-'ra-lə-tē\ *noun, plural* **-ties** (14th century)
1 a : the state of being plural **b :** the state of being numerous **c :** a large number or quantity
2 : PLURALISM 1; *also* **:** a benefice held by pluralism
3 a : a number greater than another **b :** an excess of votes over those cast for an opposing candidate **c :** a number of votes cast for a candidate in a contest of more than two candidates that is greater than the number cast for any other candidate but not more than half the total votes cast

plu·ral·ize \'plur-ə-ˌlīz\ *transitive verb* **-ized; -iz·ing** (1803)
: to make plural or express in the plural form
— **plu·ral·i·za·tion** \ˌplur-ə-lə-'zā-shən\ *noun*

plu·rip·o·tent \plu-'ri-pə-tənt\ *adjective* [Latin *plur-, plus* more + English *potent*] (1916)
: not fixed as to developmental potentialities **:** having developmental plasticity ⟨*pluripotent* stem cell⟩

¹plus \'pləs\ *adjective* [Latin, adverb, more, from neuter of *plur-, plus*, adjective; akin to Greek *pleion* more, Latin *plenus* full — more at FULL] (1579)
1 : algebraically positive
2 : having, receiving, or being in addition to what is anticipated
3 a : falling high in a specified range ⟨a grade of C *plus*⟩ **b :** greater than that specified **c :** possessing a specified quality to a high degree
4 : electrically positive
5 : relating to or being a particular one of the two mating types that are required for successful fertilization in sexual reproduction in some lower plants (as a fungus)

²plus *noun, plural* **plus·es** \'plə-səz\ *also* **plus·ses** (1654)
1 : PLUS SIGN
2 : an added quantity
3 : a positive factor or quality
4 : SURPLUS

³plus *preposition* (1668)
1 : increased by **:** with the addition of ⟨four *plus* five⟩ ⟨principal *plus* interest⟩ ⟨made twelve dollars a week *plus* room and board —E. L. Doctorow⟩
2 : BESIDES — used chiefly in speech and casual writing ⟨*plus* all this, as a sedative it has no equal —Groucho Marx⟩

⁴plus *conjunction* (circa 1950)
1 : AND ⟨the Smyth Report, *plus* an idea and some knowledge of bureaucracy, were all I needed —Pat Frank⟩ ⟨a box-office *plus* critical and artistic success —G. J. Nathan⟩ ⟨eats

alone, a hot beef sandwich *plus* a BLT *plus* apple pie —Garrison Keillor⟩
2 : in addition to which ⟨it was an achievement. *Plus*, I wrote the story and the musical score —Jackie Gleason⟩ ⟨it's also pretty on my open shelves, *plus* it smells good —Nikki Giovanni⟩ □

plus fours *noun plural* (1920)
: loose sports knickers made four inches longer than ordinary knickers

¹plush \'pləsh\ *noun* [Middle French *peluche*] (1594)
: a fabric with an even pile longer and less dense than velvet pile

²plush *adjective* (circa 1645)
1 : relating to, resembling, or made of plush
2 : notably luxurious
— **plush·ly** *adverb*
— **plush·ness** *noun*

plushy \'plə-shē\ *adjective* **plush·i·er; -est** (1611)
1 : having the texture of or covered with plush
2 : LUXURIOUS, SHOWY
— **plush·i·ness** *noun*

plus·sage \'plə-sij\ *noun* (1924)
: an amount over and above another amount

plus sign *noun* (circa 1907)
: a sign + denoting addition or a positive quantity

Plu·to \'plü-(ˌ)tō\ *noun* [Latin *Pluton-, Pluto*, from Greek *Ploutōn*]
1 : the Greek god of the underworld — compare DIS
2 [New Latin] **:** the planet with the farthest mean distance from the sun — see PLANET table

plu·toc·ra·cy \plü-'tä-krə-sē\ *noun, plural* **-cies** [Greek *ploutokratia*, from *ploutos* wealth; akin to Greek *plein* to sail, float — more at FLOW] (1652)
1 : government by the wealthy
2 : a controlling class of the wealthy
— **plu·to·crat** \'plü-tə-ˌkrat\ *noun*
— **plu·to·crat·ic** \ˌplü-tə-'kra-tik\ *adjective*
— **plu·to·crat·i·cal·ly** \-ti-k(ə-)lē\ *adverb*

plu·ton \'plü-ˌtän\ *noun* [probably back-formation from *plutonic*] (1936)
: a typically large body of intrusive igneous rock

plu·to·ni·an \plü-'tō-nē-ən\ *adjective, often capitalized* (1667)
: of, relating to, or characteristic of Pluto or the lower world **:** INFERNAL

plu·ton·ic \plü-'tä-nik\ *adjective* [Latin *Pluton-, Pluto*] (1833)
1 : formed by solidification of magma deep within the earth and crystalline throughout ⟨*plutonic* rock⟩
2 *often capitalized* **:** PLUTONIAN

plu·to·ni·um \plü-'tō-nē-əm\ *noun* [New Latin, from *Pluton-, Pluto*, the planet Pluto] (1942)
: a radioactive metallic element similar chemically to uranium that is formed as the isotope 239 by decay of neptunium and found in minute quantities in pitchblende, that undergoes slow disintegration with the emission of an alpha particle to form uranium 235, and

□ USAGE
plus The preposition *plus* has long been used with a meaning equivalent to *and* (as in "two *plus* two"); it is not, therefore, very surprising that in time people have begun to use it as a conjunction much like *and*. Sense 2 is considered to be an adverb by some commentators. It is used chiefly in speech and in informal writing.

\ə\ **abut** \ə\ **kitten** \ər\ **further** \a\ **ash** \ā\ **ace**
\ä\ **mop, mar** \au̇\ **out** \ch\ **chin** \e\ **bet** \ē\ **easy**
\g\ **go** \i\ **hit** \ī\ **ice** \j\ **job** \ŋ\ **sing** \ō\ **go**
\ȯ\ **law** \ȯi\ **boy** \th\ **thin** \th\ **the** \ü\ **loot** \u̇\ **foot**
\y\ **yet** \zh\ **vision** *see also* Guide to Pronunciation

that is fissionable with slow neutrons to yield atomic energy — see ELEMENT table

¹plu·vi·al \'plü-vē-əl\ adjective [Latin pluvialis, from pluvia rain, from feminine of pluvius rainy, from pluere to rain — more at FLOW] (circa 1656)

1 a : of or relating to rain **b :** characterized by abundant rain
2 of a geologic change **:** resulting from the action of rain

²pluvial noun (1929)
: a prolonged period of wet climate

¹ply \'plī\ verb **plied; ply·ing** [Middle English plien, short for applien to apply] (14th century)
transitive verb
1 a : to use or wield diligently ⟨busily plying his pen⟩ **b :** to practice or perform diligently ⟨ply a trade⟩
2 : to keep furnishing or supplying something to ⟨plied us with liquor⟩
3 a : to make a practice of rowing or sailing over or on ⟨the boat plies the river⟩ **b :** to go or travel regularly over, on, or through ⟨jets plying the skies⟩
intransitive verb
1 : to apply oneself steadily
2 : to go or travel regularly ⟨a steamer plying between the towns⟩

²ply noun, plural **plies** [³ply] (1532)
1 a : one of several layers (as of cloth) usually sewn or laminated together **b :** one of the strands in a yarn **c :** one of the veneer sheets forming plywood **d :** a layer of a paper or paperboard
2 : INCLINATION, BIAS

³ply transitive verb **plied; ply·ing** [Middle English plien to fold, from Middle French plier, from Latin plicare; akin to Old High German flehtan to braid, Latin plectere, Greek plekein] (circa 1909)
: to twist together ⟨ply two single yarns⟩

Plym·outh Rock \'pli-məth-\ noun [Plymouth Rock, on which the Pilgrims are supposed to have landed in 1620] (1849)
: any of an American breed of medium-sized single-combed dual-purpose domestic fowls

ply·wood \'plī-,wùd\ noun (1907)
: a structural material consisting of sheets of wood glued or cemented together with the grains of adjacent layers arranged at right angles or at a wide angle

-pnea or **-pnoea** noun combining form [New Latin, from Greek -pnoia, from pnoia, from pnein to breathe]
: breath : breathing ⟨hyperpnea⟩ ⟨apnoea⟩

pneum- or **pneumo-** combining form [New Latin, partly from Greek pneum- (from pneuma); partly from Greek pneumōn lung]
1 : air : gas ⟨pneumothorax⟩
2 : lung ⟨pneumoconiosis⟩
3 : respiration ⟨pneumograph⟩
4 : pneumonia ⟨pneumococcus⟩

pneu·ma \'nü-mə, 'nyü-\ noun [Greek] (1884)
: SOUL, SPIRIT

pneumat- or **pneumato-** combining form [Greek, from pneumat-, pneuma]
1 : air : vapor : gas ⟨pneumatolytic⟩
2 : respiration ⟨pneumatophore⟩

pneu·mat·ic \nu-'ma-tik, nyü-\ adjective [Latin pneumaticus, from Greek pneumatikos, from pneumat-, pneuma air, breath, spirit, from pnein to breathe — more at SNEEZE] (1659)
1 : of, relating to, or using gas (as air or wind): **a :** moved or worked by air pressure **b** (1) **:** adapted for holding or inflated with compressed air (2) **:** having air-filled cavities
2 : of or relating to the pneuma : SPIRITUAL
3 : having a well-proportioned feminine figure; especially **:** having a full bust
— pneu·mat·i·cal·ly \-ti-k(ə-)lē\ adverb
— pneu·ma·tic·i·ty \,nü-mə-'ti-sə-tē, ,nyü-\ noun

pneu·ma·tol·o·gy \,nü-mə-'tä-lə-jē, ,nyü-\ noun [New Latin pneumatologia, from Greek pneumat-, pneuma + New Latin -logia -logy] (1678)
: the study of spiritual beings or phenomena

pneu·ma·to·lyt·ic \,nü-mə-t⁰l-'i-tik, ,nyü-; (,)n(y)ü-,ma-\ adjective [International Scientific Vocabulary] (1896)
: formed or forming by hot vapors or superheated liquids under pressure — used especially of minerals and ores

pneu·mat·o·phore \nù-'ma-tə-,fōr, nyù-, -,fȯr\ noun [International Scientific Vocabulary] (1859)
1 : a muscular gas-containing sac that serves as a float on a siphonophore colony
2 : a root often functioning as a respiratory organ in a wetland plant

pneu·mo·coc·cus \,nü-mə-'kä-kəs, ,nyü-\ noun, plural **-coc·ci** \-'käk-,sī, -,sē; -'kä-,kī, -,kē\ [New Latin] (1890)
: a bacterium (Streptococcus pneumoniae) that causes an acute pneumonia involving one or more lobes of the lung
— pneu·mo·coc·cal \-'kä-kəl\ adjective

pneu·mo·co·ni·o·sis \,nü-mō-,kō-nē-'ō-səs, ,nyü-\ noun, plural **-o·ses** \-,sēz\ [New Latin, from pneum- + Greek konis dust — more at INCINERATE] (1881)
: a disease of the lungs caused by the habitual inhalation of irritants (as mineral or metallic particles) — compare BLACK LUNG, SILICOSIS

Pneu·mo·cys·tis ca·ri·nii pneumonia \,nü-mə-'sis-təs-kə-'rī-nē-,ē-, ,nyü-\ noun [New Latin Pneumocystis carinii, species name] (1964)
: a pneumonia that affects individuals whose immunological defenses have been compromised, that is caused by a microorganism (Pneumocystis carinii), and that attacks especially the interstitial tissue of the lungs with marked thickening of the alveolar septa and alveoli

pneu·mo·graph \'nü-mə-,graf, 'nyü-\ noun [International Scientific Vocabulary] (1878)
: an instrument for recording thoracic movements or volume change during respiration

pneu·mo·nec·to·my \,nü-mə-'nek-tə-mē, ,nyü-\ noun, plural **-mies** [Greek pneumōn + International Scientific Vocabulary -ectomy] (circa 1895)
: excision of an entire lung or of one or more lobes of a lung

pneu·mo·nia \nù-'mō-nyə, nyù-\ noun [New Latin, from Greek, from pneumōn lung, alteration of pleumōn — more at PULMONARY] (1603)
: a disease of the lungs characterized by inflammation and consolidation followed by resolution and caused by infection or irritants

pneu·mon·ic \nù-'mä-nik, nyù-\ adjective [New Latin pneumonicus, from Greek pneumonikos, from pneumōn] (1675)
1 : of, relating to, or affecting the lungs : PULMONIC, PULMONARY
2 : of, relating to, or affected with pneumonia

pneu·mo·ni·tis \,nü-mə-'nī-təs, ,nyü-\ noun [New Latin, from Greek pneumōn] (circa 1834)
: inflammation of the lungs

pneu·mo·tho·rax \,nü-mə-'thōr-,aks, ,nyü-, -'thȯr-\ noun [New Latin] (1821)
: a condition in which air or other gas is present in the pleural cavity and which occurs spontaneously as a result of disease or injury of lung tissue or puncture of the chest wall or is induced as a therapeutic measure to collapse the lung

¹poach \'pōch\ transitive verb [Middle English pochen, from Middle French pocher, from Old French pochier, literally, to put in a bag, from poche bag, pocket, of Germanic origin; akin to Old English pocca bag] (15th century)
: to cook in simmering liquid

²poach verb [Middle French pocher, of Germanic origin; akin to Middle English poken to poke] (1611)
intransitive verb
1 : to encroach upon especially for the purpose of taking something
2 : to trespass for the purpose of stealing game; also **:** to take game or fish illegally
transitive verb
1 : to trespass on ⟨a field poached too frequently by the amateur —Times Literary Supplement⟩
2 a : to take (game or fish) by illegal methods **b :** to appropriate (something) as one's own

¹poach·er \'pō-chər\ noun [²poach] (1614)
1 : one that trespasses or steals
2 : one who kills or takes wild animals (as game or fish) illegally

²poacher noun [¹poach] (1861)
1 : a covered pan containing a plate with depressions or shallow cups in each of which an egg can be cooked over steam rising from boiling water in the bottom of the pan
2 : a baking dish in which food (as fish) can be poached

po'·boy \'pō-,bȯi\ variant of POOR BOY

po·chard \'pō-chərd\ noun [origin unknown] (1552)
: any of numerous rather heavy-bodied diving ducks (especially genus Aythya) with a large head and with feet and legs placed far back under the body

¹pock \'päk\ noun [Middle English pokke, from Old English pocc; akin to Middle Low German & Middle Dutch pocke pock] (before 12th century)
: a pustule in an eruptive disease (as smallpox); also **:** a spot suggesting such a pustule

²pock transitive verb (1841)
: to mark with or as if with pocks : PIT

¹pock·et \'pä-kət\ noun [Middle English poket, from Old North French pokete, diminutive of poke bag, of Germanic origin; akin to Old English pocca bag] (15th century)
1 a : a small bag carried by a person : PURSE **b :** a small bag that is sewed or inserted in a garment so that it is open at the top or side ⟨coat pocket⟩
2 : supply of money : MEANS
3 : RECEPTACLE, CONTAINER: as **a :** an opening at the corner or side of a billiard table **b :** a superficial pouch in some animals
4 : a small often isolated area or group ⟨pockets of unemployment⟩ **: a** (1) **:** a cavity containing a deposit (as of gold, water, or gas) (2) **:** a small body of ore **b :** AIR POCKET
5 : a place for a batten made by sewing a strip on a sail
6 a : BLIND ALLEY **b :** the position of a contestant in a race hemmed in by others **c :** an area formed by blockers from which a football quarterback attempts to pass
7 : the concave area at the base of the finger sections of a baseball glove or mitt in which the ball is normally caught
— pock·et·ful \-,fùl\ noun
— in one's pocket : in one's control or possession
— in pocket 1 : provided with funds **2 :** in the position of having made a profit
— out of pocket 1 : low on money or funds **2 :** having suffered a loss

²pocket transitive verb (1589)
1 a : to put or enclose in or as if in one's pocket ⟨pocketed the change⟩ **b :** to appropriate to one's own use : STEAL **c :** to refuse assent to (a bill) by a pocket veto
2 : to put up with : ACCEPT
3 : to set aside : SUPPRESS ⟨pocketed his pride⟩
4 a : to hem in **b :** to drive (a ball) into a pocket of a pool table
5 : to cover or supply with pockets
— pock·et·able \'pä-kə-tə-bəl\ adjective

³pocket adjective (1612)

1 a : small enough to be carried in the pocket **b :** SMALL, MINIATURE ⟨a *pocket* park⟩ **2 a :** of or relating to money **b :** carried in or paid from one's own pocket

pocket battleship *noun* (1930)
: a small German battleship built so as to come within treaty limitations of tonnage and armament

pocket billiards *noun plural but usually singular in construction* (1913)
: POOL 2b

¹**pock·et·book** \'pä-kət-ˌbu̇k\ *noun* (1617)
1 *often* **pocket book :** a small especially paperback book that can be carried in the pocket
2 : a flat typically leather folding case for money or personal papers that can be carried in a pocket or handbag
3 a : PURSE **b :** HANDBAG 2
4 : financial resources : INCOME

²**pocketbook** *adjective* (1894)
: relating to or involving economic interests ⟨*pocketbook* issues⟩

pocket borough *noun* (1856)
: an English constituency controlled before parliamentary reform by a single person or family

pocket edition *noun* (1715)
1 : POCKETBOOK 1
2 : a miniature form of something

pocket gopher *noun* (1873)
: GOPHER 2a

pocket–handkerchief *noun* (1645)
: a handkerchief carried in the pocket

pock·et·knife \'pä-kət-ˌnīf\ *noun* (1727)
: a knife that has one or more blades that fold into the handle and that can be carried in the pocket

pocket money *noun* (1632)
: money for small personal expenses

pocket mouse *noun* (1884)
: any of various nocturnal burrowing rodents (family Heteromyidae) that resemble mice, live in arid parts of western North America, and have long hind legs and tail and fur-lined cheek pouches

pock·et·size \'pä-kət-ˌsīz\ *also* **pock·et·sized** \-ˌsīzd\ *adjective* (1907)
1 : of a size convenient for carrying in the pocket
2 : SMALL ⟨a *pocket-size* country⟩

pocket mouse

pocket veto *noun* (1842)
: an indirect veto of a legislative bill by an executive through retention of the bill unsigned until after adjournment of the legislature
— **pocket veto** *transitive verb*

¹**pock·mark** \'päk-ˌmärk\ *noun* (circa 1673)
: a mark, pit, or depressed scar caused by smallpox or acne; *also* : an imperfection or depression like a pockmark

²**pockmark** *transitive verb* (1756)
: to cover with or as if with pockmarks : PIT

pocky \'pä-kē\ *adjective* (14th century)
: covered with pocks

po·co \'pō-(ˌ)kō, 'pȯ-\ *adverb* [Italian, little, from Latin *paucus* — more at FEW] (1724)
: to a slight degree : SOMEWHAT — used to qualify a direction in music ⟨*poco* allegro⟩

po·co a po·co \ˌpō-kō-(ˌ)ä-'pō-(ˌ)kō, ˌpȯ-kō-(ˌ)ä-'pȯ-kō\ *adverb* [Italian] (circa 1854)
: little by little : GRADUALLY — used as a direction in music

po·co·cu·ran·te \ˌpō-kō-kyu̇-'ran-tē, -ku̇-\ *adjective* [Italian *poco curante* caring little] (1815)
: INDIFFERENT, NONCHALANT
— **po·co·cu·ran·tism** \-'ran-ˌti-zəm\ *noun*

po·co·sin \pə-'kō-sᵊn\ *noun* [probably from Virginia or North Carolina Algonquian] (1634)
: an upland swamp of the coastal plain of the southeastern U.S.

¹**pod** \'päd\ *noun* [origin unknown] (1573)

1 : a bit socket in a brace
2 : a straight groove or channel in the barrel of an auger

²**pod** *noun* [probably alteration of *cod* bag — more at CODPIECE] (1688)
1 : a dry dehiscent pericarp or fruit that is composed of one or more carpels; *especially* : LEGUME
2 a : an anatomical pouch **b :** a grasshopper egg case
3 : a tapered and roughly cylindrical body of ore or mineral
4 : a usually protective container or housing: as **a :** a streamlined compartment (as for fuel) under the wings or fuselage of an aircraft **b :** compartment (as for personnel, a power unit, or an instrument) on a ship or craft

³**pod** *intransitive verb* **pod·ded; pod·ding** (1734)
: to produce pods

⁴**pod** *noun* [origin unknown] (1832)
: a number of animals (as whales) clustered together

-**pod** *noun combining form* [Greek *-podos*, from *pod-*, *pous* foot — more at FOOT]
: foot : part resembling a foot ⟨pleo*pod*⟩

po·dag·ra \pə-'da-grə\ *noun* [Middle English, from Latin, from Greek, literally, foot trap, from *pod-*, *pous* + *agra* hunt, catch; probably akin to Greek *agein* to drive, lead — more at AGENT] (14th century)
: a painful condition of the big toe caused by gout

pod corn *noun* (1893)
: an Indian corn that has each kernel enclosed in a chaffy shell similar to that of other cereals

po·de·sta \ˌpō-dā-'stä\ *noun* [Italian *podestà*, literally, power, from Latin *potestat-*, *potestas*, irregular from *potis* able — more at POTENT] (1548)
: a chief magistrate in a medieval Italian municipality

podgy \'pä-jē\ *adjective* **podg·i·er; -est** [*podge* something pudgy] (1846)
chiefly British : PUDGY

po·di·a·try \pə-'dī-ə-trē, pō-\ *noun* [Greek *pod-*, *pous* + English *-iatry*] (1914)
: the medical care and treatment of the human foot — called also *chiropody*
— **po·di·at·ric** \ˌpō-dē-'a-trik\ *adjective*
— **po·di·a·trist** \pə-'dī-ə-trist, pō-\ *noun*

po·di·um \'pō-dē-əm\ *noun, plural* **podiums** *or* **po·dia** \-dē-ə\ [Latin — more at PEW] (1743)
1 : a low wall serving as a foundation or terrace wall: as **a :** one around the arena of an ancient amphitheater serving as a base for the tiers of seats **b :** the masonry under the stylobate of a temple
2 a : a dais especially for an orchestral conductor **b :** LECTERN □

-**podium** *noun combining form, plural* **-podia** [New Latin, from Greek *podion*, diminutive of *pod-*, *pous* foot — more at FOOT]
: foot : part resembling a foot ⟨pseudo*podium*⟩

podo·phyl·lin \ˌpä-də-'fi-lən\ *noun* [International Scientific Vocabulary, from New Latin *Podophyllum*] (1851)
: a resin obtained from podophyllum and used in medicine as a caustic

podo·phyl·lum \-'fi-ləm\ *noun, plural* **-phyl·li** \-'fi-ˌlī\ *or* **-phyllums** [New Latin, from *Podophyllum*, genus of herbs including the mayapple] (1842)
: the dried rhizome and rootlet of the mayapple that is used as a caustic or as a source of the more effective podophyllin

Po·dunk \'pō-ˌdəŋk\ *noun* [*Podunk*, village in Mass. or locality in Conn.] (1846)
: a small, unimportant, and isolated town

pod·zol *also* **pod·sol** \'päd-ˌzȯl\ *noun* [Russian] (1908)
: any of a group of zonal soils that develop in a moist climate especially under coniferous or mixed forest and have an organic mat and a thin organic-mineral layer above a light gray

leached layer resting on a dark illuvial horizon enriched with amorphous clay
— **pod·zol·ic** \päd-'zä-lik, -'zȯ-\ *adjective*

pod·zol·i·za·tion *also* **pod·sol·i·za·tion** \ˌpäd-ˌzō-lə-'zā-shən\ *noun* (1912)
: a process of soil formation especially in humid regions involving principally leaching of the upper layers with accumulation of material in lower layers and development of characteristic horizons; *specifically* : the development of a podzol
— **pod·zol·ize** \'päd-ˌzō-ˌlīz\ *verb*

po·em \'pō-əm, -im, 'pōm *also* 'pȯ(-)im, 'pō-ˌem\ *noun* [Middle French *poeme*, from Latin *poema*, from Greek *poiēma*, from *poiein*] (15th century)
1 : a composition in verse
2 : something suggesting a poem (as in expressiveness, lyricism, or formal grace) ⟨the house we stayed in . . . was itself a *poem* —H. J. Laski⟩

po·e·sy \'pō-ə-zē, -sē\ *noun, plural* **po·e·sies** [Middle English *poesie*, from Middle French, from Latin *poesis*, from Greek *poiēsis*, literally, creation, from *poiein*] (14th century)
1 a : a poem or body of poems **b :** POETRY **c :** artificial or sentimentalized poetic writing
2 : poetic inspiration

po·et \'pō-ət, -it *also* 'pȯ(-)it\ *noun* [Middle English, from Middle French *poete*, from Latin *poeta*, from Greek *poiētēs* maker, poet, from *poiein* to make; akin to Sanskrit *cinoti* he gathers, heaps up] (14th century)
1 : one who writes poetry : a maker of verses
2 : one (as a creative artist) of great imaginative and expressive capabilities and special sensitivity to the medium

po·et·as·ter \'pō-ə-ˌtas-tər\ *noun* [New Latin, from Latin *poeta* + *-aster* -aster] (1599)
: an inferior poet

po·et·ess \'pō-ə-təs, 'pō-i- *also* 'pȯ(-)i-\ *noun* (1530)
: a girl or woman who is a poet
usage see -ESS

po·et·ic \pō-'e-tik\ *adjective* (1530)
1 a : of, relating to, or characteristic of poets or poetry **b :** given to writing poetry
2 : written in verse

po·et·i·cal \-ti-kəl\ *adjective* (14th century)
1 : POETIC
2 : being beyond or above the truth of history or nature : IDEALIZED ⟨had *poetical* ideas about love⟩
— **po·et·i·cal·ly** \-k(ə-)lē\ *adverb*
— **po·et·i·cal·ness** \-ti-kəl-nəs\ *noun*

po·et·i·cism \pō-'e-tə-ˌsi-zəm\ *noun* (1847)
: an archaic, trite, or strained expression in poetry

po·et·i·cize \-,sīz\ *transitive verb* **-cized; -ciz·ing** (1804)
: to give a poetic quality to
poetic justice *noun* (circa 1890)
: an outcome in which vice is punished and virtue rewarded usually in a manner peculiarly or ironically appropriate
poetic license *noun* (1819)
: LICENSE 4
po·et·ics \pō-'e-tiks\ *noun plural but singular or plural in construction* (circa 1741)
1 a : a treatise on poetry or aesthetics **b** *also* **po·et·ic** \-tik\ : poetic theory or practice
2 : poetic feelings or utterances
po·et·ize \'pō-ə-,tīz\ *verb* **-ized; -iz·ing** (1581)
intransitive verb
: to compose poetry
transitive verb
: POETICIZE
— **po·et·iz·er** *noun*
poet laureate *noun, plural* **poets laureate** *or* **poet laureates** (15th century)
1 : a poet honored for achievement in his art
2 : a poet appointed for life by an English sovereign as a member of the royal household and formerly expected to compose poems for court and national occasions
3 : one regarded by a country or region as its most eminent or representative poet
po·et·ry \'pō-ə-trē, -i-trē *also* 'pō(-)i-trē\ *noun* (14th century)
1 a : metrical writing : VERSE **b** : the productions of a poet : POEMS
2 : writing that formulates a concentrated imaginative awareness of experience in language chosen and arranged to create a specific emotional response through meaning, sound, and rhythm
3 a : something likened to poetry especially in beauty of expression **b** : poetic quality or aspect ⟨the *poetry* of dance⟩
po–faced \'pō-,fāst\ *adjective* [perhaps from *po* chamber pot, toilet, from French *pot* pot] (1934)
British : having an assumed solemn, serious, or earnest expression or manner : piously or hypocritically solemn
pog·o·nip \'päg-ə-,nip\ *noun* [Shoshone *paɣinappih* cloud] (1865)
: a dense winter fog containing frozen particles that is formed in deep mountain valleys of the western U.S.
po·go·noph·o·ran \,pō-gə-'nä-fə-rən\ *noun* [New Latin *Pogonophora*, from Greek *pōgō-nophora*, neuter plural of *pōgōnophoros* wearing a beard, from *pōgōn* beard + *-phoros* -phore] (1963)
: any of a phylum (Pogonophora) of marine wormlike animals of uncertain systematic relationships that live in chitinous tubes, have obscure segmentation, and lack a mouth and digestive tract
— **pogonophoran** *adjective*
po·go stick \'pō-(,)gō-\ *noun* [from *Pogo*, a trademark] (1921)
: a pole with a strong spring at the bottom and two footrests on which a person stands and moves along with a series of jumps
¹**po·grom** \'pō-grəm, 'pä-; pō-'gräm, pə-\ *noun* [Yiddish, from Russian, literally, devastation] (1903)
: an organized massacre of helpless people; *specifically* : such a massacre of Jews
²**pogrom** *transitive verb* (1915)
: to massacre or destroy in a pogrom
po·grom·ist \'pō-grə-mist, 'pä-; pō-'grä-, pə-\ *noun* (1907)
: one who organizes or takes part in a pogrom
po·gy \'pō-gē\ *noun, plural* **pogies** [by shortening & alteration from *poghaden*, perhaps from Eastern Abenaki] (circa 1847)
: MENHADEN
poi \'pȯi\ *noun, plural* **poi** *or* **pois** [Hawaiian & Samoan] (1823)

: a Hawaiian food of taro root cooked, pounded, and kneaded to a paste and often allowed to ferment
-poiesis *noun combining form, plural* **-poieses** [New Latin, from Greek *poiēsis* creation — more at POESY]
: production : formation ⟨hemato*poiesis*⟩
-poietic *adjective combining form* [Greek *poiētikos* creative, from *poiētēs* maker — more at POET]
: productive : formative ⟨hemato*poietic*⟩
poi·gnan·cy \'pȯi-nyən(t)s *sometimes* 'pȯi(g)-nən(t)s\ *noun* (1769)
: POIGNANCY
poi·gnan·cy \'pȯi-nyən(t)-sē *sometimes* 'pȯi(g)-nən(t)-sē\ *noun, plural* **-cies** (1730)
1 : the quality or state of being poignant
2 : an instance of poignancy
poi·gnant \'pȯi-nyənt *sometimes* 'pȯi(g)-nənt\ *adjective* [Middle English *poinaunt*, from Middle French *poignant*, present participle of *poindre* to prick, sting, from Latin *pungere* — more at PUNGENT] (14th century)
1 : pungently pervasive ⟨a *poignant* perfume⟩
2 a (1) : painfully affecting the feelings : PIERCING (2) : deeply affecting : TOUCHING **b** : designed to make an impression : CUTTING ⟨*poignant* satire⟩
3 a : pleasurably stimulating **b** : being to the point : APT
synonym see PUNGENT, MOVING
— **poi·gnant·ly** *adverb*
poi·ki·lo·therm \pȯi-'kē-lə-,thərm, -'ki-\ *noun* [Greek *poikilos* variegated + International Scientific Vocabulary *-therm* — more at PAINT] (1920)
: an organism (as a frog) with a variable body temperature that is usually slightly higher than the temperature of its environment : a cold-blooded organism
— **poi·ki·lo·ther·mic** \,pȯi-kə-lō-'thər-mik\ *adjective*
poi·lu \pwäl-'yü, pwä-'lü; 'pwäl-,yü, 'pwä-,lü; pwä-lǖ\ *noun* [French, from *poilu* hairy, from Middle French, from *poil* hair, from Latin *pilus*] (1914)
: a French soldier; *especially* : a front-line soldier in World War I
poin·ci·ana \,pȯin(t)-sē-'a-nə, ,p(w)än(t)-\ *noun* [New Latin, from De *Poinci*, 17th century governor of part of the French West Indies] (1731)
: any of several ornamental tropical leguminous trees or shrubs (genera *Caesalpinia* and *Delonix*) formerly placed in their own genus (*Poinciana*) — compare ROYAL POINCIANA
poin·set·tia \pȯin-'se-tē-ə, ÷pȯint-, ÷-'se-tə\ *noun* [New Latin, from Joel R. *Poinsett* (died 1851) American diplomat] (1836)
: any of several spurges (genus *Euphorbia*) with flower clusters subtended by showy involucral bracts; *especially* : a showy Mexican and Central American plant (*E. pulcherrima*) with tapering usually scarlet bracts that suggest petals and surround small yellow flowers

poinsettia

¹**point** \'pȯint\ *noun* [Middle English, partly from Old French, puncture, small spot, point in time or space, from Latin *punctum*, from neuter of *punctus*, past participle of *pungere* to prick; partly from Old French *pointe* sharp end, from (assumed) Vulgar Latin *puncta*, from Latin, feminine of *punctus*, past participle — more at PUNGENT] (13th century)
1 a (1) : an individual detail : ITEM (2) : a distinguishing detail ⟨tact is one of her strong

points⟩ **b** : the most important essential in a discussion or matter ⟨missed the whole *point* of the joke⟩ **c** : COGENCY
2 *obsolete* : physical condition
3 : an end or object to be achieved : PURPOSE ⟨did not see what *point* there was in continuing the discussion⟩
4 a (1) : a geometric element of which it is postulated that at least two exist and that two suffice to determine a line (2) : a geometric element determined by an ordered set of coordinates **b** (1) : a narrowly localized place having a precisely indicated position ⟨walked to a *point* 50 yards north of the building⟩ (2) : a particular place : LOCALITY ⟨have come from distant *points*⟩ **c** (1) : an exact moment ⟨at this *point* I was interrupted⟩ (2) : a time interval immediately before something indicated : VERGE ⟨at the *point* of death⟩ **d** (1) : a particular step, stage, or degree in development ⟨had reached the *point* where nothing seemed to matter anymore⟩ (2) : a definite position in a scale
5 a : the terminal usually sharp or narrowly rounded part of something : TIP **b** : a weapon or tool having such a part and used for stabbing or piercing: as (1) : ARROWHEAD (2) : SPEARHEAD **c** (1) : the contact or discharge extremity of an electric device (as a spark plug or distributor) (2) *chiefly British* : an electric outlet
6 a : a projecting usually tapering piece of land or a sharp prominence **b** (1) : the tip of a projecting body part (2) : TINE 2 (3) *plural* : the extremities or markings of the extremities of an animal especially when of a color differing from the rest of the body **c** (1) : a railroad switch (2) : the tip of the angle between two rails in a railroad frog **d** : the head of the bow of a stringed instrument
7 : a short musical phrase; *especially* : a phrase in contrapuntal music
8 a : a very small mark **b** (1) : PUNCTUATION MARK; *especially* : PERIOD (2) : DECIMAL POINT
9 : a lace for tying parts of a garment together used especially in the 16th and 17th centuries
10 : one of usually 11 divisions of a heraldic shield that determines the position of a charge
11 a : one of the 32 equidistant spots of a compass card **b** : the difference of 11¼ degrees between two such successive points
12 : a small detachment ahead of an advance guard or behind a rear guard
13 a : NEEDLEPOINT 1 **b** : lace made with a bobbin
14 : one of 12 spaces marked off on each side of a backgammon board
15 : a unit of measurement: as **a** (1) : a unit of counting in the scoring of a game or contest (2) : a unit used in evaluating the strength of a bridge hand **b** : a unit of academic credit **c** (1) : a unit used in quoting prices (as of stocks, bonds, and commodities) (2) *plural* : a percentage of the face value of a loan often added as a placement fee or service charge (3) : a percentage of the profits of a business venture (as a motion-picture production) **d** : a unit of about ¹⁄₇₂ inch used especially to measure the size of type
16 : the action of pointing: as **a** : the rigidly intent attitude of a hunting dog marking game for a gunner **b** : the action in dancing of extending one leg and arching the foot so that only the tips of the toes touch the floor
17 : a position of a player in various games (as lacrosse); *also* : the player of such a position
18 : a number thrown on the first roll of the dice in craps which the player attempts to repeat before throwing a seven — compare MISSOUT, PASS 13
19 : credit accruing from creating a good impression ⟨scored *points* for hard work⟩
— **beside the point** : IRRELEVANT
— **in point of** : with regard to : in the matter of ⟨*in point of* law⟩ ⟨*in point of* fact⟩

— to the point : RELEVANT, PERTINENT ⟨a suggestion that was *to the point*⟩

²**point** (14th century)
transitive verb
1 a : to furnish with a point : SHARPEN ⟨*pointing* a pencil with a knife⟩ **b** : to give added force, emphasis, or piquancy to ⟨*point* up a remark⟩
2 : to scratch out the old mortar from the joints of (as a brick wall) and fill in with new material
3 a (1) : to mark the pauses or grammatical divisions in : PUNCTUATE (2) : to separate (a decimal fraction) from an integer by a decimal point — usually used with *off* **b** : to mark (as Hebrew words) with diacritics (as vowel points)
4 a (1) : to indicate the position or direction of especially by extending a finger ⟨*point* the way home⟩ (2) : to direct someone's attention to ⟨*point* the way to new knowledge —Elizabeth Hall⟩ — usually used with *out* or *up* ⟨*point* out a mistake⟩ ⟨*points* up the difference⟩ **b** *of a hunting dog* : to indicate the presence and place of (game) by a point
5 a : to cause to be turned in a particular direction ⟨*point* a gun⟩ ⟨*pointed* the boat upstream⟩ **b** : to extend (a leg) and arch (the foot) in executing a point in dancing
intransitive verb
1 a : to indicate the fact or probability of something specified ⟨everything *points* to a bright future⟩ **b** : to indicate the position or direction of something especially by extending a finger ⟨*point* at the map⟩ **c** : to direct attention ⟨can *point* with pride to their own traditions⟩ **d** : to point game ⟨a dog that *points* well⟩
2 a : to lie extended, aimed, or turned in a particular direction ⟨a directional arrow that *pointed* to the north⟩ **b** : to execute a point in dancing
3 *of a ship* : to sail close to the wind
4 : to train for a particular contest
point–blank \ˈpȯint-ˈblaŋk\ *adjective* (1591)
1 a : marked by no appreciable drop below initial horizontal line of flight **b** : so close to a target that a missile fired will travel in a straight line to the mark
2 : DIRECT, BLUNT ⟨a *point-blank* refusal⟩
— point–blank *adverb*
point count *noun* (1950)
: a method of evaluating the strength of a hand in bridge by counting points for each high card and usually for long or short suits; *also* : the value of a hand so evaluated
point d'ap·pui \ˌpwaⁿ(n)-da-ˈpwē\ *noun, plural* **points d'appui** *same*\ [French, literally, point of support] (1819)
: FOUNDATION, BASE
point–de·vice \ˌpȯint-di-ˈvīs\ *adjective* [Middle English *at point devis* at a fixed point] (1526)
archaic : marked by punctilious attention to detail : METICULOUS
— point–device *adverb, archaic*
pointe \ˈpwaⁿ(n)t\ *noun* [French *pointe* (*du pied*), literally, tiptoe] (1846)
: a ballet position in which the body is balanced on the extreme tip of the toe
¹**point·ed** \ˈpȯin-təd\ *adjective* (14th century)
1 a : having a point **b** : being an arch with a pointed crown; *also* : marked by the use of a pointed arch ⟨*pointed* architecture⟩
2 a : being to the point : PERTINENT **b** : aimed at a particular person or group
3 : CONSPICUOUS, MARKED ⟨*pointed* indifference⟩
— point·ed·ly *adverb*
— point·ed·ness *noun*
²**pointed** *adjective* [short for *appointed*] (1523)
obsolete : SET, FIXED
poin·telle \ˌpȯin-ˈtel\ *noun* [perhaps from ¹*point* + *-elle* (as in *dentelle* lace)] (1953)

: an openwork design (as in knitted fabric) typically in the shape of chevrons; *also* : a fabric with this design
point·er \ˈpȯin-tər\ *noun* (1574)
1 a *plural, capitalized* : the two stars in the Big Dipper a line through which points to the North Star **b** : one that points out; *especially* : a rod used to direct attention **c** : a computer memory address that contains another address (as of desired data)
2 : a large strong slender smooth-haired gundog that hunts by scent and indicates the presence of game by pointing
3 : one that furnishes with points
4 : a useful suggestion or hint : TIP
point estimate *noun* (1966)
: the single value assigned to a parameter in point estimation
point estimation *noun* (1962)
: estimation in which a single value is assigned to a parameter
point guard *noun* (1970)
: a guard in basketball who is chiefly responsible for running the offense
poin·til·lism \ˈpwaⁿ(n)-tē-ˌyi-zəm, ˈpȯin-tᵊl-ˌi-zəm\ *noun, often capitalized* [French *pointillisme*, from *pointiller* to stipple, from *point* spot — more at POINT] (1901)
: the theory or practice in art of applying small strokes or dots of color to a surface so that from a distance they blend together
— poin·til·list \ˌpwaⁿ(n)-tē-ˈyēst, ˈpȯin-tᵊl-ist\ *noun*
poin·til·lis·tic \ˌpwaⁿ(n)-tē-ˈyis-tik, ˌpȯin-tᵊl-ˈis-\ *also* **point·til·list** \ˌpwaⁿ(n)-tē-ˈyēst, ˈpȯin-tᵊl-ist\ *adjective* (1922)
1 : composed of many discrete details or parts
2 : of, relating to, or characteristic of pointillism or pointillists
point lace *noun* (1672)
: NEEDLEPOINT 1
point·less \ˈpȯint-ləs\ *adjective* (1726)
1 : devoid of meaning : SENSELESS ⟨a *pointless* remark⟩
2 : devoid of effectiveness : FLAT ⟨*pointless* attempts to be funny⟩
— point·less·ly *adverb*
— point·less·ness *noun*
point man *noun* (1903)
: a soldier who goes ahead of a patrol; *broadly* : one who is in the forefront (as on a political issue)
point mutation *noun* (1925)
: mutation due to intramolecular gene reorganization (as by substitution, addition, or deletion of a nucleotide)
point of accumulation (1929)
: LIMIT POINT
point of departure (1857)
: a starting point especially in a discussion
point of honor (1612)
: a matter seriously affecting one's honor
point of inflection (1743)
: INFLECTION POINT
point of no return (1941)
1 : the point in the flight of an aircraft beyond which the remaining fuel will be insufficient for a return to the starting point with the result that the craft must proceed
2 : a critical point at which turning back or reversal is not possible
point of view (1720)
: a position from which something is considered or evaluated : STANDPOINT
point set topology *noun* (1957)
: a branch of topology concerned with the properties and theory of topological spaces and metric spaces developed with emphasis on set theory
point source *noun* (1903)
: a source of radiation (as light) that is concentrated at a point and considered as having no spatial extension
point–to–point *noun* (1898)
: a cross-country steeplechase

pointy \ˈpȯin-tē\ *adjective* **point·i·er; -est** (1644)
1 : coming to a rather sharp point
2 : having parts that stick out sharply here and there
pointy–head \ˈpȯin-tē-ˌhed\ *noun* (1968)
: INTELLECTUAL — usually used disparagingly
— pointy–head·ed \-ˌhe-dəd\ *adjective*
¹**poise** \ˈpȯiz\ *noun* [Middle English *poyse* weight, heaviness, from Middle French *pois*, from Latin *pensum*, from neuter of *pensus*, past participle of *pendere* to weigh — more at PENDANT] (1555)
1 : a stably balanced state : EQUILIBRIUM ⟨a *poise* between widely divergent impulses —F. R. Leavis⟩
2 a : easy self-possessed assurance of manner : gracious tact in coping or handling; *also* : the pleasantly tranquil interaction between persons of poise ⟨no angry outbursts marred the *poise* of the meeting⟩ **b** : a particular way of carrying oneself : BEARING, CARRIAGE
synonym see TACT
²**poise** *verb* **poised; pois·ing** [Middle English, to weigh, ponder, from Middle French *pois-*, stem of *peser*, from Latin *pensare* — more at PENSIVE] (1598)
transitive verb
1 a : BALANCE; *especially* : to hold or carry in equilibrium ⟨carried a water jar *poised* on her head⟩ **b** : to hold supported or suspended without motion in a steady position ⟨*poised* her fork and gave her guest a knowing look —Louis Bromfield⟩
2 : to hold or carry (the head) in a particular way
3 : to put into readiness : BRACE
intransitive verb
1 : to become drawn up into readiness
2 : HOVER
³**poise** \ˈpwäz\ *noun* [French, from Jean Louis Marie *Poiseuille* (died 1869) French physician and anatomist] (1913)
: a centimeter-gram-second unit of viscosity equal to the viscosity of a fluid that would require a shearing force of one dyne to move a square-centimeter area of either of two parallel layers of fluid one centimeter apart with a velocity of one centimeter per second relative to the other layer with the space between the layers being filled with the fluid
poised \ˈpȯizd\ *adjective* (circa 1643)
: having poise: **a** : marked by balance or equilibrium **b** : marked by easy composure of manner or bearing
poi·sha \ˈpȯi-shə\ *noun, plural* **poisha** [Bengali, from Hindi *paisā*] (circa 1976)
: the paisa of Bangladesh
¹**poi·son** \ˈpȯi-zᵊn\ *noun* [Middle English, from Middle French, drink, poisonous drink, poison, from Latin *potion-, potio* drink — more at POTION] (13th century)
1 a : a substance that through its chemical action usually kills, injures, or impairs an organism **b** (1) : something destructive or harmful (2) : an object of aversion or abhorrence
2 : a substance that inhibits the activity of another substance or the course of a reaction or process ⟨a catalyst *poison*⟩
word history see VENOM
²**poison** *transitive verb* **poi·soned; poi·son·ing** \ˈpȯiz-niŋ, ˈpȯi-zᵊn-iŋ\ (14th century)
1 a : to injure or kill with poison **b** : to treat, taint, or impregnate with or as if with poison
2 : to exert a baneful influence on : CORRUPT ⟨*poisoned* their minds⟩
3 : to inhibit the activity, course, or occurrence of
— poi·son·er \ˈpȯiz-nər, ˈpȯi-zᵊn-ər\ *noun*
³**poison** *adjective* (1530)

\ə\ abut \ᵊ\ kitten \ər\ further \a\ ash \ā\ ace
\ä\ mop, mar \aů\ out \ch\ chin \e\ bet \ē\ easy
\g\ go \i\ hit \ī\ ice \j\ job \ŋ\ sing \ō\ go
\ȯ\ law \ȯi\ boy \th\ thin \th\ the \ü\ loot \ů\ foot
\y\ yet \zh\ vision *see also* Guide to Pronunciation

1 : POISONOUS, VENOMOUS ⟨a *poison* plant⟩ ⟨a *poison* tongue⟩
2 : impregnated with poison **:** POISONED ⟨a *poison* arrow⟩
poison gas *noun* (1915)
: a poisonous gas or a liquid or a solid giving off poisonous vapors designed (as in chemical warfare) to kill, injure, or disable by inhalation or contact
poison hemlock *noun* (circa 1818)
1 : a large branching biennial poisonous herb (*Conium maculatum*) of the carrot family with finely divided leaves and white flowers
2 : WATER HEMLOCK
poison ivy *noun* (1784)
1 a : a climbing plant (*Rhus radicans*) of the cashew family that is especially common in the eastern and central U.S., that has ternate leaves, greenish flowers, and white berries, and that produces an acutely irritating oil causing a usually intensely itching skin rash **b :** any of several

poison ivy 1a

plants (as poison oak) closely related to poison ivy
2 : a skin rash caused by poison ivy
poison oak *noun* (1743)
1 : any of several plants of the same genus (*Rhus*) as poison ivy that produce an oil with similar irritating properties: **a :** a bushy plant (*Rhus diversiloba*) of the Pacific coast **b :** a bushy plant (*Rhus toxicodendron* synonym *R. quercifolia*) of the southeastern U.S.
2 : POISON IVY 1
poi·son·ous \'pȯiz-nəs, 'pȯi-zⁿ-əs\ *adjective* (circa 1580)
1 : having the properties or effects of poison **:** VENOMOUS
2 : DESTRUCTIVE, HARMFUL
3 : SPITEFUL, MALICIOUS
— poi·son·ous·ly *adverb*
poison-pen *adjective* (1925)
: written with malice and spite and usually anonymously ⟨*poison-pen* letter⟩
poison pill *noun* (1983)
: a financial tactic (as increasing indebtedness) used by a company to deter an unwanted takeover
poison sumac *noun* (1817)
: a smooth American swamp shrub (*Rhus vernix*) that has pinnate leaves, greenish flowers, and greenish white berries and produces an irritating oil — called also *poison dogwood*
poi·son·wood \'pȯi-zⁿ-ˌwu̇d\ *noun* (1721)
: a poisonous tree (*Metopium toxiferum*) of the cashew family that is native to Florida and the West Indies and has compound leaves, greenish paniculate flowers, and orange-yellow fruits
Pois·son distribution \pwä-'sōⁿ-\ *noun* [Siméon D. *Poisson* (died 1840) French mathematician] (1922)
: a probability density function that is often used as a mathematical model of the number of outcomes obtained in a suitable interval of time and space, that has its mean equal to its variance, that is used as an approximation to the binomial distribution, and that has the form

$$f(x) = \frac{e^{-\mu}\mu^x}{x!} \text{ where } \mu$$

is the mean and *x* takes on nonnegative integral values
Poisson's ratio *noun* [S. *Poisson*] (1886)
: the ratio of transverse to longitudinal strain in a material under tension
¹poke \'pōk\ *noun* [Middle English, from Old North French — more at POCKET] (13th century)

1 *chiefly Southern & Midland* **:** BAG, SACK
2 a : WALLET **b :** PURSE
²poke *verb* **poked; pok·ing** [Middle English; akin to Middle Dutch *poken* to poke] (14th century)
transitive verb
1 a (1) **:** PROD, JAB ⟨*poked* him in the ribs⟩ (2) **:** to urge or stir by prodding or jabbing (3) **:** to cause to prod **:** THRUST ⟨*poked* a stick at the snake⟩ **b** (1) **:** PIERCE, STAB (2) **:** to produce by piercing, stabbing, or jabbing ⟨*poke* a hole⟩ **c** (1) **:** HIT, PUNCH ⟨*poked* him in the nose⟩ (2) **:** to deliver (a blow) with the fist
2 a : to cause to project ⟨*poked* her head out of the window⟩ **b :** to make (one's way) by poking ⟨*poked* his way through the ruins⟩ **c :** to interpose or interject in a meddlesome manner ⟨asked him not to *poke* his nose into other people's business⟩
intransitive verb
1 a : to make a prodding, jabbing, or thrusting movement especially repeatedly **b :** to strike out at something
2 a : to look about or through something without system **:** RUMMAGE ⟨*poking* around in the attic⟩ **b :** MEDDLE
3 : to move or act slowly or aimlessly ⟨just *poked* around and didn't accomplish much⟩
4 : to become stuck out or forward **:** PROTRUDE
— poke fun at : RIDICULE, MOCK
³poke *noun* (circa 1796)
1 a : a quick thrust **:** JAB **b :** a blow with the fist **:** PUNCH
2 : a projecting brim on the front of a woman's bonnet
⁴poke *noun* [perhaps modification of Virginia Algonquian *pocone, poughkone* puccoon] (1708)
: POKEWEED
poke·ber·ry \'pōk-ˌber-ē\ *noun* (1774)
: the berry of the pokeweed; *also* **:** POKEWEED
poke bonnet *noun* (1820)
: a woman's bonnet with a projecting brim at the front
¹pok·er \'pō-kər\ *noun* (1534)
: one that pokes; *especially* **:** a metal rod for stirring a fire
²po·ker \'pō-kər\ *noun* [probably modification of French *poque,* a card game similar to poker] (1836)
: any of several card games in which a player bets that the value of his or her hand is greater than that of the hands held by others, in which each subsequent player must either equal or raise the bet or drop out, and in which the player holding the highest hand at the end of the betting wins the pot

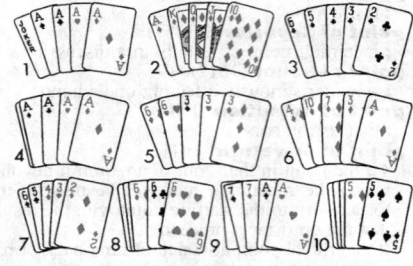

poker hands in descending value: *1* five of a kind, *2* royal flush, *3* straight flush, *4* four of a kind, *5* full house, *6* flush, *7* straight, *8* three of a kind, *9* two pairs, *10* one pair

poker face *noun* [²*poker;* from the poker player's need to conceal emotions during play] (1885)
: an inscrutable face that reveals no hint of a person's thoughts or feelings
— po·ker-faced \'pō-kər-ˌfāst\ *adjective*
poke·weed \'pōk-ˌwēd\ *noun* (1751)
: a coarse American perennial herb (*Phytolacca americana* of the family Phytolaccaceae,

the pokeweed family) with racemose white flowers, dark purple juicy berries, a poisonous root, and young shoots sometimes used as potherbs
po·key \'pō-kē\ *noun, plural* **pokeys** [origin unknown] (circa 1919)
slang **:** JAIL
poky *or* **pok·ey** \'pō-kē\ *adjective* **pok·i·er; -est** [²*poke*] (1849)
1 : small and cramped
2 : SHABBY, DULL
3 : annoyingly slow
— pok·i·ly \-kə-lē\ *adverb*
— pok·i·ness \-kē-nəs\ *noun*
pol \'päl\ *noun* (circa 1942)
: POLITICIAN
Po·la·bi·an \pō-'lä-bē-ən, -'lä-\ *noun* [*Polab,* ultimately from Polabian *po* on + *Låbí,* the Elbe River] (1866)
1 *or* **Po·lab** \pō-'läb\ **:** a member of a Slavic people formerly dwelling in the basin of the Elbe and on the Baltic coast of Germany
2 : the extinct West Slavic language of the Polabians
Po·lack \'pō-ˌläk, -ˌlak\ *noun* [Polish *polak*] (1574)
1 *obsolete* **:** a native or inhabitant of Poland
2 : a person of Polish birth or descent — usually used disparagingly
Po·land Chi·na \'pō-lən(d)-'chī-nə\ *noun* [*Poland,* Europe + *China,* Asia] (1879)
: any of an American breed of large white-marked black swine
¹po·lar \'pō-lər\ *adjective* [New Latin *polaris,* from Latin *polus* pole] (1551)
1 a : of or relating to a geographical pole or the region around it **b :** coming from or having the characteristics of such a region **c** (1) **:** passing over a celestial body's north and south poles ⟨a satellite in a *polar* orbit⟩ (2) **:** traveling in a polar orbit ⟨a *polar* satellite⟩
2 : of or relating to one or more poles (as of a magnet)
3 : serving as a guide
4 : diametrically opposite
5 : exhibiting polarity; *especially* **:** having a dipole or characterized by molecules having dipoles ⟨a *polar* solvent⟩
6 : resembling a pole or axis around which all else revolves **:** PIVOTAL
7 : of, relating to, or expressed in polar coordinates ⟨*polar* equations⟩; *also* **:** of or relating to a polar coordinate system
²polar *noun* (1848)
: a straight line related to a point; *specifically* **:** the straight line joining the points of contact of the tangents from a point exterior to a conic section
polar bear *noun* (1781)
: a large creamy-white bear (*Thalarctos maritimus* synonym *Ursus maritimus*) that inhabits arctic regions

polar bear

polar body *noun* (1888)
: a cell that separates from an oocyte during meiosis and that contains a nucleus produced in the first or second meiotic division but very little cytoplasm
polar circle *noun* (1551)
: either of the two parallels of latitude each at a distance from a pole of the earth equal to about 23 degrees 27 minutes
polar coordinate *noun* (1816)
: either of two numbers that locate a point in a plane by its distance from a fixed point on a line and the angle this line makes with a fixed line
polar front *noun* (1920)
: the boundary between the cold air of a polar region and the warmer air of lower latitudes

po·lar·im·e·ter \ˌpō-lə-'ri-mə-tər\ *noun* [International Scientific Vocabulary, from *polarization*] (circa 1859)
1 : an instrument for determining the amount of polarization of light or the proportion of polarized light in a partially polarized ray
2 : a polariscope for measuring the amount of rotation of the plane of polarization especially by liquids
— **po·lar·i·met·ric** \pō-ˌlar-ə-'me-trik\ *adjective*
— **po·lar·im·e·try** \ˌpō-lə-'ri-mə-trē\ *noun*
Po·lar·is \pə-'lar-əs, -'lär-\ *noun* [New Latin, from *polaris* polar]
: NORTH STAR
po·lar·ise *British variant of* POLARIZE
po·lar·i·scope \pō-'lar-ə-ˌskōp\ *noun* [International Scientific Vocabulary, from *polarization*] (1829)
1 : an instrument for studying the properties of or examining substances in polarized light
2 : POLARIMETER 2
— **po·lar·i·scop·ic** \-ˌlar-ə-'skä-pik\ *adjective*
po·lar·i·ty \pō-'lar-ə-tē, pə-\ *noun, plural* **-ties** (1646)
1 : the quality or condition inherent in a body that exhibits opposite properties or powers in opposite parts or directions or that exhibits contrasted properties or powers in contrasted parts or directions : the condition of having poles
2 : attraction toward a particular object or in a specific direction
3 : the particular state either positive or negative with reference to the two poles or to electrification
4 a : diametrical opposition **b** : an instance of such opposition
po·lar·i·za·tion \ˌpō-lə-rə-'zā-shən\ *noun* (1812)
1 : the action of polarizing or state of being or becoming polarized: as **a** (1) : the action or process of affecting radiation and especially light so that the vibrations of the wave assume a definite form (2) : the state of radiation affected by this process **b** : an increase in the resistance of an electrolytic cell often caused by the deposition of gas on one or both electrodes **c** : MAGNETIZATION
2 a : division into two opposites **b** : concentration about opposing extremes of groups or interests formerly ranged on a continuum
po·lar·ize \'pō-lə-ˌrīz\ *verb* **-ized; -iz·ing** [French *polariser*, from New Latin *polaris* polar] (1811)
transitive verb
1 : to cause (as light waves) to vibrate in a definite pattern
2 : to give physical polarity to
3 : to break up into opposing factions or groupings ⟨a campaign that *polarized* the electorate⟩
4 : CONCENTRATE 1 ⟨recreate a cohesive rock community by *polarizing* . . . an amorphous, fragmented audience —Ellen Willis⟩
intransitive verb
: to become polarized
— **po·lar·iz·abil·i·ty** \ˌpō-lə-ˌrī-zə-'bi-lə-tē\ *noun*
— **po·lar·iz·able** \ˌpō-lə-'rī-zə-bəl\ *adjective*
polar nucleus *noun* (1882)
: either of the two nuclei of a seed plant embryo sac that are destined to form endosperm
po·lar·og·ra·phy \ˌpō-lə-'rä-grə-fē\ *noun* [International Scientific Vocabulary, from *polarization*] (1936)
: a method of qualitative or quantitative analysis based on current-voltage curves obtained during electrolysis of a solution with a steadily increasing electromotive force
— **po·lar·o·graph·ic** \ˌpō-ˌlar-ə-'gra-fik\ *adjective*
— **po·lar·o·graph·i·cal·ly** \-fi-k(ə-)lē\ *adverb*

Po·lar·oid \'pō-lə-ˌròid\ *trademark*
— used especially for a light-polarizing material used especially in eyeglasses and lamps to prevent glare or for a camera that develops pictures instantly
po·lar·on \'pō-lə-ˌrän\ *noun* [International Scientific Vocabulary *polar* + ²*-on*] (1946)
: a conducting electron in an ionic crystal together with the induced polarization of the surrounding lattice
pol·der \'pōl-dər\ *noun* [Dutch] (1604)
: a tract of low land (as in the Netherlands) reclaimed from a body of water (as the sea)
¹pole \'pōl\ *noun* [Middle English, from Old English *pāl* stake, pole, from Latin *palus* stake; akin to Latin *pangere* to fix — more at PACT] (before 12th century)
1 a : a long slender usually cylindrical object (as a length of wood) **b** : a shaft which extends from the front axle of a wagon between wheelhorses and by which the wagon is drawn : TONGUE **c** : a long staff of wood, metal, or fiberglass used in the pole vault
2 a : a varying unit of length; *especially* : one measuring 16½ feet (5.03 meters) **b** : a unit of area equal to a square rod (25.293 square meters)
3 : a tree with a breast-high diameter of from 4 to 12 inches (10 to 30 centimeters)
4 : the inside front row position on the starting line for a race
²pole *verb* **poled; pol·ing** (1573)
transitive verb
1 : to act upon with a pole
2 : to impel or push with a pole
intransitive verb
1 : to propel a boat with a pole
2 : to use ski poles to gain speed
³pole *noun* [Middle English, from Latin *polus*, from Greek *polos* pivot, pole; akin to Greek *pelesthai* to become, Sanskrit *carati* he moves, wanders — more at WHEEL] (14th century)
1 : either extremity of an axis of a sphere and especially of the earth's axis
2 a : either of two related opposites **b** : a point of guidance or attraction
3 a : either of the two terminals of an electric cell, battery, generator, or motor **b** : one of two or more regions in a magnetized body at which the magnetic flux density is concentrated
4 : either of two morphologically or physiologically differentiated areas at opposite ends of an axis in an organism or cell — see BLASTULA illustration
5 a : the fixed point in a system of polar coordinates that serves as the origin **b** : the point of origin of two tangents to a conic section that determine a polar
— **poles apart** : as diametrically opposed as possible
Pole \'pōl\ *noun* [German, of Slavic origin; akin to Polish *polak* Pole] (1535)
1 : a native or inhabitant of Poland
2 : a person of Polish descent
¹pole·ax \'pō-ˌlaks\ *noun* [Middle English *polax, pollax*, from *pol, polle* poll + *ax*] (14th century)
1 : a battle-ax with a short handle and often a hook or spike opposite the blade; *also* : one with a long handle used as an ornamental weapon
2 : an ax used in slaughtering cattle
²poleax *transitive verb* (1882)
: to attack, strike, or fell with or as if with a poleax
pole bean *noun* (circa 1770)
: a cultivated bean that is usually trained to grow upright on supports
pole·cat \'pōl-ˌkat\ *noun, plural* **polecats** *or* **polecat** [Middle English *polcat*, probably from Middle French *poul, pol* cock + Middle English *cat*; probably from its preying on poultry — more at PULLET] (14th century)
1 : any of several carnivorous mammals (as of the genera *Mustela* or *Vormela*) of the weasel

family; *especially* : a brown to black European mammal (*M. putorius*) from which the domesticated ferret is derived
2 : SKUNK
word history *see* FERRET
poleis *plural of* POLIS
pole·less \'pōl-ləs\ *adjective* (1647)
: having no pole
po·lem·ic \pə-'le-mik\ *noun* [French *polémique*, from Middle French, from *polemique* controversial, from Greek *polemikos* warlike, hostile, from *polemos* war; perhaps akin to Greek *pelemizein* to shake, Old English ea*lfelo* baleful] (1638)
1 a : an aggressive attack on or refutation of the opinions or principles of another **b** : the art or practice of disputation or controversy — usually used in plural but singular or plural in construction
2 : an aggressive controversialist : DISPUTANT
— **po·lem·i·cist** \-'le-mə-sist\ *noun*
po·lem·i·cal \-mi-kəl\ *also* **po·lem·ic** \-mik\ *adjective* (1640)
1 : of, relating to, or being a polemic : CONTROVERSIAL
2 : engaged in or addicted to polemics : DISPUTATIOUS
— **po·lem·i·cal·ly** \-mi-k(ə-)lē\ *adverb*
po·lem·i·cize \-'le-mə-ˌsīz\ *intransitive verb* **-cized; -ciz·ing** (1950)
: to engage in controversy : deliver a polemic
po·le·mist \pə-'le-mist, 'pä-lə-mist\ *noun* (1825)
: one skilled in or given to polemics
pol·e·mize \'pä-lə-ˌmīz\ *intransitive verb* **-mized; -miz·ing** (1828)
: POLEMICIZE
pol·e·mo·ni·um \ˌpä-lə-'mō-nē-əm\ *noun* [New Latin, from Greek *polemōnion*, a plant] (1900)
: JACOB'S LADDER 1
po·len·ta \pō-'len-tə, pə-, -ˌtä\ *noun* [Italian, from Latin, crushed and hulled barley; akin to Latin *pollen* fine flour] (1764)
: mush made of chestnut meal, cornmeal, semolina, or farina
pol·er \'pō-lər\ *noun* (1848)
: one that poles; *especially* : one that poles a boat
pole·star \'pōl-ˌstär\ *noun*
1 : NORTH STAR
2 a : a directing principle : GUIDE **b** : a center of attraction
pole vault *noun* (circa 1890)
: a vault with the aid of a pole; *specifically* : a field event consisting of a vault for height over a crossbar
— **pole–vault** *intransitive verb*
— **pole–vaulter** *noun*
pole·ward \'pōl-wərd\ *adverb or adjective* (1875)
: toward or in the direction of a pole of the earth ⟨as the sun moves *poleward*⟩ ⟨*poleward* variation in temperature⟩
¹po·lice \pə-'lēs\ *transitive verb* **po·liced; po·lic·ing** [in sense 1, from Middle French *policier*, from *police* conduct of public affairs; in other senses, from ²*police*] (1589)
1 *archaic* : GOVERN
2 : to control, regulate, or keep in order by use of police
3 : to make clean and put in order
4 a : to supervise the operation, execution, or administration of to prevent or detect and prosecute violations of rules and regulations **b** : to exercise such supervision over the policies and activities of
5 : to perform the functions of a police force in or over

²**police** *noun, plural* **police** *often attributive* [French, from Late Latin *politia* government, administration, from Greek *politeia*, from *polītēs* citizen, from *polis* city, state; akin to Sanskrit *pur* rampart, Lithuanian *pilis* castle] (1716)
1 a : the internal organization or regulation of a political unit through exercise of governmental powers especially with respect to general comfort, health, morals, safety, or prosperity **b :** control and regulation of affairs affecting the general order and welfare of any unit or area **c :** the system of laws for effecting such control
2 a : the department of government concerned primarily with maintenance of public order, safety, and health and enforcement of laws and possessing executive, judicial, and legislative powers **b :** the department of government charged with prevention, detection, and prosecution of public nuisances and crimes
3 a : POLICE FORCE **b** *plural* **:** POLICE OFFICERS
4 a : a private organization resembling a police force ⟨campus *police*⟩ **b** *plural* **:** the members of a private police organization
5 a : the action or process of cleaning and putting in order **b :** military personnel detailed to perform this function
police action *noun* (1933)
: a localized military action undertaken without formal declaration of war by regular armed forces against persons (as guerrillas or aggressors) held to be violators of international peace and order
police court *noun* (1823)
: a court of record that has jurisdiction over various minor offenses (as breach of the peace) and the power to bind over for trial in a superior court or for a grand jury persons accused of more serious offenses
police dog *noun* (1908)
1 : a dog trained to assist police (as in drug detection)
2 : GERMAN SHEPHERD
police force *noun* (1838)
: a body of trained officers entrusted by a government with maintenance of public peace and order, enforcement of laws, and prevention and detection of crime
po·lice·man \pə-'lēs-mən\ *noun* (1801)
1 : a member of a police force
2 : one held to resemble a policeman ⟨making the United States the *policeman* for the whole wide world —R. B. Long⟩
police officer *noun* (1800)
: a member of a police force
police power *noun* (1827)
: the inherent power of a government to exercise reasonable control over persons and property within its jurisdiction in the interest of the general security, health, safety, morals, and welfare except where legally prohibited
police procedural *noun, plural* **police procedurals** (1967)
: a mystery story written from the point of view of the police investigating the crime
police reporter *noun* (1834)
: a reporter regularly assigned to cover police news (as crimes and arrests)
police state *noun* (1865)
: a political unit characterized by repressive governmental control of political, economic, and social life usually by an arbitrary exercise of power by police and especially secret police in place of regular operation of administrative and judicial organs of the government according to publicly known legal procedures
police station *noun* (1846)
: the headquarters of the police for a locality
po·lice·wom·an \pə-'lēs-ˌwu̇-mən\ *noun* (1853)
: a woman who is a member of a police force
¹**pol·i·cy** \'pä-lə-sē\ *noun, plural* **-cies** *often attributive* [Middle English *policie* government, policy, from Middle French, govern-

ment, regulation, from Late Latin *politia*] (15th century)
1 a : prudence or wisdom in the management of affairs **b :** management or procedure based primarily on material interest
2 a : a definite course or method of action selected from among alternatives and in light of given conditions to guide and determine present and future decisions **b :** a high-level overall plan embracing the general goals and acceptable procedures especially of a governmental body
²**policy** *noun, plural* **-cies** [alteration of earlier *police*, from Middle French, certificate, from Old Italian *polizza*, modification of Medieval Latin *apodixa* receipt, from Middle Greek *apodeixis*, from Greek, proof, from *apodeiknynai* to demonstrate — more at APODICTIC] (1565)
1 : a writing whereby a contract of insurance is made
2 a : a daily lottery in which participants bet that certain numbers will be drawn from a lottery wheel **b :** NUMBER 7a
pol·i·cy·hold·er \'pä-lə-sē-ˌhōl-dər\ *noun* (1851)
: the owner of an insurance policy
policy science *noun* (1950)
: a social science dealing with the making of high-level policy (as in a government or business)
po·lio \'pō-lē-ˌō\ *noun* (1931)
: POLIOMYELITIS
po·lio·my·eli·tis \ˌpō-lē-(ˌ)ō-ˌmī-ə-'lī-təs\ *noun* [New Latin, from Greek *polios* gray + *myelos* marrow — more at FALLOW, MYEL-] (1878)
: an acute infectious virus disease characterized by fever, motor paralysis, and atrophy of skeletal muscles often with permanent disability and deformity and marked by inflammation of nerve cells in the anterior gray matter in each lateral half of the spinal cord — called also *infantile paralysis*
po·lio·vi·rus \'pō-lē-(ˌ)ō-ˌvī-rəs\ *noun* [New Latin, from *polio*myelitis + *virus*] (1953)
: an enterovirus that occurs in several antigenically distinct forms and is the causative agent of human poliomyelitis
po·lis \'pä-ləs\ *noun, plural* **po·leis** \'pä-ˌlās\ [Greek — more at POLICE] (1894)
: a Greek city-state; *broadly* **:** a state or society especially when characterized by a sense of community
-polis *noun combining form* [Late Latin, from Greek, from *polis*]
: city ⟨megalo*polis*⟩
¹**pol·ish** \'pä-lish\ *verb* [Middle English *polisshen*, from Middle French *poliss-*, stem of *polir*, from Latin *polire*] (14th century)
transitive verb
1 : to make smooth and glossy usually by friction **:** BURNISH
2 : to smooth, soften, or refine in manners or condition
3 : to bring to a highly developed, finished, or refined state **:** PERFECT
intransitive verb
: to become smooth or glossy by or as if by friction
— pol·ish·er *noun*
²**polish** *noun* (1704)
1 a : a smooth glossy surface **:** LUSTER **b :** freedom from rudeness or coarseness **:** CULTURE **c :** a state of high development or refinement
2 : the action or process of polishing
3 : a preparation that is used to produce a gloss and often a color for the protection and decoration of a surface ⟨furniture *polish*⟩ ⟨nail *polish*⟩
¹**Pol·ish** \'pō-lish\ *adjective* [*Pole*] (1674)
: of, relating to, or characteristic of Poland, the Poles, or Polish
²**Polish** *noun* (1784)
: the Slavic language of the Poles

polish off *transitive verb* (1829)
: to finish off or dispose of rapidly or completely
po·lit·bu·ro \'pä-lət-ˌbyu̇r-(ˌ)ō, 'pō-lət-, pə-'lit-\ *noun* [Russian *politbyuro*, from *politicheskoe byuro* political bureau] (1925)
: the principal policy-making and executive committee of a Communist party
po·lite \pə-'līt\ *adjective* **po·lit·er; -est** [Latin *politus*, from past participle of *polire*] (1501)
1 a : of, relating to, or having the characteristics of advanced culture **b :** marked by refined cultural interests and pursuits especially in arts and belles lettres
2 a : showing or characterized by correct social usage **b :** marked by an appearance of consideration, tact, deference, or courtesy **c :** marked by a lack of roughness or crudities ⟨*polite* literature⟩
synonym see CIVIL
— po·lite·ly *adverb*
— po·lite·ness *noun*
po·li·tesse \ˌpä-li-'tes, ˌpȯ-\ *noun* [French, from Middle French, cleanness, from Old Italian *pulitezza*, from *pulito*, past participle of *pulire* to polish, clean, from Latin *polire*] (1717)
: formal politeness **:** DECOROUSNESS
pol·i·tic \'pä-lə-ˌtik\ *adjective* [Middle English *politik*, from Middle French *politique*, from Latin *politicus*, from Greek *politikos*, from *polītēs* citizen — more at POLICE] (15th century)
1 : POLITICAL
2 : characterized by shrewdness in managing, contriving, or dealing
3 : sagacious in promoting a policy
4 : shrewdly tactful
synonym see EXPEDIENT, SUAVE
po·lit·i·cal \pə-'li-ti-kəl\ *adjective* [Latin *politicus*] (1551)
1 a : of or relating to government, a government, or the conduct of government **b :** of, relating to, or concerned with the making as distinguished from the administration of governmental policy
2 : of, relating to, involving, or involved in politics and especially party politics
3 : organized in governmental terms ⟨*political* units⟩
4 : involving or charged or concerned with acts against a government or a political system ⟨*political* prisoners⟩
— po·lit·i·cal·ly \-k(ə-)lē\ *adverb*
political action committee *noun* (1944)
: a group formed (as by an industry or an issue-oriented organization) to raise and contribute money to the campaigns of candidates likely to advance the group's interests
political correctness *noun* (1990)
: conformity to a belief that language and practices which could offend political sensibilities should be eliminated
political economy *noun* (1740)
1 : ECONOMICS
2 : the theory or study of the role of public policy in influencing the economic and social welfare of a political unit
— political economist *noun*
po·lit·i·cal·ize \pə-'li-ti-kə-ˌlīz\ *transitive verb* **-ized; -izing** (1869)
: POLITICIZE
— po·lit·i·cal·i·za·tion \-ˌli-ti-kə-lə-'zā-shən\ *noun*
politically correct *adjective* (1936)
: conforming to a belief that language and practices which could offend political sensibilities (as in matters of sex or race) should be eliminated
political science *noun* (1779)
: a social science concerned chiefly with the description and analysis of political and especially governmental institutions and processes
— political scientist *noun*
pol·i·ti·cian \ˌpä-lə-'ti-shən\ *noun* (1589)

1 : a person experienced in the art or science of government; *especially* **:** one actively engaged in conducting the business of a government
2 a : a person engaged in party politics as a profession **b :** a person primarily interested in political office for selfish or other narrow usually short-sighted reasons
po·lit·i·cise *British variant of* POLITICIZE
po·lit·i·cize \pə-'li-tə-,sīz\ *transitive verb* **-cized; -ciz·ing** (1846)
: to give a political tone or character to ⟨an attempt to *politicize* the civil service⟩
— **po·lit·i·ci·za·tion** \-,li-tə-sə-'zā-shən\ *noun*
pol·i·tick \'pä-lə-,tik\ *intransitive verb* [backformation from *politicking*, noun, from *politics* + ³-*ing*] (circa 1934)
: to engage in often partisan political discussion or activity
— **pol·i·tick·er** *noun*
po·lit·i·co \pə-'li-ti-,kō\ *noun, plural* **-cos** *also* **-coes** [Italian *politico* or Spanish *político*, ultimately from Latin *politicus* political] (1630)
: POLITICIAN 2
pol·i·tics \'pä-lə-,tiks\ *noun plural but singular or plural in construction* [Greek *politika*, from neuter plural of *politikos* political] (circa 1529)
1 a : the art or science of government **b :** the art or science concerned with guiding or influencing governmental policy **c :** the art or science concerned with winning and holding control over a government
2 : political actions, practices, or policies
3 a : political affairs or business; *especially* **:** competition between competing interest groups or individuals for power and leadership (as in a government) **b :** political life especially as a principal activity or profession **c :** political activities characterized by artful and often dishonest practices
4 : the political opinions or sympathies of a person
5 a : the total complex of relations between people living in society **b :** relations or conduct in a particular area of experience especially as seen or dealt with from a political point of view ⟨office *politics*⟩
pol·i·ty \'pä-lə-tē\ *noun, plural* **-ties** [Late Latin *politia* — more at POLICE] (1538)
1 : political organization
2 : a specific form of political organization
3 : a politically organized unit
4 a : the form or constitution of a politically organized unit **b :** the form of government of a religious denomination
pol·ka \'pōl-kə, 'pō-kə\ *noun* [Czech, from *Polka* Polish woman, feminine of *Polák* Pole] (1844)
1 : a vivacious couple dance of Bohemian origin in duple time with a basic pattern of hop-step-close-step
2 : a lively Bohemian dance tune in ²/₄ time
— **polka** *intransitive verb*
pol·ka dot \'pō-kə-,dät\ *noun* (1884)
: a dot in a pattern of regularly distributed dots in textile design
— **polka–dot** *or* **pol·ka–dot·ted** \-,dä-təd\ *adjective*
¹poll \'pōl\ *noun* [Middle English *pol, polle*, from Middle Low German] (14th century)
1 : HEAD
2 a : the top or back of the head **b :** NAPE
3 : the broad or flat end of a striking tool (as a hammer)
4 a (1) **:** the casting or recording of the votes of a body of persons (2) **:** a counting of votes cast **b :** the place where votes are cast or recorded — usually used in plural ⟨at the *polls*⟩ **c :** the period of time during which votes may be cast at an election **d :** the total number of votes recorded ⟨a heavy *poll*⟩

5 a : a questioning or canvassing of persons selected at random or by quota to obtain information or opinions to be analyzed **b :** a record of the information so obtained
²poll (14th century)
transitive verb
1 a : to cut off or cut short the hair or wool of **:** CROP, SHEAR **b :** to cut off or cut short (as wool)
2 a : to cut off or back the top of (as a tree); *specifically* **:** POLLARD **b :** to cut off or cut short the horns of (cattle)
3 a : to receive and record the votes of **b :** to request each member of to declare a vote individually ⟨*poll* the assembly⟩
4 : to receive (as votes) in an election
5 : to question or canvass in a poll
6 : to test (as several computer terminals sharing a single line) in sequence for messages to be transmitted
intransitive verb
: to cast one's vote at a poll
— **poll·ee** \pō-'lē\ *noun*
— **poll·er** \'pō-lər\ *noun*
pol·lack *or* **pol·lock** \'pä-lək\ *noun, plural* **pollack** *or* **pollock** [Middle English *poullok*, perhaps from Scottish Gaelic *pollag* or Irish *pollóg*] (15th century)
1 : a commercially important north Atlantic food fish (*Pollachius virens*) related to and resembling the cods but darker
2 : a commercially important northern Pacific food fish (*Theragra chalcogramma*) of the cod family that closely resembles the pollack — called also *walleye pollack*
¹pol·lard \'pä-lərd\ *noun* [²*poll*] (1611)
: a tree cut back to the trunk to promote the growth of a dense head of foliage
²pollard *transitive verb* (1670)
: to make a pollard of (a tree)
polled \'pōld\ *adjective* (1584)
: having no horns
pol·len \'pä-lən\ *noun* [New Latin *pollin-, pollen*, from Latin, fine flour] (1760)
1 : a mass of microspores in a seed plant appearing usually as a fine dust
2 : a dusty bloom on the body of an insect
pollen basket *noun* (1860)
: a smooth area on each hind tibia of a bee that is edged by a fringe of stiff hairs and serves to collect and transport pollen — called also *corbicula*
pollen grain *noun* (1835)
: one of the granular microspores that occur in pollen and give rise to the male gametophyte of a seed plant
pol·len·iz·er *also* **pol·lin·iz·er** \'pä-lə-,nī-zər\ *noun* [*pollenize* to pollinate] (1897)
1 : a plant that is a source of pollen
2 : POLLINATOR a
pollen mother cell *noun* (1884)
: a cell that is derived from the hypodermis of the pollen sac and that gives rise by meiosis to four cells each of which develops into a pollen grain
pollen sac *noun* (1875)
: one of the pouches of a seed plant anther in which pollen is formed
pollen tube *noun* (1835)
: a tube that is formed by a pollen grain and conveys the sperm nuclei to the embryo sac of an angiosperm or the archegonium of a gymnosperm
pol·lex \'pä-,leks\ *noun, plural* **pol·li·ces** \'pä-lə-,sēz\ [New Latin *pollic-, pollex*, from Latin, thumb, big toe] (circa 1836)
: the first digit of the forelimb **:** THUMB
pollin- *combining form* [New Latin *pollin-, pollen*]
: pollen ⟨*pollinate*⟩
pol·li·nate \'pä-lə-,nāt\ *transitive verb* **-nat·ed; -nat·ing** (1875)
1 : to carry out the pollination of
2 : to mark or smudge with pollen
pol·li·na·tion \,pä-lə-'nā-shən\ *noun* (1875)

: the transfer of pollen from an anther to the stigma in angiosperms or from the microsporangium to the micropyle in gymnosperms
pol·li·na·tor \'pä-lə-,nā-tər\ *noun* (1903)
: one that pollinates: as **a :** an agent (as an insect) that pollinates flowers **b :** POLLENIZER 1
pol·lin·i·um \pä-'li-nē-əm\ *noun, plural* **-ia** \-nē-ə\ [New Latin, from *pollin*-] (1862)
: a coherent mass of pollen grains often with a stalk bearing an adhesive disk that clings to insects
pol·li·no·sis *or* **pol·len·osis** \,pä-lə-'nō-səs\ *noun* [New Latin *pollinosis*, from *pollin*-] (1925)
: an acute recurrent catarrhal disorder caused by allergic sensitivity to specific pollens
poll·ster \'pōl-stər\ *noun* (1939)
: one that conducts a poll or compiles data obtained by a poll
poll tax *noun* (1692)
: a tax of a fixed amount per person levied on adults
pol·lut·ant \pə-'lü-t°nt\ *noun* (1892)
: something that pollutes
pol·lute \pə-'lüt\ *transitive verb* **pol·lut·ed; pol·lut·ing** [Middle English, from Latin *pollutus*, past participle of *polluere*, from *por*- (akin to Latin *per* through) + *-luere* (akin to Latin *lutum* mud, Greek *lyma* dirt, defilement) — more at FOR] (14th century)
1 a : to make ceremonially or morally impure **:** DEFILE **b :** DEBASE 1 ⟨using language to deceive or mislead *pollutes* language —Linda C. Lederman⟩
2 a : to make physically impure or unclean **:** BEFOUL, DIRTY **b :** to contaminate (an environment) especially with man-made waste
synonym *see* CONTAMINATE
— **pol·lut·er** *noun*
— **pol·lut·ive** \-'lü-tiv\ *adjective*
pol·lu·tion \pə-'lü-shən\ *noun* (14th century)
1 : the action of polluting especially by environmental contamination with man-made waste; *also* **:** the condition of being polluted
2 : POLLUTANT
Pol·lux \'pä-ləks\ *noun* [Latin, modification of Greek *Polydeukēs*]
1 : one of the Dioscuri
2 : a first-magnitude star in the constellation Gemini
Pol·ly·an·na \,pä-lē-'a-nə\ *noun* [*Pollyanna*, heroine of the novel *Pollyanna* (1913) by Eleanor Porter (died 1920) American fiction writer] (1921)
: a person characterized by irrepressible optimism and a tendency to find good in everything
— **Pollyanna** *adjective*
— **Pol·ly·an·na·ish** \-'a-nə-ish\ *also* **Pol·ly·an·nish** \-'a-nish\ *adjective*
pol·ly·wog *or* **pol·li·wog** \'pä-lē-,wäg, -,wòg\ *noun* [alteration of Middle English *polwygle*, probably from *pol* poll + *wiglen* to wiggle] (1832)
: TADPOLE
po·lo \'pō-(,)lō\ *noun* [Balti, ball] (1872)
1 : a game played by teams of players on horseback using mallets with long flexible handles to drive a wooden ball through goalposts
2 : WATER POLO
— **po·lo·ist** \'pō-(,)lō-ist\ *noun*
polo coat *noun* (1910)
: a tailored overcoat that is made especially of tan camel's hair and often has stitched edges and a half-belt on the back
po·lo·naise \,pä-lə-'nāz, ,pō-\ *noun* [French, from feminine of *polonais* Polish, from *Pologne* Poland, from Medieval Latin *Polonia*] (1773)

\ə\ abut \ᵊ\ kitten \ər\ further \a\ ash \ā\ ace
\ä\ mop, mar \aù\ out \ch\ chin \e\ bet \ē\ easy
\g\ go \i\ hit \ī\ ice \j\ job \ŋ\ sing \ō\ go
\ò\ law \òi\ boy \th\ thin \th\ the \ü\ loot \ù\ foot
\y\ yet \zh\ vision *see also* Guide to Pronunciation

1 : an elaborate overdress with a short-sleeved fitted waist and a draped cutaway overskirt
2 a : a stately Polish processional dance popular in 19th century Europe **b :** music for this dance in moderate ¾ time

Po·lo·nia \pə-ˈlō-nē-ə, -nyə\ *noun* [New Latin, Poland, from Medieval Latin] (1944)
: people of Polish descent living outside Poland

po·lo·ni·um \pə-ˈlō-nē-əm\ *noun* [New Latin, from Medieval Latin *Polonia*] (1898)
: a radioactive metallic element that is similar chemically to tellurium and bismuth, occurs especially in pitchblende and radium-lead residues, and emits an alpha particle to form an isotope of lead — see ELEMENT table

polonaise 1

Po·lo·ni·us \pə-ˈlō-nē-əs\ *noun*
: a garrulous courtier and father of Ophelia and Laertes in Shakespeare's *Hamlet*

polo shirt *noun* (1920)
: a close-fitting pullover often knit shirt with short or long sleeves and turnover collar or banded neck

pol·ter·geist \ˈpōl-tər-ˌgīst\ *noun* [German, from *poltern* to knock + *Geist* spirit] (1848)
: a noisy usually mischievous ghost held to be responsible for unexplained noises (as rappings)

¹pol·troon \päl-ˈtrün\ *noun* [Middle French *poultron*, from Old Italian *poltrone*, probably akin to *poltro* colt, ultimately from Latin *pullus* young of an animal — more at FOAL] (circa 1529)
: a spiritless coward **:** CRAVEN

²poltroon *adjective* (1645)
: characterized by complete cowardice

pol·troon·ery \-ˈtrü-nə-rē, -ˈtrün-rē\ *noun* (1590)
: mean pusillanimity **:** COWARDICE

poly \ˈpä-lē\ *noun, plural* **pol·ys** \-lēz\ *often attributive* [short for *polymer*] (1942)
: a polymerized plastic or something made of this; *especially* **:** a polyester fiber, fabric, or garment

poly- *combining form* [Middle English, from Latin, from Greek, from *polys;* akin to Old High German *filu* many, Sanskrit *puru*, Latin *plenus* full — more at FULL]
1 : many **:** several **:** much MULTI- ⟨*poly*chotomous⟩ ⟨*poly*gyny⟩
2 a : containing an indefinite number more than one of a (specified) substance ⟨*poly*sulfide⟩ **b :** polymeric **:** polymer of a (specified) monomer ⟨*poly*ethylene⟩ ⟨*poly*adenylic acid⟩

poly·A \ˌpä-lē-ˈā\ *noun* [*poly-* + *adenylic acid*] (1957)
: RNA or a segment of RNA that is composed of a polynucleotide chain consisting entirely of adenylic acid residues and that codes for polylysine when functioning as messenger RNA in protein synthesis

poly·acryl·amide \ˌpä-lē-ə-ˈkri-lə-ˌmīd\ *noun* (1944)
: a polyamide of acrylic acid

poly·ac·ry·lo·ni·trile \ˌpä-lē-ˌa-krə-lō-ˈnī-trəl, -ˌtrēl\ *noun* (1935)
: a polymer of acrylonitrile used often as fibers

poly·ad·e·nyl·ic acid \ˌpä-lē-ˌa-dᵊn-ˈi-lik-\ *noun* (1956)
: POLYA

poly·al·co·hol \ˌpä-lē-ˈal-kə-ˌhȯl\ *noun* (1900)
: an alcohol (as a diol) that contains more than one hydroxyl group

poly·am·ide \ˌpä-lē-ˈa-ˌmīd, -məd\ *noun* [International Scientific Vocabulary] (1929)
: a compound characterized by more than one amide group; *especially* **:** a polymeric amide (as nylon)

poly·amine \ˈpä-lē-ə-ˌmēn, ˌpä-lē-ˈa-ˌmēn\ *noun* (1861)
: a compound characterized by more than one amino group

poly·an·dry \ˈpä-lē-ˌan-drē\ *noun* [Greek *polyandros*, adjective, having many husbands, from *poly-* + *andr-, anēr* man, husband — more at ANDR-] (1780)
: the state or practice of having more than one husband or male mate at one time — compare POLYGAMY, POLYGYNY
— **poly·an·drous** \ˌpä-lē-ˈan-drəs\ *adjective*

poly·an·tha \ˌpä-lē-ˈan(t)-thə\ *noun* [New Latin, from Greek *polyanthos* blooming] (1889)
: any of numerous dwarf hybrid roses characterized by many large clusters of small flowers

poly·an·thus \-ˈan(t)-thəs\ *noun, plural* **-an·thus·es** *or* **-an·thi** \-ˈan-ˌthī, -ˌthē\ [New Latin, from Greek *polyanthos* blooming, from *poly-* + *anthos* flower — more at ANTHOLOGY] (circa 1727)
1 : any of various hybrid primroses
2 : a narcissus (*Narcissus tazetta*) having small white or yellow flowers arranged in umbels and having a spreading perianth

poly·atom·ic \-ə-ˈtä-mik\ *adjective* [International Scientific Vocabulary] (1857)
: containing more than one and especially more than two atoms ⟨*polyatomic* molecules⟩

poly·bro·mi·nat·ed biphenyl \ˌpä-lē-ˈbrō-mə-ˌnā-təd-\ *noun* (1975)
: any of several compounds that are similar to polychlorinated biphenyls in environmental toxicity and in structure but that have various hydrogen atoms replaced by bromine rather than chlorine — called also *PBB*

poly·bu·ta·di·ene \-ˌbyü-tə-ˈdī-ˌēn, -ˌdī-\ *noun* (1939)
: a synthetic rubber that has a high resistance to wear and is used especially in the manufacture of tires

poly·car·bon·ate \-ˈkär-bə-ˌnāt, -nət\ *noun* (1930)
: any of various tough transparent thermoplastics characterized by high impact strength and high softening temperature

poly·cen·tric \-ˈsen-trik\ *adjective* (1887)
: having more than one center (as of development or control): as **a :** having several centromeres ⟨*polycentric* chromosomes⟩ ⟨*polycentric* cells⟩ **b :** characterized by polycentrism

poly·cen·trism \-ˈsen-ˌtri-zəm\ *noun* (1956)
: the existence of many centers of communist ideological thought; *especially* **:** the existence of a number of autonomous national communist movements

poly·chaete \ˈpä-lē-ˌkēt\ *noun* [ultimately from Greek *polychaitēs* having much hair, from *poly-* + *chaitē* long hair] (1896)
: any of a class (Polychaeta) of chiefly marine annelid worms (as clam worms) usually with paired segmental appendages, separate sexes, and a free-swimming trochophore larva
— **polychaete** *adjective*

poly·chlo·ri·nat·ed biphenyl \ˌpä-lē-ˈklōr-ə-ˌnā-təd-, -ˈklȯr-\ *noun* (1962)
: any of several compounds that are produced by replacing hydrogen atoms in biphenyl with chlorine, have various industrial applications, and are poisonous environmental pollutants which tend to accumulate in animal tissues — called also *PCB*

poly·chot·o·mous \-ˈkä-tə-məs\ *adjective* [*poly-* + *-chotomous* (as in *dichotomous*)] (circa 1858)
: dividing or marked by division into many parts, branches, or classes
— **poly·chot·o·my** \-mē\ *noun*

poly·chro·mat·ic \-krō-ˈma-tik\ *adjective* [Greek *polychrōmatos*, from *poly-* + *chrōmat-, chrōma* color — more at CHROMATIC] (circa 1841)
1 : showing a variety or a change of colors **:** MULTICOLORED
2 : being or relating to radiation that is composed of more than one wavelength

poly·chro·mato·phil·ic \-krō-ˌma-tə-ˈfi-lik\ *adjective* (1897)
: stainable with more than one type of stain and especially with both acid and basic dyes ⟨*polychromatophilic* erythroblasts⟩
— **poly·chro·mato·phil·ia** \-ˈfi-lē-ə\ *noun*

poly·chrome \ˈpä-lē-ˌkrōm\ *adjective* [Greek *polychrōmos*, from *poly-* + *chrōma*] (1837)
: relating to, made with, or decorated in several colors ⟨*polychrome* pottery⟩
— **polychrome** *transitive verb*
— **poly·chro·my** \-ˌkrō-mē\ *noun*

poly·cis·tron·ic \ˌpä-lē-sis-ˈträ-nik\ *adjective* (1963)
: containing the genetic information of a number of cistrons ⟨*polycistronic* messenger RNA⟩

poly·clin·ic \-ˈkli-nik\ *noun* [International Scientific Vocabulary] (circa 1890)
: a clinic or hospital treating diseases of many sorts

poly·clon·al \-ˈklō-nəl\ *adjective* (1914)
: produced by or being cells derived from two or more cells of different ancestry or genetic constitution ⟨*polyclonal* antibodies⟩

poly·con·den·sa·tion \-ˌkän-ˌden-ˈsā-shən, -dən-\ *noun* [International Scientific Vocabulary] (1936)
: a chemical condensation leading to the formation of a compound of high molecular weight

poly·con·ic projection \ˌpä-lē-ˈkä-nik-\ *noun* (circa 1864)
: a map projection consisting of a composite series of concentric cones each of which before being unrolled has been placed over a sphere so as to be tangent to a different parallel of latitude

poly·crys·tal·line \-ˈkris-tə-lən\ *adjective* (1918)
1 : consisting of crystals variously oriented
2 : composed of more than one crystal
— **poly·crys·tal** \ˌpä-lē-ˌkris-tᵊl\ *noun*

poly·cy·clic \ˌpä-lē-ˈsī-klik, -ˈsi-\ *adjective* [International Scientific Vocabulary] (1869)
: having more than one cyclic component; *especially* **:** having two or more rings in the molecule

poly·cys·tic \-ˈsis-tik\ *adjective* (1872)
: having or involving more than one cyst ⟨*polycystic* kidneys⟩ ⟨*polycystic* disease⟩

poly·cy·the·mia \-(ˌ)sī-ˈthē-mē-ə\ *noun* [New Latin, from *poly-* + *cyt-* + *-hemia*] (circa 1857)
: a condition marked by an abnormal increase in the number of circulating red blood cells; *specifically* **:** POLYCYTHEMIA VERA
— **poly·cy·the·mic** \-mik\ *adjective*

polycythemia ve·ra \-ˈvir-ə\ *noun* [New Latin, true polycythemia] (circa 1925)
: polycythemia of unknown cause that is characterized by increase in total blood volume and accompanied by nosebleed, distension of the circulatory vessels, and enlargement of the spleen — called also *erythremia*

poly·cyt·i·dyl·ic acid \ˌpä-lē-ˌsi-tə-ˈdi-lik-\ *noun* (1965)
: RNA or a segment of RNA that is composed of a polynucleotide chain consisting entirely of cytosine-containing nucleotides and that codes for a polypeptide chain consisting of proline residues when functioning as messenger RNA in protein synthesis

poly·dac·tyl \-ˈdak-tᵊl\ *adjective* [Greek *polydaktylos*, from *poly-* + *daktylos* digit] (circa 1890)
: having or causing polydactyly

poly·dac·ty·ly \-ˈdak-tᵊl-ē\ *noun* (1886)
: the condition of having more than the normal number of fingers or toes

poly·dip·sia \-ˈdip-sē-ə\ *noun* [New Latin, from *poly-* + Greek *dipsa* thirst] (1660)
: excessive or abnormal thirst

— **poly·dip·sic** \-sik\ *adjective*

poly·dis·perse \-dis-'pərs\ *adjective* [*poly-* + Latin *dispersus* dispersed, from past participle of *dispergere* to disperse] (1915)
: of, relating to, or characterized by or as particles of varied sizes in the dispersed phase of a disperse system
— **poly·dis·per·si·ty** \-'pər-sə-tē\ *noun*

poly·elec·tro·lyte \‚pä-lē-ə-'lek-trə-‚līt\ *noun* (circa 1947)
: a substance of high molecular weight (as a protein) that is an electrolyte

poly·em·bry·o·ny \-'em-brē-ə-nē, -(‚)em-'brī-\ *noun* [International Scientific Vocabulary *poly-* + *embryon-* + ²-y] (1849)
1 : the condition of having several embryos
2 : the production of two or more embryos from one ovule or egg
— **poly·em·bry·on·ic** \-‚em-brē-'ä-nik\ *adjective*

poly·ene \'pä-lē-‚ēn\ *noun* [International Scientific Vocabulary] (1928)
: an organic compound containing many double bonds; *especially* : one having the double bonds in a long aliphatic hydrocarbon chain
— **poly·en·ic** \‚pä-lē-'ē-nik\ *adjective*

¹**poly·es·ter** \'pä-lē-‚es-tər, ‚pä-lē-'\ *noun* [International Scientific Vocabulary] (1929)
: any of a group of polymers that consist basically of repeated units of an ester and are used especially in making fibers or plastics
— **poly·es·ter·i·fi·ca·tion** \-e‚ster-ə-fə-'kā-shən\ *noun*

²**polyester** *adjective* (1975)
: characterized by inelegant or unsophisticated middle-class taste ⟨*polyester* suburbs⟩ ⟨*polyester* folks⟩

poly·es·trous \‚pä-lē-'es-trəs\ *adjective* (1900)
: having more than one period of estrus in a year

poly·eth·yl·ene \-'e-thə-‚lēn\ *noun* (circa 1862)
: a polymer of ethylene; *especially* : any of various partially crystalline lightweight thermoplastics $(CH_2CH_2)_x$ that are resistant to chemicals and moisture, have good insulating properties, and are used especially in packaging and insulation

po·lyg·a·la \pə-'li-gə-lə\ *noun* [New Latin, genus name, from Latin, milkwort, from Greek *polygalon*, from *poly-* + *gala* milk — more at GALAXY] (1578)
: MILKWORT

poly·gam·ic \‚pä-lē-'ga-mik\ *adjective* (1819)
: POLYGAMOUS

po·lyg·a·mous \pə-'li-gə-məs\ *adjective* [Greek *polygamos*, from *poly-* + *-gamos* -gamous] (1613)
1 a : relating to or practicing polygamy **b** : having more than one mate at one time ⟨baboons are *polygamous*⟩
2 : bearing both hermaphrodite and unisexual flowers on the same plant

po·lyg·a·my \-mē\ *noun* (circa 1591)
1 : marriage in which a spouse of either sex may have more than one mate at the same time — compare POLYANDRY, POLYGYNY
2 : the state of being polygamous
— **po·lyg·a·mist** \-mist\ *noun*
— **po·lyg·a·mize** \-‚mīz\ *intransitive verb*

poly·gene \'pä-lē-‚jēn\ *noun* [International Scientific Vocabulary] (1941)
: any of a group of nonallelic genes that collectively control the inheritance of a quantitative character or modify the expression of a qualitative character
— **poly·gen·ic** \‚pä-lē-'je-nik\ *adjective*

poly·gen·e·sis \‚pä-lē-'je-nə-səs\ *noun* [New Latin] (circa 1882)
: development from more than one source

poly·ge·net·ic \-jə-'ne-tik\ *adjective* (1861)
1 : POLYPHYLETIC
2 : having many distinct sources

¹**poly·glot** \'pä-lē-‚glät\ *noun* [²*polyglot*] (circa 1645)

1 : one who is polyglot
2 *capitalized* : a book containing versions of the same text in several languages; *especially* : the Scriptures in several languages
3 : a mixture or confusion of languages or nomenclatures

²**polyglot** *adjective* [Greek *polyglōttos*, from *poly-* + *glōtta* language — more at GLOSS] (1656)
1 a : speaking or writing several languages : MULTILINGUAL **b** : composed of numerous linguistic groups ⟨a *polyglot* population⟩
2 : containing matter in several languages ⟨a *polyglot* sign⟩
3 : composed of elements from different languages
4 : being widely diverse (as in ethnic or cultural origins) ⟨*polyglot* cuisine⟩

poly·glot·ism *or* **poly·glot·tism** \-‚glä-‚ti-zəm\ *noun* (1882)
: the use of many languages : the ability to speak many languages

poly·gon \'pä-lē-‚gän\ *noun* [Late Latin *polygonum*, from Greek *polygōnon*, from neuter of *polygōnos* polygonal, from *poly-* + *gōnia* angle — more at -GON] (1571)
1 : a closed plane figure bounded by straight lines
2 : a closed figure on a sphere bounded by arcs of great circles
— **po·lyg·o·nal** \pə-'li-gə-n°l\ *adjective*
— **po·lyg·o·nal·ly** \-n°l-ē\ *adverb*

po·lyg·o·num \pə-'li-gə-nəm\ *noun* [New Latin, from Greek *polygonon* knotgrass, from *poly-* + *gony* knee — more at KNEE] (circa 1706)
: any of a genus (*Polygonum*) of herbs of the buckwheat family with a prominent tubular sheath around the base of each petiole, thickened nodes, and flowers that are solitary and axillary or in spiked racemes — called also *knotweed*

poly·graph \'pä-lē-‚graf\ *noun* (1871)
: an instrument for recording variations of several different pulsations (as of physiological variables) simultaneously; *broadly* : LIE DETECTOR
— **poly·graph·ic** \‚pä-lē-'gra-fik\ *adjective*

po·lyg·ra·pher \'pä-lē-‚gra-fər, pə-'li-grə-fər\ *noun* (circa 1934)
: one who operates a polygraph

po·lyg·ra·phist \'pä-lē-‚gra-fist, pə-'li-grə-fist\ *noun* (1954)
: POLYGRAPHER

po·lyg·y·nous \pə-'li-jə-nəs\ *adjective* (1874)
: relating to or practicing polygyny

po·lyg·y·ny \-nē\ *noun* (1780)
: the state or practice of having more than one wife or female mate at one time — compare POLYANDRY, POLYGAMY

polyhedral angle *noun* (circa 1864)
: a portion of space partly enclosed by three or more planes whose intersections meet in a vertex

poly·he·dron \‚pä-lē-'hē-drən\ *noun, plural* **-drons** *or* **-dra** \-drə\ [New Latin] (1570)
: a solid formed by plane faces
— **poly·he·dral** \-drəl\ *adjective*

poly·he·dro·sis \‚pä-lē-hē-'drō-səs\ *noun, plural* **-dro·ses** \-‚sēz\ [New Latin, from *polyhedron*] (1947)
: any of several virus diseases of insect larvae characterized by dissolution of tissues and accumulation of polyhedral granules in the resultant fluid

poly·his·tor \‚pä-lē-'his-tər\ *noun* [Greek *polyistōr* very learned, from *poly-* + *istōr*, *histōr* learned — more at HISTORY] (1588)
: POLYMATH
— **poly·his·tor·ic** \-his-'tór-ik, -'tär-\ *adjective*

poly·hy·droxy \-hī-'dräk-sē\ *adjective* (circa 1929)
: containing more than one hydroxyl group in the molecule

Poly·hym·nia \‚pä-lē-'him-nē-ə\ *noun* [Latin, from Greek *Polymnia*]
: the Greek Muse of sacred song

poly I:C \‚pä-lē-'ī-'sē\ *or* **poly I·poly C** \‚pä-lē-'ī-‚pä-lē-'sē\ *noun* [*poly-* + *inosinic acid* + *cytidylic acid*] (1969)
: a synthetic 2-stranded RNA composed of one strand of polyinosinic acid and one strand of polycytidylic acid that induces interferon formation and has been used experimentally as an anticancer and antiviral agent

poly·ino·sin·ic acid \‚pä-lē-‚i-nə-'si-nik-, -‚ī-nə-\ *noun* [*poly-* + *inosinic acid* ($C_{10}H_{13}N_4O_8P$), from Greek *in-*, *is* sinew + International Scientific Vocabulary ²-*ose* + ¹-*in* + ¹-*ic* + *acid*] (1965)
: RNA or a segment of RNA that is composed of a polynucleotide chain consisting entirely of inosinic acid residues

poly·ly·sine \‚pä-lē-'lī-‚sēn\ *noun* (1947)
: a protein whose polypeptide chain consists entirely of lysine residues

poly·math \'pä-lē-‚math\ *noun* [Greek *polymathēs* very learned, from *poly-* + *manthanein* to learn — more at MATHEMATICAL] (1621)
: a person of encyclopedic learning
— **polymath** *or* **poly·math·ic** \‚pä-lē-'ma-thik\ *adjective*
— **po·ly·ma·thy** \pə-'li-mə-thē, 'pä-lə-‚ma-thē\ *noun*

poly·mer \'pä-lə-mər\ *noun* [International Scientific Vocabulary, back-formation from *polymeric*, from Greek *polymerēs* having many parts, from *poly-* + *meros* part — more at MERIT] (1866)
: a chemical compound or mixture of compounds formed by polymerization and consisting essentially of repeating structural units
— **poly·mer·ic** \‚pä-lə-'mer-ik\ *adjective*
— **poly·mer·ism** \pə-'li-mə-‚ri-zəm, 'pä-lə-mə-\ *noun*

poly·mer·ase \'pä-lə-mə-‚rās, -‚rāz\ *noun* (1958)
: any of several enzymes that catalyze the formation of DNA or RNA from precursor substances in the presence of preexisting DNA or RNA acting as a template

polymerase chain reaction *noun* (1987)
: an in vitro technique for rapidly synthesizing large quantities of a given DNA segment that involves separating the DNA into its two complementary strands, using DNA polymerase to synthesize two-stranded DNA from each single strand, and repeating the process

po·ly·mer·i·sa·tion, po·ly·mer·ise *chiefly British variant of* POLYMERIZATION, POLYMERIZE

po·ly·mer·i·za·tion \pə-‚li-mə-rə-'zā-shən, ‚pä-lə-mə-rə-\ *noun* [International Scientific Vocabulary] (1872)
1 : a chemical reaction in which two or more molecules combine to form larger molecules that contain repeating structural units — compare ASSOCIATION 5
2 : reduplication of parts in an organism

po·ly·mer·ize \pə-'li-mə-‚rīz, 'pä-lə-mə-\ *verb* **-ized; -iz·ing** (1865)
transitive verb
: to subject to polymerization
intransitive verb
: to undergo polymerization

poly·meth·yl methacrylate \'pä-lē-‚me-thəl-\ *noun* (1936)
: a thermoplastic resin of polymerized methyl methacrylate which is characterized by its optical clarity (as in a contact lens)

poly·morph \'pä-lē-‚mórf\ *noun* [International Scientific Vocabulary] (circa 1828)
1 : a polymorphic organism; *also* : one of the several forms of such an organism

\ə\ abut \°\ kitten \ər\ further \a\ ash \ā\ ace
\ä\ mop, mar \aů\ out \ch\ chin \e\ bet \ē\ easy
\g\ go \i\ hit \ī\ ice \j\ job \ŋ\ sing \ō\ go
\ó\ law \ói\ boy \th\ thin \th\ the \ü\ loot \ů\ foot
\y\ yet \zh\ vision *see also* Guide to Pronunciation

2 : any of the crystalline forms of a polymorphic substance

poly·mor·phism \ˌpä-lē-ˈmȯr-ˌfi-zəm\ noun (1839)
: the quality or state of being able to assume different forms: as **a :** existence of a species in several forms independent of the variations of sex **b :** the property of crystallizing in two or more forms with distinct structure
— **poly·mor·phic** \-ˈfik\ adjective
— **poly·mor·phi·cal·ly** \-fi-k(ə-)lē\ adverb

poly·mor·pho·nu·cle·ar \-ˌmȯr-fə-ˈnü-klē-ər, -ˈnyü-\ adjective (1897)
of a leukocyte : having the nucleus complexly lobed
— **polymorphonuclear** noun

poly·mor·phous \-ˈmȯr-fəs\ adjective [Greek polymorphous, from poly- + -morphos -morphous] (1785)
: having, assuming, or occurring in various forms, characters, or styles : POLYMORPHIC ⟨a polymorphous rash⟩ ⟨polymorphous sexuality⟩
— **poly·mor·phous·ly** adverb

polymorphous perverse adjective (1909)
: relating to or exhibiting infantile sexual tendencies in which the genitals are not yet identified as the sole or principal sexual organs nor coitus as the goal of erotic activity

poly·myx·in \ˌpä-lē-ˈmik-sən\ noun [International Scientific Vocabulary, from New Latin polymyxa, from poly- + Greek myxa mucus — more at MUCUS] (1947)
: any of several toxic antibiotics obtained from a soil bacterium (Bacillus polymyxa) and active against gram-negative bacteria

Poly·ne·sian \ˌpä-lə-ˈnē-zhən, -shən\ noun (1807)
1 : a member of any of the indigenous peoples of Polynesia
2 : a group of Austronesian languages spoken in Polynesia
— **Polynesian** adjective

poly·neu·ri·tis \ˌpä-lē-nü-ˈrī-təs, -nyü-\ noun [New Latin] (1886)
: neuritis of several peripheral nerves at the same time

Poly·ni·ces \ˌpä-lə-ˈnī-sēz\ noun [Latin, from Greek Polyneikēs]
: a son of Oedipus for whom the Seven against Thebes mount their expedition

¹poly·no·mi·al \ˌpä-lə-ˈnō-mē-əl\ noun [poly- + -nomial (as in binomial)] (1674)
: a mathematical expression of one or more algebraic terms each of which consists of a constant multiplied by one or more variables raised to a nonnegative integral power (as $a + bx + cx^2$)

²polynomial adjective (circa 1704)
: relating to, composed of, or expressed as one or more polynomials ⟨polynomial functions⟩ ⟨polynomial equations⟩

poly·nu·cle·ar \ˌpä-lē-ˈnü-klē-ər, -ˈnyü-, ÷-kyə-lər\ adjective [International Scientific Vocabulary] (1908)
: chemically polycyclic especially with respect to the benzene ring — used chiefly of aromatic hydrocarbons that are important as pollutants and possibly as carcinogens

poly·nu·cle·o·tide \-ˈnü-klē-ə-ˌtīd, -ˈnyü-\ noun [International Scientific Vocabulary] (1911)
: a polymeric chain of nucleotides

po·lyn·ya \ˌpä-lən-ˈyä\ noun, plural **polyn·yas** also **po·lyn·yi** \-ˈyē\ [Russian polyn'ya] (1853)
: an area of open water in sea ice

poly·ole·fin \ˌpä-lē-ˈō-lə-fən\ noun (1930)
: a polymer of an alkene (as polyethylene)

poly·oma virus \ˌpä-lē-ˈō-mə-\ noun [New Latin polyoma, from poly- + -oma] (1958)
: a papovavirus of rodents that is associated with various kinds of tumors — called also polyoma

poly·on·y·mous \ˌpä-lē-ˈä-nə-məs\ adjective [Greek polyōnymos, from poly- + onoma, onyma name — more at NAME] (1678)

: having or known by various names

pol·yp \ˈpä-ləp\ noun [Middle French polype octopus, nasal tumor, from Latin polypus, from Greek polypous, from poly- + pous foot — more at FOOT] (1742)
1 : a coelenterate that has typically a hollow cylindrical body closed and attached at one end and opening at the other by a central mouth surrounded by tentacles armed with nematocysts
2 : a projecting mass of swollen and hypertrophied or tumorous membrane
— **pol·yp·oid** \-lə-ˌpȯid\ adjective

poly·pep·tide \ˌpä-lē-ˈpep-ˌtīd\ noun [International Scientific Vocabulary] (1903)
: a molecular chain of amino acids
— **poly·pep·tid·ic** \-(ˌ)pep-ˈti-dik\ adjective

poly·pet·al·ous \-ˈpe-tᵊl-əs\ adjective [New Latin polypetalus, from poly- + petalum petal] (circa 1704)
: having or consisting of separate petals

poly·pha·gia \-ˈfā-j(ē-)ə\ noun [Greek polyphagia, from polyphagos] (circa 1693)
: excessive appetite or eating

po·lyph·a·gous \pə-ˈli-fə-gəs\ adjective [Greek polyphagos eating too much, from poly- + -phagos -phagous] (1815)
: feeding on or utilizing many kinds of food
— **po·lyph·a·gy** \-jē\ noun

poly·phase \ˈpä-lē-ˌfāz\ adjective [International Scientific Vocabulary] (1891)
: having or producing two or more phases ⟨a polyphase machine⟩ ⟨a polyphase current⟩

poly·pha·sic \ˌpä-lē-ˈfā-zik\ adjective (1922)
: consisting of two or more phases

Poly·phe·mus \ˌpä-lə-ˈfē-məs\ noun [Latin, from Greek Polyphēmos]
: a Cyclops whom Odysseus blinds in order to escape from his cave

poly·phe·nol \ˌpä-lē-ˈfē-ˌnȯl, -fi-\ noun [International Scientific Vocabulary] (1894)
: a polyhydroxy phenol
— **poly·phe·no·lic** \-fi-ˈnō-lik, -ˈnä-\ adjective

poly·phil·o·pro·gen·i·tive \-ˌfi-lə-prō-ˈje-nə-tiv\ adjective (1919)
: extremely prolific : PHILOPROGENITIVE

poly·phone \ˈpä-lē-ˌfōn\ noun (1872)
: a symbol or sequence of symbols having more than one phonemic value (as a in English)

poly·phon·ic \ˌpä-lē-ˈfä-nik\ or **po·lyph·o·nous** \pə-ˈli-fə-nəs\ adjective (1782)
1 : of, relating to, or marked by polyphony
2 : being a polyphone
— **poly·phon·i·cal·ly** \ˌpä-lē-ˈfä-ni-k(ə-)lē\ or **po·lyph·o·nous·ly** adverb

polyphonic prose noun (1916)
: a freely rhythmical prose employing characteristic devices of verse (as alliteration and assonance)

po·lyph·o·ny \pə-ˈli-fə-nē\ noun [Greek polyphōnia variety of tones, from polyphōnos having many tones or voices, from poly- + phōnē voice — more at BAN] (circa 1864)
: a style of musical composition in which two or more independent melodies are juxtaposed in harmony

poly·phy·let·ic \ˌpä-lē-(ˌ)fī-ˈle-tik\ adjective [International Scientific Vocabulary, from Greek polyphylos of many tribes, from poly- + phylē tribe — more at PHYL-] (1875)
: of, relating to, or derived from different ancestral stocks; specifically : relating to or being a taxonomic group that includes members (as genera or species) from different ancestral lineages
— **poly·phy·let·i·cal·ly** \-ti-k(ə-)lē\ adverb

pol·yp·ide \ˈpä-lə-ˌpīd\ noun [polyp + Greek -idēs, patronymic suffix] (1850)
: one of the individual zooids of a bryozoan colony

poly·ploid \ˈpä-lē-ˌplȯid\ adjective [International Scientific Vocabulary] (1920)

: having or being a chromosome number that is a multiple greater than two of the monoploid number
— **polyploid** noun
— **poly·ploi·dy** \-ˌplȯi-dē\ noun

po·lyp·nea \ˌpä-ˈlip-nē-ə, pə-\ noun [New Latin] (circa 1890)
: rapid or panting respiration

poly·po·dy \ˈpä-lə-ˌpō-dē\ noun, plural **-dies** [Middle English polypodie, from Latin polypodium, from Greek polypodion, from poly- + pod-, pous foot — more at FOOT] (14th century)
: any of a genus (Polypodium) of chiefly epiphytic ferns with creeping rhizomes; especially : either of two ferns (P. vulgare of Eurasia and P. virginianum of North America) with relatively narrow entire segments

polypody

poly·pro·pyl·ene \ˌpä-lē-ˈprō-pə-ˌlēn\ noun (1935)
: any of various thermoplastic plastics or fibers that are polymers of propylene

po·lyp·tych \ˈpä-ləp-ˌtik, pə-ˈlip-tik\ noun [Greek polyptychos having many folds, from poly- + ptychē fold, from ptyssein to fold] (1859)
: an arrangement of four or more panels (as of a painting) usually hinged and folding together

poly·rhythm \ˈpä-lē-ˌri-thəm\ noun (1929)
: the simultaneous combination of contrasting rhythms in music
— **poly·rhyth·mic** \ˌpä-lē-ˈrith-mik\ adjective
— **poly·rhyth·mi·cal·ly** \-mi-k(ə-)lē\ adverb

poly·ri·bo·nu·cle·o·tide \ˌpä-lē-ˌrī-bō-ˈnü-klē-ə-ˌtīd, -ˈnyü-\ noun (1956)
: a polynucleotide in which the mononucleotides are ribonucleotides

poly·ri·bo·some \-ˈrī-bə-ˌsōm\ noun (1962)
: a cluster of ribosomes linked together by a molecule of messenger RNA and forming the site of protein synthesis
— **poly·ri·bo·som·al** \-ˌrī-bə-ˈsō-məl\ adjective

poly·sac·cha·ride \-ˈsa-kə-ˌrīd\ noun [International Scientific Vocabulary] (1892)
: a carbohydrate that can be decomposed by hydrolysis into two or more molecules of monosaccharides; especially : any of the more complex carbohydrates (as cellulose, starch, or glycogen)

po·ly·se·mous \ˌpä-lē-ˈsē-məs, pə-ˈli-sə-məs\ adjective [Late Latin polysemus, from Greek polysēmos, from poly- + sēma sign] (1884)
: having multiple meanings
— **po·ly·se·my** \-mē\ noun

poly·some \ˈpä-lē-ˌsōm\ noun (1962)
: POLYRIBOSOME

poly·sor·bate \ˌpä-lē-ˈsȯr-ˌbāt\ noun (1950)
: any of several emulsifiers used in the preparation of some pharmaceuticals or foods

po·ly·sti·chous \pə-ˈlis-ti-kəs\ adjective [Greek polystichos, from poly- + stichos row — more at DISTICH] (circa 1890)
: arranged in several rows

poly·sty·rene \ˌpä-lē-ˈstī-ˌrēn\ noun (1927)
: a polymer of styrene; especially : a rigid transparent thermoplastic that has good physical and electrical insulating properties and is used especially in molded products, foams, and sheet materials

poly·sul·fide \-ˈsəl-ˌfīd\ noun [International Scientific Vocabulary] (1849)
: a sulfide containing two or more atoms of sulfur in the molecule

poly·syl·lab·ic \-sə-ˈla-bik\ adjective [Medieval Latin polysyllabus, from Greek polysyllabos, from poly- + syllabē syllable] (1782)
1 : having more than one and usually more than three syllables

2 : characterized by words of many syllables
— **poly·syl·lab·i·cal·ly** \-bi-k(ə-)lē\ *adverb*

poly·syl·la·ble \'pä-lē-,si-lə-bəl, ,pä-lē-'\ *noun* [modification of Medieval Latin *polysyllaba*, from feminine of *polysyllabus*] (1570)
: a polysyllabic word

poly·syn·ap·tic \,pä-lē-sə-'nap-tik\ *adjective* (1964)
: involving two or more synapses in the central nervous system ⟨*polysynaptic* reflexes⟩
— **poly·syn·ap·ti·cal·ly** \-ti-k(ə-)lē\ *adverb*

poly·syn·de·ton \-'sin-də-,tän\ *noun* [New Latin, from Late Greek, neuter of *polysyndetos* using many conjunctions, from Greek *poly-* + *syndetos* bound together, conjunctive — more at ASYNDETON] (circa 1577)
: repetition of conjunctions in close succession (as in *we have ships and men and money and stores*)

¹poly·tech·nic \-'tek-nik\ *adjective* [French *polytechnique*, from Greek *polytechnos* skilled in many arts, from *poly-* + *technē* art — more at TECHNICAL] (1805)
: relating to or devoted to instruction in many technical arts or applied sciences

²polytechnic *noun* (1836)
: a polytechnic school

poly·tene \'pä-lē-,tēn\ *adjective* [International Scientific Vocabulary] (1935)
: relating to, being, or having chromosomes each of which consists of many strands with the corresponding chromomeres in contact
— **poly·te·ny** \-,tē-nē\ *noun*

poly·the·ism \'pä-lē-(,)thē-,i-zəm\ *noun* [French *polytheisme*, from Late Greek *polytheos* polytheistic, from Greek, of many gods, from *poly-* + *theos* god] (1613)
: belief in or worship of more than one god
— **poly·the·ist** \-,thē-ist\ *adjective or noun*
— **poly·the·is·tic** \,pä-lē-thē-'is-tik\ *also* **poly·the·is·ti·cal** \-'is-ti-kəl\ *adjective*

poly·thene \'pä-lə-,thēn\ *noun* [by contraction] (1939)
chiefly British **:** POLYETHYLENE

poly·to·nal·i·ty \,pä-lē-tō-'na-lə-tē\ *noun* (1923)
: the simultaneous use of two or more musical keys
— **poly·ton·al** \-'tō-n°l\ *adjective*
— **poly·ton·al·ly** \-n°l-ē\ *adverb*

poly·typ·ic \,pä-lē-'ti-pik\ *adjective* (1888)
: represented by several or many types or subdivisions ⟨a *polytypic* species of organism⟩

poly·un·sat·u·rat·ed \,pä-lē-,ən-'sa-chə-,rā-təd\ *adjective* (1932)
of an oil or fatty acid **:** having many double or triple bonds in a molecule — compare MONOUNSATURATED

poly·ure·thane \,pä-lē-'yur-ə-,thān\ *noun* [International Scientific Vocabulary] (1944)
: any of various polymers that contain NHCOO linkages and are used especially in flexible and rigid foams, elastomers, and resins (as for coatings)

poly·uria \-'yur-ē-ə\ *noun* [New Latin] (circa 1842)
: excessive secretion of urine

poly·va·lent \,pä-lē-'vā-lənt *also* pə-'li-və-lənt\ *adjective* [International Scientific Vocabulary] (1881)
1 : having a chemical valence greater usually than two
2 : effective against, sensitive toward, or counteracting more than one exciting agent (as a toxin or antigen)
— **poly·va·lence** \-lən(t)s\ *noun*

poly·vi·nyl \,pä-lē-'vī-n°l\ *adjective* [International Scientific Vocabulary] (1927)
: of, relating to, or being a polymerized vinyl compound, resin, or plastic — often used in combination

polyvinyl chloride *noun* (1933)
: a polymer of vinyl chloride used especially for electrical insulation, films, and pipes — abbreviation *PVC*

poly·wa·ter \'pä-lē-,wò-tər, -,wä-\ *noun* [*poly*-meric *water*] (1969)
: water condensed into a glass capillary tube and formerly held to be a stable form with special properties

Pom \'päm\ *noun* (1912)
Australian & New Zealand **:** POMMY — usually used disparagingly

pom·ace \'pə-məs, 'pä-\ *noun* [Middle English *pomys*, probably from Medieval Latin *pomacium* cider, from Late Latin *pomum* apple, from Latin, fruit] (15th century)
1 : the dry or pulpy residue of material (as fruit, seeds, or fish) from which a liquid (as juice or oil) has been pressed or extracted
2 : something crushed to a pulpy mass

po·ma·ceous \pō-'mā-shəs\ *adjective* [New Latin *pomaceus*, from Late Latin *pomum*] (1708)
1 : of or relating to apples
2 [*pome*] **:** resembling a pome

po·made \pō-'mād, -'mäd\ *noun* [Middle French *pommade* ointment formerly made from apples, from Italian *pomata*, from *pomo* apple, from Late Latin *pomum*] (1562)
: a perfumed ointment; *especially* **:** a fragrant hair dressing
— **pomade** *transitive verb*

po·man·der \'pō-,man-dər, pō-'\ *noun* [Middle English, modification of Middle French *pome d'ambre*, literally, apple or ball of amber] (15th century)
1 : a mixture of aromatic substances enclosed in a perforated bag or box and used to scent clothes and linens or formerly carried as a guard against infection; *also* **:** a clove-studded orange or apple used for the same purposes
2 : a box or hollow fruit-shaped ball for holding pomander

po·ma·tum \pō-'mā-təm, -'mä-\ *noun* [New Latin, from Late Latin *pomum* apple] (1562)
: POMADE

pome \'pōm\ *noun* [Middle English, from Middle French *pome, pomme* apple, pome, ball, ultimately from Late Latin *pomum*] (15th century)
: a fleshy fruit (as an apple or pear) consisting of an outer thickened fleshy layer and a central core with usually five seeds enclosed in a capsule

pome·gran·ate \'pä-mə-,gra-nət; 'päm-,gra-nət, 'pəm-\ *noun* [Middle English *poumgrenet*, from Middle French *pomme grenate*, literally, seedy apple] (14th century)
1 : a thick-skinned several-celled reddish berry that is about the size of an orange and has many seeds with pulpy crimson arils of tart flavor
2 : a widely cultivated tropical Old World tree (*Punica granatum* of the family Punicaceae) bearing pomegranates

pomegranate

pom·e·lo \'pä-mə-,lō\ *noun*, *plural* **-los** [alteration of earlier *pompelmous*, from Dutch *pompelmoes*] (1858)
1 : GRAPEFRUIT
2 : SHADDOCK

Pom·er·a·nian \,pä-mə-'rā-nē-ən, -nyən\ *noun* (1760)
1 : any of a breed of very small compact long-haired dogs
2 : a native or inhabitant of Pomerania
— **Pomeranian** *adjective*

pom·mée \pä-'mā, ,pə-\ *adjective* [French, from Middle French *pomme* apple, ball] (1725)
of a heraldic cross **:** having the end of each arm terminating in a ball or disk — see CROSS illustration

¹pom·mel \'pə-məl, 'pä-\ *noun* [Middle English *pomel*, from Middle French, from (assumed) Vulgar Latin *pomellum* ball, knob, from diminutive of Late Latin *pomum* apple] (14th century)
1 : the knob on the hilt of a sword or saber
2 : the protuberance at the front and top of a saddle
3 : either of a pair of removable rounded or U-shaped handles used on the top of a pommel horse

²pom·mel \'pə-məl\ *transitive verb* **-meled** *or* **-melled; -mel·ing** *or* **-mel·ling** \'pə-mə-liŋ, 'pəm-liŋ\ [¹*pommel*] (1530)
: PUMMEL

pommel horse *noun* (1908)
1 : a gymnastics apparatus for swinging and balancing feats that consists of a padded rectangular or cylindrical form with two pommels on the top and that is supported in a horizontal position above the floor
2 : an event in which the pommel horse is used

pommel horse 1

Pom·my *or* **Pom·mie** \'pä-mē\ *noun*, *plural* **Pommies** [by shortening & alteration from *pomegranate*, alteration of *Jimmy Grant*, rhyming slang for *immigrant*] (1912)
Australian & New Zealand **:** BRITON; *especially* **:** an English immigrant — usually used disparagingly

Po·mo \'pō-(,)mō\ *noun*, *plural* **Pomo** *or* **Pomos** (1852)
: a member of an American Indian people of northern California

po·mol·o·gy \pō-'mä-lə-jē\ *noun* [New Latin *pomologia*, from Latin *pomum* fruit + *-logia* -logy] (1818)
: the science and practice of fruit growing
— **po·mo·log·i·cal** \,pō-mə-'lä-ji-kəl\ *adjective*
— **po·mol·o·gist** \pō-'mä-lə-jist\ *noun*

pomp \'pämp\ *noun* [Middle English, from Middle French *pompe*, from Latin *pompa* procession, pomp, from Greek *pompē* act of sending, escort, procession, pomp, from *pempein* to send] (14th century)
1 : a show of magnificence **:** SPLENDOR ⟨every day begins . . . in a *pomp* of flaming colours —F. D. Ommanney⟩
2 : a ceremonial or festival display (as a train of followers or a pageant)
3 a : ostentatious display **:** VAINGLORY **b :** an ostentatious gesture or act

pom·pa·dour \'päm-pə-,dōr, -,dòr\ *noun* [Marquise de *Pompadour*] (1756)
1 a : a man's style of hairdressing in which the hair is combed into a high mound in front **b :** a woman's style of hairdressing in which the hair is brushed into a loose full roll around the face
2 : hair dressed in a pompadour
— **pom·pa·doured** \-,dōrd, -,dòrd\ *adjective*

pom·pa·no \'päm-pə-,nō, 'pəm-\ *noun*, *plural* **-no** *or* **-nos** [American Spanish *pámpano*, from Spanish, a percoid fish (*Sparus auratus*), literally, vine leaf, from Latin *pampinus*] (1778)
1 : a carangid food fish (*Trachinotus carolinus*) of the southern Atlantic and Gulf coasts of North America; *broadly* **:** any of several related fishes
2 : a small bluish or greenish butterfish (*Peprilus simillimus*) of the Pacific coast

\ə\ abut \°\ kitten \ər\ further \a\ ash \ā\ ace
\ä\ mop, mar \aù\ out \ch\ chin \e\ bet \ē\ easy
\g\ go \i\ hit \ī\ ice \j\ job \ŋ\ sing \ō\ go
\ò\ law \òi\ boy \th\ thin \t͟h\ the \ü\ loot \ù\ foot
\y\ yet \zh\ vision *see also* Guide to Pronunciation

¹pom–pom \'päm-,päm\ *noun* [alteration of *pompon*] (1897)
1 : an ornamental ball or tuft used especially on clothing, caps, or costumes
2 : a handheld usually brightly colored fluffy ball flourished by cheerleaders

²pom–pom *noun* [imitative; from the sound of its discharge] (1899)
: a multibarreled automatic antiaircraft gun of 20 to 40 millimeters mounted especially on ships

pom·pon \'päm-,pän\ *noun* [French, from Middle French *pompe* tuft of ribbons] (1753)
1 : ¹POM-POM 1
2 : a chrysanthemum or dahlia with small rounded flower heads

pom·pos·i·ty \päm-'pä-sə-tē\ *noun, plural* **-ties** (1620)
1 : pompous demeanor, speech, or behavior
2 : a pompous gesture, habit, or act

pomp·ous \'päm-pəs\ *adjective* (15th century)
1 : excessively elevated or ornate ⟨*pompous* rhetoric⟩
2 : having or exhibiting self-importance : ARROGANT ⟨a *pompous* politician⟩
3 : relating to or suggestive of pomp : MAGNIFICENT
— **pomp·ous·ly** *adverb*
— **pomp·ous·ness** *noun*

ponce \'pän(t)s\ *noun* [origin unknown] (1872) *British* : PIMP; *also* : a male homosexual — usually used disparagingly

pon·cho \'pän-(,)chō\ *noun, plural* **ponchos** [American Spanish, from Araucanian] (1717)
1 : a blanket with a slit in the middle so that it can be slipped over the head and worn as a sleeveless garment
2 : a waterproof garment resembling a poncho and having an integral hood

¹pond \'pänd\ *noun* [Middle English *ponde* artificially confined body of water, probably alteration of *pounde* enclosure — more at POUND] (14th century)
: a body of water usually smaller than a lake

²pond (1694)
transitive verb
: to block (as a stream) to create a pond
intransitive verb
: to collect in or form a pond

pon·der \'pän-dər\ *verb* **pon·dered; pon·der·ing** \-d(ə-)riŋ\ [Middle English, from Middle French *ponderer*, from Latin *ponderare* to weigh, ponder, from *ponder-, pondus* weight — more at PENDANT] (14th century)
transitive verb
1 : to weigh in the mind : APPRAISE ⟨*pondered* their chances of success⟩
2 : to think about : reflect on ⟨*pondered* the events of the day⟩
intransitive verb
: to think or consider especially quietly, soberly, and deeply ☆
— **pon·der·er** \-dər-ər\ *noun*

pon·der·a·ble \'pän-d(ə-)rə-bəl\ *adjective* [Late Latin *ponderabilis*, from *ponderare*] (1813)
: significant enough to be worth considering : APPRECIABLE
synonym see PERCEPTIBLE

pon·der·o·sa pine \,pän-də-'rō-sə-, -zə-\ *noun* [New Latin *ponderosa*, specific epithet of *Pinus ponderosa*, from Latin, feminine of *ponderosus* ponderous] (1878)
: a tall pine (*Pinus ponderosa*) of western North America with long needles usually in groups of 2 or 3; *also* : its strong reddish straight-grained wood — called also *ponderosa*

pon·der·ous \'pän-d(ə-)rəs\ *adjective* [Middle English, from Middle French *pondereux*, from Latin *ponderosus*, from *ponder-, pondus* weight] (15th century)
1 : of very great weight
2 : unwieldy or clumsy because of weight and size

3 : oppressively or unpleasantly dull : LIFELESS ⟨*ponderous* prose⟩
synonym see HEAVY
— **pon·der·ous·ly** *adverb*
— **pon·der·ous·ness** *noun*

pond lily *noun* (1748)
: WATER LILY

pond scum *noun* (circa 1890)
1 : SPIROGYRA; *also* : any of various related algae
2 : a mass of tangled algal filaments in stagnant waters

pond skater *noun* (1895)
: WATER STRIDER

pond·weed \'pänd-,wēd\ *noun* (1578)
: any of a genus (*Potamogeton* of the family Potamogetonaceae, the pondweed family) of aquatic plants with jointed usually rooting stems, 2-ranked floating or submerged leaves, and spikes of greenish flowers

pone \'pōn\ *noun* [modification of Virginia Algonquian *appone*] (1634)
Southern & Midland : CORN PONE

pon·gee \,pän-'jē, 'pän-,\ *noun, often attributive* [Chinese (Beijing) *běnjī*, from *běn* own + *jī* loom] (1711)
: a thin soft fabric of Chinese origin woven from raw silk; *also* : an imitation of this fabric in cotton or a synthetic fiber (as of polyester or rayon)

pon·gid \'pän-jəd, 'pän-gəd\ *noun* [ultimately from Kongo *mpongi* ape] (1950)
: any of a family (Pongidae) of apes that includes the chimpanzee, gorilla, and orangutan
— **pongid** *adjective*

¹pon·iard \'pän-yərd\ *noun* [Middle French *poignard*, from *poing* fist, from Latin *pugnus* fist — more at PUNGENT] (1588)
: a dagger with a usually slender blade of triangular or square cross section

²poniard *transitive verb* (1601)
: to pierce or kill with a poniard

pons \'pänz\ *noun, plural* **pon·tes** \'pän-,tēz\ [New Latin, short for *pons Varolii*] (1831)
: a broad mass of chiefly transverse nerve fibers conspicuous on the ventral surface of the brain of man and lower mammals at the anterior end of the medulla oblongata — see BRAIN illustration

pons as·i·no·rum \,pänz-,a-sə-'nōr-əm, -'nȯr-\ *noun* [New Latin, literally, asses' bridge, name applied to the proposition that the base angles of an isosceles triangle are equal] (1751)
: a critical test of ability or understanding; *also* : STUMBLING BLOCK

pons Va·ro·lii \-və-'rō-lē-,ī, -lē-,ē\ *noun* [New Latin, literally, bridge of Varoli, from Costanzo *Varoli* (died 1575) Italian surgeon and anatomist] (circa 1693)
: PONS

pon·ti·fex \'pän-tə-,feks\ *noun, plural* **pon·tif·i·ces** \pän-'ti-fə-,sēz\ [Latin *pontific-, pontifex*, from *pont-, pons* bridge + *facere* to make — more at FIND, DO] (circa 1580)
: a member of the council of priests in ancient Rome

pon·tiff \'pän-təf\ *noun* [French *pontif*, from Latin *pontific-, pontifex*] (1626)
1 : PONTIFEX
2 : BISHOP; *specifically* : POPE

¹pon·tif·i·cal \pän-'ti-fi-kəl\ *adjective* (14th century)
1 : episcopal attire; *specifically* : the insignia of the episcopal order worn by a prelate when celebrating a pontifical mass — usually used in plural
2 : a book containing the forms for sacraments and rites performed by a bishop

²pontifical *adjective* [Middle English, from Latin *pontificalis*, from *pontific-, pontifex*] (15th century)
1 a : of or relating to a pontiff or pontifex **b** : celebrated by a prelate of episcopal rank with distinctive ceremonies ⟨*pontifical* mass⟩
2 : POMPOUS
3 : pretentiously dogmatic

— **pon·tif·i·cal·ly** \-k(ə-)lē\ *adverb*

¹pon·tif·i·cate \pän-'ti-fi-kət, -,kāt\ *noun* [Middle English, from Latin *pontificatus*, from *pontific-, pontifex*] (15th century)
: the state, office, or term of office of a pontiff

²pon·tif·i·cate \pän-'ti-fə-,kāt\ *intransitive verb* **-cat·ed; -cat·ing** [Medieval Latin *pontificatus*, past participle of *pontificare*, from Latin *pontific-, pontifex*] (1818)
1 a : to officiate as a pontiff **b** : to celebrate pontifical mass
2 : to speak or express opinions in a pompous or dogmatic way
— **pon·tif·i·ca·tion** \(,)pän-,ti-fə-'kā-shən\ *noun*
— **pon·tif·i·ca·tor** \-,kā-tər\ *noun*

pon·til \'pän-t³l\ *noun* [French, perhaps from Italian *puntello*, diminutive of *punto* point, from Latin *punctus* — more at POINT] (1832)
: PUNTY — called also *pontil rod*

pon·tine \'pän-,tīn\ *adjective* [New Latin *pont-, pons* pons] (1889)
: of or relating to the pons

Pont l'É·vêque \,pōⁿ-lā-'vek\ *noun* [*Pont l'Évêque*, town in France] (circa 1889)
: a soft surface-ripened cheese firmer, yellower, and having less surface mold than Camembert

¹pon·toon \pän-'tün\ *noun* [French *ponton*, from Latin *ponton-, ponto*] (1690)
1 : a flat-bottomed boat (as a lighter); *especially* : a flat-bottomed boat or portable float used in building a floating temporary bridge
2 : a float especially of a seaplane

²pontoon *noun* [perhaps alteration of *vingt-et-un*] (circa 1917)
British : BLACKJACK 5

po·ny \'pō-nē\ *noun, plural* **ponies** [probably from obsolete French *poulenet*, diminutive of French *poulain* colt, from Medieval Latin *pullanus*, from Latin *pullus* young of an animal, foal — more at FOAL] (1659)
1 a : a small horse; *especially* : one of any of several breeds of very small stocky animals noted for their gentleness and endurance **b** : a bronco, mustang, or similar horse of the western U.S. **c** : RACEHORSE — usually used in plural
2 : something smaller than standard: as **a** : a small beer glass **b** : a small liqueur glass typically holding one ounce
3 : a literal translation of a foreign language text; *especially* : one used surreptitiously by students in preparing or reciting lessons

pony express *noun, often P&E capitalized* (1860)
: a rapid postal and express system that operated across the western U.S. in 1860–1861 by relays of horses and riders

po·ny·tail \'pō-nē-,tāl\ *noun* (1951)
: a hairstyle in which the hair is pulled together and banded at the back of the head so as to resemble a pony's tail
— **po·ny·tailed** \-,tāld\ *adjective*

po·ny up \'pō-nē-\ *verb* **po·nied up; po·ny·ing up** [origin unknown] (1824)
transitive verb

☆ SYNONYMS
Ponder, meditate, muse, ruminate mean to consider or examine attentively or deliberately. PONDER implies a careful weighing of a problem or, often, prolonged inconclusive thinking about a matter ⟨*pondered* the course of action⟩. MEDITATE implies a definite focusing of one's thoughts on something so as to understand it deeply ⟨*meditated* on the meaning of life⟩. MUSE suggests a more or less focused daydreaming as in remembrance ⟨*mused* upon childhood joys⟩. RUMINATE implies going over the same matter in one's thoughts again and again but suggests little of either purposive thinking or rapt absorption ⟨*ruminated* on past disappointments⟩.

: to pay (money) especially in settlement of an account 〈*ponied up* $12.50 for the fine —*Newsweek*〉
intransitive verb
: PAY

Pon·zi scheme \'pän-zē-\ *noun* [Charles A. Ponzi (died 1949) American (Italian-born) swindler] (1973)
: an investment swindle in which some early investors are paid off with money put up by later ones in order to encourage more and bigger risks

-poo \,pü, 'pü\ *suffix* [origin unknown]
— used as a disparaging diminutive 〈cutesy-*poo*〉

¹**pooch** \'püch\ *verb* [alteration of ¹*pouch*] (circa 1923)
chiefly dialect **:** BULGE

²**pooch** *noun* [origin unknown] (1924)
: DOG

pood \'püd, 'püt\ *noun* [Russian *pud*, from Old Russian, from Old Norse *pund* pound — more at POUND] (1554)
: a Russian unit of weight equal to about 36.11 pounds (16.38 kilograms)

poo·dle \'pü-d°l\ *noun* [German *Pudel*, short for *Pudelhund*, from *pudeln* to splash + *Hund* dog] (1820)
1 : a dog of any of three breeds of active intelligent heavy-coated solid-colored dogs — compare TOY POODLE
2 : a fabric with a nubby or coarsely looped surface that resembles a poodle's coat — called also *poodle cloth*

¹**poof** \'püf, 'pùf\ *interjection* (1824)
— used to express disdain or dismissal or to suggest instantaneous occurrence

²**poof** *also* **poove** \'püv, 'pùv\ *noun, plural* **poofs** *also* **pooves** [perhaps alteration of ²*puff*] (circa 1860)
British **:** a male homosexual — usually used disparagingly

poof·ter \'püf-tər, 'pùf-\ *also* **poof·tah** \-tə\ *noun* [by alteration] (1903)
British **:** POOF — usually used disparagingly

pooh \'pü, 'pù\ *interjection* (1602)
— used to express contempt or disapproval

pooh–bah *also* **poo-bah** \'pü-,bä, -,bȯ\ *noun, often P&B capitalized* [*Pooh-Bah,* character in Gilbert and Sullivan's opera *The Mikado* (1885) bearing the title Lord-High-Everything-Else] (1888)
1 : a person holding many public or private offices
2 : a person in high position or of great influence

pooh–pooh \'pü-(,)pü, pü-'\ *also* **pooh** \'pü\ *verb* [*pooh*] (1827)
intransitive verb
: to express contempt or impatience
transitive verb
: to express contempt for or make light of **:** PLAY DOWN, DISMISS

¹**pool** \'pü(ə)l\ *noun* [Middle English, from Old English *pōl;* akin to Old High German *pfuol* pool] (before 12th century)
1 a (1) **:** a small and rather deep body of usually fresh water (2) **:** a quiet place in a stream (3) **:** a body of water forming above a dam **b :** something resembling a pool 〈a *pool* of light〉
2 : a small body of standing liquid
3 : a continuous area of porous sedimentary rock that yields petroleum or gas
4 : SWIMMING POOL

²**pool** *intransitive verb* (1626)
1 : to form a pool
2 *of blood* **:** to accumulate or become static (as in the veins of a bodily part)

³**pool** *noun* [French *poule*, literally, hen, from Old French, feminine of *poul* cock — more at PULLET] (circa 1712)
1 a : an aggregate stake to which each player of a game has contributed **b :** all the money bet by a number of persons on a particular event

2 a : a game played on an English billiard table in which each of the players stakes a sum and the winner takes all **b :** any of various games of billiards played on an oblong table having 6 pockets with usually 15 object balls
3 : an aggregation of the interests or property of different persons made to further a joint undertaking by subjecting them to the same control and a common liability
4 : a readily available supply: as **a :** the whole quantity of a particular material present in the body and available for function or the satisfying of metabolic demands **b :** a body product (as blood) collected from many donors and stored for later use **c :** a group of people available for some purpose 〈a shrinking *pool* of applicants〉 〈typing *pool*〉
5 : GENE POOL

⁴**pool** *transitive verb* (1879)
: to combine (as resources) in a common fund or effort

pool·room \'pü(ə)l-,rüm, -,rùm\ *noun* (1861)
1 : a room in which bookmaking is carried on
2 : a room for the playing of pool

pool·side \-,sīd\ *noun* (1921)
: the area surrounding a swimming pool

¹**poop** \'püp\ *noun* [Middle English, from Middle French *poupe*, from Latin *puppis*] (15th century)
1 *obsolete* **:** STERN
2 : an enclosed superstructure at the stern of a ship above the main deck

²**poop** *transitive verb* (1748)
1 : to break over the stern of
2 : to ship (a sea or wave) over the stern

³**poop** *verb* [origin unknown] (circa 1932)
transitive verb
slang **:** to put out of breath; *also* **:** to tire out
intransitive verb
slang **:** to become exhausted 〈*poop* out〉

⁴**poop** *noun* [perhaps from ⁵*poop*] (circa 1941)
slang **:** INFORMATION, SCOOP

⁵**poop** *noun* [*poop,* verb, to defecate, break wind, from Middle English *poupen* to make a gulping sound; of imitative origin] (1965)
: EXCREMENT

poop deck *noun* (1840)
: a partial deck above a ship's main afterdeck

poop·er–scoop·er \'pü-pər-,skü-pər\ *noun* [⁵*poop*] (1976)
: a device used for picking up the droppings of a pet (as a dog) for disposal

poor \'pùr, 'pōr\ *adjective* [Middle English *poure,* from Old French *povre,* from Latin *pauper;* akin to Latin *paucus* little and to Latin *parere* to give birth to, produce — more at FEW, PARE] (13th century)
1 a : lacking material possessions **b :** of, relating to, or characterized by poverty
2 a : less than adequate **:** MEAGER **b :** small in worth
3 : exciting pity 〈you *poor* thing〉
4 a : inferior in quality or value **b :** HUMBLE, UNPRETENTIOUS **c :** MEAN, PETTY
5 : LEAN, EMACIATED
6 : BARREN, UNPRODUCTIVE — used of land
7 : INDIFFERENT, UNFAVORABLE
8 : lacking a normal or adequate supply of something specified — often used in combination 〈oil-*poor* countries〉
— **poor·ish** \-ish\ *adjective*
— **poor·ness** *noun*

poor box *noun* (1621)
: a box (as in a church) for alms for the poor

poor boy \'pō(r)-,bȯi\ *noun* (circa 1941)
: SUBMARINE 2

Poor Clare \-'klar, -'kler\ *noun* (1608)
: a member of an austere order of nuns founded by Saint Clare under the direction of Saint Francis in Assisi, Italy, in 1212

poor farm \'pùr-,färm, 'pōr-\ *noun* (1852)
: a farm maintained at public expense for the support and employment of needy persons

poor·house \-,haùs\ *noun* (1792)
: a place maintained at public expense to house needy or dependent persons

poor law *noun* (1752)
: a law providing for or regulating the public relief or support of the poor

¹**poor·ly** \'pùr-lē, 'pōr-\ *adverb* (13th century)
: in a poor condition or manner; *especially* **:** in an inferior or imperfect way **:** BADLY 〈sang *poorly*〉

²**poor·ly** *adjective* (1750)
: somewhat ill **:** INDISPOSED

poor–mouth \'pùr-,maùth, 'pōr-, -,maùth\ (1964)
intransitive verb
: to plead poverty as a defense or excuse
transitive verb
: to speak disparagingly of

poor mouth \-,maùth\ *noun* (1822)
: an exaggerated claim of poverty

poor–spir·it·ed \-'spir-ə-təd\ *adjective* (1670)
: lacking zest, confidence, or courage
— **poor–spir·it·ed·ly** *adverb*
— **poor–spir·it·ed·ness** *noun*

poor white *noun* (1819)
: a member of an inferior or underprivileged white social group — often taken to be offensive

¹**pop** \'päp\ *verb* **popped; pop·ping** [Middle English *poppen,* of imitative origin] (15th century)
transitive verb
1 : to strike or knock sharply **:** HIT
2 : to push, put, or thrust suddenly and often deftly
3 : to cause to explode or burst open
4 : to fire at **:** SHOOT
5 : to take (pills) especially frequently or habitually
6 : to open with a pop 〈*pop* a cold beer〉
intransitive verb
1 a : to go, come, or appear suddenly — often used with *up* **b :** to escape or break away from something (as a point of attachment) usually suddenly or unexpectedly
2 : to make or burst with a sharp sound **:** EXPLODE
3 : to protrude from the sockets
4 : to shoot with a firearm
5 : to hit a pop fly — often used with *up* or *out*
— **pop the question** **:** to propose marriage

²**pop** *noun* (1591)
1 : a sharp explosive sound
2 : a shot from a gun
3 : SODA POP
4 : POP FLY
— **a pop** **:** for each one **:** APIECE 〈tickets at $10 *a pop*〉

³**pop** *adverb* (1621)
: like or with a pop **:** SUDDENLY

⁴**pop** *noun* [short for *poppa*] (1838)
: FATHER

⁵**pop** *adjective* [by shortening] (1880)
1 : POPULAR 〈*pop* music〉: as **a :** of or relating to popular music 〈*pop* singer〉 **b :** of or relating to the popular culture disseminated through the mass media 〈*pop* psychology〉 〈*pop* grammarians〉 〈*pop* society〉
2 a : of or relating to pop art 〈*pop* painter〉 **b :** having, using, or imitating themes or techniques characteristic of pop art 〈*pop* movie〉

⁶**pop** *noun* (1954)
1 : pop music
2 : POP ART
3 : pop culture

pop art *noun* (1957)
: art in which commonplace objects (as road signs, hamburgers, comic strips, or soup cans)

are used as subject matter and are often physically incorporated in the work
— **pop artist** noun

pop·corn \'päp-ˌkȯrn\ noun (1823)
: an Indian corn (Zea mays praecox) whose kernels on exposure to heat burst open to form a white starchy mass; also : the kernels especially after popping

pope \'pōp\ noun [Middle English, from Old English pāpa, from Late Latin papa, from Greek pappas, papas, title of bishops, literally, papa] (before 12th century)
1 often capitalized : a prelate who as bishop of Rome is the head of the Roman Catholic Church
2 : one that resembles a pope (as in authority)
3 a : the Eastern Orthodox or Coptic patriarch of Alexandria **b** : a priest of an Eastern church

pop·ery \'pō-p(ə-)rē\ noun (circa 1534)
: ROMAN CATHOLICISM — usually disparagingly

pop eye \'päp-ˌī\ noun [back-formation from pop-eyed] (1828)
: an eye staring and bulging (as from excitement)
— **pop–eyed** \-ˌīd\ adjective

pop fly noun (1887)
: a high fly ball in baseball

pop·gun \'päp-ˌgən\ noun (1622)
: a toy gun that usually shoots a cork and produces a popping sound

pop·in·jay \'pä-pən-ˌjā\ noun [Middle English papejay parrot, from Middle French papegai, papejai, from Arabic babghā'] (1528)
: a strutting supercilious person

pop·ish \'pō-pish\ adjective [pope] (1528)
: ROMAN CATHOLIC — often used disparagingly

pop·lar \'pä-plər\ noun [Middle English poplere, from Middle French pouplier, from pouple poplar, from Latin populus] (14th century)
1 a : any of a genus (Populus) of slender catkin-bearing quick-growing trees (as an aspen or cottonwood) of the willow family **b** : the wood of a poplar
2 : TULIP TREE 1

pop·lin \'pä-plən\ noun [French papeline] (1710)
: a strong fabric in plain weave with crosswise ribs

pop·li·te·al \ˌpä-plə-'tē-əl also pä-'pli-tē-əl\ adjective [New Latin popliteus, from Latin poplit-, poples ham of the knee] (1786)
: of or relating to the back part of the leg behind the knee joint

pop off intransitive verb (1764)
1 a : to die unexpectedly **b** : to leave suddenly
2 : to talk thoughtlessly and often loudly or angrily

pop·over \'päp-ˌō-vər\ noun (1876)
: a hollow quick bread shaped like a muffin and made from a thin batter of eggs, milk, and flour

pop·pa \'pä-pə\ variant of PAPA

pop·per \'pä-pər\ noun (1750)
1 : one that pops; especially : a utensil for popping corn
2 slang : a vial of amyl nitrite or butyl nitrite especially when used illicitly as an aphrodisiac

pop·pet \'pä-pət\ noun [Middle English popet — more at PUPPET] (15th century)
1 a Midland : DOLL **b** obsolete : MARIONETTE
2 chiefly British : DEAR
3 a : an upright support or guide of a machine that is fastened at the bottom only **b** : a valve that rises perpendicularly to or from its seat

pop·pied \'pä-pēd\ adjective (1818)
1 archaic : growing or overgrown with poppies
2 : DROWSY

¹pop·ple \'pä-pəl\ noun [Middle English popul, from Old English, from Latin populus] (14th century)
chiefly dialect : POPLAR 1

²popple noun [popple, verb, from Middle English poplen to bubble, ripple, probably of imitative origin] (1875)
: a choppy sea

pop·py \'pä-pē\ noun, plural **poppies** [Middle English popi, from Old English popæg, popig, modification of Latin papaver] (before 12th century)
1 a : any of a genus (Papaver of the family Papaveraceae, the poppy family) of chiefly annual or perennial herbs with milky juice, showy regular flowers, and capsular fruits including the opium poppy and several forms cultivated as ornamentals **b** : an extract or decoction of poppy used medicinally
2 : a strong reddish orange

pop·py·cock \'pä-pē-ˌkäk\ noun [Dutch dialect pappekak, literally, soft dung, from Dutch pap pap + kak dung] (1865)
: empty talk or writing : NONSENSE

pop·py·head \-ˌhed\ noun (1839)
: a raised ornament often in the form of a finial generally used on the tops of the upright ends of seats in Gothic churches

poppy seed noun (14th century)
: the seed of a poppy used chiefly as a topping or flavoring for baked goods

pop quiz noun (circa 1960)
: an unscheduled or unannounced quiz

Pop·si·cle \'päp-ˌsi-kəl, -si-kəl\ trademark
— used for flavored and colored water frozen on a stick

pop–top \'päp-ˌtäp\ adjective (1965)
: a closure that can be pulled by hand to open a can

pop·u·lace \'pä-pyə-ləs\ noun [Middle French, from Italian popolaccio rabble, augmentative of popolo the people, from Latin populus] (1572)
1 : the common people : MASSES
2 : POPULATION

pop·u·lar \'pä-pyə-lər\ adjective [Latin popularis, from populus the people, a people] (1548)
1 : of or relating to the general public
2 : suitable to the majority : as **a** : adapted to or indicative of the understanding and taste of the majority ⟨a popular history of the war⟩ **b** : suited to the means of the majority : INEXPENSIVE ⟨sold at popular prices⟩
3 : frequently encountered or widely accepted
4 : commonly liked or approved ⟨a very popular girl⟩
synonym see COMMON
— **pop·u·lar·ly** adverb

popular front noun, often P&F capitalized (1936)
: a coalition especially of leftist political parties against a common opponent; specifically : one sponsored and dominated by Communists as a device for gaining power

pop·u·lar·ise British variant of POPULARIZE

pop·u·lar·i·ty \ˌpä-pyə-'lar-ə-tē\ noun (1601)
: the quality or state of being popular

pop·u·lar·ize \'pä-pyə-lə-ˌrīz\ verb **-ized; -izing** (1593)
intransitive verb
: to cater to popular taste
transitive verb
: to make popular: as **a** : to cause to be liked or esteemed **b** : to present in generally understandable or interesting form
— **pop·u·lar·i·za·tion** \ˌpä-pyə-lə-rə-'zā-shən\ noun
— **pop·u·lar·iz·er** \'pä-pyə-lə-ˌrī-zər\ noun

popular sovereignty noun (1848)
1 : a doctrine in political theory that government is created by and subject to the will of the people
2 : a pre-Civil War doctrine asserting the right of the people living in a newly organized territory to decide by vote of their territorial legislature whether or not slavery would be permitted there

pop·u·late \'pä-pyə-ˌlāt\ transitive verb **-lated; -lating** [Medieval Latin populatus, past participle of populare to people, from Latin populus people] (1578)
1 : to have a place in : OCCUPY, INHABIT
2 a : to furnish or provide with inhabitants : PEOPLE **b** : to provide with members

pop·u·la·tion \ˌpä-pyə-'lā-shən\ noun [Late Latin population-, populatio, from Latin populus] (1612)
1 a : the whole number of people or inhabitants in a country or region **b** : the total of individuals occupying an area or making up a whole **c** : the total of particles at a particular energy level — used especially of atoms in a laser
2 : the act or process of populating
3 a : a body of persons or individuals having a quality or characteristic in common **b** (1) : the organisms inhabiting a particular locality (2) : a group of interbreeding organisms that represents the level of organization at which speciation begins
4 : a group of individual persons, objects, or items from which samples are taken for statistical measurement
— **pop·u·la·tion·al** \-shnəl, -shə-nᵊl\ adjective

population explosion noun (1953)
: a pyramiding of numbers of a biological population; especially : the recent great increase in human numbers resulting from increased survival and exponential population growth

¹pop·u·list \'pä-pyə-list\ noun [Latin populus the people] (1892)
1 : a member of a political party claiming to represent the common people; especially, often capitalized : a member of a U.S. political party formed in 1891 primarily to represent agrarian interests and to advocate the free coinage of silver and government control of monopolies
2 : a believer in the rights, wisdom, or virtues of the common people
— **pop·u·lism** \-ˌli-zəm\ noun
— **pop·u·lis·tic** \ˌpä-pyə-'lis-tik\ adjective

²populist adjective (1893)
1 often capitalized : of, relating to, or characterized by populism
2 : POPULAR 1, 2

pop·u·lous \'pä-pyə-ləs\ adjective [Middle English, from Latin populosus, from populus people] (15th century)
1 a : densely populated **b** : having a large population
2 a : NUMEROUS **b** : filled to capacity
— **pop·u·lous·ly** adverb
— **pop·u·lous·ness** noun

pop-up \'päp-ˌəp\ noun (1906)
: POP FLY

por·bea·gle \'pȯr-ˌbē-gəl\ noun [Cornish porgh-bugel] (1758)
: a small viviparous shark (Lamna nasus) chiefly of the North Atlantic Ocean with a pointed nose and crescent-shaped tail

por·ce·lain \'pȯr-s(ə-)lən, 'pȯr-\ noun [Middle French porcelaine cowrie shell, porcelain, from Italian porcellana, from porcello vulva, literally, little pig, from Latin porcellus, diminutive of porcus pig, vulva; from the shape of the shell — more at FARROW] (circa 1530)
: a hard, fine-grained, sonorous, nonporous, and usually translucent and white ceramic ware that consists essentially of kaolin, quartz, and feldspar and is fired at high temperatures
— **por·ce·lain·like** \-ˌlīk\ adjective
— **por·ce·la·ne·ous** or **por·cel·la·ne·ous** \ˌpȯr-sə-'lā-nē-əs, ˌpȯr-\ adjective

porcelain enamel noun (1883)
: a fired-on opaque glassy coating on metal (as steel)

por·ce·lain·ize \'pȯr-s(ə-)lə-ˌnīz, 'pȯr-\ transitive verb **-ized; -iz·ing** (1951)
: to fire a glassy coating on (as steel)

porch \'pȯrch, 'pȯrch\ noun [Middle English porche, from Old French, from Latin porticus

portico, from *porta* gate; akin to Latin *portus* port — more at FORD] (14th century)
1 : a covered area adjoining an entrance to a building and usually having a separate roof
2 *obsolete* **:** PORTICO

por·cine \'pȯr-ˌsīn\ *adjective* [Latin *porcinus,* from *porcus* pig — more at FARROW] (circa 1656)
: of, relating to, or suggesting swine

por·ci·no \pȯr-'chē-(ˌ)nō\ *noun, plural* **-ni** \-(ˌ)nē\ [Italian, short for *fungo porcino,* literally, porcine mushroom] (1976)
: a wild edible boletus mushroom (especially *Boletus edulis*)

por·cu·pine \'pȯr-kyə-ˌpīn\ *noun, plural* **por·cupines** *also* **porcupine** [Middle English *porkepin,* from Middle French *porc espin,* from Old Italian *porcospino,* from Latin *porcus* pig + *spina* spine, prickle] (15th century)
: any of various relatively large rodents having stiff sharp erectile bristles mingled with the hair and constituting an Old World terrestrial family (Hystricidae) and a New World arboreal family (Erethizontidae)

porcupine fish *noun* (1681)
: any of several bony fishes (family Diodontidae) having sharp spines covering the body; *especially* **:** a spotted chiefly tropical fish (*Diodon hystrix*) that is olive to brown above with white below

¹pore \'pȯr, 'pȯr\ *intransitive verb* **pored; por·ing** [Middle English *pouren*] (13th century)
1 : to gaze intently
2 : to read studiously or attentively — usually used with *over*
3 : to reflect or meditate steadily

²pore *noun* [Middle English, from Middle French, from Latin *porus,* from Greek *poros* passage, pore — more at FARE] (14th century)
1 : a minute opening especially in an animal or plant; *especially* **:** one by which matter passes through a membrane
2 : a small interstice (as in soil) admitting absorption or passage of liquid
— **pored** \'pȯrd, 'pȯrd\ *adjective*

pore fungus *noun* (1922)
: a fungus (family Boletaceae or Polyporaceae) having the spore-bearing surface within tubes or pores

por·gy \'pȯr-gē\ *noun, plural* **porgies** *also* **porgy** [alteration of *pargo,* from Spanish & Portuguese, from Latin *phager,* from Greek *phagros*] (1671)
1 : a blue-spotted crimson food fish (*Pagrus pagrus* of the family Sparidae) of the eastern and western Atlantic; *also* **:** any of various fishes of the same family
2 [alteration of *pogy*] **:** any of various bony fishes (as a menhaden) of families other than that of the porgy

pork \'pȯrk, 'pȯrk\ *noun* [Middle English, from Old French *porc* pig, from Latin *porcus* — more at FARROW] (14th century)
1 : the fresh or salted flesh of swine when dressed for food
2 : government money, jobs, or favors used by politicians as patronage

pork barrel *noun* (1909)
: government projects or appropriations yielding rich patronage benefits; *also* **:** PORK 2

pork belly *noun* (circa 1950)
: an uncured side of pork

pork·er \'pȯr-kər, 'pȯrk-\ *noun* (1657)
: HOG; *especially* **:** a young pig fattened for table use as fresh pork

pork·pie hat \'pȯrk-ˌpī-, 'pȯrk-\ *noun* [from its shape] (1860)
: a hat with a low telescoped crown, flat top, and brim turned all around up or up in back and down in front

¹porky \'pȯr-kē, 'pȯr-\ *adjective* **pork·i·er; -est** (1852)
1 : resembling a pig **:** FAT

²por·ky \'pȯr-kē\ *noun, plural* **porkies** (1900)
: PORCUPINE

porn \'pȯrn\ *also* **por·no** \'pȯr-(ˌ)nō\ *noun, often attributive* (1962)
: PORNOGRAPHY

por·nog·ra·pher \pȯr-'nä-grə-fər\ *noun* (1850)
: one who produces pornography

por·nog·ra·phy \-fē\ *noun* [Greek *pornographos,* adjective, writing about prostitutes, from *pornē* prostitute + *graphein* to write; akin to Greek *pernanai* to sell, *poros* journey — more at FARE, CARVE] (circa 1864)
1 : the depiction of erotic behavior (as in pictures or writing) intended to cause sexual excitement
2 : material (as books or a photograph) that depicts erotic behavior and is intended to cause sexual excitement
3 : the depiction of acts in a sensational manner so as to arouse a quick intense emotional reaction ⟨the *pornography* of violence⟩
— **por·no·graph·ic** \ˌpȯr-nə-'gra-fik\ *adjective*
— **por·no·graph·i·cal·ly** \-fi-k(ə-)lē\ *adverb*

porny \'pȯr-ne\ *adjective* **porn·i·er; -est** (1961)
: of, relating to, involved in, or being pornography

po·ros·i·ty \pə-'rä-sə-tē, pȯ-\ *noun, plural* **-ties** (14th century)
1 a : the quality or state of being porous **b :** the ratio of the volume of interstices of a material to the volume of its mass
2 : PORE

po·rous \'pȯr-əs, 'pȯr-\ *adjective* (14th century)
1 a : possessing or full of pores **b :** containing vessels ⟨hardwood is *porous*⟩
2 a : permeable to fluids **b :** permeable to outside influences ⟨his imagination is astonishingly *porous* —Elizabeth Hardwick⟩
3 : capable of being penetrated ⟨*porous* national boundaries⟩ ⟨a *porous* defense⟩
— **po·rous·ly** *adverb*
— **po·rous·ness** *noun*

por·phyr·ia \pȯr-'fir-ē-ə\ *noun* [New Latin, from International Scientific Vocabulary *porphyrin*] (1923)
: any of several usually hereditary abnormalities of porphyrin metabolism characterized by excretion of excess porphyrins in the urine

por·phy·rin \'pȯr-fə-rən\ *noun* [International Scientific Vocabulary, from Greek *porphyra* purple] (1910)
: any of various compounds with a structure that consists essentially of four pyrrole rings joined by four =CH— groups; *especially* **:** one (as chlorophyll or hemoglobin) containing a central metal atom and usually exhibiting biological activity

por·phy·rit·ic \ˌpȯr-fə-'ri-tik\ *adjective* [Medieval Latin *porphyriticus,* from Greek *porphyritikos,* from *porphyritēs* (*lithos*) porphyry] (15th century)
1 : of or relating to porphyry
2 : having distinct crystals (as of feldspar) in a relatively fine-grained base

por·phy·rop·sin \ˌpȯr-fə-'räp-sən\ *noun* [Greek *porphyra* purple + English *-opsin* (as in *rhodopsin*)] (1930)
: a purple pigment in the retinal rods of freshwater fishes that resembles rhodopsin

por·phy·ry \'pȯr-f(ə-)rē\ *noun, plural* **-ries** [Middle English *porphiri,* from Medieval Latin *porphyrium,* alteration of Latin *porphyrites,* from Greek *porphyritēs* (*lithos*), literally, stone like Tyrian purple, from *porphyra* purple] (15th century)
1 : a rock consisting of feldspar crystals embedded in a compact dark red or purple groundmass
2 : an igneous rock of porphyritic texture

por·poise \'pȯr-pəs\ *noun* [Middle English

porpoys, from Middle French *porpois,* from Medieval Latin *porcopiscis,* from Latin *porcus* pig + *piscis* fish — more at FARROW, FISH] (14th century)
1 : any of a family (Phocoenidae) of small gregarious toothed whales; *especially* **:** a blunt-snouted usually largely black whale (*Phocoena phocoena*) of the North Atlantic and Pacific 5 to 8 feet (1.5 to 2.4 meters) long
2 : DOLPHIN 1a

por·rect \pə-'rekt, pä-\ *adjective* [Latin *porrectus,* past participle of *porrigere* to stretch out, from *por-* forward + *regere* to direct — more at PORTEND, RIGHT] (15th century)
: extended forward ⟨*porrect* antennae⟩

por·ridge \'pȯr-ij, 'pär-\ *noun* [alteration of *pottage*] (circa 1643)
: a soft food made by boiling meal of grains or legumes in milk or water until thick
— **por·ridgy** \-i-jē\ *adjective*

por·rin·ger \-ən-jər\ *noun* [alteration of Middle English *poteger, potinger,* from Anglo-French *potageer,* from Middle French *potager* of pottage, from *potage* pottage] (1522)
: a low usually metal bowl with a single and usually flat and pierced handle

¹port \'pȯrt, 'pȯrt\ *noun* [Middle English, from Old English & Old French, from Latin *portus* — more at FORD] (before 12th century)
1 : a place where ships may ride secure from storms **:** HAVEN
2 a : a harbor town or city where ships may take on or discharge cargo **b :** AIRPORT
3 : PORT OF ENTRY

²port *noun* [Middle English *porte,* from Middle French, gate, door, from Latin *porta* passage, gate; akin to Latin *portus* port] (before 12th century)
1 *chiefly Scottish* **:** GATE
2 a : an opening (as in a valve seat or valve face) for intake or exhaust of a fluid **b :** the area of opening in a cylinder face of a passageway for the working fluid in an engine; *also* **:** such a passageway
3 a : an opening in a vessel's side (as for admitting light or loading cargo) **b** *archaic* **:** the cover for a porthole
4 : a hole in an armored vehicle or fortification through which guns may be fired
5 : a hardware interface by which a computer communicates with another device or system

³port *noun* [Middle English, from Middle French, from *porter* to carry, from Latin *portare*] (14th century)
1 : the manner of bearing oneself
2 *archaic* **:** STATE 3
3 : the position in which a military weapon is carried at the command *port arms*

⁴port *transitive verb* [⁵*port*] (1580)
: to turn or put (a helm) to the left — used chiefly as a command

⁵port *noun* [probably from ¹*port* or ²*port*] (circa 1625)
: the left side of a ship or aircraft looking forward — called also *larboard;* compare STARBOARD
 word history *see* STARBOARD
— **port** *adjective*

⁶port *noun* [*Oporto,* Portugal] (1691)
: a sweet fortified wine of rich taste and aroma made in Portugal; *also* **:** a similar wine made elsewhere

¹por·ta·ble \'pȯr-tə-bəl, 'pȯr-\ *adjective* [Middle English, from Middle French, from Late Latin *portabilis,* from Latin *portare* to carry — more at FARE] (15th century)
1 a : capable of being carried or moved about ⟨a *portable* TV⟩ ⟨a *portable* sawmill⟩ **b :** usable on many computers without modification ⟨*portable* software⟩

\ə\ abut \ᵊ\ kitten \ər\ further \a\ ash \ā\ ace \ä\ mop, mar \au̇\ out \ch\ chin \e\ bet \ē\ easy \g\ go \i\ hit \ī\ ice \j\ job \ŋ\ sing \ō\ go \ȯ\ law \ȯi\ boy \th\ thin \th\ the \ü\ loot \u̇\ foot \y\ yet \zh\ vision *see also* Guide to Pronunciation

2 *archaic* **:** BEARABLE
 — **por·ta·bil·i·ty** \ˌpȯr-tə-'bi-lə-tē, ˌpȯr-\ *noun*
 — **por·ta·bly** \'pȯr-tə-blē, 'pȯr-\ *adverb*
²portable *noun* (1883)
: something that is portable
¹por·tage \'pȯr-tij, 'pȯr-, *3 is also* pȯr-'täzh\ *noun* [Middle English, from Middle French, from *porter* to carry] (15th century)
1 : the labor of carrying or transporting
2 *archaic* **:** the cost of carrying **:** PORTERAGE
3 a : the carrying of boats or goods overland from one body of water to another or around an obstacle (as a rapids) **b :** the route followed in making such a transfer
²por·tage \'pȯr-tij, 'pȯr-; pȯr-'täzh\ *verb* **por·taged; por·tag·ing** (1864)
transitive verb
: to carry over a portage
intransitive verb
: to move gear over a portage
¹por·tal \'pȯr-t°l, 'pȯr-\ *noun* [Middle English, from Middle French, from Medieval Latin *portale* city gate, porch, from neuter of *portalis* of a gate, from Latin *porta* gate — more at PORT] (14th century)
1 : DOOR, ENTRANCE; *especially* **:** a grand or imposing one
2 : the whole architectural composition surrounding and including the doorways and porches of a church
3 : the approach or entrance to a bridge or tunnel
4 : a communicating part or area of an organism; *specifically* **:** the point at which something (as a pathogen) enters the body
²portal *adjective* [New Latin *porta* transverse fissure of the liver, from Latin, gate] (1845)
1 : of or relating to the transverse fissure on the underside of the liver where most of the vessels enter
2 : of, relating to, or being a portal vein
portal system *noun* [*portal vein*] (1851)
: a system of veins that begins and ends in capillaries
portal–to–portal *adjective* (1943)
: of or relating to the time spent by a worker in traveling between the entrance to an employer's property and the worker's actual job site (as in a mine) ⟨*portal-to-portal* pay⟩
portal vein *noun* [²*portal*] (1845)
: a vein that collects blood from one part of the body and distributes it in another through capillaries; *especially* **:** a vein carrying blood from the digestive organs and spleen to the liver
por·ta·men·to \ˌpȯr-tə-'men-(ˌ)tō, ˌpȯr-\ *noun, plural* **-men·ti** \-(ˌ)tē\ [Italian, literally, act of carrying, from *portare* to carry, from Latin] (1771)
: a continuous gliding movement from one tone to another (as by the voice)
por·ta·pak *or* **por·ta·pack** \'pȯr-tə-ˌpak, 'pȯr-\ *noun* [*portable* + *pack*] (1970)
: a small portable combined videotape recorder and camera
port arms *noun* [from the command *port arms!*] (circa 1890)
: a position in the manual of arms in which the rifle is held diagonally in front of the body with the muzzle pointing upward to the left; *also* **:** a command to assume this position
por·ta·tive \'pȯr-tə-tiv, 'pȯr-\ *adjective* [Middle English *portatif*, from Middle French, from Latin *portatus*, past participle of *portare*] (14th century)
: PORTABLE
port·cul·lis \pȯrt-'kə-ləs, 'pȯrt-\ *noun* [Middle English *port colice*, from Middle French *porte coleïce*, literally, sliding door] (14th century)
: a grating of iron hung over the gateway of a fortified place and lowered between grooves to prevent passage
port de bras \ˌpȯr-də-'brä\ *noun* [French, literally, carriage of the arm] (1912)

: the technique and practice of arm movement in ballet
Port du Sa·lut \ˌpȯr-də-sə-'lü, -sa-; -səl-'yü, -sal-\ *noun* [French *port-du-salut, port-salut,* from *Port du Salut,* Trappist abbey in northwest France] (1881)
: a semisoft pressed ripened cheese of usually mild flavor originated by Trappist monks in France
Porte \'pȯrt, 'pȯrt\ *noun* [French, short for *Sublime Porte,* literally, sublime gate; from the gate of the sultan's palace where justice was administered] (15th century)
: the government of the Ottoman empire
porte co·chere \ˌpȯrt-kō-'sher, ˌpȯrt-\ *noun* [French *porte cochère,* literally, coach door] (1698)
1 : a passageway through a building or screen wall designed to let vehicles pass from the street to an interior courtyard
2 : a roofed structure extending from the entrance of a building over an adjacent driveway and sheltering those getting in or out of vehicles
por·tend \pȯr-'tend, pȯr-\ *transitive verb* [Middle English, from Latin *portendere,* from *por-* forward (akin to *per* through) + *tendere* to stretch — more at FOR, THIN] (15th century)
1 : to give an omen or anticipatory sign of **:** BODE
2 : INDICATE, SIGNIFY
por·tent \'pȯr-ˌtent, 'pȯr-\ *noun* [Latin *portentum,* from neuter of *portentus,* past participle of *portendere*] (circa 1587)
1 : something that foreshadows a coming event **:** OMEN
2 : prophetic indication or significance
3 : MARVEL, PRODIGY
por·ten·tous \pȯr-'ten-təs, pȯr-\ *adjective* (15th century)
1 : of, relating to, or constituting a portent
2 : eliciting amazement or wonder **:** PRODIGIOUS
3 a : being a grave or serious matter ⟨*portentous* decisions⟩ **b :** self-consciously solemn or important **:** POMPOUS **c :** ponderously excessive ⟨that discipline's overwrought, *portentous* phrases —R. M. Coles⟩
synonym see OMINOUS
 — **por·ten·tous·ly** *adverb*
 — **por·ten·tous·ness** *noun*
¹por·ter \'pȯr-tər, 'pȯr-\ *noun* [Middle English, from Old French *portier,* from Late Latin *portarius,* from Latin *porta* gate — more at PORT] (13th century)
chiefly British **:** a person stationed at a door or gate to admit or assist those entering
²porter *noun* [Middle English *portour,* from Middle French *porteour,* from Late Latin *portator,* from Latin *portare* to carry — more at FARE] (14th century)
1 : a person who carries burdens; *especially* **:** one employed to carry baggage for patrons at a hotel or transportation terminal
2 : a parlor-car or sleeping-car attendant who waits on passengers and makes up berths
3 [short for *porter's beer*] **:** a heavy dark brown beer brewed from browned or charred malt
4 : a person who does routine cleaning (as in a hospital or office)
³porter (1609)
transitive verb
: to transport or carry as or as if by a porter
intransitive verb
: to act as a porter
por·ter·age \-tə-rij\ *noun* (15th century)
: a porter's work; *also* **:** the charge for it
por·ter·house \'pȯr-tər-ˌhaus, 'pȯr-\ *noun* (circa 1758)

portcullis

1 *archaic* **:** a house where malt liquor (as porter) is sold
2 : a large steak cut from the thick end of the short loin to contain a T-shaped bone and a large piece of tenderloin — see BEEF illustration
port·fo·lio \pȯrt-'fō-lē-ˌō, pȯrt-\ *noun, plural* **-li·os** [Italian *portafoglio,* from *portare* to carry (from Latin) + *foglio* leaf, sheet, from Latin *folium* — more at BLADE] (1722)
1 : a hinged cover or flexible case for carrying loose papers, pictures, or pamphlets
2 [from the use of such a case to carry documents of state] **:** the office and functions of a minister of state or member of a cabinet
3 : the securities held by an investor **:** the commercial paper held by a financial house (as a bank)
4 : a set of pictures (as drawings or photographs) either bound in book form or loose in a folder
port·hole \'pȯrt-ˌhōl, 'pȯrt-\ *noun* [²*port*] (circa 1591)
1 : an opening (as a window) with a cover or closure especially in the side of a ship or aircraft
2 : a port through which to shoot
3 : ²PORT 2
Por·tia \'pȯr-shə, 'pȯr-\ *noun*
: the heroine in Shakespeare's *The Merchant of Venice*
por·ti·co \'pȯr-ti-ˌkō, 'pȯr-\ *noun, plural* **-coes** *or* **-cos** [Italian, from Latin *porticus* — more at PORCH] (1605)
: a colonnade or covered ambulatory especially in classical architecture and often at the entrance of a building
por·tiere \pȯr-'tyer, pȯr-, -'tir; 'pȯr-tē-ər, 'pȯr-\ *noun* [French *portière,* from Old French, feminine of *portier* porter, doorkeeper] (1843)
: a curtain hanging across a doorway
¹por·tion \'pȯr-shən, 'pȯr-\ *noun* [Middle English, from Old French, from Latin *portion-, portio;* akin to Latin *part-, pars* part] (14th century)
1 : an individual's part or share of something: as **a :** a share received by gift or inheritance **b :** DOWRY **c :** enough food especially of one kind to serve one person at one meal
2 : an individual's lot, fate, or fortune **:** one's share of good and evil
3 : an often limited part set off or abstracted from a whole ⟨give but that *portion* which yourself proposed —Shakespeare⟩
synonym see PART, FATE
²portion *transitive verb* **por·tioned; por·tion·ing** \-sh(ə-)niŋ\ (14th century)
1 : to divide into portions **:** DISTRIBUTE
2 : to allot a dowry to **:** DOWER
por·tion·less \-shən-ləs\ *adjective* (1782)
: having no portion; *especially* **:** having no dowry or inheritance
port·land cement \'pȯrt-lən(d)-, 'pȯrt-\ *noun* [Isle of *Portland,* England; from its resemblance to a limestone found there] (1824)
: a hydraulic cement made by finely pulverizing the clinker produced by calcining to incipient fusion a mixture of clay and limestone or similar materials
port·ly \'pȯrt-lē, 'pȯrt-\ *adjective* **port·li·er; -est** [³*port*] (15th century)
1 : DIGNIFIED, STATELY
2 : heavy or rotund of body **:** STOUT
 — **port·li·ness** *noun*
¹port·man·teau \pȯrt-'man-(ˌ)tō, pȯrt-\ *noun, plural* **-teaus** *or* **-teaux** \-(ˌ)tōz\ [Middle French *portemanteau,* from *porter* to carry + *manteau* mantle, from Latin *mantellum* — more at PORT] (1579)
1 : a large suitcase
2 : a word or morpheme whose form and meaning are derived from a blending of two or more distinct forms (as *smog* from *smoke* and *fog*)
²portmanteau *adjective* (1909)
1 : combining more than one use or quality

2 : being a portmanteau ⟨a *portmanteau* word⟩
port of call (1884)
1 : an intermediate port where ships customarily stop for supplies, repairs, or transshipment of cargo
2 : a stop included on an itinerary
port of entry (1840)
1 : a place where foreign goods may be cleared through a customhouse
2 : a place where an alien may be permitted to enter a country
por·trait \'pōr-trət, 'pȯr-, -ˌtrāt\ *noun* [Middle French, from past participle of *portraire*] (1570)
1 : PICTURE; *especially* **:** a pictorial representation (as a painting) of a person usually showing the face
2 : a sculptured figure **:** BUST, STATUE
3 : a graphic portrayal in words
por·trait·ist \-trə-tist, -ˌtrā-\ *noun* (1866)
: a maker of portraits
por·trai·ture \'pōr-trə-ˌchu̇r, 'pȯr-, -chər, -ˌtyu̇r, -ˌtu̇r\ *noun* (14th century)
1 : the making of portraits **:** PORTRAYAL
2 : PORTRAIT
por·tray \pȯr-'trā, pȯr-, pər-\ *transitive verb* [Middle English *portraien*, from Middle French *portraire*, from Latin *protrahere* to draw forth, reveal, expose — more at PROTRACT] (14th century)
1 : to make a picture of **:** DEPICT
2 a : to describe in words **b :** to play the role of **:** ENACT
— **por·tray·er** *noun*
por·tray·al \-'trā(-ə)l\ *noun* (circa 1847)
1 : the act or process or an instance of portraying **:** REPRESENTATION
2 : PORTRAIT
por·tress \'pōr-trəs, 'pȯr-\ *noun* (15th century)
: a female porter: as **a :** a doorkeeper in a convent or apartment house **b :** CHARWOMAN
Port Roy·al·ist \pȯrt-'rȯi-ə-list, pȯrt-\ *noun* [French *port-royaliste*, from *Port-Royal*, a convent near Versailles, France] (circa 1741)
: a member or adherent of a 17th century French Jansenist lay community noted for its logicians and educators
Port Sa·lut \ˌpȯr-sə-'lü, -sa-; -səl-'yü, -sal-\ *noun* (1902)
: PORT DU SALUT
Por·tu·guese \'pōr-chə-ˌgēz, 'pȯr-, -ˌgēs, ˌpȯr-chə-', ˌpȯr-\ *noun, plural* **Portuguese** [Portuguese *português*, adjective & noun, from *Portugal*] (1534)
1 a : a native or inhabitant of Portugal **b :** one who is of Portuguese descent
2 : the Romance language of Portugal and Brazil
— **Portuguese** *adjective*
Portuguese man–of–war *noun, plural* **Portuguese man–of–wars** *also* **Portuguese men–of–war** (1707)
: any of a genus (*Physalia*) of large tropical and subtropical pelagic siphonophores having a crested bladderlike float which bears the colony comprised of three types of zooids on the lower surface with one of the three having nematocyst-equipped tentacles
por·tu·la·ca \ˌpȯr-chə-'la-kə, ˌpȯr-\ *noun* [New Latin, from Latin, purslane, from *portula*, diminutive of *porta* gate; from the lid of its capsule — more at PORT] (1548)
: any of a genus (*Portulaca*)

Portuguese
man-of-war

of mainly tropical succulent herbs of the purslane family; *especially* **:** a widely cultivated plant (*P. grandiflora*) with showy flowers and small conical leaves
port–wine stain \'pȯrt-'wīn-, 'pȯrt-\ *noun* (circa 1909)

: a reddish purple superficial hemangioma of the skin commonly occurring as a birthmark
po·sa·da \pə-'sä-də\ *noun* [Spanish, from *posar* to lodge, from Late Latin *pausare*] (1763)
: an inn in Spanish-speaking countries
¹pose \'pōz\ *verb* **posed; pos·ing** [Middle English, from Middle French *poser*, from (assumed) Vulgar Latin *pausare*, from Late Latin, to stop, rest, pause, from Latin *pausa* pause] (14th century)
transitive verb
1 a : to present for attention or consideration ⟨let me *pose* a question⟩ **b :** to put or set forth **:** OFFER ⟨this attitude *poses* a threat to our hopes for peace⟩
2 a : to put or set in place **b :** to place (as a model) in a studied attitude
intransitive verb
1 : to assume a posture or attitude usually for artistic purposes
2 : to affect an attitude or character usually to deceive or impress
²pose *noun* (1818)
1 : a sustained posture; *especially* **:** one assumed for artistic effect
2 : an attitude, role, or characteristic assumed for effect ☆
³pose *transitive verb* **posed; pos·ing** [short for earlier *appose*, from Middle English *apposen*, alteration of *opposen* to oppose] (1593)
: PUZZLE, BAFFLE
Po·sei·don \pə-'sī-dᵊn\ *noun* [Latin, from Greek *Poseidōn*] (circa 1741)
: the Greek god of the sea — compare NEPTUNE
¹pos·er \'pō-zər\ *noun* [³pose] (1793)
: a puzzling or baffling question
²poser *noun* [¹pose] (1888)
: a person who poses
po·seur \pō-'zər\ *noun* [French, literally, poser, from *poser*] (1872)
: a person who pretends to be what he or she is not **:** an affected or insincere person
posh \'päsh\ *adjective* [origin unknown] (1918)
: ELEGANT, FASHIONABLE ◇
— **posh·ly** *adverb*
— **posh·ness** *noun*
pos·it \'pä-zət\ *transitive verb* **pos·it·ed** \'pä-zə-təd, 'päz-təd\; **pos·it·ing** \'pä-zə-tiŋ, 'päz-tiŋ\ [Latin *positus*, past participle of *ponere*] (1647)
1 : to dispose or set firmly **:** FIX
2 : to assume or affirm the existence of **:** POSTULATE
3 : to propose as an explanation **:** SUGGEST
¹po·si·tion \pə-'zi-shən\ *noun* [Middle English *posycion*, from Middle French *position*, from Latin *position-, positio*, from *ponere* to lay down, put, place, from (assumed) Old Latin *posinere*, from *po-* away (akin to Old Church Slavonic *po-*, perfective prefix, Greek *apo* away) + Latin *sinere* to leave — more at OF] (14th century)
1 : an act of placing or arranging: as **a :** the laying down of a proposition or thesis **b :** an arranging in order
2 : a point of view adopted and held to ⟨made my *position* on the issue clear⟩
3 a : the point or area occupied by a physical object ⟨took her *position* at the head of the line⟩ **b :** a certain arrangement of bodily parts ⟨rose to a standing *position*⟩
4 : a market commitment in securities or commodities; *also* **:** the inventory of a market trader
5 a : relative place, situation, or standing ⟨is now in a *position* to make decisions on his own⟩ **b :** social or official rank or status **c :** an employment for which one has been hired **:** JOB ⟨a *position* with a brokerage firm⟩ **d :** a situation that confers advantage or preference
²position *transitive verb* **po·si·tioned; po·si·tion·ing** \pə-'zi-sh(ə-)niŋ\ (1817)
: to put in proper position; *also* **:** LOCATE

po·si·tion·al \pə-'zi-sh(ə-)nəl\ *adjective* (1571)
1 : of, relating to, or fixed by position ⟨*positional* astronomy⟩
2 : involving little movement ⟨*positional* warfare⟩
3 : dependent on position or environment or context ⟨the front-articulated \k\ in \kē\ *key* and the back-articulated \k\ in \kül\ *cool* are *positional* variants⟩
— **po·si·tion·al·ly** *adverb*
positional notation *noun* (1941)
: a system of expressing numbers in which the digits are arranged in succession, the position of each digit has a place value, and the number is equal to the sum of the products of each digit by its place value
position effect *noun* (1930)
: genetic effect that is due to interaction of adjacent genes and that is modified when the spatial relationships of the genes change (as by chromosomal inversion)
position paper *noun* (1949)
: a detailed report that recommends a course of action on a particular issue
¹pos·i·tive \'pä-zə-tiv, 'päz-tiv\ *adjective* [Middle English, from Middle French *positif*,

\ə\ abut \ᵊ\ kitten \ər\ further \a\ ash \ā\ ace
\ä\ mop, mar \au̇\ out \ch\ chin \e\ bet \ē\ easy
\g\ go \i\ hit \ī\ ice \j\ job \ŋ\ sing \ō\ go
\ȯ\ law \ȯi\ boy \th\ thin \t͟h\ the \ü\ loot \u̇\ foot
\y\ yet \zh\ vision *see also* Guide to Pronunciation

from Latin *positivus,* from *positus,* past participle of *ponere*] (14th century)
1 a : formally laid down or imposed **:** PRESCRIBED ⟨*positive* laws⟩ **b :** expressed clearly or peremptorily ⟨her answer was a *positive no*⟩ **c :** fully assured **:** CONFIDENT
2 a : of, relating to, or constituting the degree of comparison that is expressed in English by the unmodified and uninflected form of an adjective or adverb and denotes no increase or diminution **b** (1) **:** independent of changing circumstances **:** UNCONDITIONED (2) **:** relating to or constituting a motion or device that is definite, unyielding, constant, or certain in its action ⟨a *positive* system of levers⟩ **c** (1) **:** INCONTESTABLE ⟨*positive* proof⟩ (2) **:** UNQUALIFIED ⟨a *positive* disgrace⟩
3 a : not fictitious **:** REAL ⟨a *positive* influence for good in the community⟩ **b :** active and effective in social or economic function rather than merely maintaining peace and order ⟨a *positive* government⟩
4 a : having or expressing actual existence or quality as distinguished from deprivation or deficiency ⟨*positive* change in temperature⟩: as (1) **:** capable of being constructively applied (2) **:** not speculative **:** EMPIRICAL **b :** having rendition of light and shade similar in tone to the tones of the original subject ⟨a *positive* photographic image⟩ **c :** that is or is generated in a direction arbitrarily or customarily taken as that of increase or progression ⟨*positive* rotation of the earth⟩ ⟨we are making some *positive* progress⟩ **d :** directed or moving toward a source of stimulation ⟨a *positive* taxis⟩ **e :** real and numerically greater than zero ⟨+2 is a *positive* integer⟩
5 a (1) **:** being, relating to, or charged with electricity of which the proton is the elementary unit and which predominates in a glass body after being rubbed with silk (2) **:** having more protons than electrons ⟨a *positive* ion⟩ **b** (1) **:** having higher electric potential and constituting the part from which the current flows to the external circuit ⟨the *positive* terminal of a discharging storage battery⟩ (2) **:** being an electron-collecting electrode of an electron tube
6 a : marked by or indicating acceptance, approval, or affirmation **b :** affirming the presence of that sought or suspected to be present ⟨a *positive* test for blood⟩
7 *of a lens* **:** converging light rays and forming a real inverted image
synonym see SURE
— **pos·i·tive·ly** \-lē, *for emphasis often* ˌpä-zə-ˈtiv-\ *adverb*
— **pos·i·tive·ness** \ˈpä-zə-tiv-nəs, ˈpäz-tiv-\ *noun*
²**positive** *noun* (1530)
: something positive: as **a** (1) **:** the positive degree of comparison in a language (2) **:** a positive form of an adjective or adverb **b :** something of which an affirmation can be made **:** REALITY **c :** a positive photograph or a print from a negative
positive definite *adjective* (1907)
1 : having a positive value for all values of the constituent variables ⟨*positive definite* quadratic forms⟩
2 *of a matrix* **:** having the characteristic roots real and positive
positive law *noun* (14th century)
: law established or recognized by governmental authority — compare NATURAL LAW
pos·i·tiv·ism \ˈpä-zə-ti-ˌvi-zəm, ˈpäz-ti-\ *noun* [French *positivisme,* from *positif* positive + *-isme* -ism] (1847)
1 a : a theory that theology and metaphysics are earlier imperfect modes of knowledge and that positive knowledge is based on natural phenomena and their properties and relations as verified by the empirical sciences **b :** LOGICAL POSITIVISM
2 : the quality or state of being positive
— **pos·i·tiv·ist** \-vist\ *adjective or noun*

— **pos·i·tiv·is·tic** \ˌpä-zə-ti-ˈvis-tik, ˌpäz-ti-\ *adjective*
— **pos·i·tiv·is·ti·cal·ly** \-ti-k(ə-)lē\ *adverb*
pos·i·tiv·i·ty \ˌpä-zə-ˈti-və-tē\ *noun, plural* **-ties** (1659)
1 : the quality or state of being positive
2 : something that is positive
pos·i·tron \ˈpä-zə-ˌträn\ *noun* [*posi*tive + -*tron* (as in *electron*)] (1933)
: a positively charged particle having the same mass and magnitude of charge as the electron and constituting the antiparticle of the electron
positron–emission tomography *noun* (1979)
: tomography in which a cross-sectional image of regional metabolism is obtained by a usually color-coded cathode-ray tube representation of the distribution of gamma radiation given off in the collision of electrons in cells with positrons emitted by radionuclides incorporated into metabolic substances
pos·i·tro·ni·um \ˌpä-zə-ˈtrō-nē-əm\ *noun* (1945)
: a short-lived system that consists of a positron and an electron bound together and is suggestive of a hydrogen atom
pos·se \ˈpä-sē\ *noun* [Medieval Latin *posse comitatus,* literally, power or authority of the county] (1645)
1 : a large group often with a common interest
2 : a body of persons summoned by a sheriff to assist in preserving the public peace usually in an emergency
3 : a group of people temporarily organized to make a search (as for a lost child)
pos·sess \pə-ˈzes *also* -ˈses\ *transitive verb* [Middle English, from Middle French *possesser* to have possession of, from Latin *possessus,* past participle of *possidēre,* from *potis* able, having the power + *sedēre* to sit — more at POTENT, SIT] (14th century)
1 a : to have and hold as property **:** OWN **b :** to have as an attribute, knowledge, or skill
2 a : to take into one's possession **b :** to enter into and control firmly **:** DOMINATE ⟨was *possessed* by demons⟩ **c :** to bring or cause to fall under the influence, possession, or control of some emotional or intellectual reaction ⟨melancholy *possesses* her⟩
3 a *obsolete* **:** to instate as owner **b :** to make the owner or holder — used in passive construction to indicate simple possession ⟨*possessed* of riches⟩ ⟨*possessed* of knowledge and experience⟩
— **pos·ses·sor** *noun*
pos·sessed *adjective* (1534)
1 a (1) **:** influenced or controlled by something (as an evil spirit or a passion) (2) **:** MAD, CRAZED **b :** urgently desirous to do or have something
2 *obsolete* **:** held as a possession
3 : SELF-POSSESSED, CALM
— **pos·sessed·ly** \-ˈze-səd-lē, -ˈzest-lē *also* -ˈse-səd- *or* -ˈsest-\ *adverb*
— **pos·sessed·ness** \-ˈze-səd-nəs, -ˈzest-nəs *also* -ˈse-səd- *or* -ˈsest-\ *noun*
pos·ses·sion \-ˈze-shən *also* -ˈse-\ *noun* (14th century)
1 a : the act of having or taking into control **b :** control or occupancy of property without regard to ownership **c :** OWNERSHIP **d :** control of the ball or puck
2 : something owned, occupied, or controlled **:** PROPERTY
3 a : domination by something (as an evil spirit, a passion, or an idea) **b :** a psychological state in which an individual's normal personality is replaced by another **c :** the fact or condition of being self-controlled
— **pos·ses·sion·al** \-ˈzesh-nəl, -ˈze-shə-n°l *also* -ˈsesh-nəl *or* -ˈse-shə-n°l\ *adjective*
— **pos·ses·sion·less** \-ˈze-shən-ləs, -ˈse-\ *adjective*
¹**pos·ses·sive** \pə-ˈze-siv *also* -ˈse-\ *adjective* (15th century)

1 : of, relating to, or constituting a word, a word group, or a grammatical case that denotes ownership or a relation analogous to ownership
2 : manifesting possession or the desire to own or dominate
— **pos·ses·sive·ly** *adverb*
— **pos·ses·sive·ness** *noun*
²**possessive** *noun* (15th century)
1 : a possessive word or word group
2 a : the possessive case **b :** a word in the possessive case
possessive adjective *noun* (1870)
: a pronominal adjective expressing possession
possessive pronoun *noun* (15th century)
: a pronoun that derives from a personal pronoun and denotes possession and analogous relationships
pos·ses·so·ry \pə-ˈze-sə-rē, -ˈzes-rē *also* -ˈse-sə-rē *or* -ˈses-rē\ *adjective* (15th century)
1 : of, arising from, or having the nature of possession ⟨*possessory* rights⟩
2 : having possession
3 : characteristic of a possessor **:** POSSESSIVE
pos·set \ˈpä-sət\ *noun* [Middle English *poshet, possot*] (15th century)
: a hot drink of sweetened and spiced milk curdled with ale or wine
pos·si·bil·i·ty \ˌpä-sə-ˈbi-lə-tē\ *noun, plural* **-ties** (14th century)
1 : the condition or fact of being possible
2 *archaic* **:** one's utmost power, capacity, or ability
3 : something that is possible
4 : potential or prospective value — usually used in plural ⟨the house had great *possibilities*⟩
pos·si·ble \ˈpä-sə-bəl\ *adjective* [Middle English, from Middle French, from Latin *possibilis,* from *posse* to be able, from *potis, pote* able + *esse* to be — more at POTENT, IS] (14th century)
1 a : being within the limits of ability, capacity, or realization **b :** being what may be done or may occur according to nature, custom, or manners
2 a : being something that may or may not occur **b :** being something that may or may not be true or actual ⟨*possible* explanation⟩
3 : having an indicated potential ⟨a *possible* housing site⟩ ☆
pos·si·bly \-blē\ *adverb* (14th century)
1 : in a possible manner **:** by any possibility
2 : by merest chance **:** PERHAPS
pos·sum \ˈpä-səm\ *noun* (1613)
: OPOSSUM
¹**post** \ˈpōst\ *noun* [Middle English, from Old English, from Latin *postis;* probably akin to Latin *por*- forward and to Latin *stare* to stand — more at PORTEND, STAND] (before 12th century)
1 : a piece (as of timber or metal) fixed firmly in an upright position especially as a stay or support **:** PILLAR, COLUMN
2 : a pole or stake set up to mark or indicate something; *especially* **:** a pole that marks the starting or finishing point of a horse race
3 : a metallic fitting attached to an electrical device (as a storage battery) for convenience in making connections

☆ SYNONYMS
Possible, practicable, feasible mean capable of being realized. POSSIBLE implies that a thing may certainly exist or occur given the proper conditions ⟨a *possible* route up the west face of the mountain⟩. PRACTICABLE implies that something may be effected by available means or under current conditions ⟨a *practicable* route up the west face of the mountain⟩. FEASIBLE applies to what is likely to work or be useful in attaining the end desired ⟨commercially *feasible* for mass production⟩.

4 : GOALPOST
5 : the metal stem of a pierced earring
²**post** *transitive verb* (1633)
1 a : to publish, announce, or advertise by or as if by use of a placard **b** : to denounce by public notice **c** : to enter on a public listing **d** : to forbid (property) to trespassers under penalty of legal prosecution by notices placed along the boundaries **e** : SCORE ⟨*posted* a 70 in the final round⟩
2 : to affix to a usual place (as a wall) for public notices : PLACARD
³**post** *noun* [Middle French *poste* relay station, courier, from Old Italian *posta* relay station, from feminine of *posto*, past participle of *porre* to place, from Latin *ponere* — more at POSITION] (1507)
1 *obsolete* : COURIER
2 *archaic* **a** : one of a series of stations for keeping horses for relays **b** : the distance between any two such consecutive stations : STAGE
3 *chiefly British* **a** : a nation's organization for handling mail; *also* : the mail handled **b** : a single dispatch of mail **c** : POST OFFICE **d** : POSTBOX
⁴**post** (1533)
intransitive verb
1 : to travel with post-horses
2 : to ride or travel with haste : HURRY
3 : to rise from the saddle and return to it in rhythm with a horse's trot
transitive verb
1 *archaic* : to dispatch in haste
2 : MAIL ⟨*post* a letter⟩
3 a : to transfer or carry from a book of original entry to a ledger **b** : to make transfer entries in
4 : to make familiar with a subject : INFORM ⟨kept her *posted* on the latest gossip⟩
⁵**post** *adverb* (1549)
: with post-horses : EXPRESS
⁶**post** *noun* [Middle French *poste*, from Old Italian *posto*, from past participle of *porre* to place] (1598)
1 a : the place at which a soldier is stationed; *especially* : a sentry's beat or station **b** : a station or task to which one is assigned **c** : the place at which a body of troops is stationed : CAMP **d** : a local subdivision of a veterans' organization **e** : one of two bugle calls sounded (as in the British army) at tattoo
2 a : an office or position to which a person is appointed **b** : a player position in basketball that is the focal point of the offense; *specifically* : PIVOT 2b
3 a : TRADING POST, SETTLEMENT **b** : a trading station on the floor of a stock exchange
⁷**post** *transitive verb* (1683)
1 a : to station in a given place ⟨guards were *posted* at the doors⟩ **b** : to carry ceremoniously to a position ⟨*posting* the colors⟩
2 *chiefly British* : to assign to a unit, position, or location (as in the military or civil service)
3 : to put up (as bond)
post- *prefix* [Middle English, from Latin, from *post*; akin to Lithuanian *pas* at, Greek *apo* away from — more at OF]
1 a : after : subsequent : later ⟨*post*date⟩ **b** : behind : posterior : following after ⟨*post*consonantal⟩
2 a : subsequent to : later than ⟨*post*operative⟩ **b** : posterior to ⟨*post*orbital⟩

post·abor·tion
post·ac·ci·dent
post·ad·o·les·cent
post·am·pu·ta·tion
post·apoc·a·lyp·tic
post·ar·rest
post·atom·ic
post·at·tack
post·bac·ca·lau·re·ate
post·base
post·bib·li·cal
post·bour·geois
post·burn
post·cap·i·tal·ist
post–Chris·tian
post·co·i·tal
post·col·lege
post·col·le·giate
post·co·lo·nial
post·con·cep·tion
post·con·cert
post·con·quest
post·con·so·nan·tal

post·con·ven·tion
post·cop·u·la·to·ry
post·cor·o·nary
post·coup
post·crash
post·cri·sis
post–Dar·win·i·an
post·dead·line
post·de·bate
post·deb·u·tante
post·de·liv·ery
post·de·po·si·tion·al
post·de·pres·sion
post·de·val·u·a·tion
post·dive
post·di·ves·ti·ture
post·di·vorce
post·drug
post·ed·it·ing
post–Ein·stein·ian
post·elec·tion
post·em·bry·o·nal
post·em·bry·on·ic
post·emer·gen·cy
post·en·ceph·a·lit·ic
post·ep·i·lep·tic
post·erup·tive
post·ex·er·cise
post·ex·pe·ri·ence
post·ex·per·i·men·tal
post·ex·po·sure
post·fault
post·fire
post·flight
post·frac·ture
post·freeze
post–Freud·ian
post·game
post·gla·cial
post·grad·u·a·tion
post·har·vest
post·hem·or·rhag·ic
post·hol·i·day
post·ho·lo·caust
post·hos·pi·tal
post·im·pact
post·im·pe·ri·al
post·in·au·gu·ral
post·in·de·pen·dence
post·in·dus·tri·al
post·in·fec·tion
post·in·jec·tion

post·in·oc·u·la·tion
post·ir·ra·di·a·tion
post·is·che·mic
post·iso·la·tion
post·land·ing
post·launch
post·lib·er·a·tion
post·mar·i·tal
post·mas·tec·to·my
post·mat·ing
post·me·di·e·val
post·mid·night
post·neo·na·tal
post·or·gas·mic
post·pol·li·na·tion
post·pres·i·den·tial
post·pri·ma·ry
post·pris·on
post·psy·cho·an·a·lyt·ic
post·pu·ber·ty
post·pu·bes·cent
post·race
post·re·ces·sion
post–Ref·or·ma·tion
post·res·ur·rec·tion
post·re·tire·ment
post·rev·o·lu·tion·ary
post·ri·ot
post·ro·man·tic
post·sea·son
post·sec·ond·ary
post·show
post·stim·u·la·tion
post·stim·u·la·to·ry
post·stim·u·lus
post·strike
post·sur·gi·cal
post·tax
post·teen
post·trau·mat·ic
post·treat·ment
post·tri·al
post·vac·ci·nal
post·vac·ci·na·tion
post·va·got·o·my
post·va·sec·to·my
post–Vic·to·ri·an
post·war
post·wean·ing
post·work·shop

post·age \'pōs-tij\ *noun* (1654)
1 : the fee for postal service
2 : adhesive stamps or printed indicia representing postal fees
postage–due stamp *noun* (1893)
: a special adhesive stamp that is applied by a post office to mail bearing insufficient postage
postage meter *noun* (1927)
: a machine that prints postal indicia on pieces of mail, records the amount of postage, and subtracts it from a total paid amount for which the machine has been set
postage–stamp *adjective* (1938)
: suggesting a postage stamp in size : very small ⟨*postage-stamp* yards⟩
postage stamp *noun* (1840)
: a government adhesive stamp or imprinted stamp for use on mail as evidence of prepayment of postage
post·al \'pōs-t²l\ *adjective* (1843)
1 : of or relating to the mails or the post office
2 : conducted by mail ⟨*postal* chess⟩
postal card *noun* (1872)
1 : a card officially stamped and issued by the government for use in the mail
2 : POSTCARD
postal order *noun* (1883)
British : MONEY ORDER
postal service *noun* (circa 1920)
: POST OFFICE 1
postal union *noun* (1875)

: an association of governments setting up uniform regulations and practices for international mail
post·ax·i·al \ˌpōst-'ak-sē-əl\ *adjective* (1872)
: of or relating to the ulnar side of the vertebrate forelimb or the fibular side of the hind limb; *also* : of or relating to the side of an animal or side of one of its limbs that is posterior to the axis of its body or limb
post·bag \'pōs(t)-ˌbag\ *noun* (1813)
1 *British* : MAILBAG
2 *British* : a single batch of mail : LETTERS
post·bel·lum \ˌpōs(t)-'be-ləm\ *adjective* [Latin *post bellum* after the war] (1874)
: of, relating to, or characteristic of the period following a war and especially following the American Civil War
post·box \'pōs(t)-ˌbäks\ *noun* (1754)
: MAILBOX; *especially* : a public mailbox
post·boy \-ˌboi\ *noun* (1707)
: POSTILION
post·card \'pōs(t)-ˌkärd\ *noun* (1870)
1 : POSTAL CARD 1
2 : a card on which a message may be written for mailing without an envelope and to which the sender must affix a stamp
— **post·card·like** \-ˌlīk\ *adjective*
post·ca·va \ˌpōs(t)-'kā-və\ *noun* [New Latin] (1882)
: the inferior vena cava of vertebrates higher than fishes
— **post·ca·val** \-vəl\ *adjective*
post chaise *noun* (1712)
: a carriage usually having a closed body on four wheels and seating two to four persons
post·clas·si·cal \ˌpōs(t)-'kla-si-kəl\ *or* **post·clas·sic** \-sik\ *adjective* (1867)
: of or relating to a period (as in art, literature, or civilization) following a classical one
post·code \'pōs(t)-ˌkōd\ *noun* (1967)
: a code (as of numbers and letters) used similarly to the zip code especially in the United Kingdom and Australia
post–com·mu·nion \ˌpōs(t)-kə-'myü-nyən\ *noun, often P&C capitalized* [Medieval Latin *postcommunion-*, *postcommunio*, from Latin *post-* + Late Latin *communio* communion] (15th century)
: a liturgically variable prayer following the communion at Mass
post·cra·ni·al \-'krā-nē-əl\ *adjective* (1913)
: of or relating to the part of the body caudal to the head ⟨*postcranial* skeleton⟩ ⟨*postcranial* fossil remains⟩
— **post·cra·ni·al·ly** *adverb*
post·date \ˌpōs(t)-'dāt, 'pōs(t)-ˌ\ *transitive verb* (1624)
1 a : to date with a date later than that of execution ⟨*postdate* a check⟩ **b** : to assign (an event) to a date subsequent to that of actual occurrence
2 : to follow in time
post·di·lu·vi·an \ˌpōs(t)-də-'lü-vē-ən, -dī-\ *adjective* [*post-* + Latin *diluvium* flood — more at DELUGE] (1680)
: of or relating to the period after the flood described in the Bible
— **postdiluvian** *noun*
¹**post·doc** \'pōs(t)-ˌdäk\ *noun* (1968)
: one engaged in postdoctoral study or research
²**postdoc** *adjective* (1970)
: POSTDOCTORAL
post·doc·tor·al \ˌpōs(t)-'däk-t(ə-)rəl, 'pōst-ˌ\ *also* **post·doc·tor·ate** \-t(ə-)rət\ *adjective* (1936)
: being beyond the doctoral level: **a** : of or relating to advanced academic or professional work beyond a doctor's degree ⟨a *postdoctoral*

fellowship⟩ **b** : engaged in such work ⟨*post-doctoral* scholars⟩

post·emer·gence \ˌpōst-i-ˈmər-jən(t)s\ *adjective* (1940)
: used or occurring in the stage between the emergence of a seedling and the maturity of a crop plant ⟨*postemergence* herbicides⟩ ⟨*postemergence* development⟩

¹post·er \ˈpōs-tər\ *noun* [⁴*post*] (1605)
archaic : a swift traveler

²poster *noun* [²*post*] (1838)
: a bill or placard for posting often in a public place; *especially* : one that is decorative or pictorial

poster color *noun* (1925)
: an opaque watercolor paint with a gum or glue-size binder sold usually in jars — called also *poster paint*

poste res·tante \ˌpōst-ˌres-ˈtänt\ *noun* [French, literally, waiting mail] (1768)
chiefly British : GENERAL DELIVERY

¹pos·te·ri·or \pō-ˈstir-ē-ər, pä-\ *adjective* [Latin, comparative of *posterus* coming after, from *post* after — more at POST-] (1534)
1 : later in time : SUBSEQUENT
2 : situated behind: as **a** : CAUDAL **b** of the human body or its parts : DORSAL
3 of a plant part : ADAXIAL, SUPERIOR
— **pos·te·ri·or·ly** *adverb*

²pos·te·ri·or \pä-ˈstir-ē-ər, pō-\ *noun* (circa 1616)
: the hinder parts of the body; *specifically* : BUTTOCKS

pos·te·ri·or·i·ty \(ˌ)pō-ˌstir-ē-ˈor-ə-tē, (ˌ)pä-, -ˈär-\ *noun* (14th century)
: the quality or state of being later or subsequent

pos·ter·i·ty \pä-ˈster-ə-tē\ *noun* [Middle English *posterite*, from Middle French *posterité*, from Latin *posteritat-*, *posteritas*, from *posterus* coming after] (14th century)
1 : the offspring of one progenitor to the furthest generation
2 : all future generations

pos·tern \ˈpōs-tərn, ˈpäs-\ *noun* [Middle English *posterne*, from Old French, alteration of *posterle*, from Late Latin *posterula*, diminutive of *postera* back door, from Latin, feminine of *posterus*] (14th century)
1 : a back door or gate
2 : a private or side entrance or way
— **postern** *adjective*

pos·tero·lat·er·al \ˌpäs-tə-rō-ˈla-t(ə-)rəl\ *adjective* [*posterior* + *-o-* + *lateral*] (1852)
: posterior and lateral in position or direction

post exchange *noun* (1892)
: a store at a military installation that sells merchandise and services to military personnel and authorized civilians

post·ex·il·ic \ˌpōst-(ˌ)eg-ˈzi-lik\ *adjective* (1871)
: of or relating to the period of Jewish history between the end of the exile in Babylon in 538 B.C. and A.D. 1

post·face \ˈpōs(t)-fəs, -ˌfās; pōs-ˈfàs\ *noun* [French, from *post-* + *-face* (as in *préface* preface)] (1782)
: a brief article or note (as of explanation) placed at the end of a publication

post·fem·i·nist \ˌpōst-ˈfe-mə-nist\ *adjective* (1983)
: of, relating to, occurring in, or being the period following widespread advocacy and acceptance of feminism

post·fix \ˈpōs(t)-ˌfiks\ *adjective* [*post-* + *-fix* (as in *prefix*)] (1973)
: characterized by placement of an operator after its operand or after its two operands if it is a binary operator — compare INFIX, PREFIX

post·free \ˈpōs(t)-ˈfrē\ *adjective* (1723)
chiefly British : POSTPAID

post·gan·gli·on·ic \ˌpōs(t)-ˌgaŋ-glē-ˈä-nik\ *adjective* (1897)
: distal to a ganglion; *specifically* : of, relating to, or being an axon arising from a cell body

within an autonomic ganglion — compare PREGANGLIONIC

¹post·grad·u·ate \-ˈgra-jə-wət, -ˌwāt, -ˈgraj-wət\ *adjective* (1858)
: GRADUATE 2

²postgraduate *noun* (circa 1890)
: a student continuing formal education after graduation from high school or college

¹post·haste \ˈpōst-ˈhāst\ *noun* [³*post*] (1545)
archaic : great haste

²posthaste *adverb* (1593)
: with all possible speed

³posthaste *adjective* (1604)
obsolete : SPEEDY, IMMEDIATE ⟨requires your . . . *posthaste* appearance —Shakespeare⟩

post hoc \ˈpōst-ˈhäk\ *adjective* [New Latin *post hoc, ergo propter hoc* after this, therefore because of this] (1704)
1 : relating to or being the fallacy of arguing from temporal sequence to a causal relation
2 : formulated after the fact ⟨a *post hoc* rationalization⟩

post·hole \ˈpōst-ˌhōl\ *noun* (1703)
: a hole dug for a post (as to support a fence or wall)

post horn *noun* (1675)
: a simple straight or coiled brass or copper wind instrument with cupped mouthpiece used especially by guards of mail coaches of the 18th and 19th centuries

post horn

post·horse \ˈpōst-ˌhors\ *noun* [³*post*] (1527)
: a horse for use especially by couriers or mail carriers

post·hu·mous \ˈpäs-chə-məs *also* -tə-, -tyə-, -thə-; päst-ˈhyü-məs, ˈpōst-, -ˈyü-\ *adjective* [Latin *posthumus*, alteration of *postumus* lateborn, posthumous, from superlative of *posterus* coming after — more at POSTERIOR] (1619)
1 : born after the death of the father
2 : published after the death of the author
3 : following or occurring after death ⟨*posthumous* fame⟩
— **post·hu·mous·ly** *adverb*
— **post·hu·mous·ness** *noun*

post·hyp·not·ic \ˌpōst-hip-ˈnä-tik, -ip-\ *adjective* [International Scientific Vocabulary] (1890)
: of, relating to, or characteristic of the period following a hypnotic trance

pos·tiche \pä-ˈtēsh\ *noun* [French, from Spanish *postizo*] (1886)
: WIG; *especially* : TOUPEE 2

pos·til·ion *or* **pos·til·lion** \pō-ˈstil-yən, pə-\ *noun* [Middle French *postillon* mail carrier using post-horses, from Italian *postiglione*, from *posta* post — more at POST] (circa 1611)
: one who rides as a guide on the near horse of one of the pairs attached to a coach or post chaise especially without a coachman

Post·im·pres·sion·ism \ˌpōst-im-ˈpre-shə-ˌni-zəm\ *noun* [French *postimpressionisme*, from *post-* + *impressionisme* impressionism] (1910)
: a theory or practice of art originating in France in the last quarter of the 19th century that in revolt against impressionism stresses variously volume, picture structure, or expressionism
— **Post·im·pres·sion·ist** \-ˈpre-sh(ə-)nist\ *adjective or noun*
— **Post·im·pres·sion·is·tic** \-ˌpre-shə-ˈnis-tik\ *adjective*

¹post·ing \ˈpōs-tiŋ\ *noun* [⁴*post*] (1682)
1 : the act of transferring an entry or item from a book of original entry to the proper account in a ledger
2 : the record in a ledger account resulting from the transfer of an entry or item from a book of original entry

²posting *noun* [⁷*post*] (1880)
: appointment to a post or a command

post–Kant·ian \ˌpōs(t)-ˈkan-tē-ən, -ˈkän-\ *adjective* (1843)
: of or relating to the idealist philosophers (as Fichte, Schelling, and Hegel) following Kant and developing some of his ideas

post·lap·sar·i·an \-ˌlap-ˈser-ē-ən\ *adjective* [*post-* + Latin *lapsus* slip, fall — more at LAPSE] (1733)
: of, relating to, or characteristic of the time or state after the fall of mankind

post·lit·er·ate \-ˈli-tə-rət *also* -ˈli-trət\ *adjective* (1965)
: relating to or occurring after the introduction of the electronic media

post·lude \ˈpōst-ˌlüd\ *noun* [*post-* + *-lude* (as in *prelude*)] (1851)
1 : a closing piece of music; *especially* : an organ voluntary at the end of a church service
2 : a closing phase (as of an epoch or a literary work)

post·man \ˈpōs(t)-mən, -ˌman\ *noun* (1529)
: MAILMAN

¹post·mark \-ˌmärk\ *noun* (1678)
: an official postal marking on a piece of mail; *specifically* : a mark showing the post office and date of mailing

²postmark *transitive verb* (1716)
: to put a postmark on

post·mas·ter \-ˌmas-tər\ *noun* (1513)
1 : one who has charge of a post office
2 : one who has charge of a station for the accommodation of travelers or who supplies post-horses
— **post·mas·ter·ship** \-ˌship\ *noun*

postmaster general *noun, plural* **postmasters general** (1626)
: an official in charge of a national post office department or agency

post·men·o·paus·al \ˌpōs(t)-ˌme-nə-ˈpo-zəl\ *adjective* (1928)
1 : having undergone menopause
2 : occurring after menopause

post me·ri·di·em \-mə-ˈri-dē-əm, -ˌem\ *adjective* [Latin] (1647)
: being after noon — abbreviation *p.m.*

post·mil·le·nar·i·an·ism \-ˌmi-lə-ˈner-ē-ə-ˌni-zəm\ *noun* (circa 1890)
: POSTMILLENNIALISM
— **postmillenarian** *adjective or noun*

post·mil·len·ni·al \-mə-ˈle-nē-əl\ *adjective* (1851)
1 : coming after or relating to the period after the millennium
2 : holding or relating to postmillennialism

post·mil·len·ni·al·ism \-ə-ˌli-zəm\ *noun* (1879)
: the theological doctrine that the second coming of Christ will occur after the millennium
— **post·mil·len·ni·al·ist** \-ə-list\ *noun*

post·mis·tress \ˈpōs(t)-ˌmis-trəs\ *noun* (1697)
: a woman who is a postmaster

post·mod·ern \ˌpōs(t)-ˈmä-dərn, ÷ˈmä-d(ə-)rən\ *adjective* (1949)
: of, relating to, or being any of several movements (as in art, architecture, or literature) that are reactions against the philosophy and practices of modern movements and are typically marked by revival of traditional elements and techniques
— **post·mod·ern·ism** \-dər-ˌni-zəm\ *noun*
— **post·mod·ern·ist** \-nist\ *adjective or noun*

¹post·mor·tem \ˌpōs(t)-ˈmor-təm\ *adjective* [Latin *post mortem* after death] (circa 1836)
1 : done, occurring, or collected after death ⟨*postmortem* tissue specimens⟩
2 : following the event

²postmortem *noun* (1850)
1 : an analysis or discussion of an event after it is over
2 : AUTOPSY 1

postmortem examination *noun* (1837)
: AUTOPSY 1

post·na·sal drip \ˈpōst-ˌnā-zəl-\ *noun* (1949)

: flow of mucous secretion from the posterior part of the nasal cavity onto the wall of the pharynx occurring usually as a chronic accompaniment of an allergic state

post·na·tal \ˌpōs(t)-ˈnā-tᵊl\ *adjective* [International Scientific Vocabulary] (circa 1859)
: occurring or being after birth; *specifically*
: of or relating to an infant immediately after birth ⟨*postnatal* care⟩
— **post·na·tal·ly** *adverb*

post·nup·tial \-ˈnəp-shəl, -chəl, ÷-chə-wəl\ *adjective* (1807)
: made or occurring after marriage or mating

post oak *noun* [¹*post*] (1775)
: an oak (*Quercus stellata*) of the eastern and central U.S. having hard durable wood

¹post–obit \ˌpōst-ˈō-bət, *especially British* -ˈä-bit\ *noun* (1751)
: POST-OBIT BOND

²post–obit *adjective* [Latin *post obitum* after death] (circa 1834)
: occurring or taking effect after death

post–obit bond *noun* (1788)
: a bond made by a reversioner to secure a loan and payable out of his reversion

post office *noun* (1652)
1 : a government department or agency handling the transmission of mail
2 : a local branch of a national post office handling the mail for a particular place or area
3 : a game in which a player acting as postmaster or postmistress may exact a kiss from one of the opposite sex as payment for the pretended delivery of a letter

post·op·er·a·tive \ˌpōst-ˈä-p(ə-)rə-tiv, -pə-ˌrā-\ *adjective* [International Scientific Vocabulary] (circa 1890)
1 : following a surgical operation ⟨*postoperative* care⟩
2 : having undergone a surgical operation ⟨a *postoperative* patient⟩
— **post·op·er·a·tive·ly** *adverb*

post·or·bit·al \-ˈȯr-bə-tᵊl\ *adjective* (circa 1836)
: situated behind the eye socket

post·paid \ˈpōs(t)-ˈpād\ *adjective* (1653)
: having the postage paid by the sender and not chargeable to the receiver

post·par·tum \ˌpōs(t)-ˈpär-təm\ *adjective* [New Latin *post partum* after birth] (1846)
1 : following parturition ⟨*postpartum* period⟩
2 : being in the postpartum period ⟨*postpartum* mothers⟩
— **postpartum** *adverb*

post·pone \(ˌ)pōs(t)-ˈpōn\ *transitive verb* **post·poned; post·pon·ing** [Latin *postponere* to place after, postpone, from *post-* + *ponere* to place — more at POSITION] (circa 1520)
1 : to put off to a later time : DEFER
2 a : to place later (as in a sentence) than the normal position in English ⟨*postpone* an adjective⟩ **b** : to place later in order of precedence, preference, or importance
synonym see DEFER
— **post·pon·able** \-ˈpō-nə-bəl\ *adjective*
— **post·pone·ment** \-ˈpōn-mənt\ *noun*
— **post·pon·er** *noun*

post·po·si·tion \ˌpōs(t)-pə-ˈzi-shən, ˈpōs(t)-pə-ˌ\ *noun* [French, from *postposer* to place after, from Latin *postponere* (perfect indicative *postposui*)] (circa 1638)
: the placing of a grammatical element after a word to which it is primarily related in a sentence; *also* : such a word or particle especially when functioning as a preposition
— **post·po·si·tion·al** \ˌpōs(t)-pə-ˈzish-nəl, -ˈzi-shə-nᵊl\ *adjective*
— **post·po·si·tion·al·ly** *adverb*

post·pos·i·tive \-ˈpä-zə-tiv, -ˈpäz-tiv\ *adjective* (1786)
: placed after or at the end of another word
— **post·pos·i·tive·ly** *adverb*

post·pran·di·al \pōs(t)-ˈpran-dē-əl\ *adjective* (1820)
: occurring after a meal

post·pro·duc·tion \ˌpōs(t)-prə-ˈdək-shən, ˈpōs(t)-prə-ˌ, -prō-\ *noun* (1953)
: the period following filming or taping in which a motion picture or television show is readied for public presentation

post road *noun* (1657)
: a route over which mail is carried

post·script \ˈpōs(t)-ˌskript\ *noun* [New Latin *postscriptum*, from Latin, neuter of *postscriptus*, past participle of *postscribere* to write after, from *post-* + *scribere* to write — more at SCRIBE] (1551)
: a note or series of notes appended to a completed letter, article, or book

post·syn·ap·tic \ˌpōs(t)-sə-ˈnap-tik\ *adjective* (1909)
1 : occurring after synapsis ⟨a *postsynaptic* chromosome⟩
2 : relating to, occurring in, or being part of a nerve cell by which a wave of excitation is conveyed away from a synapse
— **post·syn·ap·ti·cal·ly** \-ti-k(ə-)lē\ *adverb*

post·ten·sion \-ˈten(t)-shən\ *transitive verb* (1950)
: to apply tension to (reinforcing steel) after concrete has set

post·test \ˈpōs(t)-ˌtest\ *noun* (circa 1951)
: a test given to students after completion of an instructional program or segment and often used in conjunction with a pretest to measure their achievement and the effectiveness of the program

post time *noun* [¹*post*] (1941)
: the designated time for the start of a horse race

post·tran·scrip·tion·al \ˌpōs(t)-tran(t)-ˈskrip-shnəl, -shə-nᵊl\ *adjective* (1969)
: occurring, acting, or existing after genetic transcription

post·trans·fu·sion \-tran(t)s-ˈfyü-zhən\ *adjective* (1944)
1 : caused by transfused blood
2 : occurring after blood transfusion ⟨*posttransfusion* shock⟩

post·trans·la·tion·al \-tran(t)s-ˈlā-shnəl, -shə-nᵊl\ *adjective* (1975)
: occurring or existing after genetic translation

post–traumatic stress disorder *noun* (1980)
: a psychological reaction occurring after a highly stressing event that is usually characterized by depression, anxiety, flashbacks, recurrent nightmares, and avoidance of reminders of the event — called also *post-traumatic stress syndrome*

pos·tu·lan·cy \ˈpäs-chə-lən(t)-sē\ *noun, plural* **-cies** (circa 1883)
1 : the quality or state of being a postulant
2 : the period during which a person remains a postulant

pos·tu·lant \ˈpäs-chə-lənt\ *noun* [French, petitioner, candidate, postulant, from Middle French, from present participle of *postuler* to demand, solicit, from Latin *postulare*] (1759)
1 : a person admitted to a religious order as a probationary candidate for membership
2 : a person on probation before being admitted as a candidate for holy orders in the Episcopal Church

¹pos·tu·late \ˈpäs-chə-ˌlāt\ *transitive verb* **-lat·ed; -lat·ing** [Latin *postulatus*, past participle of *postulare*; akin to Latin *poscere* to ask, Old High German *forscōn* to search, Sanskrit *pṛcchati* he asks — more at PRAY] (1593)
1 : DEMAND, CLAIM
2 a : to assume or claim as true, existent, or necessary : depend upon or start from the postulate of **b** : to assume as a postulate or axiom (as in logic or mathematics)
— **pos·tu·la·tion** \ˌpäs-chə-ˈlā-shən\ *noun*
— **pos·tu·la·tion·al** \-shnəl, -shə-nᵊl\ *adjective*

²pos·tu·late \ˈpäs-chə-lət, -ˌlāt\ *noun* [Medieval Latin *postulatum*, from neuter of *postula-*

tus, past participle of *postulare* to assume, from Latin, to demand] (1646)
1 : a hypothesis advanced as an essential presupposition, condition, or premise of a train of reasoning
2 : AXIOM 3

pos·tu·la·tor \-ˌlā-tər\ *noun* (1863)
: an official who presents a plea for beatification or canonization in the Roman Catholic Church — compare DEVIL'S ADVOCATE

pos·tur·al \ˈpäs-chə-rəl\ *adjective* (1857)
: of, relating to, or involving posture

¹pos·ture \ˈpäs-chər\ *noun* [French, from Italian *postura*, from Latin *positura*, from *positus*, past participle of *ponere* to place — more at POSITION] (circa 1586)
1 a : the position or bearing of the body whether characteristic or assumed for a special purpose ⟨erect *posture*⟩ **b** : the pose of a model or artistic figure
2 : state or condition at a given time especially with respect to capability in particular circumstances ⟨maintain a competitive *posture* in the market⟩ ⟨put the country in a *posture* of defense⟩
3 : a conscious mental or outward behavioral attitude ⟨takes a neutral *posture* toward the discussions⟩

²posture *verb* **pos·tured; pos·tur·ing** (circa 1645)
transitive verb
: to cause to assume a given posture : POSE
intransitive verb
1 : to assume a posture; *especially* : to strike a pose for effect
2 : to assume an artificial or pretended attitude : ATTITUDINIZE
— **pos·tur·er** \-chər-ər\ *noun*

post·vo·cal·ic \ˌpōs(t)-vō-ˈka-lik, -və-\ *adjective* [International Scientific Vocabulary] (1892)
: immediately following a vowel

po·sy \ˈpō-zē\ *noun, plural* **posies** [alteration of *poesy*] (1533)
1 : a brief sentiment, motto, or legend
2 a : BOUQUET, NOSEGAY **b** : FLOWER

¹pot \ˈpät\ *noun* [Middle English, from Old English *pott*; akin to Middle Low German *pot* pot] (before 12th century)
1 a : a usually rounded metal or earthen container used chiefly for domestic purposes (as in cooking or for holding liquids or growing plants); *also* : any of various technical or industrial vessels or enclosures resembling or likened to a household pot ⟨the *pot* of a still⟩ **b** : POTFUL ⟨a *pot* of coffee⟩
2 : an enclosed framework of wire, wood, or wicker for catching fish or lobsters
3 a : a large amount (as of money) **b** (1) : the total of the bets at stake at one time (2) : one round in a poker game **c** : the common fund of a group
4 : POTSHOT
5 : POTBELLY
6 : RUIN ⟨gone to *pot*⟩
7 *British* : a shot in snooker in which a ball is pocketed

²pot *verb* **pot·ted; pot·ting** (1616)
transitive verb
1 a : to place in a pot **b** : to pack or preserve (as cooked and chopped meat) in a sealed pot, jar, or can often with aspic
2 : to shoot with a potshot
3 : to make or shape (earthenware) as a potter
4 : to embed (as electronic components) in a container with an insulating or protective material (as plastic)
intransitive verb
: to take a potshot

\ə\ abut	\ᵊ\ kitten	\ər\ **further**	\a\ ash	\ā\ ace	
\ä\ mop, mar	\aú\ out	\ch\ chin	\e\ bet	\ē\ easy	
\g\ go	\i\ hit	\ī\ ice	\j\ job	\ŋ\ sing	\ō\ go
\ȯ\ law	\ȯi\ boy	\th\ thin	\t̶h\ the	\ü\ loot	\ú\ foot
\y\ yet	\zh\ vision	*see also* Guide to Pronunciation			

³**pot** *noun* [perhaps modification of Mexican Spanish *potiguaya*] (1938)
: MARIJUANA

¹**po·ta·ble** \'pō-tə-bəl\ *adjective* [Middle English, from Late Latin *potabilis*, from Latin *potare* to drink; akin to Latin *bibere* to drink, Greek *pinein*] (15th century)
: suitable for drinking
— **po·ta·bil·i·ty** \,pō-tə-'bi-lə-tē\ *noun*
— **po·ta·ble·ness** \'pō-tə-bəl-nəs\ *noun*

²**potable** *noun* (1623)
: a liquid that is suitable for drinking; *especially* : an alcoholic beverage

po·tage \pȯ-'täzh\ *noun* [Middle French, from Old French, pottage] (1567)
: a thick soup

pot ale *noun* (1812)
: the residue of fermented wort left in a still after the distillation of whiskey or alcohol and used for feeding swine

pot·ash \'pät-,ash\ *noun* [singular of *pot ashes*] (circa 1648)
1 : potassium carbonate especially from wood ashes
2 : potassium or a potassium compound especially as used in agriculture or industry

po·tas·sic \pə-'ta-sik\ *adjective* (1858)
: of, relating to, or containing potassium

po·tas·si·um \pə-'ta-sē-əm\ *noun, often attributive* [New Latin, from *potassa* potash, from English *potash*] (circa 1807)
: a silver-white soft light low-melting univalent metallic element of the alkali metal group that occurs abundantly in nature especially combined in minerals — see ELEMENT table

potassium–argon *adjective* (1953)
: being or relating to a method of dating paleontological or geological materials based on the radioactive decay of potassium to argon that has taken place in a specimen

potassium bromide *noun* (1873)
: a crystalline salt KBr with a saline taste that is used as a sedative and in photography

potassium carbonate *noun* (1885)
: a white salt K_2CO_3 that forms a strongly alkaline solution and is used in making glass and soap

potassium chlorate *noun* (1885)
: a crystalline salt $KClO_3$ that is used as an oxidizing agent in matches, fireworks, and explosives

potassium chloride *noun* (1885)
: a crystalline salt KCl occurring as a mineral and in natural waters and used especially as a fertilizer

potassium cyanide *noun* (1885)
: a very poisonous crystalline salt KCN used especially in gold and silver extraction from ore

potassium dichromate *noun* (1885)
: a soluble salt $K_2Cr_2O_7$ forming large orange-red crystals used especially in dyeing, in photography, and as an oxidizing agent

potassium hydroxide *noun* (1885)
: a white deliquescent solid KOH that dissolves in water with much heat to form a strongly alkaline and caustic liquid and is used chiefly in making soap and as a reagent

potassium nitrate *noun* (1885)
: a crystalline salt KNO_3 that occurs as a product of nitrification in arable soils, is a strong oxidizer, and is used especially in making gunpowder, as a fertilizer, and in medicine

potassium permanganate *noun* (1869)
: a dark purple salt $KMnO_4$ used as an oxidizer and disinfectant

potassium sorbate *noun* (1960)
: a potassium salt $C_6H_7KO_2$ of sorbic acid used especially as a food preservative

potassium sulfate *noun* (1885)
: a white crystalline compound K_2SO_4 used especially as a fertilizer

po·ta·tion \pō-'tā-shən\ *noun* [Middle English *potacioun*, from Middle French *potation*, from Latin *potation-*, *potatio* act of drinking, from *potare* to drink — more at POTABLE] (15th century)
1 : a usually alcoholic drink or brew
2 : the act or an instance of drinking or inhaling; *also* : the portion taken in one such act

po·ta·to \pə-'tā-(,)tō, -tə, *dialect* pə-'dā-, bə-\ *noun, plural* **-toes** *often attributive* [Spanish *batata*, from Taino] (1565)
1 : SWEET POTATO
2 a : an erect South American herb (*Solanum tuberosum*) of the nightshade family widely cultivated as a vegetable crop **b** : the edible starchy tuber of a potato — called also *Irish potato, white potato*
usage see TOMATO

potato 2a

potato beetle *noun* (1821)
: COLORADO POTATO BEETLE

potato blight *noun* (1879)
: any of several destructive fungus diseases of the potato

potato bug *noun* (1799)
: COLORADO POTATO BEETLE

potato chip *noun* (1878)
: a thin slice of white potato that has been fried until crisp and then usually salted

potato leafhopper *noun* (1921)
: a small green white-spotted leafhopper (*Empoasca fabae*) of the eastern and southern U.S. that is a serious pest on many cultivated plants and especially on the potato

potato pancake *noun* (1935)
: a fried flat cake of grated potato mixed with raw egg and usually grated onion and spices

potato tu·ber·worm \-'tü-bər-,wərm, -'tyü-\ *noun* (1920)
: a grayish brown moth (*Phthorimaea operculella* of the family Gelechiidae) whose larva mines the leaves and bores in the stems especially of potato and tobacco plants and commonly overwinters in potato tubers

pot-au-feu \,pät-ō-'fə(r), pȯ-tō-fœ̄\ *noun, plural* **pot-au-feu** [French, literally, pot on the fire] (1791)
: a French boiled dinner of meat and vegetables

pot·bel·lied \'pät-,be-lēd\ *adjective* (1657)
: having a potbelly

potbellied stove *noun* (1933)
: a stove with a rounded or bulging body — called also *potbelly stove*

pot·bel·ly \'pät-,be-lē\ *noun* (circa 1714)
1 : an enlarged, swollen, or protruding abdomen
2 : POTBELLIED STOVE

pot·boil \-,bȯil\ *intransitive verb* (1867)
: to produce potboilers

pot·boil·er \-,bȯi-lər\ *noun* (1864)
: a usually inferior work (as of art or literature) produced chiefly for profit

pot–bound \'pät-,baùnd\ *adjective* (1850)
of a potted plant : having roots so densely matted as to allow little or no space for further growth

pot·boy \-,bȯi\ *noun* (1795)
: a boy who serves drinks in a tavern

pot cheese *noun* (1812)
: COTTAGE CHEESE

po·teen *also* **po·theen** \pə-'tēn, -'chēn, -'tyēn, -'thēn\ *noun* [Irish *poitín*, literally, small pot, diminutive of *pota* pot] (1812)
: whiskey illicitly distilled in Ireland

Po·tem·kin village \pə-'tem(p)-kən-\ *noun* [Grigori *Potëmkin*, who supposedly built impressive fake villages along a route Catherine the Great was to travel] (1937)
: an impressive facade or show designed to hide an undesirable fact or condition ◇

po·tence \'pō-t³n(t)s\ *noun* (15th century)
: POTENCY

po·ten·cy \'pō-t³n(t)-sē\ *noun, plural* **-cies** (15th century)

1 a : FORCE, POWER **b** : the quality or state of being potent **c** : the ability or capacity to achieve or bring about a particular result
2 : POTENTIALITY 1

¹**po·tent** \'pō-t³nt\ *adjective* [Middle English, from Latin *potent-*, *potens* (present participle of *posse* to be able), from Latin *potis*, *pote* able; akin to Gothic *brūthfaths* bridegroom, Greek *posis* husband, Sanskrit *pati* master] (15th century)
1 : having or wielding force, authority, or influence : POWERFUL
2 : achieving or bringing about a particular result : EFFECTIVE
3 a : chemically or medicinally effective ⟨a *potent* vaccine⟩ **b** : rich in a characteristic constituent
4 : able to copulate — usually used of the male
— **po·tent·ly** *adverb*

²**potent** *adjective* [obsolete English *potent* crutch] (1610)
of a heraldic cross : having flat bars across the ends of the arms — see CROSS illustration

po·ten·tate \'pō-t³n-,tāt\ *noun* (15th century)
: RULER, SOVEREIGN; *broadly* : one who wields great power or sway

¹**po·ten·tial** \pə-'ten(t)-shəl\ *adjective* [Middle English *potencial*, from Late Latin *potentialis*, from *potentia* potentiality, from Latin, power, from *potent-*, *potens*] (14th century)
1 : existing in possibility : capable of development into actuality ⟨*potential* benefits⟩
2 : expressing possibility; *specifically* : of, relating to, or constituting a verb phrase expressing possibility, liberty, or power by the use of an auxiliary with the infinitive of the verb (as in "it may rain")
synonym see LATENT
— **po·ten·tial·ly** \-'ten(t)-sh(ə-)lē\ *adverb*

²**potential** *noun* (1817)
1 a : something that can develop or become actual ⟨a *potential* for violence⟩ **b** : PROMISE 2
2 a : any of various functions from which the intensity or the velocity at any point in a field may be readily calculated **b** : the work required to move a unit positive charge from a reference point (as at infinity) to a point in question **c** : POTENTIAL DIFFERENCE

potential difference *noun* (1896)
: the difference in potential between two points that represents the work involved or the energy released in the transfer of a unit quantity of electricity from one point to the other

potential energy *noun* (1853)
: the energy that a piece of matter has because of its position or because of the arrangement of parts

po·ten·ti·al·i·ty \pə-,ten(t)-shē-'a-lə-tē\ *noun, plural* **-ties** (1625)
1 : the ability to develop or come into existence
2 : POTENTIAL 1

po·ten·ti·ate \pə-'ten(t)-shē-ˌāt\ *transitive verb* **-at·ed; -at·ing** (1817)
: to make effective or active or more effective or more active; *also* : to augment the activity of (as a drug) synergistically
— **po·ten·ti·a·tion** \-ˌten(t)-shē-'ā-shən\ *noun*
— **po·ten·ti·a·tor** \-'ten(t)-shē-ˌā-tər\ *noun*

po·ten·til·la \ˌpō-tᵊn-'ti-lə\ *noun* [New Latin, from Medieval Latin, garden heliotrope, from Latin *potent-, potens*] (1548)
: CINQUEFOIL 1

po·ten·ti·om·e·ter \pə-ˌten(t)-shē-'ä-mə-tər\ *noun* [International Scientific Vocabulary *potential* + *-o-* + *-meter*] (1881)
1 : an instrument for measuring electromotive forces
2 : VOLTAGE DIVIDER
— **po·ten·ti·o·met·ric** \-sh(ē-)ə-'me-trik\ *adjective*

pot·ful \'pät-ˌful\ *noun* (14th century)
1 : as much or as many as a pot will hold
2 : a large amount ⟨makes a *potful* of money —John Corry⟩

pot hat *noun* (1798)
: a hat with a stiff crown; *especially* : DERBY

pot·head \'pät-ˌhed\ *noun* (1959)
: a person who smokes marijuana

¹poth·er \'pä-thər\ *noun* [origin unknown] (1591)
1 a : confused or fidgety flurry or activity : COMMOTION **b** : agitated talk or controversy usually over a trivial matter
2 : a choking cloud of dust or smoke
3 : mental turmoil

²pother *verb* **poth·ered; poth·er·ing** \'pä-thə-riŋ, 'päth-riŋ\ (1692)
transitive verb
: to put into a pother
intransitive verb
: to be in a pother

pot·herb \'pät-ˌ(h)ərb, -ˌhərb\ *noun* (1538)
: a usually leafy herb that is cooked for use as greens; *also* : one (as mint) used to season food

pot holder *noun* (1944)
: a small cloth pad used for handling hot cooking utensils or containers

pot·hole \'pät-ˌhōl\ *noun* (1826)
1 a : a circular hole formed in the rocky bed of a river by the grinding action of stones or gravel whirled round by the water **b** : a sizable rounded often water-filled depression in land
2 : a pot-shaped hole in a road surface
— **pot·holed** \-ˌhōld\ *adjective*

pot·hook \-ˌhuk\ *noun* (15th century)
1 : an S-shaped hook for hanging pots and kettles over an open fire
2 : a written character resembling a pothook

pot·house \-ˌhaus\ *noun* (1724)
: TAVERN 1

pot·hunt·er \-ˌhən-tər\ *noun* (1781)
1 : one who hunts game for food
2 : an amateur archaeologist
— **pot·hunt·ing** \-tiŋ\ *noun*

po·tion \'pō-shən\ *noun* [Middle English *pocioun*, from Middle French *potion*, from Latin *potion-, potio* drink, potion, from *potare* to drink — more at POTABLE] (14th century)
: a mixture of liquids (as liquor or medicine)

¹pot·latch \'pät-ˌlach\ *noun* [Chinook Jargon *patlač*, from Nootka *p̓aƛp̓ac̓*] (circa 1861)
1 : a ceremonial feast of the American Indians of the northwest coast marked by the host's lavish distribution of gifts or sometimes destruction of property to demonstrate wealth and generosity with the expectation of eventual reciprocation
2 *Northwest* : a social event or celebration

²potlatch (1898)
transitive verb
1 : to give (as a gift) especially with the expectation of a gift in return
2 : to hold or give a potlatch for (as a tribe or group)

intransitive verb
: to hold or give a potlatch

pot lik·ker \-'li-kər\ *Southern & Midland variant of* POT LIQUOR

pot·line \'pät-ˌlīn\ *noun* (1944)
: a row of electrolytic cells used in the production of aluminum

pot liquor *noun* (1744)
: the liquid left in a pot after cooking something

pot·luck \'pät-'lək, *1b also* -ˌlək\ *noun* (1592)
1 a : the regular meal available to a guest for whom no special preparations have been made
b : a communal meal to which people bring food to share — usually used attributively ⟨a *potluck* supper⟩
2 : whatever is offered or available in given circumstances or at a given time

pot marigold *noun* (1814)
: a calendula (*Calendula officinalis*) grown especially for ornament

po·tom·e·ter \pō-'tä-mə-tər\ *noun* [Greek *poton* drink (akin to Greek *pinein* to drink) + English *-meter* — more at POTABLE] (1884)
: an apparatus for measuring the rate of transpiration in a plant by determining the amount of water absorbed

pot·pie \'pät-'pī, -ˌpī\ *noun* (circa 1792)
: pastry-covered meat and vegetables cooked in a deep dish

pot·pour·ri \ˌpō-pu̇-'rē\ *noun* [French *pot pourri*, literally, rotten pot] (1749)
1 : a mixture of flowers, herbs, and spices that is usually kept in a jar and used for scent
2 : a miscellaneous collection : MEDLEY ⟨a *potpourri* of the best songs and sketches —*Current Biography*⟩ ◇

pot roast *noun* (1881)
: a piece of beef cooked by braising usually on top of the stove

pot·sherd \'pät-ˌshərd\ *noun* [Middle English *pot-sherd*, from *pot* + *sherd* shard] (14th century)
: a pottery fragment

¹pot·shot \-ˌshät\ *noun* [from the notion that such a shot is unsportsmanlike and worthy only of one whose object is to fill the cooking pot] (1858)
1 : a shot taken from ambush or at a random or easy target
2 : a critical remark made in a random or sporadic manner

²potshot *verb* **potshot; pot·shot·ting** (1918)
intransitive verb
: to take a potshot
transitive verb
: to attack or shoot with a potshot

pot still *noun* (1799)
: a still used especially in the distillation of Irish grain whiskey and Scotch malt whiskey in which the heat of the fire is applied directly to the pot containing the mash

pot·stone \'pät-ˌstōn\ *noun* (1771)
: a more or less impure steatite used especially in prehistoric times to make cooking vessels

pot·tage \'pä-tij\ *noun* [Middle English *potage*, from Old French, from *pot* pot, of Germanic origin; akin to Old English *pott* pot] (13th century)
: a thick soup of vegetables and often meat

pot·ted \'pä-təd\ *adjective* (1646)
1 *chiefly British* : preserved in a pot, jar, or can
2 : planted or grown in a pot
3 *chiefly British* : briefly and superficially summarized ⟨a dull, pedestrian *potted* history —*Times Literary Supplement*⟩
4 *slang* : DRUNK 1a

¹pot·ter \'pä-tər\ *noun* (before 12th century)
: one that makes pottery

²potter *intransitive verb* [probably frequentative of English dialect *pote* to poke] (1829)
: PUTTER
— **pot·ter·er** \'pä-tər-ər\ *noun*
— **pot·ter·ing·ly** \'pä-tə-riŋ-lē\ *adverb*

potter's clay *noun* (15th century)
: a plastic clay suitable for making pottery — called also *potter's earth*

potter's field *noun* [from the mention in Matthew 27:7 of the purchase of a potter's field for use as a graveyard] (1777)
: a public burial place for paupers, unknown persons, and criminals

potter's wheel *noun* (circa 1741)
: a usually horizontal disk revolving on a vertical spindle and carrying the clay being shaped by a potter

pot·tery \'pä-tə-rē\ *noun, plural* **-ter·ies** (15th century)
1 : a place where clayware is made and fired
2 a : the art or craft of the potter **b** : the manufacture of clayware
3 : CLAYWARE; *especially* : earthenware as distinguished on the one hand from porcelain and stoneware and on the other from brick and tile

pot·tle \'pä-tᵊl\ *noun* [Middle English *potel*, from Middle French, from *pot*] (14th century)
: a container holding a half gallon (1.9 liters)

pot·to \'pä-(ˌ)tō\ *noun, plural* **pottos** [perhaps from Wolof *pata,* a tailless monkey] (1705)
: any of several African primates (genera *Arctocebus* and *Perodicticus*); *especially* : a West African primate (*P. potto*) that has a vestigial index finger and tail

Pott's disease \'päts-\ *noun* [Percivall *Pott* (died 1788) English surgeon] (1835)
: tuberculosis of the spine with destruction of bone resulting in curvature of the spine

¹pot·ty \'pä-tē\ *adjective* **pot·ti·er; -est** [probably from ¹*pot*] (circa 1860)
1 *British* : TRIVIAL, INSIGNIFICANT
2 *chiefly British* : slightly crazy
3 : SNOBBISH

²potty *noun, plural* **potties** (circa 1942)
: a small child's pot for urination or defecation

pot·ty–chair \-ˌcher, -ˌchar\ *noun* (1943)
: a child's chair having an open seat under which a receptacle in placed for toilet training

pot·zer \'pät-sər\ *variant of* PATZER

¹pouch \'pau̇ch\ *noun* [Middle English *pouche*, from Middle French, of Germanic origin; akin to Old English *pocca* bag] (14th century)
1 : a small drawstring bag carried on the person

◇ **WORD HISTORY**
potpourri A potpourri, which in ordinary usage alludes to a dried mixture of pleasant-smelling herbs or more broadly to any miscellaneous collection, is etymologically a "putrid pot." The original French *pot pourri* was a stew made of a variety of meats and vegetables cooked together. This was a traditional Spanish dish borrowed by the French, whose name for it is a loan translation of Spanish *olla podrida*. Just why the stew designated *olla podrida* was called "rotten" is not very clear. One explanation is that the Spanish adjective *podrido* has occasionally been used colloquially to mean "very full, teeming," a sense that would fit the nature of the dish. Though not common, similar uses of English *rotten* can be found (as, for example, in the passage "The country's rotten with money, if one could touch it" from a novel by Elizabeth Bowen). And *rotten* in the common idiom "to spoil a child rotten" means little more than "thoroughly."

2 a : a bag of small or moderate size for storing or transporting goods; *specifically* **:** a lockable bag for first-class mail or diplomatic dispatches **b** *chiefly Scottish* **:** POCKET **c :** PACKET **3 :** an anatomical structure resembling a pouch
— **pouched** \'paùcht\ *adjective*

²**pouch** (circa 1566)
transitive verb
1 : to put or form into or as if into a pouch **2 :** to transmit by pouch
intransitive verb
1 : to bulge or stick out or down in a manner suggesting a pouch ⟨*pouching* cheeks⟩ **2 :** to transmit mail or dispatches by pouch

pouchy \'paù-chē\ *adjective* **pouch·i·er; -est** (1828)
: having, tending to have, or resembling a pouch ⟨*pouchy* insomniac eyes —Graham Greene⟩

pouf *also* **pouffe** \'püf\ *noun* [French *pouf*, something inflated, of imitative origin] (1817)
1 : PUFF 3b(3)
2 : a bouffant or fluffy part of a garment or accessory
3 : OTTOMAN
— **poufed** *or* **pouffed** \'püft\ *adjective*

Pouil·ly-Fuis·sé \pü-'yē-fwē-'sā\ *noun* [Solutré-*Pouilly* and *Fuissé*, villages in France] (1927)
: a dry white burgundy from an area west of Mâcon, France

Pouil·ly-Fu·mé \pü-'yē-fü-'mā, -'fū-\ *noun* [French, from *Pouilly*-sur-Loire, village in France + *fumé*, past participle of *fumer* to smoke, from Latin *fumare*, from *fumus* smoke — more at FUME] (1935)
: a dry white wine from the Loire valley of France

pou·larde *also* **pou·lard** \pü-'lärd\ *noun* [French *poularde*] (1732)
: a pullet sterilized to produce fattening

poult \'pōlt\ *noun* [Middle English *polet, pulte* young fowl — more at PULLET] (15th century)
: a young fowl; *especially* **:** a young turkey

poul·ter·er \'pōl-tər-ər\ *noun* [alteration of Middle English *pulter,* from Middle French *pouletier*] (1638)
: one that deals in poultry

poul·ter's measure \'pōl-tərz-\ *noun* [obsolete *poulter* poulterer, from Middle English *pulter;* from the former practice of occasionally giving one or two extra when counting eggs by dozens] (1576)
: a meter in which lines of 12 and 14 syllables alternate

¹**poul·tice** \'pōl-təs\ *noun* [Middle English *pultes,* from Medieval Latin, literally, pap, from Latin, plural of *pult-, puls* porridge] (15th century)
: a soft usually heated and sometimes medicated mass spread on cloth and applied to sores or other lesions

²**poultice** *transitive verb* **-ticed; -tic·ing** (1730)
: to apply a poultice to

poul·try \'pōl-trē\ *noun* [Middle English *pultrie,* from Middle French *pouleterie,* from Old French, from *pouletier* poulterer, from *poulet* — more at PULLET] (14th century)
: domesticated birds kept for eggs or meat

poul·try·man \-mən\ *noun* (circa 1574)
1 : one who raises domestic fowls especially on a commercial scale for the production of eggs and meat **2 :** one who deals in poultry or poultry products

¹**pounce** \'paùn(t)s\ *noun* [Middle English, talon] (15th century)
: the claw of a bird of prey

²**pounce** *intransitive verb* **pounced; pounc·ing** (1744)

1 a : to swoop upon and seize something with or as if with talons **b :** to seize upon and make capital of something (as another's blunder or an opportunity) **2 :** to make a sudden assault or approach

³**pounce** *noun* (1841)
: the act of pouncing

⁴**pounce** *transitive verb* **pounced; pounc·ing** [Middle French *poncer,* from *ponce*] (1535)
: to dust, rub, finish, or stencil with pounce

⁵**pounce** *noun* [French *ponce* pumice, from Middle French, from Late Latin *pomic-, pomex,* alteration of Latin *pumic-, pumex* — more at FOAM] (1706)
1 : a fine powder formerly used to prevent ink from spreading
2 : a fine powder for making stenciled patterns

poun·cet-box \'paùn(t)-sət-\ *noun* [probably from (assumed) Middle French *poncette* small pounce bag] (1596)
archaic **:** a box for carrying pomander

¹**pound** \'paùnd\ *noun, plural* **pounds** *also* **pound** [Middle English, from Old English *pund,* from Latin *pondo* pound, from ablative of *pondus* weight — more at PENDANT] (before 12th century)
1 : any of various units of mass and weight; *specifically* **:** a unit now in general use among English-speaking peoples equal to 16 avoirdupois ounces or 7000 grains or 0.45359237 kilogram — see WEIGHT table
2 a : the basic monetary unit of the United Kingdom — called also *pound sterling* **b :** any of numerous basic monetary units of other countries — see MONEY table **c :** ²LIRA

²**pound** *noun* [Middle English, enclosure, from Old English *pund-*] (14th century)
1 a : an enclosure for animals; *especially* **:** a public enclosure for stray or unlicensed animals ⟨a dog *pound*⟩ **b :** a depot for holding impounded personal property until redeemed by the owner ⟨a car *pound*⟩ **2 :** a place or condition of confinement **3 :** an enclosure within which fish are kept or caught; *especially* **:** the inner compartment of a fish trap or pound net

³**pound** *noun* (1562)
: an act or sound of pounding

⁴**pound** *verb* [alteration of Middle English *pounen,* from Old English *pūnian*] (1594)
transitive verb
1 : to reduce to powder or pulp by beating **2 a :** to strike heavily or repeatedly **b :** to produce with or as if with repeated vigorous strokes — usually used with *out* ⟨*pound* out a story on the typewriter⟩ **c :** to inculcate by insistent repetition **:** DRIVE ⟨day after day the facts were *pounded* home to them —Ivy B. Priest⟩ **3 :** to move along heavily or persistently ⟨*pounded* the pavements looking for work⟩
intransitive verb
1 : to strike heavy repeated blows **2 :** PULSATE, THROB ⟨my heart was *pounding*⟩ **3 a :** to move with or make a heavy repetitive sound **b :** to work hard and continuously — usually used with *away*

¹**pound·age** \'paùn-dij\ *noun* (circa 1500)
1 : a charge per pound of weight **2 :** weight in pounds

²**poundage** *noun* (1554)
: IMPOUNDMENT 1

pound·al \'paùn-d²l\ *noun* [¹*pound* + *-al* (as in *quintal*)] (1879)
: a unit of force equal to the force that would give a free mass of one pound an acceleration of one foot per second per second

pound cake *noun* [from the original recipe prescribing a pound of each of the principal ingredients] (1747)
: a rich butter cake made with a large proportion of eggs and shortening

¹**pound·er** \'paùn-dər\ *noun* (before 12th century)
1 : one that pounds

2 : a tool used for pounding

²**pounder** *noun* (1684)
1 : a gun throwing a projectile of a specified weight — usually used in combination ⟨the ship was armed with six-*pounders*⟩ **2 :** one having a usually specified weight or value in pounds — usually used in combination ⟨caught a ten-*pounder*⟩

pound-fool·ish \'paùn(d)-'fü-lish\ *adjective* [from the phrase *penny-wise and pound-foolish*] (1607)
: imprudent in dealing with large sums or large matters

pound mile *noun* (1939)
: the transport of one pound of mail or express for one mile

pound net *noun* (1865)
: a fish trap consisting of a netting arranged into a directing wing and an enclosure with a narrow entrance

pound sign *noun* (1980)
1 : the symbol £
2 : the symbol #

¹**pour** \'pōr, 'pȯr\ *verb* [Middle English] (14th century)
transitive verb
1 a : to cause to flow in a stream **b :** to dispense from a container ⟨*poured* drinks for everyone⟩ **2 :** to supply or produce freely or copiously **3 :** to give full expression to **:** VENT ⟨*poured* out his feelings⟩
intransitive verb
1 : to move with a continuous flow **2 :** to rain hard **3 :** to move or come continuously **:** STREAM ⟨complaints *poured* in⟩
— **pour·able** \'pōr-ə-bəl, 'pȯr-\ *adjective*
— **pour·er** \-ər\ *noun*
— **pour·ing·ly** \-iŋ-lē\ *adverb*

²**pour** *noun* (1790)
1 : the action of pouring **:** STREAM **2 a :** an instance of pouring or an amount poured **b :** a heavy fall of rain **:** DOWNPOUR

pour·boire \pùr-'bwär\ *noun* [French, from *pour boire* for drinking] (1817)
: TIP, GRATUITY

pour·par·ler \ˌpùr-pär-'lā\ *noun* [French, from Middle French, from *pourparler* to discuss, from Old French, from *pour* for, before + *parler* to speak — more at PURCHASE, PARLEY] (1795)
: a discussion preliminary to negotiations

pour·point \'pùr-ˌpȯint, -ˌpwant\ *noun* [Middle English *purpoint,* from Middle French *pourpoint,* from Old French *porpoint,* from *porpoint,* adjective, quilted, alteration of (assumed) Vulgar Latin *perpunctus,* past participle of *perpungere* to perforate, from Latin *per* through + *pungere* to prick, pierce — more at PUNGENT] (14th century)
: a padded and quilted doublet

pour point \'pōr-ˌpȯint, 'pȯr-\ *noun* (1922)
: the lowest temperature at which a substance flows under specified conditions

pousse-ca·fé \ˌpüs-(ˌ)ka-'fā\ *noun* [French, literally, coffee chaser] (1880)
: an after-dinner drink consisting of several liqueurs of different colors and specific gravities poured so as to remain in separate layers

pous·sette \pü-'set\ *intransitive verb* **pous·sett·ed; pous·sett·ing** [French, game in which contestants cross pins with each attempting to get his pin on top, from *pousser* to push] (1812)
: to swing in a semicircle with hands joined with one's partner in a country-dance

¹**pout** \'paùt\ *verb* [Middle English] (14th century)
intransitive verb
1 a : to show displeasure by thrusting out the lips or wearing a sullen expression **b :** SULK **2 :** PROTRUDE
transitive verb
: to cause to protrude ⟨*pouted* her lips⟩

²**pout** *noun* (1591)

1 : a protrusion of the lips expressive of displeasure
2 *plural* **:** a fit of pique

³pout *noun, plural* **pout** *or* **pouts** [probably from (assumed) Middle English *poute*, a fish with a large head, from Old English *-pūte*; akin to Middle English *pouten* to pout] (1591) **:** any of several large-headed fishes (as a bullhead or eelpout)

pout·er \'paů-tər\ *noun* (1725)
1 : a domestic pigeon of a breed characterized by erect carriage and a dilatable crop
2 : one that pouts

pouty \'paů-tē\ *adjective* (1863)
1 : SULKY 1
2 : expressive of displeasure

pov·er·ty \'pä-vər-tē\ *noun, often attributive* [Middle English *poverte*, from Old French *poverté*, from Latin *paupertat-, paupertas*, from *pauper* poor — more at POOR] (12th century)
1 a : the state of one who lacks a usual or socially acceptable amount of money or material possessions **b :** renunciation as a member of a religious order of the right as an individual to own property
2 : SCARCITY, DEARTH
3 a : debility due to malnutrition **b :** lack of fertility ⟨*poverty* of the soil⟩ ☆

poverty line *noun* (1901)
: a level of personal or family income below which one is classified as poor according to governmental standards — called also *poverty level*

pov·er·ty–strick·en \-,stri-kən\ *adjective* (1803)
: very poor **:** DESTITUTE

¹pow \'pō, 'paů\ *noun* [alteration of *poll*] (1724)
: HEAD, POLL

²pow \'paů\ *noun* [imitative] (1881)
: a sound of a blow or explosion

POW \,pē-(,)ō-'də-bəl-(,)yü, -bə-(,)yü; -'dəb-(,)yü\ *noun* (circa 1919)
: PRISONER OF WAR

¹pow·der \'paů-dər\ *verb* **pow·dered; pow·der·ing** \'paů-d(ə-)riŋ\ (13th century)
transitive verb
1 : to sprinkle or cover with or as if with powder
2 : to reduce or convert to powder
3 : to hit (as a ball) very hard
intransitive verb
1 : to become powder
2 : to apply cosmetic powder
— **pow·der·er** \-dər-ər\ *noun*

²powder *noun, often attributive* [Middle English *poudre*, from Old French, from Latin *pulver-, pulvis* dust; probably akin to Sanskrit *palāva* chaff] (14th century)
1 : matter in a finely divided state **:** particulate matter
2 a : a preparation in the form of fine particles especially for medicinal or cosmetic use **b :** fine dry light snow
3 : any of various solid explosives used chiefly in gunnery and blasting
— **pow·der·less** \-ləs\ *adjective*
— **pow·der·like** \-,līk\ *adjective*

powder blue *noun* (1896)
: a pale blue

powder horn *noun* (1533)
: a flask for carrying gunpowder; *especially* **:** one made from the horn of an ox or cow

powder keg *noun* (1855)
1 : a small usually metal cask for holding gunpowder or blasting powder
2 : something liable to explode

powder metallurgy *noun* (1933)
: a branch of science or an art concerned with the production of powdered metals or of metallic objects by compressing a powdered metal or alloy with or without other materials and heating without thoroughly melting to solidify and strengthen

powder monkey *noun* (1682)

: one who carries or has charge of explosives (as in blasting operations)

powder–puff *adjective* (1939)
: of, relating to, or being a competitive activity or event for women ⟨a *powder-puff* football game⟩

powder puff *noun* (circa 1704)
: a small fluffy device (as a pad) for applying cosmetic powder

powder room *noun* (circa 1937)
1 : a rest room for women
2 : a lavatory in the main living area of a house

pow·dery \'paů-də-rē\ *adjective* (15th century)
1 a : resembling or consisting of powder ⟨*powdery* snow⟩ **b :** easily reduced to powder **:** CRUMBLING
2 : covered with or as if with powder

powdery mildew *noun* (1889)
1 : an ascomycetous fungus (family Erysiphaceae) producing abundant powdery conidia on the host
2 : a plant disease caused by a powdery mildew

¹pow·er \'paů(-ə)r\ *noun, often attributive* [Middle English, from Old French *poeir*, from *poeir* to be able, from (assumed) Vulgar Latin *potēre*, alteration of Latin *posse* — more at POTENT] (13th century)
1 a (1) **:** ability to act or produce an effect (2) **:** ability to get extra-base hits (3) **:** capacity for being acted upon or undergoing an effect **b :** legal or official authority, capacity, or right
2 a : possession of control, authority, or influence over others **b :** one having such power; *specifically* **:** a sovereign state **c :** a controlling group **:** ESTABLISHMENT — often used in the phrase *the powers that be* **d** *archaic* **:** a force of armed men **e** *chiefly dialect* **:** a large number or quantity
3 a : physical might **b :** mental or moral efficacy **c :** political control or influence
4 *plural* **:** an order of angels — see CELESTIAL HIERARCHY
5 a : the number of times as indicated by an exponent that a number occurs as a factor in a product; *also* **:** the product itself **b :** CARDINAL NUMBER 2
6 a : a source or means of supplying energy; *especially* **:** ELECTRICITY **b :** MOTIVE POWER **c :** the time rate at which work is done or energy emitted or transferred
7 : MAGNIFICATION 2b
8 : SCOPE, COMPREHENSIVENESS
9 : the probability of rejecting the null hypothesis in a statistical test when a particular alternative hypothesis happens to be true ☆ ☆

²power (1540)
transitive verb
1 : to supply with power and especially motive power
2 : to give impetus to
intransitive verb
1 : to move about by means of motive power
2 : to move with great speed or force

³power *adjective* (1949)
1 : relating to or utilizing power ⟨plays a *power* game⟩; *also* **:** POWERFUL 1 ⟨a *power* critic⟩
2 : of, relating to, or being a meal at which influential people discuss business or politics

power base *noun* (1959)
: a base of political support

pow·er·boat \'paů(-ə)r-,bōt\ *noun* (1908)
: MOTORBOAT

power broker *noun* (1961)
: a person (as in politics) able to exert strong influence through control of votes or individuals

pow·er–dive \-,dīv\ (1937)
intransitive verb
: to make a power dive
transitive verb
: to cause to power-dive

power dive *noun* (1930)
: a dive of an airplane accelerated by the power of the engine

pow·er·ful \'paů(-ə)r-fəl\ *adjective* (15th century)
1 : having great power, prestige, or influence
2 : leading to many or important deductions ⟨a *powerful* set of postulates⟩
— **pow·er·ful·ly** \-f(ə-)lē\ *adverb*

power function *noun* (1957)
1 : a function of a parameter under statistical test whose value for a particular value of the parameter is the probability of rejecting the null hypothesis if that value of the parameter happens to be true
2 : a function (as $f(x) = ax^k$) that equals the product of a constant and a power of the independent variable

pow·er·house \'paů(-ə)r-,haůs\ *noun* (circa 1890)

☆ **SYNONYMS**

Poverty, indigence, penury, want, destitution mean the state of one with insufficient resources. POVERTY may cover a range from extreme want of necessities to an absence of material comforts ⟨the extreme *poverty* of the slum dwellers⟩. INDIGENCE implies seriously straitened circumstances ⟨the *indigence* of her years as a graduate student⟩. PENURY suggests a cramping or oppressive lack of money ⟨a catastrophic illness that condemned them to years of *penury*⟩. WANT and DESTITUTION imply extreme poverty that threatens life itself through starvation or exposure ⟨lived in a perpetual state of *want*⟩ ⟨the widespread *destitution* in countries beset by famine⟩.

Power, authority, jurisdiction, control, command, sway, dominion mean the right to govern or rule or determine. POWER implies possession of ability to wield force, permissive authority, or substantial influence ⟨the *power* to mold public opinion⟩. AUTHORITY implies the granting of power for a specific purpose within specified limits ⟨gave her attorney the *authority* to manage her estate⟩. JURISDICTION applies to official power exercised within prescribed limits ⟨the bureau having *jurisdiction* over alcohol and firearms⟩. CONTROL stresses the power to direct and restrain ⟨you are responsible for the students under your *control*⟩. COMMAND implies the power to make arbitrary decisions and compel obedience ⟨the army officer in *command*⟩. SWAY suggests the extent or scope of exercised power or influence ⟨an empire that extended its *sway* over the known world⟩. DOMINION stresses sovereign power or supreme authority ⟨given *dominion* over all the animals⟩.

Power, force, energy, strength, might mean the ability to exert effort. POWER may imply latent or exerted physical, mental, or spiritual ability to act or be acted upon ⟨the awesome *power* of flowing water⟩. FORCE implies the actual effective exercise of power ⟨used enough *force* to push the door open⟩. ENERGY applies to power expended or capable of being transformed into work ⟨a worker with boundless *energy*⟩. STRENGTH applies to the quality or property of a person or thing that makes possible the exertion of force or the withstanding of strain, pressure, or attack ⟨use weight training to build your *strength*⟩. MIGHT implies great or overwhelming power or strength ⟨the belief that *might* makes right⟩.

1 a : POWER PLANT 1 **b :** a source of influence or inspiration
2 : one having great power: as **a :** one having great drive, energy, or ability **b :** an athletic team characterized by strong aggressive play
pow·er·less \-ləs\ *adjective* (15th century)
1 : devoid of strength or resources
2 : lacking the authority or capacity to act
— **pow·er·less·ly** *adverb*
— **pow·er·less·ness** *noun*
power mower *noun* (1940)
: a motor-driven lawn mower
power of attorney (1747)
: a legal instrument authorizing one to act as the attorney or agent of the grantor
power pack *noun* (1936)
: a unit for converting a power supply (as from a battery or household electrical circuit) to a voltage suitable for an electronic device
power plant *noun* (1890)
1 : an electric utility generating station
2 : an engine and related parts supplying the motive power of a self-propelled object (as a rocket or automobile)
power play *noun* (1947)
1 : a military, diplomatic, political, or administrative maneuver in which power is brought to bear
2 a : a concentrated attack in football in which the ballcarrier is preceded by a mass of blockers **b :** a situation in ice hockey in which one team temporarily has more players on the ice than the other team because of a penalty
power politics *noun plural but singular or plural in construction* (1926)
: politics based primarily on the use of power (as military and economic strength) as a coercive force rather than on ethical precepts
power series *noun* (1893)
: an infinite series whose terms are successive integral powers of a variable multiplied by constants
power shovel *noun* (1909)
: a power-operated excavating machine consisting of a boom or crane that supports a lever arm with a large bucket at the end of it
power station *noun* (1901)
: POWER PLANT 1
power steering *noun* (1932)
: automotive steering with engine power used to amplify the torque applied at the steering wheel by the driver
power structure *noun* (1950)
1 : a group of persons having control of an organization **:** ESTABLISHMENT
2 : the hierarchical interrelationships existing within a controlling group
power sweep *noun* (1964)
: SWEEP 3e
power take–off *noun* (1929)
: a supplementary mechanism (as on a tractor) enabling the engine power to be used to operate nonautomotive apparatus (as a pump or saw)
power train *noun* (1943)
: the intervening mechanism by which power is transmitted from an engine to a propeller or axle that it drives
power up *transitive verb* (1970)
: to cause to operate ⟨*power up* the computer⟩
— **pow·er-up** \'paù-(-ə)r-,əp\ *noun*
¹pow·wow \'paù-,waù\ *noun* [Narraganset *powwaw* or Massachuset *pauwau*] (1625)
1 : an American Indian medicine man
2 a : an American Indian ceremony (as for victory in war) **b :** an American Indian social gathering or fair usually including competitive dancing
3 a : a social get-together **b :** a meeting for discussion
²powwow *intransitive verb* (1642)
: to hold a powwow
¹pox \'päks\ *noun, plural* **pox** *or* **pox·es** [alteration of *pocks*, plural of *pock*] (1550)

1 a : a virus disease (as chicken pox) characterized by pustules or eruptions **b** *archaic* **:** SMALLPOX **c :** SYPHILIS
2 : a disastrous evil **:** PLAGUE, CURSE ⟨a *pox* on him⟩
²pox *transitive verb* (1601)
archaic **:** to infect with a pox and especially with syphilis
pox·vi·rus \'päks-,vī-rəs\ *noun* (1941)
: any of a group of relatively large round, brick-shaped, or ovoid DNA-containing animal viruses (as the causative agent of smallpox) that have a fluffy appearance caused by a covering of tubules and threads
poz·zo·la·na \,pät-sə-'lä-nə\ *or* **poz·zo·lan** \'pät-sə-lən\ *noun* [Italian *pozzolana*] (1706)
: finely divided siliceous or siliceous and aluminous material that reacts chemically with slaked lime at ordinary temperature and in the presence of moisture to form a strong slow-hardening cement
— **poz·zo·lan·ic** \,pät-sə-'la-nik, -'lä-\ *adjective*
PPO \,pē-(,)pē-'ō\ *noun, plural* **PPOs** [preferred provider organization] (1983)
: an organization providing health care that gives economic incentives to the individual purchaser of a health-care contract to patronize certain physicians, laboratories, and hospitals that agree to supervision and reduced fees — compare HMO
prac·ti·ca·ble \'prak-ti-kə-bəl\ *adjective* (1670)
1 : capable of being put into practice or of being done or accomplished **:** FEASIBLE
2 : capable of being used **:** USABLE
synonym see POSSIBLE
— **prac·ti·ca·bil·i·ty** \,prak-ti-kə-'bi-lə-tē\ *noun*
— **prac·ti·ca·ble·ness** \'prak-ti-kə-bəl-nəs\ *noun*
— **prac·ti·ca·bly** \-blē\ *adverb*
¹prac·ti·cal \'prak-ti-kəl\ *adjective* [Middle English, from Late Latin *practicus*, from Greek *praktikos*, from *prassein* to pass over, fare, do; akin to Greek *peran* to pass through — more at FARE] (15th century)
1 a : of, relating to, or manifested in practice or action **:** not theoretical or ideal ⟨a *practical* question⟩ ⟨for all *practical* purposes⟩ **b :** being such in practice or effect **:** VIRTUAL ⟨a *practical* failure⟩
2 : actively engaged in some course of action or occupation ⟨a *practical* farmer⟩
3 : capable of being put to use or account **:** USEFUL ⟨he had a *practical* knowledge of French⟩
4 a : disposed to action as opposed to speculation or abstraction **b** (1) **:** qualified by practice or practical training ⟨a good *practical* mechanic⟩ (2) **:** designed to supplement theoretical training by experience
5 : concerned with voluntary action and ethical decisions ⟨*practical* reason⟩
— **prac·ti·cal·i·ty** \,prak-ti-'ka-lə-tē\ *noun*
— **prac·ti·cal·ness** \'prak-ti-kəl-nəs\ *noun*
²practical *noun* (1925)
: an examination requiring demonstration of some practical skill ⟨a zoology *practical*⟩
practical art *noun* (circa 1925)
: an art (as woodworking) that serves ordinary or material needs — usually used in plural
practical joke *noun* (circa 1847)
: a prank intended to trick or embarrass someone or cause physical discomfort
— **practical joker** *noun*
prac·ti·cal·ly \'prak-ti-k(ə-)lē\ *adverb* (1623)
1 : in a practical manner ⟨look *practically* at the problem⟩
2 : ALMOST, NEARLY ⟨*practically* everyone went to the party⟩
practical nurse *noun* (1921)
: a nurse who cares for the sick professionally without having the training or experience required of a registered nurse; *especially* **:** LICENSED PRACTICAL NURSE

practical theology *noun* (circa 1909)
: the study of the institutional activities of religion (as preaching, church administration, pastoral care, and liturgics)
¹prac·tice *or* **prac·tise** \'prak-təs\ *verb* **prac·ticed** *or* **prac·tised; prac·tic·ing** *or* **prac·tis·ing** [Middle English *practisen*, from Middle French *practiser*, from *practique, pratique* practice, noun, from Late Latin *practice*, from Greek *praktikē*, from feminine of *praktikos*] (14th century)
transitive verb
1 a : CARRY OUT, APPLY ⟨*practice* what you preach⟩ **b :** to do or perform often, customarily, or habitually ⟨*practice* politeness⟩ **c :** to be professionally engaged in ⟨*practice* medicine⟩
2 a : to perform or work at repeatedly so as to become proficient ⟨*practice* the act⟩ **b :** to train by repeated exercises ⟨*practice* pupils in penmanship⟩
3 *obsolete* **:** PLOT
intransitive verb
1 : to do repeated exercises for proficiency
2 : to pursue a profession actively
3 *archaic* **:** INTRIGUE
4 : to do something customarily
5 : to take advantage of someone ⟨he *practised* on their credulity with huge success —*Times Literary Supplement*⟩
— **prac·tic·er** *noun*
²practice *also* **practise** *noun* (15th century)
1 a : actual performance or application ⟨ready to carry out in *practice* what they advocated in principle⟩ **b :** a repeated or customary action ⟨had this irritating *practice*⟩ **c :** the usual way of doing something ⟨local *practices*⟩ **d :** the form, manner, and order of conducting legal suits and prosecutions
2 a : systematic exercise for proficiency ⟨*practice* makes perfect⟩ **b :** the condition of being proficient through systematic exercise ⟨get in *practice*⟩
3 a : the continuous exercise of a profession **b :** a professional business; *especially* **:** one constituting an incorporeal property
synonym see HABIT
prac·ticed *or* **prac·tised** \'prak-təst\ *adjective* (1568)
1 : EXPERIENCED, SKILLED
2 : learned by practice
prac·tice–teach \'prak-təs-'tēch\ *intransitive verb* **-taught** \-'tȯt\; **-teach·ing** [back-formation from *practice teaching*] (1952)
: to engage in practice teaching
— **practice teacher** *noun*
practice teaching *noun* (circa 1913)
: teaching by a student under the supervision of an experienced teacher
practicing *or* **practising** *adjective* (1625)
: actively engaged in a specified career or way of life ⟨a *practicing* physician⟩
prac·ti·cum \'prak-ti-kəm\ *noun* [German *Praktikum*, from Late Latin *practicum*, neuter of *practicus* practical] (circa 1909)
: a course of study designed especially for the preparation of teachers and clinicians that involves the supervised practical application of previously studied theory
prac·ti·tion·er \prak-'ti-sh(ə-)nər\ *noun* [alteration of earlier *practician*, from Middle English (Scots) *pratician*, from Middle French *practicien*, from *pratique*] (1535)
1 : one who practices; *especially* **:** one who practices a profession
2 *Christian Science* **:** an authorized healer
prae·ci·pe \'pre-sə-,pē, 'prē-\ *noun* [Middle English *presepe*, from Medieval Latin *praecipe*, from Latin, imperative of *praecipere* to instruct — more at PRECEPT] (15th century)
1 : any of various legal writs commanding a person to do something or to appear and show cause why he or she should not
2 : a written order requesting a clerk or prothonotary of a court to issue a writ and specifying the contents of the writ
prae·di·al *variant of* PREDIAL

prae·mu·ni·re \ˌprē-myu̇-ˈnīr-ē\ *noun* [Middle English *praemunire facias,* from Medieval Latin, that you cause to warn; from prominent words in the writ] (1529)
: an offense against the English Crown punishable chiefly by forfeiture and originally committed by asserting papal legal supremacy in England

prae·no·men \prē-ˈnō-mən\ *noun, plural* **-nomens** *or* **-no·mi·na** \-ˈnä-mə-nə, -ˈnō-\ [Latin, from *prae-* pre- + *nomen* name — more at NAME] (1706)
: the first of the usual three names of an ancient Roman male

prae·sid·i·um *variant of* PRESIDIUM

prae·tor \ˈprē-tər\ *noun* [Middle English *pretor,* from Latin *praetor*] (15th century)
: an ancient Roman magistrate ranking below a consul and having chiefly judicial functions
— **prae·to·ri·al** \prē-ˈtȯr-ē-əl, -ˈtȯr-\ *adjective*
— **prae·tor·ship** \ˈprē-tər-ˌship\ *noun*

prae·to·ri·an \prē-ˈtȯr-ē-ən, -ˈtȯr-\ *adjective* (15th century)
1 *often capitalized* : of, forming, or resembling the Roman imperial bodyguard
2 : of or relating to a praetor
— **praetorian** *noun, often capitalized*

prag·mat·ic \prag-ˈma-tik\ *also* **prag·mat·i·cal** \-ti-kəl\ *adjective* [Latin *pragmaticus* skilled in law or business, from Greek *pragmatikos,* from *pragmat-, pragma* deed, from *prassein* to do — more at PRACTICAL] (1616)
1 *archaic* **a** (1) : BUSY (2) : OFFICIOUS **b** : OPINIONATED
2 : relating to matters of fact or practical affairs often to the exclusion of intellectual or artistic matters : practical as opposed to idealistic ⟨*pragmatic* men of power have had no time or inclination to deal with . . . social morality —K. B. Clark⟩
3 : relating to or being in accordance with philosophical pragmatism
— **pragmatic** *noun*
— **prag·mat·i·cal·ly** \-ti-k(ə-)lē\ *adverb*

prag·mat·i·cism \prag-ˈma-tə-ˌsi-zəm\ *noun* (1905)
: the philosophic doctrine of C. S. Peirce
— **prag·mat·i·cist** \-sist\ *noun*

prag·mat·ics \prag-ˈma-tiks\ *noun plural but singular or plural in construction* (1937)
1 : a branch of semiotic that deals with the relation between signs or linguistic expressions and their users
2 : linguistics concerned with the relationship of sentences to the environment in which they occur

pragmatic sanction *noun* (1643)
: a solemn decree of a sovereign on a matter of primary importance and with the force of fundamental law

prag·ma·tism \ˈprag-mə-ˌti-zəm\ *noun* (circa 1864)
1 : a practical approach to problems and affairs ⟨tried to strike a balance between principles and *pragmatism*⟩
2 : an American movement in philosophy founded by C. S. Peirce and William James and marked by the doctrines that the meaning of conceptions is to be sought in their practical bearings, that the function of thought is to guide action, and that truth is preeminently to be tested by the practical consequences of belief
— **prag·ma·tist** \-mə-tist\ *adjective or noun*
— **prag·ma·tis·tic** \ˌprag-mə-ˈtis-tik\ *adjective*

prai·rie \ˈprer-ē\ *noun, often attributive* [French, from (assumed) Vulgar Latin *prataria,* from Latin *pratum* meadow] (circa 1682)
1 : land or predominantly in grass
2 : a tract of grassland: as **a** : a large area of level or rolling land in the Mississippi valley that in its natural uncultivated state usually has

deep fertile soil, a cover of tall coarse grasses, and few trees **b** : one of the dry treeless plateaus east of the Rocky Mountains that merge on their east side with the prairies proper and are characterized by shorter grasses and drier less fertile soil

prairie chicken *noun* (1691)
: a grouse (*Tympanuchus cupido*) chiefly of the prairies of the central U.S.; *also* : a closely related smaller grouse (*T. pallidicinctus*)

prairie chicken

prairie dog *noun* (1774)
: any of a genus (*Cynomys*) of gregarious burrowing rodents of the squirrel family chiefly of central and western U.S. plains; *especially* : a black-tailed rodent (*C. ludovicianus*) that usually lives in extensive colonial burrows

prairie dog

prairie schooner *noun* (1841)
: a covered wagon used by pioneers in cross-country travel — called *also* prairie wagon

prairie soil *noun* (1817)
: any of a zonal group of soils developed in a temperate relatively humid climate under tall grass

prairie wolf *noun* (1804)
: COYOTE

¹praise \ˈprāz\ *verb* **praised; prais·ing** [Middle English, from Old French *preisier* to prize, praise, from Late Latin *pretiare* to prize, from Latin *pretium* price — more at PRICE] (13th century)
transitive verb
1 : to express a favorable judgment of : COMMEND
2 : to glorify (a god or saint) especially by the attribution of perfections
intransitive verb
: to express praise
— **prais·er** *noun*

²praise *noun* (14th century)
1 a : an expression of approval : COMMENDATION **b** : WORSHIP
2 a : VALUE, MERIT **b** *archaic* : one that is praised

praise·wor·thy \ˈprāz-ˌwər-the̱\ *adjective* (15th century)
: LAUDABLE
— **praise·wor·thi·ly** \-thə-lē\ *adverb*
— **praise·wor·thi·ness** \-thē-nəs\ *noun*

Pra·krit \ˈprä-ˌkrit, -krət\ *noun* [Sanskrit *prākṛta,* from *prākṛta* natural, vulgar] (1766)
: any or all of the ancient Indo-Aryan languages or dialects other than Sanskrit — see INDO-EUROPEAN LANGUAGES table

pra·line \ˈprä-ˌlēn, ˈprā-, ˈprȯ-\ *noun* [French, from Count Plessis-*Praslin* (died 1675) French soldier] (1723)
: a confection of nuts and sugar: **a** : almonds cooked in boiling sugar until brown and crisp **b** : a patty of creamy brown sugar and pecan meats

prall·tril·ler \ˈpräl-ˌtri-lər\ *noun* [German, from *prallen* to rebound + *Triller* trill] (circa 1841)
: a musical ornament made by a quick alternation of a principal tone with the tone above

¹pram \ˈpräm, ˈpram\ *noun* [Middle Dutch *praem* & Middle Low German *prām*] (1548)
: a small lightweight nearly flat-bottomed boat with a broad transom and usually squared-off bow

²pram \ˈpram\ *noun* [by shortening & alteration from *perambulator*] (1884)
chiefly British : BABY CARRIAGE

¹prance \ˈpran(t)s\ *verb* **pranced; prancing** [Middle English *prauncen*] (14th century)
intransitive verb
1 : to spring from the hind legs or move by so doing
2 : to ride on a prancing horse
3 : to walk or move in a spirited manner : STRUT; *also* : to dance about
transitive verb
: to cause (a horse) to prance
— **pranc·er** \ˈpran(t)-sər\ *noun*

²prance *noun* (1751)
: an act or instance of prancing; *specifically* : a prancing movement

pran·di·al \ˈpran-dē-əl\ *adjective* [Latin *prandium* late breakfast, luncheon] (1820)
: of or relating to a meal

prang \ˈpraŋ\ *transitive verb* [origin unknown] (1941)
chiefly British : to have an accident with : cause to crash
— **prang** *noun, chiefly British*

¹prank \ˈpraŋk\ *noun* [obsolete *prank* to play tricks] (circa 1529)
: TRICK: **a** *obsolete* : a malicious act **b** : a mildly mischievous act **c** : a ludicrous act

²prank *verb* [probably from Dutch *pronken* to strut; akin to Middle High German ge*brunkel* glitter of metal] (15th century)
intransitive verb
: to show oneself off
transitive verb
: to dress or adorn gaily or showily

prank·ish \ˈpraŋ-kish\ *adjective* (1827)
1 : full of pranks ⟨a *prankish* child⟩
2 : having the nature of a prank ⟨*prankish* acts⟩
— **prank·ish·ly** *adverb*
— **prank·ish·ness** *noun*

prank·ster \ˈpraŋ(k)-stər\ *noun* (1927)
: a person who plays pranks

prase \ˈprāz, ˈprās\ *noun* [French, from Latin *prasius,* from Greek *prasios,* from *prasios,* adjective, of the color of a leek from *prason* leek; akin to Latin *porrum* leek] (1788)
: a chalcedony that is translucent and yellowish green

pra·seo·dym·i·um \ˌprā-zē-ō-ˈdi-mē-əm, ˌprā-sē-\ *noun* [New Latin, alteration of *praseodidymium,* irregular from Greek *prasios,* adjective + New Latin *didymium* didymium] (1885)
: a yellowish white trivalent metallic element of the rare-earth group used chiefly in the form of its salts in coloring glass greenish yellow — see ELEMENT table

prate \ˈprāt\ *intransitive verb* **prat·ed; prat·ing** [Middle English, from Middle Dutch; akin to Middle Low German *pratten* to pout] (15th century)
: to talk long and idly : CHATTER
— **prate** *noun*
— **prat·er** *noun*
— **prat·ing·ly** \ˈprā-tiŋ-lē\ *adverb*

prat·fall \ˈprat-ˌfȯl\ *noun* [*prat* buttocks + *fall*] (1938)
1 : a fall on the buttocks
2 : a humiliating mishap or blunder

pra·tin·cole \ˈpra-t°n-ˌkōl, ˈprā-, -tiŋ-\ *noun* [ultimately from Latin *pratum* meadow + *incola* inhabitant, from *in-* + *colere* to cultivate — more at WHEEL] (1773)
: any of several Old World shore-inhabiting birds (genera *Glareolus* and *Stiltia* of the family Glareolidae) with a short bill and a forked tail

\ə\ abut \ᵊ\ kitten \ər\ further \a\ ash \ā\ ace \ä\ mop, mar \au̇\ out \ch\ chin \e\ bet \ē\ easy \g\ go \i\ hit \ī\ ice \j\ job \ŋ\ sing \ō\ go \ȯ\ law \ȯi\ boy \th\ thin \ṯh\ the \ü\ loot \u̇\ foot \y\ yet \zh\ vision *see also* Guide to Pronunciation

pra·tique \pra-'tēk\ *noun* [French, literally, practice — more at PRACTICE] (1609)
: clearance given an incoming ship by the health authority of a port

¹prat·tle \'pra-t°l\ *verb* **prat·tled; prat·tling** \'prat-liŋ, 'pra-t°l-iŋ\ [Low German *pratelen;* akin to Middle Dutch *praten* to prate] (1532)
intransitive verb
1 : PRATE
2 : to utter or make meaningless sounds suggestive of the chatter of children : BABBLE
transitive verb
: to say in an unaffected or childish manner
— **prat·tler** \'prat-lər, 'pra-t°l-ər\ *noun*
— **prat·tling·ly** \-liŋ-lē, -t°l-iŋ-\ *adverb*

²prattle *noun* (1555)
1 : trifling or empty talk
2 : a sound that is meaningless, repetitive, and suggestive of the chatter of children

prau \'prau̇, 'prä-,ü\ *noun* [Malay *pĕrahu*] (1582)
: any of various Indonesian boats usually without a deck that are propelled especially by sails or paddles

¹prawn \'prȯn, 'prän\ *noun* [Middle English *prane*] (15th century)
: any of numerous widely distributed edible decapod crustaceans (as of the genera *Pandalus* and *Peneus*) that resemble shrimps and have large compressed abdomens; *also* : SHRIMP

²prawn *intransitive verb* (1886)
: to fish for or with prawns
— **prawn·er** *noun*

prax·e·ol·o·gy \,prak-sē-'ä-lə-jē\ *noun* [alteration of earlier *praxiology,* from *praxis* + *-o-* + *-logy*] (1904)
: the study of human action and conduct
— **prax·e·o·log·i·cal** \-sē-ə-'lä-ji-kəl\ *adjective*

prax·is \'prak-səs\ *noun, plural* **prax·es** \-,sēz\ [Medieval Latin, from Greek, doing, action, from *prassein* to do, practice — more at PRACTICAL] (1581)
: ACTION, PRACTICE: as **a** : exercise or practice of an art, science, or skill **b** : customary practice or conduct

pray \'prā\ *verb* [Middle English, from Old French *preier,* from Latin *precari,* from *prec-, prex* request, prayer; akin to Old High German *frāgēn* to ask, Sanskrit *pṛcchati* he asks] (13th century)
transitive verb
1 : ENTREAT, IMPLORE — often used as a function word in introducing a question, request, or plea ⟨*pray* be careful⟩
2 : to get or bring by praying
intransitive verb
1 : to make a request in a humble manner
2 : to address God or a god with adoration, confession, supplication, or thanksgiving

¹prayer \'prar, 'prer\ *noun, often attributive* [Middle English, from Middle French *preiere,* from Medieval Latin *precaria,* from Latin, feminine of *precarius* obtained by entreaty, from *prec-, prex*] (14th century)
1 a (1) : an address (as a petition) to God or a god in word or thought ⟨said a *prayer* for the success of the voyage⟩ (2) : a set order of words used in praying **b** : an earnest request or wish
2 : the act or practice of praying to God or a god ⟨kneeling in *prayer*⟩
3 : a religious service consisting chiefly of prayers — often used in plural
4 : something prayed for
5 : a slight chance ⟨haven't got a *prayer*⟩

²pray·er \'prā-ər, 'pre(-ə)r\ *noun* [Middle English *prayere,* from *prayen* to pray + ²*-er*] (14th century)
: one that prays : SUPPLIANT

prayer beads \'prar-, 'prer-\ *noun plural* (1630)
: a string of beads by which prayers are counted; *specifically* : ROSARY

prayer book *noun* (circa 1597)
: a book containing prayers and often other forms and directions for worship

prayer·ful \'prar-fəl, 'prer-\ *adjective* (1626)
1 : DEVOUT
2 : EARNEST, SINCERE
— **prayer·ful·ly** \-fə-lē\ *adverb*
— **prayer·ful·ness** *noun*

prayer meeting *noun* (1780)
: a usually informal gathering for worship and prayer; *especially* : a Protestant worship service usually held on a week night — called also *prayer service*

prayer rug *noun* (circa 1890)
: a small Oriental rug used by Muslims to kneel on when praying

prayer shawl *noun* (1905)
: TALLITH

prayer wheel *noun* (1814)
: a cylinder of wood or metal that revolves on an axis and contains written prayers and that is used in praying by Tibetan Buddhists

praying mantis *noun* (circa 1890)
: MANTIS; *especially* : a European mantis (*Mantis religiosa*) that has been introduced into the U.S. — called also *praying mantid*

pre- *prefix* [Middle English, from Old French & Latin; Old French, from Latin *prae-,* from *prae* in front of, before — more at FOR]
1 a (1) : earlier than : prior to : before ⟨*Precambrian*⟩ ⟨*prehistoric*⟩ (2) : preparatory or prerequisite to ⟨*premedical*⟩ **b** : in advance : beforehand ⟨*precancel*⟩ ⟨*prepay*⟩
2 : in front of : anterior to ⟨*preaxial*⟩ ⟨*premolar*⟩

pre·ad·mis·sion
pre·adult
pre·ag·ri·cul·tur·al
pre·an·es·thet·ic
pre·an·nounce
pre·ap·prove
pre·ar·range
pre·ar·range·ment
pre·as·sem·bled
pre·as·sign
pre·bake
pre·bat·tle
pre·bib·li·cal
pre·book
pre·break·fast
pre·cap·i·tal·ist
pre·chill
pre·Christ·mas
pre·clear
pre·clear·ance
pre·code
pre·co·i·tal
pre·col·lege
pre·col·le·giate
pre·co·lo·nial
pre·com·bus·tion
pre·com·mit·ment
pre·com·pute
pre·com·put·er
pre·con·cert
pre·con·quest
pre·con·so·nan·tal
pre·con·struct·ed
pre·con·ven·tion
pre·con·vic·tion
pre·cool
pre·cop·u·la·to·ry
pre·crash
pre·crease
pre·cri·sis
pre·cut
pre·dawn
pre·de·fine
pre·de·liv·ery
pre·de·par·ture
pre·des·ig·nate
pre·de·val·u·a·tion
pre·de·vel·op·ment
pre·din·ner
pre·dis·charge

pre·dis·cov·ery
pre·dive
pre·drill
pre·dy·nas·tic
pre·elec·tion
pre·elec·tric
pre·em·bar·go
pre·em·ploy·ment
pre·en·roll·ment
pre·erect
pre·es·tab·lish
pre·eth·i·cal
pre·ex·per·i·ment
pre·fade
pre·fas·cist
pre·feu·dal
pre·fight
pre·file
pre·filled
pre·fi·nance
pre·fire
pre·flame
pre·flight
pre·for·mat
pre·for·mu·late
pre·fresh·man
pre·fro·zen
pre·game
pre·gen·i·tal
pre·har·vest
pre·head·ache
pre·hir·ing
pre·hol·i·day
pre·hu·man
pre·in·au·gu·ral
pre·in·cor·po·ra·tion
pre·in·duc·tion
pre·in·dus·tri·al
pre·in·ter·view
pre·in·va·sion
pre·kin·der·gar·ten
pre·launch
pre·life
pre·lit·er·ary
pre·log·i·cal
pre·lunch
pre·lun·cheon
pre·made
pre·man·u·fac·ture
pre·mar·i·tal

pre·mar·i·tal·ly
pre·mar·ket
pre·mar·ket·ing
pre·mar·riage
pre·meal
pre·mea·sure
pre·me·di·e·val
pre·meet
pre·mei·ot·ic
pre·men·o·paus·al
pre·merg·er
pre·mi·gra·tion
pre·mod·ern
pre·mod·i·fi·ca·tion
pre·mod·i·fy
pre·moist·en
pre·mold
pre·molt
pre·mor·al
pre·my·cot·ic
pre·noon
pre·no·ti·fi·ca·tion
pre·no·ti·fy
pre·num·ber
pre·open·ing
pre·op·er·a·tion·al
pre·or·der
pre·paste
pre·per·for·mance
pre·pill
pre·plan
pre·por·tion
pre·pre·pared
pre·pres·i·den·tial
pre·price
pre·pri·ma·ry
pre·pro·duc·tion
pre·pro·gram
pre·psy·che·del·ic
pre·pub·li·ca·tion
pre·punch
pre·pu·pal
pre·pur·chase
pre·qual·i·fi·ca·tion
pre·qual·i·fy
pre·race
pre·re·ces·sion
pre·re·cord·ed
pre·re·hears·al
pre·re·lease
pre·re·quire
pre·re·tire·ment
pre·re·turn
pre·re·view
pre·re·vi·sion·ist

pre·rev·o·lu·tion
pre·rev·o·lu·tion·ary
pre·rinse
pre·ri·ot
pre·rock
pre·ro·man·tic
pre·sale
pre·sched·ule
pre·screen
pre·sea·son
pre·sen·tence
pre·sen·tenc·ing
pre·ser·vice
pre·set
pre·set·tle·ment
pre·show
pre·slaugh·ter
pre·sleep
pre·slice
pre·song
pre·spec·i·fy
pre·split
pre·stamp
pre·ster·il·ize
pre·stor·age
pre·strike
pre·struc·ture
pre·sum·mit
pre·sur·gery
pre·sweet·en
pre·symp·tom·at·ic
pre·tape
pre·tax
pre·tech·no·log·i·cal
pre·tele·vi·sion
pre·ter·mi·na·tion
pre·the·a·ter
pre·tour·na·ment
pre·train
pre·trav·el
pre·treat
pre·treat·ment
pre·trial
pre·trimmed
pre·type
pre·uni·fi·ca·tion
pre·uni·ver·si·ty
pre·vi·a·ble
pre·war
pre·warn
pre·wash
pre·wean·ing
pre·work
pre·wrap

preach \'prēch\ *verb* [Middle English *prechen,* from Old French *prechier,* from Late Latin *praedicare,* from Latin, to proclaim publicly, from *prae-* pre- + *dicare* to proclaim — more at DICTION] (13th century)
intransitive verb
1 : to deliver a sermon
2 : to urge acceptance or abandonment of an idea or course of action; *specifically* : to exhort in an officious or tiresome manner
transitive verb
1 : to set forth in a sermon ⟨*preach* the gospel⟩
2 : to advocate earnestly ⟨*preached* revolution⟩
3 : to deliver (as a sermon) publicly
4 : to bring, put, or affect by preaching ⟨*preached* the . . . church out of debt —*American Guide Series: Virginia*⟩
— **preach·er** *noun*
— **preach·ing·ly** \'prē-chiŋ-lē\ *adverb*

preach·ify \'prē-chə-,fī\ *intransitive verb* **-ified; -ify·ing** (1775)
: to preach ineptly or tediously

preach·ment \'prēch-mənt\ *noun* (14th century)
1 : the act or practice of preaching
2 : SERMON, EXHORTATION; *specifically* : a tedious or unwelcome one

preachy \'prē-chē\ *adjective* **preach·i·er; -est** (1819)

: marked by obvious moral exhortation : DI-DACTIC
— **preach·i·ly** \-chə-lē\ *adverb*
— **preach·i·ness** \-chē-nəs\ *noun*
pre·ad·ap·ta·tion \ˌprē-ˌa-ˌdap-'tā-shən\ *noun* (1886)
1 : the possession by an organism or taxonomic group of characters that are not adapted to the ancestral environment but favor survival in some other environment
2 : a preadaptive character
pre·adapt·ed \ˌprē-ə-'dap-təd\ *adjective* (1915)
: characterized by preadaptation
pre·adap·tive \-'dap-tiv\ *adjective* (1915)
: of, relating to, or characterized by preadaptation
pre·ad·o·les·cence \ˌprē-ˌa-dᵊl-'e-sᵊn(t)s\ *noun* (1930)
: the period of human development just preceding adolescence; *specifically* : the period between the approximate ages of 9 and 12
— **pre·ad·o·les·cent** \-sᵊnt\ *adjective or noun*
pre·am·ble \'prē-ˌam-bəl, prē-'\ *noun* [Middle English, from Middle French *preamble,* from Medieval Latin *preambulum,* from Late Latin, neuter of *praeambulus* walking in front of, from Latin *prae-* + *ambulare* to walk] (14th century)
1 : an introductory statement; *especially* : the introductory part of a constitution or statute that usually states the reasons for and intent of the law
2 : an introductory fact or circumstance; *especially* : one indicating what is to follow
pre·amp \'prē-ˌamp\ *noun* (1949)
: PREAMPLIFIER
pre·am·pli·fi·er \ˌprē-'am-plə-ˌfī(-ə)r\ *noun* (1935)
: an amplifier designed to amplify extremely weak electrical signals before they are fed to additional amplifier circuits
pre·atom·ic \ˌprē-ə-'tä-mik\ *adjective* (1914)
: of or relating to a time before the use of the atomic bomb and atomic energy
pre·ax·i·al \ˌprē-'ak-sē-əl\ *adjective* (1872)
: situated in front of an axis of the body
preb·end \'pre-bənd\ *noun* [Middle English *prebende,* from Middle French, from Medieval Latin *praebenda,* from Late Latin, subsistence allowance granted by the state, from Latin, feminine of *praebendus,* gerundive of *praebēre* to offer, from *prae-* + *habēre* to hold — more at GIVE] (15th century)
1 : a stipend furnished by a cathedral or collegiate church to a clergyman (as a canon) in its chapter
2 : PREBENDARY
— **pre·ben·dal** \pri-'ben-dᵊl, 'pre-bən-\ *adjective*
preb·en·dary \'pre-bən-ˌder-ē\ *noun, plural* -dar·ies (15th century)
1 : a clergyman receiving a prebend for officiating and serving in the church
2 : an honorary canon in a cathedral chapter
pre·bi·o·log·i·cal \ˌprē-ˌbī-ə-'lä-ji-kəl\ *also* **pre·bi·o·log·ic** \-jik\ *adjective* (1953)
: of, relating to, or being chemical or environmental precursors of the origin of life ⟨*prebio-logical* molecules⟩
pre·bi·ot·ic \ˌprē-ˌbī-'ä-tik\ *adjective* (1958)
: PREBIOLOGICAL
pre·cal·cu·lus \ˌprē-'kal-kyə-ləs\ *adjective* (1964)
: relating to or being mathematical prerequisites for the study of calculus
— **precalculus** *noun*
Pre·cam·bri·an \ˌprē-'kam-brē-ən, -'käm-\ *adjective* (1864)
: of, relating to, or being the earliest era of geological history or the corresponding system of rocks characterized especially by the appearance of single-celled organisms and is equivalent to the Archean and Proterozoic eons — see GEOLOGIC TIME table

— **Precambrian** *noun*
¹pre·can·cel \ˌ(ˌ)prē-'kan(t)-səl\ *transitive verb* (1921)
: to cancel (a postage stamp) in advance of use
— **pre·can·cel·la·tion** \ˌprē-ˌkan(t)-sə-'lā-shən\ *noun*
²precancel *noun* (1929)
: a precanceled postage stamp
pre·can·cer·ous \ˌ(ˌ)prē-'kan(t)s-rəs, -'kan(t)-sə-\ *adjective* [International Scientific Vocabulary] (1882)
: tending to become cancerous ⟨a *precancerous* lesion⟩
pre·car·i·ous \pri-'kar-ē-əs, -'ker-\ *adjective* [Latin *precarius* obtained by entreaty, uncertain — more at PRAYER] (1646)
1 : depending on the will or pleasure of another
2 : dependent on uncertain premises : DUBIOUS ⟨*precarious* generalizations⟩
3 a : dependent on chance circumstances, unknown conditions, or uncertain developments **b** : characterized by a lack of security or stability that threatens with danger
synonym see DANGEROUS
— **pre·car·i·ous·ly** *adverb*
— **pre·car·i·ous·ness** *noun*
pre·cast \ˌprē-'kast, 'prē-\ *adjective* (1914)
: being concrete that is cast in the form of a structural element (as a panel or beam) before being placed in final position
prec·a·to·ry \'pre-kə-ˌtōr-ē, -ˌtȯr-\ *adjective* [Late Latin *precatorius,* from Latin *precari* to pray — more at PRAY] (1636)
: expressing a wish
pre·cau·tion \pri-'kȯ-shən\ *noun* [French *précaution,* from Late Latin *praecaution-, praecautio,* from Latin *praecavēre* to guard against, from *prae-* + *cavēre* to be on one's guard — more at HEAR] (1603)
1 : care taken in advance : FORESIGHT ⟨warned of the need for *precaution*⟩
2 : a measure taken beforehand to prevent harm or secure good : SAFEGUARD
— **pre·cau·tion·ary** \-shə-ˌner-ē\ *adjective*
pre·cede \pri-'sēd\ *verb* **pre·ced·ed; pre·ced·ing** [Middle English, from Middle French *preceder,* from Latin *praecedere,* from *prae-* pre- + *cedere* to go] (15th century) *transitive verb*
1 : to surpass in rank, dignity, or importance
2 : to be, go, or come ahead or in front of
3 : to be earlier than
4 : to cause to be preceded : PREFACE
intransitive verb
: to go or come before
pre·ce·dence \'pre-sə-dən(t)s, pri-'sē-dᵊn(t)s\ *noun* (1588)
1 a *obsolete* : ANTECEDENT **b** : the fact of preceding in time
2 a : the right to superior honor on a ceremonial or formal occasion **b** : the order of ceremonial or formal preference **c** : priority of importance ⟨your safety takes *precedence*⟩
pre·ce·den·cy \-dən(t)-sē, -dᵊn(t)-sē\ *noun* (1612)
: PRECEDENCE
¹pre·ce·dent \pri-'sē-dᵊnt, 'pre-sə-dənt\ *adjective* [Middle English, from Middle French, from Latin *praecedent-, praecedens,* present participle of *praecedere*] (15th century)
: prior in time, order, arrangement, or significance
²prec·e·dent \'pre-sə-dənt\ *noun* (15th century)
1 : an earlier occurrence of something similar
2 a : something done or said that may serve as an example or rule to authorize or justify a subsequent act of the same or an analogous kind ⟨a verdict that had no *precedent*⟩ **b** : the convention established by such a precedent or by long practice
3 : a person or thing that serves as a model
pre·ced·ing \pri-'sē-diŋ\ *adjective* (15th century)

: that immediately precedes in time or place ⟨the *preceding* day⟩ ⟨*preceding* paragraphs⟩ ☆
pre·cen·sor \ˌ(ˌ)prē-'sen(t)-sər\ *transitive verb* (1942)
: to censor (a publication or film) before its release to the public
pre·cen·tor \pri-'sen-tər\ *noun* [Late Latin *praecentor,* from Latin *praecinere* to sing before, from *prae-* + *canere* to sing — more at CHANT] (1613)
: a leader of the singing of a choir or congregation
— **pre·cen·to·ri·al** \ˌprē-ˌsen-'tōr-ē-əl, -'tȯr-\ *adjective*
— **pre·cen·tor·ship** \pri-'sen-tər-ˌship\ *noun*
pre·cept \'prē-ˌsept\ *noun* [Middle English, from Latin *praeceptum,* from neuter of *prae-ceptus,* past participle of *praecipere* to take beforehand, instruct, from *prae-* + *capere* to take — more at HEAVE] (14th century)
1 : a command or principle intended especially as a general rule of action
2 : an order issued by legally constituted authority to a subordinate official
synonym see LAW
pre·cep·tive \pri-'sep-tiv\ *adjective* (15th century)
: giving precepts : DIDACTIC
pre·cep·tor \pri-'sep-tər, 'prē-\ *noun* (15th century)
1 a : TEACHER, TUTOR **b** : the headmaster or principal of a school
2 : the head of a preceptory of Knights Templars
— **pre·cep·tor·ship** \-ˌship\ *noun*
¹pre·cep·to·ri·al \pri-ˌsep-'tōr-ē-əl, ˌprē-, -'tȯr-\ *adjective* (circa 1741)
: of, relating to, or making use of preceptors
²preceptorial *noun* (circa 1952)
: a college course that emphasizes independent reading, discussion in small groups, and individual conferences with the teacher
pre·cep·to·ry \pri-'sep-t(ə-)rē, 'prē-\ *noun, plural* -ries (1540)
1 : a subordinate house or community of the Knights Templars; *broadly* : COMMANDERY 1
2 : COMMANDERY 2
pre·cess \prē-'ses, 'prē-\ *verb* [back-formation from *precession*] (1892)
intransitive verb
: to progress with a movement of precession
transitive verb
: to cause to precess

☆ **SYNONYMS**
Preceding, antecedent, foregoing, previous, prior, former, anterior mean being before. PRECEDING usually implies being immediately before in time or in place ⟨the *preceding* sentence⟩. ANTECEDENT applies to order in time and may suggest a causal relation ⟨conditions *antecedent* to the revolution⟩. FOREGOING applies chiefly to statements ⟨the *foregoing* remarks⟩. PREVIOUS and PRIOR imply existing or occurring earlier, but PRIOR often adds an implication of greater importance ⟨a child from a *previous* marriage⟩ ⟨a *prior* obligation⟩. FORMER implies always a definite comparison or contrast with something that is latter ⟨the *former* name of the company⟩. ANTERIOR applies to position before or ahead of usually in space, sometimes in time or order ⟨the *anterior* lobe of the brain⟩.

\ə\ abut \ᵊ\ kitten \ər\ **further** \a\ ash \ā\ ace
\ä\ mop, mar \aᵘ\ **out** \ch\ chin \e\ bet \ē\ **easy**
\g\ go \i\ hit \ī\ ice \j\ job \ŋ\ sing \ō\ go
\ȯ\ law \ȯi\ boy \th\ **thin** \t̲h̲\ the \ü\ loot \u̇\ **foot**
\y\ yet \zh\ vision *see also* Guide to Pronunciation

pre·ces·sion \prē-'se-shən\ *noun* [New Latin *praecession-, praecessio,* from Medieval Latin, act of preceding, from Latin *praecedere* to precede] (1879)
: a comparatively slow gyration of the rotation axis of a spinning body about another line intersecting it so as to describe a cone
— **pre·ces·sion·al** \-'sesh-nəl, -'se-shə-n°l\ *adjective*

precession of the equinoxes (1621)
: a slow westward motion of the equinoxes along the ecliptic caused by the gravitational action of sun and moon upon the protuberant matter about the earth's equator

pre–Chel·le·an \(,)prē-'she-lē-ən\ *adjective* (1916)
: of or relating to a Lower Paleolithic culture preceding the Abbevillian and characterized by crudely flaked stone hand axes

pre–Chris·tian \-'kris-chən, -'krish-\ *adjective* (1828)
: of, relating to, or being a time before the beginning of the Christian era

pré·cieux \prā-syœ̅\ *or* **pré·cieuse** \-syœ̅z\ *adjective* [French *précieux,* masculine, & *précieuse,* feminine, literally, precious, from Middle French *precios*] (1727)
: PRECIOUS 3

pre·cinct \'prē-,siŋ(k)t\ *noun* [Middle English, from Medieval Latin *praecinctum,* from Latin, neuter of *praecinctus,* past participle of *praecingere* to gird about, from *prae-* pre- + *cingere* to gird — more at CINCTURE] (15th century)
1 : a part of a territory with definite bounds or functions often established for administrative purposes : DISTRICT: as **a** : a subdivision of a county, town, city, or ward for election purposes **b** : a division of a city for police control
2 a : an enclosure bounded by the walls of a building — often used in plural **b** : a sphere of thought, action, or influence — often used in plural
3 a *plural* : the region immediately surrounding a place : ENVIRONS **b** : PLACE, LOCALE
4 : BOUNDARY — often used in plural 〈a ruined tower within the *precincts* of the squire's grounds —T. L. Peacock〉

pre·ci·os·i·ty \,pre-shē-'ä-sə-tē, -sē-\ *noun, plural* **-ties** (1866)
1 : fastidious refinement
2 : an instance of preciosity

¹pre·cious \'pre-shəs\ *adjective* [Middle English, from Middle French *precios,* from Latin *pretiosus,* from *pretium* price — more at PRICE] (13th century)
1 : of great value or high price
2 : highly esteemed or cherished
3 : excessively refined : AFFECTED
4 : GREAT, THOROUGHGOING 〈*precious* scoundrel〉
— **pre·cious·ness** *noun*

²precious *adverb* (1595)
: VERY, EXTREMELY 〈has *precious* little to say〉

pre·cious·ly *adverb* (14th century)
1 : in a precious manner
2 : PRECIOUS

pre·ci·pe *variant of* PRAECIPE

prec·i·pice \'pre-s(ə-)pəs\ *noun* [Middle French, from Latin *praecipitium,* from *praecipit-, praeceps* headlong, from *prae-* + *caput* head — more at HEAD] (1613)
1 : a very steep or overhanging place
2 : a hazardous situation; *broadly* : BRINK

pre·cip·i·ta·ble \pri-'si-pə-tə-bəl\ *adjective* (1670)
: capable of being precipitated

pre·cip·i·tance \pri-'si-pə-tən(t)s\ *noun* (1667)
: PRECIPITANCY

pre·cip·i·tan·cy \-tən(t)-sē\ *noun* (1646)
: undue hastiness or suddenness

¹pre·cip·i·tant \-tənt\ *adjective* (1671)
: PRECIPITATE
— **pre·cip·i·tant·ly** *adverb*
— **pre·cip·i·tant·ness** *noun*

²precipitant *noun* (circa 1685)
: a precipitating agent; *especially* : one that causes the formation of a precipitate

¹pre·cip·i·tate \pri-'si-pə-,tāt\ *verb* **-tat·ed; -tat·ing** [Latin *praecipitatus,* past participle of *praecipitare,* from *praecipit-, praeceps*] (1528)
transitive verb
1 a : to throw violently : HURL 〈the quandaries into which the release of nuclear energy has *precipitated* mankind —A. B. Arons〉 **b** : to throw down
2 : to bring about especially abruptly 〈*precipitate* a scandal that would end with his expulsion —John Cheever〉
3 a : to cause to separate from solution or suspension **b** : to cause (vapor) to condense and fall or deposit
intransitive verb
1 a : to fall headlong **b** : to fall or come suddenly into some condition
2 : to move or act precipitately
3 a : to separate from solution or suspension **b** : to condense from a vapor and fall as rain or snow
— **pre·cip·i·ta·tive** \-,tā-tiv\ *adjective*
— **pre·cip·i·ta·tor** \-,tā-tər\ *noun*

²pre·cip·i·tate \pri-'si-pə-tət, -,tāt\ *noun* [New Latin *praecipitatum,* from Latin, neuter of *praecipitatus*] (1594)
1 : a substance separated from a solution or suspension by chemical or physical change usually as an insoluble amorphous or crystalline solid
2 : a product, result, or outcome of some process or action

³pre·cip·i·tate \pri-'si-pə-tət\ *adjective* (1615)
1 a : falling, flowing, or rushing with steep descent **b** : PRECIPITOUS, STEEP
2 : exhibiting violent or unwise speed ☆
— **pre·cip·i·tate·ly** *adverb*
— **pre·cip·i·tate·ness** *noun*

pre·cip·i·ta·tion \pri-,si-pə-'tā-shən\ *noun* (1502)
1 : the quality or state of being precipitate : HASTINESS
2 : an act, process, or instance of precipating; *especially* : the process of forming a precipitate
3 : something precipitated: as **a** : a deposit on the earth of hail, mist, rain, sleet, or snow; *also* : the quantity of water deposited **b** : PRECIPITATE 1

pre·cip·i·tin \pri-'si-pə-tən\ *noun* [International Scientific Vocabulary, from *precipitate*] (1900)
: an antibody that forms a precipitate when it unites with its antigen

pre·cip·i·tin·o·gen \pri-,si-pə-'ti-nə-jən\ *noun* (1904)
: an antigen that stimulates the production of a specific precipitin

pre·cip·i·tous \pri-'si-pə-təs\ *adjective* [French *précipiteux,* from Middle French, from Latin *precipitium* precipice] (1613)
1 : PRECIPITATE 2
2 a : very steep, perpendicular, or overhanging in rise or fall 〈a *precipitous* slope〉 **b** : having precipitous sides 〈a *precipitous* gorge〉 **c** : having a very steep ascent 〈a *precipitous* street〉
synonym see STEEP
— **pre·cip·i·tous·ly** *adverb*
— **pre·cip·i·tous·ness** *noun*

pré·cis \prā-'sē, 'prā-(,)sē\ *noun, plural* **pré·cis** \-'sēz, -(,)sēz\ [French, from *précis* precise] (1760)
: a concise summary of essential points, statements, or facts

pre·cise \pri-'sīs\ *adjective* [Middle English, from Middle French *precis,* from Latin *precisus,* past participle of *praecidere* to cut off, from *prae-* + *caedere* to cut] (15th century)
1 : exactly or sharply defined or stated
2 : minutely exact

3 : strictly conforming to a pattern, standard, or convention
4 : distinguished from every other 〈at just that *precise* moment〉
synonym see CORRECT
— **pre·cise·ness** *noun*

pre·cise·ly *adverb* (14th century)
: EXACTLY 〈*precisely* two o'clock〉 — sometimes used as an intensive 〈was popular *precisely* because he was so kind〉

pre·ci·sian \pri-'si-zhən\ *noun* (1571)
1 : a person who stresses or practices scrupulous adherence to a strict standard especially of religious observance or morality
2 : PURITAN 1

¹pre·ci·sion \pri-'si-zhən\ *noun* (1740)
1 : the quality or state of being precise : EXACTNESS
2 a : the degree of refinement with which an operation is performed or a measurement stated — compare ACCURACY 2b **b** : the accuracy (as in binary or decimal places) with which a number can be represented usually expressed in terms of the number of computer words available for representation 〈double *precision* arithmetic permits the representation of an expression by two computer words〉
3 : RELEVANCE 2
— **pre·ci·sion·ist** \-'si-zhə-nist, -'sizh-nist\ *noun*

²precision *adjective* (1875)
1 : adapted for extremely accurate measurement or operation
2 : held to low tolerance in manufacture
3 : marked by precision of execution

pre·clin·i·cal \(,)prē-'kli-ni-kəl\ *adjective* (1926)
1 : of, relating to, or concerned with the period preceding clinical manifestations
2 : of, relating to, or being the period in medical or dental education preceding the clinical study of medicine or dentistry

pre·clude \pri-'klüd\ *transitive verb* **preclud·ed; pre·clud·ing** [Latin *praecludere,* from *prae-* + *claudere* to close — more at CLOSE] (1629)
1 *archaic* : CLOSE
2 : to make impossible by necessary consequence : rule out in advance
— **pre·clu·sion** \-'klü-zhən\ *noun*
— **pre·clu·sive** \-'klü-siv, -ziv\ *adjective*
— **pre·clu·sive·ly** *adverb*

pre·co·cial \pri-'kō-shəl\ *adjective* [New Latin *praecoces* precocial birds, from Latin, plural of *praecoc-, precox*] (circa 1872)
: capable of a high degree of independent activity from birth 〈ducklings are *precocial*〉 — compare ALTRICIAL

pre·co·cious \pri-'kō-shəs\ *adjective* [Latin *praecoc-, praecox* early ripening, precocious, from *prae-* + *coquere* to cook — more at COOK] (1650)
1 : exceptionally early in development or occurrence
2 : exhibiting mature qualities at an unusually early age
— **pre·co·cious·ly** *adverb*
— **pre·co·cious·ness** *noun*

☆ SYNONYMS
Precipitate, headlong, abrupt, impetuous, sudden mean showing undue haste or unexpectedness. PRECIPITATE stresses lack of due deliberation and implies prematureness of action 〈the army's *precipitate* withdrawal〉. HEADLONG stresses rashness and lack of forethought 〈a *headlong* flight from arrest〉. ABRUPT stresses curtness and a lack of warning or ceremony 〈an *abrupt* refusal〉. IMPETUOUS stresses extreme impatience or impulsiveness 〈an *impetuous* lover proposing marriage〉. SUDDEN stresses unexpectedness and sharpness or violence of action 〈flew into a *sudden* rage〉.

— **pre·coc·i·ty** \pri-'kä-sə-tē\ *noun*

pre·cog·ni·tion \ˌprē-(ˌ)käg-'ni-shən\ *noun* [Late Latin *praecognition-, praecognitio,* from Latin *praecognoscere* to know beforehand, from *prae-* + *cognoscere* to know — more at COGNITION] (circa 1611)
: clairvoyance relating to an event or state not yet experienced
— **pre·cog·ni·tive** \(ˌ)prē-'käg-nə-tiv\ *adjective*

pre·Co·lum·bi·an \ˌprē-kə-'ləm-bē-ən\ *adjective* (1888)
: preceding or belonging to the time before the arrival of Columbus in America

pre·con·ceive \ˌprē-kən-'sēv\ *transitive verb* (1558)
: to form (as an opinion) prior to actual knowledge or experience ⟨*preconceived* notions⟩

pre·con·cep·tion \-kən-'sep-shən\ *noun* (1625)
1 : a preconceived idea
2 : PREJUDICE

pre·con·cert \ˌprē-kən-'sərt\ *transitive verb* (1748)
: to settle by prior agreement

¹**pre·con·di·tion** \-kən-'di-shən\ *noun* (1825)
: PREREQUISITE

²**precondition** *transitive verb* (1922)
: to put in a proper or desired condition or frame of mind especially in preparation

¹**pre·con·scious** \(ˌ)prē-'kän(t)-shəs\ *adjective* (1860)
: not present in consciousness but capable of being recalled without encountering any inner resistance or repression
— **pre·con·scious·ly** *adverb*

²**preconscious** *noun* (circa 1922)
: the preconscious part of the psyche especially in psychoanalysis

pre·con·tact \ˌprē-'kän-ˌtakt\ *adjective* (circa 1909)
: of or relating to the period before contact of an indigenous people with an outside culture

pre·cook \(ˌ)prē-'kůk\ *transitive verb* (1926)
: to cook partially or entirely before final cooking or reheating

pre·crit·i·cal \-'kri-ti-kəl\ *adjective* (1881)
: prior to the development of critical capacity

pre·cur·sor \pri-'kər-sər, 'prē-\ *noun* [Middle English *precursoure,* from Latin *praecursor,* from *praecurrere* to run before, from *prae-* pre- + *currere* to run — more at CURRENT] (15th century)
1 a : one that precedes and indicates the approach of another **b** : PREDECESSOR
2 : a substance, cell, or cellular component from which another substance, cell, or cellular component is formed
synonym SEE FORERUNNER
— **pre·cur·so·ry** \-'kərs-rē, -'kər-sə-\ *adjective*

pre·da·ceous *or* **pre·da·cious** \pri-'dā-shəs\ *adjective* [Latin *praedari* to prey upon (from *praeda* prey) + English *-aceous* or *-acious* (as in *rapacious*) — more at PREY] (1713)
1 : living by preying on other animals : PREDATORY
2 *usually* predacious : tending to devour or despoil : RAPACIOUS
— **pre·da·ceous·ness** *noun*
— **pre·dac·i·ty** \-'da-sə-tē\ *noun*

pre·date \(ˌ)prē-'dāt\ *transitive verb* (circa 1864)
: ANTEDATE

pre·da·tion \pri-'dā-shən\ *noun* [Middle English *predacion,* from Latin *praedation-, praedatio,* from *praedari*] (15th century)
1 : the act of preying or plundering : DEPREDATION
2 : a mode of life in which food is primarily obtained by the killing and consuming of animals

predation pressure *noun* (1942)

: the effects of predation on a natural community especially with respect to the survival of species preyed upon

pred·a·tor \'pre-də-tər, -ˌtȯr\ *noun* (1912)
1 : one that preys, destroys, or devours
2 : an animal that lives by predation

pred·a·to·ry \'pre-də-ˌtȯr-ē, -ˌtȯr-\ *adjective* (1589)
1 a : of, relating to, or practicing plunder, pillage, or rapine **b** : inclined or intended to injure or exploit others for personal gain or profit ⟨*predatory* pricing practices⟩
2 : living by predation : PREDACEOUS; *also* : adapted to predation

pre·de·cease \ˌprē-di-'sēs\ *verb* **-ceased; -ceas·ing** (1593)
transitive verb
: to die before (another person)
intransitive verb
: to die first
— **predecease** *noun*

pre·de·ces·sor \'pre-də-ˌse-sər, 'prē-; ˌpre-də-', ˌprē-\ *noun* [Middle English *predecessour,* from Middle French *predecesseur,* from Late Latin *praedecessor,* from Latin *prae-* pre- + *decessor* retiring governor, from *decedere* to depart, retire from office — more at DECEASE] (14th century)
1 : one that precedes; *especially* : a person who has previously occupied a position or office to which another has succeeded
2 *archaic* : ANCESTOR

pre·des·ti·nar·i·an \(ˌ)prē-ˌdes-tə-'ner-ē-ən, ˌprē-ˌdes-\ *noun* [*predestin*ation + *-arian*] (1667)
: one who believes in predestination
— **predestinarian** *adjective*
— **pre·des·ti·nar·i·an·ism** \-ē-ə-ˌni-zəm\ *noun*

¹**pre·des·ti·nate** \prē-'des-tə-nət, -ˌnāt\ *adjective* [Middle English, from Latin *praedestinatus,* past participle of *praedestinare*] (14th century)
: destined, fated, or determined beforehand

²**pre·des·ti·nate** \-ˌnāt\ *transitive verb* **-nat·ed; -nat·ing** [Middle English, from Latin *praedestinatus,* past participle] (15th century)
1 : to foreordain to an earthly or eternal lot or destiny by divine decree
2 *archaic* : PREDETERMINE

pre·des·ti·na·tion \(ˌ)prē-ˌdes-tə-'nā-shən, ˌprē-des-\ *noun* (14th century)
1 : the act of predestinating : the state of being predestinated
2 : the doctrine that God in consequence of his foreknowledge of all events infallibly guides those who are destined for salvation

pre·des·ti·na·tor \prē-'des-tə-ˌnā-tər\ *noun* (1579)
1 *archaic* : PREDESTINARIAN
2 : one that predestinates

pre·des·tine \(ˌ)prē-'des-tən\ *transitive verb* [Middle English, from Middle French or Latin; Middle French *predestiner,* from Latin *praedestinare,* from *prae-* + *destinare* to determine — more at DESTINE] (14th century)
: to destine, decree, determine, appoint, or settle beforehand; *especially* : PREDESTINATE 1

pre·de·ter·mi·na·tion \ˌprē-di-ˌtər-mə-'nā-shən\ *noun* (1647)
1 : the act of predetermining : the state of being predetermined: **a** : the ordaining of events beforehand **b** : a fixing or settling in advance
2 : a purpose formed beforehand

pre·de·ter·mine \-di-'tər-mən\ *transitive verb* [Late Latin *praedeterminare,* from Latin *prae-* + *determinare* to determine] (1625)
1 a : FOREORDAIN, PREDESTINE **b** : to determine beforehand
2 : to impose a direction or tendency on beforehand

pre·de·ter·min·er \-di-'tər-mə-nər\ *noun* (1959)

: a limiting noun modifier (as *both* or *all*) characterized by occurrence before the determiner in a noun phrase

pre·di·a·be·tes \ˌprē-ˌdī-ə-'bē-tēz, -təs\ *noun* (1935)
: an inapparent abnormal state that precedes the development of clinically evident diabetes
— **pre·di·a·bet·ic** \-'be-tik\ *adjective or noun*

pre·di·al \'prē-dē-əl\ *adjective* [Middle English *prediall,* from Medieval Latin *praedialis,* from Latin *praedium* landed property, from *praed-, praes* bondsman, from *prae-* + *vad-, vas* surety — more at WED] (15th century)
: of or relating to land or its products

¹**pred·i·ca·ble** \'pre-di-kə-bəl\ *noun* [Medieval Latin *praedicabile,* from neuter of *praedicabilis*] (1551)
: something that may be predicated; *especially* : one of the five most general kinds of attribution in traditional logic that include genus, species, difference, property, and accident

²**predicable** *adjective* [Medieval Latin *praedicabilis,* from Late Latin *praedicare* to predicate] (circa 1598)
: capable of being asserted

pre·dic·a·ment \pri-'di-kə-mənt, *1 is usually* 'pre-di-kə-\ *noun* [Middle English, from Late Latin *praedicamentum,* from *praedicare*] (14th century)
1 : the character, status, or classification assigned by a predication; *specifically* : CATEGORY 1
2 : CONDITION, STATE; *especially* : a difficult, perplexing, or trying situation

¹**pred·i·cate** \'pre-di-kət\ *noun* [Middle English, from Late Latin *praedicatum,* from neuter of *praedicatus*] (15th century)
1 a : something that is affirmed or denied of the subject in a proposition in logic **b** : a term designating a property or relation
2 : the part of a sentence or clause that expresses what is said of the subject and that usually consists of a verb with or without objects, complements, or adverbial modifiers
— **pred·i·ca·tive** \-kə-tiv, -ˌkā-\ *adjective*
— **pred·i·ca·tive·ly** *adverb*

²**pred·i·cate** \'pre-də-ˌkāt\ *transitive verb* **-cat·ed; -cat·ing** [Late Latin *praedicatus,* past participle of *praedicare* to assert, predicate logically, preach, from Latin, to proclaim publicly, assert — more at PREACH] (1552)
1 a : AFFIRM, DECLARE **b** *archaic* : PREACH
2 a : to assert to be a quality, attribute, or property — used with following *of* ⟨*predicates* intelligence of humans⟩ **b** : to make (a term) the predicate in a proposition
3 : FOUND, BASE — usually used with *on* ⟨the theory is *predicated* on recent findings⟩
4 : IMPLY

³**pred·i·cate** \'pre-di-kət\ *adjective* (1887)
: completing the meaning of a copula ⟨*predicate* adjective⟩ ⟨*predicate* noun⟩

predicate calculus *noun* (1950)
: the branch of symbolic logic that uses symbols for quantifiers and for arguments and predicates of propositions as well as for unanalyzed propositions and logical connectives — called also *functional calculus;* compare PROPOSITIONAL CALCULUS

predicate nominative *noun* (1887)
: a noun or pronoun in the nominative or common case completing the meaning of a copula

pred·i·ca·tion \ˌpre-də-'kā-shən\ *noun* [Middle English *predicacion,* from Middle French *predication,* from Latin *praedication-, praedicatio,* from *praedicare*] (14th century)
1 *archaic* **a** : an act of proclaiming or preaching **b** : SERMON

\ə\ abut \ᵊ\ kitten \ər\ further \a\ ash \ā\ ace \ä\ mop, mar \au̇\ out \ch\ chin \e\ bet \ē\ easy \g\ go \i\ hit \ī\ ice \j\ job \ŋ\ sing \ō\ go \ȯ\ law \ȯi\ boy \th\ thin \t͟h\ the \ü\ loot \u̇\ foot \y\ yet \zh\ vision *see also* Guide to Pronunciation

2 : an act or instance of predicating: as **a :** the expression of action, state, or quality by a grammatical predicate **b :** the logical affirmation of something about another; *especially* **:** assignment of something to a class

pred·i·ca·to·ry \'pre-di-kə-ˌtȯr-ē, -ˌtȯr-\ *adjective* [Late Latin *praedicatorius*, from *praedicare* to preach] (1611) **:** of or relating to preaching

pre·dict \pri-'dikt\ *verb* [Latin *praedictus*, past participle of *praedicere*, from *prae-* pre- + *dicere* to say — more at DICTION] (circa 1632)
transitive verb
: to declare or indicate in advance; *especially* **:** foretell on the basis of observation, experience, or scientific reason
intransitive verb
: to make a prediction
synonym see FORETELL
— **pre·dict·abil·i·ty** \-ˌdik-tə-'bi-lə-tē\ *noun*
— **pre·dict·able** \-'dik-tə-bəl\ *adjective*
— **pre·dic·tive** \-'dik-tiv\ *adjective*
— **pre·dic·tive·ly** \-lē\ *adverb*
— **pre·dic·tor** \-'dik-tər\ *noun*

pre·dict·ably \-'dik-tə-blē\ *adverb* (1914) **1 :** in a manner that can be predicted ⟨works quickly and *predictably*⟩ **2 :** as one could predict **:** as one would expect ⟨*predictably*, the politicians howled⟩

pre·dic·tion \pri-'dik-shən\ *noun* (1561) **1 :** an act of predicting **2 :** something that is predicted **:** FORECAST

pre·di·gest \ˌprē-dī-'jest, -də-\ *transitive verb* (1663) **1 :** to subject to predigestion **2 :** to simplify for easy use ⟨*predigested* classics for children⟩

pre·di·ges·tion \-'jes-chən, -'jesh-\ *noun* (circa 1612) **:** artificial or natural partial digestion of food ⟨enzymatic *predigestion*⟩ ⟨microbial *predigestion*⟩

pre·di·lec·tion \ˌpre-dᵊl-'ek-shən, ˌprē-\ *noun* [French *prédilection*, from Medieval Latin *praediligere* to love more, prefer, from Latin *prae-* + *diligere* to love — more at DILIGENT] (1742) **:** an established preference for something ☆

pre·dis·pose \ˌprē-di-'spōz\ (1646) *transitive verb* **1 :** to dispose in advance ⟨a good teacher *predisposes* children to learn⟩ **2 :** to make susceptible ⟨malnutrition *predisposes* one to disease⟩
intransitive verb
: to bring about susceptibility
synonym see INCLINE
— **pre·dis·po·si·tion** \ˌprē-ˌdis-pə-'zi-shən\ *noun*

pred·nis·o·lone \pred-'ni-sə-ˌlōn\ *noun* [blend of *prednisone* and ¹-*ol*] (1955) **:** a glucocorticoid $C_{21}H_{28}O_5$ that is a dehydrogenated analogue of hydrocortisone and is used especially as an anti-inflammatory drug

pred·ni·sone \'pred-nə-ˌsōn also -ˌzōn\ *noun* [probably from *pregnane* ($C_{21}H_{36}$) + *diene* (compound containing two double bonds) + *cortisone*] (1955) **:** a glucocorticoid $C_{21}H_{26}O_5$ that is a dehydrogenated analogue of cortisone and is used as an anti-inflammatory agent especially in the treatment of arthritis, as an antineoplastic agent, and as an immunosuppressant

pre·doc·tor·al \(ˌ)prē-'däk-t(ə-)rəl\ *adjective* (1937) **:** of, relating to, or engaged in academic study leading to the doctoral degree

pre·dom·i·nance \pri-'dä-mə-nən(t)s, -'dämn-ən(t)s\ *noun* (1602) **:** the quality or state of being predominant

pre·dom·i·nan·cy \-nən(t)-sē\ *noun* (1598) **:** PREDOMINANCE

pre·dom·i·nant \-nənt\ *adjective* [Middle French, from Medieval Latin *praedominant-,*

praedominans, present participle of *praedominari* to predominate, from Latin *prae-* + *dominari* to rule, govern — more at DOMINATE] (1576) **1 :** having superior strength, influence, or authority **:** PREVAILING **2 :** being most frequent or common
synonym see DOMINANT
usage see PREDOMINATE

pre·dom·i·nant·ly \-nənt-lē\ *adverb* (1681) **:** for the most part **:** MAINLY
usage see PREDOMINATE

¹pre·dom·i·nate \-nət\ *adjective* [alteration of *predominant*] (1591) **:** PREDOMINANT □
— **pre·dom·i·nate·ly** *adverb*

²pre·dom·i·nate \pri-'dä-mə-ˌnāt\ *verb* [Medieval Latin *praedominatus*, past participle of *praedominari*] (1594)
intransitive verb
1 : to hold advantage in numbers or quantity **2 :** to exert controlling power or influence **:** PREVAIL
transitive verb
: to exert control over **:** DOMINATE
— **pre·dom·i·na·tion** \-ˌdä-mə-'nā-shən\ *noun*

pree \'prē\ *transitive verb* **preed; pree·ing** [alteration of *preve* to prove, test, from Middle English *preven*, from Old French *preuv-*, stem of *prover* to prove] (1680)
Scottish **:** to taste tentatively **:** SAMPLE

pre·eclamp·sia \ˌprē-i-'klam(p)-sē-ə\ *noun* [New Latin] (1923) **:** a toxic condition developing in late pregnancy that is characterized by a sudden rise in blood pressure, excessive weight gain, generalized edema, albuminuria, severe headache, and visual disturbances
— **pre·eclamp·tic** \-'klam(p)-tik\ *adjective*

pre·emer·gence \ˌprē-ə-'mər-jən(t)s\ *adjective* (1935) **:** used or occurring before emergence of seedlings above the ground ⟨*preemergence* herbicides⟩

pre·emer·gent \-jənt\ *adjective* (1959) **:** PREEMERGENCE

pree·mie \'prē-mē\ *noun* [*prem*ature + -*ie*] (1927) **:** a premature baby

pre·em·i·nence \prē-'e-mə-nən(t)s\ *noun* (13th century) **:** the quality or state of being preeminent **:** SUPERIORITY

pre·em·i·nent \-nənt\ *adjective* [Middle English, from Late Latin *praeeminent-, praeeminens*, from Latin, present participle of *praeeminēre* to be outstanding, from *prae-* + *eminēre* to stand out — more at EMINENT] (15th century) **:** having paramount rank, dignity, or importance **:** OUTSTANDING
— **pre·em·i·nent·ly** *adverb*

pre·empt \prē-'em(p)t\ *verb* [back-formation from *preemption*] (1850)
transitive verb
1 : to acquire (as land) by preemption **2 :** to seize upon to the exclusion of others **:** take for oneself ⟨the movement was then *preempted* by a lunatic fringe⟩ **3 :** to replace with something considered to be of greater value or priority **:** take precedence over ⟨the program did not appear, having been *preempted* by a baseball game —Robert MacNeil⟩ **4 :** to gain a commanding or preeminent place in **5 :** to prevent from happening or taking place **:** FORESTALL, PRECLUDE
intransitive verb
: to make a preemptive bid in bridge
— **pre·emp·tor** \-'em(p)-tər\ *noun*

pre·emp·tion \-'em(p)-shən\ *noun* [Medieval Latin *praeemption-, praeemptio* previous purchase, from *praeemere* to buy before, from

Latin *prae-* pre- + *emere* to buy — more at REDEEM] (1602) **1 a :** the right of purchasing before others; *especially* **:** one given by the government to the actual settler upon a tract of public land **b :** the purchase of something under this right **2 :** a prior seizure or appropriation **:** a taking possession before others

pre·emp·tive \-'em(p)-tiv\ *adjective* (1855) **1 a :** of or relating to preemption **b :** having power to preempt **2** *of a bid in bridge* **:** higher than necessary and intended to shut out bids by the opponents **3 :** giving a stockholder first option to purchase new stock in an amount proportionate to his existing holdings **4 :** marked by the seizing of the initiative **:** initiated by oneself ⟨a *preemptive* attack⟩
— **pre·emp·tive·ly** *adverb*

¹preen \'prēn\ *noun* [Middle English *prene*, from Old English *prēon*; akin to Middle High German *pfrieme* awl] (before 12th century) **1** *dialect chiefly British* **:** PIN **2** *dialect chiefly British* **:** BROOCH

²preen *transitive verb* (1572) *chiefly Scottish* **:** PIN

³preen *verb* [Middle English *preinen*] (14th century)
transitive verb
1 : to dress or smooth (oneself) up **:** PRIMP **2** *of a bird* **:** to trim or dress with a bill **3 :** to pride or congratulate (oneself) for achievement
intransitive verb
1 : to make oneself sleek **2 :** GLOAT, SWELL
— **preen·er** *noun*

pre·en·gi·neered \ˌprē-ˌen-jə-'nird\ *adjective* (1951) **:** constructed of or employing prefabricated modules ⟨a *pre-engineered* building⟩

pre·ex·il·ic \ˌprē-eg-'zi-lik\ *adjective* (1880) **:** previous to the exile of the Jews to Babylon in about 600 B.C.

pre·ex·ist \ˌprē-ig-'zist\ (1599)
intransitive verb

☆ **SYNONYMS**

Predilection, prepossession, prejudice, bias mean an attitude of mind that predisposes one to favor something. PREDILECTION implies a strong liking deriving from one's temperament or experience ⟨a *predilection* for horror movies⟩. PREPOSSESSION suggests a fixed conception likely to preclude objective judgment of anything counter to it ⟨a *prepossession* against technology⟩. PREJUDICE usually implies an unfavorable prepossession and connotes a feeling rooted in suspicion, fear, or intolerance ⟨a mindless *prejudice* against the unfamiliar⟩. BIAS implies an unreasoned and unfair distortion of judgment in favor of or against a person or thing ⟨the common *bias* against overweight people⟩.

□ **USAGE**

predominate *Predominant* and *predominate* are synonymous adjectives. *Predominant* is the older and more common form. During this century a number of handbooks and commentators have held *predominate* to be a mistake—a few insisting that the word is only a verb. But they are wrong. As an adjective *predominate* is somewhat more likely to turn up in technical writing than in general writing. The adverbs *predominantly* and *predominately* are a more even match in frequency than their base adjectives are. *Predominately* seems to be more widely used than *predominate* and hence to be more often found in general writing.

: to exist earlier or before
transitive verb
: ANTEDATE

pre·ex·is·tence \-ig-'zis-tən(t)s\ *noun* (circa 1652)
: existence in a former state or previous to something else; *specifically* : existence of the soul before its union with the body
— **pre·ex·is·tent** \-tənt\ *adjective*

pre·fab \(,)prē-'fab, 'prē-,\ *noun* (1937)
: a prefabricated structure
— **prefab** *adjective*

pre·fab·ri·cate \(,)prē-'fa-bri-,kāt\ *transitive verb* (1932)
1 : to fabricate the parts of at a factory so that construction consists mainly of assembling and uniting standardized parts
2 : to produce artificially
— **pre·fab·ri·ca·tion** \,prē-,fa-bri-'kā-shən\ *noun*

¹pref·ace \'pre-fəs\ *noun* [Middle English, from Middle French, from Medieval Latin *prephatia*, alteration of Latin *praefation-*, *praefatio* foreword, from *praefari* to say beforehand, from *prae-* pre- + *fari* to say — more at BAN] (14th century)
1 *often capitalized* : a variable doxology beginning with the Sursum Corda and ending with the Sanctus in traditional eucharistic liturgies
2 : the introductory remarks of a speaker or author
3 : APPROACH, PRELIMINARY

²preface *verb* **pref·aced; pref·ac·ing** (1619)
intransitive verb
: to make introductory remarks
transitive verb
1 : to say or write as preface ⟨a note *prefaced* to the manuscript⟩
2 : PRECEDE, HERALD
3 : to introduce by or begin with a preface
4 : to stand in front of ⟨a porch *prefaces* the entrance⟩
5 : to be a preliminary to
— **pref·ac·er** *noun*

pref·a·to·ry \'pre-fə-,tōr-ē, -,tòr-\ *adjective* [Latin *praefari*] (1675)
1 : of, relating to, or constituting a preface
2 : located in front

pre·fect \'prē-,fekt\ *noun* [Middle English, from Middle French, from Latin *praefectus*, from past participle of *praeficere* to place at the head of, from *prae-* + *facere* to make — more at DO] (14th century)
1 : any of various high officials or magistrates of differing functions and ranks in ancient Rome
2 : a chief officer or chief magistrate
3 : a student monitor in a private school

prefect apostolic *noun* (circa 1888)
: a Roman Catholic clergyman and usually a priest with quasi-episcopal jurisdiction over a district of a missionary territory

pre·fec·ture \'prē-,fek-chər\ *noun* (15th century)
1 : the office or term of office of a prefect
2 : the official residence of a prefect
3 : the district governed by a prefect
— **pre·fec·tur·al** \'prē-,fek-chə-rəl, pri-'\ *adjective*

prefecture apostolic *noun* (1911)
: the district under a prefect apostolic

pre·fer \pri-'fər\ *transitive verb* **pre·ferred; pre·fer·ring** [Middle English *preferren*, from Middle French *preferer*, from Latin *praeferre* to put before, prefer, from *prae-* + *ferre* to carry — more at BEAR] (14th century)
1 : to promote or advance to a rank or position
2 : to like better or best ⟨*prefers* sports to reading⟩ ⟨*prefers* to watch TV⟩
3 : to give (a creditor) priority
4 *archaic* : to put or set forward or before someone : RECOMMEND
5 : to bring or lay against someone ⟨won't *prefer* charges⟩

6 : to bring forward or lay before one for consideration
— **pre·fer·rer** *noun*

pref·er·a·ble \'pre-f(ə-)rə-bəl, 'pre-fər-bəl *also* pri-'fər-ə-bəl\ *adjective* (1666)
: having greater value or desirability : being preferred
— **pref·er·a·bil·i·ty** \,pre-f(ə-)rə-'bi-lə-tē\ *noun*
— **pref·er·a·bly** \-blē\ *adverb*

pref·er·ence \'pre-fərn(t)s, 'pre-f(ə-)rən(t)s\ *noun* [Middle English *preferraunce*, from Middle French *preferance*, from Medieval Latin *praeferentia*, from Latin *praeferent-*, *praeferens*, present participle of *praeferre*] (15th century)
1 a : the act of preferring : the state of being preferred **b** : the power or opportunity of choosing
2 : one that is preferred
3 : the act, fact, or principle of giving advantages to some over others
4 : priority in the right to demand and receive satisfaction of an obligation
5 : ORIENTATION 2 ⟨sexual *preference*⟩
synonym see CHOICE

pref·er·en·tial \,pre-fə-'ren(t)-shəl\ *adjective* (1849)
1 : showing preference
2 : employing or creating a preference in trade relations
3 : designed to permit expression of preference among candidates ⟨a *preferential* primary⟩
4 : giving preference especially in hiring to union members ⟨a *preferential* shop⟩
— **pref·er·en·tial·ly** \-'ren(t)-sh(ə-)lē\ *adverb*

pre·fer·ment \pri-'fər-mənt\ *noun* (15th century)
1 a : advancement or promotion in dignity, office, or station **b** : a position or office of honor or profit
2 : priority or seniority in right especially to receive payment or to purchase property on equal terms with others
3 : the act of bringing forward (as charges)

preferred stock *noun* (circa 1859)
: stock guaranteed priority by a corporation's charter over common stock in the payment of dividends and usually in the distribution of assets

pre·fig·u·ra·tion \(,)prē-,fi-gyə-'rā-shən, -gə-\ *noun* (14th century)
1 : the act of prefiguring : the state of being prefigured
2 : something that prefigures

pre·fig·u·ra·tive \,prē-'fi-gyə-rə-tiv, -gə-\ *adjective* (1504)
: of, relating to, or showing by prefiguration
— **pre·fig·u·ra·tive·ly** *adverb*
— **pre·fig·u·ra·tive·ness** *noun*

pre·fig·ure \,prē-'fi-gyər, *especially British* -'fi-gər\ *transitive verb* [Middle English, from Late Latin *praefigurare*, from Latin *prae-* pre- + *figurare* to shape, picture, from *figura* figure] (15th century)
1 : to show, suggest, or announce by an antecedent type, image, or likeness
2 : to picture or imagine beforehand : FORESEE
— **pre·fig·ure·ment** \-mənt\ *noun*

¹pre·fix *transitive verb* [Middle English, from Middle French *prefixer*, from *pre-* + *fixer* to fix, from *fix* fixed, from Latin *fixus* — more at FIX] (15th century)
1 \(,)prē-'fiks\ : to fix or appoint beforehand
2 \'prē-,, prē-'\ [partly from ²*prefix*] : to place in front; *especially* : to add as a prefix ⟨*prefix* a syllable to a word⟩

²pre·fix \'prē-,fiks\ *noun* [New Latin *praefixum*, from Latin, neuter of *praefixus*, past participle of *praefigere* to fasten before, from *prae-* + *figere* to fasten — more at FIX] (1646)
1 : an affix attached to the beginning of a word, base, or phrase and serving to produce a

derivative word or an inflectional form — compare SUFFIX
2 : a title used before a person's name
— **pre·fix·al** \'prē-,fik-səl, prē-'\ *adjective*

³pre·fix *same as* ²\ *adjective* (1971)
: characterized by placement of an operator before its operand or before its two operands if it is a binary operator — compare INFIX, POSTFIX

pre·fo·cus \(,)prē-'fō-kəs\ *transitive verb* (1948)
: to focus beforehand (as automotive headlights before installation)

pre·form \'prē-,fòrm, (,)prē-'\ *transitive verb* [Latin *praeformare*, from *prae-* + *formare* to form, from *forma* form] (1601)
1 : to form or shape beforehand
2 : to bring to approximate preliminary shape and size
— **pre·form** \'prē-,fòrm\ *noun*

pre·for·ma·tion \,prē-fòr-'mā-shən\ *noun* (1732)
1 : previous formation
2 : the now discredited theory that every germ cell contains the organism of its kind fully formed and that development involves merely an increase in size — compare EPIGENESIS 1, HOMUNCULUS 2
— **pre·for·ma·tion·ist** \-sh(ə-)nist\ *noun or adjective*

¹pre·fron·tal \(,)prē-'frən-t°l\ *adjective* (1854)
: anterior to or involving the anterior part of a frontal structure ⟨a *prefrontal* bone⟩

²prefrontal *noun* (1854)
: a prefrontal part (as a bone)

pre·gan·gli·on·ic \,prē-,gaŋ-glē-'ä-nik\ *adjective* (1895)
: proximal to a ganglion; *specifically* : of, relating to, or being a usually medullated axon arising from a cell body in the central nervous system and terminating in an autonomic ganglion — compare POSTGANGLIONIC

preg·na·ble \'preg-nə-bəl\ *adjective* [alteration of Middle English *prenable*, from Middle French — more at IMPREGNABLE] (14th century)
: vulnerable to capture ⟨a *pregnable* fort⟩
— **preg·na·bil·i·ty** \,preg-nə-'bi-lə-tē\ *noun*

preg·nan·cy \'preg-nən(t)-sē\ *noun, plural* **-cies** (15th century)
1 : the quality of being pregnant (as in meaning)
2 : the condition of being pregnant : GESTATION
3 : an instance of being pregnant

¹preg·nant \'preg-nənt\ *adjective* [Middle English *pregnant*, from Middle French, from present participle of *preindre* to press, from Latin *premere* — more at PRESS] (14th century)
archaic : COGENT

²pregnant *adjective* [Middle English, from Latin *praegnant-*, *praegnans*, alteration of *praegnas*, from *prae-* pre- + *-gnas* (akin to *gignere* to give birth to) — more at KIN] (15th century)
1 : abounding in fancy, wit, or resourcefulness : INVENTIVE ⟨all this has been said . . . by great and *pregnant* artists —*Times Literary Supplement*⟩
2 : rich in significance or implication : MEANINGFUL, PROFOUND ⟨the *pregnant* phrases of the Bible —Edmund Wilson⟩ ⟨a *pregnant* pause⟩
3 : containing unborn young within the body : GRAVID
4 : having possibilities of development or consequence : involving important issues : MOMENTOUS ⟨draw inspiration from the heroic achievements of that *pregnant* age —Kemp Malone⟩

\ə\ abut \ᵊ\ kitten \ər\ further \a\ ash \ā\ ace \ä\ mop, mar \au̇\ out \ch\ chin \e\ bet \ē\ easy \g\ go \i\ hit \ī\ ice \j\ job \ŋ\ sing \ō\ go \ȯ\ law \ȯi\ boy \th\ thin \t̲h̲\ the \ü\ loot \u̇\ foot \y\ yet \zh\ vision *see also* Guide to Pronunciation

5 *obsolete* **:** INCLINED, DISPOSED ⟨your own most *pregnant* and vouchsafed ear —Shakespeare⟩
6 : FULL, TEEMING
— **preg·nant·ly** *adverb*
preg·nen·o·lone \preg-'ne-n°l-,ōn\ *noun* [International Scientific Vocabulary *pregnene* ($C_{21}H_{34}$) + ¹-*ol* + -*one*] (1936)
: an unsaturated hydroxy steroid ketone C_{21}-$H_{32}O_2$ that is formed by the oxidation of steroids (as cholesterol) and yields progesterone on dehydrogenation
pre·heat \(,)prē-'hēt\ *transitive verb* (1898)
: to heat beforehand; *especially* **:** to heat (an oven) to a designated temperature before using for cooking
— **pre·heat·er** *noun*
pre·hen·sile \prē-'hen(t)-səl, -'hen-,sīl\ *adjective* [French *préhensile*, from Latin *prehensus*, past participle of *prehendere* to seize — more at GET] (circa 1785)
1 : adapted for seizing or grasping especially by wrapping around ⟨*prehensile* tail⟩
2 : gifted with mental grasp or moral or aesthetic perception
— **pre·hen·sil·i·ty** \(,)prē-,hen-'si-lə-tē\ *noun*
pre·hen·sion \prē-'hen(t)-shən\ *noun* (circa 1828)
1 : the act of taking hold, seizing, or grasping
2 a : mental understanding **:** COMPREHENSION **b :** apprehension by the senses
pre–His·pan·ic \,prē-(h)i-'spa-nik\ *adjective* (1919)
: of, relating to, or being the time prior to Spanish conquests in the western hemisphere
pre·his·to·ri·an \,prē-(h)is-'tōr-ē-ən, -'tòr-\ *noun* (1893)
: an archaeologist who specializes in prehistory
pre·his·tor·ic \,prē-(h)is-'tór-ik, -'tär-\ *also*
pre·his·tor·i·cal \-i-kəl\ *adjective* (1851)
1 : of, relating to, or existing in times antedating written history
2 : of or relating to a language in a period of its development from which contemporary records of its sounds and forms have not been preserved
— **pre·his·tor·i·cal·ly** \-i-k(ə-)lē\ *adverb*
pre·his·to·ry \,prē-'his-t(ə-)rē\ *noun* (1871)
1 : the study of prehistoric humankind
2 : a history of the antecedents of an event, situation, or thing
3 : the prehistoric period of human evolution
pre·hom·i·nid \-'hä-mə-nəd\ *noun* [ultimately from Latin *pre-* + *homin-, homo* human being — more at HOMAGE] (1939)
: any of various extinct primates resembling or ancestral to humans
— **prehominid** *adjective*
pre·ig·ni·tion \,prē-ig-'ni-shən\ *noun* (1898)
: ignition in an internal combustion engine while the inlet valve is open or before compression is completed
pre·im·plan·ta·tion \,prē-,im-,plan-'tā-shən\ *adjective* (1945)
: of, involving, or being an embryo before uterine implantation
pre·judge \(,)prē-'jəj\ *transitive verb* [Middle French *prejuger*, from Latin *praejudicare*, from *prae-* + *judicare* to judge — more at JUDGE] (1579)
: to judge before hearing or before full and sufficient examination
— **pre·judg·er** *noun*
— **pre·judg·ment** \-'jəj-mənt\ *noun*
¹**prej·u·dice** \'pre-jə-dəs\ *noun* [Middle English, from Old French, from Latin *praejudicium* previous judgment, damage, from *prae-* + *judicium* judgment — more at JUDICIAL] (13th century)
1 : injury or damage resulting from some judgment or action of another in disregard of one's rights; *especially* **:** detriment to one's legal rights or claims

2 a (1) **:** preconceived judgment or opinion (2) **:** an adverse opinion or leaning formed without just grounds or before sufficient knowledge **b :** an instance of such judgment or opinion **c :** an irrational attitude of hostility directed against an individual, a group, a race, or their supposed characteristics
synonym see PREDILECTION
²**prejudice** *transitive verb* **-diced; -dic·ing** (15th century)
1 : to injure or damage by some judgment or action (as in a case of law)
2 : to cause to have prejudice
prej·u·diced \-dəst\ *adjective* (1579)
: resulting from or having a prejudice or bias for or especially against
prej·u·di·cial \,pre-jə-'di-shəl\ *adjective* (15th century)
1 : tending to injure or impair **:** DETRIMENTAL
2 : leading to premature judgment or unwarranted opinion
— **prej·u·di·cial·ly** \-'di-sh(ə-)lē\ *adverb*
— **prej·u·di·cial·ness** \-shəl-nəs\ *noun*
prel·a·cy \'pre-lə-sē\ *noun, plural* **-cies** (14th century)
1 : the office or dignity of a prelate
2 : episcopal church government
pre·lap·sar·i·an \,prē-,lap-'ser-ē-ən\ *adjective* [*pre-* + Latin *lapsus* slip, fall — more at LAPSE] (1879)
: characteristic of or belonging to the time or state before the fall of mankind
prel·ate \'pre-lət *also* 'prē-,lāt\ *noun* [Middle English *prelat*, from Old French, from Medieval Latin *praelatus*, literally, one receiving preferment, from Latin (past participle of *praeferre* to prefer), from *prae-* + *latus*, past participle of *ferre* to carry — more at TOLERATE, BEAR] (13th century)
: an ecclesiastic (as a bishop or abbot) of superior rank
prel·a·ture \'pre-lə-,chùr, -chər, -,tyùr, -,tùr\ *noun* (1607)
1 : PRELACY 1
2 : a body of prelates
pre·lect \pri-'lekt\ *intransitive verb* [Latin *praelectus*, past participle of *praelegere*, from *prae-* + *legere* to read — more at LEGEND] (1785)
: to discourse publicly **:** LECTURE
— **pre·lec·tion** \-'lek-shən\ *noun*
pre·li·ba·tion \,prē-lī-'bā-shən\ *noun* [Latin *praelibation-, praelibatio*, from *praelibare* to taste beforehand, from *prae-* + *libare* to pour as an offering, taste — more at LIBATION] (1526)
: FORETASTE
pre·lim \'prē-,lim, pri-'\ *noun or adjective* (1891)
: PRELIMINARY
¹**pre·lim·i·nary** \pri-'li-mə-,ner-ē\ *noun, plural* **-nar·ies** [French *préliminaires*, plural, from Medieval Latin *praeliminaris*, adjective, preliminary, from Latin *prae-* pre- + *limin-, limen* threshold] (1656)
: something that precedes or is introductory or preparatory: as **a :** a preliminary scholastic examination **b** *plural, British* **:** FRONT MATTER **c :** a preliminary heat or trial (as of a race) **d :** a minor match preceding the main event (as of a boxing card)
²**preliminary** *adjective* (circa 1667)
: coming before and usually forming a necessary prelude to something else
— **pre·lim·i·nar·i·ly** \-,li-mə-'ner-ə-lē\ *adverb*
pre·lit·er·ate \,prē-'li-t(ə-)rət\ *adjective* (1925)
1 a : not yet employing writing as a cultural medium **b :** lacking the use of writing
2 : antedating the use of writing
— **preliterate** *noun*
¹**pre·lude** \'prel-,yüd, 'prāl-; 'pre-,lüd, 'prā-; *sense 1 also* 'prē-,lüd\ *noun* [Middle French, from Medieval Latin *praeludium*, from Latin

praeludere to play beforehand, from *prae-* + *ludere* to play — more at LUDICROUS] (1561)
1 : an introductory performance, action, or event preceding and preparing for the principal or a more important matter
2 a : a musical section or movement introducing the theme or chief subject (as of a fugue or suite) or serving as an introduction to an opera or oratorio **b :** an opening voluntary **c :** a separate concert piece usually for piano or orchestra and based entirely on a short motif
²**prelude** *verb* **pre·lud·ed; pre·lud·ing** (1655)
transitive verb
1 : to serve as a prelude to
2 : to play as a prelude
intransitive verb
: to give or serve as a prelude; *especially* **:** to play a musical introduction
— **pre·lud·er** *noun*
pre·lu·sion \pri-'lü-zhən\ *noun* [Latin *praelusion-, praelusio*, from *praeludere*] (1597)
: PRELUDE, INTRODUCTION
pre·lu·sive \-'lü-siv, -ziv\ *adjective* (1605)
: constituting or having the form of a prelude **:** INTRODUCTORY
— **pre·lu·sive·ly** *adverb*
pre·ma·lig·nant \,prē-mə-'lig-nənt\ *adjective* (circa 1897)
: PRECANCEROUS
pre·man \(,)prē-'man, 'prē-,man\ *noun* (1921)
: any of several extinct primates ancestral to humans and especially recent humans
pre·ma·ture \,prē-mə-'tyùr, -'tùr, -'chùr *also* ,pre-\ *adjective* [Latin *praematurus* too early, from *prae-* + *maturus* ripe, mature] (circa 1529)
: happening, arriving, existing, or performed before the proper, usual, or intended time; *especially* **:** born after a gestation period of less than 37 weeks ⟨*premature* babies⟩
— **premature** *noun*
— **pre·ma·ture·ly** *adverb*
— **pre·ma·ture·ness** *noun*
— **pre·ma·tu·ri·ty** \-'tyùr-ə-tē, -'tùr-, -'chùr-\ *noun*
pre·max·il·la \,prē-mak-'si-lə\ *noun* [New Latin] (1866)
: either of a pair of bones of the upper jaw of vertebrates between and in front of the maxillae
— **pre·max·il·lary** \(,)prē-'mak-sə-,ler-ē, *chiefly British* ,prē-mak-'si-lə-rē\ *adjective or noun*
¹**pre·med** \(,)prē-'med, 'prē-,med\ *noun* (circa 1928)
: a premedical student or course of study
²**premed** *adjective* (1950)
: PREMEDICAL
pre·med·i·cal \(,)prē-'me-di-kəl\ *adjective* (1904)
: preceding and preparing for the professional study of medicine
pre·med·i·tate \(,)prē-'me-də-,tāt\ *verb* [Latin *praemeditatus*, past participle of *praemeditari*, from *prae-* + *meditari* to meditate] (circa 1548)
transitive verb
: to think about and revolve in the mind beforehand
intransitive verb
: to think, consider, or deliberate beforehand
— **pre·med·i·ta·tor** \-,tā-tər\ *noun*
pre·med·i·tat·ed *adjective* (1590)
: characterized by fully conscious willful intent and a measure of forethought and planning ⟨*premeditated* murder⟩
— **pre·med·i·tat·ed·ly** *adverb*
pre·med·i·ta·tion \(,)prē-,me-də-'tā-shən\ *noun* (15th century)
: an act or instance of premeditating; *specifically* **:** consideration or planning of an act beforehand that shows intent to commit that act
pre·med·i·ta·tive \(,)prē-'me-də-,tā-tiv\ *adjective* (1858)
: given to or characterized by premeditation

pre·men·stru·al \\(ˌ)prē-ˈmen(t)-strə-wəl, -strəl\\ *adjective* (1885)
: of, relating to, occurring in, or being the period just preceding menstruation ⟨*premenstrual* tension⟩ ⟨*premenstrual* women⟩
— **pre·men·stru·al·ly** *adverb*

premenstrual syndrome *noun* (1982)
: a varying group of symptoms manifested by some women prior to menstruation that may include emotional instability, irritability, insomnia, fatigue, anxiety, depression, headache, edema, and abdominal pain — abbreviation *PMS*

pre·mie *variant of* PREEMIE

¹pre·mier \\pri-ˈmir, -ˈmyir, -ˈmē-ər; ˈprē-, ˈpre-\\ *adjective* [Middle English *primier*, from Middle French *premier* first, chief, from Latin *primarius* of the first rank — more at PRIMARY] (15th century)
1 : first in position, rank, or importance
2 : first in time : EARLIEST

²premier *noun* [French, from *premier*, adjective] (1711)
: PRIME MINISTER
— **pre·mier·ship** \\-ˌship\\ *noun*

pre·mier dan·seur \\prə-myā-dä^n-ˈsœr\\ *noun* [French] (1828)
: the principal male dancer in a ballet company

¹pre·miere \\pri-ˈmyer, -ˈmir, -ˈmē-ər; ˌpri-mē-ˈer\\ *adjective* [alteration of ¹*premier*] (1768)
: PREMIER

²premiere *also* **pre·mière** *same as* ¹PREMIERE\\ *noun* [French *première*, from feminine of *premier* first] (1889)
1 : a first performance or exhibition ⟨the *premiere* of a play⟩
2 : the chief actress of a theatrical cast

³premiere *also* **pre·mière** *or* **pre·mier** *same as* ¹PREMIERE\\ *verb* **premiered** *also* **pre·mièred; pre·mier·ing** *also* **pre·mièr·ing** (1933)
transitive verb
: to give a first public performance of
intransitive verb
1 : to have a first public performance
2 : to appear for the first time as a star performer

pre·mière dan·seuse \\prə-myer-dä^n-ˈsœz\\ *noun* [French] (1828)
: PRIMA BALLERINA

pre·mil·le·nar·i·an·ism \\ˌprē-ˌmi-lə-ˈner-ē-ə-ˌni-zəm\\ *noun* (1844)
: PREMILLENNIALISM
— **pre·mil·le·nar·i·an** \\-ē-ən\\ *adjective or noun*

pre·mil·len·ni·al \\ˌprē-mə-ˈle-nē-əl\\ *adjective* (1846)
1 : coming before a millennium
2 : holding or relating to premillennialism
— **pre·mil·len·ni·al·ly** \\-nē-ə-lē\\ *adverb*

pre·mil·len·ni·al·ism \\-nē-ə-ˌli-zəm\\ *noun* (circa 1883)
: the view that Christ's return will usher in a future millennium of Messianic rule mentioned in Revelation
— **pre·mil·len·ni·al·ist** \\-nē-ə-list\\ *noun*

¹prem·ise *also* **pre·miss** \\ˈpre-məs\\ *noun* [in sense 1, from Middle English *premisse*, from Middle French, from Medieval Latin *praemissa*, from Latin, feminine of *praemissus*, past participle of *praemittere* to place ahead, from *prae-* pre- + *mittere* to send; in other senses, from Middle English *premisses*, from Medieval Latin *praemissa*, from Latin, neuter plural of *praemissus*] (14th century)
1 a : a proposition antecedently supposed or proved as a basis of argument or inference; *specifically* : either of the first two propositions of a syllogism from which the conclusion is drawn **b** : something assumed or taken for granted : PRESUPPOSITION
2 *plural* : matters previously stated; *specifically* : the preliminary and explanatory part of a deed or of a bill in equity

3 *plural* [from its being identified in the premises of the deed] **a** : a tract of land with the buildings thereon **b** : a building or part of a building usually with its appurtenances (as grounds)

²pre·mise \\ˈpre-məs *also* pri-ˈmīz\\ *transitive verb* **pre·mised; pre·mis·ing** (1526)
1 a : to set forth beforehand as an introduction or a postulate **b** : to offer as a premise in an argument
2 : POSTULATE
3 : to base on certain assumptions

¹pre·mi·um \\ˈprē-mē-əm\\ *noun* [Latin *praemium* booty, profit, reward, from *prae-* + *emere* to take, buy — more at REDEEM] (1601)
1 a : a reward or recompense for a particular act **b** : a sum over and above a regular price paid chiefly as an inducement or incentive **c** : a sum in advance of or in addition to the nominal value of something ⟨bonds callable at a *premium* of six percent⟩ **d** : something given free or at a reduced price with the purchase of a product or service
2 : the consideration paid for a contract of insurance
3 : a high value or a value in excess of that normally or usually expected ⟨put a *premium* on accuracy⟩

²premium *adjective* (1844)
: of exceptional quality or amount; *also* : higher-priced

¹pre·mix \\(ˌ)prē-ˈmiks, ˈprē-\\ *transitive verb* (1927)
: to mix before use

²pre·mix \\ˈprē-ˌmiks\\ *noun* (1937)
: a mixture of ingredients designed to be mixed with other ingredients before use

pre·mo·lar \\(ˌ)prē-ˈmō-lər\\ *adjective* (circa 1859)
: situated in front of or preceding the molar teeth; *especially* : being or relating to those teeth of a mammal in front of the true molars and behind the canines when the latter are present
— **premolar** *noun*

pre·mon·ish \\-ˈmä-nish\\ (1526)
transitive verb
archaic : FOREWARN
intransitive verb
archaic : to give warning in advance

pre·mo·ni·tion \\ˌprē-mə-ˈni-shən, ˌpre-\\ *noun* [Middle English, from Middle French, from Late Latin *praemonition-, praemonitio*, from Latin *praemonēre* to warn in advance, from *prae-* + *monēre* to warn — more at MIND] (15th century)
1 : previous notice or warning : FOREWARNING
2 : anticipation of an event without conscious reason : PRESENTIMENT

pre·mon·i·to·ry \\pri-ˈmä-nə-ˌtōr-ē, -ˌtȯr-\\ *adjective* (1647)
: giving warning ⟨a *premonitory* symptom⟩
— **pre·mon·i·to·ri·ly** \\-ˌmä-nə-ˈtōr-ə-lē, -ˈtȯr-\\ *adverb*

Pre·mon·stra·ten·sian \\ˌprē-ˌmän(t)-strə-ˈten(t)-shən\\ *noun* [Medieval Latin *praemonstratensis*, from *praemonstratensis* of Prémontré, from *Praemonstratus* Prémontré] (1695)
: a member of an order of canons regular founded by Saint Norbert at Prémontré near Laon, France, in 1120

pre·mune \\(ˌ)prē-ˈmyün\\ *adjective* [back-formation from *premunition*] (1948)
: exhibiting premunition

pre·mu·ni·tion \\ˌprē-myu̇-ˈni-shən\\ *noun* [Latin *praemunition-, praemunitio* advance fortification, from *praemunire* to fortify in advance, from *prae-* + *munire* to fortify — more at MUNITION] (1607)
1 *archaic* : an advance provision of protection
2 a : resistance to a disease due to the existence of its causative agent in a state of physiological equilibrium in the host **b** : immunity to a particular infection due to previous presence of the causative agent

pre·name \\ˈprē-ˌnām\\ *noun* (1894)
: FORENAME

pre·na·tal \\(ˌ)prē-ˈnā-t°l\\ *adjective* (1826)
1 : occurring, existing, or performed before birth ⟨*prenatal* care⟩ ⟨the *prenatal* period⟩
2 : providing or receiving prenatal medical care ⟨a *prenatal* clinic⟩ ⟨*prenatal* patients⟩
— **pre·na·tal·ly** \\-t°l-ē\\ *adverb*

¹pre·nom·i·nate \\(ˌ)prē-ˈnä-mə-nət\\ *adjective* [Late Latin *praenominatus*, past participle of *praenominare* to name before, from Latin *prae-* + *nominare* to name — more at NOMINATE] (1513)
obsolete : previously mentioned

²pre·nom·i·nate \\-ˌnāt\\ *transitive verb* (1547)
obsolete : to mention previously
— **pre·nom·i·na·tion** \\(ˌ)prē-ˌnä-mə-ˈnā-shən\\ *noun, obsolete*

pre·no·tion \\(ˌ)prē-ˈnō-shən, ˈprē-\\ *noun* [Latin *praenotion-, praenotio* preconception, from *prae-* + *notio* idea, conception — more at NOTION] (1588)
1 : PRESENTIMENT, PREMONITION
2 : PRECONCEPTION

¹pren·tice \\ˈpren-təs\\ *noun* [Middle English *prentis*, short for *apprentis*] (14th century)
: APPRENTICE 1, LEARNER
— **prentice** *adjective*

²prentice *transitive verb* **pren·ticed; pren·tic·ing** (1598)
: APPRENTICE

pre·nup·tial \\(ˌ)prē-ˈnəp-shəl, -chəl, ÷-chə-wəl\\ *adjective* (1869)
: made or occurring before marriage ⟨a *prenuptial* agreement⟩

pre·oc·cu·pan·cy \\(ˌ)prē-ˈä-kyə-pən(t)-sē\\ *noun* (circa 1755)
1 : an act or the right of taking possession before another
2 : the condition of being completely busied or preoccupied

pre·oc·cu·pa·tion \\(ˌ)prē-ˌä-kyə-ˈpā-shən\\ *noun* (1603)
1 : an act of preoccupying : the state of being preoccupied
2 a : extreme or excessive concern with something **b** : something that preoccupies one

pre·oc·cu·pied \\(ˌ)prē-ˈä-kyə-ˌpīd\\ *adjective* (1842)
1 : previously applied to another group and unavailable for use in a new sense — used of a biological generic or specific name
2 a : lost in thought; *also* : absorbed in some preoccupation **b** : already occupied

pre·oc·cu·py \\-ˌpī\\ *transitive verb* [Latin *praeoccupare*, literally, to seize in advance, from *prae-* + *occupare* to seize, occupy] (1567)
1 : to engage or engross the interest or attention of beforehand or preferentially
2 : to take possession of or fill beforehand or before another

pre·op·er·a·tive \\(ˌ)prē-ˈä-p(ə-)rə-tiv, -pə-ˌrā-\\ *adjective* (1904)
: occurring before a surgical operation
— **pre·op·er·a·tive·ly** *adverb*

pre·or·dain \\ˌprē-ȯr-ˈdān\\ *transitive verb* (1533)
: to decree or ordain in advance : FOREORDAIN
— **pre·or·dain·ment** \\-mənt\\ *noun*
— **pre·or·di·na·tion** \\(ˌ)prē-ˌȯr-d°n-ˈā-shən\\ *noun*

pre·ovu·la·to·ry \\(ˌ)prē-ˈäv-yə-lə-ˌtōr-ē, -ˌtȯr-, -ˈōv-\\ *adjective* (1935)
: occurring or existing in or typical of the period immediately preceding ovulation ⟨*preovulatory* oocytes⟩ ⟨a *preovulatory* surge of luteinizing hormone⟩

pre-owned \\(ˌ)prē-ˈōnd, ˈprē-\\ *adjective* (1964)

: SECONDHAND

¹prep \'prep\ *noun* (1862)
1 : PREPARATION
2 : PREPARATORY SCHOOL
3 : a preliminary trial for a racehorse

²prep *verb* **prepped; prep·ping** (1915)
intransitive verb
1 : to attend preparatory school
2 [short for *prepare*] : to get ready
transitive verb
: PREPARE; *especially* : to prepare for operation or examination

pre·pack·age \(,)prē-'pa-kij\ *transitive verb* (1945)
: to package (as food or a manufactured article) before offering for sale to the consumer

prep·a·ra·tion \,pre-pə-'rā-shən\ *noun* [Middle English *preparacion*, from Middle French *preparation*, from Latin *praeparation-, praeparatio*, from *praeparare* to prepare] (14th century)
1 : the action or process of making something ready for use or service or of getting ready for some occasion, test, or duty
2 : a state of being prepared : READINESS
3 : a preparatory act or measure
4 : something that is prepared; *specifically* : a medicinal substance made ready for use ⟨a *preparation* for colds⟩

¹pre·par·a·tive \pri-'par-ə-tiv\ *noun* (14th century)
: something that prepares the way for or serves as a preliminary to something else : PREPARATION

²preparative *adjective* (circa 1530)
: PREPARATORY
— **pre·par·a·tive·ly** *adverb*

pre·par·a·tor \pri-'par-ə-tər\ *noun* (1762)
: one that prepares; *specifically* : a person who prepares scientific specimens or museum displays

pre·par·a·to·ry \pri-'par-ə-,tōr-ē, -,tòr- *also* 'pre-p(ə-)rə-\ *adjective* (15th century)
: preparing or serving to prepare for something : INTRODUCTORY
— **pre·par·a·to·ri·ly** \pri-,par-ə-'tōr-ə-lē, -'tòr- *also* ,pre-p(ə-)rə-\ *adverb*

preparatory school *noun* (1822)
1 : a usually private school preparing students primarily for college
2 *British* : a private elementary school preparing students primarily for British public schools

preparatory to *preposition* (1649)
: in preparation for

pre·pare \pri-'par, -'per\ *verb* **pre·pared; pre·par·ing** [Middle English, from Middle French *preparer*, from Latin *praeparare*, from *prae-* pre- + *parare* to procure, prepare — more at PARE] (15th century)
transitive verb
1 a : to make ready beforehand for some purpose, use, or activity ⟨*prepare* food for dinner⟩ **b** : to put in a proper state of mind ⟨is *prepared* to listen⟩
2 : to work out the details of : plan in advance ⟨*preparing* strategy for the coming campaign⟩
3 a : to put together : COMPOUND ⟨*prepare* a prescription⟩ **b** : to put into written form ⟨*prepare* a report⟩
intransitive verb
: to get ready ⟨*preparing* for a career⟩
— **pre·par·er** *noun*

prepared *adjective* (1663)
: subjected to a special process or treatment
— **pre·pared·ly** \-'pärd-lē, -'perd-; -'par-əd-, -'per-\ *adverb*

pre·pared·ness \pri-'par-əd-nəs, -'per- *also* -'pärd-nəs *or* -'perd-nəs\ *noun* (1590)
: the quality or state of being prepared; *especially* : a state of adequate preparation in case of war

pre·pay \(,)prē-'pā\ *transitive verb* **-paid** \-'pād\; **-pay·ing** (1839)
: to pay or pay the charge on in advance
— **pre·pay·ment** \-'pā-mənt\ *noun*

pre·pense \pri-'pen(t)s\ *adjective* [by shortening & alteration from earlier *purpensed*, from Middle English, past participle of *purpensen* to deliberate, premeditate, from Middle French *purpenser*, from Old French, from *pur-* for + *penser* to think — more at PURCHASE, PENSIVE] (1702)
: planned beforehand : PREMEDITATED — usually used postpositively ⟨malice *prepense*⟩
— **pre·pense·ly** *adverb*

pre·plant \,prē-'plant, 'prē-\ *also* **pre·plant·ing** \-'plan-tin\ *adjective* (1961)
: occurring or used before planting a crop ⟨*preplant* soil fertilization⟩

pre·pon·der·ance \pri-'pän-d(ə-)rən(t)s\ *noun* (1681)
1 : a superiority in weight, power, importance, or strength
2 a : a superiority or excess in number or quantity **b** : MAJORITY

pre·pon·der·an·cy \-d(ə-)rən(t)-sē\ *noun* (1646)
: PREPONDERANCE

pre·pon·der·ant \pri-'pän-d(ə-)rənt\ *adjective* (15th century)
1 : having superior weight, force, or influence
2 : having greater prevalence
— **pre·pon·der·ant·ly** *adverb*

¹pre·pon·der·ate \pri-'pän-də-,rāt\ *verb* **-at·ed; -at·ing** [Latin *praeponderatus*, past participle of *praeponderare*, from *prae-* + *ponder-, pondus* weight — more at PENDANT] (1623)
intransitive verb
1 : to exceed in weight
2 : to exceed in influence, power, or importance
3 : to exceed in numbers
transitive verb
1 *archaic* : OUTWEIGH
2 *archaic* : to weigh down
— **pre·pon·der·a·tion** \-,pän-də-'rā-shən, ,prē-\ *noun*

²pre·pon·der·ate \-'pän-də-rət\ *adjective* (1802)
: PREPONDERANT
— **pre·pon·der·ate·ly** *adverb*

prep·o·si·tion \,pre-pə-'zi-shən\ *noun* [Middle English *preposicioun*, from Latin *preposition-, praepositio*, from *praeponere* to put in front, from *prae-* pre- + *ponere* to put — more at POSITION] (14th century)
: a function word that typically combines with a noun phrase to form a phrase which usually expresses a modification or predication □
— **prep·o·si·tion·al** \-'zish-nəl, -'zi-shə-n³l\ *adjective*
— **prep·o·si·tion·al·ly** *adverb*

pre·pos·i·tive \pri-'pä-zə-tiv, -'päz-tiv\ *adjective* [Late Latin *praepositivus*, from Latin *praepositus*, past participle of *praeponere*] (1583)
: put before : PREFIXED
— **pre·pos·i·tive·ly** *adverb*

pre·pos·sess \,prē-pə-'zes *also* -'ses\ *transitive verb* (1614)
1 *obsolete* : to take previous possession of
2 : to cause to be preoccupied
3 : to influence beforehand especially favorably

pre·pos·sess·ing *adjective* (1642)
1 *archaic* : creating prejudice
2 : tending to create a favorable impression : ATTRACTIVE

pre·pos·ses·sion \,prē-pə-'ze-shən *also* -'se-\ *noun* (1648)
1 *archaic* : prior possession
2 : an attitude, belief, or impression formed beforehand : PREJUDICE
3 : an exclusive concern with one idea or object : PREOCCUPATION
synonym see PREDILECTION

pre·pos·ter·ous \pri-'päs-t(ə-)rəs\ *adjective* [Latin *praeposterus*, literally, in the wrong or-

der, from *prae-* + *posterus* hinder, following — more at POSTERIOR] (1542)
: contrary to nature, reason, or common sense : ABSURD
— **pre·pos·ter·ous·ly** *adverb*
— **pre·pos·ter·ous·ness** *noun*

pre·po·ten·cy \(,)prē-'pō-t³n(t)-sē\ *noun* (1646)
1 : the quality or state of being prepotent : PREDOMINANCE
2 : unusual ability of an individual or strain to transmit its characters to offspring because of homozygosity for numerous dominant genes

pre·po·tent \-t³nt\ *adjective* [Middle English, from Latin *praepotent-, praepotens*, from *prae-* + *potens* powerful — more at POTENT] (15th century)
1 a : having exceptional power, authority, or influence **b** : exceeding others in power
2 : exhibiting genetic prepotency
— **pre·po·tent·ly** *adverb*

¹prep·py *or* **prep·pie** \'pre-pē\ *noun, plural* **prep·pies** [¹*preparatory*] (1967)
1 : a student at or a graduate of a preparatory school
2 : a person deemed to dress or behave like a preppy

²preppy *or* **preppie** *adjective* (1967)
1 : relating to, characteristic of, or being a preppy
2 : relating to or being a style of dress characterized especially by classic clothing and neat appearance
— **prep·pi·ly** \'pre-pə-lē\ *adverb*
— **prep·pi·ness** \'pre-pē-nəs\ *noun*

pre·pran·di·al \(,)prē-'pran-dē-əl\ *adjective* (1822)
: of, relating to, or suitable for the time just before dinner ⟨a *preprandial* drink⟩

pre·preg \,prē-'preg, 'prē-\ *noun* [*pre-* + im*preg*nated] (1954)
: a reinforcing or molding material (as paper or glass cloth) already impregnated with a synthetic resin

¹pre·print \'prē-,print, ,prē-'print\ *noun* (1889)
1 : an issue of a technical paper often in preliminary form before its publication in a journal
2 : something (as an advertisement) printed before the rest of the publication in which it is to appear

☐ USAGE

preposition Is it all right to end a sentence with a preposition? The answer is yes, even though many people cherish the notion that it is not. The notion of the inappropriateness of the deferred preposition goes back to the middle of the 17th century and is probably based on Latin grammar. But modern commentators know that the construction is standard. It is even required by these constructions: a restrictive clause introduced by *that* ⟨the magazine that I most wanted to have a story published *in* —Truman Capote⟩, a restrictive clause from which *that* has been omitted ⟨as soon as I finish the short story I'm working *on* —F. Scott Fitzgerald⟩, a clause introduced by *what* ⟨we can only speculate what they might have been *about* —Elizabeth Drew⟩, an infinitive clause ⟨both bought new suits to be married *in* —Russell Baker⟩, a participial clause ⟨relatively new and therefore worth keeping track *of* —Kenneth G. Wilson⟩, and a passive construction ⟨people deficient in learning were looked down *on* —Cynthia Ozick⟩. Questions, too, require the deferred preposition ⟨has the car been paid *for?*⟩ ⟨what does she look *like?*⟩. The preposition at the end is so natural that consciously avoiding it can cause mistakes ⟨a young man *with* whom most Americans could identify *with* —Herbert Warren Wind⟩.

²**pre·print** \(,)prē-'print\ *transitive verb* (1926)
: to print in advance for later use
pre·pro·cess \(,)prē-'prä-,ses, -'prō-, -səs\ *transitive verb* (1942)
: to do preliminary processing of (as data)
— **pre·pro·ces·sor** \-,se-sər; -sə-sər, -,sόr\ *noun*
pre·pro·fes·sion·al \,prē-prə-'fesh-nəl, -'fe-shə-n°l\ *adjective* (1926)
: of or relating to the period preceding specific study for or practice of a profession
prep school *noun* (1895)
: PREPARATORY SCHOOL
pre·pu·ber·al \(,)prē-'pyü-b(ə-)rəl\ *adjective* (circa 1935)
: PREPUBERTAL
pre·pu·ber·tal \-bər-t°l\ *adjective* (1859)
: of or relating to prepuberty
pre·pu·ber·ty \-bər-tē\ *noun* (1922)
: the period immediately preceding puberty
pre·pu·bes·cence \,prē-pyü-'be-s°n(t)s\ *noun* (1916)
: PREPUBERTY
pre·pu·bes·cent \-s°nt\ *adjective* (1904)
: PREPUBERTAL
— **prepubescent** *noun*
pre·puce \'prē-,pyüs\ *noun* [Middle English, from Middle French, from Latin *praeputium*] (15th century)
: FORESKIN; *also* : a similar fold investing the clitoris
— **pre·pu·tial** \prē-'pyü-shəl\ *adjective*
pre·quel \'prē-kwəl\ *noun* [*pre-* + *-quel* (as in *sequel*)] (1972)
: a literary or dramatic work whose story precedes that of an earlier work
Pre–Ra·pha·el·ite \(,)prē-'ra-fē-ə-,līt, -'rā-, -'rä-\ *noun* (1850)
1 a : a member of a brotherhood of artists formed in England in 1848 to restore the artistic principles and practices regarded as characteristic of Italian art before Raphael **b** : an artist or writer influenced by this brotherhood
2 : a modern artist dedicated to restoring early Renaissance ideals or methods
— **Pre–Raphaelite** *adjective*
— **Pre–Ra·pha·el·it·ism** \-,lī-,ti-zəm\ *noun*
pre·reg·is·tra·tion \,prē-,re-jə-'strā-shən\ *noun* (1967)
: a special registration (as for returning students) prior to an official registration period
— **pre·reg·is·ter** \(,)prē-'re-jə-stər\ *intransitive verb*
pre·req·ui·site \(,)prē-'re-kwə-zət\ *noun* (1633)
: something that is necessary to an end or to the carrying out of a function
— **prerequisite** *adjective*
pre·rog·a·tive \pri-'rä-gə-tiv\ *noun* [Middle English, from Middle French & Latin; Middle French, from Latin *praerogativa*, Roman century voting first in the comitia, privilege, from feminine of *praerogativus* voting first, from *praerogatus*, past participle of *praerogare* to ask for an opinion before another, from *prae-* + *rogare* to ask — more at RIGHT] (15th century)
1 a : an exclusive or special right, power, or privilege: as (1) : one belonging to an office or an official body (2) : one belonging to a person, group, or class of individuals (3) : one possessed by a nation as an attribute of sovereignty **b** : the discretionary power inhering in the British Crown
2 : a distinctive excellence
— **pre·rog·a·tived** \-tivd\ *adjective*
¹**pres·age** \'pre-sij, *also* pri-'sāj\ *noun* [Middle English, from Latin *praesagium*, from *praesagus* having a foreboding, from *prae-* + *sagus* prophetic — more at SEEK] (14th century)
1 : something that foreshadows or portends a future event : OMEN
2 : an intuition or feeling of what is going to happen in the future

3 *archaic* : PROGNOSTICATION
4 : warning or indication of the future
— **pre·sage·ful** \pri-'sāj-fəl\ *adjective*
²**pre·sage** \'pre-sij, pri-'sāj\ *verb* **pre·saged; pre·sag·ing** (1562)
transitive verb
1 : to give an omen or warning of : FORESHADOW
2 : FORETELL, PREDICT
intransitive verb
: to make or utter a prediction
— **pre·sag·er** *noun, obsolete*
pre·sanc·ti·fied \(,)prē-'san(k)-ti-,fīd\ *adjective* (1758)
: consecrated at a previous service — used of eucharistic elements
pres·by·ope \'prez-bē-,ōp; 'pres-bē-, -pē-\ *noun* [probably from French, from Greek *presbys* old man + *ōps* eye — more at EYE] (circa 1857)
: one affected with presbyopia
pres·by·o·pia \,prez-bē-'ō-pē-ə, ,pres-\ *noun* [New Latin] (1793)
: a visual condition which becomes apparent especially in middle age and in which loss of elasticity of the lens of the eye causes defective accommodation and inability to focus sharply for near vision
— **pres·by·o·pic** \-'ō-pik, -'ä-\ *adjective or noun*
pres·by·ter \'prez-bə-tər, 'pres-\ *noun* [Late Latin, elder, priest, from Greek *presbyteros*, comparative of *presbys* old man, elder; akin to Greek *pro* before and Greek *bainein* to go — more at FOR, COME] (1597)
1 : a member of the governing body of an early Christian church
2 : a member of the order of priests in churches having episcopal hierarchies that include bishops, priests, and deacons
3 : ELDER 4b
— **pres·byt·er·ate** \prez-'bi-tə-rət, pres-, -,rāt\ *noun*
¹**pres·by·te·ri·al** \,prez-bə-'tir-ē-əl, ,pres-\ *adjective* (circa 1600)
: of or relating to presbyters or a presbytery
— **pres·by·te·ri·al·ly** \-ē-ə-lē\ *adverb*
²**presbyterial** *noun, often capitalized* (1928)
: an organization of Presbyterian women associated with a presbytery
¹**Pres·by·te·ri·an** \-ē-ən\ *noun* (1640)
: a member of a Presbyterian church
²**Presbyterian** *adjective* (1641)
1 *often not capitalized* : characterized by a graded system of representative ecclesiastical bodies (as presbyteries) exercising legislative and judicial powers
2 : of, relating to, or constituting a Protestant Christian church that is presbyterian in government and traditionally Calvinistic in doctrine
— **Pres·by·te·ri·an·ism** \-ē-ə-,ni-zəm\ *noun*
pres·by·tery \'prez-bə-,ter-ē, 'pres-, -bə-trē\ *noun, plural* **-ter·ies** [Middle English & Late Latin; Middle English *presbytory* part of church reserved for clergy, from Late Latin *presbyterium* group of presbyters, part of church reserved for clergy, from Greek *presbyterion* group of presbyters, from *presbyteros* elder, priest] (15th century)
1 : the part of a church reserved for the officiating clergy
2 : a ruling body in presbyterian churches consisting of the ministers and representative elders from congregations within a district
3 : the jurisdiction of a presbytery
4 : the house of a Roman Catholic parish priest
¹**pre·school** \'prē-,skül, (,)prē-'\ *adjective* (1914)
: of, relating to, or constituting the period in a child's life from infancy to the age of five or six that ordinarily precedes attendance at elementary school
²**pre·school** \'prē-,skül\ *noun* (circa 1925)

: NURSERY SCHOOL, KINDERGARTEN
pre·school·er \-,skü-lər\ *noun* (1946)
1 : a child not yet old enough for school
2 : a child attending a preschool
pre·science \'pre-sh(ē-)ən(t)s, 'prē-, -s(ē-)ən(t)s\ *noun* [Middle English, from Late Latin *praescientia*, from Latin *praescient-, praesciens*, present participle of *praescire* to know beforehand, from *prae-* + *scire* to know — more at SCIENCE] (14th century)
: foreknowledge of events: **a** : divine omniscience **b** : human anticipation of the course of events : FORESIGHT
— **pre·scient** \-sh(ē-)ənt, -s(ē-)ənt\ *adjective*
— **pre·scient·ly** *adverb*
pre·sci·en·tif·ic \,prē-,sī-ən-'ti-fik\ *adjective* (1858)
: of, relating to, or having the characteristics of a period before the rise of modern science or a state prior to the application of the scientific method
pre·scind \pri-'sind\ *verb* [Latin *praescindere* to cut off in front, from *prae-* + *scindere* to cut — more at SHED] (1650)
intransitive verb
: to withdraw one's attention
transitive verb
: to detach for purposes of thought
pre·score \(,)prē-'skōr, -'skόr\ *transitive verb* (1937)
: to record (as sound) in advance for use when the corresponding scenes are photographed in making movies
pre·scribe \pri-'skrīb\ *verb* **pre·scribed; pre·scrib·ing** [Middle English, from Latin *praescribere* to write at the beginning, dictate, order, from *prae-* + *scribere* to write — more at SCRIBE] (15th century)
intransitive verb
1 : to lay down a rule : DICTATE
2 [Middle English, from Medieval Latin *praescribere*, from Latin, to write at the beginning] : to claim a title to something by right of prescription
3 : to write or give medical prescriptions
4 : to become by prescription invalid or unenforceable
transitive verb
1 a : to lay down as a guide, direction, or rule of action : ORDAIN **b** : to specify with authority
2 : to designate or order the use of as a remedy
— **pre·scrib·er** *noun*
pre·script \'prē-,skript, pri-'\ *adjective* [Middle English, from Latin *praescriptus*, past participle] (circa 1540)
: prescribed as a rule
— **pre·script** \'prē-,skript\ *noun*
pre·scrip·tion \pri-'skrip-shən\ *noun* [partly from Middle English *prescripcion* establishment of a claim, from Middle French *prescription*, from Late Latin *praescription-, praescriptio*, from Latin, act of writing at the beginning, order, limitation of subject matter, from *praescribere*; partly from Latin *praescription-, praescriptio* order] (14th century)
1 a : the establishment of a claim of title to something under common law usually by use and enjoyment for a period fixed by statute **b** : the right or title acquired under common law by such possession
2 : the process of making claim to something by long use and enjoyment
3 : the action of laying down authoritative rules or directions
4 a : a written direction for a therapeutic or corrective agent; *specifically* : one for the

preparation and use of a medicine **b** : a prescribed medicine **c** : something like a doctor's prescription ⟨*prescriptions* for economic recovery⟩
5 a : ancient or long continued custom **b** : a claim founded upon ancient custom or long continued use
6 : something prescribed as a rule
prescription drug *noun* (1951)
: a drug that can be obtained only by means of a physician's prescription
pre·scrip·tive \pri-'skrip-tiv\ *adjective* (1748)
1 : serving to prescribe ⟨*prescriptive* rules of usage⟩
2 : acquired by, founded on, or determined by prescription or by long-standing custom
— **pre·scrip·tive·ly** *adverb*
pre·se·lect \ˌprē-sə-'lekt\ *transitive verb* (circa 1859)
: to choose in advance usually on the basis of a particular criterion
— **pre·se·lec·tion** \-'lek-shən\ *noun*
pre·sell \(ˌ)prē-'sel\ *transitive verb* **-sold** \-'sōld\; **-sell·ing** (1947)
1 : to precondition (as a customer) for subsequent purchase or create advance demand for (as a product) especially through marketing strategies
2 : to sell in advance ⟨raised money to publish the book by *preselling* film rights⟩
pres·ence \'pre-z³n(t)s\ *noun* (14th century)
1 : the fact or condition of being present
2 a : the part of space within one's immediate vicinity **b** : the neighborhood of one of superior or especially royal rank
3 *archaic* : COMPANY 2a
4 : one that is present: as **a** : the actual person or thing that is present **b** : something present of a visible or concrete nature
5 a : the bearing, carriage, or air of a person; *especially* : stately or distinguished bearing **b** : a quality of poise and effectiveness that enables a performer to achieve a close relationship with his audience
6 : something (as a spirit) felt or believed to be present
presence of mind (1665)
: self-control so maintained in an emergency or in an embarrassing situation that one can say or do the right thing
¹**pres·ent** \'pre-z³nt\ *noun* [Middle English, from Old French, from *presenter*] (13th century)
: something presented : GIFT
²**pre·sent** \pri-'zent\ *verb* [Middle English, from Old French *presenter*, from Latin *praesentare*, from *praesent-, praesens*, adjective] (14th century)
transitive verb
1 a (1) : to bring or introduce into the presence of someone especially of superior rank or status (2) : to introduce socially **b** : to bring (as a play) before the public
2 : to make a gift to
3 : to give or bestow formally
4 a : to lay (as a charge) before a court as an object of inquiry **b** : to bring a formal public charge, indictment, or presentment against
5 : to nominate to a benefice
6 a : to offer to view : SHOW **b** : to bring to one's attention ⟨this *presents* a problem⟩
7 : to act the part of : PERFORM
8 : to aim, point, or direct (as a weapon) so as to face something or in a particular direction
intransitive verb
1 : to present a weapon
2 : to become manifest
3 : to come forward as a patient
4 : to make a presentation
synonym see GIVE
— **pre·sent·er** *noun*
³**pres·ent** \'pre-z³nt\ *adjective* [Middle English, from Old French, from Latin *praesent-, praesens*, from present participle of *praeesse* to be before one, from *prae-* pre- + *esse* to be — more at IS] (14th century)

1 : now existing or in progress
2 a : being in view or at hand **b** : existing in something mentioned or under consideration
3 : constituting the one actually involved, at hand, or being considered
4 : of, relating to, or constituting a verb tense that is expressive of present time or the time of speaking
5 *obsolete* : ATTENTIVE
6 *archaic* : INSTANT, IMMEDIATE
— **pres·ent·ness** *noun*
⁴**pres·ent** \'pre-z³nt\ *noun* (14th century)
1 a *obsolete* : present occasion or affair **b** *plural* : the present words or statements; *specifically* : the legal instrument or other writing in which these words are used
2 a : the present tense of a language **b** : a verb form in the present tense
3 : the present time
— **at present** : at or during this time : NOW
pre·sent·able \pri-'zen-tə-bəl\ *adjective* (circa 1626)
1 : capable of being presented
2 : being in condition to be seen or inspected especially by the critical
— **pre·sent·abil·i·ty** \-ˌzen-tə-'bi-lə-tē\ *noun*
— **pre·sent·able·ness** \-'zen-tə-bəl-nəs\ *noun*
— **pre·sent·ably** \-blē\ *adverb*
pre·sent arms \pri-'zent-\ *noun* [from the command *present arms!*] (circa 1884)
1 : a position in the manual of arms in which the rifle is held vertically in front of the body
2 : a command to assume the position of present arms or to give a hand salute
pre·sen·ta·tion \ˌprē-ˌzen-'tā-shən, ˌpre-z³n-, ˌprē-z³n-\ *noun* (15th century)
1 a : the act of presenting **b** : the act, power, or privilege especially of a patron of applying to the bishop or ordinary for instituting someone into a benefice
2 : something presented: as **a** : a symbol or image that represents something **b** : something offered or given : GIFT **c** : something set forth for the attention of the mind **d** : a descriptive or persuasive account (as by a salesman of a product)
3 : the position in which the fetus lies in the uterus in labor with respect to the mouth of the uterus
4 : an immediate object of perception, cognition, or memory
5 *often capitalized* : a church feast on November 21 celebrating the presentation of the Virgin Mary in the temple
6 : the method by which radio, navigation, or radar information is given to the operator (as the pilot of an airplane)
— **pre·sen·ta·tion·al** \-shnəl, -shə-n³l\ *adjective*
pre·sen·ta·tive \pri-'zen-tə-tiv, 'pre-z³n-ˌtā-\ *adjective* (circa 1842)
: known, knowing, or capable of being known directly rather than through cogitation
pres·ent–day \'pre-z³nt-'dā\ *adjective* (1887)
: now existing or occurring
pre·sen·tee \ˌpre-z³n-'tē, pri-ˌzen-\ *noun* (15th century)
: one who is presented or to whom something is presented
pre·sen·tient \pri-'sen(t)-sh(ē-)ənt, 'prē-; pri-'zen(t)-\ *adjective* [Latin *praesentient-, praesentiens*, present participle of *praesentire*] (1814)
: having a presentiment
pre·sen·ti·ment \pri-'zen-tə-mənt\ *noun* [French *pressentiment*, from Middle French, from *pressentir* to have a presentiment, from Latin *praesentire* to feel beforehand, from *prae-* + *sentire* to feel — more at SENSE] (1714)
: a feeling that something will or is about to happen : PREMONITION

— **pre·sen·ti·men·tal** \-ˌzen-tə-'men-t³l\ *adjective*
pres·ent·ism \'pre-z³n-ˌti-zəm\ *noun* [³*present*] (1923)
: an outlook dominated by present-day attitudes and experiences
— **pres·ent·ist** \-z³n-tist\ *adjective*
pres·ent·ly \'pre-z³nt-lē\ *adverb* (14th century)
1 a *archaic* : at once **b** : before long : without undue delay
2 : at the present time : NOW □
pre·sent·ment \pri-'zent-mənt\ *noun* (14th century)
1 : the act of presenting to an authority a formal statement of a matter to be dealt with; *specifically* : the notice taken or statement made by a grand jury of an offense from their own knowledge without a bill of indictment laid before them
2 : the act of offering at the proper time and place a document (as a bill of exchange) that calls for acceptance or payment by another
3 a : the act of presenting to view or consciousness **b** : something set forth, presented, or exhibited **c** : the aspect in which something is presented
present participle *noun* (1864)
: a participle that typically expresses present action in relation to the time expressed by the finite verb in its clause and that in English is formed with the suffix *-ing* and is used in the formation of the progressive tenses
present perfect *adjective* (1887)
: of, relating to, or constituting a verb tense that is formed in English with *have* and that expresses action or state completed at the time of speaking
— **present perfect** *noun*
present tense *noun* (14th century)
: the tense of a verb that expresses action or state in the present time and is used of what occurs or is true at the time of speaking and of what is habitual or characteristic or is always or necessarily true, that is sometimes used to refer to action in the past, and that is sometimes used for future events
present value *noun* (1831)
: the sum of money which if invested now at a given rate of compound interest will accumulate exactly to a specified amount at a specified future date
pres·er·va·tion·ist \ˌpre-zər-'vā-sh(ə-)nist\ *noun* (1927)
: one who advocates preservation (as of a biological species or a historical landmark)
¹**pre·ser·va·tive** \pri-'zər-və-tiv\ *adjective* (14th century)
: having the power of preserving
²**preservative** *noun* (15th century)
: something that preserves or has the power of preserving; *specifically* : an additive used to protect against decay, discoloration, or spoilage

¹pre·serve \pri-'zərv\ *verb* **pre·served; pre·serv·ing** [Middle English, from Middle French *preserver*, from Medieval Latin *praeservare*, from Late Latin, to observe beforehand, from Latin *prae-* + *servare* to keep, guard, observe — more at CONSERVE] (14th century)
transitive verb
1 : to keep safe from injury, harm, or destruction : PROTECT
2 a : to keep alive, intact, or free from decay **b** : MAINTAIN
3 a : to keep or save from decomposition **b** : to can, pickle, or similarly prepare for future use
4 : to keep up and reserve for personal or special use
intransitive verb
1 : to make preserves
2 : to raise and protect game for purposes of sport
3 : to be able to be preserved (as by canning)
— **pre·serv·abil·i·ty** \-,zər-və-'bi-lə-tē\ *noun*
— **pre·serv·able** \-'zər-və-bəl\ *adjective*
— **pres·er·va·tion** \,pre-zər-'vā-shən\ *noun*
— **pre·serv·er** \pri-'zər-vər\ *noun*

²preserve *noun* (1600)
1 : fruit canned or made into jams or jellies or cooked whole or in large pieces in a syrup so as to keep its shape — often used in plural
2 : an area restricted for the protection and preservation of natural resources (as animals or trees); *especially* : one used primarily for regulated hunting or fishing
3 : something regarded as reserved for certain persons

pre·shrink \(,)prē-'shriŋk, *especially Southern* -'sriŋk\ *transitive verb* **-shrank** \-'shraŋk, -'sraŋk\; **-shrunk** \-'shrəŋk, -'srəŋk\ (1926) : to shrink (as a fabric) before making into a garment so that it will not shrink much when washed

pre·side \pri-'zīd\ *intransitive verb* **pre·sid·ed; pre·sid·ing** [Latin *praesidēre* to guard, preside over, from *prae-* + *sedēre* to sit — more at SIT] (1608)
1 : to exercise guidance, direction, or control
2 a : to occupy the place of authority : act as president, chairman, or moderator **b** : to occupy a position similar to that of a president or chairman
3 : to occupy a position of featured instrumental performer — usually used with *at* ⟨*presided* at the organ⟩
— **pre·sid·er** *noun*

pres·i·den·cy \'pre-zə-dən(t)-sē, 'prez-dən(t)- *also* 'pre-zə-,den(t)-sē\ *noun, plural* **-cies** (1591)
1 a : the office of president **b** (1) : the office of president of the U.S. (2) : the American governmental institution comprising the office of president and various associated administrative and policy-making agencies
2 : the term during which a president holds office
3 : the action or function of one that presides : SUPERINTENDENCE
4 : a Mormon executive council of the church or a stake consisting of a president and two counselors

pres·i·dent \'pre-zə-dənt, 'prez-dənt, 'pre-zə-,dent *in rapid speech* 'pre-z²nt\ *noun* [Middle English, from Middle French, from Latin *praesident-, praesidens,* from present participle of *praesidēre*] (14th century)
1 : an official chosen to preside over a meeting or assembly
2 : an appointed governor of a subordinate political unit
3 : the chief officer of an organization (as a corporation or institution) usually entrusted with the direction and administration of its policies
4 : the presiding officer of a governmental body

5 a : an elected official serving as both chief of state and chief political executive in a republic having a presidential government **b** : an elected official having the position of chief of state but usually only minimal political powers in a republic having a parliamentary government
— **pres·i·den·tial** \,pre-zə-'den(t)-shəl, ,prez-'den(t)-\ *adjective*
— **pres·i·den·tial·ly** \-sh(ə-)lē\ *adverb*
— **pres·i·dent·ship** \'pre-zə-dənt-,ship, 'prez-dənt-, 'pre-zə-,dent-\ *noun*

presidential government *noun* (1902) : a system of government in which the president is constitutionally independent of the legislature

Presidents' Day *noun* (1952) : WASHINGTON'S BIRTHDAY 2

pre·sid·i·al \pri-'si-dē-əl, prī-, -'zi-\ *adjective* [Late Latin *praesidialis,* from Latin *praesidium* garrison, from *praesid-, praeses* guard, governor, from *praesidēre*] (1611)
1 [French *présidial,* from Middle French, alteration of *presidal,* from Late Latin *praesidalis* of a provincial governor, from Latin *praesid-, praeses*] : PROVINCIAL 1
2 : of, having, or constituting a garrison
3 : of or relating to a president : PRESIDENTIAL

pre·sid·i·ary \-dē-,er-ē\ *adjective* (1599) : PRESIDIAL 2

pre·si·dio \pri-'sē-dē-,ō, -'si-, -'zē-, -'zi-\ *noun, plural* **-di·os** [Spanish, from Latin *praesidium*] (1763) : a garrisoned place; *especially* : a military post or fortified settlement in areas currently or originally under Spanish control

pre·sid·i·um \pri-'si-dē-əm, prī-, -'zi-\ *noun, plural* **-ia** \-dē-ə\ *or* **-iums** [Russian *prezidium,* from Latin *praesidium* garrison] (1920)
1 : a permanent executive committee selected especially in Communist countries to act for a larger body
2 : a nongovernmental executive committee

pre·sig·ni·fy \(,)prē-'sig-nə-,fī\ *transitive verb* [Latin *praesignificare,* from *prae-* + *significare* to signify] (1586) : to intimate or signify beforehand : PRESAGE

¹pre·soak \(,)prē-'sōk\ *transitive verb* (1919) : to soak beforehand

²pre·soak \'prē-,sōk\ *noun* (1919)
1 : an instance of presoaking
2 : a preparation used in presoaking clothes

pre·So·crat·ic \,prē-sə-'kra-tik, -sō-\ *adjective* (1871) : of or relating to Greek philosophers before Socrates
— **pre·Socratic** *noun*

pre·sort \(,)prē-'sòrt\ *transitive verb* (1951) : to sort (outgoing mail) by zip code usually before delivery to a post office

¹press \'pres\ *noun* [Middle English *presse,* from Old French, from *presser* to press] (13th century)
1 a : a crowd or crowded condition : THRONG **b** : a thronging or crowding forward or together
2 a : an apparatus or machine by which a substance is cut or shaped, an impression of a body is taken, a material is compressed, pressure is applied to a body, liquid is expressed, or a cutting tool is fed into the work by pressure **b** : a building containing presses or a business using presses
3 : CLOSET, CUPBOARD
4 a : an action of pressing or pushing : PRESSURE **b** : an aggressive pressuring defense employed in basketball often over the entire court area
5 : the properly smoothed and creased condition of a freshly pressed garment ⟨out of *press*⟩
6 a : PRINTING PRESS **b** : the act or the process of printing **c** : a printing or publishing establishment
7 a : the gathering and publishing or broadcasting of news : JOURNALISM **b** : newspapers, periodicals, and often radio and television

news broadcasting **c** : news reporters, publishers, and broadcasters **d** : comment or notice in newspapers and periodicals ⟨is getting a good *press*⟩
8 : any of various pressure devices (as one for keeping sporting gear from warping when not in use)
9 : a lift in weight lifting in which the weight is raised to shoulder height and then smoothly extended overhead without assist from the legs
— compare CLEAN AND JERK, SNATCH

²press *verb* [Middle English, from Middle French *presser,* from Latin *pressare,* frequentative of *premere* to press; probably akin to Russian na*peret'* to press] (14th century)
transitive verb
1 : to act upon through steady pushing or thrusting force exerted in contact : SQUEEZE
2 a : ASSAIL, HARASS **b** : AFFLICT, OPPRESS
3 a : to squeeze out the juice or contents of **b** : to squeeze with apparatus or instruments to a desired density, smoothness, or shape
4 a : to exert influence on : CONSTRAIN **b** : to try hard to persuade : BESEECH, ENTREAT
5 : to move by means of pressure
6 a : to lay stress or emphasis on **b** : to insist on or request urgently
7 : to follow through (a course of action)
8 : to clasp in affection or courtesy
9 : to make (a phonograph record) from a matrix
intransitive verb
1 : to crowd closely : MASS
2 : to force or push one's way
3 : to seek urgently : CONTEND
4 : to require haste or speed in action
5 : to exert pressure
6 : to take or hold a press
7 : to employ a press in basketball
— **press·er** *noun*
— **press the flesh** : to greet and shake hands with people especially while campaigning for political office

³press *verb* [alteration of obsolete *prest* to enlist by giving pay in advance] (1578)
transitive verb
1 : to force into service especially in an army or navy : IMPRESS
2 a : to take by authority especially for public use : COMMANDEER **b** : to take and force into any usually emergency service
intransitive verb
: to impress men as soldiers or sailors

⁴press *noun* (1599)
1 : impressment into service especially in a navy
2 *obsolete* : a warrant for impressing recruits

press agent *noun* [¹*press*] (1883) : an agent employed to establish and maintain good public relations through publicity
— **press–agent** *verb*
— **press–agent·ry** \-'ā-jən-trē\ *noun*

press-board \'pres-,bòrd, -,bòrd\ *noun* (1849)
1 : IRONING BOARD; *especially* : a small one for sleeves
2 : a strong highly glazed composition board resembling vulcanized fiber

press box *noun* (1889) : a space reserved for reporters (as at a stadium)

press cloth *noun* (1899) : a cloth used between an iron and a garment

press conference *noun* (1937) : an interview or announcement given by a public figure to the press by appointment

press-gang \'pres-,gaŋ\ *noun* [⁴*press*] (1693) : a detachment of men under command of an officer empowered to force men into military or naval service

\ə\ abut \ᵊ\ kitten \ər\ **further** \a\ ash \ā\ ace
\ä\ mop, mar \aù\ out \ch\ chin \e\ bet \ē\ **easy**
\g\ go \i\ hit \ī\ ice \j\ job \ŋ\ sing \ō\ go
\ò\ law \òi\ boy \th\ thin \t̲h̲\ the \ü\ loot \ù\ foot
\y\ yet \zh\ vision *see also* Guide to Pronunciation

— **press–gang** *transitive verb*
press·ing *adjective* (1616)
1 : urgently important **:** CRITICAL
2 : EARNEST, WARM
— **press·ing·ly** \'pre-siŋ-lē\ *adverb*
press kit *noun* (1968)
: a collection of promotional materials for distribution to the press
press·man \'pres-mən, -,man\ *noun* (1598)
1 : an operator of a press; *especially* **:** the operator of a printing press
2 *British* **:** NEWSPAPERMAN
press·mark \-,märk\ *noun* [¹*press* (closet)] (1802)
chiefly British **:** a mark or number assigned to a book to indicate its location in a library
press of sail (1794)
: the fullest amount of sail that a ship can crowd on — called also *press of canvas*
pres·sor \'pre-,sȯr, -sər\ *adjective* [Late Latin, one that presses, from Latin *premere* to press — more at PRESS] (circa 1890)
: raising or tending to raise blood pressure; *also* **:** involving vasoconstriction
press·room \'pres-,rüm, -,rum\ *noun* (1683)
1 : a room in a printing plant containing the printing presses
2 : a room (as at the White House) for the use of members of the press
press-run \-,rən\ *noun* (1945)
: a continuous operation of a printing press producing a specified number of copies; *also* **:** the number of copies printed
press secretary *noun* (1951)
: a person officially in charge of press relations for a usually prominent public figure ⟨the President's *press secretary*⟩
press–up \'pres-(,)əp\ (1936)
British **:** PUSH-UP
¹pres·sure \'pre-shər\ *noun* [Middle English, from Late Latin *pressura*, from Latin, action of pressing, pressure, from *pressus*, past participle of *premere*] (14th century)
1 a : the burden of physical or mental distress
b : the constraint of circumstance **:** the weight of social or economic imposition
2 : the application of force to something by something else in direct contact with it **:** COMPRESSION
3 *archaic* **:** IMPRESSION, STAMP
4 a : the action of a force against an opposing force **b :** the force or thrust exerted over a surface divided by its area **c :** ELECTROMOTIVE FORCE
5 : the stress or urgency of matters demanding attention **:** EXIGENCY ⟨people who work well under *pressure*⟩
6 : the force of selection that results from one or more agents and tends to reduce a population of organisms ⟨population *pressure*⟩ ⟨predation *pressure*⟩
7 : atmospheric pressure
8 : a sensation aroused by moderate compression of a body part or surface
— **pres·sure·less** *adjective*
²pressure *transitive verb* **pres·sured; pres·sur·ing** \'pre-sh(ə-)riŋ\ (1938)
1 : to apply pressure to
2 : PRESSURIZE
3 : to cook in a pressure cooker
pressure cabin *noun* (1935)
: a pressurized cabin
pressure cooker *noun* (1915)
1 : an airtight utensil for quick cooking or preserving of foods by means of superheated steam under pressure
2 : a situation or environment that is fraught with emotional or social pressures
— **pressure–cook** *verb*
pressure gauge *noun* (1862)
: a gauge for indicating fluid pressure
pressure group *noun* (1928)
: an interest group organized to influence public and especially government policy but not to elect candidates to office

pressure point *noun* (1909)
: a point where a blood vessel runs near a bone and can be compressed (as to check bleeding) by the application of pressure against the bone
pressure suit *noun* (1936)
: an inflatable suit for high-altitude or space flight to protect the body from low pressure
pressure wave *noun* (1942)
: a wave (as a sound wave) in which the propagated disturbance is a variation of pressure in a material medium — called also *P-wave*
pres·sur·ise *British variant of* PRESSURIZE
pres·sur·ize \'pre-shə-,rīz\ *transitive verb* **-ized; -iz·ing** (1938)
1 : to confine the contents of under a pressure greater than that of the outside atmosphere; *especially* **:** to maintain near-normal atmospheric pressure in during high-altitude or spaceflight (as by means of a supercharger)
2 : to apply pressure to
3 : to design to withstand pressure
— **pres·sur·i·za·tion** \,pre-sh(ə-)rə-'zā-shən\ *noun*
— **pres·sur·iz·er** *noun*
press·work \'pres-,wərk\ *noun* (1771)
: the operation, management, or product of a printing press; *especially* **:** the branch of printing concerned with the actual transfer of ink from form or plates to paper
prest \'prest\ *adjective* [Middle English, from Old French, from Latin *praestus* — more at PRESTO] (14th century)
obsolete **:** READY
pres·ti·dig·i·ta·tion \,pres-tə-,di-jə-'tā-shən\ *noun* [French, from *prestidigitateur* prestidigitator, from *preste* nimble, quick (from Italian *presto*) + Latin *digitus* finger — more at DIGIT] (1859)
: SLEIGHT OF HAND, LEGERDEMAIN
— **pres·ti·dig·i·ta·tor** \-'di-jə-,tā-tər\ *noun*
pres·tige \pre-'stēzh, -'stēj\ *noun, often attributive* [French, from Middle French, conjuror's trick, illusion, from Latin *praestigiae*, plural, conjuror's tricks, from *praestringere* to graze, blunt, constrict, from *prae-* + *stringere* to bind tight — more at STRAIN] (1829)
1 : standing or estimation in the eyes of people **:** weight or credit in general opinion
2 : commanding position in people's minds ◆
synonym see INFLUENCE
— **pres·tige·ful** \-fəl\ *adjective*
pres·ti·gious \pre-'sti-jəs, -'stē- *also* prə-\ *adjective* [Latin *praestigiosus*, from *praestigiae*] (1546)
1 *archaic* **:** of, relating to, or marked by illusion, conjuring, or trickery
2 : having prestige **:** HONORED
— **pres·ti·gious·ly** *adverb*
— **pres·ti·gious·ness** *noun*
pres·tis·si·mo \pre-'sti-sə-,mō\ *adverb or adjective* [Italian, from *presto* + *-issimo*, suffix denoting a high degree] (circa 1724)
: faster than presto — used as a direction in music
¹pres·to \'pres-(,)tō\ *adverb or adjective* [Italian, quick, quickly, from Latin *praestus* ready, from *praesto*, adverb, on hand; akin to Latin *prae* before — more at FOR] (circa 1599)
1 : suddenly as if by magic **:** IMMEDIATELY
2 : at a rapid tempo — used as a direction in music
²presto *noun, plural* **prestos** (1869)
: a presto musical passage or movement
¹pre·stress \(,)prē-'stres\ *transitive verb* (1934)
: to introduce internal stresses into (as a structural beam) to counteract the stresses that will result from applied load (as in incorporating cables under tension in concrete)
²pre·stress \'prē-,stres, ,prē-'\ *noun* (1934)
1 : the stresses introduced in prestressing
2 : the process of prestressing

3 : the condition of being prestressed
pre·sum·able \pri-'zü-mə-bəl\ *adjective* (1692)
: capable of being presumed **:** acceptable as an assumption
pre·sum·ably \-blē\ *adverb* (1846)
: by reasonable assumption
pre·sume \pri-'züm\ *verb* **pre·sumed; pre·sum·ing** [Middle English, from Late Latin & Middle French; Late Latin *praesumere* to dare, from Latin, to anticipate, assume, from *prae-* + *sumere* to take; Middle French *presumer* to assume, from Latin *praesumere* — more at CONSUME] (14th century)
transitive verb
1 : to undertake without leave or clear justification **:** DARE
2 : to expect or assume especially with confidence
3 : to suppose to be true without proof ⟨*presumed* innocent until proved guilty⟩
4 : to take for granted **:** IMPLY
intransitive verb
1 : to act or proceed presumptuously or on a presumption
2 : to go beyond what is right or proper
— **pre·sumed·ly** \-'zü-məd-lē, -'zümd-lē\ *adverb*
— **pre·sum·er** *noun*
presuming *adjective* (15th century)
: PRESUMPTUOUS
— **pre·sum·ing·ly** \-'zü-miŋ-lē\ *adverb*
pre·sump·tion \pri-'zəm(p)-shən\ *noun* [Middle English *presumpcioun*, from Old French *presumption*, from Late Latin & Latin; Late Latin *praesumption-, praesumptio* presumptuous attitude, from Latin, assumption, from *praesumere*] (13th century)
1 : presumptuous attitude or conduct **:** AUDACITY
2 a : an attitude or belief dictated by probability **:** ASSUMPTION **b :** the ground, reason, or evidence lending probability to a belief
3 : a legal inference as to the existence or truth of a fact not certainly known that is drawn from the known or proved existence of some other fact
pre·sump·tive \-'zəm(p)-tiv\ *adjective* (15th century)
1 : based on probability or presumption
2 : giving grounds for reasonable opinion or belief
3 : being an embryonic precursor with the potential for forming a particular structure or tissue in the normal course of development ⟨*presumptive* retina⟩
— **pre·sump·tive·ly** *adverb*
pre·sump·tu·ous \pri-'zəm(p)-chə-wəs, -chəs, -shəs\ *adjective* [Middle English, from Middle French *presumptueux*, from Late Latin *praesumptuosus*, irregular from *praesumptio*] (14th century)

: overstepping due bounds (as of propriety or courtesy) **:** taking liberties
— **pre·sump·tu·ous·ly** *adverb*
— **pre·sump·tu·ous·ness** *noun*
pre·sup·pose \ˌprē-sə-'pōz\ *transitive verb* [Middle English, from Middle French *presupposer*, from Medieval Latin *praesupponere* (perfect indicative *praesupposui*), from Latin *prae-* + Medieval Latin *supponere* to suppose — more at SUPPOSE] (15th century)
1 : to suppose beforehand
2 : to require as an antecedent in logic or fact
— **pre·sup·po·si·tion** \ˌ(ˌ)prē-sə-pə-'zish-ən\ *noun*
— **pre·sup·po·si·tion·al** \-'zish-nəl, -'zish-ə-n°l\ *adjective*
pre·syn·ap·tic \ˌprē-sə-'nap-tik\ *adjective* (1909)
: situated or occurring just before a nerve synapse
— **pre·syn·ap·ti·cal·ly** \-ti-k(ə-)lē\ *adverb*
pret-a-por·ter *or* **prêt-à-por·ter** \ˌpret-ä-pȯr-'tā\ *noun* [French, ready to wear] (1959)
: ready-to-wear clothes
¹pre·teen \'prē-ˌtēn, -ˌtēn\ *noun* (1952)
: a boy or girl not yet 13 years old
²preteen *adjective* (1954)
1 : relating to or produced for children especially in the 9 to 12 year-old age group ⟨*preteen* fashions⟩
2 : being younger than 13
pre·teen-ag·er \ˌ(ˌ)prē-'tē-nā-jər\ *noun* (1965)
: PRETEEN
¹pre·tend \pri-'tend\ *verb* [Middle English, from Latin *praetendere* to allege as an excuse, literally, to stretch out, from *prae-* pre- + *tendere* to stretch — more at THIN] (15th century)
transitive verb
1 : to give a false appearance of being, possessing, or performing ⟨does not *pretend* to be a psychiatrist⟩
2 a : to make believe **:** FEIGN ⟨he *pretended* deafness⟩ **b :** to claim, represent, or assert falsely ⟨*pretending* an emotion he could not really feel⟩
3 *archaic* **:** VENTURE, UNDERTAKE
intransitive verb
1 : to feign an action, part, or role in play
2 : to put in a claim
synonym *see* ASSUME
²pretend *adjective* (1911)
: IMAGINARY, MAKE-BELIEVE
pre·tend·ed *adjective* (15th century)
: professed or avowed but not genuine ⟨*pretended* affection⟩
— **pre·tend·ed·ly** *adverb*
pre·tend·er \pri-'ten-dər\ *noun* (1609)
: one that pretends: as **a :** one who lays claim to something; *specifically* **:** a claimant to a throne who is held to have no just title **b :** one who makes a false or hypocritical show
pre·tense *or* **pre·tence** \'prē-ˌten(t)s, pri-'\ *noun* [Middle English, from Middle French *pretensse*, from (assumed) Medieval Latin *praetensa*, from Late Latin, feminine of *praetensus*, past participle of Latin *praetendere*] (15th century)
1 : a claim made or implied; *especially* **:** one not supported by fact
2 a : mere ostentation **:** PRETENTIOUSNESS ⟨confuse dignity with pomposity and *pretense* —Bennett Cerf⟩ **b :** a pretentious act or assertion
3 : an inadequate or insincere attempt to attain a certain condition or quality
4 : professed rather than real intention or purpose **:** PRETEXT ⟨was there under false *pretenses*⟩
5 : MAKE-BELIEVE, FICTION
6 : false show **:** SIMULATION ⟨saw through his *pretense* of indifference⟩

¹pre·ten·sion \pri-'ten(t)-shən\ *noun* (15th century)
1 : an allegation of doubtful value **:** PRETEXT
2 : a claim or an effort to establish a claim
3 : a claim or right to attention or honor because of merit
4 : an aspiration or intention that may or may not reach fulfillment ⟨has serious literary *pretensions*⟩
5 : VANITY, PRETENTIOUSNESS
synonym *see* AMBITION
— **pre·ten·sion·less** \-ləs\ *adjective*
²pre·ten·sion \ˌprē-'ten(t)-shən\ *transitive verb* [pre- + ²tension] (1937)
: PRESTRESS
pre·ten·tious \pri-'ten(t)-shəs\ *adjective* [French *prétentieux*, from *prétention* pretension, from Medieval Latin *praetention-, praetentio*, from Latin *praetendere*] (1837)
1 : characterized by pretension: as **a :** making usually unjustified or excessive claims (as of value or standing) ⟨the *pretentious* fraud who assumes a love of culture that is alien to him —Richard Watts⟩ **b :** expressive of affected, unwarranted, or exaggerated importance, worth, or stature ⟨*pretentious* language⟩ ⟨*pretentious* houses⟩
2 : making demands on one's skill, ability, or means **:** AMBITIOUS ⟨the *pretentious* daring of the Green Mountain Boys in crossing the lake —*American Guide Series: Vermont*⟩
synonym *see* SHOWY
— **pre·ten·tious·ly** *adverb*
— **pre·ten·tious·ness** *noun*
¹pret·er·it *or* **pret·er·ite** \'pre-tə-rət\ *adjective* [Middle English *preterit*, from Middle French, from Latin *praeteritus*, from past participle of *praeterire* to go by, pass, from *praeter* beyond, past, by (from comparative of *prae* before) + *ire* to go — more at FOR, ISSUE] (14th century)
archaic **:** BYGONE, FORMER
²preterit *or* **preterite** *noun* (14th century)
: PAST TENSE
pre·term \ˌ(ˌ)prē-'tərm, 'prē-ˌ\ *adjective* (1928)
: of, relating to, being, or brought forth by premature birth ⟨*preterm* infant⟩ ⟨*preterm* labor⟩
pre·ter·mi·nal \ˌ(ˌ)prē-'tərm-nəl, -'tər-mə-\ *adjective* (1947)
: occurring before death ⟨*preterminal* cancer⟩
pre·ter·mis·sion \ˌprē-tər-'mi-shən\ *noun* [Latin *praetermission-, praetermissio*, from *praetermittere*] (1583)
: the act or an instance of pretermitting **:** OMISSION
pre·ter·mit \-'mit\ *transitive verb* **-mit·ted; -mit·ting** [Latin *praetermittere*, from *praeter* by, past + *mittere* to let go, send] (1538)
1 : to let pass without mention or notice **:** OMIT
2 : to leave undone **:** NEGLECT
3 : SUSPEND, BREAK OFF
pre·ter·nat·u·ral \ˌprē-tər-'na-chə-rəl, -'nach-rəl\ *adjective* [Medieval Latin *praeternaturalis*, from Latin *praeter naturam* beyond nature] (1580)
1 : existing outside of nature
2 : exceeding what is natural or regular **:** EXTRAORDINARY ⟨wits trained to *preternatural* acuteness by the debates —G. L. Dickinson⟩
3 : inexplicable by ordinary means; *especially* **:** PSYCHIC ⟨*preternatural* phenomena⟩
— **pre·ter·nat·u·ral·ly** \-'na-chə-rə-lē, 'nach-rə-, 'na-chər-\ *adverb*
— **pre·ter·nat·u·ral·ness** \-'na-chə-rəl-nəs, -'nach-rəl-\ *noun*
pre·test \'prē-ˌtest\ *noun* (1926)
: a preliminary test: as **a :** a test of the effectiveness or safety of a product prior to its sale **b :** a test to evaluate the preparedness of students for further studies
— **pre·test** \ˌ(ˌ)prē-'test\ *transitive verb*
pre·text \'prē-ˌtekst\ *noun* [Latin *praetextus*, from *praetexere* to assign as a pretext, screen,

extend in front, from *prae-* + *texere* to weave — more at TECHNICAL] (1513)
: a purpose or motive alleged or an appearance assumed in order to cloak the real intention or state of affairs
synonym *see* APOLOGY
pre·tor, pre·to·ri·an *variant of* PRAETOR, PRAETORIAN
pret·ti·fy \'pri-ti-ˌfī, 'pu̇r-, 'pru̇-\ *transitive verb* **-fied; -fy·ing** (1850)
: to make pretty
— **pret·ti·fi·ca·tion** \ˌpri-ti-fə-'kā-shən, ˌpu̇r-, ˌpru̇-\ *noun*
— **pret·ti·fi·er** \'pri-ti-ˌfī(-ə)r, 'pu̇r-, 'pru̇-\ *noun*
pret·ti·ness \'pri-tē-nəs, 'pu̇r-, 'pru̇-\ *noun* (1649)
1 : the quality or state of being pretty
2 : something pretty
¹pret·ty \'pri-tē, 'pu̇r- *also* 'pru̇-\ *adjective* **pret·ti·er; -est** [Middle English *praty, pretty*, from Old English *prættig* tricky, from *prætt* trick; akin to Old Norse *prettr* trick] (15th century)
1 a : ARTFUL, CLEVER **b :** PAT, APT
2 a : pleasing by delicacy or grace **b :** having conventionally accepted elements of beauty **c :** appearing or sounding pleasant or nice but lacking strength, force, manliness, purpose, or intensity ⟨*pretty* words that make no sense —Elizabeth B. Browning⟩
3 a : MISERABLE, TERRIBLE ⟨a *pretty* mess you've gotten us into⟩ **b** *chiefly Scottish* **:** STOUT
4 : moderately large **:** CONSIDERABLE ⟨a very *pretty* profit⟩ ⟨cost a *pretty* penny⟩
synonym *see* BEAUTIFUL
— **pret·ti·ly** \-t°l-ē\ *adverb*
— **pret·ty·ish** \-tē-ish\ *adjective*
²pret·ty \'pu̇r-tē, 'pər-tē, 'pri-tē *also* 'pru̇-tē; *before* "near(ly)" *often* 'pərt *or* 'prit *or* 'pru̇t\ *adverb* (1565)
1 : in some degree **:** MODERATELY ⟨*pretty* cold weather⟩
2 : in a pretty manner **:** PRETTILY ⟨pop vocalists who can sing *pretty* —Gerald Levitch⟩ □
³pret·ty \'pri-tē, 'pu̇r-tē *also* 'pru̇-tē\ *noun, plural* **pretties** (1736)
1 *plural* **:** dainty clothes; *especially* **:** LINGERIE
2 : a pretty person or thing
⁴pret·ty *same as* ³\ *transitive verb* **pret·tied; pret·ty·ing** (1909)
: to make pretty — usually used with *up* ⟨curtains to *pretty* up the room⟩
pret·zel \'pret-səl\ *noun* [German *Brezel*, ultimately from Latin *brachiatus* having branches like arms, from *brachium* arm — more at BRACE] (circa 1838)

\ə\ abut \ᵊ\ kitten \ər\ further \a\ ash \ā\ ace \ä\ mop, mar \au̇\ out \ch\ chin \e\ bet \ē\ easy \g\ go \i\ hit \ī\ ice \j\ job \ŋ\ sing \ō\ go \ȯ\ law \ȯi\ boy \th\ thin \t͟h\ the \ü\ loot \u̇\ foot \y\ yet \zh\ vision *see also* Guide to Pronunciation

: a brittle or chewy glazed usually salted slender bread often shaped like a loose knot ◇

pre·vail \pri-'vā(ə)l\ *intransitive verb* [Middle English, from Latin *praevalēre,* from *prae-* pre- + *valēre* to be strong — more at WIELD] (15th century)
1 : to gain ascendancy through strength or superiority : TRIUMPH
2 : to be or become effective or effectual
3 : to use persuasion successfully ⟨*prevailed* on him to sing⟩
4 : to be frequent : PREDOMINATE ⟨the west winds that *prevail* in the mountains⟩
5 : to be or continue in use or fashion : PERSIST ⟨a custom that still *prevails*⟩

prev·a·lence \'pre-və-lən(t)s, 'prev-lən(t)s\ *noun* (1713)
1 : the quality or state of being prevalent
2 : the degree to which something is prevalent; *especially* : the percentage of a population that is affected with a particular disease at a given time

prev·a·lent \-lənt\ *adjective* [Latin *praevalent-, praevalens* very powerful, from present participle of *praevalēre*] (1576)
1 *archaic* : POWERFUL
2 : being in ascendancy : DOMINANT
3 : generally or widely accepted, practiced, or favored : WIDESPREAD
— **prevalent** *noun*
— **prev·a·lent·ly** *adverb*

pre·var·i·cate \pri-'var-ə-ˌkāt\ *intransitive verb* **-cat·ed; -cat·ing** [Latin *praevaricatus,* past participle of *praevaricari* to active in collusion, literally, to straddle, from *prae-* + *varicare* to straddle, from *varus* bowlegged] (circa 1631)
: to deviate from the truth : EQUIVOCATE
synonym see LIE
— **pre·var·i·ca·tion** \-ˌvar-ə-'kā-shən\ *noun*
— **pre·var·i·ca·tor** \-'var-ə-ˌkā-tər\ *noun*

pre·ve·nient \pri-'vēn-yənt\ *adjective* [Latin *praevenient-, praeveniens,* present participle of *praevenire*] (circa 1656)
: ANTECEDENT, ANTICIPATORY
— **pre·ve·nient·ly** *adverb*

pre·vent \pri-'vent\ *verb* [Middle English, to anticipate, from Latin *praeventus,* past participle of *praevenire* to come before, anticipate, forestall, from *prae-* + *venire* to come — more at COME] (15th century)
transitive verb
1 *archaic* **a** : to be in readiness for (as an occasion) **b** : to meet or satisfy in advance **c** : to act ahead of **d** : to go or arrive before
2 : to deprive of power or hope of acting or succeeding
3 : to keep from happening or existing ⟨steps to *prevent* war⟩
4 : to hold or keep back : HINDER, STOP — often used with *from*
intransitive verb
: to interpose an obstacle ☆
— **pre·vent·abil·i·ty** \-ˌven-tə-'bi-lə-tē\ *noun*
— **pre·vent·able** *also* **pre·vent·ible** \-'ven-tə-bəl\ *adjective*
— **pre·vent·er** *noun*

pre·ven·ta·tive \-'ven-tə-tiv\ *adjective or noun* (circa 1666)
: PREVENTIVE

pre·ven·tion \pri-'ven(t)-shən\ *noun* (1582)
: the act of preventing or hindering

¹pre·ven·tive \-'ven-tiv\ *noun* (circa 1639)
: something that prevents; *especially* : something used to prevent disease

²preventive *adjective* (1639)
1 : devoted to or concerned with prevention : PRECAUTIONARY ⟨*preventive* steps against soil erosion⟩
2 : undertaken to forestall anticipated hostile action ⟨a *preventive* coup⟩
— **pre·ven·tive·ly** *adverb*
— **pre·ven·tive·ness** *noun*

pre·ver·bal \(ˌ)prē-'vər-bəl\ *adjective* (1921)

1 : occurring before the verb
2 : having not yet acquired the faculty of speech ⟨a *preverbal* child⟩

¹pre·view \'prē-ˌvyü\ *transitive verb* (1607)
1 : to see beforehand; *specifically* : to view or to show in advance of public presentation
2 : to give a preliminary survey of
— **pre·view·er** \-ˌvyü-ər\ *noun*

²preview *noun* (1922)
1 : an advance showing or performance (as of a motion picture or play)
2 *also* **pre·vue** \-ˌvyü\ : a showing of snatches from a motion picture advertised for appearance in the near future — called also *trailer*
3 : an advance statement, sample, or survey

pre·vi·ous \'prē-vē-əs\ *adjective* [Latin *praevius* leading the way, from *prae-* pre- + *via* way — more at WAY] (1625)
1 : going before in time or order : PRIOR
2 : acting too soon : PREMATURE
synonym see PRECEDING
— **pre·vi·ous·ly** *adverb*
— **pre·vi·ous·ness** *noun*

previous question *noun* (circa 1715)
: a parliamentary motion to put the pending question to an immediate vote without further debate or amendment that if defeated has the effect of permitting resumption of debate

previous to *preposition* (1702)
: PRIOR TO, BEFORE

¹pre·vi·sion \prē-'vi-zhən\ *noun* [Middle English *previsioun,* from Old French *prevision,* from Late Latin *praevision-, praevisio,* from Latin *praevidēre* to foresee, from *prae-* + *vidēre* to see — more at WIT] (15th century)
1 : FORESIGHT, PRESCIENCE
2 : FORECAST, PROGNOSTICATION
— **pre·vi·sion·al** \-'vizh-nəl, -'vi-zhə-nᵊl\ *adjective*
— **pre·vi·sion·ary** \-'vi-zhə-ˌner-ē\ *adjective*

²prevision *transitive verb* **pre·vi·sioned; pre·vi·sion·ing** \-'vi-zhə-niŋ, -'vizh-niŋ\ (1891)
: FORESEE

pre·vo·cal·ic \ˌprē-vō-'ka-lik, -və-\ *adjective* [International Scientific Vocabulary] (1899)
: immediately preceding a vowel

pre·vo·ca·tion·al \ˌprē-vō-'kā-shnəl, -shə-nᵊl\ *adjective* (1914)
: given or required before admission to a vocational school

pre·writ·ing \'prē-ˌrī-tiŋ\ *noun* (1968)
: the formulation and organization of ideas preparatory to writing

prexy \'prek-sē\ *also* **prex** \'preks\ *noun, plural* **prex·ies** *also* **prex·es** [*prexy* from *prex,* by shortening & alteration from *president*] (1871)
slang : PRESIDENT — used chiefly of a college president

¹prey \'prā\ *noun, plural* **prey** *also* **preys** [Middle English *preie,* from Old French, from Latin *praeda;* akin to Latin *prehendere* to grasp, seize — more at GET] (13th century)
1 *archaic* : SPOIL, BOOTY
2 a : an animal taken by a predator as food **b** : one that is helpless or unable to resist attack : VICTIM ⟨was *prey* to his own appetites⟩
3 : the act or habit of preying

²prey *intransitive verb* **preyed; prey·ing** [Middle English, from Old French *preier,* from Latin *praedari,* from *praeda*] (14th century)
1 : to make raids for the sake of booty
2 a : to seize and devour prey **b** : to commit violence or robbery or fraud
3 : to have an injurious, destructive, or wasting effect
— **prey·er** *noun*

prez \'prez\ *noun, plural* **prez·es** \'pre-zəz\ [by shortening & alteration] (1892)
slang : PRESIDENT

Pri·am \'prī-əm, -ˌam\ *noun* [Latin *Priamus,* from Greek *Priamos*]

: the father of Hector and Paris and king of Troy during the Trojan War

pri·a·pic \prī-'ā-pik, -'a-\ *adjective* [Latin *priapus* lecher, from *Priapus*] (1786)
1 : PHALLIC
2 : relating to or preoccupied with virility

Pri·a·pus \prī-'ā-pəs\ *noun* [Latin, from Greek *Priapos*]
: a Greek and Roman god of gardens and male generative power

¹price \'prīs\ *noun* [Middle English *pris,* from Old French, from Latin *pretium* price, money; probably akin to Sanskrit *prati-* against, in return — more at PROS-] (13th century)
1 *archaic* : VALUE, WORTH
2 a : the quantity of one thing that is exchanged or demanded in barter or sale for another **b** : the amount of money given or set as consideration for the sale of a specified thing
3 : the terms for the sake of which something is done or undertaken: as **a** : an amount sufficient to bribe one ⟨believed every man had his *price*⟩ **b** : a reward for the apprehension or death of a person ⟨an outlaw with a *price* on his head⟩
4 : the cost at which something is obtained ⟨the *price* of freedom is restraint —J. Irwin Miller⟩

²price *transitive verb* **priced; pric·ing** (15th century)
1 : to set a price on
2 : to find out the price of
3 : to drive by raising prices excessively ⟨*priced* themselves out of the market⟩
— **pric·er** *noun*

price–cut·ter \'prīs-ˌkə-tər\ *noun* (1901)
: one that reduces prices especially to a level designed to cripple competition
— **price–cut·ting** \-tiŋ\ *noun*

priced \'prīst\ *adjective* (1722)
: having a specified price — used in combination ⟨low-*priced* merchandise⟩

☆ SYNONYMS
Prevent, anticipate, forestall mean to deal with beforehand. PREVENT implies taking advance measures against something possible or probable ⟨measures taken to *prevent* leaks⟩. ANTICIPATE may imply merely getting ahead of another by being a precursor or forerunner or it may imply checking another's intention by acting first ⟨*anticipated* the question by making a statement⟩. FORESTALL implies a getting ahead so as to stop or interrupt something in its course ⟨hoped to *forestall* the sale⟩.

◇ WORD HISTORY
pretzel Pretzels were apparently known to Americans by 1856, when the word *pretzel,* borrowed from German *Prezel* or *Brezel,* appears in a Sacramento, California, newspaper among a list of items claimed to be typical of German cuisine, such as wurst and lager beer. This familiar hard, knot-shaped bread has been baked, at least in Germanic countries, for centuries, as is evidenced by its appearance in a painting by the 16th century Flemish artist Pieter Brueghel. The origins of the pretzel, however, are even earlier, for the word is found in Old High German glosses as *brecila* or *brezitela.* These words were borrowed from the same vernacular Latin source that yielded Medieval Latin *bracidellus* and 15th century Italian *bracciatello.* These were names for a sweet, ring-shaped pastry—all ultimately from derivatives of Latin *brachiatus* "branched, having branches like arms." Twisted pastries were apparently so called because of the similarity between their knotted shape and a pair of folded arms.

price–earnings ratio *noun* (1961)
: a measure of the value of a common stock determined as the ratio of its market price to its earnings per share and usually expressed as a simple numeral

price–fix·ing \'prīs-,fik-siŋ\ *noun* (1920)
: the setting of prices artificially (as by producers or government) contrary to free market operations

price index *noun* (1886)
: an index number expressing the level of a group of commodity prices relative to the level of the prices of the same commodities during an arbitrarily chosen base period and used to indicate changes in the level of prices from one period to another

price·less \'prīs-ləs\ *adjective* (1593)
1 a : having a value beyond any price : IN-VALUABLE **b** : costly because of rarity or quality : PRECIOUS
2 : having worth in terms of other than market value
3 : delightfully amusing, odd, or absurd
— **price·less·ly** *adverb*

price support *noun* (1945)
: artificial maintenance of prices (as of a raw material) at some predetermined level usually through government action

price tag *noun* (1881)
1 : a tag on merchandise showing the price at which it is offered for sale
2 : PRICE, COST

price war *noun* (1925)
: commercial competition characterized by the repeated cutting of prices below those of competitors

pric·ey *also* **pricy** \'prī-sē\ *adjective* **pric·i·er; -est** (1932)
: EXPENSIVE

¹prick \'prik\ *noun* [Middle English *prikke*, from Old English *prica*; akin to Middle Dutch *pric* prick] (before 12th century)
1 : a mark or shallow hole made by a pointed instrument
2 a : a pointed instrument or weapon **b** : a sharp projecting organ or part
3 : an instance of pricking or the sensation of being pricked: as **a** : a nagging or sharp feeling of remorse, regret, or sorrow **b** : a slight sharply localized discomfort ⟨the *prick* of a needle⟩
4 : PENIS — usually considered vulgar
5 : a spiteful or contemptible man often having some authority — usually considered vulgar

²prick (before 12th century)
transitive verb
1 : to pierce slightly with a sharp point
2 : to affect with anguish, grief, or remorse ⟨doubt began to *prick* him —Philip Hale⟩
3 : to ride, guide, or urge on with or as if with spurs : GOAD
4 : to mark, distinguish, or note by means of a small mark
5 : to trace or outline with punctures
6 : to remove (a young seedling) from the seedbed to another suitable for further growth — usually used with *out*
7 : to cause to be or stand erect ⟨a dog *pricking* its ears⟩
intransitive verb
1 a : to prick something or cause a pricking sensation **b** : to feel discomfort as if from being pricked
2 a : to urge a horse with the spur **b** : to ride fast
3 : THRUST
4 : to become directed upward : POINT
— **prick up one's ears** : to listen intently

prick·er \'pri-kər\ *noun* (14th century)
1 : one that pricks: as **a** : a rider of horses **b** : a military light horseman
2 a : THORN, PRICKLE **b** : BRIER

prick·et \'pri-kət\ *noun* [Middle English *priket*, from *prikke*] (15th century)
1 a : a spike on which a candle is stuck **b** : a candlestick with such a point
2 : a buck in the second year of life

¹prick·le \'pri-kəl\ *noun* [Middle English *prikle*, from Old English *pricle*; akin to Old English *prica* prick] (15th century)
1 : a fine sharp process or projection; *especially* : a sharp pointed emergence arising from the epidermis or bark of a plant
2 : a prickling or tingling sensation

²prickle *verb* **prick·led; prick·ling** \-k(ə-)liŋ\ (1513)
transitive verb
1 : to prick slightly
2 : to produce prickles in
intransitive verb
: to cause or feel a prickling, tingling, or stinging sensation

prick·ly \'pri-k(ə-)lē\ *adjective* **prick·li·er; -est** (1578)
1 : full of or covered with prickles; *especially* : distinguished from related kinds by the presence of prickles
2 : marked by prickling : STINGING ⟨a *prickly* sensation⟩
3 a : TROUBLESOME, VEXATIOUS ⟨*prickly* issues⟩ **b** : easily irritated ⟨had a *prickly* disposition⟩
— **prick·li·ness** *noun*

prickly ash *noun* (1709)
: a prickly aromatic shrub or small tree (*Zanthoxylum americanum*) of the rue family with yellowish flowers

prickly heat *noun* (1736)
: a noncontagious cutaneous eruption of red pimples with intense itching and tingling caused by inflammation around the sweat ducts

prickly pear *noun* (1612)
1 : OPUNTIA; *especially* : any of those with flat spiny joints — called also *prickly pear cactus*; compare CHOLLA
2 : the pulpy pear-shaped edible fruit of various prickly pears (as *Opuntia ficus-indica*)

prickly poppy *noun* (1724)
: any of a genus (*Argemone*) of plants of the poppy family with white or yellow flowers and prickly leaves and fruits

prickly pear 1

¹pride \'prīd\ *noun* [Middle English, from Old English *prȳde*, from *prūd* proud — more at PROUD] (before 12th century)
1 : the quality or state of being proud: as **a** : inordinate self-esteem : CONCEIT **b** : a reasonable or justifiable self-respect **c** : delight or elation arising from some act, possession, or relationship ⟨parental *pride*⟩
2 : proud or disdainful behavior or treatment : DISDAIN
3 a : ostentatious display **b** : highest pitch : PRIME
4 : a source of pride : the best in a group or class
5 : a company of lions
6 : a showy or impressive group ⟨a *pride* of dancers⟩

²pride *transitive verb* **prid·ed; prid·ing** (13th century)
: to indulge (as oneself) in pride

pride·ful \'prīd-fəl\ *adjective* (15th century)
: full of pride: as **a** : DISDAINFUL, HAUGHTY **b** : EXULTANT, ELATED
— **pride·ful·ly** \-fə-lē\ *adverb*
— **pride·ful·ness** *noun*

pride of place (1605)
: the highest or first position

prie-dieu \(,)prē-'dyə(r), prē-dyœ̄\ *noun, plural* **prie-dieux** \-'dyə(r)(z), -dyœ̄(z)\ [French, literally, pray God] (1760)
1 : a kneeling bench designed for use by a person at prayer and fitted with a raised shelf on which the elbows or a book may be rested

2 : a low armless upholstered chair with a high straight back

prie-dieu 1

pri·er \'prī-(ə)r\ *noun* (1552)
: one that pries; *especially* : an inquisitive person

priest \'prēst\ *noun* [Middle English *preist*, from Old English *prēost*, ultimately from Late Latin *presbyter* — more at PRESBYTER] (before 12th century)
: one authorized to perform the sacred rites of a religion especially as a mediatory agent between humans and God; *specifically* : an Anglican, Eastern Orthodox, or Roman Catholic clergyman ranking below a bishop and above a deacon

priest·ess \'prēs-təs\ *noun* (1693)
1 : a woman authorized to perform the sacred rites of a religion
2 : a woman regarded as a leader (as of a movement)
usage see -ESS

priest·hood \'prēst-,hùd, 'prē-,stùd\ *noun* (before 12th century)
1 : the office, dignity, or character of a priest
2 : the whole body of priests

priest·ly \'prēst-lē\ *adjective* (before 12th century)
1 : of or relating to a priest or the priesthood : SACERDOTAL
2 : characteristic of or befitting a priest
— **priest·li·ness** *noun*

priest–rid·den \'prēst-,ri-dᵊn\ *adjective* (1653)
: controlled or oppressed by a priest

¹prig \'prig\ *noun* [*prig* to steal] (1610)
: THIEF

²prig *noun* [probably from ¹*prig*] (1676)
1 *archaic* : FOP
2 *archaic* : FELLOW, PERSON
3 : one who offends or irritates by observance of proprieties (as of speech or manners) in a pointed manner or to an obnoxious degree
— **prig·gery** \-gə-rē\ *noun*
— **prig·gish** \'pri-gish\ *adjective*
— **prig·gish·ly** *adverb*
— **prig·gish·ness** *noun*

prig·gism \'pri-,gi-zəm\ *noun* (circa 1805)
: stilted adherence to convention

¹prill \'pril\ *transitive verb* [origin unknown] (1944)
: to convert (as a molten solid) into spherical pellets usually by forming into drops in a spray and allowing the drops to solidify

²prill *noun* (1952)
: a pellet made by prilling

¹prim \'prim\ *transitive verb* **primmed; prim·ming** [origin unknown] (1706)
1 : to give a prim or demure expression to ⟨*primming* her thin lips after every mouthful —John Buchan⟩
2 : to dress primly

²prim *adjective* **prim·mer; prim·mest** (1709)
1 a : stiffly formal and proper : DECOROUS **b** : PRUDISH
2 : NEAT, TRIM ⟨*prim* hedges⟩
— **prim·ly** *adverb*
— **prim·ness** *noun*

pri·ma ballerina \'prē-mə-\ *noun* [Italian, leading ballerina] (1870)
: the principal female dancer in a ballet company

pri·ma·cy \'prī-mə-sē\ *noun* (14th century)
1 : the state of being first (as in importance, order, or rank) : PREEMINENCE ⟨the *primacy* of

intellectual and esthetic over materialistic values —T. R. McConnell
2 : the office, rank, or preeminence of an ecclesiastical primate

pri·ma don·na \ˌpri-mə-ˈdä-nə, ˌprē-\ *noun, plural* **prima donnas** [Italian, literally, first lady] (1782)
1 : a principal female singer in an opera or concert organization
2 : an extremely sensitive, vain, or undisciplined person

¹prima fa·cie \ˌprī-mə-ˈfā-shə, -shē, -sē *also* -shē-ˌē, -sē-ˌē\ *adverb* [Middle English, from Latin] (15th century)
: at first view : on the first appearance

²prima facie *adjective* (1800)
1 : true, valid, or sufficient at first impression : APPARENT ⟨the theory . . . gives a *prima facie* solution —R. J. Butler⟩
2 : SELF-EVIDENT
3 : legally sufficient to establish a fact or a case unless disproved ⟨*prima facie* evidence⟩

pri·mal \ˈprī-məl\ *adjective* [Medieval Latin *primalis*, from Latin *primus* first — more at PRIME] (1602)
1 : ORIGINAL, PRIMITIVE ⟨village life continued in its *primal* innocence —Van Wyck Brooks⟩
2 : first in importance : FUNDAMENTAL ⟨our *primal* concern⟩

pri·mal·i·ty \prī-ˈma-lə-tē\ *noun* (1919)
: the property of being a prime number

primal scream therapy *noun* (1971)
: psychotherapy in which the patient recalls and reenacts a particularly disturbing past experience usually occurring early in life and expresses normally repressed anger or frustration especially through spontaneous and unrestrained screams, hysteria, or violence — called also *primal therapy*

pri·mar·i·ly \prī-ˈmer-ə-lē *also* prə-, *chiefly British* ˈprī-mər-ə-lē\ *adverb* (1601)
1 : for the most part : CHIEFLY ⟨has now become *primarily* a residential town —S. P. B. Mais⟩
2 : in the first place : ORIGINALLY

¹pri·ma·ry \ˈprī-ˌmer-ē, ˈprī-mə-rē, ˈprim-rē\ *adjective* [Middle English, from Late Latin *primarius* basic, primary, from Latin, principal, from *primus*] (15th century)
1 a : first in order of time or development : PRIMITIVE ⟨the *primary* stage of civilization⟩ **b** : of or relating to formations of the Paleozoic and earlier periods
2 a : of first rank, importance, or value : PRINCIPAL ⟨the *primary* purpose⟩ **b** : BASIC, FUNDAMENTAL ⟨security is a *primary* need⟩ **c** : of, relating to, or constituting the principal quills of a bird's wing **d** : of or relating to agriculture, forestry, and the extractive industries or their products **e** : expressive of present or future time ⟨*primary* tense⟩ **f** : of, relating to, or constituting the strongest of the three or four degrees of stress recognized by most linguists ⟨the first syllable of *basketball* carries *primary* stress⟩
3 a : DIRECT, FIRSTHAND ⟨*primary* sources of information⟩ **b** : not derivable from other colors, odors, or tastes **c** : preparatory to something else in a continuing process ⟨*primary* instruction⟩ **d** : of or relating to a primary school ⟨*primary* education⟩ **e** : belonging to the first group or order in successive divisions, combinations, or ramifications ⟨*primary* nerves⟩ **f** : of, relating to, or constituting the inducing current or its circuit in an induction coil or transformer **g** : directly derived from ores ⟨*primary* metals⟩ **h** : of, relating to, or being the amino acid sequence in proteins ⟨*primary* protein structure⟩
4 : resulting from the substitution of one of two or more atoms or groups in a molecule; *especially* : being or characterized by a carbon atom having a bond to only one other carbon atom

5 : of, relating to, involving, or derived from primary meristem ⟨*primary* tissue⟩ ⟨*primary* growth⟩
6 : of, relating to, or involved in the production of organic substances by green plants ⟨*primary* productivity⟩

²primary *noun, plural* **-ries** (circa 1772)
1 : something that stands first in rank, importance, or value : FUNDAMENTAL — usually used in plural
2 : the celestial body around which one or more other celestial bodies revolve; *especially* : the more massive usually brighter component of a binary star system
3 : one of the usually 9 or 10 strong quills on the distal joint of a bird's wing — see WING illustration
4 a : PRIMARY COLOR **b** : a primary-color sensation
5 a : CAUCUS **b** : an election in which qualified voters nominate or express a preference for a particular candidate or group of candidates for political office, choose party officials, or select delegates for a party convention
6 : the coil that is connected to the source of electricity in an induction coil or transformer — called also *primary coil*

primary atypical pneumonia *noun* (circa 1944)
: any of a group of pneumonias (as Q fever and psittacosis) caused especially by viruses, mycoplasmas, rickettsias, and chlamydias

primary cell *noun* (1902)
: a cell that converts chemical energy into electrical energy by irreversible chemical reactions

primary color *noun* (1612)
: any of a set of colors from which all other colors may be derived

primary meristem *noun* (1875)
: meristem (as procambium) derived from the apical meristem

primary root *noun* (circa 1890)
: the root of a plant that develops first and originates from the radicle

primary school *noun* (1802)
1 : a school usually including the first three grades of elementary school but sometimes also including kindergarten
2 : ELEMENTARY SCHOOL

primary syphilis *noun* (circa 1890)
: the first stage of syphilis that is marked by the development of a chancre and the spread of the causative spirochete in the tissues of the body

primary tooth *noun* (circa 1898)
: MILK TOOTH

primary wall *noun* (circa 1933)
: the first-formed wall of a plant cell that is produced around the protoplast and usually has plasmodesmata

pri·mate \ˈprī-ˌmāt *or especially for 1* -mət\ *noun* [Middle English *primat*, from Old French, from Medieval Latin *primat-, primas* archbishop, from Latin, leader, from *primus*] (13th century)
1 *often capitalized* : a bishop who has precedence in a province, group of provinces, or a nation
2 *archaic* : one first in authority or rank : LEADER
3 [New Latin *Primates*, from Latin, plural of *primat-, primas*] : any of an order (Primates) of mammals comprising humans, apes, monkeys, and related forms (as lemurs and tarsiers)
— **pri·mate·ship** \-ˌship\ *noun*
— **pri·ma·tial** \prī-ˈmā-shəl\ *adjective*

pri·ma·tol·o·gy \ˌprī-mə-ˈtä-lə-jē\ *noun* (1926)
: the study of primates especially other than recent humans (*Homo sapiens*)
— **pri·ma·to·log·i·cal** \-mə-tᵊl-ˈä-ji-kəl\ *adjective*
— **pri·ma·tol·o·gist** \-mə-ˈtä-lə-jist\ *noun*

¹prime \ˈprīm\ *noun* [Middle English, from Old English *prīm*, from Latin *prima hora* first hour] (before 12th century)
1 a *often capitalized* : the second of the canonical hours **b** : the first hour of the day usually considered either as 6 a.m. or the hour of sunrise
2 a : the earliest stage **b** : SPRING **c** : YOUTH
3 : the most active, thriving, or successful stage or period ⟨in the *prime* of his life⟩
4 : the chief or best individual or part : PICK ⟨*prime* of the flock, and choicest of the stall —Alexander Pope⟩
5 : PRIME NUMBER
6 a : the first note or tone of a musical scale : TONIC **b** : the interval between two notes on the same staff degree
7 : the symbol ′
8 : PRIME RATE

²prime *adjective* [Middle English, from Middle French, feminine of *prin* first, from Latin *primus*; akin to Latin *prior*] (14th century)
1 : first in time : ORIGINAL
2 a : of, relating to, or being a prime number — compare RELATIVELY PRIME **b** : having no polynomial factors other than itself and no monomial factors other than 1 ⟨a *prime* polynomial⟩ **c** : expressed as a product of prime factors (as prime numbers and prime polynomials) ⟨a *prime* factorization⟩
3 a : first in rank, authority, or significance : PRINCIPAL **b** : having the highest quality or value ⟨*prime* farmland⟩ **c** : of the highest grade regularly marketed — used of meat and especially beef
4 : not deriving from something else : PRIMARY
— **prime·ly** *adverb*
— **prime·ness** *noun*

³prime *verb* **primed; prim·ing** [probably from ¹*prime*] (1513)
transitive verb
1 : FILL, LOAD
2 a : to prepare for firing by supplying with priming **b** : to insert a primer into (a cartridge case)
3 : to apply the first color, coating, or preparation to ⟨*prime* a wall⟩
4 : to put into working order by filling or charging with something ⟨*prime* a pump with water⟩
5 : to instruct beforehand : COACH ⟨*primed* the witness⟩
6 : STIMULATE
intransitive verb
: to become prime
— **prime the pump** : to take steps to encourage the growth or functioning of something

prime cost *noun* (1718)
: the combined total of raw material and direct labor costs incurred in production; *broadly* : cost less vendor's or agent's commission for charges

prime meridian *noun* (circa 1859)
: the meridian of 0 degrees longitude which runs through the original site of the Royal Observatory at Greenwich, England, and from which other longitudes are reckoned

prime minister *noun* (1655)
1 : the chief minister of a ruler or state
2 : the official head of a cabinet or ministry; *especially* : the chief executive of a parliamentary government
— **prime ministerial** *adjective*
— **prime ministership** *noun*
— **prime ministry** *noun*

prime mover *noun* [translation of Medieval Latin *primus motor*] (1809)
1 a : an initial source of motive power (as a windmill, waterwheel, turbine, or internal combustion engine) designed to receive and modify force and motion as supplied by some

natural source and apply them to drive machinery **b** : a powerful tractor or truck usually with all-wheel drive
2 : the self-moved being that is the source of all motion
3 : the original or most effective force in an undertaking or work ⟨education is . . . a *prime mover* of cultural and societal change —R. C. Buck⟩

prime number *noun* (1570)
: any integer other than 0 or ± 1 that is not divisible without remainder by any other integers except ± 1 and ± the integer itself

¹prim·er \'pri-mər, *chiefly British* 'prī-mər\ *noun* [Middle English, from Medieval Latin *primarium*, from Late Latin, neuter of *primarius* primary] (14th century)
1 : a small book for teaching children to read
2 : a small introductory book on a subject

²prim·er \'prī-mər\ *noun* (1819)
1 : a device for priming; *especially* : a cap, tube, or wafer containing percussion powder or compound used to ignite an explosive charge
2 : material used in priming a surface — called also *prime coat*
3 : a molecule (as a short strand of RNA or DNA) whose presence is required for formation of another molecule (as a longer chain of DNA)

prime rate *noun* (1958)
: an interest rate formally announced by a bank to be the lowest available at a particular time to its most credit-worthy customers — called also *prime interest rate*

pri·me·ro \pri-'mer-(,)ō, -'mir-\ *noun* [modification of Spanish *primera*, from feminine of *primer* first, from Latin *primarius*] (1533)
: a card game popular in the 16th and 17th centuries

prime time *noun* (1958)
1 : the time period when the television or radio audience is the largest; *also* : prime-time television
2 : the choicest or busiest time
— **prime–time** *adjective*

pri·me·val \prī-'mē-vəl\ *adjective* [Latin *primaevus*, from *primus* first + *aevum* age — more at AYE] (1662)
1 : of or relating to the earliest ages (as of the world or human history) : ANCIENT, PRIMITIVE ⟨100 acres of *primeval* forest which has never felt an ax —Mary R. Zimmer⟩
2 : PRIMORDIAL 1b
— **pri·me·val·ly** \-və-lē\ *adverb*

priming *noun* (15th century)
1 : the act of one that primes
2 : the explosive used in priming a charge
3 : ²PRIMER 2

pri·mip·a·ra \prī-'mi-pə-rə\ *noun, plural* **-ras** *or* **-rae** \-,rē, -,rī\ [Latin, from *primus* first + *-para* -para] (circa 1842)
1 : an individual bearing a first offspring
2 : an individual that has borne only one offspring
— **pri·mip·a·rous** \prī-'mi-pə-rəs\ *adjective*

¹prim·i·tive \'pri-mə-tiv\ *adjective* [Middle English *primitif*, from Latin *primitivus* first formed, from *primitiae* first fruits, from *primus* first — more at PRIME] (14th century)
1 a : not derived : ORIGINAL, PRIMARY **b** : assumed as a basis; *especially* : AXIOMATIC ⟨*primitive* concepts⟩
2 a : of or relating to the earliest age or period : PRIMEVAL ⟨the *primitive* church⟩ **b** : closely approximating an early ancestral type : little evolved ⟨*primitive* mammals⟩ **c** : belonging to or characteristic of an early stage of development : CRUDE, RUDIMENTARY ⟨*primitive* technology⟩ **d** : of, relating to, or constituting the assumed parent speech of related languages ⟨*primitive* Germanic⟩
3 a : ELEMENTAL, NATURAL ⟨our *primitive* feelings of vengeance —John Mackwood⟩ **b** : of, relating to, or produced by a people or culture that is nonindustrial and often nonliterate and

tribal ⟨*primitive* art⟩ **c** : NAIVE **d** (1) : SELF-TAUGHT, UNTUTORED ⟨*primitive* craftsmen⟩ (2) : produced by a self-taught artist ⟨a *primitive* painting⟩
— **prim·i·tive·ly** *adverb*
— **prim·i·tive·ness** *noun*
— **prim·i·tiv·i·ty** \,pri-mə-'ti-və-tē\ *noun*

²primitive *noun* (15th century)
1 a : something primitive; *specifically* : a primitive idea, term, or proposition **b** : a root word
2 a (1) : an artist of an early period of a culture or artistic movement (2) : a later imitator or follower of such an artist **b** (1) : a self-taught artist (2) : an artist whose work is marked by directness and naïveté **c** : a work of art produced by a primitive artist **d** : a typically rough or simple usually handmade and antique home accessory or furnishing
3 a : a member of a primitive people **b** : an unsophisticated person

prim·i·tiv·ism \'pri-mə-ti-,vi-zəm\ *noun* (1861)
1 a : belief in the superiority of a simple way of life close to nature **b** : belief in the superiority of nonindustrial society to that of the present
2 : the style of art of primitive peoples or primitive artists
— **prim·i·tiv·ist** \-vist\ *noun or adjective*
— **prim·i·tiv·is·tic** \,pri-mə-ti-'vis-tik\ *adjective*

¹pri·mo \'prē-(,)mō\ *noun, plural* **primos** [Italian, from *primo* first, from Latin *primus*] (1792)
: the first or leading part (as in a duet or trio)

²pri·mo \'prē-(,)mō, 'prī-\ *adverb* [Latin, from *primus*] (circa 1901)
: in the first place

³pri·mo \'prē-(,)mō\ *adjective* [probably from Italian, chief, first] (1972)
slang : of the finest quality : EXCELLENT

pri·mo·gen·i·tor \,prī-mō-'je-nə-tər\ *noun* [Late Latin, from Latin *primus* + *genitor* begetter, from *gignere* to beget — more at KIN] (1654)
: ANCESTOR, FOREFATHER

pri·mo·gen·i·ture \-,chùr, -chər, -,tyùr, -,tùr\ *noun* [Late Latin *primogenitura*, from Latin *primus* + *genitura* birth, from *genitus*, past participle of *gignere*] (1602)
1 : the state of being the firstborn of the children of the same parents
2 : an exclusive right of inheritance belonging to the eldest son

pri·mor·di·al \prī-'mòr-dē-əl\ *adjective* [Middle English, from Late Latin *primordialis*, from Latin *primordium* origin, from *primus* first + *ordiri* to begin — more at PRIME, ORDER] (14th century)
1 a : first created or developed : PRIMEVAL 1 b : existing in or persisting from the beginning (as of a solar system or universe) ⟨a *primordial* gas cloud⟩ **c** : earliest formed in the growth of an individual or organ : PRIMITIVE
2 : FUNDAMENTAL, PRIMARY ⟨*primordial* human joys —Sir Winston Churchill⟩
— **pri·mor·di·al·ly** \-dē-ə-lē\ *adverb*

pri·mor·di·um \-dē-əm\ *noun, plural* **-dia** \-dē-ə\ [New Latin, from Latin] (1671)
: the rudiment or commencement of a part or organ

primp \'primp\ *verb* [perhaps alteration of ¹*prim*] (1801)
transitive verb
: to dress, adorn, or arrange in a careful or finicky manner
intransitive verb
: to dress or groom oneself carefully ⟨*primps* for hours before a date⟩

prim·rose \'prim-,rōz\ *noun* [Middle English *primerose*, from Middle French, from *prime* (feminine of *prin* prime) + *rose* rose — more at PRIME, ROSE] (14th century)
: any of a genus (*Primula* of the family Primulaceae, the primrose family) of perennial herbs

with large tufted basal leaves and showy variously colored flowers — compare EVENING PRIMROSE

primrose path *noun* (1602)
1 : a path of ease or pleasure and especially sensual pleasure ⟨himself the *primrose path* of dalliance treads —Shakespeare⟩
2 : a path of least resistance

primrose yellow *noun* (1882)
1 : a light to moderate greenish yellow
2 : a light to moderate yellow

prim·u·la \'prim-yə-lə\ *noun* [Medieval Latin, from *primula veris*, literally, first fruit of spring] (1753)
: PRIMROSE

pri·mum mo·bi·le \'prī-məm-'mō-bə-lē, 'prē-\ *noun, plural* **primum mobiles** [Middle English, from Medieval Latin, literally, first moving thing] (15th century)
: the outermost concentric sphere conceived in medieval astronomy as carrying the spheres of the fixed stars and the planets in its daily revolution

pri·mus \'prī-məs\ *noun, often capitalized* [Medieval Latin, one who is first, magnate, from Latin, first — more at PRIME] (1724)
: the presiding bishop of the Scottish Episcopal Church

pri·mus in·ter pa·res \'prī-məs-,in-tər-'par-ēz, 'prē-,məs-\ *noun* [Latin] (1813)
: first among equals

prince \'prin(t)s\ *noun* [Middle English, from Old French, from Latin *princip-, princeps* leader, initiator, from *primus* first + *capere* to take — more at HEAVE] (13th century)
1 a : MONARCH, KING **b** : the ruler of a principality or state
2 : a male member of a royal family; *especially* : a son of the sovereign
3 : a nobleman of varying rank and status
4 : one likened to a prince; *especially* : a man of high rank or of high standing in his class or profession
— **prince·ship** \'prin(t)s-,ship\ *noun*

Prince Al·bert \-'al-bərt\ *noun* [*Prince Albert* Edward (later Edward VII king of England)] (1884)
: a double-breasted frock coat with the upper part fitted to the body

Prince Charming *noun* [*Prince Charming*, hero of the fairy tale *Cinderella* by Charles Perrault] (1862)
: a suitor who fulfills the dreams of his beloved; *also* : a man of often specious charm toward women

prince consort *noun, plural* **princes consort** (1861)
: the husband of a reigning queen

Prince Albert

prince·dom \'prin(t)s-dəm, -təm\ *noun* (1560)
1 : the jurisdiction, sovereignty, rank, or estate of a prince
2 : PRINCIPALITY 3 — usually used in plural

prince·let \'prin(t)s-lət\ *noun* (1682)
: PRINCELING

prince·li·ness \-lē-nəs\ *noun* (1571)
1 : princely conduct or character
2 : LUXURY, MAGNIFICENCE

prince·ling \'prin(t)s-liŋ\ *noun* (1794)
: a petty or insignificant prince

prince·ly \'prin(t)s-lē\ *adjective* **prince·li·er; -est** (15th century)
1 : of or relating to a prince : ROYAL
2 : befitting a prince : NOBLE, MAGNIFICENT ⟨*princely* manners⟩ ⟨a *princely* sum⟩
— **princely** *adverb*

\ə\ abut \ʾ\ kitten \ər\ further \a\ ash \ā\ ace \ä\ mop, mar \aù\ out \ch\ chin \e\ bet \ē\ easy \g\ go \i\ hit \ī\ ice \j\ job \ŋ\ sing \ō\ go \ò\ law \òi\ boy \th\ thin \th\ the \ü\ loot \ù\ foot \y\ yet \zh\ vision *see also* Guide to Pronunciation

Prince of Wales \-'wā(ə)lz\ (15th century)
: the male heir apparent to the British throne — used as a title only after it has been specifically conferred by the sovereign

prince's–feath·er \'prin(t)-səz-,fe-thər\ *noun* (1629)
: a showy widely cultivated annual plant (*Amaranthus hybridus erythrostachys*) of the amaranth family having dense usually red spikes of flowers

¹**prin·cess** \'prin(t)-səs, 'prin-,ses, (*British usually*) prin-'ses\ *noun* (14th century)
1 *archaic* : a woman having sovereign power
2 : a female member of a royal family; *especially* : a daughter or granddaughter of a sovereign
3 : the consort of a prince
4 : one likened to a princess; *especially* : a woman of high rank or of high standing in her class or profession ⟨a pop music *princess*⟩

²**princess** *same as* ¹\ *or* **prin·cesse** \prin-'ses\ *adjective* [French *princesse* princess, from *prince*] (1867)
: close-fitting and usually with gores from neck to flaring hemline ⟨a *princess* gown⟩

Princess Royal *noun, plural* **Princesses Royal** (circa 1649)
: the eldest daughter of a British sovereign — a title granted for life and used only after it has been specifically conferred by the sovereign

¹**prin·ci·pal** \'prin(t)-s(ə-)pəl, -sə-bəl\ *adjective* [Middle English, from Old French, from Latin *principalis,* from *princip-, princeps*] (14th century)
1 : most important, consequential, or influential : CHIEF
2 : of, relating to, or constituting principal or a principal
usage *see* PRINCIPLE
— **prin·ci·pal·ly** \-sə-p(ə-)lē, -sə-bə-lē, -splē\ *adverb*

²**principal** *noun* (14th century)
1 : a person who has controlling authority or is in a leading position: as **a** : a chief or head man or woman **b** : the chief executive officer of an educational institution **c** : one who employs another to act as agent subject to the employer's general control and instruction; *specifically* : the person from whom an agent's authority derives **d** : the chief or an actual participant in a crime **e** : the person primarily or ultimately liable on a legal obligation **f** : a leading performer : STAR
2 : a matter or thing of primary importance: as **a** (1) : a capital sum placed at interest, due as a debt, or used as a fund (2) : the corpus of an estate, portion, devise, or bequest **b** : the construction that gives shape and strength to a roof and is usually one of several trusses; *broadly* : the most important member of a piece of framing
usage *see* PRINCIPLE
— **prin·ci·pal·ship** \'prin(t)-s(ə-)pəl-,ship, -sə-bəl-\ *noun*

principal diagonal *noun* (1965)
: the diagonal in a square matrix that runs from upper left to lower right

prin·ci·pal·i·ty \,prin(t)-sə-'pa-lə-tē\ *noun, plural* **-ties** (14th century)
1 a : the state, office, or authority of a prince **b** : the position or responsibilities of a principal (as of a school)
2 : the territory or jurisdiction of a prince : the country that gives title to a prince
3 *plural* : an order of angels — *see* CELESTIAL HIERARCHY

principal parts *noun plural* (1870)
: a series of verb forms from which all the other forms of a verb can be derived including in English the infinitive, the past tense, and the present and past participles

prin·cip·i·um \prin-'si-pē-əm, prin-'ki-\ *noun, plural* **-ia** \-pē-ə\ [Latin, beginning, basis] (1600)
: a fundamental principle

prin·ci·ple \'prin(t)-s(ə-)pəl, -sə-bəl\ *noun* [Middle English, modification of Middle French *principe,* from Latin *principium* beginning, from *princip-, princeps* initiator — more at PRINCE] (14th century)
1 a : a comprehensive and fundamental law, doctrine, or assumption **b** (1) : a rule or code of conduct (2) : habitual devotion to right principles ⟨a man of *principle*⟩ **c** : the laws or facts of nature underlying the working of an artificial device
2 : a primary source : ORIGIN
3 a : an underlying faculty or endowment ⟨such *principles* of human nature as greed and curiosity⟩ **b** : an ingredient (as a chemical) that exhibits or imparts a characteristic quality
4 *capitalized, Christian Science* : a divine principle : GOD ☐
— **in principle** : with respect to fundamentals ⟨prepared to accept the proposition *in principle*⟩

prin·ci·pled \-s(ə-)pəld, -sə-bəld\ *adjective* (1642)
: exhibiting, based on, or characterized by principle — often used in combination

prin·cox \'prin-,käks, 'priŋ-\ *noun* [origin unknown] (1540)
archaic : a pert youth : COXCOMB

prink \'priŋk\ *verb* [probably alteration of ²*prank*] (1576)
: PRIMP
— **prink·er** *noun*

¹**print** \'print\ *noun* [Middle English *preinte,* from Middle French, from *preint,* past participle of *preindre* to press, from Latin *premere* — more at PRESS] (14th century)
1 a : a mark made by pressure : IMPRESSION **b** : something impressed with a print or formed in a mold
2 a : printed state or form **b** : the printing industry
3 a : PRINTED MATTER **b** *plural* : printed publications
4 : printed letters : TYPE
5 a (1) : a copy made by printing (2) : a reproduction of an original work of art (as a painting) made by a photomechanical process (3) : an original work of art (as a woodcut, etching, or lithograph) intended for graphic reproduction and produced by or under the supervision of the artist who designed it **b** : cloth with a pattern or figured design applied by printing; *also* : an article of such cloth **c** : a photographic or motion-picture copy; *especially* : one made from a negative
— **in print** : procurable from the publisher
— **out of print** : not procurable from the publisher

²**print** (14th century)
transitive verb
1 a : to impress something in or on **b** : to stamp (as a mark) in or on something
2 a : to make a copy of by impressing paper against an inked printing surface **b** (1) : to impress (as wallpaper) with a design or pattern (2) : to impress (a pattern or design) on something **c** : to publish in print **d** : PRINT OUT; *also* : to display on a surface (as a computer screen) for viewing
3 : to write in letters shaped like those of ordinary roman text type
4 : to make (a positive picture) on a sensitized photographic surface from a negative or a positive
intransitive verb
1 a : to work as a printer **b** : to produce printed matter
2 : to produce something in printed form
3 : to write or hand-letter in imitation of unjoined printed characters

³**print** *adjective* (1953)
: of, relating to, or writing for printed publications ⟨*print* journalists⟩

print·able \'prin-tə-bəl\ *adjective* (1837)
1 : capable of being printed or of being printed from

2 : considered fit to publish
— **print·abil·i·ty** \,prin-tə-'bi-lə-tē\ *noun*

printed circuit *noun* (1946)
: a circuit for electronic apparatus made by depositing conductive material in continuous paths from terminal to terminal on an insulating surface

printed matter *noun* (1876)
: matter printed by any of various mechanical processes that is eligible for mailing at a special rate

print·er \'prin-tər\ *noun* (1504)
: one that prints: as **a** : a person engaged in printing **b** : a device used for printing; *especially* : a machine for printing from photographic negatives **c** : a device (as a dot matrix printer) that produces printout

printer's devil *noun* (1763)
: an apprentice in a printing office

print·ery \'prin-tə-rē\ *noun, plural* **-er·ies** (1638)
: PRINTING OFFICE

print·head \'print-,hed\ *noun* (1968)
: a usually movable part of a computer printer that contains the printing elements

print·ing *noun* (14th century)
1 : the act or product of one that prints
2 : reproduction in printed form
3 : the art, practice, or business of a printer
4 : IMPRESSION 4c
5 *plural* : paper to be printed on

printing office *noun* (1733)
: an establishment where printing is done

printing press *noun* (1588)
: a machine that produces printed copies

print·less \'print-ləs\ *adjective* (1610)
: making, bearing, or taking no imprint

print·mak·ing \-,mā-kiŋ\ *noun* (1928)
: the design and production of prints by an artist
— **print·mak·er** \-kər\ *noun*

print·out \'print-,aut\ *noun* (1953)
: a printed record produced automatically (as by a computer)

print out *transitive verb* (1953)
: to make a printout of

pri·on \'prē-,än\ *noun* [*pro*tinaceous + *infec*tious + ²*-on*] (1982)
: a protein particle that lacks nucleic acid and is sometimes held to be the cause of various infectious diseases of the nervous system (as scrapie and Creutzfeldt-Jakob disease)

¹**pri·or** \'prī-(ə)r\ *noun* [Middle English, from Old English & Old French; both from Medieval Latin, from Late Latin, administrator, from Latin, former, superior] (before 12th century)
1 : the superior ranking next to the abbot of a monastery
2 : the superior of a house or group of houses of any of various religious communities
— **pri·or·ate** \'prī-ə-rət\ *noun*
— **pri·or·ship** \'prī-(ə)r-,ship\ *noun*

²**prior** *adjective* [Latin, former, superior, comparative of Old Latin *pri* before; akin to Latin *priscus* ancient, *prae* before — more at FOR] (1714)
1 : earlier in time or order : PREVIOUS ⟨by *prior* agreement⟩
2 : taking precedence (as in importance)
synonym *see* PRECEDING
— **pri·or·ly** *adverb*

pri·or·ess \'prī-ə-rəs\ *noun* (14th century)
: a nun corresponding in rank to a prior

☐ USAGE
principle Although nearly every handbook and many dictionaries warn against confusing *principle* and *principal,* many people still do. *Principle* is only a noun; *principal* is both adjective and noun. If you are unsure which noun you want, read the definitions in this dictionary.

pri·or·i·tize \prī-'ȯr-ə-ˌtīz, -'är-; 'prī-ə-rə-\ *transitive verb* **-tized; -tiz·ing** (1964)
: to list or rate (as projects or goals) in order of priority
usage see -IZE
— **pri·or·i·ti·za·tion** \prī-ˌȯr-ə-tə-'zā-shən, -är-; ˌprī-ə-rə-\ *noun*

pri·or·i·ty \prī-'ȯr-ə-tē, -'är-\ *noun, plural* **-ties** (14th century)
1 a (1) : the quality or state of being prior (2) : precedence in date or position of publication — used of taxa **b** (1) : superiority in rank, position, or privilege (2) : legal precedence in exercise of rights over the same subject matter
2 : a preferential rating; *especially* : one that allocates rights to goods and services usually in limited supply ⟨that project has top *priority*⟩
3 : something given or meriting attention before competing alternatives

prior restraint *noun* (1951)
: governmental prohibition imposed on expression before the expression actually takes place

prior to *preposition* (1714)
: in advance of : BEFORE □

pri·o·ry \'prī-(ə-)rē\ *noun, plural* **-ries** [Middle English *priorie*, from Anglo-French, from Medieval Latin *prioria*, from *prior*] (13th century)
: a religious house under a prior or prioress

prise \'prīz\ *chiefly British variant of* ⁵PRIZE

prism \'pri-zəm\ *noun* [Late Latin *prismat-, prisma*, from Greek, literally, anything sawn, from *priein* to saw] (1570)
1 : a polyhedron with two polygonal faces lying in parallel planes and with the other faces parallelograms
2 a : a transparent body that is bounded in part by two nonparallel plane faces and is used to refract or disperse a beam of light **b** : a prism-shaped decorative glass luster
3 : a crystal form whose faces are parallel to one axis; *especially* : one whose faces are parallel to the vertical axis
4 : a medium that distorts, slants, or colors whatever is viewed through it

pris·mat·ic \priz-'ma-tik\ *adjective* (1709)
1 : relating to, resembling, or constituting a prism
2 a : formed by a prism **b** : resembling the colors formed by refraction of light through a prism ⟨*prismatic* effects⟩
3 : highly colored : BRILLIANT ⟨*prismatic* lyrics⟩
4 : having such symmetry that a general form with faces cutting all axes at unspecified intercepts is a prism ⟨*prismatic* crystals⟩
— **pris·mat·i·cal·ly** \-ti-k(ə-)lē\ *adverb*

pris·ma·toid \'priz-mə-ˌtȯid\ *noun* [Late Latin *prismat-, prisma* prism] (circa 1890)
: a polyhedron that has all of its vertices in two parallel planes

pris·moid \'priz-ˌmȯid\ *noun* (circa 1704)
: a prismatoid whose parallel bases have the same number of sides
— **pris·moi·dal** \priz-'mȯi-dᵊl\ *adjective*

¹pris·on \'pri-zᵊn\ *noun* [Middle English, from Old French, from Latin *prehension-, prehensio* act of seizing, from *prehendere* to seize — more at GET] (12th century)
1 : a state of confinement or captivity
2 : a place of confinement especially for lawbreakers; *specifically* : an institution (as one under state jurisdiction) for confinement of persons convicted of serious crimes — compare JAIL

²prison *transitive verb* (14th century)
: IMPRISON, CONFINE

prison camp *noun* (circa 1908)
1 : a camp for the confinement of reasonably trustworthy prisoners usually employed on government projects
2 : a camp for prisoners of war or political prisoners

pris·on·er \'priz-nər, 'pri-zᵊn-ər\ *noun* (14th century)

1 : a person deprived of liberty and kept under involuntary restraint, confinement, or custody; *especially* : one on trial or in prison
2 : someone restrained as if in prison ⟨a *prisoner* of her own conscience⟩

prisoner of war (1678)
: a person captured in war; *especially* : a member of the armed forces of a nation who is taken by the enemy during combat

prisoner's base *noun* (circa 1773)
: a game in which players on each of two teams seek to tag and imprison players of the other team who have ventured out of their home territory

pris·sy \'pri-sē\ *adjective* **pris·si·er; -est** [probably blend of *prim* and *sissy*] (1895)
: being prim and precise : FINICKY
— **pris·si·ly** \'pri-sə-lē\ *adverb*
— **pris·si·ness** \'pri-sē-nəs\ *noun*

pris·tane \'pris-ˌtān\ *noun* [Latin *pristis* shark, sawfish; from its occurrence in the liver oils of sharks] (1923)
: an isoprenoid hydrocarbon $C_{19}H_{40}$ that usually accompanies phytane

pris·tine \'pris-ˌtēn, pris-'tēn, *especially British* 'pris-ˌtīn\ *adjective* [Latin *pristinus*; akin to Latin *prior*] (1534)
1 : belonging to the earliest period or state : ORIGINAL ⟨the hypothetical *pristine* lunar atmosphere⟩
2 a : not spoiled, corrupted, or polluted (as by civilization) : PURE ⟨a *pristine* forest⟩ **b** : fresh and clean as or as if new ⟨*pristine* hard-backs in uniform editions to fill our built-in bookcases —Michiko Kakutani⟩
— **pris·tine·ly** *adverb*

prith·ee \'pri-thē, -thē\ *interjection* [alteration of (*I*) *pray thee*] (circa 1591)
archaic — used to express a wish or request

pri·va·cy \'prī-və-sē, *especially British* 'pri-\ *noun, plural* **-cies** (15th century)
1 a : the quality or state of being apart from company or observation : SECLUSION **b** : freedom from unauthorized intrusion ⟨one's right to *privacy*⟩
2 *archaic* : a place of seclusion
3 a : SECRECY **b** : a private matter : SECRET

pri·vat·do·cent *or* **pri·vat·do·zent** \pri-'vät-(ˌ)dō(t)-ˌsent\ *noun* [German *Privatdozent*, from *privat* private + *Dozent* teacher, from Latin *docent-, docens*, present participle of *docēre* to teach — more at DOCILE] (1854)
: an unsalaried university lecturer or teacher in German-speaking countries remunerated directly by students' fees

¹pri·vate \'prī-vət\ *adjective* [Middle English *privat*, from Latin *privatus*, from past participle of *privare* to deprive, release, from *privus* private, individual; probably akin to Latin *pro* for, in front of — more at FOR] (14th century)
1 a : intended for or restricted to the use of a particular person, group, or class ⟨a *private* park⟩ **b** : belonging to or concerning an individual person, company, or interest ⟨a *private* house⟩ **c** (1) : restricted to the individual or arising independently of others ⟨*private* opinion⟩ (2) : carried on by the individual independently of the usual institutions ⟨*private* study⟩; *also* : being educated by independent study or a tutor or in a private school ⟨*private* students⟩ **d** : not general in effect ⟨a *private* statute⟩ **e** : of, relating to, or receiving hospital service in which the patient has more privileges than a semiprivate or ward patient
2 a (1) : not holding public office or employment ⟨a *private* citizen⟩ (2) : not related to one's official position : PERSONAL ⟨*private* correspondence⟩ **b** : being a private ⟨a *private* soldier⟩
3 a : withdrawn from company or observation : SEQUESTERED ⟨a *private* retreat⟩ **b** : not known or intended to be known publicly : SECRET **c** : preferring to keep personal affairs to oneself : valuing privacy highly **d** : unsuitable for public use or display

4 : not having shares that can be freely traded on the open market ⟨a *private* company⟩
— **pri·vate·ly** *adverb*
— **pri·vate·ness** *noun*

²private *noun* (15th century)
1 *archaic* : one not in public office
2 *obsolete* : PRIVACY
3 *plural* : PRIVATE PARTS
4 a : a person of low rank in various organizations (as a police or fire department) **b** : an enlisted man of the lowest rank in the marine corps or of one of the two lowest ranks in the army
— **in private** : not openly or in public

private detective *noun* (1868)
: PRIVATE INVESTIGATOR

private enterprise *noun* (1844)
: FREE ENTERPRISE

pri·va·teer \ˌprī-və-'tir\ *noun* (1664)
: an armed private ship licensed to attack enemy shipping; *also* : a sailor on such a ship
— **privateer** *intransitive verb*

private eye *noun* (1938)
: PRIVATE INVESTIGATOR

private first class *noun* (1918)
: an enlisted man ranking in the army above a private and below a corporal and in the marine corps above a private and below a lance corporal

private investigator *noun* (1940)
: a person not a member of a police force who is licensed to do detective work (as investigation of suspected wrongdoing or searching for missing persons)

private law *noun* (1773)
: a branch of law concerned with private persons, property, and relationships — compare PUBLIC LAW

private parts *noun plural* (1785)
: the external genital and excretory organs

private school *noun* (1857)
: a school that is established, conducted, and primarily supported by a nongovernmental agency

private treaty *noun* (1858)
: a sale of property on terms determined by conference of the seller and buyer — compare AUCTION

pri·va·tion \prī-'vā-shən\ *noun* [Middle English *privacion*, from Middle French *privation*, from Latin *privation-, privatio*, from *privare* to deprive] (14th century)
1 : an act or instance of depriving : DEPRIVATION
2 : the state of being deprived; *especially* : lack of what is needed for existence

pri·vat·ise *British variant of* PRIVATIZE

pri·vat·ism \'prī-və-ˌti-zəm\ *noun* [*private*] (1950)
: the attitude of being uncommitted to or avoiding involvement in anything beyond one's immediate interests

□ USAGE
prior to Sometimes termed pompous or affected, *prior to* is a synonym of *before* that most often appears in rather formal contexts, such as the annual reports of corporations. It may occasionally emphasize the notion of anticipation ⟨if page makeup decisions are verified and approved *prior to* typesetting, proofreading of pages afterward becomes unnecessary —*Publishers Weekly*⟩. It is also used sometimes in less formal contexts ⟨they have taught her how to walk (which I thought she did rather well *prior to* the expenditure of the 200 bucks) —Groucho Marx (letter)⟩.

\ə\ **abut** \ᵊ\ **kitten** \ər\ **further** \a\ **ash** \ā\ **ace**
\ä\ **mop, mar** \au̇\ **out** \ch\ **chin** \e\ **bet** \ē\ **easy**
\g\ **go** \i\ **hit** \ī\ **ice** \j\ **job** \ŋ\ **sing** \ō\ **go**
\ȯ\ **law** \ȯi\ **boy** \th\ **thin** \t͟h\ **the** \ü\ **loot** \u̇\ **foot**
\y\ **yet** \zh\ **vision** *see also* Guide to Pronunciation

¹priv·a·tive \'pri-və-tiv\ adjective (14th century)
: constituting or predicating privation or absence of a quality (as the prefixes a-, un-, non-)
— **priv·a·tive·ly** adverb
²priv·a·tive noun (1588)
: a privative term, expression, or proposition; also : a privative prefix or suffix
priv·at·ize \'prī-və-ˌtīz\ transitive verb (1948)
: to make private; especially : to change (as a business or industry) from public to private control or ownership
— **pri·vat·iza·tion** \ˌprī-və-tə-'zā-shən\ noun
priv·et \'pri-vət\ noun [origin unknown] (1542)
: a European deciduous shrub (Ligustrum vulgare) of the olive family with semievergreen leaves and small white flowers that is widely used for hedges; broadly : any of various congeneric shrubs
¹priv·i·lege \'priv-lij, 'pri-və-\ noun [Middle English, from Old French, from Latin privilegium law for or against a private person, from privus private + leg-, lex law] (12th century)
: a right or immunity granted as a peculiar benefit, advantage, or favor : PREROGATIVE; especially : such a right or immunity attached specifically to a position or an office
²privilege transitive verb -leged; -leg·ing (14th century)
: to grant a privilege to
priv·i·leged \-lijd\ adjective (14th century)
1 : having or enjoying one or more privileges ⟨privileged classes⟩
2 : not subject to the usual rules or penalties because of some special circumstance; especially : not subject to disclosure in a court of law ⟨a privileged communication⟩
priv·i·ty \'pri-və-tē\ noun, plural -ties [Middle English privite privacy, secret, from Old French privité, from Medieval Latin privitat-, privitas, from Latin privus private — more at PRIVATE] (1523)
1 a : a relationship between persons who successively have a legal interest in the same right or property **b** : an interest in a transaction, contract, or legal action to which one is not a party arising out of a relationship to one of the parties
2 : private or joint knowledge of a private matter; especially : cognizance implying concurrence
¹privy \'pri-vē\ adjective [Middle English prive, from Old French privé, from Latin privatus private] (14th century)
1 a : PRIVATE, WITHDRAWN **b** : SECRET
2 : belonging or relating to a person in one's individual rather than official capacity
3 : admitted as one sharing in a secret ⟨privy to the conspiracy⟩
— **priv·i·ly** \-və-lē\ adverb
²privy noun, plural priv·ies (14th century)
1 a : a small building having a bench with holes through which the user may defecate or urinate **b** : TOILET 3b
2 : a person having a legal interest of privity
privy council noun (14th century)
1 archaic : a secret or private council
2 P&C capitalized : a body of officials and dignitaries chosen by the British monarch as an advisory council to the Crown usually functioning through its committees
3 : a usually appointive advisory council to an executive
— **privy councillor** noun
privy purse noun (1765)
: an allowance for the private expenses of the British sovereign
prix fixe \'prē-'fēks, -'fiks\ noun [French, fixed price] (1883)
: a complete meal offered at a fixed price; also : the price charged

¹prize \'prīz\ noun [Middle English pris prize, price — more at PRICE]
1 : something offered or striven for in competition or in contests of chance; also : PREMIUM 1d
2 : something exceptionally desirable
3 archaic : a contest for a reward : COMPETITION
²prize adjective (1803)
1 a : awarded or worthy of a prize **b** : awarded as a prize **c** : entered for the sake of a prize ⟨a prize drawing⟩
2 : outstanding of a kind ⟨raised prize hogs⟩
³prize transitive verb prized; priz·ing [Middle English prisen, from Middle French prisier, from Late Latin pretiare, from Latin pretium price, value — more at PRICE] (14th century)
1 : to estimate the value of : RATE
2 : to value highly : ESTEEM
synonym see APPRECIATE
⁴prize noun [Middle English prise, from Middle French, act of taking, from prendre to take, from Latin prehendere — more at GET] (14th century)
1 : something taken by force, stratagem, or threat; especially : property lawfully captured at sea in time of war
2 : an act of capturing or taking; especially : the wartime capture of a ship and its cargo at sea
synonym see SPOIL
⁵prize transitive verb prized; priz·ing [prize lever] (1686)
: to press, force, or move with a lever : PRY
prize·fight \'prīz-ˌfīt\ noun (1824)
: a professional boxing match
— **prize·fight·er** \-ˌfī-tər\ noun
prize·fight·ing \-ˌfī-tiŋ\ noun (1706)
: professional boxing
prize money noun (1748)
1 : a part of the proceeds of a captured ship formerly divided among the officers and men making the capture
2 : money offered in prizes
priz·er \'prī-zər\ noun (1599)
archaic : one that contends for a prize
prize·win·ner \'prīz-ˌwi-nər\ noun (1893)
: a winner of a prize
prize·win·ning \-ˌwi-niŋ\ adjective (1919)
: having won or of a quality to win a prize ⟨a prizewinning design⟩
¹pro \'prō\ noun, plural pros [Middle English, from Latin, preposition, for — more at FOR] (15th century)
1 : an argument or evidence in affirmation ⟨an appraisal of the pros and cons⟩
2 : the affirmative side or one holding it
²pro adverb [pro-] (15th century)
: on the affirmative side : in affirmation ⟨much has been written pro and con⟩
³pro preposition [Latin] (1837)
: in favor of
⁴pro noun or adjective (1866)
: PROFESSIONAL
¹pro- prefix [Middle English, from Old French, from Latin, from Greek, before, forward, forth, for, from pro — more at FOR]
1 a : earlier than : prior to : before ⟨prothalamion⟩ **b** : rudimentary : PROT- ⟨pronucleus⟩ **c** : precursory ⟨proinsulin⟩
2 a : located in front of or at the front of : anterior to ⟨procephalic⟩ ⟨proventriculus⟩ **b** : front : anterior ⟨prothorax⟩
3 : projecting ⟨prognathous⟩
²pro- prefix [Latin pro in front of, before, for, forward — more at FOR]
1 : taking the place of : substituting for ⟨procathedral⟩ ⟨procaine⟩
2 : favoring : supporting : championing ⟨pro-American⟩
proa \'prō-ə\ variant of PRAU
pro·abor·tion \ˌprō-ə-'bȯr-shən\ adjective (1972)
: favoring the legalization of abortion
— **pro–abor·tion·ist** \-sh(ə-)nist\ noun

pro·ac·tive \(ˌ)prō-'ak-tiv\ adjective (1933)
1 [¹pro-] : relating to, caused by, or being interference between previous learning and the recall or performance of later learning ⟨proactive inhibition of memory⟩
2 [²pro- + reactive] : acting in anticipation of future problems, needs, or changes
prob·a·bi·lism \'prä-bə-bə-ˌli-zəm\ noun [French probabilisme, from Latin probabilis probable] (circa 1843)
1 : a theory that in disputed moral questions any solidly probable course may be followed even though an opposed course is or appears more probable
2 : a theory that certainty is impossible especially in the sciences and that probability suffices to govern belief and action
— **prob·a·bi·list** \-list\ adjective or noun
prob·a·bi·lis·tic \ˌprä-bə-bə-'lis-tik\ adjective (1864)
1 : of or relating to probabilism
2 : of, relating to, or based on probability
— **prob·a·bi·lis·ti·cal·ly** adverb
prob·a·bil·i·ty \ˌprä-bə-'bi-lə-tē\ noun, plural -ties (15th century)
1 : the quality or state of being probable
2 : something (as an event or circumstance) that is probable
3 a (1) : the ratio of the number of outcomes in an exhaustive set of equally likely outcomes that produce a given event to the total number of possible outcomes (2) : the chance that a given event will occur **b** : a branch of mathematics concerned with the study of probabilities
4 : a logical relation between statements such that evidence confirming one confirms the other to some degree
probability density noun (1939)
: PROBABILITY DENSITY FUNCTION; also : a particular value of a probability density function
probability density function noun (1957)
1 : PROBABILITY FUNCTION
2 : a function of a continuous random variable whose integral over an interval gives the probability that its value will fall within the interval
probability distribution noun (1937)
: PROBABILITY FUNCTION; also : PROBABILITY DENSITY FUNCTION 2
probability function noun (1906)
: a function of a discrete random variable that gives the probability that a specified value will occur
¹prob·a·ble \'prä-bə-bəl, 'prä(b)-bəl\ adjective [Middle English, provable, from Middle French, from Latin probabilis commendable, probable, from probare to test, approve, prove — more at PROVE] (1606)
1 : supported by evidence strong enough to establish presumption but not proof ⟨a probable hypothesis⟩
2 : establishing a probability ⟨probable evidence⟩
3 : likely to be or become true or real ⟨probable events⟩
²probable noun (1647)
: one that is probable
probable cause noun (circa 1676)
: a reasonable ground for supposing that a charge is well-founded
prob·a·bly \'prä-bə-blē, 'prä(b)-blē\ adverb (1613)
: insofar as seems reasonably true, factual, or to be expected : without much doubt ⟨is probably happy⟩ ⟨it will probably rain⟩
pro·band \'prō-ˌband, prō-'\ noun [Latin probandus, gerundive of probare] (circa 1929)
: SUBJECT 3c(2)
pro·bang \'prō-ˌbaŋ\ noun [origin unknown] (1657)
: a slender flexible rod with a sponge on one end used especially for removing obstructions from the esophagus
¹pro·bate \'prō-ˌbāt, British also -bit\ noun [Middle English probat, from Latin probatum,

neuter of *probatus,* past participle of *probare*] (15th century)
1 a : the action or process of proving before a competent judicial authority that a document offered for official recognition and registration as the last will and testament of a deceased person is genuine **b :** the judicial determination of the validity of a will
2 : the officially authenticated copy of a probated will
²**pro·bate** \-ˌbāt\ *transitive verb* **pro·bat·ed; pro·bat·ing** (1570)
1 : to establish (a will) by probate as genuine and valid
2 : to put (a convicted offender) on probation
probate court *noun* (circa 1847)
: a court that has jurisdiction chiefly over the probate of wills and administration of deceased persons' estates
pro·ba·tion \prō-'bā-shən\ *noun* [Middle English *probacioun,* from Middle French *probation,* from Latin *probation-, probatio,* from *probare*] (15th century)
1 : critical examination and evaluation or subjection to such examination and evaluation
2 a : subjection of an individual to a period of testing and trial to ascertain fitness (as for a job or school) **b :** the action of suspending the sentence of a convicted offender and giving the offender freedom during good behavior under the supervision of a probation officer **c :** the state or a period of being subject to probation
 — **pro·ba·tion·al** \-shnəl, -shə-nᵊl\ *adjective*
 — **pro·ba·tion·al·ly** *adverb*
 — **pro·ba·tion·ary** \-shə-ˌner-ē\ *adjective*
pro·ba·tion·er \-sh(ə-)nər\ *noun* (1603)
1 : a person (as a newly admitted student nurse) whose fitness is being tested during a trial period
2 : a convicted offender on probation
probation officer *noun* (1880)
: an officer appointed to investigate, report on, and supervise the conduct of convicted offenders on probation
pro·ba·tive \'prō-bə-tiv\ *adjective* (15th century)
1 : serving to test or try **:** EXPLORATORY
2 : serving to prove **:** SUBSTANTIATING
pro·ba·to·ry \'prō-bə-ˌtōr-ē, -ˌtȯr-\ *adjective* (1625)
: PROBATIVE
¹**probe** \'prōb\ *noun* [Medieval Latin *proba* examination, from Latin *probare*] (1580)
1 : a slender medical instrument used especially for exploration (as of a wound or bodily cavity)
2 a : any of various testing devices or substances: as (1) **:** a pointed metal tip for making electrical contact with a circuit element being checked (2) **:** a usually small object that is inserted into something so as to test conditions at a given point (3) **:** a device used to penetrate or send back information especially from outer space or a celestial body (4) **:** a device (as an ultrasound generator) or a substance (as DNA in genetic research) used to obtain specific information for diagnostic or experimental purposes **b :** a pipe on the receiving airplane thrust into the drogue of the delivering airplane in air refueling
3 a : the action of probing **b :** a penetrating or critical investigation **c :** a tentative exploratory advance or survey
²**probe** *verb* **probed; prob·ing** (1649)
transitive verb
1 : to search into and explore with great thoroughness **:** subject to a penetrating investigation
2 : to examine with a probe ⟨unmanned vehicles *probed* space⟩
intransitive verb
: to make a searching exploratory investigation
 synonym see ENTER

 — **prob·er** *noun*
pro·ben·e·cid \prō-'be-nə-səd\ *noun* [irregular from *propyl* + *benzoic acid*] (1950)
: a drug $C_{13}H_{19}NO_4S$ that acts on renal tubular function and is used to increase the concentration of some drugs (as penicillin) in the blood by inhibiting their excretion and to increase the excretion of urates in gout
prob·it \'prä-bət\ *noun* [*prob*ability un*it*] (1934)
: a unit of measurement of statistical probability based on deviations from the mean of a normal distribution
pro·bi·ty \'prō-bə-tē\ *noun* [Middle English *probite,* from Middle French *probité,* from Latin *probitat-, probitas,* from *probus* honest — more at PROVE] (15th century)
: adherence to the highest principles and ideals
: UPRIGHTNESS
 synonym see HONESTY
¹**prob·lem** \'prä-bləm, -bᵊm, -ˌblem\ *noun* [Middle English *probleme,* from Middle French, from Latin *problema,* from Greek *problēma,* literally, obstacle, from *proballein* to throw forward, from *pro-* forward + *ballein* to throw — more at PRO-, DEVIL] (14th century)
1 a : a question raised for inquiry, consideration, or solution **b :** a proposition in mathematics or physics stating something to be done
2 a : an intricate unsettled question **b :** a source of perplexity, distress, or vexation **c :** difficulty in understanding or accepting ⟨I have a *problem* with your saying that⟩
 synonym see MYSTERY
²**problem** *adjective* (1894)
1 : dealing with a problem of conduct or social relationship ⟨a *problem* play⟩
2 : difficult to deal with ⟨a *problem* child⟩
¹**prob·lem·at·ic** \ˌprä-blə-'ma-tik\ *or* **prob·lem·at·i·cal** \-ti-kəl\ *adjective* (1609)
1 a : posing a problem **:** difficult to solve or decide **b :** not definite or settled **:** UNCERTAIN ⟨their future remains *problematic*⟩ **c :** open to question or debate **:** QUESTIONABLE
2 : expressing or supporting a possibility
 synonym see DOUBTFUL
 — **prob·lem·at·i·cal·ly** \-ti-k(ə-)lē\ *adverb*
²**problematic** *noun* (1957)
: something that is problematic **:** a problematic aspect or concern
pro bono \ˌprō-'bō-(ˌ)nō\ *adjective* [Latin *pro bono publico* for the public good] (1970)
: being, involving, or doing legal work donated especially for the public good ⟨*pro bono* work⟩
pro·bos·ci·de·an \prə-ˌbä-sə-'dē-ən\ *or* **pro·bos·cid·i·an** \prə-ˌbä-'si-dē-ən, (ˌ)prō-\ *noun* [ultimately from Latin *proboscid-, proboscis*] (circa 1859)
: any of an order (Proboscidea) of large mammals comprising the elephants and extinct related forms
 — **proboscidean** *adjective*
pro·bos·cis \prə-'bä-səs, -'bäs-kəs\ *noun, plural* **-bos·cis·es** *also* **-bos·ci·des** \-'bä-sə-ˌdēz\ [Latin, from Greek *proboskis,* from *pro-* + *boskein* to feed] (1576)
1 a : the trunk of an elephant; *also :* any long flexible snout **b :** the human nose especially when prominent
2 : any of various elongated or extensible tubular processes (as the sucking organ of a butterfly) of the oral region of an invertebrate
pro·caine \'prō-ˌkān\ *noun* [International Scientific Vocabulary ²*pro-* + *-caine*] (1918)
: a basic ester $C_{13}H_{20}N_2O_2$ of para-aminobenzoic acid; *also :* its crystalline hydrochloride used as a local anesthetic
pro·cam·bi·um \(ˌ)prō-'kam-bē-əm\ *noun* [New Latin] (1875)
: the part of the primary meristem of a plant that forms cambium and primary vascular tissues
 — **pro·cam·bi·al** \-bē-əl\ *adjective*

pro·car·ba·zine \prō-'kär-bə-ˌzēn, -zən\ *noun* [*propyl* + *carb*amic *acid* + *azine*] (1965)
: an antineoplastic drug $C_{12}H_{19}N_3O$ that is a monoamine oxidase inhibitor used in the form of its hydrochloride especially in the palliative treatment of Hodgkin's disease
pro·cary·ote *variant of* PROKARYOTE
pro·ca·the·dral \ˌprō-kə-'thē-drəl\ *noun* (1868)
: a parish church used as a cathedral
¹**pro·ce·dur·al** \prə-'sē-jə-rəl, -'sēj-rəl\ *adjective* (1889)
: of or relating to procedure; *especially* **:** of or relating to the procedure used by courts or other bodies administering substantive law
 — **pro·ce·dur·al·ly** *adverb*
²**procedural** *noun* (1974)
: a realist crime novel with a specific focus ⟨a courtroom *procedural*⟩; *especially* **:** POLICE PROCEDURAL
procedural due process *noun* (1938)
: DUE PROCESS 1
pro·ce·dure \prə-'sē-jər\ *noun* [French *procédure,* from Middle French, from *proceder*] (circa 1611)
1 a : a particular way of accomplishing something or of acting **b :** a step in a procedure
2 a : a series of steps followed in a regular definite order ⟨legal *procedure*⟩ ⟨a surgical *procedure*⟩ **b :** a series of instructions for a computer that has a name by which it can be called into action
3 a : a traditional or established way of doing things **b :** PROTOCOL 3a
pro·ceed \prō-'sēd, prə-\ *intransitive verb* [Middle English *proceden,* from Middle French *proceder,* from Latin *procedere,* from *pro-* forward + *cedere* to go — more at PRO-] (14th century)
1 : to come forth from a source **:** ISSUE
2 a : to continue after a pause or interruption **b :** to go on in an orderly regulated way
3 a : to begin and carry on an action, process, or movement **b :** to be in the process of being accomplished
4 : to move along a course **:** ADVANCE
 synonym see SPRING
pro·ceed·ing *noun* (15th century)
1 : legal action ⟨a divorce *proceeding*⟩
2 : PROCEDURE
3 *plural* **:** EVENTS, HAPPENINGS
4 : TRANSACTION
5 *plural* **:** an official record of things said or done
pro·ceeds \'prō-ˌsēdz\ *noun plural* (1665)
1 : the total amount brought in ⟨the *proceeds* of a sale⟩
2 : the net amount received (as for a check or from an insurance settlement) after deduction of any discount or charges
pro·ce·phal·ic \ˌprō-sə-'fa-lik\ *adjective* (1874)
: relating to, forming, or situated on or near the front of the head
pro·cer·coid \(ˌ)prō-'sər-ˌkȯid\ *noun* [*pro-* + Greek *kerkos* tail] (1926)
: the solid first parasitic larva of some tapeworms that develops usually in the body cavity of a copepod
¹**pro·cess** \'prä-ˌses, 'prō-, -səs\ *noun, plural* **pro·cess·es** \-ˌse-səz, -sə-, -ˌsēz\ [Middle English *proces,* from Middle French, from Latin *processus,* from *procedere*] (14th century)
1 a : PROGRESS, ADVANCE ⟨in the *process* of time⟩ **b :** something going on **:** PROCEEDING
2 a (1) **:** a natural phenomenon marked by gradual changes that lead toward a particular

\ə\ abut \ᵊ\ kitten \ər\ further \a\ ash \ā\ ace
\ä\ mop, mar \au̇\ out \ch\ chin \e\ bet \ē\ easy
\g\ go \i\ hit \ī\ ice \j\ job \ŋ\ sing \ō\ go
\ȯ\ law \ȯi\ boy \th\ thin \t͟h\ the \ü\ loot \u̇\ foot
\y\ yet \zh\ vision *see also* Guide to Pronunciation

result ⟨the *process* of growth⟩ (2) **:** a natural continuing activity or function ⟨such life *processes* as breathing⟩ **b :** a series of actions or operations conducing to an end; *especially* **:** a continuous operation or treatment especially in manufacture
3 a : the whole course of proceedings in a legal action **b :** the summons, mandate, or writ used by a court to compel the appearance of the defendant in a legal action or compliance with its orders
4 : a prominent or projecting part of an organism or organic structure ⟨a bone *process*⟩
5 : ⁵CONK

²process *transitive verb* (1532)
1 a : to proceed against by law **:** PROSECUTE **b** (1) **:** to take out a summons against (2) **:** to serve a summons on
2 a : to subject to a special process or treatment (as in the course of manufacture) **b** (1) **:** to subject to or handle through an established usually routine set of procedures ⟨*process* insurance claims⟩ (2) **:** to subject to examination or analysis ⟨computers *process* data⟩ **c :** to work (hair) into a conk

³process *adjective* (1888)
1 : treated or made by a special process especially when involving synthesis or artificial modification
2 : made by or used in a mechanical or photomechanical duplicating process
3 : of or involving illusory effects usually introduced during processing of the film

⁴pro·cess \prə-ˈses\ *intransitive verb* [back-formation from ¹*procession*] (1814)
chiefly British **:** to move in a procession

process cheese *noun* (1926)
: a cheese made by blending several lots of cheese — called also *processed cheese*

pro·cess·ible or **pro·cess·able** \ˈprä-ˌse-sə-bəl, ˈprō-\ *adjective* (1954)
: suitable for processing **:** capable of being processed
— **pro·cess·ibil·i·ty** or **pro·cess·abil·i·ty** \ˌprä-ˌse-sə-ˈbi-lə-tē, ˌprō-\ *noun*

¹pro·ces·sion \prə-ˈse-shən\ *noun* [Middle English *processioun*, from Old French *procession*, from Late Latin & Latin; Late Latin *procession-*, *processio* religious procession, from Latin, act of proceeding, from *procedere*] (12th century)
1 a : a group of individuals moving along in an orderly often ceremonial way **b :** SUCCESSION, SEQUENCE
2 a : continuous forward movement **:** PROGRESSION **b :** EMANATION ⟨the Holy Spirit's *procession* from the Father⟩

²procession *intransitive verb* (1691)
archaic **:** to go in procession

¹pro·ces·sion·al \prə-ˈsesh-nəl, -ˈse-shə-nᵊl\ *noun* (15th century)
1 : a book containing material for a procession
2 : a musical composition (as a hymn) designed for a procession
3 : a ceremonial procession

²processional *adjective* (circa 1611)
: of, relating to, or moving in a procession
— **pro·ces·sion·al·ly** *adverb*

pro·ces·sor \ˈprä-ˌse-sər, ˈprō-\ *noun* (1909)
1 : one that processes ⟨scrap *processor*⟩ ⟨agricultural *processor*⟩
2 a (1) **:** COMPUTER (2) **:** the part of a computer system that operates on data — called also *central processing unit* **b :** a computer program (as a compiler) that puts another program into a form acceptable to the computer
3 : FOOD PROCESSOR

pro·cès-ver·bal \prō-ˌsā-vər-ˈbäl, -(ˌ)ver-\ *noun*, plural **pro·cès-ver·baux** \-ˈbō\ [French, literally, verbal trial] (1635)
: an official written record

pro-choice \(ˌ)prō-ˈchȯis\ *adjective* (1975)
: favoring the legalization of abortion
— **pro-choic·er** \-ˈchȯi-sər\ *noun*

pro·claim \prō-ˈklām, prə-\ *transitive verb* [Middle English *proclamen*, from Middle

French or Latin; Middle French *proclamer*, from Latin *proclamare*, from *pro-* before + *clamare* to cry out — more at PRO-, CLAIM] (14th century)
1 a : to declare publicly, typically insistently, proudly, or defiantly and in either speech or writing **:** ANNOUNCE **b :** to give outward indication of **:** SHOW
2 : to declare or declare to be solemnly, officially, or formally ⟨*proclaim* an amnesty⟩ ⟨*proclaim* the country a republic⟩
3 : to praise or glorify openly or publicly **:** EXTOL
synonym see DECLARE
— **pro·claim·er** *noun*

proc·la·ma·tion \ˌprä-klə-ˈmā-shən\ *noun* [Middle English *proclamacion*, from Middle French *proclamation*, from Latin *proclamation-*, *proclamatio*, from *proclamare*] (14th century)
1 : the action of proclaiming **:** the state of being proclaimed
2 : something proclaimed; *specifically* **:** an official formal public announcement

pro·clit·ic \(ˌ)prō-ˈkli-tik\ *noun* [New Latin *procliticus*, from Greek *pro-* + Late Latin *-cliticus* (as in *encliticus* enclitic)] (circa 1864)
: a clitic that is associated with a following word
— **proclitic** *adjective*

pro·cliv·i·ty \prō-ˈkli-və-tē\ *noun, plural* **-ties** [Latin *proclivitas*, from *proclivis* sloping, prone, from *pro-* forward + *clivus* slope — more at PRO-, DECLIVITY] (circa 1591)
: an inclination or predisposition toward something; *especially* **:** a strong inherent inclination toward something objectionable
synonym see LEANING

Proc·ne \ˈpräk-nē\ *noun* [Latin, from Greek *Proknē*]
: the wife of Tereus who is changed into a swallow while fleeing from him

pro·con·sul \(ˌ)prō-ˈkän(t)-səl\ *noun* [Middle English, from Latin, from *pro consule* for a consul] (14th century)
1 : a governor or military commander of an ancient Roman province
2 : an administrator in a modern colony, dependency, or occupied area usually with wide powers
— **pro·con·su·lar** \-s(ə-)lər\ *adjective*
— **pro·con·su·late** \-s(ə-)lət\ *noun*
— **pro·con·sul·ship** \-səl-ˌship\ *noun*

pro·cras·ti·nate \prə-ˈkras-tə-ˌnāt, prō-\ *verb* **-nat·ed; -nat·ing** [Latin *procrastinatus*, past participle of *procrastinare*, from *pro-* forward + *crastinus* of tomorrow, from *cras* tomorrow] (1588)
transitive verb
: to put off intentionally and habitually
intransitive verb
: to put off intentionally the doing of something that should be done
synonym see DELAY
— **pro·cras·ti·na·tion** \-ˌkras-tə-ˈnā-shən\ *noun*
— **pro·cras·ti·na·tor** \-ˈkras-tə-ˌnā-tər\ *noun*

pro·cre·ant \ˈprō-krē-ənt\ *adjective* (1588)
1 : producing offspring
2 *archaic* **:** of or relating to procreation

pro·cre·ate \-ˌāt\ *verb* **-at·ed; -at·ing** [Latin *procreatus*, past participle of *procreare*, from *pro-* forth + *creare* to create — more at PRO-, CREATE] (1536)
transitive verb
: to beget or bring forth (offspring) **:** PROPAGATE
intransitive verb
: to beget or bring forth offspring **:** REPRODUCE
— **pro·cre·ation** \ˌprō-krē-ˈā-shən\ *noun*
— **pro·cre·ative** \ˈprō-krē-ˌā-tiv\ *adjective*
— **pro·cre·ator** \-ˌā-tər\ *noun*

pro·crus·te·an \prə-ˈkrəs-tē-ən, prō-\ *adjective, often capitalized* (circa 1846)
1 : of, relating to, or typical of Procrustes

2 : marked by arbitrary often ruthless disregard of individual differences or special circumstances

procrustean bed *noun, often P capitalized* (1844)
: a scheme or pattern into which someone or something is arbitrarily forced

Pro·crus·tes \prə-ˈkrəs-(ˌ)tēz, prō-\ *noun* [Latin, from Greek *Prokroustēs*]
: a villainous son of Poseidon in Greek mythology who forces travelers to fit into his bed by stretching their bodies or cutting off their legs

pro·cryp·tic \(ˌ)prō-ˈkrip-tik\ *adjective* [*pro-* (as in *protect*) + *cryptic*] (1891)
: of, relating to, or being a concealing pattern or shade of coloring especially in insects

proc·to·dae·um \ˌpräk-tə-ˈdē-əm\ *noun, plural* **-daea** \-ˈdē-ə\ *or* **-dae·ums** [New Latin, from Greek *prōktos* anus + *hodos* way] (1878)
: the posterior ectodermal part of the alimentary canal formed in the embryo by invagination of the outer body wall

proc·tol·o·gy \präk-ˈtä-lə-jē\ *noun* [Greek *prōktos* + English *-logy*] (1899)
: a branch of medicine dealing with the structure and diseases of the anus, rectum, and sigmoid colon
— **proc·to·log·ic** \ˌpräk-tə-ˈlä-jik\ *or* **proc·to·log·i·cal** \-ji-kəl\ *adjective*
— **proc·tol·o·gist** \präk-ˈtä-lə-jist\ *noun*

proc·tor \ˈpräk-tər\ *noun* [Middle English *procutour* procurator, proctor, alteration of *procuratour*] (14th century)
: SUPERVISOR, MONITOR; *specifically* **:** one appointed to supervise students (as at an examination)
— **proctor** *verb*
— **proc·to·ri·al** \präk-ˈtōr-ē-əl, -ˈtȯr-\ *adjective*
— **proc·tor·ship** \ˈpräk-tər-ˌship\ *noun*

pro·cum·bent \prō-ˈkəm-bənt\ *adjective* [Latin *procumbent-*, *procumbens*, present participle of *procumbere* to fall or lean forward, from *pro-* forward + *-cumbere* to lie down] (1668)
1 : being or having stems that trail along the ground without rooting
2 : lying face down

proc·u·ra·tion \ˌprä-kyə-ˈrā-shən\ *noun* [Middle English *procuratioun*, from Middle French *procuration*, from Latin *procuration-*, *procuratio*, from *procurare*] (15th century)
1 a : the act of appointing another as one's agent or attorney **b :** the authority vested in one so appointed
2 : the action of obtaining something (as supplies) **:** PROCUREMENT

proc·u·ra·tor \ˈprä-kyə-ˌrā-tər\ *noun* (14th century)
1 : one that manages another's affairs **:** AGENT
2 : an officer of the Roman empire entrusted with management of the financial affairs of a province and often having administrative powers as agent of the emperor
— **proc·u·ra·to·ri·al** \ˌprä-kyə-rə-ˈtōr-ē-əl, -ˈtȯr-\ *adjective*

pro·cure \prə-ˈkyu̇r, prō-\ *verb* **pro·cured; pro·cur·ing** [Middle English, from Late Latin *procurare*, from Latin, to take care of, from *pro-* for + *cura* care] (14th century)
transitive verb
1 a : to get possession of **:** obtain by particular care and effort **b :** to get and make available for promiscuous sexual intercourse
2 : BRING ABOUT, ACHIEVE
intransitive verb
: to procure women
— **pro·cur·able** \-ˈkyu̇r-ə-bəl\ *adjective*
— **pro·cure·ment** \-ˈkyu̇r-mənt\ *noun*

pro·cur·er \-ˈkyu̇r-ər\ *noun* (1538)
: one that procures; *especially* **:** PANDER

Pro·cy·on \ˈprō-sē-ˌän, ˈprä-, -ən\ *noun* [Latin, from Greek *Prokyōn*, literally, fore-dog; from its rising before Sirius]

: the brightest star in the constellation Canis Minor

¹**prod** \'präd\ *verb* **prod·ded; prod·ding** [origin unknown] (1535)
transitive verb
1 a : to thrust a pointed instrument into **:** PRICK
b : to incite to action **:** STIR
2 : to poke or stir as if with a prod
intransitive verb
: to urge someone on
— **prod·der** *noun*

²**prod** *noun* (circa 1787)
1 : a pointed instrument used to prod
2 : an incitement to act

¹**prod·i·gal** \'prä-di-gəl\ *adjective* [Latin *prodigus*, from *prodigere* to drive away, squander, from *pro-, prod-* forth + *agere* to drive — more at PRO-, AGENT] (circa 1520)
1 : recklessly extravagant
2 : characterized by wasteful expenditure **:** LAVISH
3 : yielding abundantly **:** LUXURIANT — often used with *of* ⟨nature has been so *prodigal* of her bounty —H. T. Buckle⟩
synonym *see* PROFUSE
— **prod·i·gal·i·ty** \,prä-də-'ga-lə-tē\ *noun*
— **prod·i·gal·ly** \'prä-di-g(ə-)lē\ *adverb*

²**prodigal** *noun* (1596)
: one who spends or gives lavishly and foolishly

pro·di·gious \prə-'di-jəs\ *adjective* (15th century)
1 a *obsolete* **:** being an omen **:** PORTENTOUS **b** *archaic* **:** resembling or befitting a prodigy **:** STRANGE, UNUSUAL
2 : exciting amazement or wonder
3 : extraordinary in bulk, quantity, or degree **:** ENORMOUS
synonym *see* MONSTROUS
— **pro·di·gious·ly** *adverb*
— **pro·di·gious·ness** *noun*

prod·i·gy \'prä-də-jē\ *noun, plural* **-gies** [Middle English, from Latin *prodigium* omen, monster, from *pro-, prod-* + *-igium* (akin to *aio* I say) — more at ADAGE] (15th century)
1 a : a portentous event **:** OMEN **b :** something extraordinary or inexplicable
2 a : an extraordinary, marvelous, or unusual accomplishment, deed, or event **b :** a highly talented child or youth

pro·dro·mal \(,)prō-'drō-məl\ *adjective* (1716)
: PRECURSORY; *especially* **:** marked by prodromes

pro·drome \'prō-,drōm\ *noun* [French, literally, precursor, from Greek *prodromos*, from *pro-* before + *dromos* act of running, racecourse — more at PRO-, DROMEDARY] (circa 1834)
: a premonitory symptom of disease

¹**pro·duce** \prə-'düs, prō-, -'dyüs\ *verb* **pro·duced; pro·duc·ing** [Middle English (Scots), from Latin *producere*, from *pro-* forward + *ducere* to lead — more at TOW] (15th century)
transitive verb
1 : to offer to view or notice
2 : to give birth or rise to **:** YIELD
3 : to extend in length, area, or volume ⟨*produce* a side of a triangle⟩
4 : to present to the public on the stage or screen or over radio or television
5 a : to cause to have existence or to happen **:** BRING ABOUT **b :** to give being, form, or shape to **:** MAKE; *especially* **:** MANUFACTURE
6 : to compose, create, or bring out by intellectual or physical effort
7 : to cause to accrue
intransitive verb
: to bear, make, or yield something
— **pro·duc·ible** \-'dü-sə-bəl, -'dyü-\ *adjective*

²**pro·duce** \'prä-(,)düs, 'prō- *also* -(,)dyüs\ *noun* (1695)
1 a : something produced **b :** the amount produced **:** YIELD

2 : agricultural products and especially fresh fruits and vegetables as distinguished from grain and other staple crops
3 : the progeny usually of a female animal

pro·duc·er \prə-'dü-sər, prō-, -'dyü-\ *noun* (1513)
1 : one that produces; *especially* **:** one that grows agricultural products or manufactures crude materials into articles of use
2 : a furnace or apparatus that produces combustible gas to be used for fuel by circulating air or a mixture of air and steam through a layer of incandescent fuel
3 : a person who supervises or finances the production of a stage or screen production or radio or television program
4 : any of various organisms (as a green plant) which produce their own organic compounds from simple precursors (as carbon dioxide and inorganic nitrogen) and many of which are food sources for other organisms — compare CONSUMER

producer gas *noun* (1895)
: a fuel gas made in a producer and consisting chiefly of carbon monoxide, hydrogen, and nitrogen

producer goods *noun plural* (1948)
: goods (as tools and raw materials) used to produce other goods and satisfy human wants only indirectly

prod·uct \'prä-(,)dəkt\ *noun* [in sense 1, from Middle English, from Medieval Latin *productum*, from Latin, something produced, from neuter of *productus*, past participle of *producere*; in other senses, from Latin *productum*] (15th century)
1 : the number or expression resulting from the multiplication together of two or more numbers or expressions
2 a : something produced **b :** something resulting from or necessarily following from a set of conditions ⟨a *product* of his environment⟩
3 : the amount, quantity, or total produced
4 : CONJUNCTION 5

pro·duc·tion \prə-'dək-shən, prō-\ *noun* (15th century)
1 a : something produced **:** PRODUCT **b** (1) **:** a literary or artistic work (2) **:** a work presented on the stage or screen or over the air **c :** something exaggerated out of proportion to its importance
2 a : the act or process of producing **b :** the creation of utility; *especially* **:** the making of goods available for use
3 : total output especially of a commodity or an industry
— **pro·duc·tion·al** \-shnəl, -shə-nᵊl\ *adjective*

production control *noun* (1929)
: systematic planning, coordinating, and directing of all manufacturing activities and influences to insure having goods made on time, of adequate quality, and at reasonable cost

production line *noun* (1935)
: LINE 6j

pro·duc·tive \prə-'dək-tiv, prō-\ *adjective* (1612)
1 : having the quality or power of producing especially in abundance ⟨*productive* fishing waters⟩
2 : effective in bringing about ⟨investigating committees have been *productive* of much good —R. K. Carr⟩
3 a : yielding results, benefits, or profits **b :** yielding or devoted to the satisfaction of wants or the creation of utilities
4 : continuing to be used in the formation of new words or constructions ⟨*un-* is a *productive* prefix⟩
5 : raising mucus or sputum (as from the bronchi) ⟨a *productive* cough⟩
— **pro·duc·tive·ly** *adverb*
— **pro·duc·tive·ness** *noun*

pro·duc·tiv·i·ty \,prō-dək-'ti-və-tē, ,prä-, prə-, ,dək-\ *noun* (circa 1810)

1 : the quality or state of being productive
2 : rate of production especially of food by the utilization of solar energy by producer organisms

pro·em \'prō-,em, -əm\ *noun* [Middle English *proheme*, from Middle French, from Latin *prooemium*, from Greek *prooimion*, from *pro-* + *oimē* song; probably akin to Hittite *išamai-* song, Sanskrit *syati* he binds — more at SINEW] (14th century)
1 : preliminary comment **:** PREFACE
2 : PRELUDE
— **pro·emi·al** \prō-'ē-mē-əl, -'e-\ *adjective*

pro·en·zyme \(,)prō-'en-,zīm\ *noun* [International Scientific Vocabulary] (circa 1900)
: ZYMOGEN

pro·es·trus \(,)prō-'es-trəs\ *noun* [New Latin] (1923)
: a period immediately preceding estrus characterized by preparatory physiological changes

prof \'präf\ *noun* (1838)
: PROFESSOR

pro·fam·i·ly \,prō-'fam-lē, -'fa-mə-\ *adjective* (1926)
1 : favoring or encouraging traditional family structures and values
2 : opposing abortion and often birth control

prof·a·na·tion \,prä-fə-'nā-shən, ,prō-\ *noun* (1552)
: the act or an instance of profaning

pro·fa·na·to·ry \prō-'fa-nə-,tōr-ē, prə-, -'fä-, -,tȯr-\ *adjective* (1853)
: tending to profane **:** DESECRATING

¹**pro·fane** \prō-'fān, prə-\ *transitive verb* **pro·faned; pro·fan·ing** [Middle English *prophanen*, from Latin *profanare*, from *profanus*] (14th century)
1 : to treat (something sacred) with abuse, irreverence, or contempt **:** DESECRATE
2 : to debase by a wrong, unworthy, or vulgar use
— **pro·fan·er** *noun*

²**profane** *adjective* [Middle English *prophane*, from Middle French, from Latin *profanus*, from *pro-* before + *fanum* temple — more at PRO-, FEAST] (15th century)
1 : not concerned with religion or religious purposes **:** SECULAR
2 : not holy because unconsecrated, impure, or defiled **:** UNSANCTIFIED
3 : serving to debase or defile what is holy **:** IRREVERENT
4 a : not being among the initiated **b :** not possessing esoteric or expert knowledge
— **pro·fane·ly** *adverb*
— **pro·fane·ness** \-'fān-nəs\ *noun*

pro·fan·i·ty \prō-'fa-nə-tē, prə-\ *noun, plural* **-ties** (1607)
1 a : the quality or state of being profane **b :** the use of profane language
2 a : profane language **b :** an utterance of profane language

pro·fess \prə-'fes, prō-\ *verb* [in sense 1, from Middle English, from *profes*, adjective, having professed one's vows, from Middle French, from Late Latin *professus*, from Latin, past participle of *profitēri* to profess, confess, from *pro-* before + *fatēri* to acknowledge; in other senses, from Latin *professus*, past participle — more at CONFESS] (14th century)
transitive verb
1 : to receive formally into a religious community following a novitiate by acceptance of the required vows
2 a : to declare or admit openly or freely **:** AFFIRM **b :** to declare in words or appearances only **:** PRETEND, CLAIM
3 : to confess one's faith in or allegiance to

4 a : to practice or claim to be versed in (a calling or profession) **b :** to teach as a professor
intransitive verb
1 : to make a profession or avowal
2 *obsolete* **:** to profess friendship

pro·fessed \-'fest\ *adjective* (circa 1569)
1 : openly and freely declared or acknowledged **:** AFFIRMED
2 : professing to be qualified; *also* **:** EXPERT

pro·fessed·ly \prə-'fe-səd-lē, -'fest-lē\ *adverb* (1570)
1 : by profession or declaration **:** AVOWEDLY
2 : with pretense **:** ALLEGEDLY

pro·fes·sion \prə-'fe-shən\ *noun* [Middle English *professioun*, from Old French *profession*, from Late Latin & Latin; Late Latin *profession-, professio*, from Latin, public declaration, from *profitēri*] (13th century)
1 : the act of taking the vows of a religious community
2 : an act of openly declaring or publicly claiming a belief, faith, or opinion **:** PROTESTATION
3 : an avowed religious faith
4 a : a calling requiring specialized knowledge and often long and intensive academic preparation **b :** a principal calling, vocation, or employment **c :** the whole body of persons engaged in a calling

¹pro·fes·sion·al \prə-'fesh-nəl, -'fe-shə-n°l\ *adjective* (circa 1748)
1 a : of, relating to, or characteristic of a profession **b :** engaged in one of the learned professions **c** (1) **:** characterized by or conforming to the technical or ethical standards of a profession (2) **:** exhibiting a courteous, conscientious, and generally businesslike manner in the workplace
2 a : participating for gain or livelihood in an activity or field of endeavor often engaged in by amateurs ⟨a *professional* golfer⟩ **b :** having a particular profession as a permanent career ⟨a *professional* soldier⟩ **c :** engaged in by persons receiving financial return ⟨*professional* football⟩
3 : following a line of conduct as though it were a profession ⟨a *professional* patriot⟩
— **pro·fes·sion·al·ly** *adverb*

²professional *noun* (1811)
: one that is professional; *especially* **:** one that engages in a pursuit or activity professionally

professional corporation *noun* (1970)
: a corporation organized by one or more licensed individuals (as a doctor or lawyer) especially for the purpose of providing professional services and obtaining tax advantages

pro·fes·sion·al·ism \-'fesh-nə-,li-zəm, -'fe-shə-n°l-,i-\ *noun* (1856)
1 : the conduct, aims, or qualities that characterize or mark a profession or a professional person
2 : the following of a profession (as athletics) for gain or livelihood

pro·fes·sion·al·ize \-,līz, -,īz\ *transitive verb* **-ized; -iz·ing** (1856)
: to give a professional character to
— **pro·fes·sion·al·i·za·tion** \-,fesh-nə-lə-'zā-shən, -,fe-shə-n°l-ə-\ *noun*

pro·fes·sor \prə-'fe-sər\ *noun* (14th century)
1 : one that professes, avows, or declares
2 a : a faculty member of the highest academic rank at an institution of higher education **b :** a teacher at a university, college, or sometimes secondary school **c :** one that teaches or professes special knowledge of an art, sport, or occupation requiring skill
— **pro·fes·so·ri·al** \,prō-fə-'sōr-ē-əl, ,prä-, -'sòr-\ *adjective*
— **pro·fes·so·ri·al·ly** \-ē-ə-lē\ *adverb*
— **pro·fes·sor·ship** \prə-'fe-sər-,ship\ *noun*

pro·fes·sor·ate \prə-'fe-sə-rət\ *noun* (1860)
: the office, term of office, or position of a professor

pro·fes·so·ri·at \,prō-fə-'sōr-ē-ət, ,prä-, -'sòr-, -ē-,at\ *or* **pro·fes·so·ri·ate** \-ət, -,āt\ *noun* [modification of French *professorat*, from *professeur* professor, from Latin *professor*, from *profitēri*] (1858)
1 : the body of college and university teachers at an institution or in society
2 : the office, duties, or position of a professor

¹prof·fer \'prä-fər\ *transitive verb* **proffered; prof·fer·ing** \-f(ə-)riŋ\ [Middle English *profren*, from Anglo-French *profrer*, from Old French *poroffrir*, from *por-* forth (from Latin *pro-*) + *offrir* to offer — more at PRO-] (14th century)
: to present for acceptance **:** TENDER, OFFER

²proffer *noun* (14th century)
: OFFER, SUGGESTION

pro·fi·cien·cy \prə-'fi-shən(t)-sē\ *noun* (1544)
1 : advancement in knowledge or skill **:** PROGRESS
2 : the quality or state of being proficient

pro·fi·cient \-shənt\ *adjective* [Latin *proficient-, proficiens*, present participle of *proficere* to go forward, accomplish, from *pro-* forward + *facere* to make — more at PRO-, DO] (circa 1590)
: well advanced in an art, occupation, or branch of knowledge ☆
— **proficient** *noun*
— **pro·fi·cient·ly** *adverb*

¹pro·file \'prō-,fīl\ *noun* [Italian *profilo*, from *profilare* to draw in outline, from *pro-* forward (from Latin) + *filare* to spin, from Late Latin — more at FILE] (circa 1656)
1 : a representation of something in outline; *especially* **:** a human head or face represented or seen in a side view
2 : an outline seen or represented in sharp relief **:** CONTOUR
3 : a side or sectional elevation: as **a :** a drawing showing a vertical section of the ground **b :** a vertical section of a soil from the ground surface to the underlying unweathered material
4 : a set of data often in graphic form portraying the significant features of something ⟨a corporation's earnings *profile*⟩; *especially* **:** a graph representing the extent to which an individual exhibits traits or abilities as determined by tests or ratings
5 : a concise biographical sketch
6 : degree or level of public exposure ⟨trying to keep a low *profile*⟩ ⟨a job with a high *profile*⟩
synonym see OUTLINE

²profile *transitive verb* **pro·filed; pro·fil·ing** (1715)
1 : to represent in profile or by a profile **:** produce (as by drawing, writing, or graphing) a profile of
2 : to shape the outline of by passing a cutter around
— **pro·fil·er** *noun*

¹prof·it \'prä-fət\ *noun, often attributive* [Middle English, from Middle French, from Latin *profectus* advance, profit, from *proficere*] (14th century)
1 : a valuable return **:** GAIN
2 : the excess of returns over expenditure in a transaction or series of transactions; *especially* **:** the excess of the selling price of goods over their cost
3 : net income usually for a given period of time
4 : the ratio of profit for a given year to the amount of capital invested or to the value of sales
5 : the compensation accruing to entrepreneurs for the assumption of risk in business enterprise as distinguished from wages or rent
— **prof·it·less** \-ləs\ *adjective*
— **prof·it·wise** \-,wīz\ *adverb*

²profit (14th century)
intransitive verb
1 : to be of service or advantage **:** AVAIL
2 : to derive benefit **:** GAIN

3 : to make a profit
transitive verb
: to be of service to **:** BENEFIT

prof·it·able \'prä-fə-tə-bəl, 'präf-tə-bəl\ *adjective* (14th century)
: affording profits **:** yielding advantageous returns or results
— **prof·it·abil·i·ty** \,prä-fə-tə-'bi-lə-tē\ *noun*
— **prof·it·able·ness** \'prä-fə-tə-bəl-nəs\ *noun*
— **prof·it·ably** \-blē\ *adverb*

profit and loss *noun* (1588)
: a summary account used at the end of an accounting period to collect the balances of the nominal accounts so that the net profit or loss may be shown

prof·i·teer \,prä-fə-'tir\ *noun* (1912)
: one who makes what is considered an unreasonable profit especially on the sale of essential goods during times of emergency
— **profiteer** *intransitive verb*

pro·fit·er·ole \prə-'fi-tə-,rōl\ *noun* [French, perhaps from *profit* profit] (1884)
: a miniature cream puff with a sweet or savory filling

profit sharing *noun* (1881)
: a system or process under which employees receive a part of the profits of an industrial or commercial enterprise

profit system *noun* (1945)
: FREE ENTERPRISE

prof·li·ga·cy \'prä-fli-gə-sē\ *noun* (1738)
: the quality or state of being profligate

¹prof·li·gate \'prä-fli-gət, -,gāt\ *adjective* [Latin *profligatus*, from past participle of *profligare* to strike down, from *pro-* forward, down + *-fligare* (akin to *fligere* to strike); akin to Greek *phlibein* to squeeze] (1647)
1 : completely given up to dissipation and licentiousness
2 : wildly extravagant **:** PRODIGAL
— **prof·li·gate·ly** *adverb*

²profligate *noun* (1709)
: a person given to wildly extravagant and usually grossly self-indulgent expenditure

pro·flu·ent \'prä-,flü-ənt, 'prō-; prō-'flü-\ *adjective* [Middle English, from Latin *profluent-, profluens*, present participle of *profluere* to flow forth, from *pro-* forth + *fluere* to flow — more at PRO-, FLUID] (15th century)
: flowing copiously or smoothly

pro for·ma \(,)prō-'fòr-mə\ *adjective* [Latin, for form] (circa 1580)
1 : made or carried out in a perfunctory manner or as a formality
2 : provided in advance to prescribe form or describe items ⟨pro forma invoice⟩

¹pro·found \prə-'faund, prō-\ *adjective* [Middle English, from Middle French *profond* deep, from Latin *profundus*, from *pro-* before + *fundus* bottom — more at PRO-, BOTTOM] (14th century)
1 a : having intellectual depth and insight **b :** difficult to fathom or understand
2 a : extending far below the surface **b :** coming from, reaching to, or situated at a depth **:** DEEP-SEATED ⟨a *profound* sigh⟩

☆ SYNONYMS
Proficient, adept, skilled, skillful, expert mean having great knowledge and experience in a trade or profession. PROFICIENT implies a thorough competence derived from training and practice ⟨*proficient* in translating foreign languages⟩. ADEPT implies special aptitude as well as proficiency ⟨*adept* at doing long division⟩. SKILLED stresses mastery of technique ⟨a *skilled* surgeon⟩. SKILLFUL implies individual dexterity in execution or performance ⟨*skillful* drivers⟩. EXPERT implies extraordinary proficiency and often connotes knowledge as well as technical skill ⟨*expert* in the evaluation of wines⟩.

3 a : characterized by intensity of feeling or quality **b :** all encompassing **:** COMPLETE ⟨*profound* sleep⟩
— **pro·found·ly** \-'fau̇n(d)-lē\ *adverb*
— **pro·found·ness** \-'fau̇n(d)-nəs\ *noun*

²profound *noun* (1621)
archaic **:** something that is very deep; *specifically* **:** the depths of the sea

pro·fun·di·ty \prə-'fən-də-tē\ *noun, plural* **-ties** [Middle English *profundite*, from Middle French *profundité*, from Latin *profunditat-*, *profunditas* depth, from *profundus*] (15th century)
1 a : intellectual depth **b :** something profound or abstruse
2 : the quality or state of being profound or deep

pro·fuse \prə-'fyüs, prō-\ *adjective* [Middle English, from Latin *profusus*, past participle of *profundere* to pour forth, from *pro-* forth + *fundere* to pour — more at FOUND] (15th century)
1 : pouring forth liberally **:** EXTRAVAGANT ⟨*profuse* in their thanks⟩
2 : exhibiting great abundance **:** BOUNTIFUL ⟨a *profuse* harvest⟩ ☆
— **pro·fuse·ly** *adverb*
— **pro·fuse·ness** *noun*

pro·fu·sion \-'fyü-zhən\ *noun* (1545)
1 : lavish expenditure **:** EXTRAVAGANCE
2 : the quality or state of being profuse
3 : great quantity **:** lavish display or supply ⟨snow falling in *profusion*⟩

¹prog \'präg\ *intransitive verb* **progged; prog·ging** [origin unknown] (1624)
chiefly dialect **:** to search about; *especially* **:** FORAGE

²prog *noun* (1655)
chiefly dialect **:** FOOD, VICTUALS

pro·gen·i·tor \prō-'je-nə-tər, prə-\ *noun* [Middle English, from Middle French *progeniteur*, from Latin *progenitor*, from *pro-* forth + *gignere* to beget — more at KIN] (14th century)
1 a : an ancestor in the direct line **:** FOREFATHER **b :** a biologically ancestral form
2 : PRECURSOR, ORIGINATOR ⟨*progenitors* of socialist ideas —*Times Literary Supplement*⟩

prog·e·ny \'prä-jᵊn-ē\ *noun, plural* **-nies** [Middle English *progenie*, from Middle French, from Latin *progenies*, from *progignere*] (14th century)
1 a : DESCENDANTS, CHILDREN **b :** offspring of animals or plants
2 : OUTCOME, PRODUCT
3 : a body of followers, disciples, or successors

pro·ges·ta·tion·al \,prō-jes-'tā-shnəl, -shə-nᵊl\ *adjective* (1923)
: preceding pregnancy or gestation; *especially* **:** of, relating to, inducing, or constituting the modifications of the female mammalian system associated especially with ovulation and corpus luteum formation ⟨*progestational* hormones⟩

pro·ges·ter·one \prō-'jes-tə-,rōn\ *noun* [*progestin* + *-sterone*] (1935)
: a female steroid sex hormone $C_{21}H_{30}O_2$ that is secreted by the corpus luteum to prepare the endometrium for implantation and later by the placenta during pregnancy to prevent rejection of the developing embryo or fetus

pro·ges·tin \-'jes-tən\ *noun* [*pro-* + *gestation* + ¹*-in*] (1930)
: a progestational hormone; *especially* **:** PROGESTERONE

pro·ges·to·gen \-'jes-tə-jən\ *noun* [*progestational* + *-ogen* (as in *estrogen*)] (1942)
: any of several progestational steroids (as progesterone)
— **pro·ges·to·gen·ic** \-,jes-tə-'je-nik\ *adjective*

pro·glot·tid \(,)prō-'glä-təd\ *noun* [New Latin *proglottis*] (1878)
: a segment of a tapeworm containing both male and female reproductive organs

pro·glot·tis \(,)prō-'glä-təs\ *noun, plural* **-glot·ti·des** \-'glä-tə-,dēz\ [New Latin *proglottid-*, *proglottis*, from Greek *proglōttis* tip of the tongue, from *pro-* + *glōtta* tongue — more at GLOSS] (1855)
: PROGLOTTID

prog·na·thism \'präg-nə-,thi-zəm, präg-'nā-\ *noun* (circa 1864)
: prognathous condition

prog·na·thous \-thəs\ *adjective* (1836)
: having the jaws projecting beyond the upper part of the face

prog·no·sis \präg-'nō-səs\ *noun, plural* **-no·ses** \-,sēz\ [Late Latin, from Greek *prognōsis*, literally, foreknowledge, from *prognignōskein* to know before, from *pro-* + *gignōskein* to know — more at KNOW] (1655)
1 : the prospect of recovery as anticipated from the usual course of disease or peculiarities of the case
2 : FORECAST, PROGNOSTICATION

¹prog·nos·tic \präg-'näs-tik\ *noun* [Middle English *pronostique*, from Middle French, from Latin *prognosticum*, from Greek *prognōstikon*, from neuter of *prognōstikos* foretelling, from *progignōskein*] (14th century)
1 : something that foretells **:** PORTENT
2 : PROGNOSTICATION, PROPHECY

²prognostic *adjective* (1603)
: of, relating to, or serving as ground for prognostication or a prognosis ⟨*prognostic* weather charts⟩ ⟨favorable *prognostic* signs⟩

prog·nos·ti·cate \präg-'näs-tə-,kāt\ *transitive verb* **-cat·ed; -cat·ing** (15th century)
1 : to foretell from signs or symptoms **:** PREDICT
2 : PRESAGE
synonym see FORETELL
— **prog·nos·ti·ca·tive** \-,kā-tiv\ *adjective*
— **prog·nos·ti·ca·tor** \-,kā-tər\ *noun*

prog·nos·ti·ca·tion \(,)präg-,näs-tə-'kā-shən\ *noun* (15th century)
1 : an indication in advance **:** FORETOKEN
2 a : an act, the fact, or the power of prognosticating **:** FORECAST **b :** FOREBODING

pro·grade \'prō-,grād\ *adjective* [Latin *pro-* forward + English *-grade* (as in *retrograde*)] (1967)
: having or being a direction of rotation or revolution that is counterclockwise as viewed from the north pole of the sky or a planet

¹pro·gram \'prō-,gram, -grəm\ *noun* [French *programme* agenda, public notice, from Greek *programma*, from *prographein* to write before, from *pro-* before + *graphein* to write — more at CARVE] (1633)
1 [Late Latin *programma*, from Greek] **:** a public notice
2 a : a brief usually printed outline of the order to be followed, of the features to be presented, and the persons participating (as in a public exercise or performance) **b :** the performance of a program; *especially* **:** a performance broadcast on radio or television
3 : a plan or system under which action may be taken toward a goal
4 : CURRICULUM
5 : PROSPECTUS, SYLLABUS
6 a : a plan for the programming of a mechanism (as a computer) **b :** a sequence of coded instructions that can be inserted into a mechanism (as a computer); *also* **:** such a sequence that is part of an organism's genotype or behavioral repertoire

²program *also* **programme** *transitive verb* **-grammed** *or* **-gramed; -gram·ming** *or* **-gram·ing** (1896)
1 a : to arrange or furnish a program of or for **:** BILL **b :** to enter in a program
2 : to work out a sequence of operations to be performed by (a mechanism) **:** provide with a program

3 a : to insert a program for (a particular action) into or as if into a mechanism **b :** to control by or as if by a program **c** (1) **:** to code in an organism's program (2) **:** to provide with a biological program ⟨cells *programmed* to synthesize hemoglobin⟩
4 : to predetermine the thinking, behavior, or operations of as if by computer programming ⟨children are *programmed* into violence —Lisa A. Richette⟩
— **pro·gram·ma·bil·i·ty** \(,)prō-,gra-mə-'bi-lə-tē\ *noun*
— **pro·gram·ma·ble** \'prō-,gra-mə-bəl\ *adjective or noun*

program director *noun* (1953)
: one in charge of planning and scheduling program material for a radio or television station or network

pro·gram·mat·ic \,prō-grə-'ma-tik\ *adjective* (1896)
1 : relating to program music
2 : of, relating to, resembling, or having a program
— **pro·gram·mat·i·cal·ly** \-ti-k(ə-)lē\ *adverb*

programme *chiefly British variant of* PROGRAM

programmed instruction *noun* (1962)
: instruction through information given in small steps with each requiring a correct response by the learner before going on to the next step

pro·gram·mer *also* **pro·gram·er** \'prō-,gra-mər, -grə-\ *noun* (circa 1890)
: one that programs: as **a :** a person who prepares and tests programs for devices (as computers) **b :** one that programs a mechanism **c :** one that prepares instructional or educational programs

pro·gram·ming *also* **pro·gram·ing** \-miŋ\ *noun* (1940)
1 : the planning, scheduling, or performing of a program
2 a : the process of instructing or learning by means of an instructional program **b :** the process of preparing an instructional program

program music *noun* (1879)
: music intended to suggest a sequence of images or incidents

program trading *noun* (1985)
: computerized trading of large blocks of stocks in one market against stock index futures in another

¹prog·ress \'prä-grəs, -,gres, *US also & British usually* 'prō-,gres\ *noun* [Middle English, from Latin *progressus* advance, from *progredi* to go forth, from *pro-* forward + *gradi* to go — more at PRO-, GRADE] (15th century)

☆ SYNONYMS
Profuse, lavish, prodigal, luxuriant, lush, exuberant mean giving or given out in great abundance. PROFUSE implies pouring forth without restraint (uttered *profuse* apologies). LAVISH suggests an unstinted or unmeasured profusion (a *lavish* wedding reception). PRODIGAL implies reckless or wasteful lavishness threatening to lead to early exhaustion of resources (*prodigal* spending). LUXURIANT suggests a rich and splendid abundance ⟨*luxuriant* sidewhiskers⟩. LUSH suggests rich, soft luxuriance (a *lush* green lawn). EXUBERANT implies marked vitality or vigor in what produces abundantly (an *exuberant* imagination).

\ə\ **abut** \ᵊ\ **kitten** \ər\ **further** \a\ **ash** \ā\ **ace**
\ä\ **mop, mar** \au̇\ **out** \ch\ **chin** \e\ **bet** \ē\ **easy**
\g\ **go** \i\ **hit** \ī\ **ice** \j\ **job** \ŋ\ **sing** \ō\ **go**
\ȯ\ **law** \ȯi\ **boy** \th\ **thin** \t͟h\ **the** \ü\ **loot** \u̇\ **foot**
\y\ **yet** \zh\ **vision** *see also* Guide to Pronunciation

1 a (1) : a royal journey marked by pomp and pageant (2) : a state procession **b** : a tour or circuit made by an official (as a judge) **c** : an expedition, journey, or march through a region **2** : a forward or onward movement (as to an objective or to a goal) : ADVANCE **3** : gradual betterment; *especially* : the progressive development of mankind
— **in progress** : going on : OCCURRING
²**pro·gress** \prə-'gres\ *intransitive verb* (1539) **1** : to move forward : PROCEED **2** : to develop to a higher, better, or more advanced stage
pro·gres·sion \prə-'gre-shən\ *noun* (15th century) **1** : a sequence of numbers in which each term is related to its predecessor by a uniform law **2 a** : the action or process of progressing : ADVANCE **b** : a continuous and connected series : SEQUENCE **3 a** : succession of musical tones or chords **b** : the movement of musical parts in harmony **c** : SEQUENCE 2c
¹**pro·gres·sive** \prə-'gre-siv\ *adjective* (circa 1612) **1 a** : of, relating to, or characterized by progress **b** : making use of or interested in new ideas, findings, or opportunities **c** : of, relating to, or constituting an educational theory marked by emphasis on the individual child, informality of classroom procedure, and encouragement of self-expression **2** : of, relating to, or characterized by progression **3** : moving forward or onward : ADVANCING **4 a** : increasing in extent or severity ⟨a *progressive* disease⟩ **b** : increasing in rate as the base increases ⟨a *progressive* tax⟩ **5** *often capitalized* : of or relating to political Progressives **6** : of, relating to, or constituting a verb form that expresses action or state in progress at the time of speaking or a time spoken of
— **pro·gres·sive·ly** *adverb*
— **pro·gres·sive·ness** *noun*
²**progressive** *noun* (1846) **1 a** : one that is progressive **b** : one believing in moderate political change and especially social improvement by governmental action **2** *capitalized* : a member of any of various U.S. political parties: as **a** : a member of a predominantly agrarian minor party that around 1912 split off from the Republicans; *specifically* : BULL MOOSE **b** : a follower of Robert M. La Follette in the presidential campaign of 1924 **c** : a follower of Henry A. Wallace in the presidential campaign of 1948
Progressive Conservative *adjective* (1944)
: of or relating to a major political party in Canada traditionally advocating economic nationalism and close ties with the United Kingdom and the Commonwealth
— **Progressive Conservative** *noun*
pro·gres·siv·ism \prə-'gre-si-ˌvi-zəm\ *noun* (1892) **1** : the principles, beliefs, or practices of progressives **2** *capitalized* : the political and economic doctrines advocated by the Progressives **3** : the theories of progressive education
— **pro·gres·siv·ist** \-vist\ *noun or adjective*
— **pro·gres·siv·is·tic** \-ˌgre-si-'vis-tik\ *adjective*
pro·gres·siv·i·ty \ˌprō-(ˌ)gre-'si-və-tē\ *noun* (1883)
: the quality or state of being a progressive tax
pro·hib·it \prō-'hi-bət, prə-\ *transitive verb* [Middle English, from Latin *prohibitus*, past participle of *prohibēre* to keep off, from *pro-* forward + *habēre* to hold — more at PRO-, GIVE] (15th century) **1** : to forbid by authority : ENJOIN

2 a : to prevent from doing something **b** : PRECLUDE
synonym see FORBID
pro·hi·bi·tion \ˌprō-ə-'bi-shən *also* ˌprō-hə-\ *noun* (14th century) **1** : the act of prohibiting by authority **2** : an order to restrain or stop **3** *often capitalized* : the forbidding by law of the manufacture, transportation, and sale of alcoholic liquors except for medicinal and sacramental purposes
pro·hi·bi·tion·ist \-sh(ə-)nist\ *noun* (circa 1846)
: one who favors prohibition; *especially, capitalized* : a member of a minor U.S. political party advocating prohibition
pro·hib·i·tive \prō-'hi-bə-tiv, prə-\ *adjective* (15th century) **1** : tending to prohibit or restrain **2** : tending to preclude use or purchase ⟨*prohibitive* costs⟩ **3** : almost certain to perform as predicted ⟨a *prohibitive* favorite⟩
— **pro·hib·i·tive·ly** *adverb*
— **pro·hib·i·tive·ness** *noun*
pro·hib·i·to·ry \-'hi-bə-ˌtōr-ē, -ˌtȯr-\ *adjective* (circa 1591)
: PROHIBITIVE
pro·insu·lin \(ˌ)prō-'in(t)-s(ə-)lən\ *noun* (1916)
: a single-chain pancreatic polypeptide precursor of insulin that gives rise to the double chain of insulin by loss of the middle part of the molecule
¹**proj·ect** \'prä-ˌjekt, -jikt *also* 'prō-\ *noun* [Middle English *proiecte*, from Medieval Latin *projectum*, from Latin, neuter of *projectus*, past participle of *proicere* to throw forward, from *pro-* + *jacere* to throw — more at JET] (15th century) **1** : a specific plan or design : SCHEME **2** *obsolete* : IDEA **3** : a planned undertaking: as **a** : a definitely formulated piece of research **b** : a large usually government-supported undertaking **c** : a task or problem engaged in usually by a group of students to supplement and apply classroom studies **4** : a usually public housing development consisting of houses or apartments built and arranged according to a single plan
synonym see PLAN
²**pro·ject** \prə-'jekt\ *verb* [partly modification of Middle French *projeter*, from Old French *porjeter* to throw forward, from *por-* (from Latin *porro* forward; akin to Greek *pro* forward) + *jeter* to throw; partly from Latin *projectus*, past participle — more at FOR, JET] (15th century)
transitive verb **1 a** : to devise in the mind : DESIGN **b** : to plan, figure, or estimate for the future ⟨*project* expenditures for the coming year⟩ **2** : to throw or cast forward : THRUST **3** : to put or set forth : present for consideration **4** : to cause to protrude **5** : to cause (light or shadow) to fall into space or (an image) to fall on a surface ⟨*project* a beam of light⟩ **6** : to reproduce (as a point, line, or area) on a surface by motion in a prescribed direction **7** : to display outwardly especially to an audience ⟨*project* an image⟩ ⟨an actress who could *project* amorality —*Current Biography*⟩ **8** : to attribute (one's own ideas, feelings, or characteristics) to other people or to objects ⟨a nation is an entity on which one can *project* many of the worst of one's instincts —*Times Literary Supplement*⟩
intransitive verb **1** : to jut out : PROTRUDE **2 a** : to come across vividly : give an impression **b** : to make oneself heard clearly
— **pro·ject·able** \-'jek-tə-bəl\ *adjective*
¹**pro·jec·tile** \prə-'jek-t²l, -ˌtil, *chiefly British* 'prä-jik-ˌtīl\ *noun* (1665)

1 : a body projected by external force and continuing in motion by its own inertia; *especially* : a missile for a weapon (as a firearm) **2** : a self-propelling weapon (as a rocket)
²**projectile** *adjective* (1715) **1** : projecting or impelling forward ⟨a *projectile* force⟩ **2** : capable of being thrust forward
pro·jec·tion \prə-'jek-shən\ *noun* (1557) **1 a** : a systematic presentation of intersecting coordinate lines on a flat surface upon which features from the curved surface of the earth or the celestial sphere may be mapped **b** : the process or technique of reproducing a spatial object upon a plane or curved surface or a line by projecting its points; *also* : a graph or figure so formed **2** : a transforming change **3** : the act of throwing or thrusting forward **4** : the forming of a plan : SCHEMING **5 a** (1) : a jutting out (2) : a part that juts out **b** : a view of a building or architectural element **6 a** : the act of perceiving a mental object as spatially and sensibly objective; *also* : something so perceived **b** : the attribution of one's own ideas, feelings, or attitudes to other people or to objects; *especially* : the externalization of blame, guilt, or responsibility as a defense against anxiety **7** : the display of motion pictures by projecting an image from them upon a screen **8 a** : the act of projecting especially to an audience **b** : control of the volume, clarity, and distinctness of a voice to gain greater audibility **9** : an estimate of future possibilities based on a current trend ☆
— **pro·jec·tion·al** \-shnəl, -shə-nᵊl\ *adjective*
projection booth *noun* (circa 1928)
: a booth in a theater or hall for housing and operating a projector and especially a motion-picture projector
pro·jec·tion·ist \prə-'jek-sh(ə-)nist\ *noun* (1922)
: one that makes projections: as **a** : CARTOGRAPHER **b** : a person who operates a motion-picture projector or television equipment
pro·jec·tive \prə-'jek-tiv\ *adjective* (1682) **1** : relating to, produced by, or involving geometric projection **2** : of or relating to something that indicates the psychodynamic constitution of an individual ⟨*projective* tests⟩
— **pro·jec·tive·ly** *adverb*
projective geometry *noun* (1885)
: a branch of geometry that deals with the properties of configurations that are unaltered by projection
pro·jec·tor \prə-'jek-tər\ *noun* (1596) **1** : one that plans a project; *specifically* : PROMOTER **2** : one that projects: as **a** : a device for projecting a beam of light **b** : an optical instrument for projecting an image upon a surface **c** : a machine for projecting motion pictures on a screen **3** : an imagined line from an object to a surface along which projection takes place

☆ SYNONYMS
Projection, protrusion, protuberance, bulge mean an extension beyond the normal line or surface. PROJECTION implies a jutting out especially at a sharp angle ⟨those *projections* along the wall are safety hazards⟩. PROTRUSION suggests a thrusting out so that the extension seems a deformity ⟨the bizarre *protrusions* of a coral reef⟩. PROTUBERANCE implies a growing or swelling out in rounded form ⟨a skin disease marked by warty *protuberances*⟩. BULGE suggests an expansion caused by internal pressure ⟨*bulges* in the tile floor⟩.

pro·jet \prō-'zhā, 'prō-,\ *noun, plural* **projets** \-'zhā(z), -,zhā(z)\ [French, from Middle French *pourget*, from *pourjeter, projeter*] (1808)
1 : PLAN; *especially* : a draft of a proposed measure or treaty
2 : a projected or proposed design

pro·kary·ote \(,)prō-'kar-ē-,ōt\ *noun* [New Latin *Prokaryotes*, proposed subdivision of protists, from ¹*pro-* + *kary-* + *-otes*, plural noun suffix, from Greek *-ōtos* — more at -OTIC] (1963)
: a cellular organism (as a bacterium or a blue-green alga) that does not have a distinct nucleus — compare EUKARYOTE
— **pro·kary·ot·ic** \-,kar-ē-'ä-tik\ *adjective*

pro·lac·tin \prō-'lak-tən\ *noun* [²*pro-* + *lact-* + ¹*-in*] (1932)
: a protein hormone of the anterior lobe of the pituitary that induces lactation

pro·la·min *or* **pro·la·mine** \'prō-lə-mən, -,mēn\ *noun* [International Scientific Vocabulary *proline* + *ammonia* + *-in*, ²*-ine*] (1908)
: any of various simple proteins (as zein) that are found especially in seeds and are insoluble in absolute alcohol or water

pro·lan \'prō-,lan\ *noun* [German, from Latin *proles* progeny — more at PROLETARIAN] (1931)
: either of two gonadotrophic hormones: **a** : FOLLICLE-STIMULATING HORMONE **b** : LUTEINIZING HORMONE

¹**pro·lapse** \prō-'laps, 'prō-,\ *noun* [New Latin *prolapsus*, from Late Latin, fall, from Latin *prolabi* to fall or slide forward, from *pro-* forward + *labi* to slide — more at PRO-, SLEEP] (circa 1834)
: the falling down or slipping of a body part from its usual position or relations

²**pro·lapse** \prō-'laps\ *intransitive verb* **pro·lapsed; pro·laps·ing** (1876)
: to undergo prolapse

pro·late \'prō-,lāt\ *adjective* [Latin *prolatus* (past participle of *proferre* to bring forward, extend) from *pro-* forward + *latus*, past participle of *ferre* to carry — more at BEAR, TOLERATE] (1694)
: EXTENDED; *especially* : elongated in the direction of a line joining the poles ⟨a *prolate* spheroid⟩

prole \'prōl\ *noun or adjective* (1887)
: PROLETARIAN

pro·leg \'prō-,leg, -,lāg\ *noun* (1816)
: a fleshy leg that occurs on an abdominal segment of some insect larvae but not in the adult

pro·le·gom·e·non \,prō-li-'gä-mə-,nän, -nən\ *noun, plural* **-e·na** \-nə\ [Greek, neuter present passive participle of *prolegein* to say beforehand, from *pro-* before + *legein* to say — more at LEGEND] (circa 1652)
: prefatory remarks; *specifically* : a formal essay or critical discussion serving to introduce and interpret an extended work
— **pro·le·gom·e·nous** \-nəs\ *adjective*

pro·lep·sis \prō-'lep-səs\ *noun, plural* **-lep·ses** \-,sēz\ [Greek *prolēpsis*, from *prolambanein* to take beforehand, from *pro-* before + *lambanein* to take — more at LATCH] (1578)
: ANTICIPATION: as **a** : the representation or assumption of a future act or development as if presently existing or accomplished **b** : the application of an adjective to a noun in anticipation of the result of the action of the verb (as in "while yon slow oxen turn the *furrowed* plain")
— **pro·lep·tic** \-'lep-tik\ *adjective*
— **pro·lep·ti·cal·ly** \-ti-k(ə-)lē\ *adverb*

pro·le·tar·i·an \,prō-lə-'ter-ē-ən\ *noun* [Latin *proletarius*, from *proles* progeny, from *pro-* forth + *-oles* (akin to *alere* to nourish) — more at OLD] (1658)
: a member of the proletariat
— **proletarian** *adjective*

pro·le·tar·i·an·ise *British variant of* PROLETARIANIZE

pro·le·tar·i·an·ize \-'ter-ē-ə-,nīz\ *transitive verb* **-ized; -iz·ing** (1887)
: to reduce to a proletarian status or level
— **pro·le·tar·i·an·i·za·tion** \-,ter-ē-ə-nə-'zā-shən\ *noun*

pro·le·tar·i·at \,prō-lə-'ter-ē-ət, -'tar-, -ē-,at\ *noun* [French *prolétariat*, from Latin *proletarius*] (1853)
1 : the lowest social or economic class of a community
2 : the laboring class; *especially* : the class of industrial workers who lack their own means of production and hence sell their labor to live
◇

pro–life \(,)prō-'līf\ *adjective* (1961)
: ANTIABORTION
— **pro–lif·er** \-'lī-fər\ *noun*

pro·lif·er·ate \prə-'li-fə-,rāt\ *verb* **-at·ed; -at·ing** [back-formation from *proliferation*, from French *prolifération*, from *proliférer* to proliferate, from *prolifère* reproducing freely, from Latin *proles* + *-fer* -ferous] (1873)
intransitive verb
1 : to grow by rapid production of new parts, cells, buds, or offspring
2 : to increase in number as if by proliferating : MULTIPLY
transitive verb
: to cause to grow by proliferating
— **pro·lif·er·a·tion** \-,li-fə-'rā-shən\ *noun*
— **pro·lif·er·a·tive** \-'li-fə-,rā-tiv, -f(ə-)rə-tiv\ *adjective*

pro·lif·ic \prə-'li-fik\ *adjective* [French *prolifique*, from Latin *proles*] (1650)
1 : producing young or fruit especially freely : FRUITFUL
2 *archaic* : causing abundant growth, generation, or reproduction
3 : marked by abundant inventiveness or productivity ⟨a *prolific* composer⟩
synonym see FERTILE
— **pro·lif·i·ca·cy** \-'li-fi-kə-sē\ *noun*
— **pro·lif·i·cal·ly** \-fi-k(ə-)lē\ *adverb*
— **pro·lif·ic·ness** \-fik-nəs\ *noun*

pro·li·fic·i·ty \,prō-lə-'fi-sə-tē\ *noun* (1725)
: prolific power or character

pro·line \'prō-,lēn\ *noun* [German *Prolin*] (1904)
: an amino acid $C_5H_9NO_2$ that can be synthesized by animals from glutamate

pro·lix \prō-'liks, 'prō-(,)\ *adjective* [Middle English, from Middle French & Latin; Middle French *prolixe*, from Latin *prolixus* extended, from *pro-* forward + *liquēre* to be fluid — more at LIQUID] (15th century)
1 : unduly prolonged or drawn out : too long
2 : marked by or using an excess of words
synonym see WORDY
— **pro·lix·i·ty** \prō-'lik-sə-tē\ *noun*
— **pro·lix·ly** *adverb*

pro·loc·u·tor \prō-'lä-kyə-tər\ *noun* [Middle English, from Latin, from *pro-* for + *locutor* speaker, from *loqui* to speak] (15th century)
1 : one who speaks for another : SPOKESMAN
2 : presiding officer : CHAIRMAN

pro·log·ize \'prō-,lò-,gīz, -,lä-; -lə-,jīz\ *or* **pro·logu·ize** \-,lò-,gīz, -,lä-\ *intransitive verb* **-log·ized** *or* **-logu·ized; -log·iz·ing** *or* **-logu·iz·ing** (1608)
: to write or speak a prologue

pro·logue *also* **pro·log** \'prō-,lòg, -,läg\ *noun* [Middle English *prolog*, from Middle French *prologue*, from Latin *prologus* preface to a play, from Greek *prologos* part of a Greek play preceding the entry of the chorus, from *pro-* before + *legein* to speak — more at PRO-, LEGEND] (14th century)
1 : the preface or introduction to a literary work
2 a : a speech often in verse addressed to the audience by an actor at the beginning of a play **b** : the actor speaking such a prologue
3 : an introductory or preceding event or development

pro·long \prə-'lòŋ\ *transitive verb* [Middle English, from Middle French *prolonguer*, from Late Latin *prolongare*, from Latin *pro-* forward + *longus* long] (15th century)
1 : to lengthen in time : CONTINUE
2 : to lengthen in extent, scope, or range
synonym see EXTEND
— **pro·long·er** \-'lòŋ-ər\ *noun*

pro·lon·ga·tion \(,)prō-,lòŋ-'gā-shən, prə-\ *noun* (15th century)
1 : an extension or lengthening in time or duration
2 : an expansion or continuation in extent, scope, or range

pro·lu·sion \prō-'lü-zhən\ *noun* [Latin *prolusion-, prolusio*, from *proludere* to play beforehand, from *pro-* before + *ludere* to play — more at LUDICROUS] (1601)
1 : a preliminary trial or exercise : PRELUDE
2 : an introductory and often tentative discourse
— **pro·lu·so·ry** \-'lü-sə-rē, -zə-; -'lüz-rē, -'lüz-\ *adjective*

prom \'präm\ *noun* [short for *promenade*] (1894)
1 : a formal dance given by a high school or college class
2 *British* : PROMENADE 2

¹**prom·e·nade** \,prä-mə-'nād, -'näd\ *verb* **-nad·ed; -nad·ing** [²*promenade*] (1588)
intransitive verb
1 : to take or go on a promenade
2 : to perform a promenade in a dance
transitive verb
: to walk about in or on
— **prom·e·nad·er** *noun*

²**promenade** *noun* [French, from *promener* to take for a walk, from Latin *prominare* to drive forward, from *pro-* forward + *minare* to drive — more at AMENABLE] (1648)
1 : a place for strolling
2 : a leisurely walk or ride especially in a public place for pleasure or display
3 a : a ceremonious opening of a formal ball consisting of a grand march of all the guests **b** : a figure in a square dance in which couples move counterclockwise in a circle

◇ WORD HISTORY

proletariat The Latin adjective *proletarius* "pertaining to the lowest class of citizens" was a derivative of *proles* "offspring, progeny," the Roman conception apparently being that the humblest citizens had nothing to contribute to the state but their offspring. *Proletarius* was borrowed into French as *prolétaire*, which in the writing of early French socialists such as Saint-Simon was applied to the working class, that is, those people who did not own property and lived solely off their wages. In 1832 the socialist philosopher Pierre Leroux first used the derivative noun *prolétariat* to refer to this class. The concept of the proletariat was refined by Karl Marx, whose "scientific socialism" ousted French utopianism, and French *prolétariat* was borrowed into nearly every language of Europe, including English. The phrase *dictature du prolétariat* "dictatorship of the proletariat," which apparently first surfaced in Paris in 1850, in a manifesto of a revolutionary group inspired by the agitator Louis-Auguste Blanqui, was taken up by Marx in the same year and became a staple of communism. Under Lenin it was synonymous with the dictatorship of the party and became a license for ruthless suppression of dissent in the name of the proletariat.

promenade deck *noun* (1829)
: an upper deck or an area on a deck of a passenger ship where passengers stroll

Pro·me·the·an \prə-'mē-thē-ən\ *adjective* (1588)
: of, relating to, or resembling Prometheus, his experiences, or his art; *especially* : daringly original or creative

Pro·me·theus \-thē-əs, -,thyüs\ *noun* [Latin, from Greek *Promētheus*]
: a Titan who is chained and tortured by Zeus for stealing fire from heaven and giving it to mankind

pro·me·thi·um \-thē-əm\ *noun* [New Latin, from Latin *Prometheus*] (1948)
: a radioactive metallic element of the rare-earth group obtained as a fission product of uranium or from neutron-irradiated neodymium — see ELEMENT table

prom·i·nence \'prä-mə-nən(t)s, 'präm-nən(t)s\ *noun* (1598)
1 : something prominent : PROJECTION ⟨a rocky *prominence*⟩
2 : the quality, state, or fact of being prominent or conspicuous
3 : a mass of gas resembling a cloud that arises from the chromosphere of the sun

prom·i·nent \-nənt\ *adjective* [Middle English *prominent*, from Latin *prominent-, prominens*, from present participle of *prominēre* to jut forward, from *pro-* forward + *-minēre* (akin to *mont-, mons* mountain) — more at MOUNT] (15th century)
1 : standing out or projecting beyond a surface or line : PROTUBERANT
2 a : readily noticeable : CONSPICUOUS **b** : widely and popularly known : LEADING
synonym see NOTICEABLE
— **prom·i·nent·ly** *adverb*

pro·mis·cu·i·ty \,prä-mə-'skyü-ə-tē, ,prō-\ *noun, plural* **-ties** (circa 1849)
1 : a miscellaneous mixture or mingling of persons or things
2 : promiscuous sexual behavior

pro·mis·cu·ous \prə-'mis-kyə-wəs\ *adjective* [Latin *promiscuus*, from *pro-* forth + *miscēre* to mix — more at PRO-, MIX] (1603)
1 : composed of all sorts of persons or things
2 : not restricted to one class, sort, or person : INDISCRIMINATE ⟨education . . . cheapened through the *promiscuous* distribution of diplomas —Norman Cousins⟩
3 : not restricted to one sexual partner
4 : CASUAL, IRREGULAR ⟨*promiscuous* eating habits⟩
— **pro·mis·cu·ous·ly** *adverb*
— **pro·mis·cu·ous·ness** *noun*

¹prom·ise \'prä-məs\ *noun* [Middle English *promis*, from Latin *promissum*, from neuter of *promissus*, past participle of *promittere* to send forth, promise, from *pro-* forth + *mittere* to send] (15th century)
1 a : a declaration that one will do or refrain from doing something specified **b** : a legally binding declaration that gives the person to whom it is made a right to expect or to claim the performance or forbearance of a specified act
2 : reason to expect something ⟨little *promise* of relief⟩; *especially* : ground for expectation of success, improvement, or excellence ⟨shows considerable *promise*⟩
3 : something that is promised

²promise *verb* **prom·ised; prom·is·ing** (15th century)
transitive verb
1 : to pledge to do, bring about, or provide ⟨*promise* aid⟩
2 *archaic* : WARRANT, ASSURE
3 *chiefly dialect* : BETROTH
4 : to suggest beforehand : give promise of ⟨dark clouds *promise* rain⟩
intransitive verb
1 : to make a promise

2 : to give ground for expectation : be imminent
— **prom·is·ee** \,prä-mə-'sē\ *noun*
— **prom·i·sor** \-'sòr\ *also* **prom·is·er** \'prä-mə-sər\ *noun*

promised land *noun* (1667)
: something and especially a place or condition believed to promise final satisfaction or realization of hopes

prom·is·ing \'prä-mə-siŋ\ *adjective* (1601)
: full of promise : likely to succeed or to yield good results
— **prom·is·ing·ly** \-siŋ-lē\ *adverb*

prom·is·so·ry \'prä-mə-,sòr-ē, -,sòr-\ *adjective* [Middle English *promissorye*, from Medieval Latin *promissorius*, from Latin *promittere*] (15th century)
: containing or conveying a promise or assurance

promissory note *noun* (1710)
: a written promise to pay at a fixed or determinable future time a sum of money to a specified individual or to bearer

pro·mo \'prō-(,)mō\ *noun, plural* **promos** *often attributive* [short for *promotional*] (1946)
: a promotional announcement, blurb, or appearance

prom·on·to·ry \'prä-mən-,tōr-ē, -,tòr-\ *noun, plural* **-ries** [Latin *promunturium, promontorium*; probably akin to *prominēre* to jut forth — more at PROMINENT] (1548)
1 a : a high point of land or rock projecting into a body of water **b** : a prominent mass of land overlooking or projecting into a lowland
2 : a bodily prominence

pro·mote \prə-'mōt\ *transitive verb* **pro·mot·ed; pro·mot·ing** [Middle English, from Latin *promotus*, past participle of *promovēre*, literally, to move forward, from *pro-* forward + *movēre* to move] (14th century)
1 a : to advance in station, rank, or honor : RAISE **b** : to change (a pawn) into a piece in chess by moving to the eighth rank **c** : to advance (a student) from one grade to the next higher grade
2 a : to contribute to the growth or prosperity of : FURTHER ⟨*promote* international understanding⟩ **b** : to help bring (as an enterprise) into being : LAUNCH **c** : to present (merchandise) for buyer acceptance through advertising, publicity, or discounting
3 *slang* : to get possession of by doubtful means or by ingenuity
synonym see ADVANCE
— **pro·mot·abil·i·ty** \-,mō-tə-'bi-lə-tē\ *noun*
— **pro·mot·able** \-'mō-tə-bəl\ *adjective*

pro·mot·er \-'mō-tər\ *noun* (14th century)
1 : one that promotes; *especially* : one who assumes the financial responsibilities of a sporting event (as a boxing match) including contracting with the principals, renting the site, and collecting gate receipts
2 *obsolete* : PROSECUTOR
3 : a substance that in very small amounts is able to increase the activity of a catalyst
4 : a binding site in a DNA chain at which RNA polymerase binds to initiate transcription of messenger RNA by one or more nearby structural genes

pro·mo·tion \prə-'mō-shən\ *noun* (15th century)
1 : the act or fact of being raised in position or rank : PREFERMENT
2 : the act of furthering the growth or development of something; *especially* : the furtherance of the acceptance and sale of merchandise through advertising, publicity, or discounting
— **pro·mo·tion·al** \-shnəl, -shə-nʲl\ *adjective*

pro·mo·tive \-'mō-tiv\ *adjective* (1644)
: tending or serving to promote
— **pro·mo·tive·ness** *noun*

¹prompt \'präm(p)t\ *transitive verb* [Middle English, from Medieval Latin *promptare*, from Latin *promptus* prompt] (14th century)
1 : to move to action : INCITE
2 : to assist (one acting or reciting) by suggesting or saying the next words of something forgotten or imperfectly learned : CUE
3 : to serve as the inciting cause of
— **prompt·er** *noun*

²prompt *adjective* (1784)
: of or relating to prompting actors

³prompt *adjective* [Middle English, from Middle French or Latin; Middle French, from Latin *promptus* ready, prompt, from past participle of *promere* to bring forth, from *pro-* forth + *emere* to take — more at REDEEM] (15th century)
1 : being ready and quick to act as occasion demands
2 : performed readily or immediately ⟨*prompt* assistance⟩
synonym see QUICK
— **prompt·ly** \'präm(p)t-lē, 'präm-plē\ *adverb*
— **prompt·ness** \'präm(p)t-nəs, 'prämp-nəs\ *noun*

⁴prompt *noun, plural* **prompts** \'präm(p)ts, 'prämps\ (1597)
1 [¹prompt] : something that prompts : REMINDER
2 [³prompt] : a limit of time given for payment of an account for goods purchased; *also* : the contract by which this time is set

prompt·book \'präm(p)t-,bûk, 'prämp-,bùk\ *noun* (1809)
: a copy of a play with directions for performance used by a theater prompter

promp·ti·tude \'präm(p)-tə-,tüd, -,tyüd\ *noun* [Middle English, from Middle French or Late Latin; Middle French, from Late Latin *promptitudo*, from Latin *promptus*] (15th century)
: the quality or habit of being prompt : PROMPTNESS

prompt side *noun* (1824)
1 : the side of the stage adjacent to the prompter's corner
2 : the side of the stage to the right of an actor facing the audience

pro·mul·gate \'prä-məl-,gāt; prō-'məl-, prə-', 'prō-(,)\ *transitive verb* **-gat·ed; -gat·ing** [Latin *promulgatus*, past participle of *promulgare*, from *pro-* forward + *-mulgare* (probably akin to *mulgēre* to milk, extract) — more at EMULSION] (1530)
1 : to make known by open declaration : PROCLAIM
2 a : to make known or public the terms of (a proposed law) **b** : to put (a law) into action or force
synonym see DECLARE
— **pro·mul·ga·tion** \,prä-məl-'gā-shən; ,prō-(,)məl-, (,)prō-\ *noun*
— **pro·mul·ga·tor** \'prä-məl-,gā-tər; prō-'məl-, prə-', 'prō-(,)\ *noun*

pro·na·tion \prō-'nā-shən\ *noun* [*pronate*, from Late Latin *pronatus*, past participle of *pronare* to bend forward, from Latin *pronus*] (1666)
1 : rotation of the hand and forearm so that the palm faces backwards or downwards
2 : rotation of the medial bones in the midtarsal region of the foot inward and downward so that in walking the foot tends to come down on its inner margin
— **pro·nate** \'prō-,nāt\ *verb*

pro·na·tor \'prō-,nā-tər\ *noun* (circa 1741)
: a muscle that produces pronation

prone \'prōn\ *adjective* [Middle English, from Latin *pronus* bent forward, tending; akin to Latin *pro* forward — more at FOR] (14th century)
1 : having a tendency or inclination : being likely ⟨*prone* to forget names⟩ ⟨accident-*prone*⟩

2 a : having the front or ventral surface downward **b :** lying flat or prostrate ☆ □
— **prone** adverb
— **prone·ly** adverb
— **prone·ness** \'prōn-nəs\ noun
pro·neph·ros \(ˌ)prō-'ne-frəs, -ˌfräs\ noun [New Latin, from Greek pro- + nephros kidney — more at NEPHRITIS] (1881)
: either member of the first and most anterior pair of the three successive paired vertebrate renal organs that functions in the adults of amphioxus and some lampreys, functions temporarily in larval fishes and amphibians, and is present but nonfunctional in embryos of reptiles, birds, and mammals — compare MESONEPHROS, METANEPHROS
— **pro·neph·ric** \-frik\ adjective
¹prong \'prȯŋ, 'präŋ\ noun [Middle English pronge] (15th century)
1 : FORK
2 : a tine of a fork
3 : a slender pointed or projecting part: as **a** : a fang of a tooth **b** : a point of an antler
4 : something resembling a prong
²prong transitive verb (1848)
: to stab, pierce, or break up with a pronged device
pronged \'prȯŋd, 'präŋd\ adjective (1767)
1 : having a usually specified number of prongs — usually used in combination ⟨a three-*pronged* fork⟩
2 : having a usually specified number of parts or approaches ⟨a two-*pronged* strategy⟩
prong·horn \'prȯŋ-ˌhȯrn, 'präŋ-\ noun, plural **pronghorn** or **pronghorns** (1823)
: a ruminant mammal (*Antilocapra americana*) of treeless parts of western North America that resembles an antelope — called also *pronghorn antelope*

pronghorn

pro·nom·i·nal \prō-'nä-mə-nᵊl, -'näm-nᵊl\ adjective [Late Latin pronominalis, from Latin pronomin-, pronomen] (1680)
1 : of, relating to, or constituting a pronoun
2 : resembling a pronoun in identifying or specifying without describing ⟨the *pronominal* adjective *this* in *this* dog⟩
— **pro·nom·i·nal·ly** adverb
pro·noun \'prō-ˌnaun\ noun [Middle English pronom, from Latin pronomin-, pronomen, from pro- for + nomin-, nomen name — more at PRO-, NAME] (1530)
: any of a small set of words in a language that are used as substitutes for nouns or noun phrases and whose referents are named or understood in the context
pro·nounce \prə-'naun(t)s\ verb **pronounced; pro·nounc·ing** [Middle English, from Middle French prononcier, from Latin pronuntiare, from pro- forth + nuntiare to report, from nuntius messenger — more at PRO-] (14th century)
transitive verb
1 : to declare officially or ceremoniously ⟨the minister *pronounced* them husband and wife⟩
2 : to declare authoritatively or as an opinion ⟨doctors *pronounced* him fit to resume duties⟩
3 a : to employ the organs of speech to produce ⟨*pronounce* these words⟩; *especially* : to say correctly ⟨I can't *pronounce* his name⟩ **b** : to represent in printed characters the spoken counterpart of (an orthographic representation) ⟨both dictionaries *pronounce* clique the same⟩
4 : RECITE ⟨speak the speech, I pray you, as I *pronounced* it to you —Shakespeare⟩
intransitive verb
1 : to pass judgment
2 : to produce the components of spoken language

— **pro·nounce·abil·i·ty** \-ˌnaun(t)-sə-'bi-lə-tē\ noun
— **pro·nounce·able** \-'naun(t)-sə-bəl\ adjective
— **pro·nounc·er** noun
pro·nounced \-'naun(t)st\ adjective (circa 1741)
: strongly marked : DECIDED
— **pro·nounc·ed·ly** \-'naun(t)-səd-lē, -'naun(t)st-lē\ adverb
pro·nounce·ment \prə-'naun(t)s-mənt\ noun (1593)
1 : a usually formal declaration of opinion
2 : an authoritative announcement
pronouncing adjective (1764)
: relating to or indicating pronunciation ⟨a *pronouncing* dictionary⟩
pron·to \'prän-ˌtō\ adverb [Spanish, from Latin promptus prompt] (circa 1740)
: without delay
¹pro·nu·clear \(ˌ)prō-'nü-klē-ər, -'nyü-, ÷-kyə-lər\ adjective [pronucleus] (circa 1890)
: of, relating to, or resembling a pronucleus
²pronuclear adjective [²pro- + nuclear] (1971)
: advocating the use of nuclear-powered generating stations
pro·nu·cle·us \(ˌ)prō-'nü-klē-əs, -'nyü-\ noun [New Latin] (1880)
: the haploid nucleus of a male or female gamete (as an egg or sperm) up to the time of fusion with that of another gamete in fertilization
pro·nun·ci·a·men·to \prō-ˌnən(t)-sē-ə-'men-(ˌ)tō\ noun, plural **-tos** or **-toes** [modification of Spanish pronunciamiento, from pronunciar to pronounce, from Latin pronuntiare] (1835)
: PROCLAMATION, PRONOUNCEMENT
pro·nun·ci·a·tion \prə-ˌnən(t)-sē-'ā-shən also ÷-ˌnaun(t)-\ noun [Middle English pronunciacion, from Middle French prononciation, from Latin pronuntiation-, pronuntiatio, from pronuntiare] (15th century)
: the act or manner of pronouncing something □
— **pro·nun·ci·a·tion·al** \-shnəl, -shə-nᵊl\ adjective
¹proof \'prüf\ noun [Middle English, alteration of preove, from Old French preuve, from Late Latin proba, from Latin probare to prove — more at PROVE] (13th century)
1 a : the cogency of evidence that compels acceptance by the mind of a truth or a fact **b** : the process or an instance of establishing the validity of a statement especially by derivation from other statements in accordance with principles of reasoning
2 obsolete **:** EXPERIENCE
3 : something that induces certainty or establishes validity
4 archaic **:** the quality or state of having been tested or tried; *especially* : unyielding hardness
5 : evidence operating to determine the finding or judgment of a tribunal
6 a plural **proofs** or **proof :** a copy (as of typeset text) made for examination or correction **b** : a test impression of an engraving, etching, or lithograph **c** : a coin that is struck from a highly-polished die on a polished planchet, is not intended for circulation, and sometimes differs in metallic content from coins of identical design struck for circulation **d** : a test photographic print made from a negative
7 : a test applied to articles or substances to determine whether they are of standard or satisfactory quality
8 a : the minimum alcoholic strength of proof spirit **b** : strength with reference to the standard for proof spirit; *specifically* : alcoholic strength indicated by a number that is twice the percent by volume of alcohol present ⟨whiskey of 90 *proof* is 45% alcohol⟩

²proof adjective (1592)
1 : able to resist or repel ⟨boots that were . . . *proof* against cold and wet —Robertson Davies⟩ — often used in combination ⟨wind-*proof*⟩
2 : used in proving or testing or as a standard of comparison

☆ **SYNONYMS**
Prone, supine, prostrate, recumbent mean lying down. PRONE implies a position with the front of the body turned toward the supporting surface ⟨push-ups require a *prone* position⟩. SUPINE implies lying on one's back and suggests inertness or abjectness ⟨lying *supine* on the couch⟩. PROSTRATE implies lying full-length as in submission, defeat, or physical collapse ⟨a runner fell *prostrate* at the finish line⟩. RECUMBENT implies the posture of one sleeping or resting ⟨a patient comfortably *recumbent* in a hospital bed⟩. See in addition LIABLE.

□ **USAGE**
prone Most commentators insist on the distinction between *prone* and *supine* spelled out in the synonymy paragraph above. The distinction is indeed observed by those writing on physiology and anatomy, and *prone* always means lying on one's belly to those who shoot guns and write about it. But *prone* has wider application: it is used of inanimate objects to mean simply "lying flat" ⟨the *prone* golden autumn harvest of leaves —Michael P. O'Connor⟩ and is also used of the body when its orientation is uncertain or unimportant ⟨I caught sight of the large *prone* figure in bed —D. H. Lawrence⟩ ⟨I too have been *prone* on my couch this week, a victim of the common cold —Flannery O'Connor⟩. Sometimes it is used where *supine* could be used ⟨he lies *prone*, his face to the sky —James Joyce⟩; such use may come from a conscious avoidance of the pejorative overtones of sense 2 of *supine*. *Supine* is a relatively rare word, so apparently most writers find a way around it. Both *prone* and *supine* are more commonly used in their figurative senses.

pronunciation As if to prove the inherently controversial nature of English pronunciation, the very word *pronunciation* has given rise to not one, but two disputes. The first has to do with the sound of the letter *c* before *i*: should it be articulated as an \s\ as in *précis* or as an \sh\ as in *specialty*? The *ci* sequence in *species, uncial, preciosity,* and *sociologist* is heard both ways, though in many familiar words of Latin derivation the *c* before *i* is pronounced only as \sh\: *special, precious, superficial, judicious.* No fast rule obtains for the Latinate *ci,* though, and thus common usage has dictated the \s\ sound for *pronunciation.* The second issue is that some substitute the syllable \-ˌnaun(t)-\ for \-ˌnən(t)-\, perhaps wanting unconsciously to preserve the relatedness of *pronounce* and *pronunciation.* The same speakers do not, however, extend the analogy to the pronunciation of *annunciation* or *denunciation.* The \-ˌnaun(t)-\ variant has never established itself as an accepted form. Again, common usage overwhelmingly dictates the *pronunciation* \prə-ˌnən(t)-sē-'ā-shən\.

\ə\ abut \ᵊ\ kitten \ər\ further \a\ ash \ā\ ace
\ä\ mop, mar \au̇\ out \ch\ chin \e\ bet \ē\ easy
\g\ go \i\ hit \ī\ ice \j\ job \ŋ\ sing \ō\ go
\ȯ\ law \ȯi\ boy \th\ thin \t̲h̲\ the \ü\ loot \u̇\ foot
\y\ yet \zh\ vision *see also* Guide to Pronunciation

PROOFREADERS' MARKS

ℐ or ℽ or ⌐ delete; take it out	*ital* set in italic ⟨*italic*⟩
⌒ close up; print as one word	*rom* set in roman ⟨roman⟩
ℐ⌒ delete and close up	*bf* set in boldface ⟨**boldface**⟩
∧ or > or ⅄ caret; insert here ⌐something	= or -/ or ⌢ or /H/ hyphen
# insert a space	-/N or *en* or /N/ en dash ⟨1965–72⟩
eq# space evenly where indicated	-/M or *em* or /M/ em — or long — dash
stet let marked text stand as set	∨ superscript or superior ⟨²as in πr^2⟩
tr transpose; change order the	∧ subscript or inferior ⟨₂as in H_2O⟩
/ used to separate two or more marks and often as a concluding stroke at the end of an insertion	◇ or X centered ⟨◇for a centered dot in $p \cdot q$⟩
[⌐ set farther to the left	⌐ comma
] set] farther to the right	⌐ apostrophe
⌒ set æ or fl as ligatures æ or fl	⊙ period
= straighten alignment	; or ;/ semicolon
‖ ⫼ straighten or align	: or ⊙ colon
X imperfect or broken character	⌐⌐ or ⌐⌐ quotation marks
⊓ indent or insert em quad space	(/) parentheses
¶ begin a new paragraph	[/] brackets
ⓢⓟ spell out ⟨set 5 lbs as five pounds⟩	*OK/?* query to author: has this been set as intended?
cap set in capitals ⟨CAPITALS⟩	⌐ or ⌐¹ push down a work-up
sm cap or *s.c.* set in small capitals ⟨SMALL CAPITALS⟩	⊙¹ turn over an inverted letter
lc set in lowercase ⟨lowercase⟩	*wf*¹ wrong font; a character of the wrong size or esp. style

¹ The last three symbols are unlikely to be needed in marking proofs of photocomposed matter.

3 : of standard strength or quality or alcoholic content
³proof *transitive verb* (1745)
1 a : to make or take a proof or test of **b :** PROOFREAD
2 : to give a resistant quality to
3 : to activate (yeast) by mixing with water and sometimes sugar or milk
— proof·er *noun*
proof·read \ˈprüf-ˌrēd\ *transitive verb* **-read** \-ˌred\; **-read·ing** [back-formation from *proofreader*] (1920)
: to read and mark corrections in (as a proof)
proof·read·er \-ˌrē-dər\ *noun* (1832)
: a person who proofreads
proof·room \ˈprüf-ˌrüm, -ˌrum\ *noun* (1903)
: a room for proofreading
proof spirit *noun* (1790)
: an alcoholic liquor or mixture of ethanol and water that contains 50% ethanol by volume at 60°F (16°C)
¹prop \ˈpräp\ *noun* [Middle English *proppe*, from Middle Dutch, stopper; akin to Middle Low German *proppe* stopper] (15th century)
: something that props or sustains : SUPPORT
²prop *transitive verb* **propped; prop·ping** (1538)
1 a : to support by placing something under or against — often used with *up* **b :** to support by placing against something
2 : SUSTAIN, STRENGTHEN
³prop *noun* (1841)
: PROPERTY 3
⁴prop *noun* (1914)
: PROPELLER
prop- *combining form* [International Scientific Vocabulary, from *propionic (acid)*]
: related to propionic acid ⟨*propane*⟩ ⟨*propyl*⟩
pro·pae·deu·tic \ˌprō-pi-ˈdü-tik, -ˈdyü-\ *noun* [Greek *propaideuein* to teach beforehand,

from *pro-* before + *paideuein* to teach, from *paid-, pais* child — more at PRO-, FEW] (1798)
: preparatory study or instruction
— propaedeutic *adjective*
pro·pa·gan·da \ˌprä-pə-ˈgan-də, ˌprō-\ *noun* [New Latin, from *Congregatio de propaganda fide* Congregation for propagating the faith, organization established by Pope Gregory XV (died 1623)] (1718)
1 *capitalized* **:** a congregation of the Roman curia having jurisdiction over missionary territories and related institutions
2 : the spreading of ideas, information, or rumor for the purpose of helping or injuring an institution, a cause, or a person
3 : ideas, facts, or allegations spread deliberately to further one's cause or to damage an opposing cause; *also* **:** a public action having such an effect ◇
— pro·pa·gan·dist \-dist\ *noun or adjective*
— pro·pa·gan·dis·tic \-ˌgan-ˈdis-tik\ *adjective*
— pro·pa·gan·dis·ti·cal·ly \-ti-k(ə-)lē\ *adverb*
pro·pa·gan·dize \-ˈgan-ˌdīz\ *verb* **-dized; -diz·ing** (1844)
transitive verb
: to subject to propaganda; *also* **:** to carry on propaganda for
intransitive verb
: to carry on propaganda
— pro·pa·gan·diz·er \-ˌdī-zər\ *noun*
prop·a·gate \ˈprä-pə-ˌgāt\ *verb* **-gat·ed; -gat·ing** [Latin *propagatus*, past participle of *propagare* to set slips, propagate, from *pro-pages* slip, offspring, from *pro-* before + *pangere* to fasten — more at PRO-, PACT] (circa 1570)
transitive verb

1 : to cause to continue or increase by sexual or asexual reproduction
2 : to pass along to offspring
3 a : to cause to spread out and affect a greater number or greater area : EXTEND **b :** to foster

◇ **WORD HISTORY**
propaganda In 1622, in an effort to centralize the missionary activities of the Roman Catholic Church overseas, Pope Gregory XV issued a bull by which he established the *Congregatio de propaganda fide* ("Congregation for the Propagation of the Faith"), a committee of cardinals charged with the administration of ecclesiastical affairs in non-Catholic countries. The name of the office was informally shortened to *Propaganda*, a word that became current in several European vernaculars, including English. During the French Revolution, the French form *propagande* was generalized to mean any group whose purpose was to spread views or principles, especially of a political nature, and then to mean the activity of spreading such views. The latter meaning of the word was taken up by English, German, Russian, and other languages. The association of *propaganda* in various languages with the promulgation of subversive political or economic ideas by revolutionary groups gave it a negative connotation in the 19th and 20th centuries. In extremist circles of both the left and right, though, it simply came to mean "inculcation of correct political views," and German *Propaganda* was a positive term to both the Nazis and the Communist regime that succeeded the Nazis in eastern Germany.

growing knowledge of, familiarity with, or acceptance of (as an idea or belief) : PUBLICIZE **c** : to transmit (as sound or light) through a medium
intransitive verb
1 : to multiply sexually or asexually
2 : INCREASE, EXTEND
3 : to travel through space or a material — used of wave energy (as light, sound, or radio waves)
— **prop·a·ga·ble** \'prä-pə-gə-bəl\ *adjective*
— **prop·a·ga·tive** \-ˌgā-tiv\ *adjective*
— **prop·a·ga·tor** \-ˌgā-tər\ *noun*
prop·a·ga·tion \ˌprä-pə-'gā-shən\ *noun* (15th century)
: the act or action of propagating: as **a** : increase (as of a kind of organism) in numbers **b** : the spreading of something (as a belief) abroad or into new regions **c** : enlargement or extension (as of a crack) in a solid body
prop·a·gule \'prä-pə-ˌgyü(ə)l\ *noun* [New Latin *propagulum*, from Latin *propages* slip] (1858)
: a structure (as a cutting, a seed, or a spore) that propagates a plant
pro·pane \'prō-ˌpān\ *noun* [International Scientific Vocabulary *prop-* + *-ane*] (1866)
: a heavy flammable gaseous alkane C_3H_8 found in crude petroleum and natural gas and used especially as fuel and in chemical synthesis
pro·pel \prə-'pel\ *transitive verb* **pro·pelled**; **pro·pel·ling** [Middle English *propellen*, from Latin *propellere*, from *pro-* before + *pellere* to drive — more at FELT] (15th century)
: to drive forward or onward by or as if by means of a force that imparts motion
¹pro·pel·lant *also* **pro·pel·lent** \-'pe-lənt\ *adjective* (1644)
: capable of propelling
²propellant *also* **propellent** *noun* (1814)
: something that propels: as **a** : an explosive for propelling projectiles **b** : fuel plus oxidizer used by a rocket engine **c** : a gas kept under pressure in a bottle or can for expelling the contents when the pressure is released
pro·pel·ler *also* **pro·pel·lor** \prə-'pe-lər\ *noun* (1780)
: one that propels; *especially* : a device that consists of a central hub with radiating blades placed and twisted so that each forms part of a helical surface and that is used to propel a vehicle (as a ship or airplane)
pro·pend \prō-'pend\ *intransitive verb* [Latin *propendēre*, from *pro-* before + *pendēre* to hang — more at PENDANT] (1545)
obsolete : INCLINE
pro·pense \prō-'pen(t)s\ *adjective* [Latin *propensus*, past participle of *propendēre*] (1528)
archaic : leaning or inclining toward : DISPOSED
pro·pen·si·ty \prə-'pen(t)-sə-tē\ *noun, plural* **-ties** (1570)
: an often intense natural inclination or preference
synonym see LEANING
¹prop·er \'prä-pər\ *adjective* [Middle English *propre* proper, own, from Middle French, from Latin *proprius* own] (14th century)
1 a : referring to one individual only **b** : belonging to one : OWN **c** : appointed for the liturgy of a particular day **d** : represented heraldically in natural color
2 : belonging characteristically to a species or individual : PECULIAR
3 *chiefly dialect* : GOOD-LOOKING, HANDSOME
4 : very good : EXCELLENT
5 *chiefly British* : UTTER, ABSOLUTE
6 : strictly limited to a specified thing, place, or idea ⟨the city *proper*⟩
7 a : strictly accurate : CORRECT **b** *archaic* : VIRTUOUS, RESPECTABLE **c** : strictly decorous : GENTEEL
8 : marked by suitability, rightness, or appropriateness : FIT

9 : being a mathematical subset (as a subgroup) that does not contain all the elements of the inclusive set from which it is derived
synonym see FIT
— **prop·er·ly** *adverb*
— **prop·er·ness** *noun*
²proper *noun* (15th century)
1 : the parts of the Mass that vary according to the liturgical calendar
2 : the part of a missal or breviary containing the proper of the Mass and the offices proper to the holy days of the liturgical year
³proper *adverb* (15th century)
chiefly dialect : in a thorough manner : COMPLETELY
proper adjective *noun* (1905)
: an adjective that is formed from a proper noun and that is usually capitalized in English
pro·per·din \prō-'pər-d³n\ *noun* [probably from ¹*pro-* + Latin *perdere* to destroy + English ¹*-in* — more at PERDITION] (1954)
: a serum protein that participates in destruction of bacteria, neutralization of viruses, and lysis of red blood cells
proper fraction *noun* (1674)
: a fraction in which the numerator is less or of lower degree than the denominator
proper noun *noun* (circa 1890)
: a noun that designates a particular being or thing, does not take a limiting modifier, and is usually capitalized in English — called also *proper name*
prop·er·tied \'prä-pər-tēd\ *adjective* (circa 1772)
: possessing property
prop·er·ty \'prä-pər-tē\ *noun, plural* **-ties** [Middle English *proprete*, from Middle French *propreté*, from Latin *proprietat-, proprietas*, from *proprius* own] (14th century)
1 a : a quality or trait belonging and especially peculiar to an individual or thing **b** : an effect that an object has on another object or on the senses **c** : VIRTUE 3 **d** : an attribute common to all members of a class
2 a : something owned or possessed; *specifically* : a piece of real estate **b** : the exclusive right to possess, enjoy, and dispose of a thing : OWNERSHIP **c** : something to which a person or business has a legal title **d** : one (as a performer) under contract whose work is especially valuable
3 : an article or object used in a play or motion picture except painted scenery and costumes
synonym see QUALITY
— **prop·er·ty·less** \-ləs\ *adjective*
— **prop·er·ty·less·ness** \-nəs\ *noun*
property damage insurance *noun* (circa 1946)
: insurance protecting against all or part of an individual's legal liability for damage done (as by his or her automobile) to the property of another
property right *noun* (1903)
: a legal right or interest in or against specific property
property tax *noun* (1808)
: a tax levied on real or personal property
pro·phage \'prō-ˌfāj, -ˌfäzh\ *noun* (1951)
: an intracellular form of a bacteriophage in which it is harmless to the host, is usually integrated into the hereditary material of the host, and reproduces when the host does
pro·phase \-ˌfāz\ *noun* [International Scientific Vocabulary] (1884)
1 : the initial stage of mitosis and of the mitotic division of meiosis characterized by the condensation of chromosomes consisting of two chromatids, disappearance of the nucleolus and nuclear membrane, and formation of mitotic spindle
2 : the initial stage of the first division of meiosis in which the chromosomes become visible, homologous pairs of chromosomes undergo synapsis and crossing over, chiasmata appear, chromosomes condense with homo-

logues visible as tetrads, and the nuclear membrane and nucleolus disappear — compare DIAKINESIS, DIPLOTENE, LEPTOTENE, PACHYTENE, ZYGOTENE
— **pro·pha·sic** \(ˌ)prō-'fā-zik\ *adjective*
proph·e·cy *also* **proph·e·sy** \'prä-fə-sē\ *noun, plural* **-cies** *also* **-sies** [Middle English *prophecie*, from Old French, from Late Latin *prophetia*, from Greek *prophēteia*, from *prophētēs* prophet] (13th century)
1 : an inspired utterance of a prophet
2 : the function or vocation of a prophet; *specifically* : the inspired declaration of divine will and purpose
3 : a prediction of something to come
proph·e·sy \'prä-fə-ˌsī\ *verb* **-sied**; **-sy·ing** [Middle English *prophesien*, from Middle French *prophesier*, from Old French, from *prophecie*] (14th century)
transitive verb
1 : to utter by or as if by divine inspiration
2 : to predict with assurance or on the basis of mystic knowledge
3 : PREFIGURE
intransitive verb
1 : to speak as if divinely inspired
2 : to give instruction in religious matters : PREACH
3 : to make a prediction
synonym see FORETELL
— **proph·e·si·er** \-ˌsī-(-ə)r\ *noun*
proph·et \'prä-fət\ *noun* [Middle English *prophete*, from Old French, from Latin *propheta*, from Greek *prophētēs*, from *pro* for + *phanai* to speak — more at FOR, BAN] (12th century)
1 : one who utters divinely inspired revelations; *specifically, often capitalized* : the writer of one of the prophetic books of the Old Testament
2 : one gifted with more than ordinary spiritual and moral insight; *especially* : an inspired poet
3 : one who foretells future events : PREDICTOR
4 : an effective or leading spokesman for a cause, doctrine, or group
5 *Christian Science* **a** : a spiritual seer **b** : disappearance of material sense before the conscious facts of spiritual Truth
— **proph·et·hood** \-ˌhùd\ *noun*
proph·et·ess \'prä-fə-təs\ *noun* (14th century)
: a woman who is a prophet
proph·et·ic \prə-'fe-tik\ *also* **pro·phet·i·cal** \-'fe-ti-kəl\ *adjective* (15th century)
1 : of, relating to, or characteristic of a prophet or prophecy
2 : foretelling events : PREDICTIVE
— **proph·et·i·cal·ly** \-ti-k(ə-)lē\ *adverb*
Proph·ets \'prä-fəts\ *noun plural*
: the second part of the Jewish scriptures — see BIBLE table
¹pro·phy·lac·tic \ˌprō-fə-'lak-tik *also* ˌprä-\ *adjective* [Greek *prophylaktikos*, from *prophylassein* to be on guard, from *pro-* before + *phylassein* to guard, from *phylak-, phylax* guard] (1574)
1 : guarding from or preventing disease
2 : tending to prevent or ward off : PREVENTIVE
— **pro·phy·lac·ti·cal·ly** \-ti-k(ə-)lē\ *adverb*
²prophylactic *noun* (1642)
: something prophylactic; *especially* : a device and especially a condom for preventing venereal infection or conception
pro·phy·lax·is \-'lak-səs\ *noun, plural* **-lax·es** \-'lak-ˌsēz\ [New Latin, from Greek *prophylaktikos*] (circa 1842)

\ə\ abut \ᵊ\ kitten \ər\ further \a\ ash \ā\ ace
\ä\ mop, mar \aù\ out \ch\ chin \e\ bet \ē\ easy
\g\ go \i\ hit \ī\ ice \j\ job \ŋ\ sing \ō\ go
\ò\ law \òi\ boy \th\ thin \th\ the \ü\ loot \ù\ foot
\y\ yet \zh\ vision *see also* Guide to Pronunciation

: measures designed to preserve health (as of an individual or of society) and prevent the spread of disease

¹**pro·pine** \prə-'pēn, -'pīn\ *transitive verb* **pro·pined; pro·pin·ing** [Middle English, from Middle French *propiner*, from Latin *propinare* to present, drink to someone's health, from Greek *propinein* literally, to drink first, from *pro-* + *pinein* to drink — more at POTABLE] (15th century)
chiefly Scottish : to present or give especially as a token of friendship

²**propine** *noun* (15th century)
Scottish : a gift in return for a favor

pro·pin·qui·ty \prə-'piŋ-kwə-tē\ *noun* [Middle English *propinquite*, from Latin *propinquitat-, propinquitas* kinship, proximity, from *propinquus* near, akin, from *prope* near — more at APPROACH] (14th century)
1 : nearness of blood : KINSHIP
2 : nearness in place or time : PROXIMITY

pro·pi·o·nate \'prō-pē-ə-ˌnāt\ *noun* [International Scientific Vocabulary] (1862)
: a salt or ester of propionic acid

pro·pi·on·ic acid \ˌprō-pē-'ä-nik-\ *noun* [International Scientific Vocabulary ¹*pro-* + Greek *piōn* fat; akin to Sanskrit *pīvan* swelling, fat] (1850)
: a liquid sharp-odored fatty acid $C_3H_6O_2$ found in milk and distillates of wood, coal, and petroleum

pro·pi·ti·ate \prō-'pi-shē-ˌāt\ *transitive verb* **-at·ed; -at·ing** [Latin *propitiatus*, past participle of *propitiare*, from *propitius* propitious] (1583)
: to gain or regain the favor or goodwill of : APPEASE, CONCILIATE
synonym see PACIFY
— **pro·pi·ti·a·tor** \-ˌā-tər\ *noun*

pro·pi·ti·a·tion \prō-ˌpi-shē-'ā-shən\ *noun* (14th century)
1 : the act of propitiating
2 : something that propitiates; *specifically* : an atoning sacrifice

pro·pi·ti·a·to·ry \prō-'pi-sh(ē-)ə-ˌtōr-ē, -ˌtȯr-\ *adjective* (1551)
1 : intended to propitiate : EXPIATORY
2 : of or relating to propitiation

pro·pi·tious \prə-'pi-shəs\ *adjective* [Middle English *propicious*, from Latin *propitius*, probably from *pro-* for + *petere* to seek — more at PRO-, FEATHER] (15th century)
1 : favorably disposed : BENEVOLENT
2 : being of good omen : AUSPICIOUS ⟨*propitious* sign⟩
3 : tending to favor : ADVANTAGEOUS
synonym see FAVORABLE
— **pro·pi·tious·ly** *adverb*
— **pro·pi·tious·ness** *noun*

pro·plas·tid \(ˌ)prō-'plas-təd\ *noun* [International Scientific Vocabulary] (1922)
: a minute cytoplasmic body from which a plastid is formed

prop·man \'präp-ˌman\ *noun* (circa 1937)
: a man in charge of stage properties

prop·o·lis \'prä-pə-ləs\ *noun* [Middle English *propoleos*, from Medieval Latin, alteration of Latin *propolis*, from Greek, from *pro-* for + *polis* city — more at PRO-, POLICE] (15th century)
: a brownish resinous material of waxy consistency collected by bees from the buds of trees and used as a cement

pro·pone \prə-'pōn\ *transitive verb* **pro·poned; pro·pon·ing** [Middle English (Scots), from Latin *proponere* — more at PROPOUND] (14th century)
1 *Scottish* : PROPOSE, PROPOUND
2 *Scottish* : to put forward (a defense)

pro·po·nent \prə-'pō-nənt, 'prō-ˌ\ *noun* [Latin *proponent-, proponens*, present participle of *proponere*] (1588)
: one who argues in favor of something : ADVOCATE

¹**pro·por·tion** \prə-'pōr-shən, -'pȯr-\ *noun* [Middle English *proporcion*, from Middle French *proportion*, from Latin *proportion-, proportio*, from *pro* for + *portion-, portio* portion — more at FOR] (14th century)
1 : harmonious relation of parts to each other or to the whole : BALANCE, SYMMETRY
2 a : proper or equal share ⟨each did her *portion* of the work⟩ **b** : QUOTA, PERCENTAGE
3 : the relation of one part to another or to the whole with respect to magnitude, quantity, or degree : RATIO
4 : SIZE, DIMENSION
5 : a statement of equality between two ratios in which the first of the four terms divided by the second equals the third divided by the fourth (as in 4/2=10/5) — compare EXTREME 1b, MEAN 1c
— **in proportion** : PROPORTIONAL 1

²**proportion** *transitive verb* **pro·por·tioned; pro·por·tion·ing** \-sh(ə-)niŋ\ (14th century)
1 : to adjust (a part or thing) in size relative to other parts or things
2 : to make the parts of harmonious or symmetrical
3 : APPORTION, ALLOT

pro·por·tion·able \-sh(ə-)nə-bəl\ *adjective* (14th century)
: PROPORTIONAL, PROPORTIONATE
— **pro·por·tion·ably** \-blē\ *adverb, archaic*

¹**pro·por·tion·al** \prə-'pōr-shnəl, -'pȯr-, -shə-n°l\ *adjective* (14th century)
: a number or quantity in a proportion

²**proportional** *adjective* (15th century)
1 a : corresponding in size, degree, or intensity **b** : having the same or a constant ratio ⟨corresponding sides of similar triangles are *proportional*⟩
2 : regulated or determined in size or degree with reference to proportions ⟨a *proportional* system of immigration quotas⟩
— **pro·por·tion·al·i·ty** \-ˌpōr-shə-'na-lə-tē, -ˌpȯr-\ *noun*
— **pro·por·tion·al·ly** \-'pōr-shnə-lē, -'pȯr-, -shə-n°l-ē\ *adverb*

proportional parts *noun plural* (circa 1890)
: fractional parts of the difference between successive entries in a table for use in linear interpolation

proportional representation *noun* (1870)
: an electoral system designed to represent in a legislative body each political group or party in proportion to its actual voting strength in the electorate

proportional tax *noun* (circa 1943)
: a tax in which the tax rate remains constant regardless of the amount of the tax base

¹**pro·por·tion·ate** \prə-'pōr-sh(-)nət, -'pȯr-\ *adjective* (14th century)
: PROPORTIONAL 1
— **pro·por·tion·ate·ly** *adverb*

²**pro·por·tion·ate** \-shə-ˌnāt\ *transitive verb* **-at·ed; -at·ing** (1570)
: to make proportionate : PROPORTION

pro·pos·al \prə-'pō-zəl\ *noun* (1653)
1 : an act of putting forward or stating something for consideration
2 a : something proposed : SUGGESTION **b** : OFFER; *specifically* : an offer of marriage

pro·pose \prə-'pōz\ *verb* **pro·posed; pro·pos·ing** [Middle English, from Middle French *proposer*, from Latin *proponere* (perfect indicative *proposui*) — more at PROPOUND] (14th century)
intransitive verb
1 : to form or put forward a plan or intention ⟨man *proposes*, but God disposes⟩
2 *obsolete* : to engage in talk or discussion
3 : to make an offer of marriage
transitive verb
1 a : to set before the mind (as for discussion, imitation, or action) ⟨*propose* a plan for settling the dispute⟩ **b** : to set before someone and especially oneself as an aim or intent ⟨*proposed* to spend the summer in Italy⟩
2 a : to set forth for acceptance or rejection ⟨*propose* terms for peace⟩ **b** : to recommend to fill a place or vacancy : NOMINATE ⟨*propose* them for membership⟩ **c** : to offer as a toast ⟨*propose* the happiness of the couple⟩
— **pro·pos·er** *noun*

¹**prop·o·si·tion** \ˌprä-pə-'zi-shən\ *noun* (14th century)
1 a (1) : something offered for consideration or acceptance : PROPOSAL (2) : a request for sexual intercourse **b** : the point to be discussed or maintained in argument usually stated in sentence form near the outset **c** : a theorem or problem to be demonstrated or performed
2 a : an expression in language or signs of something that can be believed, doubted, or denied or is either true or false **b** : the objective meaning of a proposition
3 : something of an indicated kind ⟨getting there is a tough *proposition*⟩ ⟨the farm was never a paying *proposition*⟩
— **prop·o·si·tion·al** \-'zish-nəl, -'zi-shə-n°l\ *adjective*

²**proposition** *transitive verb* **-si·tioned; -si·tion·ing** \-'zi-sh(ə-)niŋ\ (1924)
: to make a proposal to; *especially* : to suggest sexual intercourse to

propositional calculus *noun* (1903)
: the branch of symbolic logic that uses symbols for unanalyzed propositions and logical connectives only — called also *sentential calculus*; compare PREDICATE CALCULUS

propositional function *noun* (1903)
1 : SENTENTIAL FUNCTION
2 : something that is designated or expressed by a sentential function

pro·pos·i·tus \prō-'pä-zə-təs\ *noun, plural* **-i·ti** \-ˌtī\ [New Latin, from Latin, past participle of *proponere*] (1899)
: the person immediately concerned : SUBJECT

pro·pound \prə-'paùnd\ *transitive verb* [alteration of earlier *propone*, from Middle English (Scots) *proponen*, from Latin *proponere* to display, propound, from *pro-* before + *ponere* to put, place — more at PRO-, POSITION] (1537)
: to offer for discussion or consideration
— **pro·pound·er** *noun*

pro·poxy·phene \prō-'päk-sə-ˌfēn\ *noun* [*prop-* + *oxy* + *-phene* (alteration of *phenyl*)] (1955)
: an analgesic $C_{22}H_{29}NO_2$ structurally related to methadone but less addicting that is administered in the form of its hydrochloride

pro·prae·tor *or* **pro·pre·tor** \(ˌ)prō-'prē-tər\ *noun* [Latin *propraetor*, from *pro-* (as in *proconsul*) + *praetor*] (circa 1580)
: a praetor of ancient Rome sent out to govern a province

pro·pran·o·lol \prō-'pra-nə-ˌlȯl, -ˌlōl\ *noun* [*propyl* + *propanol* + ¹*-ol*] (1964)
: a beta-adrenergic blocking agent $C_{16}H_{21}NO_2$ used in the form of its hydrochloride in the treatment of abnormal heart rhythms and angina pectoris

¹**pro·pri·e·tary** \prə-'prī-ə-ˌter-ē\ *noun, plural* **-tar·ies** (15th century)
1 : one that possesses, owns, or holds exclusive right to something; *specifically* : PROPRIETOR 1
2 : something that is used, produced, or marketed under exclusive legal right of the inventor or maker; *specifically* : a drug (as a patent medicine) that is protected by secrecy, patent, or copyright against free competition as to name, product, composition, or process of manufacture
3 : a business secretly owned by and run as a cover for an intelligence organization

²**proprietary** *adjective* [Late Latin *proprietarius*, from Latin *proprietas* property — more at PROPERTY] (1589)
1 : of, relating to, or characteristic of a proprietor ⟨*proprietary* rights⟩
2 : used, made, or marketed by one having the exclusive legal right ⟨a *proprietary* process⟩

3 : privately owned and managed and run as a profit-making organization ⟨a *proprietary* clinic⟩

pro·pri·e·tor \prə-'prī-ə-tər\ *noun* [alteration of ¹*proprietary*] (1637)
1 : one granted ownership of a colony (as one of the original American colonies) and full prerogatives of establishing a government and distributing land
2 a : one who has the legal right or exclusive title to something : OWNER **b :** one having an interest (as control or present use) less than absolute and exclusive right
— **pro·pri·e·tor·ship** \-,ship\ *noun*

pro·pri·e·to·ri·al \prə-,prī-ə-'tōr-ē-əl, prō-, -'tȯr-\ *adjective* (1851)
: PROPRIETARY 1

pro·pri·e·tress \-'prī-ə-trəs\ *noun* (1692)
: a woman who is a proprietor

pro·pri·e·ty \prə-'prī-ə-tē\ *noun, plural* **-ties** [Middle English *propriete*, from Middle French *proprieté*, *propreté* property, quality of a person or thing — more at PROPERTY] (14th century)
1 *obsolete* **:** true nature
2 *obsolete* **:** a special characteristic : PECULIARITY
3 : the quality or state of being proper : APPROPRIATENESS
4 a : conformity to what is socially acceptable in conduct or speech **b :** fear of offending against conventional rules of behavior especially between the sexes **c** *plural* **:** the customs and manners of polite society

pro·pri·o·cep·tion \,prō-prē-ō-'sep-shən\ *noun* [*proprioceptive* + *-ion*] (1906)
: the reception of stimuli produced within the organism

pro·pri·o·cep·tive \-'sep-tiv\ *adjective* [Latin *proprius* own + English *-ceptive* (as in *receptive*)] (1906)
: of, relating to, or being stimuli arising within the organism

pro·pri·o·cep·tor \-tər\ *noun* [New Latin, from Latin *proprius* + New Latin *-ceptor* (as in *receptor*)] (1906)
: a sensory receptor (as a muscle spindle) excited by proprioceptive stimuli

prop root *noun* (1905)
: a root that serves as a prop or support to the plant

prop·to·sis \präp-'tō-səs, prō-'tō-\ *noun* [New Latin, from Late Latin, falling forward, from Greek *proptōsis*, from *propiptein* to fall forward, from *pro-* forward + *piptein* to fall — more at PRO-, FEATHER] (1676)
: forward projection or displacement especially of the eyeball

pro·pul·sion \prə-'pəl-shən\ *noun* [Latin *propellere* to propel] (1626)
1 : the action or process of propelling
2 : something that propels

pro·pul·sive \-'pəl-siv\ *adjective* [Latin *propulsus*] (1758)
: tending or having power to propel

pro·pyl \'prō-pəl\ *noun, often attributive* [International Scientific Vocabulary *prop-* + *-yl*] (1850)
: either of two isomeric alkyl groups C_3H_7 derived from propane — often used in combination

pro·py·lae·um \,prä-pə-'lē-əm, ,prō-\ *noun, plural* **-laea** \-'lē-ə\ [Latin, from Greek *propylaion*, from *pro-* before + *pylē* gate — more at PRO-] (circa 1706)
: a vestibule or entrance of architectural importance before a building or enclosure — often used in plural

pro·py·lene \'prō-pə-,lēn\ *noun* (1850)
: a flammable gaseous hydrocarbon C_3H_6 obtained by cracking petroleum hydrocarbons and used chiefly in organic synthesis

propylene glycol *noun* (1885)

: a sweet hygroscopic viscous liquid $C_3H_8O_2$ made especially from propylene and used especially as an antifreeze and solvent and in brake fluids

pro ra·ta \(,)prō-'rā-tə, -'rä-, -'ra-\ *adverb* [Latin] (1575)
: proportionately according to an exactly calculable factor (as share or liability)
— **pro rata** *adjective*

pro·rate \(,)prō-'rāt, 'prō-, 'prō-,\ *verb* **pro·rat·ed; pro·rat·ing** [*pro rata*] (1860)
transitive verb
: to divide, distribute, or assess proportionately
intransitive verb
: to make a pro rata distribution
— **pro·ra·tion** \prō-'rā-shən\ *noun*

pro·ro·gate \'prō-rə-,gāt\ *transitive verb* **-gat·ed; -gat·ing** (1534)
: PROROGUE
— **pro·ro·ga·tion** \,prō-rə-'gā-shən\ *noun*

pro·rogue \prə-'rōg\ *verb* **pro·rogued; pro·rogu·ing** [Middle English *prorogen*, from Middle French *proroguer*, from Latin *prorogare*, from *pro-* before + *rogare* to ask — more at PRO-, RIGHT] (15th century)
transitive verb
1 : DEFER, POSTPONE
2 : to terminate a session of (as a British parliament) by royal prerogative
intransitive verb
: to suspend or end a legislative session

pros *plural of* PRO

pros- *prefix* [Late Latin, from Greek, from *proti*, *pros* face to face with, toward, in addition to, near; akin to Sanskrit *prati-* near, toward, against, in return, Greek *pro* before — more at FOR]
: in front ⟨*prosencephalon*⟩

pro·sa·ic \prō-'zā-ik\ *adjective* [Late Latin *prosaicus*, from Latin *prosa* prose] (circa 1656)
1 a : characteristic of prose as distinguished from poetry : FACTUAL **b :** DULL, UNIMAGINATIVE
2 : EVERYDAY, ORDINARY
— **pro·sa·i·cal·ly** \-'zā-ə-k(ə-)lē\ *adverb*

pro·sa·ism \'prō-(,)zā-,i-zəm\ *noun* (1787)
1 : a prosaic manner, style, or quality
2 : a prosaic expression

pro·sa·ist \'prō-(,)zā-ist\ *noun* [Latin *prosa* prose] (1803)
1 \'prō-(,)zā-ist, -zā-,ist\ **:** a prose writer
2 \prō-'zā-ist\ **:** a prosaic person

pro·sa·teur \,prō-zə-'tər\ *noun* [French, from Italian *prosatore*, from Medieval Latin *prosator*, from Latin *prosa*] (1880)
: a writer of prose

pro·sau·ro·pod \prō-'sȯr-ə-,päd\ *noun* [New Latin *Prosauropoda*, from ¹*pro-* + *Sauropoda* — more at SAUROPOD] (1941)
: any of a group (Prosauropoda) of chiefly herbivorous Triassic dinosaurs that are probably ancestral to sauropods

pro·sce·ni·um \prō-'sē-nē-əm\ *noun* [Latin, from Greek *proskēnion* front of the building forming the background for a dramatic performance, stage, from *pro-* + *skēnē* building forming the background for a dramatic performance — more at SCENE] (1606)
1 a : the stage of an ancient Greek or Roman theater **b :** the part of a modern stage in front of the curtain **c :** the wall that separates the stage from the auditorium and provides the arch that frames it
2 : FOREGROUND

pro·sciut·to \prō-'shü-(,)tō\ *noun, plural* **-ti** \-(,)tē\ *or* **-tos** [Italian, alteration of *presciutto*, from *pre-* (from Latin *prae-* pre-) + *asciutto* dried out, from Latin *exsuctus*, from past participle of *exsugere* to suck out, from *ex-* + *sugere* to suck — more at SUCK] (circa 1929)
: dry-cured spiced Italian ham usually sliced thin

pro·scribe \prō-'skrīb\ *transitive verb* **pro·scribed; pro·scrib·ing** [Latin *proscribere*

to publish, proscribe, from *pro-* before + *scribere* to write — more at SCRIBE] (1560)
1 : to condemn or forbid as harmful or unlawful : PROHIBIT
2 : to publish the name of as condemned to death with the property of the condemned forfeited to the state
— **pro·scrib·er** *noun*

pro·scrip·tion \prō-'skrip-shən\ *noun* [Middle English *proscripcion*, from Latin *proscription-*, *proscriptio*, from *proscribere*] (14th century)
1 : the act of proscribing : the state of being proscribed
2 : an imposed restraint or restriction : PROHIBITION
— **pro·scrip·tive** \-'skrip-tiv\ *adjective*
— **pro·scrip·tive·ly** *adverb*

¹prose \'prōz\ *noun* [Middle English, from Middle French, from Latin *prosa*, from feminine of *prorsus*, *prosus*, straightforward, being in prose, contraction of *proversus*, past participle of *provertere* to turn forward, from *pro-* forward + *vertere* to turn — more at PRO-, WORTH] (14th century)
1 a : the ordinary language people use in speaking or writing **b :** a literary medium distinguished from poetry especially by its greater irregularity and variety of rhythm and its closer correspondence to the patterns of everyday speech
2 : a prosaic style, quality, or condition

²prose *adjective* (14th century)
1 : of, relating to, or written in prose
2 : PROSAIC

³prose *intransitive verb* **prosed; pros·ing** (1642)
1 : to write prose
2 : to write or speak in a prosaic manner

pro·sec·tor \prō-'sek-tər\ *noun* [probably from French *prosecteur*, from Late Latin *prosector* anatomist, from Latin *prosecare* to cut away, from *pro-* forth + *secare* to cut — more at PRO-, SAW] (circa 1857)
: a person who makes dissections for anatomic demonstrations

pros·e·cute \'prä-si-,kyüt\ *verb* **-cut·ed; -cut·ing** [Middle English, from Latin *prosecutus*, past participle of *prosequi* to pursue — more at PURSUE] (15th century)
transitive verb
1 : to follow to the end : pursue until finished ⟨was . . . ordered to *prosecute* the war with . . . vigor —Marjory S. Douglas⟩
2 : to engage in : PERFORM
3 a : to bring legal action against for redress or punishment of a crime or violation of law ⟨*prosecuted* them for fraud⟩ **b :** to institute legal proceedings with reference to ⟨*prosecute* a claim⟩
intransitive verb
: to institute and carry on a legal suit or prosecution
— **pros·e·cut·able** \,prä-sə-'kyü-tə-bəl\ *adjective*

prosecuting attorney *noun* (1832)
: an attorney who conducts proceedings in a court on behalf of the government : DISTRICT ATTORNEY

pros·e·cu·tion \,prä-si-'kyü-shən\ *noun* (1567)
1 : the act or process of prosecuting; *specifically* **:** the institution and continuance of a criminal suit involving the process of pursuing formal charges against an offender to final judgment
2 : the party by whom criminal proceedings are instituted or conducted
3 *obsolete* **:** PURSUIT

\ə\ abut \ᵊ\ kitten \ər\ further \a\ ash \ā\ ace
\ä\ mop, mar \au̇\ out \ch\ chin \e\ bet \ē\ easy
\g\ go \i\ hit \ī\ ice \j\ job \ŋ\ sing \ō\ go
\ȯ\ law \ȯi\ boy \th\ thin \t͟h\ the \ü\ loot \u̇\ foot
\y\ yet \zh\ vision *see also* Guide to Pronunciation

pros·e·cu·tor \'prä-si-ˌkyü-tər\ noun (circa 1670)
1 : a person who institutes an official prosecution before a court
2 : PROSECUTING ATTORNEY

pros·e·cu·to·ri·al \ˌprä-si-kyü-'tōr-ē-əl, -'tȯr-\ adjective (1968)
: of, relating to, or being a prosecutor or prosecution

¹pros·e·lyte \'prä-sə-ˌlīt\ noun [Middle English proselite, from Late Latin proselytus proselyte, alien resident, from Greek prosēlytos, from pros near + -ēlytos (akin to ēlythe he went) — more at PROS-, ELASTIC] (14th century)
: a new convert; specifically **:** a convert to Judaism

²proselyte verb **-lyt·ed; -lyt·ing** (1624)
: PROSELYTIZE

pros·e·ly·tise British variant of PROSELYTIZE

pros·e·ly·tism \'prä-sə-ˌlī-ˌti-zəm, 'prä-s(ə-)lə-\ noun (circa 1660)
1 : the act of becoming or condition of being a proselyte **:** CONVERSION
2 : the act or process of proselytizing

pros·e·ly·tize \'prä-s(ə-)lə-ˌtīz\ verb **-tized; -tiz·ing** (1679)
intransitive verb
1 : to induce someone to convert to one's faith
2 : to recruit someone to join one's party, institution, or cause
transitive verb
: to recruit or convert especially to a new faith, institution, or cause
— **pros·e·ly·ti·za·tion** \ˌprä-s(ə-)lə-tə-'zā-shən, ˌprä-sə-ˌlī-tə-\ noun
— **pros·e·ly·tiz·er** \'prä-s(ə-)lə-ˌtī-zər\ noun

pro·sem·i·nar \(ˌ)prō-'se-mə-ˌnär\ noun (circa 1922)
: a directed course of study like a graduate seminar but often open to advanced undergraduates

pros·en·ceph·a·lon \ˌpräs-ˌen-'se-fə-ˌlän, -lən\ noun [New Latin] (1846)
: FOREBRAIN
— **pros·en·ce·phal·ic** \-sə-'fa-lik\ adjective

prose poem noun (1842)
: a composition in prose that has some of the qualities of a poem
— **prose poet** noun

pros·er \'prō-zər\ noun (1627)
1 : a writer of prose
2 : one who talks or writes tediously

Pro·ser·pi·na \prə-'sər-pə-nə\ or **Pros·er·pine** \'prä-sər-ˌpīn\ noun [Latin]
: PERSEPHONE

pro·sim·i·an \prō-'si-mē-ən\ noun [New Latin Prosimii, from ¹pro- + Latin simia ape — more at SIMIAN] (circa 1890)
: any of a suborder (Prosimii) of lower primates (as lemurs)
— **prosimian** adjective

pro·sit \'prō-zət, -sət\ or **prost** \'prōst\ interjection [German, from Latin prosit may it be beneficial, from prodesse to be useful — more at PROUD] (1846)
— used to wish good health especially before drinking

pro·so \'prō-(ˌ)sō\ noun [Russian] (1917)
: MILLET 1a

pros·o·branch \'prä-sə-ˌbraŋk\ noun, plural **-branchs** [New Latin Prosobranchia, from proso- in front (from Greek prosō forward) + branchia gills (from Greek)] (1851)
: any of a subclass (Prosobranchia) of gastropod mollusks that have the loop of visceral nerves twisted into a figure eight, the sexes usually separate, and usually an operculum
— **prosobranch** adjective

pro·sod·ic \prə-'sä-dik also -'zä-\ or **pro·sod·i·cal** \-di-kəl\ adjective (1774)
: of or relating to prosody
— **pro·sod·i·cal·ly** \-di-k(ə-)lē\ adverb

pros·o·dy \'prä-sə-dē, -zə-\ noun, plural **-dies** [Middle English, from Latin prosodia accent of a syllable, from Greek prosōidia song sung to instrumental music, accent, from pros in addition to + ōidē song — more at PROS-, ODE] (15th century)
1 : the study of versification; especially **:** the systematic study of metrical structure
2 : a particular system, theory, or style of versification
3 : the rhythmic and intonational aspect of language
— **pros·o·dist** \-dist\ noun

pro·so·ma \(ˌ)prō-'sō-mə\ noun [New Latin, from Greek pro- + sōma body] (1872)
: the anterior region of the body of an invertebrate when not readily analyzable into its primitive segmentation; especially **:** CEPHALOTHORAX

pros·o·pog·ra·phy \ˌprä-sə-'pä-grə-fē\ noun [New Latin prosopographia, from Greek prosōpon person + -graphia -graphy] (1929)
: a study that identifies and relates a group of persons or characters within a particular historical or literary context
— **pros·o·po·graph·i·cal** \-pə-'gra-fi-kəl\ adjective

pro·so·po·poe·ia \ˌprä-ˌsō-pə-'pē-ə, ˌprä-sə-pə-\ noun [Latin, from Greek prosōpopoiia, from prosōpon mask, person (from pros- + ōps face) + poiein to make — more at EYE, POET] (circa 1555)
1 : a figure of speech in which an imaginary or absent person is represented as speaking or acting
2 : PERSONIFICATION

¹pros·pect \'prä-ˌspekt\ noun [Middle English, from Latin prospectus view, prospect, from prospicere to look forward, exercise foresight, from pro- forward + specere to look — more at PRO-, SPY] (15th century)
1 : EXPOSURE 3b
2 a (1) : an extensive view **(2) :** a mental consideration **:** SURVEY **b :** a place that commands an extensive view **:** LOOKOUT **c :** something extended to the view **:** SCENE **d** archaic **:** a sketch or picture of a scene
3 obsolete **:** ASPECT
4 a : the act of looking forward **:** ANTICIPATION **b :** a mental picture of something to come **:** VISION **c :** something that is awaited or expected **:** POSSIBILITY **d** plural **(1) :** financial expectations **(2) :** CHANCES
5 : a place showing signs of containing a mineral deposit
6 a : a potential buyer or customer **b :** a likely candidate ☆
— **in prospect :** possible or likely for the future

²prospect \'prä-ˌspekt, chiefly British prə-'\ (1841)
intransitive verb
: to explore an area especially for mineral deposits
transitive verb
: to inspect (a region) for mineral deposits; broadly **:** EXPLORE
— **pros·pec·tor** \-ˌspek-tər, -'spek-\ noun

pro·spec·tive \prə-'spek-tiv also 'prä-ˌ, prō-', prä-'\ adjective (circa 1699)
1 : relating to or effective in the future
2 a : likely to come about **:** EXPECTED ⟨the prospective benefits of this law⟩ **b :** likely to be or become ⟨a prospective mother⟩
— **pro·spec·tive·ly** adverb

pro·spec·tus \prə-'spek-təs, prä-\ noun, plural **-tus·es** [Latin, prospect] (1765)
1 : a preliminary printed statement that describes an enterprise (as a business or publication) and that is distributed to prospective buyers, investors, or participants
2 : something (as a statement or situation) that forecasts the course or nature of something

pros·per \'prä-spər\ verb **pros·pered; pros·per·ing** \-p(ə-)riŋ\ [Middle English, from Middle French prosperer, from Latin prosper-

are to cause to succeed, from prosperus favorable] (14th century)
intransitive verb
1 : to succeed in an enterprise or activity; especially **:** to achieve economic success
2 : to become strong and flourishing
transitive verb
: to cause to succeed or thrive

pros·per·i·ty \prä-'sper-ə-tē\ noun (13th century)
: the condition of being successful or thriving; especially **:** economic well-being

Pros·pe·ro \'präs-pə-ˌrō\ noun
: the rightful duke of Milan in Shakespeare's The Tempest

pros·per·ous \'präs-p(ə-)rəs\ adjective [Middle English, from Middle French prospereus, from Latin prosperus] (15th century)
1 : AUSPICIOUS, FAVORABLE
2 a : marked by success or economic well-being **b :** enjoying vigorous and healthy growth **:** FLOURISHING
— **pros·per·ous·ly** adverb
— **pros·per·ous·ness** noun

pross \'präs\ or **pros·sie** \'prä-sē\ or **pros·tie** \'präs-tē\ noun (circa 1902)
slang **:** PROSTITUTE 1a

pros·ta·cy·clin \ˌpräs-tə-'sī-klən\ noun [prosta- (as in prostaglandin) + cycl- + ¹-in] (1976)
: a prostaglandin that is a metabolite of arachidonic acid, inhibits platelet aggregation, and dilates blood vessels

pros·ta·glan·din \ˌpräs-tə-'glan-dən\ noun [prostate gland + ¹-in; from its occurrence in the seminal fluid of animals] (1936)
: any of various oxygenated unsaturated cyclic fatty acids of animals that perform a variety of hormonelike actions (as in controlling blood pressure or smooth muscle contraction)

pros·tate \'präs-ˌtāt\ noun [New Latin prostata prostate gland, from Greek prostatēs, from proïstanai to put in front, from pro- before + histanai to cause to stand — more at PRO-, STAND] (1646)
: PROSTATE GLAND
— **pros·tat·ic** \prä-'sta-tik\ adjective

pros·ta·tec·to·my \ˌpräs-tə-'tek-tə-mē\ noun, plural **-mies** (circa 1890)
: surgical removal or resection of the prostate gland

prostate gland noun (1828)
: a firm partly muscular partly glandular body that is situated about the base of the mammalian male urethra and secretes an alkaline viscid fluid which is a major constituent of the ejaculatory fluid

pros·ta·tism \'präs-tə-ˌti-zəm\ noun (circa 1900)
: disease of the prostate; especially **:** a disorder resulting from obstruction of the bladder neck by an enlarged prostate

pros·ta·ti·tis \ˌpräs-tə-'tī-təs\ noun [New Latin] (circa 1844)
: inflammation of the prostate gland

pros·the·sis \präs-'thē-səs, 'präs-thə-\ noun, plural **-the·ses** \-ˌsēz\ [New Latin, from Greek, addition, from prostithenai to add to,

from *pros-* in addition to + *tithenai* to put — more at PROS-, DO] (circa 1900)
: an artificial device to replace a missing part of the body

pros·thet·ic \präs-'the-tik\ *adjective* (circa 1890)
1 : of or relating to a prosthesis or prosthetics
2 : of, relating to, or constituting a nonprotein group of a conjugated protein
— **pros·thet·i·cal·ly** \-ti-k(ə-)lē\ *adverb*

pros·thet·ics \-tiks\ *noun plural but singular or plural in construction* (circa 1894)
: the surgical or dental specialty concerned with the design, construction, and fitting of prostheses

pros·thet·ist \'präs-thə-tist\ *noun* (1902)
: a specialist in prosthetics

pros·tho·don·tics \,präs-thə-'dän-tiks\ *noun plural but singular or plural in construction* [New Latin *prosthodontia*, from *prosthesis* + *-odontia*] (1947)
: prosthetic dentistry

pros·tho·don·tist \-'dän-tist\ *noun* (1917)
: a specialist in prosthodontics

¹pros·ti·tute \'präs-tə-,tüt, -,tyüt\ *transitive verb* **-tut·ed; -tut·ing** [Latin *prostitutus*, past participle of *prostituere*, from *pro-* before + *statuere* to station — more at PRO-, STAT-UTE] (1530)
1 : to offer indiscriminately for sexual intercourse especially for money
2 : to devote to corrupt or unworthy purposes : DEBASE ⟨prostitute one's talents⟩
— **pros·ti·tu·tor** \-,tü-tər, -,tyü-\ *noun*

²prostitute *adjective* (1563)
: devoted to corrupt purposes : PROSTITUTED

³prostitute *noun* (1613)
1 a : a woman who engages in promiscuous sexual intercourse especially for money : WHORE **b** : a male who engages in sexual and especially homosexual practices for money
2 : a person (as a writer or painter) who deliberately debases his or her talents (as for money)

pros·ti·tu·tion \,präs-tə-'tü-shən, -'tyü-\ *noun* (1553)
1 : the act or practice of indulging in promiscuous sexual relations especially for money
2 : the state of being prostituted : DEBASEMENT

pro·sto·mi·um \prō-'stō-mē-əm\ *noun, plural* **-mia** \-mē-ə\ [New Latin, from Greek *pro-* + *stoma* mouth — more at STOMACH] (1870)
: the portion of the head of various worms that is situated in front of the mouth
— **pro·sto·mi·al** \-mē-əl\ *adjective*

¹pros·trate \'prä-,strāt\ *adjective* [Middle English *prostrat*, from Latin *prostratus*, past participle of *prosternere*, from *pro-* before + *sternere* to spread out, throw down — more at STREW] (14th century)
1 : stretched out with face on the ground in adoration or submission; *also* : lying flat
2 : completely overcome and lacking vitality, will, or power to rise ⟨was *prostrate* from the heat⟩
3 : trailing on the ground : PROCUMBENT ⟨*prostrate* shrub⟩
synonym see PRONE

²pros·trate \'prä-,strāt, *especially British* prä-'\ *transitive verb* **pros·trat·ed; pros·trat·ing** (15th century)
1 : to throw or put into a prostrate position
2 : to put (oneself) in a humble and submissive posture or state ⟨the whole town had to *prostrate* itself in official apology —Claudia Cassidy⟩
3 : to reduce to submission, helplessness, or exhaustion ⟨was *prostrated* with grief⟩

pros·tra·tion \prä-'strā-shən\ *noun* (14th century)
1 a : the act of assuming a prostrate position **b** : the state of being in a prostrate position : ABASEMENT

2 a : complete physical or mental exhaustion : COLLAPSE **b** : the process of being made powerless or the condition of powerlessness ⟨the country suffered economic *prostration* after the war⟩

prosy \'prō-zē\ *adjective* **pros·i·er; -est** [¹*prose*] (1814)
: lacking in qualities that seize the attention or strike the imagination : COMMONPLACE; *especially* : tediously dull in speech or manner
— **pros·i·ly** \-zə-lē\ *adverb*
— **pros·i·ness** \-zē-nəs\ *noun*

prot- *or* **proto-** *combining form* [Middle English *protho-*, from Middle French, from Late Latin *proto-*, from Greek *prōt-*, *prōto-*, from *prōtos*; akin to Greek *pro* before — more at FOR]
1 a : first in time ⟨*proto*history⟩ **b** : beginning : giving rise to ⟨*proto*planet⟩
2 : parent substance of a (specified) substance ⟨*prot*actinium⟩
3 : first formed : primary ⟨*proto*xylem⟩
4 *capitalized* : relating to or constituting the recorded or assumed language that is ancestral to a language or to a group of related languages or dialects ⟨*Proto*-Indo-European⟩

prot·ac·tin·i·um \,prō-,tak-'ti-nē-əm\ *noun* [New Latin] (1918)
: a shiny radioactive metallic element of relatively short life — see ELEMENT table

pro·tag·o·nist \prō-'ta-gə-nist\ *noun* [Greek *prōtagōnistēs*, from *prōt-* prot- + *agōnistēs* competitor at games, actor, from *agōnizesthai* to compete, from *agōn* contest, competition at games — more at AGONY] (1671)
1 a : the principal character in a literary work (as a drama or story) **b** : a leading actor, character, or participant in a literary work or real event
2 : a leader, proponent, or supporter of a cause : CHAMPION
3 : a muscle that by its contraction actually causes a particular movement

prot·amine \'prō-tə-,mēn\ *noun* [International Scientific Vocabulary *prot-* + *amine*] (1874)
: any of various strongly basic proteins of relatively low molecular weight that are rich in arginine and are found associated especially with DNA in place of histone in the sperm cells of various animals (as fish)

prot·a·sis \'prä-tə-səs\ *noun, plural* **-a·ses** \-,sēz\ [Late Latin, from Greek, premise of a syllogism, conditional clause, from *proteinein* to stretch out before, put forward, from *pro-* + *teinein* to stretch — more at THIN] (circa 1568)
1 : the introductory part of a play or narrative poem
2 : the subordinate clause of a conditional sentence — compare APODOSIS
— **pro·tat·ic** \prä-'ta-tik, prō-\ *adjective*

prote- *or* **proteo-** *combining form* [International Scientific Vocabulary, from French *protéine*]
: protein ⟨*proteo*lysis⟩ ⟨*proteo*se⟩

pro·tea \'prō-tē-ə\ *noun* [New Latin, from Latin *Proteus* Proteus] (1825)
: any of a genus (*Protea* of the family Proteaceae, the protea family) of evergreen shrubs often grown for their showy bracts and dense flower heads

pro·te·an \'prō-tē-ən, prō-'tē-\ *adjective* (1598)
1 : of or resembling Proteus in having a varied nature or ability to assume different forms
2 : displaying great diversity or variety : VERSATILE

protea

pro·te·ase \'prō-tē-,ās, -,āz\ *noun* [International Scientific Vocabulary] (1903)
: any of numerous enzymes that hydrolyze proteins and are classified according to the

most prominent functional group (as serine or cysteine) at the active site — called also *proteinase*

pro·tect \prə-'tekt\ *transitive verb* [Middle English, from Latin *protectus*, past participle of *protegere*, from *pro-* in front + *tegere* to cover — more at PRO-, THATCH] (15th century)
1 : to cover or shield from exposure, injury, or destruction : GUARD
2 : to maintain the status or integrity of especially through financial or legal guarantees: as **a** : to save from contingent financial loss **b** : to foster or shield from infringement or restriction ⟨salesmen with *protected* territories⟩; *specifically* : to restrict competition for (as domestic industries) by means of tariffs or trade controls
synonym see DEFEND
— **pro·tec·tive** \-'tek-tiv\ *adjective*
— **pro·tec·tive·ly** *adverb*
— **pro·tec·tive·ness** *noun*

pro·tec·tant \prə-'tek-tənt\ *noun* (1935)
: a protecting agent

pro·tec·tion \prə-'tek-shən\ *noun* (14th century)
1 : the act of protecting : the state of being protected
2 a : one that protects **b** : supervision or support of one that is smaller and weaker
3 : the freeing of the producers of a country from foreign competition in their home market by restrictions (as high duties) on foreign competitive goods
4 a : immunity from prosecution purchased by criminals through bribery **b** : money extorted by racketeers posing as a protective association
5 : COVERAGE 1a

pro·tec·tion·ist \-sh(ə-)nist\ *noun* (1844)
: an advocate of government economic protection for domestic producers through restrictions on foreign competitors
— **pro·tec·tion·ism** \-shə-,ni-zəm\ *noun*
— **protectionist** *adjective*

protective tariff *noun* (1838)
: a tariff intended primarily to protect domestic producers rather than to yield revenue

pro·tec·tor \prə-'tek-tər\ *noun* (14th century)
1 a : one that protects : GUARDIAN **b** : a device used to prevent injury : GUARD
2 a : one having the care of a kingdom during the king's minority : REGENT **b** : the executive head of the Commonwealth of England, Scotland, and Ireland from 1653 to 1659 — called also *Lord Protector of the Commonwealth*
— **pro·tec·tor·ship** \-,ship\ *noun*

pro·tec·tor·al \-'tek-t(ə-)rəl\ *adjective* (1657)
: of or relating to a protector or protectorate

pro·tec·tor·ate \-'tek-t(ə-)rət\ *noun* (1692)
1 a : government by a protector **b** *capitalized* : the government of England (1653–59) under the Cromwells **c** : the rank, office, or period of rule of a protector
2 a : the relationship of superior authority assumed by one power or state over a dependent one **b** : the dependent political unit in such a relationship

pro·tec·to·ry \-'tek-t(ə-)rē\ *noun, plural* **-ries** (1885)
: an institution for the protection and care usually of homeless or delinquent children

pro·tec·tress \-'tek-trəs\ *noun* (1570)
: a woman who is a protector

pro·té·gé \'prō-tə-,zhā, ,prō-tə-'\ *noun* [French, from past participle of *protéger* to protect, from Latin *protegere*] (1787)

: one who is protected or trained or whose career is furthered by a person of experience, prominence, or influence

pro·té·gée \'prō-tə-ˌzhā, ˌprō-tə-'\ *noun* [French, feminine of *protégé*] (1778)
: a female protégé

pro·tein \'prō-ˌtēn *also* 'prō-tē-ən\ *noun, often attributive* [French *protéine*, from Late Greek *prōteios* primary, from Greek *prōtos* first — more at PROT-] (circa 1844)
1 : any of numerous naturally occurring extremely complex substances that consist of amino-acid residues joined by peptide bonds, contain the elements carbon, hydrogen, nitrogen, oxygen, usually sulfur, and occasionally other elements (as phosphorus or iron), and include many essential biological compounds (as enzymes, hormones, or immunoglobulins)
2 : the total nitrogenous material in plant or animal substances

pro·tein·a·ceous \ˌprō-tᵊn-'ā-shəs; ˌprō-ˌtē(-ə)-'nā-shəs\ *adjective* (circa 1844)
: of, relating to, resembling, or being protein

pro·tein·ase \'prō-tᵊn-ˌās, -ˌāz; 'prō-ˌtē(-ə)-ˌnās, -ˌnāz\ *noun* [International Scientific Vocabulary] (circa 1929)
: PROTEASE

pro·tein·uria \ˌprō-tᵊn-'ûr-ē-ə, -'yûr-; ˌprō-tē(-ə)-'nûr-ē-ə, -'nyûr-\ *noun* [New Latin, from International Scientific Vocabulary *protein* + New Latin *-uria*] (1911)
: the presence of excess protein in the urine

pro tem \(ˌ)prō-'tem\ *adverb* (1828)
: PRO TEMPORE

pro tem·po·re \prō-'tem-pə-ˌrē\ *adverb* [Middle English, from Latin] (15th century)
: for the time being

pro·tend \prō-'tend\ *verb* [Middle English, from Latin *protendere*, from *pro-* + *tendere* to stretch — more at THIN] (15th century)
transitive verb
1 *archaic* : to stretch forth
2 *archaic* : EXTEND
intransitive verb
archaic : STICK OUT, PROTRUDE

pro·ten·sive \-'ten(t)-siv\ *adjective* [Latin *protensus*, past participle of *protendere*] (1671)
1 *archaic* : having continuance in time
2 *archaic* : having lengthwise extent or extensiveness
— **pro·ten·sive·ly** *adverb*

pro·teo·gly·can \ˌprō-tē-ō-'glī-ˌkan\ [International Scientific Vocabulary] (1968)
: any of a class of glycoproteins of high molecular weight that are found especially in the extracellular matrix of connective tissue

pro·te·ol·y·sis \ˌprō-tē-'ä-lə-səs\ *noun* [New Latin] (1880)
: the hydrolysis of proteins or peptides with formation of simpler and soluble products

pro·teo·lyt·ic \ˌprō-tē-ə-'li-tik\ *adjective* (1877)
: of, relating to, or producing proteolysis
— **pro·teo·lyt·i·cal·ly** \-ti-k(ə-)lē\ *adverb*

pro·te·ose \'prō-tē-ˌōs, -ˌōz\ *noun* [International Scientific Vocabulary] (circa 1890)
: any of various water-soluble protein derivatives formed by partial hydrolysis of proteins

Pro·te·ro·zo·ic \ˌprä-tə-rə-'zō-ik, ˌprō-\ *adjective* [Greek *proteros* former, earlier (from *pro* before) + International Scientific Vocabulary *-zoic* — more at FOR] (1899)
: of, relating to, or being the eon of geologic time or the corresponding system of rocks that includes the interval between the Archean and Phanerozoic eons, perhaps exceeds in length all of subsequent geological time, and is marked by rocks that contain fossils indicating the first appearance of eukaryotic organisms (as algae) — see GEOLOGIC TIME table
— **Proterozoic** *noun*

¹pro·test \'prō-ˌtest\ *noun* [Middle English, from Middle French, from *protester*] (15th century)
1 : a solemn declaration of opinion and usually of dissent: as **a** : a sworn declaration that payment of a note or bill has been refused and that all responsible signers or debtors are liable for resulting loss or damage **b** : a declaration made especially before or while paying that a tax is illegal and that payment is not voluntary
2 : the act of objecting or a gesture of disapproval ⟨resigned in *protest*⟩; *especially* : a usually organized public demonstration of disapproval
3 : a complaint, objection, or display of unwillingness usually to an idea or a course of action ⟨went under *protest*⟩
4 : an objection made to an official or a governing body of a sport

²pro·test \prə-'test, 'prō-ˌ, prō-'\ *verb* [Middle English, from Middle French *protester*, from Latin *protestari*, from *pro-* + *testari* to call to witness — more at PRO-, TESTAMENT] (15th century)
transitive verb
1 : to make solemn declaration or affirmation of ⟨*protest* my innocence⟩
2 : to execute or have executed a formal protest against (as a bill or note)
3 : to make a statement or gesture in objection to ⟨*protested* the abuses of human rights⟩
intransitive verb
1 : to make a protestation
2 : to make or enter a protest
synonym see ASSERT
— **pro·test·er** *or* **pro·tes·tor** \-'tes-tər, -ˌtes-\ *noun*

¹prot·es·tant \'prä-təs-tənt, *2 is also* prə-'tes-\ *noun* [Middle French, from Latin *protestant-, protestans,* present participle of *protestari*] (1539)
1 *capitalized* **a** : any of a group of German princes and cities presenting a defense of freedom of conscience against an edict of the Diet of Spires in 1529 intended to suppress the Lutheran movement **b** : a member of any of several church denominations denying the universal authority of the Pope and affirming the Reformation principles of justification by faith alone, the priesthood of all believers, and the primacy of the Bible as the only source of revealed truth; *broadly* : a Christian not of a Catholic or Eastern church
2 : one who makes or enters a protest
— **Prot·es·tant·ism** \'prä-təs-tən-ˌti-zəm\ *noun*

²protestant *adjective* (1539)
1 *capitalized* : of or relating to Protestants, their churches, or their religion
2 : making or sounding a protest ⟨the two *protestant* ladies up and marched out —*Time*⟩

Protestant ethic *noun* (1926)
: an ethic that stresses the virtue of hard work, thrift, and self-discipline

pro·tes·ta·tion \ˌprä-təs-'tā-shən, ˌprō-, -ˌtes-\ *noun* (14th century)
: the act of protesting : a solemn declaration or avowal

pro·te·us \'prō-tē-əs\ *noun, plural* **-tei** \-tē-ˌī\ [New Latin, from Latin, Proteus] (1896)
: any of a genus (*Proteus*) of aerobic usually motile enterobacteria that include saprophytes in decaying organic matter and forms associated with urinary tract infections

Pro·teus \'prō-ˌtyüs, -tē-əs, -ˌtüs\ *noun* [Latin, from Greek *Prōteus*]
: a Greek sea god capable of assuming different forms

pro·tha·la·mi·on \ˌprō-thə-'lā-mē-ən, -ˌän\ *or* **pro·tha·la·mi·um** \-mē-əm\ *noun, plural* **-mia** \-mē-ə\ [New Latin, from Greek *pro-* + *-thalamion* (as in *epithalamion*)] (1597)
: a song in celebration of a marriage

pro·thal·li·um \prō-'tha-lē-əm\ *noun, plural* **-thal·lia** \-lē-ə\ [New Latin, from *pro-* + *thallus*] (1858)
1 : the gametophyte of a pteridophyte (as a fern) that is typically a small flat green thallus attached to the soil by rhizoids
2 : a greatly reduced structure of a seed plant corresponding to the pteridophyte prothallium

pro·thal·lus \(ˌ)prō-'tha-ləs\ *noun* [New Latin] (1854)
: PROTHALLIUM

proth·e·sis \'prä-thə-səs\ *noun, plural* **-e·ses** \-ˌsēz\ [Late Latin, alteration of *prosthesis,* from Greek, literally, addition — more at PROSTHESIS] (circa 1550)
: the addition of a sound to the beginning of a word (as in Old French *estat*—whence English *estate*—from Latin *status*)
— **pro·thet·ic** \prä-'the-tik\ *adjective*

pro·tho·no·ta·ry \prō-'thä-nə-ˌter-ē, ˌprō-thə-'nō-tə-rē\ *or* **pro·to·no·ta·ry** \prō-'tä-nə-ˌter-ē, ˌprō-tə-'nō-tə-rē\ *noun, plural* **-ries** [Middle English *prothonotarie,* from Late Latin *protonotarius,* from *prot-* + Latin *notarius* stenographer — more at NOTARY PUBLIC] (15th century)
: a chief clerk of any of various courts of law
— **pro·tho·no·tar·i·al** \prō-ˌthä-nə-'ter-ē-əl, ˌprō-thə-nō-'ter-ē-əl\ *adjective*

pro·tho·rac·ic \ˌprō-thə-'ra-sik\ *adjective* (1826)
: of or relating to the prothorax

prothoracic gland *noun* (1887)
: one of a pair of thoracic endocrine organs in some insects that control molting

pro·tho·rax \(ˌ)prō-'thōr-ˌaks, -'thȯr-\ *noun* [New Latin *prothorac-, prothorax,* from *¹pro-* + *thorax*] (1826)
: the anterior segment of the thorax of an insect — see INSECT illustration

pro·throm·bin \(ˌ)prō-'thräm-bən\ *noun* [International Scientific Vocabulary] (1898)
: a plasma protein produced in the liver in the presence of vitamin K and converted into thrombin in the clotting of blood

pro·tist \'prō-(ˌ)tist\ *noun* [New Latin *Protista,* from Greek, neuter plural of *prōtistos* very first, primal, from superlative of *prōtos* first — more at PROT-] (1889)
: any of a taxonomic group and especially a kingdom (Protista) of unicellular, colonial, or multicellular organisms usually including the protozoans and most algae and in various classifications prokaryotes, some or all fungi, and the sponges
— **pro·tis·tan** \prō-'tis-tən\ *adjective or noun*

pro·ti·um \'prō-tē-əm, 'prō-shē-\ *noun* [New Latin, from Greek *prōtos* first] (1933)
: the ordinary light hydrogen isotope of atomic mass 1

proto- — see PROT-

pro·to·col \'prō-tə-ˌkȯl, -ˌkōl, -ˌkäl, -kəl\ *noun* [Middle French *prothocole,* from Medieval Latin *protocollum,* from Late Greek *prōtokollon* first sheet of a papyrus roll bearing data of manufacture, from Greek *prōt-* prot- + *kollan* to glue together, from *kolla* glue; perhaps akin to Middle Dutch *helen* to glue] (1541)
1 : an original draft, minute, or record of a document or transaction
2 a : a preliminary memorandum often formulated and signed by diplomatic negotiators as a basis for a final convention or treaty **b** : the records or minutes of a diplomatic conference or congress that show officially the agreements arrived at by the negotiators
3 a : a code prescribing strict adherence to correct etiquette and precedence (as in diplomatic exchange and in the military services) **b** : a set of conventions governing the treatment and especially the formatting of data in an electronic communications system

4 : a detailed plan of a scientific or medical experiment, treatment, or procedure ◆

pro·to·derm \'prō-tə-ˌdərm\ *noun* [International Scientific Vocabulary] (circa 1932)
: the outer primary meristem of a plant or plant part

pro·to·gal·axy \ˌprō-tō-'ga-lək-sē\ *noun* (1950)
: a cloud of gas believed to be the precursor to a galaxy

pro·to·his·to·ry \-'his-t(ə-)rē\ *noun* [International Scientific Vocabulary] (1903)
: the study of human beings in the times that immediately antedate recorded history
— **pro·to·his·to·ri·an** \-(h)is-'tōr-ē-ən, -'tȯr-\ *noun*
— **pro·to·his·tor·ic** \-'tȯr-ik, -'tär-\ *adjective*

pro·to·hu·man \-'hyü-mən, -'yü-\ *adjective* (circa 1909)
: of, relating to, or resembling an early hominid (as an australopithecine)
— **protohuman** *noun*

pro·to·lan·guage \'prō-tō-ˌlaŋ-gwij\ *noun* (1948)
: an assumed or recorded ancestral language

pro·to·mar·tyr \'prō-tō-ˌmär-tər\ *noun* [Middle English *prothomartir*, from Middle French, from Late Latin *protomartyr*, from Late Greek *prōtomartyr-, prōtomartys*, from Greek *prōt-* + *martyr-, martys* martyr] (15th century)
: the first martyr in a cause or region

pro·ton \'prō-ˌtän\ *noun* [Greek *prōton*, neuter of *prōtos* first — more at PROT-] (1920)
: an elementary particle that is identical with the nucleus of the hydrogen atom, that along with neutrons is a constituent of all other atomic nuclei, that carries a positive charge numerically equal to the charge of an electron, and that has a mass of 1.673×10^{-24} gram
— **pro·ton·ic** \prō-'tä-nik\ *adjective*

pro·ton·ate \'prō-tə-ˌnāt\ *verb* **-at·ed; -at·ing** (1945)
transitive verb
: to add a proton to
intransitive verb
: to acquire an additional proton
— **pro·ton·ation** \ˌprō-tə-'nā-shən\ *noun*

pro·to·ne·ma \ˌprō-tə-'nē-mə\ *noun, plural* **-ne·ma·ta** \-'nē-mə-tə, -'ne-\ [New Latin *protonemat-, protonema*, from *prot-* + Greek *nēma* thread — more at NEMAT-] (1857)
: the primary usually filamentous thalloid stage of the gametophyte in mosses and in some liverworts comparable to the prothallium in ferns
— **pro·to·ne·mal** \-'nē-məl\ *adjective*
— **pro·to·ne·ma·tal** \-'nē-mə-t°l, -'ne-\ *adjective*

protonotary apostolic *or* **prothonotary apostolic** *noun, plural* **protonotaries apostolic** *or* **prothonotaries apostolic** (1682)
: a priest of the chief college of the papal curia who keeps records of consistories and canonizations and signs papal bulls; *also* **:** an honorary member of this college

proton synchrotron *noun* (1947)
: a synchrotron in which protons are accelerated by means of frequency modulation of the radio-frequency accelerating voltage so that they have energies of billions of electron volts

pro·to·path·ic \ˌprō-tə-'pa-thik\ *adjective* [International Scientific Vocabulary, from Middle Greek *prōtopathēs* affected first, from Greek *prōt-* prot- + *pathos* experience, suffering — more at PATHOS] (1905)
: of, relating to, or being cutaneous sensory reception responsive only to rather gross stimuli

pro·to·phlo·em \-'flō-ˌem\ *noun* (1884)
: the first-formed phloem that develops from procambium, consists of narrow thin-walled cells capable of a limited amount of stretching, and is usually associated with a region of rapid growth

pro·to·plan·et \'prō-tō-ˌpla-nət\ *noun* (1949)

: a hypothetical whirling gaseous mass within a giant cloud of gas and dust that rotates around a sun and is believed to give rise to a planet
— **pro·to·plan·e·tary** \ˌprō-tō-'pla-nə-ˌter-ē\ *adjective*

pro·to·plasm \'prō-tə-ˌpla-zəm\ *noun* [German *Protoplasma*, from *prot-* + New Latin *plasma*] (1848)
1 : the organized colloidal complex of organic and inorganic substances (as proteins and water) that constitutes the living nucleus, cytoplasm, plastids, and mitochondria of the cell
2 : CYTOPLASM
— **pro·to·plas·mic** \ˌprō-tə-'plaz-mik\ *adjective*

pro·to·plast \'prō-tə-ˌplast\ *noun* [Middle French *protoplaste*, from Late Latin *protoplastus* first human, from Greek *prōtoplastos* first formed, from *prōt-* prot- + *plastos* formed, from *plassein* to mold — more at PLASTER] (1532)
1 : one that is formed first **:** PROTOTYPE
2 : a plant cell that has had its cell wall removed; *also* **:** the nucleus, cytoplasm, and plasma membrane of a cell as distinguished from inert walls and inclusions

pro·to·por·phy·rin \ˌprō-tō-'pȯr-f(ə-)rən\ *noun* [International Scientific Vocabulary] (1925)
: a purple porphyrin acid $C_{34}H_{34}N_4O_4$ obtained from hemin or heme by removal of bound iron

pro·to·star \'prō-tō-ˌstär\ *noun* (1947)
: a cloud of gas and dust in space believed to develop into a star

pro·to·stele \'prō-tə-ˌstēl, ˌprō-tə-'stē-lē\ *noun* (1901)
: a stele forming a solid rod with the phloem surrounding the xylem
— **pro·to·ste·lic** \ˌprō-tə-'stē-lik\ *adjective*

pro·to·stome \'prō-tə-ˌstōm\ *noun* [New Latin *Protostomia*, from *prot-* + Greek *stoma* mouth — more at STOMACH] (circa 1961)
: any of a major group (Protostomia) of bilateral metazoan animals (as mollusks, annelids, and arthropods) characterized in typical forms by determinate and spiral cleavage, formation of a mouth and anus directly from the blastopore, and formation of the coelom by splitting of the embryonic mesoderm — compare DEUTEROSTOME

pro·to·troph \'prō-tə-ˌtrōf, -ˌträf\ *noun* [back-formation from *prototrophic*] (1946)
: a prototrophic individual

pro·to·tro·phic \ˌprō-tə-'trō-fik\ *adjective* [International Scientific Vocabulary] (1900)
: having the nutritional requirements of the normal or wild type
— **pro·to·tro·phy** \prō-'tä-trə-fē\ *noun*

pro·to·typ·al \ˌprō-tə-'tī-pəl\ *adjective* (circa 1693)
: PROTOTYPICAL

pro·to·type \'prō-tə-ˌtīp\ *noun* [French, from Greek *prōtotypon*, from neuter of *prōtotypos* archetypal, from *prōt-* + *typos* type] (1552)
1 : an original model on which something is patterned **:** ARCHETYPE
2 : an individual that exhibits the essential features of a later type
3 : a standard or typical example
4 : a first full-scale and usually functional form of a new type or design of a construction (as an airplane)

pro·to·typ·i·cal \ˌprō-tə-'ti-pi-kəl\ *also* **pro·to·typ·ic** \-'pik\ *adjective* (1650)
: of, relating to, or being a prototype
— **pro·to·typ·i·cal·ly** \-pi-k(ə-)lē\ *adverb*

pro·to·xy·lem \ˌprō-tə-'zī-ləm, -ˌlem\ *noun* (1887)
: the first-formed xylem developing from procambium and consisting of narrow cells with annular, spiral, or scalariform wall thickenings

pro·to·zo·al \ˌprō-tə-'zō-əl\ *adjective* (1890)
: of or relating to protozoans

pro·to·zo·an \-'zō-ən\ *noun* [New Latin *Protozoa*, from *prot-* + *-zoa*] (circa 1864)
: any of a phylum or subkingdom (Protozoa) of chiefly motile and heterotrophic unicellular protists (as amoebas, trypanosomes, sporozoans, and paramecia) that are represented in almost every kind of habitat and include some pathogenic parasites of humans and domestic animals
— **protozoan** *adjective*

pro·to·zo·ol·o·gy \-zō-'ä-lə-jē, -zə-'wä-\ *noun* [New Latin *Protozoa* + International Scientific Vocabulary *-logy*] (1904)
: a branch of zoology dealing with protozoans
— **pro·to·zo·ol·o·gist** \-zō-'ä-lə-jist, -zə-'wä-\ *noun*

pro·to·zo·on \-'zō-ˌän\ *noun, plural* **-zoa** \-'zō-ə\ [New Latin, from singular of *Protozoa*] (circa 1853)
: PROTOZOAN

pro·tract \prō-'trakt, prə-\ *transitive verb* [Latin *protractus*, past participle of *protrahere*, literally, to draw forward, from *pro-* forward + *trahere* to draw — more at PRO-] (1540)
1 *archaic* **:** DELAY, DEFER
2 : to prolong in time or space **:** CONTINUE
3 : to extend forward or outward — compare RETRACT 1
synonym see EXTEND
— **pro·trac·tive** \-'trak-tiv\ *adjective*

protracted meeting *noun* (1832)
: a protracted revival meeting

pro·trac·tile \-'trak-t°l, -ˌtīl\ *adjective* [Latin *protractus*] (1828)
: capable of being thrust out ⟨*protractile* jaws⟩

pro·trac·tion \-'trak-shən\ *noun* [Late Latin *protraction-, protractio* act of drawing out, from *protrahere*] (1535)
1 : the act of protracting **:** the state of being protracted
2 : the drawing to scale of an area of land

pro·trac·tor \-'trak-tər\ *noun* (circa 1611)
1 a : one that protracts **b :** a muscle that extends a part
2 : an instrument for laying down and measuring angles in drawing and plotting

◇ **WORD HISTORY**

protocol In ancient Greece a book consisted of papyrus sheets glued together along their edges to form a roll. The first sheet in the roll was known in Late Greek as the *protokollon*, from *proto-*, "first, beginning," and *-kollon*, a derivative of Greek *kolla* "glue." From *protokollon* came Medieval Latin *protocollum* and hence Middle French *prothocole*. By the time this ancient Greek word made its way into English via French in the 16th century as *protocol*, it had come to denote a "first" document of a different kind: the original draft, minute, or record of a transaction. A century later the word referred specifically to the first draft or record of a diplomatic document, such as a treaty or declaration. The diplomatic connection was reinforced in the 19th century when the official records or minutes of a diplomatic conference or congress also came under the rubric of *protocol*. Not long afterward, the French used *protocole* in the name of a department within the Ministry of Foreign Affairs whose province was the etiquette to be observed in official ceremonies and diplomatic relations. This use by the French is responsible for what is now the most familiar meaning of *protocol* in English.

pro·trep·tic \prō-'trep-tik\ *noun* [Late Latin *protrepticus* hortatory, encouraging, from Greek *protreptikos,* from *protrepein* to turn forward, urge on, from *pro-* + *trepein* to turn] (circa 1656)
: an utterance (as a speech) designed to instruct and persuade
— **protreptic** *adjective*

pro·trude \prō-'trüd\ *verb* **pro·trud·ed; pro·trud·ing** [Latin *protrudere,* from *pro-* + *trudere* to thrust — more at THREAT] (1620)
transitive verb
1 *archaic* : to thrust forward
2 : to cause to project
intransitive verb
: to jut out from the surrounding surface or context ⟨a handkerchief *protruding* from his breast pocket⟩
— **pro·tru·si·ble** \-'trü-sə-bəl, -zə-\ *adjective*

pro·tru·sion \prō-'trü-zhən\ *noun* [Latin *protrudere*] (1646)
1 : the act of protruding : the state of being protruded
2 : something (as a part or excrescence) that protrudes
synonym see PROJECTION

pro·tru·sive \-'trü-siv, -ziv\ *adjective* (1676)
1 *archaic* : thrusting forward
2 : PROMINENT, PROTUBERANT ⟨a *protrusive* jaw⟩
3 : OBTRUSIVE, PUSHING ⟨a coarse *protrusive* manner⟩
— **pro·tru·sive·ly** *adverb*
— **pro·tru·sive·ness** *noun*

pro·tu·ber·ance \prō-'tü-b(ə-)rən(t)s, -'tyü-\ *noun* (1646)
1 : something that is protuberant
2 : the quality or state of being protuberant
synonym see PROJECTION

pro·tu·ber·ant \-b(ə-)rənt\ *adjective* [Late Latin *protuberant-, protuberans,* present participle of *protuberare* to bulge out, from Latin *pro-* forward + *tuber* excrescence, swelling; perhaps akin to Latin *tumēre* to swell — more at THUMB] (1646)
1 : thrusting out from a surrounding or adjacent surface often as a rounded mass : PROMINENT
2 : forcing itself into consciousness : OBTRUSIVE
— **pro·tu·ber·ant·ly** *adverb*

proud \'praůd\ *adjective* [Middle English, from Old English *prūd,* probably from Old French *prod, prud, prou* capable, good, valiant, from Late Latin *prode* advantage, advantageous, back-formation from Latin *prodesse* to be advantageous, from *pro-, prod-* for, in favor + *esse* to be — more at PRO-, IS] (before 12th century)
1 : feeling or showing pride: as **a** : having or displaying excessive self-esteem **b** : much pleased : EXULTANT **c** : having proper self-respect
2 a : marked by stateliness : MAGNIFICENT **b** : giving reason for pride : GLORIOUS ⟨the *proudest* moment in her life⟩
3 : VIGOROUS, SPIRITED ⟨a *proud* steed⟩
4 *chiefly British* : raised above a surrounding area ⟨a *proud* design on a stamp⟩ ☆
— **proud·ly** *adverb*

proud flesh *noun* (14th century)
: an excessive growth of granulation tissue (as in an ulcer)

proud·ful \'praůd-fəl\ *adjective* (14th century) *chiefly dialect* : marked by or full of pride

proud·heart·ed \-'här-təd\ *adjective* (14th century)
: proud in spirit : HAUGHTY

proust·ite \'prü-ˌstīt\ *noun* [French, from Joseph L. *Proust* (died 1826) French chemist] (1835)
: a mineral that consists of a red silver arsenic sulfide and occurs in crystals or massively

pro·vas·cu·lar \(ˌ)prō-'vas-kyə-lər\ *adjective* (circa 1948)

: of, relating to, or being procambium

prove \'prüv\ *verb* **proved** *or* **prov·en** \'prü-vən, *British also* 'prō-\; **prov·ing** \'prü-viŋ\ [Middle English, from Old French *prover,* from Latin *probare* to test, approve, prove, from *probus* good, honest, from *pro-* for, in favor + *-bus* (akin to Old English *bēon* to be) — more at PRO-, BE] (13th century)
transitive verb
1 *archaic* : to learn or find out by experience
2 a : to test the truth, validity, or genuineness of ⟨the exception *proves* the rule⟩ ⟨*prove* a will at probate⟩ **b** : to test the worth or quality of; *specifically* : to compare against a standard — sometimes used with *up* or *out* **c** : to check the correctness of (as an arithmetic result)
3 a : to establish the existence, truth, or validity of (as by evidence or logic) ⟨*prove* a theorem⟩ ⟨the charges were never *proved* in court⟩ **b** : to demonstrate as having a particular quality or worth ⟨the vaccine has been *proven* effective after years of tests⟩ ⟨*proved* herself a great actress⟩
4 : to show (oneself) to be worthy or capable ⟨eager to *prove* myself in the new job⟩
intransitive verb
: to turn out especially after trial or test ⟨the new drug *proved* effective⟩ □
— **prov·able** \'prü-və-bəl\ *adjective*
— **prov·able·ness** *noun*
— **prov·ably** \-blē\ *adverb*
— **prov·er** \'prü-vər\ *noun*

prov·e·nance \'präv-nən(t)s, 'prä-və-ˌnän(t)s\ *noun* [French, from *provenir* to come forth, originate, from Latin *provenire,* from *pro-* forth + *venire* to come — more at PRO-, COME] (1785)
1 : ORIGIN, SOURCE
2 : the history of ownership of a valued object or work of art or literature

¹**Pro·ven·çal** \ˌprō-ˌvän-'säl, ˌprä-vən-, *sense 1 also* prə-'ven(t)-səl\ *adjective* [Middle French, from *Provence* Provence] (1589)
1 : of, relating to, or characteristic of Provence or the people of Provence
2 *or* **Pro·ven·çale** : cooked with garlic, onion, mushrooms, tomato, olive oil, and herbs ⟨scallops *Provençal*⟩

²**Pro·ven·çal** \ˌprō-ˌvän-'säl, ˌprä-vən-\ *noun* (1600)
1 : a native or inhabitant of Provence
2 : a Romance language spoken in southern France; *especially* : the dialect of this language spoken in Provence

prov·en·der \'prä-vən-dər\ *noun* [Middle English, from Middle French *provende, provendre,* from Medieval Latin *provenda,* alteration of *praebenda* prebend] (14th century)
1 : dry food for domestic animals : FEED
2 : FOOD, VICTUALS

pro·ve·nience \prə-'vē-nyən(t)s, -nē-ən(t)s\ *noun* [alteration of *provenance*] (1882)
: ORIGIN, SOURCE

prov·en·ly \'prü-vən-lē, *British also* 'prō-\ *adverb* (1887)
: demonstrably as stated : without doubt or uncertainty

pro·ven·tric·u·lus \ˌprō-ven-'tri-kyə-ləs\ *noun, plural* **-li** \-ˌlī, -ˌlē\ [New Latin] (circa 1836)
1 : the glandular or true stomach of a bird that is situated between the crop and gizzard
2 : a muscular dilatation of the foregut in most mandibulate insects that is armed internally with chitinous teeth or plates for triturating food
3 : the thin-walled sac in front of the gizzard of an earthworm

prove out *intransitive verb* (1941)
: to turn out to be satisfactory or as expected

¹**prov·erb** \'prä-ˌvərb\ *noun* [Middle English *proverbe,* from Middle French, from Latin *proverbium,* from *pro-* + *verbum* word — more at WORD] (14th century)
1 : a brief popular epigram or maxim : ADAGE

2 : BYWORD 4

²**proverb** *transitive verb* (14th century)
1 : to speak of proverbially
2 *obsolete* : to provide with a proverb

pro–verb \'prō-ˌvərb, -'vərb\ *noun* (1907)
: a form of the verb *do* used to avoid repetition of a verb (as *do* in "act as I do")

pro·ver·bi·al \prə-'vər-bē-əl\ *adjective* (1548)
1 : of, relating to, or resembling a proverb
2 : that has become a proverb or byword : commonly spoken of ⟨the *proverbial* smoking gun⟩
— **pro·ver·bi·al·ly** \-ə-lē\ *adverb*

Prov·erbs \'prä-ˌvərbz\ *noun plural but singular in construction*
: a collection of moral sayings and counsels forming a book of canonical Jewish and Christian Scripture — see BIBLE table

pro·vide \prə-'vīd\ *verb* **pro·vid·ed; pro·vid·ing** [Middle English, from Latin *providēre,* literally, to see ahead, from *pro-* forward + *vidēre* to see — more at PRO-, WIT] (15th century)
intransitive verb
1 : to take precautionary measures ⟨*provide* for the common defense —*U.S. Constitution*⟩
2 : to make a proviso or stipulation ⟨the constitution . . . *provides* for an elected two-chamber legislature —*Current Biography*⟩
3 : to make preparation to meet a need ⟨*provide* for entertainment⟩; *especially* : to supply something for sustenance or support ⟨*provides* for the poor⟩
transitive verb
1 *archaic* : to prepare or get ready in advance

2 a : to supply or make available (something wanted or needed) ⟨*provided* new uniforms for the band⟩; *also* **:** AFFORD ⟨curtains *provide* privacy⟩ **b :** to make something available to ⟨*provide* the children with free balloons⟩
3 : to have as a condition **:** STIPULATE ⟨the contract *provides* that certain deadlines will be met⟩
provided *conjunction* [Middle English, past participle of *providen* to provide] (15th century)
: on condition that **:** with the understanding **:** IF
usage see PROVIDING
prov·i·dence \'prä-və-dən(t)s, -,den(t)s\ *noun* [Middle English, from Middle French, from Latin *providentia,* from *provident-, providens*] (14th century)
1 a *often capitalized* **:** divine guidance or care **b** *capitalized* **:** God conceived as the power sustaining and guiding human destiny
2 : the quality or state of being provident
prov·i·dent \-dənt, -,dent\ *adjective* [Middle English, from Latin *provident-, providens,* from present participle of *providēre*] (15th century)
1 : making provision for the future **:** PRUDENT
2 : FRUGAL, SAVING
— **prov·i·dent·ly** *adverb*
prov·i·den·tial \,prä-və-'den(t)-shəl\ *adjective* (1648)
1 : of, relating to, or determined by Providence
2 *archaic* **:** marked by foresight **:** PRUDENT
3 : occurring by or as if by an intervention of Providence ⟨a *providential* escape⟩
synonym see LUCKY
— **prov·i·den·tial·ly** \-'den(t)-sh(ə-)lē\ *adverb*
pro·vid·er \prə-'vī-dər\ *noun* (1523)
: one that provides; *especially* **:** BREADWINNER
providing *conjunction* [Middle English, present participle of *providen*] (15th century)
: on condition that **:** in case □
prov·ince \'prä-vən(t)s\ *noun* [Middle English, from Middle French, from Latin *provincia*] (14th century)
1 a : a country or region brought under the control of the ancient Roman government **b :** an administrative district or division of a country **c** *plural* **:** all of a country except the metropolises
2 a : a division of a country forming the jurisdiction of an archbishop or metropolitan **b :** a territorial unit of a religious order
3 a : a biogeographic division of less rank than a region **b :** an area that exhibits essential continuity of geological history; *also* **:** one characterized by particular structural or petrological features
4 a : proper or appropriate function or scope **:** SPHERE **b :** a department of knowledge or activity
synonym see FUNCTION
¹pro·vin·cial \prə-'vin(t)-shəl\ *noun* [in sense 1, from Middle English, from Middle French or Medieval Latin; Middle French, from Medieval Latin *provincialis,* from *provincia* ecclesiastical province; in other senses, from Latin *provincialis,* from *provincia* province] (14th century)
1 : the superior of a province of a Roman Catholic religious order
2 : one living in or coming from a province
3 a : a person of local or restricted interests or outlook **b :** a person lacking urban polish or refinement
²provincial *adjective* (14th century)
1 : of, relating to, or coming from a province
2 a : limited in outlook **:** NARROW **b :** lacking the polish of urban society **:** UNSOPHISTICATED
3 : of or relating to a decorative style (as in furniture) marked by simplicity, informality, and relative plainness; *especially* **:** FRENCH PROVINCIAL
— **pro·vin·cial·ly** \-'vin(t)-sh(ə-)lē\ *adverb*
pro·vin·cial·ism \-shə-,li-zəm\ *noun* (1770)

1 : a dialectal or local word, phrase, or idiom
2 : the quality or state of being provincial
pro·vin·cial·ist \-'vin(t)-sh(ə-)list\ *noun* (1656)
: a native or inhabitant of a province
pro·vin·ci·al·i·ty \prə-,vin(t)-shē-'a-lə-tē\ *noun, plural* **-ties** (1782)
1 : PROVINCIALISM 2
2 : an act or instance of provincialism
pro·vin·cial·ize \-'vin(t)-shə-,līz\ *transitive verb* **-ized; -iz·ing** (1829)
: to make provincial
— **pro·vin·cial·i·za·tion** \-,vin(t)-sh(ə-)lə-'zā-shən\ *noun*
proving ground *noun* (circa 1890)
1 : a place for scientific experimentation or testing (as of vehicles or weapons)
2 : a place where something is developed or tried out
pro·vi·rus \(,)prō-'vī-rəs\ *noun* [New Latin] (1949)
: a form of a virus that is integrated into the genetic material of a host cell and by replicating with it can be transmitted from one cell generation to the next without causing lysis
— **pro·vi·ral** \-rəl\ *adjective*
¹pro·vi·sion \prə-'vi-zhən\ *noun* [Middle English, from Middle French, from Late Latin & Latin; Late Latin *provision-, provisio* act of providing, from Latin, foresight, from *providēre* to see ahead — more at PROVIDE] (14th century)
1 a : the act or process of providing **b :** the fact or state of being prepared beforehand **c :** a measure taken beforehand to deal with a need or contingency **:** PREPARATION ⟨made *provision* for replacements⟩
2 : a stock of needed materials or supplies; *especially* **:** a stock of food — usually used in plural
3 : PROVISO, STIPULATION
²provision *transitive verb* **pro·vi·sioned; pro·vi·sion·ing** \-'vi-zhə-niŋ, -'vizh-niŋ\ (1809)
: to supply with provisions
¹pro·vi·sion·al \prə-'vizh-nəl, -'vi-zhə-nᵊl\ *adjective* (1601)
: serving for the time being **:** TEMPORARY
— **pro·vi·sion·al·ly** *adverb*
²provisional *noun* (1886)
: a postage stamp for use until a regular issue appears — compare DEFINITIVE
pro·vi·sion·ary \prə-'vi-zhə-,ner-ē\ *adjective* (1617)
: PROVISIONAL
pro·vi·sion·er \-'vi-zhə-nər, -'vizh-nər\ *noun* (1866)
: a furnisher of provisions
pro·vi·so \prə-'vī-(,)zō\ *noun, plural* **-sos** *or* **-soes** [Middle English, from Medieval Latin *proviso quod* provided that] (15th century)
1 : an article or clause (as in a contract) that introduces a condition
2 : a conditional stipulation
pro·vi·so·ry \-'vī-zə-rē, -'vīz-rē\ *adjective* (circa 1611)
1 : containing or subject to a proviso **:** CONDITIONAL
2 : PROVISIONAL
pro·vi·ta·min \(,)prō-'vī-tə-mən\ *noun* (1927)
: a precursor of a vitamin convertible into the vitamin in an organism
Pro·vo \'prō-(,)vō\ *noun, plural* **Provos** [*Provisional* I.R.A., name of the faction + ¹-*o*] (1971)
: a member of the extremist faction of the Irish Republican Army
pro·vo·ca·teur \prō-,vä-kə-'tər\ *noun* (1919)
: AGENT PROVOCATEUR
prov·o·ca·tion \,prä-və-'kā-shən\ *noun* [Middle English *provocacioun,* from Middle French *provocation,* from Latin *provocation-, provocatio,* from *provocare*] (14th century)
1 : the act of provoking **:** INCITEMENT
2 : something that provokes, arouses, or stimulates

pro·voc·a·tive \prə-'vä-kə-tiv\ *adjective* (15th century)
: serving or tending to provoke, excite, or stimulate
— **provocative** *noun*
— **pro·voc·a·tive·ly** *adverb*
— **pro·voc·a·tive·ness** *noun*
pro·voke \prə-'vōk\ *transitive verb* **pro·voked; pro·vok·ing** [Middle English, from Middle French *provoquer,* from Latin *provocare,* from *pro-* forth + *vocare* to call, from *voc-, vox* voice — more at PRO-, VOICE] (14th century)
1 a *archaic* **:** to arouse to a feeling or action **b :** to incite to anger
2 a : to call forth (as a feeling or action) **:** EVOKE ⟨*provoke* laughter⟩ **b :** to stir up purposely ⟨*provoke* a fight⟩ **c :** to provide the needed stimulus for ⟨will *provoke* a lot of discussion⟩ ☆
— **pro·vok·er** *noun*
pro·vok·ing \-'vō-kiŋ\ *adjective* (1642)
: causing mild anger **:** ANNOYING
— **pro·vok·ing·ly** \-kiŋ-lē\ *adverb*
pro·vo·lo·ne \,prō-və-'lō-nē\ *noun* [Italian, augmentative of *provola,* a kind of cheese] (1912)
: a usually firm pliant often smoked cheese of Italian origin
pro·vost \'prō-,vōst, 'prä-vəst, 'prō-vəst, *especially attributive* ,prō-(,)vō\ *noun* [Middle English, from Old English *profost* & Old French *provost,* from Medieval Latin *propositus,* alteration of *praepositus,* from Latin, one in charge, director, from past participle of *praeponere* to place at the head — more at PREPOSITION] (before 12th century)
1 : the chief dignitary of a collegiate or cathedral chapter
2 : the chief magistrate of a Scottish burgh
3 : the keeper of a prison
4 : a high-ranking university administrative officer
provost court *noun* (1864)
: a military court usually for the trial of minor offenses within an occupied hostile territory
provost guard *noun* (1862)
: a police detail of soldiers under the authority of the provost marshal
provost marshal *noun* (1535)
: an officer who supervises the military police of a command

☆ SYNONYMS
Provoke, excite, stimulate, pique, quicken mean to arouse as if by pricking. PROVOKE directs attention to the response called forth ⟨my stories usually *provoke* laughter⟩. EXCITE implies a stirring up or moving profoundly ⟨news that *excited* anger and frustration⟩. STIMULATE suggests a rousing out of lethargy, quiescence, or indifference ⟨*stimulating* conversation⟩. PIQUE suggests stimulating by mild irritation or challenge ⟨that remark *piqued* my interest⟩. QUICKEN implies beneficially stimulating and making active or lively ⟨the high salary *quickened* her desire to have the job⟩. See in addition IRRITATE.

□ USAGE
providing Although occasionally still disapproved, *providing* is as well established as a conjunction as *provided* is. *Provided* is more common.

\ə\ abut \ᵊ\ kitten \ər\ further \a\ ash \ā\ ace
\ä\ mop, mar \aů\ out \ch\ chin \e\ bet \ē\ easy
\g\ go \i\ hit \ī\ ice \j\ job \ŋ\ sing \ō\ go
\ȯ\ law \ȯi\ boy \th\ thin \t͟h\ the \ü\ loot \ů\ foot
\y\ yet \zh\ vision *see also* Guide to Pronunciation

¹prow \'praú\ *adjective* [Middle English, from Middle French *prou* — more at PROUD] (14th century)
archaic : VALIANT, GALLANT

²prow \'praú\, *archaic* 'prō\ *noun* [Middle French *proue*, probably from Old Italian dialect *prua*, from Latin *prora*, from Greek *prōira*] (1555)
1 : the bow of a ship : STEM
2 : a pointed projecting front part

prow·ess \'praú-əs *also* 'prō-\ *noun* [Middle English *prouesse*, from Old French *proesse*, from *prou*] (13th century)
1 : distinguished bravery; *especially* : military valor and skill
2 : extraordinary ability 〈his *prowess* on the football field〉

¹prowl \'praú(ə)l\ *verb* [Middle English *prollen*] (14th century)
intransitive verb
: to move about or wander stealthily in or as if in search of prey
transitive verb
: to roam over in a predatory manner
— **prowl·er** \'praú-lər\ *noun*

²prowl *noun* (1803)
: an act or instance of prowling
— **on the prowl** : in the act of prowling; *also* : in search of something 〈his fourth wife had just left him, and he was *on the prowl* again —Mary McCarthy〉

prowl car *noun* (1937)
: SQUAD CAR

prox·e·mics \präk-'sē-miks\ *noun plural but singular or plural in construction* [*proximity* + *-emics* (as in *phonemics*)] (1963)
: the study of the nature, degree, and effect of the spatial separation individuals naturally maintain (as in various social and interpersonal situations) and of how this separation relates to environmental and cultural factors
— **prox·e·mic** \-mik\ *adjective*

prox·i·mal \'präk-sə-məl\ *adjective* [Latin *proximus*] (1727)
1 : situated close to : PROXIMATE
2 : next to or nearest the point of attachment or origin, a central point, or the point of view; *especially* : located toward the center of the body — compare DISTAL
3 : of, relating to, or being the mesial and distal surfaces of a tooth
— **prox·i·mal·ly** \-mə-lē\ *adverb*

proximal convoluted tubule *noun* (circa 1899)
: the convoluted portion of the vertebrate nephron that lies between Bowman's capsule and the loop of Henle and functions especially in the resorption of sugar, sodium and chloride ions, and water from the glomerular filtrate — called also *proximal tubule*

prox·i·mate \'präk-sə-mət\ *adjective* [Latin *proximatus*, past participle of *proximare* to approach, from *proximus* nearest, next, superlative of *prope* near — more at APPROACH] (1661)
1 : immediately preceding or following (as in a chain of events, causes, or effects) 〈*proximate*, rather than ultimate, goals —Reinhold Niebuhr〉
2 a : very near : CLOSE **b** : soon forthcoming : IMMINENT
— **prox·i·mate·ly** *adverb*
— **prox·i·mate·ness** *noun*

prox·im·i·ty \präk-'si-mə-tē\ *noun* [Middle French *proximité*, from Latin *proximitat-, proximitas*, from *proximus*] (15th century)
: the quality or state of being proximate : CLOSENESS

proximity fuze *noun* (1945)
: a fuze for a projectile that uses the principle of radar to detect the presence of a target within the projectile's effective range

prox·i·mo \'präk-sə-,mō\ *adjective* [Latin *proximo mense* in the next month] (1855)
: of or occurring in the next month after the present

proxy \'präk-sē\ *noun, plural* **prox·ies** [Middle English *procucie*, contraction of *procuracie*, from Anglo-French, from Medieval Latin *procuratia*, alteration of Latin *procuratio* procuration] (15th century)
1 : the agency, function, or office of a deputy who acts as a substitute for another
2 a : authority or power to act for another **b** : a document giving such authority; *specifically* : a power of attorney authorizing a specified person to vote corporate stock
3 : a person authorized to act for another : PROCURATOR
— **proxy** *adjective*

proxy marriage *noun* (1900)
: a marriage celebrated in the absence of one of the contracting parties who is represented at the ceremony by a proxy

prude \'prüd\ *noun* [French, good woman, prudish woman, short for *prudefemme* good woman, from Old French *prode femme*] (1704)
: a person who is excessively or priggishly attentive to propriety or decorum; *especially* : a woman who shows or affects extreme modesty

pru·dence \'prü-d°n(t)s\ *noun* [Middle English, from Middle French, from Latin *prudentia*, alteration of *providentia* — more at PROVIDENCE] (14th century)
1 : the ability to govern and discipline oneself by the use of reason
2 : sagacity or shrewdness in the management of affairs
3 : skill and good judgment in the use of resources
4 : caution or circumspection as to danger or risk

pru·dent \-d°nt\ *adjective* [Middle English, from Middle French, from Latin *prudent-, prudens*, contraction of *provident-, providens* — more at PROVIDENT] (14th century)
: characterized by, arising from, or showing prudence: as **a** : marked by wisdom or judiciousness **b** : shrewd in the management of practical affairs **c** : marked by circumspection : DISCREET **d** : PROVIDENT, FRUGAL
synonym see WISE
— **pru·dent·ly** *adverb*

pru·den·tial \prü-'den(t)-shəl\ *adjective* (15th century)
1 : of, relating to, or proceeding from prudence
2 : exercising prudence especially in business matters
— **pru·den·tial·ly** \-'den(t)-sh(ə-)lē\ *adverb*

prud·ery \'prü-d(ə-)rē\ *noun, plural* **-er·ies** (1709)
1 : the characteristic quality or state of a prude
2 : a prudish act or remark

prud·ish \'prü-dish\ *adjective* (1717)
: marked by prudery : PRIGGISH
— **prud·ish·ly** *adverb*
— **prud·ish·ness** *noun*

pru·i·nose \'prü-ə-,nōs\ *adjective* [Latin *pruinosus* covered with hoarfrost, from *pruina* hoarfrost — more at FREEZE] (circa 1826)
: covered with whitish dust or bloom 〈*pruinose* stems〉

¹prune \'prün\ *noun* [Middle English, from Middle French, plum, from Latin *prunum* — more at PLUM] (14th century)
: a plum dried or capable of drying without fermentation

²prune *verb* **pruned; prun·ing** [Middle English *prouynen*, from Middle French *proignier*, probably alteration of *provigner* to layer, from *provain* layer, from Middle French *propagin-, propago*, from *pro-* forward + *pangere* to fix — more at PRO-, PACT] (15th century)
transitive verb
1 a : to reduce especially by eliminating superfluous matter 〈*pruned* the text〉 〈*prune* the budget〉 **b** : to remove as superfluous 〈*prune* away all ornamentation〉

2 : to cut off or cut back parts of for better shape or more fruitful growth
intransitive verb
: to cut away what is unwanted or superfluous
— **prun·er** *noun*

pru·nel·la \prü-'ne-lə\ *also* **pru·nelle** \-'nel\ *noun* [French *prunelle*, literally, sloe, from diminutive of *prune* plum] (1670)
1 : a twilled woolen dress fabric
2 : a heavy woolen fabric used for the uppers of shoes

pruning hook *noun* (1611)
: a pole bearing a curved blade for pruning plants

pru·nus \'prü-nəs\ *noun* [New Latin, from Latin, plum tree, from Greek *proumnē*] (1901)
: any of a genus (*Prunus*) of drupaceous trees or shrubs of the rose family that have showy clusters of usually white or pink flowers first appearing in the spring often before the leaves including many grown for ornament or for their fruit (as the plum, cherry, or apricot)

pru·ri·ence \'prúr-ē-ən(t)s\ *noun* (1781)
: the quality or state of being prurient

pru·ri·en·cy \-ən(t)-sē\ *noun* (1795)
: PRURIENCE

pru·ri·ent \-ənt\ *adjective* [Latin *prurient-, pruriens*, present participle of *prurire* to itch, crave; akin to Latin *pruna* glowing coal, Sanskrit *ploṣati* he singes, and probably to Latin *pruina* hoarfrost — more at FREEZE] (1592)
: marked by or arousing an immoderate or unwholesome interest or desire; *especially* : marked by, arousing, or appealing to unusual sexual desire
— **pru·ri·ent·ly** *adverb*

pru·ri·go \prü-'rī-(,)gō, -'rē-\ *noun* [New Latin, from Latin, itch, from *prurire*] (circa 1646)
: a chronic inflammatory skin disease marked by itching papules

pru·rit·ic \-'ri-tik\ *adjective* (1899)
: of, relating to, or marked by itching

pru·ri·tus \-'rī-təs, -'rē-\ *noun* [Latin, from *prurire*] (1653)
: ITCH 1a

Prus·sian blue \'prə-shən-\ *noun* [*Prussia*, Germany] (1724)
1 : any of numerous blue iron pigments formerly regarded as ferric ferrocyanide
2 : a dark blue crystalline hydrated ferric ferrocyanide $Fe_4[Fe(CN)_6]_3 \cdot xH_2O$ used as a test for ferric iron
3 : a greenish blue

prus·sian·ise *British variant of* PRUSSIANIZE

Prus·sian·ism \'prə-shə-,ni-zəm\ *noun* (1856)
: the practices or policies (as the advocacy of militarism) held to be typically Prussian

prus·sian·ize \-,nīz\ *transitive verb* **-ized; -iz·ing** *often capitalized* (1861)
: to make Prussian in character or principle (as in authoritarian control or rigid discipline)
— **prus·sian·i·za·tion** \,prə-shə-nə-'zā-shən\ *noun*

pru·tah *or* **pru·ta** \prü-'tä\ *noun, plural* **pru·toth** \-'tōt, -'tōth, -'tōs\ *or* **pru·tot** \-'tōt, -'tōs\ [New Hebrew *pĕrūṭāh*, from Late Hebrew, a small coin] (1949)
1 : a former monetary unit of Israel equivalent to $\frac{1}{1000}$ pound
2 : a coin representing one prutah

¹pry \'prī\ *intransitive verb* **pried; pry·ing** [Middle English *prien*] (14th century)
: to look closely or inquisitively; *also* : to make a nosy or presumptuous inquiry

²pry *transitive verb* **pried; pry·ing** [probably back-formation from ⁵*prize*] (circa 1806)
1 : to raise, move, or pull apart with a lever : PRIZE
2 : to extract, detach, or open with difficulty 〈*pried* the secret out of my sister〉

³pry *noun* (1823)
1 : a tool for prying
2 : LEVERAGE

pry·er *variant of* PRIER

prying *adjective* (1552)

: impertinently or officiously inquisitive or interrogatory
synonym see CURIOUS
— **pry·ing·ly** \-iŋ-lē\ *adverb*
Prze·wal·ski's horse \pshə-'väl-skēz-, shə-, ˌpər-zhə-'väl-\ *noun* [Nikolaĭ M. *Przhevalskiĭ* (died 1888) Russian soldier & explorer] (1881)
: a small stocky bay- or dun-colored wild horse (*Equus caballus przewalskii* synonym *E. przewalskii*) of central Asia having a large head and short erect mane — called also *Prze·wal·ski horse* \-skē-\
psalm \'säm, 'sälm, 'sȯm, 'sȯlm, *New England also* 'sȧm\ *noun, often capitalized* [Middle English, from Old English *psealm,* from Late Latin *psalmus,* from Greek *psalmos,* literally, twanging of a harp, from *psallein* to pluck, play a stringed instrument] (before 12th century)
: a sacred song or poem used in worship; *especially* : one of the biblical hymns collected in the Book of Psalms
psalm-book \-ˌbůk\ *noun* (12th century)
archaic : PSALTER
psalm·ist \'sä-mist, 'säl-, 'sȯ-, 'sȯl-, *New England also* 'sȧ-mist\ *noun* (15th century)
: a writer or composer of especially biblical psalms
psalm·o·dy \'sä-mə-dē, 'säl-, 'sȯ-, 'sȯl, *New England also* 'sȧ-mə-dē\ *noun* [Middle English *psalmodie,* from Late Latin *psalmodia,* from Late Greek *psalmōidia,* literally, singing to the harp, from Greek *psalmos* + *aidein* to sing — more at ODE] (14th century)
1 : the act, practice, or art of singing psalms in worship
2 : a collection of psalms
Psalms \'sämz, 'sälmz, 'sȯmz, 'sȯlmz, *New England also* 'sȧmz\ *noun plural but singular in construction*
: a collection of sacred poems forming a book of canonical Jewish and Christian Scripture — see BIBLE table
Psal·ter \'säl-tər, 'sȯl-\ *noun* [Middle English, from Old English *psalter* & Old French *psaltier,* from Late Latin *psalterium,* from Late Greek *psaltērion,* from Greek, psaltery] (before 12th century)
: the Book of Psalms; *also* : a collection of Psalms for liturgical or devotional use
psal·te·ri·um \säl-'tir-ē-əm, sȯl-\ *noun, plural* -**ria** \-ē-ə\ [New Latin, from Late Latin, psalter; from the resemblance of the folds to the pages of a book] (circa 1846)
: OMASUM
psal·tery *also* **psal·try** \'säl-t(ə-)rē, 'sȯl-\ *noun, plural* -**ter·ies** *also* -**tries** [Middle English *psalterie,* from Middle French, from Latin *psalterium,* from Greek *psaltērion,* from *psallein* to play on a stringed instrument] (14th century)
: an ancient musical instrument resembling the zither
p's and q's \ˌpēz-ᵊn-'kyüz\ *noun plural* [from the phrase *mind one's p's and q's,* alluding to the difficulty a child learning to write has in distinguishing between *p* and *q*] (1779)
1 : something (as one's manners) that one should be mindful of ⟨better watch his *p's and q's* when I get a six-gun of my own —Jean Stafford⟩
2 : best behavior ⟨being on her *p's and q's* for two solid days was too much —Guy McCrone⟩
pse·phol·o·gy \sē-'fä-lə-jē\ *noun* [Greek *psēphos* pebble, ballot, vote; from the use of pebbles by the ancient Greeks in voting] (1952)
: the scientific study of elections
— **pse·pho·log·i·cal** \ˌsē-fə-'lä-ji-kəl\ *adjective*
— **pse·phol·o·gist** \sē-'fä-lə-jist\ *noun*
pseud \'süd\ *noun* [short for *pseudo-intellectual*] (1964)
British : a person who pretends to be an intellectual

pseud- *or* **pseudo-** *combining form* [Middle English, from Late Latin, from Greek, from *pseudēs,* from *pseudesthai* to lie; akin to Armenian *sut* lie and probably to Greek *psychein* to breathe — more at PSYCH-]
: false : spurious ⟨*pseudo*classic⟩ ⟨*pseudo*podium⟩
pseud·ep·i·graph \sü-'de-pə-ˌgraf\ *noun* (1884)
: PSEUDEPIGRAPHON 2
pseud·epig·ra·phon \ˌsü-di-'pi-grə-ˌfän\ *noun, plural* -**pha** \-fə\ [New Latin, singular of *pseudepigrapha,* from Greek, neuter plural of *pseudepigraphos* falsely inscribed, from *pseud-* + *epigraphein* to inscribe — more at EPIGRAM] (1692)
1 *plural* : APOCRYPHA
2 : any of various pseudonymous or anonymous Jewish religious writings of the period 200 B.C. to 200 A.D.; *especially* : one of such writings (as the Psalms of Solomon) not included in any canon of biblical Scripture — usually used in plural
pseud·epig·ra·phy \-fē\ *noun* [Greek *pseudepigraphos*] (circa 1842)
: the ascription of false names of authors to works
pseu·do \'sü-(ˌ)dō\ *adjective* [Middle English, from *pseudo-*] (15th century)
: being apparently rather than actually as stated : SHAM, SPURIOUS ⟨distinction between true and *pseudo* humanism —K. F. Reinhardt⟩
pseu·do·al·lele \ˌsü-dō-ə-'lē(ə)l\ *noun* (1948)
: any of two or more closely linked genes that act usually as if a single member of an allelic pair but occasionally undergo crossing-over and recombination
pseu·do·cho·lin·es·ter·ase \'sü-dō-ˌkō-lə-'nes-tə-ˌrās, -ˌrāz\ *noun* (1943)
: CHOLINESTERASE 2
pseu·do·clas·sic \ˌsü-dō-'kla-sik\ *adjective* (1899)
: pretending to be or erroneously regarded as classic
— **pseudoclassic** *noun*
pseu·do·clas·si·cism \-'kla-sə-ˌsi-zəm\ *noun* (1871)
: imitative representation of classicism in literature and art
pseu·do·coel \'sü-də-ˌsēl\ *noun* (1887)
: a body cavity that is not a product of gastrulation and is not lined with a well-defined mesodermal membrane
pseu·do·coe·lom·ate \ˌsü-dō-'sē-lə-ˌmāt\ *noun* (1940)
: an invertebrate (as a nematode or rotifer) having a body cavity that is a pseudocoel
— **pseudocoelomate** *adjective*
pseu·do·cy·e·sis \-sī-'ē-səs\ *noun* [New Latin, from *pseud-* + *cyesis* pregnancy, from Greek *kyēsis,* from *kyein* to be pregnant — more at CYME] (circa 1817)
: a psychosomatic state that occurs without conception and is marked by some of the physical symptoms and changes in hormonal balance of pregnancy
pseu·do·mo·nad \ˌsü-də-'mō-ˌnad, -nəd\ *noun* [New Latin *Pseudomonad-, Pseudomonas*] (1921)
: any of a genus (*Pseudomonas*) of gram-negative rod-shaped motile bacteria including some that produce a greenish fluorescent water-soluble pigment and some that are saprophytes or plant or animal pathogens
pseu·do·mo·nas \-nəs\ *noun, plural* -**mo·na·des** \-'mō-nə-ˌdēz, -'mä-\ [New Latin, from *pseud-* + *monad-, monas* monad] (1903)
: PSEUDOMONAD
pseu·do·morph \'sü-də-ˌmȯrf\ *noun* [probably from French *pseudomorphe,* from *pseud-* + *-morphe* -morph] (1849)
1 : a mineral having the characteristic outward form of another species
2 : a deceptive or irregular form
— **pseu·do·mor·phic** \ˌsü-də-'mȯr-fik\ *adjective*

— **pseu·do·mor·phism** \-ˌfi-zəm\ *noun*
— **pseu·do·mor·phous** \-fəs\ *adjective*
pseu·do·nym \'sü-dᵊn-ˌim\ *noun* [French *pseudonyme,* from Greek *pseudōnymos* bearing a false name, from *pseud-* + *onyma* name — more at NAME] (1833)
: a fictitious name; *especially* : PEN NAME
pseu·do·nym·i·ty \ˌsü-dᵊn-'i-mə-tē\ *noun* (1877)
: the use of a pseudonym; *also* : the fact or state of being signed with a pseudonym
pseu·don·y·mous \sü-'dä-nə-məs\ *adjective* [Greek *pseudōnymos*] (circa 1706)
: bearing or using a fictitious name ⟨a *pseudonymous* report⟩; *also* : being a pseudonym
— **pseu·don·y·mous·ly** *adverb*
— **pseu·don·y·mous·ness** *noun*
pseu·do·pa·ren·chy·ma \ˌsü-dō-pə-'reŋ-kə-mə\ *noun* [New Latin] (1875)
: compactly interwoven short-celled filaments in a thallophyte that resemble parenchyma of higher plants
— **pseu·do·par·en·chy·ma·tous** \-ˌpar-ən-'ki-mə-təs, -'kī-\ *adjective*
pseu·do·pod \'sü-də-ˌpäd\ *noun* [New Latin *pseudopodium*] (1874)
: PSEUDOPODIUM
— **pseu·do·pod·al** \sü-'dä-pə-dᵊl\ *or* **pseu·do·po·di·al** \ˌsü-də-'pō-dē-əl\ *adjective*
pseu·do·po·di·um \ˌsü-də-'pō-dē-əm\ *noun, plural* -**po·dia** \-dē-ə\ [New Latin] (1854)
1 : a temporary protrusion or retractile process of the cytoplasm of a cell that functions (as in an amoeba) especially in a locomotor or food gathering capacity — see AMOEBA illustration
2 : a slender leafless branch of the gametophyte in various mosses that often bears gemmae
pseu·do·preg·nan·cy \ˌsü-dō-'preg-nən(t)-sē\ *noun* (1860)
1 : PSEUDOCYESIS
2 : an anestrous state resembling pregnancy that occurs in various mammals usually after an infertile copulation
— **pseu·do·preg·nant** \-nənt\ *adjective*
pseu·do·ran·dom \-'ran-dəm\ *adjective* (1949)
: being or involving entities (as numbers) that are selected by a definite computational process but that satisfy one or more standard tests for statistical randomness
pseu·do·sci·ence \ˌsü-dō-'sī-ən(t)s\ *noun* (1844)
: a system of theories, assumptions, and methods erroneously regarded as scientific
— **pseu·do·sci·en·tif·ic** \-ˌsī-ən-'ti-fik\ *adjective*
— **pseu·do·sci·en·tist** \-'sī-ən-tist\ *noun*
pseu·do·scor·pi·on \-'skȯr-pē-ən\ *noun* [New Latin *Pseudoscorpiones,* from *pseud-* + Latin *scorpion-, scorpio* scorpion] (1835)
: any of a widely distributed order (Pseudoscorpionida synonym Pseudoscorpiones) of tiny arachnids that have no caudal stinger and feed on tiny invertebrates (as insects and mites)
pseu·do·so·phis·ti·ca·tion \'sü-dō-sə-ˌfis-tə-'kā-shən\ *noun* (1965)
: false or feigned sophistication
— **pseu·do·so·phis·ti·cat·ed** \-sə-'fis-ti-ˌkā-təd\ *adjective*
pseu·do·tu·ber·cu·lo·sis \-tü-ˌbər-kyə-'lō-səs, -tyü-\ *noun* [New Latin] (1900)
: any of several diseases that are characterized by the formation of granulomas resembling tubercular nodules but are not caused by the tubercle bacillus
pshaw \'shȯ\ *interjection* (1673)

\ə\ **abut** \ᵊ\ **kitten** \ər\ **further** \a\ **ash** \ā\ **ace**
\ä\ **mop, mar** \au̇\ **out** \ch\ **chin** \e\ **bet** \ē\ **easy**
\g\ **go** \i\ **hit** \ī\ **ice** \j\ **job** \ŋ\ **sing** \ō\ **go**
\ȯ\ **law** \ȯi\ **boy** \th\ **thin** \th̶\ **the** \ü\ **loot** \u̇\ **foot**
\y\ **yet** \zh\ **vision** *see also* Guide to Pronunciation

— used to express irritation, disapproval, contempt, or disbelief

¹psi \'sī, 'psī\ *noun* [Middle English, from Medieval Latin, from Late Greek, from Greek *psei*] (15th century)
: the 23d letter of the Greek alphabet — see ALPHABET table

²psi \'sī\ *noun* [probably by shortening & alteration from *psychic*] (circa 1946)
: parapsychological psychic phenomena or powers

psi·lo·cy·bin \,sī-lə-'sī-bən\ *noun* [New Latin *Psilocybe*, fungus genus + ¹-*in*] (1958)
: a hallucinogenic indole $C_{12}H_{17}N_2O_4P$ obtained from a fungus (*Psilocybe mexicana*)

psi·lo·phyte \'sī-lə-,fīt\ *noun* [New Latin *Psilophyton*, genus of plants, from Greek *psilos* bare, mere (probably akin to Greek *psēn* to rub) + *phyton* plant — more at PHYT-] (circa 1911)
: any of an order (Psilophytales) of extinct simple dichotomously branched plants from the Paleozoic of Europe and eastern Canada that include the oldest known land plants with vascular structure
— **psi·lo·phyt·ic** \,sī-lə-'fi-tik\ *adjective*

psi particle \'sī-, 'psī-\ *noun* (1974)
: J/PSI PARTICLE

psit·ta·cine \'si-tə-,sīn\ *adjective* [Latin *psittacinus*, from *psittacus* parrot, from Greek *psittakos*] (1874)
: of or relating to the parrots
— **psittacine** *noun*

psit·ta·co·sis \,si-tə-'kō-səs\ *noun* [New Latin, from Latin *psittacus*] (1897)
: an infectious disease of birds caused by a bacterium (*Chlamydia psittaci*), marked by diarrhea and wasting, and transmissible to humans in whom it usually occurs as an atypical pneumonia accompanied by high fever
— **psit·ta·cot·ic** \-'kä-tik, -'kō-\ *adjective*

pso·cid \'sō-səd\ *noun* [ultimately from New Latin *Psocus*, genus of lice] (1891)
: any of an order (Psocoptera synonym Corrodentia) of minute usually winged primitive insects (as a book louse)

pso·ri·a·sis \sə-'rī-ə-səs\ *noun* [New Latin, from Greek *psōriasis*, from *psōrian* to have the itch, from *psōra* itch; akin to Greek *psēn* to rub] (circa 1684)
: a chronic skin disease characterized by circumscribed red patches covered with white scales
— **pso·ri·at·ic** \,sōr-ē-'a-tik, ,sòr-\ *adjective or noun*

psych *also* **psyche** \'sīk\ *transitive verb* **psyched; psych·ing** [by shortening] (1917)
1 : PSYCHOANALYZE
2 a : to anticipate correctly the intentions or actions of : OUTGUESS **b** : to analyze or figure out (as a problem or course of action) ⟨I *psyched* it all out by myself and decided —David Hulburd⟩
3 a : to make psychologically uneasy : INTIMIDATE, SCARE ⟨pressure doesn't *psych* me —Jerry Quarry⟩ — often used with *out* **b** : to make (as oneself) psychologically ready especially for performance — often used with *up* ⟨*psyched* herself up for the race⟩

psych- *or* **psycho-** *combining form* [Greek, from *psychē* breath, principle of life, life, soul, from *psychein* to breathe; akin to Sanskrit *babhasti* he blows]
1 : mind : mental processes and activities ⟨*psycho*dynamic⟩ ⟨*psycho*logy⟩
2 : psychological methods ⟨*psycho*analysis⟩ ⟨*psycho*therapy⟩
3 : brain ⟨*psycho*surgery⟩
4 : mental and ⟨*psycho*somatic⟩

psych·as·the·nia \,sī-kəs-'thē-nē-ə\ *noun* [New Latin] (1900)
: a neurotic state characterized especially by phobias, obsessions, or compulsions that one knows are irrational

— **psych·as·then·ic** \-'the-nik\ *adjective or noun*

Psy·che \'sī-kē\ *noun* [Latin, from Greek *psychē* soul]
1 : a princess loved by Cupid
2 *not capitalized* [Greek *psychē*] **a** : SOUL, SELF **b** : MIND

psy·che·de·lia \,sī-kə-'dēl-yə\ *noun* [New Latin, from English *psychedelic*] (1967)
: the world of people, phenomena, or items associated with psychedelic drugs

¹psy·che·del·ic \,sī-kə-'de-lik\ *noun* [irregular from *psych-* + Greek *dēloun* to show, from *dēlos* evident; akin to Sanskrit *dīdeti* it shines, Latin *dies* day — more at DEITY] (1956)
: a psychedelic drug (as LSD)

²psychedelic *adjective* (1957)
1 a : of, relating to, or being drugs (as LSD) capable of producing abnormal psychic effects (as hallucinations) and sometimes psychic states resembling mental illness **b** : produced by or associated with the use of psychedelic drugs ⟨a *psychedelic* experience⟩
2 : imitating, suggestive of, or reproducing effects (as distorted or bizarre images or sounds) resembling those produced by psychedelic drugs ⟨*psychedelic* color schemes⟩
— **psy·che·del·i·cal·ly** \-'de-li-k(ə-)lē\ *adverb*

psy·chi·a·try \sə-'kī-ə-trē, sī-\ *noun* [probably from French *psychiatrie*, from *psychiatre* psychiatrist, from *psych-* psych- + Greek *iatros* physician — more at -IATRY] (circa 1846)
: a branch of medicine that deals with mental, emotional, or behavioral disorders
— **psy·chi·at·ric** \,sī-kē-'a-trik\ *adjective*
— **psy·chi·at·ri·cal·ly** \-tri-k(ə-)lē\ *adverb*
— **psy·chi·a·trist** \sə-'kī-ə-trist, sī-\ *noun*

¹psy·chic \'sī-kik\ *also* **psy·chi·cal** \-ki-kəl\ *adjective* [Greek *psychikos* of the soul, from *psychē* soul] (1642)
1 : of or relating to the psyche : PSYCHOGENIC
2 : lying outside the sphere of physical science or knowledge : immaterial, moral, or spiritual in origin or force
3 : sensitive to nonphysical or supernatural forces and influences : marked by extraordinary or mysterious sensitivity, perception, or understanding
— **psy·chi·cal·ly** \-ki-k(ə-)lē\ *adverb*

²psychic *noun* (1871)
1 a : a person apparently sensitive to nonphysical forces **b** : MEDIUM 2d
2 : psychic phenomena

psy·cho \'sī-(,)kō\ *noun, plural* **psychos** [short for *psychopath*] (1942)
: a deranged or psychopathic person — not used technically
— **psycho** *adjective*

psy·cho·acous·tics \,sī-kō-ə-'kü-stiks\ *noun plural but singular in construction* (1948)
: a branch of science dealing with hearing, the sensations produced by sounds, and the problems of communication
— **psy·cho·acous·tic** \-stik\ *adjective*

psy·cho·ac·tive \,sī-kō-'ak-tiv\ *adjective* (1961)
: affecting the mind or behavior ⟨*psychoactive* drugs⟩

psy·cho·anal·y·sis \,sī-kō-ə-'na-lə-səs\ *noun* [New Latin] (1906)
: a method of analyzing psychic phenomena and treating emotional disorders that involves treatment sessions during which the patient is encouraged to talk freely about personal experiences and especially about early childhood and dreams
— **psy·cho·an·a·lyst** \-'a-nᵊl-ist\ *noun*

psy·cho·an·a·lyt·ic \-,a-nᵊl-'i-tik\ *also* **psy·cho·an·a·lyt·i·cal** \-ti-kəl\ *adjective* (1906)
: of, relating to, or employing psychoanalysis or its principles and techniques
— **psy·cho·an·a·lyt·i·cal·ly** \-ti-k(ə-)lē\ *adverb*

psy·cho·an·a·lyze \-'a-nᵊl-,īz\ *transitive verb* (1911)

: to treat by means of psychoanalysis

psy·cho·bab·ble \'sī-kō-,ba-bəl\ *noun* (1975)
: a predominantly metaphorical language for expressing one's feelings; *also* : psychological jargon
— **psy·cho·bab·bler** \-,ba-blər\ *noun*

psy·cho·bi·og·ra·phy \,sī-kō-bī-'ä-grə-fē, -bē-\ *noun* (1931)
: a biography written from a psychodynamic or psychoanalytic point of view; *also* : the application of such a point of view when writing a biography
— **psy·cho·bi·og·ra·pher** \-fər\ *noun*
— **psy·cho·bio·graph·i·cal** \-,bī-ə-'gra-fi-kəl\ *adjective*

psy·cho·bi·ol·o·gy \-bī-'ä-lə-jē\ *noun* [International Scientific Vocabulary] (1902)
: the study of mental functioning and behavior in relation to other biological processes
— **psy·cho·bi·o·log·i·cal** \-,bī-ə-'lä-ji-kəl\ *also* **psy·cho·bi·o·log·ic** \-jik\ *adjective*
— **psy·cho·bi·ol·o·gist** \-bī-'ä-lə-jist\ *noun*

psy·cho·chem·i·cal \-'ke-mi-kəl\ *noun* (1956)
: a psychoactive chemical
— **psychochemical** *adjective*

psy·cho·dra·ma \-'drä-mə, -'dra-\ *noun* (1937)
1 : an extemporized dramatization designed to afford catharsis and social relearning for one or more of the participants from whose life history the plot is abstracted
2 : a dramatic narrative or event characterized by psychological overtones
— **psy·cho·dra·mat·ic** \-drə-'ma-tik\ *adjective*

psy·cho·dy·nam·ics \-dī-'na-miks, -də-\ *noun plural but singular or plural in construction* (1874)
1 : the psychology of mental or emotional forces or processes developing especially in early childhood and their effects on behavior and mental states
2 : explanation or interpretation (as of behavior or mental states) in terms of mental or emotional forces or processes
3 : motivational forces acting especially at the unconscious level
— **psy·cho·dy·nam·ic** \-mik\ *adjective*
— **psy·cho·dy·nam·i·cal·ly** \-mi-k(ə-)lē\ *adverb*

psy·cho·gen·e·sis \-'je-nə-səs\ *noun* [New Latin] (1838)
1 : the origin and development of mental functions, traits, or states
2 : development from mental as distinguished from physical origins
— **psy·cho·ge·net·ic** \-jə-'ne-tik\ *adjective*

psy·cho·gen·ic \-'je-nik\ *adjective* (1902)
: originating in the mind or in mental or emotional conflict
— **psy·cho·gen·i·cal·ly** \-ni-k(ə-)lē\ *adverb*

psy·cho·graph \'sī-kə-,graf\ *noun* (1916)
: PSYCHOBIOGRAPHY

psy·cho·his·to·ry \'sī-kō-,his-t(ə-)rē\ *noun* (1934)
: historical analysis or interpretation employing psychological and psychoanalytic methods; *also* : a work of history employing such methods
— **psy·cho·his·to·ri·an** \,sī-kō-(h)is-'tōr-ē-ən, -'tòr-, -'tär-\ *noun*
— **psy·cho·his·to·ri·cal** \-'tòr-i-kəl, -'tär-\ *adjective*

psy·cho·ki·ne·sis \,sī-kō-kə-'nē-səs, -kī-\ *noun* [New Latin] (1914)
: movement of physical objects by the mind without use of physical means — compare PRECOGNITION, TELEKINESIS
— **psy·cho·ki·net·ic** \-'ne-tik\ *adjective*

psy·cho·lin·guis·tics \,sī-kō-liŋ-'gwis-tiks\ *noun plural but singular in construction* (1936)

: the study of the mental faculties involved in the perception, production, and acquisition of language
— **psy·cho·lin·guist** \-'liŋ-gwist\ *noun*
— **psy·cho·lin·guis·tic** \-tik\ *adjective*
psy·cho·log·i·cal \ˌsī-kə-'lä-ji-kəl\ *also* **psy·cho·log·ic** \-jik\ *adjective* (circa 1688)
1 a : of or relating to psychology **b** : MENTAL
2 : directed toward the will or toward the mind specifically in its conative function ⟨*psychological* warfare⟩
— **psy·cho·log·i·cal·ly** \-ji-k(ə-)lē\ *adverb*
psychological moment *noun* (1871)
: the occasion when the mental atmosphere is most certain to be favorable to the full effect of an action or event
psy·chol·o·gise *British variant of* PSYCHOLOGIZE
psy·chol·o·gism \sī-'kä-lə-ˌji-zəm\ *noun* (1858)
: a theory that applies psychological conceptions to the interpretation of historical events or logical thought
psy·chol·o·gize \-ˌjīz\ *verb* **-gized; -giz·ing** (1810)
intransitive verb
: to speculate in psychological terms or on psychological motivations
transitive verb
: to explain or interpret in psychological terms
psy·chol·o·gy \-jē\ *noun, plural* **-gies** [New Latin *psychologia*, from *psych-* + *-logia* -logy] (1653)
1 : the science of mind and behavior
2 a : the mental or behavioral characteristics of an individual or group **b** : the study of mind and behavior in relation to a particular field of knowledge or activity
3 : a treatise on psychology
— **psy·chol·o·gist** \-jist\ *noun*
psy·cho·met·ric \ˌsī-kə-'me-trik\ *adjective* (1854)
: of or relating to psychometrics or psychometry
— **psy·cho·met·ri·cal·ly** \-tri-k(ə-)lē\ *adverb*
psy·cho·me·tri·cian \-mə-'tri-shən\ *noun* (circa 1939)
1 : a person (as a clinical psychologist) who is skilled in the administration and interpretation of objective psychological tests
2 : a psychologist who devises, constructs, and standardizes psychometric tests
psy·cho·met·rics \-'me-triks\ *noun plural but singular in construction* (circa 1924)
: the psychological theory or technique of mental measurement
psy·chom·e·try \sī-'kä-mə-trē\ *noun* (circa 1842)
1 : divination of facts concerning an object or its owner through contact with or proximity to the object
2 : PSYCHOMETRICS
psy·cho·mo·tor \ˌsī-kə-'mō-tər\ *adjective* [International Scientific Vocabulary] (1878)
: of or relating to motor action directly proceeding from mental activity
psy·cho·neu·ro·sis \ˌsī-kō-nu̇-'rō-səs, -nyu̇-\ *noun* [New Latin] (1883)
: NEUROSIS; *especially* : a neurosis based on emotional conflict in which an impulse that has been blocked seeks expression in a disguised response or symptom
— **psy·cho·neu·rot·ic** \-'rä-tik\ *adjective or noun*
psy·cho·path \'sī-kə-ˌpath\ *noun* [International Scientific Vocabulary] (1885)
: a mentally ill or unstable person; *especially* : a person having a psychopathic personality
¹**psy·cho·path·ic** \ˌsī-kə-'pa-thik\ *adjective* (1847)
: of, relating to, or characterized by psychopathy
— **psy·cho·path·i·cal·ly** \-thi-k(ə-)lē\ *adverb*

²**psychopathic** *noun* (circa 1890)
: PSYCHOPATH
psychopathic personality *noun* (circa 1923)
1 : an emotionally and behaviorally disordered state characterized by clear perception of reality except for the individual's social and moral obligations and often by the pursuit of immediate personal gratification in criminal acts, drug addiction, or sexual perversion
2 : an individual having a psychopathic personality
psy·cho·pa·thol·o·gy \ˌsī-kō-pə-'thä-lə-jē, -pa-\ *noun* [International Scientific Vocabulary] (1847)
: the study of psychological and behavioral dysfunction occurring in mental disorder or in social disorganization; *also* : such dysfunction
— **psy·cho·path·o·log·ic** \-ˌpa-thə-'lä-jik\ *or* **psy·cho·path·o·log·i·cal** \-ji-kəl\ *adjective*
— **psy·cho·path·o·log·i·cal·ly** \-ji-k(ə-)lē\ *adverb*
— **psy·cho·pa·thol·o·gist** \-pə-'thä-jist, -pa-\ *noun*
psy·chop·a·thy \sī-'kä-pə-thē\ *noun* [International Scientific Vocabulary] (1847)
: mental disorder; *especially* : extreme mental disorder marked usually by egocentric and antisocial activity
psy·cho·phar·ma·col·o·gy \ˌsī-kō-ˌfär-mə-'kä-lə-jē\ *noun* (1920)
: the study of the effect of drugs on the mind and behavior
— **psy·cho·phar·ma·co·log·i·cal** \-mə-kə-'lä-ji-kəl\ *or* **psy·cho·phar·ma·co·log·ic** \-jik\ *adjective*
— **psy·cho·phar·ma·col·o·gist** \-'kä-lə-jist\ *noun*
psy·cho·phys·i·cal \ˌsī-kō-'fi-zi-kəl\ *adjective* (1847)
: of or relating to psychophysics; *also* : sharing mental and physical qualities
— **psy·cho·phys·i·cal·ly** \-k(ə-)lē\ *adverb*
psychophysical parallelism *noun* (1894)
: PARALLELISM 4
psy·cho·phys·ics \ˌsī-kō-'fi-ziks\ *noun plural but singular in construction* [International Scientific Vocabulary] (1878)
: a branch of psychology concerned with the effect of physical processes (as intensity of stimulation) on the mental processes of an organism
— **psy·cho·phys·i·cist** \-'fi-zə-sist, -'fiz-sist\ *noun*
psy·cho·phys·i·o·log·i·cal \ˌsī-kō-ˌfi-zē-ə-'lä-ji-kəl\ *also* **psy·cho·phys·i·o·log·ic** \-jik\ *adjective* (1839)
1 : of or relating to physiological psychology
2 : combining or involving mental and bodily processes
— **psy·cho·phys·i·o·log·i·cal·ly** \-ji-k(ə-)lē\ *adverb*
psy·cho·phys·i·ol·o·gy \-ˌfi-zē-'ä-lə-jē\ *noun* [International Scientific Vocabulary] (1839)
: PHYSIOLOGICAL PSYCHOLOGY
— **psy·cho·phys·i·ol·o·gist** \-jist\ *noun*
psy·cho·sex·u·al \-'sek-shə-wəl, -shwəl, -shəl\ *adjective* (1897)
1 : of or relating to the mental, emotional, and behavioral aspects of sexual development
2 : of or relating to mental or emotional attitudes concerning sexual activity
3 : of or relating to the physiological psychology of sex
— **psy·cho·sex·u·al·ly** *adverb*
psy·cho·sex·u·al·i·ty \-ˌsek-shə-'wa-lə-tē\ *noun* (1910)
: the psychic factors of sex
psy·cho·sis \sī-'kō-səs\ *noun, plural* **-cho·ses** \-ˌsēz\ [New Latin] (1847)
: fundamental mental derangement (as schizophrenia) characterized by defective or lost contact with reality

psy·cho·so·cial \ˌsī-kō-'sō-shəl\ *adjective* (1899)
1 : involving both psychological and social aspects ⟨*psychosocial* adjustment in marriage⟩
2 : relating social conditions to mental health ⟨*psychosocial* medicine⟩
— **psy·cho·so·cial·ly** \-'sō-sh(ə-)lē\ *adverb*
psy·cho·so·mat·ic \-sə-'ma-tik\ *adjective* [International Scientific Vocabulary] (1863)
1 : of, relating to, concerned with, or involving both mind and body ⟨the *psychosomatic* nature of man —Herbert Ratner⟩
2 : of, relating to, involving, or concerned with bodily symptoms caused by mental or emotional disturbance ⟨*psychosomatic* illness⟩ ⟨*psychosomatic* medicine⟩
— **psy·cho·so·mat·i·cal·ly** \-ti-k(ə-)lē\ *adverb*
psy·cho·so·mat·ics \-sə-'ma-tiks\ *noun plural but singular in construction* (1938)
: a branch of medical science dealing with interrelationships between the mind or emotions and the body and especially with the relation of psychic conflict to somatic symptomatology
psy·cho·sur·gery \-'sər-jə-rē, -'sərj-rē\ *noun* (1936)
: cerebral surgery employed in treating psychic symptoms
— **psy·cho·sur·geon** \-'sər-jən\ *noun*
— **psy·cho·sur·gi·cal** \-'sər-ji-kəl\ *adjective*
psy·cho·syn·the·sis \-'sin(t)-thə-səs\ *noun* (1919)
: a form of psychotherapy combining psychoanalytic techniques with meditation and exercise
psy·cho·ther·a·peu·tic \-ˌther-ə-'pyü-tik\ *adjective* [International Scientific Vocabulary] (circa 1888)
: of, relating to, or used in psychotherapy
— **psy·cho·ther·a·peu·ti·cal·ly** \-ti-k(ə-)lē\ *adverb*
psy·cho·ther·a·py \-'ther-ə-pē\ *noun* [International Scientific Vocabulary] (circa 1890)
: treatment of mental or emotional disorder or of related bodily ills by psychological means
— **psy·cho·ther·a·pist** \-pist\ *noun*
psy·chot·ic \sī-'kä-tik\ *adjective* (circa 1890)
: of, relating to, marked by, or affected with psychosis ⟨a *psychotic* patient⟩ ⟨*psychotic* behavior⟩
— **psychotic** *noun*
— **psy·chot·i·cal·ly** \-ti-k(ə-)lē\ *adverb*
psy·cho·to·mi·met·ic \ˌsī-ˌkä-tō-mə-'me-tik, -ˌmī-\ *adjective* [*psychotic* + *-o-* + *mimetic*] (1957)
: of, relating to, involving, or inducing psychotic alteration of behavior and personality ⟨*psychotomimetic* drugs⟩
— **psychotomimetic** *noun*
— **psy·cho·to·mi·met·i·cal·ly** \-ti-k(ə-)lē\ *adverb*
psy·cho·tro·pic \ˌsī-kə-'trō-pik\ *adjective* (1948)
: acting on the mind ⟨*psychotropic* drugs⟩
— **psychotropic** *noun*
psych–out \'sīk-ˌau̇t\ *noun* (1971)
: an act or an instance of psyching someone out
psychro- *combining form* [Greek, from *psychros*, from *psychein* to cool]
: cold ⟨*psychrometer*⟩
psy·chrom·e·ter \sī-'krä-mə-tər\ *noun* [International Scientific Vocabulary] (1838)
: a hygrometer consisting essentially of two similar thermometers with the bulb of one being kept wet so that the cooling that results from evaporation makes it register a lower

temperature than the dry one and with the difference between the readings constituting a measure of the dryness of the atmosphere
— **psy·chro·met·ric** \ˌsī-krə-'me-trik\ adjective
— **psy·chrom·e·try** \sī-'krä-mə-trē\ noun
psy·chro·phil·ic \ˌsī-krō-'fi-lik\ adjective (circa 1903)
: thriving at a relatively low temperature ⟨psychrophilic bacteria⟩

psyl·la \'si-lə\ noun [New Latin, genus name, from Greek, flea; akin to Latin pulex flea, Sanskrit pluṣi] (1852)
: any of various plant lice (family Psyllidae) including economically important plant pests — compare PEAR PSYLLA

psyl·lid \'si-ləd\ noun [ultimately from New Latin Psylla] (1899)
: PSYLLA
— **psyllid** adjective

psyl·li·um seed \'si-lē-əm-\ noun [New Latin psyllium, from Greek psyllion fleawort, from psylla] (1897)
: the seed of a fleawort (especially Plantago psyllium) that has the property of swelling and becoming gelatinous when moist and is used as a mild laxative — called also psyllium

psy·war \'sī-ˌwȯr\ noun [by shortening] (1951)
: psychological warfare

ptar·mi·gan \'tär-mi-gən\ noun, plural **-gan** or **-gans** [modification of Scottish Gaelic tarmachan] (1599)
: any of various grouses (genus Lagopus) of northern regions with completely feathered feet

ptarmigan: *A* summer plumage; *B* winter plumage

PT boat \ˌpē-'tē-, 'pē-ˌ\ noun [patrol torpedo] (1941)
: a small fast patrol craft usually armed with torpedoes, machine guns, and depth charges — called also PT

PTC \ˌpē-(ˌ)tē-'sē\ noun (1932)
: PHENYLTHIOCARBAMIDE

pter·an·o·don \tə-'ra-nə-ˌdän, -'rä-\ noun [New Latin, from Greek pteron wing + anodōn toothless from an- + odōn, odous tooth — more at FEATHER, TOOTH] (1897)
: any of a genus (Pteranodon) of Cretaceous pterosaurs having a backwardly directed bony crest on the skull and a wingspan of about 25 feet (7.7 meters)

pterid- or **pterido-** combining form [Greek pterid-, pteris; akin to Greek pteron wing, feather]
: fern ⟨pteridology⟩

pter·i·dine \'ter-ə-ˌdēn\ noun [International Scientific Vocabulary pterin + -idine] (circa 1943)
: a yellow crystalline bicyclic base $C_6H_4N_4$ that is a structural constituent especially of various animal pigments

pter·i·dol·o·gy \ˌter-ə-'dä-lə-jē\ noun (1855)
: the study of ferns
— **pter·i·do·log·i·cal** \ˌter-ə-də-'lä-ji-kəl\ adjective
— **pter·i·dol·o·gist** \-'dä-lə-jist\ noun

pte·ri·do·phyte \tə-'ri-də-ˌfīt, 'ter-ə-dō-\ noun [New Latin Pteridophyta, from Greek pterid-, pteris fern + phyton plant — more at PHYT-] (1880)
: any of a division (Pteridophyta) of vascular plants (as a fern) that have roots, stems, and leaves but lack flowers or seeds

pte·ri·do·sperm \tə-'ri-də-ˌspərm, 'ter-ə-dō-\ noun [International Scientific Vocabulary] (1904)
: SEED FERN

pter·in \'ter-ən\ noun [International Scientific Vocabulary pter- (from Greek pteron wing) + ¹-in; from its being a factor in the pigments of butterfly wings] (1934)
: any of various compounds that contain the bicyclic ring system characteristic of pteridine

ptero·dac·tyl \ˌter-ə-'dak-tᵊl\ noun [New Latin Pterodactylus, genus of reptiles, from Greek pteron wing + daktylos finger — more at FEATHER] (1830)
: any of various pterosaurs (suborder Pterodactyloidea) of the Late Jurassic and Cretaceous having a rudimentary tail and a beak with reduced dentition; broadly : PTEROSAUR

ptero·pod \'ter-ə-ˌpäd\ noun [New Latin Pteropoda, group name, from Greek pteron wing + New Latin -poda] (1835)
: any of the opisthobranch mollusks comprising two orders (Thecosomata and Gymnosomata) and having the anterior lobes of the foot expanded into broad thin winglike swimming organs

ptero·saur \'ter-ə-ˌsȯr\ noun [New Latin Pterosauria, from Greek pteron wing + sauros lizard] (1862)
: any of an order (Pterosauria) of extinct flying reptiles existing from the Late Triassic throughout the Jurassic and most of the Cretaceous and having a featherless wing membrane extending from the side of the body along the arm to the end of the greatly elongated fourth digit

pter·o·yl·glu·tam·ic acid \ˌter-ə-ˌwil-glü-'ta-mik-\ noun [International Scientific Vocabulary pteroyl (the radical $(C_{13}H_{11}N_6O)CO$) + glutamic acid] (1943)
: FOLIC ACID

¹pter·y·goid \'ter-ə-ˌgȯid\ adjective [New Latin pterygoides, from Greek pterygoeidēs, literally, shaped like a wing, from pteryg-, pteryx wing; akin to Greek pteron wing — more at FEATHER] (1722)
: of, relating to, or lying in the region of the inferior part of the sphenoid bone of the vertebrate skull

²pterygoid noun (1831)
: a pterygoid part (as a bone, muscle, or nerve)

pterygoid process noun (1741)
: a process extending downward from each side of the sphenoid bone in humans and other mammals

pter·y·la \'ter-ə-lə\ noun, plural **-lae** \-ˌlē, -ˌlī\ [New Latin, from Greek pteron + hylē wood, forest] (1867)
: one of the definite areas of the skin of a bird on which feathers grow

Ptol·e·ma·ic \ˌtä-lə-'mā-ik\ adjective [Greek Ptolemaikos, from Ptolemaios Ptolemy] (1674)
1 : of or relating to Ptolemy the geographer and astronomer who flourished at Alexandria about A.D. 130
2 : of or relating to the Greco-Egyptian Ptolemies ruling Egypt from 323 to 30 B.C.

Ptolemaic system noun (circa 1771)
: the system of planetary motions according to which the earth is at the center with the sun, moon, and planets revolving around it

pto·maine \'tō-ˌmān, tō-'\ noun [Italian ptomaina, from Greek ptōma fall, fallen body, corpse, from piptein to fall — more at FEATHER] (1880)
: any of various organic bases which are formed by the action of putrefactive bacteria on nitrogenous matter and some of which are poisonous

ptomaine poisoning noun (1893)
: food poisoning caused by bacteria or bacterial products

pto·sis \'tō-səs\ noun, plural **pto·ses** \-ˌsēz\ [New Latin, from Greek ptōsis act of falling, from piptein] (1743)
: a sagging or prolapse of an organ or part; especially : a drooping of the upper eyelid

pty·a·lin \'tī-ə-lən\ noun [Greek ptyalon saliva, from ptyein to spit — more at SPEW] (1845)
: an amylase found in the saliva of many animals that converts starch into sugar

pty·a·lism \-ˌli-zəm\ noun [New Latin ptyalismus, from Greek ptyalismos, from ptyalizein to salivate, from ptyalon] (1676)
: an excessive flow of saliva

p-type \'pē-ˌtīp\ adjective [positive type] (1946)
: relating to or being a semiconductor in which charge is carried by holes — compare N-TYPE

pub \'pəb\ noun (circa 1859)
1 chiefly British : PUBLIC HOUSE 2
2 : an establishment where alcoholic beverages are sold and consumed

pub crawler noun (1910)
: one who goes from bar to bar
— **pub-crawl** intransitive verb
— **pub crawl** noun

pu·ber·tal \'pyü-bər-tᵊl\ or **pu·ber·al** \'pyü-bə-rəl\ adjective [pubertal from puberty; puberal from Medieval Latin puberalis, from Latin puber] (circa 1837)
: of or relating to puberty

pu·ber·ty \'pyü-bər-tē\ noun [Middle English puberte, from Latin pubertas, from puber pubescent] (14th century)
1 : the condition of being or the period of becoming first capable of reproducing sexually marked by maturing of the genital organs, development of secondary sex characteristics, and in the human and in higher primates by the first occurrence of menstruation in the female
2 : the age at which puberty occurs often construed legally as 14 in boys and 12 in girls

pu·ber·u·lent \pyü-'ber-ə-lənt, -yə-lənt\ adjective [Latin puber pubescent + English -ulent (as in pulverulent)] (circa 1859)
: covered with fine pubescence

pu·bes \'pyü-(ˌ)bēz\ noun, plural **pubes** [New Latin, from Latin, manhood, body hair, pubic region; akin to Latin puber pubescent] (circa 1570)
1 : the hair that appears on the lower part of the hypogastric region at puberty
2 : the pubic region

pu·bes·cence \pyü-'be-sᵊn(t)s\ noun (15th century)
1 : the quality or state of being pubescent
2 : a pubescent covering or surface

pu·bes·cent \-sᵊnt\ adjective [Latin pubescent-, pubescens, present participle of pubescere to reach puberty, become covered with hair, from pubes] (1646)
1 a : arriving at or having reached puberty b : of or relating to puberty
2 : covered with fine soft short hairs — compare VILLOUS

pu·bic \'pyü-bik\ adjective (1831)
: of, relating to, or situated in or near the region of the pubes or the pubis

pu·bis \'pyü-bəs\ noun, plural **pu·bes** \-(ˌ)bēz\ [New Latin os pubis, literally, bone of the pubic region] (1597)
: the ventral and anterior of the three principal bones composing either half of the pelvis — called also pubic bone

¹pub·lic \'pə-blik\ adjective [Middle English publique, from Middle French, from Latin publicus; akin to Latin populus the people] (14th century)
1 a : exposed to general view : OPEN b : WELL-KNOWN, PROMINENT c : PERCEPTIBLE, MATERIAL
2 a : of, relating to, or affecting all the people or the whole area of a nation or state ⟨public law⟩ b : of or relating to a government c : of, relating to, or being in the service of the community or nation
3 a : of or relating to people in general : UNIVERSAL b : GENERAL, POPULAR
4 : of or relating to business or community interests as opposed to private affairs : SOCIAL

5 : devoted to the general or national welfare **:** HUMANITARIAN
6 a : accessible to or shared by all members of the community **b :** capitalized in shares that can be freely traded on the open market — often used with *go*
— **pub·lic·ness** *noun*
²**public** *noun* (15th century)
1 : a place accessible or visible to the public — usually used in the phrase *in public*
2 : the people as a whole **:** POPULACE
3 : a group of people having common interests or characteristics; *specifically* **:** the group at which a particular activity or enterprise aims
public–address system *noun* (1923)
: an apparatus including a microphone and loudspeakers used for broadcasting to a large audience in an auditorium or outdoors
pub·li·can \'pə-bli-kən\ *noun* [Middle English, from Old French, from Latin *publicanus* tax farmer, from *publicum* public revenue, from neuter of *publicus*] (13th century)
1 a : a Jewish tax collector for the ancient Romans **b :** a collector of taxes or tribute
2 *chiefly British* **:** the licensee of a public house
public assistance *noun* (1884)
: government aid to needy, blind, aged, or disabled persons and to dependent children
pub·li·ca·tion \,pə-blə-'kā-shən\ *noun* [Middle English *publicacioun*, from Middle French *publication*, from Latin *publication-*, *publicatio*, from *publicare*, from *publicus* public] (14th century)
1 : the act or process of publishing
2 : a published work
public defender *noun* (1918)
: a lawyer usually holding public office whose duty is to defend accused persons unable to pay for legal assistance
public domain *noun* (1832)
1 : land owned directly by the government
2 : the realm embracing property rights that belong to the community at large, are unprotected by copyright or patent, and are subject to appropriation by anyone
public health *noun* (1617)
: the art and science dealing with the protection and improvement of community health by organized community effort and including preventive medicine and sanitary and social science
public house *noun* (1658)
1 : INN, HOSTELRY
2 *chiefly British* **:** a licensed saloon or bar
pub·li·cise *British variant of* PUBLICIZE
pub·li·cist \'pə-blə-sist\ *noun* (1792)
1 a : an expert in international law **b :** an expert or commentator on public affairs
2 : one that publicizes; *specifically* **:** PRESS AGENT
pub·lic·i·ty \(,)pə-'bli-sə-tē, -'blis-tē\ *noun* (1791)
1 : the quality or state of being public
2 a : an act or device designed to attract public interest; *specifically* **:** information with news value issued as a means of gaining public attention or support **b :** the dissemination of information or promotional material **c :** paid advertising **d :** public attention or acclaim
pub·li·cize \'pə-blə-,sīz\ *transitive verb* **-cized; -ciz·ing** (1925)
: to bring to the attention of the public **:** ADVERTISE
public land *noun* (1789)
: land owned by a government; *specifically* **:** that part of the U.S. public domain subject to sale or disposal under the homestead laws
public law *noun* (1773)
1 : a legislative enactment affecting the public at large
2 : a branch of law concerned with regulating the relations of individuals with the government and the organization and conduct of the government itself — compare PRIVATE LAW

pub·lic·ly \'pə-bli-klē\ *also* **pub·li·cal·ly** \-li-k(ə-)lē\ *adverb* (1567)
1 : in a manner observable by or in a place accessible to the public **:** OPENLY
2 a : by the people generally **b :** by a government
public officer *noun* (1925)
: a person who has been legally elected or appointed to office and who exercises governmental functions
public relations *noun plural but usually singular in construction, often attributive* (1807)
: the business of inducing the public to have understanding for and goodwill toward a person, firm, or institution; *also* **:** the degree of understanding and goodwill achieved
public sale *noun* (1678)
: AUCTION 1
public school *noun* (1580)
1 : an endowed secondary boarding school in Great Britain offering a classical curriculum and preparation for the universities or public service
2 : a free tax-supported school controlled by a local governmental authority
public servant *noun* (1676)
: a government official or employee
public service *noun* (circa 1576)
1 : the business of supplying a commodity (as electricity or gas) or service (as transportation) to any or all members of a community
2 : a service rendered in the public interest
3 : governmental employment; *especially* **:** CIVIL SERVICE
public–service corporation *noun* (1904)
: a quasi-public corporation
public speaking *noun* (1762)
1 : the act or process of making speeches in public
2 : the art of effective oral communication with an audience
public–spirited *adjective* (1677)
: motivated by devotion to the general welfare
— **pub·lic–spir·it·ed·ness** *noun*
public television *noun* (1965)
: television supported by public funds and private contributions rather than by commercials
public utility *noun* (1903)
: a business organization (as an electric company) performing a public service and subject to special governmental regulation
public works *noun plural* (1676)
: works (as schools, highways, docks) constructed for public use or enjoyment especially when financed and owned by the government
pub·lish \'pə-blish\ *verb* [Middle English, modification of Middle French *publier*, from Latin *publicare*, from *publicus* public] (14th century)
transitive verb
1 a : to make generally known **b :** to make public announcement of
2 a : to disseminate to the public **b :** to produce or release for distribution; *specifically* **:** PRINT 2c **c :** to issue the work of (an author)
intransitive verb
1 : to put out an edition
2 : to have one's work accepted for publication
— **pub·lish·able** \-bli-shə-bəl\ *adjective*
pub·lish·er \'pə-bli-shər\ *noun* (15th century)
: one that publishes something; *especially* **:** a person or corporation whose business is publishing
pub·lish·ing \-shin\ *noun* (1580)
: the business or profession of the commercial production and issuance of literature, information, musical scores or sometimes recordings, or art 〈newspaper *publishing*〉 〈software *publishing*〉
puc·coon \(,)pə-'kün\ *noun* [Virginia Algonquian *poughkone*] (1612)
1 : any of several American plants (as bloodroot) yielding a red or yellow pigment
2 : a pigment from a puccoon

puce \'pyüs\ *noun* [French, literally, flea, from Latin *pulic-*, *pulex* — more at PSYLLA] (1882)
: a dark red
¹**puck** \'pək\ *noun* [Middle English *puke*, from Old English *pūca*; akin to Old Norse *pūki* devil] (before 12th century)
1 *archaic* **:** an evil spirit **:** DEMON
2 : a mischievous sprite **:** HOBGOBLIN; *specifically, capitalized* **:** ROBIN GOODFELLOW
²**puck** *noun* [English dialect *puck* to poke, hit, probably from Irish *poc* butt, stroke in hurling, literally, buck (male deer)] (1891)
: a vulcanized rubber disk used in ice hockey
pucka *variant of* PUKKA
¹**puck·er** \'pə-kər\ *verb* **puck·ered; puck·er·ing** \-k(ə-)riŋ\ [probably irregular from ¹*poke*] (1598)
intransitive verb
: to become wrinkled or constricted
transitive verb
: to contract into folds or wrinkles
²**pucker** *noun* (circa 1750)
: a fold or wrinkle in a normally even surface
puck·ery \'pə-k(ə-)rē\ *adjective* (1830)
: that puckers or causes puckering
puck·ish \'pə-kish\ *adjective* [¹*puck*] (1874)
: IMPISH, WHIMSICAL
— **puck·ish·ly** *adverb*
— **puck·ish·ness** *noun*
pud \'pùd\ *noun* (1706)
British **:** PUDDING
pud·ding \'pù-diŋ\ *noun* [Middle English] (13th century)
1 : BLOOD SAUSAGE
2 a (1) : a boiled or baked soft food usually with a cereal base 〈corn *pudding*〉 (2) **:** a dessert of a soft, spongy, or thick creamy consistency 〈chocolate *pudding*〉 (3) *British* **:** DESSERT **b :** a dish often containing suet or having a suet crust and originally boiled in a bag 〈steak and kidney *pudding*〉
pudding stone *noun* (1753)
: CONGLOMERATE
¹**pud·dle** \'pə-d°l\ *noun* [Middle English *podel*; akin to Low German *pudel* puddle, Old English *pudd* ditch] (14th century)
1 : a very small pool of usually dirty or muddy water
2 a : an earthy mixture (as of clay, sand, and gravel) worked while wet into a compact mass that becomes impervious to water when dry **b :** a thin mixture of soil and water for puddling plants
²**puddle** *verb* **pud·dled; pud·dling** \'pəd-liŋ, 'pə-d°l-iŋ\ (15th century)
intransitive verb
: to dabble or wade around in a puddle
transitive verb
1 : to make muddy or turbid **:** MUDDLE
2 a : to work (a wet mixture of earth or concrete) into a dense impervious mass **b :** to subject (iron) to the process of puddling
3 a : to strew with puddles **b :** to compact (soil) especially by working when too wet **c :** to dip the roots of (a plant) in a thin mud before transplanting
— **pud·dler** \'pəd-lər, 'pə-d°l-ər\ *noun*
puddle duck *noun* (1877)
: DABBLER b
puddle jumper *noun* (1942)
slang **:** LIGHTPLANE
pud·dling \'pəd-liŋ, 'pə-d°l-iŋ\ *noun* (1839)
: the process of converting pig iron into wrought iron or rarely steel by subjecting it to heat and frequent stirring in a furnace in the presence of oxidizing substances
pu·den·cy \'pyü-d°n(t)-sē\ *noun* [Latin *pudentia*, from *pudent-*, *pudens*, present participle of *pudēre* to be ashamed, make ashamed] (1611)
: MODESTY

\ə\ abut	\°\ kitten	\ər\ further	\a\ ash	\ā\ ace	
\ä\ mop, mar	\au̇\ out	\ch\ chin	\e\ bet	\ē\ easy	
\g\ go	\i\ hit	\ī\ ice	\j\ job	\ŋ\ go	
\ō\ law	\ȯi\ boy	\th\ thin	\th\ the	\ü\ loot	\u̇\ foot
\y\ yet	\zh\ vision	*see also* Guide to Pronunciation			

pu·den·dum \pyu̇-'den-dəm\ *noun, plural* **-da** \-də\ [New Latin, singular of Latin *pudenda*, from neuter plural of *pudendus*, gerundive of *pudēre* to be ashamed] (1634)
: the external genital organs of a human being and especially of a woman — usually used in plural
— **pu·den·dal** \-d°l\ *adjective*

pudgy \'pə-jē\ *adjective* **pudg·i·er; -est** [origin unknown] (1836)
: being short and plump : CHUBBY
— **pudg·i·ness** *noun*

pu·di·bund \'pyü-də-,bənd\ *adjective* [Latin *pudibundus*, from *pudēre* to be ashamed + *-bundus* (as in *moribundus* moribund)] (circa 1656)
: PRUDISH

pueb·lo \'pwe-(,)blō; pü-'e-, pyü-\ *noun, plural* **-los** [Spanish, village, literally, people, from Latin *populus*] (1808)
1 a : the communal dwelling of an Indian village of Arizona, New Mexico, and adjacent areas consisting of contiguous flat-roofed stone or adobe houses in groups sometimes several stories high **b** : an Indian village of the southwestern U.S.
2 *capitalized* : a member of a group of Indian peoples of the southwestern U.S.

pu·er·ile \'pyu̇(-ə)r-əl, -,īl\ *adjective* [French or Latin; French *puéril*, from Latin *puerilis*, from *puer* boy, child; akin to Sanskrit *putra* son, child and perhaps to Greek *pais* boy, child — more at FEW] (1661)
1 : JUVENILE
2 : CHILDISH, SILLY ⟨*puerile* remarks⟩
— **pu·er·ile·ly** \-ə(l)-lē, -,īl-lē\ *adverb*
— **pu·er·il·i·ty** \pyu̇(-ə)r-'i-lə-tē\ *noun*

pu·er·il·ism \'pyu̇(-ə)r-ə-,li-zəm, 'pyu̇(-ə)r-,ī-\ *noun* (1924)
: childish behavior especially as a symptom of mental disorder

pu·er·per·al \pyü-'ər-p(ə-)rəl\ *adjective* [Latin *puerpera* woman in childbirth, from *puer* child + *parere* to give birth to — more at PARE] (1768)
: of, relating to, or occurring during childbirth or the period immediately following ⟨*puerperal* depression⟩ ⟨*puerperal* infection⟩

puerperal fever *noun* (1768)
: an abnormal condition that results from infection of the placental site following delivery or abortion and is characterized in mild form by fever but in serious cases the infection may spread through the uterine wall or pass into the bloodstream — called also *childbed fever, puerperal sepsis*

pu·er·pe·ri·um \,pyü-ər-'pir-ē-əm\ *noun, plural* **-ria** \-ē-ə\ [Latin, from *puerpera*] (circa 1890)
: the period between childbirth and the return of the uterus to its normal size

¹puff \'pəf\ *verb* [Middle English, from Old English *pyffan*, of imitative origin] (before 12th century)
intransitive verb
1 a (1) : to blow in short gusts (2) : to exhale forcibly **b** : to breathe hard : PANT **c** : to emit small whiffs or clouds (as of smoke) often as an accompaniment to vigorous action ⟨*puff* at a pipe⟩
2 : to speak or act in a scornful, conceited, or exaggerated manner
3 a : to become distended : SWELL — usually used with *up* **b** : to open or appear in or as if in a puff
4 : to form a chromosomal puff
transitive verb
1 a : to emit, propel, blow, or expel by or as if by puffs : WAFT **b** : to draw on (as a cigar, cigarette, or pipe) with intermittent exhalations of smoke
2 a : to distend with or as if with air or gas : INFLATE **b** : to make proud or conceited : ELATE **c** (1) : to praise extravagantly and usually with exaggeration (2) : ADVERTISE

²puff *noun* (13th century)

1 a : an act or instance of puffing : WHIFF **b** : a slight explosive sound accompanying a puff **c** : a perceptible cloud or aura emitted in a puff **d** : DRAW 1a
2 : a light round hollow pastry
3 a : a slight swelling : PROTUBERANCE **b** : a fluffy mass: as (1) : POUF 2 (2) : a small fluffy pad for applying cosmetic powder (3) : a soft loose roll of hair (4) : a quilted bed covering
4 : a commendatory or promotional notice or review
5 : an enlarged region of a chromosome that is associated with intensely active genes involved in RNA synthesis
— **puff·i·ness** \'pə-fē-nəs\ *noun*
— **puffy** \'pə-fē\ *adjective*

puff adder *noun* (1789)
1 : a thick-bodied extremely venomous African viper (*Bitis arietans*)
2 : HOGNOSE SNAKE

puff·ball \'pəf-,bȯl\ *noun* (1649)
: any of various globose and often edible fungi (especially family Lycoperdaceae) that discharge ripe spores in a smokelike cloud when pressed or struck

puff·er \'pə-fər\ *noun* (1629)
1 : one that puffs
2 a : any of a family (Tetraodontidae) of chiefly tropical marine bony fishes which can distend themselves to a globular form and most of which are highly poisonous — called also *blowfish, globefish* **b** : any of various fish of the same order (Tetraodontiformes synonym Plectognathi) as the puffers

puff·ery \'pə-f(ə-)rē\ *noun* (1782)
: exaggerated commendation especially for promotional purposes : HYPE

puf·fin \'pə-fən\ *noun* [Middle English *pophyn*] (14th century)
: any of several seabirds (genera *Fratercula* and *Lunda*) having a short neck and a deep grooved parti-colored laterally compressed bill

puffin

puff pastry *noun* (1611)
: a pastry dough containing many alternating layers of butter and dough or the light flaky pastry made from it — called also *puff paste*

¹pug \'pəg\ *noun* [obsolete *pug* hobgoblin, monkey] (1789)
1 : a small sturdy compact dog of a breed of Asian origin with a close coat, tightly curled tail, and broad wrinkled face
2 a : PUG NOSE **b** : a close knot or coil of hair : BUN

²pug *transitive verb* **pugged; pug·ging** [origin unknown] (1843)
: to work and mix (as clay) when wet especially to make more homogeneous and easier to handle (as in throwing or molding wares)

³pug *noun* [by shortening & alteration from *pugilist*] (1858)
: ¹BOXER 1

⁴pug *noun* [Hindi *pag* foot] (1865)
: FOOTPRINT; *especially* : a print of a wild mammal

pug·ga·ree *or* **pug·a·ree** *or* **pug·gree** \'pə-g(ə-)rē\ *noun* [Hindi *pagrī* turban] (1665)
: a light scarf wrapped around a sun helmet or used as a hatband

pu·gi·lism \'pyü-jə-,li-zəm\ *noun* [Latin *pugil* boxer; akin to Latin *pugnus* fist — more at PUNGENT] (1791)
: ²BOXING
— **pu·gi·lis·tic** \,pyü-jə-'lis-tik\ *adjective*

pu·gi·list \'pyü-jə-list\ *noun* (1790)

: FIGHTER; *especially* : a professional boxer

pug·mark \'pəg-,märk\ *noun* (1922)
: ⁴PUG

pug mill *noun* [²*pug*] (1824)
: a machine in which materials (as clay and water) are mixed, blended, or kneaded into a desired consistency

pug·na·cious \,pəg-'nā-shəs\ *adjective* [Latin *pugnac-, pugnax*, from *pugnare* to fight — more at PUNGENT] (1642)
: having a quarrelsome or combative nature : TRUCULENT
synonym see BELLIGERENT
— **pug·na·cious·ly** *adverb*
— **pug·na·cious·ness** *noun*
— **pug·nac·i·ty** \-'na-sə-tē\ *noun*

pug nose *noun* [¹*pug*] (1778)
: a nose having a slightly concave bridge and flattened nostrils
— **pug-nosed** \'pəg-,nōzd\ *adjective*

puis·ne \'pyü-nē\ *adjective* [Middle French *puisné* younger — more at PUNY] (1688)
chiefly British : inferior in rank ⟨*puisne* judge⟩
— **puisne** *noun*

puis·sance \'pwi-s°n(t)s, 'pyü-ə-sən(t)s, pyü-'i-s°n(t)s\ *noun* [Middle English, from Middle French, from Old French, from *puissant* powerful, from *poeir* to be able, be powerful — more at POWER] (15th century)
: STRENGTH, POWER

puis·sant \-s°nt, -sənt\ *adjective* (15th century)
: having puissance : POWERFUL

puke \'pyük\ *verb* **puked; puk·ing** [origin unknown] (1600)
: VOMIT
— **puke** *noun*

puk·ka \'pə-kə\ *adjective* [Hindi *pakkā* cooked, ripe, solid, from Sanskrit *pakva;* akin to Greek *pessein* to cook — more at COOK] (1698)
: GENUINE, AUTHENTIC; *also* : FIRST-CLASS

pul \'pu̇l\ *noun, plural* **puls** \'pu̇lz\ *or* **pul** [Persian *pūl*] (1927)
— see *afghani* at MONEY table

pu·la \'pü-lə, 'pyü-\ *noun, plural* **pula** [Tswana, literally, rain (used as a greeting)] (1976)
— see MONEY table

Pu·las·ki \pə-'las-kē, pyü-\ *noun* [Edward C. Pulaski, 20th century American forest ranger] (1924)
: a single-bit ax with an adze-shaped hoe extending from the back

pul·chri·tude \'pəl-krə-,tüd, -,tyüd\ *noun* [Middle English, from Latin *pulchritudin-, pulchritudo*, from *pulchr-, pulcher* beautiful] (15th century)
: physical comeliness
— **pul·chri·tu·di·nous** \,pəl-krə-'tüd-nəs, -'tyüd-; -'tü-d°n-əs, -'tyü-\ *adjective*

pule \'pyü(ə)l\ *intransitive verb* **puled; pul·ing** [probably imitative] (1534)
: WHINE, WHIMPER

pu·li \'pu̇-lē, 'pyü-\ *noun, plural* **pu·lik** \-lik\ *or* **pulis** \-lēz\ [Hungarian] (1936)
: any of a breed of medium-sized Hungarian sheepdogs with a thick woolly coat hanging in long thin cords

Pu·lit·zer prize \'pu̇-lət-sər-, 'pyü-\ *noun* (1918)
: any of various annual prizes (as for outstanding literary or journalistic achievement) established by the will of Joseph Pulitzer — called also *Pulitzer*

¹pull \'pu̇l *also* 'pəl\ *verb* [Middle English, from Old English *pullian;* akin to Middle Low German *pulen* to shell, cull] (before 12th century)
transitive verb
1 a : to exert force upon so as to cause or tend to cause motion toward the force **b** : to stretch (cooling candy) repeatedly ⟨*pull* taffy⟩ **c** : to strain abnormally ⟨*pull* a tendon⟩ **d** : to hold back (a racehorse) from winning **e** : to work (an oar) by drawing back strongly

2 a : to draw out from the skin ⟨*pull* feathers from a rooster's tail⟩ **b :** to pluck from a plant or by the roots ⟨*pull* flowers⟩ ⟨*pull* turnips⟩ **c :** EXTRACT ⟨*pull* a tooth⟩
3 : to hit (a ball) toward the left from a right-handed swing or toward the right from a left-handed swing — compare PUSH
4 : to draw apart : REND, TEAR
5 : to print (as a proof) by impression
6 : to remove from a place or situation ⟨*pull* the engine⟩ ⟨*pulled* the pitcher in the third inning⟩ ⟨*pulled* the show⟩
7 : to bring (a weapon) into the open ⟨*pulled* a knife⟩
8 a : COMMIT, PERPETRATE ⟨*pull* a robbery⟩ ⟨*pull* a prank⟩ **b :** to carry out as an assignment or duty
9 : PUT ON, ASSUME ⟨*pull* a grin⟩
10 a : to draw the support or attention of : ATTRACT ⟨*pull* votes⟩ — often used with *in* **b :** OBTAIN, SECURE ⟨*pulled* a B in the course⟩
11 : to demand or obtain an advantage over someone by the assertion of ⟨*pull* rank⟩
intransitive verb
1 a : to use force in drawing, dragging, or tugging **b :** to move especially through the exercise of mechanical energy ⟨the car *pulled* clear of the rut⟩ **c** (1) : to take a drink (2) : to draw hard in smoking ⟨*pulled* at a pipe⟩ **d :** to strain against the bit
2 : to draw a gun
3 : to admit of being pulled
4 : to feel or express strong sympathy : ROOT ⟨*pulling* for my team to win⟩
5 *of an offensive lineman in football* : to move back from the line of scrimmage and toward one flank to provide blocking for a ballcarrier
— **pull·er** *noun*
— **pull a fast one :** to perpetrate a trick or fraud
— **pull punches** *also* **pull a punch :** to refrain from using all the force at one's disposal
— **pull oneself together :** to regain one's composure
— **pull one's leg :** to deceive someone playfully : HOAX
— **pull one's weight :** to do one's full share of the work
— **pull out all the stops :** to use all one's resources without restraint
— **pull stakes** *or* **pull up stakes :** to move out : LEAVE
— **pull strings** *also* **pull wires :** to exert hidden influence or control
— **pull the plug 1 :** to disconnect a medical life-support system **2 :** to withdraw essential and especially financial support
— **pull the rug from under :** to weaken or unsettle especially by removing support or assistance from
— **pull the string :** to throw a change-up
— **pull the wool over one's eyes :** to blind to the true situation : HOODWINK
— **pull together :** to work in harmony : COOPERATE
²**pull** *noun, often attributive* (14th century)
1 a : the act or an instance of pulling **b** (1) : a draft of liquid (2) : an inhalation of smoke **c :** the effort expended in moving ⟨a long *pull* uphill⟩ **d :** force required to overcome resistance to pulling ⟨trigger *pull*⟩
2 a : ADVANTAGE **b :** special influence
3 : PROOF 6a
4 : a device for pulling something or for operating by pulling ⟨drawer *pull*⟩
5 : a force that attracts, compels, or influences : ATTRACTION
6 : an injury resulting from abnormal straining or stretching ⟨a muscle *pull*⟩ ⟨a groin *pull*⟩
pull away *intransitive verb* (circa 1934)
1 : to draw oneself back or away : WITHDRAW
2 : to move off or ahead
pull·back \ˈpu̇l-ˌbak\ *noun* (1668)
: a pulling back; *especially* : an orderly withdrawal of troops from a position or area

pull down *transitive verb* (15th century)
1 a : DEMOLISH, DESTROY **b :** to hunt down : OVERCOME
2 a : to bring to a lower level : REDUCE **b :** to depress in health, strength, or spirits
3 : to draw as wages or salary
pul·let \ˈpu̇-lət\ *noun* [Middle English *polet* young fowl, from Middle French *poulet*, from Old French, diminutive of *poul* cock, from Late Latin *pullus*, from Latin, young of an animal, chicken, sprout — more at FOAL] (14th century)
: a young hen; *specifically* : a hen of the domestic chicken less than a year old
pul·ley \ˈpu̇-lē\ *noun, plural* **pulleys** [Middle English *pouley*, from Middle French *poulie*, probably ultimately from Greek *polos* axis, pole — more at POLE] (14th century)
1 : a sheave or small wheel with a grooved rim and with or without the block in which it runs used singly with a rope or chain to change the direction and point of application of a pulling force and in various combinations to increase the applied force especially for lifting weights
2 : a pulley or pulleys with ropes to form a tackle that constitutes one of the simple machines
3 : a wheel used to transmit power by means of a band, belt, cord, rope, or chain passing over its rim
pull in (1605)
transitive verb
1 : CHECK, RESTRAIN
2 : ARREST
intransitive verb
: to arrive at a destination or come to a stop
Pull·man \ˈpu̇l-mən\ *noun* [George M. *Pullman*] (1867)
1 : a railroad passenger car with specially comfortable furnishings for day or especially for night travel
2 : a large suitcase
pull off *transitive verb* (1883)
: to carry out despite difficulties : accomplish successfully against odds
pul·lo·rum disease \pə-ˈlȯr-əm-, -ˈlȯr-\ *noun* [New Latin *pullorum* (specific epithet of *Salmonella pullorum*), from Latin, of chickens (genitive plural of *pullus*)] (1929)
: a destructive typically diarrheal salmonellosis especially of young domestic chickens that is caused by a bacterium (*Salmonella pullorum*)
pull·out \ˈpu̇l-ˌau̇t\ *noun* (1825)
1 : the act or an instance of pulling out: as **a :** the action in which an airplane goes from a dive to horizontal flight **b :** PULLBACK
2 : something that can be pulled out
pull out *intransitive verb* (1855)
1 : LEAVE, DEPART
2 : WITHDRAW
¹**pull·over** \ˈpu̇l-ˌō-vər\ *noun* (1899)
: a pullover garment (as a sweater)
²**pullover** *adjective* (1907)
: put on by being pulled over the head
pull over (1930)
intransitive verb
: to steer one's vehicle to the side of the road
transitive verb
: to cause to pull over ⟨*pulled* him *over* for speeding⟩
pull round (1891)
intransitive verb
chiefly British : to regain one's health
transitive verb
chiefly British : to restore to good health
pull tab *noun* (1963)
: a metal tab (as on a can) pulled to open the container
pull through (1852)
intransitive verb
: to survive a dangerous or difficult situation
transitive verb
: to help survive a dangerous or difficult situation

pul·lu·late \ˈpəl-yə-ˌlāt\ *intransitive verb* **-lat·ed; -lat·ing** [Latin *pullulatus*, past participle of *pullulare*, from *pullulus*, diminutive of *pullus* chicken, sprout — more at FOAL] (1619)
1 a : GERMINATE, SPROUT **b :** to breed or produce freely
2 : SWARM, TEEM
— **pul·lu·la·tion** \ˌpəl-yə-ˈlā-shən\ *noun*
pull-up \ˈpu̇l-ˌəp\ *noun* (1938)
: CHIN-UP
pull up (1623)
transitive verb
1 : to bring to a stop : HALT
2 : CHECK, REBUKE
intransitive verb
1 a : to check oneself **b :** to come to an often abrupt halt : STOP
2 : to draw even with others in a race
pul·mo·nary \ˈpu̇l-mə-ˌner-ē, ˈpəl-\ *adjective* [Latin *pulmonarius*, from *pulmon-, pulmo* lung; akin to Greek *pleumōn* lung, Sanskrit *kloman* right lung] (1704)
1 : relating to, functioning like, or associated with the lungs
2 : PULMONATE
3 : carried on by the lungs
pulmonary artery *noun* (1704)
: an artery that conveys venous blood from the heart to the lungs — see HEART illustration
pulmonary circulation *noun* (circa 1890)
: the passage of blood from the right side of the heart through arteries to the lungs where it picks up oxygen and is returned to the left side of the heart by veins
pulmonary vein *noun* (1704)
: a valveless vein that returns oxygenated blood from the lungs to the heart
¹**pul·mo·nate** \ˈpu̇l-mə-ˌnāt, ˈpəl-\ *adjective* [Latin *pulmon-, pulmo* lung] (circa 1859)
1 : having lungs or organs resembling lungs
2 : of or relating to a subclass (Pulmonata) of gastropod mollusks having a respiratory sac and comprising most land snails and slugs and many freshwater snails
²**pulmonate** *noun* (1883)
: a pulmonate gastropod
pul·mon·ic \pu̇l-ˈmä-nik, ˌpəl-\ *adjective* [Latin *pulmon-, pulmo*] (1661)
: PULMONARY
pul·mo·tor \ˈpu̇l-ˌmō-tər, ˈpəl-\ *noun* [from *Pulmotor*, a trademark] (1911)
: a respiratory apparatus for pumping oxygen or air into and out of the lungs (as of an asphyxiated person)
¹**pulp** \ˈpəlp\ *noun* [Middle English *pulpe*, from Middle French *poulpe*, from Latin *pulpa* flesh, pulp] (14th century)
1 a (1) : the soft, succulent part of a fruit usually composed of mesocarp (2) : stem pith when soft and spongy **b :** a soft mass of vegetable matter (as of apples) from which most of the water has been extracted by pressure **c :** the soft sensitive tissue that fills the central cavity of a tooth — see TOOTH illustration **d :** a material prepared by chemical or mechanical means from various materials (as wood or rags) for use in making paper and cellulose products
2 : pulverized ore mixed with water
3 a : pulpy condition or character **b :** something in such a condition or having such a character
4 : a magazine or book printed on cheap paper (as newsprint) and often dealing with sensational material
— **pulp·i·ness** \ˈpəl-pē-nəs\ *noun*
— **pulpy** \ˈpəl-pē\ *adjective*
²**pulp** (1683)
transitive verb
1 : to reduce to pulp : cause to appear pulpy

\ə\ abut \ᵊ\ kitten \ər\ further \a\ ash \ā\ ace
\ä\ mop, mar \au̇\ out \ch\ chin \e\ bet \ē\ easy
\g\ go \i\ hit \ī\ ice \j\ job \ŋ\ sing \ō\ go
\ȯ\ law \ȯi\ boy \th\ thin \ṯh\ the \ü\ loot \u̇\ foot
\y\ yet \zh\ vision *see also* Guide to Pronunciation

2 : to deprive of the pulp
3 : to produce or reproduce (written matter) in pulp form
intransitive verb
: to become pulp or pulpy
— **pulp·er** *noun*

pulp·al \'pəl-pəl\ *adjective* (1903)
: of or relating to pulp especially of a tooth ⟨a *pulpal* abscess⟩
— **pulp·al·ly** \'pəl-pə-lē\ *adverb*

pul·pit \'pùl-,pit *also* 'pəl-, -pət\ *noun* [Middle English, from Late Latin *pulpitum,* from Latin, staging, platform] (14th century)
1 : an elevated platform or high reading desk used in preaching or conducting a worship service
2 a : the preaching profession **b :** a preaching position

pulp·wood \'pəlp-,wùd\ *noun* (1885)
: a wood (as of aspen, hemlock, pine, or spruce) used in making pulp for paper

pul·que \'pùl-,kā; 'pùl-kē, 'pùl-\ *noun* [Mexican Spanish] (1693)
: a Mexican alcoholic beverage made from the fermented sap of various agaves (as *Agave atrovirens*)

pul·sant \'pəl-sənt\ *adjective* (1709)
: pulsating with activity

pul·sar \'pəl-,sär\ *noun* [*pulse* + *-ar* (as in *quasar*)] (1968)
: a celestial source of pulsating electromagnetic radiation (as radio waves) characterized by a short relatively constant interval (as .033 second) between pulses that is held to be a rotating neutron star

pul·sate \'pəl-,sāt *also* ,pəl-'\ *intransitive verb* **pul·sat·ed; pul·sat·ing** [Latin *pulsatus,* past participle of *pulsare,* frequentative of *pellere*] (1794)
1 : to exhibit a pulse or pulsation **:** BEAT
2 : to throb or move rhythmically **:** VIBRATE

pul·sa·tile \'pəl-sə-t'l, -,tīl\ *adjective* (1541)
: of or marked by pulsation

pul·sa·tion \,pəl-'sā-shən\ *noun* (1541)
1 : rhythmical throbbing or vibrating (as of an artery); *also* **:** a single beat or throb
2 : a periodically recurring alternate increase and decrease of a quantity (as pressure, volume, or voltage)

pul·sa·tor \'pəl-,sā-tər, ,pəl-'\ *noun* (1890)
: something that beats or throbs in working

¹pulse \'pəls\ *noun* [Middle English *puls,* from Old French *pouls* porridge, from Latin *pult-, puls,* probably from Greek *poltos*] (13th century)
: the edible seeds of various leguminous crops (as peas, beans, or lentils); *also* **:** a plant yielding pulse

²pulse *noun* [Middle English *puls,* from Middle French *pouls,* from Latin *pulsus,* literally, beating, from *pellere* to drive, push, beat — more at FELT] (14th century)
1 a : a regular throbbing caused in the arteries by the contractions of the heart **b :** the palpable beat resulting from such pulse as detected in a superficial artery; *also* **:** the number of individual beats in a specified time period (as one minute) ⟨a resting *pulse* of 70⟩
2 a : underlying sentiment or opinion or an indication of it **b :** VITALITY
3 a : rhythmical beating, vibrating, or sounding **b :** BEAT, THROB
4 a : a transient variation of a quantity (as electrical current or voltage) whose value is normally constant **b** (1) **:** an electromagnetic wave or modulation thereof of brief duration (2) **:** a brief disturbance of pressure in a medium; *especially* **:** a sound wave or short train of sound waves
5 : a dose of a substance especially when applied over a short period of time ⟨*pulse*-labeled DNA⟩

³pulse *verb* **pulsed; puls·ing** (15th century)
intransitive verb
: to exhibit a pulse or pulsation **:** THROB
transitive verb

1 : to drive by or as if by a pulsation
2 : to cause to pulsate
3 a : to produce or modulate (as electromagnetic waves) in the form of pulses ⟨*pulsed* waves⟩ **b :** to cause (an apparatus) to produce pulses
— **puls·er** *noun*

pulse–jet engine \'pəls-'jet-\ *noun* (1949)
: a jet engine designed to produce a pulsating thrust by the intermittent flow of hot gases

pul·ver·a·ble \'pəl-və-rə-bəl, 'pəlv-rə-\ *adjective* (circa 1617)
: capable of being pulverized

pul·ver·ise *British variant of* PULVERIZE

pul·ver·ize \'pəl-və-,rīz\ *verb* **-ized; -iz·ing** [Middle English, from Middle French *pulveriser,* from Late Latin *pulverizare,* from Latin *pulver-, pulvis* dust, powder — more at POWDER] (15th century)
transitive verb
1 : to reduce (as by crushing, beating, or grinding) to very small particles **:** ATOMIZE
2 : ANNIHILATE, DEMOLISH
intransitive verb
: to become pulverized
— **pul·ver·iz·able** \,pəl-və-'rī-zə-bəl\ *adjective*
— **pul·ver·i·za·tion** \,pəl-və-rə-'zā-shən, ,pəlv-rə-\ *noun*
— **pul·ver·iz·er** \'pəl-və-,rī-zər\ *noun*

pul·ver·u·lent \,pəl-'ver-yə-lənt, -'ver-ə-\ *adjective* [Latin *pulverulentus* dusty, from *pulver-, pulvis*] (circa 1656)
1 : consisting of or reducible to fine powder
2 : being or looking dusty **:** CRUMBLY

pul·vil·lus \,pəl-'vi-ləs\ *noun, plural* **-vil·li** \-'vi-,lī, -(,)lē\ [New Latin, from Latin, diminutive of *pulvinus*] (circa 1826)
: one of the lobed hairy adhesive organs that terminate the feet of dipteran flies

pul·vi·nus \,pəl-'vī-nəs, -'vē-\ *noun, plural* **-vi·ni** \-'vī-,nī, -(,)nē\ [New Latin, from Latin, cushion] (1857)
: a mass of large thin-walled cells surrounding a vascular strand at the base of a petiole or petiolule and functioning in turgor movements of leaves or leaflets

pu·ma \'pü-mə, 'pyü-\ *noun, plural* **pumas** *also* **puma** [Spanish, from Quechua] (1777)
: COUGAR; *also* **:** the fur or pelt of a cougar

pum·ice \'pə-məs\ *noun* [Middle English *pomis,* from Middle French, from Latin *pumic-, pumex* — more at FOAM] (15th century)
: a volcanic glass full of cavities and very light in weight used especially in powder form for smoothing and polishing
— **pu·mi·ceous** \pyü-'mi-shəs, ,pə-\ *adjective*

pum·ic·ite \'pə-mə-,sīt\ *noun* (1916)
: PUMICE

pum·mel \'pə-məl\ *verb* **-meled** *also* **-melled; -mel·ing** *also* **-mel·ling** \'pə-mə-liŋ, 'pəm-liŋ\ [alteration of *pommel*] (1548)
: POUND, BEAT

pum·me·lo *variant of* POMELO 2

¹pump \'pəmp\ *noun* [Middle English *pumpe, pompe,* from Middle Low German *pumpe* or Middle Dutch *pompe,* perhaps from Spanish *bomba,* of imitative origin] (15th century)
1 : a device that raises, transfers, or compresses fluids or that attenuates gases especially by suction or pressure or both
2 : HEART
3 : an act or the process of pumping
4 : an energy source (as light) for pumping atoms or molecules
5 : a mechanism (as the sodium pump) for pumping atoms, ions, or molecules

²pump (1508)
intransitive verb
1 : to work a pump **:** raise or move a fluid with a pump
2 : to exert oneself to pump or as if to pump something
3 : to move in a manner that resembles the action of a pump handle

transitive verb
1 a : to raise (as water) with a pump **b :** to draw fluid from with a pump
2 : to pour forth, deliver, or draw with or as if with a pump ⟨*pumped* money into the economy⟩ ⟨*pump* new life into the classroom⟩
3 a : to question persistently **b :** to elicit by persistent questioning
4 a : to operate by manipulating a lever **b :** to manipulate as if operating a pump handle ⟨*pumped* my hand warmly⟩ **c :** to cause to move with an action resembling that of a pump handle ⟨a runner *pumping* her arms⟩
5 : to transport (as ions) against a concentration gradient by the expenditure of energy
6 a : to excite (as atoms or molecules) especially so as to cause emission of coherent monochromatic electromagnetic radiation (as in a laser) **b :** to energize (as a laser) by pumping
— **pump iron :** to lift weights

³pump *noun* [origin unknown] (1555)
: a shoe that grips the foot chiefly at the toe and heel; *especially* **:** a close-fitting woman's dress shoe with a moderate to high heel

pumped storage *noun* (1927)
: a hydroelectric system in which electricity is generated during periods of high demand by the use of water that has been pumped into a reservoir at a higher altitude during periods of low demand

pump·er \'pəm-pər\ *noun* (1660)
: one that pumps; *especially* **:** a fire truck equipped with a pump

pum·per·nick·el \'pəm-pər-,ni-kəl\ *noun* [German, from *pumpern* to break wind + *Nickel* goblin; from its reputed indigestibility] (1756)
: a dark coarse sourdough bread made of unbolted rye flour

pump·kin \'pəm(p)-kən, ÷'pəŋ-kən\ *noun, often attributive* [alteration of earlier *pumpion,* modification of French *popon, pompon* melon, pumpkin, from Latin *pepon-, pepo,* from Greek *pepōn,* from *pepōn* ripened; akin to Greek *pessein* to cook, ripen — more at COOK] (1654)
1 a : the usually round orange fruit of a vine (*Cucurbita pepo*) of the gourd family widely cultivated as food **b :** WINTER CROOKNECK **c** *British* **:** any of various large-fruited winter squashes (*C. maxima*)
2 : a usually hairy prickly vine that produces pumpkins

pump·kin·seed \-,sēd\ *noun* (1814)
: a brilliantly colored North American freshwater sunfish (*Lepomis gibbosus*) with a reddish spot on the operculum

pump priming *noun* (1936)
: government investment expenditures designed to induce a self-sustaining expansion of economic activity

pump up *transitive verb* (1791)
1 a : to fill with enthusiasm or excitement **b :** to fill with or as if with air **:** INFLATE
2 : INCREASE 1

¹pun \'pən\ *noun* [perhaps from Italian *puntiglio* fine point, quibble — more at PUNCTILIO] (1662)
: the usually humorous use of a word in such a way as to suggest two or more of its meanings or the meaning of another word similar in sound

²pun *intransitive verb* **punned; pun·ning** (1670)
: to make puns

pu·na \'pü-nə\ *noun* [American Spanish, from Quechua] (1613)
: a treeless windswept tableland or basin in the higher Andes

¹punch \'pənch\ *verb* [Middle English, from Middle French *poinçonner* to prick, stamp, from *poinçon* puncheon] (14th century)
transitive verb

1 a : PROD, POKE **b :** DRIVE, HERD ⟨*punching* cattle⟩
2 a : to strike with a forward thrust especially of the fist **b :** to drive or push forcibly by or as if by a punch **c :** to hit (a ball) with less than a full swing
3 : to emboss, cut, perforate, or make with or as if with a punch
4 a : to push down so as to produce a desired result ⟨*punch* buttons on a jukebox⟩ **b :** to hit or press down the operating mechanism of ⟨*punch* a time clock⟩ ⟨*punch* a typewriter⟩ **c :** to produce by or as if by punching keys ⟨*punch* out a tune on the piano⟩ **d :** to enter (as data) by punching keys
5 : to give emphasis to
intransitive verb
: to perform the action of punching something
— **punch·er** *noun*

²punch *noun* (14th century)
1 : the action of punching
2 : a quick blow with or as if with the fist
3 : effective energy or forcefulness ⟨a story that packs a *punch*⟩ ⟨political *punch*⟩
— **punch·less** \'pənch-ləs\ *adjective*
— **to the punch :** to the first blow or to decisive action — usually used with *beat*

³punch *noun* [probably short for *puncheon*] (14th century)
1 a : a tool usually in the form of a short rod of steel that is variously shaped at one end for different operations (as forming, perforating, embossing, or cutting) **b :** a short tapering steel rod for driving the heads of nails below a surface **c :** a steel die faced with a letter in relief that is forced into a softer metal to form an intaglio matrix from which foundry type is cast **d :** a device or machine for cutting holes or notches (as in paper or cardboard)
2 : a hole or notch from a perforating operation

⁴punch *noun* [perhaps from Hindi *pãc* five, from Sanskrit *pañca*; akin to Greek *pente* five; from its originally having five ingredients — more at FIVE] (1632)
: a hot or cold drink that is usually a combination of hard liquor, wine, or beer and nonalcoholic beverages; *also* **:** a drink that is a mixture of nonalcoholic beverages

Punch–and–Judy show \,pənch-ən-'jü-dē\ *noun* (1876)
: a traditional puppet show in which the little hook-nosed humpback Punch fights comically with his wife Judy

punch·ball \'pənch-,bòl\ *noun* (1932)
: baseball adapted for small areas in which a rubber ball is hit with a fist instead of a bat

punch·board \-,bōrd, -,bòrd\ *noun* (1912)
: a small board that has many holes each filled with a rolled-up printed slip to be punched out on payment of a nominal sum in an effort to obtain a slip that entitles the player to a designated prize

punch bowl *noun* (1692)
: a large bowl from which a beverage (as punch) is served

punch–drunk \'pənch-,drəŋk\ *adjective* [²*punch*] (1918)
1 : suffering cerebral injury from many minute brain hemorrhages as a result of repeated head blows received in boxing
2 : behaving as if punch-drunk **:** DAZED, CONFUSED

punched card \'pəncht-\ *noun* (1919)
: a card in which holes are punched in designated positions to represent data — called also *Hollerith card*, *punch card*

¹pun·cheon \'pən-chən\ *noun* [Middle English *ponson*, from Middle French *poinçon* pointed tool, king post, from (assumed) Vulgar Latin *punction-*, *punctio* pointed tool, from Latin, action of pricking, from *pungere* to prick — more at PUNGENT] (14th century)
1 : a pointed tool for piercing or for working on stone

2 a : a short upright framing timber **b :** a split log or heavy slab with the face smoothed

²puncheon *noun* [Middle English *poncion*, from Middle French *ponchon*, *poinçon*, of unknown origin] (15th century)
: a large cask of varying capacity

punch in *intransitive verb* (1926)
: to record the time of one's arrival or beginning work by punching a time clock

pun·chi·nel·lo \,pən-chə-'ne-(,)lō\ *noun* [modification of Italian dialect *polecenella*] (1666)
1 *capitalized* **:** a fat short humpbacked clown or buffoon in Italian puppet shows
2 *plural* **-los :** a squat grotesque person

punching bag *noun* (1886)
: a stuffed or inflated bag that is usually suspended for free movement and that is punched for exercise or for training in boxing

Punchinello

punch line *noun* (1921)
: the sentence, statement, or phrase (as in a joke) that makes the point

punch–out \'pənch-,aut\ *noun* (1928)
: FISTFIGHT

punch out (1973)
intransitive verb
1 : to record the time of one's stopping work or departure by punching a time clock
2 : to bail out of an aircraft using an ejection seat
transitive verb
1 : to beat up
2 : STRIKE OUT

punch press *noun* (1911)
: a press equipped with cutting, shaping, or combination dies for working on material (as metal)

punch–up \'pənch-,əp\ *noun* (1958)
chiefly British **:** FISTFIGHT

punch up *transitive verb* (circa 1959)
: to give energy or forcefulness to ⟨jokes added to *punch up* a speech⟩

punchy \'pən-chē\ *adjective* **punch·i·er; -est** (1917)
1 : having punch **:** FORCEFUL, SPIRITED
2 : PUNCH-DRUNK

punc·tate \'pəŋk-,tāt\ *adjective* [New Latin *punctatus*, from Latin *punctum* point — more at POINT] (circa 1760)
1 : marked with minute spots or depressions ⟨a *punctate* leaf⟩
2 : characterized by dots or points ⟨*punctate* skin lesions⟩
— **punc·ta·tion** \,pəŋk-'tā-shən\ *noun*

punc·til·io \,pəŋk-'ti-lē-,ō\ *noun, plural* **-i·os** [Italian & Spanish; Italian *puntiglio* point of honor, scruple, from Spanish *puntillo*, from diminutive of *punto* point, from Latin *punctum*] (1596)
1 : a minute detail of conduct in a ceremony or in observance of a code
2 : careful observance of forms (as in social conduct)

punc·til·i·ous \-lē-əs\ *adjective* (1634)
: marked by or concerned about precise accordance with the details of codes or conventions
synonym see CAREFUL
— **punc·til·i·ous·ly** *adverb*
— **punc·til·i·ous·ness** *noun*

punc·tu·al \'pəŋk-chə-wəl, -chəl\ *adjective* [Middle English, having a sharp point, from Medieval Latin *punctualis* of a point, from Latin *punctus* pricking, point, from *pungere* to prick — more at PUNGENT] (1675)

: being on time **:** PROMPT
— **punc·tu·al·i·ty** \,pəŋk-chə-'wa-lə-tē\ *noun*
— **punc·tu·al·ly** \'pəŋk-chə-wə-lē, -chə-lē\ *adverb*

punc·tu·ate \'pəŋk-chə-,wāt\ *verb* **-at·ed; -at·ing** [Medieval Latin *punctuatus*, past participle of *punctuare* to point, provide with punctuation marks, from Latin *punctus* point] (circa 1818)
transitive verb
1 : to mark or divide (written matter) with punctuation marks
2 : to break into or interrupt at intervals ⟨the steady click of her needles *punctuated* the silence —Edith Wharton⟩
3 : ACCENTUATE, EMPHASIZE
intransitive verb
: to use punctuation marks
— **punc·tu·a·tor** \-,wā-tər\ *noun*

punctuated equilibrium *noun* (1978)
: evolution that is characterized by long periods of stability in the characteristics of an organism and short periods of rapid change during which new forms appear especially from small subpopulations of the ancestral form in restricted parts of its geographic range; *also* **:** a theory or model of evolution emphasizing this — compare GRADUALISM 2

punc·tu·a·tion \,pəŋk-chə-'wā-shən\ *noun* (circa 1539)
1 : the act of punctuating **:** the state of being punctuated
2 : the act or practice of inserting standardized marks or signs in written matter to clarify the meaning and separate structural units; *also* **:** a system of punctuation
3 : something that contrasts or accentuates

punctuation mark *noun* (1860)
: any of various standardized marks or signs used in punctuation

PUNCTUATION MARKS

.	period (*or* full stop)
,	comma
;	semicolon
:	colon
'	apostrophe
' '	quotation marks, single (*or chiefly British* inverted commas)
" "	quotation marks, double (*or chiefly British* inverted commas)
« »	guillemets
?	question mark (*or* interrogation point)
¿ ?	question marks, Spanish
!	exclamation point
¡ !	exclamation points, Spanish
‽	interrobang
/	slash (*or* diagonal *or* slant *or* solidus *or* virgule)
. . . *or*	ellipsis (*or* suspension points)
-	hyphen
⸗	double hyphen
–	dash (*or* en dash)
—	dash (*or* em dash)
~	swung dash
()	parentheses (*or* brackets)
[]	brackets, square (*or* braces)
⟨ ⟩	brackets, angle
{ }	braces (*or* curly brackets)

¹punc·ture \'pəŋk-chər\ *noun* [Middle English, from Latin *punctura*, from *punctus*, past participle of *pungere*] (14th century)
1 : an act of puncturing
2 : a hole, wound, or perforation made by puncturing
3 : a minute depression

²puncture *verb* **punc·tured; punc·tur·ing** \'pəŋk-chə-riŋ, 'pəŋk-shriŋ\ (1699)
transitive verb
1 : to pierce with or as if with a pointed instrument or object
2 : to make useless or ineffective as if by a puncture : DEFLATE
intransitive verb
: to become punctured

puncture vine *noun* (1911)
: an Old World annual prostrate herb (*Tribulus terrestris*) of the caltrop family that has hard spiny pods and is a troublesome weed especially in the western U.S. — called also *caltrop, puncture-weed*

pun·dit \'pən-dət\ *noun* [Hindi *paṇḍit*, from Sanskrit *paṇḍita*, from *paṇḍita* learned] (1672)
1 : PANDIT
2 : a learned man : TEACHER
3 : one who gives opinions in an authoritative manner : CRITIC
— **pun·dit·ry** \-də-trē\ *noun*

pung \'pəŋ\ *noun* [short for earlier *tow-pong*, of Algonquian origin; akin to Micmac *tobâgun* drag made with skin] (1825)
New England : a sleigh with a box-shaped body

pun·gen·cy \'pən-jən(t)-sē\ *noun* (1649)
: the quality or state of being pungent

pun·gent \-jənt\ *adjective* [Latin *pungent-, pungens*, present participle of *pungere* to prick, sting; akin to Latin *pugnus* fist, *pugnare* to fight, Greek *pygmē* fist] (1597)
1 : sharply painful
2 : having a stiff and sharp point ⟨*pungent* leaves⟩
3 a : marked by a sharp incisive quality : CAUSTIC ⟨a *pungent* critic⟩ ⟨*pungent* language⟩ **b** : being sharp and to the point
4 : causing a sharp or irritating sensation; *especially* : ACRID ☆
— **pun·gent·ly** *adverb*

pun·gle \'pən-gəl\ *verb* **pun·gled; pun·gling** \'pən-g(ə-)liŋ\ [Spanish *póngale* put it down] (1851)
transitive verb
: to make a payment or contribution of (money) — usually used with *up*
intransitive verb
: PAY, CONTRIBUTE — usually used with *up*

¹Pu·nic \'pyü-nik\ *adjective* [Latin *punicus*, from *Poenus* inhabitant of Carthage; akin to Greek *Phoinix* Phoenician] (1533)
1 : of or relating to Carthage or the Carthaginians
2 : FAITHLESS, TREACHEROUS

²Punic *noun* (1673)
: the Phoenician dialect of ancient Carthage

pun·ish \'pə-nish\ *verb* [Middle English *punisshen*, from Middle French *puniss-*, stem of *punir*, from Latin *punire*, from *poena* penalty — more at PAIN] (14th century)
transitive verb
1 a : to impose a penalty on for a fault, offense, or violation **b** : to inflict a penalty for the commission of (an offense) in retribution or retaliation
2 a : to deal with roughly or harshly **b** : to inflict injury on : HURT
intransitive verb
: to inflict punishment ☆
— **pun·ish·abil·i·ty** \,pə-nish-ə-'bi-lə-tē\ *noun*
— **pun·ish·able** \'pə-nish-ə-bəl\ *adjective*
— **pun·ish·er** *noun*

pun·ish·ment \'pə-nish-mənt\ *noun* (15th century)
1 : the act of punishing
2 a : suffering, pain, or loss that serves as retribution **b** : a penalty inflicted on an offender through judicial procedure
3 : severe, rough, or disastrous treatment

pu·ni·tion \pyü-'ni-shən\ *noun* [Middle English *punicion*, from Middle French *punition*, from Latin *punition-, punitio*, from *punire*] (15th century)
: PUNISHMENT

pu·ni·tive \'pyü-nə-tiv\ *adjective* [French *punitif*, from Medieval Latin *punitivus*, from Latin *punitus*, past participle of *punire*] (1624)
: inflicting, involving, or aiming at punishment
— **pu·ni·tive·ly** *adverb*
— **pu·ni·tive·ness** *noun*

punitive damages *noun plural* (circa 1890)
: damages awarded in excess of normal compensation to the plaintiff to punish a defendant for a serious wrong

Pun·jabi \,pən-'jä-bē, -'ja-\ *noun* [Hindi *pañjābī*, from *pañjābī* of Punjab, from Persian *panjābī*, from *Panjāb* Punjab] (1846)
1 : PANJABI 1
2 : a native or inhabitant of the Punjab region of the northwestern Indian subcontinent
— **Punjabi** *adjective*

¹punk \'pəŋk\ *noun* [origin unknown] (1596)
1 *archaic* : PROSTITUTE
2 [probably partly from ³*punk*] : NONSENSE, FOOLISHNESS
3 a : a young inexperienced person : BEGINNER, NOVICE; *especially* : a young man **b** : a usually petty gangster, hoodlum, or ruffian **c** : a youth used as a homosexual partner
4 a : PUNK ROCK **b** : a punk rock musician **c** : one who affects punk styles

²punk *adjective* (1896)
1 : very poor : INFERIOR ⟨played a *punk* game⟩
2 : being in poor health ⟨said that she was feeling *punk*⟩
3 a : of or relating to punk rock **b** : relating to or being a style (as of dress or hair) inspired by punk rock
— **punk·ish** \'pən-kish\ *adjective*

³punk *noun* [perhaps alteration of *spunk*] (1687)
1 : wood so decayed as to be dry, crumbly, and useful for tinder
2 : a dry spongy substance prepared from fungi (genus *Fomes*) and used to ignite fuses especially in fireworks

pun·kah \'pəŋ-kə\ *noun* [Hindi *pākhā*] (1787)
: a fan used especially in India that consists of a canvas-covered frame suspended from the ceiling and that is operated by a cord

punk·er \'pəŋ-kər\ *noun* (1977)
: ¹PUNK 4b, c

pun·kie *also* **pun·ky** \'pəŋ-kē\ *noun, plural* **punkies** [New York Dutch *punki*, modification of Delaware (Munsee) *pónkwəs*] (1769)
: BITING MIDGE

pun·kin \'pəŋ-kən\ *variant of* PUMPKIN

punk rock *noun* (1971)
: rock music marked by extreme and often deliberately offensive expressions of alienation and social discontent
— **punk rocker** *noun*

¹punky \'pəŋ-kē\ *adjective* **punk·i·er; -est** [³*punk*] (1872)
: resembling punk in being soft or rotted
— **punk·i·ness** *noun*

²punky *adjective* [¹*punk*] (1972)
: resembling or typical of a punk

pun·net \'pə-nət\ *noun* [origin unknown] (circa 1822)
British : a small basket for fruits or vegetables

Pun·nett square \'pə-nət-\ *noun* [Reginald C. Punnett (died 1967) English geneticist] (1942)
: an $n \times n$ square used in genetics to calculate the frequencies of the different genotypes and phenotypes among the offspring of a cross

pun·ny \'pə-nē\ *adjective* **pun·ni·er; -est** (1947)
: constituting or involving a pun

pun·ster \'pən(t)-stər\ *noun* (1700)
: one who is given to punning

¹punt \'pənt\ *noun* [(assumed) Middle English, from Old English, from Latin *ponton-, ponto*] (before 12th century)
: a long narrow flat-bottomed boat with square ends usually propelled with a pole

²punt *transitive verb* (1816)
: to propel (as a punt) with a pole

³punt *intransitive verb* [French *ponter*, from *ponte* point in some games, play against the banker, from Spanish *punto* point, from Latin *punctum* — more at POINT] (1712)
1 : to play at a gambling game against the banker
2 *British* : GAMBLE

⁴punt *verb* [origin unknown] (1845)
transitive verb
: to kick (a football or soccer ball) with the top of the foot before the ball which is dropped from the hands hits the ground
intransitive verb
: to punt a ball

⁵punt *noun* (1845)
: the act or an instance of punting a ball

⁶punt \'pŭnt\ *noun* [Irish, pound, from English *pound*] (1975)
: the monetary pound of Ireland

punt·er \'pən-tər\ *noun* (circa 1706)
: one that punts: as **a** *chiefly British* : a person who gambles; *especially* : one who bets against a bookmaker **b** : one who uses a punt in boating **c** : one who punts a ball

punt formation *noun* (1949)
: an offensive football formation in which a back making a punt stands approximately 10 yards behind the line and the other backs are in blocking position close to the line

pun·ty \'pən-tē\ *noun, plural* **punties** [French *pontil*] (1662)
: a metal rod used for fashioning hot glass

pu·ny \'pyü-nē\ *adjective* **pu·ni·er; -est** [Middle French *puisné* younger, literally, born afterward, from *puis* afterward + *né* born] (1593)

☆ **SYNONYMS**

Pungent, piquant, poignant, racy mean sharp and stimulating to the mind or the senses. PUNGENT implies a sharp, stinging, or biting quality especially of odors ⟨a cheese with a *pungent* odor⟩. PIQUANT suggests a power to whet the appetite or interest through tartness or mild pungency ⟨a *piquant* sauce⟩. POIGNANT suggests something is sharply or piercingly effective in stirring one's consciousness or emotions ⟨felt a *poignant* sense of loss⟩. RACY implies having a strongly characteristic natural quality fresh and unimpaired ⟨spontaneous, *racy* prose⟩.

Punish, chastise, castigate, chasten, discipline, correct mean to inflict a penalty on in requital for wrongdoing. PUNISH implies subjecting to a penalty for wrongdoing ⟨*punished* for stealing⟩. CHASTISE may apply to either the infliction of corporal punishment or to verbal censure or denunciation ⟨*chastised* his son for neglecting his studies⟩. CASTIGATE usually implies a severe, typically public censure ⟨an editorial *castigating* the entire city council⟩. CHASTEN suggests any affliction or trial that leaves one humbled or subdued ⟨*chastened* by a landslide election defeat⟩. DISCIPLINE implies a punishing or chastening in order to bring under control ⟨parents must *discipline* their children⟩. CORRECT implies punishing aimed at reforming an offender ⟨the function of prison is to *correct* the wrongdoer⟩.

: slight or inferior in power, size, or importance **:** WEAK ◇
— **pu·ni·ly** \'pyü-nᵊl-ē\ *adverb*
— **pu·ni·ness** \'pyü-nē-nəs\ *noun*
¹**pup** \'pəp\ *noun* [short for *puppy*] (1773)
: a young dog; *also* : one of the young of various animals (as a seal or rat)
²**pup** *intransitive verb* **pupped; pup·ping** (1787)
: to give birth to pups
pu·pa \'pyü-pə\ *noun, plural* **pu·pae** \-(,)pē *also* -,pī\ *or* **pupas** [New Latin, from Latin *pupa* doll] (1815)
: an intermediate usually quiescent stage of a metamorphic insect (as a bee, moth, or beetle) that occurs between the larva and the imago, is usually enclosed in a cocoon or protective covering, and undergoes internal changes by which larval structures are replaced by those typical of the imago
word history see LARVA
— **pu·pal** \'pyü-pəl\ *adjective*
pu·par·i·um \pyü-'par-ē-əm, -'per-\ *noun, plural* **pu·par·ia** \-ē-ə\ [New Latin, from *pupa*] (1815)
: a rigid outer shell formed from the larval skin that covers some pupae (as of a dipteran fly)
pu·pate \'pyü-,pāt\ *intransitive verb* **pu·pat·ed; pu·pat·ing** (circa 1879)
: to become a pupa : pass through a pupal stage
— **pu·pa·tion** \pyü-'pā-shən\ *noun*
pup·fish \'pəp-,fish\ *noun* (1949)
: any of several killifishes (genus *Cyprinodon* of the family Cyprinodontidae) especially of warm streams and springs of the western U.S.
¹**pu·pil** \'pyü-pəl\ *noun* [Middle English *pupille* minor ward, from Middle French, from Latin *pupillus* male ward (from diminutive of *pupus* boy) & *pupilla* female ward, from diminutive of *pupa* girl, doll] (1536)
1 : a child or young person in school or in the charge of a tutor or instructor **:** STUDENT
2 : one who has been taught or influenced by a famous or distinguished person ◇
²**pupil** *noun* [Middle French *pupille*, from Latin *pupilla*, from diminutive of *pupa* doll; from the tiny image of oneself seen reflected in another's eye] (1567)
: the contractile aperture in the iris of the eye ◇
— **pu·pil·lary** \'pyü-pə-,ler-ē\ *adjective*
pu·pil·age *or* **pu·pil·lage** \'pyü-pə-lij\ *noun* (circa 1599)
: the state or period of being a pupil
pup·pet \'pə-pət\ *noun, often attributive* [Middle English *popet*, from Middle French *poupette*, diminutive of (assumed) *poupe* doll, from Latin *pupa*] (1538)
1 a : a small-scale figure (as of a person or animal) usually with a cloth body and hollow head that fits over and is moved by the hand **b** **:** MARIONETTE
2 **:** DOLL 1
3 : one whose acts are controlled by an outside force or influence
— **pup·pet·like** \-,līk\ *adjective*
pup·pe·teer \,pə-pə-'tir\ *noun* (circa 1923)
: one who manipulates puppets
pup·pet·ry \'pə-pə-trē\ *noun, plural* **-ries** (1528)
1 : the production or creation of puppets or puppet shows
2 : the art of manipulating puppets
pup·py \'pə-pē\ *noun, plural* **puppies** [Middle English *popi*, from Middle French *poupée* doll, toy, from (assumed) *poupe* doll] (1591)
: a young domestic dog; *specifically* : one less than a year old
— **pup·py·hood** \-,hüd\ *noun*
— **pup·py·ish** \-ish\ *adjective*
— **pup·py·like** \-,līk\ *adjective*
puppy dog *noun* (1595)
: a domestic dog; *especially* : one having the lovable attributes of a puppy
puppy love *noun* (1834)

: transitory affection felt by a boy or girl for one of the opposite sex
pup tent *noun* (1863)
: a low small tent for two persons usually consisting of two halves fastened together
Pu·ra·na \pu̇-'rä-nə\ *noun, often capitalized* [Sanskrit *purāṇa*, from *purāṇa* ancient, from *purā* formerly; akin to Sanskrit *pura* before, Greek *para* beside, *pro* before — more at FOR] (1696)
: one of a class of Hindu sacred writings chiefly from A.D. 300 to A.D. 750 comprising popular myths and legends and other traditional lore
— **Pu·ran·ic** \-nik\ *adjective*
pur·blind \'pər-,blīnd\ *adjective* [Middle English *pur blind*, from *pur* purely, wholly, from *pur* pure] (14th century)
1 a *obsolete* : wholly blind **b** : partly blind
2 : lacking in vision, insight, or understanding **:** OBTUSE
— **pur·blind·ly** \-,blīn(d)-lē\ *adverb*
— **pur·blind·ness** \-,blīn(d)-nəs\ *noun*
¹**pur·chase** \'pər-chəs\ *verb* **pur·chased; pur·chas·ing** [Middle English *purchacen*, from Old French *purchacier* to seek to obtain, from *por-, pur-* for, forward (modification of Latin *pro-*) + *chacier* to pursue, chase — more at PRO-] (14th century)
transitive verb
1 a *archaic* **:** GAIN, ACQUIRE **b** : to acquire (real estate) by means other than descent or inheritance **c** : to obtain by paying money or its equivalent **:** BUY **d** : to obtain by labor, danger, or sacrifice
2 : to apply a device for obtaining a mechanical advantage to (as something to be moved); *also* : to move by a purchase
3 : to constitute the means for buying ⟨our dollars *purchase* less each year⟩
intransitive verb
: to purchase something
— **pur·chas·able** \-chə-sə-bəl\ *adjective*
— **pur·chas·er** *noun*
²**purchase** *noun* (14th century)
1 : an act or instance of purchasing
2 : something obtained especially for a price in money or its equivalent
3 a (1) : a mechanical hold or advantage applied to the raising or moving of heavy bodies (2) : an apparatus or device by which advantage is gained **b** (1) : an advantage (as a firm hold or position) used in applying one's power ⟨clutching the steering wheel for more *purchase* —Barry Crump⟩ (2) : a means of exerting power
pur·dah \'pər-də\ *noun* [Hindi *parda*, literally, screen, veil] (1865)
1 : seclusion of women from public observation among Muslims and some Hindus especially in India
2 : a state of seclusion or concealment
pure \'pyu̇r\ *adjective* **pur·er; pur·est** [Middle English *pur*, from Old French, from Latin *purus*; akin to Old High German *fowen* to sift, Sanskrit *punāti* he cleanses, Middle Irish *úr* fresh, new] (14th century)
1 a (1) : unmixed with any other matter ⟨*pure* gold⟩ (2) : free from dust, dirt, or taint ⟨*pure* food⟩ (3) **:** SPOTLESS, STAINLESS **b** : free from harshness or roughness and being in tune — used of a musical tone **c** *of a vowel* : characterized by no appreciable alteration of articulation during utterance
2 a : being thus and no other **:** SHEER, UNMITIGATED ⟨*pure* folly⟩ **b** (1) **:** ABSTRACT, THEORETICAL (2) **:** A PRIORI ⟨*pure* mechanics⟩ **c** : not directed toward exposition of reality or solution of practical problems ⟨*pure* literature⟩ **d** : being nonobjective and to be appraised on formal and technical qualities only ⟨*pure* form⟩

3 a (1) : free from what vitiates, weakens, or pollutes (2) : containing nothing that does not properly belong **b** : free from moral fault or guilt **c** : marked by chastity **:** CONTINENT **d** (1) : of pure blood and unmixed ancestry (2) **:** homozygous in and breeding true for one or more characters **e** : ritually clean
synonym see CHASTE
— **pure·ness** *noun*
pure–blood·ed \'pyu̇r-,blə-dəd\ *or* **pure–blood** \-,bləd\ *adjective* (1821)
: FULL-BLOODED 1
— **pure–blood** \-,bləd\ *noun*
pure·bred \-'bred, -,bred\ *adjective* (1868)
: bred from members of a recognized breed, strain, or kind without admixture of other blood over many generations
— **pure·bred** \-,bred\ *noun*
pure democracy *noun* (circa 1910)
: democracy in which the power is exercised directly by the people rather than through representatives
¹**pu·ree** *or* **pu·rée** \pyu̇-'rā, -'rē\ *noun* [French *purée*, from Middle French, from feminine of *puré*, past participle of *purer* to purify, strain, from Latin *purare* to purify, from *purus*] (1707)
1 : a paste or thick liquid suspension usually made from cooked food ground finely
2 : a thick soup made of pureed vegetables
²**puree** *transitive verb* **pu·reed; pu·ree·ing** (1928)
: to make a puree of
pure imaginary *noun* (1947)

◇ WORD HISTORY
puny In medieval French *puisné*, literally "born afterward," was used to mean "younger" in reference to the relationship between two people. When borrowed into English, *puisne* and the phonetic spelling *puny* came to be used of anyone in a lesser position relative to others. From this use a specific legal sense developed. A *puisne* (or *puny*) judge became the designation for a junior or subordinate judge in the superior courts. By Shakespeare's time *puny* had largely lost its implication of relative rank and become nearly synonymous with "weak" or "feeble," a sense the word retains.

pupil If you look into another person's eyes, you see reflected within the iris a tiny image of your own face. The Romans, comparing this image of a miniature human to a doll, called the opening in the iris that seems to hold the image *pupilla*, a diminutive of the word *pupa*, meaning "doll." This Latin word, via medieval French *pupille*, was borrowed into English as *pupil*. Another sense of Latin *pupa* was "girl," and a young girl, typically an orphan, who was under the care of a guardian was called by the same diminutive form *pupilla* as the pupil of the eye. The masculine counterpart of *pupilla* was *pupillus*, a diminutive of *pupus*, meaning "boy." In medieval French and later in Middle English, the word *pupille* served for both sexes. It had about the same meaning as the Latin word, an orphan in a guardian's care, though in the 15th century *pupille* began to be used in French for any child being instructed by a tutor. English *pupil* adopted this meaning in the 16th century, but it has gradually expanded in scope to include the children under instruction in an elementary school (for which the Modern French counterpart is *élève*.)

\ə\ abut \ᵊ\ kitten \ər\ **further** \a\ ash \ā\ ace
\ä\ mop, mar \au̇\ out \ch\ chin \e\ bet \ē\ easy
\g\ go \i\ hit \ī\ ice \j\ job \ŋ\ sing \ō\ go
\ȯ\ law \ȯi\ boy \th\ thin \t͟h\ the \ü\ loot \u̇\ foot
\y\ yet \zh\ vision *see also* Guide to Pronunciation

: a complex number that is the product of a real number other than zero and the imaginary unit

— **pure imaginary** *adjective*

pure·ly \'pyu̇r-lē\ *adverb* (14th century)
1 : WHOLLY, COMPLETELY ⟨a selection based *purely* on merit⟩
2 : without admixture of anything injurious or foreign
3 : SIMPLY, MERELY ⟨read *purely* for relaxation⟩
4 : in a chaste or innocent manner

pur·fle \'pər-fəl\ *transitive verb* **pur·fled; pur·fling** \-f(ə-)liŋ\ [Middle English *purfilen*, from Middle French *porfiler*, from (assumed) Vulgar Latin *profilare*, from Latin *pro-* forward + Late Latin *filare* to spin — more at PRO-, FILE] (14th century)
: to ornament the border or edges of

— **purfle** *noun*

pur·ga·tion \ˌpər-'gā-shən\ *noun* (14th century)
: the act or result of purging

¹pur·ga·tive \'pər-gə-tiv\ *adjective* [Middle English *purgatif*, from Middle French, from Late Latin *purgativus*, from Latin *purgatus*, past participle] (15th century)
: purging or tending to purge

²purgative *noun* (1626)
: a purging medicine : CATHARTIC

pur·ga·to·ri·al \ˌpər-gə-'tōr-ē-əl, -'tȯr-\ *adjective* (15th century)
1 : of, relating to, or suggestive of purgatory
2 : cleansing of sin : EXPIATORY

pur·ga·to·ry \'pər-gə-ˌtōr-ē, -ˌtȯr-\ *noun, plural* **-ries** [Middle English, from Anglo-French or Medieval Latin; Anglo-French *purgatorie*, from Medieval Latin *purgatorium*, from Late Latin, neuter of *purgatorius* purging, from Latin *purgare*] (13th century)
1 : an intermediate state after death for expiatory purification; *specifically* : a place or state of punishment wherein according to Roman Catholic doctrine the souls of those who die in God's grace may make satisfaction for past sins and so become fit for heaven
2 : a place or state of temporary suffering or misery

¹purge \'pərj\ *verb* **purged; purg·ing** [Middle English, from Middle French *purgier*, from Latin *purigare, purgare* to purify, purge, from *purus* pure + *-igare* (akin to *agere* to drive, do) — more at ACT] (14th century)
transitive verb
1 a : to clear of guilt **b :** to free from moral or ceremonial defilement
2 a : to cause evacuation from (as the bowels) **b** (1) : to make free of something unwanted ⟨*purge* a manhole of gas⟩ ⟨*purge* yourself of fear⟩ (2) : to free (as a boiler) of sediment or relieve (as a steam pipe) of trapped air by bleeding **c** (1) : to rid (as a nation or party) by a purge (2) : to get rid of ⟨the leaders had been *purged*⟩ ⟨*purge* money-losing operations⟩
intransitive verb
1 : to become purged
2 : to have or produce frequent evacuations
3 : to cause purgation

— **purg·er** *noun*

²purge *noun* (1563)
1 : something that purges; *especially* : PURGATIVE
2 a : an act or instance of purging **b :** the removal of elements or members regarded as undesirable and especially as treacherous or disloyal

pu·ri \'pu̇r-ē\ *noun, plural* **puri** *or* **puris** [Hindi *pūrī*, from Sanskrit *pūra*] (circa 1885)
: a puffy fried wheat cake of India

pu·ri·fi·ca·tion \ˌpyu̇r-ə-fə-'kā-shən\ *noun* (14th century)
: the act or an instance of purifying or of being purified

pu·ri·fi·ca·tor \'pyu̇r-ə-fə-ˌkā-tər\ *noun* (1853)
1 : a linen cloth used to wipe the chalice after celebration of the Eucharist
2 : one that purifies

pu·ri·fi·ca·to·ry \pyu̇r-'i-fi-kə-ˌtōr-ē, 'pyu̇r-(ə-)fə-kə-, -ˌtȯr-\ *adjective* (1610)
: serving, tending, or intended to purify

pu·ri·fy \'pyu̇r-ə-ˌfī\ *verb* **-fied; -fy·ing** [Middle English *purifien*, from Middle French *purifier*, from Latin *purificare*, from *purus* + *-ificare* -ify] (14th century)
transitive verb
: to make pure: as **a :** to clear from material defilement or imperfection **b :** to free from guilt or moral or ceremonial blemish **c :** to free from undesirable elements
intransitive verb
: to grow or become pure or clean

— **pu·ri·fi·er** \-ˌfī(-ə)r\ *noun*

Pu·rim \'pu̇r-im, 'pyu̇r-, -ˌēm; pu̇·'rim, pyu̇-, -'rēm\ *noun* [Hebrew *pūrīm*, literally, lots; from the casting of lots by Haman (Esther 9:24–26)] (1535)
: a Jewish holiday celebrated on the 14th of Adar in commemoration of the deliverance of the Jews from the massacre plotted by Haman

pu·rine \'pyu̇r-ˌēn\ *noun* [German *Purin*, from Latin *purus* pure + New Latin *uricus* uric (from English *uric*) + German *-in* ²-ine] (1898)
1 : a crystalline base $C_5H_4N_4$ that is the parent of compounds of the uric-acid group
2 : a derivative of purine; *especially* : a base (as adenine or guanine) that is a constituent of DNA or RNA

pur·ism \'pyu̇r-ˌi-zəm\ *noun* (1803)
1 : an example of rigid adherence to or insistence on purity or nicety especially in use of words; *especially* : a word, phrase, or sense used chiefly by purists
2 : the quality or practice of adherence to purity especially in language

pur·ist \'pyu̇r-ist\ *noun* (circa 1706)
: one who adheres strictly and often excessively to a tradition; *especially* : one preoccupied with the purity of a language and its protection from the use of foreign or altered forms

— **pu·ris·tic** \pyu̇-'ris-tik\ *adjective*
— **pu·ris·ti·cal·ly** \-ti-k(ə-)lē\ *adverb*

¹pu·ri·tan \'pyu̇r-ə-t³n\ *noun* [probably from Late Latin *puritas* purity] (1572)
1 *capitalized* : a member of a 16th and 17th century Protestant group in England and New England opposing as unscriptural the ceremonial worship and the prelacy of the Church of England
2 : one who practices or preaches a more rigorous or professedly purer moral code than that which prevails

²puritan *adjective, often capitalized* (1589)
: of or relating to puritans, the Puritans, or puritanism

pu·ri·tan·i·cal \ˌpyu̇r-ə-'ta-ni-kəl\ *adjective* (1607)
1 : PURITAN
2 : of, relating to, or characterized by a rigid morality

— **pu·ri·tan·i·cal·ly** \-k(ə-)lē\ *adverb*

pu·ri·tan·ism \'pyu̇r-ə-t³n-ˌi-zəm\ *noun* (1573)
1 *capitalized* : the beliefs and practices characteristic of the Puritans
2 : strictness and austerity especially in matters of religion or conduct

pu·ri·ty \'pyu̇r-ə-tē\ *noun* [Middle English *purete*, from Old French *pureté*, from Late Latin *puritat-*, *puritas*, from Latin *purus* pure] (13th century)
1 : the quality or state of being pure
2 : SATURATION 4a

Pur·kin·je cell \(ˌ)pər-'kin-jē-\ *noun* [Jan *Purkinje*] (circa 1890)
: any of numerous nerve cells that occupy the middle layer of the cerebellar cortex and are characterized by a large globose body with massive dendrites directed outward and a single slender axon directed inward

Purkinje fiber *noun* (circa 1890)
: any of the modified cardiac muscle fibers that have few nuclei, granulated central cyto-

plasm, and sparse peripheral striations and make up a network of conducting tissue in the myocardium

¹purl \'pər(-ə)l\ *noun* [Middle English] (14th century)
1 : gold or silver thread or wire for embroidering or edging
2 : the intertwisting of thread that knots a stitch usually along an edge
3 : PURL STITCH

²purl (1526)
transitive verb
1 a : to embroider with gold or silver thread **b :** to edge or border with gold or silver embroidery
2 : to knit in purl stitch
intransitive verb
: to do knitting in purl stitch

³purl *noun* [perhaps of Scandinavian origin; akin to Norwegian *purla* to ripple] (circa 1522)
1 : a purling or swirling stream or rill
2 : a gentle murmur or movement (as of purling water)

⁴purl *intransitive verb* (1591)
1 : EDDY, SWIRL
2 : to make a soft murmuring sound like that of a purling stream

pur·lieu \'pərl-(ˌ)yü, 'pər-(ˌ)lü\ *noun* [Middle English *purlewe* land severed from an English royal forest by perambulation, from Anglo-French *puralé* perambulation, from Old French *puraler* to go through, from *pur-* for, through + *aler* to go — more at PURCHASE] (15th century)
1 a : an outlying or adjacent district **b** *plural* : ENVIRONS, NEIGHBORHOOD
2 a : a frequently visited place : HAUNT **b** *plural* : CONFINES, BOUNDS

pur·lin \'pər-lən\ *noun* [origin unknown] (15th century)
: a horizontal member in a roof

pur·loin \(ˌ)pər-'lȯin, 'pər-ˌ\ *transitive verb* [Middle English, to put away, misappropriate, from Anglo-French *purloigner*, from Old French *porloigner* to put off, delay, from *por-* forward + *loing* at a distance, from Latin *longe*, from *longus* long — more at PURCHASE, LONG] (15th century)
: to appropriate wrongfully and often by a breach of trust
synonym see STEAL

— **pur·loin·er** *noun*

purl stitch *noun* (1885)
: a knitting stitch usually made with the yarn at the front of the work by inserting the right needle into the front of a loop on the left needle from the right, catching the yarn with the right needle, and bringing it through to form a new loop — compare KNIT STITCH

pu·ro·my·cin \ˌpyu̇r-ə-'mī-s³n\ *noun* [*purine* + *-o-* + *-mycin*] (1953)
: an antibiotic $C_{22}H_{29}N_7O_5$ that is obtained from an actinomycete (*Streptomyces alboniger*) and is used especially as a potent inhibitor of protein synthesis

¹pur·ple \'pər-pəl\ *adjective* **pur·pler** \-p(ə-)lər\; **pur·plest** \-p(ə-)ləst\ [Middle English *purpel*, alteration of *purper*, from Old English *purpuran* of purple, genitive of *purpure* purple color, from Latin *purpura*, from Greek *porphyra*] (before 12th century)
1 : REGAL, IMPERIAL
2 : of the color purple
3 a : highly rhetorical : ORNATE **b :** marked by profanity

²purple *noun* (15th century)
1 a (1) : cloth dyed purple (2) : a garment of such color; *especially* : a purple robe worn as an emblem of rank or authority **b** (1) : TYRIAN PURPLE (2) : any of various colors that fall about midway between red and blue in hue **c** (1) : a mollusk (as of the genus *Purpura*) yielding a purple dye and especially the Tyrian purple of ancient times (2) : a pigment or dye that colors purple

2 a : imperial or regal rank or power **b** : high rank or station

³purple verb **pur·pled; pur·pling** \-p(ə-)liŋ\ (15th century)
transitive verb
: to make purple
intransitive verb
: to become purple

pur·ple·heart \'pər-pəl-ˌhärt\ noun (1796)
: a strong durable purplish wood that is obtained from various leguminous trees (genus *Peltogyne*); *also* : a tree producing such wood

Purple Heart noun (1932)
: a U.S. military decoration awarded to any member of the armed forces wounded or killed in action

purple loosestrife noun (1548)
: an Old World marsh herb (*Lythrum salicaria*) of the loosestrife family that is naturalized in the eastern U.S. and has long spikes of purple flowers

purple martin noun (1743)
: a large swallow (*Progne subis*) of North America the males of which have bluish black plumage

purple passage noun [translation of Latin *pannus purpureus* purple patch; from the traditional splendor of purple cloth as contrasted with plainer materials] (1895)
1 : a passage conspicuous for brilliance or effectiveness in a work that is dull, commonplace, or uninspired
2 *chiefly British* : a piece of obtrusively ornate writing — called also *purple patch*

purple scale noun (circa 1909)
: a brownish or purplish armored scale (*Lepidosaphes beckii*) that is destructive to citrus fruit

pur·plish \'pər-p(ə-)lish\ adjective (1562)
: somewhat purple

pur·ply \'pər-p(ə-)lē\ adjective (1725)
: PURPLISH

¹pur·port \'pər-ˌpōrt, -ˌpȯrt\ noun [Middle English, from Anglo-French, content, tenor, from *purporter* to contain, from Old French *porporter* to convey, from *por-* forward + *porter* to carry — more at PURCHASE, PORT] (15th century)
: meaning conveyed, professed, or implied : IMPORT; *also* : SUBSTANCE, GIST

²pur·port \(ˌ)pər-'pōrt, -'pȯrt\ transitive verb (1528)
1 : to have the often specious appearance of being, intending, or claiming (something implied or inferred) (a book that *purports* to be an objective analysis); *also* : CLAIM (foreign novels which he *purports* to have translated —Mary McCarthy)
2 : INTEND, PURPOSE

pur·port·ed \-'pōr-təd, -'pȯr-\ adjective (1894)
: REPUTED, ALLEGED (took gullible tourists to *purported* ancient sites)

pur·port·ed·ly \-lē\ adverb (1942)
: it is purported : OSTENSIBLY, ALLEGEDLY

¹pur·pose \'pər-pəs\ noun [Middle English *purpos*, from Old French, from *purposer* to purpose, from Latin *proponere* (perfect indicative *proposui*) to propose — more at PROPOUND] (14th century)
1 a : something set up as an object or end to be attained : INTENTION **b** : RESOLUTION, DETERMINATION
2 : a subject under discussion or an action in course of execution
synonym see INTENTION
— **on purpose** : by intent : INTENTIONALLY

²purpose transitive verb **pur·posed; pur·pos·ing** (14th century)
: to propose as an aim to oneself

pur·pose–built \ˌpər-pəs-'bilt\ adjective (1954)
chiefly British : built for a particular purpose

pur·pose·ful \'pər-pəs-fəl\ adjective (1853)
1 : having a purpose: as **a** : MEANINGFUL (*purposeful* activities) **b** : INTENTIONAL (*purposeful* ambiguity)

2 : full of determination (a *purposeful* man)
— **pur·pose·ful·ly** \-fə-lē\ adverb
— **pur·pose·ful·ness** noun

pur·pose·less \-ləs\ adjective (circa 1552)
: having no purpose : AIMLESS, MEANINGLESS
— **pur·pose·less·ly** adverb
— **pur·pose·less·ness** noun

pur·pose·ly \-lē\ adverb (15th century)
: with a deliberate or express purpose

pur·po·sive \'pər-pə-siv, (ˌ)pər-'pō-\ adjective (1855)
1 : serving or effecting a useful function though not as a result of planning or design
2 : having or tending to fulfill a conscious purpose or design : PURPOSEFUL
— **pur·po·sive·ly** adverb
— **pur·po·sive·ness** noun

pur·pu·ra \'pər-pyə-rə, -pə-rə\ noun [New Latin, from Latin, purple color] (1753)
: any of several hemorrhagic states characterized by patches of purplish discoloration resulting from extravasation of blood into the skin and mucous membranes
— **pur·pu·ric** \ˌpər-'pyu̇r-ik\ adjective

pur·pure \'pər-pyər\ noun [Middle English, from Old English, purple] (1535)
: the heraldic color purple

¹purr \'pər\ noun [imitative] (1601)
: a low vibratory murmur typical of an apparently contented or pleased cat

²purr intransitive verb (1620)
1 : to make a purr or a sound like a purr (cars *purring* along the highway)
2 a : to speak in a manner that resembles a purr **b** : to speak in a malicious catty manner
— **purr·ing·ly** \-iŋ-lē\ adverb

¹purse \'pərs\ noun [Middle English *purs*, from Old English, modification of Medieval Latin *bursa*, from Late Latin, ox hide, from Greek *byrsa*] (before 12th century)
1 a (1) : a small bag for money (2) : a receptacle (as a pocketbook) for carrying money and often other small objects **b** : a receptacle (as a pouch) shaped like a purse
2 a : RESOURCES, FUNDS **b** : a sum of money offered as a prize or present; *also* : the total amount of money offered in prizes for a given event
— **purse·like** \-ˌlīk\ adjective

²purse transitive verb **pursed; purs·ing** (14th century)
1 : to put into a purse
2 : PUCKER, KNIT

purse–proud \'pərs-ˌprau̇d\ adjective (1681)
: proud because of one's wealth especially in the absence of other distinctions

purs·er \'pər-sər\ noun [Middle English, from *purs* purse] (15th century)
1 : an official on a ship responsible for papers and accounts and on a passenger ship also for the comfort and welfare of passengers
2 : a steward on an airliner

purse seine noun (1870)
: a large seine designed to be set by two boats around a school of fish and so arranged that after the ends have been brought together the bottom can be closed

purse seine

— **purse seiner** noun
— **purse seining** noun

purse strings noun plural (15th century)
: financial resources; *also* : control over these resources

purs·lane \'pər-slən, -ˌslān\ noun [Middle English, from Middle French *porcelaine*, from Late Latin *porcillagin-, porcillago*, alteration of Latin *porcillaca*, alteration of *portulaca*] (14th century)
: any of a family (Portulacaceae, the purslane family) of cosmopolitan usually succulent herbs; *especially* : a fleshy-leaved trailing plant (*Portulaca oleracea*) with tiny yellow

flowers that is a common troublesome weed but is sometimes eaten as a potherb or in salads

pur·su·ance \pər-'sü-ən(t)s\ noun (1605)
: the act of pursuing; *especially* : a carrying out or into effect : PROSECUTION (in *pursuance* of his duties)

pur·su·ant to \-ənt-\ preposition (1648)
: in carrying out : in conformity with : ACCORDING TO

pur·sue \pər-'sü, -'syü\ verb **pur·sued; pur·su·ing** [Middle English, from Anglo-French *pursuer*, from Old French *poursuir*, from Latin *prosequi*, from *pro-* forward + *sequi* to follow — more at PRO-, SUE] (14th century)
transitive verb
1 : to follow in order to overtake, capture, kill, or defeat
2 : to find or employ measures to obtain or accomplish : SEEK (*pursue* a goal)
3 : to proceed along (*pursues* a northern course)
4 a : to engage in (*pursue* a hobby) **b** : to follow up or proceed with (*pursue* an argument)
5 : to continue to afflict : HAUNT (was *pursued* by horrible memories)
6 : ²CHASE 1c (*pursued* by dozens of fans)
intransitive verb
: to go in pursuit
synonym see CHASE
— **pur·su·er** noun

pur·suit \pər-'süt, -'syüt\ noun [Middle English, from Middle French *poursuite*, from *poursuir*] (14th century)
1 : the act of pursuing
2 : an activity that one engages in as a vocation, profession, or avocation : OCCUPATION
synonym see WORK

pursuit plane noun (circa 1918)
: a fighter plane especially of the period before World War II

pur·sui·vant \'pər-si-vənt, -swi-\ noun [Middle English *pursevant* attendant of a herald, from Middle French *poursuivant*, literally, follower, from present participle of *poursuir, poursuivre* to pursue] (14th century)
1 : an officer of arms ranking below a herald but having similar duties
2 : FOLLOWER, ATTENDANT

¹pur·sy \'pə-sē, 'pər-sē\ adjective **pur·si·er; -est** [Middle English, from Anglo-French *pursif*, alteration of Middle French *polsif*, from *poulser, polser* to beat, push, pant — more at PUSH] (15th century)
1 : short-winded especially because of corpulence
2 : FAT
— **pur·si·ness** noun

²pursy \'pər-sē\ adjective **purs·i·er; -est** [¹*purse*] (1552)
1 : having a puckered appearance
2 : PURSE-PROUD

pur·te·nance \'pərt-nən(t)s, 'pər-tᵊn-ən(t)s\ noun [Middle English, literally, appendage, modification of Middle French *partenance*, from *partenir* to pertain — more at PERTAIN] (15th century)
: ENTRAILS, PLUCK

pu·ru·lence \'pyu̇r-ə-lən(t)s, 'pyu̇r-yə-\ noun (1597)
: the quality or state of being purulent; *also* : PUS

pu·ru·lent \-lənt\ adjective [Latin *purulentus*, from *pur-, pus* pus] (1597)
1 : containing, consisting of, or being pus (a *purulent* discharge)
2 : accompanied by suppuration

pur·vey \(ˌ)pər-ˈvā, ˈpər-\ *transitive verb* **pur·veyed; pur·vey·ing** [Middle English *purveien*, from Middle French *porveeir*, from Latin *providēre* to provide] (14th century)
1 : to supply (as provisions) usually as a matter of business
2 : PEDDLE 2
pur·vey·ance \-ən(t)s\ *noun* (14th century)
: the act or process of purveying or procuring
pur·vey·or \-ər\ *noun* (14th century)
1 : one that purveys
2 : VICTUALLER, CATERER
pur·view \ˈpər-ˌvyü\ *noun* [Middle English *purveu*, from Anglo-French *purveu est* it is provided (opening phrase of a statute)] (15th century)
1 a : the body or enacting part of a statute **b** : the limit, purpose, or scope of a statute
2 : the range or limit of authority, competence, responsibility, concern, or intention
3 : range of vision, understanding, or cognizance
pus \ˈpəs\ *noun* [Latin *pur-, pus* — more at FOUL] (1541)
: thick opaque usually yellowish white fluid matter formed by suppuration and composed of exudate containing white blood cells, tissue debris, and microorganisms
Pu·sey·ism \ˈpyü-zē-ˌi-zəm, -sē-\ *noun* [Edward Bouverie *Pusey*] (1838)
: TRACTARIANISM
— **Pu·sey·ite** \-ˌīt\ *noun*
¹**push** \ˈpush\ *verb* [Middle English *pusshen*, from Middle French *poulser* to beat, push, from Old French, from Latin *pulsare*, frequentative of *pellere* to drive, strike — more at FELT] (13th century)
transitive verb
1 a : to press against with force in order to drive or impel **b** : to move or endeavor to move away or ahead by steady pressure without striking
2 a : to thrust forward, downward, or outward **b** : to cause to increase : RAISE ⟨*push* prices to record levels⟩ **c** : to hit (a ball) toward the right from a right-handed swing or toward the left from a left-handed swing — compare PULL
3 a : to press or urge forward to completion **b** : to urge or press the advancement, adoption, or practice of ⟨*pushed* a bill in the legislature⟩; *especially* : to make aggressive efforts to sell ⟨we're *pushing* ham this week⟩ **c** : to engage in the illicit sale of (narcotics)
4 : to bear hard upon so as to involve in difficulty ⟨poverty *pushed* them to the breaking point⟩
5 : to approach in age or number ⟨grandmother must be *pushing* 75⟩
intransitive verb
1 : to press against something with steady force in or as if in order to impel
2 : to press forward energetically against opposition
3 : to exert oneself continuously, vigorously, or obtrusively to gain an end ⟨*pushing* for higher wages⟩
— **push one's luck** : to take an increasing risk
²**push** *noun* (1563)
1 : a vigorous effort to attain an end : DRIVE: **a** : a military assault or offensive **b** : an advance that overcomes obstacles **c** : a campaign to promote a product
2 : a time for action : EMERGENCY
3 a : an act of pushing : SHOVE **b** (1) : a physical force steadily applied in a direction away from the body exerting it (2) : a nonphysical pressure : INFLUENCE, URGE **c** : vigorous enterprise or energy
4 a : an exertion of influence to promote another's interests **b** : stimulation to activity : IMPETUS
— **push comes to shove** : a decisive moment comes ⟨backed down when *push came to shove*⟩

push around *transitive verb* (1923)
: to impose on contemptuously
push–ball \ˈpush-ˌbȯl\ *noun* (1896)
: a game in which each of two sides endeavors to push an inflated originally leather-covered ball six feet (1.8 meters) in diameter across its opponents' goal; *also* : the ball used
push–bike \-ˌbīk\ *noun* (1913)
British : BICYCLE — called also *push bicycle*
push broom *noun* (1926)
: a long-handled wide brush that is designed to be pushed and is used for sweeping
push–button *adjective* (1916)
1 : operated or done by means of push buttons ⟨a *push-button* phone⟩
2 : using or dependent on complex and more or less self-operating mechanisms that are put in operation by a simple act comparable to pushing a button ⟨*push-button* warfare⟩
push button *noun* (1878)
: a small button or knob that when pushed operates something especially by closing an electric circuit
push·cart \ˈpush-ˌkärt\ *noun* (1893)
: a cart or barrow pushed by hand
push·chair \-ˌcher, -ˌchar\ *noun* (1921)
chiefly British : STROLLER
push·down \-ˌdaún\ *noun* (1961)
: a store of data (as in a computer) from which the most recently stored item must be the first retrieved — called also *pushdown list*, *pushdown stack*
push·er \ˈpu̇-shər\ *noun* (1591)
: one that pushes; *especially* : one that pushes illegal drugs
push·ful \-fəl\ *adjective* (1896)
chiefly British : PUSHING
— **push·ful·ness** *noun, chiefly British*
push·ing *adjective* (1692)
1 : marked by ambition, energy, enterprise, and initiative
2 : marked by tactless forwardness or officious intrusiveness
push off *intransitive verb* (1925)
: SET OUT ⟨we *pushed off* for home⟩
push on *intransitive verb* (1718)
: to continue on one's way : PROCEED
push·over \ˈpush-ˌō-vər\ *noun* (1906)
1 : something accomplished without difficulty : SNAP
2 : an opponent who is easy to defeat or a victim who is capable of no effective resistance
3 : someone unable to resist an attraction or appeal : SUCKER
push·pin \-ˌpin\ *noun* (1907)
: a pin that has a roughly cylindrical head and that is easily inserted and withdrawn (as from a bulletin board)
push–pull \-ˈpu̇l\ *adjective* (1922)
: relating to or being an arrangement of two electronic circuit elements (as transistors) such that an alternating input causes them to send current through a load alternately ⟨a *push-pull* circuit⟩
— **push–pull** *noun*
Push·tu \ˈpəsh-(ˌ)tü\ *variant of* PASHTO
Push·tun *variant of* PASHTUN
push–up \ˈpush-ˌəp\ *noun* (1942)
: a conditioning exercise performed in a prone position by raising and lowering the body with the straightening and bending of the arms while keeping the back straight and supporting the body on the hands and toes
pushy \ˈpu̇-shē\ *adjective* **push·i·er; -est** (1936)
: aggressive often to an objectionable degree : FORWARD
— **push·i·ly** \ˈpu̇-shə-lē\ *adverb*
— **push·i·ness** \ˈpu̇-shē-nəs\ *noun*
pu·sil·la·nim·i·ty \ˌpyü-sə-lə-ˈni-mə-tē *also* ˌpyü-zə-\ *noun* (14th century)
: the quality or state of being pusillanimous : COWARDLINESS
pu·sil·la·ni·mous \-ˈla-nə-məs\ *adjective* [Late Latin *pusillanimis*, from Latin *pusillus* very small (diminutive of *pusus* boy) + *animus*

spirit; perhaps akin to Latin *puer* child — more at PUERILE, ANIMATE] (1586)
: lacking courage and resolution : marked by contemptible timidity
synonym see COWARDLY
— **pu·sil·lan·i·mous·ly** *adverb*
¹**puss** \ˈpu̇s\ *noun* [origin unknown] (circa 1530)
1 : CAT
2 : GIRL
²**puss** *noun* [Irish *pus* mouth] (circa 1890)
slang : FACE
puss·ley \ˈpəs-lē\ *noun* [by alteration] (1833)
: PURSLANE
¹**puss·y** \ˈpu̇-sē\ *noun, plural* **puss·ies** [¹*puss*] (1726)
1 : CAT
2 : a catkin of the pussy willow
²**pus·sy** \ˈpu̇-sē\ *noun, plural* **pussies** [perhaps of Low German or Scandinavian origin; akin to Old Norse *püss* pocket, pouch, Low German *püse* vulva, Old English *pusa* bag] (circa 1879)
1 : VULVA — usually considered vulgar
2 a : SEXUAL INTERCOURSE — usually considered vulgar **b** : the female partner in sexual intercourse — usually considered vulgar
³**pus·sy** \ˈpə-sē\ *adjective* **pus·si·er; -est** (circa 1890)
: full of or resembling pus
⁴**pus·sy** \ˈpə-sē\ *variant of* ¹PURSY
pussy·cat \ˈpu̇-sē-ˌkat\ *noun* (1805)
1 : CAT
2 : one that is weak, compliant, or amiable : SOFTY
pussy·foot \ˈpu̇-sē-ˌfu̇t\ *intransitive verb* (1903)
1 : to tread or move warily or stealthily
2 : to refrain from committing oneself
— **pussy·foot·er** *noun*
pussy·toes \ˈpu̇-sē-ˌtōz\ *or* **puss·y's–toes** \-ˌsēz-\ *noun plural but singular or plural in construction* (1892)
: any of a genus (*Antennaria*) of woolly or hoary chiefly temperate composite herbs that have small usually whitish discoid flower heads and a pappus formed of club-shaped bristles
pussy willow \ˈpu̇-sē-\ *noun* (1869)
: a willow (as the American *Salix discolor*) having large cylindrical silky aments
¹**pus·tu·lant** \ˈpəs-chə-lənt; ˈpəs-tyə-, -tə-\ *noun* (1871)
: an agent (as a chemical) that induces pustule formation
²**pustulant** *adjective* (circa 1890)
: producing pustules
pus·tu·lar \-lər\ *adjective* (1739)
1 : of, relating to, or resembling pustules
2 : covered with pustular prominences : PUSTULATED
pus·tu·lat·ed \-ˌlā-təd\ *adjective* (1732)
: covered with pustules
pus·tu·la·tion \ˌpəs-chə-ˈlā-shən, ˌpəs-tyə-, -tə-\ *noun* (circa 1860)
1 : the act of producing pustules : the state of having pustules
2 : PUSTULE
pus·tule \ˈpəs-(ˌ)chü(ə)l, -(ˌ)tyü(ə)l, -(ˌ)tü(ə)l\ *noun* [Middle English, from Latin *pustula*; akin to Lithuanian *pusti* to blow, Greek *physa* breath] (14th century)
1 : a small circumscribed elevation of the skin containing pus and having an inflamed base
2 : a small often distinctively colored elevation or spot resembling a blister or pimple
¹**put** \ˈpu̇t\ *verb* **put; put·ting** [Middle English *putten*; akin to Old English *putung* instigation, Middle Dutch *poten* to plant] (12th century)
transitive verb

pussy willow

1 a : to place in a specified position or relationship **:** LAY ⟨*put* the book on the table⟩ **b :** to move in a specified direction **c** (1) **:** to send (as a weapon or missile) into or through something **:** THRUST (2) **:** to throw with an overhand pushing motion ⟨*put* the shot⟩ **d :** to bring into a specified state or condition ⟨a reapportionment . . . that was *put* into effect at the September primaries —*Current Biography*⟩
2 a : to cause to endure or suffer something **:** SUBJECT ⟨*put* traitors to death⟩ **b :** IMPOSE, INFLICT ⟨*put* a special tax on luxuries⟩
3 a : to set before one for judgment or decision ⟨*put* the question⟩ **b :** to call for a formal vote on ⟨*put* the motion⟩
4 a (1) **:** to convey into another form ⟨want to *put* my feelings into words⟩ (2) **:** to translate into another language or style ⟨*put* the poem into English⟩ (3) **:** ADAPT ⟨lyrics *put* to music⟩ **b :** EXPRESS, STATE ⟨*putting* it mildly⟩
5 a : to devote (oneself) to an activity or end ⟨*put* himself to winning back their confidence⟩ **b :** APPLY ⟨*put* her mind to the problem⟩ **c :** ASSIGN ⟨*put* them to work⟩ **d :** to cause to perform an action **:** URGE ⟨*put* the horse over the fence⟩ **e :** IMPEL, INCITE ⟨*put* them into a frenzy⟩
6 a : REPOSE, REST ⟨*puts* his faith in reason⟩ **b :** INVEST ⟨*put* her money in the company⟩
7 a : to give as an estimate ⟨*put* the time as about eleven⟩ **b :** ATTACH, ATTRIBUTE ⟨*puts* a high value on their friendship⟩ **c :** IMPUTE ⟨*put* the blame on the partners⟩
8 : BET, WAGER ⟨*put* $2 on the favorite⟩
intransitive verb
1 : to start in motion **:** GO; *especially* **:** to leave in a hurry
2 *of a ship* **:** to take a specified course ⟨*put* down the river⟩
— put forth 1 a : ASSERT, PROPOSE **b :** to make public **:** ISSUE **2 :** to bring into action **:** EXERT **3 :** to produce or send out by growth ⟨*put forth* leaves⟩ **4 :** to start out
— put forward : PROPOSE ⟨*put forward* a theory⟩
— put in mind : REMIND
— put one's finger on : IDENTIFY ⟨*put his finger on* the cause of the trouble⟩
— put one's foot down : to take a firm stand
— put one's foot in one's mouth : to make a tactless or embarrassing blunder
— put paid to *British* **:** to finish off **:** WIPE OUT
— put the arm on *or* **put the bite on :** to ask for money
— put the finger on : to inform on ⟨*put the finger on* . . . heroin pushers —Barrie Zwicker⟩
— put the make on : to make sexual advances toward
— put to bed : to make the final preparations for printing (as a newspaper)
— put together 1 : to create as a unified whole **:** CONSTRUCT **2 :** ADD, COMBINE
— put to it : to give difficulty to **:** press hard ⟨had been *put to it* to keep up⟩
²put *noun* (14th century)
1 : a throw made with an overhand pushing motion; *specifically* **:** the act or an instance of putting the shot
2 : an option to sell a specified amount of a security (as a stock) or commodity (as wheat) at a fixed price at or within a specified time — compare CALL 3d
³put *adjective* (1848)
: being in place **:** FIXED, SET ⟨stay *put* until I call⟩
put about (1748)
intransitive verb
of a ship **:** to change direction **:** go on another tack
transitive verb
: to cause to change course or direction
put across *transitive verb* (1919)
1 : PUT OVER 3

2 : to convey effectively or forcefully
put-and-take \ˌpu̇t-ᵊn-ˈtāk\ *noun* (1922)
: any of various games of chance played with a teetotum or with dice in which players contribute to a pool and take from it according to the instructions on the top or dice
pu·ta·tive \ˈpyü-tə-tiv\ *adjective* [Middle English, from Late Latin *putativus*, from Latin *putatus*, past participle of *putare* to think] (15th century)
1 : commonly accepted or supposed
2 : assumed to exist or to have existed
— pu·ta·tive·ly *adverb*
put away *transitive verb* (14th century)
1 a : DISCARD, RENOUNCE ⟨to *put* grief *away* is disloyal to the memory of the departed —H. A. Overstreet⟩ **b :** DIVORCE
2 : to eat or drink up **:** CONSUME
3 a : to confine especially in a mental institution **b :** BURY **c :** KILL
put by *transitive verb* (15th century)
1 *archaic* **:** REJECT
2 : to lay aside **:** SAVE
put-down \ˈpu̇t-ˌdau̇n\ *noun* (1962)
: an act or instance of putting down; *especially* **:** a humiliating remark **:** SQUELCH
put down *transitive verb* (14th century)
1 : to bring to an end **:** STOP ⟨*put down* a riot⟩
2 a : DEPOSE, DEGRADE **:** DISPARAGE, BELITTLE ⟨mentioned his poetry only to *put* it *down*⟩ **c :** DISAPPROVE, CRITICIZE ⟨was *put down* for the way she dressed⟩ **d :** HUMILIATE, SQUELCH ⟨*put* him *down* with a sharp retort⟩
3 : to make ineffective **:** CHECK ⟨*put down* the gossip⟩
4 : to do away with (as an injured, sick, or aged animal) **:** DESTROY
5 a : to put in writing ⟨*put* it *down* truthfully⟩ **b :** to enter in a list ⟨*put* me *down* for a donation⟩
6 a : to place in a category ⟨I *put* him *down* as a hypochondriac —O. S. J. Gogarty⟩ **b :** ATTRIBUTE ⟨*put* it *down* to inexperience⟩
7 : to pack or preserve for future use
8 : CONSUME ⟨*putting down* helping after helping —Carson McCullers⟩
— put down roots : to establish a permanent residence
put in (15th century)
transitive verb
1 : to make a formal offer or declaration of ⟨*put in* a plea of guilty⟩
2 : to come in with **:** INTERPOSE ⟨*put in* a word for his brother⟩
3 : to spend (time) especially at some occupation or job ⟨*put in* six hours at the office⟩
4 : PLANT ⟨*put in* a crop⟩
intransitive verb
1 : to call at or enter a place; *especially* **:** to enter a harbor or port
2 : to make an application, request, or offer — often used with *for* ⟨had to retire and *put in* for a pension —Seymour Nagan⟩
put-log \ˈpu̇t-ˌlȯg, ˈpət-, -ˌläg\ *noun* [probably alteration of earlier *putlock*, perhaps from ³*put* + ²*lock*] (1645)
: one of the short timbers that support the flooring of a scaffold
put off *transitive verb* (14th century)
1 a : DISCONCERT **b :** REPEL
2 a : to hold back to a later time **b :** to induce to wait ⟨*put* the bill collector *off*⟩
3 : to rid oneself of **:** TAKE OFF
4 : to sell or pass fraudulently
¹put-on \ˈpu̇t-ˈȯn, -ˈän\ *adjective* (1621)
: PRETENDED, ASSUMED
²put-on \ˈpu̇t-ˌȯn, -ˌän\ *noun* (circa 1927)
1 : an instance of putting someone on ⟨conversational *put-ons* are related to old-fashioned joshing —Jacob Brackman⟩
2 : PARODY, SPOOF ⟨a kind of *put-on* of every pretentious film ever made —C. A. Ridley⟩
put on *transitive verb* (15th century)
1 a : to dress oneself in **:** DON **b :** to make part of one's appearance or behavior **c :** FEIGN ⟨*put* a saintly manner *on*⟩

2 : to cause to act or operate **:** APPLY ⟨*put on* more speed⟩
3 a : ADD ⟨*put on* weight⟩ **b :** EXAGGERATE, OVERSTATE ⟨he's *putting* it *on* when he makes such claims⟩
4 : PERFORM, PRODUCE ⟨*put on* a play⟩
5 a : to mislead deliberately especially for amusement ⟨the interviewer . . . must be put down — or possibly, *put on* —Melvin Maddocks⟩ **b :** KID ⟨you're *putting* me *on*⟩
put-out \ˈpu̇t-ˌau̇t\ *noun* (1885)
: the retiring of a base runner or batter by a defensive player in baseball
put out (14th century)
transitive verb
1 : EXTINGUISH ⟨*put* the fire *out*⟩
2 : EXERT, USE ⟨*put out* considerable effort⟩
3 : PUBLISH, ISSUE
4 : to produce for sale
5 a : DISCONCERT, EMBARRASS **b :** ANNOY, IRRITATE **c :** INCONVENIENCE ⟨don't *put* yourself *out* for us⟩
6 : to cause to be out (as in baseball or cricket)
intransitive verb
1 : to set out from shore
2 : to make an effort
3 : to engage in sexual intercourse
put over *transitive verb* (1528)
1 : POSTPONE, DELAY
2 : PUT ACROSS 2
3 : to achieve or carry through by deceit or trickery ⟨*put* one *over* on me⟩
pu·tre·fac·tion \ˌpyü-trə-ˈfak-shən\ *noun* [Middle English *putrefaccion*, from Late Latin *putrefaction-, putrefactio*, from Latin *putrefacere*] (14th century)
1 : the decomposition of organic matter; *especially* **:** the typically anaerobic splitting of proteins by bacteria and fungi with the formation of foul-smelling incompletely oxidized products
2 : the state of being putrefied **:** CORRUPTION
— pu·tre·fac·tive \-ˈfak-tiv\ *adjective*
pu·tre·fy \ˈpyü-trə-ˌfī\ *verb* **-fied; -fy·ing** [Middle English *putrefien*, from Middle French & Latin; Middle French *putrefier*, from Latin *putrefacere*, from *putrēre* to be rotten + *facere* to make — more at DO] (14th century)
transitive verb
: to make putrid
intransitive verb
: to undergo putrefaction
synonym see DECAY
pu·tres·cence \pyü-ˈtre-sᵊn(t)s\ *noun* (1646)
: the state of being putrescent
pu·tres·cent \-sᵊnt\ *adjective* [Latin *putrescent-, putrescens*, present participle of *putrescere* to grow rotten, inchoative of *putrēre*] (1732)
1 : undergoing putrefaction **:** becoming putrid
2 : of or relating to putrefaction
pu·tres·ci·ble \-ˈtre-sə-bəl\ *adjective* (1797)
: liable to become putrid
pu·tres·cine \-ˈtre-ˌsēn\ *noun* [International Scientific Vocabulary, from Latin *putrescere*] (1887)
: a crystalline slightly poisonous ptomaine $C_4H_{12}N_2$ that occurs in small amounts in virtually all living things
pu·trid \ˈpyü-trəd\ *adjective* [Latin *putridus*, from *putrēre* to be rotten, from *puter, putris* rotten; akin to Latin *putēre* to stink — more at FOUL] (1598)
1 a : being in a state of putrefaction **:** ROTTEN **b :** of, relating to, or characteristic of putrefaction **:** FOUL ⟨a *putrid* odor⟩
2 a : morally corrupt **b :** totally objectionable
synonym see MALODOROUS
— pu·trid·i·ty \pyü-ˈtri-də-tē\ *noun*

\ə\ abut \ᵊ\ kitten \ər\ further \a\ ash \ā\ ace
\ä\ mop, mar \au̇\ out \ch\ chin \e\ bet \ē\ easy
\g\ go \i\ hit \ī\ ice \j\ job \ŋ\ sing \ō\ go
\ȯ\ law \ȯi\ boy \th\ thin \t͟h\ the \ü\ loot \u̇\ foot
\y\ yet \zh\ vision *see also* Guide to Pronunciation

— **pu·trid·ly** \'pyü-trəd-lē\ *adverb*

putsch \'pùch\ *noun* [German] (1920)
: a secretly plotted and suddenly executed attempt to overthrow a government

putsch·ist \'pù-chist\ *noun* (1898)
: one who takes part in a putsch

putt \'pət\ *noun* [Scots, literally, shove, gentle push, from *putt, put* to put] (1743)
: a golf stroke made on a putting green to cause the ball to roll into or near the hole
— **putt** *verb*

put·tee \pə-'tē, pù-; 'pə-tē\ *noun* [Hindi *paṭṭī* strip of cloth, from Sanskrit *paṭṭikā*] (1886)
1 : a cloth strip wrapped around the leg from ankle to knee
2 : a usually leather legging secured by a strap or catch or by laces

¹**put·ter** \'pù-tər\ *noun* (14th century)
: one that puts ⟨a *putter* of questions⟩

²**putt·er** \'pə-tər\ *noun* (1743)
1 : a golf club used in putting
2 : one that putts

³**put·ter** \'pə-tər\ *intransitive verb* [alteration of *potter*] (circa 1877)
1 : to move or act aimlessly or idly
2 : to work at random : TINKER
— **put·ter·er** \-tər-ər\ *noun*

put through *transitive verb* (1852)
1 : to carry to a successful conclusion ⟨*put through* a number of reforms⟩
2 a : to make a telephone connection for **b** : to obtain a connection for (a telephone call)

putt·ing green \'pə-tiŋ-\ *noun* (1841)
: a smooth grassy area at the end of a golf fairway containing the hole; *also* : a similar area usually with many holes that is used for practice

put·to \'pü-(,)tō\ *noun, plural* **put·ti** \-(,)tē\ [Italian, literally, boy, from (assumed) Vulgar Latin *puttus*, alteration of Latin *putus*; akin to Latin *puer* boy — more at PUERILE] (1644)
: a figure of an infant boy especially in European art of the Renaissance — usually used in plural

¹**put·ty** \'pə-tē\ *noun, plural* **putties** [French *potée* potter's glaze, literally, potful, from Old French, from *pot* pot — more at POTTAGE] (circa 1706)
1 a : a doughlike material typically made of whiting and linseed oil that is used especially to fasten glass in window frames and to fill crevices in woodwork **b** : any of various substances resembling putty in appearance, consistency, or use
2 : a light brownish gray to light grayish brown color
3 : one who is easily manipulated ⟨is *putty* in her hands⟩
— **put·ty·less** *adjective*
— **put·ty·like** *adjective*

²**putty** *transitive verb* **put·tied; put·ty·ing** (1734)
: to use putty on or apply putty to

putty knife *noun* (1858)
: an implement with a broad flat metal blade used especially for applying putty and for scraping

put·ty-root \'pə-tē-,rüt, -,rùt\ *noun* (1817)
: a North American orchid (*Aplectrum hyemale*) having a slender naked rootstock and producing a solitary leaf and a scape bearing a raceme of brownish flowers

put-up \'pùt-'əp\ *adjective* (1810)
: arranged secretly beforehand

put up (14th century)
transitive verb
1 a : to place in a container or receptacle ⟨*put* his lunch *up* in a bag⟩ **b** : to put away (a sword) in a scabbard : SHEATHE **c** : to prepare so as to preserve for later use : CAN **d** : to put in storage
2 : to start (game) from cover
3 : to nominate for election
4 : to offer up (as a prayer)
5 : SET 16

6 : to offer for public sale ⟨*put* their possessions *up* for auction⟩
7 : to give food and shelter to : ACCOMMODATE
8 : to arrange (as a plot or scheme) with others ⟨*put up* a job to steal the jewels⟩
9 : BUILD, ERECT
10 a : to make a display of ⟨*put up* a bluff⟩ **b** : to engage in ⟨*put up* a struggle against odds⟩
11 a : CONTRIBUTE, PAY **b** : to offer as a prize or stake
12 *chiefly British* : to increase the amount of : RAISE
intransitive verb
: LODGE
— **put up to** : INCITE, INSTIGATE ⟨they *put* him *up to* playing the prank⟩
— **put up with** : to endure or tolerate without complaint or attempt at reprisal

put-up·on \'pùt-ə-,pòn, -,pän\ *adjective* (1920)
: imposed upon : taken advantage of

¹**puz·zle** \'pə-zəl\ *verb* **puz·zled; puz·zling** \'pə-zə-liŋ, 'pəz-liŋ\ [origin unknown] (1602)
transitive verb
1 : to offer or represent to (as a person) a problem difficult to solve or a situation difficult to resolve : challenge mentally; *also* : to exert (as oneself) over such a problem or situation ⟨they *puzzled* their wits to find a solution⟩
2 *archaic* : COMPLICATE, ENTANGLE
3 : to solve with difficulty or ingenuity ⟨*puzzle* out an answer to a riddle⟩
intransitive verb
1 : to be uncertain as to action or choice
2 : to attempt a solution of a puzzle by guesswork or experiment ☆
— **puz·zler** \'pə-zə-lər, 'pəz-lər\ *noun*

²**puzzle** *noun* (circa 1612)
1 : the state of being puzzled : PERPLEXITY
2 a : something that puzzles **b** : a question, problem, or contrivance designed for testing ingenuity
synonym see MYSTERY

puz·zle-head·ed \'pə-zəl-,he-dəd\ *adjective* (circa 1784)
: having or based on confused attitudes or ideas
— **puz·zle-head·ed·ness** *noun*

puz·zle·ment \'pə-zəl-mənt\ *noun* (1822)
1 : the state of being puzzled : PERPLEXITY
2 : PUZZLE

puzzling *adjective* (1666)
: difficult to understand or solve
— **puz·zling·ly** *adverb*

P-wave \'pē-,wāv\ *noun* [by shortening] (1936)
: PRESSURE WAVE

py- *or* **pyo-** *combining form* [Greek, from *pyon* pus — more at FOUL]
: pus ⟨*pye*mia⟩ ⟨*pyo*rrhea⟩

pya \'pyä, pē-'ä\ *noun* [Burmese] (1952)
— see *kyat* at MONEY table

pyc·nid·i·um \pik-'ni-dē-əm\ *noun, plural* **-ia** \-dē-ə\ [New Latin, from Greek *pyknos* dense] (1857)
: a flask-shaped fruiting body bearing conidiophores and conidia on the interior and occurring in various imperfect fungi and ascomycetes
— **pyc·nid·i·al** \-dē-əl\ *adjective*

pyc·no·go·nid \pik-'nä-gə-nəd, ,pik-nə-'gänəd\ *noun* [ultimately from Greek *pyknos* + *gony* knee — more at KNEE] (1881)
: SEA SPIDER

pyc·nom·e·ter \pik-'nä-mə-tər\ *noun* [Greek *pyknos* + International Scientific Vocabulary *-meter*] (1858)
: a standard vessel often provided with a thermometer for measuring and comparing the densities of liquids or solids

pye-dog \'pī-,dòg\ *noun* [perhaps from Hindi *pāhī* outsider] (1864)
: a half-wild dog common about Asian villages

pyel- *or* **pyelo-** *combining form* [New Latin, pelvis, from Greek *pyelos* basin; akin to Greek *plynein* to wash, *plein* to sail — more at FLOW]
: renal pelvis ⟨*pyel*itis⟩

py·eli·tis \,pī-ə-'lī-təs\ *noun* [New Latin] (circa 1842)
: inflammation of the lining of the renal pelvis

py·elo·ne·phri·tis \,pī-(ə-)lō-ni-'frī-təs\ *noun* [New Latin] (1866)
: inflammation of both the lining of the pelvis and the parenchyma of the kidney
— **py·elo·ne·phrit·ic** \-'fri-tik\ *adjective*

py·emia \pī-'ē-mē-ə\ *noun* [New Latin] (circa 1857)
: septicemia caused by pus-forming bacteria and accompanied by multiple abscesses

py·gid·i·um \pī-'ji-dē-əm\ *noun, plural* **-ia** \-dē-ə\ [New Latin, from Greek *pygidion*, diminutive of *pygē* rump] (circa 1849)
: a caudal structure or the terminal body region of various invertebrates
— **py·gid·i·al** \-dē-əl\ *adjective*

pyg·mae·an *or* **pyg·me·an** \pig-'mē-ən, 'pig-mē-\ *adjective* [Latin *pygmaeus*] (1667)
: PYGMY

Pyg·ma·lion \pig-'māl-yən, -'mā-lē-ən\ *noun* [Latin, from Greek *Pygmaliōn*]
: a king of Cyprus who makes a female figure of ivory that is brought to life for him by Aphrodite

pyg·moid \'pig-,mòid\ *adjective* (circa 1930)
: resembling or having the characteristics of the Pygmies

pyg·my \'pig-mē\ *noun, plural* **pygmies** [Middle English *pigmei*, from Latin *pygmaeus* of a pygmy, dwarfish, from Greek *pygmaios*, from *pygmē* fist, measure of length — more at PUNGENT] (14th century)
1 *often capitalized* : any of a race of dwarfs described by ancient Greek authors
2 *capitalized* : any of a small people of equatorial Africa ranging under five feet (1.5 meters) in height
3 a : a short insignificant person : DWARF **b** : something very small of its kind
— **pygmy** *adjective*

pygmy chimpanzee *noun* (1962)
: an anthropoid ape (*Pan paniscus*) of Zaire that has a lighter build than the related common chimpanzee (*P. troglodytes*) — called also *pygmy chimp*

py·ja·mas \pə-'jä-məz\ *chiefly British variant of* PAJAMAS

pyk·nic \'pik-nik\ *adjective* [International Scientific Vocabulary, from Greek *pyknos* dense, stocky] (1925)

☆ **SYNONYMS**
Puzzle, perplex, bewilder, distract, nonplus, confound, dumbfound mean to baffle and disturb mentally. PUZZLE implies existence of a problem difficult to solve ⟨the persistent fever *puzzled* the doctor⟩. PERPLEX adds a suggestion of worry and uncertainty especially about making a necessary decision ⟨a behavior that *perplexed* her friends⟩. BEWILDER stresses a confusion of mind that hampers clear and decisive thinking ⟨a *bewildering* number of possibilities⟩. DISTRACT implies agitation or uncertainty induced by conflicting preoccupations or interests ⟨*distracted* by personal problems⟩. NONPLUS implies a bafflement that makes orderly planning or deciding impossible ⟨the remark left us utterly *nonplussed*⟩. CONFOUND implies temporary mental paralysis caused by astonishment or profound abasement ⟨the tragic news *confounded* us all⟩. DUMBFOUND suggests intense but momentary confounding; often the idea of astonishment is so stressed that it becomes a near synonym of *astound* ⟨was at first too *dumbfounded* to reply⟩.

: characterized by shortness of stature, broadness of girth, and powerful muscularity : EN-DOMORPHIC 2
— **pyknic** *noun*

py·lon \'pī-ˌlän, -lən\ *noun* [Greek *pylōn*, from *pylē* gate] (1850)
1 a : a usually massive gateway **b :** an ancient Egyptian gateway building in a truncated pyramidal form **c :** a monumental mass flanking an entranceway or an approach to a bridge
2 a *chiefly British* **:** a tower for supporting either end of usually a number of wires over a long span **b :** any of various towerlike structures
3 a : a post or tower marking a prescribed course of flight for an airplane **b :** TRAFFIC CONE
4 : a rigid structure on the outside of an aircraft for supporting something (as an engine or missile) — see AIRPLANE illustration

py·lo·ric \pī-'lȯr-ik, pə-, -'lȯr-\ *adjective* (1807)
: of or relating to the pylorus; *also* : of, relating to, or situated in or near the posterior part of the stomach

py·lo·rus \-əs\ *noun, plural* **py·lo·ri** \-'lȯr-ˌī, -ˌ)ē\ [Late Latin, from Greek *pylōros*, literally, gatekeeper, from *pylē*] (1615)
: the opening from the vertebrate stomach into the intestine

pyo·der·ma \ˌpī-ə-'dər-mə\ *noun* [New Latin] (1930)
: a bacterial skin inflammation marked by pus-filled lesions

pyo·gen·ic \-'je-nik\ *adjective* [International Scientific Vocabulary] (circa 1847)
: producing pus ⟨*pyogenic* bacteria⟩; *also* : marked by pus production ⟨*pyogenic* meningitis⟩

py·or·rhea \ˌpī-ə-'rē-ə\ *noun* [New Latin] (1878)
: purulent inflammation of the sockets of the teeth leading usually to loosening of the teeth

pyr- *or* **pyro-** *combining form* [Middle English, from Middle French, from Late Latin, from Greek, from *pyr* — more at FIRE]
1 : fire : heat ⟨*pyro*meter⟩ ⟨*pyr*heliometer⟩
2 a : produced by or as if by the action of heat ⟨*pyro*electricity⟩ **b :** derived from a corresponding ortho acid by loss usually of one molecule of water from two molecules of acid ⟨*pyro*phosphoric acid⟩
3 : fever ⟨*pyro*genic⟩

pyr·acan·tha \ˌpī-rə-'kan(t)-thə\ *noun* [New Latin, from Greek *pyrakantha*, a tree, from *pyr-* + *akantha* thorn] (1705)
: any of a small genus (*Pyracantha*) of Eurasian thorny evergreen or semievergreen shrubs of the rose family with alternate leaves, corymbs of white flowers, and small red or orange pomes

py·ral·id \pī-'ra-ləd\ *noun* [ultimately from Latin *pyralis*, fly fabled as living in fire, from Greek, from *pyr* fire] (circa 1890)
: any of a very large heterogeneous family (Pyralidae) of mostly small slender long-legged moths
— **pyralid** *adjective*

¹pyr·a·mid \'pir-ə-ˌmid\ *noun* [Latin *pyramid-, pyramis,* from Greek] (1549)
1 a : an ancient massive structure found especially in Egypt having typically a square ground plan, outside walls in the form of four triangles that meet in a point at the top,

pyramid 2

and inner sepulchral chambers **b :** a structure or object of similar form
2 : a polyhedron having for its base a polygon and for faces triangles with a common vertex — see VOLUME table

3 : a crystalline form each face of which intersects the vertical axis and either two lateral axes or in the tetragonal system one lateral axis
4 : an anatomical structure resembling a pyramid: **a :** any of the conical masses that project from the renal medulla into the kidney pelvis **b :** either of two large bundles of motor fibers from the cerebral cortex that reach the medulla oblongata and are continuous with the pyramidal tracts of the spinal cord
5 : an immaterial structure built on a broad supporting base and narrowing gradually to an apex ⟨the socioeconomic *pyramid*⟩
— **py·ra·mi·dal** \pə-'ra-mə-dᵊl, ˌpir-ə-'mi-\ *adjective*
— **py·ra·mi·dal·ly** *adverb*
— **pyr·a·mid·i·cal** \ˌpir-ə-'mi-di-kəl\ *adjective*

²pyramid (circa 1900)
intransitive verb
1 : to speculate (as on a security or commodity exchange) by using paper profits as margin for additional transactions
2 : to increase rapidly and progressively step by step on a broad base
transitive verb
1 : to arrange or build up as if on the base of a pyramid
2 : to use (as profits) in speculative pyramiding
3 : to increase the impact of (as a tax assessed at the production level) on the ultimate consumer by treating as a cost subject to markup

pyramidal tract *noun* (circa 1890)
: any of four columns of motor fibers that run in pairs on each side of the spinal cord and are continuations of the pyramids of the medulla oblongata

Pyr·a·mus \'pir-ə-məs\ *noun* [Latin, from Greek *Pyramos*]
: a legendary youth of Babylon who dies for love of Thisbe

py·ran \'pī-ˌran\ *noun* [International Scientific Vocabulary] (1904)
: either of two cyclic compounds C_5H_6O that contain five carbon atoms and one oxygen atom in the ring

py·ra·nose \'pī-rə-ˌnōs, -ˌnōz\ *noun* [International Scientific Vocabulary] (1927)
: a monosaccharide in the form of a cyclic hemiacetal containing a pyran ring

py·ran·o·side \pī-'ra-nə-ˌsīd\ *noun* (1932)
: a glycoside containing the pyran ring

pyr·ar·gy·rite \pī-'rär-jə-ˌrīt\ *noun* [German *Pyrargyrit,* from Greek *pyr-* + *argyros* silver — more at ARGENT] (1849)
: a mineral consisting of silver antimony sulfide that occurs in rhombohedral crystals or in massive form and has a dark red or black color or with a metallic luster

pyre \'pī(ə)r\ *noun* [Latin *pyra,* from Greek, from *pyr* fire — more at FIRE] (1658)
: a combustible heap for burning a dead body as a funeral rite; *broadly* : a pile of material to be burned ⟨a *pyre* of dead leaves⟩

py·re·noid \pī-'rē-ˌnȯid, 'pī-rə-\ *noun* [International Scientific Vocabulary, from New Latin *pyrena* stone of a fruit, from Greek *pyrēnoun;* akin to Greek *pyros* wheat grain, wheat — more at FURZE] (circa 1875)
: one of the protein bodies in the chromatophores of various lower organisms (as some algae) that act as centers for starch deposition

py·re·thrin \pī-'rē-thrən, -'re-\ *noun* [International Scientific Vocabulary, from Latin *pyrethrum*] (1924)
: either of two oily liquid esters $C_{21}H_{28}O_3$ and $C_{22}H_{28}O_5$ having insecticidal properties and occurring especially in the flowers of pyrethrum

py·re·throid \-'rē-ˌthrȯid, -'re-\ *noun* [*pyrethrin* + *-oid*] (1949)
: any of various synthetic compounds that are related to the pyrethrins and resemble them in insecticidal properties

— **pyrethroid** *adjective*

py·re·thrum \pī-'rē-thrəm, -'re-\ *noun* [Latin, pellitory, from Greek *pyrethron,* from *pyr* fire] (circa 1543)
1 : any of several chrysanthemums with finely divided often aromatic leaves including ornamentals as well as important sources of insecticides
2 : an insecticide made from the dried heads of any of several Old World chrysanthemums

py·ret·ic \pī-'re-tik\ *adjective* [New Latin *pyreticus,* from Greek *pyretikos,* from *pyretos* fever, from *pyr*] (circa 1858)
: of or relating to fever : FEBRILE

Py·rex \'pī-ˌreks\ *trademark*
— used for borosilicate glass and glassware resistant to heat, chemicals, and electricity

py·rex·ia \pī-'rek-sē-ə\ *noun* [New Latin, from Greek *pyressein* to be feverish, from *pyretos*] (1769)
: abnormal elevation of body temperature : FEVER
— **py·rex·i·al** \-sē-əl\ *adjective*
— **py·rex·ic** \-sik\ *adjective*

pyr·he·li·om·e·ter \ˌpir-ˌhē-lē-'ä-mə-tər, ˌpir-\ *noun* [International Scientific Vocabulary] (1863)
: an instrument for measuring the sun's radiant energy as received at the earth
— **pyr·he·lio·met·ric** \-lē-ə-'me-trik\ *adjective*

py·ric \'pī-rik, 'pir-ik\ *adjective* [French *pyrique,* from Greek *pyr*] (1946)
: resulting from, induced by, or associated with burning

pyr·i·dine \'pir-ə-ˌdēn\ *noun* [*pyr-* + *-ide* + *²-ine*] (1851)
: a toxic water-soluble flammable liquid base C_5H_5N of pungent odor that is the parent of many naturally occurring organic compounds and is used as a solvent and as a denaturant for alcohol and in the manufacture of pharmaceuticals and waterproofing agents

pyr·i·dox·al \ˌpir-ə-'däk-ˌsal\ *noun* [International Scientific Vocabulary, from *pyridoxine*] (1944)
: a crystalline aldehyde $C_8H_9NO_3$ of the vitamin B_6 group that occurs as a phosphate and is active as a coenzyme

pyr·i·dox·amine \ˌpir-ə-'däk-sə-ˌmēn\ *noun* [International Scientific Vocabulary *pyridox*ine + *amine*] (1944)
: a crystalline amine $C_8H_{12}N_2O_2$ of the vitamin B_6 group that occurs as a phosphate and is active as a coenzyme

pyr·i·dox·ine \ˌpir-ə-'däk-ˌsēn, -sən\ *noun* [*pyridine* + *ox-* + *²-ine*] (1939)
: a crystalline phenolic alcohol $C_8H_{11}NO_3$ of the vitamin B_6 group found especially in cereals and convertible in the organism into pyridoxal and pyridoxamine

pyr·i·form \'pir-ə-ˌfȯrm\ *adjective* [New Latin *pyriformis,* from Medieval Latin *pyrum* pear (alteration of Latin *pirum*) + Latin *-iformis* -iform] (1741)
: having the form of a pear

py·ri·meth·amine \ˌpī-rə-'me-thə-ˌmēn\ *noun* [*pyrim*idine + *ethyl* + *amine*] (1952)
: a folic acid antagonist $C_{12}H_{13}ClN_4$ used in the treatment of malaria and of toxoplasmosis

py·rim·i·dine \pī-'ri-mə-ˌdēn, pə-\ *noun* [International Scientific Vocabulary, alteration of *pyridine*] (1885)
1 : a feeble organic base $C_4H_2N_2$ of penetrating odor
2 : a derivative of pyrimidine; *especially* : a base (as cytosine, thymine, or uracil) that is a constituent of DNA or RNA

py·rite \'pī-ˌrīt\ *noun* [Latin *pyrites*] (1588)

: a common mineral that consists of iron disulfide, has a pale brass-yellow color and metallic luster, and is burned in making sulfur dioxide and sulfuric acid

py·rites \pə-'rī-tēz, pī-; 'pī-ˌrīts\ *noun, plural* **pyrites** [Latin, flint, from Greek *pyritēs* of or in fire, from *pyr* fire] (1543)
: any of various metallic-looking sulfides of which pyrite is the commonest
— **py·rit·ic** \-'ri-tik\ *adjective*

py·ro·cat·e·chol \ˌpī-rō-'ka-tə-ˌkȯl, -ˌkōl\ *noun* [International Scientific Vocabulary] (1890)
: a crystalline phenol $C_6H_6O_2$ obtained by pyrolysis of various natural substances (as resins and lignins) but usually made synthetically and used especially as a photographic developer and in organic synthesis

py·ro·clas·tic \-'klas-tik\ *adjective* (1887)
: formed by or involving fragmentation as a result of volcanic or igneous action

py·ro·elec·tric·i·ty \ˌpī-rō-ə-ˌlek-'tri-sə-tē, -'tris-tē\ *noun* [International Scientific Vocabulary] (circa 1834)
: a state of electrical polarization produced (as in a crystal) by a change of temperature
— **py·ro·elec·tric** \-'lek-trik\ *adjective*

py·ro·gal·lol \ˌpī-rō-'ga-ˌlȯl, -ˌlōl; -'gȯl-\ *noun* [International Scientific Vocabulary *pyro-* + *gallic* (acid) + [1]-*ol*] (1876)
: a poisonous bitter crystalline phenol $C_6H_6O_3$ with weak acid properties that is obtained usually by pyrolysis of gallic acid and used especially as a mild reducing agent (as in photographic developing)

py·ro·gen \'pī-rə-jən\ *noun* [International Scientific Vocabulary] (circa 1890)
: a fever-producing substance

py·ro·gen·ic \ˌpī-rō-'je-nik\ *adjective* [International Scientific Vocabulary] (1853)
1 : producing or produced by heat or fever
2 : of or relating to igneous origin
— **py·ro·ge·nic·i·ty** \ˌpī-rō-jə-'ni-sə-tē\ *noun*

py·ro·la \pī-'rō-lə\ *noun* [New Latin, probably from Latin *pirum* pear] (1578)
: WINTERGREEN 1

py·ro·lig·ne·ous acid \ˌpī-rō-'lig-nē-əs-\ *noun* [French *pyroligneux*, from *pyr-* + *ligneux* woody, from Latin *lignosus*, from *lignum* wood — more at LIGNEOUS] (circa 1790)
: an acid reddish brown aqueous liquid containing chiefly acetic acid, methanol, wood oils, and tars that is obtained by destructive distillation of wood

py·ro·lu·site \ˌpī-rō-'lü-ˌsīt\ *noun* [German *Pyrolusit*, from Greek *pyr-* + *lousis* washing, from *louein* to wash — more at LYE] (1828)
: a mineral consisting of manganese dioxide that is of an iron-black or dark steel-gray color and metallic luster, is usually soft, and is the most important ore of manganese

py·rol·y·sate \pī-'rä-lə-ˌzāt, -ˌsāt\ *or* **py·rol·y·zate** \-ˌzāt\ *noun* (1944)
: a product of pyrolysis

py·rol·y·sis \pī-'rä-lə-səs\ *noun* [New Latin] (circa 1890)
: chemical change brought about by the action of heat
— **py·ro·lyt·ic** \ˌpī-rə-'li-tik\ *adjective*
— **py·ro·lyt·i·cal·ly** \-ti-k(ə-)lē\ *adverb*

py·ro·lyze *also* **py·ro·lize** \'pī-rə-ˌlīz\ *transitive verb* **-lyzed** *also* **-lized; -lyz·ing** *also* **-liz·ing** (1932)
: to subject to pyrolysis
— **py·ro·lyz·able** \ˌpī-rə-'lī-zə-bəl\ *adjective*
— **py·ro·lyz·er** *noun*

py·ro·man·cy \-ˌman(t)-sē\ *noun* [Middle English *pyromancie*, from Middle French, from Late Latin *pyromantia*, from Greek *pyromanteia*, from *pyr* fire + *manteia* divination — more at -MANCY] (14th century)
: divination by means of fire or flames

py·ro·ma·nia \ˌpī-rō-'mā-nē-ə, -nyə\ *noun* [New Latin] (circa 1842)
: an irresistible impulse to start fires
— **py·ro·ma·ni·ac** \-nē-ˌak\ *noun*
— **py·ro·ma·ni·a·cal** \-mə-'nī-ə-kəl\ *adjective*

py·ro·met·al·lur·gy \-'me-t°l-ˌər-jē, *especially British* -mə-'ta-lər-\ *noun* [International Scientific Vocabulary] (1908)
: chemical metallurgy depending on heat action (as roasting and smelting)
— **py·ro·met·al·lur·gi·cal** \-ˌme-t°l-'ər-ji-kəl\ *adjective*

py·rom·e·ter \pī-'rä-mə-tər\ *noun* [International Scientific Vocabulary] (1796)
: an instrument for measuring temperatures especially when beyond the range of mercurial thermometers
— **py·ro·met·ric** \ˌpī-rə-'me-trik\ *adjective*
— **py·ro·met·ri·cal·ly** \-tri-k(ə-)lē\ *adverb*
— **py·rom·e·try** \pī-'rä-mə-trē\ *noun*

py·ro·mor·phite \ˌpī-rə-'mȯr-ˌfīt\ *noun* [German *Pyromorphit*, from Greek *pyr-* + *morphē* form] (circa 1814)
: a mineral consisting essentially of a lead chloride and phosphate

py·ro·nine \'pī-rə-ˌnēn\ *noun* [International Scientific Vocabulary, irregular from *pyr-* + [2]-*ine*] (1895)
: any of several basic xanthene dyes used chiefly as biological stains

py·ro·nin·o·phil·ic \ˌpī-rə-ˌnē-nə-'fi-lik\ *adjective* (1946)
: staining selectively with pyronines ⟨*pyroninophilic* cells⟩

py·rope \'pīr-ˌōp\ *noun* [Middle English *pirope*, a red gem, from Middle French, from Latin *pyropus*, a red bronze, from Greek *pyrōpos*, literally, fiery-eyed, from *pyr-* + *ōp-*, *ōps* eye — more at EYE] (1804)
: a magnesium-aluminum garnet that is deep red in color and is frequently used as a gem

py·ro·phor·ic \ˌpī-rə-'fȯr-ik, -'fär-\ *adjective* [New Latin *pyrophorus*, from Greek *pyrophoros* fire-bearing, from *pyr-* + *-phoros* carrying — more at -PHORE] (1836)
1 : igniting spontaneously
2 : emitting sparks when scratched or struck especially with steel

py·ro·phos·phate \-'fäs-ˌfāt\ *noun* (1836)
: a salt or ester of pyrophosphoric acid

py·ro·phos·pho·ric acid \-ˌfäs-'fȯr-ik, -'fär-; -'fäs-f(ə-)rik-\ *noun* [International Scientific Vocabulary] (1832)
: a crystalline acid $H_4P_2O_7$ formed when orthophosphoric acid is heated or prepared in the form of salts by heating acid salts of orthophosphoric acid

py·ro·phyl·lite \ˌpī-rō-'fi-ˌlīt, pī-'rä-fə-ˌlīt\ *noun* [German *Pyrophyllit*, from Greek *pyr-* + *phyllon* leaf — more at BLADE] (1830)
: a white or greenish mineral that is a hydrous aluminum silicate, resembles talc, occurs in a foliated form or in compact masses, and is used especially in ceramic wares

py·ro·sis \pī-'rō-səs\ *noun* [New Latin, from Greek *pyrōsis* burning, from *pyroun* to burn, from *pyr* fire — more at FIRE] (1789)
: HEARTBURN

[1]**py·ro·tech·nic** \ˌpī-rə-'tek-nik\ *also* **py·ro·tech·ni·cal** \-ni-kəl\ *adjective* [French *pyrotechnique*, from Greek *pyr* fire + *technē* art — more at TECHNICAL] (1825)
: of or relating to pyrotechnics
— **py·ro·tech·ni·cal·ly** \-ni-k(ə-)lē\ *adverb*

[2]**pyrotechnic** *noun* (1840)
1 a : FIREWORK **b** : any of various similar devices (as for igniting a rocket or producing an explosion)
2 : a combustible substance used in a firework

py·ro·tech·nics \ˌpī-rə-'tek-niks\ *noun plural* (1729)
1 *singular or plural in construction* : the art of making or the manufacture and use of fireworks
2 a : a display of fireworks **b** : a spectacular display (as of extreme virtuosity) ⟨verbal *pyrotechnics*⟩ ⟨keyboard *pyrotechnics*⟩
— **py·ro·tech·nist** \-nist\ *noun*

py·rox·ene \pī-'räk-ˌsēn, pə-\ *noun* [French *pyroxène*, from Greek *pyr-* + *xenos* stranger] (1800)
: any of a group of igneous-rock-forming silicate minerals that contain calcium, sodium, magnesium, iron, or aluminum, usually occur in short prismatic crystals or massive form, are often laminated, and vary in color from white to dark green or black
— **py·rox·e·nic** \ˌpī-räk-'sē-nik, pə-, -'se-\ *adjective*
— **py·rox·e·noid** \pī-'räk-sə-ˌnȯid, pə-\ *adjective or noun*

py·rox·e·nite \pī-'räk-sə-ˌnīt, pə-\ *noun* (circa 1862)
: an igneous rock that is free from olivine and is composed essentially of pyroxene
— **py·rox·e·nit·ic** \-ˌräk-sə-'ni-tik\ *adjective*

py·rox·y·lin \pī-'räk-sə-lən, pə-\ *noun* [International Scientific Vocabulary *pyr-* + Greek *xylon* wood] (circa 1847)
1 : a flammable mixture of nitrocelluloses used especially in making plastics and water-repellent coatings (as lacquers)
2 : a pyroxylin product

Pyr·rha \'pir-ə\ *noun* [Latin, from Greek]
: the wife of Deucalion

pyr·rhic \'pir-ik\ *noun* [Latin *pyrrhichius*, from Greek (*pous*) *pyrrhichios*, from *pyrrhichē*, a kind of dance] (1626)
: a metrical foot consisting of two short or unaccented syllables

Pyr·rhic \'pir-ik\ *adjective* [*Pyrrhus*, king of Epirus who sustained heavy losses in defeating the Romans] (1885)
: achieved or gained at excessive cost ⟨a *Pyrrhic* victory⟩; *also* : costly to the point of negating or outweighing expected benefits ⟨a great but *Pyrrhic* act of ingenuity⟩

Pyr·rho·nism \'pir-ə-ˌni-zəm\ *noun* [French *pyrrhonisme*, from *Pyrrhon* Pyrrho, 4th century B.C. Greek philosopher, from Greek *Pyrrhōn*] (circa 1670)
1 : the doctrines of a school of ancient extreme skeptics who suspended judgment on every proposition — compare ACADEMICISM
2 : total or radical skepticism
— **Pyr·rho·nist** \-nist\ *noun*

pyr·rho·tite \'pir-ə-ˌtīt\ *noun* [modification of German *Pyrrhotin*, from Greek *pyrrhotēs* redness, from *pyrrhos* red, from *pyr* fire — more at FIRE] (1868)
: a bronze-colored mineral of metallic luster that consists of ferrous sulfide and is attracted by a magnet

Pyr·rhus \'pir-əs\ *noun* [Latin, from Greek *Pyrrhos*]
: a son of Achilles and slayer of Priam at the taking of Troy

pyr·role \'pir-ˌōl\ *noun* [Greek *pyrrhos*] (1835)
: a toxic liquid heterocyclic compound C_4H_5N that has a ring consisting of four carbon atoms and one nitrogen atom, polymerizes readily in air, and is the parent compound of many biologically important substances (as bile pigments, porphyrins, and chlorophyll); *broadly* : a derivative of pyrrole
— **pyr·rol·ic** \pi-'rō-lik\ *adjective*

py·ru·vate \pī-'rü-ˌvāt\ *noun* (1855)
: a salt or ester of pyruvic acid

py·ru·vic acid \pī-'rü-vik-\ *noun* [International Scientific Vocabulary *pyr-* + Latin *uva* grapes; from its importance in fermentation — more at UVULA] (1838)
: a 3-carbon keto acid $C_3H_4O_3$ that in carbo-

hydrate metabolism is an important intermediate product formed as pyruvate by glycolysis

¹Py·thag·o·re·an \pə-ˌtha-gə-'rē-ən, (ˌ)pī-\ *noun* (1550)
: any of a group professing to be followers of the Greek philosopher Pythagoras

²Pythagorean *adjective* (circa 1580)
: of, relating to, or associated with the Greek philosopher Pythagoras, his philosophy, or the Pythagoreans

Py·thag·o·re·an·ism \-'rē-ə-ˌni-zəm\ *noun* (circa 1727)
: the doctrines and theories of Pythagoras and the Pythagoreans who developed some basic principles of mathematics and astronomy, originated the doctrine of the harmony of the spheres, and believed in metempsychosis, the eternal recurrence of things, and the mystical significance of numbers

Pythagorean theorem *noun* (circa 1909)
: a theorem in geometry: the square of the length of the hypotenuse of a right triangle equals the sum of the squares of the lengths of the other two sides

Pyth·i·ad \'pi-thē-ˌad, -əd\ *noun* [Greek *Pythia,* the Pythian games, from neuter plural of *pythios*] (1842)
: the 4-year period between celebrations of the Pythian games in ancient Greece

¹Pyth·i·an \'pi-thē-ən\ *adjective* [Latin *pythius* of Delphi, from Greek *pythios,* from *Pythō* Pytho, name for Delphi, Greece] (1603)
1 : of or relating to games celebrated at Delphi every four years
2 : of or relating to Delphi or its oracle of Apollo

²Pythian *noun* (1903)
: KNIGHT OF PYTHIAS

Pyth·i·as \'pi-thē-əs\ *noun* [Greek]
: a friend of Damon condemned to death by Dionysius of Syracuse

py·thon \'pī-ˌthän, -thən\ *noun* [Latin, monstrous serpent killed by Apollo, from Greek *Pythōn,* from *Pythō* Delphi] (1836)
: any of various large constricting snakes (as a boa); *especially* **:** any of the large oviparous snakes (subfamily Pythoninae of the family Boidae) of Africa, Asia, Australia, and adjacent islands that include some of the largest existing snakes

python

py·tho·ness \'pī-thə-nəs, 'pi-\ *noun* [Middle English *Phitonesse,* from Middle French *pithonisse,* from Late

Latin *pythonissa,* from Greek *Pythōn,* spirit of divination, perhaps from *Pythō,* seat of the Delphic oracle] (14th century)
1 : a woman who practices divination
2 : a prophetic priestess of Apollo
— **py·thon·ic** \pī-'thä-nik\ *adjective*

py·uria \pī-'yür-ē-ə\ *noun* [New Latin] (circa 1811)
: pus in the urine; *also* **:** a condition characterized by pus in the urine

pyx \'piks\ *noun* [Middle English, from Medieval Latin *pyxis,* from Latin, box, from Greek, from *pyxos* box (shrub)] (15th century)
1 : a container for the reserved host; *especially* **:** a small round metal receptacle used to carry the Eucharist to the sick
2 : a box used in a mint for deposit of sample coins reserved for testing weight and fineness

pyx·ie \'pik-sē\ *noun* [by shortening & alteration from New Latin *Pyxidanthera*] (1882)
: a creeping evergreen dicotyledonous shrub (*Pyxidanthera barbulata* of the family Diapensiaceae) of the sandy pine barrens of the Atlantic coast of the U.S. that has white or pink pentamerous flowers

pyx·is \'pik-səs\ *noun, plural* **pyx·i·des** \-sə-ˌdēz\ [New Latin, from Latin, box] (1845)
: a capsular fruit that dehisces so that the upper part falls off like a cap

Q is the seventeenth letter of the English alphabet. It comes from Phoenician qōph, *representing a guttural* k *sound, which survived in a western Greek alphabet as* koppa *and passed through Etruscan and Latin into English as* Q. *In English, as in Latin, this sign is normally used in combination with* u *to represent the sound of* kw, *as in* quiet. *In some English words of French origin, however,* qu *has the sound of plain* k, *as in antique.* Q *seldom appears without* u, *except in the transliteration of the Semitic letter* koph *(Arabic* qāf*), as in Iraq.* Q *is rarely found in Old English, where the usual spelling for the* kw- *sound was* cw *or* cu *(as in* cwēn *"queen").* Qu *became the usual form in Middle English, under the influence of French and Latin. The small form of* q *developed in the late Roman period when scribes began forming the capital letter with one pen stroke, making its tail extend vertically along the right side of the letter.*

q \'kyü\ *noun, plural* **q's** *or* **qs** \'kyüz\ *often capitalized, often attributive* (before 12th century)
1 a : the 17th letter of the English alphabet **b :** a graphic representation of this letter **c :** a speech counterpart of orthographic *q*
2 : a graphic device for reproducing the letter *q*
3 : one designated *q* especially as the 17th in order or class
4 : something shaped like the letter Q

Q–boat \'kyü-ˌbōt\ *noun* (1918)
: Q-SHIP

Q fever \'kyü-\ *noun* [query] (1937)
: a disease that is characterized by high fever, chills, and muscular pains, is caused by a rickettsial bacterium (*Coxiella burnetii*), and is transmitted by raw milk, by droplet infection, or by ticks

qin·tar \kyin-'tär, kin-\ *noun, plural* **qin·dar·ka** \-'där-kə\ *also* **qintars** *or* **qin·dars** \-'därz\ [Albanian] (circa 1929)
— see *lek* at MONEY table

qi·vi·ut \'kē-vē-ət, -vē-ˌüt\ *noun* [Inuit] (1958)
: the wool of the undercoat of the musk ox

qoph \'kōf\ *noun* [Hebrew *qōph*] (circa 1823)
: the 19th letter of the Hebrew alphabet — see ALPHABET table

Q–ship \'kyü-ˌship\ *noun* (1919)
: an armed ship disguised as a merchant or fishing ship to decoy enemy submarines into gun range

q.t. \ˌkyü-'tē\ *noun, often Q&T capitalized* [abbreviation] (circa 1887)
: QUIET — usually used in the phrase *on the q.t.*

qua \'kwä *also* 'kwā\ *preposition* [Latin, which way, as, from ablative singular feminine of *qui* who — more at WHO] (1647)
: in the capacity or character of **:** AS ⟨confusion of the role of scientist *qua* scientist with that of scientist as citizen —Philip Handler⟩

quaa·lude \'kwä-ˌlüd\ *noun* [from *Quaalude*, a trademark] (1966)
: a tablet or capsule of methaqualone

¹quack \'kwak\ *intransitive verb* [alteration of *queck* to quack, from Middle English *queken*, from *queke*, interjection, of imitative origin] (14th century)
: to make the characteristic cry of a duck

²quack *noun* (1839)
: a noise made by quacking

³quack *intransitive verb* [⁴*quack*] (1628)
: to act like a quack

⁴quack *noun* [short for *quacksalver*] (1638)
1 : CHARLATAN
2 : a pretender to medical skill
— **quack·ish** \'kwa-kish\ *adjective*

⁵quack *adjective* (1653)

: of, relating to, or characteristic of a quack; *especially* **:** pretending to cure diseases

quack·ery \'kwa-k(ə-)rē\ *noun* (circa 1711)
: the practices or pretensions of a quack

quack grass \'kwak-\ *noun* [alteration of *quick* (grass), alteration of *quitch* (grass)] (circa 1818)
: a European grass (*Agropyron repens*) that is naturalized throughout North America as a weed and spreads by creeping rhizomes — called also *couch grass, quitch, twitch, witchgrass*

quack·sal·ver \'kwak-ˌsal-vər\ *noun* [obsolete Dutch (now *kwakzalver*)] (1579)
: CHARLATAN, QUACK

¹quad \'kwäd\ *noun* (1820)
: QUADRANGLE

²quad *noun* [short for *quadrat*] (circa 1879)
: a type-metal space that is 1 en or more in width

³quad *transitive verb* **quad·ded; quad·ding** (1888)
: to fill out (as a typeset line) with blank space

⁴quad *noun* (1896)
: QUADRUPLET

⁵quad *adjective* (1970)
: QUADRAPHONIC

⁶quad *noun* (1971)
: quadraphonic sound

⁷quad *noun* [short for *quadrillion*] (1974)
: a unit of energy equal to one quadrillion British thermal units

quad·ran·gle \'kwä-ˌdraŋ-gəl\ *noun* [Middle English, from Middle French, from Late Latin *quadriangulum*, from Latin, neuter of *quadriangulus* quadrangular, from *quadri-* + *angulus* angle] (15th century)
1 : QUADRILATERAL
2 a : a 4-sided enclosure especially when surrounded by buildings **b :** the buildings enclosing a quadrangle
3 : a tract of country represented by one of a series of map sheets (as published by the U.S. Geological Survey)
— **qua·dran·gu·lar** \kwä-'draŋ-gyə-lər\ *adjective*

quad·rant \'kwä-drənt\ *noun* [Middle English, from Latin *quadrant-, quadrans* fourth part; akin to Latin *quattuor* four — more at FOUR] (15th century)
1 a : an instrument for measuring altitudes consisting commonly of a graduated arc of 90 degrees with an index or vernier and usually having a plumb line or spirit level for fixing the vertical or horizontal direc-

tion **b :** a device or mechanical part shaped like or suggestive of the quadrant of a circle
2 a : an arc of 90 degrees that is one quarter of a circle **b :** the area bounded by a quadrant and two radii
3 a : any of the four parts into which a plane is divided by rectangular coordinate axes lying in that plane **b :** any of the four quarters into which something is divided by two real or imaginary lines that intersect each other at right angles
— **qua·dran·tal** \kwä-'dran-t³l\ *adjective*

Qua·dran·tid \kwä-'dran-təd\ *noun* [New Latin in *Quadrant-, Quadrans (Muralis)* mural quadrant, a group of stars in the constellation Draco from which the shower appears to radiate]
: any of a group of meteors that appear annually about January 3

quad·ra·phon·ic *also* **quad·ri·phon·ic** \ˌkwä-drə-'fä-nik\ *adjective* [irregular from *quadri-* + *-phonic* (as in *stereophonic*)] (circa 1970)
: of, relating to, or using four channels for the transmission, recording, or reproduction of sound
— **quad·ra·phon·ics** *or* **quad·ri·phon·ics** \-niks\ *noun plural but singular in construction*

quad·rat \'kwä-drət, -ˌdrat\ *noun* [alteration of ²*quadrate*] (1683)
1 : ²QUAD
2 : a usually rectangular plot used for ecological or population studies

¹quad·rate \'kwä-ˌdrāt, -drət\ *adjective* [Middle English, from Latin *quadratus*, past participle of *quadrare* to make square, fit, from *quadrum* square; akin to Latin *quattuor* four] (14th century)
1 : being square or approximately square
2 : *of a heraldic cross* **:** expanded into a square at the junction of the arms — see CROSS illustration
3 : of, relating to, or constituting a bony or cartilaginous element of each side of the skull to which the lower jaw is articulated in most vertebrates below mammals

²quadrate *noun* (15th century)
1 : an approximately square or cubical area, space, or body
2 : a quadrate bone

qua·drat·ic \kwä-'dra-tik\ *adjective* (1668)
: involving terms of the second degree at most ⟨*quadratic* function⟩ ⟨*quadratic* equations⟩
— **quadratic** *noun*
— **qua·drat·i·cal·ly** \-ti-k(ə-)lē\ *adverb*

quadratic form *noun* (1859)
: a homogeneous polynomial (as $x^2 + 5xy + y^2$) of the second degree

quad·ra·ture \'kwä-drə-ˌchùr, -chər, -ˌtyùr, -ˌtùr\ *noun* (1591)
1 : a configuration in which two celestial bodies (as the moon and the sun) have an angular separation of 90 degrees as seen from the earth
2 : the process of finding a square equal in area to a given area

qua·dren·ni·al \kwä-'dre-nē-əl\ *adjective* (circa 1656)
1 : consisting of or lasting for four years
2 : occurring or being done every four years
— **quadrennial** *noun*
— **qua·dren·ni·al·ly** \-nē-ə-lē\ *adverb*

qua·dren·ni·um \-nē-əm\ *noun, plural* **-ni·ums** *or* **-nia** \-nē-ə\ [Latin *quadriennium*, from *quadri-* + *annus* year — more at ANNUAL] (1754)
: a period of four years

quadri- *or* **quadr-** *or* **quadru-** *combining form* [Middle English, from Latin; akin to Latin *quattuor* four]
1 a : four ⟨*quadri*lateral⟩ ⟨*quadru*manous⟩ **b :** square ⟨*quadri*c⟩
2 : fourth ⟨*quadri*centennial⟩

quad·ric \'kwä-drik\ *adjective* [International Scientific Vocabulary] (1858)

quadrant 2

: QUADRATIC ⟨*quadric* surface⟩ — used where there are more than two variables
— **quadric** *noun*

quad·ri·cen·ten·ni·al \ˌkwä-drə-sen-'te-nē-əl\ *noun* (1882)
: a 400th anniversary or its celebration

quad·ri·ceps \'kwä-drə-ˌseps\ *noun* [New Latin *quadricipit-, quadriceps*, from *quadri-* + *-cipit-, -ceps* (as in *bicipit-, biceps* biceps)] (1840)
: the greater extensor muscle of the front of the thigh that is divided into four parts

qua·dri·ga \kwä-'drē-gə\ *noun, plural* **-gae** \-ˌgī\ [Latin, singular of *quadrigae* team of four, contraction of *quadrijugae*, feminine plural of *quadrijugus* yoked four abreast, from *quadri-* + *jungere* to yoke, join — more at YOKE] (circa 1741)
: a chariot drawn by four horses abreast

¹quad·ri·lat·er·al \ˌkwä-drə-'la-t(ə-)rəl\ *noun* [Latin *quadrilaterus* four-sided, from *quadri-* + *later-, latus* side] (1650)
: a polygon of four sides

²quadrilateral *adjective* (1656)
: having four sides

¹qua·drille \kwä-'dril, kwə-, kə-\ *noun* [French, group of knights engaged in a carousel, from Spanish *cuadrilla* troop, from diminutive of *cuadra* square, from Latin *quadra, quadrum*] (1726)
1 : a four-handed variant of ombre popular especially in the 18th century
2 : a square dance for four couples made up of five or six figures chiefly in ⁶⁄₈ and ²⁄₄ time; *also* : music for this dance

²quadrille *adjective* [French *quadrillé*] (circa 1885)
: marked with squares or rectangles

qua·dril·lion \kwä-'dril-yən\ *noun* [French, from Middle French, from *quadri-* + *-illion* (as in *million*)] (1674)
— see NUMBER table
— **quadrillion** *adjective*
— **qua·dril·lionth** \-yən(t)th\ *adjective or noun*

quad·ri·par·tite \ˌkwä-drə-'pär-ˌtīt\ *adjective* [Middle English, from Latin *quadripartitus*, from *quadri-* + *partitus*, past participle of *partire* to divide, from *part-, pars* part] (15th century)
1 : consisting of or divided into four parts
2 : shared or participated in by four parties or persons ⟨a *quadripartite* agreement⟩

quad·ri·ple·gic \ˌkwä-drə-'plē-jik\ *noun* [*quadriplegia*, from New Latin] (1921)
: one affected with paralysis of both arms and both legs
— **quad·ri·ple·gia** \-j(ē-)ə\ *noun*

¹quad·ri·va·lent \ˌkwä-drə-'vā-lənt, *in sense* 2 'kwä-'dri-və-lənt\ *adjective* [International Scientific Vocabulary] (1865)
1 : TETRAVALENT
2 : composed of four homologous chromosomes synapsed in meiotic prophase

²quadrivalent *noun* (1923)
: a quadrivalent chromosomal group

qua·driv·i·al \kwä-'dri-vē-əl\ *adjective* (15th century)
1 : of or relating to the quadrivium
2 : having four ways or roads meeting in a point

qua·driv·i·um \-vē-əm\ *noun* [Late Latin, from Latin, crossroads, from *quadri-* + *via* way — more at WAY] (1804)
: a group of studies consisting of arithmetic, music, geometry, and astronomy and forming the upper division of the seven liberal arts in medieval universities — compare TRIVIUM

qua·droon \kwä-'drün\ *noun* [modification of Spanish *cuarterón*, from *cuarto* fourth, from Latin *quartus* — more at QUART] (1707)
: a person of one-quarter black ancestry

qua·dru·ma·nous \kwä-'drü-mə-nəs\ *adjective* [ultimately from Latin *quadri-* + *manus* hand — more at MANUAL] (1819)

: of, relating to, or being the primates excluding humans which are distinguished by hand-shaped feet

qua·drum·vir \kwä-'drəm-vər\ *noun* [back-formation from *quadrumvirate*] (1790)
: a member of a quadrumvirate

qua·drum·vi·rate \-və-rət\ *noun* [*quadri-* + *-umvirate* (as in *triumvirate*)] (1752)
: a group or association of four

quad·ru·ped \'kwä-drə-ˌped\ *noun* [Latin *quadruped-, quadrupes*, from *quadruped-, quadrupes*, adjective, having four feet, from *quadri-* + *ped-, pes* foot — more at FOOT] (1646)
: an animal having four feet
— **quadruped** *adjective*
— **qua·dru·pe·dal** \kwä-'drü-pə-d³l, ˌkwä-drə-'pe-\ *adjective*

¹qua·dru·ple \kwä-'drü-pəl, -'drə-; 'kwä-drə-\ *verb* **qua·dru·pled; qua·dru·pling** \-p(ə-)liŋ\ (14th century)
transitive verb
: to make four times as great or as many
intransitive verb
: to become four times as great or as numerous

²quadruple *noun* (15th century)
: a sum four times as great as another

³quadruple *adjective* [Middle French or Latin; Middle French, from Latin *quadruplus*, from *quadri-* + *-plus* multiplied by — more at -FOLD] (1557)
1 : having four units or members
2 : being four times as great or as many
3 : marked by four beats per measure ⟨*quadruple* meter⟩
— **qua·dru·ply** \-'drü-plē, -'drə-, -drə-\ *adverb*
— **qua·dru·plic·i·ty** \ˌkwä-drù-'pli-sə-tē\ *noun*

qua·dru·plet \kwä-'drü-plət, -'drə-; 'kwä-drə-plət\ *noun* (1787)
1 : one of four offspring born at one birth
2 : a combination of four of a kind
3 : a group of four musical notes to be performed in the time ordinarily given to three of the same kind

¹qua·dru·pli·cate \kwä-'drü-pli-kət\ *adjective* [Latin *quadruplicatus*, past participle of *quadruplicare* to quadruple, from *quadruplic-, quadruplex* fourfold, from *quadri-* + *-plic-, -plex* fold — more at -FOLD] (1657)
1 : consisting of or existing in four corresponding or identical parts or examples ⟨*quadruplicate* invoices⟩
2 : being the fourth of four things exactly alike

²qua·dru·pli·cate \-plə-ˌkāt\ *transitive verb* **-cat·ed; -cat·ing** (circa 1661)
1 : to make quadruple or fourfold
2 : to prepare in quadruplicate
— **qua·dru·pli·ca·tion** \-ˌdrü-plə-'kā-shən\ *noun*

³qua·dru·pli·cate \kwä-'drü-pli-kət\ *noun* (1790)
1 : four copies all alike — used with *in* ⟨typed in *quadruplicate*⟩
2 : one of four things exactly alike; *specifically* : one of four identical copies

quad·ru·pole \'kwä-drə-ˌpōl\ *noun* [International Scientific Vocabulary *quadri-* + *pole*] (1922)
: a system composed of two dipoles of equal but oppositely directed moment

quae·re \'kwir-ē, 'kwer-\ *noun* [Latin, imperative of *quaerere* to seek, question] (1589)
archaic : QUERY

quaes·tor \'kwe-stər, 'kwē-\ *noun* [Middle English *questor*, from Latin *quaestor*, from *quaerere*] (14th century)
: one of numerous ancient Roman officials concerned chiefly with financial administration

quaff \'kwäf, 'kwaf\ *verb* [origin unknown] (1523)
intransitive verb
: to drink deeply

transitive verb
: to drink (a beverage) deeply
— **quaff** *noun*
— **quaff·er** *noun*

quag \'kwag, 'kwäg\ *noun* [origin unknown] (1589)
: MARSH, BOG

quag·ga \'kwa-gə, 'kwä-\ *noun* [obsolete Afrikaans (now *kwagga*), from Khoikhoi *quácha*] (1785)
: an extinct mammal (*Equus quagga*) of southern Africa related to the zebras

quag·gy \'kwa-gē, 'kwäg-\ *adjective* (1610)
1 : MARSHY
2 : FLABBY

quag·mire \'kwag-ˌmīr, 'kwäg-\ *noun* (circa 1580)
1 : soft miry land that shakes or yields under the foot
2 : a difficult, precarious, or entrapping position : PREDICAMENT

qua·hog *also* **qua·haug** \'kō-ˌhòg, 'kwò-, 'kwō-, -ˌhäg\ *noun* [Narraganset *poquaûhock*] (1753)
: a thick-shelled edible clam (*Mercenaria mercenaria*) of the U.S.

quai \'kā\ *noun* [French, from Middle French *cai* — more at QUAY] (1862)
: QUAY

quaich *or* **quaigh** \'kwāk\ *noun* [Scottish Gaelic *cuach*] (1546)
chiefly Scottish : a small shallow drinking vessel with ears for use as handles

¹quail \'kwā(ə)l\ *noun, plural* **quail** *or* **quails** [Middle English *quaille*, from Middle French, from Medieval Latin *quaccula*, of imitative origin] (14th century)
: any of numerous small gallinaceous birds: as **a** : an Old World migratory game bird (*Coturnix coturnix*) **b** : BOB-WHITE

quail

²quail *verb* [Middle English, from Middle Dutch *quelen*] (15th century)
intransitive verb
1 **a** *chiefly dialect* : WITHER, DECLINE **b** : to give way : FALTER ⟨his courage never *quailed*⟩
2 : to recoil in dread or terror : COWER ⟨the strongest *quail* before financial ruin —Samuel Butler (died 1902)⟩
transitive verb
archaic : to make fearful
synonym *see* RECOIL

quaint \'kwānt\ *adjective* [Middle English *cointe*, from Old French, from Latin *cognitus*, past participle of *cognoscere* to know — more at COGNITION] (13th century)
1 *obsolete* : EXPERT, SKILLED
2 **a** : marked by skillful design ⟨*quaint* with many a device in India ink —Herman Melville⟩ **b** : marked by beauty or elegance
3 **a** : unusual or different in character or appearance : ODD ⟨figures of fun, *quaint* people —Herman Wouk⟩ **b** : pleasingly or strikingly old-fashioned or unfamiliar
synonym *see* STRANGE
— **quaint·ly** *adverb*
— **quaint·ness** *noun*

¹quake \'kwāk\ *intransitive verb* **quaked; quak·ing** [Middle English, from Old English *cwacian*] (before 12th century)
1 : to shake or vibrate usually from shock or instability
2 : to tremble or shudder usually from cold or fear

²quake *noun* (14th century)

\ə\ **abut** \ᵊ\ **kitten** \ər\ **further** \a\ **ash** \ā\ **ace**
\ä\ **mop, mar** \au̇\ **out** \ch\ **chin** \e\ **bet** \ē\ **easy**
\g\ **go** \i\ **hit** \ī\ **ice** \j\ **job** \ŋ\ **sing**
\ò\ **law** \ȯi\ **boy** \th\ **thin** \t͟h\ **the** \ü\ **loot** \u̇\ **foot**
\y\ **yet** \zh\ **vision** *see also* Guide to Pronunciation

: an instance of shaking or trembling (as of the earth or moon); *especially* : EARTHQUAKE

quak·er \'kwā-kər\ *noun* (1597)
1 : one that quakes
2 *capitalized* : FRIEND 5
— **Quak·er·ish** \-kwā-k(ə-)rish\ *adjective*
— **Quak·er·ism** \-kə-ri-zəm\ *noun*
— **Quak·er·ly** \-kər-lē\ *adjective*

Quaker gun *noun* [from opposition to war as a basic Quaker tenet] (1809)
: a dummy piece of artillery usually made of wood

quak·er·la·dies \,kwā-kər-'lā-dēz\ *noun plural* (1871)
: BLUETS

quaking aspen *noun* (1843)
: an aspen (*Populus tremuloides*) chiefly of the U.S. and Canada that has small nearly circular leaves with flattened petioles and finely serrate margins

qua·le \'kwä-lē, -,lā\ *noun, plural* **qua·lia** \'kwä-lē-ə\ [Latin, neuter of *qualis* of what kind] (1675)
1 : a property (as redness) considered apart from things having the property : UNIVERSAL
2 : a property as it is experienced as distinct from any source it might have in a physical object

qual·i·fi·able \,kwä-lə-'fī-ə-bəl\ *adjective* (1611)
: capable of qualifying or being qualified

qual·i·fi·ca·tion \,kwä-lə-fə-'kā-shən\ *noun* (circa 1544)
1 : a restriction in meaning or application : a limiting modification ⟨this statement stands without *qualification*⟩
2 a *obsolete* : NATURE **b** *archaic* : CHARACTERISTIC
3 a : a quality or skill that fits a person (as for an office) ⟨the applicant with the best *qualifications*⟩ **b** : a condition or standard that must be complied with (as for the attainment of a privilege) ⟨a *qualification* for membership⟩

qual·i·fied \'kwä-lə-fīd\ *adjective* (1558)
1 a : fitted (as by training or experience) for a given purpose : COMPETENT **b** : having complied with the specific requirements or precedent conditions (as for an office or employment) : ELIGIBLE
2 : limited or modified in some way ⟨*qualified* approval⟩
— **qual·i·fied·ly** \-,fī(-ə)d-lē\ *adverb*

qual·i·fi·er \-,fī(-ə)r\ *noun* (1561)
: one that qualifies: as **a** : one that satisfies requirements or meets a specified standard **b** : a word (as an adjective) or word group that limits or modifies the meaning of another word (as a noun) or word group

qual·i·fy \'kwä-lə-,fī\ *verb* **-fied; -fy·ing** [Middle French *qualifier*, from Medieval Latin *qualificare*, from Latin *qualis*] (1533)
transitive verb
1 a : to reduce from a general to a particular or restricted form : MODIFY **b** : to make less harsh or strict : MODERATE **c** : to alter the strength or flavor of **d** : to limit or modify the meaning of (as a noun)
2 : to characterize by naming an attribute : DESCRIBE ⟨cannot *qualify* it as . . . either glad or sorry —T. S. Eliot⟩
3 a : to fit by training, skill, or ability for a special purpose **b** (1) : to declare competent or adequate : CERTIFY (2) : to invest with legal capacity : LICENSE
intransitive verb
1 : to be or become fit (as for an office) : meet the required standard
2 : to acquire legal or competent power or capacity ⟨has just *qualified* as a lawyer⟩
3 a : to exhibit a required degree of ability in a preliminary contest ⟨*qualified* for the finals⟩ **b** : to shoot well enough to earn a marksmanship badge

qual·i·ta·tive \'kwä-lə-,tā-tiv\ *adjective* (1607)
: of, relating to, or involving quality or kind

— **qual·i·ta·tive·ly** *adverb*

qualitative analysis *noun* (1842)
: chemical analysis designed to identify the components of a substance or mixture

¹qual·i·ty \'kwä-lə-tē\ *noun, plural* **-ties** [Middle English *qualite*, from Old French *qualité*, from Latin *qualitat-, qualitas*, from *qualis* of what kind; akin to Latin *qui* who — more at WHO] (14th century)
1 a : peculiar and essential character : NATURE ⟨her ethereal *quality* —Gay Talese⟩ **b** : an inherent feature : PROPERTY ⟨had a *quality* of stridence, dissonance —Roald Dahl⟩ **c** : CAPACITY, ROLE ⟨in the *quality* of reader and companion —Joseph Conrad⟩
2 a : degree of excellence : GRADE ⟨the *quality* of competing air service —*Current Biography*⟩ **b** : superiority in kind ⟨merchandise of *quality*⟩
3 a : social status : RANK **b** : ARISTOCRACY
4 a : a distinguishing attribute : CHARACTERISTIC ⟨possesses many fine *qualities*⟩ **b** *archaic* : an acquired skill : ACCOMPLISHMENT
5 : the character in a logical proposition of being affirmative or negative
6 : vividness of hue
7 a : TIMBRE **b** : the identifying character of a vowel sound determined chiefly by the resonance of the vocal chambers in uttering it
8 : the attribute of an elementary sensation that makes it fundamentally unlike any other sensation ☆

²quality *adjective* (1701)
: being of high quality

quality assurance *noun* (1982)
: a program for the systematic monitoring and evaluation of the various aspects of a project, service, or facility to ensure that standards of quality are being met

quality circle *noun* (1980)
: a group of employees who volunteer to meet regularly to discuss and propose solutions to problems (as of quality or productivity) in the workplace

quality control *noun* (1935)
: an aggregate of activities (as design analysis and inspection for defects) designed to ensure adequate quality especially in manufactured products
— **quality controller** *noun*

quality point *noun* (1948)
: GRADE POINT

quality point average *noun* (circa 1972)
: GRADE POINT AVERAGE

qualm \'kwäm *also* 'kwȯm *or* 'kwälm\ *noun* [origin unknown] (circa 1530)
1 : a sudden attack of illness, faintness, or nausea
2 : a sudden access of usually disturbing emotion (as doubt or fear)
3 : a feeling of uneasiness about a point especially of conscience or propriety ☆
— **qualmy** *adjective*

qualm·ish \'kwä-mish *also* 'kwȯ- *or* 'kwäl-\ *adjective* (1548)
1 a : feeling qualms : NAUSEATED **b** : overly scrupulous : SQUEAMISH
2 : of, relating to, or producing qualms
— **qualm·ish·ly** *adverb*
— **qualm·ish·ness** *noun*

qua·mash \'kwä-mish\ *variant of* CAMAS

quan·da·ry \'kwän-d(ə-)rē\ *noun, plural* **-ries** [origin unknown] (1579)
: a state of perplexity or doubt

quan·tal \'kwän-tᵊl\ *adjective* (1933)
1 [Latin *quanti* how many, plural of *quantus*] : of, relating to, or having only two experimental alternatives (as dead or alive, all or none)
2 [*quantum*] : of or relating to a quantum

quan·ti·fi·ca·tion \,kwän-tə-fə-'kā-shən\ *noun* (circa 1840)
: the operation of quantifying
— **quan·ti·fi·ca·tion·al** \-shnəl, -shə-nᵊl\ *adjective*
— **quan·ti·fi·ca·tion·al·ly** *adverb*

quan·ti·fi·er \'kwän-tə-,fī(-ə)r\ *noun* (1876)
: one that quantifies: as **a** : a prefixed operator that binds the variables in a logical formula by specifying their quantity **b** : a limiting noun modifier (as *five* in "the five young men") expressive of quantity and characterized by occurrence before the descriptive adjectives in a noun phrase

quan·ti·fy \-,fī\ *transitive verb* **-fied; -fy·ing** [Medieval Latin *quantificare*, from Latin *quantus* how much] (circa 1840)
1 a (1) : to limit by a quantifier (2) : to bind by prefixing a quantifier **b** : to make explicit the logical quantity of
2 : to determine, express, or measure the quantity of
— **quan·ti·fi·able** \,kwän-tə-'fī-ə-bəl\ *adjective*

quan·ti·tate \'kwän-tə-,tāt\ *transitive verb* **-tat·ed; -tat·ing** [back-formation from *quantitative*] (1927)
1 : to measure or estimate the quantity of; *especially* : to measure or determine precisely
2 : to express in quantitative terms
— **quan·ti·ta·tion** \,kwän-tə-'tā-shən\ *noun*

quan·ti·ta·tive \'kwän-tə-,tā-tiv\ *adjective* [Medieval Latin *quantitativus*, from Latin *quantitat-, quantitas* quantity] (1581)
1 : of, relating to, or expressible in terms of quantity
2 : of, relating to, or involving the measurement of quantity or amount
3 : based on quantity; *specifically, of classical verse* : based on temporal quantity or duration of sounds
— **quan·ti·ta·tive·ly** *adverb*
— **quan·ti·ta·tive·ness** *noun*

quantitative analysis *noun* (circa 1847)
: chemical analysis designed to determine the amounts or proportions of the components of a substance

quantitative inheritance *noun* (circa 1929)
: genic inheritance of a character (as human skin color) controlled by polygenes

quan·ti·ty \'kwän-tə-tē\ *noun, plural* **-ties** [Middle English *quantite*, from Middle French *quantité*, from Latin *quantitat-, quantitas*, from *quantus* how much, how large; akin to Latin *quam* how, as, *quando* when, *qui* who — more at WHO] (14th century)

1 a : an indefinite amount or number **b :** a determinate or estimated amount **c :** total amount or number **d :** a considerable amount or number — often used in plural ⟨generous *quantities* of luck —H. E. Putsch⟩
2 a : the aspect in which a thing is measurable in terms of greater, less, or equal or of increasing or decreasing magnitude **b :** the subject of a mathematical operation **c :** an individual considered with respect to a given situation ⟨an unknown *quantity* . . . as attorney general —Tom Wicker⟩
3 a : duration and intensity of speech sounds as distinct from their individual quality or phonemic character; *specifically* : the relative length or brevity of a prosodic syllable in some languages (as Greek and Latin) **b :** the relative duration or time length of a speech sound or sound sequence
4 : the character of a logical proposition as being universal, particular, or singular

quantity theory *noun* (1888)
: a theory in economics: changes in the price level tend to vary directly with the amount of money in circulation and the rate of its circulation

quan·tize \ˈkwän-ˌtīz\ *transitive verb* **quantized; quan·tiz·ing** [*quantum*] (1922)
1 : to subdivide (as energy) into small but measurable increments
2 : to calculate or express in terms of quantum mechanics
— **quan·ti·za·tion** \ˌkwän-tə-ˈzā-shən\ *noun*
— **quan·tiz·er** \ˈkwän-ˌtī-zər\ *noun*

¹quan·tum \ˈkwän-təm\ *noun, plural* **quanta** \ˈkwän-tə\ [Latin, neuter of *quantus* how much] (1567)
1 a : QUANTITY, AMOUNT **b :** PORTION, PART **c :** gross quantity : BULK
2 a : any of the very small increments or parcels into which many forms of energy are subdivided **b :** any of the small subdivisions of a quantized physical magnitude (as magnetic moment)

²quantum *adjective* (1942)
: LARGE, SIGNIFICANT ⟨a *quantum* improvement⟩

quantum chromodynamics *noun plural but singular in construction* (1975)
: a theory of fundamental particles based on the assumption that quarks are distinguished by differences in color and are held together (as in hadrons) by an exchange of gluons

quantum electrodynamics *noun plural but usually singular in construction* (1927)
: quantum mechanics applied to electrical interactions (as between nuclear particles)

quantum field theory *noun* (1948)
: a theory in physics: the interaction of two separate physical systems (as particles) is attributed to a field that extends from one to the other and is manifested in a particle exchange between the two systems

quantum jump *noun* (1926)
1 : an abrupt transition (as of an electron, an atom, or a molecule) from one discrete energy state to another
2 : QUANTUM LEAP

quantum leap *noun* (1956)
: an abrupt change, sudden increase, or dramatic advance

quantum mechanics *noun plural but singular or plural in construction* (1922)
: a theory of matter that is based on the concept of the possession of wave properties by elementary particles, that affords a mathematical interpretation of the structure and interactions of matter on the basis of these properties, and that incorporates within it quantum theory and the uncertainty principle — called also *wave mechanics*
— **quantum mechanical** *adjective*
— **quantum mechanically** *adverb*

quantum number *noun* (1902)
: any of a set of integers or half odd integers that indicate the magnitude of various discrete

quantities (as electric charge) of a particle or system and that serve to define its state

quantum theory *noun* (1912)
: a theory in physics based on the concept of the subdivision of radiant energy into finite quanta and applied to numerous processes involving transference or transformation of energy in an atomic or molecular scale

¹quar·an·tine \ˈkwȯr-ən-ˌtēn, ˈkwär-\ *noun* [partly modification of French *quarantaine*, from Old French, from *quarante* forty, from Latin *quadraginta*, from *quadra-* (akin to *quattuor* four) + *-ginta* (akin to *viginti* twenty); partly modification of Italian *quarantena* quarantine of a ship, from *quaranta* forty, from Latin *quadraginta* — more at FOUR, VIGESIMAL] (1609)
1 : a period of 40 days
2 a : a term during which a ship arriving in port and suspected of carrying contagious disease is held in isolation from the shore **b :** a regulation placing a ship in quarantine **c :** a place where a ship is detained during quarantine
3 a : a restraint upon the activities or communication of persons or the transport of goods designed to prevent the spread of disease or pests **b :** a place in which those under quarantine are kept
4 : a state of enforced isolation

²quarantine *verb* **-tined; -tin·ing** (1804)
transitive verb
1 : to detain in or exclude by quarantine
2 : to isolate from normal relations or communication ⟨*quarantine* an aggressor⟩
intransitive verb
: to establish or declare a quarantine

quare \ˈkwar, ˈkwer, ˈkwär\ *dialect variant of* ¹QUEER

quark \ˈkwȯrk, ˈkwärk\ *noun* [coined by Murray Gell-Mann] (1964)
: any of several elementary particles that are postulated to come in pairs (as in the up and down varieties) of similar mass with one member having a charge of $+\frac{2}{3}$ and the other a charge of $-\frac{1}{3}$ and are held to make up hadrons ◇

¹quar·rel \ˈkwȯr(-ə)l, ˈkwär(-ə)l\ *noun* [Middle English, from Old French, square-headed arrow, building stone, from (assumed) Vulgar Latin *quadrellum*, diminutive of Latin *quadrum* square — more at QUADRATE] (13th century)
: a square-headed bolt or arrow especially for a crossbow

²quarrel *noun* [Middle English *querele*, from Middle French, complaint, from Latin *querela*, from *queri* to complain] (14th century)
1 : a ground of dispute or complaint ⟨have no *quarrel* with a different approach⟩
2 : a usually verbal conflict between antagonists : ALTERCATION

³quarrel *intransitive verb* **-reled** *or* **-relled; -rel·ing** *or* **-rel·ling** (14th century)
1 : to find fault ⟨many people *quarrel* with the idea —*Johns Hopkins Magazine*⟩
2 : to contend or dispute actively ⟨*quarreled* frequently with his superiors —*London Calling*⟩
— **quar·rel·er** *or* **quar·rel·ler** *noun*

quar·rel·some \ˈkwȯr(-ə)l-səm, ˈkwär(-ə)l-\ *adjective* (1596)
: apt or disposed to quarrel in an often petty manner : CONTENTIOUS
synonym see BELLIGERENT
— **quar·rel·some·ly** *adverb*
— **quar·rel·some·ness** *noun*

quar·ri·er \ˈkwȯr-ē-ər, ˈkwär-\ *noun* (14th century)
: a worker in a stone quarry

¹quar·ry \ˈkwȯr-ē, ˈkwär-\ *noun, plural* **quarries** [Middle English *querre* entrails of game given to the hounds, from Middle French *cuiree*, from *cuir* skin, hide (on which the entrails were placed), from Latin *corium* — more at CUIRASS] (14th century)

1 *obsolete* : a heap of the game killed in a hunt
2 : GAME; *specifically* : game hunted with hawks
3 : one that is sought or pursued : PREY ◇

²quarry *noun, plural* **quarries** [Middle English *quarey*, alteration of *quarrere*, from Middle French *quarriere*, from (assumed) Old French *quarre* squared stone, from Latin *quadrum* square] (14th century)
1 : an open excavation usually for obtaining building stone, slate, or limestone
2 : a rich source

³quarry *verb* **quar·ried; quar·ry·ing** (1774)
transitive verb
1 : to dig or take from or as if from a quarry ⟨*quarry* marble⟩
2 : to make a quarry in ⟨*quarry* a hill⟩
intransitive verb
: to delve in or as if in a quarry

⁴quarry *noun, plural* **quarries** [alteration of ¹*quarrel*] (1555)
: a diamond-shaped pane of glass, stone, or tile

quarrying *noun* (circa 1828)
: the business, occupation, or act of extracting useful material (as building stone) from quarries

quar·ry·man \ˈkwȯr-ē-mən, ˈkwär-\ *noun* (15th century)
: QUARRIER

quart \ˈkwȯrt\ *noun* [Middle English, one fourth of a gallon, from Middle French *quarte*,

\ə\ abut \ˀ\ kitten \ər\ further \a\ ash \ā\ ace \ä\ mop, mar \au̇\ out \ch\ chin \e\ bet \ē\ easy \g\ go \i\ hit \ī\ ice \j\ job \ŋ\ sing \ō\ go \ȯ\ law \ȯi\ boy \th\ thin \t̲h̲\ the \ü\ loot \u̇\ foot \y\ yet \zh\ vision *see also* Guide to Pronunciation

from Old French, from feminine of *quart,* adjective, fourth, from Latin *quartus;* akin to Latin *quattuor* four — more at FOUR] (14th century)
1 — see WEIGHT table
2 : a vessel or measure having a capacity of one quart

¹quar·tan \'kwȯr-t°n\ *adjective* [Middle English *quarteyne,* from Middle French *(fievre) quartaine* quartan fever, from Latin *(febris) quartana,* from *quartanus* of the fourth, from *quartus*] (14th century)
: occurring every fourth day reckoning inclusively; *specifically* **:** recurring at approximately 72-hour intervals

²quartan *noun* (14th century)
: an intermittent fever that recurs at approximately 72-hour intervals; *especially* **:** a quartan malaria

¹quar·ter \'kwȯ(r)-tər *also* 'kȯ(r)-\ *noun* [Middle English, from Old French *quartier,* from Latin *quartarius,* from *quartus* fourth] (14th century)
1 : one of four equal parts into which something is divisible **:** a fourth part ⟨in the top *quarter* of his class⟩
2 : any of various units of capacity or weight equal to or derived from one fourth of some larger unit
3 : any of various units of length or area equal to one fourth of some larger unit
4 : the fourth part of a measure of time: as **a :** one of a set of four 3-month divisions of a year ⟨business was up during the third *quarter*⟩ **b :** a school term of about 12 weeks **c :** QUARTER HOUR ⟨a *quarter* after three⟩
5 a : a coin worth a quarter of a dollar **b :** the sum of 25 cents
6 a : one limb of a quadruped with the adjacent parts; *especially* **:** one fourth part of the carcass of a slaughtered animal including a leg **b** *plural, British* **:** HINDQUARTER 2
7 a : the region or direction lying under any of the four divisions of the horizon **b :** one of the four parts into which the horizon is divided or the cardinal point corresponding to it **c :** a compass point or direction other than the cardinal points **d** (1) **:** an unspecified person or group ⟨financial help from many *quarters* —*Current Biography*⟩ (2) **:** a point, direction, or place not definitely identified ⟨the view to the rear *quarter* —*Consumer Reports*⟩
8 a : a division or district of a town or city ⟨he describes the immigrant *quarter* —Alfred Kazin⟩ **b :** the inhabitants of such a quarter
9 a : an assigned station or post **b** *plural* **:** an assembly of a ship's company for ceremony, drill, or emergency **c** *plural* **:** living accommodations **:** LODGINGS ⟨show you to your *quarters*⟩
10 : merciful consideration of an opponent; *specifically* **:** the clemency of not killing a defeated enemy
11 : a fourth part of the moon's period
12 : the side of a horse's hoof between the toe and the heel — see HOOF illustration
13 a : any of the four parts into which a heraldic field is divided **b :** a bearing or charge occupying the first fourth part of a heraldic field
14 : the state of two machine parts that are exactly at right angles to one another or are spaced about a circle so as to subtend a right angle at the center of the circle
15 a : the stern area of a ship's side **b :** the part of the yardarm outside the slings
16 : one side of the upper of a shoe or boot from heel to vamp
17 : one of the four equal periods into which the playing time of some games is divided

²quarter (14th century)
transitive verb
1 a : to cut or divide into four equal or nearly equal parts ⟨*quarter* an apple⟩ ⟨condemned to be hanged, drawn, and *quartered*⟩ **b** *archaic* **:** DIVIDE
2 : to provide with lodging or shelter

3 : to crisscross (an area) in many directions
4 a : to arrange or bear (as different coats of arms) quarterly on one escutcheon **b :** to add (a coat of arms) to others on one escutcheon **c :** to divide (a shield) into distinct sections (as by stripes)
5 : to adjust or locate (as cranks) at right angles in a machine
intransitive verb
1 : LODGE, DWELL
2 : to crisscross a district
3 : to change from one quarter to another ⟨the moon *quarters*⟩
4 : to strike on a ship's quarter ⟨the wind was *quartering*⟩

³quarter *adjective* (14th century)
: consisting of or equal to a quarter

quar·ter·age \'kwȯ(r)-tə-rij\ *noun* (14th century)
: a quarterly payment, tax, wage, or allowance

¹quar·ter·back \'kwȯ(r)-tər-,bak\ *noun* (1879)
1 : an offensive back in football who usually lines up behind the center, calls the signals, and directs the offensive play of the team
2 : one who gives direction and leadership

²quarterback (1944)
transitive verb
1 : to direct the offensive play of (as a football team)
2 : to give executive direction to **:** BOSS ⟨*quarterbacked* the original buying syndicate —*Time*⟩
intransitive verb
: to play quarterback

quarterback sneak *noun* (circa 1923)
: a usually quick run with the ball by a quarterback into the middle of the offensive line

quar·ter–bound \'kwȯ(r)-tər-'baùnd\ *adjective* (circa 1888)
of a book **:** bound in material of two qualities with the material of better quality on the spine only
— **quarter binding** *noun*

quarter day *noun* (15th century)
chiefly British **:** the day which begins a quarter of the year and on which a quarterly payment often falls due

quar·ter·deck \'kwȯ(r)-tər-,dek\ *noun* (1627)
1 : the stern area of a ship's upper deck
2 : a part of a deck on a naval vessel set aside by the captain for ceremonial and official use

¹quar·ter·fi·nal \,kwȯ(r)-tər-'fī-n°l\ *noun* (1927)
1 *plural* **:** a quarterfinal round
2 : a quarterfinal match
— **quar·ter·fi·nal·ist** \-n°l-ist\ *noun*

²quarterfinal *adjective* (circa 1934)
1 : immediately preceding the semifinal in an elimination tournament
2 : of or participating in a quarterfinal

quarter horse *noun* [from its high speed for distances up to a quarter of a mile] (1834)
: any of a breed of compact muscular saddle horses characterized by great endurance and by high speed for short distances

quarter horse

quarter hour *noun* (1883)
1 : any of the quarter points of an hour
2 : fifteen minutes
3 : a unit of academic credit representing an hour of class (as lecture class) or three hours of laboratory work each week for an academic quarter

¹quar·ter·ing \'kwȯ(r)-tə-riŋ\ *noun* (15th century)
1 a : the division of an escutcheon containing different coats of arms into four or more com-

partments **b :** a quarter of an escutcheon or the coat of arms on it
2 : a line of usually noble or distinguished ancestry

²quartering *adjective* (circa 1692)
1 : coming from a point well abaft the beam of a ship but not directly astern ⟨*quartering* waves⟩
2 : lying at right angles

¹quar·ter·ly \'kwȯ(r)-tər-lē\ *adverb* (14th century)
1 : in heraldic quarters or quarterings
2 : at 3-month intervals

²quarterly *adjective* (15th century)
1 : computed for or payable at 3-month intervals ⟨*quarterly* premium⟩
2 : recurring, issued, or spaced at 3-month intervals
3 : divided into heraldic quarters or compartments

³quarterly *noun, plural* **-lies** (1830)
: a periodical published four times a year

Quarterly Meeting *noun* (1675)
: an organizational unit of the Society of Friends usually composed of several Monthly Meetings

quar·ter·mas·ter \'kwȯ(r)-tər-,mas-tər\ *noun* (15th century)
1 : a petty officer who attends to a ship's helm, binnacle, and signals
2 : an army officer who provides clothing and subsistence for a body of troops

quar·tern \'kwȯ(r)-tərn\ *noun* [Middle English *quarteron,* from Old French, quarter of a pound, quarter of a hundred, from *quartier* quarter] (14th century)
: a fourth part (as of a unit of measurement)

quarter note *noun* (1763)
: a musical note with the time value of ¼ of a whole note — see NOTE illustration

quarter rest *noun* (circa 1890)
: a musical rest corresponding in time value to a quarter note — see REST illustration

quar·ter·sawn \'kwȯ(r)-tər-'sȯn\ *also* **quar·ter·sawed** \-'sȯd\ *adjective* (circa 1890)
: sawed from quartered logs so that the annual rings are nearly at right angles to the wide face — used of boards and planks

quarter section *noun* (1804)
: a tract of land that is half a mile square and contains 160 acres in the U.S. government system of land surveying

quarter sessions *noun plural* (1577)
: a former English local court with limited original and appellate criminal and sometimes civil jurisdiction and often administrative functions held quarterly usually by two justices of the peace in a county or by a recorder in a borough

quar·ter·staff \'kwȯ(r)-tər-,staf\ *noun, plural* **-staves** \-,stavz, -,stāvz\ (1550)
: a long stout staff formerly used as a weapon and wielded with one hand in the middle and the other between the middle and the end

quarter tone *noun* (circa 1776)
1 : a musical interval of one half a semitone
2 : a tone at an interval of one quarter tone

quar·tet *also* **quar·tette** \kwȯr-'tet\ *noun* [Italian *quartetto,* from *quarto* fourth, from Latin *quartus* — more at QUART] (1773)
1 : a musical composition for four instruments or voices
2 : a group or set of four; *especially* **:** the performers of a quartet

quar·tic \'kwȯr-tik\ *adjective* [Latin *quartus* fourth] (circa 1890)
: of the fourth degree ⟨*quartic* equation⟩
— **quartic** *noun*

quar·tile \'kwȯr-,tīl, -t°l\ *noun* [International Scientific Vocabulary, from Latin *quartus*] (1879)
: any of the three values that divide the items of a frequency distribution into four classes with each containing one fourth of the total population; *also* **:** any one of the four classes

quar·to \'kwȯr-(ˌ)tō\ *noun, plural* **quartos** [Latin, ablative of *quartus* fourth] (1589)
1 : the size of a piece of paper cut four from a sheet; *also* : paper or a page of this size
2 : a book printed on quarto pages

quartz \'kwȯrts\ *noun* [German *Quarz*] (circa 1631)
1 : a mineral consisting of silicon dioxide occurring in colorless and transparent or colored hexagonal crystals or in crystalline masses
2 : a quartz crystal that when placed in an electric field oscillates at a constant frequency and is used to control devices which require precise regulation ⟨a *quartz* watch⟩
— **quartz·ose** \'kwȯrt-ˌsōs\ *adjective*

quartz glass *noun* (1903)
: vitreous silica prepared from pure quartz and noted for its transparency to ultraviolet radiation

quartz heater *noun* (1980)
: a portable electric radiant heater that has heating elements sealed in quartz-glass tubes producing infrared radiation in front of a reflective backing

quartz–iodine lamp *noun* (circa 1964)
: an incandescent lamp that has a quartz bulb and a tungsten filament with the bulb containing iodine which reacts with the vaporized tungsten to prevent excessive blackening of the bulb

quartz·ite \'kwȯrt-ˌsīt\ *noun* [International Scientific Vocabulary] (circa 1847)
: a compact granular rock composed of quartz and derived from sandstone by metamorphism
— **quartz·it·ic** \kwȯrt-'si-tik\ *adjective*

qua·sar \'kwā-ˌzär *also* -ˌsär\ *noun* [*quasistellar*] (1964)
: any of a class of celestial objects that resemble stars but whose large redshift and apparent brightness imply extreme distance and huge energy output

¹**quash** \'kwäsh, 'kwȯsh\ *transitive verb* [Middle English *quashen* to smash, from Middle French *quasser, casser,* from Latin *quassare* to shake violently, shatter, frequentative of *quatere* to shake] (13th century)
: to suppress or extinguish summarily and completely ⟨*quash* a rebellion⟩

²**quash** *transitive verb* [Middle English *quassen,* from Middle French *casser, quasser* to annul, from Late Latin *cassare,* from Latin *cassus* void] (14th century)
: to nullify especially by judicial action ⟨*quash* an indictment⟩

qua·si \'kwā-ˌzī, -ˌsī; 'kwä-zē, -sē\ *adjective* [*quasi-*] (1642)
1 : having some resemblance usually by possession of certain attributes ⟨a *quasi* corporation⟩
2 : having a legal status only by operation or construction of law and without reference to intent ⟨a *quasi* contract⟩

quasi- *combining form* [Latin *quasi* as if, as it were, approximately, from *quam* as + *si* if — more at QUANTITY, SO]
1 : in some sense or degree ⟨*quasi*periodic⟩
2 : resembling in some degree ⟨*quasi*particle⟩

qua·si–ju·di·cial \ˌkwā-ˌzī-jü-'di-shəl, -ˌsī-, ˌkwä-zē-, -sē-\ *adjective* (1836)
1 : having a partly judicial character by possession of the right to hold hearings on and conduct investigations into disputed claims and alleged infractions of rules and regulations and to make decisions in the general manner of courts ⟨*quasi-judicial* bodies⟩
2 : essentially judicial in character but not within the judicial power or function especially as constitutionally defined ⟨*quasi-judicial* review⟩
— **qua·si–ju·di·cial·ly** \-'di-sh(ə-)lē\ *adverb*

qua·si–leg·is·la·tive \-'le-jəs-ˌlā-tiv\ *adjective* (circa 1934)
1 : having a partly legislative character by possession of the right to make rules and regulations having the force of law ⟨a *quasi-legislative* agency⟩
2 : essentially legislative in character but not within the legislative power or function especially as constitutionally defined ⟨*quasi-legislative* powers⟩

Qua·si·mo·do \ˌkwä-si-'mō-(ˌ)dō, ˌkwä-zi-\ *noun* [Medieval Latin *quasi modo geniti infantes* as newborn babes (words of the introit for Low Sunday)] (circa 1847)
: LOW SUNDAY

qua·si·par·ti·cle \ˌkwā-ˌzī-'pär-ti-kəl, -ˌsī-, ˌkwä-zē-, -sē-\ *noun* (1957)
: a composite entity (as a vibration in a solid) that is analogous in its behavior to a single particle

qua·si·pe·ri·od·ic \-ˌpir-ē-'ä-dik\ *adjective* (circa 1890)
: almost but not quite periodic; *especially* : periodic on a small scale but unpredictable at some larger scale
— **qua·si·pe·ri·od·ic·i·ty** \-ˌpir-ē-ə-'di-sə-tē\ *noun*

qua·si–pub·lic \-'pə-blik\ *adjective* (1888)
: essentially public (as in services rendered) although under private ownership or control

qua·si–stel·lar object \-'ste-lər-\ *noun* (1964)
: QUASAR

quas·sia \'kwä-shə\ *noun* [New Latin, genus name of a South American tree, from *Quassi* 18th century Surinam slave who discovered the medicinal value of quassia] (1770)
: a drug from the heartwood of various tropical trees of the ailanthus family used especially as a bitter tonic and remedy for roundworms in children and as an insecticide

qua·ter·cen·te·na·ry \ˌkwä-tər-sen-'te-nə-rē, -'sen-tᵊn-ˌer-ē, -sen-'tē-nə-rē\ *noun* [Latin *quater* four times + English *centenary* — more at QUATERNION] (1883)
: a year marking a 400th anniversary

¹**qua·ter·na·ry** \'kwä-tə(r)-ˌner-ē, kwə-'tər-nə-rē\ *adjective* [Latin *quaternarius,* from *quaterni* four each] (1605)
1 a : of, relating to, or consisting of four units or members **b** : of, relating to, or being a number system with a base of four
2 *capitalized* : of, relating to, or being the geological period from the end of the Tertiary to the present time or the corresponding system of rocks — see GEOLOGIC TIME table
3 : consisting of, containing, or being an atom bonded to four other atoms

²**quaternary** *noun, plural* **-ries** (1880)
1 *capitalized* : the Quaternary period or system of rocks
2 : a member of a group fourth in order or rank

quaternary ammonium compound *noun* (circa 1934)
: any of numerous strong bases and their salts derived from ammonium by replacement of the hydrogen atoms with organic radicals and important especially as surface-active agents, disinfectants, and textile

qua·ter·ni·on \kwə-'tər-nē-ən, kwä-\ *noun* [Middle English *quaternyoun,* from Late Latin *quaternion-, quaternio,* from Latin *quaterni* four each, from *quater* four times; akin to Latin *quattuor* four — more at FOUR] (14th century)
1 : a set of four parts, things, or persons
2 a : a generalized complex number that is composed of a real number and a vector and that depends on one real and three imaginary units **b** *plural* : the calculus of quaternions

qua·ter·ni·ty \kwə-'tər-nə-tē, kwä-\ *noun, plural* **-ties** [Late Latin *quaternitas,* from Latin *quaterni* four each] (1529)
: a union of a group or set of four

qua·train \'kwä-ˌtrān, kwä-'\ *noun* [Middle French, from *quatre* four, from Latin *quattuor*] (1582)
: a unit or group of four lines of verse

qua·tre·foil \'ka-tər-ˌfȯil, 'ka-trə-\ *noun* [Middle English *quaterfoil* set of four leaves, from Middle French *quatre* + Middle English *-foil* (as in *trefoil*)] (15th century)
1 : a conventionalized representation of a flower with four petals or of a leaf with four leaflets
2 : a 4-lobed foliation in architecture

quat·tro·cen·to \ˌkwä-trō-'chen-(ˌ)tō\ *noun, often capitalized* [Italian, literally, four hundred, from *quattro* four (from Latin *quattuor*) + *cento* hundred — more at CINQUECENTO] (circa 1854)
: the 15th century especially with reference to Italian literature and art

quat·tu·or·de·cil·lion \ˌkwä-tə-ˌwȯr-di-'sil-yən\ *noun, often attributive* [Latin *quattuordecim* fourteen (from *quattuor* four + *decem* ten) + English *-illion* (as in *million*) — more at TEN] (circa 1903)
— see NUMBER table

¹**qua·ver** \'kwā-vər\ *verb* **qua·vered; qua·ver·ing** \'kwā-və-riŋ, 'kwāv-riŋ\ [Middle English, frequentative of *quaven* to tremble] (15th century)
intransitive verb
1 : TREMBLE
2 : TRILL
3 : to utter sound in tremulous tones
transitive verb
: to utter quaveringly
— **qua·ver·ing·ly** *adverb*
— **qua·very** \'kwā-və-rē, 'kwāv-rē\ *adjective*

²**quaver** *noun* (1570)
1 : EIGHTH NOTE
2 : TRILL 1
3 : a tremulous sound

quay \'kē, 'kā, 'kwā\ *noun* [alteration of earlier *key,* from Middle English, from Middle French dialect *cai,* probably of Celtic origin; akin to Breton *kae* hedge, enclosure; akin to Old English *hecg* hedge] (1696)
: a structure built parallel to the bank of a waterway for use as a landing place

quay·age \-ij\ *noun* (circa 1756)
1 : a charge for use of a quay
2 : room on or for quays
3 : a system of quays

quay·side \-ˌsīd\ *noun* (1903)
: land bordering a quay

quean \'kwēn, 'kwän\ *noun* [Middle English *quene,* from Old English *cwene;* akin to Old English *cwēn* woman, queen] (before 12th century)
1 : a disreputable woman; *specifically* : PROSTITUTE
2 *chiefly Scottish* : WOMAN; *especially* : one that is young or unmarried

quea·sy *also* **quea·zy** \'kwē-zē\ *adjective* **quea·si·er; -est** [Middle English *coysy, qwesye*] (15th century)
1 a : causing nausea ⟨*queasy* motion⟩ **b** : suffering from nausea : NAUSEATED
2 : full of doubt : HAZARDOUS
3 a : causing uneasiness **b** (1) : DELICATE, SQUEAMISH (2) : ill at ease
— **quea·si·ly** \-zə-lē\ *adverb*
— **quea·si·ness** \-zē-nəs\ *noun*

Que·bec \kwi-'bek *also* ki-\ (1952)
— a communications code word for the letter *q*

Que·be·cois *or* **Qué·be·cois** *or* **Qué·be·cois** \ˌkā-bə-'kwä, -ˌbe-\ *noun, plural* **Que·be·cois** *or* **Qué·bé·cois** *or* **Qué·be·cois** \-'kwä(z)\ [French *québecois, québécois,* from *Québec* Quebec] (1873)
: a native or inhabitant of Quebec; *specifically* : a French-speaking native or inhabitant of Quebec

— Quebecois or **Québécois** or **Québecois** adjective

que·bra·cho \kā-'brä-(ˌ)chō, ki-\ noun [American Spanish, alteration of quiebracha, from Spanish quiebra it breaks + hacha ax] (circa 1881)
1 : any of several trees of southern South America with hard wood: as **a :** a tree (Aspidosperma quebracho) of the dogbane family which occurs in Argentina and Chile and whose dried bark is used as a respiratory sedative in dyspnea and in asthma **b :** a chiefly Argentine tree (Schinopsis lorentzii) of the cashew family with dense wood rich in tannins **2 a :** the wood of a quebracho **b :** a tannin-rich extract of the Argentine quebracho used in tanning leather

Que·chua \'ke-chə-wə, 'kech-wə\ noun, plural **Quechua** or **Quechuas** [Spanish, probably from Southern Peruvian Quechua qheswa (simi), literally, valley speech] (1840)
1 : a family of languages spoken by Indian peoples of Peru, Bolivia, Ecuador, Chile, and Argentina
2 a : a member of an Indian people of central Peru **b :** a group of peoples forming the dominant element of the Inca Empire
— Que·chu·an \-wən\ adjective or noun

¹queen \'kwēn\ noun [Middle English quene, from Old English cwēn woman, wife, queen; akin to Gothic qens wife, Greek gynē woman, Sanskrit jani] (before 12th century)
1 a : the wife or widow of a king **b :** the wife or widow of a tribal chief
2 a : a female monarch **b :** a female chieftain
3 a : a woman eminent in rank, power, or attractions ⟨a movie queen⟩ **b :** a goddess or a thing personified as female and having supremacy in a specified realm **c :** an attractive girl or woman; especially : a beauty contest winner
4 : the most privileged piece of each color in a set of chessmen having the power to move in any direction across any number of unoccupied squares
5 : a playing card marked with a stylized figure of a queen
6 : the fertile fully developed female of social bees, ants, and termites whose function is to lay eggs
7 : a mature female cat kept especially for breeding
8 : a male homosexual; especially : an effeminate one — often used disparagingly

²queen (1611)
intransitive verb
1 : to act like a queen; especially : to put on airs — usually used with it ⟨queens it over her friends⟩
2 : to become a queen in chess
transitive verb
: to promote (a pawn) to a queen in chess

Queen Anne \-'an\ adjective [Queen Anne of England] (1863)
1 : of, relating to, or having the characteristics of a style of furniture originating in England under Dutch influence especially during the first half of the 18th century that is marked by extensive use of upholstery, marquetry, and oriental fabrics
2 : of, relating to, or having the characteristics of a style of English building of the early 18th century characterized by modified classic ornament and the use of red brickwork in which even relief ornament is carved

Queen Anne's lace noun (1895)
: a widely naturalized Eurasian biennial herb (Daucus carota) which has a whitish acrid taproot and from which the cultivated carrot originated — called also wild carrot

queen consort noun, plural **queens consort** (1765)
: the wife of a reigning king

queen·ly \'kwēn-lē\ adjective **queen·li·er; -est** (15th century)
1 : of, relating to, or befitting a queen

2 : having royal rank
3 : MONARCHICAL
— queen·li·ness noun
— queenly adverb

queen mother noun (1577)
: a queen dowager who is mother of the reigning sovereign

queen post noun (1823)
: one of two vertical tie posts in a truss (as of a roof)

queen regnant noun, plural **queens regnant** (circa 1639)
: a queen reigning in her own right

de gf queen posts

Queen's Bench noun (circa 1809)
: a division of the English superior courts system that hears civil and criminal court cases — used during the reign of a queen

Queen's Counsel noun (circa 1860)
: a barrister selected to serve as counsel to the British crown — used during the reign of a queen

queen·ship \'kwēn-ˌship\ noun (1536)
1 : the rank, dignity, or state of being a queen
2 : a regal quality like that of a queen

queen·side \-ˌsīd\ noun (1897)
: the side of a chessboard containing the file on which the queen sits at the beginning of the game

queen–size adjective (1959)
1 : having dimensions of approximately 60 inches by 80 inches (about 1.5 by 2.0 meters) — used of a bed; compare FULL-SIZE, KING-SIZE, TWIN-SIZE
2 : of a size that fits a queen-size bed ⟨a queen-size sheet⟩

queen substance noun (1954)
: a pheromone secreted by queen bees that is consumed by worker bees and inhibits ovary development

¹queer \'kwir\ adjective [origin unknown] (1508)
1 a : WORTHLESS, COUNTERFEIT ⟨queer money⟩ **b :** QUESTIONABLE, SUSPICIOUS
2 a : differing in some odd way from what is usual or normal **b** (1) : ECCENTRIC, UNCONVENTIONAL (2) : mildly insane : TOUCHED **c :** absorbed or interested to an extreme or unreasonable degree : OBSESSED **d :** HOMOSEXUAL — usually used disparagingly
3 : not quite well
synonym see STRANGE
— queer·ish \-ish\ adjective
— queer·ly adverb
— queer·ness noun

²queer transitive verb (circa 1812)
1 : to spoil the effect or success of ⟨queer one's plans⟩
2 : to put or get into an embarrassing or disadvantageous situation

³queer noun (circa 1812)
: one that is queer; especially : HOMOSEXUAL — usually used disparagingly

¹quell \'kwel\ transitive verb [Middle English, to kill, quell, from Old English cwellan to kill; akin to Old High German quellen to torture, kill, quāla torment, Lithuanian gelti to hurt] (13th century)
1 : to thoroughly overwhelm and reduce to submission or passivity ⟨quell a riot⟩
2 : QUIET, PACIFY ⟨quell fears⟩
— quell·er noun

²quell noun [Middle English, from quellen to kill] (15th century)
1 obsolete : SLAUGHTER
2 archaic : the power of quelling

quench \'kwench\ verb [Middle English, from Old English -cwencan; akin to Old English -cwincan to vanish, Old Frisian quinka] (12th century)
transitive verb

1 a : PUT OUT, EXTINGUISH **b :** to put out the light or fire of ⟨quench glowing coals with water⟩ **c :** to cool (as heated metal) suddenly by immersion (as in oil or water) **d :** to cause to lose heat or warmth ⟨you have quenched the warmth of France toward you —Alfred Tennyson⟩
2 a : to bring (something immaterial) to an end typically by satisfying, damping, cooling, or decreasing ⟨a rational understanding of the laws of nature can quench impossible desires —Lucius Garvin⟩ ⟨the praise that quenches all desire to read the book —T. S. Eliot⟩ **b :** to terminate by or as if by destroying : ELIMINATE ⟨the Commonwealth party quenched a whole generation of play-acting —Margery Bailey⟩ ⟨quench a rebellion⟩ **c :** to relieve or satisfy with liquid ⟨quenched his thirst at a wayside spring⟩
intransitive verb
1 : to become extinguished : COOL
2 : to become calm : SUBSIDE
— quench·able \'kwen-chə-bəl\ adjective
— quench·er noun
— quench·less \'kwench-ləs\ adjective

que·nelle \kə-'nel\ noun [French, from German Knödel dumpling, from Middle High German; akin to Old High German knoto knot — more at KNOT] (1845)
: a poached oval dumpling of pureed forcemeat (as of pike) often served in a cream sauce

quer·ce·tin \'kwər-sə-tən\ noun [International Scientific Vocabulary, from Latin quercetum oak forest, from quercus oak — more at FIR] (1857)
: a yellow crystalline pigment $C_{15}H_{10}O_7$ occurring usually in the form of glycosides in various plants

quer·cit·ron \'kwər-ˌsi-trən, ˌkwər-'\ noun [blend of New Latin Quercus and International Scientific Vocabulary citron] (1794)
1 : a large timber oak (Quercus velutina) of the eastern and central U.S.
2 : the bark of the quercitron that is rich in tannin and a dye containing quercetin; also : the dye

que·rist \'kwir-əst, 'kwer-\ noun [Latin quaerere to ask] (1633)
: one who inquires

quern \'kwərn\ noun [Middle English, from Old English cweorn; akin to Old High German quirn hand mill, Old Church Slavonic žrŭny] (before 12th century)
: a primitive hand mill for grinding grain

quer·u·lous \'kwer-yə-ləs, -ə-ləs also 'kwir-\ adjective [Middle English querelose, from Latin querulus, from queri to complain] (15th century)
1 : habitually complaining
2 : FRETFUL, WHINING ⟨a querulous voice⟩
— quer·u·lous·ly adverb
— quer·u·lous·ness noun

¹que·ry \'kwir-ē, 'kwer-\ noun, plural **que·ries** [alteration of earlier quere, from Latin quaere, imperative of quaerere to ask] (circa 1635)
1 : QUESTION, INQUIRY
2 : a question in the mind : DOUBT
3 : QUESTION MARK

²query transitive verb **que·ried; que·ry·ing** (1654)
1 : to ask questions of especially with a desire for authoritative information
2 : to ask questions about especially in order to resolve a doubt
3 : to put as a question
4 : to mark with a query
synonym see ASK
— que·ri·er noun

que·sa·dil·la \ˌkā-sə-'dē-ə also -'thē- or -'thēl-yə\ noun [Mexican Spanish, from Spanish, cheese pastry, diminutive of quesada, from queso cheese, from Latin caseus] (1944)

: a wheat tortilla filled with a savory mixture, folded, fried in deep fat, and topped with cheese

¹quest \'kwest\ *noun* [Middle English, search, pursuit, investigation, from Middle French *queste* search, pursuit, from (assumed) Vulgar Latin *quaesta,* from Latin, feminine of *quaestus,* past participle of *quaerere*] (14th century)
1 a : a jury of inquest **b :** INVESTIGATION
2 : an act or instance of seeking: **a :** PURSUIT, SEARCH **b :** a chivalrous enterprise in medieval romance usually involving an adventurous journey
3 *obsolete* **:** a person or group of persons who search or make inquiry
²quest (14th century)
intransitive verb
1 *of a dog* **a :** to search a trail **b :** BAY
2 : to go on a quest
transitive verb
1 : to search for
2 : to ask for
— quest·er *noun*

¹ques·tion \'kwes-chən, 'kwesh-\ *noun* [Middle English, from Middle French, from Latin *quaestion-, quaestio,* from *quaerere* to seek, ask] (14th century)
1 a (1) **:** an interrogative expression often used to test knowledge (2) **:** an interrogative sentence or clause **b :** a subject or aspect in dispute or open for discussion **:** ISSUE; *broadly* **:** PROBLEM, MATTER **c** (1) **:** a subject or point of debate or a proposition to be voted on in a meeting (2) **:** the bringing of such to a vote **d :** the specific point at issue
2 a : an act or instance of asking **:** INQUIRY **b :** INTERROGATION; *also* **:** a judicial or official investigation **c :** torture as part of an examination **d** (1) **:** OBJECTION, DISPUTE ⟨true beyond *question*⟩ (2) **:** room for doubt or objection ⟨little *question* of his skill⟩ (3) **:** CHANCE, POSSIBILITY ⟨no *question* of escape⟩
²question (15th century)
transitive verb
1 : to ask a question of or about
2 : to interrogate intensively **:** CROSS-EXAMINE
3 a : DOUBT, DISPUTE **b :** to subject to analysis **:** EXAMINE
intransitive verb
: to ask questions **:** INQUIRE
synonym see ASK
— ques·tion·er *noun*

ques·tion·able \'kwes-chə-nə-bəl, 'kwesh-\, *in rapid speech* 'kwesh-nə-\ *adjective* (1590)
1 *obsolete* **:** inviting inquiry
2 *obsolete* **:** liable to judicial inquiry or action
3 : affording reason for being doubted, questioned, or challenged **:** not certain or exact **:** PROBLEMATIC ⟨milk of *questionable* purity⟩ ⟨a *questionable* decision⟩
4 : attended by well-grounded suspicions of being immoral, crude, false, or unsound **:** DUBIOUS ⟨*questionable* motives⟩
synonym see DOUBTFUL
— ques·tion·able·ness *noun*
— ques·tion·ably \-blē\ *adverb*
ques·tion·ary \'kwes-chə-,ner-ē, 'kwesh-\ *noun, plural* **-ar·ies** (1887)
: QUESTIONNAIRE
ques·tion·less \'kwes-chən-ləs, 'kwesh-\ *adjective* (1532)
1 : INDUBITABLE, UNQUESTIONABLE
2 : UNQUESTIONING
question mark *noun* (1869)
1 : something unknown, unknowable, or uncertain
2 : a mark ? used in writing and printing at the conclusion of a sentence to indicate a direct question
ques·tion·naire \,kwes-chə-'nar, -'ner, ,kwesh-\ *noun* [French, from *questionner* to question, from Middle French, from *question,* noun] (1899)

1 : a set of questions for obtaining statistically useful or personal information from individuals
2 : a written or printed questionnaire often with spaces for answers
3 : a survey made by the use of a questionnaire
question time *noun* (1885)
: a period in a session of a British parliamentary body during which members may put questions to ministers on matters concerning their departments
ques·tor \'kwes-tər\ *variant of* QUAESTOR
quet·zal \ket-'säl, -'sal\ *noun, plural* **quetzals** *or* **quet·za·les** \-'sä-(,)läs, -'sa-\ [American Spanish, from Nahuatl *quetzalli* tail coverts of the quetzal] (1827)
1 : a Central American trogon (*Pharomachrus mocinno*) that has brilliant green plumage above, a red breast, and in the male long upper tail coverts
2 *plural* quetzales — see MONEY table
Quet·zal·co·a·tl \,kwet-səl-kə-'wä-t°l, ,ket-, -səl-'kwä-; ket-,säl-, -,sal-\ *noun* [Nahuatl *Quetzalcōātl*]
: a chief Toltec and Aztec god identified with the wind and air and represented by a feathered serpent

quetzal 1

¹queue \'kyü\ *noun* [French, literally, tail, from Latin *cauda, coda*] (1748)
1 : a braid of hair usually worn hanging at the back of the head
2 : a waiting line especially of persons or vehicles
3 a : a sequence of messages or jobs held in auxiliary storage awaiting transmission or processing **b :** a data structure that consists of a list of records such that records are added at one end and removed from the other
²queue *verb* **queued; queu·ing** *or* **queue·ing** (1777)
transitive verb
: to arrange or form in a queue
intransitive verb
: to line up or wait in a queue — often used with *up*
— queu·er *noun*
¹quib·ble \'kwi-bəl\ *verb* **quib·bled; quib·bling** \-b(ə-)liŋ\ (1656)
intransitive verb
1 : to evade the point of an argument by caviling about words
2 a : CAVIL, CARP **b :** BICKER
transitive verb
: to subject to quibbles
— quib·bler \-b(ə-)lər\ *noun*
²quibble *noun* [probably diminutive of obsolete *quib* quibble] (1670)
1 : an evasion of or shift from the point
2 : a minor objection or criticism
quiche \'kēsh\ *noun* [French, from French dialect (Lorraine)] (1941)
: an unsweetened custard pie usually having a savory filling (as spinach, mushrooms, or ham)
quiche lor·raine \-lə-'rän, -lȯ-\ *noun, often L capitalized* [French, quiche of Lorraine] (1941)
: a quiche containing cheese and bacon bits
¹quick \'kwik\ *adjective* [Middle English *quik,* from Old English *cwic;* akin to Old Norse *kvikr* living, Latin *vivus* living, *vivere* to live, Greek *bios, zōē* life] (before 12th century)
1 : not dead **:** LIVING, ALIVE
2 : acting or capable of acting with speed: as **a** (1) **:** fast in understanding, thinking, or learning **:** mentally agile ⟨a *quick* wit⟩ ⟨*quick*

thinking⟩ (2) **:** reacting to stimuli with speed and keen sensitivity (3) **:** aroused immediately and intensely ⟨*quick* tempers⟩ **b** (1) **:** fast in development or occurrence ⟨a *quick* succession of events⟩ (2) **:** done or taking place with rapidity ⟨gave them a *quick* look⟩ **c :** marked by speed, readiness, or promptness of physical movement ⟨walked with *quick* steps⟩ **d :** inclined to hastiness (as in action or response) ⟨*quick* to criticize⟩ **e :** capable of being easily and speedily prepared ⟨a *quick* and tasty dinner⟩
3 *archaic* **a :** not stagnant **:** RUNNING, FLOWING **b :** MOVING, SHIFTING ⟨*quick* mud⟩
4 *archaic* **:** FIERY, GLOWING
5 *obsolete* **a :** PUNGENT **b :** CAUSTIC
6 *archaic* **:** PREGNANT
7 : having a sharp angle ⟨a *quick* turn in the road⟩ ☆
— quick·ly *adverb*
— quick·ness *noun*
²quick *noun* (before 12th century)
1 quick *plural* **:** living beings
2 [probably of Scandinavian origin; akin to Old Norse *kvika* sensitive flesh, from *kvikr* living] **a :** a painfully sensitive spot or area of flesh (as that underlying a fingernail or toenail) **b :** the inmost sensibilities ⟨hurt to the *quick* by the remark⟩ **c :** the very center of something **:** HEART
3 *archaic* **:** LIFE 11
³quick *adverb* (14th century)
: in a quick manner
quick assets *noun plural* (1891)
: cash, accounts receivable, and other current assets excluding inventories
quick bread *noun* (1918)
: bread made with a leavening agent (as baking powder or baking soda) that permits immediate baking of the dough or batter mixture
quick·en \'kwi-kən\ *verb* **quick·ened; quick·en·ing** \'kwi-kə-niŋ, 'kwik-niŋ\ (14th century)
transitive verb
1 a : to make alive **:** REVIVE **b :** to cause to be enlivened **:** STIMULATE
2 *archaic* **a :** KINDLE **b :** to cause to burn more intensely
3 : to make more rapid **:** HASTEN, ACCELERATE ⟨*quickened* her steps⟩
4 a : to make (a curve) sharper **b :** to make (a slope) steeper
intransitive verb
1 : to quicken something
2 : to come to life; *especially* **:** to enter into a phase of active growth and development ⟨seeds *quickening* in the soil⟩
3 : to reach the stage of gestation at which fetal motion is felt

4 : to shine more brightly ⟨watched the dawn *quickening* in the east⟩
5 : to become more rapid ⟨her pulse *quickened* at the sight⟩ ☆
— **quick·en·er** \'kwi-kə-nər, 'kwik-nər\ *noun*

quick fix *noun* (1970)
: an expedient usually temporary or inadequate solution to a problem

quick–freeze \'kwik-'frēz\ *transitive verb* **-froze** \-'frōz\; **-fro·zen** \-'frō-z°n\; **-freez·ing** (1930)
: to freeze (food) for preservation so rapidly that ice crystals formed are too small to rupture the cells and the natural juices and flavor are preserved

quick·ie \'kwi-kē\ *noun, often attributive* (circa 1926)
: something done or made in a hurry: as **a :** a quickly and usually cheaply produced work (as a motion picture or book) **b :** a hastily performed act of sexual intercourse

quick kick *noun* (circa 1940)
: a punt in football on first, second, or third down made from a running or passing formation and designed to take the opposing team by surprise

quick·lime \'kwik-ˌlīm\ *noun* (14th century)
: ¹LIME 2a

quick·sand \'kwik-ˌsand\ *noun* (14th century)
1 : sand readily yielding to pressure; *especially* **:** a deep mass of loose sand mixed with water into which heavy objects readily sink
2 : something that entraps or frustrates

quick·set \-ˌset\ *noun* (15th century)
chiefly British **:** plant cuttings set in the ground to grow especially in a hedgerow; *also* **:** a hedge or thicket especially of hawthorn grown from quickset

¹quick·sil·ver \-ˌsil-vər\ *noun* (before 12th century)
: MERCURY 2a ◇

²quicksilver *adjective* (1655)
: resembling or suggestive of quicksilver; *especially* **:** MERCURIAL 3

quick·step \-ˌstep\ *noun* (circa 1811)
: a spirited march tune usually accompanying a march in quick time

quick–tem·pered \-'tem-pərd\ *adjective* (1830)
: easily angered **:** IRASCIBLE

quick time *noun* (circa 1802)
: a rate of marching in which 120 steps each 30 inches in length are taken in one minute

quick–wit·ted \'kwik-'wi-təd\ *adjective* (1530)
: quick in perception and understanding **:** mentally alert
synonym see INTELLIGENT
— **quick–wit·ted·ly** *adverb*
— **quick–wit·ted·ness** *noun*

¹quid \'kwid\ *noun, plural* **quid** *also* **quids** [origin unknown] (1688)
British **:** a pound sterling

²quid *noun* [English dialect, cud, from Middle English *quide*, from Old English *cwidu, cwudu* — more at CUD] (circa 1727)
: a cut or wad of something chewable

quid·di·ty \'kwi-də-tē\ *noun, plural* **-ties** [Middle English *quidite*, from Medieval Latin *quidditat-, quidditas* essence, from Latin *quid* what, neuter of *quis* who — more at WHO] (14th century)
1 : whatever makes something the type that it is **:** ESSENCE
2 a : a trifling point **:** QUIBBLE **b :** CROTCHET, ECCENTRICITY

quid·nunc \'kwid-ˌnəŋk\ *noun* [Latin *quid nunc* what now?] (1709)
: a person who seeks to know all the latest news or gossip **:** BUSYBODY

quid pro quo \ˌkwid-ˌprō-'kwō\ *noun* [New Latin, something for something] (1591)
: something given or received for something else; *also* **:** a deal arranging a quid pro quo

qui·es·cence \kwī-'e-s°n(t)s, kwē-\ *noun* (circa 1631)
: the quality or state of being quiescent

qui·es·cent \-s°nt\ *adjective* [Latin *quiescent-, quiescens*, present participle of *quiescere* to become quiet, rest, from *quies*] (1605)
1 : marked by inactivity or repose **:** tranquilly at rest
2 : causing no trouble or symptoms ⟨*quiescent* gallstones⟩
synonym see LATENT
— **qui·es·cent·ly** *adverb*

¹qui·et \'kwī-ət\ *noun* [Middle English, from Latin *quiet-, quies* rest, quiet — more at WHILE] (14th century)
: the quality or state of being quiet **:** TRANQUILLITY
— **on the quiet :** in a secretive manner **:** in secret

²quiet *adjective* [Middle English, from Middle French, from Latin *quietus*, from past participle of *quiescere*] (14th century)
1 a : marked by little or no motion or activity **:** CALM ⟨a *quiet* sea⟩ **b :** GENTLE, EASYGOING ⟨a *quiet* temperament⟩ **c :** not interfered with ⟨*quiet* reading⟩ **d :** enjoyed in peace and relaxation ⟨a *quiet* cup of tea⟩
2 a : free from noise or uproar **:** STILL **b :** UNOBTRUSIVE, CONSERVATIVE ⟨*quiet* clothes⟩
3 : SECLUDED ⟨a *quiet* nook⟩
— **qui·et·ly** *adverb*
— **qui·et·ness** *noun*

³quiet *adverb* (1573)
: in a quiet manner ⟨a *quiet*-running engine⟩

⁴quiet *verb* [Middle English, from Late Latin *quietare* to set free, to calm, from Latin *quietus*] (14th century)
transitive verb
1 : to cause to be quiet **:** CALM
2 : to make secure by freeing from dispute or question ⟨*quiet* title to a property⟩
intransitive verb
: to become quiet — usually used with *down*
— **qui·et·er** *noun*

qui·et·en \'kwī-ə-t°n\ *verb* **qui·et·ened; qui·et·en·ing** \'kwī-ət-niŋ, 'kwī-ə-t°n-iŋ\ (circa 1828)
chiefly British **:** QUIET

qui·et·ism \'kwī-ə-ˌti-zəm\ *noun* (1687)
1 a : a system of religious mysticism teaching that perfection and spiritual peace are attained by annihilation of the will and passive absorption in contemplation of God and divine things **b :** a passive withdrawn attitude or policy toward the world or worldly affairs
2 : a state of calmness or passivity
— **qui·et·ist** \-tist\ *adjective or noun*
— **qui·et·is·tic** \ˌkwī-ə-'tis-tik\ *adjective*

qui·etude \'kwī-ə-ˌtüd, -ˌtyüd\ *noun* [Middle French, from Late Latin *quietudo*, from Latin *quietus*] (1597)
: a quiet state **:** REPOSE

qui·etus \kwī-'ē-təs, -'ā-\ *noun* [Middle English *quietus est*, from Medieval Latin, he is quit, formula of discharge from obligation] (1540)
1 : final settlement (as of a debt)
2 : removal from activity; *especially* **:** DEATH
3 : something that quiets or represses

quiff \'kwif\ *noun* [origin unknown] (circa 1890)
British **:** a prominent forelock

¹quill \'kwil\ *noun* [Middle English *quil* hollow reed, bobbin; akin to Middle High German *kil* large feather] (15th century)
1 a (1) **:** a bobbin, spool, or spindle on which filling yarn is wound (2) **:** a hollow shaft often surrounding another shaft and used in various mechanical devices **b :** a roll of dried bark ⟨cinnamon *quills*⟩
2 a (1) **:** the hollow horny shaft of a feather — see FEATHER illustration (2) **:** FEATHER; *especially* **:** one of the large stiff feathers of the wing or tail **b :** one of the hollow sharp spines of a porcupine or hedgehog **c :** ³PEN 3

3 : something made from or resembling the quill of a feather; *especially* **:** a pen for writing
4 : a float for a fishing line

²quill *transitive verb* (1783)
1 : to pierce with quills
2 a : to wind (thread or yarn) on a quill **b :** to make a series of small rounded ridges in (cloth)

quill·back \'kwil-ˌbak\ *noun, plural* **quillback** *or* **quillbacks** (1882)
: any of several suckers; *especially* **:** a small fish (*Carpiodes cyprinus*) of central and eastern North America that has the first ray of the dorsal fin much elongated

quill·work \-ˌwərk\ *noun* (1843)
: ornamental work in porcupine or bird quills

¹quilt \'kwilt\ *noun* [Middle English *quilte* mattress, quilt, from Old French *cuilte*, from Latin *culcita* mattress] (14th century)
1 : a bed coverlet of two layers of cloth filled with padding (as down or batting) held in place by ties or stitched designs
2 : something that is quilted or resembles a quilt

²quilt (1555)
transitive verb
1 a : to fill, pad, or line like a quilt **b** (1) **:** to stitch, sew, or cover with lines or patterns like those used in quilts (2) **:** to stitch (designs) through layers of cloth **c :** to fasten between two pieces of material
2 : to stitch or sew in layers with padding in between
intransitive verb
1 : to make quilts
2 : to do quilted work
— **quilt·er** *noun*

quilt·ing *noun* (1609)
1 : material that is quilted or used for making quilts
2 : the process of quilting

quin·a·crine \'kwi-nə-ˌkrēn\ *noun* [*quinine* + *acridine*] (circa 1934)
: an antimalarial drug derived from acridine and used especially in the form of its dihydrochloride $C_{23}H_{30}ClN_3O \cdot 2HCl \cdot 2H_2O$

quince \'kwin(t)s\ *noun* [Middle English *quynce* quinces, plural of *coyn, quyn* quince,

from Middle French *coin*, from Latin *cotoneum*, alteration *cydonium*, from Greek *kydōnion*] (14th century)
1 : the fruit of a central Asian tree (*Cydonia oblonga*) of the rose family that resembles a hard-fleshed yellow apple and is used especially in preserves
2 : a tree that bears quinces

quin·cen·te·na·ry \ˌkwin-sen-'te-nə-rē, -'sen-t°n-ˌer-ē, *especially British* -sen-'tē-nə-rē\ *noun* [Latin *quinque* five + English *centenary*] (1879)
: a 500th anniversary or its celebration
— **quincentenary** *adjective*

quin·cen·ten·ni·al \-sen-'te-nē-əl\ *noun* [Latin *quinque* five + English *centennial*] (1884)
: QUINCENTENARY
— **quincentennial** *adjective*

quin·cunx \'kwin-ˌkəŋ(k)s\ *noun* [Latin *quincunc-, quincunx*, literally, five twelfths, from *quinque* five + *uncia* twelfth part — more at FIVE, OUNCE] (1658)
: an arrangement of five things in a square or rectangle with one at each corner and one in the middle
— **quin·cun·cial** \kwin-'kən(t)-shəl\ *or* **quin·cunx·ial** \-'kəŋk-sē-əl\ *adjective*

quin·de·cil·lion \ˌkwin-di-'sil-yən\ *noun, often attributive* [Latin *quindecim* fifteen (from *quinque* five + *decem* ten) + English *-illion* (as in *million*) — more at TEN] (1903)
— see NUMBER table

quin·i·dine \'kwi-nə-ˌdēn\ *noun* [International Scientific Vocabulary, from *quinine*] (1836)
: an alkaloid $C_{20}H_{24}N_2O_2$ that is stereoisomeric with quinine and is used in treating cardiac rhythm irregularities

qui·nie·la \kwin-'ye-lə\ *or* **qui·nel·la** \kwi-'ne-lə\ *noun* [American Spanish *quiniela*, a game of chance resembling a lottery] (1905)
: a bet in which the bettor picks the first and second place finishers but need not designate their order of finish in order to win — compare PERFECTA

qui·nine \'kwī-ˌnīn *also* 'kwi- *or* kwi-'nīn *or* ki-'nēn *or* kwi-'nēn\ *noun* [Spanish *quina* cinchona, from Quechua *kina* bark] (1826)
1 : a bitter crystalline alkaloid $C_{20}H_{24}N_2O_2$ from cinchona bark used in medicine
2 : a salt of quinine used especially as an antipyretic, antimalarial, and bitter tonic

quinine water *noun* (1953)
: TONIC WATER

qui·noa \'kēn-ˌwä\ *noun* [Spanish, from Quechua *kinua*] (1625)
: a pigweed (*Chenopodium quinoa*) of the high Andes whose seeds are ground and widely used as food in Peru

quin·o·line \'kwi-n°l-ˌēn\ *noun* [International Scientific Vocabulary *quin*ine + 3-*ol* + 2-*ine*] (1845)
1 : a pungent oily nitrogenous base C_9H_7N obtained usually by distillation of coal tar or by synthesis from aniline that is the parent compound of many alkaloids, drugs, and dyes
2 : a derivative of quinoline

qui·none \kwi-'nōn, 'kwi-ˌ\ *noun* [International Scientific Vocabulary *quin*ine + -*one*] (1853)
1 : either of two isomeric cyclic crystalline compounds $C_6H_4O_2$ that are di-keto derivatives of dihydro-benzene
2 : any of various usually yellow, orange, or red quinonoid compounds including several that are biologically important as coenzymes, hydrogen acceptors, or vitamins

qui·no·noid \kwi-'nō-ˌnȯid, 'kwi-nə-\ *or* **quin·oid** \'kwi-ˌnȯid\ *adjective* (1878)

: resembling quinone especially in having a benzene nucleus containing two double bonds within the nucleus

quin·quen·ni·al \kwin-'kwe-nē-əl, kwiŋ-\ *adjective* (15th century)
1 : consisting of or lasting for five years
2 : occurring or being done every five years
— **quinquennial** *noun*
— **quin·quen·ni·al·ly** \-nē-ə-lē\ *adverb*

quin·quen·ni·um \-nē-əm\ *noun, plural* **-ni·ums** *or* **-nia** \-nē-ə\ [Latin, from *quinque* five + *annus* year — more at FIVE, ANNUAL] (1621)
: a period of five years

quin·sy \'kwin-zē\ *noun* [Middle English *quinesie*, from Middle French *quinancie*, from Late Latin *cynanche*, from Greek *kynanchē*, from *kyn-, kyōn* dog + *anchein* to strangle — more at HOUND, ANGER] (14th century)
: an abscess in the tissue around a tonsil usually resulting from bacterial infection and often accompanied by pain and fever

quint \'kwint\ *noun* (1935)
: QUINTUPLET

quin·ta \'kin-tə, 'kēn-\ *noun* [Spanish & Portuguese, *quinta*, farm rented at one fifth of its income, from Latin, feminine of *quintus* fifth] (1754)
: a country villa or estate especially in Portugal or Latin America

quin·tain \'kwin-t°n\ *noun* [Middle English *quintaine*, from Middle French, perhaps from Latin *quintana* street in a Roman camp separating the fifth maniple from the sixth where a market was held, from feminine of *quintanus* fifth in rank, from *quintus* fifth] (15th century)
: an object to be tilted at; *especially* : a post with a revolving crosspiece that has a target at one end and a sandbag at the other end

quin·tal \'kwin-t°l, 'kan-\ *noun* [Middle English, from Middle French, from Medieval Latin *quintale*, from Arabic *qinṭār*, from Late Greek *kentēnarion*, from Late Latin *centenarium*, from Latin, neuter of *centenarius* consisting of a hundred — more at CENTENARY] (15th century)
1 : HUNDREDWEIGHT
2 : a unit of weight equal to 100 kilograms (about 220 pounds)

quin·tes·sence \kwin-'te-s°n(t)s\ *noun* [Middle English, from Middle French *quinte essence*, from Medieval Latin *quinta essentia*, literally, fifth essence] (15th century)
1 : the fifth and highest element in ancient and medieval philosophy that permeates all nature and is the substance composing the celestial bodies
2 : the essence of a thing in its purest and most concentrated form
3 : the most typical example or representative
◇
— **quin·tes·sen·tial** \ˌkwin-tə-'sen(t)-shəl\ *adjective*
— **quin·tes·sen·tial·ly** *adverb*

quin·tet *also* **quin·tette** \kwin-'tet\ *noun* [*quintet* from Italian *quintetto*, from *quinto* fifth, from Italian *quintus; quintette* from French, from Italian *quintetto*] (1811)
1 : a musical composition or movement for five instruments or voices
2 : a group or set of five: as **a** : the performers of a quintet **b** : a basketball team

¹quin·tic \'kwin-tik\ *adjective* [Latin *quintus* fifth] (1853)
: of the fifth degree

²quintic *noun* (1856)
: a polynomial or a polynomial equation of the fifth degree

quin·tile \'kwin-ˌtīl\ *noun* [Latin *quintus* + English 2-*ile*] (circa 1928)
: any of the four values that divide the items of a frequency distribution into five classes with each containing one fifth of the total population; *also* : any one of the five classes

quin·til·lion \kwin-'til-yən\ *noun* [Latin *quintus* + English -*illion* (as in *million*)] (1674)

— see NUMBER table
— **quintillion** *adjective*
— **quin·til·lionth** \-yən(t)th\ *adjective or noun*

¹quin·tu·ple \kwin-'tü-pəl, -'tyü-, -'tə-; 'kwin-tə-\ *adjective* [Middle French, from Medieval Latin *quintuplus*, from Latin *quintus* fifth + -*plus* -fold; akin to Latin *quinque* five — more at FIVE, -FOLD] (1570)
1 : being five times as great or as many
2 : having five units or members
3 : marked by five beats per measure ⟨*quintuple* meter⟩
— **quintuple** *noun*

²quintuple *verb* **quin·tu·pled; quin·tu·pling** \-p(ə-)liŋ\ (1639)
transitive verb
: to make five times as great or as many
intransitive verb
: to become five times as much or as numerous

quin·tu·plet \kwin-'tə-plət, -'tü-, -'tyü-; 'kwin-tə-\ *noun* (1873)
1 : a combination of five of a kind
2 : one of five offspring born at one birth

¹quin·tu·pli·cate \kwin-'tü-pli-kət, -'tyü-\ *adjective* [Medieval Latin *quintuplicatus*, past participle of *quintuplicare* to quintuple, from *quintuplus* quintuple] (1656)
1 : consisting of or existing in five corresponding or identical parts or examples ⟨*quintuplicate* invoices⟩
2 : being the fifth of five things exactly alike ⟨file the *quintuplicate* copy⟩

²quintuplicate *noun* (1851)
1 : one of five things exactly alike; *specifically* : one of five identical copies
2 : five copies all alike — used with *in* ⟨typed in *quintuplicate*⟩

³quin·tu·pli·cate \-plə-ˌkāt\ *transitive verb* -cat·ed; -cat·ing (circa 1890)
1 : to make quintuple or fivefold
2 : to prepare in quintuplicate

¹quip \'kwip\ *noun* [earlier *quippy*, perhaps from Latin *quippe* indeed, to be sure (often ironic), from *quid* what — more at QUIDDITY] (1532)
1 a : a clever usually taunting remark : GIBE **b** : a witty or funny observation or response usually made on the spur of the moment

2 : QUIBBLE, EQUIVOCATION
3 : something strange, droll, curious, or eccentric **:** ODDITY
²quip *verb* **quipped; quip·ping** (1579)
intransitive verb
: to make quips **:** GIBE
transitive verb
: to jest or gibe at
— **quip·per** \'kwi-pər\ *noun*
quip·ster \'kwip-stər\ *noun* (1876)
: one who is given to quipping
qui·pu \'kē-(,)pü\ *noun* [Spanish *quipo,* from Quechua *khipu*] (1704)
: a device made of a main cord with smaller varicolored cords attached and knotted and used by the ancient Peruvians (as for calculating)
¹quire \'kwīr\ *noun* [Middle English *quair* four sheets of paper folded once, collection of sheets, from Middle French *quaer,* from (assumed) Vulgar Latin *quaternum* set of four, from Latin *quaterni* four each, set of four — more at QUATERNION] (15th century)
: a collection of 24 or sometimes 25 sheets of paper of the same size and quality **:** one twentieth of a ream
²quire *variant of* CHOIR
Qui·ri·nus \kwə-'rī-nəs, -'rē-\ *noun* [Latin]
: an early state god of the Romans later identified with Romulus
¹quirk \'kwərk\ *noun* [origin unknown] (1565)
1 a : an abrupt twist or curve **b :** a peculiar trait **:** IDIOSYNCRASY **c :** ACCIDENT, VAGARY ⟨a *quirk* of fate⟩
2 : a groove separating a bead or other molding from adjoining members
— **quirk·i·ly** \'kwər-kə-lē\ *adverb*
— **quirk·i·ness** \-kē-nəs\ *noun*
— **quirk·ish** \'kwər-kish\ *adjective*
— **quirky** \-kē\ *adjective*
²quirk *verb* (1596)
: CURVE, TWIST ⟨*quirked* his eyebrows⟩
¹quirt \'kwərt\ *noun* [Mexican Spanish *cuarta*] (1845)
: a riding whip with a short handle and a rawhide lash
²quirt *transitive verb* (1887)
: to strike or drive with a quirt
quis·ling \'kwiz-liŋ\ *noun, often attributive* [Vidkun *Quisling* (died 1945) Norwegian politician who collaborated with the Nazis] (1940)
: TRAITOR 2, COLLABORATOR
— **quis·ling·ism** \-liŋ-,i-zəm\ *noun*
¹quit \'kwit\ *adjective* [Middle English *quite, quit,* from Old French *quite*] (13th century)
: released from obligation, charge, or penalty; *especially* **:** FREE
²quit *verb* **quit** *also* **quit·ted; quit·ting** [Middle English *quiten, quitten,* from Middle French *quiter, quitter,* from Old French, from *quite* free of, released, literally, at rest, from Latin *quietus* quiet, at rest] (13th century)
transitive verb
1 : to make full payment of **:** PAY UP ⟨*quit* a debt⟩
2 : to set free **:** RELIEVE, RELEASE ⟨*quit* oneself of fear⟩
3 : CONDUCT, ACQUIT ⟨the youths *quit* themselves like men⟩
4 a : to depart from or out of **b :** to leave the company of **c :** GIVE UP 1, 2 ⟨*quit* a job⟩ ⟨*quit* smoking⟩
intransitive verb
1 : to cease normal, expected, or necessary action
2 : to give up employment
3 : to admit defeat **:** GIVE UP
synonym see STOP
³quit *noun* (circa 1923)
: the act or an instance of quitting a job
quitch \'kwich\ *noun* [(assumed) Middle English *quicche,* from Old English *cwice;* akin to Old High German *quecca* couch grass] (before 12th century)
: QUACK GRASS

quit·claim \'kwit-,klām\ *transitive verb* (14th century)
: to release or relinquish a legal claim to; *especially* **:** to release a claim to or convey by a quitclaim deed
— **quitclaim** *noun*
quitclaim deed *noun* (1756)
: a legal instrument used to release one person's right, title, or interest to another without providing a guarantee or warranty of title
quite \'kwīt\ *adverb* [Middle English, from *quite,* adjective, quit] (14th century)
1 : WHOLLY, COMPLETELY ⟨not *quite* finished⟩
2 : to an extreme **:** POSITIVELY ⟨*quite* sure⟩ — often used as an intensifier with *a* ⟨*quite* a swell guy⟩ ⟨*quite* a beauty⟩
3 : to a considerable extent **:** RATHER ⟨*quite* near⟩
usage see PLENTY
— **quite a bit :** a considerable amount
— **quite a few :** MANY
quit·rent \'kwit-,rent\ *noun* (15th century)
: a fixed rent payable to a feudal superior in commutation of services; *specifically* **:** a fixed rent due from a socage tenant
quits \'kwits\ *adjective* [Middle English, quit, probably from Medieval Latin *quittus,* alteration of Latin *quietus* at rest] (15th century)
: being on even terms by repayment or requital
quit·tance \'kwi-t°n(t)s\ *noun* (14th century)
1 a : discharge from a debt or an obligation **b :** a document evidencing quittance
2 : RECOMPENSE, REQUITAL
quit·ter \'kwi-tər\ *noun* (1611)
: one that quits; *especially* **:** one that gives up too easily **:** DEFEATIST
quit·tor \'kwi-tər\ *noun* [Middle English *quiture* pus, probably from Old French, act of boiling, from Latin *coctura,* from *coctus,* past participle of *coquere* to cook — more at COOK] (1703)
: a purulent inflammation of the feet especially of horses and donkeys
¹quiv·er \'kwi-vər\ *noun* [Middle English, from Middle French *quivre,* of Germanic origin; akin to Old English *cocer* quiver, Old High German *kohhari*] (14th century)
1 : a case for carrying or holding arrows
2 : the arrows in a quiver
²quiver *intransitive verb* **quiv·ered; quiv·er·ing** \'kwi-və-riŋ, 'kwiv-riŋ\ [Middle English, probably from *quiver* agile, quick; akin to Old English *cwiferlice* zealously] (15th century)
: to shake or move with a slight trembling motion
— **quiv·er·ing·ly** *adverb*
³quiver *noun* (1786)
: the act or action of quivering **:** TREMOR
qui vive \kē-'vēv\ *noun* [French *qui-vive,* from *qui vive?* long live who?, challenge of a French sentry] (1726)
: ALERT, LOOKOUT — used in the phrase *on the qui vive*
qui·xote \'kwik-sət, kē-'hō-tē, -'ō-\ *noun, often capitalized* [Don *Quixote,* hero of the novel *Don Quixote de la Mancha* (1605, 1615) by Cervantes] (1648)
: a quixotic person
— **quix·o·tism** \'kwik-sə-,ti-zəm\ *noun*
— **quix·o·try** \-sə-trē\ *noun*
quix·ot·ic \kwik-'sä-tik\ *adjective* [Don *Quixote*] (1815)
1 : foolishly impractical especially in the pursuit of ideals; *especially* **:** marked by rash lofty romantic ideas or extravagantly chivalrous action
2 : CAPRICIOUS, UNPREDICTABLE ◆
synonym see IMAGINARY
— **quix·ot·i·cal** \-ti-kəl\ *adjective*
— **quix·ot·i·cal·ly** \-ti-k(ə-)lē\ *adverb*
¹quiz \'kwiz\ *noun, plural* **quiz·zes** [origin unknown] (1749)

1 : an eccentric person
2 : PRACTICAL JOKE
3 : the act or action of quizzing; *specifically* **:** a short oral or written test
²quiz *transitive verb* **quizzed; quiz·zing** (1794)
1 : to make fun of **:** MOCK
2 : to look at inquisitively
3 : to question closely
— **quiz·zer** *noun*
quiz·mas·ter \'kwiz-,mas-tər\ *noun* (1943)
: one who puts the questions to contestants in a quiz show
quiz show *noun* (1944)
: an entertainment program (as on radio or television) in which contestants answer questions — called also *quiz program*
quiz·zi·cal \'kwi-zi-kəl\ *adjective* (1800)
1 : comically quaint
2 : mildly teasing or mocking ⟨a *quizzical* remark⟩
3 : expressive of puzzlement, curiosity, or disbelief ⟨raised a *quizzical* eyebrow⟩
— **quiz·zi·cal·i·ty** \,kwi-zə-'ka-lə-tē\ *noun*
— **quiz·zi·cal·ly** \'kwi-zi-k(ə-)lē\ *adverb*
quod \'kwäd\ *noun* [origin unknown] (circa 1700)
slang British **:** PRISON
quod·li·bet \'kwäd-lə-,bet\ *noun* [Middle English, from Medieval Latin *quodlibetum,* from Latin *quodlibet,* neuter of *quilibet* any whatever, from *qui* who, what + *libet* it pleases, from *libēre* to please — more at WHO, LOVE] (14th century)
1 : a philosophical or theological point proposed for disputation; *also* **:** a disputation on such a point
2 : a whimsical combination of familiar melodies or texts
¹quoin \'kȯin, 'kwȯin\ *noun* [alteration of ¹*coin*] (1532)
1 a : a solid exterior angle (as of a building) **b :** one of the members (as a block) forming a quoin and usually differentiated from the adjoining walls by material, texture, color, size, or projection

quoin 1b

2 : the keystone or a voussoir of an arch
3 : a wooden or expandable metal block used by printers to lock up a form within a chase
²quoin *transitive verb* (1683)
1 : to equip (a type form) with quoins
2 : to provide with quoins ⟨*quoined* walls⟩
¹quoit \'kȯit, 'kwȯit, 'kwät\ *noun* [Middle English *coite*] (15th century)
1 : a flattened ring of iron or circle of rope used in a throwing game

◇ **WORD HISTORY**
quixotic The word *quixotic* reflects the lasting place in world literature held by Miguel de Cervantes Saavedra's novel *Don Quixote de la Mancha* (1605 and 1615). The story concerns Alonso Quijano, who, inspired by the romantic ideals of the days of chivalry, sets out determined to have his own chivalric adventures and in the process undo the wrongs of the world. With the title of Don Quixote and the viewpoint of a romantic idealist, he undergoes a series of adventures that turn into comic misadventures. The would-be knight returns to his home in La Mancha a tired and disillusioned old man. *Don Quixote* was translated into English not long after its Spanish publication and within a few decades gave rise to *Quixote* as a synonym for an impractical idealist. The 19th century derivative *quixotic* now evokes the unrealizable schemes of modern Don Quixotes.

2 *plural but singular in construction* **:** a game in which the quoits are thrown at an upright pin in an attempt to ring the pin or come as near to it as possible

²quoit *transitive verb* (1597)
: to throw like a quoit

quon·dam \'kwän-dəm, -ˌdam\ *adjective* [Latin, at one time, formerly, from *quom, cum* when; akin to Latin *qui* who — more at WHO] (1539)
: FORMER, SOMETIME ⟨a *quondam* friend⟩

Quon·set \'kwän(t)-sət, 'kwän-zət\ *trademark*
— used for a prefabricated shelter set on a foundation of bolted steel trusses and built of a semicircular arching roof of corrugated metal insulated with wood fiber

quo·rum \'kwōr-əm, 'kwȯr-\ *noun* [Middle English, quorum of justices of the peace, from Latin, of whom, genitive plural of *qui* who; from the wording of the commission formerly issued to justices of the peace] (1602)
1 : a select group
2 : the number (as a majority) of officers or members of a body that when duly assembled is legally competent to transact business
3 : a Mormon body comprising those in the same grade of priesthood

quo·ta \'kwō-tə\ *noun* [Medieval Latin, from Latin *quota pars* how great a part] (1618)
1 : a proportional part or share; *especially* **:** the share or proportion assigned to each in a division or to each member of a body
2 : the number or amount constituting a proportional share

quot·able \'kwō-tə-bəl *also* 'kō-\ *adjective* (1811)
: fit for or worth quoting
— **quot·abil·i·ty** \ˌkwō-tə-'bi-lə-tē *also* ˌkō-\ *noun*

quo·ta·tion \kwō-'tā-shən *also* kō-\ *noun* (1646)
1 a : the act or process of quoting **b** (1) **:** the naming or publishing of current bids and offers or prices of securities or commodities (2) **:** the bids, offers, or prices so named or pub-

lished; *especially* **:** the highest bid and lowest offer for a particular security in a given market at a given time
2 : something that is quoted; *especially* **:** a passage referred to, repeated, or adduced

quotation mark *noun* (circa 1859)
: one of a pair of punctuation marks " " or ' ' used chiefly to indicate the beginning and the end of a quotation in which the exact phraseology of another or of a text is directly cited

¹quote \'kwōt *also* 'kōt\ *verb* **quot·ed;**
quot·ing [Medieval Latin *quotare* to mark the number of, number references, from Latin *quotus* of what number or quantity, from *quot* how many, (as) many as; akin to Latin *qui* who — more at WHO] (1582)
transitive verb
1 a : to speak or write (a passage) from another usually with credit acknowledgment **b :** to repeat a passage from especially in substantiation or illustration
2 : to cite in illustration ⟨*quote* cases⟩
3 a : to state (the current price or bid-offer spread) for a commodity, stock, or bond **b :** to give exact information on
4 : to set off by quotation marks
intransitive verb
: to inform a hearer or reader that matter following is quoted
— **quot·er** *noun*

²quote *noun* (1888)
1 : QUOTATION
2 : QUOTATION MARK — often used orally to indicate the beginning of a direct quotation

quoth \'kwōth *also* 'kōth\ *verb past* [Middle English, past of *quethen* to say, from Old English *cwethan;* akin to Old High German *quedan* to say] (before 12th century)
archaic **:** SAID — used chiefly in the first and third persons with a postpositive subject

quotha \'kwō-thə\ *interjection* [alteration of *quoth he*] (1519)
archaic — used especially to express surprise or contempt

quo·tid·i·an \kwō-'ti-dē-ən\ *adjective* [Middle

English *cotidian,* from Middle French, from Latin *quotidianus, cotidianus,* from *quotidie* every day, from *quot* (as) many as + *dies* day — more at DEITY] (14th century)
1 : occurring every day ⟨*quotidian* fever⟩
2 a : belonging to each day **:** EVERYDAY ⟨*quotidian* routine⟩ **b :** COMMONPLACE, ORDINARY ⟨*quotidian* drabness⟩
— **quotidian** *noun*

quo·tient \'kwō-shənt\ *noun* [Middle English *quocient,* modification of Latin *quotiens* how many times, from *quot* how many] (15th century)
1 : the number resulting from the division of one number by another
2 : the numerical ratio usually multiplied by 100 between a test score and a measurement on which that score might be expected largely to depend
3 : QUOTA, SHARE

quotient group *noun* (1893)
: a group whose elements are the cosets of a normal subgroup of a given group — called also *factor group*

quotient ring *noun* (circa 1958)
: a ring whose elements are the cosets of an ideal in a given ring

quo war·ran·to \ˌkwō-wə-'rän-(ˌ)tō, -'ran-; -'wȯr-ən-ˌtō, -'wär-\ *noun* [Middle English *quo waranto,* from Medieval Latin *quo warranto* by what warrant; from the wording of the writ] (15th century)
1 a : an English writ formerly requiring a person to show by what authority he exercises a public office, franchise, or liberty **b :** a legal proceeding for a like purpose begun by an information
2 : the legal action begun by a quo warranto

Qur·'an *also* **Qur·an** \kə-'ran, -'rän; kü-'ran, -'rän\ *variant of* KORAN

QWER·TY \'kwər-tē, 'kwer-\ *noun, often not capitalized* [from the first six letters in the second row of the keyboard] (1929)
: a standard typewriter keyboard — called also *QWERTY keyboard*

R *is the eighteenth letter of the English alphabet. It came through Latin by way of Etruscan from Greek* rhō, *which originated as a borrowing of Phoenician* rês. *In English* r *usually denotes the consonant shared by* run, dry, *and* very. *In words derived from Greek the letter* h *that is usually written after* r *to represent* rhō *with a rough breathing mark over it (as in* rhapsody *and* rhetoric*) does not affect the pronunciation of the English word. In many regional dialects of the United States (as those of eastern New England, metropolitan New York, and the South) and in England, an* r *sound at the end of a syllable is "dropped," that is, either it is not pronounced and the preceding vowel is lengthened slightly or it is pronounced as the neutral schwa sound with little or no* r *quality in it. The small* r *form developed in the late Roman period through the gradual degeneration of the loop and tail of the capital form.*

r \'är\ *noun, plural* **r's** *or* **rs** \'ärz\ *often capitalized, often attributive* (before 12th century)
1 a : the 18th letter of the English alphabet **b :** a graphic representation of this letter **c :** a speech counterpart of orthographic *r*
2 : a graphic device for reproducing the letter *r*
3 : one designated *r* especially as the 18th in order or class
4 : something shaped like the letter R
R *certification mark*
— used to certify that a motion picture is of such a nature that admission is restricted to persons over a specified age (as 17) unless accompanied by a parent or guardian; compare G, NC-17, PG, PG-13
Ra \'rä\ *noun* [Egyptian *rʿ*]
: the Egyptian sun-god and chief deity
ra·ba·to \rə-'bä-(,)tō\ *noun, plural* **-tos** [modification of Middle French *rabat*, literally, act of turning down, from *rabattre*] (1591)
: a wide lace-edged collar of the early 17th century often stiffened to stand high at the back
¹rab·bet \'ra-bət\ *noun* [Middle English *rabet*, from Middle French *rabat* act of beating down, from Old French *rabattre* to beat down, reduce — more at REBATE] (14th century)
: a channel, groove, or recess cut out of the edge or face of a surface; *especially* : one that is intended to receive another member (as a panel)
²rabbet (15th century)
transitive verb
1 : to unite the edges of in a rabbet joint
2 : to cut a rabbet in
intransitive verb
: to become joined by a rabbet
rabbet joint *noun* (circa 1828)
: a joint formed by fitting together rabbeted boards or timbers
rab·bi \'ra-,bī\ *noun* [Middle English, from Old English, from Late Latin, from Greek *rhabbi*, from Hebrew *rabbī* my master, from *rabh* master + *-ī* my] (before 12th century)
1 : MASTER, TEACHER — used by Jews as a term of address
2 : a Jew qualified to expound and apply the halakah and other Jewish law
3 : a Jew trained and ordained for professional religious leadership; *specifically* : the official leader of a Jewish congregation
rab·bin \'ra-bən\ *noun* [French] (1579)
: RABBI
rab·bin·ate \'ra-bə-nət, -,nāt\ *noun* (1702)

rabbet joint

1 : the office or tenure of a rabbi
2 : the whole body of rabbis
rab·bin·ic \rə-'bi-nik, ra-\ *or* **rab·bin·i·cal** \-ni-kəl\ *adjective* (1612)
1 : of or relating to rabbis or their writings
2 : of or preparing for the rabbinate
3 : comprising or belonging to any of several sets of Hebrew characters simpler than the square Hebrew letters
— **rab·bin·i·cal·ly** \-ni-k(ə-)lē\ *adverb*
Rabbinic Hebrew *noun* (circa 1909)
: the Hebrew used especially by medieval rabbis
rab·bin·ism \'ra-bə-,ni-zəm\ *noun* (1652)
: rabbinic teachings and traditions
¹rab·bit \'ra-bət\ *noun, plural* **rabbit** *or* **rabbits** *often attributive* [Middle English *rabet*, probably from Middle French dialect (Walloon) *robett*, from Middle Dutch *robe*] (14th century)
1 : any of a family (Leporidae) of long-eared short-tailed lagomorph mammals with long hind legs: **a :** any of various lagomorphs that are born naked, blind, and helpless, that are sometimes gregarious, and that include especially the cottontails of the New World and a small Old World mammal (*Oryctolagus cuniculus*) that is the source of various domestic breeds **b :** HARE
2 : the pelt of a rabbit
3 : WELSH RABBIT
4 a : a figure of a rabbit sped mechanically along the edge of a dog track as an object of pursuit **b :** a runner in a long-distance race who sets a fast pace for the field in the first part of the race
— **rab·bity** \-bə-tē\ *adjective*
²rabbit *intransitive verb* (1852)
: to hunt rabbits
— **rab·bit·er** *noun*
rab·bit-brush \'ra-bət-,brəsh\ *noun* (circa 1890)
: any of several low branching composite shrubs (genus *Chrysothamnus* and especially *C. nauseosus*) of the alkali plains of western North America that are characterized by linear entire leaves and clusters of golden yellow or white flowers
rabbit ears *noun plural* (1952)
: an indoor dipole television antenna consisting of two usually extensible rods connected to a base to form a V shape
rabbit fever *noun* (1925)
: TULAREMIA
rabbit punch *noun* (1915)
: a short chopping blow delivered to the back of the neck or the base of the skull
— **rabbit-punch** *transitive verb*
rab·bit·ry \'ra-bə-trē\ *noun, plural* **-ries** (1838)

: a place where domestic rabbits are kept; *also* : a rabbit-raising enterprise
¹rab·ble \'ra-bəl\ *noun* [Middle English *rabel* pack of animals] (14th century)
1 : a disorganized or confused collection of things
2 a : a disorganized or disorderly crowd of people : MOB **b :** the lowest class of people
²rabble *transitive verb* **rab·bled; rab·bling** \-b(ə-)liŋ\ (1644)
: to insult or assault by or as a mob
rab·ble·ment \'ra-bəl-mənt\ *noun* (1548)
1 : RABBLE
2 : DISTURBANCE
rab·ble–rous·er \'ra-bəl-,rau̇-zər\ *noun* (1843)
: one that stirs up (as to hatred or violence) the masses of the people : DEMAGOGUE
— **rab·ble–rous·ing** \-ziŋ\ *noun or adjective*
Ra·be·lai·sian \,ra-bə-'lā-zhən, -zē-ən\ *adjective* (1817)
1 : of, relating to, or characteristic of Rabelais or his works
2 : marked by gross robust humor, extravagance of caricature, or bold naturalism
Ra·bi \'rə-bē\ *noun* [Arabic *rabīʿ*] (circa 1769)
: either of two months of the Islamic year: **a :** the 3d month **b :** the 4th month — see MONTH table
ra·bic \'rā-bik\ *adjective* (1885)
: of or relating to rabies
ra·bid \'ra-bəd *also* 'rā-\ *adjective* [Latin *rabidus* mad, from *rabere*] (1611)
1 a : extremely violent : FURIOUS **b :** going to extreme lengths in expressing or pursuing a feeling, interest, or opinion
2 : affected with rabies
— **ra·bid·i·ty** \rə-'bi-də-tē, ra-, rā-\ *noun*
— **ra·bid·ly** \'ra-bəd-lē *also* 'rā-\ *adverb*
— **ra·bid·ness** *noun*
ra·bies \'rā-bēz\ *noun, plural* **rabies** [New Latin, from Latin, madness, from *rabere* to rave — more at RAGE] (circa 1598)
: an acute virus disease of the nervous system of warm-blooded animals usually transmitted through the bite of a rabid animal and typically characterized by increased salivation, abnormal behavior, and eventual paralysis and death
rac·coon \ra-'kün *also* rə-\ *noun, plural* **raccoon** *or* **raccoons** [Virginia Algonquian *raugroughcun, arocoun*] (1608)
1 a : a small nocturnal carnivore (*Procyon lotor*) of North America that is chiefly gray, has a black mask and bushy ringed tail, lives chiefly in trees, and has a varied diet including small animals, fruits, and nuts **b :** the pelt of this animal

raccoon 1a

2 : any of several animals resembling or related to the raccoon ◆
raccoon dog *noun* (1868)
: a small omnivorous canid (*Nyctereutes procyonoides*) of eastern Asia having a long yellowish brown coat and facial markings resembling that of a raccoon — called also *tanuki*
¹race \'rās\ *noun* [Middle English *ras*, from Old Norse *rās*; akin to Old English *rǣs* rush] (14th century)
1 *chiefly Scottish* : the act of running
2 a : a strong or rapid current of water flowing through a narrow channel **b :** a watercourse used industrially **c :** the current flowing in such a course

3 a : a set course or duration of time **b :** the course of life
4 a : a contest of speed **b** *plural* **:** a meeting in which several races (as for horses) are run **c :** a contest or rivalry involving progress toward a goal ⟨pennant *race*⟩
5 : a track or channel in which something rolls or slides; *specifically* **:** a groove (as for the balls) in a bearing — see ROLLER BEARING illustration

²**race** *verb* **raced; rac·ing** (15th century)
intransitive verb
1 : to compete in a race
2 : to go or move at top speed or out of control
3 : to revolve too fast under a diminished load
transitive verb
1 : to engage in a race with
2 a : to enter in a race **b :** to drive or ride at high speed **c :** to transport or propel at maximum speed
3 : to speed (as an engine) without a working load or with the transmission disengaged

³**race** *noun* [Middle French, generation, from Old Italian *razza*] (1580)
1 : a breeding stock of animals
2 a : a family, tribe, people, or nation belonging to the same stock **b :** a class or kind of people united by community of interests, habits, or characteristics ⟨the English *race*⟩
3 a : an actually or potentially interbreeding group within a species; *also* **:** a taxonomic category (as a subspecies) representing such a group **b :** BREED **c :** a division of mankind possessing traits that are transmissible by descent and sufficient to characterize it as a distinct human type
4 *obsolete* **:** inherited temperament or disposition
5 : distinctive flavor, taste, or strength

race·course \ˈrās-ˌkȯrs, -ˌkōrs\ *noun* (1764)
1 : a course for racing
2 : RACEWAY 1

race·horse \-ˌhȯrs\ *noun* (circa 1626)
: a horse bred or kept for racing

ra·ce·mate \rā-ˈsē-ˌmāt, rə-; ˈra-sə-\ *noun* (1907)
: a racemic compound or mixture

ra·ceme \rā-ˈsēm, rə-\ *noun* [Latin *racemus* bunch of grapes; probably akin to Greek *rhag-, rhax* grape] (1785)
: a simple inflorescence (as in the lily-of-the-valley) in which the flowers are borne on short stalks of about equal length at equal distances along an elongated axis and open in succession toward the apex — see INFLORESCENCE illustration

ra·ce·mic \-ˈsē-mik\ *adjective* (1892)
: of, relating to, or constituting a compound or mixture that is composed of equal amounts of dextrorotatory and levorotatory forms of the same compound and is not optically active

ra·ce·mi·za·tion \rā-ˌsē-mə-ˈzā-shən, rə-; ˌra-sə-mə-\ *noun* (1895)
: the action or process of changing from an optically active compound into a racemic compound or mixture
— **ra·ce·mize** \rā-ˈsē-ˌmīz, rə-; ˈra-sə-\ *verb*

ra·ce·mose \ˈra-sə-ˌmōs; rā-ˈsē-, rə-\ *adjective* [Latin *racemosus* full of clusters, from *racemus*] (1698)
: having or growing in the form of a raceme

rac·er \ˈrā-sər\ *noun* (1649)
1 : one that races or is used for racing
2 : any of various active American colubrid snakes (genus *Coluber* and *Mastigophis*); *especially* **:** BLACK RACER

race riot *noun* (1890)
: a riot caused by racial dissensions or hatreds

race runner *noun* (1915)
: a North American lizard (*Cnemidophorus sexlineatus*) that moves swiftly

race·track \ˈrās-ˌtrak\ *noun* (1859)
: a usually oval course for racing

race·track·er \-ˌtra-kər\ *noun* (1953)
: one who frequents a racetrack

race·walk·ing \-ˌwȯ-kiŋ\ *noun* (1962)
: the competitive sport of racing at a fast walk while maintaining continuous foot contact with the ground and keeping the supporting leg straight
— **race·walk·er** \-kər\ *noun*

race·way \-ˌwā\ *noun* (1828)
1 : a canal for a current of water
2 : a channel for loosely holding electrical wires in buildings
3 : ¹RACE 5
4 : a course for racing; *especially* **:** a track for harness racing

rach·et \ˈra-chət\ *variant of* RATCHET

ra·chis \ˈrā-kəs, ˈra-\ *noun, plural* **ra·chis·es** *also* **ra·chi·des** \ˈra-kə-ˌdēz, ˈrā-\ [New Latin *rachid-, rachis,* from Greek *rhachis;* akin to Greek *rhachos* thorn, Lithuanian *ražas* dry twig, tine] (1842)
1 : SPINAL COLUMN
2 : an axial structure: as **a** (1) **:** the elongated axis of an inflorescence (2) **:** an extension of the petiole of a compound leaf that bears the leaflets **b :** the distal part of the shaft of a feather that bears the web

ra·chit·ic \rə-ˈki-tik\ *adjective* [New Latin *rachitis* rickets, from Greek *rhachitis* spinal disease, from *rhachis*] (1797)
: RICKETY

ra·cial \ˈrā-shəl\ *adjective* (1862)
1 : of, relating to, or based on a race
2 : existing or occurring between races
— **ra·cial·ly** \-shə-lē\ *adverb*

ra·cial·ism \ˈrā-shə-ˌli-zəm\ *noun* (1907)
: RACISM
— **ra·cial·ist** \-list\ *noun or adjective*
— **ra·cial·is·tic** \ˌrā-shə-ˈlis-tik\ *adjective*

rac·ing \ˈrā-siŋ\ *noun* (1680)
: the sport or profession of engaging in or holding races

racing form *noun* (1946)
: an information sheet giving details of past performance (as for racehorses) for use by bettors

rac·ism \ˈrā-ˌsi-zəm *also* -ˌshi-\ *noun* (1936)
1 : a belief that race is the primary determinant of human traits and capacities and that racial differences produce an inherent superiority of a particular race
2 : racial prejudice or discrimination
— **rac·ist** \-sist *also* -shist\ *noun or adjective*

¹**rack** \ˈrak\ *noun* [Middle English *rak,* probably of Scandinavian origin; akin to Swedish dialect *rak* wreck; akin to Old English *wrecan* to drive — more at WREAK] (14th century)
: a wind-driven mass of high often broken clouds

²**rack** *intransitive verb* (1590)
: to fly or scud in high wind

³**rack** *noun* [Middle English, probably from Middle Dutch *rec* framework; akin to Old English *reccan* to stretch, Greek *oregein* — more at RIGHT] (14th century)
1 : a framework for holding fodder for livestock
2 : an instrument of torture on which a body is stretched
3 a (1) **:** a cause of anguish or pain (2) **:** acute suffering **b :** the action of straining or wrenching
4 : a framework, stand, or grating on or in which articles are placed
5 : a frame placed in a stream to stop fish and floating or suspended matter
6 a : a bar with teeth on one face for gearing with a pinion or worm gear to transform rotary motion to linear motion or vice versa (as in an automobile steering mechanism or microscope

drawtube) **b :** a notched bar used as a ratchet to engage with a pawl, click, or detent
7 : a pair of antlers
8 : a triangular frame used to set up the balls in a pool game; *also* **:** the balls as set up
— **rack·ful** \-ˌfu̇l\ *noun*
— **on the rack :** under great mental or emotional stress

⁴**rack** (15th century)
transitive verb
1 : to torture on the rack
2 : to cause to suffer torture, pain, or anguish
3 a : to stretch or strain violently ⟨*racked* his brains⟩ **b :** to raise (rents) oppressively **c :** to harass or oppress with high rents or extortions
4 : to work or treat (material) on a rack
5 : to work by a rack and pinion or worm so as to extend or contract ⟨*rack* a camera⟩
6 : to seize (as parallel ropes of a tackle) together
7 : to place (as pool balls) in a rack
intransitive verb
: to become forced out of shape or out of plumb
synonym see AFFLICT
— **rack·er** *noun*
— **rack·ing·ly** \ˈra-kiŋ-lē\ *adverb*

⁵**rack** *transitive verb* [Middle English *rakken,* from Old Provençal *arraca,* from *raca* stems and husks of pressed grapes] (15th century)
: to draw off (as wine) from the lees

⁶**rack** *intransitive verb* [probably alteration of ¹*rock*] (1530)
of a horse **:** to go at a rack

⁷**rack** *noun* (1580)
: either of two gaits of a horse: **a :** PACE 4b **b :** a fast showy 4-beat gait

⁸**rack** *noun* [perhaps from ³*rack*] (1570)
1 : the neck and spine of a forequarter of veal, pork, or especially mutton
2 : the rib section of a foresaddle of lamb used for chops or as a roast — see LAMB illustration

⁹**rack** *noun* [alteration of *wrack*] (1599)
: DESTRUCTION ⟨*rack* and ruin⟩

¹**rack·et** *also* **rac·quet** \ˈra-kət\ *noun* [Mid-

\a\ abut \ᵊ\ kitten \ər\ **further** \a\ ash \ā\ ace
\ä\ mop, mar \au̇\ **out** \ch\ chin \e\ bet \ē\ **easy**
\g\ go \h\ **hit** \ī\ ice \j\ job \ŋ\ **sing** \ō\ **go**
\ȯ\ law \ȯi\ **boy** \th\ **thin** \t̲h̲\ **the** \ü\ **loot** \u̇\ **foot**
\y\ **yet** \zh\ **vision** *see also* Guide to Pronunciation

dle French *raquette,* ultimately from Arabic *rāḥah* palm of the hand] (circa 1520)
1 : a lightweight implement that consists of a netting (as of nylon) stretched in a usually oval open frame with a handle attached and that is used for striking the ball or shuttlecock in various games (as tennis, racquets, or badminton)

racket 1: *A* tennis, *B* racquetball, *C* badminton

2 *usually* **racquets** *plural but singular in construction* : a game for two or four players with ball and racket on a 4-walled court
²racket *noun* [origin unknown] (1565)
1 : confused clattering noise : CLAMOR
2 a : social whirl or excitement **b** : the strain of exciting or trying experiences
3 a : a fraudulent scheme, enterprise, or activity **b** : a usually illegitimate enterprise made workable by bribery or intimidation **c** : an easy and lucrative means of livelihood **d** *slang* : OCCUPATION, BUSINESS
³racket *intransitive verb* (1609)
1 : to engage in active social life
2 : to move with or make a racket
¹rack·e·teer \,ra-kə-'tir\ *noun* (1928)
: one who obtains money by an illegal enterprise usually involving intimidation
²racketeer (1928)
intransitive verb
: to carry on a racket
transitive verb
: to practice extortion on
rack·et·y \'ra-kə-tē\ *adjective* (1773)
1 : NOISY
2 : FLASHY, ROWDY
3 : RICKETY
rack·le \'ra-kəl\ *adjective* [Middle English *rakel*] (14th century)
chiefly Scottish : IMPETUOUS
rack railway *noun* (1884)
: a railway having between its rails a rack that meshes with a gear wheel or pinion of the locomotive for traction on steep grades
rack–rent *transitive verb* (1748)
: to subject to rack rent
rack rent *noun* [⁴*rack*] (1607)
1 : an excessive or unreasonably high rent
2 *British* : the highest rent that can be earned on a property
rack–rent·er \'rak-,ren-tər\ *noun* (1680)
: one that pays or exacts rack rent
rack up *transitive verb* (1949)
: ACCUMULATE, GAIN ⟨*racked up* their tenth victory⟩
ra·clette \ra-'klet, rä-\ *noun* [French, literally, scraper, from *racler* to scrape, from Middle French *rasclar,* from Old Provençal *rasclar,* from (assumed) Vulgar Latin *rasiculare,* from Latin *rasus,* past participle of *radere* to scrape — more at RODENT] (circa 1949)
: a Swiss dish consisting of cheese melted over a fire and then scraped onto bread or boiled potatoes; *also* : the cheese used in this dish
ra·con \'rä-,kän\ *noun* [radar bea*con*] (1945)
: RADAR BEACON
ra·con·teur \,ra-,kän-'tər, -kən-\ *noun* [French, from Middle French, from *raconter* to tell, from Old French, from *re-* + *aconter, acompter* to tell, count — more at ACCOUNT] (1828)
: a person who excels in telling anecdotes
ra·coon *variant of* RACCOON
rac·quet·ball \'ra-kət-,bȯl\ *noun* (1968)
: a game similar to handball that is played on a

4-walled court with a short-handled racket and a larger ball
¹racy \'rā-sē\ *adjective* **rac·i·er; -est** [³*race*] (circa 1650)
1 a : full of zest or vigor **b** : having a strongly marked quality : PIQUANT ⟨a *racy* flavor⟩ **c** : RISQUÉ, SUGGESTIVE
2 : having the distinctive quality of something in its original or most characteristic form
synonym see PUNGENT
— **rac·i·ly** \'rā-sə-lē\ *adverb*
— **rac·i·ness** \-sē-nəs\ *noun*
²racy *adjective* **rac·i·er; -est** [¹*race*] (1841)
: having a body fitted for racing : long-bodied and lean
¹rad \'rad\ *noun* [radiation absorbed dose] (1918)
: a unit of absorbed dose of ionizing radiation equal to an energy of 100 ergs per gram of irradiated material
²rad *adjective* (1982)
slang : COOL 7, RADICAL
ra·dar \'rā-,där\ *noun, often attributive* [radio detecting and ranging] (1941)
: a device or system consisting usually of a synchronized radio transmitter and receiver that emits radio waves and processes their reflections for display and is used especially for detecting and locating objects (as aircraft) or surface features (as of a planet)
radar astronomy *noun* (1959)
: astronomy in which celestial bodies in the solar system are studied by analyzing the return of radio waves directed at them
radar beacon *noun* (1945)
: a radar transmitter that upon receiving a radar signal emits a signal which reinforces the normal reflected signal or which introduces a code into the reflected signal especially for identification purposes
ra·dar·scope \'rā-,där-,skōp\ *noun* [radar + oscillo*scope*] (1945)
: the oscilloscope or screen serving as the visual indicator in a radar receiver
¹rad·dle \'ra-dᵊl\ *noun* [Middle English *radel,* from diminutive of *rad-, red* red] (14th century)
: RED OCHER
²raddle *transitive verb* **rad·dled; rad·dling** \'rad-liŋ, 'ra-dᵊl-iŋ\ (1631)
: to mark or paint with raddle
³raddle *transitive verb* **rad·dled; rad·dling** \'rad-liŋ, 'ra-dᵊl-iŋ\ [English dialect *raddle* supple stick interwoven with others as in making a fence] (1671)
: to twist together : INTERWEAVE
rad·dled \'ra-dᵊld\ *adjective* [origin unknown] (1694)
1 : being in a state of confusion : lacking composure
2 : BROKEN-DOWN, WORN
radi- *or* **radio-** *combining form* [French, from Latin *radius* ray]
1 : radiant energy : radiation ⟨*radio*active⟩ ⟨*radio*paque⟩
2 : radioactive ⟨*radio*element⟩
3 : radium : X rays ⟨*radio*therapy⟩
4 : radioactive isotopes especially as produced artificially ⟨*radio*carbon⟩
5 : radio ⟨*radio*telegraphy⟩
¹ra·di·al \'rā-dē-əl\ *adjective* [Medieval Latin *radialis,* from Latin *radius* ray] (1570)
1 : arranged or having parts arranged like rays
2 a : relating to, placed like, or moving along a radius **b** : characterized by divergence from a center
3 : of, relating to, or adjacent to a bodily radius
4 : developing uniformly around a central axis
— **ra·di·al·ly** \-ə-lē\ *adverb*
²radial *noun* (1872)
1 a : a radial part **b** : RAY
2 : a body part (as an artery) lying near or following the course of the radius

3 : a pneumatic tire in which the ply cords that extend to the beads are laid at approximately 90 degrees to the centerline of the tread — called also *radial-ply tire, radial tire*
radial cleavage *noun* (1973)
: holoblastic cleavage that is typical of deuterostomes and that is characterized by arrangement of the blastomeres of each upper tier directly over those of the next lower tier resulting in radial symmetry around the pole to pole axis of the embryo — compare SPIRAL CLEAVAGE
radial engine *noun* (1909)
: a usually internal combustion engine with cylinders arranged radially like the spokes of a wheel
radial ker·a·tot·o·my \-,ker-ə-'tä-tə-mē\ *noun* (1980)
: multiple incision of the cornea in a radial pattern that is performed to correct myopia
radial symmetry *noun* (circa 1890)
: the condition of having similar parts regularly arranged around a central axis
— **radially symmetrical** *adjective*
ra·di·an \'rā-dē-ən\ *noun* (1879)
: a unit of plane angular measurement that is equal to the angle at the center of a circle subtended by an arc equal in length to the radius
ra·di·ance \'rā-dē-ən(t)s\ *noun* (1601)
1 : the quality or state of being radiant
2 : a deep pink
3 : the flux density of radiant energy per unit solid angle and per unit projected area of radiating surface
ra·di·an·cy \-ən(t)-sē\ *noun* (1646)
: RADIANCE
¹ra·di·ant \'rā-dē-ənt\ *adjective* (15th century)
1 a : radiating rays or reflecting beams of light **b** : vividly bright and shining : GLOWING
2 : marked by or expressive of love, confidence, or happiness ⟨a *radiant* smile⟩
3 a : emitted or transmitted by radiation **b** : emitting or relating to radiant heat
synonym see BRIGHT
— **ra·di·ant·ly** *adverb*
²radiant *noun* (circa 1741)
: something that radiates: as **a** : a point in the heavens at which the visible parallel paths of meteors appear to meet when traced backward **b** : the part of a gas or electric heater that becomes incandescent
radiant energy *noun* (circa 1890)
: energy traveling as electromagnetic waves
radiant flux *noun* (1917)
: the rate of emission or transmission of radiant energy
radiant heat *noun* (1794)
: heat transmitted by radiation as contrasted with that transmitted by conduction or convection
¹ra·di·ate \'rā-dē-,āt\ *verb* **-at·ed; -at·ing** [Latin *radiatus,* past participle of *radiare,* from *radius* ray] (circa 1619)
intransitive verb
1 : to proceed in a direct line from or toward a center
2 : to send out rays : shine brightly
3 a : to issue in or as if in rays **b** : to evolve by adaptive radiation
transitive verb
1 : to send out in or as if in rays
2 : IRRADIATE, ILLUMINATE
3 : to spread abroad or around as if from a center
²ra·di·ate \'rā-dē-ət, -,āt\ *adjective* (1668)
: having rays or radial parts: as **a** : having ray flowers **b** : characterized by radial symmetry : radially symmetrical
— **ra·di·ate·ly** *adverb*
ra·di·a·tion \,rā-dē-'ā-shən\ *noun* (15th century)
1 a : the action or process of radiating **b** : the process of emitting radiant energy in the form

of waves or particles **c** (1) **:** the combined processes of emission, transmission, and absorption of radiant energy (2) **:** the transfer of heat by radiation — compare CONDUCTION, CONVECTION

2 a : something that is radiated **b :** energy radiated in the form of waves or particles
3 : radial arrangement
4 : ADAPTIVE RADIATION
5 : RADIATOR
— **ra·di·a·tion·al** \-shnəl, -shə-n°l\ *adjective*
— **ra·di·a·tion·less** \-shən-ləs\ *adjective*
— **ra·di·a·tive** \'rā-dē-ˌā-tiv\ *adjective*

radiation sickness *noun* (1924)
: sickness that results from exposure to radiation and is commonly marked by fatigue, nausea, vomiting, loss of teeth and hair, and in more severe cases by damage to blood-forming tissue with decrease in red and white blood cells and with bleeding

ra·di·a·tor \'rā-dē-ˌā-tər, *dialect* 'ra-\ *noun* (1836)
: one that radiates: as **a :** any of various devices (as a nest of pipes or tubes) for transferring heat from a fluid within to an area or object outside **b :** a transmitting antenna

¹**rad·i·cal** \'ra-di-kəl\ *adjective* [Middle English, from Late Latin *radicalis*, from Latin *radic-, radix* root — more at ROOT] (14th century)
1 : of, relating to, or proceeding from a root: as **a** (1) **:** of or growing from the root of a plant ⟨*radical* tubers⟩ (2) **:** growing from the base of a stem, from a rootlike stem, or from a stem that does not rise above the ground ⟨*radical* leaves⟩ **b :** of, relating to, or constituting a linguistic root **c :** of or relating to a mathematical root **d :** designed to remove the root of a disease or all diseased tissue ⟨*radical* surgery⟩
2 : of or relating to the origin **:** FUNDAMENTAL
3 a : marked by a considerable departure from the usual or traditional **:** EXTREME **b :** tending or disposed to make extreme changes in existing views, habits, conditions, or institutions **c :** of, relating to, or constituting a political group associated with views, practices, and policies of extreme change **d :** advocating extreme measures to retain or restore a political state of affairs ⟨the *radical* right⟩
4 *slang* **:** EXCELLENT, COOL ◇
— **rad·i·cal·ness** *noun*

²**radical** *noun* (1641)
1 a : a root part **b :** a basic principle **:** FOUNDATION
2 a : ROOT 6 **b :** a sound or letter belonging to a radical
3 : one who is radical
4 : FREE RADICAL; *also* **:** a group of atoms bonded together that is considered an entity in various kinds of reactions
5 a : a mathematical expression indicating a root by means of a radical sign **b :** RADICAL SIGN

radical chic *noun* (1970)
: a fashionable practice among socially prominent people of associating with radicals or members of minority groups

rad·i·cal·ise *British variant of* RADICALIZE

rad·i·cal·ism \'ra-di-kə-ˌli-zəm\ *noun* (1820)
1 : the quality or state of being radical
2 : the doctrines or principles of radicals

rad·i·cal·ize \-kə-ˌlīz\ *transitive verb* **-ized; -iz·ing** (1830)
: to make radical especially in politics
— **rad·i·cal·i·za·tion** \ˌra-di-kə-lə-'zā-shən\ *noun*

rad·i·cal·ly \'ra-di-k(ə-)lē\ *adverb* (15th century)
1 : in origin or essence
2 : in a radical or extreme manner

radical sign *noun* (1668)
: the sign √ or √ placed before an expression to denote that the square root is to be ex-

tracted or that the root marked by an index (as in ∛ or ∜ for the cube root) is to be extracted

rad·i·cand \ˌra-də-'kand\ *noun* [Latin *radicandum*, neuter of *radicandus*, gerundive of *radicari*] (circa 1890)
: the quantity under a radical sign

ra·dic·chio \ra-'di-kē-ō\ *noun* [Italian, chicory, from (assumed) Vulgar Latin *radiculus*, alteration of Latin *radicula*] (1968)
: a chicory of a red variety with variegated leaves that is used as a salad green

radices *plural of* RADIX

rad·i·cle \'ra-di-kəl\ *noun* [Latin *radicula*, diminutive of *radic-, radix*] (1671)
1 : the lower part of the axis of a plant embryo or seedling : **a :** the embryonic root of a seedling **b :** HYPOCOTYL **c :** the hypocotyl and the root together
2 : RADICAL

ra·dic·u·lar \rə-'di-kyə-lər, ra-\ *adjective* (1830)
1 : of or relating to a plant radicle
2 : of, relating to, or involving a nerve root ⟨*radicular* pain⟩

radii *plural of* RADIUS

¹**ra·dio** \'rā-dē-ˌō\ *adjective* [²*radio* or *radio-*] (1887)
1 : of, relating to, or operated by radiant energy
2 : of or relating to electric currents or phenomena (as electromagnetic radiation) of frequencies between about 15,000 and 10¹¹ hertz
3 a : of, relating to, or used in radio or a radio set **b :** specializing in radio or associated with the radio industry **c** (1) **:** transmitted by radio (2) **:** making or participating in radio broadcasts **d :** controlled or directed by radio

²**radio** *noun, plural* **ra·di·os** [short for *radiotelegraphy*] (1903)
1 a : the wireless transmission and reception of electric impulses or signals by means of electromagnetic waves **b :** the use of these waves for the wireless transmission of electric impulses into which sound is converted
2 : a radio message
3 : a radio receiving set
4 a : a radio transmitting station **b :** a radio broadcasting organization **c :** the radio broadcasting industry **d :** communication by radio

³**radio** (1913)
transitive verb
1 : to send or communicate by radio
2 : to send a radio message to
intransitive verb
: to send or communicate something by radio

radio- — see RADI-

ra·dio·ac·tive \ˌrā-dē-ō-'ak-tiv\ *adjective* [International Scientific Vocabulary] (1898)
: of, caused by, or exhibiting radioactivity
— **ra·dio·ac·tive·ly** *adverb*

ra·dio·ac·tiv·i·ty \-ak-'ti-və-tē\ *noun* [International Scientific Vocabulary] (1899)
: the property possessed by some elements (as uranium) or isotopes (as carbon 14) of spontaneously emitting energetic particles (as electrons or alpha particles) by the disintegration of their atomic nuclei; *also* **:** the rays emitted

ra·dio·al·ler·go·sor·bent \ˌrā-dē-ō-ə-ˌlər-gō-'sȯr-bənt\ *adjective* [radi- + allergen + -o- + sorbent] (1967)
: relating to or being a blood analysis that tests for allergen-specific antibodies and is used to detect allergic reactions

radio astronomy *noun* (1948)
: astronomy dealing with radio waves received from outside the earth's atmosphere
— **radio astronomer** *noun*
— **radio astronomical** *adjective*

ra·dio·au·to·graph \ˌrā-dē-ō-'ȯ-tə-ˌgraf\ *noun* (1941)
: AUTORADIOGRAPH
— **ra·dio·au·to·graph·ic** \-ˌȯ-tə-'gra-fik\ *adjective*

— **ra·dio·au·tog·ra·phy** \-ȯ-'tä-grə-fē\ *noun*

radio beacon *noun* (1919)
: a radio transmitting station that transmits special radio signals for use (as on a landing field) in determining the direction or position of those receiving them

ra·dio·bi·ol·o·gy \ˌrā-dē-ō-bī-'ä-lə-jē\ *noun* (1919)
: a branch of biology dealing with the effects of radiation or radioactive materials on biological systems
— **ra·dio·bi·o·log·i·cal** \-ˌbī-ə-'lä-ji-kəl\ *also* **ra·dio·bi·o·log·ic** \-jik\ *adjective*
— **ra·dio·bi·o·log·i·cal·ly** \-ji-k(ə-)lē\ *adverb*
— **ra·dio·bi·ol·o·gist** \-bī-'ä-lə-jist\ *noun*

radio car *noun* (1925)
: an automobile equipped with radio communication

ra·dio·car·bon \ˌrā-dē-ō-'kär-bən\ *noun, often attributive* [International Scientific Vocabulary] (1939)
: radioactive carbon; *especially* **:** CARBON 14

radiocarbon dating *noun* (1951)
: CARBON DATING
— **radiocarbon–date** \-'dāt\ *transitive verb*

ra·dio·chem·is·try \ˌrā-dē-ō-'ke-mə-strē\ *noun* (1904)
: a branch of chemistry dealing with radioactive substances and phenomena including tracer studies
— **ra·dio·chem·i·cal** \-'ke-mi-kəl\ *adjective*
— **ra·dio·chem·i·cal·ly** \-k(ə-)lē\ *adverb*
— **ra·dio·chem·ist** \-'ke-mist\ *noun*

ra·dio·chro·ma·to·gram \-krō-'ma-tə-ˌgram, -krə-\ *noun* (1951)
: a chromatogram revealing one or more radioactive substances

radio compass *noun* (1918)
: a direction finder used in navigation

ra·dio·ecol·o·gy \ˌrā-dē-ō-i-'kä-lə-jē\ *noun* (1956)
: the study of the effects of radiation and radioactive substances on ecological communities

ra·dio·el·e·ment \-'e-lə-mənt\ *noun* [International Scientific Vocabulary] (1903)
: a radioactive element

radio frequency *noun* (1915)
: any of the electromagnetic wave frequencies that lie in the range extending from below 3 kilohertz to about 300 gigahertz and that in-

◇ WORD HISTORY
radical The Late Latin adjective *radicalis* "rooted, having roots," a derivative of Latin *radix* "root," was borrowed into later Middle English as *radical*. Aside from its literal meaning "of a root," *radical* in the 16th century meant "primary" or "fundamental," that is, effecting the "root" of something. In the 17th and 18th centuries *radical* increasingly began to modify nouns such as *change* or *cure* and gradually shifted from the sense "fundamental" to "thorough" and then "extreme." This shift was complete by the year 1800, when *radical reform* became a political catch-phrase, and an advocate of radical reform was called a *radical*. In the 20th century *radical*, when applied to opinions or to advocates of a particular cause, is practically synonymous with *extremist*.

\ə\ **abut** \ᵊ\ **kitten** \ər\ **further** \a\ **ash** \ā\ **ace**
\ä\ **mop, mar** \au̇\ **out** \ch\ **chin** \e\ **bet** \ē\ **easy**
\g\ **go** \i\ **hit** \ī\ **ice** \j\ **job** \ŋ\ **sing** \ō\ **go**
\ȯ\ **law** \ȯi\ **boy** \th\ **thin** \t͟h\ **the** \ü\ **loot** \u̇\ **foot**
\y\ **yet** \zh\ **vision** *see also* Guide to Pronunciation

RADIO FREQUENCIES

CLASS	ABBREVIATION	RANGE
extremely low frequency	ELF	below 3 kilohertz
very low frequency	VLF	3 to 30 kilohertz
low frequency	LF	30 to 300 kilohertz
medium frequency	MF	300 to 3000 kilohertz
high frequency	HF	3 to 30 megahertz
very high frequency	VHF	30 to 300 megahertz
ultrahigh frequency	UHF	300 to 3000 megahertz
superhigh frequency	SHF	3 to 30 gigahertz
extremely high frequency	EHF	30 to 300 gigahertz

clude the frequencies used for radio and television transmission

radio galaxy *noun* (1960)
: a galaxy that is a powerful source of radio waves

ra·dio·gen·ic \,rā-dē-ō-'je-nik\ *adjective* (1935)
: produced by or determined from radioactivity ⟨*radiogenic* isotopes⟩ ⟨*radiogenic* tumors⟩

ra·dio·gram \'rā-dē-ō-,gram\ *noun* (1896)
1 : RADIOGRAPH
2 : a message transmitted by radiotelegraphy
3 [short for *radiogramophone*] *British* **:** a combined radio receiver and record player

¹ra·dio·graph \-,graf\ *noun* (1896)
: a picture produced on a sensitive surface by a form of radiation other than visible light; *specifically* **:** an X-ray or gamma ray photograph
— **ra·dio·graph·ic** \,rā-dē-ō-'gra-fik\ *adjective*
— **ra·dio·graph·i·cal·ly** \-fi-k(ə-)lē\ *adverb*

²radiograph *transitive verb* (1896)
: to make a radiograph of

ra·di·og·ra·phy \,rā-dē-'ä-grə-fē\ *noun* [International Scientific Vocabulary] (1896)
: the art, act, or process of making radiographs

ra·dio·im·mu·no·as·say \,rā-dē-,ō-i-myə-nō-'a-,sā, -i-,myü-, -a-'sā\ *noun* (1961)
: immunoassay of a substance that has been radioactively labeled
— **ra·dio·im·mu·no·as·say·able** \-ə-bəl\ *adjective*

ra·dio·iso·tope \,rā-dē-ō-'ī-sə-,tōp\ *noun* [International Scientific Vocabulary] (1946)
: a radioactive isotope
— **ra·dio·iso·to·pic** \-,ī-sə-'tä-pik, -'tō-\ *adjective*
— **ra·dio·iso·to·pi·cal·ly** \-pi-k(ə-)lē\ *adverb*

ra·dio·la·bel \-'lā-bəl\ *transitive verb* (1953)
: to label with a radioactive atom or substance

ra·di·o·lar·i·an \,rā-dē-ō-'lar-ē-ən, -'ler-\ *noun* [ultimately from Late Latin *radiolus* small sunbeam, from diminutive of Latin *radius* ray — more at RAY] (1877)
: any of three classes (Acantharia, Polycystina, and Phaeodaria) of usually spherical marine protozoans having radiating threadlike pseudopodia and often a siliceous skeleton of spicules
— **radiolarian** *adjective*

ra·dio·log·i·cal \,rā-dē-ə-'lä-ji-kəl\ *or* **ra·dio·log·ic** \-jik\ *adjective* (1909)

1 : of or relating to radiology
2 : of or relating to nuclear radiation
— **ra·dio·log·i·cal·ly** \-k(ə-)lē\ *adverb*

ra·di·ol·o·gist \,rā-dē-'ä-lə-jist\ *noun* (1906)
: a physician specializing in the use of radiant energy for diagnostic and therapeutic purposes

ra·di·ol·o·gy \-jē\ *noun* (1900)
1 : a branch of medicine concerned with the use of radiant energy (as X rays and radium) in the diagnosis and treatment of disease
2 : the science of radioactive substances and high-energy radiations

ra·dio·lu·cent \,rā-dē-ō-'lü-s°nt\ *adjective* (1917)
: partly or wholly permeable to radiation ⟨*radiolucent* tissues⟩
— **ra·dio·lu·cen·cy** \-s°n(t)-sē\ *noun*

ra·di·ol·y·sis \,rā-dē-'ä-lə-səs\ *noun* [New Latin] (1948)
: chemical decomposition by the action of radiation
— **ra·dio·lyt·ic** \-dē-ə-'li-tik\ *adjective*

ra·dio·man \'rā-dē-ō-,man\ *noun* (1921)
: a radio operator or technician

ra·di·om·e·ter \,rā-dē-'ä-mə-tər\ *noun* (1875)
: an instrument for measuring the intensity of radiant energy by the torsional twist of suspended vanes that are blackened on one side and exposed to a source of radiant energy; *also* **:** an instrument for measuring electromagnetic or acoustic radiation
— **ra·di·om·e·try** \-mə-trē\ *noun*

radiometer

ra·dio·met·ric \,rā-dē-ō-'me-trik\ *adjective* [International Scientific Vocabulary] (1877)
1 : relating to, using, or measured by a radiometer
2 : of or relating to the measurement of geologic time by means of the rate of disintegration of radioactive elements
— **ra·dio·met·ri·cal·ly** \-tri-k(ə-)lē\ *adverb*

ra·dio·mi·met·ic \-mə-'me-tik, -mī-\ *adjective* [International Scientific Vocabulary] (1947)
: producing effects similar to those of radiation

ra·dio·nu·clide \,rā-dē-ō-'nü-,klīd, -'nyü-\ *noun* (1947)
: a radioactive nuclide

ra·di·opaque \,rā-dē-ō-'pāk\ *adjective* (circa 1923)
: being opaque to various forms of radiation (as X rays)

ra·dio·phar·ma·ceu·ti·cal \,rā-dē-ō-,fär-mə-'sü-ti-kəl\ *noun* (1952)
: a radioactive drug used for diagnostic or therapeutic purposes
— **radiopharmaceutical** *adjective*

ra·dio·phone \'rā-dē-ə-,fōn\ *noun* (1919)
: RADIOTELEPHONE

ra·dio·pho·to \,rā-dē-ō-'fō-(,)tō\ *noun* (1929)
: a picture transmitted by radio

ra·dio·pro·tec·tive \-prə-'tek-tiv\ *adjective* (1956)
: serving to protect or aiding in protecting against the injurious effect of radiations ⟨*radioprotective* drugs⟩
— **ra·dio·pro·tec·tion** \-'tek-shən\ *noun*

radio range *noun* (1929)
: a radio facility for aircraft navigation

ra·dio·sen·si·tive \,rā-dē-ō-'sen(t)-sə-tiv, -'sen(t)-stiv\ *adjective* (1920)
: sensitive to the effects of radiant energy ⟨*radiosensitive* cancer cells⟩
— **ra·dio·sen·si·tiv·i·ty** \-,sen(t)-sə-'ti-və-tē\ *noun*

ra·dio·sonde \'rā-dē-ō-,sänd\ *noun* [International Scientific Vocabulary] (1937)
: a miniature radio transmitter that is carried aloft (as by an unmanned balloon) with instruments for broadcasting the humidity, temperature, and pressure

radio spectrum *noun* (1929)
: the region of the electromagnetic spectrum usually including frequencies below 30,000 megahertz in which radio or radar transmission and detection techniques may be used

radio star *noun* (1948)
: a cosmic radio source; *especially* **:** a point source of radio emissions

ra·dio·stron·tium \,rā-dē-ō-'strän(t)-sh(ē-)əm, -'strän-tē-əm\ *noun* [New Latin] (1941)
: radioactive strontium; *especially* **:** STRONTIUM 90

ra·dio·tele·graph \-'te-lə-,graf\ *noun* [International Scientific Vocabulary] (1903)
: WIRELESS TELEGRAPHY
— **ra·dio·te·leg·ra·phy** \-tə-'le-grə-fē\ *noun*

ra·dio·te·lem·e·try \-tə-'le-mə-trē\ *noun* (1951)
1 : TELEMETRY
2 : BIOTELEMETRY
— **ra·dio·tele·met·ric** \-,te-lə-'me-trik\ *adjective*

ra·dio·tele·phone \-'te-lə-,fōn\ *noun* [International Scientific Vocabulary] (1904)
: an apparatus for carrying on wireless telephony by radio waves
— **ra·dio·te·le·pho·ny** \-tə-'le-fə-nē, -'te-lə-,fō-nē\ *noun*

radio telescope *noun* (1929)
: a radio receiver-antenna combination used for observation in radio astronomy

ra·dio·ther·a·py \,rā-dē-ō-'ther-ə-pē\ *noun* [International Scientific Vocabulary] (1903)
: the treatment of disease with radiation (as X rays)
— **ra·dio·ther·a·pist** \-pist\ *noun*

ra·dio·tho·ri·um \-'thōr-ē-əm, -'thȯr-\ *noun* [New Latin] (1905)
: a radioactive isotope of thorium with the mass number 228

ra·dio·trac·er \'rā-dē-ō-,trā-sər\ *noun* (1946)
: a radioactive tracer

ra·dio·ul·na \,rā-dē-ō-'əl-nə\ *noun* [New Latin] (1960)
: a single bone in the forelimb of an amphibian (as a frog) that represents fusion of the separate radius and ulna of higher vertebrate forms

radio wave *noun* (1916)
: an electromagnetic wave with radio frequency

rad·ish \'ra-dish *also* 're-\ *noun* [Middle English, alteration of Old English *rædic*, from Latin *radic-, radix* root, radish — more at ROOT] (15th century)
: the pungent fleshy root of a widely cultivated Eurasian plant (*Raphanus sativus*) of the mustard family usually eaten raw; *also* **:** a plant that produces radishes

ra·di·um \'rā-dē-əm\ *noun, often attributive* [New Latin, from Latin *radius* ray] (1899)
: an intensely radioactive brilliant white metallic element that resembles barium chemically, occurs in combination in minute quantities in minerals (as pitchblende or carnotite), emits alpha particles and gamma rays to form radon, and is used chiefly in luminous materials and in the treatment of cancer — see ELEMENT table

radium therapy *noun* (1904)
: RADIOTHERAPY

ra·di·us \'rā-dē-əs\ *noun, plural* **ra·dii** \-dē-,ī\ *also* **ra·di·us·es** [Latin, ray, radius] (circa 1611)
1 : a line segment extending from the center of a circle or sphere to the circumference or bounding surface
2 a : the bone on the thumb side of the human forearm; *also* **:** a corresponding part of vertebrates above fishes **b :** the third and usually largest vein of an insect's wing
3 a : the length of a radius ⟨a truck with a short turning *radius*⟩ **b :** the circular area de-

fined by a stated radius **c** : a bounded or circumscribed area
4 : a radial part
5 : the distance from a center line or point to an axis of rotation
radius of curvature (circa 1753)
: the reciprocal of the curvature of a curve
radius vector *noun* (circa 1753)
1 a : the line segment or its length from a fixed point to a variable point **b** : the linear polar coordinate of a variable point
2 : a straight line joining the center of an attracting body (as the sun) with that of a body (as a planet) in orbit around it
ra·dix \'rā-diks\ *noun, plural* **ra·di·ces** \'rā-də-ˌsēz, 'ra-\ *or* **ra·dix·es** \'rā-dik-səz\ [Latin, root — more at ROOT] (1798)
1 : the base of a number system or of logarithms
2 : the primary source
ra·dome \'rā-ˌdōm\ *noun* [radar dome] (circa 1944)
: a plastic housing sheltering the antenna assembly of a radar set especially on an airplane
ra·don \'rā-ˌdän\ *noun* [International Scientific Vocabulary, from *radium*] (1918)
: a heavy radioactive gaseous element formed by the decay of radium — see ELEMENT table
rad·u·la \'ra-jə-lə\ *noun, plural* **-lae** \-ˌlē, -ˌlī\ *also* **-las** [New Latin, from Latin, scraper, from *radere* to scrape — more at RODENT] (circa 1859)
: a horny band or ribbon in mollusks other than bivalves that bears minute teeth on its dorsal surface and tears up food and draws it into the mouth
— **rad·u·lar** \-lər\ *adjective*
rad·waste \'rad-ˌwāst\ *noun, often attributive* [by shortening] (1973)
: radioactive waste
raff \'raf\ *noun* [Middle English *raf* rubbish] (14th century)
: RIFFRAFF
raf·fia \'ra-fē-ə\ *noun* [Malagasy *rafia*] (1882)
: the fiber of the raffia palm used especially for tying plants and making baskets and hats
raffia palm *noun* (1897)
: a pinnate-leaved palm (*Raphia farinifera* synonym *R. ruffia*) of Madagascar that is valued for the fiber from its leafstalks
raf·fi·nose \'ra-fə-ˌnōs, -ˌnōz\ *noun* [French, from *raffiner* to refine, from *re-* + *affiner* to make fine, from *a-* ad- (from Latin *ad-*) + *fin* fine] (1876)
: a crystalline slightly sweet sugar $C_{18}H_{32}O_{16}$ obtained commercially from cottonseed meal and present in many plant products
raff·ish \'ra-fish\ *adjective* (1801)
1 : marked by or suggestive of flashy vulgarity or crudeness
2 : marked by a careless unconventionality : RAKISH
— **raff·ish·ly** *adverb*
— **raff·ish·ness** *noun*
¹raf·fle \'ra-fəl\ *verb* **raf·fled; raf·fling** \'ra-f(ə-)liŋ\ (circa 1680)
intransitive verb
: to engage in a raffle
transitive verb
: to dispose of by means of a raffle ⟨*raffle* off a turkey⟩
²raffle *noun* [Middle English *rafle*, a dice game, from Middle French, dice game in which all the stakes can be won in a throw, literally, rake for a fire, from Middle High German *raffel* rake for a fire, from *raffen* to snatch, gather] (1766)
: a lottery in which the prize is won by one of numerous persons buying chances
³raffle *noun* [probably from French *rafle* act of snatching, sweeping, from Middle French, rake for a fire] (1881)
: RUBBISH; *especially* : a jumble or tangle of nautical equipment
raf·fle·sia \ra-ˈflē-zh(ē-)ə, rä-\ *noun* [New Latin, from Sir Stamford *Raffles* (died 1826)

English colonial administrator] (1830)
: any of a genus (*Rafflesia* of the family Rafflesiaceae) of Malaysian dicotyledonous plants that are parasitic in other plants and have fleshy usually foul-smelling apetalous flowers emerging from the host, imbricated scales in place of leaves, and no stems
¹raft \'raft\ *noun* [Middle English *rafte* rafter, raft, from Old Norse *raptr* rafter] (15th century)
1 a : a collection of logs or timber fastened together for conveyance by water **b** : a flat structure for support or transportation on water
2 : a floating cohesive mass
3 : an aggregation of animals (as waterfowl) resting on the water
²raft (1706)
transitive verb
1 : to transport in the form of or by means of a raft; *also* : to convey (as pebbles) in floating ice or masses of organic material
2 : to make into a raft
intransitive verb
: to travel by raft
³raft *noun* [alteration of *raff* jumble] (1830)
: a large collection or number
¹raf·ter \'raf-tər\ *noun* [Middle English, from Old English *ræfter;* akin to Old Norse *raptr* rafter] (before 12th century)
: any of the parallel beams that support a roof — see RIDGEPOLE illustration
— **raf·tered** \-tərd\ *adjective*
²raft·er \'raf-tər\ *noun* [²raft] (1809)
1 : one who maneuvers logs into position and binds them into rafts
2 : one who travels by raft
rafts·man \'raf(t)s-mən\ *noun* (1776)
: a man engaged in rafting
¹rag \'rag\ *noun* [Middle English *ragge,* from (assumed) Old English *ragg,* from Old Norse *rǫgg* tuft, shagginess] (14th century)
1 a : a waste piece of cloth **b** *plural* : clothes usually in poor or ragged condition **c** : CLOTHING ⟨the *rag* trade⟩
2 : something resembling a rag
3 : NEWSPAPER
²rag *noun* [Middle English *ragge*] (14th century)
1 : any of various hard rocks
2 : a large roofing slate that is rough on one side
³rag *transitive verb* **ragged** \'ragd\; **ragging** [origin unknown] (1739)
1 : to rail at : SCOLD
2 : TORMENT, TEASE
⁴rag *noun* (1864)
chiefly British : an outburst of boisterous fun; *also* : PRANK
⁵rag *noun* [short for *ragtime*] (1897)
: a composition in ragtime
ra·ga \'rä-gə\ *noun* [Sanskrit *rāga,* literally, color, tone; akin to Sanskrit *rajyati* it reddens, Greek *rhezein* to dye] (1788)
1 : one of the ancient traditional melodic patterns or modes in Indian music
2 : an improvisation based on a traditional raga — compare TALA
rag·a·muf·fin \'ra-gə-ˌmə-fən\ *noun* [Middle English *Ragamuffyn,* name for a ragged, oafish person] (1581)
: a ragged often disreputable person; *especially* : a poorly clothed often dirty child
rag·bag \'rag-ˌbag\ *noun* (1820)
1 : a bag for scraps
2 : a miscellaneous collection
rag doll *noun* (1853)
: a stuffed usually painted cloth doll
¹rage \'rāj\ *noun* [Middle English, from Old French, from Late Latin *rabia,* from Latin *rabies* rage, madness, from *rabere* to be mad; akin to Sanskrit *rabhas* violence] (14th century)
1 a : violent and uncontrolled anger **b** : a fit of violent wrath **c** *archaic* : INSANITY
2 : violent action (as of wind or sea)
3 : an intense feeling : PASSION

4 : a fad pursued with intense enthusiasm ⟨was all the *rage*⟩
synonym see ANGER, FASHION
²rage *intransitive verb* **raged; rag·ing** (14th century)
1 : to be in a rage
2 : to be in tumult
3 : to prevail uncontrollably
rag·ged \'ra-gəd\ *adjective* (14th century)
1 : roughly unkempt
2 : having an irregular edge or outline
3 a : torn or worn to tatters **b** : worn-out from stress and strain ⟨ran herself *ragged*⟩
4 : wearing tattered clothes
5 a : STRAGGLY **b** : executed in an irregular or uneven manner **c** *of a sound* : HARSH, DISSONANT
— **rag·ged·ly** *adverb*
— **rag·ged·ness** *noun*
ragged robin *noun* (1741)
: a perennial herb (*Lychnis flos-cuculi*) cultivated for its pink flowers with narrow-lobed petals
rag·gedy \'ra-gə-dē\ *adjective* (1890)
: RAGGED
rag·gle-tag·gle \'ra-gəl-ˌta-gəl\ *adjective* [irregular from *ragtag*] (1904)
: MOTLEY
ra·gi \'ra-gē, 'rä-\ *noun* [perhaps from Deccan Hindi *rāgī*] (1792)
: an Old World cereal grass (*Eleusine coracana*) yielding a staple food crop especially in India and Africa; *also* : the seeds of ragi used for food
raging *adjective* (15th century)
1 : causing great pain or distress
2 : VIOLENT, WILD
3 : EXTRAORDINARY, TREMENDOUS ⟨a *raging* success⟩
rag·lan \'ra-glən\ *noun* [F.J.H. Somerset, Baron *Raglan* (died 1855) British field marshal] (circa 1859)
: a loose overcoat with raglan sleeves
raglan sleeve *noun* (circa 1924)
: a sleeve that extends to the neckline with slanted seams from the underarm to the neck
rag·man \'rag-ˌman\ *noun* (1586)
: a man who collects or deals in rags
Rag·na·rok \'rag-nə-ˌräk, -ˌrôk\ *noun* [Old Norse *Ragnarǫk,* literally, fate of the gods, from *ragna,* genitive plural of *regin* gods + *rǫk* fate, course (later rendered as *Ragnarøkkr,* literally, twilight of the gods)]
: the final destruction of the world in the conflict between the Aesir and the powers of Hel led by Loki — called also *Twilight of the Gods*
ra·gout \ra-ˈgü\ *noun* [French *ragoût,* from *ragoûter* to revive the taste, from Middle French *ragouster,* from *re-* + *a-* ad- (from Latin *ad-*) + *goust* taste, from Latin *gustus;* akin to Latin *gustare* to taste — more at CHOOSE] (circa 1657)
1 : well-seasoned meat and vegetables cooked in a thick sauce
2 : MIXTURE, MÉLANGE
rag·pick·er \'rag-ˌpi-kər\ *noun* (1860)
: one who collects rags and refuse for a living
rag·tag \'rag-ˌtag\ *adjective* [*ragtag and bobtail*] (1882)
1 : RAGGED, UNKEMPT
2 : MOTLEY 2 ⟨a *ragtag* bunch of misfits⟩
ragtag and bobtail *noun* [¹rag + ¹tag] (1820)
: RABBLE
rag·time \'rag-ˌtīm\ *noun* [probably from *ragged* + *time*] (1897)
1 : rhythm characterized by strong syncopation in the melody with a regularly accented accompaniment

2 : music having ragtime rhythm

rag·top \-ˌtäp\ *noun* (1953)
: a convertible automobile

rag·weed \-ˌwēd\ *noun* (1790)
: any of various chiefly North American weedy composite herbs (genus *Ambrosia*) that produce highly allergenic pollen

rag·wort \-ˌwərt, -ˌwȯrt\ *noun* (14th century)
: any of several senecios; *especially* : TANSY RAGWORT

rah \ˈrä, ˈrȯ\ *interjection* (1870)
: HURRAH — used especially to cheer on a team

rah–rah \ˈrä-ˌrä, ˈrȯ-ˌrȯ\ *adjective* [reduplication of *rah*] (1911)
: marked by the enthusiastic expression of college spirit

¹raid \ˈrād\ *noun* [Middle English (Scots) *rade*, from Old English *rād* ride, raid — more at ROAD] (15th century)
1 a : a hostile or predatory incursion **b** : a surprise attack by a small force
2 a : a brief foray outside one's usual sphere **b** : a sudden invasion by officers of the law **c** : a daring operation against a competitor **d** : the recruiting of personnel (as faculty, executives, or athletes) from competing organizations
3 : the act of mulcting public money
4 : an attempt by professional operators to depress stock prices by concerted selling

²raid (1865)
intransitive verb
: to conduct or take part in a raid
transitive verb
: to make a raid on

raid·er \ˈrā-dər\ *noun* (1863)
: one that raids: as **a** : a fast lightly armed ship operating against merchant shipping **b** : a soldier specially trained for close-range fighting **c** : one that attempts a usually hostile takeover of a business corporation (corporate *raiders*)

¹rail \ˈrā(ə)l\ *noun* [Middle English *raile*, from Middle French *reille* ruler, bar, from Latin *regula* ruler, from *regere* to keep straight, direct, rule — more at RIGHT] (14th century)
1 a : a bar extending from one post or support to another and serving as a guard or barrier **b** : a structural member or support
2 a : RAILING 1 **b** : a light structure serving as a guard at the outer edge of a ship's deck **c** : a fence bounding a racetrack
3 a : a bar of rolled steel forming a track for wheeled vehicles **b** : TRACK **c** : RAILROAD

²rail *transitive verb* (14th century)
: to provide with a railing : FENCE

³rail *noun, plural* **rail** *or* **rails** [Middle English *raile*, from Middle French *raale*] (15th century)
: any of numerous wading birds (family Rallidae, the rail family) that are of small or medium size and have short rounded wings, a short tail, and usually very long toes which enable them to run on the soft mud of marshes

rail

⁴rail *intransitive verb* [Middle English, from Middle French *railler* to mock, from Old Provençal *ralhar* to babble, joke, from (assumed) Vulgar Latin *ragulare* to bray, from Late Latin *ragere* to neigh] (15th century)
: to revile or scold in harsh, insolent, or abusive language
synonym see SCOLD
— **rail·er** *noun*

rail·bird \ˈrā(ə)l-ˌbərd\ *noun* (1892)
: a racing enthusiast who sits on or near the track rail to watch a race or workout

rail·bus \-ˌbəs\ *noun* (1933)
: a passenger car with an automotive engine for operation on rails

rail·car \-ˌkär\ *noun* (1834)
1 : a railroad car

2 : a self-propelled railroad car

rail·head \ˈrā(ə)l-ˌhed\ *noun* (1896)
: a point on a railroad at which traffic may originate or terminate

rail·ing \ˈrā-liŋ\ *noun* (15th century)
1 : a barrier consisting of a rail and supports
2 : RAILS; *also* : material for making rails

rail·lery \ˈrā-lə-rē\ *noun, plural* **-ler·ies** [French *raillerie*, from Middle French, from *railler* to mock] (1653)
1 : good-natured ridicule : BANTER
2 : JEST

¹rail·road \ˈrā(ə)l-ˌrōd, ˈre(ə)l-; ˈre-ˌrōd\ *noun* (1825)
: a permanent road having a line of rails fixed to ties and laid on a roadbed and providing a track for cars or equipment drawn by locomotives or propelled by self-contained motors; *also* : such a road and its assets constituting a single property

²railroad (1877)
transitive verb
1 a : to convict with undue haste and by means of false charges or insufficient evidence **b** : to push through hastily or without due consideration
2 : to transport by railroad
intransitive verb
: to work for a railroad company
— **rail·road·er** *noun*

railroad flat *noun* (1947)
: an apartment having a series of narrow rooms arranged in line

rail·road·ing *noun* (1870)
: construction or operation of a railroad

railroad worm *noun* (1909)
1 [probably from its dissemination by railroad] : APPLE MAGGOT
2 [from the rows of luminescent spots along its sides making it resemble a lighted train] : the larva or wingless female of any of several South American beetles (genus *Phrixothrix* of the family Cantharidae)

rail·split·ter \ˈrā(ə)l-ˌspli-tər\ *noun* (1860)
: one that makes logs into fence rails

rail·way \-ˌwā\ *noun* (1812)
: RAILROAD; *especially* : a railroad operating with light equipment or within a small area

rai·ment \ˈrā-mənt\ *noun* [Middle English *rayment*, short for *arrayment*, from *arrayen* to array] (15th century)
: CLOTHING, GARMENTS

¹rain \ˈrān\ *noun, often attributive* [Middle English *reyn*, from Old English *regn*, *rēn*; akin to Old High German *regan* rain] (before 12th century)
1 a : water falling in drops condensed from vapor in the atmosphere **b** : the descent of this water **c** : water that has fallen as rain : RAINWATER
2 a : a fall of rain : RAINSTORM **b** *plural* : the rainy season
3 : rainy weather
4 : a heavy fall of particles or bodies

²rain (before 12th century)
intransitive verb
1 : to send down rain
2 : to fall as water in drops from the clouds
3 : to fall like rain
transitive verb
1 : to pour down
2 : to bestow abundantly
— **rain cats and dogs** : to rain heavily

rain·bird \ˈrān-ˌbərd\ *noun* (1555)
: any of numerous birds (especially of the family Cuculidae) whose cries are popularly believed to augur rain

rain·bow \-ˌbō\ *noun* (before 12th century)
1 : an arc or circle that exhibits in concentric bands the colors of the spectrum and that is formed opposite the sun by the refraction and reflection of the sun's rays in raindrops, spray, or mist
2 a : a multicolored array **b** : a wide assortment or range

3 [from the impossibility of reaching the rainbow, at whose foot a pot of gold is said to be buried] : an illusory goal or hope
4 : RAINBOW TROUT
— **rain·bow·like** *adjective*

rainbow fish *noun* (1888)
: any of numerous brilliantly colored fishes (as a wrasse, parrot fish, or guppy)

rainbow runner *noun* (1940)
: a large brilliantly marked blue and yellow carangid food and sport fish (*Elagatis bipinnulata*) common in warm seas

rainbow trout *noun* (1882)
: a large stout-bodied salmonid fish (*Oncorhynchus mykiss* synonym *Salmo gairdneri*) of western North America that is related to the Pacific salmon and is typically greenish above and white on the belly with a pink, red, or lavender stripe along each side of the body and with profuse black dots — compare STEELHEAD

rainbow trout

rain check *noun* (1884)
1 : a ticket stub good for a later performance when the scheduled one is rained out
2 : an assurance of a deferred extension of an offer; *especially* : an assurance that a customer can take advantage of a sale later if the item or service offered is not available (as by being sold out)

rain·coat \ˈrān-ˌkōt\ *noun* (1830)
: a waterproof or water-resistant coat

rain·drop \-ˌdräp\ *noun* (before 12th century)
: a drop of rain

rain·fall \-ˌfȯl\ *noun* (1854)
1 : the amount of precipitation usually measured by the depth in inches
2 : RAIN 2a

rain forest *noun* (1903)
1 : a tropical woodland with an annual rainfall of at least 100 inches (254 centimeters) and marked by lofty broad-leaved evergreen trees forming a continuous canopy — called also *tropical rain forest*
2 : TEMPERATE RAIN FOREST

rain gauge *noun* (1769)
: an instrument for measuring the quantity of precipitation

rain·mak·er \ˈrān-ˌmā-kər\ *noun* (1775)
1 : a person who produces or attempts to produce rain by artificial means
2 : a person (as a partner in a law firm) who brings in new business; *also* : a person whose influence can initiate progress or ensure success
— **rain·mak·ing** \-ˌmā-kiŋ\ *noun*

rain out *transitive verb* (1928)
: to interrupt or prevent by rain

rain·proof \ˈrān-ˌprüf\ *adjective* (1831)
: impervious to rain

rain·spout \-ˌspaut\ *noun* (1922)
: GUTTER 1a; *also* : DOWNSPOUT

rain·squall \-ˌskwȯl\ *noun* (1849)
: a squall accompanied by rain

rain·storm \-ˌstȯrm\ *noun* (1816)
: a storm of or with rain

rain tree *noun* (circa 1890)
: MONKEYPOD

rain·wash \ˈrān-ˌwȯsh, -ˌwäsh\ *noun* (1876)
: the washing away of material by rain; *also* : the material so washed away

rain·wa·ter \-ˌwȯ-tər, -ˌwä-\ *noun* (before 12th century)
: water fallen as rain that has not collected soluble matter from the soil and is therefore soft

rain·wear \-ˌwar, -ˌwer\ *noun* (1939)
: waterproof or water-resistant clothing

rainy \'rā-nē\ *adjective* **rain·i·er; -est** (before 12th century)
: marked by, abounding with, or bringing rain

rainy day *noun* (circa 1580)
: a period of want or need

¹**raise** \'rāz\ *verb* **raised; rais·ing** [Middle English, from Old Norse *reisa* — more at REAR] (13th century)
transitive verb
1 : to cause or help to rise to a standing position
2 a : AWAKEN, AROUSE **b** : to stir up : INCITE ⟨*raise* a rebellion⟩ **c** : to flush (game) from cover **d** : to recall from or as if from death **e** : to establish radio communication with
3 a : to set upright by lifting or building **b** : to lift higher **c** : to place higher in rank or dignity : ELEVATE **d** : HEIGHTEN, INVIGORATE ⟨*raise* the spirits⟩ **e** : to end or suspend the operation or validity of ⟨*raise* a siege⟩
4 : to get together for a purpose : COLLECT ⟨*raise* funds⟩
5 a : to breed and bring (an animal) to maturity **b** : GROW, CULTIVATE ⟨*raise* cotton⟩ **c** : to bring up (a child) : REAR
6 a : to give rise to : PROVOKE ⟨*raise* a commotion⟩ **b** : to give voice to ⟨*raise* a cheer⟩
7 : to bring up for consideration or debate ⟨*raise* an issue⟩
8 a : to increase the strength, intensity, or pitch of **b** : to increase the degree of **c** : to cause to rise in level or amount ⟨*raise* the rent⟩ **d** (1) : to increase the amount of (a poker bet) (2) : to bet more than (a previous bettor) **e** (1) : to make a higher bridge bid in (a partner's suit) (2) : to increase the bid of (one's partner)
9 : to make light and porous ⟨*raise* dough⟩
10 : to cause to ascend
11 : to multiply (a quantity) by itself a specified number of times
12 : to bring in sight on the horizon by approaching ⟨*raise* land⟩
13 a : to bring up the nap of (cloth) **b** : to cause (as a blister) to form on the skin
14 : to increase the nominal value of fraudulently ⟨*raise* a check⟩
15 : to articulate (a sound) with the tongue in a higher position
intransitive verb
1 *dialect* : RISE
2 : to increase a bet or bid □
synonym see LIFT
— **rais·er** *noun*
— **raise Cain** *or* **raise hell 1** : to act wildly : create a disturbance **2** : to scold or upbraid someone especially loudly
— **raise eyebrows** : to cause surprise or astonishment

²**raise** *noun* (1538)
1 : an act of raising or lifting
2 : a rising stretch of road : an upward grade : RISE
3 : an increase in amount: as **a** : an increase of a bet or bid **b** : an increase in wages or salary
4 : a vertical or inclined opening or passageway connecting one mine working area with another at a higher level

raised *adjective* (1599)
1 a : done in relief **b** : having a nap
2 : leavened with yeast rather than with baking powder or baking soda

rai·sin \'rā-z²n\ *noun* [Middle English, from Middle French, grape, from Latin *racemus* cluster of grapes or berries — more at RACEME] (14th century)
: a grape of any of several varieties that has been dried in the sun or by artificial heat

rai·son d'être *also* **rai·son d'etre** \,rā-,zōⁿ-'detr²\ *noun* [French] (1864)
: reason or justification for existence

raj \'räj\ *noun* [Hindi *rāj*, from Sanskrit *rājya*; akin to Sanskrit *rājan* king] (1800)

: RULE; *especially, often capitalized* : the former British rule of the Indian subcontinent

ra·ja *or* **ra·jah** \'rä-jə, -(,)jä, -zhə, -(,)zhä\ *noun* [Hindi *rājā*, from Sanskrit *rājan* king — more at ROYAL] (1555)
1 : an Indian or Malay prince or chief
2 : the bearer of a title of nobility among the Hindus

Ra·jab \rə-'jab\ *noun* [Arabic] (circa 1771)
: the 7th month of the Islamic year — see MONTH table

Ra·jas·tha·ni \,rä-jə-'stä-nē, ,rä-zhə-\ *noun* [Hindi *Rājasthānī*, from *Rājasthān* Rajasthan] (1901)
: the Indo-Aryan dialects of Rajasthan

Raj·put *or* **Raj·poot** \'räj-,pút, 'räzh-\ *noun* [Hindi *rājpūt*, from Sanskrit *rājaputra* king's son, from *rājan* king + *putra* son — more at FEW] (1598)
: a member of a dominant military caste of northern India

¹**rake** \'rāk\ *noun* [Middle English, from Old English *racu*; akin to Old High German *rehho* rake] (before 12th century)
1 a : an implement equipped with projecting prongs to gather material (as leaves) or for loosening or smoothing the surface of the ground **b** : a machine for gathering hay
2 : an implement like a rake

²**rake** *transitive verb* **raked; rak·ing** (13th century)
1 : to gather, loosen, or smooth with or as if with a rake
2 : to gain rapidly or in abundance ⟨*rake* in a fortune⟩
3 a : to touch in passing over lightly **b** : SCRATCH
4 : to censure severely
5 : to search through : RANSACK
6 : to sweep the length of especially with gunfire : ENFILADE
7 : to glance over rapidly
— **rak·er** *noun*

³**rake** *noun* [origin unknown] (1626)
1 : inclination from the perpendicular; *especially* : the overhang of a ship's bow or stern
2 : inclination from the horizontal : SLOPE
3 : the angle between the top cutting surface of a tool and a plane perpendicular to the surface of the work
4 : the angle between a wing-tip edge that is sensibly straight in planform and the plane of symmetry of an airplane

⁴**rake** *intransitive verb* **raked; rak·ing** (1691)
: to incline from the perpendicular

⁵**rake** *noun* [short for *rakehell*] (1653)
: a dissolute person : LIBERTINE

rake·hell \'rāk-,hel\ *noun* (1554)
: LIBERTINE 2
— **rakehell** *or* **rake·helly** \-,he-lē\ *adjective*

rake–off \'rāk-,óf\ *noun* [*rake off*, verb; from the use of a rake by a croupier to collect the operator's profits in a gambling casino] (1888)
: a percentage or cut taken (as by an operator)

rake up *transitive verb* (1581)
: to make known or public : UNCOVER ⟨*rake up* a scandal⟩

ra·ki \rə-'kē; 'ra-kē, 'rä-\ *noun* [Turkish, from Arabic *'araqī*, literally, of liquor, from *'araq* liquor, arrack] (1675)
: a Turkish liqueur flavored with aniseed

¹**rak·ish** \'rā-kish\ *adjective* [⁵*rake*] (1706)
: of, relating to, or characteristic of a rake : DISSOLUTE

²**rakish** *adjective* [probably from ⁴*rake*; from the raking masts of pirate ships] (1824)
1 : having a trim or streamlined appearance suggestive of speed ⟨a *rakish* ship⟩
2 : dashingly or carelessly unconventional : JAUNTY ⟨*rakish* clothes⟩
rak·ish·ly *adverb* (1838)
: in a rakish manner

rak·ish·ness *noun* (circa 1828)
: the quality or state of being rakish

rale \'ral, 'räl\ *noun* [French *râle*, from *râler* to make a rattling sound in the throat] (1828)
: an abnormal sound heard accompanying the normal respiratory sounds on auscultation of the chest

ral·len·tan·do \,rä-lən-'tän-(,)dō\ *adverb or adjective* [Italian, literally, slowing down, verbal of *rallentare* to slow down, from *re-* + *allentare* to slow down, from Late Latin, from Latin *al-* *ad-* + *lentus* slow, pliant — more at LITHE] (circa 1811)
: RITARDANDO

¹**ral·ly** \'ra-lē\ *verb* **ral·lied; ral·ly·ing** [French *rallier*, from Old French *ralier*, from *re-* + *alier* to unite — more at ALLY] (1603)
transitive verb
1 a : to muster for a common purpose **b** : to recall to order
2 a : to arouse for action **b** : to rouse from depression or weakness
intransitive verb
1 : to come together again to renew an effort
2 : to join in a common cause
3 : RECOVER, REBOUND
4 : to engage in a rally

²**rally** *noun, plural* **rallies** (1651)
1 a : a mustering of scattered forces to renew an effort **b** : a summoning up of strength or courage after weakness or dejection **c** : a recovery of price after a decline **d** : a renewed offensive
2 : a mass meeting intended to arouse group enthusiasm

□ **USAGE**

raise Some critics still offer the prescription "raise plants and animals and rear children." What is wrong with raising children? Actually, nothing. Sense 5c of *raise* dropped out of fashionable use in England around 1800 but continued in American use. Throughout the 19th century, English reviewers, who commonly found much to fault in the writing of American authors, seem to have included this use of *raise* among other objectionable usages. American literati appear to have been somewhat sensitive to the criticism, and *raise* came to be viewed as something less than elegant. In the opinion of some New Englanders, including Noah Webster, this use of *raise* was a Southernism. The two leading 19th century American dictionaries, Webster's and Worcester's, were both edited by New Englanders, and both labeled *raise* as a Southern usage. So when the question was picked up by handbooks, the dictionaries could be cited as evidence the usage was not standard, but regional. We now know that the description of *raise* as a Southernism was not quite accurate—John Adams had used it. The usage was simply American ⟨grew up, and married, and *raised* a large family —Mark Twain⟩ ⟨the small town in which I was *raised* —Sherwood Anderson⟩ ⟨a very great advantage to have been *raised* in an atmosphere of evangelical piety — Irving Howe⟩. We now know too that *raise* was used of humans in the English of Scotland, Ireland, and some northern and eastern counties of England. And it seems not to have died entirely in the mainstream even in England ⟨she had been *raised* in virtual seclusion —Lady Antonia Fraser⟩. This sense is standard and can be used without a second thought.

\ə\ abut \ᵊ\ kitten \ər\ further \a\ ash \ā\ ace
\ä\ mop, mar \aú\ out \ch\ chin \e\ bet \ē\ easy
\g\ go \i\ hit \ī\ ice \j\ job \ŋ\ sing \ō\ go
\ó\ law \ói\ boy \th\ thin \th\ the \ü\ loot \ú\ foot
\y\ yet \zh\ vision *see also* Guide to Pronunciation

3 : a series of shots interchanged between players (as in tennis) before a point is won
4 *also* **ral·lye** [French *rallye,* from English ¹*rally*] **:** an automobile competition using public roads and ordinary traffic rules with the object of maintaining a specified average speed between checkpoints over a route unknown to the participants until the start of the event

³**rally** *transitive verb* **ral·lied; ral·ly·ing** [French *railler* to mock, rally — more at RAIL] (1668)
: to attack with raillery **:** BANTER

ral·ly·ing \'ra-lē-iŋ\ *noun* (1957)
: the sport of driving in automobile rallies

¹**ram** \'ram\ *noun* [Middle English, from Old English *ramm;* akin to Old High German *ram*] (before 12th century)
1 a : a male sheep **b** *capitalized* **:** ARIES
2 a : BATTERING RAM **b :** a warship with a heavy beak at the prow for piercing an enemy ship
3 : any of various guided pieces for exerting pressure or for driving or forcing something by impact: as **a :** the plunger of a hydrostatic press or force pump **b :** the weight that strikes the blow in a pile driver

²**ram** *verb* **rammed; ram·ming** [Middle English *rammen,* probably from *ram,* noun] (14th century)
intransitive verb
1 : to strike with violence **:** CRASH
2 : to move with extreme rapidity
transitive verb
1 : to force in by or as if by driving
2 a : to make compact (as by pounding) **b :** CRAM, CROWD
3 : to force passage or acceptance of ⟨*ram* home an idea⟩
4 : to strike against violently
— **ram·mer** *noun*

RAM \'ram\ *noun* (1957)
: RANDOM-ACCESS MEMORY

Ra·ma \'rä-mə\ *noun* [Sanskrit *Rāma*]
: a deity or deified hero of later Hinduism worshiped as an avatar of Vishnu

Ram·a·dan \'rä-mə-,dän, ,rä-mə-'-\ *noun* [Arabic *Ramaḍān*] (circa 1595)
: the 9th month of the Islamic year observed as sacred with fasting practiced daily from dawn to sunset — see MONTH table

ra·mate \'rā-,māt\ *adjective* [Latin *ramus* branch — more at RAMIFY] (1897)
: RAMOSE

¹**ram·ble** \'ram-bəl\ *verb* **ram·bled; ram·bling** \-b(ə-)liŋ\ [perhaps from Middle English *romblen,* frequentative of *romen* to roam] (1620)
intransitive verb
1 a : to move aimlessly from place to place **b :** to explore idly
2 : to talk or write in a desultory or long-winded wandering fashion
3 : to grow or extend irregularly
transitive verb
: to wander over **:** ROAM
synonym see WANDER
— **ram·bling·ly** \-b(ə-)liŋ-lē\ *adverb*

²**ramble** *noun* (1654)
: a leisurely excursion for pleasure; *especially* **:** an aimless walk

ram·bler \'ram-blər\ *noun* (1624)
1 : one that rambles
2 : any of various climbing roses with long flexible canes and rather small often double flowers in large clusters
3 : RANCH HOUSE

ram·bouil·let \,ram-bə-'lā, -bü-'yā\ *noun, often capitalized* [*Rambouillet,* France] (1906)
: any of a breed of large sturdy sheep developed in France

ram·bunc·tious \ram-'bəŋk-shəs\ *adjective* [probably alteration of *rumbustious*] (1830)
: marked by uncontrollable exuberance **:** UNRULY
— **ram·bunc·tious·ly** *adverb*
— **ram·bunc·tious·ness** *noun*

ram·bu·tan \ram-'bü-t³n\ *noun* [Malay] (1707)
: a bright red spiny Malayan fruit closely related to the litchi; *also* **:** a tree (*Nephelium lappaceum*) of the soapberry family that bears this fruit

ram·e·kin *also* **ram·e·quin** \'ram-kən, 'ra-mi-\ *noun* [French *ramequin,* from Low German *ramken,* diminutive of *ram* cream] (circa 1706)
1 : a preparation of cheese especially with bread crumbs or eggs baked in a mold or shell
2 : an individual baking dish

ra·met \'rā-,met\ *noun* [Latin *ramus* branch] (1929)
: an independent member of a clone

ra·mie \'rā-mē, 'ra-\ *noun* [Malay *rami*] (1832)
1 : an Asian perennial plant (*Boehmeria nivea*) of the nettle family
2 a : the strong lustrous bast fiber of ramie capable of being spun or woven **b :** fabric made of ramie often resembling linen or silk

ram·i·fi·ca·tion \,ra-mə-fə-'kā-shən\ *noun* (1665)
1 a : BRANCH, OFFSHOOT **b :** a branched structure
2 a : the act or process of branching **b :** arrangement of branches (as on a plant)
3 : CONSEQUENCE, OUTGROWTH ⟨the *ramifications* of a problem⟩

ram·i·fy \'ra-mə-,fī\ *verb* **-fied; -fy·ing** [Middle English *ramifien,* from Middle French *ramifier,* from Medieval Latin *ramificare,* from Latin *ramus* branch; akin to Latin *radix* root — more at ROOT] (15th century)
intransitive verb
1 : to split up into branches or constituent parts
2 : to send forth branches or extensions
transitive verb
1 : to cause to branch
2 : to separate into divisions

Ra·mism \'rā-,mi-zəm\ *noun* [Petrus *Ramus* (died 1572) French philosopher] (1710)
: the doctrines of Ramus based on opposition to Aristotelianism and advocacy of a new logic blended with rhetoric
— **Ra·mist** \-mist\ *noun or adjective*

ram·jet \'ram-,jet\ *noun* (1942)
: a jet engine that consists essentially of a hollow tube without mechanical components and depends on the aircraft's speed of flight for the air compression necessary to produce the thrust obtained from the expansion of gases caused by the combustion of fuel

ra·mose \'rā-,mōs\ *adjective* [Latin *ramosus,* from *ramus* branch] (1689)
: consisting of or having branches ⟨a *ramose* sponge⟩

¹**ramp** \'ramp\ *verb* [Middle English, from Middle French *ramper* to crawl, rear, of Germanic origin; akin to Old High German *rimpfan* to wrinkle — more at RUMPLE] (14th century)
intransitive verb
1 a : to stand or advance menacingly with forelegs or with arms raised **b :** to move or act furiously
2 : to creep up — used especially of plants
transitive verb
[⁴*ramp* (electrical waveform)] **:** to increase or decrease especially at a constant rate — usually used with *up* or *down* ⟨*ramp* up production⟩

²**ramp** *noun* (1671)
: the act or an instance of ramping

³**ramp** *noun* [back-formation from *ramps,* alteration of *rams,* from Middle English, from Old English *hramsa;* akin to Old High German *ramusia* ramp, Greek *krommyon* onion] (1598)
: any of various alliums used for food

⁴**ramp** *noun* [French *rampe,* from *ramper,* from Middle French] (1778)
1 : a short bend, slope, or curve usually in the vertical plane where a handrail or coping changes its direction
2 : a sloping way: as **a :** a sloping floor, walk, or roadway leading from one level to another **b :** a stairway for entering or leaving an airplane **c :** a slope for launching boats
3 : APRON 2h

¹**ram·page** \'ram-,pāj, (,)ram-'\ *intransitive verb* **ram·paged; ram·pag·ing** [Scots] (1808)
: to rush wildly about

²**ram·page** \'ram-,pāj\ *noun* (1861)
: a course of violent, riotous, or reckless action or behavior
— **ram·pa·geous** \ram-'pā-jəs\ *adjective*
— **ram·pa·geous·ly** *adverb*
— **ram·pa·geous·ness** *noun*

ram·pan·cy \'ram-pən(t)-sē\ *noun* (1664)
: the quality or state of being rampant

ram·pant \'ram-pənt *also* -,pant\ *adjective* [Middle English, from Middle French, present participle of *ramper*] (14th century)
1 a : rearing upon the hind legs with forelegs extended **b :** standing on one hind foot with one foreleg raised above the other and the head in profile — used of a heraldic animal
2 a : marked by a menacing wildness, extravagance, or absence of restraint **b :** WIDESPREAD
3 : having one impost or abutment higher than the other ⟨a *rampant* arch⟩
— **ram·pant·ly** *adverb*

ram·part \'ram-,pärt, -pərt\ *noun* [Middle French, from *ramparer* to fortify, from *re-* + *emparer* to defend, from Old Provençal *antparar,* from (assumed) Vulgar Latin *anteparare,* from Latin *ante* before + *parare* to prepare — more at ANTE-, PARE] (1536)
1 : a protective barrier **:** BULWARK
2 : a broad embankment raised as a fortification and usually surmounted by a parapet
3 : a wall-like ridge (as of rock fragments, earth, or debris)

ram·pike \-,pīk\ *noun* [origin unknown] (1853)
: an erect broken or dead tree

¹**ram·rod** \'ram-,räd\ *noun* (1757)
1 : a rod for ramming home the charge in a muzzle-loading firearm
2 : a cleaning rod for small arms
3 : BOSS, OVERSEER

²**ramrod** *adjective* (1905)
: marked by rigidity, severity, or stiffness

³**ramrod** *transitive verb* (circa 1940)
: to direct, supervise, and control

ram·shack·le \'ram-,sha-kəl\ *adjective* [alteration of earlier *ransackled,* from past participle of obsolete *ransackle,* frequentative of *ransack*] (1830)
1 : appearing ready to collapse **:** RICKETY
2 : carelessly or loosely constructed

rams·horn \'ramz-,hórn\ *noun* (1901)
: any of various snails (as genera *Planorbis, Helisoma,* and *Planorbarius*) often used as aquarium scavengers

ra·mus \'rā-məs\ *noun, plural* **ra·mi** \-,mī\ [New Latin, from Latin, branch — more at RAMIFY] (1803)
: a projecting part, elongated process, or branch: as **a :** the posterior more or less vertical part on each side of the lower jaw that articulates with the skull **b :** a branch of a nerve

ran *past of* RUN

¹**ranch** \'ranch\ *noun* [Mexican Spanish *rancho* small ranch, from Spanish, camp, hut & Spanish dialect, small farm, from Old Spanish *ranchearse* to take up quarters, from Middle French *se ranger* to take up a position, from *ranger* to set in a row — more at RANGE] (1831)
1 : a large farm for raising horses, beef cattle, or sheep
2 : a farm or area devoted to a particular specialty

3 : RANCH HOUSE ◆
²ranch (1866)
intransitive verb
: to live or work on a ranch
transitive verb
1 : to work as a rancher on
2 : to raise on a ranch
ranch dressing *noun* (1984)
: a creamy salad dressing usually containing milk or buttermilk and mayonnaise
ranch·er \'ran-chər\ *noun* (1836)
: one who owns or works on a ranch
ran·che·ro \ran-'cher-(ˌ)ō, rän-\ *noun, plural* **-ros** [Mexican Spanish, from *rancho*] (1826)
: RANCHER; *also* **:** RANCH 1
ranch house *noun* (1862)
1 : the main dwelling house on a ranch
2 : a one-story house typically with a low-pitched roof and an open plan
word history see RANCH
ranch·man \'ranch-mən\ *noun* (1856)
: RANCHER
ran·cho \'ran-(ˌ)chō, 'rän-\ *noun, plural* **ran·chos** [Mexican Spanish, small ranch] (1808)
: RANCH 1
word history see RANCH
ran·cid \'ran(t)-səd\ *adjective* [Latin *rancidus*, from *rancēre* to be rancid] (1646)
1 : having a rank smell or taste
2 : OFFENSIVE
— **ran·cid·i·ty** \ran-'si-də-tē\ *noun*
— **ran·cid·ness** \'ran(t)-səd-nəs\ *noun*
ran·cor \'raŋ-kər, -ˌkòr\ *noun* [Middle English *rancour*, from Middle French *ranceur*, from Late Latin *rancor* rancidity, rancor, from Latin *rancēre*] (14th century)
: bitter deep-seated ill will
synonym see ENMITY
ran·cor·ous \'raŋ-k(ə-)rəs\ *adjective* (1590)
: marked by rancor
— **ran·cor·ous·ly** *adverb*
ran·cour *British variant of* RANCOR
rand \'rand, 'ränd, 'ränt\ *noun, plural* **rand** [the *Rand*, South Africa] (circa 1932)
1 — see MONEY table
2 : a former monetary unit of Botswana, Lesotho, and Swaziland
R and D *noun* (1966)
: research and development
¹ran·dom \'ran-dəm\ *noun* [Middle English, impetuosity, from Middle French *randon*, from Old French, from *randir* to run, of Germanic origin; akin to Old High German *rinnan* to run — more at RUN] (1561)
: a haphazard course
— **at random :** without definite aim, direction, rule, or method
²random *adjective* (1565)
1 a : lacking a definite plan, purpose, or pattern **b :** made, done, or chosen at random ⟨read *random* passages from the book⟩
2 a : relating to, having, or being elements or events with definite probability of occurrence ⟨*random* processes⟩ **b :** being or relating to a set or to an element of a set each of whose elements has equal probability of occurrence ⟨a *random* sample⟩; *also* **:** characterized by procedures designed to obtain such sets or elements ⟨*random* sampling⟩ ☆
— **ran·dom·ly** *adverb*
— **ran·dom·ness** *noun*
³random *adverb* (1618)
: in a random manner
random–access *adjective* (1953)
: permitting access to stored data in any order the user desires
random–access memory *noun* (1955)
: a computer memory that provides the main internal storage available to the user for programs and data — called also *RAM;* compare READ-ONLY MEMORY
ran·dom·ize \'ran-də-ˌmīz\ *transitive verb* **-ized; -iz·ing** (1926)
: to select, assign, or arrange in a random way
— **ran·dom·i·za·tion** \ˌran-də-mə-'zā-shən\ *noun*

— **ran·dom·iz·er** *noun*
randomized block *noun* (circa 1942)
: an experimental design (as in horticulture) in which different treatments are distributed in random order in a block or plot — called also *randomized block design*
random variable *noun* (1949)
: a variable that is itself a function of the result of a statistical experiment in which each outcome has a definite probability of occurrence — called also *variate*
random walk *noun* (1941)
: a process (as Brownian motion or genetic drift) consisting of a sequence of steps (as movements or changes in gene frequency) each of whose characteristics (as magnitude and direction) is determined by chance
¹randy \'ran-dē\ *adjective* [probably from obsolete *rand* to rant] (1698)
1 *chiefly Scottish* **:** having a coarse manner
2 : LUSTFUL, LECHEROUS
²randy *noun, plural* **rand·ies** (1762)
chiefly Scottish **:** a scolding or dissolute woman
rang *past of* RING
¹range \'rānj\ *noun, often attributive* [Middle English, row of persons, from Middle French *renge*, from Old French *rengier* to range] (14th century)
1 a (1) **:** a series of things in a line **:** ROW (2) **:** a series of mountains (3) **:** one of the north-south rows of townships in a U.S. public-land survey that are numbered east and west from the principal meridian of the survey **b :** an aggregate of individuals in one order **c :** a direction line
2 : a cooking stove that has an oven and a flat top with burners or heating elements
3 a : a place that may be ranged over **b :** an open region over which animals (as livestock) may roam and feed **c :** the region throughout which a kind of organism or ecological community naturally lives or occurs
4 : the act of ranging about
5 a (1) **:** the horizontal distance to which a projectile can be propelled (2) **:** the horizontal distance between a weapon and target **b :** the maximum distance a vehicle or craft can travel without refueling **c** (1) **:** a place where shooting is practiced (2) **:** DRIVING RANGE
6 a : the space or extent included, covered, or used **:** SCOPE **b :** the extent of pitch covered by a melody or lying within the capacity of a voice or instrument
7 a : a sequence, series, or scale between limits ⟨a wide *range* of patterns⟩ **b :** the limits of a series **:** the distance or extent between possible extremes **c :** the difference between the least and greatest values of an attribute or of the variable of a frequency distribution
8 a : the set of values a function may take on **b :** the class of admissible values of a variable
9 : LINE 11 ☆
²range *verb* **ranged; rang·ing** [Middle English, from Middle French *rengier*, from Old French *renc, reng* line, place, row — more at RANK] (14th century)
transitive verb
1 a : to set in a row or in the proper order **b :** to place among others in a position or situation **c :** to assign to a category **:** CLASSIFY
2 a : to rove over or through **b :** to sail or pass along
3 : to arrange (an anchor cable) on deck
4 : to graze (livestock) on a range
5 : to determine or give the elevation necessary for (a gun) to propel a projectile to a given distance
intransitive verb
1 a : to roam at large or freely **b :** to move over an area so as to explore it
2 : to take a position
3 a : to correspond in direction or line **:** ALIGN **b :** to extend in a particular direction
4 : to have range

5 : to change or differ within limits
6 *of an organism* **:** to live or occur in or be native to a region
7 : to obtain the range of an object by instrument (as radar or laser)
word history see RANCH
range finder *noun* (1872)
1 : an instrument used in gunnery to determine the distance of a target

☆ **SYNONYMS**
Random, haphazard, casual mean determined by accident rather than design. RANDOM stresses lack of definite aim, fixed goal, or regular procedure ⟨a *random* selection of books⟩. HAPHAZARD applies to what is done without regard for regularity or fitness or ultimate consequence ⟨a *haphazard* collection of rocks⟩. CASUAL suggests working or acting without deliberation, intention, or purpose ⟨a *casual* collector⟩.

Range, gamut, compass, sweep, scope, orbit mean the extent that lies within the powers of something (as to cover or control). RANGE is a general term indicating the extent of one's perception or the extent of powers, capacities, or possibilities ⟨the entire *range* of human experience⟩. GAMUT suggests a graduated series running from one possible extreme to another ⟨a performance that ran the *gamut* of emotions⟩. COMPASS implies a sometimes limited extent of perception, knowledge, or activity ⟨your concerns lie beyond the narrow *compass* of this study⟩. SWEEP suggests extent, often circular or arc-shaped, of motion or activity ⟨the book covers the entire *sweep* of criminal activity⟩. SCOPE is applicable to an area of activity, predetermined and limited, but somewhat flexible ⟨as time went on, the *scope* of the investigation widened⟩. ORBIT suggests an often circumscribed range of activity or influence within which forces work toward accommodation ⟨within that restricted *orbit* they tried to effect social change⟩.

◇ **WORD HISTORY**
ranch Old French *renc* or *ranc* "row, line" (the source of English *rank*) gave rise to a verb *rengier* "to set in rows, place in proper order" (the source of English *range*). The reflexive form of this verb in Middle French, *se ranger*, meant "to line up, take a position." By the 16th century, *se ranger* had found its way into Spanish as *rancharse*, which meant in military contexts "to take up quarters, be billeted." The conquistadores who took this verb to the Americas were also familiar with a derivative noun *rancho*, denoting originally a camp or temporary dwelling such as a hut. The word *rancho* remains widely used in American Spanish, with much local variation in meaning. Both the general sense "habitation" and the specifically Mexican Spanish sense "small farm" were adopted into American English in the 19th century directly as *rancho* and in the Anglicized form *ranch*. By the late 19th century, *ranch* most often denoted not a small farm but a large tract of land devoted to livestock-raising—a meaning the word still maintains. The one-story, rambling dwelling typical of ranches was the prototype of that staple of American domestic architecture, the *ranch house*.

2 : a surveying instrument (as a transit) for determining quickly the distances, bearings, and elevations of distant objects
3 : a usually built-in adjustable optical device for focusing a camera that automatically indicates the correct focus (as when two parts of a split image are brought together)
range·land \'rānj-,land\ *noun* (1935)
: land used or suitable for range
rang·er \'rān-jər\ *noun* (14th century)
1 a : the keeper of a British royal park or forest **b :** FOREST RANGER
2 : one that ranges
3 a : one of a body of organized armed men who range over a region especially to enforce the law **b :** a soldier specially trained in close-range fighting and in raiding tactics
rangy \'rān-jē\ *adjective* **rang·i·er; -est** (1868)
1 : able to range for considerable distances
2 a : long-limbed and long-bodied ⟨*rangy* cattle⟩ **b :** being tall and slender
3 : having room for ranging
4 : having great scope
— **rang·i·ness** *noun*
ra·ni *or* **ra·nee** \rä-'nē, 'rä-,nē\ *noun* [Hindi *rānī*, from Sanskrit *rājñī*, feminine of *rājan* king — more at ROYAL] (1673)
: a Hindu queen : a rajah's wife
ra·nid \'ra-nəd, 'rā-\ *noun* [ultimately from Latin *rana* frog] (circa 1934)
: any of a large family (Ranidae) of frogs distinguished by slightly dilated transverse sacral processes
¹rank \'raŋk\ *adjective* [Middle English, from Old English *ranc* overbearing, strong; akin to Old Norse *rakkr* erect and perhaps to Old English *riht* right — more at RIGHT] (13th century)
1 : luxuriantly or excessively vigorous in growth
2 : offensively gross or coarse : FOUL
3 *obsolete* : grown too large
4 a : shockingly conspicuous ⟨must lecture him on his *rank* disloyalty —David Walden⟩ **b :** OUTRIGHT — used as an intensive ⟨*rank* beginners⟩
5 *archaic* : LUSTFUL, RUTTISH
6 : offensive in odor or flavor; *especially* : RANCID
7 : PUTRID, FESTERING
8 : high in amount or degree : FRAUGHT
synonym see MALODOROUS, FLAGRANT
— **rank·ly** *adverb*
— **rank·ness** *noun*
²rank *noun* [Middle English, from Middle French *renc, reng,* of Germanic origin; akin to Old High German *hring* ring — more at RING] (14th century)
1 a : ROW, SERIES **b :** a row of people **c** (1) **:** a line of soldiers ranged side by side in close order (2) *plural* : ARMED FORCES (3) *plural* : the body of enlisted personnel **d :** any of the rows of squares that extend across a chessboard perpendicular to the files **e** *British* : STAND 6
2 a : relative standing or position **b :** a degree or position of dignity, eminence, or excellence : DISTINCTION ⟨soon took *rank* as a leading attorney —J. D. Hicks⟩ **c :** high social position ⟨the privileges of *rank*⟩ **d :** a grade of official standing in a hierarchy
3 : an orderly arrangement : FORMATION
4 : an aggregate of individuals classed together — usually used in plural
5 : the order according to some statistical characteristic (as the score on a test)
6 : any of a series of classes of coal based on increasing alteration of the parent vegetable matter, increasing carbon content, and increasing fuel value
7 : the number of linearly independent rows or columns in a matrix
word history see RANCH
³rank (1573)
transitive verb
1 : to arrange in lines or in a regular formation

2 : to determine the relative position of : RATE
3 : to take precedence of
intransitive verb
1 : to form or move in ranks
2 : to take or have a position in relation to others
rank and file *noun* (1598)
1 : the enlisted personnel of an armed force
2 : the individuals who constitute the body of an organization, society, or nation as distinguished from the leaders
— **rank–and–file** \,raŋk-ᵊn-'fīl\ *adjective*
— **rank and fil·er** \-'fī-lər\ *noun*
rank correlation *noun* (1907)
: a measure of correlation depending on rank
rank·er \'raŋ-kər\ *noun* (1878)
: one who serves or has served in the ranks; *especially* : a commissioned officer promoted from the ranks
Ran·kine \'raŋ-kən\ *adjective* [William J. M. *Rankine* (died 1872) Scottish engineer & physicist] (circa 1926)
: being, according to, or relating to an absolute-temperature scale on which the unit of measurement equals a Fahrenheit degree and on which the freezing point of water is 491.67° and the boiling point 671.67°
rank·ing *adjective* (1862)
: having a high position: as **a :** FOREMOST ⟨*ranking* poet⟩ **b :** being next to the chairman in seniority ⟨*ranking* committee member⟩
ran·kle \'raŋ-kəl\ *verb* **ran·kled; ran·kling** \-k(ə-)liŋ\ [Middle English *ranclen* to fester, from Middle French *rancler,* from Old French *draoncler, raoncler,* from *draoncle, raoncle* festering sore, from Medieval Latin *dracunculus,* from Latin, diminutive of *draco* serpent — more at DRAGON] (1606)
intransitive verb
1 : to cause anger, irritation, or deep bitterness
2 : to feel anger and irritation
transitive verb
: to cause irritation or bitterness in ◇
ran·sack \'ran-,sak, (,)ran-'\ *transitive verb* [Middle English *ransaken,* from Old Norse *rannsaka,* from *rann* house + *-saka* (akin to Old English *sēcan* to seek) — more at SEEK] (13th century)
1 a : to search thoroughly **b :** to examine closely and carefully
2 : to search through to commit robbery : PLUNDER
— **ran·sack·er** *noun*
¹ran·som \'ran(t)-səm\ *noun* [Middle English *ransoun,* from Old French *rançon,* from Latin *redemption-, redemptio* — more at REDEMPTION] (13th century)
1 : a consideration paid or demanded for the release of someone or something from captivity
2 : the act of ransoming
²ransom *transitive verb* (14th century)
1 : to deliver especially from sin or its penalty
2 : to free from captivity or punishment by paying a price
synonym see RESCUE
— **ran·som·er** *noun*
¹rant \'rant\ *verb* [obsolete Dutch *ranten, randen*] (1602)
intransitive verb
1 : to talk in a noisy, excited, or declamatory manner
2 : to scold vehemently
transitive verb
: to utter in a bombastic declamatory fashion
— **rant·er** *noun*
— **rant·ing·ly** \'ran-tiŋ-lē\ *adverb*
²rant *noun* (1649)
1 a : a bombastic extravagant speech **b :** bombastic extravagant language
2 *dialect British* : a rousing good time
ran·u·la \'ran-yə-lə\ *noun* [New Latin, from Latin, swelling on the tongue of cattle, from diminutive of *rana* frog] (15th century)
: a cyst formed under the tongue by obstruction of a gland duct

ra·nun·cu·lus \rə-'nəŋ-kyə-ləs\ *noun, plural* **-lus·es** *or* **-li** \-,lī, -,lē\ [New Latin, from Latin, from diminutive of *rana* frog] (1543)
: BUTTERCUP
¹rap \'rap\ *noun* [Middle English *rappe*] (14th century)
1 : a sharp blow or knock
2 a : a sharp rebuke or criticism **b :** a negative and often undeserved reputation or charge — usually used with *bum* or *bad* ⟨given a bum *rap* by the press⟩
3 a : the responsibility for or adverse consequences of an action ⟨refused to take the *rap*⟩ **b :** a criminal charge **c :** a prison sentence
²rap *verb* **rapped; rap·ping** (14th century)
transitive verb
1 : to strike with a sharp blow
2 : to utter suddenly and forcibly
3 : to cause to be or come by raps ⟨*rap* the meeting to order⟩
4 : to criticize sharply
intransitive verb
1 : to strike a quick sharp blow
2 : to make a short sharp sound
³rap *transitive verb* **rapped** *also* **rapt** \'rapt\; **rap·ping** [back-formation from *rapt*] (1528)
1 : to snatch away or upward
2 : ENRAPTURE
⁴rap *noun* [perhaps from ¹*rap*] (1834)
: a minimum amount or degree (as of care or consideration) : the least bit ⟨doesn't care a *rap*⟩
⁵rap *intransitive verb* **rapped; rap·ping** [perhaps from ¹*rap*] (1929)
1 : to talk freely and frankly
2 : to perform rap music
⁶rap *noun* (1967)
1 : TALK, CONVERSATION; *also* : a line of talk : PATTER
2 a : a rhythmic chanting often in unison of usually rhymed couplets to a musical accompaniment **b :** a piece so performed
ra·pa·cious \rə-'pā-shəs\ *adjective* [Latin *rapac-, rapax,* from *rapere* to seize — more at RAPID] (1651)
1 : excessively grasping or covetous
2 : living on prey
3 : RAVENOUS
synonym see VORACIOUS
word history see RAPT
— **ra·pa·cious·ly** *adverb*
— **ra·pa·cious·ness** *noun*
ra·pac·i·ty \rə-'pa-sə-tē\ *noun* (1543)
: the quality of being rapacious
¹rape \'rāp\ *noun* [Middle English, from Latin *rapa, rapum* turnip, rape; akin to Old High German *rāba* turnip, rape, Lithuanian *ropė*] (14th century)
: a European herb (*Brassica napus*) of the mustard family grown as a forage crop for sheep and hogs and for its seeds which yield rapeseed oil and are a bird food — compare CANOLA

◇ WORD HISTORY
rankle The modern meaning of the verb *rankle* "to cause anger, irritation, or bitterness" is a figurative extension of the earlier meaning "to fester, swell," said of an ulcer or festering sore. The Middle English predecessor of this verb, *ranclen* or *ranklen,* was a loanword from Middle French *rancler,* contracted from Old French *draoncler* or *raoncler,* a derivative of *draoncle* "festering sore." *Draoncle* is descended from Latin *dracunculus,* which in classical Latin is a diminutive of *draco* "snake," though in spoken Latin, to judge by its offspring in Romance languages, it must also have had the meaning "festering sore." The comparison of something both painful and destructive to a biting animal is not surprising; another example is the use of *cancer* "crab" in Latin to denote gangrene or a malignant tumor.

word history see RAPT

²**rape** *transitive verb* **raped; rap·ing** [Middle English, from Latin *rapere*] (14th century)
1 a *archaic* : to seize and take away by force
b : DESPOIL
2 : to commit rape on
— **rap·er** *noun*
— **rap·ist** \'rā-pist\ *noun*

³**rape** *noun* (14th century)
1 : an act or instance of robbing or despoiling or carrying away a person by force
2 a : sexual intercourse with a woman by a man without her consent and chiefly by force or deception — compare STATUTORY RAPE **b** : unlawful sexual intercourse by force or threat other than by a man with a woman
3 : an outrageous violation

⁴**rape** *noun* [French *râpe* grape stalk] (1657)
: grape pomace

rape·seed \'rāp-ˌsēd\ *noun* (1577)
: the seed of the rape plant

rapeseed oil *noun* (1816)
: a nondrying or semidrying oil obtained from rapeseed and turnip seed and used chiefly as a lubricant, illuminant, and food — called also *rape oil*; compare CANOLA OIL

Ra·pha·el \'ra-fē-əl, 'rā-, -ˌel\ *noun* [Late Latin, from Greek *Rhaphaēl*, from Hebrew *Rĕphāʾēl*]
: one of the four archangels named in Hebrew tradition

ra·phe \'rā-(ˌ)fē\ *noun* [New Latin, from Greek *rhaphē* seam, from *rhaptein* to sew] (circa 1753)
1 : the seamlike union of the two lateral halves of a part or organ (as the tongue) having externally a ridge or furrow
2 a : the part of the stalk of an anatropous ovary that is united in growth to the outside covering and forms a ridge along the body of the ovule **b** : the median line or slit of a diatom's valve

ra·phia \'rā-fē-ə, 'ra-\ *noun* [New Latin, genus of palms, from Malagasy *rafia* raffia] (circa 1866)
: RAFFIA

raph·ide \'ra-ˌfīd\ *noun, plural* **raph·ides** \'ra-ˌfīdz, 'ra-fə-ˌdēz\ [French & New Latin; French *raphide*, from New Latin *raphides*, plural, from Greek *rhaphides*, plural of *rhaphid-, rhaphis* needle, from *rhaptein*] (circa 1842)
: any of the needle-shaped crystals usually of calcium oxalate that develop as metabolic by-products in plant cells

¹**rap·id** \'ra-pəd\ *adjective* [Latin *rapidus* seizing, sweeping, rapid, from *rapere* to seize, sweep away; akin to Lithuanian *aprėpti* to embrace] (1634)
: marked by a fast rate of motion, activity, succession, or occurrence
synonym see FAST
— **rap·id·ly** *adverb*
— **rap·id·ness** *noun*

²**rapid** *noun* (1765)
: a part of a river where the current is fast and the surface is usually broken by obstructions — usually used in plural but singular or plural in construction

rapid eye movement *noun* (1916)
: a rapid conjugate movement of the eyes associated especially with REM sleep

rapid eye movement sleep *noun* (1965)
: REM SLEEP

rap·id-fire \ˌra-pəd-'fīr\ *adjective* (1890)
1 : firing or adapted for firing shots in rapid succession
2 : marked by rapidity, liveliness, or sharpness

ra·pid·i·ty \rə-'pi-də-tē, ra-\ *noun* (1654)
: the quality or state of being rapid

rapid transit *noun* (1873)
: fast passenger transportation (as by subway) in urban areas

ra·pi·er \'rā-pē-ər\ *noun* [Middle French (*espee*) *rapiere*] (1553)
: a straight 2-edged sword with a narrow pointed blade

rap·ine \'ra-pən, -ˌpīn\ *noun* [Middle English *rapyne*, from Latin *rapina*, from *rapere* to seize, rob] (15th century)
: PILLAGE, PLUNDER

ra·pi·ni *also* **rap·pi·ni** \ra-'pē-nē\ *noun* [Italian *rapini*, plural of *rapino*, diminutive of *rapo* turnip, from Latin *rapum* — more at RAPE] (1942)
: BROCCOLI RABE

rap·pa·ree \ˌra-pə-'rē\ *noun* [Irish *rapaire, ropaire*, literally, thruster, stabber, from *rop* thrust, stab] (1690)
1 : an Irish irregular soldier or bandit
2 : VAGABOND, PLUNDERER

rap·pee \ra-'pā\ *noun* [French (*tabac*) *râpé*, literally, grated tobacco] (circa 1740)
: a pungent snuff made from dark tobacco leaves

rap·pel \ra-'pel, ra-\ *intransitive verb* **-pelled** *also* **-peled; -pel·ling** *also* **-pel·ing** [French, literally, recall, from Old French *rapel*, from *rapeler* to recall, from *re-* + *apeler* to appeal, call — more at APPEAL] (1944)
: to descend (as from a cliff) by sliding down a rope passed under one thigh, across the body, and over the opposite shoulder or through a special friction device
— **rappel** *noun*

rap·pen \'räp-ən\ *noun, plural* **rappen** [German, from German dialect, literally, raven] (1838)
: the centime of Switzerland

rap·per \'ra-pər\ *noun* (1640)
: one that raps or is used for rapping: as **a** : a door knocker **b** : a performer of rap music

rap·port \ra-'pōr, rə-, -'pȯr\ *noun* [French, from *rapporter* to bring back, refer, from Old French *raporter* to bring back, from *re-* + *aporter* to bring, from Latin *apportare*, from *ad-* ad- + *portare* to carry — more at FARE] (circa 1661)
: RELATION; *especially* : relation marked by harmony, conformity, accord, or affinity

rap·por·teur \ˌra-pōr-'tər, -ˌpȯr-\ *noun* [Middle French, from *rapporter* to bring back, report] (circa 1500)
: a person who gives reports (as at a meeting of a learned society)

rap·proche·ment \ˌra-ˌprōsh-'mäⁿ, -ˌprȯsh-; ra-'prōsh-ˌ\ *noun* [French, from *rapprocher* to bring together, from Middle French, from *re-* + *approcher* to approach, from Old French *aprochier*] (1809)
: establishment of or state of having cordial relations

rap·scal·lion \rap-'skal-yən\ *noun* [alteration of earlier *rascallion*, irregular from *rascal*] (1699)
: RASCAL, NE'ER-DO-WELL

rap sheet *noun* (1960)
: a police arrest record especially for an individual

rapt \'rapt\ *adjective* [Middle English, from Latin *raptus*, past participle of *rapere* to seize — more at RAPID] (14th century)
1 : lifted up and carried away
2 : transported with emotion : ENRAPTURED
3 : wholly absorbed : ENGROSSED ◇
— **rapt·ly** \'rap(t)-lē\ *adverb*
— **rapt·ness** \'rap(t)-nəs\ *noun*

rap·tor \'rap-tər, -ˌtȯr\ *noun* [New Latin *Raptores*, former order name, from Latin, plural of *raptor* plunderer, from *rapere*] (1873)
: BIRD OF PREY
word history see RAPT

rap·to·ri·al \rap-'tōr-ē-əl, -'tȯr-\ *adjective* (1823)
1 : PREDACEOUS 1
2 : adapted to seize prey
3 : of, relating to, or being a bird of prey

¹**rap·ture** \'rap-chər\ *noun* [Latin *raptus*] (1629)
1 a : a state or experience of being carried away by overwhelming emotion **b** : a mystical experience in which the spirit is exalted to a knowledge of divine things
2 : an expression or manifestation of ecstasy or passion
synonym see ECSTASY
word history see RAPT
— **rap·tur·ous** \'rap-chə-rəs, 'rap-shrəs\ *adjective*
— **rap·tur·ous·ly** *adverb*
— **rap·tur·ous·ness** *noun*

²**rapture** *transitive verb* **rap·tured; rap·tur·ing** (1637)
: ENRAPTURE

rapture of the deep (1953)
: NITROGEN NARCOSIS

ra·ra avis \ˌrar-ə-'ā-vəs, ˌrer-; ˌrär-ə-'ä-wəs\ *noun, plural* **ra·ra avis·es** \-'ā-və-səz\ *or* **ra·rae aves** \ˌrär-ˌī-'ä-ˌwās\ [Latin, rare bird] (1607)
: RARITY 2

¹**rare** \'rar, 'rer\ *adjective* **rar·er; rar·est** [Middle English, from Latin *rarus*] (14th century)
1 : marked by wide separation of component particles : THIN ⟨*rare* air⟩
2 a : marked by unusual quality, merit, or appeal : DISTINCTIVE **b** : superlative or extreme of its kind
3 : seldom occurring or found : UNCOMMON
synonym see CHOICE, INFREQUENT
— **rare·ness** *noun*

²**rare** *adjective* **rar·er; rar·est** [alteration of earlier *rere*, from Middle English, from Old English *hrēre* boiled lightly; akin to Old English *hrēran* to stir, Old High German *hruoren*] (1784)
: cooked so that the inside is still red ⟨*rare* roast beef⟩

rare bird *noun* (1890)
: RARITY 2, RARA AVIS

rare·bit \'rar-bət, 'rer-\ *noun* [(Welsh) rarebit] (circa 1785)
: WELSH RABBIT

rare earth *noun* (1875)
1 : any of a group of similar oxides of metals or a mixture of such oxides occurring together in widely distributed but relatively scarce minerals

◇ **WORD HISTORY**

rapt Current usage of the adjective *rapt* reflects its history only dimly. It is borrowed from Latin *raptus*, the past participle of *rapere* "to seize, carry off." This Latin verb is the ultimate source of a number of other English words, including *rapacious* and *raptor*, which still convey something of the idea of seizing, as well as *rapture*, now more usual in the figurative sense of being carried away with emotional ecstasy. In Middle English *rapt* simply functioned as the past participle of *rapen*, which meant both "to rape" or "to abduct (a woman) with the intent of raping her" and, with a wholly different connotation, "to carry off" or "to transport" by divine agency. Fifteenth century authors use the latter sense when they speak of a saint being "rapt in to paradys" or of someone whose body "was rapte up fro the erthe." In early Modern English *rape*, with its long vowel, and *rapt*, with its short vowel, went their own separate ways. While *rape* maintained its brutal literal sense, *rapt* came to mean solely "carried away in spirit" and hence "transported by emotion" or "wholly absorbed or engrossed," which are its usual modern senses.

\ə\ **abut** \ᵊ\ **kitten** \ər\ **further** \a\ **ash** \ā\ **ace** \ä\ **mop, mar** \au̇\ **out** \ch\ **chin** \e\ **bet** \ē\ **easy** \g\ **go** \i\ **hit** \ī\ **ice** \j\ **job** \ŋ\ **sing** \ō\ **go** \ȯ\ **law** \ȯi\ **boy** \th\ **thin** \t̲h̲\ **the** \ü\ **loot** \u̇\ **foot** \y\ **yet** \zh\ **vision** *see also* Guide to Pronunciation

2 : RARE EARTH ELEMENT

rare earth element *noun* (1942)
: any of a series of metallic elements of which the oxides are classed as rare earths and which include the elements of the lanthanide series and sometimes yttrium and scandium — called also *rare earth metal*

rar·ee-show \'rar-ē-,shō, 'rer-\ *noun* [alteration of *rare show*] (1684)
: a small display or scene viewed in a box : PEEP SHOW; *broadly* **:** an unusual or amazing show or spectacle

rar·e·fac·tion \,rar-ə-'fak-shən, ,rer-\ *noun* [French or Medieval Latin; French *raréfaction*, from Medieval Latin *rarefaction-, rarefactio*, from Latin *rarefacere* to rarefy] (1603)
1 : the action or process of rarefying
2 : the quality or state of being rarefied
3 : a state or region of minimum pressure in a medium traversed by compressional waves (as sound waves)
— **rar·e·fac·tion·al** \-shnəl, -shə-n°l\ *adjective*

rar·e·fied *also* **rar·i·fied** \'rar-ə-,fīd, 'rer-\ *adjective* (1941)
1 : of, relating to, or interesting to a select group : ESOTERIC
2 : very high

rar·e·fy *also* **rar·i·fy** \-ə-,fī\ *verb* **-fied; -fy·ing** [Middle English *rarefien, rarifien*, from Middle French *rarefier*, modification of Latin *rarefacere*, from *rarus* rare + *facere* to make — more at DO] (14th century)
transitive verb
1 : to make rare, thin, porous, or less dense **:** to expand without the addition of matter
2 : to make more spiritual, refined, or abstruse
intransitive verb
: to become less dense

rare·ly \'rar-lē, 'rer-\ *adverb* (1552)
1 : not often : SELDOM
2 : with rare skill : EXCELLENTLY
3 : in an extreme or exceptional manner

rare·ripe \'rar-,rīp, 'rer-\ *noun* [English dialect *rare* early + English *ripe*] (1722)
1 : an early ripening fruit or vegetable
2 *dialect* **:** GREEN ONION

rar·ing \'rar-ən, 'rer-, -iŋ\ *adjective* [from present participle of English dialect *rare* to rear, alteration of English *rear*] (1909)
: full of enthusiasm or eagerness ⟨ready and *raring* to go⟩

rar·i·ty \'rar-ə-tē, 'rer-\ *noun, plural* **-ties** (1542)
1 : the quality, state, or fact of being rare
2 : one that is rare

ras·bo·ra \raz-'bōr-ə, -'bȯr-\ *noun* [New Latin] (1931)
: any of a genus (*Rasbora*) of tiny brilliantly colored cyprinid freshwater fishes often kept in tropical aquariums

ras·cal \'ras-kəl\ *noun* [Middle English *rascaile* rabble, one of the rabble] (15th century)
1 : a mean, unprincipled, or dishonest person
2 : a mischievous person or animal
— **rascal** *adjective*

ras·cal·i·ty \ra-'ska-lə-tē\ *noun, plural* **-ties** (circa 1577)
1 : RABBLE
2 a : the character or actions of a rascal **b :** a rascally act : KNAVERY

ras·cal·ly \'ras-kə-lē\ *adjective* (1594)
: of or characteristic of a rascal
— **rascally** *adverb*

rase \'rāz\ *transitive verb* **rased; ras·ing** [Middle English, from Middle French *raser*, from (assumed) Vulgar Latin *rasare*, frequentative of Latin *radere* to scrape, shave — more at RODENT] (14th century)
1 *archaic* **:** ERASE
2 *archaic* **:** RAZE 2

¹rash \'rash\ *adverb* [Middle English (northern dialect) *rasch* quickly; akin to Old High German *rasc* fast] (15th century)
archaic **:** in a rash manner

²rash *adjective* (1509)
1 : marked by or proceeding from undue haste or lack of deliberation or caution
2 *obsolete* **:** quickly effective
synonym see ADVENTUROUS
— **rash·ly** *adverb*
— **rash·ness** *noun*

³rash *noun* [obsolete French *rache* scurf, from (assumed) Vulgar Latin *rasica*, from *rasicare* to scratch, from Latin *rasus*, past participle of *radere*] (1709)
1 : an eruption on the body
2 : a large number of instances in a short period ⟨a *rash* of complaints⟩

rash·er \'ra-shər\ *noun* [perhaps from obsolete *rash* to cut, from Middle English *rashen*] (1592)
: a thin slice of bacon or ham broiled or fried; *also* **:** a portion consisting of several such slices

¹rasp \'rasp\ *verb* [Middle English, from (assumed) Middle French *rasper*, of Germanic origin; akin to Old High German *raspōn* to scrape together] (14th century)
transitive verb
1 : to rub with something rough; *specifically* **:** to abrade with a rasp
2 : to grate upon : IRRITATE
3 : to utter in a raspy tone
intransitive verb
1 : SCRAPE
2 : to produce a grating sound
— **rasp·er** *noun*
— **rasp·ing·ly** \'ras-piŋ-lē\ *adverb*

²rasp *noun* (circa 1512)
1 : a coarse file with cutting points instead of lines
2 : something used for rasping
3 a : an act of rasping **b :** a rasping sound, sensation, or effect

rasp·ber·ry \'raz-,ber-ē, -b(ə-)rē\ *noun* [English dialect *rasp* raspberry + English *berry*] (circa 1616)
1 a : any of various usually black or red edible berries that are aggregate fruits consisting of numerous small drupes on a fleshy receptacle and that are usually rounder and smaller than the closely related blackberries **b :** a plant (genus *Rubus*) of the rose family that bears raspberries
2 [short for *raspberry tart*, rhyming slang for *fart*] **:** a sound of contempt made by protruding the tongue between the lips and expelling air forcibly to produce a vibration; *broadly* **:** an expression of disapproval or contempt

raspy \'ras-pē\ *adjective* (1838)
1 : HARSH, GRATING
2 : IRRITABLE

Ras·ta \'ras-tə, 'räs-\ *noun* (1955)
: RASTAFARIAN
— **Rasta** *adjective*

Ras·ta·far·i·an \,ras-tə-'far-ē-ən, ,räs-tə-'fär-\ *noun* [*Ras Tafari*, precoronation name of Haile Selassie] (1955)
: an adherent of Rastafarianism
— **Rastafarian** *adjective*

Ras·ta·far·i·an·ism \-ē-ə-,ni-zəm\ *noun* (1968)
: a religious cult among black Jamaicans that teaches the eventual redemption of blacks and their return to Africa, employs the ritualistic use of marijuana, forbids the cutting of hair, and venerates Haile Selassie as a god

ras·ter \'ras-tər\ *noun* [German, from Latin *raster, rastrum* rake, from *radere* to scrape] (1934)
: a scan pattern (as of the electron beam in a cathode-ray tube) in which an area is scanned from side to side in lines from top to bottom; *also* **:** a pattern of closely spaced rows of dots that form the image on a cathode-ray tube (as of a television or computer display)

ra·sure \'rā-shər, -zhər\ *noun* [Middle French, from Latin *rasura*, from *rasus*, past participle of *radere*] (1508)
: ERASURE, OBLITERATION

¹rat \'rat\ *noun* [Middle English, from Old English *ræt*; akin to Old High German *ratta* rat and perhaps to Latin *rodere* to gnaw — more at RODENT] (before 12th century)
1 a : any of numerous rodents (*Rattus* and related genera) differing from the related mice by considerably larger size and by structural details (as of the teeth) **b :** any of various similar rodents
2 : a contemptible person: as **a :** one who betrays or deserts friends or associates **b :** SCAB 3b **c :** INFORMER 2
3 : a pad over which a woman's hair is arranged
4 : a person who spends much time especially idly in a specified place ⟨a mall *rat*⟩
— **rat·like** \-,līk\ *adjective*

²rat *verb* **rat·ted; rat·ting** (1812)
intransitive verb
1 : to betray, desert, or inform on one's associates — usually used with *on*
2 : to catch or hunt rats
3 : to work as a scab
transitive verb
: to give (hair) the effect of greater quantity by use of a rat

rat·able *or* **rate·able** \'rā-tə-bəl\ *adjective* (1503)
: capable of being rated, estimated, or apportioned
— **rat·ably** \-blē\ *adverb*

rat·a·fia \,ra-tə-'fē-ə\ *noun* [French] (1699)
1 : a liqueur made from an infusion of macerated fruit or fruit juice in a liquor (as brandy) and often flavored with almonds
2 : a sweet biscuit made of almond paste

rat·a·plan \'ra-tə-,plan\ *noun* [French, of imitative origin] (circa 1848)
: the iterative sound of beating ⟨a rolling *rataplan* of drums —*Time*⟩

rat-a-tat \'ra-tə-,tat\ *or* **rat-a-tat-tat** \,ra-tə-,ta(t)-'tat\ *noun* [imitative] (1681)
: a rapid succession of knocking, tapping, or cracking sounds

ra·ta·tou·ille \,ra-,tə-'twē, ,rä-,tä-, -'tü-ē\ *noun* [French, from blend of *ratouiller* to disturb, shake and *tatouiller* to stir] (circa 1877)
: a seasoned stew made of eggplant, tomatoes, green peppers, squash, and sometimes meat

rat·bag \'rat-,bag\ *noun* (1890)
chiefly Australian **:** a stupid, eccentric, or disagreeable person

rat-bite fever *noun* (1910)
: either of two febrile bacterial diseases of humans usually transmitted by the bite of a rat

rat cheese *noun* (1939)
: CHEDDAR

¹ratch·et \'ra-chət\ *noun* [alteration of earlier *rochet*, from French, alteration of Middle French *rocquet* ratchet, bobbin, of Germanic origin; akin to Old High German *rocko* distaff — more at ROCK] (1654)
1 : a mechanism that consists of a bar or wheel having inclined teeth into which a pawl drops so that motion can be imparted to the wheel or bar, governed, or prevented and that is used in a hand tool (as a wrench or screwdriver) to allow effective motion in one direction only
2 : a pawl or detent for holding or propelling a ratchet wheel

²ratchet (1973)
transitive verb
: to cause to move by steps or degrees — usually used with *up* or *down* ⟨tried to *ratchet* down the debt⟩
intransitive verb
: to proceed by steps or degrees

ratchet wheel *noun* (1777)
: a toothed wheel held in position or turned by an engaging pawl

ratchet wheel:
1 wheel, *2* reciprocating lever, *3* pawl for communicating motion, *4* pawl for preventing backward motion

¹rate \'rāt\ *verb* **rat·ed; rat·ing** [Middle English] (14th century)
transitive verb
1 : to rebuke angrily or violently
2 *obsolete* **:** to drive away by scolding
intransitive verb
: to voice angry reprimands

²rate *noun* [Middle English, from Middle French, from Medieval Latin *rata*, from Latin (*pro*) *rata* (*parte*) according to a fixed proportion] (15th century)
1 a : reckoned value **:** VALUATION **b** *obsolete* **:** ESTIMATION
2 *obsolete* **:** a fixed quantity
3 a : a fixed ratio between two things **b :** a charge, payment, or price fixed according to a ratio, scale, or standard: as (1) **:** a charge per unit of a public-service commodity (2) **:** a charge per unit of freight or passenger service (3) **:** a unit charge or ratio used by a government for assessing property taxes (4) *British* **:** a local tax
4 a : a quantity, amount, or degree of something measured per unit of something else **b :** an amount of payment or charge based on another amount; *specifically* **:** the amount of premium per unit of insurance
5 : relative condition or quality **:** CLASS
— at any rate : in any case **:** ANYWAY

³rate *verb* **rat·ed; rat·ing** (15th century)
transitive verb
1 *obsolete* **:** ALLOT
2 a : to set an estimate on **:** VALUE, ESTEEM ⟨black is *rated* very high this season⟩ **b :** to determine or assign the relative rank or class of **:** GRADE ⟨*rate* a seaman⟩ **c :** to estimate the normal capacity or power of
3 : CONSIDER, REGARD ⟨was *rated* an excellent pianist⟩
4 : to fix the amount of premium to be charged per unit of insurance on
5 : to have a right to **:** DESERVE ⟨she *rated* special privileges⟩
intransitive verb
: to enjoy a status of special privilege ⟨really *rates* with the boss⟩
synonym see ESTIMATE

ra·tel \'rä-t⁰l, 'rā-\ *noun* [Afrikaans, literally, rattle, from Dutch, from Middle Dutch — more at RATTLE] (1777)
: an African or Asian nocturnal carnivorous mammal (*Mellivora capensis*) of the weasel family that resembles a badger

rate-me·ter \'rāt-ˌmē-tər\ *noun* (1949)
: an instrument that indicates the counting rate of an electronic counter

rate of change (circa 1939)
: a value that results from dividing the change in a function of a variable by the change in the variable ⟨velocity is the *rate of change* in distance with respect to time⟩

rate of exchange (circa 1741)
: the amount of one currency that will buy a given amount of another

rate of interest (1785)
: the percentage usually on an annual basis that is paid for the use of money borrowed from another

rate-pay·er \'rāt-ˌpā-ər\ *noun* (1845)
1 *British* **:** TAXPAYER
2 : one who pays for the consumption of electricity according to established rates

rat·er \'rā-tər\ *noun* (1611)
1 : one that rates; *specifically* **:** a person who estimates or determines a rating
2 : one having a specified rating or class — usually used in combination ⟨first-*rater*⟩

rat fink *noun* (1964)
: FINK, INFORMER

rat·fish \'rat-ˌfish\ *noun* (1882)
: CHIMAERA; *especially* **:** a silvery iridescent white-spotted chimaera (*Hydrolagus colliei*) of cold deep waters of the Pacific coast of North America

rathe \'rāth, 'rath\ *adjective* [Middle English, quick, from Old English *hræth*, alteration of

hræd; akin to Old High German *hrad* quick] (14th century)
archaic **:** EARLY ⟨bring the *rathe* primrose that forsaken dies —John Milton⟩

rath·er \'ra-thər, 'rä-, 'rə- *also* 're-; *interjectionally* 'ra-'thər, 'rä-, 'rə-\ *adverb* [Middle English, from Old English *hrathor*, comparative of *hrathe* quickly; akin to Old High German *rado* quickly, Old English *hræd* quick] (before 12th century)
1 : with better reason or more propriety **:** more properly ⟨this you should pity *rather* than despise —Shakespeare⟩
2 : more readily or willingly **:** PREFERABLY ⟨I'd *rather* not go⟩ ⟨would *rather* read than watch television⟩ — often used interjectionally to express affirmation
3 : more correctly speaking ⟨my father, or *rather* my stepfather⟩
4 : to the contrary **:** INSTEAD ⟨was no better but *rather* grew worse —Mark 5:26 (Revised Standard Version)⟩
5 : in some degree **:** SOMEWHAT ⟨it's *rather* warm⟩ — often used as a mild intensive ⟨spent *rather* a lot of money⟩
— the rather *archaic* **:** the more quickly or readily

rather than *conjunction* (14th century)
: and not ⟨obscures *rather than* resolves the problem⟩ ⟨why do one thing *rather than* another?⟩

raths·kel·ler \'rät-ˌske-lər, 'rat-, 'rath-\ *noun* [obsolete German (now *Ratskeller*), city-hall basement restaurant, from *Rat* council + *Keller* cellar] (1900)
: a usually basement tavern or restaurant

rat·i·cide \'ra-tə-ˌsīd\ *noun* (1908)
: a substance for killing rats

rat·i·fy \'ra-tə-ˌfī\ *transitive verb* **-fied; -fy·ing** [Middle English *ratifien*, from Middle French *ratifier*, from Medieval Latin *ratificare*, from Latin *ratus* determined, from past participle of *reri* to calculate — more at REASON] (14th century)
: to approve and sanction formally **:** CONFIRM ⟨*ratify* a treaty⟩
— rat·i·fi·ca·tion \ˌra-tə-fə-'kā-shən\ *noun*
— rat·i·fi·er \'ra-tə-ˌfī(-ə)r\ *noun*

ra·ti·né \ˌra-tə-'nā\ *or* **ra·tine** \ˌra-tə-'nā, ra-'tēn\ *noun* [French *ratiné*] (circa 1914)
1 : a nubby ply yarn of various fibers made by twisting under tension a thick and a thin yarn
2 : a rough bulky fabric usually woven loosely in plain weave from ratiné yarns

rat·ing \'rā-tiŋ\ *noun* (1702)
1 : a classification according to grade; *specifically* **:** a military or naval specialist classification
2 *chiefly British* **:** a naval enlisted man
3 a : a relative estimate or evaluation **:** STANDING ⟨the school has a good academic *rating*⟩ **b :** an estimate of an individual's or business's credit and responsibility **c :** an estimate of the percentage of the public listening to or viewing a particular radio or television program
4 : a stated operating limit of a machine expressible in power terms (as kilowatts of a direct-current generator) or in characteristics (as voltage)

ra·tio \'rā-(ˌ)shō, -shē-ˌō\ *noun, plural* **ra·tios** [Latin, computation, reason — more at REASON] (1660)
1 a : the indicated quotient of two mathematical expressions **b :** the relationship in quantity, amount, or size between two or more things **:** PROPORTION
2 : the expression of the relative values of gold and silver as determined by a country's currency laws

ra·ti·o·ci·nate \ˌra-tē-'ō-s⁰n-ˌāt, ˌra-shē-, -'ä-\ *intransitive verb* **-nat·ed; -nat·ing** [Latin *ratiocinatus*, past participle of *ratiocinari* to reckon, from *ratio* + *-cinari* (as in *vaticinari* to prophesy) — more at VATICINATE] (1643)
: REASON
— ra·ti·o·ci·na·tor \-ˌā-tər\ *noun*

ra·ti·o·ci·na·tion \-ˌō-s⁰n-'ā-shən, -ˌä-\ *noun* (circa 1530)
1 : the process of exact thinking **:** REASONING
2 : a reasoned train of thought
— ra·ti·o·ci·na·tive \-'ō-s⁰n-ˌā-tiv, -'ä-\ *adjective*

¹ra·tion \'ra-shən, 'rā-\ *noun* [French, from Latin *ration-, ratio* computation, reason] (circa 1711)
1 a : a food allowance for one day **b** *plural* **:** FOOD, PROVISIONS
2 : a share especially as determined by supply

²ration *transitive verb* **ra·tioned; ra·tion·ing** \'ra-sh(ə-)niŋ, 'rā-\ (1859)
1 : to supply with or put on rations
2 a : to distribute as rations — often used with *out* **b :** to distribute equitably **c :** to use sparingly

¹ra·tio·nal \'rash-nəl, 'ra-shə-n⁰l\ *adjective* [Middle English *racional*, from Latin *rationalis*, from *ration-, ratio*] (14th century)
1 a : having reason or understanding **b :** relating to, based on, or agreeable to reason **:** REASONABLE ⟨a *rational* explanation⟩ ⟨*rational* behavior⟩
2 : involving only multiplication, division, addition, and subtraction and only a finite number of times
3 : relating to, consisting of, or being one or more rational numbers ⟨a *rational* root of an equation⟩
— ra·tio·nal·ly *adverb*
— ra·tio·nal·ness *noun*

²rational *noun* (1606)
: something rational; *specifically* **:** RATIONAL NUMBER

ra·tio·nale \ˌra-shə-'nal\ *noun* [Latin, neuter of *rationalis*] (1657)
1 : an explanation of controlling principles of opinion, belief, practice, or phenomena
2 : an underlying reason **:** BASIS

rational function *noun* (1885)
: a function that is the quotient of two polynomials; *also* **:** POLYNOMIAL

ra·tio·nal·ise *British variant of* RATIONALIZE

ra·tio·nal·ism \'rash-nə-ˌli-zəm, 'ra-shə-n⁰l-ˌi-\ *noun* (1827)
1 : reliance on reason as the basis for establishment of religious truth
2 a : a theory that reason is in itself a source of knowledge superior to and independent of sense perceptions **b :** a view that reason and experience rather than the nonrational are the fundamental criteria in the solution of problems
3 : FUNCTIONALISM
— ra·tio·nal·ist \-nə-list, -n⁰l-ist\ *noun*
— rationalist *or* **ra·tio·nal·is·tic** \ˌrash-nə-'lis-tik, ˌra-shə-n⁰l-'is-\ *adjective*
— ra·tio·nal·is·ti·cal·ly \-ti-k(ə-)lē\ *adverb*

ra·tio·nal·i·ty \ˌra-shə-'na-lə-tē\ *noun, plural* **-ties** (1628)
1 : the quality or state of being rational
2 : the quality or state of being agreeable to reason **:** REASONABLENESS
3 : a rational opinion, belief, or practice — usually used in plural

ra·tio·nal·ize \'rash-nə-ˌlīz, 'ra-shə-n⁰l-ˌīz\ *verb* **-ized; -iz·ing** (1803)
transitive verb
1 : to free (a mathematical expression) from irrational parts ⟨*rationalize* a denominator⟩
2 : to bring into accord with reason or cause something to seem reasonable: as **a :** to substitute a natural for a supernatural explanation of

⟨*rationalize* a myth⟩ **b** : to attribute (one's actions) to rational and creditable motives without analysis of true and especially unconscious motives ⟨*rationalized* his dislike of his brother⟩
3 : to apply the principles of scientific management to (as an industry or its operations) for a desired result (as increased efficiency) *intransitive verb*
: to provide plausible but untrue reasons for conduct
— **ra·tio·nal·iz·able** \,rash-nə-'lī-zə-bəl, ,ra-shə-nᵊl-ī-\ *adjective*
— **ra·tio·nal·i·za·tion** \,rash-nə-lə-'zā-shən, ,ra-shə-nᵊl-ə-\ *noun*
— **ra·tio·nal·iz·er** \'rash-nə-,līz-ər, 'ra-shə-nᵊl-,ī-\ *noun*
rational number *noun* (1904)
: an integer or the quotient of an integer divided by a nonzero integer
rat·ite \'ra-,tīt\ *noun* [ultimately from Latin *ratitus* marked with the figure of a raft, from *ratis* raft] (circa 1890)
: a bird with a flat breastbone; *especially* : any of various mostly flightless birds (as an ostrich, rhea, emu, moa, or kiwi) with small or rudimentary wings and no keel on the sternum that are probably of polyphyletic origin and are assigned to a number of different orders
— **ratite** *adjective*
rat·line \'rat-lən\ *noun* [Middle English *radelyng*] (15th century)
: any of the small transverse ropes attached to the shrouds of a ship so as to form the steps of a rope ladder

¹ra·toon \ra-'tün\ *noun* [Spanish *retoño*, from *retoñar* to sprout, from *re-* (from Latin) + *otoñar* to grow in autumn, from *otoño* autumn, from Latin *autumnus*] (1631)
1 : a shoot of a perennial plant (as sugarcane)
2 : a crop (as of bananas) produced on ratoons

ratline

²ratoon (1756)
intransitive verb
: to sprout or spring up from the root
transitive verb
: to grow or produce (a crop) from or on ratoons
rat race *noun* (1939)
: strenuous, wearisome, and usually competitive activity or rush
rats \'rats\ *interjection* (1890)
— used to express disappointment, frustration, or disgust
rat snake *noun* (1860)
: any of numerous large harmless rat-eating colubrid snakes (especially genus *Elaphe*) — called also *chicken snake*
rat·tail \'rat-,tāl\ *noun* (1705)
1 : a horse's tail with little or no hair
2 : GRENADIER 2
rattail cactus *noun* (1900)
: a commonly cultivated tropical American cactus (*Aporocactus flagelliformis*) with showy crimson flowers
rat–tail file *noun* (1744)
: a round slender tapered file
rat·tan \ra-'tan, rə-\ *noun* [Malay *rotan*] (1660)
1 : a rattan cane or switch
2 a : a climbing palm (especially of the genera *Calamus* and *Daemonorops*) with very long tough stems **b** : a part of the stem of a rattan used especially for walking sticks and wickerwork
rat·teen \ra-'tēn\ *noun* [French *ratine*] (1685)
archaic : a coarse woolen fabric

rat·ter \'ra-tər\ *noun* (1857)
: one that catches rats; *specifically* : a rat-catching dog or cat
¹rat·tle \'ra-tᵊl\ *verb* **rat·tled**; **rat·tling** \'rat-liŋ, 'ra-tᵊl-iŋ\ [Middle English *ratelen*; akin to Middle Dutch *ratel* rattle] (14th century)
intransitive verb
1 : to make a rapid succession of short sharp noises ⟨the windows *rattled* in the wind⟩
2 : to chatter incessantly and aimlessly
3 : to move with a clatter or rattle; *also* : to be or move about in a place or station too large or grand ⟨*rattled* around the big old house⟩
transitive verb
1 : to say, perform, or affect in a brisk lively fashion ⟨*rattled* off four magnificent backhands —Kim Chapin⟩
2 : to cause to make a rattling sound
3 : ROUSE; *specifically* : to beat (a cover) for game
4 : to upset to the point of loss of poise and composure
synonym see EMBARRASS
²rattle *noun* (1519)
1 a : a device that produces a rattle; *specifically* : a case containing pellets used as a baby's toy **b** : the sound-producing organ on a rattlesnake's tail
2 a : a rapid succession of sharp clattering sounds **b** : NOISE, RACKET
3 : a throat noise caused by air passing through mucus and heard especially at the approach of death
³rattle *transitive verb* **rat·tled**; **rat·tling** \'rat-liŋ, 'ra-tᵊl-iŋ\ [irregular from *ratline*] (1729)
: to furnish with ratlines
rat·tle·brain \'ra-tᵊl-,brān\ *noun* (1709)
: a flighty or thoughtless person
— **rat·tle-brained** \-,brānd\ *adjective*
rat·tler \'rat-lər, 'ra-tᵊl-ər\ *noun* (15th century)
1 : one that rattles
2 : RATTLESNAKE
rat·tle·snake \'ra-tᵊl-,snāk\ *noun* (1630)
: any of the American pit vipers comprising two genera (*Crotalus* and *Sistrurus*) and having horny interlocking joints at the end of the tail that make a sharp rattling sound when shaken

rattlesnake

rattlesnake plantain *noun* (1778)
: an orchid (genus *Goodyera*) with checked or mottled leaves
rattlesnake root *noun* (1682)
: any of various plants formerly believed to be distasteful to rattlesnakes or effective against their venom: as **a** : any of a genus (*Prenanthes* and especially *P. altissima*) of composite plants that have lobed or pinnatifid leaves and small heads of drooping ligulate flowers **b** : SENECA SNAKEROOT
rattlesnake weed *noun* (1760)
: a hawkweed (*Hieracium venosum*) with purple-veined leaves
rat·tle·trap \'ra-tᵊl-,trap\ *noun* (1822)
: something rattly or rickety; *especially* : an old car
— **rattletrap** *adjective*
¹rat·tling \'rat-liŋ\ *adjective* (1560)
1 : LIVELY, BRISK ⟨moved at a *rattling* pace⟩
2 : extraordinarily good : SPLENDID
— **rat·tling·ly** \-liŋ-lē\ *adverb*
²rattling *adverb* (1829)
: to an extreme degree : VERY ⟨a *rattling* good argument —E. A. Betts⟩
rat·tly \'rat-lē, 'ra-tᵊl-ē\ *adjective* (1881)
: likely to rattle : making a rattle
rat·ton \'ra-tᵊn, 'rä-\ *noun* [Middle English *ratoun*, from Middle French *raton*, diminutive of

rat, probably of Germanic origin; akin to Old English *ræt* rat] (14th century)
chiefly dialect : RAT
rat·trap \'ra(t)-,trap\ *noun* (15th century)
1 : a trap for rats
2 : a dirty dilapidated structure
3 : a hopeless situation
rat trap cheese *noun* (1927)
: CHEDDAR
rat·ty \'ra-tē\ *adjective* **rat·ti·er; -est** (1865)
1 a : infested with rats **b** : of, relating to, or suggestive of a rat
2 : SHABBY, UNKEMPT ⟨a *ratty* brown overcoat —John Lardner⟩
3 a : DESPICABLE, TREACHEROUS **b** : IRRITABLE ⟨feeling *ratty* as hell —Richard Bissell⟩
rau·cous \'ró-kəs\ *adjective* [Latin *raucus* hoarse; akin to Latin *ravis* hoarseness] (1769)
1 : disagreeably harsh or strident : HOARSE ⟨*raucous* voices⟩
2 : boisterously disorderly ⟨a . . . *raucous* frontier town —Truman Capote⟩
synonym see LOUD
— **rau·cous·ly** *adverb*
— **rau·cous·ness** *noun*
raunch \'rónch, 'ränch\ *noun* [back-formation from *raunchy*] (1964)
: VULGARITY, LEWDNESS
raun·chy \'rón-chē, 'rän-\ *adjective* **raun·chi·er; -est** [origin unknown] (1939)
1 : SLOVENLY, DIRTY ⟨a *raunchy* panhandler⟩; *also* : very smelly ⟨*raunchy* sneakers⟩
2 : OBSCENE, SMUTTY ⟨*raunchy* jokes⟩
— **raun·chi·ly** \'rón-chə-lē, 'rän-\ *adverb*
— **raun·chi·ness** \-chē-nəs\ *noun*
rau·wol·fia \raú-'wùl-fē-ə, ró-\ *noun* [New Latin, from Leonhard *Rauwolf* (died 1596) German botanist] (1752)
1 : any of a large pantropical genus (*Rauvolfia* synonym *Rauwolfia*) of somewhat poisonous trees and shrubs of the dogbane family that yield emetic and purgative substances
2 : a medicinal extract from the root of an Asian rauwolfia (*Rauvolfia serpentina*) used in the treatment of hypertension and mental disorders
¹rav·age \'ra-vij\ *noun* [French, from Middle French, from *ravir* to ravish — more at RAVISH] (circa 1611)
1 : an act or practice of ravaging
2 : damage resulting from ravaging : violently destructive effect ⟨the *ravages* of time⟩
²ravage *verb* **rav·aged; rav·ag·ing** (circa 1611)
transitive verb
: to wreak havoc on : affect destructively
intransitive verb
: to commit destructive actions ☆
— **rav·age·ment** \-vij-mənt\ *noun*
— **rav·ag·er** *noun*
¹rave \'rāv\ *verb* **raved; rav·ing** [Middle English] (14th century)
intransitive verb

1 a : to talk irrationally in or as if in delirium **b** : to speak out wildly **c** : to talk with extreme enthusiasm ⟨*raved* about its beauty⟩ **2** : to move or advance violently : STORM ⟨the iced gusts still *rave* and beat —John Keats⟩
transitive verb
: to utter in madness or frenzy
— rav·er *noun*

²rave *noun* (1598)
1 : an act or instance of raving **2** : an extravagantly favorable criticism ⟨the play received the critics' *raves*⟩

¹rav·el \'ra-vəl\ *verb* **-eled** *or* **-elled; -el·ing** *or* **-el·ling** \'rav-liŋ, 'ra-və-\ [Dutch *rafelen*, from *rafel* loose thread] (1582)
transitive verb
1 a : to separate or undo the texture of : UN-RAVEL **b** : to undo the intricacies of : DISEN-TANGLE
2 : ENTANGLE, CONFUSE
intransitive verb
1 *obsolete* : to become entangled or confused **2** : to become unwoven, untwisted, or un-wound : FRAY
3 : BREAK UP, CRUMBLE
— rav·el·er \'rav-lər, 'ra-və-\ *noun*
— rav·el·ment \'ra-vəl-mənt\ *noun*

²ravel *noun* (1634)
: an act or result of raveling: as **a** : something tangled **b** : something raveled out; *specifically* : a loose thread

rav·el·ing *or* **rav·el·ling** *noun* (1658)
: RAVEL b

¹ra·ven \'rā-vən\ *noun* [Middle English, from Old English *hræfn;* akin to Old High German *hraban* raven, Latin *corvus,* Greek *korax*] (before 12th century)
: a large glossy black corvine bird (*Corvus corax*) of Europe, Asia, northern Africa, and America

raven

²raven *adjective* (1634)
: shiny and black like a raven's feathers ⟨*raven* hair⟩

³rav·en \'ra-vən\ *verb* **rav·ened; rav·en·ing** \'ra-və-niŋ, 'rav-niŋ\ [Middle French *raviner* to rush, take by force, from *ravine* rapine] (1530)
transitive verb
1 : to devour greedily
2 : DESPOIL ⟨men . . . *raven* the earth, destroying its resources —*New Yorker*⟩
intransitive verb
1 : to feed greedily
2 : to prowl for food : PREY
3 : PLUNDER
— rav·en·er \'ra-və-nər, 'rav-nər\ *noun*

rav·en·ous \'ra-və-nəs, 'rav-nəs\ *adjective* (15th century)
1 : RAPACIOUS ⟨*ravenous* wolves⟩
2 : very eager or greedy for food, satisfaction, or gratification ⟨a *ravenous* appetite⟩
synonym see VORACIOUS
— rav·en·ous·ly *adverb*
— rav·en·ous·ness *noun*

rav·in \'ra-vən\ *noun* [Middle English, from Middle French *ravine*] (14th century)
1 : PLUNDER, PILLAGE
2 a : an act or habit of preying **b** : something seized as prey

ra·vine \rə-'vēn\ *noun* [French, from Middle French, rapine, rush, from Latin *rapina* rapine] (1760)
: a small narrow steep-sided valley that is larger than a gully and smaller than a canyon and that is usually worn by running water

rav·ined \'ra-vənd\ *adjective* (1606)
obsolete : RAPACIOUS, RAVENOUS

¹rav·ing \'rā-viŋ\ *noun* (14th century)

: irrational, incoherent, wild, or extravagant utterance or declamation — usually used in plural

²raving *adjective* (15th century)
1 : talking wildly or irrationally ⟨a *raving* lunatic⟩
2 : RAVISHING ⟨a *raving* beauty⟩

rav·i·o·li \,ra-vē-'ō-lē, ,rä-\ *noun, plural* **ra·violi** *also* **rav·i·o·lis** \-lēz\ [Italian, from Italian dialect, plural of *raviolo,* literally, little turnip, diminutive of *rava* turnip, from Latin *rapa* — more at RAPE] (circa 1611)
: pasta in the form of little cases of dough containing a savory filling (as of meat or cheese)

rav·ish \'ra-vish\ *transitive verb* [Middle English *ravisshen,* from Middle French *raviss-,* stem of *ravir,* from (assumed) Vulgar Latin *rapire,* alteration of Latin *rapere* to seize, rob — more at RAPID] (14th century)
1 a : to seize and take away by violence **b** : to overcome with emotion (as joy or delight) ⟨*ravished* by the scenic beauty⟩ **c** : RAPE 2
2 : PLUNDER, ROB
— rav·ish·er *noun*
— rav·ish·ment \-mənt\ *noun*

rav·ish·ing \'ra-vi-shiŋ\ *adjective* (14th century)
: unusually attractive, pleasing, or striking
— rav·ish·ing·ly \-shiŋ-lē\ *adverb*

¹raw \'rȯ\ *adjective* **raw·er** \'rȯ(-ə)r\; **raw·est** \'rȯ-əst\ [Middle English, from Old English *hrēaw;* akin to Old High German *hrō* raw, Latin *crudus* raw, *cruor* blood, Greek *kreas* flesh] (before 12th century)
1 : not cooked
2 a (1) : being in or nearly in the natural state : not processed or purified ⟨*raw* fibers⟩ ⟨*raw* sewage⟩ (2) : not diluted or blended ⟨*raw* spirits⟩ **b** : unprepared or imperfectly prepared for use **c** : not being in polished, finished, or processed form ⟨*raw* data⟩ ⟨a *raw* draft of a thesis⟩
3 a (1) : having the surface abraded or chafed (2) : very irritated ⟨a *raw* sore throat⟩ **b** : lacking covering : NAKED **c** : not protected : susceptible to hurt ⟨*raw* emotions⟩
4 a : lacking experience or understanding : GREEN ⟨a *raw* recruit⟩ **b** (1) : marked by absence of refinements (2) : VULGAR, COARSE **c** : not tempered : UNBRIDLED ⟨*raw* power⟩
5 : disagreeably damp or cold
synonym see RUDE
— raw·ly *adverb*
— raw·ness *noun*

²raw *noun* (1823)
: a raw place or state
— in the raw 1 : in a natural, unrefined, or crude state **2** : NAKED ⟨slept *in the raw*⟩

raw bar *noun* (1943)
: a counter (as in a restaurant) that serves raw shellfish

raw·boned \'rȯ-,bōnd\ *adjective* (1591)
: relatively thin with prominent bone structure; *also* : heavy-framed and rugged but not attractively built
synonym see LEAN

raw deal *noun* (circa 1912)
: an instance of unfair treatment

¹raw·hide \'rȯ-,hīd\ *noun* (1829)
1 : a whip of untanned hide
2 : untanned cattle skin

²rawhide *transitive verb* **raw·hid·ed; raw·hid·ing** (1858)
1 : to whip or drive with or as if with a rawhide
2 : CHASTISE 2

ra·win·sonde \'rā-wən-,sänd\ *noun* [radar + wind + radio*sonde*] (1946)
: a radiosonde tracked by a radio direction-finding device to determine the velocity of winds aloft

raw material *noun* (1796)
: crude or processed material that can be converted by manufacture, processing, or combination into a new and useful product ⟨wheat . . . is *raw material* for the flour mill —C. A.

Koepke); *broadly* : something with a potential for improvement, development, or elaboration ⟨perplexities are often the *raw material* of discoveries —Agnes M. Clerke⟩

raw score *noun* (1920)
: an individual's actual achievement score (as on a test) before being adjusted for relative position in the test group

rax \'raks\ *verb* [Middle English (northern dialect) *raxen,* from Old English *raxan;* akin to Old English *reccan* to stretch — more at RACK] (before 12th century)
chiefly Scottish : STRETCH

¹ray \'rā\ *noun* [Middle English *raye,* from Middle French *raie,* from Latin *raia*] (14th century)
: any of an order (Rajiformes) of cartilaginous fishes (as stingrays and skates) having the body flattened dorsoventrally, the eyes on the upper surface, and enlarged pectoral fins fused with the head

²ray *noun* [Middle English, from Middle French *rai,* from Latin *radius* rod, ray] (14th century)
1 a : any of the lines of light that appear to radiate from a bright object **b** : a beam of radiant energy (as light) of small cross section **c** (1) : a stream of material particles traveling in the same line (as in radioactive phenomena) (2) : a single particle of such a stream
2 a : light cast by rays : RADIANCE **b** : a moral or intellectual light
3 : a thin line suggesting a ray: as **a** : any of a group of lines diverging from a common center **b** : HALF LINE
4 a : one of the bony rods that extend and support the membrane in the fin of a fish **b** : one of the radiating divisions of the body of a radiate animal (as a starfish)
5 a : a branch or flower stalk of an umbel **b** (1) : MEDULLARY RAY (2) : VASCULAR RAY **c** : RAY FLOWER 1
6 : PARTICLE, TRACE ⟨*ray* of hope⟩
— rayed \'rād\ *adjective*

³ray (1598)
intransitive verb
1 a : to shine in or as if in rays **b** : to issue as rays
2 : to extend like the radii of a circle : RADIATE
transitive verb
1 : to emit in rays
2 : to furnish or mark with rays

ray flower *noun* (1842)
1 : one of the marginal flowers of the head in a composite plant (as the aster) that also has disk flowers
2 : the entire head in a plant (as chicory) that lacks disk flowers

Ray·leigh scattering \'rā-lē-\ *noun* [John W. S. *Rayleigh*] (1937)
: scattering of light by particles small enough to render the effect selective so that different colors are deflected through different angles

ray·less \'rā-ləs\ *adjective* (1747)
: having, admitting, or emitting no rays; *especially* : DARK
— ray·less·ness *noun*

rayless goldenrod *noun* (1923)
: a shrubby to herbaceous composite plant (*Haplopappus heterophyllus* synonym *Isocoma wrightii*) especially of open saline ground from Texas to Arizona and northern Mexico that lacks ray flowers and causes trembles in cattle

ray·on \'rā-,än\ *noun* [irregular from ²*ray*] (1924)
1 : any of a group of smooth textile fibers made from regenerated cellulose by extrusion through minute holes
2 : a rayon yarn, thread, or fabric

\ə\ abut \ᵊ\ kitten \ər\ further \a\ ash \ā\ ace \ä\ mop, mar \au̇\ out \ch\ chin \e\ bet \ē\ easy \g\ go \i\ hit \ī\ ice \j\ job \ŋ\ sing \ō\ go \ȯ\ law \ȯi\ boy \th\ thin \th\ the \ü\ loot \u̇\ foot \y\ yet \zh\ vision *see also* Guide to Pronunciation

raze \'rāz\ *transitive verb* **razed; raz·ing** [alteration of *rase*] (1536)
1 a *archaic* : ERASE **b** : to scrape, cut, or shave off
2 : to destroy to the ground : DEMOLISH
— **raz·er** *noun*

ra·zee \rā-'zē\ *noun* [French (*vaisseau*) *rasé*, literally, cut-off ship] (1794)
: a wooden warship with the upper deck cut away

ra·zor \'rā-zər\ *noun* [Middle English *rasour*, from Old French *raseor*, from *raser* to raze, shave — more at RASE] (14th century)
: a keen-edged cutting instrument for shaving or cutting hair

ra·zor·back \'rā-zər-ˌbak\ *noun* (1849)
: a thin-bodied long-legged feral hog chiefly of the southeastern U.S.

ra·zor–backed \-ˌbakt\ *or* **ra·zor·back** \-ˌbak\ *adjective* (1829)
: having a sharp narrow back ⟨a *razor-backed* horse⟩

ra·zor·bill \-ˌbil\ *noun* (1674)
: a North Atlantic auk (*Alca torda*) with the plumage black above and white below and a compressed sharp-edged bill — called also *razor-billed auk*

razor clam *noun* (1882)
: any of a family (Solenidae) of marine bivalve mollusks having a long narrow thin shell

¹razz \'raz\ *noun* [short for *razzberry* sound of contempt, alteration of *raspberry*] (circa 1919)
: RASPBERRY 2

²razz *transitive verb* (1921)
: HECKLE, DERIDE ⟨the fans *razzed* the visiting players⟩

razz·a·ma·tazz \ˌra-zə-mə-'taz\ *chiefly British variant of* RAZZMATAZZ

razz·le–daz·zle \ˌra-zəl-'da-zəl\ *noun* [reduplication of *dazzle*] (1889)
1 : a state of confusion or hilarity
2 : a complex maneuver (as in sports) designed to confuse an opponent
3 : a confusing or colorful often gaudy action or display
— **razzle–dazzle** *adjective*

razz·ma·tazz \ˌraz-mə-'taz\ *noun* [probably alteration of *razzle-dazzle*] (1942)
1 : RAZZLE-DAZZLE 3
2 : DOUBLE-TALK 2
3 : VIM, ZING

RBI \ˌär-(ˌ)bē-'ī, 'ri-bē\ *noun, plural* **RBIs** *or* **RBI** [*run batted in*] (1948)
: a run in baseball that is driven in by a batter; *also* : official credit to a batter for driving in a run ⟨led the league in *RBIs*⟩

r color *noun* (1937)
: an acoustic effect of a simultaneously articulated \r\ imparted to a vowel by retroflexion or constriction of the tongue
— **r–col·ored** \'är-ˌkə-lərd\ *adjective*

-rd *symbol*
— used after the figure 3 to indicate the ordinal number *third* ⟨3rd⟩ ⟨83rd⟩

¹re \'rā\ *noun* [Medieval Latin, from the syllable sung to this note in a medieval hymn to Saint John the Baptist] (14th century)
: the 2d tone of the diatonic scale in solmization

²re \'rā, 'rē\ *preposition* [Latin, ablative of *res* thing — more at REAL] (1707)
: with regard to : IN RE

re- *prefix* [Middle English, from Old French, from Latin *re-, red-* back, again, against]
1 : again : anew ⟨retell⟩
2 : back : backward ⟨recall⟩

re·ac·cel·er·ate
re·ac·cept
re·ac·ces·sion
re·ac·cli·ma·tize
re·ac·cred·it
re·ac·cred·i·ta·tion
re·ac·quaint
re·ac·quire
re·ac·qui·si·tion
re·ac·ti·vate
re·ac·ti·va·tion
re·ad·dress
re·ad·just
re·ad·just·ment
re·ad·mis·sion
re·ad·mit
re·adopt
re·af·firm

re·af·fir·ma·tion
re·af·fix
re·al·lo·cate
re·al·lo·ca·tion
re·anal·y·sis
re·an·a·lyze
re·an·i·mate
re·an·i·ma·tion
re·an·nex
re·an·nex·a·tion
re·ap·pear
re·ap·pear·ance
re·ap·pli·ca·tion
re·ap·ply
re·ap·point
re·ap·point·ment
re·ap·prais·al
re·ap·praise
re·ap·pro·pri·ate
re·ap·prove
re·ar·gue
re·ar·gu·ment
re·arous·al
re·arouse
re·ar·range
re·ar·range·ment
re·ar·rest
re·ar·tic·u·late
re·as·cend
re·as·cent
re·as·sem·blage
re·as·sem·ble
re·as·sem·bly
re·as·sert
re·as·ser·tion
re·as·sess
re·as·sess·ment
re·as·sign
re·as·sign·ment
re·as·sume
re·at·tach
re·at·tach·ment
re·at·tain
re·at·tempt
re·at·tri·bute
re·at·tri·bu·tion
re·au·tho·ri·za·tion
re·au·tho·rize
re·awak·en
re·bait
re·bal·ance
re·bap·tism
re·bap·tize
re·be·gin
re·bid
re·bind
re·blend
re·bloom
re·board
re·boil
re·book
re·boot
re·bore
re·bot·tle
re·breed
re·buri·al
re·bury
re·buy
re·cal·cu·late
re·cal·cu·la·tion
re·cal·i·brate
re·cal·i·bra·tion
re·cen·tral·i·za·tion
re·cen·tri·fuge
re·cer·ti·fi·ca·tion
re·cer·ti·fy
re·chal·lenge
re·chan·nel
re·char·ter
re·check
re·cho·reo·graph
re·chris·ten
re–Chris·tian·ize
re·chro·mato·graph
re·chro·ma·tog·ra·phy

re·af·fir·ma·tion
re·cir·cu·late
re·cir·cu·la·tion
re·clad
re·clas·si·fi·ca·tion
re·clas·si·fy
re·clothe
re·cock
re·cod·i·fi·ca·tion
re·cod·i·fy
re·col·o·ni·za·tion
re·col·o·nize
re·col·or
re·com·bine
re·com·mence
re·com·mence·ment
re·com·mis·sion
re·com·pi·la·tion
re·com·pile
re·com·pu·ta·tion
re·com·pute
re·con·ceive
re·con·cen·trate
re·con·cen·tra·tion
re·con·cep·tion
re·con·cep·tu·al·i·za·tion
re·con·cep·tu·al·ize
re·con·dense
re·con·fig·u·ra·tion
re·con·fig·ure
re·con·nect
re·con·nec·tion
re·con·quer
re·con·quest
re·con·se·crate
re·con·se·cra·tion
re·con·sol·i·date
re·con·tact
re·con·tam·i·nate
re·con·tam·i·na·tion
re·con·tex·tu·al·ize
re·con·tour
re·con·vene
re·con·ver·sion
re·con·vert
re·con·vict
re·con·vic·tion
re·con·vince
re·copy
re·cork
re·cross
re·cul·ti·vate
re·date
re·ded·i·cate
re·ded·i·ca·tion
re·de·fect
re·de·liv·er
re·de·liv·ery
re·de·pos·it
re·de·ter·mi·na·tion
re·de·ter·mine
re·di·ges·tion
re·dis·cov·er
re·dis·cov·ery
re·dis·cuss
re·dis·play
re·dis·pose
re·dis·po·si·tion
re·dis·solve
re·dis·till
re·dis·til·la·tion
re·di·vide
re·di·vi·sion
re·don
re·draft
re·draw
re·dream
re·drill
re·dub
re·el·i·gi·bil·i·ty
re·el·i·gi·ble
re·emerge
re·emer·gence
re·emis·sion
re·emit
re·em·pha·sis

re·em·pha·size
re·em·ploy
re·em·ploy·ment
re·en·coun·ter
re·en·dow
re·en·er·gize
re·en·gage
re·en·gage·ment
re·en·gi·neer
re·en·grave
re·en·list
re·en·list·ment
re·en·roll
re·en·throne
re·equip
re·equip·ment
re·erect
re·es·ca·late
re·es·ca·la·tion
re·es·tab·lish
re·es·tab·lish·ment
re·es·ti·mate
re·eval·u·ate
re·eval·u·a·tion
re·ex·am·i·na·tion
re·ex·am·ine
re·ex·pe·ri·ence
re·ex·plore
re·ex·port
re·ex·por·ta·tion
re·ex·pose
re·ex·po·sure
re·ex·press
re·face
re·feed
re·feel
re·fence
re·fight
re·fig·ure
re·file
re·find
re·fire
re·fix
re·float
re·fold
re·forge
re·for·mat
re·for·mu·late
re·for·mu·la·tion
re·for·ti·fi·ca·tion
re·for·ti·fy
re·found
re·foun·da·tion
re·frame
re·freeze
re·fry
re·fur·nish
re·gain
re·gath·er
re·gear
re·gild
re·give
re·glaze
re·grade
re·graft
re·grant
re·green
re·grind
re·groom
re·groove
re·growth
re·han·dle
re·hang
re·heat
re·hinge
re·hire
re·hos·pi·tal·i·za·tion
re·hos·pi·tal·ize
re·hu·man·ize
re·hyp·no·tize
re·iden·ti·fy
re·ig·nite
re·ig·ni·tion
re·im·age
re·im·merse
re·im·plant

re·im·plan·ta·tion
re·im·port
re·im·por·ta·tion
re·im·pose
re·im·po·si·tion
re·in·cor·po·rate
re·in·cor·po·ra·tion
re·in·dict
re·in·dict·ment
re·in·fes·ta·tion
re·in·flate
re·in·fla·tion
re·in·hab·it
re·ini·tiate
re·in·ject
re·in·jec·tion
re·in·jure
re·in·ju·ry
re·ink
re·in·ner·vate
re·in·ner·va·tion
re·in·oc·u·late
re·in·oc·u·la·tion
re·in·sert
re·in·ser·tion
re·in·spect
re·in·spec·tion
re·in·spire
re·in·stall
re·in·stal·la·tion
re·in·sti·tute
re·in·sti·tu·tion·al·i·za·tion
re·in·ter
re·in·ter·view
re·in·tro·duce
re·in·tro·duc·tion
re·in·vade
re·in·va·sion
re·in·ves·ti·gate
re·in·ves·ti·ga·tion
re·in·vig·o·rate
re·in·vig·o·ra·tion
re·in·vig·o·ra·tor
re·jack·et
re·judge
re·jug·gle
re·key
re·key·board
re·kin·dle
re·knit
re·la·bel
re·lac·quer
re·land·scape
re·launch
re·learn
re·lend
re·li·cense
re·li·cen·sure
re·light
re·link
re·liq·ue·fy
re·load
re·lock
re·look
re·lu·bri·cate
re·lu·bri·ca·tion
re·mar·ket
re·mar·riage
re·mar·ry
re·mate
re·ma·te·ri·al·ize
re·mea·sure
re·mea·sure·ment
re·meet
re·melt
re·merge
re·mi·gra·tion
re·mil·i·ta·ri·za·tion
re·mil·i·ta·rize
re·mix
re·mo·bi·li·za·tion
re·mo·bi·lize
re·moist·en
re·mold
re·mon·e·ti·za·tion

re·mon·e·tize
re·mo·ti·vate
re·mo·ti·va·tion
re·my·thol·o·gize
re·nail
re·name
re·na·tion·al·i·za·tion
re·na·tion·al·ize
re·nest
re·num·ber
re·ob·serve
re·oc·cu·pa·tion
re·oc·cu·py
re·oc·cur
re·oc·cur·rence
re·oil
re·op·er·ate
re·op·er·a·tion
re·or·ches·trate
re·or·ches·tra·tion
re·ori·ent
re·ori·en·tate
re·ori·en·ta·tion
re·out·fit
re·ox·i·da·tion
re·ox·i·dize
re·pack
re·paint
re·park
re·patch
re·pat·tern
re·pave
re·peg
re·peo·ple
re·pho·to·graph
re·phrase
re·plan
re·plas·ter
re·plate
re·pledge
re·plot
re·plumb
re·pol·ish
re·poll
re·pop·u·lar·ize
re·pop·u·late
re·pop·u·la·tion
re·pot
re·pres·sur·ize
re·price
re·pri·vat·i·za·tion
re·pri·vat·ize
re·pro·vi·sion
re·pump
re·punc·tu·a·tion
re·pur·chase
re·pu·ri·fy
re·rack
re·raise
re·read
re·read·ing
re·re·cord
re·reg·is·ter
re·reg·is·tra·tion
re·reg·u·late
re·reg·u·la·tion
re·re·lease
re·re·mind
re·re·peat
re·re·view
re·rig
re·roof
re·route
re·sail
re·sam·ple
re·saw
re·school
re·score
re·screen
re·sculpt
re·seal
re·seal·able
re·sea·son
re·seat
re·se·cure
re·see

re·seg·re·gate
re·seg·re·ga·tion
re·sell
re·sell·er
re·sen·si·tize
re·sen·tence
re·ser·vice
re·set·tle
re·set·tle·ment
re·sew
re·shin·gle
re·shoe
re·shoot
re·show
re·sight
re·sil·ver
re·site
re·size
re·slate
re·soak
re·so·cial·i·za·tion
re·so·cial·ize
re·sod
re·sol·der
re·sole
re·so·lid·i·fi·ca·tion
re·so·lid·i·fy
re·sow
re·spir·i·tu·al·ize
re·spot
re·spray
re·sprout
re·sta·bi·lize
re·stack
re·stage
re·stamp
re·stim·u·late
re·stim·u·la·tion
re·stock
re·stoke
re·strength·en
re·stress
re·study
re·stuff
re·style
re·sub·mis·sion
re·sub·mit
re·sum·mon
re·sup·ply
re·sur·vey
re·syn·the·sis
re·syn·the·size
re·sys·tem·a·tize
re·tack·le
re·tag
re·tar·get
re·taste
re·teach
re·team
re·test
re·tex·ture
re·thread
re·tie
re·tight·en
re·tile
re·time
re·trace
re·trans·fer
re·trans·form
re·trans·for·ma·tion
re·trans·mis·sion
re·trans·mit
re·try
re·tune
re·type
re·uni·fy
re·uni·fi·ca·tion
re·up·hol·ster
re·uti·li·za·tion
re·uti·lize
re·vac·ci·nate
re·vac·ci·na·tion
re·val·i·date
re·val·i·da·tion
re·val·o·ri·za·tion
re·val·o·rize

re·vict·ual
re·vi·su·al·i·za·tion
re·vote
re·warm
re·wash
re·weave

re·weigh
re·wet
re·wire
re·wrap
re·zone

¹re \(ə)r\ *verb* (1591)
: ARE ⟨you*'re* right⟩

re·ab·sorb \ˌrē-əb-'sȯrb, -'zȯrb\ *transitive verb* (circa 1774)
: to take up (something previously secreted or emitted) ⟨sugars *reabsorbed* in the kidney⟩; *also* : RESORB 2

¹reach \'rēch\ *verb* [Middle English *rechen*, from Old English *ræcan;* akin to Old High German *reichen* to reach, Lithuanian *raižytis* to stretch oneself] (before 12th century)
transitive verb
1 a : to stretch out : EXTEND **b :** THRUST
2 a : to touch or grasp by extending a part of the body (as a hand) or an object ⟨couldn't *reach* the apple⟩ **b :** to pick up and draw toward one : TAKE **c** (1) : to extend to ⟨the shadow *reached* the wall⟩ (2) : to get up to or as far as : come to ⟨your letter *reached* me yesterday⟩ ⟨his voice *reached* the last rows⟩ ⟨they hoped to *reach* an agreement⟩ **d** (1) : ENCOMPASS (2) : to make an impression on (3) : to communicate with
3 : to hand over : PASS
intransitive verb
1 a : to make a stretch with or as if with one's hand **b :** to strain after something
2 a : PROJECT, EXTEND ⟨his land *reaches* to the river⟩ **b :** to arrive at or come to something ⟨as far as the eye could *reach*⟩
3 : to sail on a reach
— **reach·able** \'rē-chə-bəl\ *adjective*
— **reach·er** *noun*
²reach *noun* (1536)
1 : a continuous stretch or expanse; *especially* : a straight portion of a stream or river
2 a (1) : the action or an act of reaching (2) : an individual part of a progression or journey **b** (1) : a reachable distance ⟨within *reach*⟩ : ability to reach ⟨had a long *reach*⟩ **c :** an extent or range especially of knowledge or comprehension
3 : a bearing shaft or coupling pole; *especially* : the rod joining the hind axle to the forward bolster of a wagon
4 : the tack sailed by a ship with the wind coming just forward of the beam or with the wind directly abeam or abaft the beam
5 : ECHELON, LEVEL — usually used in plural ⟨the higher *reaches* of academic life⟩

reach-me-down \'rēch-mē-ˌdaûn\ *adjective or noun* (1862)
chiefly British : HAND-ME-DOWN

re·act \rē-'akt\ *verb* [New Latin *reactus,* past participle of *reagere,* from Latin *re-* + *agere* to act — more at AGENT] (1644)
intransitive verb
1 : to exert a reciprocal or counteracting force or influence — often used with *on* or *upon*
2 : to respond to a stimulus
3 : to act in opposition to a force or influence — usually used with *against*
4 : to move or tend in a reverse direction
5 : to undergo chemical reaction
transitive verb
: to cause to react

re·ac·tance \rē-'ak-tən(t)s\ *noun* (1893)
: the part of the impedance of an alternating-current circuit that is due to capacitance or inductance or both and that is expressed in ohms

re·ac·tant \-tənt\ *noun* (circa 1920)
: a substance that enters into and is altered in the course of a chemical reaction

re·ac·tion \rē-'ak-shən\ *noun* (circa 1611)
1 a : the act or process or an instance of reacting **b :** resistance or opposition to a force, influence, or movement; *especially* : tendency toward a former and usually outmoded political or social order or policy

2 : a response to some treatment, situation, or stimulus ⟨her stunned *reaction* to the news⟩; *also* : such a response expressed verbally ⟨critical *reaction* to the play⟩
3 : bodily response to or activity aroused by a stimulus: **a :** an action induced by vital resistance to another action; *especially* : the response of tissues to a foreign substance (as an antigen or infective agent) **b :** depression or exhaustion due to excessive exertion or stimulation **c :** heightened activity and overaction succeeding depression or shock **d :** a mental or emotional disorder forming an individual's response to his or her life situation
4 : the force that a body subjected to the action of a force from another body exerts in the opposite direction
5 a (1) : chemical transformation or change : the interaction of chemical entities (2) : the state resulting from such a reaction **b :** a process involving change in atomic nuclei

re·ac·tion·ary \rē-'ak-shə-ˌner-ē\ *adjective* (1840)
: relating to, marked by, or favoring reaction; *especially* : ultraconservative in politics
— **reactionary** *noun*
— **re·ac·tion·ary·ism** \-ˌi-zəm\ *noun*
re·ac·tive \rē-'ak-tiv\ *adjective* (1794)
1 : of, relating to, or marked by reaction or reactance
2 a : readily responsive to a stimulus **b :** occurring as a result of stress or emotional upset ⟨*reactive* depression⟩
— **re·ac·tive·ly** *adverb*
— **re·ac·tive·ness** *noun*
— **re·ac·tiv·i·ty** \(ˌ)rē-ˌak-'ti-və-tē\ *noun*
re·ac·tor \rē-'ak-tər\ *noun* (circa 1904)
1 : one that reacts
2 : a device (as a coil, winding, or conductor of small resistance) used to introduce reactance into an alternating-current circuit
3 a : a vat for an industrial chemical reaction **b :** a device for the controlled release of nuclear energy (as for producing heat)

¹read \'rēd\ *verb* **read** \'red\; **read·ing** \'rē-diη\ [Middle English *reden* to advise, interpret, read, from Old English *rǣdan;* akin to Old High German *rātan* to advise, Sanskrit *rādhnoti* he achieves, prepares] (before 12th century)
transitive verb
1 a : to receive or take in the sense of (as letters or symbols) especially by sight or touch (2) : to study the movements of (as lips) with mental formulation of the communication expressed (3) : to utter aloud the printed or written words of ⟨*read* them a story⟩ **b :** to learn from what one has seen or found in writing or printing **c :** to deliver aloud by or as if by reading; *specifically* : to utter interpretively **d** (1) : to become acquainted with or look over the contents of (as a book) (2) : to make a study of ⟨*read* law⟩ (3) : to read the works of **e :** to check (as copy or proof) for errors **f** (1) : to receive and understand (a voice message) by radio (2) : UNDERSTAND, COMPREHEND
2 a : to interpret the meaning or significance of ⟨*read* palms⟩ **b :** FORETELL, PREDICT ⟨able to *read* his fortune⟩
3 : to recognize or interpret as if by reading: as **a :** to learn the nature of by observing outward expression or signs ⟨*reads* him like a book⟩ **b :** to note the action or characteristics of in order to anticipate what will happen ⟨a good canoeist *reads* the rapids⟩ ⟨a golfer *reading* a green⟩; *also* : to predict the movement of (a putt) by reading a green **c :** to anticipate by observation of an opponent's position or movement ⟨*read* a blitz⟩

\ə\ abut \ᵊ\ kitten \ər\ further \a\ ash \ā\ ace
\ä\ mop, mar \aù\ out \ch\ chin \e\ bet \ē\ easy
\g\ go \i\ hit \ī\ ice \j\ job \η\ sing \ō\ go
\ȯ\ law \ȯi\ boy \th\ thin \t͟h\ the \ü\ loot \ù\ foot
\y\ yet \zh\ vision *see also* Guide to Pronunciation

4 a : to attribute a meaning to (as something read) **:** INTERPRET ⟨how do you *read* this passage⟩ **b :** to attribute (a meaning) to something read or considered ⟨*read* a nonexistent meaning into her words⟩ **5 :** to use as a substitute for or in preference to another word or phrase in a particular passage, text, or version ⟨*read* hurry for *harry*⟩ — often used to introduce a clarifying substitute for a euphemistic or misleading word or phrase ⟨a friendly, *read* nosy, coworker⟩ **6 :** INDICATE ⟨the thermometer *reads* zero⟩ **7 :** to interpret (a musical work) in performance **8 a :** to acquire (information) from storage; *especially* **:** to sense the meaning of (data) in recorded and coded form — used of a computer or data processor **b :** to read the coded information on (as a floppy disk) ~ *intransitive verb* **1 a :** to perform the act of reading words **:** read something **b** (1) **:** to learn something by reading (2) **:** to pursue a course of study **2 a :** to yield a particular meaning or impression when read **b :** to be readable or read in a particular manner or to a particular degree ⟨this book *reads* smoothly⟩ **3 :** to consist of specific words, phrases, or other similar elements ⟨a passage that *reads* differently in older versions⟩ — **read between the lines :** to understand more than is directly stated — **read the riot act 1 :** to order a mob to disperse **2 a :** to order or warn to cease something **b :** to protest vehemently **c :** to reprimand severely

²read \'red\ *adjective* (1586) **:** instructed by or informed through reading

³read \'red\ *noun* (1825) **1** *chiefly British* **:** a period of reading ⟨it was a night . . . for a *read* and a long sleep —William Sansom⟩ **2 :** something (as a book) that is read ⟨a novel that's a good *read*⟩ **3 :** the action or an instance of reading

read·able \'rē-də-bəl\ *adjective* (15th century) **:** able to be read easily: as **a :** LEGIBLE **b :** interesting to read — **read·abil·i·ty** \,rē-də-'bi-lə-tē\ *noun* — **read·able·ness** \'rē-də-bəl-nəs\ *noun* — **read·ably** \-blē\ *adverb*

read·er \'rē-dər\ *noun* (before 12th century) **1 a :** one that reads **b :** one appointed to read to others: as (1) **:** LECTOR (2) **:** one chosen to read aloud selected material in a Christian Science church or society **c** (1) **:** PROOFREADER (2) **:** one who evaluates manuscripts (3) **:** one who reads periodical literature to discover items of special interest or value **d :** an employee who reads and records the indications of meters **e :** a teacher's assistant who reads and marks student papers **2** *British* **:** one who reads lectures or expounds subjects to students **3 a :** a device for projecting a readable image of a transparency **b :** a unit that scans material recorded (as on punched cards) for storage or computation **4 a :** a book for instruction and practice especially in reading **b :** ANTHOLOGY

read·er·ly \-lē\ *adjective* (1959) **:** of, relating to, or typical of a reader

read·er·ship \-,ship\ *noun* (1719) **1 a :** the quality or state of being a reader **b :** the office or position of a reader **2 :** the mass or a particular group of readers ⟨a magazine's *readership*⟩

read·i·ly \'re-d²l-ē\ *adverb* (14th century) **:** in a ready manner: as **a :** without hesitating **:** WILLINGLY ⟨*readily* accepted advice⟩ **b :** without much difficulty **:** EASILY ⟨for reasons that anyone could *readily* understand⟩

read·ing \'rē-diŋ\ *noun* (before 12th century) **1 :** the act of reading

2 a : material read or for reading **b :** extent of material read **3 a :** a particular version **b :** data indicated by an instrument **4 a :** a particular interpretation of something (as a law) **b :** a particular performance of something (as a musical work) **5 :** an indication of a certain state of affairs ⟨a study to get some *reading* of shoppers' preferences⟩

reading desk *noun* (1703) **:** LECTERN

reading frame *noun* (1965) **:** any of the three possible ways of reading a sequence of nucleotides as a series of triplets

read–only memory *noun* (1961) **:** a usually small computer memory that contains special-purpose information (as a program) which cannot be altered — called also *ROM*; compare RANDOM-ACCESS MEMORY

read·out \'rēd-,aůt\ *noun* (1652) **1 :** the process of reading **2 a :** the process of removing information from an automatic device (as an electronic computer) and displaying it in an understandable form **b :** the information removed from such a device and displayed or recorded (as by magnetic tape or printing device) **c :** an electronic device that presents information in visual form **3 :** the radio transmission of data or pictures from a space vehicle

read out *transitive verb* (1600) **1 a :** to read aloud **b :** to produce a readout of **2 :** to expel from an organization or group

¹ready \'re-dē\ *adjective* **read·i·er; -est** [Middle English *redy;* akin to Old English *gerǣde* ready, Gothic *garaiths* arranged] (13th century) **1 a :** prepared mentally or physically for some experience or action **b :** prepared for immediate use ⟨dinner is *ready*⟩ **2 a :** willingly disposed **:** INCLINED ⟨*ready* to agree to his proposal⟩ **b :** likely to do something indicated ⟨a house that looks *ready* to collapse⟩ **3 :** displayed readily and spontaneously ⟨a *ready* wit⟩ **4 :** immediately available ⟨had little *ready* cash⟩ ~ *synonym* see QUICK — **read·i·ness** *noun* — **at the ready :** ready for immediate use ⟨kept their guns *at the ready*⟩

²ready *transitive verb* **read·ied; ready·ing** (14th century) **:** to make ready

ready box *noun* (1942) **:** a box placed near a gun (as on a ship) to hold ammunition kept ready for immediate use

¹ready–made \,red-ē-'mād\ *adjective* (15th century) **1 :** made beforehand especially for general sale ⟨*ready-made* suits⟩ **2 :** lacking originality or individuality **3 :** readily available ⟨her illness provided a *ready-made* excuse⟩

²ready–made *noun* (1882) **1 :** something (as a garment) that is ready-made **2** *usually* **ready·made** [French *ready-made,* from English] **:** a commonplace artifact (as a comb or a pair of ice tongs) selected and displayed as a work of art

ready room *noun* (1941) **:** a room in which pilots or astronauts are briefed and await orders

ready–to–wear *adjective* (1895) **1** *of clothing* **:** READY-MADE **2 :** dealing in ready-made clothes ⟨*ready-to-wear* stores⟩ — **ready–to–wear** *noun*

ready–wit·ted \,re-dē-'wi-təd\ *adjective* (1581) **:** QUICK-WITTED

re·af·for·es·ta·tion \,rē-ə-,fȯr-ə-'stā-shən, -,fär-\ *noun* (1884) *chiefly British* **:** REFORESTATION — **re·af·for·est** \-'fȯr-əst, -'fär-\ *transitive verb, chiefly British*

re·agent \rē-'ā-jənt\ *noun* [New Latin *reagent-, reagens,* present participle of *reagere* to react — more at REACT] (1797) **:** a substance used (as in detecting or measuring a component, in preparing a product, or in developing photographs) because of its chemical or biological activity

re·ag·gre·gate \(,)rē-'a-gri-,gāt\ *transitive verb* (1849) **:** to cause to re-form into an aggregate or a whole — **re·ag·gre·gate** \-gət\ *noun* — **re·ag·gre·ga·tion** \-,a-gri-'gā-shən\ *noun*

re·agin \rē-'ā-jən, -gən\ *noun* [International Scientific Vocabulary, from *reagent*] (circa 1911) **1 :** a substance in the blood of persons with syphilis responsible for positive serological reactions for syphilis **2 :** an antibody in the blood of individuals with some forms of allergy possessing the power of passively sensitizing the skin of normal individuals — **re·agin·ic** \,rē-ə-'ji-nik, -'gi-\ *adjective*

¹re·al \'rē(-ə)l, 'ri(-ə)l\ *adjective* [Middle English, real, relating to things (in law), from Middle French, from Medieval Latin & Late Latin; Medieval Latin *realis* relating to things (in law), from Late Latin, real, from Latin *res* thing, fact; akin to Sanskrit *rayi* property] (14th century) **1 :** of or relating to fixed, permanent, or immovable things (as lands or tenements) **2 a :** not artificial, fraudulent, illusory, or apparent **:** GENUINE ⟨*real* gold⟩; *also* **:** being precisely what the name implies ⟨a *real* professional⟩ **b** (1) **:** occurring in fact ⟨a story of *real* life⟩ (2) **:** of or relating to practical or everyday concerns or activities ⟨left school to live in the *real* world⟩ (3) **:** existing as a physical entity and having properties that deviate from an ideal, law, or standard ⟨a *real* gas⟩ — compare IDEAL 3b **c :** having objective independent existence ⟨unable to believe that what he saw was *real*⟩ **d :** FUNDAMENTAL, ESSENTIAL **e** (1) **:** belonging to or having elements or components that belong to the set of real numbers ⟨the *real* roots of an equation⟩ ⟨a *real* matrix⟩ (2) **:** concerned with or containing real numbers ⟨*real* analysis⟩ (3) **:** REAL-VALUED ⟨*real* variable⟩ **f :** measured by purchasing power ⟨*real* income⟩ ⟨*real* dollars⟩ **g :** COMPLETE, UTTER ⟨a *real* fiasco⟩ **3** *of a particle* **:** capable of being detected — compare VIRTUAL 3 — **re·al·ness** *noun* — **for real 1 :** in earnest **:** SERIOUSLY ⟨fighting *for real*⟩ **2 :** GENUINE ⟨couldn't believe the threats were *for real*⟩

²real *noun* (circa 1626) **:** a real thing; *especially* **:** a mathematically real quantity

³real *adverb* (1718) **:** VERY ⟨he was *real* cool —H. M. McLuhan⟩ □

□ USAGE
real Most handbooks consider the adverb *real* to be informal and more suitable to speech than writing. Our evidence shows these observations to be true in the main, but *real* is becoming increasingly common in writing of an informal, conversational style. It is used as an intensifier only and is not interchangeable with *really* except in that use.

⁴**re·al** \rā-'äl\ *noun, plural* **reals** *or* **re·ales** \-'ä-(,)lās\ [Spanish, from *real* royal, from Latin *regalis* — more at ROYAL] (1555)
: a former monetary unit and coin of Spain and its possessions

⁵**re·al** \rā-'äl\ *noun, plural* **reals** *or* **reis** \'räsh, 'räs, 'räzh, 'räz\ [Portuguese, from *real* royal, from Latin *regalis*] (1951)
1 : a former monetary unit and coin of Portugal
2 — see MONEY table

real estate *noun* (1666)
: property in buildings and land

real focus *noun* (1909)
: a point at which rays (as of light) converge or from which they diverge

re·al·gar \rē-'al-,gär, -gər\ *noun* [Middle English, from Medieval Latin, from Catalan, from Arabic *rahj al-ghār* powder of the mine] (15th century)
: an orange-red mineral consisting of arsenic sulfide and having a resinous luster

re·a·lia \rē-'a-lē-ə, -'ä-\ *noun plural* [Late Latin, neuter plural of *realis* real] (1937)
: objects or activities used to relate classroom teaching to the real life especially of peoples studied

re·align \,rē-ə-'līn\ *transitive verb* (1899)
: to align again; *especially* : to reorganize or make new groupings of
— **re·align·ment** \-mənt\ *noun*

real image *noun* (1899)
: an optical image formed of real foci

re·al·ism \'rē-ə-,li-zəm, 'ri-ə-\ *noun* (1817)
1 : concern for fact or reality and rejection of the impractical and visionary
2 a : a doctrine that universals exist outside the mind; *specifically* : the conception that an abstract term names an independent and unitary reality **b** : the conception that objects of sense perception or cognition exist independently of the mind — compare NOMINALISM
3 : fidelity in art and literature to nature or to real life and to accurate representation without idealization
— **re·al·ist** \-list\ *adjective or noun*
— **re·al·is·tic** \,rē-ə-'lis-tik, ,ri-ə-\ *adjective*
— **re·al·is·ti·cal·ly** \-ti-k(ə-)lē\ *adverb*

re·al·i·ty \rē-'a-lə-tē\ *noun, plural* **-ties** (1550)
1 : the quality or state of being real
2 a (1) : a real event, entity, or state of affairs ⟨his dream became a *reality*⟩ (2) : the totality of real things and events ⟨trying to escape from *reality*⟩ **b** : something that is neither derivative nor dependent but exists necessarily
— **in reality** : in actual fact

reality check *noun* (1986)
: something that clarifies or serves as a reminder of reality often by correcting a misconception

re·al·i·za·tion \,rē-ə-lə-'zā-shən, ,ri-ə-\ *noun* (circa 1611)
1 : the action of realizing : the state of being realized
2 : something realized

re·al·ize \'rē-ə-,līz, 'ri-ə-\ *transitive verb* **-ized; -iz·ing** [French *réaliser*, from Middle French *realiser*, from *real* real] (circa 1611)
1 a : to bring into concrete existence : ACCOMPLISH ⟨finally *realized* her goal⟩ **b** : to cause to seem real : make appear real ⟨a book in which the characters are carefully *realized*⟩
2 a : to convert into actual money ⟨*realized* assets⟩ **b** : to bring or get by sale, investment, or effort : GAIN
3 : to conceive vividly as real : be fully aware of ⟨did not *realize* the risk she was taking⟩
synonym see THINK
— **re·al·iz·able** \,rē-ə-'lī-zə-bəl, ,ri-ə-\ *adjective*
— **re·al·iz·er** *noun*

real–life *adjective* (1938)

: existing or occurring in reality : drawn from or drawing on actual events or situations ⟨*real-life* problems⟩ ⟨*real-life* drama⟩

re·al·ly \'rē-(ə-)lē, 'ri-\ *adverb* (15th century)
1 a : in reality : ACTUALLY ⟨things as they *really* are⟩ ⟨there was nothing peculiar about her doing this, *really* —Peter Taylor⟩ **b** : TRULY, UNQUESTIONABLY — used as an intensifier ⟨a *really* beautiful day⟩
2 — used to emphasize an assertion ⟨you *really* should read Yeats⟩ ⟨*really*, you're being ridiculous⟩

realm \'relm\ *noun* [Middle English *realme*, from Old French *reialme*, alteration of *reiame*, from Latin *regimen* rule — more at REGIMEN] (13th century)
1 : KINGDOM 2
2 : SPHERE, DOMAIN ⟨within the *realm* of possibility⟩
3 : a primary marine or terrestrial biogeographic division of the earth's surface

real number *noun* (1909)
: one of the numbers that have no imaginary parts and comprise the rationals and the irrationals

real part *noun* (1949)
: the term in a complex number (as 2 in 2 + 3i) that does not contain the imaginary unit as a factor

re·al·po·li·tik \rā-'äl-,pō-li-,tēk\ *noun, often capitalized* [German, from *real* actual + *Politik* politics] (1914)
: politics based on practical and material factors rather than on theoretical or ethical objectives

real presence *noun, often R&P capitalized* (1559)
: the doctrine that Christ is actually present in the Eucharist

real time *noun* (1953)
: the actual time during which something takes place ⟨the computer may partly analyze the data in *real time* (as it comes in) —R. H. March⟩
— **real–time** *adjective*

Re·al·tor \'rē-(ə-)l-tər, -,tór, ÷'rē-lə-tər\ *also* rē-'al-tər\ *collective mark*
— used for a real estate agent who is a member of the National Association of Realtors

re·al·ty \'rē-(ə-)l-tē\ *noun* [*real* + *-ty* (as in *property*)] (1670)
: REAL ESTATE

real–valued *adjective* (1965)
: taking on only real numbers for values

real–world *adjective* (1963)
: REAL-LIFE

¹**ream** \'rēm\ *noun* [Middle English *reme*, from Middle French *raime*, from Arabic *rizmah*, literally, bundle] (14th century)
1 : a quantity of paper being 20 quires or variously 480, 500, or 516 sheets
2 : a great amount — usually used in plural

²**ream** *transitive verb* [perhaps from (assumed) Middle English *remen*, from Old English *rēman*; akin to Old English *rȳman* to open up, *rūm* space — more at ROOM] (1815)
1 a : to widen the opening of (a hole) : COUNTERSINK **b** (1) : to enlarge or dress out (a hole) with a reamer (2) : to enlarge the bore of (as a gun) in this way **c** : to remove by reaming
2 a : to press out with a reamer **b** : to press out the juice of (as an orange) with a reamer
3 : CHEAT, VICTIMIZE
4 : REPRIMAND

ream·er \'rē-mər\ *noun* (1825)
: one that reams: as **a** : a rotating finishing tool with cutting edges used to enlarge or shape a hole **b** : a fruit juice extractor with a ridged and pointed center rising from a shallow dish

reap \'rēp\ *verb* [Middle English *repen*, from Old English *reopan*] (before 12th century)
transitive verb
1 a (1) : to cut with a sickle, scythe, or reaping

machine (2) : to clear of a crop by reaping **b** : to gather by reaping : HARVEST
2 : OBTAIN, WIN
intransitive verb
: to reap something

reap·er \'rē-pər\ *noun* (before 12th century)
: one that reaps; *especially* : any of various machines for reaping grain

reap–hook \'rēp-,húk\ *noun* (1591)
: a hand implement with a hook-shaped blade used in reaping

re·ap·por·tion \,rē-ə-'pōr-shən, -'pór-\ (circa 1828)
transitive verb
: to apportion (as a house of representatives) anew
intransitive verb
: to make a new apportionment
— **re·ap·por·tion·ment** \-shən-mənt\ *noun*

¹**rear** \'rir, *transitive verb* 4 & *intransitive verb* 2 are also 'rar *or* 'rer\ *verb* [Middle English *reren*, from Old English *ræran*; akin to Old Norse *reisa* to raise, Old English *rīsan* to rise] (before 12th century)
transitive verb
1 : to erect by building : CONSTRUCT
2 : to raise upright
3 a : to breed and raise (an animal) for use or market (2) : BRING UP 1 **b** : to cause (as plants) to grow
4 : to cause (a horse) to rise up on the hind legs
intransitive verb
1 : to rise high
2 *of a horse* : to rise up on the hind legs
synonym see LIFT
— **rear·er** *noun*

²**rear** \'rir\ *noun* [Middle English *rere*, short for *rerewarde* rearward] (14th century)
1 : the back part of something: as **a** : the unit (as of an army) or area farthest from the enemy **b** : the part of something located opposite its front ⟨the *rear* of a house⟩ **c** : BUTTOCKS
2 : the space or position at the back ⟨moved to the *rear*⟩

³**rear** \'rir\ *adjective* [Middle English *rere-*, from Middle French *rere* backward, behind, from Latin *retro-* — more at RETRO] (14th century)
: being at the back

⁴**rear** \'rir\ *adverb* (1855)
: toward or from the rear — usually used in combination ⟨a *rear*-driven car⟩

rear admiral *noun* (1589)
: a commissioned officer in the navy who ranks above a commodore and in the coast guard who ranks above a captain and whose insignia is two stars

rear echelon *noun* (circa 1934)
: an element of a military headquarters or unit located at a considerable distance from the front and concerned especially with administrative and supply duties

rear–end \'rir-'end, -,end\ *transitive verb* (1957)
: to crash into the back of (as an automobile)

rear end *noun* (circa 1930)
: BUTTOCKS

rear·guard \'rir-,gärd\ *adjective* (1898)
: of or relating to resistance especially to sweeping social forces ⟨fought a *rearguard* action against automation⟩

rear guard \-'gärd, -,gärd\ *noun* [Middle French *reregarde*, from Old French, from *rere* + *garde* guard] (1659)
: a military detachment detailed to bring up and protect the rear of a main body or force

re·arm \(ˌ)rē-'ärm\ (1871)
transitive verb
: to arm (as a nation or a military force) again with new or better weapons
intransitive verb
: to become armed again
— **re·arma·ment** \-'ärm-ə-mənt\ *noun*
rear·most \'rir-ˌmōst\ *adjective* (1718)
: farthest in the rear : LAST
rear·view mirror \'rir-ˌvyü-\ *noun* (1926)
: a mirror (as in an automobile) that gives a view of the area behind a vehicle
¹**rear·ward** \'rir-wȯrd\ *noun* [Middle English rerewarde, from Anglo-French; akin to Old French reregarde rear guard] (14th century)
: REAR; *especially* : the rear division (as of an army)
²**rear·ward** \-wərd\ *adjective* [²rear + -ward] (1598)
1 : located at, near, or toward the rear
2 : directed toward the rear
³**rear·ward** \-wərd\ *also* **rear·wards** \-wərdz\ *adverb* (1625)
: at, near, or toward the rear : BACKWARD
¹**rea·son** \'rē-z°n\ *noun* [Middle English resoun, from Old French raison, from Latin ration-, ratio reason, computation, from reri to calculate, think; probably akin to Gothic rathjo account, explanation] (13th century)
1 a : a statement offered in explanation or justification ⟨gave reasons that were quite satisfactory⟩ b : a rational ground or motive ⟨a good reason to act soon⟩ c : a sufficient ground of explanation or of logical defense; especially : something (as a principle or law) that supports a conclusion or explains a fact ⟨the reasons behind her client's action⟩ d : the thing that makes sense but intelligible : CAUSE ⟨the reason for earthquakes⟩ ⟨the real reason why he wanted me to stay —Graham Greene⟩
2 a (1) : the power of comprehending, inferring, or thinking especially in orderly rational ways : INTELLIGENCE (2) : proper exercise of the mind (3) : SANITY b : the sum of the intellectual powers
3 archaic : treatment that affords satisfaction
☐
— **in reason** : RIGHTLY, JUSTIFIABLY
— **within reason** : within reasonable limits
— **with reason** : with good cause
²**reason** verb **rea·soned; rea·son·ing** \'rēz-niŋ, 'rē-z°n-iŋ\ (15th century)
intransitive verb
1 a obsolete : to take part in conversation, discussion, or argument b : to talk with another so as to influence his actions or opinions ⟨can't reason with her⟩
2 : to use the faculty of reason so as to arrive at conclusions
transitive verb
1 archaic : to justify or support with reasons
2 : to persuade or influence by the use of reason
3 : to discover, formulate, or conclude by the use of reason ⟨a carefully reasoned analysis⟩
synonym see THINK
— **rea·son·er** \'rēz-nər, 'rē-z°n-ər\ noun
rea·son·able \'rēz-nə-bəl, 'rē-z°n-ə-bəl\ adjective (14th century)
1 a : being in accordance with reason ⟨a reasonable theory⟩ b : not extreme or excessive ⟨reasonable requests⟩ c : MODERATE, FAIR ⟨a reasonable chance⟩ ⟨a reasonable price⟩ d : INEXPENSIVE
2 a : having the faculty of reason b : possessing sound judgment
— **rea·son·abil·i·ty** \ˌrēz-nə-'bi-lə-tē, ˌrē-z°n-ə-\ noun
— **rea·son·able·ness** \'rēz-nə-bəl-nəs, 'rē-z°n-ə-\ noun
— **rea·son·ably** \-blē\ adverb
reasoning noun (14th century)
1 : the use of reason; especially : the drawing of inferences or conclusions through the use of reason

2 : an instance of the use of reason : ARGUMENT
rea·son·less \'rē-z°n-ləs\ adjective (14th century)
1 : not having the faculty of reason ⟨a reasonless brute⟩
2 : not reasoned : SENSELESS ⟨reasonless hostility⟩
3 : not based on or supported by reasons ⟨a reasonless accusation⟩
— **rea·son·less·ly** adverb
re·as·sur·ance \ˌrē-ə-'shu̇r-ən(t)s\ noun (circa 1611)
1 : the action of reassuring : the state of being reassured
2 : REINSURANCE
re·as·sure \ˌrē-ə-'shu̇r\ transitive verb (1598)
1 : to assure anew ⟨reassured him that the work was on schedule⟩
2 : to restore to confidence ⟨felt reassured by their earnest promise to do better⟩
3 : REINSURE
— **re·as·sur·ing·ly** \-'shu̇r-iŋ-lē\ adverb
re·ata \rē-'a-tə, -'ä-\ noun [American Spanish — more at LARIAT] (1846)
: LARIAT
Re·au·mur \ˌrā-ō-'myu̇r, 'rā-ō-,\ adjective [René Antoine Ferchault de Réaumur] (1814)
: relating to or conforming to a thermometric scale on which the boiling point of water is at 80° above the zero of the scale and the freezing point is at zero
¹**reave** \'rēv\ verb **reaved** or **reft** \'reft\; **reav·ing** [Middle English reven, from Old English rēafian; akin to Old High German roubōn to rob, Latin rumpere to break] (before 12th century)
intransitive verb
: PLUNDER, ROB
transitive verb
1 archaic a (1) : ROB, DESPOIL (2) : to deprive one of b : SEIZE
2 archaic : to carry or tear away
— **reav·er** noun
²**reave** transitive verb **reaved** or **reft** \'reft\; **reav·ing** [Middle English reven, probably modification of Old Norse rīfa to rive] (13th century)
archaic : BURST
reb \'reb\ noun [short for rebel] (1862)
: JOHNNY REB
Reb \'reb\ noun [Yiddish, from Hebrew rabbī my master, rabbi] (1882)
: RABBI, MISTER — used as a title
re·bar \'rē-ˌbär\ noun [reinforcing bar] (1953)
: a steel rod with ridges for use in reinforced concrete
re·bar·ba·tive \ri-'bär-bə-tiv\ adjective [French rébarbatif, from Middle French, from rebarber to be repellent, from re- + barbe beard, from Latin barba — more at BEARD] (1892)
: REPELLENT, IRRITATING
— **re·bar·ba·tive·ly** adverb
¹**re·bate** \'rē-ˌbāt, ri-'\ verb **re·bat·ed; re·bat·ing** [Middle English, from Middle French rabattre to beat down again, from Old French, from re- + abattre to beat down, from a- (from Latin ad-) + battre to beat, from Latin battuere] (14th century)
transitive verb
1 : to reduce the force or activity of : DIMINISH
2 : to reduce the sharpness of : BLUNT
3 a : to make a rebate of b : to give a rebate to
intransitive verb
: to give rebates
— **re·bat·er** noun
²**re·bate** \'rē-ˌbāt\ noun (1656)
: a return of a part of a payment
³**re·bate** \'ra-bət, 'rē-ˌbāt\ chiefly British variant of RABBET

re·ba·to \ri-'bä-(ˌ)tō\ variant of RABATO
reb·be \'re-bə\ noun [Yiddish rebe, from Hebrew rabbī rabbi] (1881)
: a Jewish spiritual leader or teacher : RABBI
re·bec or **re·beck** \'rē-ˌbek, 'rē-(ˌ)bek\ noun [Middle English rebecke, from Middle French rebec, alteration of Old French rebebe, from Old Provençal rebeb, from Arabic rabāb] (15th century)
: an ancient bowed usually 3-stringed musical instrument with a pear-shaped body and slender neck
Re·bek·ah \ri-'be-kə\ noun [Hebrew Ribhqāh]
: the wife of Isaac

rebec

¹**reb·el** \'re-bəl\ adjective [Middle English, from Old French rebelle, from Latin rebellis, from re- + bellum war, from Old Latin duellum] (14th century)
1 a : opposing or taking arms against a government or ruler b : of or relating to rebels ⟨the rebel camp⟩
2 : DISOBEDIENT, REBELLIOUS
²**rebel** noun (14th century)
: one who rebels or participates in a rebellion
³**re·bel** \ri-'bel\ intransitive verb **re·belled; re·bel·ling** (14th century)
1 a : to oppose or disobey one in authority or control b : to renounce and resist by force the authority of one's government
2 a : to act in or show opposition or disobedience ⟨rebelled against the conventions of polite society⟩ b : to feel or exhibit anger or revulsion ⟨rebelled at the injustice of life⟩
re·bel·lion \ri-'bel-yən\ noun (14th century)
1 : opposition to one in authority or dominance
2 a : open, armed, and usually unsuccessful defiance of or resistance to an established gov-

☐ USAGE
reason *The reason is because* is a short way of referring to a number of locutions in which a primary clause with reason as its subject is followed by a subordinate clause introduced by because ⟨the reason I didn't answer the other letter was because mine was already on the way to you —Ernest Hemingway⟩. This locution has been used in standard English since the 16th century at least, but it has been attacked since a commentator named Robert Baker decided it made no sense in 1770. Modern objections are that the expression is redundant or illogical (which follows Baker) or that it is ungrammatical (which is incorrect). The universal recommendation is to replace *the reason is because* with *the reason is that*. Our evidence shows that *the reason is that* is more often used in edited prose than *the reason is because*; the latter is the more common in speech. We find because quite common in informal prose ⟨the reason the story has never been made into a film is because I won't sign a contract —E. B. White⟩ ⟨the reason I had not seen the nomination in the Tazewell paper was . . . because I did not then, as I do not now, take that paper —Abraham Lincoln⟩ ⟨the only reason my appearances are rare . . . is because nobody asks me oftener —Groucho Marx⟩ ⟨now the reason hair falls off is because it hangs down —Lewis Carroll⟩. Although this locution is perfectly ordinary, perfectly understandable, and perfectly standard, the handbooks continue to advise against it. They omit, however, Baker's other observation, that "there are scarce any even of our greatest authors, that avoid this way of speaking."

ernment **b :** an instance of such defiance or resistance ☆

re·bel·lious \-yəs\ *adjective* (15th century) **1 a :** given to or engaged in rebellion ⟨*rebellious* troops⟩ **b :** of, relating to, or characteristic of a rebel or rebellion ⟨a *rebellious* speech⟩ **2 :** resisting treatment or management **:** REFRACTORY
— **re·bel·lious·ly** *adverb*
— **re·bel·lious·ness** *noun*

rebel yell *noun* (1863)
: a prolonged high-pitched yell often uttered by Confederate soldiers in the U.S. Civil War

re·birth \(ˌ)rē-'bərth, 'rē-ˌ\ *noun* (1837) **1 a :** a new or second birth **:** METEMPSYCHOSIS **b :** spiritual regeneration **2 :** RENAISSANCE, REVIVAL ⟨a *rebirth* of nationalism⟩

Re·blo·chon \rə-blȯ-'shōⁿ\ *noun* [French *reblochon,* from French dialect (Savoy)] (1908)
: a semisoft creamy mild-flavored French cheese

reb·o·ant \'re-bə-wənt\ *adjective* [Latin *reboant-, reboans,* present participle of *reboare* to resound, from *re-* + *boare* to cry aloud, roar, from Greek *boan,* of imitative origin] (1830)
: marked by reverberation

re·born \(ˌ)rē-'bȯrn\ *adjective* (1598)
: born again **:** REGENERATED, REVIVED

¹re·bound \'rē-ˌbau̇nd, ri-'\ *verb* [Middle English, from Middle French *rebondir,* from Old French, from *re-* + *bondir* to bound — more at BOUND] (14th century)
intransitive verb
1 a : to spring back on or as if on collision or impact with another body **b :** to recover from setback or frustration **2 :** REECHO **3 :** to gain possession of a rebound in basketball
transitive verb
: to cause to rebound
— **re·bound·er** \'rē-ˌbau̇n-dər, ri-'\ *noun*

²re·bound \'rē-ˌbau̇nd, ri-'\ *noun* (1530) **1 a :** the action of rebounding **:** RECOIL **b :** an upward leap or movement **:** RECOVERY ⟨a sharp *rebound* in prices⟩ **2 a :** a basketball or hockey puck that rebounds **b :** the act or an instance of gaining possession of a basketball rebound ⟨leads the league in *rebounds*⟩ **3 :** a reaction to setback, frustration, or crisis ⟨on the *rebound* from an unhappy love affair⟩

re·bo·zo \ri-'bō-(ˌ)zō, -(ˌ)sō\ *noun, plural* **-zos** [Spanish, shawl, from *rebozar* to muffle, alteration of *embozar* to muffle, probably from (assumed) Vulgar Latin *imbucciare,* from Latin *in-* + *bucca* cheek] (1807)
: a long scarf worn chiefly by Mexican women

re·branch \(ˌ)rē-'branch\ *intransitive verb* (1888)
: to form secondary branches

re·broad·cast \(ˌ)rē-'brȯd-ˌkast\ *transitive verb* **-cast; -cast·ing** (1923) **1 :** to broadcast again ⟨a radio or television program being simultaneously received from another source⟩ **2 :** to repeat (a broadcast) at a later time
— **rebroadcast** *noun*

re·buff \ri-'bəf\ *transitive verb* [Middle French *rebuffer,* from Old Italian *ribuffare* to reprimand, from *ribuffo* reprimand] (circa 1586)
: to reject or criticize sharply **:** SNUB
— **rebuff** *noun*

re·build \(ˌ)rē-'bild\ *verb* **-built** \-'bilt\; **-build·ing** (1537)
transitive verb
1 a : to make extensive repairs to **:** RECONSTRUCT ⟨*rebuild* a war-torn city⟩ **b :** to restore to a previous state ⟨*rebuild* inventories⟩ **2 :** to make extensive changes in **:** REMODEL ⟨*rebuild* society⟩

intransitive verb
: to build again ⟨planned to *rebuild* after the fire⟩
synonym see MEND

¹re·buke \ri-'byük\ *transitive verb* **re·buked; re·buk·ing** [Middle English, from Old North French *rebuker*] (14th century) **1 a :** to criticize sharply **:** REPRIMAND **b :** to serve as a rebuke to **2 :** to turn back or keep down **:** CHECK
synonym see REPROVE
— **re·buk·er** *noun*

²rebuke *noun* (15th century)
: an expression of strong disapproval **:** REPRIMAND

re·bus \'rē-bəs\ *noun* [Latin, by things, ablative plural of *res* thing — more at REAL] (1605)
: a representation of words or syllables by pictures of objects or by symbols whose names resemble the intended words or syllables in sound; *also* **:** a riddle made up of such pictures or symbols

rebus

re·but \ri-'bət\ *verb* **re·but·ted; re·but·ting** [Middle English, from Middle French *reboter,* from *re-* + *boter* to butt — more at BUTT] (14th century)
transitive verb
1 : to drive or beat back **:** REPEL **2 a :** to contradict or oppose by formal legal argument, plea, or countervailing proof **b :** to expose the falsity of **:** REFUTE
intransitive verb
: to make or furnish an answer or counter proof
— **re·but·ta·ble** \-'bə-tə-bəl\ *adjective*

re·but·tal \ri-'bə-t⁰l\ *noun* (1830)
: the act of rebutting especially in a legal suit; *also* **:** argument or proof that rebuts

¹re·but·ter \-'bə-tər\ *noun* [Anglo-French *rebuter,* from Old French *reboter* to rebut] (1540)
: the answer of a defendant in matter of fact to a plaintiff's surrejoinder

²rebutter *noun* (1794)
: one that rebuts

re·cal·ci·trance \ri-'kal-sə-trən(t)s\ *noun* (1856)
: the state of being recalcitrant

re·cal·ci·tran·cy \-trən(t)-sē\ *noun* (1869)
: RECALCITRANCE

re·cal·ci·trant \-trənt\ *adjective* [Late Latin *recalcitrant-, recalcitrans,* present participle of *recalcitrare* to be stubbornly disobedient, from Latin, to kick back, from *re-* + *calcitrare* to kick, from *calc-, calx* heel] (1843) **1 :** obstinately defiant of authority or restraint **2 a :** difficult to manage or operate **b :** not responsive to treatment **c :** RESISTANT ⟨this subject is *recalcitrant* both to observation and to experiment —G. G. Simpson⟩ ◇
synonym see UNRULY
— **recalcitrant** *noun*

¹re·call \ri-'kȯl\ *transitive verb* (1582) **1 a :** to call back ⟨was *recalled* to active duty⟩ **b :** to bring back to mind ⟨*recall* those early years⟩ **c :** to remind one of **:** RESEMBLE ⟨a playwright who *recalls* the Elizabethan dramatists⟩ **2 :** CANCEL, REVOKE **3 :** RESTORE, REVIVE
synonym see REMEMBER
— **re·call·abil·i·ty** \-ˌkȯ-lə-'bi-lə-tē\ *noun*
— **re·call·able** \-'kȯ-lə-bəl\ *adjective*
— **re·call·er** *noun*

²re·call \ri-'kȯl, 'rē-ˌ\ *noun* (1611) **1 :** a call to return ⟨a *recall* of workers after a layoff⟩ **2 :** the right or procedure by which an official may be removed by vote of the people **3 :** remembrance of what has been learned or experienced **4 :** the act of revoking

5 : a public call by a manufacturer for the return of a product that may be defective or contaminated

re·ca·mier \ˌrā-käm-'yā\ *noun* [from its appearance in a portrait of Mme. Récamier by Jacques-Louis David] (1924)
: a sometimes backless couch with a high curved headrest and low footrest

recamier

re·can·a·li·za·tion \(ˌ)rē-ka-n⁰l-ə-'zā-shən\ *noun* (1953)
: the process of restoring flow to or reuniting an interrupted channel of a bodily tube (as a blood vessel or vas deferens)
— **re·can·a·lize** \-kə-'na-ˌlīz, -'ka-n⁰l-ˌīz\ *transitive verb*

re·cant \ri-'kant\ *verb* [Latin *recantare,* from *re-* + *cantare* to sing — more at CHANT] (1535)
transitive verb
1 : to withdraw or repudiate (a statement or belief) formally and publicly **:** RENOUNCE **2 :** REVOKE
intransitive verb
: to make an open confession of error
synonym see ABJURE
— **re·can·ta·tion** \ˌrē-ˌkan-'tā-shən\ *noun*

¹re·cap \'rē-ˌkap\ *noun* [by shortening] (circa 1926)

☆ **SYNONYMS**

Rebellion, revolution, uprising, revolt, insurrection, mutiny mean an outbreak against authority. REBELLION implies an open formidable resistance that is often unsuccessful ⟨open *rebellion* against the officers⟩. REVOLUTION applies to a successful rebellion resulting in a major change (as in government) ⟨a political *revolution* that toppled the monarchy⟩. UPRISING implies a brief, limited and often immediately ineffective rebellion ⟨quickly put down the *uprising*⟩. REVOLT and INSURRECTION imply an armed uprising that quickly fails or succeeds ⟨a *revolt* by the Young Turks that surprised party leaders⟩ ⟨an *insurrection* of oppressed laborers⟩. MUTINY applies to group insubordination or insurrection especially against naval authority ⟨a *mutiny* led by the ship's cook⟩.

◇ **WORD HISTORY**

recalcitrant Underlying the word *recalcitrant* is the image of a stubborn beast of burden kicking back at its handlers. The rather uncommon Latin word *calcitrare* "to kick with the heels" was a derivative of an unattested noun *calcitrum,* which presumably meant "kick" and was itself formed from the well-attested *calx* "heel." The verb *recalcitrare* "to kick back," formed from *calcitrare* with the addition of the prefix *re-* "back," is known only once from classical Latin. But in the Latin of the church fathers the verb occurs more frequently and in the figurative usage "to be disobedient, rebel," in part as a loan translation of the Greek verb *apolaktizein.* The now rare English word *recalcitrate* "to show opposition to" was borrowed from Latin *recalcitrare* in the 17th century, but much more common now is *recalcitrant* (based on the present participle of *recalcitrare*), which is not attested until the 19th century.

\ə\ **abut** \ᵊ\ **kitten** \ər\ **further** \a\ **ash** \ā\ **ace**
\ä\ **mop, mar** \au̇\ **out** \ch\ **chin** \e\ **bet** \ē\ **easy**
\g\ **go** \i\ **hit** \ī\ **ice** \j\ **job** \ŋ\ **sing** \ō\ **go**
\ȯ\ **law** \ȯi\ **boy** \th\ **thin** \th\ **the** \ü\ **loot** \u̇\ **foot**
\y\ **yet** \zh\ **vision** *see also* Guide to Pronunciation

: RECAPITULATION

²re·cap \'rē-ˌkap, ri-'\ *verb* **re·capped; re·cap·ping** (1945)
: RECAPITULATE

³re·cap \'rē-ˌkap\ *noun* [⁴recap] (1940)
: RETREAD 1

⁴re·cap \(ˌ)rē-'kap\ *transitive verb* **re·capped; re·cap·ping** [re- + ¹cap] (1941)
: RETREAD
— **re·cap·pa·ble** \-'ka-pə-bəl\ *adjective*

re·cap·i·tal·i·za·tion \(ˌ)rē-ˌka-pə-t°l-ə-'zā-shən, -ˌkap-t°l-\ *noun* (1920)
: a revision of the capital structure of a corporation

re·cap·i·tal·ize \(ˌ)rē-'ka-pə-t°l-ˌīz, -'kap-t°l-\ *transitive verb* (1904)
: to change the capital structure of

re·ca·pit·u·late \ˌrē-kə-'pi-chə-ˌlāt\ *verb* **-lat·ed; -lat·ing** [Late Latin *recapitulatus,* past participle of *recapitulare* to restate by heads, sum up, from Latin *re- + capitulum* division of a book — more at CHAPTER] (1570)
transitive verb
: to repeat the principal points or stages of
: SUMMARIZE
intransitive verb
: SUM UP

re·ca·pit·u·la·tion \-ˌpi-chə-'lā-shən\ *noun* (14th century)
1 : a concise summary
2 : the hypothetical occurrence in an individual organism's development of successive stages resembling the series of ancestral types from which it has descended so that the ontogeny of the individual is a recapitulation of the phylogeny of its group
3 : the third section of a sonata form

¹re·cap·ture \(ˌ)rē-'kap-chər\ *noun* (1752)
1 a : the act of retaking **b** : an instance of being retaken
2 : the retaking of a prize or goods under international law
3 : a government seizure under law of earnings or profits beyond a fixed amount

²recapture *transitive verb* (1799)
1 a : to capture again **b** : to experience again ⟨by no effort of the imagination could she *recapture* the ecstasy —Ellen Glasgow⟩
2 : to take (as a portion of earnings or profits above a fixed amount) by law or through negotiations under law

re·cast \(ˌ)rē-'kast\ *transitive verb* **-cast; -cast·ing** (1603)
: to cast again ⟨*recast* a gun⟩ ⟨*recast* a play⟩; *also* : REMODEL, REFASHION ⟨*recasts* his political image to fit the times⟩
— **re·cast** \'rē-ˌkast, (ˌ)rē-'\ *noun*

rec·ce \'re-kē\ *noun, often attributive* [by shortening & alteration] (1941)
: RECONNAISSANCE

¹re·cede \ri-'sēd\ *intransitive verb* **re·ced·ed; re·ced·ing** [Middle English, from Latin *recedere* to go back, from *re- + cedere* to go] (15th century)
1 a : to move back or away : WITHDRAW **b** : to slant backward
2 : to grow less or smaller : DIMINISH, DECREASE ☆

²re·cede \(ˌ)rē-'sēd\ *transitive verb* [re- + cede] (1771)
: to cede back to a former possessor

¹re·ceipt \ri-'sēt\ *noun* [Middle English *receite,* from Old North French, from Medieval Latin *recepta,* probably from Latin, neuter plural of *receptus,* past participle of *recipere* to receive] (14th century)
1 : RECIPE
2 a *obsolete* : RECEPTACLE **b** *archaic* : a revenue office
3 : the act or process of receiving
4 : something received — usually used in plural
5 : a writing acknowledging the receiving of goods or money

²receipt *transitive verb* (1787)
1 : to give a receipt for or acknowledge the receipt of
2 : to mark as paid

re·ceiv·able \ri-'sē-və-bəl\ *adjective* (14th century)
1 : capable of being received
2 : subject to call for payment ⟨notes *receivable*⟩

re·ceiv·ables \-bəlz\ *noun plural* (1863)
: amounts of money receivable

re·ceive \ri-'sēv\ *verb* **re·ceived; re·ceiv·ing** [Middle English, from Old North French *receivre,* from Latin *recipere,* from *re- + capere* to take — more at HEAVE] (14th century)
transitive verb
1 : to come into possession of : ACQUIRE ⟨*receive* a gift⟩
2 a : to act as a receptacle or container for ⟨the cistern *receives* water from the roof⟩ **b** : to assimilate through the mind or senses ⟨*receive* new ideas⟩
3 a : to permit to enter : ADMIT **b** : WELCOME, GREET **c** : to react to in a specified manner
4 : to accept as authoritative, true, or accurate : BELIEVE
5 a : to support the weight or pressure of : BEAR **b** : to take (a mark or impression) from the weight of something ⟨some clay *receives* clear impressions⟩ **c** : ACQUIRE, EXPERIENCE ⟨*received* his early schooling at home⟩ **d** : to suffer the hurt or injury of ⟨*received* a broken nose⟩
intransitive verb
1 : to be a recipient
2 : to be at home to visitors ⟨*receives* on Tuesdays⟩
3 : to convert incoming radio waves into perceptible signals
4 : to prepare to take possession of the ball from a kick in football

received *adjective* (15th century)
: generally accepted : COMMON ⟨a healthy skepticism about *received* explanations —B. K. Lewalski⟩

Received Pronunciation *noun* (1869)
: the pronunciation of Received Standard

Received Standard *noun* (1913)
: a traditionally prestigious form of English spoken at the English public schools, at the universities of Oxford and Cambridge, and by many educated British people elsewhere

re·ceiv·er \ri-'sē-vər\ *noun* (14th century)
: one that receives: as **a** : TREASURER **b** (1) : a person appointed to hold in trust and administer property under litigation (2) : a person appointed to settle the affairs of a business involving a public interest or to manage a corporation during reorganization **c** : one that receives stolen goods : FENCE **d** : a device for converting signals (as electromagnetic waves) into audio or visual form: as (1) : a device in a telephone for converting electric impulses or varying current into sound (2) : a radio receiver with a tuner and amplifier on one chassis **e** (1) : CATCHER (2) : a member of the offensive team in football eligible to catch a forward pass

receiver general *noun, plural* **receivers general** (15th century)
: a public officer in charge of the treasury (as of Massachusetts)

re·ceiv·er·ship \ri-'sē-vər-ˌship\ *noun* (15th century)
1 : the office or function of a receiver
2 : the state of being in the hands of a receiver

receiving blanket *noun* (1926)
: a small lightweight blanket to wrap an infant (as after bathing)

receiving end *noun* (1937)
: the position of being a recipient or especially a victim — usually used in the phrase *on the receiving end*

receiving line *noun* (1933)
: a group of people who stand in a line and individually welcome guests (as at a wedding reception)

re·cen·cy \'rē-s°n(t)-sē\ *noun* (1612)
: the quality or state of being recent

re·cen·sion \ri-'sen(t)-shən\ *noun* [Latin *recension-, recensio* enumeration, from *recensēre* to review, from *re- + censēre* to assess, tax — more at CENSOR] (circa 1828)
1 : a critical revision of a text
2 : a text established by critical revision

re·cent \'rē-s°nt\ *adjective* [Middle English, from Middle French or Latin; Middle French, from Latin *recent-, recens;* perhaps akin to Greek *kainos* new] (15th century)
1 a : having lately come into existence : NEW, FRESH **b** : of or relating to a time not long past
2 *capitalized* : HOLOCENE
— **re·cent·ness** *noun*

re·cent·ly *adverb* (1533)
: during a recent period of time : LATELY

re·cep·ta·cle \ri-'sep-ti-kəl\ *noun* [Middle English, from Latin *receptaculum,* from *receptare* to receive, frequentative of *recipere* to receive] (15th century)
1 : one that receives and contains something : CONTAINER
2 [New Latin *receptaculum,* from Latin] **a** : the end of the flower stalk upon which the floral organs are borne **b** : a modified branch bearing sporangia in a cryptogamous plant
3 : a mounted female electrical fitting that contains the live parts of the circuit

re·cep·tion \ri-'sep-shən\ *noun* [Middle English *recepcion,* from Middle French or Latin; Middle French *reception,* from Latin *reception-, receptio,* from *recipere*] (15th century)
1 : the act or action or an instance of receiving: as **a** : RECEIPT ⟨the *reception* and distribution of funds⟩ **b** : ADMISSION ⟨*reception* into the church⟩ **c** : RESPONSE, REACTION ⟨the play met with a mixed *reception*⟩ **d** : the receiving of a radio or television broadcast **e** : the catching of a forward pass by a receiver
2 : a social gathering often for the purpose of extending a formal welcome

re·cep·tion·ist \-sh(ə-)nist\ *noun* (1901)
: a person employed to greet telephone callers, visitors, patients, or clients

re·cep·tive \ri-'sep-tiv\ *adjective* (15th century)
1 : able or inclined to receive; *especially* : open and responsive to ideas, impressions, or suggestions
2 a *of a sensory end organ* : fit to receive and transmit stimuli **b** : SENSORY
— **re·cep·tive·ly** *adverb*
— **re·cep·tive·ness** *noun*
— **re·cep·tiv·i·ty** \ˌrē-ˌsep-'ti-və-tē, ri-\ *noun*

re·cep·tor \ri-'sep-tər\ *noun* (1898)
: RECEIVER: as **a** : a cell or group of cells that receives stimuli : SENSE ORGAN **b** : a chemical group or molecule (as a protein) on the cell surface or in the cell interior that has an affinity for a specific chemical group, molecule, or virus

¹re·cess \'rē-ˌses, ri-'\ *noun* [Latin *recessus,* from *recedere* to recede] (1531)
1 : the action of receding : RECESSION
2 : a hidden, secret, or secluded place or part
3 a : INDENTATION, CLEFT ⟨a deep *recess* in the hill⟩ **b** : ALCOVE ⟨a *recess* lined with books⟩

☆ SYNONYMS
Recede, retreat, retract, back mean to move backward. RECEDE implies a gradual withdrawing from a forward or high fixed point in time or space ⟨the flood waters gradually *receded*⟩. RETREAT implies withdrawal from a point or position reached ⟨*retreating* soldiers⟩. RETRACT implies drawing back from an extended position ⟨a cat *retracting* its claws⟩. BACK is used with *up, down, out,* or *off* to refer to any retrograde motion ⟨*backed* off on the throttle⟩.

4 : a suspension of business or procedure often for rest or relaxation ⟨children playing at *recess*⟩
²recess (1809)
transitive verb
1 : to put into a recess ⟨*recessed* lighting⟩
2 : to make a recess in
3 : to interrupt for a recess
intransitive verb
: to take a recess
¹re·ces·sion \ri-'se-shən\ *noun* (circa 1652)
1 : the act or action of receding **:** WITHDRAWAL
2 : a departing procession (as of clergy and choir at the end of a church service)
3 : a period of reduced economic activity
— **re·ces·sion·ary** \-shə-ˌner-ē\ *adjective*
²re·ces·sion \(ˌ)rē-'se-shən\ *noun* [re- + cession] (1828)
: the act of ceding back to a former possessor
¹re·ces·sion·al \ri-'sesh-nəl, -'se-shə-nᵊl\ *adjective* (1867)
: of or relating to a withdrawal
²recessional *noun* (1867)
1 : a hymn or musical piece at the conclusion of a service or program
2 : ¹RECESSION 2
¹re·ces·sive \ri-'se-siv\ *adjective* (circa 1673)
1 a : tending to recede **b :** WITHDRAWN 2
2 a : producing little or no phenotypic effect when occurring in heterozygous condition with a contrasting allele ⟨*recessive* genes⟩ **b :** expressed only when the determining gene is in the homozygous condition ⟨*recessive* traits⟩
— **re·ces·sive·ly** *adverb*
— **re·ces·sive·ness** *noun*
²recessive *noun* (1900)
1 : an organism possessing one or more recessive characters
2 : a recessive character or gene
re·charge \(ˌ)rē-'chärj\ (1598)
intransitive verb
1 : to make a new attack
2 : to regain energy or spirit
transitive verb
1 : to charge again; *especially* **:** to restore anew the active materials in (a storage battery)
2 : to inspire or invigorate afresh **:** RENEW
— **re·charge** \(ˌ)rē-'chärj\ *noun*
— **re·charge·able** \(ˌ)rē-'chär-jə-bəl\ *adjective*
— **re·charg·er** \-jər\ *noun*
ré·chauf·fé \ˌrā-shō-'fā, -'shō-ˌ\ *noun* [French, from *réchauffé* warmed-over, from past participle of *réchauffer* to warm over, from *ré*- re- + *chauffer* to warm, from Middle French *chaufer* — more at CHAFE] (1805)
1 : REHASH
2 : a warmed-over dish of food
re·cheat \ri-'chēt\ *noun* [Middle English *rechate*, from *rechaten* to blow the recheat, from Middle French *rachater* to assemble, rally, from *re*- + *achater* to acquire, from (assumed) Vulgar Latin *accaptare* — more at CATE] (15th century)
: a hunting call sounded on a horn to assemble the hounds
re·cher·ché \rə-ˌsher-'shā, -'sher-ˌ\ *adjective* [French, from past participle of *rechercher* to seek out, from Middle French *recherchier* — more at RESEARCH] (1722)
1 a : EXQUISITE, CHOICE **b :** EXOTIC, RARE
2 : excessively refined **:** AFFECTED
3 : PRETENTIOUS, OVERBLOWN
re·cid·i·vism \ri-'si-də-ˌvi-zəm\ *noun* (1886)
: a tendency to relapse into a previous condition or mode of behavior; *especially* **:** relapse into criminal behavior
re·cid·i·vist \-vist\ *noun* [French *récidiviste*, from *récidiver* to relapse, from Medieval Latin *recidivare*, from Latin *recidivus* recurring, from *recidere* to fall back, from *re*- + *cadere* to fall — more at CHANCE] (1880)
: one who relapses; *specifically* **:** an habitual criminal

— **recidivist** *adjective*
— **re·cid·i·vis·tic** \-ˌsi-də-'vis-tik\ *adjective*
rec·i·pe \'re-sə-(ˌ)pē\ *noun* [Latin, take, imperative of *recipere* to take, receive — more at RECEIVE] (1584)
1 : PRESCRIPTION 4a
2 : a set of instructions for making something from various ingredients
3 : a formula or procedure for doing or attaining something ⟨a *recipe* for success⟩
re·cip·i·ent \ri-'si-pē-ənt\ *noun* [Latin *recipient-, recipiens*, present participle of *recipere*] (1558)
: one that receives **:** RECEIVER
— **recipient** *adjective*
¹re·cip·ro·cal \ri-'si-prə-kəl\ *adjective* [Latin *reciprocus* returning the same way, alternating] (1570)
1 a : inversely related **:** OPPOSITE **b :** of, constituting, or resulting from paired crosses in which the kind that supplies the male parent of the first cross supplies the female parent of the second cross and vice versa
2 : shared, felt, or shown by both sides
3 : serving to reciprocate **:** consisting of or functioning as a return in kind ⟨the *reciprocal* devastation of nuclear war⟩
4 a : mutually corresponding ⟨agreed to extend *reciprocal* privileges to each other's citizens⟩ **b :** marked by or based on reciprocity ⟨*reciprocal* trade agreements⟩
— **re·cip·ro·cal·ly** \-k(ə-)lē\ *adverb*
²reciprocal *noun* (1570)
1 : something in a reciprocal relationship to another
2 : either of a pair of numbers (as ⅔ and 3⁄2 or 9 and ⅑) whose product is one; *broadly* **:** MULTIPLICATIVE INVERSE
reciprocal pronoun *noun* (1844)
: a pronoun (as *each other*) used when its referents are predicated to bear the same relationship to one another
re·cip·ro·cate \ri-'si-prə-ˌkāt\ *verb* **-cat·ed; -cat·ing** (1607)
transitive verb
1 : to give and take mutually
2 : to return in kind or degree ⟨*reciprocate* a compliment gracefully⟩
intransitive verb
1 : to make a return for something ⟨we hope to *reciprocate* for your kindness⟩
2 : to move forward and backward alternately ⟨a *reciprocating* valve⟩ ☆
— **re·cip·ro·ca·tor** \-ˌkā-tər\ *noun*
reciprocating engine *noun* (1822)
: an engine in which the to-and-fro motion of one or more pistons is transformed into the rotary motion of a crankshaft
re·cip·ro·ca·tion \ri-ˌsi-prə-'kā-shən\ *noun* (1561)
1 a : a mutual exchange **b :** a return in kind or of like value
2 : an alternating motion
— **re·cip·ro·ca·tive** \-'si-prə-ˌkā-tiv, -kə-\ *adjective*
rec·i·proc·i·ty \ˌre-sə-'prä-s(ə-)tē\ *noun, plural* **-ties** (1766)
1 : the quality or state of being reciprocal **:** mutual dependence, action, or influence
2 : a mutual exchange of privileges; *specifically* **:** a recognition by one of two countries or institutions of the validity of licenses or privileges granted by the other
re·ci·sion \ri-'si-zhən\ *noun* [Middle French, alteration of *rescision*, from Late Latin *rescission-, rescissio* rescission] (1611)
: an act of rescinding **:** CANCELLATION
re·cit·al \ri-'sī-tᵊl\ *noun* (1536)
1 a : a detailed account **:** ENUMERATION ⟨a *recital* of names and dates⟩ **b :** the act or process

or an instance of reciting **c :** DISCOURSE, NARRATION ⟨a colorful *recital* of a night on the town⟩
2 a : a concert given by an individual musician or dancer or by a dance troupe **b :** a public exhibition of skill given by music or dance pupils
— **re·cit·al·ist** \-t°l-ist\ *noun*
rec·i·ta·tion \ˌre-sə-'tā-shən\ *noun* (15th century)
1 : the act of enumerating ⟨a *recitation* of relevant details⟩
2 : the act or an instance of reading or repeating aloud something publicly
3 a : a student's oral reply to questions **b :** a class period especially in association with and for review of a lecture
rec·i·ta·tive \ˌre-sə-tə-'tēv, ˌres-tə-\ *noun* [Italian *recitativo*, from *recitare* to recite, from Latin] (1656)
1 : a rhythmically free vocal style that imitates the natural inflections of speech and that is used for dialogue and narrative in operas and oratorios; *also* **:** a passage to be delivered in this style
2 : RECITATION 2
— **recitative** *adjective*
rec·i·ta·ti·vo \-'tē-(ˌ)vō\ *noun, plural* **-vi** \-(ˌ)vē\ *or* **-vos** [Italian] (1645)
: RECITATIVE 1
re·cite \ri-'sīt\ *verb* **re·cit·ed; re·cit·ing** [Middle English, to state formally, from Middle French or Latin; Middle French *reciter* to recite, from Latin *recitare*, from *re*- + *citare* to summon — more at CITE] (15th century)
transitive verb
1 : to repeat from memory or read aloud publicly
2 a : to relate in full ⟨*recites* dull anecdotes⟩ **b :** to give a recital of **:** DETAIL ⟨*recited* a catalog of offenses⟩
3 : to repeat or answer questions about (a lesson)
intransitive verb
1 : to repeat or read aloud something memorized or prepared
2 : to reply to a teacher's question on a lesson
— **re·cit·er** *noun*
reck \'rek\ *verb* [Middle English, to take heed, from Old English *reccan;* akin to Old High German *ruohhen* to take heed] (before 12th century)
intransitive verb
1 : WORRY, CARE
2 *archaic* **:** to be of account or interest **:** MATTER
transitive verb
1 *archaic* **:** to care for **:** REGARD
2 *archaic* **:** to matter to **:** CONCERN
reck·less \'re-kləs\ *adjective* (before 12th century)

☆ **SYNONYMS**
Reciprocate, retaliate, requite, return mean to give back usually in kind or in quantity. RECIPROCATE implies a mutual or equivalent exchange or a paying back of what one has received ⟨*reciprocated* their hospitality by inviting them for a visit⟩. RETALIATE usually implies a paying back of injury in exact kind, often vengefully ⟨the enemy *retaliated* by executing their prisoners⟩. REQUITE implies a paying back according to one's preference and often not equivalently ⟨*requited* her love with cold indifference⟩. RETURN implies a paying or giving back ⟨*returned* their call⟩ ⟨*return* good for evil⟩.

1 : marked by lack of proper caution **:** careless of consequences
2 : IRRESPONSIBLE 〈*reckless* charges〉
synonym see ADVENTUROUS
— **reck·less·ly** *adverb*
— **reck·less·ness** *noun*

reck·on \'re-kən\ *verb* **reck·oned; reck·on·ing** \'re-kə-niŋ, 'rek-niŋ\ [Middle English *rekenen,* from Old English *-recenian* (as in *gerecenian* to narrate); akin to Old English *reccan*] (13th century)
transitive verb
1 a : COUNT 〈*reckon* the days till Christmas〉 **b :** ESTIMATE, COMPUTE 〈*reckon* the height of a building〉 **c :** to determine by reference to a fixed basis 〈the existence of the U.S. is *reckoned* from the Declaration of Independence〉
2 : to regard or think of as **:** CONSIDER
3 *chiefly dialect* **:** THINK, SUPPOSE 〈I *reckon* I've outlived my time —Ellen Glasgow〉
intransitive verb
1 : to settle accounts
2 : to make a calculation
3 a : JUDGE **b** *chiefly dialect* **:** SUPPOSE, THINK
4 : to accept something as certain **:** place reliance 〈I *reckon* on your promise to help〉
— **reckon with :** to take into consideration
— **reckon without :** to fail to consider **:** IGNORE

reckoning *noun* (14th century)
1 : the act or an instance of reckoning: as **a :** ACCOUNT, BILL **b :** COMPUTATION **c :** calculation of a ship's position
2 : a settling of accounts 〈day of *reckoning*〉
3 : a summing up

re·claim \ri-'klām\ *transitive verb* [Middle English *reclamen,* from Middle French *reclamer* to call back, from Latin *reclamare* to cry out against, from *re-* + *clamare* to cry out — more at CLAIM] (14th century)
1 a : to recall from wrong or improper conduct **:** REFORM **b :** TAME, SUBDUE
2 a : to rescue from an undesirable state **b :** to make available for human use by changing natural conditions 〈*reclaim* swampland〉
3 : to obtain from a waste product or by-product **:** RECOVER
4 a : to demand or obtain the return of **b :** to regain possession of
synonym see RESCUE
— **re·claim·able** \-'klā-mə-bəl\ *adjective*

rec·la·ma·tion \,re-klə-'mā-shən\ *noun* [French *réclamation,* from Latin *reclamation-, reclamatio,* from *reclamare*] (1633)
: the act or process of reclaiming: as **a :** REFORMATION, REHABILITATION **b :** restoration to use **:** RECOVERY

ré·clame \rā-'kläm\ *noun* [French, advertising, from *réclamer* to appeal, from Middle French *reclamer*] (1883)
1 : a gift for dramatization or publicity **:** SHOWMANSHIP
2 : public acclaim **:** VOGUE

re·cline \ri-'klīn\ *verb* **re·clined; re·clin·ing** [Middle English, from Middle French or Latin; Middle French *recliner,* from Latin *reclinare,* from *re-* + *clinare* to bend — more at LEAN] (15th century)
transitive verb
: to cause or permit to incline backwards
intransitive verb
1 : to lean or incline backwards
2 : REPOSE, LIE

re·clin·er \-'klī-nər\ *noun* (1928)
: a chair with an adjustable back and footrest

re·clos·able \(,)rē-'klō-zə-bəl\ *adjective* (1965)
: capable of being tightly closed again after opening 〈*reclosable* packages of bacon〉

¹**re·cluse** \'re-,klüs, ri-'klüs, 're-,klüz\ *adjective* [Middle English, from Old French *reclus,* literally, shut up, from Late Latin *reclusus,* past participle of *recludere* to shut up, from Latin *re-* + *claudere* to close — more at CLOSE] (13th century)

: marked by withdrawal from society **:** SOLITARY
— **re·clu·sive** \ri-'klü-siv, -ziv\ *adjective*
— **re·clu·sive·ly** *adverb*
— **re·clu·sive·ness** *noun*

²**recluse** *noun* (13th century)
: a person who leads a secluded or solitary life

re·clu·sion \ri-'klü-zhən\ *noun* (15th century)
: the state of being recluse

rec·og·nise *chiefly British variant of* RECOGNIZE

rec·og·ni·tion \,re-kig-'ni-shən, -kəg-\ *noun* [Middle English *recognicion,* from Latin *recognition-, recognitio,* from *recognoscere*] (15th century)
1 : the action of recognizing **:** the state of being recognized: as **a :** ACKNOWLEDGMENT; *especially* **:** formal acknowledgment of the political existence of a government or nation **b :** knowledge or feeling that someone or something present has been encountered before
2 : special notice or attention
3 : the sensing and encoding of printed or written data by a machine 〈optical character *recognition*〉 〈magnetic ink character *recognition*〉

re·cog·ni·zance \ri-'käg-nə-zən(t)s, -'kä-nə-\ *noun* [Middle English, alteration of *reconissaunce,* from Middle French *reconoissance* recognition, from *reconoistre* to recognize] (14th century)
1 a : an obligation of record entered into before a court or magistrate requiring the performance of an act (as appearance in court) usually under penalty of a money forfeiture 〈released on his own *recognizance*〉 **b :** the sum liable to forfeiture upon such an obligation
2 *archaic* **:** TOKEN, PLEDGE

rec·og·nize \'re-kig-,nīz, -kəg-\ *transitive verb* **-nized; -niz·ing** [modification of Middle French *reconoiss-,* stem of *reconoistre,* from Latin *recognoscere,* from *re-* + *cognoscere* to know — more at COGNITION] (circa 1532)
1 : to acknowledge formally: as **a :** to admit as being lord or sovereign **b :** to admit as being of a particular status **c :** to admit as being one entitled to be heard **:** give the floor to **d :** to acknowledge the de facto existence or the independence of
2 : to acknowledge or take notice of in some definite way: as **a :** to acknowledge with a show of appreciation 〈*recognize* an act of bravery with the award of a medal〉 **b :** to acknowledge acquaintance with 〈*recognize* a neighbor with a nod〉
3 a : to perceive to be something or someone previously known 〈*recognized* the word〉 **b :** to perceive clearly **:** REALIZE
— **rec·og·niz·abil·i·ty** \,re-kig-,nī-zə-'bi-lə-tē, -kəg-\ *noun*
— **rec·og·niz·able** \'re-kəg-,nī-zə-bəl, -kig-\ *adjective*
— **rec·og·niz·ably** \-blē\ *adverb*
— **rec·og·niz·er** *noun*

¹**re·coil** \ri-'kȯi(ə)l\ *intransitive verb* [Middle English *reculen,* from Middle French *reculer,* from *re-* + *cul* backside — more at CULET] (14th century)
1 a : to fall back under pressure **b :** to shrink back physically or emotionally
2 : to spring back to or as if to a starting point **:** REBOUND
3 *obsolete* **:** DEGENERATE ☆
²**re·coil** \'rē-,kȯil, ri-'kȯi(ə)l\ *noun* (14th century)
1 : the act or action of recoiling; *especially* **:** the kickback of a gun upon firing
2 : REACTION 〈the *recoil* from the rigors of Calvinism —Edmund Wilson〉

re·coil·less \-,kȯil-ləs, -'kȯi(ə)l-\ *adjective* (1943)
: venting expanding propellant gas before recoil is produced 〈*recoilless* rifle〉 〈*recoilless* airgun〉

recoil–operated *adjective* (1942)
of a firearm **:** utilizing the movement of parts in recoil to operate the action

re·coin \(,)rē-'kȯin\ *transitive verb* (1685)
: to coin again or anew; *especially* **:** REMINT
— **re·coin·age** \-'kȯi-nij\ *noun*

rec·ol·lect \,re-kə-'lekt\ *verb* [Medieval Latin *recollectus,* past participle of *recolligere,* from Latin, to gather again] (1559)
transitive verb
1 : to bring back to the level of conscious awareness **:** REMEMBER 〈trying to *recollect* the name〉
2 : to remind (oneself) of something temporarily forgotten
intransitive verb
: to call something to mind
synonym see REMEMBER

re·col·lect \,rē-kə-'lekt\ *transitive verb* [partly from Latin *recollectus,* past participle of *recolligere,* from *re-* + *colligere* to collect; partly from *re-* + *collect*] (1604)
: to collect again; *especially* **:** RALLY, RECOVER

re·col·lect·ed \,rē-kə-'lek-təd\ *adjective* (1627)
: COMPOSED, CALM

rec·ol·lec·tion \,re-kə-'lek-shən\ *noun* (1624)
1 a : tranquillity of mind **b :** religious contemplation
2 a : the action or power of recalling to mind **b :** something recalled to the mind
synonym see MEMORY

re·com·bi·nant \(,)rē-'käm-bə-nənt\ *adjective* (1942)
1 : relating to or exhibiting genetic recombination 〈*recombinant* progeny〉
2 : relating to or containing recombinant DNA; *also* **:** produced by recombinant DNA technology
— **recombinant** *noun*

recombinant DNA *noun* (1975)
: genetically engineered DNA prepared in vitro by cutting up DNA molecules and splicing together specific DNA fragments usually from more than one species of organism

re·com·bi·na·tion \,rē-,käm-bə-'nā-shən\ *noun* (1903)
: the formation by the processes of crossing-over and independent assortment of new combinations of genes in progeny that did not occur in the parents
— **re·com·bi·na·tion·al** \-shnəl, -shə-nᵊl\ *adjective*

rec·om·mend \,re-kə-'mend\ *transitive verb* [Middle English, to praise, from Medieval Latin *recommendare,* from Latin *re-* + *commendare* to commend] (14th century)
1 a : to present as worthy of acceptance or trial 〈*recommended* the medicine〉 **b :** to endorse as fit, worthy, or competent 〈*recommends* her for the position〉
2 : ENTRUST, COMMIT 〈*recommended* his soul to God〉

☆ **SYNONYMS**
Recoil, shrink, flinch, wince, blench, quail mean to draw back in fear or distaste. RECOIL implies a start or movement away through shock, fear, or disgust 〈*recoiled* at the suggestion of stealing〉. SHRINK suggests an instinctive recoil through sensitiveness, scrupulousness, or cowardice 〈*shrank* from the unpleasant truth〉. FLINCH implies a failure to endure pain or face something dangerous or frightening with resolution 〈faced her accusers without *flinching*〉. WINCE suggests a slight involuntary physical reaction (as a start or recoiling) 〈*winced* in pain〉. BLENCH implies fainthearted flinching 〈stood their ground without *blenching*〉. QUAIL suggests shrinking and cowering in fear 〈*quailed* before the apparition〉.

3 : to make acceptable ⟨has other points to *recommend* it⟩
4 : ADVISE ⟨*recommend* that the matter be dropped⟩
— **rec·om·mend·able** \-'men-də-bəl\ *adjective*
— **rec·om·men·da·to·ry** \-də-ˌtȯr-ē, -ˌtȯr-\ *adjective*
rec·om·men·da·tion \ˌre-kə-mən-'dā-shən, -ˌmen-\ *noun* (15th century)
1 a : the act of recommending **b :** something (as a procedure) recommended
2 : something that recommends or expresses commendation
re·com·mit \ˌrē-kə-'mit\ *transitive verb* (1621)
1 : to refer (as a bill) back to a committee
2 : to entrust or consign again
— **re·com·mit·ment** \-mənt\ *noun*
— **re·com·mit·tal** \-'mi-t°l\ *noun*
¹rec·om·pense \'re-kəm-ˌpen(t)s\ *transitive verb* **-pensed; -pens·ing** [Middle English, from Middle French *recompenser*, from Late Latin *recompensare*, from Latin *re-* + *compensare* to compensate] (15th century)
1 a : to give something to by way of compensation (as for a service rendered or damage incurred) **b :** to pay for
2 : to return in kind **:** REQUITE
synonym see PAY
²recompense *noun* (15th century)
: an equivalent or a return for something done, suffered, or given **:** COMPENSATION ⟨offered in *recompense* for injuries⟩
re·com·pose \ˌrē-kəm-'pōz\ *transitive verb* (1611)
1 : to compose again **:** REARRANGE
2 : to restore to composure
— **re·com·po·si·tion** \(ˌ)rē-ˌkäm-pə-'zi-shən\ *noun*
re·con \ri-'kän, 'rē-ˌkän\ *noun* (1918)
: RECONNAISSANCE
rec·on·cile \'re-kən-ˌsīl\ *verb* **-ciled; -cil·ing** [Middle English, from Middle French or Latin; Middle French *reconcilier*, from Latin *reconciliare*, from *re-* + *conciliare* to conciliate] (14th century)
transitive verb
1 a : to restore to friendship or harmony ⟨*reconciled* the factions⟩ **b :** SETTLE, RESOLVE ⟨*reconcile* differences⟩
2 : to make consistent or congruous ⟨*reconcile* an ideal with reality⟩
3 : to cause to submit to or accept something unpleasant ⟨was *reconciled* to hardship⟩
4 a : to check (a financial account) against another for accuracy **b :** to account for
intransitive verb
: to become reconciled
synonym see ADAPT
— **rec·on·cil·abil·i·ty** \ˌre-kən-ˌsī-lə-'bi-lə-tē\ *noun*
— **rec·on·cil·able** \ˌre-kən-'sī-lə-bəl, 're-kən-ˌ\ *adjective*
— **rec·on·cile·ment** \'re-kən-ˌsīl-mənt\ *noun*
— **rec·on·cil·er** *noun*
rec·on·cil·i·a·tion \ˌre-kən-ˌsi-lē-'ā-shən\ *noun* [Middle English, from Latin *reconciliation-, reconciliatio*, from *reconciliare*] (14th century)
1 : the action of reconciling **:** the state of being reconciled
2 : the Roman Catholic sacrament of penance
— **rec·on·cil·ia·to·ry** \-'sil-yə-ˌtȯr-ē, -'si-lē-ə-, -ˌtȯr-\ *adjective*
re·con·dite \'re-kən-ˌdīt, ri-'kän-\ *adjective* [Latin *reconditus*, past participle of *recondere* to conceal, from *re-* + *condere* to store up, from *com-* + *-dere* to put — more at COM-, DO] (1649)
1 : hidden from sight **:** CONCEALED

2 : difficult or impossible for one of ordinary understanding or knowledge to comprehend **:** DEEP ⟨a *recondite* subject⟩
3 : of, relating to, or dealing with something little known or obscure ⟨*recondite* fact about the origin of the holiday —Floyd Dell⟩
— **re·con·dite·ly** *adverb*
— **re·con·dite·ness** *noun*
re·con·di·tion \ˌrē-kən-'di-shən\ *transitive verb* (1920)
1 : to restore to good condition (as by replacing parts)
2 : to condition (as a person or a person's attitudes) anew; *also* **:** to reinstate (a response) in an organism
re·con·firm \ˌrē-kən-'fərm\ *transitive verb* (1611)
: to confirm again; *also* **:** to establish more strongly
— **re·con·fir·ma·tion** \(ˌ)rē-ˌkän-fər-'mā-shən\ *noun*
re·con·nais·sance \ri-'kä-nə-zən(t)s, -sən(t)s\ *noun* [French, literally, recognition, from Middle French *reconoissance* — more at RECOGNIZANCE] (1810)
: a preliminary survey to gain information; *especially* **:** an exploratory military survey of enemy territory
re·con·noi·ter *or* **re·con·noi·tre** \ˌrē-kə-'nȯi-tər, ˌre-kə-\ *verb* **-noi·tered** *or* **-noi·tred; -noi·ter·ing** *or* **-noi·tring** \-'nȯi-tə-riŋ, -'nȯi-triŋ\ [obsolete French *reconnoître*, literally, to recognize, from Middle French *reconoistre* — more at RECOGNIZE] (1707)
transitive verb
: to make a reconnaissance of
intransitive verb
: to engage in reconnaissance
re·con·sid·er \ˌrē-kən-'si-dər\ (1571)
transitive verb
: to consider again especially with a view to changing or reversing
intransitive verb
: to consider something again
— **re·con·sid·er·a·tion** \-ˌsi-də-'rā-shən\ *noun*
re·con·sti·tute \(ˌ)rē-'kän(t)-stə-ˌtüt, -ˌtyüt\ *transitive verb* (1812)
: to constitute again or anew; *especially* **:** to restore to a former condition by adding water
— **re·con·sti·tu·tion** \(ˌ)rē-ˌkän(t)-stə-'tü-shən, -'tyü-\ *noun*
re·con·struct \ˌrē-kən-'strəkt\ *transitive verb* (1768)
: to construct again: as **a :** to establish or assemble again **b :** to build up again mentally **:** RE-CREATE ⟨*reconstructing* a lost civilization⟩
— **re·con·struct·ible** \-'strək-tə-bəl\ *adjective*
— **re·con·struc·tive** \-tiv\ *adjective*
— **re·con·struc·tor** \-tər\ *noun*
re·con·struc·tion \ˌrē-kən-'strək-shən\ *noun* (1791)
1 a : the action of reconstructing **:** the state of being reconstructed **b** *often capitalized* **:** the reorganization and reestablishment of the seceded states in the Union after the American Civil War
2 : something reconstructed
re·con·struc·tion·ism \-shə-ˌni-zəm\ *noun, often capitalized* (1942)
1 : a movement in 20th century American Judaism that advocates a creative adjustment to contemporary conditions through the cultivation of traditions and folkways shared by all Jews
2 : advocacy of post-Civil War reconstruction
— **re·con·struc·tion·ist** \-sh(ə-)nist\ *adjective or noun, often capitalized*
reconstructive surgery *noun* (1943)
: surgery to restore function or normal appearance by remaking defective organs or parts

re·con·vey \ˌrē-kən-'vā\ *transitive verb* (1506)
: to convey back to a previous position or owner
— **re·con·vey·ance** \-'vā-ən(t)s\ *noun*
¹re·cord \ri-'kȯrd\ *verb* [Middle English, literally, to recall, from Old French *recorder*, from Latin *recordari*, from *re-* + *cord-, cor* heart — more at HEART] (14th century)
transitive verb
1 a (1) : to set down in writing **:** furnish written evidence of **(2) :** to deposit an authentic official copy of ⟨*record* a deed⟩ **b :** to state for or as if for the record ⟨voted in favor but *recorded* certain reservations⟩ **c (1) :** to register permanently by mechanical means ⟨earthquake shocks *recorded* by a seismograph⟩ **(2) :** INDICATE, READ ⟨the thermometer *recorded* 90°⟩
2 : to give evidence of
3 : to cause (as sound, visual images, or data) to be registered on something (as a disc or magnetic tape) in reproducible form
intransitive verb
: to record something
— **re·cord·able** \-'kȯr-də-bəl\ *adjective*
²rec·ord \'re-kərd *also* -ˌkȯrd\ *noun* (14th century)
1 : the state or fact of being recorded
2 : something that records: as **a :** something that recalls or relates past events **b :** an official document that records the acts of a public body or officer **c :** an authentic official copy of a document deposited with a legally designated officer **d :** the official copy of the papers used in a law case
3 a (1) : a body of known or recorded facts about something or someone especially with reference to a particular sphere of activity that often forms a discernible pattern ⟨a good academic *record*⟩ ⟨a liberal voting *record*⟩ **(2) :** a collection of related items of information (as in a database) treated as a unit **b (1) :** an attested top performance **(2) :** an unsurpassed statistic
4 : something on which sound or visual images have been recorded; *specifically* **:** a disc with a spiral groove carrying recorded sound for phonograph reproduction
— **for the record :** for public knowledge **:** on the record
— **off the record :** not for publication ⟨spoke *off the record*⟩ ⟨remarks that were *off the record*⟩
— **of record :** being documented or attested ⟨a partner *of record* in several firms⟩
— **on record 1 :** in the position of having publicly declared oneself ⟨went *on record* as opposed to higher taxes⟩ **2 :** being known, published, or documented ⟨the judge's opinion is *on record*⟩
— **on the record :** for publication
³record *same as* ²\ *adjective* (1893)
: of, relating to, or being one that is extraordinary among or surpasses others of its kind
re·cor·da·tion \ˌre-ˌkȯr-'dā-shən; ˌrē-, ri-\ *noun* (circa 1812)
: the action or process of recording
record changer *noun* (1931)
: a phonograph with a device that automatically positions and plays successively each of a stack of records; *also* **:** the automatic device on a record changer
re·cord·er \ri-'kȯr-dər\ *noun* (15th century)
1 a : the chief judicial magistrate of some British cities and boroughs **b :** a municipal judge with criminal jurisdiction of first instance and sometimes limited civil jurisdiction
2 : one that records
3 : any of a group of wind instruments ranging from soprano to bass that are characterized by

a conical tube, a whistle mouthpiece, and eight finger holes ◇

recorder 3

re·cord·ing \ri-'kȯr-diŋ\ *noun* (1932)
: RECORD 4

re·cord·ist \ri-'kȯr-dist\ *noun* (circa 1930)
: one who records sound (as on magnetic tape)

¹re·count \ri-'kaȯnt\ *transitive verb* [Middle English, from Middle French *reconter*, from *re-* + *conter* to count, relate — more at COUNT] (15th century)
: to relate in detail : NARRATE
— **re·count·er** *noun*

²re·count \(,)rē-'kaȯnt\ *transitive verb* [*re-* + *count*] (1764)
: to count again

³re·count \'rē-,kaȯnt, (,)rē-'\ *noun* (1884)
: a second or fresh count

re·coup \ri-'küp\ *verb* [French *recouper* to cut back, from Old French, from *re-* + *couper* to cut — more at COPE] (1628)
transitive verb
1 a : to get an equivalent for (as losses) : make up for **b** : REIMBURSE, COMPENSATE ⟨*recoup* a person for losses⟩
2 : REGAIN ⟨an attempt to *recoup* his fortune⟩
intransitive verb
: to make good or make up for something lost; *also* : RECUPERATE
— **re·coup·able** \-'kü-pə-bəl\ *adjective*
— **re·coup·ment** \-'küp-mənt\ *noun*

re·course \'rē-,kȯrs, -,kȯrs, ri-'\ *noun* [Middle English *recours*, from Middle French, from Late Latin *recursus*, from Latin, act of running back, from *recurrere* to run back — more at RECUR] (14th century)
1 a : a turning to someone or something for help or protection **b** : a source of help or strength : RESORT
2 : the right to demand payment from the maker or endorser of a negotiable instrument (as a check)

re·cov·er \ri-'kə-vər\ *verb* **re·cov·ered; re·cov·er·ing** \-'kə-və-riŋ, -'kəv-riŋ\ [Middle English, from Middle French *recoverer*, from Latin *recuperare*, from *re-* + (assumed) Latin *caperare*, from *capere* to take — more at HEAVE] (14th century)
transitive verb
1 : to get back : REGAIN
2 a : to bring back to normal position or condition ⟨stumbled, then *recovered* himself⟩ **b** *archaic* : RESCUE
3 a : to make up for ⟨*recover* increased costs through higher prices⟩ **b** : to gain by legal process
4 *archaic* : REACH
5 : to find or identify again ⟨*recover* a comet⟩
6 a : to obtain from an ore, a waste product, or a by-product **b** : to save from loss and restore to usefulness : RECLAIM
intransitive verb
1 : to regain a normal position or condition (as of health) ⟨*recovering* from a cold⟩
2 : to obtain a final legal judgment in one's favor
— **re·cov·er·abil·i·ty** \-,kə-və-rə-'bi-lə-tē, -,kəv-rə-\ *noun*
— **re·cov·er·able** \-'kə-və-rə-bəl, -'kəv-rə-\ *adjective*
— **re·cov·er·er** \-'kə-vər-ər\ *noun*

re–cov·er \(,)rē-'kə-vər\ *transitive verb* (15th century)
: to cover again or anew

re·cov·ery \ri-'kə-və-rē, -'kəv-rē\ *noun, plural* **-er·ies** (15th century)
: the act, process, or an instance of recovering; *especially* : an economic upturn (as after a depression)

recovery room *noun* (1916)

: a hospital room equipped for meeting post-operative emergencies

¹rec·re·ant \'re-krē-ənt\ *adjective* [Middle English, from Middle French, from present participle of *recroire* to renounce one's cause in a trial by battle, from *re-* + *croire* to believe, from Latin *credere* — more at CREED] (14th century)
1 : crying for mercy : COWARDLY
2 : unfaithful to duty or allegiance

²recreant *noun* (15th century)
1 : COWARD
2 : APOSTATE, DESERTER

rec·re·ate \'re-krē-,āt\ *verb* **-at·ed; -at·ing** [Latin *recreatus*, past participle of *recreare*] (1530)
transitive verb
: to give new life or freshness to : REFRESH
intransitive verb
: to take recreation
— **rec·re·a·tive** \-,ā-tiv\ *adjective*

re–cre·ate \,rē-krē-'āt\ *transitive verb* (1587)
: to create again; *especially* : to form anew in the imagination
— **re–cre·at·able** \-'ā-tə-bəl\ *adjective*
— **re–cre·a·tion** \-'ā-shən\ *noun*
— **re–cre·a·tive** \-'ā-tiv\ *adjective*
— **re–cre·a·tor** \-'ā-tər\ *noun*

rec·re·a·tion \,re-krē-'ā-shən\ *noun* [Middle English *recreacion*, from Middle French *recreation*, from Latin *recreation-, recreatio* restoration to health, from *recreare* to create anew, restore, refresh, from *re-* + *creare* to create] (15th century)
: refreshment of strength and spirits after work; *also* : a means of refreshment or diversion : HOBBY
— **rec·re·a·tion·al** \-shnəl, -shə-n°l\ *adjective*

recreational vehicle *noun* (1966)
: a vehicle designed for recreational use (as in camping); *especially* : MOTOR HOME

rec·re·a·tion·ist \-sh(ə-)nist\ *noun* (1904)
: a person who seeks recreation especially in the outdoors

recreation room *noun* (1854)
1 : a room (as a rumpus room) used for recreation and relaxation — called also *rec room*
2 : a public room (as in a hospital) for recreation and social activities

re·crim·i·na·tion \ri-,kri-mə-'nā-shən\ *noun* [Medieval Latin *recrimination-, recriminatio*, from *recriminare* to make a retaliatory charge, from Latin *re-* + *criminari* to accuse — more at CRIMINATE] (circa 1611)
: a retaliatory accusation; *also* : the making of such accusations ⟨endless *recrimination*⟩
— **re·crim·i·nate** \-'kri-mə-,nāt\ *intransitive verb*
— **re·crim·i·na·tive** \-,nā-tiv\ *adjective*
— **re·crim·i·na·to·ry** \-'kri-mə-nə-,tōr-ē, -'krim-nə-, -,tȯr\ *adjective*

re·cru·desce \,rē-krü-'des\ *intransitive verb* **-desced; -desc·ing** [Latin *recrudescere* to become raw again, from *re-* + *crudescere* to become raw, from *crudus* raw — more at RAW] (1884)
: to break out or become active again

re·cru·des·cence \-'de-s°n(t)s\ *noun* (circa 1721)
: a new outbreak after a period of abatement or inactivity : RENEWAL

re·cru·des·cent \-s°nt\ *adjective* (circa 1727)
: breaking out again : RENEWING

¹re·cruit \ri-'krüt\ (1643)
transitive verb
1 a (1) : to fill up the number of (as an army) with new members : REINFORCE (2) : to enlist as a member of an armed service **b** : to increase or maintain the number of ⟨America *recruited* her population from Europe⟩ **c** : to secure the services of : ENGAGE, HIRE **d** : to seek to enroll ⟨*recruit* students⟩
2 : REPLENISH
3 : to restore or increase the health, vigor, or intensity of

intransitive verb
: to enlist new members
— **re·cruit·er** *noun*

²recruit *noun* [French *recrute, recrue* fresh growth, new levy of soldiers, from Middle French, from *recroistre* to grow up again, from Latin *recrescere*, from *re-* + *crescere* to grow — more at CRESCENT] (circa 1645)
1 : a fresh or additional supply
2 : a newcomer to a field or activity; *specifically* : a newly enlisted or drafted member of the armed forces
3 : a former enlisted man of the lowest rank in the army

re·cruit·ment \ri-'krüt-mənt\ *noun* (circa 1828)
1 : the action or process of recruiting
2 : the process of adding new individuals to a population or subpopulation (as of breeding individuals) by growth, reproduction, immigration, and stocking; *also* : a measure (as in numbers or biomass) of recruitment

re·crys·tal·lize \(,)rē-'kris-tə-,līz\ *verb* (1797)
: to crystallize again or repeatedly
— **re·crys·tal·li·za·tion** \(,)rē-,kris-tə-lə-'zā-shən\ *noun*

rec·tal \'rek-t°l\ *adjective* (circa 1859)
: relating to, affecting, or being near the rectum
— **rec·tal·ly** *adverb*

rect·an·gle \'rek-,taŋ-gəl\ *noun* [Medieval Latin *rectangulus* having a right angle, from Latin *rectus* right + *angulus* angle — more at RIGHT, ANGLE] (1571)
: a parallelogram all of whose angles are right angles; *especially* : one with adjacent sides of unequal length

rect·an·gu·lar \rek-'taŋ-gyə-lər\ *adjective* (1624)
1 : shaped like a rectangle ⟨a *rectangular* area⟩
2 a : crossing, lying, or meeting at a right angle ⟨*rectangular* axes⟩ **b** : having edges, surfaces, or faces that meet at right angles : having faces or surfaces shaped like rectangles ⟨*rectangular* parallelepipeds⟩ ⟨a *rectangular* solid⟩
— **rect·an·gu·lar·i·ty** \(,)rek-,taŋ-gyə-'lar-ə-tē\ *noun*
— **rect·an·gu·lar·ly** \rek-'taŋ-gyə-lər-lē\ *adverb*

rectangular coordinate *noun* (circa 1864)
: a Cartesian coordinate of a Cartesian coordinate system whose straight-line axes or coordinate planes are perpendicular

◇ WORD HISTORY
recorder There is little obvious connection between the sweet-sounding wind instrument called the recorder and modern electronic devices that copy sound and image. In actuality, the origin of the woodwind's name is rather mysterious, and it has no relation to current senses of the verb *record*. The customary, though not totally satisfactory, solution is to see it as a derivative of Middle English *recorden* "to repeat, rehearse," one of several early senses that Modern English *record* has not retained. In Elizabethan English *record* could mean "to play (a tune)," but this more appropriate sense may come from the instrument's name. The oldest reference to the name appears to be a Latin notation in the household accounts of Henry, Earl of Derby, dated 1388, that mentions a *fistula nomine Ricordo* ("pipe called Ricordo"). If this is a hint of the word's origin, it sends us off in a quite different direction, for "Ricordo" appears to be Italian *ricordo* "remembrance, memento." Other languages offer no illumination, since their names for the instrument simply consist of the word for "flute" with some modifier, such as German *Blockflöte* ("fipple flute") or French *flûte à neuf trous* ("flute with nine holes").

rec·ti·fi·able \'rek-tə-ˌfī-ə-bəl\ adjective [rectify (to determine the length of an arc)] (1816)
: having finite length ⟨a rectifiable curve⟩
— **rec·ti·fi·abil·i·ty** \ˌrek-tə-ˌfī-ə-'bi-lə-tē\ noun

rec·ti·fi·er \'rek-tə-ˌfī(-ə)r\ noun (1611)
: one that rectifies; specifically : a device for converting alternating current into direct current

rec·ti·fy \'rek-tə-ˌfī\ transitive verb **-fied; -fy·ing** [Middle English rectifien, from Middle French rectifier, from Medieval Latin rectificare, from Latin rectus right — more at RIGHT] (14th century)
1 : to set right : REMEDY
2 : to purify (as alcohol) especially by repeated or fractional distillation
3 : to correct by removing errors : ADJUST ⟨rectify the calendar⟩
4 : to make (an alternating current) unidirectional
synonym see CORRECT
— **rec·ti·fi·ca·tion** \ˌrek-tə-fə-'kā-shən\ noun

rec·ti·lin·e·ar \ˌrek-tə-'li-nē-ər\ adjective [Late Latin rectilineus, from Latin rectus + linea line] (1659)
1 : moving in or forming a straight line ⟨rectilinear motion⟩
2 : characterized by straight lines
3 : PERPENDICULAR 3
— **rec·ti·lin·e·ar·ly** adverb

rec·ti·tude \'rek-tə-ˌtüd, -ˌtyüd\ noun [Middle English, from Middle French, from Late Latin rectitudo, from Latin rectus straight, right] (15th century)
1 : the quality or state of being straight
2 : moral integrity : RIGHTEOUSNESS
3 : the quality or state of being correct in judgment or procedure

rec·ti·tu·di·nous \ˌrek-tə-'tüd-nəs, -'tyüd-; -'tü-də-nəs, -'tyü-\ adjective [Late Latin rectitudin-, rectitudo rectitude] (1897)
1 : characterized by rectitude
2 : piously self-righteous

rec·to \'rek-ˌtō\ noun, plural **rectos** [New Latin recto (folio) on the right-hand leaf] (1824)
1 : the side of a leaf (as of a manuscript) that is to be read first
2 : a right-hand page — compare VERSO

rec·tor \'rek-tər\ noun [Middle English, from Latin, from regere to direct — more at RIGHT] (14th century)
1 : one that directs : LEADER
2 a : a clergyman (as of the Protestant Episcopal Church) in charge of a parish **b** : an incumbent of a Church of England benefice in full possession of its rights **c** : a Roman Catholic priest directing a church with no pastor or one whose pastor has other duties
3 : the head of a university or school
— **rec·tor·ate** \-t(ə-)rət\ noun
— **rec·to·ri·al** \rek-'tōr-ē-əl, -'tòr-\ adjective
— **rec·tor·ship** \'rek-tər-ˌship\ noun

rec·to·ry \'rek-t(ə-)rē\ noun, plural **-ries** (1594)
1 : a benefice held by a rector
2 : a residence of a rector or a parish priest

rec·trix \'rek-triks\ noun, plural **rec·tri·ces** \'rek-trə-ˌsēz, rek-'trī-(ˌ)sēz\ [New Latin, from Latin, feminine of rector one that directs] (1768)
: any of the quill feathers of a bird's tail that are important in controlling flight direction — see BIRD illustration

rec·tum \'rek-təm\ noun, plural **rectums** or **rec·ta** \-tə\ [Middle English, from Medieval Latin, from rectum intestinum, literally, straight intestine] (15th century)
: the terminal part of the intestine from the sigmoid flexure to the anus

rec·tus \'rek-təs\ noun, plural **rec·ti** \-ˌtī, -ˌtē\ [New Latin, from rectus musculus straight muscle] (circa 1704)

: any of several straight muscles (as of the abdomen)

re·cum·ben·cy \ri-'kəm-bən(t)-sē\ noun, plural **-cies** (1646)
: the state of leaning, resting, or reclining : REPOSE; also : a recumbent position

re·cum·bent \-bənt\ adjective [Latin recumbent-, recumbens, present participle of recumbere to lie down, from re- + -cumbere to lie down; akin to Latin cubare to lie] (1705)
1 a : suggestive of repose : LEANING, RESTING **b** : lying down
2 : representing a person lying down ⟨a recumbent statue⟩
synonym see PRONE

re·cu·per·ate \ri-'kü-pə-ˌrāt, -'kyü-\ verb **-at·ed; -at·ing** [Latin recuperatus, past participle of recuperare — more at RECOVER] (1542)
transitive verb
: to get back : REGAIN
intransitive verb
: to regain a former state or condition; especially : to recover health or strength
— **re·cu·per·a·tion** \-ˌkü-pə-'rā-shən, -ˌkyü-\ noun

re·cu·per·a·tive \-'kü-pə-ˌrā-tiv, -'kyü-, -p(ə-)rə-tiv\ adjective (circa 1828)
1 : of or relating to recuperation ⟨recuperative powers⟩
2 : aiding in recuperation : RESTORATIVE

re·cur \ri-'kər\ intransitive verb **re·curred; re·cur·ring** [Middle English recurren to return, from Latin recurrere, literally, to run back, from re- + currere to run — more at CAR] (1529)
1 : to have recourse : RESORT
2 : to go back in thought or discourse
3 a : to come up again for consideration **b** : to come again to mind
4 : to occur again after an interval : occur time after time
— **re·cur·rence** \-'kər-ən(t)s, -'kə-rən(t)s\ noun

re·cur·rent \-'kər-ənt, -'kə-rənt\ adjective [Latin recurrent-, recurrens, present participle of recurrere] (1611)
1 : running or turning back in a direction opposite to a former course — used of various nerves and branches of vessels in the arms and legs
2 : returning or happening time after time ⟨recurrent complaints⟩
— **re·cur·rent·ly** adverb

recurring decimal noun (1801)
: REPEATING DECIMAL

re·cur·sion \ri-'kər-zhən\ noun [Late Latin recursion-, recursio, from recurrere] (1616)
1 : RETURN
2 : the determination of a succession of elements (as numbers or functions) by operation on one or more preceding elements according to a rule or formula involving a finite number of steps
3 : a computer programming technique involving the use of a procedure, subroutine, function, or algorithm that calls itself in a step having a termination condition so that successive repetitions are processed up to the critical step until the condition is met at which time the rest of each repetition is processed from the last one called to the first — compare ITERATION

re·cur·sive \ri-'kər-siv\ adjective (1934)
1 : of, relating to, or involving recursion ⟨a recursive function in a computer program⟩
2 : of, relating to, or constituting a procedure that can repeat itself indefinitely ⟨a recursive rule in a grammar⟩
— **re·cur·sive·ly** adverb
— **re·cur·sive·ness** noun

re·curved \(ˌ)rē-'kərvd\ adjective (1597)
: curved backward or inward

re·cu·san·cy \'re-kyə-zən(t)-sē, ri-'kyü-\ noun (circa 1600)
: the act or state of being a recusant

re·cu·sant \-zənt\ noun [Latin recusant-, recusans, present participle of recusare to refuse, from re- + causari to give a reason, from causa cause, reason] (circa 1553)
1 : an English Roman Catholic of the time from about 1570 to 1791 who refused to attend services of the Church of England and thereby committed a statutory offense
2 : one who refuses to accept or obey established authority
— **recusant** adjective

re·cuse \ri-'kyüz\ transitive verb **re·cused; re·cus·ing** [Middle English, to refuse, from Middle French recuser, from Latin recusare] (1949)
: to disqualify (oneself) as judge in a particular case; broadly : to remove (oneself) from participation to avoid a conflict of interest
— **re·cus·al** \-'kyü-zəl\ noun

re·cut \(ˌ)rē-'kət, 'rē-\ transitive verb (1664)
1 : to cut again
2 : to edit (as a film) anew

¹re·cy·cle \(ˌ)rē-'sī-kəl\ (1926)
transitive verb
1 : to pass again through a series of changes or treatments: as **a** : to process (as liquid body waste, glass, or cans) in order to regain material for human use **b** : RECOVER 6
2 : to adapt to a new use : ALTER
3 : to bring back : REUSE ⟨recycles a number of good anecdotes —Larry McMurtry⟩
4 : to make ready for reuse ⟨a plan to recycle vacant tenements⟩
intransitive verb
1 : to return to an earlier point in a countdown
2 : to return to an original condition so that operation can begin again — used of an electronic device
— **re·cy·cla·ble** \-k(ə-)lə-bəl\ adjective or noun
— **re·cy·cler** \-k(ə-)lər\ noun

²recycle noun (1926)
: the process of recycling

¹red \'red\ adjective **red·der; red·dest** [Middle English, from Old English rēad; akin to Old High German rōt red, Latin ruber & rufus, Greek erythros] (before 12th century)
1 a : of the color red **b** : having red as a distinguishing color
2 a (1) : flushed especially with anger or embarrassment (2) : RUDDY, FLORID (3) : being or having skin of a coppery hue **b** : BLOODSHOT ⟨eyes red from crying⟩ **c** : in the color range between a moderate orange and russet or bay **d** : tinged with red : REDDISH
3 : heated to redness : GLOWING
4 a : inciting or endorsing radical social or political change especially by force **b** often capitalized : COMMUNIST **c** often capitalized : of or relating to a communist country and especially to the U.S.S.R.

²red noun (before 12th century)
1 : a color whose hue resembles that of blood or of the ruby or is that of the long-wave extreme of the visible spectrum
2 : red clothing ⟨the lady in red⟩
3 : one that is of a red or reddish color: as **a** : RED WINE **b** : an animal with a red or reddish coat
4 a : a pigment or dye that colors red **b** : a shade or tint of red
5 a : one who advocates the violent overthrow of an existing social or political order **b** capitalized : COMMUNIST
6 [from the bookkeeping practice of entering debit items in red ink] : the condition of showing a loss — usually used with the ⟨in the red⟩; compare BLACK

\ə\ abut	\ᵊ\ kitten	\ər\ further	\a\ ash	\ā\ ace	
\ä\ mop, mar		\aù\ out	\ch\ chin	\e\ bet	\ē\ easy
\g\ go	\i\ hit	\ī\ ice	\j\ job		\ŋ\ sing
\ō\ law	\òi\ boy	\th\ thin	\ṯh\ the	\ü\ loot	\ù\ foot
\y\ yet	\zh\ vision		see also Guide to Pronunciation		

re·dact \ri-'dakt\ *transitive verb* [Middle English, from Latin *redactus,* past participle of *redigere*] (15th century)
1 : to put in writing : FRAME
2 : to select or adapt for publication : EDIT

re·dac·tion \-'dak-shən\ *noun* [French *rédaction,* from Late Latin *redaction-, redactio* act of reducing, compressing, from Latin *redigere* to bring back, reduce, from *re-, red-* re- + *agere* to lead — more at AGENT] (1785)
1 : an act or instance of redacting something
2 : a work that has been redacted : EDITION, VERSION
— **re·dac·tion·al** \-shnəl, -shə-nᵊl\ *adjective*

re·dac·tor \-'dak-tər\ *noun* (1816)
: one who redacts a work; *especially* : EDITOR

red admiral *noun* (1840)
: a nymphalid butterfly (*Vanessa atalanta*) that is common in both Europe and America, has broad orange-red bands on the forewings, and feeds chiefly on nettles in the larval stage

red admiral

red alert *noun* (circa 1951)
: the final stage of alert in which enemy attack appears imminent; *broadly* : a state of alert brought on by impending danger

red alga *noun* (1852)
: any of a division (Rhodophyta) of chiefly marine algae that have predominantly red pigmentation

red ant *noun* (1667)
: any of various reddish ants (as the pharaoh ant)

red·ar·gue \ri-'där-(,)gyü\ *transitive verb* **-gued; -gu·ing** [Middle English, from Latin *redarguere,* from *red-* + *arguere* to demonstrate, prove — more at ARGUE] (1627)
archaic : CONFUTE, DISPROVE

red–bait \'red-,bāt\ *verb, often R capitalized* (1940)
transitive verb
: to subject (as a person or group) to red-baiting
intransitive verb
: to engage in red-baiting
— **red–bait·er** *noun, often R capitalized*

red–bait·ing *noun, often R capitalized* (1928)
: the act of attacking or persecuting as a Communist or as communistic

red bay *noun* (circa 1730)
: a small tree (*Persea borbonia*) of the southern U.S. that has dark red heartwood

red·bel·ly dace \'red-'be-lē-\ *noun* (1884)
: either of two small brightly marked North American cyprinid fishes (*Phoxinus eos* and *P. erythrogaster*) — called also *red·bel·lied dace* \-lēd-\

red·bird \'red-,bərd\ *noun* (1669)
: any of several birds (as a cardinal, several tanagers, or the bullfinch) with predominantly red plumage

red blood cell *noun* (1910)
: any of the hemoglobin-containing cells that carry oxygen to the tissues and are responsible for the red color of vertebrate blood — called also *erythrocyte, red blood corpuscle, red cell, red corpuscle*

red·blood·ed \'red-'blə-dəd\ *adjective* (1881)
: VIGOROUS, LUSTY

red·bone \'red-,bōn\ *noun* (1916)
: any of a breed of moderate-sized speedy dark red or red and tan coonhounds of American origin

red·breast \'red-,brest\ *noun* (15th century)
1 : a bird (as a robin) with a reddish breast
2 : a reddish-bellied sunfish (*Lepomis auritus*) of the eastern U.S. — called also *red-breasted bream*

red·brick \-,brik\ *adjective* (1943)
1 : built of red brick

2 *often capitalized* [from the common use of red brick in constructing the buildings of recently founded universities] : of, relating to, or being the British Universities founded in the 19th or early 20th century — compare OXBRIDGE, PLATEGLASS

red bud \-,bəd\ *noun* (1705)
: any of several leguminous trees (genus *Cercis*) with usually pale rosy pink flowers

red bug *noun* (1804)
Southern & Midland : CHIGGER 2

red·cap \'red-,kap\ *noun* (1918)
: a baggage porter (as at a railroad station) — compare SKYCAP

red–carpet *adjective* [from the traditional laying down of a red carpet for important guests to walk on] (1952)
: marked by ceremonial courtesy ⟨*red-carpet* treatment⟩

red carpet *noun* (1951)
: a greeting or reception marked by ceremonial courtesy — usually used in the phrase *roll out the red carpet*

red cedar *noun* (1682)
1 : a common juniper (*Juniperus virginiana*) chiefly of the eastern U.S. that has dark green closely imbricated scalelike leaves; *also* : a related tree (*J. silicicola*) of the southeastern U.S.
2 : an arborvitae (*Thuja plicata*) of the Pacific Northwest
3 : the red or reddish brown wood of a red cedar

red cent *noun* (circa 1839)
: PENNY — used for emphasis in negative constructions

red clover *noun* (before 12th century)
: a Eurasian clover (*Trifolium pratense*) that has globose heads of reddish purple flowers and is widely cultivated as a hay, forage, and cover crop

red·coat \'red-,kōt\ *noun* (1520)
: a British soldier especially in America during the Revolutionary War

red coral *noun* (circa 1864)
: a gorgonian (*Corallium nobile*) of the Mediterranean and adjacent parts of the Atlantic having a hard stony skeleton of a delicate red or pink color used for ornaments and jewelry

Red Cross *noun* (1863)
: a red Greek cross on a white background used as the emblem of the International Red Cross

red currant *noun* (1622)
: either of two currants (*Ribes sativum* and *R. rubrum*) often cultivated for their fruit; *also* : the fruit

¹redd \'red\ *verb* **redd·ed** *or* **redd; redd·ing** [Middle English (Scots), to clear, perhaps alteration of *ridden* — more at RID] (circa 1520)
transitive verb
chiefly dialect : to set in order — usually used with *up* or *out*
intransitive verb
chiefly dialect : to make things tidy — usually used with *up*

²redd *noun* [origin unknown] (1808)
: the spawning ground or nest of various fishes

red deer *noun* (15th century)
: ELK 1b — used for one of the Old World elk

red·den \'re-dᵊn\ *verb* **red·dened; red·den·ing** \'red-niŋ, 're-dᵊn-iŋ\ (circa 1611)
transitive verb
: to make red or reddish
intransitive verb
: to become red; *especially* : BLUSH

red·dish \'re-dish\ *adjective* (14th century)
: tinged with red
— **red·dish·ness** *noun*

red dog *noun* (1953)
: BLITZ 2b
— **red dog** *verb*

red drum *noun* (1709)
: CHANNEL BASS

¹rede \'rēd\ *transitive verb* [Middle English — more at READ] (before 12th century)
1 *dialect* : to give counsel to : ADVISE
2 *dialect* : INTERPRET, EXPLAIN

²rede *noun* (before 12th century)
1 *chiefly dialect* : COUNSEL, ADVICE
2 *archaic* : ACCOUNT, STORY

red·ear \'red-,ir\ *noun* (circa 1948)
: a common sunfish (*Lepomis microlophus*) of the southern and eastern U.S. resembling the bluegill but having the back part of the operculum bright orange-red — called also *redear sunfish, shellcracker*

re·dec·o·rate \(,)rē-'de-kə-,rāt\ (circa 1611) *transitive verb*
: to freshen or change in appearance : REFURBISH
intransitive verb
: to freshen or change a decorative scheme
— **re·dec·o·ra·tion** \(,)rē-,de-kə-'rā-shən\ *noun*
— **re·dec·o·ra·tor** \(,)rē-'de-kə-,rā-tər\ *noun*

re·deem \ri-'dēm\ *transitive verb* [Middle English *redemen,* modification of Middle French *redimer,* from Latin *redimere,* from *re-, red-* re- + *emere* to take, buy; akin to Lithuanian *imti* to take] (15th century)
1 a : to buy back : REPURCHASE **b** : to get or win back
2 : to free from what distresses or harms: as **a** : to free from captivity by payment of ransom **b** : to extricate from or help to overcome something detrimental **c** : to release from blame or debt : CLEAR **d** : to free from the consequences of sin
3 : to change for the better : REFORM
4 : REPAIR, RESTORE
5 a : to free from a lien by payment of an amount secured thereby **b** (1) : to remove the obligation of by payment ⟨the U.S. Treasury *redeems* savings bonds on demand⟩ (2) : to exchange for something of value ⟨*redeem* trading stamps⟩ **c** : to make good : FULFILL
6 a : to atone for : EXPIATE **b** (1) : to offset the bad effect of (2) : to make worthwhile : RETRIEVE
synonym see RESCUE
— **re·deem·able** \-'dē-mə-bəl\ *adjective*

re·deem·er \-'dē-mər\ *noun* (15th century)
: a person who redeems; *especially, capitalized* : JESUS

re·deem·ing \-'dē-miŋ\ *adjective* (1631)
: serving to offset or compensate for a defect ⟨her performance is the film's *redeeming* feature⟩

re·de·fine \,rē-di-'fīn\ *transitive verb* (1872)
1 : to define (as a concept) again : REFORMULATE ⟨had to *redefine* their terms⟩
2 a : to reexamine or reevaluate especially with a view to change **b** : TRANSFORM 1c
— **re·def·i·ni·tion** \(,)rē-,de-fə-'ni-shən\ *noun*

re·demp·tion \ri-'dem(p)-shən\ *noun* [Middle English *redempcioun,* from Middle French *redemption,* from Latin *redemption-, redemptio,* from *redimere* to redeem] (14th century)
: the act, process, or an instance of redeeming

re·demp·tion·er \-sh(ə-)nər\ *noun* (1771)
: an immigrant to America in the 18th and 19th centuries who obtained passage by becoming an indentured servant

re·demp·tive \-'dem(p)-tiv\ *adjective* (15th century)
: of, relating to, or bringing about redemption

Re·demp·tor·ist \ri-'dem(p)-t(ə-)rist\ *noun* [French *rédemptoriste,* from Late Latin *redemptor* redeemer, from Latin, contractor, from *redimere*] (circa 1842)
: a member of the Congregation of the Most Holy Redeemer founded by Saint Alphonsus Liguori in Scala, Italy, in 1732 and devoted to preaching

re·demp·to·ry \ri-'dem(p)-t(ə-)rē\ *adjective* (1602)
: serving to redeem

re·de·ploy \ˌrē-di-'plöi\ (1945)
transitive verb
: to transfer from one area or activity to another
intransitive verb
: to relocate men or equipment
— **re·de·ploy·ment** \-mənt\ *noun*

re·de·scribe \ˌrē-di-'skrīb\ *transitive verb* (1871)
: to describe anew or again; *especially* **:** to give a new and more complete description to (a biological taxon)

re·de·scrip·tion \-'skrip-shən\ *noun* (1884)
: a new and more complete description especially of a biological taxon

re·de·sign \ˌrē-di-'zīn\ *transitive verb* (1891)
: to revise in appearance, function, or content
— **redesign** *noun*

re·de·vel·op \ˌrē-di-'ve-ləp\ *transitive verb* (1882)
: to develop again; *especially* **:** REDESIGN, REBUILD
— **re·de·vel·op·er** *noun*

re·de·vel·op·ment \-mənt\ *noun* (1873)
: the act or process of redeveloping; *especially* **:** renovation of a blighted area

red–eye \'red-ˌī\ *noun* (1819)
1 : cheap whiskey
2 : a late night or overnight flight

red–eye gravy \'red-ˌī-\ *noun* (1947)
: gravy made from the juices of ham and often flavored with coffee

red fescue *noun* (1900)
: a perennial pasture and turf grass (*Festuca rubra*) of Eurasia and North America with creeping rootstocks, erect culms, and reddish spikelets

red·fish \'red-ˌfish\ *noun* (15th century)
: any of various reddish fishes: as **a** (1) **:** a marine scorpaenid food fish (*Sebastes marinus*) of the northern coasts of Europe and North America that is usually bright rose-red when mature — called also *rosefish* (2) **:** a fish (*Sebastes mentella*) related to the redfish **b** **:** CHANNEL BASS

red flag *noun* (1777)
1 : a warning signal
2 : something that attracts usually irritated attention

red flannel hash *noun* (circa 1907)
: hash made especially from beef, potatoes, and beets

red fox *noun* (1778)
: a usually orange-red to reddish brown Holarctic fox (*Vulpes vulpes*) that has a white-tipped tail

red giant *noun* (1916)
: a star that has low surface temperature and a diameter that is large relative to the sun

red fox

red–green blindness *noun* (1888)
: dichromatism in which the spectrum is seen in tones of yellow and blue — called also *red-green color blindness*

Red Guard *noun* (1966)
: a member of a paramilitary youth organization in China in the 1960s

red gum *noun* (1788)
1 a : any of several Australian eucalyptus trees (especially *Eucalyptus camaldulensis, E. amygdalina,* and *E. calophylla*) **b :** eucalyptus gum
2 : SWEET GUM

red–hand·ed \'red-'han-dəd\ *adverb or adjective* (1819)
: in the act of committing a crime or misdeed ⟨caught *red-handed*⟩

red·head \'red-ˌhed\ *noun* (1664)
1 : a person having red hair
2 : a North American duck (*Aythya americana*) resembling the related canvasback but having a shorter bill with a black tip and in the male a brighter reddish head

red·head·ed \-ˌhe-dəd\ *adjective* (1565)
: having red hair or a red head

red heat *noun* (1686)
: the state of being red-hot; *also* **:** the temperature at which a substance is red-hot

red herring *noun* (15th century)
1 : a herring cured by salting and slow smoking to a dark brown color
2 [from the practice of drawing a red herring across a trail to confuse hunting dogs] **:** something that distracts attention from the real issue

red·horse \'red-ˌhors\ *noun* (1796)
: any of numerous large suckers (genus *Moxostoma*) of North American rivers and lakes with the males having red fins especially in the breeding season

red–hot \'red-'hät\ *adjective* (14th century)
: extremely hot: as **a :** glowing with heat **b :** exhibiting or marked by intense emotion, enthusiasm, or violence ⟨a *red-hot* campaign⟩ **c :** FRESH, NEW ⟨*red-hot* news⟩ **d :** extremely popular

red hot *noun* (1835)
1 : one who shows intense emotion or partisanship
2 : HOT DOG 1
3 : a small red candy strongly flavored with cinnamon

re·dia \'rē-dē-ə\ *noun, plural* **re·di·ae** \-dē-ˌē\ *also* **re·di·as** [New Latin, from Francesco Redi (died 1698?) Italian naturalist] (1877)
: a larva produced within the sporocyst of many trematodes that produces another generation of rediae or develops into a cercaria
— **re·di·al** \-dē-əl\ *adjective*

re·dial \'rē-ˌdī(-ə)l, rē-'\ *noun* (1980)
: a function on a telephone that automatically repeats the dialing of the last number called; *also* **:** a button that invokes this function
— **re·dial** *verb*

Red Indian *noun* (1831)
chiefly British **:** AMERICAN INDIAN

red·in·gote \'re-diŋ-ˌgōt\ *noun* [French, modification of English *riding coat*] (1793)
: a fitted outer garment: as **a :** a double-breasted coat with wide flat cuffs and collar worn by men in the 18th century **b :** a woman's lightweight coat open at the front **c :** a dress with a front gore of contrasting material

redingote a

red ink *noun* [from the use of red ink in financial statements to indicate a loss] (1926)
1 : a business loss **:** DEFICIT
2 : the condition of showing a business loss

red·in·te·grate \ri-'din-tə-ˌgrāt, re-\ *transitive verb* [Middle English, from Latin *redintegratus,* past participle of *redintegrare,* from *re-, red-* + *integrare* to make complete — more at INTEGRATE] (15th century)
archaic **:** to restore to a former and especially sound state

red·in·te·gra·tion \ri-ˌdin-tə-'grā-shən, re-\ *noun* (15th century)
1 *archaic* **:** restoration to a former state
2 a : revival of the whole of a previous mental state when a phase of it recurs **b :** arousal of any response by a part of the complex of stimuli that originally aroused that response
— **red·in·te·gra·tive** \-'din-tə-ˌgrā-tiv\ *adjective*

re·di·rect \ˌrē-də-'rekt, ˌre-(ˌ)dī-\ *transitive verb* (1844)
: to change the course or direction of
— **re·di·rec·tion** \-'rek-shən\ *noun*

¹re·dis·count \(ˌ)rē-'dis-ˌkaunt, ˌrē-dis-'\ *transitive verb* (1866)
: to discount again (as commercial paper)
— **re·dis·count·able** \-ˌkaun-tə-bəl, -'kaun-\ *adjective*

²re·dis·count \(ˌ)rē-'dis-ˌkaunt\ *noun* (1892)
1 : the act or process of rediscounting
2 : negotiable paper that is rediscounted

re·dis·trib·ute \ˌrē-də-'stri-byət\ *transitive verb* (1611)
1 : to alter the distribution of **:** REALLOCATE
2 : to spread to other areas
— **re·dis·tri·bu·tion** \(ˌ)rē-ˌdis-trə-'byü-shən\ *noun*
— **re·dis·tri·bu·tion·al** \-shnəl, -shə-n°l\ *adjective*
— **re·dis·trib·u·tive** \ˌrē-də-'stri-byə-tiv\ *adjective*

re·dis·tri·bu·tion·ist \(ˌ)rē-ˌdis-trə-'byü-sh(ə-)nist\ *noun* (1979)
: one that believes in or advocates a welfare state

re·dis·trict \(ˌ)rē-'dis-(ˌ)trikt\ *transitive verb* (1850)
: to divide anew into districts; *specifically* **:** to revise the legislative districts of
intransitive verb
: to revise legislative districts

red·i·vi·vus \ˌre-də-'vī-vəs, -'vē-\ *adjective* [Late Latin, from Latin, reused] (1675)
: brought back to life **:** REBORN — used postpositively

red lead *noun* (15th century)
: an orange-red to brick-red lead oxide Pb_3O_4 used in storage-battery plates, in glass and ceramics, and as a paint pigment

red leaf *noun* (1909)
: any of several plant diseases characterized by reddening of the foliage

red·leg \'red-ˌleg, -ˌlāg\ *noun* (1900)
: ARTILLERYMAN

red–legged grasshopper *noun* (1867)
: a widely distributed and sometimes highly destructive small North American grasshopper (*Melanoplus femur-rubrum*) with red hind legs — called also *red-legged locust*

red–let·ter \'red-ˌle-tər\ *adjective* [from the practice of marking holy days in red letters in church calendars] (1704)
: of special significance
word history SEE RUBRIC

red light *noun* (1849)
: a warning signal; *especially* **:** a red traffic signal

red–light district *noun* (1900)
: a district in which houses of prostitution are numerous

¹red·line \'red-'līn\ *noun* (1952)
: a recommended safety limit **:** the fastest, farthest, or highest point or degree considered safe; *also* **:** the red line which marks this point on a gauge

²red·line \'red-ˌlīn, -'līn\ (1968)
intransitive verb
: to withhold home-loan funds or insurance from neighborhoods considered poor economic risks
transitive verb
: to discriminate against in housing or insurance

red·ly \'red-lē\ *adverb* (1611)
: in a red manner **:** with red color

red man *noun* (1725)
1 : AMERICAN INDIAN
2 *R&M capitalized* [Improved Order of *Red Men*] **:** a member of a major benevolent and fraternal order

red maple *noun* (1770)
: a common tree (*Acer rubrum*) of the eastern and central U.S. that grows chiefly on moist soils, has reddish twigs and flowers, and yields a lighter and softer wood than the sugar maple

red marrow *noun* (1900)

\ə\ abut \°\ kitten \ər\ further \a\ ash \ā\ ace
\ä\ mop, mar \au\ out \ch\ chin \e\ bet \ē\ easy
\g\ go \i\ hit \ī\ ice \j\ job \ŋ\ sing \ō\ go
\o\ law \oi\ boy \th\ thin \th\ the \ü\ loot \u\ foot
\y\ yet \zh\ vision *see also* Guide to Pronunciation

: reddish bone marrow that is the seat of blood-cell production

red mass *noun, often R&M capitalized* (1889)
: a votive mass of the Holy Spirit celebrated in red vestments especially at the opening of courts and congresses

red mite *noun* (1894)
: any of several mites having a red color: as **a** : EUROPEAN RED MITE **b** : CITRUS RED MITE

red mulberry *noun* (1717)
: a North American forest tree (*Morus rubra*) with toothed leaves and soft durable wood; *also* : its edible usually purple fruit

red mullet *noun* (1762)
: GOATFISH

red·neck \'red-ˌnek\ *noun* (1830)
1 : a white member of the Southern rural laboring class — sometimes used disparagingly
2 : a person whose behavior and opinions are similar to those attributed to rednecks — often used disparagingly
— **redneck** *also* **red·necked** \-ˌnekt\ *adjective*

red·ness \-nəs\ *noun* (before 12th century)
: the quality or state of being red or red-hot

re·do \(ˌ)rē-'dü\ *transitive verb* **-did** \-'did\; **-done** \-'dən\; **-do·ing** \-'dü-iŋ\; **-does** \-'dəz\ (1597)
1 : to do over or again
2 : REDECORATE
— **re-do** \'rē-ˌdü, ˌrē-'dü\ *noun*

red oak *noun* (1634)
1 : any of numerous American oaks (as *Quercus rubra* and *Quercus falcata*) that have four stamens in each floret, acorns with the inner surface of the shell lined with woolly hairs, the acorn cap covered with thin scales, and leaf veins that usually run beyond the margin of the leaf to form bristles
2 : the wood of red oak

red ocher *noun* (1572)
: a red earthy hematite used as a pigment

red·o·lence \'re-dᵊl-ən(t)s\ *noun* (15th century)
1 : an often pungent or agreeable odor
2 : the quality or state of being redolent
synonym *see* FRAGRANCE

red·o·lent \-ənt\ *adjective* [Middle English, from Middle French, from Latin *redolent-, redolens*, present participle of *redolēre* to emit a scent, from *re-, red-* + *olēre* to smell — more at ODOR] (15th century)
1 : exuding fragrance : AROMATIC
2 a : full of a specified fragrance : SCENTED ⟨air *redolent* of seaweed⟩ **b** : EVOCATIVE, SUGGESTIVE ⟨a city *redolent* of antiquity⟩
synonym *see* ODOROUS
— **red·o·lent·ly** *adverb*

red osier *noun* (1807)
: a common shrubby North American dogwood (*Cornus sericea* synonym *C. stolonifera*) with reddish purple twigs, white flowers, and globose blue or whitish fruit

re·dou·ble \(ˌ)rē-'də-bəl\ (15th century)
transitive verb
1 : to make twice as great in size or amount; *broadly* : INTENSIFY, STRENGTHEN
2 a *obsolete* : to echo back **b** *archaic* : REPEAT
intransitive verb
1 : to become redoubled
2 *archaic* : RESOUND
3 : to double an opponent's double in bridge
— **redouble** *noun*

re·doubt \ri-'daut\ *noun* [French *redoute*, from Italian *ridotto*, from Medieval Latin *reductus* secret place, from Latin, withdrawn, from past participle of *reducere* to lead back — more at REDUCE] (circa 1608)
1 a : a small usually temporary enclosed defensive work **b** : a defended position : protective barrier
2 : a secure retreat : STRONGHOLD

re·doubt·able \ri-'dau-tə-bəl\ *adjective* [Middle English *redoutable*, from Middle French,

from *redouter* to dread, from *re-* + *douter* to doubt] (15th century)
1 : causing fear or alarm : FORMIDABLE
2 : ILLUSTRIOUS, EMINENT; *broadly* : worthy of respect
— **re·doubt·ably** \-blē\ *adverb*

re·dound \ri-'daund\ *intransitive verb* [Middle English, from Middle French *redonder*, from Latin *redundare*, from *re-, red-* re- + *unda* wave — more at WATER] (14th century)
1 *archaic* : to become swollen : OVERFLOW
2 : to have an effect for good or ill ⟨new power alignments which may or may not *redound* to the faculty's benefit —G. W. Bonham⟩
3 : to become transferred or added : ACCRUE
4 : REBOUND, REFLECT

red-out \'red-ˌaut\ *noun* (1942)
: a condition in which centripetal acceleration (as that created when an aircraft abruptly enters a dive) drives blood to the head and causes reddening of the visual field and headache

re·dox \'rē-ˌdäks\ *adjective* [*reduction* + *oxidation*] (1928)
: of or relating to oxidation-reduction

red panda *noun* (1955)
: PANDA 1

red–pen·cil \'red-ˌpen(t)-səl\ *transitive verb* (1946)
1 : CENSOR
2 : CORRECT, REVISE

red pepper *noun* (circa 1591)
: CAYENNE PEPPER

red pine *noun* (1809)
1 : a North American pine (*Pinus resinosa*) that has reddish bark and two long needles in each cluster
2 : the relatively hard wood of the red pine that consists chiefly of sapwood

red·poll \'red-ˌpōl\ *noun* (1738)
: either of two small finches (genus *Carduelis* synonym *Acanthis*) having brownish streaked plumage and a red or rosy crown; *especially* : one (*C. flammea*) found in northern regions of both the New and Old World

red poll *noun, often R&P capitalized* [alteration of *red polled*] (1891)
: any of a breed of large hornless red beef cattle of English origin

¹**re·dress** \ri-'dres\ *transitive verb* [Middle English, from Middle French *redresser*, from Old French *redrecier*, from *re-* + *drecier* to make straight — more at DRESS] (14th century)
1 a (1) : to set right : REMEDY (2) : to make up for : COMPENSATE **b** : to remove the cause of (a grievance or complaint) **c** : to exact reparation for : AVENGE
2 *archaic* **a** : to requite (a person) for a wrong or loss **b** : HEAL
synonym *see* CORRECT
— **re·dress·er** *noun*

²**re·dress** \ri-'dres, 'rē-\ *noun* (14th century)
1 a : relief from distress **b** : means or possibility of seeking a remedy ⟨without *redress*⟩
2 : compensation for wrong or loss : REPARATION
3 a : an act or instance of redressing **b** : RETRIBUTION, CORRECTION

red ribbon *noun* (1927)
: a red ribbon usually with appropriate words or markings awarded the second-place winner in a competition

red-root \'red-ˌrüt, -ˌrut\ *noun* (1709)
1 : a perennial herb (*Lachnanthes caroliniana* synonym *L. tinctoria*) of the bloodwort family of the eastern U.S. whose red root is the source of a dye
2 : NEW JERSEY TEA
3 : BLOODROOT
4 : a pigweed (*Amaranthus retroflexus*) that bears greenish flowers in dense spikes with bracts almost twice as long as the sepals

red rust *noun* (1846)
1 : the uredinial stage of a rust
2 : the diseased condition produced by red rust

red salmon *noun* (1881)

: SOCKEYE

red–shaft·ed flicker \'red-'shaf-təd-\ *noun* (1846)
: a flicker of western North America with light red on the underside of the tail and wings, a gray nape with no red, and in the male red on each cheek

red·shank \'red-ˌshaŋk\ *noun* (1525)
: a common Old World sandpiper (*Tringa totanus*) with pale red legs and feet

red·shift \'red-'shift\ *noun* (1923)
: a displacement of the spectrum of a celestial body toward longer wavelengths that is a consequence of the Doppler effect or the gravitational field of the source
— **red·shift·ed** *adjective*

red·shirt \'red-ˌshərt\ *noun* [from the red jersey commonly worn by such a player in practice scrimmages against the regulars] (1955)
: a college athlete who is kept out of varsity competition for a year in order to extend eligibility
— **redshirt** *verb*

red–shoul·dered hawk \-ˌshōl-dərd-\ *noun* (1812)
: a common North American hawk (*Buteo lineatus*) that has a banded tail and a light spot on the underside of the wings toward the tips

red sin·dhi \-'sin-dē\ *noun* [¹*red* + *sindhi* one belonging to Sind, Pakistan] (1946)
: any of a breed of humped rather small red dairy cattle developed in southwestern Asia and extensively used for crossbreeding with European stock in tropical areas

red siskin *noun* (1948)
: a finch (*Carduelis cucullata*) of northern South America that is scarlet with black head, wings, and tail

red·skin \'red-ˌskin\ *noun* (1699)
: AMERICAN INDIAN — usually taken to be offensive

red snapper *noun* (1755)
: any of various reddish fishes (as of the genera *Lutjanus* and *Sebastes*) including several food fishes

red snow *noun* (1678)
: snow colored by various airborne dusts or by a growth of algae (as of the genus *Chlamydomonas*) that contain red pigment and live in the upper layer of snow; *also* : an alga causing red snow

red soil *noun* (1889)
: any of a group of zonal soils that develop in a warm temperate moist climate under deciduous or mixed forests and that have thin organic and organic-mineral layers overlying a yellowish brown leached layer resting on an illuvial red horizon — called also *red podzolic soil*

red spider *noun* (1646)
: SPIDER MITE

red spruce *noun* (1777)
: a spruce (*Picea rubens*) of eastern North America that has pubescent twigs and yellowish green needles and is an important source of lumber and pulpwood

red squill *noun* (1738)
1 : a red-bulbed form of squill (*Urginea maritima*)
2 : a rat poison derived from the bulb of red squill

red squirrel *noun* (1682)
: a common and widely distributed North American squirrel (*Tamiasciurus hudsonicus*) that has reddish upper parts and is smaller than the gray squirrel

red star *noun* (1903)
: a star having a very low surface temperature and a red color

red-start \'red-ˌstärt\ *noun* [*red* + obsolete *start* handle, tail] (circa 1570)
1 : a small Old World songbird (*Phoenicurus phoenicurus* of the family Turdidae) with the male having a white brow, black throat, and chestnut breast and tail

2 : an American warbler (*Setophaga ruticilla* of the family Parulidae) with a black and orange male

red–tailed hawk \'red-ˌtāld-\ *noun* (1805)
: a widely distributed chiefly rodent-eating New World hawk (*Buteo jamaicensis*) that is usually mottled dusky above and white streaked dusky and tinged with buff below and has a rather short typically reddish tail — called also *redtail*

red-tailed hawk

red tape *noun* [from the red tape formerly used to bind legal documents in England] (1736)
: official routine or procedure marked by excessive complexity which results in delay or inaction

red tide *noun* (1904)
: seawater discolored by the presence of large numbers of dinoflagellates (especially of the genera *Gonyaulax* and *Gymnodinium*) which produce a toxin poisonous especially to many forms of marine vertebrate life and to humans who consume contaminated shellfish — compare SAXITOXIN

red-top \'red-ˌtäp\ *noun* (1790)
: any of various grasses (genus *Agrostis*) with usually reddish panicles; *especially* : an important forage and lawn grass (*A. alba* synonym *A. gigantea*) of eastern North America

re-duce \ri-'düs, -'dyüs\ *verb* **re-duced; re-duc-ing** [Middle English, to lead back, from Latin *reducere*, from *re-* + *ducere* to lead — more at TOW] (14th century)
transitive verb
1 a : to draw together or cause to converge : CONSOLIDATE ⟨*reduce* all the questions to one⟩ **b** (1) : to diminish in size, amount, extent, or number ⟨*reduce* taxes⟩ ⟨*reduce* the likelihood of war⟩ (2) : to decrease the volume and concentrate the flavor of by boiling ⟨add the wine and *reduce* the sauce for two minutes⟩ **c :** to narrow down : RESTRICT ⟨the Indians were *reduced* to small reservations⟩ **d :** to make shorter : ABRIDGE
2 *archaic* **:** to restore to righteousness : SAVE
3 : to bring to a specified state or condition ⟨the impact of the movie *reduced* them to tears⟩
4 a : to force to capitulate **b :** FORCE, COMPEL
5 a : to bring to a systematic form or character ⟨*reduce* natural events to laws⟩ **b :** to put down in written or printed form ⟨*reduce* an agreement to writing⟩
6 : to correct (as a fracture) by bringing displaced or broken parts back into their normal positions
7 a : to lower in grade or rank : DEMOTE **b :** to lower in condition or status : DOWNGRADE
8 a : to diminish in strength or density **b :** to diminish in value
9 a (1) : to change the denominations or form of without changing the value (2) : to construct a geometrical figure similar to but smaller than (a given figure) **b :** to transpose from one form into another : CONVERT **c :** to change (an expression) to an equivalent but more fundamental expression ⟨*reduce* a fraction⟩
10 : to break down (as by crushing or grinding) : PULVERIZE
11 a : to bring to the metallic state by removal of nonmetallic elements ⟨*reduce* an ore by heat⟩ **b :** DEOXIDIZE **c :** to combine with or subject to the action of hydrogen **d** (1) : to change (an element or ion) from a higher to a lower oxidation state (2) : to add one or more electrons to (an atom or ion or molecule)
12 : to change (a stressed vowel) to an unstressed vowel
intransitive verb

1 a (1) : to become diminished or lessened; *especially* : to lose weight by dieting (2) : to become reduced ⟨ferrous iron *reduces* to ferric iron⟩ **b :** to become concentrated or consolidated **c :** to undergo meiosis
2 : to become converted or equated
synonym *see* DECREASE, CONQUER
— **re-duc-er** *noun*
— **re-duc-ibil-i-ty** \-ˌdü-sə-'bi-lə-tē, -ˌdyü-\ *noun*
— **re-duc-ible** \-'dü-sə-bəl, -'dyü-\ *adjective*
— **re-duc-ibly** \-blē\ *adverb*

reducing agent *noun* (1885)
: a substance that reduces a chemical compound usually by donating electrons

re-duc-tant \ri-'dək-tənt\ *noun* (1925)
: REDUCING AGENT

re-duc-tase \-ˌtās, -ˌtāz\ *noun* (1902)
: an enzyme that catalyzes reduction

re-duc-tio ad ab-sur-dum \ri-'dək-tē-ˌō-ˌad-əb-'sər-dəm, -'dək-sē-ō-, -shē-, -'zər-\ *noun* [Late Latin, literally, reduction to the absurd] (1741)
1 : disproof of a proposition by showing an absurdity to which it leads when carried to its logical conclusion
2 : the carrying of something to an absurd extreme

re-duc-tion \ri-'dək-shən\ *noun* [Middle English *reduccion* restoration, from Middle French *reduction*, from Late Latin & Latin; Late Latin *reduction-, reductio* reduction (in a syllogism), from Latin, restoration, from *reducere*] (1546)
1 : the act or process of reducing : the state of being reduced
2 a : something made by reducing **b :** the amount by which something is reduced
3 [Spanish *reducción*, from Latin *reduction-, reductio*] : a South American Indian settlement directed by Jesuit missionaries
4 : MEIOSIS 2; *specifically* : production of the gametic chromosome number in the first meiotic division
— **re-duc-tion-al** \-shnəl, -shə-nᵊl\ *adjective*

reduction division *noun* (1891)
: the usually first division of meiosis in which chromosome reduction occurs; *also* : MEIOSIS 2

reduction gear *noun* (1896)
: a combination of gears used to reduce the input speed (as of a marine turbine) to a lower output speed (as of a ship's propeller)

re-duc-tion-ism \ri-'dək-shə-ˌni-zəm\ *noun* (1943)
1 : the attempt to explain all biological processes by the same explanations (as by physical laws) that chemists and physicists use to interpret inanimate matter; *also* : the theory that complete reductionism is possible
2 : a procedure or theory that reduces complex data or phenomena to simple terms; *especially* : OVERSIMPLIFICATION
— **re-duc-tion-ist** \-sh(ə-)nist\ *noun or adjective*
— **re-duc-tion-is-tic** \-ˌdək-shə-'nis-tik\ *adjective*

re-duc-tive \ri-'dək-tiv\ *adjective* (1633)
1 : of, relating to, causing, or involving reduction
2 : of or relating to reductionism : REDUCTIONISTIC
— **re-duc-tive-ly** *adverb*
— **re-duc-tive-ness** *noun*

re-dun-dan-cy \ri-'dən-dən(t)-sē\ *noun, plural* **-cies** (circa 1602)
1 a : the quality or state of being redundant : SUPERFLUITY **b :** the use of redundant components; *also* : such components **c** *chiefly British* : dismissal from a job especially by layoff
2 : PROFUSION, ABUNDANCE
3 a : superfluous repetition : PROLIXITY **b :** an act or instance of needless repetition
4 : the part of a message that can be eliminated without loss of essential information

re-dun-dant \-dənt\ *adjective* [Latin *redundant-, redundans*, present participle of *redundare* to overflow — more at REDOUND] (1594)
1 a : exceeding what is necessary or normal : SUPERFLUOUS **b :** characterized by or containing an excess; *specifically* : using more words than necessary **c :** characterized by similarity or repetition ⟨a group of particularly redundant brick buildings⟩ **d** *chiefly British* : no longer needed for a job and hence laid off
2 : PROFUSE, LAVISH
3 : serving as a duplicate for preventing failure of an entire system (as a spacecraft) upon failure of a single component
— **re-dun-dant-ly** *adverb*

re-du-pli-cate \ri-'dü-pli-ˌkāt, 'rē-, -'dyü-\ *transitive verb* [Late Latin *reduplicatus*, past participle of *reduplicare*, from Latin *re-* + *duplicare* to double — more at DUPLICATE] (circa 1570)
1 : to make or perform again : COPY, REPEAT
2 : to form (a word) by reduplication
— **re-du-pli-cate** \-kət\ *adjective*

re-du-pli-ca-tion \ri-ˌdü-pli-'kā-shən, ˌrē-, -'dyü-\ *noun* (1555)
1 : an act or instance of doubling or reiterating
2 a : an often grammatically functional repetition of a radical element or a part of it occurring usually at the beginning of a word and often accompanied by change of the radical vowel **b** (1) : a word or form produced by reduplication (2) : the repeated element in such a word or form
3 : ANADIPLOSIS
— **re-du-pli-ca-tive** \ri-'dü-pli-ˌkā-tiv, 'rē-, -'dyü-\ *adjective*
— **re-du-pli-ca-tive-ly** *adverb*

re-du-vi-id \ri-'dü-vē-əd, -'dyü-\ *noun* [ultimately from Latin *reduvia* hangnail] (1888)
: ASSASSIN BUG
— **reduviid** *adjective*

re-dux \(ˌ)rē-'dəks, 'rē-\ *adjective* [Latin, returning, from *reducere* to lead back] (1873)
: brought back — used postpositively

red-ware \'red-ˌwar, -ˌwer\ *noun* (circa 1797)
: earthenware pottery made of clay containing considerable iron oxide

red water *noun* (1594)
: any of several cattle diseases characterized by hematuria

red wheat *noun* (1523)
: a wheat that has red grains

red wine *noun* (circa 1754)
: a wine with a predominantly red color derived during fermentation from the natural pigment in the skins of dark-colored grapes

red-wing \'red-ˌwiŋ\ *noun* (1657)
1 : a European thrush (*Turdus iliacus* synonym *T. musicus*) having the underwing coverts red
2 : RED-WINGED BLACKBIRD

red–winged blackbird \'red-ˌwiŋd-\ *noun* (1797)
: a North American blackbird (*Agelaius phoeniceus*) of which the adult male is black with a patch of bright scarlet at the bend of the wings bordered behind with yellow or buff — called also *redwing blackbird*

red wolf *noun* (1840)
: a wolf (*Canis rufus* synonym *C. niger*) originally of the southeastern U.S.

red-wood \'red-ˌwùd\ *noun* (1634)
1 : any of various woods yielding a red dye
2 : a tree that yields a red dyewood or produces red or reddish wood
3 a : a commercially important coniferous timber tree (*Sequoia sempervirens*) of the bald cypress family that grows chiefly in coastal California and sometimes reaches a height of

\ə\ abut \ᵊ\ kitten \ər\ further \a\ ash \ā\ ace
\ä\ mop, mar \aú\ out \ch\ chin \e\ bet \ē\ easy
\g\ go \i\ hit \ī\ ice \j\ job \ŋ\ sing \ō\ go
\ò\ law \òi\ boy \th\ thin \t̲h̲\ the \ü\ loot \ù\ foot
\y\ yet \zh\ vision *see also* Guide to Pronunciation

360 feet (110 meters) — called also *coast redwood* **b** : its brownish red durable wood

red worm *noun* (1935)
: BLOODWORM

re·echo \(ˌ)rē-'e-(ˌ)kō\ (1590)
intransitive verb
: to repeat or return an echo : echo again or repeatedly : REVERBERATE
transitive verb
: to echo back : REPEAT

¹**reed** \'rēd\ *noun* [Middle English *rede*, from Old English *hrēod*; akin to Old High German *hriot* reed] (before 12th century)
1 a : any of various tall grasses with slender often prominently jointed stems that grow especially in wet areas **b** : a stem of a reed **c** : a person or thing too weak to rely on : one easily swayed or overcome

reed 6a

2 : a growth or mass of reeds; *specifically* : reeds for thatching
3 : ARROW
4 : a wind instrument made from the hollow joint of a plant
5 : an ancient Hebrew unit of length equal to 6 cubits
6 a : a thin elastic tongue (as of cane, wood, metal, or plastic) fastened at one end over an air opening in a wind instrument (as a clarinet, organ pipe, or accordion) and set in vibration by an air current **b** : a woodwind instrument that produces sound by the vibrating of a reed against the mouthpiece ⟨the *reeds* of an orchestra⟩
7 : a device on a loom resembling a comb and used to space warp yarns evenly
8 : REEDING 1a
— **reed·like** \-ˌlīk\ *adjective*

²**reed** *transitive verb* (1951)
: MILL 2

reed·buck \'rēd-ˌbək\ *noun, plural* **reedbuck** *also* **reedbucks** (1834)
: any of a genus (*Redunca*) of fawn-colored African antelopes in which the females are hornless

reed·ed \'rē-dəd\ *adjective* (1829)
: decorated with reeds or reeding ⟨a bed with *reeded* posts⟩

re·ed·i·fy \(ˌ)rē-'e-də-ˌfī\ *transitive verb* **-fied; -fy·ing** [Middle English *reedifien*, from Middle French *reedifier*, from Late Latin *reaedificare*, from Latin *re-* + *aedificare* to build — more at EDIFY] (15th century)
British : REBUILD

reed·ing \'rē-diŋ\ *noun* (1815)
1 a : a small convex molding — see MOLDING illustration **b** : decoration by series of reedings
2 : MILLING

re·edit \(ˌ)rē-'e-dət\ *transitive verb* (1797)
: to edit again : make a new edition of
— **re·edi·tion** \-'di-shən\ *noun*

reed·man \'rēd-ˌman\ *noun* (1938)
: one who plays a reed instrument

reed organ *noun* (1851)
: a keyboard wind instrument in which the wind acts on a set of free reeds

reed pipe *noun* (circa 1741)
: a pipe-organ pipe producing its tone by vibration of a beating reed in a current of air

re·ed·u·cate \(ˌ)rē-'e-jə-ˌkāt\ *transitive verb* (1808)
: to train again; *especially* : to rehabilitate through education
— **re·ed·u·ca·tion** \(ˌ)rē-ˌe-jə-'kā-shən\ *noun*
— **re·ed·u·ca·tive** \(ˌ)rē-'e-jə-ˌkā-tiv\ *adjective*

reedy \'rē-dē\ *adjective* **reed·i·er; -est** (14th century)
1 : abounding in or covered with reeds

2 : made of or resembling reeds; *especially* : SLENDER, FRAIL
3 : having the tone quality of a reed instrument
— **reed·i·ness** \-nəs\ *noun*

¹**reef** \'rēf\ *noun* [Middle English *riff*, from Old Norse *rif*; akin to Old English *ribb* rib] (14th century)
1 : a part of a sail taken in or let out in regulating size
2 : reduction in sail area by reefing

²**reef** (1667)
transitive verb
1 : to reduce the area of (a sail) by rolling or folding a portion
2 : to lower or bring inboard (a spar) wholly or partially
intransitive verb
: to reduce a sail by taking in a reef
— **reef·able** \'rē-fə-bəl\ *adjective*

³**reef** *noun* [Dutch *rif*, probably of Scandinavian origin; akin to Old Norse *rif* reef of a sail] (1584)
1 a : a chain of rocks or coral or a ridge of sand at or near the surface of water **b** : a hazardous obstruction
2 : LODE, VEIN
— **reefy** \'rē-fē\ *adjective*

¹**reef·er** \'rē-fər\ *noun* (1818)
1 : one that reefs
2 : a close-fitting usually double-breasted jacket or coat of thick cloth

²**ree·fer** \'rē-fər\ *noun* [by shortening & alteration] (1914)
1 : REFRIGERATOR
2 : a refrigerator car, truck, trailer, or ship

³**ree·fer** *noun* [probably modification of Mexican Spanish *grifa*] (1931)
: a marijuana cigarette; *also* : MARIJUANA 2

reef knot *noun* (1841)
: a square knot used in reefing a sail

¹**reek** \'rēk\ *noun* [Middle English *rek*, from Old English *rēc*; akin to Old High German *rouh* smoke] (before 12th century)
1 *chiefly dialect* : SMOKE
2 : VAPOR, FOG
3 : a strong or disagreeable fume or odor

²**reek** (before 12th century)
intransitive verb
1 : to emit smoke or vapor
2 a : to give off or become permeated with a strong or offensive odor **b** : to give a strong impression of some constituent quality or feature ⟨a neighborhood that *reeks* of poverty⟩
3 : EMANATE
transitive verb
1 : to subject to the action of smoke or vapor
2 : EXUDE, GIVE OFF ⟨a politician who *reeks* charm⟩
— **reek·er** *noun*
— **reeky** \'rē-kē\ *adjective*

¹**reel** \'rē(ə)l\ *noun* [Middle English, from Old English *hrēol*; akin to Old Norse *hrǣll* weaver's reed, Greek *krekein* to weave] (before 12th century)
1 : a revolvable device on which something flexible is wound: as **a** : a small windlass at the butt of a fishing rod for the line **b** *chiefly British* : a spool or bobbin for sewing thread **c** : a flanged spool for photographic film; *especially* : one for motion pictures
2 : a quantity of something wound on a reel

²**reel** (14th century)
transitive verb
1 : to wind on or as if on a reel
2 : to draw by reeling a line ⟨*reel* a fish in⟩
intransitive verb
: to turn a reel
— **reel·able** \'rē-lə-bəl\ *adjective*

³**reel** *verb* [Middle English *relen*, probably from *reel*, noun] (14th century)
intransitive verb
1 a : to turn or move round and round **b** : to be in a whirl
2 : to behave in a violent disorderly manner
3 : to waver or fall back (as from a blow)

4 : to walk or move unsteadily
transitive verb
: to cause to reel

⁴**reel** *noun* (1572)
: a reeling motion

⁵**reel** *noun* [probably from ⁴*reel*] (circa 1585)
1 : a lively Scottish-Highland dance; *also* : the music for this dance
2 : VIRGINIA REEL

re·elect \ˌrē-ə-'lekt\ *transitive verb* (1601)
: to elect for another term in office
— **re·elec·tion** \-'lek-shən\ *noun*

reel·er \'rē-lər\ *noun* (circa 1598)
1 : one that reels
2 : a motion picture having a specified number of reels ⟨a two-*reeler*⟩

reel off *transitive verb* (1837)
1 : to tell or recite readily and usually at length ⟨*reel off* a few jokes to break the ice⟩
2 : to chalk up usually as a series

reel-to-reel *adjective* (1961)
: of, relating to, or utilizing magnetic tape that requires threading on a take-up reel ⟨a *reel-to-reel* tape recorder⟩

re·em·broi·der \ˌrē-əm-'brȯi-dər\ *transitive verb* (1927)
: to outline a design (as on lace) with embroidery stitching

re·en·act \ˌrē-ə-'nakt\ *transitive verb* (circa 1676)
1 : to enact (as a law) again
2 : to act or perform again
3 : to repeat the actions of (an earlier event or incident)
— **re·en·act·ment** \-'nak(t)-mənt\ *noun*

re·en·force \ˌrē-ən-'fȯrs, -'fȯrs\ *variant of* REINFORCE

re·en·ter \(ˌ)rē-'en-tər\ (15th century)
transitive verb
1 : to enter (something) again
2 : to return to and enter
intransitive verb
: to enter again

re·en·trance \(ˌ)rē-'en-trən(t)s\ *noun* (1594)
: REENTRY

¹**re·en·trant** \-trənt\ *adjective* (1781)
: directed inward

²**reentrant** *noun* (1899)
1 : one that reenters
2 : one that is reentrant
3 : an indentation in a landform

re·en·try \(ˌ)rē-'en-trē\ *noun* (15th century)
1 : a retaking possession; *especially* : entry by a lessor on leased premises on the tenant's failure to perform the conditions of the lease
2 : a second or new entry
3 : a playing card that will enable a player to regain the lead
4 : the action of reentering the earth's atmosphere after travel in space

reest \'rēst\ *intransitive verb* [probably short for Scots *arreest* to arrest, from Middle English (Scots) *arreisten*, from Middle French *arester* — more at ARREST] (1786)
chiefly Scottish : BALK

¹**reeve** \'rēv\ *noun* [Middle English *reve*, from Old English *gerēfa*, from *ge-* (associative prefix) + *-rōfa* number, Old High German *ruova*) — more at CO-] (before 12th century)
1 : a local administrative agent of an Anglo-Saxon king
2 : a medieval English manor officer responsible chiefly for overseeing the discharge of feudal obligations
3 a : the council president in some Canadian municipalities **b** : a local official charged with enforcement of specific regulations ⟨deer *reeve*⟩

²**reeve** *verb* **rove** \'rōv\ *or* **reeved; reev·ing** [origin unknown] (1627)
transitive verb
1 : to pass (as a rope) through a hole or opening
2 : to fasten by passing through a hole or around something

3 : to pass a rope through
intransitive verb
of a rope **:** to pass through a block or similar device

³**reeve** *noun* [origin unknown] (1634)
: the female of the ruff (sandpiper)

ref \'ref\ *noun* (1899)
: a referee in a game or sport

re·fash·ion \(ˌ)rē-'fa-shən\ *transitive verb* (1803)
: REMAKE, ALTER

re·fect \ri-'fekt\ *transitive verb* [Latin *refectus*, past participle of *reficere*] (14th century)
archaic **:** to refresh with food or drink

re·fec·tion \ri-'fek-shən\ *noun* [Middle English *refeccioun*, from Middle French *refection*, from Latin *refection-, refectio*, from *reficere* to restore, from *re-* + *facere* to make — more at DO] (14th century)
1 : refreshment of mind, spirit, or body; *especially* **:** NOURISHMENT
2 a : the taking of refreshment **b :** food and drink together **:** REPAST

re·fec·to·ry \ri-'fek-t(ə-)rē\ *noun, plural* **-ries** [Late Latin *refectorium*, from Latin *reficere*] (15th century)
: a dining hall (as in a monastery or college)

refectory table *noun* (1923)
: a long table with heavy legs

re·fel \ri-'fel\ *transitive verb* **re·felled; re·fel·ling** [Latin *refellere* to prove false, refute, from *re-* + *fallere* to deceive] (1530)
obsolete **:** REJECT, REPULSE

re·fer \ri-'fər\ *verb* **re·ferred; re·fer·ring** [Middle English *referren*, from Latin *referre* to bring back, report, refer, from *re-* + *ferre* to carry — more at BEAR] (14th century)
transitive verb
1 a (1) **:** to think of, regard, or classify within a general category or group (2) **:** to explain in terms of a general cause **b :** to allot to a particular place, stage, or period **c :** to regard as coming from or located in a specific area
2 a : to send or direct for treatment, aid, information, or decision ⟨*refer* a patient to a specialist⟩ ⟨*refer* a bill back to a committee⟩ **b :** to direct for testimony or guaranty as to character or ability
intransitive verb
1 a : to have relation or connection **:** RELATE **b :** to direct attention usually by clear and specific mention ⟨no one *referred* to yesterday's quarrel⟩
2 : to have recourse **:** glance briefly ⟨*referred* frequently to his notes while speaking⟩
— **re·fer·able** \'re-f(ə-)rə-bəl, ri-'fər-ə-\ *adjective*
— **re·fer·rer** \ri-'fər-ər\ *noun*

¹**ref·er·ee** \ˌre-fə-'rē\ *noun* (1621)
1 : one to whom a thing is referred: as **a :** a person to whom a legal matter if referred for investigation and report or for settlement **b :** a person who reviews a paper and especially a technical paper and recommends that it should or should not be published **c** *chiefly British* **:** REFERENCE 4a
2 : a sports official usually having final authority in administering a game

²**referee** *verb* **-eed; -ee·ing** (1889)
transitive verb
1 : to conduct (as a match or game) as referee
2 a : to arbitrate (as a legal matter) as a judge or third party **b :** to review (as a technical paper) before publication
intransitive verb
: to act as a referee

¹**ref·er·ence** \'re-fərn(t)s, 're-f(ə-)rən(t)s\ *noun* (1589)
1 : the act of referring or consulting
2 : a bearing on a matter **:** RELATION ⟨in *reference* to your recent letter⟩
3 : something that refers: as **a :** ALLUSION, MENTION **b :** something (as a sign or indication) that refers a reader or consulter to another source of information (as a book or pas-

sage) **c :** consultation of sources of information
4 : one referred to or consulted: as **a :** a person to whom inquiries as to character or ability can be made **b :** a statement of the qualifications of a person seeking employment or appointment given by someone familiar with the person **c** (1) **:** a source of information (as a book or passage) to which a reader or consulter is referred (2) **:** a work (as a dictionary or encyclopedia) containing useful facts or information **d :** DENOTATION, MEANING

²**reference** *adjective* (1856)
: used or usable for reference; *especially* **:** constituting a standard for measuring or constructing

³**reference** *transitive verb* **-enced; -enc·ing** (1891)
1 a : to supply with references **b :** to cite in or as a reference
2 : to put in a form (as a table) adapted to easy reference

reference mark *noun* (1856)
: a conventional mark (as *, †, or ‡) placed in written or printed text to direct the reader's attention especially to a footnote

ref·er·en·dum \ˌre-fə-'ren-dəm\ *noun, plural* **-da** \-də\ *or* **-dums** [New Latin, from Latin, neuter of *referendus*, gerundive of *referre* to refer] (1847)
1 a : the principle or practice of submitting to popular vote a measure passed on or proposed by a legislative body or by popular initiative **b :** a vote on a measure so submitted
2 : a diplomatic agent's note asking for government instructions

ref·er·ent \'re-f(ə-)rənt\ *noun* [Latin *referent-, referens*, present participle of *referre*] (1844)
: one that refers or is referred to; *especially* **:** the thing that a symbol (as a word or sign) stands for
— **referent** *adjective*

ref·er·en·tial \ˌre-fə-'ren(t)-shəl\ *adjective* (1660)
: of, containing, or constituting a reference
— **ref·er·en·tial·i·ty** \-ˌren(t)-shē-'a-lə-tē\ *noun*
— **ref·er·en·tial·ly** \-'ren(t)-sh(ə-)lē\ *adverb*

re·fer·ral \ri-'fər-əl\ *noun* (1927)
1 : the act, action, or an instance of referring ⟨gave the patient a *referral* to a specialist⟩
2 : one that is referred

¹**re·fill** \(ˌ)rē-'fil\ (1681)
transitive verb
: to fill again **:** REPLENISH
intransitive verb
: to become filled again
— **re·fill·able** \-'fi-lə-bəl\ *adjective*

²**re·fill** \'rē-ˌfil\ *noun* (1886)
1 : a product or a container and a product used to refill the exhausted supply of a device
2 : something provided again; *especially* **:** a second or later filling of a medical prescription

re·fi·nance \ˌrē-fə-'nan(t)s, (ˌ)rē-'fī-, ˌrē-(ˌ)fī-'\ (1908)
transitive verb
: to renew or reorganize the financing of
intransitive verb
: to finance something anew

re·fine \ri-'fīn\ *verb* **re·fined; re·fin·ing** (1582)
transitive verb
1 : to free (as metal, sugar, or oil) from impurities or unwanted material
2 : to free from moral imperfection **:** ELEVATE
3 : to improve or perfect by pruning or polishing ⟨*refine* a poetic style⟩
4 : to reduce in vigor or intensity
5 : to free from what is coarse, vulgar, or uncouth
intransitive verb
1 : to become pure or perfected
2 : to make improvement by introducing subtleties or distinctions

— **re·fin·er** *noun*

re·fined \ri-'fīnd\ *adjective* (1588)
1 : FASTIDIOUS, CULTIVATED
2 : free from impurities
3 : PRECISE, EXACT ⟨a *refined* test for radioactivity⟩

re·fine·ment \ri-'fīn-mənt\ *noun* (circa 1611)
1 : the action or process of refining
2 : the quality or state of being refined **:** CULTIVATION
3 a : a refined feature or method **b :** a highly refined distinction **:** SUBTLETY **c :** a contrivance or device intended to improve or perfect

re·fin·ery \ri-'fī-nə-rē, -'fīn-rē\ *noun, plural* **-er·ies** (circa 1741)
: a building and equipment for refining or processing (as oil or sugar)

re·fin·ish \(ˌ)rē-'fi-nish\ (1931)
transitive verb
: to give (as furniture) a new surface
intransitive verb
: to refinish furniture
— **re·fin·ish·er** *noun*

¹**re·fit** \(ˌ)rē-'fit\ (1666)
transitive verb
: to fit out or supply again
intransitive verb
: to obtain repairs or fresh supplies or equipment

²**re·fit** \'rē-ˌfit, (ˌ)rē-'\ *noun* (1799)
: the action of refitting; *especially* **:** a refitting and renovating of a ship

re·fla·tion \(ˌ)rē-'flā-shən\ *noun* [*re-* + *-flation* (as in *deflation*)] (1932)
: restoration of deflated prices to a desirable level
— **re·flate** \(ˌ)rē-'flāt\ *verb*
— **re·fla·tion·ary** \-shə-ˌner-ē\ *adjective*

re·flect \ri-'flekt\ *verb* [Middle English, from Latin *reflectere* to bend back, from *re-* + *flectere* to bend] (15th century)
transitive verb
1 *archaic* **:** to turn into or away from a course **:** DEFLECT
2 : to prevent passage of and cause to change direction ⟨a mirror *reflects* light⟩
3 : to bend or fold back
4 : to give back or exhibit as an image, likeness, or outline **:** MIRROR ⟨the clouds were *reflected* in the water⟩
5 : to bring or cast as a result ⟨his attitude *reflects* little credit on his judgment⟩
6 : to make manifest or apparent **:** SHOW ⟨the pulse *reflects* the condition of the heart⟩
7 : REALIZE, CONSIDER
intransitive verb
1 : to throw back light or sound
2 a : to think quietly and calmly **b :** to express a thought or opinion resulting from reflection
3 a : to tend to bring reproach or discredit ⟨an investigation that *reflects* on all the members of the department⟩ **b :** to bring about a specified appearance or characterization ⟨an act which *reflects* well on him⟩ **c :** to have a bearing or influence
synonym see THINK

re·flec·tance \ri-'flek-tən(t)s\ *noun* (1926)
: the fraction of the total radiant flux incident upon a surface that is reflected and that varies according to the wavelength distribution of the incident radiation — called also *re·flec·tiv·i·ty* \ˌrē-ˌflek-'ti-və-tē, ri-\

reflecting telescope *noun* (circa 1704)
: REFLECTOR 2

re·flec·tion \ri-'flek-shən\ *noun* [Middle English, alteration of *reflexion*, from Late Latin *reflexion-, reflexio* act of bending back, from Latin *reflectere*] (14th century)
1 : an instance of reflecting; *especially* **:** the return of light or sound waves from a surface

2 : the production of an image by or as if by a mirror
3 a : the action of bending or folding back **b :** a reflected part **:** FOLD
4 : something produced by reflecting: as **a :** an image given back by a reflecting surface **b :** an effect produced by an influence ⟨the high crime rate is a *reflection* of our violent society⟩
5 : an often obscure or indirect criticism **:** RE-PROACH ⟨a *reflection* on his character⟩
6 : a thought, idea, or opinion formed or a re-mark made as a result of meditation
7 : consideration of some subject matter, idea, or purpose
8 *obsolete* **:** turning back **:** RETURN
9 a : a transformation of a figure in which each point is replaced by a point symmetric with respect to a line or plane **b :** a transfor-mation that involves reflection in more than one axis of a rectangular coordinate system
— **re·flec·tion·al** \-shnəl, -shə-nᵊl\ *adjec-tive*

re·flec·tive \ri-'flek-tiv\ *adjective* (1627)
1 : capable of reflecting light, images, or sound waves
2 : marked by reflection **:** THOUGHTFUL, DELIB-ERATIVE
3 : of, relating to, or caused by reflection ⟨*re-flective* glare⟩
4 : REFLEXIVE 3
— **re·flec·tive·ly** *adverb*
— **re·flec·tive·ness** *noun*
re·flec·tom·e·ter \ˌrē-ˌflek-'tä-mə-tər, ri-\ *noun* (1891)
: a device for measuring the reflectance of ra-diant energy (as light)
— **re·flec·tom·e·try** \-mə-trē\ *noun*
re·flec·tor \ri-'flek-tər\ *noun* (1665)
1 : one that reflects; *especially* **:** a polished surface for reflecting light or other radiation
2 : a telescope in which the principal focusing element is a mirror
re·flec·tor·ize \-tə-ˌrīz\ *transitive verb* **-ized; -iz·ing** (1940)
1 : to make reflecting
2 : to provide with reflectors
¹**re·flex** \'rē-ˌfleks\ *noun* [Latin *reflexus,* past participle of *reflectere* to reflect] (1508)
1 a : reflected heat, light, or color **b :** a mir-rored image **c :** a copy exact in essential or peculiar features
2 a : an automatic and often inborn response to a stimulus that involves a nerve impulse passing inward from a receptor to a nerve cen-ter and thence outward to an effector (as a muscle or gland) without reaching the level of consciousness — compare HABIT **b :** the pro-cess that culminates in a reflex and comprises reception, transmission, and reaction — called also *reflex action* **c** *plural* **:** the power of acting or responding with adequate speed **d :** a way of thinking or behaving
3 : a linguistic element (as a word or sound) or system (as writing) that is derived from a prior and especially an older element or sys-tem ⟨*boat* is the *reflex* of Old English *bāt*⟩
²**reflex** *adjective* [Latin *reflexus*] (1649)
1 : directed back on the mind or its operations **:** INTROSPECTIVE
2 : bent, turned, or directed back **:** REFLECTED ⟨a stem with *reflex* leaves⟩
3 : produced or carried out in reaction, resis-tance, or return
4 *of an angle* **:** being between 180° and 360°
5 : of, relating to, or produced by a reflex without intervention of consciousness
— **re·flex·ly** *adverb*
reflex arc *noun* (1882)
: the complete nervous path involved in a re-flex
re·flexed \'rē-ˌflekst, ri-'\ *adjective* [Latin *re-flexus* + English ¹-ed] (1733)
: bent or curved backward or downward ⟨*re-flexed* petals⟩ ⟨*reflexed* leaves⟩

re·flex·ion *chiefly British variant of* REFLEC-TION
¹**re·flex·ive** \ri-'flek-siv\ *adjective* [Medieval Latin *reflexivus,* from Latin *reflexus*] (1640)
1 a : directed or turned back on itself **b :** marked by or capable of reflection **:** REFLEC-TIVE
2 : of, relating to, characterized by, or being a relation that exists between an entity and itself ⟨the relation "is equal to" is *reflexive* but the relation "is the father of" is not⟩
3 : of, relating to, or constituting an action (as in "he perjured himself") directed back on the agent or the grammatical subject
4 : characterized by habitual and unthinking behavior
— **re·flex·ive·ly** *adverb*
— **re·flex·ive·ness** *noun*
— **re·flex·iv·i·ty** \ˌrē-ˌflek-'si-və-tē, ri-\ *noun*
²**reflexive** *noun* (1866)
: REFLEXIVE PRONOUN
reflexive pronoun *noun* (1867)
: a pronoun referring to the subject of the sen-tence, clause, or verbal phrase in which it stands; *specifically* **:** a personal pronoun com-pounded with *-self*
re·flex·ol·o·gy \ˌrē-ˌflek-'sä-lə-jē\ *noun* [Inter-national Scientific Vocabulary] (1923)
1 : the study and interpretation of behavior in terms of simple and complex reflexes
2 : massage of the hands or feet based on the belief that pressure applied to specific points on these extremities benefits other parts of the body
re·flow \(ˌ)rē-'flō\ *intransitive verb* (14th cen-tury)
1 : to flow back **:** EBB
2 : to flow in again
— **re·flow** \'rē-ˌflō\ *noun*
ref·lu·ence \'re-ˌflü-ən(t)s, re-'flü-\ *noun* (15th century)
archaic **:** REFLUX 1
re·flu·ent \-ənt\ *adjective* [Middle English, from Latin *refluent-, refluens,* present partici-ple of *refluere* to flow back, from *re-* + *fluere* to flow — more at FLUID] (15th century)
: flowing back
¹**re·flux** \'rē-ˌfləks\ *noun* [Middle English, from Medieval Latin *refluxus,* from Latin *re-* + *fluxus* flow — more at FLUX] (15th centu-ry)
1 : a flowing back **:** EBB
2 : a process of refluxing or condition of being refluxed
²**re·flux** \ri-'fləks, 'rē-\ *transitive verb* (1926)
: to cause to flow back or return; *especially* **:** to heat so that the vapors formed condense and return to be heated again
re·fo·cus \(ˌ)rē-'fō-kəs\ (circa 1865)
transitive verb
1 : to focus again
2 : to change the emphasis or direction of ⟨had *refocused* his life⟩
intransitive verb
1 : to focus something again
2 : to change emphasis or direction
re·for·es·ta·tion \(ˌ)rē-ˌfȯr-ə-'stā-shən, -ˌfär-\ *noun* (1887)
: the action of renewing forest cover by plant-ing seeds or young trees
— **re·for·est** \(ˌ)rē-'fȯr-əst, -'fär-\ *transitive verb*
¹**re·form** \ri-'fȯrm\ *verb* [Middle English, from Middle French *reformer,* from Latin *refor-mare,* from *re-* + *formare* to form, from *forma* form] (14th century)
transitive verb
1 a : to put or change into an improved form or condition **b :** to amend or improve by change of form or removal of faults or abuses
2 : to put an end to (an evil) by enforcing or introducing a better method or course of ac-tion
3 : to induce or cause to abandon evil ways ⟨*reform* a drunkard⟩

4 a : to subject (hydrocarbons) to cracking **b :** to produce (as gasoline or gas) by cracking
intransitive verb
: to become changed for the better
synonym see CORRECT
— **re·form·abil·i·ty** \-ˌfȯr-mə-'bi-lə-tē\ *noun*
— **re·form·able** \-'fȯr-mə-bəl\ *adjective*
²**reform** *noun* (1663)
1 : amendment of what is defective, vicious, corrupt, or depraved
2 : a removal or correction of an abuse, a wrong, or errors
3 *capitalized* **:** REFORM JUDAISM
³**reform** *adjective* (1819)
: relating to or favoring reform
re·form \(ˌ)rē-'fȯrm\ (14th century)
transitive verb
: to form again
intransitive verb
: to take form again ⟨the ice *re-formed* on the lake⟩
re·for·mate \ri-'fȯr-ˌmāt, -mət\ *noun* (1949)
: a product of hydrocarbon reforming
ref·or·ma·tion \ˌre-fər-'mā-shən\ *noun* (15th century)
1 : the act of reforming **:** the state of being re-formed
2 *capitalized* **:** a 16th century religious move-ment marked ultimately by rejection or modi-fication of some Roman Catholic doctrine and practice and establishment of the Protestant churches
— **ref·or·ma·tion·al** \-shnəl, -shə-nᵊl\ *ad-jective*
re·for·ma·tive \ri-'fȯr-mə-tiv\ *adjective* (1593)
: intended or tending to reform
¹**re·for·ma·to·ry** \ri-'fȯr-mə-ˌtōr-ē, -ˌtȯr-\ *ad-jective* (1589)
: REFORMATIVE
²**reformatory** *noun, plural* **-ries** (1834)
: a penal institution to which especially young or first offenders are committed for training and reformation
re·formed *adjective* (1563)
1 : changed for the better
2 *capitalized* **:** PROTESTANT; *specifically* **:** of or relating to the chiefly Calvinist Protestant churches formed in various continental Euro-pean countries
reformed spelling *noun* (circa 1934)
: any of several methods of spelling English words that use letters with more phonetic con-sistency than conventional spelling and that usually discard some silent letters (as in *peda-gog* for *pedagogue*)
re·form·er \ri-'fȯr-mər\ *noun* (1548)
1 : one that works for or urges reform
2 *capitalized* **:** a leader of the Protestant Ref-ormation
3 : an apparatus for cracking oils or gases to form specialized products
re·form·ism \ri-'fȯr-ˌmi-zəm\ *noun* (1904)
: a doctrine, policy, or movement of reform
— **re·form·ist** \-mist\ *noun or adjective*
Reform Judaism *noun* (circa 1905)
: Judaism marked by a liberal approach in nonobservance of much legal tradition regard-ed as irrelevant to the present and in shorten-ing and simplification of traditional ritual — compare CONSERVATIVE JUDAISM, ORTHODOX JU-DAISM
reform school *noun* (circa 1859)
: a reformatory for boys or girls
re·fract \ri-'frakt\ *transitive verb* [Latin *re-fractus,* past participle of *refringere* to break open, break up, from *re-* + *frangere* to break — more at BREAK] (1612)
1 a : to subject (as a ray of light) to refraction **b :** to alter or distort as if by refraction ⟨to *re-fract* that familiar world through the mind and heart of a romantic . . . woman —Anton Myrer⟩
2 : to determine the refracting power of

re·frac·tile \-'frak-t³l, -,tīl\ *adjective* (circa 1849)
: capable of refracting : REFRACTIVE

refracting telescope *noun* (1764)
: REFRACTOR

re·frac·tion \ri-'frak-shən\ *noun* (1603)
1 : deflection from a straight path undergone by a light ray or energy wave in passing obliquely from one medium (as air) into another (as glass) in which its velocity is different

2 : the change in the apparent position of a celestial body due to bending of the light rays emanating from it as they pass through the atmosphere; *also*

refraction 1: *a* light ray, *b* reflected ray, *c* refracted ray

: the correction to be applied to the apparent position of a body because of this bending
3 : the action of distorting an image by viewing through a medium; *also* : an instance of this

re·frac·tive \ri-'frak-tiv\ *adjective* (1673)
1 : having power to refract
2 : relating or due to refraction
— **re·frac·tive·ly** *adverb*
— **re·frac·tive·ness** *noun*
— **re·frac·tiv·i·ty** \,rē-,frak-'ti-və-tē, ri-\ *noun*

refractive index *noun* (1839)
: INDEX OF REFRACTION

re·frac·tom·e·ter \,rē-,frak-'tä-mə-tər, ri-\ *noun* [International Scientific Vocabulary] (circa 1859)
: an instrument for measuring indices of refraction
— **re·frac·to·met·ric** \ri-,frak-tə-'me-trik\ *adjective*
— **re·frac·tom·e·try** \,rē-,frak-'tä-mə-trē, ri-\ *noun*

re·frac·tor \ri-'frak-tər\ *noun* (1769)
: a telescope whose principal focusing element is a lens

¹re·frac·to·ry \ri-'frak-t(ə-)rē\ *adjective* [alteration of *refractary*, from Latin *refractarius*, irregular from *refragari* to oppose, from *re-* + *-fragari* (as in *suffragari* to support with one's vote)] (1606)
1 : resisting control or authority : STUBBORN, UNMANAGEABLE
2 a : resistant to treatment or cure ⟨a *refractory* lesion⟩ **b** : unresponsive to stimulus **c** : IMMUNE, INSUSCEPTIBLE ⟨after recovery they were *refractory* to infection⟩
3 : difficult to fuse, corrode, or draw out; *especially* : capable of enduring high temperature
synonym see UNRULY
— **re·frac·to·ri·ly** \-t(ə-)rə-lē; ,rē-,frak-'tōr-ə-lē, ri-, -'tòr-\ *adverb*
— **re·frac·to·ri·ness** \ri-'frak-t(ə-)rē-nəs\ *noun*

²refractory *noun, plural* **-ries** (1627)
: a refractory person or thing; *especially* : a heat-resisting ceramic material

refractory period *noun* (circa 1880)
: the brief period immediately following the response especially of a muscle or nerve before it recovers the capacity to make a second response — called also *refractory phase*

¹re·frain \ri-'frān\ *verb* [Middle English *refreynen*, from Middle French *refreiner, refrener*, from Latin *refrenare*, from *re-* + *frenum* bridle — more at FRENUM] (14th century)
transitive verb
archaic : CURB, RESTRAIN
intransitive verb
: to keep oneself from doing, feeling, or indulging in something and especially from following a passing impulse
— **re·frain·ment** \-mənt\ *noun*

²refrain *noun* [Middle English *refreyn*, from Middle French *refrain*, from *refraindre, refreindre* to resound, from Latin *refringere* to break up] (14th century)
: a regularly recurring phrase or verse especially at the end of each stanza or division of a poem or song : CHORUS; *also* : the musical setting of a refrain

re·fran·gi·ble \ri-'fran-jə-bəl\ *adjective* [irregular from Latin *refringere* to break up] (1673)
: capable of being refracted
— **re·fran·gi·bil·i·ty** \-,fran-jə-'bi-lə-tē\ *noun*
— **re·fran·gi·ble·ness** \-'fran-jə-bəl-nəs\ *noun*

re·fresh \ri-'fresh\ *verb* [Middle English *refresshen*, from Middle French *refreschir*, from Old French, from *re-* + *freis* fresh — more at FRESH] (14th century)
transitive verb
1 : to restore strength and animation to : REVIVE
2 : to freshen up : RENOVATE
3 a : to restore or maintain by renewing supply : REPLENISH **b** : AROUSE, STIMULATE ⟨let me *refresh* your memory⟩
4 : to run water over or restore water to
intransitive verb
1 : to become refreshed
2 : to take refreshment
3 : to lay in fresh provisions
synonym see RENEW

re·fresh·en \ri-'fre-shən, ,rē-\ *transitive verb* [*re-* + *freshen*] (1782)
: REFRESH

re·fresh·er \ri-'fre-shər\ *noun* (15th century)
1 : something (as a drink) that refreshes
2 : REMINDER
3 : review or instruction designed especially to keep one abreast of professional developments ⟨*refresher* course⟩

re·fresh·ing \-shiŋ\ *adjective* (circa 1580)
: serving to refresh; *especially* : agreeably stimulating because of freshness or newness
— **re·fresh·ing·ly** \-shiŋ-lē\ *adverb*

re·fresh·ment \ri-'fresh-mənt\ *noun* (14th century)
1 : the act of refreshing : the state of being refreshed
2 a : something (as food or drink) that refreshes **b** *plural* (1) : a light meal (2) : assorted light foods

re·fried beans \'rē-,frīd-\ *noun plural* (1957)
: beans cooked with seasonings, fried, then mashed and fried again

¹re·frig·er·ant \ri-'fri-jə-rənt, -'frij-rənt\ *adjective* (1599)
: allaying heat or fever

²refrigerant *noun* (1676)
: a refrigerant agent or agency: as **a** : a medication for reducing body heat **b** : a substance used in refrigeration

re·frig·er·ate \ri-'fri-jə-,rāt\ *transitive verb* **-at·ed; -at·ing** [Latin *refrigeratus*, past participle of *refrigerare*, from *re-* + *frigerare* to cool, from *frigor-, frigus* cold — more at FRIGID] (1534)
: to make or keep cold or cool; *specifically* : to freeze or chill (as food) for preservation
— **re·frig·er·a·tion** \-,fri-jə-'rā-shən\ *noun*

re·frig·er·a·tor \ri-'fri-jə-,rā-tər\ *noun* (1803)
: something that refrigerates; *especially* : a room or appliance for keeping food or other items cool

reft *past of* REAVE

re·fu·el \(,)rē-'fyü(-ə)l\ (1811)
transitive verb
: to provide with additional fuel
intransitive verb
: to take on additional fuel

¹ref·uge \'re-(,)fyüj *also* -(,)fyüzh\ *noun* [Middle English, from Middle French, from Latin *refugium*, from *refugere* to escape, from *re-* + *fugere* to flee — more at FUGITIVE] (14th century)

1 : shelter or protection from danger or distress
2 : a place that provides shelter or protection
3 : something to which one has recourse in difficulty

²refuge *verb* **ref·uged; ref·ug·ing** (1594)
transitive verb
: to give refuge to
intransitive verb
: to seek or take refuge

ref·u·gee \,re-fyù-'jē, 're-fyù-,\ *noun* [French *réfugié*, past participle of (*se*) *réfugier* to take refuge, from Latin *refugium*] (1685)
: one that flees; *especially* : a person who flees to a foreign country or power to escape danger or persecution
— **ref·u·gee·ism** \-,i-zəm\ *noun*

re·fu·gi·um \ri-'fyü-jē-əm\ *noun, plural* **-gia** \-jē-ə\ [New Latin, from Latin, refuge] (1943)
: an area of relatively unaltered climate that is inhabited by plants and animals during a period of continental climatic change (as a glaciation) and remains as a center of relict forms from which a new dispersion and speciation may take place after climatic readjustment

re·ful·gence \ri-'fùl-jən(t)s, -'fəl-\ *noun* [Latin *refulgentia*, from *refulgent-, refulgens*, present participle of *refulgēre* to shine brightly, from *re-* + *fulgēre* to shine — more at FULGENT] (1634)
: a radiant or resplendent quality or state : BRILLIANCE
— **re·ful·gent** \-jənt\ *adjective*

¹re·fund \ri-'fənd, 'rē-,\ *transitive verb* [Middle English, from Middle French & Latin; Middle French *refonder*, from Latin *refundere*, literally, to pour back, from *re-* + *fundere* to pour — more at FOUND] (15th century)
1 : to give or put back
2 : to return (money) in restitution, repayment, or balancing of accounts
— **re·fund·abil·i·ty** \ri-,fən-də-'bi-lə-tē, (,)rē-\ *noun*
— **re·fund·able** \-'fən-də-bəl\ *adjective*

²re·fund \'rē-,fənd\ *noun* (1866)
1 : the act of refunding
2 : a sum refunded

³re·fund \(,)rē-'fənd\ *transitive verb* [*re-* + *²fund*] (circa 1860)
: to fund again

re·fur·bish \ri-'fər-bish\ *transitive verb* (1611)
: to brighten or freshen up : RENOVATE
— **re·fur·bish·er** *noun*
— **re·fur·bish·ment** \-bish-mənt\ *noun*

re·fus·al \ri-'fyü-zəl\ *noun* (15th century)
1 : the act of refusing or denying
2 : the opportunity or right of refusing or taking before others

¹re·fuse \ri-'fyüz\ *verb* **re·fused; re·fus·ing** [Middle English, from Middle French *refuser*, from (assumed) Vulgar Latin *refusare*, perhaps blend of Latin *refutare* to refute and *recusare* to demur — more at RECUSE] (14th century)
transitive verb
1 : to express oneself as unwilling to accept ⟨*refuse* a gift⟩ ⟨*refuse* a promotion⟩
2 a : to show or express unwillingness to do or comply with ⟨*refused* to answer the question⟩ **b** : DENY ⟨they were *refused* admittance to the game⟩
3 *obsolete* : GIVE UP, RENOUNCE
4 *of a horse* : to decline to jump or leap over
intransitive verb
: to withhold acceptance, compliance, or permission
synonym see DECLINE
— **re·fus·er** *noun*

²ref·use \'re-ˌfyüs, -ˌfyüz\ *noun* [Middle English, from Middle French *refus* rejection, from Old French, from *refuser*] (14th century)
1 : the worthless or useless part of something
: LEAVINGS
2 : TRASH, GARBAGE

³ref·use \'re-ˌfyüs, -ˌfyüz\ *adjective* (15th century)
: thrown aside or left as worthless

re·fuse·nik *also* **re·fus·nik** \ri-'fyüz-(ˌ)nik\ *noun* [part translation of Russian *otkaznik*, from *otkaz* refusal] (1974)
: a Soviet citizen and especially a Jew refused permission to emigrate

ref·u·ta·tion \ˌre-fyù-'tā-shən\ *noun* (circa 1548)
: the act or process of refuting

re·fute \ri-'fyüt\ *transitive verb* **re·fut·ed**; **re·fut·ing** [Latin *refutare* to check, suppress, refute] (1597)
1 : to prove wrong by argument or evidence : show to be false or erroneous
2 : to deny the truth or accuracy of ⟨*refuted* the allegations⟩
— **re·fut·able** \-'fyü-tə-bəl\ *adjective*
— **re·fut·ably** \-blē\ *adverb*
— **re·fut·er** *noun*

reg \'reg\ *noun* [by shortening] (circa 1925)
: REGULATION (federal *regs*)

re·gal \'rē-gəl\ *adjective* [Middle English, from Middle French or Latin; Middle French, from Latin *regalis* — more at ROYAL] (14th century)
1 : of, relating to, or suitable for a king
2 : of notable excellence or magnificence : SPLENDID
— **re·gal·i·ty** \ri-'ga-lə-tē\ *noun*
— **re·gal·ly** \'rē-gə-lē\ *adverb*

¹re·gale \ri-'gā(ə)l\ *verb* **re·galed**; **re·gal·ing** [French *régaler*, from Middle French, from *regale*, noun] (circa 1656)
transitive verb
1 : to entertain sumptuously : feast with delicacies
2 : to give pleasure or amusement to ⟨*regaled* us with tall tales⟩
intransitive verb
: to feast oneself : FEED

²regale *noun* [French *régal*, from Middle French *regale*, from *re-* + *galer* to have a good time — more at GALLANT] (1670)
1 : a sumptuous feast
2 : a choice piece especially of food

re·ga·lia \ri-'gāl-yə\ *noun plural* [Medieval Latin, from Latin, neuter plural of *regalis*] (circa 1540)
1 : royal rights or prerogatives
2 a : the emblems, symbols, or paraphernalia indicative of royalty **b** : decorations or insignia indicative of an office or membership
3 : special dress; *especially* : FINERY

¹re·gard \ri-'gärd\ *noun* [Middle English, from Middle French, from Old French, from *re-garder*] (14th century)
1 *archaic* : APPEARANCE
2 a : ATTENTION, CONSIDERATION ⟨due *regard* should be given to all facets of the question⟩ **b** : a protective interest : CARE ⟨ought to have more *regard* for his health⟩
3 : LOOK, GAZE
4 a : the worth or estimation in which something or someone is held ⟨a man of small *regard*⟩ **b** (1) : a feeling of respect and affection : ESTEEM ⟨his hard work won him the *regard* of his colleagues⟩ (2) *plural* : friendly greetings implying such feeling ⟨give him my *regards*⟩
5 : a basis of action or opinion : MOTIVE
6 : an aspect to be taken into consideration : RESPECT ⟨is a small school, and is fortunate in this *regard*⟩
7 *obsolete* : INTENTION
— **in regard to** : with respect to : CONCERNING
— **with regard to** : in regard to

²regard *verb* [Middle English, from Middle French *regarder* to look back at, regard, from

Old French, from *re-* + *garder* to guard, look at — more at GUARD] (14th century)
transitive verb
1 : to consider and appraise usually from a particular point of view ⟨is highly *regarded* as a mechanic⟩
2 : to pay attention to : take into consideration or account
3 a : to show respect or consideration for **b** : to hold in high esteem
4 : to look at
5 *archaic* : to relate to
intransitive verb
1 : to look attentively : GAZE
2 : to pay attention : HEED ☆
— **as regards** : with respect to : CONCERNING

re·gar·dant \ri-'gär-dᵊnt\ *adjective* [Middle English *regardand*, from Middle French *regardant*, present participle of *regarder*] (15th century)
: looking backward over the shoulder — used of a heraldic animal

re·gard·ful \ri-'gärd-fəl\ *adjective* (circa 1586)
1 : HEEDFUL, OBSERVANT
2 : full or expressive of regard or respect : RESPECTFUL
— **re·gard·ful·ly** \-fə-lē\ *adverb*
— **re·gard·ful·ness** *noun*

re·gard·ing *preposition* (1866)
: with respect to : CONCERNING

¹re·gard·less \ri-'gärd-ləs\ *adjective* (1591)
: HEEDLESS, CARELESS
— **re·gard·less·ly** *adverb*
— **re·gard·less·ness** *noun*

²regardless *adverb* (1872)
: despite everything ⟨went ahead with their plans *regardless*⟩
usage see IRREGARDLESS

regardless of *preposition* (1784)
: without taking into account ⟨accepts all *regardless of* age⟩; *also* : in spite of ⟨*regardless of* our mistakes⟩

re·gat·ta \ri-'gä-tə, -'ga-\ *noun* [Italian *regata*] (1652)
: a rowing, speedboat, or sailing race or a series of such races

re·gen·cy \'rē-jən(t)-sē\ *noun, plural* **-cies** (15th century)
1 : the office, jurisdiction, or government of a regent or body of regents
2 : a body of regents
3 : the period of rule of a regent or body of regents

Regency *adjective* (1880)
: of, relating to, or characteristic of the styles of George IV's regency as Prince of Wales during the period 1811–20

re·gen·er·a·cy \ri-'je-nə-rə-sē, -'jen-rə-\ *noun* (1626)
: the state of being regenerated

¹re·gen·er·ate \-rət\ *adjective* [Middle English *regenerat*, from Latin *regeneratus*, past participle of *regenerare* to regenerate, from *re-* + *generare* to beget — more at GENERATE] (15th century)
1 : formed or created again
2 : spiritually reborn or converted
3 : restored to a better, higher, or more worthy state
— **re·gen·er·ate·ly** *adverb*
— **re·gen·er·ate·ness** *noun*

²re·gen·er·ate \ri-'je-nə-ˌrāt\ (1541)
intransitive verb
1 : to become formed again
2 : to become regenerate : REFORM
3 : to undergo regeneration
transitive verb
1 a : to subject to spiritual regeneration **b** : to change radically and for the better
2 a : to generate or produce anew; *especially* : to replace (a body part) by a new growth of tissue **b** : to produce again chemically sometimes in a physically changed form
3 : to restore to original strength or properties

— **re·gen·er·a·ble** \-'je-nə-rə-bəl, -'jen-rə-\ *adjective*

³re·gen·er·ate \same as ¹\ *noun* (circa 1569)
: one that is regenerated: as **a** : an individual who is spiritually reborn **b** (1) : an organism that has undergone regeneration (2) : a regenerated body part

regenerated cellulose *noun* (1904)
: cellulose obtained in a changed form by chemical treatment (as of a cellulose solution or derivative)

re·gen·er·a·tion \ri-ˌje-nə-'rā-shən, ˌrē-\ *noun* (14th century)
1 : an act or the process of regenerating : the state of being regenerated
2 : spiritual renewal or revival
3 : renewal or restoration of a body or bodily part after injury or as a normal process
4 : utilization by special devices of heat or other products that would ordinarily be lost

re·gen·er·a·tive \ri-'je-nə-ˌrā-tiv, -'je-nə-rə-, -'jen-rə-\ *adjective* (14th century)
1 : of, relating to, or marked by regeneration
2 : tending to regenerate

re·gen·er·a·tor \ri-'je-nə-ˌrā-tər\ *noun* (circa 1550)
1 : one that regenerates
2 : a device used especially with hot-air engines or gas furnaces in which incoming air or gas is heated by contact with masses (as of brick) previously heated by outgoing hot air or gas

re·gent \'rē-jənt\ *noun* [Middle English, from Middle French or Medieval Latin; Middle French, from Medieval Latin *regent-, regens*, from Latin, present participle of *regere* to rule — more at RIGHT] (15th century)
1 : one who governs a kingdom in the minority, absence, or disability of the sovereign
2 : one who rules or reigns : GOVERNOR
3 : a member of a governing board (as of a state university)
— **regent** *adjective*
— **re·gent·al** \-jən-tᵊl\ *adjective*

reg·gae \'re-(ˌ)gā, 'rā-\ *noun* [origin unknown] (1968)
: popular music of Jamaican origin that combines native styles with elements of rock and soul music and is performed at moderate tempos with the accent on the offbeat

reg·i·cide \'re-jə-ˌsīd\ *noun* [Latin *reg-, rex* king + English *-cide* — more at ROYAL] (circa 1548)
1 : one who kills a king
2 : the killing of a king
— **reg·i·ci·dal** \ˌre-jə-'sī-dᵊl\ *adjective*

re·gime *also* **ré·gime** \rā-'zhēm, ri- *also* ri-'jēm\ *noun* [French *régime*, from Latin *regimin-, regimen*] (1776)
1 a : REGIMEN 1 **b** : a regular pattern of occurrence or action (as of seasonal rainfall) **c** : the characteristic behavior or orderly procedure of a natural phenomenon or process
2 a : mode of rule or management **b** : a form of government ⟨a socialist *regime*⟩ **c** : a government in power ⟨predicted that the new *regime* would fall⟩ **d** : a period of rule

☆ **SYNONYMS**
Regard, respect, esteem, admire
mean to recognize the worth of a person or thing. REGARD is a general term that is usually qualified ⟨he is highly *regarded* in the profession⟩. RESPECT implies a considered evaluation or estimation ⟨after many years they came to *respect* her views⟩. ESTEEM implies greater warmth of feeling accompanying a high valuation ⟨no citizen of the town was more highly *esteemed*⟩. ADMIRE suggests usually enthusiastic appreciation and often deep affection ⟨a friend that I truly *admire*⟩.

reg·i·men \'re-jə-mən *also* 're-zhə-\ *noun* [Middle English, from Latin *regimin-, regimen* rule, from *regere* to rule] (14th century) **1 a :** a systematic plan (as of diet, therapy, or medication) especially when designed to improve and maintain the health of a patient **b :** a regular course of action and especially of strenuous training ⟨the daily *regimen* of a top ballet dancer⟩ **2 :** GOVERNMENT, RULE **3 :** REGIME 1c

¹**reg·i·ment** \'re-jə-mənt, 'rej-mənt\ *noun* [Middle English, from Middle French, from Late Latin *regimentum,* from Latin *regere*] (14th century) **1** *archaic* **:** governmental rule **2 :** a military unit consisting usually of a number of battalions

²**reg·i·ment** \'re-jə-,ment\ *transitive verb* (1617) **1 :** to form into or assign to a regiment **2 a :** to organize rigidly especially for the sake of regulation or control ⟨*regiment* an entire country⟩ **b :** to subject to order or uniformity — **reg·i·men·ta·tion** \,re-jə-mən-'tā-shən, -,men-\ *noun*

reg·i·men·tal \,re-jə-'men-t°l\ *adjective* (1659) **1 :** of or relating to a regiment **2 :** AUTHORITATIVE, DICTATORIAL

reg·i·men·tals \-t°lz\ *noun plural* (1742) **1 :** a regimental uniform **2 :** military dress

re·gion \'rē-jən\ *noun* [Middle English, from Middle French, from Latin *region-, regio,* from *regere* to rule] (14th century) **1 :** an administrative area, division, or district; *especially* **:** the basic administrative unit for local government in Scotland **2 a :** an indefinite area of the world or universe ⟨few unknown *regions* left on earth⟩ **b :** a broad geographical area distinguished by similar features ⟨the Appalachian *region*⟩ **c** (1) **:** a major world area that supports a characteristic fauna (2) **:** an area characterized by the prevalence of one or more vegetational climax types **3 a :** any of the major subdivisions into which the body or one of its parts is divisible **b :** an indefinite area surrounding a specified body part ⟨a pain in the *region* of the heart⟩ **4 :** a sphere of activity or interest **:** FIELD **5 :** any of the zones into which the atmosphere is divided according to height or the sea according to depth **6 :** an open connected set together with none, some, or all of the points on its boundary ⟨a simple closed curve divides a plane into two *regions*⟩

¹**re·gion·al** \'rēj-nəl, 'rē-jə-n°l\ *adjective* (15th century) **1 :** affecting a particular region **:** LOCALIZED **2 :** of, relating to, characteristic of, or serving a region ⟨a *regional* high school⟩ **3 :** marked by regionalism ⟨*regional* art⟩

²**regional** *noun* (1936) **:** something (as a branch of an organization or an edition of a magazine) that serves a region

re·gion·al·ism \'rēj-nə-,li-zəm, 'rē-jə-n°l-,i-\ *noun* (1881) **1 a :** consciousness of and loyalty to a distinct region with a homogeneous population **b :** development of a political or social system based on one or more such areas **2 :** emphasis on regional locale and characteristics in art or literature **3 :** a characteristic feature (as of speech) of a geographic area — **re·gion·al·ist** \-list, -ist\ *noun or adjective* — **re·gion·al·is·tic** \,rēj-nə-'lis-tik, ,rē-jə-n°l-'is-\ *adjective*

re·gion·al·ize \'rēj-nə-,līz, 'rē-jə-n°l-,īz\ *transitive verb* **-ized; -iz·ing** (1921) **:** to divide into regions or administrative districts **:** arrange regionally

— **re·gion·al·i·za·tion** \,rēj-nə-lə-'zā-shən, ,rē-jə-n°l-ə-\ *noun*

re·gion·al·ly \'rēj-nə-lē, 'rē-jə-n°l-ē\ *adverb* (1879) **:** on a regional basis

re·gis·seur *or* **ré·gis·seur** \,rā-zhi-'sər\ *noun* [French *régisseur,* from *régir* to direct, from Latin *regere* to rule] (1828) **:** a director responsible for staging a theatrical work (as a ballet)

¹**reg·is·ter** \'re-jə-stər\ *noun* [Middle English *registre,* from Middle French, from Medieval Latin *registrum,* alteration of Late Latin *regesta,* plural, register, from Latin, neuter plural of *regestus,* past participle of *regerere* to bring back, pile up, collect, from *re-* + *gerere* to bear] (14th century) **1 :** a written record containing regular entries of items or details **2 a :** a book or system of public records **b :** a roster of qualified or available individuals ⟨a civil service *register*⟩ **3 :** an entry in a register **4 a :** a set of organ pipes of like quality **:** STOP **b** (1) **:** the range of a human voice or a musical instrument (2) **:** a portion of such a range similarly produced or of the same quality **c :** any of the varieties of a language that a speaker uses in a particular social context **5 a :** a device regulating admission of air to fuel **b :** a grille often with shutters for admitting heated air or for ventilation **6 :** REGISTRATION, REGISTRY **7 a :** an automatic device registering a number or a quantity **b :** a number or quantity so registered **8 :** a condition of correct alignment or proper relative position **9 :** a device (as in a computer) for storing small amounts of data; *especially* **:** one in which data can be both stored and operated on

²**register** *verb* **reg·is·tered; reg·is·ter·ing** \-st(ə-)riŋ\ (14th century) *transitive verb* **1 a :** to make or secure official entry of in a register **b :** to enroll formally especially as a voter or student **c :** to record automatically **:** INDICATE **d :** to make a record of **:** NOTE **e :** PERCEIVE; *also* **:** COMPREHEND **2 :** to make or adjust so as to correspond exactly **3 :** to secure special protection for (a piece of mail) by prepayment of a fee **4 :** to convey an impression of **:** EXPRESS **5 :** ACHIEVE ⟨*registered* an impressive victory⟩ *intransitive verb* **1 a :** to enroll one's name in a register ⟨*registered* at the hotel⟩ **b :** to enroll one's name officially as a prerequisite for voting **c :** to enroll formally as a student **2 a :** to correspond exactly **b :** to be in correct alignment or register **3 :** to make or convey an impression

³**register** *noun* [probably alteration of Middle English *registrer*] (circa 1532) **:** REGISTRAR

registered *adjective* (1861) **1 a :** having the owner's name entered in a register ⟨*registered* security⟩ **b :** recorded as the owner of a security **2 :** recorded on the basis of pedigree or breed characteristics in the studbook of a breed association **3 :** qualified formally or officially

registered mail *noun* (1886) **:** mail recorded in the post office of mailing and at each successive point of transmission and guaranteed special care in delivery

registered nurse *noun* (1896) **:** a graduate trained nurse who has been licensed by a state authority after qualifying for registration

register ton *noun* (circa 1909) **:** TON 1a

reg·is·tra·ble \'re-jə-strə-bəl\ *also* **reg·is·ter·able** \-st(ə-)rə-bəl\ *adjective* (1765)

: capable of being registered

reg·is·trant \'re-jə-strənt\ *noun* (circa 1890) **:** one that registers or is registered

reg·is·trar \'re-jə-,strär\ *noun* [alteration of Middle English *registrer,* from Middle French *registreur,* from *registrer* to register, from Medieval Latin *registrare,* from *registrum*] (1675) **:** an official recorder or keeper of records: as **a :** an officer of an educational institution responsible for registering students, keeping academic records, and corresponding with applicants and evaluating their credentials **b :** an admitting officer at a hospital **c** *chiefly British* **:** RESIDENT 3

reg·is·tra·tion \,re-jə-'strā-shən\ *noun* (circa 1566) **1 :** the act of registering **2 :** an entry in a register **3 :** the number of individuals registered **:** ENROLLMENT **4 a :** the art or act of selecting and adjusting pipe organ stops **b :** the combination of stops selected for performing a particular organ work **5 :** a document certifying an act of registering

reg·is·try \'re-jə-strē\ *noun, plural* **-tries** (1589) **1 :** REGISTRATION, ENROLLMENT **2 :** the nationality of a ship according to its entry in a register **:** FLAG **3 :** a place of registration **4 a :** an official record book **b :** an entry in a registry

re·gius professor \'rē-j(ē-)əs-\ *noun* [New Latin, royal professor] (1621) **:** a holder of a professorship founded by royal subsidy at a British university

reg·let \'re-glət\ *noun* [French *réglet,* from Middle French *reglet* straightedge, from *regle* rule, from Latin *regula* — more at RULE] (1664) **1 :** a flat narrow architectural molding **2 :** a strip of wood used like a lead between lines of type

reg·nal \'reg-n°l\ *adjective* [Medieval Latin *regnalis,* from Latin *regnum* reign — more at REIGN] (1612) **:** of or relating to a king or his reign; *specifically* **:** calculated from a monarch's accession to the throne ⟨in his eighth *regnal* year⟩

reg·nant \'reg-nənt\ *adjective* [Latin *regnant-, regnans,* present participle of *regnare* to reign, from *regnum*] (1600) **1 :** exercising rule **:** REIGNING **2 a :** having the chief power **:** DOMINANT **b :** of common or widespread occurrence

reg·num \'reg-nəm\ *noun, plural* **reg·na** \-nə\ [Latin] (circa 1890) **:** KINGDOM

reg·o·lith \'re-gə-,lith\ *noun* [Greek *rhēgos* blanket + English *-lith;* akin to Greek *rhezein* to dye — more at RAGA] (1897) **:** unconsolidated residual or transported material that overlies the solid rock on the earth, moon, or a planet

reg·o·sol \'re-gə-,säl, -,sȯl\ *noun* [*rego-* (as in *regolith*) + Latin *solum* soil — more at SOLE] (1949) **:** any of a group of azonal soils consisting chiefly of imperfectly consolidated material and having no clear-cut and specific morphology

re·greet \(,)rē-'grēt\ *transitive verb* (1593) *archaic* **:** to greet in return

regreets *noun plural* (1596) *obsolete* **:** GREETINGS

¹**re·gress** \'rē-,gres\ *noun* [Middle English, from Latin *regressus,* from *regredi* to go back, from *re-* + *gradi* to go — more at GRADE] (14th century)

1 a : an act or the privilege of going or coming back **b :** REENTRY 1
2 : movement backward to a previous and especially worse or more primitive state or condition
3 : the act of reasoning backward
²**re·gress** \ri-'gres\ (1552)
intransitive verb
1 a : to make or undergo regress **:** RETRO-GRADE **b :** to be subject to or exhibit regression
2 : to tend to approach or revert to a mean
transitive verb
: to induce a state of psychological regression in
— **re·gres·sor** \-'gre-sər\ *noun*
re·gres·sion \ri-'gre-shən\ *noun* (1597)
1 : the act or an instance of regressing
2 : a trend or shift toward a lower or less perfect state: as **a :** progressive decline of a manifestation of disease **b** (1) **:** gradual loss of differentiation and function by a body part especially as a physiological change accompanying aging (2) **:** gradual loss of memories and acquired skills **c :** reversion to an earlier mental or behavioral level **d :** a functional relationship between two or more correlated variables that is often empirically determined from data and is used especially to predict values of one variable when given values of the others ⟨the *regression* of *y* on *x* is linear⟩; *specifically* **:** a function that yields the mean value of a random variable under the condition that one or more independent variables have specified values
3 : retrograde motion
re·gres·sive \ri-'gre-siv\ *adjective* (1634)
1 : tending to regress or produce regression
2 : being, characterized by, or developing in the course of an evolutionary process involving increasing simplification of bodily structure
3 : decreasing in rate as the base increases ⟨a *regressive* tax⟩
— **re·gres·sive·ly** *adverb*
— **re·gres·sive·ness** *noun*
— **re·gres·siv·i·ty** \ˌrē-gre-'si-və-tē\ *noun*
¹**re·gret** \ri-'gret\ *verb* **re·gret·ted; re·gret·ting** [Middle English *regretten*, from Middle French *regreter*, from Old French, from *re-* + *-greter* (perhaps of Germanic origin; akin to Old Norse *grāta* to weep) — more at GREET] (14th century)
transitive verb
1 a : to mourn the loss or death of **b :** to miss very much
2 : to be very sorry for ⟨*regrets* his mistakes⟩
intransitive verb
: to experience regret
— **re·gret·ter** *noun*
²**regret** *noun* (1590)
1 : sorrow aroused by circumstances beyond one's control or power to repair
2 a : an expression of distressing emotion (as sorrow or disappointment) **b** *plural* **:** a note politely declining an invitation
synonym see SORROW
— **re·gret·ful** \-'gret-fəl\ *adjective*
— **re·gret·ful·ness** *noun*
re·gret·ful·ly \ri-'gret-fə-lē\ *adverb* (1682)
1 : with regret
2 : it is to be regretted
re·gret·ta·ble \ri-'gre-tə-bəl\ *adjective* (1603)
: deserving regret
re·gret·ta·bly \-blē\ *adverb* (1866)
1 : to a regrettable extent ⟨a *regrettably* steep decline in wages⟩
2 : it is to be regretted ⟨*regrettably*, they could not attend⟩
re·group \(ˌ)rē-'grüp\ (1885)
transitive verb
: to form into a new grouping ⟨in order to subtract 129 from 531 *regroup* 531 into 5 hundreds, 2 tens, and 11 ones⟩ ⟨*regroup* military forces⟩
intransitive verb

1 : to reorganize (as after a setback) for renewed activity
2 : to alter the tactical formation of a military force
re·grow \(ˌ)rē-'grō\ *verb* **-grew** \-'grü\; **-grown** \-'grōn\; **-grow·ing** (1872)
transitive verb
: to grow (as a missing part) anew
intransitive verb
: to continue growth after interruption or injury
¹**reg·u·lar** \'re-gyə-lər, 're-g(ə-)lər\ *adjective* [Middle English *reguler*, from Middle French, from Late Latin *regularis* regular, from Latin, of a bar, from *regula* rule — more at RULE] (14th century)
1 : belonging to a religious order
2 a : formed, built, arranged, or ordered according to some established rule, law, principle, or type **b** (1) **:** both equilateral and equiangular ⟨a *regular* polygon⟩ (2) **:** having faces that are congruent regular polygons and all the polyhedral angles congruent ⟨a *regular* polyhedron⟩ **c** *of a flower* **:** having the arrangement of floral parts exhibiting radial symmetry with members of the same whorl similar in form
3 a : ORDERLY, METHODICAL ⟨*regular* habits⟩ **b :** recurring, attending, or functioning at fixed or uniform intervals ⟨a *regular* income⟩ ⟨a *regular* churchgoer⟩
4 a : constituted, conducted, or done in conformity with established or prescribed usages, rules, or discipline **b :** NORMAL, STANDARD: as (1) **:** ABSOLUTE, COMPLETE ⟨a *regular* fool⟩ ⟨the office seemed like a *regular* madhouse⟩ (2) **:** thinking or behaving in an acceptable, normal, or agreeable manner ⟨was a *regular* guy⟩ **c** (1) **:** conforming to the normal or usual manner of inflection (2) **:** WEAK 7 **d** *of a postage stamp* **:** issued in large numbers over a long period for general use in prepayment of postage
5 : of, relating to, or constituting the permanent standing military force of a state ⟨*regular* army⟩ ⟨*regular* soldiers⟩ ☆
²**regular** *noun* (15th century)
1 : one who is regular: as **a :** one of the regular clergy **b :** a soldier in a regular army **c :** one who can be trusted or depended on ⟨a party *regular*⟩ **d :** a player on an athletic team who usually starts every game **e :** one who is usually present or participating; *especially* **:** a long-standing regular customer
2 : something of average or medium size; *especially* **:** a clothing size designed to fit a person of average height
reg·u·lar·i·ty \ˌre-gyə-'lar-ə-tē\ *noun, plural* **-ties** (1603)
1 : the quality or state of being regular
2 : something that is regular
reg·u·lar·ize \'re-gyə-lə-ˌrīz\ *transitive verb* **-ized; -iz·ing** (1833)
: to make regular by conformance to law, rules, or custom
— **reg·u·lar·i·za·tion** \ˌre-gyə-lə-rə-'zā-shən\ *noun*
reg·u·lar·ly \'re-gyə-lər-lē, 're-gyə(r)-lē\ *adverb* (14th century)
1 : in a regular manner
2 : on a regular basis **:** at regular intervals
regular solid *noun* (1841)
: any of the five possible regular polyhedrons that include the regular forms of the tetrahedron, hexahedron, octahedron, dodecahedron, and icosahedron
reg·u·late \'re-gyə-ˌlāt\ *transitive verb* **-lat·ed; -lat·ing** [Middle English, from Late Latin *regulatus*, past participle of *regulare*, from Latin *regula* rule] (15th century)
1 a : to govern or direct according to rule **b** (1) **:** to bring under the control of law or constituted authority (2) **:** to make regulations for or concerning ⟨*regulate* the industries of a country⟩

2 : to bring order, method, or uniformity to ⟨*regulate* one's habits⟩
3 : to fix or adjust the time, amount, degree, or rate of ⟨*regulate* the pressure of a tire⟩
— **reg·u·la·tive** \-ˌlā-tiv\ *adjective*
— **reg·u·la·to·ry** \-lə-ˌtōr-ē, -ˌtòr-\ *adjective*
¹**reg·u·la·tion** \ˌre-gyə-'lā-shən, ˌre-gə-\ *noun* (1665)
1 : the act of regulating **:** the state of being regulated
2 a : an authoritative rule dealing with details or procedure ⟨safety *regulations*⟩ **b :** a rule or order issued by an executive authority or regulatory agency of a government and having the force of law
3 a : the process of redistributing material (as in an embryo) to restore a damaged or lost part independent of new tissue growth **b :** the mechanism by which an early embryo maintains normal development
synonym see LAW
²**regulation** *adjective* (circa 1839)
: conforming to regulations **:** OFFICIAL
reg·u·la·tor \'re-gyə-ˌlā-tər\ *noun* (1655)
1 : one that regulates
2 : REGULATORY GENE
regulatory gene *or* **regulator gene** *noun* (1961)
: a gene that regulates the expression of one or more structural genes by controlling the production of a protein (as a genetic repressor) which regulates their rate of transcription
reg·u·lus \'re-gyə-ləs\ *noun* [New Latin, from Latin, petty king, from *reg-, rex* king — more at ROYAL]
1 *capitalized* **:** a first-magnitude star in the constellation Leo
2 [Medieval Latin, metallic antimony, from Latin] **:** the more or less impure mass of metal formed beneath the slag in smelting and reducing ores
re·gur·gi·tate \(ˌ)rē-'gər-jə-ˌtāt\ *verb* **-tat·ed; -tat·ing** [Medieval Latin *regurgitatus*, past participle of *regurgitare*, from Latin *re-* + Late Latin *gurgitare* to engulf, from Latin *gurgit-, gurges* whirlpool — more at VORACIOUS] (1653)
intransitive verb
: to become thrown or poured back
transitive verb
: to throw or pour back or out from or as if from a cavity ⟨*regurgitate* food⟩ ⟨memorized facts to *regurgitate* on the exam⟩
re·gur·gi·ta·tion \(ˌ)rē-ˌgər-jə-'tā-shən\ *noun* (1601)
: an act of regurgitating: as **a :** the casting up of incompletely digested food (as by some birds in feeding their young) **b :** the backward flow of blood through a defective heart valve
re·hab \'rē-ˌhab\ *noun, often attributive* [short for *rehabilitation* or *rehabilitate*] (1941)
1 : the action or process of rehabilitating **:** REHABILITATION
2 : a rehabilitated building or dwelling
— **rehab** *transitive verb*
— **re·hab·ber** \-ˌha-bər\ *noun*

☆ **SYNONYMS**
Regular, normal, typical, natural mean being of the sort or kind that is expected as usual, ordinary, or average. REGULAR stresses conformity to a rule, standard, or pattern ⟨the club's *regular* monthly meeting⟩. NORMAL implies lack of deviation from what has been discovered or established as the most usual or expected ⟨*normal* behavior for a two-year-old⟩. TYPICAL implies showing all important traits of a type, class, or group and may suggest lack of strong individuality ⟨a *typical* small town⟩. NATURAL applies to what conforms to a thing's essential nature, function, or mode of being ⟨the *natural* love of a mother for her child⟩.

re·ha·bil·i·tant \ˌrē-ə-ˈbi-lə-tənt, ˌrē-hə-\ *noun* (1961)
: a disabled person undergoing rehabilitation

re·ha·bil·i·tate \ˌrē-ə-ˈbi-lə-ˌtāt, ˌrē-hə-\ *transitive verb* **-tat·ed; -tat·ing** [Medieval Latin *rehabilitatus,* past participle of *rehabilitare,* from Latin *re-* + Late Latin *habilitare* to habilitate] (circa 1581)
1 a : to restore to a former capacity : REINSTATE **b :** to restore to good repute : reestablish the good name of
2 a : to restore to a former state (as of efficiency, good management, or solvency) ⟨*rehabilitate* slum areas⟩ **b :** to restore or bring to a condition of health or useful and constructive activity
— **re·ha·bil·i·ta·tion** \-ˌbi-lə-ˈtā-shən\ *noun*
— **re·ha·bil·i·ta·tive** \-ˈbi-lə-ˌtā-tiv\ *adjective*
— **re·ha·bil·i·ta·tor** \-ˌtā-tər\ *noun*

¹**re·hash** \(ˌ)rē-ˈhash\ *transitive verb* (circa 1822)
1 : to talk over or discuss again
2 : to present or use again in another form without substantial change or improvement

²**re·hash** \ˈrē-ˌhash\ *noun* (1849)
1 : something that is rehashed
2 : the action or process of rehashing

re·hear \(ˌ)rē-ˈhir\ *transitive verb* **-heard** \-ˈhərd\; **-hear·ing** \-ˈhir-iŋ\ (1756)
: to hear again or anew especially judicially
rehearing *noun* (1686)
: a second or new hearing by the same tribunal

re·hears·al \ri-ˈhər-səl\ *noun* (14th century)
1 : something recounted or told again : RECITAL
2 a : a private performance or practice session preparatory to a public appearance **b :** a practice exercise : TRIAL

re·hearse \ri-ˈhərs\ *verb* **re·hearsed; re·hears·ing** [Middle English *rehersen,* from Middle French *rehercier,* literally, to harrow again, from *re-* + *hercier* to harrow, from *herce* harrow — more at HEARSE] (14th century)
transitive verb
1 a : to say again : REPEAT **b :** to recite aloud in a formal manner
2 : to present an account of : RELATE ⟨*rehearse* a familiar story⟩
3 : to recount in order : ENUMERATE ⟨*rehearsed* their demands⟩
4 a : to give a rehearsal of **b :** to train or make proficient by rehearsal
5 : to perform or practice as if in a rehearsal
intransitive verb
: to engage in a rehearsal
word history see HEARSE
— **re·hears·er** *noun*

re·house \(ˌ)rē-ˈhaúz\ *transitive verb* (1820)
: to house again or anew; *especially* : to establish in a new or different housing unit of a better quality

re·hy·drate \(ˌ)rē-ˈhī-ˌdrāt\ *transitive verb* (1943)
: to restore fluid to (something dehydrated)
— **re·hy·drat·able** \-ˌdrā-tə-bəl\ *adjective*
— **re·hy·dra·tion** \ˌrē-ˌhī-ˈdrā-shən\ *noun*

reichs·mark \ˈrīks-ˌmärk\ *noun, plural* **reichs·marks** *also* **reichsmark** [German, from *Reich* empire, kingdom + *Mark* mark] (1924)
: the German mark from 1925 to 1948

re·ifi·ca·tion \ˌrā-ə-fə-ˈkā-shən, ˌrē-\ *noun* (1846)
: the process or result of reifying

re·ify \ˈrā-ə-ˌfī, ˈrē-\ *transitive verb* **re·ified; re·ify·ing** [Latin *res* thing — more at REAL] (1854)
: to regard (something abstract) as a material or concrete thing

¹**reign** \ˈrān\ *noun* [Middle English *regne,* from Old French, from Latin *regnum,* from *reg-, rex* king — more at ROYAL] (13th century)
1 a : royal authority : SOVEREIGNTY ⟨under the reign of the Stuart kings⟩ **b :** the dominion, sway, or influence of one resembling a monarch ⟨the *reign* of the Puritan ministers⟩
2 : the time during which one (as a sovereign) reigns

²**reign** *intransitive verb* (14th century)
1 a : to possess or exercise sovereign power : RULE **b :** to hold office as chief of state although possessing little governing power ⟨in England the sovereign *reigns* but does not rule⟩
2 : to exercise authority in the manner of a monarch
3 : to be predominant or prevalent ⟨chaos *reigned* in the classroom⟩

reign of terror [*Reign of Terror,* a period of the French Revolution that was conspicuous for mass executions of political suspects] (1801)
: a state or a period of time marked by violence often committed by those in power that produces widespread terror

re·imag·ine \ˌrē-i-ˈma-jən\ *transitive verb* (circa 1934)
: to imagine again or anew; *especially* : to form a new conception of : RE-CREATE

re·im·burse \ˌrē-əm-ˈbərs\ *transitive verb* **-bursed; -burs·ing** [*re-* + obsolete English *imburse* to put in the pocket, pay, from Medieval Latin *imbursare,* from Latin *in-* in- + Medieval Latin *bursa* purse — more at PURSE] (1611)
1 : to pay back to someone : REPAY ⟨*reimburse* travel expenses⟩
2 : to make restoration or payment of an equivalent to ⟨*reimburse* him for his traveling expenses⟩
synonym see PAY
— **re·im·burs·able** \-ˈbər-sə-bəl\ *adjective*
— **re·im·burse·ment** \-ˈbərs-mənt\ *noun*

re·im·pres·sion \ˌrē-əm-ˈpre-shən\ *noun* (1684)
: REPRINT a

¹**rein** \ˈrān\ *noun* [Middle English *reine,* from Middle French *rene,* from (assumed) Vulgar Latin *retina,* from Latin *retinēre* to restrain — more at RETAIN] (14th century)
1 : a strap fastened to a bit by which a rider or driver controls an animal — usually used in plural
2 a : a restraining influence : CHECK ⟨kept a tight *rein* on the proceedings⟩ **b :** controlling or guiding power — usually used in plural ⟨the *reins* of government⟩
3 : opportunity for unhampered activity or use ⟨gave full *rein* to her imagination⟩

²**rein** (15th century)
transitive verb
1 : to control or direct with or as if with reins
2 : to check or stop by or as if by a pull at the reins ⟨*reined* in her horse⟩ ⟨couldn't *rein* his impatience⟩
intransitive verb
1 *archaic* : to submit to the use of reins
2 : to stop or slow up one's horse or oneself by or as if by pulling the reins

re·in·car·nate \ˌrē-ən-ˈkär-ˌnāt, (ˌ)rē-ˈin-\ *transitive verb* (1858)
: to incarnate again

re·in·car·na·tion \ˌrē-(ˌ)in-(ˌ)kär-ˈnā-shən\ *noun* (1858)
1 a : the action of reincarnating : the state of being reincarnated **b :** rebirth in new bodies or forms of life; *especially* : a rebirth of a soul in a new human body
2 : a fresh embodiment

rein·deer \ˈrān-ˌdir\ *noun* [Middle English *reindere,* from Old Norse *hreinn* reindeer + Middle English *deer* animal, deer] (14th century)
: CARIBOU — used especially for the Old World caribou

reindeer moss *noun* (circa 1753)
: a gray, erect, tufted, and much-branched lichen (*Cladonia rangiferina*) that forms extensive patches in arctic and north-temperate regions, constitutes a large part of the food of caribou, and is sometimes eaten by humans — called also *reindeer lichen*

re·in·dus·tri·al·i·za·tion \ˌrē-in-ˌdəs-trē-ə-lə-ˈzā-shən\ *noun* (1979)
: a policy of stimulating economic growth especially through government aid to revitalize and modernize aging industries and encourage growth of new ones
— **re·in·dus·tri·al·ize** \-ˈdəs-trē-ə-ˌlīz\ *verb*

re·in·fec·tion \ˌrē-ən-ˈfek-shən\ *noun* (1882)
: infection following recovery from or superimposed on infection of the same type

re·in·force \ˌrē-ən-ˈfōrs, -ˈfòrs\ *verb* [*re-* + *inforce,* alteration of *enforce*] (1600)
transitive verb
1 : to strengthen or increase by fresh additions ⟨*reinforce* our troops⟩ ⟨were *reinforcing* their pitching staff⟩
2 : to strengthen by additional assistance, material, or support : make stronger or more pronounced ⟨*reinforce* levees⟩ ⟨*reinforce* the elbows of a jacket⟩ ⟨*reinforce* ideas⟩
3 : to stimulate (as an experimental animal or a student) with a reinforcer; *also* : to encourage (a response) with a reinforcer
intransitive verb
: to seek or get reinforcements
— **re·in·force·able** \-ˈfōr-sə-bəl, -ˈfòr-\ *adjective*

reinforced concrete *noun* (1902)
: concrete in which metal (as steel) is embedded so that the two materials act together in resisting forces

re·in·force·ment \ˌrē-ən-ˈfōrs-mənt, -ˈfòrs-\ *noun* (1617)
1 : the action of reinforcing : the state of being reinforced
2 : something that reinforces

re·in·forc·er \-ˈfōr-sər, -ˈfòr-\ *noun* (1955)
: a stimulus (as a reward or the removal of an electric shock) that increases the probability of a desired response in operant conditioning by being applied or effected following the desired response

reins \ˈrānz\ *noun plural* [Middle English, from Middle French & Latin; Middle French, from Latin *renes*] (14th century)
1 a : KIDNEYS **b :** the region of the kidneys : LOINS
2 : the seat of the feelings or passions

reins·man \ˈrānz-mən\ *noun* (1855)
: a skilled driver or rider of horses

re·in·state \ˌrē-ən-ˈstāt\ *transitive verb* **-stat·ed; -stat·ing** (1628)
1 : to place again (as in possession or in a former position)
2 : to restore to a previous effective state
— **re·in·state·ment** \-ˈstāt-mənt\ *noun*

re·in·sur·ance \ˌrē-ən-ˈshùr-ən(t)s *also* (ˌ)rē-ˈin-\ *noun* (1755)
: insurance by another insurer of all or a part of a risk previously assumed by an insurance company

re·in·sure \ˌrē-ən-ˈshùr\ (1755)
transitive verb
1 : to insure again by transferring to another insurance company all or a part of a liability assumed
2 : to insure again by assuming all or a part of the liability of an insurance company already covering a risk
intransitive verb
: to provide increased insurance
— **re·in·sur·er** *noun*

re·in·te·grate \(ˌ)rē-ˈin-tə-ˌgrāt\ *transitive verb* [Medieval Latin *reintegratus,* past participle of *reintegrare* to renew, reinstate, from Latin *re-* + *integrare* to integrate] (1626)

: to integrate again into an entity : restore to unity

— **re·in·te·gra·tion** \(,)rē-,in-tə-'grā-shən\ noun

— **re·in·te·gra·tive** \(,)rē-'in-tə-,grā-tiv\ adjective

re·in·ter·pret \,rē-ən-'tər-prət, -pət\ transitive verb (1611)
: to interpret again; specifically : to give a new or different interpretation to

— **re·in·ter·pre·ta·tion** \-,tər-prə-'tā-shən, -pə-\ noun

re·in·vent \,rē-ən-'vent\ transitive verb (1686)
1 : to make as if for the first time something already invented ⟨reinvent the wheel⟩
2 : to remake or redo completely
3 : to bring into use again

— **re·in·ven·tion** \-'ven(t)-shən\ noun

re·in·vest \,rē-ən-'vest\ transitive verb (1611)
1 : to invest again or anew
2 a : to invest (as income from investments) in additional securities **b** : to invest (as earnings) in a business rather than distribute as dividends or profits

re·in·vest·ment \-'ves(t)-mənt\ noun (1611)
1 : the action of reinvesting : the state of being reinvested
2 : a second or repeated investment

reis plural of REAL

re·is·sue \(,)rē-'i-(,)shü, chiefly British -'is-(,)yü\ (circa 1618)
intransitive verb
: to come forth again
transitive verb
: to issue again; especially : to cause to become available again

— **reissue** noun

re·it·er·ate \rē-'i-tə-,rāt\ transitive verb **-at·ed; -at·ing** [Middle English, from Latin reiteratus, past participle of reiterare to repeat, from re- + iterare to iterate] (15th century)
: to state or do over again or repeatedly sometimes with wearying effect

— **re·it·er·a·tion** \(,)rē-,i-tə-'rā-shən\ noun

— **re·it·er·a·tive** \rē-'i-tə-,rā-tiv, -t(ə-)rə-tiv\ adjective

— **re·it·er·a·tive·ly** adverb

Rei·ter's syndrome \'rī-tərz-\ noun [Hans Reiter (died 1969) German physician] (circa 1947)
: a disease that is usually initiated by infection in genetically predisposed individuals and is characterized usually by recurrence of arthritis, conjunctivitis, and urethritis — called also Reiter's disease

reive \'rēv\ verb **reived; reiv·ing** [Middle English (Scots) reifen, from Old English rēafian to rob — more at REAVE] (before 12th century)
Scottish : RAID

— **reiv·er** noun, Scottish

¹re·ject \ri-'jekt\ transitive verb [Middle English, from Latin rejectus, past participle of reicere, from re- + jacere to throw — more at JET] (15th century)
1 a : to refuse to accept, consider, submit to, take for some purpose, or use ⟨rejected the suggestion⟩ ⟨reject a manuscript⟩ **b** : to refuse to hear, receive, or admit : REBUFF, REPEL ⟨parents who reject their children⟩ **c** : to refuse as lover or spouse
2 obsolete : to cast off
3 : THROW BACK, REPULSE
4 : to spew out
5 : to subject to immunological rejection
synonym see DECLINE

— **re·ject·er** or **re·jec·tor** \-'jek-tər\ noun

— **re·ject·ing·ly** \-'tiŋ-lē\ adverb

— **re·jec·tive** \-'jek-tiv\ adjective

²re·ject \'rē-,jekt\ noun (circa 1555)
: a rejected person or thing; especially : one rejected as not wanted, unsatisfactory, or not fulfilling standard requirements

re·ject·ee \ri-,jek-'tē, ,rē-\ noun (1941)
: one that is rejected; especially : a person rejected as unfit for military service

re·jec·tion \ri-'jek-shən\ noun (circa 1552)
1 a : the action of rejecting : the state of being rejected **b** : the immunological process of sloughing off foreign tissue or an organ (as a transplant) by the recipient organism
2 : something rejected

rejection slip noun (1906)
: a printed slip enclosed with a rejected manuscript returned by an editor to an author

re·jig·ger \(,)rē-'ji-gər\ transitive verb [re- + ³jigger] (1942)
: ALTER, REARRANGE

re·joice \ri-'jȯis\ verb **re·joiced; re·joic·ing** [Middle English, from Middle French rejoiss-, stem of rejoir, from re- + joir to rejoice, from Latin gaudēre — more at JOY] (14th century)
transitive verb
: to give joy to : GLADDEN
intransitive verb
: to feel joy or great delight

— **re·joic·er** noun

— **re·joic·ing·ly** \-'jȯi-siŋ-lē\ adverb

— **rejoice in** : HAVE, POSSESS

rejoicing noun (14th century)
1 : the action of one that rejoices
2 : an instance, occasion, or expression of joy : FESTIVITY

re·join \ri-'jȯin, transitive verb 1 is (,)rē-\ verb [Middle English, from Middle French rejoin-, stem of rejoindre, from re- + Old French joindre to join — more at JOIN] (15th century)
intransitive verb
1 : to join again
2 : to say often sharply or critically in response especially as a reply to a reply
synonym see ANSWER

re·join·der \ri-'jȯin-dər\ noun [Middle English rejoiner, from Middle French rejoindre to rejoin] (15th century)
1 : the defendant's answer to the plaintiff's replication
2 : REPLY; specifically : an answer to a reply

re·ju·ve·nate \ri-'jü-və-,nāt\ verb **-nat·ed; -nat·ing** [re- + Latin juvenis young — more at YOUNG] (1807)
transitive verb
1 a : to make young or youthful again : give new vigor to **b** : to restore to an original or new state ⟨rejuvenate old cars⟩
2 a : to stimulate (a stream) to renewed erosive activity especially by uplift **b** : to develop youthful features of topography in
intransitive verb
: to cause or undergo rejuvenescence
synonym see RENEW

— **re·ju·ve·na·tion** \ri-,jü-və-'nā-shən, ,rē-\ noun

— **re·ju·ve·na·tor** \ri-'jü-və-,nā-tər\ noun

re·ju·ve·nesce \,ri-,jü-və-'ne-sən(t)s, ,rē-\ noun [Medieval Latin rejuvenescere to become young again, from Latin re- + juvenescere to become young, from juvenis] (circa 1631)
: a renewal of youthfulness or vigor : REJUVENATION

— **re·ju·ve·nes·cent** \-s°nt\ adjective

¹re·lapse \ri-'laps, 'rē-,\ noun [Middle English, from Medieval Latin relapsus, from Latin relabi to slide back, from re- + labi to slide — more at SLEEP] (15th century)
1 : the act or an instance of backsliding, worsening, or subsiding
2 : a recurrence of symptoms of a disease after a period of improvement

²re·lapse \ri-'laps\ intransitive verb **re·lapsed; re·laps·ing** (1568)
1 : to slip or fall back into a former worse state
2 : SINK, SUBSIDE ⟨relapse into deep thought⟩

— **re·laps·er** noun

relapsing fever noun (1849)
: a variable acute epidemic disease that is marked by recurring high fever usually lasting 3 to 7 days and is caused by a spirochete (genus Borrelia) transmitted by the bites of lice and ticks

re·late \ri-'lāt\ verb **re·lat·ed; re·lat·ing** [Latin relatus (past participle of referre to carry back), from re- + latus, past participle of ferre to carry — more at TOLERATE, BEAR] (1530)
transitive verb
1 : to give an account of : TELL
2 : to show or establish logical or causal connection between ⟨seeks to relate crime to poverty⟩
intransitive verb
1 : to apply or take effect retroactively
2 : to have relationship or connection ⟨the readings relate to his lectures⟩
3 : to have or establish a relationship : INTERACT ⟨the way a child relates to a teacher⟩
4 : to respond especially favorably ⟨can't relate to that kind of music⟩

— **re·lat·able** \-'lā-tə-bəl\ adjective

— **re·lat·er** or **re·la·tor** \-'lā-tər\ noun

related adjective (circa 1663)
1 : connected by reason of an established or discoverable relation
2 : connected by common ancestry or sometimes by marriage
3 : having close harmonic connection — used of tones, chords, or tonalities

— **re·lat·ed·ly** adverb

— **re·lat·ed·ness** noun

re·la·tion \ri-'lā-shən\ noun [Middle English relacioun, from Middle French relation, from Latin relation-, relatio, from referre (past participle relatus) to carry back] (14th century)
1 : the act of telling or recounting : ACCOUNT
2 : an aspect or quality (as resemblance) that connects two or more things or parts as being or belonging or working together or as being of the same kind ⟨the relation of time and space⟩; specifically : a property (as one expressed by is equal to, is less than, or is the brother of) that holds between an ordered pair of objects
3 : the referring by a legal fiction of an act to a prior date as the time of its taking effect
4 a (1) : a person connected by consanguinity or affinity : RELATIVE (2) : a person legally entitled to a share of property of an intestate **b** : relationship by consanguinity or affinity : KINSHIP
5 : REFERENCE, RESPECT ⟨in relation to⟩
6 : the attitude or stance which two or more persons or groups assume toward one another ⟨race relations⟩
7 a : the state of being mutually or reciprocally interested (as in social or commercial matters) **b** plural (1) : DEALINGS, AFFAIRS ⟨foreign relations⟩ (2) : INTERCOURSE (3) : SEXUAL INTERCOURSE

re·la·tion·al \-shnəl, -shə-n°l\ adjective (1662)
1 : of or relating to kinship
2 : characterized or constituted by relations
3 : having the function chiefly of indicating a relation of syntax ⟨has is notional in he has luck, relational in he has gone⟩
4 : relating to, using, or being a method of organizing data in a database so that it is perceived by the user as a set of tables

— **re·la·tion·al·ly** adverb

relational grammar noun (1982)
: a grammar based on a theory in which grammatical relations (as subject or object) are primitives in terms of which syntactic operations are defined

re·la·tion·ship \-shən-,ship\ noun (circa 1744)
1 : the state of being related or interrelated ⟨studied the relationship between the variables⟩
2 : the relation connecting or binding participants in a relationship: as **a** : KINSHIP **b** : a specific instance or type of kinship

3 a : a state of affairs existing between those having relations or dealings ⟨had a good *relationship* with his family⟩ **b :** a romantic or passionate attachment

¹rel·a·tive \'re-lə-tiv\ *noun* (14th century)
1 : a word referring grammatically to an antecedent
2 : a thing having a relation to or connection with or necessary dependence on another thing
3 a : a person connected with another by blood or affinity **b :** an animal or plant related to another by common descent
4 : a relative term

²relative *adjective* (15th century)
1 : introducing a subordinate clause qualifying an expressed or implied antecedent ⟨*relative* pronoun⟩; *also* **:** introduced by such a connective ⟨*relative* clause⟩
2 : RELEVANT, PERTINENT ⟨matters *relative* to world peace⟩
3 : not absolute or independent **:** COMPARATIVE ⟨the *relative* isolation of life in the country⟩
4 : having the same key signature — used of major and minor keys and scales
5 : expressed as the ratio of the specified quantity (as an error in measuring) to the total magnitude (as the value of a measured quantity) or to the mean of all the quantities involved

relative humidity *noun* (1820)
: the ratio of the amount of water vapor actually present in the air to the greatest amount possible at the same temperature

rel·a·tive·ly *adverb* (1561)
: to a relative degree or extent **:** SOMEWHAT

relatively prime *adjective* (circa 1890)
of integers **:** having no common factors except +1 and −1 ⟨12 and 25 are *relatively prime*⟩

relative to *preposition* (1660)
: with regard to **:** in connection with

relative wind *noun* (circa 1918)
: the motion of the air relative to a body in it

rel·a·tiv·ism \'re-lə-ti-ˌvi-zəm\ *noun* (1865)
1 a : a theory that knowledge is relative to the limited nature of the mind and the conditions of knowing **b :** a view that ethical truths depend on the individuals and groups holding them
2 : RELATIVITY
— **rel·a·tiv·ist** \-vist\ *noun*

rel·a·tiv·is·tic \ˌre-lə-ti-'vis-tik\ *adjective* (1886)
1 : of, relating to, or characterized by relativity or relativism
2 : moving at a velocity such that there is a significant change in properties (as mass) in accordance with the theory of relativity ⟨a *relativistic* electron⟩
— **rel·a·tiv·is·ti·cal·ly** \-'vis-ti-k(ə-)lē\ *adverb*

rel·a·tiv·i·ty \ˌre-lə-'ti-və-tē\ *noun, plural* **-ties** (circa 1834)
1 a : the quality or state of being relative **b :** something that is relative
2 : the state of being dependent for existence on or determined in nature, value, or quality by relation to something else
3 a : a theory which is based on the two postulates (1) that the speed of light in a vacuum is constant and independent of the source or observer and (2) that the mathematical forms of the laws of physics are invariant in all inertial systems and which leads to the assertion of the equivalence of mass and energy and of change in mass, dimension, and time with increased velocity — called also *special relativity, special theory of relativity* **b :** an extension of the theory to include gravitation and related acceleration phenomena — called also *general relativity, general theory of relativity*
4 : RELATIVISM 1b

rel·a·tiv·ize \'re-lə-tə-ˌvīz\ *transitive verb* **-ized; -iz·ing** (1935)
: to treat or describe as relative

re·lax \ri-'laks\ *verb* [Middle English, from Latin *relaxare*, from *re-* + *laxare* to loosen, from *laxus* loose — more at SLACK] (15th century)
transitive verb
1 : to make less tense or rigid **:** SLACKEN ⟨*relaxed* his grip⟩
2 : to make less severe or stringent **:** MODIFY ⟨*relax* immigration laws⟩
3 : to make soft or enervated
4 : to relieve from nervous tension
intransitive verb
1 : to become lax, weak, or loose **:** REST
2 : to become less intense or severe ⟨hoped the committee would *relax* in its opposition⟩
3 *of a muscle or muscle fiber* **:** to become inactive and lengthen
4 : to cast off social restraint, nervous tension, or anxiety ⟨couldn't *relax* in crowds⟩
5 : to seek rest or recreation ⟨*relax* at the seashore⟩
6 : to relieve constipation
7 : to attain equilibrium following the abrupt removal of some influence (as light, high temperature, or stress)
— **re·lax·er** *noun*

¹re·lax·ant \ri-'lak-sənt\ *adjective* (1771)
: of, relating to, or producing relaxation ⟨an anesthetic and *relaxant* agent⟩

²relaxant *noun* (circa 1847)
: a substance (as a drug) that relaxes; *specifically* **:** one that relieves muscular tension

re·lax·a·tion \ˌrē-ˌlak-'sā-shən, ri-ˌlak-, *especially British* ˌre-lək-\ *noun* (1548)
1 : the act of relaxing or state of being relaxed
2 : a relaxing or recreative state, activity, or pastime **:** DIVERSION
3 : the lengthening that characterizes inactive muscle fibers or muscles

re·laxed \ri-'lakst\ *adjective* (1623)
1 : freed from or lacking in precision or stringency
2 : set or being at rest or at ease
3 : easy of manner **:** INFORMAL
— **re·laxed·ly** \-'lak-səd-lē, -'lakst-lē\ *adverb*
— **re·laxed·ness** \-'lak-səd-nəs, -'laks(t)-nəs\ *noun*

re·lax·in \ri-'lak-sən\ *noun* (1930)
: a sex hormone of the corpus luteum that facilitates birth by causing relaxation of the pelvic ligaments

¹re·lay \'rē-ˌlā\ *noun* (1659)
1 a : a supply (as of horses) arranged beforehand for successive relief **b :** a number of persons who relieve others in some work ⟨worked in *relays* around the clock⟩
2 a : a race between teams in which each team member successively covers a specified portion of the course **b :** one of the divisions of a relay
3 : an electromagnetic device for remote or automatic control that is actuated by variation in conditions of an electric circuit and that operates in turn other devices (as switches) in the same or a different circuit
4 : SERVOMOTOR
5 : the act of passing along (as a message or ball) by stages; *also* **:** one of such stages

²re·lay \'rē-ˌlā, ri-'lā\ *transitive verb* **re·layed; re·lay·ing** [Middle English, to hunt with relays, from Middle French *relaier*, from Old French, from *re-* + *laier* to leave — more at DELAY] (1788)
1 a : to place or dispose in relays **b :** to provide with relays
2 : to pass along by relays ⟨news was *relayed* to distant points⟩
3 : to control or operate by a relay

³re·lay \ˌ(ˌ)rē-'lā\ *transitive verb* **-laid** \-'lād\; **-lay·ing** [*re-* + ¹*lay*] (1757)
: to lay again ⟨*relay* track⟩

¹re·lease \ri-'lēs\ *transitive verb* **re·leased; re·leas·ing** [Middle English *relesen*, from Middle French *relessier*, from Latin *relaxare* to relax] (14th century)

1 : to set free from restraint, confinement, or servitude ⟨*release* hostages⟩ ⟨*release* pent-up emotions⟩ ⟨*release* the brakes⟩; *also* **:** to let go **:** DISMISS ⟨*released* from her job⟩
2 : to relieve from something that confines, burdens, or oppresses ⟨was *released* from her promise⟩
3 : to give up in favor of another **:** RELINQUISH ⟨*release* a claim to property⟩
4 : to give permission for publication, performance, exhibition, or sale of; *also* **:** to make available to the public ⟨the commission *released* its findings⟩ ⟨*release* a new movie⟩
synonym see FREE
— **re·leas·able** \-'lē-sə-bəl\ *adjective*

²release *noun* (14th century)
1 : relief or deliverance from sorrow, suffering, or trouble
2 a : discharge from obligation or responsibility **b** (1) **:** relinquishment of a right or claim (2) **:** an act by which a legal right is discharged; *specifically* **:** a conveyance of a right in lands or tenements to another having an estate in possession
3 a : the act or an instance of liberating or freeing (as from restraint) **b :** the act or manner of concluding a musical tone or phrase **c :** the act or manner of ending a sound **:** the movement of one or more vocal organs in quitting the position for a speech sound
4 : an instrument effecting a legal release
5 : the state of being freed
6 : a device adapted to hold or release a mechanism as required
7 a : the act of permitting performance or publication; *also* **:** PERFORMANCE, PUBLICATION ⟨became a best-seller on its *release*⟩ **b :** the matter released; *especially* **:** a statement prepared for the press

re–lease \ˌ(ˌ)rē-'lēs\ *transitive verb* (1828)
: to lease again

released time *noun* (1941)
: time off from regularly scheduled activities (as school) given to take part in some other specified activity

release print *noun* (1937)
: a motion-picture film released for public showing

re·leas·er \ri-'lē-sər\ *noun* (15th century)
: one that releases; *specifically* **:** a stimulus that serves as the initiator of complex reflex behavior

rel·e·gate \'re-lə-ˌgāt\ *transitive verb* **-gat·ed; -gat·ing** [Latin *relegatus*, past participle of *relegare*, from *re-* + *legare* to send with a commission — more at LEGATE] (1599)
1 : to send into exile **:** BANISH
2 : ASSIGN: as **a :** to assign to a place of insignificance or of oblivion **:** put out of sight or mind **b :** to assign to an appropriate place or situation on the basis of classification or appraisal **c :** to submit to someone or something for appropriate action **:** DELEGATE
synonym see COMMIT
— **rel·e·ga·tion** \ˌre-lə-'gā-shən\ *noun*

re·lent \ri-'lent\ *verb* [Middle English, to melt, soften, from Anglo-French *relenter*, from *re-* + Latin *lentare* to bend, from *lentus* soft, pliant, slow — more at LITHE] (1526)
intransitive verb
1 a : to become less severe, harsh, or strict usually from reasons of humanity **b :** to cease resistance **:** GIVE IN
2 : LET UP, SLACKEN
transitive verb
obsolete **:** SOFTEN, MOLLIFY
synonym see YIELD

re·lent·less \-ləs\ *adjective* (1592)

\ə\ abut \ᵊ\ kitten \ər\ further \a\ ash \ā\ ace
\ä\ mop, mar \au̇\ out \ch\ chin \e\ bet \ē\ easy
\g\ go \i\ hit \ī\ ice \j\ job \ŋ\ sing \ō\ go
\ȯ\ law \ȯi\ boy \th\ thin \t͟h\ the \ü\ loot \u̇\ foot
\y\ yet \zh\ vision *see also* Guide to Pronunciation

: showing or promising no abatement of severity, intensity, strength, or pace : UNRELENTING ⟨*relentless* pressure⟩ ⟨a *relentless* campaign⟩
— **re·lent·less·ly** *adverb*
— **re·lent·less·ness** *noun*

rel·e·vance \'re-lə-vən(t)s\ *noun* (1733)
1 a : relation to the matter at hand **b :** practical and especially social applicability : PERTINENCE ⟨giving *relevance* to college courses⟩
2 : the ability (as of an information retrieval system) to retrieve material that satisfies the needs of the user

rel·e·van·cy \-vən(t)-sē\ *noun, plural* **-cies** (1561)
: RELEVANCE; *also* : something relevant

rel·e·vant \'re-lə-vənt\ *adjective* [Medieval Latin *relevant-, relevans*, from Latin, present participle of *relevare* to raise up — more at RELIEVE] (1560)
1 a : having significant and demonstrable bearing on the matter at hand **b :** affording evidence tending to prove or disprove the matter at issue or under discussion ⟨*relevant* testimony⟩ **c :** having social relevance
2 : PROPORTIONAL, RELATIVE ☆
— **rel·e·vant·ly** *adverb*

re·li·abil·i·ty \ri-,lī-ə-'bi-lə-tē\ *noun* (1816)
1 : the quality or state of being reliable
2 : the extent to which an experiment, test, or measuring procedure yields the same results on repeated trials

¹re·li·able \ri-'lī-ə-bəl\ *adjective* (1569)
1 : suitable or fit to be relied on : DEPENDABLE
2 : giving the same result on successive trials
— **re·li·able·ness** *noun*
— **re·li·ably** \-blē\ *adverb*

²reliable *noun* (1890)
: one that is reliable

re·li·ance \ri-'lī-ən(t)s\ *noun* (1607)
1 : the act of relying : the state of being reliant
2 : something or someone relied on

re·li·ant \-ənt\ *adjective* (1859)
: having reliance on something or someone : DEPENDENT
— **re·li·ant·ly** *adverb*

rel·ic \'re-lik\ *noun* [Middle English *relik*, from Old French *relique*, from Medieval Latin *reliquia*, from Late Latin *reliquiae*, plural, remains of a martyr, from Latin, remains, from *relinquere* to leave behind — more at RELINQUISH] (13th century)
1 a : an object esteemed and venerated because of association with a saint or martyr **b :** SOUVENIR, MEMENTO
2 *plural* **:** REMAINS, CORPSE
3 : a survivor or remnant left after decay, disintegration, or disappearance
4 : a trace of some past or outmoded practice, custom, or belief

¹rel·ict \'re-likt\ *noun* [in sense 1, from Middle English *relicte*, from Late Latin *relicta*, from Latin, feminine of *relictus*, past participle of *relinquere*; in senses 2 & 3, from *relict* residual, adjective, from Latin *relictus*] (15th century)
1 : WIDOW
2 : a persistent remnant of an otherwise extinct flora or fauna or kind of organism
3 a : a relief feature or rock remaining after other parts have disappeared **b :** something left unchanged

²relict *adjective* (15th century)
: of, relating to, or being a relict ⟨*relict* populations⟩

re·lic·tion \ri-'lik-shən\ *noun* [Latin *reliction-, relictio* act of leaving behind, from *relinquere*] (circa 1676)
1 : the gradual recession of water leaving land permanently uncovered
2 : land uncovered by reliction

¹re·lief \ri-'lēf\ *noun* [Middle English, from Middle French, from Old French, from *relever* to relieve] (14th century)
1 : a payment made by a feudal tenant to a lord on succeeding to an inherited estate

2 a : removal or lightening of something oppressive, painful, or distressing **b :** WELFARE
2a **c :** military assistance to an endangered post or force **d :** means of breaking or avoiding monotony or boredom : DIVERSION
3 : release from a post or from the performance of duty

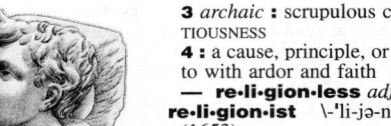
relief 6b

4 : one that takes the place of another on duty
5 : legal remedy or redress
6 [French] **a :** a mode of sculpture in which forms and figures are distinguished from a surrounding plane surface **b :** sculpture or a sculptural form executed in this mode **c :** projecting detail, ornament, or figures
7 : sharpness of outline due to contrast ⟨a roof in bold *relief* against the sky⟩
8 : the elevations or inequalities of a land surface
9 : the pitching done by a relief pitcher ⟨two innings of hitless *relief*⟩

²relief *adjective* (1838)
1 : providing relief
2 : characterized by surface inequalities
3 : of or used in letterpress

relief map *noun* (1876)
: a map representing topographic relief

relief pitcher *noun* (circa 1949)
: a baseball pitcher who takes over for another during a game

relief printing *noun* (1875)
: LETTERPRESS 1

re·lieve \ri-'lēv\ *verb* **re·lieved; re·liev·ing** [Middle English *releven*, from Middle French *relever* to raise, relieve, from Latin *relevare*, from *re-* + *levare* to raise — more at LEVER] (14th century)
transitive verb
1 a : to free from a burden : give aid or help to **b :** to set free from an obligation, condition, or restriction **c :** to ease of a burden, wrong, or oppression by judicial or legislative interposition
2 a : to bring about the removal or alleviation of : MITIGATE **b :** ROB, DEPRIVE
3 a : to release from a post, station, or duty **b :** to take the place of
4 : to remove or lessen the monotony of
5 a : to set off by contrast **b :** to raise in relief
6 : to discharge the bladder or bowels of (oneself)
intransitive verb
1 : to bring or give relief
2 : to stand out in relief
3 : to serve as a relief pitcher ☆
— **re·liev·able** \-'lē-və-bəl\ *adjective*

re·lieved \ri-'lēvd\ *adjective* (1869)
: experiencing or showing relief especially from anxiety or pent-up emotions
— **re·liev·ed·ly** \-'lē-vəd-lē\ *adverb*

re·liev·er \ri-'lē-vər\ *noun* (15th century)
: one that relieves; *especially* : RELIEF PITCHER

re·lie·vo \ri-'lē-(,)vō, rēl-'yā-(,)vō\ *noun, plural* **-vos** [Italian *rilievo*, from *rilevare* to raise, from Latin *relevare*] (1625)
: RELIEF 6

re·li·gio- \ri-'li-j(ē-)ō\ *combining form*
: religion and ⟨*religio*-political⟩

re·li·gion \ri-'li-jən\ *noun* [Middle English *religioun*, from Old French *religion-, religio* supernatural constraint, sanction, religious practice, perhaps from *religare* to restrain, tie back — more at RELY] (13th century)
1 a : the state of a religious ⟨a nun in her 20th year of *religion*⟩ **b** (1) **:** the service and worship of God or the supernatural (2) **:** commitment or devotion to religious faith or observance
2 : a personal set or institutionalized system of religious attitudes, beliefs, and practices

3 *archaic* **:** scrupulous conformity : CONSCIENTIOUSNESS
4 : a cause, principle, or system of beliefs held to with ardor and faith
— **re·li·gion·less** *adjective*

re·li·gion·ist \-'li-jə-nist, -'lij-nist\ *noun* (1653)
: a person adhering to a religion; *especially* : a religious zealot

re·li·gi·ose \ri-'li-jē-,ōs\ *adjective* [*religion* + *¹-ose*] (1853)
: RELIGIOUS; *especially* : excessively, obtrusively, or sentimentally religious
— **re·li·gi·os·i·ty** \-,li-jē-'ä-sə-tē\ *noun*

¹re·li·gious \ri-'li-jəs\ *adjective* [Middle English, from Old French *religieus*, from Latin *religiosus*, from *religio*] (13th century)
1 : relating to or manifesting faithful devotion to an acknowledged ultimate reality or deity ⟨a *religious* person⟩ ⟨*religious* attitudes⟩
2 : of, relating to, or devoted to religious beliefs or observances
3 a : scrupulously and conscientiously faithful **b :** FERVENT, ZEALOUS
— **re·li·gious·ly** *adverb*
— **re·li·gious·ness** *noun*

²religious *noun, plural* **religious** [Middle English, from Old French *religieus*, from *religieus*, adjective] (13th century)
: a member of a religious order under monastic vows

re·line \(,)rē-'līn\ *transitive verb* (1851)
: to put new lines on or a new lining in

re·lin·quish \ri-'liŋ-kwish, -'lin-\ *transitive verb* [Middle English *relinquisshen*, from Middle French *relinquiss-*, stem of *relinquir*, from Latin *relinquere* to leave behind, from *re-* + *linquere* to leave — more at LOAN] (15th century)
1 : to withdraw or retreat from : leave behind
2 : GIVE UP ⟨*relinquish* a title⟩

3 a : to stop holding physically **: RELEASE** ⟨slowly *relinquished* his grip on the bar⟩ **b :** to give over possession or control of ⟨few leaders willingly *relinquish* power⟩ ☆ — **re·lin·quish·ment** \-mənt\ *noun*

rel·i·quary \'re-lə-,kwer-ē\ *noun, plural* **-quar·ies** [French *reliquaire*, from Medieval Latin *reliquiarium*, from *reliquia* relic — more at RELIC] (circa 1656) **:** a container or shrine in which sacred relics are kept

re·lique \ri-'lēk, 're-lik\ *archaic variant of* REL-IC

re·liq·ui·ae \ri-'li-kwē-,ī, -kwē-,ē\ *noun plural* [Latin — more at RELIC] (1654) **:** remains of the dead **: RELICS**

¹**rel·ish** \'re-lish\ *noun* [alteration of Middle English *reles* taste, from Old French, something left behind, release, from *relessier* to release] (1530) **1 :** characteristic flavor; *especially* **:** pleasing or zestful flavor **2 :** a quantity just sufficient to flavor or characterize **: TRACE** **3 a :** enjoyment of or delight in something that satisfies one's tastes, inclinations, or desires ⟨eat with great *relish*⟩ **b :** a strong liking **: INCLINATION** ⟨has little *relish* for sports⟩ **4 a :** something adding a zestful flavor; *especially* **:** a condiment (as of pickles or green tomatoes) eaten with other food to add flavor **b :** APPETIZER, HORS D'OEUVRE

²**relish** (1586) *transitive verb* **1 :** to add relish to **2 :** to be pleased or gratified by **: ENJOY** **3 :** to eat or drink with pleasure **4 :** to appreciate with taste and discernment *intransitive verb* **:** to have a characteristic or pleasing taste — **rel·ish·able** \'re-li-shə-bəl\ *adjective*

re·live \(,)rē-'liv\ (1548) *intransitive verb* **:** to live again *transitive verb* **:** to live over again; *especially* **:** to experience again in the imagination

re·lo·cate \(,)rē-'lō-,kāt, ,rē-lō-'\ (1834) *transitive verb* **:** to locate again **:** establish or lay out in a new place *intransitive verb* **:** to move to a new location — **re·lo·cat·able** \-'lō-,kā-tə-bəl, -,lō-'kā-\ *adjective* — **re·lo·ca·tion** \,rē-lō-'kā-shən\ *noun*

re·lo·cat·ee \,rē-lə-,kā-'tē, ,rē-,lō-kə-'tē\ *noun* (1954) **:** one who moves to a new location **:** one that is relocated

re·lu·cent \ri-'lü-sᵊnt\ *adjective* [Latin *re-lucent-, relucens*, past participle of *relucēre* to shine back, from *re-* + *lucēre* to shine — more at LIGHT] (15th century) **:** reflecting light **:** SHINING

re·luct \ri-'ləkt\ *intransitive verb* [Latin *reluctari*] (1547) **:** to show reluctance

re·luc·tance \ri-'lək-tən(t)s\ *noun* (1710) **1 :** the quality or state of being reluctant **2 :** the opposition offered in a magnetic circuit to magnetic flux; *specifically* **:** the ratio of the magnetic potential difference to the corresponding flux

re·luc·tan·cy \-tən(t)-sē\ *noun* (1634) **:** RELUCTANCE

re·luc·tant \ri-'lək-tənt\ *adjective* [Latin *reluctant-, reluctans*, present participle of *reluctari* to struggle against, from *re-* + *luctari* to struggle] (1667) **:** feeling or showing aversion, hesitation, or unwillingness ⟨*reluctant* to get involved⟩; *also* **:** having or assuming a specified role unwillingly ⟨a *reluctant* hero⟩ **synonym** see DISINCLINED — **re·luc·tant·ly** *adverb*

re·luc·tate \ri-'lək-,tāt\ *intransitive verb* **-tat·ed; -tat·ing** (1643) **:** RELUCT — **re·luc·ta·tion** \ri-,lək-'tā-shən, ,rē-\ *noun*

re·lume \(,)rē-'lüm\ *transitive verb* **re·lumed; re·lum·ing** [irregular from Late Latin *reluminare*, from Latin *re-* + *luminare* to light up — more at ILLUMINATE] (1604) *archaic* **:** to light or light up again **:** REKINDLE

re·ly \ri-'lī\ *intransitive verb* **re·lied; re·ly·ing** [Middle English *relien* to rally, from Middle French *relier* to connect, rally, from Latin *religare* to tie back, from *re-* + *ligare* to tie — more at LIGATURE] (1574) **1 :** to be dependent ⟨the system on which we *rely* for water⟩ **2 :** to have confidence based on experience ⟨someone you can *rely* on⟩ — **re·li·er** \-'lī(-ə)r\ *noun*

rem \'rem\ *noun* [roentgen equivalent *man*] (1947) **:** the dosage of an ionizing radiation that will cause the same biological effect as one roentgen of X-ray or gamma-ray exposure

REM \'rem\ *noun* (1957) **:** RAPID EYE MOVEMENT

¹**re·main** \ri-'mān\ *intransitive verb* [Middle English, from Middle French, from Latin *remanēre*, from *re-* + *manēre* to remain — more at MANSION] (14th century) **1 a :** to be a part not destroyed, taken, or used up ⟨only a few ruins *remain*⟩ **b :** to be something yet to be shown, done, or treated ⟨it *remains* to be seen⟩ **2 :** to stay in the same place or with the same person or group; *especially* **:** to stay behind **3 :** to continue unchanged ⟨the fact *remains* that we can't go⟩

²**remain** *noun* (15th century) **1** *obsolete* **:** STAY **2 :** a remaining part or trace — usually used in plural **3** *plural* **:** a dead body

¹**re·main·der** \ri-'mān-dər\ *noun* [Middle English, from Anglo-French, from Middle French *remaindre*] (14th century) **1 :** an interest or estate in property that follows and is dependent on the termination of a prior intervening possessory estate created at the same time by the same instrument **2 a :** a remaining group, part, or trace **b** (1) **:** the number left after a subtraction (2) **:** the final undivided part after division that is less or of lower degree than the divisor **3 :** a book sold at a reduced price by the publisher after sales have slowed

²**remainder** *adjective* (1567) **:** LEFTOVER, REMAINING

³**remainder** *transitive verb* **-dered; -der·ing** \-d(ə-)riŋ\ (1904) **:** to dispose of as remainders

remainder theorem *noun* (1886) **:** a theorem in algebra: if $f(x)$ is a polynomial in x then the remainder on dividing $f(x)$ by $x - a$ is $f(a)$

¹**re·make** \(,)rē-'māk\ *transitive verb* **-made** \-'mād\; **-mak·ing** (circa 1635) **:** to make anew or in a different form — **re·mak·er** \-'mā-kər\ *noun*

²**re·make** \'rē-,māk\ *noun* (1936) **:** one that is remade; *especially* **:** a new version of a motion picture

re·man \(,)rē-'man\ *transitive verb* (1666) **1 :** to man again or anew **2 :** to imbue with courage again

re·mand \ri-'mand\ *transitive verb* [Middle English *remaunden*, from Middle French *remander*, from Late Latin *remandare* to send back word, from Latin *re-* + *mandare* to order — more at MANDATE] (15th century) **:** to order back: as **a :** to send back (a case) to another court or agency for further action **b :** to return to custody pending trial or for further detention — **remand** *noun*

rem·a·nence \'re-mə-nən(t)s, ri-'mā-\ *noun* (circa 1880) **:** the magnetic induction remaining in a magnetized substance no longer under external magnetic influence

rem·a·nent \-nənt\ *adjective* [Middle English, from Latin *remanent-, remanens*, present participle of *remanēre* to remain] (15th century) **1 :** RESIDUAL, REMAINING **2 :** of, relating to, or characterized by remanence

re·man·u·fac·ture \(,)rē-,ma-nyə-'fak-chər, -,ma-nə-\ *transitive verb* (1851) **:** to manufacture into a new product — **remanufacture** *noun* — **re·man·u·fac·tur·er** \-chər-ər\ *noun*

re·map \(,)rē-'map\ *transitive verb* (1931) **:** to map again; *also* **:** to lay out in a new pattern

¹**re·mark** \ri-'märk\ *noun* [French *remarque*, from Middle French, from *remarquer* to remark, from *re-* re- + *marquer* to mark — more at MARQUE] (1660) **1 :** the act of remarking **: NOTICE** **2 :** an expression of opinion or judgment **3 :** mention of that which deserves attention or notice

²**remark** (1675) *transitive verb* **1 :** to take notice of **: OBSERVE** **2 :** to express as an observation or comment **: SAY** *intransitive verb* **:** to notice something and comment thereon — used with *on* or *upon*

re·mark·able \ri-'mär-kə-bəl\ *adjective* (circa 1604) **:** worthy of being or likely to be noticed especially as being uncommon or extraordinary **synonym** see NOTICEABLE — **re·mark·able·ness** *noun*

re·mark·ably \-blē\ *adverb* (1638) **1 :** in a remarkable manner ⟨*remarkably* talented⟩ **2 :** as is remarkable ⟨*remarkably*, no one was hurt⟩

re·marque \ri-'märk\ *noun* [French *remarque* remark, note, from Middle French, from *remarquer*] (1882) **1 :** a drawn, etched, or incised scribble or sketch done on the margin of a plate or stone and removed before the regular printing **2 :** a proof taken before remarques have been removed

re·mas·ter \(,)rē-'mas-tər\ *transitive verb* (1964) **:** to create a new master of especially by altering or enhancing the sound quality of an older recording

re·match \(,)rē-'mach, 'rē-,\ *noun* (1941)

☆ **SYNONYMS**
Relinquish, yield, resign, surrender, abandon, waive mean to give up completely. RELINQUISH usually does not imply strong feeling but may suggest some regret, reluctance, or weakness ⟨*relinquished* her crown⟩. YIELD implies concession or compliance or submission to force ⟨the troops *yielded* ground grudgingly⟩. RESIGN emphasizes voluntary relinquishment or sacrifice without struggle ⟨*resigned* her position⟩. SURRENDER implies a giving up after a struggle to retain or resist ⟨*surrendered* their claims⟩. ABANDON stresses finality and completeness in giving up ⟨*abandoned* all hope⟩. WAIVE implies conceding or forgoing with little or no compulsion ⟨*waived* the right to a trial by jury⟩.

\ə\ abut \ᵊ\ kitten \ər\ **further** \a\ ash \ā\ **ace** \ä\ mop, mar \aů\ **out** \ch\ **chin** \e\ bet \ē\ **easy** \g\ **go** \i\ hit \ī\ **ice** \j\ **job** \ŋ\ **sing** \ō\ **go** \ȯ\ law \ȯi\ **boy** \th\ **thin** \t͟h\ **the** \ü\ **loot** \ů\ **foot** \y\ **yet** \zh\ **vision** *see also* Guide to Pronunciation

: a second match between the same contestants or teams

re·me·di·a·ble \ri-'mē-dē-ə-bəl\ *adjective* (15th century)
: capable of being remedied
— **re·me·di·abil·i·ty** \ri-,mē-dē-ə-'bi-lə-tē\ *noun*

re·me·di·al \ri-'mē-dē-əl\ *adjective* (1651)
1 : intended as a remedy
2 : concerned with the correction of faulty study habits and the raising of a pupil's general competence ⟨*remedial* reading courses⟩; *also* : receiving or requiring remedial instruction ⟨*remedial* students⟩
— **re·me·di·al·ly** \-ə-lē\ *adverb*

re·me·di·ate \ri-'mē-dē-ət\ *adjective* (1605)
archaic : REMEDIAL

re·me·di·a·tion \ri-,mē-dē-'ā-shən\ *noun* (1818)
: the act or process of remedying ⟨*remediation* of reading problems⟩
— **re·me·di·ate** \-'mē-dē-,āt\ *transitive verb*

¹rem·e·dy \'re-mə-dē\ *noun, plural* **-dies** [Middle English *remedie*, from Anglo-French, from Latin *remedium*, from *re-* + *mederi* to heal — more at MEDICAL] (13th century)
1 : a medicine, application, or treatment that relieves or cures a disease
2 : something that corrects or counteracts
3 : the legal means to recover a right or to prevent or obtain redress for a wrong
— **rem·e·di·less** *adjective*

²remedy *transitive verb* **-died; -dy·ing** (15th century)
: to provide or serve as a remedy for : RELIEVE ⟨*remedy* a social evil⟩
synonym see CORRECT

re·mem·ber \ri-'mem-bər\ *verb* **-bered; -ber·ing** \-b(ə-)riŋ\ [Middle English *remembren*, from Middle French *remembrer*, from Late Latin *rememorari*, from Latin *re-* + Late Latin *memorari* to be mindful of, from Latin *memor* mindful — more at MEMORY] (14th century)
transitive verb
1 : to bring to mind or think of again ⟨*remembers* the old days⟩
2 *archaic* **a** : BETHINK 1b **b** : REMIND
3 a : to keep in mind for attention or consideration ⟨*remembers* friends at Christmas⟩ **b** : REWARD ⟨was *remembered* in the will⟩
4 : to retain in the memory ⟨*remember* the facts until the test is over⟩
5 : to convey greetings from ⟨*remember* me to her⟩
6 : RECORD, COMMEMORATE
intransitive verb
1 : to exercise or have the power of memory
2 : to have a recollection or remembrance ☆
— **re·mem·ber·abil·i·ty** \-,mem-b(ə-)rə-'bi-lə-tē\ *noun*
— **re·mem·ber·able** \-'mem-b(ə-)rə-bəl\ *adjective*
— **re·mem·ber·er** \-bər-ər\ *noun*

re·mem·brance \ri-'mem-brən(t)s *also* -bə-rən(t)s\ *noun* (14th century)
1 : the state of bearing in mind
2 a : the ability to remember : MEMORY **b** : the period over which one's memory extends
3 : an act of recalling to mind
4 : a memory of a person, thing, or event
5 a : something that serves to keep in or bring to mind : REMINDER **b** : COMMEMORATION, MEMORIAL **c** : a greeting or gift recalling or expressing friendship or affection
synonym see MEMORY

Remembrance Day *noun* (1918)
: November 11 set aside in commemoration of the end of hostilities in 1918 and 1945 and observed as a legal holiday in Canada; *also* : REMEMBRANCE SUNDAY

re·mem·branc·er \ri-'mem-brən(t)-sər\ *noun* (15th century)
1 : any of several English officials
2 : one that reminds

Remembrance Sunday *noun* (1942)
: a Sunday that is usually closest to November 11 and that in Great Britain is set aside in commemoration of the end of hostilities in 1918 and 1945

re·mex \'rē-,meks\ *noun, plural* **rem·i·ges** \'re-mə-,jēz\ [New Latin *remig-, remex*, from Latin, oarsman, from *remus* oar + *agere* to drive — more at ROW, AGENT] (1767)
: a primary or secondary quill feather of the wing of a bird

re·mind \ri-'mīnd\ *transitive verb* (1660)
: to put in mind of something : cause to remember
synonym see REMEMBER
— **re·mind·er** *noun*

re·mind·ful \-'mīn(d)-fəl\ *adjective* (1810)
1 : MINDFUL
2 : tending to remind : SUGGESTIVE, EVOCATIVE

rem·i·nisce \,re-mə-'nis\ *intransitive verb* **-nisced; -nisc·ing** [back-formation from *reminiscence*] (1829)
: to indulge in reminiscence
synonym see REMEMBER
— **rem·i·nis·cer** \-'ni-sər\ *noun*

rem·i·nis·cence \-'ni-s°n(t)s\ *noun* (1589)
1 : apprehension of a Platonic idea as if it had been known in a previous existence
2 a : recall to mind of a long-forgotten experience or fact **b** : the process or practice of thinking or telling about past experiences
3 a : a remembered experience **b** : an account of a memorable experience — often used in plural
4 : something so like another as to be regarded as an unconscious repetition, imitation, or survival
synonym see MEMORY

rem·i·nis·cent \-s°nt\ *adjective* [Latin *reminiscent-, reminiscens*, present participle of *reminisci* to remember, from *re-* + *-minisci* (akin to Latin *ment-, mens* mind) — more at MIND] (1765)
1 : of the character of or relating to reminiscence
2 : marked by or given to reminiscence
3 : tending to remind : SUGGESTIVE
— **rem·i·nis·cent·ly** *adverb*

rem·i·nis·cen·tial \,re-mə-(,)ni-'sen(t)-shəl\ *adjective* (1646)
: REMINISCENT

re·mint \(,)rē-'mint\ *transitive verb* (1823)
: to melt down (old or worn coin) and make into new coin

re·mise \ri-'mīz\ *transitive verb* **re·mised; re·mis·ing** [Middle English, from Middle French *remis*, past participle of *remettre* to put back, from Latin *remittere* to send back] (15th century)
: to give, grant, or release a claim to : DEED

re·miss \ri-'mis\ *adjective* [Middle English, from Latin *remissus*, from past participle of *remittere* to send back, relax] (15th century)
1 : negligent in the performance of work or duty : CARELESS
2 : showing neglect or inattention : LAX
synonym see NEGLIGENT
— **re·miss·ly** *adverb*
— **re·miss·ness** *noun*

re·mis·si·ble \ri-'mi-sə-bəl\ *adjective* (1577)
: capable of being forgiven ⟨*remissible* sins⟩
— **re·mis·si·bly** \-blē\ *adverb*

re·mis·sion \ri-'mi-shən\ *noun* (13th century)
1 : the act or process of remitting
2 : a state or period during which something is remitted

¹re·mit \ri-'mit\ *verb* **re·mit·ted; re·mit·ting** [Middle English *remitten*, from Latin *remittere* to send back, from *re-* + *mittere* to send] (14th century)
transitive verb
1 a : to lay aside (a mood or disposition) partly or wholly **b** : to desist from (an activity) **c** : to let (as attention or diligence) slacken : RELAX

2 a : to release from the guilt or penalty of ⟨*remit* sins⟩ **b** : to refrain from exacting ⟨*remit* a tax⟩ **c** : to cancel or refrain from inflicting ⟨*remit* the penalty⟩ **d** : to give relief from (suffering)
3 : to submit or refer for consideration, judgment, decision, or action; *specifically* : REMAND
4 : to restore or consign to a former status or condition
5 : POSTPONE, DEFER
6 : to send (money) to a person or place especially in payment of a demand, account, or draft
intransitive verb
1 a : to abate in force or intensity : MODERATE **b** *of a disease or abnormality* : to abate symptoms for a period
2 : to send money (as in payment)
— **re·mit·ment** \-'mit-mənt\ *noun*
— **re·mit·ta·ble** \-'mi-tə-bəl\ *adjective*
— **re·mit·ter** *noun*

²re·mit \ri-'mit, 'rē-,\ *noun* (15th century)
1 : an act of remitting
2 : something remitted to another person or authority

re·mit·tal \ri-'mi-t°l\ *noun* (1596)
: REMISSION

re·mit·tance \ri-'mi-t°n(t)s\ *noun* (1705)
1 a : a sum of money remitted **b** : an instrument by which money is remitted
2 : transmittal of money (as to a distant place)

remittance man *noun* (1886)
: one living abroad on remittances from home

re·mit·tent \ri-'mi-t°nt\ *adjective* [Latin *remittent-, remittens*, present participle of *remittere*] (1693)
of a disease : marked by alternating periods of abatement and increase of symptoms

¹rem·nant \'rem-nənt\ *noun* [Middle English, contraction of *remenant*, from Middle French, from present participle of *remenoir* to remain, from Latin *remanēre* — more at REMAIN] (14th century)
1 a : a usually small part, member, or trace remaining **b** : a small surviving group — often used in plural
2 : an unsold or unused end of piece goods

²remnant *adjective* (1550)
: still remaining

re·mod·el \(,)rē-'mä-d°l\ *transitive verb* (1789)
: to alter the structure of : REMAKE

re·mon·strance \ri-'män(t)-strən(t)s\ *noun* (1585)
1 : an earnest presentation of reasons for opposition or grievance; *especially* : a document formally stating such points
2 : an act or instance of remonstrating

re·mon·strant \-strənt\ *adjective* (1641)
: vigorously objecting or opposing
— **remonstrant** *noun*
— **re·mon·strant·ly** *adverb*

re·mon·strate \'re-mən-,strāt, ri-'män-\ *verb* **-strat·ed; -strat·ing** [Medieval Latin *remonstratus*, past participle of *remonstrare* to

☆ SYNONYMS
Remember, recollect, recall, remind, reminisce mean to bring an image or idea from the past into the mind. REMEMBER implies a keeping in memory that may be effortless or unwilled ⟨*remembers* that day as though it were yesterday⟩. RECOLLECT implies a bringing back to mind what is lost or scattered ⟨as near as I can *recollect*⟩. RECALL suggests an effort to bring back to mind and often to re-create in speech ⟨can't *recall* the words of the song⟩. REMIND suggests a jogging of one's memory by an association or similarity ⟨that *reminds* me of a story⟩. REMINISCE implies a casual often nostalgic recalling of experiences long past and gone ⟨old college friends like to *reminisce*⟩.

demonstrate, from Latin *re-* + *monstrare* to show — more at MUSTER] (1695)
intransitive verb
: to present and urge reasons in opposition **:** EXPOSTULATE — usually used with *with*
transitive verb
: to say or plead in protest, reproof, or opposition
— **re·mon·stra·tion** \,re-mən-'strā-shən, ri-'man-\ *noun*
— **re·mon·stra·tive** \ri-'män(t)-strə-tiv\ *adjective*
— **re·mon·stra·tive·ly** *adverb*
— **re·mon·stra·tor** \'re-mən-,strā-tər, ri-'män-\ *noun*

rem·o·ra \'re-mə-rə *also* ri-'mȯr-ə *or* -'mȯr-\ *noun* [Late Latin, from Latin, delay, from *remorari* to delay, from *re-* + *morari* to delay — more at MORATORIUM] (1567)
1 : any of a family (Echeneididae) of marine bony fishes that have the anterior dorsal fin modified into a suctorial disk on the head by means of which they especially cling to other fishes
2 : HINDRANCE, DRAG

remoras on tiger shark

re·morse \ri-'mȯrs\ *noun* [Middle English, from Middle French *remors*, from Medieval Latin *remorsus*, from Late Latin, act of biting again, from Latin *remordēre* to bite again, from *re-* + *mordēre* to bite — more at MORDANT] (14th century)
1 : a gnawing distress arising from a sense of guilt for past wrongs **:** SELF-REPROACH
2 *obsolete* **:** COMPASSION ◇
synonym see PENITENCE

re·morse·ful \-'mȯrs-fəl\ *adjective* (1592)
: motivated or marked by remorse
— **re·morse·ful·ly** \-fə-lē\ *adverb*
— **re·morse·ful·ness** *noun*

re·morse·less \-ləs\ *adjective* (1593)
1 : having no remorse **:** MERCILESS
2 : RELENTLESS
— **re·morse·less·ly** *adverb*
— **re·morse·less·ness** *noun*

¹re·mote \ri-'mōt\ *adjective* **re·mot·er; -est** [Middle English, from Latin *remotus*, from past participle of *removēre* to remove] (15th century)
1 : separated by an interval or space greater than usual ⟨an involucre *remote* from the flower⟩
2 : far removed in space, time, or relation **:** DIVERGENT ⟨the *remote* past⟩ ⟨comments *remote* from the truth⟩
3 : OUT-OF-THE-WAY, SECLUDED ⟨a *remote* cabin in the hills⟩
4 : acting, acted on, or controlled indirectly or from a distance ⟨*remote* computer operation⟩; *also* **:** relating to the acquisition of information about a distant object (as by radar or photography) without coming into physical contact with it ⟨*remote* sensing⟩
5 : not arising from a primary or proximate action
6 : small in degree **:** SLIGHT ⟨a *remote* possibility⟩
7 : distant in manner **:** ALOOF
— **re·mote·ly** *adverb*
— **re·mote·ness** *noun*

²remote *noun* (1937)
1 : a radio or television program or a portion of a program originating outside the studio
2 : REMOTE CONTROL 2

remote control *noun* (1904)
1 : control (as by radio signal) of operation from a point at some distance removed

2 : a device or mechanism for controlling something from a distance

re·mo·tion \ri-'mō-shən\ *noun* (15th century)
1 : the quality or state of being remote
2 : the act of removing **:** REMOVAL
3 *obsolete* **:** DEPARTURE

¹re·mount \(,)rē-'maůnt\ *verb* [Middle English, partly from *re-* + *mounten* to mount, partly from Middle French *remonter*, from *re-* + *monter* to mount] (15th century)
transitive verb
1 : to mount (something) again ⟨*remount* a picture⟩
2 : to furnish remounts to
intransitive verb
1 : to mount again
2 : REVERT

²re·mount \'rē-,maůnt, (,)rē-'\ *noun* (1781)
: a fresh horse to replace one no longer available

re·mov·al \ri-'mü-vəl\ *noun* (1597)
: the act or process of removing **:** the fact of being removed

¹re·move \ri-'müv\ *verb* **re·moved; re·mov·ing** [Middle English, from Old French *removoir*, from Latin *removēre*, from *re-* + *movēre* to move] (14th century)
transitive verb
1 a : to change the location, position, station, or residence of ⟨*remove* soldiers to the front⟩ **b :** to transfer (a legal proceeding) from one court to another
2 : to move by lifting, pushing aside, or taking away or off ⟨*remove* your hat⟩
3 : to dismiss from office
4 : to get rid of **:** ELIMINATE ⟨*remove* a tumor surgically⟩
intransitive verb
1 : to change location, station, or residence ⟨*removing* from the city to the suburbs⟩
2 : to go away
3 : to be capable of being removed
— **re·mov·abil·i·ty** \-,mü-və-'bi-lə-tē\ *noun*
— **re·mov·able** *also* **re·move·able** \ri-'mü-və-bəl\ *adjective*
— **re·mov·able·ness** \-'mü-və-bəl-nəs\ *noun*
— **re·mov·ably** \-blē\ *adverb*
— **re·mov·er** *noun*

²remove *noun* (1553)
1 : REMOVAL; *specifically* **:** MOVE 2c
2 a : a distance or interval separating one person or thing from another **b :** a degree or stage of separation

removed *adjective* (circa 1548)
1 a : distant in degree of relationship **b :** of a younger or older generation ⟨a second cousin's child is a second cousin once *removed*⟩
2 : separate or remote in space, time, or character

REM sleep *noun* (1965)
: a state of sleep that recurs cyclically several times during a normal period of sleep and that is characterized by increased neuronal activity of the forebrain and midbrain, by depressed muscle tone, and especially in humans by dreaming, rapid eye movements, and vascular congestion of the sex organs — called also *paradoxical sleep, rapid eye movement sleep*

re·mu·da \ri-'mü-də, -'myü-\ *noun* [American Spanish, relay of horses, from Spanish, exchange, from *remudar* to exchange, from *re-* + *mudar* to change, from Latin *mutare* — more at MUTABLE] (circa 1892)
: the herd of horses from which those to be used for the day are chosen

re·mu·ner·ate \ri-'myü-nə-,rāt\ *transitive verb* **-at·ed; -at·ing** [Latin *remuneratus*, past participle of *remunerare* to recompense, from *re-* + *munerare* to give, from *muner-, munus* gift — more at MEAN] (1523)
1 : to pay an equivalent for ⟨their services were generously *remunerated*⟩

2 : to pay an equivalent to for a service, loss, or expense **:** RECOMPENSE
synonym see PAY
— **re·mu·ner·a·tor** \-,rā-tər\ *noun*
— **re·mu·ner·a·to·ry** \-rə-,tȯr-ē, -,tȯr-\ *adjective*

re·mu·ner·a·tion \ri-,myü-nə-'rā-shən\ *noun* (15th century)
1 : something that remunerates **:** RECOMPENSE, PAY
2 : an act or fact of remunerating

re·mu·ner·a·tive \ri-'myü-nə-rə-tiv, -,rā-\ *adjective* (circa 1677)
1 : serving to remunerate
2 : providing remuneration **:** PROFITABLE
— **re·mu·ner·a·tive·ly** *adverb*
— **re·mu·ner·a·tive·ness** *noun*

Re·mus \'rē-məs\ *noun* [Latin]
: a son of Mars slain by his twin brother Romulus

re·nais·sance \,re-nə-'sän(t)s, -'zän(t)s, -'säⁿs, -'zäⁿs, 're-nə-,, *chiefly British* ri-'nā-sⁿn(t)s\ *noun, often attributive* [French, from Middle French, rebirth, from *renaistre* to be born again, from Latin *renasci*, from *re-* + *nasci* to be born — more at NATION] (1845)
1 *capitalized* **a :** the transitional movement in Europe between medieval and modern times beginning in the 14th century in Italy, lasting into the 17th century, and marked by a humanistic revival of classical influence expressed in a flowering of the arts and literature and by the beginnings of modern science **b :** the period of the Renaissance **c :** the neoclassic style of architecture prevailing during the Renaissance
2 *often capitalized* **:** a movement or period of vigorous artistic and intellectual activity
3 : REBIRTH, REVIVAL

Renaissance man *noun* (1906)
: a person who has wide interests and is expert in several areas

re·nal \'rē-nᵊl\ *adjective* [French or Late Latin; French *rénal*, from Late Latin *renalis*, from Latin *renes* kidneys] (circa 1656)
: relating to, involving, or located in the region of the kidneys **:** NEPHRITIC

renal clearance *noun* (1948)
: CLEARANCE 3

re·na·scence \ri-'na-sⁿn(t)s, -'nā-\ *noun, often capitalized* (1727)
: RENAISSANCE

re·na·scent \-sⁿnt\ *adjective* [Latin *renascent-, renascens*, present participle of *renasci*] (circa 1727)

◇ **WORD HISTORY**
remorse *Remorse* is a gnawing distress that arises from a sense of guilt. In the light of its etymology, "gnawing" is a description of special relevance, for *remorse* is borrowed from Medieval Latin *remorsus*, a noun derivative of Latin *remordere* "to bite again, vex persistently." When a monk known to us as Dan Michel of Northgate, in the year 1340, finished his English translation of a French manual on sin and penitence, he called it *Ayenbite of Inwyt*—which we would render in Modern English as "Remorse of Conscience." The word *ayenbite* was Dan Michel's piece-by-piece translation of Latin *remorsus*, with *ayen-* ("again" in Modern English) rendering *re-* and *bite* rendering *morsus*. Similar loan translations of Latin words with *ayen-* for *re-* were quite popular in Middle English, though they have not survived. In many cases we have simply borrowed the Latin word, as has happened with *remorse*.

\ə\ abut \ᵊ\ kitten \ər\ further \a\ ash \ā\ ace
\ä\ mop, mar \aů\ out \ch\ chin \e\ bet \ē\ easy
\g\ go \i\ hit \ī\ ice \j\ job \ŋ\ sing \ō\ go
\ȯ\ law \ȯi\ boy \th\ thin \t̲h̲\ the \ü\ loot \ů\ foot
\y\ yet \zh\ vision *see also* Guide to Pronunciation

: rising again into being or vigor

re·na·ture \(ˌ)rē-'nā-chər\ *transitive verb* **re·na·tured; re·na·tur·ing** \-'nā-chə-riŋ, -'nāch-riŋ\ [*re-* + *denature*] (1926)
: to restore (as a denatured protein) to an original or normal condition
— **re·na·tur·ation** \(ˌ)rē-ˌnā-chə-'rā-shən\ *noun*

ren·con·tre \rän-'kōⁿtrᵊ, ren-'kän-tər\ *or* **ren·coun·ter** \ren-'kaůn-tər\ *noun* [*rencounter* from Middle French *rencontre*, from *rencontrer; rencontre* from French] (1523)
1 : a hostile meeting or a contest between forces or individuals : COMBAT
2 : a casual meeting

ren·coun·ter \ren-'kaůn-tər\ *transitive verb* [Middle French *rencontrer* to meet by chance or in hostility, from *re-* + *encontrer* to encounter] (1549)
archaic : to meet casually

rend \'rend\ *verb* **rent** \'rent\ *also* **rend·ed** \'ren-dəd\; **rend·ing** [Middle English, from Old English *rendan;* akin to Old Frisian *renda* to tear and perhaps to Sanskrit *randhra* hole] (before 12th century)
transitive verb
1 : to remove from place by violence : WREST
2 : to split or tear apart or in pieces by violence
3 : to tear (the hair or clothing) as a sign of anger, grief, or despair
4 a : to lacerate mentally or emotionally **b** : to pierce with sound **c** : to divide (as a nation) into contesting factions
intransitive verb
1 : to perform an act of tearing or splitting
2 : to become torn or split
synonym see TEAR

¹ren·der \'ren-dər\ *verb* **ren·dered; ren·der·ing** \-d(ə-)riŋ\ [Middle English *rendren,* from Middle French *rendre* to give back, yield, from (assumed) Vulgar Latin *rendere,* alteration of Latin *reddere,* partly from *re-* + *dare* to give & partly from *re-* + *-dere* to put — more at DATE, DO] (14th century)
transitive verb
1 a : to melt down ⟨*render* suet⟩; *also* : to extract by melting ⟨*render* lard⟩ **b** : to treat so as to convert into industrial fats and oils or fertilizer
2 a : to transmit to another : DELIVER **b** : GIVE UP, YIELD **c** : to furnish for consideration, approval, or information: as (1) : to hand down (a legal judgment) (2) : to agree on and report (a verdict)
3 a : to give in return or retribution **b** (1) : GIVE BACK, RESTORE (2) : REFLECT, ECHO **c** : to give in acknowledgment of dependence or obligation : PAY **d** : to do (a service) for another
4 a (1) : to cause to be or become : MAKE ⟨enough rainfall . . . to *render* irrigation unnecessary —P. E. James⟩ ⟨*rendered* him helpless⟩ (2) : IMPART **b** (1) : to reproduce or represent by artistic or verbal means : DEPICT (2) : to give a performance of (3) : to produce a copy or version of ⟨the documents are *rendered* in the original French⟩ (4) : to execute the motions of ⟨*render* a salute⟩ **c** : TRANSLATE
5 : to direct the execution of : ADMINISTER ⟨*render* justice⟩
6 : to apply a coat of plaster or cement directly to
intransitive verb
: to give recompense
— **ren·der·able** \-d(ə-)rə-bəl\ *adjective*
— **ren·der·er** \-dər-ər\ *noun*

²render *noun* (1647)
: a return especially in goods or services due from a feudal tenant to his lord

¹ren·dez·vous \'rän-di-ˌvü, -dā-\ *noun, plural* **ren·dez·vous** \-ˌvüz\ [Middle French, from *rendez vous* present yourselves] (1591)
1 a : a place appointed for assembling or meeting **b** : a place of popular resort : HAUNT
2 : a meeting at an appointed place and time

3 : the process of bringing two spacecraft together

²rendezvous *verb* **-voused** \-ˌvüd\; **-vous·ing** \-ˌvü-iŋ\; **-vouses** \-ˌvüz\ (circa 1645)
intransitive verb
: to come together at a rendezvous
transitive verb
1 : to bring together at a rendezvous
2 : to meet at a rendezvous

ren·di·tion \ren-'di-shən\ *noun* [obsolete French, from Middle French, alteration of *reddition,* from Late Latin *reddition-, redditio,* from Latin *reddere* to return] (1601)
: the act or result of rendering: as **a** : SURRENDER **b** : TRANSLATION **c** : PERFORMANCE, INTERPRETATION

ren·dzi·na \ren-'jē-nə\ *noun* [Polish *rędzina* rich limy soil] (1922)
: any of a group of dark grayish brown intrazonal soils developed in grassy regions of high to moderate humidity from soft calcareous marl or chalk

¹ren·e·gade \'re-ni-ˌgād\ *noun* [Spanish *renegado,* from Medieval Latin *renegatus,* from past participle of *renegare* to deny, from Latin *re-* + *negare* to deny — more at NEGATE] (1583)
1 : a deserter from one faith, cause, or allegiance to another
2 : an individual who rejects lawful or conventional behavior

²renegade *intransitive verb* **-gad·ed; -gad·ing** (circa 1611)
: to become a renegade

³renegade *adjective* (1705)
1 : having deserted a faith, cause, or religion for a hostile one
2 : having rejected tradition : UNCONVENTIONAL

re·nege \ri-'nig, -'neg, -'nēg, -'näg\ *verb* **re·neged; re·neg·ing** [Medieval Latin *renegare*] (1548)
transitive verb
: DENY, RENOUNCE
intransitive verb
1 *obsolete* : to make a denial
2 : REVOKE
3 : to go back on a promise or commitment
— **re·neg·er** *noun*

re·ne·go·tia·ble \ˌrē-ni-'gō-sh(ē-)ə-bəl\ *adjective* (1943)
: subject to renegotiation ⟨*renegotiable* mortgages⟩ ⟨*renegotiable* rates⟩

re·ne·go·ti·ate \ˌrē-ni-'gō-shē-ˌāt\ *transitive verb* (circa 1934)
: to negotiate again (as to adjust interest rates or repayments or to get more money) ⟨*renegotiate* a loan⟩ ⟨*renegotiate* a contract⟩
— **re·ne·go·ti·a·tion** \ˌrē-ni-ˌgō-shē-'ā-shən, -sē-'ā-\ *noun*

re·new \ri-'nü, -'nyü\ *verb* (14th century)
transitive verb
1 : to make like new : restore to freshness, vigor, or perfection ⟨as we *renew* our strength in sleep⟩
2 : to make new spiritually : REGENERATE
3 a : to restore to existence : REVIVE **b** : to make extensive changes in : REBUILD
4 : to do again : REPEAT
5 : to begin again : RESUME
6 : REPLACE, REPLENISH ⟨*renew* water in a tank⟩
7 a : to grant or obtain an extension of or on ⟨*renew* a license⟩ **b** : to grant or obtain an extension on the loan of ⟨*renew* a library book⟩
intransitive verb
1 : to become new or as new
2 : to begin again : RESUME
3 : to make a renewal (as of a lease) ☆
— **re·new·er** *noun*

re·new·able \-'nü-ə-bəl, -'nyü-\ *adjective* (1727)
1 : capable of being renewed ⟨*renewable* contracts⟩
2 : capable of being replaced by natural ecological cycles or sound management practices ⟨*renewable* resources⟩

— **re·new·abil·i·ty** \-ˌnü-ə-'bi-lə-tē, -ˌnyü-\ *noun*
— **re·new·ably** \-'nü-ə-blē, -'nyü-\ *adverb*

re·new·al \ri-'nü-əl, -'nyü-\ *noun* (circa 1686)
1 : the act or process of renewing : REPETITION
2 : the quality or state of being renewed
3 : something (as a subscription to a magazine) renewed
4 : something used for renewing; *specifically* : an expenditure that betters existing fixed assets
5 : the rebuilding of a large area (as of a city) by a public authority

reni- *or* **reno-** *combining form* [Latin *renes* kidneys]
: kidney ⟨*reniform*⟩

re·ni·form \'rē-nə-ˌförm, 'rē-\ *adjective* [New Latin *reniformis,* from *reni-* + *-formis* -form] (circa 1753)
: suggesting a kidney in outline

re·nin \'rē-nən, 'rē-\ *noun* [International Scientific Vocabulary, from Latin *renes*] (1906)
: a proteolytic enzyme of the kidney that plays a major role in the release of angiotensin

re·ni·ten·cy \'re-nə-tən(t)-sē, ri-'nī-tᵊn(t)-\ *noun* (1613)
: RESISTANCE, OPPOSITION

re·ni·tent \'re-nə-tənt, ri-'nī-tᵊnt\ *adjective* [French or Latin; French *rénitent,* from Latin *renitent-, renitens,* present participle of *reniti* to resist, from *re-* + *niti* to strive — more at NISUS] (1701)
1 : resisting physical pressure
2 : resisting constraint or compulsion : RECALCITRANT

ren·min·bi \'ren-ˌmin-'bē\ *noun plural* [Chinese (Beijing) *rénmínbì,* from *rénmín* people + *bì* currency] (1957)
: the currency of the People's Republic of China consisting of yuan

ren·net \'re-nət\ *noun* [Middle English, from (assumed) Middle English *rennen* to cause to coagulate, from Old English *gerennan,* from *ge-* together + (assumed) Old English *rennan* to cause to run; akin to Old High German *rennen* to cause to run, Old English *rinnan* to run — more at CO-, RUN] (15th century)
1 a : the contents of the stomach of an unweaned animal and especially a calf **b** : the lining membrane of a stomach or one of its compartments (as the fourth of a ruminant) used for curdling milk; *also* : a preparation of the stomach of animals used for this purpose
2 a : RENNIN **b** : a substitute for rennin

ren·nin \'re-nən\ *noun* [*rennet* + ¹*-in*] (1897)
: an enzyme that coagulates milk and is used in making cheese and junkets; *especially* : one from the mucous membrane of the stomach of a calf

re·no·gram \'rē-nə-ˌgram\ *noun* (1952)
: a photographic depiction of the course of renal excretion of a radioactively labeled substance

— **re·no·graph·ic** \ˌrē-nə-'gra-fik\ *adjective*
— **re·nog·ra·phy** \rē-'nä-grə-fē\ *noun*

re·nom·i·nate \(ˌ)rē-ˈnä-mə-ˌnāt\ *transitive verb* (1864)
: to nominate again especially for a succeeding term
— **re·nom·i·na·tion** \(ˌ)rē-ˌnä-mə-ˈnā-shən\ *noun*

re·nounce \ri-ˈnaủn(t)s\ *verb* **re·nounced; re·nounc·ing** [Middle English, from Middle French *renoncer,* from Latin *renuntiare,* from *re-* + *nuntiare* to report, from *nuntius* messenger] (14th century)
transitive verb
1 : to give up, refuse, or resign usually by formal declaration ⟨*renounce* his errors⟩
2 : to refuse to follow, obey, or recognize any further : REPUDIATE ⟨*renounce* the authority of the church⟩
intransitive verb
1 : to make a renunciation
2 : to fail to follow suit in a card game
synonym see ABDICATE, ABJURE
— **re·nounce·ment** \-ˈnaủn(t)s-mənt\ *noun*
— **re·nounc·er** *noun*

re·no·vas·cu·lar \ˌrē-nō-ˈvas-kyə-lər\ *adjective* (1961)
: of, relating to, or involving the blood vessels of the kidneys ⟨*renovascular* hypertension⟩

ren·o·vate \ˈre-nə-ˌvāt\ *transitive verb* **-vat·ed; -vat·ing** [Latin *renovatus,* past participle of *renovare,* from *re-* + *novare* to make new, from *novus* new — more at NEW] (circa 1522)
1 : to restore to a former better state (as by cleaning, repairing, or rebuilding)
2 : to restore to life, vigor, or activity : REVIVE ⟨the church was *renovated* by a new ecumenical spirit⟩
synonym see RENEW
— **ren·o·va·tion** \ˌre-nə-ˈvā-shən\ *noun*
— **ren·o·va·tive** \ˈre-nə-ˌvā-tiv\ *adjective*
— **ren·o·va·tor** \-ˌvā-tər\ *noun*

¹re·nown \ri-ˈnaủn\ *noun* [Middle English, from Middle French *renon,* from Old French, from *renomer* to celebrate, from *re-* + *nomer* to name, from Latin *nominare,* from *nomin-, nomen* name — more at NAME] (14th century)
1 : a state of being widely acclaimed and highly honored : FAME
2 *obsolete* : REPORT, RUMOR

²renown *transitive verb* (15th century)
: to give renown to

re·nowned *adjective* (14th century)
: having renown : CELEBRATED
synonym see FAMOUS

¹rent \ˈrent\ *noun* [Middle English *rente,* from Old French, income from a property, from (assumed) Vulgar Latin *rendita,* from feminine of *renditus,* past participle of *rendere* to yield — more at RENDER] (12th century)
1 : property (as a house) rented or for rent
2 a : a usually fixed periodical return made by a tenant or occupant of property to the owner for the use and possession thereof; *especially* : an agreed sum paid at fixed intervals by a tenant to the landlord **b** : the amount paid by a hirer of personal property to the owner for the use thereof
3 a : the portion of the income of an economy (as of a nation) attributable to land as a factor of production in addition to capital and labor **b** : ECONOMIC RENT
— **for rent** : available for use or service in return for payment

²rent (15th century)
transitive verb
1 : to grant the possession and enjoyment of in exchange for rent
2 : to take and hold under an agreement to pay rent
intransitive verb
1 : to be for rent

2 a : to obtain the possession and use of a place or article in exchange for rent **b** : to allow the possession and use of property in exchange for rent
synonym see HIRE
— **rent·abil·i·ty** \ˌren-tə-ˈbi-lə-tē\ *noun*
— **rent·able** \ˈren-tə-bəl\ *adjective*

³rent *past and past participle of* REND

⁴rent *noun* [English dialect *rent* to rend, from Middle English, alteration of *renden* — more at REND] (1535)
1 : an opening made by or as if by rending
2 : a split in a party or organized group : SCHISM
3 : an act or instance of rending

rent-a-car \ˈrent-ə-ˌkär\ *noun* (1935)
: a rented car

¹rent·al \ˈren-t³l\ *noun* (14th century)
1 : an amount paid or collected as rent
2 : something that is rented
3 : an act of renting
4 : a business that rents something

²rental *adjective* (15th century)
1 a : of or relating to rent **b** : available for rent
2 : dealing in rental property ⟨a *rental* agency⟩

rental library *noun* (1928)
: a commercially operated library (as in a store) that lends books at a fixed charge per book per day — called also *lending library*

rent control *noun* (1931)
: government regulation of the amount charged as rent for housing and often also of eviction
— **rent-controlled** *adjective*

rente \ˈrän(t)\ *noun* [French] (1873)
: a government security (as in France) paying interest; *also* : the interest paid

rent·er \ˈren-tər\ *noun* (1655)
: one that rents; *specifically* : the lessee or tenant of property

ren·tier \rä⁰-tyā\ *noun* [French, from Old French, from *rente*] (circa 1847)
: a person who lives on income from property or securities

rent strike *noun* (1964)
: a refusal by a group of tenants to pay rent (as in protest against high rates)

re·nun·ci·a·tion \ri-ˌnən(t)-sē-ˈā-shən\ *noun* [Middle English, from Latin *renuntiation-, renuntiatio,* from *renuntiare* to renounce] (14th century)
: the act or practice of renouncing : REPUDIATION; *specifically* : ascetic self-denial
— **re·nun·ci·a·tive** \ri-ˈnən(t)-sē-ˌā-tiv\ *adjective*
— **re·nun·ci·a·to·ry** \-sē-ə-ˌtȯr-ē, -ˌtȯr-\ *adjective*

re·of·fer \(ˌ)rē-ˈȯ-fər, -ˈä-\ *transitive verb* (1920)
: to offer (a security issue) for public sale

re·open \(ˌ)rē-ˈō-pən, -ˈō-p³m\ (1733)
transitive verb
1 : to open again
2 a : to take up again : RESUME ⟨*reopen* discussion⟩ **b** : to resume discussion or consideration of ⟨*reopen* a contract⟩
3 : to begin again
intransitive verb
: to open again ⟨school *reopens* in September⟩

¹re·or·der \(ˌ)rē-ˈȯr-dər\ (1656)
transitive verb
1 : to arrange in a different way
2 : to give a reorder for
intransitive verb
: to place a reorder

²reorder *noun* (1901)
: an order like a previous order placed with the same supplier

re·or·ga·ni·za·tion \(ˌ)rē-ˌȯr-gə-nə-ˈzā-shən, -ˌȯrg-nə-\ *noun* (1813)
: the act or process of reorganizing : the state of being reorganized; *especially* : the financial reconstruction of a business concern
— **re·or·ga·ni·za·tion·al** \-shnəl, -shə-n³l\ *adjective*

re·or·ga·nize \(ˌ)rē-ˈȯr-gə-ˌnīz\ (circa 1686)

transitive verb
: to organize again or anew
intransitive verb
: to reorganize something
— **re·or·ga·niz·er** *noun*

reo·vi·rus \ˌrē-ō-ˈvī-rəs\ *noun* [respiratory enteric orphan (i.e., unidentified) *virus*] (1959)
: any of a group of double-stranded RNA viruses lacking a lipoprotein envelope that includes many pathogens of plants or animals

¹rep \ˈrep\ *noun* (circa 1705)
slang : REPUTATION; *especially* : status in a group (as a gang)

²rep *noun* (1848)
: REPRESENTATIVE ⟨sales *reps*⟩

³rep *or* **repp** \ˈrep\ *noun* [French *reps,* modification of English *ribs,* plural of *rib*] (1860)
: a plain-weave fabric with prominent rounded crosswise ribs

⁴rep *noun* (1925)
: REPERTORY 2b, 3

⁵rep *noun* [**r**oentgen **e**quivalent **p**hysical] (1947)
: the dosage of an ionizing radiation that will develop the same amount of energy upon absorption in human tissue as one roentgen of X-ray or gamma-ray exposure

⁶rep *noun* [short for *repetition*] (1978)
: a repetition of a specified movement or exercise (as in weight lifting)

re·pack·age \(ˌ)rē-ˈpa-kij\ *transitive verb* (1946)
: to package again or anew; *specifically* : to put into a more efficient or attractive form
— **re·pack·ag·er** *noun*

¹re·pair \ri-ˈpar, -ˈper\ *intransitive verb* [Middle English, from Middle French *repairier* to go back to one's country, from Late Latin *repatriare,* from Latin *re-* + *patria* native country — more at EXPATRIATE] (14th century)
1 a : to betake oneself : GO ⟨*repaired* to the judge's chambers⟩ **b** : to come together : RALLY
2 *obsolete* : RETURN

²repair *noun* (14th century)
1 : the act of repairing : RESORT
2 : a popular gathering place

³repair *verb* [Middle English, from Middle French *reparer,* from Latin *reparare,* from *re-* + *parare* to prepare — more at PARE] (14th century)
transitive verb
1 a : to restore by replacing a part or putting together what is torn or broken : FIX ⟨*repair* a shoe⟩ **b** : to restore to a sound or healthy state : RENEW ⟨*repair* his strength⟩
2 : to make good : compensate for : REMEDY ⟨*repair* a gap in my reading⟩
intransitive verb
: to make repairs
synonym see MEND
— **re·pair·abil·i·ty** \-ˌpar-ə-ˈbi-lə-tē, -ˌper-\ *noun*
— **re·pair·able** \-ˈpar-ə-bəl, -ˈper-\ *adjective*
— **re·pair·er** \-ˈpar-ər, -ˈper-\ *noun*

⁴repair *noun* (15th century)
1 a : an instance or result of repairing **b** : the act or process of repairing **c** : the replacement of destroyed cells or tissues by new formations
2 a : relative condition with respect to soundness or need of repairing **b** : the state of being in good or sound condition

re·pair·man \ri-ˈpar-ˌman, -ˈper-, -mən\ *noun* (1871)
: one who repairs; *specifically* : one whose occupation is to make repairs in a mechanism

\ə\ **abut**	\³\ **kitten** \ər\ **further**	\a\ **ash** \ā\ **ace**
\ä\ **mop, mar**	\aủ\ **out** \ch\ **chin**	\e\ **bet** \ē\ **easy**
\g\ **go**	\i\ **hit** \ī\ **ice** \j\ **job**	\ŋ\ **sing** \ō\ **go**
\ȯ\ **law**	\ȯi\ **boy** \th\ **thin**	\th̲\ **the** \ü\ **loot** \ủ\ **foot**
\y\ **yet**	\zh\ **vision**	*see also* Guide to Pronunciation

re·pand \ri-'pand\ *adjective* [Latin *repandus* spread out, from *repandere* to open wide, from *re-* + *pandere* to spread — more at FATHOM] (circa 1760)
: having a slightly undulating margin 〈a *repand* leaf〉 〈a *repand* colony of bacteria〉

rep·a·ra·ble \'re-p(ə-)rə-bəl\ *adjective* (1570)
: capable of being repaired

rep·a·ra·tion \,re-pə-'rā-shən\ *noun* [Middle English, from Anglo-French, from Late Latin *reparation-, reparatio*, from Latin *reparare*] (14th century)
1 a : a repairing or keeping in repair **b** *plural*
: REPAIRS
2 a : the act of making amends, offering expiation, or giving satisfaction for a wrong or injury **b :** something done or given as amends or satisfaction
3 : the payment of damages **:** INDEMNIFICATION; *specifically* **:** compensation in money or materials payable by a defeated nation for damages to or expenditures sustained by another nation as a result of hostilities with the defeated nation — usually used in plural

re·par·a·tive \ri-'par-ə-tiv\ *adjective* (1656)
1 : of, relating to, or effecting repair
2 : serving to make amends

rep·ar·tee \,re-pər-'tē, -,pär-, -'tā\ *noun* [French *repartie*, from *repartir* to retort, from Middle French, from *re-* + *partir* to divide — more at PART] (circa 1645)
1 a : a quick and witty reply **b :** a succession or interchange of clever retorts **:** amusing and usually light sparring with words
2 : adroitness and cleverness in reply **:** skill in repartee
synonym see WIT

¹re·par·ti·tion \,re-,pär-'ti-shən, ,rē-\ *noun* [probably from Spanish *repartición*, from *repartir* to distribute, from *re-* + *partir* to divide, from Latin *partire* — more at PART] (1555)
: DISTRIBUTION

²re·par·ti·tion \,rē-,pär-'ti-shən\ *noun* [*re-* + *partition*] (1835)
: a second or additional dividing or distribution

re·pass \(,)rē-'pas\ *verb* [Middle English, from Middle French *repasser*, from Old French, from *re-* + *passer* to pass] (15th century)
intransitive verb
: to pass again especially in the opposite direction **:** RETURN
transitive verb
1 : to pass through, over, or by again 〈*repass* the house〉
2 : to cause to pass again
3 : to adopt again 〈*repassed* the resolution〉
— **re·pas·sage** \-'pa-sij\ *noun*

¹re·past \ri-'past, 'rē-,\ *noun* [Middle English, from Middle French, from Old French, from *repaistre* to feed, from *re-* + *paistre* to feed, from Latin *pascere* — more at FOOD] (14th century)
1 : something taken as food **:** MEAL
2 : the act or time of taking food

²re·past \ri-'past\ (15th century)
transitive verb
obsolete **:** FEED
intransitive verb
: to take food **:** FEAST

re·pa·tri·ate \(,)rē-'pā-trē-,āt, -'pa-\ *transitive verb* **-at·ed; -at·ing** [Late Latin *repatriatus*, past participle of *repatriare* to go back to one's country — more at REPAIR] (1611)
: to restore or return to the country of origin, allegiance, or citizenship 〈*repatriate* prisoners of war〉
— **re·pa·tri·ate** \-trē-ət, -trē-,āt\ *noun*
— **re·pa·tri·a·tion** \(,)rē-,pā-trē-'ā-shən, -,pa-\ *noun*

re·pay \(,)rē-'pā\ *verb* **-paid** \-'pād\; **-pay·ing** (15th century)
transitive verb
1 a : to pay back 〈*repay* a loan〉 **b :** to give or inflict in return or requital 〈*repay* evil for evil〉
2 : to make a return payment to **:** COMPENSATE, REQUITE
3 : to make requital for **:** RECOMPENSE 〈the success that *repays* hard work〉
intransitive verb
: to make return payment or requital
synonym see PAY
— **re·pay·able** \-'pā-ə-bəl\ *adjective*
— **re·pay·ment** \-'pā-mənt\ *noun*

re·peal \ri-'pē(ə)l\ *transitive verb* [Middle English *repelen*, from Middle French *repeler*, from Old French, from *re-* + *apeler* to appeal, call] (14th century)
1 : to rescind or annul by authoritative act; *especially* **:** to revoke or abrogate by legislative enactment
2 : ABANDON, RENOUNCE
3 *obsolete* **:** to summon to return **:** RECALL
— **repeal** *noun*
— **re·peal·able** \-'pē-lə-bəl\ *adjective*

re·peal·er \ri-'pē-lər\ *noun* (1765)
: one that repeals; *specifically* **:** a legislative act that abrogates an earlier act

¹re·peat \ri-'pēt\ *verb* [Middle English *repeten*, from Middle French *repeter*, from Latin *repetere* to return to, repeat, from *re-* + *petere* to go to, seek — more at FEATHER] (14th century)
transitive verb
1 a : to say or state again **b :** to say over from memory **:** RECITE **c :** to say after another
2 a : to make, do, or perform again 〈*repeat* an experiment〉 **b :** to make appear again 〈the curtains *repeat* the wallpaper pattern〉 〈will *repeat* the program tomorrow〉 **c :** to go through or experience again 〈had to *repeat* third grade〉
3 : to express or present (oneself) again in the same words, terms, or form
intransitive verb
: to say, do, or accomplish something again; *especially* **:** to win (as a sports championship) another time in succession
— **re·peat·abil·i·ty** \-,pē-tə-'bi-lə-tē\ *noun*
— **re·peat·able** \-'pē-tə-bəl\ *adjective*

²re·peat \ri-'pēt, 'rē-\ *noun* (15th century)
1 a : something repeated **:** REPETITION **b :** a musical passage to be repeated in performance; *also* **:** a sign placed before and after such a passage **c :** a usually transcribed repetition of a radio or television program **d :** a genetic duplication in which the duplicated parts are adjacent to each other along the chromosome
2 : the act of repeating

re·peat·ed \ri-'pē-təd\ *adjective* (1611)
1 : renewed or recurring again and again 〈*repeated* changes of plan〉
2 : said, done, or presented again

re·peat·ed·ly *adverb* (circa 1718)
: AGAIN AND AGAIN

re·peat·er \ri-'pē-tər\ *noun* (1598)
: one that repeats: as **a :** one who relates or recites **b :** a watch or clock with a striking mechanism that upon pressure of a spring will indicate the time in hours or quarters and sometimes minutes **c :** a firearm having a magazine that holds a number of cartridges loaded one at a time into the chamber by the action of the piece **d :** an habitual violator of the laws **e :** one who votes illegally by casting more than one ballot in an election **f :** a student enrolled in a class or course for a second or subsequent time **g :** a device for receiving electronic communication signals and delivering corresponding amplified ones

re·peat·ing *adjective* (1824)
of a firearm **:** designed to load cartridges from a magazine

repeating decimal *noun* (1773)
: a decimal in which after a certain point a particular digit or sequence of digits repeats itself indefinitely — compare TERMINATING DECIMAL

re·pe·chage \,re-pə-'shäzh, 'rē-pə-,\ *noun* [French *repêchage* second chance, reexamination for a candidate who has failed, from *repêcher* to fish out, rescue, from *re-* + *pêcher* to fish, from Latin *piscari* — more at PISCATORY] (1928)
: a trial heat (as in rowing) in which first-round losers are given another chance to qualify for the semifinals

re·pel \ri-'pel\ *verb* **re·pelled; re·pel·ling** [Middle English *repellen*, from Latin *repellere*, from *re-* + *pellere* to drive — more at FELT] (15th century)
transitive verb
1 a : to drive back **:** REPULSE **b :** to fight against **:** RESIST
2 : TURN AWAY, REJECT 〈*repelled* the insinuation〉
3 a : to drive away **:** DISCOURAGE 〈foul words and frowns must not *repel* a lover —Shakespeare〉 **b :** to be incapable of adhering to, mixing with, taking up, or holding **c :** to force away or apart or tend to do so by mutual action at a distance
4 : to cause aversion in **:** DISGUST
intransitive verb
: to cause aversion
— **re·pel·ler** *noun*

re·pel·len·cy \ri-'pe-lən(t)-sē\ *noun* (1747)
: the quality or capacity of repelling

¹re·pel·lent *also* **re·pel·lant** \ri-'pe-lənt\ *adjective* [Latin *repellent-, repellens*, present participle of *repellere*] (1643)
1 : serving or tending to drive away or ward off — often used in combination 〈a mosquito-*repellent* spray〉
2 : arousing aversion or disgust **:** REPULSIVE
— **re·pel·lent·ly** *adverb*

²repellent *also* **repellant** *noun* (1661)
: something that repels; *especially* **:** a substance that repels insects

¹re·pent \ri-'pent\ *verb* [Middle English, from Old French *repentir*, from *re-* + *pentir* to be sorry, from Latin *paenitēre* — more at PENITENT] (14th century)
intransitive verb
1 : to turn from sin and dedicate oneself to the amendment of one's life
2 a : to feel regret or contrition **b :** to change one's mind
transitive verb
1 : to cause to feel regret or contrition
2 : to feel sorrow, regret, or contrition for
— **re·pent·er** *noun*

²re·pent \'rē-pənt\ *adjective* [Latin *repent-, repens*, present participle of *repere* to creep — more at REPTILE] (1669)
: CREEPING, PROSTRATE 〈*repent* stems〉

re·pen·tance \ri-'pen-t°n(t)s\ *noun* (14th century)
: the action or process of repenting especially for misdeeds or moral shortcomings
synonym see PENITENCE

re·pen·tant \-t°nt\ *adjective* (13th century)
1 : experiencing repentance **:** PENITENT
2 : expressive of repentance
— **re·pen·tant·ly** *adverb*

re·per·cus·sion \,rē-pər-'kə-shən, ,re-\ *noun* [Latin *repercussion-, repercussio*, from *repercutere* to drive back, from *re-* + *percutere* to beat — more at PERCUSSION] (1536)
1 : REFLECTION, REVERBERATION
2 a : an action or effect given or exerted in return **:** a reciprocal action or effect **b :** a widespread, indirect, or unforeseen effect of an act, action, or event — usually used in plural
— **re·per·cus·sive** \-'kə-siv\ *adjective*

rep·er·toire \'re-pə(r)-,twär\ *noun* [French *répertoire*, from Late Latin *repertorium*] (1847)
1 a : a list or supply of dramas, operas, pieces, or parts that a company or person is prepared to perform **b :** a supply of skills, devices, or expedients 〈part of the *repertoire* of a quarterback〉; *broadly* **:** AMOUNT, SUPPLY 〈an endless

repeat 1b

repertoire of summer clothes⟩ **c :** a list or supply of capabilities ⟨the instruction *repertoire* of a computer⟩
2 a : the complete list or supply of dramas, operas, or musical works available for performance ⟨our modern orchestral *repertoire*⟩ **b :** the complete list or supply of skills, devices, or ingredients used in a particular field, occupation, or practice ⟨the *repertoire* of literary criticism⟩

rep·er·to·ry \'re-pə(r)-ˌtōr-ē, -ˌtȯr-\ *noun, plural* **-ries** [Late Latin *repertorium* list, from Latin *reperire* to find, from *re-* + *parere* to produce — more at PARE] (1593)
1 : a place where something may be found **:** REPOSITORY
2 a : REPERTOIRE **b :** a company that presents several different plays, operas, or pieces usually alternately in the course of a season at one theater **c :** a theater housing such a company
3 : the production and presentation of plays by a repertory company ⟨acting in *repertory*⟩

rep·e·tend \'re-pə-ˌtend\ *noun* [Latin *repetendus* to be repeated, gerundive of *repetere* to repeat] (1874)
: a repeated sound, word, or phrase; *specifically* **:** REFRAIN

rep·e·ti·tion \ˌre-pə-'ti-shən\ *noun* [Middle English *repeticioun*, from Latin *repetition-, repetitio,* from *repetere* to repeat] (15th century)
1 : the act or an instance of repeating or being repeated
2 : MENTION, RECITAL
— **rep·e·ti·tion·al** \-'tish-nəl, -'ti-shə-n°l\ *adjective*

rep·e·ti·tious \-'ti-shəs\ *adjective* (1675)
: characterized or marked by repetition; *especially* **:** tediously repeating
— **rep·e·ti·tious·ly** *adverb*
— **rep·e·ti·tious·ness** *noun*

re·pet·i·tive \ri-'pe-tə-tiv\ *adjective* (1839)
1 : containing repetition
2 : REPETITIOUS
— **re·pet·i·tive·ly** *adverb*
— **re·pet·i·tive·ness** *noun*

re·pine \ri-'pīn\ *intransitive verb* (circa 1530)
1 : to feel or express dejection or discontent
2 : to long for something
— **re·pin·er** *noun*

re·place \ri-'plās\ *transitive verb* (1595)
1 : to restore to a former place or position ⟨*replace* cards in a file⟩
2 : to take the place of especially as a substitute or successor
3 : to put something new in the place of ⟨*replace* a worn carpet⟩ ☆
— **re·place·able** \-'plā-sə-bəl\ *adjective*
— **re·plac·er** *noun*

re·place·ment \ri-'plās-mənt\ *noun* (circa 1790)
1 : the action or process of replacing **:** the state of being replaced
2 : one that replaces another especially in a job or function

replacement set *noun* (1959)
: a set of elements any one of which may be used to replace a given variable or placeholder in a mathematical sentence or expression (as an equation)

re·plant \(ˌ)rē-'plant\ *transitive verb* (1575)
1 : to plant again or anew
2 : to provide with new plants
3 : to subject to replantation

re·plan·ta·tion \ˌrē-(ˌ)plan-'tā-shən\ *noun* (1870)
: reattachment or reinsertion of a bodily part (as a limb or tooth) after separation from the body

¹re·play \(ˌ)rē-'plā\ *transitive verb* (1884)
: to play again or over

²re·play \'rē-ˌplā\ *noun* (1895)
1 a : an act or instance of replaying **b :** the playing of a tape (as a videotape)
2 : REPETITION, REENACTMENT ⟨don't want a *replay* of our old mistakes⟩

re·plead·er \(ˌ)rē-'plē-dər\ *noun* [*replead* to plead again + *-er* (as in *misnomer*)] (1607)
1 : a second legal pleading
2 : the right of pleading again granted usually when the issue raised is immaterial or insufficient

re·plen·ish \ri-'ple-nish\ *verb* [Middle English *replenisshen*, from Middle French *repleniss-*, stem of *replenir* to fill, from Old French, from *re-* + *plein* full, from Latin *plenus* — more at FULL] (14th century)
transitive verb
1 a : to fill with persons or animals **:** STOCK **b** *archaic* **:** to supply fully **:** PERFECT **c :** to fill with inspiration or power **:** NOURISH
2 a : to fill or build up again ⟨*replenished* his glass⟩ **b :** to make good **:** REPLACE
intransitive verb
: to become full **:** fill up again
— **re·plen·ish·able** \-ni-shə-bəl\ *adjective*
— **re·plen·ish·er** *noun*
— **re·plen·ish·ment** \-nish-mənt\ *noun*

re·plete \ri-'plēt\ *adjective* [Middle English, from Middle French & Latin; Middle French *replet*, from Latin *repletus*, past participle of *replēre* to fill up, from *re-* + *plēre* to fill — more at FULL] (14th century)
1 : fully or abundantly provided or filled ⟨a book *replete* with . . . delicious details —William Safire⟩
2 a : abundantly fed **b :** FAT, STOUT
3 : COMPLETE
synonym see FULL
— **re·plete·ness** *noun*

re·ple·tion \ri-'plē-shən\ *noun* (14th century)
1 : the act of eating to excess **:** the state of being fed to excess **:** SURFEIT
2 : the condition of being filled up or overcrowded
3 : fulfillment of a need or desire **:** SATISFACTION

¹re·plev·in \ri-'ple-vən\ *noun* [Middle English, from Anglo-French *replevine*, from *replevir* to give security, from Old French, from *re-* + *plevir* to pledge, from (assumed) Late Latin *plebere* — more at PLEDGE] (15th century)
1 : the recovery by a person of goods or chattels claimed to be wrongfully taken or detained upon the person's giving security to try the matter in court and return the goods if defeated in the action
2 : the writ or the common-law action whereby goods and chattels are replevied

²replevin *transitive verb* (1678)
: REPLEVY

¹re·plevy \ri-'ple-vē\ *noun, plural* **re·plev·ies** [Middle English, from Anglo-French *replevir*, verb] (15th century)
: REPLEVIN

²replevy *transitive verb* **re·plev·ied; re·plevy·ing** (1596)
: to take or get back by a writ for replevin
— **re·plevi·able** \-vē-ə-bəl\ *adjective*

rep·li·ca \'re-pli-kə\ *noun* [Italian, repetition, from *replicare* to repeat, from Late Latin, from Latin, to fold back — more at REPLY] (1824)
1 : an exact reproduction (as of a painting) executed by the original artist ⟨a *replica* of this was painted . . . this year —Constance Strachey⟩
2 : a copy exact in all details ⟨DNA makes a *replica* of itself⟩ ⟨sailed a *replica* of the Viking ship⟩; *broadly* **:** COPY ⟨this faithful, pathetic *replica* of a Midwestern suburb —G. F. Kennan⟩ □
synonym see REPRODUCTION

rep·li·ca·ble \'re-plə-kə-bəl\ *adjective* (1950)
: capable of replication ⟨*replicable* experimental results⟩
— **rep·li·ca·bil·i·ty** \ˌre-plə-kə-'bi-lə-tē\ *noun*

rep·li·case \'re-pli-ˌkās, -ˌkāz\ *noun* [*replication* + *-ase*] (1963)

: a polymerase that promotes synthesis of a particular RNA in the presence of a template of RNA

¹rep·li·cate \'re-plə-ˌkāt\ *verb* **-cat·ed; -cat·ing** [Late Latin *replicatus*, past participle of *replicare*] (15th century)
transitive verb
: DUPLICATE, REPEAT ⟨*replicate* a statistical experiment⟩
intransitive verb
: to undergo replication **:** produce a replica of itself ⟨virus particles *replicating* in cells⟩

²rep·li·cate \-kət\ *adjective* (1922)
: MANIFOLD, REPEATED

³rep·li·cate \-kət\ *noun* (1929)
: one of several identical experiments, procedures, or samples

rep·li·ca·tion \ˌre-plə-'kā-shən\ *noun* (14th century)
1 a : ANSWER, REPLY **b** (1) **:** an answer to a reply **:** REJOINDER (2) **:** a plaintiff's reply to a defendant's plea, answer, or counterclaim
2 : ECHO, REVERBERATION
3 a : COPY, REPRODUCTION **b :** the action or process of reproducing
4 : performance of an experiment or procedure more than once; *especially* **:** systematic or random repetition of agricultural test rows or plats to reduce error

rep·li·ca·tive \'re-pli-ˌkā-tiv\ *adjective* (circa 1890)
: of, relating to, involved in, or characterized by replication ⟨the *replicative* form of tobacco mosaic virus⟩

rep·li·con \'re-pli-ˌkän\ *noun* [*replicate* + *²-on*] (1963)
: a linear or circular section of DNA or RNA which replicates sequentially as a unit

¹re·ply \ri-'plī\ *verb* **re·plied; re·ply·ing** [Middle English *replien*, from Middle French *replier* to fold again, from Latin *replicare* to fold back, from *re-* + *plicare* to fold — more at PLY] (14th century)
intransitive verb
1 a : to respond in words or writing **b :** ECHO, RESOUND **c :** to make a legal replication

\ə\ abut \ᵊ\ kitten \ər\ further \a\ ash \ā\ ace
\ä\ mop, mar \aù\ out \ch\ chin \e\ bet \ē\ easy
\g\ go \i\ hit \ī\ ice \j\ job \ŋ\ sing \ō\ go
\ȯ\ law \ȯi\ boy \th\ thin \th̲\ the \ü\ loot \ù\ foot
\y\ yet \zh\ vision *see also* Guide to Pronunciation

2 : to do something in response; *specifically*
: to return gunfire or an attack
transitive verb
: to give as an answer
synonym see ANSWER
— **re·pli·er** \-'plī-(-ə)r\ *noun*
²**reply** *noun, plural* **replies** (1560)
1 : something said, written, or done in answer or response
2 : REPLICATION 1b(2)
re·po \'rē-ˌpō\ *noun, plural* **repos** [by shortening & alteration] (1963)
: REPURCHASE AGREEMENT
re·po·lar·i·za·tion \ˌrē-ˌpō-lə-rə-'zā-shən\ *noun* (1922)
: polarization of a muscle fiber, cell, or membrane following depolarization
— **re·po·lar·ize** \(ˌ)rē-'pō-lə-ˌrīz\ *verb*
¹**re·port** \ri-'pōrt, -'pȯrt\ *noun* [Middle English, from Middle French, from Old French, from *reporter* to report, from Latin *reportare*, from *re-* + *portare* to carry — more at FARE] (14th century)
1 a : common talk or an account spread by common talk : RUMOR **b** : quality of reputation ⟨a witness of good *report*⟩
2 a : a usually detailed account or statement ⟨a news *report*⟩ **b** : an account or statement of a judicial opinion or decision **c** : a usually formal record of the proceedings of a meeting or session
3 : an explosive noise
— **on report** : subject to disciplinary action
²**report** (14th century)
transitive verb
1 a : to give an account of : RELATE **b** : to describe as being in a specified state ⟨*reported* him much improved⟩
2 a : to serve as carrier of (a message) **b** : to relate the words or sense of (something said) **c** : to make a written record or summary of **d** (1) : to watch for and write about the newsworthy aspects or developments of : COVER (2) : to prepare or present an account of for broadcast
3 a (1) : to give a formal or official account or statement of ⟨the treasurer *reported* a balance of ten dollars⟩ (2) : to return or present (a matter referred for consideration) with conclusions or recommendations **b** : to announce or relate as the result of investigation ⟨*reported* no sign of disease⟩ **c** : to announce the presence, arrival, or sighting of **d** : to make known to the proper authorities ⟨*report* a fire⟩ **e** : to make a charge of misconduct against
intransitive verb
1 a : to give an account : TELL **b** : to present oneself **c** : to account for oneself ⟨*reported* sick on Friday⟩
2 : to make, issue, or submit a report
3 : to act in the capacity of a reporter
re·port·able \ri-'pōr-tə-bəl, -'pȯr-\ *adjective* (1858)
1 : worth reporting ⟨*reportable* news⟩
2 : required by law to be reported ⟨*reportable* income⟩ ⟨*reportable* diseases⟩
re·port·age \ri-'pōr-tij, -'pȯr-, *especially for 2* ˌre-pər-'täzh, ˌre-ˌpȯr-\ *noun* [French, from *reporter* to report] (circa 1864)
1 a : the act or process of reporting news **b** : something (as news) that is reported
2 : writing intended to give an account of observed or documented events
report card *noun* (1920)
1 : a report on a student that is periodically submitted by a school to the student's parents or guardian
2 : an evaluation of performance
re·port·ed·ly \ri-'pōr-təd-lē, -'pȯr-\ *adverb* (1901)
: according to report
re·port·er \ri-'pōr-tər, -'pȯr-\ *noun* (14th century)
: one that reports: as **a** : one who makes authorized statements of law decisions or legisla-

tive proceedings **b** : one who makes a shorthand record of a speech or proceeding **c** (1) : one employed by a newspaper, magazine, or television company to gather and report news (2) : one who broadcasts news
— **re·por·to·ri·al** \ˌre-pə(r)-'tōr-ē-əl, ˌrē-, -'tȯr-\ *adjective*
— **re·por·to·ri·al·ly** \-ē-ə-lē\ *adverb*
report out *transitive verb* (1907)
: to return after consideration and often with revisions to a legislative body for action ⟨after much debate the committee *reported* the bill *out*⟩
report stage *noun* (circa 1906)
: the stage in the British legislative process preceding the third reading and concerned especially with amendments and details
re·pos·al \ri-'pō-zəl\ *noun* (1605)
obsolete : the act of reposing
¹**re·pose** \ri-'pōz\ *verb* **re·posed; re·pos·ing** [Middle English, from Middle French *reposer*, from Old French, from Late Latin *repausare* to stop, from Latin *re-* + Late Latin *pausare* to stop, from Latin *pausa* pause] (15th century)
transitive verb
: to lay at rest
intransitive verb
1 a : to lie at rest **b** : to lie dead ⟨*reposing* in state⟩ **c** : to remain still or concealed
2 : to take a rest
3 *archaic* : RELY
4 : to rest for support : LIE
²**repose** *noun* (1509)
1 a : a state of resting after exertion or strain; *especially* : rest in sleep **b** : eternal or heavenly rest ⟨pray for the *repose* of a soul⟩
2 a : a place of rest **b** : PEACE, TRANQUILLITY ⟨the *repose* of the bayous⟩ **c** : a harmony in the arrangement of parts and colors that is restful to the eye
3 a : lack of activity : QUIESCENCE **b** : cessation or absence of activity, movement, or animation ⟨the face in *repose* is grave and thoughtful⟩
4 : composure of manner : POISE
³**re·pose** *transitive verb* **re·posed; re·pos·ing** [Middle English, to replace, from Latin *reponere* (perfect indicative *reposui*)] (15th century)
1 *archaic* : to put away or set down : DEPOSIT
2 a : to place (as confidence or trust) in someone or something **b** : to place for control, management, or use
re·pose·ful \ri-'pōz-fəl\ *adjective* (1852)
: of a kind to induce ease and relaxation
— **re·pose·ful·ly** \-fə-lē\ *adverb*
— **re·pose·ful·ness** *noun*
re·pos·it *transitive verb* **re·pos·it·ed** \-'pä-zə-təd, -'päz-təd\; **re·pos·it·ing** \-'pä-zə-tiŋ, -'päz-tiŋ\ [Latin *repositus*, past participle of *reponere* to replace, from *re-* + *ponere* to place — more at POSITION] (circa 1641)
1 \ri-'pä-zət\ : DEPOSIT, STORE
2 \(ˌ)rē-\ : to put back in place : REPLACE
¹**re·po·si·tion** \ˌrē-pə-'zi-shən, ˌre-\ *noun* (1588)
: the act of repositing : the state of being reposited
²**re·po·si·tion** \ˌrē-pə-'zi-shən\ *transitive verb* (circa 1859)
1 : to change the position of
2 : to revise the marketing strategy of (a product or a company) so as to increase sales
¹**re·pos·i·to·ry** \ri-'pä-zə-ˌtōr-ē, -ˌtȯr-\ *noun, plural* **-ries** (15th century)
1 : a place, room, or container where something is deposited or stored : DEPOSITORY
2 : a side altar in a Roman Catholic church where the consecrated Host is reserved from Maundy Thursday until Good Friday
3 : one that contains or stores something nonmaterial ⟨considered the book a *repository* of knowledge⟩
4 : a place or region richly supplied with a natural resource

5 : a person to whom something is confided or entrusted
²**repository** *adjective* (1950)
of a drug : designed to act over a prolonged period ⟨*repository* penicillin⟩
re·pos·sess \ˌrē-pə-'zes *also* -'ses\ *transitive verb* (15th century)
1 a : to regain possession of **b** : to resume possession of in default of the payment of installments due
2 : to restore to possession
— **re·pos·ses·sion** \-'ze-shən *also* -'se-\ *noun*
— **re·pos·ses·sor** \-'ze-sər *also* -'se-\ *noun*
¹**re·pous·sé** \rə-ˌpü-'sā, -'pü-ˌ\ *adjective* [French, literally, pushed back] (1858)
1 : shaped or ornamented with patterns in relief made by hammering or pressing on the reverse side — used especially of metal
2 : formed in relief
²**repoussé** *noun* (1858)
1 : repoussé work
2 : repoussé decoration
re·pow·er \(ˌ)rē-'pau̇(-ə)r\ *transitive verb* (1954)
: to provide again or anew with power; *especially* : to provide (as a boat) with a new engine
repp *variant of* REP
rep·re·hend \ˌre-pri-'hend\ *transitive verb* [Middle English, from Latin *reprehendere*, literally, to hold back, from *re-* + *prehendere* to grasp — more at GET] (14th century)
: to voice disapproval of : CENSURE
synonym see CRITICIZE
rep·re·hen·si·ble \ˌre-pri-'hen(t)-sə-bəl\ *adjective* (14th century)
: worthy of or deserving reprehension : CULPABLE
— **rep·re·hen·si·bil·i·ty** \-ˌhen(t)-sə-'bi-lə-tē\ *noun*
— **rep·re·hen·si·ble·ness** \-'hen(t)-sə-bəl-nəs\ *noun*
— **rep·re·hen·si·bly** \-blē\ *adverb*
rep·re·hen·sion \-'hen(t)-shən\ *noun* [Middle English *reprehension*, from Middle French or Latin; Middle French *reprehension*, from Latin *reprehension-, reprehensio*, from *reprehendere*] (14th century)
: the act of reprehending : CENSURE
rep·re·hen·sive \-'hen(t)-siv\ *adjective* (1589)
: serving to reprehend : conveying reprehension or reproof
rep·re·sent \ˌre-pri-'zent\ *verb* [Middle English, from Middle French *representer*, from Latin *repraesentare*, from *re-* + *praesentare* to present] (14th century)
transitive verb
1 : to bring clearly before the mind : PRESENT ⟨a book which *represents* the character of early America⟩
2 : to serve as a sign or symbol of ⟨the flag *represents* our country⟩
3 : to portray or exhibit in art : DEPICT
4 : to serve as the counterpart or image of : TYPIFY ⟨a movie hero who *represents* the ideals of the culture⟩
5 a : to produce on the stage **b** : to act the part or role of
6 a (1) : to take the place of in some respect (2) : to act in the place of or for usually by legal right **b** : to serve especially in a legislative body by delegated authority usually resulting from election
7 : to describe as having a specified character or quality ⟨*represents* himself as a friend⟩
8 a : to give one's impression and judgment of : state in a manner intended to affect action or judgment **b** : to point out in protest or remonstrance
9 : to serve as a specimen, example, or instance of

10 a : to form an image or representation of in the mind **b** (1) **:** to apprehend (an object) by means of an idea (2) **:** to recall in memory **11 :** to correspond to in essence **:** CONSTITUTE *intransitive verb*
: to make representations against something **:** PROTEST
— **rep·re·sent·able** \-'zen-tə-bəl\ *adjective*
— **rep·re·sent·er** *noun*
re–pre·sent \ˌrē-pri-'zent\ *transitive verb* (1564)
: to present again or anew
— **re–pre·sen·ta·tion** \ˌrē-ˌprē-ˌzen-'tā-shən, -ˌpre-zᵊn-, -ˌprē-zᵊn-\ *noun*
rep·re·sen·ta·tion \ˌre-pri-ˌzen-'tā-shən, -zən-\ *noun* (15th century)
1 : one that represents: as **a :** an artistic likeness or image **b** (1) **:** a statement or account made to influence opinion or action (2) **:** an incidental or collateral statement of fact on the faith of which a contract is entered into **c :** a dramatic production or performance **d** (1) **:** a usually formal statement made against something or to effect a change (2) **:** a usually formal protest
2 : the act or action of representing **:** the state of being represented: as **a :** REPRESENTATIONALISM 2 **b** (1) **:** the action or fact of one person standing for another so as to have the rights and obligations of the person represented (2) **:** the substitution of an individual or class in place of a person (as a child for a deceased parent) **c :** the action of representing or the fact of being represented especially in a legislative body
3 : the body of persons representing a constituency
— **rep·re·sen·ta·tion·al** \-shnəl, -shə-nᵊl\ *adjective*
— **rep·re·sen·ta·tion·al·ly** *adverb*
rep·re·sen·ta·tion·al·ism \-shnə-ˌli-zəm, -shə-nᵊl-ˌi-\ *noun* (1899)
1 : the doctrine that the immediate object of knowledge is an idea in the mind distinct from the external object which is the occasion of perception
2 : the theory or practice of realistic representation in art
— **rep·re·sen·ta·tion·al·ist** \-list, -ist\ *noun*
¹**rep·re·sen·ta·tive** \ˌre-pri-'zen-tə-tiv\ *adjective* (1532)
1 : serving to represent
2 a : standing or acting for another especially through delegated authority **b :** of, based on, or constituting a government in which the many are represented by persons chosen from among them usually by election
3 : serving as a typical or characteristic example ⟨a *representative* moviegoer⟩
4 : of or relating to representation or representationalism
— **rep·re·sen·ta·tive·ly** *adverb*
— **rep·re·sen·ta·tive·ness** *noun*
— **rep·re·sen·ta·tiv·i·ty** \-ˌzen-tə-'ti-və-tē\ *noun*
²**representative** *noun* (1647)
1 : a typical example of a group, class, or quality **:** SPECIMEN
2 : one that represents another or others: as **a** (1) **:** one that represents a constituency as a member of a legislative body (2) **:** a member of the house of representatives of the U.S. Congress or a state legislature **b :** one that represents another as agent, deputy, substitute, or delegate usually being invested with the authority of the principal **c :** one that represents a business organization **d :** one that represents another as successor or heir
re·press \ri-'pres\ *verb* [Middle English, from Latin *repressus,* past participle of *reprimere* to check, from *re-* + *premere* to press — more at PRESS] (14th century)
transitive verb

1 a : to check by or as if by pressure **:** CURB ⟨*injustice* was *repressed*⟩ **b :** to put down by force **:** SUBDUE ⟨*repress* a disturbance⟩
2 a : to hold in by self-control ⟨*repressed* a laugh⟩ **b :** to prevent the natural or normal expression, activity, or development of ⟨*repressed* her anger⟩
3 : to exclude from consciousness
4 : to inactivate (a gene or formation of a gene product) by allosteric combination at a DNA binding site
intransitive verb
: to take repressive action
— **re·press·ibil·i·ty** \-ˌpre-sə-'bi-lə-tē\ *noun*
— **re·press·ible** \-'pre-sə-bəl\ *adjective*
— **re·pres·sive** \-'pre-siv\ *adjective*
— **re·pres·sive·ly** *adverb*
— **re·pres·sive·ness** *noun*
re–press \ˌ(ˌ)rē-'pres\ *transitive verb* (14th century)
: to press again ⟨*re-press* a record⟩
re·pressed \ri-'prest\ *adjective* (1665)
1 : subjected to or marked by repression
2 : characterized by restraint
re·pres·sion \ri-'pre-shən\ *noun* (1533)
1 a : the action or process of repressing **:** the state of being repressed ⟨*repression* of unpopular opinions⟩ **b :** an instance of repressing ⟨racial *repressions*⟩
2 a : a process by which unacceptable desires or impulses are excluded from consciousness and left to operate in the unconscious **b :** an item so excluded
— **re·pres·sion·ist** \-sh(ə-)nist\ *adjective*
re·pres·sor \ri-'pre-sər\ *noun* [New Latin] (1611)
: one that represses; *especially* **:** a protein that is determined by a regulatory gene, binds to a genetic operator, and inhibits the initiation of transcription of messenger RNA
re·priev·al \ri-'prē-vəl\ *noun* (circa 1586)
archaic **:** REPRIEVE
¹**re·prieve** \ri-'prēv\ *transitive verb* **re·prieved; re·priev·ing** [alteration of earlier *repry,* perhaps from Middle French *repris,* past participle of *reprendre* to take back] (1596)
1 : to delay the punishment of (as a condemned prisoner)
2 : to give relief or deliverance to for a time
²**reprieve** *noun* (1592)
1 a : the act of reprieving **:** the state of being reprieved **b :** a formal temporary suspension of the execution of a sentence especially of death
2 : an order or warrant for a reprieve
3 : a temporary respite (as from pain or trouble)
¹**rep·ri·mand** \'re-prə-ˌmand\ *noun* [French *réprimande,* from Latin *reprimenda,* feminine of *reprimendus,* gerundive of *reprimere* to check — more at REPRESS] (1636)
: a severe or formal reproof
²**reprimand** *transitive verb* (1681)
: to reprove sharply or censure formally usually from a position of authority
synonym SEE REPROVE
¹**re·print** \ˌ(ˌ)rē-'print\ *transitive verb* (1551)
: to print again **:** make a reprint of
²**re·print** \'rē-ˌprint, ˌ(ˌ)rē-'\ *noun* (1611)
: a reproduction of printed matter: as **a :** a subsequent printing of a book already published that preserves the identical text of the previous printing **b :** OFFPRINT **c :** matter (as an article) that has appeared in print before
re·print·er \ˌ(ˌ)rē-'prin-tər\ *noun* (1689)
: one that publishes a reprint
re·pri·sal \ri-'prī-zəl\ *noun* [Middle English *reprisail,* from Middle French *reprisaille,* from Old Italian *ripresaglia,* from *ripreso,* past participle of *riprendere* to take back, from *ri-* re- (from Latin *re-*) + *prendere* to take, from Latin *prehendere* — more at GET] (15th century)
1 a : the act or practice in international law of resorting to force short of war in retaliation for

damage or loss suffered **b :** an instance of such action
2 *obsolete* **:** PRIZE
3 : the regaining of something (as by recapture)
4 : something (as a sum of money) given or paid in restitution — usually used in plural
5 : a retaliatory act
¹**re·prise** \ri-'prēz, *1 is also* -'prīz\ *noun* [Middle English, from Middle French, literally, action of taking back, from Old French, from *reprendre* to take back, from *re-* + *prendre* to take, from Latin *prehendere*] (15th century)
1 : a deduction or charge made yearly out of a manor or estate — usually used in plural
2 : a recurrence, renewal, or resumption of an action
3 a : a musical repetition: (1) **:** the repetition of the exposition preceding the development (2) **:** RECAPITULATION **b :** a repeated performance **:** REPETITION
²**re·prise** \ri-'prēz, *3 is* -'prēz\ *transitive verb* **re·prised; re·pris·ing** [Middle French *reprise* action of taking back] (15th century)
1 *archaic* **:** TAKE BACK; *especially* **:** to recover by force
2 *archaic* **:** COMPENSATE
3 a : to repeat the performance of **b :** RECAPITULATE
re·pris·ti·nate \ˌ(ˌ)rē-'pris-tə-ˌnāt\ *transitive verb* **-nat·ed; -nat·ing** [*re-* + *pristine* + ⁴*-ate*] (1659)
: to restore to an original state or condition
— **re·pris·ti·na·tion** \ˌ(ˌ)rē-ˌpris-tə-'nā-shən\ *noun*
re·pro \'rē-(ˌ)prō\ *noun, plural* **repros** [short for *reproduction*] (1946)
1 : a clear sharp proof made especially from a letterpress printing surface to serve as photographic copy for a printing plate
2 : REPRODUCTION 2
¹**re·proach** \ri-'prōch\ *noun* [Middle English *reproche,* from Middle French, from Old French, from *reprochier* to reproach, from (assumed) Vulgar Latin *repropiare,* from Latin *re-* + *prope* near — more at APPROACH] (14th century)
1 : an expression of rebuke or disapproval
2 : the act or action of reproaching or disapproving ⟨was beyond *reproach*⟩
3 a : a cause or occasion of blame, discredit, or disgrace **b :** DISCREDIT, DISGRACE
4 *obsolete* **:** one subjected to censure or scorn
— **re·proach·ful** \-fəl\ *adjective*
— **re·proach·ful·ly** \-fə-lē\ *adverb*
— **re·proach·ful·ness** *noun*
²**reproach** *transitive verb* (14th century)
1 : to express disappointment in or displeasure with (a person) for conduct that is blameworthy or in need of amendment
2 : to make (something) a matter of reproach
3 : to bring into discredit
synonym SEE REPROVE
— **re·proach·able** \-'prō-chə-bəl\ *adjective*
— **re·proach·er** *noun*
— **re·proach·ing·ly** \-'prō-chiŋ-lē\ *adverb*
rep·ro·bance \'re-prə-bən(t)s\ *noun* (1604)
archaic **:** REPROBATION
¹**rep·ro·bate** \'re-prə-ˌbāt\ *transitive verb* **-bat·ed; -bat·ing** [Middle English, from Late Latin *reprobatus,* past participle of *reprobare* — more at REPROVE] (15th century)
1 : to condemn strongly as unworthy, unacceptable, or evil ⟨*reprobating* the laxity of the age⟩
2 : to foreordain to damnation
3 : to refuse to accept **:** REJECT
synonym SEE CRITICIZE
— **rep·ro·ba·tive** \'re-prə-ˌbā-tiv\ *adjective*

\ə\ **abut** \ᵊ\ **kitten** \ər\ **further** \a\ **ash** \ā\ **ace** \ä\ **mop, mar** \au̇\ **out** \ch\ **chin** \e\ **bet** \ē\ **easy** \g\ **go** \i\ **hit** \ī\ **ice** \j\ **job** \ŋ\ **sing** \ō\ **go** \o̅\ **law** \o̅i\ **boy** \th\ **thin** \t̲h̲\ **the** \ü\ **loot** \u̇\ **foot** \y\ **yet** \zh\ **vision** *see also* Guide to Pronunciation

— **rep·ro·ba·to·ry** \-bə-ˌtōr-ē, -ˌtȯr-\ adjective

²**reprobate** adjective (15th century)
1 archaic : rejected as worthless or not standing a test : CONDEMNED
2 a : foreordained to damnation **b :** morally corrupt : DEPRAVED
3 : expressing or involving reprobation
4 : of, relating to, or characteristic of a reprobate

³**reprobate** noun (1545)
: a reprobate person

rep·ro·ba·tion \ˌre-prə-'bā-shən\ noun (14th century)
: the act of reprobating or the state of being reprobated

re·pro·cess \(ˌ)rē-'prä-ˌses, -'prō-, -səs\ transitive verb (1921)
: to subject to a special process or treatment in preparation for reuse; especially : to extract uranium and plutonium from (the spent fuel rods of a nuclear reactor) for use again as fuel

re·pro·duce \ˌrē-prə-'düs, -'dyüs\ (1611)
transitive verb
: to produce again: as **a :** to produce (new individuals of the same kind) by a sexual or asexual process **b :** to cause to exist again or anew ⟨reproduce water from steam⟩ **c :** to imitate closely ⟨sound-effects can reproduce the sound of thunder⟩ **d :** to present again **e :** to make a representation (as an image or copy) of ⟨reproduce a face on canvas⟩ **f :** to revive mentally : RECALL **g :** to translate (a recording) into sound
intransitive verb
1 : to undergo reproduction
2 : to produce offspring
— **re·pro·duc·er** noun
— **re·pro·duc·ibil·i·ty** \-ˌdü-sə-'bi-lə-tē, -ˌdyü-\ noun
— **re·pro·duc·ible** \-'dü-sə-bəl, -'dyü-\ adjective or noun
— **re·pro·duc·ibly** \-blē\ adverb

re·pro·duc·tion \ˌrē-prə-'dək-shən\ noun (1659)
1 : the act or process of reproducing; specifically : the process by which plants and animals give rise to offspring and which fundamentally consists of the segregation of a portion of the parental body by a sexual or asexual process and its subsequent growth and differentiation into a new individual
2 : something reproduced : COPY
3 : young seedling trees in a forest ☆

reproduction proof noun (1945)
: REPRO 1

¹**re·pro·duc·tive** \ˌrē-prə-'dək-tiv\ adjective (1753)
: of, relating to, or capable of reproduction
— **re·pro·duc·tive·ly** adverb

²**reproductive** noun (1934)
: an actual or potential parent; specifically : a sexually functional social insect

re·pro·gram \(ˌ)rē-'prō-ˌgram, -grəm\ (1959)
transitive verb
: to program anew; especially : to write new programs for (as a computer)
intransitive verb
: to rewrite or revise a program especially of a computer
— **re·pro·gram·ma·ble** \-'prō-ˌgra-mə-bəl, -ˌprō-'gra-\ adjective

re·prog·ra·phy \ri-'prä-grə-fē\ noun [reproduction + -graphy] (1956)
: facsimile reproduction (as by photocopying) of graphic matter
— **re·prog·ra·pher** \-grə-fər\ noun
— **re·pro·graph·ic** \ˌrē-prə-'gra-fik, ˌre-\ adjective
— **re·pro·graph·ics** \-fiks\ noun plural

re·proof \ri-'prüf\ noun [Middle English reprof, from Middle French reprove, from Old French, from reprover] (14th century)
: criticism for a fault : REBUKE

re·prove \ri-'prüv\ verb **re·proved; re·prov·ing** [Middle English, from Middle

French reprover, from Late Latin reprobare to disapprove, condemn, from Latin re- + probare to test, approve — more at PROVE] (14th century)
transitive verb
1 : to scold or correct usually gently or with kindly intent
2 : to express disapproval of : CENSURE ⟨it is not for me to reprove popular taste —D. W. Brogan⟩
3 obsolete : DISPROVE, REFUTE
4 obsolete : CONVINCE, CONVICT
intransitive verb
: to express rebuke or reproof ☆
— **re·prov·er** noun
— **re·prov·ing·ly** \-'prü-viŋ-lē\ adverb

¹**rep·tile** \'rep-ˌtīl, -t²l\ noun [Middle English reptil, from Middle French or Late Latin; Middle French reptile (feminine), from Late Latin reptile (neuter), from neuter of reptilis creeping, from Latin reptus, past participle of repere to crawl; akin to Lithuanian rėplioti to crawl] (14th century)
1 : an animal that crawls or moves on its belly (as a snake) or on small short legs (as a lizard)
2 : any of a class (Reptilia) of air-breathing vertebrates that include the alligators and crocodiles, lizards, snakes, turtles, and extinct related forms (as dinosaurs and pterosaurs) and are characterized by a completely ossified skeleton with a single occipital condyle, a distinct quadrate bone usually immovably articulated with the skull, ribs attached to the sternum, and a body usually covered with scales or bony plates
3 : a groveling or despised person

²**reptile** adjective (1607)
: characteristic of a reptile : REPTILIAN

¹**rep·til·ian** \rep-'ti-lē-ən, -'til-yən\ adjective (circa 1846)
1 : resembling or having the characteristics of the reptiles
2 : of or relating to the reptiles
3 : cold-bloodedly treacherous ⟨a reptilian villain —Theodore Dreiser⟩

²**reptilian** noun (circa 1847)
: REPTILE 2

re·pub·lic \ri-'pə-blik\ noun [French république, from Middle French republique, from Latin respublica, from res thing, wealth + publica, feminine of publicus public — more at REAL, PUBLIC] (1604)
1 a (1) : a government having a chief of state who is not a monarch and who in modern times is usually a president (2) : a political unit (as a nation) having such a form of government **b** (1) : a government in which supreme power resides in a body of citizens entitled to vote and is exercised by elected officers and representatives responsible to them and governing according to law (2) : a political unit (as a nation) having such a form of government **c :** a usually specified republican government of a political unit ⟨the French Fourth Republic⟩
2 : a body of persons freely engaged in a specified activity ⟨the republic of letters⟩
3 : a constituent political and territorial unit of the former nations of Czechoslovakia, the U.S.S.R., or Yugoslavia

¹**re·pub·li·can** \ri-'pə-bli-kən\ noun (1697)
1 : one that favors or supports a republican form of government
2 capitalized **a :** a member of a political party advocating republicanism **b :** a member of the Democratic-Republican party or of the Republican party of the U.S.

²**republican** adjective (1712)
1 a : of, relating to, or having the characteristics of a republic **b :** favoring, supporting, or advocating a republic **c :** belonging or appropriate to one living in or supporting a republic ⟨republican simplicity⟩
2 capitalized **a :** DEMOCRATIC-REPUBLICAN **b :** of, relating to, or constituting the one of the

two major political parties evolving in the U.S. in the mid-19th century that is usually primarily associated with business, financial, and some agricultural interests and is held to favor a restricted governmental role in economic life

re·pub·li·can·ism \ri-'pə-bli-kə-ˌni-zəm\ noun (1689)
1 : adherence to or sympathy for a republican form of government
2 : the principles or theory of republican government
3 capitalized **a :** the principles, policy, or practices of the Republican party of the U.S. **b :** the Republican party or its members

re·pub·li·can·ize \-kə-ˌnīz\ transitive verb **-ized; -iz·ing** (1797)
: to make republican in character, form, or principle

re·pub·li·ca·tion \(ˌ)rē-ˌpə-blə-'kā-shən\ noun (1730)
1 : the act or action of republishing : the state of being republished
2 : something that has been republished

re·pub·lish \(ˌ)rē-'pə-blish\ transitive verb (1592)
1 : to publish again or anew
2 : to execute (a will) anew
— **re·pub·lish·er** noun

re·pu·di·ate \ri-'pyü-dē-ˌāt\ transitive verb **-at·ed; -at·ing** [Latin repudiatus, past participle of repudiare, from repudium rejection of a prospective spouse, divorce, probably from re- + pudēre to shame] (1545)
1 : to divorce or separate formally from (a woman)
2 : to refuse to have anything to do with : DISOWN
3 a : to refuse to accept; especially : to reject as unauthorized or as having no binding force **b :** to reject as untrue or unjust ⟨repudiate a charge⟩
4 : to refuse to acknowledge or pay
synonym see DECLINE
— **re·pu·di·a·tor** \-ˌā-tər\ noun

re·pu·di·a·tion \ri-ˌpyü-dē-ˈā-shən\ *noun* (1545)
: the act of repudiating : the state of being repudiated; *especially* : the refusal of public authorities to acknowledge or pay a debt
— **re·pu·di·a·tion·ist** \-sh(ə-)nist\ *noun*

re·pugn \ri-ˈpyün\ *verb* [Middle English, from Middle French & Latin; Middle French *repugner*, from Latin *repugnare*] (14th century) *intransitive verb*
archaic : to offer opposition, objection, or resistance
transitive verb
: to contend against : OPPOSE

re·pug·nance \ri-ˈpəg-nən(t)s\ *noun* (15th century)
1 a : the quality or fact of being contradictory or inconsistent **b** : an instance of such contradiction or inconsistency
2 : strong dislike, distaste, or antagonism

re·pug·nan·cy \-nən(t)-sē\ *noun, plural* **-cies** (15th century)
: REPUGNANCE

re·pug·nant \-nənt\ *adjective* [Middle English, opposed, contradictory, incompatible, from Middle French, from Latin *repugnant-, repugnans*, present participle of *repugnare* to fight against, from *re- + pugnare* to fight — more at PUNGENT] (15th century)
1 : INCOMPATIBLE, INCONSISTENT
2 *archaic* : HOSTILE
3 : exciting distaste or aversion
— **re·pug·nant·ly** *adverb*

¹re·pulse \ri-ˈpəls\ *transitive verb* **re·pulsed; re·puls·ing** [Latin *repulsus*, past participle of *repellere* to repel] (15th century)
1 : to drive or beat back : REPEL
2 : to repel by discourtesy, coldness, or denial
3 : to cause repulsion in

²repulse *noun* (1533)
1 : REBUFF, REJECTION
2 : the action of repelling an attacker : the fact of being repelled

re·pul·sion \ri-ˈpəl-shən\ *noun* (15th century)
1 : the action of repulsing : the state of being repulsed
2 : the action of repelling : the force with which bodies, particles, or like forces repel one another
3 : a feeling of aversion : REPUGNANCE

re·pul·sive \-siv\ *adjective* (1598)
1 : tending to repel or reject : COLD, FORBIDDING
2 : serving or able to repulse
3 : arousing aversion or disgust
— **re·pul·sive·ly** *adverb*
— **re·pul·sive·ness** *noun*

re·pur·chase agreement \(ˌ)rē-ˈpər-chəs-\ *noun* (1952)
: a contract giving the seller of securities (as treasury bills) the right to repurchase after a stated period and the buyer the right to retain interest earnings

rep·u·ta·ble \ˈre-pyə-tə-bəl\ *adjective* (1674)
1 : enjoying good repute : held in esteem
2 : employed widely or sanctioned by good writers
— **rep·u·ta·bil·i·ty** \ˌre-pyə-tə-ˈbi-lə-tē\ *noun*
— **rep·u·ta·bly** \ˈre-pyə-tə-blē\ *adverb*

rep·u·ta·tion \ˌre-pyə-ˈtā-shən\ *noun* [Middle English *reputacioun*, from Latin *reputation-, reputatio* consideration, from *reputare*] (14th century)
1 a : overall quality or character as seen or judged by people in general **b** : recognition by other people of some characteristic or ability ⟨has the *reputation* of being clever⟩
2 : a place in public esteem or regard : good name
— **rep·u·ta·tion·al** \-shnəl, -shə-nᵊl\ *adjective*

¹re·pute \ri-ˈpyüt\ *transitive verb* **re·put·ed; re·put·ing** [Middle English, from Middle French *reputer*, from Latin *reputare* to reckon

up, think over, from *re- + putare* to reckon] (15th century)
: BELIEVE, CONSIDER

²repute *noun* (1551)
1 : the character or status commonly ascribed to one : REPUTATION
2 : the state of being favorably known, spoken of, or esteemed

reputed *adjective* (1549)
1 : having a good repute : REPUTABLE
2 : being such according to reputation or popular belief

re·put·ed·ly *adverb* (1687)
: according to reputation or general belief

¹re·quest \ri-ˈkwest\ *noun* [Middle English *requeste*, from Middle French, from (assumed) Vulgar Latin *requaesta*, from feminine of *requaestus*, past participle of *requaerere* to require] (14th century)
1 : the act or an instance of asking for something
2 : something asked for
3 : the condition or fact of being requested ⟨available on *request*⟩
4 : the state of being sought after : DEMAND

²request *transitive verb* (1533)
1 : to make a request to or of ⟨*requested* her to write a paper⟩
2 : to ask as a favor or privilege ⟨*requests* to be excused⟩
3 *obsolete* : to ask (a person) to come or go to a thing or place
4 : to ask for ⟨*requested* a brief delay⟩
synonym see ASK
— **re·quest·er** *or* **re·quest·or** \-ˈkwes-tər\ *noun*

re·qui·em \ˈre-kwē-əm *also* ˈrā- *or* ˈrē-\ *noun* [Middle English, from Latin (first word of the introit of the requiem mass), accusative of *requies* rest, from *re- + quies* quiet, rest — more at WHILE] (14th century)
1 : a mass for the dead
2 a : a solemn chant (as a dirge) for the repose of the dead **b** : something that resembles such a solemn chant
3 a : a musical setting of the mass for the dead **b** : a musical composition in honor of the dead

requiem shark *noun* [obsolete French *requiem* shark, alteration of French *requin*] (1900)
: any of a family (Carcharhinidae) of sharks (as the tiger shark) that includes some dangerous to humans

re·qui·es·cat \ˌre-kwē-ˈes-ˌkät, -ˌkat; ˌrā-kwē-ˈes-ˌkät\ *noun* [Latin, may he (or she) rest, from *requiescere* to rest, from *re- + quiescere* to be quiet, from *quies*] (1824)
: a prayer for the repose of a dead person

re·quire \ri-ˈkwīr\ *verb* **re·quired; re·quir·ing** [Middle English *requeren*, from Middle French *requerre*, from (assumed) Vulgar Latin *requaerere* to seek for, need, require, alteration of Latin *requirere*, from *re- + quaerere* to seek, ask] (14th century)
transitive verb
1 a : to claim or ask for by right and authority **b** *archaic* : REQUEST
2 a : to call for as suitable or appropriate ⟨the occasion *requires* formal dress⟩ **b** : to demand as necessary or essential : have a compelling need for ⟨all living beings *require* food⟩
3 : to impose a compulsion or command on : COMPEL
4 *chiefly British* : to feel or be obliged — used with a following infinitive ⟨one does not *require* to be a specialist —Elizabeth Bowen⟩
intransitive verb
archaic : ASK
synonym see DEMAND

re·quire·ment \-ˈkwīr-mənt\ *noun* (1662)
: something required: **a** : something wanted or needed : NECESSITY ⟨production was not sufficient to satisfy military *requirements*⟩ **b** : something essential to the existence or occurrence of something else : CONDITION ⟨failed to meet the school's *requirements* for graduation⟩

req·ui·site \ˈre-kwə-zət\ *adjective* [Middle English, from Latin *requisitus*, past participle of *requirere*] (15th century)
: ESSENTIAL, NECESSARY
— **requisite** *noun*
— **req·ui·site·ness** *noun*

req·ui·si·tion \ˌre-kwə-ˈzi-shən\ *noun* [Middle English *requisicion*, from Middle French or Medieval Latin; Middle French *requisition*, from Medieval Latin *requisition-, requisitio*, from Latin, act of searching, from *requirere*] (15th century)
1 a : the act of formally requiring or calling upon someone to perform an action **b** : a formal demand made by one nation upon another for the surrender or extradition of a fugitive from justice
2 a : the act of requiring something to be furnished **b** : a demand or application made usually with authority: as (1) : a demand made by military authorities upon civilians for supplies or other needs (2) : a written request for something authorized but not made available automatically
3 : the state of being in demand or use
— **requisition** *transitive verb*

re·quit·al \ri-ˈkwī-tᵊl\ *noun* (1582)
1 : something given in return, compensation, or retaliation
2 : the act or action of requiting : the state of being requited

re·quite \ri-ˈkwīt\ *transitive verb* **re·quit·ed; re·quit·ing** [*re-* + obsolete *quite* to quit, pay, from Middle English *quiten* — more at QUIT] (1529)
1 a : to make return for : REPAY **b** : to make retaliation for : AVENGE
2 : to make suitable return to for a benefit or service or for an injury
synonym see RECIPROCATE
— **re·quit·er** *noun*

re·ra·di·ate \(ˌ)rē-ˈrā-dē-ˌāt\ *transitive verb* (1913)
: to radiate again or anew; *especially* : to emit (energy) in the form of radiation after absorbing incident radiation
— **re·ra·di·a·tion** \(ˌ)rē-ˌrā-dē-ˈā-shən\ *noun*

rere·dos \ˈrer-ə-ˌdäs *also* ˈrir-ə-ˌdäs *or* ˈrir-ˌdäs\ *noun* [Middle English, from Anglo-French *areredos*, from Middle French *arrere* behind + *dos* back, from Latin *dorsum* — more at ARREAR] (14th century)
: a usually ornamental wood or stone screen or partition wall behind an altar

rere·ward *noun* [Middle English *rerewarde*, from Anglo-French, from Old French *rere* behind + Old North French *warde* guard; akin to Old French *garde* guard — more at REAR GUARD] (14th century)
obsolete : REAR GUARD

¹re·run \(ˌ)rē-ˈrən\ *transitive verb* **-ran** \-ˈran\; **-run; -run·ning** (1804)
: to run again or anew

²re·run \ˈrē-ˌrən, (ˌ)rē-ˈ\ *noun* (circa 1934)
: the act or action or an instance of rerunning : REPETITION; *especially* : a movie or television show that is rerun

res \ˈrās, ˈrēz\ *noun, plural* **res** [Latin — more at REAL] (1851)
: a particular thing : MATTER — used especially in legal phrases

res ad·ju·di·ca·ta \ˈrēz-ə-ˌjü-di-ˈkä-tə\ *noun* [Late Latin] (1902)
: RES JUDICATA

re·sal·able \(ˌ)rē-ˈsā-lə-bəl\ *adjective* (1866)
: fit for resale

re·sale \ˈrē-ˌsāl, (ˌ)rē-ˈsā(ə)l\ *noun* (1625)
1 : the act of selling again usually to a new party

2 a : a secondhand sale **b :** an additional sale to the same buyer

re·scale \(,)rē-'skā(ə)l\ *transitive verb* (1944) **:** to plan, establish, or formulate on a new and usually smaller scale

re·sched·ule \(,)rē-'ske-(,)jü(ə)l, -jəl, *Canadian also* -'she-, *British usually* -'she-(,)dyü(ə)l\ *transitive verb* (1965) **:** to schedule or plan again according to a different timetable; *especially* **:** to defer required payment of (a debt or loan)

re·scind \ri-'sind\ *transitive verb* [Latin *rescindere* to annul, from *re-* + *scindere* to cut — more at SHED] (1643) **1 :** to take away **:** REMOVE **2 a :** TAKE BACK, CANCEL ⟨refused to *rescind* the order⟩ **b :** to abrogate (a contract) and restore the parties to the positions they would have occupied had there been no contract **3 :** to make void (as an act) by action of the enacting authority or a superior authority **:** REPEAL
 — **re·scind·er** *noun*
 — **re·scind·ment** \-'sin(d)-mənt\ *noun*

re·scis·sion \ri-'si-zhən\ *noun* [Late Latin *rescission-, rescissio,* from Latin *rescindere*] (1611) **:** an act of rescinding

re·scis·so·ry \-'si-zə-rē, -'si-sə-\ *adjective* (1605) **:** relating to or tending to or having the effect of rescission

re·script \'rē-,skript\ *noun* [Middle English *rescripte,* from Latin *rescriptum,* from neuter of *rescriptus,* past participle of *rescribere* to write in reply, from *re-* + *scribere* to write — more at SCRIBE] (15th century) **1 :** a written answer of a Roman emperor or of a pope to a legal inquiry or petition **2 :** an official or authoritative order, decree, edict, or announcement **3 :** an act or instance of rewriting

res·cue \'res-(,)kyü\ *transitive verb* **res·cued; res·cu·ing** [Middle English, from Middle French *rescourre,* from Old French, from *re-* + *escourre* to shake out, from Latin *excutere,* from *ex-* + *quatere* to shake] (14th century) **:** to free from confinement, danger, or evil **:** SAVE, DELIVER: as **a :** to take (as a prisoner) forcibly from custody **b :** to recover (as a prize) by force **c :** to deliver (as a place under siege) by armed force ☆
 — **res·cu·able** \-ə-bəl\ *adjective*
 — **rescue** *noun*
 — **res·cu·er** *noun*

rescue mission *noun* (1902) **:** a city religious mission seeking to convert and rehabilitate the down-and-out

¹re·search \ri-'sərch, 'rē-,\ *noun* [Middle French *recerche,* from *recerchier* to investigate thoroughly, from Old French, from *re-* + *cerchier* to search — more at SEARCH] (1577) **1 :** careful or diligent search **2 :** studious inquiry or examination; *especially* **:** investigation or experimentation aimed at the discovery and interpretation of facts, revision of accepted theories or laws in the light of new facts, or practical application of such new or revised theories or laws **3 :** the collecting of information about a particular subject

²research (1593) *transitive verb* **1 :** to search or investigate exhaustively ⟨*research* a problem⟩ **2 :** to do research for ⟨*research* a book⟩ *intransitive verb* **:** to engage in research
 — **re·search·able** \ri-'sər-chə-bəl, 'rē-,\ *adjective*
 — **re·search·er** *noun*

re·search·ist \ri-'sər-chist, 'rē-,sər-\ *noun* (1921) **:** one engaged in research

re·seau \rā-'zō, ri-\ *noun, plural* **re·seaux** \-'zōz\ [French *réseau,* from Old French *resel,* diminutive of *rais* net, from Latin *retis, rete*] (1578) **1 :** a net ground or foundation in lace **2 :** a grid photographed by a separate exposure onto a plate containing star images to facilitate astronomical measurements

re·sect \ri-'sekt\ *transitive verb* [Latin *resectus,* past participle of *resecare* to cut off, from *re-* + *secare* to cut — more at SAW] (1846) **:** to perform resection on
 — **re·sect·abil·i·ty** \-,sek-tə-'bi-lə-tē\ *noun*
 — **re·sect·able** \-'sek-tə-bəl\ *adjective*

re·sec·tion \ri-'sek-shən\ *noun* (1775) **:** the surgical removal of part of an organ or structure

re·se·da \'rā-zə-,dä\ *noun* [French *réséda,* from *réséda,* a mignonette] (1873) **:** a grayish green color

re·seed \(,)rē-'sēd\ (1888) *transitive verb* **1 :** to sow seed on again or anew **2 :** to maintain (itself) by self-sown seed *intransitive verb* **:** to maintain itself by self-sown seed

re·sem·blance \ri-'zem-blən(t)s\ *noun* (14th century) **1 a :** the quality or state of resembling; *especially* **:** correspondence in appearance or superficial qualities **b :** a point of likeness **:** SIMILARITY **2 :** REPRESENTATION, IMAGE **3** *archaic* **:** characteristic appearance **4** *obsolete* **:** PROBABILITY
 synonym see LIKENESS

re·sem·blant \-blənt\ *adjective* (14th century) **:** marked by or showing resemblance

re·sem·ble \ri-'zem-bəl\ *transitive verb* **re·sem·bled; re·sem·bling** \-b(ə-)liŋ\ [Middle English, from Middle French *resembler, ressembler,* from Old French, from *re-* + *sembler* to be like, seem, from Latin *similare* to copy, from *similis* like — more at SAME] (14th century) **1 :** to be like or similar to **2** *archaic* **:** to represent as like

re·send \(')rē-'send\ *transitive verb* **-sent** \-'sent\; **-send·ing** (1554) **:** to send again or back

re·sent \ri-'zent\ *transitive verb* [French *ressentir* to be emotionally sensible of, from Old French, from *re-* + *sentir* to feel, from Latin *sentire* — more at SENSE] (1628) **:** to feel or express annoyance or ill will at

re·sent·ful \-fəl\ *adjective* (1656) **1 :** full of resentment **:** inclined to resent **2 :** caused or marked by resentment
 — **re·sent·ful·ly** \-fə-lē\ *adverb*
 — **re·sent·ful·ness** *noun*

re·sent·ment \ri-'zent-mənt\ *noun* (1619) **:** a feeling of indignant displeasure or persistent ill will at something regarded as a wrong, insult, or injury
 synonym see OFFENSE

re·ser·pine \ri-'sər-,pēn, -pən\ *noun* [German *Reserpin,* probably irregular from New Latin *Rauwolfia serpentina,* a species of rauwolfia] (1952) **:** an alkaloid $C_{33}H_{40}N_2O_9$ extracted especially from the root of rauwolfias and used in the treatment of hypertension, mental disorders, and tension states

res·er·va·tion \,re-zər-'vā-shən\ *noun* (15th century) **1 :** an act of reserving something: as **a** (1) **:** the act or fact of a grantor's reserving some newly created thing out of the thing granted (2) **:** the right or interest so reserved **b :** the setting of limiting conditions or withholding from complete exposition ⟨answered without *reservation*⟩ **c :** an arrangement to have something (as a hotel room) held for one's use; *also* **:** a promise, guarantee, or record of such engagement

2 a : a limiting condition ⟨agreed, but with *reservations*⟩ **b :** DOUBT, MISGIVING ⟨had serious *reservations* about marriage⟩ **3 :** something reserved: as **a :** a tract of public land set aside (as for use by American Indians) **b :** an area in which hunting is not permitted; *especially* **:** one set aside as a secure breeding place
 — **res·er·va·tion·ist** \-sh(ə-)nist\ *noun*

¹re·serve \ri-'zərv\ *transitive verb* **re·served; re·serv·ing** [Middle English, from Middle French *reserver,* from Latin *reservare,* literally, to keep back, from *re-* + *servare* to keep — more at CONSERVE] (14th century) **1 a :** to hold in reserve **:** keep back ⟨*reserve* grain for seed⟩ **b :** to set aside (part of the consecrated elements) at the Eucharist for future use **c :** to retain or hold over to a future time or place **:** DEFER ⟨*reserve* one's judgment on a plan⟩ **d :** to make legal reservation of **2 :** to set or have set aside or apart ⟨*reserve* a hotel room⟩
 synonym see KEEP
 — **re·serv·able** \-'zər-və-bəl\ *adjective*

²reserve *noun, often attributive* (1648) **1 :** something reserved or set aside for a particular purpose, use, or reason: as **a** (1) **:** a military force withheld from action for later decisive use — usually used in plural (2) **:** forces not in the field but available (3) **:** the military forces of a country not part of the regular services; *also* **:** RESERVIST **b :** a tract (as of public land) set apart **:** RESERVATION **2 :** something stored or kept available for future use or need **:** STOCK **3 :** an act of reserving **:** QUALIFICATION **4 a :** restraint, closeness, or caution in one's words and actions **b :** forbearance from making a full explanation, complete disclosure, or free expression of one's mind **5** *archaic* **:** SECRET **6 a :** money or its equivalent kept in hand or set apart usually to meet liabilities **b :** the liquid resources of a nation for meeting international payments **7 :** SUBSTITUTE **8 :** RESERVE PRICE **9 :** a wine made from select grapes, bottled on the maker's premises, and aged specially and often longer
 — **in reserve :** held back for future or special use

reserve bank *noun* (1905) **:** a central bank holding reserves of other banks

reserve clause *noun* (1944) **:** a clause formerly placed in a professional athlete's contract that reserved for the club the exclusive right automatically to renew the

contract and that bound the athlete to the club until retirement or until the athlete was traded or released

re·served \ri-'zərvd\ *adjective* (1601)
1 : restrained in words and actions
2 : kept or set apart or aside for future or special use
synonym see SILENT
— **re·serv·ed·ly** \-'zər-vəd-lē\ *adverb*
— **re·serv·ed·ness** \-'zər-vəd-nəs\ *noun*
reserved power *noun* (1838)
: a political power reserved by a constitution to the exclusive jurisdiction of a specified political authority
reserve price *noun* (1919)
: a price announced at an auction as the lowest that will be considered
re·serv·ist \ri-'zər-vist\ *noun* (1876)
: a member of a military reserve
res·er·voir \'re-zə-,vwär, -zər-, -,vwȯr *also* -,vȯi\ *noun* [French *réservoir*, from Middle French, from *reserver*] (1690)
1 : a place where something is kept in store: as **a** : an artificial lake where water is collected and kept in quantity for use **b** : a part of an apparatus in which a liquid is held **c** : SUPPLY, STORE ⟨a large *reservoir* of educated people⟩
2 : an extra supply : RESERVE
3 : an organism in which a parasite that is pathogenic for some other species lives and multiplies without damaging its host; *also* : a noneconomic organism within which a pathogen of economic or medical importance flourishes
re·set \(,)rē-'set\ *transitive verb* **-set; -set·ting** (1655)
1 : to set again or anew ⟨*reset* type⟩ ⟨*reset* a diamond⟩ ⟨*reset* a circuit breaker⟩
2 : to change the reading of often to zero ⟨*reset* an odometer⟩
— **re·set** \'rē-,set\ *noun*
— **re·set·table** \-'se-tə-bəl\ *adjective*
res ges·tae \'räs-'ges-,tī, 'rēz-'jes-(,)tē\ *noun plural* [Latin] (1616)
: things done; *especially* : the facts that form the environment of a litigated issue and are admissible in evidence
resh \'räsh\ *noun* [Hebrew *rēsh*] (circa 1823)
: the 20th letter of the Hebrew alphabet — see ALPHABET table
re·shape \(,)rē-'shāp\ *transitive verb* (1827)
: to give a new form or orientation to : REORGANIZE
— **re·shap·er** *noun*
re·shuf·fle \(,)rē-'shə-fəl\ *transitive verb* (1830)
1 : to shuffle (as cards) again
2 : to reorganize usually by the redistribution of existing elements ⟨the cabinet was *reshuffled* by the prime minister⟩
— **reshuffle** *noun*
re·sid \ri-'zid\ *noun* (1967)
: RESIDUAL OIL
re·side \ri-'zīd\ *intransitive verb* **re·sid·ed; re·sid·ing** [Middle English, from Middle French or Latin; Middle French *resider*, from Latin *residēre* to sit back, remain, abide, from *re-* + *sedēre* to sit — more at SIT] (15th century)
1 a : to be in residence as the incumbent of a benefice or office **b** : to dwell permanently or continuously : occupy a place as one's legal domicile
2 a : to be present as an element or quality **b** : to be vested as a right
— **re·sid·er** *noun*
res·i·dence \'re-zə-dən(t)s, 'rez-dən(t)s, 're-zə-,den(t)s\ *noun* (14th century)
1 a : the act or fact of dwelling in a place for some time **b** : the act or fact of living or regularly staying at or in some place for the discharge of a duty or the enjoyment of a benefit
2 a (1) : the place where one actually lives as distinguished from one's domicile or a place of temporary sojourn (2) : DOMICILE 2a **b** : the place where a corporation is actually or offi-

cially established **c** : the status of a legal resident
3 a : a building used as a home : DWELLING **b** : housing or a unit of housing provided for students
4 a : the period or duration of abode in a place **b** : a period of active and especially full-time study, research, or teaching at a college or university
— **in residence** : engaged to live and work at a particular place often for a specified time ⟨poet *in residence* at a university⟩
residence time *noun* (1954)
: the duration of persistence of a mass or substance in a medium or place
res·i·den·cy \'re-zə-dən(t)s-sē, 'rez-dən(t)-, 're-zə-,den(t)-\ *noun, plural* **-cies** (1579)
1 : a usually official place of residence
2 : a territory in a protected state in which the powers of the protecting state are executed by a resident agent
3 : a period of advanced training in a medical specialty after graduation from medical school and licensing to practice medicine
¹**res·i·dent** \'re-zə-dənt, 'rez-dənt, 're-zə-,dent\ *adjective* [Middle English, from Latin *resident-, residens,* present participle of *residēre*] (14th century)
1 a : living in a place for some length of time : RESIDING **b** : serving in a regular or full-time capacity ⟨the *resident* engineer for a highway department⟩; *also* : being in residence
2 : PRESENT, INHERENT
3 : not migratory
²**resident** *noun* (15th century)
1 : one who resides in a place
2 : a diplomatic agent residing at a foreign court or seat of government; *especially* : one exercising authority in a protected state as representative of the protecting power
3 : a physician serving a residency
resident commissioner *noun* (1902)
1 : a nonvoting representative of a dependency in the U.S. House of Representatives
2 : a resident administrator in a British colony or possession
res·i·den·tial \,re-zə-'den(t)-shəl, ,rez-'den(t)-\ *adjective* (1654)
1 a : used as a residence or by residents **b** : providing living accommodations for students ⟨a *residential* college⟩
2 : restricted to or occupied by residences ⟨a *residential* neighborhood⟩
3 : of or relating to residence or residences
— **res·i·den·tial·ly** \-'den(t)-sh(ə-)lē\ *adverb*
¹**re·sid·u·al** \ri-'zi-jə-wəl, -jəl; -'zij-wəl\ *noun* [Latin *residuum* residue] (1557)
1 : REMAINDER, RESIDUUM: as **a** : the difference between results obtained by observation and by computation from a formula or between the mean of several observations and any one of them **b** : a residual product or substance **c** : an internal aftereffect of experience or activity that influences later behavior; *especially* : a disability remaining from a disease or operation
2 : a payment (as to an actor or writer) for each rerun after an initial showing (as of a TV show)
²**residual** *adjective* (1570)
1 : of, relating to, or constituting a residue
2 : leaving a residue that remains effective for some time
— **re·sid·u·al·ly** *adverb*
residual oil *noun* (circa 1948)
: fuel oil that remains after the removal of valuable distillates (as gasoline) from petroleum and that is used especially by industry — called also *resid*
residual power *noun* (1919)
: power held to remain at the disposal of a governmental authority after an enumeration or delegation of specified powers to other authorities
re·sid·u·ary \ri-'zi-jə-,wer-ē\ *adjective* (1726)

: of, relating to, or constituting a residue ⟨*residuary* estate⟩
res·i·due \'re-zə-,dü, -,dyü\ *noun* [Middle English, from Middle French *residu*, from Latin *residuum*, from neuter of *residuus* left over, from *residēre* to remain] (14th century)
: something that remains after a part is taken, separated, or designated : REMNANT, REMAINDER: as **a** : the part of a testator's estate remaining after the satisfaction of all debts, charges, allowances, and previous devises and bequests **b** : the remainder after subtracting a multiple of a modulus from an integer or a power of the integer that can appear as the second of the two terms in an appropriate congruence ⟨2 and 7 are *residues* of 12 modulo 5⟩ **c** : a constituent structural unit (as a group or monomer) of a usually complex molecule ⟨amino acid *residues* from hydrolysis of protein⟩
residue class *noun* (1948)
: the set of elements (as integers) that leave the same remainder when divided by a given modulus
re·sid·u·um \ri-'zi-jə-wəm\ *noun, plural* **re·sid·ua** \-wə\ [Latin] (1672)
: something residual: as **a** : RESIDUE a **b** : a residual product (as from the distillation of petroleum)
re·sign \ri-'zīn\ *verb* [Middle English, from Middle French *resigner*, from Latin *resignare*, literally, to unseal, cancel, from *re-* + *signare* to sign, seal — more at SIGN] (14th century)
transitive verb
1 : RELEGATE, CONSIGN; *especially* : to give (oneself) over without resistance ⟨*resigned* herself to her fate⟩
2 : to give up deliberately; *especially* : to renounce (as a right or position) by a formal act
intransitive verb
1 : to give up one's office or position : QUIT
2 : to accept something as inevitable : SUBMIT
synonym see RELINQUISH, ABDICATE
— **re·sign·ed·ly** \-'zī-nəd-lē\ *adverb*
— **re·sign·ed·ness** \-'zī-nəd-nəs\ *noun*
— **re·sign·er** \-'zī-nər\ *noun*
re–sign \(,)rē-'sīn\ (1805)
transitive verb
: to sign again
intransitive verb
: to sign up again
res·ig·na·tion \,re-zig-'nā-shən\ *noun* (14th century)
1 a : an act or instance of resigning something : SURRENDER **b** : a formal notification of resigning
2 : the quality or state of being resigned : SUBMISSIVENESS
re·sile \ri-'zī(ə)l\ *intransitive verb* **re·siled; re·sil·ing** [Late Latin & Latin; Late Latin *resilire* to withdraw, from Latin, to recoil] (1529)
: RECOIL, RETRACT; *especially* : to return to a prior position
re·sil·ience \ri-'zil-yən(t)s\ *noun* (1824)
1 : the capability of a strained body to recover its size and shape after deformation caused especially by compressive stress
2 : an ability to recover from or adjust easily to misfortune or change
re·sil·ien·cy \-yən(t)-sē\ *noun* (circa 1836)
: RESILIENCE
re·sil·ient \-yənt\ *adjective* [Latin *resilient-, resiliens,* present participle of *resilire* to jump back, recoil, from *re-* + *salire* to leap — more at SALLY] (1674)

\ə\ **abut** \ᵊ\ **kitten** \ər\ **further** \a\ **ash** \ā\ **ace**
\ä\ **mop, mar** \aú\ **out** \ch\ **chin** \e\ **bet** \ē\ **easy**
\g\ **go** \i\ **hit** \ī\ **ice** \j\ **job** \ŋ\ **sing** \ō\ **go**
\ȯ\ **law** \ȯi\ **boy** \th\ **thin** \th\ **the** \ü\ **loot** \ú\ **foot**
\y\ **yet** \zh\ **vision** *see also* Guide to Pronunciation

: characterized or marked by resilience: as **a** : capable of withstanding shock without permanent deformation or rupture **b** : tending to recover from or adjust easily to misfortune or change

synonym see ELASTIC

— **re·sil·ient·ly** adverb

¹**res·in** \'re-z°n\ noun [Middle English, from Middle French resine, from Latin resina; akin to Greek rhētinē pine resin] (14th century) **1 a** : any of various solid or semisolid amorphous fusible flammable natural organic substances that are usually transparent or translucent and yellowish to brown, are formed especially in plant secretions, are soluble in organic solvents (as ether) but not in water, are electrical nonconductors, and are used chiefly in varnishes, printing inks, plastics, and sizes and in medicine **b** : ROSIN **2 a** : any of a large class of synthetic products that have some of the physical properties of natural resins but are different chemically and are used chiefly in plastics **b** : any various products made from a natural resin or a natural polymer

— **res·in·ous** \'re-z°n-əs, 'rez-nəs\ adjective

²**resin** transitive verb **res·ined; res·in·ing** \'re-z°n-iŋ, 'rez-niŋ\ (1865)
: to treat with resin

res·in·ate \'re-z°n-ˌāt\ transitive verb **-at·ed; -at·ing** (circa 1890)
: to impregnate or flavor with resin

resin canal noun (1884)
: a tubular intercellular space in gymnosperms and some angiosperms that is lined with epithelial cells which secrete resin — called also *resin duct*

res·in·oid \'re-z°n-ˌoid\ noun (1880)
: GUM RESIN

¹**re·sist** \ri-'zist\ verb [Middle English, from Middle French or Latin; Middle French resister, from Latin resistere, from re- + sistere to take a stand; akin to Latin stare to stand — more at STAND] (14th century)
intransitive verb
: to exert force in opposition
transitive verb
1 : to exert oneself so as to counteract or defeat
2 : to withstand the force or effect of
synonym see OPPOSE

²**resist** noun (1836)
: something (as a coating) that protects against a chemical, electrical, or physical action

re·sis·tance \ri-'zis-tən(t)s\ noun (14th century)
1 a : an act or instance of resisting : OPPOSITION **b** : a means of resisting
2 : the ability to resist; *especially* : the inherent capacity of a living being to resist untoward circumstances (as disease, malnutrition, or toxic agents)
3 : an opposing or retarding force
4 a : the opposition offered by a body or substance to the passage through it of a steady electric current **b** : a source of resistance
5 *often capitalized* : an underground organization of a conquered or nearly conquered country engaging in sabotage and secret operations against occupation forces and collaborators

¹**re·sis·tant** \-tənt\ adjective (15th century)
: giving or capable of resistance — often used in combination ⟨wrinkle-*resistant* clothes⟩

²**resistant** noun (1600)
: one that resists : RESISTER

re·sist·er \ri-'zis-tər\ noun (14th century)
: one that resists; *especially* : one who actively opposes the policies of a government

re·sist·ibil·i·ty \ri-ˌzis-tə-'bi-lə-tē\ noun (1617)
1 : the quality or state of being resistible
2 : ability to resist

re·sist·ible \ri-'zis-tə-bəl\ adjective (1608)
: capable of being resisted

re·sis·tive \ri-'zis-tiv\ adjective (1603)

: marked by resistance — often used in combination ⟨fire-*resistive* material⟩

— **re·sis·tive·ly** adverb
— **re·sis·tive·ness** noun

re·sis·tiv·i·ty \ri-ˌzis-'ti-və-tē, ˌrē-\ noun, plural **-ties** (1885)
1 : the longitudinal electrical resistance of a uniform rod of unit length and unit cross-sectional area : the reciprocal of conductivity
2 : capacity for resisting : RESISTANCE

re·sist·less \ri-'zist-ləs\ adjective (1586)
1 : IRRESISTIBLE
2 : offering no resistance

— **re·sist·less·ly** adverb
— **re·sist·less·ness** noun

re·sis·tor \ri-'zis-tər\ noun (1905)
: a device that has electrical resistance and that is used in an electric circuit for protection, operation, or current control

re·sit·ting \(ˌ)rē-'si-tiŋ\ noun (1661)
: a sitting (as of a legislature) for a second time : another sitting

res ju·di·ca·ta \'rēz-ˌjü-di-'kä-tə\ noun [Latin, judged matter] (1693)
: a matter finally decided on its merits by a court having competent jurisdiction and not subject to litigation again between the same parties

re·sol·u·ble \ri-'zäl-yə-bəl\ adjective [Late Latin resolubilis, from Latin resolvere to resolve, unloose] (1602)
: capable of being resolved

¹**res·o·lute** \'re-zə-ˌlüt, -lət\ adjective [Latin resolutus, past participle of resolvere] (1533)
1 : marked by firm determination : RESOLVED
2 : BOLD, STEADY
synonym see FAITHFUL

— **res·o·lute·ly** \-ˌlüt-lē, -lət-; ˌre-zə-'lüt-\ adverb

— **res·o·lute·ness** \-ˌlüt-nəs, -lət-, -'lüt-\ noun

²**resolute** noun (1602)
: a resolute person

res·o·lu·tion \ˌre-zə-'lü-shən\ noun [Middle English, from Middle French or Latin; Middle French resolution, from Latin resolution-, resolutio, from resolvere] (14th century)
1 : the act or process of reducing to simpler form: as **a** : the act of analyzing a complex notion into simpler ones **b** : the act of answering : SOLVING **c** : the act of determining **d** : the passing of a voice part from a dissonant to a consonant tone or the progression of a chord from dissonance to consonance **e** : the separating of a chemical compound or mixture into its constituents **f** (1) : the division of a prosodic element into its component parts (2) : the substitution in Greek or Latin prosody of two short syllables for a long syllable **g** : the analysis of a vector into two or more vectors of which it is the sum **h** : the process or capability of making distinguishable the individual parts of an object, closely adjacent optical images, or sources of light
2 : the subsidence of a pathological state (as inflammation)
3 a : something that is resolved ⟨made a *resolution* to mend my ways⟩ **b** : firmness of resolve
4 : a formal expression of opinion, will, or intent voted by an official body or assembled group
5 : the point in a literary work at which the chief dramatic complication is worked out
synonym see COURAGE

¹**re·solve** \ri-'zälv, -'zölv also -'zäv or -'zöv\ verb **re·solved; re·solv·ing** [Middle English, from Latin resolvere to unloose, dissolve, from re- + solvere to loosen, release — more at SOLVE] (14th century)
transitive verb
1 obsolete : DISSOLVE, MELT
2 a : BREAK UP, SEPARATE ⟨the prism *resolved* the light into a play of color⟩; *also* : to change

by disintegration **b** : to reduce by analysis ⟨*resolve* the problem into simple elements⟩ **c** : to distinguish between or make independently visible adjacent parts of **d** : to separate (a racemic compound or mixture) into the two components
3 : to cause resolution of (a pathological state)
4 a : to deal with successfully : clear up ⟨*resolve* doubts⟩ ⟨*resolve* a dispute⟩ **b** : to find an answer to **c** : to make clear or understandable **d** : to find a mathematical solution of **e** : to split up (as a vector) into two or more components especially in assigned directions
5 : to reach a firm decision about ⟨*resolve* to get more sleep⟩ ⟨*resolve* disputed points in a text⟩
6 a : to declare or decide by a formal resolution and vote **b** : to change by resolution or formal vote ⟨the house *resolved* itself into a committee⟩
7 : to make (as voice parts) progress from dissonance to consonance
8 : to work out the resolution of (as a play)
intransitive verb
1 : to become separated into component parts; *also* : to become reduced by dissolving or analysis
2 : to form a resolution : DETERMINE
3 : CONSULT, DELIBERATE
4 : to progress from dissonance to consonance
synonym see DECIDE

— **re·solv·able** \-'zäl-və-bəl, -'zöl- also -'zä-və- or -'zö-və-\ adjective

— **re·solv·er** noun

²**resolve** noun (1591)
1 : fixity of purpose : RESOLUTENESS
2 : something that is resolved
3 : a legal or official determination; *especially* : a formal resolution

re·sol·vent \ri-'zäl-vənt, -'zöl-\ noun (1851)
: a means of solving something (as an equation)

— **resolvent** adjective

resolving power noun (1879)
1 : the ability of an optical system to form distinguishable images of objects separated by small angular distances
2 : the ability of a photographic film or plate to reproduce the fine detail of an optical image

res·o·nance \'re-z°n-ən(t)s, 'rez-nən(t)s\ noun (15th century)
1 a : the quality or state of being resonant **b** (1) : a vibration of large amplitude in a mechanical or electrical system caused by a relatively small periodic stimulus of the same or nearly the same period as the natural vibration period of the system (2) : the state of adjustment that produces resonance in a mechanical or electrical system
2 a : the intensification and enriching of a musical tone by supplementary vibration **b** : a quality imparted to voiced sounds by vibration in anatomical resonating chambers or cavities (as the mouth or the nasal cavity) **c** : a quality of richness or variety **d** : a quality of evoking response ⟨how much *resonance* the scandal seems to be having —U.S. News & World Report⟩
3 : the sound elicited on percussion of the chest
4 : the conceptual alternation of a chemical species (as a molecule or ion) between two or more equivalent allowed structural representations differing only in the placement of electrons that aids in understanding the actual state of the species as an amalgamation of its possible structures and the usually higher-than-expected stability of the species
5 a : the enhancement of an atomic, nuclear, or particle reaction or a scattering event by excitation of internal motion in the system **b** : MAGNETIC RESONANCE
6 : an extremely short-lived elementary particle
7 : a synchronous gravitational relationship of two celestial bodies (as moons) that orbit a

res·o·nant \'re-z°n-ənt, 'rez-nənt\ *adjective* (1592)
1 : continuing to sound : ECHOING
2 a : capable of inducing resonance **b** : relating to or exhibiting resonance
3 a : intensified and enriched by or as if by resonance **b** : marked by grandiloquence
— **resonant** *noun*
— **res·o·nant·ly** *adverb*

res·o·nate \'re-z°n-ˌāt\ *verb* **-nat·ed; -nat·ing** [Latin *resonatus*, past participle of *resonare* to resound — more at RESOUND] (1873)
intransitive verb
1 : to produce or exhibit resonance
2 : to respond as if by resonance ⟨*resonate* to the music⟩; *also* : to have a repetitive pattern that resembles resonance
3 : to relate harmoniously
transitive verb
: to subject to resonating

res·o·na·tor \-ˌā-tər\ *noun* (circa 1869)
: something that resounds or resonates: as **a** : a hollow metallic container for producing microwaves or a piezoelectric crystal put into oscillation by the oscillations of an outside source **b** : a device for increasing the resonance of a musical instrument

re·sorb \(ˌ)rē-'sorb, -'zorb\ *verb* [Latin *resorbēre*, from *re-* + *sorbēre* to suck up — more at ABSORB] (1640)
transitive verb
1 : to swallow or suck in again
2 : to break down and assimilate (something previously differentiated)
intransitive verb
: to undergo resorption

res·or·cin \rə-'sor-s°n\ *noun* [International Scientific Vocabulary *res-* (from Latin *resina* resin) + *orcin*, a phenol ($C_7H_8O_2$)] (circa 1868)
: RESORCINOL

res·or·cin·ol \-ˌol, -ˌōl\ *noun* (1881)
: a crystalline phenol $C_6H_6O_2$ obtained from various resins or artificially and used especially in making dyes, pharmaceuticals, and resins

re·sorp·tion \(ˌ)rē-'sorp-shən, -'zorp-\ *noun* [Latin *resorbēre*] (circa 1820)
: the action or process of resorbing something
— **re·sorp·tive** \-tiv\ *adjective*

¹re·sort \ri-'zort\ *noun* [Middle English, from Middle French, resource, recourse, from *resortir* to rebound, resort, from Old French, from *re-* + *sortir* to escape, sally] (14th century)
1 a : one that affords aid or refuge : RESOURCE ⟨went to them as a last *resort*⟩ **b** : RECOURSE
2 a : frequent, habitual, or general visiting ⟨a place of popular *resort*⟩ **b** : persons who frequent a place : THRONG **c** (1) : a frequently visited place : HAUNT (2) : a place providing recreation and entertainment especially to vacationers
synonym see RESOURCE

²resort *intransitive verb* (15th century)
1 : to go especially frequently or habitually : REPAIR
2 : to have recourse ⟨*resort* to force⟩

re-sort \(ˌ)rē-'sort\ *transitive verb* (1889)
: to sort again

re·sort·er \ri-'zor-tər\ *noun* (1917)
: a frequenter of resorts

re·sound \ri-'zaund *also* -'saund\ *verb* [Middle English *resounen*, from Middle French *resoner*, from Latin *resonare*, from *re-* + *sonare* to sound — more at SOUND] (14th century)
intransitive verb
1 : to become filled with sound : REVERBERATE
2 a : to sound loudly **b** : to produce a sonorous or echoing sound
3 : to become renowned
transitive verb
1 : to extol loudly or widely : CELEBRATE
2 : ECHO, REVERBERATE

3 : to sound or utter in full resonant tones

re·sound·ing *adjective* (15th century)
1 : producing or characterized by resonant sound : RESONATING
2 a : impressively sonorous **b** : EMPHATIC, UNEQUIVOCAL ⟨a *resounding* success⟩
— **re·sound·ing·ly** \-'zaun-diŋ-lē *also* -'saun-\ *adverb*

re·source \'rē-ˌsors, -ˌsors, -ˌzors, -ˌzors, ri-'\ *noun* [French *ressource*, from Old French *ressourse* relief, resource, from *resourdre* to relieve, literally, to rise again, from Latin *resurgere* — more at RESURRECTION] (1611)
1 a : a source of supply or support : an available means — usually used in plural **b** : a natural source of wealth or revenue — often used in plural **c** : computable wealth — usually used in plural **d** : a source of information or expertise
2 : something to which one has recourse in difficulty : EXPEDIENT
3 : a possibility of relief or recovery
4 : a means of spending one's leisure time
5 : an ability to meet and handle a situation
: RESOURCEFULNESS ☆

re·source·ful \ri-'sors-fəl, -'sors-, -'zors-, -'zors-\ *adjective* (1851)
: able to meet situations : capable of devising ways and means
— **re·source·ful·ly** \-fə-lē\ *adverb*
— **re·source·ful·ness** *noun*

¹re·spect \ri-'spekt\ *noun* [Middle English, from Latin *respectus*, literally, act of looking back, from *respicere* to look back, regard, from *re-* + *specere* to look — more at SPY] (14th century)
1 : a relation or reference to a particular thing or situation ⟨remarks having *respect* to an earlier plan⟩
2 : an act of giving particular attention : CONSIDERATION
3 a : high or special regard : ESTEEM **b** : the quality or state of being esteemed **c** *plural* : expressions of respect or deference ⟨paid our *respects*⟩
4 : PARTICULAR, DETAIL ⟨a good plan in some *respects*⟩
— **in respect of** *chiefly British* : with respect to : CONCERNING
— **in respect to** : with respect to : CONCERNING
— **with respect to** : with reference to : in relation to

²respect *transitive verb* (1560)
1 a : to consider worthy of high regard : ESTEEM **b** : to refrain from interfering with
2 : to have reference to : CONCERN
synonym see REGARD
— **re·spect·er** *noun*

¹re·spect·able \ri-'spek-tə-bəl\ *adjective* (1599)
1 : worthy of respect : ESTIMABLE
2 : decent or correct in character or behavior : PROPER
3 a : fair in size or quantity ⟨*respectable* amount⟩ **b** : moderately good : TOLERABLE
4 : fit to be seen : PRESENTABLE ⟨*respectable* clothes⟩
— **re·spect·abil·i·ty** \-ˌspek-tə-'bi-lə-tē\ *noun*
— **re·spect·able·ness** \-'spek-tə-bəl-nəs\ *noun*
— **re·spect·ably** \-blē\ *adverb*

²respectable *noun* (1814)
: a respectable person

re·spect·ful \ri-'spekt-fəl\ *adjective* (1687)
: marked by or showing respect or deference
— **re·spect·ful·ly** \-fə-lē\ *adverb*
— **re·spect·ful·ness** *noun*

re·spect·ing *preposition* (1611)
1 : in view of : CONSIDERING
2 : with respect to : CONCERNING

re·spec·tive \ri-'spek-tiv\ *adjective* (1592)
1 *obsolete* : PARTIAL, DISCRIMINATIVE
2 : PARTICULAR, SEPARATE ⟨their *respective* homes⟩

— **re·spec·tive·ness** *noun*
re·spec·tive·ly *adverb* (1605)
1 : in particular : SEPARATELY ⟨could not recognize the solutions as salty or sour, *respectively*⟩
2 : in the order given ⟨Mary and Anne were *respectively* 12 and 16 years old⟩

re·spell \(ˌ)rē-'spel\ *transitive verb* (1806)
: to spell again or in another way; *especially* : to spell out according to a phonetic system
— **re·spell·ing** \-'spe-liŋ\ *noun*

re·spi·ra·ble \'res-p(ə-)rə-bəl, ri-'spī-rə-\ *adjective* (1779)
: fit for breathing; *also* : capable of being taken in by breathing ⟨*respirable* particles of ash⟩

res·pi·ra·tion \ˌres-pə-'rā-shən\ *noun* [Middle English *respiracioun*, from Latin *respiration-, respiratio*, from *respirare*] (15th century)
1 a : the placing of air or dissolved gases in intimate contact with the circulating medium of a multicellular organism (as by breathing) **b** : a single complete act of breathing
2 : the physical and chemical processes by which an organism supplies its cells and tissues with the oxygen needed for metabolism and relieves them of the carbon dioxide formed in energy-producing reactions
3 : any of various energy-yielding oxidative reactions in living matter
— **re·spi·ra·to·ry** \'res-p(ə-)rə-ˌtor-ē, ri-'spī-rə-, -ˌtor-\ *adjective*

res·pi·ra·tor \'res-pə-ˌrā-tər\ *noun* (1836)
1 : a device worn over the mouth or nose for protecting the respiratory tract
2 : a device for maintaining artificial respiration

respiratory pigment *noun* (1896)
: any of various permanently or intermittently colored conjugated proteins and especially hemoglobin that function in the transfer of oxygen in cellular respiration

respiratory quotient *noun* (circa 1890)
: a ratio indicating the relation of the volume of carbon dioxide given off in respiration to that of the oxygen consumed

respiratory system *noun* (1940)
: a system of organs subserving the function of respiration and in air-breathing vertebrates consisting typically of the lungs and their nervous and circulatory supply and the channels by which these are continuous with the outer air

re·spire \ri-'spīr\ *verb* **re·spired; re·spir·ing** [Middle English, from Latin *respirare*, from *re-* + *spirare* to blow, breathe] (15th century)
intransitive verb

☆ **SYNONYMS**
Resource, resort, expedient, shift, makeshift, stopgap mean something one turns to in the absence of the usual means or source of supply. RESOURCE and RESORT apply to anything one falls back upon (exhausted all of their *resources*) ⟨a last *resort*⟩. EXPEDIENT may apply to any device or contrivance used when the usual one is not at hand or not possible ⟨a flimsy *expedient*⟩. SHIFT implies a tentative or temporary imperfect expedient ⟨desperate *shifts* to stave off foreclosure⟩. MAKESHIFT implies an inferior expedient adopted because of urgent need or countenanced through indifference ⟨old equipment employed as a *makeshift*⟩. STOPGAP applies to something used temporarily as an emergency measure ⟨a new law intended only as a *stopgap*⟩.

\ə\ **abut** \ᵊ\ **kitten** \ər\ **further** \a\ **ash** \ā\ **ace**
\ä\ **mop, mar** \au\ **out** \ch\ **chin** \e\ **bet** \ē\ **easy**
\g\ **go** \i\ **hit** \ī\ **ice** \j\ **job** \ŋ\ **sing** \ō\ **go**
\o\ **law** \oi\ **boy** \th\ **thin** \th\ **the** \ü\ **loot** \u\ **foot**
\y\ **yet** \zh\ **vision** *see also* Guide to Pronunciation

1 : BREATHE; *specifically* : to inhale and exhale air successively
2 *of a cell or tissue* : to take up oxygen and produce carbon dioxide through oxidation ~ *transitive verb* : BREATHE
— **res·pi·rom·e·ter** \ˌres-pə-'rä-mə-tər\ *noun* (circa 1883)
: an instrument for studying the character and extent of respiration
— **res·pi·ro·met·ric** \-rō-'me-trik\ *adjective*
— **res·pi·rom·e·try** \-'rä-mə-trē\ *noun*
¹re·spite \'res-pət *also* ri-'spīt, *British usually* 'res-ˌpīt\ *noun* [Middle English *respit,* from Old French, from Medieval Latin *respectus,* from Latin, act of looking back — more at RESPECT] (13th century)
1 : a period of temporary delay; *especially* : REPRIEVE 1b
2 : an interval of rest or relief
²respite *transitive verb* **re·spit·ed; re·spit·ing** (14th century)
1 : to grant a respite to
2 : PUT OFF, DELAY
re·splen·dence \ri-'splen-dən(t)s\ *noun* (15th century)
: the quality or state of being resplendent : SPLENDOR
re·splen·den·cy \-dən(t)-sē\ *noun* (1611)
: RESPLENDENCE
re·splen·dent \-dənt\ *adjective* [Latin *resplendent-, resplendens,* present participle of *resplendēre* to shine back, from *re-* + *splendēre* to shine — more at SPLENDID] (15th century)
: shining brilliantly : characterized by a glowing splendor ⟨meadows *resplendent* with wildflowers —*Outdoor World*⟩
synonym see SPLENDID
— **re·splen·dent·ly** *adverb*
¹re·spond \ri-'spänd\ *noun* (15th century)
: an engaged pillar supporting an arch or closing a colonnade or arcade
²respond *verb* [Middle French *respondre,* from Latin *respondēre* to promise in return, answer, from *re-* + *spondēre* to promise — more at SPOUSE] (1719)
intransitive verb
1 : to say something in return : make an answer ⟨*respond* to criticism⟩
2 a : to react in response ⟨*responded* to a call for help⟩ **b** : to show favorable reaction ⟨*respond* to surgery⟩
3 : to be answerable ⟨*respond* in damages⟩
~ *transitive verb* : REPLY
synonym see ANSWER
— **re·spond·er** \-'spän-dər\ *noun*
¹re·spon·dent \ri-'spän-dənt\ *noun* [Latin *respondent-, respondens,* present participle of *respondēre*] (1528)
1 : one who responds: as **a** : one who maintains a thesis in reply **b** (1) : one who answers in various legal proceedings (as in equity cases) (2) : the prevailing party in the lower court **c** : a person who responds to a poll
2 : a reflex that occurs in response to a specific external stimulus — compare OPERANT
²respondent *adjective* (1726)
1 : making response : RESPONSIVE; *especially* : being a respondent at law
2 : relating to or being behavior or responses to a stimulus that are followed by a reward ⟨*respondent* conditioning⟩ — compare OPERANT 3
re·sponse \ri-'spän(t)s\ *noun* [Middle English & Latin; Middle English *respounse,* from Middle French *respons,* from Latin *responsum* reply, from neuter of *responsus,* past participle of *respondēre*] (14th century)
1 : an act of responding
2 : something constituting a reply or a reaction: as **a** : a verse, phrase, or word sung or said by the people or choir after or in reply to

the officiant in a liturgical service **b** : the activity or inhibition of previous activity of an organism or any of its parts resulting from stimulation **c** : the output of a transducer or detecting device resulting from a given input
re·spon·si·bil·i·ty \ri-ˌspän(t)-sə-'bi-lə-tē\ *noun, plural* **-ties** (1787)
1 : the quality or state of being responsible: as **a** : moral, legal, or mental accountability **b** : RELIABILITY, TRUSTWORTHINESS
2 : something for which one is responsible : BURDEN
re·spon·si·ble \ri-'spän(t)-sə-bəl\ *adjective* (1643)
1 a : liable to be called on to answer **b** (1) : liable to be called to account as the primary cause, motive, or agent ⟨a committee *responsible* for the job⟩ (2) : being the cause or explanation ⟨mechanical defects were *responsible* for the accident⟩ **c** : liable to legal review or in case of fault to penalties
2 a : able to answer for one's conduct and obligations : TRUSTWORTHY **b** : able to choose for oneself between right and wrong
3 : marked by or involving responsibility or accountability ⟨*responsible* financial policies⟩ ⟨a *responsible* job⟩
4 : politically answerable; *especially* : required to submit to the electorate if defeated by the legislature — used especially of the British cabinet ☆
— **re·spon·si·ble·ness** *noun*
— **re·spon·si·bly** \-blē\ *adverb*
re·spon·sions \ri-'spän(t)-shənz\ *noun plural* [Middle English *responcioun* response, sum to be paid, from Middle French or Medieval Latin; Middle French *responsion,* from Medieval Latin *responsion-, responsio,* from Latin, answer, from *respondēre*] (1813)
: an examination required for matriculation as an undergraduate at Oxford
re·spon·sive \ri-'spän(t)-siv\ *adjective* (15th century)
1 : giving response : constituting a response : ANSWERING ⟨a *responsive* glance⟩ ⟨*responsive* aggression⟩
2 : quick to respond or react appropriately or sympathetically : SENSITIVE
3 : using responses ⟨*responsive* worship⟩
— **re·spon·sive·ly** *adverb*
— **re·spon·sive·ness** *noun*
re·spon·so·ry \ri-'spän(t)s-(ə-)rē\ *noun, plural* **-ries** [Middle English, from Medieval Latin *responsorius,* from Latin *respondēre*] (15th century)
: a set of versicles and responses sung or said after or during a lection
re·spon·sum \ri-'spän(t)-səm\ *noun, plural* **-sa** \-sə\ [New Latin, from Latin, reply, response] (1896)
: a written decision from a rabbinic authority in response to a submitted question or problem
res pu·bli·ca \'räs-'pü-bli-ˌkä\ *noun* [Latin — more at REPUBLIC] (circa 1898)
1 : COMMONWEALTH, STATE, REPUBLIC
2 : COMMONWEAL
res·sen·ti·ment \rə-ˌsäⁿ-tē-'mäⁿ\ *noun* [French, resentment, from *ressentir* to resent — more at RESENT] (1941)
: deep-seated resentment, frustration, and hostility accompanied by a sense of being powerless to express these feelings directly
¹rest \'rest\ *noun* [Middle English, from Old English; akin to Old High German *rasta* rest and perhaps to Old High German *ruowa* calm] (before 12th century)
1 : REPOSE, SLEEP; *specifically* : a bodily state characterized by minimal functional and metabolic activities
2 a : freedom from activity or labor **b** : a state of motionlessness or inactivity **c** : the repose of death
3 : a place for resting or lodging
4 : peace of mind or spirit

5 a (1) : a rhythmic silence in music (2) : a character representing such a silence **b** : a brief pause in reading
6 : something used for support
— **at rest 1** : resting or reposing especially in sleep or death **2** : QUIESCENT, MOTIONLESS **3** : free of anxieties

rest 5a(2): *1* whole, *2* half, *3* quarter, *4* eighth, *5* sixteenth

²rest (before 12th century)
intransitive verb
1 a : to get rest by lying down; *especially* : SLEEP **b** : to lie dead
2 : to cease from action or motion : refrain from labor or exertion
3 : to be free from anxiety or disturbance
4 : to sit or lie fixed or supported ⟨a column *rests* on its pedestal⟩
5 a : to remain confident : TRUST ⟨cannot *rest* on that assumption⟩ **b** : to be based or founded ⟨the verdict *rested* on several sound precedents⟩
6 : to remain for action or accomplishment ⟨the answer *rests* with you⟩
7 *of farmland* : to remain idle or uncropped
8 : to bring to an end voluntarily the introduction of evidence in a law case
~ *transitive verb*
1 : to give rest to
2 : to set at rest
3 : to place on or against a support
4 : to cause to be firmly fixed ⟨*rested* all hope in his child⟩
5 : to stop voluntarily from presenting evidence pertinent to (a case at law)
— **rest·er** *noun*
³rest *noun* [Middle English *reste,* literally, stoppage, short for *areste,* from Middle French, from Old French, from *arester* to arrest] (14th century)
: a projection or attachment on the side of the breastplate of medieval armor for supporting the butt of a lance
⁴rest *noun* [Middle English, from Middle French *reste,* from *rester* to remain, from Latin *restare,* from *re-* + *stare* to stand — more at STAND] (15th century)
: something that remains over : REMAINDER ⟨ate the *rest* of the candy⟩
— **for the rest** : with regard to remaining issues or needs
re·start \(ˌ)rē-'stärt\ (1845)
transitive verb
1 : to start anew
2 : to resume (as an activity) after interruption
intransitive verb
: to resume operation
— **re·start** \'rē-ˌstärt, (ˌ)re-'\ *noun*

— **re·start·able** \-'stär-tə-bəl\ *adjective*

re·state \(ˌ)rē-'stāt\ *transitive verb* (circa 1713)
: to state again or in another way

re·state·ment \-mənt\ *noun* (1803)
1 : something that is restated
2 : the act of restating

res·tau·rant \'res-t(ə-)rənt, -tə-ˌränt, -ˌtränt, -tərnt\ *noun* [French, from present participle of *restaurer* to restore, from Latin *restaurare*] (1827)
: a business establishment where meals or refreshments may be procured ◇

res·tau·ra·teur \ˌres-tə-rə-'tər\ *also* **res·tau·ran·teur** \-ˌrän-\ *noun* [French *restaurateur*, from Late Latin *restaurator* restorer, from Latin *restaurare*] (1796)
: the operator or proprietor of a restaurant

rest·ful \'rest-fəl\ *adjective* (14th century)
1 : marked by, affording, or suggesting rest and repose ⟨a *restful* color scheme⟩
2 : being at rest : QUIET
synonym *see* COMFORTABLE
— **rest·ful·ly** \-fə-lē\ *adverb*
— **rest·ful·ness** *noun*

rest home *noun* (1926)
: an establishment that provides housing and general care for the aged or the convalescent

rest house *noun* (1807)
: a building used for shelter by travelers

rest·ing *adjective* (14th century)
1 : being or characterized by dormancy : QUIESCENT ⟨a *resting* spore⟩ ⟨bulbs in the *resting* state⟩
2 : not undergoing or marked by division : VEGETATIVE ⟨a *resting* nucleus⟩

res·ti·tute \'res-tə-ˌtüt, -ˌtyüt\ *verb* **-tut·ed; -tut·ing** [Latin *restitutus*, past participle of *restituere*] (circa 1500)
transitive verb
1 : to restore to a former state or position
2 : GIVE BACK; *especially* : REFUND
intransitive verb
: to undergo restitution

res·ti·tu·tion \ˌres-tə-'tü-shən, -'tyü-\ *noun* [Middle English, from Middle French, from Latin *restitution-, restitutio,* from *restituere* to restore, from *re-* + *statuere* to set up — more at STATUTE] (14th century)
1 : an act of restoring or a condition of being restored: as **a** : a restoration of something to its rightful owner **b** : a making good of or giving an equivalent for some injury
2 : a legal action serving to cause restoration of a previous state

res·tive \'res-tiv\ *adjective* [Middle English *restyf,* from Middle French *restif,* from *rester* to stop behind, remain] (15th century)
1 : stubbornly resisting control : BALKY
2 : marked by impatience : FIDGETY
synonym *see* CONTRARY
— **res·tive·ly** *adverb*
— **res·tive·ness** *noun*

rest·less \'rest-ləs\ *adjective* (before 12th century)
1 : lacking or denying rest : UNEASY ⟨a *restless* night⟩
2 : continuously moving : UNQUIET ⟨the *restless* sea⟩
3 : characterized by or manifesting unrest especially of mind ⟨*restless* pacing⟩; *also* : CHANGEFUL, DISCONTENTED
— **rest·less·ly** *adverb*
— **rest·less·ness** *noun*

rest mass *noun* (1914)
: the mass of a body exclusive of additional mass the body acquires by its motion according to the theory of relativity

re·stor·able \ri-'stōr-ə-bəl, -'stȯr-\ *adjective* (1611)
: fit for restoring or reclaiming

re·stor·al \-əl\ *noun* (1611)
: RESTORATION

res·to·ra·tion \ˌres-tə-'rā-shən\ *noun* (14th century)

1 : an act of restoring or the condition of being restored: as **a** : a bringing back to a former position or condition : REINSTATEMENT ⟨the *restoration* of peace⟩ **b** : RESTITUTION **c** : a restoring to an unimpaired or improved condition ⟨the *restoration* of a painting⟩ **d** : the replacing of missing teeth or crowns
2 : something that is restored; *especially* : a representation or reconstruction of the original form (as of a fossil or a building)
3 *capitalized* **a** : the reestablishing of the monarchy in England in 1660 under Charles II **b** : the period in English history usually held to coincide with the reign of Charles II but sometimes to extend through the reign of James II

¹**re·stor·ative** \ri-'stōr-ə-tiv, -'stȯr-\ *adjective* (14th century)
: of or relating to restoration; *especially* : having power to restore

²**restorative** *noun* (15th century)
: something that serves to restore to consciousness, vigor, or health

re·store \ri-'stōr, -'stȯr\ *transitive verb* **re·stored; re·stor·ing** [Middle English, from Old French *restorer,* from Latin *restaurare* to renew, rebuild, alteration of *instaurare* to renew] (14th century)
1 : GIVE BACK, RETURN
2 : to put or bring back into existence or use
3 : to bring back to or put back into a former or original state : RENEW
4 : to put again in possession of something
synonym *see* RENEW
— **re·stor·er** *noun*

re·strain \ri-'strān\ *transitive verb* [Middle English *restraynen,* from Middle French *restraindre,* from Latin *restringere* to restrain, restrict, from *re-* + *stringere* to bind tight — more at STRAIN] (14th century)
1 a : to prevent from doing, exhibiting, or expressing something ⟨*restrained* the child from jumping⟩ **b** : to limit, restrict, or keep under control ⟨try to *restrain* your anger⟩
2 : to moderate or limit the force, effect, development, or full exercise of ⟨*restrain* trade⟩
3 : to deprive of liberty; *especially* : to place under arrest or restraint ☆
— **re·strain·able** \-'strā-nə-bəl\ *adjective*
— **re·strain·er** *noun*

re·strained \ri-'strānd\ *adjective* (14th century)
: marked by restraint : being without excess or extravagance
— **re·strain·ed·ly** \-'strā-nəd-lē\ *adverb*

restraining order *noun* (circa 1876)
1 : a preliminary legal order sometimes issued to keep a situation unchanged pending decision upon an application for an injunction
2 : a legal order issued against an individual to restrict or prohibit access or proximity to another specified individual

re·straint \ri-'strānt\ *noun* [Middle English, from Middle French *restrainte,* from *restraindre*] (15th century)
1 a : an act of restraining : the state of being restrained **b** (1) : a means of restraining : a restraining force or influence (2) : a device that restricts movement ⟨a *restraint* for children riding in cars⟩
2 : a control over the expression of one's emotions or thoughts

re·strict \ri-'strikt\ *transitive verb* [Latin *restrictus,* past participle of *restringere*] (1535)
1 : to confine within bounds : RESTRAIN
2 : to place under restrictions as to use or distribution
synonym *see* LIMIT

re·strict·ed *adjective* (circa 1828)
: subject or subjected to restriction: as **a** : not general : LIMITED ⟨the decision had a *restricted* effect⟩ **b** : available to the use of particular groups or specifically excluding others ⟨a *restricted* country club⟩ **c** : not intended for general circulation or release ⟨a *restricted* document⟩

— **re·strict·ed·ly** *adverb*

re·stric·tion \ri-'strik-shən\ *noun* [Middle English *restriccioun,* from Late Latin *restriction-, restrictio,* from Latin *restringere*] (15th century)
1 : something that restricts: as **a** : a regulation that restricts or restrains ⟨*restrictions* for hunters⟩ **b** : a limitation on the use or enjoyment of property or a facility
2 : an act of restricting : the condition of being restricted

restriction enzyme *noun* (1965)
: any of various enzymes that break DNA into fragments at specific sites in the interior of the molecule — called also *restriction endonuclease*

re·stric·tion·ism \-shə-ˌni-zəm\ *noun* (1937)
: a policy or philosophy favoring restriction (as of trade or immigration)
— **re·stric·tion·ist** \-sh(ə-)nist\ *adjective or noun*

re·stric·tive \ri-'strik-tiv\ *adjective* (1579)
1 a : of or relating to restriction **b** : serving or tending to restrict ⟨*restrictive* regulations⟩
2 : limiting the reference of a modified word or phrase
3 : prohibiting further negotiation
— **restrictive** *noun*
— **re·stric·tive·ly** *adverb*
— **re·stric·tive·ness** *noun*

☆ **SYNONYMS**
Restrain, check, curb, bridle mean to hold back from or control in doing something. RESTRAIN suggests holding back by force or persuasion from acting or from going to extremes ⟨*restrained* themselves from laughing⟩. CHECK implies restraining or impeding a progress, activity, or impetus ⟨trying to *check* government spending⟩. CURB suggests an abrupt or drastic checking ⟨learn to *curb* your appetite⟩. BRIDLE implies keeping under control by subduing or holding in ⟨*bridle* an impulse to throw the book down⟩.

◇ **WORD HISTORY**
restaurant The *restaurant*—both word and institution—allegedly originated in Paris in the second half of the 18th century. According to an oft-repeated account first published in 1853, the first *restaurant* was opened in 1765 by a Parisian named Boulanger, though the word is not definitely attested in French before 1803. Boulanger's establishment offered to its customers *bouillons restaurants* ("restorative broths," from which the name *restaurant* supposedly derived), fowl, and eggs under the Latin motto *Venite ad me omnes qui stomacho laboratis et ego vos restaurabo* ("Come to me all who suffer from pain of the stomach and I will restore you"), which punningly alludes to both *restaurant* and the invitation of Matthew 11:28 (Revised Standard Version) "Come to me all who labor and are heavy-laden, and I will give you rest." Similar but more elaborate establishments soon opened, though cooked meat dishes (*ragoûts*) briefly remained the domain of someone called a *traiteur* "treater," a sort of caterer who had preceded the *restaurateur* in providing food to Frenchmen who did not have their own kitchens. (*Traiteur* was borrowed into Italian as *trattore,* the base of *trattoria,* a common Italian word for "restaurant" now familiar to many English-speaking diners.)

restrictive clause *noun* (circa 1895)
: a descriptive clause that is essential to the definiteness of the word it modifies (as *that you ordered* in "the book that you ordered is out of print")

re·strike \(ˌ)rē-ˈstrīk, ˈrē-\ *noun* (1899)
: a coin or medal struck from an original die at some time after the original issue

rest room *noun* (1899)
: a room or suite of rooms providing toilets and lavatories

re·struc·ture \(ˌ)rē-ˈstrək-chər\ (1942)
transitive verb
: to change the makeup, organization, or pattern of
intransitive verb
: to restructure something

¹re·sult \ri-ˈzəlt\ *intransitive verb* [Middle English, from Medieval Latin *resultare*, from Latin, to rebound, from *re-* + *saltare* to leap — more at SALTATION] (15th century)
1 a : to proceed or arise as a consequence, effect, or conclusion ⟨death *resulted* from the disease⟩ **b** : to have an issue or result ⟨the disease *resulted* in death⟩
2 : REVERT 2

²result *noun* (1647)
1 : something that results as a consequence, issue, or conclusion; *also* : beneficial or tangible effect : FRUIT
2 : something obtained by calculation or investigation
— **re·sult·ful** \-fəl\ *adjective*
— **re·sult·less** \-ləs\ *adjective*

¹re·sul·tant \ri-ˈzəl-tᵊnt\ *adjective* (1639)
: derived from or resulting from something else
— **re·sul·tant·ly** *adverb*

²resultant *noun* (1815)
: something that results : OUTCOME; *specifically* : the single vector that is the sum of a given set of vectors

re·sume \ri-ˈzüm\ *verb* **re·sumed; re·sum·ing** [Middle English, from Middle French or Latin; Middle French *resumer*, from Latin *resumere*, from *re-* + *sumere* to take up, take — more at CONSUME] (15th century)
transitive verb
1 : to assume or take again : REOCCUPY ⟨*resumed* his seat by the fire —Thomas Hardy⟩
2 : to return to or begin again after interruption ⟨*resumed* her work⟩
3 : to take back to oneself
4 : to pick up again
5 : REITERATE, SUMMARIZE
intransitive verb
: to begin again something interrupted

ré·su·mé *or* **re·su·me** *or* **re·su·mé** \ˈre-zə-ˌmā, ˌre-zə-ˈ\ *also* ˈrā- *or* ˌrā-\ *noun* [French *résumé*, from past participle of *résumer* to resume, summarize, from Middle French *resumer*] (1804)
1 : SUMMARY
2 : CURRICULUM VITAE

re·sump·tion \ri-ˈzəm(p)-shən\ *noun* [Middle English, from Middle French or Late Latin; Middle French *resomption*, from Late Latin *resumption-*, *resumptio*, from Latin *resumere*] (15th century)
1 : an act or instance of resuming : RECOMMENCEMENT
2 : a return to payment in specie

re·su·pi·nate \ri-ˈsü-pə-ˌnāt\ *adjective* [Latin *resupinatus*, past participle of *resupinare* to bend back to a supine position, from *re-* + *supinus* supine] (circa 1776)
1 : inverted in position ⟨*resupinate* orchid flowers⟩
2 : having or being a fruiting body lying flat on the substrate with the hymenium at the periphery or over the whole surface ⟨*resupinate* fungi⟩ ⟨*resupinate* sporophores⟩

re·sur·face \(ˌ)rē-ˈsər-fəs\ (1894)
transitive verb
: to provide with a new or fresh surface

: to come again to the surface (as of the water); *broadly* : to appear or show up again
— **re·sur·fac·er** \-fə-sər\ *noun*

re·surge \ri-ˈsərj\ *intransitive verb* **re·surged; re·surg·ing** [Latin *resurgere*] (1575)
: to undergo a resurgence

re·sur·gence \ri-ˈsər-jən(t)s\ *noun* (circa 1834)
: a rising again into life, activity, or prominence : RENASCENCE

re·sur·gent \-jənt\ *adjective* [Latin *resurgent-, resurgens*, present participle of *resurgere*] (1808)
: undergoing or tending to produce resurgence

res·ur·rect \ˌre-zə-ˈrekt\ *transitive verb* [back-formation from *resurrection*] (1772)
1 : to raise from the dead
2 : to bring to view, attention, or use again

res·ur·rec·tion \ˌre-zə-ˈrek-shən\ *noun* [Middle English, from Late Latin *resurrection-, resurrectio* act of rising from the dead, from *resurgere* to rise from the dead, from Latin, to rise again, from *re-* + *surgere* to rise — more at SURGE] (14th century)
1 a *capitalized* : the rising of Christ from the dead **b** *often capitalized* : the rising again to life of all the human dead before the final judgment **c** : the state of one risen from the dead
2 : RESURGENCE, REVIVAL
3 *Christian Science* : a spiritualization of thought : material belief that yields to spiritual understanding
— **res·ur·rec·tion·al** \-shnəl, -shə-nᵊl\ *adjective*

res·ur·rec·tion·ist \-sh(ə-)nist\ *noun* (1776)
1 : BODY SNATCHER
2 : one who resurrects

re·sus·ci·tate \ri-ˈsə-sə-ˌtāt\ *verb* **-tat·ed; -tat·ing** [Latin *resuscitatus*, past participle of *resuscitare* to reawaken, from *re-* + *suscitare* to rouse, from *sub-, sus-* up + *citare* to put in motion, stir — more at SUB-, CITE] (1532)
transitive verb
: to revive from apparent death or from unconsciousness; *also* : REVITALIZE
intransitive verb
: COME TO, REVIVE
— **re·sus·ci·ta·tion** \ri-ˌsə-sə-ˈtā-shən, ˌrē-\ *noun*
— **re·sus·ci·ta·tive** \ri-ˈsə-sə-ˌtā-tiv\ *adjective*

re·sus·ci·ta·tor \ri-ˈsə-sə-ˌtā-tər\ *noun* (circa 1843)
: one that resuscitates; *specifically* : an apparatus used to restore respiration (as to a partially asphyxiated person)

ret \ˈret\ *verb* **ret·ted; ret·ting** [Middle English, from Middle Dutch] (14th century)
transitive verb
: to soak (as flax) to loosen the fiber from the woody tissue
intransitive verb
: to become retted

re·ta·ble \ˈrē-ˌtā-bəl, rē-ˈ\ *noun* [French, from Middle French, modification of Old Provençal *retaule*, alteration of *reretaule*, ultimately from Latin *retro-* + *tabula* board, tablet] (circa 1823)
: a raised shelf above an altar for the altar cross, the altar lights, and flowers

¹re·tail \ˈrē-ˌtāl, especially for 2 also ri-ˈtā(ə)l\ *verb* [Middle English, from Middle French *retaillier* to cut back, divide into pieces, from Old French, from *re-* + *taillier* to cut — more at TAILOR] (15th century)
transitive verb
1 : to sell in small quantities directly to the ultimate consumer
2 : TELL, RETELL
intransitive verb
: to sell at retail
— **re·tail·er** *noun*

²re·tail \ˈrē-ˌtāl\ *noun* (15th century)

: the sale of commodities or goods in small quantities to ultimate consumers; *also* : the industry of such selling
— **at retail 1** : at a retailer's price **2** : ⁴RETAIL

³re·tail \ˈrē-ˌtāl\ *adjective* (1601)
: of, relating to, or engaged in the sale of commodities at retail ⟨*retail* trade⟩

⁴re·tail \ˈrē-ˌtāl\ *adverb* (1784)
: in small quantities : from a retailer

re·tail·ing \ˈrē-ˌtā-liŋ\ *noun* (14th century)
: the activities involved in the selling of goods to ultimate consumers for personal or household consumption

re·tain \ri-ˈtān\ *transitive verb* [Middle English *reteinen, retainen*, from Middle French *retenir*, from Latin *retinēre* to hold back, keep, restrain, from *re-* + *tenēre* to hold — more at THIN] (15th century)
1 a : to keep in possession or use **b** : to keep in one's pay or service; *specifically* : to employ by paying a retainer **c** : to keep in mind or memory : REMEMBER
2 : to hold secure or intact
synonym see KEEP

retained object *noun* (circa 1904)
: an object of a verb in the predicate of a passive construction (as *me* in "a book was given me" and *book* in "I was given a book")

¹re·tain·er \ri-ˈtā-nər\ *noun* (1540)
1 a : a person attached or owing service to a household; *especially* : SERVANT **b** : EMPLOYEE
2 : one that retains
3 : any of various devices used for holding something

²retainer *noun* [Middle English *reteiner* act of withholding, from *reteinen* + Anglo-French *-er* (as in *weyver* waiver)] (1775)
1 : the act of a client by which the services of a lawyer, counselor, or adviser are engaged
2 : a fee paid to a lawyer or professional adviser for advice or services or for a claim on services when needed

¹re·take \(ˌ)rē-ˈtāk\ *transitive verb* **-took** \-ˈtuk\; **-tak·en** \-ˈtā-kən\; **-tak·ing** (15th century)
1 : to take or receive again
2 : RECAPTURE
3 : to photograph again

²re·take \ˈrē-ˌtāk\ *noun* (1916)
: a subsequent filming, photographing, or recording undertaken to improve upon the first; *also* : an instance of this

re·tal·i·ate \ri-ˈta-lē-ˌāt\ *verb* **-at·ed; -at·ing** [Late Latin *retaliatus*, past participle of *retaliare*, from Latin *re-* + *talio* legal retaliation] (1611)
transitive verb
: to repay (as an injury) in kind
intransitive verb
: to return like for like; *especially* : to get revenge
synonym see RECIPROCATE
— **re·tal·i·a·tion** \ri-ˌta-lē-ˈā-shən, ˌrē-\ *noun*
— **re·tal·i·a·tive** \ri-ˈta-lē-ˌā-tiv\ *adjective*
— **re·tal·ia·to·ry** \-ˈtal-yə-ˌtōr-ē, -ˈta-lē-ə-, -ˌtȯr-\ *adjective*

¹re·tard \ri-ˈtärd\ *verb* [Middle English, from Middle French or Latin; Middle French *retarder*, from Latin *retardare*, from *re-* + *tardus* slow] (15th century)
transitive verb
1 : to slow up especially by preventing or hindering advance or accomplishment : IMPEDE
2 : to delay academic progress by failure to promote
intransitive verb
: to undergo retardation
synonym see DELAY
— **re·tard·er** *noun*

²re·tard *noun* (1788)
1 \ri-ˈtärd\ : a holding back or slowing down
: RETARDATION

2 \'rē-ˌtärd\ : a retarded person; *also* : a person held to resemble a retarded person in behavior — often taken to be offensive

re·tar·dant \ri-'tär-dᵊnt\ *adjective* (1642)
: serving or tending to retard ⟨a growth-*retardant* substance⟩
— **retardant** *noun*

re·tar·date \-'tär-ˌdāt, -dət\ *noun* (1915)
: a mentally retarded person

re·tar·da·tion \ˌrē-ˌtär-'dā-shən, ri-\ *noun* (15th century)
1 : an act or instance of retarding
2 : the extent to which something is retarded
3 : a musical suspension; *specifically* : one that resolves upward
4 a : an abnormal slowness of thought or action; *also* : less than normal intellectual competence usually characterized by an IQ of less than 70 **b** : slowness in development or progress

re·tard·ed \ri-'tär-dəd\ *adjective* (1895)
: slow or limited in intellectual or emotional development or academic progress

retch \'rech, *especially British* 'rēch\ *verb* [(assumed) Middle English *rechen* to spit, retch, from Old English *hrǣcan* to spit, hawk; akin to Old Norse *hrækja* to spit] (circa 1798)
transitive verb
: VOMIT 1
intransitive verb
: to make an effort to vomit; *also* : VOMIT
— **retch** *noun*

re·te \'rē-tē, 'rā-\ *noun, plural* **re·tia** \'rē-tē-ə, 'rā-\ [New Latin, from Latin, net] (1541)
1 : a network especially of blood vessels or nerves : PLEXUS
2 : an anatomical part resembling or including a network

re·tell \(ˌ)rē-'tel\ *transitive verb* **-told** \-'tōld\; **-tell·ing** (1593)
1 : to tell again or in another form
2 : to count again

re·tell·ing *noun* (1883)
: a new version of a story ⟨a *retelling* of a Greek legend⟩

re·ten·tion \ri-'ten(t)-shən\ *noun* [Middle English *retencioun*, from Latin *retention-, retentio*, from *retinēre* to retain — more at RETAIN] (14th century)
1 a : the act of retaining : the state of being retained **b** : abnormal retaining of a fluid or secretion in a body cavity
2 a : power of retaining : RETENTIVENESS **b** : an ability to retain things in mind; *specifically* : a preservation of the aftereffects of experience and learning that makes recall or recognition possible
3 : something retained

re·ten·tive \-'ten-tiv\ *adjective* [Middle English *retentif*, from Middle French & Medieval Latin; Middle French, from Medieval Latin *retentivus*, from Latin *retentus*, past participle of *retinēre*] (14th century)
: having the power, property, or capacity of retaining ⟨soils *retentive* of moisture⟩; *especially* : retaining knowledge easily
— **re·ten·tive·ly** *adverb*
— **re·ten·tive·ness** *noun*

re·ten·tiv·i·ty \ˌrē-ˌten-'ti-və-tē, ri-\ *noun* (1881)
: the power of retaining; *specifically* : the capacity for retaining magnetism after the action of the magnetizing force has ceased

re·think \(ˌ)rē-'thiŋk\ *verb* **-thought** \-'thȯt\; **-think·ing** (1700)
transitive verb
: to think about again : RECONSIDER
intransitive verb
: to engage in reconsideration
— **re·think** \'rē-ˌthiŋk, -'thiŋk\ *noun*
— **re·think·er** *noun*

ret·i·cence \'re-tə-sən(t)s\ *noun* (1603)
1 : the quality or state of being reticent : RESERVE, RESTRAINT
2 : an instance of being reticent
3 : RELUCTANCE 1

ret·i·cen·cy \-sən(t)-sē\ *noun, plural* **-cies** (1617)
: RETICENCE

ret·i·cent \-sənt\ *adjective* [Latin *reticent-, reticens*, present participle of *reticēre* to keep silent, from *re-* + *tacēre* to be silent — more at TACIT] (circa 1834)
1 : inclined to be silent or uncommunicative in speech : RESERVED
2 : restrained in expression, presentation, or appearance ⟨the room has an aspect of *reticent* dignity —A. N. Whitehead⟩
3 : RELUCTANT
synonym see SILENT
— **ret·i·cent·ly** *adverb*

ret·i·cle \'re-ti-kəl\ *noun* [Latin *reticulum* network] (circa 1731)
: a scale on transparent material (as in an optical instrument) used especially for measuring or aiming

re·tic·u·lar \ri-'ti-kyə-lər\ *adjective* (1597)
1 a : RETICULATE **b** : of, relating to, or forming a reticulum
2 : INTRICATE

reticular formation *noun* (1887)
: a mass of nerve cells and fibers situated primarily in the brain stem and functioning upon stimulation especially in arousal of the organism

¹re·tic·u·late \-lət, -ˌlāt\ *adjective* [Latin *reticulatus*, from *reticulum*] (1658)
1 : resembling a net; *especially* : having veins, fibers, or lines crossing ⟨a *reticulate* leaf⟩
2 : being or involving evolutionary change dependent on genetic recombination involving diverse interbreeding populations
— **re·tic·u·late·ly** *adverb*

²re·tic·u·late \-ˌlāt\ *verb* **-lat·ed; -lat·ing** [back-formation from *reticulated*, adjective, reticulate] (1787)
transitive verb
: to divide, mark, or construct so as to form a network
intransitive verb
: to become reticulated

re·tic·u·la·tion \ri-ˌti-kyə-'lā-shən\ *noun* (1671)
: a reticulated formation : NETWORK; *also* : something reticulated

ret·i·cule \'re-ti-ˌkyü(ə)l\ *noun* [French *réticule*, from Latin *reticulum* network, network bag, from diminutive of *rete* net] (circa 1738)
1 : RETICLE
2 : a woman's drawstring bag used especially as a carryall

re·tic·u·lo·cyte \ri-'ti-kyə-lō-ˌsīt\ *noun* [New Latin *reticulum* + International Scientific Vocabulary *-cyte*] (1922)
: an immature red blood cell that appears especially during regeneration of lost blood and has a fine basophilic reticulum formed of ribosomal remains

re·tic·u·lo·en·do·the·li·al \ri-ˌti-kyə-lō-ˌen-də-'thē-lē-əl\ *adjective* [New Latin *reticulum* + *endothelium*] (circa 1923)
: of, relating to, or being the reticuloendothelial system

reticuloendothelial system *noun* (circa 1923)
: a diffuse system of cells arising from mesenchyme and comprising all the phagocytic cells of the body except the circulating white blood cells

re·tic·u·lum \ri-'ti-kyə-ləm\ *noun* [New Latin, from Latin, network] (circa 1658)
1 : the second compartment of the stomach of a ruminant in which folds of the mucous membrane form hexagonal cells — compare ABOMASUM, OMASUM, RUMEN
2 : a reticular structure : NETWORK; *especially* : interstitial tissue composed of reticulum cells

reticulum cell *noun* (1912)
: one of the branched anastomosing reticuloendothelial cells that form an intricate interstitial network ramifying through other tissues and organs

retin- *or* **retino-** *combining form* [*retina*]
1 : retina ⟨*retinitis*⟩ ⟨*retinoscopy*⟩
2 : retinol ⟨*retinoid*⟩

ret·i·na \'re-tᵊn-ə, 're-tnə\ *noun, plural* **reti·nas** *or* **ret·i·nae** \-tᵊn-ˌē, -ˌī\ [Middle English *rethina*, from Medieval Latin *retina*, probably from Latin *rete* net] (14th century)
: the sensory membrane that lines the eye, is composed of several layers including one containing the rods and cones, and functions as the immediate instrument of vision by receiving the image formed by the lens and converting it into chemical and nervous signals which reach the brain by way of the optic nerve — see EYE illustration

ret·i·nac·u·lum \ˌre-tᵊn-'a-kyə-ləm\ *noun, plural* **-la** \-lə\ [New Latin, from Latin, halter, cable, from *retinēre* to hold back — more at RETAIN] (circa 1825)
: a small structure on the forewings of many lepidopterous insects (as a noctuid moth) that catches and holds the frenulum

¹ret·i·nal \'re-tᵊn-əl, 're-tnəl\ *adjective* (1838)
: of, relating to, involving, or being a retina

²ret·i·nal \'re-tᵊn-al, -ˌȯl\ *noun* [retin- + ³-al] (1944)
: a yellowish to orange aldehyde $C_{20}H_{28}O$ derived from vitamin A that in combination with proteins forms the visual pigments of the retinal rods and cones

ret·i·nene \'re-tᵊn-ˌēn\ *noun* (1934)
: RETINAL

ret·i·ni·tis \ˌre-tᵊn-'ī-təs\ *noun* [New Latin] (1861)
: inflammation of the retina

retinitis pig·men·to·sa \-ˌpig-mən-'tō-sə, -(ˌ)men-, -zə\ *noun* [New Latin, pigmented retinitis] (1861)
: any of several hereditary progressive degenerative diseases of the eye marked by night blindness in the early stages, atrophy and pigment changes in the retina, constriction of the visual field, and eventual blindness

ret·i·no·blas·to·ma \ˌre-tᵊn-ō-ˌblas-'tō-mə\ *noun* [retin- + *blast-* + *-oma*] (1924)
: a malignant tumor of the retina that develops during childhood, is derived from retinal germ cells, and is associated with a chromosomal abnormality

ret·i·no·ic acid \ˌre-tᵊn-'ō-ik-\ *noun* (1965)
: an acid $C_{20}H_{28}O_2$ derived from vitamin A and used especially in the treatment of acne

ret·i·noid \'re-tᵊn-ˌȯid\ *noun* (1976)
: any of various synthetic or naturally occurring analogues of vitamin A

ret·i·nol \'re-tᵊn-ˌȯl, -ˌōl\ *noun* [retin- + ¹-ol; from its being the source of retinal] (1960)
: the chief and typical vitamin A

ret·i·nop·a·thy \ˌre-tᵊn-'ä-pə-thē\ *noun* (1932)
: any of various noninflammatory disorders of the retina including some that cause blindness

ret·i·nos·co·py \ˌre-tᵊn-'äs-kə-pē\ *noun* (1884)
: observation of the retina of the eye especially to determine the state of refraction

ret·i·no·tec·tal \ˌre-tᵊn-ō-'tek-təl\ *adjective* [retin- + *tectum* + ¹-al] (1951)
: of, relating to, or being the nerve fibers connecting the retina and the tectum of the midbrain ⟨*retinotectal* pathways⟩

ret·i·nue \'re-tᵊn-ˌü, -ˌyü\ *noun* [Middle English *retenue*, from Middle French, from feminine of *retenu*, past participle of *retenir* to retain] (14th century)
: a group of retainers or attendants

re·tin·u·la \re-'tin-yə-lə\ *noun, plural* **-lae** \-ˌlē, -ˌlī\ *also* **-las** [New Latin, diminutive of Medieval Latin *retina*] (1878)
: the neural receptor of a single facet of an arthropod compound eye

— **re·tin·u·lar** \-lər\ *adjective*

re·tir·ant \ri-'tī-rənt\ *noun* (1948)
: RETIREE

re·tire \ri-'tīr\ *verb* **re·tired; re·tir·ing**
[Middle French *retirer,* from *re-* + *tirer* to draw] (1533)
intransitive verb
1 : to withdraw from action or danger **:** RE-TREAT
2 : to withdraw especially for privacy
3 : to move back **:** RECEDE
4 : to withdraw from one's position or occupation **:** conclude one's working or professional career
5 : to go to bed
transitive verb
1 : WITHDRAW: as **a :** to march (a military force) away from the enemy **b :** to withdraw from circulation or from the market **:** RECALL **c :** to withdraw from usual use or service
2 : to cause to retire from one's position or occupation
3 a : to put out (a batter or batsman) in baseball or cricket **b :** to cause (a side) to end a turn at bat in baseball
4 : to win permanent possession of (as a trophy)

re·tired \ri-'tīrd\ *adjective* (1590)
1 : SECLUDED ⟨*retired* village⟩
2 : withdrawn from one's position or occupation **:** having concluded one's working or professional career
3 : received by or due to one in retirement
— **re·tired·ly** \-'tī-rəd-lē, -'tīrd-\ *adverb*
— **re·tired·ness** \-'tīrd-nəs\ *noun*

re·tir·ee \ri-ˌtī-'rē\ *noun* (1945)
: a person who has retired from a working or professional career

¹re·tire·ment \ri-'tīr-mənt\ *noun* (1596)
1 a : an act of retiring **:** the state of being retired **b :** withdrawal from one's position or occupation or from active working life **c :** the age at which one normally retires ⟨reaches *retirement* in May⟩
2 : a place of seclusion or privacy

²retirement *adjective* (1919)
: of, relating to, or designed for retired persons

re·tir·ing \ri-'tīr-iŋ\ *adjective* (1766)
: RESERVED, SHY
— **re·tir·ing·ly** \-iŋ-lē\ *adverb*
— **re·tir·ing·ness** *noun*

re·tool \(ˌ)rē-'tül\ *transitive verb* (1927)
1 : to reequip with tools
2 : REORGANIZE

¹re·tort \ri-'tȯrt\ *verb* [Latin *retortus,* past participle of *retorquēre,* literally, to twist back, hurl back, from *re-* + *torquēre* to twist — more at TORTURE] (circa 1557)
transitive verb
1 : to pay or hurl back **:** RETURN ⟨*retort* an insult⟩
2 a : to make a reply to **b :** to say in reply
3 : to answer (as an argument) by a counter argument
intransitive verb
1 : to answer back usually sharply
2 : to return an argument or charge
3 : RETALIATE
synonym see ANSWER

²retort *noun* (1600)
: a quick, witty, or cutting reply; *especially* : one that turns back or counters the first speaker's words

³re·tort \ri-'tȯrt, 'rē-ˌ\ *noun* [Middle French *retorte,* from Medieval Latin *retorta,* from Latin, feminine of *retortus;* from its shape] (1605)
: a vessel or chamber in which substances are distilled or decomposed by heat

⁴re·tort \ri-'tȯrt, 'rē-ˌ\ *transitive verb* (1850)
: to treat (as oil shale) by heating in a retort

retort

re·tort pouch \ri-'tȯrt-, 'rē-ˌ\ *noun* (1977)
: a flexible package in which prepared food is hermetically sealed for long-term unrefrigerated storage

¹re·touch \(ˌ)rē-'təch\ *verb* [French *retoucher,* from Middle French, from *re-* + *toucher* to touch] (1685)
transitive verb
1 : to rework in order to improve **:** TOUCH UP
2 : to alter (as a photographic negative) to produce a more desirable appearance
3 : to color (new growth of hair) to match previously dyed, tinted, or bleached hair
intransitive verb
: to make or give retouches
— **re·touch·er** *noun*

²re·touch \'rē-ˌtəch, (ˌ)rē-'\ *noun* (1703)
: the act, process, or an instance of retouching; *especially* : the retouching of a new growth of hair

re·tract \ri-'trakt\ *verb* [Middle English, from Latin *retractus,* past participle of *retrahere* — more at RETREAT] (15th century)
transitive verb
1 : to draw back or in ⟨cats *retract* their claws⟩
2 a : TAKE BACK, WITHDRAW ⟨*retract* a confession⟩ **b :** DISAVOW
intransitive verb
1 : to draw or pull back
2 : to recant or disavow something
synonym see ABJURE, RECEDE
— **re·tract·able** \-'trak-tə-bəl\ *adjective*

re·trac·tile \ri-'trak-t⁹l, -ˌtīl\ *adjective* (1777)
: capable of being drawn back or in ⟨*retractile* claws⟩
— **re·trac·til·i·ty** \ˌrē-ˌtrak-'ti-lə-tē, ri-\ *noun*

re·trac·tion \ri-'trak-shən\ *noun* (14th century)
1 : an act of recanting; *specifically* : a statement made by one retracting
2 : an act of retracting **:** the state of being retracted
3 : the ability to retract

re·trac·tor \ri-'trak-tər\ *noun* (1837)
: one that retracts: as **a :** a surgical instrument for holding open the edges of a wound **b :** a muscle that draws in an organ or part

re·train \(ˌ)rē-'trān\ (1918)
transitive verb
: to train again or anew
intransitive verb
: to become trained again
— **re·train·able** \-'trā-nə-bəl\ *adjective*

re·tral \'rē-trəl, 'rē-\ *adjective* [Latin *retro* back — more at RETRO-] (1875)
1 : situated at or toward the back **:** POSTERIOR
2 : BACKWARD, RETROGRADE
— **re·tral·ly** \-trə-lē\ *adverb*

re·trans·late \ˌrē-tran(t)s-'lāt, -tranz-\ (1860)
transitive verb
: to translate (a translation) into another language; *also* : to give a new form to
intransitive verb
: to retranslate something
— **re·trans·la·tion** \-'lā-shən\ *noun*

¹re·tread \(ˌ)rē-'tred\ *transitive verb* **re·tread·ed; re·tread·ing** (1907)
1 : to bond or vulcanize a new tread to the prepared surface of (a worn tire)
2 : to make over as if new ⟨*retread* an old plot⟩

²re·tread \'rē-ˌtred\ *noun* (1914)
1 : a retreaded tire
2 : something made or done again especially in slightly revised form **:** REMAKE
3 a : one (as a retired person) who is retrained for work **b :** one (as an athlete) who has previously held the same or a similar position

re–tread \(ˌ)rē-'tred\ *transitive verb* **-trod** \-'träd\; **-trod·den** \-'trä-d⁹n\ *or* **-trod; -tread·ing** (1598)
: to tread again

¹re·treat \ri-'trēt\ *noun* [Middle English *retret,* from Middle French *retrait,* from past partici-

ple of *retraire* to withdraw, from Latin *retrahere,* from *re-* + *trahere* to draw] (14th century)
1 a (1) **:** an act or process of withdrawing especially from what is difficult, dangerous, or disagreeable (2) **:** the process of receding from a position or state attained ⟨the *retreat* of a glacier⟩ ⟨the slow *retreat* of an epidemic⟩ **b** (1) **:** the usually forced withdrawal of troops from an enemy or from an advanced position (2) **:** a signal for retreating **c** (1) **:** a signal given by bugle at the beginning of a military flag-lowering ceremony (2) **:** a military flag-lowering ceremony
2 : a place of privacy or safety **:** REFUGE
3 : a period of group withdrawal for prayer, meditation, study, and instruction under a director

²retreat (15th century)
intransitive verb
1 : to make a retreat **:** WITHDRAW
2 : to slope backward
transitive verb
: to draw or lead back **:** REMOVE; *specifically* : to move (a piece) back in chess
synonym see RECEDE
— **re·treat·er** *noun*

re·treat·ant \ri-'trē-t⁹nt\ *noun* (1880)
: a person on a religious retreat

re·trench \ri-'trench\ *verb* [obsolete French *retrencher* (now *retrancher*), from Middle French *retrenchier,* from *re-* + *trenchier* to cut] (1625)
transitive verb
1 a : CUT DOWN, REDUCE **b :** to cut out **:** EXCISE
2 : to pare away **:** REMOVE
intransitive verb
: to make retrenchments; *specifically* : ECONOMIZE
synonym see SHORTEN

re·trench·ment \-mənt\ *noun* (circa 1600)
: REDUCTION, CURTAILMENT; *specifically* : a cutting of expenses

re·tri·al \(ˌ)rē-'trī(-ə)l\ *noun* (1875)
: a second trial, experiment, or test; *specifically* : a second judicial trial

ret·ri·bu·tion \ˌre-trə-'byü-shən\ *noun* [Middle English *retribucioun,* from Middle French *retribution,* from Late Latin *retribution-, retributio,* from Latin *retribuere* to pay back, from *re-* + *tribuere* to pay — more at TRIBUTE] (14th century)
1 : RECOMPENSE, REWARD
2 : the dispensing or receiving of reward or punishment especially in the hereafter
3 : something given or exacted in recompense; *especially* : PUNISHMENT

re·trib·u·tive \ri-'tri-byə-tiv\ *adjective* (1678)
: of, relating to, or marked by retribution
— **re·trib·u·tive·ly** *adverb*

re·trib·u·to·ry \-byə-ˌtȯr-ē, -ˌtȯr-\ *adjective* (circa 1615)
: RETRIBUTIVE

re·triev·al \ri-'trē-vəl\ *noun* (circa 1643)
1 : an act or process of retrieving
2 : possibility of being retrieved or of recovering ⟨beyond *retrieval*⟩

¹re·trieve \ri-'trēv\ *verb* **re·trieved; re·triev·ing** [Middle English *retreven,* modification of Middle French *retrouver* to find again, from *re-* + *trouver* to find, from (assumed) Vulgar Latin *tropare* to find, compose — more at TROUBADOUR] (15th century)
transitive verb
1 : to discover and bring in (killed or wounded game)
2 : to call to mind again
3 : to get back again **:** REGAIN
4 a : RESCUE, SALVAGE **b :** to return (as a ball or shuttlecock that is difficult to reach) successfully
5 : RESTORE, REVIVE ⟨his writing *retrieves* the past⟩
6 : to remedy the evil consequences of **:** CORRECT

7 : to get and bring back; *especially* **:** to recover (as information) from storage
intransitive verb
: to bring in game ⟨a dog that *retrieves* well⟩; *also* **:** to bring back an object thrown by a person
— **re·triev·abil·i·ty** \-ˌtrē-və-ˈbi-lə-tē\ *noun*
— **re·triev·able** \-ˈtrē-və-bəl\ *adjective*
²**retrieve** *noun* (1575)
1 : RETRIEVAL
2 : the successful return of a ball that is difficult to reach or control (as in tennis)
re·triev·er \ri-ˈtrē-vər\ *noun* (15th century)
: one that retrieves; *especially* **:** a dog of any of several breeds (as a golden retriever) having a heavy water-resistant coat and used especially for retrieving game
ret·ro \ˈre-(ˌ)trō\ *adjective* [French *rétro*, short for *rétrospectif* retrospective] (1974)
: relating to, reviving, or being the styles or especially the fashions of the past **:** fashionably nostalgic or old-fashioned ⟨a *retro* look⟩
retro- *prefix* [Middle English, from Latin, from *retro*, from *re-* + *-tro* (as in *intro* within) — more at INTRO-]
1 : backward **:** back ⟨*retro*-rocket⟩
2 : situated behind ⟨*retro*peritoneal⟩
ret·ro·ac·tion \ˌre-trō-ˈak-shən\ *noun* (circa 1738)
1 [*retroactive*] **:** retroactive operation (as of a law or tax)
2 [*retro-* + *action*] **:** a reciprocal action **:** REACTION
ret·ro·ac·tive \-ˈak-tiv\ *adjective* [French *rétroactif*, from Latin *retroactus*, past participle of *retroagere* to drive back, reverse, from *retro-* + *agere* to drive — more at AGENT] (1611)
: extending in scope or effect to a prior time or to conditions that existed or originated in the past; *especially* **:** made effective as of a date prior to enactment, promulgation, or imposition ⟨*retroactive* tax⟩
— **ret·ro·ac·tive·ly** *adverb*
— **ret·ro·ac·tiv·i·ty** \-ˌak-ˈti-və-tē\ *noun*
ret·ro·cede \ˌre-trō-ˈsēd\ *verb* **-ced·ed; -ced·ing** [Latin *retrocedere*, from *retro-* + *cedere* to go, cede] (1654)
intransitive verb
: to go back **:** RECEDE
transitive verb
[French *rétrocéder*, from Medieval Latin *retrocedere*, from Latin *retro-* + *cedere* to cede] **:** to cede back (as a territory)
— **ret·ro·ces·sion** \-ˈse-shən\ *noun*
ret·ro·dict \ˌre-trə-ˈdikt\ *transitive verb* [*retro-* + pre*dict*] (1949)
: to utilize present information or ideas to infer or explain (a past event or state of affairs) ⟨*retrodict* past eclipses⟩
— **ret·ro·dic·tion** \-ˈdik-shən\ *noun*
— **ret·ro·dic·tive** \-ˈdik-tiv\ *adjective*
ret·ro·engine \ˈre-trō-ˌen-jən\ *noun* (1965)
: RETRO-ROCKET
ret·ro·fire \-ˌfīr\ (1961)
transitive verb
: to cause (a retro-rocket) to become ignited
intransitive verb
of a retro-rocket **:** to become ignited
— **retrofire** *noun*
ret·ro·fit \ˌre-trō-ˈfit\ *transitive verb* (1953)
1 : to furnish (as a computer, airplane, or building) with new or modified parts or equipment not available or considered necessary at the time of manufacture
2 : to install (new or modified parts or equipment) in something previously manufactured or constructed
— **retrofit** *noun*
ret·ro·flex \ˈre-trə-ˌfleks\ *adjective* [New Latin *retroflexus*, from Latin *retro-* + *flexus*, past participle of *flectere* to bend] (1776)
1 : turned or bent abruptly backward

2 : articulated with the tongue tip turned up or curled back just under the hard palate ⟨*retroflex* vowel⟩
ret·ro·flex·ion *or* **ret·ro·flec·tion** \ˌre-trə-ˈflek-shən\ *noun* (1845)
1 : the state of being bent back; *especially* **:** the bending back of an organ (as a uterus) upon itself
2 : the act or process of bending back
3 : retroflex articulation
ret·ro·gra·da·tion \ˌre-trō-grā-ˈdā-shən, -grə-\ *noun* (circa 1545)
: the action or process of retrograding
¹**ret·ro·grade** \ˈre-trə-ˌgrād\ *adjective* [Middle English, from Latin *retrogradus*, from *retrogradi*] (14th century)
1 a (1) *of a celestial body* **:** having a direction contrary to that of the general motion of similar bodies (2) **:** having or being a direction of rotation or revolution that is clockwise as viewed from the north pole of the sky or a planet **b :** moving, occurring, or performed in a backward direction or opposite to the usual direction ⟨a *retrograde* step⟩ ⟨*retrograde* peristalsis⟩ **c :** contrary to the normal order **:** INVERSE
2 : tending toward or resulting in a worse or previous state
3 *archaic* **:** CONTRADICTORY, OPPOSED
4 : characterized by retrogression
5 : affecting a period prior to a precipitating cause ⟨*retrograde* amnesia⟩
6 : RETRO
— **ret·ro·grade·ly** *adverb*
²**retrograde** *adverb* (circa 1619)
: BACKWARD, REVERSELY
³**retrograde** *verb* [Latin *retrogradi*, from *retro-* + *gradi* to go — more at GRADE] (1582)
transitive verb
archaic **:** to turn back **:** REVERSE
intransitive verb
1 a : to go back **:** RETREAT **b :** to go back over or recapitulate something
2 : to decline to a worse condition
ret·ro·gress \ˌre-trə-ˈgres\ *intransitive verb* [Latin *retrogressus*, past participle of *retrogradi*] (1819)
: to move backward **:** REVERT
ret·ro·gres·sion \-ˈgre-shən\ *noun* (1646)
1 : REGRESSION 3
2 : return to a former and less complex level of development or organization
ret·ro·gres·sive \-ˈgre-siv\ *adjective* (1802)
: characterized by retrogression: as **a :** going or directed backward **b :** declining from a better to a worse state **c :** passing from a higher to a lower level of organization ⟨*retrogressive* evolution⟩
— **ret·ro·gres·sive·ly** *adverb*
ret·ro·pack \ˈre-trō-ˌpak\ *noun* (1962)
: a system of auxiliary rockets on a spacecraft that produces thrust in the direction opposite to the motion of the spacecraft and that is used to reduce speed
ret·ro·per·i·to·ne·al \ˌre-trō-ˌper-ə-tᵊn-ˈē-əl\ *adjective* (1874)
: situated behind the peritoneum
— **ret·ro·per·i·to·ne·al·ly** \-ə-lē\ *adverb*
ret·ro·re·flec·tion \ˌre-trō-ri-ˈflek-shən\ *noun* (circa 1965)
: the action or use of a retroreflector
— **ret·ro·re·flec·tive** \-ˈflek-tiv\ *adjective*
ret·ro·re·flec·tor \-ˈflek-tər\ *noun* (1946)
: a device that reflects radiation (as light) so that the paths of the rays are parallel to those of the incident rays
ret·ro·rock·et \ˈre-trō-ˌrä-kət\ *noun* (1957)
: an auxiliary rocket engine (as on a spacecraft) used in decelerating
re·trorse \ˈrē-ˌtrȯrs\ *adjective* [Latin *retrorsus*, contraction of *retroversus*] (circa 1825)
: bent backward or downward
¹**ret·ro·spect** \ˈre-trə-ˌspekt\ *noun* [probably from *retro-* + pro*spect*] (1602)

1 *archaic* **:** reference to or regard of a precedent or authority
2 : a review of or meditation on past events
— **in retrospect :** in considering the past or a past event
²**retrospect** *adjective* (1709)
: RETROSPECTIVE
³**retrospect** (1659)
intransitive verb
1 : to engage in retrospection
2 : to refer back **:** REFLECT
transitive verb
: to go back over in thought
ret·ro·spec·tion \ˌre-trə-ˈspek-shən\ *noun* (1674)
: the act or process or an instance of surveying the past
¹**ret·ro·spec·tive** \-ˈspek-tiv\ *adjective* (1664)
1 a (1) **:** of, relating to, or given to retrospection (2) **:** based on memory ⟨a *retrospective* report⟩ **b :** being a retrospective ⟨a *retrospective* exhibition⟩
2 : affecting things past **:** RETROACTIVE
— **ret·ro·spec·tive·ly** *adverb*
²**retrospective** *noun* (1932)
: a generally comprehensive exhibition or performance of the work of an artist over a span of years
re·trous·sé \rə-ˌtrü-ˈsā, rə-ˈtrü-ˌ, ˌre-trù-ˈ\ *adjective* [French, from past participle of *retrousser* to tuck up, from Middle French, from *re-* + *trousser* to truss, tuck up — more at TRUSS] (1802)
: turned up ⟨*retroussé* nose⟩
ret·ro·ver·sion \ˌre-trō-ˈvər-zhən *also* -shən\ *noun* [Latin *retroversus* turned backward, from *retro-* + *versus*, past participle of *vertere* to turn — more at WORTH] (1776)
1 : the bending backward of the uterus and cervix
2 : the act or process of turning back or regressing
ret·ro·vi·rus \ˈre-trō-ˌvī-rəs\ *noun* (1975)
: any of a group of RNA-containing viruses (as HIV) that produce reverse transcriptase by means of which DNA is produced using their RNA as a template and incorporated into the genome of infected cells and that include numerous tumorigenic viruses
— **ret·ro·vi·ral** \-rəl\ *adjective*
ret·si·na \ret-ˈsē-nə\ *noun* [New Greek, perhaps from Italian *resina* resin, from Latin — more at RESIN] (1940)
: a resin-flavored Greek wine
¹**re·turn** \ri-ˈtərn\ *verb* [Middle English *retournen*, from Middle French *retourner*, from *re-* + *tourner* to turn — more at TURN] (14th century)
intransitive verb
1 a : to go back or come back again ⟨*return* home⟩ **b :** to go back in thought or practice **:** REVERT ⟨soon *returned* to her old habit⟩
2 : to pass back to an earlier possessor
3 : REPLY, RETORT
transitive verb
1 a : to give (as an official account) to a superior **b** *British* **:** to elect (a candidate) as attested by official report or returns **c :** to bring back (as a writ or verdict) to an office or tribunal
2 a : to bring, send, or put back to a former or proper place ⟨*return* the gun to its holster⟩ **b :** to restore to a former or to a normal state
3 a : to send back **:** VISIT — usually used with *on* or *upon* **b** *obsolete* **:** RETORT
4 : to bring in (as profit) **:** YIELD
5 a : to give or perform in return **:** REPAY ⟨*return* a compliment⟩ **b :** to give back to the owner **c :** REFLECT ⟨*return* an echo⟩

\ə\ abut \ᵊ\ kitten \ər\ further \a\ ash \ā\ ace \ä\ mop, mar \au̇\ out \ch\ chin \e\ bet \ē\ easy \g\ go \i\ hit \ī\ ice \j\ job \ŋ\ sing \ō\ go \ȯ\ law \ȯi\ boy \th\ thin \t͟h\ the \ü\ loot \u̇\ foot \y\ yet \zh\ vision *see also* Guide to Pronunciation

6 : to cause (as a wall) to continue in a different direction (as at a right angle)
7 : to lead (a specified suit or specified card of a suit) in response to a partner's earlier lead
8 a : to hit back (a ball or shuttlecock) **b :** to run with (a football) after a change of possession (as by a punt or a fumble)
synonym see RECIPROCATE
— re·turn·er *noun*
²return *noun* (14th century)
1 a : the act of coming back to or from a place or condition **b :** a regular or frequent returning **:** RECURRENCE
2 a (1) **:** the delivery of a legal order (as a writ) to the proper officer or court (2) **:** an endorsed certificate stating an official's action in the execution of such an order (3) **:** the sending back of a commission with the certificate of the commissioners **b :** an account or formal report **c** (1) **:** a report of the results of balloting — usually used in plural 〈election *returns*〉 (2) **:** an official declaration of the election of a candidate (3) *chiefly British* **:** ELECTION **d** (1) **:** a formal statement on a required legal form showing taxable income, allowable deductions and exemptions, and the computation of the tax due (2) **:** a list of taxable property
3 a : the continuation usually at a right angle of the face or of a member of a building or of a molding or group of moldings **b :** a turn, bend, or winding back (as in a rod, stream, or trench) **c :** a means for conveying something (as water) back to its starting point
4 a : a quantity of goods, consignment, or cargo coming back in exchange for goods sent out as a mercantile venture **b :** the value of or profit from such venture **c** (1) **:** the profit from labor, investment, or business **:** YIELD (2) *plural* **:** RESULTS **d :** the rate of profit in a process of production per unit of cost
5 a : the act of returning something to a former place, condition, or ownership **:** RESTITUTION **b :** something returned; *especially, plural* **:** unsold publications returned to the publisher for cash or credit
6 a : something given in repayment or reciprocation **b :** ANSWER, RETORT
7 : an answering play: as **a :** a lead in a suit previously led by one's partner in a card game **b :** the action or an instance of returning a ball (as in football or tennis)
— in return : in compensation or repayment
³return *adjective* (1676)
1 a : having or formed by a change of direction 〈a *return* facade〉 **b :** doubled on itself 〈a *return* flue〉
2 : played, delivered, or given in return **:** taking place for the second time 〈a *return* meeting for the two champions〉
3 : used or taken on returning 〈the *return* road〉
4 : returning or permitting return 〈a *return* valve〉
5 : of, relating to, or causing a return to a place or condition
¹re·turn·able \ri-ˈtər-nə-bəl\ *adjective* (15th century)
1 : legally required to be returned, delivered, or argued at a specified time or place 〈a writ *returnable* on the date indicated〉
2 a : capable of returning or of being returned (as for reuse) **b :** permitted to be returned
²returnable *noun* (1963)
: something designed to be returned (as for recycling); *especially* **:** a returnable beverage container
re·turn·ee \ri-ˌtər-ˈnē\ *noun* (1944)
: one who returns; *especially* **:** one returning to the U.S. after military service overseas
re·tuse \ri-ˈtüs, -ˈtyüs\ *adjective* [Latin *retusus* blunted, from past participle of *retundere* to pound back, blunt, from *re-* + *tundere* to beat, pound — more at CONTUSION] (circa 1753)

: having the apex rounded or obtuse with a slight notch
¹Reu·ben \ˈrü-bən\ *noun* [Hebrew *Rĕ'ûbhēn*]
: a son of Jacob and the traditional eponymous ancestor of one of the tribes of Israel
²Reuben *noun* [probably from *Reuben* Kulakofsky (died 1960) American grocer] (1956)
: a grilled sandwich of corned beef, Swiss cheese, and sauerkraut usually on rye bread ◆
³Reuben *noun* [*Reuben* L. Goldberg (died 1970) American cartoonist] (1958)
: a statuette awarded annually by a professional organization for notable achievement in cartoon artistry
re·union \(ˌ)rē-ˈyün-yən\ *noun* (1610)
1 : an act of reuniting **:** the state of being reunited
2 : a reuniting of persons after separation
re·union·ist \-yə-nist\ *noun* (1866)
: an advocate of reunion (as of sects or parties)
— re·union·is·tic \(ˌ)rē-ˌyün-yə-ˈnis-tik\ *adjective*
re·unite \ˌrē-yü-ˈnīt\ *verb* [Medieval Latin *reunitus*, past participle of *reunire*, from Latin *re-* + Late Latin *unire* to unite — more at UNITE] (15th century)
transitive verb
: to bring together again
intransitive verb
: to come together again **:** REJOIN
re–up \(ˌ)rē-ˈəp\ *intransitive verb* [*re-* + sign *up*] (circa 1906)
: to enlist again
re·us·able \(ˌ)rē-ˈyü-zə-bəl\ *adjective* (1943)
: capable of being used again or repeatedly
— re·us·abil·i·ty \(ˌ)rē-ˌyü-zə-ˈbi-lə-tē\ *noun*
¹re·use \(ˌ)rē-ˈyüz\ *transitive verb* (1843)
: to use again especially after reclaiming or reprocessing 〈the need to *reuse* scarce resources〉
²reuse \-ˈyüs\ *noun* (1866)
: further or repeated use
¹rev \ˈrev\ *noun* [short for *revolution*] (circa 1890)
: a revolution of a motor
²rev *verb* **revved; rev·ving** (1920)
transitive verb
1 a : to step up the number of revolutions per minute of — often used with *up* 〈*rev* up the engine〉 **b :** INCREASE — used with *up* 〈*rev* up production〉
2 : to drive or operate especially at high speed — often used with *up*
3 : to make more active or effective — used with *up*
4 : to stir up **:** EXCITE — usually used with *up*
intransitive verb
1 : to operate at an increased speed of revolution — usually used with *up*
2 : to increase in amount or activity — used with *up*
re·val·u·ate \(ˌ)rē-ˈval-yə-ˌwāt\ *transitive verb* [back-formation from *revaluation*] (1921)
: REVALUE; *specifically* **:** to increase the value of (as currency)
— re·val·u·a·tion \(ˌ)rē-ˌval-yə-ˈwā-shən\ *noun*
re·val·ue \(ˌ)rē-ˈval-(ˌ)yü\ *transitive verb* (1592)
1 : to value (as currency) anew
2 : to make a new valuation of **:** REAPPRAISE
re·vamp \(ˌ)rē-ˈvamp\ *transitive verb* (1850)
1 : REMAKE, REVISE
2 : RENOVATE, RECONSTRUCT
— re·vamp \ˈrē-, ri-\ *noun*
re·vanche \rə-ˈvä ⁿsh\ *noun* [French, from Middle French, alteration of *revenche* — more at REVENGE] (1882)
: REVENGE; *especially* **:** a usually political policy designed to recover lost territory or status
— re·vanch·ism \-ˈvä ⁿ-ˌshi-zəm\ *noun*
¹re·vanch·ist \-ˈvä ⁿ-shist\ *noun* (1926)
: one who advocates a policy of revanche
²revanchist *adjective* (1948)
: of or relating to a policy of revanche

re·vas·cu·lar·i·za·tion \ˌrē-ˌvas-kyə-lə-rə-ˈzā-shən\ *noun* (1951)
: a surgical procedure for the provision of a new, additional, or augmented blood supply to a body part or organ
¹re·veal \ri-ˈvē(ə)l\ *transitive verb* [Middle English *revelen*, from Middle French *reveler*, from Latin *revelare* to uncover, reveal, from *re-* + *velare* to cover, veil, from *velum* veil] (14th century)
1 : to make known through divine inspiration
2 : to make (something secret or hidden) publicly or generally known 〈*reveal* a secret〉
3 : to open up to view **:** DISPLAY 〈the uncurtained window *revealed* a cluttered room〉 ☆
— re·veal·able \-ˈvē-lə-bəl\ *adjective*
— re·veal·er *noun*
²reveal *noun* [alteration of earlier *revale*, from Middle English *revalen* to lower, from Middle French *revaler*, from *re-* + *val* valley — more at VALE] (1688)
: the side of an opening (as for a window) between a frame and the outer surface of a wall; *also* **:** JAMB
re·veal·ing *adjective* (circa 1925)
: allowing a look at or an understanding of something inner or hidden **:** INSIGHTFUL
— re·veal·ing·ly *adverb*
re·veal·ment \ri-ˈvē(ə)l-mənt\ *noun* (1584)

☆ **SYNONYMS**
Reveal, disclose, divulge, tell, betray mean to make known what has been or should be concealed. REVEAL may apply to supernatural or inspired revelation of truths beyond the range of ordinary human vision or reason 〈divine will as *revealed* in sacred writings〉. DISCLOSE may imply a discovering but more often an imparting of information previously kept secret 〈candidates must *disclose* their financial assets〉. DIVULGE implies a disclosure involving some impropriety or breach of confidence 〈refused to *divulge* an anonymous source〉. TELL implies an imparting of necessary or useful information 〈*told* them what he had overheard〉. BETRAY implies a divulging that represents a breach of faith or an involuntary or unconscious disclosure 〈a blush that *betrayed* her embarrassment〉.

◇ **WORD HISTORY**
Reuben The history of American culinary items can be difficult to trace once we confront people's sometimes unconsciously embellished recollections with documentary evidence. One difficult item is the Reuben, winner of a national sandwich contest in 1956 after being submitted by Fern Snider, a waitress from Omaha, Nebraska. Ms. Snider had acquired the recipe from a former employer, the Schimmel family, who had for a number of years managed the Blackstone Hotel in downtown Omaha. According to local tradition, the combination of rye bread, corned beef, Swiss cheese, and sauerkraut had been dreamed up in the 1920's to feed participants in a late-night poker game at the hotel by Reuben Kulakofsky, an Omaha grocer. Charles Schimmel, the hotel's owner, was so taken with the sandwich that he then put it on their restaurant menu designated by its inventor's name. Is this tale fact or folklore? We can say for certain that there was a Reuben Kulakofsky—his 1960 obituary appeared in the *Omaha World-Herald*—and a sandwich called the "rueben" (not further described, hence presumably familiar to habitués) appears on a Blackstone Hotel menu datable to about 1944. The argument for the Reuben's Nebraskan origin is hence fairly convincing.

: an act of revealing

re·veg·e·tate \(ˌ)rē-'ve-jə-ˌtāt\ *transitive verb* (1804)
: to provide (barren or denuded land) with a new vegetative cover
— **re·veg·e·ta·tion** \(ˌ)rē-ˌve-jə-'tā-shən\ *noun*

rev·eil·le \'re-və-lē, *British* ri-'va-li *or* -'ve-\ *noun* [modification of French *réveillez*, imperative plural of *réveiller* to awaken, from Middle French *reveiller*, from *re-* + *eveiller* to awaken, from (assumed) Vulgar Latin *exvigilare*, from Latin *ex-* + *vigilare* to keep watch, stay awake — more at VIGILANT] (1644)
1 : a signal to get up mornings
2 : a bugle call at about sunrise signaling the first military formation of the day; *also* : the formation so signaled

¹**rev·el** \'re-vəl\ *intransitive verb* **-eled** *or* **-elled; el·ing** *or* **el·ling** \'re-və-liŋ, 'rev-liŋ\ [Middle English, from Middle French *reveler*, literally, to rebel, from Latin *rebellare*] (14th century)
1 : to take part in a revel : CAROUSE
2 : to take intense pleasure or satisfaction

²**revel** *noun* (14th century)
: a usually wild party or celebration

rev·e·la·tion \ˌre-və-'lā-shən\ *noun* [Middle English, from Middle French, from Late Latin *revelation-, revelatio*, from Latin *revelare* to reveal] (14th century)
1 a : an act of revealing or communicating divine truth **b** : something that is revealed by God to humans
2 a : an act of revealing to view or making known **b** : something that is revealed; *especially* : an enlightening or astonishing disclosure ⟨shocking *revelations*⟩ **c** : a pleasant often enlightening surprise ⟨her talent was a *revelation*⟩
3 *capitalized* : an apocalyptic writing addressed to early Christians of Asia Minor and included as a book in the New Testament — called also *Apocalypse*; see BIBLE table

Rev·e·la·tions \-shənz\ *noun plural but singular in construction*
: REVELATION 3

rev·e·la·tor \'re-və-ˌlā-tər\ *noun* (1801)
: one that reveals; *especially* : one that reveals the will of God

re·ve·la·to·ry \'re-və-lə-ˌtōr-ē, -ˌtor-, ri-'ve-lə-\ *adjective* (1882)
: of or relating to revelation : serving to reveal something

rev·el·er *or* **rev·el·ler** \'re-və-lər, 'rev-lər\ *noun* (14th century)
: one who engages in revelry

rev·el·ry \'re-vəl-rē\ *noun* (15th century)
: noisy partying or merrymaking

rev·e·nant \'re-və-ˌnäⁿ, -nənt\ *noun* [French, from present participle of *revenir* to return] (1827)
: one that returns after death or a long absence
— **revenant** *adjective*

¹**re·venge** \ri-'venj\ *transitive verb* **re·venged; re·veng·ing** [Middle English, from Middle French *revengier*, from Old French, from *re-* + *vengier* to avenge — more at VENGEANCE] (14th century)
1 : to avenge (as oneself) usually by retaliating in kind or degree
2 : to inflict injury in return for ⟨*revenge* an insult⟩
— **re·veng·er** *noun*

²**revenge** *noun* [Middle French *revenge, revenche*, from *revengier, revenchier* to revenge] (circa 1547)
1 : a desire for revenge
2 : an act or instance of retaliating in order to get even
3 : an opportunity for getting satisfaction

re·venge·ful \ri-'venj-fəl\ *adjective* (circa 1586)
: full of or prone to revenge : determined to get even
— **re·venge·ful·ly** \-fə-lē\ *adverb*

— **re·venge·ful·ness** *noun*

rev·e·nue \'re-və-ˌnü, -ˌnyü\ *noun, often attributive* [Middle English, from Middle French, from *revenir* to return, from Latin *revenire*, from *re-* + *venire* to come — more at COME] (15th century)
1 : the total income produced by a given source ⟨a property expected to yield a large annual *revenue*⟩
2 : the gross income returned by an investment
3 : the yield of sources of income (as taxes) that a political unit (as a nation or state) collects and receives into the treasury for public use
4 : a government department concerned with the collection of the national revenue

revenue bond *noun* (1856)
: a bond issued by a public agency authorized to build, acquire, or improve a revenue-producing property (as a toll road) and payable out of revenue derived from such property

rev·e·nu·er \'re-və-ˌnü-ər, -ˌnyü-\ *noun* (1880)
: a revenue officer or boat

revenue stamp *noun* (1862)
: a stamp (as on a cigar box) for use as evidence of payment of a tax

revenue tariff *noun* (1820)
: a tariff intended wholly or primarily to produce public revenue — compare PROTECTIVE TARIFF

re·verb \ri-'vərb, 'rē-\ *noun* [short for *reverberation*] (1953)
: an electronically produced echo effect in recorded music; *also* : a device for producing reverb

re·ver·ber·ant \ri-'vər-b(ə-)rənt\ *adjective* (circa 1798)
1 : tending to reverberate
2 : marked by reverberation : RESONANT
— **re·ver·ber·ant·ly** *adverb*

¹**re·ver·ber·ate** \-bə-ˌrāt\ *verb* **-at·ed; -at·ing** [Latin *reverberatus*, past participle of *reverberare*, from *re-* + *verberare* to lash, from *verber* rod — more at VERVAIN] (15th century)
transitive verb
1 : REFLECT
2 : REPEL
3 : ECHO
intransitive verb
1 a : to become driven back **b** : to become reflected
2 : to continue in or as if in a series of echoes : RESOUND

²**re·ver·ber·ate** \-b(ə-)rət\ *adjective* (1603)
: REVERBERANT

re·ver·ber·a·tion \ri-ˌvər-bə-'rā-shən\ *noun* (14th century)
1 : an act of reverberating : the state of being reverberated
2 a : something that is reverberated **b** : an effect or impact that resembles an echo

re·ver·ber·a·tive \ri-'vər-bə-ˌrā-tiv, -b(ə-)rə-\ *adjective* (1716)
1 : constituting reverberation
2 : tending to reverberate : REVERBERANT

re·ver·ber·a·to·ry \ri-'vər-b(ə-)rə-ˌtōr-ē, -bə-ˌtōr-, -ˌtor-\ *adjective* (1605)
: acting by reverberation

reverberatory furnace *noun* (1672)
: a furnace in which heat is radiated from the roof onto the material treated

¹**re·vere** \ri-'vir\ *transitive verb* **re·vered; re·ver·ing** [Latin *revereri*, from *re-* + *vereri* to fear, respect — more at WARY] (circa 1661)
: to show devoted deferential honor to : regard as worthy of great honor ⟨*revere* the aged⟩ ⟨*revere* tradition⟩ ☆

²**revere** *noun* [by alteration] (circa 1934)
: REVERS

¹**rev·er·ence** \'rev-rən(t)s, 're-və-; 're-vərn(t)s\ *noun* (14th century)

1 : honor or respect felt or shown : DEFERENCE; *especially* : profound adoring awed respect
2 : a gesture of respect (as a bow)
3 : the state of being revered
4 : one held in reverence — used as a title for a clergyman
synonym see HONOR

²**reverence** *transitive verb* **-enced; -enc·ing** (14th century)
: to regard or treat with reverence
synonym see REVERE
— **rev·er·enc·er** *noun*

¹**rev·er·end** \'rev-rənd, 're-və-; 're-vərnd\ *adjective* [Middle English, from Middle French, from Latin *reverendus*, gerundive of *revereri*] (15th century)
1 : worthy of reverence : REVERED
2 a : of or relating to the clergy **b** : being a member of the clergy — used as a title ⟨the *Reverend* Mr. Doe⟩ ⟨the *Reverend* John Doe⟩ ⟨the *Reverend* Mrs. Jane Doe⟩

²**reverend** *noun* (1608)
: a member of the clergy — sometimes used in plural as a title

rev·er·ent \'rev-rənt, 're-və-; 're-vərnt\ *adjective* [Middle English, from Latin *reverent-, reverens*, present participle of *revereri*] (14th century)
: expressing or characterized by reverence : WORSHIPFUL
— **rev·er·ent·ly** *adverb*

rev·er·en·tial \ˌre-və-'ren(t)-shəl\ *adjective* (circa 1555)
1 : expressing or having a quality of reverence ⟨*reverential* awe⟩
2 : inspiring reverence
— **rev·er·en·tial·ly** \-'ren(t)-sh(ə)lē\ *adverb*

rev·er·ie *also* **rev·ery** \'re-və-rē, 'rev-rē\ *noun, plural* **rev·er·ies** [French *rêverie*, from Middle French, delirium, from *resver, rever* to wander, be delirious] (1657)
1 : DAYDREAM
2 : the condition of being lost in thought

re·vers \ri-'vir, -'ver\ *noun, plural* **re·vers** \-'virz, -'verz\ [French, literally, reverse, from Middle French, from *revers*, adjective] (1869)
: a lapel especially on a woman's garment

re·ver·sal \ri-'vər-səl\ *noun* (15th century)
1 : an act or the process of reversing
2 : a conversion of a photographic positive into a negative or vice versa
3 : a change of fortune usually for the worse

¹**re·verse** \ri-'vərs\ *adjective* [Middle English *revers*, from Middle French, from Latin *reversus*, past participle of *revertere* to turn back — more at REVERT] (14th century)

1 a : opposite or contrary to a previous or normal condition ⟨*reverse* order⟩ **b :** having the back presented to the observer or opponent **2 :** coming from the rear of a military force **3 :** acting, operating, or arranged in a manner contrary to the usual **4 :** effecting reverse movement ⟨*reverse* gear⟩ **5 :** so made that the part which normally prints in color appears white against a colored background
— **re·verse·ly** *adverb*

²reverse *verb* **re·versed; re·vers·ing** (14th century)
transitive verb
1 a : to turn completely about in position or direction **b :** to turn upside down **:** INVERT **2 :** ANNUL: as **a :** to overthrow, set aside, or make void (a legal decision) by a contrary decision **b :** to cause to take an opposite point of view **c :** to change to the contrary ⟨*reverse* a policy⟩ **3 :** to cause to go in the opposite direction; *especially* **:** to cause (as an engine) to perform its action in the opposite direction
intransitive verb
1 : to turn or move in the opposite direction **2 :** to put a mechanism (as an engine) in reverse ☆
— **re·vers·er** *noun*
— **reverse field :** to make a sudden reversal in direction or opinion

³reverse *noun* (14th century)
1 : something directly contrary to something else **:** OPPOSITE
2 : an act or instance of reversing; *especially* **:** DEFEAT, SETBACK
3 : the back part of something
4 a (1) **:** a gear that reverses something; *also* **:** the whole mechanism brought into play when such a gear is used (2) **:** movement in reverse **b :** an offensive play in football in which a back moving in one direction gives the ball to a player moving in the opposite direction
— **in reverse :** in an opposite manner or direction

reverse discrimination *noun* (1969)
: discrimination against whites or males (as in employment or education)

reverse osmosis *noun* (1955)
: the movement of fresh water through a semipermeable membrane when pressure is applied to a solution (as seawater) on one side of it

reverse tran·scrip·tase \-ˌtran-ˈskrip-ˌtās, -(ˌ)tāz\ *noun* (1971)
: a polymerase that catalyzes the formation of DNA using RNA as a template and that is found especially in retroviruses

reverse transcription *noun* (1971)
: the process of synthesizing double-stranded DNA using RNA as a template and reverse transcriptase as a catalyst

¹re·vers·ible \ri-ˈvər-sə-bəl\ *adjective* (1648)
: capable of being reversed or of reversing: as **a :** capable of going through a series of actions (as changes) either backward or forward ⟨a *reversible* chemical reaction⟩ **b :** having two finished usable sides ⟨*reversible* fabric⟩ **c :** wearable with either side out ⟨a *reversible* coat⟩
— **re·vers·ibil·i·ty** \-ˌvər-sə-ˈbi-lə-tē\ *noun*
— **re·vers·ibly** \-ˈvər-sə-blē\ *adverb*

²reversible *noun* (1863)
: a reversible cloth or article of clothing

re·ver·sion \ri-ˈvər-zhən, -shən\ *noun* [Middle English, from Middle French, from Latin *reversion-, reversio* act of returning, from *revertere*] (15th century)
1 a : the part of a simple estate remaining in the control of its owner after the owner has granted therefrom a lesser particular estate **b :** a future interest in property left in the control of a grantor or the grantor's successor
2 : the right of succession or future possession or enjoyment

3 a : an act or the process of returning (as to a former condition) **b :** a return toward an ancestral type or condition **:** reappearance of an ancestral character
4 : an act or instance of turning the opposite way **:** the state of being so turned
5 : a product of reversion; *specifically* **:** an organism with an atavistic character **:** THROWBACK

re·ver·sion·al \-ˈvərzh-nəl, -ˈvərsh-; -ˈvər-zhə-nᵊl, -shə-\ *adjective* (1675)
: REVERSIONARY

re·ver·sion·ary \-ˈvər-zhə-ˌner-ē, -shə-\ *adjective* (1720)
: of, relating to, constituting, or involving especially a legal reversion

re·ver·sion·er \-ˈvərzh-nər, -ˈvərsh-; -ˈvər-zhə-nər, -shə-\ *noun* (1614)
: one that has or is entitled to a reversion; *broadly* **:** one having a vested right to a future estate

re·vert \ri-ˈvərt\ *intransitive verb* [Middle English, from Middle French *revertir*, from Latin *revertere*, transitive verb, to turn back & *reverti*, intransitive verb, to return, come back, from *re- + vertere, verti* to turn — more at WORTH] (15th century)
1 : to come or go back (as to a former condition, period, or subject)
2 : to return to the proprietor or his heirs at the end of a reversion
3 : to return to an ancestral type
— **re·vert·er** *noun*
— **re·vert·ible** \-ˈvər-tə-bəl\ *adjective*

re·ver·tant \ri-ˈvər-tᵊnt\ *noun* (1955)
: a mutant gene, individual, or strain that regains a former capability (as the production of a particular protein) by undergoing further mutation ⟨yeast *revertants*⟩
— **revertant** *adjective*

re·vest \(ˌ)rē-ˈvest\ *transitive verb* (1561)
: REINSTATE, REINVEST

re·vet \ri-ˈvet\ *transitive verb* **re·vet·ted; re·vet·ting** [French *revêtir*, literally, to clothe again, dress up, from Latin *revestire*, from *re- + vestire* to clothe — more at VEST] (1812)
: to face (as an embankment) with a revetment

re·vet·ment \-ˈvet-mənt\ *noun* (1779)
1 : a facing (as of stone or concrete) to sustain an embankment
2 : EMBANKMENT; *especially* **:** a barricade to provide shelter (as against bomb fragments or strafing)

¹re·view \ri-ˈvyü\ *noun* [Middle English, from Middle French *reveue*, from *revoir* to look over, from *re- + voir* to see — more at VIEW] (15th century)
1 a : a formal military inspection **b :** a military ceremony honoring a person or an event
2 : REVISION 1a
3 : a general survey (as of the events of a period)
4 : an act or the process of reviewing
5 : judicial reexamination (as of the proceedings of a lower tribunal by a higher)
6 a : a critical evaluation (as of a book or play) **b :** a magazine devoted chiefly to reviews and essays
7 a : a retrospective view or survey (as of one's life) **b** (1) **:** renewed study of material previously studied (2) **:** an exercise facilitating such study
8 : REVUE

²re·view \ri-ˈvyü, *1 is also* \rē-\ *verb* [in senses 1 & 2, from *re- + view*; in other senses, from ¹*review*] (1576)
transitive verb
1 : to view or see again
2 : to examine or study again; *especially* **:** to reexamine judicially
3 : to look back on **:** take a retrospective view of
4 a : to go over or examine critically or deliberately ⟨*reviewed* the results of the study⟩ **b :** to give a critical evaluation of ⟨*review* a novel⟩

5 : to hold a review of ⟨*review* troops⟩
intransitive verb
1 : to study material again **:** make a review ⟨*review* for a test⟩
2 : to write reviews
— **re·view·able** \ri-ˈvyü-ə-bəl\ *adjective*

re·view·er \ri-ˈvyü-ər\ *noun* (1651)
: one that reviews; *especially* **:** a writer of critical reviews

re·vile \ri-ˈvī(ə)l\ *verb* **re·viled; re·vil·ing** [Middle English, from Middle French *reviler* to despise, from *re- + vil* vile] (14th century)
transitive verb
: to subject to verbal abuse **:** VITUPERATE
intransitive verb
: to use abusive language **:** RAIL
synonym *see* SCOLD
— **re·vile·ment** \-ˈvī(ə)l-mənt\ *noun*
— **re·vil·er** *noun*

re·vis·al \ri-ˈvī-zəl\ *noun* (1612)
: an act of revising **:** REVISION

¹re·vise \ˈrē-ˌvīz, ri-\ *noun* (1591)
1 : an act of revising **:** REVISION
2 : a printing proof that incorporates changes marked in a previous proof

²re·vise \ri-ˈvīz\ *verb* **re·vised; re·vis·ing** [Middle French *reviser*, from Latin *revisere* to look at again, frequentative of *revidēre* to see again, from *re- + vidēre* to see — more at WIT] (1596)
transitive verb
1 a : to look over again in order to correct or improve ⟨*revise* a manuscript⟩ **b** *British* **:** to study again **:** REVIEW
2 a : to make a new, amended, improved, or up-to-date version of ⟨*revise* a dictionary⟩ **b :** to provide with a new taxonomic arrangement ⟨*revising* the alpine ferns⟩
intransitive verb
British **:** REVIEW 1
synonym *see* CORRECT
— **re·vis·able** \-ˈvī-zə-bəl\ *adjective*
— **re·vis·er** *or* **re·vi·sor** \-ˈvī-zər\ *noun*

Revised Standard Version *noun* (1946)
: a revision of the American Standard Version of the Bible published in 1946 and 1952

Revised Version *noun* (1880)
: a British revision of the Authorized Version of the Bible published in 1881 and 1885

re·vi·sion \ri-ˈvi-zhən\ *noun* (1611)
1 a : an act of revising **b :** a result of revising **:** ALTERATION
2 : a revised version
— **re·vi·sion·ary** \-zhə-ˌner-ē\ *adjective*

re·vi·sion·ism \ri-ˈvi-zhə-ˌni-zəm\ *noun* (1903)
1 : a movement in revolutionary Marxian socialism favoring an evolutionary rather than a revolutionary spirit
2 : advocacy of revision (as of a doctrine or policy or in historical analysis)
— **re·vi·sion·ist** \-nist\ *noun or adjective*

¹re·vis·it \(ˌ)rē-ˈvi-zət\ *transitive verb* (15th century)
: to visit again **:** return to ⟨*revisit* the old neighborhood⟩; *also* **:** to consider or take up again ⟨reluctant to *revisit* past disputes⟩

²revisit *noun* (1623)
: a second or subsequent visit

re·vi·so·ry \ri-ˈvī-zə-rē, -ˈvīz-rē\ *adjective* (circa 1841)

☆ **SYNONYMS**
Reverse, transpose, invert mean to change to the opposite position. REVERSE is the most general term and may imply change in order, side, direction, meaning ⟨*reversed* his position on the trade agreement⟩. TRANSPOSE implies a change in order or relative position of units often through exchange of position ⟨*transposed* the letters to form an anagram⟩. INVERT applies chiefly to turning upside down or inside out ⟨a stamp with an *inverted* picture of an airplane⟩.

: having the power or purpose to revise ⟨a *revisory* committee⟩ ⟨a *revisory* function⟩

re·vi·tal·ise *British variant of* REVITALIZE

re·vi·tal·ize \(ˌ)rē-ˈvī-t⁹l-ˌīz\ *transitive verb* **-ized; -iz·ing** (1869)
: to give new life or vigor to
— **re·vi·tal·i·za·tion** \(ˌ)rē-ˌvī-t⁹l-ə-ˈzā-shən\ *noun*

re·viv·al \ri-ˈvī-vəl\ *noun* (1651)
1: an act or instance of reviving : the state of being revived: as **a**: renewed attention to or interest in something **b**: a new presentation or publication of something old **c** (1): a period of renewed religious interest (2): an often highly emotional evangelistic meeting or series of meetings
2: restoration of force, validity, or effect (as to a contract)

re·viv·al·ism \-ˈvī-və-ˌli-zəm\ *noun* (1815)
1: the spirit or methods characteristic of religious revivals
2: a tendency or desire to revive or restore

re·viv·al·ist \-ˈvī-və-list, -ˈvīv-list\ *noun* (1820)
1: one who conducts religious revivals; *specifically*: a clergyman who travels about to conduct revivals
2: one who revives or restores something disused
— **revivalist** *adjective*
— **re·viv·al·is·tic** \-ˌvī-və-ˈlis-tik\ *adjective*

re·vive \ri-ˈvīv\ *verb* **re·vived; re·viv·ing** [Middle English, from Middle French *revivre*, from Latin *revivere* to live again, from *re-* + *vivere* to live — more at QUICK] (15th century)
intransitive verb
: to return to consciousness or life : become active or flourishing again
transitive verb
1: to restore to consciousness or life
2: to restore from a depressed, inactive, or unused state : bring back
3: to renew in the mind or memory
— **re·viv·able** \-ˈvī-və-bəl\ *adjective*
— **re·viv·er** *noun*

re·viv·i·fy \rē-ˈvi-və-ˌfī\ *transitive verb* [French *révivifier*, from Late Latin *revivificare*, from Latin *re-* + Late Latin *vivificare* to vivify] (1675)
: to give new life to : REVIVE
— **re·viv·i·fi·ca·tion** \-ˌvi-və-fə-ˈkā-shən\ *noun*

re·vi·vis·cence \ˌrē-ˌvī-ˈvi-s⁹n(t)s, ri-\ *noun* [Latin *reviviscere* to come to life again, from *re-* + *viviscere* to come to life, from *vivus* alive, living — more at QUICK] (1626)
: an act of reviving : the state of being revived
— **re·vi·vis·cent** \-s⁹nt\ *adjective*

rev·o·ca·ble \ˈre-və-kə-bəl *also* ri-ˈvō-\ *also* **re·vok·able** \ri-ˈvō-kə-bəl\ *adjective* [Middle English, from Middle French, from Latin *revocabilis*, from *revocare*] (15th century)
: capable of being revoked

rev·o·ca·tion \ˌre-və-ˈkā-shən; ri-ˌvō-, ˌrē-\ *noun* [Middle English, from Middle French, from Latin *revocation-, revocatio*, from *revocare*] (15th century)
: an act or instance of revoking

¹re·voke \ri-ˈvōk\ *verb* **re·voked; re·vok·ing** [Middle English, from Middle French *revoquer*, from Latin *revocare*, from *re-* + *vocare* to call, from *voc-, vox* voice — more at VOICE] (14th century)
transitive verb
1: to annul by recalling or taking back : RESCIND ⟨*revoke* a will⟩
2: to bring or call back
intransitive verb
: to fail to follow suit when able in a card game in violation of the rules
— **re·vok·er** *noun*

²revoke *noun* (1709)
: an act or instance of revoking in a card game

¹re·volt \ri-ˈvōlt *also* -ˈvȯlt\ *verb* [Middle French *revolter*, from Old Italian *rivoltare* to

overthrow, from (assumed) Vulgar Latin *revolvitare*, frequentative of Latin *revolvere* to revolve, roll back] (1539)
intransitive verb
1: to renounce allegiance or subjection (as to a government) : REBEL
2 a: to experience disgust or shock **b**: to turn away with disgust
transitive verb
: to cause to turn away or shrink with disgust or abhorrence
— **re·volt·er** *noun*

²revolt *noun* (1560)
1: a renouncing of allegiance (as to a government or party); *especially*: a determined armed uprising
2: a movement or expression of vigorous dissent
synonym see REBELLION

re·volt·ing *adjective* (1806)
: extremely offensive
— **re·volt·ing·ly** *adverb*

rev·o·lute \ˈre-və-ˌlüt\ *adjective* [Latin *revolutus*, past participle of *revolvere*] (circa 1753)
: rolled backward or downward ⟨a leaf with *revolute* margins⟩

rev·o·lu·tion \ˌre-və-ˈlü-shən\ *noun* [Middle English *revolucioun*, from Middle French *revolution*, from Late Latin *revolution-, revolutio*, from Latin *revolvere* to revolve] (14th century)
1 a (1): the action by a celestial body of going round in an orbit or elliptical course; *also*: apparent movement of such a body round the earth (2): the time taken by a celestial body to make a complete round in its orbit (3): the rotation of a celestial body on its axis **b**: completion of a course (as of years); *also*: the period made by the regular succession of a measure of time or by a succession of similar events **c** (1): a progressive motion of a body round an axis so that any line of the body parallel to the axis returns to its initial position while remaining parallel to the axis in transit and usually at a constant distance from it (2): motion of any figure about a center or axis ⟨*revolution* of a right triangle about one of its legs generates a cone⟩ (3): ROTATION 1b
2 a: a sudden, radical, or complete change **b**: a fundamental change in political organization; *especially*: the overthrow or renunciation of one government or ruler and the substitution of another by the governed **c**: activity or movement designed to effect fundamental changes in the socioeconomic situation **d**: a fundamental change in the way of thinking about or visualizing something : a change of paradigm ⟨the Copernican *revolution*⟩ **e**: a changeover in use or preference especially in technology ⟨the computer *revolution*⟩ ⟨the foreign car *revolution*⟩
synonym see REBELLION

¹rev·o·lu·tion·ary \-shə-ˌner-ē\ *adjective* (1774)
1 a: of, relating to, or constituting a revolution ⟨*revolutionary* war⟩ **b**: tending to or promoting revolution ⟨a *revolutionary* party⟩ **c**: constituting or bringing about a major or fundamental change ⟨*revolutionary* styling⟩ ⟨a *revolutionary* new product⟩
2 *capitalized*: of or relating to the American Revolution or to the period in which it occurred
— **rev·o·lu·tion·ar·i·ly** \-ˌlü-shə-ˈner-ə-lē\ *adverb*
— **rev·o·lu·tion·ar·i·ness** \-ˈlü-shə-ˌner-ē-nəs\ *noun*

²revolutionary *noun, plural* **-ar·ies** (1850)
1: one engaged in a revolution
2: an advocate or adherent of revolutionary doctrines

rev·o·lu·tion·ise *British variant of* REVOLUTIONIZE

rev·o·lu·tion·ist \ˌre-və-ˈlü-sh(ə-)nist\ *noun* (1710)
: REVOLUTIONARY

— **revolutionist** *adjective*

rev·o·lu·tion·ize \-shə-ˌnīz\ *verb* **-ized; -iz·ing** (1797)
transitive verb
1: to overthrow the established government of
2: to imbue with revolutionary doctrines
3: to change fundamentally or completely
intransitive verb
: to engage in revolution
— **rev·o·lu·tion·iz·er** *noun*

re·volve \ri-ˈvälv, -ˈvȯlv *also* -ˈväv *or* -ˈvȯv\ *verb* **re·volved; re·volv·ing** [Middle English, from Latin *revolvere* to roll back, cause to return, from *re-* + *volvere* to roll — more at VOLUBLE] (15th century)
transitive verb
1: to turn over at length in the mind : PONDER ⟨*revolve* a scheme⟩
2 a *obsolete*: to cause to go round in an orbit **b**: ROTATE 1
intransitive verb
1: RECUR
2 a: to ponder something **b**: to remain under consideration ⟨ideas *revolved* in his mind⟩
3 a: to move in a curved path round a center or axis **b**: to turn or roll round on an axis
4: to come to a main or central point : CENTER ⟨the dispute *revolved* around wages⟩
— **re·volv·able** \-ˈväl-və-bəl, -ˈvȯl- *also* -ˈvä-və- *or* -ˈvȯ-və-\ *adjective*

re·volv·er \ri-ˈväl-vər, -ˈvȯl- *also* -ˈvä-vər *or* -ˈvȯ-vər\ *noun* (circa 1835)
1: one that revolves
2: a handgun with a cylinder of several chambers brought successively into line with the barrel and discharged with the same hammer

revolving *adjective* (1599)
1: tending to revolve or recur; *especially*: recurrently available
2: turning around on or as if on an axis ⟨a *revolving* platform⟩

revolving charge account *noun* (1967)
: a charge account under which payment is made in monthly installments and includes a carrying charge

revolving credit *noun* (1919)
: a credit which may be used repeatedly up to the limit specified after partial or total repayments have been made

revolving–door *adjective* (1973)
: characterized by a frequently repeated cycle of leaving and returning ⟨*revolving-door* governments⟩

revolving fund *noun* (1920)
: a fund set up for specified purposes with the proviso that repayments to the fund may be used again for these purposes

re·vue \ri-ˈvyü\ *noun* [French, from Middle French *reveue* review — more at REVIEW] (1872)
: a theatrical production consisting typically of brief loosely connected often satirical skits, songs, and dances

re·vulsed \ri-ˈvəlst\ *adjective* [Latin *revulsus*, past participle of *revellere* + English *-ed*] (circa 1934)
: affected with or having undergone revulsion

re·vul·sion \ri-ˈvəl-shən\ *noun* [Latin *revulsion-, revulsio* act of tearing away, from *revellere* to pluck away, from *re-* + *vellere* to pluck — more at VULNERABLE] (1609)
1: a strong pulling or drawing away : WITHDRAWAL
2 a: a sudden or strong reaction or change **b**: a sense of utter distaste or repugnance
— **re·vul·sive** \-ˈvəl-siv\ *adjective*

revved *past and past participle of* REV
revving *present participle of* REV

re·wake \(ˌ)rē-'wāk\ *verb* **-waked** *or* **-woke** \-'wōk\; **-waked** *or* **-wo·ken** \-'wō-kən\ *or* **-woke; -wak·ing** (1593)
transitive verb
: to waken again or anew
intransitive verb
: to become awake again
re·wak·en \(ˌ)rē-'wā-kən\ *verb* (1638)
: REWAKE
¹re·ward \ri-'wȯrd\ *transitive verb* [Middle English, from Old North French *rewarder* to regard, reward, from *re-* + *warder* to watch, guard, of Germanic origin; akin to Old High German *wartēn* to watch — more at WARD] (14th century)
1 : to give a reward to or for
2 : RECOMPENSE
— **re·ward·able** \-'wȯr-də-bəl\ *adjective*
— **re·ward·er** *noun*
²reward *noun* (14th century)
1 : something that is given in return for good or evil done or received and especially that is offered or given for some service or attainment
2 : a stimulus administered to an organism following a correct or desired response that increases the probability of occurrence of the response
re·ward·ing *adjective* (1697)
1 : yielding or likely to yield a reward **:** VALUABLE, SATISFYING ⟨a *rewarding* experience⟩
2 : serving as a reward ⟨a *rewarding* smile of thanks⟩
— **re·ward·ing·ly** *adverb*
¹re·wind \(ˌ)rē-'wīnd\ *transitive verb* **-wound** \-'waȯnd\; **-wind·ing** (1717)
: to wind again; *especially* **:** to reverse the winding of (as film)
²re·wind \'rē-ˌwīnd, (ˌ)rē-\ *noun* (1926)
1 : something that rewinds or is rewound
2 : an act of rewinding
re·word \(ˌ)rē-'wərd\ *transitive verb* (1602)
1 : to repeat in the same words
2 : to alter the wording of; *also* **:** to restate in other words
re·work \(ˌ)rē-'wərk\ *transitive verb* (1842)
: to work again or anew: as **a :** REVISE **b :** to reprocess (as used material) for further use
¹re·write \(ˌ)rē-'rīt\ *verb* **-wrote** \-'rōt\; **-writ·ten** \-'ri-tᵊn\; **-writ·ing** \-'rī-tiŋ\ (1567)
transitive verb
1 : to write in reply
2 : to make a revision of (as a story) **:** cause to be revised: as **a :** to put (contributed material) into form for publication **b :** to alter (previously published material) for use in another publication
intransitive verb
: to revise something previously written
— **re·writ·er** *noun*
²re·write \'rē-ˌrīt\ *noun* (1914)
1 : a piece of writing (as a news story) constructed by rewriting
2 : an act or instance of rewriting
re·write man \'rē-ˌrīt-ˌman\ *noun* (1901)
: a newspaperman who specializes in rewriting
re·write rule \'rē-ˌrīt-\ *noun* (1961)
: a rule in a grammar which specifies the constituents of a single symbol
rex \'reks\ *noun, plural* **rex·es** *or* **rex** [modification of French *castorrex, castorex*, a variety of rabbit, perhaps from Latin *castor* beaver + *rex* king — more at CASTOR, ROYAL] (1920)
: an animal (as a domestic rabbit) showing a genetic recessive variation in which the guard hairs are very short or entirely lacking; *especially* **:** any of the slender domestic cats having a short

rex

curly undercoat and no guard hairs and belonging to either of two breeds
Reye's syndrome \'rīz-, 'rāz-\ *noun* [R.D.K. *Reye* (died 1977) Australian pathologist] (1965)
: an often fatal encephalopathy especially of childhood characterized by fever, vomiting, fatty infiltration of the liver, and swelling of the kidneys and brain — called also *Reye syndrome*
rey·nard \'rā-nərd, 'rē-, -ˌnär(d)\ *noun, often capitalized* [Middle English *Renard*, name of the fox who is hero of the French beast epic *Roman de Renart*, from Middle French *Renart, Renard*] (14th century)
: FOX
Rey·nolds number \'re-nᵊldz-\ *noun* [Osborne *Reynolds* (died 1912) English physicist] (1910)
: a number characteristic of the flow of a fluid in a pipe or past an obstruction
R factor \'är-\ *noun* [*r*esistance] (1962)
: a group of genes present in some bacteria that provide a basis for resistance to antibiotics and can be transferred from cell to cell by conjugation
Rh \'är-'āch\ *adjective* (1940)
: of, relating to, or being an Rh factor ⟨*Rh* antigens⟩ ⟨*Rh* sensitization in pregnancy⟩
rhabdo- *combining form* [Late Greek, from Greek *rhabdos* rod — more at VERVAIN]
: rodlike structure ⟨*rhabdo*virus⟩
rhab·do·coele \'rab-də-ˌsēl\ *noun* [New Latin *Rhabdocoela*, from *rhabdo-* + New Latin *-coela* -coele] (circa 1909)
: a turbellarian worm (order Rhabdocoela) with an unbranched intestine
rhab·dom \'rab-ˌdäm, -dəm\ *or* **rhab·dome** \-ˌdōm\ *noun* [New Latin, from Late Greek *rhabdōma* bundle of rods, from Greek *rhabdos* rod] (1878)
: one of the minute rodlike structures in the retinulae in the compound eyes of arthropods
rhab·do·man·cy \'rab-də-ˌman(t)-sē\ *noun* [Late Greek *rhabdomanteia*, from Greek *rhabdos* rod + *-manteia* -mancy] (1646)
: divination by rods or wands
— **rhab·do·man·cer** \-ˌman(t)-sər\ *noun*
rhab·do·mere \-ˌmir\ *noun* (circa 1884)
: a division of a rhabdom
rhab·do·myo·sar·co·ma \'rab-(ˌ)dō-ˌmī-ə-sär-'kō-mə\ *noun, plural* **-mas** *or* **-ma·ta** \-mə-tə\ [New Latin, from *rhabdo-* + *my-* + *sarcoma*] (1898)
: a malignant tumor composed of striated muscle fibers
rhab·do·vi·rus \-ˌvī-rəs\ *noun* [New Latin] (1966)
: any of a group of RNA-containing rod- or bullet-shaped viruses found in plants and animals and including the causative agents of rabies and vesicular stomatitis
rhad·a·man·thine \ˌra-də-'man(t)-thən, -'man-ˌthīn\ *adjective, often capitalized* [*Rhadamanthus*] (1840)
: rigorously strict or just
Rhad·a·man·thus \ˌra-də-'man(t)-thəs\ *noun*
: a judge of the underworld in Greek mythology
Rhae·to-Ro·mance \ˌrē-tō-rō-'man(t)s, -tō-rə-; -'rō-ˌman(t)s\ *also* **Rhae·to-Ro·man·ic** \-rō-'ma-nik\ *noun* [Latin *Rhaetus* of Rhaetia, ancient Roman province] (1867)
: a group of Romance languages spoken in eastern Switzerland and northeastern Italy
rham·nose \'ram-ˌnōs, -ˌnōz\ *noun* [International Scientific Vocabulary, from New Latin *Rhamnus*, genus of the buckthorn; from its being produced from a plant of this genus] (1888)
: a crystalline sugar $C_6H_{12}O_5$ that occurs usually in the form of a glycoside in many plants and is obtained in the common dextrorotatory L form
rhap·sode \'rap-ˌsōd\ *noun* [French, from Greek *rhapsōidos*] (1834)

: RHAPSODIST
rhap·sod·ic \rap-'sä-dik\ *also* **rhap·sod·i·cal** \-di-kəl\ *adjective* (1782)
1 : extravagantly emotional **:** RAPTUROUS
2 : resembling or characteristic of a rhapsody
— **rhap·sod·i·cal·ly** \-di-k(ə-)lē\ *adverb*
rhap·so·dist \'rap-sə-dist\ *noun* (circa 1656)
1 : a professional reciter of epic poems
2 : one who writes or speaks rhapsodically
rhap·so·dize \-sə-ˌdīz\ *intransitive verb* **-dized; -diz·ing** (1806)
: to speak or write in a rhapsodic manner ⟨*rhapsodize* about a new book⟩
rhap·so·dy \'rap-sə-dē\ *noun, plural* **-dies** [Latin *rhapsodia*, from Greek *rhapsōidia* recitation of selections from epic poetry, rhapsody, from *rhapsōidos* rhapsodist, from *rhaptein* to sew, stitch together + *aidein* to sing — more at ODE] (1542)
1 : a portion of an epic poem adapted for recitation
2 *archaic* **:** a miscellaneous collection
3 a (1) **:** a highly emotional utterance (2) **:** a highly emotional literary work (3) **:** effusively rapturous or extravagant discourse **b :** RAPTURE, ECSTASY
4 : a musical composition of irregular form having an improvisatory character
rhat·a·ny \'ra-tᵊn-ē\ *noun* [Spanish *ratania* & Portuguese *ratânhia*] (1808)
1 : the dried root of either of two South American shrubs (*Krameria triandra* and *K. argentea* of the family Krameriaceae) used as an astringent
2 : a plant yielding rhatany
rhea \'rē-ə\ *noun* [New Latin, genus of birds, probably from Latin *Rhea*, mother of Zeus, from Greek] (1797)
: either of two South American ratite birds (*Rhea americana* and *Pterocnemia pennata* of the family Rheidae) that resemble but are smaller than the African ostrich and that have three toes, a fully feathered head and neck, an undeveloped tail, and pale gray to brownish feathers that droop over the rump and back

rhea

rhe·bok \'rē-ˌbäk\ *noun* [Afrikaans *reebok*, from Dutch, male roe deer, from *ree* roe + *boc* buck] (1834)
: a brownish gray antelope (*Pelea capreolus*) of southern Africa
rhe·ni·um \'rē-nē-əm\ *noun* [New Latin, from Latin *Rhenus* Rhine River] (1925)
: a rare heavy metallic element that resembles manganese, is obtained either as a powder or as a silver-white hard metal, and is used in catalysts and thermocouples — see ELEMENT table
rheo- *combining form* [Greek *rhein* to flow — more at STREAM]
: flow **:** current ⟨*rheo*stat⟩
rhe·ol·o·gy \rē-'ä-lə-jē\ *noun* [International Scientific Vocabulary] (1929)
: a science dealing with the deformation and flow of matter; *also* **:** the ability to flow or be deformed
— **rhe·o·log·i·cal** \ˌrē-ə-'lä-ji-kəl\ *adjective*
— **rhe·o·log·i·cal·ly** \-k(ə-)lē\ *adverb*
— **rhe·ol·o·gist** \rē-'ä-lə-jist\ *noun*
rhe·om·e·ter \rē-'ä-mə-tər\ *noun* [International Scientific Vocabulary] (circa 1859)
: an instrument for measuring flow (as of viscous substances)
rheo·stat \'rē-ə-ˌstat\ *noun* (1843)
: a resistor for regulating a current by means of variable resistances
— **rheo·stat·ic** \ˌrē-ə-'sta-tik\ *adjective*

rhe·sus monkey \'rē-səs-\ *noun* [New Latin *Rhesus*, genus of monkeys, from Latin, a mythical king of Thrace, from Greek *Rhēsos*] (1841)
: a pale brown Asian macaque (*Macaca mulatta*) often used in medical research

rhe·tor \'rē-,tȯr, 're-; 'rē-tər, 'rē-\ *noun* [Middle English *rethor*, from Latin *rhetor*, from Greek *rhētōr*] (14th century)
: RHETORICIAN 1

rhet·o·ric \'re-tə-rik\ *noun* [Middle English *rethorik*, from Middle French *rethorique*, from Latin *rhetorica*, from Greek *rhētorikē*, literally, art of oratory, from feminine of *rhētorikos* of an orator, from *rhētōr* orator, rhetorician, from *eirein* to say, speak — more at WORD] (14th century)
1 : the art of speaking or writing effectively: as **a** : the study of principles and rules of composition formulated by critics of ancient times **b** : the study of writing or speaking as a means of communication or persuasion
2 a : skill in the effective use of speech **b** : a type or mode of language or speech; *also* : insincere or grandiloquent language
3 : verbal communication : DISCOURSE

rhe·tor·i·cal \ri-'tȯr-i-kəl, -'tär-\ *also* **rhe·tor·ic** \ri-'tȯr-ik, -'tär-\ *adjective* (15th century)
1 a : of, relating to, or concerned with rhetoric **b** : employed for rhetorical effect; *especially* : asked merely for effect with no answer expected ⟨a *rhetorical* question⟩
2 a : given to rhetoric : GRANDILOQUENT **b** : VERBAL
— **rhe·tor·i·cal·ly** \-i-k(ə-)lē\ *adverb*

rhet·o·ri·cian \,re-tə-'ri-shən\ *noun* (15th century)
1 a : a master or teacher of rhetoric **b** : ORATOR
2 : an eloquent or grandiloquent writer or speaker

rheum \'rüm\ *noun* [Middle English *reume*, from Middle French, from Latin *rheuma*, from Greek, literally, flow, flux, from *rhein* to flow — more at STREAM] (14th century)
1 : a watery discharge from the mucous membranes especially of the eyes or nose
2 *archaic* : TEARS
— **rheumy** \'rü-mē\ *adjective*

¹rheu·mat·ic \rü-'ma-tik\ *adjective* [Middle English *rewmatik* subject to rheum, from Latin *rheumaticus*, from Greek *rheumatikos*, from *rheumat-, rheuma*] (1711)
: of, relating to, characteristic of, or affected with rheumatism
— **rheu·mat·i·cal·ly** \-ti-k(ə-)lē\ *adverb*

²rheumatic *noun* (1884)
: one affected with rheumatism

rheumatic fever *noun* (1782)
: an acute disease that occurs chiefly in children and young adults and is characterized by fever, by inflammation and pain in and around the joints, and by inflammatory involvement of the pericardium and heart valves

rheu·ma·tism \'rü-mə-,ti-zəm, 'rü-\ *noun* [Latin *rheumatismus* flux, rheum, from Greek *rheumatismos*, from *rheumatizesthai* to suffer from a flux, from *rheumat-, rheuma* flux] (1677)
1 : any of various conditions characterized by inflammation or pain in muscles, joints, or fibrous tissue ⟨muscular *rheumatism*⟩
2 : RHEUMATOID ARTHRITIS

rheu·ma·tiz \-'tiz\ *noun* (1760)
chiefly dialect : RHEUMATISM

rheu·ma·toid \-,tȯid\ *adjective* [International Scientific Vocabulary, from *rheumatism*] (1871)
: characteristic of or affected with rheumatoid arthritis

rheumatoid arthritis *noun* (1859)
: a usually chronic disease of unknown cause that is characterized especially by pain, stiffness, inflammation, swelling, and sometimes destruction of joints

rheumatoid factor *noun* (1960)
: an autoantibody of high molecular weight that is usually present in rheumatoid arthritis

rheu·ma·tol·o·gy \,rü-mə-'tä-lə-jē, ,rü-\ *noun* (circa 1941)
: a medical science dealing with rheumatic diseases
— **rheu·ma·tol·o·gist** \-jist\ *noun*

Rh factor \,är-'āch-\ *noun* [*rh*esus monkey (in which it was first detected)] (1942)
: any of one or more genetically determined antigens present in the red blood cells of most persons and of higher animals and capable of inducing intense immunogenic reactions

rhin- *or* **rhino-** *combining form* [New Latin, from Greek, from *rhin-, rhis*]
: nose ⟨*rhino*plasty⟩

rhi·nal \'rī-n°l\ *adjective* (circa 1859)
: of or relating to the nose : NASAL

rhin·en·ceph·a·lon \,rī-(,)nen-'se-fə-,län, -lən\ *noun* [New Latin] (1846)
: the chiefly olfactory part of the forebrain
— **rhin·en·ce·phal·ic** \,rī-,nen-sə-'fa-lik\ *adjective*

rhine·stone \'rīn-,stōn\ *noun* [*Rhine* River] (circa 1888)
: a colorless imitation stone of high luster made of glass, paste, or gem quartz
— **rhine·stoned** \-,stōnd\ *adjective*

Rhine wine \'rīn-\ *noun* (1843)
1 : a usually white wine produced in the Rhine valley
2 : a wine similar to Rhine wine produced elsewhere

rhi·ni·tis \rī-'nī-təs\ *noun* [New Latin] (circa 1884)
: inflammation of the mucous membrane of the nose

¹rhi·no \'rī-(,)nō\ *noun* [origin unknown] (1670)
: MONEY, CASH

²rhino *noun, plural* **rhino** *or* **rhinos** (1884)
: RHINOCEROS

rhi·noc·er·os \rī-'näs-rəs, rə-, -'nä-sə-\ *noun, plural* **-noc·er·os·es** *or* **-noc·er·os** *or* **-noc·eri** \-'nä-sə-,rī\ [Middle English *rinoceros*, from Latin *rhinocerot-, rhinoceros*, from Greek *rhinokerōt-, rhinokerōs*, from *rhin- + keras* horn — more at HORN] (14th century)
: any of a family (Rhinocerotidae) of large heavyset herbivorous perissodactyl mammals of Africa and Asia that have one or two upright keratinous horns on the snout and thick gray to brown skin with little hair
word history SEE UNICORN

rhinoceros beetle *noun* (1681)
: any of various large chiefly tropical scarab beetles (subfamily Dynastinae) having projecting horns on thorax and head

rhinoceros beetle

rhi·no·plas·ty \'rī-nō-,plas-tē\ *noun, plural* **-ties** (1842)
: plastic surgery on the nose usually for cosmetic purposes

rhi·nos·co·py \rī-'näs-kə-pē\ *noun* [International Scientific Vocabulary] (1861)
: examination of the nasal passages

rhi·no·vi·rus \,rī-nō-'vī-rəs\ *noun* [New Latin] (1961)
: any of a group of picornaviruses that are related to the enteroviruses and are associated with disorders of the upper respiratory tract (as the common cold)

rhiz- *or* **rhizo-** *combining form* [New Latin, from Greek, from *rhiza* — more at ROOT]
: root ⟨*rhizo*plane⟩

-rhiza *or* **-rrhiza** *noun combining form, plural* **-zae** *or* **-zas** [New Latin, from Greek *rhiza*]
: root : part resembling or connected with a root ⟨coleo*rhiza*⟩ ⟨myco*rrhiza*⟩

rhi·zo·bi·um \rī-'zō-bē-əm\ *noun, plural* **-bia** \-bē-ə\ [New Latin, from *rhiz-* + Greek *bios* life — more at QUICK] (1921)
: any of a genus (*Rhizobium*) of small heterotrophic soil bacteria capable of forming symbiotic nodules on the roots of leguminous plants and of there becoming bacteroids that fix atmospheric nitrogen
— **rhi·zo·bi·al** \-bē-əl\ *adjective*

rhi·zoc·to·nia \,rī-,zäk-'tō-nē-ə\ *noun* [New Latin, from *rhiz-* + Greek *-ktonos* killing, from *kteinein* to kill; akin to Sanskrit *kṣaṇoti* he wounds] (1897)
: any of a form genus (*Rhizoctonia*) of imperfect fungi that includes major plant pathogens

rhi·zoid \'rī-,zȯid\ *noun* (1875)
: a rootlike structure
— **rhi·zoi·dal** \rī-'zȯi-d°l\ *adjective*

rhi·zo·ma·tous \rī-'zō-mə-təs\ *adjective* [International Scientific Vocabulary, from New Latin *rhizomat-, rhizoma*] (1847)
: having, resembling, or being a rhizome ⟨*rhizomatous* plants⟩

rhi·zome \'rī-,zōm\ *noun* [New Latin *rhizomat-, rhizoma*, from Greek *rhizōmat-, rhizōma* mass of roots, from *rhizoun* to cause to take root, from *rhiza* root — more at ROOT] (1845)
: a somewhat elongate usually horizontal subterranean plant stem that is often thickened by deposits of reserve food material, produces shoots above and roots below, and is distinguished from a true root in possessing buds, nodes, and usually scalelike leaves
— **rhi·zo·mic** \rī-'zō-mik, -'zä-\ *adjective*

rhi·zo·plane \'rī-zə-,plān\ *noun* (1949)
: the external surface of roots together with closely adhering soil particles and debris

rhi·zo·pod \'rī-zə-,päd\ *noun* [New Latin *Rhizopoda*, from *rhiz-* + *-poda* -pod] (1851)
: any of a superclass (Rhizopoda) of usually creeping protozoans (as an amoeba or a foraminifer) having lobate or rootlike pseudopodia

rhi·zo·pus \'rī-zə-pəs, -,pùs\ *noun* [New Latin, from *rhiz-* + Greek *pous* foot — more at FOOT] (1887)
: any of a genus (*Rhizopus*) of mold fungi including some economically valuable forms and some plant or animal pathogens (as a bread mold)

rhi·zo·sphere \-,sfir\ *noun* [International Scientific Vocabulary] (1929)
: soil that surrounds and is influenced by the roots of a plant

rhi·zot·o·my \rī-'zä-tə-mē\ *noun, plural* **-mies** [International Scientific Vocabulary] (1911)
: the operation of cutting the anterior or posterior spinal nerve roots

Rh–neg·a·tive \,är-,āch-'ne-gə-tiv\ *adjective* (1945)
: lacking Rh factor in the blood

rho \'rō\ *noun* [Greek *rhō*, of Semitic origin; akin to Hebrew *rēsh* resh] (15th century)
: the 17th letter of the Greek alphabet — see ALPHABET table

rhod- *or* **rhodo-** *combining form* [New Latin, from Latin, from Greek, from *rhodon* rose — more at ROSE]
: rose : red ⟨*rhodo*lite⟩

rho·da·mine \'rō-də-,mēn\ *noun, often capitalized* [International Scientific Vocabulary] (1888)
: any of a group of yellowish red to blue fluorescent dyes; *especially* : a brilliant bluish red dye made by fusing an amino derivative of phenol with phthalic anhydride and used especially in coloring paper and as a biological stain

\ə\ abut \°\ kitten \ər\ further \a\ ash \ā\ ace
\ä\ mop, mar \aù\ out \ch\ chin \e\ bet \ē\ easy
\g\ go \i\ hit \ī\ ice \j\ job \ŋ\ sing \ō\ go
\ȯ\ law \ȯi\ boy \th\ thin \t͟h\ the \ü\ loot \ù\ foot
\y\ yet \zh\ vision *see also* Guide to Pronunciation

Rhode Island Red *noun* [*Rhode Island*, U.S. state] (1896)
: any of an American breed of general-purpose domestic fowls having a long heavy body, smooth yellow or reddish legs, and rich brownish red plumage

Rhode Island White *noun* (circa 1923)
: any of an American breed of domestic fowls resembling Rhode Island Reds but having pure white plumage

Rhodes grass \'rōdz-\ *noun* [Cecil J. *Rhodes*] (1915)
: an African perennial grass (*Chloris gayana*) widely cultivated as a forage grass especially in dry regions

Rho·de·sian man \rō-'dē-zh(ē-)ən-\ *noun* [Northern *Rhodesia*, Africa] (1921)
: an extinct African hominid (*Homo sapiens rhodesiensis*) having long bones of modern type, a skull with prominent brow ridges and large face but human palate and dentition, and a simple but relatively large brain

Rhodesian Ridge·back \-'rij-,bak\ *noun* (1925)
: any of an African breed of powerful long-bodied hunting dogs having a dense harsh short tan coat with a characteristic crest of reversed hair along the spine

Rhodes scholar \'rōd(z)-\ *noun* (1902)
: a holder of one of numerous scholarships founded under the will of Cecil J. Rhodes that can be used at Oxford University for two or three years and are open to candidates from the Commonwealth and the U.S.

rho·di·um \'rō-dē-əm\ *noun* [New Latin, from Greek *rhodon* rose] (1804)
: a white hard ductile metallic element that is resistant to acids, occurs in platinum ores, and is used in alloys with platinum — see ELEMENT table

rho·do·chro·site \,rō-də-'krō-,sīt\ *noun* [German *Rhodocrosit*, from Greek *rhodochrōs* rose-colored, from *rhod-* + *chrōs* color — more at CHROMATIC] (1836)
: a rose red mineral consisting essentially of manganese carbonate

rho·do·den·dron \,rō-də-'den-drən\ *noun* [New Latin, from Latin, oleander, from Greek, from *rhod-* + *dendron* tree — more at DENDR-] (1664)
: any of a genus (*Rhododendron*) of the heath family of widely cultivated shrubs and trees with alternate leaves and showy flowers; *especially* : one with leathery evergreen leaves as distinguished from a deciduous azalea

rho·do·lite \'rō-dᵊl-,īt\ *noun* (1897)
: a pink or purple garnet used as a gem

rho·do·mon·tade *variant of* RODOMONTADE

rho·do·nite \'rō-dᵊn-,īt\ *noun* [German *Rhodonit*, from Greek *rhodon* rose] (1823)
: a pale red triclinic mineral that consists essentially of manganese silicate and is used as an ornamental stone

rho·dop·sin \rō-'däp-sən\ *noun* [International Scientific Vocabulary *rhod-* + Greek *opsis* sight, vision + International Scientific Vocabulary ¹*-in* — more at OPTIC] (1886)
: a red photosensitive pigment in the retinal rods of marine fishes and most higher vertebrates that is important in vision in dim light — called also *visual purple*

rho·do·ra \rō-'dōr-ə, -'dor-\ *noun* [New Latin, alteration of Latin *rodarum*, a plant] (circa 1731)
: an azalea (*Rhododendron canadense*) of northeastern North America that has spring-flowering pink blossoms

rhomb \'räm(b)\ *noun, plural* **rhombs** \'rämz\ [Middle French *rhombe*, from Latin *rhombus*] (circa 1578)
1 : RHOMBUS
2 : RHOMBOHEDRON

rhomb- *or* **rhombo-** *combining form* [New Latin, from Greek *rhombos*]
: rhombus ⟨*rhomb*encephalon⟩

rhomb·en·ceph·a·lon \,räm-(,)ben-'se-fə-,län, -lən\ *noun* [New Latin] (1897)
: HINDBRAIN 1

rhom·bic \'räm-bik\ *adjective* (1701)
1 : having the form of a rhombus
2 : ORTHORHOMBIC

rhom·bo·he·dron \,räm-bō-'hē-drən\ *noun, plural* **-drons** *or* **-dra** \-drə\ [New Latin] (1836)
: a parallelepiped whose faces are rhombuses
— **rhom·bo·he·dral** \-drəl\ *adjective*

¹rhom·boid \'räm-,boid\ *noun* [Middle French *rhomboïde*, from Latin *rhomboides*, from Greek *rhomboeidēs* resembling a rhombus, from *rhombos*] (1570)
: a parallelogram with no right angles and with adjacent sides of unequal length

²rhom·boid \'räm-,boid\ *or* **rhom·boi·dal** \räm-'boi-dᵊl\ *adjective* (1693)
: shaped somewhat like a rhombus or rhomboid

rhomboid

rhom·boi·de·us \räm-'boi-dē-əs\ *noun, plural* **-dei** \-dē-,ī\ [New Latin, from Latin *rhomboides* rhomboid] (circa 1836)
: either of two muscles that lie beneath the trapezius muscle and connect the spinous processes of various vertebrae with the medial border of the scapula

rhom·bus \'räm-bəs\ *noun, plural* **rhom·bus·es** *or* **rhom·bi** \-,bī, -,bē\ [Latin, from Greek *rhombos* piece of wood whirled on a string, lozenge, from *rhembein* to whirl] (circa 1567)
: a parallelogram with four equal sides and sometimes one with no right angles

rhon·chus \'rän-kəs\ *noun, plural* **rhon·chi** \'rän-,kī\ [Late Latin, from *rhenchein* to snore, wheeze; probably akin to Old Irish *sreinnid* he snores] (1829)
: a whistling or snoring sound heard on auscultation of the chest when the air channels are partly obstructed

Rh–pos·i·tive \,är-,āch-'pä-zə-tiv, -'päz-tiv\ *adjective* (1942)
: containing Rh factor in the red blood cells

rhu·barb \'rü-,bärb\ *noun* [Middle English *rubarbe*, from Middle French *reubarbe*, from Medieval Latin *reubarbarum*, alteration of *rha barbarum*, literally, barbarian rhubarb] (15th century)
1 : any of a genus (*Rheum*) of Asian plants of the buckwheat family having large leaves with thick succulent petioles often used as food
2 : the dried rhizome and roots of any of several rhubarbs grown in China and Tibet and used as a purgative and stomachic
3 : a heated dispute or controversy

rhumb \'rəm(b)\ *noun, plural* **rhumbs** \'rəmz\ [Spanish *rumbo* rhumb, rhumb line] (1578)
1 : a line or course on a single bearing
2 : any of the points of the mariner's compass

rhumba *variant of* RUMBA

rhumb line *noun* [Spanish *rumbo*] (circa 1795)
: a line on the surface of the earth that follows a single compass bearing and makes equal oblique angles with all meridians — called also *loxodrome*

rhus \'rüs\ *noun, plural* **rhus·es** *or* **rhus** [New Latin, from Latin, sumac, from Greek *rhous*] (circa 1611)
: any of a genus (*Rhus*) of shrubs and trees (as sumac or poison ivy) of the cashew family that are native to temperate and warm regions, have compound trifoliolate or pinnate leaves, and sometimes produce substances causing dermatitis

¹rhyme \'rīm\ *noun* [Middle English *rime*, from Old French] (13th century)
1 a (1) : rhyming verse (2) : POETRY **b** : a composition in verse that rhymes
2 a : correspondence in terminal sounds of units of composition or utterance (as two or

more words or lines of verse) **b** : one of two or more words thus corresponding in sound **c** : correspondence of other than terminal word sounds: as (1) : ALLITERATION (2) : INTERNAL RHYME
3 : RHYTHM, MEASURE
— **rhyme·less** *adjective*

²rhyme *verb* **rhymed; rhym·ing** (14th century)
transitive verb
1 : to relate or praise in rhyming verse
2 a : to put into rhyme **b** : to compose (verse) in rhyme **c** : to cause to rhyme : use as rhyme
intransitive verb
1 : to make rhymes; *also* : to compose rhyming verse
2 *of a word or verse* : to end in syllables that are rhymes
3 : to be in accord : HARMONIZE
— **rhym·er** *noun*

rhyme or reason *noun* (15th century)
: good sense or reason

rhyme royal \-'rȯi-(-ə)l\ *noun* (circa 1841)
: a stanza of seven lines in iambic pentameter with a rhyme scheme of *ababbcc*

rhyme scheme *noun* (1917)
: the arrangement of rhymes in a stanza or a poem

rhyme·ster \'rīm(p)-stər\ *noun* (1589)
: an inferior poet

rhyming slang *noun* (1859)
: slang in which the word intended is replaced by a word or phrase that rhymes with it (as *loaf of bread* for *head*) or the first part of the phrase (as *loaf* for *head*)

rhyn·cho·ce·pha·lian \,riŋ-kō-sə-'fāl-yən\ *noun* [ultimately from Greek *rhynchos* beak, snout + *kephalē* head — more at CEPHALIC] (1886)
: any of an order (Rhynchocephalia) of reptiles resembling lizards that includes the tuatara as the only living member
— **rhynchocephalian** *adjective*

rhy·o·lite \'rī-ə-,līt\ *noun* [German *Rhyolith*, from Greek *rhyax* stream, stream of lava (from *rhein*) + German *-lith* -lite] (1868)
: a very acid volcanic rock that is the lava form of granite
— **rhy·o·lit·ic** \,rī-ə-'li-tik\ *adjective*

rhythm \'ri-thəm\ *noun* [Middle French & Latin; Middle French *rhythme*, from Latin *rhythmus*, from Greek *rhythmos*, probably from *rhein* to flow — more at STREAM] (1560)
1 a : an ordered recurrent alternation of strong and weak elements in the flow of sound and silence in speech **b** : a particular example or form of rhythm ⟨iambic *rhythm*⟩
2 a : the aspect of music comprising all the elements (as accent, meter, and tempo) that relate to forward movement **b** : a characteristic rhythmic pattern ⟨rumba *rhythm*⟩; *also* : ¹METER 2 **c** : the group of instruments in a band supplying the rhythm — called also *rhythm section*
3 a : movement or fluctuation marked by the regular recurrence or natural flow of related elements **b** : the repetition in a literary work of phrase, incident, character type, or symbol
4 : a regularly recurrent quantitative change in a variable biological process ⟨a circadian *rhythm*⟩ — compare BIORHYTHM
5 : the effect created by the elements in a play, movie, or novel that relate to the temporal development of the action
6 : RHYTHM METHOD

rhythm and blues *noun* (1949)
: popular music typically including elements of blues and black folk music and marked by a strong beat and simple chord structure

rhythm band *noun* (circa 1943)
: a band usually composed of schoolchildren who play simple percussion instruments (as rhythm sticks, sleigh bells, or tambourines) to learn fundamentals of coordination and music

rhyth·mic \'rith-mik\ *adjective* **or** **rhyth·mi·cal** \-mi-kəl\ *adjective* (1589)

1 : marked by or moving in pronounced rhythm
2 : of, relating to, or involving rhythm
— **rhyth·mi·cal·ly** \-mi-k(ə-)lē\ *adverb*

rhyth·mic·i·ty \rith-'mi-sə-tē\ *noun* (1901)
: the state of being rhythmic or of responding rhythmically

rhyth·mics \'rith-miks\ *noun plural but singular or plural in construction* (circa 1859)
: the science or theory of rhythms

rhyth·mist \'ri-thə-mist, 'rith-mist\ *noun* (1864)
: one who studies or has a feeling for rhythm

rhyth·mize \-ˌmīz\ *transitive verb* **-mized; -miz·ing** (1885)
: to order or compose rhythmically
— **rhyth·mi·za·tion** \ˌri-thə-mə-'zā-shən, ˌrith-mə-\ *noun*

rhythm method *noun* (1940)
: a method of birth control involving continence during the period in which ovulation is most likely to occur

rhythm stick *noun* (1952)
: one of a pair of plain or notched wood sticks that are struck or rubbed together to produce various percussive sounds and are used especially by young children in rhythm bands

rhyt·i·dome \'ri-tə-ˌdōm, 'rī-\ *noun* [Greek *rhytidōma* wrinkle, from *rhytidoun* to wrinkle, from *rhytid-, rhytis* wrinkle] (1881)
: the bark external to the last formed periderm

rhy·ton \'rī-ˌtän\ *noun* [Greek, neuter of *rhytos* flowing, from *rhein* to flow — more at STREAM] (1850)
: any of various ornate drinking vessels of ancient times typically shaped in part like an animal or animal's head

¹ri·al \rē-'ól, -'äl\ *noun* [Persian, from Arabic *riyāl* riyal] (1932)
— see MONEY table

²rial *variant of* RIYAL

ri·al·to \rē-'al-(ˌ)tō\ *noun, plural* **-tos** [*Rialto*, island and district in Venice] (1549)
1 : EXCHANGE, MARKETPLACE
2 : a theater district

ri·ant \'rī-ənt, 'rē-; rē-'äⁿ\ *adjective* [Middle French, present participle of *rire* to laugh, from Latin *ridēre*] (1567)
: GAY, MIRTHFUL
— **ri·ant·ly** \'rī-ənt-lē, 'rē-\ *adverb*

ri·a·ta \rē-'a-tə, -'ä-\ *noun* [modification of American Spanish *reata*] (1846)
: LARIAT

¹rib \'rib\ *noun* [Middle English, from Old English *ribb*; akin to Old High German *rippi* rib, Old Church Slavonic *rebro*, and probably to Greek *erephein* to roof over] (before 12th century)
1 a : any of the paired curved bony or partly cartilaginous rods that stiffen the walls of the body of most vertebrates and protect the viscera **b :** a cut of meat including a rib — see BEEF illustration **c** [from the account of Eve's creation from Adam's rib in Genesis 2:21–22] : WIFE
2 : something resembling a rib in shape or function: as **a** (1) : a traverse member of the frame of a ship that runs from keel to deck (2) : a light fore-and-aft member in an airplane's wing **b :** one of the stiff strips supporting an umbrella's fabric **c :** one of the arches in Romanesque and Gothic vaulting meeting and crossing one another and dividing the whole vaulted space into triangles
3 : an elongated ridge: as **a** (1) : a vein of an insect's wing (2) : one of the primary veins of a leaf **b :** one of the ridges in a knitted or woven fabric

rib 1a

²rib *transitive verb* **ribbed; rib·bing** (circa 1547)
1 : to furnish or enclose with ribs
2 : to form vertical ridges in in knitting
— **rib·ber** *noun*

³rib *noun* [⁴*rib*] (1929)
1 : JOKE
2 : PARODY

⁴rib *transitive verb* **ribbed; rib·bing** [probably from ³*rib*; from the tickling of the ribs to cause laughter] (1930)
: to poke fun at : KID
— **rib·ber** *noun*

¹rib·ald \'ri-bəld *also* 'ri-ˌbóld, 'rī-ˌbóld\ *noun* [Middle English, from Middle French *ribaut, ribauld* wanton, rascal, from *riber* to be wanton, of Germanic origin; akin to Old High German *rīban* to be wanton, literally, to rub] (13th century)
: a ribald person

²ribald *adjective* (1508)
1 : CRUDE, OFFENSIVE ⟨*ribald* language⟩
2 : characterized by or using coarse indecent humor
synonym see COARSE

rib·ald·ry \'ri-bəl-drē *also* 'rī-\ *noun, plural* **-ries** (14th century)
1 : a ribald quality or element
2 a : ribald language or humor **b :** an instance of ribald language or humor

rib·and \'ri-bənd\ *noun* [Middle English, alteration of *riban*] (15th century)
: a ribbon used especially as a decoration

ri·ba·vi·rin \ˌrī-bə-'vī-rən\ *noun* [perhaps from *ribonucleic acid* + *virus* + *-in*] (1976)
: a synthetic broad-spectrum antiviral nucleoside $C_8H_{12}N_4O_5$

rib·band \'ri(b)-ˌband, 'ri-bən(d)\ *noun* [¹*rib* + ¹*band*] (1711)
: a long narrow strip or bar used in shipbuilding; *especially* : one bent and bolted longitudinally to the frames to hold them in position during construction

rib·bing \'ri-biŋ\ *noun* (1564)
: an arrangement of ribs

¹rib·bon \'ri-bən\ *noun* [Middle English *riban*, from Middle French *riban, ruban*] (14th century)
1 a : a flat or tubular narrow closely woven fabric (as of silk or rayon) used for trimmings or knitting **b :** a narrow fabric used for tying packages **c :** a piece of usually multicolored ribbon worn as a military decoration or in place of a medal **d :** a strip of colored satin given for winning a place in a competition
2 : a strip of inked fabric (as in a typewriter)
3 *plural* : reins for controlling an animal
4 : TATTER, SHRED — usually used in plural
5 : RIBBAND
— **rib·bon·like** \-ˌlīk\ *adjective*

²ribbon *transitive verb* (1716)
1 a : to adorn with ribbons **b :** to divide into ribbons **c :** to cover with or as if with ribbons
2 : to rip to shreds

ribbon development *noun* (1927)
: a system of buildings built side by side along a road

rib·bon·fish \'ri-bən-ˌfish\ *noun* (circa 1798)
: any of a family (Trachipteridae) of elongate greatly compressed marine bony fishes (as a dealfish)

ribbon worm *noun* (1855)
: NEMERTEAN

rib·by \'ri-bē\ *adjective* (1849)
: showing or marked by ribs

rib cage *noun* (1909)
: the bony enclosing wall of the chest consisting chiefly of the ribs and the structures connecting them

ri·bes \'rī-(ˌ)bēz\ *noun, plural* **ribes** [New Latin, from Medieval Latin, currant, from Arabic *rībās* rhubarb] (1543)
: any of a genus (*Ribes*) of shrubs (as a currant or a gooseberry) of the saxifrage family that have small racemose variously colored flowers and pulpy two-seeded to many-seeded berries

rib eye *noun* (1926)
: the large piece of meat that lies along the outer side of the rib (as of a steer)

rib·grass \'rib-ˌgras\ *noun* (circa 1500)
: ¹PLANTAIN; *especially* : an Old World plantain (*Plantago lanceolata*) with long narrow ribbed leaves

rib·let \'ri-blət\ *noun* (1943)
: one of the rib ends in the strip of breast of lamb or veal — see LAMB illustration

ribo- *combining form* [*ribose*]
1 : ribose ⟨*ribo*flavin⟩
2 : ribonucleic acid ⟨*ribo*some⟩

ri·bo·fla·vin \ˌrī-bō-'flā-vən, 'rī-bə-ˌ\ *noun* [International Scientific Vocabulary *ribo-* + Latin *flavus* yellow — more at BLUE] (1935)
: a yellow crystalline compound $C_{17}H_{20}N_4O_6$ that is a growth-promoting member of the vitamin B complex and occurs both free (as in milk) and combined (as in liver) — called also *vitamin B₂, vitamin G*

ri·bo·nu·cle·ase \ˌrī-bō-'nü-klē-ˌās, -'nyü-, -ˌāz\ *noun* (1942)
: an enzyme that catalyzes the hydrolysis of RNA

ri·bo·nu·cle·ic acid \ˌrī-bō-nü-'klē-ik-, -nyü-, -ˌklā-\ *noun* (1931)
: RNA

ri·bo·nu·cleo·pro·tein \-ˌnü-klē-ō-'prō-ˌtēn, -ˌprō-tē-ən\ *noun* (1940)
: a nucleoprotein that contains RNA

ri·bo·nu·cle·o·side \-'nü-klē-ə-ˌsīd, -'nyü-\ *noun* (1931)
: a nucleoside that contains ribose

ri·bo·nu·cle·o·tide \-ˌtīd\ *noun* (1929)
: a nucleotide that contains ribose and occurs especially as a constituent of RNA

ri·bose \'rī-ˌbōs, -ˌbōz\ *noun* [International Scientific Vocabulary, from *ribonic acid* (an acid $C_5H_{10}O_6$ obtained by oxidation of ribose)] (1892)
: a pentose $C_5H_{10}O_5$ found especially in the dextrorotatory form and obtained especially from RNA

ribosomal RNA *noun* (1961)
: RNA that is a fundamental structural element of ribosomes

ri·bo·some \'rī-bə-ˌsōm\ *noun* (1958)
: any of the RNA-rich cytoplasmic granules that are sites of protein synthesis — see CELL illustration
— **ri·bo·som·al** \ˌrī-bə-'sō-məl\ *adjective*

rib roast *noun* (circa 1890)
: a cut of meat containing the large piece that lies along the outer side of the rib — see BEEF illustration

rib·wort \'rib-ˌwərt, -ˌwórt\ *noun* (14th century)
: RIBGRASS

rice \'rīs\ *noun* [Middle English *rys*, from Old French *ris*, from Old Italian *riso*, from Greek *oryza, oryzon*, of Iranian origin; akin to Pashto *wriže* rice; akin to Sanskrit *vrīhi* rice] (13th century)
: the starchy seeds of an annual cereal grass (*Oryza sativa*) that are cooked and used for food; *also* : this cereal grass that occurs in southeastern Asia and is widely cultivated in warm climates for its seeds and by-products

rice-bird \'rīs-ˌbərd\ *noun* (1731)
: any of several small birds common in rice fields; *especially* : BOBOLINK

rice paper *noun* [from its resemblance to paper made from rice straw] (1822)

\ə\ abut \ᵊ\ kitten \ər\ **further** \a\ **ash** \ā\ **ace**
\ä\ mop, mar \au̇\ **out** \ch\ **chin** \e\ **bet** \ē\ **easy**
\g\ go \i\ **hit** \ī\ **ice** \j\ **job** \ŋ\ **sing** \ō\ **go**
\ȯ\ **law** \ȯi\ **boy** \th\ **thin** \t͟h\ **the** \ü\ **loot** \u̇\ **foot**
\y\ **yet** \zh\ **vision** *see also* Guide to Pronunciation

: a thin papery material made from the pith of a small Asian tree or shrub (*Tetrapanax papyriferum*) of the ginseng family

rice polishings *noun plural* (circa 1934)
: the inner bran layer of rice rubbed off in milling

ric·er \'rī-sər\ *noun* (1896)
: a kitchen utensil in which soft foods are pressed through a perforated container to produce strings

ri·cer·car \,rē-(,)chər-'kär\ *or* **ri·cer·ca·re** \-'kä-(,)rā\ *noun, plural* **ricercars** *or* **ri·cer·ca·ri** \-'kä-(,)rē\ [Italian, from *ricercare* to seek again, seek out, from *ri-* re- (from Latin *re-*) + *cercare* to seek, from Late Latin *circare* to go about — more at SEARCH] (1789)
: any of various usually keyboard musical forms especially of the 16th and 17th centuries in either quasi-improvisatory toccata style or strict polyphonic fugal style

rich \'rich\ *adjective* [Middle English *riche*, from Old English *rīce;* akin to Old High German *rīhhi* rich, Old English *rīce* kingdom, Old High German *rīhhi,* noun; all from prehistoric Germanic words borrowed from Celtic words akin to Old Irish *rí* (genitive *ríg*) king — more at ROYAL] (before 12th century)
1 : having abundant possessions and especially material wealth
2 a : having high value or quality **b** : well supplied ⟨a city *rich* in traditions⟩
3 : magnificently impressive : SUMPTUOUS
4 a : vivid and deep in color ⟨a *rich* red⟩ **b** : full and mellow in tone and quality ⟨a *rich* voice⟩ **c** : having a strong fragrance ⟨*rich* perfumes⟩
5 : highly productive or remunerative ⟨a *rich* mine⟩
6 a : having abundant plant nutrients ⟨*rich* soil⟩ **b** : highly seasoned, fatty, oily, or sweet ⟨*rich* foods⟩ **c** : high in the combustible component ⟨a *rich* fuel mixture⟩ **d** : high in some component ⟨cholesterol-*rich* foods⟩
7 a : ENTERTAINING; *also* : LAUGHABLE **b** : MEANINGFUL, SIGNIFICANT ⟨*rich* allusions⟩ **c** : LUSH ⟨*rich* meadows⟩
8 : pure or nearly pure ⟨*rich* lime⟩ ☆
— rich·ness *noun*

Rich·ard Roe \,rich-ərd-'rō\ *noun* (1768)
: a party to legal proceedings whose true name is unknown — compare JOHN DOE

rich·en \'ri-chən\ *transitive verb* **rich·ened; rich·en·ing** \'ri-chə-niŋ, 'rich-niŋ\ (1878)
: to make rich or richer

rich·es \'ri-chəz\ *noun plural* [Middle English, singular or plural, from *richesse,* literally, richness, from Old French, from *riche* rich, of Germanic origin; akin to Old English *rīce* rich] (13th century)
: things that make one rich : WEALTH

rich·ly \'rich-lē\ *adverb* [Middle English *richely,* from Old English *rīclīce,* from *rīce* rich] (before 12th century)
1 : in a rich manner
2 : in full measure : AMPLY ⟨praise *richly* deserved⟩

Rich·ter scale \'rik-tər-\ *noun* [Charles F. *Richter*] (1938)
: an open-ended logarithmic scale for expressing the magnitude of a seismic disturbance (as an earthquake) in terms of the energy dissipated in it with 1.5 indicating the smallest earthquake that can be felt, 4.5 an earthquake causing slight damage, and 8.5 a very devastating earthquake

ri·cin \'rī-sⁿn, 'ri-\ *noun* [Latin *ricinus* castor-oil plant] (1896)
: a poisonous protein in the castor bean

ri·cin·ole·ic acid \,rī-sⁿn-ō-'lē-ik-, ,ri-, -'lā-\ *noun* [Latin *ricin*us + English *oleic acid*] (1848)
: an oily unsaturated hydroxy fatty acid

$C_{18}H_{34}O_3$ that occurs in castor oil as a glyceride and yields esters important as plasticizers

¹rick \'rik\ *noun* [Middle English *reek,* from Old English *hrēac;* akin to Old Norse *hraukr* rick] (before 12th century)
1 : a stack (as of hay) in the open air
2 : a pile of material (as cordwood) split from short logs

²rick *transitive verb* (1623)
: to pile (as hay) in ricks

³rick *transitive verb* [perhaps from Middle English *wrikken* to move unsteadily] (1798)
chiefly British : WRENCH, SPRAIN

rick·ets \'ri-kəts\ *noun plural but singular in construction* [origin unknown] (1634)
: a deficiency disease that affects the young during the period of skeletal growth, is characterized especially by soft and deformed bones, and is caused by failure to assimilate and use calcium and phosphorus normally due to inadequate sunlight or vitamin D

rick·ett·sia \ri-'ket-sē-ə\ *noun, plural* **-si·as** *or* **-si·ae** \-sē-,ē, -,ī\ *also* **-sia** [New Latin, genus name, from Howard T. *Ricketts* (died 1910) American pathologist] (1919)
: any of a family (Rickettsiaceae) of rod-shaped, coccoid, or diplococcus-shaped, often pleomorphic bacteria that cause various diseases (as typhus)
— rick·ett·si·al \-sē-əl\ *adjective*

rick·ety \'ri-kə-tē\ *adjective* (1683)
1 : affected with rickets
2 a : lacking stability or firmness : SHAKY 2a ⟨a *rickety* coalition⟩ **b** : in unsound physical condition ⟨*rickety* veterans⟩ ⟨*rickety* stairs⟩

rick·ey \'ri-kē\ *noun, plural* **rickeys** [probably from the name *Rickey*] (1895)
: a drink containing liquor, lime juice, sugar, and soda water; *also* : a similar drink without liquor

rick·rack *or* **ric·rac** \'rik-,rak\ *noun* [reduplication of ⁴*rack*] (1884)
: a flat braid woven to form zigzags and used especially as trimming on clothing

rick·sha *or* **rick·shaw** \'rik-,shȯ\ *noun* [alteration of *jinrikisha*] (1887)
: a small covered 2-wheeled vehicle usually for one passenger that is pulled by one man and that was used originally in Japan

¹ric·o·chet \'ri-kə-,shā, *British also* -,shet\ *noun* [French] (1769)
: a glancing rebound (as of a projectile off a flat surface); *also* : an object that ricochets

²ricochet *intransitive verb* **-cheted** \-,shād\ *or* **-chet·ted** \-,she-təd\; **-chet·ing** \-,shā-iŋ\ *or* **-chet·ting** \-,she-tiŋ\ (1828)
: to skip with or as if with glancing rebounds

ri·cot·ta \ri-'kä-tə, -'kȯ-\ *noun* [Italian, from feminine of past participle of *ricuocere* to cook again, from Latin *recoquere,* from *re-* + *coquere* to cook — more at COOK] (1877)
: a white unripened whey cheese of Italy that resembles cottage cheese; *also* : a similar cheese made in the U.S. from whole or skim milk

ric·tal \'rik-tⁿl\ *adjective* (1825)
: of or relating to the rictus

ric·tus \'rik-təs\ *noun* [New Latin, from Latin, open mouth, from *ringi* to open the mouth; akin to Old Church Slavonic *rǫgŭ* mockery] (1827)
1 : the gape of a bird's mouth
2 a : the mouth orifice **b** : a gaping grin or grimace

rid \'rid\ *transitive verb* **rid** *also* **rid·ded; rid·ding** [Middle English *ridden* to clear, from Old Norse *rythja;* akin to Old High German *riutan* to clear land] (13th century)
1 *archaic* : SAVE, RESCUE
2 : to make free : RELIEVE, DISENCUMBER ⟨*rid* the language of impropriety⟩ ⟨be *rid* of worries⟩ ⟨get *rid* of that junk⟩

rid·dance \'ri-dⁿn(t)s\ *noun* (1533)
1 : an act of ridding

2 : DELIVERANCE, RELIEF — often used in the phrase *good riddance*

rid·den \'ri-dⁿn\ *adjective* (1653)
1 : harassed, oppressed, or obsessed by — usually used in combination ⟨guilt-*ridden*⟩ ⟨debt-*ridden*⟩
2 : excessively full of or supplied with — usually used in combination ⟨slum-*ridden*⟩

¹rid·dle \'ri-dⁿl\ *noun* [Middle English *redels, ridel,* from Old English *rǣdelse* opinion, conjecture, riddle; akin to Old English *rǣdan* to interpret — more at READ] (before 12th century)
1 : a mystifying, misleading, or puzzling question posed as a problem to be solved or guessed : CONUNDRUM, ENIGMA
2 : something or someone difficult to understand
synonym see MYSTERY

²riddle *verb* **rid·dled; rid·dling** \'rid-liŋ, 'ri-dⁿl-iŋ\ (1571)
intransitive verb
: to speak in or propound riddles
transitive verb
1 : to find the solution of : EXPLAIN
2 : to set a riddle for : PUZZLE
— rid·dler \'rid-lər, 'ri-dⁿl-ər\ *noun*

³riddle *noun* [Middle English *riddil,* from Old English *hriddel;* akin to Latin *cribrum* sieve, *cernere* to sift — more at CERTAIN] (before 12th century)
: a coarse sieve

⁴riddle *transitive verb* **rid·dled; rid·dling** \'rid-liŋ, 'ri-dⁿl-iŋ\ (13th century)
1 : to separate (as grain from chaff) with a riddle : SCREEN
2 : to pierce with many holes ⟨*riddled* the car with bullets⟩
3 : to spread through : PERMEATE ⟨a book *riddled* with errors⟩

rid·dling \'rid-liŋ, 'ri-dⁿl-iŋ\ *adjective* (1591)
: containing or presenting riddles

¹ride \'rīd\ *verb* **rode** \'rōd\ *or chiefly dialect* **rid** \'rid\; **rid·den** \'ri-dⁿn\ *or chiefly dialect* **rid** *or* **rode; rid·ing** \'rī-diŋ\ [Middle English, from Old English *rīdan;* akin to Old High German *rītan* to ride, Middle Irish *réidid* he rides] (before 12th century)
intransitive verb
1 a : to sit and travel on the back of an animal that one directs **b** : to travel in or on a conveyance
2 : to travel as if on a conveyance : be borne ⟨*rode* on a wave of popularity⟩
3 a : to lie moored or anchored ⟨a ship *rides* at anchor⟩ **b** : SAIL **c** : to move like a floating object ⟨the moon *rode* in the sky⟩
4 : to become supported on a point or surface
5 a : to travel over a surface ⟨the car *rides* well⟩ **b** : to move on the body ⟨shorts that *ride* up⟩
6 : to continue without interference ⟨let it *ride*⟩
7 a : to be contingent : DEPEND ⟨plans on which the future *rides*⟩ **b** : to become bet ⟨a lot of money *riding* on the favorite⟩
transitive verb
1 a : to travel on ⟨*ride* a bike⟩ ⟨*ride* the bus⟩ **b** : to move with like a rider ⟨*ride* the waves⟩

2 a : to traverse by conveyance ⟨*rode* 500 miles⟩ **b :** to ride a horse in ⟨*ride* a race⟩
3 : SURVIVE, OUTLAST — usually used with *out* ⟨*rode* out the gale⟩
4 : to traverse on horseback to inspect or maintain ⟨*ride* fence⟩
5 : to mount in copulation
6 a : OBSESS, OPPRESS ⟨*ridden* by anxiety⟩ **b :** to harass persistently **: NAG c : TEASE, RIB**
7 : CARRY, CONVEY
8 : to project over **: OVERLAP**
9 : to give with (a punch) to soften the impact
10 : to keep in partial engagement by resting a foot continuously on the pedal ⟨*ride* the brakes⟩
— **rid·able** *or* **ride·able** \ˈrī-də-bəl\ *adjective*
— **ride circuit :** to hold court in the various towns of a judicial circuit
— **ride for a fall :** to court disaster
— **ride herd on :** to keep a check on
— **ride high :** to experience success
— **ride shotgun :** to ride in the front passenger seat of a motor vehicle

²ride *noun* (1759)
1 : an act of riding; *especially* **:** a trip on horseback or by vehicle
2 : a way (as a road or path) suitable for riding
3 : any of various mechanical devices (as at an amusement park) for riding on
4 a : a trip on which gangsters take a victim to murder him **b :** something likened to such a trip ⟨take the taxpayers for a *ride*⟩
5 : a means of transportation
6 : the qualities of travel comfort in a vehicle

rid·er \ˈrī-dər\ *noun* (14th century)
1 : one that rides
2 a : an addition to a document often attached on a separate piece of paper **b :** a clause appended to a legislative bill to secure a usually distinct object
3 : something used to overlie another or to move along on another piece
— **rid·er·less** \-ləs\ *adjective*

rid·er·ship \ˈrī-dər-ˌship\ *noun* (1968)
: the number of persons who ride a system of public transportation

¹ridge \ˈrij\ *noun* [Middle English *rigge*, from Old English *hrycg*; akin to Old High German *hrukki* ridge, back] (before 12th century)
1 : an elevated body part (as along the backbone)
2 a : a range of hills or mountains **b :** an elongate elevation on an ocean bottom
3 : an elongate crest or a linear series of crests
4 : a raised strip (as of plowed ground)
5 : the line of intersection at the top between the opposite slopes or sides of a roof
— **ridged** \ˈrijd\ *adjective*

²ridge *verb* **ridged; ridg·ing** (1523)
transitive verb
: to form into a ridge
intransitive verb
: to extend in ridges

ridge·line \ˈrij-ˌlīn\ *noun* (1833)
: a line marking or following a ridge top

ridge·ling *or* **ridg·ling** \ˈrij-liŋ\ *noun* [perhaps from ¹*ridge*; from the supposition that the undescended testis remains near the animal's back] (1555)
1 : a partially castrated male animal
2 : a male animal having one or both testes retained in the inguinal canal

ridge·pole \ˈrij-ˌpōl\ *noun* (1788)
1 : the horizontal pole at the top of a tent
2 : the highest horizontal timber in a roof against which the upper ends of the rafters are fixed

ridgy \ˈri-jē\ *adjective* (1697)
: having or rising in ridges

1 ridgepole, 2 rafters

¹rid·i·cule \ˈri-də-ˌkyü(ə)l\ *noun* [French or Latin; French, from Latin *ridiculum* jest] (1690)
: the act of exposing to laughter **: DERISION, MOCKERY**

²ridicule *transitive verb* **-culed; -cul·ing** (circa 1700)
: to make fun of ☆
— **rid·i·cul·er** *noun*

ri·dic·u·lous \rə-ˈdi-kyə-ləs\ *adjective* [Latin *ridiculosus* (from *ridiculum* jest, from neuter of *ridiculus*) or *ridiculus*, literally, laughable, from *ridēre* to laugh] (1550)
: arousing or deserving ridicule **: ABSURD, PREPOSTEROUS**
synonym see LAUGHABLE
— **ri·dic·u·lous·ly** *adverb*
— **ri·dic·u·lous·ness** *noun*

¹rid·ing \ˈrī-diŋ\ *noun* (14th century)
: the action or state of one that rides
²rid·ing *adjective* (15th century)
1 : used for or when riding ⟨a *riding* horse⟩ ⟨*riding* boots⟩
2 : operated by a rider ⟨a *riding* mower⟩

³rid·ing \ˈrī-diŋ\ *noun* [Middle English *-redying* or *trithing*, alteration of (assumed) Old English *thriding*, from Old Norse *thrithjungr* third part, from *thrithi* third; akin to Old English *thridda* third — more at THIRD] (15th century)
1 : one of the three administrative jurisdictions into which Yorkshire, England, was formerly divided
2 : an administrative jurisdiction or electoral district in a British dominion (as Canada)

rid·ley \ˈrid-lē\ *noun* [origin unknown] (1926)
: either of two sea turtles **: a :** one (*Lepidochelys kempii*) of the Gulf of Mexico and the Atlantic coast of the U.S. — called also *Kemp's ridley* **b :** one (*L. olivacea*) of the Pacific, Atlantic, and Indian oceans

ri·dot·to \ri-ˈdä-(ˌ)tō\ *noun, plural* **-tos** [Italian, retreat, place of entertainment, redoubt — more at REDOUBT] (1722)
: a public entertainment consisting of music and dancing often in masquerade popular in 18th century England

ri·el \rē-ˈel\ *noun* [origin unknown] (1956)
— see MONEY table

Rie·mann·ian geometry \rē-ˈmä-nē-ən-\ *noun* [G. F. B. *Riemann*] (1904)
: a non-Euclidean geometry in which straight lines are geodesics and in which the parallel postulate is replaced by the postulate that every pair of straight lines intersects

Rie·mann integral \ˈrē-ˌmän-, -mən-\ *noun* (1914)
: a definite integral defined as the limit of sums found by partitioning the interval comprising the domain of definition into subintervals, by finding the sum of products each of which consists of the width of a subinterval multiplied by the value of the function at some point in it, and by letting the maximum width of the subintervals approach zero

Ries·ling \ˈrēz-liŋ, ˈrēs-\ *noun* [German] (1833)
: a white wine that ranges from dry to very sweet and is made from a single variety of grape originally grown in Germany; *also* **:** the grape

ri·fam·pin \rī-ˈfam-pən\ *or* **ri·fam·pi·cin** \rī-ˈfam-pə-sən\ *noun* [International Scientific Vocabulary, alteration of *rifamycin*, antibiotic derived from *Streptomyces mediterranei*] (1966)
: a semisynthetic antibiotic $C_{43}H_{58}N_4O_{12}$ that acts against some viruses and bacteria especially by inhibiting RNA synthesis

rife \ˈrīf\ *adjective* [Middle English *ryfe*, from Old English *rȳfe*; akin to Old Norse *rīfr* abundant] (12th century)
1 : prevalent especially to an increasing degree ⟨fear was *rife* in the people⟩
2 : ABUNDANT, COMMON

3 : copiously supplied **: ABOUNDING** — usually used with *with* ⟨*rife* with rumors⟩
— **rife** *adverb*
— **rife·ly** *adverb*

¹riff \ˈrif\ *noun* [probably by shortening & alteration from *refrain*] (1935)
1 : an ostinato phrase (as in jazz) typically supporting a solo improvisation; *also* **:** a piece based on such a phrase
2 : a short succinct usually witty comment; *also* **: BIT, ROUTINE**

²riff *intransitive verb* (1950)
: to perform a riff

³riff *verb* [short for *riffle*] (1952)
: RIFFLE, SKIM ⟨*riff* pages⟩

Riff \ˈrif\ *noun, plural* **Riffs** *or* **Riffi** \ˈri-fē\ *or* **Riff** (1903)
: a Berber of the Rif Mountains in northern Morocco

Riff·ian \ˈri-fē-ən\ *noun* (1867)
: RIFF

¹rif·fle \ˈri-fəl\ *verb* **rif·fled; rif·fling** \ˈri-f(ə-)liŋ\ [²*riffle*] (1752)
intransitive verb
1 : to form, flow over, or move in riffles
2 : to flip cursorily **: THUMB** ⟨*riffle* through the catalog⟩
transitive verb
1 : to ruffle slightly **: RIPPLE**
2 a : to leaf through hastily; *specifically* **:** to leaf (as a stack of paper) by sliding a thumb along the edge of the leaves **b :** to shuffle (playing cards) by separating the deck into two parts and riffling with the thumbs so the cards intermix
3 : to manipulate (small objects) idly between the fingers

²riffle *noun* [perhaps alteration of *ruffle*] (1785)
1 a : a shallow extending across a streambed and causing broken water **b :** a stretch of water flowing over a riffle
2 : a small wave or succession of small waves **: RIPPLE**
3 a : any of various contrivances (as blocks or rails) laid on the bottom of a sluice or launder to make a series of grooves or interstices to catch and retain a mineral (as gold) **b :** a groove or interstice so formed
4 : a cleat or bar fastened to an inclined surface in a gold-washing apparatus to catch and hold mineral grains
5 : [¹*riffle*] **a :** the act or process of shuffling (as cards) **b :** the sound made while doing this

rif·fler \ˈri-flər\ *noun* [French *rifloir*, from *rifler* to file, rifle] (circa 1797)
: a small filing or scraping tool

riff·raff \ˈrif-ˌraf\ *noun* [Middle English *ryffe raffe*, from *rif and raf* every single one, from Middle French *rif et raf* completely, from *rifler* to scratch, plunder + *raffe* act of sweeping] (15th century)
1 a : disreputable persons **b : RABBLE c :** one of the riffraff

\ə\ abut	\ᵊ\ kitten	\ər\ further	\a\ ash	\ā\ ace	
\ä\ mop, mar	\aú\ out	\ch\ chin	\e\ bet	\ē\ easy	
\g\ go	\i\ hit	\ī\ ice	\j\ job	\ŋ\ sing	\ō\ go
\ò\ law	\ói\ boy	\th\ thin	\th\ the	\ü\ loot	\ú\ foot
\y\ yet	\zh\ vision	*see also* Guide to Pronunciation			

2 : REFUSE, RUBBISH ◆
— **riffraff** *adjective*

¹**ri·fle** \'rī-fəl\ *verb* **ri·fled; ri·fling** \-f(ə-)liŋ\ [Middle English, from Middle French *rifler* to scratch, file, plunder, of Germanic origin; akin to Old High German *riffilōn* to saw, obsolete Dutch *riffelen* to scrape] (14th century)
transitive verb
1 : to ransack especially with the intent to steal
2 : to steal and carry away
intransitive verb
: to engage in ransacking and stealing
— **ri·fler** \-f(ə-)lər\ *noun*

²**rifle** *transitive verb* **ri·fled; ri·fling** \-f(ə-)liŋ\ [perhaps from French *rifler* to scratch, file] (1635)
: to cut spiral grooves into the bore of ⟨*rifled* arms⟩ ⟨*rifled* pipe⟩

³**rifle** *noun* (1770)
1 a : a shoulder weapon with a rifled bore **b :** a rifled artillery piece
2 *plural* **:** soldiers armed with rifles
word history see MUSKET

⁴**rifle** *transitive verb* **ri·fled; ri·fling** \-f(ə-)liŋ\ [³*rifle*] (1937)
: to propel (as a ball) with great force or speed

ri·fle·bird \'rī-fəl-,bərd\ *noun* (1831)
: any of several birds of paradise (genus *Ptiloris*)

ri·fle·man \-mən\ *noun* (1775)
1 : a soldier armed with a rifle
2 : one skilled in shooting with a rifle

ri·fle·ry \'rī-fəl-rē\ *noun* (1935)
: the practice of shooting at targets with a rifle

ri·fling \'rī-f(ə-)liŋ\ *noun* (1797)
1 : the act or process of making spiral grooves
2 : a system of spiral grooves in the surface of the bore of a gun causing a projectile when fired to rotate about its longer axis

¹**rift** \'rift\ *noun* [Middle English, of Scandinavian origin; akin to Danish & Norwegian *rift* fissure, Old Norse *rīfa* to rive — more at RIVE] (14th century)
1 a : FISSURE, CREVASSE **b :** FAULT 5
2 : a clear space or interval
3 : BREACH, ESTRANGEMENT

²**rift** (14th century)
intransitive verb
: to burst open
transitive verb
1 : CLEAVE, DIVIDE ⟨hills were *rifted* by the earthquake⟩
2 : PENETRATE

rift valley *noun* (1894)
: an elongated valley formed by the depression of a block of the earth's crust between two faults or groups of faults of approximately parallel strike

¹**rig** \'rig\ *transitive verb* **rigged; rig·ging** [Middle English *riggen*] (15th century)
1 : to fit out (as a ship) with rigging
2 : CLOTHE, DRESS — usually used with *out*
3 : to furnish with special gear **:** EQUIP
4 a : to put in condition or position for use **:** ADJUST, ARRANGE ⟨a car *rigged* for manual control⟩ **b :** CONSTRUCT ⟨*rig* up a temporary shelter⟩

²**rig** *noun* (1822)
1 : the distinctive shape, number, and arrangement of sails and masts of a ship
2 : EQUIPAGE; *especially* **:** a carriage with its horse
3 : CLOTHING, DRESS
4 : tackle, equipment, or machinery fitted for a specified purpose ⟨an oil-drilling *rig*⟩
5 : a tractor-trailer combination

³**rig** *transitive verb* **rigged; rig·ging** [*rig*, noun, a swindle] (1851)
1 : to manipulate or control usually by deceptive or dishonest means ⟨*rig* an election⟩
2 : to fix in advance for a desired result ⟨*rig* a quiz program⟩

rig·a·doon \,ri-gə-'dün\ *or* **ri·gau·don** \rē-gō-dōⁿ\ *noun* [French *rigaudon*] (1691)

: a lively dance of the 17th and 18th centuries; *also* **:** the music for a rigadoon

rig·a·ma·role *variant of* RIGMAROLE

rig·a·to·ni \,ri-gə-'tō-nē\ *noun* [Italian, plural, from *rigato* furrowed, fluted, from past participle of *rigare* to furrow, flute, from *riga* line, of Germanic origin; akin to Old High German *rīga* line — more at ROW] (circa 1923)
: pasta made in short wide fluted tubes

Ri·gel \'rī-jəl, -gəl; 'ri-jəl\ *noun* [Arabic *Rijl*, literally, foot]
: a first-magnitude star in the left foot of the constellation Orion

rig·ger \'ri-gər\ *noun* (1611)
1 : one that rigs
2 : a long slender pointed sable paintbrush

rig·ging \'ri-giŋ, -gən\ *noun* (1594)
1 a : lines and chains used aboard a ship especially in working sail and supporting masts and spars **b :** a similar network (as in theater scenery) used for support and manipulation
2 : CLOTHING

¹**right** \'rīt\ *adjective* [Middle English, from Old English *riht*; akin to Old High German *reht* right, Latin *rectus* straight, right, *regere* to lead straight, direct, rule, *rogare* to ask, Greek *oregein* to stretch out] (before 12th century)
1 : RIGHTEOUS, UPRIGHT
2 : being in accordance with what is just, good, or proper ⟨*right* conduct⟩
3 a : agreeable to a standard **b :** conforming to facts or truth **:** CORRECT ⟨the *right* answer⟩
4 : SUITABLE, APPROPRIATE ⟨the *right* man for the job⟩
5 : STRAIGHT ⟨a *right* line⟩
6 : GENUINE, REAL
7 a : of, relating to, situated on, or being the side of the body which is away from the heart and on which the hand is stronger in most people **b :** located nearer to the right hand than to the left **c :** located to the right of an observer facing the object specified or directed as the right arm would point when raised out to the side **d (1) :** located on the right of an observer facing in the same direction as the object specified ⟨stage *right*⟩ **(2) :** located on the right when facing downstream ⟨the *right* bank of a river⟩
8 : having the axis perpendicular to the base ⟨*right* cone⟩
9 : of, relating to, or constituting the principal or more prominent side of an object ⟨made sure the socks were *right* side out⟩
10 : acting or judging in accordance with truth or fact ⟨time proved her *right*⟩
11 a : being in good physical or mental health or order ⟨not in his *right* mind⟩ **b :** being in a correct or proper state ⟨put things *right*⟩
12 : most favorable or desired **:** PREFERABLE; *also* **:** socially acceptable ⟨knew all the *right* people⟩
13 *often capitalized* **:** of, adhering to, or constituted by the Right especially in politics
synonym see CORRECT
— **right·ness** *noun*

²**right** *noun* [Middle English, from Old English *riht*, from *riht*, adjective] (before 12th century)
1 : qualities (as adherence to duty or obedience to lawful authority) that together constitute the ideal of moral propriety or merit moral approval
2 : something to which one has a just claim: as **a :** the power or privilege to which one is justly entitled **b (1) :** the interest that one has in a piece of property — often used in plural ⟨mineral *rights*⟩ **(2)** *plural* **:** the property interest possessed under law or custom and agreement in an intangible thing especially of a literary and artistic nature ⟨film *rights* of the novel⟩
3 : something that one may properly claim as due
4 : the cause of truth or justice
5 a : RIGHT HAND 1a; *also* **:** a blow struck with this hand ⟨gave him a hard *right* on the jaw⟩ **b :** the location or direction of the right side

⟨woods on his *right*⟩ **c :** the part on the right side **d :** RIGHT FIELD
6 a : the true account or correct interpretation **b :** the quality or state of being factually correct
7 *often capitalized* **a :** the part of a legislative chamber located to the right of the presiding officer **b :** the members of a continental European legislative body occupying the right as a result of holding more conservative political views than other members
8 a *often capitalized* **:** individuals sometimes professing opposition to change in the established order and favoring traditional attitudes and practices and sometimes advocating the forced establishment of an authoritarian order (as in government) **b** *often capitalized* **:** a conservative position
9 a : a privilege given stockholders to subscribe pro rata to a new issue of securities generally below market price **b :** the negotiable certificate evidencing such privilege — usually used in plural
— **right·most** \-,mōst\ *adjective*
— **by rights :** with reason or justice **:** PROPERLY
— **in one's own right :** by virtue of one's own qualifications or properties
— **of right 1 :** as an absolute right **2 :** legally or morally exactable
— **to rights :** into proper order

³**right** *adverb* (before 12th century)
1 : according to right ⟨live *right*⟩
2 : in the exact location, position, or moment **:** PRECISELY ⟨*right* at his fingertips⟩ ⟨quit *right* then and there⟩
3 : in a suitable, proper, or desired manner ⟨knew he wasn't doing it *right*⟩
4 : in a direct line, course, or manner **:** DIRECTLY, STRAIGHT ⟨go *right* home⟩ ⟨came *right* out and said it⟩
5 : according to fact or truth **:** TRULY ⟨guessed *right*⟩
6 a : all the way ⟨windows *right* to the floor⟩ **b :** in a complete manner ⟨felt *right* at home⟩
7 : without delay **:** IMMEDIATELY ⟨*right* after lunch⟩
8 : to a great degree **:** VERY ⟨a *right* pleasant day⟩
9 : on or to the right ⟨looked left and *right*⟩

⁴**right** (before 12th century)
transitive verb
1 a : to do justice to **:** redress the injuries of ⟨so just is God to *right* the innocent —Shakespeare⟩ **b :** JUSTIFY, VINDICATE ⟨felt the need to *right* himself in court⟩
2 : AVENGE ⟨vows to *right* the injustice done to his family⟩

◇ WORD HISTORY
riffraff The word *riffraff* seems to represent a triumph of sound over sense, for it is a compound of two quite different words that have little semantic connection. In Middle French the verb *rifler* meant "to scratch" or "to plunder" and the noun *rafle* or *raffe* meant "the act of sweeping or snatching." From these words about the late 13th century the French contrived the phrase *rif et raf*, used to mean "completely," "altogether." Later variants such as *rifle ou* [or] *rafle* and *rif ny* [nor] *raf* show that the phrase most likely also meant "anything" or with a negative adverb "nothing." Medieval French *rif et raf* was thus borrowed into Middle English as *rif and raf*, in the sense "one and all, every single one." No doubt it was the lack of exclusivity implied by "every single one" that led to *ryffe raffe* being used in early Modern English as a collective noun for the multitude of people of the lowest or most disreputable sort.

3 a : to adjust or restore to the proper state or condition ⟨*right* the economy⟩ **b :** to bring or restore to an upright position ⟨*right* a capsized boat⟩
intransitive verb
: to become upright
— **right·er** *noun*
right and left *adverb* (1829)
: on both or all sides **:** in every direction **:** EVERYWHERE
right angle *noun* (15th century)
: the angle bounded by two lines perpendicular to each other **:** an angle of 90° or ½ π radians
— **right–an·gled** \'rīt-'aŋ-gəld\ *or* **right-an·gle** \-gəl\ *adjective*
right ascension *noun* (15th century)
: the arc of the celestial equator between the vernal equinox and the point where the hour circle through the given body intersects the equator reckoned eastward commonly in terms of the corresponding interval of sidereal time in hours, minutes, and seconds
right away *adverb* (1818)
: without delay or hesitation **:** IMMEDIATELY
right circular cone *noun* (circa 1889)
: CONE 1a
right circular cylinder *noun* (1877)
: a cylinder with the bases circular and with the axis joining the two centers of the bases perpendicular to the planes of the two bases

right·eous \'rī-chəs\ *adjective* [alteration of earlier *rightuous*, alteration of Middle English *rightwise*, *rightwos*, from Old English *rihtwīs*, from *riht*, *noun*, right + *wīs* wise] (1535)
1 : acting in accord with divine or moral law **:** free from guilt or sin
2 a : morally right or justifiable ⟨a *righteous* decision⟩ **b :** arising from an outraged sense of justice or morality ⟨*righteous* indignation⟩
3 *slang* **:** GENUINE, GOOD
synonym see MORAL
— **righ·teous·ly** *adverb*
— **righ·teous·ness** *noun*
right field *noun* (1857)
1 : the part of the baseball outfield to the right looking out from home plate
2 : the position of the player defending right field
— **right fielder** *noun*
right·ful \'rīt-fəl\ *adjective* (14th century)
1 : JUST, EQUITABLE
2 a : having a just or legally established claim **:** LEGITIMATE ⟨the *rightful* owner⟩ **b :** held by right or just claim **:** LEGAL ⟨*rightful* authority⟩
3 : PROPER, FITTING ⟨assured of his *rightful* place in history —Brian Duff⟩
— **right·ful·ly** \-fə-lē\ *adverb*
— **right·ful·ness** *noun*
right–hand \'rīt-,hand\ *adjective* (1592)
1 : situated on the right
2 : RIGHT-HANDED
3 : chiefly relied on ⟨*right-hand* man⟩
right hand *noun* (before 12th century)
1 a : the hand on a person's right side **b :** an indispensable person
2 a : the right side **b :** a place of honor
right–hand·ed \-'han-dəd\ *adjective* (14th century)
1 : using the right hand habitually or more easily than the left; *also* **:** swinging from right to left ⟨a *right-handed* batter⟩
2 : relating to, designed for, or done with the right hand
3 a : having the same direction or course as the movement of the hands of a watch viewed from in front **:** CLOCKWISE **b :** having a spiral structure or form that ascends or advances to

the right ⟨a *right-handed* screw⟩ ⟨a *right-handed* double helix of DNA⟩
4 *of a door* **:** opening to the right away from one
— **right–handed** *adverb*
— **right–hand·ed·ly** *adverb*
— **right–hand·ed·ness** *noun*
right–hand·er \-'han-dər\ *noun* (1857)
1 : a blow struck with the right hand
2 : a right-handed person; *especially* **:** a right-handed pitcher
right·ism \'rīt-,i-zəm\ *noun, often capitalized* (1939)
1 : the principles and views of the Right
2 : advocacy of or adherence to the doctrines of the Right
— **right·ist** \'rī-tist\ *noun or adjective, often capitalized*
right·ly \'rīt-lē\ *adverb* (before 12th century)
1 : in accordance with right conduct **:** FAIRLY, JUSTLY
2 : in the right or proper manner **:** PROPERLY, FITTINGLY
3 : according to truth or fact **:** CORRECTLY, EXACTLY
right–mind·ed \-'mīn-dəd\ *adjective* (circa 1586)
: having a right or honest mind ⟨a *right-minded* citizen⟩
— **right–mind·ed·ness** *noun*
right now *adverb* (14th century)
1 : RIGHT AWAY
2 : at present
righto \,rīt-'ō, 'rī-(,)tō\ *interjection* (1896)
— used to express cheerful concurrence, assent, or understanding
right off *adverb* (1790)
: RIGHT AWAY **:** at once
— **right off the bat :** RIGHT OFF
right–of–way \,rīt-ə(v)-'wā\ *noun, plural* **rights–of–way** *also* **right–of–ways** (1768)
1 : a legal right of passage over another person's ground
2 a : the area over which a right-of-way exists **b :** the strip of land over which is built a public road **c :** the land occupied by a railroad especially for its main line **d :** the land used by a public utility (as for a transmission line)
3 a : a precedence in passing accorded to one vehicle over another by custom, decision, or statute **b :** the right of traffic to take precedence **c :** the right to take precedence over others ⟨gave the bill the *right-of-way* in the Senate⟩
right on *adjective* (1925)
1 : exactly correct — often used interjectionally to express agreement
2 *usually* **right-on :** attuned to the spirit of the times
Right Reverend (15th century)
— used as a title for high ecclesiastical officials
right shoulder arms *noun* (1902)
: a position in the manual of arms in which the butt of the rifle is held in the right hand with the barrel resting on the right shoulder; *also* **:** a command to assume this position
right–to–life \'rīt-tə-'līf\ *adjective* (1973)
: opposed to abortion
— **right–to–lif·er** \-'lī-fər\ *noun*
right–to–work *adjective* (1949)
: opposing or banning the closed shop and the union shop
right triangle *noun* (1924)
: a triangle having a right angle — see TRIANGLE illustration
right·ward \'rīt-wərd\ *adverb* (1825)
: being toward or on the right
right whale *noun* (1725)
: any of a family (Balaenidae) of baleen whales having very long baleen, a large head on a stocky body, a smooth throat, and short broad rounded flippers
right wing *noun* (1905)
1 : the rightist division of a group or party

2 : RIGHT 8
— **right–wing** \'rīt-'wiŋ, -,wiŋ\ *adjective*
— **right–wing·er** \'rīt-'wiŋ-ər, ,rīt-\ *noun*
righty \'rī-tē\ *noun, plural* **right·ies** (1949)
: RIGHT-HANDER 2

right whale

rig·id \'ri-jəd\ *adjective* [Middle English *rigide*, from Middle French or Latin; Middle French, from Latin *rigidus*, from *rigēre* to be stiff] (15th century)
1 a : deficient in or devoid of flexibility ⟨*rigid* price controls⟩ ⟨a *rigid* bar of metal⟩ **b :** appearing stiff and unyielding ⟨his face *rigid* with pain⟩
2 a : inflexibly set in opinion **b :** strictly observed ⟨adheres to a *rigid* schedule⟩
3 : firmly inflexible rather than lax or indulgent ⟨a *rigid* disciplinarian⟩
4 : precise and accurate in procedure ⟨*rigid* control of the manufacturing process⟩
5 *of an airship* **:** having the outer shape maintained by a fixed framework ☆
— **rig·id·ly** *adverb*
— **rig·id·ness** *noun*
rig·id·i·fy \rə-'ji-də-,fī\ *verb* **-fied; -fy·ing** (1842)
transitive verb
: to make rigid
intransitive verb
: to become rigid
— **rig·id·i·fi·ca·tion** \-,ji-də-fə-'kā-shən\ *noun*
ri·gid·i·ty \rə-'ji-də-tē\ *noun, plural* **-ties** (1624)
1 : the quality or state of being rigid
2 : one that is rigid (as in form or conduct)
rig·ma·role \'ri-gə-mə-,rōl, 'rig-mə-\ *noun* [alteration of obsolete *ragman roll* long list, catalog] (circa 1736)
1 : confused or meaningless talk
2 : a complex and ritualistic procedure
rig·or \'ri-gər\ *noun* [Middle English *rigour*, from Middle French *rigueur*, from Latin *rigor*, literally, stiffness, from *rigēre* to be stiff] (14th century)
1 a (1) **:** harsh inflexibility in opinion, temper, or judgment **:** SEVERITY (2) **:** the quality of being unyielding or inflexible **:** STRICTNESS (3) **:** severity of life **:** AUSTERITY **b :** an act or instance of strictness, severity, or cruelty
2 : a tremor caused by a chill
3 : a condition that makes life difficult, challenging, or uncomfortable; *especially* **:** extremity of cold
4 : strict precision **:** EXACTNESS ⟨logical *rigor*⟩
5 a *obsolete* **:** RIGIDITY, STIFFNESS **b :** rigidness or torpor of organs or tissue that prevents response to stimuli
rig·or·ism \'ri-gə-,ri-zəm\ *noun* (1704)
: rigidity in principle or practice

☆ **SYNONYMS**
Rigid, rigorous, strict, stringent mean extremely severe or stern. RIGID implies uncompromising inflexibility ⟨*rigid* rules of conduct⟩. RIGOROUS implies the imposition of hardship and difficulty ⟨the *rigorous* training of recruits⟩. STRICT emphasizes undeviating conformity to rules, standards, or requirements ⟨*strict* enforcement of the law⟩. STRINGENT suggests severe, tight restriction or limitation ⟨*stringent* standards of admission⟩. See in addition STIFF.

— **rig·or·ist** \-rist\ *noun or adjective*
— **rig·or·is·tic** \ˌri-gə-ˈris-tik\ *adjective*
rig·or mor·tis \ˌri-gər-ˈmȯr-təs *also chiefly British* ˌrī-ˌgȯr-\ *noun* [New Latin, stiffness of death] (circa 1847)
: temporary rigidity of muscles occurring after death
rig·or·ous \ˈri-g(ə-)rəs\ *adjective* (15th century)
1 : manifesting, exercising, or favoring rigor : very strict
2 a : marked by extremes of temperature or climate **b** : HARSH, SEVERE
3 : scrupulously accurate : PRECISE
synonym see RIGID
— **rig·or·ous·ly** *adverb*
— **rig·or·ous·ness** *noun*
rig·our *chiefly British variant of* RIGOR
rijst·ta·fel \ˈrīs-ˌtä-fəl\ *noun* [Dutch, from *rijst* rice + *tafel* table] (1889)
: an Indonesian meal consisting of rice and a variety of accompanying dishes (as meat, seafood, and vegetables)
Riks·mål *or* **Riks·maal** \ˈriks-ˌmȯl, ˈrēks-\ *noun* [Norwegian, from *rik* kingdom + *mål* speech] (1913)
: BOKMÅL
rile \ˈrī(ə)l\ *transitive verb* **riled; ril·ing** [variant of *roil*] (1825)
1 : to make agitated and angry : UPSET
2 : ROIL 1 ◇
synonym see IRRITATE
ril·ey \ˈrī-lē\ *adjective* (1805)
1 : TURBID
2 : ANGRY
¹rill \ˈril\ *noun* [Dutch *ril* or Low German *rille;* akin to Old English *rīth* rivulet] (1538)
: a very small brook
²rill *intransitive verb* (1610)
: to flow like a rill
³rill \ˈril\ *or* **rille** \ˈril, ˈri-lə\ *noun* [German *Rille,* literally, channel made by a small stream, from Low German, rill] (1868)
: any of several long narrow valleys on the moon's surface
rill·et \ˈri-lət\ *noun* (1538)
: a little rill
ril·lettes \ri-ˈlets, -ˈyet\ *noun plural* [French, plural, diminutive of *rille,* singular, piece of pork, from Middle French, dialect variant of *reille* board, lath, from Latin *regula* straightedge — more at RULE] (1889)
: cooked shredded meat (as pork or duck) or fish preserved in fat
¹rim \ˈrim\ *noun* [Middle English, from Old English *rima;* akin to Old Norse *rimi* strip of land] (13th century)
1 a : BRINK **b** : the outer often curved or circular edge or border of something
2 a : the outer part of a wheel joined to the hub usually by spokes **b** : a removable outer metal band on an automobile wheel to which the tire is attached
3 : FRAME 4c(1)
— **rim·less** \-ləs\ *adjective*
²rim *verb* **rimmed; rim·ming** (1794)
transitive verb
1 : to serve as a rim for : BORDER ⟨cliffs *rimming* the camp⟩
2 : to run around the rim of ⟨putts that *rim* the cup⟩
intransitive verb
: to form or show a rim
¹rime \ˈrīm\ *noun* [Middle English *rim,* from Old English *hrīm;* akin to Old Norse *hrīm* frost] (before 12th century)
1 : FROST 1b
2 : an accumulation of granular ice tufts on the windward sides of exposed objects that is formed from supercooled fog or cloud and built out directly against the wind
3 : CRUST, INCRUSTATION ⟨a *rime* of snow⟩
²rime *transitive verb* **rimed; rim·ing** (circa 1755)
: to cover with or as if with rime

³rime, rime·ster *variant of* RHYME, RHYMESTER
rim·fire \ˈrim-ˌfīr\ *adjective* (1868)
of a cartridge : having the priming distributed in the rim of the shell
— **rimfire** *noun*
rim·land \ˈrim-ˌland\ *noun* (1944)
: a region on the periphery of the heartland
rimmed \ˈrimd\ *adjective* (1729)
: having a rim — usually used in combination ⟨dark-*rimmed* glasses⟩ ⟨red-*rimmed* eyes⟩
rim·rock \ˈrim-ˌräk\ *noun* (1860)
1 : a top stratum or overlying strata of resistant rock of a plateau that outcrops to form a vertical face
2 : the edge or face of a rimrock outcrop
rimy \ˈrī-mē\ *adjective* **rim·i·er; -est** [Old English *hrūmig,* from *hrūm*] (before 12th century)
: covered with rime : FROSTY
rind \ˈrīnd, *dialect* ˈrīn\ *noun* [Middle English, from Old English; akin to Old High German *rinda* bark, and probably to Old English *rendan* to rend] (before 12th century)
1 : the bark of a tree
2 : a usually hard or tough outer layer : PEEL, CRUST ⟨grated lemon *rind*⟩
— **rind·ed** \ˈrīn-dəd\ *adjective*
rin·der·pest \ˈrin-dər-ˌpest\ *noun* [German, from *Rinder,* plural, cattle + *Pest* pestilence] (1865)
: an acute infectious febrile disease of ruminant mammals (as cattle) that is caused by a virus and is marked by diarrhea and inflammation of mucous membranes
¹ring \ˈriŋ\ *noun* [Middle English, from Old English *hring;* akin to Old High German *hring* ring, Old Church Slavonic *krǫgŭ* circle] (before 12th century)
1 : a circular band for holding, connecting, hanging, pulling, packing, or sealing ⟨a key *ring*⟩ ⟨a towel *ring*⟩
2 : a circlet usually of precious metal worn on the finger
3 a : a circular line, figure, or object ⟨smoke *ring*⟩ **b** : an encircling arrangement ⟨a *ring* of suburbs⟩ **c** : a circular or spiral course — often used in plural in the phrase *run rings around*
4 a (1) : an often circular space especially for exhibitions or competitions; *especially* : such a space at a circus (2) : a structure containing such a ring **b** : a square enclosure in which boxers or wrestlers contest
5 : a band believed to be composed of rocky fragments revolving around a planet (as Saturn)
6 : ANNUAL RING
7 a : an exclusive combination of persons for a selfish and often corrupt purpose (as to control a market) ⟨a wheat *ring*⟩ **b** : GANG
8 : the field of a political contest : RACE
9 : food in the shape of a circle
10 : an arrangement of atoms represented in formulas or models in a cyclic manner — called also *cycle*
11 : a set of mathematical elements that is closed under two binary operations of which the first forms a commutative group with the set and the second is associative over the set and is distributive with respect to the first operation
12 *plural* **a** : a pair of usually rubber-covered metal rings suspended from a ceiling or crossbar to a height of approximately eight feet above the floor and used for hanging, swinging, and balancing feats in gymnastics **b** : an event in gymnastics competition in which the rings are used
13 : ²BOXING ⟨ended his *ring* career⟩
— **ring·like** \ˈriŋ-ˌlīk\ *adjective*
²ring *verb* **ringed; ring·ing** \ˈriŋ-iŋ\ (14th century)
transitive verb
1 : to provide with a ring

2 : to place or form a ring around : ENCIRCLE ⟨police *ringed* the building⟩
3 : GIRDLE 2
4 : to throw a ringer over (the peg) in a game (as horseshoes or quoits)
intransitive verb
1 a : to move in a ring **b** : to rise in the air spirally
2 : to form or take the shape of a ring
³ring *verb* **rang** \ˈraŋ\; **rung** \ˈrəŋ\; **ring·ing** \ˈriŋ-iŋ\ [Middle English, from Old English *hringan;* akin to Old Norse *hringja* to ring] (before 12th century)
intransitive verb
1 : to sound resonantly or sonorously ⟨the doorbell *rang*⟩ ⟨cheers *rang* out⟩
2 a : to be filled with a reverberating sound : RESOUND ⟨the halls *rang* with laughter⟩ **b** : to have the sensation of being filled with a humming sound ⟨his ears *rang*⟩
3 : to cause something to ring ⟨*ring* for the butler⟩
4 a : to be filled with talk or report ⟨the whole land *rang* with her fame⟩ **b** : to have great renown **c** : to sound repetitiously ⟨their praise *rang* in his ears⟩
5 : to have a sound or character expressive of some quality ⟨a story that *rings* true⟩
6 *chiefly British* : to make a telephone call — usually used with *up*
transitive verb
1 : to cause to sound especially by striking
2 : to make (a sound) by or as if by ringing a bell
3 : to announce by or as if by ringing
4 : to repeat often, loudly, or earnestly
5 a : to summon especially by bell **b** *chiefly British* : TELEPHONE — usually used with *up*
— **ring a bell** : to arouse a response ⟨that name *rings a bell*⟩
— **ring down the curtain** : to conclude a performance or an action
— **ring off the hook** : to ring frequently or constantly with incoming calls ⟨the telephone was *ringing off the hook*⟩
— **ring the changes** *or* **ring changes** : to run through the range of possible variations
— **ring up the curtain** : to begin a performance or an action
⁴ring *noun* (1549)
1 : a set of bells
2 : a clear resonant sound made by or resembling that made by vibrating metal
3 : resonant tone : SONORITY

◇ **WORD HISTORY**
rile English words that now have the sound \ȯi\ such as *boil* and *voice* fall into two major groups of distinct historical origin. The diphthong (vowel combination) of the *voice* group had a sound in early Modern English nearly the same as present-day \ȯi\; the *boil* group, on the other hand, had a sound close to \əi\. Because the \əi\ sound of the *boil* words was virtually identical to the sound that *i* had come to acquire in words such as *price* and *write,* the two merged, so that *boil* rhymed with *bile* and *toil* with *tile.* This pronunciation remained standard into the 18th century, though literate people, under the influence of English spelling, had begun to pronounce *boil* and *toil* with the diphthong of *toy* and *choice.* By the 19th century, standard pronunciation had shifted completely, and spellings such as *pizen* or *pison* for *poison* were used by Mark Twain and other American authors to characterize uneducated rural speech. The word *roil* underwent a unique development: in the sense "to make angry" it was disassociated from the spelling *roil* and written *rile,* becoming thereby a different word. Originally a colloquialism, it has since become standard written English.

4 : a loud sound continued, repeated, or reverberated

5 : a sound or character expressive of some particular quality ⟨the story had a familiar *ring*⟩

6 a : the act or an instance of ringing **b** : a telephone call ⟨give me a *ring* in the morning⟩

ring·a·le·vio \ˌriŋ-ə-'lē-vē-ˌō\ *or* **ring–a–lie·vo** \-'lē-(ˌ)vō\ *noun* [alteration of earlier *ring relievo*, from ¹*ring* + *relieve*] (circa 1901)
: a game in which players on one team are given time to hide and are then sought out by members of the other team who try to capture them, keep them in a place of confinement, and keep them from being released by their teammates

ring–around–a–rosy \ˌriŋ-ə-ˌraun-də-'rō-zē\ *or* **ring–around–the–rosy** \-ˌraun(d)-thə-\ *noun* (circa 1886)
: a children's singing game in which players dance around in a circle and at a given signal squat — called also *ring-a-rosy* \ˌriŋ-ə-'rō-zē\

ring·bark \'riŋ-ˌbärk\ *transitive verb* (1892)
: GIRDLE 2

ring binder *noun* (1929)
: a loose-leaf binder in which split metal rings attached to a metal back hold the perforated sheets of paper

ring·bolt \'riŋ-ˌbōlt\ *noun* (1599)
: an eyebolt with a ring through its eye

ring·bone \-ˌbōn\ *noun* (1523)
: a bony outgrowth on the pastern bones of the horse usually producing lameness

ring dance *noun* (1600)
: ROUND DANCE 1

ring·dove \'riŋ-ˌdəv\ *noun* (1538)
1 : a chiefly European pigeon (*Columba palumbus*) with a whitish patch on each side of the neck and wings edged with white
2 : a small dove (*Streptopelia risoria*) of southeastern Europe and Asia — called also *ringed turtle dove*

ringed \'riŋd\ *adjective* (14th century)
1 : encircled or marked with or as if with rings
2 : composed or formed of rings

¹ring·er \'riŋ-ər\ *noun* (15th century)
1 : one that sounds especially by ringing
2 a (1) : one that enters a competition under false representations (2) : IMPOSTER, FAKE **b** : one that strongly resembles another — often used with *dead* ⟨he's a dead *ringer* for the senator⟩

²ringer *noun* (1863)
: one that encircles or puts a ring around (as a quoit or horseshoe that lodges so as to surround the peg)

Ring·er's solution \'riŋ-ərz-\ *noun* [Sidney Ringer (died 1910) English physician] (1893)
: a balanced aqueous solution that contains chloride, sodium, potassium, calcium, bicarbonate, and phosphate ions and that is used in physiological experiments to provide a medium essentially isotonic to many animal tissues — called also *Ringer solution*

ring finger *noun* (before 12th century)
: the third finger especially of the left hand counting the forefinger as the first

ring·git \'riŋ-git\ *noun, plural* **ringgit** *or* **ringgits** [Malay, literally, toothed, serrated] (1967)
— see MONEY table

ring·ing \'riŋ-iŋ\ *adjective* (14th century)
1 : clear and full in tone : RESOUNDING ⟨a *ringing* baritone⟩
2 : vigorously unequivocal : DECISIVE ⟨a *ringing* condemnation of immorality⟩
— **ring·ing·ly** \-iŋ-lē\ *adverb*

ring·lead·er \'riŋ-ˌlē-dər\ *noun* (1503)
: a leader of a ring of individuals engaged especially in improper or unlawful activities

ring·let \'riŋ-lət\ *noun* (1555)
1 : a small ring or circle
2 : CURL; *especially* : a long curl of hair

ring·mas·ter \'riŋ-ˌmas-tər\ *noun* (1873)

: one in charge of performances in a ring (as of a circus); *broadly* : a supervisor or moderator especially of a performance or presentation

ring·neck \-ˌnek\ *noun* (1791)
: a ring-necked animal

ring–necked \'riŋ-ˌnekt\ *or* **ring–neck** \'riŋ-ˌnek\ *adjective* (1817)
: having a ring of color about the neck

ring–necked duck *noun* (1831)
: an American scaup duck (*Aythya collaris*) that has a white ring around the bill and in the male a faint narrow chestnut ring encircling the neck

ring–necked pheasant *noun* (1834)
: a Eurasian pheasant (*Phasianus colchicus*) that has been widely introduced as a game bird in North America and that has a white neck ring and an iridescent green and purplish head with red wattles around the eyes

ring-necked pheasant

ring off *intransitive verb* (1882)
chiefly British : HANG UP 1

ring–po·rous \'riŋ-ˌpōr-əs, -ˌpȯr-\ *adjective* (1902)
: having vessels more numerous and usually larger in cross section in the springwood with a resulting more or less distinct line between the springwood and the last season's wood — compare DIFFUSE-POROUS

ring road *noun* (1928)
chiefly British : a highway skirting an urban area

¹ring·side \'riŋ-ˌsīd\ *noun* (1866)
1 : the area just outside a ring especially in which a contest occurs
2 : a place from which one may have a close view

²ringside *adjective* (1896)
: being at the ringside ⟨a *ringside* seat⟩

ring spot *noun* (1923)
1 : a lesion of plant tissue consisting of yellowish, purplish, or necrotic, often concentric rings
2 : a viral disease of plants that is characterized by ring spots

ring stand *noun* (circa 1865)
: a metal stand consisting of a long upright rod attached to a heavy rectangular base that is used with rings and clamps for supporting laboratory apparatus

ring–straked \'riŋ-ˌstrākt\ *adjective* (1611)
archaic : marked with circular stripes

ring·tail \-ˌtāl\ *noun* (1844)
1 : RACCOON
2 : a carnivore (*Bassariscus astutus*) of the western U.S. and Mexico that is related to and resembles the raccoon — called also *cacomistle, civet cat, ringtail cat, ringtailed cat*
3 : CAPUCHIN 3

ring–tailed \-ˌtā(ə)ld\ *adjective* (1729)
1 : having a tail marked with rings of differing colors
2 : having a tail carried in a form approximating a circle ⟨a *ring-tailed* Afghan hound⟩

ring·taw \-ˌtȯ\ *noun* (1828)
: a game of marbles in which marbles are placed in a circle on the ground and shot at from the edge of the circle with the object being to knock them out of the circle

ring·toss \-ˌtȯs, -ˌtäs\ *noun* (1871)
: a game in which the object is to toss a ring so that it will fall over an upright stick

ring up *transitive verb* (1937)
1 : to total and record especially by means of a cash register
2 : ACHIEVE ⟨*rang up* many social triumphs⟩

ring·worm \'riŋ-ˌwərm\ *noun* (15th century)
: any of several contagious fungal diseases of the skin, hair, or nails of humans and domestic

animals that are characterized by ring-shaped discolored skin patches covered with vesicles and scales

rink \'riŋk\ *noun* [Middle English (Scots) *rinc* area in which a contest takes place, from Middle French *renc* place, row — more at RANK] (1787)
1 a : a smooth extent of ice marked off for curling or ice hockey **b** : a surface of ice for ice-skating; *also* : a building containing such a rink **c** : an enclosure for roller-skating
2 : an alley for lawn bowling
3 : a team in bowls or curling

rinky–dink \'riŋ-kē-ˌdiŋk\ *adjective* [origin unknown] (1913)
1 : SMALL-TIME
2 : OLD-FASHIONED

¹rinse \'rin(t)s, *especially dialect* 'rench\ *transitive verb* **rinsed; rins·ing** [Middle English *rincen*, from Middle French *rincer*, from (assumed) Vulgar Latin *recentiare*, from Latin *recent-, recens* fresh, recent] (14th century)
1 : to cleanse by flushing with liquid (as water) — often used with *out* ⟨*rinse* out the mouth⟩
2 a : to cleanse (as of soap used in washing) by clear water **b** : to treat (hair) with a rinse
3 : to remove (dirt or impurities) by washing lightly or in water only
— **rins·er** *noun*

²rinse *noun* (1837)
1 : the act or process of rinsing
2 a : liquid used for rinsing **b** : a solution that temporarily tints hair

rins·ing *noun* (1818)
1 : DREGS, RESIDUE — usually used in plural
2 : water that has been used for rinsing — usually used in plural

rio·ja \rē-'ō-(ˌ)hä\ *noun, often capitalized* (1907)
: a wine from the Rioja region of Spain; *especially* : a dry red wine from this region

¹ri·ot \'rī-ət\ *noun* [Middle English, from Old French, dispute, from *rioter* to quarrel] (13th century)
1 *archaic* **a** : profligate behavior : DEBAUCHERY **b** : unrestrained revelry **c** : noise, uproar, or disturbance made by revelers
2 a : public violence, tumult, or disorder **b** : a violent public disorder; *specifically* : a tumultuous disturbance of the public peace by three or more persons assembled together and acting with a common intent
3 : a random or disorderly profusion ⟨the woods were a *riot* of color⟩
4 : one that is wildly amusing ⟨the new comedy is a *riot*⟩

²riot *intransitive verb* (14th century)
1 : to indulge in revelry or wantonness
2 : to create or engage in a riot
— **ri·ot·er** *noun*

riot act *noun* [the *Riot Act*, English law of 1715 providing for the dispersal of riots upon command of legal authority] (1819)
: a vigorous reprimand or warning — used in the phrase *read the riot act*

riot gun *noun* (1916)
: a small arm used to disperse rioters rather than to inflict serious injury or death; *especially* : a short-barreled shotgun

ri·ot·ous \'rī-ə-təs\ *adjective* (15th century)
1 a : of the nature of a riot : TURBULENT **b** : participating in riot
2 : ABUNDANT, EXUBERANT ⟨the garden was *riotous* with flowers⟩
— **ri·ot·ous·ly** *adverb*
— **ri·ot·ous·ness** *noun*

¹rip \'rip\ *verb* **ripped; rip·ping** [probably from Flemish *rippen* to strip off roughly] (15th century)

\ə\ abut \ᵊ\ kitten \ər\ further \a\ ash \ā\ ace
\ä\ mop, mar \au̇\ out \ch\ chin \e\ bet \ē\ easy
\g\ go \i\ hit \ī\ ice \j\ job \ŋ\ sing \ō\ go
\ȯ\ law \ȯi\ boy \th\ thin \th\ the \ü\ loot \u̇\ foot
\y\ yet \zh\ vision *see also* Guide to Pronunciation

transitive verb
1 a : to tear or split apart or open **b :** to saw or split (wood) with the grain
2 : to slash or slit with or as if with a sharp blade
3 : to hit sharply ⟨*ripped* a double to left field⟩
4 : to utter violently **:** spit out ⟨*ripped* out an oath⟩
5 : CRITICIZE, PUT DOWN
intransitive verb
1 : to become ripped **:** REND
2 : to rush headlong ⟨*ripped* past second base⟩
synonym see TEAR
— **rip into :** to tear into **:** ATTACK
²rip *noun* (1711)
1 : a rent made by ripping **:** TEAR
2 : CUT 5b
³rip *noun* [perhaps from ²*rip*] (1775)
1 : a body of water made rough by the meeting of opposing tides, currents, or winds
2 : a current of water roughened by passing over an irregular bottom
3 : RIP CURRENT
⁴rip *noun* [perhaps by shortening & alteration from *reprobate*] (1797)
: a dissolute person **:** LIBERTINE
ri·par·i·an \rə-'per-ē-ən, rī-\ *adjective* [Latin *riparius* — more at RIVER] (circa 1841)
: relating to or living or located on the bank of a natural watercourse (as a river) or sometimes of a lake or a tidewater
riparian right *noun* (circa 1860)
: a right (as access to or use of the shore, bed, and water) of one owning riparian land
rip cord *noun* (1907)
1 : a cord by which the gasbag of a balloon may be ripped open for a limited distance to release the gas quickly and so cause immediate descent
2 : a cord or wire pulled in making a descent to release the pilot parachute which lifts the main parachute out of its container
rip current *noun* (1936)
: a strong usually narrow surface current flowing outward from a shore that results from the return flow of waves and wind-driven water
ripe \'rīp\ *adjective* **rip·er; rip·est** [Middle English, from Old English *rīpe;* akin to Old English *rīpan, reopan* to reap] (before 12th century)
1 : fully grown and developed **:** MATURE
2 : having mature knowledge, understanding, or judgment
3 : of advanced years **:** LATE ⟨lived to a *ripe* old age⟩
4 a : SUITABLE, APPROPRIATE ⟨the time seemed *ripe* for the experiment⟩ **b :** fully prepared **:** READY ⟨the colonies were *ripe* for revolution⟩
5 a : brought by aging to full flavor or the best state **:** MELLOW ⟨*ripe* cheese⟩ **b :** SMELLY, STINKING
6 : ruddy, plump, or full like ripened fruit
7 : INDECENT ⟨*ripe* language⟩
— **ripe·ly** *adverb*
— **ripe·ness** *noun*
rip·en \'rī-pən, 'rī-pᵊm\ *verb* **rip·ened; rip·en·ing** \'rī-pə-niŋ, 'rīp-niŋ\ (1561)
intransitive verb
: to grow or become ripe
transitive verb
1 : to make ripe
2 a : to bring to completeness or perfection **b :** to age or cure (cheese) to develop characteristic flavor, odor, body, texture, and color **c :** to improve flavor and tenderness of (beef or game) by aging under refrigeration
— **rip·en·er** \'rī-pə-nər, 'rīp-nər\ *noun*
ri·pie·no \ri-'pyā-(ˌ)nō, -'pye-\ *noun, plural* **-ni** \-(ˌ)nē\ *or* **-nos** [Italian, literally, filled up] (circa 1930)
: TUTTI
rip-off \'rip-ˌóf\ *noun* (1969)
1 : an act or instance of stealing **:** THEFT; *also* **:** a financial exploitation
2 : a usually cheap exploitive imitation
rip off *transitive verb* (1967)

1 a : ROB; *also* **:** CHEAT, DEFRAUD **b :** STEAL
2 : to copy or imitate blatantly or unscrupulously
3 : to perform, achieve, or score quickly or easily ⟨*ripped off* 10 straight points⟩
ri·poste \ri-'pōst\ *noun* [French, modification of Italian *risposta,* literally, answer, from *rispondere* to respond, from Latin *respondēre*] (1707)
1 : a fencer's quick return thrust following a parry
2 : a retaliatory verbal sally **:** RETORT
3 : a retaliatory maneuver or measure
— **riposte** *verb*
ripped \'ript\ *adjective* (1970)
slang **:** being under the influence of alcohol or drugs **:** HIGH, STONED
rip·per \'ri-pər\ *noun* (1611)
1 : one that rips; *especially* **:** a machine used to break up solid material (as rock or ore)
2 : an excellent example or instance of its kind
rip·ping \'ri-piŋ\ *adjective* [probably from present participle of ¹*rip*] (1846)
chiefly British **:** EXCELLENT, DELIGHTFUL ⟨wrote me some *ripping* letters⟩ ⟨had a *ripping* time⟩
¹rip·ple \'ri-pəl\ *verb* **rip·pled; rip·pling** \-p(ə-)liŋ\ [perhaps frequentative of ¹*rip*] (circa 1671)
intransitive verb
1 a : to become lightly ruffled or covered with small waves **b :** to flow in small waves **c :** to fall in soft undulating folds ⟨the scarf *rippled* to the floor⟩
2 : to flow with a light rise and fall of sound or inflection ⟨laughter *rippled* over the audience⟩
3 : to move with an undulating motion or so as to cause ripples ⟨the canoe *rippled* through the water⟩
4 : to have or produce a ripple effect **:** SPREAD ⟨the news *rippled* outwards⟩
transitive verb
1 : to stir up small waves on
2 : to impart a wavy motion or appearance to ⟨*rippling* his arm muscles⟩
3 : to utter or play with a slight rise and fall of sound
— **rip·pler** \-p(ə-)lər\ *noun*
²ripple *noun* (1755)
1 a : a shallow stretch of rough water in a stream **b** (1) **:** the ruffling of the surface of water (2) **:** a small wave
2 a : RIPPLE MARK **b :** a sound like that of rippling water ⟨a *ripple* of laughter⟩ **c :** a usually slight noticeable effect or reaction
— **rip·ply** \'ri-p(ə-)lē\ *adjective*
ripple effect *noun* (1966)
: a spreading, pervasive, and usually unintentional effect or influence ⟨the automotive industry has a *ripple effect* on many other industries⟩ — compare DOMINO EFFECT
ripple mark *noun* (1833)
1 : one of a series of small ridges produced especially on sand by the action of wind, a current of water, or waves
2 : a striation across the grain of wood especially on the tangential surface
— **rip·ple-marked** \'ri-pəl-ˌmärkt\ *adjective*
¹rip·rap \'rip-ˌrap\ *noun* [obsolete *riprap* sound of rapping] (1833)
1 : a foundation or sustaining wall of stones or chunks of concrete thrown together without order (as in deep water); *also* **:** a layer of this or similar material on an embankment slope to prevent erosion
2 : material used for riprap
²riprap *transitive verb* (1848)
1 : to form a riprap in or upon
2 : to strengthen or support with a riprap
rip-roar·ing \'rip-'rōr-iŋ, -'rór-\ *adjective* (1834)
: noisily excited or exciting
rip·saw \'rip-ˌsó\ *noun* (1846)

: a coarse-toothed saw used to cut wood in the direction of the grain — compare CROSSCUT SAW
rip·snort·er \'rip-'snór-tər\ *noun* (1840)
: something extraordinary **:** HUMDINGER ⟨the finale was a *ripsnorter*⟩
— **rip·snort·ing** \-tiŋ\ *adjective*
rip·stop \'rip-ˌstäp\ *adjective* (1949)
: of, relating to, or being a fabric woven with a double thread at regular intervals so that small tears do not spread ⟨*ripstop* nylon⟩
— **ripstop** *noun*
rip·tide \'rip-ˌtīd\ *noun* (1862)
: RIP CURRENT
Rip·u·ar·i·an \ˌri-pyə-'wer-ē-ən\ *adjective* [Medieval Latin *Ripuarius*] (1781)
: of, relating to, or constituting a group of Franks settling in the 4th century on the Rhine near Cologne
Rip van Win·kle \ˌrip-(ˌ)van-'wiŋ-kəl, -vən-\ *noun*
: a ne'er-do-well in a story in Washington Irving's *Sketch Book* who sleeps for 20 years
¹rise \'rīz\ *intransitive verb* **rose** \'rōz\; **ris·en** \'ri-zᵊn\; **ris·ing** \'rī-ziŋ\ [Middle English, from Old English *rīsan;* akin to Old High German *rīsan* to rise] (before 12th century)
1 a : to assume an upright position especially from lying, kneeling, or sitting **b :** to get up from sleep or from one's bed
2 : to return from death
3 : to take up arms ⟨*rise* in rebellion⟩
4 : to respond warmly **:** APPLAUD — usually used with *to* ⟨the audience *rose* to her verve and wit⟩
5 *chiefly British* **:** to end a session **:** ADJOURN
6 : to appear above the horizon ⟨the sun *rises* at six⟩
7 a : to move upward **:** ASCEND **b :** to increase in height, size, or volume ⟨the river *rose* after the heavy rains⟩
8 : to extend above other objects ⟨mountain peaks *rose* to the west⟩
9 a : to become heartened or elated ⟨his spirits *rose*⟩ **b :** to increase in fervor or intensity ⟨my anger *rose* as I thought about the insult⟩
10 a : to attain a higher level or rank ⟨officers who *rose* from the ranks⟩ **b :** to increase in quantity or number
11 a : to take place **:** HAPPEN **b :** to come into being **:** ORIGINATE
12 : to follow as a consequence **:** RESULT
13 : to exert oneself to meet a challenge ⟨*rise* to the occasion⟩
synonym see SPRING
²rise \'rīz *also* 'rīs\ *noun* (15th century)
1 a : a spot higher than surrounding ground **:** HILLTOP **b :** an upward slope ⟨a *rise* in the road⟩
2 : an act of rising or a state of being risen: as **a :** a movement upward **:** ASCENT **b :** emergence (as of the sun) above the horizon **c :** the upward movement of a fish to seize food or bait
3 : BEGINNING, ORIGIN ⟨the river had its *rise* in the mountain⟩
4 : the distance or elevation of one point above another
5 a : an increase especially in amount, number, or volume **b** *chiefly British* **:** RAISE 3b **c :** an increase in price, value, rate, or sum ⟨a *rise* in the cost of living⟩
6 : an angry reaction ⟨got a *rise* out of him⟩
7 : the distance from the crotch to the waistline on pants
ris·er \'rī-zər\ *noun* (15th century)
1 : one that rises (as from sleep)
2 : the upright member between two stair treads
3 : a stage platform on which performers are placed for greater visibility
4 : a vertical pipe (as for water or gas) or a vertical portion of an electric wiring system
5 : one of the straps that connects a parachutist's harness with the shroud lines

ris·i·bil·i·ty \,ri-zə-'bi-lə-tē\ *noun, plural* **-ties** (1620)
1 : LAUGHTER
2 : the ability or inclination to laugh — often used in plural ⟨our *risibilities* support us as we skim over the surface of a deep issue —J. A. Pike⟩

ris·i·ble \'ri-zə-bəl\ *adjective* [Late Latin *risibilis,* from Latin *risus,* past participle of *ridēre* to laugh] (1557)
1 a : capable of laughing **b** : disposed to laugh
2 : arousing or provoking laughter; *especially* : LAUGHABLE
3 : associated with, relating to, or used in laughter ⟨*risible* muscles⟩

ris·i·bles \-bəlz\ *noun plural* (1785)
: sense of the ridiculous : sense of humor

¹ris·ing \'rī-ziŋ\ *noun* (14th century)
: INSURRECTION, UPRISING

²rising *adverb* (circa 1772)
: approaching a stated age : NEARLY ⟨a red cow *rising* four years old —*Lancaster (Pennsylvania) Journal*⟩

rising diphthong *noun* (1888)
: a diphthong in which the second element is more sonorous than the first (as \wi\ in \'kwit\ *quit*)

rising rhythm *noun* (1881)
: rhythm with stress occurring regularly on the last syllable of each foot — compare FALLING RHYTHM

¹risk \'risk\ *noun* [French *risque,* from Italian *risco*] (circa 1661)
1 : possibility of loss or injury : PERIL
2 : someone or something that creates or suggests a hazard
3 a : the chance of loss or the perils to the subject matter of an insurance contract; *also* : the degree of probability of such loss **b** : a person or thing that is a specified hazard to an insurer ⟨a poor *risk* for insurance⟩ **c** : an insurance hazard from a specified cause or source ⟨war *risk*⟩
— risk·less \'ris-kləs\ *adjective*
— at risk : exposed to a usually specified danger or loss ⟨patients *at risk* of infection⟩

²risk *transitive verb* (circa 1687)
1 : to expose to hazard or danger ⟨*risked* her life⟩
2 : to incur the risk or danger of ⟨*risked* breaking his neck⟩
— risk·er *noun*

risk capital *noun* (1944)
: VENTURE CAPITAL

risky \'ris-kē\ *adjective* **risk·i·er; -est** (1827)
: attended with risk or danger : HAZARDOUS
synonym see DANGEROUS
— risk·i·ness *noun*

ri·sor·gi·men·to \(,)rē-,zȯr-ji-'men-(,)tō, -,sȯr-\ *noun, plural* **-tos** [Italian, literally, rising again, from *risorgere* to rise again, from Latin *resurgere* — more at RESURRECTION] (1902)
: a time of renewal or renaissance : REVIVAL; *specifically* : the 19th century movement for Italian political unity

ri·sot·to \ri-'sȯ-(,)tō, -'zȯ-\ *noun, plural* **-tos** [Italian, from *riso* rice — more at RICE] (1855)
: rice cooked in meat stock and seasoned (as with Parmesan cheese or saffron)

ris·qué \ri-'skā\ *adjective* [French, from past participle of *risquer* to risk, from *risque*] (1867)
: verging on impropriety or indecency : OFF-COLOR

Rit·a·lin \'ri-tə-lən\ *trademark*
— used for methylphenidate

ri·tard \ri-'tärd\ *noun* (circa 1890)
: RITARDANDO

¹ri·tar·dan·do \ri-,tär-'dän-(,)dō, -,rē-\ *adverb or adjective* [Italian, from Latin *retardandum,* gerund of *retardare* to retard] (circa 1811)
: with a gradual slackening in tempo — used as a direction in music

²ritardando *noun, plural* **-dos** (1889)

: a ritardando passage

rite \'rīt\ *noun* [Middle English, from Latin *ritus;* akin to Greek *arithmos* number — more at ARITHMETIC] (14th century)
1 a : a prescribed form or manner governing the words or actions for a ceremony **b** : the liturgy of a church or group of churches
2 : a ceremonial act or action ⟨initiation *rites*⟩
3 : a division of the Christian church using a distinctive liturgy

rite de pas·sage \,rēt-də-pa-'säzh, -pä-\ *noun, plural* **rites de passage** \,rēt(s)-də-\ [French] (1911)
: RITE OF PASSAGE

rite of passage (1909)
: a ritual associated with a crisis or a change of status (as marriage, illness, or death) for an individual

ri·tor·nel·lo \,ri-tər-'ne-(,)lō, ,ri-,tȯr-\ *noun, plural* **-nel·li** \-'ne-(,)lē\ *or* **-nellos** [Italian, diminutive of *ritorno* return, from *ritornare* to return, from *ri-* re- + *tornare* to turn, from Latin, to turn on a lathe — more at TURN] (1675)
1 a : a short recurrent instrumental passage in a vocal composition **b** : an instrumental interlude in early opera
2 : a tutti passage in a concerto or rondo refrain

¹rit·u·al \'ri-chə-wəl, -chəl; 'rich-wəl\ *adjective* [Latin *ritualis,* from *ritus* rite] (1570)
1 : of or relating to rites or a ritual : CEREMONIAL ⟨a *ritual* dance⟩
2 : according to religious law or social custom ⟨*ritual* purity⟩
— rit·u·al·ly *adverb*

²ritual *noun* (1649)
1 : the established form for a ceremony; *specifically* : the order of words prescribed for a religious ceremony
2 a : ritual observance; *specifically* : a system of rites **b** : a ceremonial act or action **c** : a customarily repeated often formal act or series of acts

rit·u·al·ism \'ri-chə-wə-,li-zəm, -chə-,li-; 'rich-wə-\ *noun* (1843)
1 : the use of ritual
2 : excessive devotion to ritual
— rit·u·al·ist \-list\ *noun*
— rit·u·al·is·tic \,ri-chə-wə-'lis-tik, -chə-'lis-; ,rich-wə-\ *adjective*
— rit·u·al·is·ti·cal·ly \-ti-k(ə-)lē\ *adverb*

rit·u·al·ize \-,līz\ *verb* **-ized; -iz·ing** (1842)
intransitive verb
: to practice ritualism
transitive verb
1 : to make a ritual of
2 : to impose a ritual on
— rit·u·al·i·za·tion \,ri-chə-wə-lə-'zā-shən, -chə-lə-; ,rich-wə-\ *noun*

ritzy \'rit-sē\ *adjective* **ritz·i·er; -est** [*Ritz* hotels, noted for their opulence] (1920)
1 : SNOBBISH
2 : ostentatiously smart : FASHIONABLE, POSH
— ritz·i·ness *noun*

¹ri·val \'rī-vəl\ *noun* [Middle French or Latin; Middle French, from Latin *rivalis* one using the same stream as another, rival in love, from *rivalis* of a stream, from *rivus* stream — more at RUN] (1577)
1 a : one of two or more striving to reach or obtain something that only one can possess **b** : one striving for competitive advantage
2 *obsolete* : COMPANION, ASSOCIATE
3 : one that equals another in desired qualities : PEER ◇

²rival *adjective* (1590)
: having the same pretensions or claims : COMPETING

³rival *verb* **ri·valed** *or* **ri·valled; ri·val·ing** *or* **ri·val·ling** \'rīv-(ə-)liŋ\ (1605)
intransitive verb
: to act as a rival : COMPETE
transitive verb
1 : to be in competition with
2 : to strive to equal or excel : EMULATE

3 : to possess qualities or aptitudes that approach or equal (those of another)

ri·val·rous \'rī-vəl-rəs\ *adjective* (1812)
: given to rivalry : COMPETITIVE

ri·val·ry \'rī-vəl-rē\ *noun, plural* **-ries** (1598)
: the act of rivaling : the state of being a rival : COMPETITION

rive \'rīv\ *verb* **rived** \'rīvd\; **riv·en** \'ri-vən\ *also* **rived; riv·ing** \'rī-viŋ\ [Middle English, from Old Norse *rīfa;* akin to Greek *ereipein* to tear down] (14th century)
transitive verb
1 a : to wrench open or tear apart or to pieces : REND **b** : to split with force or violence ⟨lightning *rived* the tree⟩
2 a : to divide into pieces : SHATTER **b** : FRACTURE
intransitive verb
: to become split : CRACK
synonym see TEAR

riv·er \'ri-vər\ *noun, often attributive* [Middle English *rivere,* from Old French, from (assumed) Vulgar Latin *riparia,* from Latin, feminine of *riparius* riparian, from *ripa* bank, shore; perhaps akin to Greek *ereipein* to tear down] (14th century)
1 a : a natural stream of water of usually considerable volume **b** : WATERCOURSE
2 a : something resembling a river ⟨a *river* of lava⟩ **b** *plural* : large or overwhelming quantities ⟨drank *rivers* of coffee⟩
word history see RIVAL
— up the river : to or in prison ⟨takes the rap and goes *up the river* —Nigel Balchin⟩

riv·er·bank \'ri-vər-,baŋk\ *noun* (1565)
: the bank of a river

riv·er·bed \-,bed\ *noun* (1833)
: the channel occupied by a river

river blindness *noun* (1953)
: ONCHOCERCIASIS

riv·er·boat \-,bōt\ *noun* (1565)
: a boat for use on a river

river duck *noun* (1837)
: DABBLER b

riv·er·front \-,frənt\ *noun* (1855)
: the land or area along a river

river horse *noun* (1601)
: HIPPOPOTAMUS

riv·er·ine \'ri-və-,rīn, -,rēn\ *adjective* (1860)
1 : relating to, formed by, or resembling a river
2 : living or situated on the banks of a river

riv·er·side \'ri-vər-,sīd\ *noun* (14th century)

◇ WORD HISTORY
rival *Rival* is borrowed, directly or indirectly through French, from Latin *rivalis,* which, as an adjective derivative of *rivus* "brook or stream," meant "of a brook or stream." As a noun, *rivalis* occurs only in its plural forms in Latin texts, referring literally to those who used the same stream as a source of water. Just as neighbors are likely to dispute each other's rights to a common source of water, so too contention is inevitable when two or more persons strive to obtain something that only one can possess. Thus Latin *rivalis* also developed a sense relating to competition in other areas, especially love, and in this sense it came into French and English. Despite its aquatic background, *rival* is unrelated to *river,* which descends ultimately not from Latin *rivus,* but rather from an unrelated word *ripa* "bank, shore." The Old French word *rivere* or *riviere* (from an unattested spoken Latin word *riparia*) meant "riverbank" or "land along a river" as well as "watercourse, stream."

: the side or bank of a river

riv·er·ward \-wərd\ *or* **riv·er·wards** \-wərdz\ *adverb or adjective* (1833)
: toward a river

¹riv·et \'ri-vət\ *noun* [Middle English *ryvette*, from Middle French *rivet*, from *river* to attach] (15th century)
: a headed pin or bolt of metal used for uniting two or more pieces by passing the shank through a hole in each piece and then beating or pressing down the plain end so as to make a second head

²rivet *transitive verb* (15th century)
1 : to fasten with or as if with rivets
2 : to upset the end or point of (as a metallic pin, rod, or bolt) by beating or pressing so as to form a head
3 : to fasten firmly ⟨they *rivet* these feelings . . . tightly together —Michael Novak⟩
4 : to attract and hold (as the attention) completely
— **riv·et·er** *noun*

riv·et·ing \'ri-və-tiŋ\ *adjective* (1677)
: having the power to fix the attention : ENGROSSING, FASCINATING
— **riv·et·ing·ly** \-lē\ *adverb*

riv·i·era \ˌri-vē-'er-ə, ri-'vyer-\ *noun, often capitalized* [from the *Riviera*, region in southeastern France and northwestern Italy] (1766)
: a coastal region frequented as a resort area and usually marked by a mild climate

ri·vi·ère \ˌri-vē-'er, ri-'vyer\ *noun* [French, literally, river, from Old French *rivere*] (1879)
: a necklace of precious stones (as diamonds)

riv·u·let \'ri-vyə-lət, -və-\ *noun* [Italian *rivoletto*, diminutive of *rivolo*, from Latin *rivulus*, diminutive of *rivus* stream — more at RUN] (1587)
: a small stream

¹ri·yal \rē-'yäl, -'yal\ *noun* [Arabic *riyāl*, from Spanish *real* real] (1928)
— see MONEY table

²riyal *variant of* RIAL

RN \ˌär-'en\ *noun* (1903)
: REGISTERED NURSE

RNA \ˌär-(ˌ)en-'ā\ *noun* [ribonucleic acid] (1948)
: any of various nucleic acids that contain ribose and uracil as structural components and are associated with the control of cellular chemical activities — compare MESSENGER RNA, RIBOSOMAL RNA, TRANSFER RNA

RNA polymerase *noun* (circa 1962)
: any of a group of enzymes that promote the synthesis of RNA using DNA or RNA as a template

RN·ase \ˌär-'en-ˌās, -ˌāz\ *or* **RNA·ase** \ˌär-(ˌ)en-'ā-ˌās, -'ā-ˌāz\ *noun* [*RNA* + *-ase*] (1957)
: RIBONUCLEASE

¹roach \'rōch\ *noun, plural* **roach** *also* **roach·es** [Middle English *roche*, from Middle French] (13th century)
1 : a silver-green European freshwater cyprinid fish (*Rutilus rutilus*); *also* : any of various related fishes (as some shiners)
2 : any of several American freshwater sunfishes (family Centrarchidae)

²roach *noun* [origin unknown] (1794)
1 : a curved cut in the edge of a sail to prevent chafing or to secure a better fit
2 : a roll of hair brushed straight back from the forehead or side of the head

³roach *transitive verb* (1818)
1 : to cut (as a horse's mane) so that the remainder stands upright
2 : to cause to arch; *specifically* : to brush (the hair) in a roach — often used with *up*

⁴roach *noun* [by shortening] (circa 1848)
1 : COCKROACH
2 : the butt of a marijuana cigarette

roach back *noun* (1874)
: an arched back (as of a dog)

roach clip *noun* (1968)
: a metal clip that resembles tweezers and is used by marijuana smokers to hold a roach — called also *roach holder*

road \'rōd\ *noun* [Middle English *rode*, from Old English *rād* ride, journey; akin to Old English *rīdan* to ride] (14th century)
1 : ROADSTEAD — often used in plural
2 a : an open way for vehicles, persons, and animals; *especially* : one lying outside of an urban district : HIGHWAY **b** : ROADBED 2b
3 : ROUTE, PATH
4 : RAILWAY
5 : a series of scheduled visits or appearances (as games or performances) in several locations or the travel necessary to make these visits ⟨the team is on the *road*⟩ ⟨on tour with the musical's *road* company⟩
— **road·less** \'rōd-ləs\ *adjective*
— **down the road** : in or into the future

road·abil·i·ty \ˌrō-də-'bi-lə-tē\ *noun* (circa 1914)
: the qualities (as steadiness and balance) desirable in an automobile on the road

road agent *noun* (1863)
: a highwayman who formerly operated especially on stage routes in unsettled districts

road·bed \'rōd-ˌbed\ *noun* (circa 1840)
1 a : the bed on which the ties, rails, and ballast of a railroad rest **b** : the ballast or the upper surface of the ballast on which the ties rest
2 a : the earth foundation of a road prepared for surfacing **b** : the part of the surface of a road traveled by vehicles

road·block \-ˌbläk\ *noun* (1940)
1 a : a barricade often with traps or mines for holding up an enemy at a point on a road covered by fire **b** : a road barricade set up especially by law enforcement officers
2 : an obstruction in a road
3 : something (as a fact, condition, or countermeasure) that blocks progress or prevents accomplishment of an objective
— **roadblock** *transitive verb*

road hog *noun* (1891)
: a driver of an automotive vehicle who obstructs others especially by occupying part of another's traffic lane

road·hold·ing \'rōd-ˌhōl-diŋ\ *noun* (1932)
chiefly British : the qualities of an automobile that tend to make it respond precisely to the driver's steering

road·house \'rōd-ˌhau̇s\ *noun* (1857)
: an inn or tavern usually outside city limits providing liquor and usually meals, dancing, and often gambling

road·ie \'rō-dē\ *noun* [*road* + *-ie*] (1969)
: one who works (as by moving heavy equipment) for traveling entertainers

road·kill \'rōd-ˌkil\ *noun* (1979)
: an animal that has been killed on a road by a motor vehicle
— **road–killed** \-ˌkild\ *adjective*

road map *noun* (1883)
1 : a map showing roads especially for automobile travel
2 a : a detailed plan to guide progress toward a goal **b** : a detailed explanation

road metal *noun* (1818)
: broken stone or cinders used in making and repairing roads or ballasting railroads

road racing *noun* (1828)
: racing over public roads; *especially* : automobile racing over roads or over a closed course designed to simulate public roads
— **road race** *noun*

road roller *noun* (circa 1876)
: one that rolls roadways; *specifically* : a machine with heavy wide smooth rollers for compacting roadbeds

road·run·ner \'rōd-ˌrə-nər\ *noun* (1856)

roach back

roadrunner

: a largely terrestrial bird (*Geococcyx californianus*) of the cuckoo family that has a long tail and a crest, is a speedy runner, and ranges from the southwestern U.S. to Mexico; *also* : a closely related bird (*G. velox*) of Mexico and Central America

road show *noun* (1908)
1 : a theatrical performance given by a troupe on tour
2 : a special engagement of a new motion picture usually at increased prices
3 : a promotional presentation or meeting conducted in a series of locations

road·side \'rōd-ˌsīd\ *noun* (1744)
: the strip of land along a road : the side of a road
— **roadside** *adjective*

road·stead \'rōd-ˌsted\ *noun* (1556)
: a place less enclosed than a harbor where ships may ride at anchor

road·ster \'rōd-stər\ *noun* (1818)
1 a : a horse for riding or driving on roads **b** : a utility saddle horse of the hackney type
2 a : a light carriage : BUGGY **b** : an automobile with an open body that seats two and has a folding fabric top and a luggage compartment in the rear

road test *noun* (1906)
1 : a test of a vehicle under practical operating conditions on the road
2 : a test on the road of a person's driving ability as a requirement for a driver's license
— **road test** *transitive verb*

road·way \'rōd-ˌwā\ *noun* (1600)
1 a : the strip of land over which a road passes **b** : ROAD; *specifically* : ROADBED 2b
2 : the part of a bridge used by vehicles

road·work \-ˌwərk\ *noun* (1869)
1 : work done in constructing or repairing roads
2 : conditioning for an athletic contest (as a boxing match) consisting mainly of long runs

road·wor·thy \-ˌwər-thē\ *adjective* (1819)
: fit for use on the road
— **road·wor·thi·ness** *noun*

roam \'rōm\ *verb* [Middle English *romen*] (14th century)
intransitive verb
1 : to go from place to place without purpose or direction : WANDER
2 : to travel purposefully unhindered through a wide area ⟨cattle *roaming* in search of water⟩
transitive verb
: to range or wander over
synonym see WANDER
— **roam** *noun*
— **roam·er** *noun*

¹roan \'rōn *also* 'rō-ən\ *adjective* [Middle French, from Old Spanish *roano*] (1530)
: having the base color (as red, black, or brown) muted and lightened by admixture of white hairs ⟨a *roan* horse⟩ ⟨a *roan* calf⟩

²roan *noun* (1580)
1 : an animal (as a horse) with a roan coat — usually used of a red roan when unqualified
2 : the color of a roan horse — used especially when the base color is red

³roan *noun* [origin unknown] (1818)
: sheepskin tanned with sumac and colored and finished to imitate morocco

¹roar \'rōr, 'ror\ *verb* [Middle English *roren*, from Old English *rārian*; akin to Old High German *rērēn* to bleat] (before 12th century)
intransitive verb
1 a : to utter or emit a full loud prolonged sound **b** : to sing or shout with full force
2 a : to make or emit a loud confused sound (as background reverberation or rumbling) **b** : to laugh loudly

3 a : to be boisterous or disorderly **b :** to proceed or rush with great noise or commotion **4 :** to make a loud noise during inhalation (as that of a horse affected with roaring) *transitive verb* **1 :** to utter or proclaim with a roar **2 :** to cause to roar
²**roar** *noun* (14th century) **1 :** the deep cry of a wild animal **2 :** a loud deep cry (as of pain or anger) **3 :** a loud continuous confused sound ⟨the *roar* of the crowd⟩ **4 :** a boisterous outcry
roar·er \'rȯr-ər, 'rȯr-\ *noun* (14th century) **1 :** one that roars **2 :** a horse subject to roaring
¹**roar·ing** \'rȯr-iŋ, 'rȯr-\ *adjective* (14th century) **1 :** making or characterized by a sound resembling a roar : LOUD ⟨*roaring* applause⟩ **2 :** marked by prosperity especially of a temporary nature : BOOMING **3 :** INTENSE, UTTER ⟨in the *roaring* heat⟩ ⟨a *roaring* success⟩ — **roar·ing·ly** *adverb*
²**roaring** *adverb* (1697) **:** EXTREMELY ⟨was *roaring* hungry —Herman Wouk⟩
³**roaring** *noun* (1823) **:** noisy inhalation in a horse caused by nerve paralysis and muscular atrophy and constituting an unsoundness
roaring boy *noun* (circa 1590) **:** a noisy street bully especially of Elizabethan and Jacobean England who intimidated passersby
¹**roast** \'rōst\ *verb* [Middle English *rosten*, from Old French *rostir*, of Germanic origin; akin to Old High German *rōsten* to roast] (13th century) *transitive verb* **1 a :** to cook by exposing to dry heat (as in an oven or before a fire) or by surrounding with hot embers, sand, or stones ⟨*roast* a potato in ashes⟩ **b :** to dry and parch by exposure to heat ⟨*roast* coffee⟩ **2 :** to heat (inorganic material) with access of air and without fusing to effect change (as expulsion of volatile matter, oxidation, or removal of sulfur from sulfide ores) **3 :** to heat to excess ⟨*roasted* by the summer sun⟩ **4 :** to subject to severe criticism or ridicule ⟨films have been *roasted* by most critics —H. J. Seldes⟩ **5 :** to honor (a person) at a roast *intransitive verb* **1 :** to cook food by heat **2 :** to undergo being roasted
²**roast** *noun* (14th century) **1 :** a piece of meat suitable for roasting **2 :** a gathering at which food is roasted before an open fire or in hot ashes or sand **3 :** an act or process of roasting; *specifically* **:** severe banter or criticism **4 :** a banquet honoring a person (as a celebrity) who is subjected to humorous tongue-in-cheek ridicule by friends
³**roast** *adjective* (14th century) **:** that has been roasted ⟨*roast* beef⟩
roast·er \'rōs-tər\ *noun* (15th century) **1 :** one that roasts **2 :** a device for roasting **3 :** something adapted to roasting: as **a :** a suckling pig **b :** a bird fit for roasting; *especially* **:** a young chicken of more than four pounds (1.8 kilograms) dressed weight
roast·ing ear \'rōs-tiŋ-,ir, *sense 2 usually* 'rō-sⁿn-,ir *or* 'rōs-,nir\ *noun* (1650) **1 :** an ear of young corn roasted or suitable for roasting usually in the husk **2** *chiefly Southern & Midland* **:** an ear of corn suitable for boiling or steaming
rob \'räb\ *verb* **robbed; rob·bing** [Middle English *robben*, from Old French *rober*, of

Germanic origin; akin to Old High German *roubōn* to rob — more at REAVE] (13th century) *transitive verb* **1 a** (1) **:** to take something away from by force : steal from (2) **:** to take personal property from by violence or threat **b** (1) **:** to remove valuables without right from (a place) (2) **:** to take the contents of (a receptacle) **c :** to take away as loot : STEAL ⟨*rob* jewelry⟩ **2 a :** to deprive of something due, expected, or desired **b :** to withhold unjustly or injuriously *intransitive verb* **:** to commit robbery □ — **rob·ber** *noun*
ro·ba·lo \rō-'bä-(,)lō\ *noun, plural* **-los** *or* **-lo** [Spanish] (circa 1890) **:** SNOOK 1
ro·band \'rō-,band, -bənd\ *noun* [probably from Middle Dutch *rabant*] (1762) **:** a piece of spun yarn or marline used to fasten the head of a sail to a spar
robber baron *noun* (1878) **:** an American capitalist of the latter part of the 19th century who became wealthy through exploitation (as of natural resources, governmental influence, or low wage scales)
robber fly *noun* (1871) **:** any of a family (Asilidae) of predaceous flies including some closely resembling bumblebees
rob·bery \'rä-b(ə-)rē\ *noun, plural* **-ber·ies** (13th century) **:** the act or practice of robbing; *specifically* **:** larceny from the person or presence of another by violence or threat
¹**robe** \'rōb\ *noun* [Middle English, from Old French, robe, booty, of Germanic origin; akin to Old High German *roubōn* to rob] (13th century) **1 a :** a long flowing outer garment; *especially* **:** one used for ceremonial occasions or as a symbol of office or profession **b :** a loose garment (as a bathrobe) for informal wear especially at home **2 :** COVERING, MANTLE ⟨peaks on the axis of the range in their *robes* of snow and light —John Muir (died 1914)⟩ **3 :** a covering of pelts or fabric for the lower body used while driving or at outdoor events
²**robe** *verb* **robed; rob·ing** (14th century) *transitive verb* **:** to clothe or cover with or as if with a robe *intransitive verb* **1 :** to put on a robe **2 :** DRESS
robe de cham·bre \,rōb-də-'shäⁿbrᵉ, -'shäm-brə\ *noun, plural* **robes de chambre** \,rōb(z)-\ [French] (1731) **:** DRESSING GOWN
rob·in \'rä-bən\ *noun* [short for *robin redbreast*] (1549) **1 a :** a small chiefly European thrush (*Erithacus rubecula*) resembling a warbler and having a brownish olive back and orangish face and breast **b :** any of various Old World songbirds that are related to or resemble the European robin **2 :** a large North American thrush (*Turdus migratorius*) with olivaceous to slate gray upperparts, blackish head and tail, black and whitish streaked throat, and dull reddish breast and underparts
Rob·in Good·fel·low \'rä-bən-'gùd,fe-(,)lō\ *noun* **:** a mischievous sprite in English folklore
Robin Hood \-,hùd\ *noun* [*Robin Hood*, legendary English outlaw who gave to the poor what he stole from the rich] (1597) **:** a person or group likened to a heroic outlaw; *especially* **:** one that robs the rich and gives to the poor
robin red·breast \-'red-,brest\ *noun* [Middle English, from *Robin*, nickname for *Robert*] (15th century)

: ROBIN
Rob·in·son Cru·soe \'rä-bə(n)-sən-'krü-(,)sō\ *noun* **:** a shipwrecked sailor in Defoe's *Robinson Crusoe* who lives for many years on a desert island
Rob·in·son projection \'rä-bən-sən-\ *noun* [Arthur H. *Robinson* (born 1915) American geographer] (1978) **:** a compromise map projection showing the poles as lines rather than points and more accurately portraying high latititude lands and water to land ratio
ro·ble \'rō-(,)blā\ *noun* [American Spanish, from Spanish, oak, from Latin *robur*] (1864) **:** any of several oaks of California and Mexico
ro·bot \'rō-,bät, -bət\ *noun* [Czech, from *robota* compulsory labor; akin to Old High German *arabeit* trouble, Latin *orbus* orphaned — more at ORPHAN] (1923) **1 a :** a machine that looks like a human being and performs various complex acts (as walking or talking) of a human being; *also* **:** a similar but fictional machine whose lack of capacity for human emotions is often emphasized **b :** an efficient insensitive person who functions automatically **2 :** a device that automatically performs complicated often repetitive tasks **3 :** a mechanism guided by automatic controls ◇ — **ro·bot·ism** \'rō-,bä-,ti-zəm, -bə-\ *noun*
ro·bot·ic \rō-'bä-tik, rə-\ *adjective* (1941) **1 :** of or relating to mechanical robots **2 :** having the characteristics of a robot ⟨performs with *robotic* consistency⟩ — **ro·bot·i·cal·ly** \-ti-k(ə-)lē\ *adverb*

□ **USAGE**
rob Sense *transitive verb* 1c, in which the direct object is the thing stolen, is sometimes considered to be wrong, or perhaps archaic. The sense has been in use since the 13th century and is found in earlier literature ⟨contrive to *rob* the honey and subvert the hive —John Dryden⟩. It is still in use though not as common as other senses ⟨then robbed $100 after the clerk fled —*Springfield (Massachusetts) Morning Union*⟩.

◇ **WORD HISTORY**
robot In 1923 the play *R.U.R.*, by Czech author Karel Čapek, opened in London and New York. The title in the Czech version as well as its English translation stands for "Rossum's Universal Robots." In Čapek's drama this is the name of a company formed by Rossum, an English scientist, to manufacture "robots," humanlike machines that do manual labor. Another scientist decides to make the machines more human, which he does by gradually adding such traits as the capacity to feel pain. Eventually the robots, created to serve humans, come to dominate them completely. Čapek based his coinage *robot* on the Czech word *robota* "compulsory labor." Highly successful in its day, his play caught the imagination of the public. *Robot* was soon used generically for a humanoid machine but then also for a human who has become machinelike and stolid as a result of performing mindless tasks. Appropriately, given the origin of *robot,* the word *robotics* was also first used in a work of fiction, by the American writer Isaac Asimov.

\ə\ **abut** \ᵊ\ **kitten** \ər\ **further** \a\ **ash** \ā\ **ace** \ä\ **mop, mar** \aù\ **out** \ch\ **chin** \e\ **easy** \g\ **go** \i\ **hit** \ī\ **ice** \j\ **job** \ŋ\ **sing** \ō\ **go** \ò\ **law** \òi\ **boy** \th\ **thin** \th\ **the** \ü\ **loot** \ù\ **foot** \y\ **yet** \zh\ **vision** *see also* Guide to Pronunciation

ro·bot·ics \rō-'bä-tiks\ *noun plural but singular in construction* (1941)
: technology dealing with the design, construction, and operation of robots in automation
word history *see* ROBOT
ro·bot·i·za·tion \,rō-,bä-tə-'zā-shən, -bə-\ *noun* (circa 1927)
1 : AUTOMATION
2 : the process of turning a human being into a robot
ro·bot·ize \'rō-,bä-,tīz, -bə-\ *transitive verb* **-ized; -iz·ing** (1927)
1 : to make automatic : equip with robots
2 : to turn (a human being) into a robot
Rob Roy \'räb-'rói\ *noun* [*Rob Roy*, nickname of Robert McGregor (died 1734) Scottish freebooter] (1919)
: a manhattan made with Scotch whisky
ro·bust \rō-'bəst, 'rō-(,)bəst\ *adjective* [Latin *robustus* oaken, strong, from *robor-*, *robur* oak, strength] (1549)
1 a : having or exhibiting strength or vigorous health **b** : having or showing vigor, strength, or firmness ⟨a *robust* debate⟩ ⟨a *robust* faith⟩ **c** : strongly formed or constructed : STURDY ⟨a *robust* plastic⟩
2 : ROUGH, RUDE ⟨stories . . . laden with *robust*, down-home imagery —*Playboy*⟩
3 : requiring strength or vigor ⟨*robust* work⟩
4 : FULL-BODIED ⟨*robust* coffee⟩; *also* : HEARTY ⟨a *robust* dinner⟩
5 : relating to, resembling, or being any of the primitive, relatively large, heavyset hominids (genus *Australopithecus* and especially *A. robustus* and *A. boisei*) characterized especially by heavy molars and small incisors adapted to a vegetarian diet — compare GRACILE 3
synonym *see* HEALTHY
— **ro·bust·ly** *adverb*
— **ro·bust·ness** \-'bəs(t)-nəs, -(,)bəs(t)-\ *noun*
ro·bus·ta \rō-'bəs-tə\ *noun, often attributive* [New Latin *robusta*, specific epithet of *Coffea robusta*, synonym of *Coffea canephora*] (1909)
1 : a coffee (*Coffea canephora*) that is indigenous to central Africa but has been introduced elsewhere (as in Java)
2 a : the seed of robusta coffee **b** : coffee brewed from the seed of robusta coffee
ro·bus·tious \rō-'bəs-chəs\ *adjective* (circa 1548)
1 : ROBUST
2 : vigorous in a rough or unrefined way : BOISTEROUS
— **ro·bus·tious·ly** *adverb*
— **ro·bus·tious·ness** *noun*
roc \'räk\ *noun* [Arabic *rukhkh*]
: a legendary bird of great size and strength believed to inhabit the Indian Ocean area
ro·caille \rō-'kī, rä-\ *noun* [French, literally, stone debris, from Middle French *roquailles*, plural, rocky terrain, from *roc* rock, alteration of *roche*, from (assumed) Vulgar Latin *rocca*] (1856)
1 : a style of ornament developed in the 18th century and characterized by sinuous foliate forms
2 : ROCOCO
Roche limit \'rōsh-, 'rōsh-\ *noun* [E. A. *Roche* (died 1883) French mathematician] (1889)
: the distance between a planet's center and its satellite within which the satellite cannot approach without becoming disrupted
Ro·chelle salt \rō-'shel-\ *noun* [La *Rochelle*, France] (1753)
: a crystalline salt $KNaC_4H_4O_6 \cdot 4H_2O$ that is a mild purgative
roche mou·ton·née \'rōsh-,mü-t³n-'ā, 'rōsh-\ *noun, plural* **roches mou·ton·nées** *same or* -'āz\ [French, literally, fleecy rock] (1843)
: an elongate rounded ice-sculptured hillock of bedrock
roch·et \'rä-chət\ *noun* [Middle English, from Middle French, from Old French, from (as-

sumed) Old French *roc* coat, of Germanic origin; akin to Old High German *roc* coat] (13th century)
: a white linen vestment resembling a surplice with close-fitting sleeves worn especially by bishops and privileged prelates
¹rock \'räk\ *verb* [Middle English *rokken*, from Old English *roccian*; akin to Old High German *rucken* to cause to move] (12th century)
transitive verb
1 a : to move back and forth in or as if in a cradle **b** : to wash (placer gravel) in a cradle
2 a : to cause to sway back and forth ⟨a boat *rocked* by the waves⟩ **b** (1) : to cause to shake violently (2) : to daze with or as if with a vigorous blow ⟨a hard right *rocked* the contender⟩ (3) : to astonish or disturb greatly ⟨the scandal *rocked* the community⟩
intransitive verb
1 : to become moved backward and forward under often violent impact; *also* : to move gently back and forth
2 : to move forward at a steady pace; *also* : to move forward at a high speed ⟨the train *rocked* through the countryside⟩
3 : to sing, dance to, or play rock music
synonym *see* SHAKE
— **rock the boat** : to do something that disturbs the equilibrium of a situation
²rock *noun, often attributive* (1823)
1 : a rocking movement
2 : popular music usually played on electronically amplified instruments and characterized by a persistent heavily accented beat, much repetition of simple phrases, and often country, folk, and blues elements
³rock *noun* [Middle English *roc*, from Middle Dutch *rocke*; akin to Old High German *rocko* distaff] (14th century)
1 : DISTAFF
2 : the wool or flax on a distaff
⁴rock *noun* [Middle English *rokke*, from Old North French *roque*, from (assumed) Vulgar Latin *rocca*] (14th century)
1 : a large mass of stone forming a cliff, promontory, or peak
2 : a concreted mass of stony material; *also* : broken pieces of such masses
3 : consolidated or unconsolidated solid mineral matter; *also* : a particular mass of it
4 a : something like a rock in firmness: (1) : FOUNDATION, SUPPORT (2) : REFUGE ⟨a *rock* of independent thought . . . in an ocean of parochialism —Thomas Molnar⟩ **b** : something that threatens or causes disaster — often used in plural
5 a : a flavored stick candy with color running through **b** : ROCK CANDY 2
6 *slang* **a** : GEM **b** : DIAMOND
7 a : a small crystallized mass of crack cocaine **b** : CRACK 9
— **rock** *adjective*
— **rock·like** \'räk-,līk\ *adjective*
— **between a rock and a hard place** *also* **between the rock and the hard place** : in a difficult or uncomfortable position with no attractive way out
— **on the rocks 1** : in or into a state of destruction or wreckage ⟨their marriage went *on the rocks*⟩ **2** : on ice cubes ⟨bourbon *on the rocks*⟩
rock·a·bil·ly \'rä-kə-,bi-lē\ *noun* [²*rock* + -a- (as in *rock-a-bye*, phrase used to put a child to sleep) + hill*billy*] (1956)
: pop music marked by features of rock and country music
rock and roll *noun* (1954)
: ²ROCK 2
rock and roller *noun* (1956)
: ROCKER 3
rock·a·way \'rä-kə-,wä\ *noun* [perhaps from *Rockaway*, New Jersey] (1846)
: a light low four-wheel carriage with a fixed top and open sides
rock bass *noun* (1811)

: a brown spotted sunfish (*Ambloplites rupestris*) found especially in the upper Mississippi valley and Great Lakes region
rock–bottom *adjective* (1884)
: being the very lowest ⟨*rock-bottom* offseason rates⟩; *also* : FUNDAMENTAL ⟨the *rock-bottom* question⟩
rock bottom *noun* (1890)
: the lowest or most fundamental part or level
rock·bound \'räk-,baùnd\ *adjective* (1840)
: fringed, surrounded, or covered with rocks : ROCKY
rock brake *noun* (circa 1850)
: any of several ferns that grow chiefly on or among rocks
rock candy *noun* (1723)
1 : boiled sugar crystallized in large masses on string
2 : ⁴ROCK 5a
rock climbing *noun* (1892)
: mountain climbing on rocky cliffs
— **rock climb** *intransitive verb*
— **rock climber** *noun*
Rock Cornish *noun* (1956)
: a crossbred domestic fowl produced by interbreeding Cornish and white Plymouth Rock fowls and used especially for small roasters
rock crystal *noun* (1666)
: CRYSTAL 1
rock dove *noun* (1655)
: a bluish gray dove (*Columba livia*) of Europe and Asia that is the ancestor of many domesticated pigeons and of the feral pigeons found in cities and towns throughout most of the world — called also *rock pigeon*
rock·er \'rä-kər\ *noun* (1760)
1 a : either of two curving pieces of wood or metal on which an object (as a cradle) rocks **b** : any of various objects (as a rocking chair or an infant's toy having a seat placed between side pieces) that rock on rockers **c** : any of various objects in the form of a rocker or with parts resembling a rocker (as a skate with a curved blade) **d** (1) : any of the curved stripes at the lower part of a chevron worn by a noncommissioned officer above the rank of sergeant (2) : the curved stripe at the upper part of a chevron worn by a chief petty officer
2 : any of various devices that work with a rocking motion
3 : a rock performer, song, or enthusiast
— **off one's rocker** : in a state of extreme confusion or insanity ⟨went *off her rocker*, and had to be put away —Mervyn Wall⟩
rocker arm *noun* (1860)
: a center-pivoted lever to push an automotive engine valve down
rock·ery \'rä-k(ə-)rē\ *noun, plural* **-er·ies** [⁴*rock* + -*ery*] (1845) *chiefly British* : ROCK GARDEN
¹rock·et \'rä-kət, rä-'ket\ *noun* [Middle French *roquette*, from Old Italian *rochetta*, diminutive of *ruca* arugula, from Latin *eruca*] (1530)
: any of several plants of the mustard family: as **a** : ARUGULA **b** : DAME'S ROCKET
²rock·et \'rä-kət\ *noun, often attributive* [Italian *rocchetta*, literally, small distaff, from diminutive of *rocca* distaff, of Germanic origin; akin to Old High German *rocko* distaff] (1611)
1 a : a firework consisting of a case partly filled with a combustible composition fastened to a guiding stick and propelled through the air by the rearward discharge of the gases liberated by combustion **b** : a similar device used as an incendiary weapon or as a propelling unit (as for a lifesaving line)
2 : a jet engine that operates on the same principle as the firework rocket, consists essentially of a combustion chamber and an exhaust nozzle, carries either liquid or solid propellants which provide the fuel and oxygen needed for combustion and thus make the engine independent of the oxygen of the air, and is used especially for the propulsion of a missile (as a bomb or shell) or a vehicle (as an airplane)

3 : a rocket-propelled bomb, missile, or projectile

³**rock·et** \'rä-kət\ (1837)
transitive verb
: to convey or propel by means of or as if by a rocket
intransitive verb
1 : to rise up swiftly, spectacularly, and with force
2 : to travel rapidly in or as if in a rocket

rock·e·teer \,rä-kə-'tir\ *noun* (1832)
1 : one who fires, pilots, or rides in a rocket
2 : a scientist who specializes in rocketry

rocket plane *noun* (1928)
: an airplane propelled by rockets

rock·et·ry \'rä-kə-trē\ *noun* (1930)
: the study of, experimentation with, or use of rockets

rocket ship *noun* (1927)
: a rocket-propelled spaceship

rocket sled *noun* (1954)
: a rocket-propelled vehicle that runs usually on a single rail and that is used especially in aeronautical experimentation

rock·fall \'räk-,fòl\ *noun* (1924)
: a mass of falling or fallen rocks

rock·fish \-,fish\ *noun* (1598)
: any of various important market fishes that live among rocks or on rocky bottoms: as **a :** any of numerous scorpaenid fishes (especially genus *Sebastes*) **b :** STRIPED BASS **c :** any of several groupers

rock garden *noun* (1836)
: a garden laid out among rocks or decorated with rocks and adapted for the growth of particular kinds of plants (as alpines)

rock hind *noun* (circa 1867)
: a red-spotted tan to olive brown grouper (*Epinephelus adscensionis*) of the Atlantic especially from Massachusetts to southeastern Brazil

rock·hop·per \'räk-,hä-pər\ *noun* (1875)
: a small penguin (*Eudyptes crestatus*) with a short thick bill and a yellow crest

rock hound *noun* (1915)
1 : a specialist in geology
2 : an amateur rock and mineral collector
— **rock·hound·ing** \'räk-,haùn-diŋ\ *noun*

rock·i·ness \'rä-kē-nəs\ *noun* (1611)
: the quality or state of being rocky

rocking chair *noun* (1766)
: a chair mounted on rockers

rocking horse *noun* (1724)
: a toy horse mounted on rockers — called also *hobbyhorse*

rock·ling \'rä-kliŋ\ *noun* (1602)
: any of several small rather elongate marine bony fishes (especially genera *Enchelyopus* and *Gaidropsarus*) of the cod family

rock lobster *noun* (1884)
1 : SPINY LOBSTER
2 : the flesh of a spiny lobster especially when canned or frozen for use as food

rock maple *noun* (1775)
: SUGAR MAPLE 1

rock 'n' roll, rock 'n' roller *variant of* ROCK AND ROLL, ROCK AND ROLLER

rock oil *noun* (1668)
: PETROLEUM

rock pigeon *noun* (1611)
: ROCK DOVE

rock rabbit *noun* (1840)
1 : HYRAX
2 : PIKA

rock–ribbed \'räk-'ribd\ *adjective* (1776)
1 : ¹ROCKY 1
2 : firm and inflexible in doctrine or integrity ⟨a *rock-ribbed* conservative community —John Hale⟩

rock·rose \'räk-,rōz\ *noun* (1731)
: any of various shrubs or woody herbs (family Cistaceae, the rockrose family) with simple entire leaves and a capsular fruit

rock salt *noun* (1707)

: common salt occurring in solid form as a mineral; *also* **:** salt artificially prepared in large crystals or masses

rock·shaft \'räk-,shaft\ *noun* (circa 1864)
: a shaft that oscillates on its journals instead of revolving

rock tripe *noun* (1854)
: any of various dark leathery umbilicate foliose lichens (as of the genus *Umbilicaria*) that are widely distributed on rocks in boreal and alpine areas and are sometimes used as food

rock wallaby *noun* (1841)
: any of various medium-sized kangaroos (genus *Petrogale*)

rock·weed \'räk-,wēd\ *noun* (1626)
: any of various coarse brown algae (family Fucaceae, especially genera *Fucus* and *Ascophyllum*) growing in marine environments attached to rocks

rock wool *noun* (circa 1909)
: mineral wool made by blowing a jet of steam through molten rock (as limestone or siliceous rock) or through slag and used chiefly for heat and sound insulation

¹**rocky** \'rä-kē\ *adjective* **rock·i·er; -est** [Middle English *rokky*, from *rokke* rock] (15th century)
1 : abounding in or consisting of rocks
2 : difficult to impress or affect **:** INSENSITIVE
3 : firmly held **:** STEADFAST

²**rocky** *adjective* **rock·i·er; -est** [¹*rock*] (1737)
1 : UNSTABLE, WOBBLY
2 : physically upset or mentally confused (as from drinking excessively)
3 : marked by obstacles **:** DIFFICULT ⟨a financially *rocky* year —Michael Murray⟩

Rocky Mountain sheep *noun* [*Rocky Mountains*, North America] (1817)
: BIGHORN

Rocky Mountain spotted fever *noun* (1905)
: an acute disease that is characterized by chills, fever, prostration, pains in muscles and joints, and a red to purple eruption and that is caused by a rickettsia (*Rickettsia rickettii*) usually transmitted by an ixodid tick and especially either the American dog tick or a wood tick (*Dermacentor andersoni*)

¹**ro·co·co** \rə-'kō-(,)kō, rō-kə-'kō\ *noun* (1840)
: rococo work or style

²**rococo** *adjective* [French, irregular from *rocaille* rocaille] (1841)
1 a : of or relating to an artistic style especially of the 18th century characterized by fanciful curved asymmetrical forms and elaborate ornamentation **b :** of or relating to an 18th century musical style marked by light gay ornamentation and departure from thorough-bass and polyphony
2 : excessively ornate or intricate

rod \'räd\ *noun* [Middle English, from Old English *rodd*; akin to Old Norse *rudda* club] (before 12th century)
1 a (1) **:** a straight slender stick growing on or cut from a tree or bush (2) **:** OSIER (3) **:** a stick or bundle of twigs used to punish; *also* **:** PUNISHMENT (4) **:** a shepherd's cudgel (5) **:** a pole with a line and usually a reel attached for fishing **b** (1) **:** a slender bar (as of wood or metal) (2) **:** a bar or staff for measuring (3) **:** SCEPTER; *also* **:** a wand or staff carried as a badge of office (as of marshal)
2 a : a unit of length — see WEIGHT table **b :** a square rod
3 : any of the long rod-shaped photosensitive receptors in the retina responsive to faint light — compare CONE 3a
4 : a rod-shaped bacterium
5 *slang* **:** HANDGUN
— **rod·less** \-ləs\ *adjective*
— **rod·like** \-,līk\ *adjective*

rode *past and chiefly dialect past participle of* RIDE

ro·dent \'rō-d°nt\ *noun* [ultimately from Latin *rodent-, rodens*, present participle of *rodere* to

gnaw; akin to Latin *radere* to scrape, scratch, Sanskrit *radati* he gnaws] (1859)
1 : any of an order (Rodentia) of relatively small gnawing mammals (as a mouse, a squirrel, or a beaver) that have in both jaws a single pair of incisors with a chisel-shaped edge
2 : a small mammal (as a rabbit or a shrew) other than a true rodent
— **rodent** *adjective*

ro·den·ti·cide \rō-'den-tə-,sīd\ *noun* (circa 1935)
: an agent that kills, repels, or controls rodents

rodent ulcer *noun* [Latin *rodent-, rodens* gnawing] (1853)
: a chronic persisting ulcer of the exposed skin and especially of the face that is destructive locally, spreads slowly, and is usually a carcinoma derived from basal cells — called also *rodent cancer*

¹**ro·deo** \'rō-dē-,ō, rə-'dā-(,)ō\ *noun, plural* **ro·de·os** [Spanish, from *rodear* to surround, from *rueda* wheel, from Latin *rota* — more at ROLL] (1834)
1 : ROUNDUP
2 a : a public performance featuring bronco riding, calf roping, steer wrestling, and Brahma bull riding **b :** a contest resembling a rodeo

²**rodeo** *intransitive verb* (1951)
: to participate in a rodeo

rod·man \'räd-mən, -,man\ *noun* (1853)
: a surveyor's assistant who holds the leveling rod

ro·do·mon·tade \,rä-də-mən-'tād, ,rō-, -'täd\ *noun* [Middle French, from Italian *Rodomonte*, character in *Orlando Innamorato* by Matteo M. Boiardo] (1612)
1 : a bragging speech
2 : vain boasting or bluster **:** RANT
— **rodomontade** *adjective*

¹**roe** \'rō\ *noun, plural* **roe** *or* **roes** [Middle English *ro*, from Old English *rā*; akin to Old High German *rēh* roe] (before 12th century)
: DOE

²**roe** *noun* [Middle English *roof, roughe, row*; akin to Old Norse *hrogn* roe and probably to Lithuanian *kurkulai* frog's eggs] (15th century)
1 : the eggs of a fish especially when still enclosed in the ovarian membrane
2 : the eggs or ovaries of an invertebrate (as the coral of a lobster)

roe·buck \'rō-,bək\ *noun, plural* **roebuck** *or* **roebucks** (14th century)
: ROE DEER; *especially* **:** the male roe deer

roe deer *noun* (1575)
: either of two small European or Asian deer (*Capreolus capreolus* and *C. pygarus*) that have erect cylindrical antlers forked at the summit, are reddish brown in summer and grayish in winter, have a white rump patch, and are noted for their nimbleness and grace

roe deer

¹**roent·gen** \'rent-gən, 'rənt-, -jən, -shən\ *adjective* [International Scientific Vocabulary, from Wilhelm *Röntgen*] (1896)
: of or relating to X rays ⟨*roentgen* examinations⟩

²**roentgen** *noun* (1922)
: the international unit of x-radiation or gamma radiation equal to the amount of radiation that produces in one cubic centimeter of dry air at 0°C and standard atmospheric pressure

ionization of either sign equal to one electro-static unit of charge

roent·gen·o·gram \-gə-nə-,gram, -jə-, -shə-\ *noun* [International Scientific Vocabulary] (circa 1904)
: a photograph made with X rays

roent·gen·og·ra·phy \,rent-gə-'nä-grə-fē, ,rənt-, -jə-, -shə-\ *noun* [International Scientific Vocabulary] (1905)
: photography by means of X rays
— **roent·gen·o·graph·ic** \-nə-'gra-fik\ *adjective*
— **roent·gen·o·graph·i·cal·ly** \-fi-k(ə-)lē\ *adverb*

roent·gen·ol·o·gy \-'nä-lə-jē\ *noun* [International Scientific Vocabulary] (1905)
: a branch of radiology that deals with the use of X rays for diagnosis or treatment of disease
— **roent·gen·o·log·ic** \-nə-'lä-jik\ *or* **roent·gen·o·log·i·cal** \-ji-kəl\ *adjective*
— **roent·gen·o·log·i·cal·ly** \-ji-k(ə-)lē\ *adverb*
— **roent·gen·ol·o·gist** \-'nä-lə-jist\ *noun*

roentgen ray *noun, often 1st R capitalized* (circa 1890)
: X RAY

ro·ga·tion \rō-'gā-shən\ *noun* [Middle English *rogacion*, from Late Latin *rogation-, rogatio*, from Latin, questioning, from *rogare* to ask — more at RIGHT] (14th century)
1 : LITANY, SUPPLICATION
2 : the religious observance of the Rogation Days — often used in plural

Rogation Day *noun* (15th century)
: any of the days of prayer especially for the harvest observed on the three days before Ascension Day and by Roman Catholics also on April 25

rog·er \'rä-jər\ *interjection* [from *Roger*, former communications code word for the letter *r*] (circa 1941)
— used especially in radio and signaling to indicate that a message has been received and understood

¹rogue \'rōg\ *noun* [origin unknown] (1561)
1 : VAGRANT, TRAMP
2 : a dishonest or worthless person : SCOUNDREL
3 : a mischievous person : SCAMP
4 : a horse inclined to shirk or misbehave
5 : an individual exhibiting a chance and usually inferior biological variation
— **rogu·ish** \'rō-gish\ *adjective*
— **rogu·ish·ly** *adverb*
— **rogu·ish·ness** *noun*

²rogue *intransitive verb* **rogued; rogu·ing** *or* **rogue·ing** (1766)
: to weed out inferior, diseased, or nontypical individuals from a crop plant or a field

³rogue *adjective* (1872)
1 *of an animal* : being vicious and destructive
2 : resembling or suggesting a rogue elephant especially in being isolated and dangerous or uncontrollable ⟨capsized by a *rogue* wave⟩

rogue elephant *noun* (1859)
: a vicious elephant that separates from the herd and roams alone

rogu·ery \'rō-g(ə-)rē\ *noun, plural* **-er·ies** (1592)
1 : an act or behavior characteristic of a rogue
2 : mischievous play

rogues' gallery *noun* (1859)
: a collection of pictures of persons arrested as criminals; *also* : a collection or list likened to a rogues' gallery ⟨a *rogues' gallery* of infectious diseases⟩

roil \'rȯi(ə)l, *verb transitive 2 is also* 'rī(ə)l\ *verb* [origin unknown] (1590)
transitive verb
1 a : to make turbid by stirring up the sediment or dregs of **b** : to stir up : DISTURB, DISORDER
2 : RILE 1
intransitive verb
: to move turbulently : be in a state of turbulence or agitation

word history see RILE

roily \'rȯi-lē\ *adjective* (1823)
1 : full of sediment or dregs : MUDDY
2 : TURBULENT ⟨*roily* waters⟩

¹rois·ter \'rȯi-stər\ *noun* [Middle French *rustre* lout, alteration of *ruste*, from *ruste*, adjective, rude, rough, from Latin *rusticus* rural — more at RUSTIC] (1551)
archaic : one that roisters : ROISTERER

²roister *intransitive verb* **rois·tered; rois·ter·ing** \-st(ə-)riŋ\ (1582)
: to engage in noisy revelry : CAROUSE
— **rois·ter·er** \-stər-ər\ *noun*
— **rois·ter·ous** \-st(ə-)rəs\ *adjective*
— **rois·ter·ous·ly** *adverb*

Ro·land \'rō-lənd\ *noun* [French]
: a stalwart defender of the Christians against the Saracens in the Charlemagne legends who is killed at Roncesvalles

role *also* **rôle** \'rōl\ *noun* [French *rôle*, literally, roll, from Old French *rolle*] (1606)
1 a (1) : a character assigned or assumed (2) : a socially expected behavior pattern usually determined by an individual's status in a particular society **b** : a part played by an actor or singer
2 : a function or part performed especially in a particular operation or process ⟨played a major *role* in the negotiations⟩
3 : an identifier attached to an index term to show functional relationships between terms

role model *noun* (1957)
: a person whose behavior in a particular role is imitated by others

role–play \'rōl-,plā, -'plā\ (1949)
transitive verb
: ACT OUT ⟨students were asked to *role-play* the thoughts and feelings of each character —R. G. Lambert⟩
intransitive verb
: to play a role

rolf \'rȯlf *also* 'rȯf\ *transitive verb, often capitalized* (1970)
: to practice Rolfing on
— **rolf·er** \'rȯl-fər *also* 'rȯ-\ *noun, often capitalized*

Rolf·ing \'rȯl-fiŋ *also* 'rȯ-\ *service mark*
— used for a system of muscle massage intended to serve as both physical and emotional therapy

¹roll \'rōl\ *noun* [Middle English *rolle*, from Old French, from Latin *rotulus*, diminutive of *rota* wheel; akin to Old High German *rad* wheel, Welsh *rhod*, Sanskrit *ratha* wagon] (13th century)
1 a (1) : a written document that may be rolled up : SCROLL; *specifically* : a document containing an official or formal record ⟨the *rolls* of parliament⟩ (2) : a manuscript book **b** : a list of names or related items : CATALOG **c** : an official list: as (1) : MUSTER ROLL (2) : a list of members of a school or class or of members of a legislative body
2 : something that is rolled up into a cylinder or ball or rounded as if rolled: as **a** : a quantity (as of fabric or paper) rolled up to form a single package **b** : a hairdo in which some or all of the hair is rolled or curled up or under ⟨a pageboy *roll*⟩ **c** : any of various food preparations rolled up for cooking or serving; *especially* : a small piece of baked yeast dough **d** : a cylindrical twist of tobacco **e** : a flexible case (as of leather) in which articles may be rolled and fastened by straps or clasps **f** (1) : paper money folded or rolled into a wad (2) *slang* : BANKROLL
3 : something that performs a rolling action or movement : ROLLER: as **a** : a wheel for making decorative lines on book covers; *also* : a design impressed by such a tool **b** : a typewriter platen

²roll *verb* [Middle English, from Middle French *roller*, from (assumed) Vulgar Latin *rotulare*, from Latin *rotulus*] (14th century)
transitive verb

1 a : to impel forward by causing to turn over and over on a surface **b** : to cause to revolve by turning over and over on or as if on an axis **c** : to cause to move in a circular manner **d** : to form into a mass by turning over and over **e** : to impel forward with an easy continuous motion
2 a : to put a wrapping around : ENFOLD, ENVELOP **b** : to wrap round on itself : shape into a ball or roll; *also* : to produce by such shaping ⟨*rolled* his own cigarettes⟩
3 a : to press, spread, or level with a roller : make smooth, even, or compact ⟨hulled and *rolled* oats⟩ **b** : to spread out : EXTEND ⟨*roll* out the red carpet⟩
4 a : to move on rollers or wheels **b** : to cause to begin operating or moving ⟨*roll* the cameras⟩
5 a : to sound with a full reverberating tone ⟨*rolled* out the words⟩ **b** : to make a continuous beating sound upon : sound a roll upon ⟨*rolled* their drums⟩ **c** : to utter with a trill ⟨*rolled* his *r*'s⟩ **d** : to play (a chord) in arpeggio style
6 : to rob (a drunk, sleeping, or unconscious person) usually by going through the pockets
intransitive verb
1 a : to move along a surface by rotation without sliding **b** (1) : to turn over and over ⟨the children *rolled* in the grass⟩ (2) : to luxuriate in an abundant supply : WALLOW ⟨fairly *rolling* in money⟩
2 a : to move onward or around as if by completing a revolution : ELAPSE, PASS ⟨the months *roll* on⟩ **b** : to shift the gaze continually ⟨eyes *rolling* in terror⟩ **c** : to revolve on an axis
3 : to move about : ROAM, WANDER
4 a : to go forward in an easy, gentle, or undulating manner ⟨the waves *rolled* in⟩ **b** : to flow in a continuous stream : POUR ⟨money was *rolling* in⟩ **c** : to flow as part of a stream of words **d** : to have an undulating contour ⟨*rolling* prairie⟩ **e** : to lie extended : STRETCH
5 a : to travel in a vehicle **b** : to become carried on a stream **c** : to move on wheels
6 a : to make a deep reverberating sound ⟨the thunder *rolls*⟩ **b** : TRILL
7 a : to swing from side to side ⟨the ship heaved and *rolled*⟩ **b** : to walk with a swinging gait : SWAY **c** : to move so as to lessen the impact of a blow — used with *with* ⟨*rolled* with the punch⟩
8 a : to take the form of a cylinder or ball **b** : to respond to rolling in a specified way
9 a : to get under way : begin to move or operate **b** : to move forward : develop and maintain impetus; *especially* : to proceed or progress with notable ease or success ⟨the team was *rolling*⟩
10 a : BOWL **b** : to execute a somersault
11 *of a football quarterback* : to run toward one flank usually parallel to the line of scrimmage especially before throwing a pass — often used with *out*
— **roll the bones** : to shoot craps

³roll *noun* (1688)
1 a : a sound produced by rapid strokes on a drum **b** : a sonorous and often rhythmical flow of speech **c** : a heavy reverberatory sound ⟨the *roll* of cannon⟩ **d** : a chord in arpeggio style **e** : a trill of some birds (as a canary)
2 : a rolling movement or an action or process involving such movement ⟨an airplane's takeoff *roll*⟩: as **a** : a swaying movement of the body **b** : a side-to-side movement (as of a ship or train) **c** (1) : a flight maneuver in which a complete revolution about the longitudinal axis of an airplane is made with the horizontal direction of flight being approximately maintained (2) : the motion of an aircraft or spacecraft about its longitudinal axis **d** : SOMERSAULT **e** : the movement of a curling stone after impact with another stone

— on a roll : in the midst of a series of successes **:** on a hot streak — sometimes used with a modifier ⟨has been *on a brilliant roll*⟩

roll·back \'rōl-ˌbak\ *noun* (1942)
: the act or an instance of rolling back ⟨a government-ordered *rollback* of gasoline prices⟩

roll back *transitive verb* (1942)
1 : to reduce (as a commodity price) to or toward a previous level on a national scale
2 : to cause to retreat or withdraw **:** push back
3 : RESCIND ⟨attempted to *roll back* antipollution standards⟩

roll bar *noun* (circa 1952)
: an overhead metal bar on an automobile that is designed to protect the occupant in case of a rollover

roll cage *noun* (1966)
: a protective framework of metal bars encasing the driver of a vehicle (as a racing car)

roll call *noun* (1775)
1 : the act or an instance of calling off a list of names (as for checking attendance); *also* **:** a time for a roll call
2 : ⁶LIST 1

¹roll·er \'rō-lər\ *noun* (13th century)
1 a : a revolving cylinder over or on which something is moved or which is used to press, shape, spread, or smooth something **b :** a cylinder or rod on which something (as a shade) is rolled up
2 a : a long heavy ocean wave **b :** a tumbler pigeon
3 : one that rolls or performs a rolling operation
4 : a slowly rolling ground ball

²roll·er \'rō-lər\ *noun* [German, from *rollen* to roll, reverberate, from Middle French *roller* — more at ROLL] (1678)
1 : any of numerous mostly brightly colored nonpasserine Old World birds (family Coraciidae) that perform rolling aerial dives during courtship displays
2 : a canary having a song in which the notes are soft and run together

roller bearing *noun* (1857)
: a bearing in which the journal rotates in peripheral contact with a number of rollers usually contained in a cage

roll·er-coast·er \'rō-lər-ˌkō-stər, 'rō-lə-ˌkō-\ *adjective* (1940)
: marked by numerous ups and downs ⟨an entertainer's *roller-coaster* career⟩

roller bearing: *1* outer race, *2* cage, *3* roller, *4* inner race

roll·er coast·er \'rō-lər-ˌkō-stər, 'rō-lē-ˌkō-\ *noun* (1888)
1 : an elevated railway (as in an amusement park) constructed with sharp curves and steep inclines on which cars roll
2 : something resembling a roller coaster; *especially* **:** behavior, events, or experiences characterized by sudden and extreme changes ⟨an emotional *roller coaster*⟩

Roller Derby *service mark*
— used for an entertainment involving two roller-skating teams on an oval track in which each team attempts to maneuver a skater into position to score points by circling the track and lapping opponents within a given time period

roller rink *noun* (1885)
: RINK 1c

roller skate *noun* (1863)
: a shoe with a set of wheels attached for skating over a flat surface; *also* **:** a metal frame with wheels attached that can be fitted to the sole of a shoe
— roller-skate *intransitive verb*
— roller skater *noun*

roller towel *noun* (1845)
: an endless towel hung from a roller

Rolle's theorem \'rōlz-, 'rōlz-\ *noun* [Michel *Rolle* (died 1719) French mathematician] (circa 1891)
: a theorem in mathematics: if a curve is continuous, crosses the x-axis at two points, and has a tangent at every point between the two intercepts, its tangent is parallel to the x-axis at some point between the intercepts

roll film *noun* (1895)
: a strip of film for still camera use wound on a spool

rol·lick \'rä-lik\ *intransitive verb* [origin unknown] (1826)
: to move or behave in a carefree joyous manner **:** FROLIC
— rollick *noun*

rol·lick·ing \'rä-li-kiŋ\ *adjective* (1811)
: boisterously carefree, joyful, or high-spirited ⟨a *rollicking* adventure film⟩

rolling hitch *noun* (circa 1769)
: a hitch for fastening a line to a spar or to the standing part of another line that will not slip when the pull is parallel to the spar or line — see KNOT illustration

rolling mill *noun* (1787)
: an establishment where metal is rolled into plates and bars

rolling pin *noun* (circa 1589)
: a long cylinder for rolling out dough

rolling stock *noun* (1853)
: the wheeled vehicles owned and used by a railroad or motor carrier

roll-neck \'rōl-ˌnek\ *noun, often attributive* (1943)
British **:** TURTLENECK
— roll-necked \-ˌnekt\ *adjective*

roll-off \'rō-ˌlȯf\ *noun* (1947)
: a play-off match in bowling

roll-out \'rō-ˌlaut\ *noun* (1952)
1 : the public introduction of a new aircraft; *broadly* **:** the widespread public introduction of a new product
2 : a football play in which the quarterback rolls to the left or right

roll out (1884)
intransitive verb
: to get out of bed
transitive verb
: to introduce (as a new product) especially for widespread sale to the public

roll·over \'rō-ˌlō-vər\ *noun* (1945)
1 : the act or process of rolling over
2 : a motor vehicle accident in which the vehicle overturns

roll over *transitive verb* (1949)
1 a : to defer payment of (an obligation) **b :** to renegotiate the terms of (a financial agreement)
2 : to place (invested funds) in a new investment of the same kind **:** REINVEST ⟨*roll over* IRA funds⟩

roll-over arm *noun* (circa 1925)
: a fully upholstered chair or sofa arm curving outward from the seat

roll·top desk \'rōl-ˌtäp-\ *noun* (1887)
: a writing desk with a sliding cover often of parallel slats fastened to a flexible backing

roll up (1859)
transitive verb
: to increase or acquire by successive accumulations **:** ACCUMULATE ⟨*rolled up* a large majority⟩
intransitive verb
1 : to become larger by successive accumulations
2 : to arrive in a vehicle

rolltop desk

¹ro·ly-po·ly \ˌrō-lē-'pō-lē\ *adjective* [reduplication of *roly*, from ²*roll*] (1820)
: being short and pudgy **:** ROTUND

²roly-poly *noun, plural* **-lies** (1836)
1 : a roly-poly person or thing

2 *British* **:** a sweet dough spread with a filling, rolled, and baked or steamed — called also *roly-poly pudding*

Rom \'räm\ *noun, plural* **Rom** *also* **Roma** \'rō-mə\ [Romany, married man, husband, male Gypsy, from Sanskrit *ḍomba, ḍoma* low caste male musician] (1841)
: GYPSY 1

ROM \'räm\ *noun* (1966)
: READ-ONLY MEMORY

Ro·ma·ic \rō-'mā-ik\ *noun* [New Greek *Rhōmaiïkos*, from Greek *Rhōmaïkos* Roman, from *Rhōmē* Rome] (1810)
: the modern Greek vernacular
— Romaic *adjective*

ro·maine \rō-'mān, 'rō-ˌ\ *noun* [French, from feminine of *romain* Roman, from Latin *Romanus*] (1907)
: a lettuce that belongs to a cultivar of garden lettuce (*Lactuca sativa*) and has long crisp leaves and columnar heads — called also *cos lettuce*

ro·man \rō-'mäⁿ\ *noun* [French, from Old French *romans* romance] (1765)
: a metrical romance

¹Ro·man \'rō-mən\ *noun* [partly from Middle English, from Old English, from Latin *Romanus*, adjective & noun, from *Roma* Rome; partly from Middle English *Romain*, from Old French, from Latin *Romanus*] (before 12th century)
1 : a native or resident of Rome
2 : ROMAN CATHOLIC — often taken to be offensive
3 : *not capitalized* **:** roman letters or type

²Roman *adjective* (14th century)
1 : of or relating to Rome or the people of Rome; *specifically* **:** characteristic of the ancient Romans ⟨*Roman* fortitude⟩
2 a : LATIN 1a **b :** of or relating to the Latin alphabet
3 : *not capitalized* **:** of or relating to a type style with upright characters — compare ITALIC
4 : of or relating to the see of Rome or the Roman Catholic Church
5 : having a semicircular intrados ⟨*Roman* arch⟩
6 : having a prominent slightly aquiline bridge ⟨*Roman* nose⟩

ro·man à clef \rō-ˌmä(ⁿ)n-(ˌ)ä-ˈklā\ *noun, plural* **romans à clef** \-ˌmä(ⁿ)-(ˌ)zä-\ [French, literally, novel with a key] (1893)
: a novel in which real persons or actual events figure under disguise

Roman candle *noun* (1834)
: a cylindrical firework that discharges at intervals balls or stars of fire

¹Roman Catholic *noun* (1605)
: a member of the Roman Catholic Church

²Roman Catholic *adjective* (1614)
: of, relating to, or being a Christian church having a hierarchy of priests and bishops under the pope, a liturgy centered in the Mass, veneration of the Virgin Mary and saints, clerical celibacy, and a body of dogma including transubstantiation and papal infallibility

Roman Catholicism *noun* (circa 1823)
: the faith, doctrine, or polity of the Roman Catholic Church

¹ro·mance \rō-'man(t)s, rə-; 'rō-ˌ\ *noun* [Middle English *romauns*, from Old French *romans* French, something written in French, from Latin *romanice* in the Roman manner, from *romanicus* Roman, from *Romanus*] (14th century)
1 a (1) : a medieval tale based on legend, chivalric love and adventure, or the supernatural **(2) :** a prose narrative treating imaginary characters involved in events remote in time or place and usually heroic, adventurous, or

mysterious (3) **:** a love story **b :** a class of such literature
2 : something (as an extravagant story or account) that lacks basis in fact
3 : an emotional attraction or aura belonging to an especially heroic era, adventure, or activity
4 : LOVE AFFAIR
5 capitalized **:** the Romance languages ◇
²**romance** verb **ro·manced; ro·manc·ing** (1671)
intransitive verb
1 : to exaggerate or invent detail or incident
2 : to entertain romantic thoughts or ideas
transitive verb
1 : to try to influence or curry favor with especially by lavishing personal attention, gifts, or flattery
2 : to carry on a love affair with
³**romance** noun (circa 1854)
: a short instrumental piece in ballad style
Ro·mance \rō-'man(t)s, rə-; 'rō-\ adjective (1690)
: of, relating to, or being any of several languages developed from Latin (as Italian, French, and Spanish)
ro·manc·er \rō-'man(t)-sər, rə-; 'rō-\ noun (1654)
1 : a writer of romance
2 : one that romances
Roman collar noun (circa 1890)
: CLERICAL COLLAR
Ro·man·esque \,rō-mə-'nesk\ adjective (1819)
: of or relating to a style of architecture developed in Italy and western Europe between the Roman and the Gothic styles and characterized in its development after 1000 by the use of the round arch and vault, substitution of piers for columns, decorative use of arcades, and profuse ornament
— **Romanesque** noun
ro·man-fleuve \rō-,mäⁿ-'flœv, -'flə(r)v\ noun, plural **ro·mans-fleuves** \-,mäⁿ-'flœv, 'flə(r)v(z)\ [French, literally, river novel] (1935)
: a novel in the form of a long usually easygoing chronicle of a social group (as a family or a community)
Roman holiday noun (1886)
1 : a time of debauchery or of sadistic enjoyment
2 : a destructive or tumultuous disturbance **:** RIOT
Ro·ma·nian \ru̇-'mā-nē-ən, rō-, -nyən\ noun (1868)
1 : a native or inhabitant of Romania
2 : the Romance language of the Romanians
Ro·man·ic \rō-'ma-nik\ adjective (1708)
: ROMANCE
— **Romanic** noun
ro·man·ise British variant of ROMANIZE
Ro·man·ism \'rō-mə-,ni-zəm\ noun (1674)
: ROMAN CATHOLICISM — often taken to be offensive
Ro·man·ist \-nist\ noun (1523)
1 : ROMAN CATHOLIC — often taken to be offensive
2 : a specialist in the language, culture, or law of ancient Rome
— **Romanist** or **Ro·man·is·tic** \,rō-mə-'nis-tik\ adjective
ro·man·ize \'rō-mə-,nīz\ transitive verb **-ized; -iz·ing** (1607)
1 often capitalized **:** to make Roman in character
2 : to write or print (as a language) in the Latin alphabet (romanize Chinese)
3 capitalized **a :** to convert to Roman Catholicism **b :** to give a Roman Catholic character to
— **ro·man·i·za·tion** \,rō-mə-nə-'zā-shən\ noun, often capitalized
roman law noun, often R capitalized (1660)
: the legal system of the ancient Romans that includes written and unwritten law, is based

on the traditional law and the legislation of the city of Rome, and in form comprises legislation of the assemblies, resolves of the senate, enactments of the emperors, edicts of the praetors, writings of the jurisconsults, and the codes of the later emperors
Roman numeral noun (1735)
: a numeral in a system of notation that is based on the ancient Roman system — see NUMBER table
Ro·ma·no \rə-'mä-(,)nō, rō-\ noun [Italian, Roman, from Latin Romanus] (1908)
: a hard sharp cheese of Italian origin that is often served grated
Ro·mans \'rō-mənz\ noun plural but singular in construction
: a letter on doctrine written by Saint Paul to the Christians of Rome and included as a book in the New Testament — see BIBLE table
Ro·mansh or **Ro·mansch** \rō-'mänch, -'manch\ noun [Romansh romonsch] (1663)
: the Rhaeto-Romance dialects spoken in the Grisons, Switzerland
¹**ro·man·tic** \rō-'man-tik, rə-\ adjective [French romantique, from obsolete romant romance, from Old French romans] (1650)
1 : consisting of or resembling a romance
2 : having no basis in fact **:** IMAGINARY
3 : impractical in conception or plan **:** VISIONARY
4 a : marked by the imaginative or emotional appeal of what is heroic, adventurous, remote, mysterious, or idealized **b** often capitalized **:** of, relating to, or having the characteristics of romanticism **c :** of or relating to music of the 19th century characterized by an emphasis on subjective emotional qualities and freedom of form; also **:** of or relating to a composer of this music
5 a : having an inclination for romance **:** responsive to the appeal of what is idealized, heroic, or adventurous **b :** marked by expressions of love or affection **c :** conducive to or suitable for lovemaking
6 : of, relating to, or constituting the part of the hero especially in a light comedy
— **ro·man·ti·cal·ly** \-ti-k(ə-)lē\ adverb
²**romantic** noun (1679)
1 : a romantic person, trait, or component
2 capitalized **:** a romantic writer, artist, or composer
ro·man·ti·cise British variant of ROMANTICIZE
ro·man·ti·cism \rō-'man-tə-,si-zəm, rə-\ noun (1823)
1 often capitalized **a** (1) **:** a literary, artistic, and philosophical movement originating in the 18th century, characterized chiefly by a reaction against neoclassicism and an emphasis on the imagination and emotions, and marked especially in English literature by sensibility and the use of autobiographical material, an exaltation of the primitive and the common man, an appreciation of external nature, an interest in the remote, a predilection for melancholy, and the use in poetry of older verse forms (2) **:** an aspect of romanticism **b :** adherence to a romantic attitude or style
2 : the quality or state of being romantic
— **ro·man·ti·cist** \-sist\ noun, often capitalized
ro·man·ti·cize \-'man-tə-,sīz\ verb **-cized; -ciz·ing** (1818)
transitive verb
: to make romantic **:** treat as idealized or heroic
intransitive verb
1 : to hold romantic ideas
2 : to present details, incidents, or people in a romantic way
— **ro·man·ti·ci·za·tion** \-,man-tə-sə-'zā-shən\ noun
Ro·ma·ny \'rä-mə-nē, 'rō-\ noun, plural **Ro·manies** [Romany romani, feminine of romano, adjective, Gypsy, from rom Gypsy man — more at ROM] (circa 1812)

1 : GYPSY 1
2 : the Indo-Aryan language of the Gypsies
— **Romany** adjective
ro·maunt \rō-'mȯnt, -'mänt\ noun [Middle English, from Middle French romant] (1530)
archaic **:** ROMANCE 1a(1)
rom·el·dale \'rä-məl-,dāl\ noun, often capitalized [blend of Romney (Marsh), Rambouillet, and Corriedale] (circa 1948)
: any of an American breed of utility sheep yielding a heavy fleece of fine wool and producing a quickly maturing high-grade market lamb
¹**Ro·meo** \'rō-mē-,ō, in Shakespeare also 'rōm-(,)yō\ noun, plural **Ro·me·os**
1 : the hero of Shakespeare's Romeo and Juliet who dies for love of Juliet
2 : a male lover
²**Romeo** (1952)
— a communications code word for the letter r
Rom·ish \'rō-mish\ adjective (1531)
: ROMAN CATHOLIC — usually used disparagingly
— **Rom·ish·ly** adverb
— **Rom·ish·ness** noun
Rom·ney Marsh \'räm-nē-, 'rəm-\ noun [Romney Marsh, pasture tract in England] (1832)
: any of a British breed of hardy long-wooled mutton-type sheep especially adapted to damp or marshy regions — called also Romney
¹**romp** \'rämp, 'rȯmp\ noun [partly alteration of ²ramp; partly alteration of ramp bold woman] (1706)
1 : one that romps; especially **:** a romping girl or woman
2 a : high-spirited, carefree, and boisterous play **b :** something suggestive of such play: as (1) **:** a light fast-paced narrative, dramatic, or musical work usually in a comic mood (2) **:** an episode of lovemaking
3 : an easy winning pace; also **:** RUNAWAY
²**romp** intransitive verb [alteration of ¹ramp] (1709)
1 : to run or play in a lively, carefree, or boisterous manner
2 : to move or proceed in a brisk, easy, or playful manner
3 : to win a contest easily
romp·er \'räm-pər, 'rȯm-\ noun (1842)
1 : one that romps
2 : a one-piece garment especially for children with the lower part shaped like bloomers — usually used in plural

◇ WORD HISTORY
romance The Latin word Romanus "of Rome, Roman" was used by the inhabitants of Gaul in the declining years of the Roman Empire to refer to their own Latin-derived speech, Gallo-Romance, as opposed to the language of the Franks and other Germanic peoples who had overwhelmed Gaul by the end of the 5th century. In the Middle Ages, the Latin adverb Romanice, a derivative of Romanus, meant "in the vernacular," alluding to the languages that had developed out of Gallo-Romance (namely Old French in the north of what had been Gaul and Old Occitan in the south), as opposed to Latin, the language of the church and of most formal writing. The Old French outcome of Romanice was romans or romanz, which was used as a noun referring not only to Old French, but to works composed in it, and then specifically to a verse narrative in the vernacular, typically one dealing with chivalric love and adventure. Middle English romaunce was borrowed from Old French with all these senses. The close association of the word with tales of love has led to the use of Modern English romance for both love stories in fiction and real love affairs.

Rom·u·lus \'räm-yə-ləs\ *noun* [Latin]
: a son of Mars and legendary founder of Rome

ron·deau \'rän-(ˌ)dō, rän-'dō\ *noun, plural* **ron·deaux** \-(ˌ)dōz, -'dōz\ [Middle French *rondel, rondeau*] (1525)
1 a : a fixed form of verse based on two rhyme sounds and consisting usually of 13 lines in three stanzas with the opening words of the first line of the first stanza used as an independent refrain after the second and third stanzas **b** : a poem in this form
2 : a monophonic trouvère song with a 2-part refrain

ron·del \'rän-dᵊl, rän-'del\ *or* **ron·delle** \rän-'del\ *noun* [Middle English, from Old French, literally, small circle — more at ROUNDEL] (14th century)
1 *usually* **rondelle** : a circular object; *especially* : a circular jewel or jeweled ring
2 a *usually* **rondel** : a fixed form of verse based on two rhyme sounds and consisting usually of 14 lines in three stanzas in which the first two lines of the first stanza are repeated as the refrain of the second and third stanzas **b** : a poem in this form **c** : RONDEAU 1

ron·de·let \ˌrän-də-'let, -'lā\ *noun* (15th century)
: a modified rondeau consisting usually of seven lines in which the first line of four syllables is repeated as the third line and as the final line or refrain and the remaining lines are made up of eight syllables each

ron·do \'rän-(ˌ)dō, rän-'dō\ *noun, plural* **ron·dos** [Italian *rondò*, from Middle French *rondeau*] (1797)
1 : an instrumental composition typically with a refrain recurring four times in the tonic and with three couplets in contrasting keys
2 : the musical form of a rondo used especially for a movement in a concerto or sonata

ron·dure \'rän-jər, -(ˌ)dyu̇r, -(ˌ)du̇r\ *noun* [French *rondeur* roundness, from Middle French, from *rond* round, from Old French *roont* — more at ROUND] (circa 1600)
1 : ROUND 1a
2 : gracefully rounded curvature

ron·yon \'rən-yən, 'rän-\ *noun* [perhaps modification of Middle French *rogne* scab] (1598)
obsolete : a mangy or scabby creature

rood \'rüd\ *noun* [Middle English, from Old English *rōd* rod, rood; akin to Old High German *ruota* rod and perhaps to Old Russian *ratĭšte* lance] (before 12th century)
1 : a cross or crucifix symbolizing the cross on which Jesus Christ died; *specifically* : a large crucifix on a beam or screen at the entrance of the chancel of a medieval church
2 a : any of various units of land area; *especially* : a British unit equal to ¼ acre **b** : any of various units of length; *especially* : a British unit equal to seven or eight yards or sometimes a rod

¹roof \'rüf, 'ru̇f\ *noun, plural* **roofs** \'rüfs, 'ru̇fs *also* 'rüvz, 'ru̇vz\ [Middle English, from Old English *hrōf*; akin to Old Norse *hrōf* roof of a boathouse and perhaps to Old Church Slavonic *stropŭ* roof] (before 12th century)
1 a (1) : the cover of a building (2) : material used for a roof : ROOFING **b** : the roof of a dwelling conventionally designating the home itself ⟨didn't have a *roof* over my head⟩ ⟨they share the same *roof*⟩
2 a : the highest point : SUMMIT **b** : an upper limit : CEILING
3 a : the vaulted upper boundary of the mouth **b** : a covering structure of any of various parts of the body ⟨*roof* of the skull⟩
4 : something suggesting a roof: as **a** : a canopy of leaves and branches **b** : the top over the passenger section of a vehicle
— **roofed** \'rüft, 'ru̇ft\ *adjective*
— **roof·less** \'rü-fləs, 'ru̇-\ *adjective*
— **roof·like** \-ˌlīk\ *adjective*

²roof *transitive verb* (15th century)

roof 1a(1): *1* gambrel, *2* mansard, *3* hip, *4* lean-to

1 a : to cover with or as if with a roof **b** : to provide with a particular kind of roof or roofing — often used in combination ⟨slate-roofed houses⟩
2 : to constitute a roof over
— **roof·er** *noun*

roof garden *noun* (1893)
: a restaurant or nightclub at the top of a building often in connection with or decorated to suggest an outdoor garden

roof·ing *noun* (15th century)
: material for a roof

roof·line \'rüf-ˌlīn, 'ru̇f-\ *noun* (1857)
: the profile of a roof (as of a house)

¹roof·top \-ˌtäp\ *noun* (1611)
: ROOF; *especially* : the outer surface of a usually flat roof ⟨sunning themselves on the *rooftop*⟩

²rooftop *adjective* (1935)
: situated or taking place on a rooftop

roof·tree \'rüf-ˌtrē, 'ru̇f-\ *noun* (14th century)
: RIDGEPOLE

¹rook \'ru̇k\ *noun* [Middle English, from Old English *hrōc*; akin to Old High German *hruoch* rook] (before 12th century)
: a common Old World gregarious bird (*Corvus frugilegus*) about the size and color of the related American crow but having a bare patch of skin at the base of the bill

²rook *transitive verb* (circa 1590)
: to defraud by cheating or swindling

rook

³rook *noun* [Middle English *rok*, from Middle French *roc*, from Arabic *rukhkh*, from Persian *rukh*] (14th century)
: either of two pieces of the same color in a set of chessmen having the power to move along the ranks or files across any number of unoccupied squares — called also *castle*

rook·ery \'ru̇-kə-rē\ *noun, plural* **-er·ies** (1725)
1 a : the nests or breeding place of a colony of rooks; *also* : a colony of rooks **b** : a breeding ground or haunt especially of gregarious birds or mammals; *also* : a colony of such birds or mammals
2 : a crowded dilapidated tenement or group of dwellings
3 : a place teeming with like individuals

rook·ie \'ru̇-kē\ *noun* [perhaps alteration of *recruit*] (1892)
1 : RECRUIT; *also* : NOVICE
2 : a first-year participant in a major professional sport

rooky \'ru̇-kē\ *adjective* (1605)
: full of or containing rooks

¹room \'rüm, 'ru̇m\ *noun* [Middle English, from Old English *rūm*; akin to Old High German *rūm* room, Latin *rur-, rus* open land] (before 12th century)
1 : an extent of space occupied by or sufficient or available for something ⟨in the country where there is *room* to run and play⟩

2 a *obsolete* : an appropriate or designated position, post, or station **b** : PLACE, STEAD ⟨in whose *room* I am now assuming the pen —Sir Walter Scott⟩
3 a : a partitioned part of the inside of a building; *especially* : such a part used as a lodging **b** : the people in a room
4 : a suitable or fit occasion or opportunity : CHANCE ⟨left no *room* for doubt⟩
— **roomed** \'rümd, 'ru̇md\ *adjective*

²room (1817)
intransitive verb
: to occupy a room especially as a lodger
transitive verb
: to accommodate with lodgings

room and board *noun* (1955)
: lodging and food usually furnished for a set price or as part of wages

room·er \'rü-mər, 'ru̇-\ *noun* (circa 1871)
: one who occupies a rented room in another's house

room·ette \rü-'met, ru̇-\ *noun* (1937)
: a small private single room on a railroad sleeping car

room·ful \'rüm-ˌfu̇l, 'ru̇m-\ *noun* (1710)
: as much or as many as a room will hold; *also* : the persons or objects in a room

rooming house *noun* (1893)
: a house where lodgings are provided for rent

rooming–in \'rü-miŋ-'in, 'ru̇-\ *noun* (1943)
: an arrangement in a hospital whereby a newborn infant is kept in a crib at the mother's bedside instead of in a nursery

room·mate \'rüm-ˌmāt, 'ru̇m-\ *noun* (1789)
: one of two or more persons sharing the same room or living quarters — called also *room·ie* \'rü-mē, 'ru̇-\

room service *noun* (1930)
: service provided to hotel guests in their rooms; *also* : the hotel department responsible for such service ⟨ordered a meal from *room service*⟩

roomy \'rü-mē, 'ru̇-\ *adjective* **room·i·er; -est** (1627)
1 : having ample room : SPACIOUS
2 *of a female mammal* : having a large or well-proportioned body suited for breeding
— **room·i·ness** *noun*

roor·back \'ru̇r-ˌbak\ *noun* [from an attack on James K. Polk in 1844 purporting to quote from an invented book by a Baron von *Roorback*] (1855)
: a defamatory falsehood published for political effect

roose \'rüz\ *transitive verb* [Middle English *rusen*, from Old Norse *hrōsa*] (14th century)
chiefly dialect : PRAISE

¹roost \'rüst\ *noun* [Middle English, from Old English *hrōst*; akin to Old Saxon *hrōst* attic] (before 12th century)
1 a : a support on which birds rest **b** : a place where winged animals and especially birds customarily roost
2 : a group of birds (as fowl) roosting together

²roost (1530)
intransitive verb
1 : to settle down for rest or sleep : PERCH
2 : to settle oneself as if on a roost
transitive verb
: to supply a roost for or put to roost

roost·er \'rüs-tər *also* 'ru̇s-\ *noun* (1772)
1 a : an adult male domestic fowl : COCK **b** : an adult male of various birds other than the domestic fowl
2 : a cocky or vain man

rooster tail *noun* (1946)
: a high arching spray of water thrown up behind a fast-moving motorboat

¹root \'rüt, 'ru̇t\ *noun, often attributive* [Middle English, from Old English *rōt*, from Old

\ə\ abut \ᵊ\ kitten \ər\ further \a\ ash \ā\ ace
\ä\ mop, mar \au̇\ out \ch\ chin \e\ bet \ē\ easy
\g\ go \i\ hit \ī\ ice \j\ job \ŋ\ sing \ō\ go
\o̅\ law \o̅i\ boy \th\ thin \t̲h̲\ the \ü\ loot \u̇\ foot
\y\ yet \zh\ vision *see also* Guide to Pronunciation

Norse; akin to Old English *wyrt* root, Latin *radix*, Greek *rhiza*] (12th century)
1 a : the usually underground part of a seed plant body that originates usually from the hypocotyl, functions as an organ of absorption, aeration, and food storage or as a means of anchorage and support, and differs from a stem especially in lacking nodes, buds, and leaves **b :** any subterranean plant part (as a true root or a bulb, tuber, rootstock, or other modified stem) especially when fleshy and edible
2 a : the part of a tooth within the socket; *also* **:** any of the processes into which this part is often divided — see TOOTH illustration **b :** the enlarged basal part of a hair within the skin **c :** the proximal end of a nerve **d :** the part of an organ or physical structure by which it is attached to the body ⟨the *root* of the tongue⟩
3 a : something that is an origin or source (as of a condition or quality) ⟨the love of money is the *root* of all evil —1 Timothy 6:10 (Authorized Version)⟩ **b :** one or more progenitors of a group of descendants — usually used in plural **c :** an underlying support **:** BASIS **d :** the essential core **:** HEART — often used in the phrase *at root* **e :** close relationship with an environment **:** TIE — usually used in plural
4 a : a quantity taken an indicated number of times as an equal factor ⟨2 is a fourth *root* of 16⟩ **b :** a number that reduces an equation to an identity when it is substituted for one variable
5 a : the lower part **:** BASE **b :** the part by which an object is attached to something else
6 : the simple element inferred as the basis from which a word is derived by phonetic change or by extension (as composition or the addition of an affix or inflectional ending)
7 : the tone from whose overtones a chord is composed **:** the lowest tone of a chord in normal position
synonym see ORIGIN
— **root·ed** \'rü-təd, 'ru̇-\ *adjective*
— **root·less** \'rüt-ləs, 'ru̇t-\ *adjective*
— **root·less·ness** *noun*
— **root·like** \-,līk\ *adjective*
²**root** (14th century)
transitive verb
1 a : to furnish with or enable to develop roots **b :** to fix or implant by or as if by roots **2 :** to remove altogether by or as if by pulling out by the roots — usually used with *out* ⟨*root* out dissenters⟩
intransitive verb
1 : to grow roots or take root **2 :** to have an origin or base
³**root** *verb* [alteration of *wroot,* from Middle English *wroten,* from Old English *wrōtan;* akin to Old High German *ruozzan* to root] (1532)
intransitive verb
1 : to turn up or dig in the earth with the snout **:** GRUB
2 : to poke or dig about
transitive verb
: to turn over, dig up, or discover and bring to light — usually used with *out* ⟨*root* out the cause of the problem⟩
⁴**root** \'rüt *also* 'ru̇t\ *intransitive verb* [perhaps alteration of ²*rout*] (1889)
1 : to noisily applaud or encourage a contestant or team **:** CHEER
2 : to wish the success of or lend support to someone or something
— **root·er** *noun*
root·age \'rü-tij, 'ru̇-\ *noun* (circa 1895)
1 : a developed system of roots
2 : ROOT 3a
root beer *noun* (1843)
: a sweetened carbonated beverage flavored with extracts of roots (as sarsaparilla) and herbs
root canal *noun* (1893)
: the part of the pulp cavity lying in the root of a tooth; *also* **:** a dental operation to save a

tooth by removing the contents of its root canal and filling the cavity with a protective substance
root cap *noun* (1875)
: a protective cap of parenchyma cells that covers the terminal meristem in most root tips
root cellar *noun* (1822)
: a pit used for the storage especially of root crops
root crop *noun* (1834)
: a crop (as turnips) grown for its enlarged roots
root·ed·ness \'rü-təd-nəs, 'ru̇-\ *noun* (1642)
: the quality or state of having roots
root hair *noun* (1857)
: a filamentous extension of an epidermal cell near the tip of a rootlet that functions in absorption of water and minerals
root·hold \'rüt-,hōld, 'ru̇t-\ *noun* (1864)
1 : the anchorage of a plant to soil through the growing and spreading of roots
2 : a place where plants may obtain a roothold
root knot *noun* (1889)
: a plant disease caused by nematodes that produce characteristic enlargements on the roots and stunt the growth of the plant
root–knot nematode *noun* (1922)
: any of several small plant-parasitic nematodes (genus *Meloidogyne*) that cause root knot
root·let \'rüt-lət, 'ru̇t-\ *noun* (circa 1793)
: a small root
root–mean–square *noun* (1895)
: the square root of the arithmetic mean of the squares of a set of numbers
root pressure *noun* (1875)
: the chiefly osmotic pressure by which water rises into the stems of plants from the roots
root rot *noun* (1883)
: any of various plant diseases characterized by decay of the roots and caused especially by fungi
root·stock \'rüt-,stäk, 'ru̇t-\ *noun* (1832)
1 : a rhizomatous underground part of a plant
2 : a stock for grafting consisting of a root or a piece of root; *broadly* **:** STOCK 3b
rooty \'rü-tē, 'ru̇-\ *adjective* (15th century)
: full or consisting of roots ⟨*rooty* soil⟩
¹**rope** \'rōp\ *noun* [Middle English, from Old English *rāp;* akin to Old High German *reif* hoop] (before 12th century)
1 a : a large stout cord of strands of fibers or wire twisted or braided together **b :** a long slender strip of material used as rope ⟨rawhide *rope*⟩ **c :** a hangman's noose **d :** LARIAT
2 : a row or string consisting of things united by or as if by braiding, twining, or threading
3 *plural* **:** special or basic techniques or procedures ⟨show him the *ropes*⟩
4 : LINE DRIVE
— **rope·like** \-,līk\ *adjective*
— **on the ropes :** in a defensive and often helpless position
²**rope** *verb* **roped; rop·ing** (14th century)
transitive verb
1 a : to bind, fasten, or tie with a rope or cord **b :** to partition, separate, or divide by a rope ⟨*rope* off the street⟩ **c :** LASSO
2 : to draw as if with a rope **:** LURE
intransitive verb
: to take the form of or twist in the manner of rope
— **rop·er** *noun*
rope·danc·er \'rōp-,dan(t)-sər\ *noun* (1648)
: one that dances, walks, or performs acrobatic feats on a rope high in the air
— **rope·danc·ing** \-siŋ\ *noun*
rop·ery \'rō-p(ə-)rē\ *noun* [probably from the thought that the perpetrator deserved the gallows] (1592)
archaic **:** roguish tricks or banter
rope tow *noun* (1948)
: SKI TOW 1
rope·walk \'rōp-,wȯk\ *noun* (1672)
: a long covered walk, building, or room where ropes are manufactured

rope·walk·er \-,wȯ-kər\ *noun* (1615)
: an acrobat who walks on a rope high in the air
rope·way \-,wā\ *noun* (1889)
1 : an endless aerial cable moved by a stationary engine and used to transport freight (as logs and ore)
2 : a fixed cable or a pair of fixed cables between supporting towers serving as a track for suspended passenger or freight carriers
ropy *also* **rop·ey** \'rō-pē\ *adjective* **rop·i·er; -est** (15th century)
1 a : capable of being drawn into a thread **:** VISCOUS; *also* **:** tending to adhere in stringy masses **b :** having a gelatinous or slimy quality from bacterial or fungal contamination ⟨*ropy* milk⟩ ⟨*ropy* flour⟩
2 a : resembling rope **b :** MUSCULAR, SINEWY
3 *usually* **ropey,** *slang* **:** extremely unsatisfactory **:** LOUSY
— **rop·i·ness** *noun*
roque \'rōk\ *noun* [alteration of *croquet*] (1899)
: croquet played on a hard-surfaced court with a raised border
Roque·fort \'rōk-fərt\ *trademark*
— used for a pungent French blue cheese made from sheep's milk
ro·que·laure \,rō-kə-'lȯr, ,rä-, -'lȯr\ *noun* [French, from the Duc de *Roquelaure* (died 1738) French marshal] (1716)
: a knee-length cloak worn especially in the 18th and 19th centuries
ror·qual \'rȯr-kwəl, -,kwȯl\ *noun* [French, from Norwegian *rørhval,* from Old Norse *reytharhvalr,* from *reythr* rorqual + *hvalr* whale] (1827)
: any of a family (Balaenopteridae) of large baleen whales (as a blue whale or humpback whale) having the skin of the throat marked with deep longitudinal furrows
Ror·schach \'rȯr-,shäk\ *adjective* (1927)
: of, relating to, used in connection with, or resulting from the Rorschach test
Rorschach test *noun* [Hermann *Rorschach* (died 1922) Swiss psychiatrist] (1927)
: a personality and intelligence test in which a subject interprets inkblot designs in terms that reveal intellectual and emotional factors — called also *Rorschach, Rorschach inkblot test*
ro·sa·ceous \rō-'zā-shəs\ *adjective* [ultimately from Latin *rosa*] (1731)
1 : of or relating to the rose family
2 : of, relating to, or resembling a rose especially in having a 5-petaled regular corolla
ro·sar·i·an \rō-'zar-ē-ən, -'zer-\ *noun* (1864)
: a cultivator of roses
ro·sa·ry \'rō-zə-rē, 'rōz-rē\ *noun, plural* **-ries** [Medieval Latin *rosarium,* from Latin, rose garden, from neuter of *rosarius* of roses, from *rosa* rose] (1547)
1 *often capitalized* **:** a Roman Catholic devotion consisting of meditation on usually five sacred mysteries during recitation of five decades of Hail Marys of which each begins with an Our Father and ends with a Gloria Patri
2 : a string of beads used in counting prayers especially of the Roman Catholic rosary
rosary pea *noun* (circa 1866)
1 : a tropical leguminous twining herb (*Abrus precatorius*) that bears jequirity beans and has a root used as a substitute for licorice — called also *Indian licorice, jequirity bean*
2 : JEQUIRITY BEAN 1
ros·coe \'räs-(,)kō\ *noun* [probably from the name *Roscoe*] (circa 1914)
slang **:** HANDGUN
¹**rose** *past of* RISE
²**rose** \'rōz\ *noun* [Middle English, from Old English, from Latin *rosa;* akin to Greek *rhodon* rose, Persian *gul*] (before 12th century)
1 a : any of a genus (*Rosa* of the family Rosaceae, the rose family) of usually prickly shrubs with pinnate leaves and showy flowers

having five petals in the wild state but being often double or partly double under cultivation
b : the flower of a rose
2 : something resembling a rose in form: as **a** (1) **:** COMPASS CARD (2) **:** a circular card with radiating lines used in other instruments **b :** a rosette especially in a shoe **c :** ROSE CUT
3 *plural* **:** a comfortable situation or an easily accomplished task ⟨it was not all sunshine and roses —Anthony Lewis⟩
4 : a moderate purplish red
5 : a plane curve which consists of three or more loops meeting at the origin and whose equation in polar coordinates is of the form $\rho = a \sin n\theta$ or $\rho = a \cos n\theta$ where n is an integer greater than zero
— **rose-like** \-,līk\ *adjective*
— **under the rose :** SUB ROSA
³rose *adjective* (14th century)
1 a : containing or used for roses **b :** of or relating to a rose **c :** flavored, scented, or colored with or like roses
2 : of the color rose
ro·sé \rō-'zā\ *noun* [French] (1897)
: a light pink table wine made from red grapes by removing the skins after fermentation has begun
ro·se·ate \'rō-zē-ət, -zē-,āt\ *adjective* [Latin *roseus* rosy, from *rosa*] (1589)
1 : resembling a rose especially in color
2 : overly optimistic **:** viewed favorably
— **ro·se·ate·ly** *adverb*
roseate spoonbill *noun* (circa 1785)
: a spoonbill (*Ajaia ajaja*) that is found from the southern U.S. to Patagonia and has chiefly pink plumage
rose·bay \'rōz-,bā\ *noun* (1760)
1 : RHODODENDRON; *especially* **:** GREAT LAUREL
2 : FIREWEED b
rosebay rhododendron *noun* (circa 1949)
: GREAT LAUREL
rose–breast·ed grosbeak \'rōz-,bres-təd-\ *noun* (1810)
: a grosbeak (*Pheucticus ludovicianus*) chiefly of eastern North America that in the male is chiefly black and white with a rose-red breast and in the female is grayish brown with a streaked breast
rose·bud \'rōz-,bəd\ *noun* (15th century)
: the bud of a rose
rose·bush \-,bùsh\ *noun* (1587)
: a shrub that produces roses
rose chafer *noun* (1704)
: a common North American beetle (*Macrodactylus subspinosus*) that feeds on plant roots as a larva and on leaves and flowers (as of rose or grapevines) as an adult — called also *rose bug*
rose–col·ored \'rōz-,kə-lərd\ *adjective* (1526)
1 : having a rose color
2 : seeing or seen in a promising light **:** OPTIMISTIC
rose–colored glasses *noun plural* (1950)
: favorably disposed opinions **:** optimistic eyes ⟨views the world through *rose-colored glasses*⟩
rose cut *noun* (circa 1842)
: a form in which gems (as diamonds) are cut that usually has a flat circular base and facets in two ranges rising to a point
— **rose–cut** *adjective*
rose fever *noun* (1851)
: hay fever occurring in the spring or early summer — called also *rose cold*
rose·fish \'rōz-,fish\ *noun* (1731)
: REDFISH
rose geranium *noun* (1832)
: any of several pelargoniums grown for their fragrant 3- to 5-lobed leaves and small pink flowers
rose hip *noun* (1857)
: the ripened accessory fruit of a rose that consists of a fleshy receptacle enclosing numerous achenes

ro·se·ma·ling \'rō-zə-,mä-liŋ, -sə-\ *noun* [Norwegian, from *rose* rose + *maling* painting] (1942)
: painted or sometimes carved decoration (as on furniture, walls, or wooden dinnerware) in Scandinavian peasant style that consists especially of floral designs and inscriptions
rose mallow *noun* (1857)
: any of several hibiscuses with large rose-colored flowers; *especially* **:** a showy plant (*Hibiscus moscheutos*) of the salt marshes of the eastern U.S.
rose·mary \'rōz-,mer-ē\ *noun, plural* **-mar·ies** [Middle English *rosmarine*, from Latin *rosmarinus*, from *ror-, ros* dew + *marinus* of the sea; akin to Sanskrit *rasa* sap, juice — more at MARINE] (14th century)
: a fragrant shrubby mint (*Rosmarinus officinalis*) of southern Europe and Asia Minor; *also* **:** its leaves used as a seasoning
rose of Jer·i·cho \-'jer-i-,kō\ [Middle English, from *Jericho*, ancient city in Palestine] (15th century)
: an Asian plant (*Anastatica hierochuntica*) of the mustard family that rolls up when dry and expands when moistened
rose of Shar·on \-'shar-ən, -'sher-\ [Plain of *Sharon*, Palestine] (circa 1847)
: a commonly cultivated Asian shrub or small tree (*Hibiscus syriacus*) having showy bell-shaped rose, purple, or white flowers
rose oil *noun* (1552)
: a fragrant essential oil obtained from roses and used chiefly in perfumery and in flavoring
ro·se·o·la \,rō-zē-'ō-lə, rō-'zē-ə-lə\ *noun* [New Latin, from Latin *roseus* rosy, from *rosa* rose] (circa 1818)
: a rose-colored eruption in spots or a disease marked by such an eruption; *especially* **:** ROSEOLA INFANTUM
— **ro·se·o·lar** \-lər\ *adjective*
roseola in·fan·tum \-in-'fan-təm\ *noun* [Latin, infant roseola] (circa 1935)
: a mild disease of infants and children characterized by fever lasting usually three days followed by an eruption of rose-colored spots
rose pink *noun* (circa 1859)
: a moderate pink
rose slug *noun* (1877)
: the slimy green larva of either of two sawflies (*Claudius isomerus* and *Endelomyia aethiops*) that feed on the parenchyma of and skeletonize the leaves of roses
ro·set \'rō-zət\ *noun* [alteration of Middle English *rosin*] (14th century)
chiefly Scottish **:** RESIN
Ro·set·ta stone \rō-'ze-tə-\ *noun* [*Rosetta*, Egypt] (circa 1859)
1 : a black basalt stone found in 1799 that bears an inscription in hieroglyphics, demotic characters, and Greek and is celebrated for having given the first clue to the decipherment of Egyptian hieroglyphics
2 : one that gives a clue to understanding
ro·sette \rō-'zet\ *noun* [French, literally, small rose, from Old French, from *rose*, from Latin *rosa*] (1790)
1 : an ornament usually made of material gathered or pleated so as to resemble a rose and worn as a badge of office, as evidence of having won a decoration (as the Medal of Honor), or as trimming
2 : a disk of foliage or a floral design usually in relief used as a decorative motif
3 : a structure or color marking on an animal suggestive of a rosette; *especially* **:** one of the groups of spots on a leopard
4 : a cluster of leaves in crowded circles or spirals arising basally from a crown (as in the

rosette 2

dandelion) or apically from an axis with greatly shortened internodes (as in many tropical palms)
5 : a food decoration or garnish in the shape of a rose ⟨icing *rosettes*⟩ ⟨carrot *rosettes*⟩
rose-wa·ter \'rōz-,wo-tər, -,wä-\ *adjective* (1840)
1 : affectedly nice or delicate
2 : having the odor of rose water
rose water *noun* (14th century)
: a watery solution of the odoriferous constituents of the rose used as a perfume or a flavoring
rose window *noun* (1773)
: a circular window filled with tracery
rose·wood \'rōz-,wùd\ *noun* (1660)
: any of various tropical trees especially genus *Dalbergia* yielding valuable cabinet woods of a dark red or purplish color streaked and variegated with black; *also* **:** the wood

rose window

Rosh Ha·sha·nah \,räsh-(h)ə-'shä-nə, ,rōsh-, -'shō-\ *noun* [Late Hebrew *rōsh hashshānāh*, literally, beginning of the year] (1846)
: the Jewish New Year observed on the first and by Orthodox and Conservative Jews also on the second of Tishri
Ro·si·cru·cian \,rō-zə-'krü-shən, ,rä-\ *noun* [Christian *Rosenkreutz* (New Latin *Rosae Crucis*) reputed 15th century founder of the movement] (1624)
1 : an adherent of a 17th and 18th century movement devoted to esoteric wisdom with emphasis on psychic and spiritual enlightenment
2 : a member of one of several organizations held to be descended from the Rosicrucians
— **Rosicrucian** *adjective*
— **Ro·si·cru·cian·ism** \-shə-,ni-zəm\ *noun*
ros·i·ly \'rō-zə-lē\ *adverb* (1809)
1 : in an optimistic manner
2 : with a rosy color or tinge
¹ros·in \'rä-z°n, 'rō-, *dialect* 'ro-zəm\ *noun* [Middle English, modification of Middle French *resine* resin] (13th century)
: a translucent amber-colored to almost black brittle friable resin that is obtained by chemical means from the oleoresin or deadwood of pine trees or from tall oil and used especially in making varnish, paper size, soap, and soldering flux and in rosining violin bows
²rosin *transitive verb* **ros·ined; ros·in·ing** \'räz-niŋ, 'rōz-; 'rä-z°n-iŋ, 'rō-\ (15th century)
: to rub or treat (as the bow of a violin) with rosin
ros·in·weed \'rä-z°n-,wēd, 'rō-\ *noun* (1831)
: any of several American plants (as the compass plant) having resinous foliage or a resinous odor
ros·tel·lum \rä-'ste-ləm\ *noun* [New Latin, from Latin, diminutive of *rostrum* beak] (circa 1826)
: a small process resembling a beak **:** a diminutive rostrum: as **a :** an extension of the stigma of an orchid flower **b :** an anterior prolongation of the head of a tapeworm bearing hooks
— **ros·tel·lar** \rä-'ste-lər\ *adjective*
ros·ter \'räs-tər *also* 'ròs- *or* 'rōs-\ *noun* [Dutch *rooster*, literally, gridiron; from the parallel lines] (1727)

1 a : a roll or list of personnel **b :** such a list giving the order in which a duty is to be performed ⟨duty *roster*⟩ **c :** the persons listed on a roster
2 : an itemized list

ros·tral \'räs-trəl *also* 'ròs-\ *adjective* [New Latin *rostralis*, from Latin *rostrum*] (1709)
1 : of or relating to a rostrum
2 : situated toward the oral or nasal region: as **a** of a part of the spinal cord **:** SUPERIOR 6a **b** of a part of the brain **:** ANTERIOR, VENTRAL
— **ros·tral·ly** \-trə-lē\ *adverb*

ros·trate \'räs-,trāt, -trət *also* 'ròs-\ *adjective* (circa 1819)
: having a rostrum

ros·trum \'räs-trəm *also* 'ròs-\ *noun, plural* **ros·tra** \-trə\ *or* **rostrums** [Latin, beak, ship's beak, from *rodere* to gnaw — more at RODENT] (1542)
1 [Latin *Rostra*, plural, a platform for speakers in the Roman Forum decorated with the beaks of captured ships, from plural of *rostrum*] **a :** an ancient Roman platform for public orators **b :** a stage for public speaking **c :** a raised platform on a stage
2 : the curved end of a ship's prow; *especially* **:** the beak of a war galley
3 : a bodily part or process suggesting a bird's bill: as **a :** the beak, snout, or proboscis of any of various insects or arachnids **b :** the often spinelike anterior median prolongation of the carapace of a crustacean (as a crayfish or lobster) ◊

rosy \'rō-zē\ *adjective* **ros·i·er; -est** (14th century)
1 a : of the color rose **b :** having a pinkish usually healthy-looking complexion **:** BLOOMING **c :** marked by blushes
2 : characterized by or tending to promote optimism
— **ros·i·ness** *noun*

¹rot \'rät\ *verb* **rot·ted; rot·ting** [Middle English *roten*, from Old English *rotian*; akin to Old High German *rōzzēn* to rot] (before 12th century)
intransitive verb
1 a : to undergo decomposition from the action of bacteria or fungi **b :** to become unsound or weak (as from use or chemical action)
2 a : to go to ruin **:** DETERIORATE **b :** to become morally corrupt **:** DEGENERATE
transitive verb
: to cause to decompose or deteriorate with or as if with rot
synonym *see* DECAY

²rot *noun* (14th century)
1 a : the process of rotting **:** the state of being rotten **:** DECAY **b :** something rotten or rotting
2 a *archaic* **:** a wasting putrescent disease **b :** any of several parasitic diseases especially of sheep marked by necrosis and wasting **c :** plant disease marked by breakdown of tissues and caused especially by fungi or bacteria
3 : NONSENSE — often used interjectionally

ro·ta \'rō-tə\ *noun* [Latin, wheel — more at ROLL] (1673)
1 *chiefly British* **a :** a fixed order of rotation (as of persons or duties) **b :** a roll or list of persons **:** ROSTER
2 *capitalized* [Medieval Latin, from Latin] **:** a tribunal of the papal curia exercising jurisdiction especially in matrimonial cases appealed from diocesan courts

ro·ta·me·ter \'rō-tə-,mē-tər, rō-'ta-mə-tər\ *noun* [Latin *rota* + English *-meter*] (1907)
: a gauge that consists of a graduated glass tube containing a free float for measuring the flow of a fluid

Ro·tar·i·an \rō-'ter-ē-ən\ *noun* [*Rotary* (club)] (1911)
: a member of a major national and international service club

¹ro·ta·ry \'rō-tə-rē\ *adjective* [Medieval Latin *rotarius*, from Latin *rota* wheel] (circa 1731)

1 a : turning on an axis like a wheel **b :** taking place about an axis ⟨*rotary* motion⟩
2 : having an important part that turns on an axis ⟨*rotary* cutter⟩
3 : characterized by rotation
4 : of, relating to, or being a press in which paper is printed by rotation in contact with a curved printing surface attached to a cylinder

²rotary *noun, plural* **-ries** (circa 1888)
1 : a rotary machine
2 : a road junction formed around a central circle about which traffic moves in one direction only — called also *circle, traffic circle*

rotary cultivator *noun* (1926)
: ROTOTILLER

rotary engine *noun* (1837)
1 : any of various engines (as a turbine) in which power is applied to vanes or similar parts constrained to move in a circular path
2 : a radial engine in which the cylinders revolve about a stationary crankshaft

rotary–wing aircraft *noun* (1935)
: ROTORCRAFT; *specifically* **:** HELICOPTER — usually used in plural

¹ro·tate \'rō-,tāt\ *adjective* [Latin *rota*] (1785)
: having the parts flat and spreading or radiating like the spokes of a wheel ⟨*rotate* blue flowers⟩

²ro·tate \'rō-,tāt, *especially British* rō-'\ *verb*
ro·tat·ed; ro·tat·ing [Latin *rotatus*, past participle of *rotare*, from *rota* wheel — more at ROLL] (1808)
intransitive verb
1 : to turn about an axis or a center **:** REVOLVE; *especially* **:** to move in such a way that all particles follow circles with a common angular velocity about a common axis
2 a : to perform an act, function, or operation in turn **b :** to pass or alternate in a series
transitive verb
1 a : to cause to turn or move about an axis or a center **b :** to cause (a plane region or line) to sweep out a volume or surface by moving around an axis so that each of its points remains at a constant distance from the axis ⟨*generate a torus by* rotating *a circle about an external line*⟩
2 : to cause to grow in rotation ⟨*rotate* crops⟩
3 : to cause to pass or act in a series **:** ALTERNATE
4 : to exchange (individuals or units) with others
— **ro·tat·able** \'rō-,tā-tə-bəl *also* rō-'\ *adjective*

ro·ta·tion \rō-'tā-shən\ *noun* (1555)
1 a (1) **:** the action or process of rotating on or as if on an axis or center (2) **:** the act or an instance of rotating something **b :** one complete turn **:** the angular displacement required to return a rotating body or figure to its original orientation
2 a : return or succession in a series ⟨*rotation* of the seasons⟩ **b :** the growing of different crops in succession in one field usually in a regular sequence
3 : the turning of a body part about its long axis as if on a pivot
4 : a game of pool in which all 15 object balls are shot in numerical order
5 : the series of pitchers on a baseball team who regularly start successive games in turn
— **ro·ta·tion·al** \-shnəl, -shə-n°l\ *adjective*

ro·ta·tive \'rō-,tā-tiv *also* rō-'\ *adjective* (1778)
1 : turning like a wheel **:** ROTARY
2 : relating to, occurring in, or characterized by rotation
— **ro·ta·tive·ly** *adverb*

ro·ta·tor \'rō-,tā-tər *also* rō-'\ *noun* (1676)
: one that rotates or causes rotation; *especially, plural* **-tors** *or* **-tor·es** \,rō-tə-'tòr-,ēz, -'tòr-\ **:** a muscle that partially rotates a part on its axis

rotator cuff *noun* (1961)
: a supporting and strengthening structure of the shoulder joint that is made up of the cap-

sule of the shoulder joint blended with tendons and muscles as they pass to the capsule or across it to insert on the head of the humerus

ro·ta·to·ry \'rō-tə-,tòr-ē, -,tòr-, *British* -t(ə-)ri *also* rō-'tā-tə-ri\ *adjective* (1755)
1 : of, relating to, or producing rotation
2 : occurring in rotation

ro·ta·vi·rus \'rō-tə-,vī-rəs\ *noun* [New Latin, from Latin *rota* wheel + New Latin *virus*] (1974)
: a reovirus that has a double-layered capsid and that causes diarrhea especially in infants

¹rote \'rōt\ *noun* [Middle English, from Middle French, of Germanic origin; akin to Old High German *hruozza* crowd] (14th century)
: ³CROWD 1

²rote *noun* [Middle English] (14th century)
1 : the use of memory usually with little intelligence ⟨learn by *rote*⟩
2 : routine or repetition carried out mechanically or unthinkingly ⟨a joyless sense of order, *rote*, and commercial hustle —L. L. King⟩

³rote *adjective* (1641)
1 : learned or memorized by rote
2 : MECHANICAL 3a

⁴rote *noun* [perhaps of Scandinavian origin; akin to Old Norse *rauta* to roar — more at ROUT] (1610)
: the noise of surf on the shore

ro·te·none \'rō-t°n-,ōn\ *noun* [International Scientific Vocabulary, from Japanese *roten* derris plant] (1924)
: a crystalline insecticide $C_{23}H_{22}O_6$ that is obtained from the roots of several tropical plants (as a derris) and is of low toxicity for warm-blooded animals and is used especially in home gardens

rot·gut \'rät-,gət\ *noun* (1633)
: cheap or inferior liquor

ro·ti \'rō-tē\ *noun* [Hindi *roṭī* bread; akin to Sanskrit *roṭika*, kind of bread] (1920)
: a round soft flat unleavened bread; *also* **:** such a bread wrapped around a filling and eaten as a sandwich

ro·ti·fer \'rō-tə-fər\ *noun* [ultimately from Latin *rota* + *-fer*] (1793)
: any of a class (Rotifera of the phylum Aschelminthes) of minute usually microscopic but many-celled chiefly freshwater aquatic invertebrates having the anterior end modified into a retractile disk bearing circles of strong cilia that often give the appearance of rapidly revolving wheels

ro·tis·ser·ie \rō-'tis-rē, -'ti-sə-\ *noun* [French *rôtisserie*, from Middle French *rostisserie*, from *rostir* to roast — more at ROAST] (circa 1920)
1 : a restaurant specializing in broiled and barbecued meats
2 : an appliance fitted with a spit on which food is rotated before or over a source of heat

ro·to \'rō-(,)tō\ *noun, plural* **rotos** (1926)
: ROTOGRAVURE

◊ **WORD HISTORY**
rostrum In Latin the primary meaning of *rostrum* was "beak," the noun having been derived from the verb *rodere*, meaning "to gnaw." Eventually *rostrum* came to be used metaphorically for a metal-pointed beam projecting from a galley's bow and used for ramming enemy ships. (Using the same metaphor, English calls this beam a *beak*.) In 338 B.C. the beaks of ships captured from the people of Antium (now called Anzio) were used to decorate the orators' platform in the Roman Forum. According to tradition this event gave to the platform the name *Rostra* (the plural of *rostrum*). Later *rostra* was applied to other platforms from which a speaker addressed an assembly. It was in this general sense that the singular form *rostrum* was first used in English in the 18th century.

ro·to·gra·vure \ˌrō-tə-grə-'vyùr\ *noun* [German *Rotogravur*, blend of Latin *rota* wheel and German *Photogravur* photogravure] (1913)
1 : PHOTOGRAVURE
2 : a section of a newspaper devoted to rotogravure pictures

ro·tor \'rō-tər\ *noun* [contraction of *rotator*] (1903)
1 : a part that revolves in a stationary part; *especially* : the rotating member of an electrical machine
2 : a complete system of horizontal rotating blades that supplies lift for a rotorcraft

ro·tor·craft \-ˌkraft\ *noun, plural* **rotorcraft** (1940)
: an aircraft (as a helicopter) whose lift is derived principally from rotating airfoils

ro·to·till \'rō-tə-ˌtil\ *transitive verb* [back-formation from *rototiller*] (1939)
: to till or plow (soil) with a rototiller

ro·to·till·er \-ˌti-lər\ *noun* [from *Rototiller*, a trademark] (1923)
: a landscaping implement with engine-powered rotating blades used to lift and turn over soil

¹rot·ten \'rä-t³n\ *adjective* [Middle English *roten*, from Old Norse *rotinn*; akin to Old English *rotian* to rot] (13th century)
1 : having rotted : PUTRID
2 : morally corrupt
3 : extremely unpleasant or inferior ⟨a *rotten* day⟩ ⟨a *rotten* job⟩
4 : very uncomfortable ⟨feeling *rotten*⟩
5 : of very poor quality : LOUSY, ABOMINABLE ⟨a *rotten* show⟩ ⟨what *rotten* luck⟩
— **rot·ten·ly** *adverb*
— **rot·ten·ness** \-t³n-(n)əs\ *noun*

²rotten *adverb* (1880)
: to an extreme degree ⟨spoiled *rotten*⟩

rotten borough *noun* (1812)
: an election district that has many fewer inhabitants than other election districts with the same voting power

rot·ten·stone \'rä-t³n-ˌstōn\ *noun* (1677)
: a decomposed siliceous limestone used for polishing

rot·ter \'rä-tər\ *noun* (1894)
: a thoroughly objectionable person

rott·wei·ler \'rät-ˌwī-lər, 'rót-ˌvī-\ *noun, often capitalized* [German, from *Rottweil*, city in Germany] (1907)
: any of a breed of tall powerful black-and-tan short-haired dogs of German origin that are commonly used as guard dogs

rottweiler

ro·tund \rō-'tənd, 'rō-ˌ\ *adjective* [Latin *rotundus*, probably alteration of (assumed) Old Latin *retundus*; akin to Latin *rota* wheel — more at ROLL] (1705)
1 : marked by roundness : ROUNDED
2 : marked by fullness of sound or cadence : OROTUND, SONOROUS ⟨a master of *rotund* phrase⟩
3 : notably plump : CHUBBY
— **ro·tun·di·ty** \rō-'tən-də-tē\ *noun*
— **ro·tund·ly** \-'tən(d)-lē, 'rō-ˌ\ *adverb*
— **ro·tund·ness** \rō-'tən(d)-nəs, 'rō-ˌ\ *noun*

ro·tun·da \rō-'tən-də\ *noun* [Italian *rotonda*, from Latin *rotunda*, feminine of *rotundus*] (circa 1700)
1 : a round building; *especially* : one covered by a dome
2 a : a large round room **b** : a large central area (as in a hotel)

ro·tu·ri·er \rō-'tùr-ē-ˌā, -'tyùr-\ *noun* [Middle French] (1586)
: a person not of noble birth

rou·ble *variant of* RUBLE

roué \rü-'ā\ *noun* [French, literally, broken on the wheel, from past participle of *rouer* to break on the wheel, from Medieval Latin *rotare*, from Latin, to rotate; from the feeling that such a person deserves this punishment] (1800)
: a man devoted to a life of sensual pleasure : RAKE ◆

¹rouge \'rüzh, *especially Southern* 'rüj\ *noun* [French, from Middle French, from *rouge* red, from Latin *rubeus* reddish — more at RUBY] (1753)
1 : any of various cosmetics for coloring the cheeks or lips red
2 : a red powder consisting essentially of ferric oxide used in polishing glass, metal, or gems and as a pigment

²rouge *verb* **rouged; roug·ing** (1777)
transitive verb
1 : to apply rouge to
2 : to cause to redden
intransitive verb
: to use rouge

¹rough \'rəf\ *adjective* **rough·er; rough·est** [Middle English, from Old English *rūh*; akin to Old High German *rūh* rough, Lithuanian *raukas* wrinkle] (before 12th century)
1 a : marked by inequalities, ridges, or projections on the surface : COARSE **b** : covered with or made up of coarse and often shaggy hair ⟨*rough*-coated collie⟩ — compare SMOOTH, WIREHAIRED **c** (1) : having a broken, uneven, or bumpy surface ⟨*rough* terrain⟩ (2) : difficult to travel through or penetrate : WILD ⟨into the *rough* woods —P. B. Shelley⟩
2 a : TURBULENT, TEMPESTUOUS ⟨*rough* seas⟩ **b** (1) : characterized by harshness, violence, or force (2) : presenting a challenge : DIFFICULT ⟨*rough* to deal with —R. M. McAlmon⟩
3 : coarse or rugged in character or appearance: as **a** : harsh to the ear **b** : crude in style or expression **c** : INDELICATE **d** : marked by a lack of refinement or grace : UNCOUTH
4 a : CRUDE, UNFINISHED ⟨*rough* carpentry⟩ **b** : executed or ventured hastily, tentatively, or imperfectly ⟨a *rough* draft⟩ ⟨*rough* estimate⟩; *also* : APPROXIMATE ⟨this gives a *rough* idea⟩ ☆
— **rough·ish** \'rə-fish\ *adjective*
— **rough·ness** \'rəf-nəs\ *noun*

²rough *adverb* (14th century)
: ROUGHLY 1

³rough *noun* (15th century)
1 : uneven ground covered with high grass, brush, and stones; *specifically* : such ground bordering a golf fairway
2 : the rugged or disagreeable side or aspect ⟨hiking-camping admirers of nature in the *rough* —Eleanor Stirling⟩
3 a : something in a crude, unfinished, or preliminary state **b** : broad outline : general terms ⟨the question . . . has been discussed in *rough* —*Manchester Guardian Weekly*⟩ **c** : a hasty preliminary drawing or layout
4 : ROWDY

⁴rough *transitive verb* (1763)
1 : ROUGHEN
2 a : to subject to abuse : MANHANDLE, BEAT — usually used with *up* **b** : to subject to unnecessary and intentional violence in a sport
3 : to calk or otherwise roughen (a horse's shoes) to prevent slipping
4 a : to shape, make, or dress in a rough or preliminary way **b** : to indicate the chief lines of ⟨*rough* out the structure of a building⟩
— **rough·er** *noun*
— **rough it** : to live under harsh or primitive conditions

rough·age \'rə-fij\ *noun* (circa 1900)
: FIBER 1d; *also* : food containing much indigestible material acting as fiber

rough–and–ready \ˌrə-fən-'re-dē\ *adjective* (1810)
: crude in nature, method, or manner but effective in action or use

¹rough–and–tum·ble \-'təm-bəl\ *noun* (1792)
: rough disorderly unrestrained fighting or struggling; *also* : INFIGHTING

²rough–and–tumble *adjective* (1832)
1 : marked by rough-and-tumble ⟨grew up in a *rough-and-tumble* atmosphere —E. J. Kahn⟩; *also* : ROUGH-AND-READY
2 : put together haphazardly : MAKESHIFT ⟨a *rough-and-tumble* fence⟩

rough bluegrass *noun* (circa 1925)
: a forage grass (*Poa trivialis*) of Eurasia and northern Africa that is naturalized in North America

rough breathing *noun* (1899)
1 : a mark ʽ used in Greek over some initial vowels to show that they are aspirated or over ρ to show that it is voiceless
2 : the sound indicated by a mark ʽ over a Greek vowel or ρ

¹rough·cast \'rəf-ˌkast, *for 2 also* -'kast\ *transitive verb* **-cast; -cast·ing** (1565)
1 : to plaster (as a wall) with roughcast
2 : to shape or form roughly

²rough·cast \-ˌkast\ *noun* (1579)
1 : a rough model
2 : a plaster of lime mixed with shells or pebbles used for covering buildings
3 : a rough surface finish (as of a plaster wall)

rough cut *noun* (1937)

: a print of an incompletely edited motion picture

¹rough–dry \'rəf-'drī\ *transitive verb* (1837)
: to dry (laundry) without smoothing or ironing

²rough–dry *adjective* (1856)
: being dry after laundering but not ironed or smoothed over ⟨*rough-dry* clothes⟩

rough·en \'rə-fən\ *verb* **rough·ened; rough·en·ing** \'rə-fə-niŋ, 'rəf-niŋ\ (1582)
transitive verb
: to make rough or rougher ⟨her hands were *roughened* by work —Ellen Glasgow⟩
intransitive verb
: to become rough

rough fish *noun* (1843)
: a fish that is neither a sport fish nor an important food for sport fishes

rough–hew \'rəf-'hyü\ *transitive verb* **-hewed; -hewn** \-'hyün\; **-hew·ing** (1530)
1 : to hew (as timber) coarsely without smoothing or finishing
2 : to form crudely

rough–hewn \-'hyün\ *adjective* (1530)
1 : being in a rough, unsmoothed, or unfinished state : crudely formed ⟨*rough-hewn* beams⟩
2 : lacking refinement ⟨he was rather attractive, in a *rough-hewn* kind of way —Jan Speas⟩

¹rough·house \'rəf-,haús\ *noun* (1887)
: violence or rough boisterous play

²rough·house \-,haús, -,haúz\ *verb* **rough·housed; rough·hous·ing** (1902)
transitive verb
: to treat in a boisterously rough manner
intransitive verb
: to engage in roughhouse

rough·leg \'rəf-,leg, -,lāg\ *noun* (1895)
: ROUGH-LEGGED HAWK

rough–legged hawk *noun* (1811)
: a large circumpolar arctic hawk (*Buteo lagopus*) that winters southward and typically has a white tail with a wide black band or bands at the tip

rough lemon *noun* (1900)
1 : a hybrid lemon that forms a large spreading thorny tree, bears rough-skinned nearly globular acid fruit, and is important chiefly as a rootstock for other citrus trees
2 : the fruit of a rough lemon

rough·ly \'rə-flē\ *adverb* (14th century)
1 : in a rough manner: as **a** : with harshness or violence ⟨treated the prisoner *roughly*⟩ **b** : in crude fashion : IMPERFECTLY ⟨*roughly* dressed lumber⟩
2 : without completeness or exactness : APPROXIMATELY ⟨*roughly* 20 percent⟩

¹rough·neck \'rəf-,nek\ *noun* (1836)
1 **a** : a rough or uncouth person **b** : ROWDY, TOUGH
2 : a worker of an oil-well-drilling crew other than the driller

²roughneck *adjective* (1916)
: having the characteristics of or suitable for a roughneck

rough·ri·der \'rəf-'rī-dər\ *noun* (1733)
1 : one who is accustomed to riding unbroken or little-trained horses
2 *usually* **Rough Rider** : a member of the 1st U.S. Volunteer Cavalry regiment in the Spanish-American War commanded by Theodore Roosevelt

¹rough·shod \-,shäd\ *adjective* (circa 1688)
1 : shod with calked shoes
2 : marked by tyrannical force ⟨*roughshod* rule⟩

²roughshod *adverb* (1813)
: in a roughshod manner ⟨rode *roughshod* over the opposition⟩

rough trade *noun* (circa 1935)
: male homosexuals who are or affect to be rugged and potentially violent; *also* : such a homosexual

rouille \'rü-ē, rüy\ *noun* [French, literally, rust; from its color] (1951)

: a peppery garlic sauce

rou·lade \rü-'läd\ *noun* [French, literally, act of rolling] (circa 1706)
1 : a florid vocal embellishment sung to one syllable
2 : a slice of usually stuffed meat that is rolled, browned, and steamed or braised

rou·leau \rü-'lō\ *noun, plural* **rou·leaux** \-'lōz\ [French] (1693)
: a little roll; *especially* : a roll of coins put up in paper

¹rou·lette \rü-'let\ *noun* [French, literally, small wheel, from Old French *roelete*, diminutive of *roele* small wheel, from Late Latin *rotella*, diminutive of Latin *rota* wheel — more at ROLL] (1745)
1 : a gambling game in which players bet on which compartment of a revolving wheel a small ball will come to rest in
2 **a** : any of various toothed wheels or disks (as for producing rows of dots on engraved plates or for making short consecutive incisions in paper to facilitate subsequent division) **b** : tiny slits between rows of stamps in a sheet that are made by a roulette and serve as an aid in separation — compare PERFORATION

²roulette *transitive verb* **rou·lett·ed; rou·lett·ing** (1867)
: to make roulettes in

Rou·ma·nian \rú-'mā-nē-ən, -nyən\ *variant of* RUMANIAN

¹round \raúnd\ *adjective* [Middle English, from Old French *roont*, from Latin *rotundus* — more at ROTUND] (14th century)
1 **a** (1) : having every part of the surface or circumference equidistant from the center (2) : CYLINDRICAL ⟨a *round* peg⟩ **b** : approximately round ⟨a *round* face⟩
2 : well filled out : PLUMP, SHAPELY
3 **a** : COMPLETE, FULL ⟨a *round* dozen⟩ ⟨a *round* ton⟩ **b** : approximately correct; *especially* : exact only to a specific decimal or place (use the *round* number 1400 for the exact figure 1411) **c** : substantial in amount : AMPLE ⟨a good *round* price —T. B. Costain⟩
4 : direct in utterance : OUTSPOKEN ⟨a *round* oath⟩
5 : moving in or forming a circle
6 **a** : brought to completion or perfection : FINISHED **b** : presented with lifelike fullness or vividness
7 : delivered with a swing of the arm ⟨a *round* blow⟩
8 **a** : having full or unimpeded resonance or tone : SONOROUS **b** : pronounced with rounded lips : LABIALIZED
9 : of or relating to handwriting predominantly curved rather than angular
— **round·ness** \'raún(d)-nəs\ *noun*

²round *adverb* (14th century)
: AROUND 1, 2b, 3, 4, 5

³round *noun* (14th century)
1 **a** : something (as a circle, globe, or ring) that is round **b** (1) : a knot of people (2) : a circle of things
2 : ROUND DANCE 1
3 : a musical canon sung in unison in which each part is continuously repeated
4 **a** : a rung of a ladder or a chair **b** : a rounded molding
5 **a** : a circling or circuitous path or course **b** : motion in a circle or a curving path
6 **a** : a route or circuit habitually covered (as by a security guard or police officer) **b** : a series of similar or customary calls or stops ⟨making the *rounds* of his friends —*Current Biography*⟩; *especially* : a series of regularly scheduled professional calls on hospital patients made by a doctor or nurse — usually used in plural
7 : a drink of liquor apiece served at one time to each person in a group ⟨I'll buy the next *round*⟩
8 : a sequence of recurring routine or repetitive actions or events ⟨went about my *round* of chores⟩ ⟨the newest *round* of talks⟩

9 : a period of time that recurs in a fixed pattern ⟨the daily *round*⟩
10 **a** : one shot fired by a weapon or by each man in a military unit **b** : a unit of ammunition consisting of the parts necessary to fire one shot
11 **a** : a unit of action in a contest or game which comprises a stated period, covers a prescribed distance, includes a specified number of plays, or gives each player one turn **b** : a division of a tournament in which each contestant plays an opponent
12 : a prolonged burst (as of applause)
13 **a** : a cut of meat (as beef) especially between the rump and the lower leg — see BEEF illustration **b** : a slice of food ⟨a *round* of bread⟩
14 : a rounded or curved part
— **in the round** 1 : in full sculptured form unattached to a background 2 : with an inclusive or comprehensive view or representation 3 : with a center stage surrounded by an audience ⟨theater *in the round*⟩

⁴round (14th century)
transitive verb
1 **a** : to make round **b** (1) : to make (the lips) round and protruded (as in the pronunciation of \ü\) (2) : to pronounce with lip rounding : LABIALIZE
2 **a** : GO AROUND **b** : to pass part of the way around
3 : ENCIRCLE, ENCOMPASS
4 : to bring to completion or perfection — often used with *off* or *out*
5 : to express as a round number — often used with *off* ⟨11.3572 *rounded* off to two decimal places becomes 11.36⟩
intransitive verb
1 **a** : to become round, plump, or shapely **b** : to reach fullness or completion
2 : to follow a winding course : BEND
— **round on** : to turn against : ASSAIL

⁵round *preposition* (1602)
1 : AROUND
2 : all during : THROUGHOUT ⟨*round* the year⟩

⁶round *transitive verb* [alteration of Middle English *rounen*, from Old English *rūnian*; akin to Old English *rūn* mystery — more at RUNE] (circa 1529)
1 *archaic* : WHISPER
2 *archaic* : to speak to in a whisper

¹round·about \'raún-də-,baút\ *adjective* (1608)
: CIRCUITOUS, INDIRECT ⟨had to take a *roundabout* course⟩
— **round·about·ness** *noun*

²roundabout *noun* (1755)
1 : a circuitous route : DETOUR
2 *British* : MERRY-GO-ROUND
3 : a short close-fitting jacket worn by men and boys especially in the 19th century
4 *British* : ROTARY 2

round angle *noun* (circa 1934)
: an angle of 360° or 2 π radians

round clam *noun* (circa 1843)
: QUAHOG

round dance *noun* (1683)
1 : a folk dance in which participants form a ring and move in a prescribed direction
2 : a ballroom dance in which couples progress around the room
3 : a series of movements performed by a bee to indicate that a source of food is nearby

round·ed \'raún-dəd\ *adjective* (1712)
1 : made round : flowing rather than jagged or angular
2 : fully developed
— **round·ed·ness** *noun*

roun·del \'raún-d°l\ *noun* [Middle English, from Old French *rondel*, from *roont* round — more at ROUND] (14th century)
1 : a round figure or object (as a circular panel, window, or niche)
2 **a** : RONDEL 2a **b** : an English modified rondeau

roun·de·lay \'raün-də-ˌlā\ *noun* [Middle English, modification of Middle French *rondelet*, diminutive of *rondel*] (15th century)
1 : a simple song with a refrain
2 : a poem with a refrain recurring frequently or at fixed intervals as in a rondel
round·er \'raün-dər\ *noun* (1828)
1 *plural but singular in construction* : a game of English origin that is played with ball and bat and that somewhat resembles baseball
2 : a dissolute person : WASTREL
3 : one that rounds by hand or by machine
4 : a boxing match lasting a specified number of rounds — usually used in combination ⟨a 10-*rounder*⟩
Round·head \'raund-ˌhed\ *noun* [from the Puritans' cropping their hair short in contrast to the Cavaliers] (1642)
1 : a member of the parliamentary party in England at the time of Charles I and Oliver Cromwell
2 : PURITAN 1
round·head·ed \-'he-dəd\ *adjective* (1729)
: having a round head; *specifically* : BRACHYCEPHALIC
— round·head·ed·ness *noun*
round·house \'raund-ˌhaus\ *noun* (1589)
1 *archaic* : LOCKUP
2 : a circular building for housing and repairing locomotives
3 : a blow delivered with a wide swing
round·ish \'raün-dish\ *adjective* (1545)
: somewhat round
round lot *noun* (circa 1902)
: the standard unit of trading in a security market usually amounting to 100 shares of stock
round·ly \'raün(d)-lē\ *adverb* (15th century)
1 a : in a complete or thorough manner : THOROUGHLY ⟨*roundly* disliked⟩ ⟨*roundly* satisfying⟩ **b** : by nearly everyone : WIDELY ⟨*roundly* praised⟩
2 : in a plainspoken manner : BLUNTLY ⟨told them *roundly* they would get no help⟩
3 : with vigor or asperity ⟨*roundly* attacked the plan⟩
round–rob·in \'raund-ˌrä-bən\ *noun* [from the name *Robin*] (1730)
1 a : a written petition, memorial, or protest to which the signatures are affixed in a circle so as not to indicate who signed first **b** : a statement signed by several persons **c** : something (as a letter) sent in turn to the members of a group each of whom signs and forwards it sometimes after adding comment
2 : ROUND TABLE 2
3 : a tournament in which every contestant meets every other contestant in turn
4 : SERIES, ROUND
round–shoul·dered \'raün(d)-ˌshōl-dərd\ *adjective* (1586)
: having the shoulders stooping or rounded
rounds·man \'raün(d)z-mən\ *noun* (1795)
1 : one that makes rounds
2 : a supervisory police officer of the grade of sergeant or just below
round steak *noun* (1876)
: a steak cut from the round of beef — see BEEF illustration
round ta·ble \'raün(d)-ˌtā-bəl\ *noun* (14th century)
1 a *R&T capitalized* : the large circular table of King Arthur and his knights **b** : the knights of King Arthur
2 *usually* **round-ta·ble** : a conference for discussion or deliberation by several participants; *also* : the participants in such a conference
round–the–clock *adjective* (1937)
: AROUND-THE-CLOCK
round–trip \'raün(d)-ˌtrip\ *noun, often attributive* (1860)
: a trip to a place and back usually over the same route
round–up \'raün-ˌdəp\ *noun* (1873)
1 a (1) : the act or process of collecting animals (as cattle) by riding around them and driving them in (2) : the cowboys and ranch personnel engaged in a cattle roundup **b** : a gathering in of scattered persons or things ⟨a *roundup* of all suspects⟩
2 : a summary of information ⟨a *roundup* of the news⟩
round up *transitive verb* (1844)
1 : to collect (as cattle) by means of a roundup
2 : to gather in or bring together from various quarters
round window *noun* (circa 1903)
: FENESTRA 1b
round·wood \'raund-ˌwud\ *noun* (1910)
: timber used (as for poles) without being squared by sawing or hewing
round·worm \'raund-ˌwərm\ *noun* (1565)
: NEMATODE; *also* : a related round-bodied unsegmented worm (as a spiny-headed worm) as distinguished from a flatworm
roup \'rüp, 'raüp\ *noun* [origin unknown] (circa 1808)
: TRICHOMONIASIS c
¹rouse \'rauz\ *verb* **roused; rous·ing** [Middle English, to shake the feathers] (1531)
transitive verb
1 *archaic* : to cause to break from cover
2 a : to stir up : EXCITE ⟨was *roused* to fury⟩ **b** : to arouse from or as if from sleep or repose : AWAKEN
intransitive verb
1 : to become aroused : AWAKEN
2 : to become stirred
— rouse·ment \'rauz-mənt\ *noun*
— rous·er *noun*
²rouse *noun* (circa 1802)
: an act or instance of rousing; *especially* : an excited stir
³rouse *noun* [alteration (from misdivision of *to drink carouse*) of *carouse*] (1602)
1 *obsolete* : DRINK, TOAST
2 *archaic* : CAROUSAL
rouse·about \'rau-zə-ˌbaut\ *noun* (1861)
Australian : an unskilled worker
rous·ing \'rau-zin\ *adjective* (1641)
1 a : giving rise to excitement : STIRRING **b** : BRISK, LIVELY
2 : EXCEPTIONAL, SUPERLATIVE
— rous·ing·ly *adverb*
Rous sarcoma \'raus-\ *noun* [F. Peyton Rous (died 1970) American physician] (circa 1925)
: a readily transplantable malignant fibrosarcoma of chickens that is caused by a specific carcinogenic virus
Rous·seau·ism \rü-'sō-ˌi-zəm\ *noun* (1865)
1 : the philosophical, educational, and political doctrines of Jean Jacques Rousseau
2 : the return to or glorification of a simpler and more primitive way of life
— Rous·seau·ist \-ist\ *noun*
— Rous·seau·is·tic \ˌrü-sō-'is-tik, rü-\ *adjective*
roust \'raust\ *transitive verb* [alteration of ¹*rouse*] (1658)
: to drive (as from bed) roughly or unceremoniously
roust·about \'raus-tə-ˌbaut\ *noun* (1868)
1 a : DECKHAND **b** : LONGSHOREMAN
2 : an unskilled or semiskilled laborer especially in an oil field or refinery
3 : a circus worker who erects and dismantles tents, cares for the grounds, and handles animals and equipment
roust·er \'raus-tər\ *noun* (1883)
1 : DECKHAND
2 : LONGSHOREMAN
¹rout \'raut\ *noun* [Middle English *route*, from Middle French, troop, defeat, from (assumed) Vulgar Latin *rupta*, from Latin, feminine of *ruptus*, past participle of *rumpere* to break — more at REAVE] (13th century)
1 : a crowd of people : THRONG; *specifically* : RABBLE 2b
2 a : DISTURBANCE **b** *archaic* : FUSS
3 : a fashionable gathering
²rout \'rōt, 'rüt\ *intransitive verb* [Middle English *rowten*, from Old Norse *rauta*; akin to

Old English *rēotan* to weep, Latin *rudere* to roar] (14th century)
dialect chiefly British : to low loudly : BELLOW — used of cattle
³rout \'raut\ *verb* [alteration of ³*root*] (circa 1564)
intransitive verb
1 : to poke around with the snout : ROOT ⟨pigs *routing* in the earth⟩
2 : to search haphazardly
transitive verb
1 a *archaic* : to dig up with the snout **b** : to gouge out or make a furrow in (as wood or metal)
2 a : to force out as if by digging — usually used with *out* **b** : to cause to emerge especially from bed
3 : to come up with : UNCOVER
⁴rout \'raut\ *noun* [Middle French *route* troop, defeat] (1598)
1 : a state of wild confusion or disorderly retreat
2 a : a disastrous defeat : DEBACLE **b** : a precipitate flight
⁵rout \'raut\ *transitive verb* (1600)
1 a : to disorganize completely : DEMORALIZE **b** : to put to precipitate flight **c** : to defeat decisively or disastrously ⟨the discomfiture of seeing his party *routed* at the polls —A. N. Holcombe⟩
2 : to drive out : DISPEL
¹route \'rüt, 'raut\ *noun* [Middle English, from Old French, from (assumed) Vulgar Latin *rupta* (via), literally, broken way, from Latin *rupta*, feminine of *ruptus*, past participle] (13th century)
1 a : a traveled way : HIGHWAY ⟨the main *route* north⟩ **b** : a means of access : CHANNEL ⟨the *route* to social mobility —T. F. O'Dea⟩
2 : a line of travel : COURSE
3 a : an established or selected course of travel or action **b** : an assigned territory to be systematically covered ⟨a newspaper *route*⟩
²route *transitive verb* **rout·ed; rout·ing** (1832)
1 : to send by a selected route : DIRECT ⟨was *routed* along the scenic shore road⟩
2 : to divert in a specified direction
route·man \'rüt-mən, 'raut-ˌman\ *noun* (1918)
: one who is responsible for making sales or deliveries on an assigned route
¹rout·er \'rau-tər\ *noun* (1846)
: one that routs: as **a** : a routing plane **b** : a machine with a revolving vertical spindle and cutter for milling out the surface of wood or metal
²rout·er \'rü-tər, 'rau-\ *noun* (1903)
: one that routes
³rout·er \'rü-tər, 'rau-\ *noun* [*route* (race of a mile or more)] (circa 1951)
: a horse trained for distance races
route step *noun* (1867)
: a style of marching in which troops maintain prescribed intervals but are not required to keep in step or to maintain silence — called also *route march*
route·way \'rüt-ˌwā, 'raut-\ *noun* (1946)
chiefly British : ROUTE 3a
routh \'rauth, 'rüth\ *noun* [origin unknown] (circa 1689)
chiefly Scottish : PLENTY
¹rou·tine \rü-'tēn\ *noun* [French, from Middle French, from *route* traveled way] (1676)
1 a : a regular course of procedure ⟨if resort to legal action becomes a campus *routine* —J. A. Perkins⟩ **b** : habitual or mechanical performance of an established procedure ⟨the *routine* of factory work⟩
2 : a reiterated speech or formula ⟨the old "After you" *routine* —Ray Russell⟩

3 : a worked-out part (as of an entertainment or sports contest) that may be often repeated ⟨a dance *routine*⟩ ⟨a gymnastic *routine*⟩; *especially* **:** a theatrical number
4 : a sequence of computer instructions for performing a particular task
²**rou·tine** \rü-'tēn, 'rü-,\ *adjective* (1817)
1 : of a commonplace or repetitious character **:** ORDINARY
2 : of, relating to, or being in accordance with established procedure ⟨*routine* business⟩
— **rou·tine·ly** *adverb*
rou·tin·ize \rü-'tē-,nīz, 'rü-t³n-,īz\ *transitive verb* **-ized; -iz·ing** (1921)
: to discipline in or reduce to a routine
— **rou·tin·i·za·tion** \(,)rü-,tē-nə-'zā-shən, ,rü-t³n-ə-\ *noun*
roux \'rü\ *noun, plural* **roux** \'rüz\ [French, from *beurre roux* brown butter] (1813)
: a cooked mixture of flour and fat used as a thickening agent in a soup or a sauce
¹**rove** \'rōv\ *verb* **roved; rov·ing** [Middle English *roven* to shoot at random, wander] (1536)
intransitive verb
: to move aimlessly **:** ROAM
transitive verb
: to wander through or over
synonym see WANDER
²**rove** *noun* (1606)
: an act or instance of wandering
³**rove** *past and past participle of* REEVE
⁴**rove** *transitive verb* **roved; rov·ing** [origin unknown] (1789)
: to join (textile fibers) with a slight twist and draw out into roving
⁵**rove** *noun* (1789)
: ROVING
rove beetle *noun* [perhaps from ¹*rove*] (circa 1771)
: any of a family (Staphylinidae) of often predatory active beetles having a long body and very short wing covers beneath which the wings are folded transversely — called also *staphylinid*
¹**ro·ver** \'rō-vər\ *noun* [Middle English, from Middle Dutch, from *roven* to rob; akin to Old English *rēafian* to reave — more at REAVE] (14th century)
: PIRATE
²**rov·er** \'rō-vər\ *noun* [Middle English, from *roven*] (15th century)
1 : a random or long-distance mark in archery — usually used in plural
2 : WANDERER, ROAMER
3 : a player who is not assigned to a specific position on a team and who plays wherever needed
4 : a vehicle for exploring the surface of an extraterrestrial body (as the moon or Mars)
¹**rov·ing** \'rō-viŋ\ *adjective* [¹*rove*] (1596)
1 a : capable of being shifted from place to place **:** MOBILE **b :** not restricted as to location or area of concern
2 : inclined to ramble or stray ⟨a *roving* fancy⟩
²**roving** *noun* [⁴*rove*] (1802)
: a slightly twisted roll or strand of usually textile fibers
¹**row** \'rō\ *verb* [Middle English, from Old English *rōwan;* akin to Middle High German *rüejen* to row, Latin *remus* oar] (before 12th century)
intransitive verb
1 : to propel a boat by means of oars
2 : to move by or as if by the propulsion of oars
transitive verb
1 a : to propel with or as if with oars **b :** to be equipped with (a specified number of oars) **c** (1) **:** to participate in (a rowing match) (2) **:** to compete against in rowing (3) **:** to pull (an oar) in a crew
2 : to transport in an oar-propelled boat
— **row·er** \'rō-(ə)r\ *noun*
²**row** *noun* (1832)
: an act or instance of rowing

³**row** *noun* [Middle English *rawe;* akin to Old English *rǣw* row, Old High German *rīga* line, and perhaps to Sanskrit *rikhati* he scratches] (13th century)
1 : a number of objects arranged in a usually straight line ⟨a *row* of bottles⟩; *also* **:** the line along which such objects are arranged ⟨planted the corn in parallel *rows*⟩
2 a : WAY, STREET **b :** a street or area dominated by a specific kind of enterprise or occupancy ⟨doctors' *row*⟩
3 : TWELVE-TONE ROW
4 a : a continuous strip usually running horizontally or parallel to a base line **b :** a horizontal arrangement of items
— **in a row :** one after another **:** SUCCESSIVELY
⁴**row** *transitive verb* (1657)
: to form into rows
⁵**row** \'raù\ *noun* [origin unknown] (1746)
: a noisy disturbance or quarrel
⁶**row** \'raù\ *intransitive verb* (1797)
: to engage in a row **:** have a quarrel
row·an \'raù-ən, 'rō-ən\ *noun* [of Scandinavian origin; akin to Old Norse *reynir* rowan; akin to Old English *rēad* red — more at RED] (1804)
1 a : a Eurasian mountain ash (*Sorbus aucuparia*) with flat corymbs of white flowers followed by small red pomes **b :** an American mountain ash (*Sorbus americana*) with flat corymbs of white flowers followed by small orange red pomes
2 : the fruit of a rowan

rowan 1b: leaves and fruit

row·an·ber·ry \-,ber-ē\ *noun* (1814)
: ROWAN 2
row·boat \'rō-,bōt\ *noun* (1538)
: a small boat designed to be rowed
¹**row·dy** \'raù-dē\ *adjective* **row·di·er; -est** [perhaps irregular from ⁵*row*] (1819)
: coarse or boisterous in behavior **:** ROUGH; *also* **:** characterized by such behavior ⟨*rowdy* local bars⟩
— **row·di·ly** \'raù-d³l-ē\ *adverb*
— **row·di·ness** \'raù-dē-nəs\ *noun*
— **row·dy·ish** \-ish\ *adjective*
²**rowdy** *noun, plural* **rowdies** (1819)
: a rowdy person **:** TOUGH
row·dy·ism \'raù-dē-,i-zəm\ *noun* (1842)
: rowdy character or behavior
¹**row·el** \'raù-(ə)l\ *noun* [Middle English *rowelle,* from Middle French *rouelle* small wheel, from Old French *roele* — more at ROULETTE] (15th century)
: a revolving disk with sharp marginal points at the end of a spur
²**rowel** *transitive verb* **-eled** *or* **-elled; -el·ing** *or* **-el·ling** (1599)
1 : to goad with or as if with a rowel
2 : VEX, TROUBLE
row·en \'raù-ən\ *noun* [Middle English *rowein,* from (assumed) Old North French *rewain;* akin to Old French *regaïn* aftermath, from *re-* + *gaïn* aftermath, of Germanic origin; akin to Old High German *weida* pasture, *weidanōn* to hunt for food — more at GAIN] (15th century)
: AFTERMATH 1
row house *noun* (1936)
: one of a series of houses connected by common sidewalls and forming a continuous group
row·ing \'rō-iŋ\ *noun* (before 12th century)
1 : the propelling of a boat by means of oars **:** the action of one that rows
2 : the sport of racing in shells
rowing boat *noun* (1820)
chiefly British **:** ROWBOAT
rowing machine *noun* (1848)

: an exercise machine that simulates the action of rowing
row·lock \'rä-lək, 'rə-; 'rō-,läk\ *noun* [probably by alteration] (circa 1750)
chiefly British **:** OARLOCK
¹**roy·al** \'ròi(-ə)l\ *adjective* [Middle English *roial,* from Middle French, from Latin *regalis,* from *reg-, rex* king; akin to Old Irish *rī* (genitive *rīg*) king, Sanskrit *rājan,* Latin *regere* to rule — more at RIGHT] (14th century)
1 a : of kingly ancestry ⟨the *royal* family⟩ **b :** of, relating to, or subject to the crown ⟨the *royal* estates⟩ **c :** being in the crown's service ⟨*Royal* Air Force⟩
2 a : suitable for royalty **:** MAGNIFICENT **b :** requiring no exertion **:** EASY ⟨there is no *royal* road to logic —Justus Buchler⟩
3 a : of superior size, magnitude, or quality ⟨a patronage of *royal* dimensions —J. H. Plumb⟩ — often used as an intensive ⟨a *royal* pain⟩ **b :** established or chartered by the crown
4 : of, relating to, or being a part (as a mast, sail, or yard) next above the topgallant
— **roy·al·ly** \'ròi-ə-lē\ *adverb*
²**royal** *noun* (14th century)
1 : a person of royal blood
2 : a small sail on the royal mast immediately above the topgallant sail
3 : a stag of 8 years or more having antlers with at least 12 points
royal blue *noun* (1789)
: a vivid purplish blue
royal flush *noun* (circa 1868)
: a straight flush having an ace as the highest card — see POKER illustration
roy·al·ism \'ròi-ə-,li-zəm\ *noun* (1793)
: MONARCHISM
roy·al·ist \-list\ *noun* (1643)
1 *often capitalized* **:** an adherent of a king or of monarchical government: as **a :** CAVALIER 3 **b :** TORY 4
2 : a reactionary business tycoon
— **royalist** *adjective*
royal jelly *noun* (1817)
: a highly nutritious secretion of the pharyngeal glands of the honeybee that is fed to the very young larvae in a colony and to all queen larvae
royal palm *noun* (1861)
: any of a genus (*Roystonea*) of palms chiefly of the Caribbean region; *especially* **:** a tall graceful pinnate-leaved palm (*R. regia*) native to Cuba that is widely planted for ornament
royal poinciana *noun* (circa 1900)
: a showy tropical tree (*Delonix regia* synonym *Poinciana regia*) widely planted for its immense racemes of scarlet and orange flowers — called also *flamboyant, peacock flower*
royal purple *noun* (1661)
: a dark reddish purple
roy·al·ty \'ròi-(ə)l-tē\ *noun, plural* **-ties** [Middle English *roialte,* from Middle French *roialté,* from Old French, from *roial*] (14th century)
1 a : royal status or power **:** SOVEREIGNTY **b :** a right or perquisite of a sovereign (as a percentage paid to the crown of gold or silver taken from mines)
2 : regal character or bearing **:** NOBILITY
3 a : persons of royal lineage **b :** a person of royal rank ⟨how to address *royalties* —George Santayana⟩ **c :** a privileged class
4 : a right of jurisdiction granted to an individual or corporation by a sovereign
5 a : a share of the product or profit reserved by the grantor especially of an oil or mining lease **b :** a payment made to an author or composer for each copy of a work sold or to an inventor for each article sold under a patent
royster *variant of* ROISTER
roz·zer \'rä-zər\ *noun* [origin unknown] (1893)
slang British **:** POLICE OFFICER
RPG \,är-(,)pē-'jē\ *noun* [*r*eport *p*rogram *g*enerator] (1966)

: a computer language that generates programs from the user's specifications especially to produce business reports

RPV \ˌär-ˌ)pē-'vē\ *noun* [*r*emotely *p*iloted *v*ehicle] (1970)
: an unmanned aircraft flown by remote control and used especially for reconnaissance

-rrhagia *noun combining form* [New Latin, from Greek, from *rhēgnynai* to break, burst; probably akin to Lithuanian *rèžti* to cut]
: abnormal or excessive discharge or flow ⟨metro*rrhagia*⟩

-rrhea *noun combining form* [Middle English *-ria*, from Late Latin *-rrhoea*, from Greek *-rrhoia*, from *rhoia*, from *rhein* to flow — more at STREAM]
: flow : discharge ⟨logo*rrhea*⟩ ⟨leuko*rrhea*⟩

-rrhiza — see -RHIZA

-rrhoea *chiefly British variant of* -RRHEA

rRNA \ˌär-ˌ)är-ˌ)en-'ā\ *noun* (circa 1965)
: RIBOSOMAL RNA

ru·a·na \rü-'ä-nə\ *noun* [American Spanish, from Spanish, woolen fabric] (1903)
: a woolen covering resembling a poncho

¹rub \'rəb\ *verb* **rubbed; rub·bing** [Middle English *rubben;* akin to Icelandic *rubba* to scrape] (14th century)
intransitive verb
1 a : to move along the surface of a body with pressure : GRATE **b** (1) : to fret or chafe with or as if with friction (2) : to cause discontent, irritation, or anger
2 : to continue in a situation usually with slight difficulty ⟨in spite of financial difficulties, he is *rubbing* along⟩
3 : to admit of being rubbed (as for erasure or obliteration)
transitive verb
1 a : to subject to or as if to the action of something moving especially back and forth with pressure and friction **b** (1) : to cause (a body) to move with pressure and friction along a surface (2) : to treat in any of various ways by rubbing **c** : to bring into reciprocal back-and-forth or rotary contact
2 : ANNOY, IRRITATE
— **rub elbows** *or* **rub shoulders :** to associate closely : MINGLE
— **rub one's nose in :** to bring forcefully or repeatedly to one's attention
— **rub the wrong way :** to arouse the antagonism or displeasure of : IRRITATE

²rub *noun* (1586)
1 a : an unevenness of surface (as of the ground in lawn bowling) **b :** OBSTRUCTION, DIFFICULTY ⟨the *rub* is that so few of the scholars have any sense of this truth themselves —Benjamin Farrington⟩ **c :** something grating to the feelings (as a gibe or harsh criticism) **d :** something that mars serenity
2 : the application of friction with pressure ⟨an alcohol *rub*⟩

Ru·bai·yat stanza \'rü-bē-ˌät-, -ˌbī-, -ˌat-\ *noun* [*The Rubáiyát of Omar Khayyám*, quatrains translated by Edward FitzGerald (1859)] (1940)
: an iambic pentameter quatrain with a rhyme scheme *aaba*

ru·basse \rü-'bas, 'rü-ˌ\ *noun* [French *rubace*, irregular from *rubis* ruby — more at RUBY] (circa 1890)
: a quartz stained a ruby red

ru·ba·to \rü-'bä-(ˌ)tō\ *noun, plural* **-tos** [Italian, literally, robbed] (circa 1883)
: a fluctuation of tempo within a musical phrase often against a rhythmically steady accompaniment

¹rub·ber \'rə-bər\ *noun* (1536)
1 a : one that rubs **b :** an instrument or object (as a rubber eraser) used in rubbing, polishing, scraping, or cleaning **c :** something that prevents rubbing or chafing
2 [from its use in erasers] **a :** an elastic substance that is obtained by coagulating the milky juice of any of various tropical plants (as of the genera *Hevea* and *Ficus*), is essen-

tially a polymer of isoprene, and is prepared as sheets and then dried — called also *caoutchouc, india rubber* **b :** any of various synthetic rubberlike substances **c :** natural or synthetic rubber modified by chemical treatment to increase its useful properties (as toughness and resistance to wear) and used especially in tires, electrical insulation, and waterproof materials
3 : something made of or resembling rubber: as **a :** a rubber overshoe **b** (1) : a rubber tire (2) : the set of tires on a vehicle **c :** a rectangular slab of white rubber in the middle of a baseball infield on which a pitcher stands while pitching **d :** CONDOM
— **rubber** *adjective*

²rubber *noun* [origin unknown] (1599)
1 : a contest consisting of an odd number of games won by the side that takes a majority (as two out of three)
2 : an odd game played to determine the winner of a tie

rubber band *noun* (1886)
: a continuous band of rubber used in various ways (as for holding together a sheaf of papers)

rubber bridge *noun* (1936)
: a form of contract bridge in which settlement is made at the end of each rubber

rubber cement *noun* (1886)
: an adhesive consisting typically of a dispersion of vulcanized rubber in an organic solvent

rubber check *noun* [from its coming back like a bouncing rubber ball] (1926)
: a check returned by a bank because of insufficient funds in the payer's account

rub·ber·ized \'rə-bə-ˌrīzd\ *adjective* (1908)
: coated or saturated with rubber or a rubber solution

rub·ber·like \'rə-bər-ˌlīk\ *adjective* (1922)
: resembling rubber especially in physical properties (as elasticity and toughness)

¹rub·ber·neck \-ˌnek\ *noun* (circa 1896)
1 : an overly inquisitive person
2 : TOURIST; *especially* : one on a guided tour

²rubberneck *intransitive verb* (1896)
1 : to look about, stare, or listen with exaggerated curiosity
2 : to go on a tour : SIGHTSEE
— **rub·ber·neck·er** \-ˌne-kər\ *noun*

rubber plant *noun* (1888)
: a plant that yields rubber; *especially* : a tall tropical Asian tree (*Ficus elastica*) of the mulberry family that is frequently dwarfed as an ornamental

rubber–stamp *transitive verb* (1918)
1 : to approve, endorse, or dispose of as a matter of routine or at the command of another
2 : to mark with a rubber stamp

rubber stamp *noun* (1881)
1 : a stamp of rubber for making imprints
2 a : a person who echoes or imitates others **b :** a body or person that approves or endorses a program or policy with little or no dissent or discussion
3 a : a stereotyped copy or expression ⟨the usual *rubber stamps* of criticism —H. L. Mencken⟩ **b :** a routine endorsement or approval
— **rubber–stamp** *adjective*

rubber tree *noun* (1847)
: a tree that yields rubber; *especially* : a South American tree (*Hevea brasiliensis*) of the spurge family that is cultivated in plantations and is a chief source of rubber

rub·bery \'rə-b(ə-)rē\ *adjective* (1907)
: resembling rubber (as in elasticity, consistency, or texture) ⟨*rubbery* legs⟩

rubber tree

rub·bing \'rə-biŋ\ *noun* (1845)
: an image of a raised, incised, or textured surface obtained by placing paper over it and rubbing the paper with a colored substance

rubbing alcohol *noun* (circa 1931)
: a cooling and soothing liquid for external application that contains approximately 70 percent denatured ethyl alcohol or isopropanol

rub·bish \'rə-bish, *dialect* -bij\ *noun* [Middle English *robys*] (15th century)
1 : useless waste or rejected matter : TRASH
2 : something that is worthless or nonsensical ⟨few real masterpieces are forgotten and not much *rubbish* survives —William Bridges-Adams⟩
— **rub·bishy** \-bə-shē\ *adjective*

¹rub·ble \'rə-bəl\ *noun* [Middle English *robyl*] (14th century)
1 a : broken fragments (as of rock) resulting from the decay or destruction of a building ⟨fortifications knocked into *rubble* —C. S. Forester⟩ **b :** a miscellaneous confused mass or group of usually broken or worthless things ⟨lay in a pile of *rubble*, only this time there was more of it, additional gear having hit the deck —K. M. Dodson⟩
2 : waterworn or rough broken stones or bricks used in coarse masonry or in filling courses of walls
3 : rough stone as it comes from the quarry

²rubble *transitive verb* **rub·bled; rub·bling** \-b(ə-)liŋ\ (1926)
: to reduce to rubble

rub·down \'rəb-ˌdaùn\ *noun* (1896)
: a brisk rubbing of the body

rube \'rüb\ *noun* [*Rube*, nickname for *Reuben*] (1896)
: an awkward unsophisticated person : RUSTIC

¹ru·be·fa·cient \ˌrü-bə-'fā-shənt\ *adjective* [Latin *rubefacient-, rubefaciens*, present participle of *rubefacere* to make red, from *rubeus* reddish + *facere* to make — more at RUBY, DO] (1804)
: causing redness (as of the skin)

²rubefacient *noun* (1805)
: a substance for external application that produces redness of the skin

Rube Gold·berg \'rüb-'gōl(d)-ˌbərg\ *also* **Rube Gold·berg·i·an** \-ˌbər-gē-ən, -ˌbərg-yən\ *adjective* [Reuben (*Rube*) L. *Goldberg* (died 1970) American cartoonist] (1931)
: accomplishing by complex means what seemingly could be done simply ⟨a kind of *Rube Goldberg* contraption . . . with five hundred moving parts —L. T. Grant⟩; *also* : characterized by such complex means

ru·bel·la \rü-'be-lə\ *noun* [New Latin, from Latin, feminine of *rubellus* reddish, from *ruber* red — more at RED] (1883)
: GERMAN MEASLES

ru·bel·lite \rü-'be-ˌlīt, 'rü-bə-ˌlīt\ *noun* [Latin *rubellus*] (circa 1796)
: a red tourmaline used as a gem

Ru·ben·esque \ˌrü-bə-'nesk\ *adjective* (1925)
: of, relating to, or suggestive of the painter Rubens or his works; *especially* : plump or rounded usually in a pleasing or attractive way ⟨a *Rubenesque* figure⟩

ru·be·o·la \ˌrü-bē-'ō-lə, rü-'bē-ə-lə\ *noun* [New Latin, from neuter plural of (assumed) New Latin *rubeolus* reddish, from Latin *rubeus*] (1803)
: MEASLES

Ru·bi·con \'rü-bi-ˌkän\ *noun* [Latin *Rubicon-, Rubico*, river of northern Italy forming part of the boundary between Cisalpine Gaul and Italy whose crossing by Julius Caesar in 49 B.C. was regarded by the Senate as an act of war] (1626)

: a bounding or limiting line; *especially* : one that when crossed commits a person irrevocably

ru·bi·cund \'rü-bi-(,)kənd\ *adjective* [Middle English *rubicunde*, from Latin *rubicundus*, from *rubēre* to be red; akin to Latin *rubeus*] (15th century)
: RUDDY
— **ru·bi·cun·di·ty** \,rü-bi-'kən-də-tē\ *noun*

ru·bid·i·um \rü-'bid-ē-əm\ *noun* [New Latin, from Latin *rubidus* red, from *rubēre*] (1861)
: a soft silvery metallic element of the alkali metal group that reacts violently with water and bursts into flame spontaneously in air — see ELEMENT table

rub in *transitive verb* (1851)
: to harp on (as something unpleasant) : EMPHASIZE

ru·bi·ous \'rü-bē-əs\ *adjective* (1601)
: RED, RUBY

ru·ble \'rü-bəl\ *noun* [Russian *rubl'*] (1554)
— see MONEY table

rub off *intransitive verb* (1950)
: to become transferred ⟨bad habits *rubbed off* on them⟩ ⟨carbon *rubs off* on your hands⟩
— **rub–off** \'rəb-,óf\ *noun*

rub out *transitive verb* (14th century)
1 : to obliterate or extinguish by or as if by rubbing
2 : to destroy completely; *specifically* : KILL, MURDER ⟨somebody *rubbed* him *out* . . . with a twenty-two —Raymond Chandler⟩
— **rub–out** \'rəb-,aút\ *noun*

ru·bric \'rü-brik, -,brik\ *noun* [Middle English *rubrike* red ocher, heading in red letters of part of a book, from Middle French *rubrique*, from Latin *rubrica*, from *rubr-, ruber* red] (14th century)
1 a : an authoritative rule; *especially* : a rule for conduct of a liturgical service b (1) : NAME, TITLE; *specifically* : the title of a statute (2) : something under which a thing is classed : CATEGORY ⟨the sensations falling under the general *rubric*, "pressure" —F. A. Geldard⟩ c : an explanatory or introductory commentary : GLOSS; *specifically* : an editorial interpolation
2 : a heading of a part of a book or manuscript done or underlined in a color (as red) different from the rest
3 : an established rule, tradition, or custom ◆
— **rubric** *or* **ru·bri·cal** \-bri-kəl\ *adjective*
— **ru·bri·cal·ly** \-bri-k(ə-)lē\ *adverb*

ru·bri·cate \'rü-bri-,kāt\ *transitive verb* **-cat·ed; -cat·ing** (1570)
1 : to write or print as a rubric
2 : to provide with a rubric
— **ru·bri·ca·tion** \,rü-bri-'kā-shən\ *noun*
— **ru·bri·ca·tor** \'rü-bri-,kā-tər\ *noun*

rub up *transitive verb* (1572)
1 : to revive or refresh knowledge of : RECALL
2 : to improve the keenness of (a mental faculty)

ru·bus \'rü-bəs\ *noun, plural* **rubus** [New Latin, from Latin, blackberry] (circa 1921)
: any of a genus (*Rubus*) of plants (as a blackberry or a raspberry) of the rose family having 3- to 7-foliolate or simple lobed leaves, white or pink flowers, and a mass of carpels ripening into an aggregate fruit composed of many drupelets

¹ru·by \'rü-bē\ *noun, plural* **rubies** [Middle English, from Middle French *rubis, rubi*, alteration of *robin*, from Medieval Latin *rubinus*, from Latin *rubeus* reddish; akin to Latin *ruber* red — more at RED] (14th century)
1 a : a precious stone that is a red corundum b : something (as a watch bearing) made of ruby
2 a : the dark red color of the ruby b : something resembling a ruby in color

²ruby *adjective* (1508)
: of the color ruby

ruby glass *noun* (1797)
: glass of a deep red color containing selenium, an oxide of copper, or a chloride of gold

ruby spinel *noun* (1839)
: a usually red spinel used as a gem

ru·by–throat \'rü-bē-,thrōt\ *noun* (circa 1783)
: RUBY-THROATED HUMMINGBIRD

ru·by–throat·ed hummingbird \'rü-bē-,thrō-təd-\ *noun* (circa 1782)
: a hummingbird (*Archilochus colubris*) of eastern North America having a bright green back, whitish underparts, and in the adult male a red throat with metallic reflections

ruche \'rüsh\ *or* **ruch·ing** \'rü-shiŋ\ *noun* [French *ruche* literally, beehive, from Medieval Latin *rusca* bark] (1827)
: a pleated, fluted, or gathered strip of fabric used for trimming
— **ruched** \'rüsht\ *adjective*

¹ruck \'rək\ *noun* [Middle English, of Scandinavian origin; akin to Old Norse *hraukr* rick — more at RICK] (15th century)
1 a : the usual run of persons or things : GENERALITY ⟨trying to rise above the *ruck* —Richard Holt⟩ b : an indistinguishable gathering : JUMBLE
2 : the persons or things following the vanguard ⟨finished the race in the *ruck*⟩

²ruck *verb* [*ruck*, noun, wrinkle] (1812)
: PUCKER, WRINKLE

ruck·sack \'rək-,sak, 'rùk-\ *noun* [German, from German dialect, from *Rucken* back + *Sack* sack] (1866)
: KNAPSACK

ruck·us \'rə-kəs *also* 'rü- *or* 'rù-\ *noun* [probably blend of *ruction* and *rumpus*] (circa 1890)
: ROW, DISTURBANCE ⟨raise a *ruckus*⟩

ruc·tion \'rək-shən\ *noun* [perhaps by shortening & alteration from *insurrection*] (circa 1825)
1 : a noisy fight
2 : DISTURBANCE, UPROAR

rud·beck·ia \,rəd-'be-kē-ə, rüd-\ *noun* [New Latin, from Olof *Rudbeck* (died 1702) Swedish scientist] (circa 1759)
: any of a genus (*Rudbeckia*) of North American perennial composite herbs having showy flower heads with mostly yellow ray flowers and a conical chaffy receptacle

rudd \'rəd, 'rùd\ *noun* [probably from *rud* redness, rud ocher, from Middle English *rude*, from Old English *rudu* — more at RUDDY] (1526)
: a freshwater European cyprinid fish (*Scardinius erythrophthalmus*) resembling the roach

rud·der \'rə-dər\ *noun* [Middle English *rother*, from Old English *rōther* paddle; akin to Old English *rōwan* to row] (14th century)
1 : a flat piece or structure of wood or metal attached upright to the stern of a boat or ship so that it can be turned causing the vessel's head to turn in the same direction
2 : a movable auxiliary airfoil on an airplane usually attached at the rear end that serves to control direction of flight in the horizontal plane — see AIRPLANE illustration
3 : a guiding force or strategy
— **rud·der·less** \-ləs\ *adjective*

rud·der·post \-,pōst\ *noun* (1691)
1 : the shaft of a rudder
2 : an additional sternpost in a ship with a single screw propeller to which the rudder is attached

¹rud·dle \'rə-d°l\ *noun* [diminutive of *rud* red ocher] (1538)
: RED OCHER

²ruddle *transitive verb* **rud·dled; rud·dling** \'rəd-liŋ, 'rə-d°l-iŋ\ (1718)
: to color with or as if with red ocher : REDDEN

rud·dock \'rə-dək, 'rù-\ *noun* [Middle English *ruddok*, from Old English *rudduc*; akin to Old English *rudu*] (before 12th century)
archaic : ROBIN 1a

rud·dy \'rə-dē\ *adjective* **rud·di·er; -est** [Middle English *rudi*, from Old English *rudig*, from *rudu* redness; akin to Old English *rēad* red — more at RED] (before 12th century)
1 : having a healthy reddish color
2 : RED, REDDISH

3 *British* — used as an intensive ⟨bellowed like a *ruddy* bull when she wanted food —Doreen Tovey⟩
— **rud·di·ly** \'rə-d°l-ē\ *adverb*
— **rud·di·ness** \'rə-dē-nəs\ *noun*

ruddy duck *noun* (1814)
: an American duck (*Oxyura jamaicensis*) which has a wedge-shaped tail of stiff sharp feathers, a broad bill, and white cheeks and the adult male of which has rich brownish red on the upper side and a blue bill during breeding season

rude \'rüd\ *adjective* **rud·er; rud·est** [Middle English, from Middle French, from Latin *rudis*; probably akin to Latin *rudus* rubble] (14th century)
1 a : being in a rough or unfinished state : CRUDE ⟨*rude* line illustrations⟩ b : NATURAL, RAW ⟨*rude* cotton⟩ c : PRIMITIVE, UNDEVELOPED ⟨peasants use *rude* wooden plows —Jack Raymond⟩ d : SIMPLE, ELEMENTAL ⟨landscape done in *rude* whites, blacks, deep browns —Richard Harris⟩
2 : lacking refinement or delicacy: a : IGNORANT, UNLEARNED b : INELEGANT, UNCOUTH c : offensive in manner or action : DISCOURTEOUS d : UNCIVILIZED, SAVAGE e : COARSE, VULGAR
3 : marked by or suggestive of lack of training or skill : INEXPERIENCED ⟨*rude* workmanship⟩
4 : ROBUST, STURDY ⟨in *rude* health⟩
5 : occurring abruptly and disconcertingly ⟨a *rude* awakening⟩ ☆
— **rude·ly** *adverb*

rude·ness *noun* (14th century)
1 : the quality or state of being rude
2 : a rude action

¹ru·der·al \'rü-də-rəl\ *adjective* [New Latin *ruderalis*, from Latin *ruder-, rudus* rubble] (circa 1858)
: growing where the natural vegetational cover has been disturbed by humans ⟨*ruderal* weeds of old fields and roadsides⟩

²ruderal *noun* (circa 1928)
: a weedy and commonly introduced plant growing where the vegetational cover has been interrupted

ru·di·ment \'rü-də-mənt\ *noun* [Latin *rudimentum* beginning, from *rudis* raw, rude] (1548)

☆ SYNONYMS
Rude, rough, crude, raw mean lacking in social refinement. RUDE implies ignorance of or indifference to good form; it may suggest intentional discourtesy ⟨*rude* behavior⟩. ROUGH is likely to stress lack of polish and gentleness ⟨*rough* manners⟩. CRUDE may apply to thought or behavior limited to the gross, the obvious, or the primitive and ignorant of civilized amenities ⟨a *crude* joke⟩. RAW suggests being untested, inexperienced, or unfinished ⟨turning *raw* youths into polished performers⟩.

◇ WORD HISTORY
rubric Descended ultimately from Latin *rubrica*, a derivative of *ruber* "red," the word *rubric* was used in Middle English to designate red ocher, a red, earthy hematite used as a pigment. Yet it also meant "heading for part of a treatise," the predecessor of present-day English *rubric* in the sense "category, something under which a thing is classed." This semantic transformation derives from the ancient practice of putting chapter headings or explanatory notes in a manuscript in red to contrast with the black ink of the text. Similarly, red ink was used to enter saints' names and holy days in calendars, and we still speak of a day with special significance as a "red-letter day."

1 : a basic principle or element or a fundamental skill — usually used in plural ⟨teaching themselves the *rudiments* of rational government —G. B. Galanti⟩
2 a : something unformed or undeveloped **:** BEGINNING — usually used in plural ⟨the *rudiments* of a plan⟩ **b** (1) **:** a body part so deficient in size or structure as to be entirely unable to perform its normal function (2) **:** an organ just beginning to develop **:** ANLAGE
— **ru·di·men·tal** \ˌrü-də-ˈmen-tᵊl\ *adjective*
ru·di·men·ta·ry \ˌrü-də-ˈmen-tə-rē, -ˈmen-trē\ *adjective* (1839)
1 : consisting in first principles **:** FUNDAMENTAL ⟨had only a *rudimentary* formal education —D. J. Boorstin⟩
2 : of a primitive kind ⟨the equipment of these past empire-builders was *rudimentary* —A. J. Toynbee⟩
3 : very imperfectly developed or represented only by a vestige ⟨the *rudimentary* tail of a hyrax⟩
— **ru·di·men·tar·i·ly** \-ˌmen-ˈter-ə-lē, -ˈmen-trə-lē\ *adverb*
— **ru·di·men·ta·ri·ness** \-ˈmen-tə-rē-nəs, -ˈmen-trē-\ *noun*
¹rue \ˈrü\ *noun* [Middle English *rewe*, from Old English *hrēow*; akin to Old High German *hriuwa* sorrow] (before 12th century)
: REGRET, SORROW
²rue *verb* **rued; ru·ing** (12th century)
transitive verb
: to feel penitence, remorse, or regret for
intransitive verb
: to feel sorrow, remorse, or regret
³rue *noun* [Middle English, from Middle French, from Latin *ruta*, from Greek *rhytē*] (13th century)
: a European strong-scented perennial woody herb (*Ruta graveolens* of the family Rutaceae, the rue family) that has bitter leaves used medicinally
rue anemone *noun* (circa 1818)
: a delicate vernal North American herb (*Anemonella thalictroides*) of the buttercup family with white flowers resembling those of the wood anemone
rue·ful \ˈrü-fəl\ *adjective* (13th century)
1 : exciting pity or sympathy **:** PITIABLE ⟨*rueful* squalid poverty . . . by every wayside —John Morley⟩
2 : MOURNFUL, REGRETFUL ⟨troubled her with a *rueful* disquiet —W. M. Thackeray⟩
— **rue·ful·ly** \-fə-lē\ *adverb*
— **rue·ful·ness** *noun*
ru·fes·cent \rü-ˈfe-sᵊnt\ *adjective* [Latin *rufescent-, rufescens*, present participle of *rufescere* to become reddish, from *rufus* red — more at RED] (1817)
: REDDISH
¹ruff *also* **ruffe** \ˈrəf\ *noun* [Middle English *ruf*] (15th century)
: a small freshwater European perch (*Acerina cernua*)
²ruff *noun* [probably back-formation from *ruffle*] (1555)
1 : a large round collar of pleated muslin or linen worn by men and women of the late 16th and early 17th centuries
2 : a fringe or frill of long hairs or feathers growing around or on the neck
3 : a common Eurasian sandpiper (*Philomachus pugnax*) whose male during the breeding season has a large ruff of erectile feathers on the neck
— **ruffed** \ˈrəft\ *adjective*
³ruff *verb* [Middle French *roffler*] (1598)
intransitive verb
: to take a trick with a trump

ruff 1

transitive verb
: to play a trump on (a card previously led or played)
⁴ruff *noun* (circa 1828)
: the act of trumping
ruffed grouse *noun* (circa 1782)
: a North American grouse (*Bonasa umbellus*) of heavy forests that has a ruff of erectile black feathers in the male that is lighter and less conspicuous in the female
ruf·fi·an \ˈrə-fē-ən\ *noun* [Middle French *rufian*] (1531)
: a brutal person **:** BULLY
— **ruffian** *adjective*
— **ruf·fi·an·ism** \-ə-ˌni-zəm\ *noun*
— **ruf·fi·an·ly** *adjective*
¹ruf·fle \ˈrə-fəl\ *verb* **ruf·fled; ruf·fling** \-f(ə-)liŋ\ [Middle English *ruffelen*; akin to Low German *ruffelen* to crumple] (14th century)
transitive verb
1 a : ROUGHEN, ABRADE **b :** TROUBLE, VEX ⟨is not *ruffled* by such barbs —Bruce Anderson⟩
2 : to erect (as feathers) in or like a ruff
3 a : to flip through (as pages) **b :** SHUFFLE
4 : to make into a ruffle
intransitive verb
: to become ruffled ⟨their dispositions *ruffle* perceptibly —*Life*⟩
²ruffle *noun* (1534)
1 : COMMOTION, BRAWL
2 : a state or cause of irritation
3 a : a strip of fabric gathered or pleated on one edge **b :** ²RUFF 2
4 : an unevenness or disturbance of surface **:** RIPPLE
— **ruf·fly** \ˈrə-f(ə-)lē\ *adjective*
³ruffle *noun* [*ruff* a drumbeat] (circa 1802)
: a low vibrating drumbeat less loud than a roll
ru·fi·yaa \ˈrü-fē-ˌyä\ *noun, plural* **rufiyaa** [probably from Divehi (Indo-Aryan language of the Maldive Islands), from Hindi *rupīyā, rūpaiyā* rupee] (1982)
— see MONEY table
RU 486 \ˈär-ˌyü-ˌfōr-ˌā-tē-ˈsiks, -ˌfȯr-\ *noun* [*Roussel-UCLAF*, the drug's French manufacturer + *486*, laboratory serial number] (1983)
: a drug $C_{29}H_{35}NO_2$ taken orally to induce abortion especially early in pregnancy by blocking the body's use of progesterone
ru·fous \ˈrü-fəs\ *adjective* [Latin *rufus* red — more at RED] (1782)
: REDDISH
rug \ˈrəg\ *noun* [(assumed) Middle English, rag, tuft, of Scandinavian origin; akin to Old Norse *rǫgg* tuft] (1591)
1 : LAP ROBE
2 : a piece of thick heavy fabric that usually has a nap or pile and is used as a floor covering
3 : a floor mat of an animal pelt ⟨a bearskin *rug*⟩
4 *slang* **:** TOUPEE 2
5 *British* **:** a blanket for an animal (as a horse or dog)
ru·ga \ˈrü-gə\ *noun, plural* **ru·gae** \-ˌgī, -ˌgē, -ˌjē\ [New Latin, from Latin, wrinkle — more at CORRUGATE] (1775)
: an anatomical fold or wrinkle especially of the viscera — usually used in plural
rug·by \ˈrəg-bē\ *noun, often capitalized* [*Rugby* School, Rugby, England] (1864)
: a football game in which play is continuous without time-outs or substitutions, interference and forward passing are not permitted, and kicking, dribbling, lateral passing, and tackling are featured
rug·ged \ˈrə-gəd\ *adjective* [Middle English, from (assumed) Middle English *rug*] (14th century)
1 *obsolete* **:** SHAGGY, HAIRY
2 : having a rough uneven surface **:** JAGGED ⟨*rugged* mountains⟩
3 : TURBULENT, STORMY ⟨*rugged* weather⟩

4 a : seamed with wrinkles and furrows **:** WEATHERED — used of a human face **b :** showing facial signs of strength ⟨*rugged* good looks⟩
5 a : AUSTERE, STERN **b :** COARSE, RUDE **c :** rough and strong in character
6 a : presenting a severe test of ability, stamina, or resolution **b :** strongly built or constituted **:** ROBUST ⟨those that survive are stalwart, *rugged* men —L. D. Stamp⟩
synonym SEE ROUGH
— **rug·ged·ly** *adverb*
— **rug·ged·ness** *noun*
rug·ged·ize \ˈrə-gə-ˌdīz\ *transitive verb* **-ized; -iz·ing** (1950)
: to strengthen (as a machine) for better resistance to wear, stress, and abuse ⟨a *ruggedized* camera⟩
— **rug·ged·i·za·tion** \ˌrə-gə-də-ˈzā-shən\ *noun*
rug·ger \ˈrə-gər\ *noun* [by alteration] (1893)
British **:** RUGBY; *also* **:** a rugby player
ru·go·la \ˈrü-gə-lə\ *noun* [probably from Italian dialect; akin to Italian dialect *ruga* arugula, Italian *ruca* — more at ROCKET] (1973)
: ARUGULA
ru·go·sa rose \rü-ˈgō-sə-, -zə-\ *noun* [New Latin *rugosa*, specific epithet of *Rosa rugosa* rugose rose] (1892)
: any of various garden roses descended from a rose (*Rosa rugosa*) introduced from China and Japan — called also *rugosa*
ru·gose \ˈrü-ˌgōs\ *adjective* [Latin *rugosus*, from *ruga*] (1676)
1 : full of wrinkles ⟨*rugose* cheeks⟩
2 : having the veinlets sunken and the spaces between elevated ⟨*rugose* leaves of the sage⟩
— **ru·gos·i·ty** \rü-ˈgä-sə-tē\ *noun*
ru·gu·lose \ˈrü-gyə-ˌlōs\ *adjective* [New Latin *rugula*, diminutive of Latin *ruga*] (circa 1819)
: having small rugae **:** finely wrinkled
¹ru·in \ˈrü-ən, -ˌin; ˈrün\ *noun* [Middle English *ruine*, from Middle French, from Latin *ruina*, from *ruere* to rush headlong, fall, collapse] (12th century)
1 a *archaic* **:** a falling down **:** COLLAPSE ⟨from age to age . . . the crash of *ruin* fitfully resounds —William Wordsworth⟩ **b :** physical, moral, economic, or social collapse
2 a : the state of being ruined — archaic except in plural ⟨the city lay in *ruins*⟩ **b :** the remains of something destroyed — usually used in plural ⟨the *ruins* of an ancient temple⟩ ⟨the *ruins* of his life⟩
3 : a cause of destruction
4 a : the action of destroying, laying waste, or wrecking **b :** DAMAGE, INJURY
5 : a ruined building, person, or object
— **ru·in·ate** \ˈrü-ə-ˌnāt, -nət\ *adjective*
— **ruinate** \-ˌnāt\ *transitive verb*
²ruin (1585)
transitive verb
1 : to reduce to ruins **:** DEVASTATE
2 a : to damage irreparably **b :** BANKRUPT, IMPOVERISH ⟨*ruined* by stock speculation⟩
3 : to subject to frustration, failure, or disaster ⟨will *ruin* your chances of promotion⟩
intransitive verb
: to become ruined
— **ru·in·er** *noun*
ru·in·a·tion \ˌrü-ə-ˈnā-shən\ *noun* (1664)
: RUIN, DESTRUCTION
ru·in·ous \ˈrü-ə-nəs\ *adjective* (14th century)
1 : DILAPIDATED, RUINED
2 : causing or tending to cause ruin
— **ru·in·ous·ly** *adverb*
— **ru·in·ous·ness** *noun*
¹rule \ˈrül\ *noun* [Middle English *reule*, from Old French, from Latin *regula* straightedge,

\ə\ abut \ᵊ\ kitten \ər\ further \a\ ash \ā\ ace
\ä\ mop, mar \au̇\ out \ch\ chin \e\ bet \ē\ easy
\g\ go \i\ hit \ī\ ice \j\ job \ŋ\ sing \ō\ go
\ȯ\ law \ȯi\ boy \th\ thin \t͟h\ the \ü\ loot \u̇\ foot
\y\ yet \zh\ vision *see also* Guide to Pronunciation

rule, from *regere* to direct — more at RIGHT] (13th century)

1 a : a prescribed guide for conduct or action **b :** the laws or regulations prescribed by the founder of a religious order for observance by its members **c :** an accepted procedure, custom, or habit **d** (1) **:** a usually written order or direction made by a court regulating court practice or the action of parties (2) **:** a legal precept or doctrine **e :** a regulation or bylaw governing procedure or controlling conduct **2 a** (1) **:** a usually valid generalization (2) **:** a generally prevailing quality, state, or mode ⟨fair weather was the *rule* yesterday —*N.Y. Times*⟩ **b :** a standard of judgment **:** CRITERION **c :** a regulating principle **d :** a determinate method for performing a mathematical operation and obtaining a certain result **3 a :** the exercise of authority or control **:** DOMINION **b :** a period during which a specified ruler or government exercises control **4 a :** a strip of material marked off in units used especially for measuring **:** RULER 3, TAPE MEASURE **b :** a metal strip with a type-high face that prints a linear design; *also* **:** a linear design produced by or as if by such a strip
synonym see LAW
— **as a rule :** for the most part **:** GENERALLY
²**rule** *verb* **ruled; rul·ing** (13th century)
transitive verb
1 a : to exert control, direction, or influence on ⟨the passions that *rule* our minds⟩ **b :** to exercise control over especially by curbing or restraining ⟨*rule* a fractious horse⟩ ⟨*ruled* his appetites firmly⟩ **2 a :** to exercise authority or power over often harshly or arbitrarily ⟨the speaker *ruled* the legislature with an iron hand⟩ **b :** to be preeminent in **:** DOMINATE **3 :** to determine and declare authoritatively; *especially* **:** to command or determine judicially **4 a** (1) **:** to mark with lines drawn along or as if along the straight edge of a ruler (2) **:** to mark (a line) on a paper with a ruler **b :** to arrange in a line
intransitive verb
1 a : to exercise supreme authority **b :** to be first in importance or prominence **:** PREDOMINATE ⟨the physical did not *rule* in her nature —Sherwood Anderson⟩ **2 :** to exist in a specified state or condition **3 :** to lay down a legal rule
synonym see DECIDE
ruled surface *noun* (1862)
: a surface generated by a moving straight line with the result that through every point on the surface a line can be drawn lying wholly in the surface
rule·less \'rül-ləs\ *adjective* (15th century)
: not restrained or regulated by law
rule of the road (1871)
: a customary practice (as driving always on a particular side of the road or yielding the right of way) developed in the interest of safety and often subsequently reinforced by law; *especially* **:** any of the rules making up a code governing ships in matters relating to mutual safety
rule of thumb (1692)
1 : a method of procedure based on experience and common sense
2 : a general principle regarded as roughly correct but not intended to be scientifically accurate
rule out *transitive verb* (1869)
1 : EXCLUDE, ELIMINATE
2 : to make impossible **:** PREVENT ⟨heavy rain *ruled out* the picnic⟩
rul·er \'rü-lər\ *noun* (14th century)
1 : one that rules; *specifically* **:** SOVEREIGN
2 : a worker or a machine that rules paper
3 : a smooth-edged strip (as of wood or metal) that is usually marked off in units (as inches) and is used as a straightedge or for measuring
— **rul·er·ship** \-,ship\ *noun*

¹**rul·ing** \'rü-liŋ\ *noun* (15th century)
: an official or authoritative decision, decree, statement, or interpretation (as by a judge on a point of law)
²**ruling** *adjective* (1593)
1 a : exerting power or authority ⟨the *ruling* party⟩ **b :** CHIEF, PREDOMINATING ⟨a *ruling* passion⟩
2 : generally prevailing
ru·ly \'rü-lē\ *adjective* [back-formation from *unruly*] (15th century)
: OBEDIENT, ORDERLY ⟨a *ruly* crowd⟩
¹**rum** \'rəm\ *noun* [probably short for obsolete *rumbullion* rum] (1654)
1 : an alcoholic beverage distilled from a fermented cane product (as molasses)
2 : alcoholic liquor ⟨the demon *rum*⟩
²**rum** *adjective* **rum·mer; rum·mest** [origin unknown] (1752)
1 *chiefly British* **:** QUEER, ODD ⟨writing is a *rum* trade . . . and what is all right one day is all wrong the next —Angela Thirkell⟩
2 *chiefly British* **:** DIFFICULT, DANGEROUS
ru·ma·ki \rə-'mä-kē\ *noun* [perhaps modification of Japanese *harumaki*, translation of Chinese (Beijing) *chūnjuǎn* spring roll] (1961)
: a cooked appetizer made of pieces of usually marinated chicken liver wrapped together with sliced water chestnuts in bacon slices
Ru·ma·nian \rú-'mā-nē-ən, -nyən\ *noun* (1878)
: ROMANIAN
— **Rumanian** *adjective*
rum·ba \'rəm-bə, 'rúm-, 'rüm-\ *noun* [American Spanish] (1922)
: a ballroom dance of Cuban origin in ¾ or ⁴⁄₄ time with a basic pattern of step-close-step and marked by a delayed transfer of weight and pronounced hip movements; *also* **:** the music for this dance
¹**rum·ble** \'rəm-bəl\ *verb* **rum·bled; rum·bling** \-b(ə-)liŋ\ [Middle English; akin to Middle High German *rummeln* to rumble] (14th century)
intransitive verb
1 : to make a low heavy rolling sound ⟨thunder *rumbling* in the distance⟩
2 : to travel with a low reverberating sound ⟨wagons *rumbled* into town⟩
3 : to speak in a low rolling tone
4 : to engage in a rumble
transitive verb
1 : to utter or emit in a low rolling voice
2 *British* **:** to reveal or discover the true character of
— **rum·bler** \-b(ə-)lər\ *noun*
²**rumble** *noun* (14th century)
1 a : a low heavy continuous reverberating often muffled sound (as of thunder) **b :** low frequency noise in phonographic playback caused by the transmission of mechanical vibrations by the turntable to the pickup
2 : a seat for servants behind the body of a carriage
3 a : widespread expression of dissatisfaction or unrest **b :** a street fight especially among gangs
rumble seat *noun* (1912)
: a folding seat in the back of an automobile (as a coupe or roadster) not covered by the top
rum·bling \'rəm-bliŋ\ *noun* (14th century)
1 : RUMBLE
2 : general but unofficial talk or opinion often of dissatisfaction — usually used in plural ⟨*rumblings* of political trouble —Anthony Burgess⟩
rum·bly \'rəm-b(ə-)lē\ *adjective* (1874)
: tending to rumble or rattle
rum·bus·tious \,rəm-'bəs-chəs\ *adjective* [alteration of *robustious*] (1778)
chiefly British **:** RAMBUNCTIOUS
— **rum·bus·tious·ly** *adverb, chiefly British*
— **rum·bus·tious·ness** *noun, chiefly British*

ru·men \'rü-mən\ *noun, plural* **ru·mi·na** \-mə-nə\ *or* **rumens** [New Latin *rumin-, rumen*, from Latin] (circa 1728)
: the large first compartment of the stomach of a ruminant in which cellulose is broken down by the action of symbiotic microorganisms — compare ABOMASUM, OMASUM, RETICULUM
— **ru·mi·nal** \-mə-n°l\ *adjective*
¹**ru·mi·nant** \'rü-mə-nənt\ *noun* (1661)
: a ruminant mammal
²**ruminant** *adjective* (1691)
1 a (1) **:** chewing the cud (2) **:** characterized by chewing again what has been swallowed **b :** of or relating to a suborder (Ruminantia) of even-toed hoofed mammals (as sheep, giraffes, deer, and camels) that chew the cud and have a complex usually 4-chambered stomach **2 :** given to or engaged in contemplation **:** MEDITATIVE ⟨stood there with her hands clasped in this attitude of *ruminant* relish —Thomas Wolfe⟩
— **ru·mi·nant·ly** *adverb*
ru·mi·nate \'rü-mə-,nāt\ *verb* **-nat·ed; -nat·ing** [Latin *ruminatus*, past participle of *ruminari* to chew the cud, muse upon, from *rumin-, rumen* rumen; perhaps akin to Sanskrit *romantha* act of chewing the cud] (1533)
transitive verb
1 : to go over in the mind repeatedly and often casually or slowly
2 : to chew repeatedly for an extended period
intransitive verb
1 : to chew again what has been chewed slightly and swallowed **:** chew the cud
2 : to engage in contemplation **:** REFLECT ◇
synonym see PONDER
— **ru·mi·na·tion** \,rü-mə-'nā-shən\ *noun*
— **ru·mi·na·tive** \'rü-mə-,nā-tiv\ *adjective*
— **ru·mi·na·tive·ly** *adverb*
— **ru·mi·na·tor** \-,nā-tər\ *noun*
¹**rum·mage** \'rə-mij\ *verb* **rum·maged; rum·mag·ing** [²*rummage*] (circa 1595)
intransitive verb
1 : to make a thorough search or investigation
2 : to engage in an undirected or haphazard search
transitive verb
1 : to make a thorough search through **:** RANSACK ⟨*rummaged* the attic⟩
2 : to examine minutely and completely
3 : to discover by searching
— **rum·mag·er** *noun*
²**rummage** *noun* [obsolete English *rummage* act of packing cargo, modification of Middle French *arrimage*] (1598)
1 a : a confused miscellaneous collection **b :** items for sale at a rummage sale
2 : a thorough search especially among a confusion of objects
rummage sale *noun* (circa 1858)

◇ **WORD HISTORY**

ruminate Hoofed animals such as deer, sheep, and domestic cattle digest their food in stages, first swallowing the vegetation that they crop into a special stomach, where it is partially digested, then bringing it back up for some further leisurely chewing. This process is known as chewing the cud, and the animals that engage in it are called *ruminants*, from the present participle of the Latin verb *ruminari* "to chew the cud," a derivative of *rumen*, the Latin name for a ruminant's first stomach. The similarity between recalling food to the mouth for further chewing and recalling an idea to the mind for further thought—as well, perhaps, as the contemplative expression characteristic of a cow in mid-chew—led the Romans to use *ruminari* in an extended sense "to think over, meditate on." The English verb *ruminate*, from the past participle of *ruminari*, retains both the literal and figurative applications of its Latin source.

: a usually informal sale of miscellaneous goods; *especially* : a sale of donated articles conducted by a nonprofit organization (as a church or charity) to help support its programs

rum·mer \'rə-mər\ *noun* [German or Dutch; German *Römer*, from Dutch *roemer*] (1654)
: a large-bowled footed drinking glass often elaborately etched or engraved

¹rum·my \'rə-mē\ *adjective* **rum·mi·er; -est** [²*rum*] (1828)
: QUEER, ODD ⟨were still feeling a little *rummy* from our trip up the escalator —*New Yorker*⟩

²rummy *noun, plural* **rummies** [¹*rum*] (1851)
: DRUNKARD

³rummy *noun* [perhaps from ¹*rummy*] (1915)
: any of several card games for two or more players in which each player tries to assemble groups of three or more cards of the same rank or suit and to be the first to meld them all

¹ru·mor \'rü-mər\ *noun* [Middle English *rumour*, from Middle French, from Latin *rumor* clamor, gossip; akin to Old English *rēon* to lament, Sanskrit *rauti* he roars] (14th century)
1 : talk or opinion widely disseminated with no discernible source
2 : a statement or report current without known authority for its truth
3 *archaic* : talk or report of a notable person or event
4 : a soft low indistinct sound : MURMUR

²rumor *transitive verb* **ru·mored; ru·mor·ing** (1594)
: to tell or spread by rumor

ru·mor·mon·ger \-,mən-gər, -,mäŋ-\ *noun* (1884)
: a person who spreads rumors
— **ru·mor·mon·ger·ing** \-gər-iŋ\ *noun*

ru·mour \'rü-mər\ *chiefly British variant of* RU-MOR

rump \'rəmp\ *noun* [Middle English, of Scandinavian origin; akin to Icelandic *rumpr* rump; akin to Middle High German *rumph* torso] (15th century)
1 a : the upper rounded part of the hindquarters of a quadruped mammal **b** : BUTTOCKS **c** : the sacral or dorsal part of the posterior end of a bird
2 : a cut of meat (as beef) between the loin and round — see BEEF illustration
3 : a small or inferior remnant or offshoot; *especially* : a group (as a parliament) carrying on in the name of the original body after the departure or expulsion of a large number of its members

¹rum·ple \'rəm-pəl\ *noun* (circa 1520)
: FOLD, WRINKLE

²rumple *verb* **rum·pled; rum·pling** \-p(ə-)liŋ\ [Dutch *rompelen*; akin to Old High German *rimpfan* to wrinkle] (1603)
transitive verb
1 : WRINKLE, CRUMPLE
2 : to make unkempt : TOUSLE
intransitive verb
: to become rumpled

rum·ply \'rəm-p(ə-)lē\ *adjective* **rum·pli·er; -est** (1833)
: having rumples

rum·pus \'rəm-pəs\ *noun* [origin unknown] (1764)
: a usually noisy commotion

rumpus room *noun* (1939)
: a room usually in the basement of a home that is used for games, parties, and recreation

rum·run·ner \'rəm-,rə-nər\ *noun* (1920)
: a person or ship engaged in bringing prohibited liquor ashore or across a border
— **rum–run·ning** \-,rə-niŋ\ *adjective or noun*

¹run \'rən\ *verb* **ran** \'ran\ *also chiefly dialect* **run; run; run·ning** [Middle English *rennen*, alteration of *rinnen*, intransitive verb (from Old English *iernan, rinnan* & Old Norse *rinna*) & of *rennen*, transitive verb, from Old Norse *renna*; akin to Old High German *rinnan*, intransitive verb, to run, Sanskrit *riṇāti*

he causes to flow, and probably to Latin *rivus* stream] (before 12th century)
intransitive verb
1 a : to go faster than a walk; *specifically* : to go steadily by springing steps so that both feet leave the ground for an instant in each step **b** *of a horse* : to move at a fast gallop **c** : FLEE, RETREAT, ESCAPE ⟨dropped the gun and *ran*⟩ **d** : to utilize a running play on offense — used of a football team
2 a : to go without restraint : move freely about at will ⟨let chickens *run* loose⟩ **b** : to keep company : CONSORT ⟨a ram *running* with ewes⟩ ⟨*ran* with a wild crowd when he was young⟩ **c** : to sail before the wind in distinction from reaching or sailing close-hauled **d** : ROAM, ROVE ⟨*running* about with no overcoat⟩
3 a : to go rapidly or hurriedly : HASTEN ⟨*run* and fetch the doctor⟩ **b** : to go in urgency or distress : RESORT ⟨*runs* to mother at every little difficulty⟩ **c** : to make a quick, easy, or casual trip or visit ⟨*ran* over to borrow some sugar⟩
4 a : to contend in a race **b** : to enter into an election contest
5 a : to move on or as if on wheels : GLIDE ⟨file drawers *running* on ball bearings⟩ **b** : to roll forward rapidly or freely **c** : to pass or slide freely ⟨a rope *runs* through the pulley⟩ **d** : to ravel lengthwise ⟨stockings guaranteed not to *run*⟩
6 : to sing or play a musical passage quickly ⟨*run* up the scale⟩
7 a : to go back and forth : PLY ⟨the train *runs* between New York and Washington⟩ **b** *of fish* : to migrate or move in considerable numbers; *especially* : to move up or down a river to spawn
8 a : TURN, ROTATE ⟨a swiftly *running* grindstone⟩ **b** : FUNCTION, OPERATE ⟨the engine *runs* on gasoline⟩
9 a (1) : to continue in force, operation, or production ⟨the contract has two more years to *run*⟩ ⟨the play *ran* for six months⟩ (2) : to have a specified duration, extent, or length ⟨the manuscript *runs* nearly 500 pages⟩ **b** : to accompany as a valid obligation or right ⟨a right-of-way that *runs* with the land⟩ **c** : to continue to accrue or become payable ⟨interest on the loan *runs* from July 1st⟩
10 : to pass from one state to another ⟨*run* into debt⟩
11 a : to flow rapidly or under pressure **b** : MELT, FUSE **c** : SPREAD, DISSOLVE ⟨colors guaranteed not to *run*⟩ **d** : to discharge pus or serum ⟨a *running* sore⟩
12 a : to develop rapidly in some specific direction; *especially* : to throw out an elongated shoot of growth **b** : to tend to produce or develop a specified quality or feature ⟨they *run* to big noses in that family⟩
13 a : to lie in or take a certain direction ⟨the boundary line *runs* east⟩ **b** : to lie or extend in relation to something **c** : to go back : REACH **d** (1) : to be in a certain form or expression ⟨the letter *runs* as follows⟩ (2) : to be in a certain order of succession
14 a : to occur persistently ⟨musical talent *runs* in the family⟩ **b** (1) : to remain of a specified size, amount, character, or quality ⟨profits were *running* high⟩ (2) : to have or maintain a relative position or condition ⟨as in a race⟩ ⟨*ran* third⟩ ⟨*running* late⟩ **c** : to exist or occur in a continuous range of variation ⟨shades *run* from white to dark gray⟩
15 a : to spread or pass quickly from point to point ⟨chills *ran* up her spine⟩ **b** : to be current : CIRCULATE ⟨speculation *ran* rife⟩
transitive verb
1 a : to cause (an animal) to go rapidly : ride or drive fast **b** : to bring to a specified condition by or as if by running ⟨*ran* himself to death⟩ **c** : to go in pursuit of : HUNT, CHASE ⟨dogs that *run* deer⟩ **d** : to follow the trail of backward : TRACE ⟨*ran* the rumor to its source⟩

e : to enter, register, or enroll as a contestant in a race **f** : to put forward as a candidate for office
2 a : to drive (livestock) especially to a grazing place **b** : to provide pasturage for (livestock) **c** : to keep or maintain (livestock) on or as if on pasturage
3 a : to pass over or traverse with speed **b** : to accomplish or perform by or as if by running ⟨*ran* a great race⟩ ⟨*running* errands for a bank⟩ **c** : to slip or go through or past ⟨*run* a blockade⟩ ⟨*run* a red light⟩
4 a : to cause to penetrate or enter : THRUST ⟨*ran* a splinter into her toe⟩ **b** : STITCH **c** : to cause to pass : LEAD ⟨*run* a wire in from the antenna⟩ **d** : to cause to collide ⟨*ran* his head into a post⟩ **e** : SMUGGLE ⟨*run* guns⟩
5 : to cause to pass lightly or quickly over, along, or into something ⟨*ran* her eye down the list⟩
6 a : to cause or allow (as a vehicle or a vessel) to go in a specified manner or direction ⟨*ran* the car off the road⟩ **b** : OPERATE ⟨*run* a lathe⟩ **c** : to direct the business or activities of : MANAGE, CONDUCT ⟨*run* a factory⟩
7 a : to be full of or drenched with ⟨streets *ran* blood⟩ **b** : CONTAIN, ASSAY
8 a : to cause to move or flow in a specified way or into a specified position ⟨*run* cards into a file⟩ **b** : to cause to produce a flow (as of water) ⟨*run* the faucet⟩; *also* : to prepare by running a faucet ⟨*run* a hot bath⟩
9 a : to melt and cast in a mold ⟨*run* bullets⟩ **b** : TREAT, PROCESS, REFINE ⟨*run* oil in a still⟩ ⟨*run* a problem through a computer⟩
10 : to make oneself liable to : INCUR ⟨*ran* the risk of discovery⟩
11 : to mark out : DRAW ⟨*run* a contour line on a map⟩
12 a : to permit (as charges) to accumulate before settling ⟨*run* an account at the grocery⟩ — often used with *up* ⟨*run* up a large phone bill⟩ **b** : COST 1 ⟨rooms that *run* $50 a night⟩
13 a : to produce by or as if by printing — usually used with *off* ⟨*ran* off 10,000 copies of the first edition⟩ **b** : to carry in a printed medium : PRINT ⟨every newspaper *ran* the story⟩
14 a : to make (a series of counts) without a miss ⟨*run* 19 in an inning in billiards⟩ **b** : to lead winning cards of (a suit) successively **c** : to alter by addition ⟨*ran* his record to six wins and four losses⟩
15 : to make (a golf ball) roll forward after alighting ▫
— **run across** : to meet with or discover by chance
— **run a fever** *or* **run a temperature** : to have a fever
— **run after 1** : PURSUE, CHASE; *especially* : to seek the company of **2** : to take up with : FOLLOW ⟨*run after* new theories⟩
— **run against 1** : to meet suddenly or unexpectedly **2** : to work or take effect unfavorably to : DISFAVOR, OPPOSE
— **run foul of 1** : to collide with ⟨*ran foul of* a hidden reef⟩ **2** : to come into conflict with ⟨*run foul of* the law⟩

\ə\ abut \ᵊ\ kitten \ər\ **further** \a\ ash \ā\ **ace** \ä\ mop, mar \au̇\ **out** \ch\ **chin** \e\ bet \ē\ **easy** \g\ go \i\ hit \ī\ **ice** \j\ **job** \ŋ\ sing \ō\ **go** \ȯ\ law \ȯi\ **boy** \th\ **thin** \t͟h\ **the** \ü\ **loot** \u̇\ **foot** \y\ yet \zh\ vision *see also* Guide to Pronunciation

— **run into 1 a :** to change or transform into **:** BECOME **b :** to merge with **c :** to mount up to 〈their yearly income often *runs into* six figures〉 **2 a :** to collide with **b :** to meet by chance 〈*ran into* an old classmate the other day〉

— **run low on :** to approach running out of 〈*running low on* options〉

— **run rings around :** to show marked superiority over **:** defeat decisively or overwhelmingly

— **run riot 1 :** to act wildly or without restraint **2 :** to occur in profusion 〈daffodils *running riot*〉

— **run short :** to become insufficient

— **run short of :** to use up **:** run low on

— **run to :** to mount up to 〈the book *runs to* 500 pages〉

— **run upon :** to run across **:** meet with

²**run** *noun* (14th century)
1 a : an act or the action of running **:** continued rapid movement **b :** a quickened gallop **c :** a migration of fish (as up or down a river) especially to spawn; *also* **:** such fish in the process of migration **d :** a running race 〈a mile *run*〉 **e :** a score made in baseball by a runner reaching home plate safely **f :** strength or ability to run **g :** a gain of a usually specified distance made on a running play in football 〈scored on a 25-yard *run*〉; *also* **:** a running play **h :** a sustained usually aggressive effort (as to win or obtain something) 〈making a *run* at the championship〉
2 a *chiefly Midland* **:** CREEK **2 b :** something that flows in the course of an operation or during a particular time 〈the first *run* of sap in sugar maples〉
3 a : the stern of the underwater body of a ship from where it begins to curve or slope upward and inward **b :** the direction in which a vein of ore lies **c :** a direction of secondary or minor cleavage 〈the *run* of a mass of granite〉 **d :** a horizontal distance (as that covered by a flight of steps) **e :** general tendency or direction
4 : a continuous period or series especially of things of identical or similar sort 〈a *run* of bad luck〉: as **a :** a rapid passage up or down a scale in vocal or instrumental music **b :** a number of rapid small dance steps executed in even tempo **c :** the act of making successively a number of successful shots or strokes; *also* **:** the score thus made 〈a *run* of 20 in billiards〉 **d :** an unbroken course of performances or showings **e :** a set of consecutive measurements, readings, or observations **f :** persistent and heavy demands from depositors, creditors, or customers 〈a *run* on a bank〉 **g :** SEQUENCE 2b
5 : the quantity of work turned out in a continuous operation 〈a press *run* of 10,000 copies〉
6 : the usual or normal kind, character, type, or group 〈the average *run* of students〉
7 a : the distance covered in a period of continuous traveling or sailing **b :** a course or trip especially if mapped out and traveled with regularity **c :** a news reporter's regular territory **:** BEAT **d :** freedom of movement in or access to a place or area 〈has the *run* of the house〉
8 a : the period during which a machine or plant is in continuous operation **b :** the use of machinery for a single set of processing procedures 〈a computer *run*〉
9 a : a way, track, or path frequented by animals **b :** an enclosure for domestic animals where they may feed or exercise **c** *Australian* (1) **:** a large area of land used for grazing 〈a sheep *run*〉 (2) **:** RANCH, STATION 〈*run*-holder〉 **d :** an inclined passageway
10 a : an inclined course (as for skiing or bobsledding) **b :** a support (as a track, pipe, or trough) on which something runs
11 a : a ravel in a knitted fabric (as in hosiery) caused by the breaking of stitches **b :** a paint defect caused by excessive flow

12 *plural but singular or plural in construction* **:** DIARRHEA — used with *the*

— **on the run 1 :** in haste **:** without pausing 〈ate lunch *on the run*〉 **2 :** in retreat **:** in flight (as from the law) 〈an escaped convict *on the run*〉

³**run** *adjective* (1774)
1 a : being in a melted state 〈*run* butter〉 **b :** made from molten material **:** cast in a mold 〈*run* metal〉
2 *of fish* **:** having made a migration or spawning run 〈a fresh *run* salmon〉
3 : exhausted or winded from running

run·about \'rə-nə-ˌbaut\ *noun* (1549)
1 : one who wanders about **:** STRAY
2 : a light usually open wagon, car, or motorboat

run·a·gate \'rə-nə-ˌgāt\ *noun* [alteration of *renegate*, from Medieval Latin *renegatus* — more at RENEGADE] (1547)
1 : VAGABOND
2 : FUGITIVE, RUNAWAY

run along *intransitive verb* (1902)
: to go away **:** be on one's way **:** DEPART

run·around \'rə-nə-ˌraund\ *noun* (1915)
1 : deceptive or delaying action especially in response to a request 〈tired of getting the *runaround*〉
2 : matter typeset in shortened measure to run around something (as a cut)

¹**run·away** \'rə-nə-ˌwā\ *noun* (1547)
1 : one that runs away from danger, duty, or restraint **:** FUGITIVE
2 : the act of running away out of control; *also* **:** something (as a horse) that is running out of control
3 : a one-sided or overwhelming victory

²**runaway** *adjective* (1548)
1 a : running away **:** FUGITIVE **b :** leaving to gain special advantages (as lower wages) or avoid disadvantages (as governmental or union restrictions) 〈*runaway* shipping firms〉 〈a *runaway* shop〉
2 : accomplished by elopement or during flight
3 : won by or having a long lead 〈a *runaway* success〉; *also* **:** extremely successful 〈a *runaway* best-seller〉
4 : subject to uncontrolled changes 〈*runaway* inflation〉
5 : being or operating out of control 〈a *runaway* oil well〉 〈a *runaway* nuclear reactor〉

run away *intransitive verb* (13th century)
1 a : to leave quickly in order to avoid or escape something **b :** to leave home; *especially* **:** ELOPE
2 : to run out of control **:** STAMPEDE, BOLT
3 : to gain a substantial lead **:** win by a large margin

— **run away with 1 :** to take away in haste or secretly; *especially* **:** STEAL **2 :** to outshine the others in (a theatrical performance) **3 :** to carry or drive beyond prudent or reasonable limits 〈your imagination *ran away with* you〉

run·back \'rən-ˌbak\ *noun* (1929)
: a run made in football after catching an opponent's kick or intercepting a pass

run·ci·ble spoon \'rən(t)-sə-bəl-\ *noun* [coined with an obscure meaning by Edward Lear] (1871)
: a sharp-edged fork with three broad curved prongs

run·ci·nate \'rən(t)-sə-ˌnāt\ *adjective* [Latin *runcinatus*, past participle of *runcinare* to plane off, from *runcina* plane] (1776)
: pinnately cut with the lobes pointing downward 〈*runcinate* leaves of the dandelion〉 — see LEAF illustration

run·dle \'rən-dᵊl\ *noun* [Middle English *roundel* circle — more at ROUNDEL] (1565)
1 : a step of a ladder
2 : the drum of a windlass or capstan

rund·let *or* **run·let** \'rən(d)-lət\ *noun* [Middle English *roundelet*, from Middle French *rondelet* — more at ROUNDELAY] (14th century)
: a small barrel **:** KEG

run·down \'rən-ˌdaun\ *noun* (1908)
1 : a play in baseball in which a base runner who is caught off base is chased by two or more opposing players who throw the ball from one to another in an attempt to tag the runner out
2 : an item-by-item report or review **:** SUMMARY

run–down \'rən-'daun\ *adjective* (1866)
1 : WORN-OUT, EXHAUSTED
2 : completely unwound
3 : being in poor repair **:** DILAPIDATED

run down (circa 1578)
transitive verb
1 a : to collide with and knock down **b :** to run against and cause to sink
2 a : to chase to exhaustion or until captured **b :** to trace the source of **c :** to tag out (a base runner) between bases on a rundown
3 : DISPARAGE
intransitive verb
1 : to cease to operate because of the exhaustion of motive power 〈the clock *ran down*〉
2 : to decline in physical condition or vigor

rune \'rün\ *noun* [Old Norse & Old English *rūn* mystery, runic character, writing; akin to Old High German *rūna* secret discussion, Old Irish *rún* mystery] (1690)
1 : any of the characters of any of several alphabets used by the Germanic peoples from about the 3d to the 13th centuries
2 : MYSTERY, MAGIC
3 [Finnish *runo*, of Germanic origin; akin to Old Norse *rūn*] **a :** a Finnish or Old Norse poem **b :** POEM, SONG
— **ru·nic** \'rü-nik\ *adjective*

rune 1: Anglo-Saxon runic alphabet

¹**rung** *past participle of* RING

²**rung** \'rəŋ\ *noun* [Middle English, from Old English *hrung* crossbar; akin to Gothic *hrunga* staff and perhaps to Old English *hring* ring — more at RING] (14th century)
1 a : a rounded part placed as a crosspiece between the legs of a chair **b :** one of the crosspieces of a ladder
2 *Scottish* **:** a heavy staff or cudgel
3 : a spoke of a wheel
4 : a level in a hierarchy 〈rise a few *rungs* on the social scale —H. W. Van Loon〉

run-in \'rən-ˌin\ *noun* (1857)
1 *British* **:** the final part of a race or racetrack
2 : ALTERCATION, QUARREL
3 : something inserted as a substantial addition in copy or typeset matter

run in (1817)
transitive verb
1 a : to insert as additional matter **b :** to make (typeset matter) continuous without a paragraph or other break
2 : to arrest for a usually minor offense
3 *chiefly British* **:** to operate (a new machine) carefully until there is efficient running
intransitive verb
: to pay a casual visit

run·less \'rən-ləs\ *adjective* (1921)
: scoring or allowing no runs

run·let \'rən-lət\ *noun* (circa 1755)
: RIVULET, STREAMLET

run·nel \'rə-nᵊl\ *noun* [alteration of Middle English *rinel*, from Old English *rynel*; akin to Old English *rinnan* to run — more at RUN] (before 12th century)
: RIVULET, STREAMLET

run·ner \'rə-nər\ *noun* (14th century)
1 a : one that runs **:** RACER **b :** BASE RUNNER **c :** BALLCARRIER
2 a : MESSENGER **b :** one that smuggles or distributes illicit or contraband goods (as drugs, liquor, or guns)
3 : any of several large active carangid fishes

4 a : either of the longitudinal pieces on which a sled or sleigh slides **b :** the part of a skate that slides on the ice **:** BLADE **c :** the support of a drawer or a sliding door
5 a : a growth produced by a plant in running; *especially* **:** STOLON 1a **b :** a plant that forms or spreads by means of runners **c :** a twining vine (as a scarlet runner)
6 a : a long narrow carpet for a hall or staircase **b :** a narrow decorative cloth cover for a table or dresser top

runner bean *noun* (1882)
chiefly British **:** SCARLET RUNNER

run·ner–up \ˈrə-nə-ˌrəp, ˌrə-nə-ˈ\ *noun, plural* **run·ners–up** \-nər-ˌzəp, -ˈzəp\ *also* **runner–ups** (1842)
: the competitor that does not win first place in a contest; *especially* **:** one that finishes in second place

¹run·ning \ˈrə-niŋ\ *noun* (before 12th century)
1 a : the action of running **b :** RACE
2 : physical condition for running
3 : MANAGEMENT, CARE
— in the running 1 : competing in a contest **2 :** having a chance to win a contest
— out of the running 1 : not competing in a contest **2 :** having no chance of winning a contest

²running *adjective* (14th century)
1 : CURSIVE, FLOWING
2 : FLUID, RUNNY
3 a : INCESSANT, CONTINUOUS (a *running* battle) **b :** made during the course of a process or activity (a *running* commentary on the game)
4 : measured in a straight line (cost of lumber per *running* foot)
5 a : initiated or performed while running or with a running start (*running* catch) **b :** of, relating to, or being a football play in which the ball is advanced by running rather than by passing (their *running* game was off) **c :** designed for use by runners (a *running* track) (*running* shoes)
6 : fitted or trained for running rather than walking, trotting, or jumping (a *running* horse)

³running *adverb* (1719)
: in succession **:** CONSECUTIVELY (three days *running*)

running back *noun* (1924)
: a football back (as a halfback or fullback) who carries the ball on running plays

running board *noun* (1817)
: a footboard especially at the side of an automobile

running dog *noun* (1927)
: one who does someone else's bidding **:** LACKEY

running board

running gear *noun* (1662)
1 : the working and carrying parts of a machine (as a locomotive)
2 : the parts of an automobile chassis not used in developing, transmitting, and controlling power

running hand *noun* (1648)
: handwriting in which the letters are usually slanted and the words formed without lifting the pen

running head *noun* (1839)
: a headline repeated on consecutive pages (as of a book) — called also *running headline*

running knot *noun* (1648)
: a knot that slips along the rope or line round which it is tied; *especially* **:** an overhand slipknot

running light *noun* (1881)
: any of the lights carried by a vehicle (as a ship) under way at night that indicate size, position, and course

running mate *noun* (1868)
1 : a horse entered in a race to set the pace for a horse of the same owner or stable

2 : a candidate running for a subordinate place on a ticket; *especially* **:** the candidate for vice-president
3 : COMPANION

running start *noun* (1926)
: FLYING START 1

running stitch *noun* (1848)
: a small even stitch run in and out in cloth

running title *noun* (1668)
: the title or short title of a volume printed at the top of left-hand text pages or sometimes of all text pages

running water *noun* (1912)
: water distributed through pipes and fixtures (a cabin with hot and cold *running water*)

run·ny \ˈrə-nē\ *adjective* (1817)
: having a tendency to run: as **a :** extremely or excessively soft and liquid (a *runny* dough) **b :** secreting a thin flow of mucus (a *runny* nose)

run·off \ˈrən-ˌȯf\ *noun* (1873)
1 : a final race, contest, or election to decide an earlier one that has not resulted in a decision in favor of any one competitor
2 : the portion of precipitation on land that ultimately reaches streams often with dissolved or suspended material

run off (1683)
transitive verb
1 a : to recite, compose, or produce rapidly **b :** to cause to be run or played to a finish **c :** to decide (as a race) by a runoff **d :** CARRY OUT
2 : to drain off **:** DRAW OFF
3 a : to drive off (as trespassers) **b :** to steal (as cattle) by driving away
intransitive verb
: RUN AWAY 1
— run off with : to carry off **:** STEAL

run–of–paper \ˌrən-əv-ˈpā-pər\ *adjective* (circa 1923)
: to be placed anywhere in a newspaper at the option of the editor (*run-of-paper* advertisement)

run–of–the–mill \ˌrən-ə(v)-thə-ˈmil\ *adjective* (1930)
: not outstanding in quality or rarity **:** AVERAGE, ORDINARY

run–of–the–mine \-ˈmīn\ *or* **run–of–mine** \-əv-ˈmīn\ *adjective* (1903)
1 : not graded (*run-of-the-mine* coal)
2 : RUN-OF-THE-MILL

¹run–on \ˈrən-ˌȯn, -ˌän\ *adjective* (1877)
: continuing without rhetorical pause from one line of verse into another

²run–on \-ˌȯn, -ˌän\ *noun* (circa 1909)
: something (as a dictionary entry) that is run on

run on (15th century)
intransitive verb
1 : to talk or narrate at length
2 : to keep going **:** CONTINUE
transitive verb
1 : to continue (matter in type) without a break or a new paragraph **:** RUN IN
2 : to place or add (as an entry in a dictionary) at the end of a paragraphed item

run–on sentence *noun* (1914)
: a sentence containing a comma splice

run out (14th century)
intransitive verb
1 a : to come to an end **:** EXPIRE (time *ran out*)
b : to become exhausted or used up (the gasoline *ran out*)
2 : to jut out
transitive verb
1 : to finish out (as a course, series, or contest) **:** COMPLETE
2 a : to fill out (a typeset line) with quads, leaders, or ornaments **b :** to set (as the first line of a paragraph) with a hanging indention
3 : to exhaust (oneself) in running
4 : to cause to leave by force or coercion **:** EXPEL
— run out of : to use up the available supply of
— run out on : DESERT

run·over \ˈrən-ˌō-vər\ *noun* (1927)

: matter for publication that exceeds the space allotted

run–over \ˈrən-ˌō-vər\ *adjective* (circa 1934)
: extending beyond the allotted space

run over (15th century)
intransitive verb
1 : to exceed a limit
2 : OVERFLOW
transitive verb
1 : to go over, examine, repeat, or rehearse quickly
2 : to collide with, knock down, and often drive over (*ran over* a dog)

runt \ˈrənt\ *noun* [origin unknown] (1501)
1 *chiefly Scottish* **:** a hardened stalk or stem of a plant
2 : an animal unusually small of its kind; *especially* **:** the smallest of a litter of pigs
3 : a person of small stature
— runt·i·ness \ˈrən-tē-nəs\ *noun*
— runt·ish \-tish\ *adjective*
— runty \-tē\ *adjective*

run–through \ˈrən-ˌthrü\ *noun* (1923)
: a usually cursory reading, summary, or rehearsal

run through *transitive verb* (15th century)
1 : PIERCE
2 : to spend or consume wastefully and rapidly
3 : to read or rehearse without pausing
4 a : CARRY OUT, DO **b :** to subject to a process

run–up \ˈrən-ˌəp\ *noun* (1834)
1 : the act of running up something
2 : a usually sudden increase in volume or price
3 *chiefly British* **:** a period immediately preceding an action or event

run up (1664)
intransitive verb
: to grow rapidly **:** shoot up
transitive verb
1 : to increase by bidding **:** bid up
2 : to stitch together quickly
3 : to erect hastily
4 : to achieve by accumulating (*ran up* a big lead)

run·way \ˈrən-ˌwā\ *noun* (1833)
1 a : a beaten path made by animals **b :** a passageway for animals
2 : a paved strip of ground on a landing field for the landing and takeoff of airplanes
3 a : a narrow platform from a stage into an auditorium **b :** a platform along which models walk in a fashion show
4 : RUN 10b
5 : the area or path along which a jumper, pole vaulter, or javelin thrower runs

ru·pee \rü-ˈpē, ˈrü-ˌpē\ *noun* [Hindi *rūpaiyā*, from Sanskrit *rūpya* coined silver] (1610)
— see MONEY table

ru·pi·ah \rü-ˈpē-ə\ *noun, plural* **rupiah** *or* **ru·piahs** [Malay, from Hindi *rūpaiyā* rupee] (1947)
— see MONEY table

¹rup·ture \ˈrəp(t)-shər\ *noun* [Middle English *ruptur,* from Middle French or Latin; Middle French *rupture,* from Latin *ruptura* fracture, from *ruptus,* past participle of *rumpere* to break — more at REAVE] (15th century)
1 : breach of peace or concord; *specifically* **:** open hostility or war between nations
2 a : the tearing apart of a tissue (*rupture* of the heart muscle) (*rupture* of an intervertebral disk) **b :** HERNIA
3 : a breaking apart or the state of being broken apart

²rupture *verb* **rup·tured; rup·tur·ing** \-sh(ə-)riŋ\ (1739)
transitive verb

1 a : to part by violence **:** BREAK, BURST **b :** to create or induce a breach of
2 : to produce a rupture in
intransitive verb
: to have or undergo a rupture
ru·ral \'rùr-əl\ *adjective* [Middle English, from Middle French, from Latin *ruralis*, from *rur-*, *rus* open land — more at ROOM] (15th century)
: of or relating to the country, country people or life, or agriculture
 — **ru·ral·i·ty** \rù-'ra-lə-tē\ *noun*
 — **ru·ral·ly** \'rùr-ə-lē\ *adverb*
rural dean *noun* (circa 1628)
: DEAN 1b
rural free delivery *noun* (1892)
: free delivery of mail to a rural area — called also *rural delivery*
ru·ral·ist \'rùr-ə-list\ *noun* (1739)
: one who lives in a rural area
rural route *noun* (1898)
: a mail-delivery route in a rural free delivery area
rur·ban \'rər-bən, 'rùr-\ *adjective* [blend of *rural* and *urban*] (1918)
: of, relating to, or constituting an area which is chiefly residential but where some farming is carried on
Ru·ri·tan \'rùr-ə-tən\ *noun* [*Ruritan National,* a service club] (1968)
: a member of a major national service club
Ru·ri·ta·ni·an \'rùr-ə-,tā-nē-ən, ,rùr-ə-'\ *adjective* [*Ruritania,* fictional kingdom in the novel *Prisoner of Zenda* (1894) by Anthony Hope] (1896)
: of, relating to, or having the characteristics of an imaginary place of high romance
ruse \'rüs, 'rüz\ *noun* [French, from Middle French, from *ruser* to dodge, deceive] (1625)
: a wily subterfuge
 synonym see TRICK
¹rush \'rəsh\ *noun* [Middle English, from Old English *rysc*; akin to Middle High German *rusch* rush, Lithuanian *rezgti* to knit] (before 12th century)
: any of various monocotyledonous often tufted marsh plants (as of the genera *Juncus* and *Scirpus* of the family Juncaceae, the rush family) with cylindrical often hollow stems which are used in bottoming chairs and plaiting mats
 — **rushy** \'rə-shē\ *adjective*
²rush *verb* [Middle English *russhen*, from Middle French *ruser* to put to flight, repel, deceive, from Latin *recusare* to refuse — more at RECUSANT] (14th century)
intransitive verb
1 : to move forward, progress, or act with haste or eagerness or without preparation
2 : to advance a football by running plays ⟨*rushed* for a total of 150 yards⟩
transitive verb
1 : to push or impel on or forward with speed, impetuosity, or violence
2 : to perform in a short time or at high speed
3 : to urge to an unnatural or extreme speed ⟨don't *rush* me⟩
4 : to run toward or against in attack **:** CHARGE
5 a : to carry (a ball) forward in a running play **b :** to move in quickly on (a kicker or passer) to hinder, prevent, or block a kick or pass — used especially of defensive linemen
6 a : to lavish attention on **:** COURT **b :** to try to secure a pledge of membership (as in a fraternity) from
³rush *noun* (14th century)
1 a : a violent forward motion **b :** ATTACK, ONSET **c :** a surging of emotion
2 a : a burst of activity, productivity, or speed **b :** a sudden insistent demand
3 : a thronging of people usually to a new place in search of wealth ⟨gold *rush*⟩
4 a : the act of carrying a football during a game **:** running play **b :** the action or an instance of rushing a passer or kicker in football ⟨pass *rush*⟩

5 a : a round of attention usually involving extensive social activity **b :** a drive by a fraternity or sorority to recruit new members
6 : a print of a motion-picture scene processed directly after the shooting for review by the director or producer — usually used in plural
7 a : the immediate pleasurable feeling produced by a drug (as heroin or amphetamine) — called also *flash* **b :** a sudden feeling of intense pleasure or euphoria **:** THRILL
⁴rush *adjective* (1887)
: requiring or marked by special speed or urgency ⟨*rush* orders⟩ ⟨the *rush* season⟩ ⟨a *rush* job⟩
rush candle *noun* (1591)
: RUSHLIGHT
rush·ee \,rə-'shē\ *noun* (circa 1916)
: a college or university student who is being rushed by a fraternity or sorority
rush·er \'rə-shər\ *noun* (1654)
: one that rushes; *especially* **:** BALLCARRIER
rush hour *noun* (1898)
: a period of the day when the demands especially of traffic or business are at a peak
rush·ing *noun* (1883)
: the act of advancing a football by running plays **:** the use of running plays; *also* **:** yardage gained by running plays
rush·light \'rəsh-,līt\ *noun* (1710)
: a candle that consists of the pith of a rush dipped in grease
rusk \'rəsk\ *noun* [modification of Spanish & Portuguese *rosca* coil, twisted roll] (1595)
1 : hard crisp bread originally used as ship's stores
2 : a sweet or plain bread baked, sliced, and baked again until dry and crisp
Russ \'rəs, 'rüs, 'rùs\ *noun, plural* **Russian** *or* **Russ·es** [ultimately from Old Russian *Rus'* the East Slavic-speaking lands] (1537)
: RUSSIAN
 — **Russ** *adjective*
¹rus·set \'rə-sət\ *noun* [Middle English, from Old French *rousset,* from *rousset,* adjective, russet, from *rous* russet, from Latin *russus* red; akin to Latin *ruber* red — more at RED] (13th century)
1 : coarse homespun usually reddish brown cloth
2 : a strong brown
3 : any of various winter apples having russet rough skins
4 : IDAHO
²russet *adjective* (15th century)
: of the color russet
rus·set·ing *also* **rus·set·ting** \'rə-sə-tiŋ\ *noun* (1912)
: a brownish roughened area on the skin of fruit (as apples) caused by injury
Rus·sia leather \'rə-shə-\ *noun* [*Russia,* Europe] (1658)
: leather made by tanning various skins with willow, birch, or oak and then rubbing the flesh side with a phenolic oil distilled from a European birch — called also *Russia calf*
Rus·sian \'rə-shən\ *noun* (1538)
1 a : a native or inhabitant of Russia **b :** a member of the dominant Slavic-speaking ethnic group of Russia **c :** a person of Russian descent
2 : a Slavic language of the Russian people spoken as a second language by many non-Russian ethnic groups of the Soviet Union and its successor states
 — **Russian** *adjective*
 — **Rus·sian·ness** \-nəs\ *noun*
Russian blue *noun, often B capitalized* (1889)
: any of a breed of slender long-bodied large-eared domestic cats with short silky bluish gray fur
Russian dressing *noun* (1922)
: a dressing (as of mayonnaise or oil and vinegar) with added chili sauce, chopped pickles, or pimientos

Rus·sian·ize \'rə-shə-,nīz\ *transitive verb* **-ized; -iz·ing** (1831)
: to make Russian
 — **Rus·sian·i·za·tion** \,rə-shə-nə-'zā-shən\ *noun*
Russian olive *noun* (1913)
: a chiefly silvery Eurasian large shrub or small tree (*Elaeagnus angustifolia* of the family Elaeagnaceae) cultivated especially as a shelterbelt plant
Russian roulette *noun* (1937)
1 : an act of bravado consisting of spinning the cylinder of a revolver loaded with one cartridge, pointing the muzzle at one's own head, and pulling the trigger
2 : something resembling Russian roulette in its potential for disaster ⟨taking cocaine is playing *Russian roulette* —Jonathan Nicholas⟩
Russian thistle *noun* (1894)
: a prickly European saltwort (*Salsola kali*) that is a serious pest in North America — called also *Russian tumbleweed*
Russian wolfhound *noun* (1872)
: BORZOI
Rus·si·fy \'rə-sə-,fī\ *transitive verb* **-fied; -fy·ing** (1865)
: RUSSIANIZE
 — **Rus·si·fi·ca·tion** \,rə-sə-fə-'kā-shən\ *noun*
Russ·ki *or* **Russ·ky** *or* **Russ·kie** \'rəs-kē, 'rùs-\ *noun, plural* **Russkies** *or* **Russkis** [Russian *russkiĭ,* adjective & noun, Russian, from Old Russian, from *Rus'*] (1858)
: RUSSIAN 1
Rus·so- \'rə-(,)sō, ,rə-, -(,)shō\ *combining form* [*Russia* & *Russian*]
: Russian and ⟨the *Russo*-Japanese war⟩
¹rust \'rəst\ *noun* [Middle English, from Old English *rūst;* akin to Old English *rēad* red — more at RED] (before 12th century)
1 a : the reddish brittle coating formed on iron especially when chemically attacked by moist air and composed essentially of hydrated ferric oxide **b :** a comparable coating produced on a metal other than iron by corrosion **c :** something resembling rust **:** ACCRETION
2 : corrosive or injurious influence or effect
3 : any of numerous destructive diseases of plants produced by fungi (order Uredinales) and characterized by usually reddish brown pustular lesions; *also* **:** a fungus causing this
4 : a strong reddish brown
²rust (13th century)
intransitive verb
1 : to form rust **:** become oxidized ⟨iron *rusts*⟩
2 : to degenerate especially from inaction, lack of use, or passage of time ⟨most men would . . . have allowed their faculties to *rust* —T. B. Macaulay⟩
3 : to become reddish brown as if with rust ⟨the leaves slowly *rusted*⟩
4 : to be affected with a rust fungus
transitive verb
1 : to cause (a metal) to form rust ⟨keep up your bright swords, for the dew will *rust* them —Shakespeare⟩
2 : to impair or corrode by or as if by time, inactivity, or deleterious use
3 : to cause to become reddish brown **:** turn the color of rust
rust belt *noun, often R&B capitalized* (1983)
: the northeastern and midwestern states of the U.S. in which heavy industry has declined
rust bucket *noun* (1945)
: an old and dilapidated ship
¹rus·tic \'rəs-tik\ *also* **rus·ti·cal** \-ti-kəl\ *adjective* [Middle English *rustik,* from Middle French *rustique,* from Latin *rusticus,* from *rus* open land — more at ROOM] (15th century)
1 : of, relating to, or suitable for the country **:** RURAL
2 a : made of the rough limbs of trees ⟨*rustic* furniture⟩ **b :** finished by rusticating ⟨a *rustic* joint in masonry⟩

3 a : characteristic of or resembling country people **b :** lacking in social graces or polish
4 : appropriate to the country (as in plainness or sturdiness) ⟨heavy *rustic* boots⟩
— **rus·ti·cal·ly** \-ti-k(ə-)lē\ *adverb*
— **rus·tic·i·ty** \ˌrəs-'ti-sə-tē\ *noun*
²**rustic** *noun* (circa 1550)
1 : an inhabitant of a rural area
2 a : an awkward coarse person **b :** an unsophisticated rural person
rus·ti·cate \'rəs-ti-ˌkāt\ *verb* **-cat·ed; -cat·ing** (1660)
intransitive verb
: to go into or reside in the country **:** follow a rustic life
transitive verb
1 *chiefly British* **:** to suspend from school or college
2 : to build or face with usually rough-surfaced masonry blocks having beveled or rebated edges producing pronounced joints ⟨a *rusticated* facade⟩
3 a : to compel to reside in the country **b :** to cause to become rustic **:** implant rustic mannerisms in
— **rus·ti·ca·tion** \ˌrəs-ti-'kā-shən\ *noun*
— **rus·ti·ca·tor** \'rəs-ti-ˌkā-tər\ *noun*
¹**rus·tle** \'rə-səl\ *verb* **rus·tled; rus·tling** \'rə-s(ə-)liŋ\ [Middle English *rustelen*] (14th century)
intransitive verb
1 : to make or cause a rustle
2 a : to act or move with energy or speed **b :** to forage food
3 : to steal cattle
transitive verb
1 : to cause to rustle
2 a : to obtain by one's own exertions — often used with *up* ⟨able to *rustle* up $5,000 bail —Jack McCallum⟩ **b :** FORAGE
3 : to steal (as livestock) especially from a farm or ranch
— **rus·tler** \-s(ə-)lər\ *noun*
²**rustle** *noun* (1759)
: a quick succession or confusion of small sounds
rust mite *noun* (1884)
: any of various small gall mites that burrow in the surface of leaves or fruits usually producing brown or reddish patches
rust·proof \'rəst-ˌprüf\ *adjective* (1691)
: incapable of rusting
¹**rusty** \'rəs-tē\ *adjective* **rust·i·er; -est** (before 12th century)
1 : affected by or as if by rust; *especially* **:** stiff with or as if with rust
2 : inept and slow through lack of practice or old age
3 a : of the color rust **b :** dulled in color or appearance by age and use ⟨a *rusty* old suit of clothes⟩
4 : OUTMODED
5 : HOARSE, GRATING
— **rust·i·ly** \-tə-lē\ *adverb*

— **rust·i·ness** \-tē-nəs\ *noun*
²**rus·ty** \'rəs-tē\ *adjective* **rus·ti·er; -est** [alteration of *restive*] (1625)
chiefly dialect **:** ILL-NATURED, SURLY
¹**rut** \'rət\ *noun* [Middle English *rutte*, from Middle French *rut* roar, from Late Latin *rugitus*, from Latin *rugire* to roar; akin to Middle Irish *rucht* roar, Old Church Slavonic *ružati* to neigh] (15th century)
1 : an annually recurrent state of sexual excitement in the male deer; *broadly* **:** sexual excitement in a mammal (as estrus in the female) especially when periodic
2 : the period during which rut normally occurs — often used with *the*
²**rut** *intransitive verb* **rut·ted; rut·ting** (1625)
: to be in or enter into a state of rut
³**rut** *noun* [perhaps modification of Middle French *route* way, route] (1580)
1 a : a track worn by a wheel or by habitual passage **b :** a groove in which something runs **c :** CHANNEL, FURROW
2 : a usual or fixed practice; *especially* **:** a monotonous routine ⟨fall easily into a conversational *rut*⟩
⁴**rut** *transitive verb* **rut·ted; rut·ting** (1607)
: to make a rut in **:** FURROW
ru·ta·ba·ga \ˌrü-tə-'bā-gə, ˌrü-, -'be-; 'rü-tə-ˌ, 'rü-\ *noun* [Swedish dialect *rotabagge*, from *rot* root + *bagge* bag] (1799)
: a turnip (*Brassica napus napobrassica*) that usually produces a large yellowish root
ruth \'rüth\ *noun* [Middle English *ruthe*, from *ruen* to rue] (13th century)
1 : compassion for the misery of another
2 : sorrow for one's own faults **:** REMORSE
Ruth \'rüth\ *noun* [Hebrew *Rūth*]
1 : a Moabite woman who accompanied Naomi to Bethlehem and became the ancestress of David
2 : a short narrative book of canonical Jewish and Christian Scriptures — see BIBLE table
ru·the·ni·um \rü-'thē-nē-əm\ *noun* [New Latin, from Medieval Latin *Ruthenia* Ruthenia] (1848)
: a hard brittle grayish polyvalent rare metallic element occurring in platinum ores and used in hardening platinum alloys — see ELEMENT table
ruth·er·ford·ium \ˌrə-thə(r)-'fȯr-dē-əm\ *noun* [New Latin, from Ernest *Rutherford*] (1969)
: UNNILQUADIUM
ruth·ful \'rüth-fəl\ *adjective* (13th century)
1 : full of ruth **:** TENDER
2 : full of sorrow **:** WOEFUL
3 : causing sorrow
— **ruth·ful·ly** \-fə-lē\ *adverb*
— **ruth·ful·ness** *noun*
ruth·less \'rüth-ləs *also* 'rüth-\ *adjective* (14th century)
: having no ruth **:** MERCILESS, CRUEL
— **ruth·less·ly** *adverb*
— **ruth·less·ness** *noun*

ru·ti·lant \'rü-t⁸l-ənt\ *adjective* [Middle English *rutilaunt*, from Latin *rutilant-, rutilans*, past participle of *rutilare* to glow reddish, from *rutilus* ruddy; probably akin to Latin *ruber* red — more at RED] (15th century)
: having a reddish glow
ru·tile \'rü-ˌtēl\ *noun* [German *Rutil*, from Latin *rutilus*] (1803)
: a mineral that consists of titanium dioxide usually with a little iron, is typically of a reddish brown color but sometimes deep red or black, and has a brilliant metallic or adamantine luster
rut·tish \'rə-tish\ *adjective* (1601)
: inclined to rut **:** LUSTFUL
— **rut·tish·ly** *adverb*
— **rut·tish·ness** *noun*
rut·ty \'rə-tē\ *adjective* **rut·ti·er; -est** (1596)
: full of ruts
RV \ˌär-'vē\ *noun* (1967)
: RECREATIONAL VEHICLE
R-value \'är-ˌval-(ˌ)yü\ *noun* [probably from thermal resistance] (1948)
: a measure of resistance to the flow of heat through a given thickness of a material (as insulation) with higher numbers indicating better insulating properties — compare U-VALUE
Rx \ˌär-'eks\ *noun* [alteration of ℞, symbol used at the beginning of a prescription, abbreviation for Latin *recipe*, literally, take — more at RECIPE] (1926)
: a medical prescription
-ry *noun suffix* [Middle English *-rie*, from Old French, short for *-erie* -ery]
: -ERY ⟨wizard*ry*⟩ ⟨citizen*ry*⟩ ⟨ancient*ry*⟩
rya \'rē-ə\ *noun* [*Rya*, village in southwest Sweden] (1945)
: a Scandinavian handwoven rug with a deep resilient comparatively flat pile; *also* **:** the weave typical of this rug
¹**rye** \'rī\ *noun* [Middle English, from Old English *ryge*; akin to Old High German *rocko* rye, Lithuanian *rugys*] (before 12th century)
1 : a hardy annual grass (*Secale cereale*) that is widely grown for grain and as a cover crop
2 : the seeds of rye
3 : RYE BREAD
4 : RYE WHISKEY
²**rye** *noun* [Romany *rai* gentleman, master, from Sanskrit *rājan* king — more at ROYAL] (1851)
: a male Gypsy
rye bread *noun* (1579)
: bread made wholly or in part of rye flour; *especially* **:** a light bread often with caraway seeds
rye·grass \'rī-ˌgras\ *noun* (1747)
: any of several grasses (genus *Lolium*); *especially* **:** either of two grasses (*Latin perenne* and *Latin multiflorum*) that are used especially for pasture, a cover crop, or lawn grass
rye whiskey *noun* (1785)
: a whiskey distilled from rye or from rye and malt

\ə\ abut \ᵊ\ kitten \ər\ **further** \a\ ash \ā\ ace
\ä\ mop, mar \au̇\ **out** \ch\ **chin** \e\ bet \ē\ **easy**
\g\ go \i\ hit \ī\ **ice** \j\ **job** \ŋ\ **sing** \ō\ **go**
\ȯ\ **law** \ȯi\ **boy** \th\ **thin** \t̲h̲\ **the** \ü\ loot \u̇\ **foot**
\y\ yet \zh\ **vision** *see also* Guide to Pronunciation

S

S *is the nineteenth letter of the English alphabet. It came through Latin via Etruscan from Greek* sigma, *which borrowed the character from the Phoenician* šîn, *pronounced "sh." In English,* s *usually represents the sibilant sound in* soon, hates, *and* hats. *In certain positions, however,* s *may represent the sound of* z *(as in* deserve; loves; heads*), and it sometimes has the value of* sh *or* zh, *as in* sure *and* measure. *In a few words it is silent (as* isle *and* debris*). With the letter* h *it forms the digraph* sh, *as in* ship. *In related languages, English* s *corresponds to German* s, *Latin* s *or* r, *Greek* s *or* h *(rough breathing), and Sanskrit* s *or* ṣ. *For example, English* sit *is historically related to German* sitzen, *Latin* sedere, *Greek* hezesthai, *and Sanskrit* sadas *("a seat"). The small form of* s *began as a simple reduction in size of the capital form. In printing, the "long* s*" (ſ), formerly much used, now appears only rarely, usually joined with a following consonant such as* s *or* t.

s \'es\ *noun, plural* **s's** *or* **ss** \'e-səz\ *often capitalized, often attributive* (before 12th century)
1 a : the 19th letter of the English alphabet **b :** a graphic representation of this letter **c :** a speech counterpart of orthographic *s*
2 : a graphic device for reproducing the letter *s*
3 : one designated *s* especially as the 19th in order or class
4 [abbreviation for *satisfactory*] **a :** a grade rating a student's work as satisfactory **b :** one graded or rated with an S
5 : something shaped like the letter S
¹-s \s\ *after a voiceless consonant, z after a voiced consonant or a vowel\ noun plural suffix* [Middle English *-es, -s,* from Old English *-as,* nominative & accusative plural ending of some masculine nouns; akin to Old Saxon *-os*]
— used to form the plural of most nouns that do not end in *s, z, sh, ch,* or postconsonantal *y* ⟨heads⟩ ⟨books⟩ ⟨boys⟩ ⟨beliefs⟩, to form the plural of proper nouns that end in postconsonantal *y* ⟨Marys⟩, and with or without a preceding apostrophe to form the plural of abbreviations, numbers, letters, and symbols used as nouns ⟨MCs⟩ ⟨PhD's⟩ ⟨4s⟩ ⟨the 1940's⟩ ⟨$s⟩ ⟨B's⟩; compare ¹-ES
²-s *adverb suffix* [Middle English *-es, -s,* plural ending of nouns, from *-es,* genitive singular ending of nouns (functioning adverbially), from Old English *-es*]
— used to form adverbs denoting usual or repeated action or state ⟨always at home Sundays⟩ ⟨mornings he stops by the newsstand⟩
³-s *verb suffix* [Middle English (Northern & North Midland dialect) *-es,* from Old English (Northumbrian dialect) *-es, -as,* probably from Old English *-es, -as,* 2d singular present indicative ending — more at -EST]
— used to form the third person singular present of most verbs that do not end in *s, z, sh, ch,* or postconsonantal *y* ⟨falls⟩ ⟨takes⟩ ⟨plays⟩; compare ²-ES
¹'s *same as* -'s\ *verb* [contraction of *is, has, does*] (1584)
1 a : IS ⟨she's here⟩ **b :** WAS ⟨when's the last time you ate?⟩
2 : HAS ⟨he's seen them⟩
3 : DOES ⟨what's he want?⟩
²'s \s\ *pronoun* [by contraction] (1588)
: US — used with *let* ⟨let's⟩
-'s \s\ *after voiceless consonants other than* s, sh, ch; z *after vowels and voiced consonants other than* z, zh, j; *also after* s, sh, ch, z, zh, j\ *noun suffix or pronoun suffix* [Middle English *-es, -s,* genitive singular ending, from Old English *-es;* akin to Old High German *-es,* genitive singular ending, Greek *-oio, -ou,* Sanskrit *-asya*]
— used to form the possessive of singular nouns ⟨boy's⟩, of plural nouns not ending in *s*

⟨children's⟩, of some pronouns ⟨anyone's⟩, and of word groups functioning as nouns ⟨the man in the corner's hat⟩ or pronouns ⟨someone else's⟩
Saa·nen \'sä-nən, 'zä-\ *noun* [*Saanen,* locality in southwest Switzerland] (1906)
: any of a Swiss breed of usually white and hornless short-haired dairy goats
sab·a·dil·la \,sa-bə-'di-lə, -'dē-yə\ *noun* [Spanish *cebadilla*] (1812)
: a Mexican plant (*Schoenocaulon officinalis*) of the lily family; *also* : its seeds that are used as a source of veratrine and in insecticides
sa·ba·yon \sà-bà-yōⁿ\ *noun* [French, modification of Italian *zabaione*] (1906)
: ZABAGLIONE
sab·bat \'sa-bət\ *noun, often capitalized* [French, literally, sabbath, from Latin *sabbatum*] (1652)
: a midnight assembly of diabolists (as witches and sorcerers) held especially in medieval and Renaissance times to renew allegiance to the devil through mystic rites and orgies
¹Sab·ba·tar·i·an \,sa-bə-'ter-ē-ən\ *noun* [Latin *sabbatarius,* from *sabbatum* sabbath] (1613)
1 : one who observes the Sabbath on Saturday in conformity with the letter of the fourth commandment
2 : an adherent of Sabbatarianism
²Sabbatarian *adjective* (circa 1631)
1 : of or relating to the Sabbath
2 : of or relating to the Sabbatarians or Sabbatarianism
Sab·ba·tar·i·an·ism \,sa-bə-'ter-ē-ə-,ni-zəm\ *noun* (circa 1674)
: strict and often rigorous observance of the Sabbath
Sab·bath \'sa-bəth\ *noun* [Middle English *sabat,* from Old French & Old English, from Latin *sabbatum,* from Greek *sabbaton,* from Hebrew *shabbāth,* literally, rest] (before 12th century)
1 a : the seventh day of the week observed from Friday evening to Saturday evening as a day of rest and worship by Jews and some Christians **b :** Sunday observed among Christians as a day of rest and worship
2 : a time of rest
¹sab·bat·i·cal \sə-'ba-ti-kəl\ *or* **sab·bat·ic** \-'tik\ *adjective* [Late Latin *sabbaticus,* from Greek *sabbatikos,* from *sabbaton*] (1645)
1 : of or relating to the sabbath ⟨*sabbatical* laws⟩
2 : of or relating to a sabbatical year
²sabbatical *noun* (1903)
1 : SABBATICAL YEAR 2
2 : LEAVE 1b
3 : a break or change from a normal routine (as of employment)
sabbatical year *noun* (1599)

1 *often S capitalized* **:** a year of rest for the land observed every seventh year in ancient Judea
2 : a leave often with pay granted usually every seventh year (as to a college professor) for rest, travel, or research — called also *sabbatical leave*
Sa·bel·li·an \sə-'be-lē-ən\ *noun* [Latin *Sabellus* Sabine] (1601)
1 : a member of one of a group of early Italian peoples including Sabines and Samnites
2 : one or all of several little known languages or dialects of ancient Italy presumably closely related to Oscan and Umbrian
— **Sabellian** *adjective*
¹sa·ber *or* **sa·bre** \'sā-bər\ *noun* [French *sabre,* modification of German dialect *Sabel,* from Middle High German, probably of Slavic origin; akin to Russian *sablya* saber] (1680)
1 : a cavalry sword with a curved blade, thick back, and guard
2 a : a light fencing or dueling sword having an arched guard that covers the back of the hand and a tapering flexible blade with a full cutting edge along one side and a partial cutting edge on the back at the tip — compare ÉPÉE, FOIL **b :** the sport of fencing with the saber

saber 1

²saber *or* **sabre** *transitive verb* **sa·bered** *or* **sa·bred; sa·ber·ing** *or* **sa·bring** \-b(ə-)riŋ\
: to strike, cut, or kill with a saber
sa·ber·met·rics \,sā-bər-'me-triks\ *noun plural but singular in construction* [*saber-* (from *Society for American Baseball Research*) + *-metrics* (as in *econometrics*)] (1982)
: the statistical analysis of baseball data
— **sa·ber·me·tri·cian** \,sā-bər-mə-'tri-shən\ *noun*
saber rattling *noun* (1922)
: ostentatious display of military power
saber saw *noun* (1953)
: a light portable electric saw with a pointed reciprocating blade
sa·ber-toothed \'sā-bər-,tütht\ *adjective* (1849)
: having long sharp canine teeth
saber-toothed tiger *noun* (1849)
: any of numerous extinct cats (as genus *Smilodon*) widely distributed from the Oligocene through the Pleistocene and characterized by long curving upper canines — called also *saber-toothed cat*
sa·bin \'sā-bən\ *noun* [Wallace C. W. *Sabine* (died 1919) American physicist] (1934)
: a unit of acoustic absorption equivalent to the absorption by one square foot of a perfect absorber
Sa·bine \'sā-,bīn, *especially British* 'sa-\ *noun* [Middle English *Sabin,* from Latin *Sabinus*] (14th century)
1 : a member of an ancient people of the Apennines northeast of Latium
2 : the Italic language of the Sabine people
— **Sabine** *adjective*
¹sa·ble \'sā-bəl\ *noun, plural* **sables** [Middle English, sable or its fur, the heraldic color black, black, from Middle French, sable or its fur, the heraldic color black, from Middle Low German *sabel* sable or its fur, from Middle High German *zobel,* of Slavic origin; akin to Russian *sobol'* sable or its fur] (14th century)
1 a : the color black **b :** black clothing worn in mourning — usually used in plural
2 a *or plural* **sable** (1) **:** a carnivorous mammal (*Martes zibellina*) of the weasel family that occurs chiefly in northern Asia (2) **:** any of various animals related to the sable **b :** the fur or pelt of a sable

3 a : the usually dark brown color of the fur of the sable **b** : a grayish yellowish brown

²**sable** *adjective* (15th century)
1 : of the color black
2 : DARK, GLOOMY

sa·ble·fish \ˈsā-bəl-ˌfish\ *noun* (1917)
: a large spiny-finned gray to blackish bony fish (*Anoplopoma fimbria* of the family Anoplomatidae) of the Pacific coast that is an important food fish and has a liver rich in vitamins

sa·bot \sa-ˈbō, ˈsa-(ˌ)bō, *for 1b also* ˈsa-bət\ *noun* [French] (1607)
1 a : a wooden shoe worn in various European countries **b** (1) : a strap across the instep in a shoe especially of the sandal type (2) : a shoe having a sabot strap
2 : a thrust-transmitting carrier that positions a missile in a gun barrel or launching tube and that prevents the escape of gas ahead of the missile
3 : SHOE 6

¹**sab·o·tage** \ˈsa-bə-ˌtäzh\ *noun* [French, from *saboter* to clatter with sabots, botch, sabotage, from *sabot*] (1910)
1 : destruction of an employer's property (as tools or materials) or the hindering of manufacturing by discontented workers
2 : destructive or obstructive action carried on by a civilian or enemy agent to hinder a nation's war effort
3 a : an act or process tending to hamper or hurt **b** : deliberate subversion ◇

²**sabotage** *transitive verb* **-taged; -tag·ing** (1913)
: to practice sabotage on

sab·o·teur \ˌsa-bə-ˈtər, -ˈtůr, -ˈtyůr\ *noun* [French, from *saboter*] (1921)
: one that practices sabotage

sa·bra \ˈsä-brə\ *noun, often capitalized* [New Hebrew *ṣabhār*, literally, prickly pear] (1945)
: a native-born Israeli

sac \ˈsak\ *noun* [French, literally, bag, from Latin *saccus* — more at SACK] (1741)
: a pouch within an animal or plant often containing a fluid ⟨a synovial *sac*⟩
— **sac·like** \-ˌlīk\ *adjective*

Sac \ˈsak, ˈsȯk\ *variant of* SAUK

sa·ca·huis·te \ˌsa-kə-ˈwis-tə, ˌsä-, -tē\ *or* **sa·ca·huis·ta** \-tə\ *noun* [Mexican Spanish *zacahuiscle*, from (assumed) Nahuatl *zacahuiztli*, from Nahuatl *zacatl* grass, hay + *huiztli* thorn] (1896)
: a bear grass (*Nolina texana*) that may cause poisoning in livestock

sac·a·ton \ˈsa-kə-ˌtōn\ *noun* [American Spanish *zacatón*, from *zacate* coarse grass, from Nahuatl *zacatl*] (1846)
: a coarse perennial grass (*Sporobolus wrightii*) of the southwestern U.S. that is used for hay in alkaline regions

sac·cade \sa-ˈkäd\ *noun* [French, twitch, jerk, from Middle French, from *saquer* to pull, draw] (1938)
: a small rapid jerky movement of the eye especially as it jumps from fixation on one point to another (as in reading)
— **sac·cad·ic** \-ˈkä-dik\ *adjective*

sac·cate \ˈsa-ˌkāt\ *adjective* [New Latin *saccatus*, from Latin *saccus*] (1830)
: having the form of a sac or pouch ⟨*saccate* pollen grains⟩

sacchar- *or* **sacchari-** *or* **saccharo-** *combining form* [Latin *saccharon*, from Greek *sakcharon*, from Prakrit *sakkharā*, from Sanskrit *śarkarā* gravel, sugar]
: sugar ⟨*sacchari*fy⟩ ⟨*saccharo*meter⟩

sac·cha·rase \ˈsa-kə-ˌrās, -ˌrāz\ *noun* [International Scientific Vocabulary] (1920)
: INVERTASE

sac·cha·ride \ˈsa-kə-ˌrīd\ *noun* (1895)
: a simple sugar, combination of sugars, or polymerized sugar : CARBOHYDRATE

sac·char·i·fi·ca·tion \sə-ˌkar-ə-fə-ˈkā-shən\ *noun* (1839)

: the process of breaking a complex carbohydrate (as starch or cellulose) into simple sugars
— **sac·char·i·fy** \sə-ˈkar-ə-ˌfī, sa-\ *transitive verb*

sac·cha·rim·e·ter \ˌsa-kə-ˈri-mə-tər\ *noun* [International Scientific Vocabulary] (1874)
: a device for measuring the amount of sugar in a solution; *specifically* : a polarimeter so used

sac·cha·rin \ˈsa-k(ə-)rən\ *noun* [International Scientific Vocabulary] (1885)
: a crystalline compound $C_7H_5NO_3S$ that is unrelated to the carbohydrates, is several hundred times sweeter than cane sugar, and is used as a calorie-free sweetener

sac·cha·rine \ˈsa-k(ə-)rən, -kə-ˌrēn, -kə-ˌrīn\ *adjective* [Latin *saccharum*] (circa 1674)
1 a : of, relating to, or resembling that of sugar ⟨*saccharine* taste⟩ **b** : yielding or containing sugar ⟨*saccharine* vegetables⟩
2 : overly or sickishly sweet ⟨*saccharine* flavor⟩
3 : ingratiatingly or affectedly agreeable or friendly
4 : overly sentimental : MAWKISH
— **sac·cha·rin·i·ty** \ˌsa-kə-ˈri-nə-tē\ *noun*

sac·cha·roi·dal \ˌsa-kə-ˈrȯi-d⁰l\ *adjective* (1838)
: having or being a fine granular texture like that of loaf sugar ⟨*saccharoidal* marble⟩

sac·cha·rom·e·ter \-ˈrä-mə-tər\ *noun* (1784)
: SACCHARIMETER; *especially* : a hydrometer with a special scale

sac·cha·ro·my·ces \-rō-ˈmī-(ˌ)sēz\ *noun* [New Latin, from *sacchar-* + *-myces* fungus, from Greek *mykēs* — more at MYC-] (1873)
: any of a genus (*Saccharomyces* of the family Saccharomycetaceae) of usually unicellular yeasts (as a brewer's yeast) that are distinguished by their sparse or absent mycelium and by their facility in reproducing asexually by budding

sac·cu·lar \ˈsa-kyə-lər\ *adjective* (circa 1859)
: resembling a sac ⟨a *saccular* aneurysm⟩

sac·cu·lat·ed \-ˌlā-təd\ *also* **sac·cu·late** \-ˌlāt, -lət\ *adjective* (circa 1836)
: having or formed of a series of saccular expansions
— **sac·cu·la·tion** \ˌsa-kyə-ˈlā-shən\ *noun*

sac·cule \ˈsa-(ˌ)kyü(ə)l\ *noun* [New Latin *sacculus*, from Latin, diminutive of *saccus* bag — more at SACK] (circa 1839)
: a little sac; *specifically* : the smaller chamber of the membranous labyrinth of the ear

sac·cu·lus \ˈsa-kyə-ləs\ *noun, plural* **-li** \-ˌlī, -ˌlē\ [New Latin] (1748)
: SACCULE

sac·er·do·tal \ˌsa-sər-ˈdō-t⁰l, ˌsa-kər-\ *adjective* [Middle English, from Middle French, from Latin *sacerdotalis*, from *sacerdot-, sacerdos* priest, from *sacer* sacred + *-dot-, -dos* (akin to *facere* to make) — more at SACRED, DO] (15th century)
1 : of or relating to priests or a priesthood : PRIESTLY
2 : of, relating to, or suggesting sacerdotalism
— **sac·er·do·tal·ly** \-t⁰l-ē\ *adverb*

sac·er·do·tal·ism \-t⁰l-ˌi-zəm\ *noun* (1856)
: religious belief emphasizing the powers of priests as essential mediators between God and mankind
— **sac·er·do·tal·ist** \-t⁰l-ist\ *noun*

sac fungus *noun* (circa 1929)
: ASCOMYCETE

sa·chem \ˈsā-chəm, ˈsa-\ *noun* [Narraganset *sâchim*] (1622)
1 : a North American Indian chief; *especially* : the chief of a confederation of the Algonquian tribes of the North Atlantic coast
2 : a Tammany leader
— **sa·chem·ic** \sā-ˈche-mik, sa-\ *adjective*

Sa·cher torte \ˈsä-kər-, ˈzä-\ *noun* [German *Sachertorte*, from *Sacher* (name of a family of 19th and 20th century Austrian restaurant proprietors) + German *Torte* torte] (1906)

: a rich chocolate torte with an apricot jam filling

sa·chet \sa-ˈshā\ *noun* [Middle French, from Old French, diminutive of *sac* bag — more at SAC] (15th century)
1 : a small bag or packet
2 : a small bag containing a perfumed powder or potpourri used to scent clothes and linens
— **sa·cheted** \-ˈshād\ *adjective*

¹**sack** \ˈsak\ *noun* [Middle English *sak* bag, sackcloth, from Old English *sacc,* from Latin *saccus* bag & Late Latin *saccus* sackcloth, both from Greek *sakkos* bag, sackcloth, of Semitic origin; akin to Hebrew *śaq* bag, sackcloth] (before 12th century)
1 : a usually rectangular-shaped bag (as of paper, burlap, or canvas)
2 : the amount contained in a sack; *especially* : a fixed amount of a commodity used as a unit of measure
3 a : a woman's loose-fitting dress **b** : a short usually loose-fitting coat for women and children **c** : SACQUE 2
4 : DISMISSAL
5 a : HAMMOCK, BUNK **b** : BED
6 : a base in baseball
7 : an instance of sacking the quarterback in football
— **sack·ful** \-ˌfůl\ *noun*

²**sack** *transitive verb* (14th century)
1 : to put in or as if in a sack
2 : to dismiss especially summarily
3 : to tackle (the quarterback) behind the line of scrimmage in football
— **sack·er** *noun*

³**sack** *noun* [modification of Middle French *sec* dry, from Latin *siccus;* probably akin to Old High German *sīhan* to filter, Sanskrit *siñcati* he pours] (circa 1532)
: any of several white wines imported to England from Spain and the Canary Islands during the 16th and 17th centuries

⁴**sack** *transitive verb* [⁵*sack*] (circa 1547)
1 : to plunder (as a town) especially after capture
2 : to strip of valuables : LOOT
synonym see RAVAGE
— **sack·er** *noun*

◇ WORD HISTORY

sabotage Because the word *sabotage* appears to have some relation to French *sabot* "wooden shoe," the suggestion has often been made that *sabotage* in France originally alluded to disgruntled industrial workers throwing their sabots into machinery in order to damage it. In fact, there is no evidence to support such an etymology. The meaning "to damage an employer's property" of the French verb *saboter*, attested in the first decade of our century, is clearly built on an older sense "to perform haphazardly, botch, bungle," first attested in 1808. This meaning is in turn usually explained as proceeding from a yet older sense, "to make a clattering noise with sabots," on the premise that walking with wooden shoes suggests clumsy performance. Though the hypothesis is not implausible, *saboter* is attested in the 17th century with the sense "to torment," and as early as the 14th century in the meaning "to shake, knock." It is difficult to determine if these diverse meanings constitute a single line of development, or if the many associations evoked in Frenchmen by this piece of peasant footwear caused repeated episodes of verb creation from the same noun.

⁵sack *noun* [Middle French *sac*, from Old Italian *sacco*, literally, bag, from Latin *saccus*] (1549)
: the plundering of a captured town

sack·but \'sak-(ˌ)bət\ *noun* [Middle French *saqueboute*, literally, hooked lance, from Old French *saquer* to pull + *boter* to push — more at BUTT] (1533)
: the medieval and Renaissance trombone

sack·cloth \'sa(k)-ˌklȯth\ *noun* [¹*sack*] (13th century)
1 : a coarse cloth of goat or camel's hair or of flax, hemp, or cotton
2 : a garment of sackcloth worn as a sign of mourning or penitence

sack coat *noun* (1847)
: a man's jacket with a straight back

sack·ing \'sa-kiŋ\ *noun* (1707)
: material for sacks; *especially* : a coarse fabric (as burlap)

sack out *intransitive verb* [¹*sack*] (1946)
: to go to bed : go to sleep

sack race *noun* (1859)
: a jumping race in which each contestant's legs are enclosed in a sack

sacque \'sak\ *noun* [alteration of ¹*sack*] (1846)
1 : SACK 3a, b
2 : an infant's usually short jacket that fastens at the neck

¹sa·cral \'sa-krəl, 'sā-\ *adjective* (1767)
: of, relating to, or lying near the sacrum

²sa·cral \'sā-krəl, 'sa-\ *adjective* [Latin *sacr-*, *sacer* — more at SACRED] (1882)
: HOLY, SACRED

sac·ra·ment \'sa-krə-mənt\ *noun* [Middle English *sacrement*, *sacrament*, from Old French & Late Latin; Old French, from Late Latin *sacramentum*, from Latin, oath of allegiance, obligation, from *sacrare* to consecrate] (13th century)
1 a : a Christian rite (as baptism or the Eucharist) that is believed to have been ordained by Christ and that is held to be a means of divine grace or to be a sign or symbol of a spiritual reality **b** : a religious rite or observance comparable to a Christian sacrament
2 *capitalized* **a** : COMMUNION 2a **b** : BLESSED SACRAMENT
3 : something likened to a religious sacrament ⟨saw voting as a *sacrament* of democracy⟩

¹sac·ra·men·tal \ˌsa-krə-'men-t²l\ *adjective* (15th century)
1 : of, relating to, or having the character of a sacrament
2 : suggesting a sacrament (as in sacredness)
— **sac·ra·men·tal·ly** \-t²l-ē\ *adverb*

²sacramental *noun* (15th century)
: an action or object (as the rosary) of ecclesiastical origin that serves to express or increase devotion

sac·ra·men·tal·ism \-t²l-ˌi-zəm\ *noun* (1861)
: belief in or use of sacramental rites, acts, or objects; *specifically* : belief that the sacraments are inherently efficacious and necessary for salvation

sac·ra·men·tal·ist \-t²l-ist\ *noun* (1840)
1 : SACRAMENTARIAN
2 : an adherent of sacramentalism

Sac·ra·men·tar·i·an \ˌsa-krə-ˌmen-'ter-ē-ən, -mən-\ *noun* (1535)
1 : one who interprets sacraments as merely visible symbols
2 : SACRAMENTALIST
— **Sacramentarian** *adjective*
— **Sac·ra·men·tar·i·an·ism** \-ē-ə-ˌni-zəm\ *noun*

sa·crar·i·um \sə-'krer-ē-əm, sa-, sā-\ *noun, plural* **-ia** \-ē-ə\ [Medieval Latin, from Latin, shrine, from *sacr-*, *sacer* sacred] (1727)
1 a : SANCTUARY 1b **b** : SACRISTY **c** : PISCINA
2 : an ancient Roman shrine or sanctuary in a temple or a home holding sacred objects

sa·cred \'sā-krəd\ *adjective* [Middle English, from past participle of *sacren* to consecrate,

from Old French *sacrer*, from Latin *sacrare*, from *sacr-*, *sacer* sacred; akin to Latin *sancire* to make sacred, Hittite *šaklāi-* rite] (14th century)
1 a : dedicated or set apart for the service or worship of a deity ⟨a tree *sacred* to the gods⟩ **b** : devoted exclusively to one service or use (as of a person or purpose) ⟨a fund *sacred* to charity⟩
2 a : worthy of religious veneration : HOLY **b** : entitled to reverence and respect
3 : of or relating to religion : not secular or profane ⟨*sacred* music⟩
4 *archaic* : ACCURSED
5 a : UNASSAILABLE, INVIOLABLE **b** : highly valued and important ⟨a *sacred* responsibility⟩
— **sa·cred·ly** *adverb*
— **sa·cred·ness** *noun*

sacred baboon *noun* [from its veneration by the ancient Egyptians] (circa 1890)
: HAMADRYAS BABOON

sacred cow *noun* [from the veneration of the cow by Hindus] (1910)
: one that is often unreasonably immune from criticism or opposition

sacred mushroom *noun* (1930)
1 : any of various New World hallucinogenic fungi (genus *Psilocybe*) used especially in some Indian ceremonies
2 : MESCAL BUTTON

¹sac·ri·fice \'sa-krə-ˌfīs, *also* -fəs *or* -ˌfīz\ *noun* [Middle English, from Old French, from Latin *sacrificium*, from *sacr-*, *sacer* + *facere* to make — more at DO] (13th century)
1 : an act of offering to a deity something precious; *especially* : the killing of a victim on an altar
2 : something offered in sacrifice
3 a : destruction or surrender of something for the sake of something else **b** : something given up or lost ⟨the *sacrifices* made by parents⟩
4 : LOSS ⟨goods sold at a *sacrifice*⟩
5 : SACRIFICE HIT

²sacrifice *verb* **-ficed; -fic·ing** (14th century)
transitive verb
1 : to offer as a sacrifice
2 : to suffer loss of, give up, renounce, injure, or destroy especially for an ideal, belief, or end
3 : to sell at a loss
intransitive verb
1 : to make or perform the rites of a sacrifice
2 : to make a sacrifice hit in baseball
— **sac·ri·fic·er** *noun*

sacrifice fly *noun* (1944)
: an outfield fly in baseball caught by a fielder after which a runner scores

sacrifice hit *noun* (1880)
: a bunt in baseball that allows a runner to advance one base while the batter is put out

sac·ri·fi·cial \ˌsa-krə-'fi-shəl\ *adjective* (1607)
1 : of, relating to, of the nature of, or involving sacrifice
2 : of or relating to a metal that serves as the anode and is electrolytically consumed instead of another metal that is present
— **sac·ri·fi·cial·ly** \-shə-lē\ *adverb*

sac·ri·lege \'sa-krə-lij\ *noun* [Middle English, from Middle French, from Latin *sacrilegium*, from *sacrilegus* one who steals sacred things, from *sacr-*, *sacer* + *legere* to gather, steal — more at LEGEND] (14th century)
1 : a technical and not necessarily intrinsically outrageous violation (as improper reception of a sacrament) of what is sacred because consecrated to God
2 : gross irreverence toward a hallowed person, place, or thing
— **sac·ri·le·gious** \÷ˌsa-krə-'li-jəs *also* -'lē-\ *adjective*
— **sac·ri·le·gious·ly** *adverb*
— **sac·ri·le·gious·ness** *noun*

sac·ris·tan \'sa-krə-stən\ *noun* [Middle English, from Medieval Latin *sacristanus*, from Latin *sacr-*, *sacer*] (14th century)

: a person in charge of the sacristy and ceremonial equipment; *also* : SEXTON

sac·ris·ty \'sa-krə-stē\ *noun, plural* **-ties** [Middle English *sacristie*, from Medieval Latin *sacristia*, from *sacrista* sacristan, from Latin *sacr-*, *sacer*] (15th century)
: a room in a church where sacred vessels and vestments are kept and where the clergy vests

¹sa·cro·il·i·ac \ˌsa-krō-'i-lē-ˌak, ˌsā-\ *adjective* [probably from French *sacro-iliaque*, from New Latin *sacrum* + French *iliaque* iliac] (1831)
: of, relating to, or being the region of juncture of the sacrum and ilium

²sacroiliac *noun* (1936)
: the sacroiliac region; *also* : its firm fibrous cartilage

sac·ro·sanct \'sa-krō-ˌsaŋ(k)t\ *adjective* [Latin *sacrosanctus*, probably from *sacro sanctus* hallowed by a sacred rite] (1601)
1 : most sacred or holy : INVIOLABLE
2 : treated as if holy : immune from criticism or violation ⟨politically *sacrosanct* programs⟩
— **sac·ro·sanc·ti·ty** \ˌsa-krō-'saŋ(k)-tə-tē\ *noun*

sa·crum \'sa-krəm, 'sā-\ *noun, plural* **sa·cra** \'sa-krə, 'sā-\ [New Latin, from Late Latin *os sacrum* last bone of the spine, literally, holy bone, translation of Greek *hieron osteon*] (1753)
: the part of the vertebral column that is directly connected with or forms a part of the pelvis and in humans consists of five fused vertebrae

sad \'sad\ *adjective* **sad·der; sad·dest** [Middle English, from Old English *sæd* sated; akin to Old High German *sat* sated, Latin *satis* enough] (13th century)
1 a : affected with or expressive of grief or unhappiness : DOWNCAST **b** (1) : causing or associated with grief or unhappiness : DEPRESSING ⟨*sad* news⟩ (2) : REGRETTABLE, DEPLORABLE ⟨a *sad* relaxation of morals —C. W. Cunnington⟩ **c** : of little worth
2 : of a dull somber color ◇
— **sad·ly** *adverb*
— **sad·ness** *noun*

sad·den \'sa-d²n\ *verb* **sad·dened; sad·den·ing** \'sad-niŋ, 'sa-d²n-iŋ\ (1628)
transitive verb
: to make sad
intransitive verb
: to become sad

◇ WORD HISTORY
sad The word *sad* goes back to the remote Germanic past of the English language, though the ordinary modern meanings of the word, such as "downcast," "depressing," or "deplorable," give little hint of its history. Its Old English ancestor *sæd* meant "filled, full, satiated," a meaning matched by cognate words in other early Germanic languages, and continued by Modern German *satt* "full, having had enough to eat." In Middle English, though *sad* continued to have the Old English sense "full, sated," it underwent a great burst of semantic diversification. Common senses were "firmly established, fixed," "solid, weighty," "sober, serious," "powerful, strong," "hard, stout (of a blow)," "true, real," "deep, intense (of a color)." The meaning "sorrowful" was in use fairly early, by about 1300, though peculiarly it alone has been retained, as virtually all the other senses developed in Middle English gradually fell from use in early Modern English. The sense "sober, serious" occurs notably in Samuel Taylor Coleridge's poem "The Rime of the Ancient Mariner" ("A sadder and a wiser man,/He rose the following morn"), though Coleridge may also have been employing it as a conscious archaism.

¹sad·dle \'sa-dᵊl\ *noun, often attributive* [Middle English *sadel,* from Old English *sadol;* akin to Old High German *satul* saddle] (before 12th century)
1 a (1) : a girthed usually padded and leather-covered seat for the rider of an animal (as a horse) (2) : a part of a driving harness comparable to a saddle that is used to keep the breeching in place **b** : a seat to be straddled by the rider of a vehicle (as a bicycle)
2 : a device mounted as a support and often shaped to fit the object held
3 a : a ridge connecting two higher elevations **b** : a pass in a mountain range
4 a : both sides of the unsplit back of a carcass including both loins **b** : a colored marking on the back of an animal **c** : the rear part of a male fowl's back extending to the tail — see DUCK illustration
5 : the central part of the backbone of the binding of a book
6 : a piece of leather across the instep of a shoe
— **sad·dle·less** \-dᵊl-(l)əs\ *adjective*
— **in the saddle** : in control

saddle 1a(1): *1* western,
2 English

²saddle *verb* **sad·dled; sad·dling** \'sad-liŋ, 'sa-dᵊl-iŋ\ (before 12th century)
transitive verb
1 : to put a saddle on
2 a : to place under a burden or encumbrance **b** : to place (an onerous responsibility) on a person or group
intransitive verb
: to mount a saddled horse

sad·dle·bag \'sa-dᵊl-,bag\ *noun* (1773)
: one of a pair of covered pouches laid across the back of a horse behind the saddle or hanging over the rear wheel of a bicycle or motorcycle

saddle blanket *noun* (1737)
: a folded blanket or pad under a saddle to prevent galling the horse

sad·dle·bow \'sa-dᵊl-,bō\ *noun* (before 12th century)
: the arch in or the pieces forming the front of a saddle

sad·dle·bred \-,bred\ *noun* (1948)
: AMERICAN SADDLEBRED

sad·dle·cloth \-,klȯth\ *noun* (15th century)
: a cloth placed under or over a saddle

sad·dled prominent \'sa-dᵊld-\ *noun* [from the hump or prominence on the back of the larva] (1910)
: a moth (*Heterocampa guttivitta*) whose larva is a serious defoliator of hardwood trees in the eastern and midwestern U.S.

saddle horn *noun* (1856)
: a hornlike prolongation of the pommel of a stock saddle

saddle horse *noun* (1662)
: a horse suited for or trained for riding

saddle leather *noun* (1832)
: leather made of cowhide that is vegetable tanned and used especially for saddlery; *also*
: smooth polished leather simulating this

sad·dler \'sad-lər\ *noun* (14th century)
: one that makes, repairs, or sells saddles and other furnishings for horses

sad·dlery \'sad-lə-rē, 'sa-dᵊl-rē\ *noun, plural* **-dler·ies** (15th century)
: the trade, articles of trade, or shop of a saddler

saddle seat *noun* (1895)
: a slightly concave chair seat (as of a Windsor chair) with sometimes a thickened ridge at the center front

saddle shoe *noun* (1939)
: an oxford-style shoe having a saddle of contrasting color or leather — called also *saddle oxford*

saddle soap *noun* (1889)
: a mild soap used for cleansing and conditioning leather

saddle sore *noun* (1946)
1 : a gall or open sore developing on the back of a horse at points of pressure from an ill-fitting or ill-adjusted saddle
2 : an irritation or sore on parts of the rider chafed by the saddle

sad·dle·tree \'sa-dᵊl-,trē\ *noun* (15th century)
: the frame of a saddle

Sad·du·ce·an \,sa-jə-'sē-ən, ,sa-dyə-\ *adjective* (1593)
: of or relating to the Sadducees

Sad·du·cee \'sa-jə-,sē, 'sa-dyə-\ *noun* [Middle English *saducee,* from Old English *sadduce,* from Late Latin *sadducaeus,* from Greek *saddoukaios,* from Late Hebrew *ṣāddūqi*] (before 12th century)
: a member of a Jewish party of the intertestamental period consisting of a traditional ruling class of priests and rejecting doctrines not in the Law (as resurrection, retribution in a future life, and the existence of angels)
— **Sad·du·cee·ism** \-,i-zəm\ *noun*

sa·dhe \'(t)sä-də, -dē\ *noun* [Hebrew *ṣādhē*] (circa 1899)
: the 18th letter of the Hebrew alphabet — see ALPHABET table

sa·dhu *also* **sad·dhu** \'sä-(,)dü\ *noun* [Sanskrit *sādhu*] (1845)
: a usually Hindu mendicant ascetic

sad·iron \'sad-,ī(-ə)rn\ *noun* [*sad* (compact, heavy) + *iron*] (1761)
: a flatiron pointed at both ends and having a removable handle

sa·dism \'sā-,di-zəm, 'sa-\ *noun* [International Scientific Vocabulary, from Marquis de *Sade*] (1888)
1 : a sexual perversion in which gratification is obtained by the infliction of physical or mental pain on others (as on a love object) — compare MASOCHISM
2 a : delight in cruelty **b** : excessive cruelty
— **sa·dist** \'sā-dist, 'sa-\ *noun*
— **sa·dis·tic** \sə-'dis-tik *also* sā- *or* sa-\ *adjective*
— **sa·dis·ti·cal·ly** \-ti-k(ə)lē\ *adverb*

sa·do·mas·och·ism \,sā-(,)dō-'ma-sə-,ki-zəm, ,sa-, -'ma-zə-\ *noun* [International Scientific Vocabulary *sad*ism + *-o-* + *masochism*] (1922)
: the derivation of pleasure from the infliction of physical or mental pain either on others or on oneself
— **sa·do·mas·och·ist** \-kist\ *noun or adjective*
— **sa·do·mas·och·is·tic** \-,ma-sə-'kis-tik, -,ma-zə-\ *adjective*

sad sack *noun* (1943)
: an inept person; *especially* : an inept soldier
— **sad–sack** *adjective*

Sa·far \sə-'fär\ *noun* [Arabic *ṣafar*] (circa 1771)
: the 2d month of the Islamic year — see MONTH table

sa·fa·ri \sə-'fär-ē, -'far-\ *noun* [Arabic *safarīy* of a trip] (1896)
1 : the caravan and equipment of a hunting expedition especially in eastern Africa; *also* : such a hunting expedition
2 : JOURNEY, EXPEDITION ⟨an arctic *safari*⟩
— **safari** *intransitive verb*

safari jacket *noun* (1951)
: a usually belted shirt jacket with pleated expansible pockets

safari suit *noun* (1967)
: a safari jacket with matching pants

¹safe \'sāf\ *adjective* **saf·er; saf·est** [Middle English *sauf,* from Old French, from Latin *salvus* safe, healthy; akin to Latin *solidus* solid, Greek *holos* whole, safe, Sanskrit *sarva* entire] (14th century)
1 : free from harm or risk : UNHURT
2 a : secure from threat of danger, harm, or loss **b** : successful at getting to a base in baseball without being put out
3 : affording safety or security from danger, risk, or difficulty
4 *obsolete* : *of mental or moral faculties* : HEALTHY, SOUND
5 a : not threatening danger : HARMLESS **b** : unlikely to produce controversy or contradiction
6 a : not likely to take risks : CAUTIOUS **b** : TRUSTWORTHY, RELIABLE
— **safe** *or* **safe·ly** *adverb*
— **safe·ness** *noun*

²safe *noun* (15th century)
1 : a place or receptacle to keep articles (as valuables) safe
2 : CONDOM

safe–con·duct \'sāf-'kän-(,)dəkt\ *noun* [Middle English *sauf conduit,* from Old French, safe conduct] (14th century)
1 : protection given a person passing through a military zone or occupied area
2 : a document authorizing safe-conduct

safe–crack·er \'sāf-,kra-kər\ *noun* (circa 1825)
: one that breaks open safes to steal
— **safe–crack·ing** \-kiŋ\ *noun*

safe–deposit box *noun* (1882)
: a box (as in the vault of a bank) for safe storage of valuables — called also *safety-deposit box*

¹safe·guard \'sāf-,gärd\ *noun* [Middle English *saufgarde,* from Middle French *saufegarde,* from Old French, from *sauve* safe + *garde* guard] (14th century)
1 a : PASS, SAFE-CONDUCT **b** : CONVOY, ESCORT
2 a : a precautionary measure, stipulation, or device **b** : a technical contrivance to prevent accident

²safeguard *transitive verb* (15th century)
1 : to provide a safeguard for
2 : to make safe : PROTECT
synonym see DEFEND

safe house *noun* (1946)
: a place where one may engage in secret activities or take refuge

safe·keep·ing \'sāf-'kē-piŋ\ *noun* (15th century)
1 : the act or process of preserving in safety
2 : the state of being preserved in safety

safe·light \'sāf-,līt\ *noun* (1903)
: a darkroom lamp with a filter to screen out rays that are harmful to sensitive film or paper

safe sex *noun* (1985)
: sexual activity and especially sexual intercourse in which various measures (as the use of latex condoms or the practice of monogamy) are taken to avoid disease (as AIDS) transmitted by sexual contact

¹safe·ty \'sāf-tē\ *noun, plural* **safeties** [Middle English *saufte,* from Middle French *sauveté,* from Old French, from *sauve,* feminine of *sauf* safe] (14th century)
1 : the condition of being safe from undergoing or causing hurt, injury, or loss
2 : a device (as on a weapon or a machine) designed to prevent inadvertent or hazardous operation
3 a (1) : a situation in football in which a member of the offensive team is tackled behind its own goal line that counts two points for the defensive team — compare TOUCHBACK (2) : a member of a defensive backfield in football who occupies the deepest position in order to receive a kick, defend against a forward pass, or stop a ballcarrier **b** : a billiard shot made with no attempt to score or so as to

leave the balls in an unfavorable position for the opponent **c :** BASE HIT

²safety *transitive verb* **safe·tied; safe·ty·ing** (1940)
: to protect against failure, breakage, or accident ⟨*safety* a rifle⟩

safety belt *noun* (circa 1858)
: a belt fastening a person to an object (as a car seat) to prevent falling or injury

safety glass *noun* (1919)
: transparent material that is made by laminating a sheet of transparent plastic between sheets of clear glass and is used especially for windows (as of automobiles) likely to be subjected to shock or impact

safety lamp *noun* (1816)
: a miner's lamp constructed to avoid explosion in an atmosphere containing flammable gas usually by enclosing the flame in fine wire gauze

safe·ty·man \'sāf-tē-‚man\ *noun* (1927)
: SAFETY 3a(2)

safety match *noun* (1863)
: a match capable of being struck and ignited only on a specially prepared friction surface

safety net *noun* (1950)
: something that provides security against misfortune or difficulty

safety pin *noun* (1857)
: a pin in the form of a clasp with a guard covering its point when fastened

safety razor *noun* (circa 1875)
: a razor provided with a guard for the blade to prevent deep cuts in the skin

safety valve *noun* (1813)
1 : an automatic escape or relief valve (as for a steam boiler)
2 : an outlet for pent-up energy or emotion
3 : something that relieves the pressure of overcrowding

saf·flow·er \'sa-‚flaù(-ə)r\ *noun* [Middle French *safleur,* from Old Italian *saffiore,* from Arabic *aṣfar,* a yellow plant] (1642)
: a widely cultivated Old World composite herb (*Carthamus tinctorius*) with large orange or red flower heads and seeds rich in oil; *also* **:** a red dyestuff prepared from the flower heads

safflower oil *noun* (circa 1857)
: an edible drying oil obtained from the seeds of the safflower

saf·fron \'sa-frən\ *noun* [Middle English, from Old French *safran,* from Medieval Latin *safranum,* from Arabic *za'farān*] (13th century)
1 a : the deep orange aromatic pungent dried stigmas of a purple-flowered crocus (*Crocus sativus*) used to color and flavor foods and formerly as a dyestuff and in medicine **b :** the crocus supplying saffron
2 : a moderate to orange yellow

saf·ra·nine \'sa-frə-‚nēn, -nən\ *or* **saf·ra·nin** \-nən\ *noun* [International Scientific Vocabulary, from French *safran* saffron] (1868)
1 : any of various usually red synthetic dyes that are amino derivatives of bases
2 : any of various mixtures of safranine salts used in dyeing and as biological stains

saf·role \'saf-‚rōl\ *noun* [International Scientific Vocabulary, from *sassafras* + *-ole*] (1869)
: a poisonous oily cyclic ether $C_{10}H_{10}O_2$ that is the principal component of sassafras oil and is used chiefly in perfumery

¹sag \'sag\ *verb* **sagged; sag·ging** [Middle English *saggen,* probably of Scandinavian origin; akin to Swedish *sacka* to sag] (14th century)
intransitive verb
1 : to droop, sink, or settle from or as if from pressure or loss of tautness
2 a : to lose firmness, resiliency, or vigor ⟨spirits *sagging* from overwork⟩ **b :** to decline especially from a thriving state
3 : DRIFT
4 : to fail to stimulate or retain interest

transitive verb
: to cause to sag **:** leave slack in

²sag *noun* (1580)
1 : a tendency to drift (as of a ship to leeward)
2 a : a sagging part ⟨the *sag* in a rope⟩ **b :** a drop or depression below the surrounding area **c :** an instance or amount of sagging
3 : a temporary decline (as in the price of a commodity)

sa·ga \'sä-gə *also* 'sa-\ *noun* [Old Norse — more at SAW] (1709)
1 : a prose narrative recorded in Iceland in the 12th and 13th centuries of historic or legendary figures and events of the heroic age of Norway and Iceland
2 : a modern heroic narrative resembling the Icelandic saga
3 : a long detailed account ⟨a *saga* of the Old South⟩

sa·ga·cious \sə-'gā-shəs, si-\ *adjective* [Latin *sagac-, sagax, sagire* to perceive keenly; akin to Latin *sagus* prophetic — more at SEEK] (1607)
1 *obsolete* **:** keen in sense perception
2 a : of keen and farsighted penetration and judgment **:** DISCERNING ⟨*sagacious* judge of character⟩ **b :** caused by or indicating acute discernment ⟨*sagacious* purchase of stock⟩
synonym see SHREWD
— **sa·ga·cious·ly** *adverb*
— **sa·ga·cious·ness** *noun*

sa·gac·i·ty \sə-'ga-sə-tē, si-\ *noun* (15th century)
: the quality of being sagacious

sag·a·more \'sa-gə-‚mōr, -‚mȯr\ *noun* [Eastern Abenaki *sàkəmə*] (1613)
1 : a subordinate chief of the Algonquian Indians of the North Atlantic coast
2 : SACHEM 1

saga novel *noun* (circa 1938)
: ROMAN-FLEUVE

¹sage \'sāj\ *adjective* **sag·er; sag·est** [Middle English, from Old French, from (assumed) Vulgar Latin *sapius,* from Latin *sapere* to taste, have good taste, be wise; akin to Oscan *sipus* knowing, Old Saxon an *sebbian* to perceive] (14th century)
1 a : wise through reflection and experience **b** *archaic* **:** GRAVE, SOLEMN
2 : proceeding from or characterized by wisdom, prudence, and good judgment ⟨*sage* advice⟩
synonym see WISE
— **sage·ly** *adverb*
— **sage·ness** *noun*

²sage *noun* (14th century)
1 : one (as a profound philosopher) distinguished for wisdom
2 : a mature or venerable man of sound judgment

³sage *noun* [Middle English, from Middle French *sauge,* from Latin *salvia,* from *salvus* healthy; from its use as a medicinal herb — more at SAFE] (14th century)
1 : a mint (*Salvia officinalis*) with grayish green aromatic leaves used especially in flavoring meats; *broadly* **:** SALVIA
2 : SAGEBRUSH

sage·brush \'sāj-‚brəsh\ *noun* (1850)
: any of several North American hoary composite subshrubs (genus *Artemisia*); *especially* **:** one (*A. tridentata*) having a bitter juice and an odor resembling sage and often covering vast tracts of alkaline plains in the western U.S.

sage cheese *noun* (1699)
: a cheese similar to mild cheddar flecked with green and flavored with sage

sage grouse *noun* (1876)
: a large grouse (*Centrocercus urophasianus*) of the dry sagebrush plains of western North America that has mottled gray and buff plumage with a contrasting black belly

sag·ger *or* **sag·gar** \'sa-gər\ *noun* [probably alteration of *safeguard*] (1752)

: a box made of fireclay in which delicate ceramic pieces are fired

sag·it·tal \'sa-jə-t°l\ *adjective* [Middle English *sagittale,* from Medieval Latin *sagittalis,* from Latin *sagitta* arrow] (14th century)
1 : of or relating to the suture between the parietal bones of the skull
2 : of, relating to, situated in, or being the median plane of the body or any plane parallel thereto
— **sag·it·tal·ly** \-t°l-ē\ *adverb*

Sag·it·tar·i·an \‚sa-jə-'ter-ē-ən\ *noun* (1911)
: SAGITTARIUS 2b

Sag·it·tar·i·us \-ē-əs\ *noun* [Latin (genitive *Sagittarii*), literally, archer, from *sagitta*]
1 : a southern zodiacal constellation pictured as a centaur shooting an arrow and containing the point in the sky where the center of the Milky Way galaxy is located
2 a : the 9th sign of the zodiac in astrology — see ZODIAC table **b :** one born under the sign of Sagittarius

sag·it·tate \'sa-jə-‚tāt\ *adjective* [Latin *sagitta*] (1760)
: shaped like an arrowhead; *specifically* **:** elongated, triangular, and having the two basal lobes prolonged downward ⟨*sagittate* leaf⟩ — see LEAF illustration

sa·go \'sā-(‚)gō\ *noun, plural* **sagos** [Malay *sagu* sago palm] (circa 1580)
: a dry granulated or powdered starch prepared from the pith of a sago palm and used in foods and as textile stiffening

sago palm *noun* (1769)
: a plant that yields sago; *especially* **:** any of various lofty pinnate-leaved Indian and Malaysian palms (genus *Metroxylon*)

sa·gua·ro \sə-'wär-ə, -'gwär-, -ō\ *noun, plural* **-ros** [Mexican Spanish] (1856)
: an arborescent cactus (*Carnegiea gigantea*) of desert regions of the southwestern U.S. and Mexico that has a tall columnar simple or sparsely branched trunk of up to 60 feet (18 meters) and bears white flowers and edible fruit

Sa·hap·ti·an \sə-'hap-tē-ən\ *variant of* SHAHAPTIAN

sa·hib \'sä-‚(h)ib, -‚(h)ēb, ‚sä-'\ *noun* [Hindi *sāheb,* from Arabic *ṣāḥib*] (1673)
: SIR, MASTER — used especially among the native inhabitants of colonial India when addressing or speaking of a European of some social or official status

¹said *past and past participle of* SAY

²said \'sed\ *adjective* [past participle of *say*] (14th century)
: AFOREMENTIONED

¹sail \'sā(ə)l, *as last element in compounds often* səl\ *noun* [Middle English, from Old English *segl;* akin to Old High German *segal* sail] (before 12th century)
1 a (1) : an extent of fabric (as canvas) by means of which wind is used to propel a ship through water **(2) :** the sails of a ship **b** *plural usually* **sail :** a ship equipped with sails
2 : an extent of fabric used in propelling a wind-driven vehicle (as an iceboat)

saguaro

sail 1a (of a schooner): *1 flying jib, 2 jib, 3 forestaysail, 4 foresail, 5 fore gaff-topsail, 6 main-topmast staysail, 7 mainsail, 8 main gaff-topsail*

3 : something that resembles a sail; *especially*
: a streamlined conning tower on a submarine
4 : a passage by a sailing craft : CRUISE
— **sailed** \'sā\ld\ *adjective*
— **under sail** : in motion with sails set
²**sail** (before 12th century)
intransitive verb
1 a : to travel on water in a ship **b** : YACHT
2 a : to travel on water by the action of wind upon sails or by other means **b** : to move or proceed easily, gracefully, nonchalantly, or without resistance ⟨*sails* through all sorts of contradictions —Vicki Hearne⟩ ⟨the bill *sailed* through the legislature⟩
3 : to begin a water voyage ⟨*sail* with the tide⟩
transitive verb
1 a : to travel on (water) by means of motive power (as sail) **b** : to glide through
2 : to direct or manage the motion of (as a ship)
— **sail·able** \'sā-lə-bəl\ *adjective*
— **sail into** : to attack vigorously or sharply ⟨*sailed* into me for being late⟩
sail·board \'sā(ə)l-,bȯrd, -,bȯrd\ *noun* (1962)
: a modified surfboard having a mast mounted on a universal joint and sailed by one person standing up
— **sail·board·ing** *noun*
sail·boat \'sā(ə)l-,bōt\ *noun* (1798)
: a boat usually propelled by sail
— **sail·boat·er** \-,bō-tər\ *noun*
— **sail·boat·ing** *noun*
sail·cloth \-,klȯth\ *noun* (13th century)
: a heavy canvas used for sails, tents, or upholstery; *also* : a lightweight canvas used for clothing
sail·er \'sā-lər\ *noun* (15th century)
: a ship or boat especially having specified sailing qualities
sail·fish \'sā(ə)l-,fish\ *noun* (1879)
: any of a genus (*Istiophorus* and especially *I. platypterus*) of billfishes having a very large dorsal fin
sail·ing \'sā-liŋ\ *noun* (before 12th century)
1 a : the technical skill of managing a ship : NAVIGATION **b** : the method of determining the course to be followed to reach a given point
2 a : the sport of handling or riding in a sailboat **b** : a departure from a port
sail·or \'sā-lər\ *noun* [alteration of *sailer*] (circa 1642)
1 a : one that sails; *especially* : MARINER **b** (1) : a member of a ship's crew (2) : SEAMAN 2b
2 : a traveler by water
3 : a stiff straw hat with a low flat crown and straight circular brim
sailor collar *noun* (1895)
: a broad collar having a square flap across the back and tapering to a V in the front
sail·or's–choice \,sā-lərz-'chȯis\ *noun* (1850)
: any of several small grunts of the Western Atlantic: as **a** : PINFISH **b** : PIGFISH
sail·plane \'sā(ə)l-,plān\ *noun* (1922)
: a glider of such design that it is able to rise in an upward air current
— **sailplane** *intransitive verb*
— **sail·plan·er** *noun*
sai·min \'sī-'min\ *noun* [probably from Chinese (Guangdong) *sai mihn* fine noodles] (1949)
: a Hawaiian noodle soup
sain \'sān\ *transitive verb* [Middle English, from Old English *segnian*, from Late Latin *signare*, from Latin, to mark — more at SIGN] (before 12th century)
1 *dialect British* : to make the sign of the cross on (oneself)
2 *dialect British* : BLESS
sain·foin \'sān-,fȯin, 'san-\ *noun* [French, from Middle French *sain* healthy (from Latin *sanus*) + *foin* hay, from Latin *fenum*] (1626)
: a pink-flowered Eurasian perennial leguminous herb (*Onobrychis viciaefolia* synonym *O. viciifolia*) grown for forage

¹**saint** \'sānt, *before a name* (,)sānt *or* sənt\ *noun* [Middle English, from Old French, from Late Latin *sanctus*, from Latin, sacred, from past participle of *sancire* to make sacred — more at SACRED] (13th century)
1 : one officially recognized especially through canonization as preeminent for holiness
2 a : one of the spirits of the departed in heaven **b** : ANGEL 1a
3 a : one of God's chosen and usually Christian people **b** *capitalized* : a member of any of various Christian bodies; *specifically* : LATTER-DAY SAINT
4 : one eminent for piety or virtue
5 : an illustrious predecessor
— **saint·dom** \'sānt-dəm\ *noun*
— **saint·like** \-,līk\ *adjective*
²**saint** \'sānt\ *transitive verb* (13th century)
: to recognize or designate as a saint; *specifically* : CANONIZE
Saint Ag·nes' Eve \-'ag-nə-səz-, -'ag-nəs-\ *noun* [*Saint Agnes*] (1820)
: the night of January 20 when a woman is traditionally held to have a revelation of her future husband
Saint An·drew's cross \-'an-,drüz-\ *noun* [*Saint Andrew* (died about A.D. 60), apostle who, according to tradition, was crucified on a cross of this type] (1615)
: a figure of a cross that has the form of two intersecting oblique bars — see CROSS illustration
Saint An·tho·ny's cross \-'an(t)-thə-nēz-, *chiefly British* -'an-tə-\ *noun* [*Saint Anthony*] (1885)
: TAU CROSS
Saint Anthony's fire *noun* (14th century)
: any of several inflammations or gangrenous conditions (as erysipelas or ergotism) of the skin
saint au·gus·tine grass \-'ȯ-gə-,stēn-\ *noun, often S&A capitalized* [probably from *Saint Augustine*, Fla.] (1900)
: a perennial much-branched creeping grass (*Stenotaphrum secundatum*) of the southern U.S. that is valuable as a sand binder and as sod grass
Saint Ber·nard \-bər-'närd\ *noun* [the hospice of Grand *Saint Bernard*, where such dogs were first bred] (1839)
: any of a Swiss alpine breed of tall powerful working dogs used especially formerly in aiding lost travelers
saint·ed \'sān-təd\ *adjective* (1598)
1 : befitting or relating to a saint
2 : SAINTLY, PIOUS
3 : entered into heaven : DEAD
4 : much admired : IDOLIZED

Saint Bernard

Saint El·mo's fire \'sānt-'el-(,)mōz-\ *noun* [*Saint Elmo* (*Erasmus*) (died 303) Italian bishop & patron saint of sailors] (1814)
: a flaming phenomenon sometimes seen in stormy weather at prominent points on an airplane or ship and on land that is of the nature of a brush discharge of electricity — called also *Saint Elmo's light*
Saint Emi·lion \,saⁿ-tā-mēl-'yōⁿ\ *noun* [*Saint-Émilion*, village in SW France] (1833)
: a red Bordeaux wine
saint·hood \'sānt-,húd\ *noun* (1550)
1 : the quality or state of being a saint
2 : saints as a group
Saint John's bread \-'jänz-,bred\ *noun* (1591)
: CAROB 2
Saint–John's–wort \-,wərt, -,wȯrt\ *noun* [*Saint John* the Baptist] (15th century)

: any of a genus (*Hypericum* of the family Guttiferae, the Saint-John's-wort family) of herbs and shrubs with showy pentamerous yellow flowers
Saint Lou·is encephalitis \-'lü-əs-\ *noun* [*Saint Louis*, Mo.] (1934)
: a North American viral encephalitis that is transmitted by several culex mosquitoes
saint·ly \'sānt-lē\ *adjective* **saint·li·er; -est** (1534)
: relating to, resembling, or befitting a saint : HOLY
— **saint·li·ness** *noun*
Saint Mar·tin's summer \-'mär-t²nz-\ *noun* [*Saint Martin's* Day, November 11] (1591)
: Indian summer when occurring in November
Saint Pat·rick's Day \-'pa-triks-\ *noun* (1844)
: March 17 observed by the Roman Catholic Church in honor of Saint Patrick and celebrated in Ireland in commemoration of his death
saint's day *noun* (15th century)
: a day in a church calendar on which a saint is commemorated
saint·ship \'sānt-,ship\ *noun* (1631)
: SAINTHOOD 1
Saint Val·en·tine's Day \-'va-lən-,tīnz-\ *noun* [*Saint Valentine* (died about 270) Italian priest] (14th century)
: February 14 observed in honor of Saint Valentine and as a time for sending valentines
Saint Vi·tus' dance \-'vī-təs-, -'vī-tə-səz-\ *noun* [*Saint Vitus*, 3d century Christian child martyr] (1621)
: CHOREA — called also *Saint Vitus's dance* *same*\
saith \'seth, 'sā-əth\ *archaic present 3d singular of* SAY
saithe \'sāth, 'sāth\ *noun, plural* **saithe** [of Scandinavian origin; akin to Old Norse *seithr* coalfish] (1632)
: POLLACK
Sai·va \'sī-və, 'shī-\ *noun* [Sanskrit *Śaiva*, from *Śiva* Siva] (1810)
: a member of a major Hindu sect devoted to the cult of Siva
— **Sai·vism** \-,vi-zəm\ *noun*
¹**sake** \'sāk\ *noun* [Middle English, dispute, guilt, purpose, from Old English *sacu* guilt, action at law; akin to Old High German *sahha* action at law, cause, Old English *sēcan* to seek — more at SEEK] (13th century)
1 : END, PURPOSE ⟨for the *sake* of argument⟩
2 a : the good, advantage, or enhancement of some entity (as an ideal) ⟨free to pursue learning for its own *sake* —M. S. Eisenhower⟩ **b** : personal or social welfare, safety, or benefit
²**sa·ke** *or* **sa·ki** \'sä-kē\ *noun* [Japanese *sake*] (1687)
: a Japanese alcoholic beverage of fermented rice usually served hot
sa·ker \'sā-kər\ *noun* [Middle English *sagre*, from Middle French *sacre*, from Arabic *ṣaqr*] (15th century)
: an Old World falcon (*Falco cherrug*) used in falconry
Sak·ti \'säk-tē, 'shäk-\, **Sak·tism** *variant of* SHAKTI, SHAKTISM
sal \'sal\ *noun* [Middle English, from Latin — more at SALT] (14th century)
: SALT
¹**sa·laam** \sə-'läm\ *noun* [Arabic *salām*, literally, peace] (1613)
1 : a salutation or ceremonial greeting in the East
2 : an obeisance performed by bowing very low and placing the right palm on the forehead
²**salaam** (1693)
transitive verb
: to greet or pay homage to with a salaam

intransitive verb
: to perform a salaam

sal·able *or* **sale·able** \'sā-lə-bəl\ *adjective* (1530)
: capable of being or fit to be sold : MARKET-ABLE
— **sal·abil·i·ty** \ˌsā-lə-'bi-lə-tē\ *noun*

sa·la·cious \sə-'lā-shəs\ *adjective* [Latin *salac-, salax*, from *salire* to move spasmodically, leap — more at SALLY] (circa 1645)
1 : arousing or appealing to sexual desire or imagination : LASCIVIOUS
2 : LECHEROUS, LUSTFUL
— **sa·la·cious·ly** *adverb*
— **sa·la·cious·ness** *noun*

sal·ad \'sa-ləd\ *noun* [Middle English *salade*, from Middle French, from Old Provençal *salada*, from *salar* to salt, from *sal* salt, from Latin] (14th century)
1 a : green vegetables (as lettuce, endive, or romaine) and often tomatoes, cucumbers, or radishes served with dressing **b** : a dish of meat, fish, shellfish, eggs, fruits, or vegetables singly or in combination usually served cold with a dressing
2 : a green vegetable or herb grown for salad; *especially* : LETTUCE
3 : a usually incongruous mixture : HODGE-PODGE

salad bar *noun* (1973)
: a self-service counter (as in a restaurant) featuring an array of salad makings and dressings

salad days *noun plural* (1606)
: time of youthful inexperience or indiscretion ⟨my *salad days* when I was green in judgment —Shakespeare⟩; *also* : an early flourishing period : HEYDAY

salad dressing *noun* (circa 1839)
: a dressing either uncooked (as French dressing) or cooked (as a boiled dressing) that is used for salad

salad oil *noun* (1537)
: an edible vegetable oil suitable for use in salad dressings

sa·lal \sə-'lal, sa-\ *noun* [Chinook Jargon, from Lower Chinook *sálal*] (1825)
: a small shrub (*Gaultheria shallon*) of the heath family found on the Pacific coast of North America and bearing edible grape-sized dark purple berries

sal·a·man·der \'sa-lə-ˌman-dər *also* ˌsa-lə-'\ *noun* [Middle English *salamandre*, from Middle French, from Latin *salamandra*, from Greek] (14th century)
1 : a mythical animal having the power to endure fire without harm
2 : an elemental being in the theory of Paracelsus inhabiting fire
3 : any of numerous amphibians (order Caudata) superficially resembling lizards but scaleless and covered with a soft moist skin and breathing by gills in the larval stage
4 : an article used in connection with fire: as **a** : a cooking utensil for browning a food (as pastry or pudding) **b** : a portable stove **c** : a cooking device with an overhead heat source like a broiler
— **sal·a·man·drine** \ˌsa-lə-'man-drən\ *adjective*

sa·la·mi \sə-'lä-mē\ *noun* [Italian, plural of *salame* salami, from *salare* to salt, from *sale* salt, from Latin *sal* — more at SALT] (1852)
: a highly seasoned sausage of pork and beef either dried or fresh

sal ammoniac *noun* [Middle English *sal armoniak*, from Latin *sal ammoniacus*, literally, salt of Ammon] (14th century)
: AMMONIUM CHLORIDE

sa·lar·i·at \sə-'lar-ē-ət, -'ler-\ *noun* [French, from *salaire* salary (from Latin *salarium*) + *-ariat* (as in *prolétariat* proletariat)] (1917)
: the class or body of salaried persons usually as distinguished from wage earners

sal·a·ry \'sal-rē, 'sa-lə-\ *noun, plural* **-ries** [Middle English *salarie*, from Latin *salarium*

pension, salary, from neuter of *salarius* of salt, from *sal* salt — more at SALT] (13th century)
: fixed compensation paid regularly for services ◇
— **sal·a·ried** \-rēd\ *adjective*

sal·a·ry·man \-ˌman\ *noun* [Japanese *sararī-man*, from English *salary* + *man*] (1962)
: a Japanese white-collar businessman

sal·chow \'sal-ˌkau̇, -ˌkȯv, -ˌ(ˌ)kō\ *noun* [Ulrich Salchow (died 1949) Swedish figure skater] (1940)
: a figure-skating jump with a takeoff from the back inside edge of one skate followed by a full turn in the air and a landing on the back outside edge of the opposite skate

sale \'sā(ə)l\ *noun* [Middle English, from Old English *sala*, from Old Norse — more at SELL] (before 12th century)
1 : the act of selling; *specifically* : the transfer of ownership of and title to property from one person to another for a price
2 a : opportunity of selling or being sold : DEMAND **b** : distribution by selling
3 : public disposal to the highest bidder : AUCTION
4 : a selling of goods at bargain prices
5 *plural* **a** : operations and activities involved in promoting and selling goods or services ⟨vice-president in charge of *sales*⟩ **b** : gross receipts
— **for sale** : available for purchase
— **on sale 1** : for sale **2** : available for purchase at a reduced price

sa·lep \'sa-ləp, sə-'lep\ *noun* [French or Spanish, both from Arabic dialect *saḥlab*, perhaps alteration of Arabic (*khuṣy ath-*)*tha'lab*, literally, testicles of the fox] (1736)
: the starchy or mucilaginous dried tubers of various Old World orchids (especially genus *Orchis*) used for food or in medicine

sal·e·ra·tus \ˌsa-lə-'rā-təs\ *noun* [New Latin *sal aeratus* aerated salt] (1837)
: a leavening agent consisting of potassium or sodium bicarbonate

sale·room \'sā(ə)l-ˌrüm, -ˌru̇m\ *chiefly British variant of* SALESROOM

sales \'sā(ə)lz\ *adjective* (1913)
: of, relating to, or used in selling

sales·clerk \'sā(ə)lz-ˌklərk\ *noun* (1926)
: a retail salesperson

sales·girl \-ˌgər(-ə)l\ *noun* (1887)
: SALESWOMAN

Sa·le·sian \sə-'lē-zhən, sā-\ *noun* (1884)
: a member of the Society of Saint Francis de Sales founded by Saint John Bosco in Turin, Italy in the 19th century and devoted chiefly to education

sales·la·dy \'sā(ə)lz-ˌlā-dē\ *noun* (1856)
: SALESWOMAN

sales·man \'sā(ə)lz-mən\ *noun* (1523)
: one who sells in a given territory, in a store, or by telephone

sales·man·ship \-ˌship\ *noun* (1880)
1 : the skill or art of selling
2 : ability or effectiveness in selling or in presenting persuasively ⟨political *salesmanship*⟩

sales·peo·ple \-ˌpē-pəl\ *noun plural* (1876)
: persons employed to sell goods or services

sales·per·son \-ˌpər-sᵊn\ *noun* (1901)
: a salesman or saleswoman

sales·room \'sā(ə)lz-ˌrüm, -ˌru̇m\ *noun* (1840)
: a place where goods are displayed for sale; *especially* : an auction room

sales slip *noun* (1926)
: a receipt for a purchase

sales tax *noun* (1921)
: a tax levied on the sale of goods and services that is usually calculated as a percentage of the purchase price and collected by the seller

sales·wom·an \'sā(ə)lz-ˌwu̇-mən\ *noun* (1704)
: a woman who sells in a given territory, in a store, or by telephone

sal·ic \'sa-lik\ *adjective* [by alteration] (1902)
: SIALIC

Sa·lic \'sā-lik, 'sa-\ *adjective* [Middle French or Medieval Latin; Middle French *salique*, from Medieval Latin *Salicus*, from Late Latin *Salii* Salic Franks] (circa 1548)
: of, relating to, or being a Frankish people that settled on the IJssel river early in the 4th century

sal·i·cin \'sa-lə-sən\ *noun* [French *salicine*, from Latin *salic-, salix* willow — more at SALLOW] (1830)
: a bitter white crystalline glucoside $C_{13}H_{18}O_7$ found in the bark and leaves of several willows and poplars and used in medicine like salicylic acid

Salic law *noun* (1599)
1 : a rule held to derive from the legal code of the Salic Franks excluding females from the line of succession to a throne
2 : the legal code of the Salic Franks

sa·lic·y·late \sə-'li-sə-ˌlāt\ *noun* (1842)
: a salt or ester of salicylic acid

sal·i·cyl·ic acid \ˌsa-lə-'si-lik-\ *noun* [International Scientific Vocabulary, from *salicyl* (the group HOC_6H_4CO)] (1840)
: a crystalline phenolic acid $C_7H_6O_3$ used especially in the form of salts and other derivatives as an analgesic and antipyretic

sa·lience \'sā-lyən(t)s, -lē-ən(t)s\ *noun* (1836)
1 : the quality or state of being salient
2 : a striking point or feature : HIGHLIGHT

sa·lien·cy \-lyən(t)-sē, -lē-ən(t)-\ *noun, plural* **-cies** (1664)
: SALIENCE

¹sa·lient \'sā-lyənt, -lē-ənt\ *adjective* [Latin *salient-, saliens*, present participle of *salire* to leap — more at SALLY] (1646)
1 : moving by leaps or springs : JUMPING
2 : jetting upward ⟨a *salient* fountain⟩
3 a : projecting beyond a line, surface, or level **b** : standing out conspicuously : PROMINENT; *especially* : of notable significance ⟨similar to . . . Prohibition, but there are a couple of *salient* differences —Tony Gibbs⟩
synonym see NOTICEABLE
— **sa·lient·ly** *adverb*

²salient *noun* (1828)
: something (as a promontory) that projects outward or upward from its surroundings; *especially* : an outwardly projecting part of a fortification, trench system, or line of defense

¹sa·line \'sā-ˌlēn, -ˌlīn\ *adjective* [Middle English, from Latin *salinus*, from *sal* salt — more at SALT] (15th century)
1 : consisting of or containing salt ⟨a *saline* solution⟩
2 : of, relating to, or resembling salt : SALTY ⟨a *saline* taste⟩

3 : consisting of or relating to the salts of the alkali metals or of magnesium ⟨a *saline* cathartic⟩
— **sa·lin·i·ty** \sā-'li-nə-tē, sə-\ *noun*

²saline *noun* (1662)
1 : a metallic salt; *especially* : a salt of potassium, sodium, or magnesium with a cathartic action
2 : a saline solution; *especially* : one isotonic with body fluids

sa·li·nize \'sa-lə-ˌnīz *also* 'sā-\ *transitive verb* **-nized; -niz·ing** (1926)
: to treat or impregnate with salt
— **sa·li·ni·za·tion** \ˌsa-lə-nə-'zā-shən *also* ˌsā-\ *noun*

sa·li·nom·e·ter \ˌsa-lə-'nä-mə-tər, ˌsā-\ *noun* [International Scientific Vocabulary *saline* + *-o-* + *-meter*] (1844)
: an instrument (as a hydrometer) for measuring the amount of salt in a solution

Sa·lique \'sā-lik, 'sa-; sə-'lēk, sā-\ *variant of* SALIC

Salis·bury steak \'sȯlz-ˌber-ē-, 'salz-, -b(ə-)rē-\ *noun* [J. H. *Salisbury*, 19th century English physician] (1897)
: ground beef mixed with egg, milk, bread crumbs, and seasonings and formed into a large patty and cooked

Sa·lish \'sā-lish\ *noun* (1831)
1 : a group of American Indian peoples of British Columbia and the northwestern U.S.
2 : the family of languages spoken by the Salish peoples
— **Sa·lish·an** \-li-shən\ *adjective or noun*

sa·li·va \sə-'lī-və\ *noun* [Latin] (15th century)
: a slightly alkaline secretion of water, mucin, protein, salts, and often a starch-splitting enzyme (as ptyalin) that is secreted into the mouth by salivary glands, lubricates ingested food, and often begins the breakdown of starches

sal·i·vary \'sa-lə-ˌver-ē\ *adjective* (1709)
: of or relating to saliva or the glands that secrete it; *especially* : producing or carrying saliva

sal·i·vate \'sa-lə-ˌvāt\ *intransitive verb* **-vat·ed; -vat·ing** (circa 1706)
1 : to have a flow of saliva especially in excess
2 : DROOL 2
— **sal·i·va·tion** \ˌsa-lə-'vā-shən\ *noun*
— **sal·i·va·tor** \'sa-lə-ˌvā-tər\ *noun*

Salk vaccine \'sȯk-, 'sȯlk-\ *noun* [Jonas *Salk*] (1954)
: a vaccine consisting of poliomyelitis virus inactivated with formaldehyde

sal·let \'sa-lət\ *noun* [Middle English, from Middle French *sallade*] (15th century)
: a light 15th century helmet with or without a visor and with a projection over the neck

¹sal·low \'sa-(ˌ)lō\ *noun* [Middle English, from Old English *sealh*; akin to Old High German *salha* sallow, Latin *salix* willow] (before 12th century)
: any of several Old World broad-leaved willows (as *Salix caprea*) including important sources of charcoal and tanbark

²sallow *adjective* [Middle English *salowe*, from Old English *salu*; akin to Old High German *salo* murky, Russian *solovyĭ* yellowish gray] (before 12th century)
: of a grayish greenish yellow color
— **sal·low·ish** \'sa-lō-wish\ *adjective*
— **sal·low·ness** \'sa-lō-nəs, -lə-\ *noun*

¹sal·ly \'sa-lē\ *noun, plural* **sallies** [Middle French *saillie*, from Old French, from *saillir* to rush forward, from *saillir* to leap; akin to Greek *hallesthai* to leap] (1560)
1 : an action of rushing or bursting forth; *especially* : a sortie of troops from a defensive position to attack the enemy
2 a : a brief outburst : OUTBURST **b** : a witty or imaginative saying : QUIP
3 : a venture or excursion usually off the beaten track : JAUNT

²sally *intransitive verb* **sal·lied; sal·ly·ing** (1560)
1 : to leap out or burst forth suddenly
2 : SET OUT, DEPART — often used with *forth*

Sal·ly Lunn \ˌsa-lē-'lən\ *noun* [*Sally Lunn*, 18th century English baker] (1780)
: a slightly sweetened yeast-leavened bread

sally port *noun* (1649)
: a gate or passage in a fortified place for use by troops making a sortie

sal·ma·gun·di \ˌsal-mə-'gən-dē\ *noun* [French *salmigondis*] (circa 1674)
1 : a salad plate of chopped meats, anchovies, eggs, and vegetables arranged in rows for contrast and dressed with a salad dressing
2 : a heterogeneous mixture : POTPOURRI

sal·mi \'sal-mē\ *noun* [French *salmis*, short for *salmigondis*] (1759)
: a ragout of partly roasted game stewed in a rich sauce

salm·on \'sa-mən\ *noun, plural* **salmon** *also* **salmons** [Middle English *samon*, from Middle French, from Latin *salmon-, salmo*] (13th century)
1 a : a large anadromous salmonid fish (*Salmo salar*) of the North Atlantic noted as a game and food fish — called also *Atlantic salmon*
b : any of various anadromous salmonid fishes other than the salmon; *especially* : PACIFIC SALMON **c** : a fish (as a barramunda) resembling a salmon
2 : the variable color of salmon's flesh averaging a strong yellowish pink

salm·on·ber·ry \-ˌber-ē\ *noun* (1844)
: a showy red-flowered raspberry (*Rubus spectabilis*) of the Pacific coast; *also* : its edible salmon-colored fruit

sal·mo·nel·la \ˌsal-mə-'ne-lə\ *noun, plural* **-nel·lae** \-'ne-(ˌ)lē, -ˌlī\ *or* **-nellas** *or* **-nella** [New Latin, from Daniel E. *Salmon* (died 1914) American veterinarian] (1913)
: any of a genus (*Salmonella*) of usually motile enterobacteria that are pathogenic for humans and other warm-blooded animals and cause food poisoning, gastrointestinal inflammation, typhoid fever, or septicemia

sal·mo·nel·lo·sis \ˌsal-mə-(ˌ)ne-'lō-səs\ *noun, plural* **-lo·ses** \-ˌsēz\ [New Latin] (circa 1913)
: infection with or disease caused by salmonellae

sal·mo·nid \'sa-mə-nid, 'sal-\ *noun* [New Latin *Salmonidae*, from *Salmon-, Salmo*, genus name, from Latin *salmo* salmon] (1868)
: any of a family (Salmonidae) of elongate bony fishes (as a salmon or trout) that have the last three vertebrae upturned
— **salmonid** *adjective*

salm·on·oid \'sa-mə-ˌnȯid\ *noun* (circa 1842)
: SALMONID; *also* : a related fish
— **salmonoid** *adjective*

salmon pink *noun* (1882)
: a strong yellowish pink

Sa·lo·me \sə-'lō-mē, 'sa-lə-(ˌ)mā\ *noun* [Late Latin, from Greek *Salōmē*]
: a niece of Herod Antipas given the head of John the Baptist as a reward for her dancing

sa·lom·e·ter \sā-'lä-mə-tər, sə-\ *noun* [Latin *sal* salt + English *-o-* + *-meter*] (1860)
: a hydrometer for indicating the percentage of salt in a solution

sa·lon \sə-'län, 'sa-ˌlän, sa-'lōⁿ\ *noun* [French] (1699)
1 : an elegant apartment or living room (as in a fashionable home)
2 : a fashionable assemblage of notables (as literary figures, artists, or statesmen) held by custom at the home of a prominent person
3 a : a hall for exhibition of art **b** *capitalized* : an annual exhibition of works of art
4 : a stylish business establishment or shop ⟨a beauty *salon*⟩

sa·loon \sə-'lün\ *noun* [French *salon*, from Italian *salone*, augmentative of *sala* hall, of Germanic origin; akin to Old High German *sal* hall; akin to Lithuanian *sala* village] (1728)

1 a *chiefly British* : SALON 1 **b** *chiefly British* : an often elaborately decorated public hall **c** (1) : a usually large public cabin on a ship (as for dining) (2) : the living area on a yacht **d** *chiefly British* : SALON 4 **e** : BARROOM
2 : SALON 2
3 *British* **a** : PARLOR CAR **b** : SEDAN 2a — called also *saloon car*

salp \'salp\ *also* **sal·pa** \'sal-pə\ *noun* [New Latin, from Latin, a kind of deep-sea fish, from Greek *salpē*] (1835)
: any of various transparent barrel-shaped or fusiform free-swimming tunicates (class Thaliacea) abundant in warm seas

sal·pi·glos·sis \ˌsal-pə-'glä-səs\ *noun* [New Latin, irregular from Greek *salpinx* trumpet + *glōssa* tongue — more at GLOSS] (1827)
: any of a small genus (*Salpiglossis*) of Chilean herbs of the nightshade family with large funnel-shaped varicolored flowers often strikingly marked

sal·pin·gi·tis \ˌsal-pən-'jī-təs\ *noun* [New Latin, from *salping-, salpinx* fallopian or eustachian tube, from Greek, trumpet] (1860)
: inflammation of a fallopian or eustachian tube

sal·sa \'sȯl-sə, 'säl-\ *noun* [Spanish, literally, sauce, from Latin, feminine of *salsus* salted — more at SAUCE] (circa 1962)
1 : a spicy sauce of tomatoes, onions, and hot peppers
2 : popular music of Latin American origin that has absorbed characteristics of rhythm and blues, jazz, and rock

sal·si·fy \'sal-sə-fē, -ˌfī\ *noun* [French *salsifis*, from Italian *salsefica, sassefrica*] (circa 1706)
: a European biennial composite herb (*Tragopogon porrifolius*) with a long fusiform edible root — called also *oyster plant, vegetable oyster*

sal soda *noun* (15th century)
: WASHING SODA

¹salt \'sȯlt\ *noun* [Middle English, from Old English *sealt*; akin to Old High German *salz* salt, Lithuanian *saldus* sweet, Latin *sal* salt, Greek *hals* salt, sea] (before 12th century)
1 a : a crystalline compound NaCl that consists of sodium chloride, is abundant in nature, and is used especially to season or preserve food or in industry — called also *common salt* **b** : a substance (as washing soda) resembling common salt **c** *plural* (1) : a mineral or saline mixture (as Epsom salts) used as an aperient or cathartic (2) : SMELLING SALTS **d** : any of numerous compounds that result from replacement of part or all of the acid hydrogen of an acid by a metal or a group acting like a metal : an ionic crystalline compound
2 : a container for salt at table — often used in the phrases *above the salt* and *below the salt* alluding to the former custom of seating persons of higher rank above and those of lower rank below a saltcellar placed in the middle of a long table
3 a : an ingredient that gives savor, piquancy, or zest : FLAVOR ⟨a people . . . full of life, vigor, and the *salt* of personality —Clifton Fadiman⟩ **b** : sharpness of wit : PUNGENCY **c** : COMMON SENSE **d** : RESERVE, SKEPTICISM — usually used in the phrases *with a grain of salt* and *with a pinch of salt* **e** : a dependable steadfast person or group of people — usually used in the phrase *salt of the earth*
4 : SAILOR ⟨a tale worthy of an old *salt*⟩
5 : KEEP 3 — usually used in the phrase *worth one's salt*
— **salt·like** \-ˌlīk\ *adjective*

²salt *transitive verb* (before 12th century)

1 a : to treat, provide, or season with common salt **b :** to preserve (food) with salt or in brine **c :** to supply (as an animal) with salt **2 :** to give flavor or piquancy to (as a story) **3 :** to enrich (as a mine) artificially by secretly placing valuable mineral in some of the working places **4 :** to sprinkle with or as if with a salt — **salt·er** \'sȯl-tər\ *noun*

³salt *adjective* (before 12th century) **1 a :** SALINE, SALTY **b :** being or inducing the one of the four basic taste sensations that is suggestive of seawater — compare BITTER, SOUR, SWEET **2 :** cured or seasoned with salt **:** SALTED **3 :** overflowed with salt water ⟨a *salt* pond⟩ **4 :** SHARP, PUNGENT — **salt·ness** *noun*

⁴salt *adjective* [by shortening & alteration from *assaut*, from Middle English *a sawt*, from Middle French *a saut*, literally, on the jump] (1598) *obsolete* **:** LUSTFUL, LASCIVIOUS

salt–and–pepper *adjective* (1915) **:** having black-and-white or dark and light color or intermingled in small flecks ⟨a *salt-and-pepper* suit⟩

sal·ta·rel·lo \ˌsal-tə-'re-(ˌ)lō, ˌsäl-\ *noun, plural* **-los** [Italian, from *saltare* to jump, from Latin] (circa 1724) **:** an Italian dance with a lively hop step beginning each measure

sal·ta·tion \sal-'tā-shən, sȯl-\ *noun* [Latin *saltation-, saltatio*, from *saltare* to leap, dance, frequentative of *salire* to leap — more at SALLY] (1646) **1 a :** the action or process of leaping or jumping **b :** DANCE **2 a :** the origin of a new species or a higher taxon in essentially a single evolutionary step that in some especially former theories is held to be due to a major mutation or to unknown causes — compare DARWINISM, NEO-DARWINISM, PUNCTUATED EQUILIBRIUM **b :** MUTATION — used especially of bacteria and fungi

sal·ta·to·ri·al \ˌsal-tə-'tōr-ē-əl, ˌsȯl-, -'tȯr-\ *adjective* (1789) **:** relating to, marked by, or adapted for leaping ⟨*saltatorial* legs of a grasshopper⟩

sal·ta·to·ry \'sal-tə-ˌtōr-ē, 'sȯl-, -ˌtȯr-\ *adjective* (1656) **1** *archaic* **:** of or relating to dancing **2 :** proceeding by leaps rather than by gradual transitions **:** DISCONTINUOUS

salt away *transitive verb* (circa 1890) **:** to lay away (as money) safely **:** SAVE

salt·box \'sȯlt-ˌbäks\ *noun* (1876) **:** a frame dwelling with two stories in front and one behind and a roof with a long rear slope

saltbox

salt·bush \-ˌbu̇sh\ *noun* (1863) **:** any of various shrubby plants of the goosefoot family that thrive in dry alkaline soil; *especially* **:** any of numerous oraches that are important browse plants in dry regions

salt·cel·lar \'sȯlt-ˌse-lər\ *noun* [Middle English *salt saler*, from *salt* + *saler* saltcellar, from Middle French, from Latin *salarius* of salt — more at SALARY] (14th century) **:** a small container for holding salt at the table

salt dome *noun* (1908) **:** a domical anticline in sedimentary rock that has a mass of rock salt as its core

salt flat *noun* (1816) **:** a salt-encrusted flat area resulting from evaporation of a former body of water

salt gland *noun* (1950) **:** a gland (as of a marine bird) capable of excreting a concentrated salt solution

salt grass *noun* (1704)

: a grass (especially *Distichlis spicata*) native to an alkaline habitat (as a salt marsh)

sal·tim·boc·ca \ˌsȯl-təm-'bä-kə\ *noun* [Italian, from *saltare* to jump + *in* in + *bocca* mouth] (1937) **:** scallops of veal prepared with sage, slices of ham, and sometimes cheese and served with a wine sauce

sal·tine \sȯl-'tēn\ *noun* (1907) **:** a thin crisp cracker usually sprinkled with salt

salt·ing \'sȯl-tiŋ\ *noun* (1712) *chiefly British* **:** land flooded regularly by tides — usually used in plural

sal·tire \'sȯl-ˌtīr, 'sal-\ *noun* [Middle English *sautire*, from Middle French *saultoir* X-shaped animal barricade that can be jumped over by people, saltire, from *saulter* to jump, from Latin *saltare* — more at SALTATION] (14th century) **:** a heraldic charge consisting of a cross formed by a bend and a bend sinister crossing in the center

salt lake *noun* (1763) **:** a landlocked body of water that has become salty through evaporation

salt·less \'sȯlt-ləs\ *adjective* (14th century) **1 :** having no salt **2 :** INSIPID

salt lick *noun* (1751) **:** LICK 3

salt marsh *noun* (before 12th century) **:** flat land subject to overflow by salt water

salt out (1939) *transitive verb* **:** to precipitate, coagulate, or separate (as a dissolved substance or lyophilic sol) especially from a solution by the addition of salt *intransitive verb* **:** to become salted out

salt pan *noun* (15th century) **:** an undrained natural depression in which water gathers and leaves a deposit of salt on evaporation

salt·pe·ter \'sȯlt-'pē-tər\ *noun* [Middle English *salt petre*, alteration of *salpetre*, from Middle French, from Medieval Latin *sal petrae*, literally, salt of the rock] (14th century) **1 :** POTASSIUM NITRATE **2 :** SODIUM NITRATE

salt pork *noun* (1723) **:** fat pork cured in salt or brine

salt·shak·er \'sȯlt-ˌshā-kər\ *noun* (1895) **:** a container with a perforated top for sprinkling salt

salt·wa·ter \'sȯlt-ˌwȯ-tər, -ˌwä-\ *adjective* (before 12th century) **:** relating to, living in, located near, or consisting of salt water

salt·works \'sȯlt-ˌwərks\ *noun plural but singular or plural in construction* (1565) **:** a plant where salt is prepared commercially

salt·wort \-ˌwərt, -ˌwȯrt\ *noun* (1568) **1 :** any of a genus (*Salsola*) of plants (as the Russian thistle) of the goosefoot family of which some have been used in making soda ash **2 :** a low-growing strong-smelling coastal shrub (*Batis maritima* of the family Bataceae) of warm parts of the New World

salty \'sȯl-tē\ *adjective* **salt·i·er; -est** (15th century) **1 :** of, seasoned with, or containing salt **2 :** smacking of the sea or nautical life **3 a :** PIQUANT **b :** EARTHY, CRUDE ⟨*salty* language⟩ — **salt·i·ly** \-tə-lē\ *adverb* — **salt·i·ness** \-tē-nəs\ *noun*

sa·lu·bri·ous \sə-'lü-brē-əs\ *adjective* [Latin *salubris;* akin to *salvus* safe, healthy — more at SAFE] (1547) **:** favorable to or promoting health or well-being *synonym* see HEALTHFUL — **sa·lu·bri·ous·ly** *adverb* — **sa·lu·bri·ous·ness** *noun*

sa·lu·bri·ty \-brə-tē\ *noun*

sa·lu·ki \sə-'lü-kē\ *noun* [Arabic *salūqīy* of Saluq, from *Salūq* Saluq, ancient city in Arabia] (1809) **:** any of an ancient northern African and Asian breed of tall swift slender hunting dogs having long narrow heads, long silky ears, and a smooth silky coat

saluki

sal·u·tary \'sal-yə-ˌter-ē\ *adjective* [Middle French *salutaire*, from Latin *salutaris*, from *salut-, salus* health] (15th century) **1 :** producing a beneficial effect **:** REMEDIAL ⟨*salutary* influences⟩ **2 :** promoting health **:** CURATIVE *synonym* see HEALTHFUL — **sal·u·tar·i·ly** \ˌsal-yə-'ter-ə-lē\ *adverb* — **sal·u·tar·i·ness** \'sal-yə-ˌter-ē-nəs\ *noun*

sal·u·ta·tion \ˌsal-yə-'tā-shən\ *noun* (14th century) **1 a :** an expression of greeting, goodwill, or courtesy by word, gesture, or ceremony **b** *plural* **:** REGARDS **2 :** the word or phrase of greeting (as *Gentlemen* or *Dear Sir* or *Madam*) that conventionally comes immediately before the body of a letter — **sal·u·ta·tion·al** \-shnəl, -shə-n³l\ *adjective*

sa·lu·ta·to·ri·an \sə-ˌlü-tə-'tōr-ē-ən, -'tȯr-\ *noun* (circa 1847) **:** the student usually having the second highest rank in a graduating class who delivers the salutatory address at the commencement exercises

¹sa·lu·ta·to·ry \sə-'lü-tə-ˌtōr-ē, -ˌtȯr-\ *adjective* (1702) **:** of or relating to a salutation **:** expressing or containing a welcome or greeting

²salutatory *noun, plural* **-ries** (1779) **:** an address or statement of welcome or greeting

¹sa·lute \sə-'lüt\ *verb* **sa·lut·ed; sa·lut·ing** [Middle English, from Latin *salutare*, from *salut-, salus* health, safety, greeting, from *salvus* safe, healthy — more at SAFE] (14th century) *transitive verb* **1 a :** to address with expressions of kind wishes, courtesy, or honor **b :** to give a sign of respect, courtesy, or goodwill to **:** GREET **2 :** to become apparent to (one of the senses) **3 a :** to honor (as a person, nation, or event) by a conventional military or naval ceremony **b :** to show respect and recognition to (a military superior) by assuming a prescribed position **c :** to express commendation of **:** PRAISE *intransitive verb* **:** to make a salute — **sa·lut·er** *noun*

²salute *noun* (14th century) **1 :** GREETING, SALUTATION **2 a :** a sign, token, or ceremony expressing goodwill, compliment, or respect ⟨the festival was a *salute* to the arts⟩ **b :** the position (as of the hand) or the entire attitude of a person saluting a superior **3 :** FIRECRACKER

sal·u·tif·er·ous \ˌsal-yə-'ti-f(ə-)rəs\ *adjective* [Latin *salutifer*, from *salut-, salus* + *-i-* + *-fer* -ferous] (circa 1540) **:** SALUTARY

salv·able \'sal-və-bəl\ *adjective* [Late Latin *salvare* to save — more at SAVE] (1667) **:** capable of being saved or salvaged

¹sal·vage \'sal-vij\ *noun* [French, from Middle French, from *salver* to save — more at SAVE] (1645) **1 a :** compensation paid for saving a ship or its cargo from the perils of the sea or for the

lives and property rescued in a wreck **b** : the act of saving or rescuing a ship or its cargo **c** : the act of saving or rescuing property in danger (as from fire)
2 a : property saved from destruction in a calamity (as a wreck or fire) **b** : something extracted (as from rubbish) as valuable or useful
²**salvage** transitive verb **sal·vaged; salvag·ing** (1889)
: to rescue or save especially from wreckage or ruin
— **sal·vage·abil·i·ty** \ˌsal-vi-jə-'bi-lə-tē\ noun
— **sal·vage·able** \'sal-vi-jə-bəl\ adjective
— **sal·vag·er** noun
sal·var·san \'sal-vər-ˌsan\ noun [from Salvarsan, a trademark] (1909)
: ARSPHENAMINE
sal·va·tion \sal-'vā-shən\ noun [Middle English, from Old French, from Late Latin salvation-, salvatio, from salvare to save — more at SAVE] (13th century)
1 a : deliverance from the power and effects of sin **b** : the agent or means that effects salvation **c** Christian Science : the realization of the supremacy of infinite Mind over all bringing with it the destruction of the illusion of sin, sickness, and death
2 : liberation from ignorance or illusion
3 a : preservation from destruction or failure **b** : deliverance from danger or difficulty
— **sal·va·tion·al** \-shnəl, -shə-n°l\ adjective
Salvation Army noun (1878)
: an international religious and charitable group organized on military lines and founded in 1865 by William Booth for evangelizing and social betterment (as of the poor)
sal·va·tion·ism \sal-'vā-shə-ˌni-zəm\ noun (1883)
: religious teaching emphasizing the saving of the soul
Sal·va·tion·ist \-sh(ə-)nist\ noun (1882)
1 : a soldier or officer of the Salvation Army
2 often not capitalized : EVANGELIST
— **salvationist** adjective, often capitalized
¹**salve** \'sav, 'säv, 'såv, 'salv, 'sälv\ noun [Middle English, from Old English sealf; akin to Old High German salba salve, Greek olpē oil flask] (before 12th century)
1 : an unctuous adhesive substance for application to wounds or sores
2 : a remedial or soothing influence or agency ⟨a salve to their hurt feelings⟩
²**salve** transitive verb **salved; salv·ing** (before 12th century)
1 : to remedy (as disease) with or as if with a salve
2 : QUIET, ASSUAGE ⟨give him a raise in salary to salve his feelings —Upton Sinclair⟩
³**salve** \'salv\ transitive verb **salved; salv·ing** [back-formation from salvage] (circa 1706)
: SALVAGE
— **sal·vor** \'sal-vər\ noun
sal·ver \'sal-vər\ noun [modification of French salve, from Spanish salva sampling of food to detect poison, tray, from salvar to save, sample food to detect poison, from Late Latin salvare to save — more at SAVE] (circa 1661)
: a tray especially for serving food or beverages
sal·ver·form \'sal-vər-ˌfòrm\ adjective (1821)
: tubular with a spreading limb — used of a gamopetalous corolla
sal·via \'sal-vē-ə\ noun [New Latin, from Latin, sage — more at SAGE] (1601)
: any of a large and widely distributed genus (Salvia) of herbs and shrubs of the mint family having a 2-lipped open calyx and two anthers; especially : one (S. splendens) with scarlet flowers
sal·vif·ic \sal-'vi-fik\ adjective [Late Latin salvificus, from Latin salvus safe + -ficus -fic] (1591)

: having the intent or power to save or redeem ⟨the salvific life and death of Christ —E. A. Walsh⟩
¹**sal·vo** \'sal-(ˌ)vō\ noun, plural **salvos** or **salvoes** [Italian salva, from French salve, from Latin, hail!, from salvus healthy — more at SAFE] (1591)
1 a : a simultaneous discharge of two or more guns in military action or as a salute **b** : the release all at one time of a rack of bombs or rockets (as from an airplane) **c** : a series of shots by an artillery battery with each gun firing one round in turn after a prescribed interval **d** : the bombs or projectiles released in a salvo
2 : something suggestive of a salvo: as **a** : a sudden burst ⟨a salvo of cheers⟩ **b** : a spirited attack ⟨the first salvo of a political campaign⟩
²**salvo** (1839)
transitive verb
: to release a salvo of
intransitive verb
: to fire a salvo
³**salvo** noun, plural **salvos** [Medieval Latin salvo jure with the right reserved] (1621)
1 : a mental reservation : PROVISO
2 : a means of safeguarding one's name or honor or allaying one's conscience : SALVE
sal vo·la·ti·le \ˌsal-və-'la-t°l-ē\ noun [New Latin, literally, volatile salt] (1654)
: SMELLING SALTS
SAM \'sam, ˌes-(ˌ)ā-'em\ noun (1950)
: a surface-to-air missile
sa·ma·ra \'sa-mə-rə; sə-'mar-ə, -'mär-\ noun [New Latin, from Latin, seed of the elm] (1577)
: a dry indehiscent usually one-seeded winged fruit (as of an ash or elm tree) — called also key
Sa·mar·i·tan \sə-'mar-ə-t°n, -'mer-\ noun [Middle English, from Old English, from Late Latin samaritanus, noun & adjective, from Greek samaritēs inhabitant of Samaria, from Samaria] (before 12th century)
1 : a native or inhabitant of Samaria
2 [from the parable of the good Samaritan in Luke 10:30–37] : one ready and generous in helping those in distress
— **samaritan** adjective, often capitalized
sa·mar·i·um \sə-'mer-ē-əm, -'mar-\ noun [New Latin, from French samarskite] (1879)
: a pale gray lustrous metallic element used especially in alloys that form permanent magnets — see ELEMENT table
sa·mar·skite \sə-'mär-ˌskīt, 'sa-mər-\ noun [German Samarskit, from V. E. Samarskiĭ-Bykhovets (died 1870) Russian mining engineer] (1849)
: a black or brownish black orthorhombic mineral that is a complex oxide of rare earths, uranium, iron, lead, thorium, niobium, tantalum, titanium, and tin
sam·ba \'sam-bə, 'säm-\ noun [Portuguese] (1885)
: a Brazilian dance of African origin with a basic pattern of step-close-step-close and characterized by a dip and spring upward at each beat of the music; also : the music for this dance
— **samba** intransitive verb
sam·bar or **sam·bur** \'säm-bär, 'sam-\ noun [Hindi sãbar, from Sanskrit śambara] (1698)
: a large Asian deer (Cervus unicolor) with the male having strong 3-pointed antlers and long coarse hair on the throat
sam·bo \'sam-(ˌ)bō, 'säm-\ noun [Russian, from samozashchita bez oruzhiya self-defense without weapons] (1972)
: an international style of wrestling employing judo techniques
Sam Browne \'sam-'braùn\ noun [Sir Samuel James Browne (died 1901) British army officer] (1915)
: a leather belt for a dress uniform supported by a light strap passing over the right shoulder

¹**same** \'sām\ adjective [Middle English, from Old Norse samr; akin to Old High German sama same, Latin simulis like, simul together, at the same time, similis like, sem- one, Greek homos same, hama together, hen-, heis one] (13th century)
1 a : resembling in every relevant respect **b** : conforming in every respect — used with as
2 a : being one without addition, change, or discontinuance : IDENTICAL **b** : being the one under discussion or already referred to
3 : corresponding so closely as to be indistinguishable
4 : equal in size, shape, value, or importance — usually used with the or a demonstrative (as that, those) in all senses ☆
²**same** pronoun (14th century)
1 : something identical with or similar to another
2 : something or someone previously mentioned or described — often used with the or a demonstrative (as that, those) in both senses
— **all the same** or **just the same** : despite everything : NEVERTHELESS
³**same** adverb (1766)
: in the same manner — used with the or a demonstrative (as that, those)
sa·mekh \'sä-ˌmek\ noun [Hebrew sāmekh] (1823)
: the 15th letter of the Hebrew alphabet — see ALPHABET table
same·ness \'sām-nəs\ noun (1581)
1 : the quality or state of being the same : IDENTITY, SIMILARITY
2 : MONOTONY, UNIFORMITY
sam·i·sen \'sa-mə-ˌsen\ noun [Japanese] (1864)
: a 3-stringed Japanese musical instrument resembling a banjo
sa·mite \'sa-ˌmīt, 'sā-\ noun [Middle English samit, from Middle French, from Medieval Latin examitum, samitum, from Middle Greek hexamiton, from Greek, neuter of hexamitos of six threads, from hexa- + mitos thread of the warp] (13th century)
: a rich medieval silk fabric interwoven with gold or silver
sa·miz·dat \'sä-mēz-ˌdät\ noun [Russian, from sam- self- + izdatel'stvo publishing house] (1967)
: a system in the U.S.S.R. and countries within its orbit by which government-suppressed literature was clandestinely printed and distributed; also : such literature
sam·let \'sam-lət\ noun [irregular from salmon + -let] (1655)
: PARR

☆ SYNONYMS
Same, selfsame, very, identical, equivalent, equal mean not different or not differing from one another. SAME may imply and SELFSAME always implies that the things under consideration are one thing and not two or more things ⟨took the same route⟩ (derived from the selfsame source). VERY, like SELFSAME, may imply identity, or, like SAME, may imply likeness in kind ⟨the very point I was trying to make⟩. IDENTICAL may imply selfsameness or suggest absolute agreement in all details ⟨their test answers were identical⟩. EQUIVALENT implies amounting to the same thing in worth or significance ⟨two houses equivalent in market value⟩. EQUAL implies being identical in value, magnitude, or some specified quality ⟨equal shares in the business⟩.

Sam·ma·ri·nese \(ˌ)sa(m)-ˌmar-ə-ˈnēz, -ˈnēs\ *noun, plural* **-ne·si** \-ˈnä-zē\ [Italian *sammarinese,* from *San Marino*] (1938)
: a native or inhabitant of San Marino
Sam·nite \ˈsam-ˌnīt\ *noun* [*Samnium,* Italy] (14th century)
: a member of an ancient people of central Italy
Sa·mo·an \sə-ˈmō-ən\ *noun* (1846)
1 : the Polynesian language of the Samoans
2 : a native or inhabitant of Samoa
— **Samoan** *adjective*
Samoa time *noun* (1983)
: the time of the 11th time zone west of Greenwich that includes American Samoa
sam·o·var \ˈsa-mə-ˌvär\ *noun* [Russian, from *samo-* self + *varit'* to boil] (1830)
1 : an urn with a spigot at its base used especially in Russia to boil water for tea
2 : an urn similar to a Russian samovar with a device for heating the contents
Sam·o·yed *also* **Sam·o·yede** \ˈsa-mə-ˌyed, -ˌmȯi-\ *noun* [Russian *samoed*] (1589)
1 : a member of any of a group of peoples inhabiting the far north of European Russia and parts of northwestern Siberia
2 : the family of Uralic languages spoken by the Samoyed people
3 : any of a Siberian breed of medium-sized white or cream-colored sled dogs
— **Samoyed** *adjective*
— **Sam·o·yed·ic** \ˌsa-mə-ˈye-dik, -ˌmȯi-\ *adjective*
samp \ˈsamp\ *noun* [modification of Narraganset *nasàump* corn mush] (1643)
: coarse hominy or a boiled cereal made from it
sam·pan \ˈsam-ˌpan\ *noun* [Chinese (Guangdong) *sàambáan,* from *sàam* three + *báan* board, plank] (1620)
: a flat-bottomed Chinese skiff usually propelled by two short oars
sam·phire \ˈsam-ˌfīr\ *noun* [alteration of earlier *sampiere,* from Middle French (*herbe de*) *Saint Pierre,* literally, Saint Peter's herb] (1545)
1 : a fleshy European seacoast plant (*Crithmum maritimum*) of the carrot family that is sometimes pickled
2 : a common glasswort (*Salicornia europaea*) that is sometimes pickled
¹sam·ple \ˈsam-pəl\ *noun* [Middle English, from Middle French *essample,* from Latin *exemplum* — more at EXAMPLE] (15th century)
1 : a representative part or a single item from a larger whole or group especially when presented for inspection or shown as evidence of quality : SPECIMEN
2 : a finite part of a statistical population whose properties are studied to gain information about the whole
synonym see INSTANCE
²sample *transitive verb* **sam·pled; sampling** \-p(ə-)liŋ\ (1767)
: to take a sample of or from; *especially* : to judge the quality of by a sample : TEST ⟨*sampled* his output for defects⟩ ⟨*sample* a wine⟩
³sample *adjective* (1820)
: serving as an illustration or example ⟨*sample* questions⟩
¹sam·pler \ˈsam-plər\ *noun* (1523)
: a decorative piece of needlework typically having letters or verses embroidered on it in various stitches as an example of skill
²sam·pler \-p(ə-)lər\ *noun* (1778)
1 : one that collects, prepares, or examines samples
2 : something containing representative specimens or selections ⟨a *sampler* of nineteen poets —K. E. Judd⟩; *also* : ASSORTMENT
sample space *noun* (1951)

: a set in which all of the possible outcomes of a statistical experiment are represented as points
sam·pling \ˈsam-pliŋ, *for 1 & 3* -p(ə-)liŋ\ *noun* (1778)
1 : the act, process, or technique of selecting a suitable sample; *specifically* : the act, process, or technique of selecting a representative part of a population for the purpose of determining parameters or characteristics of the whole population
2 : a small part selected as a sample for inspection or analysis ⟨ask a *sampling* of people which candidate they favor⟩
3 : the introduction or promotion of a product by distributing trial packages of it
sam·sa·ra \səm-ˈsär-ə\ *noun* [Sanskrit *saṁsāra,* literally, passing through] (1886)
: the indefinitely repeated cycles of birth, misery, and death caused by karma
Sam·son \ˈsam(p)-sən\ *noun* [Late Latin, from Greek *Sampsōn,* from Hebrew *Shimshōn*]
: a Hebrew hero who wreaked havoc among the Philistines by means of his great strength
Sam·so·ni·an \sam(p)-ˈsō-nē-ən\ *adjective* [*Samson*] (circa 1623)
: of heroic strength or proportions : MIGHTY
Sam·u·el \ˈsam-yə-wəl, -yəl\ *noun* [Late Latin, from Greek *Samouēl,* from Hebrew *Shĕmūʾēl*]
1 : the early Hebrew judge who successively anointed Saul and David king
2 : either of two narrative and historical books of canonical Jewish and Christian Scriptures — see BIBLE table
sam·u·rai \ˈsa-mə-ˌrī, ˈsam-yə-\ *noun, plural* **samurai** [Japanese] (1727)
1 : a military retainer of a Japanese daimyo practicing the code of conduct of Bushido
2 : the warrior aristocracy of Japan
San \ˈsän\ *noun* (1876)
1 *plural in construction* : BUSHMEN
2 : BUSHMAN 2
san·a·tive \ˈsa-nə-tiv\ *adjective* [Middle English *sanatif,* from Middle French, from Late Latin *sanativus,* from Latin *sanatus,* past participle of *sanare* to cure, from *sanus* healthy] (15th century)
: having the power to cure or heal : CURATIVE, RESTORATIVE
san·a·to·ri·um \ˌsa-nə-ˈtȯr-ē-əm, -ˈtȯr-\ *noun, plural* **-riums** *or* **-ria** \-ē-ə\ [New Latin, from Late Latin, neuter of *sanatorius* curative, from *sanare*] (1839)
1 : an establishment that provides therapy combined with a regimen (as of diet and exercise) for treatment or rehabilitation
2 a : an institution for rest and recuperation (as of convalescents) **b** : an establishment for the treatment of the chronically ill
san·be·ni·to \ˌsan-bə-ˈnē-(ˌ)tō, ˌsam-\ *noun, plural* **-tos** [Spanish *sambenito,* from *San Benito* Saint Benedict of Nursia] (circa 1560)
1 : a sackcloth coat worn by penitents on being reconciled to the church
2 : a Spanish Inquisition garment resembling a scapular and being either yellow with red crosses for the penitent or black with painted devils and flames for the impenitent condemned to an auto-da-fé
San·cerre \säⁿ-ˈser\ *noun* [*Sancerre,* village in France] (circa 1946)
: a dry white wine from the Loire valley of France
San·cho Pan·za \ˌsan-chō-ˈpan-zə, ˌsän-chō-ˈpän-\ *noun* [Spanish]
: the squire of Don Quixote in Cervantes' *Don Quixote*
sanc·ti·fi·ca·tion \ˌsaŋ(k)-tə-fə-ˈkā-shən\ *noun* (14th century)
1 : an act of sanctifying
2 a : the state of being sanctified **b** : the state of growing in divine grace as a result of Christian commitment after baptism or conversion
sanc·ti·fi·er \ˈsaŋ(k)-tə-ˌfī-(ə-)r\ *noun* (1548)

: one that sanctifies; *specifically, capitalized* : HOLY SPIRIT
sanc·ti·fy \-ˌfī\ *transitive verb* **-fied; -fy·ing** [Middle English *sanctifien,* from Middle French *sanctifier,* from Late Latin *sanctificare,* from Latin *sanctus* sacred — more at SAINT] (14th century)
1 : to set apart to a sacred purpose or to religious use : CONSECRATE
2 : to free from sin : PURIFY
3 a : to impart or impute sacredness, inviolability, or respect to **b** : to give moral or social sanction to
4 : to make productive of holiness or piety ⟨observe the day of the sabbath, to *sanctify* it —Deuteronomy 5:12 (Douay Version)⟩
sanc·ti·mo·nious \ˌsaŋ(k)-tə-ˈmō-nē-əs, -nyəs\ *adjective* (1603)
1 : affecting piousness : hypocritically devout; *also* : indicative of affected piousness ⟨the king's *sanctimonious* rebuke —G. B. Shaw⟩
2 *obsolete* : possessing sanctity : HOLY
— **sanc·ti·mo·nious·ly** *adverb*
— **sanc·ti·mo·nious·ness** *noun*
sanc·ti·mo·ny \ˈsaŋ(k)-tə-ˌmō-nē\ *noun, plural* **-nies** [Middle French *sanctimonie,* from Latin *sanctimonia,* from *sanctus*] (circa 1541)
1 *obsolete* : HOLINESS
2 : affected or hypocritical holiness
¹sanc·tion \ˈsaŋ(k)-shən\ *noun* [Middle French or Latin; Middle French, from Latin *sanction-, sanctio,* from *sancire* to make holy — more at SACRED] (15th century)
1 : a formal decree; *especially* : an ecclesiastical decree
2 a *obsolete* : a solemn agreement : OATH **b** : something that makes an oath binding
3 : the detriment, loss of reward, or coercive intervention annexed to a violation of a law as a means of enforcing the law
4 a : a consideration, principle, or influence (as of conscience) that impels to moral action or determines moral judgment **b** : a mechanism of social control for enforcing a society's standards **c** : explicit or official approval, permission, or ratification : APPROBATION
5 : an economic or military coercive measure adopted usually by several nations in concert for forcing a nation violating international law to desist or yield to adjudication
²sanction *transitive verb* **sanc·tioned; sanc·tion·ing** \-sh(ə-)niŋ\ (1778)
1 : to make valid or binding usually by a formal procedure (as ratification)
2 : to give effective or authoritative approval or consent to
synonym see APPROVE
— **sanc·tion·able** \-sh(ə-)nə-bəl\ *adjective*
sanc·ti·ty \ˈsaŋ(k)-tə-tē\ *noun, plural* **-ties** [Middle English *saunctite,* from Middle French *sainctete,* from Latin *sanctitat-, sanctitas,* from *sanctus* sacred] (14th century)
1 : holiness of life and character : GODLINESS
2 a : the quality or state of being holy or sacred : INVIOLABILITY **b** *plural* : sacred objects, obligations, or rights
sanc·tu·ary \ˈsaŋ(k)-chə-ˌwer-ē\ *noun, plural* **-ar·ies** [Middle English *sanctuarie,* from Middle French *sainctuarie,* from Late Latin *sanctuarium,* from Latin *sanctus*] (14th century)
1 : a consecrated place: as **a** : the ancient Hebrew temple at Jerusalem or its holy of holies **b** (1) : the most sacred part of a religious building (as the part of a Christian church in which the altar is placed) (2) : the room in which general worship services are held (3) : a place (as a church or a temple) for worship
2 a (1) : a place of refuge and protection (2) : a refuge for wildlife where predators are controlled and hunting is illegal **b** : the immunity from law attached to a sanctuary
sanc·tum \ˈsaŋ(k)-təm\ *noun, plural* **sanc·tums** *also* **sanc·ta** \-tə\ [Late Latin, neuter of *sanctus* sacred] (1577)
1 : a sacred place

samovar 1

2 : a place where one is free from intrusion ⟨an editor's *sanctum*⟩ ⟨the inner *sanctums* of research⟩

sanc·tum sanc·to·rum \ˌsaŋ(k)-təm-ˌsaŋ(k)-ˈtōr-əm, -ˈtȯr-\ *noun* [Late Latin] (1558)

1 : HOLY OF HOLIES
2 : SANCTUM 2

Sanc·tus \ˈsaŋ(k)-təs; ˈsäŋ(k)-təs, -ˌtüs\ *noun* [Middle English, from Late Latin *Sanctus, sanctus, sanctus* Holy, holy, holy, opening of a hymn sung by the angels in Isaiah 6:3] (15th century)
: an ancient Christian hymn of adoration sung or said immediately before the prayer of consecration in traditional liturgies

Sanctus bell *noun* (15th century)
: a bell rung by the server at several points (as at the Sanctus) during the mass

¹sand \ˈsand\ *noun* [Middle English, from Old English; akin to Old High German *sant* sand, Latin *sabulum,* Greek *psammos*] (before 12th century)
1 a : a loose granular material that results from the disintegration of rocks, consists of particles smaller than gravel but coarser than silt, and is used in mortar, glass, abrasives, and foundry molds **b :** soil containing 85 percent or more of sand and a maximum of 10 percent of clay; *broadly :* sandy soil
2 a : a tract of sand : BEACH **b :** a sandbank or sandbar
3 : the sand in an hourglass; *also :* the moments of a lifetime — usually used in plural ⟨the *sands* of this government run out very rapidly —H. J. Laski⟩
4 : an oil-producing formation of sandstone or unconsolidated sand
5 : firm resolution
6 : a yellowish gray color

²sand *transitive verb* (14th century)
1 : to sprinkle or dust with or as if with sand
2 : to cover or fill with sand
3 : to smooth or dress by grinding or rubbing with an abrasive (as sandpaper)

san·dal \ˈsan-dᵊl\ *noun* [Middle English *sandalie,* from Latin *sandalium,* from Greek *sandalion,* diminutive of *sandalon* sandal] (14th century)
1 : a shoe consisting of a sole strapped to the foot
2 : a low-cut shoe that fastens by an ankle strap
3 : a strap to hold on a slipper or low shoe
4 : a rubber overshoe cut very low
— **san·daled** \ˈsan-dᵊld\ *adjective*

san·dal·wood \-ˌwu̇d\ *noun* [*sandal* sandalwood (from Middle English, from Middle French, from Medieval Latin *sandalum,* from Late Greek *santalon,* ultimately from Sanskrit *candana,* of Dravidian origin; akin to Tamil *cāntu* sandalwood tree) + ²*wood*] (circa 1511)
1 : the compact close-grained fragrant yellowish heartwood of a parasitic tree (*Santalum album* of the family Santalaceae, the sandalwood family) of southern Asia much used in ornamental carving and cabinetwork; *also :* the tree that yields this wood
2 : any of various trees other than the sandalwood some of which yield dyewoods; *also :* the fragrant wood of such a tree

sandalwood oil *noun* (1851)
: an essential oil obtained from sandalwood: as **a :** a pale yellow somewhat viscous aromatic liquid obtained from a sandalwood (*Santalum album*) and used chiefly in perfumes and soaps **b :** an oil obtained from a sandalwood (*Eucarya spicata*) of Australia

san·da·rac \ˈsan-də-ˌrak\ *noun* [Latin *sandaraca* red coloring, from Greek *sandarakē* realgar, red pigment from realgar] (1543)
: a brittle faintly aromatic translucent resin obtained from a northern African tree (*Tetraclinis articulata*) of the cypress family and used chiefly in making varnish and as incense; *also*

: a similar resin obtained from any of several Australian trees (genus *Callitris*) of the same family

¹sand·bag \ˈsan(d)-ˌbag\ *noun* (1590)
: a bag filled with sand and used in fortifications, as ballast, or as a weapon

²sandbag *transitive verb* (1860)
1 : to bank, stop up, or weight with sandbags
2 a : to hit or stun with or as if with a sandbag **b :** to treat unfairly or harshly **c :** to coerce by crude means ⟨are raiding the Treasury and *sandbagging* the government —C. W. Ferguson⟩ **d :** to conceal or misrepresent one's true position, potential, or intent especially in order to take advantage of
— **sand·bag·ger** *noun*

sand·bank \ˈsan(d)-ˌbaŋk\ *noun* (15th century)
: a large deposit of sand forming a mound, hillside, bar, or shoal

sand·bar \-ˌbär\ *noun* (1766)
: a ridge of sand built up by currents especially in a river or in coastal waters

¹sand·blast \-ˌblast\ *noun* (1871)
: a stream of sand projected by compressed air (as for engraving, cutting, or cleaning glass or stone)

²sandblast *transitive verb* (1888)
: to affect or treat with or as if with a sandblast
— **sand·blast·er** *noun*

sand–blind \ˈsan(d)-ˌblīnd\ *adjective* [Middle English, probably from (assumed) Middle English *samblind,* from Old English *sam-* half (akin to Old High German *sāmi-* half) + *blind* — more at SEMI-] (15th century)
: having poor eyesight : PURBLIND

sand bluestem *noun* (circa 1946)
: a tall rhizomatous grass (*Andropogon hallii*) of the western U.S. used for forage and as a soil binder

sand·box \ˈsan(d)-ˌbäks\ *noun* (1688)
: a box or receptacle containing loose sand: as **a :** a shaker for sprinkling sand on wet ink **b :** a box that contains sand for children to play in

sand·bur \ˈsan(d)-ˌbər\ *noun* (1830)
: any of a genus (*Cenchrus*) of grasses producing spikelets enclosed in ovoid spiny involucres that form burs; *also :* one of these burs

sand·cast \-ˌkast\ *transitive verb* **-cast; -cast·ing** (1928)
: to make (a casting) by pouring metal in a sand mold

sand casting *noun* (1926)
: a casting made in a mold of sand

sand crack *noun* (1754)
: a fissure in the wall of a horse's hoof often causing lameness

sand dab *noun* (1946)
: any of several Pacific flounders (genus *Citharichthys* of the family Bothidae); *especially* **:** a common food fish (*C. sordidus*)

sand dollar *noun* (1884)
: any of numerous flat circular sea urchins (order Clypeasteroida) that live chiefly in shallow water on sandy bottoms

sand·er \ˈsan-dər\ *noun* (1627)
: one that sands: as **a :** a device for spreading sand on newly surfaced or icy roads; *also :* the device together with the truck that bears it **b :** a machine or device that smooths, polishes, or scours by means of abrasive material usually in the form of a disk or belt — called also *sanding machine*

sand·er·ling \ˈsan-dər-liŋ\ *noun* [*sand* + *-erling,* perhaps from Old English *yrthling,* kind of bird found in fields, literally, plowman, from *yrth,* earth plowing, from *erian* to plow — more at ARABLE] (1602)
: a small widely distributed sandpiper (*Calidris alba*) with pale gray and white plumage in winter

sand flea *noun* (1796)
1 : a flea (as a chigoe) found in sandy places
2 : BEACH FLEA

sand fly *noun* (1736)
: any of various small biting dipteran flies (families Psychodidae, Simuliidae, and Ceratopogonidae)

sand–fly fever \ˈsan(d)-ˌflī-\ *noun* (1910)
: a virus disease of brief duration that is characterized by fever, headache, pain in the eyes, malaise, and leukopenia and is transmitted by the bite of a sand fly (*Phlebotomus papatasii*) — called also *phlebotomus fever*

sand·glass \ˈsan(d)-ˌglas\ *noun* (1556)
: an instrument (as an hourglass) for measuring time by the running of sand

sand·grouse \-ˌgrau̇s\ *noun* (1783)
: any of numerous birds (family Pteroclidae) of arid parts of southern Europe, Asia, and Africa that are closely related to the pigeons but have precocial downy young

san·dhi \ˈsan-dē, ˈsän-, ˈsən-\ *noun* [Sanskrit *saṃdhi,* literally, placing together] (1806)
: modification of the sound of a morpheme (as a word or affix) conditioned by syntactic context in which it is uttered (as pronunciation of *-ed* as \d\ in *glazed* and as \t\ in *paced* or occurrence of *a* in *a cow* and of *an* in *an old cow*)

sand·hill crane \ˈsand-ˌhil-\ *noun* (1805)
: a crane (*Grus canadensis*) of North America and Siberia that has a red crown and is chiefly bluish gray tinged with a sandy yellow

sand·hog \ˈsand-ˌhȯg, -ˌhäg\ *noun* (1903)
: a laborer who works in a caisson in driving underwater tunnels

San·di·nis·ta \ˌsan-də-ˈnēs-tə, ˌsän-\ *noun* [American Spanish, from Augusto César Sandino (died 1933) Nicaraguan rebel leader] (1974)
: a member of a military and political coalition taking power in Nicaragua in 1979

S and L *noun* (1951)
: SAVINGS AND LOAN ASSOCIATION

sand lance *noun* (1776)
: any of several small elongate marine bony fishes (genus *Ammodytes* of the family Ammodytidae) that associate in large schools and remain buried in sandy beaches at ebb tide — called also *sand eel, sand launce*

sand lily *noun* (circa 1900)
: a western North American spring herb (*Leucocrinum montanum*) of the lily family with narrow linear leaves and fragrant salverform flowers

sand·lot \ˈsan(d)-ˌlät\ *noun* (1878)
: a vacant lot especially when used (as by children) for usually unorganized sports
— **sandlot** *adjective*
— **sand·lot·ter** \-ˌlä-tər\ *noun*

sand·man \ˈsan(d)-ˌman\ *noun*
: a genie in folklore who makes children sleepy by sprinkling sand in their eyes

sand myrtle *noun* (1814)
: a variable low-branching evergreen upland shrub (*Leiophyllum buxifolium*) of the heath family found in the southeastern U.S.

sand·paint·ing \ˈsan(d)-ˌpān-tiŋ\ *noun* (1900)
: a Navajo and Pueblo Indian ceremonial design made of various materials (as colored sands) on a flat surface of sand or buckskin

¹sand·pa·per \-ˌpā-pər\ *noun* (1825)
: paper covered on one side with abrasive material (as sand) glued fast and used for smoothing and polishing
— **sand·pa·pery** \-p(ə-)rē\ *adjective*

²sandpaper *transitive verb* (1846)
: to rub with or as if with sandpaper

sand·pile \ˈsan(d)-ˌpīl\ *noun* (1901)
: a pile of sand; *especially :* sand for children to play in

\ə\ abut \ᵊ\ kitten \ər\ further \a\ ash \ā\ ace
\ä\ mop, mar \au̇\ out \ch\ chin \e\ bet \ē\ easy
\g\ go \i\ hit \ī\ ice \j\ job \ŋ\ sing \ō\ go
\ȯ\ law \ȯi\ boy \th\ thin \t͟h\ the \ü\ loot \u̇\ foot
\y\ yet \zh\ vision *see also* Guide to Pronunciation

sand·pip·er \-ˌpī-pər\ *noun* (1674)
: any of numerous small shorebirds (family Scolopacidae) distinguished from the related plovers chiefly by the longer and soft-tipped bill

sandpiper

sand·pit \-ˌpit\ *noun* (1898)
b *British* : SANDBOX

sand·shoe \-ˌshü\ *noun* (1855)
chiefly Australian & New Zealand : TENNIS SHOE

sand·soap \ˈsan(d)-ˌsōp\ *noun* (1854)
: a gritty soap for all-purpose cleaning

sand·spur \-ˌspər\ *noun* (circa 1898)
: SANDBUR

sand·stone \-ˌstōn\ *noun* (1668)
: a sedimentary rock consisting of usually quartz sand united by some cement (as silica or calcium carbonate)

sand·storm \-ˌstȯrm\ *noun* (1774)
: a windstorm (as in a desert) driving clouds of sand before it

sand table *noun* (1812)
1 : a table holding sand for children to mold
2 : a table bearing a relief model of a terrain built to scale for study or demonstration especially of military tactics

sand trap *noun* (1922)
: an artificial hazard on a golf course consisting of a depression containing sand

sand verbena *noun* (1898)
: any of several western North American herbs (genus *Abronia*) of the four-o'clock family with flowers like the verbena; *especially* : either of two plants (*A. latifolia* and *A. umbellata*) of the Pacific coast

¹**sand·wich** \ˈsan(d)-ˌwich, ˈsam-\ *noun* [John Montagu, 4th Earl of *Sandwich* (died 1792) English diplomat] (1762)
1 a : two or more slices of bread or a split roll having a filling in between **b** : one slice of bread covered with food
2 : something resembling a sandwich; *especially* : composite structural material consisting of layers often of high-strength facings bonded to a low strength central core ◆

²**sandwich** *transitive verb* (1861)
1 : to make into or as if into a sandwich; *especially* : to insert or enclose between usually two things of another quality or character
2 : to make a place for — often used with *in* or *between*

sandwich board *noun* (1897)
: two usually hinged boards designed for hanging from the shoulders with one board before and one behind and used especially for advertising or picketing

sandwich coin *noun* (1965)
: a clad coin

sandwich man *noun* (1864)
: one who wears a sandwich board

sand·worm \ˈsan(d)-ˌwərm\ *noun* (1776)
: any of various sand-dwelling polychaete worms: as **a** : any of several large burrowing worms (especially genus *Nereis*) often used as bait **b** : LUGWORM

sand·wort \ˈsan(d)-ˌwərt, -ˌwȯrt\ *noun* (1597)
: any of a genus (*Arenaria*) of low tufted herbs of the pink family growing usually in dry sandy regions

sandy \ˈsan-dē\ *adjective* **sand·i·er; -est** (before 12th century)
1 a : consisting of or containing sand : full of sand **b** : sprinkled with sand
2 : of the color sand
— **sand·i·ness** *noun*

sane \ˈsān\ *adjective* **san·er; san·est** [Latin *sanus* healthy, sane] (1628)
1 : proceeding from a sound mind : RATIONAL
2 : mentally sound; *especially* : able to anticipate and appraise the effect of one's actions

3 : healthy in body
synonym see WISE
— **sane·ly** *adverb*
— **sane·ness** \ˈsān-nəs\ *noun*

San·for·ized \ˈsan-fə-ˌrīzd\ *trademark*
— used for fabrics that are shrunk by a mechanical process before being manufactured into articles (as clothing)

sang *past of* SING

san·ga·ree \ˌsaŋ-gə-ˈrē\ *noun* [Spanish *sangría*, literally, act of bleeding, from *sangre* blood, from Latin *sanguin-, sanguis*] (1736)
1 : a sweetened iced drink of wine or sometimes of ale, beer, or liquor garnished with nutmeg
2 : SANGRIA

sang·froid \ˈsäⁿ-ˈf(r)wä\ *noun* [French *sang-froid*, literally, cold blood] (1750)
: self-possession or imperturbability especially under strain
synonym see EQUANIMITY

San·greal \ˈsan-ˈgrā(ə)l, ˈsaŋ-\ *noun* [Middle English *Sangrayll*, from Middle French *Saint Graal* Holy Grail]
: GRAIL

san·gria \saŋ-ˈgrē-ə, san-\ *noun* [Spanish] (1736)
: a usually iced punch made of red wine, fruit juice, and soda water

san·gui·nar·ia \ˌsaŋ-gwə-ˈner-ē-ə, -ˈnar-\ *noun* [New Latin, from Latin, an herb that stanches blood, from feminine of *sanguinarius* sanguinary] (1808)
1 : BLOODROOT
2 : the rhizome and roots of a bloodroot used as an expectorant and emetic

san·gui·nary \ˈsaŋ-gwə-ˌner-ē\ *adjective* [Latin *sanguinarius*, from *sanguin-, sanguis* blood] (1623)
1 : BLOODTHIRSTY, MURDEROUS ⟨*sanguinary* hatred⟩
2 : attended by bloodshed : BLOODY ⟨this bitter and *sanguinary* war —T. H. D. Mahoney⟩
3 : consisting of blood ⟨a *sanguinary* stream⟩
synonym see BLOODY
— **san·gui·nar·i·ly** \ˌsaŋ-gwə-ˈner-ə-lē\ *adverb*

¹**san·guine** \ˈsaŋ-gwən\ *adjective* [Middle English *sanguin*, from Middle French, from Latin *sanguineus*, from *sanguin-, sanguis*] (14th century)
1 : BLOODRED
2 a : consisting of or relating to blood **b** : BLOODTHIRSTY, SANGUINARY **c** *of the complexion* : RUDDY
3 : having blood as the predominating bodily humor; *also* : having the bodily conformation and temperament held characteristic of such predominance and marked by sturdiness, high color, and cheerfulness
4 : CONFIDENT, OPTIMISTIC
— **san·guine·ly** *adverb*
— **san·guine·ness** \-gwən-nəs\ *noun*
— **san·guin·i·ty** \saŋ-ˈgwi-nə-tē, san-\ *noun*

²**sanguine** *noun* (1500)
: a moderate to strong red

san·guin·e·ous \san-ˈgwi-nē-əs, saŋ-\ *adjective* [Latin *sanguineus*] (circa 1520)
1 : BLOODRED
2 : of, relating to, or involving bloodshed : BLOODTHIRSTY
3 : of, relating to, or containing blood

San·he·drin \san-ˈhe-drən, sän-; san-ˈhē-, ˈsa-nə-\ *noun* [Late Hebrew *sanhedhrīn* (*gĕdhōlāh*) (great) Sanhedrin, from Greek *synedrion* council, from *synedros* sitting in council, from *syn-* + *hedra* seat — more at SIT] (1588)
: the supreme council and tribunal of the Jews during postexilic times headed by a High Priest and having religious, civil, and criminal jurisdiction

san·i·cle \ˈsa-ni-kəl\ *noun* [Middle English, from Middle French, from Medieval Latin *sanicula*] (14th century)
: any of several plants sometimes held to have healing powers; *especially* : a plant (genus *Sanicula*) of the carrot family with a root used in folk medicine as an anodyne or astringent

san·i·tar·i·an \ˌsa-nə-ˈter-ē-ən\ *noun* (1859)
: a specialist in sanitary science and public health ⟨milk *sanitarian*⟩

san·i·tar·i·um \ˌsa-nə-ˈter-ē-əm\ *noun, plural* **-i·ums** *or* **-ia** \-ē-ə\ [New Latin, from Latin *sanitat-, sanitas* health] (1851)
: SANATORIUM

san·i·tary \ˈsa-nə-ˌter-ē\ *adjective* [French *sanitaire*, from Latin *sanitas*] (1842)
1 : of or relating to health ⟨*sanitary* measures⟩
2 : of, relating to, or used in the disposal especially of domestic waterborne waste ⟨*sanitary* sewage⟩
3 : characterized by or readily kept in cleanliness ⟨*sanitary* packages⟩
— **san·i·tar·i·ly** \ˌsa-nə-ˈter-ə-lē\ *adverb*

sanitary landfill *noun* (1968)
: LANDFILL

sanitary napkin *noun* (1917)
: a disposable absorbent pad used postpartum or during menstruation to absorb the uterine flow

sanitary ware *noun* (1872)
: ceramic plumbing fixtures (as sinks, lavatories, or toilet bowls)

san·i·tate \ˈsa-nə-ˌtāt\ *transitive verb* **-tated; -tat·ing** [back-formation from *sanitation*] (1882)
: to make sanitary especially by providing with sanitary appliances or facilities

san·i·ta·tion \ˌsa-nə-ˈtā-shən\ *noun* (1848)
1 : the act or process of making sanitary
2 : the promotion of hygiene and prevention of disease by maintenance of sanitary conditions

san·i·tize \ˈsa-nə-ˌtīz\ *transitive verb* **-tized; -tiz·ing** [Latin *sanitas*] (1836)
1 : to make sanitary (as by cleaning or sterilizing)
2 : to make more acceptable by removing unpleasant or undesired features ⟨*sanitize* a document⟩
— **san·i·ti·za·tion** \ˌsa-nə-tə-ˈzā-shən\ *noun*

san·i·to·ri·um \ˌsa-nə-ˈtȯr-ē-əm, -ˈtȯr-\ *noun, plural* **-ri·ums** *or* **-ria** \-ē-ə\ [by alteration (influenced by *sanitarium*)] (1917)
: SANATORIUM

san·i·ty \ˈsa-nə-tē\ *noun* [Middle English *sanite*, from Latin *sanitat-, sanitas* health, sanity, from *sanus* healthy, sane] (15th century)

: the quality or state of being sane; *especially*
: soundness or health of mind

San Ja·cin·to Day \,san-jə-'sin-tə-, -hə-,sin-\ *noun* (1907)
: April 21 observed as a legal holiday in Texas in commemoration of the battle of San Jacinto in 1836 by which independence from Mexico was won

San Jo·se scale \,sa-nə-'zā-, ,san-(h)ō-\ *noun* [*San Jose,* Calif.] (1887)
: a scale insect (*Quadraspidiotus perniciosus*) probably of Asian origin that is naturalized in the U.S. and is destructive to fruit trees

sank *past of* SINK

San·khya \'sän-kyə\ *noun* [Sanskrit *sāṁkhya,* literally, based on calculation] (1788)
: an orthodox Hindu philosophy teaching salvation through knowledge of the dualism of matter and souls

sann hemp \'sən-, 'sän-\ *noun* [Hindi *san*] (1939)
: SUNN

san·nup \'sa-nəp\ *noun* [Eastern Abenaki *sénape* man, male human] (1628)
: a married male American Indian

sann·ya·si \(,)sən-'yä-sē\ *or* **sann·ya·sin** \-'yä-sⁿn\ *noun* [Hindi *sannyāsī,* from Sanskrit *sannyāsin*] (1613)
: a Hindu mendicant ascetic

¹sans \'sanz\ *preposition* [Middle English *saun, sans,* from Middle French *san, sans,* modification of Latin *sine* without — more at SUNDER] (14th century)
: WITHOUT ⟨my love to thee is sound, *sans* crack or flaw —Shakespeare⟩

²sans \'sanz\ *noun, plural* **sans** (circa 1909)
: SANS SERIF

sans·cu·lotte \,sanz-kù-'lät, -kyù-\ *noun* [French *sans-culotte,* literally, without breeches] (1790)
1 : an extreme radical republican in France at the time of the Revolution
2 : a radical or violent extremist in politics
— **sans·cu·lott·ic** \-'lä-tik\ *adjective*
— **sans·cu·lott·ish** \-tish\ *adjective*
— **sans·cu·lott·ism** \-,ti-zəm\ *noun*

san·sei \'san-'sā, 'sän-\ *noun, plural* **sansei** *often capitalized* [Japanese *san* third + *sei* generation] (1940)
: a son or daughter of nisei parents who is born and educated in America and especially in the U.S.

san·se·vie·ria \,san(t)-sə-'vir-ē-ə\ *noun* [New Latin, from Raimondo di Sangro, prince of *San Severo* (died 1774) Italian scholar] (1804)
: any of a genus (*Sansevieria*) of tropical herbs of the agave family with showy mottled sword-shaped leaves usually yielding a strong fiber

San·skrit \'san-,skrit, 'san(t)-skrət\ *noun* [Sanskrit *saṁskṛta,* literally, perfected, from *sam* together + *karoti* he makes] (1696)
1 : an ancient Indo-Aryan language that is the classical language of India and of Hinduism
2 : classical Sanskrit together with the older Vedic and various later modifications of classical Sanskrit — see INDO-EUROPEAN LANGUAGES table
— **Sanskrit** *adjective*
— **San·skrit·ic** \san-'skri-tik\ *adjective*
— **San·skrit·ist** \-,skri-tist\ *noun*

sans ser·if *or* **san-ser·if** \san-'ser-əf, 'sanz-\ *noun* [probably from *sans* + modification of Dutch *schreef* stroke — more at SERIF] (1830)
: a letter or typeface with no serifs

San·ta Ana \,san-tə-'a-nə\ *noun* [*Santa Ana* Mountains in southern Calif.] (1880)
: a strong hot dry foehn wind from the north, northeast, or east in southern California

San·ta Claus \'san-tə-,klöz *also* 'san-tē-\ *noun* [modification of Dutch *Sinterklaas,* alteration of *Sint Nikolaas* Saint Nicholas]
: a plump white-bearded and red-suited old man in modern folklore who delivers presents to good children at Christmastime — called also *Santa*

San·ta Ger·tru·dis \,san-tə-(,)gər-'trü-dəs\ *noun* [*Santa Gertrudis,* section of the King Ranch, Kingsville, Texas] (1942)
: any of a breed of red beef cattle developed from a Brahman-shorthorn cross and valued for their hardiness in hot climates

Santa Gertrudis

San·te·ria *also* **San·te·ría** \,san-tə-'rē-ə, san-\ *noun* [American Spanish *santería,* from *santero* practitioner of Santeria, from *santo* Yoruba deity, literally, saint's image, saint, from Spanish] (1950)
: a religion practiced originally in Cuba in which Yoruba deities are identified with Roman Catholic saints

san·tir \san-'tir\ *or* **san·tour** \-'tùr\ *noun* [Arabic *ṣanṭīr, ṣanṭūr,* from Greek *psaltērion* psaltery] (1853)
: a Persian dulcimer

san·to \'sän-(,)tō\ *noun, plural* **santos** [Spanish, literally, saint, from Late Latin *sanctus* — more at SAINT] (1834)
: a painted or carved wooden image of a saint common especially in Mexico and the southwestern U.S.

san·to·li·na \,san-tⁿl-'ē-nə\ *noun* [New Latin, alteration of Latin *santonica,* an herb, feminine of *santonicus* of the Santoni, from *Santoni,* a people of Aquitania] (1578)
: any of a genus (*Santolina*) of Mediterranean composite subshrubs that have dissected leaves and clustered flower heads lacking ray flowers

san·to·nin \'san-tⁿn-ən, san-'tä-nən\ *noun* [International Scientific Vocabulary, from New Latin *santonica,* from Latin] (1838)
: a poisonous slightly bitter crystalline compound $C_{15}H_{18}O_3$ found especially in the unopened flower heads of several artemisias (especially *Artemisia maritima*) and used as an anthelmintic

¹sap \'sap\ *noun* [Middle English, from Old English *sæp;* akin to Old High German *saf* sap] (before 12th century)
1 a : the fluid part of a plant; *specifically* : a watery solution that circulates through a plant's vascular system **b** (1) : a body fluid (as blood) essential to life, health, or vigor (2) : bodily health and vigor
2 : a foolish gullible person
3 : BLACKJACK, BLUDGEON
— **sap·less** \'sa-pləs\ *adjective*
— **sap·less·ness** \-nəs\ *noun*

²sap *transitive verb* **sapped; sap·ping** (1725)
1 : to drain or deprive of sap
2 : to knock out with a sap

³sap *verb* **sapped; sap·ping** [Middle French *sapper,* from Old Italian *zappare,* from *zappa* hoe] (1598)
intransitive verb
: to proceed by digging a sap
transitive verb
1 : to subvert by digging or eroding the substratum or foundation : UNDERMINE
2 a : to gradually diminish the supply or intensity of ⟨*sapped* her strength⟩ **b** : to weaken or exhaust the energy or vitality of
3 : to operate against or pierce by a sap
synonym see WEAKEN

⁴sap *noun* [Middle French *sape,* from *saper*] (1642)
: the extension of a trench to a point beneath an enemy's fortifications

sap green *noun* (1578)
: a strong yellow green

sap·head \'sap-,hed\ *noun* (1798)
: a weak-minded stupid person : SAP
— **sap·head·ed** \-'he-dəd\ *adjective*

sa·phe·nous \sə-'fē-nəs, 'sa-fə-nəs\ *adjective* [*saphena* saphenous vein, from Middle English, from Medieval Latin, from Arabic *ṣāfin*] (1840)
: of, relating to, associated with, or being either of the two chief superficial veins of the leg ⟨*saphenous* nerve⟩

sap·id \'sa-pəd\ *adjective* [Latin *sapidus* tasty, from *sapere* to taste — more at SAGE] (1623)
1 : having flavor : FLAVORFUL
2 *archaic* : agreeable to the mind
— **sa·pid·i·ty** \sa-'pi-də-tē\ *noun, archaic*

sa·pi·ence \'sā-pē-ən(t)s, 'sa-\ *noun* [Middle English, from Middle French, from Latin *sapientia,* from *sapient-, sapiens,* present participle] (14th century)
: WISDOM, SAGACITY

sa·pi·ens \'sa-pē-ənz, 'sā-, -,enz\ *adjective* [New Latin (specific epithet of *Homo sapiens*), from Latin, present participle of *sapere*] (1939)
: of, relating to, or being recent humans (*Homo sapiens*) as distinguished from various fossil hominids

sa·pi·ent \'sā-pē-ənt, 'sa-\ *adjective* [Middle English, from Middle French, from Latin *sapient-, sapiens,* from present participle of *sapere* to taste, be wise — more at SAGE] (15th century)
: possessing or expressing great sagacity
synonym see WISE
— **sa·pi·ent·ly** *adverb*

sap·ling \'sa-pliŋ, -plən\ *noun* (14th century)
1 : a young tree; *specifically* : one not over four inches in diameter at breast height
2 : YOUTH 2a

sap·o·dil·la \,sa-pə-'di-lə, -'dē-yə\ *noun* [Spanish *zapotillo,* diminutive of *zapote* sapodilla, from Nahuatl *tzapotl*] (1697)
: a tropical evergreen tree (*Manilkara zapota* synonym *Achras zapota* of the family Sapotaceae, the sapodilla family) with hard reddish wood, a latex that yields chicle, and a rough-skinned brownish edible fruit; *also* : its fruit

sa·po·ge·nin \,sa-pə-'je-nən, sə-'pä-jə-nən\ *noun* [International Scientific Vocabulary *saponin* + *-genin* (compound formed from another compound)] (circa 1862)
: a nonsugar portion of a saponin that is typically obtained by hydrolysis, has either a complex terpenoid or a steroidal structure, and in the latter case forms a practicable starting point in the synthesis of steroid hormones

sap·o·na·ceous \,sa-pə-'nā-shəs\ *adjective* [New Latin *saponaceus,* from Latin *sapon-, sapo* soap, of Germanic origin; akin to Old English *sāpe* soap] (1710)
: resembling or having the qualities of soap
— **sap·o·na·ceous·ness** *noun*

sa·pon·i·fy \sə-'pä-nə-,fī\ *verb* **-fied; -fy·ing** [French *saponifier,* from Latin *sapon-, sapo*] (1821)
transitive verb
: to convert (as fat) into soap; *specifically* : to hydrolyze (a fat) with alkali to form a soap and glycerol
intransitive verb
: to undergo saponifying
— **sa·pon·i·fi·able** \-,fī-ə-bəl\ *adjective*
— **sa·pon·i·fi·ca·tion** \-,pä-nə-fə-'kā-shən\ *noun*

\ə\ abut \ᵊ\ kitten \ər\ further \a\ ash \ā\ ace
\ä\ mop, mar \aù\ out \ch\ chin \e\ bet \ē\ easy
\g\ go \i\ hit \ī\ ice \j\ job \ŋ\ sing \ō\ go
\ò\ law \òi\ boy \th\ thin \th\ the \ü\ loot \ù\ foot
\y\ yet \zh\ vision *see also* Guide to Pronunciation

— sa·pon·i·fi·er \-'pä-nə-ˌfī(-ə)r\ *noun*
sa·po·nin \'sa-pə-nən, sə-'pō-\ *noun* [French *saponine*, from Latin *sapon-, sapo*] (1831)
: any of various mostly toxic glucosides that occur in plants (as soapwort or soapbark) and are characterized by the property of producing a soapy lather **: especially :** a hygroscopic amorphous saponin mixture used especially as a foaming and emulsifying agent and detergent
sap·o·nite \'sa-pə-ˌnīt\ *noun* [Swedish *saponit*, from Latin *sapon-, sapo* soap] (circa 1849)
: a hydrous magnesium aluminum silicate occurring in soft soapy amorphous masses and filling veins and cavities (as in serpentine)
sap·per \'sa-pər\ *noun* (1626)
1 : a military specialist in field fortification work (as sapping)
2 : a military demolitions specialist
¹sap·phic \'sa-fik\ *adjective* (1501)
1 *capitalized* **:** of or relating to the Greek lyric poet Sappho
2 : of, relating to, or consisting of a 4-line strophe made up of chiefly trochaic and dactylic feet
3 : LESBIAN 2
²sapphic *noun* (1586)
1 : a verse having the metrical pattern of one of the first three lines of a sapphic strophe
2 : a sapphic strophe
sap·phire \'sa-ˌfīr\ *noun* [Middle English *safir*, from Old French, from Latin *sapphirus*, from Greek *sappheiros*, perhaps of Semitic origin; akin to Hebrew *sappīr* sapphire] (13th century)
1 a : a gem variety of corundum in transparent or translucent crystals of a color other than red; *especially* **:** one of a transparent rich blue
b : a gem of such color
2 : a deep purplish blue color
— sapphire *adjective*
sap·phi·rine \'sa-fə-ˌrīn, -ˌrēn, 'sa-ˌfīr-ˌēn, sa-'fī-rən\ *adjective* (15th century)
1 : made of sapphire
2 : resembling sapphire especially in color
sap·phism \'sa-ˌfi-zəm\ *noun* [*Sappho* + *-ism*; from the belief that Sappho was homosexual] (circa 1890)
: LESBIANISM
sap·pi·ness \'sa-pē-nəs\ *noun* (1552)
1 : the state of being full of or smelling of sap
2 : the quality or state of being sappy **:** FOOLISHNESS
sap·py \'sa-pē\ *adjective* **sap·pi·er; -est** (12th century)
1 : abounding with sap
2 : resembling or consisting largely of sapwood
3 a : overly sweet or sentimental **b :** lacking in good sense **:** SILLY
sapr- *or* **sapro-** *combining form* [New Latin, from Greek *sapros* rotten]
1 : dead or decaying organic matter ⟨*sapro*phyte⟩
2 : decay **:** putrefaction ⟨*sapro*genic⟩
sap·ro·gen·ic \ˌsa-prə-'je-nik\ *adjective* (1876)
: of, causing, or resulting from putrefaction
— sap·ro·ge·nic·i·ty \-jə-'ni-sə-tē\ *noun*
sap·ro·lite \'sa-prə-ˌlīt\ *noun* (1894)
: disintegrated rock that lies in its original place
sa·proph·a·gous \sa-'prä-fə-gəs\ *adjective* [New Latin *saprophagus*, from *sapr-* + *-phagous* -phagous] (1819)
: feeding on decaying matter
sap·ro·phyte \'sa-prə-ˌfīt\ *noun* [International Scientific Vocabulary] (1875)
: a saprophytic organism; *especially* **:** a plant living on dead or decaying organic matter
sap·ro·phyt·ic \ˌsa-prə-'fi-tik\ *adjective* (1882)
: obtaining food by absorbing dissolved organic material; *especially* **:** obtaining nourishment

osmotically from the products of organic breakdown and decay
— sap·ro·phyt·i·cal·ly \-ti-k(ə-)lē\ *adverb*
sap·ro·zo·ic \ˌsa-prə-'zō-ik\ *adjective* (circa 1920)
: SAPROPHYTIC — used of animals (as protozoans)
sap·sa·go \sap-'sā-(ˌ)gō, 'sap-sə-ˌgō\ *noun* [modification of German *Schabziger*] (circa 1846)
: a very hard green skim-milk cheese flavored with the powdered leaves of an aromatic legume (*Trigonella coerulea*)
sap·suck·er \'sap-ˌsə-kər\ *noun* (1805)
: any of a genus (*Sphyrapicus*) of small North American woodpeckers that drill holes in trees in order to obtain sap and insects for food
sap·wood \-ˌwu̇d\ *noun* (1791)
: the younger softer living or physiologically active outer portion of wood that lies between the cambium and the heartwood and is more permeable, less durable, and usually lighter in color than the heartwood
sar·a·band *or* **sar·a·bande** \'sar-ə-ˌband\ *noun* [French *sarabande*, from Spanish *zarabanda*] (1616)
1 : a stately court dance of the 17th and 18th centuries resembling the minuet
2 : the music for the saraband in slow triple time with accent on the second beat
Sar·a·cen \'sar-ə-sən\ *noun* [Middle English, from Old English, from Late Latin *Saracenus*, from Late Greek *Sarakēnos*] (before 12th century)
: a member of a nomadic people of the deserts between Syria and Arabia; *broadly* **:** ARAB
— Saracen *adjective*
— Sar·a·cen·ic \ˌsar-ə-'se-nik\ *adjective*
Sa·rah \'ser-ə, 'sar-ə, 'sā-rə\ *noun* [Hebrew *Śārāh*]
1 : the wife of Abraham and mother of Isaac
2 : a kinswoman of Tobias married to him
sa·ran \sə-'ran\ *noun* [from *Saran*, a trademark] (1940)
: a tough flexible thermoplastic resin
sarape \sə-'rä-pē\ *variant of* SERAPE
Sar·a·to·ga trunk \ˌsar-ə-'tō-gə-\ *noun* [*Saratoga* Springs, N.Y.] (1858)
: a large traveling trunk usually with a rounded top
sarc- *or* **sarco-** *combining form* [Greek *sark-, sarko-*, from *sark-, sarx*]
1 : flesh ⟨*sarc*oid⟩
2 : striated muscle ⟨*sarco*lemma⟩
sar·casm \'sär-ˌka-zəm\ *noun* [French or Late Latin; French *sarcasme*, from Late Latin *sarcasmos*, from Greek *sarkasmos*, from *sarkazein* to tear flesh, bite the lips in rage, sneer, from *sark-, sarx* flesh; probably akin to Avestan *thwaras-* to cut] (1550)
1 : a sharp and often satirical or ironic utterance designed to cut or give pain ⟨tired of continual *sarcasms*⟩
2 a : a mode of satirical wit depending for its effect on bitter, caustic, and often ironic language that is usually directed against an individual **b :** the use or language of sarcasm ⟨this is no time to indulge in *sarcasm*⟩
synonym see WIT
sar·cas·tic \sär-'kas-tik\ *adjective* (1695)
1 : having the character of sarcasm ⟨*sarcastic* criticism⟩
2 : given to the use of sarcasm **:** CAUSTIC ⟨a *sarcastic* critic⟩ ☆
— sar·cas·ti·cal·ly \-ti-k(ə-)lē\ *adverb*
¹sarce·net \'sär-snət\ *noun* [Middle English, from Anglo-French *sarzinett*] (15th century)
: a soft thin silk in plain or twill weaves; *also* **:** a garment made of this
²sarcenet *adjective* (1521)
1 *archaic* **:** made of sarcenet
2 *archaic* **:** soft like sarcenet
sar·coid \'sär-ˌkȯid\ *noun* (1899)
1 : any of various diseases characterized especially by the formation of nodules in the skin

2 : a nodule characteristic of sarcoid or of sarcoidosis
sar·coid·o·sis \ˌsär-ˌkȯi-'dō-səs\ *noun*, *plural* **-o·ses** \-ˌsēz\ [New Latin] (1936)
: a chronic disease of unknown cause that is characterized by the formation of nodules especially in the lymph nodes, lungs, bones, and skin
sar·co·lem·ma \ˌsär-kə-'le-mə\ *noun* [New Latin, from *sarc-* + Greek *lemma* husk — more at LEMMA] (1840)
: the thin transparent homogeneous sheath enclosing a striated muscle fiber
— sar·co·lem·mal \-məl\ *adjective*
sar·co·ma \sär-'kō-mə\ *noun*, *plural* **-mas** *also* **-ma·ta** \-mə-tə\ [New Latin, from Greek *sarkōmat-, sarkōma* fleshy growth, from *sark-oun* to grow flesh, from *sark-, sarx*] (1804)
: a malignant neoplasm arising in tissue of mesodermal origin (as connective tissue, bone, cartilage, or striated muscle)
— sar·co·ma·tous \sär-'kō-mə-təs\ *adjective*
sar·co·ma·to·sis \(ˌ)sär-ˌkō-mə-'tō-səs\ *noun*, *plural* **-to·ses** \-ˌsēz\ [New Latin] (circa 1890)
: a disease characterized by the presence and spread of sarcomas
sar·co·mere \'sär-kə-ˌmir\ *noun* (1891)
: any of the repeating structural units of striated muscle fibrils
sar·coph·a·gus \sär-'kä-fə-gəs\ *noun*, *plural* **-gi** \-ˌgī, -ˌjī, -ˌgē\ *also* **-gus·es** [Latin *sarcophagus (lapis)* limestone used for coffins, from Greek (*lithos*) *sarkophagos*, literally, flesh-eating stone, from *sark-* sarc- + *phagein* to eat — more at BAKSHEESH] (1619)
: a stone coffin; *broadly* **:** COFFIN
sar·co·plasm \'sär-kə-ˌpla-zəm\ *noun* [New Latin *sarcoplasma*] (1899)
: the cytoplasm of a striated muscle fiber
— sar·co·plas·mic \-'plaz-mik\ *adjective*
sarcoplasmic reticulum *noun* (1953)
: the specialized endoplasmic reticulum of cardiac muscle and skeletal striated muscle that functions especially as a storage and release area for calcium
sar·cop·tic mange \(ˌ)sär-ˌkäp-tik-\ *noun* [New Latin *Sarcoptes*, from *sarc-* + Greek *koptein* to cut — more at CAPON] (1886)
: mange caused by mites (genus *Sarcoptes*) burrowing in the skin especially of the head and face
sar·co·some \'sär-kə-ˌsōm\ *noun* [New Latin *sarcosoma*, from *sarc-* + *-soma* -some] (1899)
: a mitochondrion of a striated muscle fiber
— sar·co·som·al \ˌsär-kə-'sō-məl\ *adjective*
sard \'särd\ *noun* [French *sarde*, from Latin *sarda*] (14th century)
: a reddish brown variety of chalcedony sometimes classified as a variety of carnelian
sardar *variant of* SIRDAR
sar·dine \sär-'dēn\ *noun*, *plural* **sardines** *also* **sardine** [Middle English *sardeine*, from

Middle French *sardine,* from Latin *sardina*] (14th century)
1 : any of several small or immature clupeid fishes; *especially* **:** the young of the European pilchard (*Sardina pilchardus*) when of a size suitable for preserving for food
2 : any of various small fishes (as an anchovy) resembling the true sardines or similarly preserved for food
Sar·din·ian \sär-'di-nē-ən, -'din-yən\ *noun* (1598)
1 : a native or inhabitant of Sardinia
2 : the Romance language of central and southern Sardinia
— Sardinian *adjective*
sar·don·ic \sär-'dä-nik\ *adjective* [French *sardonique,* from Greek *sardonios*] (1638)
: disdainfully or skeptically humorous **:** derisively mocking ⟨a *sardonic* comment⟩ ⟨his *sardonic* expression⟩
synonym see SARCASTIC
— sar·don·i·cal·ly \-ni-k(ə-)lē\ *adverb*
sar·don·i·cism \sär-'dä-nə-,si-zəm\ *noun* (1926)
: sardonic quality or humor
sar·don·yx \sär-'dä-niks *also* 'sär-d°n-iks\ *noun* [Middle English *sardonix,* from Latin *sardonyx,* from Greek] (14th century)
: an onyx having parallel layers of sard
sar·gas·so \sär-'ga-(,)sō\ *noun, plural* **-sos** [Portuguese *sargaço*] (1598)
1 : GULFWEED, SARGASSUM
2 : a mass of floating vegetation and especially sargassums
sar·gas·sum \sär-'ga-səm\ *noun* [New Latin, genus name, from International Scientific Vocabulary *sargasso*] (circa 1890)
: any of a genus (*Sargassum*) of brown algae that have a branching thallus with lateral outgrowths differentiated as leafy segments, air bladders, or spore-bearing structures **:** GULFWEED
sarge \'särj\ *noun* [by shortening & alteration] (1867)
: SERGEANT
sa·ri *also* **sa·ree** \'sär-ē\ *noun* [Hindi *sāṛī,* from Sanskrit *śāṭī* strip of cloth] (1785)
: a garment of southern Asian women that consists of several yards of lightweight cloth draped so that one end forms a skirt and the other a head or shoulder covering
sa·rin \'sär-ən, zä-'rēn\ *noun* [German] (1951)
: an extremely toxic chemical warfare agent $C_4H_{10}FO_2P$ that is a powerful cholinesterase inhibitor
sark \'särk\ *noun* [Middle English (Scots) *serk,* from Old English *serc;* akin to Old Norse *serkr* shirt] (before 12th century)
dialect chiefly British **:** SHIRT
sa·rod *also* **sa·rode** \sə-'rōd\ *noun* [Hindi *sarod,* from Persian] (1865)
: a lute of northern India
— sa·rod·ist \-'rō-dist\ *noun*
sa·rong \sə-'ròŋ, -'räŋ\ *noun* [Malay] (1830)
: a loose garment made of a long strip of cloth wrapped around the body that is worn as a skirt or dress by men and women chiefly of the Malay Archipelago and the Pacific islands
Sar·pe·don \sär-'pē-d°n\ *noun* [Latin, from Greek *Sarpēdōn*]
: a son of Zeus and Europa and king of Lycia killed in the Trojan War
sar·ra·ce·nia \,sar-ə-'sē-nē-ə, -'se-\ *noun* [New Latin, from Michel *Sarrazin* (died 1734) French physician & naturalist] (1884)
: any of a genus (*Sarracenia* of the family Sarraceniaceae) that includes the insectivorous bog pitcher plants of eastern North America
sar·sa·pa·ril·la \,sas-pə-'ri-lə, ,särs-, -'re-, ,sa-sə-, ,sär-sə-\ *noun* [Spanish *zarzaparrilla,*

from *zarza* bush + *parrilla,* diminutive of *parra* vine] (1577)
1 a : any of various tropical American greenbriers **b :** the dried roots of a sarsaparilla used especially as a flavoring
2 : any of various plants (as wild sarsaparilla) that resemble or are used as a substitute for sarsaparilla
3 : a sweetened carbonated beverage flavored with sassafras and oil distilled from a European birch
sarsenet *variant of* SARCENET
sar·to·ri·al \sär-'tòr-ē-əl, sə(r)-, -'tòr-\ *adjective* [Medieval Latin *sartor*] (1823)
: of or relating to a tailor or tailored clothes; *broadly* **:** of or relating to clothes
— sar·to·ri·al·ly \-ē-ə-lē\ *adverb*
sar·to·ri·us \sär-'tòr-ē-əs, -'tòr-\ *noun, plural* **-rii** \-ē-,ī, -ē-,ē\ [New Latin, from Medieval Latin *sartor* tailor, from Latin *sarcire* to mend] (1704)
: a muscle that crosses the front of the thigh obliquely, assists in rotating the leg to the cross-legged position in which the knees are spread wide apart, and in humans is the longest muscle
Sar·um \'sar-əm, 'ser-\ *adjective* [*Sarum,* old borough near Salisbury, England] (1570)
: of or relating to the Roman rite as modified in Salisbury and used in England, Wales, and Ireland before the Reformation
¹sash \'sash\ *noun* [Arabic *shāsh* muslin] (1681)
: a band worn about the waist or over one shoulder and used as a dress accessory or the emblem of an honorary or military order
— sashed \'sasht\ *adjective*
²sash *noun, plural* **sash** *also* **sash·es** [probably modification of French *châssis* chassis (taken as plural)] (1681)
: the framework in which panes of glass are set in a window or door; *also* **:** such a framework together with its panes forming a usually movable part of a window
¹sa·shay \sa-'shā *also* sī-\ *intransitive verb* [alteration of *chassé*] (1836)
1 : to make a chassé
2 a : WALK, GLIDE, GO **b :** to strut or move about in an ostentatious or conspicuous manner **c :** to proceed or move in a diagonal or sideways manner
²sashay *noun* [by alteration] (1900)
1 : TRIP, EXCURSION
2 : a square-dance figure in which partners sidestep in a circle around each other with the man moving behind the woman
3 : CHASSÉ
sa·shi·mi \'sä-shə-mē\ *noun* [Japanese] (1880)
: a Japanese dish consisting of thinly sliced raw fish served with a sauce for dipping
sas·ka·toon \,sas-kə-'tün\ *noun* [modification of Cree *misa·skwato·min* serviceberry fruit] (1810)
: SERVICEBERRY
Sas·quatch \'sas-,kwach, -,kwäch\ *noun* [Halkomelem (Salishan language of southwestern British Columbia) *sésq̓ac*] (1929)
: a hairy creature like a human being reported to exist in the northwestern U.S. and western Canada and said to be a primate between 6 and 15 feet (1.8 and 4.6 meters) tall — called *also* bigfoot
¹sass \'sas\ *noun* [alteration of ¹*sauce*] (1835)
: impudent speech ◇
²sass *transitive verb* (1856)
: to talk impudently or disrespectfully to
sas·sa·fras \'sa-sə-,fras\ *noun* [Spanish *sasafrás*] (1577)
1 : an eastern North American tree (*Sassafras albidum*) of the laurel family having both ovate and lobed aromatic leaves
2 : the carcinogenic dried root bark of the sassafras used formerly as a diaphoretic or flavoring agent
¹Sas·sa·ni·an *or* **Sa·sa·ni·an** \sə-'sā-nē-ən, sa-'sā-\ *adjective* (1788)

: of, relating to, or having the characteristics of the Sassanid dynasty of ancient Persia or its art or architecture
²Sassanian *or* **Sasanian** *noun* (1855)
: SASSANID
Sas·sa·nid *or* **Sa·sa·nid** \sə-'sä-nəd, -'sa-; 'sa-s°n-əd\ *noun* [New Latin *Sassanidae* Sassanids, from *Sassan,* founder of the dynasty] (1776)
: a member of a dynasty of Persian kings of the 3d to 7th centuries
— Sassanid *or* **Sasanid** *adjective*
sassy \'sa-sē\ *adjective* **sass·i·er; -est** [alteration of *saucy*] (1833)
1 : IMPUDENT, SAUCY
2 : VIGOROUS, LIVELY
3 : distinctively smart and stylish ⟨a *sassy* black-and-white bow tie —Jean Stafford⟩
sat *past and past participle of* SIT
Sa·tan \'sā-t°n\ *noun* [Middle English, from Old English, from Late Latin, from Greek, from Hebrew *śāṭān* adversary] (before 12th century)
: the adversary of God and lord of evil in Judaism and Christianity
sa·tang \sə-'täŋ\ *noun, plural* **satang** *or* **satangs** [Thai *sataŋ*] (circa 1915)
— see *baht* at MONEY table
sa·tan·ic \sə-'ta-nik, sā-\ *adjective* (1667)
1 : of, relating to, or characteristic of Satan or satanism ⟨*satanic* pride⟩ ⟨*satanic* rites⟩
2 : characterized by extreme cruelty or viciousness
— sa·tan·i·cal·ly \-ni-k(ə-)lē\ *adverb*
sa·tan·ism \'sā-t°n-,i-zəm\ *noun, often capitalized* (1565)
1 : innate wickedness **:** DIABOLISM
2 : obsession with or affinity for evil; *specifically* **:** the worship of Satan marked by the travesty of Christian rites
— sa·tan·ist \-ist\ *noun, often capitalized*
satch·el \'sa-chəl\ *noun* [Middle English *sachel,* from Middle French, from Late Latin *saccellum,* diminutive of Latin *sacculus,* diminutive of *saccus* bag — more at SACK] (14th century)
: a small bag often with a shoulder strap
— satch·el·ful \-,fúl\ *noun*
¹sate \'sāt, 'sat\ *archaic past of* SIT

◇ **WORD HISTORY**

sass The pronunciation of the *au* in *sauce, saucer,* and *sausage* with \a\ rather than the \ò\ that most Americans and Britons have in these words is the result of a change that took place in English toward the end of the Middle Ages, when the diphthong (vowel combination) \aú\ that *au* then represented lost its final element and changed to a short *a* sound. By the 17th century, some Englishmen were pronouncing *sauce* to rhyme with *pass.* This pronunciation was brought to the thirteen American colonies, where the spelling *sas* appears for *sauce* by 1775. This word differed not only in pronunciation but in meaning from what we now think of as *sauce:* it usually denoted a side dish of vegetables or stewed fruit rather than a liquid garnish. In the 19th century United States there was *long sass* (carrots, parsnips, and beets) and *short sass* (potatoes, onions, and turnips). Aside from *applesauce* and *cranberry sauce* these usages are now passing away, but *sass* in the sense "impudent speech," along with its derivative *sassy,* still survives, and many people no longer associate the two words *sass* and *sauce.*

²sate \'sāt\ *transitive verb* **sat·ed; sat·ing** [probably by shortening & alteration from *satiate*] (1602)
1 : to cloy with overabundance **:** GLUT
2 : to appease (as a thirst) by indulging to the full
synonym see SATIATE

sa·teen \sa-'tēn, sə-\ *noun* [alteration of *satin*] (circa 1878)
: a smooth durable lustrous fabric usually made of cotton in satin weave

sat·el·lite \'sa-t°l-,īt\ *noun* [Middle French, from Latin *satellit-, satelles* attendant] (circa 1548)
1 : a hired agent or obsequious follower **:** MINION, SYCOPHANT
2 a : a celestial body orbiting another of larger size **b :** a manufactured object or vehicle intended to orbit the earth, the moon, or another celestial body
3 : someone or something attendant, subordinate, or dependent; *especially* **:** a country politically and economically dominated or controlled by another more powerful country
4 : a usually independent urban community situated near but not immediately adjacent to a large city
— **satellite** *adjective*

satellite DNA *noun* (1969)
: a fraction of a eukaryotic organism's DNA that differs in density from most of its DNA as determined by centrifugation, that apparently consists of short repetitive nucleotide sequences, that does not undergo transcription, and that in some organisms (as the mouse) is found especially in centromeric regions

sa·tem \'sä-təm\ *adjective* [Avestan *satəm* hundred; from the fact that its initial sound (derived from an alveolar fricative) is the representative of an Indo-European palatal stop — more at HUNDRED] (1901)
: of, relating to, or constituting an Indo-European language group in which the palatal stops became in prehistoric times palatal or alveolar fricatives — compare CENTUM

sa·ti \(,)sə-'tē, 'sə-,tē\ *variant of* SUTTEE

sa·tia·ble \'sā-shə-bəl\ *adjective* (1570)
: capable of being appeased or satisfied

¹sa·tiate \'sā-sh(ē-)ət\ *adjective* (15th century)
: filled to satiety

²sa·ti·ate \'sā-shē-,āt\ *transitive verb* **-at·ed; -at·ing** [Latin *satiatus*, past participle of *satiare*, from *satis* enough — more at SAD] (15th century)
: to satisfy (as a need or desire) fully or to excess ☆
— **sa·ti·a·tion** \,sā-shē-'ā-shən, ,sā-sē-\ *noun*

sa·ti·ety \sə-'tī-ə-tē *also* 'sā-sh(ē-)ə-\ *noun* [Middle French *satieté*, from Latin *satietat-, satietas*, from *satis*] (1533)
1 : the quality or state of being fed or gratified to or beyond capacity **:** SURFEIT, FULLNESS
2 : the revulsion or disgust caused by overindulgence or excess

¹sat·in \'sa-t°n\ *noun* [Middle English, from Middle French, probably from Arabic *zaytūnī*, literally, of Zaytūn, seaport in China during the Middle Ages] (14th century)
: a fabric (as of silk) in satin weave with lustrous face and dull back

²satin *adjective* (1521)
1 : made of or covered with satin
2 : suggestive of satin especially in smooth lustrous appearance or sleekness to touch

sat·in·et \,sa-t°n-'et\ *noun* (1703)
1 : a thin silk satin or imitation satin
2 : a variation of satin weave used in making satinet

satin stitch *noun* (1684)
: an embroidery stitch nearly alike on both sides and worked so closely as to resemble satin

satin weave *noun* (circa 1883)

: a weave in which warp threads interlace with filling threads to produce a smooth-faced fabric

satin stitch

sat·in·wood \'sa-t°n-,wùd\ *noun* (1792)
1 a : an East Indian tree (*Chloroxylon swietenia*) of the rue family that yields a lustrous yellowish brown wood **b :** a tree (as *Zanthoxylum flavum* of the rue family) with wood resembling true satinwood
2 : the wood of a satinwood

sat·iny \'sat-nē, 'sa-t°n-ē\ *adjective* (1786)
: having or resembling the soft usually lustrous smoothness of satin

sat·ire \'sa-,tīr\ *noun* [Middle French or Latin; Middle French, from Latin *satura, satira*, perhaps from (*lanx*) *satura* dish of mixed ingredients, from feminine of *satur* well-fed; akin to Latin *satis* enough — more at SAD] (1501)
1 : a literary work holding up human vices and follies to ridicule or scorn
2 : trenchant wit, irony, or sarcasm used to expose and discredit vice or folly
synonym see WIT

sa·tir·ic \sə-'tir-ik\ *or* **sa·tir·i·cal** \-i-kəl\ *adjective* (1509)
1 : of, relating to, or constituting satire ⟨*satiric* writers⟩
2 : manifesting or given to satire
synonym see SARCASTIC
— **sa·tir·i·cal·ly** \-i-k(ə-)lē\ *adverb*

sat·i·rise *British variant of* SATIRIZE

sat·i·rist \'sa-tə-rist\ *noun* (1589)
: one that satirizes; *especially* **:** a writer of satire

sat·i·rize \-,rīz\ *verb* **-rized; -riz·ing** (1601)
intransitive verb
: to utter or write satire
transitive verb
: to censure or ridicule by means of satire
— **sat·i·ri·za·ble** \,sa-tə-'rī-zə-bəl\ *adjective*

sat·is·fac·tion \,sa-təs-'fak-shən\ *noun* [Middle English, from Middle French, from Late Latin *satisfaction-, satisfactio*, from Latin, reparation, amends, from *satisfacere* to satisfy] (14th century)
1 a : the payment through penance of the temporal punishment incurred by a sin **b :** reparation for sin that meets the demands of divine justice
2 a : fulfillment of a need or want **b :** the quality or state of being satisfied **:** CONTENTMENT **c :** a source or means of enjoyment **:** GRATIFICATION
3 a : compensation for a loss or injury **:** ATONEMENT, RESTITUTION **b :** the discharge of a legal obligation or claim **c :** VINDICATION
4 : convinced assurance or certainty ⟨proved to the *satisfaction* of the court⟩

sat·is·fac·to·ry \,sa-təs-'fak-t(ə-)rē\ *adjective* (15th century)
: giving satisfaction **:** ADEQUATE
— **sat·is·fac·to·ri·ly** \-t(ə-)rə-lē\ *adverb*
— **sat·is·fac·to·ri·ness** *noun*

sat·is·fi·able \'sa-təs-,fī-ə-bəl\ *adjective* (1609)
: capable of being satisfied

sat·is·fy \'sa-təs-,fī\ *verb* **-fied; -fy·ing** [Middle English *satisfien*, from Middle French *satisfier*, modification of Latin *satisfacere*, from *satis* enough + *facere* to do, make — more at SAD, DO] (15th century)
transitive verb
1 a : to carry out the terms of (as a contract) **:** DISCHARGE **b :** to meet a financial obligation to
2 : to make reparation to (an injured party) **:** INDEMNIFY
3 a : to make happy **:** PLEASE **b :** to gratify to the full **:** APPEASE
4 a : CONVINCE **b :** to put an end to (doubt or uncertainty) **:** DISPEL

5 a : to conform to (as specifications) **:** be adequate to (an end in view) **b :** to make true by fulfilling a condition ⟨values that *satisfy* an equation⟩ ⟨*satisfy* a hypothesis⟩
intransitive verb
: to be adequate **:** SUFFICE; *also* **:** PLEASE
synonym see PAY
— **sat·is·fy·ing·ly** \-iŋ-lē\ *adverb*

sa·to·ri \sə-'tōr-ē, sä-, -'tòr-\ *noun* [Japanese] (1727)
: a state of intuitive illumination sought in Zen Buddhism

sa·trap \'sā-,trap *also* 'sa-,trap *or* 'sa-trəp\ *noun* [Middle English, from Latin *satrapes*, from Greek *satrapēs*, from Old Persian *khshathrapāvan*, literally, protector of the dominion] (14th century)
1 : the governor of a province in ancient Persia
2 a : RULER **b :** a subordinate official **:** HENCHMAN

sa·tra·py \'sā-trə-pē, 'sa-, -,tra-pē\ *noun, plural* **-pies** (1603)
: the territory or jurisdiction of a satrap

sat·su·ma \sat-'sü-mə, 'sat-sə-\ *noun* [*Satsuma*, former province in Kyushu, Japan] (1882)
1 : any of several cultivated mandarin trees that bear medium-sized largely seedless fruits with thin smooth skin
2 : the fruit of a satsuma

sat·u·ra·ble \'sach-rə-bəl, 'sa-chə-\ *adjective* (1570)
: capable of being saturated

sat·u·rant \-rənt\ *noun* (circa 1775)
: something that saturates

¹sat·u·rate \'sa-chə-,rāt\ *transitive verb* **-rat·ed; -rat·ing** [Latin *saturatus*, past participle of *saturare*, from *satur* well-fed — more at SATIRE] (1538)
1 : to satisfy fully **:** SATIATE
2 : to treat, furnish, or charge with something to the point where no more can be absorbed, dissolved, or retained ⟨water *saturated* with salt⟩
3 a : to fill completely with something that permeates or pervades ⟨book is *saturated* with Hollywood, old and new —Newgate Callendar⟩ **b :** to load to capacity
4 : to cause to combine till there is no further tendency to combine
synonym see SOAK
— **sat·u·ra·tor** \-,rā-tər\ *noun*

²sat·u·rate \'sach-rət, 'sa-chə-\ *adjective* (1782)
: SATURATED

sat·u·rat·ed \'sa-chə-,rā-təd\ *adjective* (1728)
1 : full of moisture **:** made thoroughly wet
2 a : being a solution that is unable to absorb or dissolve any more of a solute at a given temperature and pressure **b :** being an organic compound having no double or triple bonds between carbon atoms
3 *of a color* **:** having high saturation **:** PURE

sat·u·ra·tion \,sa-chə-'rā-shən\ *noun* (circa 1554)
1 a : the act of saturating **:** the state of being saturated **b :** SATIETY, SURFEIT
2 : conversion of an unsaturated to a saturated chemical compound (as by hydrogenation)
3 : a state of maximum impregnation: as **a :** complete infiltration **:** PERMEATION **b :** the presence in air of the most water possible under existent pressure and temperature **c :** magnetization to the point beyond which a further increase in the intensity of the magnetizing force will produce no further magnetization
4 a : chromatic purity **:** freedom from dilution with white **b** (1) **:** degree of difference from the gray having the same lightness — used of an object color (2) **:** degree of difference from the achromatic light-source color of the same brightness — used of a light-source color; compare HUE 2c
5 : the supplying of a market with as much of a product as it will absorb
6 : an overwhelming concentration of military forces or firepower
Sat·ur·day \'sa-tər-dē, -(,)dā\ *noun* [Middle English *saterday*, from Old English *sæterndæg* (akin to Old Frisian *sāterdei*), from Latin *Saturnus* Saturn + Old English *dæg* day] (before 12th century)
: the seventh day of the week
— **Sat·ur·days** \-dēz, -(,)dāz\ *adverb*
Saturday night special *noun* (1968)
: a cheap easily concealed handgun
Sat·urn \'sa-tərn\ *noun* [Latin *Saturnus*]
1 : a Roman god of agriculture and father by Ops of Jupiter
2 : the planet 6th in order from the sun — see PLANET table
sat·ur·na·lia \,sa-tər-'nāl-yə, -'nā-lē-ə\ *noun plural but singular or plural in construction* [Latin, from neuter plural of *saturnalis* of Saturn, from *Saturnus*] (1591)
1 *capitalized* **:** the festival of Saturn in ancient Rome beginning on Dec. 17
2 *singular, plural* **saturnalias** *also* **saturnalia a :** an unrestrained often licentious celebration **:** ORGY **b :** EXCESS, EXTRAVAGANCE
— **sat·ur·na·lian** \-'nāl-yən, -'nā-lē-ən\ *adjective*
— **sat·ur·na·lian·ly** *adverb*
Sa·tur·ni·an \sa-'tər-nē-ən, sə-\ *adjective* (1557)
1 : of, relating to, or influenced by the planet Saturn
2 *archaic* **:** of or relating to the god Saturn or the golden age of his reign
sa·tur·ni·id \-nē-əd\ *noun* [New Latin *Saturniidae*, from *Saturnia*, genus of moths, from Latin, daughter of the god Saturn] (circa 1909)
: any of a family (Saturniidae) of usually large stout strong-winged moths (as a luna moth or a cecropia moth) with hairy bodies
— **saturniid** *adjective*
sat·ur·nine \'sa-tər-,nīn\ *adjective* (15th century)
1 : born under or influenced astrologically by the planet Saturn
2 a : cold and steady in mood **:** slow to act or change **b :** of a gloomy or surly disposition **c :** having a sardonic aspect ⟨a *saturnine* smile⟩
synonym SEE SULLEN
sat·urn·ism \'sa-tər-,ni-zəm\ *noun* [*saturn* lead] (1855)
: LEAD POISONING
sa·tya·gra·ha \(,)sə-'tyä-grə-hə, 'sə-tyə-\ *noun* [New Sanskrit *satyāgraha*, from Sanskrit *satya* truth + *āgraha* persistence] (1920)
: pressure for social and political reform through friendly passive resistance practiced by M. K. Gandhi and his followers in India
sa·tyr \'sā-tər, *chiefly British* 'sa-\ *noun* [Middle English, from Latin *satyrus*, from Greek *satyros*]
1 *often capitalized* **:** a sylvan deity in Greek mythology having certain characteristics of a horse or goat and fond of Dionysian revelry

2 a : a lecherous man **b :** one having satyriasis
3 : any of various usually brown and gray satyrid butterflies
— **sa·tyr·ic** \sə-'tir-ik, sə-, sa-\ *adjective*
sa·ty·ri·a·sis \,sā-tə-'rī-ə-səs, ,sa-\ *noun* [Late Latin, from Greek, from *satyros*] (15th century)
: excessive or abnormal sexual craving in the male
sa·ty·rid \sə-'tī-rəd\ *noun* [New Latin *Satyridae*, ultimately from Greek *satyros*] (1901)
: any of a family (Satyridae) of usually brownish butterflies that feed on grasses as larvae and have one or more forewing veins swollen basally
— **satyrid** *adjective*
satyr play *noun* (1929)
: a comic play of ancient Greece burlesquing a mythological subject and having a chorus representing satyrs
¹sauce \'sȯs, *usually* 'sas *for 4*\ *noun* [Middle English, from Middle French, from Latin *salsa*, feminine of *salsus* salted, from past participle of *sallere* to salt, from *sal* salt — more at SALT] (14th century)
1 : a condiment or relish for food; *especially* **:** a fluid dressing or topping
2 : something that adds zest or piquancy
3 : stewed fruit eaten with other food or as a dessert
4 : pert or impudent language or actions
5 *slang* **:** LIQUOR — used with *the*
²sauce \'sȯs, *usually* 'sas *for 3*\ *transitive verb* **sauced; sauc·ing** (15th century)
1 a : to dress with relish or seasoning **b :** to cover or serve with a sauce
2 a *archaic* **:** to modify the harsh or unpleasant characteristics of **b :** to give zest or piquancy to
3 : to be rude or impudent to
sauce·boat \'sȯs-,bōt\ *noun* (1747)
: a low boat-shaped pitcher for serving sauces and gravies
sauce·box \'sȯs-,bäks, 'sas-\ *noun* (1588)
: a saucy impudent person
sauce·pan \'sȯs-,pan, *especially British* -pən\ *noun* (1686)
: a small deep cooking pan with a handle
sau·cer \'sȯ-sər\ *noun* [Middle English, plate containing sauce, from Middle French *saussier*, from *sausse, sauce*] (1607)
1 : a small shallow dish in which a cup is set at table
2 : something resembling a saucer especially in shape; *especially* **:** FLYING SAUCER
— **sau·cer·like** \-,līk\ *adjective*
saucy \'sȯ-sē, 'sa-\ *adjective* **sauc·i·er; -est** (1508)
1 : served with or having the consistency of sauce
2 a : impertinently bold and impudent **b :** amusingly forward and flippant **:** IRREPRESSIBLE
3 : SMART, TRIM ⟨a *saucy* little hat⟩
— **sauc·i·ly** \-sə-lē\ *adverb*
— **sauc·i·ness** \-sē-nəs\ *noun*
sau·er·bra·ten \'saú-(ə)r-,brä-t⁰n\ *noun* [German, from *sauer* sour + *Braten* roast meat] (1889)
: oven-roasted or pot-roasted beef marinated before cooking in vinegar with peppercorns, garlic, onions, and bay leaves
sau·er·kraut \'saú-(ə)r-,kraút\ *noun* [German, from *sauer* sour + *Kraut* greens] (1617)
: cabbage cut fine and fermented in a brine made of its own juice with salt
sau·ger \'sȯ-gər\ *noun* [origin unknown] (1882)
: a pike perch (*Stizostedion canadense*) similar to but smaller than the walleye
saugh *or* **sauch** \'säk, 'sȯk\ *noun* [Middle English (Scots) *sauch*, from Old English *salh*, alteration of *sealh* — more at SALLOW] (before 12th century)
chiefly Scottish **:** SALLOW

Sauk \'sȯk\ *noun, plural* **Sauk** *or* **Sauks** (1762)
: a member of an American Indian people formerly living in what is now Wisconsin
Saul \'sȯl\ *noun* [Late Latin *Saulus*, from Greek *Saulos*, from Hebrew *Shā'ūl*]
1 : the first king of Israel
2 : the apostle Paul — called also *Saul of Tarsus*
sau·na \'sȯ-nə, 'saú-nə\ *noun* [Finnish] (1891)
1 : a Finnish steam bath in which the steam is provided by water thrown on hot stones; *also* **:** a bathhouse or room used for such a bath
2 : a dry heat bath; *also* **:** a room or cabinet used for such a bath
saun·ter \'sȯn-tər, 'sän-\ *intransitive verb* [probably from Middle English *santren* to muse] (circa 1667)
: to walk about in an idle or leisurely manner **:** STROLL
— **saunter** *noun*
— **saun·ter·er** \-tər-ər\ *noun*
sau·rel \sȯ-'rel\ *noun* [French, from Late Latin *saurus* horse mackerel, from Greek *sauros* horse mackerel, lizard] (1882)
: JACK MACKEREL
sau·ri·an \'sȯr-ē-ən\ *noun* [New Latin *Sauria*, from New Latin *saurus* lizard, from Greek *sauros*] (circa 1829)
: any of a suborder (Sauria) of reptiles including the lizards and in older classifications the crocodiles and various extinct forms (as the dinosaurs and ichthyosaurs) that resemble lizards
— **saurian** *adjective*
sau·ris·chi·an \(,)sȯ-'ris-kē-ən\ *noun* [New Latin *Saurischia*, from Greek *sauros* lizard + New Latin *ischium* ischium] (circa 1891)
: any of an order (Saurischia) of herbivorous or carnivorous dinosaurs (as a brontosaurus) that have a triradiate pelvis with the pubis typically pointed forward — compare ORNITHISCHIAN
— **saurischian** *adjective*
sau·ro·pod \'sȯr-ə-,päd\ *noun* [New Latin *Sauropoda*, from Greek *sauros* lizard + New Latin *-poda*] (circa 1891)
: any of a suborder (Sauropoda) of quadrupedal saurischian dinosaurs comprising herbivorous forms with a long neck and tail, small head, and more or less plantigrade 5-toed limbs
— **sauropod** *adjective*
sau·ry \'sȯr-ē\ *noun, plural* **sauries** [New Latin *saurus* lizard] (circa 1771)
1 : a slender long-beaked fish (*Scombresox saurus*) related to the needlefishes and found in temperate parts of the Atlantic
2 : a widely distributed fish (*Cololabris saira*) of the Pacific similar to the related Atlantic saury
sau·sage \'sȯ-sij\ *noun* [Middle English *sausige*, from Old North French *saussiche*, from Late Latin *salsicia*, from Latin *salsus* salted — more at SAUCE] (15th century)
: a highly seasoned minced meat (as pork) usually stuffed in casings of prepared animal intestine; *also* **:** a link or patty of sausage
¹sau·té *also* **sau·te** \sȯ-'tā, sō-\ *noun* [French, from past participle of *sauter* to jump, from Latin *saltare* — more at SALTATION] (1813)
: a sautéed dish
— **sauté** *adjective*
²sauté *also* **saute** *transitive verb* **sau·téed** *or* **sau·téd; sau·té·ing** (1859)
: to fry in a small amount of fat
sau·ternes \sō-'tərn, sȯ-, -'tern\ *noun, often capitalized* [French, from *Sauternes*, commune in France] (1711)

\ə\ abut \ᵊ\ kitten \ər\ further \a\ ash \ā\ ace
\ä\ mop, mar \aú\ out \ch\ chin \e\ bet \ē\ easy
\g\ go \i\ hit \ī\ ice \j\ job \ŋ\ sing \ō\ go
\ȯ\ law \ȯi\ boy \th\ thin \t͟h\ the \ü\ loot \ú\ foot
\y\ yet \zh\ vision *see also* Guide to Pronunciation

1 : a full-bodied sweet white wine from the Bordeaux region of France

2 *usually* **sauterne** : a semidry to semisweet American white wine that is a blend of several grapes

sau·vi·gnon blanc \ˌsō-vēn-'yōⁿ-'blä\ *noun* [French, white sauvignon (variety of grape)] (1941)

: a dry white wine made from a grape originally grown in Bordeaux and the Loire valley

¹**sav·age** \'sa-vij\ *adjective* [Middle English *sauvage*, from Middle French, from Medieval Latin *salvaticus*, alteration of Latin *silvaticus* of the woods, wild, from *silva* wood, forest] (13th century)

1 a : not domesticated or under human control : UNTAMED ⟨*savage* beasts⟩ **b** : lacking the restraints normal to civilized human beings : FIERCE, FEROCIOUS

2 : WILD, UNCULTIVATED ⟨seldom have I seen such *savage* scenery —Douglas Carruthers⟩

3 a : BOORISH, RUDE ⟨the *savage* bad manners of most motorists —M. P. O'Connor⟩ **b** : MALICIOUS

4 : lacking complex or advanced culture : UNCIVILIZED ◇

synonym see FIERCE

— **sav·age·ly** *adverb*

— **sav·age·ness** *noun*

²**savage** *noun* (15th century)

1 : a person belonging to a primitive society

2 : a brutal person

3 : a rude or unmannerly person

³**savage** *transitive verb* **sav·aged; sav·ag·ing** (1880)

: to attack or treat brutally

sav·age·ry \'sa-vij-rē, -vi-jə-\ *noun, plural* **-ries** (1595)

1 a : the quality of being savage **b** : an act of cruelty or violence

2 : an uncivilized state

sav·ag·ism \'sa-vi-ˌji-zəm\ *noun* (1796)
: SAVAGERY

sa·van·na *also* **sa·van·nah** \sə-'va-nə\ *noun* [Spanish *zavana*, from Taino *zabana*] (1555)

1 : a treeless plain especially in Florida

2 : a tropical or subtropical grassland containing scattered trees and drought-resistant undergrowth

sa·vant \sa-'vänt, sə-, -'väⁿ; sə-'vant, 'sa-vənt\ *noun* [French, from Middle French, from present participle of *savoir* to know, from Latin *sapere* to be wise — more at SAGE] (1719)

1 : a person of learning; *especially* : one with detailed knowledge in some specialized field (as of science or literature)

2 : IDIOT SAVANT 1

sav·a·rin \'sa-və-rən\ *noun* [French, from Anthelme Brillat-*Savarin* (died 1826) French politician, writer, and gourmet] (1877)

: a rich yeast cake baked in a ring mold and soaked in a rum or kirsch syrup

sa·vate \sə-'vät, sa-, -'vat\ *noun* [French, literally, old shoe] (1862)

: a form of boxing in which blows are delivered with either the hands or the feet

¹**save** \'sāv\ *verb* **saved; sav·ing** [Middle English, from Old French *salver*, from Late Latin *salvare*, from Latin *salvus* safe — more at SAFE] (13th century)

transitive verb

1 a : to deliver from sin **b** : to rescue or deliver from danger or harm **c** : to preserve or guard from injury, destruction, or loss

2 a : to put aside as a store or reserve : ACCUMULATE **b** : to spend less by ⟨*save* 25%⟩

3 a : to make unnecessary : AVOID ⟨it *saves* an hour's driving⟩ **b** (1) : to keep from being lost to an opponent (2) : to prevent an opponent from scoring or winning

4 : MAINTAIN, PRESERVE ⟨*save* appearances⟩

intransitive verb

1 : to rescue or deliver someone

2 a : to put aside money **b** : to avoid unnecessary waste or expense : ECONOMIZE **c** : to spend less money ⟨buy now and *save*⟩

3 : to make a save

synonym see RESCUE

— **sav·able** *or* **save·able** \'sā-və-bəl\ *adjective*

— **sav·er** *noun*

²**save** *noun* (1890)

1 : a play that prevents an opponent from scoring or winning

2 : the action of a relief pitcher in baseball in successfully protecting a team's lead

³**save** *preposition* [Middle English *sauf*, from Middle French, from *sauf*, adjective, safe — more at SAFE] (14th century)

: other than : BUT, EXCEPT ⟨no hope *save* one⟩

⁴**save** *conjunction* (14th century)

1 : except for the fact that : ONLY — used with *that* ⟨of his earlier years little is known, *save* that he studied violin —J. N. Burk⟩

2 : BUT, EXCEPT — used before a word often taken to be the subject of a clause ⟨no one knows about it *save* she⟩

save-all \'sā-və-ˌvȯl\ *noun* (circa 1645)

: something that prevents waste, loss, or damage (as a receptacle for catching waste products for further utilization)

sav·e·loy \'sa-və-ˌlȯi\ *noun* [modification of French *cervelas*, from Middle French, from Old Italian *cervellata*, literally, pig's brains, from *cervello* brain, from Latin *cerebellum* — more at CEREBELLUM] (1837)

British : a ready-cooked highly seasoned dry sausage

sav·in \'sa-vən\ *noun* [Middle English, from Middle French *savine*, from Latin (*herba*) *sabina*, literally, Sabine plant] (14th century)

1 : a Eurasian juniper (*Juniperus sabina*) with dark foliage and small yellowish green berries

2 : RED CEDAR 1

¹**sav·ing** \'sā-viŋ\ *noun* [Middle English, from gerund of *saven* to save] (14th century)

1 : preservation from danger or destruction : DELIVERANCE

2 : the act or an instance of economizing

3 a *plural* : money put by **b** : the excess of income over consumption expenditures — often used in plural **c** : a usually specified lower cost — often used in plural ⟨a *savings* of 50%⟩

²**saving** *preposition* [Middle English, from present participle of *saven*] (14th century)

1 : EXCEPT, SAVE

2 : without disrespect to

³**saving** *conjunction* (15th century)
: EXCEPT, SAVE

saving grace *noun* (1597)
: a redeeming quality or factor

savings account *noun* (1911)

: an account (as in a bank) on which interest is usually paid and from which withdrawals can be made usually only by presentation of a passbook or by written authorization on a prescribed form

savings and loan association *noun* (circa 1924)

: a cooperative association organized to hold savings of members in the form of dividend-bearing shares and to invest chiefly in home mortgage loans

savings bank *noun* (1817)

: a bank organized to hold funds of individual depositors in interest-bearing accounts and to make long-term investments (as in home mortgage loans)

savings bond *noun* (1948)

: a nontransferable registered U.S. bond issued in denominations of $50 to $10,000

sav·ior *or* **sav·iour** \'sāv-yər *also* -ˌyȯr\ *noun* [Middle English *saveour*, from Middle French, from Late Latin *salvator*, from *salvare* to save] (14th century)

1 : one that saves from danger or destruction

2 : one who brings salvation; *specifically, capitalized* : JESUS 1

sa·voir faire \ˌsav-ˌwär-'far, -'fer\ *noun* [French *savoir-faire*, literally, knowing how to do] (1815)

: capacity for appropriate action; *especially* : a polished sureness in social behavior

synonym see TACT

¹**sa·vor** *also* **sa·vour** \'sā-vər\ *noun* [Middle English, from Old French, from Latin *sapor*, from *sapere* to taste — more at SAGE] (13th century)

1 : the taste or smell of something

2 : a particular flavor or smell

3 : a distinctive quality

— **sa·vor·less** \-ləs\ *adjective*

— **sa·vor·ous** \'sā-vər-əs, 'säv-rəs\ *adjective*

²**savor** *also* **savour** *verb* **sa·vored; sa·vor·ing** \'sā-vər-iŋ, 'säv-riŋ\ (14th century)

intransitive verb

: to have a specified smell or quality : SMACK

transitive verb

1 : to give flavor to : SEASON

2 a : to have experience of : TASTE **b** : to taste or smell with pleasure : RELISH **c** : to delight in : ENJOY

— **sa·vor·er** \'sā-vər-ər\ *noun*

¹**sa·vory** *also* **sa·voury** \'sā-və-rē, 'säv-rē\ *adjective* (13th century)

: having savor: as **a** : piquantly pleasant to the mind ⟨a *savory* collection of essays⟩ **b** : morally exemplary : EDIFYING ⟨his reputation was anything but *savory*⟩ **c** : pleasing to the sense of taste especially by reason of effective seasoning

synonym see PALATABLE

— **sa·vor·i·ly** \-rə-lē\ *adverb*

— **sa·vor·i·ness** \-rē-nəs\ *noun*

²**savory** *also* **savoury** *noun, plural* **sa·vor·ies** (1661)

British : a dish of stimulating flavor served usually at the end of dinner but sometimes as an appetizer

³**sa·vo·ry** \'sā-və-rē, 'säv-rē\ *noun, plural* **-ries** [Middle English *saverey*] (14th century)

: either of two aromatic mints: **a** : SUMMER SAVORY **b** : WINTER SAVORY

Sa·voy·ard \sə-'vȯi-ˌärd, ˌsa-ˌvȯi-'ärd, ˌsav-ˌwä-'yär(d)\ *noun* [*Savoy* Theater, London, built for the presentation of Gilbert and Sullivan operas] (1890)

: a devotee, performer, or producer of the comic operas of W. S. Gilbert and A. S. Sullivan

sa·voy cabbage \sə-'vȯi-, 'sa-ˌvȯi-\ *noun, often S capitalized* [translation of French *chou de Savoie* cabbage of Savoy] (1707)

: a cabbage with compact heads of wrinkled and curled leaves

¹**sav·vy** \'sa-vē\ *verb* **sav·vied; sav·vy·ing** [alteration of *sabi* know (in English-based creoles and pidgins), from Portuguese *sabe* he knows, from *saber* to know, from Latin *sapere* to be wise — more at SAGE] (1785)

◇ **WORD HISTORY**

savage In Latin the adjective *silvaticus*, a derivative of *silva* "forest," meant, when applied to animals or plants, "growing or living in the forest." Because forest life is wild rather than domesticated, the adjective easily acquired the meaning "wild, uncultivated" in literary Late Latin as well as the spoken Latin of the declining Roman Empire. Old French inherited Late Latin *silvaticus*, altered to *salvaticus*, as *salvage*. In later medieval French this became *sauvage*, which was borrowed into Middle English in the 13th century. The Old French adjective retained the source meanings "wild, uncultivated (of fruit)" and "untamed (of animals)." But *sauvage* could also be applied to humans, in which case its meanings could range from "lacking civilization, barbarous" to "fierce, cruel." English *savage* has had all these meanings at some point in its history, though the "fierce" sense is the one we now perhaps associate most closely with the word.

: UNDERSTAND

²savvy *noun* (circa 1785)
: practical know-how ⟨political *savvy*⟩
— **savvy** *adjective*

¹saw *past of* SEE

²saw \'sȯ\ *noun* [Middle English *sawe,* from Old English *sagu;* akin to Old High German *sega* saw, Latin *secare* to cut] (before 12th century)
: a hand or power tool or a machine used to cut hard material (as wood, metal, or bone) and equipped usually with a toothed blade or disk
— **saw·like** \-ˌlīk\ *adjective*

³saw *verb* **sawed** \'sȯd\; **sawed** *or* **sawn** \'sȯn\; **saw·ing** \'sȯ(-)iŋ\ (13th century)
transitive verb
1 : to cut with a saw
2 : to produce or form by cutting with a saw
3 : to slash as though with a saw
intransitive verb
1 a : to use a saw **b** : to cut with or as if with a saw
2 : to undergo cutting with a saw
3 : to make motions as though using a saw ⟨*sawed* at the reins⟩
— **saw·er** \'sȯ(-ə)r\ *noun*

⁴saw *noun* [Middle English *sawe,* from Old English *sagu* discourse; akin to Old High German & Old Norse *saga* tale, Old English *secgan* to say — more at SAY] (before 12th century)
: MAXIM, PROVERB

saw·bones \'sȯ-ˌbōnz\ *noun, plural* **saw·bones** *or* **saw·bones·es** (1837)
slang : PHYSICIAN, SURGEON

saw·buck \'sȯ-ˌbək\ *noun* (1850)
1 *slang* : a 10-dollar bill
2 : SAWHORSE; *especially* : one with X-shaped ends

saw·dust \'sȯ-(ˌ)dəst\ *noun* (1530)
: fine particles (as of wood) made by a saw in cutting

sawed–off \'sȯ-ˌdȯf\ *adjective* (1869)
1 : having an end sawed off ⟨a *sawed-off* shotgun⟩
2 : of less than average height

saw·fish \'sȯ-ˌfish\ *noun* (1664)
: any of a family (Pristidae) of large elongate rays that resemble sharks but have a long flattened snout with a row of serrate structures along each edge and that live in tropical and subtropical shallow seas and in or near the mouths of rivers

saw·fly \-ˌflī\ *noun* (1773)
: any of numerous hymenopterous insects (superfamily Tenthredinoidea) with the female usually having a sawlike ovipositor and with the larva resembling a plant-feeding caterpillar

saw grass *noun* (1822)
: any of various sedges (as of the genus *Cladium*) having the edges of the leaves set with minute sharp teeth

saw·horse \'sȯ-ˌhȯrs\ *noun* (1778)
: a frame on which wood is laid for sawing by hand; *especially* : HORSE 2b
word history
see EASEL

sawhorses

saw·log \-ˌlȯg, -ˌläg\ *noun* (1756)
: a log of suitable size for sawing into lumber

saw·mill \-ˌmil\ *noun* (1553)
: a mill or machine for sawing logs

saw·ney \'sȯ-nē\ *noun* [perhaps from *sawney* Scotsman, from Scots, alteration of *Sandy,* short for *Alexander*] (circa 1700)
chiefly British : FOOL, SIMPLETON
— **sawney** *adjective*

saw palmetto *noun* (1797)
: any of several shrubby palms chiefly of the southern U.S. and West Indies that have spiny-toothed petioles; *especially* : a common palm

(*Serenoa repens*) of the southeastern U.S. with a usually creeping stem

saw set *noun* (1846)
: an instrument used to set the teeth of saws

saw·tim·ber \'sȯ-ˌtim-bər\ *noun* (1901)
: timber suitable for sawing into lumber

saw·tooth \-ˌtüth\ *adjective* (circa 1859)
: having serrations : arranged or having parts arranged like the teeth of a saw ⟨a *sawtooth* roof⟩

saw–toothed \-ˈtütht\ *adjective* (circa 1857)
1 : having teeth like those of a saw ⟨a *saw-toothed* shark⟩
2 : SAWTOOTH

saw–whet owl \'sȯ-ˌhwet, -ˌwet-\ *noun* [from the supposed resemblance of its cry to the sound made in filing a saw] (1834)
: a very small harsh-voiced North American owl (*Aegolius acadicus*) that is largely dark brown above and chestnut streaked with white beneath — called also *saw-whet*

saw·yer \'sȯ-yər, 'sȯi-ər\ *noun* (13th century)
1 : one that saws
2 : any of several large longicorn beetles whose larvae bore large holes in timber or dead wood
3 : a tree fast in the bed of a stream with its branches projecting to the surface

sax \'saks\ *noun* (circa 1923)
: SAXOPHONE

sax·horn \'saks-ˌhȯrn\ *noun* [Antoine *Sax* (died 1894) Belgian instrument maker + English *horn*] (1844)
: any of a group of valved brass instruments ranging from soprano to bass and characterized by a conical tube, oval shape, and cup-shaped mouthpiece

sax·ic·o·lous \sak-'si-kə-ləs\ *adjective* [Latin *saxum* rock (akin to Latin *secare* to cut) + English *-colous* — more at SAW] (1856)
: inhabiting or growing among rocks ⟨*saxicolous* lichens⟩

sax·i·frage \'sak-sə-frij, -ˌfrāj\ *noun* [Middle English, from Middle French, from Late Latin *saxifraga,* from Latin, feminine of *saxifragus* breaking rocks, from *saxum* rock + *frangere* to break — more at BREAK] (14th century)
: any of a genus (*Saxifraga* of the family Saxifragaceae, the saxifrage family) of chiefly perennial herbs with showy pentamerous flowers and often with basal tufted leaves

sax·i·tox·in \ˌsak-sə-'täk-sən\ *noun* [*saxi-* (from New Latin *Saxidomus giganteus,* species of butter clam from which it is isolated) + *toxin*] (1962)
: a potent nonprotein neurotoxin $C_{10}H_{17}N_7O_4 \cdot 2HCl$ that originates in dinoflagellates (genus *Gonyaulax*) found in red tides and that sometimes occurs in and renders toxic normally edible mollusks which feed on them

Sax·on \'sak-sən\ *noun* [Middle English, from Late Latin *Saxones* Saxons, of Germanic origin; akin to Old English *Seaxan* Saxons] (13th century)
1 a (1) : a member of a Germanic people that entered and conquered England with the Angles and Jutes in the 5th century A.D. and merged with them to form the Anglo-Saxon people (2) : an Englishman or lowlander as distinguished from a Welshman, Irishman, or Highlander **b** : a native or inhabitant of Saxony
2 a : the Germanic language or dialect of any of the Saxon peoples **b** : the Germanic element in the English language especially as distinguished from the French and Latin
— **Saxon** *adjective*

sax·o·ny \'sak-s(ə-)nē\ *noun, plural* **-nies** *often capitalized* [*Saxony,* Germany] (1842)
1 a : a fine soft woolen fabric **b** : a fine closely twisted knitting yarn
2 : a Wilton jacquard carpet

sax·o·phone \'sak-sə-ˌfōn\ *noun* [French, from Antoine *Sax* (died 1894) Belgian instrument maker + French *-phone*] (1851)

: one of a group of single-reed woodwind instruments ranging from soprano to bass and characterized by a conical metal tube and finger keys
— **sax·o·phon·ic** \ˌsak-sə-'fä-nik, -'fä-\ *adjective*
— **sax·o·phon·ist** \'sak-sə-ˌfō-nist, *especially British* sak-'sä-fə-\ *noun*

sax·tu·ba \'saks-ˌtü-bə, -ˌtyü-\ *noun* [Antoine *Sax* + English *tuba*] (1856)
: a bass saxhorn

saxophone

¹say \'sā, *Southern also* 'se\ *verb* **said** \'sed, *especially when subject follows* səd\; **say·ing** \'sā-iŋ\; **says** \'sez, *sometimes* 'sāz, *especially when subject follows* səz\ [Middle English, from Old English *secgan;* akin to Old High German *sagēn* to say, Lithuanian *sakyti,* Greek *ennepein* to speak, tell] (before 12th century)
transitive verb
1 a : to express in words : STATE **b** : to state as opinion or belief : DECLARE
2 a : UTTER, PRONOUNCE **b** : RECITE, REPEAT ⟨*say* your prayers⟩
3 a : INDICATE, SHOW ⟨the clock *says* five minutes after twelve⟩ **b** : to give expression to : COMMUNICATE ⟨a glance that *said* all that was necessary⟩
intransitive verb
: to express oneself : SPEAK
— **say·er** \'sā-ər, 'se(-ə)r\ *noun*
— **say uncle** : to admit defeat
— **that is to say** : in other words : in effect

²say *noun, plural* **says** \'sāz, *Southern also* 'sez\ (1571)
1 *archaic* : something that is said : STATEMENT
2 : an expression of opinion ⟨had my *say*⟩
3 : a right or power to influence action or decision; *especially* : the authority to make final decisions

³say *adverb* [from imperative of ¹*say*] (1596)
1 : ABOUT, APPROXIMATELY ⟨the property is worth, *say,* four million dollars⟩
2 : for example : AS ⟨if we compress any gas, *say* oxygen⟩

say·able \'sā-ə-bəl, 'se-\ *adjective* (1856)
1 : capable of being said
2 : capable of being spoken effectively or easily ⟨readings in *sayable* Chinese —*Linguistic Reporter*⟩

say·est \'sā-əst\ *archaic 2d person singular of* SAY

say·ing \'sā-iŋ, 'se-\ *noun* (14th century)
: something said; *especially* : ADAGE

say–so \'sā-(ˌ)sō, 'se-\ *noun* (1637)
1 a : one's unsupported assertion or assurance **b** : an authoritative pronouncement ⟨left the hospital on the *say-so* of his doctor⟩
2 : a right of final decision ⟨has the ultimate *say-so* on what will be taught⟩

say·yid \'sī-yəd, 'sā-; 'sīd, 'sād\ *noun* [Arabic] (1788)
1 : an Islamic chief or leader
2 : LORD, SIR — used as a courtesy title for a Muslim of rank or lineage

Saz·e·rac \'sa-zə-ˌrak\ *trademark*
— used for a cocktail with a whiskey base

¹scab \'skab\ *noun* [Middle English, of Scandinavian origin; akin to Old Swedish *skabber* scab; akin to Old English *sceabb* scab, Latin *scabere* to scratch — more at SHAVE] (13th century)
1 : scabies of domestic animals
2 : a crust of hardened blood and serum over a wound

\ə\ abut \ᵊ\ kitten \ər\ further \a\ ash \ā\ ace
\ä\ mop, mar \aú\ out \ch\ chin \e\ bet \ē\ easy
\g\ go \i\ hit \ī\ ice \j\ job \ŋ\ sing \ō\ go
\ȯ\ law \ȯi\ boy \th\ thin \th\ the \ü\ loot \ú\ foot
\y\ yet \zh\ vision *see also* Guide to Pronunciation

3 a : a contemptible person **b** (1) **:** a worker who refuses to join a labor union (2) **:** a union member who refuses to strike or returns to work before a strike has ended (3) **:** a worker who accepts employment or replaces a union worker during a strike (4) **:** one who works for less than union wages or on nonunion terms **4 :** any of various bacterial or fungus diseases of plants characterized by crustaceous spots; *also* **:** one of the spots

²**scab** *intransitive verb* **scabbed; scabbing** (1683)
1 : to become covered with a scab
2 : to act as a scab

scab·bard \'ska-bərd\ *noun* [Middle English *scaubert*, from Anglo-French *escaubers*] (13th century)
: a sheath for a sword, dagger, or bayonet
— **scabbard** *transitive verb*

scab·by \'ska-bē\ *adjective* **scab·bi·er; -est** (15th century)
1 a : covered with or full of scabs ⟨*scabby* skin⟩ **b :** diseased with scab ⟨a *scabby* animal⟩ ⟨*scabby* potatoes⟩
2 : MEAN, CONTEMPTIBLE ⟨a *scabby* trick⟩

sca·bies \'skā-bēz\ *noun, plural* **scabies** [Latin, from *scabere* to scratch] (1814)
: contagious itch or mange especially with exudative crusts that is caused by parasitic mites (especially *Sarcoptes scabiei*)
— **sca·bi·et·ic** \,skā-bē-'e-tik\ *adjective*

¹**sca·bi·ous** \'skā-bē-əs, 'ska-\ *noun* [Middle English *scabiose*, from Medieval Latin *scabiosa*, from Latin, feminine of *scabiosus*, adjective] (14th century)
: any of a genus (*Scabiosa*) of Old World herbs of the teasel family with terminal flower heads subtended by a leafy involucre

²**scabious** *adjective* [Latin *scabiosus*, from *scabies*] (1603)
1 : SCABBY
2 : of, relating to, or resembling scabies ⟨*scabious* eruptions⟩

scab·land \'skab-,land\ *noun* (1904)
: a region characterized by elevated tracts of rocky land with little or no soil cover and traversed or isolated by postglacial dry stream channels — usually used in plural

sca·brous \'ska-brəs *also* 'skā-\ *adjective* [Latin *scabr-, scaber* rough, scurfy; akin to Latin *scabere* to scratch — more at SCAB] (1646)
1 : DIFFICULT, KNOTTY ⟨a *scabrous* problem⟩
2 : rough to the touch: as **a :** having small raised dots, scales, or points ⟨a *scabrous* leaf⟩ **b :** covered with raised, roughened, or unwholesome patches ⟨*scabrous* paint⟩ ⟨yellowed *scabrous* skin⟩
3 : dealing with suggestive, indecent, or scandalous themes **:** SALACIOUS; *also* **:** SQUALID
synonym SEE ROUGH
— **sca·brous·ly** *adverb*
— **sca·brous·ness** *noun*

¹**scad** \'skad\ *noun, plural* **scad** *also* **scads** [origin unknown] (1602)
: any of several carangid fishes (especially of the genus *Decapterus*)

²**scad** *noun* [probably alteration of English dialect *scald* a multitude] (1869)
: a large number or quantity — usually used in plural ⟨*scads* of money⟩

scaf·fold \'ska-fəld *also* -,fōld\ *noun* [Middle English, from Old North French *escafaut*, modification of (assumed) Vulgar Latin *catafalicum*, from Greek *kata-* cata- + Latin *fala* siege tower] (14th century)
1 a : a temporary or movable platform for workers (as bricklayers, painters, or miners) to stand or sit on when working at a height above the floor or ground **b :** a platform on which a criminal is executed (as by hanging or beheading) **c :** a platform at a height above ground or floor level
2 : a supporting framework

scaf·fold·ing \-fəl-diŋ, -,fōl-\ *noun* (14th century)

: a system of scaffolds; *also* **:** material for scaffolds

scag \'skag\ *noun* [origin unknown] (1967)
slang **:** HEROIN

sca·glio·la \skal-'yō-lə, -'yò-\ *noun, often attributive* [Italian, literally, little chip] (1747)
: an imitation marble used for floors, columns, and ornamental interior work

scal·able \'skā-lə-bəl\ *adjective* (circa 1580)
: capable of being scaled

sca·lade \skə-'lād, -'läd\ *or* **sca·la·do** \-'lā-(,)dō, -'lä-\ *noun, plural* **-lades** *or* **-la·dos** [obsolete Italian *scalada*, from *scalare* to scale, from *scala* ladder, staircase, from Late Latin — more at SCALE] (1591)
archaic **:** ESCALADE

¹**sca·lar** \'skā-lər, -,lär\ *adjective* [Latin *scalaris*, from *scalae* stairs, ladder — more at SCALE] (circa 1656)
1 : having an uninterrupted series of steps **:** GRADUATED ⟨*scalar* chain of authority⟩ ⟨*scalar* cells⟩
2 a : capable of being represented by a point on a scale ⟨*scalar* quantity⟩ **b :** of or relating to a scalar or scalar product ⟨*scalar* multiplication⟩

²**scalar** *noun* (1846)
1 : a real number rather than a vector
2 : a quantity (as mass or time) that has a magnitude describable by a real number and no direction

sca·la·re \skə-'lar-ē, -'ler-, -'lär-\ *noun* [New Latin, specific epithet, from Latin, neuter of *scalaris;* from the barred pattern on its body] (1928)
: a black and silver laterally compressed South American cichlid fish (*Pterophyllum scalare*) popular in aquariums

sca·lar·i·form \skə-'lar-ə-,form\ *adjective* [New Latin *scalariformis*, from Latin *scalaris* + *-iformis* -iform] (1836)
: resembling a ladder especially in having transverse bars or markings like the rungs of a ladder ⟨*scalariform* cells in plants⟩
— **sca·lar·i·form·ly** *adverb*

scalar product *noun* (1878)
: a real number that is the product of the lengths of two vectors and the cosine of the angle between them — called also *dot product, inner product*

scal·a·wag \'ska-li-,wag\ *noun* [origin unknown] (circa 1848)
1 : SCAMP, REPROBATE
2 : a white Southerner acting in support of the reconstruction governments after the American Civil War often for private gain

¹**scald** \'skold\ *verb* [Middle English, from Old North French *escalder*, from Late Latin *excaldare* to wash in warm water, from Latin *ex-* + *calida, calda* warm water, from feminine of *calidus* warm, from *calēre* to be warm — more at LEE] (13th century)
transitive verb
1 : to burn with or as if with hot liquid or steam
2 a : to subject to the action of boiling water or steam **b :** to bring to a temperature just below the boiling point ⟨*scald* milk⟩
3 : SCORCH
intransitive verb
1 : to scald something
2 : to become scalded

²**scald** *noun* (1601)
1 : an injury to the body caused by scalding
2 : an act or process of scalding
3 : any of various conditions or diseases of plants or fruits marked especially by a usually brownish discoloration of tissue

³**scald** *adjective* [*scall* + ¹*-ed*] (1561)
1 *archaic* **:** SCABBY, SCURFY
2 *archaic* **:** SHABBY, CONTEMPTIBLE

⁴**scald** \'skold, 'skäld\ *variant of* SKALD

⁵**scald** \'skold\ *adjective* [alteration of *scalded*] (1791)
: subjected to scalding ⟨coffee . . . with *scald* cream —Charles Kingsley⟩

scald·ing \'skol-diŋ\ *adjective* (13th century)
1 : hot enough to scald ⟨*scalding* water⟩
2 a : having or producing the feeling of being burned ⟨*scalding* sun⟩ ⟨*scalding* sand⟩ **b** **:** SCATHING ⟨*scalding* criticism⟩

¹**scale** \'skā(ə)l\ *noun* [Middle English, bowl, scale of a balance, from Old Norse *skāl;* akin to Old Norse *skel* shell — more at SHELL] (14th century)
1 a : either pan or tray of a balance **b :** a beam that is supported freely in the center and has two pans of equal weight suspended from its ends — usually used in plural
2 : an instrument or machine for weighing

²**scale** *verb* **scaled; scal·ing** (1603)
transitive verb
: to weigh in scales
intransitive verb
: to have a specified weight on scales

³**scale** *noun* [Middle English, from Middle French *escale*, of Germanic origin; akin to Old English *scealu* shell, husk — more at SHELL] (14th century)
1 a : a small, flattened, rigid, and definitely circumscribed plate forming part of the external body covering especially of a fish **b :** a small thin plate suggesting a fish scale ⟨*scales* of mica⟩ ⟨the *scales* on a moth's wing⟩ **c :** the scaly covering of a scaled animal
2 : a small thin dry lamina shed (as in many skin diseases) from the skin
3 : a thin coating, layer, or incrustation: **a :** a usually black scaly coating of oxide forming on the surface of a metal (as iron) when it is heated for processing **b :** a hard incrustation usually rich in sulfate of calcium that is deposited on the inside of a vessel (as a boiler) in which water is heated
4 a : a modified leaf protecting a seed plant bud before expansion **b :** a thin, membranous, chaffy, or woody bract
5 a : any of the small overlapping usually metal pieces forming the outer surface of scale armor **b :** SCALE ARMOR
6 a : SCALE INSECT **b :** infestation with or disease caused by scale insects
— **scaled** \'skā(ə)ld\ *adjective*
— **scale·less** \'skā(ə)l-ləs\ *adjective*

⁴**scale** *verb* **scaled; scal·ing** (15th century)
transitive verb
1 : to remove the scale or scales from (as by scraping) ⟨*scale* a fish⟩
2 : to take off in thin layers or scales
3 : to form scale on ⟨hard water *scales* a boiler⟩
4 : to throw (as a thin flat stone) so that the edge cuts the air or so that it skips on water **:** SKIM
intransitive verb
1 : to separate and come off in scales **:** FLAKE
2 : to shed scales ⟨*scaling* skin⟩
3 : to become encrusted with scale

⁵**scale** *verb* **scaled; scal·ing** [Middle English, from ⁶*scale*] (14th century)
transitive verb
1 a : to attack or take by means of scaling ladders ⟨*scale* a castle wall⟩ **b :** to climb up or reach by means of a ladder **c :** to reach the highest point of **:** SURMOUNT
2 a : to arrange in a graduated series ⟨*scale* a test⟩ **b** (1) **:** to measure by or as if by a scale (2) **:** to measure or estimate the sound content of (as logs) **c :** to pattern, make, regulate, set, or estimate according to some rate or standard **:** ADJUST ⟨a production schedule *scaled* to actual need⟩ — often used with *down* or *up* ⟨*scale* down imports⟩
intransitive verb
1 : to climb by or as if by a ladder
2 : to rise in a graduated series
3 : MEASURE

⁶**scale** *noun* [Middle English, from Late Latin *scala* ladder, staircase, from Latin *scalae*, plural, stairs, rungs, ladder; akin to Latin *scandere* to climb — more at SCAN] (15th century)

1 a *obsolete* **:** LADDER **b** *archaic* **:** a means of ascent
2 : a graduated series of musical tones ascending or descending in order of pitch according to a specified scheme of their intervals
3 : something graduated especially when used as a measure or rule: as **a :** a series of marks or points at known intervals used to measure distances (as the height of the mercury in a thermometer) **b :** an indication of the relationship between the distances on a map and the corresponding actual distances **c :** RULER 3
4 a : a graduated series or scheme of rank or order (a *scale* of taxation) **b :** MINIMUM WAGE 2
5 a : a proportion between two sets of dimensions (as between those of a drawing and its original) **b :** a distinctive relative size, extent, or degree (projects done on a large *scale*)
6 : a graded series of tests or of performances used in rating individual intelligence or achievement
— **scale** *adjective*
— **to scale :** according to the proportions of an established scale of measurement (floor plans drawn *to scale*)

⁷scale *noun* [⁵*scale*] (circa 1587)
1 *obsolete* **:** ESCALADE
2 : an estimate of the amount of sound lumber in logs or standing timber
scale armor *noun* (1842)
: armor of small metallic scales on leather or cloth
scale-down \'skā(ə)l-,daùn\ *noun* (1931)
: a reduction according to a fixed ratio (a *scale-down* of debts)
scale insect *noun* (1840)
: any of numerous small but very prolific homopterous insects (superfamily Coccoidea) that have winged males, wingless scale-covered females attached to the host plant, and young that suck the juices of plants and some of which are economic pests — compare LAC
scale-like \'skā(ə)l-,līk\ *adjective* (1883)
: resembling a scale (*scalelike* design); *specifically* **:** reduced to a minute appressed element resembling a scale
sca-lene \'skā-,lēn, skā-'\ *adjective* [Late Latin *scalenus*, from Greek *skalēnos*, literally, uneven; perhaps akin to Greek *skolios* crooked, *skelos* leg — more at ISOSCELES] (1734)
of a triangle **:** having the three sides of unequal length — see TRIANGLE illustration
scal-er \'skā-lər\ *noun* (1568)
1 : one that scales
2 : a dental instrument for removing tartar from teeth
3 : an electronic device that operates a recorder or produces an output pulse after a specified number of input impulses
scale-up \'skā-,ləp\ *noun* (1945)
: an increase according to a fixed ratio
scall \'skól\ *noun* [Middle English, from Old Norse *skalli* bald head; akin to Swedish *skulle* skull] (14th century)
: a scurf or scabby disorder (as of the scalp)
scal-lion \'skal-yən\ *noun* [Middle English *scaloun*, from Anglo-French *scalun*, from (assumed) Vulgar Latin *escalonia*, from Latin *ascalonia* (*caepa*) onion of Ascalon, from feminine of *ascalonius* of Ascalon, from *Ascalon-*, *Ascalo* Ascalon, seaport in southern Palestine] (14th century)
1 : SHALLOT
2 : LEEK
3 : an onion forming a thick basal portion without a bulb; *also* **:** GREEN ONION
¹scal-lop \'skä-ləp, 'ska-, 'skó-\ *noun* [Middle English *scalop*, from Middle French *escalope* shell, of Germanic origin; akin to Middle Dutch *schelpe* shell] (15th century)
1 a : any of numerous marine bivalve lamellibranch mollusks (family Pectinidae) that have a radially ribbed shell with the edge undulated and that swim by opening and closing the valves **b :** the adductor muscle of a scallop as an article of food

2 a : a valve or shell of a scallop **b :** a baking dish shaped like a valve of a scallop
3 : one of a continuous series of circle segments or angular projections forming a border
4 : PATTYPAN
5 [French *escalope*, probably from Middle French, shell] **:** a thin slice of boneless meat (as veal)
²scallop (1737)
transitive verb
1 [from the use of a scallop shell as a baking dish] **:** to bake in a sauce usually covered with seasoned bread or cracker crumbs (*scalloped* potatoes)
2 a : to shape, cut, or finish in scallops **b :** to form scallops in
intransitive verb
: to gather or dredge scallops
scal-lop-er \-lə-pər\ *noun* (circa 1881)
1 : a person who dredges for or gathers scallops
2 : a boat equipped and used to dredge for scallops
scal-lo-pi-ni *or* **sca-lop-pi-ne** \,skä-lə-'pē-nē, ,ska-\ *noun* [Italian *scaloppine*, ultimately from French *escalope* thin slice of meat, probably from Middle French, shell] (1946)
: thin slices of meat (as veal) sautéed or coated with flour and fried
scal-ly-wag *variant of* SCALAWAG
sca-lo-gram \'skā-lə-,gram\ *noun* [⁶*scale* + *-o-* + *-gram*] (1944)
: an arrangement of items (as problems on a test or features of speech) in ascending order so that the presence or accomplishment of an item at one level implies the presence of or the capability to accomplish items at all lower levels
¹scalp \'skalp\ *noun* [Middle English, of Scandinavian origin; akin to Old Norse *skálpr* sheath; akin to Middle Dutch *schelpe* shell] (14th century)
1 a : the part of the integument of the human head usually covered with hair in both sexes **b :** the part of an animal (as a wolf or fox) corresponding to the human scalp
2 a : a part of the human scalp with attached hair cut or torn from an enemy as a token of victory (as by Indian warriors of North America) **b :** a trophy of victory or accomplishment
3 *chiefly Scottish* **:** a projecting mass of bare ground or rock
²scalp (1676)
transitive verb
1 a : to deprive of the scalp **b :** to remove an upper part from
2 : to remove a desired constituent from and discard the rest
3 : to buy and sell so as to make small quick profits (*scalp* stocks) (*scalp* grain); *especially* **:** to resell at greatly increased prices (*scalp* theater tickets)
intransitive verb
1 : to take scalps
2 : to profit by slight market fluctuations
— **scalp-er** *noun*
scal-pel \'skal-pəl *also* skal-'pel\ *noun* [Latin *scalpellus*, *scalpellum*, diminutive of *scalper*, *scalprum* chisel, knife, from *scalpere* to scratch, carve] (1742)
: a small straight thin-bladed knife used especially in surgery
scalp lock *noun* (1826)
: a long tuft of hair on the crown of the otherwise shaved head especially of a warrior of some American Indian tribes
scaly \'skā-lē\ *adjective* **scal-i-er; -est** (14th century)
1 a : covered with, composed of, or rich in scale or scales **b :** FLAKY
2 : of or relating to scaly animals
3 : DESPICABLE, POOR
4 : infested with scale insects (*scaly* fruit)
— **scal-i-ness** *noun*
scaly anteater *noun* (1840)

: PANGOLIN
scam \'skam\ *noun* [origin unknown] (1963)
: a fraudulent or deceptive act or operation (an insurance *scam*)
scam-mo-ny \'ska-mə-nē\ *noun, plural* **-nies** [Middle English *scamonie*, from Old English *scammoniam*, from Latin *scammonia*, from Greek *skammōnia*] (before 12th century)
1 : a twining convolvulus (*Convolvulus scammonia*) of Asia Minor with a large thick root
2 a : the dried root of scammony **b :** a cathartic resin obtained from scammony
¹scamp \'skamp\ *noun* [obsolete *scamp* to roam about or idly] (1808)
1 : RASCAL, ROGUE
2 : an impish or playful young person
— **scamp-ish** \'skam-pish\ *adjective*
²scamp *transitive verb* [origin unknown] (1837)
: to perform or deal with in a hasty, neglectful, or imperfect manner
¹scam-per \'skam-pər\ *intransitive verb* **scam-pered; scam-per-ing** \-p(ə-)riŋ\ [probably from obsolete Dutch *schampen* to flee, from Middle French *escamper*, from Italian *scampare*, from (assumed) Vulgar Latin *excampare* to decamp, from Latin *ex-* + *campus* field] (1691)
: to run nimbly and usually playfully about
²scamper *noun* (1697)
: a playful or hurried run or movement
scam-pi \'skam-pē, 'skäm-\ *noun, plural* **scampi** [Italian, plural of *scampo*, a European lobster] (1925)
: SHRIMP; *especially* **:** large shrimp prepared with a garlic-flavored sauce
¹scan \'skan\ *verb* **scanned; scan-ning** [Middle English *scannen*, from Late Latin *scandere*, from Latin, to climb; akin to Middle Irish *sceinnid* he springs, Sanskrit *skandati* he leaps] (14th century)
transitive verb
1 : to read or mark so as to show metrical structure
2 : to examine by point-by-point observation or checking: **a :** to investigate thoroughly by checking point by point and often repeatedly (a fire lookout *scanning* the hills with binoculars) **b :** to glance from point to point of often hastily, casually, or in search of a particular item (*scan* the want ads looking for a job)
3 a : to examine especially systematically with a sensing device (as a photometer or a beam of radiation) usually to obtain information **b :** to pass an electron beam over and convert (an image) into variations of electrical properties (as voltage) that convey information electronically **c :** to pass over in the formation of an image (the electron beam *scans* the picture tube)
intransitive verb
1 : to scan verse
2 : to conform to a metrical pattern
synonym SEE SCRUTINIZE
— **scan-na-ble** \'ska-nə-bəl\ *adjective*
²scan *noun* (1706)
1 : the act or process of scanning
2 : a radar or television trace
3 a : a depiction (as a photograph) of the distribution of a radioactive material in something (as a bodily organ) **b :** an image of a bodily part produced (as by computer) by combining radiographic data obtained from several angles or sections
¹scan-dal \'skan-dºl\ *noun* [Middle English, from Late Latin *scandalum* stumbling block, offense, from Greek *skandalon* trap, stumbling block, offense; akin to Latin *scandere* to climb] (13th century)

\ə\ *abut*	\ə\ *kitten*	\ər\ *further*	\a\ *ash*	\ā\ *ace*	
\ä\ *mop, mar*	\aù\ *out*	\ch\ *chin*	\e\ *bet*	\ē\ *easy*	
\g\ *go*	\i\ *hit*	\ī\ *ice*	\j\ *job*	\ŋ\ *sing*	\ō\ *go*
\ò\ *law*	\òi\ *boy*	\th\ *thin*	\th\ *the*	\ü\ *loot*	\ù\ *foot*
\y\ *yet*	\zh\ *vision*	*see also* Guide to Pronunciation			

1 a : discredit brought upon religion by unseemly conduct in a religious person **b** : conduct that causes or encourages a lapse of faith or of religious obedience in another
2 : loss of or damage to reputation caused by actual or apparent violation of morality or propriety : DISGRACE
3 a : a circumstance or action that offends propriety or established moral conceptions or disgraces those associated with it **b** : a person whose conduct offends propriety or morality
4 : malicious or defamatory gossip
5 : indignation, chagrin, or bewilderment brought about by a flagrant violation of morality, propriety, or religious opinion
synonym see OFFENSE
²**scandal** *transitive verb* (1592)
1 *obsolete* : DISGRACE
2 *chiefly dialect* : DEFAME, SLANDER
scan·dal·ise *chiefly British variant of* SCANDALIZE
scan·dal·ize \'skan-də-,līz\ *transitive verb* **-ized; -iz·ing** (1566)
1 : to speak falsely or maliciously of
2 *archaic* : to bring into reproach
3 : to offend the moral sense of : SHOCK
scan·dal·mon·ger \'skan-d°l-,məŋ-gər, -,mäŋ-\ *noun* (1721)
: a person who circulates scandal
— **scan·dal·mon·ger·ing** \-g(ə-)riŋ\ *noun*
scan·dal·ous \'skan-d°l-əs\ *adjective* (1603)
1 : LIBELOUS, DEFAMATORY
2 : offensive to propriety or morality : SHOCKING
— **scan·dal·ous·ly** *adverb*
— **scan·dal·ous·ness** *noun*
scandal sheet *noun* (1904)
: a newspaper or periodical dealing to a large extent in scandal and gossip
scan·dent \'skan-dənt\ *adjective* [Latin *scandent-, scandens*, present participle of *scandere* to climb — more at SCAN] (circa 1682)
: characterized by a climbing mode of growth ⟨*scandent* stems⟩ ⟨*scandent* vines⟩
Scan·di·an \'skan-dē-ən\ *adjective* [Latin *Scandia*] (1668)
1 : SCANDINAVIAN
2 : of or relating to the languages of Scandinavia
— **Scandian** *noun*
Scan·di·na·vian \,skan-də-'nā-vē-ən, -vyən\ *noun* (1766)
1 : the North Germanic languages
2 a : a native or inhabitant of Scandinavia **b** : a person of Scandinavian descent
— **Scandinavian** *adjective*
scan·di·um \'skan-dē-əm\ *noun* [New Latin, from Latin *Scandia*, ancient name of southern Scandinavian peninsula] (1879)
: a white metallic element found in association with rare earth elements — see ELEMENT table
scan·ner \'ska-nər\ *noun* (1557)
: one that scans: as **a** : a device for sensing recorded data **b** : a device (as a CAT scanner) used for scanning something (as the human body)
scanning electron microscope *noun* (1953)
: an electron microscope in which a beam of focused electrons moves across the object with the secondary electrons produced by the object and the electrons scattered by the object being collected to form a three-dimensional image on a cathode-ray tube — called also *scanning microscope*
— **scanning electron microscopy** *noun*
scanning tunneling microscope *noun* (1983)
: a microscope that makes use of the phenomenon of electron tunneling to map the positions of individual atoms in a surface or to move atoms around on a surface
— **scanning tunneling microscopy** *noun*

scan·sion \'skan(t)-shən\ *noun* [Late Latin *scansion-, scansio*, from Latin, act of climbing, from *scandere*] (1671)
: the analysis of verse to show its meter
¹**scant** \'skant\ *adjective* [Middle English, from Old Norse *skamt*, neuter of *skammr* short] (14th century)
1 *dialect* **a** : excessively frugal **b** : not prodigal : CHARY
2 a : barely or scarcely sufficient; *especially* : not quite coming up to a stated measure **b** : lacking in amplitude or quantity
3 : having a small or insufficient supply ⟨he's fat, and *scant* of breath —Shakespeare⟩
synonym see MEAGER
— **scant·ly** *adverb*
— **scant·ness** *noun*
²**scant** *adverb* (15th century)
dialect : SCARCELY, HARDLY
³**scant** *transitive verb* (circa 1580)
1 : to provide an incomplete supply of
2 : to make small, narrow, or meager
3 : to give scant attention to : SLIGHT
4 : to provide with a meager or inadequate portion or supply : STINT
scant·ies \'skan-tēz\ *noun plural* [blend of ¹*scant* and *panties*] (1929)
: abbreviated panties for women
scant·ling \'skant-liŋ, -lən\ *noun* [alteration of Middle English *scantilon*, literally, mason's or carpenter's gauge, from Old North French *escantillon*] (1555)
1 a : the dimensions of timber and stone used in building **b** : the dimensions of a frame or strake used in shipbuilding
2 : a small quantity, amount, or proportion : MODICUM
3 : a small piece of lumber (as an upright piece in house framing)
scanty \'skan-tē\ *adjective* **scant·i·er; -est** [English dialect *scant* scanty supply, from Middle English, from Old Norse *skamt*, from neuter of *skammr* short] (1660)
: limited or less than sufficient in degree, quantity, or extent
synonym see MEAGER
— **scant·i·ly** \'skan-t°l-ē\ *adverb*
— **scant·i·ness** \'skan-tē-nəs\ *noun*
¹**scape** \'skāp\ *verb* **scaped; scap·ing** [Middle English, short for *escapen*] (13th century)
: ESCAPE
²**scape** *noun* [Latin *scapus* shaft, stalk — more at SHAFT] (1601)
1 : a peduncle arising at or beneath the surface of the ground in an acaulescent plant (as the tulip); *broadly* : a flower stalk
2 : the shaft of an animal part (as an antenna or feather)
³**scape** *noun* [*landscape*] (1773)
: a view or picture of a scene — usually used in combination ⟨city*scape*⟩
word history see LANDSCAPE
¹**scape·goat** \'skāp-,gōt\ *noun* [¹*scape*; intended as translation of Hebrew *'azāzēl* (probably name of a demon), as literally, ⟨*'ēz 'ōzēl* goat that departs—Leviticus 16:8 (Authorized Version)] (1530)
1 : a goat upon whose head are symbolically placed the sins of the people after which he is sent into the wilderness in the biblical ceremony for Yom Kippur
2 a : one that bears the blame for others **b** : one that is the object of irrational hostility ◇
²**scapegoat** *transitive verb* (1943)
: to make a scapegoat of
— **scape·goat·ism** \-,gō-,ti-zəm\ *noun*
scape·grace \'skāp-,grās\ *noun* [¹*scape*] (1809)
: an incorrigible rascal
scaph·oid \'ska-,fȯid\ *noun* [New Latin *scaphoides*, from Greek *skaphoeidēs*, from *skaphos* boat] (1846)
: the bone of the thumb side of the carpus that is the largest in the proximal row; *also* : the navicular bone of the tarsus

— **scaphoid** *adjective*
scap·o·lite \'ska-pə-,līt\ *noun* [French, from Latin *scapus* shaft + French *-o-* + *-lite;* from the prismatic shape of its crystals] (1802)
: any of a group of minerals that are essentially complex silicates of aluminum, calcium, and sodium and that include some used as semiprecious stones
sca·pose \'skā-,pōs\ *adjective* (circa 1903)
: bearing, resembling, or consisting of a scape ⟨the terminal *scapose* flowers of a pyrola⟩
scap·u·la \'ska-pyə-lə\ *noun, plural* **-lae** \-,lē, -,lī\ *or* **-las** [New Latin, from Latin, shoulder blade, shoulder] (1578)
: either of a pair of large triangular bones lying one in each dorsal lateral part of the thorax, being the principal bone of the corresponding half of the shoulder girdle, and articulating with the corresponding clavicle or coracoid — called also *shoulder blade*
¹**scap·u·lar** \-lər\ *noun* [Middle English *scapulare*, from Late Latin, from Latin *scapula* shoulder] (15th century)
1 a : a long wide band of cloth with an opening for the head worn front and back over the shoulders as part of a monastic habit **b** : a pair of small cloth squares joined by shoulder tapes and worn under the clothing on the breast and back as a sacramental and often also as a badge of a third order or confraternity
2 a : SCAPULA **b** : one of the feathers covering the base of a bird's wing — see BIRD illustration
²**scapular** *adjective* [New Latin *scapularis*, from *scapula*] (1713)
: of or relating to the shoulder, the scapula, or scapulars
scapular medal *noun* (1912)
: a medal worn in place of a sacramental scapular
¹**scar** \'skär\ *noun* [Middle English *skere*, from Old Norse *sker* skerry; probably akin to Old Norse *skera* to cut — more at SHEAR] (14th century)
1 : an isolated or protruding rock
2 : a steep rocky eminence : a bare place on the side of a mountain
²**scar** *noun* [Middle English *escare, scar*, from Middle French *escare* scab, from Late Latin *eschara*, from Greek, hearth, brazier, scab] (14th century)
1 : a mark left (as in the skin) by the healing of injured tissue

◇ **WORD HISTORY**
scapegoat An ancient Hebrew custom called for the high priest on Yom Kippur, the Jewish Day of Atonement, to take two goats, one to be sacrificed to the Lord, the other to carry the sins of the people away into the desert. After the Lord's goat had been sacrificed, the priest confessed the sins of the people over the head of the live goat, which was then released "to Azazel." Modern commentators have usually interpreted Azazel as the name of a demon living in the desert, but the name was interpreted by ancient Biblical translators as referring to the goat itself, and hence being a form of the Hebrew phrase *'ez 'ōzēl*, which means "goat that departs." In the Greek translation of the passage referring to Azazel's goat, the goat became *tragos apopompaios* "goat sent out," and in the Latin Vulgate the animal became *caper emissarius* "emissary goat." Perpetuating the tradition, William Tyndale in his 1530 English translation of the Pentateuch rendered the Latin as *scapegoat*, that is, "escape goat." Although the goat for Azazel did in fact escape sacrifice, he bore the heavy burden of the people's sins. It is for this reason that we call anyone who bears the blame for others' transgressions or mistakes a *scapegoat*.

2 a : a mark left on a stem or branch by a fallen leaf or harvested fruit **b :** CICATRIX 2
3 : a mark or indentation resulting from damage or wear
4 : a lasting moral or emotional injury ⟨one of his men had been killed . . . in a manner that left a *scar* upon his mind —H. G. Wells⟩
— **scar·less** \-ləs\ *adjective*

³**scar** *verb* **scarred; scar·ring** (1555)
transitive verb
1 : to mark with a scar
2 : to do lasting injury to
intransitive verb
1 : to form a scar
2 : to become scarred

scar·ab \'skar-əb\ *noun* [Middle French *scarabee*, from Latin *scarabaeus*] (1579)
1 : any of a family (Scarabaeidae) of stout-bodied beetles (as a dung beetle) with lamellate or flabellate antennae
2 : a stone or faience beetle used in ancient Egypt as a talisman, ornament, and a symbol of resurrection

scar·a·bae·us \,skar-ə-'bē-əs\ *noun* [Latin] (1664)
: SCARAB 2

scar·a·mouch *or* **scar·a·mouche** \'skar-ə-,müsh, -,müch, -,maùch\ *noun* [French *Scaramouche*, from Italian *Scaramuccia*, from *scaramuccia* skirmish] (1662)
1 *capitalized* **:** a stock character in the Italian commedia dell'arte that burlesques the Spanish don and is characterized by boastfulness and cowardliness
2 a : a cowardly buffoon **b :** RASCAL, SCAMP

¹**scarce** \'skers, 'skars\ *adjective* **scarc·er; scarc·est** [Middle English *scars*, from Old North French *escars*, from (assumed) Vulgar Latin *excarpsus*, literally, plucked out, past participle of Latin *excerpere* to pluck out — more at EXCERPT] (14th century)
1 : deficient in quantity or number compared with the demand **:** not plentiful or abundant
2 : intentionally absent ⟨made himself *scarce* at inspection time⟩
synonym see INFREQUENT
— **scarce·ness** *noun*

²**scarce** *adverb* (15th century)
: SCARCELY, HARDLY

scarce·ly *adverb* (14th century)
1 a : by a narrow margin **:** only just ⟨had *scarcely* rung the bell when the door flew open —Agnes S. Turnbull⟩ **b :** almost not ⟨could *scarcely* see for the fog⟩
2 a : certainly not ⟨could *scarcely* interfere⟩ **b :** probably not ⟨there could *scarcely* have been found a leader better equipped —V. L. Parrington⟩

scar·ci·ty \'sker-sə-tē, 'skar-, -stē\ *noun, plural* **-ties** (14th century)
: the quality or state of being scarce; *especially* **:** want of provisions for the support of life

¹**scare** \'sker, 'skar\ *verb* **scared; scar·ing** [Middle English *skerren*, from Old Norse *skirra*, from *skjarr* shy, timid] (13th century)
transitive verb
: to frighten especially suddenly **:** ALARM
intransitive verb
: to become scared
— **scar·er** *noun*

²**scare** *noun* (circa 1548)
1 : a sudden fright
2 : a widespread state of alarm **:** PANIC
— **scare** *adjective*

scare·crow \'sker-,krō, 'skar-\ *noun* (1573)
1 a : an object usually suggesting a human figure that is set up to frighten birds away from crops **b :** something frightening but harmless
2 : a skinny or ragged person

scared *adjective* (1590)
: thrown into or being in a state of fear, fright, or panic ⟨*scared* of snakes⟩ ⟨*scared* to go out⟩

scaredy–cat \'sker-dē-,kat, 'skar-\ *noun* [*scared* (past participle of *scare*) + ¹-*y* + *cat*] (1948)

: an unduly fearful person

scare·head \'sker-,hed, 'skar-\ *noun* (1887)
: a big, sensational, or alarming newspaper headline

scare·mon·ger \-,mən-gər, -,mäŋ-\ *noun* (1888)
: one inclined to raise or excite alarms especially needlessly

scare up *transitive verb* (1841)
: to find or get together with considerable labor or difficulty **:** scrape up ⟨managed to *scare up* the money⟩

¹**scarf** \'skärf\ *noun, plural* **scarfs** [Middle English *skarf*, probably of Scandinavian origin; akin to Old Norse *skarfr* scarf] (15th century)
1 : either of the chamfered or cutaway ends that fit together to form a scarf joint
2 : a joint made by chamfering, halving, or notching two pieces to correspond and lapping and bolting them — called also *scarf joint*

¹scarf 2

²**scarf** *also* **scarph** \'skärf\ *transitive verb* (1627)
1 : to unite by a scarf joint
2 : to form a scarf on

³**scarf** *noun, plural* **scarves** \'skärvz\ *or* **scarfs** [Old North French *escarpe* sash, sling] (1555)
1 a : a military or official sash usually indicative of rank **b** *archaic* **:** TIPPET 3
2 : a broad band of cloth worn about the shoulders, around the neck, or over the head
3 : RUNNER 6b

⁴**scarf** *transitive verb* (1598)
1 : to wrap, cover, or adorn with or as if with a scarf
2 : to wrap or throw on (a scarf or mantle) loosely

⁵**scarf** *transitive verb* [by alteration] (circa 1960)
: ³SCOFF 1 ⟨*scarfed* down my sandwich⟩

scarf·pin \'skärf-,pin\ *noun* (1859)
: TIEPIN

scarf·skin \'skärf-,skin\ *noun* [³*scarf*] (1615)
: EPIDERMIS; *especially* **:** that forming the cuticle of a nail

scar·i·fi·ca·tion \,skar-ə-fə-'kā-shən, ,sker-\ *noun* (14th century)
1 : the act or process of scarifying
2 : a mark or marks made by scarifying

¹**scar·i·fy** \'skar-ə-,fī, 'sker-\ *transitive verb* **-fied; -fy·ing** [Middle English *scarifien*, from Middle French *scarifier*, from Late Latin *scarificare*, alteration of Latin *scarifare*, from Greek *skariphasthai* to scratch an outline, sketch — more at SCRIBE] (14th century)
1 : to make scratches or small cuts in (as the skin) ⟨*scarify* an area for vaccination⟩
2 : to lacerate the feelings of
3 : to break up and loosen the surface of (as a field or road)
4 : to cut or soften the wall of (a hard seed) to hasten germination
— **scar·i·fi·er** \-,fī(-ə)r\ *noun*

²**scarify** *transitive verb* **-fied; -fy·ing** (1794)
: SCARE, FRIGHTEN
— **scar·i·fy·ing·ly** \-,fī-iŋ-lē\ *adverb*

scar·i·ous \'skar-ē-əs, 'sker-\ *adjective* [New Latin *scariosus*] (circa 1806)
: dry and membranous in texture ⟨a *scarious* bract⟩

scar·la·ti·na \,skär-lə-'tē-nə\ *noun* [New Latin, from Medieval Latin *scarlata* scarlet] (1803)
: SCARLET FEVER
— **scar·la·ti·nal** \-'tē-nᵊl\ *adjective*

¹**scar·let** \'skär-lət\ *noun* [Middle English *scarlat, scarlet*, from Old French or Medieval Latin; Old French *escarlate*, from Medieval

Latin *scarlata*, from Persian *saqalāt*, a kind of rich cloth] (13th century)
1 : scarlet cloth or clothes
2 : any of various bright reds

²**scarlet** *adjective* (14th century)
1 : of the color scarlet
2 a : grossly and glaringly offensive ⟨sinning in flagrant and *scarlet* fashion —G. W. Johnson⟩ **b** [from the use of the word in Isaiah 1:18 & Revelation 17:1–6 (Authorized Version)] **:** of, characterized by, or associated with sexual immorality ⟨a *scarlet* woman⟩

scarlet fever *noun* (1676)
: an acute contagious febrile disease caused by hemolytic streptococci (especially various strains of *Streptococcus pyogenes*) and characterized by inflammation of the nose, throat, and mouth, generalized toxemia, and a red rash

scarlet letter *noun* [from such a letter in the novel *The Scarlet Letter* (1850) by Nathaniel Hawthorne] (1850)
: a scarlet A worn as a punitive mark of adultery

scarlet pimpernel *noun* (1855)
1 : a common pimpernel (*Anagallis arvensis*) having scarlet, white, or purplish flowers that close in cloudy weather
2 [*Scarlet Pimpernel*, assumed name of the hero of *The Scarlet Pimpernel* (1905), novel by Baroness Orczy] **:** a person who rescues others from mortal danger by smuggling them across a border

scarlet runner *noun* (1806)
: a tropical American high-climbing bean (*Phaseolus coccineus*) that has large bright red flowers and red-and-black seeds and is grown widely as an ornamental and as a food bean — called also *scarlet runner bean*

scarlet sage *noun* (circa 1890)
: a garden salvia (*Salvia splendens*) of Brazil with long racemes of intense typically scarlet flowers

scarlet tanager *noun* (1810)
: a common American tanager (*Piranga olivacea*) with the male having scarlet plumage and black wings during the breeding season and the female having chiefly olive plumage

scarp \'skärp\ *noun* [Italian *scarpa*] (1589)
1 : the inner side of a ditch below the parapet of a fortification
2 a : a line of cliffs produced by faulting or erosion — see FAULT illustration **b :** a low steep slope along a beach caused by wave erosion
— **scarped** *adjective*

scar·per \'skär-pər\ *intransitive verb* [probably ultimately from Italian *scappare*, from (assumed) Vulgar Latin *excappare* — more at ESCAPE] (circa 1846)
British **:** FLEE, RUN AWAY; *broadly* **:** LEAVE, DEPART

scar·ry \'skär-ē\ *adjective* [²*scar*] (1653)
: bearing marks of wounds **:** SCARRED

¹**scart** \'skärt\ *verb* [Middle English, alteration of *scratten* to scratch] (14th century)
chiefly Scottish **:** SCRATCH, SCRAPE

²**scart** *noun* (circa 1585)
chiefly Scottish **:** SCRATCH, MARK; *especially* **:** one made in writing

scar tissue *noun* (1875)
: the connective tissue forming a scar and composed chiefly of fibroblasts in recent scars and largely of dense collagenous fibers in old scars

scary \'sker-ē, 'skar-\ *adjective* **scar·i·er; -est** (1582)
1 : causing fright **:** ALARMING ⟨a *scary* story⟩
2 : easily scared **:** TIMID
3 : feeling alarm or fright **:** FRIGHTENED

\ə\ **abut** \ᵊ\ **kitten** \ər\ **further** \a\ **ash** \ā\ **ace**
\ä\ **mop, mar** \aù\ **out** \ch\ **chin** \e\ **bet** \ē\ **easy**
\g\ **go** \i\ **hit** \ī\ **ice** \j\ **job** \ŋ\ **sing** \ō\ **go**
\ò\ **law** \òi\ **boy** \th\ **thin** \th\ **the** \ü\ **loot** \ù\ **foot**
\y\ **yet** \zh\ **vision** *see also* Guide to Pronunciation

— **scar·i·ly** \'sker-ə-lē, 'skar-\ *adverb*

¹**scat** \'skat\ *intransitive verb* **scat·ted; scat·ting** [*scat,* interjection used to drive away a cat] (1838)
1 : to go away quickly
2 : to move fast **:** SCOOT

²**scat** *noun* [perhaps from Greek *skat-, skōr* excrement — more at SCATOLOGY] (1927)
: an animal fecal dropping

³**scat** *noun* [origin unknown] (1929)
: jazz singing with nonsense syllables

⁴**scat** *intransitive verb* **scat·ted; scat·ting** (1935)
: to improvise nonsense syllables usually to an instrumental accompaniment **:** sing scat

scat·back \'skat-ˌbak\ *noun* [¹*scat* + *back*] (1945)
: an offensive back in football who is an especially fast and elusive ballcarrier

¹**scathe** \'skāth, 'skäth\ *noun* [Middle English *skathe,* from Old Norse *skathi;* akin to Old English *sceatha* injury, Greek *askēthēs* unharmed] (13th century)
: HARM, INJURY
— **scathe·less** \-ləs\ *adjective*

²**scathe** \'skāth\ *transitive verb* **scathed; scath·ing** (13th century)
1 : to do harm to; *specifically* **:** SCORCH, SEAR
2 : to assail with withering denunciation

scath·ing \'skā-thin\ *adjective* (1794)
: bitterly severe ⟨a *scathing* condemnation⟩
synonym see CAUSTIC
— **scath·ing·ly** \-thin-lē\ *adverb*

sca·tol·o·gy \ska-'tä-lə-jē, skə-\ *noun* [Greek *skat-, skōr* excrement; akin to Old English *scearn* dung, Latin m*uscerdae* mouse droppings] (1876)
1 : interest in or treatment of obscene matters especially in literature
2 : the biologically oriented study of excrement (as for taxonomic purposes or for the determination of diet)
— **scat·o·log·i·cal** \ˌska-tᵊl-'ä-ji-kəl\ *adjective*

scatt \'skat\ *noun* [Middle English *scat,* from Old Norse *skattr;* akin to Old English *sceat* property, money, a small coin, Old Church Slavonic *skotŭ* domestic animal] (13th century)
archaic **:** TAX, TRIBUTE

¹**scat·ter** \'ska-tər\ *verb* [Middle English *scateren*] (14th century)
transitive verb
1 a : to cause to separate widely **b :** to cause to vanish
2 *archaic* **:** to fling away heedlessly **:** SQUANDER
3 : to distribute irregularly
4 : to sow by casting in all directions **:** STREW
5 a : to reflect irregularly and diffusely **b :** to cause (a beam of radiation) to diffuse or disperse
6 : to divide into ineffectual small portions
intransitive verb
1 : to separate and go in various directions **:** DISPERSE
2 : to occur or fall irregularly or at random ☆
— **scat·ter·er** \-tər-ər\ *noun*

²**scatter** *noun* (1642)
1 : the act of scattering
2 : a small quantity or number irregularly distributed or strewn about **:** SCATTERING
3 : the state or extent of being scattered; *especially* **:** DISPERSION

scat·ter·ation \ˌska-tə-'rā-shən\ *noun* (1776)
1 : the act or process of scattering **:** the state of being scattered
2 : the movement of people and industry away from the city; *also* **:** the resulting regional urbanization
3 : a policy of distributing funds and energies in too many ineffectively small units

scat·ter·brain \'ska-tər-ˌbrān\ *noun* (1790)
: a giddy heedless person

scat·ter·brained \-ˌbrānd\ *adjective* (1747)
: having the characteristics of a scatterbrain

scatter diagram *noun* (1925)
: a two-dimensional graph in rectangular coordinates consisting of points whose coordinates represent values of two variables under study

scat·ter·good \'ska-tər-ˌgùd\ *noun* (1577)
: a wasteful person **:** SPENDTHRIFT

scat·ter·gram \-ˌgram\ *noun* (1938)
: SCATTER DIAGRAM

scat·ter·gun \-ˌgən\ *noun or adjective* (1836)
: SHOTGUN

¹**scat·ter·ing** *noun* (14th century)
1 : an act or process in which something scatters or is scattered
2 : something scattered: as **a :** a small number or quantity interspersed here and there ⟨a *scattering* of visitors⟩ **b :** the random change in direction of the particles constituting a beam or wave front due to collision with particles of the medium traversed

²**scattering** *adjective* (15th century)
1 : going in various directions
2 : found or placed far apart and in no order
3 : divided among many or several ⟨*scattering* votes⟩
— **scat·ter·ing·ly** \'ska-tə-riŋ-lē\ *adverb*

scatter rug *noun* (1926)
: a rug of such a size that several can be used in a room

scat·ter·shot \'ska-tər-ˌshät\ *adjective* (1951)
: broadly and often randomly inclusive **:** SHOTGUN

scat·ty \'ska-tē\ *adjective* **scat·ti·er; -est** [probably from *scatterbrain* + ¹-*y*] (1911)
chiefly British **:** CRAZY

scaup \'skóp\ *noun, plural* **scaup** *or* **scaups** [short for *scaup duck; scaup* probably alteration of *scalp* bed of shellfish] (1797)
: either of two diving ducks (*Aythya affinis* or *A. marila*) with the male having a glossy purplish or greenish head and a black breast and tail

scav·enge \'ska-vənj, -vinj\ *verb* **scav·enged; scav·eng·ing** [back-formation from *scavenger*] (circa 1644)
transitive verb
1 a (1) **:** to remove (as dirt or refuse) from an area (2) **:** to clean away dirt or refuse from **:** CLEANSE ⟨*scavenge* a street⟩ **b :** to feed on (carrion or refuse)
2 a : to remove (burned gases) from the cylinder of an internal combustion engine after a working stroke **b :** to remove (as an undesirable constituent) from a substance or region by chemical or physical means **c :** to clean and purify (molten metal) by taking up foreign elements in chemical union
3 : to salvage from discarded or refuse material; *also* **:** to salvage usable material from
intransitive verb
: to work or act as a scavenger

scav·en·ger \'ska-vən-jər\ *noun* [alteration of earlier *scavager,* from Middle English *skawager* customs collector, from *skawage* customs, from Old North French *escauwage* inspection, from *escauwer* to inspect, of Germanic origin; akin to Old English *scēawian* to look at — more at SHOW] (1530)
1 *chiefly British* **:** a person employed to remove dirt and refuse from streets
2 : one that scavenges: as **a :** a garbage collector **b :** a junk collector **c :** a chemically active substance acting to make innocuous or remove an undesirable substance
3 : an organism that feeds habitually on refuse or carrion

scavenger hunt *noun* (1936)
: a game in which players try to acquire without buying specified items within a time limit

sce·na \'shā-ˌnä\ *noun* [Italian, literally, scene, from Latin] (1819)

: an elaborate solo vocal composition that consists of a recitative usually followed by one or more aria sections

sce·nar·io \sə-'nar-ē-ˌō, -'ner-\ *noun, plural* **-i·os** [Italian, from Latin *scaenarium* place for erecting stages, from *scaena* stage] (1878)
1 a : an outline or synopsis of a play; *especially* **:** a plot outline used by actors of the commedia dell'arte **b :** the libretto of an opera
2 a : SCREENPLAY **b :** SHOOTING SCRIPT
3 : a sequence of events especially when imagined; *especially* **:** an account or synopsis of a possible course of action or events ⟨his *scenario* for a settlement envisaged . . . reunification —Selig Harrison⟩

sce·nar·ist \-'nar-ist, -'ner-\ *noun* (1920)
: a writer of scenarios

scend \'send\ *noun* [perhaps short for *ascend*] (circa 1883)
1 : the lift of a wave **:** SEND
2 : the upward movement of a pitching ship

scene \'sēn\ *noun* [Middle French, stage, from Latin *scena, scaena* stage, scene, probably from Etruscan, from Greek *skēnē* shelter, tent, building forming the background for a dramatic performance, stage; perhaps akin to Greek *skia* shadow — more at SHINE] (1540)
1 : one of the subdivisions of a play: as **a :** a division of an act presenting continuous action in one place **b :** a single situation or unit of dialogue in a play ⟨the love *scene*⟩ **c :** a motion-picture or television episode or sequence
2 a : a stage setting **b :** a real or imaginary prospect suggesting a stage setting ⟨a sylvan *scene*⟩
3 : the place of an occurrence or action **:** LOCALE ⟨*scene* of the crime⟩
4 : an exhibition of anger or indecorous behavior ⟨make a *scene*⟩
5 a : sphere of activity ⟨the drug *scene*⟩ **b :** SITUATION ⟨a bad *scene*⟩
— **behind the scenes 1 :** out of public view; *also* **:** in secret **2 :** in a position to see the hidden workings ⟨taken *behind the scenes* and told just how in fact the actual government . . . has operated —William Clark⟩

scen·ery \'sē-nə-rē, 'sēn-rē\ *noun, plural* **-er·ies** (1770)
1 : the painted scenes or hangings and accessories used on a theater stage
2 : a picturesque view or landscape

scene-shift·er \'sēn-ˌshif-tər\ *noun* (1752)
: a worker who moves the scenes in a theater

scene-steal·er \-ˌstē-lər\ *noun* (1949)
: an actor who attracts attention when another is intended to be the center of attention

sce·nic \'sē-nik *also* 'se-\ *also* **sce·ni·cal** \-ni-kəl\ *adjective* (1623)
1 : of or relating to the stage, a stage setting, or stage representation
2 : of or relating to natural scenery ⟨a *scenic* view⟩
3 : representing graphically an action, event, or episode ⟨a *scenic* bas-relief⟩
— **sce·ni·cal·ly** \-ni-k(ə-)lē\ *adverb*

scenic railway *noun* (1894)
chiefly British **:** a miniature railway (as in an amusement park) with artificial scenery along the way

☆ **SYNONYMS**
Scatter, disperse, dissipate, dispel
mean to cause to separate or break up. SCATTER implies a force that drives parts or units irregularly in many directions ⟨the bowling ball *scattered* the pins⟩. DISPERSE implies a wider separation and a complete breaking up of a mass or group ⟨police *dispersed* the crowd⟩. DISSIPATE stresses complete disintegration or dissolution and final disappearance ⟨the fog was *dissipated* by the morning sun⟩. DISPEL stresses a driving away or getting rid of as if by scattering ⟨an authoritative statement that *dispelled* all doubt⟩.

sce·nog·ra·phy \sē-'nä-grə-fē\ *noun* [Greek *skēnographia* painting of scenery, from *skēnē* + *-graphia* -graphy] (1645)
: the art of perspective representation especially as applied to the painting of stage scenery (as by the ancient Greeks)
— **sce·nog·ra·pher** \-grə-fər\ *noun*
— **sce·no·graph·ic** \ˌsē-nə-'gra-fik\ *adjective*

¹**scent** \'sent\ *noun* [Middle English *sent*, from *senten*] (14th century)
1 : effluvia from a substance that affect the sense of smell: as **a** : an odor left by an animal on a surface passed over **b** : a characteristic or particular odor; *especially* : one that is agreeable
2 a : power of smelling : sense of smell ⟨a keen *scent*⟩ **b** : power of detection : NOSE ⟨a *scent* for heresy⟩
3 : a course of pursuit or discovery ⟨throw one off the *scent*⟩
4 : INKLING, INTIMATION ⟨a *scent* of trouble⟩
5 : PERFUME 2
6 : bits of paper dropped in the game of hare and hounds
7 : a mixture prepared for use as a lure in hunting or fishing
synonym see FRAGRANCE, SMELL
— **scent·less** \'sent-ləs\ *adjective*

²**scent** *verb* [Middle English *senten*, from Middle French *sentir* to feel, smell, from Latin *sentire* to perceive, feel — more at SENSE] (15th century)
transitive verb
1 a : to perceive by the olfactory organs : SMELL **b** : to get or have an inkling of ⟨*scent* trouble⟩
2 : to imbue or fill with odor ⟨*scented* the air with perfume⟩
intransitive verb
1 : to yield an odor of some specified kind ⟨this *scents* of sulfur⟩; *also* : to bear indication or suggestions
2 : to use the nose in seeking or tracking prey

scent·ed *adjective* (1666)
: having scent: as **a** : having the sense of smell **b** : having a perfumed smell **c** : having or exhaling an odor

¹**scep·ter** \'sep-tər\ *noun* [Middle English *sceptre*, from Middle French *ceptre*, from Latin *sceptrum*, from Greek *skēptron* staff, scepter, from *skēptesthai* to prop oneself — more at SHAFT] (14th century)
1 : a staff or baton borne by a sovereign as an emblem of authority
2 : royal or imperial authority : SOVEREIGNTY

²**scepter** *transitive verb* **scep·tered; scep·ter·ing** \-t(ə-)riŋ\ (1526)
: to invest with the scepter in token of royal authority

scep·tered \'sep-tərd\ *adjective* (1513)
1 : invested with a scepter or sovereign authority
2 : of or relating to a sovereign or to royalty

scep·tic, scep·ti·cal, scep·ti·cism *variant of* SKEPTIC, SKEPTICAL, SKEPTICISM

sceptre *British variant of* SCEPTER

scha·den·freu·de \'shä-d°n-ˌfrȯi-də\ *noun, often capitalized* [German, from *Schaden* damage + *Freude* joy] (1895)
: enjoyment obtained from the troubles of others

¹**sched·ule** \'ske-(ˌ)jü(ə)l, -jəl, *Canadian also* 'she-, *British usually* 'she-(ˌ)dyü(ə)l\ *noun* [alteration of Middle English *cedule*, from Middle French, slip of paper, note, from Late Latin *schedula* slip of paper, diminutive of (assumed) Latin *scheda* strip of papyrus, probably back-formation from Latin *schedium* impromptu speech, from Greek *schedion*, from neuter of *schedios* casual; akin to Greek *schedon* near at hand, *echein* to seize, have] (1560)

1 a *obsolete* : a written document **b** : a statement of supplementary details appended to a legal or legislative document
2 : a written or printed list, catalog, or inventory; *also* : TIMETABLE 1
3 : PROGRAM; *especially* : a procedural plan that indicates the time and sequence of each operation ⟨finished on *schedule*⟩
4 : a body of items to be dealt with : AGENDA
5 : a governmental list of drugs all subject to the same legal restrictions and controls □

²**schedule** *transitive verb* **sched·uled; sched·ul·ing** (1862)
1 a : to place in a schedule **b** : to make a schedule of
2 : to appoint, assign, or designate for a fixed time
— **sched·ul·er** *noun*

schee·lite \'shā-ˌlīt\ *noun* [German *Scheelit*, from Karl W. *Scheele* (died 1786) Swedish chemist] (circa 1837)
: a mineral consisting of the tungstate of calcium that is a source of tungsten and its compounds

Sche·her·a·zade \shə-ˌher-ə-'zäd; -'zä-də, -dē\ *noun* [German *Scheherezade*, from Persian *Shīrazād*]
: the fictional wife of an oriental king and the narrator of the tales in the *Arabian Nights' Entertainments*

sche·ma \'skē-mə\ *noun, plural* **sche·ma·ta** \-mə-tə\ *also* **schemas** [Greek *schēmat-*, *schēma*] (circa 1890)
1 : a diagrammatic presentation; *broadly* : a structured framework or plan : OUTLINE
2 : a mental codification of experience that includes a particular organized way of perceiving cognitively and responding to a complex situation or set of stimuli

¹**sche·mat·ic** \ski-'ma-tik\ *adjective* [New Latin *schematicus*, from Greek *schēmat-*, *schēma*] (1701)
: of or relating to a scheme or schema
— **sche·mat·i·cal·ly** \-ti-k(ə-)lē\ *adverb*

²**schematic** *noun* (1929)
: a schematic drawing or diagram

sche·ma·tism \'skē-mə-ˌti-zəm\ *noun* (1660)
: the disposition of constituents in a pattern or according to a scheme : DESIGN; *also* : a particular systematic disposition of parts

sche·ma·tize \'skē-mə-ˌtīz\ *transitive verb* **-tized; -tiz·ing** [Greek *schēmatizein*, from *schēmat-*, *schēma*] (1828)
1 : to form or to form into a scheme or systematic arrangement
2 : to express or depict schematically
— **sche·ma·ti·za·tion** \ˌskē-mə-tə-'zā-shən\ *noun*

¹**scheme** \'skēm\ *noun* [Latin *schemat-*, *schema* arrangement, figure, from Greek *schēmat-*, *schēma*, from *echein* to have, hold, be in (such) a condition; akin to Old English *sige* victory, Sanskrit *sahate* he prevails] (1610)
1 a *archaic* (1) : a mathematical or astronomical diagram (2) : a representation of the astrological aspects of the planets at a particular time **b** : a graphic sketch or outline
2 : a concise statement or table : EPITOME
3 : a plan or program of action; *especially* : a crafty or secret one
4 : a systematic or organized framework : DESIGN
synonym see PLAN

²**scheme** *verb* **schemed; schem·ing** (1767)
transitive verb
: to form a scheme for
intransitive verb
: to form plans; *also* : PLOT, INTRIGUE
— **schem·er** *noun*

schem·ing *adjective* (circa 1828)
: given to forming schemes; *especially* : shrewdly devious and intriguing

¹**scher·zan·do** \skert-'sän-(ˌ)dō\ *adverb or*
adjective [Italian, from verbal of *scherzare* to joke, of Germanic origin; akin to Middle High German *scherzen* to leap for joy, joke; perhaps akin to Greek *skairein* to gambol] (circa 1811)
: in sportive manner : PLAYFULLY — used as a direction in music indicating style and tempo ⟨allegretto *scherzando*⟩

²**scherzando** *noun, plural* **-dos** (circa 1876)
: a passage or movement in scherzando style

scher·zo \'skert-(ˌ)sō\ *noun, plural* **scher·zos** *or* **scher·zi** \-(ˌ)sē\ [Italian, literally, joke, from *scherzare*] (1852)
: a sprightly humorous instrumental musical composition or movement commonly in quick triple time

Schick test \'shik-\ *noun* [Béla *Schick*] (1916)
: a serological test for susceptibility to diphtheria by cutaneous injection of a diluted diphtheria toxin that causes an area of reddening and induration in susceptible individuals

Schiff's reagent \'shifs-\ *noun* [Hugo *Schiff* (died 1915) German chemist] (1897)
: a solution of fuchsine decolorized by treatment with sulfur dioxide that gives a useful test for aldehydes because they restore the dye's color — called also *Schiff reagent* \'shif-\; compare FEULGEN REACTION

schil·ler \'shi-lər\ *noun* [German] (1885)
: a bronzy iridescent luster (as of a mineral)

schil·ling \'shi-liŋ\ *noun* [German, from Old High German *skilling*, a gold coin — more at SHILLING] (1753)
— see MONEY table

schip·per·ke \'ski-pər-kē, 'shi-, -kə; -pərk\ *noun* [Flemish, diminutive of *schipper* skipper; from its use as a watchdog on boats — more at SKIPPER] (1887)
: any of a Belgian breed of small stocky black dogs with foxy head and heavy coat

schipperke

schism \'si-zəm, 'ski- *also* 'shi-; *among clergy usually* 'si-\ *noun* [Middle English *scisme*, from Middle French *cisme*, from Late Latin *schismat-*, *schisma*, from Greek, cleft, division, from *schizein* to split — more at SHED] (14th century)
1 : DIVISION, SEPARATION; *also* : DISCORD, DISHARMONY

\ə\ abut \ᵊ\ kitten \ər\ further \a\ ash \ā\ ace
\ä\ mop, mar \au̇\ out \ch\ chin \e\ bet \ē\ easy
\g\ go \i\ hit \ī\ ice \j\ job \ŋ\ sing \ō\ go
\ȯ\ law \ȯi\ boy \th\ thin \t̲h̲\ the \ü\ loot \u̇\ foot
\y\ yet \zh\ vision *see also* Guide to Pronunciation

2 a : formal division in or separation from a church or religious body **b :** the offense of promoting schism □

¹**schis·mat·ic** \siz-'ma-tik, ski-\ *noun* (14th century)
: one who creates or takes part in schism

²**schismatic** *also* **schis·mat·i·cal** \-ti-kəl\ *adjective* (15th century)
: of, relating to, or guilty of schism
— **schis·mat·i·cal·ly** \-ti-k(ə-)lē\ *adverb*

schis·ma·tize \'siz-mə-ˌtīz, 'skiz-\ *verb* **-tized; -tiz·ing** (1601)
intransitive verb
: to take part in schism; *especially* **:** to make a breach of union (as in the church)
transitive verb
: to induce into schism

schist \'shist\ *noun* [French *schiste*, from Latin *schistos* (*lapis*), literally, fissile stone, from Greek *schistos* that may be split, from *schizein*] (circa 1782)
: a metamorphic crystalline rock that has a closely foliated structure and can be split along approximately parallel planes

schis·tose \'shis-ˌtōs\ *adjective* (1794)
: of or relating to schist **:** having the character or structure of a schist
— **schis·tos·i·ty** \shis-'tä-sə-tē\ *noun*

schis·to·some \'shis-tə-ˌsōm\ *noun* [New Latin *Schistosoma*, from Greek *schistos* + *sōma* body] (1905)
: any of a genus (*Schistosoma*) of elongated trematode worms with the sexes separate that parasitize the blood vessels of birds and mammals and cause a destructive human schistosomiasis; *broadly* **:** a worm of the family (Schistosomatidae) that includes this genus
— **schis·to·som·al** \ˌshis-tə-'sō-məl\ *adjective*
— **schistosome** *adjective*

schis·to·so·mi·a·sis \ˌshis-tə-sō-'mī-ə-səs\ *noun, plural* **-a·ses** \-ˌsēz\ [New Latin, from *Schistosoma*] (1906)
: infestation with or disease caused by schistosomes; *specifically* **:** a severe endemic disease of humans in much of Asia, Africa, and South America marked especially by blood loss and tissue damage

schiz- *or* **schizo-** *combining form* [New Latin, from Greek *schizo-*, from *schizein* to split — more at SHED]
1 : split **:** cleft ⟨*schizo*carp⟩
2 : characterized by or involving cleavage ⟨*schizo*gony⟩
3 : schizophrenia ⟨*schiz*oid⟩

schizo \'skit-(ˌ)sō\ *noun, plural* **schiz·os** (1945)
: a schizophrenic individual

schizo·carp \'ski-zə-ˌkärp, 'skit-sə-\ *noun* [International Scientific Vocabulary] (1870)
: a dry compound fruit that splits at maturity into several indehiscent one-seeded carpels

schi·zog·o·ny \ski-'zä-gə-nē, skit-'sä-\ *noun* [New Latin *schizogonia*, from *schiz-* + Latin *-gonia -gony*] (1887)
: asexual reproduction by multiple segmentation characteristic of sporozoans (as the malaria parasite)
— **schizo·gon·ic** \ˌski-zə-'gä-nik, ˌskit-sə-\ *or* **schi·zog·o·nous** \ski-'zä-gə-nəs, skit-'sä-gə-\ *adjective*

schiz·oid \'skit-ˌsȯid\ *adjective* [International Scientific Vocabulary] (1924)
: characterized by, resulting from, tending toward, or suggestive of schizophrenia
— **schizoid** *noun*

schiz·ont \'ski-ˌzänt, 'skit-ˌsänt\ *noun* [International Scientific Vocabulary] (1900)
: a multinucleate sporozoan that reproduces by schizogony

schizo·phrene \'skit-sə-ˌfrēn\ *noun* [International Scientific Vocabulary, probably back-formation from New Latin *schizophrenia*] (1925)
: one affected with schizophrenia **:** SCHIZOPHRENIC

schizo·phre·nia \ˌskit-sə-'frē-nē-ə\ *noun* [New Latin] (1912)
1 : a psychotic disorder characterized by loss of contact with the environment, by noticeable deterioration in the level of functioning in everyday life, and by disintegration of personality expressed as disorder of feeling, thought (as in hallucinations and delusions), and conduct — called also *dementia praecox*
2 : contradictory or antagonistic qualities or attitudes ⟨both parties . . . have exhibited *schizophrenia* over the desired outcome —Elizabeth Drew⟩
— **schizo·phren·ic** \-'fre-nik\ *adjective or noun*
— **schizo·phren·i·cal·ly** \-ni-k(ə-)lē\ *adverb*

schizy *or* **schiz·zy** \'skit-sē\ *adjective* [by shortening & alteration] (1927)
: SCHIZOID

schle·miel \shlə-'mē(ə)l\ *noun* [Yiddish *shlemil*] (1892)
: an unlucky bungler **:** CHUMP

schlepp *or* **schlep** \'shlep\ *verb* [Yiddish *shlepn*, from Middle High German *slepen*, from Middle Low German *slēpen*] (1922)
transitive verb
: DRAG, HAUL
intransitive verb
: to proceed or move slowly, tediously, or awkwardly

schlie·ren \'shlir-ən\ *noun plural* [German] (1898)
1 : small masses or streaks in an igneous rock that differ in composition from the main body
2 : regions of varying refraction in a transparent medium often caused by pressure or temperature differences and detectable especially by photographing the passage of a beam of light
— **schlie·ric** \'shlir-ik\ *adjective*

schlock \'shläk\ *also* **schlocky** \'shlä-kē\ *adjective* [perhaps from Yiddish *shlak* evil, nuisance, literally, blow, from Middle High German *slag, slac*, from Old High German *slag*, from *slahan* to strike — more at SLAY] (1915)
: of low quality or value
— **schlock** *noun*

schm- *or* **shm-** \shm\ *prefix* [Yiddish *shm-*]
— used to form a rhyming term of derision by replacing the initial consonant or consonant cluster of a word or by preceding the initial vowel ⟨fancy, *schm*ancy, I prefer plain⟩ ⟨Godfather—*shm*odfather—enough already —Judith Crist⟩

schmaltz *also* **schmalz** \'shmȯlts, 'shmälts\ *noun* [Yiddish *shmalts*, literally, rendered fat, from Middle High German *smalz*; akin to Old High German *smelzan* to melt — more at SMELT] (1935)
1 : sentimental or florid music or art
2 : SENTIMENTALITY
— **schmaltzy** \'shmȯlt-sē, 'shmält-\ *adjective*

schmear *or* **schmeer** \'shmir\ *noun* [Yiddish *shmir* smear; akin to Old High German *smero* grease — more at SMEAR] (1965)
: an aggregate of related things ⟨the whole *schmear*⟩

Schmidt camera \'shmit-\ *noun* [B. Schmidt (died 1935) German optical scientist] (1936)
: a photographic telescope with specialized optics that correct for spherical aberration and coma — called also *Schmidt telescope*

schmo *or* **schmoe** \'shmō\ *noun, plural* **schmoes** [origin unknown] (1947)
slang **:** JERK 4

schmooze *or* **shmooze** \'shmüz\ *intransitive verb* [Yiddish *shmuesn*, from *shmues* talk, from Hebrew *shĕmu'ōth* news, rumor] (1897)
: to converse informally **:** CHAT

schmuck \'shmək\ *noun* [Yiddish *shmok*, literally, penis] (1892)
slang **:** JERK 4

schnapps \'shnaps\ *noun, plural* **schnapps** [German *Schnaps*, literally, dram of liquor, from Low German *snaps* dram, mouthful, from *snappen* to snap] (1818)
: any of various liquors of high alcoholic content; *especially* **:** strong Holland gin

schnau·zer \'shnaût-sər, 'shnaû-zər\ *noun* [German, from *Schnauze* snout — more at SNOUT] (1923)
: a dog of any of three breeds that originated in Germany and are characterized by a wiry coat, long head, small ears, heavy eyebrows, and long hair on the muzzle: **a :** STANDARD SCHNAUZER **b :** GIANT SCHNAUZER **c :** MINIATURE SCHNAUZER

schnit·zel \'shnit-səl\ *noun* [German, literally, shaving, chip, diminutive of *Schnitz* slice, from Middle High German *snitz*; akin to Old High German *snīdan* to cut, Old English *snīthan*, and perhaps to Czech *snět* bough] (1854)
: a seasoned and garnished veal cutlet

schnook \'shnùk\ *noun* [origin unknown] (1940)
slang **:** a stupid or unimportant person **:** DOLT

schnor·kel \'shnȯr-kəl\ *variant of* SNORKEL

schnor·rer \'shnȯr-ər, 'shnōr-\ *noun* [Yiddish *shnorer*] (1892)
: BEGGAR; *especially* **:** one who wheedles others into supplying his wants

schnoz·zle \'shnä-zəl\ *noun* [probably modification of Yiddish *shnoitsl*, diminutive of *shnoits* snout; akin to German *Schnauze* snout, muzzle — more at SNOUT] (1937)
slang **:** NOSE

scho·la can·to·rum \ˌskō-lə-kan-'tōr-əm, -'tȯr-\ *noun, plural* **scho·lae can·torum** \-ˌlē, -ˌlā-, -ˌlī-\ [Medieval Latin, school of singers] (1782)
1 : a singing school especially for church choristers; *specifically* **:** the choir or choir school of a monastery or of a cathedral
2 : an enclosure designed for a choir and located in the center of the nave in early church buildings

schol·ar \'skä-lər\ *noun* [Middle English *scoler*, from Old English *scolere* & Old French *escoler*, from Medieval Latin *scholaris*, from Late Latin, of a school, from Latin *schola* school] (before 12th century)
1 : one who attends a school or studies under a teacher **:** PUPIL
2 a : one who has done advanced study in a special field **b :** a learned person
3 : a holder of a scholarship

schol·ar·ly \-lē\ *adjective* (1638)
: of, characteristic of, or suitable to learned persons **:** LEARNED, ACADEMIC

□ USAGE

schism With the rebirth of classical learning in the Renaissance came a "silent" revolution in English spelling, whereby words formerly spelled as they were pronounced (like *onur, douten, indite,* and *receite*) were given extra letters to match their ancestral forms in Latin and Greek (yielding *honor, doubt, indict,* and *receipt*). The modern spelling of Middle English *scisme* is a product of this reform, as is the modern confusion over its pronunciation. The \'ski-zəm\ variant is a spelling pronunciation, the \'shi-zəm\ variant is another spelling pronunciation following the conventions of modern French or German, and the \'si-zəm\ variant retains the original Middle English and Middle French sound. Some insist the original \'si-zəm\ alone is correct, but these critics are not similarly exercised by the modern spelling pronunciations of *hermit* and *hostage*, which like *schism* originally had no *h* in spelling or pronunciation. Many educated speakers today use the fully acceptable spelling pronunciation \'ski-zəm\.

schol·ar·ship \-,ship\ *noun* (circa 1536)
1 : a grant-in-aid to a student (as by a college or foundation)
2 : the character, qualities, activity, or attainments of a scholar : LEARNING
3 : a fund of knowledge and learning ⟨drawing on the *scholarship* of the ancients⟩
synonym see KNOWLEDGE
Scholarship level *noun* (1947)
: S LEVEL
¹scho·las·tic \skə-'las-tik\ *adjective* [Medieval Latin & Latin; Medieval Latin *scholasticus* of the schoolmen, from Latin, of a school, from Greek *scholastikos,* from *scholazein* to keep a school, from *scholē* school] (1596)
1 a *often capitalized* : of or relating to Scholasticism ⟨*scholastic* theology⟩ ⟨*scholastic* philosophy⟩ **b** : suggestive or characteristic of a scholastic especially in subtlety or aridity : PEDANTIC ⟨dull *scholastic* reports⟩
2 : of or relating to schools or scholars; *especially* : of or relating to high school or secondary school
— **scho·las·ti·cal·ly** \-ti-k(ə-)lē\ *adverb*
²scholastic *noun* (1644)
1 a *capitalized* : a Scholastic philosopher **b** : PEDANT, FORMALIST
2 [New Latin *scholasticus,* from Latin *scholasticus,* adjective] : a student in a scholasticate
3 : one who adopts academic or traditional methods in art
scho·las·ti·cate \skə-'las-tə-,kāt, -ti-kət\ *noun* [New Latin *scholasticatus,* from *scholasticus* student in a scholasticate] (1875)
: a college-level school of general study for those preparing for membership in a Roman Catholic religious order
scho·las·ti·cism \skə-'las-tə-,si-zəm\ *noun* (circa 1782)
1 *capitalized* **a** : a philosophical movement dominant in western Christian civilization from the 9th until the 17th century and combining religious dogma with the mystical and intuitional tradition of patristic philosophy especially of Saint Augustine and later with Aristotelianism **b** : NEO-SCHOLASTICISM
2 a : close adherence to the traditional teachings or methods of a school or sect **b** : pedantic adherence to scholarly methods
scho·li·ast \'skō-lē-,ast, -lē-əst\ *noun* [Middle Greek *scholiastēs,* from *scholiazein* to write scholia on, from Greek *scholion*] (1583)
: a maker of scholia : COMMENTATOR, ANNOTATOR
— **scho·li·as·tic** \,skō-lē-'as-tik\ *adjective*
scho·li·um \'skō-lē-əm\ *noun, plural* **-lia** \-lē-ə\ *or* **-li·ums** [New Latin, from Greek *scholion* comment, scholium, from diminutive of *scholē* lecture] (1535)
1 : a marginal annotation or comment (as on the text of a classic by an early grammarian)
2 : a remark or observation subjoined but not essential to a demonstration or a train of reasoning
¹school \'skül\ *noun* [Middle English *scole,* from Old English *scōl,* from Latin *schola,* from Greek *scholē* leisure, discussion, lecture, school; perhaps akin to Greek *echein* to hold — more at SCHEME] (before 12th century)
1 : an organization that provides instruction: as **a** : an institution for the teaching of children **b** : COLLEGE, UNIVERSITY **c** (1) : a group of scholars and teachers pursuing knowledge together that with similar groups constituted a medieval university (2) : one of the four faculties of a medieval university (3) : an institution for specialized higher education often associated with a university ⟨the *school* of engineering⟩ **d** : an establishment offering specialized instruction ⟨a secretarial *school*⟩ ⟨driving *schools*⟩

2 a (1) : the process of teaching or learning especially at a school (2) : attendance at a school (3) : a session of a school **b** : a school building **c** : the students attending a school; *also* : its teachers and students
3 : a source of knowledge ⟨experience was his *school*⟩
4 a : persons who hold a common doctrine or follow the same teacher (as in philosophy, theology, or medicine) ⟨the Aristotelian *school*⟩ **b** : a group of artists under a common influence **c** : persons of similar opinions or behavior ⟨other *schools* of thought⟩
5 : the regulations governing military drill of individuals or units; *also* : the exercises carried out ⟨the *school* of the soldier⟩ ◇
²school *transitive verb* (15th century)
1 a : to teach or drill in a specific knowledge or skill ⟨well *schooled* in languages⟩ **b** : to discipline or habituate to something ⟨*school* oneself in patience⟩
2 : to educate in an institution of learning
synonym see TEACH
³school *noun* [Middle English *scole,* from Middle Dutch *schole;* akin to Old English *scolu* multitude and probably to Old English *scylian* to separate — more at SKILL] (15th century)
: a large number of fish or aquatic animals of one kind swimming together
⁴school *intransitive verb* (1597)
: to swim or feed in a school ⟨bluefish are *schooling*⟩
school–age *adjective* (1741)
: old enough to go to school ⟨*school-age* children⟩
school·bag \'skül-,bag\ *noun* (1895)
: a bag for carrying schoolbooks and school supplies
school board *noun* (1836)
: a board in charge of local public schools
school·book \-,buk\ *noun* (1745)
: a school textbook
¹school·boy \-,boi\ *noun* (1588)
: a boy attending school
²schoolboy *adjective* (1687)
1 : of, relating to, or characteristic of a schoolboy ⟨*schoolboy* pranks⟩
2 : of, relating to, or being a sport for high school or prep school boys; *also* : being one who participates in such sports ⟨a former *schoolboy* and collegiate goalie —D. J. Barr⟩
school·boy·ish \-,boi-ish\ *adjective* (1831)
: SCHOOLBOY 1
school bus *noun* (1908)
: a vehicle used for transporting children to or from school or on activities connected with school
school·child \'skül-,chīld\ *noun* (1840)
: a child attending school
school committee *noun* (1787)
: SCHOOL BOARD
school district *noun* (1809)
: a unit for administration of a public-school system often comprising several towns within a state
school·fel·low \'skül-,fe-(,)lō\ *noun* (15th century)
: SCHOOLMATE
school·girl \-,gər(-ə)l\ *noun* (1777)
: a girl attending school
school·house \-,haús\ *noun* (14th century)
: a building used as a school and especially as an elementary school
school·ing *noun* (15th century)
1 a : instruction in school : EDUCATION **b** : training, guidance, or discipline derived from experience
2 *archaic* : REPROOF
3 : the cost of instruction and maintenance at school
4 : the training of a horse to service; *especially* : the teaching and exercising of horse and rider in the formal techniques of equitation

school·kid \'skül-,kid\ *noun* (1938)
: a child or teenager attending school
school–leav·er \'skül-,lē-vər\ *noun* (1925)
British : one who has left school usually after completing a course of study
school·man \'skül-mən, -,man\ *noun* (circa 1540)
1 a : one skilled in academic disputation **b** *capitalized* : SCHOLASTIC 1a
2 : EDUCATOR 1, 2b
school·marm \-,mä(r)m\ *or* **school·ma'am** \-,mäm, -,mam\ *noun* [*school* + *marm,* alteration of *ma'am*] (1831)
1 : a woman schoolteacher especially in a rural or small-town school
2 : a person who exhibits characteristics attributed to schoolteachers (as strict adherence to arbitrary rules)
— **school·marm·ish** \-,mä(r)-mish\ *adjective*
school·mas·ter \-,mas-tər\ *noun* (13th century)
1 : a man who teaches school
2 : one that disciplines or directs
3 : a reddish brown edible snapper (*Lutjanus apodus*) of the tropical Atlantic and the Gulf of Mexico
— **school·mas·ter·ish** \-tə-rish\ *adjective*
— **school·mas·ter·ly** *adjective*
school·mate \-,māt\ *noun* (1563)
: a companion at school
school·mis·tress \-,mis-trəs\ *noun* (15th century)
: a woman who teaches school
school·room \-,rüm, -,rúm\ *noun* (1773)
: CLASSROOM
school·teach·er \-,tē-chər\ *noun* (circa 1847)
: one who teaches school
school·time \-,tīm\ *noun* (1740)
1 : the time for beginning a session of school or during which school is held
2 : the period of life spent in school or in study
school·work \-,wərk\ *noun* (1857)
: lessons done in class or assigned to be done at home

◇ **WORD HISTORY**
school The work we associate with elementary education today may make it hard to believe that the Greek ancestor of the word *school* meant "leisure," but such is the case. Ancient Greek *scholē* "rest, leisure" came to be applied to the learned discussions and philosophical disputations in which the cream of Greek society spent their free time (of which they had much). Its use was then extended to groups who listened to the lectures of a particular philosopher, and finally, in Hellenistic and later Greek, to the set of beliefs held by a particular philosophical group. When Latin *schola* was borrowed from Greek, the emphasis fell more on the place where a particular teacher expounded his views. The Romans later generalized *schola* to "place of instruction" and applied it to an establishment where a scholar tutored young students in the basics of writing and rhetoric. (The earlier Latin word for "place of instruction" was usually *ludus,* which had originally meant, ironically, "play, sport.") *Schola* also was applied in Latin to assembly places for fraternities of priests or other groups; a distant reflection of this sense, filtered through centuries of Jewish history, is the use of *shul* in Yiddish to mean "synagogue."

\ə\ abut \ə\ kitten \ər\ further \a\ ash \ā\ ace
\ä\ mop, mar \aú\ out \ch\ chin \e\ bet \ē\ easy
\g\ go \i\ hit \ī\ ice \j\ job \ŋ\ sing \ō\ go
\ò\ law \òi\ boy \th\ thin \th\ the \ü\ loot \ú\ foot
\y\ yet \zh\ vision *see also* Guide to Pronunciation

schoo·ner \'skü-nər\ *noun* [origin unknown] (1716)
1 : a typically 2-masted fore-and-aft rigged vessel with a foremast and a mainmast stepped nearly amidships
2 : a larger-than-usual drinking glass (as for beer)
3 : PRAIRIE SCHOONER

schooner 1

schooner rig *noun* (1866)
: FORE-AND-AFT RIG
— **schoo·ner–rigged** \'skü-nə(r)-'rigd\ *adjective*

schorl \'shȯr(ə)l\ *noun* [German *Schörl*] (1779)
: TOURMALINE; *especially* : tourmaline of the black variety

schot·tische \'shä-tish, shä-'tēsh\ *noun* [German, from *schottisch* Scottish, from *Schotte* Scotsman; akin to Old English *Scottas* Scots] (1849)
1 : a round dance resembling a slow polka
2 : music for the schottische

schrod *variant of* SCROD

Schrö·ding·er equation \'shrä-diŋ-ər, 'shrœ̄-, 'shrə(r)-\ *noun* [Erwin *Schrödinger*] (1936)
: an equation that describes the wave nature of elementary particles and is fundamental to the description of the properties of all matter

schtick *variant of* SHTICK

schuss \'shús, 'shüs\ *intransitive verb* [*schuss*, noun, from German *Schuss*, literally, shot, from Old High German *scuz* — more at SHOT] (1940)
: to ski directly down a slope at high speed
— **schuss** *noun*

schuss·boom·er \-ˌbü-mər\ *noun* (1953)
: a skier who schusses

schwa \'shwä\ *noun* [German, from Hebrew *schĕwā'*] (1895)
1 : an unstressed mid-central vowel (as the usual sound of the first and last vowels of the English word *America*)
2 : the symbol ə used for the schwa sound and less widely for a similarly articulated stressed vowel (as in *cut*)

Schwann cell \'shwän-\ *noun* [Theodor *Schwann* (died 1882) German naturalist] (circa 1909)
: the myelin-secreting cell surrounding a myelinated nerve fiber between two nodes of Ranvier

schwar·me·rei \ˌshver-mə-'rī\ *noun* [German *Schwärmerei*, from *schwärmen* to be enthusiastic, literally, to swarm] (1845)
: excessive or unwholesome sentiment

sci·at·ic \sī-'a-tik\ *adjective* [Middle French *sciatique*, from Late Latin *sciaticus*, alteration of Latin *ischiadicus* of sciatica, from Greek *ischiadikos*, from *ischiad-, ischias* sciatica, from *ischion* ischium] (1586)
1 : of, relating to, or situated near the hip
2 : of, relating to, or caused by sciatica ⟨*sciatic* pains⟩

sci·at·i·ca \sī-'a-ti-kə\ *noun* [Middle English, from Medieval Latin, from Late Latin, feminine of *sciaticus*] (14th century)
: pain along the course of a sciatic nerve especially in the back of the thigh; *broadly* : pain in the lower back, buttocks, hips, or adjacent parts

sciatic nerve *noun* (1741)
: either of the pair of largest nerves in the body that arise one on each side from the nerve plexus supplying the posterior limb and pelvic region and that pass out of the pelvis and down the back of the thigh

sci·ence \'sī-ən(t)s\ *noun* [Middle English, from Middle French, from Latin *scientia*, from

scient-, sciens having knowledge, from present participle of *scire* to know; probably akin to Sanskrit *chyati* he cuts off, Latin *scindere* to split — more at SHED] (14th century)
1 : the state of knowing : knowledge as distinguished from ignorance or misunderstanding
2 a : a department of systematized knowledge as an object of study ⟨the *science* of theology⟩ **b** : something (as a sport or technique) that may be studied or learned like systematized knowledge ⟨have it down to a *science*⟩
3 a : knowledge or a system of knowledge covering general truths or the operation of general laws especially as obtained and tested through scientific method **b** : such knowledge or such a system of knowledge concerned with the physical world and its phenomena : NATURAL SCIENCE
4 : a system or method reconciling practical ends with scientific laws ⟨culinary *science*⟩
5 *capitalized* : CHRISTIAN SCIENCE

science fiction *noun* (1851)
: fiction dealing principally with the impact of actual or imagined science on society or individuals or having a scientific factor as an essential orienting component

sci·en·tial \sī-'en(t)-shəl\ *adjective* (15th century)
1 : relating to or producing knowledge or science
2 : having efficient knowledge : CAPABLE

sci·en·tif·ic \ˌsī-ən-'ti-fik\ *adjective* [Medieval Latin *scientificus* producing knowledge, from Latin *scient-, sciens* + *-i-* + *-ficus* -fic] (1589)
: of, relating to, or exhibiting the methods or principles of science
— **sci·en·tif·i·cal·ly** \-fi-k(ə-)lē\ *adverb*

scientific method *noun* (1854)
: principles and procedures for the systematic pursuit of knowledge involving the recognition and formulation of a problem, the collection of data through observation and experiment, and the formulation and testing of hypotheses

scientific notation *noun* (circa 1934)
: a widely used floating-point system in which numbers are expressed as products consisting of a number between 1 and 10 multiplied by an appropriate power of 10

sci·en·tism \'sī-ən-ˌti-zəm\ *noun* (1877)
1 : methods and attitudes typical of or attributed to the natural scientist
2 : an exaggerated trust in the efficacy of the methods of natural science applied to all areas of investigation (as in philosophy, the social sciences, and the humanities)

sci·en·tist \'sī-ən-tist\ *noun* [Latin *scientia*] (1834)
1 : a person learned in science and especially natural science : a scientific investigator
2 *capitalized* : CHRISTIAN SCIENTIST

sci·en·tize \'sī-ən-ˌtīz\ *transitive verb* **-tized; -tiz·ing** (1917)
: to treat with a scientific approach ⟨the attempt to *scientize* reality, to name it and classify it —John Fowles⟩

sci-fi \'sī-ˈfī\ *adjective* [*sci*ence *fi*ction] (1955)
: of, relating to, or being science fiction ⟨a *sci-fi* film⟩
— **sci-fi** *noun*

sci·li·cet \'skē-li-ˌket; 'sī-lə-ˌset, 'si-\ *adverb* [Middle English, from Latin, surely, to wit, from *scire* to know + *licet* it is permitted, from *licēre* to be permitted — more at LICENSE] (14th century)
: TO WIT, NAMELY

scil·la \'si-lə, 'ski-\ *noun* [New Latin, from Latin, squill — more at SQUILL] (1824)
: any of a genus (*Scilla*) of Old World bulbous herbs of the lily family with narrow basal leaves and pink, blue, or white racemose flowers

scim·i·tar \'si-mə-tər, -ˌtär\ *noun* [Italian *scimitarra*] (circa 1548)

: a saber having a curved blade with the edge on the convex side and used chiefly by Arabs and Turks

scin·tig·ra·phy \sin-'ti-grə-fē\ *noun* [*scinti*llation + *-graphy*; from the scintillation counter used to record radiation on the picture] (1958)
: a diagnostic technique in which a two-dimensional picture of a bodily radiation source is obtained by the use of radioisotopes
— **scin·ti·graph·ic** \ˌsin-tə-'gra-fik\ *adjective*

scin·til·la \sin-'ti-lə\ *noun* [Latin] (1692)
: SPARK, TRACE

scin·til·lant \sin-'t°l-ənt\ *adjective* (1737)
: that scintillates : SPARKLING
— **scin·til·lant·ly** *adverb*

scin·til·late \'sin-t°l-ˌāt\ *verb* **-lat·ed; -lat·ing** [Latin *scintillatus*, past participle of *scintillare* to sparkle, from *scintilla* spark] (circa 1623)
intransitive verb
1 : to emit sparks : SPARK
2 : to emit quick flashes as if throwing off sparks : SPARKLE
transitive verb
: to throw off as a spark or as sparkling flashes ⟨*scintillate* witticisms⟩
— **scin·til·la·tor** \-ˌā-tər\ *noun*

scin·til·lat·ing *adjective* (1883)
: brilliantly lively, stimulating, or witty ⟨*scintillating* conversation⟩

scin·til·la·tion \ˌsin-t°l-'ā-shən\ *noun* (circa 1623)
1 : an act or instance of scintillating; *especially* : rapid changes in the brightness of a celestial body
2 a : a spark or flash emitted in scintillating **b** : a flash of light produced in a phosphor by an ionizing event
3 : a brilliant outburst (as of wit)
4 : a flash of the eye

scintillation counter *noun* (1948)
: a device for detecting and registering individual scintillations (as in radioactive emission)

scin·til·lom·e·ter \ˌsin-t°l-'ä-mə-tər\ *noun* [Latin *scintilla* + International Scientific Vocabulary *-o-* + *-meter*] (1877)
: SCINTILLATION COUNTER

sci·o·lism \'sī-ə-ˌli-zəm\ *noun* [Late Latin *sciolus* smatterer, from diminutive of Latin *scius* knowing, from *scire* to know — more at SCIENCE] (1816)
: a superficial show of learning
— **sci·o·list** \-list\ *noun*
— **sci·o·lis·tic** \ˌsī-ə-'lis-tik\ *adjective*

sci·on \'sī-ən\ *noun* [Middle English, from Middle French *cion*, of Germanic origin; akin to Old High German *chīnan* to sprout, split open, Old English *cīnan* to gape] (13th century)
1 : a detached living portion of a plant joined to a stock in grafting and usually supplying solely aerial parts to a graft
2 : DESCENDANT, CHILD

sci·re fa·cias \ˌsī-rē-'fā-sh(ē-)əs\ *noun* [Middle English, from Medieval Latin, you should cause to know] (15th century)
1 : a judicial writ founded on some matter of record and requiring the party proceeded against to show cause why the record should not be enforced, annulled, or vacated
2 : a legal proceeding instituted by a scire facias

sci·roc·co \shi-'rä-(ˌ)kō, sə-\ *variant of* SIROCCO

scir·rhous \'sir-əs, 'skir-\ *adjective* [New Latin *scirrhosus*, from *scirrhus* scirrhous tumor, from Greek *skiros, skirrhos* overgrown land, hardened tumor] (1563)
: of, relating to, or being a hard slow-growing malignant tumor having a preponderance of fibrous tissue

scis·sile \'si-səl, -ˌsīl\ *adjective* [French, from Latin *scissilis*, from *scissus*, past participle of *scindere* to split — more at SHED] (1621)

: capable of being cut smoothly or split easily ⟨a *scissile* peptide bond⟩

scis·sion \'si-zhən\ *noun* [Middle English *scissione,* from Middle French *scission,* from Late Latin *scission-, scissio,* from Latin *scindere*] (15th century)
1 : a division or split in a group or union : SCHISM
2 : an action or process of cutting, dividing, or splitting : the state of being cut, divided, or split

¹scis·sor \'si-zər\ *noun* [Middle English *sisoure,* from Middle French *cisoire,* from Late Latin *cisorium* cutting instrument, irregular from Latin *caedere* to cut] (15th century)
: SCISSORS

²scissor *transitive verb* **scis·sored; scis·sor·ing** \'si-zə-riŋ, 'siz-riŋ\ (1612)
: to cut, cut up, or cut off with scissors or shears

scis·sors \'si-zərz\ *noun plural but singular or plural in construction* (14th century)
1 : a cutting instrument having two blades whose cutting edges slide past each other
2 a : a gymnastic feat in which the leg movements suggest the opening and closing of scissors **b** : SCISSORS HOLD

scissors–and–paste *adjective* (1902)
: being a compilation rather than an effort of original and independent investigation

scissors hold *noun* (1909)
: a wrestling hold in which the legs are locked around the head or body of an opponent

scissors kick *noun* (circa 1930)
: a swimming kick used especially in sidestrokes in which the legs move like scissors

scis·sor–tailed flycatcher \'si-zər-ˌtāld-\ *noun* (circa 1909)
: a flycatcher (*Muscivora forficata*) of the southern U.S., Mexico, and Central America that has a deeply forked tail — called also *scissortail*

sclaff \'sklaf\ *intransitive verb* [Scots, from *sclaff,* noun, literally, blow with the palm; probably of imitative origin] (1893)
: to scrape the ground instead of hitting the ball cleanly on a golf stroke
— **sclaff** *noun*
— **sclaff·er** *noun*

scler- *or* **sclero-** *combining form* [New Latin, from Greek *sklēr-, sklēro-,* from *sklēros* — more at SKELETON]
1 : hard ⟨*scler*ite⟩ ⟨*sclero*derma⟩
2 : hardness ⟨*sclero*meter⟩

scle·ra \'skler-ə\ *noun* [New Latin, from Greek *sklēros*] (1888)
: the dense fibrous opaque white outer coat enclosing the eyeball except the part covered by the cornea — see EYE illustration
— **scler·al** \-əl\ *adjective*

scler·e·id \'skler-ē-əd\ *noun* [International Scientific Vocabulary, irregular from Greek *sklēros*] (circa 1900)
: a variably shaped sclerenchymatous cell of a higher plant that is often nearly isodiametric

scle·ren·chy·ma \sklə-'reŋ-kə-mə\ *noun* [New Latin] (1875)
: a protective or supporting tissue in higher plants composed of cells with walls thickened and often lignified
— **scler·en·chy·ma·tous** \ˌskler-ən-'kima-təs, -'kī-\ *adjective*

scler·ite \'skler-ˌīt\ *noun* [International Scientific Vocabulary] (1861)
: a hard chitinous or calcareous plate, piece, or spicule (as of the arthropod integument)

sclero·der·ma \ˌskler-ə-'dər-mə\ *noun* [New Latin] (1860)
: a usually slowly progressive disease marked by the deposition of fibrous connective tissue in the skin and often in internal organs

scle·rom·e·ter \sklə-'rä-mə-tər\ *noun* [International Scientific Vocabulary] (circa 1879)
: an instrument for determining the relative hardnesses of materials

sclero·pro·tein \ˌskler-ō-'prō-ˌtēn, -'prō-tē-ən\ *noun* [International Scientific Vocabulary] (1907)
: any of various fibrous proteins especially from connective and skeletal tissues

scle·ros·ing \sklə-'rō-siŋ, -ziŋ\ *adjective* [New Latin *sclerosis* + English ¹-*ing*] (1885)
: causing or characterized by sclerosis ⟨*sclerosing* agents⟩

scle·ro·sis \sklə-'rō-səs\ *noun* [Middle English *sclirosis* tumor, from Medieval Latin, from Greek *sklērōsis* hardening, from *sklēroun* to harden, from *sklēros*] (1846)
: pathological hardening of tissue especially from overgrowth of fibrous tissue or increase in interstitial tissue; *also* : a disease characterized by sclerosis

¹scle·rot·ic \sklə-'rä-tik\ *adjective* (1543)
1 : being or relating to the sclera
2 : of, relating to, or affected with sclerosis
3 : grown rigid or unresponsive especially with age ⟨*sclerotic* institutions⟩

²sclerotic *noun* [Medieval Latin *sclerotica,* from (assumed) Greek *sklērōtos,* verbal of Greek *sklēroun* to harden] (1690)
: SCLERA

sclerotic coat *noun* (1741)
: SCLERA

scler·o·tin \'skler-ə-tən, sklə-'rō-tᵊn\ *noun* [probably *scler-* + -*tin* (as in *chitin*)] (1940)
: an insoluble tanned protein permeating and stiffening the chitin of the cuticle of arthropods

scle·ro·tium \sklə-'rō-sh(ē-)əm\ *noun, plural* -**tia** \-sh(ē-)ə\ [New Latin, from (assumed) Greek *sklērōtos*] (1871)
: a compact mass of hardened mycelium stored with reserve food material that in some higher fungi becomes detached and remains dormant until a favorable opportunity for growth occurs
— **scle·ro·tial** \-'rō-shəl\ *adjective*

scler·o·tized \'skler-ə-ˌtīzd\ *adjective* [¹*sclerotic* + -*ize* + ¹-*ed*] (circa 1890)
: hardened especially by the formation of sclerotin ⟨*sclerotized* insect cuticle⟩
— **scler·o·ti·za·tion** \ˌskler-e-tə-'zā-shən\ *noun*

¹scoff \'skäf, 'skȯf\ *noun* [Middle English *scof,* probably of Scandinavian origin; akin to obsolete Danish *skof* jest; akin to Old Frisian *skof* mockery] (14th century)
1 : an expression of scorn, derision, or contempt : GIBE
2 : an object of scorn, mockery, or derision

²scoff (14th century)
intransitive verb
: to show contempt by derisive acts or language
transitive verb
: to treat or address with derision : MOCK ☆
— **scoff·er** *noun*

³scoff *verb* [alteration of dialect *scaff* to eat greedily] (1846)
transitive verb
1 : to eat greedily
2 : SEIZE — often used with *up*
intransitive verb
: to eat something greedily

scoff·law \-ˌlȯ\ *noun* (1924)
: a contemptuous law violator

¹scold \'skōld\ *noun* [Middle English *scald, scold,* perhaps of Scandinavian origin; akin to Old Norse *skāld* poet, skald, Icelandic *skālda* to make scurrilous verse] (12th century)
1 a : one who scolds habitually or persistently **b** : a woman who disturbs the public peace by noisy and quarrelsome or abusive behavior
2 : SCOLDING

²scold (14th century)
intransitive verb
1 *obsolete* : to quarrel noisily
2 : to find fault noisily or angrily
transitive verb
: to censure severely or angrily : REBUKE ☆
— **scold·er** *noun*

scold·ing *noun* (1547)
1 : the action of one who scolds
2 : a harsh reproof

sco·le·cite \'skä-lə-ˌsīt, 'skō-\ *noun* [German *Skolezit,* from Greek *skōlēk-, skōlēx* worm; from the motion of some forms when heated] (circa 1823)
: a zeolite mineral that is a hydrous calcium aluminum silicate and occurs in radiating groups of crystals, in fibrous masses, and in nodules

sco·lex \'skō-ˌleks\ *noun, plural* **sco·li·ces** \-lə-ˌsēz\ *also* **sco·le·ces** \'skō-lə-ˌsēz, 'skä-\ [New Latin *scolic-, scolex,* from Greek *skōlēk-, skōlēx* worm; akin to Greek *skolios* crooked, *skelos* leg — more at ISOSCELES] (1855)
: the head of a tapeworm either in the larva or adult stage

sco·li·o·sis \ˌskō-lē-'ō-səs\ *noun, plural* -**o·ses** \-ˌsēz\ [New Latin, from Greek *skoliōsis* crookedness of a bodily part, from *skolios*] (circa 1706)
: a lateral curvature of the spine
— **sco·li·ot·ic** \-'ä-tik\ *adjective*

scol·lop \'skä-ləp, 'skȯ-\ *variant of* SCALLOP

scol·o·pen·dra \ˌskä-lə-'pen-drə\ *noun* [New Latin, genus of centipedes, from Latin, a kind of millipede, from Greek *skolopendra*] (1608)
: CENTIPEDE

scom·broid \'skäm-ˌbrȯid\ *noun* [ultimately from Greek *skombros* mackerel] (circa 1842)
: any of a suborder (Scombroidei) of marine bony fishes (as mackerels, tunas, albacores, bonitos, and swordfishes) of great economic importance as food fishes
— **scombroid** *adjective*

¹sconce \'skän(t)s\ *noun* [Middle English, from Middle French *esconse* screened lantern, from Old French, from feminine of *escons,*

☆ **SYNONYMS**
Scoff, jeer, gibe, fleer, sneer, flout
mean to show one's contempt in derision or mockery. SCOFF stresses insolence, disrespect, or incredulity as motivating the derision ⟨*scoffed* at their concerns⟩. JEER suggests a coarser more undiscriminating derision ⟨the crowd *jeered* at the prisoners⟩. GIBE implies taunting either good-naturedly or in sarcastic derision ⟨hooted and *gibed* at the umpire⟩. FLEER suggests grinning or grimacing derisively ⟨the saucy jackanapes *fleered* at my credulity⟩. SNEER stresses insulting by contemptuous facial expression, phrasing, or tone of voice ⟨*sneered* at anything romantic⟩. FLOUT stresses contempt shown by refusal to heed ⟨*flouted* the conventions of polite society⟩.

Scold, upbraid, berate, rail, revile, vituperate mean to reproach angrily and abusively. SCOLD implies rebuking in irritation or ill temper justly or unjustly ⟨angrily *scolding* the children⟩. UPBRAID implies censuring on definite and usually justifiable grounds ⟨*upbraided* her assistants for poor research⟩. BERATE suggests prolonged and often abusive scolding ⟨*berated* continually by an overbearing boss⟩. RAIL (*at* or *against*) stresses an unrestrained berating ⟨*railed* loudly at their insolence⟩. REVILE implies a scurrilous, abusive attack prompted by anger or hatred ⟨an alleged killer *reviled* in the press⟩. VITUPERATE suggests a violent reviling ⟨was *vituperated* for betraying his friends⟩.

\ə\ abut \ᵊ\ kitten \ər\ further \a\ ash \ā\ ace
\ä\ mop, mar \au̇\ out \ch\ chin \e\ bet \ē\ easy
\g\ go \i\ hit \ī\ ice \j\ job \ŋ\ sing \ō\ go
\ȯ\ law \ȯi\ boy \th\ thin \t͟h\ the \ü\ loot \u̇\ foot
\y\ yet \zh\ vision *see also* Guide to Pronunciation

past participle of *escondre* to hide, from Latin *abscondere* — more at ABSCOND] (15th century)
1 : a bracket candlestick or group of candlesticks; *also* **:** an electric light fixture patterned on a candle sconce
2 : HEAD, SKULL
²sconce *noun* [Dutch *schans,* from German *Schanze*] (1571)
: a detached defensive work
scone \'skōn, 'skän\ *noun* [perhaps from Dutch *schoonbrood* fine white bread, from *schoon* pure, clean + *brood* bread] (1513)
: a rich quick bread cut into usually triangular shapes and cooked on a griddle or baked on a sheet
¹scoop \'sküp\ *noun* [Middle English *scope,* from Middle Dutch *schope;* akin to Old High German *skepfen* to shape — more at SHAPE] (14th century)
1 a : a large ladle **b :** a deep shovel or similar implement for digging, dipping, or shoveling **c :** a usually hemispherical utensil for dipping food **d :** a small spoon-shaped utensil or instrument for cutting or gouging
2 : the action of scooping
3 a : a hollow place **:** CAVITY **b :** a part forming or surrounding an opening for channeling a fluid (as air) into a desired path
4 a : information especially of immediate interest **b :** BEAT 5b
5 : a rounded and usually low-cut neckline on a woman's garment — called also *scoop neck*
— **scoop·ful** \-,fu̇l\ *noun*
²scoop *transitive verb* (14th century)
1 a : to take out or up with or as if with a scoop **:** DIP **b :** to pick up quickly or surreptitiously with or as if with a sweep of the hand — often used with *up*
2 : to empty by ladling out the contents
3 : to make hollow **:** DIG OUT
4 : BEAT 5a(2)
— **scoop·er** *noun*
scoot \'sküt\ *intransitive verb* [perhaps of Scandinavian origin; akin to Old Norse *skjōta* to shoot — more at SHOOT] (1758)
1 : to move swiftly
2 : to slide especially while seated ⟨*scoot* over and let me sit down⟩
— **scoot** *noun*
scoot·er \'skü-tər\ *noun* (1916)
1 : a child's foot-operated vehicle consisting of a narrow footboard mounted between two wheels tandem with an upright steering handle attached to the front wheel
2 : MOTOR SCOOTER
scop \'shōp, 'skōp, 'skäp\ *noun* [Old English; akin to Old High German *schof* poet] (before 12th century)
: an Old English bard or poet
¹scope \'skōp\ *noun* [Italian *scopo* purpose, goal, from Greek *skopos;* akin to Greek *skeptesthai* to watch, look at — more at SPY] (circa 1555)
1 : INTENTION, OBJECT
2 : space or opportunity for unhampered motion, activity, or thought
3 : extent of treatment, activity, or influence
4 : range of operation: as **a :** the range of a logical operator **:** a string in predicate calculus that is governed by a quantifier **b :** a grammatical constituent that determines the interpretation of a predicate or quantifier
synonym see RANGE
²scope *noun* [-*scope*] (1872)
1 : an instrument (as a telescope or radarscope) for viewing
2 : HOROSCOPE
³scope *transitive verb* **scoped; scop·ing** [perhaps from ²*scope*] (1974)
: to look at especially for the purpose of evaluation — often used with *out* ⟨*scoped* her out from across the room —Tim Allis⟩

-scope *noun combining form* [New Latin *-scopium,* from Greek *-skopion;* akin to Greek *skeptesthai*]
: means (as an instrument) for viewing or observing ⟨endo*scope*⟩ ⟨spectro*scope*⟩
sco·pol·amine \skō-'pä-lə-,mēn, -mən\ *noun* [German *Scopolamin,* from New Latin *Scopolia,* genus of plants + German *Amin* amine] (1892)
: a poisonous alkaloid $C_{17}H_{21}NO_4$ found in various plants (as jimsonweed) of the nightshade family and used especially as a truth serum or usually with morphine as a sedative in surgery and obstetrics — called also *hyoscine*
-scopy *noun combining form* [Greek *-skopia,* from *skeptesthai*]
: viewing **:** observation ⟨spectro*scopy*⟩
scor·bu·tic \skȯr-'byü-tik\ *adjective* [New Latin *scorbuticus,* from *scorbutus* scurvy, probably of Germanic origin; akin to Old English *scurf* scurf] (1655)
: of, relating to, producing, or affected with scurvy
¹scorch \'skȯrch\ *verb* [Middle English; akin to Middle English *scorcnen,* probably of Scandinavian origin; akin to Old Norse *skorpna* to shrivel up — more at SHRIMP] (14th century)
transitive verb
1 : to burn a surface of so as to change its color and texture
2 : to dry or shrivel with or as if with intense heat **:** PARCH **b :** to afflict painfully with censure or sarcasm
3 : DEVASTATE; *especially* **:** to destroy (as property of possible use to an advancing enemy) before abandoning — used in the phrase *scorched earth*
intransitive verb
1 : to become scorched
2 : to travel at great and usually excessive speed
3 : to cause intense heat or mental anguish ⟨*scorching* sun⟩ ⟨*scorching* fury⟩
— **scorch·ing·ly** \'skȯr-chiŋ-lē\ *adverb*
²scorch *noun* (15th century)
1 : a result of scorching
2 : a browning of plant tissues usually from disease or heat
³scorch *transitive verb* [Middle English, perhaps blend of *scoren* to score and *scocchen* to scotch] (14th century)
dialect British **:** CUT, SLASH
scorched *adjective* (1590)
: parched or discolored by scorching
scorch·er \'skȯr-chər\ *noun* (1842)
: one that scorches; *especially* **:** a very hot day
¹score \'skōr, 'skȯr\ *noun, plural* **scores** [Middle English *scor,* from Old Norse *skor* notch, tally, twenty; akin to Old English *scieran* to cut — more at SHEAR] (14th century)
1 *or plural* **score a :** TWENTY **b :** a group of 20 things — often used in combination with a cardinal number ⟨four*score*⟩ **c :** an indefinitely large number
2 a : a line (as a scratch or incision) made with or as if with a sharp instrument **b (1) :** a mark used as a starting point or goal **(2) :** a mark used for keeping account
3 a : an account or reckoning originally kept by making marks on a tally **b :** amount due **:** INDEBTEDNESS
4 : GRUDGE ⟨a *score* to settle⟩
5 a : REASON, GROUND **b :** SUBJECT, TOPIC
6 a : the copy of a musical composition in written or printed notation **b :** a musical composition; *specifically* **:** the music for a movie or theatrical production **c :** a complete description of a dance composition in choreographic notation
7 a : a number that expresses accomplishment (as in a game or test) or excellence (as in quality) either absolutely in points gained or by comparison to a standard **b :** an act (as a goal, run, or touchdown) in any of various games or contests that gains points

8 : success in obtaining something (as money or drugs) especially through illegal or irregular means
9 : the stark inescapable facts of a situation ⟨knows the *score*⟩
²score *verb* **scored; scor·ing** (14th century)
transitive verb
1 a : to keep a record or account of by or as if by notches on a tally **:** RECORD **b :** to enter in a record **c :** to mark with significant lines or notches (as in keeping account)
2 : to mark with lines, grooves, scratches, or notches
3 : BERATE, SCOLD; *also* **:** DENOUNCE
4 a (1) : to make (a score) in a game or contest ⟨*scored* a touchdown⟩ ⟨*scored* three points⟩ **(2) :** to enable (a base runner) to make a score **(3) :** to have as a value in a game or contest **:** COUNT ⟨a touchdown *scores* six points⟩ **b (1) :** ACHIEVE, WIN ⟨*scored* a dazzling success⟩ **(2) :** ACQUIRE ⟨help a traveler *score* local drugs —Poitor Koper⟩
5 : to determine the merit of **:** GRADE
6 a : to write or arrange (music) for a specific performance medium **b :** to make an orchestration of **c :** to compose a score for (a movie)
intransitive verb
1 : to keep score in a game or contest
2 : to make a score in a game or contest
3 a : to gain or have the advantage **b :** to be successful: as **(1) :** to succeed in having sexual intercourse **(2) :** to manage to obtain illicit drugs **c :** ³RATE
— **scor·er** *noun*
— **score points :** to gain favor, status, or advantage
score·board \'skōr-,bōrd, 'skȯr-,bȯrd\ *noun* (1826)
: a large board for displaying the score of a game or match
score·card \-,kärd\ *noun* (circa 1877)
: a card for recording the score of a game
score·keep·er \-,kē-pər\ *noun* (1880)
: one that keeps score; *specifically* **:** an official who records the score during a game or contest
score·less \-ləs\ *adjective* (1885)
: having no score
sco·ria \'skōr-ē-ə, 'skȯr-\ *noun, plural* **-ri·ae** \-ē-,ē, -ē-,ī\ [Middle English, from Latin, from Greek *skōria,* from *skōr* excrement — more at SCATOLOGY] (14th century)
1 : the refuse from melting of metals or reduction of ores **:** SLAG
2 : rough vesicular cindery lava
— **sco·ri·a·ceous** \,skōr-ē-'ā-shəs, ,skȯr-\ *adjective*
¹scorn \'skȯrn\ *noun* [Middle English, from Old French *escarn,* of Germanic origin; akin to Old High German *scern* jest] (13th century)
1 : open dislike and disrespect or derision often mixed with indignation
2 : an expression of contempt or derision
3 : an object of extreme disdain, contempt, or derision **:** something contemptible
²scorn (13th century)
transitive verb
: to treat with scorn **:** reject or dismiss as contemptible or unworthy ⟨*scorned* the traditions of their ancestors⟩ ⟨*scorned* to reply to the charge⟩
intransitive verb
: to show disdain or derision **:** SCOFF
synonym see DESPISE
— **scorn·er** *noun*
scorn·ful \'skȯrn-fəl\ *adjective* (14th century)
: full of scorn **:** CONTEMPTUOUS
— **scorn·ful·ly** \-fə-lē\ *adverb*
— **scorn·ful·ness** *noun*
scor·pae·nid \skȯr-'pē-nəd\ *noun* [ultimately from Greek *skorpaina,* a kind of fish] (1885)
: any of a family (Scorpaenidae) of marine spiny-finned fishes that includes the scorpion fishes

— **scorpaenid** *adjective*

Scor·pio \ˈskȯr-pē-ˌō\ *noun* [Latin (genitive *Scorpionis*), from Greek *Skorpios*, literally, scorpion]
1 : SCORPIUS
2 a : the 8th sign of the zodiac in astrology — see ZODIAC table **b** : one born under this sign

scor·pi·on \ˈskȯr-pē-ən\ *noun* [Middle English, from Old French, from Latin *scorpion-, scorpio,* from Greek *skorpios*] (12th century)
1 a : any of an order (Scorpionida) of nocturnal arachnids that have an elongated body and a narrow segmented tail bearing a venomous stinger at the tip **b** *capitalized* : SCORPIO
2 : a scourge probably studded with metal
3 : something that incites to action like the sting of an insect

scorpion fish *noun* (1661)
: any of various scorpaenid fishes; *especially* : one (as genus *Scorpaena*) with a venomous spine on the dorsal fin

scorpion 1a

scorpion fly *noun* (1668)
: any of a family (Panorpidae) of insects that have cylindrical bodies, a long beak with biting mouthparts, and the male genitalia enlarged into a swollen bulb; *broadly* : an insect of the order (Mecoptera) that includes this family

Scor·pi·us \ˈskȯr-pē-əs\ *noun* [Latin (genitive *Scorpii*), from Greek *Skorpios*, literally, scorpion]
: a southern zodiacal constellation partly in the Milky Way and between Libra and Sagittarius

scot \ˈskät\ *noun* [Middle English, from Old Norse *skot* shot, contribution — more at SHOT] (14th century)
: money assessed or paid

Scot \ˈskät\ *noun* [Middle English *Scottes* Scots, from Old English *Scottas* from Late Latin *Scotus*] (before 12th century)
1 : a member of a Celtic people of northern Ireland settling in Scotland about A.D. 500
2 a : a native or inhabitant of Scotland **b** : a person of Scottish descent

scot and lot *noun* (15th century)
1 : a parish assessment formerly laid on subjects in Great Britain according to their ability to pay
2 : obligations of all kinds taken as a whole

¹**scotch** \ˈskäch\ *transitive verb* [Middle English *scocchen* to gash] (15th century)
1 *archaic* : CUT, GASH, SCORE; *also* : WOUND ⟨we have *scotched* the snake, not killed it —Shakespeare⟩
2 : to put an end to ⟨*scotched* rumors of a military takeover⟩

²**scotch** *noun* (15th century)
: a superficial cut : SCORE

³**scotch** *noun* [origin unknown] (1639)
: a chock to prevent rolling or slipping

⁴**scotch** *transitive verb* (1642)
1 : to block with a chock
2 : HINDER, THWART

¹**Scotch** \ˈskäch\ *adjective* [contraction of *Scottish*] (1591)
1 : SCOTTISH
2 : inclined to frugality □

²**Scotch** *noun* (circa 1700)
1 : SCOTS
2 *plural in construction* : the people of Scotland
3 *often not capitalized* : whiskey distilled in Scotland especially from malted barley — called also *Scotch whisky*

³**Scotch** *trademark*
— used for any of numerous adhesive tapes

Scotch broom *noun* (circa 1818)
: a deciduous broom (*Cytisus scoparius*) of western Europe that is widely cultivated for its bright yellow or partly red flowers and that has become a pest in some areas (as California)

Scotch broth *noun* (1834)
: a soup made from beef or mutton and vegetables and thickened with barley

Scotch egg *noun* (1809)
: a hard-boiled egg wrapped in sausage meat, covered with bread crumbs, and fried

Scotch–Irish *adjective* (1744)
: of, relating to, or descended from Scottish settlers in northern Ireland

Scotch·man \ˈskäch-mən\ *noun* (15th century)
: SCOTSMAN

Scotch pine *noun* (1731)
: a pine (*Pinus sylvestris*) of northern Europe and Asia with spreading or pendulous branches, short rigid twisted needles, and hard yellow wood that provides valuable timber

Scotch terrier *noun* (1810)
: SCOTTISH TERRIER

Scotch verdict *noun* (1912)
1 : a verdict of not proven that is allowed by Scottish criminal law in some cases instead of a verdict of not guilty
2 : an inconclusive decision or pronouncement

Scotch·wom·an \ˈskäch-ˌwu̇-mən\ *noun* (1818)
: SCOTSWOMAN

Scotch woodcock *noun* (1879)
: buttered toast spread with anchovy paste and scrambled egg

sco·ter \ˈskō-tər\ *noun, plural* **scoters** *or* **scoter** [origin unknown] (circa 1674)
: any of a genus (*Melanitta*) of sea ducks especially of northern coasts of Europe and North America that have males with chiefly black plumage

scot–free \ˈskät-ˈfrē\ *adjective* [*scot*] (1528)
: completely free from obligation, harm, or penalty

sco·tia \ˈskō-sh(ē-)ə, -tē-ə\ *noun* [Latin, from Greek *skotia*, from feminine of *skotios* dark, shadowy, from *skotos* darkness — more at SHADE] (1563)
: a concave molding used especially in classical architecture in the bases of columns — see BASE illustration

Scot·ic \ˈskä-tik\ *adjective* (1796)
: of or relating to the ancient Scots

Sco·tism \ˈskō-ˌti-zəm\ *noun* (circa 1871)
: the doctrines of Duns Scotus
— **Sco·tist** \ˈskō-tist\ *noun*

Scot·land Yard \ˌskät-lən(d)-ˈyärd\ *noun* [*Scotland Yard*, street in London, formerly the headquarters of the metropolitan police] (1864)
: the detective department of the London metropolitan police

sco·to·ma \skə-ˈtō-mə\ *noun, plural* **-mas** *or* **-ma·ta** \-mə-tə\ [New Latin, from Medieval Latin, dimness of vision, from Greek *skotōmat-, skotōma,* from *skotoun* to darken, from *skotos*] (1875)
: a blind or dark spot in the visual field

sco·to·pic \skə-ˈtō-pik, -ˈtä-\ *adjective* [New Latin *scotopia* scotopic vision, from Greek *skotos* darkness + New Latin *-opia*] (1915)
: relating to or being vision in dim light with dark-adapted eyes which involves only the retinal rods as light receptors

¹**Scots** \ˈskäts\ *adjective* [Middle English *Scottis,* alteration of *Scottish*] (14th century)
: SCOTTISH — used especially of the people and language and in legal context
usage see SCOTCH

²**Scots** *noun* (1542)
: the English language of Scotland

Scots·man \ˈskäts-mən\ *noun* (14th century)
: a native or inhabitant of Scotland

Scots pine *noun* (1797)
chiefly British : SCOTCH PINE

Scots·wom·an \ˈskäts-ˌwu̇-mən\ *noun* (1820)
: a woman who is a native or inhabitant of Scotland

Scot·ti·cism \ˈskä-tə-ˌsi-zəm\ *noun* [Late Latin *scotticus* of the ancient Scots, from *Scotus* Scot] (1706)
: a word, phrase, or expression characteristic of Scottish English

Scot·tie \ˈskä-tē\ *noun* (circa 1896)
1 : SCOTSMAN
2 : SCOTTISH TERRIER

¹**Scot·tish** \ˈskä-tish\ *adjective* [Middle English, from *Scottes* Scotsmen] (13th century)
: of, relating to, or characteristic of Scotland, Scots, or the Scots
usage see SCOTCH
— **Scot·tish·ness** \-nəs\ *noun*

²**Scottish** *noun* (1759)
: SCOTS

Scottish deerhound *noun* (1891)
: any of an old breed of dogs of Scottish origin that have the general form of a greyhound but are larger and taller with a rough coat

Scottish Gaelic *noun* (1956)
: the Gaelic language of Scotland

Scottish rite *noun* (1903)
1 : a ceremonial observed by one of the Masonic systems
2 : a system or organization that observes the Scottish rite and confers the 4th through the 33d degrees

Scottish terrier *noun* (1837)
: any of an old Scottish breed of terrier that has short legs, a large head with small erect ears and a powerful muzzle, a broad deep chest, and a very hard coat of wiry hair

Scottish terrier

scoun·drel \ˈskau̇n-drəl\ *noun* [origin unknown] (1589)
: a disreputable person : RASCAL
— **scoundrel** *adjective*
— **scoun·drel·ly** \-drə-lē\ *adjective*

¹**scour** \ˈskau̇(-ə)r\ *verb* [Middle English, probably from Middle Dutch *schuren,* from Old French *escurer,* from Late Latin *excurare* to clean off, from Latin, to take good care of, from *ex-* + *curare* to care for, from *cura* care] (13th century)
transitive verb
1 a : to rub hard especially with a rough material for cleansing **b** : to remove by rubbing hard and washing
2 *archaic* : to clear (a region) of enemies or outlaws
3 : to clean by purging : PURGE
4 : to remove dirt and debris from (as a pipe or ditch)
5 : to free from foreign matter or impurities by or as if by washing ⟨*scour* wool⟩

□ USAGE
Scotch In Scotland *Scottish* is the preferred adjective, *Scotch* is usually limited to familiar compounds like *Scotch pine* and *Scotch whiskey,* and *Scots* refers to language and law. In North America *Scotch* is commonly used in all adjectival applications, partly because *Scotch* was the usual adjective in the 18th and 19th centuries when many Scots immigrated here. A rule of thumb which works well for Americans who do not want to offend but do not know the finer points of Scottish practice is to use *Scottish* for people and *Scotch* for things.

\ə\ abut \ᵊ\ kitten \ər\ further \a\ ash \ā\ ace
\ä\ mop, mar \au̇\ out \ch\ chin \e\ bet \ē\ easy
\g\ go \i\ hit \ī\ ice \j\ job \ŋ\ sing \ō\ go
\ȯ\ law \ȯi\ boy \th\ thin \t͟h\ the \ü\ loot \u̇\ foot
\y\ yet \zh\ vision *see also* Guide to Pronunciation

6 : to clear, dig, or remove by or as if by a powerful current of water
intransitive verb
1 : to perform a process of scouring
2 : to suffer from diarrhea or dysentery
3 : to become clean and bright by rubbing
— **scour·er** *noun*

²scour *noun* (1681)
1 : a place scoured by running water
2 : scouring action (as of a glacier)
3 : DIARRHEA, DYSENTERY — usually used in plural but singular or plural in construction
4 : SCOURING 1; *also* : damage done by scouring action

³scour *verb* [Middle English *scuren*, probably of Scandinavian origin; akin to Swedish *skura* to rush] (14th century)
intransitive verb
: to move about quickly especially in search
transitive verb
: to go through or range over in or as if in a search

¹scourge \'skərj *also* 'skōrj, 'skȯrj, 'skȯŗj\ *noun* [Middle English, from Anglo-French *escorge, from (assumed) Old French *escorgier* to whip, from Old French *es-* ex- + Latin *corrigia* whip] (13th century)
1 : WHIP; *especially* : one used to inflict pain or punishment
2 : an instrument of punishment or criticism
3 : a cause of widespread or great affliction

²scourge *transitive verb* **scourged; scourg·ing** (13th century)
1 : FLOG, WHIP
2 a : to punish severely **b :** AFFLICT **c :** to drive as if by blows of a whip **d :** CHASTISE
— **scourg·er** *noun*

scour·ing \'skau̇r-iŋ\ *noun* (1588)
1 : material removed by scouring or cleaning
2 : the lowest rank of society — usually used in plural

scouring rush *noun* (circa 1818)
: EQUISETUM; *especially* : one (*Equisetum hyemale*) with strongly siliceous stems formerly used for scouring

scouse \'skau̇s\ *noun* (1840)
1 : LOBSCOUSE
2 *capitalized* **a :** SCOUSER **b :** a dialect of English spoken in Liverpool

Scous·er \'skau̇-sər\ *noun* (1959)
: a native or inhabitant of Liverpool, England

¹scout \'skau̇t\ *verb* [Middle English, from Middle French *escouter* to listen, from Latin *auscultare* — more at AUSCULTATION] (14th century)
intransitive verb
1 : to explore an area to obtain information (as about an enemy)
2 a : to make a search **b :** to work as a talent scout
transitive verb
1 : to observe in order to obtain information or evaluate
2 : to explore in order to obtain information
3 : to find by making a search — often used with *up*

²scout *noun* (1534)
1 a : one sent to obtain information; *especially* **:** a soldier, ship, or plane sent out in war to reconnoiter **b :** WATCHMAN, LOOKOUT **c :** TALENT SCOUT
2 a : the act of scouting **b :** a scouting expedition : RECONNAISSANCE
3 *often capitalized* **:** a member of any of various scouting movements: as **a :** BOY SCOUT **b :** GIRL SCOUT
4 : INDIVIDUAL, PERSON — used chiefly in the phrase *good scout*

³scout *verb* [probably of Scandinavian origin; akin to Old Norse *skūti* taunt; akin to Old English *scēotan* to shoot — more at SHOOT] (1605)
transitive verb
1 : MOCK
2 : to reject scornfully

intransitive verb
: SCOFF

scout car *noun* (1933)
1 : a military reconnaissance vehicle
2 : SQUAD CAR

scout·craft \'skau̇t-,kraft\ *noun* (1908)
: the craft, skill, or practice of a scout

scout·er \'skau̇-tər\ *noun* (1642)
1 : one that scouts
2 *often capitalized* **:** an adult leader in the Boy Scouts of America

scouth \'skütth, 'skau̇th\ *noun* [origin unknown] (1591)
Scottish **:** PLENTY

scout·ing \'skau̇-tiŋ\ *noun* (1644)
1 : the action of one that scouts
2 *often capitalized* **:** the activities of various national and worldwide organizations for youth directed to developing character, citizenship, and individual skills

scout·mas·ter \'skau̇t-,mas-tər\ *noun* (1579)
: the leader of a band of scouts; *specifically* **:** the adult leader of a troop of Boy Scouts

scow \'skau̇\ *noun* [Dutch *schouw*; akin to Old High German *scalta* punt pole] (1669)
: a large flat-bottomed boat with broad square ends used chiefly for transporting bulk material (as ore, sand, or refuse)

¹scowl \'skau̇(ə)l\ *verb* [Middle English *skoulen*, probably of Scandinavian origin; akin to Danish *skule* to scowl] (14th century)
intransitive verb
1 : to contract the brow in an expression of displeasure
2 : to exhibit a threatening aspect
transitive verb
: to express with a scowl
— **scowl·er** *noun*
— **scowl·ing·ly** \'skau̇-liŋ-lē\ *adverb*

²scowl *noun* (1500)
: a facial expression of displeasure : FROWN

¹scrab·ble \'skra-bəl\ *verb* **scrab·bled; scrab·bling** \-b(ə-)liŋ\ [Dutch *schrabbelen* to scratch] (1537)
intransitive verb
1 : SCRAWL, SCRIBBLE
2 : to scratch, claw, or grope about clumsily or frantically
3 a : SCRAMBLE, CLAMBER **b :** to struggle by or as if by scraping or scratching 〈*scrabble* for survival〉
transitive verb
1 : SCRAMBLE
2 : SCRIBBLE
— **scrab·bler** \-b(ə-)lər\ *noun*

²scrabble *noun* (1842)
1 : SCRIBBLE
2 : a repeated scratching or clawing
3 : SCRAMBLE

scrab·bly \'skra-b(ə-)lē\ *adjective* (1945)
1 : SCRATCHY, RASPY
2 : SPARSE, SCRUBBY

¹scrag \'skrag\ *noun* [perhaps alteration of ²*crag*] (1542)
1 : a rawboned or scrawny person or animal
2 : the lean end of a neck of mutton or veal; *broadly* : NECK — called also *scrag end*

²scrag *transitive verb* **scragged; scrag·ging** (1756)
1 a : to execute by hanging or garroting **b :** to wring the neck of
2 a : CHOKE **b :** MANHANDLE 1 **c :** KILL, MURDER

scrag·gly \'skra-g(ə)lē\ *adjective* (1869)
: irregular in form or growth 〈*scraggly* hills〉 〈a *scraggly* beard〉 **:** UNKEMPT

¹scrag·gy \'skra-gē\ *adjective* **scrag·gi·er; -est** [Middle English *scraggi*; akin to English dialect *scrag* tree stump, uneven ground, Middle English *scrogge* bush] (13th century)
: ROUGH, JAGGED; *also* : SCRAGGLY

²scraggy *adjective* **scrag·gi·er; -est** [¹*scrag*] (1611)
: being lean and long : SCRAWNY

¹scram \'skram\ *intransitive verb* **scrammed; scram·ming** [short for *scramble*] (circa 1928)

: to go away at once 〈*scram*, you're not wanted〉

²scram *noun* (1953)
: a rapid emergency shutdown of a nuclear reactor

¹scram·ble \'skram-bəl\ *verb* **scram·bled; scram·bling** \-b(ə-)liŋ\ [perhaps alteration of ¹*scrabble*] (circa 1586)
intransitive verb
1 a : to move or climb hastily on all fours **b :** to move with urgency or panic
2 a : to struggle eagerly or unceremoniously for possession of something 〈*scramble* for front seats〉 **b :** to get or gather something with difficulty or in irregular ways 〈*scramble* for a living〉
3 : to spread or grow irregularly : SPRAWL, STRAGGLE
4 : to take off quickly in response to an alert
5 *of a football quarterback* **:** to run with the ball after the pass protection breaks down
transitive verb
1 : to collect by scrambling
2 a : to toss or mix together : JUMBLE **b :** to prepare (eggs) by stirring during frying
3 : to cause or order (a fighter-interceptor group) to scramble
4 : to disarrange the elements of a transmission (as a telephone or television signal) in order to make unintelligible to interception
— **scram·bler** \-b(ə-)lər\ *noun*

²scramble *noun* (1674)
1 : the act or an instance of scrambling
2 : a disordered mass : JUMBLE 〈a . . . *scramble* of patterns and textures —*Vogue*〉
3 : a rapid emergency takeoff of fighter-interceptor planes

scran·nel \'skra-nᵊl\ *adjective* [origin unknown] (1637)
: HARSH, UNMELODIOUS

¹scrap \'skrap\ *noun, often attributive* [Middle English, from Old Norse *skrap* scraps; akin to Old Norse *skrapa* to scrape] (14th century)
1 *plural* **:** fragments of discarded or leftover food
2 a : a small detached piece 〈a *scrap* of paper〉 **b :** a fragment of something written, printed, or spoken 〈*scraps* of conversation〉 **c :** the least bit 〈not a *scrap* of evidence〉
3 *plural* **:** CRACKLINGS
4 a : fragments of stock removed in manufacturing **b :** manufactured articles or parts rejected or discarded and useful only as material for reprocessing; *especially* : waste and discarded metal

²scrap *transitive verb* **scrapped; scrap·ping** (circa 1891)
1 : to convert into scrap
2 : to abandon or get rid of as no longer of enough worth or effectiveness to retain 〈*scrap* outworn methods〉
synonym see DISCARD

³scrap *noun* [origin unknown] (circa 1889)
: FIGHT

⁴scrap *intransitive verb* **scrapped; scrap·ping** (circa 1895)
: QUARREL, FIGHT

scrap·book \'skrap-,bu̇k\ *noun* (1825)
: a blank book in which miscellaneous items (as newspaper clippings or pictures) are collected and preserved

¹scrape \'skrāp\ *verb* **scraped; scrap·ing** [Middle English, from Old Norse *skrapa*; akin to Old English *scrapian* to scrape, Latin *scrobis* ditch, Russian *skresti* to scrape] (14th century)
transitive verb
1 a : to remove from a surface by usually repeated strokes of an edged instrument **b :** to make (a surface) smooth or clean with strokes of an edged instrument or an abrasive
2 a : to grate harshly over or against **b :** to damage or injure the surface of by contact with a rough surface **c :** to draw roughly or noisily over a surface

3 : to collect by or as if by scraping — often used with *up* or *together* ⟨*scrape* up the price of a ticket⟩
intransitive verb
1 : to move in sliding contact with a rough surface
2 : to accumulate money by small economies
3 : to draw back the foot along the ground in making a bow
4 : to make one's way with difficulty or succeed by a narrow margin ⟨just *scraped* by at school⟩
— **scrap·er** *noun*
— **scrape a leg :** to make a low bow
²scrape *noun* (15th century)
1 a : the act or process of scraping **b :** a sound made by scraping **c :** damage or injury caused by scraping **:** ABRASION ⟨bumps and *scrapes*⟩
2 : a bow made with a drawing back of the foot along the ground
3 a : a distressing encounter ⟨a *scrape* with death⟩ **b :** QUARREL, FIGHT
scrap heap *noun* (circa 1902)
1 : a pile of discarded metal
2 : the place where useless things are discarded
scra·pie \'skrā-pē\ *noun* [¹*scrape*] (1910)
: a usually fatal disease of the nervous system especially of sheep that is characterized by twitching, intense itching, excessive thirst, emaciation, weakness, and finally paralysis
scrap·page \'skra-pij\ *noun* (circa 1909)
1 : the scrapping of discarded objects (as automobiles)
2 : the rate at which objects are scrapped
scrap·per \'skra-pər\ *noun* (1874)
: FIGHTER, QUARRELER
scrap·pi·ly \'skra-pə-lē\ *adverb* (1886)
: in a scrappy manner
scrap·pi·ness \'skra-pē-nəs\ *noun* (1867)
: the quality or state of being scrappy
scrap·ple \'skra-pəl\ *noun* [diminutive of ¹*scrap*] (1855)
: a seasoned mixture of ground meat (as pork) and cornmeal set in a mold and served sliced and fried
¹scrap·py \'skra-pē\ *adjective* **scrap·pi·er; -est** [¹*scrap*] (1837)
: consisting of scraps ⟨*scrappy* meals⟩
²scrappy *adjective* **scrap·pi·er; -est** [³*scrap*] (circa 1896)
1 : QUARRELSOME
2 : having an aggressive and determined spirit **:** FEISTY
¹scratch \'skrach\ *verb* [Middle English *scracchen*, probably blend of *scratten* to scratch and *cracchen* to scratch] (15th century)
transitive verb
1 : to scrape or dig with the claws or nails
2 : to rub and tear or mark the surface of with something sharp or jagged
3 : to scrape or rub lightly (as to relieve itching)
4 : to scrape together **:** collect with difficulty or by effort
5 : to write or draw on a surface
6 a : to cancel or erase by or as if by drawing a line through **b :** to withdraw (an entry) from competition
7 : SCRIBBLE, SCRAWL
8 : to scrape along a rough surface ⟨*scratch* a match⟩
intransitive verb
1 : to use the claws or nails in digging, tearing, or wounding
2 : to scrape or rub oneself lightly (as to relieve itching)
3 : to gather money or get a living by hard work and especially through irregular means and sacrifice
4 : to make a thin grating sound
5 : to withdraw from a contest or engagement
6 : to make a scratch in billiards or pool
— **scratch·er** *noun*

— **scratch one's back :** to accommodate with a favor especially in expectation of like return
— **scratch the surface :** to make a superficial effort or modest start
²scratch *noun* (circa 1586)
1 : a mark or injury produced by scratching; *also* **:** a slight wound
2 : SCRAWL, SCRIBBLE
3 : the sound made by scratching
4 a : the starting line in a race **b :** a point at the beginning of a project at which nothing has been done ahead of time ⟨build a school system from *scratch*⟩
5 a : a test of courage **b :** satisfactory condition, level, or performance ⟨not up to *scratch*⟩
6 : a contestant whose name is withdrawn
7 : poultry feed (as mixed grains) scattered on the litter or ground especially to induce birds to exercise — called also *scratch feed*
8 a : a shot in billiards or pool that ends a player's turn; *specifically* **:** a shot in pool in which the cue ball falls into the pocket **b :** a shot that scores by chance **:** FLUKE
9 *slang* **:** MONEY, FUNDS
³scratch *adjective* (1897)
1 : made as or used for a tentative effort
2 : made or done by chance and not as intended ⟨a *scratch* shot⟩
3 : arranged or put together with little selection **:** HAPHAZARD ⟨a *scratch* team⟩
4 : having no handicap or allowance ⟨a *scratch* golfer⟩
5 : made from scratch **:** made with basic ingredients ⟨a *scratch* cake⟩
scratch·board \'skrach-,bōrd, -,bȯrd\ *noun* (circa 1908)
: a black-surfaced cardboard having an undercoat of white clay on which an effect resembling engraving is achieved by scratching away portions of the surface to produce white lines
scratch hit *noun* (1903)
: a batted ball not solidly hit yet credited to the batter as a base hit
scratch pad *noun* (1895)
: a pad of scratch paper
scratch paper *noun* (1899)
: paper that may be used for casual writing
scratch sheet *noun* (1939)
: a racing publication listing competitors scratched from races and giving odds
scratch test *noun* (1937)
: a test for allergic susceptibility made by rubbing an extract of an allergy-producing substance into small breaks or scratches in the skin
scratchy \'skra-chē\ *adjective* **scratch·i·er; -est** (1827)
1 : marked or made with scratches ⟨*scratchy* drawing⟩ ⟨*scratchy* handwriting⟩
2 : likely to scratch **:** PRICKLY ⟨*scratchy* undergrowth⟩
3 : making a scratching noise
4 : uneven in quality **:** RAGGED
5 : causing tingling or itching **:** IRRITATING ⟨*scratchy* wool⟩
— **scratch·i·ly** \-chə-lē\ *adverb*
— **scratch·i·ness** \-chē-nəs\ *noun*
scrawl \'skrȯl\ *verb* [origin unknown] (1612)
transitive verb
: to write or draw awkwardly, hastily, or carelessly
intransitive verb
: to write awkwardly or carelessly
— **scrawl** *noun*
— **scrawl·er** *noun*
— **scrawly** \'skrȯ-lē\ *adjective*
scraw·ny \'skrȯ-nē\ *adjective* **scraw·ni·er; -est** [origin unknown] (1833)
: exceptionally thin and slight or meager in body ⟨*scrawny* scrub cattle⟩
synonym see LEAN
— **scraw·ni·ness** *noun*

screak \'skrēk\ *intransitive verb* [of Scandinavian origin; akin to Old Norse *skrækja* to screech] (circa 1500)
: to make a harsh shrill noise **:** SCREECH
— **screak** *noun*
— **screaky** \'skrē-kē\ *adjective*
¹scream \'skrēm\ *verb* [Middle English *scremen*; akin to Middle Dutch *schreem* scream] (12th century)
intransitive verb
1 a (1) **:** to voice a sudden sharp loud cry (2) **:** to produce harsh high tones **b :** to make a noise resembling a scream ⟨a *screaming* siren⟩ **c :** to move with great rapidity
2 a : to speak or write with intense or hysterical emotion **b :** to protest or complain vehemently **c :** to laugh hysterically
3 : to produce a vivid startling effect
transitive verb
: to utter with or as if with a scream
²scream *noun* (1605)
1 : a loud sharp penetrating cry or noise
2 : one that is very funny
scream·er \'skrē-mər\ *noun* (1712)
1 : one that screams
2 : any of a small family (Anhimidae) of South American wetland birds having a large body, long legs, and spurred wings
3 : a sensationally startling headline
scream·ing *adjective* (1848)
1 : so striking or conspicuous as to attract notice as if by screaming ⟨*screaming* headlines⟩ ⟨a *screaming* need for reform⟩ ⟨dressed in *screaming* red⟩
2 : so funny as to provoke screams of laughter ⟨a *screaming* farce⟩
— **scream·ing·ly** *adverb*
screaming mee·mies \-'mē-mēz\ *noun plural but singular in construction* [origin unknown] (1942)
: nervous hysteria **:** JITTERS
scree \'skrē\ *noun* [of Scandinavian origin; akin to Old Norse *skritha* landslide, from *skrītha* to creep; akin to Old High German *scrītan* to go, Lithuanian *skriesti* to turn] (circa 1781)
: an accumulation of loose stones or rocky debris lying on a slope or at the base of a hill or cliff **:** TALUS
¹screech \'skrēch\ *noun* (1560)
1 : a high shrill piercing cry usually expressing pain or terror
2 : a sound resembling a screech
²screech *verb* [alteration of earlier *scritch*, from Middle English *scrichen*; akin to Old Norse *skrækja* to screech] (1577)
intransitive verb
1 : to utter a high shrill piercing cry **:** make an outcry usually in terror or pain
2 : to make a shrill high-pitched sound resembling a screech; *also* **:** to move with such a sound ⟨the car *screeched* to a stop⟩
transitive verb
: to utter with or as if with a screech
— **screech·er** *noun*
screech owl *noun* (1593)
1 : BARN OWL
2 : any of numerous New World owls (genus *Otus*); *especially* **:** a small North American owl (*O. asio*) with a pair of tufts of lengthened feathers on the head resembling ears
screechy \'skrē-chē\ *adjective* (circa 1830)
: producing a screech
screed \'skrēd\ *noun* [Middle English *screde* fragment, alteration of Old English *scrēade* — more at SHRED] (circa 1789)
1 a : a lengthy discourse **b :** an informal piece of writing
2 : a strip (as of plaster of the thickness planned for the coat) laid on as a guide

3 : a leveling device drawn over freshly poured concrete

¹screen \'skrēn\ *noun* [Middle English *screne,* from Middle French *escren,* from Middle Dutch *scherm;* akin to Old High German *skirm* shield; probably akin to Sanskrit *carman* skin, *kṛnāti* he injures — more at SHEAR] (14th century)
1 : a protective or ornamental device (as a movable partition) shielding an area from heat or drafts or from view
2 : something that shelters, protects, or hides: as **a :** a growth or stand of trees, shrubs, or plants **b :** a protective formation of troops, ships, or planes **c :** something that covers or disguises the true nature (as of an activity or feeling) ⟨greets strangers with a *screen* of excessive friendliness —Tony Schwartz⟩ **d** (1) : a maneuver in various sports (as basketball or ice hockey) whereby an opponent is legally impeded or his view of the play is momentarily blocked (2) : SCREEN PASS
3 a : a perforated plate or cylinder or a meshed wire or cloth fabric usually mounted and used to separate coarser from finer parts **b :** a system for examining and separating into different groups **c :** a piece of apparatus designed to prevent agencies in one part from affecting other parts ⟨an optical *screen*⟩ ⟨an electric *screen*⟩ ⟨a magnetic *screen*⟩ **d :** a frame holding a usually metallic netting used especially in a window or door to exclude pests (as insects)
4 a : a flat surface on which a picture or series of pictures is projected or reflected **b :** the surface on which the image appears in an electronic display (as in a television set, radar receiver, or computer terminal)
5 : a glass plate ruled with crossing opaque lines through which an image is photographed in making a halftone
6 : the motion-picture medium or industry

²screen (15th century)
transitive verb
1 : to guard from injury or danger
2 a : to give shelter or protection to with or as if with a screen **b :** to separate with or as if with a screen; *also* : to shield (an opponent) from a play or from view of a play
3 a : to pass (as coal, gravel, or ashes) through a screen to separate the fine part from the coarse; *also* : to remove by a screen **b** (1) : to examine usually methodically in order to make a separation into different groups (2) : to select or eliminate by a screening process
4 : to provide with a screen to keep out pests (as insects)
5 a (1) : to present (as a motion picture) for viewing on a screen (2) : to view the presentation of (as a motion picture) **b :** to present in a motion picture
intransitive verb
1 : to appear on a motion-picture screen
2 : to provide a screen in a game or sport
synonym see HIDE
— **screen·able** \'skrē-nə-bəl\ *adjective*
— **screen·er** *noun*

screen·ing \'skrē-niŋ\ *noun* (1725)
1 : the act or process of one that screens
2 *plural but singular or plural in construction* **:** material (as waste or fine coal) separated out by means of a screen
3 : metal or plastic mesh (as for window screens)
4 : a showing of a motion picture

screen·land \'skrēn-,land\ *noun* (1925)
: FILMDOM

screen memory *noun* (1923)
: a recollection of early childhood that may be falsely recalled or magnified in importance and that masks another memory of deep emotional significance

screen pass *noun* (circa 1949)
: a forward pass in football to a receiver at or behind the line of scrimmage who is protected by a screen of blockers

screen·play \'skrēn-,plā\ *noun* (1916)
: the script and often shooting directions of a story prepared for motion-picture production

screen test *noun* (1927)
: a short film sequence for assessing the ability or suitability of a person for a motion-picture role
— **screen–test** *transitive verb*

screen·writ·er \'skrēn-,rī-tər\ *noun* (1921)
: a writer of screenplays

¹screw \'skrü\ *noun* [Middle English, from Middle French *escroe* female screw, nut, from Medieval Latin *scrofa,* from Latin, sow] (15th century)
1 a : a simple machine of the inclined plane type consisting of a spirally grooved solid cylinder and a correspondingly grooved hollow cylinder into which it fits **b :** a nail-shaped or rod-shaped piece with a spiral groove and a slotted or recessed head designed to be inserted into material by rotating (as with a screwdriver) and used for fastening pieces of solid material together
2 a : a screwlike form : SPIRAL **b :** a turn of a screw; *also* : a twist like the turn of a screw **c :** a screwlike device (as a corkscrew)
3 : a worn-out horse
4 *chiefly British* **:** a small packet (as of tobacco)
5 : a prison guard
6 : one who bargains shrewdly; *also* : SKINFLINT
7 : a propeller especially of a ship
8 a : THUMBSCREW 2 **b :** pressure or punitive measures intended to coerce — used chiefly in the phrase *put the screws on* or *put the screws to*
9 a : an act of sexual intercourse — usually considered vulgar **b :** a partner in sexual intercourse — usually considered vulgar
— **screw·like** \-,līk\ *adjective*
— **have a screw loose :** to be mentally unbalanced

²screw (1605)
transitive verb
1 a (1) : to attach, fasten, or close by means of a screw (2) : to unite or separate by means of a screw or a twisting motion ⟨*screw* the two pieces together⟩ (3) : to press tightly in a device (as a vise) operated by a screw (4) : to operate, tighten, or adjust by means of a screw (5) : to torture by means of a thumbscrew **b :** to cause to rotate spirally about an axis
2 a (1) : to twist into strained configurations : CONTORT ⟨*screwed* up his face⟩ (2) : SQUINT (3) : CRUMPLE **b :** to furnish with a spiral groove or ridge : THREAD
3 : to increase the intensity, quantity, or capability of ⟨trying to *screw* up courage to confess —Will Scott⟩
4 a (1) : to mistreat or exploit through extortion, trickery, or unfair actions; *especially* : to deprive of or cheat out of something due or expected ⟨*screwed* out of a job⟩ (2) : to treat so as to bring about injury or loss (as to a person's reputation) ⟨use the available Federal machinery to *screw* our political enemies —J. W. Dean III⟩ — often used as a generalized curse ⟨*screw* you!⟩ **b :** to extract by pressure or threat
5 : to copulate with — usually considered vulgar
intransitive verb
1 : to rotate like or as a screw
2 : to turn or move with a twisting or writhing motion
3 : COPULATE — usually considered vulgar
— **screw·er** *noun*

screw around *intransitive verb* (1939)
1 : to waste time with unproductive activity : DALLY
2 : to have sexual relations with someone outside of a marriage or steady relationship : be sexually promiscuous

¹screw·ball \'skrü-,bȯl\ *noun* (1928)

1 : a baseball pitch that spins and breaks in the opposite direction to a curve
2 : a whimsical, eccentric, or crazy person : ZANY

²screwball *adjective* (circa 1936)
: crazily eccentric or whimsical : ZANY

screw·bean \'skrü-,bēn\ *noun* (1866)
1 : a leguminous shrub or small tree (*Prosopis pubescens*) of the southwestern U.S. and northern Mexico — called also *screwbean mesquite*
2 : a spirally twisted sweet pod that is the fruit of the screwbean

screw·driv·er \'skrü-,drī-vər\ *noun* (1779)
1 : a tool for turning screws
2 : vodka and orange juice served with ice

screw eye *noun* (1873)
: a wood screw with a head in the form of a loop

screw jack *noun* (1719)
: a screw-operated jack for lifting, exerting pressure, or adjusting position (as of a machine part)

screw pine *noun* (1836)
: any of a genus (*Pandanus* of the family Pandanaceae, the screw-pine family) of tropical monocotyledonous Old World plants with slender palmlike stems, often huge prop roots, and terminal crowns of swordlike leaves

screw propeller *noun* (1839)
: PROPELLER

screw thread *noun* (circa 1812)
1 : the projecting helical rib of a screw
2 : one complete turn of a screw thread

screw·up \'skrü-,əp\ *noun* (circa 1960)
1 : one who screws up
2 : BOTCH, BLUNDER

screw up (1680)
transitive verb
1 : to tighten, fasten, or lock by or as if by a screw
2 a : BUNGLE, BOTCH **b :** to cause to act or function in a crazy or confused way : CONFOUND, DISTURB
intransitive verb
: to botch an activity or undertaking

screw·worm \'skrü-,wərm\ *noun* (1879)
1 : a blowfly (*Cochliomyia hominivorax*) of the warmer parts of America whose larva develops in sores or wounds or in the nostrils of mammals including humans with serious or sometimes fatal results; *especially* : its larva
2 : any of several flies other than the screwworm and especially their larvae which parasitize the flesh of mammals

screwy \'skrü-ē\ *adjective* **screw·i·er; -est** (1887)
1 : crazily absurd, eccentric, or unusual
2 : CRAZY, INSANE
— **screw·i·ness** *noun*

scrib·al \'skrī-bəl\ *adjective* (1857)
: of, relating to, or due to a scribe

scrib·ble \'skri-bəl\ *verb* **scrib·bled; scrib·bling** \-b(ə-)liŋ\ [Middle English *scriblen,* from Medieval Latin *scribillare,* from Latin *scribere* to write] (15th century)
transitive verb
1 : to write hastily or carelessly without regard to legibility or form
2 : to cover with careless or worthless writings or drawings
intransitive verb
: to write or draw hastily and carelessly
— **scribble** *noun*

scrib·bler \'skri-b(ə-)lər\ *noun* (circa 1553)
1 : one that scribbles
2 : a minor or insignificant author

¹scribe \'skrīb\ *noun* [Middle English, from Latin *scriba* official writer, from *scribere* to write; akin to Greek *skariphasthai* to scratch an outline] (14th century)
1 : one of a learned class in ancient Israel through New Testament times studying the Scriptures and serving as copyists, editors, teachers, and jurists

2 a : an official or public secretary or clerk **b** : a copier of manuscripts
3 : WRITER; *specifically* : JOURNALIST
²scribe *intransitive verb* **scribed; scrib·ing** (1782)
: to work as a scribe : WRITE
³scribe *transitive verb* **scribed; scrib·ing** [probably short for *describe*] (1678)
1 : to mark a line on by cutting or scratching with a pointed instrument
2 : to make by cutting or scratching
⁴scribe *noun* (1812)
: SCRIBER
scrib·er \'skrī-bər\ *noun* (circa 1836)
: a sharp-pointed tool for making marks and especially for marking off material (as wood or metal) to be cut
scrieve \'skrēv\ *intransitive verb* [of Scandinavian origin; akin to Old Norse *skrefa* to stride] (1785)
Scottish : to move along swiftly and smoothly
scrim \'skrim\ *noun* [origin unknown] (1792)
1 : a durable plain-woven usually cotton fabric for use in clothing, curtains, building, and industry
2 : a theater drop that appears opaque when a scene in front is lighted and transparent or translucent when a scene in back is lighted
3 : something likened to a theater scrim
¹scrim·mage \'skri-mij\ *noun* [Middle English *scrymmage*, alteration of *skyrmissh* skirmish] (15th century)
1 a : a minor battle : SKIRMISH **b :** a confused fight : SCUFFLE
2 a : the interplay between two football teams that begins with the snap of the ball and continues until the ball is dead **b :** practice play (as in football or basketball) between two squads
²scrimmage *verb* **scrim·maged; scrim·mag·ing** (circa 1825)
intransitive verb
: to take part in a scrimmage
transitive verb
: to play a scrimmage against
— scrim·mag·er *noun*
scrimmage line *noun* (circa 1909)
: LINE OF SCRIMMAGE
scrimp \'skrimp\ *verb* [perhaps of Scandinavian origin; akin to Swedish *skrympa* to shrink, Middle Low German *schrempen* to contract — more at SHRIMP] (circa 1774)
transitive verb
1 : to be stingy in providing for
2 : to make too small, short, or scanty
intransitive verb
: to be frugal or stingy
— scrimpy \'skrim-pē\ *adjective*
scrim·shan·der \'skrim-,shan-dər\ *noun* [origin unknown] (1851)
: a person who creates scrimshaw
¹scrim·shaw \'skrim-,shȯ\ *verb* [origin unknown] (circa 1826)
transitive verb
: to carve or engrave into scrimshaw
intransitive verb
: to produce scrimshaw
²scrimshaw *noun* (circa 1864)
1 : any of various carved or engraved articles made originally by American whalers usually from baleen or whale ivory
2 : scrimshawed work
3 : the art, practice, or technique of producing scrimshaw
¹scrip \'skrip\ *noun* [Middle English *scrippe*, from Medieval Latin *scrippum* pilgrim's knapsack] (13th century)
archaic : a small bag or wallet
²scrip *noun* [alteration of *script*] (1590)
1 : a short writing (as a certificate, schedule, or list)
2 : a small piece
3 : any of various documents used as evidence that the holder or bearer is entitled to receive something (as a fractional share of

stock or an allotment of land) **b :** paper currency or a token issued for temporary use in an emergency
¹script \'skript\ *noun* [Middle English, from Latin *scriptum* thing written, from neuter of *scriptus*, past participle of *scribere* to write — more at SCRIBE] (14th century)
1 a : something written : TEXT **b :** an original or principal instrument or document **c** (1) : MANUSCRIPT 1 (2) : the written text of a stage play, screenplay, or broadcast; *specifically* : the one used in production or performance
2 a : a style of printed letters that resembles handwriting **b :** written characters : HANDWRITING **c :** ALPHABET
3 : a plan of action
²script *transitive verb* (1935)
1 : to prepare a script for or from
2 : to provide carefully considered details for (as a plan of action)
script·er \'skrip-tər\ *noun* (1939)
: SCRIPTWRITER
scrip·to·ri·um \skrip-'tȯr-ē-əm, -'tȯr-\ *noun*, *plural* **-ria** \-ē-ə\ [Medieval Latin, from Latin *scribere*] (1774)
: a copying room for the scribes in a medieval monastery
scrip·tur·al \'skrip(t)-sh(ə-)rəl\ *adjective* (1641)
: of, relating to, contained in, or according to a sacred writing; *especially* : BIBLICAL
— scrip·tur·al·ly *adverb*
scrip·ture \'skrip(t)-shər\ *noun* [Middle English, from Late Latin *scriptura*, from Latin, act or product of writing, from *scriptus*] (14th century)
1 a (1) *capitalized* : the books of the Bible — often used in plural (2) *often capitalized* : a passage from the Bible **b :** a body of writings considered sacred or authoritative
2 : something written (the primitive man's awe for any *scripture* —George Santayana)
script·writ·er \'skrip(t)-,rī-tər\ *noun* (1935)
: a person who writes scripts
scriv·en·er \'skriv-nər, 'skri-və-\ *noun* [Middle English *scriveiner*, alteration of *scrivein*, from Middle French *escrivein*, from (assumed) Vulgar Latin *scriban-, scriba*, alteration of Latin *scriba* scribe] (14th century)
1 : a professional or public copyist or writer : SCRIBE
2 : NOTARY PUBLIC
scrod \'skräd\ *noun* [origin unknown] (1841)
: a young fish (as a cod or haddock); *especially* : one split and boned for cooking
scrof·u·la \'skrȯ-fyə-lə, 'skrä-\ *noun* [New Latin, back-formation from Late Latin *scrofulae*, plural, swellings of the lymph nodes of the neck, from plural of *scrofula*, diminutive of Latin *scrofa* breeding sow] (1791)
: tuberculosis of lymph nodes especially in the neck
scrof·u·lous \-ləs\ *adjective* (1612)
1 : of, relating to, or affected with scrofula
2 a : having a diseased run-down appearance **b :** morally contaminated
¹scroll \'skrōl\ *noun* [Middle English *scrowle*, blend of *rolle* roll and *scrowe* scrap, scroll (from Middle French *escroue*, of Germanic origin; akin to Old English *scrēade* shred)] (15th century)
1 a : a roll (as of papyrus, leather, or parchment) for writing a document **b** *archaic* : a written message **c :** ROSTER, LIST **d :** a riband with rolled ends often inscribed with a motto
2 a : something resembling a scroll in shape; *especially* : a spiral or convoluted form in ornamental design derived from the curves of a loosely or partly rolled parchment scroll **b :** the curved head of a bowed stringed musical instrument — see VIOLIN illustration
²scroll (1973)

intransitive verb
: to move text or graphics up or down or across a display screen as if by unrolling a scroll
transitive verb
: to cause (text or graphics on a display screen) to move in scrolling
scroll saw *noun* (1851)
1 : FRETSAW
2 : JIGSAW 1
scroll·work \'skrōl-,wərk\ *noun* (1739)
: ornamentation characterized by scrolls; *especially* : fancy designs in wood often made with a scroll saw
scrooge \'skrüj\ *noun*, *often capitalized* [Ebenezer *Scrooge*, character in the story *A Christmas Carol* (1843) by Charles Dickens] (1899)
: a miserly person
scro·tum \'skrō-təm\ *noun*, *plural* **scro·ta** \-tə\ *or* **scrotums** [Latin; akin to Latin *scrautum* quiver] (1597)
: the external pouch that in most mammals contains the testes
— scro·tal \'skrō-t³l\ *adjective*
scrouge \'skraůj, 'skrüj\ *verb* **scrouged; scroug·ing** [alteration of English dialect *scruze* to squeeze] (1755)
chiefly dialect : CROWD, PRESS
scrounge \'skraůnj\ *verb* **scrounged; scroung·ing** [alteration of English dialect *scrunge* to wander about idly] (circa 1909)
transitive verb
1 : STEAL, SWIPE
2 a : to get as needed by or as if by foraging, scavenging, or borrowing **b :** FINAGLE, WHEEDLE — often used with *up*
intransitive verb
: to search about and turn up something needed from whatever source is available; *also* : to actively seek money, work, or sustenance from any available source
— scroung·er *noun*
scroungy \'skraůn-jē\ *adjective* **scroung·i·er; -est** (circa 1960)
: being shabby, dirty, or unkempt
¹scrub \'skrəb\ *noun*, *often attributive* [Middle English, alteration of *schrobbe* shrub — more at SHRUB] (14th century)
1 a : a stunted tree or shrub **b :** vegetation consisting chiefly of scrubs **c :** a tract covered with scrub
2 : a domestic animal of mixed or unknown parentage and usually inferior conformation : MONGREL
3 : a person of insignificant size or standing
4 : a player not belonging to the first string
²scrub *verb* **scrubbed; scrub·bing** [of Low German or Scandinavian origin; akin to Middle Low German & Middle Dutch *schrubben* to scrub, Swedish *skrubba*] (circa 1595)
transitive verb
1 a (1) : to clean with hard rubbing : SCOUR (2) : to remove by scrubbing **b :** to subject to friction : RUB
2 : WASH 6c(2)
3 : CANCEL, ELIMINATE
intransitive verb
1 : to use hard rubbing in cleaning
2 : to prepare for surgery by scrubbing oneself
— scrub·ba·ble \'skrə-bə-bəl\ *adjective*
³scrub *noun* (1621)
1 : an act or instance of scrubbing; *especially* : CANCELLATION
2 : one that scrubs
¹scrubbed \'skrə-bəd\ *adjective* [¹*scrub*] (1596)
archaic : SCRUBBY 1

scroll 1

\ə\ abut \ᵊ\ kitten \ər\ further \a\ ash \ā\ ace
\ä\ mop, mar \aů\ out \ch\ chin \e\ bet \ē\ easy
\g\ go \i\ hit \ī\ ice \j\ job \ŋ\ sing \ō\ go
\ȯ\ law \ȯi\ boy \th\ thin \t̶h\ the \ü\ loot \ů\ foot
\y\ yet \zh\ vision *see also* Guide to Pronunciation

²scrubbed \'skrəbd\ *adjective* [from past participle of ²*scrub*] (1948)
: giving the impression of being clean or wholesome as if from scrubbing ⟨days when studios manufactured *scrubbed* public images for their stars —Sally Helgesen⟩

scrub·ber \'skrə-bər\ *noun* (1839)
: one that scrubs; *especially* : an apparatus for removing impurities especially from gases

scrub brush *noun* (1897)
: a brush with hard bristles for heavy cleaning — called also *scrubbing brush*

scrub·by \'skrə-bē\ *adjective* **scrub·bi·er; -est** [¹*scrub*] (1591)
1 : inferior in size or quality : STUNTED ⟨*scrubby* cattle⟩
2 : covered with or consisting of scrub
3 : SHABBY, PALTRY

scrub·land \'skrəb-ˌland\ *noun* (1779)
: land covered with scrub

scrub nurse *noun* (1905)
: a nurse who assists the surgeon in an operating room

scrub oak *noun* (1766)
: any of various chiefly American oaks (as *Quercus ilicifolia* of the northeastern U.S.) of small size and usually shrubby habit

scrub pine *noun* (1791)
: a pine of dwarf, straggly, or scrubby growth usually by reason of environmental conditions; *specifically* : a pine tree unsuitable for lumber by reason of inferior or defective growth

scrub typhus *noun* (1929)
: TSUTSUGAMUSHI DISEASE

scrub·wom·an \'skrəb-ˌwu̇-mən\ *noun* (1873)
: CHARWOMAN

scruff \'skrəf\ *noun* [alteration of earlier *scuff*, of unknown origin] (1790)
: the back of the neck : NAPE

scruffy \'skrə-fē\ *adjective* **scruff·i·er; -est** [English dialect *scruff* something worthless] (1871)
: UNKEMPT, SLOVENLY, SHAGGY
— **scruff·i·ly** \-fə-lē\ *adverb*
— **scruff·i·ness** \-fē-nəs\ *noun*

scrum \'skrəm\ *noun* [short for *scrummage*, alteration of *scrimmage*] (1857)
1 *or* **scrum·mage** \'skrə-mij\ : a rugby play in which the forwards of each side come together in a tight formation and struggle to gain possession of the ball when it is tossed in among them
2 *British* : MADHOUSE 2
— **scrummage** *intransitive verb*

scrump·tious \'skrəm(p)-shəs\ *adjective* [perhaps alteration of *sumptuous*] (1830)
: DELIGHTFUL, EXCELLENT; *especially* : DELICIOUS
— **scrump·tious·ly** *adverb*

¹scrunch \'skrənch, 'skrünch\ *verb* [alteration of ¹*crunch*] (circa 1790)
transitive verb
1 : CRUNCH, CRUSH
2 a : to draw or squeeze together tightly **b** : CRUMPLE — often used with *up* **c** : to cause (as one's features) to draw together — usually used with *up*
intransitive verb
1 : to move with or make a crunching sound
2 : CROUCH, HUNCH; *also* : SQUEEZE

²scrunch *noun* (1857)
: a crunching sound

¹scru·ple \'skrü-pəl\ *noun* [Middle English *scriple*, from Latin *scrupulus* a unit of weight, diminutive of *scrupus* sharp stone] (14th century)
1 — see WEIGHT table
2 : a minute part or quantity : IOTA

²scruple *noun* [Middle English *scrupul*, from Middle French *scrupule*, from Latin *scrupulus*, diminutive of *scrupus* source of uneasiness, literally, sharp stone] (15th century)
1 : an ethical consideration or principle that inhibits action
2 : the quality or state of being scrupulous

3 : mental reservation ◆
synonym see QUALM

³scruple *intransitive verb* **scru·pled; scru·pling** \-p(ə-)liŋ\ (1627)
1 : to have scruples
2 : to show reluctance on grounds of conscience : HESITATE

scru·pu·los·i·ty \ˌskrü-pyə-'lä-sə-tē\ *noun* (1526)
1 : the quality or state of being scrupulous
2 : ²SCRUPLE 1

scru·pu·lous \'skrü-pyə-ləs\ *adjective* [Middle English, from Latin *scrupulosus*, from *scrupulus*] (15th century)
1 : having moral integrity : acting in strict regard for what is considered right or proper
2 : punctiliously exact : PAINSTAKING ⟨working with *scrupulous* care⟩
synonym see UPRIGHT, CAREFUL
word history see SCRUPLE
— **scru·pu·lous·ly** *adverb*
— **scru·pu·lous·ness** *noun*

scru·ta·ble \'skrü-tə-bəl\ *adjective* [Late Latin *scrutabilis* searchable, from Latin *scrutari*] (circa 1600)
: capable of being deciphered : COMPREHENSIBLE

scru·ti·neer \ˌskrü-t³n-'ir\ *noun* (1557)
1 : one that examines
2 *British* : one who takes or counts votes

scru·ti·nise *British variant of* SCRUTINIZE

scru·ti·nize \'skrü-t³n-ˌīz\ *verb* **-nized; -nizing** (1671)
transitive verb
: to examine closely and minutely
intransitive verb
: to make a scrutiny ☆
— **scru·ti·niz·er** *noun*

scru·ti·ny \'skrü-t³n-ē, 'skrüt-nē\ *noun, plural* **-nies** [Latin *scrutinium*, from *scrutari* to search, examine, probably from *scruta* trash] (1604)
1 : a searching study, inquiry, or inspection : EXAMINATION
2 : a searching look
3 : close watch : SURVEILLANCE

scu·ba \'skü-bə\ *noun, often attributive* [*self-contained underwater breathing apparatus*] (1952)
: an apparatus utilizing a portable supply of compressed gas (as air) supplied at a regulated pressure and used for breathing while swimming underwater

scuba diver *noun* (1958)
: one who swims underwater with the aid of scuba gear
— **scuba dive** *intransitive verb*

¹scud \'skəd\ *intransitive verb* **scud·ded; scud·ding** [probably of Scandinavian origin; akin to Norwegian *skudda* to push] (1532)
1 : to move or run swiftly especially as if driven forward
2 : to run before a gale

²scud *noun* (1609)
1 : the action of scudding : RUSH
2 a : loose vapory clouds driven swiftly by the wind **b** (1) : a slight sudden shower (2) : mist, rain, snow, or spray driven by the wind **c** : a gust of wind

scu·do \'skü-(ˌ)dō\ *noun, plural* **scu·di** \-(ˌ)dē\ [Italian, literally, shield, from Latin *scutum* — more at ESQUIRE] (1644)
1 : a gold or silver coin formerly used in Italy
2 : a unit of value equivalent to a scudo

¹scuff \'skəf\ *verb* [probably of Scandinavian origin; akin to Swedish *skuffa* to push] (1768)
intransitive verb
1 a : to walk without lifting the feet : SHUFFLE **b** : to poke or shuffle a foot in exploration or embarrassment
2 : to become scratched, chipped, or roughened by wear

transitive verb
1 : ³CUFF
2 a : to scrape (the feet) along a surface while walking or back and forth while standing **b** : to poke at with the toe
3 : to scratch, gouge, or wear away the surface of

²scuff *noun* (1899)
1 a : a noise of or as if of scuffing **b** : the act or an instance of scuffing **c** : a mark or injury caused by scuffing
2 : a flat-soled slipper without quarter or heel strap — compare MULE

scuf·fle \'skə-fəl\ *intransitive verb* **scuf·fled; scuf·fling** \-f(ə-)liŋ\ [probably of Scandinavian origin; akin to Swedish *skuffa* to push] (1590)
1 a : to struggle at close quarters with disorder and confusion **b** : to struggle (as by working odd jobs) to get by
2 a : to move with a quick shuffling gait : SCURRY **b** : SHUFFLE
— **scuffle** *noun*

scuffle hoe *noun* (1856)
: a garden hoe that has both edges sharpened and can be pushed forward or drawn back

¹scull \'skəl\ *noun* [Middle English *sculle*] (14th century)
1 a : an oar used at the stern of a boat to propel it forward with a thwartwise motion **b** : either of a pair of oars usually less than 10 feet (3 meters) in length and operated by one person
2 : a racing shell propelled by one or two persons using sculls

²scull *noun* (1624)
transitive verb
: to propel (a boat) by sculls or by a large oar worked thwartwise
intransitive verb
: to scull a boat
— **scull·er** *noun*

scul·lery \'skə-lə-rē, 'skəl-rē\ *noun, plural* **-ler·ies** [Middle English, department of household in charge of dishes, from Middle French *escuelerie*, from *escuelle* bowl, from Latin *scutella* drinking bowl — more at SCUTTLE] (15th century)

☆ **SYNONYMS**
Scrutinize, scan, inspect, examine mean to look at or over. SCRUTINIZE stresses close attention to minute detail ⟨*scrutinized* the hospital bill⟩. SCAN implies a surveying from point to point often suggesting a cursory overall observation ⟨*scanned* the wine list⟩. INSPECT implies scrutinizing for errors or defects ⟨*inspected* my credentials⟩. EXAMINE suggests a scrutiny in order to determine the nature, condition, or quality of a thing ⟨*examined* the specimens⟩.

◇ **WORD HISTORY**
scruple In Latin *scrupus* meant literally "sharp stone" and metaphorically "source of uneasiness," alluding to the way a sharp pebble that has worked its way into one's shoe becomes a nagging cause of discomfort. The much more commonly used diminutive form *scrupulus* had the same metaphorical meaning "source of anxiety." The derived adjective *scrupulosus* had likewise both a concrete meaning, "full of sharp rocks, jagged," and a metaphorical one—not "full of sources of anxiety," as one might expect, but "marked by careful attention to detail, taking precautions." Thus it denoted the attitude of someone following a rocky path and trying to avoid a spill. Both *scrupulus* and *scrupulosus* found their way into English in their metaphorical senses, respectively as *scruple* "an ethical consideration" and *scrupulous*.

: a room for cleaning and storing dishes and cooking utensils and for doing messy kitchen work

scul·lion \'skəl-yən\ *noun* [Middle English *sculion*, from Middle French *escouillon* dishcloth, alteration of *escouvillon*, from *escouve* broom, from Latin *scopae*, literally, twigs bound together] (15th century)
: a kitchen helper

scul·pin \'skəl-pən\ *noun, plural* **sculpins** *also* **sculpin** [origin unknown] (1672)
1 : any of a family (Cottidae) of spiny large-headed broad-mouthed often scaleless bony fishes
2 : a scorpion fish (*Scorpaena guttata*) of the southern California coast caught for food and sport

sculpin 1

sculpt \'skəlpt\ *verb* [French *sculpter*, alteration of obsolete *sculper*, from Latin *sculpere*] (1864)
: CARVE, SCULPTURE

sculp·tor \'skəlp-tər\ *noun* [Latin, from *sculpere*] (1634)
: an artist who makes sculptures

sculp·tress \-trəs\ *noun* (1662)
: a woman artist who makes sculptures

sculp·tur·al \'skəlp-chə-rəl, 'skəlp-shrəl\ *adjective* (1819)
1 : of or relating to sculpture
2 : resembling sculpture : SCULPTURESQUE
— **sculp·tur·al·ly** *adverb*

¹sculp·ture \'skəlp-chər\ *noun* [Middle English, from Latin *sculptura*, from *sculptus*, past participle of *sculpere* to carve, alteration of *scalpere* to scratch, carve] (14th century)
1 a : the action or art of processing (as by carving, modeling, or welding) plastic or hard materials into works of art **b** (1) : work produced by sculpture (2) : a three-dimensional work of art (as a statue)
2 : impressed or raised markings or a pattern of such especially on a plant or animal part

²sculpture *verb* **sculp·tured; sculp·tur·ing** \'skəlp-chə-riŋ, 'skəlp-shriŋ\ (1645)
transitive verb
1 a : to form an image or representation of from solid material (as wood or stone) **b** : to form into a three-dimensional work of art
2 : to change (the form of the earth's surface) by natural processes (as erosion and deposition)
3 : to shape by or as if by carving or molding
intransitive verb
: to work as a sculptor

sculp·tur·esque \,skəlp-chə-'resk\ *adjective* (1835)
: done in the manner of or resembling sculpture
— **sculp·tur·esque·ly** *adverb*

¹scum \'skəm\ *noun* [Middle English, from Middle Dutch *schum*; akin to Old High German *scūm* foam] (14th century)
1 a : extraneous matter or impurities risen to or formed on the surface of a liquid often as a foul filmy covering **b** : the scoria of metals in a molten state : DROSS **c** : a slimy film on a solid or gelatinous object
2 a : REFUSE **b** : a low, vile, or worthless person or group of people
— **scum·my** \'skə-mē\ *adjective*

²scum *intransitive verb* **scummed; scum·ming** (1661)
: to become covered with or as if with scum

scum·bag \'skəm-,bag *also* -,bäg\ *noun* (1967)
slang : a dirty or despicable person

¹scum·ble \'skəm-bəl\ *transitive verb* **scum·bled; scum·bling** \-b(ə-)liŋ\ [perhaps frequentative of ²*scum*]
1 a : to make (as color or a painting) less brilliant by covering with a thin coat of opaque or semiopaque color **b** : to apply (a color) in this manner

2 : to soften the lines or colors of (a drawing) by rubbing lightly

²scumble *noun* (1834)
1 : the act or effect of scumbling
2 : a material used for scumbling

scun·gil·li \skün-'jē-lē, -'gē-, -'ji-\ *noun* [Italian dialect (Neapolitan) *scuncigli*, plural of *scunciglio* conch] (1945)
: conch used as food

¹scun·ner \'skə-nər\ *intransitive verb* [Middle English (Scots) *skunniren*] (14th century)
chiefly Scottish : to be in a state of disgusted irritation

²scunner *noun* (circa 1520)
: an unreasonable or extreme dislike or prejudice

scup \'skəp\ *noun, plural* **scup** *also* **scups** [short for *scuppaug*, modification of Narraganset *mishcùppaûog*] (circa 1848)
: a porgy (*Stenotomus chrysops*) occurring along the Atlantic coast of the U.S. chiefly from North Carolina to Maine and used as a panfish

¹scup·per \'skə-pər\ *noun* [Middle English *skopper*] (15th century)
1 : an opening cut through the bulwarks of a ship so that water falling on deck may flow overboard
2 : an opening in the wall of a building through which water can drain from a floor or flat roof

²scupper *transitive verb* [origin unknown] (1899)
British : to defeat or put an end to : DO IN 1a

scup·per·nong \-,nȯŋ, -,näŋ\ *noun* [*Scuppernong*, river and lake in North Carolina] (1811)
1 : MUSCADINE; *especially* : a cultivated muscadine with yellowish green plum-flavored fruits
2 : a sweet aromatic amber-colored wine made from scuppernongs

scurf \'skərf\ *noun* [Middle English, from Old English, of Scandinavian origin; akin to Icelandic *skurfa* scurf; akin to Old High German *scorf* scurf, Old English *sceorfan* to scarify] (before 12th century)
1 : thin dry scales detached from the epidermis especially in an abnormal skin condition; *specifically* : DANDRUFF
2 a : something like flakes or scales adhering to a surface **b** : the foul remains of something adherent
3 a : a scaly deposit or covering on some plant parts; *also* : a localized or general darkening and roughening of a plant surface usually more pronounced than russeting **b** : a plant disease characterized by scurf
— **scurfy** \'skər-fē\ *adjective*

scur·rile *or* **scur·ril** \'skər-əl, 'skə-rəl\ *adjective* [Middle French *scurrile*, from Latin *scurrilis*, from *scurra* buffoon] (1567)
: SCURRILOUS

scur·ril·i·ty \skə-'ri-lə-tē\ *noun, plural* **-ties** (1508)
1 : the quality or state of being scurrilous
2 a : scurrilous or abusive language **b** : an offensively rude or abusive remark

scur·ri·lous \'skər-ə-ləs, 'skə-rə-\ *adjective* (1576)
1 a : using or given to coarse language **b** : being vulgar and evil ⟨*scurrilous* imposters who used a religious exterior to rob poor people —Edwin Benson⟩
2 : containing obscenities, abuse, or slander ⟨a . . . campaign filled with *scurrilous* charges and countercharges —A. D. Graeff⟩
— **scur·ri·lous·ly** *adverb*
— **scur·ri·lous·ness** *noun*

scur·ry \'skər-ē, 'skə-rē\ *intransitive verb* **scur·ried; scur·ry·ing** [short for *hurry-scurry*, reduplication of *hurry*] (1810)
1 : to move in or as in a brisk pace : SCAMPER
2 : to move around in an agitated, confused, or fluttering manner
— **scurry** *noun*

¹scur·vy \'skər-vē\ *noun* [²*scurvy*] (circa 1565)
: a disease marked by spongy gums, loosening of the teeth, and a bleeding into the skin and mucous membranes and caused by a lack of vitamin C

²scurvy *adjective* [*scurf*] (1579)
: disgustingly mean or contemptible : DESPICABLE ⟨a *scurvy* trick⟩
synonym see CONTEMPTIBLE
— **scur·vi·ly** \-və-lē\ *adverb*
— **scur·vi·ness** \-vē-nəs\ *noun*

scurvy grass *noun* (1597)
: a cruciferous herb (as *Cochlearia officinalis*) formerly believed useful in preventing or treating scurvy

scut \'skət\ *noun* [origin unknown] (circa 1530)
: a short erect tail (as of a hare)

scu·tage \'skü-tij, 'skyü-\ *noun* [Middle English, from Medieval Latin *scutagium*, from Latin *scutum* shield — more at ESQUIRE] (15th century)
: a tax levied on a vassal or a knight in lieu of military service

¹scutch \'skəch\ *transitive verb* [obsolete French *escoucher*, from (assumed) Vulgar Latin *excuticare* to beat out, from Latin *excutere*, from *ex-* + *quatere* to shake, strike] (1733)
: to separate the woody fiber from (flax or hemp) by beating

²scutch *noun* (circa 1791)
1 : SCUTCHER
2 : a bricklayer's hammer for cutting, trimming, and dressing bricks

scutch·eon \'skə-chən\ *noun* [Middle English *scochon*, from Middle French *escuchon*] (14th century)
: ESCUTCHEON

scutch·er \'skə-chər\ *noun* (1776)
: an implement or machine for scutching flax or cotton

scute \'sküt, 'skyüt\ *noun* [New Latin *scutum*, from Latin, shield — more at ESQUIRE] (1898)
: an external bony or horny plate or large scale

scu·tel·late \skü-'te-lət, skyü-; 'sk(y)ü-t°l-,āt\ *or* **scu·tel·lat·ed** \'sk(y)ü-t°l-,ā-təd\ *adjective* (1785)
: having or covered with scutella

scu·tel·lum \skü-'te-ləm, skyü-\ *noun, plural* **-la** \-lə\ [New Latin, diminutive of Latin *scutum* shield] (circa 1760)
1 : a hard plate or scale (as on the thorax of an insect or the tarsus of a bird)
2 : the shield-shaped cotyledon of a monocotyledon (as a grass)
— **scu·tel·lar** \-lər\ *adjective*

scut·ter \'skə-tər\ *intransitive verb* [alteration of ⁵*scuttle*] (1781)
: SCURRY, SCAMPER

¹scut·tle \'skə-t°l\ *noun* [Middle English *scutel*, from Latin *scutella* drinking bowl, tray, diminutive of *scutra* platter] (15th century)
1 : a shallow open basket for carrying something (as grain or garden produce)
2 : a metal pail that usually has a bail and a sloped lip and is used especially for carrying coal

²scuttle *noun* [Middle English *skottell*] (15th century)
1 : a small opening in a wall or roof furnished with a lid: as **a** : a small opening or hatchway in the deck of a ship large enough to admit a person and with a lid for covering it **b** : a small hole in the side or bottom of a ship fitted with a covering or glazed
2 : a covering that closes a scuttle

³scuttle *transitive verb* **scut·tled; scut·tling** \'skət-liŋ, 'skə-t°l-iŋ\ (1642)

1 : to cut a hole through the bottom, deck, or side of (a ship); *specifically* **:** to sink or attempt to sink by making holes through the bottom
2 : DESTROY, WRECK; *also* **:** SCRAP 2

⁴scuttle *noun* [perhaps blend of *scud* and *shuttle*] (1623)
1 : a quick shuffling pace
2 : a short swift run

⁵scuttle *intransitive verb* **scut·tled; scut·tling** \'skət-liŋ, 'skə-t²l-iŋ\ (1657)
: SCURRY

scut·tle·butt \'skə-t²l-ˌbət\ *noun* [²*scuttle* + ³*butt*] (1805)
1 a : a cask on shipboard to contain fresh water for a day's use **b :** a drinking fountain on a ship or at a naval or marine installation
2 : RUMOR, GOSSIP

scu·tum \'skü-təm, 'skyü-\ *noun, plural* **scu·ta** \-tə\ [New Latin, from Latin, shield — more at ESQUIRE] (1771)
: a bony, horny, or chitinous plate **:** SCUTE

scut work \'skət-\ *noun* [probably from medical argot *scut* junior intern] (circa 1962)
: routine and often menial labor

scuz·zy \'skə-zē\ *adjective* **scuz·zi·er; -est** [origin unknown] (1969)
slang **:** dirty, shabby, or foul in condition or character

Scyl·la \'si-lə\ *noun* [Latin, from Greek *Skyllē*]
: a nymph changed into a monster in Greek mythology who terrorizes mariners in the Strait of Messina
— between Scylla and Charybdis **:** between two equally hazardous alternatives

scy·phis·to·ma \sī-'fis-tə-mə\ *noun, plural* **-mae** \-ˌmē\ *also* **-mas** [New Latin, from Latin *scyphus* cup + Greek *stoma* mouth — more at STOMACH] (1878)
: a sexually produced scyphozoan larva that ultimately repeatedly constricts transversely to form free-swimming medusae

scy·pho·zo·an \ˌsī-fə-'zō-ən\ *noun* [New Latin *Scyphozoa*, from Latin *scyphus* + New Latin *-zoa*] (circa 1909)
: any of a class (Scyphozoa) of coelenterates that comprise jellyfishes lacking a true polyp and usually a velum
— scyphozoan *adjective*

¹scythe \'sīth, 'sī\ *noun* [Middle English *sithe,* from Old English *sīthe;* akin to Old English *sagu* saw — more at SAW] (before 12th century)
: an implement used for mowing (as grass) and composed of a long curving blade fastened at an angle to a long handle

²scythe *verb* **scythed; scyth·ing** (circa 1580)
intransitive verb
: to use a scythe
transitive verb
: to cut with or as if with a scythe

scythe

Scyth·i·an \'si-thē-ən, -thē-\ *noun* [Latin *Scytha,* from Greek *Skythēs*] (15th century)
1 : a member of an ancient nomadic people inhabiting Scythia
2 : the Iranian language of the Scythians
— Scythian *adjective*

sea \'sē\ *noun* [Middle English *see,* from Old English *sǣ;* akin to Old High German *sē* sea, Gothic *saiws*] (before 12th century)
1 a : a great body of salty water that covers much of the earth; *broadly* **:** the waters of the earth as distinguished from the land and air **b :** a body of salt water of second rank more or less landlocked ⟨the Mediterranean *sea*⟩ **c :** OCEAN **d :** an inland body of water — used especially for names of such bodies ⟨the Caspian *Sea*⟩ ⟨the *Sea* of Galilee⟩
2 a : surface motion on a large body of water or its direction; *also* **:** a large swell or wave

— often used in plural ⟨heavy *seas*⟩ **b :** the disturbance of the ocean or other body of water due to the wind
3 : something likened to the sea especially in vastness ⟨the crowd was a *sea* of faces⟩
4 : the seafaring life
5 : ³MARE
— sea *adjective*
— at sea 1 : on the sea; *specifically* **:** on a sea voyage **2 :** LOST, BEWILDERED
— to sea : to or on the open waters of the sea

sea anchor *noun* (1769)
: a drag typically of canvas thrown overboard to retard the drifting of a ship or seaplane and to keep its head to the wind

sea anemone *noun* (1742)
: any of numerous usually solitary anthozoan polyps (order Actiniaria) whose form, bright and varied colors, and cluster of tentacles superficially resemble a flower

sea·bag \'sē-ˌbag\ *noun* (1919)
: a cylindrical canvas bag used especially by a sailor for clothes and other gear

sea bass *noun* (1765)
1 : any of numerous marine bony fishes (family Serranidae) that are usually smaller and more active than the groupers; *especially* **:** a food and sport fish (*Centropristis striata*) of the Atlantic coast of the U.S.
2 : any of numerous croakers or drums including noted sport and food fishes

sea·bed \-ˌbed\ *noun* (1838)
: the floor of a sea or ocean

Sea·bee \'sē-(ˌ)bē\ *noun* [alteration of *cee* + *bee;* from the initials of *construction battalion*] (1942)
: a member of one of the U.S. Navy construction battalions for building naval shore facilities in combat zones

sea·bird \'sē-ˌbərd\ *noun* (1589)
: a bird (as a gull or albatross) frequenting the open ocean

sea biscuit *noun* (circa 1690)
: HARDTACK 1

sea·board \'sē-ˌbōrd, -ˌbȯrd\ *noun* (1788)
: SEACOAST; *also* **:** the country bordering a seacoast
— seaboard *adjective*

sea·boot \-ˌbüt\ *noun* (1851)
: a very high waterproof boot used especially by sailors and fishermen

sea·borg·i·um \sē-'bȯr-gē-əm\ *noun* [New Latin, from Glenn T. *Seaborg*] (1994)
: UNNILHEXIUM

sea·borne \-ˌbōrn, -ˌbȯrn\ *adjective* (1823)
1 : borne over or on the sea ⟨a *seaborne* invasion⟩
2 : carried on by oversea shipping ⟨*seaborne* trade⟩

sea bream *noun* (circa 1530)
: any of numerous marine bony fishes (as of the family Sparidae)

sea breeze *noun* (1697)
: a cooling breeze blowing generally in the daytime inland from the sea

sea captain *noun* (1612)
: the master especially of a merchant vessel

sea change *noun* (1610)
1 *archaic* **:** a change brought about by the sea
2 : a marked change **:** TRANSFORMATION

sea chest *noun* (1669)
: a sailor's storage chest for personal property

sea·coast \'sē-ˌkōst\ *noun* (14th century)
: the shore or border of the land adjacent to the sea

sea cow *noun* (1613)
: SIRENIAN

sea·craft \'sē-ˌkraft\ *noun* (1727)
1 : skill in navigation
2 : seagoing ships

sea crayfish *noun* (1601)
: SPINY LOBSTER

sea cucumber *noun* (1601)
: any of a class (Holothurioidea) of echinoderms having a tough muscular elongate body

with tentacles surrounding the mouth — called also *holothurian*

sea devil *noun* (1634)
: DEVILFISH 1

sea dog *noun* (1823)
: a veteran sailor

sea duck *noun* (1753)
: a diving duck (as a scoter, merganser, or eider) that frequents the sea

sea duty *noun* (1946)
: duty in the U.S. Navy performed with a deployable unit (as a ship or aircraft squadron)

sea eagle *noun* (1668)
: any of various fish-eating eagles (especially genus *Haliaeetus*)

Sea Explorer *noun* (1948)
: an Explorer in a scouting program that teaches seamanship

sea fan *noun* (1633)
: a gorgonian with a fan-shaped skeleton; *especially* **:** one (*Gorgonia flabellum*) of Florida and the West Indies

sea·far·er \'sē-ˌfar-ər, -ˌfer-\ *noun* [*sea* + ¹*fare* + ²*-er*] (1513)
: MARINER

sea·far·ing \-ˌfar-iŋ, -ˌfer-\ *noun* (1592)
: the use of the sea for travel or transportation
— seafaring *adjective*

sea fire *noun* (1814)
: marine bioluminescence

sea·floor \'sē-ˌflōr, -ˌflȯr\ *noun* (1855)
: SEABED

sea·food \-ˌfüd\ *noun* (1836)
: edible marine fish and shellfish

sea·fowl \-ˌfau̇l\ *noun* (14th century)
: SEABIRD

sea·front \-ˌfrənt\ *noun* (1879)
: the waterfront of a seaside place

sea·girt \'sē-ˌgərt\ *adjective* (1616)
: surrounded by the sea

sea·go·ing \-ˌgō-iŋ, -ˌgȯ(-)iŋ\ *adjective* (1828)
: OCEANGOING

sea grape *noun* (1806)
: a tree (*Coccoloba uvifera*) of the buckwheat family that inhabits sandy shores from Florida to South America, has rounded leaves, and bears clusters of purple to whitish edible berries

sea grass *noun* (1578)
: any of various grasslike plants that inhabit coastal areas; *especially* **:** EELGRASS 1

sea green *noun* (1598)
1 : a moderate green or bluish green
2 : a moderate yellow green

sea·gull \'sē-ˌgəl\ *noun* (1542)
: a gull frequenting the sea; *broadly* **:** GULL

sea hare *noun* (1593)
: any of various large opisthobranch mollusks (especially genus *Aplysia*) that have an arched back and two anterior tentacles and have the shell much reduced or missing

sea holly *noun* (1548)
: a European coastal herb (*Eryngium maritimum*) of the carrot family with spiny leaves and pale blue flowers

sea horse *noun* (circa 1500)
1 : WALRUS
2 : a mythical creature half horse and half fish
3 : any of a genus (*Hippocampus* of the family Syngnathidae) of small bony fishes that have the head angled downward toward the body which is carried vertically and are equipped with a prehensile tail

sea island cotton
noun, often S&I capitalized [Sea Islands, chain of islands off the southeastern U.S. coast] (1805)
: a cotton (*Gossypium barbadense*) with especially long silky fiber — called also *sea island*

sea horse 3

sea kale *noun* (1699)
: a succulent Eurasian perennial herb (*Crambe maritima*) of the mustard family used as a potherb

sea king *noun* (1819)
: a Norse pirate chief

¹**seal** \'sē(ə)l\ *noun, plural* **seals** *also* **seal** [Middle English *sele,* from Old English *seolh;* akin to Old High German *selah* seal] (before 12th century)
1 : any of numerous carnivorous marine mammals (families Phocidae and Otariidae) that live chiefly in cold regions and have limbs modified into webbed flippers adapted primarily to swimming; *especially* : a fur seal or hair seal as opposed to a sea lion
2 a : the pelt of a fur seal **b** : leather made from the skin of a seal
3 : a dark brown

²**seal** *intransitive verb* (1828)
: to hunt seals

³**seal** *noun* [Middle English *seel,* from Old French, from Latin *sigillum* seal, from diminutive of *signum* sign, seal — more at SIGN] (13th century)
1 a : something that confirms, ratifies, or makes secure : GUARANTEE, ASSURANCE **b** (1) : a device with a cut or raised emblem, symbol, or word used especially to certify a signature or authenticate a document (2) : a medallion or ring face bearing such a device incised so that it can be impressed on wax or moist clay; *also* : a piece of wax or a wafer bearing such an impression **c** : an impression, device, or mark given the effect of a common-law seal by statute law or by American local custom recognized by judicial decision **d** : a usually ornamental adhesive stamp that may be used to close a letter or package; *especially* : one given in a fund-raising campaign
2 a : something that secures (as a wax seal on a document) **b** : a closure that must be broken to be opened and that thus reveals tampering **c** (1) : a tight and perfect closure (as against the passage of gas or water) (2) : a device to prevent the passage or return of gas or air into a pipe or container
3 : a seal that is a symbol or mark of office
— **under seal** : with an authenticating seal affixed

⁴**seal** *transitive verb* (14th century)
1 a : to confirm or make secure by or as if by a seal **b** : to solemnize for eternity (as a marriage) by a Mormon rite
2 a : to set or affix an authenticating seal to; *also* : AUTHENTICATE, RATIFY **b** : to mark with a stamp or seal usually as an evidence of standard exactness, legal size, weight, or capacity, or merchantable quality
3 a : to fasten with or as if with a seal to prevent tampering **b** : to close or make secure against access, leakage, or passage by a fastening or coating **c** : to fix in position or close breaks in with a filling (as of plaster)
4 : to determine irrevocably or indisputably ⟨that answer *sealed* our fate⟩

sea lamprey *noun* (1879)
: a large anadromous lamprey (*Petromyzon marinus*) that has a mottled upper surface, is an ectoparasite of fish, and is sometimes used as food

sea–lane \'sē-,lān\ *noun* (1927)
: an established sea route

seal·ant \'sē-lənt\ *noun* (1944)
: a sealing agent ⟨radiator *sealant*⟩

sea lavender *noun* (1597)
: any of a genus (*Limonium*) of chiefly perennial herbs of the plumbago family with small flowers and basal leaves

sea lawyer *noun* (1848)
: an argumentative captious sailor

sealed–beam \'sē(ə)l(d)-'bēm\ *adjective* (1939)
: being an electric lamp with a prefocused reflector and lens sealed in the lamp vacuum

sea legs *noun plural* (1712)

: bodily adjustment to the motion of a ship indicated especially by ability to walk steadily and by freedom from seasickness

¹**seal·er** \'sē-lər\ *noun* (15th century)
1 : an official who attests or certifies conformity to a standard of correctness
2 : a coat (as of size) applied to prevent subsequent coats of paint or varnish from sinking in

²**sealer** *noun* (1842)
: a person or a ship engaged in hunting seals

sea lettuce *noun* (1668)
: any of a genus (*Ulva*) of seaweeds with green fronds sometimes eaten as salad

sea level *noun* (1806)
: the level of the surface of the sea especially at its mean position midway between mean high and low water

sea lily *noun* (1876)
: CRINOID; *especially* : a stalked crinoid

sealing wax *noun* (14th century)
: a resinous composition that is plastic when warm and is used for sealing (as letters, dry cells, or cans)

sea lion *noun* (1697)
: any of several Pacific eared seals (as genera *Eumetopias* and *Zalophus*) that are usually larger than the related fur seals and lack a thick underfur

seal off *transitive verb* (1931)
: to close tightly

seal point *noun* [¹*seal* (the color)] (1939)
: a coat color of cats characterized by a cream or fawn body with dark brown points; *also* : a Siamese cat with such coloring

seal ring *noun* (1608)
: a finger ring engraved with a seal : SIGNET RING

seal·skin \'sē(ə)l-,skin\ *noun* (14th century)
1 : the fur or pelt of a fur seal
2 : a garment (as a jacket, coat, or cape) of sealskin
— **sealskin** *adjective*

Sea·ly·ham terrier \'sē-lē-,ham-, *especially British* -lē-əm-\ *noun* [*Sealyham,* Pembrokeshire, Wales] (1907)
: any of a breed of short-legged long-headed strong-jawed heavy-boned chiefly white terriers developed in Wales

¹**seam** \'sēm\ *noun* [Middle English *seem,* from Old English *sēam;* akin to Old English *sīwian* to sew — more at SEW] (before 12th century)
1 a : the joining of two pieces (as of cloth or leather) by sewing usually near the edge **b** : the stitching used in such a joining
2 : the space between adjacent planks or strakes of a ship
3 a : a line, groove, or ridge formed by the abutment of edges **b** : a thin layer or stratum (as of rock) between distinctive layers; *also* : a bed of valuable mineral and especially coal irrespective of thickness **c** : a line left by a cut or wound; *also* : WRINKLE
4 : a weak or vulnerable area or gap ⟨found a *seam* in the zone defense⟩
— **seam·like** \-,līk\ *adjective*
— **at the seams** : ENTIRELY, COMPLETELY ⟨falling apart *at the seams*⟩

²**seam** (1582)
transitive verb
1 a : to join by sewing **b** : to join as if by sewing (as by welding, riveting, or heat-sealing)
2 : to mark with lines suggesting seams
intransitive verb
: to become fissured or ridgy
— **seam·er** *noun*

sea–maid \'sē-,mād\ *or* **sea–maid·en** \-,mād-ᵊn\ *noun* (1590)
: MERMAID; *also* : a goddess or nymph of the sea

sea·man \'sē-mən\ *noun* (before 12th century)
1 : SAILOR, MARINER
2 a : any of the three ranks below petty officer in the navy or coast guard **b** : an enlisted man in the navy or coast guard ranking above a seaman apprentice and below a petty officer

seaman apprentice *noun* (1947)
: an enlisted man in the navy or coast guard ranking above a seaman recruit and below a seaman

sea·man·like \'sē-mən-,līk\ *adjective* (1796)
: characteristic of or befitting a competent seaman

sea·man·ly \-lē\ *adjective* (1798)
: SEAMANLIKE

seaman recruit *noun* (1947)
: an enlisted man of the lowest rank in the navy or coast guard

sea·man·ship \'sē-mən-,ship\ *noun* (1766)
: the art or skill of handling, working, and navigating a ship

sea·mark \-,märk\ *noun* (15th century)
1 : a line on a coast marking the tidal limit
2 : an elevated object serving as a beacon to mariners

sea mew *noun* (15th century)
: SEAGULL; *especially* : a common gull (*Larus canus*) chiefly of Europe and northwestern North America

sea mile *noun* (1796)
: NAUTICAL MILE

seam·less \'sēm-ləs\ *adjective* (15th century)
1 : having no seams
2 : having no awkward transitions or indications of disparity : perfectly smooth ⟨a *seamless* fusion of beauty and intelligence —Jack Kroll *et al.*⟩
— **seam·less·ly** \-lē\ *adverb*
— **seam·less·ness** \-nəs\ *noun*

sea·mount \'sē-,mau̇nt\ *noun* (1941)
: a submarine mountain rising above the deep-sea floor

sea mouse *noun* (circa 1520)
: any of various large broad marine polychaete worms (especially genus *Aphrodite*) covered with hairlike setae

seam·ster \'sēm(p)-stər *also* 'sem(p)-\ *noun* [Middle English *semester, semster,* from Old English *sēamestre* seamstress, tailor, from *sēam* seam] (before 12th century)
: a person employed at sewing; *especially* : TAILOR

seam·stress \-strəs\ *noun* (1644)
: a woman whose occupation is sewing

seamy \'sē-mē\ *adjective* **seam·i·er; -est** (1604)
1 *archaic* : having the rough side of the seam showing
2 a : UNPLEASANT **b** : DEGRADED, SORDID
— **seam·i·ness** *noun*

sé·ance \'sā-,än(t)s, -,äⁿs, sā-'\ *noun* [French, from *seoir* to sit, from Latin *sedēre* — more at SIT] (1803)
1 : SESSION, SITTING
2 : a spiritualist meeting to receive spirit communications

sea nettle *noun* (1601)
: a stinging jellyfish; *especially* : one (*Chrysaora quinquecirrha*) occurring especially in Atlantic estuaries from Cape Cod to the West Indies

sea oats *noun plural but singular or plural in construction* (1894)
: a tall grass (*Uniola paniculata*) that has panicles resembling those of the oat, grows chiefly on the coast of the southern U.S., and is useful as a sand binder

sea onion *noun* (14th century)
: SQUILL 1a

sea otter *noun* (1664)
: a rare marine otter (*Enhydra lutris*) of the northern Pacific coasts that may attain a length of six feet (two meters), is chiefly brown but with lighter coloration on the back of the head and neck, and feeds largely on shellfish

sea pen *noun* (1763)

: any of numerous anthozoans (order Pennatulacea) growing in colonies with a feathery form

sea·piece \'sē-ˌpēs\ *noun* (1656)
: SEASCAPE 2

sea pink (1731)
1 : THRIFT 4
2 : any of a genus (*Sabatia*) of smooth slender North American herbs of the gentian family typically having pink or white cymose flowers

sea·plane \-ˌplān\ *noun* (1913)
: an airplane designed to take off from and land on the water

sea·port \'sē-ˌpōrt, -ˌpórt\ *noun* (1596)
: a port, harbor, or town accessible to seagoing ships

sea power *noun* (1849)
1 : a nation having formidable naval strength
2 : naval strength

sea puss \-ˌpús\ *noun* [alteration of dialect *seapoose* tidal stream, from Unquachog (Algonquian language of Long Island) *seépus* river] (circa 1891)
: a swirling or along shore undertow

sea·quake \'sē-ˌkwāk\ *noun* [*sea* + *earthquake*] (1680)
: a submarine earthquake

¹sear *variant of* SERE

²sear \'sir\ *verb* [Middle English *seren*, from Old English *sēarian* to become sere, from *sēar* sere] (before 12th century)
intransitive verb
: to cause withering or drying
transitive verb
1 : to make withered and dry : PARCH
2 : to burn, scorch, or injure with or as if with sudden application of intense heat
— **sear·ing·ly** \-iŋ-lē\ *adverb*

³sear *noun* (1874)
: a mark or scar left by searing

⁴sear *noun* [probably from Middle French *serre* grasp, from *serrer* to press, grasp, from Late Latin *serare* to bolt, latch, from Latin *sera* bar for fastening a door] (1596)
: the catch that holds the hammer of a gun's lock at cock or half cock

¹search \'sərch\ *verb* [Middle English *cerchen*, from Middle French *cerchier* to go about, survey, search, from Late Latin *circare* to go about, from Latin *circum* round about — more at CIRCUM-] (14th century)
transitive verb
1 : to look into or over carefully or thoroughly in an effort to find or discover something: as **a** : to examine in seeking something ⟨*searched* the north field⟩ **b** : to look through or explore by inspecting possible places of concealment or investigating suspicious circumstances **c** : to read thoroughly : CHECK; *especially* : to examine a public record or register for information about ⟨*search* land titles⟩ **d** : to examine for articles concealed on the person **e** : to look at as if to discover or penetrate intention or nature
2 : to uncover, find, or come to know by inquiry or scrutiny — usually used with *out*
intransitive verb
1 : to look or inquire carefully ⟨*searched* for the papers⟩
2 : to make painstaking investigation or examination
— **search·able** \'sər-chə-bəl\ *adjective*
— **search·er** *noun*
— **search·ing·ly** \-chiŋ-lē\ *adverb*

²search *noun* (15th century)
1 a : an act of searching ⟨a *search* for food⟩ ⟨go in *search* of help⟩ **b** : an act of boarding and inspecting a ship on the high seas in exercise of right of search
2 *obsolete* : a party that searches
3 : power or range of penetrating; *also* : a penetrating effect

search·less \'sərch-ləs\ *adjective* (1605)
: INSCRUTABLE, IMPENETRABLE

search·light \-ˌlīt\ *noun* (1883)

: an apparatus for projecting a powerful beam of light; *also* : a beam of light projected by it

search warrant *noun* (1818)
: a warrant authorizing a search (as of a house) for stolen goods or unlawful possessions

sea robin *noun* (1814)
: any of a family (Triglidae) of marine bony fishes typically having a spiny armored head and the bottom three rays of the pectoral fin on each side free of membrane and modified for use as feelers or in crawling — called also *gurnard*

sea room *noun* (circa 1554)
: room for maneuver at sea

sea rover *noun* (circa 1580)
: one that roves the sea; *specifically* : PIRATE

sea–run \'sē-ˌrən\ *adjective* (1885)
: ANADROMOUS ⟨a *sea-run* salmon⟩

sea·scape \'sē-ˌskāp\ *noun* (1799)
1 : a view of the sea
2 : a picture representing a scene at sea
word history see LANDSCAPE

sea scorpion *noun* (1896)
1 : SCULPIN 1
2 : EURYPTERID

Sea Scout *noun* (1911)
: SEA EXPLORER

sea serpent *noun* (1774)
: a large marine animal resembling a serpent often reported to have been seen but never proved to exist

sea·shell \'sē-ˌshel\ *noun* (before 12th century)
: the shell of a marine animal and especially a mollusk

sea·shore \-ˌshōr, -ˌshór\ *noun* (1526)
1 a : land adjacent to the sea : SEACOAST **b** : NATIONAL SEASHORE
2 : all the ground between the ordinary high-water and low-water marks : FORESHORE

sea·sick \-ˌsik\ *adjective* (circa 1566)
: affected with or suggestive of seasickness

sea·sick·ness \-nəs\ *noun* (1625)
: motion sickness experienced on the water

sea·side \'sē-ˌsīd\ *noun* (13th century)
: the district or land bordering the sea : country adjacent to the sea : SEASHORE
— **seaside** *adjective*

sea slug *noun* (1779)
1 : HOLOTHURIAN
2 : a naked marine gastropod; *specifically* : NUDIBRANCH

sea snake *noun* (1755)
1 : SEA SERPENT
2 : any of numerous venomous aquatic chiefly viviparous elapid snakes of warm seas

¹sea·son \'sē-zᵊn\ *noun* [Middle English, from Middle French *saison*, from Old French, from Latin *sation-, satio* action of sowing, from *serere* to sow — more at SOW] (14th century)
1 a : a time characterized by a particular circumstance or feature ⟨in a *season* of religious awakening —F. A. Christie⟩ **b** : a suitable or natural time or occasion ⟨when my *season* comes to sit on David's throne —John Milton⟩ **c** : an indefinite period of time : WHILE ⟨sent home again to her father for a *season* —Francis Hackett⟩
2 a : a period of the year characterized by or associated with a particular activity or phenomenon ⟨hay fever *season*⟩: as (1) : a period associated with some phase or activity of agriculture (as growth or harvesting) (2) : a period in which an animal engages in some activity (as migrating or mating); *also* : ESTRUS, HEAT (3) : the period normally characterized by a particular kind of weather ⟨a long rainy *season*⟩ (4) : a period marked by special activity especially in some field ⟨the theatrical *season*⟩ ⟨tourist *season*⟩ (5) : a period in which a place is most frequented **b** : one of the four quarters into which the year is commonly divided **c** : the time of a major holiday
3 : YEAR ⟨a boy of seven *seasons*⟩
4 [Middle English *sesoun*, from *sesounen*] : SEASONING

5 : the schedule of official games played or to be played by a sports team during a playing season ⟨try to get through the *season* undefeated⟩
6 : OFF-SEASON ⟨closed for the *season*⟩
— **in season 1** : at the right time **2** : at the stage of greatest fitness (as for eating) ⟨peaches are *in season*⟩ **3** : legally available to be hunted or caught
— **out of season** : not in season

²season *verb* **sea·soned; sea·son·ing** \'sēz-niŋ, 'sē-zᵊn-iŋ\ [Middle English *sesounen*, from Middle French *assaisoner* to ripen, season, from Old French, from *a-* (from Latin *ad-*) + *saison* season] (14th century)
transitive verb
1 a : to give (food) more flavor or zest by adding seasoning or savory ingredients **b** : to give a distinctive quality to as if by seasoning; *especially* : to make more agreeable ⟨advice *seasoned* with wit⟩ **c** *archaic* : to qualify by admixture : TEMPER
2 a : to treat (as wood or a skillet) so as to prepare for use **b** : to make fit by experience ⟨a *seasoned* veteran⟩
intransitive verb
: to become seasoned

sea·son·a·ble \'sēz-nə-bəl, 'sē-zᵊn-ə-bəl\ *adjective* (14th century)
1 : suitable to the season or circumstances : TIMELY ⟨a *seasonable* frost⟩
2 : occurring in good or proper time : OPPORTUNE ⟨a *seasonable* time for discussion⟩
— **sea·son·a·ble·ness** *noun*
— **sea·son·a·bly** \-blē\ *adverb*

sea·son·al \'sēz-nəl, 'sē-zᵊn-əl\ *adjective* (1838)
1 : of, relating to, or varying in occurrence according to the season ⟨*seasonal* storms⟩ ⟨*seasonal* fruits⟩
2 : affected or caused by seasonal need or availability ⟨*seasonal* unemployment⟩ ⟨*seasonal* industries⟩
— **sea·son·al·i·ty** \ˌsē-zᵊn-'a-lə-tē\ *noun*
— **sea·son·al·ly** \'sēz-nə-lē, 'sē-zᵊn-ə-lē\ *adverb*

seasonal affective disorder *noun* (1985)
: depression that tends to recur as the days grow shorter during the fall and winter

sea·son·er \'sēz-nər, 'sē-zᵊn-ər\ *noun* (1598)
: one that seasons: as **a** : a user of seasonings ⟨a heavy *seasoner*⟩ **b** : SEASONING

sea·son·ing \'sēz-niŋ, 'sē-zᵊn-iŋ\ *noun* (1580)
: something that serves to season; *especially* : an ingredient (as a condiment, spice, or herb) added to food primarily for the savor that it imparts

sea·son·less \'sē-zᵊn-ləs\ *adjective* (1816)
1 : exhibiting no seasonal changes
2 : not restricted to a particular season; *especially* : suitable for wearing in any season ⟨*seasonless* fabrics⟩

season ticket *noun* (1820)
: a ticket (as to all of a club's home games or for specified daily transportation) valid during a specified time

sea spider *noun* (1666)
: any of various small long-legged marine arthropods (class Pycnogonida) that superficially resemble spiders

sea squirt *noun* (1850)
: ASCIDIAN

sea star *noun* (1569)
: STARFISH

sea stores *noun plural* (1659)
: supplies (as of foodstuffs) laid in before starting on a sea voyage

sea·strand \'sē-ˌstrand\ *noun* (before 12th century)
: SEASHORE

¹seat \'sēt\ *noun* [Middle English *sete*, from Old Norse *sæti*; akin to Old English *gesete* seat, *sittan* to sit] (13th century)

1 a : a special chair of one in eminence; *also* **:** the status represented by it **b :** a chair, stool, or bench intended to be sat in or on **c :** the particular part of something on which one rests in sitting ⟨the *seat* of a chair⟩ ⟨trouser *seat*⟩ **d :** BUTTOCKS
2 a : a seating accommodation ⟨a *seat* for the game⟩ ⟨a 200-*seat* restaurant⟩ **b :** a right of sitting ⟨lost his *seat* in Congress⟩ **c :** membership on an exchange
3 a : a place where something specified is prevalent **:** CENTER ⟨a *seat* of learning⟩ **b :** a place from which authority is exercised ⟨the county *seat*⟩ **c :** a bodily part in which some function or condition is centered ⟨the brain as the *seat* of the mind⟩
4 : posture in or way of sitting on horseback
5 a : a part at or forming the base of something **b :** a part (as a socket) or surface on or in which another part or surface rests
— **by the seat of one's pants :** using experience and intuition rather than mechanical aids or formal theory

²**seat** (1593)
transitive verb
1 a : to install in a seat of dignity or office **b** (1) **:** to cause to sit or assist in finding a seat (2) **:** to provide seats for ⟨a theater *seating* 1000 persons⟩ **c :** to put in a sitting position
2 : to repair the seat of or provide a new seat for
3 : to fit to or with a seat ⟨*seat* a valve⟩
intransitive verb
1 *archaic* **:** to take one's seat or place
2 : to fit correctly on a seat

seat belt *noun* (1932)
: an arrangement of straps designed to hold a person steady in a seat (as in an airplane or automobile)

seat·er \'sē-tər\ *noun* (1693)
1 : one that seats
2 : one that has a specified number of seats — used in combination ⟨a two-*seater* jet⟩

seat·ing \'sē-tiŋ\ *noun* (circa 1859)
1 : the act of providing with seats
2 a : material for covering or upholstering seats **b :** a seat on or in which something rests ⟨a valve *seating*⟩

seat·mate \'sēt-ˌmāt\ *noun* (1859)
: one with whom one shares a seat (as in a vehicle with double or paired seats)

seat–of–the–pants *adjective* (1942)
: employing or based on personal experience, judgment, and effort rather than technological aids or formal theory ⟨*seat-of-the-pants* navigation⟩ ⟨a *seat-of-the-pants* decision⟩

sea·train \'sē-ˌtrān\ *noun* (1932)
: a seagoing ship equipped for carrying a train of railroad cars

sea trout *noun* (1745)
1 : any of various trouts or chars that as adults inhabit the sea but ascend rivers to spawn
2 : any of various marine fishes resembling trouts: as **a :** WEAKFISH 1 **b :** SPOTTED SEA TROUT

sea turtle *noun* (1612)
: any of two families (Cheloniidae and Dermochelyidae) of widely distributed marine turtles with the feet modified into paddles that include the green turtle, leatherback, hawksbill, loggerhead, and ridley

sea urchin *noun* (1591)
: any of numerous echinoderms (class Echinoidea) that are usually enclosed in thin brittle globular tests covered with movable spines

sea·wall \'sē-ˌwȯl\ *noun* (15th century)
: a wall or embankment to protect the shore from erosion or to act as a breakwater

¹**sea·ward** \'sē-wərd\ *noun* (14th century)
: the direction or side away from land and toward the open sea

²**seaward** *also* **sea·wards** \-wərdz\ *adverb* (1517)
: toward the sea

³**seaward** *adjective* (circa 1621)
1 : directed or situated toward the sea

2 : coming from the sea ⟨a *seaward* wind⟩

sea wasp *noun* (1910)
: any of various scyphozoan jellyfishes (order or suborder Cubomedusae) that sting virulently and sometimes fatally

sea·wa·ter \'sē-ˌwȯ-tər, -ˌwä-\ *noun* (before 12th century)
: water in or from the sea

sea·way \-ˌwā\ *noun* (before 12th century)
1 : the sea as a route for travel; *also* **:** an ocean traffic lane
2 : a moderate or rough sea
3 : a deep inland waterway that admits ocean shipping

sea·weed \-ˌwēd\ *noun* (1577)
1 : a mass or growth of marine plants
2 : a plant growing in the sea; *especially* **:** a marine alga (as a kelp)

sea whip *noun* (1775)
: any of various gorgonian corals with elongated flexible unbranched or little-branched skeletons

sea·wor·thy \'sē-ˌwər-thē\ *adjective* (1807)
: fit or safe for a sea voyage ⟨a *seaworthy* ship⟩
— **sea·wor·thi·ness** \-thē-nəs\ *noun*

sea wrack *noun* (1551)
: SEAWEED; *especially* **:** seaweed cast ashore in masses

se·ba·ceous \si-'bā-shəs\ *adjective* [Latin *sebaceus* made of tallow, from *sebum* tallow] (1728)
1 : secreting sebum ⟨*sebaceous* glands⟩
2 : of, relating to, or being fatty material **:** FATTY ⟨a *sebaceous* exudate⟩

se·ba·cic acid \si-'ba-sik-, -ˌsē-, -'bā-\ *noun* [International Scientific Vocabulary, from Latin *sebaceus*] (1790)
: a crystalline dicarboxylic acid $C_{10}H_{18}O_4$ used especially in the manufacture of synthetic resins

seb·or·rhea \ˌse-bə-'rē-ə\ *noun* [New Latin, from Latin *sebum* + New Latin *-rrhea*] (circa 1860)
: abnormally increased secretion and discharge of sebum
— **seb·or·rhe·ic** \-'rē-ik\ *adjective*

se·bum \'sē-bəm\ *noun* [Latin, tallow, grease] (circa 1860)
: fatty lubricant matter secreted by sebaceous glands of the skin

sec \'sek\ *adjective* [French, literally, dry — more at SACK] (1863)
of champagne **:** moderately dry

se·cant \'sē-ˌkant, -kənt\ *noun* [New Latin *secant-, secans*, from Latin, present participle of *secare* to cut — more at SAW] (1593)
1 : a straight line cutting a curve at two or more points — see CIRCLE illustration
2 : a straight line drawn from the center of a circle through one end of a circular arc to a tangent drawn from the other end of the arc
3 a : a trigonometric function that for an acute angle is the ratio of the hypotenuse of a right triangle of which the angle is considered part and the leg adjacent to the angle **b :** a trigonometric function sec θ that is the reciprocal of the cosine for all real numbers θ for which the cosine is not zero and that is exactly equal to the secant of an angle of measure θ in radians

se·ca·teur \ˌse-kə-'tər, 'se-kə-ˌ\ *noun* [French *sécateur*, from Latin *secare* to cut] (1881)
chiefly British **:** pruning shears — usually used in plural

¹**sec·co** \'se-(ˌ)kō\ *noun* [Italian, from *secco* dry, from Latin *siccus* — more at SACK] (1852)
: the art of painting on dry plaster

²**secco** *adjective or adverb* [Italian, literally, dry] (circa 1854)
1 : short and very staccato — used as a direction in music
2 *of a recitative* **:** accompanied only by the instruments playing the continuo

se·cede \si-'sēd\ *intransitive verb* **se·ced·ed; se·ced·ing** [Latin *secedere*, from *sed-*,

se- apart (from *sed, se* without) + *cedere* to go — more at SUICIDE] (circa 1755)
: to withdraw from an organization (as a religious communion or political party or federation)
— **se·ced·er** *noun*

se·cern \si-'sərn\ *transitive verb* [Latin *secernere* to separate — more at SECRET] (circa 1656)
: to discriminate in thought **:** DISTINGUISH

se·ces·sion \si-'se-shən\ *noun* [Latin *secession-, secessio*, from *secedere*] (1604)
1 : withdrawal into privacy or solitude **:** RETIREMENT
2 : formal withdrawal from an organization

se·ces·sion·ist \-'se-sh(ə-)nist\ *noun* (circa 1860)
: one who joins in a secession or maintains that secession is a right
— **se·ces·sion·ism** \-shə-ˌni-zəm\ *noun*
— **secessionist** *adjective*

se·clude \si-'klüd\ *transitive verb* **se·clud·ed; se·clud·ing** [Middle English, to keep away, from Latin *secludere* to separate, seclude, from *se-* apart + *claudere* to close — more at SECEDE, CLOSE] (circa 1533)
1 *obsolete* **:** to exclude from a privilege, rank, or dignity **:** DEBAR
2 : to remove or separate from intercourse or outside influence **:** ISOLATE
3 : SHUT OFF, SCREEN

secluded *adjective* (1604)
1 : screened or hidden from view **:** SEQUESTERED ⟨a *secluded* valley⟩
2 : living in seclusion **:** SOLITARY ⟨*secluded* monks⟩
— **se·clud·ed·ly** *adverb*
— **se·clud·ed·ness** *noun*

se·clu·sion \si-'klü-zhən\ *noun* [Medieval Latin *seclusion-, seclusio*, from Latin *secludere*] (circa 1616)
1 : the act of secluding **:** the condition of being secluded
2 : a secluded or isolated place
synonym see SOLITUDE
— **se·clu·sive** \-'klü-siv, -ziv\ *adjective*
— **se·clu·sive·ly** *adverb*
— **se·clu·sive·ness** *noun*

seco·bar·bi·tal \ˌse-kō-'bär-bə-ˌtȯl\ *noun* [from *Seconal*, a trademark + *barbital*] (1951)
: a barbiturate $C_{12}H_{18}N_2O_3$ that is used chiefly in the form of its bitter hygroscopic sodium salt as a hypnotic and sedative

Sec·o·nal \'se-kə-ˌnȯl, -ˌnal, -n°l\ *trademark*
— used for a preparation of secobarbital

¹**sec·ond** \'se-kənd *also* -kənt, *especially before a consonant* -kən, -k°ŋ\ *adjective* [Middle English, from Old French, from Latin *secundus* second, following, favorable, from *sequi* to follow — more at SUE] (13th century)
1 a : next to the first in place or time ⟨was *second* in line⟩ **b** (1) **:** next to the first in value, excellence, or degree ⟨his *second* choice of schools⟩ (2) **:** INFERIOR, SUBORDINATE ⟨was *second* to none⟩ **c :** ranking next below the top of a grade or degree in authority or precedence ⟨*second* mate⟩ **d :** ALTERNATE, OTHER ⟨elects a mayor every *second* year⟩ **e :** resembling or suggesting a prototype **:** ANOTHER ⟨a *second* Thoreau⟩ **f :** ingrained by discipline, training, or effort **:** ACQUIRED ⟨*second* nature⟩ **g :** being the forward gear or speed next higher than first in a motor vehicle
2 : relating to or having a part typically subordinate to and lower in pitch than the first part in concerted or ensemble music
— **second** *or* **sec·ond·ly** *adverb*

²**second** *noun* (14th century)

1 a — see NUMBER table **b :** one that is next after the first in rank, position, authority, or precedence ⟨the *second* in line⟩
2 : one that assists or supports another; *especially* **:** the assistant of a duelist or boxer
3 a : the musical interval embracing two diatonic degrees **b :** a tone at this interval; *specifically* **:** SUPERTONIC **c :** the harmonic combination of two tones a second apart
4 a *plural* **:** merchandise that is usually slightly flawed and does not meet the manufacturer's standard for firsts or irregulars **b :** an article of such merchandise
5 : the act or declaration by which a parliamentary motion is seconded
6 : a place next below the first in a competition, examination, or contest
7 : SECOND BASE
8 : the second forward gear or speed of a motor vehicle
9 *plural* **:** a second helping of food
³**second** *noun* [Middle English *secunde,* from Medieval Latin *secunda,* from Latin, feminine of *secundus* second; from its being the second sexagesimal division of a unit, as a minute is the first] (14th century)
1 a : the 60th part of a minute of angular measure **b :** the 60th part of a minute of time **:** 1/86,400 part of the mean solar day; *specifically* **:** the base unit of time in the International System of Units that is equal to the duration of 9,192,631,770 periods of the radiation corresponding to the transition between the two hyperfine levels of the ground state of the cesium-133 atom
2 : an instant of time **:** MOMENT
⁴**second** *transitive verb* [Latin *secundare,* from *secundus* second, favorable] (circa 1586)
1 a : to give support or encouragement to **:** ASSIST **b :** to support (a fighting person or group) in combat **:** bring up reinforcements for
2 a : to support or assist in contention or debate **b :** to endorse (a motion or a nomination) so that debate or voting may begin
3 \si-'känd\ *chiefly British* **:** to release (as a military officer) from a regularly assigned position for temporary duty with another unit or organization
— **sec·ond·er** *noun*
¹**sec·ond·ary** \'se-kən-ˌder-ē\ *adjective* (14th century)
1 a : of second rank, importance, or value **b :** of, relating to, or constituting the second strongest of the three or four degrees of stress recognized by most linguists ⟨the fourth syllable of *basketball team* carries *secondary* stress⟩ **c** *of a tense* **:** expressive of past time
2 a : immediately derived from something original, primary, or basic **b :** of, relating to, or being the induced current or its circuit in an induction coil or transformer ⟨*secondary* voltage⟩ **c :** characterized by or resulting from the substitution of two atoms or groups in a molecule ⟨a *secondary* salt⟩; *especially* **:** being, characterized by, or attached to a carbon atom having bonds to two other carbon atoms **d** (1) **:** not first in order of occurrence or development (2) **:** produced by activity of formative tissue and especially cambium other than that at a growing point ⟨*secondary* growth⟩ ⟨*secondary* phloem⟩
3 a : of, relating to, or being the second order or stage in a series **b :** of, relating to, or being the second segment of the wing of a bird or the quills of this segment **c :** of or relating to a secondary school ⟨*secondary* education⟩
— **sec·ond·ar·i·ly** \ˌse-kən-'der-ə-lē\ *adverb*
— **sec·ond·ar·i·ness** \'se-kən-ˌder-ē-nəs\ *noun*
²**secondary** *noun, plural* **-ar·ies** (15th century)
1 : one occupying a subordinate or auxiliary position rather than that of a principal
2 : a defensive football backfield

3 : the coil through which the secondary current passes in an induction coil or transformer — called also *secondary coil*
4 : any of the quill feathers of the forearm of a bird — see WING illustration
secondary cell *noun* (circa 1909)
: STORAGE BATTERY
secondary color *noun* (1831)
: a color formed by mixing primary colors in equal or equivalent quantities
secondary emission *noun* (1931)
: the emission of electrons from a surface that is bombarded by particles (as electrons or ions) from a primary source
secondary radiation *noun* (1900)
: radiation emitted by molecules or atoms after bombardment by a primary radiation
secondary road *noun* (1903)
1 : a road not of primary importance
2 : a feeder road
secondary root *noun* (1861)
: one of the branches of a primary root
secondary school *noun* (1835)
: a school intermediate between elementary school and college and usually offering general, technical, vocational, or college-preparatory courses
secondary sex characteristic *noun* (1927)
: a physical characteristic (as the breasts of a female mammal or the breeding plumage of a male bird) that appears in members of one sex at puberty or in seasonal breeders at the breeding season and is not directly concerned with reproduction — called also *secondary sexual characteristic*
secondary syphilis *noun* (1885)
: the second stage of syphilis that appears from 2 to 6 months after primary infection, that is marked by lesions especially in the skin but also in organs and tissues, and that lasts from 3 to 12 weeks
second banana *noun* (1953)
: a comedian who plays a supporting role to a top banana; *broadly* **:** a person in a subservient position
second base *noun* (1845)
1 : the base that must be touched second by a base runner in baseball
2 : the player position for defending the area on the first-base side of second base
— **second baseman** *noun*
sec·ond–best \ˌse-kən(d)-'best, -kᵊŋ-\ *adjective* (14th century)
: next to the best
¹**second best** *noun* (1708)
: one that is below or after the best
²**second best** *adverb* (1777)
: in second place
second blessing *noun* (1891)
: sanctification as a second gift of the Holy Spirit that follows an initial experience of conversion
second childhood *noun* (1641)
: DOTAGE
second–class *adjective* (circa 1838)
1 : of or relating to a second class
2 : MEDIOCRE; *also* **:** socially, politically, or economically deprived
second class *noun* (1810)
1 : the second and usually next to highest group in a classification
2 : CABIN CLASS
3 : a class of U.S. or Canadian mail comprising periodicals sent to regular subscribers
Second Coming *noun* (1644)
: the coming of Christ as judge on the last day
second–degree burn *noun* (1937)
: a burn marked by pain, blistering, and superficial destruction of dermis with edema and hyperemia of the tissues beneath the burn
Second Empire *adjective* (1873)
: of, relating to, or characteristic of a style (as of furniture) developed in France under Napoleon III and marked by heavy ornate modification of Empire styles

second estate *noun, often S&E capitalized* (circa 1935)
: the second of the traditional political classes; *specifically* **:** NOBILITY
second fiddle *noun* (1809)
: one that plays a supporting or subservient role
second growth *noun* (1829)
: forest trees that come up naturally after removal of the first growth by cutting or by fire
sec·ond–guess \ˌse-kᵊŋ-'ges, -kən(d)-\ *transitive verb* (1941)
1 : to criticize or question actions or decisions of (someone) often after the results of those actions or decisions are known ⟨meet almost every morning and, over coffee, *second-guess* the local coach —Bruce Newman⟩; *also* **:** to engage in such criticism of (an action or decision) ⟨*second-guess* the general's strategy⟩
2 : to seek to anticipate or predict ⟨lived royally by his ability to *second-guess* the stock market —*Time*⟩
— **sec·ond–guess·er** *noun*
¹**sec·ond·hand** \'se-kən(d)-'hand\ *adjective* (1654)
1 a : received from or through an intermediary **:** BORROWED **b :** DERIVATIVE ⟨*secondhand* ideas⟩
2 a : acquired after being used by another **:** not new ⟨*secondhand* books⟩ **b :** dealing in secondhand merchandise ⟨a *secondhand* bookstore⟩
²**secondhand** *adverb* (1849)
: at second hand **:** INDIRECTLY
¹**second hand** \ˌse-kən(d)-'hand\ *noun* (1588)
: an intermediate person or means **:** INTERMEDIARY — usually used in the phrase *at second hand*
²**second hand** \'sek-ən(d)-ˌ\ *noun* (1759)
: the hand marking seconds on a timepiece
secondhand smoke *noun* (1976)
: tobacco smoke that is exhaled by smokers and inhaled by persons nearby
second lieutenant *noun* (1702)
: a commissioned officer of the lowest rank in the army, air force, or marine corps
second mortgage *noun* (1912)
: a mortgage the lien of which is subordinate to that of a first mortgage
se·con·do \si-'kōn-(ˌ)dō, -'kän-\ *noun, plural* **-di** \-(ˌ)dē\ [Italian, from *secondo,* adjective, second, from Latin *secundus*] (1792)
: the second part in a concerted piece; *especially* **:** the lower part (as in a piano duet)
second person *noun* (1672)
1 a : a set of linguistic forms (as verb forms, pronouns, and inflectional affixes) referring to the person or thing addressed in the utterance in which they occur **b :** a linguistic form belonging to such a set
2 : reference of a linguistic form to the person or thing addressed in the utterance in which it occurs
sec·ond–rate \ˌse-kən(d)-'rāt\ *adjective* (1669)
: of second or inferior quality or value **:** MEDIOCRE
— **sec·ond–rate·ness** *noun*
— **sec·ond–rat·er** \-'rā-tər\ *noun*
Second Reader *noun* (1895)
: a member of a Christian Science church or society chosen for a term of office to assist the First Reader in conducting services by reading aloud selections from the Bible
second reading *noun* (1647)
1 : the stage in the British legislative process following the first reading and usually providing for debate on the principal features of a bill before its submission to a committee for consideration of details
2 : the stage in the U.S. legislative process that occurs when a bill has been reported back from committee and that provides an opportunity for full debate and amendment before a vote is taken on the question of a third reading
second sight *noun* (1616)

: the capacity to see remote or future objects or events : CLAIRVOYANCE, PRECOGNITION

second–story man *noun* (1886)
: a burglar who enters a house by an upstairs window

sec·ond–string \,se-kən(d)-'striŋ, ,se-k°ŋ-\ *adjective* [from the reserve bowstring carried by an archer in case the first breaks] (1922)
: being a substitute as distinguished from a regular (as on a ball team)

second thought *noun* (1633)
: reconsideration or a revised opinion of a previous often hurried decision ⟨began to have *second thoughts*⟩

second wind *noun* (1824)
: renewed energy or endurance

second world *noun, often S&W capitalized* [after *third world*] (1973)
: the Communist nations as a political and economic bloc

se·cre·cy \'sē-krə-sē\ *noun, plural* **-cies** [alteration of earlier *secretie*, from Middle English *secretee*, from *secre* secret, from Middle French *secré*, from Latin *secretus*] (1575)
1 : the condition of being hidden or concealed
2 : the habit or practice of keeping secrets or maintaining privacy or concealment

¹**se·cret** \'sē-krət\ *adjective* [Middle English, from Middle French, from Latin *secretus*, from past participle of *secernere* to separate, distinguish, from *se-* apart + *cernere* to sift — more at SECEDE, CERTAIN] (14th century)
1 a : kept from knowledge or view : HIDDEN **b** : marked by the habit of discretion : CLOSE-MOUTHED **c** : working with hidden aims or methods : UNDERCOVER ⟨a *secret* agent⟩ **d** : not acknowledged : UNAVOWED ⟨a *secret* bride⟩ **e** : conducted in secret ⟨a *secret* trial⟩
2 : remote from human frequentation or notice : SECLUDED
3 : revealed only to the initiated : ESOTERIC
4 : constructed so as to elude observation or detection ⟨a *secret* panel⟩
5 : containing information whose unauthorized disclosure could endanger national security — compare CONFIDENTIAL, TOP SECRET ☆
— **se·cret·ly** *adverb*

²**secret** *noun* (14th century)
1 a : something kept hidden or unexplained : MYSTERY **b** : something kept from the knowledge of others or shared only confidentially with a few **c** : a method, formula, or process used in an art or a manufacturing operation and divulged only to those of one's own company or craft **d** *plural* : the practices or knowledge making up the shared discipline or culture of an esoteric society
2 : a prayer traditionally said inaudibly by the celebrant just before the preface of the mass
3 : something taken to be a specific or key to a desired end ⟨the *secret* of longevity⟩
— **in secret** : in a private place or manner

se·cre·ta·gogue \si-'krē-tə-,gäg\ *noun* [*secretion* + *-agogue*] (1919)
: a substance stimulating secretion (as by the stomach or pancreas)

sec·re·tar·i·at \,se-krə-'ter-ē-ət, -ē-,at\ *noun* [French *secrétariat*, from Medieval Latin *secretariatus*, from *secretarius*] (1811)
1 : the office of secretary
2 : a secretarial corps; *specifically* : the clerical staff of an organization
3 : the administrative department of a governmental organization

sec·re·tary \'se-krə-,ter-ē, 'se-kə-,ter-, *in rapid speech also* 'sek-,ter-, *especially British* 'sek(r)ə-trē\ *noun, plural* **-tar·ies** [Middle English *secretarie*, from Medieval Latin *secretarius*, confidential employee, secretary, from Latin *secretum* secret, from neuter of *secretus*] (15th century)
1 : one employed to handle correspondence and manage routine and detail work for a superior
2 a : an officer of a business concern who may keep records of directors' and stockhold-

ers' meetings and of stock ownership and transfer and help supervise the company's legal interests **b** : an officer of an organization or society responsible for its records and correspondence
3 : an officer of state who superintends a government administrative department
4 a : WRITING DESK, ESCRITOIRE **b** : a writing desk with a top section for books

secretary 4b

— **sec·re·tar·i·al** \,se-krə-'ter-ē-əl\ *adjective*
— **sec·re·tary·ship** \'se-krə-,ter-ē-,ship\ *noun*

secretary bird *noun* [probably from the resemblance of its crest to a bunch of quill pens stuck behind the ear] (1824)
: a large long-legged African bird of prey (*Sagittarius serpentarius* of the family Sagittariidae) that feeds largely on reptiles

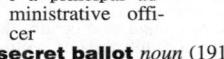

secretary bird

secretary–general *noun, plural* **secretaries–general** (1701)
: a principal administrative officer

secret ballot *noun* (1917)
: AUSTRALIAN BALLOT

¹**se·crete** \si-'krēt\ *transitive verb* **se·cret·ed; se·cret·ing** [back-formation from *secretion*] (1707)
: to form and give off (a secretion)

²**se·crete** \si-'krēt, 'sē-krət\ *transitive verb* **se·cret·ed; se·cret·ing** [alteration of obsolete *secret*, from ¹*secret*] (1741)
1 : to deposit or conceal in a hiding place
2 : to appropriate secretly : ABSTRACT
synonym see HIDE

se·cre·tin \si-'krē-t°n\ *noun* [*secretion* + ¹*-in*] (1902)
: an intestinal proteinaceous hormone capable of stimulating secretion by the pancreas and liver

se·cre·tion \si-'krē-shən\ *noun* [French *sécrétion*, from Latin *secretion-, secretio* separation, from *secernere* to separate — more at SECRET] (1646)
1 a : the process of segregating, elaborating, and releasing some material either functionally specialized (as saliva) or isolated for excretion (as urine) **b** : a product of secretion formed by an animal or plant; *especially* : one performing a specific useful function in the organism
2 [²*secrete*] : the act of hiding something : CONCEALMENT
— **se·cre·tion·ary** \-shə-,ner-ē\ *adjective*

se·cre·tive \'sē-krə-tiv, si-'krē-\ *adjective* [back-formation from *secretiveness*, part translation of French *secrétivité*] (1853)
: disposed to secrecy : not open or outgoing in speech, activity, or purposes
synonym see SILENT
— **se·cre·tive·ly** *adverb*
— **se·cre·tive·ness** *noun*

se·cre·tor \si-'krē-tər\ *noun* (1941)
: an individual of blood group A, B, or AB who secretes the antigens characteristic of these blood groups in bodily fluids (as saliva)

se·cre·to·ry \'sē-krə-,tōr-ē, *especially British* si-'krē-t(ə-)rē\ *adjective* (1692)
: of, relating to, or promoting secretion; *also* : produced by secretion

secret partner *noun* (circa 1909)

: a partner whose membership in a partnership is kept secret from the public

secret police *noun* (1823)
: a police organization operating for the most part in secrecy and especially for the political purposes of its government often with terroristic methods

secret service *noun* (1737)
1 : a governmental service of a secret nature
2 *both Ss capitalized* : a division of the U.S. Treasury Department charged chiefly with the suppression of counterfeiting and the protection of the president

secret society *noun* (1829)
: any of various oath-bound societies often devoted to brotherhood, moral discipline, and mutual assistance

sect \'sekt\ *noun* [Middle English *secte*, from Middle French & Late Latin & Latin; Middle French, group, sect, from Late Latin *secta* organized ecclesiastical body, from Latin, course of action, way of life, probably from *sectari* to pursue, frequentative of *sequi* to follow — more at SUE] (14th century)
1 a : a dissenting or schismatic religious body; *especially* : one regarded as extreme or heretical **b** : a religious denomination
2 *archaic* : SEX 1 ⟨so is all her *sect* —Shakespeare⟩
3 a : a group adhering to a distinctive doctrine or to a leader **b** : PARTY **c** : FACTION

¹**sec·tar·i·an** \sek-'ter-ē-ən\ *adjective* (1649)
1 : of, relating to, or characteristic of a sect or sectarian
2 : limited in character or scope : PAROCHIAL
— **sec·tar·i·an·ism** \-ē-ə-,ni-zəm\ *noun*

²**sectarian** *noun* (1819)
1 : an adherent of a sect
2 : a narrow or bigoted person

sec·tar·i·an·ize \sek-'ter-ē-ə-,nīz\ *verb* **-ized; -iz·ing** (1842)
intransitive verb
: to act as sectarians
transitive verb
: to make sectarian

sec·ta·ry \'sek-tə-rē\ *noun, plural* **-ries** (1556)
: a member of a sect

sec·tile \'sek-t°l, -,tīl\ *adjective* [Latin *sectilis*, from *sectus*, past participle of *secare*] (1805)
: capable of being severed by a knife with a smooth cut
— **sec·til·i·ty** \sek-'ti-lə-tē\ *noun*

☆ SYNONYMS
Secret, covert, stealthy, furtive, clandestine, surreptitious, underhanded mean done without attracting observation. SECRET implies concealment on any grounds for any motive (met at a *secret* location). COVERT stresses the fact of not being open or declared ⟨*covert* intelligence operations⟩. STEALTHY suggests taking pains to avoid being seen or heard especially in some misdoing ⟨the *stealthy* step of a burglar⟩. FURTIVE implies a sly or cautious stealthiness ⟨lovers exchanging *furtive* glances⟩. CLANDESTINE implies secrecy usually for an evil, illicit, or unauthorized purpose and often emphasizes the fear of being discovered ⟨a *clandestine* meeting of conspirators⟩. SURREPTITIOUS applies to action or behavior done secretly often with skillful avoidance of detection and in violation of custom, law, or authority ⟨the *surreptitious* stockpiling of weapons⟩. UNDERHANDED stresses fraud or deception ⟨an *underhanded* trick⟩.

\ə\ abut \ª\ kitten \ər\ further \a\ ash \ā\ ace
\ä\ mop, mar \aù\ out \ch\ chin \e\ bet \ē\ easy
\g\ go \i\ hit \ī\ ice \j\ job \ŋ\ sing \ō\ go
\ò\ law \òi\ boy \th\ thin \th\ the \ü\ loot \ù\ foot
\y\ yet \zh\ vision *see also* Guide to Pronunciation

¹sec·tion \'sek-shən\ *noun* [Latin *section-, sectio,* from *secare* to cut — more at SAW] (1559)
1 a : the action or an instance of cutting or separating by cutting **b :** a part set off by or as if by cutting
2 : a distinct part or portion of something written (as a chapter, law, or newspaper)
3 a : the profile of something as it would appear if cut through by an intersecting plane **b :** the plane figure resulting from the cutting of a solid by a plane
4 : a natural subdivision of a taxonomic group
5 : a character § used as a mark for the beginning of a section and as a reference mark
6 : a piece of land one square mile in area forming one of the 36 subdivisions of a township
7 : a distinct part of a territorial or political area, community, or group of people
8 a : a part that may be, is, or is viewed as separated ⟨chop the stalks into *sections*⟩ ⟨the northern *section* of the route⟩ **b :** one segment of a fruit **:** CARPEL
9 : a basic military unit usually having a special function
10 : a very thin slice (as of tissue) suitable for microscopic examination
11 a : one of the classes formed by dividing the students taking a course **b :** one of the discussion groups into which a conference or organization is divided
12 a : a part of a permanent railroad way under the care of a particular crew **b :** one of two or more vehicles or trains which run on the same schedule
13 : one of several component parts that may be assembled or reassembled ⟨a bookcase in *sections*⟩
14 : a division of an orchestra composed of one class of instruments
15 : SIGNATURE 3b
synonym see PART
²section *verb* **sec·tioned; sec·tion·ing** \-sh(ə-)niŋ\ (1819)
transitive verb
1 : to cut or separate into sections
2 : to represent in sections
intransitive verb
: to become cut or separated into parts
¹sec·tion·al \'sek-shnəl, -shə-n°l\ *adjective* (1806)
1 a : of or relating to a section **b :** local or regional rather than general in character ⟨*sectional* interests⟩
2 : consisting of or divided into sections ⟨*sectional* furniture⟩
— **sec·tion·al·ly** *adverb*
²sectional *noun* (1901)
: a piece of furniture made up of modular units capable of use separately or in various combinations
sec·tion·al·ism \'sek-shnə-,li-zəm, -shə-n°l-,i-\ *noun* (1855)
: an exaggerated devotion to the interests of a region
Section Eight *noun* [*Section VIII,* Army Regulation 615-360, in effect from December 1922 to July 1944] (1943)
: a discharge from the U.S. Army for military inaptitude or undesirable habits or traits of character; *also* : a soldier receiving such a discharge
section gang *noun* (1890)
: a crew of track workers employed to maintain a railroad section
section hand *noun* (1873)
: a laborer belonging to a section gang
¹sec·tor \'sek-tər, -,tȯr\ *noun* [Late Latin, from Latin, cutter, from *secare* to cut — more at SAW] (1570)
1 a : a geometric figure bounded by two radii and the included arc of a circle **b (1) :** a subdivision of a defensive military position **(2) :** a portion of a military front or area of operation

c : an area or portion resembling a sector ⟨bilingual *sector* of town —David Kleinberg⟩ **d :** a sociological, economic, or political subdivision of society ⟨greater cooperation between the public and private *sectors* —Peter Chapman⟩
2 : a mathematical instrument consisting of two rulers connected at one end by a joint and marked with several scales
3 : a subdivision of a track on a computer disk
²sec·tor \-tər\ *transitive verb* **sec·tored; sec·tor·ing** \-t(ə-)riŋ\ (1884)
: to divide into or furnish with sectors
sec·to·ri·al \sek-'tȯr-ē-əl, -'tȯr-\ *adjective* (1803)
1 : of, relating to, or having the shape of a sector of a circle
2 *of a chimera* **:** having a sector of variant growth interposed in an otherwise normal body of tissue
¹sec·u·lar \'se-kyə-lər\ *adjective* [Middle English, from Old French *seculer,* from Late Latin *saecularis,* from *saeculum* the present world, from Latin, generation, age, century, world; akin to Welsh *hoedl* lifetime] (14th century)
1 a : of or relating to the worldly or temporal ⟨*secular* concerns⟩ **b :** not overtly or specifically religious ⟨*secular* music⟩ **c :** not ecclesiastical or clerical ⟨*secular* courts⟩ ⟨*secular* landowners⟩
2 : not bound by monastic vows or rules; *specifically* **:** of, relating to, or forming clergy not belonging to a religious order or congregation ⟨a *secular* priest⟩
3 a : occurring once in an age or a century **b :** existing or continuing through ages or centuries **c :** of or relating to a long term of indefinite duration
— **sec·u·lar·i·ty** \,se-kyə-'lar-ə-tē\ *noun*
— **sec·u·lar·ly** \'se-kyə-lər-lē\ *adverb*
²secular *noun,* *plural* **seculars** *or* **secular** (14th century)
1 : a secular ecclesiastic (as a diocesan priest)
2 : LAYMAN
secular humanism *noun* (1933)
: HUMANISM 3; *especially* **:** humanistic philosophy viewed as a nontheistic religion antagonistic to traditional religion
— **secular humanist** *noun or adjective*
sec·u·lar·ism \'se-kyə-lə-,ri-zəm\ *noun* (1851)
: indifference to or rejection or exclusion of religion and religious considerations
— **sec·u·lar·ist** \-rist\ *noun*
— **secularist** *or* **sec·u·lar·is·tic** \,se-kyə-lə-'ris-tik\ *adjective*
sec·u·lar·ize \'se-kyə-lə-,rīz\ *transitive verb* **-ized; -iz·ing** (1611)
1 : to make secular
2 : to transfer from ecclesiastical to civil or lay use, possession, or control
3 : to convert to or imbue with secularism
— **sec·u·lar·i·za·tion** \,se-kyə-lə-rə-'zā-shən\ *noun*
— **sec·u·lar·iz·er** *noun*
se·cund \si-'kənd, 'sē-\ *adjective* [Latin *secundus* following — more at SECOND] (circa 1777)
: having some part or element arranged on one side only
¹se·cure \si-'kyur\ *adjective* **se·cur·er; -est** [Latin *securus* safe, secure, from *se* without + *cura* care — more at SUICIDE] (circa 1533)
1 a *archaic* **:** unwisely free from fear or distrust **:** OVERCONFIDENT **b :** easy in mind **:** CONFIDENT **c :** assured in opinion or expectation **:** having no doubt
2 a : free from danger **b :** free from risk of loss **c :** affording safety ⟨a *secure* hideaway⟩ **d :** TRUSTWORTHY, DEPENDABLE ⟨*secure* foundation⟩
3 : ASSURED 1 ⟨*secure* victory⟩
— **se·cure·ly** *adverb*
— **se·cure·ness** *noun*

²secure *verb* **se·cured; se·cur·ing** (1593)
transitive verb
1 a : to relieve from exposure to danger **:** act to make safe against adverse contingencies ⟨*secure* a supply line from enemy raids⟩ **b :** to put beyond hazard of losing or of not receiving **:** GUARANTEE ⟨*secure* the blessings of liberty —U.S. Constitution⟩ **c :** to give pledge of payment to (a creditor) or of (an obligation) ⟨*secure* a note by a pledge of collateral⟩
2 a : to take (a person) into custody **:** hold fast **:** PINION **b :** to make fast **:** SEAL ⟨*secure* a door⟩
3 a : to get secure usually lasting possession or control of ⟨*secure* a job⟩ **b :** BRING ABOUT, EFFECT
4 : to release (naval personnel) from work or duty
intransitive verb
1 *of naval personnel* **:** to stop work **:** go off duty
2 *of a ship* **:** to tie up **:** BERTH
synonym see ENSURE
— **se·cur·er** *noun*
se·cure·ment \si-'kyur-mənt\ *noun* (1622)
1 *obsolete* **:** PROTECTION
2 : the act or process of securing
se·cu·ri·tize \si-'kyur-ə-,tīz\ *transitive verb* **-tized; -tiz·ing** (1981)
: to consolidate (as mortgage loans) and sell to other investors for resale to the public in the form of securities
— **se·cu·ri·ti·za·tion** \-,kyur-ə-tə-'zā-shən\ *noun*
se·cu·ri·ty \si-'kyur-ə-tē\ *noun,* *plural* **-ties** (15th century)
1 : the quality or state of being secure: as **a :** freedom from danger **:** SAFETY **b :** freedom from fear or anxiety **c :** freedom from the prospect of being laid off ⟨*job security*⟩
2 a : something given, deposited, or pledged to make certain the fulfillment of an obligation **b :** SURETY
3 : an evidence of debt or of ownership (as a stock certificate or bond)
4 a : something that secures **:** PROTECTION **b (1) :** measures taken to guard against espionage or sabotage, crime, attack, or escape **(2) :** an organization or department whose task is security
security blanket *noun* (1968)
1 : a blanket carried by a child as a protection against anxiety
2 : a usually familiar object whose presence dispels anxiety
Security Council *noun* (1944)
: a permanent council of the United Nations with primary responsibility for maintaining peace and security
security interest *noun* (1951)
: the rights that a creditor has in the personal property of a debtor that secures an obligation **:** LIEN
security police *noun* (1920)
1 : police engaged in counterespionage
2 : AIR POLICE
se·dan \si-'dan\ *noun* [origin unknown] (1635)
1 : a portable often covered chair that is designed to carry one person and that is borne on poles by two men
2 a : a 2- or 4-door automobile seating 4 or more persons and usually having a permanent top — compare COUPE **b :** a motorboat having one passenger compartment
¹se·date \si-'dāt\ *adjective* [Latin *sedatus,* from past participle of *sedare* to calm; akin to *sedēre* to sit — more at SIT] (1663)
: keeping a quiet steady attitude or pace **:** UNRUFFLED
synonym see SERIOUS
— **se·date·ly** *adverb*
— **se·date·ness** *noun*
²sedate *transitive verb* **se·dat·ed; se·dat·ing** [back-formation from *sedative*] (1945)
: to dose with sedatives
se·da·tion \si-'dā-shən\ *noun* (1543)

1 : the inducing of a relaxed easy state especially by the use of sedatives
2 : a state resulting from or as if from sedation
¹**sed·a·tive** \'se-də-tiv\ adjective [Middle English, alleviating pain, from Middle French sedatif, from Medieval Latin sedativus, from Latin sedatus] (1795)
: tending to calm, moderate, or tranquilize nervousness or excitement
²**sedative** noun (1797)
: a sedative agent or drug
sed·en·tary \'se-dᵊn-ˌter-ē\ adjective [Middle French sedentaire, from Latin sedentarius, from sedent-, sedens, present participle of sedēre to sit — more at SIT] (1598)
1 : not migratory : SETTLED ⟨sedentary birds⟩
2 : doing or requiring much sitting
3 : permanently attached ⟨sedentary barnacles⟩
se·der \'sā-dər\ noun, often capitalized [Hebrew sēdher order] (1865)
: a Jewish home or community service including a ceremonial dinner held on the first or first and second evenings of the Passover in commemoration of the exodus from Egypt
se·de·runt \sə-'dir-ənt, -'der-\ noun [Latin, there (they) sat (from sedēre to sit), word used to introduce list of those attending a session — more at SIT] (1825)
: a prolonged sitting (as for discussion)
sedge \'sej\ noun [Middle English segge, from Old English secg; akin to Middle High German segge sedge, Old English sagu saw — more at SAW] (before 12th century)
: any of a family (Cyperaceae, the sedge family) of usually tufted marsh plants differing from the related grasses in having achenes and solid stems; especially : any of a cosmopolitan genus (Carex)
— **sedgy** \'se-jē\ adjective
se·di·lia \sə-'dēl-yə, -'dil-, especially British -'dīl-\ noun plural [Latin, plural of sedile seat, from sedēre] (1793)
: seats on the south side of the chancel for the celebrant, deacon, and subdeacon
¹**sed·i·ment** \'se-də-mənt\ noun [Middle French, from Latin sedimentum settling, from sedēre to sit, sink down] (1547)
1 : the matter that settles to the bottom of a liquid
2 : material deposited by water, wind, or glaciers
²**sed·i·ment** \-ˌment\ (1859)
transitive verb
: to deposit as sediment
intransitive verb
1 : to settle to the bottom in a liquid
2 : to deposit sediment
sed·i·ment·able \ˌse-də-'men-tə-bəl\ adjective (1943)
: capable of being sedimented by centrifugation ⟨sedimentable ribosomal particles⟩
sed·i·men·ta·ry \ˌse-də-'men-tə-rē, -'men-trē\ adjective (1830)
1 : of, relating to, or containing sediment ⟨sedimentary deposits⟩
2 : formed by or from deposits of sediment ⟨sedimentary rock⟩
sed·i·men·ta·tion \ˌse-də-mən-'tā-shən, -ˌmen-\ noun (1874)
: the action or process of forming or depositing sediment : SETTLING
sed·i·men·tol·o·gy \ˌse-də-mən-'tä-lə-jē, -ˌmen-\ noun (1932)
: a branch of science that deals with sedimentary rocks and their inclusions
— **sed·i·men·to·log·ic** \-ˌmen-tᵊl-'ä-jik\ or **sed·i·men·to·log·i·cal** \-ji-kəl\ adjective
— **sed·i·men·to·log·i·cal·ly** \-ji-k(ə-)lē\ adverb
— **sed·i·men·tol·o·gist** \-mən-'tä-lə-jist, -ˌmen-\ noun
se·di·tion \si-'di-shən\ noun [Middle English, from Middle French, from Latin sedition-, seditio, literally, separation, from se- apart +

ition-, itio act of going, from ire to go — more at SECEDE, ISSUE] (14th century)
: incitement of resistance to or insurrection against lawful authority
se·di·tious \si-'di-shəs\ adjective (15th century)
1 : disposed to arouse or take part in or guilty of sedition
2 : of, relating to, or tending toward sedition
— **se·di·tious·ly** adverb
— **se·di·tious·ness** noun
se·duce \si-'düs, -'dyüs\ transitive verb **se·duced; se·duc·ing** [Middle English, from Late Latin seducere, to lead away, from se- apart + ducere to lead — more at TOW] (15th century)
1 : to persuade to disobedience or disloyalty
2 : to lead astray usually by persuasion or false promises
3 : to carry out the physical seduction of : entice to sexual intercourse
4 : ATTRACT
synonym see LURE
— **se·duc·er** noun
se·duce·ment \-mənt\ noun (1586)
1 : SEDUCTION
2 : something that serves to seduce
se·duc·tion \si-'dək-shən\ noun [Middle French, from Late Latin seduction-, seductio, from Latin, act of leading aside, from seducere] (1526)
1 : the act of seducing to wrong; especially : the often unlawful enticement of a female to sexual intercourse
2 : something that seduces : TEMPTATION
3 : something that attracts or charms
se·duc·tive \-'dək-tiv\ adjective (1771)
: tending to seduce : having alluring or tempting qualities ⟨a seductive, sometimes disingenuous man —Thatcher Freund⟩ ⟨a seductive spring morning⟩
— **se·duc·tive·ly** adverb
— **se·duc·tive·ness** noun
se·duc·tress \-'dək-trəs\ noun [obsolete seductor male seducer, from Late Latin, from seducere to seduce] (1803)
: a woman who seduces
se·du·li·ty \si-'dü-lə-tē, -'dyü-\ noun (1542)
: sedulous activity : DILIGENCE
sed·u·lous \'se-jə-ləs\ adjective [Latin sedulus, from sedulo sincerely, diligently, from se without + dolus guile — more at SUICIDE] (1540)
1 : involving or accomplished with careful perseverance ⟨sedulous craftsmanship⟩
2 : diligent in application or pursuit ⟨a sedulous student⟩
synonym see BUSY
— **sed·u·lous·ly** adverb
— **sed·u·lous·ness** noun
se·dum \'sē-dəm\ noun [New Latin, from Latin, houseleek] (1760)
: any of a genus (Sedum) of fleshy widely distributed herbs of the orpine family — compare STONECROP
¹**see** \'sē\ verb saw \'so\; seen \'sēn\; see·ing \'sē-iŋ\ [Middle English seen, from Old English sēon; akin to Old High German sehan to see and perhaps to Latin sequi to follow — more at SUE] (before 12th century)
transitive verb
1 a : to perceive by the eye **b** : to perceive or detect as if by sight
2 a : to have experience of : UNDERGO ⟨see army service⟩ **b** : to come to know : DISCOVER **c** : to be the setting or time of ⟨the last fifty years have seen a sweeping revolution in science —Barry Commoner⟩
3 a : to form a mental picture of : VISUALIZE ⟨can still see her as she was years ago⟩ **b** : to perceive the meaning or importance of : UNDERSTAND **c** : to be aware of : RECOGNIZE ⟨sees only our faults⟩ **d** : to imagine as a possibility : SUPPOSE ⟨couldn't see him as a crook⟩

4 a : EXAMINE, WATCH ⟨want to see how she handles the problem⟩ **b** (1) : READ (2) : to read of **c** : to attend as a spectator ⟨see a play⟩
5 a : to take care of : provide for ⟨had enough money to see us through⟩ **b** : to make sure ⟨see that order is kept⟩
6 a : to regard as : JUDGE **b** : to prefer to have ⟨I'll see him hanged first⟩ ⟨I'll see you dead before I accept your terms⟩ **c** : to find acceptable or attractive ⟨can't understand what he sees in her⟩
7 a : to call on : VISIT **b** (1) : to keep company with especially in courtship or dating ⟨had been seeing each other for a year⟩ (2) : to grant an interview to : RECEIVE ⟨the president will see you now⟩
8 : ACCOMPANY, ESCORT ⟨see the guests to the door⟩
9 : to meet (a bet) in poker or to equal the bet of (a player) : CALL
intransitive verb
1 a : to give or pay attention **b** : to look about
2 a : to have the power of sight **b** : to apprehend objects by sight **c** : to perceive objects as if by sight
3 : to grasp something mentally
4 : to make investigation or inquiry
— **see·able** \-ə-bəl\ adjective
— **see after** : to attend to : care for
— **see eye to eye** : to have a common viewpoint : AGREE
— **see things** : HALLUCINATE
— **see through** : to grasp the true nature of ⟨saw through the scheme⟩
— **see to** : to attend to : care for
²**see** noun [Middle English se, from Old French, from Latin sedes seat; akin to Latin sedēre to sit — more at SIT] (14th century)
1 a archaic : CATHEDRA **b** : a cathedral town **c** : a seat of a bishop's office, power, or authority
2 : the authority or jurisdiction of a bishop
¹**seed** \'sēd\ noun, plural **seed** or **seeds** [Middle English, from Old English sǣd; akin to Old High German sāt seed, Old English sāwan to sow — more at SOW] (before 12th century)
1 a (1) : the grains or ripened ovules of plants used for sowing (2) : the fertilized ripened ovule of a flowering plant containing an embryo and capable normally of germination to produce a new plant; broadly : a propagative plant structure (as a spore or small dry fruit) **b** : a propagative animal structure: (1) : MILT, SEMEN (2) : a small egg (as of an insect) (3) : a developmental form of a lower animal suitable for transplanting; specifically : SPAT **c** : the condition or stage of bearing seed ⟨in seed⟩
2 : PROGENY
3 : a source of development or growth : GERM ⟨sowed the seeds of discord⟩
4 : something (as a tiny particle or a bubble in glass) that resembles a seed in shape or size
5 : a competitor who has been seeded in a tournament
— **seed** adjective
— **seed·ed** \'sē-dəd\ adjective
— **seed·less** \'sēd-ləs\ adjective
— **seed·like** \-ˌlīk\ adjective
— **go to seed** or **run to seed 1** : to develop seed **2** : DECAY
²**seed** (14th century)
intransitive verb
1 : to bear or shed seed
2 : to sow seed : PLANT
transitive verb

1 a : to plant seeds in **:** SOW ⟨*seed* land to grass⟩ **b :** to furnish with something that causes or stimulates growth or development **c :** INOCULATE **d :** to supply with nuclei (as of crystallization or condensation); *especially* **:** to treat (a cloud) with solid particles to convert water droplets into ice crystals in an attempt to produce precipitation **e :** to cover or permeate by or as if by scattering something ⟨*seeded* [the] sea-lanes with thousands of magnetic mines —Otto Friedrich⟩
2 : PLANT 1a
3 : to extract the seeds from (as raisins)
4 a : to schedule (tournament players or teams) so that superior ones will not meet in early rounds **b :** to rank (a contestant) relative to others in a tournament on the basis of previous record ⟨the top-*seeded* tennis star⟩

seed·bed \'sēd-,bed\ *noun* (1660)
1 : soil or a bed of soil prepared for planting seed
2 : a place or source of growth or development

seed·cake \-,kāk\ *noun* (1573)
1 : a cake or cookie containing aromatic seeds (as sesame or caraway)
2 : OIL CAKE

seed coat *noun* (1796)
: an outer protective covering of a seed

seed·eat·er \'sēd-,ē-tər\ *noun* (circa 1879)
: a bird (as a finch) whose diet consists basically of seeds

seed·er \'sē-dər\ *noun* (1868)
1 : an implement for planting or sowing seeds
2 : a device for seeding fruit
3 : one that seeds clouds

seed fern *noun* (1927)
: any of an order (Pteridospermales) of extinct cycadophytes with foliage like that of ferns and with naked seeds

seed leaf *noun* (circa 1693)
: COTYLEDON 2

seed·ling \'sēd-liŋ\ *noun* (1660)
1 : a young plant grown from seed
2 a : a young tree before it becomes a sapling **b :** a nursery plant not yet transplanted
— **seedling** *adjective*

seed money *noun* (1943)
: money used for setting up a new enterprise

seed oyster *noun* (1885)
: a young oyster especially of a size for transplantation

seed pearl *noun* (1553)
1 : a very small and often irregular pearl
2 : minute pearls imbedded in some binding material

seed plant *noun* (1707)
: a plant that bears seeds; *specifically* **:** SPERMATOPHYTE

seed·pod \'sēd-,päd\ *noun* (1718)
: ²POD 1

seeds·man \'sēdz-mən\ *noun* (1601)
1 : one who sows seeds
2 : a dealer in seeds

seed stock *noun* (1926)
: a supply (as of seed) for planting; *broadly* **:** a source of new individuals ⟨a *seed stock* of trout in the streams⟩

seed tick *noun* (1705)
: the 6-legged larva of a tick

seed·time \'sēd-,tīm\ *noun* (before 12th century)
1 : the season of sowing
2 : a period of original development

seedy \'sē-dē\ *adjective* **seed·i·er; -est** (1574)
1 : containing or full of seeds ⟨a *seedy* fruit⟩
2 : inferior in condition or quality: as **a :** SHABBY, RUN-DOWN ⟨*seedy* clothes⟩ **b :** somewhat disreputable **:** SQUALID ⟨a *seedy* district⟩ ⟨*seedy* entertainment⟩ **c :** slightly unwell **:** DEBILITATED ⟨felt *seedy* and went home early⟩
— **seed·i·ly** \'sē-dᵊl-ē\ *adverb*
— **seed·i·ness** \'sē-dē-nəs\ *noun*

¹see·ing \'sē-iŋ\ *conjunction* (1503)
: INASMUCH AS — often used with *as* or *that*

²seeing *noun* (1903)
: the quality of the images of celestial bodies observed telescopically

Seeing Eye *trademark*
— used for a guide dog trained to lead the blind

seek \'sēk\ *verb* **sought** \'sȯt\; **seek·ing** [Middle English *seken*, from Old English *sēcan;* akin to Old High German *suohhen* to seek, Latin *sagus* prophetic, Greek *hēgeisthai* to lead] (before 12th century)
transitive verb
1 : to resort to **:** go to
2 a : to go in search of **:** look for **b :** to try to discover
3 : to ask for **:** REQUEST ⟨*seeks* advice⟩
4 : to try to acquire or gain **:** aim at ⟨*seek* fame⟩
5 : to make an attempt **:** TRY — used with *to* and an infinitive ⟨governments . . . *seek* to keep the bulk of their people contented —D. M. Potter⟩
intransitive verb
1 : to make a search or inquiry
2 a : to be sought **b :** to be lacking ⟨in critical judgment . . . they were sadly to *seek* —*Times Literary Supplement*⟩
— **seek·er** *noun*

seel \'sē(ə)l\ *transitive verb* [Middle English *selen*, alteration of *silen*, from Middle French *siller*, from Medieval Latin *ciliare*, from Latin *cilium* eyelid] (15th century)
1 : to close the eyes of (as a hawk) by drawing threads through the eyelids
2 *archaic* **:** to close up (one's eyes)

see·ly \'sē-lē\ *adjective* [Middle English *sely* — more at SILLY] (14th century)
archaic **:** pitiable especially because of weak physical or mental condition **:** FRAIL

seem \'sēm\ *intransitive verb* [Middle English *semen*, of Scandinavian origin; akin to Old Norse *sœma* to honor, *sœmr* fitting, *samr* same — more at SAME] (13th century)
1 : to appear to the observation or understanding
2 : to give the impression of being

¹seem·ing *noun* (15th century)
: external appearance as distinguished from true character **:** LOOK

²seeming *adjective* (circa 1557)
: having an often deceptive or delusive appearance on superficial examination ⟨their wealth gave them a *seeming* security⟩
synonym see APPARENT
— **seem·ing·ly** \'sē-miŋ-lē\ *adverb*

seem·ly \'sēm-lē\ *adjective* **seem·li·er; -est** [Middle English *semely*, from Old Norse *sœmiligr*, from *sœmr* fitting] (13th century)
1 a : GOOD-LOOKING, HANDSOME **b :** agreeably fashioned **:** ATTRACTIVE
2 : conventionally proper **:** DECOROUS
3 : suited to the occasion, purpose, or person **:** FIT
— **seem·li·ness** *noun*
— **seemly** *adverb*

seen *past participle of* SEE

¹seep \'sēp\ *intransitive verb* [alteration of earlier *sipe*, from Middle English *sipen*, from Old English *sipian;* akin to Middle Low German *sipen* to seep] (1790)
1 : to flow or pass slowly through fine pores or small openings **:** OOZE ⟨water *seeped* in through a crack⟩
2 a : to enter or penetrate slowly ⟨fear of nuclear war had *seeped* into the national consciousness —Tip O'Neill⟩ **b :** to become diffused or spread ⟨a sadness *seeped* through his being —Agnes S. Turnbull⟩

²seep *noun* (circa 1825)
1 a : a spot where a fluid (as water, oil, or gas) contained in the ground oozes slowly to the surface and often forms a pool **b :** a small spring
2 : SEEPAGE
— **seepy** \'sē-pē\ *adjective*

seep·age \'sē-pij\ *noun* (circa 1825)

1 : the process of seeping **:** OOZING
2 : a quantity of fluid that has seeped (as through porous material)

¹seer \'sir, 'sē-ər\ *noun* (14th century)
1 : one that sees
2 a : one that predicts events or developments **b :** a person credited with extraordinary moral and spiritual insight
3 : one that practices divination especially by concentrating on a glass or crystal globe

²seer *noun, plural* **seers** *or* **seer** [Hindi *ser*] (1618)
: an Indian unit of weight equal to 2.057 pounds (0.9330 kilograms)

seer·ess \'sir-əs, 'sē-ər-əs\ *noun* (1845)
: a woman who predicts events or developments **:** PROPHETESS

seer·suck·er \'sir-,sə-kər\ *noun* [Hindi *sīrśaker*, from Persian *shīr-o-shakar*, literally, milk and sugar] (1722)
: a light fabric of linen, cotton, or rayon usually striped and slightly puckered

¹see·saw \'sē-,sȯ\ *noun* [probably from reduplication of ³*saw*] (1704)
1 : an alternating up-and-down or backward-and-forward motion or movement; *also* **:** a contest or struggle in which now one side now the other has the lead
2 a : a pastime in which two children or groups of children ride on opposite ends of a plank balanced in the middle so that one end goes up as the other goes down **b :** the plank or apparatus so used
— **seesaw** *adjective*

²seesaw (1712)
intransitive verb
1 a : to move backward and forward or up and down **b :** to play at seesaw
2 : ALTERNATE
transitive verb
: to cause to move in seesaw fashion

¹seethe \'sēth\ *verb* **seethed; seeth·ing** [Middle English *sethen*, from Old English *sēothan;* akin to Old High German *siodan* to seethe] (before 12th century)
transitive verb
1 *archaic* **:** BOIL, STEW
2 : to soak or saturate in a liquid
intransitive verb
1 *archaic* **:** BOIL
2 a : to be in a state of rapid agitated movement **b :** to churn or foam as if boiling
3 : to suffer violent internal excitement

²seethe *noun* (1816)
: a state of seething **:** EBULLITION

seething *adjective* (14th century)
1 : intensely hot **:** BOILING ⟨a *seething* inferno⟩
2 : constantly moving or active **:** AGITATED

see–through \'sē-,thrü\ *adjective* (1945)
: TRANSPARENT 1

¹seg·ment \'seg-mənt\ *noun* [Latin *segmentum*, from *secare* to cut — more at SAW] (1570)
1 a : a separate piece of something **:** BIT, FRAGMENT ⟨chop the stalks into short *segments*⟩ **b :** one of the constituent parts into which a body, entity, or quantity is divided or marked off by or as if by natural boundaries ⟨all *segments* of the population agree⟩
2 : a portion cut off from a geometric figure by one or more points, lines, or planes: as **a :** the part of a circular area bounded by a chord and an arc of that circle or so much of the area as is cut off by the chord **b :** the part of a sphere cut off by a plane or included between two parallel planes **c :** the finite part of a line between two points in the line
synonym see PART
— **seg·men·tary** \-mən-,ter-ē\ *adjective*

²seg·ment \'seg-,ment\ *transitive verb* (1859)
: to separate into segments **:** give off as segments

seg·men·tal \seg-'men-tᵊl\ *adjective* (1816)
1 : of, relating to, or having the form of a segment and especially the sector of a circle ⟨*segmental* fanlight⟩

2 : of, relating to, or composed of somites or metameres **:** METAMERIC
3 a : divided into segments ⟨*segmental* knowledge⟩ **b :** PARTIAL, INCOMPLETE **c :** resulting from segmentation
— **seg·men·tal·ly** \-t³l-ē\ *adverb*
seg·men·ta·tion \ˌseg-mən-'tā-shən, -ˌmen-\ *noun* (1851)
: the process of dividing into segments; *especially* **:** the formation of many cells from a single cell (as in a developing egg)
segmentation cavity *noun* (1888)
: BLASTOCOEL
seg·ment·ed \'seg-ˌmen-təd, seg-'\ *adjective* (1854)
: divided into or composed of segments or sections ⟨*segmented* worms⟩
se·gno \'sān-(ˌ)yō\ *noun, plural* **segnos** [Italian, sign, from Latin *signum* — more at SIGN] (1908)
: a notational sign; *specifically* **:** the sign that marks the beginning or end of a musical repeat
se·go lily \'sē-(ˌ)gō-\ *noun* [*sego* the bulb of the sego lily, from Southern Paiute *siɣoʔo*] (1913)
: a mariposa lily (*Calochortus nuttallii*) of western North America having mostly white or in some areas mostly yellow flowers mottled with a darker color

sego lily

seg·re·gant \'se-gri-gənt\ *noun* (1926)
: a genetic segregate
¹seg·re·gate \'se-gri-ˌgāt\ *verb* **-gat·ed; -gat·ing** [Latin *segregatus*, past participle of *segregare*, from *se-* apart + *greg-, grex* herd — more at SECEDE] (1542)
transitive verb
1 : to separate or set apart from others or from the general mass **:** ISOLATE
2 : to cause or force the separation of (as from the rest of society)
intransitive verb
1 : SEPARATE, WITHDRAW
2 : to practice or enforce a policy of segregation
3 : to undergo genetic segregation
— **seg·re·ga·tive** \-ˌgā-tiv\ *adjective*
²seg·re·gate \'se-gri-gət, -ˌgāt\ *noun* (1871)
: one that is in some respect segregated; *especially* **:** one that differs genetically from the parental line because of genetic segregation
segregated *adjective* (1652)
1 a : set apart or separated from others of the same kind or group ⟨a *segregated* account in a bank⟩ **b :** divided in facilities or administered separately for members of different groups or races ⟨*segregated* education⟩ **c :** restricted to members of one group or one race by a policy of segregation ⟨*segregated* schools⟩
2 : practicing or maintaining segregation especially of races ⟨*segregated* states⟩
seg·re·ga·tion \ˌse-gri-'gā-shən\ *noun* (1555)
1 : the act or process of segregating **:** the state of being segregated
2 a : the separation or isolation of a race, class, or ethnic group by enforced or voluntary residence in a restricted area, by barriers to social intercourse, by separate educational facilities, or by other discriminatory means **b :** the separation for special treatment or observation of individuals or items from a larger group ⟨*segregation* of gifted children into accelerated classes⟩
3 : the separation of allelic genes that occurs typically during meiosis
seg·re·ga·tion·ist \-sh(ə-)nist\ *noun* (1913)
: a person who believes in or practices segregation especially of races
— **segregationist** *adjective*

¹se·gue \'se-(ˌ)gwā, 'sā-\ *imperative verb* [Italian, there follows, from *seguire* to follow, from Latin *sequi* — more at SUE] (circa 1740)
1 : proceed to what follows without pause — used as a direction in music
2 : perform the music that follows like that which has preceded — used as a direction in music
²segue *intransitive verb* **se·gued; se·gue·ing** (circa 1913)
1 : to proceed without pause from one musical number or theme to another
2 : to make a transition without interruption from one activity, topic, scene, or part to another
³segue *noun* (circa 1937)
: the act or an instance of segueing
se·gui·di·lla \ˌse-gə-'dē-yə, -'dēl-yə\ *noun* [Spanish, diminutive of *seguida*, a dance, literally, sequence, from *seguido*, past participle of *seguir* to follow, from Latin *sequi*] (1763)
1 a : a Spanish dance with many regional variations **b :** the music for such a dance
2 : a Spanish stanza of four or seven short partly assonant verses
sei·cen·to \sā-'chen-(ˌ)tō\ *noun* [Italian, literally, six-hundred, from *sei* six (from Latin *sex*) + *cento* hundred — more at SIX, CINQUECENTO] (circa 1902)
: the 17th century; *specifically* **:** the 17th century period in Italian literature and art
seiche \'sāsh, 'sēch\ *noun* [French] (circa 1839)
: an oscillation of the surface of a landlocked body of water (as a lake) that varies in period from a few minutes to several hours
sei·del \'sī-d³l, 'zī-\ *noun* [German, from Middle High German *sīdel*, from Latin *situla* bucket] (1908)
: a large glass for beer
Seid·litz powders \'sed-ləts-\ *noun plural* [*Sedlitz*, (Sedlčany), village in Bohemia; from the similarity of their effect to that of the water of the village] (1815)
: effervescing salts consisting of one powder of sodium bicarbonate and Rochelle salt and another of tartaric acid that are mixed in water and drunk as a mild cathartic
sei·gneur \sān-'yər\ *noun, often capitalized* [Middle French, from Medieval Latin *senior*, from Latin, adjective, elder — more at SENIOR] (1592)
1 : a man of rank or authority; *especially* **:** the feudal lord of a manor
2 : a member of the landed gentry of Canada
sei·gneur·ial \-'yùr-ē-əl, -'yər-\ *adjective* (1656)
: of, relating to, or befitting a seigneur
sei·gneury \'sān-yə-rē\ *noun, plural* **-gneur·ies** (1683)
1 a : the territory under the government of a feudal lord **b :** a landed estate held in Canada by feudal tenure until 1854
2 : the manor house of a Canadian seigneur
sei·gnior \sān-'yór, 'sān-ˌ\ *noun* [Middle English *seigniour*, from Middle French *seigneur*] (15th century)
: SEIGNEUR 1
sei·gnior·age *or* **sei·gnor·age** \'sān-yə-rij\ *noun* [Middle English *seigneurage*, from Middle French, right of the lord (especially to coin money), from *seigneur*] (15th century)
: a government revenue from the manufacture of coins calculated as the difference between the face value and the metal value of the coins
sei·gniory *or* **sei·gnory** \'sān-yə-rē\ *noun, plural* **-gnior·ies** *or* **-gnor·ies** (14th century)
1 : LORDSHIP, DOMINION; *specifically* **:** the power or authority of a feudal lord
2 : the territory over which a lord holds jurisdiction
sei·gno·ri·al \sān-'yōr-ē-əl, -'yór-\ *adjective* (1818)

: of, relating to, or befitting a seignior **:** MANORIAL
¹seine \'sān\ *noun* [Middle English, from Old English *segne*, from Latin *sagena*, from Greek *sagēnē*] (before 12th century)
: a large net with sinkers on one edge and floats on the other that hangs vertically in the water and is used to enclose fish when its ends are pulled together or are drawn ashore
²seine *verb* **seined; sein·ing** (1836)
intransitive verb
: to fish with or catch fish with a seine
transitive verb
: to fish for or in with a seine
sein·er \'sā-nər\ *noun* (1602)
1 : one who fishes with a seine
2 : a boat used for seining
sei·sin *or* **sei·zin** \'sē-z³n\ *noun* [Middle English *seisine*, from Old French *saisine*, from *saisir* to seize — more at SEIZE] (14th century)
1 : the possession of land or chattels
2 : the possession of a freehold estate in land by one having title thereto
seis·mic \'sīz-mik, 'sīs-\ *adjective* [Greek *seismos* shock, earthquake, from *seiein* to shake; probably akin to Avestan *thwaēshō* fear] (1858)
1 : of, subject to, or caused by an earthquake; *also* **:** of or relating to an earth vibration caused by something else (as an explosion or the impact of a meteorite)
2 : of or relating to a vibration on a celestial body (as the moon) comparable to a seismic event on earth
3 : having a strong or widespread impact **:** EARTHSHAKING ⟨*seismic* social changes⟩
— **seis·mi·cal·ly** \-mi-k(ə-)lē\ *adverb*
seis·mic·i·ty \sīz-'mi-sə-tē, sīs-\ *noun* (1902)
: the relative frequency and distribution of earthquakes
seismo- *combining form* [Greek, from *seismos*]
: earthquake **:** vibration ⟨*seismo*meter⟩
seis·mo·gram \'sīz-mə-ˌgram, 'sīs-\ *noun* [International Scientific Vocabulary] (circa 1891)
: the record of an earth tremor by a seismograph
seis·mo·graph \-ˌgraf\ *noun* [International Scientific Vocabulary] (1858)
: an apparatus to measure and record vibrations within the earth and of the ground
— **seis·mog·ra·pher** \sīz-'mä-grə-fər, sīs-\ *noun*
— **seis·mo·graph·ic** \ˌsīz-mə-'gra-fik, ˌsīs-\ *adjective*
— **seis·mog·ra·phy** \sīz-'mä-grə-fē, sīs-\ *noun*
seis·mol·o·gy \sīz-'mä-lə-jē, sīs-\ *noun* [International Scientific Vocabulary] (1858)
: a science that deals with earthquakes and with artificially produced vibrations of the earth
— **seis·mo·log·i·cal** \ˌsīz-mə-'lä-ji-kəl, ˌsīs-\ *adjective*
— **seis·mol·o·gist** \sīz-'mä-lə-jist, sīs-\ *noun*
seis·mom·e·ter \sīz-'mä-mə-tər, sīs-\ *noun* (1841)
: a seismograph measuring the actual movements of the ground (as on the earth or the moon)
— **seis·mo·met·ric** \ˌsīz-mə-'me-trik, ˌsīs-\ *adjective*
seis·mom·e·try \sīz-'mä-mə-trē, sīs-\ *noun* [International Scientific Vocabulary] (1858)
: the scientific study of earthquakes
sei whale \'sā-, 'sī-\ *noun* [part translation of Norwegian *seihval*, from *sei* coalfish + *hval* whale] (1912)

: a common and widely distributed dark gray rorqual (*Balaenoptera borealis*) that has a ridge on the top of the head and grows to a length of nearly 60 feet (18 meters) — called also *sei*

seize \'sēz\ *verb* **seized; seiz·ing** [Middle English *saisen,* from Old French *saisir* to put in possession of, from Medieval Latin *sacire,* of Germanic origin; perhaps akin to Old High German *sezzen* to set — more at SET] (14th century)
transitive verb
1 a *usually* **seise** \'sēz\ : to vest ownership of a freehold estate in **b** *often* **seise** : to put in possession of something ⟨the biographer will be *seized* of all pertinent papers⟩
2 a : to take possession of : CONFISCATE **b** : to take possession of by legal process
3 a : to possess or take by force : CAPTURE **b** : to take prisoner : ARREST
4 a : to take hold of : CLUTCH **b** : to possess oneself of : GRASP **c** : to understand fully and distinctly : APPREHEND
5 a : to attack or overwhelm physically : AFFLICT ⟨suddenly *seized* with an acute illness —H. G. Armstrong⟩ **b** : to possess (as one's mind) completely or overwhelmingly ⟨*seized* the popular imagination —Basil Davenport⟩
6 : to bind or fasten together with a lashing of small stuff (as yarn, marline, or fine wire)
intransitive verb
1 : to take or lay hold suddenly or forcibly
2 a : to cohere to a relatively moving part through excessive pressure, temperature, or friction — used especially of machine parts (as bearings, brakes, or pistons) **b** : to fail to operate due to the seizing of a part — used of an engine
synonym see TAKE
— **seiz·er** *noun*

seizing *noun* (14th century)
1 a : the cord or lashing used in binding or fastening **b** : the fastening so made — see KNOT illustration
2 : the operation of fastening together or lashing with tarred small stuff

sei·zure \'sē-zhər\ *noun* (15th century)
1 a : the act, action, or process of seizing : the state of being seized **b** : the taking possession of person or property by legal process
2 : a sudden attack (as of disease) ⟨an epileptic *seizure*⟩

se·jant \'sē-jənt\ *adjective* [modification of Middle French *seant,* present participle of *seoir* to sit, from Latin *sedēre* — more at SIT] (circa 1500)
: SITTING — used of a heraldic animal

sel \'sel\ *chiefly Scottish variant of* SELF

se·la·chi·an \sə-'lā-kē-ən\ *noun* [ultimately from Greek *selachos* cartilaginous phosphorescent fish; akin to Greek *selas* brightness] (1835)
: any of a variously defined group (Selachii) of cartilaginous fishes that includes all the elasmobranchs or all elasmobranchs except the chimaeras, the existing sharks and rays or in its most restricted use the existing sharks as distinguished from the rays
— **selachian** *adjective*

se·lag·i·nel·la \sə-,la-jə-'ne-lə\ *noun* [New Latin, from Latin *selagin-, selago,* a plant resembling the savin] (1835)
: any of a genus (*Selaginella*) of mossy lower tracheophytes that are related to or grouped with the club mosses and have branching stems and scalelike leaves and produce one-celled sporangia containing both megaspores and microspores

se·lah \'sē-lə, -,lä\ *interjection* [Hebrew *selāh*] (1530)
— a term of uncertain meaning found in the Hebrew text of the Psalms and Habakkuk carried over untranslated into some English versions

sel·couth \'sel-,küth\ *adjective* [Middle English, from Old English *seldcūth,* from *seldan*

seldom + *cūth* known — more at UNCOUTH] (before 12th century)
archaic : UNUSUAL, STRANGE

¹**sel·dom** \'sel-dəm\ *adverb* [Middle English, from Old English *seldan;* akin to Old High German *seltan* seldom] (before 12th century)
: in few instances : RARELY, INFREQUENTLY

²**seldom** *adjective* (13th century)
: RARE, INFREQUENT

¹**se·lect** \sə-'lekt\ *adjective* [Latin *selectus,* past participle of *seligere* to select, from *se-* apart (from *sed, se* without) + *legere* to gather, select — more at SUICIDE, LEGEND] (1565)
1 : chosen from a number or group by fitness or preference
2 a : of special value or excellence : SUPERIOR, CHOICE **b** : exclusively or fastidiously chosen often with regard to social, economic, or cultural characteristics
3 : judicious or restrictive in choice : DISCRIMINATING ⟨pleased with the *select* appreciation of his books —Osbert Sitwell⟩
— **se·lect·able** \sə-'lek-tə-bəl\ *adjective*
— **se·lect·ness** \sə-'lek(t)-nəs\ *noun*
— **se·lec·tor** \sə-'lek-tər\ *noun*

²**select** (1567)
transitive verb
: to choose (as by fitness or excellence) from a number or group : pick out
intransitive verb
: to make a choice

³**select** *noun* (1610)
: one that is select — often used in plural

se·lect·ed *adjective* (1590)
: SELECT; *specifically* : of a higher grade or quality than the ordinary

se·lect·ee \sə-,lek-'tē\ *noun* (1940)
1 : one inducted into military service under selective service
2 : one who is chosen from a group by fitness or preference

se·lec·tion \sə-'lek-shən\ *noun* (circa 1623)
1 : the act or process of selecting : the state of being selected
2 : one that is selected : CHOICE; *also* : a collection of selected things
3 : a natural or artificial process that results or tends to result in the survival and propagation of some individuals or organisms but not of others with the result that the inherited traits of the survivors are perpetuated — compare DARWINISM, NATURAL SELECTION
synonym see CHOICE

se·lec·tion·ist \-sh(ə-)nist\ *noun* (1892)
: one who considers natural selection a fundamental factor in evolution
— **selectionist** *adjective*

se·lec·tive \sə-'lek-tiv\ *adjective* (1625)
1 : of, relating to, or characterized by selection : selecting or tending to select
2 : highly specific in activity or effect ⟨*selective* pesticides⟩ ⟨*selective* absorption⟩
— **se·lec·tive·ly** *adverb*
— **se·lec·tive·ness** *noun*
— **se·lec·tiv·i·ty** \sə-,lek-'ti-və-tē, ,sē-\ *noun*

selective service *noun* (1917)
: a system under which men are called up for military service : DRAFT

se·lect·man \si-'lek(t)-,man, -,lek(t)-'man, -'lek(t)-mən; 'sē-,lek(t)-,man\ *noun* (1635)
: one of a board of officials elected in towns of all New England states except Rhode Island to serve as the chief administrative authority of the town

¹**selen-** *or* **seleno-** *combining form* [Latin *selen-,* from Greek *selēn-,* from *selēnē* — more at SELENIUM]
: moon ⟨*selenium*⟩ ⟨*selenology*⟩

²**selen-** *or* **seleni-** *combining form* [Swedish, from New Latin *selenium*]
: selenium ⟨*seleniferous*⟩

se·le·nate \'se-lə-,nāt\ *noun* [Swedish *selenat,* from *selen* of or containing selenium, from New Latin *selenium*] (1818)
: a salt containing the anion SeO_4^{2-}

Se·le·ne \sə-'lē-nē\ *noun*
: the Greek goddess of the moon

sel·e·nide \'se-lə-,nīd\ *noun* (1849)
: a binary compound of selenium with a more electropositive element or group

sel·e·nif·er·ous \,se-lə-'ni-f(ə-)rəs\ *adjective* (1823)
: containing or yielding selenium ⟨*seleniferous* vegetation⟩ ⟨*seleniferous* soils⟩

sel·e·nite \'se-lə-,nīt\ *noun* [Middle English *selinete,* from Latin *selenites,* from Greek *selēnitēs (lithos),* literally, stone of the moon, from *selēnē;* from the belief that it waxed and waned with the moon] (15th century)
: a variety of gypsum occurring in transparent crystals or crystalline masses

se·le·ni·um \sə-'lē-nē-əm\ *noun* [New Latin, from Greek *selēnē* moon, from *selas* brightness] (1818)
: a nonmetallic element that resembles sulfur and tellurium chemically, is obtained chiefly as a by-product in copper refining, and is a photoconductive semiconductor in its crystalline form — see ELEMENT table

selenium cell *noun* (1880)
: an insulated strip of selenium mounted with electrodes and used as a photoconductive element

se·le·no·cen·tric \sə-,lē-nə-'sen-trik\ *adjective* [International Scientific Vocabulary] (circa 1852)
: of or relating to the center of the moon; *also* : referred to or involving the moon as a center

sel·e·nol·o·gy \,se-lə-'nä-lə-jē\ *noun* (1821)
: a branch of astronomy that deals with the moon
— **se·le·no·log·i·cal** \,se-lə-nō-'lä-ji-kəl, sə-,lē-n°l-'ä-\ *adjective*
— **sel·e·nol·o·gist** \,se-lə-'nä-lə-jist\ *noun*

Se·leu·cid \sə-'lü-səd, sə-'lyü-\ *noun* [New Latin *seleucides,* from *Seleucus I*] (1851)
: a member of a Greek dynasty ruling Syria and at various times other Asian territories from 312 B.C. to 64 B.C.
— **Seleucid** *adjective*

¹**self** \'self, *Southern also* 'sef\ *pronoun* [Middle English (intensive pronoun), from Old English; akin to Old High German *selb,* intensive pronoun, and probably to Latin *suus* one's own — more at SUICIDE] (before 12th century)
: MYSELF, HIMSELF, HERSELF ⟨check payable to *self*⟩

²**self** *adjective* (before 12th century)
1 *obsolete* : IDENTICAL, SAME
2 *obsolete* : belonging to oneself : OWN
3 a : having a single character or quality throughout; *specifically* : having one color only ⟨a *self* flower⟩ **b** : of the same kind (as in color, material, or pattern) as something with which it is used ⟨*self* trimming⟩

³**self** *noun, plural* **selves** \'selvz, *Southern also* 'sevz\ (13th century)
1 a : the entire person of an individual **b** : the realization or embodiment of an abstraction
2 a (1) : an individual's typical character or behavior ⟨her true *self* was revealed⟩ (2) : an individual's temporary behavior or character ⟨his better *self*⟩ **b** : a person in prime condition ⟨feel like my old *self* today⟩
3 : the union of elements (as body, emotions, thoughts, and sensations) that constitute the individuality and identity of a person
4 : personal interest or advantage
5 : material that is part of an individual organism ⟨ability of the immune system to distinguish *self* from nonself⟩

⁴**self** (1914)
transitive verb
1 : INBREED
2 : to pollinate with pollen from the same flower or plant
intransitive verb
: to undergo self-pollination

self- *combining form* [Middle English, from Old English, from *self*]

1 a : oneself or itself ⟨*self*-supporting⟩ **b :** of oneself or itself ⟨*self*-abasement⟩ **c :** by oneself or itself ⟨*self*-propelled⟩ ⟨*self*-acting⟩
2 a : to, with, for, or toward oneself or itself ⟨*self*-consistent⟩ ⟨*self*-addressed⟩ ⟨*self*-love⟩ **b :** of or in oneself or itself inherently ⟨*self*-evident⟩ **c :** from or by means of oneself or itself ⟨*self*-fertile⟩

self–abase·ment
self–ab·ne·gat·ing
self–ab·ne·ga·tion
self–ac·cel·er·at·ing
self–ac·cep·tance
self–ac·cu·sa·tion
self–ac·cu·sa·to·ry
self–ac·cus·ing
self–ac·knowl·edged
self–ad·just·ing
self–ad·min·is·ter
self–ad·min·is·tra·tion
self–ad·mit·ted
self–ad·mit·ted·ly
self–ad·u·la·to·ry
self–ad·vance·ment
self–ad·ver·tise·ment
self–ad·ver·tis·er
self–af·fir·ma·tion
self–ag·gran·dize·ment
self–ag·gran·diz·ing
self–alien·ation
self–anoint·ed
self–ap·prais·al
self–ap·pro·ba·tion
self–as·sess·ment
self–as·sign·ment
self–au·then·ti·cat·ing
self–avowed
self–bet·ter·ment
self–can·cel
self–care
self–car·i·ca·ture
self–cas·ti·gate
self–cas·ti·ga·tion
self–cen·sor·ship
self–char·ac·ter·i·za·tion
self–clas·si·fi·ca·tion
self–clean·ing
self–com·mand
self–com·mun·ing
self–com·mu·nion
self–com·pla·cen·cy
self–com·pla·cent
self–con·dem·na·tion
self–con·demned
self–con·firm·ing
self–con·se·cra·tion
self–con·sti·tut·ed
self–con·sum·ing
self–con·tempt
self–cre·at·ed
self–cre·a·tion
self–crit·i·cal
self–crit·i·cism
self–cri·tique
self–cul·ti·va·tion
self–cul·ture
self–damn·ing
self–de·base·ment
self–de·ceit
self–de·ceive
self–de·cep·tion
self–de·feat·ing
self–de·lud·ed
self–de·lud·ing
self–de·lu·sion
self–den·i·grat·ing
self–den·i·gra·tion
self–de·pen·dence
self–de·pen·dent

self–dep·re·cat·ing
self–dep·re·cat·ing·ly
self–dep·re·ca·tion
self–dep·re·ca·to·ry
self–de·pre·ci·a·tion
self–de·scribed
self–de·scrip·tion
self–de·scrip·tive
self–de·vel·op·ment
self–de·vour·ing
self–dif·fer·en·ti·a·tion
self–di·rect·ed
self–di·rect·ing
self–di·rec·tion
self–di·rec·tive
self–dis·gust
self–dis·play
self–dis·sat·is·fac·tion
self–doubt
self–ed·u·cat·ed
self–ed·u·cat·ing
self–ed·u·ca·tion
self–ef·face·ment
self–ef·fac·ing
self–eman·ci·pa·tion
self–emas·cu·la·tion
self–en·closed
self–en·grossed
self–en·hance·ment
self–eval·u·ate
self–eval·u·a·tion
self–ex·clu·sion
self–ex·cul·pa·tion
self–ex·hi·bi·tion
self–ex·is·tence
self–ex·is·tent
self–ex·plain·ing
self–ex·tinc·tion
self–fi·nance
self–formed
self–gen·er·ate
self–giv·ing
self–guid·ed
self–hate
self–hat·ing
self–ha·tred
self–heal·ing
self–help
self–hum·bling
self–hu·mil·i·a·tion
self–hyp·no·sis
self–idol·a·try
self–im·posed
self–im·prove·ment
self–im·prov·er
self–in·du·ced
self–in·fat·u·at·ed
self–in·fla·tion
self–in·flict·ed
self–ini·ti·at·ed
self–in·struct·ed
self–in·struc·tion
self–in·struc·tion·al
self–in·ter·view
self–in·vent·ed
self–in·ven·tion
self–iso·la·tion
self–la·beled
self–lac·er·at·ing
self–lac·er·a·tion
self–loath·ing
self–lock·ing
self–lu·bri·cat·ing
self–lu·mi·nous

self–main·te·nance
self–man·age·ment
self–mas·tery
self–med·i·ca·tion
self–mock·ery
self–mock·ing
self–mor·ti·fi·ca·tion
self–mo·ti·vat·ed
self–mu·ti·lat·ing
self–mu·ti·la·tion
self–ne·gat·ing
self–ob·sessed
self–op·er·at·ing
self–or·dained
self–ori·ent·ed
self–par·o·dist
self–par·o·dy
self–penned
self–per·pet·u·at·ing
self–per·pet·u·a·tion
self–pla·gia·rism
self–pleas·ing
self–po·lic·ing
self–praise
self–pre·oc·cu·pa·tion
self–pre·oc·cu·pied
self–pre·serv·ing
self–pro·claimed
self–pro·duced
self–pro·fessed
self–pro·mot·er
self–pro·mot·ing
self–pro·mo·tion
self–pro·tec·tion
self–pro·tec·tive
self–pro·tec·tive·ness
self–pun·ish·ing

self–pun·ish·ment
self–raised
self–re·crim·i·na·tion
self–ref·er·en·tial
self–re·fer·ring
self–re·flex·ive
self–ref·or·ma·tion
self–reg·u·la·tion
self–reg·u·la·tive
self–reg·u·la·to·ry
self–re·in·forc·ing
self–re·new·al
self–re·new·ing
self–re·nounc·ing
self–re·nun·ci·a·tion
self–re·proach
self–re·proach·ful
self–re·proof
self–re·prov·ing
self–re·straint
self–rid·i·cule
self–sat·i·riz·ing
self–se·lect·ed
self–se·lec·tion
self–set
self–sur·ren·der
self–sus·tained
self–ther·a·py
self–tor·ment
self–tor·men·tor
self–tor·ture
self–tran·scen·dence
self–trans·for·ma·tion
self–un·der·stand·ing
self–val·i·dat·ing
self–wor·ship
self–wor·ship·er

self–aban·doned \ˌself-ə-'ban-dənd\ *adjective* (1791)
: abandoned by oneself; *especially* **:** given up to one's impulses
self–aban·don·ment \-dən-mənt\ *noun* (1818)
1 : a surrender of one's selfish interests or desires
2 : a lack of self-restraint
self–ab·sorbed \-əb-'sȯrbd, -'zȯrbd\ *adjective* (1847)
: absorbed in one's own thoughts, activities, or interests
self–ab·sorp·tion \-'sȯrp-shən, -'zȯrp-\ *noun* (1862)
: preoccupation with oneself
self–abuse \-ə-'byüs\ *noun* (1605)
1 : reproach of oneself
2 : MASTURBATION
3 : abuse of one's body or health
self–act·ing \-'ak-tiŋ\ *adjective* (circa 1680)
: acting or capable of acting of or by itself **:** AUTOMATIC
self–ac·tiv·i·ty \-ˌak-'ti-və-tē\ *noun* (1644)
: independent and especially self-determined activity
self–ac·tu·al·ize \-'ak-ch(ə-w)ə-ˌlīz, -sh(ə-w)ə-ˌlīz\ *intransitive verb* (1874)
: to realize fully one's potential
— **self–ac·tu·al·i·za·tion** \-ˌak-ch(ə-w)ə-lə-'zā-shən, -sh(ə-w)ə-lə-\ *noun*
self–ad·dressed \-ə-'drest, -'a-ˌdrest\ *adjective* (1904)
: addressed for return to the sender ⟨a *self-addressed* envelope⟩
self–ad·he·sive \-əd-'hē-siv, -ziv\ *adjective* (1958)
: having a side coated with an adhesive that sticks without wetting ⟨*self-adhesive* labels⟩
self–ad·just·ment \-ə-'jəs(t)-mənt\ *noun* (1848)
: adjustment to oneself or one's environment
self–ad·mi·ra·tion \-ˌad-mə-'rā-shən\ *noun* (1661)
: SELF-CONCEIT
self–af·fect·ed \-ə-'fek-təd\ *adjective* (1606)

: CONCEITED, SELF-LOVING
self–anal·y·sis \-ə-'na-lə-səs\ *noun* (1860)
: a systematic attempt by an individual to understand his or her own personality without the aid of another person
self–an·a·lyt·i·cal \-ˌa-nᵊl-'i-ti-kəl\ *also* **self–an·a·lyt·ic** *adjective* (1943)
: using self-analysis
self–an·ni·hi·la·tion \-ə-ˌnī-ə-'lā-shən\ *noun* (1647)
: annihilation of the self (as in mystical contemplation of God)
self–ap·plaud·ing \-ə-'plȯ-diŋ\ *adjective* (1654)
: marked by self-applause
self–ap·plause \-'plȯz\ *noun* (1678)
: an expression or feeling of approval of oneself
self–ap·point·ed \-ə-'pȯin-təd\ *adjective* (1799)
: appointed by oneself **:** SELF-STYLED
self–as·sem·bly \-ə-'sem-blē\ *noun* (1966)
: the process by which a complex macromolecule (as collagen) or a supramolecular system (as a virus) spontaneously assembles itself from its components
— **self–as·sem·ble** \-ə-'sem-bəl\ *intransitive verb*
self–as·sert·ing \-ə-'sər-tiŋ\ *adjective* (1837)
1 : asserting oneself or one's own rights, claims, or opinions
2 a : SELF-ASSURED, CONFIDENT **b :** ARROGANT
— **self–as·sert·ing·ly** \-tiŋ-lē\ *adverb*
self–as·ser·tion \-ə-'sər-shən\ *noun* (1806)
1 : the act of asserting oneself or one's own rights, claims, or opinions
2 : the act of asserting one's superiority over others
self–as·ser·tive \-'sər-tiv\ *adjective* (1865)
: given to or characterized by self-assertion
synonym see AGGRESSIVE
— **self–as·ser·tive·ly** *adverb*
— **self–as·ser·tive·ness** *noun*
self–as·sump·tion \-ə-'səm(p)-shən\ *noun* (1606)
: SELF-CONCEIT
self–as·sur·ance \-ə-'shȯr-ən(t)s\ *noun* (1594)
: SELF-CONFIDENCE
self–as·sured \-'shȯrd\ *adjective* (1711)
: sure of oneself **:** SELF-CONFIDENT
— **self–as·sured·ly** \-'shȯr-əd-lē, -'shȯrd-\ *adverb*
— **self–as·sured·ness** \-'shȯr-əd-nəs, -'shȯrd-\ *noun*
self–aware \-ə-'war, -'wer\ *adjective* (circa 1934)
: characterized by self-awareness
self–aware·ness *noun* (1880)
: an awareness of one's own personality or individuality
self–belt \'self-'belt\ *noun* (1965)
: a belt made of the same material as the garment with which it is worn
— **self–belt·ed** \-'bel-təd\ *adjective*
self–be·tray·al \ˌself-bi-'trā-(ə)l\ *noun* (1857)
: SELF-REVELATION
self–born \-'bȯrn\ *adjective* (1587)
1 : arising within the self ⟨*self-born* sorrows⟩
2 : springing from a prior self ⟨phoenix rising *self-born* from the fire⟩
self–ca·ter·ing \-'kā-tər-iŋ\ *adjective* (1970)
British **:** provided with lodging and cooking facilities but not meals ⟨*self-catering* holiday cottages⟩
self–cen·tered \-'sen-tərd\ *adjective* (circa 1764)
1 : independent of outside force or influence **:** SELF-SUFFICIENT

\ə\ abut \ᵊ\ kitten \ər\ further \a\ ash \ā\ ace \ä\ mop, mar \au̇\ out \ch\ chin \e\ bet \ē\ easy \g\ go \i\ hit \ī\ ice \j\ job \ŋ\ sing \ō\ go \ȯ\ law \ȯi\ boy \th\ thin \t̶h̶\ the \ü\ loot \u̇\ foot \y\ yet \zh\ vision *see also* Guide to Pronunciation

2 : concerned solely with one's own desires, needs, or interests
— **self·cen·tered·ly** adverb
— **self·cen·tered·ness** noun
self·clos·ing \-'klō-ziŋ\ adjective (circa 1875)
: closing or shutting automatically after being opened
self·cock·ing \-'kä-kiŋ\ adjective (1862)
of a firearm **:** cocked by the operation of some part of the action ⟨self-cocking on pushing the bolt forward⟩
self·col·lect·ed \-kə-'lek-təd\ adjective (circa 1711)
: SELF-POSSESSED
self·col·ored \-'kə-lərd\ adjective (1759)
: of a single color ⟨a self-colored flower⟩
self·com·pat·i·ble \-kəm-'pa-tə-bəl\ adjective (1922)
: capable of effective self-pollination that results in the production of seeds and fruits
— **self·com·pat·i·bil·i·ty** \-,pa-tə-'bi-lə-tē\ noun
self·com·posed \-kəm-'pōzd\ adjective (circa 1934)
: having control over one's emotions **:** CALM
— **self·com·pos·ed·ly** \-'pō-zəd-lē\ adverb
— **self·com·posed·ness** \-'pō-zəd-nəs, -'pōz(d)-nəs\ noun
self·con·ceit \-kən-'sēt\ noun (circa 1589)
: an exaggerated opinion of one's own qualities or abilities **:** VANITY
— **self·con·ceit·ed** \-'sē-təd\ adjective
self·con·cept \'self-'kän-,sept\ noun (1925)
: the mental image one has of oneself
self·con·cep·tion \,self-kən-'sep-shən\ noun (1950)
: SELF-CONCEPT
self·con·cern \-'sərn\ noun (1681)
: a selfish or morbid concern for oneself
— **self·con·cerned** \-'sərnd\ adjective
self·con·fessed \-'fest\ adjective (circa 1900)
: openly acknowledged by oneself **:** AVOWED
— **self·con·fess·ed·ly** \-'fe-səd-lē, -'fest-lē\ adverb
self·con·fes·sion \-'fe-shən\ noun (circa 1961)
: open acknowledgment **:** AVOWAL
self·con·fi·dence \-'kän-fə-dən(t)s, -,den(t)s\ noun (1637)
: confidence in oneself and in one's powers and abilities
— **self·con·fi·dent** \-fə-dənt, -,dent\ adjective
— **self·con·fi·dent·ly** adverb
self·con·fron·ta·tion \-,kän-(,)frən-'tā-shən\ noun (1961)
: SELF-ANALYSIS
self·con·grat·u·la·tion \-kən-,gra-chə-'lā-shən, -,gra-jə-\ noun (1712)
: congratulation of oneself; especially **:** a complacent acknowledgment of one's own superiority or good fortune
self·con·grat·u·la·to·ry \-'gra-chə-lə-,tōr-ē, -,gra-jə-, -,tor-\ adjective (1877)
: expressive of self-congratulation ⟨self-congratulatory memoirs⟩
self·con·scious \-'kän(t)-shəs\ adjective (circa 1680)
1 a : conscious of one's own acts or states as belonging to or originating in oneself **:** aware of oneself as an individual **b :** intensely aware of oneself **:** CONSCIOUS ⟨a rising and self-conscious social class⟩; also **:** produced or done with such awareness ⟨self-conscious art⟩
2 : uncomfortably conscious of oneself as an object of the observation of others **:** ILL AT EASE
— **self·con·scious·ly** adverb
— **self·con·scious·ness** noun
self·con·se·quence \-'kän(t)-sə-,kwen(t)s, -si-kwən(t)s\ noun (1778)
: SELF-IMPORTANCE

self·con·sis·ten·cy \-kən-'sis-tən(t)-sē\ noun (1692)
: the quality or state of being self-consistent
self·con·sis·tent \-tənt\ adjective (1683)
: having each part logically consistent with the rest
self·con·tained \-kən-'tānd\ adjective (1591)
1 a : complete in itself **:** INDEPENDENT ⟨a self-contained machine⟩ ⟨a self-contained program of study⟩ **b :** BUILT-IN ⟨a lectern with a self-contained light fixture⟩
2 a : showing self-control **b :** formal and reserved in manner
— **self·con·tained·ly** \-'tā-nəd-lē, -'tānd-lē\ adverb
— **self·con·tained·ness** \-'tā-nəd-nəs, -'tān(d)-nəs\ noun
— **self·con·tain·ment** \-'tān-mənt\ noun
self·con·tam·i·na·tion \-kən-,ta-mə-'nā-shən\ noun (1955)
1 : contamination by oneself
2 : contamination from within
self·con·tent \-kən-'tent\ noun (1654)
: SELF-SATISFACTION
self·con·tent·ed \-'ten-təd\ adjective (1818)
: SELF-SATISFIED
— **self·con·tent·ed·ly** adverb
— **self·con·tent·ed·ness** noun
self·con·tent·ment \-'tent-mənt\ noun (1815)
: SELF-SATISFACTION
self·con·tra·dic·tion \-,kän-trə-'dik-shən\ noun (1658)
1 : contradiction of oneself
2 : a self-contradictory statement or proposition
self·con·tra·dic·to·ry \-'dik-t(ə-)rē\ adjective (1657)
: consisting of two contradictory members or parts
self·con·trol \-kən-'trōl\ noun (1711)
: restraint exercised over one's own impulses, emotions, or desires
— **self·con·trolled** \-'trōld\ adjective
self·cor·rect·ing \-kə-'rek-tiŋ\ adjective (1939)
: correcting or compensating for one's own errors or weaknesses
self·cor·rec·tive \-'rek-tiv\ adjective (circa 1925)
: SELF-CORRECTING
self·deal·ing \'self-'dē-liŋ\ noun (1940)
: financial dealing that is not at arm's length; especially **:** borrowing from or lending to a company by a controlling individual primarily to the individual's own advantage
self·de·fense \-di-'fen(t)s\ noun (1651)
1 : a plea of justification for the use of force or for homicide
2 : the act of defending oneself, one's property, or a close relative
self·de·fen·sive \-'fen(t)-siv\ adjective (1828)
: of, relating to, or given to self-defense ⟨a self-defensive person⟩ ⟨a self-defensive attitude⟩
self·def·i·ni·tion \-,de-fə-'ni-shən\ noun (1957)
: the evaluation by oneself of one's worth as an individual in distinction from one's interpersonal or social roles
self·de·ni·al \-di-'nī(-ə)l\ noun (1642)
: a restraint or limitation of one's own desires or interests
self·de·ny·ing \-'nī-iŋ\ adjective (1632)
: showing self-denial
— **self·de·ny·ing·ly** \-iŋ-lē\ adverb
self·de·spair \-di-'spar, -'sper\ noun (1677)
: despair of oneself **:** HOPELESSNESS
self·de·stroy·er \-di-'strói(-ə)r\ noun (1654)
: one who destroys oneself
self·de·stroy·ing \-'strói-iŋ\ adjective (1645)
: SELF-DESTRUCTIVE
self·de·struct \-di-'strəkt\ intransitive verb (1968)
: to destroy oneself or itself

self·de·struct adjective
self·de·struc·tion \-'strək-shən\ noun (circa 1586)
: destruction of oneself; especially **:** SUICIDE
self·de·struc·tive \-'strək-tiv\ adjective (1654)
: acting or tending to harm or destroy oneself; also **:** SUICIDAL
— **self·de·struc·tive·ness** noun
self·de·ter·mi·na·tion \-di-,tər-mə-'nā-shən\ noun (circa 1670)
1 : free choice of one's own acts or states without external compulsion
2 : determination by the people of a territorial unit of their own future political status
self·de·ter·mined \-'tər-mənd\ adjective (circa 1670)
: determined by oneself
self·de·ter·min·ing \-'tər-mə-niŋ, -'tərm-niŋ\ adjective (1662)
: capable of determining one's or its own acts
self·de·ter·min·ism \-'tər-mə-,ni-zəm\ noun (1936)
: a doctrine that the actions of a self are determined by itself
self·de·vot·ed \-di-'vō-təd\ adjective (1713)
: characterized by total devotion of oneself (as to a cause)
— **self·de·vot·ed·ness** noun
self·dis·ci·pline \-'di-sə-plən\ noun (1838)
: correction or regulation of oneself for the sake of improvement
self·dis·ci·plined \-plənd\ adjective (1932)
: capable of or subject to self-discipline
self·dis·cov·ery \-dis-'kə-v(ə-)rē\ noun (1924)
: the act or process of achieving self-knowledge
self·dis·trust \-'trəst\ noun (1789)
: a lack of confidence in oneself **:** DIFFIDENCE
— **self·dis·trust·ful** \-fəl\ adjective
self·dra·ma·ti·za·tion \,self-,dra-mə-tə-'zā-shən, -,drä-\ noun (1937)
: the act or an instance of dramatizing oneself
self·dra·ma·tiz·ing \-'dra-mə-,tī-ziŋ, -'drä-\ adjective (1938)
: seeing and presenting oneself as an important or dramatic figure
self·drive \'self-'drīv\ adjective (1929)
chiefly British **:** being a rental car
self·elect·ed \,self-ə-'lek-təd\ adjective (1818)
: SELF-APPOINTED
self·em·ployed \-im-'plóid\ adjective (1946)
: earning income directly from one's own business, trade, or profession rather than as a specified salary or wages from an employer
— **self·employed** noun
self·em·ploy·ment \-'plói-mənt\ noun (1745)
: the state of being self-employed
self·en·er·giz·ing \-'e-nər-,jī-ziŋ\ adjective (1931)
: containing means for augmentation of power within itself ⟨a self-energizing brake⟩
self·en·forc·ing \-in-'fór-siŋ, -'for-\ adjective (1952)
: containing in itself the authority or means that provide for its enforcement
self·en·rich·ment \-in-'rich-mənt\ noun (1920)
: the act or process of increasing one's intellectual or spiritual resources
self·es·teem \-ə-'stēm\ noun (1657)
1 : a confidence and satisfaction in oneself **:** SELF-RESPECT
2 : SELF-CONCEIT
self·ev·i·dence \-'e-və-dən(t)s, -,den(t)s\ noun (1671)
: the quality or state of being self-evident
self·ev·i·dent \-dənt, -,dent\ adjective (1671)
: evident without proof or reasoning
— **self·ev·i·dent·ly** adverb
self·ex·am·i·na·tion \-ig-,za-mə-'nā-shən\ noun (1647)

1 : a reflective examination (as of one's beliefs or motives) : INTROSPECTION
2 : examination of one's body especially for evidence of disease
self·ex·cit·ed \-ik-'sī-təd\ *adjective* (circa 1896)
: excited by a current produced by the generator itself ⟨*self-excited* generators⟩
self·ex·e·cut·ing \-'ek-sə-,kyü-tiŋ\ *adjective* (1868)
: taking effect immediately without implementing legislation ⟨a *self-executing* treaty⟩
self·ex·iled \-'eg-,zīld, -'ek-,sīld\ *adjective* (1737)
: exiled by one's own wish or decision
self·ex·plan·a·to·ry \ik-'spla-nə-,tȯr-ē, -,tȯr-\ *adjective* (1898)
: explaining itself : capable of being understood without explanation
self·ex·plo·ra·tion \-,ek-splə-'rā-shən, -,splȯ-\ *noun* (1959)
: the examination and analysis of one's own unrealized spiritual or intellectual capacities
self·ex·pres·sion \-ik-'spre-shən\ *noun* (1892)
: the expression of one's own personality : assertion of one's individual traits
— **self·ex·pres·sive** \-'spre-siv\ *adjective*
self-feed \'self-'fēd\ *transitive verb* **-fed** \-'fed\; **-feed·ing** (circa 1924)
: to provide rations to (animals) in bulk so as to permit feeding as wanted
self-feed·er \-'fē-dər\ *noun* (1924)
: a device for providing feed to livestock that is equipped with a feed hopper that automatically supplies a trough below
self-feel·ing \'self-'fē-liŋ\ *noun* (1879)
: self-centered emotion
self-fer·tile \,self-'fər-t°l\ *adjective* (1865)
: fertile by means of its own pollen or sperm
— **self-fer·til·i·ty** \-(,)fər-'ti-lə-tē\ *noun*
self-fer·til·i·za·tion \-,fər-t°l-ə-'zā-shən\ *noun* (1859)
: fertilization effected by union of ova with pollen or sperm from the same individual
self-fer·til·ized \-'fər-t°l-,īzd\ *adjective* (1871)
: fertilized by one's own pollen or sperm
self-fer·til·iz·ing \-,ī-ziŋ\ *adjective* (1859)
: SELF-FERTILIZED
self-flag·el·la·tion \-,fla-jə-'lā-shən\ *noun* (1845)
: extreme criticism of oneself
self-flat·ter·ing \-'fla-tə-riŋ\ *adjective* (circa 1586)
: given to self-flattery
self-flat·tery \-tə-rē\ *noun* (1680)
: the glossing over of one's own weaknesses or mistakes and the exaggeration of one's own good qualities and achievements
self-for·get·ful \-fər-'get-fəl\ *adjective* (1848)
: having or showing no thought of self or selfish interests
— **self-for·get·ful·ly** \-fə-lē\ *adverb*
— **self-for·get·ful·ness** *noun*
self-for·get·ting \-'ge-tiŋ\ *adjective* (1847)
: SELF-FORGETFUL
— **self-for·get·ting·ly** \-tiŋ-lē\ *adverb*
self–fruit·ful \'self-'früt-fəl\ *adjective* (1940)
: capable of setting a crop of self-pollinated fruit
— **self–fruit·ful·ness** *noun*
self–ful·fill·ing \,self-fül-'fi-liŋ\ *adjective* (1949)
1 : marked by or achieving self-fulfillment
2 : becoming real or true by virtue of having been predicted or expected ⟨a *self-fulfilling* prophecy⟩
self–ful·fill·ment \-'fil-mənt\ *noun* (circa 1864)
: fulfillment of oneself
self-giv·en \-'gi-vən\ *adjective* (1742)
1 : derived from itself ⟨a *self-given* entity⟩
2 : given by oneself ⟨*self-given* authority⟩

self-glo·ri·fi·ca·tion \-,glȯr-ə-fə-'kā-shən, -,glȯr-\ *noun* (1838)
: a feeling or expression of one's own superiority
self-glo·ri·fy·ing \-'glȯr-ə-,fī-iŋ, -'glȯr-\ *adjective* (1860)
: given to or marked by boasting : BOASTFUL
self-glo·ry \-'glȯr-ē, -'glȯr-ē\ *noun* (1647)
: personal vanity : PRIDE
self-gov·er·nance \-'gə-vər-nən(t)s\ *noun* (1964)
: SELF-GOVERNMENT 2
self-gov·erned \-'gə-vərnd\ *adjective* (1709)
1 : not influenced or controlled by others
2 : exercising self-control
self-gov·ern·ing \-'gə-vər-niŋ\ *adjective* (1845)
: having control or rule over oneself; *specifically* : having self-government : AUTONOMOUS
self-gov·ern·ment \-'gə-vər(n)-mənt, -'gə-v°m-ənt\ *noun* (1734)
1 : SELF-COMMAND, SELF-CONTROL
2 : government under the control and direction of the inhabitants of a political unit rather than by an outside authority; *broadly* : control of one's own affairs
self-grat·i·fi·ca·tion \-,gra-tə-fə-'kā-shən\ *noun* (1677)
: the act of pleasing oneself or of satisfying one's desires; *especially* : the satisfying of one's own sexual urges
self-grat·u·la·tion \-,gra-chə-'lā-shən\ *noun* (1802)
: SELF-CONGRATULATION
self-grat·u·la·to·ry \-'gra-chə-lə-,tȯr-ē, -,tȯr-\ *adjective* (1859)
: SELF-CONGRATULATORY
self-heal \'self-,hēl\ *noun* (14th century)
: a blue-flowered Eurasian mint (*Prunella vulgaris*) naturalized throughout North America and formerly considered to have medicinal properties
self-hood \-,hùd\ *noun* (1649)
1 : INDIVIDUALITY
2 : the quality or state of being selfish
self-iden·ti·cal \,self-ī-'den-ti-kəl, -ə-'den-\ *adjective* (1877)
: having self-identity
self-iden·ti·fi·ca·tion \-,den-tə-fə-'kā-shən\ *noun* (1941)
: identification with someone or something outside oneself
self-iden·ti·ty \-'den-tə-tē, -'de-nə-tē\ *noun* (1866)
1 : sameness of a thing with itself
2 : INDIVIDUALITY ⟨self-understanding is the necessary condition of a sense of *self-identity* —J. C. Murray⟩
self-ig·nite \-ig-'nīt\ *intransitive verb* (1943)
: to become ignited without flame or spark (as under high compression)
self-ig·ni·tion \-'ni-shən\ *noun* (1903)
: ignition without flame or spark
self-im·age \'self-'i-mij\ *noun* (1939)
: one's conception of oneself or of one's role
self-im·mo·la·tion \,self-,i-mə-'lā-shən\ *noun* (1817)
: a deliberate and willing sacrifice of oneself often by fire
— **self-im·mo·late** \-'i-mə-,lāt\ *verb*
self-im·por·tance \-im-'pȯr-t°n(t)s, -t°n(t)s\ *noun* (circa 1775)
1 : an exaggerated estimate of one's own importance : SELF-CONCEIT
2 : arrogant or pompous behavior
self-im·por·tant \-t°nt, -tənt\ *adjective* (circa 1775)
: having or showing self-importance
— **self-im·por·tant·ly** *adverb*
self-in·clu·sive \-in-'klü-siv, -ziv\ *adjective* (circa 1909)
1 : enclosing itself
2 : complete in itself
self-in·com·pat·i·ble \-,in-kəm-'pa-tə-bəl\ *adjective* (1922)
: incapable of effective self-pollination

— **self-in·com·pat·i·bil·i·ty** \-,pa-tə-'bi-lə-tē\ *noun*
self-in·crim·i·nat·ing \-in-'kri-mə-,nā-tiŋ\ *adjective* (1931)
: serving or tending to incriminate oneself
self-in·crim·i·na·tion \-,kri-mə-'nā-shən\ *noun* (1911)
: incrimination of oneself; *specifically* : the giving of testimony which will likely subject one to criminal prosecution
self-in·duc·tance \-'dək-tən(t)s\ *noun* (1865)
: inductance in which an electromotive force is produced by self-induction
self-in·duc·tion \-'dək-shən\ *noun* (1873)
: induction of an electromotive force in a circuit by a varying current in the same circuit
self-in·dul·gence \-'dəl-jən(t)s\ *noun* (1753)
: excessive or unrestrained gratification of one's own appetites, desires, or whims
— **self-in·dul·gent** \-jənt\ *adjective*
— **self-in·dul·gent·ly** *adverb*
self-in·sur·ance \in-'shùr-ən(t)s, -'in-,\ *noun* (circa 1897)
: insurance of oneself or of one's own interests by the setting aside of money at regular intervals to provide a fund to cover possible losses
self-insure \-in-'shùr\ *verb* (1932)
: to insure oneself; *especially* : to practice self-insurance
— **self-insurer** \-'shùr-ər\ *noun*
self-in·ter·est \-'in-t(ə-)rəst, -'in-tə-,rest, -,trest; -'in-tərst\ *noun* (1649)
1 : a concern for one's own advantage and well-being ⟨acted out of *self-interest* and fear⟩
2 : one's own interest or advantage ⟨*self-interest* requires that we be generous in foreign aid⟩
— **self-in·ter·est·ed** *adjective*
— **self-in·ter·est·ed·ness** *noun*
self-in·volved \-in-'välvd, -'vȯlvd also -'vävd or 'vȯvd\ *adjective* (1842)
: SELF-ABSORBED
self·ish \'sel-fish\ *adjective* (1640)
1 : concerned excessively or exclusively with oneself : seeking or concentrating on one's own advantage, pleasure, or well-being without regard for others
2 : arising from concern with one's own welfare or advantage in disregard of others ⟨a *selfish* act⟩
— **self·ish·ly** *adverb*
— **self·ish·ness** *noun*
self-jus·ti·fi·ca·tion \,self-,jəs-tə-fə-'kā-shən\ *noun* (circa 1775)
: the act or an instance of making excuses for oneself
self-jus·ti·fy·ing \-'jəs-tə-,fī-iŋ\ *adjective* (1740)
: seeking to justify oneself
self-know·ing \-'nō-iŋ\ *adjective* (1667)
: having self-knowledge
self-knowl·edge \-'nä-lij\ *noun* (circa 1613)
: knowledge or understanding of one's own capabilities, character, feelings, or motivations
self·less \'sel-fləs\ *adjective* (1825)
: having no concern for self : UNSELFISH
— **self·less·ly** *adverb*
— **self·less·ness** *noun*
self-lim·it·ed \,self-'li-mə-təd\ *adjective* (1845)
: limited by one's or its own nature; *specifically* : running a definite and limited course ⟨a *self-limited* disease⟩
self-lim·it·ing \-tiŋ\ *adjective* (1863)
: limiting oneself or itself; *especially*, *of a disease* : SELF-LIMITED
self-liq·ui·dat·ing \-'li-kwə-,dā-tiŋ\ *adjective* (1915)

\ə\ abut \°\ kitten \ər\ **further** \a\ ash \ā\ ace
\ä\ mop, mar \au̇\ **out** \ch\ **chin** \e\ bet \ē\ **easy**
\g\ go \i\ hit \ī\ ice \j\ **job** \ŋ\ sing \ō\ **go**
\ȯ\ law \ȯi\ **boy** \th\ **thin** \t̲h̲\ **the** \ü\ **loot** \u̇\ **foot**
\y\ **yet** \zh\ **vision** *see also* Guide to Pronunciation

1 : of or relating to a commercial transaction in which goods are converted into cash in a short time
2 : generating funds from its own operations to repay the investment made to create it ⟨a *self-liquidating* housing project⟩

self–load·er \-'lō-dər\ *noun* (circa 1936)
: a semiautomatic firearm
self–load·ing \-diŋ\ *adjective* (1899)
of a firearm : SEMIAUTOMATIC
self–love \'self-'ləv\ *noun* (1563)
: love of self: **a** : CONCEIT **b** : regard for one's own happiness or advantage
— **self–lov·ing** \-'lə-viŋ\ *adjective*
self–made \'self-'mād\ *adjective* (1615)
: made such by one's own actions; *especially* : having achieved success or prominence by one's own efforts ⟨a *self-made* man⟩
self–mail·er \-'mā-lər\ *noun* (circa 1942)
: a folder that can be sent by mail without enclosure in an envelope by use of a gummed sticker or a precanceled stamp to hold the leaves together
self–mail·ing \-liŋ\ *adjective* (circa 1948)
: capable of being mailed without being enclosed in an envelope
self–moved \'self-'müvd\ *adjective* (circa 1670)
: moved by inherent power
self–mur·der \-'mər-dər\ *noun* (1563)
: SELF-DESTRUCTION, SUICIDE
self–ness \'self-nəs\ *noun* (circa 1586)
1 : EGOISM, SELFISHNESS
2 : PERSONALITY, SELFHOOD
self–ob·ser·va·tion \,self-,äb-sər-'vā-shən, -zər-\ *noun* (1832)
1 : INTROSPECTION
2 : observation of one's own appearance
self–opin·ion \-ə-'pin-yən\ *noun* (circa 1580)
: high or exaggerated opinion of oneself
: SELF-CONCEIT
self–opin·ion·at·ed \-yə-,nā-təd\ *adjective* (1671)
1 : CONCEITED
2 : stubbornly holding to one's own opinion
: OPINIONATED
— **self–opin·ion·at·ed·ness** *noun*
self–or·ga·ni·za·tion \-,or-gə-nə-'zā-shən, -,org-nə-\ *noun* (1898)
: organization of oneself or itself; *specifically* : the act or process of forming or joining a labor union
self–paced \'self-'pāst\ *adjective* (1962)
: designed to permit learning at the student's own pace ⟨*self-paced* mathematician course⟩
self–par·tial·i·ty \,self-,pär-shē-'a-lə-tē, -,pär-'sha-\ *noun* (1628)
1 : an excessive estimate of oneself as compared with others
2 : a prejudice in favor of one's own claims or interests
self–per·cep·tion \-pər-'sep-shən\ *noun* (1678)
: perception of oneself; *especially* : SELF-CONCEPT
self–pity \'self-'pi-tē\ *noun* (1621)
: pity for oneself; *especially* : a self-indulgent dwelling on one's own sorrows or misfortunes
— **self–pity·ing** \-tē-iŋ\ *adjective*
— **self–pity·ing·ly** \-iŋ-lē\ *adverb*
self–pleased \-'plēzd\ *adjective* (1748)
: SELF-SATISFIED
self–poise \-'pȯiz\ *noun* (1854)
: the quality or state of being self-poised
self–poised \-'pȯizd\ *adjective* (1621)
: having poise through self-command
self–pol·li·nate \'self-'pä-lə-,nāt\ (1890)
transitive verb
: SELF 2
intransitive verb
: to undergo self-pollination
self–pol·li·na·tion \,self-,pä-lə-'nā-shən\ *noun* (1872)
: the transfer of pollen from the anther of a flower to the stigma of the same flower or

sometimes to that of a genetically identical flower (as of the same plant or clone)
self–por·trait \-'pōr-trət, -'pȯr-, -,trāt\ *noun* (1831)
: a portrait of oneself done by oneself
self–pos·sessed \-pə-'zest *also* -'sest\ *adjective* (1818)
: having or showing self-possession : composed in mind or manner : CALM
— **self–pos·sessed·ly** \-'ze-səd-lē, -'se-; -'zest-lē, -'sest-\ *adverb*
self–pos·ses·sion \-pə-'ze-shən *also* -'se-\ *noun* (1745)
: control of one's emotions or reactions especially when under stress : PRESENCE OF MIND, COMPOSURE
synonym see CONFIDENCE
self–pres·er·va·tion \-,pre-zər-'vā-shən\ *noun* (circa 1614)
1 : preservation of oneself from destruction or harm
2 : a natural or instinctive tendency to act so as to preserve one's own existence
self–pride \'self-'prīd\ *noun* (circa 1586)
: pride in oneself or in that which relates to oneself
self–pro·pelled \,self-prə-'peld\ *adjective* (1899)
1 : containing within itself the means for its own propulsion ⟨a *self-propelled* vehicle⟩
2 : mounted on or fired from a moving vehicle ⟨a *self-propelled* gun⟩
self–pro·pel·ling \-'pe-liŋ\ *adjective* (1862)
: SELF-PROPELLED 1
self–pro·pul·sion \-'pəl-shən\ *noun* (circa 1934)
: propulsion by one's own power
self–pub·lished \-'pə-blisht\ *adjective* (1975)
: published by the author ⟨*self-published* book⟩
self–pu·ri·fi·ca·tion \-,pyùr-ə-fə-'kā-shən\ *noun* (1919)
1 : purification by natural process ⟨*self-purification* of water⟩
2 : purification of oneself
self–ques·tion \'self-'kwes-chən, -'kwesh-\ *noun* (1917)
: a question asked of oneself by oneself
self–ques·tion·ing \-chə-niŋ\ *noun* (1856)
: examination of one's own actions and motives
self–rat·ing \-'rā-tiŋ\ *noun* (1925)
: determination of one's own rating with reference to a standard scale
self–re·al·i·za·tion \-,rē-ə-lə-'zā-shən, -,ri-ə-\ *noun* (1874)
: fulfillment by oneself of the possibilities of one's character or personality
self–re·al·i·za·tion·ism \-shə-,ni-zəm\ *noun* (circa 1874)
: the ethical theory that the highest good for a person consists in realizing or fulfilling oneself usually on the assumption that one has certain inborn abilities constituting one's real or ideal self
— **self–re·al·i·za·tion·ist** \-sh(ə-)nist\ *noun*
self–rec·og·ni·tion \-,re-kig-'ni-shən, -kəg-\ *noun* (1946)
1 : recognition of one's own self
2 : the process by which the immune system of an organism distinguishes between the body's own chemicals, cells, and tissues and those of foreign organisms and agents
self–re·cord·ing \-ri-'kȯr-diŋ\ *adjective* (1875)
: making an automatic record ⟨*self-recording* instruments⟩
self–re·flec·tion \-ri-'flek-shən\ *noun* (1652)
: SELF-EXAMINATION 1
self–re·flec·tive \-ri-'flek-tiv\ *adjective* (1875)
: marked by or engaging in self-reflection
self–re·gard \-ri-'gärd\ *noun* (1595)
: regard for or consideration of oneself or one's own interests

self–re·gard·ing \-ri-'gär-diŋ\ *adjective* (1789)
: concerned with oneself or one's own interests
self–reg·u·lat·ing \-'re-gyə-,lā-tiŋ\ *adjective* (1837)
: regulating oneself or itself; *especially* : AUTOMATIC ⟨a *self-regulating* mechanism⟩
self–re·li·ance \-ri-'lī-ənts\ *noun* (1833)
: reliance on one's own efforts and abilities
self–re·li·ant \-ənt\ *adjective* (1848)
: having confidence in and exercising one's own powers or judgment
self–rep·li·cat·ing \-'re-plə-,kā-tiŋ\ *adjective* (1946)
: reproducing itself autonomously ⟨DNA is a *self-replicating* molecule⟩
— **self–rep·li·ca·tion** \-,re-plə-'kā-shən\ *noun*
self–re·spect \-ri-'spekt\ *noun* (circa 1814)
1 : a proper respect for oneself as a human being
2 : regard for one's own standing or position
self–re·spect·ing \-ri-'spek-tiŋ\ *adjective* (1786)
: having or characterized by self-respect
self–re·veal·ing \-ri-'vē-liŋ\ *adjective* (1839)
: marked by self-revelation
self–rev·e·la·tion \-,re-və-'lā-shən\ *noun* (1852)
: revelation of one's own thoughts, feelings, and attitudes especially without deliberate intent
self–re·ward·ing \-ri-'wȯr-diŋ\ *adjective* (1740)
: containing or producing its own reward ⟨virtue is *self-rewarding*⟩
self–righ·teous \-'rī-chəs\ *adjective* (circa 1680)
: convinced of one's own righteousness especially in contrast with the actions and beliefs of others : narrow-mindedly moralistic
— **self–righ·teous·ly** *adverb*
— **self–righ·teous·ness** *noun*
self–ris·ing flour \'self-'rī-ziŋ-\ *noun* (1854)
: a commercially prepared mixture of flour, salt, and a leavening agent
self–rule \'self-'rül\ *noun* (circa 1855)
: SELF-GOVERNMENT
self–rul·ing \-'rü-liŋ\ *adjective* (circa 1680)
: SELF-GOVERNING
self–sac·ri·fice \'self-'sa-krə-,fīs *also* -fəs *or* -,fīz\ *noun* (1805)
: sacrifice of oneself or one's interest for others or for a cause or ideal
self–sac·ri·fic·er \-,fī-sər *also* -fə- *or* -,fī-\ *noun* (1668)
: one that practices self-sacrifice
self–sac·ri·fic·ing \-,fīs-iŋ *also* -fə- *or* -,fī-\ *adjective* (1817)
: sacrificing oneself for others
— **self–sac·ri·fic·ing·ly** \-siŋ-lē\ *adverb*
self·same \'self-,sām\ *adjective* (15th century)
: being the one mentioned or in question : IDENTICAL ⟨left the *selfsame* day⟩
synonym see SAME
— **self·same·ness** \-,sām-nəs, -'sām-\ *noun*
self–sat·is·fac·tion \,self-,sa-təs-'fak-shən\ *noun* (1739)
: a usually smug satisfaction with oneself or one's position or achievements
self–sat·is·fied \'self-'sa-təs-,fīd\ *adjective* (1734)
: feeling or showing self-satisfaction
self–scru·ti·ny \'self-'skrü-t°n-ē, -'skrüt-nē\ *noun* (circa 1711)
: SELF-EXAMINATION
self–seal·ing \'self-'sē-liŋ\ *adjective* (1924)
1 : capable of sealing itself (as after puncture) ⟨a *self-sealing* tire⟩
2 : capable of being sealed by pressure without the addition of moisture ⟨*self-sealing* envelopes⟩
self–search·ing \-'sər-chiŋ\ *noun* (1687)

: SELF-QUESTIONING
self-seek·er \-'sē-kər\ *noun* (1632)
: a self-seeking person
¹**self-seek·ing** \-kiŋ\ *noun* (circa 1586)
: the act or practice of selfishly advancing one's own ends
²**self-seeking** *adjective* (circa 1628)
: seeking only to further one's own interests
self-serve \'self-'sərv\ *adjective* (1926)
: permitting self-service
self-ser·vice \'self-'sər-vəs\ *noun* (1919)
: the serving of oneself (as in a restaurant or service station) with goods or services to be paid for at a cashier's desk or by means of a coin-operated mechanism
— **self-service** *adjective*
self-serv·ing \-'sər-viŋ\ *adjective* (1827)
: serving one's own interests often in disregard of the truth or the interests of others
— **self-serv·ing·ly** *adverb*
self-slaugh·ter \-'slȯ-tər\ *noun* (1602)
: SUICIDE 1a
self-slaugh·tered \-tərd\ *adjective* (1593)
: killed by oneself
self-sow \'self-'sō\ *intransitive verb* **-sowed** \-'sōd\; **-sown** \-'sōn\ *or* **-sowed; -sow·ing** (1608)
: to sow itself by dropping seeds or by natural action (as of wind or water)
self-start·er \,self-'stär-tər\ *noun* (1894)
 1 : STARTER 3a
 2 : a person who has initiative
self-start·ing \-'stär-tiŋ\ *adjective* (1866)
: capable of starting by oneself or itself
self-ster·ile \-'ster-əl\ *adjective* (1876)
: sterile to its own pollen or sperm
— **self-ste·ril·i·ty** \-stə-'ri-lə-tē\ *noun*
self-stick \'self-'stik\ *adjective* (1947)
: capable of adhering to a surface by application of pressure without the addition of moisture
self-stim·u·la·tion \,self-,stim-yə-'lā-shən\ *noun* (1947)
: stimulation of oneself as a result of one's own activity or behavior (electrical *self-stimulation* of the brain); *especially* : MASTURBATION
— **self-stim·u·la·to·ry** \-'stim-yə-lə-,tōr-ē, -,tȯr-\ *adjective*
self-study \-'stə-dē\ *noun* (1683)
: study of oneself; *also* : a record of observations from such study
self-styled \-'stī(ə)ld\ *adjective* (1823)
: called by oneself (*self-styled* experts)
self-sub·sis·tent \,self-səb-'sis-tənt\ *adjective* (1647)
: subsisting independently of anything external to itself
— **self-sub·sis·tence** \-tən(t)s\ *noun*
self-sub·sist·ing \-'sis-tiŋ\ *adjective* (1654)
: SELF-SUBSISTENT
self-suf·fi·cien·cy \-sə-'fi-shən(t)-sē\ *noun* (1623)
: the quality or state of being self-sufficient
self-suf·fi·cient \-'fi-shənt\ *adjective* (1589)
 1 : able to maintain oneself or itself without outside aid : capable of providing for one's own needs
 2 : having an extreme confidence in one's own ability or worth : HAUGHTY, OVERBEARING
self-suf·fic·ing \-'fī-siŋ *also* -ziŋ\ *adjective* (1687)
: SELF-SUFFICIENT
— **self-suf·fic·ing·ly** *adverb*
— **self-suf·fic·ing·ness** *noun*
self-sug·ges·tion \-səg-'jes-chən, -sə-', -'jesh-\ *noun* (1892)
: AUTOSUGGESTION
self-sup·port \,self-sə-'pōrt, -'pȯrt\ *noun* (1774)
: independent support of oneself or itself
— **self-sup·port·ed** *adjective*
self-supporting *adjective* (1829)

: characterized by self-support: as **a** : meeting one's needs by one's own efforts or output **b** : supporting itself or its own weight (a *self-supporting* wall)
self-sus·tain·ing \-sə-'stā-niŋ\ *adjective* (1844)
 1 : maintaining or able to maintain oneself or itself by independent effort
 2 : maintaining or able to maintain itself once commenced (a *self-sustaining* nuclear reaction)
self-taught \'self-'tȯt\ *adjective* (1725)
 1 : having knowledge or skills acquired by one's own efforts without formal instruction (a *self-taught* musician)
 2 : learned by oneself (*self-taught* knowledge)
self-tol·er·ance \-'tä-lə-rən(t)s, -'täl-rən(t)s\ *noun* (1964)
: the physiological state that exists in an organism when its immune system has proceeded far enough in the process of self-recognition to lose the capacity to attack and destroy its own bodily constituents
self-treat·ment \-'trēt-mənt\ *noun* (1886)
: medication of oneself or treatment of one's own disease or condition without medical supervision or prescription
self-trust \-'trəst\ *noun* (1583)
: SELF-CONFIDENCE
self-will \-'wil\ *noun* (14th century)
: stubborn or willful adherence to one's own desires or ideas : OBSTINACY
self-willed \-'wild\ *adjective* (14th century)
: governed by one's own will : not yielding to the wishes of others : OBSTINATE
— **self-willed·ly** \-'wild-lē\ *adverb*
— **self-willed·ness** \-'wild-nəs\ *noun*
self-wind·ing \-'wīn-diŋ\ *adjective* (1825)
: not needing to be wound by hand (a *self-winding* watch)
self-worth \-'wərth\ *noun* (1944)
: SELF-ESTEEM
Sel·juk \'sel-,jük, sel-'\ *or* **Sel·ju·ki·an** \sel-'jü-kē-ən\ *adjective* [Turkish *Selçuk*, eponymous ancestor of the dynasties] (1834)
 1 : of or relating to any of several Turkish dynasties ruling over a great part of western Asia in the 11th, 12th, and 13th centuries
 2 : of, relating to, or characteristic of a Turkish people ruled over by a Seljuk dynasty
— **Seljuk** *or* **Seljukian** *noun*
¹**sell** \'sel\ *verb* **sold** \'sōld\; **sell·ing** [Middle English, from Old English *sellan*; akin to Old High German *sellen* to sell, Old Norse *sala* sale, Greek *helein* to take] (before 12th century)
transitive verb
 1 : to deliver or give up in violation of duty, trust, or loyalty : BETRAY — often used with *out*
 2 a (1) : to give up (property) to another for something of value (as money) (2) : to offer for sale **b** : to give up in return for something else especially foolishly or dishonorably (*sold* his birthright for a mess of pottage) **c** : to exact a price for (*sold* their lives dearly)
 3 a : to deliver into slavery for money **b** : to give into the power of another (*sold* his soul to the devil) **c** : to deliver the personal services of for money
 4 : to dispose of or manage for profit instead of in accordance with conscience, justice, or duty (*sold* their votes)
 5 a : to develop a belief in the truth, value, or desirability of : gain acceptance for (trying to *sell* a program to the Congress) **b** : to persuade or influence to a course of action or to the acceptance of something (*sell* children on reading)
 6 : to impose on : CHEAT
 7 a : to cause or promote the sale of (using television advertising to *sell* cereal) **b** : to make or attempt to make sales to **c** : to influence or induce to make a purchase
 8 : to achieve a sale of (*sold* a million copies)
intransitive verb

 1 : to dispose of something by sale
 2 : to achieve a sale; *also* : to achieve satisfactory sales (hoped that the new line would *sell*)
 3 : to have a specified price
— **sell·able** \'se-lə-bəl\ *adjective*
— **sell down the river** : to betray the faith of
— **sell short 1** : to make a short sale **2** : to fail to value properly : UNDERESTIMATE
²**sell** *noun* (1838)
 1 : a deliberate deception : HOAX
 2 : the act or an instance of selling
³**sell** *or* **selle** \'sel\ *noun* [Middle English *selle*, from Middle French, from Latin *sella* — more at SETTLE] (15th century)
archaic : SADDLE
⁴**sell** *chiefly Scottish variant of* SELF
sell·er \'se-lər\ *noun* (13th century)
 1 : one that offers for sale
 2 : a product offered for sale and selling well, to a specified extent, or in a specified manner (a million-copy *seller*) (a poor *seller*)
seller's market *noun* (1932)
: a market in which goods are scarce, buyers have a limited range of choice, and prices are high — compare BUYER'S MARKET
selling climax *noun* (circa 1949)
: a sharp decline in stock prices for a short time on very heavy trading volume followed by a rally
sell·ing–plat·er \'se-liŋ-,plā-tər\ *noun* (1886)
: a horse that runs in selling races
selling point *noun* (1923)
: an aspect or detail of something that is emphasized (as in selling or promoting)
selling race *noun* (1898)
: a claiming race in which the winning horse is put up for auction
sell-off \'sel-,ȯf\ *noun* (1937)
: a usually sudden sharp decline in security prices accompanied by increased volume of trading
sell off *intransitive verb* (circa 1700)
: to suffer a drop in prices
sell-out \'sel-,aȯt\ *noun* (1859)
 1 : the act or an instance of selling out
 2 : something sold out; *especially* : something (as a concert or contest) for which all tickets are sold
 3 : one who sells out
sell out (1796)
transitive verb
 1 : to sell the goods of (a debtor) in order to satisfy creditors
 2 : to sell security or commodity holdings of usually to satisfy an uncovered margin
 3 a : to sell all the available tickets for **b** : to sell all of (the merchandise was quickly *sold out*)
intransitive verb
 1 : to dispose of one's goods by sale; *especially* : to sell one's business
 2 : to betray one's cause or associates
 3 : to be or achieve a sellout
sel·syn \'sel-,sin\ *noun* [*self-*synchronizing] (1926)
: a system comprising a generator and a motor so connected by wire that angular rotation or position in the generator is reproduced simultaneously in the motor — called also *synchro*
selt·zer \'selt-sər\ *noun* [modification of German *Selterser* (*Wasser*) water of Selters, from Nieder *Selters*, Germany] (1775)
: artificially carbonated water
sel·vage *or* **sel·vedge** \'sel-vij\ *noun* [Middle English *selvage*, probably from Middle Dutch *selvegge*, *selvage*, from *selv* self + *egge* edge; akin to Old English *self* and to Old English *ecg* edge — more at EDGE] (15th century)

1 a : the edge on either side of a woven or flat-knitted fabric so finished as to prevent raveling; *specifically* **:** a narrow border often of different or heavier threads than the fabric and sometimes in a different weave **b :** an edge (as of fabric or paper) meant to be cut off and discarded

2 : an outer or peripheral part **:** BORDER, EDGE

— **sel·vaged** *or* **sel·vedged** \-vijd\ *adjective*

selves *plural of* SELF

se·man·tic \si-'man-tik\ *also* **se·man·ti·cal** \-ti-kəl\ *adjective* [Greek *sēmantikos* significant, from *sēmainein* to signify, mean, from *sēma* sign, token] (1894)

1 : of or relating to meaning in language

2 : of or relating to semantics

— **se·man·ti·cal·ly** \-ti-k(ə-)lē\ *adverb*

se·man·ti·cist \-'man-tə-sist\ *noun* (1902)

: a specialist in semantics

se·man·tics \si-'man-tiks\ *noun plural but singular or plural in construction* (1893)

1 : the study of meanings: **a :** the historical and psychological study and the classification of changes in the signification of words or forms viewed as factors in linguistic development **b** (1) **:** SEMIOTIC (2) **:** a branch of semiotic dealing with the relations between signs and what they refer to and including theories of denotation, extension, naming, and truth

2 : GENERAL SEMANTICS

3 a : the meaning or relationship of meanings of a sign or set of signs; *especially* **:** connotative meaning **b :** the language used (as in advertising or political propaganda) to achieve a desired effect on an audience especially through the use of words with novel or dual meanings

¹sem·a·phore \'se-mə-ˌfōr, -ˌfȯr\ *noun* [Greek *sēma* sign, signal + International Scientific Vocabulary *-phore*] (1816)

1 : an apparatus for visual signaling (as by the position of one or more movable arms)

2 : a system of visual signaling by two flags held one in each hand

semaphore 2: alphabet; 3 positions following Z: error, end of word, numerals follow; numerals 1, 2, 3, 4, 5, 6, 7, 8, 9, 0 same as A through J

²semaphore *verb* **-phored; -phor·ing** (1893)

transitive verb

: to convey (information) by or as if by semaphore

intransitive verb

: to send signals by or as if by semaphore

se·ma·si·ol·o·gy \si-ˌmā-sē-'ä-lə-jē, -ˌmā-zē-\ *noun* [International Scientific Vocabulary, from Greek *sēmasia* meaning, from *sēmainein* to mean] (1857)

: SEMANTICS 1

— **se·ma·si·o·log·i·cal** \-sē-ə-'lä-ji-kəl, -zē-\ *adjective*

¹sem·bla·ble \'sem-blə-bəl\ *adjective* [Middle English, from Middle French, from Old French, from *sembler* to be like, seem] (14th century)

1 : SIMILAR

2 : SUITABLE

3 : APPARENT, SEEMING

— **sem·bla·bly** \-blə-blē\ *adverb*

²semblable *noun* (15th century)

1 *archaic* **:** something similar **:** LIKE

2 : one that is like oneself **:** one's fellow

sem·blance \'sem-blən(t)s\ *noun* [Middle English, from Middle French, from Old French *sembler* to be like, seem — more at RESEMBLE] (14th century)

1 a : outward and often specious appearance or show **:** FORM ⟨wrapped in a *semblance* of composure —Harry Hervey⟩ **b :** MODICUM ⟨has been struggling to get some *semblance* of justice for his people —Bayard Rustin⟩

2 : ASPECT, COUNTENANCE

3 a : a phantasmal form **:** APPARITION **b :** IMAGE, LIKENESS

4 : actual or apparent resemblance

seme \'sēm\ *noun* [Greek *sēma* sign] (circa 1866)

1 : a linguistic sign

2 : any of the basic components of the meaning of a morpheme

se·mei·ol·o·gy *variant of* SEMIOLOGY

se·mei·ot·ic *variant of* SEMIOTIC

Sem·e·le \'se-mə-ˌlē\ *noun* [Latin, from Greek *Semelē*]

: a daughter of Cadmus consumed by flames when visited by Zeus in his divine splendor

sem·eme \'se-ˌmēm\ *noun* [International Scientific Vocabulary, from Greek *sēma* + International Scientific Vocabulary *-eme*] (1913)

1 : the meaning of a morpheme

2 a : SEME 2 **b :** a class of related semes

— **se·me·mic** \sə-'mē-mik\ *adjective*

se·men \'sē-mən\ *noun* [Middle English, from Latin, seed, semen; akin to Old High German *sāmo* seed, Latin *serere* to sow — more at SOW] (14th century)

: a viscid whitish fluid of the male reproductive tract consisting of spermatozoa suspended in secretions of accessory glands

se·mes·ter \sə-'mes-tər\ *noun* [German, from Latin *semestris* half-yearly, from *sex* six + *mensis* month — more at SIX, MOON] (1827)

1 : either of the two usually 18-week periods of instruction into which an academic year is often divided

2 : a period of six months

— **se·mes·tral** \-trəl\ *or* **se·mes·tri·al** \-trē-əl\ *adjective*

semester hour *noun* (1922)

: a unit of academic credit representing an hour of class (as lecture class) or three hours of laboratory work each week for an academic semester

¹semi \'se-mē *also* -ˌmī\ *noun, plural* **sem·is** [short for *semidetached*] (1912)

chiefly British **:** a semidetached house

²semi \'se-ˌmī *also* -mē\ *noun, plural* **sem·is** (1942)

: SEMITRAILER

³semi *same as* ²\ *noun, plural* **sem·is** (1942)

: SEMIFINAL — often used in plural

semi- \ˌse-mē, -ˌmī, -mi\ *prefix* [Middle English, from Latin; akin to Old High German *sāmi-* half, Greek *hēmi-*]

1 a : precisely half of: (1) **:** forming a bisection of ⟨*semi*diameter⟩ (2) **:** being a usually vertically bisected form of (a specified architectural feature) ⟨*semi*dome⟩ **b :** half in quantity or value **:** half of or occurring halfway through a specified period of time ⟨*semi*annual⟩ ⟨*semi*monthly⟩ — compare BI-

2 : to some extent **:** partly **:** incompletely ⟨*semi*civilized⟩ ⟨*semi*-independent⟩ ⟨*semi*dry⟩ — compare DEMI-, HEMI-

3 a : partial **:** incomplete ⟨*semi*consciousness⟩ ⟨*semi*darkness⟩ **b :** having some of the characteristics of ⟨*semi*porcelain⟩ **c :** QUASI- ⟨*semi*governmental⟩ ⟨*semi*monastic⟩

semi·ab·stract \-ab-'strakt, -'ab-ˌ\ *adjective* (1871)

: having subject matter that is easily recognizable although the form is stylized ⟨*semiab*stract* art⟩

— **semi·ab·strac·tion** \-ab-'strak-shən\ *noun*

semi·an·nu·al \-'an-yə(-wə)l\ *adjective* (1794)

: occurring every six months or twice a year

— **semi·an·nu·al·ly** *adverb*

semi·an·tique \-an-'tēk\ *adjective* (circa 1930)

: being approximately 50 to 100 years old ⟨a *semi-antique* carpet⟩

— **semi·antique** *noun*

semi·aquat·ic \-ə-'kwä-tik, -'kwa-\ *adjective* (1833)

: growing equally well in or adjacent to water; *also* **:** frequenting but not living wholly in water

semi·ar·bo·re·al \-är-'bōr-ē-əl, -'bȯr-\ *adjective* (1938)

: often inhabiting and frequenting trees but not completely arboreal

semi·ar·id \-'ar-əd\ *adjective* (1898)

: characterized by light rainfall; *especially* **:** having from about 10 to 20 inches (25 to 51 centimeters) of annual precipitation

— **semi·arid·i·ty** \-ə-'ri-də-tē, -a-'ri-\ *noun*

semi·au·to·bio·graph·i·cal \-ˌȯ-tə-ˌbī-ə-'gra-fi-kəl\ *adjective* (1939)

: partly autobiographical ⟨a *semiautobiographical* comedy⟩

semi·au·to·mat·ic \-ˌȯ-tə-'ma-tik\ *adjective* (1890)

: not fully automatic: as **a :** operated partly automatically and partly by hand **b** *of a firearm* **:** employing gas pressure or force of recoil and mechanical spring action to eject the empty cartridge case after the first shot and load the next cartridge from the magazine but requiring release and another pressure of the trigger for each successive shot

— **semiautomatic** *noun*

— **semi·au·to·mat·i·cal·ly** \-ti-k(ə-)lē\ *adverb*

semi·au·ton·o·mous \-ȯ-'tä-nə-məs\ *adjective* (1915)

: largely self-governing within a larger political or organizational entity

semi·breve \'se-mē-ˌbrēv, 'se-ˌmī-, -mi-, -ˌbrev\ *noun* (15th century)

: WHOLE NOTE

semi·cen·ten·ni·al \-sen-'te-nē-əl\ *noun* (1859)

: a 50th anniversary or its celebration

— **semicentennial** *adjective*

semi·cir·cle \'se-mē-ˌsər-kəl, 'se-ˌmī-, -mi-\ *noun* [Latin *semicirculus*, from *semi-* + *circulus* circle] (1526)

1 : a half of a circle

2 : an object or arrangement of objects in the form of a half circle

— **semi·cir·cu·lar** \ˌse-mē-'sər-kyə-lər\ *adjective*

semicircular canal *noun* (1748)

: any of the loop-shaped tubular parts of the labyrinth of the ear that together constitute a sensory organ associated with the maintenance of bodily equilibrium — see EAR illustration

semi·civ·i·lized \ˌse-mē-'si-və-ˌlīzd, ˌse-ˌmī-, -mi-\ *adjective* (1836)

: partly civilized

semi·clas·sic \-'kla-sik\ *noun* (1843)

: a semiclassical work (as of music)

semi·clas·si·cal \-si-kəl\ *adjective* (1904)

: having some of the characteristics of the classical: as **a :** of, relating to, or being a musical composition that acts as a bridge between

classical and popular music **b :** of, relating to, or being a classical composition that has developed popular appeal

semi·co·lon \'se-mē-ˌkō-lən, 'se-ˌmī-, -mi-\ *noun* (1644)
: a punctuation mark ; used chiefly in a coordinating function between major sentence elements (as independent clauses of a compound sentence)

semi·co·lo·nial \ˌse-mē-kə-'lō-nyəl, ˌse-ˌmī-, -mi-, -nē-əl\ *adjective* (1932)
1 : nominally independent but actually under foreign domination
2 : dependent on foreign nations as suppliers of manufactured goods and as purchasers of raw materials
— **semi·co·lo·nial·ism** \-nyə-ˌli-zəm, -nē-ə-\ *noun*

semi·col·o·ny \-'kä-lə-nē\ *noun* (1945)
: a semicolonial state

semi·com·mer·cial \-kə-'mər-shəl\ *adjective* (1926)
: of, relating to, adapted to, or characterized by limited marketing of an experimental product

semi·con·duct·ing \ˌse-mē-kən-'dək-tiŋ, ˌse-ˌmī-, -mi-\ *adjective* (1782)
: of, relating to, or having the characteristics of a semiconductor

semi·con·duc·tor \-'dək-tər\ *noun* (1838)
: any of a class of solids (as germanium or silicon) whose electrical conductivity is between that of a conductor and that of an insulator in being nearly as great as that of a metal at high temperatures and nearly absent at low temperatures

semi·con·scious \-'kän(t)-shəs\ *adjective* (1839)
: incompletely conscious **:** imperfectly aware or responsive
— **semi·con·scious·ness** *noun*

semi·con·ser·va·tive \-kən-'sər-və-tiv\ *adjective* (1957)
: relating to or being genetic replication in which a double-stranded molecule of nucleic acid separates into two single strands each of which serves as a template for the formation of a complementary strand that together with the template forms a complete molecule
— **semi·con·ser·va·tive·ly** *adverb*

semi·crys·tal·line \-'kris-tə-lən\ *adjective* (1816)
: incompletely or imperfectly crystalline

semi·cy·lin·dri·cal \-sə-'lin-dri-kəl\ *adjective* (circa 1731)
: having the shape of a longitudinal half of a cylinder

semi·dark·ness \-'därk-nəs\ *noun* (1849)
: partial darkness

semi·de·ify \-'dē-ə-ˌfī, -'dā-\ *transitive verb* (1953)
: to regard as somewhat godlike

semi·des·ert \-'de-zərt\ *noun* (1849)
: an arid area that has some of the characteristics of a desert but has greater annual precipitation

semi·de·tached \-di-'tacht\ *adjective* (1859)
: forming one of a pair of residences joined into one building by a common sidewall

semi·di·am·e·ter \-dī-'a-mə-tər\ *noun* (14th century)
: RADIUS; *specifically* **:** the apparent radius of a generally spherical celestial body

semi·di·ur·nal \-dī-'ər-n°l\ *adjective* (1594)
1 : relating to or accomplished in half a day
2 : occurring twice a day
3 : occurring approximately every half day ⟨the *semidiurnal* tides⟩

semi·di·vine \-də-'vīn\ *adjective* (1600)
: more than mortal but not fully divine

semi·doc·u·men·ta·ry \-ˌdä-kyə-'men-tə-rē, -'men-trē\ *noun* (1939)
: a motion picture that uses many details taken from actual events or situations in presenting a fictional story
— **semidocumentary** *adjective*

semi·dome \'se-mē-ˌdōm, 'se-ˌmī-, -mi-\ *noun* (1788)
: a roof or ceiling covering a semicircular or nearly semicircular room or recess
— **semi·domed** \-ˌdōmd\ *adjective*

semi·do·mes·ti·ca·tion \ˌse-mē-də-ˌmes-ti-'kā-shən, ˌse-ˌmī-, -mi-\ *noun* (circa 1835)
: a captive state of a wild animal in which its living conditions and often its breeding are controlled by humans
— **semi·do·mes·ti·cat·ed** \-də-'mes-ti-ˌkā-təd\ *adjective*

semi·dom·i·nant \-'dä-mə-nənt, -'däm-nənt\ *adjective* (1942)
: producing an intermediate phenotype in the heterozygous condition ⟨a *semidominant* mutant gene⟩

semi·dry \-'drī\ *adjective* (1878)
: moderately dry

semi·dry·ing \-'drī-iŋ\ *adjective* (1905)
: that dries imperfectly or slowly — used of some oils (as cottonseed oil)

semi·dwarf \-'dwȯrf\ *adjective* (1959)
: of or being a plant of a variety that is undersized but larger than a dwarf ⟨*semidwarf* wheats⟩
— **semidwarf** *noun*

semi·em·pir·i·cal \-im-'pir-ə-kəl, -em-\ *adjective* (1935)
: partly empirical; *especially* **:** involving assumptions, approximations, or generalizations designed to simplify calculation or to yield a result in accord with observation

semi·erect \-ə-'rekt\ *adjective* (1822)
1 : incompletely upright in bodily posture ⟨*semierect* primates⟩
2 : erect for half the length ⟨*semierect* stems⟩

semi·ev·er·green \-'e-vər-ˌgrēn\ *adjective* (1901)
1 : having functional and persistent foliage during part of the winter or dry season
2 : tending to be evergreen in a mild climate but deciduous in a rigorous climate

semi·feu·dal \-'fyü-d°l\ *adjective* (1898)
: having some characteristics of feudalism

¹semi·fi·nal \-'fī-n°l\ *adjective* (1884)
1 : being next to the last in an elimination tournament
2 : of or participating in a semifinal

²semi·fi·nal \'se-mē-ˌfī-n°l, 'se-ˌmī-, -mi-\ *noun* (1895)
1 : a semifinal match
2 : a semifinal round
— **semi·fi·nal·ist** \ˌse-mē-'fī-n°l-ist, ˌse-ˌmī-, -mi-\ *noun*

semi·fin·ished \ˌse-mē-'fi-nisht, ˌse-ˌmī-, -mi-\ *adjective* (1902)
: partially finished or processed; *especially, of steel* **:** rolled from raw ingots into shapes (as bars, billets, or plates) suitable for further processing

semi·fit·ted \-'fi-təd\ *adjective* (circa 1950)
: conforming somewhat to the lines of the body

semi·flex·i·ble \-'flek-sə-bəl\ *adjective* (1925)
1 : somewhat flexible
2 *of a book cover* **:** having a thin board stiffener under the covering material

semi·flu·id \-'flü-əd\ *adjective* (circa 1735)
: having the qualities of both a fluid and a solid **:** VISCOUS ⟨fluid and *semifluid* lubricants⟩
— **semifluid** *noun*

semi·for·mal \-'fȯr-məl\ *adjective* (1906)
: being or suitable for an occasion of moderate formality ⟨a *semiformal* dinner⟩ ⟨*semiformal* gowns⟩

semi·gloss \'se-mē-ˌgläs, 'se-ˌmī-, -mi-, -ˌglȯs\ *adjective* (1937)
: having a low luster; *specifically* **:** producing a finish midway between gloss and flat

semi·gov·ern·men·tal \ˌse-mē-ˌgəv-ər(n)-'men-t°l, -ˌse-ˌmī-, -mi-, -ˌgə-v°m-'en-\ *adjective* (1919)
: having some governmental functions and powers

semi·group \'se-mē-ˌgrüp, 'se-ˌmī-, -mi-\ *noun* (1904)
: a mathematical set that is closed under an associative binary operation

semi·in·de·pen·dent \-ˌin-də-'pen-dənt\ *adjective* (1860)
: partially independent; *specifically* **:** SEMIAUTONOMOUS

semi·leg·end·ary \-'le-jən-ˌder-ē\ *adjective* (1878)
: having historical foundation but elaborated in legend

semi·le·thal \-'lē-thəl\ *noun* (1919)
: a mutation that in the homozygous condition produces more than 50 percent mortality but not complete mortality
— **semilethal** *adjective*

semi·liq·uid \-'li-kwəd\ *adjective* (1684)
: having the qualities of both a liquid and a solid **:** SEMIFLUID ⟨*semiliquid* manure⟩
— **semiliquid** *noun*

semi·lit·er·ate \-'li-tə-rət *also* -'li-trət\ *adjective* (1927)
1 a : able to read and write on an elementary level **b :** able to read but unable to write
2 : having limited knowledge or understanding **:** not well-versed
— **semiliterate** *noun*

semi·log \-'lȯg, -'läg\ *adjective* (1921)
: SEMILOGARITHMIC

semi·log·a·rith·mic \-ˌlȯ-gə-'rith-mik, -ˌlä-\ *adjective* (1919)
: having one scale logarithmic and the other arithmetic — used of graph paper or of a graph on such paper

semi·lu·nar \-'lü-nər\ *adjective* [New Latin *semilunaris*, from Latin *semi-* + *lunaris* lunar] (1597)
: shaped like a crescent

semilunar valve *noun* (circa 1719)
: any of the crescent-shaped cusps that occur as a set of three between the heart and the aorta and another of three between the heart and the pulmonary artery, are forced apart by pressure in the ventricles during systole and pushed together by pressure in the arteries during diastole, and prevent regurgitation of blood into the ventricles; *also* **:** either set of three cusps

semi·lus·trous \-'ləs-trəs\ *adjective* (1953)
: slightly lustrous

semi·ma·jor axis \-'mā-jər\ *noun* (1899)
: one half of the major axis of an ellipse (as that formed by the orbit of a planet)

semi·matte *also* **semi·mat** *or* **semi·matt** \-'mat\ *adjective* [*semi-* + *²matte*] (1937)
: having a slight luster

semi·met·al \-'me-t°l\ *noun* (1661)
: an element (as arsenic) possessing metallic properties in an inferior degree and not malleable
— **semi·me·tal·lic** \-mə-'ta-lik\ *adjective*

semi·mi·cro \-'mī-(ˌ)krō\ *adjective* (1935)
: of, relating to, or dealing with quantities intermediate between those treated as micro and macro ⟨*semimicro* analysis for chlorine⟩ ⟨a *semimicro* balance⟩

semi·mi·nor axis \-'mī-nər-\ *noun* (1909)
: one half of the minor axis of an ellipse (as that formed by the orbit of a planet)

semi·moist \-'mȯist\ *adjective* (1903)
: slightly moist

semi·mo·nas·tic \-mə-'nas-tik\ *adjective* (1911)
: having some features characteristic of a monastic order

¹semi·month·ly \-'mən(t)th-lē\ *noun* (1851)
: a semimonthly publication

²semimonthly *adjective* (1860)
: occurring twice a month

³semimonthly *adverb* (circa 1890)
: twice a month
semi·mys·ti·cal \-'mis-ti-kəl\ *adjective* (1890)
: having some of the qualities of mysticism
sem·i·nal \'se-mə-nᵊl\ *adjective* [Middle English, from Middle French, from Latin *seminalis,* from *semin-, semen* seed — more at SEMEN] (14th century)
1 : of, relating to, or consisting of seed or semen
2 : containing or contributing the seeds of later development : CREATIVE, ORIGINAL ⟨a *seminal* book⟩ ⟨one of the most *seminal* of the great poets⟩
— **sem·i·nal·ly** \-nᵊl-ē\ *adverb*
seminal duct *noun* (circa 1909)
: a tube or passage serving especially or exclusively as an efferent duct of the testis and in the human male being made up of the tubules of the epididymis, the vas deferens, and the ejaculatory duct
seminal fluid *noun* (circa 1929)
1 : SEMEN
2 : the part of the semen that is produced by various accessory glands : semen excepting the spermatozoa
seminal vesicle *noun* (circa 1890)
: either of a pair of glandular pouches that lie one on either side of the male reproductive tract and in the human male secrete a sugar- and protein-containing fluid into the ejaculatory duct
sem·i·nar \'se-mə-,när\ *noun* [German, from Latin *seminarium* nursery] (1889)
1 : a group of advanced students studying under a professor with each doing original research and all exchanging results through reports and discussions
2 a (1) : a course of study pursued by a seminar (2) : an advanced or graduate course often featuring informality and discussion **b** : a scheduled meeting of a seminar or a room for such meetings
3 : a meeting for giving and discussing information
sem·i·nar·i·an \,se-mə-'ner-ē-ən\ *noun* (1794)
: a student in a seminary especially of the Roman Catholic Church
sem·i·na·rist \'se-mə-nə-rist\ *noun* (1835)
: SEMINARIAN
sem·i·nary \'se-mə-,ner-ē\ *noun, plural* **-nar·ies** [Middle English, seedbed, nursery, from Latin *seminarium,* from *semin-, semen* seed] (1542)
1 : an environment in which something originates and from which it is propagated ⟨a *seminary* of vice and crime⟩
2 a : an institution of secondary or higher education **b** : an institution for the training of candidates for the priesthood, ministry, or rabbinate ◇
semi·nat·u·ral \,se-mē-'na-chə-rəl, ,se-,mī-, -mi-, -'nach-rəl\ *adjective* (circa 1962)
: modified by human influence but retaining many natural features ⟨a *seminatural* park⟩
sem·i·nif·er·ous \,se-mə-'ni-f(ə-)rəs\ *adjective* [Latin *semin-, semen* seed + English *-iferous*] (1692)
: producing or bearing seed or semen
seminiferous tubule *noun* (1860)
: any of the coiled threadlike tubules that make up the bulk of the testis and are lined with a layer of epithelial cells from which the spermatozoa are produced
Sem·i·nole \'se-mə-,nōl\ *noun, plural* **Seminoles** *or* **Seminole** [Creek *simanó'li* fugitive, wild, alteration of *simaló'ni,* from American Spanish *cimarrón* wild] (1771)
: a member of any of the groups of American Indians that emigrated to Florida from Georgia and Alabama in the 18th century and that are now located in southern Florida and Oklahoma
semi·no·mad \,se-mē-'nō-,mad, ,se-,mī-, -mi-\ *noun* (circa 1934)
: a member of a people living usually in portable or temporary dwellings and practicing seasonal migration but having a base camp at which some crops are cultivated
— **semi·no·mad·ic** \,se-mē-nō-'ma-dik\ *adjective*
semi·nude \-'nüd, -'nyüd\ *adjective* (1849)
: partially nude
— **semi·nu·di·ty** \-'nü-də-tē, -'nyü-\ *noun*
semi·of·fi·cial \-ə-'fi-shəl\ *adjective* (1806)
: having some official authority or standing
— **semi·of·fi·cial·ly** \-'fi-sh(ə-)lē\ *adverb*
se·mi·ol·o·gy \,sē-mē-'ä-lə-jē, ,se-mē-, ,sē-,mī-\ *noun* [Greek *sēmeion* sign] (circa 1890)
: the study of signs; *especially* : SEMIOTIC
— **se·mi·o·log·i·cal** \(,)sē-,mī-ə-'lä-ji-kəl, ,se-mē-ə-\ *adjective*
— **se·mi·o·log·i·cal·ly** \-ə-'lä-ji-k(ə-)lē\ *adverb*
— **se·mi·ol·o·gist** \-'ä-lə-jist\ *noun*
semi·opaque \,se-mē-ō-'pāk, ,se-,mī-, -mi-\ *adjective* (1691)
: nearly opaque
se·mi·o·sis \,sē-mē-'ō-səs, ,se-mē-, ,sē-,mī-\ *noun* [New Latin, from Greek *sēmeiōsis* observation of signs, from *sēmeioun* to observe signs, from *sēmeion*] (circa 1907)
: a process in which something functions as a sign to an organism
se·mi·ot·ic \-'ä-tik\ *or* **se·mi·ot·ics** \-tiks\ *noun, plural* **semiotics** [Greek *sēmeiōtikos* observant of signs, from *sēmeiousthai* to interpret signs, from *sēmeion* sign, from *sēma* sign] (1880)
: a general philosophical theory of signs and symbols that deals especially with their function in both artificially constructed and natural languages and comprises syntactics, semantics, and pragmatics
— **semiotic** *adjective*
— **se·mi·o·ti·cian** \-ə-'ti-shən\ *noun*
— **se·mi·ot·i·cist** \-'ä-tə-sist\ *noun*
semi·pal·mat·ed \,se-mē-'pal-,mā-təd, ,se-,mī-, -mi-, -'päl-, -'pä-\ *adjective* (1785)
: having the toes joined only part way down with a web ⟨a plover with *semipalmated* feet⟩
semi·par·a·sit·ic \-,par-ə-'si-tik\ *adjective* (circa 1880)
: of, relating to, or being a parasitic plant that contains some chlorophyll and is capable of photo-synthesis
— **semi·par·a·site** \-'par-ə-,sīt\ *noun*
semi·per·ma·nent \-'pər-mə-nənt, -'pərm-nənt\ *adjective* (circa 1890)
: lasting or intended to last for a long time but not permanent
semi·per·me·able \-'pər-mē-ə-bəl\ *adjective* (1888)
: partially but not freely or wholly permeable; *specifically* : permeable to some usually small molecules but not to other usually larger particles ⟨a *semipermeable* membrane⟩
— **semi·per·me·abil·i·ty** \-,pər-mē-ə-'bi-lə-tē\ *noun*
semi·po·lit·i·cal \-pə-'li-ti-kəl\ *adjective* (1857)
: of, relating to, or involving some political features or activity
semi·pop·u·lar \-'pä-pyə-lər\ *adjective* (1860)
: somewhat popular
semi·por·ce·lain \-'pōr-s(ə-)lən, -'pȯr-\ *noun* (1880)
: any of several ceramic wares resembling or imitative of porcelain; *especially* : a relatively high-fired and hard-glazed white earthenware widely used for tableware
semi·por·no·graph·ic \-,pȯr-nə-'gra-fik\ *adjective* (1964)
: somewhat pornographic
— **semi·por·nog·ra·phy** \-pȯr-'nä-grə-fē\ *noun*
semi·post·al \-'pōs-tᵊl\ *noun* (1927)
: a postage stamp sold at a premium over its postal value especially for a humanitarian purpose

semi·pre·cious \-'pre-shəs\ *adjective* (circa 1890)
of a gemstone : of less commercial value than a precious stone
semi·pri·vate \-'prī-vət\ *adjective* (1876)
: of, receiving, or associated with hospital service giving a patient more privileges than a ward patient but fewer than a private patient
semi·pro \'se-mē-,prō, 'se-,mī-, -mi-\ *adjective or noun* (1908)
: SEMIPROFESSIONAL
¹semi·pro·fes·sion·al \,se-mē-prə-'fesh-nəl, ,se-,mī-, -mi-, -'fe-shə-nᵊl\ *noun* (1897)
: one who engages in an activity (as a sport) semiprofessionally
²semiprofessional *adjective* (1900)
1 : engaging in an activity for pay or gain but not as a full-time occupation
2 : engaged in by semiprofessional players ⟨*semiprofessional* baseball⟩
— **semi·pro·fes·sion·al·ly** *adverb*
semi·pub·lic \-'pə-blik\ *adjective* (1804)
1 : open to some persons outside the regular constituency
2 : having some features of a public institution; *specifically* : maintained as a public service by a private nonprofit organization
semi·quan·ti·ta·tive \-'kwän-tə-,tā-tiv\ *adjective* (1927)
: constituting or involving less than quantitative precision
— **semi·quan·ti·ta·tive·ly** *adverb*
semi·qua·ver \'se-mē-,kwā-vər, 'se-,mī-, -mi-\ *noun* (1576)
: SIXTEENTH NOTE
semi·re·li·gious \,se-mē-ri-'li-jəs, ,se-,mī-, -mi-\ *adjective* (1864)
: somewhat religious
semi·re·tired \-ri-'tīrd\ *adjective* (1937)
: working only part-time especially because of age or ill health
semi·re·tire·ment \-'tīr-mənt\ *noun* (1923)
: the state or condition of being semiretired
semi·rig·id \-'ri-jəd\ *adjective* (1908)
1 : rigid to some degree or in some parts
2 *of an airship* : having a flexible cylindrical gas container with an attached stiffening keel that carries the load
semi·rur·al \-'rùr-əl\ *adjective* (1835)
: somewhat rural
semi·sa·cred \-'sā-krəd\ *adjective* (1898)
: SEMIRELIGIOUS
semi·se·cret \-'sē-krət\ *adjective* (1917)
: not publicly announced but widely known nevertheless

◇ WORD HISTORY
seminary The English word *seminary* and its Latin source *seminarium,* a derivative of *semen* "seed," both originally denoted a nursery for young plants. Though the classical Latin word was sometimes used figuratively, English has gone much further in metaphorical extensions of the word, with the old sense "nursery" is now long obsolete. The use of *seminary* in reference to training schools for the clergy was an outgrowth of 16th century reforms in the Roman Catholic Church: decrees of the Council of Trent (1545–63) applied the Latin word *seminarium* to newly established institutes for educating priests, which were meant to raise the educational level of the clergy as well as train missionaries to non-Catholic countries. In application to such schools, English *seminary* long retained a strong association with Roman Catholicism; now the word refers equally to Catholic, Protestant, or Jewish colleges for training priests, ministers, or rabbis. *Seminary* has also been applied to other kinds of schools since the 16th century. When they were first formed in the 19th century, women's colleges were called "female seminaries" or "seminaries for young ladies."

semi·sed·en·tary \-'se-d°n-,ter-ē\ *adjective* (circa 1930)
: sedentary during part of the year and nomadic otherwise ⟨*semisedentary* tribes⟩

semi·shrub·by \'se-mē-,shrə-bē, 'se-,mī-, -mi-, *especially Southern* -,srə-\ *adjective* (1930)
: resembling or being a subshrub

semi·skilled \,se-mē-'skild, ,se-,mī-, -mi-\ *adjective* (1916)
: having or requiring less training than skilled labor and more than unskilled labor

semi·soft \-'sȯft\ *adjective* (circa 1903)
: moderately soft; *specifically* : firm but easily cut ⟨*semisoft* cheese⟩

semi·sol·id \-'sä-ləd\ *adjective* (1834)
: having the qualities of both a solid and a liquid : highly viscous
— **semisolid** *noun*

semi·sub·mers·ible \-səb-'mər-sə-bəl\ *adjective* (1962)
: being a floating deepwater drilling platform that is towed to a desired location and then partially flooded for stabilization and usually anchored
— **semisubmersible** *noun*

semi·sweet \-'swēt\ *adjective* (1943)
: slightly sweetened ⟨*semisweet* chocolate⟩

semi·syn·thet·ic \-sin-'the-tik\ *adjective* (1937)
1 : produced by chemical alteration of a natural starting material ⟨*semisynthetic* penicillins⟩
2 : containing both chemically identified and complex natural ingredients ⟨a *semisynthetic* diet⟩

Sem·ite \'se-,mīt, *especially British* 'sē-,mīt\ *noun* [French *sémite*, from *Semitic* Shem, from Late Latin, from Greek *Sēm*, from Hebrew *Shēm*] (1848)
1 a : a member of any of a number of peoples of ancient southwestern Asia including the Akkadians, Phoenicians, Hebrews, and Arabs **b** : a descendant of these peoples
2 : a member of a modern people speaking a Semitic language

semi·ter·res·tri·al \,se-mē-tə-'res-trē-əl, ,se-,mī-, -mi-, -'res-chəl, -'resh-\ *adjective* (1919)
1 : growing on boggy ground
2 : frequenting but not living wholly on land

¹Se·mit·ic \sə-'mi-tik *also* -'me-\ *adjective* [German *semitisch*, from *Semit*, *Semite* Semite, probably from New Latin *Semita*, from Late Latin *Semitic* Shem] (1813)
1 : of, relating to, or constituting a subfamily of the Afro-Asiatic language family that includes Hebrew, Aramaic, Arabic, and Amharic
2 : of, relating to, or characteristic of the Semites
3 : JEWISH

²Semitic *noun* (1875)
: any or all of the Semitic languages

Se·mit·i·cist \sə-'mi-tə-sist\ *noun* (1956)
: SEMITIST

Se·mit·ics \-'mi-tiks\ *noun plural but singular in construction* (1895)
: the study of the language, literature, and history of Semitic peoples; *specifically* : Semitic philology

Sem·i·tism \'se-mə-,ti-zəm\ *noun* (1851)
1 a : Semitic character or qualities **b** : a characteristic feature of a Semitic language occurring in another language
2 : policy favorable to Jews : predisposition in favor of Jews

Sem·i·tist \-tist\ *noun* (1885)
1 : a scholar of the Semitic languages, cultures, or histories
2 *often not capitalized* : a person favoring or disposed to favor the Jews

semi·ton·al \,se-mē-'tō-n°l, ,se-,mī-, -mi-\ *adjective* (1863)
: CHROMATIC 3a, SEMITONIC
— **semi·ton·al·ly** *adverb*

semi·tone \'se-mē-,tōn, 'se-,mī-, -mi-\ *noun* (15th century)

: the tone at a half step; *also* : HALF STEP
— **semi·ton·ic** \,se-mē-'tä-nik, ,se-,mī-, -mi-\ *adjective*
— **semi·ton·i·cal·ly** \-ni-k(ə-)lē\ *adverb*

semi·trail·er \'se-,mī-,trā-lər, 'se-mē-, -mi-\ *noun* (1919)
1 : a freight trailer that when attached is supported at its forward end by the fifth wheel device of the truck tractor
2 : a trucking rig made up of a tractor and a semitrailer

semi·trans·lu·cent \,se-mē-,tran(t)s-'lü-s°nt, ,se-,mī-, -mi-, -,tranz-\ *adjective* (1832)
: somewhat translucent

semi·trans·par·ent \-,tran(t)s-'par-ənt, -'per-\ *adjective* (circa 1793)
: imperfectly transparent

semi·trop·i·cal \-'trä-pi-kəl\ *also* **semi·trop·ic** \-pik\ *adjective* (1853)
: SUBTROPICAL

semi·trop·ics \-piks\ *noun plural* (1908)
: SUBTROPICS

semi·vow·el \'se-mē-,vaů(-ə)l, 'se-,mī-, -mi-\ *noun* (1530)
1 : a speech sound (as \y\, \w\, or \r\) that has the articulation of a vowel but that is shorter in duration and is treated as a consonant in syllabication
2 : a letter representing a semivowel

¹semi·week·ly \,se-mē-'wē-klē, ,se-,mī-, -mi-\ *adjective* (1791)
: occurring twice a week
— **semiweekly** *adverb*

²semiweekly *noun* (1833)
: a semiweekly publication

semi·works \'se-mē-,wərks, 'se-,mī-, -mi-\ *noun plural, often attributive* (1926)
: a manufacturing plant operating on a limited commercial scale to provide final tests of a new product or process

semi·year·ly \,se-mē-'yir-lē, ,se-,mī-, -mi-\ *adjective* (circa 1928)
: occurring twice a year

sem·o·li·na \,se-mə-'lē-nə\ *noun* [Italian *semolino*, diminutive of *semola* bran, from Latin *simila* wheat flour] (1797)
: the purified middlings of hard wheat (as durum) used especially for pasta (as macaroni or spaghetti)

sem·per·vi·vum \,sem-pər-'vī-vəm\ *noun* [New Latin, from Latin, neuter of *sempervivus* ever-living, from *semper* ever + *vivus* living — more at QUICK] (1591)
: any of a large genus (*Sempervivum*) of Old World fleshy herbs of the orpine family often grown as ornamentals

sem·pi·ter·nal \,sem-pi-'tər-n°l\ *adjective* [Middle English, from Late Latin *sempiternalis*, from Latin *sempiternus*, from *semper* ever, always, from *sem-* one, same (akin to Old Norse *samr* same) + *per* through — more at SAME, FOR] (15th century)
: of never-ending duration : ETERNAL
— **sem·pi·ter·nal·ly** *adverb*

sem·pi·ter·ni·ty \-'tər-nə-tē\ *noun* (1599)
: ETERNITY

sem·ple \'sem-pəl\ *adjective* [alteration of *simple*] (1759)
Scottish : of humble birth

sem·pli·ce \'sem-pli-,chā\ *adjective or adverb* [Italian, from Latin *simplic-, simplex* — more at SIMPLE] (circa 1740)
: SIMPLE — used as a direction in music

sem·pre \'sem-(,)prā\ *adverb* [Italian, from Latin *semper*] (circa 1801)
: ALWAYS — used in music directions ⟨*sempre* legato⟩

semp·stress \'sem(p)-strəs\ *variant of* SEAMSTRESS

¹sen \'sen\ *noun, plural* **sen** [Japanese] (1875)
— see *yen* at MONEY table

²sen *noun, plural* **sen** [Malay, probably from English *century*] (1952)
— see *dollar, ringgit, rupiah* at MONEY table

³sen *noun, plural* **sen** [Khmer *sein*, probably from French *century*, abbreviation of *centime* centime] (1964)
— see *riel* at MONEY table

se·nar·i·us \si-'nar-ē-əs, -'ner-\ *noun, plural* **se·nar·ii** \-ē-,ī, -ē-,ē\ [Latin, from *senarius* consisting of six each, from *seni* six each, from *sex* six — more at SIX] (1540)
: a verse consisting of six feet especially in Latin prosody

se·na·ry \'se-nə-rē, 'sē-\ *adjective* [Latin *senarius* consisting of six] (1661)
: of, based on, or characterized by six : compounded of six things or six parts ⟨*senary* scale⟩ ⟨*senary* division⟩

sen·ate \'se-nət\ *noun* [Middle English *senat*, from Old French, from Latin *senatus*, from *sen-, senex* old, old man — more at SENIOR] (13th century)
1 : an assembly or council usually possessing high deliberative and legislative functions: as **a** : the supreme council of the ancient Roman republic and empire **b** : the second chamber in the bicameral legislature of a major political unit (as a nation, state, or province)
2 : the hall or chamber in which a senate meets
3 : a governing body of some universities charged with maintaining academic standards and regulations and usually composed of the principal or representative members of the faculty

sen·a·tor \'se-nə-tər\ *noun* [Middle English *senatour*, from Old French *senateur*, from Latin *senator*, from *senatus*] (13th century)
: a member of a senate
— **sen·a·tor·ship** \-,ship\ *noun*

sen·a·to·ri·al \,se-nə-'tȯr-ē-əl, -'tȯr-\ *adjective* (1740)
: of, relating to, or befitting a senator or a senate ⟨*senatorial* office⟩ ⟨*senatorial* rank⟩

senatorial courtesy *noun* (1884)
: a custom of the U.S. Senate of refusing to confirm a presidential appointment of an official in or from a state when the appointment is opposed by the senators or senior senator of the president's party from that state

senatorial district *noun* (1785)
: a territorial division from which a senator is elected — compare CONGRESSIONAL DISTRICT

sen·a·to·ri·an \,se-nə-'tȯr-ē-ən, -'tȯr-\ *adjective* (1614)
: SENATORIAL; *specifically* : of or relating to the ancient Roman senate

se·na·tus con·sul·tum \sə-,nä-təs-kən-'səl-təm, -'sůl-\ *noun, plural* **senatus con·sul·ta** \-tə\ [Latin, decree of the senate] (1696)
: a decree of the ancient Roman senate

¹send \'send\ *verb* **sent** \'sent\; **send·ing** [Middle English, from Old English *sendan*; akin to Old High German *sendan* to send, Old English *sith* road, journey, Old Irish *sét* path, way] (before 12th century)
transitive verb
1 : to cause to go: as **a** : to propel or throw in a particular direction **b** : DELIVER ⟨*sent* a blow to the chin⟩ **c** : DRIVE ⟨*sent* the ball between the goalposts⟩
2 : to cause to happen ⟨whatever fate may *send*⟩
3 : to dispatch by a means of communication
4 a : to direct, order, or request to go **b** : to permit or enable to attend a term or session ⟨*send* a daughter to college⟩ **c** : to direct by advice or reference **d** : to cause or order to depart : DISMISS
5 a : to force to go : drive away **b** : to cause to assume a specified state ⟨*sent* them into a rage⟩

6 : to cause to issue: as **a :** to pour out **:** DIS-CHARGE ⟨clouds *sending* forth rain⟩ **b :** UTTER ⟨*send* forth a cry⟩ **c :** EMIT ⟨*sent* out waves of perfume⟩ **d :** to grow out (parts) in the course of development ⟨a plant *sending* forth shoots⟩ **7 :** to cause to be carried to a destination; *especially* **:** to consign to death or a place of punishment **8 :** to convey or cause to be conveyed or transmitted by an agent ⟨*send* a package by mail⟩ ⟨*sent* out invitations⟩ **9 :** to strike or thrust so as to impel violently ⟨*sent* him sprawling⟩ **10 :** DELIGHT, THRILL *intransitive verb* **1 a :** to dispatch someone to convey a message or do an errand — often used with *out* ⟨*send* out for pizza⟩ **b :** to dispatch a request or order — often used with *away* **2 :** SCEND **3 :** TRANSMIT — **send·er** *noun* — **send for :** to request by message to come **:** SUMMON — **send packing :** to send off or dismiss roughly or in disgrace

²send *noun* (1726)
: the lift of a wave

send down *transitive verb* (1853)
British **:** to suspend or expel from a university

send in (1715)
transitive verb
1 : to cause to be delivered ⟨*send in* a letter of complaint⟩ **2 :** to give (one's name or card) to a servant when making a call **3 :** to send (a player) into an athletic contest

send–off \'send-ˌȯf\ *noun* (1872)
: a demonstration of goodwill and enthusiasm for the beginning of a new venture (as a trip)

send–up \-ˌəp\ *noun* (1958)
: PARODY, TAKEOFF

send up *transitive verb* (1852)
1 : to sentence to imprisonment **:** send to jail **2 :** to make fun of **:** SATIRIZE, PARODY

se·ne \'sā-(ˌ)nā\ *noun, plural* **sene** [Samoan, from English *century*] (1967)
— see *tala* at MONEY table

Sen·e·ca \'se-ni-kə\ *noun, plural* **Seneca** or **Senecas** [Dutch *Sennecaas*, plural, of the Iroquois living west of the Mohawks] (circa 1616)
1 : a member of an American Indian people of what is now western New York **2 :** the Iroquoian language of the Seneca people

seneca snakeroot *noun* (1789)
: a milkwort (*Polygala senega*) of eastern North America having racemes of small white flowers — called also *rattlesnake root, senega root*; compare SENEGA

se·ne·cio \si-'nē-sh(ē-ˌ)ō\ *noun, plural* **-cios** [New Latin, from Latin, old man, groundsel (from its hoary pappus), from *sen-, senic-, senex* old man] (circa 1890)
: any of a genus (*Senecio*) of widely distributed composite plants that have alternate or basal leaves and flower heads usually with yellow ray flowers

seneca snakeroot

se·nec·ti·tude \si-'nek-tə-ˌtüd, -ˌtyüd\ *noun* [Medieval Latin *senectitudo*, alteration of Latin *senectus* old age, from *sen-, senic-, senex* old, old man — more at SENIOR] (1796)
: the final stage of the normal life span

sen·e·ga \'se-ni-gə\ *noun* (1748)
: the dried root of seneca snakeroot that contains an irritating saponin and is used medicinally

senega root *noun* [alteration of *Seneca root*; from its use by the Seneca as a remedy for snakebite] (circa 1846)

1 : SENECA SNAKEROOT
2 : SENEGA

se·nes·cence \si-'ne-sᵊn(t)s\ *noun* [*senescent*, from Latin *senescent-, senescens*, present participle of *senescere* to grow old, from *sen-, senex* old] (1695)
1 : the state of being old **:** the process of becoming old **2 :** the growth phase in a plant or plant part (as a leaf) from full maturity to death — **se·nes·cent** \-sᵊnt\ *adjective*

sen·e·schal \'se-nə-shəl\ *noun* [Middle English, from Middle French, of Germanic origin; akin to Gothic *sineigs* old and to Old High German *scalc* servant — more at SENIOR] (14th century)
: an agent or steward in charge of a lord's estate in feudal times

se·nhor \si-'nyȯr, -'nyȯr\ *noun, plural* **sen·hors** or **se·nho·res** \-'nyȯr-ēsh, -'nyȯr-, -ēzh, -ēs, -ēz\ [Portuguese, from Medieval Latin *senior* superior, lord, from Latin, adjective, elder] (1795)
: a Portuguese or Brazilian man — used as a title equivalent to *Mr.*

se·nho·ra \-'nyȯr-ə, -'nyȯr-\ *noun* [Portuguese, feminine of *senhor*] (1802)
: a married Portuguese or Brazilian woman — used as a title equivalent to *Mrs.*

se·nho·ri·ta \ˌsē-nyə-'rē-tə\ *noun* [Portuguese, from diminutive of *senhora*] (1874)
: an unmarried Portuguese or Brazilian girl or woman — used as a title equivalent to *Miss*

se·nile \'sē-ˌnīl *also* 'se-\ *adjective* [Latin *senilis*, from *sen-, senex* old, old man] (1661)
1 : of, relating to, exhibiting, or characteristic of old age ⟨*senile* weakness⟩; *especially* **:** exhibiting a loss of mental faculties associated with old age **2 :** approaching the end of a geological cycle of erosion — **se·nile·ly** \-ˌnīl-lē\ *adverb*

senile dementia *noun* (circa 1851)
: a mental disorder of old age especially of the degenerative type associated with Alzheimer's disease

se·nil·i·ty \si-'ni-lə-tē *also* se-\ *noun* (1791)
: the quality or state of being senile; *specifically* **:** the physical and mental infirmity of old age

¹se·nior \'sē-nyər\ *noun* [Middle English, from Latin, from *senior*, adjective] (14th century)
1 : a person older than another ⟨five years my *senior*⟩ **2 a :** a person with higher standing or rank **b :** a senior fellow of a college at an English university **c :** a student in the year preceding graduation from a school of secondary or higher level **3** *capitalized* **:** a member of a program of the Girl Scouts for girls in the ninth through twelfth grades in school **4 :** SENIOR CITIZEN

²senior *adjective* [Middle English, from Latin, older, elder, comparative of *sen-, senex* old; akin to Gothic *sineigs* old, Greek *henos*] (14th century)
1 : of prior birth, establishment, or enrollment — often used to distinguish a father with the same given name as his son **2 :** higher ranking **:** SUPERIOR ⟨*senior* officers⟩ **3 :** of or relating to seniors ⟨the *senior* class⟩ **4 :** having a claim on corporate assets and income prior to other securities

senior airman *noun* (circa 1977)
: an enlisted man in the air force who ranks above an airman first class but who has not been made sergeant

senior chief petty officer *noun* (circa 1960)
: an enlisted man in the navy or coast guard ranking above a chief petty officer and below a master chief petty officer

senior citizen *noun* (1938)

: an elderly person; *especially* **:** one who has retired

senior high school *noun* (1909)
: a school usually including grades 10 to 12

se·nior·i·ty \sēn-'yȯr-ə-tē, -'yär-\ *noun* (15th century)
1 : the quality or state of being senior **:** PRIORITY **2 :** a privileged status attained by length of continuous service (as in a company)

senior master sergeant *noun* (circa 1962)
: a noncommissioned officer in the air force ranking above a master sergeant and below a chief master sergeant

sen·i·ti \'se-nə-tē\ *noun, plural* **seniti** [Tongan, modification of English *century*] (1967)
— see *pa'anga* at MONEY table

sen·na \'se-nə\ *noun* [New Latin, from Arabic *sanā*] (1543)
1 : any of a genus (*Cassia*) of leguminous herbs, shrubs, and trees native to warm regions; *especially* **:** one used medicinally **2 :** the dried leaflets or pods of various sennas (especially *Cassia acutifolia* and *C. angustifolia*) used as a purgative

sen·net \'se-nət\ *noun* [probably alteration of obsolete *signet* signal] (circa 1590)
: a signal call on a trumpet or cornet for entrance or exit on the stage

sen·night *also* **se'n·night** \'se-ˌnīt\ *noun* [Middle English, from Old English *seofon nihta* seven nights] (15th century)
archaic **:** the space of seven nights and days **:** WEEK

sen·nit \'se-nət\ *noun* [origin unknown] (circa 1769)
1 : a braided cord or fabric (as of plaited rope yarns) **2 :** a straw or grass braid for hats

se·nor or **se·ñor** \sān-'yȯr\ *noun, plural* **se·nors** or **se·ño·res** \-'yȯr-(ˌ)ās, -'yȯr-\ [Spanish *señor*, from Medieval Latin *senior* superior, lord, from Latin, adjective, elder] (1622)
: a Spanish or Spanish-speaking man — used as a title equivalent to *Mr.*

se·no·ra or **se·ño·ra** \sān-'yȯr-ə, -'yȯr-\ *noun* [Spanish *señora*, feminine of *señor*] (1579)
: a married Spanish or Spanish-speaking woman — used as a title equivalent to *Mrs.*

se·no·ri·ta or **se·ño·ri·ta** \ˌsān-yə-'rē-tə\ *noun* [Spanish *señorita*, from diminutive of *señora*] (1823)
: an unmarried Spanish or Spanish-speaking girl or woman — used as a title equivalent to *Miss*

sen·ryu \'sen-rē-(ˌ)ü\ *noun, plural* **senryu** [Japanese] (1938)
: a 3-line unrhymed Japanese poem structurally similar to haiku but treating human nature usually in an ironic or satiric vein

sensa *plural of* SENSUM

sen·sate \'sen-ˌsāt\ *adjective* [Middle English *sensat*, from Medieval Latin *sensatus*, from Late Latin, endowed with sense, from Latin *sensus* sense] (15th century)
1 : relating to or apprehending or apprehended through the senses **2 :** preoccupied with things that can be experienced through a sense modality — **sen·sate·ly** *adverb*

sen·sa·tion \sen-'sā-shən, sən-\ *noun* [Medieval Latin *sensation-, sensatio*, from Late Latin, understanding, idea, from Latin *sensus*] (1615)
1 a : a mental process (as seeing, hearing, or smelling) due to immediate bodily stimulation often as distinguished from awareness of the process — compare PERCEPTION **b :** awareness (as of heat or pain) due to stimulation of a sense organ **c :** a state of consciousness of a kind usually due to physical objects or internal bodily changes ⟨a burning *sensation* in his chest⟩ **d :** an indefinite bodily feeling ⟨a *sensation* of buoyancy⟩

2 : something (as a physical object, sense-datum, pain, or afterimage) that causes or is the object of sensation
3 a : a state of excited interest or feeling ⟨their elopement caused a *sensation*⟩ **b :** a cause of such excitement ⟨the show was the musical *sensation* of the season⟩; *especially* **:** one (as a person) in some respect exceptional or outstanding ⟨the rookie hitting *sensation* of the American League⟩
sen·sa·tion·al \-shnəl, -shə-n°l\ *adjective* (1840)
1 : of or relating to sensation or the senses
2 : arousing or tending to arouse (as by lurid details) a quick, intense, and usually superficial interest, curiosity, or emotional reaction
3 : exceedingly or unexpectedly excellent or great
— **sen·sa·tion·al·ly** *adverb*
sen·sa·tion·al·ise *British variant of* SENSATIONALIZE
sen·sa·tion·al·ism \-shnə-ˌli-zəm, -shə-n°l-ˌi-zəm\ *noun* (1846)
1 : empiricism that limits experience as a source of knowledge to sensation or sense perceptions
2 : the use or effect of sensational subject matter or treatment
— **sen·sa·tion·al·ist** \-list, -ist\ *adjective or noun*
— **sen·sa·tion·al·is·tic** \-ˌsā-shnə-ˈlis-tik, -shən-°l-ˈis-tik\ *adjective*
sen·sa·tion·al·ize \-ˌlīz, -ˌīz\ *transitive verb* **-ized; -iz·ing** (1869)
: to present in a sensational manner
¹sense \ˈsen(t)s\ *noun* [Middle English, from Middle French or Latin; Middle French *sens* sensation, feeling, mechanism of perception, meaning, from Latin *sensus*, from *sentire* to perceive, feel; perhaps akin to Old High German *sinnan* to go, strive, Old English *sith* journey — more at SEND] (14th century)
1 : a meaning conveyed or intended **:** IMPORT, SIGNIFICATION; *especially* **:** one of a set of meanings a word or phrase may bear especially as segregated in a dictionary entry
2 a : the faculty of perceiving by means of sense organs **b :** a specialized animal function or mechanism (as sight, hearing, smell, taste, or touch) basically involving a stimulus and a sense organ **c :** the sensory mechanisms constituting a unit distinct from other functions (as movement or thought)
3 : conscious awareness or rationality — usually used in plural ⟨finally came to his *senses*⟩
4 a : a particular sensation or kind or quality of sensation ⟨a good *sense* of balance⟩ **b :** a definite but often vague awareness or impression ⟨felt a *sense* of insecurity⟩ ⟨a *sense* of danger⟩ **c :** a motivating awareness ⟨a *sense* of shame⟩ **d :** a discerning awareness and appreciation ⟨her *sense* of humor⟩
5 : CONSENSUS ⟨the *sense* of the meeting⟩
6 a : capacity for effective application of the powers of the mind as a basis for action or response **:** INTELLIGENCE **b :** sound mental capacity and understanding typically marked by shrewdness and practicality; *also* **:** agreement with or satisfaction of such power ⟨this decision makes *sense*⟩
7 : one of two opposite directions especially of motion (as of a point, line, or surface) ☆
²sense *transitive verb* **sensed; sens·ing** (circa 1531)
1 a : to perceive by the senses **b :** to be or become conscious of ⟨*sense* danger⟩
2 : GRASP, COMPREHEND
3 : to detect automatically especially in response to a physical stimulus (as light or movement)
sense–datum *noun, plural* **sense–data** (1882)
: an immediate unanalyzable private object of sensation
sense·ful \ˈsen(t)s-fəl\ *adjective* (1591)

: REASONABLE, JUDICIOUS
sense·less \ˈsen(t)s-ləs\ *adjective* (1557)
: destitute of, deficient in, or contrary to sense: as **a :** UNCONSCIOUS ⟨knocked *senseless*⟩ **b :** FOOLISH, STUPID ⟨it was some *senseless* practical joke —A. Conan Doyle⟩ **c :** MEANINGLESS, PURPOSELESS ⟨a *senseless* murder⟩
— **sense·less·ly** *adverb*
— **sense·less·ness** *noun*
sense organ *noun* (1854)
: a bodily structure that receives a stimulus (as heat or sound waves) and is affected in such a manner as to initiate a wave of excitation in associated sensory nerve fibers which convey specific impulses to the central nervous system where they are interpreted as corresponding sensations **:** RECEPTOR
sen·si·bil·ia \ˌsen(t)-sə-ˈbi-lē-ə, -ˈbil-yə\ *noun plural* [Late Latin, from neuter plural of Latin *sensibilis* sensible] (1856)
: what may be sensed
sen·si·bil·i·ty \ˌsen(t)-sə-ˈbi-lə-tē\ *noun, plural* **-ties** (15th century)
1 : ability to receive sensations **:** SENSITIVENESS ⟨tactile *sensibility*⟩
2 : peculiar susceptibility to a pleasurable or painful impression (as from praise or a slight) — often used in plural
3 : awareness of and responsiveness toward something (as emotion in another)
4 : refined or excessive sensitiveness in emotion and taste with especial responsiveness to the pathetic
¹sen·si·ble \ˈsen(t)-sə-bəl\ *adjective* [Middle English, from Middle French, from Latin *sensibilis*, from *sensus*, past participle of *sentire* to feel] (14th century)
1 : of a kind to be felt or perceived: as **a :** perceptible to the senses or to reason or understanding ⟨felt a *sensible* chill⟩ ⟨her distress was *sensible* from her manner⟩ **b** *archaic* **:** perceptibly large **:** CONSIDERABLE **c** (1) **:** perceptible as real or material **:** SUBSTANTIAL ⟨the *sensible* world in which we live⟩ (2) **:** of a kind to arouse emotional response ⟨his whipping was a *sensible* expression of his father's anger⟩
2 a : capable of receiving sensory impressions ⟨*sensible* to pain⟩ **b :** receptive to external influences **:** SENSITIVE ⟨the most *sensible* reaches of the spirit⟩
3 a : perceiving through the senses or mind **:** COGNIZANT ⟨*sensible* of the increasing heat⟩; *also* **:** convinced by perceived evidence **:** SATISFIED ⟨*sensible* of my error⟩ **b :** emotionally aware and responsive ⟨we are *sensible* of your problems⟩ **c :** CONSCIOUS
4 : having, containing, or indicative of good sense or reason **:** RATIONAL, REASONABLE ⟨*sensible* people⟩ ⟨made a *sensible* answer⟩
synonym see MATERIAL, PERCEPTIBLE, AWARE, WISE
— **sen·si·ble·ness** *noun*
— **sen·si·bly** \-blē\ *adverb*
²sensible *noun* (1589)
: something that can be sensed
sen·sil·lum \sen-ˈsi-ləm\ *also* **sen·sil·la** \-ˈsi-lə\ *noun, plural* **-sil·la** \-ˈsi-lə\ *also* **-sil·lae** \-ˈsi-(ˌ)lē\ [New Latin *sensillum*, diminutive of Medieval Latin *sensus* sense organ, from Latin, sense] (1925)
: a simple epithelial sense organ of an invertebrate (as an insect) usually in the form of a spine, plate, rod, cone, or peg that is composed of one or a few cells with a nerve connection
sen·si·ti·sa·tion, sen·si·tise *British variant of* SENSITIZATION, SENSITIZE
¹sen·si·tive \ˈsen(t)-sə-tiv, ˈsen(t)s-təv\ *adjective* [Middle English, from Middle French *sensitif*, from Medieval Latin *sensitivus*, probably alteration of *sensativus*, from *sensatus* sensate] (15th century)
1 : SENSORY 2
2 a : receptive to sense impressions **b :** capable of being stimulated or excited by external agents (as light, gravity, or contact) ⟨a photo-

graphic emulsion *sensitive* to red light⟩ ⟨*sensitive* protoplasm⟩
3 : highly responsive or susceptible: as **a** (1) **:** easily hurt or damaged; *especially* **:** easily hurt emotionally (2) **:** delicately aware of the attitudes and feelings of others **b :** excessively or abnormally susceptible **:** HYPERSENSITIVE ⟨*sensitive* to egg protein⟩ **c :** readily fluctuating in price or demand ⟨*sensitive* commodities⟩ **d :** capable of indicating minute differences **:** DELICATE ⟨*sensitive* scales⟩ **e :** readily affected or changed by various agents (as light or mechanical shock) **f :** highly radiosensitive
4 a : concerned with highly classified government information or involving discretionary authority over important policy matters ⟨*sensitive* documents⟩ **b :** calling for tact, care, or caution in treatment **:** TOUCHY ⟨a *sensitive* issue like race relations⟩
synonym see LIABLE
— **sen·si·tive·ly** *adverb*
— **sen·si·tive·ness** *noun*
²sensitive *noun* (1850)
1 : a person having occult or psychical abilities
2 : a sensitive person
sensitive plant *noun* (1659)
: any of several mimosas (especially *Mimosa pudica*) with leaves that fold or droop when touched; *broadly* **:** a plant responding to touch with movement
sen·si·tiv·i·ty \ˌsen(t)-sə-ˈti-və-tē\ *noun, plural* **-ties** (1803)
: the quality or state of being sensitive: as **a :** the capacity of an organism or sense organ to respond to stimulation **:** IRRITABILITY **b :** the quality or state of being hypersensitive **c :** the degree to which a radio receiving set responds to incoming waves **d :** the capacity of being easily hurt **e :** awareness of the needs and emotions of others ⟨a book written with just the right mix of empathy and *sensitivity* —L.C. Brown⟩
sen·si·ti·za·tion \ˌsen(t)-sə-tə-ˈzā-shən, ˌsen(t)-tə-ˈzā-\ *noun* (1887)
1 : the action or process of sensitizing
2 : the quality or state of being sensitized (as to an antigen)
sen·si·tize \ˈsen(t)-sə-ˌtīz\ *verb* **-tized; -tiz·ing** [*sensitive* + *-ize*] (circa 1859)
transitive verb
: to make sensitive or hypersensitive
intransitive verb
: to become sensitive
— **sen·si·tiz·er** *noun*
sen·si·tom·e·ter \ˌsen(t)-sə-ˈtä-mə-tər\ *noun* [International Scientific Vocabulary *sensitive* + *-o-* + *-meter*] (1880)
: an instrument for measuring sensitivity of photographic material
— **sen·si·to·met·ric** \ˌsen(t)-sə-tə-ˈme-trik\ *adjective*

☆ **SYNONYMS**
Sense, common sense, judgment, wisdom mean ability to reach intelligent conclusions. SENSE implies a reliable ability to judge and decide with soundness, prudence, and intelligence ⟨a choice showing good *sense*⟩. COMMON SENSE suggests an average degree of such ability without sophistication or special knowledge ⟨*common sense* tells me it's wrong⟩. JUDGMENT implies sense tempered and refined by experience, training, and maturity ⟨they relied on her *judgment* for guidance⟩. WISDOM implies sense and judgment far above average ⟨a leader of rare *wisdom*⟩.

\ə\ abut \ə\ kitten \ər\ further \a\ ash \ā\ ace
\ä\ mop, mar \au̇\ out \ch\ chin \e\ bet \ē\ easy
\g\ go \i\ hit \ī\ ice \j\ job \ŋ\ sing \ō\ go
\ȯ\ law \ȯi\ boy \th\ thin \ṯh\ the \ü\ loot \u̇\ foot
\y\ yet \zh\ vision *see also* Guide to Pronunciation

sen·si·tom·e·try \-sə-'tä-mə-trē\ *noun*

sen·sor \'sen-ˌsȯr, 'sen(t)-sər\ *noun* [Latin *sentire* to perceive + English ¹*-or* — more at SENSE] (circa 1928)
: a device that responds to a physical stimulus (as heat, light, sound, pressure, magnetism, or a particular motion) and transmits a resulting impulse (as for measurement or operating a control); *also* : SENSE ORGAN

sen·so·ri·al \sen-'sȯr-ē-əl, -'sȯr-\ *adjective* (1768)
: SENSORY
— **sen·so·ri·al·ly** \-ə-lē\ *adverb*

sen·so·ri·mo·tor \ˌsen(t)s-rē-'mō-tər, ˌsen(t)-sə-\ *adjective* [*sensory* + *motor*] (1855)
: of, relating to, or functioning in both sensory and motor aspects of bodily activity

sen·so·ri·neu·ral \-'nùr-əl, -'nyùr-\ *adjective* (circa 1977)
: of, relating to, or involving the aspects of sense perception mediated by nerves ⟨*sensorineural* hearing loss⟩

sen·so·ri·um \sen-'sȯr-ē-əm, -'sȯr-\ *noun, plural* **-ri·ums** *or* **-ria** \-ē-ə\ [Late Latin, sense organ, from Latin *sentire*] (1647)
: the parts of the brain or the mind concerned with the reception and interpretation of sensory stimuli; *broadly* : the entire sensory apparatus

sen·so·ry \'sen(t)s-rē, 'sen(t)-sə-rē\ *adjective* (1749)
1 : of or relating to sensation or to the senses
2 : conveying nerve impulses from the sense organs to the nerve centers : AFFERENT

sensory area *noun* (1896)
: an area of the cerebral cortex that receives afferent nerve fibers from lower sensory or motor areas

sen·su·al \'sen(t)-sh(ə-)wəl, -shəl\ *adjective* [Middle English, from Late Latin *sensualis*, from Latin *sensus* sense] (15th century)
1 : relating to or consisting in the gratification of the senses or the indulgence of appetite : FLESHLY
2 : SENSORY
3 a : devoted to or preoccupied with the senses or appetites **b** : VOLUPTUOUS **c** : deficient in moral, spiritual, or intellectual interests : WORLDLY; *especially* : IRRELIGIOUS
synonym see CARNAL, SENSUOUS
— **sen·su·al·i·ty** \ˌsen(t)-shə-'wa-lə-tē\ *noun*
— **sen·su·al·ly** \'sen(t)-sh(ə-)wə-lē, 'sen-shə-lē\ *adverb*

sen·su·al·ism \'sen(t)-sh(ə-)wə-ˌli-zəm, 'sen-shə-ˌli-\ *noun* (1813)
: persistent or excessive pursuit of sensual pleasures and interests
— **sen·su·al·ist** \-list\ *noun*
— **sen·su·al·is·tic** \ˌsen(t)-sh(ə-)wə-'lis-tik, ˌsen-shə-'lis-\ *adjective*

sen·su·al·ize \'sen(t)-sh(ə-)wə-ˌlīz, 'sen-shə-ˌlīz\ *transitive verb* **-ized; -iz·ing** (circa 1687)
: to make sensual
— **sen·su·al·i·za·tion** \ˌsen(t)-sh(ə-)wə-lə-'zā-shən, ˌsen-shə-lə-\ *noun*

sen·sum \'sen(t)-səm\ *noun, plural* **sen·sa** \-sə\ [Medieval Latin, from Latin, neuter of *sensus*, past participle of *sentire* to feel — more at SENSE] (1868)
: SENSE-DATUM

sen·su·ous \'sen(t)-sh(ə-)wəs\ *adjective* [Latin *sensus* sense + English *-ous*] (1640)
1 a : of or relating to the senses or sensible objects **b** : producing or characterized by gratification of the senses : having strong sensory appeal ⟨*sensuous* pleasure⟩
2 : characterized by sense impressions or imagery aimed at the senses ⟨*sensuous* verse⟩
3 : highly susceptible to influence through the senses ☆
— **sen·su·os·i·ty** \ˌsen(t)-shə-'wä-sə-tē\ *noun*
— **sen·su·ous·ly** \'sen(t)-shə-wəs-lē\ *adverb*
— **sen·su·ous·ness** *noun*

sen·su stric·to \'sen-ˌsü-'strik-(ˌ)tō\ *adverb* [New Latin] (1902)
: in a narrow or strict sense

sent *past and past participle of* SEND

sen·te \'sen-tē\ *noun, plural* **li·cen·te** *or* **li·sen·te** \li-'sen-tē\ [Sesotho, from English *century*] (1966)
— see *loti* at MONEY table

¹sen·tence \'sen-t²n(t)s, -t²nz\ *noun* [Middle English, from Middle French, from Latin *sententia* feeling, opinion, from (assumed) *sentent-, sentens*, irregular present participle of *sentire* to feel — more at SENSE] (14th century)
1 *obsolete* : OPINION; *especially* : a conclusion given on request or reached after deliberation
2 a : JUDGMENT 2a; *specifically* : one formally pronounced by a court or judge in a criminal proceeding and specifying the punishment to be inflicted upon the convict **b** : the punishment so imposed ⟨serve out a *sentence*⟩
3 *archaic* : MAXIM, SAW
4 a : a word, clause, or phrase or a group of clauses or phrases forming a syntactic unit which expresses an assertion, a question, a command, a wish, an exclamation, or the performance of an action, that in writing usually begins with a capital letter and concludes with appropriate end punctuation, and that in speaking is distinguished by characteristic patterns of stress, pitch, and pauses **b** : a mathematical or logical statement (as an equation or a proposition) in words or symbols
5 : PERIOD 2b

²sentence *transitive verb* **sen·tenced; sen·tenc·ing** (1592)
1 : to impose a sentence on
2 : to cause to suffer something ⟨*sentenced* these most primitive cultures to extinction —E. W. Count⟩

sentence fragment *noun* (1947)
: a word, phrase, or clause that usually has in speech the intonation of a sentence but lacks the grammatical structure usually found in the sentences of formal and especially written composition

sentence stress *noun* (1884)
: the manner in which stresses are distributed on the syllables of words assembled into sentences — called also *sentence accent*

sen·ten·tia \sen-'ten-sh(ē-)ə\ *noun, plural* **-ti·ae** \-shē-ˌē\ [Latin, literally, feeling, opinion] (1917)
: APHORISM — usually used in plural

sen·ten·tial \sen-'ten(t)-shəl\ *adjective* (1646)
1 : of or relating to a sentence ⟨a relative clause with a *sentential* antecedent⟩
2 : of, relating to, or involving a proposition in logic ⟨*sentential* connective⟩

sentential calculus *noun* (1937)
: PROPOSITIONAL CALCULUS

sentential function *noun* (1937)
: an expression that contains one or more variables and becomes a declarative sentence when constants are substituted for the variables

sen·ten·tious \sen-'ten(t)-shəs\ *adjective* [Middle English, full of meaning, from Latin *sententiosus*, from *sententia* sentence, maxim] (1509)
1 a : given to or abounding in aphoristic expression **b** : given to or abounding in excessive moralizing
2 : terse, aphoristic, or moralistic in expression : PITHY, EPIGRAMMATIC
— **sen·ten·tious·ly** *adverb*
— **sen·ten·tious·ness** *noun*

sen·tience \'sen(t)-sh(ē-)ən(t)s, 'sen-tē-ən(t)s\ *noun* (1839)
1 : a sentient quality or state
2 : feeling or sensation as distinguished from perception and thought

sen·tient \'sen(t)-sh(ē-)ənt, 'sen-tē-ənt\ *adjective* [Latin *sentient-, sentiens*, present participle of *sentire* to perceive, feel] (1632)
1 : responsive to or conscious of sense impressions
2 : AWARE
3 : finely sensitive in perception or feeling
— **sen·tient·ly** *adverb*

sen·ti·ment \'sen-tə-mənt\ *noun* [French or Medieval Latin; French, from Medieval Latin *sentimentum*, from Latin *sentire*] (1639)
1 a : an attitude, thought, or judgment prompted by feeling : PREDILECTION **b** : a specific view or notion : OPINION
2 a : EMOTION **b** : refined feeling : delicate sensibility especially as expressed in a work of art **c** : emotional idealism **d** : a romantic or nostalgic feeling verging on sentimentality
3 a : an idea colored by emotion **b** : the emotional significance of a passage or expression as distinguished from its verbal context
synonym see FEELING, OPINION

sen·ti·men·tal \ˌsen-tə-'men-t²l\ *adjective* (1749)
1 a : marked or governed by feeling, sensibility, or emotional idealism **b** : resulting from feeling rather than reason or thought
2 : having an excess of sentiment or sensibility
— **sen·ti·men·tal·ly** *adverb*

sen·ti·men·tal·ise *British variant of* SENTIMENTALIZE

sen·ti·men·tal·ism \ˌsen-tə-'men-t²l-ˌi-zəm\ *noun* (1817)
1 : the disposition to favor or indulge in sentimentality
2 : an excessively sentimental conception or statement
— **sen·ti·men·tal·ist** \-t²l-ist\ *noun*

sen·ti·men·tal·i·ty \ˌsen-tə-ˌmen-'ta-lə-tē, -mən-\ *noun, plural* **-ties** (1770)
1 : the quality or state of being sentimental especially to excess or in affectation
2 : a sentimental idea or its expression

sen·ti·men·tal·ize \-'men-t²l-ˌīz\ *verb* **-ized; -iz·ing** (1788)
intransitive verb
: to indulge in sentiment
transitive verb
: to look upon or imbue with sentiment
— **sen·ti·men·tal·i·za·tion** \-ˌmen-t²l-ə-'zā-shən\ *noun*

sen·ti·mo \sen-'tē-(ˌ)mō\ *noun, plural* **-mos** [Tagalog, from Spanish *céntimo*] (1968)
— see *peso* at MONEY table

¹sen·ti·nel \'sent-nəl, 'sen-t²n-əl\ *noun* [Middle French *sentinelle*, from Old Italian *sentinella*, from *sentina* vigilance, from *sentire* to perceive, from Latin] (1579)
: SENTRY

²sentinel *transitive verb* **-neled** *or* **-nelled; -nel·ing** *or* **-nel·ling** (1593)
1 : to watch over as a sentinel
2 : to furnish with a sentinel
3 : to post as sentinel

sen·try \'sen-trē\ *noun, plural* **sentries** [perhaps from obsolete *sentry* sanctuary, watchtower] (1632)
: GUARD, WATCH; *especially* : a soldier standing guard at a point of passage (as a gate)

☆ SYNONYMS
Sensuous, sensual, luxurious, voluptuous mean relating to or providing pleasure through gratification of the senses. SENSUOUS implies gratification of the senses for the sake of aesthetic pleasure ⟨the *sensuous* delights of great music⟩. SENSUAL tends to imply the gratification of the senses or the indulgence of the physical appetites as ends in themselves ⟨a life devoted to *sensual* pleasures⟩. LUXURIOUS suggests the providing of or indulgence of sensuous pleasure inducing bodily ease and languor ⟨a *luxurious* hotel⟩. VOLUPTUOUS implies more strongly an abandonment especially to sensual pleasure ⟨a *voluptuous* feast⟩.

sentry box *noun* (circa 1728)
: a shelter for a sentry on his post

se·pal \'sē-pəl, 'se-\ *noun* [New Latin *sepalum,* from *sep-* (irregular from Greek *skepē* covering) + *-alum* (as in *petalum* petal)] (1821)
: one of the modified leaves comprising a calyx — see FLOWER illustration

se·pal·oid \-pə-ˌlȯid\ *adjective* (1830)
: resembling or functioning as a sepal

sep·a·ra·ble \'se-p(ə-)rə-bəl\ *adjective* [Middle English, from Latin *separabilis,* from *separare*] (14th century)
1 : capable of being separated or dissociated
2 *obsolete* : causing separation
— **sep·a·ra·bil·i·ty** \ˌse-p(ə-)rə-'bi-lə-tē\ *noun*
— **sep·a·ra·ble·ness** *noun*

¹**sep·a·rate** \'se-p(ə-)ˌrāt\ *verb* **-rat·ed; -rat·ing** [Middle English, from Latin *separatus,* past participle of *separare,* from *se-* apart + *parare* to prepare, procure — more at SE-CEDE, PARE] (15th century)
transitive verb
1 a : to set or keep apart : DISCONNECT, SEVER **b** : to make a distinction between : DISCRIMINATE, DISTINGUISH ⟨*separate* religion from magic⟩ **c** : SORT ⟨*separate* mail⟩ **d** : to disperse in space or time : SCATTER ⟨widely *separated* homesteads⟩
2 *archaic* : to set aside for a special purpose : CHOOSE, DEDICATE
3 : to part by a legal separation: **a** : to sever conjugal ties with **b** : to sever contractual relations with : DISCHARGE ⟨*separated* from the army⟩
4 : to block off : SEGREGATE
5 a : to isolate from a mixture : EXTRACT ⟨*separate* cream from milk⟩ **b** : to divide into constituent parts
6 : to dislocate (as a shoulder) especially in sports
intransitive verb
1 : to become divided or detached
2 a : to sever an association : WITHDRAW **b** : to cease to live together as a married couple
3 : to go in different directions
4 : to become isolated from a mixture ☆

²**sep·a·rate** \'se-p(ə-)rət\ *adjective* (15th century)
1 a : set or kept apart : DETACHED **b** *archaic* : SOLITARY, SECLUDED **c** : IMMATERIAL, DISEMBODIED
2 a : not shared with another : INDIVIDUAL ⟨*separate* rooms⟩ **b** *often capitalized* : estranged from a parent body ⟨*separate* churches⟩
3 a : existing by itself : AUTONOMOUS **b** : dissimilar in nature or identity
synonym see DISTINCT
— **sep·a·rate·ly** \-p(ə-)rət-lē, 'se-pərt-lē\ *adverb*
— **sep·a·rate·ness** \-nəs\ *noun*

³**sep·a·rate** \'se-p(ə-)rət\ *noun* (1886)
1 : OFFPRINT
2 : an article of dress designed to be worn interchangeably with others to form various costume combinations — usually used in plural

sep·a·ra·tion \ˌse-pə-'rā-shən\ *noun* (14th century)
1 : the act or process of separating : the state of being separated
2 a : a point, line, or means of division **b** : an intervening space : GAP
3 a : cessation of cohabitation between a married couple by mutual agreement or judicial decree **b** : termination of a contractual relationship (as employment or military service)

sep·a·ra·tion·ist \-sh(ə-)nist\ *noun* (1831)
: SEPARATIST

sep·a·rat·ism \'se-p(ə-)rə-ˌti-zəm\ *noun* (1628)
: a belief in, movement for, or state of separation (as schism, secession, or segregation)

sep·a·rat·ist \'se-p(ə-)rə-tist, 'se-pə-ˌrā-\ *noun* (1608)

: one that favors separatism: as **a** *capitalized* : one of a group of 16th and 17th century English Protestants preferring to separate from rather than to reform the Church of England **b** : an advocate of independence or autonomy for a part of a political unit (as a nation) **c** : an advocate of racial or cultural separation
— **separatist** *adjective*
— **sep·a·ra·tis·tic** \ˌse-p(ə-)rə-'tis-tik\ *adjective*

sep·a·ra·tive \'se-pə-ˌrā-tiv, 'se-p(ə-)rə-\ *adjective* (1592)
: tending toward, causing, or expressing separation

sep·a·ra·tor \'se-p(ə-)ˌrā-tər\ *noun* (1607)
: one that separates; *especially* : a device for separating liquids of different specific gravities (as cream from milk) or liquids from solids

Se·phar·di \sə-'fär-dē\ *noun, plural* **Se·phar·dim** \-'fär-dəm\ [Late Hebrew *sĕphāradhī,* from *sĕphāradh* Spain, from Hebrew, region where Jews were once exiled (Obadiah 1:20)] (1851)
: a member of the occidental branch of European Jews settling in Spain and Portugal and later in the Balkans, the Levant, England, the Netherlands, and the Americas; *also* : one of their descendants — compare ASHKENAZI
— **Se·phar·dic** \-'fär-dik\ *adjective*

¹**se·pia** \'sē-pē-ə\ *noun* [Latin, cuttlefish, ink, from Greek *sēpia*] (1821)
1 a : the inky secretion of a cuttlefish **b** : a brown melanin-containing pigment from the ink of cuttlefishes
2 : a print or photograph of a brown color resembling sepia
3 : a brownish gray to dark olive brown color

²**sepia** *adjective* (1827)
1 : made of or done in sepia
2 : of the color sepia

se·pi·o·lite \'sē-pē-ə-ˌlīt\ *noun* [German *Sepiolith,* from Greek *sēpion* cuttlebone (from *sē-pia*) + German *-lith* -lite] (1854)
: MEERSCHAUM 1

se·poy \'sē-ˌpȯi\ *noun* [Portuguese *sipai,* from Hindi *sipāhī,* from Persian, cavalryman] (circa 1718)
: a native of India employed as a soldier by a European power

sep·pu·ku \se-'pü-(ˌ)kü, 'se-pə-ˌkü\ *noun* [Japanese] (1871)
: HARA-KIRI 1

sep·sis \'sep-səs\ *noun, plural* **sep·ses** \'sep-ˌsēz\ [New Latin, from Greek *sēpsis* decay, from *sēpein* to putrefy] (1876)
: a toxic condition resulting from the spread of bacteria or their products from a focus of infection; *especially* : SEPTICEMIA

sept \'sept\ *noun* [perhaps from Latin *septum, saeptum* enclosure, fold — more at SEPTUM] (1517)
: a branch of a family; *especially* : CLAN

sep·tal \'sep-t°l\ *adjective* (circa 1847)
: of or relating to a septum

sep·tate \'sep-ˌtāt\ *adjective* (1846)
: divided by or having a septum

Sep·tem·ber \sep-'tem-bər, səp-\ *noun* [Middle English *Septembre,* from Old French & Old English, both from Latin *September* (seventh month), from *septem* seven — more at SEVEN] (before 12th century)
: the 9th month of the Gregorian calendar ◆

sep·te·nar·i·us \ˌsep-tə-'nar-ē-əs, -'ner-\ *noun, plural* **-nar·ii** \-ē-ˌī, -ē-ˌē\ [Latin, from *septenarius* of seven, from *septeni* seven each, from *septem* seven] (1819)
: a verse consisting of seven feet especially in Latin prosody

sep·ten·de·cil·lion \(ˌ)sep-ˌten-di-'sil-yən\ *noun, often attributive* [Latin *septendecim* seventeen (from *septem* seven + *decem* ten) + English *-illion* (as in *million*) — more at TEN] (circa 1938)
— see NUMBER table

sep·ten·ni·al \sep-'te-nē-əl\ *adjective* [Late Latin *septennium* period of seven years, from Latin *septem* + *-ennium* (as in *biennium*)] (1640)
1 : occurring or being done every seven years
2 : consisting of or lasting for seven years
— **sep·ten·ni·al·ly** \-ə-lē\ *adverb*

sep·ten·tri·on \sep-'ten-trē-ˌän, -trē-ən\ *noun* [Middle English, from Middle French, from Latin *septentriones,* plural, the seven stars of Ursa Major or Ursa Minor, from *septem* seven + *triones* plowing oxen] (14th century)
obsolete : the northern regions : NORTH

sep·ten·tri·o·nal \-trē-ə-n°l\ *adjective* (14th century)
: NORTHERN

sep·tet \sep-'tet\ *noun* [German, from Latin *septem*] (1828)
1 : a musical composition for seven instruments or voices
2 : a group or set of seven; *especially* : the performers of a septet

☆ **SYNONYMS**

Separate, part, divide, sever, sunder, divorce mean to become or cause to become disunited or disjointed. SEPARATE may imply any of several causes such as dispersion, removal of one from others, or presence of an intervening thing ⟨*separated* her personal life from her career⟩. PART implies the separating of things or persons in close union or association ⟨vowed never to *part*⟩. DIVIDE implies separating into pieces or sections by cutting or breaking ⟨civil war *divided* the nation⟩. SEVER implies violence especially in the removal of a part or member ⟨a *severed* limb⟩. SUNDER suggests violent rending or wrenching apart ⟨a city *sundered* by racial conflict⟩. DIVORCE implies separating two things that commonly interact and belong together ⟨cannot *divorce* scientific research from moral responsibility⟩.

◇ **WORD HISTORY**

September The earliest Roman calendar appears to have had just ten lunar months, March to December, with an uncounted intervening gap in the winter. The names of the last four months, in Latin *September, October, November,* and *December,* were formed, appropriately enough, from the numerals *septem* "seven," *octo* "eight," *novem* "nine," and *decem* "ten." The original names of *September, November,* and *December* were presumably compounds made up with the aid of an unattested element *mensri-,* itself derived from *mensis* "month" and a suffix *ri-.* Through a series of sound changes, *mensri-* became *membri-.* The resulting words should have been *Septemmember, Novemmember,* and *Decemmember,* but these likewise unattested forms appear to have undergone contraction by dropping one pair of the identical sounds found next to each other (a process called haplology) to give *September, November,* and *December. October* was simply formed by analogy to fit the shape of the other three words; its earlier name in Latin is unknown. The subsequent changes in the calendar that added two months, January and February, and made January rather than March the beginning of the year rendered the numerical sequence incorrect, but the Romans retained the old names, which we have inherited.

sep·tic \'sep-tik\ *adjective* [Latin *septicus,* from Greek *sēptikos,* from *sēpein* to putrefy] (1605)
1 : of, relating to, or causing putrefaction
2 : relating to, involving, or characteristic of sepsis

sep·ti·ce·mia \ˌsep-tə-'sē-mē-ə\ *noun* [New Latin, from Latin *septicus* + New Latin *-emia*] (circa 1860)
: invasion of the bloodstream by virulent microorganisms from a local seat of infection accompanied especially by chills, fever, and prostration — called also *blood poisoning*; compare SEPSIS
— **sep·ti·ce·mic** \-'sē-mik\ *adjective*

sep·ti·ci·dal \ˌsep-tə-'sī-dᵊl\ *adjective* [New Latin *septum* + Latin *-cidere* to cut, from *caedere*] (1819)
: dehiscent longitudinally at or along a septum ⟨a *septicidal* fruit⟩

septic sore throat *noun* (1924)
: STREP THROAT

septic tank *noun* (circa 1902)
: a tank in which the solid matter of continuously flowing sewage is disintegrated by bacteria

sep·til·lion \sep-'til-yən\ *noun, often attributive* [French, from Latin *septem* + French *-illion* (as in *million*) — more at SEVEN] (1690)
— see NUMBER table

sep·tu·a·ge·nar·i·an \ˌ(ˌ)sep-tü-ə-jə-'ner-ē-ən, -ˌtyü-, -ˌchü-\ *noun* [Late Latin *septuagenarius* seventy years old, from Latin, of or containing seventy, from *septuageni* seventy each, from *septuaginta*] (1805)
: a person whose age is in the seventies
— **septuagenarian** *adjective*

Sep·tu·a·ge·si·ma \ˌsep-tə-wə-'je-sə-mə, -'jā-zə-\ *noun* [Middle English, from Late Latin, from Latin, feminine of *septuagesimus* seventieth, from *septuaginta* seventy; from its being approximately seventy days before Easter] (14th century)
: the third Sunday before Lent

Sep·tu·a·gint \sep-'tü-ə-jənt, -'tyü-; 'sep-tə-wə-ˌjint\ *noun* [Late Latin *Septuaginta,* from Latin, seventy, irregular from *septem* seven + *-ginta* (akin to Latin vi*ginti* twenty); from the approximate number of its translators — more at SEVEN, VIGESIMAL] (1633)
: a Greek version of the Jewish Scriptures redacted in the 3d and 2d centuries B.C. by Jewish scholars and adopted by Greek-speaking Christians
— **Sep·tu·a·gin·tal** \ˌ(ˌ)sep-ˌtü-ə-'jin-tᵊl, -ˌtyü-; ˌsep-tə-wə-\ *adjective*

sep·tum \'sep-təm\ *noun, plural* **sep·ta** \-tə\ [New Latin, from Latin *saeptum* enclosure, fence, wall, from *saepire* to fence in, from *saepes* fence, hedge] (1698)
: a dividing wall or membrane especially between bodily spaces or masses of soft tissue
— compare DISSEPIMENT

se·pul·chral \sə-'pəl-krəl *also* -'pul-\ *adjective* (1615)
: suited to or suggestive of a sepulchre **:** FUNEREAL, MORTUARY
— **se·pul·chral·ly** \-krə-lē\ *adverb*

¹sep·ul·chre *or* **sep·ul·cher** \'se-pəl-kər\ *noun* [Middle English *sepulcre,* from Old French, from Latin *sepulcrum, sepulchrum,* from *sepelire* to bury; akin to Greek *hepein* to care for, Sanskrit *saparyati* he honors] (13th century)
1 : a place of burial **:** TOMB
2 : a receptacle for religious relics especially in an altar

²sepulchre *or* **sepulcher** *transitive verb* **-chred** *or* **-chered; -chring** *or* **-chering** \-k(ə-)riŋ\ (1591)
1 *archaic* **:** to place in or as if in a sepulchre **:** BURY

2 *archaic* **:** to serve as a sepulchre for

sep·ul·ture \'se-pəl-ˌchùr\ *noun* [Middle English, from Old French, from Latin *sepultura,* from *sepultus,* past participle of *sepelire*] (14th century)
1 : BURIAL
2 : SEPULCHRE

se·qua·cious \si-'kwā-shəs\ *adjective* [Latin *sequac-, sequax* inclined to follow, from *sequi*] (1643)
1 *archaic* **:** SUBSERVIENT, TRACTABLE
2 : intellectually servile
— **se·qua·cious·ly** *adverb*
— **se·quac·i·ty** \-'kwa-sə-tē\ *noun*

se·quel \'sē-kwəl *also* -ˌkwel\ *noun* [Middle English, from Middle French *sequelle,* from Latin *sequela,* from *sequi* to follow — more at SUE] (15th century)
1 : CONSEQUENCE, RESULT
2 a : subsequent development **b :** the next installment (as of a speech or story); *especially* **:** a literary or cinematic work continuing the course of a story begun in a preceding one

se·quela \si-'kwe-lə\ *noun, plural* **se·quel·ae** \-'kwe-(ˌ)lē\ [New Latin, from Latin, *sequel*] (circa 1793)
1 : an aftereffect of disease or injury
2 : a secondary result

¹se·quence \'sē-kwən(t)s, -ˌkwen(t)s\ *noun* [Middle English, from Medieval Latin *sequentia,* from Late Latin, sequel, literally, act of following, from Latin *sequent-, sequens,* present participle of *sequi*] (14th century)
1 : a hymn in irregular meter between the gradual and Gospel in masses for special occasions (as Easter)
2 a : a continuous or connected series: as **a :** an extended series of poems united by a single theme ⟨a sonnet *sequence*⟩ **b :** three or more playing cards usually of the same suit in consecutive order of rank **c :** a succession of repetitions of a melodic phrase or harmonic pattern each in a new position **d :** a set of elements ordered so that they can be labeled with the positive integers **e** (1) **:** a succession of related shots or scenes developing a single subject or phase of a film story (2) **:** EPISODE
3 a : order of succession **b :** an arrangement of the tenses of successive verbs in a sentence designed to express a coherent relationship especially between main and subordinate parts
4 a : CONSEQUENCE, RESULT **b :** a subsequent development
5 : continuity of progression

²sequence *transitive verb* **se·quenced; se·quenc·ing** (1941)
1 : to arrange in a sequence
2 : to determine the sequence of chemical constituents (as amino-acid residues) in ⟨*sequenced* biological macromolecules⟩

se·quenc·er \'sē-kwən(t)-sər, -ˌkwen(t)-\ *noun* (1949)
: one that sequences: as **a :** a device for arranging (as events in the ignition of a rocket) in a sequence **b :** a device for determining the order of occurrence of amino acids in a protein

se·quen·cy \'sē-kwən(t)-sē\ *noun* [Late Latin *sequentia*] (1818)
: SEQUENCE 3a, 5

se·quent \'sē-kwənt\ *adjective* [Latin *sequent-, sequens,* present participle] (1601)
1 : CONSECUTIVE, SUCCEEDING
2 : CONSEQUENT, RESULTANT

se·quen·tial \si-'kwen(t)-shəl\ *adjective* (1854)
1 : of, relating to, or arranged in a sequence **:** SERIAL ⟨*sequential* file systems⟩
2 : following in sequence
3 : relating to or based on a method of testing a statistical hypothesis that involves examination of a sequence of samples for each of which the decision is made to accept or reject the hypothesis or to continue sampling

se·quen·tial·ly \-'kwen(t)-sh(ə-)lē\ *adverb*

¹se·ques·ter \si-'kwes-tər *transitive verb* **-tered; -ter·ing** \-t(ə-)riŋ\ [Middle English *sequestren,* from Middle French *sequestrer,* from Latin *sequestrare* to hand over to a trustee, from *sequester* third party to whom disputed property is entrusted, agent, from *secus* beside, otherwise; akin to Latin *sequi* to follow] (14th century)
1 a : to set apart **:** SEGREGATE **b :** SECLUDE, WITHDRAW
2 a : to seize especially by a writ of sequestration **b :** to place (property) in custody especially in sequestration
3 : to hold (as a metallic ion) in solution usually by inclusion in an appropriate coordination complex

²sequester *noun* (1604)
obsolete **:** SEPARATION, ISOLATION

se·ques·trate \'sē-kwəs-ˌtrāt, 'se-; si-'kwes-\ *transitive verb* **-trat·ed; -trat·ing** [Latin *sequestratus,* past participle of *sequestrare*] (15th century)
: SEQUESTER

se·ques·tra·tion \ˌsē-kwəs-'trā-shən, ˌse-; ˌ(ˌ)sē-ˌkwes-\ *noun* (15th century)
1 : the act of sequestering **:** the state of being sequestered
2 a : a legal writ authorizing a sheriff or commissioner to take into custody the property of a defendant who is in contempt until the orders of a court are complied with **b :** a deposit whereby a neutral depositary agrees to hold property in litigation and to restore it to the party to whom it is adjudged to belong

se·ques·trum \si-'kwes-trəm\ *noun, plural* **-trums** *also* **-tra** \-trə\ [New Latin, from Latin, legal sequestration, from *sequester*] (1831)
: a fragment of dead bone detached from adjoining sound bone

se·quin \'sē-kwən\ *noun* [French, from Italian *zecchino,* from *zecca* mint, from Arabic *sikkah* die, coin] (1617)
1 : an old gold coin of Italy and Turkey
2 : a small plate of shining metal or plastic used for ornamentation especially on clothing
se·quined *or* **se·quinned** \-kwənd\ *adjective* (1894)
: ornamented with or as if with sequins

se·qui·tur \'se-kwə-tər, -ˌtùr\ *noun* [Latin, it follows, 3d person singular present indicative of *sequi* to follow — more at SUE] (1836)
: the conclusion of an inference **:** CONSEQUENCE

se·quoia \si-'kwòi-ə\ *noun* [New Latin, genus name, from *Sequoya* (George Guess)] (circa 1866)
: either of two huge coniferous California trees of the bald cypress family that may reach a height of over 300 feet (90 meters): **a :** BIG TREE **b :** REDWOOD 3a

sera *plural of* SERUM

se·rac \sə-'rak, sā-\ *noun* [French *sérac,* literally, a kind of white cheese, from Medieval Latin *seracium* whey, from Latin *serum* whey — more at SERUM] (1860)
: a pinnacle, sharp ridge, or block of ice among the crevasses of a glacier

se·ra·glio \sə-'ral-(ˌ)yō, -'räl-\ *noun, plural* **-glios** [Italian *serraglio,* modification of Turkish *saray* palace] (1581)
1 : HAREM 1a
2 : a palace of a sultan

se·rai \sə-'rī\ *noun* [Turkish & Persian; Turkish *saray* mansion, palace, from Persian *sarāī* mansion, inn] (1609)
1 : CARAVANSARY
2 : SERAGLIO 2

ser·al \'sir-əl\ *adjective* (1916)
: of, relating to, or constituting an ecological sere

se·ra·pe \sə-'rä-pē, -'ra-\ *noun* [Mexican Spanish *sarape*] (1834)

: a colorful woolen shawl worn over the shoulders especially by Mexican men

ser·aph \'ser-əf\ *noun, plural* **ser·a·phim** \-ə-,fim, -,fēm\ *or* **seraphs** [assumed singular of Hebrew *śĕrāphīm*] (1667)
: SERAPHIM 2

ser·a·phim \'ser-ə-,fim, -,fēm\ *noun plural* [Late Latin *seraphim*, plural, seraphs, from Hebrew *śĕrāphīm*] (12th century)
1 : an order of angels — see CELESTIAL HIERARCHY
2 *singular, plural* **seraphim** : one of the 6-winged angels standing in the presence of God
— **se·raph·ic** \sə-'ra-fik\ *adjective*
— **se·raph·i·cal·ly** \-fi-k(ə-)lē\ *adverb*

serape

Se·ra·pis \sə-'rā-pəs\ *noun* [Latin, from Greek *Sarapis*]
: an Egyptian god combining attributes of Osiris and Apis and having a widespread cult in Ptolemaic Egypt and ancient Greece

Serb \'sərb\ *noun* [ultimately from Serbo-Croatian *srb*] (1860)
1 : a native or inhabitant of Serbia
2 : SERBIAN 2
— **Serb** *adjective*

Ser·bi·an \'sər-bē-ən\ *noun* (1848)
1 : SERB 1
2 a : the Serbo-Croatian language as spoken in Serbia **b** : a literary form of Serbo-Croatian using the Cyrillic alphabet
— **Serbian** *adjective*

Ser·bo–Cro·a·tian \,sər-(,)bō-krō-'ā-shən\ *noun* (1883)
1 : a Slavic language spoken in Croatia, Bosnia and Herzegovina, Serbia, and Montenegro
2 : a person whose native language is Serbo-Croatian
— **Serbo–Croatian** *adjective*

¹sere \'sir\ *adjective* [Middle English, from Old English *sēar* dry; akin to Old High German *sōrēn* to wither, Greek *hauos* dry, Lithuanian *sausas*] (before 12th century)
1 : being dried and withered
2 *archaic* : THREADBARE

²sere *noun* [Latin *series* series] (1916)
: a series of ecological communities formed in ecological succession

¹ser·e·nade \,ser-ə-'nād\ *noun* [French *sérénade*, from Italian *serenata*, from *sereno* clear, calm (of weather), from Latin *serenus* serene] (1649)
1 a : a complimentary vocal or instrumental performance; *especially* : one given outdoors at night for a woman being courted **b** : a work so performed
2 : an instrumental composition in several movements, written for a small ensemble, and midway between the suite and the symphony in style

²serenade *verb* **-nad·ed; -nad·ing** (1668)
intransitive verb
: to play a serenade
transitive verb
: to perform a serenade in honor of
— **ser·e·nad·er** *noun*

ser·e·na·ta \,ser-ə-'nä-tə\ *noun* [Italian, serenade] (circa 1724)
: an 18th century secular cantata of a dramatic character usually composed in honor of an individual or event

ser·en·dip·i·tous \,ser-ən-'di-pə-təs\ *adjective* (1943)
: obtained or characterized by serendipity ⟨*serendipitous* discoveries⟩
— **ser·en·dip·i·tous·ly** *adverb*

ser·en·dip·i·ty \-'di-pə-tē\ *noun* [from its possession by the heroes of the Persian fairy tale *The Three Princes of Serendip*] (1754)
: the faculty or phenomenon of finding valuable or agreeable things not sought for

¹se·rene \sə-'rēn\ *adjective* [Latin *serenus* clear, cloudless, untroubled] (15th century)
1 a : clear and free of storms or unpleasant change ⟨*serene* skies⟩ **b** : shining bright and steady (the moon, *serene* in glory —Alexander Pope)
2 : AUGUST — used as part of a title ⟨His *Serene* Highness⟩
3 : marked by or suggestive of utter calm and unruffled repose or quietude ⟨a *serene* smile⟩
synonym see CALM
— **se·rene·ly** *adverb*
— **se·rene·ness** \-'rēn-nəs\ *noun*

²serene *noun* (1644)
1 *archaic* : a serene condition or expanse (as of sky, sea, or light)
2 *archaic* : SERENITY, TRANQUILLITY

se·ren·i·ty \sə-'re-nə-tē\ *noun* (15th century)
: the quality or state of being serene

serf \'sərf\ *noun* [French, from Old French, from Latin *servus* slave] (1611)
: a member of a servile feudal class bound to the soil and subject to the will of his lord
— **serf·age** \'sər-fij\ *noun*
— **serf·dom** \'sərf-dəm, -təm\ *noun*

serge \'sərj\ *noun* [Middle English *sarge*, from Middle French, from (assumed) Vulgar Latin *sarica*, alteration of Latin *serica*, feminine of *sericus* silken — more at SERICEOUS] (14th century)
: a durable twilled fabric having a smooth clear face and a pronounced diagonal rib on the front and the back

ser·gean·cy \'sär-jən(t)-sē\ *noun* (circa 1670)
: the function, office, or rank of a sergeant

ser·geant \'sär-jənt\ *noun* [Middle English, servant, attendant, sergeant, from Middle French *sergent, serjant*, from Latin *servient-, serviens*, present participle of *servire* to serve] (13th century)
1 : SERGEANT AT ARMS
2 *obsolete* : an officer who enforces the judgments of a court or the commands of one in authority
3 : a noncommissioned officer ranking in the army and marine corps above a corporal and below a staff sergeant and in the air force above an airman first class or senior airman and below a staff sergeant; *broadly* : NONCOMMISSIONED OFFICER
4 : an officer in a police force ranking in the U.S. just below captain or sometimes lieutenant and in England just below inspector

sergeant at arms (14th century)
: an officer of an organization (as a legislative body or court of law) who preserves order and executes commands

sergeant first class *noun* (1948)
: a noncommissioned officer in the army ranking above a staff sergeant and below a master sergeant

sergeant fish *noun* (1873)
1 : COBIA
2 : SNOOK 1

sergeant major *noun, plural* **sergeants major** *or* **sergeant majors** (1802)
1 : a noncommissioned officer in the army, air force, or marine corps serving as chief administrative assistant in a headquarters
2 : a noncommissioned officer in the marine corps ranking above a first sergeant
3 : a bluish green to yellow bony fish (*Abudefduf saxatilis* of the family Pomacentridae) with black vertical stripes on the sides that is widely distributed in the western tropical Atlantic Ocean

sergeant major of the army (1966)
: the ranking noncommissioned officer of the army serving as adviser to the chief of staff

sergeant major of the marine corps (circa 1971)
: the ranking noncommissioned officer of the marine corps serving as adviser to the commandant

ser·geanty \'sär-jən-tē\ *noun, plural* **-geant·ies** [Middle English *sergeantie*, from Middle French *sergentie*, from *sergent* sergeant] (15th century)
: any of numerous feudal services of a personal nature by which an estate is held of the king or other lord distinct from military tenure and from socage tenure

serg·ing \'sər-jiŋ\ *noun* [*serge*] (circa 1909)
: the process of overcasting the raw edges of a piece of fabric (as a carpet) to prevent raveling

¹se·ri·al \'sir-ē-əl\ *adjective* (1840)
1 : of, relating to, consisting of, or arranged in a series, rank, or row ⟨*serial* order⟩
2 : appearing in successive parts or numbers ⟨a *serial* story⟩
3 : belonging to a series maturing periodically rather than on a single date ⟨*serial* bonds⟩
4 : of, relating to, or being music based on a series of tones in a chosen pattern without regard for traditional tonality
5 a : effecting a series of similar acts over a period of time ⟨a *serial* killer⟩ **b** : occurring in such a series ⟨a *serial* murder⟩
6 : relating to or being a connection in a computer system in which the bits of a byte are transmitted sequentially over a single wire — compare PARALLEL
— **se·ri·al·ly** \-ə-lē\ *adverb*

²serial *noun* (1846)
1 a : a work appearing (as in a magazine or on television) in parts at intervals **b** : one part of a serial work : INSTALLMENT
2 : a publication (as a newspaper or journal) issued as one of a consecutively numbered and indefinitely continued series

se·ri·al·ise *British variant of* SERIALIZE

se·ri·al·ism \'sir-ē-ə-,li-zəm\ *noun* (1958)
: serial music; *also* : the theory or practice of composing serial music

se·ri·al·ist \-list\ *noun* (1846)
1 : a writer of serials
2 : a composer of serial music

se·ri·al·ize \-,līz\ *transitive verb* **-ized; -iz·ing** (1857)
: to arrange or publish in serial form
— **se·ri·al·i·za·tion** \,sir-ē-ə-lə-'zā-shən\ *noun*

serial number *noun* (1896)
: a number indicating place in a series and used as a means of identification

¹se·ri·ate \'sir-ē-,āt, -ē-ət\ *adjective* [Latin *series*] (1846)
: arranged in a series or succession
— **se·ri·ate·ly** *adverb*

²se·ri·ate \'sir-ē-,āt\ *transitive verb* **-at·ed; -at·ing** (circa 1899)
: to arrange in a series

¹se·ri·a·tim \,sir-ē-'ā-təm, -'a-\ *adverb* [Medieval Latin, from Latin *series*] (1680)
: in a series

²seriatim *adjective* (1871)
: following seriatim

se·ri·ceous \sə-'ri-shəs\ *adjective* [Late Latin *sericeus* silken, from Latin *sericum* silk garment, silk, from neuter of *sericus* silken, from Greek *sērikos*, from *Sēres*, an eastern Asian people, probably the Chinese] (circa 1777)
: covered with fine silky hair ⟨*sericeous* leaf⟩

ser·i·cin \'ser-ə-sən\ *noun* [International Scientific Vocabulary, from Latin *sericum* silk] (circa 1868)
: a gelatinous protein that cements the two fibroin filaments in a silk fiber

seri·cul·ture \'ser-ə-,kəl-chər\ *noun* [Latin *sericum* silk + English *culture*] (circa 1854)
: the production of raw silk by raising silkworms
— **seri·cul·tur·al** \-'kəl-chə-rəl, -'kəlch-rəl\ *adjective*

\ə\ abut \ᵊ\ kitten \ər\ further \a\ ash \ā\ ace
\ä\ mop, mar \aù\ out \ch\ chin \e\ bet \ē\ easy
\g\ go \i\ hit \ī\ ice \j\ job \ŋ\ sing \ō\ go
\ò\ law \òi\ boy \th\ thin \th\ the \ü\ loot \ù\ foot
\y\ yet \zh\ vision *see also* Guide to Pronunciation

— **se·ri·cul·tur·ist** \-rist\ *noun*

se·ries \'sir-(,)ēz\ *noun, plural* **series** *often attributive* [Latin, from *serere* to join, link together; akin to Greek *eirein* to string together, *hormos* chain, necklace, and perhaps to Latin *sort-, sors* lot] (1611)
1 a : a number of things or events of the same class coming one after another in spatial or temporal succession ⟨a concert *series*⟩ ⟨the hall opened into a *series* of small rooms⟩ **b :** a set of regularly presented television programs each of which is complete in itself
2 : the indicated sum of a usually infinite sequence of numbers
3 a : the coins or currency of a particular country and period **b :** a group of postage stamps in different denominations
4 : a succession of volumes or issues published with related subjects or authors, similar format and price, or continuous numbering
5 : a division of rock formations that is smaller than a system and comprises rocks deposited during an epoch
6 : a group of chemical compounds related in composition and structure
7 : an arrangement of the parts of or elements in an electric circuit whereby the whole current passes through each part or element without branching — compare PARALLEL
8 : a set of vowels connected by ablaut (as *i, a, u* in *ring, rang, rung*)
9 : a number of games (as of baseball) played usually on consecutive days between two teams ⟨in town for a 3-game *series*⟩
10 : a group of successive coordinate sentence elements joined together
11 : SOIL SERIES
12 : three consecutive games in bowling
— **in series :** in a serial arrangement

ser·if \'ser-əf\ *noun* [probably from Dutch *schreef* stroke, line, from Middle Dutch, from *schriven* to write, from Latin *scribere* — more at SCRIBE] (1841)
: any of the short lines stemming from and at an angle to the upper and lower ends of the strokes of a letter
— **ser·ifed** *or* **ser·iffed** \-əft\ *adjective*

seri·graph \'ser-ə-,graf\ *noun* [Latin *sericum* silk + Greek *graphein* to write, draw — more at CARVE] (1940)
: an original silk-screen color print
— **se·rig·ra·pher** \sə-'ri-grə-fər\ *noun*
— **se·rig·ra·phy** \-fē\ *noun*

se·rin \sə-'raⁿ\ *noun* [French] (1530)
: a small yellow and grayish Old World finch (*Serinus serinus*) that is related to the canary

ser·ine \'ser-,ēn\ *noun* [International Scientific Vocabulary *sericin* + [2]*-ine*] (1880)
: a crystalline nonessential amino acid $C_3H_7NO_3$ that occurs especially as a structural part of many proteins

se·rio·com·ic \,sir-ē-ō-'kä-mik\ *adjective* [*serious* + *-o-* + *comic*] (1783)
: having a mixture of the serious and the comic ⟨a *seriocomic* novel⟩
— **se·rio·com·i·cal·ly** \-mi-k(ə-)lē\ *adverb*

se·ri·ous \'sir-ē-əs\ *adjective* [Middle English *seryows*, from Middle French or Late Latin; Middle French *serieux*, from Late Latin *seriosus*, alteration of Latin *serius* weighty, serious; probably akin to Old English *swær* heavy, sad] (15th century)
1 : thoughtful or subdued in appearance or manner **:** SOBER
2 a : requiring much thought or work ⟨*serious* study⟩ **b :** of or relating to a matter of importance ⟨a *serious* play⟩
3 a : not joking or trifling **:** being in earnest **b** *archaic* **:** PIOUS **c :** deeply interested **:** DEVOTED ⟨a *serious* musician⟩

4 a : not easily answered or solved ⟨*serious* objections⟩ **b :** having important or dangerous possible consequences ⟨a *serious* injury⟩
5 : excessive or impressive in quantity, extent, or degree **:** CONSIDERABLE ⟨making *serious* money⟩ ⟨*serious* drinking⟩ ☆
— **se·ri·ous·ness** *noun*

se·ri·ous·ly *adverb* (1509)
1 : in a sincere manner **:** EARNESTLY
2 : to a serious extent **:** SEVERELY

se·ri·ous–mind·ed \,sir-ē-əs-'mīn-dəd\ *adjective* (1845)
: having a serious disposition or trend of thought
— **se·ri·ous–mind·ed·ly** *adverb*
— **se·ri·ous–mind·ed·ness** *noun*

ser·jeant, ser·jeanty *variant of* SERGEANT, SERGEANTY

ser·jeant–at–law \,sär-jənt-ət-'lò\ *noun, plural* **ser·jeants–at–law** (1503)
: a member of a former class of barristers of the highest rank

ser·mon \'sər-mən\ *noun* [Middle English, from Old French, from Medieval Latin *sermon-, sermo*, from Latin, speech, conversation, from *serere* to link together — more at SERIES] (13th century)
1 : a religious discourse delivered in public usually by a clergyman as a part of a worship service
2 : a speech on conduct or duty
— **ser·mon·ic** \,sər-'mä-nik\ *adjective*

ser·mon·ette \,sər-mə-'net\ *noun* (1814)
: a short sermon

ser·mon·ize \'sər-mə-,nīz\ *verb* **-ized; -iz·ing** (1635)
intransitive verb
1 : to compose or deliver a sermon
2 : to speak didactically or dogmatically
transitive verb
: to preach to or on at length
— **ser·mon·iz·er** *noun*

Sermon on the Mount
: an ethical discourse delivered by Jesus and recorded in Matthew 5–7 and paralleled briefly in Luke 6:20–49

sero- *combining form* [Latin *serum*]
: serum ⟨*serology*⟩

se·ro·con·ver·sion \,sir-ō-kən-'vər-zhən, -shən\ *noun* (1963)
: the production of antibodies in response to an antigen

se·ro·di·ag·no·sis \-,dī-ig-'nō-səs\ *noun* [New Latin] (1896)
: diagnosis by the use of serum (as in the Wassermann test)
— **se·ro·di·ag·nos·tic** \-'näs-tik\ *adjective*

se·rol·o·gy \sə-'rä-lə-jē, si-\ *noun* [International Scientific Vocabulary] (1909)
: a science dealing with serums and especially their reactions and properties
— **se·ro·log·i·cal** \,sir-ə-'lä-ji-kəl\ *or* **se·ro·log·ic** \-jik\ *adjective*
— **se·ro·log·i·cal·ly** \-ji-k(ə-)lē\ *adverb*
— **se·rol·o·gist** \sə-'rä-lə-jist, si-\ *noun*

se·ro·neg·a·tive \,sir-ō-'ne-gə-tiv\ *adjective* (1927)
: having or being a negative serum reaction especially in a test for the presence of an antibody
— **se·ro·neg·a·tiv·i·ty** \-,ne-gə-'ti-və-tē\ *noun*

se·ro·pos·i·tive \-'pä-zə-tiv, -'päz-tiv\ *adjective* (circa 1930)
: having or being a positive serum reaction especially in a test for the presence of an antibody
— **se·ro·pos·i·tiv·i·ty** \-,pä-zə-'ti-və-tē\ *noun*

se·ro·pu·ru·lent \-'pyur-ə-lənt, ,ser-, -'pyur-yə-\ *adjective* (circa 1836)
: consisting of a mixture of serum and pus ⟨*seropurulent* exudate⟩

se·ro·sa \sə-'rō-zə\ *noun* [New Latin, from feminine of *serosus* serous, from Latin *serum*] (circa 1890)

: a usually enclosing serous membrane
— **se·ro·sal** \-zəl\ *adjective*

se·ro·ti·nal \sə-'rät-nəl, -'rä-t°n-əl; ,ser-ə-'tī-n°l\ *adjective* [Latin *serotinus* coming late] (1898)
: of or relating to the latter and usually drier part of summer

se·rot·i·nous \sə-'rät-nəs, -'rä-t°n-əs; ,ser-ə-'tī-nəs\ *adjective* [Latin *serotinus* coming late, from *sero* late — more at SOIREE] (circa 1656)
: remaining closed on the tree with seed dissemination delayed or occurring gradually ⟨*serotinous* cones⟩

se·ro·to·ner·gic \,sir-ə-tə-'nər-jik\ *also* **se·ro·to·nin·er·gic** \,sir-ə-,tō-nə-'nər-jik\ *adjective* [*serotonin* + *-ergic*] (1957)
: liberating, activated by, or involving serotonin in the transmission of nerve impulses ⟨*serotonergic* pathways⟩

se·ro·to·nin \,sir-ə-'tō-nən, ,ser-\ *noun* [*sero-* + *tonic* + [1]*-in*] (1948)
: a phenolic amine neurotransmitter $C_{10}H_{12}N_2O$ that is a powerful vasoconstrictor and is found especially in the brain, blood serum, and gastric mucosa of mammals

se·ro·type \'sir-ə-,tīp, 'ser-\ *noun* (1946)
: a group of intimately related microorganisms distinguished by a common set of antigens; *also* **:** the set of antigens characteristic of such a group

se·rous \'sir-əs\ *adjective* [Middle English, from Medieval Latin *serosus*, from Latin *serum*] (15th century)
: of, relating to, or resembling serum; *especially* **:** of thin watery constitution ⟨a *serous* exudate⟩

serous membrane *noun* (circa 1852)
: a thin membrane (as the peritoneum) with cells that secrete a serous fluid; *especially* **:** SEROSA

se·row \sə-'rō\ *noun* [Lepcha *să-ro* long-haired Tibetan goat] (1847)
: any of several artiodactyl mammals (genus *Capricornis*) of eastern Asia that are usually rather dark and heavily built and some of which have distinct manes

ser·pent \'sər-pənt\ *noun* [Middle English, from Middle French, from Latin *serpent-, serpens*, from present participle of *serpere* to creep; akin to Greek *herpein* to creep, Sanskrit *sarpati* he creeps] (13th century)
1 a *archaic* **:** a noxious creature that creeps, hisses, or stings **b :** SNAKE
2 : DEVIL 1
3 : a treacherous person

[1]**ser·pen·tine** \'sər-pən-,tēn, -,tīn\ *adjective* [Middle English, from Middle French *serpentin*, from Late Latin *serpentinus*, from Latin *serpent-, serpens*] (15th century)
1 : of or resembling a serpent (as in form or movement)
2 : subtly wily or tempting

1 serif

A B C

3 a : winding or turning one way and another **b :** having a compound curve whose central curve is convex
— **ser·pen·tine·ly** *adverb*
²**serpentine** *noun* (1519)
: something that winds sinuously
³**ser·pen·tine** \-ˌtēn\ *noun* [Middle English, from Medieval Latin *serpentina, serpentinum,* from Late Latin, feminine & neuter of *serpentinus* resembling a serpent] (15th century)
: a mineral or rock consisting essentially of a hydrous magnesium silicate usually having a dull green color and often a mottled appearance
ser·pig·i·nous \(ˌ)sər-'pi-jə-nəs\ *adjective* [Middle English *serpiginose,* from Medieval Latin *serpiginosus,* from *serpigin-, serpigo* creeping skin disease, from Latin *serpere* to creep] (15th century)
: CREEPING, SPREADING; *especially* : healing over in one portion while continuing to advance in another ⟨*serpiginous* ulcer⟩
— **ser·pig·i·nous·ly** *adverb*
ser·ra·nid \'ser-ə-nəd, 'ser-ə-nəd\ *noun* [ultimately from Latin *serra* saw) (circa 1900)
: any of a large family (Serranidae) of carnivorous marine bony fishes which have an oblong compressed body covered with usually ctenoid scales and many of which are important food and sport fishes (as the sea basses) especially of warm seas
— **serranid** *adjective*
ser·ra·no \sə-'rä-(ˌ)nō, si-\ *noun, plural* **-nos** [probably from Mexican Spanish, from Spanish *serrano,* adjective, montane, highland, from *sierra* mountain range — more at SIERRA] (circa 1972)
: a small Mexican hot pepper
¹**ser·rate** \'ser-ˌāt, sə-'rāt\ *adjective* [Latin *serratus,* from *serra* saw] (1668)
: notched or toothed on the edge; *specifically* : having marginal teeth pointing forward or toward the apex ⟨a *serrate* leaf⟩
²**ser·rate** \sə-'rāt, 'ser-ˌāt\ *transitive verb* **ser·rat·ed; ser·rat·ing** [Late Latin *serratus,* past participle of *serrare* to saw, from Latin *serra*] (1750)
: to mark or make with serrations ⟨a *serrated* knife⟩
ser·ra·tion \sə-'rā-shən, se-\ *noun* (1842)
1 : the condition of being serrate
2 : a formation resembling the toothed edge of a saw
3 : one of the teeth in a serrate margin
ser·ried \'ser-ēd\ *adjective* (1667)
1 : crowded or pressed together : COMPACT ⟨the crowd collected in a *serried* mass —W. S. Maugham⟩
2 [by alteration] : marked by ridges : SERRATE ⟨the *serried* contours of the . . . mountains —*American Guide Series: Oregon*⟩
— **ser·ried·ly** *adverb*
— **ser·ried·ness** *noun*
ser·ry \'ser-ē\ *verb* **ser·ried; ser·ry·ing** [Middle French *serré,* past participle of *serrer* to press, crowd — more at SEAR] (1581)
intransitive verb
archaic : to press together especially in ranks
transitive verb
: to crowd together
Ser·to·li cell \ˌsər-'tō-lē-\ *noun* [Enrico *Sertoli* (died 1910) Italian histologist] (1888)
: one of the elongated striated cells lining the seminiferous tubules that support and apparently nourish the spermatids
Ser·to·man \(ˌ)sər-'tō-mən\ *noun* [*Sertoma* (Club)] (1956)
: a member of a major international service club
se·rum \'sir-əm\ *noun, plural* **serums** *or* **se·ra** \-ə\ [Latin, whey, wheylike fluid; akin to Greek *oros* whey] (1665)
1 : the watery portion of an animal fluid remaining after coagulation: **a** (1) : BLOOD SERUM (2) : ANTISERUM **b :** WHEY **c :** a normal or pathological serous fluid (as in a blister)

2 : the watery part of a plant fluid
serum albumin *noun* (1879)
: a crystallizable albumin or mixture of albumins that normally constitutes more than half of the protein in blood serum and serves to maintain the osmotic pressure of the blood
serum globulin *noun* (circa 1890)
: a globulin or mixture of globulins occurring in blood serum and containing most of the antibodies of the blood
serum hepatitis *noun* (1932)
: HEPATITIS B
serum sickness *noun* (circa 1913)
: an allergic reaction to the injection of foreign serum manifested by urticaria, swelling, eruption, arthritis, and fever
ser·val \'sər-vəl, (ˌ)sər-'val\ *noun* [French, from Portuguese *lobo cerval* lynx, from Medieval Latin *lupus cervalis,* literally, deerlike wolf] (1771)
: a long-legged African wildcat (*Felis serval*) having large ears and a tawny black-spotted coat

serval

ser·vant \'sər-vənt\ *noun* [Middle English, from Old French, from present participle of *servir*] (13th century)
: one that serves others ⟨a public *servant*⟩; *especially* : one that performs duties about the person or home of a master or personal employer
— **ser·vant·hood** \-ˌhùd\ *noun*
— **ser·vant·less** *adjective*
¹**serve** \'sərv\ *verb* **served; serv·ing** [Middle English, from Middle French *servir,* from Old French, from Latin *servire* to be a slave, serve, from *servus* slave, servant] (13th century)
intransitive verb
1 a : to be a servant **b :** to do military or naval service
2 : to assist a celebrant as server at mass
3 a : to be of use ⟨in a day when few people could write, seals *served* as signatures —Elizabeth W. King⟩ **b :** to be favorable, opportune, or convenient **c :** to be worthy of reliance or trust ⟨if memory *serves*⟩ **d :** to hold an office : discharge a duty or function ⟨*serve* on a jury⟩
4 : to prove adequate or satisfactory : SUFFICE
5 : to help persons to food: as **a :** to wait at table **b :** to set out portions of food or drink
6 : to wait on customers
7 : to put the ball or shuttlecock in play in various games (as tennis, volleyball, or badminton)
transitive verb
1 a : to be a servant to : ATTEND **b :** to give the service and respect due to (a superior) **c :** to comply with the commands or demands of : GRATIFY **d :** to give military or naval service to **e :** to perform the duties of (an office or post)
2 : to act as server at (mass)
3 *archaic* : to pay a lover's or suitor's court to (a lady) ⟨that gentle lady, whom I love and *serve* —Edmund Spenser⟩
4 a : to work through (a term of service) **b :** to put in (a term of imprisonment)
5 a : to wait on at table **b :** to bring (food) to a diner **c :** PRESENT, PROVIDE — usually used with *up* ⟨the novel *served* up many laughs⟩
6 a : to furnish or supply with something needed or desired **b :** to wait on (a customer) in a store **c :** to furnish professional service to
7 a : to answer the needs of **b :** to be enough for : SUFFICE **c :** to contribute or conduce to : PROMOTE
8 : to treat or act toward in a specified way ⟨he *served* me ill⟩

9 a : to bring to notice, deliver, or execute as required by law **b :** to make legal service upon (a person named in a process)
10 *of a male animal* : to copulate with
11 : to wind yarn or wire tightly around (a rope or stay) for protection
12 : to provide services that benefit or help
13 : to put (the ball or shuttlecock) in play (as in tennis or badminton)
— **serve one right :** to be deserved
²**serve** *noun* (1688)
: the act or action of putting the ball or shuttlecock in play in various games (as volleyball, badminton, or tennis); *also* : a turn to serve
serv·er \'sər-vər\ *noun* (15th century)
1 : one that serves food or drink
2 : the player who serves (as in tennis)
3 : something used in serving food or drink
4 : one that serves legal processes upon another
5 : the celebrant's assistant at low mass
6 : a computer in a network that is used to provide services (as access to files or shared peripherals or the routing of electronic mail) to other computers in the network
¹**ser·vice** \'sər-vəs\ *noun* [Middle English, from Middle French, from Latin *servitium* condition of a slave, body of slaves, from *servus* slave] (13th century)
1 a : the occupation or function of serving ⟨in active *service*⟩ **b :** employment as a servant ⟨entered his *service*⟩
2 a : the work performed by one that serves ⟨good *service*⟩ **b :** HELP, USE, BENEFIT ⟨glad to be of *service*⟩ **c :** contribution to the welfare of others **d :** disposal for use ⟨I'm entirely at your *service*⟩
3 a : a form followed in worship or in a religious ceremony ⟨the burial *service*⟩ **b :** a meeting for worship — often used in plural ⟨held evening *services*⟩
4 : the act of serving: as **a :** a helpful act ⟨did him a *service*⟩ **b :** useful labor that does not produce a tangible commodity — usually used in plural ⟨charge for professional *services*⟩ **c :** SERVE
5 : a set of articles for a particular use ⟨a silver tea *service*⟩
6 a : an administrative division (as of a government or business) ⟨the consular *service*⟩ **b :** one of a nation's military forces (as the army or navy)
7 a : a facility supplying some public demand ⟨telephone *service*⟩ ⟨bus *service*⟩ **b :** a facility providing maintenance and repair ⟨television *service*⟩
8 : the materials (as spun yarn, small lines, or canvas) used for serving a rope
9 : the act of bringing a legal writ, process, or summons to notice as prescribed by law
10 : the act of copulating with a female animal
11 : a branch of a hospital medical staff devoted to a particular specialty ⟨obstetrical *service*⟩
²**service** *transitive verb* **ser·viced; ser·vic·ing** (1528)
: to perform services for: as **a :** to repair or provide maintenance for **b :** to meet interest and sinking fund payments on (as government debt) **c :** to perform any of the business functions auxiliary to production or distribution of **d** *of a male animal* : SERVE 10
— **ser·vic·er** *noun*
³**service** *adjective* (1837)
1 : of or relating to the armed services
2 : used in serving or supplying ⟨delivery men use the *service* entrance⟩
3 : intended for hard or everyday use

\ə\ **abut** \ᵊ\ **kitten** \ər\ **further** \a\ **ash** \ā\ **ace** \ä\ **mop, mar** \aù\ **out** \ch\ **chin** \e\ **bet** \ē\ **easy** \g\ **go** \i\ **hit** \ī\ **ice** \j\ **job** \ŋ\ **sing** \ō\ **go** \ò\ **law** \òi\ **boy** \th\ **thin** \t̲h̲\ **the** \ü\ **loot** \ù\ **foot** \y\ **yet** \zh\ **vision** *see also* Guide to Pronunciation

4 a : providing services 〈the *service* trades—from filling stations to universities —John Fischer〉 **b :** offering repair, maintenance, or incidental services

⁴ser·vice \'sər-vəs\ *noun* [Middle English *serves*, plural of *serve* fruit of the service tree, service tree, from Old English *syrfe*, from (assumed) Vulgar Latin *sorbea*, from Latin *sorbus* service tree] (1530)
: an Old World tree (*Sorbus domestica*) resembling the related mountain ashes but having larger flowers and larger edible fruit; *also* **:** a related Old World tree (*S. torminalis*) with bitter fruits

ser·vice·able \'sər-və-sə-bəl\ *adjective* (14th century)
1 : HELPFUL, USEFUL
2 : fit for use 〈her *serviceable* but not exceptional voice —Irving Kolodin〉
— **ser·vice·abil·i·ty** \,sər-və-sə-'bi-lə-tē\ *noun*
— **ser·vice·able·ness** \'sər-və-sə-bəl-nəs\ *noun*
— **ser·vice·ably** \-blē\ *adverb*

ser·vice·ber·ry \'sər-vəs-,ber-ē *also* 'sär-\ *noun* [⁴*service*] (1784)
1 : the edible purple or red fruit of any of various North American trees or shrubs (genus *Amelanchier*) of the rose family
2 : a tree or shrub that produces serviceberries and has showy white flowers in the spring — called also *Juneberry, shadblow, shadbush*

service book *noun* (1580)
: a book setting forth forms of worship used in religious services

service box *noun* (circa 1898)
: the area in which a player stands while serving in various court games (as squash or handball)

service cap *noun* (circa 1908)
: a flat-topped visor cap worn as part of a military uniform — compare GARRISON CAP

service ceiling *noun* (1920)
: the altitude at which under standard air conditions a particular airplane can no longer rise at a rate greater than a small designated rate (as 100 feet per minute)

service charge *noun* (1917)
: a fee charged for a particular service often in addition to a standard or basic fee — called also *service fee*

service club *noun* (1926)
1 : a club of business or professional men or women organized for their common benefit and active in community service
2 : a recreation center for enlisted personnel provided by one of the armed services

service court *noun* (circa 1878)
: a part of the court into which the ball or shuttlecock must be served

service line *noun* (1875)
: a line marked on a court in various games (as handball or tennis) parallel to the front wall or to the net to mark a boundary of the service area or service court

ser·vice·man \'sər-vəs-,man, -mən\ *noun* (1899)
1 : a male member of the armed forces
2 : a man employed to repair or maintain equipment
3 : a service station attendant

service mark *noun* (1945)
: a mark or device used to identify a service (as transportation or insurance) offered to customers

service medal *noun* (circa 1934)
: a medal awarded to an individual for military service in a specified war or campaign

service module *noun* (1961)
: a space vehicle module that contains oxygen, water, fuel cells, propellant tanks, and the main rocket engine

service road *noun* (1921)
: FRONTAGE ROAD
service station *noun* (1916)

1 : a retail station for servicing motor vehicles especially with gasoline and oil
2 : a place at which some service is offered

service stripe *noun* (circa 1920)
: a stripe worn on an enlisted man's left sleeve to indicate three years of service in the army or four years in the navy

service tree *noun* (1600)
: ⁴SERVICE

ser·vice·wom·an \'sər-vəs-,wu̇-mən\ *noun* (1943)
: a female member of the armed forces

ser·vi·ette \,sər-vē-'et\ *noun* [French, from Middle French, from *servir* to serve] (1818) *chiefly British* **:** a table napkin

ser·vile \'sər-vəl, -,vīl\ *adjective* [Middle English, from Latin *servilis*, from *servus* slave] (15th century)
1 : of or befitting a slave or a menial position
2 : meanly or cravenly submissive **:** ABJECT
synonym see SUBSERVIENT
— **ser·vile·ly** \-və(l)-lē, -,vīl-lē\ *adverb*
— **ser·vile·ness** \-vəl-nəs, -,vīl-\ *noun*
— **ser·vil·i·ty** \(,)sər-'vi-lə-tē\ *noun*

serv·ing \'sər-viŋ\ *noun* (1864)
: a helping of food or drink

Ser·vite \'sər-,vīt\ *noun* [Medieval Latin *Servitae*, plural, Servites, from Latin *servus*] (circa 1550)
: a member of the mendicant Order of Servants of Mary founded in Florence, Italy, in 1233
— **Servite** *adjective*

ser·vi·tor \'sər-və-tər, -,tȯr\ *noun* [Middle English *servitour*, from Middle French, from Late Latin *servitor*, from Latin *servire* to serve] (14th century)
: a male servant

ser·vi·tude \'sər-və-,tüd, -,tyüd\ *noun* [Middle English, from Middle French, from Latin *servitudo* slavery, from *servus* slave] (15th century)
1 : a condition in which one lacks liberty especially to determine one's course of action or way of life
2 : a right by which something (as a piece of land) owned by one person is subject to a specified use or enjoyment by another

ser·vo \'sər-(,)vō\ *noun, plural* **servos** (1947)
1 : SERVOMOTOR
2 : SERVOMECHANISM

ser·vo·mech·a·nism \'sər-vō-,me-kə-,ni-zəm\ *noun* [*servo-* (as in *servomotor*) + *mechanism*] (1926)
: an automatic device for controlling large amounts of power by means of very small amounts of power and automatically correcting the performance of a mechanism

ser·vo·mo·tor \'sər-vō-,mō-tər\ *noun* [French *servo-moteur*, from Latin *servus* slave, servant + French *-o-* + *moteur* motor, from Latin *motor* one that moves — more at MOTOR] (1889)
: a power-driven mechanism that supplements a primary control operated by a comparatively feeble force (as in a servomechanism)

-ses *plural of* -SIS

ses·a·me \'se-sə-mē *also* 'se-zə-\ *noun* [alteration of earlier *sesam, sesama*, from Latin *sesamum, sesama*, from Greek *sēsamon, sēsamē*, of Semitic origin; akin to Akkadian *šamaššamu* sesame] (1682)
1 : a widely cultivated chiefly tropical or subtropical annual erect herb (*Sesamum indicum* of the family Pedaliaceae); *also* **:** its small seeds used especially as a source of oil and a flavoring agent
2 : OPEN SESAME

sesame oil *noun* (1870)
: a pale yellow bland semidrying fatty oil obtained from sesame seeds and used chiefly as an edible

sesame 1

oil, as a vehicle for various pharmaceuticals, and in cosmetics and soaps

ses·a·moid \'se-sə-,mȯid\ *noun* [Greek *sēsamoeidēs*, literally, resembling sesame seed, from *sēsamon*] (circa 1696)
: a nodular mass of bone (as the patella) or cartilage in a tendon especially at a joint or bony prominence
— **sesamoid** *adjective*

Se·so·tho \se-'sō-(,)thō, -(,)tō\ *noun* [Sesotho] (1846)
: the Bantu language of the Basotho people

sesqui- *combining form* [Latin, one and a half, half again, literally, and a half, from *semis* half of an as, one half (probably from *semi-* + *as* as) + *-que* (enclitic) and; akin to Greek *te* and, Sanskrit *ca*, Gothic *-h, -uh*]
1 : one and a half times 〈*sesqui*centennial〉
2 : containing half again as many atoms 〈*sesqui*terpene〉
3 : intermediate **:** combination 〈*sesqui*carbonate〉

ses·qui·car·bon·ate \,ses-kwi-'kär-bə-,nāt, -nət\ *noun* (1825)
: a salt that is neither a simple normal carbonate nor a simple bicarbonate but often (as $Na_2CO_3 \cdot NaHCO_3 \cdot 2H_2O$) a combination of the two

ses·qui·cen·te·na·ry \-kwi-sen-'te-nə-rē, -'sen-tⁿn-,er-ē, -sen-'tē-nə-rē\ *noun* (1954)
: SESQUICENTENNIAL

ses·qui·cen·ten·ni·al \-sen-'te-nē-əl\ *noun* (1880)
: a 150th anniversary or its celebration
— **sesquicentennial** *adjective*

ses·qui·pe·da·lian \,ses-kwə-pə-'dāl-yən\ *adjective* [Latin *sesquipedalis*, literally, a foot and a half long, from *sesqui-* + *ped-, pes* foot — more at FOOT] (1656)
1 : having many syllables **:** LONG 〈*sesquipedalian* terms〉
2 : given to or characterized by the use of long words 〈a *sesquipedalian* television commentator〉

ses·qui·ter·pene \,ses-kwə-'tər-,pēn\ *noun* (circa 1888)
: any of a class of terpenes $C_{15}H_{24}$; *also* **:** a derivative of such a terpene

ses·sile \'se-,sīl, -səl\ *adjective* [Latin *sessilis* of or fit for sitting, low, dwarf (of plants), from *sessus*, past participle of *sedēre*] (1753)
1 : attached directly by the base **:** not raised upon a stalk or peduncle 〈a *sessile* leaf〉 〈*sessile* bubbles〉
2 : permanently attached or established **:** not free to move about 〈*sessile* polyps〉

ses·sion \'se-shən\ *noun* [Middle English, from Middle French, from Latin *session-, sessio*, literally, act of sitting, from *sedēre* to sit — more at SIT] (14th century)
1 : a meeting or series of meetings of a body (as a court or legislature) for the transaction of business 〈morning *session*〉
2 *plural* **a** (1) **:** a sitting of English justices of peace in execution of the powers conferred by their commissions (2) **:** an English court holding such sessions **b :** any of various courts similar to the English sessions
3 : the period between the first meeting of a legislative or judicial body and the prorogation or final adjournment
4 : the ruling body of a Presbyterian congregation consisting of the elders in active service
5 : the period during the year or day in which a school conducts classes
6 : a meeting or period devoted to a particular activity 〈a recording *session*〉
— **ses·sion·al** \'sesh-nəl, 'se-shə-nⁿl\ *adjective*

session man *noun* (1958)
: a studio musician who backs up a performer at a recording session

ses·terce \'ses-,tərs\ *noun* [Latin *sestertius*, from *sestertius* two and a half times as great (from its being equal originally to two and a

half asses), from *semis* half of an as, one half + *tertius* third — more at SESQUI-, THIRD] (1598)
: an ancient Roman coin equal to ¼ denarius

ses·ter·tium \se-'stər-sh(ē-)əm\ *noun, plural* **-tia** \-sh(ē-)ə\ [Latin, from genitive plural of *sestertius* (in the phrase *milia sestertium* thousands of sesterces)] (circa 1541)
: a unit of value in ancient Rome equal to 1000 sesterces

ses·tet \ses-'tet\ *noun* [Italian *sestetto,* from *sesto* sixth, from Latin *sextus* — more at SEXT] (1859)
: a stanza or a poem of six lines; *specifically* **:** the last six lines of an Italian sonnet

ses·ti·na \se-'stē-nə\ *noun* [Italian, from *sesto* sixth] (circa 1586)
: a lyrical fixed form consisting of six 6-line usually unrhymed stanzas in which the end words of the first stanza recur as end words of the following five stanzas in a successively rotating order and as the middle and end words of the three verses of the concluding tercet

¹set \'set\ *verb* **set; set·ting** [Middle English *setten,* from Old English *settan;* akin to Old High German *sezzen* to set, Old English *sittan* to sit] (before 12th century)
transitive verb
1 : to cause to sit **:** place in or on a seat
2 a : to put (a fowl) on eggs to hatch them **b :** to put (eggs) for hatching under a fowl or into an incubator
3 : to place (oneself) in position to start running in a race
4 a : to place with care or deliberate purpose and with relative stability ⟨*set* a ladder against the wall⟩ ⟨*set* a stone on the grave⟩ **b :** TRANSPLANT 1 ⟨*set* seedlings⟩ **c** (1) **:** to make (as a trap) ready to catch prey (2) **:** to fix (a hook) firmly into the jaw of a fish **d :** to put aside (as dough containing yeast) for fermenting
5 : to direct with fixed attention ⟨*set* your mind to it⟩
6 a : to cause to assume a specified condition, relation, or occupation ⟨slaves were *set* free⟩ ⟨*set* the house on fire⟩ **b :** to cause the start of ⟨*set* a fire⟩
7 a : to appoint or assign to an office or duty **b :** POST, STATION
8 : to cause to assume a specified posture or position ⟨*set* the door ajar⟩
9 a : to fix as a distinguishing imprint, sign, or appearance ⟨the years have *set* their mark on him⟩ **b :** AFFIX **c :** APPLY ⟨*set* a match to kindling⟩
10 : to fix or decide on as a time, limit, or regulation **:** PRESCRIBE ⟨*set* a wedding day⟩ ⟨*set* the rules for the game⟩
11 a : to establish as the highest level or best performance ⟨*set* a record for the half mile⟩ **b :** to furnish as a pattern or model ⟨*set* an example of generosity⟩ **c :** to allot as a task ⟨*setting* lessons for the children to work upon at home —*Manchester Examiner*⟩
12 a : to adjust (a device and especially a measuring device) to a desired position ⟨*set* the alarm for 7:00⟩ ⟨*set* a thermostat at 68⟩; *also* **:** to adjust (as a clock) in conformity with a standard **b :** to restore to normal position or connection when dislocated or fractured ⟨*set* a broken bone⟩ **c :** to spread to the wind ⟨*set* the sails⟩
13 a : to put in order for use ⟨*set* a place for a guest⟩ **b :** to make scenically ready for a performance ⟨*set* the stage⟩ **c** (1) **:** to arrange (type) for printing ⟨*set* type by hand⟩ (2) **:** to put into type or its equivalent (as on film) ⟨*set* the first word in italic⟩
14 a : to put a fine edge on by grinding or honing ⟨*set* a razor⟩ **b :** to bend slightly the tooth points of (a saw) alternately in opposite directions **c :** to sink (the head of a nail) below the surface
15 : to fix in a desired position (as by heating or stretching)

16 : to arrange (hair) in a desired style by using implements (as curlers, rollers, or clips) and gels or lotions
17 a : to adorn with something affixed or infixed **:** STUD, DOT ⟨clear sky *set* with stars⟩ **b :** to fix (as a precious stone) in a border of metal **:** place in a setting
18 a : to hold something in regard or esteem at the rate of ⟨*sets* a great deal by daily exercise⟩ **b :** to place in a relative rank or category ⟨*set* duty before pleasure⟩ **c :** to fix at a certain amount ⟨*set* bail at $500⟩ **d :** VALUE, RATE ⟨their promises were *set* at naught⟩ **e :** to place as an estimate of worth ⟨*set* a high value on life⟩
19 : to place in relation for comparison or balance ⟨theory *set* against practice⟩
20 a : to direct to action **b :** to incite to attack or antagonism ⟨war *sets* brother against brother⟩
21 a : to place by transporting ⟨was *set* ashore on the island⟩ **b :** to put in motion **c :** to put and fix in a direction ⟨*set* our faces toward home once more⟩ **d** *of a dog* **:** to point out the position of (game) by holding a fixed attitude
22 : to defeat (an opponent or a contract) in bridge
23 a : to fix firmly **:** make immobile **:** give rigid form or condition to ⟨*set* her jaw in determination⟩ **b :** to make unyielding or obstinate
24 : to cause to become firm or solid ⟨*set* milk for cheese⟩
25 : to cause (as fruit) to develop
intransitive verb
1 *chiefly dialect* **:** SIT
2 : to be becoming **:** be suitable **:** FIT ⟨the coat *sets* well⟩
3 : to cover and warm eggs to hatch them
4 a : to become lodged or fixed ⟨the pudding *set* heavily on my stomach⟩ **b :** to place oneself in position in preparation for an action (as running)
5 *of a plant part* **:** to undergo development usually as a result of pollination
6 a : to pass below the horizon **:** go down ⟨the sun *sets*⟩ **b :** to come to an end ⟨this century *sets* with little mirth —Thomas Fuller⟩
7 : to apply oneself to some activity ⟨*set* to work⟩
8 : to have a specified direction in motion **:** FLOW, TEND ⟨the wind was *setting* from Pine Hill to the farm —Esther Forbes⟩
9 *of a dog* **:** to indicate the position of game by crouching or pointing
10 : to dance face to face with another in a square dance ⟨*set* to your partner and turn⟩
11 a : to become solid or thickened by chemical or physical alteration ⟨the cement *sets* rapidly⟩ **b** *of a dye or color* **:** to become permanent **c** *of a bone* **:** to become whole by knitting **d** *of metal* **:** to acquire a permanent twist or bend from strain ☐
— **set about :** to begin to do
— **set apart 1 :** to reserve to a particular use **2 :** to make noticeable or outstanding
— **set aside 1 :** to put to one side **:** DISCARD **2 :** to reserve for a purpose **:** SAVE **3 :** DISMISS **4 :** ANNUL, OVERRULE
— **set at :** to mount an attack on **:** ASSAIL ⟨would go although . . . devils should *set at* me —Charlotte Yonge⟩
— **set eyes on :** to catch sight of
— **set foot in :** ENTER
— **set foot on :** to step onto
— **set forth 1 :** to give an account or statement of **2 :** to start out on a journey
— **set forward 1 :** FURTHER **2 :** to start out on a journey
— **set in motion :** to give impulse to ⟨*sets* the story *in motion* vividly —Howard Thompson⟩
— **set one's hand to :** to become engaged in
— **set one's heart on :** RESOLVE *verb transitive* **5** ⟨she *set her heart on* going to medical school⟩

— **set one's house in order :** to organize one's affairs
— **set one's sights on :** to determine to pursue
— **set one's teeth on edge :** IRRITATE, ANNOY
— **set one straight :** to correct someone by providing accurate information
— **set sail :** to start out on a course; *especially* **:** to begin a voyage ⟨*set sail* for Bermuda⟩
— **set store by** *or* **set store on :** to consider valuable, trustworthy, or worthwhile
— **set the stage :** to provide the basis or background ⟨this trend will *set the stage* for higher earnings⟩
— **set to music :** to provide music or instrumental accompaniment for (a text)
— **set upon :** to attack usually with violence ⟨the dogs *set upon* the trespassers⟩

²set *noun* (14th century)
1 a : the act or action of setting **b :** the condition of being set
2 : a number of things of the same kind that belong or are used together ⟨an electric train *set*⟩
3 a : mental inclination, tendency, or habit **:** BENT ⟨a *set* toward mathematics⟩ **b :** a state of psychological preparedness usually of limited duration for action in response to an anticipated stimulus or situation ⟨the influence of mental *set* on the effect experienced with marijuana⟩
4 : direction of flow ⟨the *set* of the wind⟩
5 : form or carriage of the body or of its parts ⟨her face took on a cynical *set* —Raymond Kennedy⟩
6 : the manner of fitting or of being placed or suspended ⟨in order to give the skirt a pretty *set* —Mary J. Howell⟩
7 : amount of deflection from a straight line ⟨*set* of a saw's teeth⟩

\ə\ abut	\ᵊ\ kitten \ər\ **further** \a\ ash \ā\ ace
\ä\ mop, mar	\au̇\ out \ch\ chin \e\ bet \ē\ easy
\g\ go	\i\ hit \ī\ ice \j\ job \ŋ\ sing \ō\ go
\ȯ\ law	\ȯi\ boy \th\ thin \th\ the \ü\ loot \u̇\ foot
\y\ yet	\zh\ vision *see also* Guide to Pronunciation

8 : permanent change of form (as of metal) due to repeated or excessive stress
9 : the act or result of arranging hair by curling or waving
10 *also* **sett** \'set\ **a :** a young plant or rooted cutting ready for transplanting **b :** a small bulb, corm, or tuber or a piece of tuber used for propagation ⟨onion *sets*⟩
11 *or* **sett :** the burrow of a badger
12 : the width of the body of a piece of type
13 : an artificial setting for a scene of a theatrical or film production
14 *also* **sett :** a rectangular paving stone of sandstone or granite
15 : a division of a tennis match won by the side that wins at least six games beating the opponent by two games or by winning a tie-breaker
16 : a collection of books or periodicals forming a unit
17 : a clutch of eggs
18 : the basic formation in a country-dance or square dance
19 : a session of music (as jazz or dance music) usually followed by an intermission; *also* **:** the music played at one session
20 : a group of persons associated by common interests
21 : a collection of elements and especially mathematical ones (as numbers or points) — called also *class*
22 : an apparatus of electronic components assembled so as to function as a unit ⟨a television *set*⟩
23 : a usually offensive formation in football or basketball
24 : a group of a specific number of repetitions of a particular exercise
³**set** *adjective* [Middle English *sett*, from Old English *gesett*, past participle of *settan*] (14th century)
1 : INTENT, DETERMINED ⟨*set* upon going⟩
2 : INTENTIONAL, PREMEDITATED ⟨did it of *set* purpose⟩
3 : fixed by authority or appointment **:** PRESCRIBED, SPECIFIED ⟨*set* hours of study⟩
4 : reluctant to change ⟨*set* in their ways⟩
5 a : IMMOVABLE, RIGID ⟨*set* frown⟩ **b :** BUILT-IN ⟨a *set* tub⟩
6 : SETTLED, PERSISTENT ⟨*set* defiance⟩
7 : being in readiness **:** PREPARED ⟨*set* for an early morning start⟩
se·ta \'sē-tə\ *noun, plural* **se·tae** \'sē-,tē\ [New Latin, from Latin *saeta, seta* bristle] (circa 1793)
: a slender usually rigid or bristly and springy organ or part of an animal or plant
— **se·tal** \'sē-t⁰l\ *adjective*
se·ta·ceous \si-'tā-shəs\ *adjective* [Latin *saeta, seta*] (1664)
1 : set with or consisting of bristles
2 : resembling a bristle in form or texture
set–aside \'set-ə-,sīd\ *noun* (1943)
: something (as a portion of receipts or production) that is set aside for a specified purpose
set·back \'set-,bak\ *noun* (1674)
1 : a checking of progress
2 : DEFEAT, REVERSE
3 : ⁴PITCH 7
4 : a placing of the face of a building on a line some distance to the rear of the building line or of the wall below; *also* **:** the rooftop area produced by a setback
5 : automatic scheduled adjustment to a lower temperature setting of a thermostat
set back *transitive verb* (1600)
1 : to slow the progress of **:** HINDER, DELAY
2 : COST ⟨a new suit will *set* you *back* $200⟩
set by *transitive verb* (1595)
: to set apart for future use
set down *transitive verb* (15th century)
1 : to cause to sit down **:** SEAT
2 : to place at rest on a surface or on the ground
3 : to suspend (a jockey) from racing

4 : to cause or allow to get off a vehicle **:** DELIVER
5 : to land (an airplane) on the ground or water
6 a : ORDAIN, ESTABLISH **b :** to put in writing
7 a : REGARD, CONSIDER ⟨*set* him *down* as a liar⟩ **b :** ATTRIBUTE
se·te·nant \sə-'te-nənt, sē-; ,se-tə-'nän\ *adjective* [French, literally, holding one another] (circa 1911)
of postage stamps **:** joined together as in the original sheet but differing in design, overprint, color, or perforation
Seth \'seth\ *noun* [Hebrew *Shēth*]
: a son of Adam and Eve
¹**set-in** \'set-'in\ *adjective* (1534)
1 : placed, located, or built as a part of some other construction ⟨a *set-in* bookcase⟩ ⟨a *set-in* washbasin⟩
2 : cut separately and stitched in ⟨*set-in* sleeves⟩
²**set-in** \'set-,in\ *noun* (1953)
: INSERT
set in (15th century)
transitive verb
: INSERT; *especially* **:** to stitch (a small part) within a large article ⟨*set in* a sleeve of a dress⟩
intransitive verb
: to become established
set·line \'set-,līn\ *noun* (1865)
: a long heavy fishing line to which several hooks are attached in series
set·off \'set-,óf\ *noun* (1621)
1 : something that is set off against another thing: **a :** DECORATION, ORNAMENT **b :** COMPENSATION, COUNTERBALANCE
2 : the discharge of a debt by setting against it a distinct claim in favor of the debtor; *also* **:** the claim itself
3 : OFFSET 7a
set off (1596)
transitive verb
1 a : to put in relief **:** show up by contrast **b :** ADORN, EMBELLISH **c :** to set apart **:** make distinct or outstanding
2 a : OFFSET, COMPENSATE ⟨more variety in the Lancashire weather to *set off* its most disagreeable phases —*Geographical Journal*⟩ **b :** to make a setoff of ⟨the respective totals shall be *set off* against one another —O. R. Hobson⟩
3 a : to set in motion **:** cause to begin **b :** to cause to explode
4 : to measure off on a surface
intransitive verb
: to start out on a course or a journey ⟨*set off* for home⟩
set on (14th century)
transitive verb
1 : ATTACK
2 a *obsolete* **:** PROMOTE **b :** to urge (as a dog) to attack or pursue **c :** to incite to action **:** INSTIGATE **d :** to set to work
intransitive verb
: GO ON, ADVANCE
se·tose \'sē-,tōs\ *adjective* [Latin *saetosus*, from *saeta*] (1661)
: SETACEOUS, BRISTLY
set·out \'set-,aùt\ *noun* (1537)
1 a (1) **:** ARRAY, DISPLAY (2) **:** ARRANGEMENT, LAYOUT **b :** BUFFET, SPREAD **c :** TURNOUT 5
2 : PARTY, ENTERTAINMENT
3 : BEGINNING, OUTSET
set out (14th century)
transitive verb
1 a : to arrange and present graphically or systematically **b :** to mark out (as a design) **:** lay out the plan of
2 : to state, describe, or recite at length ⟨distributed copies of a pamphlet *setting out* his ideas in full —S. F. Mason⟩
3 : to begin with a definite purpose **:** INTEND, UNDERTAKE
intransitive verb
: to start out on a course, a journey, or a career
set piece *noun* (circa 1909)

1 : a realistic piece of stage scenery standing by itself
2 a : a composition (as in literature, art, or music) executed in a fixed or ideal form often with studied artistry and brilliant effect **b :** a scene, depiction, speech, or event that is obviously designed to have an imposing effect
3 : a precisely planned and conducted military operation
— **set–piece** *adjective*
set point *noun* (1928)
: a situation (as in tennis) in which one player will win the set by winning the next point; *also* **:** the point won
set·screw \'set-,skrü\ *noun* (circa 1855)
1 : a screw screwed through one part tightly upon or into another part to prevent relative movement
2 : a screw for regulating a valve opening or a spring tension
set shot *noun* (1937)
: a two-handed shot in basketball taken from a stationary position
sett *variant of* SET
set·tee \se-'tē\ *noun* [alteration of *settle*] (1716)
1 : a long seat with a back
2 : a medium-sized sofa with arms and a back
set·ter \'se-tər\ *noun* (15th century)
1 : one that sets
2 : a large bird dog of a type trained to point on finding game
set theory *noun* (1936)
: a branch of mathematics or of symbolic logic that deals with the nature and relations of sets
— **set theoretic** *adjective*
set·ting \'se-tiŋ\ *noun* (14th century)
1 : the manner, position, or direction in which something is set
2 : the frame or bed in which a gem is set; *also* **:** style of mounting
3 a : the time, place, and circumstances in which something occurs or develops **b :** the time and place of the action of a literary, dramatic, or cinematic work **c :** the scenery used in a theatrical or film production
4 : the music composed for a text (as a poem)
5 : the articles of tableware for setting a place at table ⟨two *settings* of sterling silver⟩
6 : a batch of eggs for incubation
synonym see BACKGROUND
setting circle *noun* (circa 1891)
: a graduated scale or wheel on the mounting of an equatorial telescope for indicating right ascension or declination
setting–up exercise *noun* (circa 1900)
: any of a series of gymnastic exercises used to give an erect carriage, supple muscles, and easy control of the limbs
¹**set·tle** \'se-t⁰l\ *verb* **set·tled; set·tling** \'set-liŋ, 'se-t⁰l-iŋ\ [Middle English, to seat, bring to rest, come to rest, from Old English *setlan*, from *setl* seat] (1515)
transitive verb
1 : to place so as to stay
2 a : to establish in residence **b :** to furnish with inhabitants **:** COLONIZE
3 a : to cause to pack down **b :** to clarify by causing dregs or impurities to sink
4 : to make quiet or orderly
5 a : to fix or resolve conclusively ⟨*settle* the question⟩ **b :** to establish or secure permanently ⟨*settle* the order of royal succession⟩ **c :** to conclude (a lawsuit) by agreement between parties usually out of court **d :** to close (as an account) by payment often of less than is due
6 : to arrange in a desired position
7 : to make or arrange for final disposition of ⟨*settled* his affairs⟩
8 *of an animal* **:** IMPREGNATE
intransitive verb
1 : to come to rest
2 a : to sink gradually or to the bottom **b :** to become clear by the deposit of sediment or scum **c :** to become compact by sinking

3 a : to become fixed, resolved, or established ⟨a cold *settled* in his chest⟩ **b** : to establish a residence or colony ⟨*settled* in Wisconsin⟩ — often used with *down*

4 a : to become quiet or orderly **b** : to take up an ordered or stable life — often used with *down* ⟨marry and *settle* down⟩

5 a : to adjust differences or accounts **b** : to come to a decision — used with *on* or *upon* ⟨*settleed* on a new plan⟩ **c** : to conclude a lawsuit by agreement out of court

6 *of an animal* : CONCEIVE

synonym *see* DECIDE

— **set·tle·able** \'se-t°l-ə-bəl, 'set-lə-bəl\ *adjective*

— **settle for** : to be content with

— **settle one's hash** : to silence or subdue someone by decisive action

— **settle the stomach** : to remove or relieve the distress or nausea of indigestion

²**set·tle** *noun* [Middle English, place for sitting, seat, chair, from Old English *setl*; akin to Old High German *sezzal* seat, Latin *sella* seat, chair, Old English *sittan* to sit] (1553)

: a wooden bench with arms, a high solid back, and an enclosed foundation which can be used as a chest

set·tle·ment \'se-t°l-mənt\ *noun* (1648)

1 : the act or process of settling

2 a : an act of bestowing or giving possession under legal sanction **b** : the sum, estate, or income secured to one by such a settlement

3 a : occupation by settlers **b** : a place or region newly settled **c** : a small village

4 : SETTLEMENT HOUSE

5 : an agreement composing differences

6 : payment or adjustment of an account

settlement house *noun* (1907)

: an institution providing various community services especially to large city populations

set·tler \'set-lər, 'se-t°l-ər\ *noun* (1696)

: one that settles (as a new region)

set·tling \'set-liŋ, 'se-t°l-iŋ\ *noun* (1594)

: SEDIMENT, DREGS — usually used in plural

set·tlor \'set-,lòr, 'se-t°l-,òr\ *noun* (1818)

: one that makes a settlement or creates a trust of property

set-to \'set-,tü\ *noun, plural* **set-tos** (1743)

: a usually brief and vigorous fight or debate

set to *intransitive verb* (circa 1525)

1 : to begin actively and earnestly

2 : to begin fighting

set-up \'set-,əp\ *noun* (1890)

1 a : carriage of the body; *especially* : erect and soldierly bearing **b** : CONSTITUTION, MAKE-UP

2 a : the assembly and arrangement of the tools and apparatus required for the performance of an operation **b** : the preparation and adjustment of machines for an assigned task

3 a : a table setting **b** : glass, ice, and mixer served to patrons who supply their own liquor

4 a : a camera position from which a scene is filmed; *also* : the footage taken from one camera position **b** : the final arrangement of the scenery and properties for a scene of a theatrical or cinematic production

5 a : a position of the balls in billiards or pool from which it is easy to score **b** : a task or contest purposely made easy **c** : something easy to get or accomplish **d** : something (as a plot) that has been constructed or contrived **e** : the execution of a planned scoring play in sports

6 a : the manner in which the elements or components of a machine, apparatus, or mechanical, electrical, or hydraulic system are arranged, designed, or assembled **b** : the patterns within which political, social, or administrative forces operate : customary or established practice

7 : PROJECT, PLAN

8 : something done by deceit or trickery in order to compromise or frame someone

set up (13th century)

transitive verb

1 a : to raise to and place in a high position **b** : to place in view : POST **c** : to put forward (as a plan) for acceptance

2 a : to place upright : ERECT ⟨*set up* a statue⟩ **b** : to assemble the parts of and erect in position ⟨*set up* a printing press⟩ **c** : to put (a machine) in readiness or adjustment for a tooling operation

3 a : CAUSE, CREATE ⟨*set up* a clamor⟩ **b** : BRING ABOUT

4 : to place in power or in office ⟨*set up* the general as dictator⟩

5 a : to raise from depression : ELATE, GRATIFY **b** : to make proud or vain

6 a : to put forward or extol as a model **b** : to claim oneself to be ⟨*sets* himself *up* as an authority⟩

7 : FOUND, INAUGURATE ⟨*set up* a home for orphans⟩

8 a : to provide with means of making a living ⟨*set* him *up* in business⟩ **b** : to bring or restore to normal health **c** : to cause (one) to take on a soldierly or athletic appearance especially through drill

9 : to erect (a perpendicular or a figure) on a base in a drawing

10 a : to make taut (a stay or hawser) **b** : to tighten firmly

11 : to make carefully worked out plans for ⟨*set up* a bank robbery⟩

12 a : to pay for (drinks) **b** : to treat (someone) to something

13 a : to put in a compromising or dangerous position usually by trickery or deceit **b** : FRAME 3

14 : to execute one or more plays in preparation for scoring

intransitive verb

1 : to come into active operation or use

2 : to begin business

3 : to make pretensions ⟨has never *set up* to be a wise man —Thomas Rogers⟩

4 : to become firm or consolidated : HARDEN

— **set up housekeeping** : to establish one's living quarters

— **set up shop** : to establish one's business

sev·en \'se-vən, 'se-b°m\ *noun* [Middle English, from *seven*, adjective, from Old English *seofon*; akin to Old High German *sibun* seven, Latin *septem*, Greek *hepta*] (before 12th century)

1 — *see* NUMBER table

2 : the seventh in a set or series ⟨the *seven* of diamonds⟩

3 : something having seven units or members

— **seven** *adjective*

— **seven** *pronoun, plural in construction*

sev·en·fold \-,fōld\ *adjective* (before 12th century)

1 : having seven units or members

2 : being seven times as great or as many

— **sevenfold** *adverb*

seven seas *noun plural* (1872)

: all the waters or oceans of the world

sev·en·teen \,se-vən-'tēn, ,se-b°m-\ *noun* [*seventeen*, adjective, from Middle English *seventene*, from Old English *seofontēne*; akin to Old English *tīen* ten] (14th century)

— *see* NUMBER table

— **seventeen** *adjective*

— **seventeen** *pronoun, plural in construction*

— **sev·en·teenth** \-'tēn(t)th\ *adjective or noun*

seventeen-year locust *noun* (1817)

: a cicada (*Magicicada septendecim*) of the U.S. that has in the North a life of seventeen years and in the South of thirteen years of which most is spent underground as a nymph and only a few weeks as a winged adult

sev·enth \'se-vən(t)th, 'se-b°m(t)th\ *noun, plural* **sevenths** \'se-vən(t)s, -vən(t)ths; 'se-b°m(t)s, -b°m(t)ths\ (12th century)

1 — *see* NUMBER table

2 a : a musical interval embracing seven diatonic degrees **b** : a tone at this interval; *specifically* : LEADING TONE **c** : the harmonic combination of two tones a seventh apart

— **seventh** *adjective or adverb*

seventh chord *noun* (circa 1909)

: a chord comprising a fundamental tone with its third, fifth, and seventh

Seventh–Day *adjective* (1684)

: advocating or practicing observance of Saturday as the Sabbath

seventh heaven *noun* [from the seventh being the highest of the seven heavens of Islamic and cabalist doctrine] (1818)

: a state of extreme joy

sev·en·ty \'se-vən-tē, 'se-b°m-, -dē\ *noun, plural* **-ties** [*seventy*, adjective, from Middle English, from Old English *seofontig*, short for *hundseofontig*, from *hundseofontig*, noun, group of seventy, from *hund* hundred + *seofon* seven + -*tig* group of ten; akin to Old English *tīen* ten] (13th century)

1 — *see* NUMBER table

2 *plural* : the numbers 70 to 79; *specifically* : the years 70 to 79 in a lifetime or century

3 *capitalized* : a Mormon elder ordained for missionary work under the apostles

— **sev·en·ti·eth** \-tē-əth, -dē-\ *adjective or noun*

— **seventy** *adjective*

— **seventy** *pronoun, plural in construction*

sev·en·ty-eight \,se-vən-tē-'āt, ,se-b°m-, -dē-'āt\ *noun* (circa 1934)

1 — *see* NUMBER table

2 : a phonograph record designed to be played at 78 revolutions per minute — usually written 78

— **seventy–eight** *adjective*

— **seventy–eight** *pronoun, plural in construction*

sev·en-up \,se-və-'nəp, ,se-b°m-'əp\ *noun* (1830)

: an American variety of all fours in which a total of seven points constitutes game

sev·er \'se-vər\ *verb* **sev·ered; sev·er·ing** \'sev-riŋ, 'se-və-\ [Middle English, from Middle French *severer*, from Latin *separare* — more at SEPARATE] (14th century)

transitive verb

: to put or keep apart : DIVIDE; *especially* : to remove (as a part) by or as if by cutting

intransitive verb

: to become separated

synonym *see* SEPARATE

sev·er·able \'sev-rə-bəl, 'se-və-\ *adjective* (1548)

: capable of being severed; *especially* : capable of being divided into legally independent rights or obligations

— **sev·er·abil·i·ty** \,sev-rə-'bi-lə-tē, ,se-və-\ *noun*

¹**sev·er·al** \'sev-rəl, 'se-və-\ *adjective* [Middle English, from Anglo-French, from Medieval Latin *separalis*, from Latin *separ* separate, back-formation from *separare* to separate] (15th century)

1 a : separate or distinct from one another ⟨federal union of the *several* states⟩ **b** (1) : individually owned or controlled : EXCLUSIVE ⟨a *several* fishery⟩ — compare COMMON (2) **c** : of or relating separately to each individual involved ⟨a *several* judgment⟩ **c** : being separate and distinctive : RESPECTIVE ⟨specialists in their *several* fields⟩

2 a : more than one ⟨*several* pleas⟩ **b** : more than two but fewer than many ⟨moved *several*

\ə\ abut \°\ kitten \ər\ further \a\ ash \ā\ ace
\ä\ mop, mar \aù\ out \ch\ chin \e\ bet \ē\ easy
\g\ go \i\ hit \ī\ ice \j\ job \ŋ\ sing \ō\ go
\ò\ law \òi\ boy \th\ thin \th\ the \ü\ loot \ù\ foot
\y\ yet \zh\ vision *see also* Guide to Pronunciation

inches⟩ **c** *chiefly dialect* **:** being a great many

²several *pronoun, plural in construction* (1686)
: an indefinite number more than two and fewer than many ⟨*several* of the guests⟩

sev·er·al·fold \,sev-rəl-'fōld, ,se-və-\ *adjective* (1738)
1 : having several parts or aspects
2 : being several times as large, as great, or as many as some understood size, degree, or amount
— **severalfold** *adverb*

sev·er·al·ly \'sev-rə-lē, 'se-və-\ *adverb* (14th century)
1 : one at a time **:** each by itself **:** SEPARATELY
2 : apart from others **:** INDEPENDENTLY

sev·er·al·ty \'sev-rəl-tē, 'se-və-\ *noun* [Middle English *severalte*, from Anglo-French *severalté*, from *several*] (15th century)
1 : the quality or state of being several **:** DISTINCTNESS, SEPARATENESS
2 a : a sole, separate, and exclusive possession, dominion, or ownership **:** one's own right without a joint interest in any other person ⟨tenants in *severalty*⟩ **b :** the quality or state of being individual or particular
3 a : land owned in severalty **b :** the quality or state of being held in severalty

sev·er·ance \'sev-rən(t)s, 'se-və-\ *noun* (15th century)
: the act or process of severing **:** the state of being severed

severance pay *noun* (1943)
: an allowance usually based on length of service that is payable to an employee on termination of employment

severance tax *noun* (1928)
: a tax levied by a state on the extractor of oil, gas, or minerals intended for consumption in other states — compare ROYALTY 5a

se·vere \sə-'vir\ *adjective* **se·ver·er; -est** [Middle French or Latin; Middle French, from Latin *severus*] (1548)
1 a : strict in judgment, discipline, or government **b :** of a strict or stern bearing or manner **:** AUSTERE
2 : rigorous in restraint, punishment, or requirement **:** STRINGENT, RESTRICTIVE
3 : strongly critical or condemnatory **:** CENSORIOUS ⟨a *severe* critic⟩
4 a : maintaining a scrupulously exacting standard of behavior or self-discipline **b :** establishing exacting standards of accuracy and integrity in intellectual processes ⟨a *severe* logician⟩
5 : sober or restrained in decoration or manner **:** PLAIN
6 a : inflicting physical discomfort or hardship **:** HARSH ⟨*severe* winters⟩ **b :** inflicting pain or distress **:** GRIEVOUS ⟨a *severe* wound⟩
7 : requiring great effort **:** ARDUOUS ⟨a *severe* test⟩
8 : of a great degree **:** SERIOUS ⟨*severe* depression⟩ ☆
— **se·vere·ly** *adverb*
— **se·vere·ness** *noun*
— **se·ver·i·ty** \sə-'ver-ə-tē\ *noun*

severe combined immunodeficiency *noun* (1974)
: a rare congenital disorder of the immune system that is characterized by inability to produce a normal complement of antibodies and T cells and that usually results in early death — called also *severe combined immune deficiency*

se·vi·che \sə-'vē-(,)chā, -chē\ *noun* [American Spanish] (1952)
: a dish of raw fish marinated in lime or lemon juice often with oil, onions, peppers, and seasonings and served especially as an appetizer

Sevres *or* **Sèvres** \'sev-rə, 'sev(r°)\ *noun* [*Sèvres*, France] (1786)
: an often elaborately decorated French porcelain

sev·ru·ga \sə-'vrü-gə, se-\ *noun* [Russian *sevryuga*, a species of sturgeon] (1591)

: a light to dark gray caviar from a sturgeon (*Acipenser sevru*) of the Caspian Sea that has very small roe; *also* **:** the fish

sew \'sō\ *verb* **sewed; sewn** \'sōn\ *or* **sewed; sew·ing** [Middle English, from Old English *sīwian*; akin to Old High German *siuwen* to sew, Latin *suere*] (before 12th century)
transitive verb
1 : to unite or fasten by stitches
2 : to close or enclose by sewing ⟨*sew* the money in a bag⟩
intransitive verb
: to practice or engage in sewing
— **sew·abil·i·ty** \,sō-ə-'bi-lə-tē\ *noun*
— **sew·able** \'sō-ə-bəl\ *adjective*

sew·age \'sü-ij\ *noun* [³*sewer*] (1834)
: refuse liquids or waste matter carried off by sewers

¹sew·er \'sü-ər, 'sù(-ə)r\ *noun* [Middle English, from Anglo-French *asseour*, literally, seater, from Old French *asseoir* to seat — more at ASSIZE] (14th century)
: a medieval household officer often of high rank in charge of serving the dishes at table and sometimes of seating and tasting

²sew·er \'sō(-ə)r\ *noun* (14th century)
: one that sews

³sew·er \'sü-ər, 'sù(-ə)r\ *noun* [Middle English, from Middle French *essewer, seweur*, from *essewer* to drain, from (assumed) Vulgar Latin *exaquare*, from Latin *ex- + aqua* water — more at ISLAND] (15th century)
: an artificial usually subterranean conduit to carry off sewage and sometimes surface water (as from rainfall)

sew·er·age \'sü-ə-rij, 'sù(-ə)r-ij\ *noun* (1834)
1 : the removal and disposal of sewage and surface water by sewers
2 : a system of sewers
3 : SEWAGE

sew·ing \'sō-iŋ\ *noun* (14th century)
1 : the act, method, or occupation of one that sews
2 : material that has been or is to be sewed

sew up *transitive verb* (15th century)
1 : to mend completely by sewing
2 : to get exclusive use or control of
3 : to make certain of **:** ASSURE

¹sex \'seks\ *noun* [Middle English, from Latin *sexus*] (14th century)
1 : either of the two major forms of individuals that occur in many species and that are distinguished respectively as female or male
2 : the sum of the structural, functional, and behavioral characteristics of living things that are involved in reproduction by two interacting parents and that distinguish males and females
3 a : sexually motivated phenomena or behavior **b :** SEXUAL INTERCOURSE
4 : GENITALIA

²sex *transitive verb* (1884)
1 : to identify the sex of ⟨*sex* chicks⟩
2 a : to increase the sexual appeal of — often used with *up* **b :** to arouse the sexual desires of

sex·a·ge·nar·i·an \,sek-sə-jə-'ner-ē-ən\ *noun* [Latin *sexagenarius* of or containing sixty, sixty years old, from *sexageni* sixty each, from *sexaginta* sixty, from *sex* six + *-ginta* (akin to Latin *viginti* twenty) — more at SIX, VIGESIMAL] (1738)
: a person whose age is in the sixties
— **sexagenarian** *adjective*

¹sex·a·ges·i·mal \-'je-sə-məl\ *adjective* [Latin *sexagesimus* sixtieth, from *sexaginta* sixty] (1685)
: of, relating to, or based on the number 60

²sexagesimal *noun* (1685)
: a sexagesimal fraction

sex appeal *noun* (1924)
1 : personal appeal or physical attractiveness for members of the opposite sex
2 : general attractiveness

sex cell *noun* (1889)
: GAMETE; *also* **:** its cellular precursor

sex chromatin *noun* (1952)
: BARR BODY

sex chromosome *noun* (1906)
: a chromosome that is inherited differently in the two sexes, that is concerned directly with the inheritance of sex, and that is the seat of factors governing the inheritance of various sex-linked and sex-limited characters

sex·de·cil·lion \,seks-di-'sil-yən\ *noun, often attributive* [Latin *sedecim, sexdecim* sixteen (from *sex* six + *decem* ten) + English *-illion* (as in *million*) — more at TEN] (circa 1934)
— see NUMBER table

sexed \'sekst\ *adjective* (circa 1891)
1 : having sex or sexual instincts
2 : having sex appeal

sex gland *noun* (1935)
: GONAD

sex hormone *noun* (1917)
: a hormone (as from the gonads or adrenal cortex) that affects the growth or function of the reproductive sex organs or the development of secondary sex characteristics

sex·ism \'sek-,si-zəm\ *noun* [¹*sex* + *-ism* (as in *racism*)] (1968)
1 : prejudice or discrimination based on sex; *especially* **:** discrimination against women
2 : behavior, conditions, or attitudes that foster stereotypes of social roles based on sex
— **sex·ist** \'sek-sist\ *adjective or noun*

sex kitten *noun* (1958)
: a young woman with conspicuous sex appeal

sex·less \'seks-ləs\ *adjective* (1598)
1 : lacking sex **:** NEUTER
2 : devoid of sexual interest or activity ⟨a *sexless* relationship⟩
— **sex·less·ly** *adverb*
— **sex·less·ness** *noun*

sex·lim·it·ed \'seks-'li-mə-təd\ *adjective* (1923)
: expressed in the phenotype of only one sex

sex–link·age \-,liŋ-kij\ *noun* (1912)
: the quality or state of being sex-linked

sex–linked \-,liŋ(k)t\ *adjective* (1912)
1 : located on a sex chromosome ⟨a *sex-linked* gene⟩
2 : mediated by a sex-linked gene ⟨a *sex-linked* character⟩

sex object *noun* (1911)
: a person regarded especially exclusively as an object of sexual interest

sex·ol·o·gy \sek-'sä-lə-jē\ *noun* (1902)
: the study of sex or of the interaction of the sexes especially among human beings
— **sex·ol·o·gist** \-jist\ *noun*

sex·ploi·ta·tion \,seks-,plói-'tā-shən\ *noun* [blend of *sex* and *exploitation*] (circa 1942)
: the exploitation of sex in the media and especially in film

sex·pot \'seks-,pät\ *noun* (1948)
: a conspicuously sexy woman

sex symbol *noun* (circa 1911)
: a usually renowned person (as an entertainer) noted and admired for conspicuous sex appeal

sext \'sekst\ *noun, often capitalized* [Middle English *sexte*, from Late Latin *sexta*, from

☆ **SYNONYMS**
Severe, stern, austere, ascetic mean given to or marked by strict discipline and firm restraint. SEVERE implies standards enforced without indulgence or laxity and may suggest harshness ⟨*severe* military discipline⟩. STERN stresses inflexibility and inexorability of temper or character ⟨*stern* arbiters of public morality⟩. AUSTERE stresses absence of warmth, color, or feeling and may apply to rigorous restraint, simplicity, or self-denial ⟨living an *austere* life in the country⟩. ASCETIC implies abstention from pleasure and comfort or self-indulgence as spiritual discipline ⟨the *ascetic* life of the monastic orders⟩.

Latin, sixth hour of the day, from feminine of *sextus* sixth, from *sex* six] (15th century)
: the fourth of the canonical hours

Sex·tans \'seks-ˌtanz\ *noun* [New Latin (genitive *Sextantis*), literally, sextant]
: a constellation on the equator south of Leo

sex·tant \'seks-tənt\ *noun* [New Latin *sextant-, sextans* sixth part of a circle, from Latin, sixth part, from *sextus* sixth] (1628)
: an instrument for measuring angular distances used especially in navigation to observe altitudes of celestial bodies (as in ascertaining latitude and longitude)

sextant

sex·tet \seks-'tet\ *noun* [alteration of *sestet*] (1841)
1 : a musical composition for six instruments or voices
2 : a group or set of six: as **a** : the performers of a sextet **b** : a hockey team

sex·til·lion \seks-'til-yən\ *noun, often attributive* [French, irregular from *sex-* (from Latin *sex*) + *-illion* (as in *million*)] (1690)
— see NUMBER table

sex·to \'seks-(ˌ)tō\ *noun, plural* **sextos** [Latin *sexto*, ablative of *sextus* sixth] (1847)
: SIXMO

sex·to·dec·i·mo \ˌseks-tə-'de-sə-ˌmō\ *noun, plural* **-mos** [Latin, ablative of *sextus decimus* sixteenth, from *sextus* sixth + *decimus* tenth — more at DIME] (1688)
: SIXTEENMO

sex·ton \'seks-tən\ *noun* [Middle English *secresteyn, sexteyn*, from Middle French *secrestain*, from Medieval Latin *sacristanus* — more at SACRISTAN] (14th century)
: a church officer or employee who takes care of the church property and performs related minor duties (as ringing the bell for services and digging graves)

*¹***sex·tu·ple** \seks-'tü-pəl, -'tyü-, -'tə-; 'seks-tə-\ *adjective* [probably from Medieval Latin *sextuplus*, from Latin *sextus* sixth + *-plus* multiplied by; akin to Latin *-plex* -plex — more at -FOLD] (1626)
1 : having six units or members
2 : being six times as great or as many
3 : marked by six beats per measure of music ⟨*sextuple* time⟩
— **sextuple** *noun*

*²***sextuple** *verb* **sex·tu·pled; sex·tu·pling** \-p(ə-)liŋ\ (1632)
transitive verb
: to make six times as much or as many
intransitive verb
: to become six times as much or as numerous

sex·tu·plet \seks-'tə-plət, -'tü-; -'tyü-; 'seks-t(y)ə-\ *noun* (1852)
1 : a combination of six of a kind
2 : one of six offspring born at one birth
3 : a group of six equal musical notes performed in the time ordinarily given to four of the same value

*¹***sex·tu·pli·cate** \seks-'tü-pli-kət, -'tyü-\ *adjective* [blend of *sextuple* and *-plicate* (as in *duplicate*)] (1657)
1 : repeated six times
2 : SIXTH ⟨file the *sextuplicate* copy⟩
— **sextuplicate** *noun*

*²***sex·tu·pli·cate** \-plə-ˌkāt\ *transitive verb* **-cat·ed; -cat·ing** (circa 1934)
1 : SEXTUPLE
2 : to provide in sextuplicate

sex·u·al \'sek-sh(ə-)wəl, 'sek-shəl\ *adjective* [Late Latin *sexualis*, from Latin *sexus* sex] (1651)
1 : of, relating to, or associated with sex or the sexes ⟨*sexual* differentiation⟩ ⟨*sexual* conflict⟩
2 : having or involving sex ⟨*sexual* reproduction⟩

— **sex·u·al·ly** \'sek-sh(ə-)wə-lē, 'sek-sh(ə-)lē\ *adverb*

sexual generation *noun* (1880)
: the generation of an organism with alternation of generations that reproduces sexually

sexual harassment *noun* (1975)
: uninvited and unwelcome verbal or physical conduct directed at an employee because of his or her sex

sexual intercourse *noun* (1799)
1 : heterosexual intercourse involving penetration of the vagina by the penis : COITUS
2 : intercourse involving genital contact between individuals other than penetration of the vagina by the penis

sex·u·al·i·ty \ˌsek-shə-'wa-lə-tē\ *noun* (circa 1800)
: the quality or state of being sexual: **a** : the condition of having sex **b** : sexual activity **c** : expression of sexual receptivity or interest especially when excessive

sex·u·al·ize \'sek-sh(ə-)wə-ˌlīz, 'sek-shə-ˌlīz\ *transitive verb* **-ized; -iz·ing** (1839)
: to make sexual : endow with a sexual character or cast

sexual relations *noun plural* (1950)
: COITUS

sexual selection *noun* (1859)
: natural selection for characters that confer success in competition for a mate as distinguished from competition with other species; *also* : the choice of a mate based on a preference for certain characteristics (as color or bird song)

sexy \'sek-sē\ *adjective* **sex·i·er; -est** (1925)
1 : sexually suggestive or stimulating : EROTIC
2 : generally attractive or interesting : APPEALING ⟨a *sexy* stock⟩
— **sex·i·ly** \-sə-lē\ *adverb*
— **sex·i·ness** \-sē-nəs\ *noun*

Sey·fert galaxy \'sē-fərt- *also* 'sī-\ *noun* [Carl K. *Seyfert* (died 1960) American astronomer] (1959)
: any of a class of spiral galaxies that have small compact bright nuclei characterized by variability in light intensity, emission of radio waves, and spectra which indicate hot gases in rapid motion — called also *Seyfert*

sfer·ics \'sfir-iks, 'sfer-\ *noun plural* [by shortening & alteration] (1945)
: ATMOSPHERICS

*¹***sfor·zan·do** \sfȯrt-'sän-(ˌ)dō, -'san-\ *adjective or adverb* [Italian, verbal of *sforzare* to force] (circa 1801)
: played with prominent stress or accent — used as a direction in music

*²***sforzando** *noun, plural* **-dos** *or* **-di** \-(ˌ)dē\ (1890)
: an accented tone or chord

sfu·ma·to \sfü-'mä-(ˌ)tō\ *noun* [Italian, from past participle of *sfumare* to evaporate] (1909)
: the definition of form in painting without abrupt outline by the blending of one tone into another

sgraf·fi·to \zgra-'fē-(ˌ)tō, skra-\ *noun, plural* **-ti** \-(ˌ)tē\ [Italian, from past participle of *sgraffire* to scratch, produce sgraffito] (circa 1730)
1 : decoration by cutting away parts of a surface layer (as of plaster or clay) to expose a different colored ground — compare GRAFFITO
2 : something (as traditional Pennsylvania Dutch pottery) decorated with sgraffito

sh \sh *often prolonged*\ *interjection* (1847)
— used often in prolonged or rapidly repeated form to urge or command silence or less noise

Sha·'ban \shə-'bän\ *noun* [Arabic *sha'bān*] (circa 1771)
: the 8th month of the Islamic year — see MONTH table

Shab·bat \shə-'bät, 'shä-bəs\ *noun* [Hebrew *shabbāth*] (circa 1905)
: the Jewish Sabbath

shab·by \'sha-bē\ *adjective* **shab·bi·er; -est** [obsolete English *shab* a low fellow] (1669)

1 : clothed with worn or seedy garments ⟨a *shabby* hobo⟩
2 a : threadbare and faded from wear ⟨a *shabby* sofa⟩ **b** : ill-kept : DILAPIDATED ⟨a *shabby* neighborhood⟩
3 a : MEAN, DESPICABLE, CONTEMPTIBLE ⟨must feel *shabby* . . . because of his compromises —Nat Hentoff⟩ **b** : UNGENEROUS, UNFAIR ⟨laments the *shabby* way in which this country often treated a poet —Paul Engle⟩ **c** : inferior in quality ⟨*shabby* reasoning⟩
— **shab·bi·ly** \'sha-bə-lē\ *adverb*
— **shab·bi·ness** \'sha-bē-nəs\ *noun*

Sha·bu·oth \shə-'vü-ˌōt, -ˌōth, -ˌōs, -əs\ *noun* [Hebrew *shābhū'ōth*, literally, weeks] (circa 1903)
: a Jewish holiday observed on the 6th and 7th of Sivan in commemoration of the revelation of the Ten Commandments at Mount Sinai — called also *Pentecost*

shack \'shak\ *noun* [probably back-formation from English dialect *shackly* rickety] (1878)
1 : HUT, SHANTY
2 : a room or similar enclosed structure for a particular person or use ⟨a guard *shack*⟩

*¹***shack·le** \'sha-kəl\ *noun* [Middle English *schakel*, from Old English *sceacul*; akin to Old Norse *skǫkull* pole of a cart] (before 12th century)
1 : something (as a manacle or fetter) that confines the legs or arms
2 : something that checks or prevents free action as if by fetters — usually used in plural
3 : a usually U-shaped fastening device secured by a bolt or pin through holes in the end of the two arms
4 : a length of cable or anchor chain of usually 15 fathoms

*²***shackle** *transitive verb* **shack·led; shack·ling** \-k(ə-)liŋ\ (15th century)
1 a : to bind with shackles : FETTER **b** : to make fast with or as if with a shackle
2 : to deprive of freedom especially of action by means of restrictions or handicaps : IMPEDE
synonym see HAMPER
— **shack·ler** \-k(ə-)lər\ *noun*

shack·le·bone \'sha-kəl-ˌbōn, 'shā-\ *noun* (1571)
Scottish : WRIST

shack up *intransitive verb* (1935)
: to sleep or live together as unmarried sexual partners

shad \'shad\ *noun, plural* **shad** [(assumed) Middle English, from Old English *sceadd*] (before 12th century)
: any of several clupeid fishes (especially genus *Alosa*) that differ from the typical herrings in having a relatively deep body and in being anadromous and that include some important food fishes of Europe and North America

shad·ber·ry \-ˌber-ē\ *noun* (1847)
: SERVICEBERRY

shad·blow \'shad-ˌblō\ *noun* (1846)
: SERVICEBERRY 2

shad·bush \-ˌbush\ *noun* (circa 1818)
: SERVICEBERRY 2

shad·dock \'sha-dək\ *noun* [Captain *Shaddock*, 17th century English ship commander] (1696)
: a very large thick-rinded usually pear-shaped citrus fruit differing from the closely related grapefruit especially in its loose rind and often coarse dry pulp; *also* : the tree (*Citrus maxima* synonym *C. grandis*) that bears it

*¹***shade** \'shād\ *noun* [Middle English, from Old English *sceadu*; akin to Old High German *scato* shadow, Greek *skotos* darkness] (before 12th century)

\ə\ abut \ᵊ\ kitten \ər\ further \a\ ash \ā\ ace
\ä\ mop, mar \au̇\ out \ch\ chin \e\ bet \ē\ easy
\g\ go \h\ hit \ī\ ice \j\ job \ŋ\ sing
\ō\ law \ȯi\ boy \th\ thin \th\ the \ü\ loot \u̇\ foot
\y\ yet \zh\ vision *see also* Guide to Pronunciation

1 a : comparative darkness or obscurity owing to interception of the rays of light **b :** relative obscurity or retirement
2 a : shelter (as by foliage) from the heat and glare of sunlight **b :** a place sheltered from the sun
3 : an evanescent or unreal appearance
4 *plural* **a :** the shadows that gather as darkness comes on **b :** NETHERWORLD, HADES
5 a : a disembodied spirit **:** GHOST **b** — used to signal the similarity between a previously encountered person or situation and one at hand; usually used in plural ⟨*shades* of my childhood⟩
6 : something that intercepts or shelters from light, sun, or heat: as **a :** a device partially covering a lamp so as to reduce glare **b :** a flexible screen usually mounted on a roller for regulating the light or the view through a window **c** *plural* **:** SUNGLASSES
7 a : the reproduction of the effect of shade in painting or drawing **b :** a subdued or somber feature
8 a : a color produced by a pigment or dye mixture having some black in it **b :** a color slightly different from the one under consideration
9 a : a minute difference or variation **:** NUANCE **b :** a minute degree or quantity
10 : a facial expression of sadness or displeasure
— **shade·less** \-ləs\ *adjective*
²**shade** *verb* **shad·ed; shad·ing** (14th century)
transitive verb
1 a : to shelter or screen by intercepting radiated light or heat **b :** to cover with a shade
2 : to hide partly by or as if by a shadow
3 : to darken with or as if with a shadow
4 : to better or exceed by a shade **:** SURPASS, ECLIPSE
5 a : to represent the effect of shade or shadow on **b :** to add shading to **c :** to color so that the shades pass gradually from one to another
6 : to change by gradual transition or qualification
7 : to reduce slightly (as a price)
8 : SLANT, BIAS
intransitive verb
1 : to pass by slight changes or imperceptible degrees
2 : to undergo or exhibit minute difference or variation
— **shad·er** *noun*
shade–grown \'shād-ˌgrōn\ *adjective* (1922) **:** grown in the shade; *specifically* **:** grown under cloth ⟨*shade-grown* tobacco⟩
shade tree *noun* (1806) **:** a tree grown primarily to produce shade
shad·ing \'shā-diŋ\ *noun* (1663)
1 : the use of marking made within outlines to suggest three-dimensionality, shadow, or degrees of light and dark in a picture or drawing
2 : an interpretative effect in music gained especially by subtle changes in dynamics
sha·doof *also* **sha·duf** \shə-'düf, sha-\ *noun* [Arabic *shādūf*] (1836) **:** a counterbalanced sweep used since ancient times especially in Egypt for raising water (as for irrigation)
¹**shad·ow** \'sha-(ˌ)dō\ *noun* [Middle English *shadwe*, from Old English *sceaduw-, sceadu* shade] (before 12th century)
1 : partial darkness or obscurity within a part of space from which rays from a source of light are cut off by an interposed opaque body
2 : a reflected image
3 : shelter from danger or observation
4 a : an imperfect and faint representation **b :** an imitation of something **:** COPY
5 : the dark figure cast upon a surface by a body intercepting the rays from a source of light
6 : PHANTOM
7 *plural* **:** DARK 1a
8 : a shaded or darker portion of a picture

9 : an attenuated form or a vestigial remnant
10 a : an inseparable companion or follower **b :** one (as a spy or detective) that shadows
11 : a small degree or portion **:** TRACE
12 : a source of gloom or unhappiness
13 a : an area near an object **:** VICINITY **b :** pervasive and dominant influence
14 : a state of ignominy or obscurity
— **shad·ow·less** \'sha-dō-ləs, -də-ləs\ *adjective*
— **shad·ow·like** \-ˌlīk\ *adjective*
²**shadow** (before 12th century)
transitive verb
1 *archaic* **:** SHELTER, PROTECT
2 : to cast a shadow upon **:** CLOUD
3 *obsolete* **:** to shelter from the sun
4 *obsolete* **:** CONCEAL
5 : to represent or indicate obscurely or faintly — often used with *forth* or *out*
6 : to follow especially secretly **:** TRAIL
7 *archaic* **:** SHADE 5
intransitive verb
1 : to pass gradually or by degrees
2 : to become overcast with or as if with shadows
— **shad·ow·er** \-dō-ər, -də-wər\ *noun*
³**shadow** *adjective* (1906)
1 : of, relating to, or resembling a shadow cabinet ⟨*shadow* minister of defense⟩
2 a : having an indistinct pattern ⟨*shadow* plaid⟩ **b :** having darker sections of design ⟨*shadow* lace⟩
shadow band *noun* (1900) **:** one of a series of dark narrow parallel bands that appear to rush swiftly across the landscape just before or after totality in a solar eclipse
shad·ow·box \'sha-dō-ˌbäks, -də-ˌbäks\ *intransitive verb* (1919) **:** to box with an imaginary opponent especially as a form of training
shadow box *noun* (circa 1909) **:** a shallow enclosing case usually with a glass front in which something is set for protection and display
shadow cabinet *noun* (1906) **:** a group of leaders of a parliamentary opposition who constitute the probable membership of the cabinet when their party is returned to power
shadow dance *noun* (circa 1909) **:** a dance shown by throwing the shadows of dancers on a screen
shad·ow·graph \'sha-dō-ˌgraf, -də-ˌgraf\ *noun* (1888)
1 : SHADOW PLAY
2 : a photographic image resembling a shadow
— **shad·ow·graphy** \-ˌgra-fē\ *noun*
shadow mask *noun* (1951) **:** a metal plate in a color television tube that contains minute apertures permitting passage of electron beams to specific phosphors on the screen during a scan
shadow play *noun* (1895) **:** a drama exhibited by throwing shadows of puppets or actors on a screen — called also *shadow show*
shad·owy \'sha-dō-ē, -də-wē\ *adjective* (14th century)
1 a : of the nature of or resembling a shadow **:** UNSUBSTANTIAL **b :** faintly perceptible **:** INDISTINCT, VAGUE
2 : being in or obscured by shadow ⟨deep *shadowy* interiors⟩
3 : SHADY 1, 3
— **shad·ow·i·ly** \-wə-lē\ *adverb*
— **shad·ow·i·ness** \-wē-nəs\ *noun*
shady \'shā-dē\ *adjective* **shad·i·er; -est** (1579)
1 : producing or affording shade
2 : sheltered from the sun's rays
3 a : of questionable merit **:** UNCERTAIN, UNRELIABLE **b :** DISREPUTABLE
— **shad·i·ly** \'shā-d'l-ē\ *adverb*
— **shad·i·ness** \'shā-dē-nəs\ *noun*

¹**shaft** \'shaft\ *noun, plural* **shafts** \'shaf(t)s, *for 1b usually* 'shavz\ [Middle English, from Old English *sceaft*; akin to Old High German *scaft* shaft, Latin *scapus* shaft, stalk, Greek *skēptesthai* to prop oneself, lean] (before 12th century)
1 a (1) **:** the long handle of a spear or similar weapon (2) **:** SPEAR, LANCE **b** *or plural* **shaves** \'shavz\ **:** POLE; *specifically* **:** either of two long pieces of wood between which a horse is hitched to a vehicle **c** (1) **:** an arrow especially for a longbow (2) **:** the body or stem of an arrow extending from the nock to the head
2 : a sharply delineated beam of light shining through an opening
3 : something suggestive of the shaft of a spear or arrow especially in long slender cylindrical form: as **a :** the trunk of a tree **b :** the cylindrical pillar between the capital and the base **c :** the handle of a tool or instrument (as a golf club) **d :** a commonly cylindrical bar used to support rotating pieces or to transmit power or motion by rotation **e :** the stem or central axis of a feather **f :** the upright member of a cross especially below the arms **g :** a small architectural column (as at each side of a doorway) **h :** a column, obelisk, or other spire-shaped or columnar monument **i :** a vertical or inclined opening of uniform and limited cross section made for finding or mining ore, raising water, or ventilating underground workings (as in a cave) **j :** a vertical opening or passage through the floors of a building
4 a : a projectile thrown like a spear or shot like an arrow **b :** a scornful, satirical, or pithily critical remark or attack **c :** harsh or unfair treatment — usually used with *the*
²**shaft** *transitive verb* (1611)
1 : to fit with a shaft
2 : to treat unfairly or harshly
shaft horsepower *noun* (1908) **:** horsepower transmitted by an engine shaft
shaft·ing \'shaf-tiŋ\ *noun* (1825) **:** shafts or material for shafts
¹**shag** \'shag\ *noun* [[assumed] Middle English *shagge*, from Old English *sceacga*; akin to Old Norse *skegg* beard, *skaga* to project] (before 12th century)
1 a : a shaggy tangled mass or covering (as of hair) **b :** long coarse or matted fiber, nap, or pile
2 : tobacco cut into fine shreds
3 : CORMORANT 1
²**shag** *adjective* (1592) **:** SHAGGY
³**shag** *verb* **shagged; shag·ging** (1596)
intransitive verb **:** to fall or hang in shaggy masses
transitive verb **:** to make rough or shaggy
⁴**shag** *transitive verb* **shagged; shag·ging** [origin unknown] (1904)
1 a : to chase after; *especially* **:** to chase after and return (a ball) hit usually out of play **b :** to catch (a fly) in baseball practice
2 : to chase away
⁵**shag** *intransitive verb* **shagged; shag·ging** [perhaps alteration of *shack* to lumber along] (1914)
1 : to move or lope along
2 : to dance the shag
⁶**shag** *noun* (1932) **:** a dance step executed by hopping livelily on each foot in turn
shag·bark \'shag-ˌbärk\ *noun* (1777) **:** SHAGBARK HICKORY
shagbark hickory *noun* (1751) **:** a hickory (*Carya ovata*) with sweet edible nuts and a gray shaggy outer bark that peels off in long strips; *also* **:** its wood
shag·gy \'sha-gē\ *adjective* **shag·gi·er; -est** (circa 1590)

1 a : covered with or consisting of long, coarse, or matted hair **b :** covered with or consisting of thick, tangled, or unkempt vegetation **c :** having a rough nap, texture, or surface **d :** having hairlike processes
2 a : UNKEMPT **b :** confused or unclear in conception or thinking
— **shag·gi·ly** \'sha-gə-lē\ *adverb*
— **shag·gi·ness** \'sha-gē-nəs\ *noun*
shag·gy–dog story \ˌsha-gē-'dȯg-\ *noun* (1946)
: a long-drawn-out circumstantial story concerning an inconsequential happening that impresses the teller as humorous but the hearer as boring and pointless; *also* **:** a similar humorous story whose humor lies in the pointlessness or irrelevance of the punch line
shag·gy·mane \'sha-gē-ˌmān\ *noun* (circa 1909)
: a common edible mushroom (*Coprinus comatus*) having an elongated shaggy white pileus with deliquescing gills and black spores — called also *shaggy cap*

shaggymane

sha·green \sha-'grēn, shə-\ *noun* [by folk etymology from French *chagrin,* modification of Turkish *saġrı*] (1677)
1 : an untanned leather covered with small round granulations and usually dyed green
2 : the rough skin of various sharks and rays when covered with small close-set tubercles
— **shagreen** *adjective*
shah \'shä, 'shȯ\ *noun, often capitalized* [Persian *shāh* king — more at CHECK] (1566)
: a sovereign of Iran
— **shah·dom** \'shä-dəm, 'shȯ-\ *noun*
Sha·hap·ti·an \shə-'hap-tē-ən\ *noun, plural* **Shahaptian** *or* **Shahaptians** (1836)
1 : a member of a group of American Indian peoples who formerly inhabited a large territory along the Columbia River and its tributaries
2 : the language of the Shahaptian people including Nez Percé and Yakima
shai·tan \shä-'tän, shī-\ *noun* [Arabic *shaytān*] (1638)
: an evil spirit; *specifically* **:** an evil jinni
¹shake \'shāk\ *verb* **shook** \'shùk\ **shak·en** \'shā-kən\ **shak·ing** [Middle English, from Old English *sceacan;* akin to Old Norse *skaka* to shake] (before 12th century)
intransitive verb
1 : to move irregularly to and fro
2 : to vibrate especially as the result of a blow or shock
3 : to tremble as a result of physical or emotional disturbance
4 : to experience a state of instability **:** TOTTER
5 : to briskly move something to and fro or up and down especially in order to mix
6 : to clasp hands
7 : ³TRILL
transitive verb
1 : to brandish, wave, or flourish often in a threatening manner
2 : to cause to move in a usually quick jerky manner
3 : to cause to quake, quiver, or tremble
4 a : to free oneself from ⟨*shake* a habit⟩ ⟨*shake* off a cold⟩ **b :** to get away from **:** get rid of ⟨can you *shake* your friend? I want to talk to you alone —Elmer Davis⟩
5 : to lessen the stability of **:** WEAKEN ⟨*shake* one's faith⟩
6 : to bring to a specified condition by or as if by repeated quick jerky movements ⟨*shook* himself loose from the man's grasp⟩
7 : to dislodge or eject by quick jerky movements of the support or container ⟨*shook* the dust from the cloth⟩
8 : to clasp (hands) in greeting or farewell or as a sign of goodwill or agreement
9 : to stir the feelings of **:** UPSET ⟨*shook* her up⟩

10 : ³TRILL ☆
— **shak·able** *or* **shake·able** \'shā-kə-bəl\ *adjective*
— **shake a leg 1 :** DANCE **2 :** to hurry up
²shake *noun* (1581)
1 : an act of shaking: as **a :** an act of shaking hands **b :** an act of shaking oneself
2 a : a blow or shock that upsets the equilibrium or disturbs the balance of something **b :** EARTHQUAKE
3 *plural* **a :** a condition of trembling or nervousness; *specifically* **:** DELIRIUM TREMENS **b :** MALARIA 2a
4 : something produced by shaking: as **a :** a fissure separating annual rings of growth in timber **b** (1) **:** MILK SHAKE (2) **:** a beverage resembling a milk shake but made without milk
5 : a wavering, quivering, or alternating motion caused by a blow or shock
6 : TRILL
7 : a very brief period of time
8 *plural* **:** one that is exceptional especially in importance, ability, or merit — usually used in the phrase *no great shakes*
9 : a shingle split from a piece of log usually three or four feet (about one meter) long
10 : ³DEAL 3 ⟨a fair *shake*⟩
shake·down \'shāk-ˌdaùn\ *noun* (circa 1730)
1 : an improvised bed (as one made up on the floor)
2 : a boisterous dance
3 : an act or instance of shaking someone down; *especially* **:** EXTORTION
4 : a thorough search
5 : a process or period of adjustment
6 : a testing under operating conditions of something new (as a ship) for possible faults and defects and for familiarizing the operators with it
shake down (circa 1859)
intransitive verb
1 a : to take up temporary quarters **b :** to occupy an improvised or makeshift bed
2 a : to become accustomed especially to new surroundings or duties **b :** to settle down
transitive verb
1 : to obtain money from in a deceitful or illegal manner
2 : to make a thorough search of
3 : to bring about a reduction of
4 : to give a shakedown test to
shake·out \'shā-ˌkaùt\ *noun* (1895)
1 : the failure or retrenchment of a significant number of firms in the economy or a sector or an industry that usually results in a depressed market
2 : a period or process in which the relatively weak or unessential are eliminated
shak·er \'shā-kər\ *noun* (15th century)
1 : one that shakes: as **a :** a utensil or machine used in shaking ⟨cocktail *shaker*⟩ **b :** one that incites, promotes, or directs action ⟨a mover and *shaker*⟩
2 *capitalized* [from a dance with shaking movements performed as part of worship] **:** a member of a millenarian sect originating in England in 1747 and practicing celibacy and an ascetic communal life
— **Shaker** *adjective*
— **Shak·er·ism** \-kə-ˌri-zəm\ *noun*
¹Shake·spear·ean *or* **Shake·spear·ian** *also* **Shak·sper·ean** *or* **Shak·sper·ian** \shāk-'spir-ē-ən\ *adjective* (1755)
1 : of, relating to, or having the characteristics of Shakespeare or his writings
2 : evocative of a theme, setting, or event from a work of Shakespeare ⟨*Shakespearean* pageantry⟩
²Shakespearean *or* **Shakespearian** *also* **Shaksperean** *or* **Shaksperian** *noun* (1837)
: an authority on or devotee of Shakespeare
Shake·spear·eana *or* **Shake·spear·iana** \ˌ(ˌ)shāk-ˌspir-ē-'a-nə, -'ä-, -'ā-\ *noun plural* (1718)

: collected items by, about, or relating to Shakespeare
Shakespearean sonnet *noun* (1903)
: ENGLISH SONNET
shake–up \'shā-ˌkəp\ *noun* (1847)
: an act or instance of shaking up; *specifically* **:** an extensive and often drastic reorganization
shake up *transitive verb* (1538)
1 *obsolete* **:** CHIDE, SCOLD
2 : to jar by or as if by a physical shock ⟨the collision *shook up* both drivers⟩
3 : to effect an extensive and often drastic reorganization
shaking palsy *noun* (1615)
: PARKINSON'S DISEASE
sha·ko \'sha-(ˌ)kō, 'shä-, 'shä-\ *noun, plural* **shakos** *or* **shakoes** [French, from Hungarian *csákó*] (1815)
: a stiff military hat with a high crown and plume
Shak·ta \'shäk-tə, 'säk-\ *noun or adjective* [Sanskrit *śākta,* from *Śakti*] (1810)
: an adherent of Shaktism
Shak·ti \-tē\ *noun* [Sanskrit *Śakti*] (1810)
: the dynamic energy of a Hindu god personified as his female consort; *broadly* **:** cosmic energy as conceived in Hindu thought
Shak·tism \-ˌti-zəm\ *noun* (1877)
: a Hindu sect worshiping Shakti under various names (as Kali or Durga) in a cult of devotion to the female principle often with magical or orgiastic rites
shaky \'shā-kē\ *adjective* **shak·i·er; -est** (1703)
1 : characterized by shakes ⟨*shaky* timber⟩
2 a : lacking stability **:** PRECARIOUS **b :** lacking in firmness (as of beliefs or principles) **c :** lacking in authority or reliability **:** QUESTIONABLE
3 a : somewhat unsound in health **b :** characterized by shaking
4 : likely to give way or break down
— **shak·i·ly** \-kə-lē\ *adverb*
— **shak·i·ness** \-kē-nəs\ *noun*
shale \'shā(ə)l\ *noun* [probably from obsolete or dialect *shale* scale, shell, from Middle English, from Old English *scealu* — more at SHELL] (1747)
: a fissile rock that is formed by the consolidation of clay, mud, or silt, has a finely stratified or laminated structure, and is composed of minerals essentially unaltered since deposition
— **shal·ey** \'shā-lē\ *adjective*
shale oil *noun* (1857)
: a crude dark oil obtained from oil shale by heating
shall \shəl, 'shal\ *verb, past* **should** \shəd, 'shùd\; *present singular & plural* **shall** [Middle English *shal* (1st & 3d singular present indicative), from Old English *sceal;* akin to Old High German *scal* (1st & 3d singular present indicative) ought to, must, Lithuanian *skola* debt] (before 12th century)

\ə\ abut \ᵊ\ kitten \ər\ further \a\ ash \ā\ ace
\ä\ mop, mar \aù\ out \ch\ chin \e\ bet \ē\ easy
\g\ go \i\ hit \ī\ ice \j\ job \ŋ\ sing \ō\ go
\ȯ\ law \ȯi\ boy \th\ thin \th\ the \ü\ loot \ù\ foot
\y\ yet \zh\ vision *see also* Guide to Pronunciation

verbal auxiliary

1 *archaic* **a :** will have to **:** MUST **b :** will be able to **:** CAN

2 a — used to express a command or exhortation ⟨you *shall* go⟩ **b** — used in laws, regulations, or directives to express what is mandatory ⟨it *shall* be unlawful to carry firearms⟩

3 a — used to express what is inevitable or seems likely to happen in the future ⟨we *shall* have to be ready⟩ ⟨we *shall* see⟩ **b** — used to express simple futurity ⟨when *shall* we expect you⟩

4 — used to express determination ⟨they *shall* not pass⟩

intransitive verb

archaic **:** will go ⟨he to England *shall* along with you —Shakespeare⟩ □

shal·loon \shə-'lün, sha-\ *noun* [*Châlons-sur-Marne, France*] (1678)
: a lightweight twilled fabric of wool or worsted used chiefly for the linings of coats and uniforms

shal·lop \'sha-ləp\ *noun* [Middle French *chaloupe*] (circa 1578)
1 : a usually 2-masted ship with lugsails
2 : a small open boat propelled by oars or sails and used chiefly in shallow waters

shal·lot \shə-'lät *also* 'sha-lət\ *noun* [modification of French *échalote*, from Middle French *eschalotte*, alteration of *eschaloigne*, from (assumed) Vulgar Latin *escalonia* — more at SCALLION] (1664)
1 : a bulbous perennial herb (*Allium cepa aggregatum*) that resembles an onion and produces small clustered bulbs used in seasoning
2 : GREEN ONION

¹shal·low \'sha-(ˌ)lō\ *adjective* [Middle English *schalowe;* probably akin to Old English *sceald* shallow — more at SKELETON] (14th century)
1 : having little depth ⟨*shallow* water⟩
2 : having little extension inward or backward ⟨office buildings have taken the form of *shallow* slabs —Lewis Mumford⟩
3 a : penetrating only the easily or quickly perceived ⟨*shallow* generalizations⟩ **b :** lacking in depth of knowledge, thought, or feeling ⟨a *shallow* demagogue⟩
4 : displacing comparatively little air **:** WEAK ⟨*shallow* breathing⟩
synonym see SUPERFICIAL
— **shal·low·ly** \-lō-lē, -lə-lē\ *adverb*
— **shal·low·ness** *noun*

²shallow (1510)
transitive verb
: to make shallow
intransitive verb
: to become shallow

³shallow *noun* (1571)
: a shallow place or area in a body of water — usually used in plural but singular or plural in construction

sha·lom \shä-'lōm, shə-\ *interjection* [Hebrew *shālōm* peace] (1904)
— used as a Jewish greeting and farewell

sha·lom aleichem \ˌshò-ləm-ə-'lā-kəm, ˌshō-, -kəm\ *interjection* [Hebrew *shālōm 'alēkhem* peace unto you] (1881)
— used as a traditional Jewish greeting

shalt \shəlt, 'shalt\ *archaic present 2d singular of* SHALL

¹sham \'sham\ *noun* [perhaps from English dialect *sham* shame, alteration of English *shame*] (1677)
1 : a trick that deludes **:** HOAX
2 : cheap falseness **:** HYPOCRISY
3 : an ornamental covering for a pillow
4 : an imitation or counterfeit purporting to be genuine
5 : a person who shams
synonym see IMPOSTURE

²sham *adjective* (1681)
1 : not genuine **:** FALSE, FEIGNED
2 : having such poor quality as to seem false

³sham *verb* **shammed; sham·ming** (1755)
transitive verb
: to go through the external motions necessary to counterfeit
intransitive verb
: to act intentionally so as to give a false impression **:** FEIGN
— **sham·mer** \'sha-mər\ *noun*
synonym see ASSUME

sha·man \'shä-mən, 'shā- *also* shə-'män\ *noun, plural* **shamans** [ultimately from Evenki (Tungusic language of Siberia) *šamán*] (1698)
1 : a priest or priestess who uses magic for the purpose of curing the sick, divining the hidden, and controlling events
2 : one who resembles a shaman; *especially* **:** HIGH PRIEST 3
— **sha·man·ic** \shə-'ma-nik, -'mä-\ *adjective*

sha·man·ism \-ˌni-zəm\ *noun* (1780)
: a religion practiced by indigenous peoples of far northern Europe and Siberia that is characterized by belief in an unseen world of gods, demons, and ancestral spirits responsive only to the shamans; *also* **:** any similar religion
— **sha·man·ist** \-nist\ *noun*
— **sha·man·is·tic** \ˌshä-mə-'nis-tik, ˌshä-mə-\ *adjective*

sham·ble \'sham-bəl\ *intransitive verb* **sham·bled; sham·bling** \-b(ə-)liŋ\ [*shamble* bowed, malformed] (1681)
: to walk awkwardly with dragging feet **:** SHUFFLE
— **shamble** *noun*

sham·bles \'sham-bəlz\ *noun plural but singular or plural in construction* [Middle English *shameles*, plural of *schamel* vendor's table, footstool, from Old English *sceamol* stool, from Latin *scamillum*, diminutive of *scamnum* stool, bench; perhaps akin to Sanskrit *skambha* pillar] (15th century)
1 *archaic* **:** a meat market
2 : SLAUGHTERHOUSE
3 a : a place of mass slaughter or bloodshed **b :** a scene or a state of great destruction **:** WRECKAGE **c** (1) **:** a scene or a state of great disorder or confusion (2) **:** great confusion **:** MESS

sham·bling *adjective* (1592)
: characterized by slow awkward movement

sham·bol·ic \sham-'bä-lik\ *adjective* [probably from *shambles*] (1970)
chiefly British **:** obviously disorganized or confused

¹shame \'shām\ *noun* [Middle English, from Old English *scamu;* akin to Old High German *scama* shame] (before 12th century)
1 a : a painful emotion caused by consciousness of guilt, shortcoming, or impropriety **b :** the susceptibility to such emotion
2 : a condition of humiliating disgrace or disrepute **:** IGNOMINY
3 a : something that brings censure or reproach; *also* **:** something to be regretted **:** PITY ⟨it's a *shame* you can't go⟩ **b :** a cause of feeling shame

²shame *transitive verb* **shamed; sham·ing** (13th century)
1 : to bring shame to **:** DISGRACE
2 : to put to shame by outdoing
3 : to cause to feel shame
4 : to force by causing to feel guilty ⟨*shamed* into confessing⟩

shame·faced \'shām-ˌfāst\ *adjective* [alteration of *shamefast*] (1593)
1 : showing modesty **:** BASHFUL
2 : showing shame **:** ASHAMED ◆
— **shame·faced·ly** \-ˌfā-səd-lē, -ˌfāst-lē\ *adverb*
— **shame·faced·ness** \-ˌfā-səd-nəs, -ˌfās(t)-nəs\ *noun*

shame·fast \'shām-ˌfast\ *adjective* [Middle English, from Old English *scamfæst*, from *scamu* + *fæst* fixed, fast] (before 12th century)

archaic **:** SHAMEFACED

shame·ful \'shām-fəl\ *adjective* (13th century)
1 a : bringing shame **:** DISGRACEFUL **b :** arousing the feeling of shame
2 *archaic* **:** full of the feeling of shame **:** ASHAMED
— **shame·ful·ly** \-fə-lē\ *adverb*
— **shame·ful·ness** *noun*

shame·less \'shām-ləs\ *adjective* (before 12th century)
1 : having no shame **:** insensible to disgrace
2 : showing lack of shame **:** DISGRACEFUL
— **shame·less·ly** *adverb*
— **shame·less·ness** *noun*

sham·mes \'shä-məs\ *noun, plural* **sham·mo·sim** \shä-'mò-səm\ [Yiddish *shames*, from Late Hebrew *shammāsh*] (1650)
1 : the sexton of a synagogue
2 : the candle or taper used to light the other candles in a Hanukkah menorah

sham·my \'sha-mē\ *variant of* CHAMOIS

¹sham·poo \sham-'pü\ *transitive verb* [Hindi *cāpo*, imperative of *cāpnā* to press, shampoo] (1762)
1 *archaic* **:** MASSAGE
2 a : to wash (as the hair) with soap and water or with a special preparation **b :** to wash the hair of
— **sham·poo·er** *noun*

²shampoo *noun, plural* **shampoos** (1838)
1 : an act or instance of shampooing
2 : a preparation used in shampooing

sham·rock \'sham-ˌräk\ *noun* [Irish *seamróg*, diminutive of *seamar* clover] (1577)
: a trifoliolate plant used as a floral emblem by the Irish: as **a :** a yellow-flowered clover (*Trifolium dubium*) often regarded as the true shamrock **b :** WOOD SORREL **c :** WHITE CLOVER

sha·mus \'shä-məs, 'shā-\ *noun* [perhaps from Yiddish *shames* shammes; from a jocular comparison of the duties of a sexton and those of a store detective] (1925)

□ USAGE
shall From the reams of pronouncements written about the distinction between *shall* and *will*—dating back as far as the 17th century—it is clear that the rules laid down have never very accurately reflected actual usage. The nationalistic statements of 18th and 19th century British grammarians, who commonly cited the misuses of the Irish, the Scots, and occasionally the Americans, suggest that the traditional rules may have come closest to the usage of southern England. Some modern commentators believe that English usage is still the closest to the traditionally prescribed norms. Most modern commentators allow that *will* is more common in nearly all uses. The entries for *shall* and *will* in this dictionary show current usage.

◇ WORD HISTORY
shamefaced Old English *scamfæst* meant "bashful" or "modest" or, more literally, "held fast by shame." The second element of *shamefaced* was thus originally the same as that of *steadfast*, meaning "fixed in place." While we can be sure that the similarity of consonant sounds between *-fast* and *-faced* contributed to the alteration of *shamefast* to *shamefaced*, the belief that modesty or bashfulness is reflected in a person's face probably had some influence too. For instance, we find this sentence in a 15th century English translation from a Latin text: "Tho that haue the face sumwhate ruddy bene schamefast." (Those who have a somewhat ruddy face are shamefast.) Around the middle of the 16th century the alteration to *shamefaced* began to appear in print, and since then the folk etymology has been firmly established.

1 *slang* : POLICE OFFICER
2 *slang* : PRIVATE INVESTIGATOR
Shan \'shän, 'shan\ *noun, plural* **Shan** *or* **Shans** (1795)
1 : a member of a people living primarily in Myanmar and southern China
2 : the Thai language of the Shan
shan·dy \'shan-dē\ *noun, plural* **shandies** (1888)
1 : SHANDYGAFF
2 : a drink consisting of beer and lemonade
shan·dy·gaff \'shan-dē-,gaf\ *noun* [origin unknown] (1853)
: beer diluted with a nonalcoholic drink (as ginger beer)
Shang \'shän\ *noun* [Chinese (Beijing) *Shāng*] (1669)
: a Chinese dynasty traditionally dated 1766–1122 B.C. and known especially for bronze work
shang·hai \shaŋ-'hī\ *transitive verb* **shang·haied; shang·hai·ing** [*Shanghai*, China; from the formerly widespread use of this method to secure sailors for voyages to the Orient] (1871)
1 a : to put aboard a ship by force often with the help of liquor or a drug **b** : to put by force or threat of force into or as if into a place of detention
2 : to put by trickery into an undesirable position
— **shang·hai·er** \-'hī-(-ə)r\ *noun*
Shan·gri–la \,shaŋ-gri-'lä\ *noun* [*Shangri-La*, imaginary land depicted in the novel *Lost Horizon* (1933) by James Hilton] (1940)
1 : a remote beautiful imaginary place where life approaches perfection : UTOPIA
2 : a remote usually idyllic hideaway
1shank \'shaŋk\ *noun* [Middle English *shanke*, from Old English *scanca*; akin to Old Norse *skakkr* crooked, Greek *skazein* to limp] (before 12th century)
1 a : the part of the leg between the knee and the ankle in humans or the corresponding part in various other vertebrates **b** : LEG **c** : a cut of beef, veal, mutton, or lamb from the upper or the lower part of the leg : SHIN — see BEEF illustration
2 : a straight narrow usually essential part of an object: as **a** : the straight part of a nail or pin **b** : a straight part of a plant : STEM, STALK **c** : the part of an anchor between the ring and the crown — see ANCHOR illustration **d** : the part of a fishhook between the eye and the bend **e** : the part of a key between the handle and the bit **f** : the stem of a tobacco pipe or the part between the stem and the bowl **g** : TANG 1 **h** (1) : the narrow part of the sole of a shoe beneath the instep (2) : SHANKPIECE
3 : a part of an object by which it can be attached: as **a** (1) : a projection on the back of a solid button (2) : a short stem of thread that holds a sewn button away from the cloth **b** : the end (as of a drill bit) that is gripped in a chuck
4 a : the latter part of a period of time **b** : the early or main part of a period of time
5 *slang* : an often homemade knife
— **shanked** \'shaŋ(k)t\ *adjective*
2shank *transitive verb* (1927)
: to hit (a golf ball or shot) with the extreme heel of the club so that the ball goes off in an unintended direction; *also* : to kick (a football) in an unintended direction
shank·piece \'shaŋk-,pēs\ *noun* (1885)
: a support for the arch of the foot inserted in the shank of a shoe
shank's mare *noun* (circa 1795)
: one's own legs ⟨traveling by *shank's mare*⟩
shan't \'shant, 'shänt\ (1664)
: shall not
shan·tung \(,)shan-'təŋ\ *noun* [*Shantung* (Shandong), China] (circa 1882)
: a fabric in plain weave having a slightly irregular surface due to uneven slubbed filling yarns

1shan·ty \'shan-tē\ *variant of* CHANTEY
2shanty *noun, plural* **shanties** [probably from Canadian French *chantier* lumber camp, hut, from French, gantry, from Latin *cantherius* rafter, trellis] (1820)
: a small crudely built dwelling or shelter usually of wood
shan·ty·man \-mən, -,man\ *noun* (circa 1858)
: one who lives in a shanty
shan·ty·town \-,taün, -\ *noun* (1876)
: a usually poor town or section of a town consisting mostly of shanties
shap·able *or* **shape·able** \'shā-pə-bəl\ *adjective* (1647)
1 : capable of being shaped
2 : SHAPELY
1shape \'shāp\ *verb* **shaped; shap·ing** [Middle English, alteration of Old English *scieppan*; akin to Old High German *skepfen* to shape] (before 12th century)
transitive verb
1 : FORM, CREATE; *especially* : to give a particular form or shape to
2 *obsolete* : ORDAIN, DECREE
3 : to adapt in shape so as to fit neatly and closely ⟨a dress *shaped* to her figure⟩
4 a : DEVISE, PLAN **b** : to embody in definite form ⟨*shaping* a folktale into an epic⟩
5 a : to make fit for (as a particular use or purpose) : ADAPT **b** : to determine or direct the course or character of (as life) **c** : to modify (behavior) by rewarding changes that tend toward a desired response
intransitive verb
1 : HAPPEN, BEFALL
2 : to take on or approach a mature or definite form — often used with *up*
— **shap·er** *noun*
2shape *noun* (before 12th century)
1 a : the visible makeup characteristic of a particular item or kind of item **b** (1) : spatial form or contour (2) : a standard or universally recognized spatial form
2 : the appearance of the body as distinguished from that of the face : FIGURE
3 a : PHANTOM, APPARITION **b** : assumed appearance : GUISE
4 : form of embodiment
5 : a mode of existence or form of being having identifying features
6 : something having a particular form
7 : the condition in which someone or something exists at a particular time ⟨the car was in fine *shape*⟩
— **shaped** \,shāpt\ *adjective*
— **in shape** : in an original, normal, or fit condition ⟨exercises to keep *in shape*⟩
shape·less \'shā-pləs\ *adjective* (14th century)
1 : having no definite shape
2 a : deprived of usual or normal shape : MISSHAPEN ⟨a *shapeless* old hat⟩ **b** : not shapely
— **shape·less·ly** *adverb*
— **shape·less·ness** *noun*
shape·ly \'shā-plē\ *adjective* **shape·li·er; -est** (14th century)
1 : having a regular or pleasing shape
2 : orderly and consistent in arrangement or plan
— **shape·li·ness** *noun*
shap·en \'shā-pən\ *adjective* [Middle English, from past participle of *shapen* to shape] (14th century)
: fashioned in or provided with a definite shape — usually used in combination ⟨an ill-*shapen* body⟩
shape note *noun* (1932)
: one of a system of seven notes showing the musical scale degree by the shape of the note head
shape–shift·er \'shāp-,shif-tər\ *noun* (1887)
: one that seems able to change form at will
shape–up \'shāp-,əp\ *noun* (1940)
: a system of hiring workers and especially longshoremen by the day or shift by having

applicants gather for each day's selection; *also* : an instance of such hiring practice
shape up (circa 1920)
intransitive verb
: to improve to a good or acceptable condition or standard of behavior
transitive verb
: to bring to a good or acceptable condition or standard of behavior
shard \'shärd\ *also* **sherd** \'shərd\ *noun* [Middle English, from Old English *sceard*; akin to Old English *scieran* to cut — more at SHEAR] (before 12th century)
1 a : a piece or fragment of a brittle substance; *broadly* : a small piece or part **b** : SHELL, SCALE; *especially* : ELYTRON
2 *usually* **sherd** : fragments of pottery vessels found on sites and in refuse deposits where pottery-making peoples have lived
3 : highly angular curved glass fragments of tuffaceous sediments
1share \'shar, 'sher\ *noun* [Middle English *schare*, from Old English *scear*; akin to Old High German *scaro* plowshare, Old English *scieran* to cut — more at SHEAR] (before 12th century)
: PLOWSHARE
2share *noun* [Middle English, from Old English *scearu* cutting, tonsure; akin to Old English *scieran* to cut] (14th century)
1 a : a portion belonging to, due to, or contributed by an individual or group **b** : one's full or fair portion
2 a : the part allotted or belonging to one of a number owning together property or interest **b** : any of the equal portions into which property or invested capital is divided; *specifically* : any of the equal interests or rights into which the entire capital stock of a corporation is divided and ownership of which is regularly evidenced by one or more certificates **c** *plural*, *chiefly British* : STOCK 7c(1)
3share *verb* **shared; shar·ing** (1590)
transitive verb
1 : to divide and distribute in shares : APPORTION — usually used with *out* or *with*
2 a : to partake of, use, experience, occupy, or enjoy with others **b** : to have in common
3 : to grant or give a share in
intransitive verb
1 : to have a share — used with *in*
2 : to apportion and take shares of something ☆
— **shar·er** *noun*
share·able *or* **shar·able** \'sher-ə-bəl, 'shar-\ *adjective* (1920)
: capable of being shared
— **share·abil·i·ty** \,sher-ə-'bi-lə-tē, ,shar-\ *noun*
share·crop \'sher-,kräp, 'shar-\ *verb* [back-formation from *sharecropper*] (circa 1930)
intransitive verb
: to farm as a sharecropper

☆ **SYNONYMS**
Share, participate, partake mean to have, get, or use in common with another or others. SHARE usually implies that one as the original holder grants to another the partial use, enjoyment, or possession of a thing ⟨*shared* my toys with the others⟩. PARTICIPATE implies a having or taking part in an undertaking, activity, or discussion ⟨*participated* in sports⟩. PARTAKE implies accepting or acquiring a share especially of food or drink ⟨*partook* freely of the refreshments⟩.

\ə\ abut \ᵊ\ kitten \ər\ further \a\ ash \ā\ ace
\ä\ mop, mar \aü\ out \ch\ chin \e\ bet \ē\ easy
\g\ go \h\ hit \ī\ ice \j\ job \ŋ\ sing \ō\ go
\ò\ law \òi\ boy \th\ thin \t͟h\ the \ü\ loot \ù\ foot
\y\ yet \zh\ vision *see also* Guide to Pronunciation

transitive verb
: to farm (land) or produce (a crop) as a share-cropper

share·crop·per \-ˌkrä-pər\ *noun* (1923)
: a tenant farmer especially in the southern U.S. who is provided with credit for seed, tools, living quarters, and food, who works the land, and who receives an agreed share of the value of the crop minus charges

share·hold·er \-ˌhōl-dər\ *noun* (circa 1828)
: one that holds or owns a share in property; *especially* **:** STOCKHOLDER

share·ware \-ˌwar, -ˌwer\ *noun* (1983)
: software with usually limited capability or incomplete documentation which is available for trial use at little or no cost but which can be upgraded upon payment of a fee to the author

sha·rif \shə-ˈrēf\ *noun* [Arabic *sharīf*, literally, illustrious] (1599)
: a descendant of the prophet Muhammad through his daughter Fatima; *broadly* **:** one of noble ancestry or political preeminence in predominantly Islamic countries
— **sha·rif·ian** \-ˈrē-fē-ən\ *adjective*

¹shark \ˈshärk\ *noun* [Middle English] (15th century)
: any of numerous mostly marine cartilaginous fishes of medium to large size that have a fusiform body, lateral branchial clefts, and a tough usually dull gray skin roughened by minute tubercles and are typically active predators sometimes dangerous to humans
— **shark·like** \ˈshärk-ˌlīk\ *adjective*

shark: *1* mako, *2* tiger, *3* thresher, *4* hammerhead, *5* great white

²shark *noun* [probably modification of German *Schurke* scoundrel] (1599)
1 : a rapacious crafty person who preys upon others through usury, extortion, or trickery
2 : one who excels greatly especially in a particular field

³shark (1602)
transitive verb
1 *archaic* **:** to gather hastily
2 *archaic* **:** to obtain by some irregular means
intransitive verb
1 *archaic* **:** to practice fraud or trickery
2 *archaic* **:** SNEAK

shark·skin \ˈshärk-ˌskin\ *noun* (1851)
1 : the hide of a shark or leather made from it
2 a : a smooth durable woolen or worsted suiting in twill or basket weave with small woven designs **b :** a smooth crisp fabric with a dull finish made usually of rayon in basket weave

shark sucker *noun* (circa 1850)
: REMORA 1

¹sharp \ˈshärp\ *adjective* [Middle English, from Old English *scearp*; akin to Old High German *scarf* sharp and perhaps to Old English *scrapian* to scrape — more at SCRAPE] (before 12th century)

1 : adapted to cutting or piercing: as **a :** having a thin keen edge or fine point **b :** briskly or bitingly cold **:** NIPPING ⟨a *sharp* wind⟩
2 a : keen in intellect **:** QUICK-WITTED **b :** keen in perception **:** ACUTE ⟨*sharp* sight⟩ **c :** keen in attention **:** VIGILANT ⟨keep a *sharp* lookout⟩ **d :** keen in attention to one's own interest sometimes to the point of being unethical ⟨a *sharp* trader⟩
3 : keen in spirit or action: as **a :** full of activity or energy **:** BRISK ⟨*sharp* blows⟩ **b :** capable of acting or reacting strongly; *especially* **:** CAUSTIC
4 : SEVERE, HARSH: as **a :** inclined to or marked by irritability or anger ⟨a *sharp* temper⟩ **b :** causing intense mental or physical distress ⟨a *sharp* pain⟩ **c :** cutting in language or import ⟨a *sharp* rebuke⟩
5 : affecting the senses or sense organs intensely: as **a** (1) **:** having a strong odor or flavor ⟨*sharp* cheese⟩ (2) **:** ACRID **b :** having a strong piercing sound **c :** having the effect of or involving a sudden brilliant display of light ⟨a *sharp* flash⟩
6 a : terminating in a point or edge ⟨*sharp* features⟩ **b :** involving an abrupt or marked change especially in direction ⟨a *sharp* turn⟩ **c :** clear in outline or detail **:** DISTINCT ⟨a *sharp* image⟩ **d :** set forth with clarity and distinctness ⟨*sharp* contrast⟩
7 a *of a tone* **:** raised a half step in pitch **b :** higher than the proper pitch **c :** MAJOR, AUGMENTED — used of an interval in music
8 : STYLISH, DRESSY ☆
— **sharp·ly** *adverb*
— **sharp·ness** *noun*

²sharp *adverb* (before 12th century)
1 : in a sharp manner
2 : EXACTLY ⟨1:15 *sharp*⟩

³sharp *noun* (14th century)
: one that is sharp: as **a :** a sharp edge or point **b** (1) **:** a musical note or tone one half step higher than a note or tone named (2) **:** a character ♯ on a line or space of the musical staff indicating a pitch a half step higher than the degree would indicate without it **c :** a needle with a small eye for sewing by hand **d :** a real or self-styled expert; *also* **:** SHARPER

⁴sharp (1662)
transitive verb
: to raise (as a musical tone) in pitch; *especially* **:** to raise in pitch by a half step
intransitive verb
: to sing or play above the proper pitch

shar·pei \ˌshär-ˈpā, ˌshär-\ *noun, plural* **shar·peis** [Chinese (Guangdong) *sà* sand + *péi* fur] (1975)
: any of an ancient breed of dogs originating in China that have loose wrinkled skin especially when young, a short bristly coat, blue-black tongue, and wide blunt muzzle

sharp·en \ˈshär-pən\ *verb* **sharp·ened; sharp·en·ing** \ˈshärp-niŋ, ˈshär-pə-\ (15th century)
transitive verb
: to make sharp or sharper; *especially* **:** HONE
intransitive verb
: to become sharp or sharper
— **sharp·en·er** \ˈshärp-nər, ˈshär-pə-\ *noun*

sharp·er \ˈshär-pər\ *noun* (1681)
: CHEAT, SWINDLER; *especially* **:** a cheating gambler

sharp–eyed \ˈshärp-ˈīd\ *adjective* (1670)
: having keen sight; *also* **:** keen in observing or penetrating

sharp·ie *or* **sharpy** \ˈshär-pē\ *noun, plural* **sharp·ies** (circa 1859)
1 : a long narrow shallow-draft boat with flat or slightly V-shaped bottom and one or two masts each carrying a triangular sail
2 a : SHARPER **b :** an exceptionally keen or alert person

sharp–nosed \ˈshärp-ˈnōzd\ *adjective* (1561)
1 : keen in smelling
2 : having a pointed nose or snout

sharp practice *noun* (1845)
: the act of dealing in which advantage is taken or sought unscrupulously

sharp–set \ˈshärp-ˈset\ *adjective* (1540)
: eager in appetite or desire

sharp–shinned hawk \ˈshärp-ˈshind-\ *noun* (circa 1812)
: a common widely distributed American accipiter (*Accipiter striatus*) that is grayish above, has a chestnut breast, short rounded wings, and a tail with a notched or square tip when folded — called also *sharp-shin*

sharp·shoot·er \ˈshärp-ˌshü-tər\ *noun* (1802)
: a good marksman

sharp·shoot·ing \-ˌshü-tiŋ\ *noun* (1806)
1 : shooting with great precision
2 : accurate and usually unexpected attack (as in words)

sharp–sight·ed \-ˈsī-təd\ *adjective* (1571)
1 : having acute sight
2 : mentally keen or alert
— **sharp–sight·ed·ly** *adverb*
— **sharp–sight·ed·ness** *noun*

sharp–tongued \-ˈtəŋd\ *adjective* (1837)
: having a sharp tongue **:** harsh or bitter in speech or language

sharp–wit·ted \-ˈwi-təd\ *adjective* (circa 1586)
: having an acute mind

shash·lik *also* **shash·lick** *or* **shas·lik** \shäsh-ˈlik, ˈshäsh-lik\ *noun* [Russian *shashlyk*, probably modification of Crimean Tatar *šišlik*, from *šiš* skewer] (1926)
: KABOB

Shas·ta daisy \ˈshas-tə-\ *noun* [Mount *Shasta*, California] (circa 1893)
: a large-flowered garden daisy (*Chrysanthemum superbum* synonym *C. maximum*) that resembles the oxeye daisy

shat *past and past participle of* SHIT

¹shat·ter \ˈsha-tər\ *verb* [Middle English *schateren*] (14th century)
transitive verb
1 : to cause to drop or be dispersed
2 a : to break at once into pieces **b :** to damage badly **:** RUIN
3 : to cause the disruption or annihilation of **:** DEMOLISH
intransitive verb
1 : to break apart **:** DISINTEGRATE
2 : to drop off parts (as leaves, petals, or fruit)
— **shat·ter·ing·ly** \-tə-riŋ-lē\ *adverb*

²shatter *noun* (circa 1640)
1 : FRAGMENT, SHRED — usually used in plural ⟨the broken vase lay in *shatters*⟩
2 : an act of shattering **:** the state of being shattered
3 : a result of shattering **:** SHOWER

shatter cone *noun* (1933)
: a conical fragment of rock that has striations radiating from the apex and that is formed by high pressure (as from volcanism or meteorite impact)

shat·ter·proof \ˈsha-tər-ˌprüf\ *adjective* (1930)
: proof against shattering

¹shave \ˈshāv\ *verb* **shaved; shaved** *or* **shav·en** \ˈshā-vən\; **shav·ing** [Middle English, from Old English *scafan*; akin to Lithuanian *skobti* to pluck, Latin *scabere* to scratch, and perhaps to Greek *koptein* to cut — more at CAPON] (before 12th century)

transitive verb
1 a : to remove a thin layer from **b :** to cut off in thin layers or shreds **:** SLICE **c :** to cut off closely
2 a : to sever the hair from (the head or another part of the body) close to the roots **b :** to cut off (hair or beard) close to the skin
3 a : to discount (a note) at an exorbitant rate **b :** DEDUCT, REDUCE
4 : to come close to or touch lightly in passing
intransitive verb
1 : to cut off hair or beard close to the skin
2 : to proceed with difficulty **:** SCRAPE

²shave *noun* (before 12th century)
1 : SHAVER 3
2 : a thin slice **:** SHAVING
3 : an act or the process of shaving

shave·ling \'shāv-liŋ\ *noun* (1529)
1 : a tonsured clergyman **:** PRIEST — usually used disparagingly
2 : YOUTH, STRIPLING

shav·er \'shā-vər\ *noun* (15th century)
1 : a person who shaves
2 *archaic* **:** one who swindles
3 : a tool or machine for shaving; *especially* **:** an electric razor
4 : BOY, YOUNGSTER

shaves *plural of* SHAFT

shave·tail \'shāv-ˌtāl\ *noun* [from the practice of shaving the tails of newly broken mules to distinguish them from seasoned ones] (1846)
1 : a pack mule especially when newly broken in
2 : SECOND LIEUTENANT — usually used disparagingly

Sha·vi·an \'shā-vē-ən\ *noun* [New Latin *Shavius*, Latinized form of George Bernard *Shaw*] (1905)
: an admirer or devotee of G. B. Shaw, his writings, or his social and political theories
— **Shavian** *adjective*

shav·ie \'shā-vē\ *noun* [*shave* (swindle) + *-ie*] (1737)
Scottish **:** PRANK

shav·ing \'shā-viŋ\ *noun* (14th century)
1 : the act of one that shaves
2 : something shaved off (wood *shavings*)

¹shaw \'shȯ\ *noun* [Middle English, from Old English *sceaga*; akin to Old Norse *skegg* beard — more at SHAG] (before 12th century)
dialect **:** COPPICE, THICKET

²shaw *noun* [probably alteration of *show*] (1726)
chiefly British **:** the tops and stalks of a cultivated crop (as potatoes or turnips)

¹shawl \'shȯl\ *noun* [Persian *shāl*] (1662)
: a square or oblong usually fabric garment or wrapper used especially as a covering for the head or shoulders

²shawl *transitive verb* (1812)
: to wrap in or as if in a shawl

shawl collar *noun* (circa 1908)
: a turned-over collar of a garment that combines with lapels forming an unbroken curving line

shawl collar

shawm \'shȯm\ *noun* [Middle English *schalme*, from Middle French *chalemie*, from Old French, alteration of *chalemel*, from Late Latin *calamellus*, diminutive of Latin *calamus* reed — more at CALAMUS] (14th century)
: an early double-reed woodwind instrument

Shaw·nee \shȯ-'nē, shä-\ *noun, plural* **Shawnee** *or* **Shawnees** [back-formation from obsolete English *Shawnese*, ultimately from Shawnee *ša'wano'ki*, literally, southerners] (1769)
1 : a member of an American Indian people originally of the central Ohio valley
2 : the Algonquian language of the Shawnee people

Shaw·wal \shȯ-'wäl\ *noun* [Arabic *shawwāl*] (circa 1771)
: the 10th month of the Islamic year — see MONTH table

shay \'shā\ *noun* [back-formation from *chaise*, taken as plural] (1717)
chiefly dialect **:** CHAISE 1

¹she \'shē\ *pronoun* [Middle English, probably alteration of *hye*, alteration of Old English *hēo* she — more at HE] (12th century)
1 : that female one who is neither speaker nor the one addressed (*she* is my wife) — compare HE, HER, HERS, IT, THEY
2 — used to refer to one regarded as feminine (as by personification) (*she* was a fine ship)
usage see HE

²she *noun* (14th century)
: a female person or animal — often used in combination (*she*-cat) (*she*-cousin)

s/he \'shē-'hē; 'shē-ər-'hē; 'shē-ˌslash-'hē\ *pronoun* (1973)
: she or he — used in writing as a pronoun of common gender

shea butter \'shē-, 'shā-\ *noun* (1847)
: a pale solid fat from the seeds of the shea tree used in food, soap, and candles

sheaf \'shēf\ *noun, plural* **sheaves** \'shēvz\ [Middle English *sheef*, from Old English *scēaf*; akin to Old High German *scoub* sheaf, Russian *chub* forelock] (before 12th century)
1 : a quantity of the stalks and ears of a cereal grass or sometimes other plant material bound together
2 : something resembling a sheaf of grain (a *sheaf* of papers)
— **sheaf·like** \'shēf-ˌlīk\ *adjective*

shea nut *noun* (1919)
: the seed of the shea tree

¹shear \'shir\ *verb* **sheared; sheared** *or* **shorn** \'shȯrn, 'shȯrn\; **shear·ing** [Middle English *sheren*, from Old English *scieran*; akin to Old Norse *skera* to cut, Latin *curtus* shortened, Greek *keirein* to cut, shear, Sanskrit *kṛṇāti* he injures] (before 12th century)
transitive verb
1 a : to cut off the hair from (with crown *shorn*) **b :** to cut or clip (as hair or wool) from someone or something; *also* **:** to cut something from (*shear* a lawn) **c** *chiefly Scottish* **:** to reap with a sickle **d :** to cut or trim with shears or a similar instrument
2 : to cut with something sharp
3 : to deprive of something as if by cutting
4 a : to subject to a shear force **b :** to cause (as a rock mass) to move along the plane of contact
intransitive verb
1 : to cut through something with or as if with a sharp instrument
2 *chiefly Scottish* **:** to reap crops with a sickle
3 : to become divided under the action of a shear (the bolt may *shear* off)
— **shear·er** *noun*

²shear *noun* (before 12th century)
1 a (1) : a cutting implement similar or identical to a pair of scissors but typically larger — usually used in plural **(2) :** one blade of a pair of shears **b :** any of various cutting tools or machines operating by the action of opposed cutting edges of metal — usually used in plural **c (1) :** something resembling a shear or a pair of shears **(2) :** a hoisting apparatus consisting of two or sometimes more upright spars fastened together at their upper ends and having tackle for masting or dismasting ships or lifting heavy loads (as guns) — usually used in plural but singular or plural in construction
2 *chiefly British* **:** the action or process or an instance of shearing — used in combination to indicate the approximate age of sheep in terms of shearings undergone
3 a : internal force tangential to the section on which it acts — called also *shearing force* **b :** an action or stress resulting from applied forces that causes or tends to cause two contiguous parts of a body to slide relatively to each other in a direction parallel to their plane of contact

sheared *adjective* (1616)
: formed or finished by shearing; *especially* **:** cut to uniform length (a *sheared* rug)

shear·ling \'shir-liŋ\ *noun* (14th century)
: skin from a recently sheared sheep or lamb that has been tanned and dressed with the wool left on

shear pin *noun* (circa 1931)
: an easily replaceable pin inserted at a critical point in a machine and designed to break when subjected to excess stress

shear·wa·ter \'shir-ˌwȯ-tər, -ˌwä-\ *noun* (circa 1671)
: any of numerous oceanic birds (especially genus *Puffinus*) that are related to the petrels and usually skim close to the waves in flight

sheath \'shēth\ *noun, plural* **sheaths** \'shēthz, 'shēths\ [Middle English *shethe*, from Old English *scēath*; akin to Old High German *sceida* sheath and perhaps to Latin *scindere* to split — more at SHED] (before 12th century)
1 : a case for a blade (as of a knife)
2 : an investing cover or case of a plant or animal body or body part: as **a :** the tubular fold of skin into which the penis of many mammals is retracted **b (1) :** the lower part of a leaf (as of a grass) when surrounding the stem **(2) :** an ensheathing spathe
3 : any of various covering or supporting structures that are applied like or resemble in appearance or function the sheath of a blade: as **a :** SHEATHING 2 **b :** a woman's close-fitting dress usually worn without a belt **c** *British* **:** CONDOM

sheath·bill \'shēth-ˌbil\ *noun* (circa 1781)
: either of two white shorebirds (*Chionis alba* and *C. minor* of the family Chionididae) of colder parts of the southern hemisphere that have a horny sheath over the base of the upper mandible and suggest the pigeons in general appearance

sheathe \'shēth\ *also* **sheath** \'shēth\ *transitive verb* **sheathed; sheath·ing** [Middle English *shethen*, from *shethe* sheath] (15th century)
1 : to put into or furnish with a sheath
2 : to plunge or bury (as a sword) in flesh
3 : to withdraw (a claw) into a sheath
4 : to case or cover with something (as sheets of metal) that protects
— **sheath·er** \'shē-thər, -thər\ *noun*

sheath·ing \'shē-thiŋ, -thiŋ\ *noun* (15th century)
1 : the action of one that sheathes something
2 : material used to sheathe something; *especially* **:** the first covering of boards or of waterproof material on the outside wall of a frame house or on a timber roof

sheath knife *noun* (1837)
: a knife having a fixed blade and designed to be carried in a sheath

shea tree \'shē-, 'shā-\ *noun* [Bambara *si*] (1799)
: a tropical African tree (*Vitellaria paradoxa* synonym *Butyrospermum parkii*) of the sapodilla family with fatty nuts that yield shea butter

¹sheave \'shiv, 'shēv\ *noun* [Middle English *sheve*; akin to Old High German *scība* disk] (14th century)
: a grooved wheel or pulley (as of a pulley block)

²sheave \'shēv\ *transitive verb* **sheaved; sheav·ing** [*sheaf*] (1598)
: to gather and bind into a sheaf

she·bang \shi-'baŋ\ *noun* [origin unknown] (1869)

\ə\ abut \ˀ\ kitten \ər\ further \a\ ash \ā\ ace \ä\ mop, mar \au̇\ out \ch\ chin \e\ bet \ē\ easy \g\ go \i\ hit \ī\ ice \j\ job \ŋ\ sing \ō\ go \ȯ\ law \ȯi\ boy \th\ thin \th\ the \ü\ loot \u̇\ foot \y\ yet \zh\ vision *see also* Guide to Pronunciation

: everything involved in what is under consideration — usually used in the phrase *the whole shebang*

She·bat \shə-'bät, -'vät\ *noun* [Hebrew *shĕbḥāt*] (1535)
: the 5th month of the civil year or the 11th month of the ecclesiastical year in the Jewish calendar — see MONTH table

she·been \shə-'bēn\ *noun* [Irish *síbín* illicit whiskey, shebeen] (circa 1787)
chiefly Irish : an unlicensed or illegally operated drinking establishment

She·chi·nah \shə-'kē-nə, -'kē-nə, -'kī-nə\ *noun* [Hebrew *shĕkhīnāh*] (1663)
: the presence of God in the world as conceived in Jewish theology

¹**shed** \'shed\ *verb* **shed; shed·ding** [Middle English, to divide, separate, from Old English *scēadan*; akin to Old High German *skeidan* to separate, Latin *scindere* to split, cleave, Greek *schizein* to split] (before 12th century)
transitive verb
1 *chiefly dialect* : to set apart : SEGREGATE
2 : to cause to be dispersed without penetrating ⟨duck's plumage *sheds* water⟩
3 a : to cause (blood) to flow by cutting or wounding **b** : to pour forth in drops ⟨*shed* tears⟩ **c** : to give off in a stream ⟨fish *shedding* their eggs in spawning⟩ **d** : to give off or out ⟨*sheds* some light on the subject⟩
4 a (1) : to cast off (as a body covering) : MOLT (2) : to let fall (as leaves) (3) : to eject (as seed or spores) from a natural receptacle **b** : to rid oneself of temporarily or permanently as superfluous or unwanted ⟨*shed* her inhibitions⟩ ⟨the company *shed* 100 jobs⟩
intransitive verb
1 : to pour out : SPILL
2 : to become dispersed : SCATTER
3 : to cast off some natural covering (as fur or skin) ⟨the cat is *shedding*⟩
synonym see DISCARD
— **shed blood** : to cause death by violence

²**shed** *noun* (12th century)
1 *obsolete* : DISTINCTION, DIFFERENCE
2 : something (as the skin of a snake) that is discarded in shedding
3 : a divide of land

³**shed** *noun* [alteration of earlier *shadde*, probably from Middle English *shade* shade] (1557)
1 a : a slight structure built for shelter or storage; *especially* : a single-storied building with one or more sides unenclosed **b** : a building that resembles a shed
2 *archaic* : HUT
— **shed·like** \-,līk\ *adjective*

⁴**shed** *transitive verb* **shed·ded; shed·ding** (1850)
: to put or house in a shed

she'd \'shēd\ (1609)
: she had : she would

shed·der \'she-dər\ *noun* (14th century)
: one that sheds something: as **a** : a crab or lobster about to molt **b** : a newly molted crab

shed dormer *noun* (1948)
: a dormer with a roof sloping in the same direction as the roof from which the dormer projects

¹**sheen** \'shēn\ *adjective* [Middle English *shene*, from Old English *scīene*; akin to Old English *scēawian* to look — more at SHOW] (before 12th century)
1 *archaic* : BEAUTIFUL
2 *archaic* : SHINING, RESPLENDENT

²**sheen** *intransitive verb* (14th century)
: to be bright : show a sheen

³**sheen** *noun* (1602)
1 a : a bright or shining condition : BRIGHTNESS **b** : a subdued glitter approaching but short of optical reflection **c** : a lustrous surface imparted to textiles through finishing processes or use of shiny yarns
2 : a textile exhibiting notable sheen
— **sheeny** \'shē-nē\ *adjective*

sheep \'shēp\ *noun, plural* **sheep** *often attributive* [Middle English, from Old English *scēap*; akin to Old High German *scāf* sheep] (before 12th century)
1 : any of various ruminant mammals (genus *Ovis*) related to the goats but stockier and lacking a beard in the male; *specifically* : one (*O. aries*) long domesticated especially for its flesh and wool
2 a : a timid defenseless creature **b** : a timid docile person; *especially* : one easily influenced or led
3 : leather prepared from the skins of sheep : SHEEPSKIN

sheep·ber·ry \-,ber-ē\ *noun* (circa 1818)
: an often shrubby North American viburnum (*Viburnum lentago*) with white flowers in flat cymes

sheep·cote \-,kōt, -,kät\ *noun* (15th century)
chiefly British : SHEEPFOLD

sheep—dip \-,dip\ *noun* (1865)
: a liquid preparation of usually toxic chemicals into which sheep are plunged especially to destroy parasitic arthropods

sheep·dog \-,dȯg\ *noun* (circa 1774)
: a dog (as a Border collie) used to tend, drive, or guard sheep

sheep fescue *noun* (1945)
: a hardy fine-foliaged perennial grass (*Festuca ovina*) widely used as a pasture grass — called also *sheep's fescue*

sheep·fold \'shēp-,fōld\ *noun* (15th century)
: a pen or shelter for sheep

sheep·herd·er \'shēp-,hər-dər\ *noun* (1871)
: a worker in charge of sheep especially on open range

sheep·herd·ing \-,hər-diŋ\ *noun* (1891)
: the activities of a worker engaged in tending sheep

sheep·ish \'shē-pish\ *adjective* (13th century)
1 : resembling a sheep in meekness, stupidity, or timidity
2 : affected by or showing embarrassment caused by consciousness of a fault ⟨a *sheepish* grin⟩
— **sheep·ish·ly** *adverb*
— **sheep·ish·ness** *noun*

sheep ked \'shēp-,ked\ *noun* [sheep + ked sheep ked, of unknown origin] (1925)
: a wingless bloodsucking dipteran fly (*Melophagus ovinus*) that feeds chiefly on sheep and is a vector of sheep trypanosomiasis — called also *sheep tick*

sheep laurel *noun* (1810)
: a dwarf shrub (*Kalmia angustifolia*) of the eastern U.S. that is poisonous to young stock and resembles mountain laurel but has narrower leaves and smaller bright red flowers — called also *lambkill*

sheep's eye *noun* (circa 1529)
: a shy longing usually amorous glance — usually used in plural

sheep·shank \'shēp-,shaŋk\ *noun* (1627)
1 : a knot for shortening a line — see KNOT illustration
2 *Scottish* : something of no worth or importance

sheeps·head \'shēps-,hed\ *noun* (1643)
1 : a marine bony fish (*Archosargus probatocephalus* of the family Sparidae) of the Atlantic and Gulf coasts of the U.S. that has broad incisor teeth and is used for food
2 : FRESHWATER DRUM
3 : a largely red or rose California wrasse (*Semicossyphus pulcher*)

sheep·shear·er \'shēp-,shir-ər\ *noun* (1539)
: one that shears sheep

sheep·shear·ing \'shēp-,shir-iŋ\ *noun* (1586)
1 : the act of shearing sheep
2 : the time or season for shearing sheep

sheep·skin \-,skin\ *noun* (13th century)
1 a : the skin of a sheep; *also* : leather prepared from it **b** : PARCHMENT **c** : a garment made of or lined with sheepskin
2 : DIPLOMA

sheep sorrel *noun* (1806)

: a small dock (*Rumex acetosella*) of acidic soils

sheep walk *noun* (1586)
chiefly British : a pasture or range for sheep

¹**sheer** \'shir\ *verb* [perhaps alteration of ¹*shear*] (1539)
intransitive verb
: to deviate from a course : SWERVE
transitive verb
: to cause to sheer

²**sheer** *noun* (1670)
1 : a turn, deviation, or change in a course (as of a ship)
2 : the position of a ship riding to a single anchor and heading toward it

³**sheer** *adjective* [Middle English *schere* freed from guilt, probably alteration of *skere*, from Old Norse *skærr* pure; akin to Old English *scīnan* to shine] (circa 1568)
1 *obsolete* : BRIGHT, SHINING
2 : of very thin or transparent texture : DIAPHANOUS
3 a : UNQUALIFIED, UTTER ⟨*sheer* folly⟩ ⟨*sheer* ignorance⟩ **b** : being free from an adulterant : PURE, UNMIXED **c** : viewed or acting in dissociation from all else ⟨in terms of *sheer* numbers⟩
4 : marked by great and continuous steepness
synonym see STEEP
— **sheer·ly** *adverb*
— **sheer·ness** *noun*

⁴**sheer** *adverb* (circa 1600)
1 : in a complete manner : ALTOGETHER
2 : straight up or down without a break : PERPENDICULARLY

⁵**sheer** *noun* (circa 1920)
: a sheer fabric; *also* : an article of such a fabric

⁶**sheer** *noun* [perhaps alteration of ²*shear*] (1691)
: the fore-and-aft curvature from bow to stern of a ship's deck as shown in side elevation

sheer·legs \'shir-,legz, -,lāgz\ *noun plural but singular or plural in construction* (circa 1860)
: SHEAR 1c(2)

¹**sheet** \'shēt\ *noun* [Middle English *shete*, from Old English *scȳte*; akin to Old English *scēat* edge, Old High German *scōz* flap, skirt] (before 12th century)
1 a : a broad piece of cloth; *especially* : BEDSHEET **b** : SAIL 1a(1)
2 a (1) : a usually rectangular piece of paper; *especially* : one manufactured for printing (2) : a rectangular piece of heavy paper with a plant specimen mounted on it ⟨an herbarium of 100,000 *sheets*⟩ **b** : a printed signature for a book especially before it has been folded, cut, or bound — usually used in plural **c** : a newspaper, periodical, or occasional publication ⟨a gossip *sheet*⟩ **d** : the unseparated postage stamps printed by one impression of a plate on a single piece of paper; *also* : a pane of stamps
3 : a broad stretch or surface of something ⟨a *sheet* of ice⟩
4 : a suspended or moving expanse (as of fire or rain)
5 a : a portion of something that is thin in comparison to its length and breadth **b** : a flat baking pan of tinned metal ⟨a cookie *sheet*⟩
6 : a surface or part of a surface in which it is possible to pass from any one point of it to any other without leaving the surface ⟨a hyperboloid of two *sheets*⟩
— **sheet·like** \-,līk\ *adjective*

²**sheet** *adjective* (1582)
1 : rolled or spread out in a sheet
2 : of, relating to, or concerned with the making of sheet metal

³**sheet** (1606)
transitive verb
1 : to cover with a sheet : SHROUD
2 : to furnish with sheets
3 : to form into sheets

intransitive verb
: to fall, spread, or flow in a sheet ⟨the rain *sheeted* against the windows⟩
— **sheet·er** *noun*
— **sheet home 1 :** to extend (a sail) and set as flat as possible by hauling upon the sheets **2 :** to fix the responsibility for **:** bring home to one

⁴sheet *noun* [Middle English *shete,* from Old English *scēata* lower corner of a sail; akin to Old English *scȳte* sheet] (13th century)
1 : a rope or chain that regulates the angle at which a sail is set in relation to the wind
2 *plural* **:** the spaces at either end of an open boat not occupied by thwarts **:** foresheets and stern sheets together
— **three sheets in the wind** *or* **three sheets to the wind :** DRUNK 1a

sheet anchor *noun* (15th century)
1 : a large strong anchor formerly carried in the waist of a ship and used as a spare in an emergency
2 : something that constitutes a main support or dependence especially in danger

sheet bend *noun* (circa 1823)
: a bend or hitch used for temporarily fastening a rope to the bight of another rope or to an eye — see KNOT illustration

sheet·fed \'shēt-ˌfed\ *adjective* (1926)
: of, relating to, being, or printed by a press that prints on paper in sheet form

sheet glass *noun* (1805)
: glass made in large sheets directly from the furnace or by making a cylinder and then flattening it

sheet·ing \'shē-tiŋ\ *noun* (1711)
1 : material in the form of sheets or suitable for forming into sheets
2 : a lining (as wood or steel) used to support an embankment or the walls of an excavation

sheet lightning *noun* (1794)
: lightning in diffused or sheet form due to reflection and diffusion by the clouds and sky

sheet metal *noun* (circa 1909)
: metal in the form of a sheet

sheet music *noun* (1857)
: music printed on large unbound sheets of paper

Sheet·rock \'shēt-ˌräk\ *trademark*
— used for plasterboard

sheikh *or* **sheik** \'shēk, *also* 'shāk *for 1*\ *noun* [Arabic *shaykh*] (1577)
1 : an Arab chief
2 *usually* **sheik :** a man held to be irresistibly attractive to romantic young women

sheikh·dom *or* **sheik·dom** \-dəm, -təm\ *noun* (1860)
: a region under the rule of a sheikh

shei·la \'shē-lə\ *noun* [probably from *Sheila,* female given name] (circa 1919)
Australian & New Zealand **:** a girl or young woman

shek·el \'she-kəl\ *noun* [Hebrew *sheqel*] (15th century)
1 a : any of various ancient units of weight; *especially* **:** a Hebrew unit equal to about 252 grains troy **b :** a unit of value based on a shekel weight of gold or silver
2 : a coin weighing one shekel
3 *plural* **:** MONEY
4 — see MONEY table

Shekinah *variant of* SHECHINAH

shel·drake \'shel-ˌdrāk\ *noun* [Middle English, from *sheld-* (akin to Middle Dutch *schillede* parti-colored) + *drake*] (14th century)
1 : SHELDUCK
2 : MERGANSER

shel·duck \-ˌdək\ *noun* [*shel-* (as in *sheldrake*) + *duck*] (1707)
: any of various Old World ducks (genus *Tadorna*); *especially* **:** a common mostly black-and-white duck (*T. tadorna*) slightly larger than the mallard

shelf \'shelf\ *noun, plural* **shelves** \'shelvz\ [Middle English, probably from Old English

scylfe; akin to Old Norse *hlīth·skjalf* Odin's seat] (14th century)
1 a : a thin flat usually long and narrow piece of material (as wood) fastened horizontally (as on a wall) at a distance from the floor to hold objects **b :** one of several similar pieces in a closet, bookcase, or similar structure **c :** the contents of a shelf
2 : something resembling a shelf in form or position: as **a :** a sandbank or ledge of rocks usually partially submerged **b :** a flat projecting layer of rock **c :** the submerged gradually sloping border of a continent or island **:** CONTINENTAL SHELF
— **shelf·ful** \'shelf-ˌfül\ *noun*
— **shelf-like** \'shelf-ˌlīk\ *adjective*
— **off the shelf :** available from stock **:** not made to order ⟨*off the shelf* equipment⟩
— **on the shelf :** in a state of inactivity or uselessness

shelf fungus *noun* (circa 1903)
: BRACKET FUNGUS

shelf ice *noun* (1910)
: an extensive ice sheet originating on land but continuing out to sea beyond the depths at which it rests on the sea bottom

shelf life *noun* (1927)
: the period of time during which a material may be stored and remain suitable for use; *broadly* **:** the period of time during which something lasts or remains popular

¹shell \'shel\ *noun* [Middle English, from Old English *sciell;* akin to Old English *scealu* shell, Old Norse *skel,* Lithuanian *skelti* to split, Greek *skallein* to hoe] (before 12th century)
1 a : a hard rigid usually largely calcareous covering or support of an animal **b :** the hard or tough often thin outer covering of an egg (as of a bird or reptile) — see EGG illustration
2 : the covering or outside part of a fruit or seed especially when hard or fibrous
3 : shell material (as of mollusks or turtles) or their substance
4 : something that resembles a shell: as **a :** a framework or exterior structure; *especially* **:** a building with an unfinished interior **b** (1) **:** an external case or outside covering ⟨the *shell* of a ship⟩ (2) **:** a thin usually spherical layer or surface enclosing a space or surrounding an object ⟨an expanding *shell* of gas around a neutron star⟩ **c :** a casing without substance ⟨mere effigies and *shells* of men —Thomas Carlyle⟩ **d :** an edible crust for holding a filling ⟨a pastry *shell*⟩ **e :** BAND SHELL **f :** a small beer glass **g :** an unlined article of outerwear
5 : a shell-bearing mollusk
6 : an impersonal attitude or manner that conceals the presence or absence of feeling ⟨he retreated into his *shell*⟩
7 : a narrow light racing boat propelled by one or more persons pulling oars or sculls
8 : any of the spaces occupied by the orbits of a group of electrons of approximately equal energy surrounding the nucleus of an atom
9 a : a projectile for cannon containing an explosive bursting charge **b :** a metal or paper case which holds the charge of powder and shot or bullet used with breech-loading small arms
10 : a plain usually sleeveless blouse or sweater
11 : a company or corporation that exists without assets or independent operations as a legal entity through which another company or corporation can conduct various dealings
— **shell** *adjective*

²shell (1562)

shelduck

transitive verb
1 a : to take out of a natural enclosing cover (as a shell, husk, pod, or capsule) ⟨*shell* peanuts⟩ **b :** to separate the kernels of (as an ear of Indian corn, wheat, or oats) from the cob, ear, or husk
2 : to throw shells at, upon, or into **:** BOMBARD
3 : to score heavily against (as an opposing pitcher in baseball)
intransitive verb
1 : to fall or scale off in thin pieces
2 : to cast the shell or exterior covering **:** fall out of the pod or husk ⟨nuts which *shell* in falling⟩
3 : to gather shells (as from a beach) **:** collect shells

she'll \'shē(ə)l, shil\ (circa 1590)
: she will **:** she shall

¹shel·lac \shə-'lak\ *noun* [¹*shell* + *lac*] (1713)
1 : purified lac usually prepared in thin orange or yellow flakes by heating and filtering and often bleached white
2 : a preparation of lac dissolved usually in alcohol and used chiefly as a wood filler and finish
3 a : a composition containing shellac formerly used for making phonograph records **b :** an old 78 rpm phonograph record

²shellac *transitive verb* **shel·lacked; shel·lack·ing** (1876)
1 : to coat or otherwise treat with shellac or a shellac varnish
2 : to defeat decisively

shellacking *noun* (1931)
: a decisive defeat **:** DRUBBING

shell·back \'shel-ˌbak\ *noun* (1853)
1 : an old or veteran sailor
2 : a person who has crossed the equator and been initiated in the traditional ceremony

shell bean *noun* (1868)
1 : a bean grown primarily for its edible seeds
— compare SNAP BEAN
2 : the edible seed of a bean

shell·crack·er \'shel-ˌkra-kər\ *noun* (circa 1890)
: REDEAR

shelled \'sheld\ *adjective* (15th century)
1 : having a shell especially of a specified kind — often used in combination ⟨pink-*shelled*⟩ ⟨thick-*shelled*⟩
2 a : having the shell removed ⟨*shelled* oysters⟩ ⟨*shelled* nuts⟩ **b :** removed from the cob ⟨*shelled* corn⟩

shell·er \'she-lər\ *noun* (1694)
1 : one that shells ⟨a peanut *sheller*⟩
2 : a person who collects seashells

shell·fish \-ˌfish\ *noun* (before 12th century)
: an aquatic invertebrate animal with a shell; *especially* **:** an edible mollusk or crustacean

shell·fish·ery \-ˌfi-shə-rē, -ˌfish-rē\ *noun* (1885)
: a commercially exploited population of shellfish

shell game *noun* (1890)
1 : thimblerig played especially with three walnut shells
2 : FRAUD; *especially* **:** a swindle involving the substitution of something of little or no value for a valuable item

shell jacket *noun* (1840)
1 : a short tight military jacket worn buttoned up the front
2 : MESS JACKET

shell out *verb* (1801)
: PAY

shell pink *noun* (1887)
: a light yellowish pink

shell-proof \'shel-ˌprüf\ *adjective* (circa 1859)
: capable of resisting shells or bombs

shell shock *noun* (1915)

: post-traumatic stress disorder in soldiers as a result of combat experience

shell–shocked *adjective* (1918)
1 : affected with shell shock
2 : mentally confused, upset, or exhausted as a result of excessive stress

shell steak *noun* (circa 1968)
: the part of a short loin of beef that contains no tenderloin

shell·work \'shel-ˌwərk\ *noun* (1611)
: work adorned with shells or composed of a pattern of shells

shelly \'she-lē\ *adjective* **shell·i·er; -est** (1555)
1 : abounding in or covered with shells ⟨a *shelly* shore⟩
2 : of, relating to, or resembling a shell

¹**shel·ter** \'shel-tər\ *noun* [origin unknown] (1585)
1 a : something that covers or affords protection ⟨a bomb *shelter*⟩ **b** : an establishment providing food and shelter (as to the homeless) **c** : an establishment that houses and feeds stray animals
2 : a position or the state of being covered and protected ⟨took *shelter*⟩
— **shel·ter·less** \-ləs\ *adjective*

²**shelter** *verb* **shel·tered; shel·ter·ing** \-t(ə-)riŋ\ (1590)
transitive verb
1 : to constitute or provide a shelter for : PROTECT ⟨has led a *sheltered* life⟩
2 : to place under shelter or protection ⟨*sheltered* himself in a mountain cave⟩
3 : to protect (income) from taxation
intransitive verb
: to take shelter
— **shel·ter·er** \-tər-ər\ *noun*

shel·ter·belt \'shel-tər-ˌbelt\ *noun* (1868)
: a barrier of trees and shrubs that protects (as crops) from wind and storm and lessens erosion

shelter half *noun* (1911)
: one of the halves of a shelter tent

shelter tent *noun* (1862)
: a small tent usually consisting of two interchangeable pieces : PUP TENT

shel·tie *or* **shel·ty** \'shel-tē\ *noun, plural* **shelties** [probably from Old Norse *Hjalti* Shetlander] (1650)
1 : SHETLAND PONY
2 : SHETLAND SHEEPDOG

shelve \'shelv\ *verb* **shelved; shelv·ing** [*shelf*] (1598)
transitive verb
1 : to furnish with shelves
2 : to place on a shelf
3 a : to remove from active service **b** : to put off or aside ⟨*shelve* a project⟩
intransitive verb
: to slope in a formation like a shelf
— **shelv·er** *noun*

¹**shelv·ing** \'shel-viŋ\ *noun* (1687)
1 : the state or degree of sloping
2 : a sloping surface or place

²**shelving** *noun* (1817)
1 : material for shelves
2 : SHELVES

Shem \'shem\ *noun* [Hebrew *Shēm*]
: the eldest son of Noah held to be the progenitor of the Semitic peoples

She·ma \shə-'mä\ *noun* [Hebrew *shēma'* hear, first word of Deuteronomy 6:4] (1706)
: the Jewish confession of faith made up of Deuteronomy 6:4–9 and 11:13–21 and Numbers 15:37–41

She·mi·ni Atze·reth \shə-ˌmē-nē-ät-'ser-ət, -əth, -əs\ *noun* [Late Hebrew *shēmīnī 'ăsereth*, from Hebrew *shēmīnī* eighth + *'ăsereth* assembly] (circa 1905)
: a Jewish festival following the seventh day of Sukkoth and marked by a special prayer for seasonal rain

Shem·ite \'she-ˌmīt\ *noun* [*Shem*] (1659)
archaic : SEMITE

— **She·mit·ic** \shə-'mi-tik\ *or* **Shem·it·ish** \'she-ˌmī-tish\ *adjective, archaic*

she·nan·i·gan \shə-'na-ni-gən\ *noun* [origin unknown] (1855)
1 : a devious trick used especially for an underhand purpose
2 a : tricky or questionable practices or conduct — usually used in plural **b** : high-spirited or mischievous activity — usually used in plural

shend \'shend\ *transitive verb* **shent** \'shent\; **shend·ing** [Middle English, from Old English *scendan*; akin to Old English *scamu* shame — more at SHAME] (before 12th century)
1 *archaic* : to put to shame or confusion
2 *archaic* : REPROVE, REVILE
3 *chiefly dialect* **a** : INJURE, MAR **b** : RUIN, DESTROY

she–oak \'shē-ˌōk\ *noun* (1792)
: any of several casuarinas

She·ol \shē-'ōl, 'shē-ˌ\ *noun* [Hebrew *Shě'ōl*] (1599)
: the abode of the dead in early Hebrew thought

¹**shep·herd** \'she-pərd\ *noun* [Middle English *sheepherde*, from Old English *scēaphyrde*, from *scēap* sheep + *hierde* herdsman; akin to Old English *heord* herd] (before 12th century)
1 : one who tends sheep
2 : PASTOR
3 : GERMAN SHEPHERD

²**shepherd** *transitive verb* (1790)
1 : to tend as a shepherd
2 : to guide or guard in the manner of a shepherd ⟨*shepherded* the bill through Congress⟩

shepherd dog *noun* (15th century)
: SHEEPDOG

shep·herd·ess \'she-pər-dəs\ *noun* (14th century)
: a woman or girl who tends sheep; *also* : a rural girl or woman

shepherd's check *noun* (1896)
: a pattern of small even black-and-white checks; *also* : a fabric woven in this pattern — called also *shepherd's plaid*

shepherd's pie *noun* (1877)
: a meat pie with a mashed potato crust

shepherd's check

shepherd's purse *noun* (15th century)
: a white-flowered weedy annual herb (*Capsella bursa-pastoris*) of the mustard family with flat heart-shaped pods

sheq·el \'she-kəl\ *noun, plural* **sheq·a·lim** \she-'kä-lim\ *variant of* SHEKEL

Sher·a·ton \'sher-ə-tᵊn\ *adjective* [Thomas *Sheraton*] (1883)
: of, relating to, or being a style of furniture that originated in England around 1800 and is characterized by straight lines and graceful proportions

sher·bet \'shər-bət\ *also* **sher·bert** \-bərt\ *noun* [Turkish & Persian; Turkish *şerbet*, from Persian *sharbat*, from Arabic *sharbah* drink] (1603)
1 : a cold drink of sweetened and diluted fruit juice
2 : an ice with milk, egg white, or gelatin added

sherd *variant of* SHARD

sher·got·tite \'shər-gə-ˌtīt\ *noun* [*Shergotty* (Sherghati), town in India] (circa 1911)
: any of a class of rare achondritic geologically young meteorites that are apparently composed of solidified lava from celestial bodies other than earth

she·rif \shə-'rēf\ *variant of* SHARIF

sher·iff \'sher-əf\ *noun* [Middle English *shir-reve*, from Old English *scīrgerēfa*, from *scīr* shire + *gerēfa* reeve — more at SHIRE, REEVE] (before 12th century)

: an important official of a shire or county charged primarily with judicial duties (as executing the processes and orders of courts and judges)
— **sher·iff·dom** \-əf-dəm, -təm\ *noun*

sher·lock \'shər-ˌläk, -lək\ *noun, often capitalized* [*Sherlock* Holmes, detective in stories by Sir Arthur Conan Doyle] (1903)
: DETECTIVE

Sher·pa \'sher-pə, 'shər-\ *noun* (1847)
: a member of a Tibetan people living on the high southern slopes of the Himalayas in eastern Nepal who provide support for foreign trekkers and mountain climbers

sher·ris \'sher-is\ *archaic variant of* SHERRY

sher·ry \'sher-ē\ *noun, plural* **sherries** [alteration of earlier *sherris* (taken as plural), from *Xeres* (now *Jerez*), Spain] (1597)
: a Spanish fortified wine with a distinctive nutty flavor; *also* : a similar wine produced elsewhere ◊

she's \'shēz\ (circa 1592)
: she is : she has

Shet·land \'shet-lənd\ *noun* (1836)
1 a : SHETLAND PONY **b** : SHETLAND SHEEPDOG
2 *often not capitalized* **a** : a lightweight loosely twisted yarn of Shetland wool used for knitting and weaving **b** : a fabric or a garment made from Shetland wool

Shetland pony *noun* (1801)
: any of a breed of small stocky hardy ponies that originated in the Shetland Islands

Shetland sheepdog *noun* (1909)
: any of a breed of small heavy-coated dogs developed in the Shetland Islands that resemble miniature collies

Shetland wool *noun* (1790)
: fine wool from sheep raised in the Shetland Islands; *also* : yarn spun from this

sheugh \'shük\ *noun* [Middle English *sogh* swamp; akin to Middle Low German *sō* gutter] (1501)
chiefly Scottish : DITCH, TRENCH

shew \'shō\ *British variant of* SHOW

shew·bread \'shō-ˌbred\ *noun* [translation of German *Schaubrot*] (1530)
: consecrated unleavened bread ritually placed by the Jewish priests of ancient Israel on a table in the sanctuary of the Tabernacle on the Sabbath

Shia \'shē-(ˌ)ä\ *noun* [Arabic *shī'ah* sect] (1626)
1 : the Muslims of the branch of Islam comprising sects believing in Ali and the Imams as the only rightful successors of Muhammad and in the concealment and messianic return of the last recognized Imam — compare SUNNI
2 : SHIITE
3 : the branch of Islam formed by the Shia

◊ **WORD HISTORY**
sherry Wines and distilled spirits are often named after the places where they are made. The region around the town of Jerez (formerly Xeres) in southern Spain produced a type of fortified wine with a rather nutty flavor that was introduced into England in the 16th century. The name *Xeres* was rendered *Sherries* or *Sherris* in English—the initial *sh* was a good approximation of the contemporary pronunciation of the Spanish sound represented by *x* (which has since changed to a \k\ or \h\ sound). Consequently, the wine from Xeres was sold under the name *sherris*. Some English speakers, however, believing that *sherris* was a plural noun, created a singular form *sherry*, which has since become standard. Other English words created by this process of back-formation from a presumed plural form are *pea* from *pease* and *cherry* from *cherise*, a northern dialectal form of Old French *cerise* "cherry."

shi·at·su *also* **shi·at·zu** \shē-'ät-(,)sü\ *noun, often capitalized* [short for Japanese *shiatsuryōhō*, from *shi-* finger + *-atsu* pressure + *ryōhō* treatment] (1967)
: a massage with the fingers applied to those specific areas of the body used in acupuncture

shib·bo·leth \'shi-bə-ləth *also* -ˌleth\ *noun* [Hebrew *shibbōleth* stream; from the use of this word in Judges 12:6 as a test to distinguish Gileadites from Ephraimites, who pronounced it *sibbōleth*] (1638)
1 a : a word or saying used by adherents of a party, sect, or belief and usually regarded by others as empty of real meaning ⟨the old *shibboleths* come rolling off their lips —Joseph Epstein⟩ **b** : a widely held belief ⟨today this book publishing *shibboleth* is a myth —L. A. Wood⟩ **c** : TRUISM, PLATITUDE ⟨some truth in the *shibboleth* that crime does not pay —Lee Rogow⟩
2 a : a use of language regarded as distinctive of a particular group ⟨accent was . . . a *shibboleth* of social class —Vivian Ducat⟩ **b** : a custom or usage regarded as distinguishing one group from others ⟨for most of the well-to-do in the town, dinner was a *shibboleth*, its hour dividing mankind —Osbert Sitwell⟩ ◆

shiel \'shē(ə)l\ *noun* [Middle English (northern dialect) *schele*] (13th century)
chiefly Scottish : SHIELING

¹shield \'shē(ə)ld\ *noun* [Middle English *sheld*, from Old English *scield*; akin to Old High German *scilt* shield and probably to Old English *sciell* shell] (before 12th century)
1 : a broad piece of defensive armor carried on the arm
2 : one that protects or defends : DEFENSE
3 : DRESS SHIELD
4 a : a device or part that serves as a protective cover or barrier **b** : a protective structure (as a carapace, scale, or plate) of some animals
5 : ESCUTCHEON; *especially* : one that is wide at the top and rounds to a point at the bottom
6 : the Precambrian nuclear mass of a continent that is surrounded and sometimes covered by sedimentary rocks
7 : something resembling a shield: as **a** : APOTHECIUM **b** : a police officer's badge **c** : a decorative or identifying emblem

²shield *transitive verb* (before 12th century)
1 a : to protect with or as if with a shield : provide with a protective cover or shelter **b** : to cut off from observation : HIDE
2 *obsolete* : FORBID
synonym see DEFEND
— **shield·er** *noun*

shield law *noun* (1971)
: a law that protects journalists from forced disclosure of confidential news sources

shield volcano *noun* (1911)
: a broad rounded volcano that is built up by successive outpourings of very fluid lava

shiel·ing \'shē-lən, -liŋ\ *noun* (1568)
1 *British* : a mountain hut used as a shelter by shepherds
2 *dialect British* : a summer pasture in the mountains

shier *comparative of* SHY
shiest *superlative of* SHY

¹shift \'shift\ *verb* [Middle English, from Old English *sciftan* to divide, arrange; akin to Old Norse *skipa* to arrange, assign] (13th century)
transitive verb
1 : to exchange for or replace by another : CHANGE
2 a : to change the place, position, or direction of : MOVE **b** : to make a change in (place)
3 : to change phonetically
intransitive verb
1 a : to change place or position **b** : to change direction ⟨the wind *shifted*⟩ **c** : to change gears **d** : to depress the shift key (as on a typewriter)
2 a : to assume responsibility ⟨had to *shift* for themselves⟩ **b** : to resort to expedients

3 a : to go through a change **b** : to change one's clothes **c** : to become changed phonetically
— **shift·able** \'shif-tə-bəl\ *adjective*
— **shift·er** *noun*
— **shift gears** : to make a change

²shift *noun* (1523)
1 a : a means or device for effecting an end **b** (1) : a deceitful or underhand scheme : DODGE (2) : an expedient tried in difficult circumstances : EXTREMITY
2 a *chiefly dialect* : a change of clothes **b** (1) *chiefly dialect* : SHIRT (2) : a woman's slip or chemise (3) : a usually loose-fitting or semifitted dress
3 a : a change in direction ⟨a *shift* in the wind⟩ **b** : a change in emphasis, judgment, or attitude
4 a : a group of people who work or occupy themselves in turn with other groups **b** (1) : a change of one group of people (as workers) for another in regular alternation (2) : a scheduled period of work or duty
5 : a change in place or position: as **a** : a change in the position of the hand on a fingerboard (as of a violin) **b** (1) : FAULT 5 (2) : the relative displacement of rock masses on opposite sides of a fault or fault zone **c** (1) : a simultaneous change of position in football by two or more players from one side of the line to the other (2) : a change of positions made by one or more players in baseball to provide better defense against a particular hitter **d** : a change in frequency resulting in a change in position of a spectral line or band — compare DOPPLER EFFECT **e** : a movement of bits in a computer register a specified number of places to the right or left
6 : a removal from one person or thing to another : TRANSFER
7 : CONSONANT SHIFT
8 : a bid in bridge in a suit other than the suit one's partner has bid — compare JUMP
9 : GEARSHIFT
synonym see RESOURCE

shift key *noun* (1893)
: a key on a keyboard (as of a typewriter) that when pressed enables an alternate set of characters to be printed

shift·less \'shif(t)-ləs\ *adjective* [*shift* (resourcefulness)] (1584)
1 : lacking in resourcefulness : INEFFICIENT
2 : lacking in ambition or incentive : LAZY
— **shift·less·ly** *adverb*
— **shift·less·ness** *noun*

shifty \'shif-tē\ *adjective* **shift·i·er; -est** (circa 1570)
1 : full of or ready with expedients : RESOURCEFUL
2 a : given to deception, evasion, or fraud : TRICKY **b** : capable of evasive movement : ELUSIVE ⟨a *shifty* boxer⟩
3 : indicative of a tricky nature ⟨*shifty* eyes⟩
— **shift·i·ly** \-tə-lē\ *adverb*
— **shift·i·ness** \-tē-nəs\ *noun*

shi·gel·la \shi-'ge-lə\ *noun, plural* **-gel·lae** \-'ge-(,)lē, -(,)lī\ *also* **-gellas** [New Latin, from Kiyoshi *Shiga* (died 1957) Japanese bacteriologist] (1937)
: any of a genus (*Shigella*) of nonmotile rod-shaped bacteria that cause dysenteries in animals and especially humans

shig·el·lo·sis \ˌshi-gə-'lō-səs\ *noun, plural* **-lo·ses** \-'lō-ˌsēz\ [New Latin] (1944)
: dysentery caused by shigellae

shih tzu \'shēd-'zü, 'shēt-'sü\ *noun, plural* **shih tzus** *also* **shih tzu** *often S&T capitalized* [Chinese (Beijing) *shīzi* (*gǒu*), from *shīzi* lion + *gǒu* dog] (1921)
: any of a breed of small short-legged dogs of Chinese origin that have a short muzzle and a long dense coat

Shi·ism \'shē-ˌi-zəm\ *noun* (circa 1883)
: Islam as taught by the Shia

shii·ta·ke \shē-'tä-kē\ *noun* [Japanese, from *shii*, the Japanese chinquapin + *take* mushroom] (1877)
: a dark Oriental mushroom (*Lentinus edodes* of the family Agaricaceae) widely cultivated especially on woods of the beech family for its edible flavorful cap

Shi·ite \'shē-ˌīt\ *noun* (1728)
: a Muslim of the Shia branch of Islam

¹shi·kar \shi-'kär\ *noun* [Hindi *shikār*, from Persian] (circa 1610)
India : HUNTING

²shikar *verb* **shi·karred; shi·kar·ring** (1872)
India : HUNT

shi·ka·ri \shi-'kär-ē, -'kar-\ *noun* [Hindi *shikārī*, from Persian, from *shikār*] (1827)
India : a big game hunter; *especially* : a professional hunter or guide

shik·sa *or* **shik·se** \'shik-sə\ *noun* [Yiddish *shikse*, feminine of *sheygets* non-Jewish boy, from Hebrew *sheqeṣ* blemish, abomination] (1892)
1 : a non-Jewish girl or woman — often used disparagingly
2 : a Jewish girl or woman who does not observe Jewish precepts — used especially by Orthodox Jews

¹shill \'shil\ *intransitive verb* [²*shill*] (circa 1914)
1 : to act as a shill
2 : to act as a spokesperson or promoter ⟨the eminent Shakespearean producer, director, actor and star . . . is now *shilling* for a brokerage house —Andy Rooney⟩

²shill *noun* [perhaps short for *shillaber*, of unknown origin] (circa 1916)
1 : one who acts as a decoy (as for a pitchman or gambler); *also* : one who makes a sales pitch
2 : PITCH 8a

shil·le·lagh *also* **shil·la·lah** \shə-'lā-lē\ *noun* [*Shillelagh*, town in Ireland] (1772)
: CUDGEL

shil·ling \'shi-liŋ\ *noun* [Middle English, from Old English *scilling*; akin to Old High German *skilling*, a gold coin] (before 12th century)
1 a : a former monetary unit of the United Kingdom equal to 12 pence or 1/20 pound **b** : a former monetary unit equal to 1/20 pound of any of various countries in or formerly in the Commonwealth
2 : a coin representing one shilling
3 : any of several early American coins

\ə\ **abut** \ᵊ\ **kitten** \ər\ **further** \a\ **ash** \ā\ **ace**
\ä\ **mop, mar** \au\ **out** \ch\ **chin** \e\ **bet** \ē\ **easy**
\g\ **go** \i\ **hit** \ī\ **ice** \j\ **job** \ŋ\ **sing** \ō\ **go**
\o\ **law** \oi\ **boy** \th\ **thin** \t͟h\ **the** \ü\ **loot** \u̇\ **foot**
\y\ **yet** \zh\ **vision** *see also* Guide to Pronunciation

4 — see MONEY table

Shil·luk \shi-'lük\ *noun, plural* **Shilluk** *or* **Shilluks** (1790)
1 : a member of a Nilotic people of the Sudan dwelling mainly on the west bank of the White Nile
2 : the language of the Shilluk people

¹**shilly–shally** \'shi-lē-,sha-lē\ *adverb* [irregular reduplication of *shall I*] (1700)
: in an irresolute, undecided, or hesitating manner

²**shilly–shally** *adjective* (1734)
: IRRESOLUTE, VACILLATING

³**shilly–shally** *noun* (1755)
: INDECISION, IRRESOLUTION

⁴**shilly–shally** *intransitive verb* **shilly–shall·ied; shilly–shally·ing** (1782)
1 : to show hesitation or lack of decisiveness or resolution
2 : DAWDLE

shil·pit \'shil-pət\ *adjective* [origin unknown] (1812)
1 *Scottish* **:** pinched and starved in appearance
2 *Scottish* **:** WEAK, INSIPID — used of drink

¹**shim** \'shim\ *noun* [origin unknown] (1860)
: a thin often tapered piece of material (as wood, metal, or stone) used to fill in space between things (as for support, leveling, or adjustment of fit)

²**shim** *transitive verb* **shimmed; shim·ming** (circa 1890)
: to fill out or level up by the use of a shim

¹**shim·mer** \'shi-mər\ *verb* **shim·mered; shim·mer·ing** \'shi-mə-riŋ, 'shim-riŋ\ [Middle English *schimeren*, from Old English *scimerian*; akin to Old English *scīnan* to shine — more at SHINE] (before 12th century)
intransitive verb
1 : to shine with a soft tremulous or fitful light
: GLIMMER
2 : to reflect a wavering sometimes distorted visual image
transitive verb
: to cause to shimmer
synonym see FLASH

²**shimmer** *noun* (1821)
1 : a light that shimmers **:** subdued sparkle or sheen **:** GLIMMER
2 : a wavering sometimes distorted visual image usually resulting from heat-induced changes in atmospheric refraction
— **shim·mery** \'shi-mə-rē, 'shim-rē\ *adjective*

¹**shim·my** \'shi-mē\ *noun, plural* **shimmies** (1837)
1 [by alteration] **:** CHEMISE
2 [short for *shimmy-shake*] **:** a jazz dance characterized by a shaking of the body from the shoulders down
3 : an abnormal vibration especially in the front wheels of a motor vehicle

²**shimmy** *intransitive verb* **shim·mied; shim·my·ing** (1919)
1 : to shake, quiver, or tremble in or as if in dancing a shimmy
2 : to vibrate abnormally — used especially of automobiles

¹**shin** \'shin\ *noun* [Middle English *shine*, from Old English *scinu*; akin to Old High German *scina* shin, Old English *scīa* shin, leg] (before 12th century)
: the front part of the vertebrate leg below the knee

²**shin** *verb* **shinned; shin·ning** (1829)
intransitive verb
1 : to move oneself up or down something vertical (as a pole) especially by alternately hugging it with the arms or hands and the legs
2 : to move forward rapidly on foot
transitive verb
1 : to kick or strike on the shins
2 : to climb by shinning

³**shin** \'shēn, 'shin\ *noun* [Hebrew *shīn*] (circa 1823)
: the 22d letter of the Hebrew alphabet — see ALPHABET table

Shin \'shin, 'shēn\ *noun* [Japanese, literally, truth] (1877)
: a major Japanese Buddhist sect that emphasizes salvation by faith in exclusive worship of Amida Buddha

Shi·na \'shē-nə\ *noun* (1854)
: an Indo-Aryan language spoken in Gilgit in northern Kashmir

shin·bone \'shin-,bōn\ *noun* (before 12th century)
: TIBIA 1

shin·dig \'shin-,dig\ *noun* [probably alteration of *shindy*] (1871)
1 a : a social gathering with dancing **b :** a usually large or lavish party
2 : SHINDY 2

shin·dy \'shin-dē\ *noun, plural* **shindys** *or* **shindies** [probably alteration of ¹*shinny*] (1821)
1 : SHINDIG 1
2 : FRACAS, UPROAR

¹**shine** \'shīn\ *verb* **shone** \'shōn, *especially Canadian & British* 'shän\ *or* **shined; shin·ing** [Middle English, from Old English *scīnan*; akin to Old High German *skīnan* to shine and perhaps to Greek *skia* shadow] (before 12th century)
intransitive verb
1 : to emit rays of light
2 : to be bright by reflection of light
3 : to be eminent, conspicuous, or distinguished ⟨*shines* in math⟩
4 : to have a bright glowing appearance ⟨his face *shone* with enthusiasm⟩
5 : to be conspicuously evident or clear
transitive verb
1 a : to cause to emit light **b :** to throw or direct the light of
2 *past & past part* **shined :** to make bright by polishing ⟨*shined* his shoes⟩

²**shine** *noun* (15th century)
1 : brightness caused by the emission of light
2 : brightness caused by the reflection of light
: LUSTER
3 : BRILLIANCE, SPLENDOR
4 : fair weather **:** SUNSHINE ⟨rain or *shine*⟩
5 : TRICK, CAPER — usually used in plural
6 : LIKING, FANCY ⟨took a *shine* to him⟩
7 a : a polish or gloss given to shoes **b :** a single polishing of a pair of shoes

shin·er \'shī-nər\ *noun* (14th century)
1 : one that shines
2 : a silvery fish; *especially* **:** any of numerous small freshwater American cyprinid fishes (especially genus *Notropis*) — compare GOLDEN SHINER
3 : BLACK EYE 1

¹**shin·gle** \'shiŋ-gəl\ *noun* [Middle English *schingel*] (13th century)
1 : a small thin piece of building material often with one end thicker than the other for laying in overlapping rows as a covering for the roof or sides of a building
2 : a small signboard especially designating a professional office — used chiefly in the phrase *hang out one's shingle*
3 : a woman's haircut with the hair trimmed short from the back of the head to the nape

²**shingle** *transitive verb* **shin·gled; shin·gling** \-g(ə-)liŋ\ (1562)
1 : to cover with or as if with shingles
2 : to bob and shape (the hair) in a shingle
3 : to lay out or arrange so as to overlap
— **shin·gler** \-g(ə-)lər\ *noun*

³**shingle** *noun* [probably of Scandinavian origin; akin to Norwegian *singel* coarse gravel] (15th century)
1 : coarse rounded detritus or alluvial material especially on the seashore that differs from ordinary gravel only in the larger size of the stones
2 : a place strewn with shingle
— **shin·gly** \-g(ə-)lē\ *adjective*

shin·gles \'shiŋ-gəlz\ *noun plural but singular in construction* [Middle English *schingles*, by folk etymology from Medieval Latin *cingulus*,

from Latin *cingulum* girdle — more at CINGULUM] (14th century)
: HERPES ZOSTER

Shin·gon \'shin-,gän, 'shēn-\ *noun* [Japanese] (1727)
: an esoteric Japanese Buddhist sect claiming the achievement of Buddhahood in this life through prescribed rituals

shin·ing \'shī-niŋ\ *adjective* (before 12th century)
1 : emitting or reflecting light
2 : bright and often splendid in appearance
: RESPLENDENT
3 : possessing a distinguished quality **:** ILLUSTRIOUS
4 : full of sunshine

shin·leaf \'shin-,lēf\ *noun, plural* **shinleafs** (circa 1818)
: any of several wintergreens (especially *Pyrola elliptica*) with lustrous evergreen basal leaves and racemose white or pinkish flowers

shin·nery \'shi-nə-rē\ *noun, plural* **-ner·ies** [modification of Louisiana French *chênière*, from French *chêne* oak] (1901)
: a dense growth of small trees or an area of such growth; *especially* **:** one of scrub oak in the West and Southwest

¹**shin·ny** *also* **shin·ney** \'shi-nē\ *noun* [perhaps from ¹*shin*] (1672)
: a variation of hockey played by children with a curved stick and a ball or block of wood; *also* **:** the stick used

²**shinny** *intransitive verb* **shin·nied; shin·ny·ing** [alteration of ²*shin*] (1851)
: SHIN 1

shin·plas·ter \'shin-,plas-tər\ *noun* (1824)
1 : a piece of privately-issued paper currency; *especially* **:** one poorly secured and depreciated in value
2 : a piece of fractional currency

shin·splints \'shin-,splin(t)s\ *noun plural but singular or plural in construction* (circa 1930)
: injury to and inflammation of the tibial and toe extensor muscles or their fasciae caused by repeated minimal traumas (as by running)

Shin·to \'shin-(,)tō\ *noun* [Japanese *shintō*] (1727)
: the indigenous religion of Japan consisting chiefly in the cultic devotion to deities of natural forces and veneration of the Emperor as a descendant of the sun goddess
— **Shinto** *adjective*
— **Shin·to·ism** \-(,)tō-,i-zəm\ *noun*
— **Shin·to·ist** \-,tō-ist\ *noun or adjective*
— **Shin·to·is·tic** \,shin-tō-'is-tik\ *adjective*

shiny \'shī-nē\ *adjective* **shin·i·er; -est** (1590)
1 a : bright with the rays of the sun **:** SUNSHINY
b : filled with light
2 : bright in appearance **:** POLISHED ⟨*shiny* new shoes⟩
3 : rubbed or worn smooth
4 : lustrous with natural secretions ⟨a *shiny* nose⟩
— **shin·i·ness** *noun*

¹**ship** \'ship\ *noun, often attributive* [Middle English, from Old English *scip*; akin to Old High German *skif* ship] (before 12th century)
1 a : a large seagoing vessel **b :** a sailing vessel having a bowsprit and usually three masts each composed of a lower mast, a topmast, and a topgallant mast
2 : BOAT; *especially* **:** one propelled by power or sail
3 : a ship's crew
4 : FORTUNE 3 ⟨when their *ship* comes in they'll be able to live in better style⟩
5 : AIRSHIP, AIRPLANE, SPACECRAFT

²**ship** *verb* **shipped; ship·ping** (14th century)
transitive verb
1 a : to place or receive on board a ship for transportation by water **b :** to cause to be transported ⟨*shipped* him off to prep school⟩
2 *obsolete* **:** to provide with a ship

3 : to put in place for use ⟨*ship* the tiller⟩
4 : to take into a ship or boat ⟨*ship* the gang-plank⟩
5 : to engage for service on a ship
6 : to take (as water) over the side — used of a boat or a ship
intransitive verb
1 : to embark on a ship
2 a : to go or travel by ship — often used with *out* **b :** to proceed by ship or other means under military orders — often used with *out*
3 : to engage to serve on shipboard
— **ship·pa·ble** \'shi-pə-bəl\ *adjective*

-ship *noun suffix* [Middle English, from Old English *-scipe*; akin to Old High German *-scaft* -ship, Old English *scieppan* to shape — more at SHAPE]
1 : state : condition : quality ⟨friend*ship*⟩
2 : office : dignity : profession ⟨clerk*ship*⟩
3 : art : skill ⟨horseman*ship*⟩
4 : something showing, exhibiting, or embodying a quality or state ⟨town*ship*⟩
5 : one entitled to a (specified) rank, title, or appellation ⟨his Lord*ship*⟩
6 : the body of persons participating in a specified activity ⟨reader*ship*⟩ ⟨listener*ship*⟩

ship biscuit *noun* (1799)
: HARDTACK — called also *ship bread*

¹ship·board \'ship-ˌbȯrd, -ˌbȯrd\ *noun* (13th century)
1 : the side of a ship
2 : SHIP ⟨met on *shipboard*⟩

²shipboard *adjective* (1857)
: existing or taking place on board a ship

ship·borne \'ship-ˌbȯrn, -ˌbȯrn\ *adjective* (circa 1835)
: transported or designed to be transported by ship ⟨*shipborne* aircraft⟩

ship·build·er \'ship-ˌbil-dər\ *noun* (circa 1700)
: one who designs or constructs ships
— **ship·build·ing** \-diŋ\ *noun*

ship·fit·ter \'ship-ˌfi-tər\ *noun* (1941)
1 : one that fits together the structural members of ships and puts them into position for riveting or welding
2 : a naval enlisted man who works in sheet metal and performs the work of a plumber aboard ship

ship·lap \-ˌlap\ *noun* (1895)
: wooden sheathing in which the boards are rabbeted so that the edges of each board lap over the edges of adjacent boards to make a flush joint

ship·load \-ˌlōd, -ˌlȯd\ *noun* (1639)
1 : as much or as many as will fill or load a ship
2 : an indefinitely large amount or number

ship·man \-mən\ *noun* (before 12th century)
1 : SAILOR, SEAMAN
2 : SHIPMASTER

ship·mas·ter \-ˌmas-tər\ *noun* (14th century)
: the master or commander of a ship other than a warship

ship·mate \-ˌmāt\ *noun* (1748)
: a fellow sailor

ship·ment \-mənt\ *noun* (1802)
1 : the act or process of shipping
2 : the goods shipped

ship of state *noun* (1847)
: the affairs of a state symbolized as a ship on a course

ship of the line (1706)
: a warship large enough to have a place in the line of battle

ship·own·er \'ship-ˌō-nər\ *noun* (circa 1530)
: the owner of a ship or of a share in a ship

ship·per \'shi-pər\ *noun* (1755)
: one that sends goods by any form of conveyance

ship·ping \'shi-piŋ\ *noun* (14th century)
1 a : passage on a ship **b :** SHIPS **c :** the body of ships in one place or belonging to one port or country
2 : the act or business of one that ships

shipping clerk *noun* (circa 1858)

: one who is employed in a shipping room to assemble, pack, and send out or receive goods

ship·shape \ˌship-'shāp, 'ship-ˌ\ *adjective* [short for earlier *shipshapen*, from *ship* + *shapen*, archaic past participle of *shape*] (1644)
: TRIM, TIDY

ship·side \'ship-ˌsīd\ *noun* (15th century)
: the area adjacent to a ship; *specifically* : a dock at which a ship loads or unloads passengers and freight

ship's papers *noun plural*
: the papers a ship is legally required to carry for due inspection to show the character of the ship and cargo

ship·way \'ship-ˌwā\ *noun* (1834)
: the ways on which a ship is built

ship·worm \-ˌwərm\ *noun* (circa 1778)
: any of various elongated marine clams (especially family Teredinidae) that resemble worms, burrow in submerged wood, and damage wharf piles and wooden ships

¹ship·wreck \-ˌrek\ *noun* [alteration of earlier *shipwrack*, from Middle English *schipwrak*, from Old English *scipwræc*, from *scip* ship + *wræc* something driven by the sea — more at WRACK] (12th century)
1 : a wrecked ship or its parts
2 : the destruction or loss of a ship
3 : an irretrievable loss or failure

²shipwreck *transitive verb* (1589)
1 a : to cause to experience shipwreck **b :** RUIN
2 : to destroy (a ship) by grounding or foundering

ship·wright \'ship-ˌrīt\ *noun* (before 12th century)
: a carpenter skilled in ship construction and repair

ship·yard \-ˌyärd\ *noun* (circa 1700)
: a yard, place, or enclosure where ships are built or repaired

shire \'shīr, *in place-name compounds* ˌshir, shər\ *noun* [Middle English, from Old English *scīr* office, shire; akin to Old High German *scīra* care] (before 12th century)
1 : an administrative subdivision; *especially* : a county in England
2 : any of a breed of large heavy draft horses of British origin that have heavily feathered legs

shire town *noun* (15th century)
1 *British* : a town that is the seat of the government of a shire
2 *New England* : a town where a court of superior jurisdiction (as a circuit court or a court with a jury) sits

shirk \'shərk\ *verb* [origin unknown] (1681)
intransitive verb
1 : to go stealthily : SNEAK
2 : to evade the performance of an obligation
transitive verb
: AVOID, EVADE ⟨*shirk* one's duty⟩
— **shirk·er** *noun*

shirr \'shər\ *transitive verb* [origin unknown] (1891)
1 : to draw (as cloth) together in a shirring
2 : to bake (eggs removed from the shell) until set

shirr·ing \'shər-iŋ\ *noun* (circa 1882)
: a decorative gathering (as of cloth) made by drawing up the material along two or more parallel lines of stitching

shirt \'shərt\ *noun* [Middle

English *shirte*, from Old English *scyrte*; akin to Old Norse *skyrta* shirt, Old English *scort* short] (before 12th century)
1 : a garment for the upper part of the body: as **a :** a cloth garment usually having a collar, sleeves, a front opening, and a tail long enough to be tucked inside trousers or a skirt **b :** UNDERSHIRT
2 : all or a large part of one's money or resources ⟨lost his *shirt* on that business deal⟩
— **shirt·less** \-ləs\ *adjective*

shirt·dress \-ˌdres\ *noun* (1943)
: a tailored dress patterned after a shirt and having buttons down the front

shirt·front \-ˌfrənt\ *noun* (1838)
: the front of a shirt; *also* : the part of a man's shirt not covered by coat or vest

shirt·ing \'shər-tiŋ\ *noun* (1604)
: fabric suitable for shirts

shirt jacket *noun* (1879)
: a jacket designed in the style of a shirt — called also *shirt-jac*

shirt·mak·er \'shərt-ˌmā-kər\ *noun* (circa 1858)
: one that makes shirts

¹shirt·sleeve \-ˌslēv\ *noun* (circa 1566)
: the sleeve of a shirt
— **in shirtsleeves** : wearing a shirt but no coat

²shirtsleeve *also* **shirt·sleeves** \-ˌslēvz\ *or* **shirt·sleeved** \-ˌslēvd\ *adjective* (1864)
1 a : being without a coat ⟨a *shirtsleeve* spectator⟩ **b :** calling for the removal of coats for the sake of comfort or efficiency ⟨*shirtsleeve* weather⟩
2 : marked by informality and directness ⟨*shirtsleeve* diplomacy⟩

¹shirt·tail \'shərt-ˌtāl\ *adjective* (1845)
1 : very young : IMMATURE ⟨*shirttail* boys fishing in the creek⟩
2 : distantly and indefinitely related ⟨a *shirttail* cousin on her father's side⟩
3 : small, trivial, or short typically to the point of inadequacy ⟨has a gullied *shirttail* ranch in the hills⟩

²shirttail *noun* (1873)
1 : the part of a shirt that reaches below the waist especially in the back
2 : something small or inadequate

shirt·waist \'shərt-ˌwāst\ *noun* (1879)
: a woman's tailored garment (as a blouse or dress) with details copied from men's shirts

shirty \'shər-tē\ *adjective* (1846)
chiefly British : ANGRY, IRRITATED

shish ke·bab \'shish-kə-ˌbäb\ *noun* [Turkish *şişkebabı*, from *şiş* spit + *kebap* roast meat] (1914)
: kabob cooked on skewers

¹shit \'shit, *interjectionally also* 'shē-ət\ *noun* [(assumed) Middle English, from Old English *scite*; akin to Old English *-scītan* to defecate] (circa 1585)
1 : EXCREMENT — usually considered vulgar
2 : an act of defecation — usually considered vulgar
3 : NONSENSE, CRAP — usually considered vulgar
4 : any of several intoxicating or narcotic drugs; *especially* : HEROIN — usually considered vulgar
5 : DAMN 2 — usually considered vulgar
6 : a worthless, offensive, or detestable person — usually considered vulgar
— **shit·ty** \'shi-tē\ *adjective*

²shit \'shit\ *verb* **shit** *or* **shat** \'shat\; **shitting** [alteration of earlier *shite*, from Middle English *shiten*, from Old English *-scītan*; akin to Old High German *scīzan* to defecate and probably to Old English *scēadan* to separate — more at SHED] (circa 1720)

shire 2

\ə\ **abut** \ᵊ\ **kitten** \ər\ **further** \a\ **ash** \ā\ **ace**
\ä\ **mop, mar** \au̇\ **out** \ch\ **chin** \e\ **bet** \ē\ **easy**
\g\ **go** \i\ **hit** \ī\ **ice** \j\ **job** \ŋ\ **sing** \ō\ **go**
\ȯ\ **law** \ȯi\ **boy** \th\ **thin** \th\ **the** \ü\ **loot** \u̇\ **foot**
\y\ **yet** \zh\ **vision** *see also* Guide to Pronunciation

intransitive verb
: DEFECATE — usually considered vulgar
transitive verb
1 : to defecate in — usually considered vulgar
2 : to attempt to deceive **:** BULLSHIT — usually considered vulgar
shi·ta·ke *variant of* SHIITAKE
shit·tah \'shi-tə\ *noun, plural* **shittahs** *or* **shit·tim** \'shi-təm\ [Hebrew *shiṭṭāh*] (1611)
: a tree of uncertain identity but probably an acacia (as *Acacia seyal*) from the wood of which the ark and fittings of the Hebrew tabernacle were made
shit·tim·wood \'shi-təm-ˌwu̇d\ *noun* [Hebrew *shiṭṭīm* (plural of *shiṭṭāh*) + English *wood*] (1588)
1 : the wood of the shittah tree
2 : any of several trees (genus *Bumelia*, especially *B. lanuginosa*) of the sapodilla family of the southern U.S.; *also* **:** their hard heavy dense wood
shiv \'shiv\ *noun* [alteration of *chiv*, of unknown origin] (1674)
slang **:** KNIFE
Shi·va \'shi-və, 'shē-\ *variant of* SIVA
shi·vah *or* **shi·va** *also* **shi·ve** \'shi-və\ *noun* [Hebrew *shibh'āh* seven (days)] (1892)
: a traditional seven-day period of mourning the dead that is observed in Jewish homes — often used in the phrase *sit shivah*
shiv·a·ree \ˌshi-və-'rē, 'shi-və-ˌ\ *noun* [modification of French *charivari* — more at CHARIVARI] (1843)
: a noisy mock serenade to a newly married couple ◇
— **shivaree** *transitive verb*
¹shiv·er \'shi-vər\ *noun* [Middle English; akin to Old High German *scivaro* splinter] (13th century)
: one of the small pieces into which a brittle thing is broken by sudden violence
²shiver *verb* **shiv·ered; shiv·er·ing** \'shi-və-riŋ, 'shiv-riŋ\ (13th century)
: to break into many small pieces **:** SHATTER
³shiver *verb* **shiv·ered; shiv·er·ing** \'shi-və-riŋ, 'shiv-riŋ\ [Middle English, alteration of *chiveren*] (15th century)
intransitive verb
1 : to undergo trembling **:** QUIVER
2 : to tremble in the wind as it strikes first one and then the other side (of a sail)
transitive verb
: to cause (a sail) to shiver by steering close to the wind
⁴shiver *noun* (1727)
1 : an instance of shivering **:** TREMBLE
2 : an intense shivery sensation especially of fear — often used in plural with *the* ⟨horror movies give him the *shivers*⟩
¹shiv·ery \'shi-və-rē, 'shiv-rē\ *adjective* (1683)
: easily broken into shivers
²shivery *adjective* (1747)
1 : characterized by shivers
2 : causing shivers
shle·miehl *variant of* SCHLEMIEL
shlep, shlepp *variant of* SCHLEPP
shlock *variant of* SCHLOCK
shm- — see SCHM-
¹shoal \'shōl\ *adjective* [alteration of Middle English *shold*, from Old English *sceald* — more at SKELETON] (1554)
: SHALLOW
²shoal *noun* (1555)
1 : SHALLOW
2 : a sandbank or sandbar that makes the water shallow; *specifically* **:** an elevation which is not rocky and on which there is a depth of water of six fathoms (11 meters) or less
³shoal (1574)
intransitive verb
: to become shallow
transitive verb
1 : to come to a shallow or less deep part of
2 : to cause to become shallow or less deep

⁴shoal *noun* [(assumed) Middle English *shole*, from Old English *scolu* multitude — more at SCHOOL] (1579)
: a large group or number **:** CROWD ⟨a *shoal* of fish⟩
⁵shoal (1610)
intransitive verb
: THRONG, SCHOOL
shoat \'shōt\ *noun* [Middle English *shote*; akin to Flemish *schote* shoat] (15th century)
: a young hog usually less than one year old
¹shock \'shäk\ *noun* [Middle English; akin to Middle High German *schoc* heap] (14th century)
: a pile of sheaves of grain or stalks of Indian corn set up in a field with the butt ends down
²shock *transitive verb* (15th century)
: to collect into shocks
³shock *noun, often attributive* [Middle French *choc*, from *choquer* to strike against, from Old French *choquier*, probably of Germanic origin; akin to Middle Dutch *schocken* to jolt] (1565)
1 : the impact or encounter of individuals or groups in combat
2 a : a violent shake or jar **:** CONCUSSION **b :** an effect of such violence
3 a (1) **:** a disturbance in the equilibrium or permanence of something (2) **:** a sudden or violent mental or emotional disturbance **b :** something that causes such disturbance **c :** a state of being so disturbed
4 : a state of profound depression of the vital processes associated with reduced blood volume and pressure and caused usually by severe especially crushing injuries, hemorrhage, or burns
5 : sudden stimulation of the nerves and convulsive contraction of the muscles caused by the discharge of electricity through the animal body
6 a : STROKE 5 **b :** CORONARY THROMBOSIS
7 : SHOCK ABSORBER
⁴shock (1576)
transitive verb
1 a : to strike with surprise, terror, horror, or disgust **b :** to cause to undergo a physical or nervous shock **c :** to subject to the action of an electrical discharge
2 : to drive by or as if by a shock
intransitive verb
1 : to meet with a shock **:** COLLIDE
2 : to cause surprise or shock
— **shock·able** \'shä-kə-bəl\ *adjective*
⁵shock *adjective* [perhaps from ¹*shock*] (1681)
: BUSHY, SHAGGY
⁶shock *noun* (1819)
: a thick bushy mass (as of hair)
shock absorber *noun* (1906)
: any of several devices for absorbing the energy of sudden impulses or shocks in machinery or structures
shock·er \'shä-kər\ *noun* (circa 1824)
: one that shocks; *especially* **:** something horrifying or offensive (as a sensational film or work of fiction)
shock front *noun* (1949)
: the advancing edge of a shock wave
shock·ing \'shä-kiŋ\ *adjective* (1703)
: extremely startling, distressing, or offensive
— **shock·ing·ly** \-kiŋ-lē\ *adverb*
shocking pink *noun* (1938)
: a striking, vivid, bright, or intense pink
shock·proof \'shäk-ˌpru̇f\ *adjective* (1911)
1 : incapable of being shocked
2 a : resistant to damage by shock **b :** unlikely to cause shock **:** protectively insulated ⟨a *shockproof* switch⟩
shock therapy *noun* (1917)
: the treatment of mental disorder by the artificial induction of coma or convulsions through use of drugs or electric current — called also *shock treatment*
shock troops *noun plural* (1917)
1 : troops especially suited and chosen for offensive work because of their high morale, training, and discipline

2 : a group of people militant in pressing for a cause
shock tube *noun* (1949)
: a usually enclosed tube in which experimental shock waves are produced as a result of the rupturing of a diaphragm separating two chambers containing a gas or gases at differential pressure
shock wave *noun* (1907)
1 : a compressional wave of high amplitude caused by a shock (as from an earthquake or explosion) to the medium through which the wave travels
2 : a violent often pulsating disturbance or reaction ⟨*shock waves* of rebellion⟩
shod \'shäd\ *adjective* [Middle English, from past participle of *shoen* to shoe, from Old English *scōgan*, from *scōh* shoe — more at SHOE] (13th century)
1 a : wearing footgear (as shoes) **b :** equipped with tires
2 : furnished or equipped with a shoe
¹shod·dy \'shä-dē\ *noun* [origin unknown] (1832)
1 a : a reclaimed wool from materials that are not felted or that is of better quality and longer staple than mungo **b :** a fabric of inferior quality manufactured wholly or partly from reclaimed wool
2 a : inferior, imitative, or pretentious articles or matter **b :** pretentious vulgarity
²shoddy *adjective* **shod·di·er; -est** (1847)
1 : made wholly or partly of shoddy
2 a : cheaply imitative **:** vulgarly pretentious **b :** hastily or poorly done **:** INFERIOR **c :** SHABBY
— **shod·di·ly** \'shä-dᵊl-ē\ *adverb*
— **shod·di·ness** \'shä-dē-nəs\ *noun*
¹shoe \'shü\ *noun* [Middle English *shoo*, from Old English *scōh*; akin to Old High German *scuoh* shoe] (before 12th century)
1 a : an outer covering for the human foot typically having a thick or stiff sole with an attached heel and an upper part of lighter material (as leather) **b :** a metal plate or rim for the hoof of an animal
2 : something resembling a shoe in function or placement
3 *plural* **:** another's place, function, or viewpoint ⟨steps from assistant stage manager into the star's *shoes* —Steven Fuller⟩

◇ WORD HISTORY
shivaree In 19th century rural America, a newly wed couple—often one whose marriage was because of discrepancy in age or some other cause considered incongruous by the local community—might have their wedding night interrupted by an unwanted disturbance. A motley band of revelers outside the windows of their home would treat them to a cacophonous serenade, delivered in derision on a battery of pots, pans, cowbells, and other ersatz musical instruments. In the eastern U.S. this custom, imported from rural England, was simply called a *serenade* or known under a variety of colorful local names. In much of the central U.S. and Canada, however, it was called a *shivaree*, a loan from French *charivari*, a word that denotes the same folk custom in France. American English *shivaree* is part of our small linguistic heritage from Mississippi Valley French, the language of French pioneers who explored and settled the Mississippi and its tributaries. The greater part of this heritage consists of place names, from the obvious (*St. Louis* and *New Orleans*) to the buried (*Ozark*, a phonetic rendering of French *Aux Arcs* "At the Arcs," *Arcs* being a French name for several tribes of Indians living in that area).

4 : a device that retards, stops, or controls the motion of an object; *especially* **:** the part of a brake that presses on the brake drum
5 a : any of various devices that are inserted in or run along a track or groove to guide a movement, provide a contact or friction grip, or protect against wear, damage, or slipping **b :** a device (as a clip or track) on a camera that permits attachment of an accessory item (as a flash unit)
6 : a dealing box designed to hold several decks of playing cards
— **shoe·less** *adjective*

²**shoe** *transitive verb* **shod** \'shäd\ *also* **shoed** \'shüd\; **shoe·ing** \'shü-iŋ\ (before 12th century)
1 : to furnish with a shoe
2 : to cover for protection, strength, or ornament

shoe·bill \'shü-ˌbil\ *noun* (1874)
: a large broad-billed wading bird (*Balaeniceps rex*) of the valley of the White Nile that is related to the storks and herons

shoe·black \-ˌblak\ *noun* (1778)
: BOOTBLACK

¹**shoe·horn** \-ˌhȯrn\ *noun* (1589)
: a curved piece (as of horn, wood, or metal) used in putting on a shoe

²**shoehorn** *transitive verb* (1926)
: to force into a small, narrow, or insufficient space **:** SQUEEZE ⟨*shoehorn* the past, present, and future into about 500 pages —Otis Port⟩

shoe·lace \'shü-ˌlās\ *noun* (circa 1647)
: a lace or string for fastening a shoe

shoe·mak·er \-ˌmā-kər\ *noun* (14th century)
: one whose occupation is making or repairing shoes

shoe·pac *or* **shoe·pack** \'shü-ˌpak\ *noun* [by folk etymology from Delaware Jargon (Delaware-based pidgin) *seppock* shoe, from Delaware (Unami dialect) *čípahkɔ* shoes] (1755)
: a waterproof laced boot worn especially over heavy socks in cold weather

¹**shoe·string** \'shü-ˌstriŋ\ *noun* (1616)
1 : SHOELACE
2 [from shoestrings being a typical item sold by itinerant vendors] **:** a small sum of money **:** capital inadequate or barely adequate to the needs of a transaction ⟨started the business on a *shoestring*⟩

²**shoestring** *adjective* (1878)
1 : narrow and long like a shoestring ⟨a *shoestring* tie⟩
2 : operating on, accomplished by, or consisting of a small amount of money or capital ⟨a *shoestring* budget⟩

shoestring catch *noun* (1926)
: a catch (as in baseball) made very close to the feet

shoe tree *noun* (1827)
: a foot-shaped device for inserting in a shoe to preserve its shape

sho·far \'shō-ˌfär, -fər\ *noun, plural* **sho·froth** \shō-ˈfrōt, -ˈfrōth, -ˈfrōs\ [Hebrew *shōphār*] (1833)
: a ram's-horn trumpet blown by the ancient Hebrews in battle and high religious observances and used in synagogues before and during Rosh Hashanah and at the conclusion of Yom Kippur

¹**shog** \'shäg\ *intransitive verb* **shogged**; **shog·ging** [Middle English *shoggen*] (15th century)
chiefly dialect **:** to move along

²**shog** *noun* (1611)
chiefly dialect **:** SHAKE, JOLT

sho·gun \'shō-gən\ *noun* [Japanese *shōgun* general] (1727)

shofar

: one of a line of military governors ruling Japan until the revolution of 1867–68
— **sho·gun·al** \'shō-gə-nəl\ *adjective*
— **sho·gun·ate** \'shō-gə-nət, -ˌnāt\ *noun*

sho·ji \'shō-(ˌ)jē\ *noun, plural* **shoji** *also* **shojis** [Japanese *shōji*] (1880)
: a paper screen serving as a wall, partition, or sliding door

sho·lom \shä-'lōm, shə-\ *variant of* SHALOM

Sho·na \'shō-nə\ *noun, plural* **Shona** *or* **Shonas** (circa 1895)
1 : a member of any of a group of Bantu peoples of Zimbabwe and southern Mozambique
2 : the group of languages spoken by the Shona

shone *past and past participle of* SHINE

¹**shoo** \'shü\ *interjection* [Middle English *schowe*] (15th century)
— used especially in driving away an unwanted animal

²**shoo** *transitive verb* (circa 1798)
: to scare, drive, or send away by or as if by crying *shoo*

shoo·fly \'shü-ˌflī\ *noun* [¹*shoo* + *fly*] (1887)
1 : a child's rocker having the seat built on or usually between supports representing an animal figure
2 : any of several plants held to repel flies

shoofly pie *noun* (1926)
: a rich pie of Pennsylvania-Dutch origin made of molasses or brown sugar sprinkled with a crumbly mixture of flour, sugar, and butter

shoo·in \'shü-ˌin\ *noun* (1937)
: one that is a certain and easy winner

¹**shook** *past or chiefly dialect past participle of* SHAKE

²**shook** \'shuk\ *noun* [origin unknown] (1796)
1 a : a set of staves and headings for one hogshead, cask, or barrel **b :** a bundle of parts (as of boxes) ready to be put together
2 : ¹SHOCK

shook–up \ˌshuk-'əp\ *adjective* (1897)
: nervously upset **:** AGITATED

shoon \'shün, 'shȯn\ *chiefly dialect plural of* SHOE

¹**shoot** \'shüt\ *verb* **shot** \'shät\; **shoot·ing** [Middle English *sheten, shuten*, from Old English *scēotan*; akin to Old Norse *skjóta* to shoot] (before 12th century)
transitive verb
1 a (1) **:** to eject or impel or cause to be ejected or impelled by a sudden release of tension (as of a bowstring or slingshot or by a flick of a finger) ⟨*shoot* an arrow⟩ ⟨*shoot* a spitball⟩ ⟨*shoot* a marble⟩ (2) **:** to drive forth or cause to be driven forth by an explosion (as of a powder charge in a firearm or of ignited fuel in a rocket) (3) **:** to drive forth or cause to be driven forth by a sudden release of gas or air ⟨*shoot* darts from a blowgun⟩ ⟨a steam catapult *shoots* planes from a carrier⟩ (4) **:** to propel (a ball or puck) toward a goal by striking or pushing with part of the body (as the hand or foot) or with an implement; *also* **:** to score by so doing ⟨*shoot* the winning goal⟩ ⟨*shoot* a basket⟩ (5) **:** to throw or cast off or out often with force ⟨*shoot* dice⟩ ⟨the horse *shot* his rider out of the saddle⟩ **b :** to cause (as a gun or bow) to propel a missile **c** (1) **:** to utter (as words or sounds) rapidly or suddenly or with force ⟨*shoot* out a stream of invective⟩ (2) **:** to emit (as light, flame, or fumes) suddenly and rapidly (3) **:** to send forth with suddenness or intensity ⟨*shoot* a look of anger at them⟩ **d :** to discharge, dump, or empty especially by overturning, upending, or directing into a slide
2 : to affect by shooting: as **a :** to strike with a missile especially from a bow or gun; *especially* **:** to wound or kill with a missile discharged from a bow or firearm **b :** to remove or destroy by use of firearms ⟨*shot* out the light⟩; *also* **:** WRECK, EXPLODE
3 a : to push or slide (as the bolt of a door or lock) into or out of a fastening **b :** to push or thrust forward **:** stick out ⟨toads *shooting* out

their tongues⟩ **c :** to put forth in growing **d :** to place, send, or bring into position abruptly
4 a : to engage in (a sport or game or a portion of a game that involves shooting) **:** PLAY ⟨*shoot* pool⟩ ⟨*shoot* a round of golf⟩ ⟨*shoot* craps⟩ **b** (1) **:** to place or offer (a bet) on the result of casting dice ⟨*shoot* $5⟩ (2) **:** to use up by or as if by betting **:** EXHAUST ⟨*shot* his whole wad on a shady deal⟩
5 a : to engage in the hunting and killing of (as game) with firearms especially as a sport ⟨*shoot* woodcock⟩ **b :** to hunt over ⟨*shoot* a tract of woodland⟩
6 a : to cause to move suddenly or swiftly forward ⟨*shot* the car onto the highway⟩ **b :** to send or carry quickly **:** DISPATCH ⟨*shoot* the letter on to me as soon as you receive it⟩
7 : to variegate as if by sprinkling color in streaks, flecks, or patches
8 : to pass swiftly by, past, or along ⟨*shooting* rapids⟩
9 : to plane (as the edge of a board) straight or true
10 a : SET OFF, DETONATE, IGNITE ⟨*shoot* a charge of dynamite⟩ **b :** to effect by blasting
11 : to determine the altitude of
12 : to take a picture or series of pictures or television images of **:** PHOTOGRAPH, FILM
13 a : to give an injection to **b :** to inject (an illicit drug) especially into the bloodstream
intransitive verb
1 a : to go or pass rapidly and precipitately ⟨sparks *shooting* all over⟩ ⟨his feet *shot* out from under him⟩ **b :** to move ahead by force of momentum **c :** to stream out suddenly **:** SPURT **d :** to dart in or as if in rays from a source of light **e :** to dart with a piercing sensation ⟨pain *shot* up my arm⟩
2 a : to cause an engine or weapon to discharge a missile **b :** to use a firearm or bow especially for sport (as in hunting)
3 : to propel a missile ⟨guns that *shoot* many miles⟩
4 : PROTRUDE, PROJECT
5 a : to grow or sprout by or as if by putting forth shoots **b :** DEVELOP, MATURE **c :** to spring or rise rapidly or suddenly — often used with *up* ⟨in a burst of growth he *shot* up to six feet tall⟩ ⟨prices *shot* up⟩
6 a : to propel an object (as a ball) in a particular way **b :** to drive the ball or puck toward a goal
7 : to cast dice
8 : to slide into or out of a fastening ⟨a bolt that *shoots* in either direction⟩
9 : to record something (as on film or videotape) with a camera
10 : to begin to speak — usually used as an imperative ⟨OK, *shoot*, what do you have to say⟩
— **shoot at** *or* **shoot for :** to aim at **:** strive for
— **shoot from the hip :** to act or speak hastily without consideration of the consequences
— **shoot one's bolt :** to exhaust one's capabilities and resources
— **shoot oneself in the foot :** to act against one's own best interests
— **shoot the breeze :** to converse idly **:** GOSSIP
— **shoot the works 1 :** to venture all one's capital on one play **2 :** to put forth all one's efforts

²**shoot** *noun* (15th century)
1 : a sending out of new growth or the growth sent out: as **a :** a stem or branch with its leaves and appendages especially when not yet mature **b :** OFFSHOOT

\ə\ abut \ᵊ\ kitten \ər\ further \a\ ash \ā\ ace \ä\ mop, mar \au̇\ out \ch\ chin \e\ bet \ē\ easy \g\ go \i\ hit \ī\ ice \j\ job \ŋ\ sing \ō\ go \ȯ\ law \ȯi\ boy \th\ thin \th\ the \ü\ loot \u̇\ foot \y\ yet \zh\ vision *see also* Guide to Pronunciation

2 a : an act of shooting (as with a bow or a firearm): **(1) :** SHOT **(2) :** the firing of a missile especially by artillery **b (1) :** a hunting trip or party **(2) :** the right to shoot game in a particular area or land over which it is held **c (1) :** a shooting match ⟨skeet *shoot*⟩ **(2) :** a round of shots in a shooting match **d :** the action or an instance of shooting with a camera **:** a session or a series of sessions of photographing or filming ⟨a movie *shoot*⟩
3 a : a motion or movement of rapid thrusting: as **(1) :** a sudden or rapid advance **(2) :** a momentary darting sensation **:** TWINGE **(3) :** THRUST 2b **(4) :** the pace between strokes in rowing **b :** a bar of rays **:** BEAM ⟨a *shoot* of sunlight⟩
4 [probably by folk etymology from French *chute* — more at CHUTE] **a :** a rush of water down a steep or rapid **b :** a place where a stream runs or descends swiftly

³shoot *interjection* [euphemism for *shit*] (1876)
— used to express annoyance or surprise

shoot down *transitive verb* (1845)
1 : to cause to fall by shooting ⟨enemy aircraft *shot down* the helicopter⟩; *especially* **:** to kill in this way ⟨was *shot down* in cold blood⟩
2 : to put an end to **:** DEFEAT
3 : DEFLATE, RIDICULE
4 : DISCREDIT 2 ⟨*shoot down* a theory⟩

shoot–'em–up \'shüt-əm-ˌəp\ *noun* (1947)
: a movie or television show with much shooting and bloodshed

shoot·er \'shü-tər\ *noun* (13th century)
1 : one that shoots: as **a :** a person who fires a missile-discharging device (as a rifle or bow) **b :** the person who is shooting or whose turn it is to shoot
2 : something that is used in shooting: as **a :** a marble shot from the hand **b :** REVOLVER — usually used in combination ⟨six-*shooter*⟩
3 : a shot of whiskey or whiskey diluted with something (as soda); *also* **:** a shot glass containing a bit of food (as a raw oyster)

shooting gallery *noun* (1836)
1 : a usually covered range equipped with targets for practice with firearms
2 *slang* **:** a place where one can obtain narcotics and shoot up

shooting iron *noun* (1775)
: FIREARM

shooting script *noun* (1929)
1 : the final completely detailed version of a motion-picture script in which scenes are grouped in the order most convenient for shooting
2 : the final version of a television script used in the production of a program

shooting star *noun* (1593)
1 : a visual meteor appearing as a temporary streak of light in the night sky
2 : any of several North American perennial herbs (genus *Dodecatheon*, especially *D. meadia*) of the primrose family that have entire oblong leaves and showy flowers with reflexed petals

shooting stick *noun* (1926)
: a spiked stick with a top that opens into a seat

shoot–out \'shüt-ˌaut\ *noun* (1948)
1 : a battle fought with handguns or rifles
2 : something resembling a shoot-out; *broadly* **:** SHOWDOWN

shoot–the–chutes \ˌshüt-thə-'shüts\ *noun plural but singular in construction* (1920)
: an amusement ride consisting of a steep incline down which boats slide into a pool at the bottom

shoot up (1890)
transitive verb
1 : to shoot or shoot at especially indiscriminately or recklessly ⟨cowboys *shooting up* the town⟩
2 : to inject (a narcotic drug) into a vein
intransitive verb
: to inject a narcotic into a vein

— **shoot-up** \'shüt-ˌəp\ *noun*

¹shop \'shäp\ *noun, often attributive* [Middle English *shoppe*, from Old English *sceoppa* booth; akin to Old High German *scopf* shed] (14th century)
1 : a handicraft establishment **:** ATELIER
2 a : a building or room stocked with merchandise for sale **:** STORE **b** *or* **shoppe** \'shäp\ **:** a small retail establishment or a department in a large one offering a specified line of goods or services ⟨a millinery *shop*⟩ ⟨a sandwich *shop*⟩
3 : a commercial establishment for the making or repair of goods or machinery ⟨machine *shop*⟩ ⟨repair *shop*⟩
4 a : a school laboratory equipped for manual training **b :** the art or science of working with tools and machinery
5 a : a business establishment **:** OFFICE **b :** SHOPTALK

²shop *verb* **shopped; shop·ping** (1764)
intransitive verb
1 a : to examine goods or services with intent to buy **b :** to hunt through a market in search of the best buy
2 : to make a search **:** HUNT
transitive verb
: to examine the stock or offerings of ⟨*shop* the stores for Christmas gift ideas⟩

shop·keep·er \'shäp-ˌkē-pər\ *noun* (1530)
: STOREKEEPER 2

shop·lift \-ˌlift\ *verb* [back-formation from *shoplifter*] (1820)
intransitive verb
: to steal displayed goods from a store
transitive verb
: to steal (displayed goods) from a store

shop·lift·er \-ˌlif-tər\ *noun* (1680)
: one who shoplifts

shop·per \'shä-pər\ *noun* (1860)
1 : one that shops
2 : one whose occupation is shopping as an agent for customers or for an employer
3 : a usually free paper carrying advertising and sometimes local news

shopping bag *noun* (1886)
: a bag (as of strong paper) that has handles and is intended for carrying purchases

shopping center *noun* (1898)
: a group of retail stores and service establishments usually with ample parking facilities and usually designed to serve a community or neighborhood — called also *shopping plaza*

shopping list *noun* (1913)
: a list of items to be purchased; *broadly* **:** a list of related items ⟨the biggest possible *shopping list* of budget cuts —Leonard Silk⟩

shopping mall *noun* (1959)
: MALL 3

shop steward *noun* (1904)
: a union member elected as the union representative of a shop or department in dealings with the management

shop·talk \'shäp-ˌtok\ *noun* (1881)
: the jargon or subject matter peculiar to an occupation or a special area of interest

shop·win·dow \-ˌwin-(ˌ)dō\ *noun* (15th century)
: a display window of a store

shop·worn \-ˌwōrn, -ˌwȯrn\ *adjective* (1838)
1 : faded, soiled, or otherwise impaired by remaining too long in a store
2 : stale from excessive use or familiarity ⟨*shopworn* clichés⟩
3 : WORN-OUT ⟨think of himself as a *shopworn* Hollywood cynic —A. H. Johnston⟩

¹shore \'shōr, 'shȯr\ *noun, often attributive* [Middle English, from (assumed) Old English *scor*; akin to Middle Low German *schōr* foreland and perhaps to Old English *scieran* to cut — more at SHEAR] (14th century)
1 : the land bordering a usually large body of water; *specifically* **:** COAST
2 : a boundary or the country or place that it bounds ⟨hold him accountable for difficulties

beyond our *shores* that he could do nothing about —Dorothy Fosdick⟩
3 : land as distinguished from the sea ⟨shipboard and *shore* duty⟩

²shore *transitive verb* **shored; shor·ing** [Middle English; akin to Old Norse *skortha* to prop] (14th century)
1 : to support by a shore **:** PROP
2 : to give support to **:** BRACE — usually used with *up*

³shore *noun* (14th century)
: a prop for preventing sinking or sagging

shore·bird \'shōr-ˌbərd, 'shȯr-\ *noun* (circa 1672)
: any of a suborder (Charadrii) of birds (as a plover or snipe) that frequent the seashore

shore dinner *noun* (1892)
: a dinner consisting chiefly of seafoods

shore·front \-ˌfrənt\ *noun* (1919)
: land along a shore; *specifically* **:** BEACHFRONT

shore leave *noun* (1888)
: a leave of absence to go on shore granted to a sailor or naval officer

shore·line \-ˌlīn\ *noun* (1852)
1 : the line where a body of water and the shore meet
2 : the strip of land along the shoreline

shore patrol *noun* (1917)
1 : a branch of a navy that exercises guard and police functions — compare MILITARY POLICE
2 : petty officers detailed to perform police duty while a ship is in port

shore·side \-ˌsīd\ *adjective* (1883)
: situated at or near a shore

shore·ward \-wərd\ *or* **shore·wards** \-wərdz\ *adverb* (circa 1691)
: toward the shore

shor·ing \'shōr-iŋ, 'shȯr-\ *noun* (15th century)
1 : the act of supporting with or as if with a prop
2 : a system or group of shores

shorn *past participle of* SHEAR

¹short \'shȯrt\ *adjective* [Middle English, from Old English *sceort*; akin to Old High German *scurz* short, Old Norse *skortr* lack] (before 12th century)
1 a : having little length **b :** not tall or high **:** LOW
2 a : not extended in time **:** BRIEF ⟨a *short* vacation⟩ **b :** not retentive ⟨a *short* memory⟩ **c :** EXPEDITIOUS, QUICK ⟨made *short* work of the problem⟩ **d :** seeming to pass quickly ⟨made great progress in just a few *short* years⟩
3 a *of a speech sound* **:** having a relatively short duration **b :** being the member of a pair of similarly spelled vowel or vowel-containing sounds that is descended from a vowel that was short in duration but is no longer so and that does not necessarily have duration as its chief distinguishing feature ⟨*short i* in *sin*⟩ **c** *of a syllable in prosody* **(1) :** of relatively brief duration **(2) :** UNSTRESSED
4 : limited in distance ⟨a *short* trip⟩
5 a : not coming up to a measure or requirement **:** INSUFFICIENT ⟨in *short* supply⟩ **b :** not reaching far enough ⟨the throw to first was *short*⟩ **c :** enduring privation **d :** insufficiently supplied ⟨*short* of cash⟩ ⟨*short* on brains⟩
6 a : ABRUPT, CURT **b :** quickly provoked
7 : CHOPPY 2
8 : payable at an early date
9 a : containing or cooked with shortening; *also* **:** FLAKY ⟨*short* pastry⟩ **b** *of metal* **:** brittle under certain conditions
10 a : not lengthy or drawn out **b :** made briefer **:** ABBREVIATED
11 a : not having goods or property that one has sold in anticipation of a fall in prices **b :** consisting of or relating to a sale of securities or commodities that the seller does not possess or has not contracted for at the time of the sale ⟨*short* sale⟩
12 : near the end of a tour of duty
— **short·ish** \'shȯr-tish\ *adjective*
— **in short order :** with dispatch **:** QUICKLY

²short *adverb* (14th century)

1 : in a curt manner
2 : for or during a brief time ⟨*short*-lasting⟩
3 : at a disadvantage **:** UNAWARES ⟨caught *short*⟩
4 : in an abrupt manner **:** SUDDENLY ⟨the car stopped *short*⟩
5 : at some point or degree before a goal or limit aimed at or under consideration ⟨the shells fell *short*⟩ ⟨quit a month *short* of graduation⟩
6 : clean across ⟨the axle was snapped *short*⟩
7 : by or as if by a short sale
³short *noun* (circa 1586)
1 : the sum and substance **:** UPSHOT
2 a : a short syllable **b :** a short sound or signal
3 *plural* **a :** a by-product of wheat milling that includes the germ, fine bran, and some flour **b :** refuse, clippings, or trimmings discarded in various manufacturing processes
4 a : knee-length or less than knee-length trousers — usually used in plural **b** *plural* **:** short drawers **c :** a size in clothing for short men
5 a : one who operates on the short side of the market **b** *plural* **:** short-term bonds
6 *plural* **:** DEFICIENCIES
7 : SHORT CIRCUIT
8 : SHORTSTOP
9 a : SHORT SUBJECT **b :** a brief story or article (as in a newspaper)
— **for short :** as an abbreviation ⟨named Katherine or Kate *for short*⟩
— **in short :** by way of summary **:** BRIEFLY
⁴short *transitive verb* (1904)
1 : SHORT-CIRCUIT
2 : SHORTCHANGE, CHEAT
short account *noun* (circa 1902)
: the total of open short sales in a given subject of trade or in the market as a whole
short·age \'shȯr-tij\ *noun* (1868)
: LACK, DEFICIT
short ballot *noun* (1909)
: a ballot limiting the number of elective offices to the most important legislative and executive posts and leaving minor positions to be filled by appointment
short·bread \'shȯrt-ˌbred\ *noun* (1801)
: a thick cookie made of flour, sugar, and a large amount of shortening
short·cake \-ˌkāk\ *noun* (1594)
1 : a crisp and often unsweetened biscuit or cookie
2 a : a dessert made typically of very short baking-powder-biscuit dough spread with sweetened fruit **b :** a dish consisting of a rich biscuit split and covered with a meat mixture
short·change \-'chānj\ *transitive verb* (1903)
1 : to give less than the correct amount of change to
2 : to deprive of or give less than something due **:** CHEAT
— **short·chang·er** *noun*
short·cir·cuit *transitive verb* (1867)
1 : to apply a short circuit to or establish a short circuit in
2 : BYPASS
3 : FRUSTRATE, IMPEDE
short circuit *noun* (1854)
: a connection of comparatively low resistance accidentally or intentionally made between points on a circuit between which the resistance is normally much greater
short·com·ing \'shȯrt-ˌkə-miŋ, ˌshȯrt-'\ *noun* (15th century)
: DEFICIENCY, DEFECT
¹short·cut \'shȯrt-ˌkət *also* -'kət\ *noun* (1637)
1 : a route more direct than the one ordinarily taken
2 : a method of doing something more directly and quickly than and often not so thoroughly as by ordinary procedure
²shortcut *verb* **-cut; -cut·ting** (1915)
transitive verb
: to shorten (as a way or procedure) by use of a shortcut; *also* **:** CIRCUMVENT

intransitive verb
: to take or use a shortcut
short–day \'shȯrt-ˌdā\ *adjective* (1920)
: responding to or relating to a short photoperiod — used especially of a plant; compare DAY-NEUTRAL, LONG-DAY
short division *noun* (circa 1890)
: mathematical division in which the successive steps are performed without writing out the remainders
short–eared owl \'shȯrt-ˌird-\ *noun* (1766)
: a medium-sized nearly cosmopolitan owl (*Asio flammeus*) that has very short ear tufts and usually nests on the ground
short·en \'shȯr-t°n\ *verb* **short·ened; short·en·ing** \'shȯrt-niŋ, 'shȯr-t°n-iŋ\ (14th century)
transitive verb
1 a : to reduce the length or duration of **b :** to cause to seem short
2 a : to reduce in power or efficiency ⟨is my hand *shortened*, that it cannot redeem —Isaiah 50:2 (Revised Standard Version)⟩ **b** *obsolete* **:** to deprive of effect
3 : to add fat to (as pastry dough) in order to make tender and flaky
intransitive verb
: to become short or shorter ☆
— **short·en·er** \'shȯrt-nər, 'shȯr-t°n-ər\ *noun*
short·en·ing \'shȯrt-niŋ, 'shȯr-t°n-iŋ\ *noun* (1538)
1 : the action or process of making or becoming short; *specifically* **:** the dropping of the latter part of a word so as to produce a new and shorter word of the same meaning
2 : an edible fat used to shorten baked goods
short·fall \'shȯrt-ˌfȯl\ *noun* (1895)
: a failure to come up to expectation or need; *also* **:** the amount of such failure
short–grass prairie \'shȯrt-ˌgras-\ *noun* (1844)
: PRAIRIE 2b
short·hair \-ˌhar, -ˌher\ *noun* (1903)
: a domestic cat with a short thick coat; *especially* **:** a member of any of several breeds of muscular medium- to large-sized cats with a short plushy coat
— **short·haired** *adjective*
short·hand \-ˌhand\ *noun* (1636)
1 : a method of writing rapidly by substituting characters, abbreviations, or symbols for letters, sounds, words, or phrases **:** STENOGRAPHY
2 : a system or instance of rapid or abbreviated communication or representation
— **shorthand** *adjective*
short·hand·ed \ˌshȯrt-'han-dəd\ *adjective* (1794)
: having, working with, or done with fewer than the regular or necessary number of people
short–haul \'shȯrt-ˌhȯl\ *adjective* (1895)
: traveling or involving a short distance ⟨*short-haul* flights⟩
short·horn \-ˌhȯrn\ *noun, often capitalized* (1847)
: any of a breed of red, roan, or white beef cattle originating in the north of England and including good milk-producing strains — called also *Durham*

shorthorn

short–horned grasshopper \'shȯrt-ˌhȯrn(d)-\ *noun* (circa 1890)
: any of a family (Acrididae) of grasshoppers with short antennae
short hundredweight *noun* (1924)
: HUNDREDWEIGHT 1
short–leaf pine \'shȯrt-ˌlēf-\ *noun* (1796)
: a pine (*Pinus echinata*) of the southeastern U.S. that has short flexible needles usually in

clusters of two and reddish brown bark; *also* **:** its yellow wood
short line *noun* (circa 1917)
: a transportation system (as a railroad) operating over a relatively short distance
short·list \'shȯrt-ˌlist\ *noun* (1927)
: a list of candidates for final consideration (as for a position or a prize)
— **short-list** *transitive verb, chiefly British*
short–lived \'shȯrt-'livd *also* -'līvd\ *adjective* (1588)
: not living or lasting long ⟨*short-lived* insects⟩ ⟨*short-lived* joy⟩
usage see LONG-LIVED
short loin *noun* (circa 1923)
: a portion of the hindquarter of beef immediately behind the ribs that is usually cut into steaks — see BEEF illustration
short·ly \'shȯrt-lē\ *adverb* (before 12th century)
1 a : in a few words **:** BRIEFLY **b :** in an abrupt manner
2 a : in a short time ⟨we will be there *shortly*⟩ **b :** at a short interval ⟨*shortly* after sunset⟩
short·ness \-nəs\ *noun* (before 12th century)
: the quality or state of being short
short–nosed cattle louse \'shȯrt-ˌnōz(d)-\ *noun* (1942)
: a large bluish sucking louse (*Haematopinus eurysternus*) that attacks domestic cattle
short–order \'shȯrt-ˌȯr-dər, -ˌȯr-\ *adjective* (1920)
: preparing or serving food that can be cooked quickly to a customer's order ⟨a *short-order* cook⟩
short–range \'shȯrt-'rānj\ *adjective* (1869)
1 : involving or taking into account a short period of time ⟨*short-range* plans⟩
2 : relating to or fit for short distances
short ribs *noun plural* (1912)
: a cut of beef consisting of rib ends between the rib roast and the plate — see BEEF illustration
short run *noun* (1879)
: a relatively brief period of time — often used in the phrase *in the short run*
— **short–run** *adjective*
short shrift *noun* (1594)
1 : barely adequate time for confession before execution
2 a : little or no attention or consideration **b :** quick work — usually used in the phrase *make short shrift of*
short sight *noun* (circa 1829)
: MYOPIA
short·sight·ed \'shȯrt-ˌsī-təd\ *adjective* (circa 1649)
1 : NEARSIGHTED
2 : lacking foresight
— **short·sight·ed·ly** *adverb*

☆ **SYNONYMS**
Shorten, curtail, abbreviate, abridge, retrench mean to reduce in extent. SHORTEN implies reduction in length or duration (*shorten* a speech). CURTAIL adds an implication of cutting that in some way deprives of completeness or adequacy (ceremonies *curtailed* because of rain). ABBREVIATE implies a making shorter usually by omitting some part (using an *abbreviated* title). ABRIDGE implies a reduction in compass or scope with retention of essential elements and a relative completeness in the result (the *abridged* version of the novel). RETRENCH suggests a reduction in extent or costs of something felt to be excessive (declining business forced the company to *retrench*).

— **short·sight·ed·ness** *noun*

short–spo·ken \-ˌspō-kən\ *adjective* (1865)
: CURT

short·stop \-ˌstäp\ *noun* (1857)
1 : the player position in baseball for defending the infield area on the third-base side of second base
2 : the player stationed in the shortstop position

short–stop \-ˌstäp\ *noun* (1936)
: STOP BATH

short story *noun* (1877)
: an invented prose narrative shorter than a novel usually dealing with a few characters and aiming at unity of effect and often concentrating on the creation of mood rather than plot

short subject *noun* (1944)
: a brief often documentary or educational film

short–tem·pered \ˌshȯrt-ˈtem-pərd\ *adjective* (1900)
: having a quick temper

short–term \ˈshȯrt-ˌtərm\ *adjective* (1901)
1 : occurring over or involving a relatively short period of time
2 a : of, relating to, or constituting a financial operation or obligation based on a brief term and especially one of less than a year **b** : generated by assets held for less than six months

short ton *noun* (1881)
— see WEIGHT table

short·wave \ˈshȯrt-ˌwāv\ *noun, often attributive* (1902)
1 : a radio wave having a wavelength between 10 and 100 meters
2 : a radio transmitter using shortwaves
3 : electromagnetic radiation having a wavelength equal to or less than that of visible light

short–weight \ˈshȯrt-ˈwāt\ *transitive verb* (1926)
: to defraud with short weight

short weight \ˈshȯrt-ˈwāt\ *noun* (1789)
: weight less than the stated weight or less than one is charged for

short–wind·ed \ˌshȯrt-ˈwin-dəd\ *adjective* (15th century)
1 : affected with or characterized by shortness of breath
2 a : BRIEF **b** : broken up into short units

shorty *or* **short·ie** \ˈshȯr-tē\ *noun, plural* **short·ies** (1888)
: one that is short

Sho·shone \shə-ˈshōn, -ˈshō-nē; ˈshō-ˌshōn\ *or* **Sho·sho·ni** \shə-ˈshō-nē\ *noun, plural* **Shoshones** *or* **Shoshoni** *also* **Shoshone** *or* **Shoshonis** (1805)
1 : a member of a group of American Indian peoples originally ranging through California, Idaho, Nevada, Utah, and Wyoming
2 : the Uto-Aztecan language of the Shoshones

¹shot \ˈshät\ *noun* [Middle English, from Old English *scot*; akin to Old Norse *skot* shot, Old High German *scuz*, Old English *scēotan* to shoot — more at SHOOT] (before 12th century)
1 a : an action of shooting **b** : a directed propelling of a missile; *specifically* : a directed discharge of a firearm **c** : a stroke or throw in an attempt to score points in a game (as tennis, pool, or basketball); *also* : HOME RUN **d** : BLAST **e** : a medical or narcotics injection
2 a *plural* **shot** : something propelled by shooting; *especially* : small lead or steel pellets especially forming a charge for a shotgun **b** : a metal sphere of iron or brass that is heaved in the shot put
3 a : the distance that a missile is or can be thrown **b** : RANGE, REACH
4 : a charge to be paid : SCOT
5 : one that shoots; *especially* : MARKSMAN
6 a : ATTEMPT, TRY **b** : GUESS, CONJECTURE **c** : CHANCE **d** : a single appearance as an entertainer (did a guest *shot* for the program)
7 : an effective remark

8 a : a single photographic exposure; *especially* : SNAPSHOT **b** : a single sequence of a motion picture or a television program shot by one camera without interruption
9 : a charge of explosives
10 a : a small measure or serving (as one ounce) of undiluted liquor **b** : a small amount applied at one time : DOSE
11 shot *plural* : SPRINKLES, JIMMIES
— **a shot** : for each one : APIECE
— **like a shot** : very rapidly
— **shot in the arm** : STIMULUS, BOOST
— **shot in the dark 1** : a wild guess **2** : an attempt that has little chance of success

²shot *past and past participle of* SHOOT

³shot *adjective* (1763)
1 a *of a fabric* : having contrasting and changeable color effects : IRIDESCENT **b** : suffused or streaked with a color (hair *shot* with gray) **c** : infused or permeated with a quality or element (*shot* through with wit)
2 : having the form of pellets resembling shot
3 : reduced to a state of ruin, prostration, or uselessness (his nerves are *shot*)

¹shot·gun \ˈshät-ˌgən\ *noun* (1776)
1 : a smoothbore shoulder weapon for firing shot at short ranges
2 : an offensive football formation in which the quarterback plays a few yards behind the line of scrimmage and the other backs are scattered as flankers or slotbacks
— **shotgun** *transitive verb*
— **shot·gun·ner** \-ˌgə-nər\ *noun*

²shotgun *adjective* (1892)
1 : of, relating to, or using a shotgun
2 : involving coercion
3 : covering a wide field with hit-or-miss effectiveness

shotgun house *noun* (1940)
: a house in which all the rooms are in direct line with each other usually front to back — called also *shotgun cottage*; compare RAILROAD FLAT

shotgun marriage *noun* (1929)
1 : a marriage forced or required because of pregnancy — called also *shotgun wedding*
2 : a forced union (a spate of brokerage mergers . . . hastily arranged *shotgun marriages* —John Brooks)

shot hole *noun* (1875)
1 : a drilled hole in which a charge of dynamite is exploded
2 : the dropping out of small rounded fragments of leaves that produces a shot-riddled appearance and is caused especially by parasitic action

shot put *noun* (1894)
: a field event in which a shot is heaved for distance
— **shot–put·ter** \ˈshät-ˌpu̇-tər\ *noun*

shot·ten \ˈshä-tᵊn\ *adjective* [Middle English *shotyn*, from past participle of *shuten* to shoot] (15th century)
: having ejected the spawn and so of inferior food value (*shotten* herring)

should \shəd, ˈshu̇d\ [Middle English *sholde*, from Old English *sceolde* owed, was obliged to, ought to] *past of* SHALL (before 12th century)
1 — used in auxiliary function to express condition (if he *should* leave his father, his father would die —Genesis 44:22 (Revised Standard Version))
2 — used in auxiliary function to express obligation, propriety, or expediency ('tis commanded I *should* do so —Shakespeare) (this is as it *should* be —H. L. Savage) (you *should* brush your teeth after each meal)
3 — used in auxiliary function to express futurity from a point of view in the past (realized that she *should* have to do most of her farm work before sunrise —Ellen Glasgow)
4 — used in auxiliary function to express what is probable or expected (with an early start, they *should* be here by noon)

5 — used in auxiliary function to express a request in a polite manner or to soften direct statement (I *should* suggest that a guide . . . is the first essential —L. D. Reddick)

¹shoul·der \ˈshōl-dər\ *noun* [Middle English *sholder*, from Old English *sculdor*; akin to Old High German *scultra* shoulder] (before 12th century)
1 a : the laterally projecting part of the human body formed of the bones and joints with their covering tissue by which the arm is connected with the trunk **b** : the region of the body of nonhuman vertebrates that corresponds to the shoulder but is less projecting
2 a : the two shoulders and the upper part of the back — usually used in plural **b** *plural* : capacity for bearing a task or blame (placed the guilt squarely on his *shoulders*)
3 : a cut of meat including the upper joint of the foreleg and adjacent parts — see LAMB illustration
4 : the part of a garment at the wearer's shoulder
5 : an area adjacent to or along the edge of a higher, more prominent, or more important part: as **a** (1) : the part of a hill or mountain near the top (2) : a lateral protrusion or extension of a hill or mountain **b** : either edge of a roadway; *specifically* : the part of a roadway outside of the traveled way
6 : a rounded or sloping part (as of a stringed instrument or a bottle) where the neck joins the body
— **shoul·dered** \-dərd\ *adjective*

²shoulder *verb* **shoul·dered; shoul·der·ing** \-d(ə-)riŋ\ (14th century)
transitive verb
1 : to push or thrust with or as if with the shoulder : JOSTLE (*shouldered* his way through the crowd)
2 a : to place or bear on the shoulder (*shouldered* her knapsack and took off) **b** : to assume the burden or responsibility of (*shoulder* the blame)
intransitive verb
: to push with or as if with the shoulders aggressively

shoulder bag *noun* (1912)
: a handbag looped over the shoulder by a strap

shoulder belt *noun* (1967)
: an automobile safety belt worn across the torso and over the shoulder — called also *shoulder harness*

shoulder blade *noun* (14th century)
: SCAPULA

shoulder board *noun* (1945)
: one of a pair of broad pieces of stiffened cloth worn on the shoulders of a military uniform and carrying insignia

shoulder girdle *noun* (1868)
: PECTORAL GIRDLE

shoulder knot *noun* (1676)
1 : an ornamental knot of ribbon or lace worn on the shoulder in the 17th and 18th centuries
2 : a detachable ornament of braided wire cord worn on ceremonial occasions on the shoulders of a uniform by a commissioned officer

shoulder patch *noun* (1945)
: a cloth patch bearing an identifying mark and worn on one sleeve of a uniform below the shoulder

shoulder strap *noun* (1688)
: a strap that passes across the shoulder and holds up an article or garment

should·est \ˈshu̇-dəst\ *archaic past 2d singular of* SHOULD

shouldn't \ˈshu̇-dᵊnt, -dᵊn, *dialect also* ˈshu̇-tᵊn(t) *or* ˈshu̇nt\ (1848)
: should not

shouldst \shədst, ˈshu̇dst, shətst, ˈshu̇tst\ *archaic past 2d singular of* SHALL

¹shout \ˈshau̇t\ *verb* [Middle English] (14th century)
intransitive verb
1 : to utter a sudden loud cry

2 : to command attention as if by shouting ⟨a quality that *shouts* from good novels —John Gardner⟩
transitive verb
1 : to utter in a loud voice
2 : to cause to be, come, or stop by or as if by shouting ⟨*shouted* himself hoarse⟩ ⟨the proponents *shouted* down the opposition⟩
— **shout·er** *noun*
²**shout** *noun* (14th century)
: a loud cry or call
shouting distance *noun* (1930)
: a short distance **:** easy reach — usually used with *within* ⟨lived within *shouting distance* of her cousins⟩
shout song *noun* (1925)
: a rhythmic song sung at religious services especially by black Americans and characterized by responsive singing or shouting between leader and congregation
¹**shove** \'shəv\ *verb* **shoved; shov·ing** [Middle English, from Old English *scūfan* to thrust away; akin to Old High German *scioban* to push and probably to Lithuanian *skubti* to hurry] (before 12th century)
transitive verb
1 : to push along
2 : to push or put in a rough, careless, or hasty manner **:** THRUST
3 : to force by other than physical means **:** COMPEL ⟨*shove* a bill through the legislature⟩
intransitive verb
1 : to move by forcing a way ⟨bargain hunters *shoving* up to the counter⟩
2 a : to move something by exerting force **b :** LEAVE — usually used with *off* ⟨*shoved* off for home⟩
— **shov·er** *noun*
²**shove** *noun* (14th century)
: an act or instance of shoving **:** a forcible push
¹**shov·el** \'shə-vəl\ *noun* [Middle English, from Old English *scofl*; akin to Old High German *scūfla* shovel, Old English *scūfan* to thrust away] (before 12th century)
1 a : a hand implement consisting of a broad scoop or a more or less hollowed out blade with a handle used to lift and throw material **b :** something that resembles a shovel **c :** an excavating machine; *especially* **:** an hydraulic diesel-engine driven power shovel
2 : SHOVELFUL
²**shovel** *verb* **-eled** *or* **-elled; -el·ing** *or* **-el·ling** \'shə-və-liŋ, 'shəv-liŋ\ (15th century)
transitive verb
1 : to take up and throw with a shovel
2 : to dig or clean out with a shovel
3 : to throw or convey roughly or in a mass as if with a shovel ⟨*shoveled* his food into his mouth⟩
intransitive verb
: to use a shovel
shov·el·er *or* **shov·el·ler** \'shə-və-lər, 'shəv-lər\ *noun* (15th century)
1 : one that shovels
2 : any of several river ducks (genus *Anas*) having a large and very broad bill
shov·el·ful \'shə-vəl-,fùl\ *noun, plural* **shov·elfuls** \-,fùlz\ *also* **shov·els·ful** \-vəlz-,fùl\ (1533)
: as much as a shovel will hold
shovel hat *noun* (1829)
: a shallow-crowned hat with a wide brim curved up at the sides that is worn by some clergymen
shov·el·nose \-,nōz\ *noun* (1709)
: SHOVEL-NOSED animal and especially a fish
shov·el·nosed \'shə-vəl-,nōzd\ *adjective* (1707)
: having a broad flat head, nose, or beak
¹**show** \'shō\ *verb* **showed** \'shōd\; **shown** \'shōn\ *or* **showed; show·ing** [Middle English *shewen, showen,* from Old English *scēawian* to look, look at, see; akin to Old High German *scouwōn* to look, look at, and

probably to Latin *cavēre* to be on one's guard] (12th century)
transitive verb
1 : to cause or permit to be seen **:** EXHIBIT ⟨*showed* pictures of the baby⟩
2 : to offer for sale ⟨stores were *showing* new spring suits⟩
3 : to present as a public spectacle **:** PERFORM
4 : to reveal by one's condition, nature, or behavior ⟨*showed* themselves to be cowards⟩
5 : to give indication or record of ⟨an anemometer *shows* wind speed⟩
6 a : to point out **:** direct attention to ⟨*showed* the view from the terrace⟩ **b :** CONDUCT, USHER ⟨*showed* me to an aisle seat⟩
7 : ACCORD, BESTOW ⟨*shows* them no mercy⟩
8 a : to set forth **:** DECLARE **b :** ALLEGE, PLEAD — used especially in law ⟨*show* cause⟩
9 a : to demonstrate or establish by argument or reasoning ⟨*show* a plan to be faulty⟩ **b :** INFORM, INSTRUCT ⟨*showed* me how to solve the problem⟩
10 : to present (an animal) for judging in a show
intransitive verb
1 a : to be or come in view ⟨3:15 *showed* on the clock⟩ **b :** to put in an appearance ⟨failed to *show*⟩
2 a : to appear in a particular way ⟨anger *showed* in their faces⟩ **b :** SEEM, APPEAR
3 a : to give a theatrical performance **b :** to be staged or presented
4 a : to appear as a contestant **b :** to present an animal in a show
5 : to finish third or at least third (as in a horse race)
6 : to exhibit one's artistic work ☆ ☆
— **show·able** \'shō-ə-bəl\ *adjective*
— **show one's hand 1 :** to display one's cards faceup **2 :** to declare one's intentions or reveal one's resources
— **show one the door :** to tell someone to get out
²**show** *noun, often attributive* (13th century)
1 : a demonstrative display ⟨a *show* of strength⟩
2 a *archaic* **:** outward appearance **b :** a false semblance **:** PRETENSE ⟨made a *show* of friendship⟩ **c :** a more or less true appearance of something **:** SIGN **d :** an impressive display ⟨his role as househusband . . . was purely for *show* —John Lahr⟩ **e :** OSTENTATION
3 : CHANCE ⟨gave him a *show* in spite of his background⟩
4 : something exhibited especially for wonder or ridicule **:** SPECTACLE
5 a : a large display or exhibition arranged to arouse interest or stimulate sales ⟨the national auto *show*⟩ **b :** a competitive exhibition of animals (as dogs) to demonstrate quality in breeding
6 a : a theatrical presentation **b :** a radio or television program **c :** ENTERTAINMENT 3a
7 : ENTERPRISE, AFFAIR ⟨they ran the whole *show*⟩
8 : an indication of metal in a mine or of gas or oil in a well
9 : third place at the finish (as of a horse race)
show–and–tell \'shō-ən(d)-'tel\ *noun* (1950)
1 : a classroom exercise in which children display an item and talk about it
2 : a public display or demonstration
show bill *noun* (1801)
: an advertising poster
show·biz \'shō-,biz\ *noun, often attributive* [by shortening & alteration] (1945)
: SHOW BUSINESS; *also* **:** RAZZLE-DAZZLE 3
— **show·biz·zy** \-,bi-zē\ *adjective*
¹**show·boat** \'shō-,bōt\ *noun* (1869)
1 : a river steamship containing a theater and carrying a troupe of actors to give plays at river communities
2 : one who tries to attract attention by conspicuous behavior
²**showboat** *intransitive verb* (1951)

: to behave in a conspicuous or ostentatious manner **:** SHOW OFF
showbread *variant of* SHEWBREAD
show business *noun* (1850)
: the arts, occupations, and businesses (as theater, motion pictures, and television) that comprise the entertainment industry
¹**show·case** \'shō-,kās\ *noun* (1835)
1 : a glazed case, box, or cabinet for displaying and protecting wares in a store or articles in a museum
2 : a setting, occasion, or medium for exhibiting something or someone especially in an attractive or favorable aspect
²**showcase** *transitive verb* **show·cased; show·cas·ing** (1945)
: to exhibit especially in an attractive or favorable aspect ⟨*showcase* new talent⟩
show·down \'shō-,daùn\ *noun* (1884)
1 : the placing of poker hands faceup on the table to determine the winner of a pot
2 : a decisive confrontation or contest
¹**show·er** \'shaù(-ə)r\ *noun* [Middle English *shour*, from Old English *scūr*; akin to Old High German *scūr* shower, storm, Latin *caurus* northwest wind] (before 12th century)
1 a : a fall of rain of short duration **b :** a similar fall of sleet, hail, or snow
2 : something resembling a rain shower ⟨a *shower* of statistics⟩; *especially* **:** a fall of meteors which belong to a single group and whose trails appear to originate at the same point in space
3 : a party given by friends who bring gifts often of a particular kind
4 : a bath in which water is showered on the body; *also* **:** the apparatus that provides a shower
— **show·er·less** \-ləs\ *adjective*
— **show·ery** \'shaù(-ə)-rē\ *adjective*

☆ **SYNONYMS**
Show, exhibit, display, expose, parade, flaunt mean to present so as to invite notice or attention. SHOW implies no more than enabling another to see or examine ⟨*showed* her snapshots to the whole group⟩. EXHIBIT stresses putting forward prominently or openly ⟨*exhibit* paintings at a gallery⟩. DISPLAY emphasizes putting in a position where others may see to advantage ⟨*display* sale items⟩. EXPOSE suggests bringing forth from concealment and displaying ⟨sought to *expose* the hypocrisy of the town fathers⟩. PARADE implies an ostentatious or arrogant displaying ⟨*parading* their piety for all to see⟩. FLAUNT suggests a shameless, boastful, often offensive parading ⟨nouveaux riches *flaunting* their wealth⟩.

Show, manifest, evidence, evince, demonstrate mean to reveal outwardly or make apparent. SHOW is the general term but sometimes implies that what is revealed must be gained by inference from acts, looks, or words ⟨careful not to *show* his true feelings⟩. MANIFEST implies a plainer, more immediate revelation ⟨*manifested* musical ability at an early age⟩. EVIDENCE suggests serving as proof of the actuality or existence of something ⟨a commitment *evidenced* by years of loyal service⟩. EVINCE implies a showing by outward marks or signs ⟨*evinced* not the slightest fear⟩. DEMONSTRATE implies showing by action or by display of feeling ⟨*demonstrated* their approval by loud applause⟩.

\ə\ **abut** \'ə\ **kitten** \ər\ **further** \a\ **ash** \ā\ **ace**
\ä\ **mop, mar** \aù\ **out** \ch\ **chin** \e\ **bet** \ē\ **easy**
\g\ **go** \i\ **hit** \ī\ **ice** \j\ **job** \ŋ\ **sing** \ō\ **go**
\ò\ **law** \òi\ **boy** \th\ **thin** \th\ **the** \ü\ **loot** \ù\ **foot**
\y\ **yet** \zh\ **vision** *see also* Guide to Pronunciation

— to the showers : out of the ball game
²**shower** (15th century)
intransitive verb
1 : to rain or fall in or as if in a shower ⟨letters *showered* on him in praise and protest⟩
2 : to bathe in a shower
transitive verb
1 a : to wet (as with water) in a spray, fine stream, or drops **b** (1) : to cause to fall in a shower ⟨factory chimneys *showered* soot on the district⟩ (2) : to cause a shower to fall on ⟨*showered* the newlyweds with rice⟩
2 : to give in abundance ⟨*showered* the writer with honors⟩
— show·er·er \'shaủ(-ə)r-ər\ *noun*
³**show·er** \'shō-(ə)r\ *noun* (14th century)
: one that shows : EXHIBITOR
shower bath *noun* (1785)
: SHOWER 4
show·er·head \'shaủ(-ə)r-,hed\ *noun* (1925)
: a fixture for directing the spray of water in a bathroom shower
show·girl \'shō-,gər(-ə)l\ *noun* (1836)
: a chorus girl in a musical comedy or night-club show
show·ing \'shō-iŋ\ *noun* (before 12th century)
1 : an act or an instance of putting something (as an artist's work) on view : DISPLAY
2 : PERFORMANCE, RECORD ⟨made a good *showing* in competition⟩
3 a : a statement or presentation of a case **b** : APPEARANCE, EVIDENCE
show jumping *noun* (1929)
: the competitive riding of horses one at a time over a set course of obstacles in which the winner is judged according to ability and speed
— show jumper *noun*
show·man \'shō-mən\ *noun* (circa 1734)
1 : the producer of a play or theatrical show
2 : an individual having a sense or knack for dramatically effective presentation
— show·man·ship \-,ship\ *noun*
show–me \'shō-mē\ *adjective* (1909)
: insistent on proof or evidence
show–off \'shō-,óf\ *noun, often attributive* (1843)
1 : the act of showing off
2 : one that shows off : EXHIBITIONIST
— show–offy \-,ó-fē\ *adjective*
show off (circa 1793)
transitive verb
: to display proudly ⟨wanted to *show* our new car *off*⟩
intransitive verb
: to seek to attract attention by conspicuous behavior ⟨boys *showing off* for the girls⟩
show·piece \'shō-,pēs\ *noun* (1885)
: a prime or outstanding example used for exhibition
show·place \-,plās\ *noun* (1794)
: a place (as an estate or building) that is regarded as an example of beauty or excellence
show·ring \-,riŋ\ *noun* (1926)
: a ring (as at a cattle show) where animals are displayed
show·room \-,rüm, -,rủm\ *noun* (1616)
: a room where merchandise is exhibited for sale or where samples are displayed
show·stop·per \-,stä-pər\ *noun* (1926)
1 : an act, song, or performer that wins applause so prolonged as to interrupt a performance
2 : something or someone exceptionally arresting or attractive ⟨the gold crown was the *showstopper* of the exhibition⟩
— show·stop·ping \-,stä-piŋ\ *adjective*
show trial *noun* (1937)
: a trial (as of political opponents) in which the verdict is rigged and a public confession is often extracted
show up (1826)
transitive verb
1 : to expose or discredit especially by revealing faults ⟨*showed* them *up* as frauds⟩

2 : to embarrass or cause to look bad especially by comparison ⟨trying to *show up* the boss⟩
3 : REVEAL ⟨*showed up* my ignorance⟩
intransitive verb
1 : ARRIVE, APPEAR ⟨*showed up* late for his own wedding⟩
2 : to be plainly evident
show window *noun* (1826)
1 : an outside display window in which a store exhibits merchandise
2 : a sample or setting used to exhibit or illustrate something at its best
showy \'shō-ē\ *adjective* **show·i·er; -est** (1712)
1 : making an attractive show : STRIKING ⟨a *showy* orchid⟩
2 : given to or marked by a flashy often tasteless display ☆
— show·i·ly \'shō-ə-lē\ *adverb*
— show·i·ness \'shō-ē-nəs\ *noun*
sho·yu \'shō-(,)yü\ *noun* [Japanese *shōyu*] (1727)
: SOY 1
shrank *past of* SHRINK
shrap·nel \'shrap-nəl, *especially Southern* 'srap-\ *noun, plural* **shrapnel** [Henry *Shrapnel* (died 1842) English artillery officer] (1806)
1 : a projectile that consists of a case provided with a powder charge and a large number of usually lead balls and that is exploded in flight
2 : bomb, mine, or shell fragments
¹**shred** \'shred, *especially Southern* 'sred\ *noun* [Middle English *shrede*, from Old English *scrēade*; akin to Old High German *scrōt* piece cut off] (before 12th century)
1 a : a long narrow strip cut or torn off **b** *plural* : a shredded, damaged, disrupted, or ruined condition ⟨torn to *shreds* by an air attack⟩
2 : PARTICLE, SCRAP ⟨not a *shred* of evidence⟩
²**shred** *verb* **shred·ded; shred·ding** (before 12th century)
transitive verb
1 *archaic* : to cut off
2 : to cut or tear into shreds ⟨*shredded* the documents⟩
3 : DEMOLISH 2 ⟨sharp lawyers *shredding* hapless witnesses —Charles Krauthammer⟩
intransitive verb
: to come apart in or break up into shreds
— shred·der *noun*
shredded wheat *noun* (1898)
: a breakfast cereal made from cooked partially dried wheat that is shredded and molded into biscuits which are then oven-baked and toasted
¹**shrew** \'shrü, *especially Southern* 'srü\ *noun* [Middle English *shrewe* evil or scolding person, from Old English *scrēawa* shrew (animal)] (before 12th century)
1 : any of a family (Soricidae) of small chiefly nocturnal insectivores related to the moles and distinguished by a long pointed snout, very small eyes, and velvety fur
2 : an ill-tempered scolding woman
— shrew·like \-,līk\ *adjective*
²**shrew** *transitive verb* (14th century)
obsolete : CURSE
shrewd \'shrüd, *especially Southern* 'srüd\ *adjective* [Middle English *shrewed*, from *shrewe* + ¹*-ed*] (13th century)
1 *archaic* : MISCHIEVOUS
2 *obsolete* : ABUSIVE, SHREWISH
3 *obsolete* : OMINOUS, DANGEROUS
4 a : SEVERE, HARD ⟨a *shrewd* knock⟩ **b** : SHARP, PIERCING ⟨a *shrewd* wind⟩
5 a : marked by clever discerning awareness and hardheaded acumen ⟨*shrewd* common sense⟩ **b** : given to wily and artful ways or dealing ⟨a *shrewd* operator⟩ ☆
— shrewd·ly *adverb*
— shrewd·ness *noun*
shrew·ish \'shrü-ish, *especially Southern* 'srü-\ *adjective* (1565)
: ILL-NATURED, INTRACTABLE
— shrew·ish·ly *adverb*

— shrew·ish·ness *noun*
shri \'shrē, 'srē\ *variant of* SRI
¹**shriek** \'shrēk, *especially Southern* 'srēk\ *verb* [Middle English *shreken*, probably irregular from *shriken* to shriek; akin to Old Norse *skrækja* to shriek] (15th century)
intransitive verb
1 : to utter a sharp shrill sound
2 a : to cry out in a high-pitched voice : SCREECH **b** : to suggest such a cry (as by vividness of expression) ⟨neon colors *shrieked* for attention —Calvin Tomkins⟩
transitive verb
1 : to utter with a shriek or sharply and shrilly ⟨*shriek* an alarm⟩
2 : to express in a manner suggestive of a shriek
²**shriek** *noun* (1590)
1 : a shrill usually wild or involuntary cry
2 : a sound resembling a shriek ⟨the *shriek* of chalk on the blackboard⟩
shrie·val \'shrē-vəl, *especially Southern* 'srē-\ *adjective* [obsolete *shrieve* sheriff, from Middle English *shirreve* — more at SHERIFF] (1681)
chiefly British : of or relating to a sheriff
shrie·val·ty \-vəl-tē\ *noun* (1502)
chiefly British : the office, term of office, or jurisdiction of a sheriff
shrieve \'shrēv, *especially Southern* 'srēv\ *archaic variant of* SHRIVE
shrift \'shrift, *especially Southern* 'srift\ *noun* [Middle English, from Old English *scrift*, from *scrīfan* to shrive — more at SHRIVE] (before 12th century)
1 *archaic* **a** : a remission of sins pronounced by a priest in the sacrament of reconciliation **b** : the act of shriving : CONFESSION
2 *obsolete* : CONFESSIONAL
shrike \'shrīk, *especially Southern* 'srīk\ *noun* [perhaps from (assumed) Middle English *shrik*, from Old English *scrīc* thrush; akin to Middle English *shriken* to shriek] (1544)
: any of numerous usually largely gray or brownish oscine birds (family Laniidae) that have a hooked bill, feed chiefly on insects, and often impale their prey on thorns
¹**shrill** \'shril, *especially Southern* 'sril\ *verb* [Middle English; probably akin to Old English *scrallettan* to resound loudly — more at SKIRL] (13th century)
transitive verb
: SCREAM

☆ **SYNONYMS**
Showy, pretentious, ostentatious mean given to excessive outward display. SHOWY implies an imposing or striking appearance but usually suggests cheapness or poor taste ⟨the performers' *showy* costumes⟩. PRETENTIOUS implies an appearance of importance not justified by the thing's value or the person's standing ⟨a *pretentious* parade of hard words⟩. OSTENTATIOUS stresses vainglorious display or parade ⟨the *ostentatious* summer homes of the rich⟩.

Shrewd, sagacious, perspicacious, astute mean acute in perception and sound in judgment. SHREWD stresses practical, hardheaded cleverness and judgment ⟨a *shrewd* judge of character⟩. SAGACIOUS suggests wisdom, penetration, and farsightedness ⟨*sagacious* investors got in on the ground floor⟩. PERSPICACIOUS implies unusual power to see through and understand what is puzzling or hidden ⟨a *perspicacious* counselor saw through the child's facade⟩. ASTUTE suggests shrewdness, perspicacity, and diplomatic skill ⟨an *astute* player of party politics⟩.

intransitive verb
: to utter or emit an acute piercing sound
²shrill *adjective* (14th century)
1 a : having or emitting a sharp high-pitched tone or sound **:** PIERCING **b :** accompanied by sharp high-pitched sounds or cries ⟨*shrill* gaiety⟩
2 : having a sharp or vivid effect on the senses ⟨*shrill* light⟩
3 : STRIDENT, INTEMPERATE ⟨*shrill* anger⟩ ⟨*shrill* criticism⟩
— **shrill** *adverb*
— **shrill·ness** *noun*
— **shril·ly** \'shril-lē, *especially Southern* 'sril-\ *adverb*
³shrill *noun* (1591)
: a shrill sound ⟨the *shrill* of the ship's whistle⟩
¹shrimp \'shrimp, *especially Southern* 'srimp\ *noun, plural* **shrimps** *or* **shrimp** [Middle English *shrimpe;* akin to Middle Low German *schrempen* to contract, wrinkle, Old Norse *skorpna* to shrivel up] (14th century)
1 : any of numerous mostly small and marine decapod crustaceans (suborders Dendrobranchiata and Pleocyemata) having a slender elongated body, a compressed abdomen, and a long spiny rostrum; *also* **:** a small crustacean (as an amphipod or a branchiopod) resembling the true shrimps
2 : a very small or puny person or thing
— **shrimp·like** \-,līk\ *adjective*
— **shrimpy** \'shrim-pē, 'srim-\ *adjective*
²shrimp *intransitive verb* (circa 1859)
: to fish for or catch shrimps
shrimp·er \'shrim-pər, *especially Southern* 'srim-\ *noun* (1851)
1 : a shrimp fisherman
2 : a boat engaged in shrimping
shrimp pink *noun* (1882)
: a deep pink
¹shrine \'shrīn, *especially Southern* 'srīn\ *noun* [Middle English, from Old English *scrīn,* from Latin *scrinium* case, chest] (before 12th century)
1 a : a case, box, or receptacle; *especially* **:** one in which sacred relics (as the bones of a saint) are deposited **b :** a place in which devotion is paid to a saint or deity **:** SANCTUARY **c :** a niche containing a religious image
2 : a receptacle (as a tomb) for the dead
3 : a place or object hallowed by its associations
²shrine *transitive verb* **shrined; shrin·ing** (14th century)
: ENSHRINE
Shrin·er \'shrī-nər, *especially Southern* 'srī-\ *noun* [Ancient Arabic Order of Nobles of the Mystic *Shrine*] (1886)
: a member of a secret fraternal society that is non-Masonic but admits only Knights Templars and 32d-degree Masons to membership
¹shrink \'shriŋk, *especially Southern* 'sriŋk\ *verb* **shrank** \'shraŋk, 'sraŋk\ *also* **shrunk** \'shrəŋk, 'srəŋk\; **shrunk** *or* **shrunk·en** \'shrəŋ-kən, 'srəŋ-\; **shrink·ing** [Middle English, from Old English *scrincan;* akin to Middle Dutch *schrinken* to draw back] (before 12th century)
intransitive verb
1 : to contract or curl up the body or part of it **:** HUDDLE, COWER
2 a : to contract to less extent or compass **b :** to become smaller or more compacted **c :** to lose substance or weight **d :** to lessen in value **:** DWINDLE
3 : to recoil instinctively (as from something painful or horrible) ⟨*shrank* from the challenge⟩
transitive verb
: to cause to contract or shrink; *specifically* **:** to compact (cloth) by causing to contract when subjected to washing, boiling, steaming, or other processes
synonym see CONTRACT, RECOIL

— **shrink·able** \'shriŋ-kə-bəl, 'sriŋ-\ *adjective*
— **shrink·er** *noun*
²shrink *noun* (1590)
1 : the act of shrinking
2 : SHRINKAGE
3 [short for *headshrinker*] **:** a clinical psychiatrist or psychologist ⟨regaling us with all the stories he never told his *shrink* —*Rolling Stone*⟩
shrink·age \'shriŋ-kij, *especially Southern* 'sriŋ-\ *noun* (1800)
1 : the act or process of shrinking
2 : the loss in weight of livestock during shipment and in the process of preparing the meat for consumption
3 : the amount lost by shrinkage
shrinking violet *noun* (1915)
: a bashful or retiring person
shrink–wrap \'shriŋk-,rap, *especially Southern* 'sriŋk-\ *transitive verb* (1966)
: to wrap (as a book or meat) in tough clear plastic film that is then shrunk (as by heating) to form a tightly fitting package
— **shrink–wrap** *noun*
shrive \'shrīv, *especially Southern* 'srīv\ *verb* **shrived** *or* **shrove** \'shrōv, 'srōv\; **shriv·en** \'shri-vən, 'sri-\ *or* **shrived; shriv·ing** [Middle English, from Old English *scrīfan* to shrive, prescribe (akin to Old High German *scrīban* to write), from Latin *scribere* to write — more at SCRIBE] (before 12th century)
transitive verb
1 : to administer the sacrament of reconciliation to
2 : to free from guilt
intransitive verb
archaic **:** to confess one's sins especially to a priest
shriv·el \'shri-vəl, *especially Southern* 'sri-\ *verb* **-eled** *or* **-elled; -el·ing** *or* **-el·ling** \'shri-vəl-iŋ, 'sri-; 'shriv-liŋ, 'sriv-\ [origin unknown] (1588)
intransitive verb
1 : to draw into wrinkles especially with a loss of moisture
2 a : to become reduced to inanition, helplessness, or inefficiency **b :** DWINDLE
transitive verb
: to cause to shrivel
shroff \'shräf, 'shrȯf, *especially Southern* 'sräf, 'srȯf\ *noun* [Hindi *śarāf,* from Arabic *ṣarrāf*] (1618)
: a banker or money changer in the Far East; *especially* **:** one who tests and evaluates coin
Shrop·shire \'shräp-,shir, -,shər, *especially US* -,shir, *especially Southern* 'sräp-\ *noun* [*Shropshire,* England] (1803)
: any of a breed of dark-faced hornless sheep of English origin that are raised for both mutton and wool
¹shroud \'shraủd, *especially Southern* 'sraủd\ *noun* [Middle English, garment, from Old English *scrūd;* akin to Old English *scrēade* shred — more at SHRED] (14th century)
1 *obsolete* **:** SHELTER, PROTECTION
2 : something that covers, screens, or guards: as
a : one of two flanges that give peripheral support to turbine or fan bedding **b :** a usually fiberglass guard that protects a spacecraft from the heat of launching
3 : burial garment **:** WINDING-SHEET, CEREMENT
4 a : one of the ropes leading usually in pairs from a ship's mastheads to give lateral support to the masts **b :** one of the cords that suspend the harness of a parachute from the canopy
²shroud (14th century)
transitive verb

1 a *archaic* **:** to cover for protection **b** *obsolete* **:** CONCEAL
2 a : to cut off from view **:** OBSCURE ⟨trees *shrouded* by a heavy fog⟩ **b :** to veil under another appearance (as by obscuring or disguising) ⟨*shrouded* the decision in a series of formalities⟩
3 : to dress for burial
intransitive verb
archaic **:** to seek shelter
Shrove·tide \'shrōv-,tīd, *especially Southern* 'srōv-\ *noun* [Middle English *schroftide,* from *schrof-* (from *shriven* to shrive) + *tide*] (15th century)
: the period usually of three days immediately preceding Ash Wednesday
Shrove Tuesday \'shrōv-, *especially Southern* 'srōv-\ *noun* [Middle English *schroftewesday,* from *schrof-* (as in *schroftide*) + *tewesday* Tuesday] (15th century)
: the Tuesday before Ash Wednesday
¹shrub \'shrəb, *especially Southern* 'srəb\ *noun* [Middle English *schrobbe,* from Old English *scrybb* brushwood; akin to Norwegian *skrubbebær* a cornel of a dwarf species] (before 12th century)
: a low usually several-stemmed woody plant
²shrub *noun* [Arabic *sharāb* beverage] (1747)
1 : an aged blend of fruit juice, sugar, and spirits served chilled and diluted with water
2 : a beverage made by adding acidulated fruit juice to iced water
shrub·bery \'shrə-b(ə-)rē, *especially Southern* 'srə-\ *noun, plural* **-ber·ies** (1748)
: a planting or growth of shrubs
shrub·by \'shrə-bē, *especially Southern* 'srə-\ *adjective* **shrub·bi·er; -est** (1540)
1 : consisting of or covered with shrubs
2 : resembling a shrub
¹shrug \'shrəg, *especially Southern* 'srəg\ *verb* **shrugged; shrug·ging** [Middle English *schruggen*] (14th century)
intransitive verb
: to raise or draw in the shoulders especially to express aloofness, indifference, or uncertainty
transitive verb
: to lift or contract (the shoulders) especially to express aloofness, indifference, or uncertainty
²shrug *noun* (1594)
1 : an act of shrugging
2 : a woman's small waist-length or shorter jacket
shrug off *transitive verb* (1904)
1 : to brush aside **:** MINIMIZE ⟨*shrugs off* the problem⟩
2 : to shake off ⟨*shrugging off* sleep⟩
3 : to remove (a garment) by wriggling out
shtetl *also* **shte·tel** \'shte-t°l, 'shtā-\ *noun, plural* **shtetl·ach** \'shtet-,läk, 'shtāt-\ *also* **shtetels** [Yiddish *shtetl,* from Middle High German *stetel,* diminutive of *stat* place, town, city, from Old High German, place — more at STEAD] (1949)
: a small Jewish town or village formerly found in Eastern Europe

1 shroud 4a

□ **USAGE**
shrink Although some people have apparently been taught that it is wrong, the past tense *shrunk* is perfectly standard if less common than *shrank* ⟨we watched fascinated, until the wolves *shrunk* to dots in the fog —Lyn Hancock⟩ ⟨the nodes *shrunk,* and for a year she was apparently free of disease —Elisabeth Rosenthal⟩ ⟨he and his chief operating officer . . . *shrunk* the headquarters staff further —*Business Week*⟩.

\ə\ abut \ᵊ\ kitten \ər\ **further** \a\ **ash** \ā\ **ace**
\ä\ **mop, mar** \aủ\ **out** \ch\ **chin** \e\ **bet** \ē\ **easy**
\g\ **go** \i\ **hit** \ī\ **ice** \j\ **job** \ŋ\ **sing** \ō\ **go**
\ȯ\ **law** \ȯi\ **boy** \th\ **thin** \th\ **the** \ü\ **loot** \ủ\ **foot**
\y\ **yet** \zh\ **vision** *see also* Guide to Pronunciation

shtick *also* **shtik** \'shtik\ *noun* [Yiddish *shtik* pranks, literally, piece, from Middle High German *stücke,* from Old High German *stucki;* akin to Old English *stycce* piece, Old High German *stoc* stick — more at STOCK] (1959) **1** : a show-business routine, gimmick, or gag : BIT **2** : one's special trait, interest, or activity : BAG ⟨he's alive and well and now doing his *shtick* out in Hollywood —Robert Daley⟩

¹shuck \'shək\ *noun* [origin unknown] (circa 1674) **1** : SHELL, HUSK: as **a** : the outer covering of a nut or of Indian corn **b** : the shell of an oyster or clam **2** : something of little value — usually used in plural often interjectionally ⟨not worth *shucks*⟩ ⟨*shucks,* it was nothing⟩

²shuck *transitive verb* (1772) **1** : to strip of shucks **2 a** : to peel off (as clothing) — often used with *off* **b** : to lay aside — often used with *off* ⟨bad habits are being *shucked* off —A. W. Smith⟩
— **shuck·er** *noun*

¹shud·der \'shə-dər\ *intransitive verb* **shud·dered; shud·der·ing** \-d(ə-)riŋ\ [Middle English *shoddren;* akin to Old High German *skutten* to shake and perhaps to Lithuanian *kutéti* to shake up] (13th century) **1** : to tremble convulsively : SHIVER **2** : QUIVER

²shudder *noun* (1607) : an act of shuddering
— **shud·dery** \-d(ə-)rē\ *adjective*

¹shuf·fle \'shə-fəl\ *verb* **shuf·fled; shuf·fling** \-f(ə-)liŋ\ [perhaps irregular from ¹*shove*] (1570) *transitive verb* **1** : to mix in a mass confusedly : JUMBLE **2** : to put or thrust aside or under cover ⟨*shuffled* the whole matter out of his mind⟩ **3 a** : to rearrange (as playing cards, dominoes, or tiles) to produce a random order **b** : to move about, back and forth, or from one place to another : SHIFT ⟨*shuffle* funds among various accounts⟩ **4 a** : to move (as the feet) by sliding along or back and forth without lifting **b** : to perform (as a dance) with a dragging, sliding step *intransitive verb* **1** : to work into or out of trickily ⟨*shuffled* out of the difficulty⟩ **2** : to act or speak in a shifty or evasive manner **3 a** : to move or walk in a sliding dragging manner without lifting the feet **b** : to dance in a lazy nonchalant manner with sliding and tapping motions of the feet **c** : to execute in a perfunctory or clumsy manner **4** : to mix playing cards or counters by shuffling
— **shuf·fler** \-f(ə-)lər\ *noun*

²shuffle *noun* (1628) **1** : an evasion of the issue : EQUIVOCATION **2 a** : an act of shuffling (as of cards) **b** : a right or turn to shuffle ⟨was reminded that it was his *shuffle*⟩ **c** : JUMBLE ⟨lost in the *shuffle* of papers⟩ **3 a** : a dragging sliding movement; *specifically* : a sliding or scraping step in dancing **b** : a dance characterized by such a step

shuf·fle·board \'shə-fəl-ˌbōrd, -ˌbȯrd\ *noun* [alteration of obsolete English *shove-board*] (1836) **1** : a game in which players use long-handled cues to shove disks into scoring areas of a diagram marked on a smooth surface **2** : a diagram on which shuffleboard is played

shul \'shùl\ *noun* [Yiddish, school, synagogue, from Middle High German *schuol* school] (circa 1874) : SYNAGOGUE

shun \'shən\ *transitive verb* **shunned; shun·ning** [Middle English *shunnen,* from Old English *scunian*] (before 12th century) : to avoid deliberately and especially habitually
synonym see ESCAPE
— **shun·ner** *noun*

shun-pike \'shən-ˌpīk\ *noun* (1862) : a side road used to avoid the toll on or the speed and traffic of a superhighway
— **shun·pik·er** \-ˌpī-kər\ *noun*
— **shun·pik·ing** \-kiŋ\ *noun*

¹shunt \'shənt\ *verb* [Middle English, to flinch] (13th century) *transitive verb* **1 a** : to turn off to one side : SHIFT ⟨was *shunted* aside⟩ **b** : to switch (as a train) from one track to another **2** : to provide with or divert by means of an electrical shunt **3** : to divert (blood) from one part to another by a surgical shunt **4** : SHUTTLE ⟨*shunted* the missiles from shelter to shelter⟩ *intransitive verb* **1** : to move to the side **2** : to travel back and forth ⟨*shunted* between the two towns⟩
— **shunt·er** *noun*

²shunt *noun* (circa 1859) **1** : a means or mechanism for turning or thrusting aside: as **a** *chiefly British* : a railroad switch **b** : a conductor joining two points in an electrical circuit so as to form a parallel or alternative path through which a portion of the current may pass (as for regulating the amount passing in the main circuit) **c** : a surgical passage created between two blood vessels to divert blood from one part to another **2** : an accident (as a collision between two cars) especially in auto racing

shush \'shəsh, 'shùsh\ *transitive verb* [imitative] (1925) : to urge to be quiet : HUSH
— **shush** *noun*

¹shut \'shət\ *verb* **shut; shut·ting** [Middle English *shutten,* from Old English *scyttan;* akin to Middle Dutch *schutten* to shut in, Old English *scēotan* to shoot — more at SHOOT] (before 12th century) *transitive verb* **1 a** : to move into position to close an opening ⟨*shut* the lid⟩ **b** : to prevent entrance to or passage to or from **2** : to confine by or as if by enclosure ⟨*shut* herself in her study⟩ **3** : to fasten with a lock or bolt **4** : to close by bringing enclosing or covering parts together ⟨*shut* the eyes⟩ **5** : to cause to cease or suspend an operation or activity — often used with *down* *intransitive verb* **1** : to close itself or become closed ⟨flowers that *shut* at night⟩ **2** : to cease or suspend an operation or activity — often used with *down*

²shut *adjective* (15th century) **1** : closed, fastened, or folded together **2** : RID, CLEAR, FREE — usually used with *of*

³shut *noun* (1667) : the act of shutting

shut·down \'shət-ˌdaùn\ *noun* (1888) : the cessation or suspension of an operation or activity

shut down *intransitive verb* (1779) : to settle so as to obscure vision : CLOSE IN ⟨the night *shut down* early⟩

shute *variant of* CHUTE

shut–eye \'shət-ˌī\ *noun* (1899) : SLEEP ⟨get some *shut-eye*⟩

¹shut-in \'shət-ˌin\ *noun* (1903) **1** : an invalid confined to home, a room, or bed **2** : a narrow gorge-shaped part of an otherwise wide valley **3** : available oil or gas which is not being produced from an existing well

²shut-in \'shət-'in\ *adjective* (1909) **1** : confined to one's home or an institution by illness or incapacity **2 a** : SECRETIVE, BROODING ⟨a bitter, *shut-in* face —Claudia Cassidy⟩ **b** : tending to avoid social contact ⟨the *shut-in* personality type —S. K. Weinberg⟩

shut in *transitive verb* (14th century) **1** : CONFINE, ENCLOSE **2** : to prevent production of (oil or gas) by closing down a well

shut-off \'shət-ˌȯf\ *noun* (1869) **1** : something (as a valve) that shuts off **2** : STOPPAGE, INTERRUPTION

shut off (1824) *transitive verb* **1 a** : to cut off (as flow or passage) : STOP ⟨*shuts off* the oxygen supply⟩ **b** : to stop the operation of (as a machine) ⟨*shut* the motor *off*⟩ **2** : to close off : SEPARATE — usually used with *from* ⟨*shut off* from the rest of the world⟩ *intransitive verb* : to cease operating : STOP ⟨*shuts off* automatically⟩

shut·out \'shət-ˌaùt\ *noun* (1889) **1** : a game or contest in which one side fails to score **2** : a preemptive bid in bridge

shut out *transitive verb* (14th century) **1** : EXCLUDE **2** : to prevent (an opponent) from scoring in a game or contest **3** : to forestall the bidding of (bridge opponents) by making a high or preemptive bid

¹shut·ter \'shə-tər\ *noun* (1542) **1** : one that shuts **2** : a usually movable cover or screen for a window or door **3** : a mechanical device that limits the passage of light; *especially* : a camera attachment that exposes the film or plate by opening and closing an aperture **4** : the movable louvers in a pipe organ by which the swell box is opened
— **shut·ter·less** \-ləs\ *adjective*

²shutter *transitive verb* (1826) **1** : to close by or as if by shutters **2** : to furnish with shutters

shut·ter·bug \'shə-tər-ˌbəg\ *noun* (1940) : a photography enthusiast

¹shut·tle \'shə-t°l\ *noun* [Middle English *shittle,* probably from Old English *scytel* bar, bolt; akin to Old Norse *skutill* bolt, Old English *scēotan* to shoot — more at SHOOT] (14th century) **1 a** : a device used in weaving for passing the thread of the weft between the threads of the warp **b** : a spindle-shaped device holding the thread in tatting, knotting, or netting **c** : a sliding thread holder for the lower thread of a sewing machine that carries the lower thread through a loop of the upper thread to make a stitch **2** : SHUTTLECOCK **3 a** : a going back and forth regularly over an often short route used by a vehicle **b** : an established route used in a shuttle; *also* : a vehicle used in a shuttle **c** : SPACE SHUTTLE
— **shut·tle·less** *adjective*

²shuttle *verb* **shut·tled; shut·tling** \'shət-liŋ, 'shə-t°l-iŋ\ (1550) *transitive verb* **1** : to cause to move or travel back and forth frequently **2** : to transport in, by, or as if by a shuttle *intransitive verb* **1** : to move or travel back and forth frequently **2** : to move by or as if by a shuttle

¹shut·tle·cock \'shə-t°l-ˌkäk\ *noun* (1522) : a lightweight conical object with a rounded often rubber-covered nose that is used in badminton

shuttlecock

²shuttlecock *transitive verb* (1687) : to send or toss to and fro : BANDY

shuttle diplomacy *noun* (1974)
: negotiations especially between nations carried on by an intermediary who shuttles back and forth between the disputants

shut up (1814)
transitive verb
: to cause (a person) to stop talking
intransitive verb
: to cease writing or speaking

¹shy \'shī\ *adjective* **shi·er** *or* **shy·er** \'shī-(ə)r\; **shi·est** *or* **shy·est** \'shī-əst\ [Middle English *schey,* from Old English *scēoh;* akin to Old High German *sciuhen* to frighten off] (before 12th century)
1 : easily frightened : TIMID
2 : disposed to avoid a person or thing ⟨publicity *shy*⟩ ⟨book-*shy* children⟩
3 : hesitant in committing oneself : CIRCUMSPECT
4 : sensitively diffident or retiring : RESERVED ⟨a *shy* seclusive person⟩; *also* : expressive of such a state or nature ⟨spoke in a *shy* voice⟩
5 : SECLUDED, HIDDEN
6 : having less than the full or specified amount or number : SHORT ⟨just *shy* of six feet tall⟩ ⟨the stew is a little *shy* of seasoning⟩
7 : DISREPUTABLE ⟨gambling hells and *shy* saloons —*Blackwood's*⟩ ☆
— **shy·ly** *adverb*
— **shy·ness** *noun*

²shy *intransitive verb* **shied; shy·ing** (1650)
1 : to develop or show a dislike or distaste — usually used with *from* or *away from* ⟨an author who *shies* away from publicity⟩
2 : to start suddenly aside through fright or alarm

³shy *noun, plural* **shies** (1791)
: a sudden start aside (as from fright)

⁴shy *verb* **shied; shy·ing** [perhaps from ¹*shy*] (1787)
intransitive verb
: to make a sudden throw
transitive verb
: to throw (an object) with a jerk : FLING

⁵shy *noun, plural* **shies** (1791)
1 : the act of shying : TOSS, THROW
2 : a verbal fling or attack
3 : COCKSHY

¹shy·lock \'shī-ˌläk\ *noun*
1 *capitalized* : the Jewish usurer and antagonist of Antonio in Shakespeare's *The Merchant of Venice*
2 : an extortionate creditor : LOAN SHARK

²shylock *intransitive verb* (circa 1934)
: to lend money at high rates of interest ⟨exposé of systematic thievery . . . *shylocking,* and murder —*Current Biography*⟩

shy·ster \'shīs-tər\ *noun* [probably from German *Scheisser,* literally, defecator] (1844)
: one who is professionally unscrupulous especially in the practice of law or politics : PETTIFOGGER ◆

si \'sē\ *noun* [Italian] (1728)
: ²TI

si·al·a·gogue \sī-'a-lə-ˌgäg\ *noun* [New Latin *sialagogus* promoting the expulsion of saliva, from Greek *sialon* saliva + New Latin *-agogus* -agogue] (circa 1783)
: an agent that promotes the flow of saliva

si·al·ic \sī-'a-lik\ *adjective* [International Scientific Vocabulary *sil*icon + *al*uminum] (1924)
: of, relating to, or being relatively light rock that is rich in silica and alumina and is typical of the outer layers of the earth

sialic acid *noun* [Greek *sialon* saliva] (1952)
: any of a group of reducing amido acids that are essentially carbohydrates and are found especially as components of blood glycoproteins and mucoproteins

si·a·mang \'sē-ə-ˌmaŋ, 'sī-\ *noun* [Malay] (1822)
: a black gibbon (*Hylobates syndactylus*) of Sumatra and the Malay Peninsula that is the largest of the gibbons

¹Si·a·mese \ˌsī-ə-'mēz, -'mēs\ *adjective* [*Siam* (Thailand); in senses 2 & 3, from *Siamese twin*] (1693)
1 : of, relating to, or characteristic of Thailand, the Thais, or their language
2 : exhibiting great resemblance : very like
3 *not capitalized* : connecting two or more pipes or hoses so as to permit discharge in a single stream

²Siamese *noun, plural* **Siamese** (1693)
1 : THAI 2
2 : THAI 3
3 : SIAMESE CAT

Siamese cat *noun* (1871)
: any of a breed of slender blue-eyed short-haired domestic cats of oriental origin with pale fawn or gray body and darker ears, paws, tail, and face

Siamese fighting fish *noun* (1933)
: a brightly colored betta (*Betta splendens*) that has highly aggressive males and is a popular aquarium fish

Siamese fighting fish

Siamese twin *noun* [from Chang (died 1874) and Eng (died 1874) congenitally united twins born in Siam] (1829)
: one of a pair of congenitally united twins in humans or other vertebrates

sib \'sib\ *adjective* [Middle English, from Old English *sibb,* from *sibb* kinship; akin to Old High German *sippa* kinship, family, Latin *sodalis* comrade, Greek *ēthos* custom, character, Latin *suus* one's own — more at SUICIDE] (before 12th century)
: related by blood : AKIN

²sib *noun* (before 12th century)
1 a : KINDRED, RELATIVES **b** : a blood relation : KINSMAN
2 : a brother or sister considered irrespective of sex; *broadly* : any plant or animal of a group sharing a degree of genetic relationship corresponding to that of human sibs
3 : a group of persons unilaterally descended from a real or supposed ancestor

Si·be·ri·an husky \sī-'bir-ē-ən-\ *noun* (1930)
: any of a breed of medium-sized thick-coated compact dogs that were developed in Siberia for use as sled dogs and that have erect ears and a bushy tail

Siberian husky

sib·i·lance \'si-bə-lən(t)s\ *noun* (1823)
: a sibilant quality or sound

¹sib·i·lant \'si-bə-lənt\ *adjective* [Latin *sibilant-, sibilans,* present participle of *sibilare* to hiss, whistle, of imitative origin] (1669)
: having, containing, or producing the sound of or a sound resembling that of the *s* or the *sh* in *sash* ⟨a *sibilant* affricate⟩ ⟨a *sibilant* snake⟩
— **sib·i·lant·ly** *adverb*

²sibilant *noun* (1788)
: a sibilant speech sound (as English \s\, \z\, \sh\, \zh\, \ch(=tsh)\, or \j(=dzh)\)

sib·i·late \'si-bə-ˌlāt\ *verb* **-lat·ed; -lat·ing** [Latin *sibilatus,* past participle of *sibilare*] (circa 1656)
intransitive verb
1 : HISS
2 : to utter an initial sibilant : prefix an \s\ sound
transitive verb
1 : HISS
2 : to pronounce with an initial sibilant : prefix an \s\-sound to
— **sib·i·la·tion** \ˌsi-bə-'lā-shən\ *noun*

sib·ling \'si-bliŋ\ *noun* (before 12th century)

1 : SIB 2; *also* : one of two or more individuals having one common parent
2 : one of two or more things related by a common tie or characteristic

sibling species *noun* (1940)
: one of two or more species that are nearly indistinguishable morphologically

sib·yl \'si-bəl\ *noun, often capitalized* [Middle English *sibile, sybylle,* from Middle French & Latin; Middle French *sibile,* from Latin *sibylla,* from Greek] (14th century)
1 : any of several prophetesses usually accepted as 10 in number and credited to widely separate parts of the ancient world (as Babylonia, Egypt, Greece, and Italy)
2 a : a female prophet **b** : FORTUNE-TELLER
— **si·byl·ic** *or* **si·byl·lic** \sə-'bi-lik\ *adjective*
— **sib·yl·line** \'si-bə-ˌlīn, -ˌlēn\ *adjective*

¹sic \'sik\ *chiefly Scottish variant of* SUCH

²sic *also* **sick** \'sik\ *transitive verb* **sicced** *also* **sicked** \'sikt\; **sic·cing** *also* **sick·ing** [alteration of *seek*] (1845)
1 : CHASE, ATTACK — usually used as a command especially to a dog ⟨*sic* 'em⟩
2 : to incite or urge to an attack, pursuit, or harassment : SET

³sic \'sik, 'sēk\ *adverb* [Latin, so, thus — more at SO] (circa 1859)

◇ **WORD HISTORY**
shyster The early history of *shyster* has prompted much speculation concerning its etymology, the origin of the word having been attributed to any number of languages or to any of various eponyms. The earliest known instance of *shyster* in print occurred in 1843, in the pages of *The Subterranean,* a New York City weekly that concerned itself with the goings-on in and about the Tombs (the city jail) and the local courts. Among the favorite targets of the muckraking paper's publisher and chief writer, Mike Walsh, were the unlicensed and unprincipled men who haunted the courthouse, pretending to be lawyers. After lambasting them as "pettifoggers," Walsh was approached by one of them—a Cornelius Terhune—who asked that the past masters of pettifoggery (himself included) not be lumped together with the amateurs. Terhune dismissed these lesser practitioners as *shiseters* (Walsh's spelling; he also used *shyseters*). Terhune's epithet was probably derived from the German vulgarism *Scheisser,* the literal meaning of which is "one that defecates." Walsh's repeated use of *shyster* (his final spelling) in *The Subterranean* led to the adoption of the word by other newspapers.

\ə\ abut \ᵊ\ kitten \ər\ further \a\ ash \ā\ ace \ä\ mop, mar \aú\ out \ch\ chin \e\ bet \ē\ easy \g\ go \i\ hit \ī\ ice \j\ job \ŋ\ sing \ō\ go \ó\ law \ói\ boy \th\ thin \th\ the \ü\ loot \ú\ foot \y\ yet \zh\ vision *see also* Guide to Pronunciation

: intentionally so written — used after a printed word or passage to indicate that it is intended exactly as printed or to indicate that it exactly reproduces an original ⟨said he seed [*sic*] it all⟩

Sichuan *variant of* SZECHUAN

sick \'sik\ *adjective* [Middle English *sek, sik,* from Old English *sēoc;* akin to Old High German *sioh* sick] (before 12th century)
1 a (1) : affected with disease or ill health : AILING (2) : of, relating to, or intended for use in sickness ⟨*sick* pay⟩ ⟨a *sick* ward⟩ **b** : QUEASY, NAUSEATED ⟨*sick* to one's stomach⟩ ⟨was *sick* in the car⟩ **c** : undergoing menstruation
2 : spiritually or morally unsound or corrupt
3 a : sickened by strong emotion ⟨*sick* with fear⟩ ⟨worried *sick*⟩ **b** : having a strong distaste from surfeit : SATIATED ⟨*sick* of flattery⟩ **c** : filled with disgust or chagrin ⟨gossip makes me *sick*⟩ **d** : depressed and longing for something ⟨*sick* for one's home⟩
4 a : mentally or emotionally unsound or disordered : MORBID ⟨*sick* thoughts⟩ **b** : MACABRE, SADISTIC ⟨*sick* jokes⟩
5 : lacking vigor : SICKLY: as **a** : badly outclassed ⟨looked *sick* in the contest⟩ **b** : incapable of yielding a profitable crop especially because of buildup of disease organisms ⟨clover-*sick* soils⟩

sick and tired *adjective* (1783)
: thoroughly fatigued or bored; *also* : FED UP

sick bay *noun* (1813)
: a compartment in a ship used as a dispensary and hospital; *broadly* : a place for the care of the sick or injured

sick·bed \'sik-,bed\ *noun* (14th century)
: the bed on which one lies sick

sick call *noun* (1836)
: a scheduled time at which individuals (as soldiers) may report as sick to the medical officer

sick day *noun* (1968)
: a paid day of sick leave

sick·en \'si-kən\ *verb* **sick·ened; sick·en·ing** \'si-kə-niŋ, 'si-niŋ\ (13th century)
intransitive verb
1 : to become sick
2 : to become weary or satiated
transitive verb
1 : to make sick
2 : to cause revulsion in as a result of weariness or satiety
— **sick·en·er** \'si-kə-nər, 'si-nər\ *noun*

sick·en·ing \-niŋ\ *adjective* (1789)
: causing sickness or disgust ⟨a *sickening* odor⟩ ⟨a *sickening* display⟩
— **sick·en·ing·ly** \-niŋ-lē\ *adverb*

sick·er \'si-kər\ *adjective* [Middle English *siker,* from Old English *sicor,* from Latin *securus* secure] (before 12th century)
chiefly Scottish : SECURE, SAFE; *also* : DEPENDABLE
— **sicker** *adverb, chiefly Scottish*
— **sick·er·ly** *adverb, chiefly Scottish*

sick headache *noun* (1778)
: MIGRAINE

sick·ie \'si-kē\ *noun* (1967)
: a person who is mentally or morally sick

sick·ish \'si-kish\ *adjective* (1581)
1 *archaic* : somewhat ill : SICKLY
2 : somewhat nauseated : QUEASY
3 : somewhat sickening ⟨a *sickish* odor⟩
— **sick·ish·ly** *adverb*
— **sick·ish·ness** *noun*

¹sick·le \'si-kəl\ *noun* [Middle English *sikel,* from Old English *sicol,* from Latin *secula* sickle, from *secare* to cut — more at SAW] (before 12th century)
1 : an agricultural implement consisting of a curved metal blade with a short handle fitted on a tang

¹sickle 1

2 : the cutting mechanism (as of a reaper, combine, or mower) consisting of a bar with a series of cutting elements

²sickle *adjective* (1688)
: having the form of a sickle blade : having a curve similar to that of a sickle blade ⟨the *sickle* moon⟩

³sickle *verb* **sick·led; sick·ling** \'si-k(ə-)liŋ\ (1922)
transitive verb
1 : to mow or reap with a sickle
2 : to change (a red blood cell) into a sickle cell
intransitive verb
: to change into a sickle cell ⟨the ability of red blood cells to *sickle*⟩

sick leave *noun* (1840)
1 : an absence from work permitted because of illness
2 : the number of days per year for which an employer agrees to pay employees who are sick

sickle cell *noun* (1923)
: an abnormal red blood cell of crescent shape

sickle–cell anemia *noun* (1922)
: a chronic inherited anemia in which a large proportion or the majority of the red blood cells tend to sickle, which occurs primarily in individuals of African, Mediterranean, or southwest Asian ancestry, and which results from homozygosity for a semidominant gene — called also *sickle-cell disease*

sickle–cell trait *noun* (1928)
: an inherited blood condition in which some red blood cells tend to sickle but usually not enough to produce anemia, which occurs primarily in individuals of African, Mediterranean, or southwest Asian ancestry, and which results from heterozygosity for a semidominant gene

sick·le·mia \,si-kə-'lē-mē-ə\ *noun* [New Latin, from English *sickle* (cell) + New Latin *-emia*] (1932)
: SICKLE-CELL TRAIT

¹sick·ly \'si-klē\ *adjective* (14th century)
1 : somewhat unwell; *also* : habitually ailing
2 : produced by or associated with sickness ⟨a *sickly* complexion⟩ ⟨a *sickly* appetite⟩
3 : producing or tending to produce disease : UNWHOLESOME ⟨a *sickly* climate⟩
4 a : appearing as if sick **b** : lacking in vigor : WEAK ⟨a *sickly* plant⟩
5 : SICKENING ⟨a *sickly* odor⟩ ⟨a *sickly* green⟩
— **sick·li·ness** *noun*
— **sickly** *adverb*

²sickly *transitive verb* **sick·lied; sick·ly·ing** (1763)
: to make sick or sickly

sick·ness \'sik-nəs\ *noun* (before 12th century)
1 a : ill health : ILLNESS **b** : a disordered, weakened, or unsound condition
2 : a specific disease
3 : NAUSEA, QUEASINESS

sicko \'si-(,)kō\ *noun, plural* **sick·os** (1963)
: SICKIE

sick–out \'sik-,aut\ *noun* (1951)
: an organized absence from work by workers on the pretext of sickness

sick pay *noun* (1887)
: salary or wages paid to an employee while on sick leave

sick·room \'sik-,rüm, -,rum\ *noun* (1749)
: a room in which a person is confined by sickness

sic pas·sim \'sik-'pa-səm, 'sēk-'pä-sim\ *adverb* [Latin] (1921)
: so throughout — used of a word or idea to be found throughout a book or a writer's work

sid·dur \'si-dər, -,dur\ *noun, plural* **sid·du·rim** \sə-'dur-əm\ [Late Hebrew *siddūr,* literally, order, arrangement] (1864)
: a Jewish prayer book containing liturgies for daily, Sabbath, and holiday observances

¹side \'sīd\ *noun* [Middle English, from Old English *sīde;* akin to Old High German *sīta* side, Old English *sīd* ample, wide] (before 12th century)
1 a : the right or left part of the wall or trunk of the body ⟨a pain in the *side*⟩ **b** (1) : one of the halves of the animal body on either side of the mesial plane (2) : a cut of meat including that about the ribs of one half of the body — used chiefly of smoked pork products **c** : one longitudinal half of a hide
2 : a place, space, or direction with respect to a center or to a line of division (as of an aisle, river, or street)
3 a : one of the longer bounding surfaces or lines of an object especially contrasted with the ends ⟨the *side* of a barn⟩ **b** : a line or surface forming a border or face of an object ⟨a die has six *sides*⟩ ⟨the back *side* of the moon⟩ **c** : either surface of a thin object ⟨one *side* of a record⟩ ⟨right *side* of the cloth⟩ **d** : a bounding line of a geometric figure ⟨*side* of a triangle⟩
4 a : the space beside one ⟨stood by my *side*⟩ **b** : an area next to something — usually used in combination ⟨a pool*side* interview⟩
5 : a slope (as of a hill) considered as opposed to another slope ⟨the far *side* of the hill⟩
6 a : the attitude or activity of one person or group with respect to another : PART ⟨there was no malice on my *side*⟩ **b** : a position that is opposite to or contrasted with another ⟨two *sides* to every question⟩ ⟨came down on the *side* of law and order⟩ **c** : a body of partisans or contestants ⟨victory for neither *side*⟩ **d** : TEAM ⟨11 players on each *side*⟩
7 : a line of descent traced through one's parent ⟨grandfather on his mother's *side*⟩
8 : an aspect or part of something contrasted with some other real or implied aspect or part ⟨the better *side* of his nature⟩ ⟨the sales *side* of the business⟩ ⟨the seasoning is a bit on the heavy *side*⟩
9 *British* : sideways spin imparted to a billiard or snooker ball
10 : a sheet containing the lines and cues for a single theatrical role
11 : a recording of music
12 : a side order or dish ⟨a *side* of fries⟩
— **on the side 1** : in addition to the main portion **2** : in addition to a principal occupation
— **this side of** : short of : ALMOST ⟨an attitude just *this side of* scandalous⟩

²side *adjective* (14th century)
1 a : situated on the side ⟨*side* window⟩ **b** : of or relating to the side
2 a : directed toward or from the side ⟨*side* thrust⟩ ⟨*side* wind⟩ **b** : INCIDENTAL, INDIRECT ⟨*side* issue⟩ ⟨*side* remark⟩ **c** : made on the side ⟨*side* payment⟩ **d** : additional to the main portion ⟨*side* order of french fries⟩

³side *verb* **sid·ed; sid·ing** (1591)
transitive verb
1 : to agree with : SUPPORT
2 : to be side by side with
3 : to set or put aside : clear away ⟨*side* the dishes⟩
4 : to furnish with sides or siding ⟨*side* a house⟩
intransitive verb
: to take sides : join or form sides ⟨*sided* with the rebels⟩

⁴side *noun* [obsolete English *side* proud, boastful] (1878)
chiefly British : swaggering or arrogant manner : PRETENTIOUSNESS

side·arm \'sīd-,ärm\ *adjective* (1908)
: of, relating to, using, or being a baseball pitching style in which the arm is not raised above the shoulder and the ball is thrown with a sideways sweep of the arm between shoulder and hip ⟨*sidearm* delivery⟩
— **sidearm** *adverb*

side arm *noun* (1689)

: a weapon (as a sword, revolver, or bayonet) worn at the side or in the belt

side·band \-,band\ *noun* (1922)
: the band of frequencies (as of radio waves) on either side of the carrier frequency produced by modulation

side·bar \-,bär\ *noun* (1945)
: a short news story accompanying and presenting sidelights of a major story

side bearing *noun* (circa 1894)
: the space provided at each side of a typeset letter to prevent its touching adjoining letters

side·board \'sīd-,bōrd, -,bòrd\ *noun* (1671)
: a piece of dining-room furniture having compartments and shelves for holding articles of table service

side·burns
\-,bərnz\ *noun plural* [anagram of *burnsides*] (1887)
1 : SIDE-WHISKERS
2 : continuations of the hairline in front of the ears ◇
— **side·burned** \-,bərnd\ *adjective*

side by side *adverb* (13th century)
1 : beside one another
2 : in the same place, time, or circumstance ⟨lived peacefully *side by side* for many years⟩
— **side–by–side** *adjective*

side·car \'sīd-,kär\ *noun* (1904)
1 : a car attached to the side of a motorcycle for a passenger
2 : a cocktail consisting of a liqueur with lemon juice and brandy

side chain *noun* (1886)
: a shorter chain or group of atoms attached to a principal chain or to a ring in a molecule

side chair *noun* (1925)
: a chair without arms used usually in a dining room

sid·ed \'sī-dəd\ *adjective* (15th century)
: having sides often of a specified number or kind ⟨one-*sided*⟩ ⟨glass-*sided*⟩
— **sid·ed·ness** *noun*

side dish *noun* (1725)
: a food served separately along with the main course

side·dress \'sīd-,dres\ *noun* (1966)
: SIDE-DRESSING
— **side–dress** \'sīd-,dres\ *transitive verb*

side–dress·ing \-,dre-siŋ\ *noun* (1935)
1 : plant nutrients placed on or in the soil near the roots of a growing crop often by means of a cultivator having a fertilizer-distributing attachment
2 : the act or process of applying side-dressing to a crop

side drum *noun* (circa 1800)
: SNARE DRUM

side effect *noun* (1884)
: a secondary and usually adverse effect (as of a drug) ⟨toxic *side effects*⟩ — called also *side reaction*

side–glance \'sīd-,glan(t)s\ *noun* (1611)
1 : a glance directed to the side
2 : a passing allusion : an indirect or slight reference

side·hill \-,hil\ *noun* (1674)
: HILLSIDE
— **sidehill** *adjective*

side horse *noun* (circa 1934)
: POMMEL HORSE

side·kick \'sīd-,kik\ *noun* (1906)
: a person closely associated with another as subordinate or partner

side·light \-,līt\ *noun* (1610)
1 a : light coming or produced from the side b : incidental light or information
2 : the red light on the port bow or the green light on the starboard bow carried by ships under way at night

¹**side·line** \-,līn\ *noun* (1862)

1 : a line at right angles to a goal line or end line and marking a side of a court or field of play for athletic games
2 a : a line of goods sold in addition to one's principal line b : a business or activity pursued in addition to one's regular occupation
3 a : the space immediately outside the lines along either side of an athletic field or court b : a sphere of little or no participation or activity — usually used in plural

²**sideline** *transitive verb* (1943)
: to put out of action : put on the sidelines

side·lin·er \'sīd-,lī-nər\ *noun* (1947)
: one that remains on the sidelines during an activity : one that does not participate

¹**side·ling** \'sīd-liŋ\ *adverb* [Middle English *sidling*, from ¹*side* + ²-*ling*] (14th century)
archaic : in a sidelong direction : SIDEWAYS

²**sideling** *adjective* (1611)
1 *archaic* : directed toward one side : OBLIQUE
2 *archaic* : having an inclination : SLOPING ⟨*sideling* ground⟩

¹**side·long** \'sīd-,lòŋ\ *adverb* [alteration of ¹*sideling*] (14th century)
1 : SIDEWAYS, OBLIQUELY
2 *archaic* : on the side

²**sidelong** *adjective* (1597)
1 : lying or inclining to one side : SLANTING
2 a : directed to one side ⟨*sidelong* looks⟩ b : indirect rather than straightforward

side·man \'sīd-,man\ *noun* (1936)
: a member of a band or orchestra and especially of a jazz or swing orchestra

side·piece \-,pēs\ *noun* (1802)
: a piece forming or contained in the side of something ⟨the *sidepiece* of a carriage⟩

sider- *or* **sidero-** *combining form* [Middle French, from Latin, from Greek *sidēr-*, *sidēro-*, from *sidēros*]
: iron ⟨hemo*siderin*⟩ ⟨*sidero*lite⟩

-sid·er \'sī-dər\ *combining form*
: one placed or living in a usually specified side (as a section of the city) ⟨an east-*sider*⟩

si·de·re·al \sī-'dir-ē-əl, sə-\ *adjective* [Latin *sidereus*, from *sider-*, *sidus* star, constellation] (1647)
: of, relating to, or expressed in relation to stars or constellations : ASTRAL

sidereal day *noun* (1794)
: the interval between two successive transits of a point on the celestial sphere (as the vernal equinox) over the upper meridian of a place
: 23 hours, 56 minutes, 4.1 seconds of mean time

sidereal hour *noun* (circa 1891)
: the 24th part of a sidereal day

sidereal minute *noun* (circa 1909)
: the 60th part of a sidereal hour

sidereal month *noun* (1868)
: the mean time of the moon's revolution in its orbit with reference to a star's position : 27 days, 7 hours, 43 minutes, 11.5 seconds of mean time

sidereal second *noun* (circa 1909)
: the 60th part of a sidereal minute

sidereal time *noun* (1812)
1 : time based on the sidereal day
2 : the hour angle of the vernal equinox at a place

sidereal year *noun* (1681)
: the time in which the earth completes one revolution in its orbit around the sun measured with respect to the fixed stars : 365 days, 6 hours, 9 minutes, and 9.5 seconds of mean time

¹**sid·er·ite** \'si-də-,rīt\ *noun* [German *Siderit*, from Greek *sidēros* iron] (1850)
: a native ferrous carbonate $FeCO_3$ that is a valuable iron ore

²**siderite** *noun* (1875)
: a nickel-iron meteorite

side road *noun* (1854)
: a smaller road off a main road

si·de·ro·lite \sī-'dir-ə-,līt, 'si-də-rə-\ *noun* (1863)
: a stony iron meteorite

side·sad·dle \'sīd-,sa-d°l\ *noun* (15th century)
: a saddle for women in which the rider sits with both legs on the same side of the horse
— **sidesaddle** *adverb*

side–scan sonar \-,skan-\ *noun* (1967)
: a sonar that scans the ocean floor to the side of a ship's track and is used especially for mapping the ocean bottom

side·show \-,shō\ *noun* (1846)
1 : a minor show offered in addition to a main exhibition (as of a circus)
2 : an incidental diversion or spectacle

side·slip \-,slip\ *intransitive verb* (1887)
1 : to skid or slide sideways
2 : to slide sideways through the air in a downward direction in an airplane along an inclined lateral axis
— **sideslip** *noun*

side·spin \-,spin\ *noun* (1926)
: a rotary motion that causes a ball to revolve horizontally

side·split·ting \-,spli-tiŋ\ *adjective* (1856)
: extremely funny
— **side·split·ting·ly** *adverb*

side·step \-,step\ (1901)
intransitive verb
1 : to take a side step
2 : to avoid an issue or decision
transitive verb
1 : to move out of the way of : AVOID ⟨*sidestep* a blow⟩
2 : BYPASS, EVADE ⟨*sidestep* a question⟩
— **side·step·per** *noun*

side step *noun* (1789)
1 : a step aside (as in boxing to avoid a blow)
2 : a step taken sideways (as when climbing on skis)

side–strad·dle hop \'sīd-,stra-d°l-\ *noun* (1952)
: JUMPING JACK 2

side·stream \-,strēm\ *adjective* (1951)
: relating to or being tobacco smoke that is emitted from the lighted end of a cigarette or cigar

side street *noun* (1617)
: a street joining and often terminated by a main thoroughfare

side·stroke \'sīd-,strōk\ *noun* (1867)
: a swimming stroke which is executed on the side and in which the arms are swept in separate strokes towards the feet and downward and the legs do a scissors kick

¹**side·swipe** \-,swīp\ *transitive verb* (1904)
: to strike with a glancing blow along the side ⟨*sideswiped* a parked car⟩

²**sideswipe** *noun* (1917)
1 a : the action of sideswiping b : an instance of sideswiping : a glancing blow

◇ WORD HISTORY
sideburns During the American Civil War, Union general Ambrose Everett Burnside (1824–1881) cultivated long bushy side-whiskers. His appearance first struck the fancy of Washingtonians as he conducted parades and maneuvers with his regiment of Rhode Island volunteers in the early days of the war. Despite a later military career that had its ups and downs, this early popularity fostered the fashion for such whiskers in 19th century America, which originally were called *burnsides*. By the 1880s the order of the two words comprising *burnsides* was reversed to give *sideburns*, most likely by analogy with *side-whiskers*. And whereas the general's whiskers were flamboyantly bushy, today sideburns can be of any length or fullness.

\ə\ abut \°\ kitten \ər\ **further** \a\ ash \ā\ ace
\ä\ mop, mar \aù\ out \ch\ chin \e\ bet \ē\ **easy**
\g\ go \i\ hit \ī\ ice \j\ job \ŋ\ sing \ō\ **go**
\ò\ law \òi\ boy \th\ thin \<u>th</u>\ the \ü\ loot \ù\ **foot**
\y\ yet \zh\ vision *see also* Guide to Pronunciation

2 : an incidental deprecatory remark, allusion, or reference

side table *noun* (14th century)
: a table designed to be placed against a wall

¹side·track \'sīd-,trak\ *noun* (1835)
1 : SIDING 2
2 : a position or condition of secondary importance to which one may be diverted

²sidetrack *transitive verb* (1880)
1 : to shunt aside (as to a railroad siding)
2 a : to turn aside from a purpose **:** DEFLECT **b :** to prevent action on by diversionary tactics ⟨*sidetrack* an issue⟩

side·walk \'sīd-,wók\ *noun* (1739)
: a usually paved walk for pedestrians at the side of a street

sidewalk superintendent *noun* (1940)
: a spectator at a building or demolition job

side·wall \'sīd-,wól\ *noun* (14th century)
1 : a wall forming the side of something
2 : the side of an automotive tire between the tread shoulder and the rim bead

side·ward \'sīd-wərd\ *or* **side·wards** \-wərdz\ *adverb* (15th century)
: toward a side

side·way \'sīd-,wā\ *adverb or adjective* (1612)
: SIDEWAYS

side·ways \-,wāz\ *adverb or adjective* (1577)
1 : from one side
2 : with one side forward ⟨turn *sideways*⟩
3 a : in a lateral direction or downward to one side ⟨hopped *sideways*⟩ ⟨slump *sideways*⟩ **b :** ASKANCE ⟨look *sideways* at someone⟩

side–wheel \'sīd-,hwēl, -,wēl\ *adjective* (1857)
: of or being a steamer having a paddle wheel on each side

— side–wheel·er \-,hwē-lər, -,wē-\ *noun*

side–whis·kers \'sīd-,hwis-kərz, -,wis-\ *noun plural* (1888)
: whiskers on the side of the face usually worn long

— side–whis·kered \-kərd\ *adjective*

side–wind·er \'sīd-,wīn-dər\ *noun* (1840)
1 : a heavy swinging blow from the side
2 : a small pale-colored desert rattlesnake (*Crotalus cerastes*) of the southwestern U.S. that moves by thrusting its body diagonally forward in a series of flat S-shaped curves

sidewinder 2

side·wise \'sīd-,wīz\ *adverb* (1571)
: SIDEWAYS

sid·ing \'sī-diŋ\ *noun* (1603)
1 *archaic* **:** the taking of sides **:** PARTISANSHIP
2 : a short railroad track connected with the main track
3 : material (as boards or metal pieces) forming the exposed surface of outside walls of frame buildings

si·dle \'sī-d'l\ *verb* **si·dled; si·dling** \'sīd-liŋ, 'sī-d'l-iŋ\ [probably back-formation from ²*sideling*] (1697)
intransitive verb
: to go or move with one side foremost especially in a furtive advance
transitive verb
: to cause to move or turn sideways
— sidle *noun*

siege \'sēj *also* 'sēzh\ *noun* [Middle English *sege*, from Old French, seat, blockade, from *siegier* to seat, settle, from (assumed) Vulgar Latin *sedicare*, from Latin *sedēre* to sit — more at SIT] (13th century)
1 *obsolete* **:** a seat of distinction **:** THRONE
2 a : a military blockade of a city or fortified place to compel it to surrender **b :** a persistent or serious attack (as of illness)

— siege *transitive verb*
— lay siege to 1 : to besiege militarily **2 :** to pursue diligently or persistently

siege mentality *noun* (1953)
: a defensive or overly fearful attitude

Siege Perilous *noun*
: a seat at King Arthur's Round Table reserved for the knight destined to achieve the quest of the Holy Grail and fatal to any other occupying it

Sieg·fried \'sig-,frēd, 'sēg-\ *noun* [German]
: a hero in Germanic legend who slays a dragon guarding a gold hoard and wakes Brunhild from her enchanted sleep

Siegfried line *noun* [*Siegfried*] (1918)
: a line of German defensive fortifications facing the Maginot Line

sie·mens \'sē-mənz, 'zē-\ *noun, plural* **siemens** [Werner von *Siemens* (died 1892) German electrical engineer] (circa 1933)
: a unit of conductance in the meter-kilogram-second system equivalent to one ampere per volt

si·en·na \sē-'e-nə\ *noun* [Italian *terra di Siena*, literally, Siena earth, from *Siena*, Italy] (1787)
: an earthy substance containing oxides of iron and usually of manganese that is brownish yellow when raw and orange red or reddish brown when burnt and is used as a pigment

si·er·o·zem \sē-'er-ə-,zem, sē-,er-ə-'zyóm\ *noun* [Russian *serozem*, from *seryĭ* gray + *zemlya* earth; akin to Latin *humus* earth — more at HUMBLE] (1934)
: any of a group of zonal soils brownish gray at the surface and lighter below, based in a carbonate or hardpan layer, and characteristic of temperate to cool arid regions

si·er·ra \sē-'er-ə\ *noun* [Spanish, literally, saw, from Latin *serra*] (1600)
1 a : a range of mountains especially with a serrated or irregular outline **b :** the country about a sierra
2 : any of several large fishes (genus *Scomberomorus*) related to the mackerel

Sierra (1952)
: a communications code word for the letter *s*

si·er·ran \sē-'er-ən\ *adjective* (1873)
1 : of or relating to a sierra ⟨*sierran* foothills⟩
2 *capitalized* **:** of or relating to the Sierra Nevada Mountains of the western U.S.

Sierran *noun* (1906)
: a native or inhabitant of the region around the Sierra Nevada Mountains

si·es·ta \sē-'es-tə\ *noun* [Spanish, from Latin *sexta* (*hora*) noon, literally, sixth hour — more at SEXT] (1655)
: an afternoon nap or rest

sie·va bean \'sē-və-, 'si-və-\ *noun* [origin unknown] (1888)
: a bean plant (*Phaseolus lunatus*) of tropical America that is closely related to and sometimes classified with the lima bean; *also* **:** its flat edible seed

¹sieve \'siv\ *noun* [Middle English *sive*, from Old English *sife*; akin to Old High German *sib* sieve] (before 12th century)
: a device with meshes or perforations through which finer particles of a mixture (as of ashes, flour, or sand) of various sizes may be passed to separate them from coarser ones, through which the liquid may be drained from liquid-containing material, or through which soft materials may be forced for reduction to fine particles

²sieve *verb* **sieved; siev·ing** (15th century)
: SIFT

sieve of Er·a·tos·the·nes \-,er-ə-'täs-thə-,nēz\ (1803)
: a procedure for finding prime numbers that involves writing down the odd numbers from 2 up in succession and lining out every third number after 3, every fifth after 5 including those already lined out, every seventh after 7, and so on with each successive number which

has not been lined out with every number that is not lined out being prime

sieve plate *noun* (1875)
: a perforated wall or part of a wall at the end of one of the individual cells making up a sieve tube

sieve tube *noun* (1875)
: a tube consisting of an end-to-end series of thin-walled living plant cells characteristic of the phloem and held to function chiefly in translocation of organic solutes

si·fa·ka \sə-'fa-kə\ *noun* [Malagasy] (1845)
: any of several diurnal mostly black and white lemurs (genus *Propithecus*) with a long tail and silky fur

sift \'sift\ *verb* [Middle English, from Old English *siftan*; akin to Old English *sife* sieve] (before 12th century)
transitive verb
1 a : to put through a sieve ⟨*sift* flour⟩ **b :** to separate or separate out by or as if by putting through a sieve
2 : to go through especially to sort out what is useful or valuable ⟨*sifted* the evidence⟩ — often used with *through* ⟨*sift* through a pile of old letters⟩
3 : to scatter by or as if by sifting ⟨*sift* sugar on a cake⟩
intransitive verb
1 : to use a sieve
2 : to pass or fall as if through a sieve
— sift·er *noun*

sift·ing *noun* (15th century)
1 : the act or process of sifting
2 *plural* **:** sifted material

¹sigh \'sī\ *verb* [Middle English *sihen*, alteration of *sichen*, from Old English *sīcan*; akin to Middle Dutch ver*siken* to sigh] (13th century)
intransitive verb
1 : to take a deep audible breath (as in weariness or relief)
2 : to make a sound like sighing ⟨wind *sighing* in the branches⟩
3 : GRIEVE, YEARN ⟨*sighing* for days gone by⟩
transitive verb
1 : to express by sighs
2 *archaic* **:** to utter sighs over **:** MOURN
— sigh·er \'sī-(ə)r\ *noun*

²sigh *noun* (14th century)
1 : an often involuntary act of sighing especially when expressing an emotion or feeling (as weariness or relief)
2 : the sound of gently moving or escaping air ⟨*sighs* of the summer breeze⟩

¹sight \'sīt\ *noun* [Middle English, from Old English *gesiht* faculty or act of sight, thing seen; akin to Old High German *gisiht* sight, Old English *sēon* to see] (before 12th century)
1 : something that is seen **:** SPECTACLE
2 a : a thing regarded as worth seeing — usually used in plural ⟨the *sights* of the city⟩ **b :** something ludicrous or disorderly in appearance ⟨you look a *sight*⟩
3 a *chiefly dialect* **:** a great number or quantity **b :** a good deal **:** LOT ⟨a far *sight* better⟩ ⟨not by a damn *sight*⟩
4 a : the process, power, or function of seeing; *specifically* **:** the animal sense of which the end organ is the eye and by which the position, shape, and color of objects are perceived **b :** mental or spiritual perception **c :** mental view; *specifically* **:** JUDGMENT
5 a : the act of looking at or beholding **b :** INSPECTION, PERUSAL **c :** VIEW, GLIMPSE **d :** an observation to determine direction or position (as by a navigator)
6 a : a perception of an object by or as if by the eye ⟨never lost *sight* of the objective⟩ **b :** the range of vision ⟨was nowhere in *sight*⟩
7 : presentation of a note or draft to the maker or draftee **:** DEMAND
8 a : a device that aids the eye in aiming or in finding the direction of an object **b** *plural* **:** ASPIRATION ⟨set her *sights* on a medical career⟩

— **in sight :** at or within a reasonable distance or time
— **on sight :** as soon as seen ⟨ordered to shoot *on sight*⟩
— **out of sight 1 :** beyond comparison **2 :** beyond all expectation or reason **3** — used as a generalized expression of approval
— **sight for sore eyes :** one whose appearance or arrival is an occasion for joy or relief

²**sight** (1602)
transitive verb
1 : to get or catch sight of ⟨several whales were *sighted*⟩
2 : to look at through or as if through a sight; *especially* **:** to test for straightness
3 : to aim by means of sights
4 a : to equip with sights **b :** to adjust the sights of
intransitive verb
1 : to take aim
2 : to look carefully in a particular direction
³**sight** *adjective* (1801)
1 : based on recognition or comprehension without previous study ⟨*sight* translation⟩
2 : payable on presentation ⟨a *sight* draft⟩
sight·ed \'sī-təd\ *adjective* (1552)
: having sight ⟨clear-*sighted*⟩ ⟨a *sighted* person⟩
sight gag *noun* (1949)
: a comic bit or episode whose effect is produced by pantomime or camera shot rather than by words
sight·less \'sīt-ləs\ *adjective* (13th century)
1 : lacking sight **:** BLIND
2 : INVISIBLE 1
— **sight·less·ly** *adverb*
— **sight·less·ness** *noun*
sight line *noun* (1859)
: a line extending from an observer's eye to a viewed object or area (as a stage) ⟨a theater with excellent *sight lines*⟩
sight·ly \-lē\ *adjective* (1534)
1 : pleasing to the sight **:** ATTRACTIVE
2 : affording a fine view
— **sight·li·ness** *noun*
— **sightly** *adverb*
sight–read \-,rēd\ *verb* **-read** \-,red\; **-read·ing** \-,rē-diŋ\ [back-formation from *sight reader*] (1903)
transitive verb
: to read (as a foreign language) or perform (music) without previous preparation or study
intransitive verb
: to read at sight; *especially* **:** to perform music at sight
— **sight reader** *noun*
sight rhyme *noun* (circa 1936)
: EYE RHYME
sight–see \'sīt-,sē\ *intransitive verb, past* **-saw** *present participle* **-see·ing** [back-formation from *sight-seeing*] (1824)
: to go about seeing sights of interest
— **sight–seer** \-,sē-ər, -,sir\ *noun*
sight–see·ing \'sīt-,sē-iŋ\ *adjective* (1827)
: devoted to or used for seeing sights
— **sight–seeing** *noun*
sight unseen *adverb* (1892)
: without inspection or appraisal
sig·il \'si-jil\ *noun* [Middle English *sigulle*, from Latin *sigillum* — more at SEAL] (15th century)
1 : SEAL, SIGNET
2 : a sign, word, or device held to have occult power in astrology or magic
sig·ma \'sig-mə\ *noun* [Greek] (1607)
1 : the 18th letter of the Greek alphabet — see ALPHABET table
2 : STANDARD DEVIATION
sig·moid \'sig-,móid\ *also* **sig·moi·dal** \sig-'mói-d³l\ *adjective* [Greek *sigmoeidēs*, from *sigma*; from a common form of sigma shaped like the Roman letter C] (1670)
1 a : curved like the letter C **b :** curved in two directions like the letter S

2 : of, relating to, or being the sigmoid flexure of the intestine
— **sig·moi·dal·ly** \sig-'mói-d³l-ē\ *adverb*
sigmoid flexure *noun* (1786)
: the contracted and crooked part of the colon immediately above the rectum — called also *sigmoid colon*
sig·moid·os·co·py \,sig-,mói-'däs-kə-pē\ *noun* (circa 1900)
: the process of using a long hollow tubular instrument passed through the anus for inspection, diagnosis, treatment, and photography especially of the sigmoid flexure
¹**sign** \'sīn\ *noun* [Middle English *signe*, from Old French, from Latin *signum* mark, token, sign, image, seal; perhaps akin to Latin *secare* to cut — more at SAW] (13th century)
1 a : a motion or gesture by which a thought is expressed or a command or wish made known **b :** SIGNAL 2a **c :** a fundamental linguistic unit that designates an object or relation or has a purely syntactic function **d :** one of a set of gestures used to represent language; *also* **:** SIGN LANGUAGE
2 : a mark having a conventional meaning and used in place of words or to represent a complex notion
3 : one of the 12 divisions of the zodiac
4 a (1) **:** a character (as a flat or sharp) used in musical notation (2) **:** SEGNO **b :** a character (as ÷) indicating a mathematical operation; *also* **:** one of two characters + and − that form part of the symbol of a number and characterize it as positive or negative
5 a : a display (as a lettered board or a configuration of neon tubing) used to identify or advertise a place of business or a product **b :** a posted command, warning, or direction **c :** SIGNBOARD
6 a : something material or external that stands for or signifies something spiritual **b :** something indicating the presence or existence of something else ⟨*signs* of success⟩ ⟨a *sign* of the times⟩ **c :** PRESAGE, PORTENT ⟨*signs* of an early spring⟩ **d :** an objective evidence of plant or animal disease
7 *plural usually* **sign :** traces of a usually wild animal ⟨red fox *sign*⟩ ☆
— **signed** *adjective*
²**sign** *verb* [Middle English, from Middle French *signer*, from Latin *signare* to mark, sign, seal, from *signum*] (13th century)
transitive verb
1 a : CROSS 2 **b :** to place a sign on **c :** to represent or indicate by a sign
2 a : to affix a signature to **:** ratify or attest by hand or seal ⟨*sign* a bill into law⟩ ⟨the prisoner *signed* a confession⟩ **b :** to assign or convey formally ⟨*signed* over his property to his brother⟩ **c :** to write down (one's name)
3 : to communicate by making a sign or by sign language
4 : to engage or hire by securing the signature of on a contract of employment — often used with *up* or *on*
intransitive verb
1 : to write one's name in token of assent, responsibility, or obligation
2 a : to make a sign or signal **b :** to use sign language
— **sign·ee** \,sī-'nē\ *noun*
— **sign·er** \'sī-nər\ *noun*
sign·age \'sī-nij\ *noun* (1976)
: signs (as of identification, warning, or direction) or a system of such signs
¹**sig·nal** \'sig-n³l\ *noun* [Middle English, from Middle French, from Medieval Latin *signale*, from Late Latin, neuter of *signalis* of a sign, from Latin *signum*] (14th century)
1 : SIGN, INDICATION
2 a : an act, event, or watchword that has been agreed on as the occasion of concerted action **b :** something that incites to action
3 : something (as a sound, gesture, or object) that conveys notice or warning

4 a : an object used to transmit or convey information beyond the range of human voice **b :** the sound or image conveyed in telegraphy, telephony, radio, radar, or television **c :** a detectable physical quantity or impulse (as a voltage, current, or magnetic field strength) by which messages or information can be transmitted
²**signal** *verb* **sig·naled** *or* **sig·nalled; sig·nal·ing** *or* **sig·nal·ling** \-nə-liŋ\ (1805)
transitive verb
1 : to notify by a signal ⟨*signal* the fleet to turn back⟩
2 a : to communicate or indicate by or as if by signals ⟨*signaled* the end of an era⟩ **b :** to constitute a characteristic feature of (a meaningful linguistic form)
intransitive verb
: to make or send a signal
— **sig·nal·er** *or* **sig·nal·ler** *noun*
³**signal** *adjective* [modification of French *signalé*, past participle of *signaler* to distinguish, from Old Italian *segnalare* to signal, distinguish, from *segnale* signal, from Medieval Latin *signale*] (1641)
: distinguished from the ordinary ⟨*signal* achievement⟩
sig·nal·ise *British variant of* SIGNALIZE
sig·nal·ize \'sig-nə-,līz\ *transitive verb* **-ized; -iz·ing** (1654)
1 : to make conspicuous **:** DISTINGUISH
2 : to point out carefully or distinctly
3 : to make signals to **:** SIGNAL; *also* **:** INDICATE
4 : to place traffic signals at or on
— **sig·nal·i·za·tion** \,sig-nə-lə-'zā-shən\ *noun*
sig·nal·ly \'sig-nə-lē\ *adverb* (1641)
: in a signal manner **:** NOTABLY
sig·nal·man \'sig-n³l-mən, -,man\ *noun* (1737)
: a person who signals or works with signals (as on a railway)
sig·nal·ment \-mənt\ *noun* [French *signalement*, from *signaler*] (1778)
: description by peculiar, appropriate, or characteristic marks; *specifically* **:** the systematic description of a person for purposes of identification
sig·na·to·ry \'sig-nə-,tōr-ē, -,tór-\ *noun, plural* **-ries** [Latin *signatorius* of sealing, from *signare*] (1866)
: a signer with another or others ⟨*signatories* to a petition⟩; *especially* **:** a government bound with others by a signed convention
— **signatory** *adjective*
sig·na·ture \'sig-nə-,chúr, -chər, -,tyúr, -,túr\ *noun* [Middle French or Medieval Latin; Middle French, from Medieval Latin *signatura*, from Latin *signatus*, past participle of *signare* to sign, seal] (1536)

\ə\ abut \'ə\ kitten \ər\ further \a\ ash \ā\ ace
\ä\ mop, mar \aú\ out \ch\ chin \e\ bet \ē\ easy
\g\ go \i\ hit \ī\ ice \j\ job \ŋ\ sing \ō\ go
\ó\ law \ói\ boy \th\ thin \th\ the \ü\ loot \ú\ foot
\y\ yet \zh\ vision *see also* Guide to Pronunciation

1 a : the act of signing one's name **b :** the name of a person written with his or her own hand
2 : a feature in the appearance or qualities of a natural object formerly held to indicate its utility in medicine
3 a : a letter or figure placed usually at the bottom of the first page on each sheet of printed pages (as of a book) as a direction to the binder in arranging and gathering the sheets **b :** a folded sheet that is one unit of a book
4 a : KEY SIGNATURE **b :** TIME SIGNATURE
5 : the part of a medical prescription that contains the directions to the patient
6 : something (as a tune, style, or logo) that serves to identify; *also* : a characteristic mark
sign·board \'sīn-,bōrd, -,bȯrd\ *noun* (1632)
: a board bearing a notice or sign
signed \'sīnd\ *adjective* (1873)
: having a sign and especially a plus or minus sign ⟨*signed* numbers like +6 and −4⟩
¹sig·net \'sig-nət\ *noun* [Middle English, from Middle French, diminutive of *signe* sign, seal] (14th century)
1 : a seal used officially to give personal authority to a document in lieu of signature
2 : the impression made by or as if by a signet
3 : a small intaglio seal (as in a finger ring)
²signet *transitive verb* (15th century)
: to stamp or authenticate with a signet
signet ring *noun* (1681)
: a finger ring engraved with a signet, seal, or monogram : SEAL RING
sig·nif·i·cance \sig-'ni-fi-kən(t)s\ *noun* (13th century)
1 a : something that is conveyed as a meaning often obscurely or indirectly **b :** the quality of conveying or implying
2 a : the quality of being important : MOMENT **b :** the quality of being statistically significant
synonym see IMPORTANCE
significance level *noun* (1947)
: LEVEL OF SIGNIFICANCE
sig·nif·i·can·cy \sig-'ni-fi-kən(t)-sē\ *noun* (circa 1595)
: SIGNIFICANCE
sig·nif·i·cant \-kənt\ *adjective* [Latin *significant-, significans,* present participle of *significare* to signify] (1579)
1 : having meaning; *especially* : SUGGESTIVE ⟨a *significant* glance⟩
2 a : having or likely to have influence or effect : IMPORTANT ⟨a *significant* piece of legislation⟩; *also* : of a noticeably or measurably large amount ⟨a *significant* number of layoffs⟩ ⟨producing *significant* profits⟩ **b :** probably caused by something other than mere chance ⟨statistically *significant* correlation between vitamin deficiency and disease⟩
significant digit *noun* (1923)
: one of the digits of a number beginning with the digit farthest to the left that is not zero and ending with the last digit farthest to the right that is not zero or is a zero considered to be exact — called also *significant figure*
sig·nif·i·cant·ly \sig-'ni-fi-kənt-lē\ *adverb* (1577)
1 : in a significant manner : to a significant degree
2 : it is significant
significant other *noun* (1953)
: a person who is important to one's well-being; *especially* : a spouse or one in a similar relationship
sig·ni·fi·ca·tion \,sig-nə-fə-'kā-shən\ *noun* (14th century)
1 a : the act or process of signifying by signs or other symbolic means **b :** a formal notification
2 : PURPORT; *especially* : the meaning that a term, symbol, or character regularly conveys or is intended to convey
3 *chiefly dialect* : IMPORTANCE, CONSEQUENCE
sig·nif·i·ca·tive \sig-'ni-fə-,kā-tiv\ *adjective* (15th century)
1 : SIGNIFICANT, SUGGESTIVE

2 : INDICATIVE ⟨symptoms *significative* of malaria⟩
sig·nif·ics \sig-'ni-fiks\ *noun plural but singular or plural in construction* [*signify*] (1896)
: SEMIOTIC, SEMANTICS
signified *noun* (1939)
: a concept or meaning as distinguished from the sign through which it is communicated — compare SIGNIFIER 2
sig·ni·fi·er \'sig-nə-,fī(-ə)r\ *noun* (1532)
1 : one that signifies
2 : a symbol, sound, or image (as a word) that represents an underlying concept or meaning — compare SIGNIFIED
sig·ni·fy \'sig-nə-,fī\ *verb* **-fied; -fy·ing** [Middle English *signifien,* from Old French *signifier,* from Latin *significare* to indicate, signify, from *signum* sign] (13th century)
transitive verb
1 a : to be a sign of : MEAN **b :** IMPLY
2 : to show especially by a conventional token (as word, signal, or gesture)
intransitive verb
1 : to have significance : MATTER
2 : to engage in signifying
sig·ni·fy·ing \'sig-nə-,fī-iŋ\ *noun* (1959)
: a good-natured needling or goading especially among urban blacks by means of indirect gibes and clever often preposterous put-downs; *also* : DOZENS
sign in (1930)
intransitive verb
: to make a record of arrival by signing a register or punching a time clock
transitive verb
: to record arrival of (a person) or receipt of (an article) by signing
sign language *noun* (1847)
1 : a formal language employing a system of hand gestures for communication (as by the deaf)
2 : an unsystematic method of communicating chiefly by manual gestures used by people speaking different languages
sign of aggregation (circa 1942)
: any of various conventional devices (as braces, brackets, parentheses, or vinculums) used in mathematics to indicate that two or more terms are to be treated as one quantity
sign off *intransitive verb* (1926)
1 : to announce the end of something (as a message or broadcast)
2 : to approve or acknowledge something by or as if by a signature ⟨*sign off* on a memo⟩
— **sign-off** \'sī-,nȯf\ *noun*
sign of the cross (14th century)
: a gesture of the hand forming a cross especially on forehead, breast, and shoulders to profess Christian faith or invoke divine protection or blessing
sign on *intransitive verb* (1885)
1 : to engage oneself by or as if by a signature
2 : to announce the start of broadcasting for the day
— **sign-on** \'sī-,nȯn, -,nän\ *noun*
si·gnor *also* **si·gnior** \sēn-'yȯr, -'yōr\ *noun, plural* **signors** *or* **si·gno·ri** \sēn-'yōr-(,)ē, -'yȯr-\ *also* **signiors** [Italian *signore, signor,* from Medieval Latin *senior* superior, lord — more at SENOR] (circa 1580)
: an Italian man usually of rank or gentility — used as a title equivalent to *Mister*
si·gno·ra \sēn-'yōr-ə, -'yȯr-\ *noun, plural* **si·gno·ras** *or* **si·gno·re** \-'yōr-(,)ā, -'yȯr-\ [Italian, feminine of *signore, signor*] (1763)
: a married Italian woman usually of rank or gentility — used as a title equivalent to *Mrs.*
si·gno·re \sēn-'yōr-(,)ā, -'yȯr-\ *noun, plural* **si·gno·ri** \-'yōr-(,)ē, -'yȯr-\ [Italian] (1594)
: SIGNOR
si·gno·ri·na \,sē-nyə-'rē-nə *noun, plural* **-nas** *or* **-ne** \-(,)nā\ [Italian, from diminutive of *signora*] (1820)
: an unmarried Italian woman — used as a title equivalent to *Miss*

si·gnory *or* **si·gniory** \'sē-nyə-rē\ *noun, plural* **si·gnor·ies** *or* **si·gnior·ies** [Middle English *signorie,* from Middle French *seigneurie*] (14th century)
: SEIGNIORY
sign out (1948)
intransitive verb
: to indicate departure by signing a register
transitive verb
: to record or approve the release or departure of
— **sign-out** \'sī-,naút\ *noun or adjective*
¹sign-post \'sīn-,pōst\ *noun* (1620)
1 : a post (as at the fork of a road) with signs on it to direct travelers
2 : GUIDE, BEACON
²signpost *transitive verb* (1895)
: to provide with signposts or guides
sign up *intransitive verb* (1903)
: to sign one's name (as to a contract) in order to obtain, do, or join something ⟨*sign up* for insurance⟩ ⟨*sign up* for classes⟩
— **sign-up** \'sī-,nəp\ *noun or adjective*
Sig·urd \'si-gúrd, -gərd\ *noun* [Old Norse *Sigurthr*]
: a hero in Norse mythology who slays the dragon Fafnir
sike \'sīk\ *noun* [Middle English, from Old English *sīc;* akin to Old Norse *sīk* slow stream, Old English *sicerian* to trickle] (before 12th century)
1 *dialect chiefly British* : a small stream; *especially* : one that dries up in summer
2 *dialect chiefly British* : DITCH
¹Sikh \'sēk\ *noun* [Hindi, literally, disciple] (1756)
: an adherent of a monotheistic religion of India founded about 1500 by Guru Nānak and marked by rejection of idolatry and caste
— **Sikh·ism** \'sē-,ki-zəm\ *noun*
²Sikh *adjective* (1845)
: of or relating to Sikhs or Sikhism
si·lage \'sī-lij\ *noun* [short for *ensilage*] (1884)
: fodder converted into succulent feed for livestock through processes of anaerobic acid fermentation (as in a silo)
si·lane \'si-,lān, 'sī-\ *noun* [International Scientific Vocabulary *sil*icon + meth*ane*] (1916)
: any of various compounds of hydrogen and silicon that have the general formula Si_nH_{2n+2} and are analogous to alkanes
Si·las·tic \sə-'las-tik, sī-\ *trademark*
— used for a soft pliable plastic
sild \'sil(d)\ *noun, plural* **sild** *or* **silds** [Norwegian] (1921)
: a young herring other than a brisling that is canned as a sardine in Norway
¹si·lence \'sī-lən(t)s\ *noun* [Middle English, from Old French, from Latin *silentium,* from *silent-, silens*] (13th century)
1 : forbearance from speech or noise : MUTENESS — often used interjectionally
2 : absence of sound or noise : STILLNESS
3 : absence of mention: **a :** OBLIVION, OBSCURITY **b :** SECRECY ⟨weapons research was conducted in *silence*⟩
²silence *transitive verb* **si·lenced; si·lenc·ing** (1597)
1 : to compel or reduce to silence : STILL
2 : to restrain from expression : SUPPRESS
3 : to cause to cease hostile firing or criticism
si·lenc·er \'sī-lən(t)-sər\ *noun* (1600)
: one that silences: as **a** *chiefly British* : the muffler of an internal combustion engine **b :** a silencing device for small arms
¹si·lent \'sī-lənt\ *adjective* [Middle English *sylent,* from Latin *silent-, silens,* from present participle of *silēre* to be silent; akin to Gothic *anasilan* to cease, grow calm] (15th century)
1 a : making no utterance : MUTE, SPEECHLESS **b :** indisposed to speak : not loquacious
2 : free from sound or noise : STILL
3 : performed or borne without utterance : UNSPOKEN ⟨*silent* prayer⟩ ⟨*silent* grief⟩

4 a : making no mention ⟨history is *silent* about this person⟩ **b :** not widely or generally known or appreciated ⟨the *silent* pressures on a person in public office⟩ **c :** making no protest or outcry ⟨the *silent* majority⟩ **5 :** UNPRONOUNCED ⟨*silent b* in *doubt*⟩ **6 :** not exhibiting the usual signs or symptoms of presence ⟨a *silent* infection⟩ **7 a :** made without spoken dialogue ⟨*silent* movies⟩ **b :** of or relating to silent movies ☆
— **si·lent·ly** *adverb*
— **si·lent·ness** *noun*

²**silent** *noun* (1929)
: a motion picture made without spoken dialogue — usually used in plural

silent auction *noun* (1952)
: an auction in which sealed bids are submitted beforehand

silent butler *noun* (1937)
: a receptacle with hinged lid for collecting table crumbs and the contents of ashtrays

silent partner *noun* (1828)
1 : a partner who is known to the public but has no voice in the conduct of a firm's business
2 : SECRET PARTNER

silent service *noun* (circa 1929)
1 : NAVY — used with *the*
2 : the submarine service — used with *the*

silent treatment *noun* (1947)
: an act of completely ignoring a person or thing by resort to silence especially as a means of expressing contempt or disapproval

si·le·nus \sī-'lē-nəs\ *noun, plural* **-ni** \-,nī\ *often capitalized* [Latin, from Greek *silēnos,* from *Silēnos* foster father of Dionysus]
: a minor woodland deity and companion of Dionysus in Greek mythology with a horse's ears and tail

si·lex \'sī-,leks\ *noun* [Latin *silic-, silex* hard stone, flint] (circa 1592)
: silica or a siliceous material (as powdered tripoli) especially for use as a filler in paints or wood

¹**sil·hou·ette** \,si-lə-'wet\ *noun* [French, from Étienne de *Silhouette* (died 1767) French controller general of finances; perhaps from his ephemeral tenure] (1783)
1 : a likeness cut from dark material and mounted on a light ground or one sketched in outline and solidly colored in
2 : the outline of a body viewed as circumscribing a mass ⟨the *silhouette* of a bird⟩
synonym see OUTLINE

²**silhouette** *transitive verb* **-ett·ed; -ett·ing** (1876)
: to represent by a silhouette; *also* : to project on a background like a silhouette
— **sil·hou·et·tist** \-'we-tist\ *noun*

sil·i·ca \'si-li-kə\ *noun* [New Latin, from Latin *silic-, silex* hard stone, flint] (circa 1801)
: silicon dioxide SiO_2 occurring in crystalline, amorphous, and impure forms (as in quartz, opal, and sand respectively)

silica gel *noun* (1919)
: colloidal silica resembling coarse white sand in appearance but possessing many fine pores and therefore extremely adsorbent

sil·i·cate \'si-lə-,kāt, -kət\ *noun* [*silicic* (acid)] (1811)
: a salt or ester derived from a silicic acid; *especially* : any of numerous insoluble often complex metal salts that contain silicon and oxygen in the anion, constitute the largest class of minerals, and are used in building materials (as cement, bricks, and glass)

si·li·ceous *or* **si·li·cious** \sə-'li-shəs\ *adjective* [Latin *siliceus* of flint, from *silic-, silex* hard stone, flint] (circa 1656)
: of, relating to, or containing silica or a silicate ⟨*siliceous* limestone⟩

si·lic·ic \sə-'li-sik\ *adjective* [New Latin *silica* & New Latin *silicium* silicon (from *silica*)] (1817)
: of, relating to, or derived from silica or silicon

silicic acid *noun* (1817)
: any of various weakly acid substances obtained as gelatinous masses by treating silicates with acids

sil·i·cide \'si-lə-,sīd\ *noun* [International Scientific Vocabulary *silicon* + *-ide*] (circa 1868)
: a binary compound of silicon with a more electropositive element or group

si·lic·i·fi·ca·tion \sə-,li-sə-fə-'kā-shən\ *noun* (1830)
: the action or process of silicifying : the state of being silicified

si·lic·i·fy \sə-'li-sə-,fī\ *verb* **-fied; -fy·ing** (circa 1828)
transitive verb
: to convert into or impregnate with silica
intransitive verb
: to become silicified

sil·i·con \'si-li-kən, 'si-lə-,kän\ *noun* [New Latin *silica* + English *-on* (as in *carbon*)] (1817)
: a tetravalent nonmetallic element that occurs combined as the most abundant element next to oxygen in the earth's crust and is used especially in alloys and electronic devices — see ELEMENT table

silicon carbide *noun* (1893)
: a very hard dark crystalline compound SiC of silicon and carbon that is used as an abrasive and as a refractory and in electric resistors

sil·i·cone \'si-lə-,kōn\ *noun* [*silicon* + *-one*] (1943)
: any of various polymeric organic silicon compounds obtained as oils, greases, or plastics and used especially for water-resistant and heat-resistant lubricants, varnishes, binders, and electric insulators

silicone rubber *noun* (1944)
: rubber made from silicone elastomers and noted for its retention of flexibility, resilience, and tensile strength over a wide temperature range

sil·i·con·ized \'si-lə-kə-,nīzd, -,kō-\ *adjective* (1949)
: treated or coated with a silicone ⟨*siliconized* glassware⟩

silicon nitride *noun* (1903)
: any of several compounds of silicon and nitrogen; *specifically* : a compound Si_3N_4 that is a hard ceramic used in high-temperature applications and in composites

sil·i·co·sis \,si-lə-'kō-səs\ *noun* [New Latin, from *silica* + *-osis*] (1881)
: pneumoconiosis characterized by massive fibrosis of the lungs resulting in shortness of breath and caused by prolonged inhalation of silica dusts
— **sil·i·cot·ic** \-'kä-tik\ *adjective or noun*

si·lique \sə-'lēk\ *noun* [French, from New Latin *siliqua,* from Latin, pod, husk] (1785)
: a narrow elongated two-valved usually many-seeded capsule that is characteristic of the mustard family, opens by sutures at either margin, and has two parietal placentas

¹**silk** \'silk\ *noun, often attributive* [Middle English, from Old English *seolc,* probably ultimately from Greek *sērikos* silken — more at SERICEOUS] (before 12th century)
1 : a fine continuous protein fiber produced by various insect larvae usually for cocoons; *especially* : a lustrous tough elastic fiber produced by silkworms and used for textiles
2 : thread, yarn, or fabric made from silk filaments
3 a : a garment of silk **b** (1) **:** a distinctive silk gown worn by a King's or Queen's Counsel (2) **:** a King's or Queen's Counsel **c** *plural* **:** the colored cap and blouse of a jockey or harness horse driver made in the registered racing color of the employing stable
4 a : a filament resembling silk; *especially* : one produced by a spider **b :** silky material ⟨milkweed *silk*⟩; *especially* : the styles of an ear of Indian corn
5 : PARACHUTE

— **silk·like** \-,līk\ *adjective*
²**silk** *intransitive verb* (1783)
of corn : to develop the silk

silk·a·line *or* **silk·o·line** \,sil-kə-'lēn\ *noun* [¹*silk* + *-oline* (as in *crinoline*)] (1896)
: a soft light cotton fabric with a smooth lustrous finish like that of silk

silk cotton *noun* (1697)
: the silky or cottony covering of seeds of various silk-cotton trees; *especially* : KAPOK

silk–cotton tree *noun* (1712)
: any of various tropical trees (family Bombacaceae, the silk-cotton family) with palmate leaves and large fruits with the seeds enveloped by silk cotton; *especially* : CEIBA 1

silk·en \'sil-kən\ *adjective* (before 12th century)
1 : made or consisting of silk
2 : resembling silk: as **a :** SOFT, LUSTROUS **b** (1) **:** agreeably smooth : HARMONIOUS (2) **:** SUAVE, INGRATIATING
3 a : dressed in silk ⟨*silken* ankles⟩ **b :** LUXURIOUS 2, 3

silk gland *noun* (1870)
: a gland that produces a viscid fluid which is extruded in filaments and hardens into silk on exposure to air: as **a :** either of a pair of greatly enlarged and modified salivary glands of an insect larva that produce a compound filament from which a larval or pupal cover (as a cocoon) is spun **b :** any of two or more abdominal glands of a spider that open through spinnerets and produce a filament used chiefly in the spinning of webs

silk hat *noun* (1834)
: a hat with a tall cylindrical crown and a silk-plush finish worn by men as a dress hat

silk oak *noun* (1866)
: any of various Australian timber trees (especially genus *Grevillea*) of the protea family that have mottled wood used in cabinetmaking and veneering — called also *silky oak*

silk screen *noun* (1930)
: a stencil process in which coloring matter is forced onto the material to be printed through the meshes of a silk or organdy screen so prepared as to have pervious printing areas and impervious nonprinting areas; *also* : a print made by this process
— **silk–screen** *transitive verb*

silk–stock·ing \'silk-'stä-kiŋ\ *adjective* (1798)
1 : ARISTOCRATIC, WEALTHY ⟨a *silk-stocking* district⟩
2 : fashionably dressed ⟨a *silk-stocking* audience⟩
3 : of or relating to the American Federalist party

☆ SYNONYMS
Silent, taciturn, reticent, reserved, secretive mean showing restraint in speaking. SILENT implies a habit of saying no more than is needed ⟨the strong, *silent* type⟩. TACITURN implies a temperamental disinclination to speech and usually connotes unsociability ⟨*taciturn* villagers⟩. RETICENT implies a reluctance to speak out or at length, especially about one's own affairs ⟨was *reticent* about his plans⟩. RESERVED implies reticence and suggests the restraining influence of caution or formality in checking easy informal conversational exchange ⟨greetings were brief, formal, and *reserved*⟩. SECRETIVE, too, implies reticence but usually carries a suggestion of deviousness and lack of frankness or of an often ostentatious will to conceal ⟨the *secretive* research and development division⟩.

\ə\ abut \ᵊ\ kitten \ər\ further \a\ ash \ā\ ace
\ä\ mop, mar \au̇\ out \ch\ chin \e\ bet \ē\ easy
\g\ go \i\ hit \ī\ ice \j\ job \ŋ\ sing \ō\ go
\ȯ\ law \ȯi\ boy \th\ thin \t̲h̲\ the \ü\ loot \u̇\ foot
\y\ yet \zh\ vision *see also* Guide to Pronunciation

silk stocking *noun* (1891)
1 : an aristocratic or wealthy person
2 : a fashionably dressed person
3 : FEDERALIST 2

silk tree *noun* (circa 1852)
: a leguminous Asian tree (*Albizia julibrissin*) having pink flowers with long silky stamens — called also *mimosa*

silk·weed \'silk-ˌwēd\ *noun* (1784)
: MILKWEED

silk·worm \-ˌwərm\ *noun* (before 12th century)
: a moth whose larva spins a large amount of strong silk in constructing its cocoon; *especially* **:** an Asian moth (*Bombyx mori* of the family Bombycidae) whose rough wrinkled hairless yellowish caterpillar produces the silk of commerce

silky \'sil-kē\ *adjective* **silk·i·er; -est** (1611)
1 : SILKEN 1, 2
2 : having or covered with fine soft hairs, plumes, or scales
— **silk·i·ly** \-kə-lē\ *adverb*
— **silk·i·ness** \-kē-nəs\ *noun*

silky terrier *noun* (1959)
: any of a breed of low-set toy terriers of Australian origin that have a flat silky glossy coat colored blue with tan on the head, chest, and legs — called also *silky*

silky terrier

sill \'sil\ *noun* [Middle English *sille*, from Old English *syll*; akin to Old High German *swelli* beam, threshold] (before 12th century)
1 : a horizontal piece (as a timber) that forms the lowest member or one of the lowest members of a framework or supporting structure: as **a :** the horizontal member at the base of a window **b :** the threshold of a door
2 : a tabular body of igneous rock injected while molten between sedimentary or volcanic beds or along foliation planes of metamorphic rocks
3 : a submerged ridge at relatively shallow depth separating the basins of two bodies of water

sillabub *variant of* SYLLABUB

sil·li·man·ite \'si-lə-mə-ˌnīt\ *noun* [Benjamin Silliman (died 1864) American geologist] (circa 1830)
: a brown, grayish, or pale green mineral that consists of an aluminum silicate in orthorhombic crystals often occurring in fibrous or columnar forms

sil·ly \'si-lē\ *adjective* **sil·li·er; -est** [Middle English *sely, silly* happy, innocent, pitiable, feeble, from Old English *sǣlig*, from Old English *sǣl* happiness; akin to Old High German *sālig* happy] (14th century)
1 *archaic* **:** HELPLESS, WEAK
2 a : RUSTIC, PLAIN **b** *obsolete* **:** lowly in station **:** HUMBLE
3 a : weak in intellect **:** FOOLISH **b :** exhibiting or indicative of a lack of common sense or sound judgment ⟨a very *silly* mistake⟩ **c :** TRIFLING, FRIVOLOUS
4 : being stunned or dazed ⟨scared *silly*⟩ ⟨knocked me *silly*⟩ ◇
synonym see SIMPLE
— **sil·li·ly** \'si-lə-lē\ *adverb*
— **sil·li·ness** \'si-lē-nəs\ *noun*
— **silly** *noun or adverb*

silly season *noun* (1861)
1 : a period (as late summer) when newspapers often resort to trivial or frivolous matters for lack of major news stories
2 : a period marked by frivolous, outlandish, or illogical activity or behavior

si·lo \'sī-(ˌ)lō\ *noun, plural* **silos** [Spanish] (1881)
1 : a trench, pit, or especially a tall cylinder (as of wood or concrete) usually sealed to exclude air and used for making and storing silage
2 a : a deep bin for storing material (as cement or coal) **b :** an underground structure for housing a guided missile

silo 1

si·lox·ane \sə-'läk-ˌsān, sī-\ *noun* [*silicon* + *oxygen* + meth*ane*] (1917)
: any of various compounds containing alternate silicon and oxygen atoms in either a linear or cyclic arrangement usually with one or two organic groups attached to each silicon atom

¹silt \'silt\ *noun* [Middle English *cylte*, probably of Scandinavian origin; akin to Danish *sylt* salt marsh; akin to Old High German *sulza* salt marsh, Old English *sealt* salt] (15th century)
1 : loose sedimentary material with rock particles usually 1/20 millimeter or less in diameter; *also* **:** soil containing 80 percent or more of such silt and less than 12 percent of clay
2 : a deposit of sediment (as by a river)
— **silty** \'sil-tē\ *adjective*

²silt (1799)
intransitive verb
: to become choked or obstructed with silt — often used with *up* ⟨the channel *silted* up⟩
transitive verb
: to choke, fill, cover, or obstruct with silt or mud ⟨the beaver had *silted* the creek —Hugh Fosburgh⟩
— **sil·ta·tion** \sil-'tā-shən\ *noun*

silt·stone \'silt-ˌstōn\ *noun* (circa 1920)
: a rock composed chiefly of indurated silt

Sil·u·res \'sil-yə-ˌrēz\ *noun* [Latin] (circa 1895)
: a people of ancient Britain described by Tacitus as occupying chiefly southern Wales

Si·lu·ri·an \sī-'lur-ē-ən, sə-\ *adjective* [Latin *Silures*] (1708)
1 : of or relating to the Silures or their place of habitation
2 : of, relating to, or being a period of the Paleozoic era between the Ordovician and Devonian or the corresponding system of rocks marked by numerous eurypterid crustaceans and the appearance of the first land plants — see GEOLOGIC TIME table
— **Silurian** *noun*

sil·va \'sil-və\ *noun* [New Latin, from Latin, wood, forest] (circa 1848)
: the forest trees of a region or country

silvan *variant of* SYLVAN

¹sil·ver \'sil-vər\ *noun* [Middle English, from Old English *seolfor*; akin to Old High German *silbar* silver, Lithuanian *sidabras*] (before 12th century)
1 : a white metallic element that is sonorous, ductile, very malleable, capable of a high degree of polish, and chiefly univalent in compounds, and that has the highest thermal and electric conductivity of any substance — see ELEMENT table
2 : silver as a commodity ⟨the value of *silver* has risen⟩
3 : coin made of silver
4 : articles (as hollowware or table flatware) made of or plated with silver; *also* **:** similar articles and especially flatware of other metals (as stainless steel)
5 : a nearly neutral slightly brownish medium gray

²silver *adjective* (before 12th century)
1 : made of silver

2 : resembling silver: as **a :** having a white lustrous sheen **b :** giving a soft resonant sound **:** dulcet in tone **c :** eloquently persuasive
3 : consisting of or yielding silver
4 : of, relating to, or characteristic of silver
5 : advocating the use of silver as a standard of currency
6 : of, relating to, or being a 25th anniversary or its celebration

³silver *transitive verb* **sil·vered; sil·ver·ing** \'sil-v(ə-)riŋ\ (14th century)
1 a : to cover with silver (as by electroplating) **b :** to coat with a substance (as a metal) resembling silver
2 a : to give a silvery luster to **b :** to make white like silver
— **sil·ver·er** \'sil-vər-ər\ *noun*

silver age *noun* (1565)
: an historical period of achievement secondary to that of a golden age

sil·ver·back \'sil-vər-ˌbak\ *noun* (1963)
: an older adult usually dominant male gorilla having gray or whitish hair on the back

silver bell *noun* (1785)
: any of a genus (*Halesia*) of trees and shrubs of the storax family; *especially* **:** one (*H. carolina*) of the southeastern U.S. cultivated for its bell-shaped white flowers

sil·ver·ber·ry \'sil-vər-ˌber-ē\ *noun* (1856)
: a silvery North American shrub (*Elaeagnus commutata*) of the oleaster family

silver bromide *noun* (1885)
: a compound AgBr that is extremely sensitive to light and is much used in the preparation of sensitive emulsion coatings for photographic materials

silver bullet *noun* (1935)
: something that acts as a magical weapon; *especially* **:** one that instantly solves a long-standing problem

silver certificate *noun* (1882)
: a certificate formerly issued against the deposit of silver coin as legal tender in the U.S. and its possessions

silver chloride *noun* (1885)
: a compound AgCl sensitive to light and used especially for photographic materials

silver cord *noun* [*The Silver Cord* (1926), play by Sidney Howard] (1942)
: the emotional tie between mother and child and especially son

silver fir *noun* (1707)
: any of various firs (genus *Abies*) with leaves that are white or silvery white beneath; *especially* **:** a valuable European timber tree (*A. alba*)

sil·ver·fish \'sil-vər-ˌfish\ *noun* (1703)

1 : any of various silvery fishes (as a tarpon or silversides)

2 : any of various small wingless insects (order Thysanura); *especially* : one (*Lepisma saccharina*) found in houses and sometimes injurious especially to sized papers or starched clothes

silver fox *noun* (circa 1792)
: a genetically determined color phase of the common red fox in which the fur is black tipped with white

silver hake *noun* (1884)
: a common hake (*Merluccius bilinearis*) of the northern Atlantic coast of the U.S. that is an important food fish

silver iodide *noun* (1885)
: a compound AgI that darkens on exposure to light and is used in photography, rainmaking, and medicine

silver lining *noun* [from the phrase "every cloud has a *silver lining*"] (1871)
: a consoling or hopeful prospect

sil·ver·ly \'sil-vər-lē\ *adverb* (1595)
: with silvery appearance or sound

silver maple *noun* (1765)
1 : a common maple (*Acer saccharinum*) of eastern North America with deeply cut leaves that are light green above and silvery white below
2 : the hard close-grained but brittle light brown wood of the silver maple

sil·vern \'sil-vərn\ *adjective* (before 12th century)
1 : made of silver
2 : resembling or characteristic of silver : SILVERY

silver nitrate *noun* (1885)
: an irritant compound AgNO$_3$ that in contact with organic matter turns black and is used as a chemical reagent, in photography, and in medicine especially as an antiseptic and caustic

silver paper *noun* (circa 1875)
: TIN FOIL

silver perch *noun* (1820)
: any of various somewhat silvery fishes that resemble perch: as **a** : a drum (*Bairdiella chrysoura*) that occurs especially along the more southern Atlantic coast of the U.S. — called also *mademoiselle, yellowtail* **b** : WHITE PERCH 1

silver plate *noun* (1610)
1 : domestic flatware and hollowware of silver or of a silver-plated base metal
2 : a plating of silver

sil·ver·point \'sil-vər-,pȯint\ *noun* (1882)
: a drawing technique utilizing a pencil of silver usually on specially prepared paper or parchment

silver protein *noun* (1928)
: any of several colloidal light-sensitive preparations of silver and protein used in aqueous solution on mucous membranes as antiseptics

silver salmon *noun* (1878)
: COHO

silver screen *noun* (1918)
1 : a motion-picture screen
2 : MOTION PICTURES

sil·ver·side \'sil-vər-,sīd\ *noun* (1820)
: SILVERSIDES

sil·ver·sides \'sil-vər-,sīdz\ *noun plural but singular or plural in construction* (1851)
: any of various small bony fishes (family Atherinidae) with a silvery stripe along each side of the body

sil·ver·smith \-,smith\ *noun* (before 12th century)
: an artisan who makes articles of silverware
— **sil·ver·smith·ing** *noun*

silver spoon *noun* [from the phrase "born with a *silver spoon* in one's mouth" (born wealthy)] (1801)
: WEALTH; *especially* : inherited wealth

silver standard *noun* (1860)
: a monetary standard under which the currency unit is defined by a stated quantity of silver

Silver Star Medal *noun* (1932)
: a U.S. military decoration awarded for gallantry in action

sil·ver·tongued \'sil-vər-,təŋd\ *adjective* (1592)
: marked by convincing and eloquent expression

sil·ver·ware \'sil-vər-,war, -,wer\ *noun* (1860)
1 : SILVER PLATE 1
2 : FLATWARE

sil·ver·weed \-,wēd\ *noun* (1578)
: any of several cinquefoils with leaves silvery or white-tomentose beneath; *especially* : one (*Potentilla anserina*) with silky hairs over the entire plant

sil·very \'sil-v(ə-)rē\ *adjective* (14th century)
1 : having the luster of silver
2 : having a soft clear musical tone : RESONANT ⟨a *silvery* voice⟩
3 : containing or consisting of silver
— **sil·ver·i·ness** *noun*

sil·vex \'sil-,veks\ *noun* [probably from Latin *silva* wood + English *exterminator*] (1961)
: a selective herbicide C$_9$H$_7$Cl$_3$O$_3$ especially effective in controlling woody plants but toxic to animals

sil·vi·cul·ture \'sil-və-,kəl-chər\ *noun* [French, from Latin *silva* + *cultura* culture] (1880)
: a branch of forestry dealing with the development and care of forests
— **sil·vi·cul·tur·al** \,sil-və-'kəlch-rəl, -'kəl-chə-\ *adjective*
— **sil·vi·cul·tur·al·ly** \-rə-lē\ *adverb*
— **sil·vi·cul·tur·ist** \,sil-və-'kəlch-rist, -'kəl-chə-\ *noun*

si·ma·zine \'sī-mə-,zēn\ *noun* [*sim-* (probably alteration of *sym-* symmetrical, prefix used in names of organic compounds) + tri*azine*] (1956)
: a selective herbicide C$_7$H$_{12}$N$_5$Cl used to control weeds especially among crop plants

Sim·chas To·rah \,sim-kəs-'tōr-ə, -'tȯr-\ *noun* [Hebrew *śimḥath tōrāh* rejoicing of the Torah] (1891)
: a Jewish holiday observed on the 23d of Tishri in celebration of the completion of the annual reading of the Torah

Sim·e·on \'si-mē-ən\ *noun* [Late Latin, from Greek *Symeōn*, from Hebrew *Shim'ōn*]
1 : a son of Jacob and the traditional eponymous ancestor of one of the tribes of Israel
2 : a devout man of Jerusalem held to have uttered the Nunc Dimittis on seeing the infant Jesus in the temple

¹sim·i·an \'si-mē-ən\ *adjective* [Latin *simia* ape, from *simus* snub-nosed, from Greek *simos*] (1607)
: of, relating to, or resembling monkeys or apes

²simian *noun* (1880)
: MONKEY, APE

sim·i·lar \'si-mə-lər, 'sim-lər\ *adjective* [French *similaire*, from Latin *similis* like, similar — more at SAME] (1611)
1 : having characteristics in common : strictly comparable
2 : alike in substance or essentials : CORRESPONDING ⟨no two animal habitats are exactly *similar* —W. H. Dowdeswell⟩
3 : not differing in shape but only in size or position ⟨*similar* triangles⟩ ⟨*similar* polygons⟩
☆
— **sim·i·lar·ly** *adverb*

sim·i·lar·i·ty \,si-mə-'lar-ə-tē\ *noun, plural* **-ties** (1664)
1 : the quality or state of being similar : RESEMBLANCE
2 : a comparable aspect : CORRESPONDENCE
synonym see LIKENESS

sim·i·le \'si-mə-(,)lē\ *noun* [Middle English, from Latin, comparison, from neuter of *similis*] (14th century)
: a figure of speech comparing two unlike things that is often introduced by *like* or *as* (as in *cheeks like roses*) — compare METAPHOR

si·mil·i·tude \sə-'mi-lə-,tüd, -,tyüd\ *noun* [Middle English, from Middle French, resemblance, likeness, from Latin *similitudo*, from *similis*] (14th century)
1 a : COUNTERPART, DOUBLE **b** : a visible likeness : IMAGE
2 : an imaginative comparison : SIMILE
3 a : correspondence in kind or quality **b** : a point of comparison
synonym see LIKENESS

Sim·men·tal *also* **Sim·men·thal** \'zi-mən-,täl\ *noun* [*Simmental*, valley of the Simme River in Switzerland] (1906)
: any of a breed of large buff or dull red and white cattle of Swiss origin that are used widely throughout the world for meat and milk

¹sim·mer \'si-mər\ *verb* **sim·mered; sim·mer·ing** \'si-mə-riŋ, 'sim-riŋ\ [alteration of English dialect *simper*, from Middle English *simperen*, of imitative origin] (1653)
intransitive verb
1 : to stew gently below or just at the boiling point
2 a : to be in a state of incipient development : FERMENT ⟨ideas *simmering* in the back of my mind⟩ **b** : to be in inward turmoil : SEETHE
transitive verb
: to cook slowly in a liquid just below the boiling point

²simmer *noun* (1809)
: the state of simmering

simmer down *intransitive verb* (1871)
1 : to become calm or peaceful
2 : to become reduced by or as if by simmering

sim·nel \'sim-nᵊl\ *noun* [Middle English *simenel*, from Middle French, ultimately from Latin *simila* wheat flour] (13th century)
1 : a bun or bread of fine wheat flour
2 *British* : a rich fruitcake sometimes coated with almond paste and baked for mid-Lent, Easter, and Christmas

si·mo·le·on \sə-'mō-lē-ən\ *noun* [origin unknown] (1896)
slang : DOLLAR

Si·mon \'sī-mən\ *noun* [Greek *Simōn*, from Hebrew *Shim'ōn*]
1 : PETER — called also *Simon Peter*
2 : one of the twelve disciples of Jesus — called also *Simon the Zealot*
3 : a kinsman of Jesus
4 : a Cyrenian constrained to help Jesus bear his cross to his place of crucifixion — called also *Simon the Cyrenian*
5 : SIMON MAGUS

si·mo·ni·ac \sī-'mō-nē-,ak, sə-\ *noun* [Middle English, from Middle French or Medieval Latin; Middle French *simoniaque*, from Medieval Latin *simoniacus*, from Late Latin *simonia* simony] (14th century)
: one who practices simony
— **simoniac** *or* **si·mo·ni·a·cal** \,sī-mə-'nī-ə-kəl, ,si-\ *adjective*
— **si·mo·ni·a·cal·ly** \-k(ə-)lē\ *adverb*

☆ SYNONYMS
Similar, analogous, parallel mean closely resembling each other. SIMILAR implies the possibility of being mistaken for each other ⟨all the houses in the development are *similar*⟩. ANALOGOUS applies to things belonging in essentially different categories but nevertheless having many similarities ⟨*analogous* political systems⟩. PARALLEL suggests a marked likeness in the development of two things ⟨the *parallel* careers of two movie stars⟩.

\ə\ abut \ᵊ\ kitten \ər\ further \a\ ash \ā\ ace
\ä\ mop, mar \au̇\ out \ch\ chin \e\ bet \ē\ easy
\g\ go \i\ hit \ī\ ice \j\ job \ŋ\ sing \ō\ go
\ȯ\ law \ȯi\ boy \th\ thin \th\ the \ü\ loot \u̇\ foot
\y\ yet \zh\ vision *see also* Guide to Pronunciation

si·mo·nize \'sī-mə-ˌnīz\ *transitive verb* **-nized; -niz·ing** [from *Simoniz*, a trademark] (1934)
: to polish with or as if with wax

Si·mon Le·gree \ˌsī-mən-lə-'grē\ *noun*
: a slave owner who has Tom flogged to death in Harriet B. Stowe's novel *Uncle Tom's Cabin*

Simon Ma·gus \-'mā-gəs\ *noun*
: a Samaritan sorcerer converted by the apostle Philip and severely rebuked by Peter for offering money for the gifts of the Holy Ghost

si·mon–pure \ˌsī-mən-'pyůr\ *adjective* [from *the real Simon Pure*, alluding to a character impersonated by another in the play *A Bold Stroke for a Wife* (1718) by Susannah Centlivre (died 1723) English dramatist and actress] (1840)
: of untainted purity or integrity; *also* : pretentiously or hypocritically pure

si·mo·ny \'sī-mə-nē, 'si-\ *noun* [Middle English *symonie*, from Late Latin *simonia*, from *Simon* Magus, Samaritan sorcerer in Acts 8: 9–24] (13th century)
: the buying or selling of a church office or ecclesiastical preferment

si·moom \sə-'müm, sī-\ *or* **si·moon** \-'mün\ *noun* [Arabic *samūm*] (1790)
: a hot dry violent dust-laden wind from Asian and African deserts

simp \'simp\ *noun* (1903)
: SIMPLETON

sim·pa·ti·co \sim-'pä-ti-ˌkō, -'pa-\ *adjective* [Italian *simpatico* & Spanish *simpático*, ultimately from Latin *sympathia* sympathy] (1864)
1 : AGREEABLE, LIKABLE
2 : being on the same wavelength : CONGENIAL, SYMPATHETIC

¹sim·per \'sim-pər\ *verb* **sim·pered; sim·per·ing** \-p(ə-)riŋ\ [perhaps of Scandinavian origin; akin to Danish dialect *simper* affected, coy] (circa 1563)
intransitive verb
: to smile in a silly manner
transitive verb
: to say with a simper ⟨*simpered* an apology⟩
— **sim·per·er** \-pər-ər\ *noun*

²simper *noun* (1599)
: a silly smile : SMIRK

¹sim·ple \'sim-pəl\ *adjective* **sim·pler** \-p(ə-)lər\; **sim·plest** \-p(ə-)ləst\ [Middle English, from Old French, plain, uncomplicated, artless, from Latin *simplus, simplex*, literally, single; Latin *simplus* from *sem-, sim-* one + *-plus* multiplied by; Latin *simplic-, simplex* from *sem-, sim-* + *-plic-, -plex* -fold — more at SAME, -FOLD] (13th century)
1 : free from guile : INNOCENT
2 a : free from vanity : MODEST **b** : free from ostentation or display
3 : of humble origin or modest position ⟨a *simple* farmer⟩
4 a : lacking in knowledge or expertise ⟨a *simple* amateur of the arts⟩ **b** : STUPID; *especially* : mentally retarded **c** : not socially or culturally ly sophisticated *also* : CREDULOUS
5 a : SHEER, UNMIXED ⟨*simple* honesty⟩ **b** : free of secondary complications ⟨a *simple* vitamin deficiency⟩ **c** (1) : having only one main clause and no subordinate clauses ⟨a *simple* sentence⟩ (2) *of a subject or predicate* : having no modifiers, complements, or objects **d** : constituting a basic element : FUNDAMENTAL **e** : not made up of many like units ⟨a *simple* eye⟩
6 : free from elaboration or figuration ⟨*simple* harmony⟩
7 a (1) : not subdivided into branches or leaflets ⟨a *simple* stem⟩ ⟨a *simple* leaf⟩ (2) : consisting of a single carpel **b** : developing from a single ovary ⟨a *simple* fruit⟩ **b** : controlled by a single gene ⟨*simple* inherited characters⟩
8 : not limited or restricted : UNCONDITIONAL ⟨a *simple* obligation⟩

9 : readily understood or performed ⟨*simple* directions⟩ ⟨the adjustment was *simple* to make⟩
10 *of a statistical hypothesis* : specifying exact values for one or more statistical parameters — compare COMPOSITE 3 ☆
— **sim·ple·ness** \-pəl-nəs\ *noun*

²simple *noun* (14th century)
1 a : a person of humble birth : COMMONER ⟨thought very little of anybody, *simples* or gentry —Virginia Woolf⟩ **b** (1) : a rude or credulous person : IGNORAMUS (2) : a mentally retarded person
2 a : a medicinal plant **b** : a vegetable drug having only one ingredient
3 : one component of a complex; *specifically* : an unanalyzable constituent

simple closed curve *noun* (1919)
: a closed plane curve (as a circle or an ellipse) that does not intersect itself — called also *Jordan curve*

simple equation *noun* (1798)
: a linear equation

simple fraction *noun* (1910)
: a fraction having whole numbers for the numerator and denominator — compare COMPLEX FRACTION

simple fracture *noun* (1685)
: a bone fracture that does not form an open wound in the skin — compare COMPOUND FRACTURE

simple interest *noun* (1798)
: interest paid or computed on the original principal only of a loan or on the amount of an account

simple machine *noun* (1704)
: any of various elementary mechanisms formerly considered as the elements of which all machines are composed and including the lever, the wheel and axle, the pulley, the inclined plane, the wedge, and the screw

sim·ple·mind·ed \ˌsim-pəl-'mīn-dəd, 'sim-pəl-ˌ\ *adjective* (1744)
: devoid of subtlety : UNSOPHISTICATED; *also* : FOOLISH
— **sim·ple·mind·ed·ly** *adverb*
— **sim·ple·mind·ed·ness** *noun*

simple protein *noun* (circa 1909)
: a protein (as a globulin) that yields amino acids as the chief or only products of complete hydrolysis — compare CONJUGATED PROTEIN

simple sugar *noun* (1942)
: MONOSACCHARIDE

sim·ple·ton \'sim-pəl-tən\ *noun* [¹*simple* + *-ton* (as in surnames such as *Washington*)] (1650)
: a person lacking in common sense

simple vow *noun* (1759)
: a public vow taken by a religious in the Roman Catholic Church under which retention of property by the individual is permitted and marriage though illicit is valid under canon law

¹sim·plex \'sim-ˌpleks\ *adjective* [Latin *simplic-, simplex* — more at SIMPLE] (1594)
1 : SIMPLE, SINGLE
2 : allowing telecommunication in only one direction at a time ⟨*simplex* system⟩

²simplex *noun, plural* **sim·plex·es** (1892)
1 *or plural* **sim·pli·ces** \-plə-ˌsēz\ *or* **sim·pli·cia** \sim-'pli-sh(ē-)ə\ : a simple word
2 : a spatial configuration of *n* dimensions determined by *n* + 1 points in a space of dimension equal to or greater than *n* ⟨a triangle together with its interior determined by its three vertices is a two-dimensional *simplex* in the plane or any space of higher dimension⟩

sim·pli·cial \sim-'pli-shəl\ *adjective* (1926)
: of or relating to simplexes
— **sim·pli·cial·ly** \-shə-lē\ *adverb*

sim·plic·i·ty \sim-'pli-sə-tē, -'plis-tē\ *noun* [Middle English *simplicite*, from Middle French *simplicité*, from Latin *simplicitat-, simplicitas*, from *simplic-, simplex*] (14th century)
1 : the state of being simple, uncomplicated, or uncompounded

2 a : lack of subtlety or penetration : INNOCENCE, NAIVETÉ **b** : FOLLY, SILLINESS
3 : freedom from pretense or guile : CANDOR
4 a : directness of expression : CLARITY **b** : restraint in ornamentation : AUSTERITY

sim·pli·fy \'sim-plə-ˌfī\ *transitive verb* **-fied; -fy·ing** [French *simplifier*, from Medieval Latin *simplificare*, from Latin *simplus* simple] (1759)
: to make simple or simpler: as **a** : to reduce to basic essentials **b** : to diminish in scope or complexity : STREAMLINE ⟨was urged to *simplify* management procedures⟩ **c** : to make more intelligible : CLARIFY
— **sim·pli·fi·ca·tion** \ˌsim-plə-fə-'kā-shən\ *noun*
— **sim·pli·fi·er** \'sim-plə-ˌfī-(ə-)r\ *noun*

sim·plism \'sim-ˌpli-zəm\ *noun* (circa 1882)
: the act or an instance of oversimplifying; *especially* : the reduction of a problem to a false simplicity by ignoring complicating factors

sim·plis·tic \sim-'plis-tik\ *adjective* (circa 1881)
1 : SIMPLE
2 : of, relating to, or characterized by simplism : OVERSIMPLE ⟨adequate, if occasionally *simplistic*, historical background —Harlow Robinson⟩
— **sim·plis·ti·cal·ly** \-ti-k(ə-)lē\ *adverb*

sim·ply \'sim-plē, *for 1 also* -pə-lē\ *adverb* (14th century)
1 a : without ambiguity : CLEARLY **b** : without embellishment : PLAINLY **c** : DIRECTLY, CANDIDLY
2 a : SOLELY, MERELY ⟨eats *simply* to keep alive⟩ ⟨*simply* cleaned it up and went to bed —Garrison Keillor⟩ **b** : REALLY, LITERALLY ⟨the concert was *simply* marvelous⟩ — often used as an intensive ⟨*simply* crawling with geniuses —F. Scott Fitzgerald⟩

simply connected *adjective* (1893)
: being or characterized by a surface that is divided into two separate parts by every closed curve it contains

simply ordered *adjective* (circa 1909)
: having any two elements connected by a relationship that is reflexive, antisymmetric, and transitive

Simp·son's rule \'sim(p)-sənz-\ *noun* [Thomas *Simpson* (died 1761) English mathematician] (1875)
: a method for approximating the area under a curve over a given interval that involves partitioning the interval by an odd number *n* + 1 of equally spaced ordinates and adding the areas of the *n*/2 figures formed by pairs of successive odd-numbered ordinates and the parabolas which they determine with their included even-numbered ordinates

sim·u·la·cre \'sim-yə-ˌlā-kər, -ˌla-\ *noun* [Middle English, from Middle French, from Latin *simulacrum*] (14th century)
archaic : SIMULACRUM

☆ **SYNONYMS**
Simple, foolish, silly, fatuous, asinine mean actually or apparently deficient in intelligence. SIMPLE implies a degree of intelligence inadequate to cope with anything complex or involving mental effort (considered people *simple* who had trouble with computers). FOOLISH implies the character of being or seeming unable to use judgment, discretion, or good sense ⟨*foolish* stunts⟩. SILLY suggests failure to act as a rational being especially by ridiculous behavior ⟨the *silly* antics of revelers⟩. FATUOUS implies foolishness, inanity, and disregard of reality ⟨*fatuous* conspiracy theories⟩. ASININE suggests utter and contemptible failure to use normal rationality or perception ⟨an *asinine* plot⟩. See in addition EASY.

sim·u·la·crum \ˌsim-yə-'la-krəm, -'lā-\ *noun, plural* **-cra** \-krə\ *also* **-crums** [Middle English, from Latin, from *simulare*] (15th century)

1 : IMAGE, REPRESENTATION ⟨a reasonable *simulacrum* of reality —Martin Mayer⟩

2 : an insubstantial form or semblance of something : TRACE

¹**sim·u·lar** \'sim-yə-lər, -,lär\ *noun* [irregular from Latin *simulare* to simulate] (1526)
archaic : one that simulates : DISSEMBLER

²**simular** *adjective* (1611)
archaic : COUNTERFEIT, PRETENDED

sim·u·late \'sim-yə-,lāt\ *transitive verb* **-lat·ed; -lat·ing** [Latin *simulatus*, past participle of *simulare* to copy, represent, feign, from *similis* like — more at SAME] (1652)

1 : to give or assume the appearance or effect of often with the intent to deceive : IMITATE

2 : to make a simulation of (as a physical system)
synonym see ASSUME
— **sim·u·la·tive** \-,lā-tiv\ *adjective*

simulated *adjective* (1622)
: made to look genuine : FAKE ⟨*simulated* pearls⟩

sim·u·la·tion \ˌsim-yə-'lā-shən\ *noun* [Middle English *simulacion*, from Middle French, from Latin *simulation-, simulatio*, from *simulare*] (14th century)

1 : the act or process of simulating

2 : a sham object : COUNTERFEIT

3 a : the imitative representation of the functioning of one system or process by means of the functioning of another ⟨a computer *simulation* of an industrial process⟩ **b** : examination of a problem often not subject to direct experimentation by means of a simulating device

sim·u·la·tor \'sim-yə-,lā-tər\ *noun* (1835)
: one that simulates; *especially* : a device that enables the operator to reproduce or represent under test conditions phenomena likely to occur in actual performance

si·mul·cast \'sī-məl-,kast *also* 'si-\ *verb* [*simultaneous* broad*cast*] (1948)
intransitive verb
: to broadcast simultaneously (as by radio and television)
transitive verb
: to broadcast (a program) by simulcasting
— **simulcast** *noun*

si·mul·ta·neous \ˌsī-məl-'tā-nē-əs, -nyəs *also* ,si-\ *adjective* [Latin *simul* at the same time + English *-taneous* (as in *instantaneous*) — more at SAME] (circa 1660)

1 : existing or occurring at the same time : exactly coincident

2 : satisfied by the same values of the variables ⟨*simultaneous* equations⟩
synonym see CONTEMPORARY
— **si·mul·ta·ne·ity** \-tə-'nē-ə-tē, -'nā-\ *noun*
— **si·mul·ta·neous·ly** \-'tā-nē-əs-lē, -nyəs-\ *adverb*
— **si·mul·ta·neous·ness** *noun*

¹**sin** \'sin\ *noun* [Middle English *sinne*, from Old English *synn*; akin to Old High German *sunta* sin; probably akin to Latin *sont-, sons* guilty, *est* is — more at IS] (before 12th century)

1 a : an offense against religious or moral law **b** : an action that is or is felt to be highly reprehensible ⟨it's a *sin* to waste food⟩ **c** : an often serious shortcoming : FAULT

2 a : transgression of the law of God **b** : a vitiated state of human nature in which the self is estranged from God
synonym see OFFENSE

²**sin** *intransitive verb* **sinned; sin·ning** (before 12th century)

1 : to commit a sin

2 : to commit an offense or fault

³**sin** \'sēn, 'sin\ *noun* [Hebrew *śīn*] (circa 1823)
: the 21st letter of the Hebrew alphabet — see ALPHABET table

Sin·an·thro·pus \sī-'nan(t)-thrə-pəs, sə-; ,sī-,nan-'thrō-, ,si-\ *noun* [New Latin, from Late Latin *Sinae*, plural, Chinese + Greek *anthrōpos* man — more at SINO-] (1928)
: PEKING MAN

Sin·bad *or* **Sind·bad** \'sin-,bad\ *noun*
: a citizen of Baghdad whose adventures at sea are told in the *Arabian Nights' Entertainments*

¹**since** \'sin(t)s\ *adverb* [Middle English *sins*, contraction of *sithens*, from *sithen*, from Old English *siththan*, from *sīth tham* after that, from *sīth* after, late + *tham*, dative of *thæt* that; akin to Old High German *sīd* later and perhaps to Latin *setius* to a lesser degree] (before 12th century)

1 : from a definite past time until now ⟨has stayed there ever *since*⟩

2 : before the present time : AGO ⟨long *since* dead⟩

3 : after a time in the past : SUBSEQUENTLY ⟨has *since* become rich⟩

²**since** *conjunction* (15th century)

1 : at a time in the past after or later than ⟨has held two jobs *since* he graduated⟩ : from the time in the past when ⟨ever *since* I was a child⟩

2 *obsolete* : WHEN

3 : in view of the fact that : BECAUSE ⟨*since* it was raining she took an umbrella⟩

³**since** *preposition* (circa 1530)
: in the period after a specified time in the past : from a specified time in the past

sin·cere \sin-'sir, sən-\ **sin·cer·er; sin·cer·est** *adjective* [Middle French, from Latin *sincerus* whole, pure, genuine, probably from *sem-* one + *-cerus* (akin to Latin *crescere* to grow) — more at SAME, CRESCENT] (1533)

1 a : free of dissimulation : HONEST ⟨*sincere* interest⟩ **b** : free from adulteration : PURE ⟨a *sincere* doctrine⟩ ⟨*sincere* wine⟩

2 : marked by genuineness : TRUE ☆
— **sin·cere·ly** *adverb*
— **sin·cere·ness** *noun*

sin·cer·i·ty \-'ser-ə-tē, -'sir-\ *noun* (15th century)
: the quality or state of being sincere : honesty of mind : freedom from hypocrisy

sin·cip·i·tal \sin-'si-pə-t³l\ *adjective* (1653)
: of or relating to the sinciput

sin·ci·put \'sin(t)-sə-(,)pət\ *noun, plural* **sin·ciputs** *or* **sin·cip·i·ta** \sin-'si-pə-tə\ [Latin *sincipit-, sinciput*, from *semi-* + *caput* head — more at HEAD] (1578)

1 : FOREHEAD

2 : the upper half of the skull

Sind·hi \'sin-dē\ *noun, plural* **Sindhi** *or* **Sindhis** [Arabic *Sindi*] (1815)

1 : a member of a mostly Muslim people of Sind

2 : the Indo-Aryan language of the Sindhi people

sine \'sīn\ *noun* [Medieval Latin *sinus*, from Latin, curve] (1593)

1 : the trigonometric function that for an acute angle is the ratio between the leg opposite the angle when it is considered part of a right angle and the hypotenuse

2 : a trigonometric function sin θ that for all real numbers θ is exactly equal to the sine of an angle of measure θ in radians and that is given by the sum of the alternating series

$$\sin \theta = \theta - \frac{\theta^3}{3!} + \frac{\theta^5}{5!} - \frac{\theta^7}{7!} + \frac{\theta^9}{9!} - \cdots$$

si·ne·cure \'sī-ni-,kyür, 'si-\ *noun* [Medieval Latin *sine cura* without cure (of souls)] (1662)

1 *archaic* : an ecclesiastical benefice without cure of souls

2 : an office or position that requires little or no work and that usually provides an income

sine curve *noun* (1902)
: the graph in rectangular coordinates of the equation y=a sin bx where a and b are constants

sine curve: graph of
y=*a* sin *bx* where
a=1, *b*=1

si·ne die \ˌsī-ni-'dī(-,ē), ,si-nā-'dē-,ā\ *adverb* [Latin, without day] (1607)
: without any future date being designated (as for resumption) : INDEFINITELY ⟨the meeting adjourned *sine die*⟩

si·ne qua non \ˌsi-ni-,kwä-'nän, -'nōn *also* ,sē-; *also* ,sī-ni-,kwä-'nän\ *noun, plural* **sine qua nons** *or* **sine qui·bus non** \-,kwi-(,)bùs- *also* -,kwī-\ [Late Latin, without which not] (1602)
: something absolutely indispensable or essential

¹**sin·ew** \'sin-(,)yü *also* 'si-(,)nü\ *noun* [Middle English *sinewe*, from Old English *seono*; akin to Old High German *senawa* sinew, Sanskrit *syati* he binds] (before 12th century)

1 : TENDON; *especially* : one dressed for use as a cord or thread

2 *obsolete* : NERVE

3 a : solid resilient strength : POWER ⟨astonishing intellectual *sinew* and clarity —Reynolds Price⟩ **b** : the chief supporting force : MAINSTAY — usually used in plural ⟨providing the *sinews* of better living —Sam Pollock⟩

²**sinew** *transitive verb* (circa 1614)
: to strengthen as if with sinews

sine wave *noun* (1893)
: a waveform that represents periodic oscillations in which the amplitude of displacement at each point is proportional to the sine of the phase angle of the displacement and that is visualized as a sine curve : SINE CURVE; *also* : a wave so represented

sin·ewy \'sin-yə-wē *also* 'si-nə-\ *adjective* (14th century)

1 : full of sinews: as **a** : TOUGH, STRINGY ⟨*sinewy* meat⟩ **b** : STRONG ⟨*sinewy* arms⟩

2 : marked by the strength of sinews ⟨a demanding *sinewy* intelligence —Helen Dudar⟩

sin·fo·nia \ˌsin-fə-'nē-ə\ *noun, plural* **-nie** \-'nē-,ā\ [Italian, from Latin *symphonia* symphony] (1773)

1 : an orchestral musical composition serving as an introduction to choral works (as opera) especially in the 18th century : OVERTURE

2 : RITORNELLO 1, SYMPHONY 2c

sinfonia con·cer·tante \-,kän(t)-sər-'tän-tē, -shər-, -,tā\ *noun* [Italian, literally, symphony in concerto style] (circa 1903)
: a concerto for more than one solo instrument

\ə\ abut \ᵊ\ kitten \ər\ further \a\ ash \ā\ ace
\ä\ mop, mar \aù\ out \ch\ chin \e\ bet \ē\ easy
\g\ go \i\ hit \ī\ ice \j\ job \ŋ\ sing \ō\ go
\ò\ law \òi\ boy \th\ thin \th\ the \ü\ loot \ù\ foot
\y\ yet \zh\ vision *see also* Guide to Pronunciation

sin·fo·niet·ta \,sin-fən-'ye-tə, -fōn-\ *noun* [Italian, diminutive of *sinfonia*] (circa 1907) **1** : a symphony of less than standard length or for fewer instruments **2 a** : a small symphony orchestra; *especially* : an orchestra of strings only

sin·ful \'sin-fəl\ *adjective* (before 12th century) **1** : tainted with, marked by, or full of sin : WICKED **2** : such as to make one feel guilty ⟨a *sinful* chocolate cake⟩ — **sin·ful·ly** \-fə-lē\ *adverb* — **sin·ful·ness** *noun*

¹sing \'sin\ *verb* **sang** \'san\ *or* **sung** \'sən\; **sung; sing·ing** \'sin-in\ [Middle English, from Old English *singan*; akin to Old High German *singan* to sing, Greek *omphē* voice] (before 12th century) *intransitive verb* **1 a** : to produce musical tones by means of the voice **b** : to utter words in musical tones and with musical inflections and modulations **c** : to deliver songs as a trained or professional singer **2** : to make a shrill whining or whistling sound **3 a** : to relate or celebrate something in verse **b** : to compose poetry **c** : to create in or through words a feeling or sense of song ⟨prose that *sings*⟩ **4** : to produce musical or harmonious sounds **5** : BUZZ, RING **6** : to make a cry : CALL **7** : to give information or evidence *transitive verb* **1** : to utter with musical inflections; *especially* : to interpret in musical tones produced by the voice **2** : to relate or celebrate in verse **3** : CHANT, INTONE **4** : to bring or accompany to a place or state by singing ⟨*sings* the child to sleep⟩ — **sing·able** \'sin-ə-bəl\ *adjective*

²sing *noun* (1850) : a session of group singing

sing–along \'sin-ə-,lȯn\ *noun* (1966) : SONGFEST; *also* : a song appropriate for a sing-along

¹singe \'sinj\ *transitive verb* **singed; singe·ing** \'sin-jin\ [Middle English *sengen*, from Old English *sengan*; akin to Old High German bi*sengan* to singe, Old Church Slavonic *isęknǫti* to dry up] (before 12th century) : to burn superficially or lightly : SCORCH; *especially* : to remove the hair, down, or fuzz from usually by passing rapidly over a flame

²singe *noun* (1658) : a slight burn : SCORCH

¹sing·er \'sin-ər\ *noun* (14th century) : one that sings

²sing·er \'sin-jər\ *noun* (circa 1875) : one that singes

singing game *noun* (1881) : a children's game in which the players accompany their actions with the singing of a narrative song

¹sin·gle \'sin-gəl\ *adjective* [Middle English, from Middle French, from Latin *singulus* one only; akin to Latin *sem-* one — more at SAME] (14th century) **1 a** : not married **b** : of or relating to celibacy **2** : unaccompanied by others : LONE, SOLE ⟨the *single* survivor of the disaster⟩ **3 a** (1) : consisting of or having only one part, feature, or portion ⟨*single* consonants⟩ (2) : consisting of one as opposed to or in contrast with many : UNIFORM ⟨a *single* standard for men and women⟩ (3) : consisting of only one in number ⟨holds to a *single* ideal⟩ **b** : having but one whorl of petals or ray flowers ⟨a *single* rose⟩ **4** : consisting of a separate unique whole : INDIVIDUAL ⟨every *single* citizen⟩ **b** : of, relating to, or involving only one person **5 a** : FRANK, HONEST ⟨a *single* devotion⟩ **b** : exclusively attentive ⟨an eye *single* to the truth⟩

6 : UNBROKEN, UNDIVIDED **7** : having no equal or like : SINGULAR **8** : designed for the use of one person only ⟨a *single* room⟩ ⟨*single* bed⟩

²single *verb* **sin·gled; sin·gling** \-g(ə-)lin\ (1628) *transitive verb* **1** : to select or distinguish from a number or group — usually used with *out* **2 a** : to advance or score (a base runner) by a single **b** : to bring about the scoring of (a run) by a single *intransitive verb* : to make a single in baseball

³single *noun* (1646) **1 a** : a separate individual person or thing **b** : an unmarried person and especially one young and socially active — usually used in plural **c** : a recording having one short tune on each side **2** : a base hit that allows the batter to reach first base **3 a** *plural* : a tennis match or similar game with one player on each side **b** : a golf match between two players — usually used in plural **4** : a room (as in a hotel) for one guest — compare DOUBLE 7

sin·gle–ac·tion \'sin-gəl-'ak-shən\ *adjective* (1900) *of a revolver* : that can be cocked only by manually retracting the hammer

sin·gle–blind \'sin-gəl-,blīnd\ *adjective* (1963) : of, relating to, or being an experimental procedure in which the experimenters but not the subjects know the makeup of the test and control groups during the actual course of the experiments — compare DOUBLE-BLIND

single bond *noun* (1903) : a chemical bond in which one pair of electrons is shared by two atoms in a molecule especially when the atoms can share more than one pair of electrons — compare DOUBLE BOND, TRIPLE BOND

sin·gle–breast·ed \'sin-gəl-'bres-təd\ *adjective* (1796) : having a center closing with one row of buttons and no lap ⟨a *single-breasted* coat⟩

single combat *noun* (1610) : combat between two persons

single cross *noun* (1940) : a first-generation hybrid between two selected and usually inbred lines — compare DOUBLE CROSS 2

single entry *noun* (1826) : a method of bookkeeping that recognizes only one side of a business transaction and usually consists only of a record of cash and personal accounts with debtors and creditors

single file *noun* (1670) : ⁶FILE 1 — **single file** *adverb*

¹sin·gle–foot \'sin-gəl-,fùt\ *noun, plural* **single–foots** (1867) : ⁷RACK b

²single–foot *intransitive verb* (1890) *of a horse* : to go at a rack — **sin·gle–foot·er** *noun*

¹sin·gle–hand·ed \,sin-gəl-'han-dəd\ *adjective* (1709) **1** : managed or done by one person or with one on a side **2** : working alone or unassisted by others — **sin·gle–hand·ed·ly** *adverb*

²single–handed *adverb* (1815) : in a single-handed manner

sin·gle–hand·er \-'han-dər\ *noun* (1946) : a person who sails single-handed

sin·gle–heart·ed \,sin-gəl-'här-təd\ *adjective* (1577) : characterized by sincerity and unity of purpose or dedication — **sin·gle–heart·ed·ly** *adverb* — **sin·gle–heart·ed·ness** *noun*

single knot *noun* (circa 1930)

: OVERHAND KNOT

single–lens reflex \'sin-gəl-'lenz-\ *noun* (1940) : a camera having a single lens that forms an image which is reflected to the viewfinder or recorded on film

sin·gle–mind·ed \,sin-gəl-'mīn-dəd, 'sin-gəl-,\ *adjective* (1860) : having one driving purpose or resolve : DETERMINED, DEDICATED — **sin·gle–mind·ed·ly** *adverb* — **sin·gle–mind·ed·ness** *noun*

sin·gle·ness \'sin-gəl-nəs\ *noun* (1560) : the quality or state of being single

sin·gle–phase \'sin-gəl-'fāz\ *adjective* (1900) : of or relating to a circuit energized by a single alternating electromotive force

sin·gle–space \-'spās\ *transitive verb* (1928) : to type or print with no blank lines between lines of text

sin·gle·stick \-,stik\ *noun* (1771) : fighting or fencing with a wooden stick or sword held in one hand; *also* : the weapon used

sin·glet \'sin-glət\ *noun* (circa 1746) **1** [from its having only one thickness of cloth] *chiefly British* : an athletic jersey : UNDERSHIRT **2** : an atom or molecule that has no net electronic magnetic moment; *also* : an excited state of an atom or molecule that is a singlet

single tax *noun* (1853) : a tax to be levied on a single item (as real estate) as the sole source of public revenue

sin·gle·ton \'sin-gəl-tən\ *noun* [French, from English *single*] (1876) **1** : a card that is the only one of its suit originally dealt to a player **2 a** : an individual member or thing distinct from others grouped with it **b** : an offspring born singly ⟨*singletons* are more common than twins⟩

sin·gle–track \'sin-gəl-'trak\ *adjective* (1849) **1** : having only one track **2** : lacking intellectual range, receptiveness, or flexibility : ONE-TRACK

sin·gle–tree \'sin-gəl-(,)trē\ *noun* (circa 1841) : WHIFFLETREE

sin·gle–val·ued \,sin-gəl-'val-(,)yüd\ *adjective* (1879) : having one and only one value of the range associated with each value of the domain ⟨a *single-valued* function⟩ — compare MULTIPLE-VALUED

single wing *noun* (1945) : an offensive football formation in which one back plays as a flanker and two backs line up four or five yards behind the line in position to receive a direct snap from center

sin·gly \'sin-g(ə-)lē\ *adverb* (14th century) **1** : without the company of others : INDIVIDUALLY **2** : SINGLE-HANDED

¹sing·song \'sin-,sȯn\ *noun* (1609) **1** : verse with marked and regular rhythm and rhyme **2** : a voice delivery marked by a narrow range or monotonous pattern of pitch **3** *British* : SONGFEST — **sing·songy** \-,sȯn-ē\ *adjective*

²singsong *adjective* (1734) : having a monotonous cadence or rhythm

sing·spiel \'sin-,spēl, 'zin-,shpēl\ *noun* [German, from *singen* to sing + *Spiel* play] (1876) : a musical work popular in Germany especially in the latter part of the 18th century characterized by spoken dialogue interspersed with popular or folk songs

¹sin·gu·lar \'sin-gyə-lər\ *adjective* [Middle English *singuler*, from Middle French, from Latin *singularis*, from *singulus* only one — more at SINGLE] (14th century) **1 a** : of or relating to a separate person or thing : INDIVIDUAL **b** : of, relating to, or being a word form denoting one person, thing, or instance **c** : of or relating to a single instance or to something considered by itself

2 : distinguished by superiority : EXCEPTIONAL ⟨an artist of *singular* attainments⟩
3 : being out of the ordinary : UNUSUAL ⟨on the way home we had a *singular* adventure⟩
4 : departing from general usage or expectation : PECULIAR, ODD ⟨the air had a *singular* chill⟩
5 a *of a matrix* : having a determinant equal to zero **b** *of a linear transformation* : having the property that the matrix of coefficients of the new variables has a determinant equal to zero
synonym see STRANGE
— **sin·gu·lar·ly** *adverb*
²**singular** *noun* (14th century)
1 : the singular number, the inflectional form denoting it, or a word in that form
2 : a singular term
sin·gu·lar·i·ty \ˌsiŋ-gyə-ˈlar-ə-tē\ *noun, plural* **-ties** (14th century)
1 : something that is singular: as **a** : a separate unit **b** : unusual or distinctive manner or behavior : PECULIARITY
2 : the quality or state of being singular
3 : a point at which the derivative of a given function of a complex variable does not exist but every neighborhood of which contains points for which the derivative exists
4 : a point or region of infinite mass density at which space and time are infinitely distorted by gravitational forces and which is held to be the final state of matter falling into a black hole
sin·gu·lar·ize \ˈsiŋ-gyə-lə-ˌrīz\ *transitive verb* **-ized; -iz·ing** (1589)
: to make singular
singular point *noun* (circa 1856)
: SINGULARITY 3
Sin·ha·la \sin-ˈhä-lä, siŋ-\ *noun* [Sanskrit *Siṁhala* Sri Lanka] (circa 1954)
: SINHALESE 2
Sin·ha·lese *or* **Sin·gha·lese** \ˌsin-gə-ˈlēz, ˌsin-(h)ə-, -ˈlēs\ *noun, plural* **Sinhalese** *or* **Singhalese** (1598)
1 : a member of a people that inhabit Sri Lanka and form a major part of its population
2 : the Indo-Aryan language of the Sinhalese people
— **Sinhalese** *or* **Sin·ghalese** *adjective*
si·ni·cize \ˈsī-nə-ˌsīz, ˈsi-\ *transitive verb* **-cized; -ciz·ing** *often capitalized* [Medieval Latin *sinicus* Chinese, from Late Latin *Sinae*, plural, Chinese — more at SINO-] (1889)
: to modify by Chinese influence
sin·is·ter \ˈsi-nəs-tər, *archaic* sə-ˈnis-\ *adjective* [Middle English *sinistre*, from Latin *sinistr-, sinister* on the left side, unlucky, inauspicious] (15th century)
1 *archaic* : UNFAVORABLE, UNLUCKY
2 *archaic* : FRAUDULENT
3 : singularly evil or productive of evil
4 a : of, relating to, or situated to the left or on the left side of something; *especially* : being or relating to the side of a heraldic shield at the left of the person bearing it **b** : of ill omen by reason of being on the left
5 : presaging ill fortune or trouble
6 : accompanied by or leading to disaster ☆ ◇
— **sin·is·ter·ly** *adverb*
— **sin·is·ter·ness** *noun*
si·nis·tral \ˈsi-nəs-trəl, sə-ˈnis-\ *adjective* (1803)
: of, relating to, or inclined to the left: as **a** : LEFT-HANDED **b** *of a gastropod shell* : having the whorls coiling counterclockwise down the spire when viewed with the apex toward the observer and having the aperture situated on the left of the axis when held with the spire uppermost and with the aperture opening toward the observer — compare DEXTRAL b
si·nis·trous \ˈsi-nəs-trəs, sə-ˈnis-\ *adjective* (circa 1575)
archaic : SINISTER
Si·nit·ic \sī-ˈni-tik, sə-\ *adjective* [Late Latin *Sinae*, plural, Chinese + English *-itic* (as in *Semitic*) — more at SINO-] (circa 1895)

: of or relating to the Chinese, their language, or their culture
¹**sink** \ˈsiŋk\ *verb* **sank** \ˈsaŋk\ *or* **sunk** \ˈsəŋk\; **sunk; sink·ing** [Middle English, from Old English *sincan*; akin to Old High German *sinkan* to sink] (before 12th century)
intransitive verb
1 a : to go to the bottom : SUBMERGE **b** : to become partly buried (as in mud) **c** : to become engulfed
2 a (1) : to fall or drop to a lower place or level (2) : to flow at a lower depth or level (3) : to burn with lower intensity (4) : to fall to a lower pitch or volume ⟨his voice *sank* to a whisper⟩ **b** : to subside gradually : SETTLE **c** : to disappear from view **d** : to slope gradually : DIP
3 a : to soak or become absorbed : PENETRATE **b** : to become impressively known or felt ⟨the lesson had *sunk* in⟩
4 : to become deeply absorbed ⟨*sank* into reverie⟩
5 a : to go downward in quality, state, or condition **b** : to grow less in amount or worth
6 a : to fall or drop slowly for lack of strength **b** : to become depressed **c** : to fail in health or strength
transitive verb
1 a : to cause to sink ⟨*sink* a battleship⟩ **b** : to force down especially below the earth's surface **c** : to cause (something) to penetrate
2 : to engage deeply the attention of : IMMERSE
3 a : to dig or bore (a well or shaft) in the earth : EXCAVATE **b** : to form by cutting or excising ⟨*sink* words in stone⟩
4 : to cast down or bring to a low condition or state : OVERWHELM, DEFEAT
5 : to lower in standing or reputation : ABASE
6 a : to lessen in value or amount **b** : to lower or soften (the voice) in speaking
7 : RESTRAIN, SUPPRESS ⟨*sinks* her pride and approaches the despised neighbor —Richard Harrison⟩
8 : to pay off (as a debt) : LIQUIDATE
9 : INVEST
10 : DROP 7c ⟨*sink* a putt⟩
— **sink·able** \ˈsiŋ-kə-bəl\ *adjective*
²**sink** *noun* (15th century)
1 a : a pool or pit for the deposit of waste or sewage : CESSPOOL **b** : a ditch or tunnel for carrying off sewage : SEWER **c** : a stationary basin connected with a drain and usually a water supply for washing and drainage
2 : a place where vice, corruption, or evil collects
3 : SUMP 3
4 a : a depression in the land surface; *especially* : one having a saline lake with no outlet **b** : SINKHOLE
5 : a body or process that acts as a storage device or disposal mechanism: as **a** : HEAT SINK; *broadly* : a device that collects or dissipates energy (as radiation) **b** : a reactant with or absorber of a substance
sink·age \ˈsiŋ-kij\ *noun* (1883)
1 : the process or degree of sinking
2 : DEPRESSION, INDENTATION
3 : the distance from the top line of a full page to the first line of sunk matter
sink·er \ˈsiŋ-kər\ *noun* (1708)
1 : one that sinks; *specifically* : a weight for sinking a fishing line, seine, or sounding line
2 : DOUGHNUT
3 : a fastball that sinks as it reaches the plate — called also *sinker ball*
sink·hole \ˈsiŋk-ˌhōl\ *noun* (15th century)
1 : a hollow place or depression in which drainage collects
2 : a hollow in a limestone region that communicates with a cavern or passage
3 : SINK 2
sinking fund *noun* (1724)
: a fund set up and accumulated by usually regular deposits for paying off the principal of a debt when it falls due

sin·less \ˈsin-ləs\ *adjective* (before 12th century)
: free from sin : IMPECCABLE
— **sin·less·ly** *adverb*
— **sin·less·ness** *noun*
sin·ner \ˈsi-nər\ *noun* (14th century)
1 : one that sins
2 : REPROBATE, SCAMP
Si·no- \ˈsī-(ˌ)nō, ˈsī-, -nə\ *combining form* [French, from Late Latin *Sinae*, plural, Chinese, from Greek *Sinai*, probably of Indo-Aryan origin; akin to Sanskrit *Cīnā*, plural, Chinese]
1 : Chinese ⟨*sino*logy⟩
2 : Chinese and ⟨*Sino*-Tibetan⟩
si·no·atri·al \ˌsī-nō-ˈā-trē-əl\ *adjective* [New Latin *sinus* + *atrium*] (1913)
: of, involving, or being the sinoatrial node ⟨*sinoatrial* block⟩
sinoatrial node *noun* (1913)
: a small mass of tissue that is embedded in the musculature of the right atrium of higher vertebrates and that originates the impulses stimulating the heartbeat
si·no·logue \ˈsī-nᵊl-ˌóg, ˈsi-, -ˌäg\ *noun* [French, from Late Latin *Sinae* + French *-logue*] (1853)
: a specialist in sinology
si·nol·o·gy \sī-ˈnä-lə-jē, sə-\ *noun* [probably from French *sinologie*, from *sino-* + *-logie* -logy] (circa 1882)
: the study of the Chinese and especially their language, literature, history, and culture
— **si·no·log·i·cal** \ˌsī-nᵊl-ˈä-ji-kəl, ˌsi-\ *adjective*

☆ **SYNONYMS**
Sinister, baleful, malign mean seriously threatening evil or disaster. SINISTER suggests a general or vague feeling of fear or apprehension on the part of the observer ⟨a *sinister* aura haunts the place⟩. BALEFUL imputes perniciousness or destructiveness to something whether working openly or covertly ⟨exerting a corrupt and *baleful* influence⟩. MALIGN applies to what is inherently evil or harmful ⟨the *malign* effects of racism⟩.

◇ **WORD HISTORY**
sinister Words for "left" and "right" in a wide variety of languages betray an ancient prejudice toward left-handers. Because most people are right-handed and use their left hand much less deftly, the left side is typically associated with clumsiness or weakness; and in the primitive, male-dominated world of farmers, warriors, and hunters from which we all ultimately descend, an attack by a wild animal or another warrior on one's weaker left side could be fatal, so that left-handedness was also associated with evil and ill fortune. The "right" word, on the other hand, is often, as in English, associated with correctness and moral rectitude. The Latin words *sinister*, *scaevus*, and *laevus* all had both the literal meaning "on the left" and various negative meanings: "unlucky," "harmful," or "perverted." Idiosyncratically, Latin *sinister* could also mean "favorable" in reference to an omen, because a Roman augur, when following the Etruscan method of doing divinations, faced the south as he stood in a ritually prescribed space, and favorable omens, such as the flight of a bird, were thought to appear from the east, the augur's left side.

— **si·nol·o·gist** \sī-'nä-lə-jist, sə-\ *noun*

si·no·pia \sə-'nō-pē-ə\ *noun, plural* **-pi·as** *or* **-pie** \-pē-,ā\ [Italian, from Latin *sinopis*, from Greek *sinōpis*, from *Sinōpē* Sinop, ancient seaport in Asia Minor] (1844)
1 : a red to reddish brown earth pigment used by the ancients that depends for its color on its content of red ferric oxide
2 : a preliminary drawing for a fresco done in sinopia

Si·no–Ti·bet·an \,sī-nō-tə-'be-t°n, 'sī-\ *noun* (1920)
: a language family comprising Tibeto-Burman and Chinese

sin·se·mil·la \,sin-sə-'mē-lə, -'mi-; -'mē-yə, -'mēl\ *noun* [American Spanish, from *sin* without + *semilla* seed] (1975)
: highly potent marijuana from female plants that are specially tended and kept seedless by preventing pollination in order to induce a high resin content; *also* **:** a female hemp plant grown to produce sinsemilla

sin·syne \'sin-,sīn\ *adverb* [Middle English (Scots) *sensyne*, from *sen* since (contraction of Middle English *sithen*) + *syne* since — more at SINCE, SYNE] (14th century)
chiefly Scottish **:** since that time

sin tax *noun* (1964)
: a tax on substances or activities considered sinful or harmful (as tobacco, alcohol, or gambling)

sin·ter \'sin-tər\ *verb* [German *Sinter* slag, cinder, from Old High German *sintar* — more at CINDER] (1871)
transitive verb
: to cause to become a coherent mass by heating without melting
intransitive verb
: to undergo sintering
— **sinter** *noun*
— **sin·ter·abil·i·ty** \,sin-tə-rə-'bi-lə-tē\ *noun*

sin·u·ate \'sin-yə-wət, -,wāt\ *adjective* [Latin *sinuatus*, past participle of *sinuare* to bend, from *sinus* curve] (1688)
: having the margin wavy with strong indentations ⟨*sinuate* leaves⟩

sin·u·os·i·ty \,sin-yə-'wä-sə-tē\ *noun, plural* **-ties** (1598)
1 : the quality or state of being sinuous
2 : something that is sinuous

sin·u·ous \'sin-yə-wəs\ *adjective* [Latin *sinuosus*, from *sinus*] (1578)
1 a : of a serpentine or wavy form **:** WINDING **b :** marked by strong lithe movements
2 : INTRICATE, COMPLEX
— **sin·u·ous·ly** *adverb*
— **sin·u·ous·ness** *noun*

si·nus \'sī-nəs\ *noun* [Middle English, from Medieval Latin, from Latin, curve, fold, hollow] (15th century)
: CAVITY, HOLLOW: as **a :** a narrow elongated tract extending from a focus of suppuration and serving for the discharge of pus **b** (1) **:** a cavity in the substance of a bone of the skull that usually communicates with the nostrils and contains air (2) **:** a channel for venous blood (3) **:** a dilatation in a bodily canal or vessel **c :** a cleft or indentation between adjoining lobes (as of a leaf or corolla)

si·nus·i·tis \,sīn-yə-'sī-təs, ,sī-nə-\ *noun* (1896)
: inflammation of a sinus of the skull

si·nu·soid \'sīn-yə-,sóid, 'sī-nə-\ *noun* [Medieval Latin *sinus* sine] (1823)
1 : SINE CURVE, SINE WAVE
2 [New Latin *sinus*] **:** a minute endothelium-lined space or passage for blood in the tissues of an organ (as the liver)

si·nu·soi·dal \,sīn-yə-'sói-d°l, ,sī-nə-\ *adjective* (1878)
: of, relating to, shaped like, or varying according to a sine curve or sine wave ⟨*sinusoidal* motion⟩ ⟨*sinusoidal* grooves⟩
— **si·nu·soi·dal·ly** \-d°l-ē\ *adverb*

sinusoidal projection *noun* (1944)
: an equal-area map projection capable of showing the entire surface of the earth with all parallels as straight lines evenly spaced, the central meridian as one half the length of the equator, and all other meridians as curved lines

si·nus ve·no·sus \'sī-nəs-vi-'nō-səs\ *noun* [New Latin, venous sinus] (circa 1839)
: an enlarged pouch that adjoins the heart, is formed by the union of the large systemic veins, and is the passage through which venous blood enters the heart in lower vertebrates and in embryos of higher forms

Si·on \'sī-ən\ *variant of* ZION

Siou·an \'sü-ən\ *noun* (1889)
1 : an American Indian language family of central and southeastern North America
2 : a member of any of the peoples speaking Siouan languages

Sioux \'sü\ *noun, plural* **Sioux** \'sü, 'süz\ [French, short for *Nadouessioux*, from Ojibwa *na·towe·ssiw-*] (1712)
1 : DAKOTA
2 : SIOUAN

¹sip \'sip\ *verb* **sipped; sip·ping** [Middle English *sippen*; akin to Low German *sippen* to sip] (14th century)
intransitive verb
: to take a sip of something especially repeatedly
transitive verb
1 : to drink in small quantities
2 : to take sips from
— **sip·per** *noun*

²sip *noun* (15th century)
1 : a small draft taken with the lips
2 : the act of sipping

¹si·phon \'sī-fən\ *noun* [French *siphon*, from Latin *siphon-, sipho* tube, pipe, siphon, from Greek *siphōn*] (1659)
1 a : a tube bent to form two legs of unequal length by which a liquid can be transferred to a lower level over an intermediate elevation by the pressure of the

siphon 1a

atmosphere in forcing the liquid up the shorter branch of the tube immersed in it while the excess of weight of the liquid in the longer branch when once filled causes a continuous flow **b** *usually* **syphon :** a bottle for holding aerated water that is driven out through a bent tube in its neck by the pressure of the gas when a valve in the tube is opened
2 : any of various tubular organs in animals and especially mollusks or arthropods that are used for drawing in or ejecting fluids — see CLAM illustration

²siphon *verb* **si·phoned; si·phon·ing** \'sī-fə-niŋ, 'sīf-niŋ\ (1859)
transitive verb
: to convey, draw off, or empty by or as if by a siphon — often used with *off*
intransitive verb
: to pass by or as if by a siphon

si·pho·no·phore \sī-'fä-nə-,fōr, 'sī-fə-nə-, -,fór\ *noun* [ultimately from Greek *siphōn* + *pherein* to carry — more at BEAR] (1883)
: any of an order (Siphonophora) of compound free-swimming or floating pelagic hydrozoans that are mostly delicate, transparent, and colored and have specialized zooids

si·pho·no·stele \sī-'fä-nə-,stēl, ,sī-fə-nə-'stē-lē\ *noun* [Greek *siphōn* tube, siphon] (1902)
: a stele consisting of vascular tissue surrounding a central core of pith parenchyma

sip·pet \'si-pət\ *noun* [alteration of *sop*] (1530)
chiefly British **:** a small bit of toast or fried bread especially for garnishing

sir \'sər\ *noun* [Middle English, from *sire*] (13th century)
1 a : a man entitled to be addressed as *sir* — used as a title before the given name of a knight or baronet and formerly sometimes before the given name of a priest **b :** a man of rank or position
2 a : used as a usually respectful form of address **b** *capitalized* — used as a conventional form of address in the salutation of a letter

Si·rach \'sī-rak *also* sə-'räk\ *noun* [Greek *Seirach*]
: a didactic book of the Roman Catholic canon of the Old Testament

sir·dar \'sər-,där, sər-\ *noun* [Hindi *sardār*, from Persian] (1595)
1 a : a person of high rank (as an hereditary noble) especially in India **b :** the commander of the Anglo-Egyptian army
2 : one (as a foreman) holding a responsible position especially in India

¹sire \'sīr\ *noun* [Middle English, from Old French, from Latin *senior* older — more at SENIOR] (13th century)
1 a : FATHER **b** *archaic* **:** male ancestor **:** FOREFATHER **c :** AUTHOR, ORIGINATOR
2 a *archaic* **:** a man of rank or authority; *especially* **:** LORD — used formerly as a form of address and as a title **b** *obsolete* **:** an elderly man **:** SENIOR
3 : the male parent of an animal and especially of a domestic animal

²sire *transitive verb* **sired; sir·ing** (1611)
1 : BEGET — used especially of male domestic animals
2 : to bring into being **:** ORIGINATE

¹si·ren \'sī-rən, *for 3 also* sī-'rēn\ *noun* [Middle English, from Middle French & Latin; Middle French *sereine*, from Late Latin *sirena*, from Latin *siren*, from Greek *seirēn*] (14th century)
1 *often capitalized* **:** any of a group of female and partly human creatures in Greek mythology that lured mariners to destruction by their singing
2 a : a woman who sings with bewitching sweetness **b :** TEMPTRESS
3 a : an apparatus producing musical tones especially in acoustical studies by the rapid interruption of a current of air, steam, or fluid by a perforated rotating disk **b :** a device often electrically operated for producing a penetrating warning sound ⟨ambulance *siren*⟩ ⟨air-raid *siren*⟩
4 [New Latin, from Latin] **:** either of two North American eel-shaped amphibians that constitute a genus (*Siren*) and have small forelimbs but neither hind legs nor pelvis and have permanent external gills as well as lungs

²si·ren \'sī-rən\ *adjective* (1568)
: resembling that of a siren **:** ENTICING

si·re·ni·an \sī-'rē-nē-ən\ *noun* [New Latin *Sirenia*, from Latin *siren*] (1883)
: any of an order (Sirenia) of aquatic herbivorous mammals including the manatee, dugong, and Steller's sea cow

siren song *noun* (1568)
: an alluring utterance or appeal; *especially* **:** one that is seductive or deceptive

Sir·i·us \'sir-ē-əs\ *noun* [Middle English, from Latin, from Greek *Seirios*]
: a star of the constellation Canis Major that is the brightest star in the heavens — called also *Dog Star*

sir·loin \'sər-,lóin\ *noun* [alteration of earlier *surloin*, modification of Middle French *surlonge*, from *sur* over (from Latin *super*) + *loigne, longe* loin — more at OVER, LOIN] (1554)
: a cut of meat and especially of beef from the part of the hindquarter just in front of the round — see BEEF illustration

si·roc·co \sə-'rä-(,)kō, shə-\ *noun, plural* **-cos** [Italian *scirocco, sirocco*, from Arabic *sharq* east] (1617)

1 a : a hot dust-laden wind from the Libyan deserts that blows on the northern Mediterranean coast chiefly in Italy, Malta, and Sicily **b** : a warm moist oppressive southeast wind in the same regions
2 : a hot or warm wind of cyclonic origin from an arid or heated region

sir·rah also **sir·ra** \'sir-ə\ noun [alteration of sir] (1526)
obsolete — used as a form of address implying inferiority in the person addressed

sir·ree also **sir·ee** \(ˌ)sər-'ē\ noun [by alteration] (1823)
: SIR — used as an emphatic form usually after yes or no

sir-reverence noun [probably alteration of save-reverence, translation of Medieval Latin salva reverentia saving (your) reverence] (1575)
1 obsolete — used as an expression of apology before a statement that might be taken as offensive
2 obsolete : human feces; also : a lump of human feces

Sir Rog·er de Cov·er·ley \sə(r)-ˌrä-jər-di-'kə-vər-lē\ noun [alteration of roger of coverley, probably from Roger, male given name + of + Coverley, a fictitious place name] (1804)
: an English country-dance that resembles the Virginia reel

sirup variant of SYRUP

sir·vente \sir-'vänt\ or **sir·ven·tes** \-'ven-təs\ noun, plural **sir·ventes** \-'vänt, -'vän(t)s, -'ven-təs\ [French, from Provençal sirventes, literally, servant's song, from sirvent servant, from Latin servient-, serviens, present participle of servire to serve] (1819)
: a usually moral or religious song of the Provençal troubadours satirizing social vices

sis \'sis\ noun (1656)
: SISTER — usually used in direct address

-sis noun suffix, plural **-ses** [Latin, from Greek, feminine suffix of action]
: process : action ⟨peristalsis⟩

si·sal \'sī-səl, -zəl\ noun [Sisal, port in Yucatán, Mexico] (1843)
1 a : a strong durable white fiber used especially for hard fiber cordage and twine — called also sisal hemp **b** : a widely cultivated Mexican agave (Agave sisalana) whose leaves yield sisal
2 : any of several fibers similar to true sisal

sis·kin \'sis-kən\ noun [German dialect Sisschen, diminutive of Middle High German zīse siskin, of Slavic origin; akin to Czech čížek siskin] (1562)
: a small chiefly greenish and yellowish finch (Carduelis spinus) of Europe, Asia, and northern Africa that is related to the goldfinch — compare PINE SISKIN, RED SISKIN

sis·si·fied \'si-si-ˌfīd\ adjective (circa 1903)
: of, relating to, or having the characteristics of a sissy

sis·sy \'si-sē\ noun, plural **sissies** [sis] (1891)
: an effeminate man or boy; also : a timid or cowardly person
— **sissy** adjective

sis·ter \'sis-tər\ noun [Middle English suster, sister, partly from Old English sweostor and partly from Scandinavian origin; akin to Old Norse systir sister; akin to Latin soror sister, Sanskrit svasṛ] (before 12th century)
1 : a female who has one or both parents in common with another
2 often capitalized **a** : a member of a women's religious order (as of nuns or deaconesses); especially : one of a Roman Catholic congregation under simple vows **b** : a woman or girl who is a member of a Christian church
3 : a woman regarded as a comrade ⟨my Korean sisters —Alice Walker⟩
4 : one that is closely similar to or associated with another ⟨sister schools⟩ ⟨sister cities⟩
5 chiefly British : NURSE

6 a : GIRL, WOMAN; especially : a girl or woman who is black **b** : PERSON — usually used in the phrase weak sister
7 : a member of a sorority

sis·ter·hood \-ˌhu̇d\ noun (1609)
1 a : the state of being a sister **b** : sisterly relationship
2 : a community or society of sisters; especially : a society of women religious
3 : the solidarity of women based on shared conditions, experiences, or concerns

sis·ter-in-law \'sis-t(ə-)rən-ˌlȯ, -tərn-ˌlȯ\ noun, plural **sis·ters-in-law** \-tər-zən-\ (15th century)
1 : the sister of one's spouse
2 a : the wife of one's brother **b** : the wife of one's spouse's brother

sis·ter·ly \'sis-tər-lē\ adjective (circa 1570)
: of, relating to, or having the characteristics of a sister
— **sisterly** adverb

Sis·tine \'sis-ˌtēn, sis-'\ adjective [Italian sistino, from New Latin sixtinus, from Sixtus, name of some popes] (circa 1864)
1 : of or relating to any of the popes named Sixtus
2 [from Pope Sixtus IV (died 1484)] : of or relating to the Sistine chapel in the Vatican

Sis·y·phe·an \ˌsi-sə-'fē-ən\ or **Si·syph·i·an** \si-'si-fē-ən\ adjective (1635)
: of, relating to, or suggestive of the labors of Sisyphus

Sis·y·phus \'si-sə-fəs\ noun [Latin, from Greek Sisyphos]
: a legendary king of Corinth condemned eternally to repeat the cycle of rolling a heavy rock up a hill in Hades only to have it roll down again as it nears the top

¹sit \'sit\ verb **sat** \'sat\; **sit·ting** [Middle English sitten, from Old English sittan; akin to Old High German sizzen to sit, Latin sedēre, Greek hezesthai to sit, hedra seat] (before 12th century)
intransitive verb
1 a : to rest on the buttocks or haunches ⟨sit in a chair⟩ — often used with down **b** : PERCH, ROOST
2 : to occupy a place as a member of an official body ⟨sit in Congress⟩
3 : to hold a session : be in session for official business
4 : to cover eggs for hatching : BROOD
5 a : to take a position for having one's portrait painted or for being photographed **b** : to serve as a model
6 archaic : to have one's dwelling place : DWELL
7 a : to lie or hang relative to a wearer ⟨the collar sits awkwardly⟩ **b** : to affect one with or as if with weight ⟨the food sat heavily on his stomach⟩
8 : LIE, REST ⟨a kettle sitting on the stove⟩
9 a : to have a location ⟨the house sits well back from the road⟩ **b** of wind : to blow from a certain direction
10 : to remain inactive or quiescent ⟨the car sits in the garage⟩
11 : to take an examination
12 : BABY-SIT
13 : to please or agree with one — used with with and an adverb ⟨the decision did not sit well with me⟩
transitive verb
1 : to cause to be seated : place on or in a seat — often used with down
2 : to sit on (eggs)
3 : to keep one's seat on ⟨sit a horse⟩
4 : to provide seats or seating room for ⟨the car will sit six people⟩
usage see SET
— **sit on 1** : to hold deliberations concerning **2** : REPRESS, SQUELCH **3** : to delay action or decision concerning
— **sit pretty** : to be in a highly favorable situation

— **sit tight 1** : to maintain one's position without change **2** : to remain quiet in or as if in hiding
— **sit under** : to attend religious service under the instruction or ministrations of; also : to attend the classes or lectures of

²sit noun (1776)
1 : the manner in which a garment fits
2 : an act or period of sitting

si·tar \si-'tär, 'si-ˌ\ noun [Hindi sitār, from Persian, a three-stringed lute, from sih three + tār string, thread] (1845)
: an Indian lute with a long neck and a varying number of strings
— **si·tar·ist** \-ist\ noun

sit·com \'sit-ˌkäm\ noun [situation comedy] (1964)
: SITUATION COMEDY

¹sit-down \'sit-ˌdau̇n\ adjective (circa 1837)
: served to seated diners ⟨a sit-down dinner⟩; also : of, relating to, or serving sit-down meals ⟨a sit-down restaurant⟩

²sit-down \'sit-ˌdau̇n\ noun (1936)
1 : a cessation of work by employees while maintaining continuous occupation of their place of employment as a protest and means toward forcing compliance with demands
2 : a mass obstruction of an activity by sitting down to demonstrate a grievance or to get the activity modified or halted

¹site \'sīt\ noun [Middle English, place, position, from Middle French or Latin; Middle French, from Latin situs, from sinere to leave, allow] (14th century)
1 a : the spatial location of an actual or planned structure or set of structures (as a building, town, or monuments) **b** : a space of ground occupied or to be occupied by a building
2 : the place, scene, or point of something

²site transitive verb **sit·ed; sit·ing** (15th century)
: to place on a site or in position : LOCATE

sith \'sith\ or **sith·ence** \'si-thən(t)s\ or **sith·ens** \'si-thənz\ archaic variant of SINCE

sit-in \'sit-ˌin\ noun (1937)
1 : SIT-DOWN 1
2 a : an act of occupying seats in a racially segregated establishment in organized protest against discrimination **b** : an act of sitting in the seats or on the floor of an establishment as a means of organized protest

sit in intransitive verb (1868)
1 : to take part in or be present at a session of music or discussion as a visitor
2 : to participate in a sit-in

Sit·ka spruce \'sit-kə-\ noun [Sitka, Alaska] (1895)
: a tall spruce (Picea sitchensis) of the northern Pacific coast that has thin reddish brown bark, flat needles, and cones with slightly toothed scales

si·tos·ter·ol \sī-'täs-tə-ˌrȯl, sə-, -ˌrōl\ noun [Greek sitos grain + English sterol] (1898)
: any of several sterols that are widespread especially in plant products (as wheat germ or soy bean oil) and are used as starting materials for the synthesis of steroid hormones

sit out transitive verb (1659)
: to refrain from participating in ⟨sit out the next dance⟩

sit·ter \'si-tər\ noun (14th century)
: one that sits; especially : one who baby-sits children

sitar

¹sit·ting \'si-tiŋ\ noun (13th century)
1 a : the act of one that sits **b :** a single occasion of continuous sitting (as for a portrait or meal)
2 a : a brooding over eggs for hatching **b :** SETTING 6
3 : SESSION ⟨a sitting of the legislature⟩

²sitting adjective (15th century)
1 : that is setting ⟨a sitting hen⟩
2 : occupying a judicial, legislative, or executive seat **:** being in office
3 : easily hit or played ⟨a sitting target⟩
4 a : used in or for sitting ⟨a sitting position⟩ **b :** performed while sitting ⟨a sitting shot⟩

sitting duck noun (1942)
: an easy or defenseless target for attack or criticism or unscrupulous dealings

sitting room noun (1771)
: LIVING ROOM 1

¹sit·u·ate \'si-chə-wət, -ˌwāt; 'sich-wət\ adjective [Middle English, from Late Latin situatus, from Latin situs] (15th century)
: having a site **:** LOCATED

²sit·u·ate \'si-chə-ˌwāt\ transitive verb -at·ed; -at·ing (circa 1532)
: to place in a site, situation, context, or category **:** LOCATE

situated adjective (15th century)
1 : having a site, situation, or location **:** LOCATED
2 : provided with money or possessions ⟨comfortably situated⟩

sit·u·a·tion \ˌsi-chə-'wā-shən\ noun (15th century)
1 a : the way in which something is placed in relation to its surroundings **b :** SITE **c** archaic **:** LOCALITY
2 archaic **:** state of health
3 a : position or place of employment **:** POST, JOB **b :** position in life **:** STATUS
4 : position with respect to conditions and circumstances ⟨the military situation remains obscure⟩
5 a : relative position or combination of circumstances at a certain moment **b :** a critical, trying, or unusual state of affairs **:** PROBLEM **c :** a particular or striking complex of affairs at a stage in the action of a narrative or drama

sit·u·a·tion·al \-shnəl, -shə-nºl\ adjective (1903)
1 : of, relating to, or appropriate to a situation
2 : of or relating to situation ethics
— **sit·u·a·tion·al·ly** adverb

situation comedy noun (1946)
: a radio or television comedy series that involves a continuing cast of characters in a succession of episodes

situation ethics noun (1955)
: a system of ethics by which acts are judged within their contexts instead of by categorical principles

sit–up \'sit-ˌəp\ noun (1938)
: a conditioning exercise performed from a supine position by raising the trunk to a sitting position without lifting the feet and returning to the original position

sit up intransitive verb (13th century)
1 a : to rise from a lying to a sitting position **b :** to sit with the back erect
2 : to show interest, alertness, or surprise ⟨sit up and take notice⟩
3 : to stay up after the usual time for going to bed ⟨sat up late to watch the movie⟩

si·tus \'sī-təs\ noun [Latin — more at SITE] (1701)
: the place where something exists or originates; specifically **:** the place where something (as a right) is held to be located in law

sitz bath \'sits-\ noun [part translation of German Sitzbad, from Sitz act of sitting + Bad bath] (1849)
: a tub in which one bathes in a sitting posture; also **:** a bath so taken especially therapeutically

sitz·mark \'sits-ˌmärk, 'zits-\ noun [part translation of German Sitzmarke, from Sitz + Marke mark] (1935)
: a depression left in the snow by a skier falling backward

Si·va \'si-və, 'shi-, 'sē-, 'shē-\ noun [Sanskrit Śiva] (1788)
: the god of destruction and regeneration in the Hindu sacred triad — compare BRAHMA, VISHNU

Si·van \'si-vən\ noun [Hebrew Sīwān] (1535)
: the 9th month of the civil year or the 3d month of the ecclesiastical year in the Jewish calendar — see MONTH table

Si·wash \'sī-ˌwȯsh, -ˌwäsh\ noun [Siwash, fictional college in stories by George Fitch (died 1915) American author] (1936)
: a small usually inland college that is notably provincial in outlook ⟨cheer for dear old Siwash⟩

six \'siks\ noun [Middle English, from six, adjective, from Old English siex; akin to Old High German sehs six, Latin sex, Greek hex] (before 12th century)
1 — see NUMBER table
2 : the sixth in a set or series ⟨the six of spades⟩
3 : something having six units or members: as **a :** an ice-hockey team **b :** a 6-cylinder engine or automobile
— **six** adjective
— **six** pronoun, plural in construction
— **at sixes and sevens :** being in disorder

six·fold \'siks-ˌfōld, -'fōld\ adjective (before 12th century)
1 : having six units or members
2 : being six times as great or as many
— **six·fold** \-'fōld\ adverb

six–gun \'siks-ˌgən\ noun (1912)
: a 6-chambered revolver

six·mo \'siks-(ˌ)mō\ noun, plural sixmos (1924)
: the size of a piece of paper cut six from a sheet; also **:** a book, a page, or paper of this size

six–o–six or 606 \ˌsiks-ˌō-'siks\ noun [from its having been the 606th compound tested and introduced by Paul Ehrlich (died 1915)] (1910)
: ARSPHENAMINE

six–pack \'siks-ˌpak\ noun (1952)
1 : six bottles or cans (as of beer) packaged and purchased as a unit
2 : the contents of a six-pack

six·pence \'siks-pən(t)s, US also -ˌpen(t)s\ noun (14th century)
1 : a former British monetary unit equal to six pennies
2 plural **sixpence** or **six·penc·es :** a coin worth sixpence

six·pen·ny \'siks-pə-nē, US also -ˌpe-nē\ adjective (15th century)
: costing or worth sixpence

sixpenny bit noun (circa 1887)
: SIXPENCE 2

six·pen·ny nail \'siks-ˌpe-nē-\ noun (15th century)
: a nail about two inches long

six–shoot·er \'sik(s)-ˌshü-tər\ noun (1844)
: SIX-GUN

six·teen \ˌsik-'stēn, 'siks-ˌtēn\ noun [Middle English sixtene, from Old English sixtȳne, adjective, from six six + -tȳne (akin to Old English tīen ten) — more at TEN] (before 12th century)
— see NUMBER table
— **sixteen** adjective
— **sixteen** pronoun, plural in construction
— **six·teenth** \-'stēn(t)th, -ˌtēn(t)th\ adjective or noun

six·teen·mo \ˌsik-'stēn-(ˌ)mō\ noun, plural -mos (1847)
: the size of a piece of paper cut 16 from a sheet; also **:** a book, a page, or paper of this size

sixteenth note noun (circa 1861)
: a musical note with the time value of $1/16$ of a whole note — see NOTE illustration

sixteenth rest noun (circa 1890)
: a musical rest corresponding in time value to a sixteenth note — see REST illustration

sixth \'siks(t)th, 'siks(t)\ noun, plural sixths \'siks(ts), 'siks(t)ths\ (12th century)
1 — see NUMBER table
2 a : a musical interval embracing six diatonic degrees **b :** a tone at this interval; specifically **:** SUBMEDIANT **c :** the harmonic combination of two tones a sixth apart
— **sixth** adjective or adverb
— **sixth·ly** \'siksth-lē, 'sikst-\ adverb

sixth chord noun (circa 1903)
: a musical chord consisting of a tone with its third and its sixth above and usually being the first inversion of a triad

sixth sense noun (1761)
: a power of perception like but not one of the five senses **:** a keen intuitive power

Six·tine \'sik-ˌstīn, -ˌstēn\ adjective variant of SISTINE

six·ty \'siks-tē\ noun, plural sixties [Middle English, from sixty, adjective, from Old English siextig, noun, group of sixty, from siex six + -tig group of ten; akin to Old English tīen ten] (14th century)
1 — see NUMBER table
2 plural **:** the numbers 60 to 69; specifically **:** the years 60 to 69 in a lifetime or century
— **six·ti·eth** \'siks-tē-əth\ adjective or noun
— **sixty** adjective
— **sixty** pronoun, plural in construction
— **six·ty·ish** \'siks-tē-ish\ adjective

sixty–fourth note \ˌsiks-tē-'fōrth-, -'fȯrth-\ noun (circa 1890)
: a musical note with the time value of $1/64$ of a whole note — see NOTE illustration

sixty–fourth rest noun (circa 1903)
: a musical rest corresponding in time value to a sixty-fourth note

six·ty–nine \ˌsiks-tē-'nīn\ noun (1924)
1 — see NUMBER table
2 : mutual cunnilingus and fellatio **:** mutual fellatio **:** mutual cunnilingus

siz·able or size·able \'sī-zə-bəl\ adjective (1613)
: fairly large **:** CONSIDERABLE
— **siz·able·ness** noun
— **siz·ably** \-blē\ adverb

siz·ar also siz·er \'sī-zər\ noun [sizar alteration of sizer, from ¹size] (1588)
: a student (as in the university of Cambridge) who receives an allowance toward college expenses and who originally acted as a servant to other students in return for this allowance

¹size \'sīz\ noun [Middle English sise assize, from Middle French, from Old French, short for assise — more at ASSIZE] (13th century)
1 dialect British **:** ASSIZE 2a — usually used in plural
2 obsolete **:** a fixed portion of food or drink
3 a : physical magnitude, extent, or bulk **:** relative or proportionate dimensions **b :** relative aggregate amount or number **c :** considerable proportions **:** BIGNESS
4 : one of a series of graduated measures especially of manufactured articles (as of clothing) conventionally identified by numbers or letters ⟨a size 7 hat⟩
5 : character, quality, or status of a person or thing especially with reference to importance, relative merit, or correspondence to needs ⟨try this idea on for size⟩
6 : actual state of affairs ⟨that's about the size of it⟩

²size verb sized; siz·ing (1609)
transitive verb
1 : to make a particular size **:** bring to proper or suitable size
2 : to arrange, grade, or classify according to size or bulk

intransitive verb
: to equal in size or other particular characteristic : COMPARE — usually used with *up* and often with *to* or *with*

³size \'sīz, ,sīz\ *adjective* (1924)
: SIZED — usually used in combination ⟨bite-*size*⟩

⁴size \'sīz\ *noun* [Middle English *sise*] (15th century)
: any of various glutinous materials (as preparations of glue, flour, varnish, or resins) used for filling the pores in surfaces (as of paper, textiles, leather, or plaster) or for applying color or metal leaf (as to book edges or covers)

⁵size *transitive verb* **sized; siz·ing** (1667)
: to cover, stiffen, or glaze with or as if with size

sized \'sīzd, ,sīzd\ *adjective* (1582)
1 : having a specified size or bulk — usually used in combination ⟨a small-*sized* house⟩
2 : arranged or adjusted according to size

size up *transitive verb* (1884)
: to form a judgment of

siz·ing \'sī-ziŋ\ *noun* (1825)
: ⁴SIZE

¹siz·zle \'si-zəl\ *verb* **siz·zled; siz·zling** \'si-zə-liŋ, 'siz-liŋ\ [perhaps frequentative of *siss* to hiss] (1603)
transitive verb
: to burn up or sear with or as if with a hissing sound
intransitive verb
1 : to make a hissing sound in or as if in burning or frying
2 : to seethe with deep anger or resentment

²sizzle *noun* (circa 1823)
: a hissing sound (as of something frying over a fire)

siz·zler \'si-zə-lər, 'siz-lər\ *noun* (1848)
: one that sizzles; *especially* : SCORCHER

ska \'skä\ *noun* [origin unknown] (1969)
: popular music of Jamaican origin that combines elements of traditional Caribbean rhythms and jazz

skag *variant of* SCAG

skald \'skȯld, 'skäld\ *noun* [Old Norse *skāld*] (1780)
: an ancient Scandinavian poet; *broadly* : BARD
— **skald·ic** \'skȯl-dik, 'skäl-\ *adjective*

skat \'skät, 'skat\ *noun* [German, modification of Italian *scarto* discard, from *scartare* to discard, from *s-* (from Latin *ex-*) + *carta* card — more at CARD] (1864)
1 : a three-handed card game played with 32 cards in which players bid for the privilege of attempting any of several contracts
2 : a widow of two cards in skat that may be used by the winner of the bid

¹skate \'skāt\ *noun, plural* **skates** *also* **skate** [Middle English *scate,* from Old Norse *skata*] (14th century)
: any of a family (Rajidae, especially genus *Raja*) of rays with the pectoral fins greatly developed giving the fish a flat diamond shape

²skate *noun* [modification of Dutch *schaats* stilt, skate, from Old North French *escache* stilt, probably of Germanic origin; akin to Old English *scēacan* to shake — more at SHAKE] (1684)
1 a : a metal frame that can be fitted to the sole of a shoe and to which is attached a runner or a set of wheels for gliding over ice or a surface other than ice **b** : ROLLER SKATE **c** : ICE SKATE
2 : a period of skating

³skate *verb* **skat·ed; skat·ing** (1696)

skate

intransitive verb
1 : to glide along on skates propelled by the alternate action of the legs
2 : to slip or glide as if on skates
3 : to proceed in a superficial or blithe manner
transitive verb
: to go along or through by skating

⁴skate *noun* [probably alteration of English dialect *skite* an offensive person] (1894)
1 : a thin awkward-looking or decrepit horse : NAG
2 : FELLOW 4c

skate·board \'skāt-,bōrd, -,bȯrd\ *noun* (1964)
: a short board mounted on small wheels that is used for coasting and often for performing athletic stunts
— **skate·board·er** \-,bōr-dər, -,bȯr-\ *noun*
— **skate·board·ing** \-diŋ\ *noun*

skat·er \'skā-tər\ *noun* (1700)
1 : one that skates
2 : WATER STRIDER

skat·ing \'skā-tiŋ\ *noun* (1723)
: the act, art, or sport of gliding on skates

ska·tole \'ska-,tōl, 'skā-\ *also* **ska·tol** \-,tȯl, -,tōl\ *noun* [International Scientific Vocabulary, from Greek *skat-, skōr* excrement — more at SCATOLOGY] (1879)
: a foul-smelling compound C_9H_9N found in the intestines and feces, in civet, and in several plants or made synthetically and used in perfumes as a fixative

¹skean *or* **skeane** *variant of* SKEIN

²skean *or* **skene** \'skē(-ə)n\ *noun* [Middle English *skene,* from Irish *scian* & Scottish Gaelic *sgian,* from Old Irish *scían;* probably akin to Sanskrit *chyati* he cuts off — more at SCIENCE] (15th century)
: DAGGER, DIRK

ske·dad·dle \ski-'da-dᵊl\ *intransitive verb* **ske·dad·dled; ske·dad·dling** \-'dad-liŋ, -'da-dᵊl-iŋ\ [origin unknown] (1861)
: RUN AWAY, SCRAM; *especially* : to flee in a panic
— **ske·dad·dler** \-'dad-lər, -'da-dᵊl-ər\ *noun*

skeet \'skēt\ *noun* [perhaps from Norwegian *skyte* to shoot] (1926)
: trapshooting in which clay targets are thrown in such a way as to simulate the angles of flight of birds

¹skee·ter \'skē-tər\ *noun* [by shortening & alteration] (1839)
1 : MOSQUITO
2 : an iceboat 16 feet (5 meters) or more in length equipped with a single sail

²skeet·er \'skē-tər\ *noun* (1926)
: a skeet shooter

skeg \'skeg\ *also* **skag** \'skag\ *noun* [Middle English *skegge,* from Old Norse *skegg* cutwater, literally, beard — more at SHAG] (13th century)
1 : the stern of the keel of a ship near the sternpost; *especially* : the part connecting the keel with the bottom of the rudderpost in a single-screw ship
2 : a fin situated on the rear bottom of a surfboard that is used for steering and stability

skeigh \'skēḵ\ *adjective* [perhaps of Scandinavian origin; akin to Swedish *skygg* shy; akin to Old English *scēoh* shy — more at SHY] (1508)
chiefly Scottish : proudly spirited : SKITTISH

¹skein \'skān\ *noun* [Middle English *skeyne,* from Middle French *escaigne*] (14th century)
1 *or* **skean** *or* **skeane** \'skān\ : a loosely coiled length of yarn or thread wound on a reel
2 : something suggesting the twists or coils of a skein : TANGLE
3 : a flock of wildfowl (as geese or ducks) in flight

²skein *transitive verb* (circa 1775)
: to wind into skeins ⟨*skein* yarn⟩

skel·e·tal \'ske-lə-t°l\ *adjective* (1854)
: of, relating to, forming, attached to, or resembling a skeleton

— **skel·e·tal·ly** \-t°l-ē\ *adverb*

skeletal muscle *noun* (1877)
: striated muscle that is usually attached to the skeleton and is usually under voluntary control

¹skel·e·ton \'ske-lə-t°n\ *noun* [New Latin, from Greek, neuter of *skeletos* dried up; akin to Greek *skellein* to dry up, *sklēros* hard and perhaps to Old English *sceald* shallow] (1578)
1 : a usually rigid supportive or protective structure or framework of an organism; *especially* : the bony or more or less cartilaginous framework supporting the soft tissues and protecting the internal organs of a vertebrate
2 : something reduced to its minimum form or essential parts
3 : an emaciated person or animal
4 a : something forming a structural framework
b : the straight or branched chain or ring of atoms that forms the basic structure of an organic molecule
5 : something shameful and kept secret (as in a family) — often used in the phrase *skeleton in the closet*
— **ske·le·ton·ic** \,ske-lə-'tä-nik\ *adjective*

²skeleton *adjective* (1778)
: of, consisting of, or resembling a skeleton

skeleton 1: *1* skull, *2* clavicle, *3* scapula, *4* sternum, *5* humerus, *6* rib, *7* pelvis, *8* radius, *9* ulna, *10* carpus, *11* metacarpal bones, *12* phalanges (fingers), *13* femur, *14* patella, *15* tibia, *16* fibula, *17* tarsus, *18* metatarsal bones, *19* phalanges (toes), *20* spinal column

skel·e·ton·ise *British variant of* SKELETONIZE
skel·e·ton·ize \-,īz\ *transitive verb* **-ized; -iz·ing** (1644)
: to produce in or reduce to skeleton form ⟨*skeletonize* a leaf⟩ ⟨*skeletonize* a news story⟩ ⟨*skeletonize* a regiment⟩

skel·e·ton·iz·er \-,ī-zər\ *noun* (circa 1891)
: any of various lepidopterous larvae that eat the parenchyma of leaves reducing them to a skeleton of veins

skeleton key *noun* (1810)
: a key with a large part of the bit filed away to enable it to open low quality locks as a master key

skel·lum \'ske-ləm\ *noun* [Dutch *schelm,* from Low German; akin to Old High German *skelmo* person deserving death] (1611)
chiefly Scottish : SCOUNDREL, RASCAL

¹skelp \'skelp\ *verb* **skelped** \'skelpt\ *also* **skel·pit** \'skel-pət\; **skelp·ing** [Middle English] (15th century)
transitive verb
dialect British : STRIKE, SLAP, BEAT
intransitive verb
: to step lively : HUSTLE

²skelp *noun* (15th century)
dialect British : a smart blow : SLAP

skel·ter \'skel-tər\ *intransitive verb* **skel·tered; skel·ter·ing** \-t(ə-)riŋ\ [from -*skelter* (in *helter-skelter*)] (1852)

\ə\ abut \ᵊ\ kitten \ər\ **further** \a\ **ash** \ā\ **ace**
\ä\ **mop, mar** \aů\ **out** \ch\ **chin** \e\ **bet** \ē\ **easy**
\g\ **go** \i\ **hit** \ī\ **ice** \j\ **job** \ŋ\ **sing** \ō\ **go**
\ȯ\ **law** \ȯi\ **boy** \th\ **thin** \ṯh\ **the** \ü\ **loot** \ů\ **foot**
\y\ **yet** \zh\ **vision** *see also* Guide to Pronunciation

: SCURRY

Skel·ton·ics \skel-'tä-niks\ *noun plural* [John *Skelton*] (1898)
: short verses of an irregular meter with two or three stresses sometimes in falling and sometimes in rising rhythm and usually with rhymed couplets

skep \'skep\ *noun* [Middle English *skeppe* basket, beehive, from Old English *sceppe* basket, from Old Norse *skeppa* bushel; akin to Old High German *sceffil* bushel, *scaf* tub] (15th century)
: BEEHIVE; *especially* : a domed hive made of twisted straw

skep·sis \'skep-səs\ *noun* [New Latin, from Greek *skepsis* examination, doubt, skeptical philosophy, from *skeptesthai*] (circa 1864)
: philosophic doubt as to the objective reality of phenomena; *broadly* : a skeptical outlook or attitude

skep·tic \'skep-tik\ *noun* [Latin or Greek; Latin *scepticus*, from Greek *skeptikos*, from *skeptikos* thoughtful, from *skeptesthai* to look, consider — more at SPY] (1587)
1 : an adherent or advocate of skepticism
2 : a person disposed to skepticism especially regarding religion or religious principles
skep·ti·cal \-ti-kəl\ *adjective* (1639)
: relating to, characteristic of, or marked by skepticism ⟨a *skeptical* listener⟩
— **skep·ti·cal·ly** \-k(ə-)lē\ *adverb*
skep·ti·cism \'skep-tə-,si-zəm\ *noun* (1646)
1 : an attitude of doubt or a disposition to incredulity either in general or toward a particular object
2 a : the doctrine that true knowledge or knowledge in a particular area is uncertain **b** : the method of suspended judgment, systematic doubt, or criticism characteristic of skeptics
3 : doubt concerning basic religious principles (as immortality, providence, and revelation)
synonym see UNCERTAINTY

sker·ry \'sker-ē\ *noun, plural* **skerries** [of Scandinavian origin; akin to Old Norse *sker* skerry and to Old Norse *ey* island; akin to Latin *aqua* water — more at SCAR, ISLAND] (1612)
: a rocky isle : REEF

¹sketch \'skech\ *noun* [Dutch *schets*, from Italian *schizzo*, literally, splash, from *schizzare* to splash, of imitative origin] (1668)
1 a : a rough drawing representing the chief features of an object or scene and often made as a preliminary study (as for a literary work) **b** : a tentative draft (as for a literary work)
2 : a brief description (as of a person) or outline
3 a : a short literary composition somewhat resembling the short story and the essay but intentionally slight in treatment, discursive in style, and familiar in tone **b** : a short instrumental composition usually for piano **c** : a slight theatrical piece having a single scene; *especially* : a comic variety act

²sketch (1694)
transitive verb
: to make a sketch, rough draft, or outline of
intransitive verb
: to draw or paint a sketch
— **sketch·er** *noun*

sketch·book \'skech-,bùk\ *noun* (1820)
: a book of or for sketches

sketchy \'ske-chē\ *adjective* **sketch·i·er; -est** (1805)
1 : of the nature of a sketch : roughly outlined
2 : wanting in completeness, clearness, or substance : SLIGHT, SUPERFICIAL
— **sketch·i·ly** \'ske-chə-lē\ *adverb*
— **sketch·i·ness** \'ske-chē-nəs\ *noun*

¹skew \'skyü\ *verb* [Middle English, to escape, skew, from Old North French *escuer* to shun, of Germanic origin; akin to Old High German *sciuhen* to frighten off — more at SHY] (15th century)
intransitive verb

1 : to take an oblique course
2 : to look askance
transitive verb
1 : to make, set, or cut on the skew
2 : to distort especially from a true value or symmetrical form ⟨*skewed* statistical data⟩

²skew *adjective* (1609)
1 : set, placed, or running obliquely : SLANTING
2 : more developed on one side or in one direction than another : not symmetrical

³skew *noun* (1688)
: a deviation from a straight line : SLANT

skew·back \'skyü-,bak\ *noun* (1703)
: a course of masonry, a stone, or an iron plate having an inclined face against which the voussoirs of an arch abut

¹skew·bald \-,bòld\ *adjective* [*skewed* (skewbald) + *bald*] (1654)
of an animal : marked with patches of white and any other color but black

²skewbald *noun* (1863)
: a skewbald horse

skew curve *noun* (circa 1889)
: a curve in three-dimensional space that does not lie in a single plane

skew distribution *noun* (circa 1931)
: an unsymmetrical frequency distribution having the mode at a different value from the mean

¹skew·er \'skyü-ər, 'skyù(-ə)r\ *noun* [Middle English *skeuier*] (15th century)
1 : a pin of wood or metal for fastening meat to keep it in form while roasting or to hold small pieces of meat or vegetables for broiling
2 : any of various things shaped or used like a meat skewer

²skewer *transitive verb* (1701)
1 : to fasten or pierce with or as if with a skewer
2 : to criticize or ridicule sharply and effectively

skew lines *noun plural* (1952)
: straight lines that do not intersect and are not in the same plane

skew·ness \'skyü-nəs\ *noun* (1894)
: lack of straightness or symmetry : DISTORTION; *especially* : lack of symmetry in a frequency distribution

¹ski \'skē, *British sometimes* 'shē\ *noun, plural* **skis** *also* **ski** [Norwegian, from Old Norse *skīth* stick of wood, ski; akin to Old English *scīd* board, *scēadan* to divide — more at SHED] (1755)
1 a : one of a pair of narrow strips of wood, metal, or plastic curving upward in front that are used especially for gliding over snow **b** : WATER SKI
2 : a piece of material that resembles a ski and is used as a runner on a vehicle

²ski *verb* **skied** \'skēd, 'shēd\; **ski·ing** (circa 1890)
intransitive verb
: to glide on skis in travel or as a sport
transitive verb
: to travel or pass over on skis
— **ski·able** \'skē-ə-bəl\ *adjective*
— **ski·er** *noun*

skia·gram \'skī-ə-,gram\ *noun* [International Scientific Vocabulary, from Greek *skia* shadow + International Scientific Vocabulary *-gram* — more at SCENE] (1801)
1 : a figure formed by shading in the outline of a shadow
2 : RADIOGRAPH

ski·bob \'skē-,bäb\ *noun* [¹*ski* + ⁷*bob*] (1966)
: a vehicle that resembles a bicycle with two short skis in place of wheels and that is used for gliding downhill over snow by a rider wearing miniature skis for balance
— **ski·bob·ber** \-,bä-bər\ *noun*
— **ski·bob·bing** \-,bä-biŋ\ *noun*

ski boot *noun* (1907)
: a rigid padded shoe that extends just above the ankle, is securely fastened to the foot (as

with laces, buckles, or clasps), and is locked into position in a ski binding

¹skid \'skid\ *noun* [perhaps of Scandinavian origin; akin to Old Norse *skīth* stick of wood — more at SKI] (circa 1610)
1 : one of a group of objects (as planks or logs) used to support or elevate a structure or object
2 : a wooden fender hung over a ship's side to protect it in handling cargo
3 : a usually iron shoe or clog attached to a chain and placed under a wheel to prevent its turning when descending a steep hill : DRAG
4 : a timber, bar, rail, pole, or log used in pairs or sets to form a slideway (as for an incline from a truck to the sidewalk)
5 : the act of skidding : SLIP, SIDESLIP
6 : a runner used as a member of the landing gear of an airplane or helicopter
7 a *plural* : a route to defeat or downfall ⟨on the *skids*⟩ ⟨his career hit the *skids*⟩ **b** : a losing streak ⟨a five-game *skid*⟩
8 : a low platform mounted (as on wheels) on which material is set for handling and moving; *also* : PALLET 3
— **skidproof** *adjective*

²skid *verb* **skid·ded; skid·ding** (1674)
transitive verb
1 : to apply a brake or skid to : slow or halt by a skid
2 a : to haul (as logs) by dragging ⟨cutting and *skidding* firewood⟩ **b** : to haul along, slide, hoist, or store on skids
intransitive verb
1 : to slide without rotating (as a wheel held from turning while a vehicle moves onward)
2 a : to fail to grip the roadway; *especially* : to slip sideways on the road **b** *of an airplane* : to slide sideways away from the center of curvature when turning **c** : SLIDE, SLIP
3 : to fall rapidly, steeply, or far

skid·der \'ski-dər\ *noun* (1870)
1 : one that skids or uses a skid
2 : a tractor used especially for hauling logs

skid·doo *or* **ski·doo** \ski-'dü, skē-\ *intransitive verb* [probably alteration of *skedaddle*] (1903)
: to go away : DEPART

skid·dy \'ski-dē\ *adjective* **skid·di·er; -est** (1902)
: likely to skid or cause skidding ⟨a wet *skiddy* road⟩

skid road *noun* (1880)
1 : a road along which logs are skidded
2 a *West* : the part of a town frequented by loggers **b** : SKID ROW

skid row \-'rō\ *noun* [alteration of *skid road*] (circa 1931)
: a district of cheap saloons and flophouses frequented by vagrants and alcoholics

ski·ey *variant of* SKYEY

skiff \'skif\ *noun* [Middle English *skif*, from Middle French or Old Italian; Middle French *esquif*, from Old Italian *schifo*, of Germanic origin; akin to Old English *scip* ship] (15th century)
: any of various small boats; *especially* : a flat-bottomed rowboat

skif·fle \'ski-fəl\ *noun* [origin unknown] (1926)
: American jazz or folk music played entirely or in part on nonstandard instruments (as jugs, washboards, or Jew's harps); *also* : a derivative form of music formerly popular in Great Britain featuring vocals with a simple instrumental accompaniment

ski·ing *noun* (1893)
: the art or sport of sliding and jumping on skis

ski·jor·ing \'skē-,jōr-iŋ, -,jòr-, (,)skē-\ *noun* [modification of Norwegian *skikjøring*, from *ski* + *kjøring* driving] (1910)
: a winter sport in which a person wearing skis is drawn over snow or ice (as by a horse or vehicle)

ski jump *noun* (1907)

: a jump made by a person wearing skis; *also*
: a course or track especially prepared for such jumping
— **ski jump** *intransitive verb*
— **ski jumper** *noun*

skil·ful *chiefly British variant of* SKILLFUL

ski lift *noun* (1939)
: a motor-driven conveyor consisting usually of a series of bars or seats suspended from an overhead moving cable and used for transporting skiers or sightseers up a long slope

¹**skill** \'skil\ *intransitive verb* [Middle English *skilen*, from Old Norse *skilja* to separate, divide; akin to Old Norse *skil* distinction] (13th century)
archaic : to make a difference : MATTER, AVAIL

²**skill** *noun* [Middle English *skil*, from Old Norse, distinction, knowledge; probably akin to Old English *scylian* to separate, *sciell* shell — more at SHELL] (13th century)
1 *obsolete* : CAUSE, REASON
2 a : the ability to use one's knowledge effectively and readily in execution or performance **b** : dexterity or coordination especially in the execution of learned physical tasks
3 : a learned power of doing something competently : a developed aptitude or ability ⟨language *skills*⟩
synonym see ART
— **skill–less** *or* **skil·less** \'skil-ləs\ *adjective*
— **skill–less·ness** *or* **skil·less·ness** *noun*

skilled \'skild\ *adjective* (1552)
1 : having acquired mastery of or skill in something (as a technique or a trade)
2 : of, relating to, or requiring workers or labor with skill and training in a particular occupation, craft, or trade
synonym see PROFICIENT

skil·let \'ski-lət\ *noun* [Middle English *skelet*] (15th century)
1 *chiefly British* : a small kettle or pot usually having three or four often long feet and used for cooking on the hearth
2 : FRYING PAN

skill·ful \'skil-fəl\ *adjective* (14th century)
1 : possessed of or displaying skill : EXPERT
2 : accomplished with skill
synonym see PROFICIENT
— **skill·ful·ly** \-fə-lē\ *adverb*
— **skill·ful·ness** *noun*

skil·ling \'ski-liŋ, 'shi-\ *noun* [Swedish, Norwegian, & Danish, from Old Norse *skillingr*, a gold coin; akin to Old English *scilling* shilling] (1793)
: any of various old Scandinavian units of value or the coins representing them

¹**skim** \'skim\ *verb* **skimmed; skim·ming** [Middle English *skymmen*] (14th century)
transitive verb
1 a : to clear (a liquid) of scum or floating substance ⟨*skim* boiling syrup⟩ **b** : to remove (as film or scum) from the surface of a liquid **c** : to remove cream from by skimming **d** : to remove the best or most easily obtainable contents from
2 : to read, study, or examine superficially and rapidly; *especially* : to glance through (as a book) for the chief ideas or the plot
3 : to throw in a gliding path; *especially* : to throw so as to ricochet along the surface of water
4 : to cover with or as if with a film, scum, or coat
5 : to pass swiftly or lightly over
6 : to remove or conceal (as a portion of casino profits) to avoid payment of taxes
intransitive verb
1 a : to pass lightly or hastily : glide or skip along, above, or near a surface **b** : to give a cursory glance, consideration, or reading
2 : to become coated with a thin layer of film or scum
3 : to put on a finishing coat of plaster

²**skim** *noun* (14th century)

1 : a thin layer, coating, or film
2 : the act of skimming
3 : something skimmed; *specifically* : SKIM MILK

³**skim** *adjective* (1794)
1 : having the cream removed by skimming
2 : made of skim milk ⟨*skim* cheese⟩

ski mask *noun* (1966)
: a knit fabric mask that covers the head, has openings for the eyes, mouth, and sometimes the nose, and is worn especially by skiers for protection from the cold

skim·ble–skam·ble \,skim-bəl-'skam-bəl\ *adjective* [reduplication of English dialect *scamble* to stumble along] (1596)
: rambling and confused : SENSELESS

skim·mer \'ski-mər\ *noun* (14th century)
1 : one that skims; *specifically* : a flat perforated scoop or spoon used for skimming
2 : any of a small genus (*Rynchops*) of long-winged marine birds that have the lower mandible longer than the upper
3 : a usually straw flat-crowned hat with a wide straight brim
4 : a fitted sleeveless dress with a usually flaring skirt

skim milk *noun* (1596)
: milk from which the cream has been taken — called also *skimmed milk*

skimming *noun* (15th century)
: that which is skimmed from a liquid

ski·mo·bile \'skē-mō-,bēl\ *noun* (1944)
: SNOWMOBILE

¹**skimp** \'skimp\ *adjective* [perhaps alteration of *scrimp*] (1775)
: SKIMPY

²**skimp** (circa 1879)
transitive verb
: to give insufficient or barely sufficient attention or effort to or funds for
intransitive verb
: to save by or as if by skimping

skimpy \'skim-pē\ *adjective* **skimp·i·er; -est** (1842)
: deficient in supply or execution especially through skimping : SCANTY
synonym see MEAGER
— **skimp·i·ly** \-pə-lē\ *adverb*
— **skimp·i·ness** \-pē-nəs\ *noun*

¹**skin** \'skin\ *noun, often attributive* [Middle English, from Old Norse *skinn;* akin to Old English *scinn* skin, Middle High German *schint* fruit peel] (13th century)
1 a (1) : the integument of an animal (as a fur-bearing mammal or a bird) separated from the body usually with its hair or feathers (2) : a usually unmounted specimen of a vertebrate (as in a museum) **b** : the hide or pelt of a game or domestic animal **c** (1) : the pelt of an animal prepared for use as a trimming or in a garment — compare ⁴HIDE (2) : a sheet of parchment or vellum made from a hide (3) : BOTTLE 1b
2 a : the external limiting tissue layer of an animal body especially when forming a tough but flexible cover relatively impermeable from without while intact **b** : any of various outer or surface layers (as a rind, husk, or pellicle)
3 : the life or physical well-being of a person ⟨saved his own *skin*⟩
4 : a sheathing or casing forming the outside surface of a structure (as a ship or airplane)
— **skin·less** \-ləs\ *adjective*
— **by the skin of one's teeth** : by a very narrow margin
— **under one's skin** : so deeply penetrative as to irritate, stimulate, provoke thought, or otherwise excite
— **under the skin** : beneath apparent or surface differences : at heart

²**skin** *verb* **skinned; skin·ning** (14th century)
transitive verb

1 a : to strip, scrape, or rub off an outer covering (as the skin or rind) of **b** : to strip or peel off **c** : to cut, chip, or damage the surface of ⟨fell and *skinned* my knee⟩
2 a : to cover with or as if with skin **b** : to heal over with skin
3 a : to strip of money or property : FLEECE **b** : to defeat badly **c** : CENSURE, CASTIGATE
4 : to urge on and direct the course of (as a draft animal)
intransitive verb
1 : to become covered with or as if with skin
2 a : SHIN 1 **b** : to pass or get by with scant room to spare

³**skin** *adjective* (circa 1935)
: involving subjects who are nude ⟨expected to conduct *skin* searches for weapons —Diane K. Shah⟩; *especially* : devoted to showing nudes ⟨*skin* magazines⟩

skin–deep \'skin-'dēp\ *adjective* (1613)
1 : as deep as the skin
2 : not thorough or lasting in impression : SUPERFICIAL

skin diving *noun* (1938)
: the sport of swimming under water with a face mask and flippers and especially without a portable breathing device
— **skin–dive** *intransitive verb*
— **skin diver** *noun*

skin effect *noun* (1891)
: an effect characteristic of current distribution in a conductor at high frequencies by virtue of which the current density is greater near the surface of the conductor than in its interior

skin·flint \'skin-,flint\ *noun* (circa 1700)
: a person who would save, gain, or extort money by any means : MISER, NIGGARD

skin·ful \-,fúl\ *noun* (1788)
1 : a large or satisfying quantity especially of liquor
2 : the contents of a skin bottle

skin game *noun* (1868)
: a swindling game or trick

skin graft *noun* (1871)
: a piece of skin that is taken from a donor area to replace skin in a defective or denuded area (as one that has been burned)
— **skin grafting** *noun*

skin·head \'skin-,hed\ *noun* (circa 1953)
1 : a person whose hair is cut very short
2 : a usually white male belonging to any of various sometimes violent youth gangs whose members have close-shaven hair and often espouse white-supremacist beliefs

¹**skink** \'skiŋk\ *transitive verb* [Middle English, from Middle Dutch *schenken;* akin to Old English *scencan* to pour out drink and probably to *scanca* shank] (15th century)
chiefly dialect : to draw, pour out, or serve (drink)

²**skink** *noun* [Latin *scincus*, from Greek *skinkos*] (1590)
: any of a family (Scincidae) of typically small insectivorous lizards with long tapering bodies

skink·er \'skiŋ-kər\ *noun* (1586)
: one that serves liquor : BARTENDER

skinned \'skind\ *adjective* (15th century)
: having skin especially of a specified kind — usually used in combination ⟨dark-*skinned*⟩

skin·ner \'ski-nər\ *noun* (14th century)
1 a : one that deals in skins, pelts, or hides **b** : one that removes, cures, or dresses skins
2 : SHARPER
3 : a driver of draft animals : TEAMSTER

Skin·ner box \'ski-nər-,bäks\ *noun* [B. F. Skinner] (1940)
: a laboratory apparatus in which an animal is caged for experiments in operant conditioning and which typically contains a lever that must

\ə\ abut \ᵊ\ kitten \ər\ **further** \a\ ash \ā\ ace \ä\ mop, mar \aú\ **out** \ch\ **chin** \e\ bet \ē\ **easy** \g\ go \i\ **hit** \ī\ ice \j\ **job** \ŋ\ sing \ō\ go \ò\ **law** \òi\ **boy** \th\ **thin** \t̲h̲\ **the** \ü\ **loot** \ú\ **foot** \y\ **yet** \zh\ **vision** *see also* Guide to Pronunciation

be pressed by the animal to gain reward or avoid punishment

¹skin·ny \'ski-nē\ *adjective* **skin·ni·er; -est** (1573)
1 : resembling skin : MEMBRANOUS
2 a : lacking sufficient flesh : very thin : EMACIATED **b** : lacking usual or desirable bulk, quantity, qualities, or significance
synonym see LEAN
— **skin·ni·ness** *noun*

²skinny *noun* [perhaps from ¹skin + ⁴-y] (1938)
slang : inside information : DOPE ⟨the straight *skinny* on what's going on —John Geary⟩

skin·ny–dip \'ski-nē-ˌdip\ *intransitive verb* (1964)
: to swim in the nude
— **skinny–dip** *noun*
— **skin·ny–dip·per** \-ˌdi-pər\ *noun*

skin–pop \'skin-ˈpäp\ (circa 1952)
intransitive verb
: to inject a drug subcutaneously rather than into a vein
transitive verb
: to inject (a drug) by skin-popping
— **skin–pop·per** \-ˌpä-pər\ *noun*

skint \'skint\ *adjective* [alteration of *skinned*, past participle of ²skin] (circa 1925)
chiefly British : PENNILESS

skin test *noun* (1925)
: a test (as a scratch test) performed on the skin and used in detecting allergic hypersensitivity

skin·tight \'skin-ˈtīt\ *adjective* (1885)
: closely fitted to the figure

¹skip \'skip\ *verb* **skipped; skip·ping** [Middle English *skippen*, perhaps of Scandinavian origin; akin to Swedish dialect *skopa* to hop] (14th century)
intransitive verb
1 a : to move or proceed with leaps and bounds or with a skip **b** : to bound off one point after another : RICOCHET
2 : to leave hurriedly or secretly ⟨*skipped* out without paying their bill⟩
3 a : to pass over or omit an interval, item, or step **b** : to omit a grade in school in advancing to the next **c** : MISFIRE 1
transitive verb
1 a : to pass over without notice or mention : OMIT **b** : to pass by or leave out (a step in a progression or series)
2 a : to cause to skip (a grade in school) **b** : to cause to bound or skim over a surface ⟨*skip* a stone across a pond⟩
3 : to leap over lightly and nimbly
4 a : to depart from quickly and secretly ⟨*skipped* town⟩ **b** : to fail to attend or participate in ⟨*skip* the tournament⟩ ⟨*skip* the meeting⟩
— **skip·pa·ble** \'ski-pə-bəl\ *adjective*
— **skip bail** : to jump bail
— **skip rope** : to use a jump rope (as for exercise or a game)

²skip *noun* (15th century)
1 a : a light bounding step **b** : a gait composed of alternating hops and steps
2 : an act of omission or the thing omitted

³skip *noun* [short for ²*skipper*] (1830)
1 : the captain of a side in a game (as curling or lawn bowling) who advises the team as to the play and controls the action
2 : ²SKIPPER

⁴skip *transitive verb* **skipped; skip·ping** (1900)
: to act as skipper of

skip bomb *transitive verb* (1943)
: to attack by releasing delayed-action bombs from a low-flying airplane so that they skip along a land or water surface and strike a target

skip·jack \'skip-ˌjak\ *noun, plural* **skip·jacks** *or* **skipjack** (1703)
1 : any of various food fishes (as a ladyfish or bluefish) that jump above or are active at the surface of the water; *especially* : SKIPJACK TUNA

2 : a sailboat with vertical sides and a bottom similar to a flat V

skipjack tuna *noun* (1950)
: a relatively small scombroid food and sport fish (*Katsuwonus pelamis* synonym *Euthynnus pelamis*) that is bluish above and silvery below with oblique dark stripes on the sides and belly

ski pole *noun* (1920)
: one of a pair of lightweight poles used in skiing that have a handgrip and usually a wrist strap at one end and an encircling disk set above the point at the other end

¹skip·per \'ski-pər\ *noun* (13th century)
1 : any of various erratically active insects (as a click beetle or a water strider)
2 : one that skips
3 : SAURY
4 : any of a superfamily (Hesperioidea, especially family Hesperiidae) of stout-bodied lepidopterous insects that differ from the typical butterflies especially in wing venation and the form of the antennae

²skipper *noun* [Middle English, from Middle Dutch *schipper*, from *schip* ship; akin to Old English *scip* ship — more at SHIP] (14th century)
1 : the master of a ship; *especially* : the master of a fishing, small trading, or pleasure boat
2 : the captain or first pilot of an airplane
3 : a person in a position of leadership; *especially* : a baseball team's manager

³skip·per *transitive verb* **skip·pered; skip·per·ing** \'ski-p(ə-)riŋ\ (1893)
1 : to act as skipper of (as a boat)
2 : to act as coach of (as a team)

¹skirl \'skər(-ə)l, 'skir(-ə)l\ *verb* [Middle English (Scots) *skrillen, skirlen* to scream, shriek, of Scandinavian origin; akin to Old Swedish *skrælla* to rattle; akin to Old English *scrallettan* to resound loudly] (circa 1665)
intransitive verb
of a bagpipe : to emit the high shrill tone of the chanter; *also* : to give forth music
transitive verb
: to play (music) on the bagpipe

²skirl *noun* (1856)
: a high shrill sound produced by the chanter of a bagpipe

¹skir·mish \'skər-mish\ *noun* [Middle English *skyrmissh*, alteration of *skarmish*, from Middle French *escarmouche*, from Old Italian *scaramuccia*] (14th century)
1 : a minor fight in war usually incidental to larger movements
2 a : a brisk preliminary verbal conflict **b** : a minor dispute or contest between opposing parties
— **skir·mish·er** *noun*

²skirmish *intransitive verb* (14th century)
1 : to engage in a skirmish
2 : to search about (as for supplies) : scout around

¹skirr \'skər, 'skir\ *verb* [perhaps alteration of ³*scour*] (circa 1548)
intransitive verb
1 : to leave hastily : FLEE ⟨birds *skirred* off from the bushes —D. H. Lawrence⟩
2 : to run, fly, sail, or move along rapidly
transitive verb
1 : to search about in ⟨*skirr* the country round —Shakespeare⟩
2 a : to pass rapidly over : SKIM **b** *dialect* : to cause to skim

²skirr *noun* [probably imitative] (circa 1870)
: WHIR, ROAR

¹skirt \'skərt\ *noun* [Middle English, from Old Norse *skyrta* shirt, kirtle — more at SHIRT] (14th century)
1 a (1) : a free-hanging part of an outer garment or undergarment extending from the waist down (2) : a separate free-hanging outer garment or undergarment usually worn by women and girls covering some or all of the

body from the waist down **b** : either of two usually leather flaps on a saddle covering the bars on which the stirrups are hung **c** : a cloth facing that hangs loosely and usually in folds or pleats from the bottom edge or across the front of a piece of furniture **d** : the lower branches of a tree when near the ground
2 a : the rim, periphery, or environs of an area **b** *plural* : outlying parts (as of a town or city)
3 : a part or attachment serving as a rim, border, or edging
4 : a girl or woman
— **skirt·ed** *adjective*

²skirt (1602)
transitive verb
1 : to form or run along the border or edge of : BORDER
2 a : to provide a skirt for **b** : to furnish a border or shield for
3 a : to go or pass around or about; *specifically* : to go around or keep away from in order to avoid danger or discovery **b** : to avoid especially because of difficulty or fear of controversy ⟨*skirted* the issue⟩ **c** : to evade or miss by a narrow margin ⟨having *skirted* disaster —Edith Wharton⟩
intransitive verb
: to be, lie, or move along an edge or border
— **skirt·er** *noun*

skirt·ing \'skər-tiŋ\ *noun* (1764)
1 : something that skirts: as **a** : BORDER, EDGING **b** *chiefly British* : BASEBOARD
2 : fabric suitable for skirts

skirt steak *noun* (circa 1909)
: a boneless strip of beef cut from the plate

ski run *noun* (1924)
: a slope or trail suitable for skiing

skit \'skit\ *noun* [origin unknown] (circa 1727)
1 : a jeering or satirical remark : TAUNT
2 a : a satirical or humorous story or sketch **b** (1) : a brief burlesque or comic sketch included in a dramatic performance (as a revue) (2) : a short serious dramatic piece; *especially* : one done by amateurs

ski touring *noun* (1935)
: cross-country skiing for pleasure

ski tow *noun* (1935)
1 : a motor-driven conveyor that is used for pulling skiers up a slope and that consists usually of an endless moving rope which a skier grasps
2 : SKI LIFT

skit·ter \'ski-tər\ *verb* [probably frequentative of English dialect *skite* to move quickly] (1845)
intransitive verb
1 : to glide or skip lightly or quickly
2 : to twitch the hook of a fishing line through or along the surface of water
transitive verb
: to cause to skitter

skit·tery \'ski-tə-rē\ *adjective* (1941)
: SKITTISH

skit·tish \'ski-tish\ *adjective* [Middle English] (15th century)
1 a : lively or frisky in action : CAPRICIOUS **b** : VARIABLE, FLUCTUATING
2 : easily frightened : RESTIVE ⟨a *skittish* horse⟩
3 a : COY, BASHFUL **b** : marked by extreme caution : WARY
— **skit·tish·ly** *adverb*
— **skit·tish·ness** *noun*

skit·tle \'ski-t°l\ *noun* [perhaps of Scandinavian origin; akin to Old Norse *skutill* bolt — more at SHUTTLE] (1634)
1 *plural but singular in construction* : English ninepins played with a wooden disk or ball
2 : one of the pins used in skittles

skive \'skīv\ *transitive verb* **skived; skiving** [probably of Scandinavian origin; akin to Old Norse *skīfa* to slice] (circa 1825)
: to cut off (as leather or rubber) in thin layers or pieces : PARE

skiv·er \'skī-vər\ *noun* (1800)

1 : a thin soft leather made of the grain side of a split sheepskin, usually tanned in sur ac and dyed
2 : one that skives something (as leather)
Skiv·vies \'ski-vēz\ *trademark*
— used for men's underwear
skiv·vy \'ski-vē\ *noun, plural* **skivvies** [origin unknown] (circa 1902)
British : a female domestic servant
ski·wear \'skē-,war, -,wer\ *noun* (1961)
: clothing suitable for wear while skiing
sklent \'sklent\ *verb* [Middle English *sclenten* to strike obliquely, alteration of *slenten* — more at SLANT] (1805)
intransitive verb
1 *chiefly Scottish* : to look askance
2 *chiefly Scottish* : to cast aspersions
transitive verb
Scottish : to direct sideways : SLANT
skoal \'skōl\ *noun* [Danish *skaal,* literally, cup; akin to Old Norse *skāl* bowl — more at SCALE] (1600)
: TOAST, HEALTH — often used interjectionally
skosh \'skōsh\ *noun* [Japanese *sukoshi*] (1952)
: a small amount : BIT, SMIDGEN — used adverbially with *a* ⟨just a *skosh* bit shook —Josiah Bunting⟩
skua \'skyü-ə\ *noun* [New Latin, from Faeroese *skūgvur;* akin to Old Norse *skūfr* tassel, skua, Old English *scēaf* sheaf — more at SHEAF] (1678)
: either of two seabirds related to the jaegers:
a : GREAT SKUA **b** : a bird (*Catharacta maccormicki*) that resembles but is slightly smaller than the great skua and that breeds in the Antarctic
skul·dug·gery *or* **skull·dug·gery** \,skəl-'də-g(ə-)rē, ,skəl-,\ *noun, plural* **-ger·ies** [origin unknown] (1867)
: a devious device or trick; *also* : underhanded or unscrupulous behavior
¹skulk \'skəlk\ *intransitive verb* [Middle English, of Scandinavian origin; akin to Danish *skulke* to shirk, play truant] (13th century)
1 : to move in a stealthy or furtive manner
2 a : to hide or conceal something (as oneself) often out of cowardice or fear or with sinister intent **b** *chiefly British* : MALINGER
synonym see LURK
— **skulk·er** *noun*
²skulk *noun* (14th century)
1 : one that skulks
2 : a group of foxes
skull \'skəl\ *noun* [Middle English *skulle,* of Scandinavian origin; akin to Swedish *skulle* skull] (13th century)
1 : the skeleton of the head of a vertebrate forming a bony or cartilaginous case that encloses and protects the brain and chief sense organs and supports the jaws
2 : the seat of understanding or intelligence : MIND
— **skulled** \'skəld\ *adjective*
skull and cross·bones \-'krȯs-,bōnz\ *noun, plural* **skulls and crossbones** (1826)
: a representation of a human skull over crossbones usually used as a warning of danger to life
skull·cap \'skəl-,kap\ *noun* (1682)
1 : a close-fitting cap; *especially* : a light cap without brim for indoor wear
2 : any of various mints (genus *Scutellaria*) having a calyx that when inverted resembles a helmet
3 : the upper portion of the skull : CALVARIUM
skull session *noun* (1937)
1 : a strategy class for an athletic team
2 : a meeting for consultation, discussion, or the interchange of ideas or information — called also *skull practice*
¹skunk \'skəŋk\ *noun, plural* **skunks** *also* **skunk** [of Algonquian origin; akin to Eastern Abenaki *segankŵ* skunk] (1634)
1 a : any of various common omnivorous black-and-white New World mammals (especially genus *Mephitis*) of the weasel family

that have a pair of perineal glands from which a secretion of pungent and offensive odor is ejected **b** : the fur of a skunk
2 : an obnoxious or disliked person
²skunk *transitive verb* (1843)
1 a : DEFEAT **b** : to shut out in a game
2 : to fail to pay; *also* : CHEAT
skunk cabbage *noun* (1751)
: either of two North American perennial herbs of the arum family that occur in shaded wet to swampy areas and have a fetid odor suggestive of a skunk: **a** : one (*Symplocarpus foetidus*) of eastern North America that sends up in spring a cowl-shaped brownish purple spathe **b** : one (*Lysichitum americana*) chiefly of the Pacific coast region that has a large yellow spathe

skunk cabbage

skunk works *noun plural but singular or plural in construction* [from the *Skonk Works,* illicit distillery in the comic strip *Li'l Abner* by Al Capp] (circa 1974)
: a usually small and often isolated department or facility (as for engineering research and development) that functions with minimal supervision within a company or corporation
¹sky \'skī\ *noun, plural* **skies** [Middle English, cloud, sky, from Old Norse *skȳ* cloud; akin to Old English *scēo* cloud] (13th century)
1 : the upper atmosphere or expanse of space that constitutes an apparent great vault or arch over the earth
2 : HEAVEN 2
3 a : weather in the upper atmosphere **b** : CLIMATE ⟨temperate English *skies* —G. G. Coulton⟩
²sky *transitive verb* **skied** *or* **skyed; sky·ing** (1802)
1 *chiefly British* : to throw or toss up : FLIP
2 : to hang (as a painting) above the line of vision
3 : to hit (a ball) high into the air
sky blue *noun* (1738)
: a pale to light blue color
sky·borne \'skī-,bȯrn, -,bȯrn\ *adjective* (1589)
: AIRBORNE ⟨*skyborne* troops⟩
sky·box \-,bäks\ *noun* (1974)
: a roofed enclosure of private seats situated high in a sports stadium and typically featuring luxurious amenities
sky·cap \-,kap\ *noun* [¹*sky* + -*cap* (as in *redcap*)] (1941)
: one employed to carry hand luggage at an airport — compare REDCAP
sky·div·ing \-,dī-viŋ\ *noun* (1957)
: the sport of jumping from an airplane at a moderate altitude (as 6000 feet) and executing various body maneuvers before pulling the rip cord of a parachute
— **sky diver** *noun*
Skye terrier \'skī-\ *noun* [*Skye,* Scotland] (1847)
: any of a Scottish breed of terriers with a long low body and long straight coat
sky·ey \'skī-ē\ *adjective* (1603)
: of or resembling the sky : ETHEREAL
¹sky–high \'skī-'hī\ *adverb* (1818)
1 a : high into the air **b** : to a high or exorbitant level or degree
2 : in an enthusiastic manner
3 : to bits : APART ⟨blown *sky-high*⟩
²sky–high *adjective* (1945)
: excessively expensive : EXORBITANT
sky·hook \-,hůk\ *noun* (1915)
: a hook conceived as being suspended from the sky
sky·jack \'skī-,jak\ *transitive verb* [¹*sky* + -*jack* (as in *hijack*)] (1961)

: to commandeer (an airplane in flight) by the threat of violence
— **sky·jack·er** \-,ja-kər\ *noun*
— **sky·jack·ing** \-kiŋ\ *noun*
¹sky·lark \'skī-,lärk\ *noun* (1686)
1 : a common largely brown Old World lark (*Alauda arvensis*) noted for its song especially as uttered in flight
2 : any of various birds resembling the skylark
²skylark *intransitive verb* (1809)
1 : to run up and down the rigging of a ship in sport
2 : FROLIC, SPORT
— **sky·lark·er** *noun*
sky·light \'skī-,līt\ *noun* (1679)
1 : the diffused and reflected light of the sky
2 : an opening in a house roof or ship's deck that is covered with translucent or transparent material and that is designed to admit light
sky·light·ed \-,lī-təd\ *also* **sky·lit** \-,lit\ *adjective* (1849)
: having a skylight
sky·line \-,līn\ *noun* (1824)
1 : the apparent juncture of earth and sky : HORIZON
2 : an outline (as of buildings or a mountain range) against the background of the sky
sky marshal *noun* (1968)
: an armed federal plainclothesman assigned to prevent skyjackings
sky pilot *noun* (1883)
: CLERGYMAN; *specifically* : CHAPLAIN
¹sky·rock·et \'skī-,rä-kət\ *noun* (1688)
: ²ROCKET 1a
²skyrocket (1851)
transitive verb
1 : to cause to rise or increase abruptly and rapidly
2 : CATAPULT
intransitive verb
: to shoot up abruptly ⟨prices are *skyrocketing*⟩
sky·sail \'skī-,sāl, -səl\ *noun* (1829)
: the sail above the royal
sky·scrap·er \-,skrā-pər\ *noun* (1883)
: a very tall building
sky·walk \-,wȯk\ *noun* (1953)
: a usually enclosed aerial walkway connecting two buildings
sky·ward \-wərd\ *adverb* (1582)
1 : toward the sky
2 : UPWARD
sky wave *noun* (1928)
: a radio wave that is propagated by means of the ionosphere
sky·way \'skī-,wā\ *noun* (1919)
1 : a route used by airplanes : AIR LANE
2 : an elevated highway
3 : SKYWALK
sky·write \-,rīt\ *verb* **-wrote** \-,rōt\; **-written** \-,ri-t²n\; **-writ·ing** \-,rī-tiŋ\ [back-formation from *skywriting*] (1926)
transitive verb
: to letter by skywriting
intransitive verb
: to do skywriting
— **sky·writ·er** *noun*
sky·writ·ing \-,rī-tiŋ\ *noun* (1922)
: writing formed in the sky by means of a visible substance (as smoke) emitted from an airplane
¹slab \'slab\ *noun* [Middle English *slabbe*] (14th century)
1 : a thick plate or slice (as of stone, wood, or bread): as **a** : the outside piece cut from a log in squaring it **b** : concrete pavement (as of a road); *specifically* : a strip of concrete pavement laid as a single unjointed piece **c** (1) : a flat rectangular architectural element that is usually formed of a single piece or mass ⟨a

concrete foundation *slab*⟩ (2) **:** a rectangular building having little width with respect to its length and usually height
2 : something that resembles a slab (as in size) ⟨backed up by a solid *slab* of reference material —*Times Literary Supplement*⟩
— **slab·like** \-,līk\ *adjective*

²**slab** *transitive verb* **slabbed; slab·bing** (1703)
1 a : to remove an outer slab from (as a log) **b :** to divide or form into slabs
2 : to cover or support (as a roadbed or roof) with slabs
3 : to put on thickly

³**slab** *adjective* [probably of Scandinavian origin; akin to obsolete Danish *slab* slippery] (1605)
dialect chiefly English **:** THICK, VISCOUS

¹**slab·ber** \'sla-bər\ *verb* **slab·bered; slab·ber·ing** \-b(ə-)riŋ\ [probably from Dutch *slabberen*, frequentative of *slabben* to slaver — more at SLAVER] (1542)
: SLOBBER, DROOL

²**slabber** *noun* (1718)
: SLOBBER, SLAVER

slab–sid·ed \'slab-'sī-dəd\ *adjective* (1817)
: having flat sides; *also* **:** being tall or long and lank

¹**slack** \'slak\ *adjective* [Middle English *slak*, from Old English *sleac*; akin to Old High German *slah* slack, Latin *laxus* slack, loose, *languēre* to languish, Greek *lagnos* lustful and perhaps to Greek *lēgein* to stop] (before 12th century)
1 : not using due diligence, care, or dispatch **:** NEGLIGENT
2 a : characterized by slowness, sluggishness, or lack of energy ⟨a *slack* pace⟩ **b :** moderate in some quality; *especially* **:** moderately warm ⟨a *slack* oven⟩ **c :** blowing or flowing at low speed ⟨the tide was *slack*⟩
3 a : not tight or taut ⟨a *slack* rope⟩ **b :** lacking in usual or normal firmness and steadiness **:** WEAK ⟨*slack* muscles⟩ ⟨*slack* supervision⟩
4 : wanting in activity **:** DULL ⟨a *slack* market⟩
5 : lacking in completeness, finish, or perfection ⟨a very *slack* piece of work⟩
synonym see NEGLIGENT
— **slack·ly** *adverb*
— **slack·ness** *noun*

²**slack** (13th century)
intransitive verb
1 : to be or become slack
2 : to shirk or evade work or duty
transitive verb
1 a : to be slack or negligent in performing or doing **b :** LESSEN, MODERATE
2 : to release tension on **:** LOOSEN
3 a : to cause to abate **b :** SLAKE 3

³**slack** *noun* (1756)
1 : cessation in movement or flow
2 : a part of something that hangs loose without strain ⟨take up the *slack* of a rope⟩
3 : trousers especially for casual wear — usually used in plural
4 : a dull season or period
5 a : a part that is available but not used ⟨some *slack* in the budget⟩ **b :** a part that is wanted but not supplied **:** SHORTFALL ⟨take up the *slack* in supplying oil⟩

⁴**slack** *noun* [Middle English *slak*, from Old Norse *slakki*] (14th century)
dialect English **:** a pass between hills

⁵**slack** *noun* [Middle English *sleck*] (15th century)
: the finest screenings of coal produced at a mine unusable as fuel unless cleaned

slack·en \'sla-kən\ *verb* **slack·ened; slack·en·ing** \'sla-k°n-iŋ\ (15th century)
transitive verb
1 : to make less active **:** slow up ⟨*slacken* speed at a crossing⟩
2 : to make slack (as by lessening tension or firmness) ⟨*slacken* sail⟩
intransitive verb

1 : to become slack or slow or negligent **:** slow down
2 : to become less active **:** SLACK
synonym see DELAY

slack·er \'sla-kər\ *noun* (1898)
: a person who shirks work or obligation; *especially* **:** one who evades military service in time of war

slack water *noun* (circa 1769)
: the period at the turn of the tide when there is little or no horizontal motion of tidal water — called also *slack tide*

slag \'slag\ *noun* [Middle Low German *slagge*] (1552)
: the dross or scoria of a metal

slain *past participle of* SLAY

slake \'slāk, *intransitive verb 2 & transitive verb 3 are also* 'slak\ *verb* **slaked; slak·ing** [Middle English, from Old English *slacian*, from *sleac* slack] (14th century)
intransitive verb
1 *archaic* **:** SUBSIDE, ABATE
2 : to become slaked **:** CRUMBLE ⟨lime may *slake* spontaneously in moist air⟩
transitive verb
1 *archaic* **:** to lessen the force of **:** MODERATE
2 : SATISFY, QUENCH ⟨*slake* your thirst⟩ ⟨will *slake* your curiosity⟩
3 : to cause (as lime) to heat and crumble by treatment with water **:** HYDRATE

¹**sla·lom** \'slä-ləm\ *noun, often attributive* [Norwegian *slalåm*, literally, sloping track] (1921)
1 : skiing in a zigzag or wavy course between upright obstacles (as flags)
2 : a timed race (as on skis or in an automobile or kayak) over a winding or zigzag course past a series of flags or markers; *broadly* **:** movement over a zigzag route

²**slalom** *intransitive verb* (1932)
: to move over a zigzag course in or as if in a slalom

¹**slam** \'slam\ *noun* [origin unknown] (1660)
1 : GRAND SLAM
2 : LITTLE SLAM

²**slam** *noun* [probably of Scandinavian origin; akin to Icelandic *slæma* to slam] (1672)
1 : a heavy blow or impact
2 a : a noisy violent closing **b :** a banging noise; *especially* **:** one made by the slam of a door
3 : a cutting or violent criticism
4 : SLAMMER

³**slam** *verb* **slammed; slam·ming** (circa 1691)
transitive verb
1 : to strike or beat hard **:** KNOCK
2 : to shut forcibly and noisily **:** BANG
3 a : to set or slap down violently or noisily ⟨*slammed* down the phone⟩ **b :** to propel, thrust, or produce by or as if by striking hard ⟨*slam* on the brakes⟩ ⟨*slammed* the car into a wall⟩
4 : to criticize harshly
intransitive verb
1 : to make a banging noise
2 : to function (as in moving) with emphatic and usually noisy vigor ⟨the hurricane *slammed* into the coast⟩ ⟨*slammed* out of the room⟩
3 : to utter verbal abuse or harsh criticism

slam–bang \'slam-'baŋ\ *adjective* (circa 1823)
1 : unduly loud or violent ⟨a *slam-bang* clatter⟩
2 : having fast-paced often nonstop action ⟨a *slam-bang* adventure novel⟩
3 : vigorously enthusiastic ⟨made a *slam-bang* effort to win⟩

slam dunk *noun* (1972)
: DUNK SHOT
— **slam–dunk** *verb*

slam·mer \'sla-mər\ *noun* (1952)
: JAIL, PRISON

¹**slan·der** \'slan-dər\ *transitive verb* **slan·dered; slan·der·ing** \-d(ə-)riŋ\ (13th century)

: to utter slander against **:** DEFAME
synonym see MALIGN
— **slan·der·er** \-dər-ər\ *noun*

²**slander** *noun* [Middle English *sclaundre*, *slaundre*, from Old French *esclandre*, from Late Latin *scandalum* stumbling block, offense — more at SCANDAL] (14th century)
1 : the utterance of false charges or misrepresentations which defame and damage another's reputation
2 : a false and defamatory oral statement about a person — compare LIBEL
— **slan·der·ous** \-d(ə-)rəs\ *adjective*
— **slan·der·ous·ly** *adverb*
— **slan·der·ous·ness** *noun*

¹**slang** \'slaŋ\ *noun* [origin unknown] (1756)
1 : language peculiar to a particular group: as **a :** ARGOT **b :** JARGON 2
2 : an informal nonstandard vocabulary composed typically of coinages, arbitrarily changed words, and extravagant, forced, or facetious figures of speech
— **slang** *adjective*
— **slang·i·ly** \'slaŋ-ə-lē\ *adverb*
— **slang·i·ness** \'slaŋ-ē-nəs\ *noun*
— **slangy** \'slaŋ-ē\ *adjective*

²**slang** (1828)
intransitive verb
: to use slang or vulgar abuse
transitive verb
: to abuse with harsh or coarse language

slanging match *noun* (1896)
chiefly British **:** a heated exchange of abuse

slan·guage \'slaŋ-gwij\ *noun* [blend of *slang* and *language*] (1879)
: slangy speech or writing

¹**slant** \'slant\ *noun* (1655)
1 : a slanting direction, line, or plane **:** SLOPE
2 a : something that slants **b :** DIAGONAL 3 **c :** a football running play in which the ballcarrier runs obliquely toward the line of scrimmage
3 a : a peculiar or personal point of view, attitude, or opinion **b :** a slanting view **:** GLANCE
— **slant** *adjective*
— **slant·ways** \-,wāz\ *adverb*
— **slant·wise** \-,wīz\ *adverb or adjective*
— **slanty** \'slan-tē\ *adjective*

²**slant** *verb* [Middle English *slenten* to fall obliquely, of Scandinavian origin; akin to Swedish *slinta* to slide] (1692)
intransitive verb
1 : to take a diagonal course, direction, or path
2 : to turn or incline from a right line or a level **:** SLOPE
transitive verb
1 : to give an oblique or sloping direction to
2 : to interpret or present in line with a special interest **:** ANGLE ⟨stories *slanted* toward youth⟩; *especially* **:** to maliciously or dishonestly distort or falsify
— **slant·ing·ly** \'slan-tiŋ-lē\ *adverb*

slant height *noun* (1798)
1 : the length of an element of a right circular cone
2 : the altitude of a side of a regular pyramid

¹**slap** \'slap\ *noun* [Middle English *slop*, from Middle Dutch; akin to Middle Dutch *slippen* to slip] (14th century)
dialect British **:** OPENING, BREACH

²**slap** *transitive verb* **slapped; slap·ping** [akin to Low German *slapp*, noun blow] (15th century)
1 a : to strike sharply with or as if with the open hand **b :** to cause to strike with a motion or sound like that of a blow with the open hand
2 : to put, place, or throw with careless haste or force ⟨*slapped* on a coat of paint⟩
3 : to assail verbally **:** INSULT
4 : to subject to a penalty — usually used with *with* ⟨*slapped* him with a $10 fine⟩

³**slap** *noun* (1648)
1 a : a blow with the open hand **b :** a quick sharp blow
2 : a noise like that of a slap

3 : REBUFF, INSULT
— slap on the wrist : a gentle usually ineffectual reprimand
⁴slap *adverb* [probably from Low German *slapp*, from *slapp*, noun] (1672)
: DIRECTLY, SMACK
slap·dash \'slap-'dash, -,dash\ *adjective* (circa 1792)
: HAPHAZARD, SLIPSHOD
slap down *transitive verb* (1842)
1 : to prohibit or restrain usually abruptly and with censure from acting in a specified way **:** SQUELCH
2 : to put an abrupt stop to **:** SUPPRESS
slap·hap·py \'slap-,ha-pē\ *adjective* (1936)
1 : PUNCH-DRUNK
2 : buoyantly or recklessly carefree or foolish **:** HAPPY-GO-LUCKY
slap·jack \-,jak\ *noun* [²*slap* + *-jack* (as in *flapjack*)] (1796)
1 : PANCAKE
2 : a card game in which each player tries to be the first to slap a hand on any jack that appears faceup
slap shot *noun* (1942)
: a shot in ice hockey made with a swinging stroke
slap·stick \'slap-,stik\ *noun* (1896)
1 : a device made of two flat pieces of wood fastened at one end so as to make a loud noise when used by an actor to strike a person
2 : comedy stressing farce and horseplay; *also* **:** activity resembling slapstick
— slapstick *adjective*
slap-up \'slap-,əp\ *adjective* (circa 1823)
chiefly British **:** FIRST-RATE, BANG-UP
¹slash \'slash\ *verb* [origin unknown] (1548)
intransitive verb
: to lash out, cut, or thrash about with or as if with an edged blade
transitive verb
1 : to cut with or as if with rough sweeping strokes
2 : CANE, LASH
3 : to cut slits in (as a garment) so as to reveal a color beneath
4 : to criticize cuttingly
5 : to reduce sharply **:** CUT
— slash·er *noun*
²slash *noun* (1576)
1 : the act of slashing; *also* **:** a long cut or stroke made by or as if by slashing
2 : an ornamental slit in a garment
3 a : an open tract in a forest strewn with debris (as from logging) **b :** the debris in such a tract
4 : DIAGONAL 3 — called also *slash mark*
³slash *noun* [origin unknown] (1652)
: a low swampy area often overgrown with brush
slash–and–burn *adjective* (1939)
: characterized or developed by felling and burning trees to clear land especially for temporary agriculture
¹slash·ing \'sla-shiŋ\ *adjective* (1593)
1 : incisively satiric or critical
2 : DRIVING, PELTING
3 : VIVID, BRILLIANT
— slash·ing·ly \-shiŋ-lē\ *adverb*
²slashing *noun* (1596)
1 : the act or process of slashing
2 : an insert or layer of contrasting color revealed by a slash (as in a garment)
3 : SLASH 3
slash pine *noun* [³*slash*] (1882)
: a pine (*Pinus elliottii*) of the southeastern U.S. that has two or three needles in a cluster and is a source of turpentine and lumber
slash pocket *noun* (1799)
: a pocket suspended on the wrong side of a garment from a finished slit on the right side that serves as its opening
¹slat \'slat\ *transitive verb* **slat·ted; slat·ting** [probably of Scandinavian origin; akin to Old Norse *sletta* to slap, throw] (1611)
1 : to hurl or throw smartly

2 : STRIKE, PUMMEL
²slat *noun* [Middle English, slate, from Middle French *esclat* splinter, from Old French, from *esclater* to burst, splinter] (1764)
1 : a thin narrow flat strip especially of wood or metal
2 *plural, slang* **:** RIBS
3 : an auxiliary airfoil at the leading edge of the wing of an airplane
— slat *adjective*
— slat·ted \'sla-təd\ *adjective*
³slat *transitive verb* **slat·ted; slat·ting** (1886)
: to make or equip with slats
¹slate \'slāt\ *noun* [Middle English, from Middle French *esclat* splinter] (14th century)
1 : a piece of construction material (as laminated rock) prepared as a shingle for roofing and siding
2 : a dense fine-grained metamorphic rock produced by the compression of various sediments (as clay or shale) so as to develop a characteristic cleavage
3 : a tablet (as of slate) used for writing on
4 a : a written or unwritten record (as of deeds) ⟨started with a clean *slate*⟩ **b :** a list of candidates for nomination or election
5 a : a dark purplish gray **b :** any of various grays similar in color to common roofing slates
— slate *adjective*
— slate·like \-,līk\ *adjective*
²slate *transitive verb* **slat·ed; slat·ing** (15th century)
1 : to cover with slate or a slatelike substance ⟨*slate* a roof⟩
2 : to designate for a specified purpose or action **:** SCHEDULE ⟨was *slated* to direct the play⟩
³slate *transitive verb* **slat·ed; slat·ing** [probably alteration of ¹*slat*] (1825)
1 : to thrash or pummel severely
2 *chiefly British* **:** to criticize or censure severely
slate black *noun* (circa 1890)
: a nearly neutral slightly purplish black
slate blue *noun* (1796)
: a grayish blue color
slat·er \'slā-tər\ *noun* (14th century)
1 : one that slates
2 [¹*slate;* from its color] **a :** WOOD LOUSE **b :** any of various marine isopods
¹slath·er \'sla-thər\ *noun* [origin unknown] (1857)
: a great quantity — often used in plural
²slather *transitive verb* **slath·ered; slath·er·ing** \'sla-thə-riŋ, 'slath-riŋ\ (1866)
1 : to use or spend in a wasteful or lavish manner **:** SQUANDER
2 a : to spread thickly or lavishly **b :** to spread something thickly or lavishly on
slat·ing \'slā-tiŋ\ *noun* (15th century)
: the work of a slater
¹slat·tern \'sla-tərn\ *noun* [probably from German *schlottern* to hang loosely, slouch; akin to Dutch *slodderen* to hang loosely, *slodder* slut] (circa 1639)
: an untidy slovenly woman; *also* **:** SLUT, PROSTITUTE
²slattern *adjective* (1716)
: SLATTERNLY
slat·tern·ly \'sla-tərn-lē\ *adjective* (circa 1680)
1 : untidy and dirty through habitual neglect; *also* **:** CARELESS, DISORDERLY
2 : of, relating to, or characteristic of a slut or prostitute
— slat·tern·li·ness *noun*
slaty *also* **slat·ey** \'slā-tē\ *adjective* (circa 1529)
: of, containing, or characteristic of slate; *also* **:** gray like slate
¹slaugh·ter \'slò-tər\ *noun* [Middle English, of Scandinavian origin; akin to Old Norse *slātra* to slaughter; akin to Old English *sleaht* slaughter, *slēan* to slay — more at SLAY] (14th century)

1 : the act of killing; *specifically* **:** the butchering of livestock for market
2 : killing of great numbers of human beings (as in battle or a massacre) **:** CARNAGE
²slaughter *transitive verb* (1535)
1 : to kill (animals) for food **:** BUTCHER
2 a : to kill in a bloody or violent manner **:** SLAY **b :** to kill in large numbers **:** MASSACRE
3 : to discredit or demolish completely
— slaugh·ter·er \-tər-ər\ *noun*
slaugh·ter·house \'slò-tər-,haús\ *noun* (14th century)
: an establishment where animals are butchered
slaugh·ter·ous \'slò-tə-rəs\ *adjective* (1582)
: of or relating to slaughter **:** MURDEROUS
— slaugh·ter·ous·ly *adverb*
Slav \'släv, 'slav\ *noun* [Middle English *Sclav,* from Medieval Latin *Sclavus,* from Late Greek *Sklabos,* from *Sklabēnoi* Slavs, of Slavic origin; akin to Old Russian *Slověne,* an East Slavic tribe] (14th century)
: a person whose native tongue is a Slavic language
word history SEE SLAVE
— Slav *adjective*
¹slave \'slāv\ *noun* [Middle English *sclave,* from Old French or Medieval Latin; Old French *esclave,* from Medieval Latin *sclavus,* from *Sclavus* Slav; from the frequent enslavement of Slavs in central Europe] (14th century)
1 : a person held in servitude as the chattel of another
2 : one that is completely subservient to a dominating influence
3 : a device (as the printer of a computer) that is directly responsive to another
4 : DRUDGE, TOILER ◇
— slave *adjective*
²slave *verb* **slaved; slav·ing** (1602)
transitive verb
1 *archaic* **:** ENSLAVE
2 : to make directly responsive to another mechanism
intransitive verb
1 : to work like a slave **:** DRUDGE

◇ **WORD HISTORY**
slave The words *Slav* and *slave* both come ultimately from a Slavic word that various groups of early medieval Slavs used in order to distinguish themselves from their neighbors. An early form of this word was *Slověne,* applied to 9th century Slavs living outside the Greek city of Thessaloniki in South Slavic versions of the life of St. Cyril, the missionary who introduced Christianity and literacy to Slavic lands. *Slověne* is the likely source of Medieval Greek *Sklabēnoi,* from which shortened Medieval Latin *Sclavus* and hence the word for "Slav" in Western European languages derive. In Medieval Latin *Sclavus* shifted in sense from "Slav" to "Slav in servitude" to "slave" in the 10th century, when German princes in central Europe were expanding their territories eastward at the expense of West Slavic tribes too decentralized to resist invasion. Many Slavic prisoners of war were sold into slavery, often ending up in Muslim Spain, then the wealthiest part of western Europe. Captives were also taken from among Balkan Slavs by the Byzantine Greeks, especially after the fall of the first Bulgarian Empire in 1018, and were sold throughout the Mediterranean. Such traffic probably led to the adoption of Medieval Latin *sclavus* into Romance languages.

\ə\ abut \ə\ kitten \ər\ further \a\ ash \ā\ ace
\ä\ mop, mar \aú\ out \ch\ chin \e\ bet \ē\ easy
\g\ go \i\ hit \ī\ ice \j\ job \ŋ\ sing \ō\ go
\ò\ law \òi\ boy \th\ thin \th\ the \ü\ loot \ú\ foot
\y\ yet \zh\ vision *see also* Guide to Pronunciation

2 : to traffic in slaves
slave driver *noun* (1807)
1 : a supervisor of slaves at work
2 : a harsh taskmaster
slave·hold·er \'slāv-,hōl-dər\ *noun* (1776)
: an owner of slaves
 — **slave·hold·ing** \-diŋ\ *adjective or noun*
slave-mak·ing ant \'slāv-,mā-kiŋ-\ *noun* (1817)
: an ant that attacks the colonies of ants of other species and carries off the larvae and pupae to be reared in its own nest as slaves
¹**sla·ver** \'sla-vər, 'slā-, 'slä-\ *verb* **sla·vered; sla·ver·ing** \-v(ə-)riŋ\ [Middle English, of Scandinavian origin; akin to Old Norse *slafra* to slaver; akin to Middle Dutch *slabben* to slaver] (14th century)
intransitive verb
: DROOL, SLOBBER
transitive verb
archaic : to smear with or as if with saliva
²**slaver** *noun* (14th century)
: saliva dribbling from the mouth
³**slav·er** \'slā-vər\ *noun* [¹*slave*] (1827)
1 a : a person engaged in the slave trade **b** : a ship used in the slave trade
2 : WHITE SLAVER
slav·ery \'slā-v(ə-)rē\ *noun* (1551)
1 : DRUDGERY, TOIL
2 : submission to a dominating influence
3 a : the state of a person who is a chattel of another **b** : the practice of slaveholding
slave state *noun* (1809)
1 : a state of the U.S. in which slavery was legal until the Civil War
2 : a nation subjected to totalitarian rule
slave trade *noun* (1734)
: traffic in slaves; *especially* : the buying and selling of blacks for profit prior to the American Civil War
slav·ey \'slā-vē\ *noun, plural* **slaveys** (circa 1812)
: DRUDGE; *especially* : a household servant who does general housework
¹**Slav·ic** \'slä-vik, 'sla-\ *noun* (1812)
: a branch of the Indo-European language family containing Belorussian, Bulgarian, Czech, Polish, Serbo-Croatian, Slovene, Russian, and Ukrainian — see INDO-EUROPEAN LANGUAGES table
²**Slavic** *adjective* (1813)
: of, relating to, or characteristic of the Slavs or their languages
Slav·i·cist \'slä-və-sist, 'sla-\ *noun* (1930)
: a specialist in the Slavic languages or literatures
slav·ish \'slā-vish *sometimes* 'sla-\ *adjective* (1565)
1 a : of or characteristic of a slave; *especially* : basely or abjectly servile **b** *archaic* : DESPICABLE, LOW
2 *archaic* : OPPRESSIVE, TYRANNICAL
3 : copying obsequiously or without originality : IMITATIVE
synonym see SUBSERVIENT
 — **slav·ish·ly** *adverb*
 — **slav·ish·ness** *noun*
Slav·ist \'slä-vist, 'sla-\ *noun* (1863)
: SLAVICIST
slav·oc·ra·cy \slä-'vä-krə-sē\ *noun* (1840)
: a faction of slaveholders and advocates of slavery in the South before the Civil War
¹**Sla·von·ic** \slə-'vä-nik\ *adjective* [New Latin *slavonicus*, from Medieval Latin *Sclavonia, Slavonia*, the Slavic-speaking countries, from *Sclavus* Slav] (circa 1645)
: SLAVIC
²**Slavonic** *noun* (1668)
1 : SLAVIC
2 : OLD CHURCH SLAVONIC
Slav·o·phile \'slä-və-,fīl, 'sla-\ *or* **Slav·o·phil** \-,fil\ *noun* (1877)
: an admirer of the Slavs : an advocate of Slavophilism
Slav·oph·i·lism \sla-'vä-fə-,li-zəm; 'sla-və-,fī-,li-, 'slä-\ *noun* (1877)

: advocacy of Slavic and specifically Russian culture over western European culture especially as practiced among some members of the Russian intelligentsia in the middle 19th century
slaw \'slȯ\ *noun* (1861)
: COLESLAW
slay \'slā\ *verb* **slew** \'slü\ *also especially in sense 2* **slayed; slain** \'slān\; **slay·ing** [Middle English *slen*, from Old English *slēan* to strike, slay; akin to Old High German *slahan* to strike, Middle Irish *slachta* stricken] (before 12th century)
transitive verb
1 : to kill violently, wantonly, or in great numbers; *broadly* : to strike down : KILL
2 : to delight or amuse immensely ⟨*slayed* the audience⟩
intransitive verb
: KILL, MURDER
synonym see KILL
 — **slay·er** *noun*
¹**sleave** \'slēv\ *noun* [²*sleave*] (1591)
archaic : SKEIN ⟨sleep that knits up the raveled *sleave* of care —Shakespeare⟩
²**sleave** *transitive verb* [(assumed) Middle English *sleven*, from Old English -*slǣfan* to cut] (circa 1628)
obsolete : to separate (silk thread) into filaments
sleave silk *noun* (1588)
obsolete : floss silk that is easily separated into filaments for embroidery
sleaze \'slēz *also* 'slāz\ *noun* [back-formation from *sleazy*] (1954)
1 : sleazy quality, appearance, or behavior; *also* : sleazy material
2 : a sleazy person
sleaze·bag \-,bag *also* -,bȧg\ *noun* (1983)
slang : a sleazy person
sleaze·ball \-,bȯl\ *noun* (1981)
slang : a sleazy person
sleazo \'slē-(,)zō\ *adjective* (1972)
slang : SLEAZY
slea·zy \'slē-zē *also* 'slā-\ *adjective* **slea·zi·er; -est** [origin unknown] (circa 1645)
1 a : lacking firmness of texture : FLIMSY **b** : carelessly made of inferior materials : SHODDY
2 a : marked by low character or quality ⟨*sleazy* tabloids⟩ **b** : SQUALID, DILAPIDATED ⟨*sleazy* bars⟩
 — **slea·zi·ly** \-zə-lē\ *adverb*
 — **slea·zi·ness** \-zē-nəs\ *noun*
¹**sled** \'sled\ *noun* [Middle English *sledde*, from Middle Dutch; akin to Old English *slīdan* to slide] (14th century)
1 : a vehicle on runners for transportation especially on snow or ice; *especially* : a small steerable one used especially by children for coasting down snow-covered hills
2 : ROCKET SLED
²**sled** *verb* **sled·ded; sled·ding** (1706)
transitive verb
: SLEDGE
intransitive verb
: to ride on a sled or sleigh
 — **sled·der** *noun*
sledding *noun* (15th century)
1 a : the use of a sled **b** : the conditions under which one may use a sled
2 : GOING 4 ⟨tough *sledding*⟩
sled dog *noun* (1692)
: a dog trained to draw a sledge especially in the Arctic regions — called also *sledge dog*
¹**sledge** \'slej\ *noun* [Middle English *slegge*, from Old English *slecg*; akin to Old Norse *sleggja* sledgehammer, Old English *slēan* to strike — more at SLAY] (before 12th century)
: SLEDGEHAMMER
²**sledge** *verb* **sledged; sledg·ing** (1654)
³**sledge** *noun* [Dutch dialect *sleedse*; akin to Middle Dutch *sledde* sled] (1617)
1 *British* : SLEIGH
2 : a strong heavy sled

⁴**sledge** *verb* **sledged; sledg·ing** (1853)
intransitive verb
1 : to travel with a sledge
2 *British* : to ride in a sleigh
transitive verb
: to transport on a sledge
¹**sledge·ham·mer** \'slej-,ha-mər\ *noun* (15th century)
: a large heavy hammer that is wielded with both hands; *also* : something that resembles a sledgehammer in action
²**sledgehammer** (1834)
transitive verb
: to strike with or as if with a sledgehammer
intransitive verb
: to strike blows with or as if with a sledgehammer
³**sledgehammer** *adjective* (1843)
: marked by heavy-handed directness or hard-hitting force ⟨trusting in *sledgehammer* warfare —C. J. Rolo⟩
¹**sleek** \'slēk\ *verb* [Middle English *sleken*, alteration of *sliken* — more at SLICK] (15th century)
transitive verb
1 : SLICK ⟨grooms *sleeking* cooled horses —Sunset⟩
2 : to cover up : gloss over
intransitive verb
: SLICK
²**sleek** *adjective* [alteration of ²*slick*] (1589)
1 a : smooth and glossy as if polished ⟨*sleek* dark hair⟩ **b** : having a smooth well-groomed look ⟨*sleek* cattle⟩ **c** : healthy-looking
2 : smooth in speech or manner; *also* : UNCTUOUS
3 a : having a prosperous air ⟨a *sleek* apartment building with a pool on the roof⟩ **b** : having trim graceful lines ⟨a *sleek* car⟩ **c** : ELEGANT, STYLISH ⟨*sleek* restaurants⟩ ☆
 — **sleek·ly** *adverb*
 — **sleek·ness** *noun*
sleek·en \'slē-kən\ *transitive verb* **sleek·ened; sleek·en·ing** \'slē-kə-niŋ, 'slēk-niŋ\ (1621)
: to make sleek
sleek·it \'slē-kət\ *adjective* [Scots, from past participle of ¹*sleek*] (1513)
1 *chiefly Scottish* : SLEEK, SMOOTH
2 *chiefly Scottish* : CRAFTY, DECEITFUL
¹**sleep** \'slēp\ *noun* [Middle English *slepe*, from Old English *slǣp*; akin to Old High German *slāf* sleep and perhaps to Latin *labi* to slip, slide] (before 12th century)
1 : the natural periodic suspension of consciousness during which the powers of the body are restored
2 : a state resembling sleep: as **a** : a state of torpid inactivity **b** : DEATH ⟨put a pet cat to *sleep*⟩; *also* : TRANCE, COMA **c** : the closing of leaves or petals especially at night **d** : a state marked by a diminution of feeling followed by tingling ⟨my foot's gone to *sleep*⟩ **e** : the state of an animal during hibernation
3 a : a period spent sleeping **b** : NIGHT **c** : a day's journey
 — **sleep·like** \-,līk\ *adjective*
²**sleep** *verb* **slept** \'slept\; **sleep·ing** (before 12th century)
intransitive verb
1 : to rest in a state of sleep
2 : to be in a state (as of quiescence or death) resembling sleep

☆ **SYNONYMS**
Sleek, slick, glossy mean having a smooth bright surface or appearance. SLEEK suggests a smoothness or brightness resulting from attentive grooming or physical conditioning ⟨a *sleek* racehorse⟩. SLICK suggests extreme smoothness that results in a slippery surface ⟨slipped and fell on the *slick* floor⟩. GLOSSY suggests a highly reflective surface ⟨photographs having a *glossy* finish⟩.

3 : to have sexual relations — usually used with *with*
transitive verb
1 : to be slumbering in ⟨*slept* the sleep of the dead⟩
2 : to get rid of or spend in or by sleep ⟨*sleep* away the hours⟩ ⟨*sleep* off a drunk⟩
3 : to provide sleeping accommodations for ⟨the boat *sleeps* six⟩
sleep around *intransitive verb* (1928)
: to engage in sex promiscuously
sleep·er \'slē-pər\ *noun* (12th century)
1 : one that sleeps
2 : a piece of timber, stone, or steel on or near the ground to support a superstructure, keep railroad rails in place, or receive floor joists **:** STRINGPIECE
3 : SLEEPING CAR
4 : someone or something unpromising or unnoticed that suddenly attains prominence or value ⟨the low-budget film became the summer's *sleeper*⟩
5 : children's pajamas usually with feet — usually used in plural
6 *chiefly British* **:** a small earring or stud worn to keep the hole of a pierced ear from closing
7 : MOLE 4
sleep–in \'slēp-ˌin\ *adjective* (1951)
: that lives at the place of employment ⟨a *sleep-in* maid⟩
sleep in *intransitive verb* (1827)
1 : to sleep where one is employed
2 a : OVERSLEEP **b :** to sleep late intentionally
sleeping bag *noun* (1850)
: a bag that is warmly lined or padded for sleeping outdoors or in a camp or tent
Sleeping Beauty *noun*
: a princess of a fairy tale who is wakened from an enchanted sleep by the kiss of a prince
sleeping car *noun* (1839)
: a railroad passenger car having berths for sleeping
sleeping partner *noun* (circa 1785)
chiefly British **:** SILENT PARTNER
sleeping pill *noun* (1664)
: a drug and especially a barbiturate that is taken as a tablet or capsule to induce sleep — called also *sleeping tablet*
sleeping porch *noun* (1915)
: a porch or room having open sides or many windows arranged to permit sleeping in the open air
sleeping sickness *noun* (1875)
1 : a serious disease that is prevalent in much of tropical Africa, is marked by fever, protracted lethargy, tremors, and loss of weight, is caused by either of two trypanosomes (*Trypanosoma brucei gambiense* and *T. b. rhodesiense*), and is transmitted by tsetse flies
2 : any of various viral encephalitides or encephalomyelitides of which lethargy or somnolence is a prominent feature
sleep·less \'slēp-ləs\ *adjective* (15th century)
1 : not able to sleep ⟨lay *sleepless* with fever⟩
2 : affording no sleep ⟨*sleepless* nights⟩
3 : unceasingly active or operative ⟨*sleepless* casinos⟩
— **sleep·less·ly** *adverb*
— **sleep·less·ness** *noun*
sleep out *intransitive verb* (1908)
: to sleep outdoors
sleep·over \'slēp-ō-vər\ *noun* (1965)
1 : an overnight stay (as at another's home)
2 : an instance of hosting a sleepover in one's home
sleep·walk·er \'slēp-ˌwȯ-kər\ *noun* (1747)
: one that walks while or as if while asleep **:** SOMNAMBULIST
— **sleep·walk** \-ˌwȯk\ *intransitive verb or noun*
sleep·wear \-ˌwar, -ˌwer\ *noun* (1935)
: NIGHTCLOTHES
sleepy \'slē-pē\ *adjective* **sleep·i·er; -est** (13th century)

1 a : ready to fall asleep **b :** of, relating to, or characteristic of sleep
2 : sluggish as if from sleep **:** LETHARGIC; *also* **:** having little activity ⟨a *sleepy* coastal village⟩
3 : sleep-inducing
— **sleep·i·ly** \-pə-lē\ *adverb*
— **sleep·i·ness** \-pē-nəs\ *noun*
sleepy·head \'slē-pē-ˌhed\ *noun* (1577)
: a sleepy person
¹**sleet** \'slēt\ *noun* [Middle English *slete;* akin to Middle High German *slōz* hailstone] (13th century)
: frozen or partly frozen rain
— **sleety** \'slē-tē\ *adjective*
²**sleet** *intransitive verb* (14th century)
: to shower sleet
sleeve \'slēv\ *noun* [Middle English *sleve,* from Old English *slīefe;* perhaps akin to Old English *slēfan* to slip (clothes) on, *slūpan* to slip, Old High German *sliofan,* Latin *lubricus* slippery] (before 12th century)
1 a : a part of a garment covering an arm **b :** SLEEVELET
2 a : a tubular part (as a hollow axle or a bushing) designed to fit over another part **b :** an open-ended flat or tubular packaging or cover; *especially* **:** JACKET 3c(2)
— **sleeved** \'slēvd\ *adjective*
— **sleeve·less** \'slēv-ləs\ *adjective*
— **up one's sleeve :** held secretly in reserve
sleeve·let \'slēv-lət\ *noun* (1889)
: a covering for the forearm to protect clothing from wear or dirt
¹**sleigh** \'slā\ *noun* [Dutch *slee,* alteration of *slede;* akin to Middle Dutch *sledde* sled] (1703)
: an open usually horse-drawn vehicle with runners for use on snow or ice

sleigh

²**sleigh** *intransitive verb* (circa 1729)
: to drive or travel in a sleigh
sleigh bed *noun* (1902)
: a bed common especially in the first half of the 19th century having a solid headboard and footboard that roll outward at the top
sleigh bell *noun* (1772)
: any of various bells commonly attached to a sleigh or to the harness of a horse drawing a sleigh: as **a :** CASCABEL 2 **b :** a hemispherical bell with an attached clapper
sleight \'slīt\ *noun* [Middle English, from Old Norse *slægth,* from *slægr* sly — more at SLY] (14th century)
1 : deceitful craftiness; *also* **:** STRATAGEM
2 : DEXTERITY, SKILL
sleight of hand *noun* (circa 1605)
1 a : a conjuring trick requiring manual dexterity **b :** a cleverly executed trick or deception
2 a : skill and dexterity in conjuring tricks **b :** adroitness in deception
slen·der \'slen-dər\ *adjective* [Middle English *sclendre, slendre*] (14th century)
1 a : spare in frame or flesh; *especially* **:** gracefully slight **b :** small or narrow in circumference or width in proportion to length or height
2 : limited or inadequate in amount or scope **:** MEAGER ⟨people of *slender* means⟩
synonym see THIN
— **slen·der·ly** *adverb*
— **slen·der·ness** *noun*
slen·der·ize \-də-ˌrīz\ *transitive verb* **-ized; -iz·ing** (1923)
: to make slender
¹**sleuth** \'slüth\ *noun* [short for *sleuthhound*] (1872)
: DETECTIVE ◆
²**sleuth** (1900)
intransitive verb

: to act as a detective **:** search for information
transitive verb
: to search for and discover
sleuth·hound \'slüth-ˌhau̇nd\ *noun* [Middle English *sleuth hund,* a kind of bloodhound, from *sleuth* track of an animal or person (from Old Norse *slōth*) + *hund* hound] (1856)
: DETECTIVE
S level *noun* (1951)
1 : the highest of three standardized British examinations in a secondary school subject used as a qualification for university entrance; *also* **:** successful completion of an S-level examination in a particular subject — called also *Scholarship level;* compare A LEVEL, O LEVEL
2 a : the level of education required to pass an S-level examination **b :** a course leading to an S-level examination
¹**slew** \'slü\ *past of* SLAY
²**slew** *variant of* SLOUGH
³**slew** *verb* [origin unknown] (circa 1769)
transitive verb
1 : to turn (as a telescope or a ship's spar) about a fixed point that is usually the axis
2 : to cause to skid **:** VEER ⟨*slew* a car around a turn⟩
intransitive verb
1 : to turn, twist, or swing about **:** PIVOT
2 : SKID
⁴**slew** *noun* [perhaps from Irish *slua* army, host, throng, from Old Irish *slúag;* akin to Lithuanian *slaugyti* to tend] (1839)
: a large number ⟨a *slew* of books⟩
¹**slice** \'slīs\ *verb* **sliced; slic·ing** [Middle English *sklicen,* from Middle French *esclicier* to splinter, from Old French, of Germanic origin; akin to Old High German *slīzan* to tear apart — more at SLIT] (1551)
transitive verb
1 : to cut with or as if with a knife
2 : to stir or spread with a slice
3 : to hit (a ball) so that a slice results
intransitive verb
1 : to slice something
2 : to move with a cutting action ⟨the ship *sliced* through the waves⟩
— **slice·able** \'slī-sə-bəl\ *adjective*
— **slic·er** *noun*
²**slice** *noun* [Middle English *sklice,* from Middle French *esclice* splinter, from Old French, from *esclicier*] (1613)
1 a : a thin flat piece cut from something **b :** a wedge-shaped piece (as of pie or cake)
2 : a spatula for spreading paint or ink

\ə\ abut \ᵊ\ kitten \ər\ further \a\ ash \ā\ ace
\ä\ mop, mar \au̇\ out \ch\ chin \e\ bet \ē\ easy
\g\ go \i\ hit \ī\ ice \j\ job \ŋ\ sing \ō\ go
\ȯ\ law \ȯi\ boy \th\ thin \t͟h\ the \ü\ loot \u̇\ foot
\y\ yet \zh\ vision *see also* Guide to Pronunciation

3 : a serving knife with wedge-shaped blade ⟨a fish *slice*⟩
4 : a flight of a ball that deviates from a straight course in the direction of the dominant hand of the player propelling it; *also* : a ball following such a course — compare HOOK
5 : PORTION, SHARE ⟨a *slice* of the profits⟩
slice–of–life *adjective* (1895)
: of, relating to, or marked by the accurate transcription (as into drama) of a segment of actual life experience
¹slick \ˈslik\ *verb* [Middle English *sliken*; akin to Old High German *slīhhan* to glide] (14th century)
transitive verb
: to make sleek or smooth
intransitive verb
: SPRUCE — usually used with *up*
²slick *adjective* (14th century)
1 a : having a smooth surface : SLIPPERY ⟨*slick* wet leaves⟩ **b :** having surface plausibility or appeal : GLIB, GLOSSY ⟨*slick* advertising⟩ **c :** based on stereotype : TRITE ⟨*slick* stories soon forgotten⟩
2 *archaic* : SLEEK 1
3 a : characterized by subtlety or nimble wit : CLEVER; *especially* : WILY ⟨a reputation as a *slick* operator⟩ **b :** DEFT, SKILLFUL ⟨a *slick* ball-player⟩
4 : extremely good : FIRST-RATE
synonym see SLEEK, SLY
— **slick** *adverb*
— **slick·ly** *adverb*
— **slick·ness** *noun*
³slick *noun* (1849)
1 a : something that is smooth or slippery; *especially* : a smooth patch of water covered with a film of oil **b :** a film of oil
2 : an implement for producing a slick surface: as **a :** a flat paddle usually of steel for smoothing a sample of flour **b :** a foundry tool for smoothing the surface of a sand mold or unbaked core
3 : a shrewd untrustworthy person
4 : a popular magazine printed on coated stock and intended to appeal to sophisticated readers
5 : an automobile tire made without a tread for maximum traction (as in drag racing)
slick–ear \ˈslik-ˌir\ *noun* (1914)
: a range animal lacking an earmark
slick·en·side \ˈsli-kən-ˌsīd\ *noun* [English dialect *slicken* smooth (alteration of English ²*slick*) + English *side*] (1822)
: a smooth often striated surface produced on rock by movement along a fault or a subsidiary fracture — usually used in plural
slick·er \ˈsli-kər\ *noun* (1881)
1 [²*slick*] : OILSKIN; *broadly* : RAINCOAT
2 [*slick* to defraud cleverly] **a :** a clever crook : SWINDLER **b :** a city dweller especially of natty appearance or sophisticated mannerisms
slick·rock \ˈslik-ˌräk\ *noun* (1925)
: smooth wind-polished rock
¹slide \ˈslīd\ *verb* **slid** \ˈslid\; **slid·ing** \ˈslī-diŋ\ [Middle English, from Old English *slīdan*; akin to Middle High German *slīten* to slide] (before 12th century)
intransitive verb
1 a : to move smoothly along a surface : SLIP **b :** to coast over snow or ice **c** *of a base runner in baseball* : to fall or dive feetfirst or headfirst when approaching a base
2 a : to slip or fall by loss of footing **b :** to change position or become dislocated : SHIFT
3 a : to slither along the ground : CRAWL **b :** to stream along : FLOW
4 a : to move or pass smoothly or easily ⟨*slid* into the prepared speech⟩ **b :** to pass unnoticed or unremarked ⟨could have responded but let it *slide*⟩
5 a : to pass unobtrusively : STEAL **b :** to pass by gradations especially downward ⟨the economy *slid* from recession to depression⟩
transitive verb
1 a : to cause to glide or slip **b :** to traverse in a sliding manner

2 : to put unobtrusively or stealthily ⟨*slid* the bill into his hand⟩
²slide *noun* (1570)
1 a : an act or instance of sliding **b** (1) : a musical grace of two or more small notes (2) : PORTAMENTO
2 : a sliding part or mechanism: as **a** (1) : a U-shaped section of tube in the trombone that is pushed out and in to produce the tones between the fundamental and its harmonics (2) : a short U-shaped section of tube in a brass instrument that is used to adjust the pitch of the instrument or of individual valves **b** (1) : a moving piece (as the ram of a punch press) that is guided by a part along which it slides (2) : a guiding surface (as a feeding mechanism) along which something slides **c :** SLIDING SEAT
3 a : the descent of a mass of earth, rock, or snow down a hill or mountainside **b :** a dislocation in which one rock mass in a mining lode has slid on another : FAULT
4 a (1) : a slippery surface for coasting (2) : a chute with a slippery bed down which children slide in play **b :** a channel or track on which something is slid **c :** a sloping trough down which objects are carried by gravity ⟨a log *slide*⟩
5 a : a flat piece of glass on which an object is mounted for microscopic examination **b :** a photographic transparency on a small plate or film mounted for projection
6 : BOTTLENECK 3
slide fastener *noun* (1934)
: ZIPPER
slid·er \ˈslī-dər\ *noun* (1530)
1 : one that slides
2 : a fast baseball pitch that breaks slightly in the same direction as a curve
slide rule *noun* (1663)
: a manual device used for calculation that consists in its simple form of a ruler and a movable middle piece which are graduated with similar logarithmic scales
slide valve *noun* (1802)
: a valve that opens and closes a passageway by sliding over a port; *specifically* : such a valve often used in steam engines for admitting steam to the piston and releasing it
slide·way \ˈslīd-ˌwā\ *noun* (1856)
: a way along which something slides
sliding scale *noun* (1842)
1 : a wage scale geared to the selling price of the product or to the consumer price index but usually guaranteeing a minimum below which the wage will not fall
2 a : a system for raising or lowering tariffs in accord with price changes **b :** a flexible scale (as of fees or subsidies) adjusted to the needs or income of individuals ⟨the *sliding scale* of medical fees⟩
sliding seat *noun* (1874)
: a rower's seat (as in a racing shell) that slides fore and aft — called also *slide*
slier *comparative of* SLY
sliest *superlative of* SLY
¹slight \ˈslīt\ *adjective* [Middle English, smooth, slight, probably from Middle Dutch *slicht*; akin to Old High German *slīhhan* to glide — more at SLICK] (14th century)
1 a : having a slim or delicate build : not stout or massive in body **b :** lacking in strength or substance : FLIMSY, FRAIL **c :** deficient in weight, solidity, or importance : TRIVIAL
2 : small of its kind or in amount : SCANTY, MEAGER
synonym see THIN
— **slight·ly** *adverb*
— **slight·ness** *noun*
²slight *transitive verb* (1597)
1 : to treat as slight or unimportant : make light of
2 : to treat with disdain or indifference
3 : to perform or attend to carelessly and inadequately

4 : ³SLUR 3
synonym see NEGLECT
³slight *noun* (1701)
1 : an act or an instance of slighting
2 : an instance of being slighted : a humiliating discourtesy
slight·ing *adjective* (1632)
: characterized by disregard or disrespect : DISPARAGING ⟨a *slighting* remark⟩
— **slight·ing·ly** \ˈslī-tiŋ-lē\ *adverb*
sli·ly *variant of* SLYLY
¹slim \ˈslim\ *adjective* **slim·mer; slim·mest** [Dutch, bad, inferior, from Middle Dutch *slim* crooked, bad; akin to Middle High German *slimp* awry] (1657)
1 : of small diameter or thickness in proportion to the height or length : SLENDER
2 a : MEAN, WORTHLESS **b :** ADROIT, CRAFTY
3 a : inferior in quality or amount : SLIGHT **b :** SCANTY, SMALL ⟨a *slim* chance⟩
synonym see THIN
— **slim·ly** *adverb*
— **slim·ness** *noun*
²slim *verb* **slimmed; slim·ming** (1862)
transitive verb
: to make slender : decrease the size of
intransitive verb
: to become slender
¹slime \ˈslīm\ *noun* [Middle English, from Old English *slīm*; akin to Middle High German *slīm* slime, Latin *limus* mud — more at LIME] (before 12th century)
1 : soft moist earth or clay; *especially* : viscous mud
2 : a viscous or glutinous substance: as **a :** a mucous or mucoid secretion of various animals (as slugs and catfishes) **b :** a product of wet crushing consisting of ore ground so fine as to pass a 200-mesh screen
3 : a repulsive or odious person
²slime *verb* **slimed; slim·ing** (1628)
transitive verb
1 : to smear or cover with slime
2 : to remove slime from (as fish for canning)
intransitive verb
: to become slimy
slime·ball \ˈslīm-ˌbȯl\ *noun* (1986)
slang : SLIME 3
slime mold *noun* (1880)
: any of a group (Myxomycetes or Mycetozoa) of organisms usually held to be lower fungi but sometimes considered protozoans that exist vegetatively as mobile plasmodia and reproduce by spores
slim–jim \ˈslim-ˈjim, -ˌjim\ *adjective* [¹*slim* + *Jim*, nickname for *James*] (1889)
: notably slender
slim·mer \ˈsli-mər\ *noun* (1967)
chiefly British : a person dieting to lose weight : DIETER
slim·nas·tics \ˌslim-ˈnas-tiks\ *noun plural but singular in construction* [¹*slim* + *gymnastics*] (1967)
: exercises designed to reduce one's weight
slim·sy *or* **slimp·sy** \ˈslim-zē, ˈslim(p)-sē\ *adjective* [blend of *slim* and *flimsy*] (1845)
: FLIMSY, FRAIL
slimy \ˈslī-mē\ *adjective* **slim·i·er; -est** (14th century)
1 : of, relating to, or resembling slime : VISCOUS; *also* : covered with or yielding slime
2 : VILE, OFFENSIVE
— **slim·i·ly** \-mə-lē\ *adverb*
— **slim·i·ness** \-mē-nəs\ *noun*
¹sling \ˈsliŋ\ *transitive verb* **slung** \ˈsləŋ\; **sling·ing** \ˈsliŋ-iŋ\ [Middle English, probably from Old Norse *slyngva* to hurl; akin to Old English & Old High German *slingan* to worm, twist, Lithuanian *slinkti*] (14th century)
1 : to cast with a sudden and usually sweeping or swirling motion ⟨*slung* the sack over my shoulder⟩
2 : to throw with or as if with a sling ⟨*slinging* punches⟩ ⟨*sling* mud⟩
synonym see THROW
— **sling·er** \ˈsliŋ-ər\ *noun*

²sling *noun* (14th century)
1 a : an instrument for throwing stones that usually consists of a short strap with strings fastened to its ends and is whirled round to discharge its missile by centrifugal force **b :** SLINGSHOT 1
2 a : a usually looped line (as of strap, chain, or rope) used to hoist, lower, or carry something; *especially* **:** a hanging bandage suspended from the neck to support an arm or hand **b :** a chain or rope attached to a lower yard at the middle and passing around a mast near the masthead to support a yard **c :** a chain hooked at the bow and stern of a boat for lowering or hoisting **d :** a device (as a rope net) for enclosing material to be hoisted by a tackle or crane
3 : a slinging or hurling of or as if of a missile

³sling *transitive verb* **slung** \'sləŋ\; **sling·ing** \'sliŋ-iŋ\ (1522)
1 : to place in a sling for hoisting or lowering
2 : to suspend by or as if by a sling

⁴sling *noun* [origin unknown] (1768)
: an alcoholic drink that is served hot or cold and that usually consists of liquor, sugar, lemon juice, and plain or carbonated water ⟨gin *sling*⟩ ⟨rum *sling*⟩

slings and arrows *noun plural* [from the phrase "the slings and arrows of outrageous fortune" in Shakespeare's *Hamlet*] (1963)
: pointed often acerbic critical attacks ⟨has suffered the *slings and arrows* of detractors —Roland Gelatt⟩

sling·shot \'sliŋ-ˌshät\ *noun* (1849)
1 : a forked stick with an elastic band attached for shooting small stones
2 a : a maneuver in auto racing in which a drafting car accelerates past the car in front by taking advantage of reserve power **b :** a dragster in which the driver sits behind the rear wheels

¹slink \'sliŋk\ *verb* **slunk** \'sləŋk\ *also* **slinked** \'sliŋ(k)t\; **slink·ing** [Middle English, from Old English *slincan* to creep; akin to Old English *slingan* to worm, twist] (14th century)
intransitive verb
1 : to go or move stealthily or furtively (as in fear or shame) **:** STEAL
2 : to move in a sinuous provocative manner
transitive verb
: to give premature birth to — used especially of a domestic animal ⟨a cow that *slinks* her calf⟩
synonym see LURK

²slink *noun* (1607)
: the young of an animal (as a calf) brought forth prematurely; *also* **:** the flesh or skin of such an animal

³slink *adjective* (1750)
: born prematurely or abortively ⟨a *slink* calf⟩

slinky \'sliŋ-kē\ *adjective* **slink·i·er; -est** (1918)
1 : characterized by slinking **:** stealthily quiet ⟨*slinky* movements⟩
2 : sleek and sinuous in movement or outline; *especially* **:** following the lines of the figure in a gracefully flowing manner ⟨a *slinky* evening gown⟩
— **slink·i·ly** \-kə-lē\ *adverb*
— **slink·i·ness** \-kē-nəs\ *noun*

¹slip \'slip\ *verb* **slipped; slip·ping** [Middle English *slippen*, from Middle Dutch or Middle Low German; akin to Middle High German *slipfen* to slide, Old High German *slīfan* to smooth, and perhaps to Greek *olibros* slippery] (14th century)
intransitive verb
1 a : to move with a smooth sliding motion **b :** to move quietly and cautiously **:** STEAL **c :** ELAPSE, PASS
2 a (1) **:** to escape from memory or consciousness (2) **:** to become uttered through inadvertence **b :** to pass quickly or easily away **:** become lost ⟨let an opportunity *slip*⟩
3 : to fall into error or fault **:** LAPSE

4 a : to slide out of place or away from a support or one's grasp **b :** to slide on or down a slippery surface ⟨*slip* on the stairs⟩ **c :** to flow smoothly
5 : to get speedily into or out of clothing ⟨*slipped* into his coat⟩
6 : to fall off from a standard or accustomed level by degrees **:** DECLINE
7 : SIDESLIP
transitive verb
1 : to cause to move easily and smoothly **:** SLIDE
2 a : to get away from **:** ELUDE, EVADE ⟨*slipped* his pursuers⟩ **b :** to free oneself from ⟨the dog *slipped* its collar⟩ **c :** to escape from ⟨one's memory or notice⟩ ⟨their names *slip* my mind⟩
3 : SHED, CAST ⟨the snake *slipped* its skin⟩
4 : to put on (a garment) quickly — usually used with *on* ⟨*slip* on a coat⟩
5 a : to let loose from a restraining leash or grasp **b :** to cause to slip open **:** RELEASE, UNDO ⟨*slip* a lock⟩ **c :** to let go of **d :** to disengage from (an anchor) instead of hauling
6 a : to insert, place, or pass quietly or secretly **b :** to give or pay on the sly
7 : SLINK, ABORT
8 : DISLOCATE ⟨*slipped* his shoulder⟩
9 : to transfer (a stitch) from one needle to another without working a stitch
10 : to avoid (a punch) by moving the body or head quickly to one side

²slip *noun* (15th century)
1 a : a sloping ramp extending out into the water to serve as a place for landing or repairing ships **b :** a ship's or boat's berth between two piers
2 : the act or an instance of departing secretly or hurriedly ⟨gave his pursuer the *slip*⟩
3 a : a mistake in judgment, policy, or procedure **b :** an unintentional and trivial mistake or fault **:** LAPSE ⟨a *slip* of the tongue⟩
4 : a leash so made that it can be quickly slipped
5 a : the act or an instance of slipping down or out of a place ⟨a *slip* on the ice⟩; *also* **:** a sudden mishap **b :** a movement dislocating parts (as of a rock or soil mass); *also* **:** the result of such movement **c :** a fall from some level or standard **:** DECLINE ⟨a *slip* in stock prices⟩
6 a : an undergarment made in dress length with shoulder straps; *also* **:** HALF-SLIP **b :** a case into which something is slipped; *specifically* **:** PILLOWCASE
7 a : the motion of the center of resistance of the float of a paddle wheel or the blade of an oar through the water horizontally **b :** retrograde movement of a belt on a pulley **c :** the amount of leakage past the piston of a pump or the impellers of a blower
8 : a disposition or tendency to slip easily
9 : the action of sideslipping **:** an instance of sideslipping
synonym see ERROR

³slip *noun* [Middle English *slippe*, probably from Middle Dutch or Middle Low German, split, slit, flap] (15th century)
1 a : a small shoot or twig cut for planting or grafting **:** SCION **b :** DESCENDANT, OFFSPRING
2 a : a long narrow strip of material **b :** a small piece of paper
3 : a young and slender person ⟨a *slip* of a girl⟩
4 : a long seat or narrow pew

⁴slip *transitive verb* **slipped; slip·ping** (1530)
: to take cuttings from (a plant) **:** divide into slips ⟨*slip* a geranium⟩

⁵slip *noun* [Middle English *slyp* slime, from Old English *slypa* slime, paste; akin to Old English *slūpan* to slip — more at SLEEVE] (1640)
: a mixture of finely divided clay and water used by potters (as for casting or decorating wares or in cementing separately formed parts)

slip·case \'slip-ˌkās\ *noun* (circa 1925)
: a protective container with one open end for books
— **slip·cased** \-ˌkāst\ *adjective*

slip·cov·er \'slip-ˌkə-vər\ *noun* (1886)
: a cover that may be slipped off and on; *specifically* **:** a removable covering for an article of furniture

slip·form \'slip-ˌform\ *transitive verb* (1962)
: to construct with the use of a slip form

slip form *noun* (1949)
: a form that is moved slowly as concrete is placed during construction (as of a building or pavement)

slip·knot \'slip-ˌnät\ *noun* (1659)
: a knot that slips along the rope or line around which it is made; *especially* **:** one made by tying an overhand knot around the standing part of a rope — see KNOT illustration

slip noose (1847)
: a noose with a slipknot

slip–on \'slip-ˌȯn, -ˌän\ *noun* (1815)
: an article of clothing that is easily slipped on or off: as **a :** a glove or shoe without fastenings **b :** a garment (as a girdle) that one steps into and pulls up **c :** PULLOVER

slip·over \-ˌō-vər\ *noun* (1917)
: a garment or cover that slips on and off easily; *specifically* **:** a pullover sweater

slip·page \'sli-pij\ *noun* (1850)
1 : an act, instance, or process of slipping
2 : a loss in transmission of power; *also* **:** the difference between theoretical and actual output (as of power)

slipped disk *noun* (1942)
: a protrusion of one of the cartilage disks between vertebrae with pressure on spinal nerves resulting in low back pain or sciatic pain

¹slip·per \'sli-pər\ *adjective* [Middle English, from Old English *slipor;* akin to Middle Low German *slipper* slippery, *slippen* to slip] (before 12th century)
chiefly dialect **:** SLIPPERY

²slipper *noun* [Middle English, from *slippen* to slip] (15th century)
: a light low-cut shoe that is easily slipped on the foot
— **slip·pered** \-pərd\ *adjective*

slip·pery \'sli-p(ə-)rē\ *adjective* **slip·per·i·er; -est** [alteration of Middle English *slipper*] (circa 1500)
1 a : causing or tending to cause something to slide or fall ⟨*slippery* roads⟩ **b :** tending to slip from the grasp
2 : not firmly fixed **:** UNSTABLE
3 : not to be trusted **:** TRICKY
— **slip·per·i·ness** *noun*

slippery elm *noun* (1748)
: a large-leaved elm (*Ulmus rubra* synonym *U. fulva*) of eastern North America that has hard wood and fragrant mucilaginous inner bark; *also* **:** the bark

slip·py \'sli-pē\ *adjective* **slip·pi·er; -est** (1548)
: SLIPPERY

slip ring *noun* [²slip] (1898)
: one of two or more continuous conducting rings from which the brushes take or to which they deliver current in a generator or motor

slip–sheet \'slip-ˌshēt\ *transitive verb* (circa 1909)
: to insert slip sheets between (newly printed sheets)

slip sheet *noun* [¹slip] (1903)
: a sheet of paper placed between newly printed sheets to prevent offsetting

slip·shod \'slip-ˌshäd\ *adjective* [¹slip] (1580)
1 a : wearing loose shoes or slippers **b :** down at the heel **:** SHABBY
2 : CARELESS, SLOVENLY

\ə\ abut \ᵊ\ kitten \ər\ further \a\ ash \ā\ ace
\ä\ mop, mar \au̇\ out \ch\ chin \e\ bet \ē\ easy
\g\ go \i\ hit \ī\ ice \j\ job \ŋ\ sing \ō\ go
\ȯ\ law \ȯi\ boy \th\ thin \ṯh\ the \ü\ loot \u̇\ foot
\y\ yet \zh\ vision *see also* Guide to Pronunciation

slip·slop \-,släp\ *noun* [reduplication of ²*slop*] (1675)
1 *archaic* **:** watery food **:** SLOPS
2 *archaic* **:** shallow talk or writing
— **slip–slop** *adjective*
slip·sole \-,sōl\ *noun* (circa 1908)
1 : a thin insole
2 : a half sole inserted between the insole or welt and the outsole of a shoe to give additional height — called also *slip tap*
slip stitch *noun* (circa 1882)
1 : a concealed stitch for sewing folded edges (as hems) made by alternately running the needle into the fold and picking up a thread or two from the body of the article
2 : an unworked stitch; *especially* **:** a knitting stitch that is shifted from one needle to another without knitting it
¹slip·stream \'slip-,strēm\ *noun* (1913)
1 : a stream of fluid (as air or water) driven aft by a propeller
2 : an area of reduced air pressure and forward suction immediately behind a rapidly moving vehicle
²slipstream *intransitive verb* (1957)
: to drive in the slipstream of a vehicle
slip·up \'slip-,əp\ *noun* (1854)
1 : MISTAKE
2 : MISCHANCE
slip up *intransitive verb* (1909)
: to make a mistake **:** BLUNDER
slip·ware \'slip-,war, -,wer\ *noun* (1883)
: pottery coated with slip to improve or decorate the surface
slip·way \-,wā\ *noun* (1840)
: an inclined usually concrete surface for a ship being built or repaired
¹slit \'slit\ *noun* [Middle English, from *slitten*] (12th century)
: a long narrow cut or opening
— **slit** *adjective*
— **slit·less** \'slit-ləs\ *adjective*
²slit *transitive verb* **slit; slit·ting** [Middle English *slitten;* akin to Middle High German *slitzen* to slit, Old High German *slīzan* to tear apart, Old English *sciell* shell — more at SHELL] (14th century)
1 a : to make a slit in **b :** to cut off or away **:** SEVER **c :** to form into a slit
2 : to cut into long narrow strips
— **slit·ter** *noun*
slith·er \'sli-thər\ *verb* [Middle English *slideren,* from Old English *slidrian,* frequentative of *slīdan* to slide] (before 12th century)
intransitive verb
1 : to slide on or as if on a loose gravelly surface
2 : to slip or slide like a snake
transitive verb
: to cause to slide
slith·ery \'sli-thə-rē\ *adjective* (circa 1825)
: having a slippery surface, texture, or quality
slit trench *noun* (1942)
: a narrow trench especially for shelter in battle from bomb and shell fragments
¹sliv·er \'sli-vər, *2 is usually* 'slī-\ *noun* [Middle English *slivere,* from *sliven* to slice off, from Old English -*slīfan;* akin to Old English -*slǣfan* to cut] (14th century)
1 a : a long slender piece cut or torn off **:** SPLINTER **b :** a small and narrow portion ⟨a *sliver* of land⟩ **c :** PARTICLE, SCRAP ⟨not a *sliver* of evidence⟩
2 : an untwisted strand or rope of textile fiber produced by a carding or combing machine and ready for drawing, roving, or spinning
²sliv·er \'sli-vər\ *verb* **sliv·ered; sliv·er·ing** \'sli-və-riŋ, 'sliv-riŋ\ (1605)
transitive verb
: to cut into slivers **:** SPLINTER
intransitive verb
: to become split into slivers
sliv·o·vitz \'sli-və-,vits, 'slē-, -,wits\ *noun* [Serbo-Croatian *šljivovica,* from *šljiva, sliva* plum; akin to Russian *sliva* plum — more at LIVID] (1885)

: a dry usually colorless plum brandy made especially in the Balkan countries
slob \'släb\ *noun* [Irish *slab* mud, ooze, slovenly person] (1861)
: a slovenly or boorish person
— **slob·bish** \'slä-bish\ *adjective*
— **slob·by** \-bē\ *adjective*
¹slob·ber \'slä-bər\ *verb* **slob·bered; slob·ber·ing** \-b(ə-)riŋ\ [Middle English *sloberen* to eat in a slovenly manner; akin to Low German *slubberen* to sip] (1733)
intransitive verb
1 : to let saliva dribble from the mouth **:** DROOL
2 : to indulge the feelings effusively and without restraint
transitive verb
: to smear with or as if with dribbling saliva or food
— **slob·ber·er** \-bər-ər\ *noun*
²slobber *noun* (circa 1755)
1 : saliva drooled from the mouth
2 : driveling, sloppy, or incoherent utterance
— **slob·bery** \'slä-b(ə-)rē\ *adjective*
sloe \'slō\ *noun* [Middle English *slo,* from Old English *slāh;* akin to Old High German *slēha* sloe and probably to Russian *sliva* plum — more at LIVID] (before 12th century)
: the small dark globose astringent fruit of the blackthorn; *also* **:** BLACKTHORN
sloe–eyed \'slō-,īd\ *adjective* (1867)
1 : having soft dark bluish or purplish black eyes
2 : having slanted eyes
sloe gin *noun* (1895)
: a sweet reddish liqueur consisting of grain spirits flavored chiefly with sloes
¹slog \'släg\ *verb* **slogged; slog·ging** [origin unknown] (1824)
transitive verb
1 : to hit hard **:** BEAT
2 : to plod (one's way) perseveringly especially against difficulty
intransitive verb
1 : to plod heavily **:** TRAMP ⟨*slogged* through the snow⟩
2 : to work hard and steadily **:** PLUG
— **slog·ger** *noun*
²slog *noun* (1888)
1 : hard persistent work
2 : a hard dogged march or tramp
slo·gan \'slō-gən\ *noun* [alteration of earlier *slogorn,* from Scottish Gaelic *sluagh-ghairm,* from *sluagh* army, host + *gairm* cry] (1513)
1 a : a war cry or rallying cry especially of a Scottish clan **b :** a word or phrase used to express a characteristic position or stand or a goal to be achieved
2 : a brief attention-getting phrase used in advertising or promotion ◇
slo·gan·eer \,slō-gə-'nir\ *noun* (1922)
: a maker or user of slogans
— **sloganeer** *intransitive verb*
slo·gan·ize \'slō-gə-,nīz\ *transitive verb* **-ized; -iz·ing** (1926)
: to express as a slogan
sloop \'slüp\ *noun* [Dutch *sloep*] (1629)
: a fore-and-aft rigged boat with one mast and a single jib
sloop of war (1704)
: a small warship with guns on only one deck
¹slop \'släp\ *noun* [Middle English *sloppe,* probably from Middle Dutch *slop;* akin to Old English *oferslop* surplice] (14th century)
1 : a loose smock or overall

sloop

2 *plural* **:** short full breeches worn by men in the 16th century
3 *plural* **:** articles (as clothing) sold to sailors
²slop *noun* [Middle English *sloppe*] (15th century)
1 : soft mud **:** SLUSH
2 : thin tasteless drink or liquid food — usually used in plural
3 : liquid spilled or splashed
4 a : food waste (as garbage) fed to animals **:** SWILL 2a **b :** excreted body waste — usually used in plural
5 : sentimental effusiveness in speech or writing **:** GUSH
³slop *verb* **slopped; slop·ping** (1557)
transitive verb
1 a : to spill from a container **b :** to splash or spill liquid on **c :** to cause (a liquid) to splash
2 : to dish out messily
3 : to eat or drink greedily or noisily
4 : to feed slop to ⟨*slop* the hogs⟩
intransitive verb
1 : to tramp in mud or slush
2 : to become spilled or splashed
3 : to be effusive **:** GUSH
4 : to pass beyond or exceed a boundary or limit
slop basin *noun* (1731)
British **:** SLOP BOWL
slop bowl *noun* (1810)
: a bowl for receiving the leavings of tea or coffee cups at table
slop chest *noun* [¹*slop*] (1840)
: a store of clothing and personal requisites (as tobacco) carried on merchant ships for issue to the crew usually as a charge against their wages
¹slope \'slōp\ *adjective* [Middle English *slope,* adverb, obliquely] (1502)
: that slants **:** SLOPING — often used in combination ⟨*slope*-sided⟩
²slope *verb* **sloped; slop·ing** (1591)
intransitive verb
1 : to take an oblique course
2 : to lie or fall in a slant **:** INCLINE
3 : GO, TRAVEL ⟨*slopes* off into the night —Wolcott Gibbs⟩
transitive verb
: to cause to incline or slant
— **slop·er** *noun*
³slope *noun* (circa 1611)
1 : upward or downward slant or inclination or degree of slant
2 : ground that forms a natural or artificial incline
3 : the part of a continent draining to a particular ocean ⟨Alaska's North *Slope*⟩
4 a : the tangent of the angle made by a straight line with the x-axis **b :** the slope of the line tangent to a plane curve at a point

slope–intercept form *noun* (circa 1942)
: the equation of a straight line in the form $y = mx + b$ where m is the slope of the line and b is the point on the y-axis through which the line passes

slo–pitch \'slō-'pich, -ˌpich\ *noun* [alteration of *slow pitch*] (1967)
: SLOW-PITCH

slop jar *noun* (1855)
: a large pail used as a chamber pot or to receive waste water from a washbowl or the contents of chamber pots

slop pail *noun* (1864)
: a pail for toilet or household slops

slop·py \'slä-pē\ *adjective* **slop·pi·er; -est** (1707)
1 a : wet so as to spatter easily **:** SLUSHY ⟨a *sloppy* racetrack⟩ **b :** wet or smeared with or as if with something slopped over
2 : SLOVENLY, CARELESS ⟨a *sloppy* dresser⟩ ⟨did *sloppy* work⟩
3 : disagreeably effusive ⟨*sloppy* sentimentalism⟩
— **slop·pi·ly** \'slä-pə-lē\ *adverb*
— **slop·pi·ness** *noun*

sloppy joe \-'jō\ *noun* [probably from the name *Joe*, nickname for *Joseph*] (1961)
: ground beef cooked in a thick spicy sauce and usually served on a bun

slop·work \'släp-ˌwərk\ *noun* (1849)
1 : the manufacture of cheap ready-made clothing
2 : hasty slovenly work

¹slosh \'släsh, 'slȯsh\ *noun* [probably blend of *slop* and *slush*] (1814)
1 : SLUSH
2 : the slap or splash of liquid

²slosh (1844)
intransitive verb
1 : to flounder or splash through water, mud, or slush
2 : to move with a splashing motion ⟨the water *sloshed* around him —Bill Alcine⟩
transitive verb
1 : to splash about in liquid
2 : to splash (a liquid) about or on something
3 : to splash with liquid

sloshed \'släsht, 'slȯsht\ *adjective* (circa 1946)
slang **:** DRUNK, INTOXICATED

¹slot \'slät\ *noun* [Middle English, the hollow running down the middle of the breast, from Middle French *esclot*] (1523)
1 a : a narrow opening or groove **:** SLIT, NOTCH ⟨a mail *slot* in a door⟩ **b :** a narrow passage or enclosure **c :** a passage through the wing of an airplane or of a missile that is located usually near the leading edge and formed between a main and an auxiliary airfoil for improving flow conditions over the wing so as to increase lift and delay stalling of the wing
2 : a place or position in an organization or sequence **:** NICHE
3 : SLOT MACHINE
4 : a gap between an end and a tackle in an offensive football line

²slot *transitive verb* **slot·ted; slot·ting** (1747)
1 : to cut a slot in
2 : to place in or assign to a slot

³slot *noun, plural* **slot** [Middle French *esclot* track] (1575)
: the track of an animal (as a deer)

slot·back \'slät-ˌbak\ *noun* (1959)
: an offensive football halfback who lines up just behind the slot between an offensive end and tackle

slot car *noun* (1966)
: an electric toy racing car with a pin underneath that fits into a groove on a track for guidance

sloth \'slȯth, 'släth *also* 'slōth\ *noun, plural* **sloths** \with ths *or* thz\ [Middle English *slouthe*, from *slow* slow] (12th century)
1 a : disinclination to action or labor **:** INDOLENCE **b :** spiritual apathy and inactivity ⟨the deadly sin of *sloth*⟩

2 : any of the slow-moving arboreal edentate mammals that comprise two genera (*Bradypus* and *Choloepus*), inhabit tropical forests of South and Central America, hang from the branches back downward, and feed on leaves, shoots, and fruits — compare THREE-TOED SLOTH, TWO-TOED SLOTH

sloth 2

sloth·ful \'slȯth-fəl, 'släth- *also* 'slōth-\ *adjective* (15th century)
: inclined to sloth **:** INDOLENT
synonym see LAZY
— **sloth·ful·ly** \-fə-lē\ *adverb*
— **sloth·ful·ness** *noun*

slot machine *noun* (1891)
1 : a machine whose operation is begun by dropping a coin into a slot
2 : a coin-operated gambling machine that pays off according to the matching of symbols on wheels spun by a handle — called also *one-armed bandit*

slot racing *noun* (1965)
: the racing of slot cars
— **slot racer** *noun*

¹slouch \'slau̇ch\ *noun* [origin unknown] (1515)
1 a : an awkward fellow **:** LOUT **b :** one that is unimpressive; *especially* **:** a lazy or incompetent person — used in negative constructions ⟨was no *slouch* at cooking⟩
2 : a gait or posture characterized by an ungainly stooping of the head and shoulders or excessive relaxation of body muscles

²slouch (1754)
intransitive verb
1 : to walk, stand, or sit with a slouch **:** assume a slouch
2 : DROOP
transitive verb
: to cause to droop ⟨*slouched* his shoulders⟩
— **slouch·er** *noun*

slouch hat *noun* (1837)
: a soft usually felt hat with a wide flexible brim

slouchy \'slau̇-chē\ *adjective* **slouch·i·er; -est** (circa 1693)
: lacking erectness or stiffness (as in form or posture) ⟨a *slouchy* sweater⟩ ⟨*slouchy* figures waiting in line⟩
— **slouch·i·ly** \-chə-lē\ *adverb*
— **slouch·i·ness** \-chē-nəs\ *noun*

¹slough \'slü, 'slau̇; *in the US (except New England)* 'slü *is usual for sense 1 with those to whom the sense is familiar; British usually* 'slau̇ *for both senses*\ *noun* [Middle English *slogh*, from Old English *slōh*; akin to Middle High German *slouche* ditch] (before 12th century)
1 a : a place of deep mud or mire **b** (1) **:** SWAMP (2) **:** an inlet on a river; *also* **:** BACKWATER (3) **:** a creek in a marsh or tide flat
2 : a state of moral degradation or spiritual dejection
— **sloughy** \-ē\ *adjective*

²slough (1846)
transitive verb
: to engulf in a slough
intransitive verb
: to plod through or as if through mud **:** SLOG

³slough \'sləf\ *also* **sluff** *noun* [Middle English *slughe*; akin to Middle High German *slūch* snakeskin] (14th century)
1 : the cast-off skin of a snake
2 : a mass of dead tissue separating from an ulcer
3 : something that may be shed or cast off

⁴slough \'sləf\ *also* **sluff** (1720)
intransitive verb
1 a : to become shed or cast off **b :** to cast off one's skin **c :** to separate in the form of dead tissue from living tissue
2 : to crumble slowly and fall away
transitive verb
1 : to cast off
2 a : to get rid of or discard as irksome, objectionable, or disadvantageous — usually used with *off* **b :** to dispose of (a losing card in bridge) by discarding
synonym see DISCARD

slough of de·spond \ˌslau̇-əv-di-'spänd, ˌslü-\ [from the *Slough of Despond*, deep bog into which Christian falls on the way from the City of Destruction and from which Help saves him in the allegory *Pilgrim's Progress* (1678) by John Bunyan] (1776)
: a state of extreme depression

Slo·vak \'slō-ˌväk, -ˌvak\ *noun* [Slovak *slovák*] (1829)
1 : a member of a Slavic people of Slovakia
2 : the Slavic language of the Slovak people
— **Slovak** *adjective*
— **Slo·va·ki·an** \slō-'vä-kē-ən, -'va-\ *adjective or noun*

¹slov·en \'slə-vən\ *noun* [Middle English *sloveyn* rascal, perhaps from Flemish *sloovin* woman of low character] (15th century)
: one habitually negligent of neatness or cleanliness especially in personal appearance

²sloven *adjective* (1815)
: SLOVENLY

Slo·vene \'slō-ˌvēn\ *noun* [German *Slowene* from Slovene *Slovenec*] (1883)
1 : a member of a Slavic people living largely in Slovenia
2 : the language of the Slovenes
— **Slovene** *adjective*
— **Slo·ve·nian** \slō-'vē-nē-ən, -nyən\ *adjective or noun*

slov·en·ly \'slə-vən-lē *also* 'slä-\ *adjective* (circa 1568)
1 a : untidy especially in personal appearance **b :** lazily slipshod ⟨*slovenly* in thought⟩
2 : characteristic of a sloven ⟨*slovenly* habits⟩
— **slo·ven·li·ness** *noun*
— **slovenly** *adverb*

¹slow \'slō\ *adjective* [Middle English, from Old English *slāw*; akin to Old High German *slēo* dull] (before 12th century)
1 a : mentally dull **:** STUPID ⟨a *slow* student⟩ **b :** naturally inert or sluggish
2 a : lacking in readiness, promptness, or willingness **b :** not hasty or precipitate ⟨was *slow* to anger⟩
3 a : moving, flowing, or proceeding without speed or at less than usual speed ⟨traffic was *slow*⟩ **b :** exhibiting or marked by low speed ⟨he moved with *slow* deliberation⟩ **c :** not acute ⟨a *slow* disease⟩ **d :** LOW, GENTLE ⟨*slow* fire⟩
4 : requiring a long time **:** GRADUAL ⟨a *slow* recovery⟩
5 : having qualities that hinder rapid progress or action ⟨a *slow* track⟩
6 a : registering behind or below what is correct ⟨the clock is *slow*⟩ **b :** less than the time indicated by another method of reckoning **c :** that is behind the time at a specified time or place
7 a : lacking in life, animation, or gaiety **:** BORING **b :** marked by reduced sales or patronage ⟨business was *slow*⟩
— **slow·ish** \'slō-ish\ *adjective*
— **slow·ness** *noun*

²slow *adverb* (15th century)

: SLOWLY □
³slow (1557)
transitive verb
: to make slow or slower : slacken the speed of ⟨*slow* a car⟩ — often used with *down* or *up*
intransitive verb
: to go or become slower ⟨production of new cars *slowed* sharply⟩
 synonym see DELAY
slow·down \'slō-ˌdau̇n\ *noun* (1897)
: a slowing down ⟨a business *slowdown*⟩
slow–foot·ed \-ˌfu̇-təd\ *adjective* (1642)
: moving at a very slow pace : PLODDING ⟨a *slow-footed* novel⟩ ⟨a *slow-footed* ship⟩
 — **slow–foot·ed·ness** *noun*
slow·ly \-lē\ *adverb* (13th century)
: in a slow manner : not quickly, fast, early, rashly, or readily
 usage see SLOW
slow match *noun* (circa 1802)
: a match or fuse made so as to burn slowly and evenly and used for firing (as of blasting charges)
slow–motion \'slō-'mō-shən\ *adjective* (1923)
: of, relating to, or being motion-picture or video photography in which the action that has been photographed is made to appear to occur slower than it actually occurred ⟨a *slow-motion* replay⟩; *also* : slowly moving ⟨a *slow-motion* dance⟩
slow motion *noun* (1924)
: slow-motion photography
slow–pitch \'slō-ˌpich\ *noun* (1967)
: softball which is played with 10 players on each side and in which each pitch must have an arc 3 to 10 feet high and base stealing is not allowed
slow–poke \'slō-ˌpōk\ *noun* [¹*slow* + *poke* annoyingly stupid person] (1848)
: a very slow person
slow–twitch \'slō-ˌtwich\ *adjective* (1971)
: of, relating to, or being muscle fiber that contracts slowly especially during sustained physical activity requiring endurance — compare FAST-TWITCH
slow virus *noun* (1954)
: any of various viruses with a long incubation period between infection and development of a degenerative disease (as kuru or Creutzfeldt-Jakob disease)
slow–wit·ted \-'wi-təd\ *adjective* (1571)
: mentally slow : DULL
slow–worm \'slō-ˌwərm\ *noun* [Middle English *sloworm*, from Old English *slāwyrm*, from *slā* (akin to Swedish *slå* earthworm) + *wyrm* worm] (before 12th century)
: a burrowing limbless European lizard (*Anguis fragilis*) with small eyes — called also *blindworm*
¹slub \'sləb\ *transitive verb* **slubbed; slubbing** [back-formation from *slubbing*] (1834)
: to draw out and twist (as slivers of wool) slightly
²slub *noun* (1851)
: a soft thick uneven section in a yarn or thread
slub·ber \'slə-bər\ *transitive verb* **slubbered; slub·ber·ing** \-b(ə-)riŋ\ [probably from obsolete Dutch *slubberen*] (1530)
1 *dialect chiefly English* : STAIN, SULLY
2 : to perform in a slipshod fashion
slub·bing \'slə-biŋ\ *noun* [origin unknown] (1786)
: ROVING
sludge \'sləj\ *noun* [Middle English *slugge*, perhaps alteration of *slicche* mud, slush; akin to Old High German *slīh* mire] (15th century)
1 : MUD, MIRE; *especially* : a muddy deposit (as on a riverbed) : OOZE
2 : a muddy or slushy mass, deposit, or sediment: as **a** : precipitated solid matter produced by water and sewage treatment processes **b** : muddy sediment in a steam boiler **c** : a precipitate or settling (as a mixture of impurities and acid) from a mineral oil
3 : SLUSH 5

— **sludgy** \'slə-jē\ *adjective*
¹slue \'slü\ *variant of* ¹SLOUGH
²slue *variant of* ³SLEW
³slue *noun* [²*slue*] (circa 1860)
1 : position or inclination after slewing
2 : SKID 5
¹slug \'sləg\ *noun* [Middle English *slugge*, of Scandinavian origin; akin to Norwegian dialect *slugga* to walk sluggishly] (15th century)
1 : SLUGGARD
2 : a lump, disk, or cylinder of material (as plastic or metal): as **a** (1) : a musket ball (2) : BULLET **b** : a piece of metal roughly shaped for subsequent processing **c** : a $50 gold piece **d** : a disk for insertion in a slot machine; *especially* : one used illegally instead of a coin

slug 3

3 : any of numerous chiefly terrestrial pulmonate gastropods (order Stylommatophora) that are found in most parts of the world where there is a reasonable supply of moisture and are closely related to the land snails but are long and wormlike and have only a rudimentary shell often buried in the mantle or entirely absent
4 : a smooth soft larva of a sawfly or moth that creeps like a mollusk
5 a : a quantity of liquor drunk in one swallow **b** : a detached mass of fluid (as water vapor or oil) that causes impact (as in a circulating system)
6 a : a strip of metal thicker than a printer's lead **b** : a line of type cast as one piece **c** : a usually temporary type line serving to instruct or identify
7 : the gravitational unit of mass in the foot-pound-second system to which a pound force can impart an acceleration of one foot per second per second and which is equal to the mass of an object weighing 32 pounds
²slug *transitive verb* **slugged; slug·ging** (1912)
1 : to add a printer's slug to
2 : to drink in gulps — often used with *down*
³slug *noun* [perhaps from *slug* to load with slugs] (1830)
: a heavy blow especially with the fist
⁴slug *transitive verb* **slugged; slug·ging** (circa 1861)
1 : to strike heavily with or as if with the fist or a bat
2 : FIGHT 4b — usually used in the phrase *slug it out*
slug·abed \'slə-gə-ˌbed\ *noun* (1592)
: a person who stays in bed after the usual or proper time to get up; *broadly* : SLUGGARD
slug·fest \'sləg-ˌfest\ *noun* (1916)
: a fight marked by the exchange of heavy blows; *also* : a heated dispute ⟨a vocal *slugfest*⟩
¹slug·gard \'slə-gərd\ *noun* [Middle English *sluggart*] (14th century)
: an habitually lazy person
²sluggard *adjective* (1593)
: SLUGGARDLY
— **slug·gard·ness** *noun*
slug·gard·ly \'slə-gərd-lē\ *adjective* (1865)
: lazily inactive
slug·ger \'slə-gər\ *noun* (1877)
: one that strikes hard or with heavy blows: as **a** : a prizefighter who punches hard but has usually little defensive skill **b** : a hard-hitting batter in baseball
slugging percentage *noun* (circa 1949)
: the ratio (as a rate per thousand) of the total number of bases reached on base hits to official times at bat for a baseball player — called also *slugging average*
slug·gish \'slə-gish\ *adjective* (15th century)
1 : averse to activity or exertion : INDOLENT; *also* : TORPID

2 : slow to respond (as to stimulation or treatment)
3 a : markedly slow in movement, flow, or growth **b** : economically inactive or slow
— **slug·gish·ly** *adverb*
— **slug·gish·ness** *noun*
¹sluice \'slüs\ *noun* [Middle English *sluse*, alteration of *scluse*, from Middle French *escluse*, from Late Latin *exclusa*, from Latin, feminine of *exclusus*, past participle of *excludere* to exclude] (15th century)
1 a : an artificial passage for water (as in a millstream) fitted with a valve or gate for stopping or regulating flow **b** : a body of water pent up behind a floodgate
2 : a dock gate : FLOODGATE
3 a : a stream flowing through a floodgate **b** : a channel to drain or carry off surplus water
4 : a long inclined trough usually on the ground; *especially* : such a contrivance paved usually with riffles to hold quicksilver for catching gold
²sluice *verb* **sluiced; sluic·ing** (1593)
transitive verb
1 : to draw off by or through a sluice
2 a : to wash with or in water running through or from a sluice **b** : to drench with a sudden flow : FLUSH
3 : to transport (as logs) in a sluice
intransitive verb
: to pour as if from a sluice
sluice·way \'slüs-ˌwā\ *noun* (1779)
: an artificial channel into which water is let or through which it flows
sluicy \'slü-sē\ *adjective* (1697)
: falling copiously or in streams : STREAMING
¹slum \'sləm\ *noun, often attributive* [origin unknown] (1825)
: a densely populated usually urban area marked by crowding, dirty run-down housing, poverty, and social disorganization
²slum *intransitive verb* **slummed; slum·ming** (1884)
: to visit slums especially out of curiosity; *broadly* : to go somewhere or do something that might be considered beneath one's station — sometimes used with *it* ⟨*slumming* it in a cabin without plumbing⟩
— **slum·mer** *noun*
¹slum·ber \'sləm-bər\ *intransitive verb* **slum·bered; slum·ber·ing** \-b(ə-)riŋ\ [Middle English, frequentative of *slumen* to doze, probably from *slume* slumber, from Old English *slūma*; akin to Middle High German *slumen* to slumber] (13th century)
1 a : to sleep lightly : DOZE **b** : SLEEP
2 a : to be in a torpid, slothful, or negligent state **b** : to lie dormant or latent
— **slum·ber·er** \-bər-ər\ *noun*
²slumber *noun* (14th century)
1 a : SLEEP **b** : a light sleep

□ USAGE
slow Some commentators claim that careful writers avoid the adverb *slow*, in spite of the fact that it has had over four centuries of usage ⟨have a continent forbearance till the speed of his rage goes *slower* —Shakespeare⟩. In actual practice, *slow* and *slowly* are not used in quite the same way. *Slow* is almost always used with verbs that denote movement or action, and it regularly follows the verb it modifies ⟨beans . . . are best cooked long and *slow* —Louise Prothro⟩. *Slowly* is used before the verb ⟨a sense of outrage, which *slowly* changed to shame —Paul Horgan⟩ and with participial adjectives ⟨a *slowly* dawning awareness . . . of the problem —*American Labor*⟩. *Slowly* is used after verbs where *slow* might also be used ⟨burn *slow* or *slowly*⟩ and after verbs where *slow* would be unidiomatic ⟨the leadership turned *slowly* toward bombing as a means of striking back —David Halberstam⟩.

2 : LETHARGY, TORPOR
slum·ber·ous *or* **slum·brous** \'sləm-b(ə-)rəs\ *adjective* (15th century)
1 : heavy with sleep **:** SLEEPY
2 : inducing sleep **:** SOPORIFIC
3 : marked by or suggestive of a state of sleep or lethargy ⟨a *slumberous* state of peace⟩
slumber party *noun* (1925)
: an overnight gathering especially of teenage girls usually at one of their homes
slum·bery \'sləm-b(ə-)rē\ *adjective* (14th century)
archaic **:** SLUMBEROUS
slum·gul·lion \'sləm-,gəl-yən, ,sləm-'\ *noun* [perhaps from *slum* slime + English dialect *gullion* mud, cesspool] (1902)
: a meat stew
slum·lord \'sləm-,lȯrd\ *noun* [¹*slum* + land*lord*] (1953)
: a landlord who receives unusually large profits from substandard properties
slum·my \'slə-mē\ *adjective* **slum·mi·er; -est** (1873)
: of, relating to, or suggestive of a slum ⟨*slummy* streets⟩
¹**slump** \'sləmp\ *intransitive verb* [probably of Scandinavian origin; akin to Norwegian *slumpa* to fall] (circa 1677)
1 a : to fall or sink suddenly **b :** to drop or slide down suddenly **:** COLLAPSE ⟨*slumped* to the floor⟩
2 : to assume a drooping posture or carriage **:** SLOUCH
3 : to go into a slump ⟨sales *slumped*⟩
²**slump** *noun* (1887)
1 a : a marked or sustained decline especially in economic activity or prices ⟨a post-election *slump*⟩ **b :** a period of poor or losing play by a team or individual ⟨one spring I was in a batting *slump* —Ted Williams⟩
2 : a downward slide of a mass of rock or land
slump·fla·tion \,sləmp-'flā-shən\ *noun* [²*slump* + in*flation*] (1974)
: a state or period of combined economic decline and rising inflation
slung *past and past participle of* SLING
slung·shot \'sləŋ-,shät\ *noun* (1842)
: a striking weapon consisting of a small mass of metal or stone fixed on a flexible handle or strap
slunk *past and past participle of* SLINK
¹**slur** \'slər\ *noun* [obsolete English dialect *slur* thin mud, from Middle English *sloor*; akin to Middle High German *slier* mud] (1609)
1 a : an insulting or disparaging remark or innuendo **:** ASPERSION **b :** a shaming or degrading effect **:** STAIN, STIGMA
2 : a blurred spot in printed matter **:** SMUDGE
²**slur** *verb* **slurred; slur·ring** (1660)
transitive verb
1 : to cast aspersions on **:** DISPARAGE
2 : to make indistinct **:** OBSCURE
intransitive verb
: to slip so as to cause a slur — used of a sheet being printed
³**slur** *verb* **slurred; slur·ring** [probably from Low German *slurrn* to shuffle; akin to Middle English *sloor* mud] (1660)
transitive verb
1 a : to slide or slip over without due mention, consideration, or emphasis ⟨*slurred* over certain facts⟩ **b :** to perform hurriedly **:** SKIMP ⟨let him not *slur* his lesson —R. W. Emerson⟩
2 : to perform (successive tones of different pitch) in a smooth or connected manner
3 a : to reduce, make a substitution for, or omit (sounds that would normally occur in an utterance) **b :** to utter with such reduction, substitution, or omission of sounds ⟨his speech was *slurred*⟩
intransitive verb
1 *dialect chiefly English* **:** SLIP, SLIDE
2 : DRAG, SHUFFLE
⁴**slur** *noun* (circa 1801)
1 a : a curved line connecting notes to be sung to the same syllable or performed without a

break **b :** the combination of two or more slurred tones
2 : a slurring manner of speech
slurp \'slərp\ *verb* [Dutch *slurpen*; akin to Middle Low German *slorpen* to slurp] (1648)
intransitive verb
: to make a sucking noise while eating or drinking
transitive verb
: to eat or drink noisily or with a sucking sound
— **slurp** *noun*
¹**slur·ry** \'slər-ē, 'slə-rē\ *noun, plural* **slur·ries** [Middle English *slory*] (15th century)
: a watery mixture of insoluble matter (as mud, lime, or plaster of paris)
²**slurry** *transitive verb* **slur·ried; slur·ry·ing** (1947)
: to convert into a slurry
¹**slush** \'sləsh\ *noun* [perhaps of Scandinavian origin; akin to Norwegian *slusk* slush] (1641)
1 a : partly melted or watery snow **b :** loose ice crystals formed during the early stages of freezing of salt water
2 : soft mud **:** MIRE
3 : refuse grease and fat from cooking especially on shipboard
4 : paper pulp in water suspension
5 : trashy and usually cheaply sentimental material
6 : unsolicited writings submitted (as to a magazine) for publication
²**slush** (1807)
transitive verb
: to wet, splash, or paint with slush
intransitive verb
1 : to make one's way through slush
2 : to make a splashing sound
slush fund *noun* (1864)
1 : a fund raised from the sale of refuse to obtain small luxuries or pleasures for a warship's crew
2 : a fund for bribing public officials or carrying on corruptive propaganda
slushy \'slə-shē\ *adjective* **slush·i·er; -est** (1791)
: being, involving, or resembling slush: as **a :** full of or covered with slush ⟨*slushy* streets⟩ **b :** made up of or having the consistency of slush ⟨*slushy* snow⟩ ⟨a *slushy* mixture⟩ **c :** having a cheaply sentimental quality **:** TRASHY ⟨a *slushy* novel⟩
— **slush·i·ness** *noun*
slut \'slət\ *noun* [Middle English *slutte*] (15th century)
1 *chiefly British* **:** a slovenly woman
2 a : a promiscuous woman; *especially* **:** PROSTITUTE **b :** a saucy girl **:** MINX
— **slut·tish** \'slə-tish\ *adjective*
— **slut·tish·ly** *adverb*
— **slut·tish·ness** *noun*
— **slut·ty** \'slə-tē\ *adjective*
sly \'slī\ *adjective* **sli·er** *or* **sly·er** \'slī-(ə)r\; **sli·est** *or* **sly·est** \'slī-əst\ [Middle English *sli*, from Old Norse *slœgr*; akin to Old English *slēan* to strike — more at SLAY] (13th century)
1 *chiefly dialect* **a :** wise in practical affairs **b :** displaying cleverness **:** INGENIOUS
2 a : clever in concealing one's aims or ends **:** FURTIVE ⟨the *sly* fox⟩ **b :** lacking in straightforwardness and candor **:** DISSEMBLING ⟨a *sly* scheme⟩
3 : lightly mischievous **:** ROGUISH ⟨a *sly* jest⟩ ⟨a *sly* smile⟩ ☆
— **sly·ly** *adverb*
— **sly·ness** *noun*
— **on the sly :** in a manner intended to avoid notice
sly·boots \'slī-,büts\ *noun plural but singular in construction* (1700)
: a sly tricky person; *especially* **:** one who is cunning or mischievous in an engaging way
¹**smack** \'smak\ *noun* [Middle English, from Old English *smæc*; akin to Old High German

smac taste and probably to Lithuanian *smaguris* sweet tooth] (before 12th century)
1 : characteristic taste or flavor; *also* **:** a perceptible taste or tincture
2 : a small quantity
²**smack** *intransitive verb* (13th century)
1 : to have a taste or flavor
2 : to have a trace, vestige, or suggestion ⟨a proposal that *smacks* of treason⟩
³**smack** *noun* [Dutch *smak* or Low German *smack*] (1533)
: a sailing ship (as a sloop or cutter) used chiefly in coasting and fishing
⁴**smack** *verb* [akin to Middle Dutch *smacken* to strike] (1557)
transitive verb
1 : to close and open (lips) noisily and in rapid succession especially in eating
2 a : to kiss with or as if with a smack **b :** to strike so as to produce a smack
intransitive verb
: to make or give a smack
⁵**smack** *noun* (1570)
1 : a quick sharp noise made by rapidly compressing and opening the lips
2 : a loud kiss
3 : a sharp slap or blow
⁶**smack** *adverb* (1782)
: squarely and sharply **:** DIRECTLY ⟨*smack* in the middle⟩
⁷**smack** *noun* [perhaps from Yiddish *shmek* sniff, whiff, pinch (of snuff)] (circa 1960)
slang **:** HEROIN
smack–dab \'smak-'dab\ *adverb* (1892)
: EXACTLY, SQUARELY
smack·er \'sma-kər\ *noun* (1611)
1 : one that smacks
2 *slang* **:** DOLLAR
smack·ing \'sma-kiŋ\ *adjective* (1820)
: BRISK, LIVELY ⟨a *smacking* breeze⟩
¹**small** \'smȯl\ *adjective* [Middle English *smal*, from Old English *smæl*; akin to Old High German *smal* small, Greek *mēlon* small domestic animal] (before 12th century)
1 a : having comparatively little size or slight dimensions **b :** LOWERCASE
2 a : minor in influence, power, or rank **b :** operating on a limited scale
3 : lacking in strength ⟨a *small* voice⟩
4 a : little or close to zero in an objectively measurable aspect (as quantity, amount, or value) **b :** made up of few or little units

☆ SYNONYMS
Sly, cunning, crafty, wily, tricky, foxy, artful, slick mean attaining or seeking to attain one's ends by guileful or devious means. SLY implies furtiveness, lack of candor, and skill in concealing one's aims and methods ⟨a *sly* corporate raider⟩. CUNNING suggests the inventive use of sometimes limited intelligence in overreaching or circumventing ⟨the *cunning* fox avoided the trap⟩. CRAFTY implies cleverness and subtlety of method ⟨a *crafty* lefthander⟩. WILY implies skill and deception in maneuvering ⟨the *wily* fugitive escaped the posse⟩. TRICKY is more likely to suggest shiftiness and unreliability than skill in deception and maneuvering ⟨a *tricky* political operative⟩. FOXY implies a shrewd and wary craftiness usually involving devious dealing ⟨a *foxy* publicity man planting stories⟩. ARTFUL implies indirectness in dealing and often connotes sophistication or cleverness ⟨elicited the information by *artful* questioning⟩. SLICK emphasizes smoothness and guile ⟨*slick* operators selling time-sharing⟩.

\ə\ abut \ᵊ\ kitten \ər\ further \a\ ash \ā\ ace
\ä\ mop, mar \au̇\ out \ch\ chin \e\ bet \ē\ easy
\g\ go \i\ hit \ī\ ice \j\ job \ŋ\ sing \ō\ go
\ȯ\ law \ȯi\ boy \th\ thin \th\ the \ü\ loot \u̇\ foot
\y\ yet \zh\ vision *see also* Guide to Pronunciation

5 a : of little consequence **:** TRIVIAL, INSIGNIFI-
CANT **b :** HUMBLE, MODEST ⟨a *small* beginning⟩
6 : limited in degree
7 a : MEAN, PETTY **b :** reduced to a humiliating
position ☆
— **small·ish** \'smȯ-lish\ *adjective*
— **small·ness** \'smȯl-nəs\ *noun*
²**small** *adverb* (before 12th century)
1 : in or into small pieces
2 : without force or loudness ⟨speak as *small*
as you will —Shakespeare⟩
3 : in a small manner
³**small** *noun* (14th century)
1 : a part smaller and especially narrower than
the remainder ⟨the *small* of the back⟩
2 a *plural* **:** small-sized products **b** *plural,
chiefly British* **:** SMALLCLOTHES; *especially*
: UNDERWEAR
small arm *noun* (1689)
: a handheld firearm (as a handgun or shoulder
arm) — usually used in plural
small beer *noun* (1568)
1 : weak or inferior beer
2 : something of small importance **:** TRIVIA
— **small–beer** *adjective*
small calorie *noun* (circa 1889)
: CALORIE 1a
small capital *noun* (1770)
: a letter having the form of but smaller than a
capital letter (as in THESE WORDS) — called
also *small cap*
small change *noun* (1819)
1 : coins of low denomination
2 : something trifling or petty
small–claims court *noun* (1925)
: a special court intended to simplify and ex-
pedite the handling of small claims on debts
— called also *small-debts court*
small·clothes \'smȯl-ˌklō(th)z\ *noun plural*
(1796)
1 : close-fitting knee breeches worn in the
18th century
2 : small articles of clothing (as underclothing
or handkerchiefs)
smaller European elm bark beetle *noun*
(circa 1945)
: ELM BARK BEETLE b
small–fry \'smȯl-ˌfrī\ *adjective* (1817)
1 : MINOR, UNIMPORTANT ⟨a *small-fry* politician⟩
2 : of, relating to, or intended for children
: CHILDISH
small·hold·ing \-ˌhōl-diŋ\ *noun* (1892)
chiefly British **:** a small farm
— **small·hold·er** \-dər\ *noun*
small hours *noun plural* (circa 1837)
: the early morning hours
small intestine *noun* (1767)
: the part of the intestine that lies between the
stomach and colon, consists of duodenum, je-
junum, and ileum, secretes digestive enzymes,
and is the chief site of the absorption of di-
gested nutrients
small–mind·ed \'smȯl-'mīn-dəd\ *adjective*
(1847)
1 : having narrow interests, sympathies, or
outlook
2 : typical of a small-minded person **:** marked
by pettiness, narrowness, or meanness ⟨*small-
minded* conduct⟩
— **small–mind·ed·ly** *adverb*
— **small–mind·ed·ness** *noun*
small–mouth bass \'smȯl-ˌmau̇th-\ *noun*
(1938)
: a black bass
(*Micropterus do-
lomieu*) of clear
rivers and lakes
that is bronzy
green above and
lighter below
and has the ver-
tex of the angle of the jaw falling below the
eye — called also *smallmouth, smallmouth
black bass*
small octave *noun* (circa 1890)

smallmouth bass

: the musical octave that begins on the first C
below middle C — see PITCH illustration
small potato *noun* (1831)
: one that is of trivial importance or worth —
usually used in plural but singular or plural in
construction
small·pox \'smȯl-ˌpäks\ *noun* (1518)
: an acute contagious febrile disease caused by
a poxvirus and characterized by skin eruption
with pustules, sloughing, and scar formation
small–scale \-'skā(ə)l\ *adjective* (1852)
1 : small in scope; *especially* **:** small in output
or operation
2 *of a map* **:** having a scale (as one inch to 25
miles) that permits plotting of comparatively
little detail and shows mainly large features
small screen *noun* (1956)
: TELEVISION
small stuff *noun* (circa 1857)
: small rope (as spun yarn or marline) usually
identified by the number of threads or yarns
which it contains
small·sword \'smȯl-ˌsōrd, -ˌsȯrd\ *noun*
(1687)
: a light tapering sword for thrusting used
chiefly in dueling and fencing
small talk *noun* (1751)
: light or casual conversation **:** CHITCHAT
small–time \'smȯl-'tīm\ *adjective* (1910)
: insignificant in performance, scope, or stand-
ing **:** PETTY ⟨*small-time* thieves⟩
— **small–tim·er** \-'tī-mər\ *noun*
smalt \'smȯlt\ *noun* [Middle French, from Old
Italian *smalto,* of Germanic origin; akin to Old
High German *smelzan* to melt — more at
SMELT] (1558)
: a deep blue pigment used especially as a ce-
ramic color and prepared by fusing together
silica, potash, and oxide of cobalt and grinding
to powder the resultant glass
smalt·ite \'smȯl-ˌtīt\ *noun* [alteration of *smal-
tine,* from French, from *smalt,* from Middle
French] (1868)
: a bluish white or gray isometric mineral of
metallic luster that is essentially an arsenide of
cobalt and nickel
smal·to \'smȯl-(ˌ)tō, 'smȯl-\ *noun, plural*
smal·ti \-(ˌ)tē\ [Italian, smalt, smalto] (1705)
: colored glass or enamel or a piece of either
used in mosaic work
sma·ragd \'smə-ˌragd, 'smar-ˌagd\ *noun* [Mid-
dle English *smaragde,* from Latin *smaragdus*]
(13th century)
: EMERALD
— **sma·rag·dine** \smə-'rag-dən, 'smar-əg-
ˌdīn\ *adjective*
sma·rag·dite \smə-'rag-ˌdīt, 'smar-əg-ˌdīt\
noun [French, from Latin *smaragdus* emerald
— more at EMERALD] (1804)
: a green foliated amphibole
smarm \'smärm\ *noun* [back-formation from
smarmy] (1937)
: smarmy language or behavior
smarmy \'smär-mē\ *adjective* [*smarm* to gush,
slobber] (1924)
1 : revealing or marked by a smug, ingratiat-
ing, or false earnestness ⟨a tone of *smarmy*
self-satisfaction —*New Yorker*⟩
2 : of low sleazy taste or quality ⟨*smarmy*
eroticism⟩
— **smarm·i·ly** \-mə-lē\ *adverb*
— **smarm·i·ness** \-mē-nəs\ *noun*
¹**smart** \'smärt\ *adjective* (before 12th century)
1 : making one smart **:** causing a sharp sting-
ing
2 : marked by often sharp forceful activity or
vigorous strength ⟨a *smart* pull of the starter
cord⟩
3 : BRISK, SPIRITED
4 a : mentally alert **:** BRIGHT **b :** KNOWLEDGE-
ABLE **c :** SHREWD ⟨a *smart* investment⟩
5 a : WITTY, CLEVER **b :** PERT, SAUCY ⟨don't get
smart with me⟩

6 a : NEAT, TRIM **b :** stylish or elegant in dress
or appearance **c** (1) **:** SOPHISTICATED (2) **:** char-
acteristic of or patronized by fashionable soci-
ety
7 a : being a guided missile ⟨a laser-guided
smart bomb⟩ **b :** operating by automation ⟨a
smart machine tool⟩ **c :** INTELLIGENT 3
— **smart·ly** *adverb*
— **smart·ness** *noun*
²**smart** *intransitive verb* [Middle English
smerten, from Old English *smeortan;* akin to
Old High German *smerzan* to pain] (13th cen-
tury)
1 : to cause or be the cause or seat of a sharp
poignant pain; *also* **:** to feel or have such a
pain
2 a : to feel or endure distress, remorse, or
embarrassment ⟨*smarting* from wounded vani-
ty —W. L. Shirer⟩ **b :** to pay a heavy or sting-
ing penalty ⟨would have to *smart* for this fool-
ishness⟩
³**smart** *noun* (13th century)
1 : a smarting pain; *especially* **:** a stinging lo-
cal pain
2 : poignant grief or remorse ⟨was not the sort
to get over *smarts* —Sir Winston Churchill⟩
3 : an affectedly witty or fashionable person
4 *plural, slang* **:** INTELLIGENCE, KNOW-HOW
⁴**smart** *adverb* (13th century)
: in a smart manner **:** SMARTLY
smart al·eck *also* **smart al·ec** \'smärt-ˌa-
lik, -ˌe-\ *noun* [*Aleck,* nickname for *Alexander*]
(1865)
: an obnoxiously conceited and self-assertive
person with pretensions to smartness or clev-
erness
— **smart–aleck** *adjective*
— **smart–al·ecky** \-ˌa-lə-kē, -ˌe-\ *adjective*
smart–ass \-ˌas\ *noun* (1964)
: SMART ALECK
— **smart–ass** *adjective*
— **smart–assed** \-ˌast\ *adjective*
smart card *noun* (1980)
: a small plastic card that has a built-in micro-
processor to store and process data and
records
smart·en \'smär-t°n\ *verb* **smart·ened;
smart·en·ing** \'smärt-niŋ, 'smär-t°n-iŋ\
(1815)
transitive verb
: to make smart or smarter; *especially* **:** SPRUCE
— usually used with *up*
intransitive verb
: to smarten oneself — used with *up*
¹**smart money** \'smärt-ˌmə-nē\ *noun* [³*smart*]
(1693)
: PUNITIVE DAMAGES
²**smart money** \-'mə-nē, -ˌmə-nē\ *noun*
[¹*smart*] (1926)
1 : money ventured by one having inside in-
formation or much experience
2 : well-informed bettors or speculators
smart·weed \'smärt-ˌwēd\ *noun* (circa 1787)

☆ SYNONYMS
**Small, little, diminutive, minute, tiny,
miniature** mean noticeably below average
in size. SMALL and LITTLE are often inter-
changeable, but SMALL applies more to rela-
tive size determined by capacity, value, num-
ber ⟨a relatively *small* backyard⟩. LITTLE is
more absolute in implication often carrying
the idea of petiteness, pettiness, insignifi-
cance, or immaturity ⟨your pathetic *little*
smile⟩. DIMINUTIVE implies abnormal small-
ness ⟨*diminutive* bonsai plants⟩. MINUTE im-
plies extreme smallness ⟨a *minute* amount of
caffeine in the soda⟩. TINY is an informal
equivalent to MINUTE ⟨*tiny* cracks formed in
the painting⟩. MINIATURE applies to an exactly
proportioned reproduction on a very small
scale ⟨a dollhouse complete with *miniature*
furnishings⟩.

: any of various polygonums with strong acid juice

smart·y *or* **smart·ie** \'smär-tē\ *noun, plural* **smart·ies** (1861)
: SMART ALECK

smarty–pants \-ˌpan(t)s\ *noun plural but singular in construction* (1941)
: SMART ALECK
— **smarty–pants** *adjective*

¹smash \'smash\ *noun* [perhaps blend of ⁴*smack* and ²*mash*] (1725)
1 a : a smashing blow or attack **b :** a hard overhand stroke (as in tennis or badminton)
2 a : the action or sound of smashing; *especially* **:** a wreck due to collision **:** CRASH **b :** utter collapse **:** RUIN
3 : a striking success

²smash (1778)
transitive verb
1 : to break or crush by violence
2 a : to drive or throw violently especially with a shattering or battering effect; *also* **:** to effect in this way **b :** to hit violently **:** BATTER **c** (1) **:** to hit (as a tennis ball) with a hard overhand stroke (2) **:** to drive (a ball) with a forceful stroke
3 : to destroy utterly **:** WRECK
intransitive verb
1 : to move or become propelled with violence or crashing effect ⟨*smashed* into a tree⟩
2 : to become wrecked
3 : to go to pieces suddenly under collision or pressure
— **smash·er** *noun*

³smash *adjective* (1923)
: being a smash **:** OUTSTANDING ⟨a *smash* hit⟩

smashed \'smasht\ *adjective* (circa 1959)
slang **:** DRUNK, INTOXICATED

smash·ing \'sma-shiŋ\ *adjective* (1833)
1 : that smashes **:** CRUSHING ⟨a *smashing* defeat⟩
2 : extraordinarily impressive or effective ⟨a *smashing* performance⟩
— **smash·ing·ly** \-shiŋ-lē\ *adverb*

smash–up \'smash-ˌəp\ *noun* (1856)
1 : a collision between vehicles
2 : a complete collapse

¹smat·ter \'sma-tər\ *verb* [Middle English *smateren*] (15th century)
intransitive verb
: to talk superficially **:** BABBLE
transitive verb
1 : to speak with spotty or superficial knowledge ⟨*smatters* French⟩
2 : to dabble in
— **smat·ter·er** \-tər-ər\ *noun*

²smatter *noun* (1668)
: SMATTERING

smat·ter·ing \'sma-tə-riŋ\ *noun* (1538)
1 : superficial piecemeal knowledge ⟨a *smattering* of carpentry, house painting, bricklaying —Alva Johnston⟩
2 : a small scattered number or amount ⟨a *smattering* of spectators⟩

¹smear \'smir\ *noun* [Middle English *smere*, from Old English *smeoru*; akin to Old High German *smero* grease and probably to Old Irish *smiur* marrow] (before 12th century)
1 a : a viscous or sticky substance **b :** a spot made by or as if by an unctuous or adhesive substance
2 : material smeared on a surface (as of a microscopic slide); *also* **:** a preparation made by smearing material on a surface ⟨a vaginal *smear*⟩
3 : a usually unsubstantiated charge or accusation against a person or organization

²smear *transitive verb* (before 12th century)
1 a : to overspread with something unctuous, viscous, or adhesive **:** DAUB **b :** to spread over a surface
2 a : to stain, smudge, or dirty by or as if by smearing **b :** SULLY, BESMIRCH; *specifically* **:** to vilify especially by secretly and maliciously spreading grave charges and imputations

3 : to obliterate, obscure, blur, blend, wipe out, or defeat by or as if by smearing
— **smear·er** *noun*

smear·case *also* **smier·case** \'smir-ˌkās\ *noun* [modification of German *Schmierkäse*, from *schmieren* to smear + *Käse* cheese] (1829)
chiefly Midland **:** COTTAGE CHEESE

smeary \'smir-ē\ *adjective* (circa 1529)
1 : marked by or covered with smears
2 : liable to cause smears ⟨*smeary* lipstick⟩

smec·tic \'smek-tik\ *adjective* [Latin *smecticus* cleansing, having the properties of soap, from Greek *smēktikos*, from *smēchein* to clean] (1923)
: of, relating to, or being the phase of a liquid crystal characterized by arrangement of molecules in layers with the long molecular axes in a given layer being parallel to one another and those of other layers and perpendicular or slightly inclined to the plane of the layer — compare CHOLESTERIC, NEMATIC

smec·tite \'smek-ˌtīt\ *noun* [*smectis* fuller's earth, modification of Greek *smēktris* kind of fuller's earth, from *smēchein* to clean] (1811)
: MONTMORILLONITE
— **smec·tit·ic** \(ˌ)smek-'ti-tik\ *adjective*

smeg·ma \'smeg-mə\ *noun* [New Latin, from Latin, detergent, soap, from Greek *smēgma*, from *smēchein* to wash off, clean] (circa 1819)
: the secretion of a sebaceous gland; *specifically* **:** the cheesy sebaceous matter that collects between the glans penis and the foreskin or around the clitoris and labia minora

¹smell \'smel\ *verb* **smelled** \'smeld\ *or* **smelt** \'smelt\; **smell·ing** [Middle English] (12th century)
transitive verb
1 : to perceive the odor or scent of through stimuli affecting the olfactory nerves **:** get the odor or scent of with the nose
2 : to detect or become aware of as if by the sense of smell
3 : to emit the odor of
intransitive verb
1 : to exercise the sense of smell
2 a (1) **:** to have an odor or scent (2) **:** to have a characteristic aura or atmosphere **:** SMACK ⟨the accounts . . . seemed to me to *smell* of truth —R. S. Bourne⟩; *also* **:** SEEM, APPEAR ⟨the story didn't *smell* right⟩ **b** (1) **:** to have an offensive odor **:** STINK (2) **:** to be of bad or questionable quality ⟨all this from the moral point of view *smells* —A. F. Wills⟩
— **smell·er** *noun*
— **smell a rat :** to have a suspicion of something wrong

²smell *noun* (12th century)
1 : the property of a thing that affects the olfactory organs **:** ODOR
2 a : the process, function, or power of smelling **b :** the special sense concerned with the perception of odor
3 a : a very small amount **:** TRACE ⟨add only a *smell* of garlic⟩ **b :** a pervading or characteristic quality **:** AURA ⟨the *smell* of affluence, of power —Harry Hervey⟩
4 : an act or instance of smelling ☆

smelling salts *noun plural but singular or plural in construction* (1840)
: a usually scented aromatic preparation of ammonium carbonate and ammonia water used as a stimulant and restorative

smelly \'sme-lē\ *adjective* **smell·i·er; -est** (1862)
: having a smell; *especially* **:** MALODOROUS

¹smelt \'smelt\ *noun, plural* **smelts** *or* **smelt** [Middle English, from Old English; akin to Norwegian *smelte* whiting] (before 12th century)
: any of a family (Osmeridae) of small salmonoid fishes that closely resemble the trouts in general structure, live along coasts and ascend rivers to spawn or are landlocked, and have delicate oily flesh with a distinctive odor and taste

²smelt *transitive verb* [Dutch or Low German *smelten*; akin to Old High German *smelzan* to melt, Old English *meltan* — more at MELT] (1543)
1 : to melt or fuse (as ore) often with an accompanying chemical change usually to separate the metal
2 : REFINE, REDUCE

smelt·er \'smel-tər\ *noun* (15th century)
: one that smelts: **a :** a worker who smelts ore **b :** an owner or operator of a smeltery **c** *or* **smelt·ery** \-t(ə-)rē\ **:** an establishment for smelting

smew \'smyü\ *noun* [akin to Middle High German *smiehe* smew] (1674)
: a small Eurasian merganser (*Mergus albellus*) with the male being white, gray, and black and the female chiefly gray but with a chestnut and white head

smid·gen *also* **smid·geon** *or* **smid·gin** \'smi-jən\ *or* **smidge** \'smij\ *noun* [probably alteration of English dialect *smitch* soiling mark] (1845)
: a small amount **:** BIT

smi·lax \'smī-ˌlaks\ *noun* [Latin, bindweed, yew, from Greek] (1601)
1 : GREENBRIER
2 : a tender twining plant (*Asparagus asparagoides*) of the lily family that has ovate bright green cladophylls and is often grown in greenhouses

¹smile \'smī(ə)l\ *verb* **smiled; smil·ing** [Middle English; akin to Old English *smerian* to laugh, Sanskrit *smayate* he smiles] (14th century)
intransitive verb
1 : to have, produce, or exhibit a smile
2 a : to look or regard with amusement or ridicule ⟨*smiled* at his own folly —Martin Gardner⟩ **b :** to bestow approval ⟨feeling that Heaven *smiled* on his labors —Sheila Rowlands⟩ **c :** to appear pleasant or agreeable
transitive verb
1 : to affect with or by smiling
2 : to express by a smile
— **smil·er** *noun*
— **smil·ey** \'smī-lē\ *adjective*
— **smil·ing·ly** \'smī-liŋ-lē\ *adverb*

²smile *noun* (15th century)
1 : a facial expression in which the eyes brighten and the corners of the mouth curve slightly upward and which expresses especially amusement, pleasure, approval, or sometimes scorn
2 : a pleasant or encouraging appearance
— **smile·less** \'smī(ə)l-ləs\ *adjective*

smirch \'smərch\ *transitive verb* [Middle English *smorchen*] (15th century)
1 a : to make dirty, stained, or discolored **:** SULLY **b :** to smear with something that stains or dirties
2 : to bring discredit or disgrace on
— **smirch** *noun*

☆ **SYNONYMS**
Smell, scent, odor, aroma mean the quality that makes a thing perceptible to the olfactory sense. SMELL implies solely the sensation without suggestion of quality or character ⟨an odd *smell* permeated the room⟩. SCENT applies to the characteristic smell given off by a substance, an animal, or a plant ⟨the *scent* of lilacs⟩. ODOR may imply a stronger or more readily distinguished scent or it may be equivalent to SMELL ⟨a cheese with a strong *odor*⟩. AROMA suggests a somewhat penetrating usually pleasant odor ⟨the *aroma* of freshly ground coffee⟩.

\ə\ abut \ᵊ\ kitten \ər\ further \a\ ash \ā\ ace
\ä\ mop, mar \au̇\ out \ch\ chin \e\ bet \ē\ easy
\g\ go \i\ hit \ī\ ice \j\ job \ŋ\ sing \ō\ go
\ȯ\ law \ȯi\ boy \th\ thin \th\ the \ü\ loot \u̇\ foot
\y\ yet \zh\ vision *see also* Guide to Pronunciation

smirk \'smərk\ *intransitive verb* [Middle English, from Old English *smearcian* to smile; akin to Old English *smerian* to laugh] (before 12th century)
: to smile in an affected or smug manner **:** SIMPER
— **smirk** *noun*

smirky \'smər-kē\ *adjective* (1728)
: that smirks **:** SMIRKING

smite \'smīt\ *verb* **smote** \'smōt\; **smit·ten** \'smi-t°n\ *or* **smote**; **smit·ing** \'smī-tiŋ\ [Middle English, from Old English *smītan* to smear, defile; akin to Old High German bi*smīzan* to defile] (12th century)
transitive verb
1 : to strike sharply or heavily especially with the hand or an implement held in the hand
2 a : to kill or severely injure by smiting **b :** to attack or afflict suddenly and injuriously ⟨*smitten* by disease⟩
3 : to cause to strike
4 : to affect as if by striking ⟨children *smitten* with the fear of hell —V. L. Parrington⟩
5 : CAPTIVATE, TAKE ⟨*smitten* with her beauty⟩
intransitive verb
: to deliver or deal a blow with or as if with the hand or something held
— **smit·er** \'smī-tər\ *noun*

smith \'smith\ *noun* [Middle English, from Old English; akin to Old High German *smid* smith and probably to Greek *smilē* wood-carving knife] (before 12th century)
1 : a worker in metals **:** BLACKSMITH
2 : MAKER — often used in combination ⟨gun*smith*⟩ ⟨tune*smith*⟩

smith·er·eens \ˌsmi-thə-'rēnz\ *noun plural* [perhaps from Irish *smidiríní*] (1829)
: FRAGMENTS, BITS ⟨the house was blown to *smithereens* by the explosion⟩

smith·ery \'smi-thə-rē\ *noun, plural* **-er·ies** (1625)
1 : the work, art, or trade of a smith
2 : SMITHY 1

Smith·field ham \'smith-ˌfēld-\ *noun* (1908)
: a Virginia ham produced in or near Smithfield, Va.

smith·son·ite \'smith-sə-ˌnīt\ *noun* [James Smithson] (1856)
: a mineral that is a carbonate of zinc and constitutes an important ore of zinc

smithy \'smi-thē *also* -thē\ *noun, plural* **smith·ies** (13th century)
1 : the workshop of a smith
2 : BLACKSMITH

¹smock \'smäk\ *noun* [Middle English *smok*, from Old English *smoc*; akin to Old High German *smocco* adornment] (before 12th century)
1 *archaic* **:** a woman's undergarment; *especially* **:** CHEMISE
2 : a light loose garment worn especially for protection of clothing while working

²smock *transitive verb* (1888)
: to embroider or shirr with smocking

smock frock *noun* (circa 1800)
: a loose outer garment worn by workmen especially in Europe

smock·ing \'smä-kiŋ\ *noun* (1888)
: a decorative embroidery or shirring made by gathering cloth in regularly spaced round tucks

smog \'smäg, 'smog\ *noun* [*smoke* + *fog*] (1905)
: a fog made heavier and darker by smoke and chemical fumes; *also* **:** a photochemical haze caused by the action of solar ultraviolet radiation on atmosphere polluted with hydrocarbons and oxides of nitrogen from automobile exhaust
— **smog·less** \'smäg-ləs, 'smog-\ *adjective*

smog·gy \'smä-gē, 'smog-\ *adjective* **smog·gier; -est** (1905)
: characterized by or abounding in smog

smok·able *or* **smoke·able** \'smō-kə-bəl\ *adjective* (1839)
: fit for smoking

¹smoke \'smōk\ *noun* [Middle English, from Old English *smoca*; akin to Old English *smēocan* to emit smoke, Middle High German *smouch* smoke, and probably to Greek *smychein* to smolder] (before 12th century)
1 a : the gaseous products of burning materials especially of organic origin made visible by the presence of small particles of carbon **b :** a suspension of particles in a gas
2 a : a mass or column of smoke **b :** SMUDGE
3 : fume or vapor often resulting from the action of heat on moisture
4 : something of little substance, permanence, or value
5 : something that obscures
6 a (1) **:** something (as a cigarette) to smoke (2) **:** MARIJUANA 2 **b :** an act or spell of smoking tobacco
7 a : a pale blue **b :** any of the colors of smoke
8 : pitches that are fastballs ⟨if a guy's going to hit you . . . he certainly isn't going to throw a spitter—he gives you *smoke* —Tony Conigliaro⟩
— **smoke·less** \'smō-kləs\ *adjective*
— **smoke·like** \'smōk-ˌlīk\ *adjective*

²smoke *verb* **smoked; smok·ing** (before 12th century)
intransitive verb
1 a : to emit or exhale smoke **b :** to emit excessive smoke
2 *archaic* **:** to undergo punishment **:** SUFFER
3 : to spread or rise like smoke
4 : to inhale and exhale the fumes of burning plant material and especially tobacco; *especially* **:** to smoke tobacco habitually
transitive verb
1 a : FUMIGATE **b :** to drive (as mosquitoes) away by smoke **c :** to blacken or discolor with smoke ⟨*smoked* glasses⟩ **d :** to cure by exposure to smoke **e :** to stupefy (as bees) by smoke
2 *archaic* **:** SUSPECT
3 : to inhale and exhale the smoke of
4 *archaic* **:** RIDICULE

smoke and mirrors *noun plural* (1982)
: something intended to disguise or draw attention away especially from an embarrassing or unpleasant issue — usually hyphenated when used attributively

smoke detector *noun* (circa 1927)
: an alarm that activates automatically when it detects smoke

smoke–filled room \'smōk-'fild-\ *noun* (1920)
: a room (as in a hotel) in which a small group of politicians carry on negotiations

smoke·house \'smōk-ˌhaus\ *noun* (1746)
: a building where meat or fish is cured by means of dense smoke

smoke·jack \-ˌjak\ *noun* (1675)
: a device for turning a spit by a fly or wheel moved by rising gases in a chimney

smoke jumper *noun* (1927)
: a forest firefighter who parachutes to locations otherwise difficult to reach

smokeless powder *noun* (1890)
: any of a class of explosive propellants that produce comparatively little smoke on explosion and consist mostly of gelatinized nitrocellulose

smokeless tobacco *noun* (1981)
: pulverized or shredded tobacco chewed or placed between cheek and gum

smoke out *transitive verb* (1593)
1 : to drive out by or as if by smoke
2 : to cause to be made public

smok·er \'smō-kər\ *noun* (1599)
1 : one that smokes
2 : a railroad car or compartment in which smoking is allowed
3 : an informal social gathering for men

smoke screen *noun* (1915)
1 : a screen of smoke to hinder enemy observation of a military force, area, or activity
2 : something designed to obscure, confuse, or mislead

¹smoke·stack \'smōk-ˌstak\ *noun* (1859)
: a pipe or funnel through which smoke and gases are discharged

²smokestack *adjective* (1926)
: of, relating to, being, or characterized by manufacturing and especially heavy industry ⟨*smokestack* industries⟩

smoke tree *noun* (1846)
: either of two small shrubby trees (genus *Cotinus*) of the cashew family with large panicles of minute flowers that suggest a cloud of smoke: **a :** one (*C. coggygria*) of the Old World that is widely planted in the eastern U.S. **b :** one (*C. obovatus*) of the southeastern U.S. and Texas

smoking gun *noun* (1974)
: something that serves as conclusive evidence or proof especially of a crime

smoking jacket *noun* (1878)
: a loose-fitting jacket or short robe for wear at home

smoking lamp *noun* (circa 1881)
: a lamp on a ship kept lighted during the hours when smoking is allowed

smoking room *noun* (1689)
: a room (as in a hotel or club) set apart for smokers

smoky *also* **smok·ey** \'smō-kē\ *adjective* **smok·i·er; -est** (14th century)
1 : emitting smoke especially in large quantities
2 a : having the characteristics of or resembling smoke **b :** suggestive of smoke especially in flavor or odor
3 a : filled with smoke **b :** made dark or black by or as if by smoke
— **smok·i·ly** \-kə-lē\ *adverb*
— **smok·i·ness** \-kē-nəs\ *noun*

smoky quartz *noun* (1837)
: CAIRNGORM

smoky topaz *noun* (1797)
: CAIRNGORM

smol·der *or* **smoul·der** \'smōl-dər\ *intransitive verb* **smol·dered** *or* **smoul·dered; smol·der·ing** *or* **smoul·der·ing** \-d(ə-)riŋ\ [Middle English *smolderen* to smother, from *smolder* smoke, smudge; akin to Middle Dutch *smölen* to smolder] (1529)
1 a : to burn sluggishly, without flame, and often with much smoke **b :** to be consumed by smoldering — often used with *out*
2 : to exist in a state of suppressed activity ⟨hostilities *smoldered* for years⟩
3 : to show suppressed anger, hate, or jealousy ⟨eyes *smoldering* with hate⟩

smolt \'smōlt\ *noun* [Middle English (Scots)] (15th century)
: a young salmon or sea trout about two years old that is at the stage of development when it assumes the silvery color of the adult and is ready to migrate to the sea

¹smooch \'smüch\ *noun* (1578)
: KISS

²smooch *intransitive verb* [alteration of *smouch* to kiss loudly] (1588)
: KISS, PET

³smooch *transitive verb* [probably alteration of *smutch*, verb] (1631)
: SMUDGE, SMEAR

⁴smooch *noun* (1825)
: SMUDGE, SMEAR
— **smoochy** \'smü-chē\ *adjective*

¹smooth \'smüth\ *adjective* [Middle English *smothe*, from Old English *smōth*; akin to Old Saxon *smōthi* smooth] (before 12th century)
1 a (1) **:** having a continuous even surface (2) *of a curve* **:** being the representation of a function with a continuous first derivative **:** having or being a short even coat of hair ⟨a *smooth* collie⟩ — compare ROUGH, WIREHAIRED **b :** being without hair **c :** GLABROUS ⟨a *smooth* leaf⟩ **d :** causing no resistance to sliding

2 : free from difficulties or impediments 〈the *smooth* course of his life〉
3 : even and uninterrupted in flow or flight
4 : excessively and often artfully suave **:** INGRATIATING 〈a *smooth* operator〉
5 a : SERENE, EQUABLE 〈a *smooth* disposition〉 **b :** AMIABLE, COURTEOUS
6 a : not sharp or harsh 〈a *smooth* sherry〉 **b :** free from lumps
synonym see LEVEL, EASY, SUAVE
— **smooth** *adverb*
— **smooth·ly** *adverb*
— **smooth·ness** *noun*
²**smooth** *verb* **smoothed; smooth·ing; smooths** *also* **smoothes** (15th century)
transitive verb
1 : to make smooth
2 a : to free from what is harsh or disagreeable **:** POLISH 〈*smoothed* out his style〉 **b :** SOOTHE
3 : to minimize (as a fault) especially in order to allay anger or ill will 〈his main job is to *smooth* over the friction that so often arises —Brian Crozier〉
4 : to free from obstruction or difficulty
5 a : to press flat **b :** to remove expression from (one's face) **:** COMPOSE
6 : to cause to lie evenly and in order **:** PREEN
7 : to free (as a graph or data) from irregularities
intransitive verb
: to become smooth
— **smooth·er** *noun*
³**smooth** *noun* (15th century)
1 : a smooth part
2 : the act of smoothing
3 : a smoothing implement
smooth-bore \'smüth-'bōr, -'bȯr\ *adjective* (1799)
of a firearm **:** having a barrel with an unrifled bore
— **smoothbore** \-,bōr, -,bȯr\ *noun*
smooth breathing *noun* (circa 1888)
1 : a mark ' placed over some initial vowels in Greek to show that they are not aspirated (as in ἐκεῖ pronounced \e-'kā\)
2 : the absence of aspiration indicated by a mark '
smooth·en \'smü-thən\ *verb* **smooth·ened; smooth·en·ing** \'smü-thə-niŋ, 'smüth-niŋ\ (1635)
transitive verb
: to make smooth
intransitive verb
: to become smooth
smooth hound *noun* [from the absence of a spine in front of the dorsal fin] (1603)
: any of several dogfishes (genus *Mustelus*) closely related to or included with the requiem sharks
smooth muscle *noun* (circa 1890)
: muscle tissue that lacks cross striations, that is made up of elongated spindle-shaped cells having a central nucleus, and that is found in vertebrate visceral structures (as the stomach and bladder) as thin sheets performing functions not subject to conscious control by the mind and in all or most of the musculature of invertebrates other than arthropods — compare STRIATED MUSCLE
smooth–tongued \'smüth-'təŋd\ *adjective* (1592)
: ingratiating in speech
smoothy *or* **smooth·ie** \'smü-thē\ *noun, plural* **smooth·ies** (1904)
1 : a smooth-tongued person
2 a : a person with polished manners **b :** one who behaves or performs with deftness, assurance, and easy competence; *especially* **:** a man with an ingratiating manner toward women
smor·gas·bord \'smȯr-gəs-,bȯrd, -,bȯrd\ *noun* [Swedish *smörgåsbord,* from *smörgås* open sandwich + *bord* table] (1893)
1 : a luncheon or supper buffet offering a variety of foods and dishes (as hors d'oeuvres, hot

and cold meats, smoked and pickled fish, cheeses, salads, and relishes)
2 : a heterogeneous mixture **:** MÉLANGE ◇
smote *past of* SMITE
¹**smoth·er** \'smə-thər\ *noun* [Middle English, alteration of *smorther,* from *smoren* to smother, from Old English *smorian* to suffocate; akin to Middle Dutch *smoren* to suffocate] (13th century)
1 a : thick stifling smoke or smudge **b :** a state of being stifled or suppressed
2 : a dense cloud (as of fog, spray, or dust)
3 : a confused multitude of things **:** WELTER
— **smoth·ery** \'smə-thə-rē, 'smə̇th-rē\ *adjective*
²**smother** *verb* **smoth·ered; smoth·er·ing** \'smə-thə-riŋ, 'smə̇th-riŋ\ (circa 1520)
intransitive verb
: to be overcome or killed through or as if through lack of air
transitive verb
1 : to overcome or kill with smoke or fumes
2 a : to destroy the life of by depriving of air **b :** to overcome or discomfit through or as if through lack of air **c :** to suppress (a fire) by excluding oxygen
3 a : to cause to smolder **b :** to suppress expression or knowledge of 〈*smothered* his rage〉 **c :** to stop or prevent the growth or activity of 〈*smother* a child with too much care〉; *also* **:** OVERWHELM **d :** to cover thickly **:** BLANKET 〈snow *smothered* the trails〉 **e :** to overcome or vanquish quickly or decisively
4 : to cook in a covered pan or pot with little liquid over low heat
¹**smudge** \'sməj\ *verb* **smudged; smudg·ing** [Middle English *smogen*] (15th century)
transitive verb
1 a : to make a smudge on **b :** to soil as if by smudging
2 a : to rub, daub, or wipe in a smeary manner **b :** to make indistinct **:** BLUR
3 : to smoke or protect by means of a smudge
intransitive verb
1 : to make a smudge
2 : to become smudged
²**smudge** *noun* (circa 1774)
1 a : a blurry spot or streak **b :** an immaterial stain 〈cleanse him of every last *smudge* of im­propriety —Richard Hanser〉 **c :** an indistinct mass **:** BLUR
2 : a smoldering mass placed on the windward side (as to protect from frost)
3 : a bid of 4 in pitch that if made wins the game
— **smudg·i·ly** \'smə-jə-lē\ *adverb*
— **smudg·i·ness** \'smə-jē-nəs\ *noun*
— **smudgy** \-jē\ *adjective*
smug \'sməg\ *adjective* **smug·ger; smug·gest** [probably modification of Low German *smuck* neat, from Middle Low German, from *smucken* to dress; akin to Old English *smoc* smock] (1551)
1 : trim or smart in dress **:** SPRUCE
2 : scrupulously clean, neat, or correct **:** TIDY
3 : highly self-satisfied
— **smug·ly** *adverb*
— **smug·ness** *noun*
smug·gle \'smə-gəl\ *verb* **smug·gled; smug·gling** \-g(ə-)liŋ\ [Low German *smuggeln* & Dutch *smokkelen*] (1687)
transitive verb
1 : to import or export secretly contrary to the law and especially without paying duties imposed by law
2 : to convey or introduce surreptitiously
intransitive verb
: to import or export something in violation of the customs laws
— **smug·gler** \'smə-glər\ *noun*
¹**smut** \'smət\ *verb* **smut·ted; smut·ting** [probably alteration of earlier *smot* to stain, from Middle English *smotten;* akin to Middle High German *smutzen* to stain] (1587)
transitive verb
1 : to stain or taint with smut

2 : to affect (a crop or plant) with smut
intransitive verb
: to become affected by smut
²**smut** *noun* (1664)
1 : matter that soils or blackens; *specifically* **:** a particle of soot
2 : any of various destructive diseases especially of cereal grasses caused by parasitic fungi (order Ustilaginales) and marked by transformation of plant organs into dark masses of spores; *also* **:** a fungus causing a smut
3 : obscene language or matter
smutch \'sməch\ *noun* [akin to Middle English *smogen* to smudge] (1530)
: a dark stain **:** SMUDGE
— **smutch** *transitive verb*
— **smutchy** \'smə-chē\ *adjective*
smut·ty \'smə-tē\ *adjective* **smut·ti·er; -est** (1597)
1 : soiled or tainted with smut; *especially* **:** affected with smut fungus
2 : OBSCENE, INDECENT
3 : resembling smut in appearance **:** SOOTY
— **smut·ti·ly** \'smə-t³l-ē\ *adverb*
— **smut·ti·ness** \'smə-tē-nəs\ *noun*
¹**snack** \'snak\ *noun* [Middle English *snak* bite, from *snaken* to bite, perhaps from Middle Dutch *snacken* to snap at — more at SNATCH] (1757)
: a light meal **:** food eaten between regular meals; *also* **:** food suitable for snacking
²**snack** *intransitive verb* (1807)
: to eat a snack
snack bar *noun* (1930)
: a public eating place where snacks are served usually at a counter
¹**snaf·fle** \'sna-fəl\ *noun* [origin unknown] (1533)
: a simple usually jointed bit for a bridle
²**snaffle** *transitive verb* **snaf·fled; snaf·fling** \'sna-f(ə-)liŋ\ [origin unknown] (1724)
: to obtain especially by devious or irregular means
¹**sna·fu** \sna-'fü, 'sna-,fü\ *noun* [situation normal *all fucked up* (fouled *up*)] (circa 1941)
: CONFUSION, MUDDLE
²**snafu** *adjective* (1943)
: snarled or stalled in confusion **:** AWRY
³**snafu** *transitive verb* (1943)
: to bring into a state of confusion
¹**snag** \'snag\ *noun* [of Scandinavian origin; akin to Old Norse *snagi* clothes peg] (circa 1587)

◇ WORD HISTORY
smorgasbord In Swedish the word *smörgås* literally means "butter goose." *Smör* simply means "butter," and *gås* has the literal meaning "goose" and the figurative sense "a lump of butter," the result of a fancied resemblance between a buttery lump and a goose. In Swedish *smörgås* also has the extended senses "bread and butter" and "open-faced sandwich." It is in the latter sense that *smörgås* forms part of *smörgåsbord,* the name for the traditional Swedish buffet of delicacies, which are typically assembled by diners into open-faced sandwiches. (The *bord* of *smörgåsbord* is related to English *board* and simply means "table.") Swedish-style buffets first gained popularity among American diners in the early decades of the 20th century. By the 1940s *smorgasbord,* stripped of its Swedish diacritics, was sufficiently established in English to have given rise to the figurative sense "a heterogeneous mixture."

\ə\ abut \ᵊ\ kitten \ər\ further \a\ ash \ā\ ace
\ä\ mop, mar \aú\ out \ch\ chin \e\ bet \ē\ easy
\g\ go \i\ hit \ī\ ice \j\ job \ŋ\ sing \ō\ go
\ȯ\ law \ȯi\ boy \th\ thin \t̲h̲\ the \ü\ loot \ú\ foot
\y\ yet \zh\ vision *see also* Guide to Pronunciation

1 a : a tree or branch embedded in a lake or stream bed and constituting a hazard to navigation **b :** a standing dead tree
2 : a rough sharp or jagged projecting part **:** PROTUBERANCE: as **a :** a projecting tooth; *also* **:** a stump of a tooth **b :** one of the secondary branches of an antler
3 : a concealed or unexpected difficulty or obstacle
4 : a jagged tear made by or as if by catching on a snag ⟨a *snag* in her stocking⟩
— **snag·gy** \'sna-gē\ *adjective*
²**snag** *transitive verb* **snagged; snag·ging** (1807)
1 a : to catch and usually damage on or as if on a snag **b :** to halt or impede as if by catching on a snag
2 : to hew, trim, or cut roughly or jaggedly
3 : to clear (as a river) of snags
4 : to catch or obtain by quick action or good fortune
snag·gle·tooth \'sna-gəl-,tüth\ *noun* [English dialect *snaggle* irregularly shaped tooth + English *tooth*] (circa 1825)
: an irregular, broken, or projecting tooth
— **snag·gle·toothed** \-,tütht\ *adjective*
¹**snail** \'snā(ə)l\ *noun* [Middle English, from Old English *snægl;* akin to Old High German *snecko* snail, *snahhan* to creep] (before 12th century)
1 : a gastropod mollusk especially when having an external enclosing spiral shell
2 : a slow-moving or sluggish person or thing
— **snail·like** \'snā(ə)l-,līk\ *adjective*
²**snail** *intransitive verb* (1582)
: to move, act, or go slowly or lazily
snail darter *noun* (1975)
: a darter (*Percina tanasi*) of the Tennessee River drainage system of eastern Tennessee and northern Georgia
snail fever *noun* [from the snails which serve as intermediate hosts to the schistosomes causing the disease] (1947)
: SCHISTOSOMIASIS
snail–paced \'snā(ə)l-,pāst\ *adjective* (1594)
: moving very slowly
snail's pace *noun* (15th century)
: an extremely slow pace
¹**snake** \'snāk\ *noun* [Middle English, from Old English *snaca;* akin to Old Norse *snakr* snake, Old High German *snahhan* to crawl] (before 12th century)
1 : any of numerous limbless scaled reptiles (suborder Serpentes synonym Ophidia) with a long tapering body and with salivary glands often modified to produce venom which is injected through grooved or tubular fangs
2 : a worthless or treacherous fellow
3 : something (as a plumber's snake) resembling a snake
— **snake·like** \-,līk\ *adjective*
²**snake** *verb* **snaked; snak·ing** (1653)
transitive verb
1 : to wind (as one's way) in the manner of a snake
2 : to move (as logs) by dragging
intransitive verb
: to crawl, move, or extend silently, secretly, or sinuously
snake·bird \'snāk-,bərd\ *noun* (1791)
: ANHINGA
snake·bit \-,bit\ *or* **snake·bit·ten** \-,bi-t⁸n\ *adjective* (1957)
: UNLUCKY 1, 3
snake·bite \-,bīt\ *noun* (1839)
: the bite of a snake and especially a venomous snake
snake charmer *noun* (1836)
: an entertainer who exhibits a professed power to charm or fascinate venomous snakes
snake–dance *intransitive verb* (1922)
: to engage in a snake dance
snake dance *noun* (1772)
1 : a ceremonial dance in which snakes or their images are handled, invoked, or symbolically imitated by individual sinuous actions

2 : a group progression in a single-file serpentine path (as in celebration of an athletic victory)
snake doctor *noun* (1862)
1 : DRAGONFLY
2 : HELLGRAMMITE
snake fence *noun* (1805)
: WORM FENCE
snake in the grass (1696)
: a secretly faithless friend
snake oil *noun* (1927)
1 : any of various substances or mixtures sold (as by a traveling medicine show) as medicine usually without regard to their medical worth or properties
2 : POPPYCOCK, BUNKUM
snake pit *noun* (1946)
1 : a hospital for mental diseases
2 : a place or state of chaotic disorder and distress
snake·root \'snāk-,rüt, -,rut\ *noun* (1635)
: any of numerous plants (as seneca snakeroot) most of which have roots sometimes believed to cure snakebites; *also* **:** the root of such a plant
snake·skin \'snāk-,skin\ *noun* (1825)
: leather prepared from the skin of a snake
snake·weed \-,wēd\ *noun* (1597)
: any of various plants popularly associated with snakes (as in appearance, habitat, or the treatment of snakebite); *especially* **:** any of an American genus (*Gutierrezia*) of composite herbs or low shrubs with clustered yellow flower heads
snaky *also* **snak·ey** \'snā-kē\ *adjective* (1567)
1 : of, formed of, or entwined with snakes ⟨the Gorgon with *snaky* hair —Joseph Addison⟩
2 : SERPENTINE, SNAKELIKE ⟨*snaky* coils⟩
3 : suggestive of a snake ⟨the oiliness and *snaky* insinuation of his demeanor —Thomas DeQuincy⟩
4 : abounding in snakes
— **snak·i·ly** \-kə-lē\ *adverb*
¹**snap** \'snap\ *verb* **snapped; snap·ping** [Dutch or Low German *snappen;* akin to Middle High German *snappen* to snap] (1530)
intransitive verb
1 a : to make a sudden closing of the jaws **:** seize something sharply with the mouth ⟨fish *snapping* at the bait⟩ **b :** to grasp at something eagerly **:** make a pounce or snatch ⟨*snap* at any chance⟩
2 : to utter sharp biting words **:** bark out irritable or peevish retorts
3 a : to break suddenly with a sharp sound ⟨the twig *snapped*⟩ **b :** to give way suddenly under strain
4 : to make a sharp or crackling sound
5 : to close or fit in place with an abrupt movement or sharp sound ⟨the lock *snapped* shut⟩
6 a : to move briskly or sharply ⟨*snaps* to attention⟩ **b :** to undergo a sudden and rapid change (as from one condition to another) ⟨*snap* out of it⟩ ⟨*snapped* awake⟩
7 : SPARKLE, FLASH ⟨eyes *snapping* with fury⟩
transitive verb
1 : to seize with or as if with a snap of the jaws
2 : to take possession or advantage of suddenly or eagerly — usually used with *up* ⟨shoppers *snapping* up bargains⟩
3 a : to retort to or interrupt curtly and irritably **b :** to utter curtly or abruptly
4 : to break suddenly **:** break short or in two
5 a : to cause to make a snapping sound ⟨*snap* a whip⟩ **b :** to put into or remove from a particular position by a sudden movement or with a sharp sound ⟨*snap* the lock shut⟩
6 a : to project with a snap **b :** to put (a football) in play with a snap **c** (1) **:** to take photographically ⟨*snapping* exclusive news pictures —*Current Biography*⟩ (2) **:** to take a snapshot of
²**snap** *noun* (1555)

1 : an abrupt closing (as of the mouth in biting or of scissors in cutting)
2 a *archaic* **:** a share of profits or booty **b :** something that brings quick and easy profit or advantage **c :** something that is easy and presents no problems **:** CINCH
3 : a small amount **:** BIT
4 a : an act or instance of seizing abruptly **:** a sudden snatching at something **b :** a quick short movement ⟨lithe *snaps* of its body —Barbara Taylor⟩ **c :** a sudden sharp breaking
5 a : a sound made by snapping something ⟨shut the book with a *snap*⟩ **b :** a brief sharp and usually irritable speech or retort
6 : a sudden spell of weather ⟨a cold *snap*⟩
7 : a catch or fastening that closes or locks with a click ⟨the *snap* of a bracelet⟩
8 : a flat brittle cookie — compare GINGER-SNAP
9 : SNAPSHOT
10 a : the condition of being vigorous in body, mind, or spirit **:** ALERTNESS, ENERGY **b :** a pleasing vigorous quality
11 : the act of a center's putting the football in play from its position on the ground by quickly passing it between his legs to a teammate (as a quarterback) standing behind him
³**snap** *adverb* (1583)
: with a snap
⁴**snap** *adjective* (1739)
1 : done, made, or carried through suddenly or without deliberation ⟨a *snap* judgment⟩
2 : called or taken without prior warning ⟨a *snap* election⟩
3 : fastening with a snap ⟨a *snap* lock⟩
4 : unusually easy or simple ⟨a *snap* course⟩
snap·back \'snap-,bak\ *noun* (1887)
1 : a football snap
2 : a sudden rebound or recovery ⟨a *snapback* of prices on the stock exchange⟩
snap back *intransitive verb* (1945)
: to make a quick or vigorous recovery
snap bean *noun* (1770)
: a bean grown primarily for its pods that are usually broken in pieces and cooked as a vegetable while young and tender and before the seeds have become enlarged — compare SHELL BEAN
snap–brim \'snap-,brim\ *noun, often attributive* (1908)
: a usually felt hat with brim turned up in back and down in front and with a dented crown
snap·drag·on \'snap-,dra-gən\ *noun* [from the fancied resemblance of the flowers to the face of a dragon] (1593)
: any of a genus (*Antirrhinum* and especially the widely cultivated *A. majus* of the family Scrophulariaceae, the snapdragon family) of herbs having showy white, crimson, or yellow bilabiate flowers
snap–on \'snap-,ȯn, -,än\ *adjective* (1925)
: designed to snap into position and fit tightly ⟨*snap-on* cuffs⟩
snap pea *noun* (1980)
: a cultivated pea that has edible usually round pods easily snapped like beans and that is classified with the snow pea as a variety (*Pisum sativum macrocarpon*) — called also *sugar snap pea*

snapdragon

snap·per \'sna-pər\ *noun, plural* **snappers** (circa 1587)
1 : one that snaps: as **a :** something (as a remark) that gives new orientation to a situation or utterance **b** (1) **:** SNAPPING TURTLE (2) **:** CLICK BEETLE
2 *plural also* **snapper a :** any of numerous active carnivorous fishes (family Lutjanidae) of warm seas important as food and often as sport fishes **b :** any of several immature fishes (as the young of the bluefish) that resemble a snapper
snap·per–back \-,bak\ *noun* (1887)

: a football center

snapping turtle *noun* (1784)

: either of two large American aquatic turtles (family Chelydridae) with powerful jaws and a strong musky odor: **a** : one

snapping turtle

(*Chelydra serpentina*) that has the head covered with smooth skin, has large plates in a double row on the underside of the tail, and is distributed from eastern Canada to Central America **b** : ALLIGATOR SNAPPER

snap·pish \'sna-pish\ *adjective* (1542)

1 a : given to curt irritable speech **b** : arising from annoyance or irascibility

2 : inclined to bite ⟨a *snappish* dog⟩

— **snap·pish·ly** *adverb*

— **snap·pish·ness** *noun*

snap·py \'sna-pē\ *adjective* **snap·pi·er; -est** (1746)

1 : SNAPPISH 1

2 a : quickly made or done **b** : marked by vigor or liveliness **c** : briskly cold **d** : STYLISH, SMART ⟨a *snappy* dresser⟩

— **snap·pi·ly** \'sna-pə-lē\ *adverb*

— **snap·pi·ness** \'sna-pē-nəs\ *noun*

snap roll *noun* (circa 1934)

: an airplane maneuver in which a rapid full revolution is completed about the plane's longitudinal axis while an approximately level line of flight is maintained

snap·shoot·er \'snap-ˌshü-tər\ *noun* (1896)

: a person who takes snapshots

snap·shot \'snap-ˌshät\ *noun* (1890)

1 : a casual photograph made typically by an amateur with a small handheld camera

2 : an impression or view of something brief or transitory

¹snare \'snar, 'sner\ *noun* [Middle English, from Old English *sneare*, from Old Norse *snara;* akin to Old High German *snuor* cord and perhaps to Greek *narkē* numbness] (before 12th century)

1 a (1) : a contrivance often consisting of a noose for entangling birds or mammals (2) : TRAP, GIN **b** (1) : something by which one is entangled, involved in difficulties, or impeded (2) : something deceptively attractive

2 [probably from Dutch *snaar*, literally, cord; akin to Old High German *snuor*] **a** : one of the catgut strings or metal spirals of a snare drum **b** : SNARE DRUM

3 : a surgical instrument consisting usually of a wire loop constricted by a mechanism in the handle and used for removing tissue masses (as tonsils)

²snare *transitive verb* **snared; snar·ing** (14th century)

1 a : to capture by or as if by use of a snare **b** : to win or attain by artful or skillful maneuvers

2 : to entangle or hold as if in a snare ⟨any object that *snared* his eye —*Current Biography*⟩

synonym see CATCH

— **snar·er** *noun*

snare drum *noun* (circa 1859)

: a small double-headed drum with one or more snares stretched across its lower head — see DRUM illustration

snarky \'snär-kē\ *adjective* [dialect *snark* to annoy, perhaps alteration of *nark* to irritate] (1906)

: CROTCHETY, SNAPPISH

¹snarl \'snär(-ə)l\ *verb* [²*snarl*] (14th century)

transitive verb

1 : to cause to become knotted and intertwined : TANGLE

2 : to make excessively complicated

intransitive verb

: to become snarled

— **snarl·er** *noun*

²snarl *noun* [Middle English *snarle*, probably diminutive of *snare*] (1609)

1 : a tangle especially of hairs or thread : KNOT

2 : a tangled situation ⟨traffic *snarls*⟩

— **snarly** \'snär-lē\ *adjective*

³snarl *verb* [frequentative of obsolete English *snar* to growl] (1589)

intransitive verb

1 : to growl with a snapping or gnashing of teeth

2 : to give vent to anger in surly language

transitive verb

: to utter or express with a snarl or by snarling

— **snarl·er** *noun*

⁴snarl *noun* (1613)

: a surly angry growl

— **snarly** \'snär-lē\ *adjective*

¹snatch \'snach\ *verb* [Middle English *snacchen* to give a sudden snap, seize; akin to Middle Dutch *snacken* to snap at] (13th century)

intransitive verb

: to attempt to seize something suddenly

transitive verb

: to take or grasp abruptly or hastily; *also* : to seize or grab suddenly without permission, ceremony, or right

synonym see TAKE

— **snatch·er** *noun*

²snatch *noun* (1563)

1 a : a brief period ⟨caught *snatches* of sleep⟩ **b** : a brief, fragmentary, or hurried part : BIT ⟨caught *snatches* of the conversation⟩

2 a : a snatching at or of something **b** *slang* : an act or instance of kidnapping

3 : a lift in weight lifting in which the weight is raised from the floor directly to an overhead position in a single motion — compare CLEAN AND JERK, PRESS

4 : the female pudenda — usually considered vulgar

snatch block *noun* (circa 1625)

: a block that can be opened on one side to receive the bight of a rope

snath \'snath, 'sneth\ *or* **snathe** \'snāth, 'snäth\ *noun* [Middle English *snede,* from Old English *snæd*] (1574)

: the handle of a scythe

snaz·zy \'sna-zē\ *adjective* **snaz·zi·er; -est** [origin unknown] (circa 1932)

: conspicuously or flashily attractive : FANCY

¹sneak \'snēk\ *verb* **sneaked** \'snēkt\ *or* **snuck** \'snək\; **sneak·ing** [akin to Old English *snīcan* to sneak along, Old Norse *snīkja*] (1596)

intransitive verb

1 : to go stealthily or furtively : SLINK

2 : to act in or as if in a furtive manner

3 : to carry the football on a quarterback sneak

transitive verb

: to put, bring, or take in a furtive or artful manner ⟨*sneak* a smoke⟩ □

synonym see LURK

— **sneak up on** : to approach or act on stealthily

²sneak *noun* (circa 1643)

1 : a person who acts in a stealthy, furtive, or shifty manner

2 a : a stealthy or furtive move **b** : an unobserved departure or escape

3 : SNEAKER 2

4 : QUARTERBACK SNEAK

³sneak *adjective* (circa 1859)

1 : carried on secretly : CLANDESTINE

2 : occurring without warning : SURPRISE ⟨a *sneak* attack⟩

sneak·er \'snē-kər\ *noun* (1598)

1 : one that sneaks

2 : a usually canvas sports shoe with a pliable rubber sole

— **sneak·ered** \-kərd\ *adjective*

sneak·ing \'snē-kiŋ\ *adjective* (1582)

1 : MEAN, CONTEMPTIBLE

2 : characteristic of a sneak : FURTIVE, UNDERHANDED

3 a : not openly expressed or acknowledged ⟨he has a *sneaking* respect for culture —H. A. Burton⟩ **b** : that is a persistent conjecture ⟨a *sneaking* suspicion⟩

— **sneak·ing·ly** \-kiŋ-lē\ *adverb*

sneak preview *noun* (circa 1937)

: a special advance showing of a motion picture usually announced but not named

sneak thief *noun* (circa 1859)

: a thief who steals whatever is readily available without using violence or forcibly breaking into buildings

sneaky \'snē-kē\ *adjective* **sneak·i·er; -est** (1833)

: marked by stealth, furtiveness, or shiftiness

— **sneak·i·ly** \-kə-lē\ *adverb*

— **sneak·i·ness** \-kē-nəs\ *noun*

¹sneap \'snēp\ *transitive verb* [Middle English *snaipen*, probably of Scandinavian origin; akin to Icelandic *sneypa* to scold — more at SNUB] (14th century)

1 *archaic* : to blast or blight with cold : NIP

2 *dialect English* : CHIDE

²sneap *noun* (1597)

archaic : REBUKE, SNUB

sneck \'snek\ *noun* [Middle English *snekke*] (14th century)

chiefly dialect : LATCH

¹sneer \'snir\ *verb* [probably akin to Middle High German *snerren* to chatter, gossip — more at SNORE] (1680)

intransitive verb

1 : to smile or laugh with facial contortions that express scorn or contempt

2 : to speak or write in a scornfully jeering manner

transitive verb

: to utter with a sneer

synonym see SCOFF

— **sneer·er** *noun*

²sneer *noun* (1707)

: the act of sneering; *also* : a sneering expression or remark

¹sneeze \'snēz\ *intransitive verb* **sneezed; sneez·ing** [Middle English *snesen*, alteration of *fnesen*, from Old English *fnēosan;* akin to Middle High German *pfnūsen* to snort, sneeze, Greek *pnein* to breathe] (14th century)

: to make a sudden violent spasmodic audible expiration of breath through the nose and mouth especially as a reflex act

— **sneez·er** *noun*

— **sneeze at** : to make light of

²sneeze *noun* (1646)

: an act or instance of sneezing

sneeze·weed \'snēz-ˌwēd\ *noun* (circa 1837)

: any of several composite plants; *especially* : a North American perennial herb (*Helenium autumnale*) with yellow ray flowers and a darker globose disk

sneezy \'snē-zē\ *adjective* (1839)

: given to or causing sneezing

¹snell \'snel\ *adjective* [Middle English, from Old English; akin to Old High German *snel* bold, agile] (before 12th century)

1 *chiefly Scottish* : QUICK, ACUTE

\ə\ **abut** \ᵊ\ **kitten** \ər\ **further** \a\ **ash** \ā\ **ace**
\ä\ **mop, mar** \aù\ **out** \ch\ **chin** \e\ **bet** \ē\ **easy**
\g\ **go** \i\ **hit** \ī\ **ice** \j\ **job** \ŋ\ **sing** \ō\ **go**
\ò\ **law** \òi\ **boy** \th\ **thin** \t̲h̲\ **the** \ü\ **loot** \ù\ **foot**
\y\ **yet** \zh\ **vision** *see also* Guide to Pronunciation

2 *chiefly Scottish* **:** KEEN, PIERCING ⟨a *snell* wind smote us —*Scotsman*⟩
3 *chiefly Scottish* **:** GRIEVOUS, SEVERE

²snell *noun* [origin unknown] (1846)
: a short line (as of gut) by which a fishhook is attached to a longer line

¹snick \'snik\ *verb* [probably from obsolete *snick or snee* to engage in cut-and-thrust fighting — more at SNICKERSNEE] (circa 1700)
transitive verb
1 *archaic* **:** to cut through
2 : to cut slightly **:** NICK
intransitive verb
: to perform a light cutting action

²snick *noun* (circa 1775)
: a small cut **:** NICK

³snick *verb* [imitative] (1828)
: CLICK

⁴snick *noun* (circa 1886)
: a slight often metallic sound **:** CLICK

¹snick·er \'sni-kər\ *intransitive verb* **snick·ered; snick·er·ing** \-k(ə-)riŋ\ [origin unknown] (1694)
: to laugh in a covert or partly suppressed manner **:** TITTER
— **snick·er·er** \-kər-ər\ *noun*
— **snick·ery** \-k(ə-)rē\ *adjective*

²snicker *noun* (1835)
: an act or sound of snickering

snick·er·snee \'sni-kə(r)-,snē\ *noun* [obsolete *snick or snee* to engage in cut-and-thrust fighting, alteration of earlier *steake or snye*, from Dutch *steken of snijden* to thrust or cut] (circa 1775)
: a large knife

snide \'snīd\ *adjective* [origin unknown] (circa 1859)
1 a : FALSE, COUNTERFEIT **b :** practicing deception **:** DISHONEST ⟨a *snide* merchant⟩
2 : unworthy of esteem **:** LOW ⟨a *snide* trick⟩
3 : slyly disparaging **:** INSINUATING ⟨*snide* remarks⟩
— **snide·ly** *adverb*
— **snide·ness** *noun*

¹sniff \'snif\ *verb* [Middle English] (14th century)
intransitive verb
1 : to draw air audibly up the nose especially for smelling ⟨*sniffed* at the flowers⟩
2 : to show or express disdain or scorn
transitive verb
1 : to smell or take by inhalation through the nose
2 : to utter contemptuously
3 : to recognize or detect by or as if by smelling ⟨*sniff* out trouble⟩

²sniff *noun* (1767)
1 : an act or sound of sniffing
2 : a quantity that is sniffed

sniff·er *noun* (1864)
: one that sniffs; *especially* **:** one who takes drugs illicitly by sniffing

sniff·ish \'sni-fish\ *adjective* (1923)
: having or expressing a haughty attitude **:** DISDAINFUL, SUPERCILIOUS
— **sniff·ish·ly** *adverb*
— **sniff·ish·ness** *noun*

¹snif·fle \'sni-fəl\ *intransitive verb* **snif·fled; snif·fling** \-f(ə-)liŋ\ [frequentative of *sniff*] (1632)
1 : to sniff repeatedly **:** SNUFFLE
2 : to speak with or as if with sniffling
— **snif·fler** \-f(ə-)lər\ *noun*

²sniffle *noun* (circa 1825)
1 *plural* **:** a head cold marked by nasal discharge
2 : an act or sound of sniffling

sniffy \'sni-fē\ *adjective* **sniff·i·er; -est** (1871)
: SNIFFISH, SUPERCILIOUS
— **sniff·i·ly** \'sni-fə-lē\ *adverb*
— **sniff·i·ness** \'sni-fē-nəs\ *noun*

snif·ter \'snif-tər\ *noun* [English dialect, *sniff, snort*, from Middle English, to sniff, snort] (1844)
1 : a small drink of distilled liquor

2 : a short-stemmed goblet with a bowl narrowing toward the top

¹snig·ger \'sni-gər\ *intransitive verb* **sniggered; snig·ger·ing** \-g(ə-)riŋ\ [by alteration] (circa 1706)
: SNICKER
— **snig·ger·er** \-gər-ər\ *noun*

²snigger *noun* (circa 1823)
: SNICKER

snig·gle \'sni-gəl\ *verb* **snig·gled; snig·gling** \-g(ə-)liŋ\ [English dialect *snig* small eel, from Middle English *snygge*] (1653)
intransitive verb
: to fish for eels by thrusting a baited hook or needle into their hiding places
transitive verb
: to catch (an eel) by sniggling

¹snip \'snip\ *noun* [from or akin to Dutch & Low German *snip*; akin to Middle High German *snipfen* to snap the fingers] (1558)
1 a : a small piece that is snipped off; *also* **:** FRAGMENT, BIT **b :** a cut or notch made by snipping **c :** an act or sound of snipping
2 : a white or light mark; *especially* **:** a white spot between the nostrils of a horse
3 : a presumptuous or impertinent person; *especially* **:** an impertinent or saucy girl
4 *British* **:** BARGAIN, BUY

²snip *verb* **snipped; snip·ping** (1586)
transitive verb
: to cut or cut off with or as if with shears or scissors; *specifically* **:** to clip suddenly or by bits
intransitive verb
: to make a short quick cut with or as if with shears or scissors
— **snip·per** *noun*

¹snipe \'snīp\ *noun, plural* **snipes** [Middle English, of Scandinavian origin; akin to Old Norse *snīpa* snipe; akin to Old High German *snepfa* snipe] (14th century)
1 *or plural* **snipe :** any of various usually slender-billed birds of the same family as the sandpipers; *especially* **:** any of several game birds (especially genus *Gallinago*) especially of marshy areas
2 : a contemptible person

²snipe *intransitive verb* **sniped; snip·ing** (1832)
1 : to shoot at exposed individuals (as of an enemy's forces) from a usually concealed point of vantage
2 : to aim a carping or snide attack
— **snip·er** *noun*

snip·er·scope \'snī-pər-,skōp\ *noun* (1941)
: an optical device for use especially with a rifle that allows a person to see targets better in the dark

snip·per·snap·per \'sni-pər-,sna-pər\ *noun* [origin unknown] (circa 1590)
: WHIPPERSNAPPER

snip·pet \'sni-pət\ *noun* [¹*snip*] (1664)
: a small part, piece, or thing; *especially* **:** a brief quotable passage

snip·pe·ty \-pə-tē\ *adjective* (1864)
1 : made up of snippets
2 [probably from ²*snip* + *-ety* (as in *pernickety*)] **:** SNIPPY

snip·py \'sni-pē\ *adjective* **snip·pi·er; -est** [²*snip*] (circa 1848)
1 : SHORT-TEMPERED, SNAPPISH
2 : unduly brief or curt
3 : putting on airs **:** SNIFFY
— **snip·pi·ly** \'sni-pə-lē\ *adverb*

snips \'snips\ *noun plural but singular or plural in construction* (circa 1846)
: hand shears used especially for cutting sheet metal

snit \'snit\ *noun* [origin unknown] (1939)
: a state of agitation

¹snitch \'snich\ *noun* [origin unknown] (circa 1785)
: one that snitches **:** TATTLETALE

²snitch *intransitive verb* (1801)
: INFORM, TATTLE
— **snitch·er** *noun*

³snitch *transitive verb* [probably alteration of *snatch*] (1904)
: to take by stealth **:** PILFER

¹sniv·el \'sni-vəl\ *intransitive verb* **-eled** *or* **-elled; -el·ing** *or* **-el·ling** \'sni-və-liŋ, 'sniv-liŋ\ [Middle English, from (assumed) Old English *snyflan*; akin to Dutch *snuffelen* to snuffle, *snuffen* to sniff] (14th century)
1 : to run at the nose
2 : to snuff mucus up the nose audibly **:** SNUFFLE
3 : to cry or whine with snuffling
4 : to speak or act in a whining, sniffling, tearful, or weakly emotional manner
— **sniv·el·er** \'sni-və-lər, 'sniv-lər\ *noun*

²snivel *noun* (1600)
1 *plural, dialect* **:** HEAD COLD
2 : an act or instance of sniveling

snob \'snäb\ *noun* [origin unknown] (1781)
1 *British* **:** COBBLER
2 : one who blatantly imitates, fawningly admires, or vulgarly seeks association with those regarded as social superiors
3 a : one who tends to rebuff, avoid, or ignore those regarded as inferior **b :** one who has an offensive air of superiority in matters of knowledge or taste

snob appeal *noun* (1933)
: qualities in a product that appeal to the snobbery in a purchaser

snob·bery \'snä-b(ə-)rē\ *noun, plural* **-ber·ies** (1843)
1 : snobbish conduct or character **:** SNOBBISHNESS
2 : an instance of snobbery

snob·bish \'snä-bish\ *adjective* (1840)
: being, characteristic of, or befitting a snob
— **snob·bish·ly** *adverb*
— **snob·bish·ness** *noun*

snob·bism \'snä-,bi-zəm\ *noun* (1845)
: SNOBBERY

snob·by \'snä-bē\ *adjective* **snob·bi·er; -est** (1846)
: characterized by snobbery

sno–cone *variant of* SNOW CONE

snol·ly·gos·ter \'snä-lē-,gäs-tər\ *noun* [probably alteration of *snallygaster* a mythical creature that preys on poultry and children] (circa 1860)
: a shrewd unprincipled person

¹snood \'snüd\ *noun* [(assumed) Middle English, from Old English *snōd*] (before 12th century)
1 a *Scottish* **:** a fillet or band for a woman's hair **b :** a net or fabric bag pinned or tied on at the back of a woman's head for holding the hair
2 : SNELL

snood 1b

²snood *transitive verb* (1714)
: to secure with a snood

¹snook \'snúk, 'snük\ *noun, plural* **snook** *or* **snooks** [Dutch *snoek* pike, snook] (1697)
1 : a large vigorous bony fish (*Centropomus undecimalis* of the family Centropomidae) of warm seas and rivers that is a prized food and sport fish
2 : any of various marine fishes of the same family as the snook

²snook *noun* [origin unknown] (1879)
: a gesture of derision made by thumbing the nose

¹snook·er \'snú-kər\ *noun* [origin unknown] (1889)
: a variation of pool played with 15 red balls and 6 variously colored balls

²snooker *transitive verb* (1925)
: to make a dupe of **:** HOODWINK

¹snoop \'snüp\ *intransitive verb* [Dutch *snoepen* to buy or eat on the sly; akin to Dutch *snappen* to snap] (1832)
: to look or pry especially in a sneaking or meddlesome manner
— **snoop·er** *noun*

²**snoop** *noun* (circa 1890)
: one that snoops
snoopy \'snü-pē\ *adjective* (circa 1895)
: given to snooping especially for personal information about others
— **snoop·i·ly** \-pə-lē\ *adverb*
¹**snoot** \'snüt\ *noun* [Middle English *snute*] (1861)
1 a : SNOUT **b :** NOSE
2 : a grimace expressive of contempt
3 : a snooty person : SNOB
²**snoot** *transitive verb* (1928)
: to treat with disdain : look down one's nose at
snooty \'snü-tē\ *adjective* **snoot·i·er; -est** (1919)
1 : looking down the nose : showing disdain ⟨*snooty* people who won't speak to their neighbors⟩
2 : characterized by snobbery ⟨a *snooty* store⟩
— **snoot·i·ly** \'snü-t°l-ē\ *adverb*
— **snoot·i·ness** \'snü-tē-nəs\ *noun*
¹**snooze** \'snüz\ *intransitive verb* **snoozed; snooz·ing** [origin unknown] (1788)
: to take a nap : DOZE
— **snooz·er** *noun*
²**snooze** *noun* (1793)
: NAP
snoo·zle \'snü-zəl\ *verb* **snoo·zled; snoo·zling** \'snü-zə-liŋ, 'snüz-liŋ\ [perhaps blend of *snooze* and *nuzzle*] (1831)
chiefly dialect : NUZZLE
¹**snore** \'snōr, 'snȯr\ *verb* **snored; snor·ing** [Middle English; akin to Middle Low German *snorren* to drone, Middle High German *snerren* to chatter] (15th century)
intransitive verb
: to breathe during sleep with a rough hoarse noise due to vibration of the soft palate
transitive verb
: to spend (time) in snoring or sleeping
— **snor·er** *noun*
²**snore** *noun* (1605)
1 : an act of snoring
2 : a noise of or as if of snoring
¹**snor·kel** \'snȯr-kəl\ *noun* [German *Schnorchel*] (1944)
1 : a tube housing air intake and exhaust pipes for a submarine's diesel engine that can be extended above the water's surface so that the engines can be operated while the submarine is submerged
2 : any of various devices (as for an underwater swimmer) resembling a snorkel in function
²**snorkel** *intransitive verb* **snor·keled; snor·kel·ing** \-k(ə-)liŋ\ (1949)
: to operate or swim submerged with only a snorkel above water
— **snor·kel·er** \-k(ə-)lər\ *noun*
¹**snort** \'snȯrt\ *verb* [Middle English] (14th century)
intransitive verb
1 a : to force air violently through the nose with a rough harsh sound **b :** to express scorn, anger, indignation, or surprise by a snort
2 : to emit explosive sounds resembling snorts
3 : to take in a drug by inhalation
transitive verb
1 : to utter with or express by a snort
2 : to expel or emit with or as if with snorts
3 : to take in (a drug) by inhalation
²**snort** *noun* (1808)
1 : an act or sound of snorting
2 : a drink of usually straight liquor taken in one draft
snort·er \'snȯr-tər\ *noun* (1601)
1 : one that snorts
2 : something that is extraordinary or prominent : HUMDINGER
3 : SNORT 2
snot \'snät\ *noun* [Middle English, from Old English *gesnot;* akin to Old High German *snuzza* nasal mucus] (15th century)
1 : nasal mucus
2 : a snotty person

snot·ty \'snä-tē\ *adjective* **snot·ti·er; -est** (circa 1570)
1 : foul with nasal mucus
2 : annoyingly or spitefully unpleasant
— **snot·ti·ly** \'snä-t°l-ē\ *adverb*
— **snot·ti·ness** \'snä-tē-nəs\ *noun*
snout \'snaȯt\ *noun* [Middle English *snute;* akin to Middle Dutch *snūt* snout, German *Schnauze*] (13th century)
1 a (1) : a long projecting nose (as of a swine) **(2) :** an anterior prolongation of the head of various animals (as a weevil) : ROSTRUM **b :** the human nose especially when large or grotesque
2 : something resembling an animal's snout in position, function, or shape: as **a :** PROW **b :** NOZZLE **c :** the terminal face of a glacier
— **snout·ed** \'snaȯ-təd\ *adjective*
— **snout·ish** \-tish\ *adjective*
— **snouty** \-tē\ *adjective*
snout beetle *noun* (1862)
: WEEVIL
¹**snow** \'snō\ *noun, often attributive* [Middle English, from Old English *snāw;* akin to Old High German *snēo* snow, Latin *niv-, nix,* Greek *nipha* (accusative)] (before 12th century)
1 a : precipitation in the form of small white ice crystals formed directly from the water vapor of the air at a temperature of less than 32°F (0°C) **b (1) :** a descent or shower of snow crystals **(2) :** a mass of fallen snow crystals
2 : something resembling snow: as **a :** a dessert made of stiffly beaten whites of eggs, sugar, and fruit pulp ⟨apple *snow*⟩ **b :** a usually white crystalline substance that condenses from a fluid phase as snow does ⟨ammonia *snow*⟩ **c** *slang* **(1) :** COCAINE **(2) :** HEROIN **d :** small transient light or dark spots on a television screen
— **snow·less** \-ləs\ *adjective*
²**snow** (14th century)
intransitive verb
: to fall in or as snow
transitive verb
1 : to cause to fall like or as snow
2 a : to cover, shut in, or imprison with or as if with snow **b :** to deceive, persuade, or charm glibly
3 : to whiten like snow
¹**snow·ball** \'snō-bȯl\ *noun* (15th century)
1 a : a round mass of snow pressed or rolled together **b :** shaved ice molded into a ball and flavored with a syrup
2 : any of several cultivated shrubs (genus *Viburnum*) with clusters of white sterile flowers — called also *snowball bush*
²**snowball** (1854)
transitive verb
1 : to throw snowballs at
2 : to cause to increase or multiply at a rapidly accelerating rate
intransitive verb
1 : to engage in throwing snowballs
2 : to increase, accumulate, expand, or multiply at a rapidly accelerating rate
snow·bank \'snō-,baŋk\ *noun* (1779)
: a mound or slope of snow
snow·belt \-,belt\ *noun, often capitalized* (1874)
: a region that receives an appreciable amount of annual snowfall
snow·ber·ry \-,ber-ē\ *noun* (1760)
: any of several white-berried shrubs (especially genus *Symphoricarpos* of the honeysuckle family); *especially* : a low-growing North American shrub (*S. albus*) with pink flowers in small axillary clusters
snow·bird \-,bərd\ *noun* (1674)
1 : any of several birds (as a junco or fieldfare) seen chiefly in winter
2 : one who travels to warm climes for the winter
snow blindness *noun* (1748)

: inflammation and photophobia caused by exposure of the eyes to ultraviolet rays reflected from snow or ice
— **snow–blind** \'snō-,blīnd\ *or* **snow–blind·ed** \-,blīn-dəd\ *adjective*
snow·blow·er \'snō-,blō-(ə)r\ *noun* (1950)
: SNOW THROWER
snow·board \-,bōrd, -,bȯrd\ *noun* (1981)
: a board like a wide ski ridden in a surfing position downhill over snow
— **snow·board·er** *noun*
— **snow·board·ing** *noun*
snow·bound \-'baȯnd\ *adjective* (1814)
: shut in or blockaded by snow
snow·brush \-,brəsh\ *noun* (circa 1923)
: a spreading white-flowered western North American shrub (*Ceanothus velutinus*) of the buckthorn family with scented leaves and panicles of small flowers
snow·cap \-,kap\ *noun* (1871)
: a covering cap of snow (as on a mountain peak)
— **snow·capped** \-,kapt\ *adjective*
snow cone *noun* (1964)
: SNOWBALL 1b
snow crab *noun* (1974)
: either of two crabs (*Chionoecetes opilio* and *C. bairdi*) of the northern Pacific Ocean and especially Alaska marketed for food
snow·drift \'snō-,drift\ *noun* (14th century)
: a bank of drifted snow
snow·drop \-,dräp\ *noun* (1664)
: a bulbous European herb (*Galanthus nivalis*) of the amaryllis family bearing nodding white flowers that often appear while the snow is on the ground
snow·fall \-,fȯl\ *noun* (1821)
: a fall of snow; *specifically* : the amount of snow that falls in a single storm or in a given period
snow fence *noun* (1872)
: a usually slatted fence placed across the path of prevailing winds to protect (as a building, road, or railroad track) from drifting snow by disrupting the flow of wind and causing the snow to be deposited on the lee side of the fence
snow·field \'snō-,fēld\ *noun* (1845)
: a broad level expanse of snow; *especially* : a mass of perennial snow at the head of a glacier
snow·flake \-,flāk\ *noun* (1734)
1 : a flake or crystal of snow
2 : any of a genus (*Leucojum*) of bulbous plants of the amaryllis family; *especially* : one (*L. vernum*) resembling the snowdrop
snow goose *noun* (1771)
: a wild goose (*Anser caerulescens* synonym *Chen caerulescens*) that has a pinkish bill and exists either as a white form with black primaries or as a grayish black form with a white head
snow job *noun* (1943)
: an intensive effort at persuasion or deception
snow leopard *noun* (1866)
: a large cat (*Panthera uncia*) of upland central Asia with long heavy grayish white fur irregularly marked with brownish black spots, rosettes, and rings

snow leopard

snow line *noun* (circa 1835)
: the lower margin of a perennial snowfield
snow·mak·er \'snō-,mā-kər\ *noun* (1954)
: a device for making snow artificially
snow·mak·ing \-,mā-kiŋ\ *adjective* (1953)

: used for the production of artificial snow usually for ski slopes ⟨*snowmaking* machines⟩

snow·man \-ˌman\ *noun* (1827)
: snow shaped to resemble a human figure

snow·melt \-ˌmelt\ *noun* (circa 1946)
: runoff produced by the melting of snow

snow·mo·bile \ˈsnō-mō-ˌbēl\ *noun* (1923)
: any of various automotive vehicles for travel on snow; *specifically* : an open vehicle for usually one or two persons with steerable skis on the front and an endless belt at the rear

snow·mo·bil·ing \-ˌbē-liŋ\ *noun* (1964)
: the sport of driving a snowmobile
— **snow·mo·bil·er** \-lər\ *also* **snow·mo·bil·ist** \-list\ *noun*

snow–on–the–mountain *noun* (1873)
: a spurge (*Euphorbia marginata*) of the central and western U.S. that has showy white-bracted flower clusters and is grown as an ornamental

snow·pack \ˈsnō-ˌpak\ *noun* (circa 1946)
: a seasonal accumulation of slow-melting packed snow

snow pea *noun* (1949)
: a cultivated pea with flat edible pods that is classified with the snap pea as a variety (*Pisum sativum macrocarpon*)

snow plant *noun* (1846)
: a fleshy bright-red saprophytic chiefly California herb (*Sarcodes sanguinea*) of the wintergreen family that grows in high-altitude coniferous woods and often appears before the snow melts

¹snow·plow \ˈsnō-ˌplaù\ *noun* (1792)
1 : any of various devices used for clearing away snow
2 : a stemming with both skis used for coming to a stop, slowing down, or descending slowly

²snowplow *intransitive verb* (1904)
: to execute a snowplow ⟨*snowplowed* to a stop⟩

snow pudding *noun* (1876)
: a pudding made very fluffy and light by the addition of whipped egg whites and gelatin

snow·scape \ˈsnō-ˌskāp\ *noun* (1886)
: a landscape covered with snow

snow·shed \-ˌshed\ *noun* (1868)
: a shelter against snowslides

¹snow·shoe \-ˌshü\ *noun* (1666)
: a light oval frame that is strengthened by two crosspieces, strung with thongs, and attached to the foot and that is used to enable a person to walk on soft snow without sinking

²snowshoe *intransitive verb* **snow·shoed; snow·shoe·ing** (1880)
: to travel on snowshoes
— **snow·sho·er** \-ˌshü-ər\ *noun*

snowshoe hare *noun* (circa 1890)
: a hare (*Lepus americanus*) of northern North America with heavy fur on the hind feet and a coat that in most populations is brown in the summer but usually white in the winter — called also *snowshoe rabbit, varying hare*

snowshoe hare

snow·slide \ˈsnō-ˌslīd\ *noun* (1841)
: an avalanche of snow

snow·storm \-ˌstòrm\ *noun* (1771)
1 : a storm of or with snow
2 : something that resembles a snowstorm

snow·suit \-ˌsüt\ *noun* (1937)
: a one-piece or two-piece lined garment for winter wear by children

snow thrower *noun* (1954)
: a machine for removing snow (as from a driveway or sidewalk) in which a rotating spiral blade picks up and propels the snow aside

snow tire *noun* (1943)

: an automotive tire with a tread designed to give added traction on snow

snow under *transitive verb* (1880)
1 : to overwhelm especially in excess of capacity to absorb or deal with something
2 : to defeat by a large margin

snow–white \ˈsnō-ˈhwīt, -ˈwīt\ *adjective* (before 12th century)
: white as snow

snowy \ˈsnō-ē\ *adjective* **snow·i·er; -est** (before 12th century)
1 a : composed of snow or melted snow **b** : marked by or covered with snow
2 a : whitened by snow **b** : SNOW-WHITE
— **snow·i·ly** \ˈsnō-ə-lē\ *adverb*
— **snow·i·ness** \ˈsnō-ē-nəs\ *noun*

snowy egret *noun* (1869)
: a white American egret (*Egretta thula*) having a slender black bill, black legs, and yellow feet

snowy owl *noun* (1781)
: a large ground-nesting diurnal arctic owl (*Nyctea scandiaca*) that enters the chiefly northern parts of the U.S. in winter and has plumage that is sometimes nearly pure white but usually with brownish spots or bars

snowy owl

¹snub \ˈsnəb\ *transitive verb* **snubbed; snub·bing** [Middle English *snubben,* of Scandinavian origin; akin to Old Norse *snubba* to scold; akin to Icelandic *sneypa* to scold] (13th century)
1 : to check or stop with a cutting retort : REBUKE
2 a : to check (as a line) suddenly while running out especially by turning around a fixed object (as a post); *also* : to check the motion of by snubbing a line ⟨*snub* a horse to a tree⟩ **b** : to restrain the action of : SUPPRESS ⟨*snub* a vibration⟩
3 : to treat with contempt or neglect
4 : to extinguish by stubbing ⟨*snub* out a cigarette⟩

²snub *noun* (14th century)
: an act or an instance of snubbing; *especially* : SLIGHT

³snub *adjective* (1724)
1 *or* **snubbed** \ˈsnəbd\ : BLUNT, STUBBY ⟨a *snub* nose⟩
2 : used in snubbing ⟨*snub* line⟩
— **snub·ness** *noun*

snub·ber \ˈsnə-bər\ *noun* (1853)
1 : one that snubs
2 : SHOCK ABSORBER

snub·by \ˈsnə-bē\ *adjective* (1828)
1 : SNUB
2 : SNUB-NOSED
— **snub·bi·ness** *noun*

snub–nosed \ˈsnəb-ˌnōzd\ *adjective* (1725)
1 : having a stubby and usually slightly turned-up nose
2 : having a very short barrel ⟨a *snub-nosed* revolver⟩

snuck *past and past participle of* SNEAK

¹snuff \ˈsnəf\ *noun* [Middle English *snoffe*] (14th century)
1 : the charred part of a candlewick
2 a *obsolete* : UMBRAGE, OFFENSE **b** *chiefly Scottish* : HUFF

²snuff *transitive verb* (15th century)
1 : to crop the snuff of (a candle) by pinching or by the use of snuffers so as to brighten the light
2 a : to extinguish by or as if by the use of a snuffer — often used with *out* **b** : to make extinct : put an end to — usually used with *out* ⟨an accident that *snuffed* out a life⟩

³snuff *adjective* (1975)
: characterized by the sensationalistic depiction of violence; *especially* : featuring a real rather than a staged murder ⟨*snuff* movies⟩

⁴snuff *verb* [akin to Dutch *snuffen* to sniff, snuff — more at SNIVEL] (1527)
transitive verb
1 : to draw forcibly through or into the nostrils
2 : SCENT, SMELL
3 : to sniff at in order to examine — used of an animal
intransitive verb
1 : to inhale through the nose noisily and forcibly; *also* : to sniff or smell inquiringly
2 *obsolete* : to sniff loudly in or as if in disgust
3 : to take snuff

⁵snuff *noun* (1570)
: the act of snuffing : SNIFF

⁶snuff *noun* [Dutch *snuf,* short for *snuftabak,* from *snuffen* to snuff + *tabak* tobacco] (1683)
1 : a preparation of pulverized tobacco to be inhaled through the nostrils, chewed, or placed against the gums
2 : the amount of snuff taken at one time
— **up to snuff** : of sufficient quality : meeting an applicable standard

snuff·box \ˈsnəf-ˌbäks\ *noun* (circa 1687)
: a small box for holding snuff usually carried about the person

¹snuff·er \ˈsnə-fər\ *noun* (15th century)
1 : a device similar to a pair of scissors for cropping and holding the snuff of a candle — usually used in plural but singular or plural in construction
2 : a device for extinguishing candles

²snuffer *noun* (circa 1610)
: one that snuffs or sniffs

¹snuf·fle \ˈsnə-fəl\ *verb* **snuf·fled; snuf·fling** \-f(ə-)liŋ\ [akin to Dutch *snuffelen* to snuffle — more at SNIVEL] (circa 1600)
intransitive verb
1 : to snuff or sniff usually audibly and repeatedly
2 : to breathe through an obstructed nose with a sniffing sound
3 : to speak through or as if through the nose : WHINE
transitive verb
: to seek or test by or as if by repeated sniffs
— **snuf·fler** \-f(ə-)lər\ *noun*

²snuffle *noun* (circa 1764)
1 : the act or sound of snuffling
2 : a nasal twang
3 *plural* : SNIFFLES

¹snuffy \ˈsnə-fē\ *adjective* [⁴*snuff*] (1678)
1 : quick to become annoyed or take offense
2 : marked by snobbery

²snuffy *adjective* [⁶*snuff*] (1787)
1 : resembling snuff
2 a : addicted to the use of snuff **b** : having unpleasant habits
3 : soiled with snuff

¹snug \ˈsnəg\ *verb* **snugged; snug·ging** [²*snug*] (1583)
intransitive verb
: SNUGGLE
transitive verb
1 : to cause to fit closely
2 : to make snug
3 : HIDE
4 : to secure by fastening or lashing down

²snug *adjective* **snug·ger; snug·gest** [perhaps of Scandinavian origin; akin to Swedish *snygg* tidy] (circa 1595)
1 a *of a ship* : manifesting seaworthiness : TAUT **b** : TRIM, NEAT **c** : fitting closely and comfortably ⟨a *snug* coat⟩
2 a : enjoying or affording warm secure shelter or cover and opportunity for ease and contentment **b** : marked by cordiality and secure privacy
3 : affording a degree of comfort and ease
4 : offering safe concealment ⟨a *snug* hideout⟩
synonym see COMFORTABLE
— **snug** *adverb*
— **snug·ly** *adverb*
— **snug·ness** *noun*

³snug *noun* [short for *snuggery*] (1860)

British **:** a small private room or compartment in a pub

snug·gery \'snə-g(ə-)rē\ *noun, plural* **-ger·ies** (1812)
chiefly British **:** a snug cozy place; *especially*
: a small room

snug·gle \'snə-gəl\ *verb* **snug·gled; snug·gling** \-g(ə-)liŋ\ [frequentative of ¹*snug*] (1687)
intransitive verb
: to curl up comfortably or cozily
transitive verb
1 : to draw close especially for comfort or in affection
2 : to make snug
— **snuggle** *noun*

¹so \'sō, *especially before adjective or adverb followed by "that"* sə\ *adverb* [Middle English, from Old English *swā;* akin to Old High German *sō* so, Latin *sic* so, thus, *si* if, Greek *hōs* so, thus, Latin *suus* one's own — more at SUICIDE] (before 12th century)
1 a : in a manner or way indicated or suggested ⟨do you really think *so*⟩ — often used as a substitute for a preceding clause ⟨are you ready? I think *so*⟩ ⟨I didn't like it and I told her *so*⟩ **b :** in the same manner or way **:** ALSO ⟨worked hard and *so* did she⟩ **c :** THUS ⟨for *so* the Lord said —Isaiah 18:4 (Authorized Version)⟩ **d :** THEN, SUBSEQUENTLY ⟨and *so* home and to bed⟩
2 a : to an indicated or suggested extent or degree ⟨had never been *so* happy⟩ **b :** to a great extent or degree **:** VERY, EXTREMELY ⟨loves her *so*⟩ **c :** to a definite but unspecified extent or degree ⟨can only do *so* much in a day⟩ **d :** most certainly **:** INDEED ⟨you did *so* do it⟩
3 : THEREFORE, CONSEQUENTLY ⟨the witness is biased and *so* unreliable⟩ ▫
²so *conjunction* (before 12th century)
1 a : with the result that ⟨the acoustics are good, *so* every note is clear⟩ **b :** in order that ⟨be quiet *so* he can sleep⟩
2 *archaic* **:** provided that
3 a : for that reason **:** THEREFORE ⟨don't want to go, *so* I won't⟩ **b** (1) — used as an introductory particle ⟨*so* here we are⟩ often to belittle a point under discussion ⟨*so* what?⟩ (2) — used interjectionally to indicate awareness of a discovery ⟨*so*, that's who did it⟩ or surprised dissent ▫
³so *adjective* (before 12th century)
1 : conforming with actual facts **:** TRUE ⟨said things that were not *so*⟩
2 : marked by a desired order ⟨his books are always just *so*⟩
3 — used to replace a preceding adjective ⟨was witty by adult standards and of course doubly *so* by mine —Sally Kempton⟩
⁴so *pronoun* (before 12th century)
1 : such as has been specified or suggested **:** the same ⟨if you have to file a claim, do *so* as soon as possible⟩
2 — used in the phrase *or so* to indicate an estimate, approximation, or conjecture ⟨stayed a week or *so*⟩ ⟨cost $15 or *so*⟩
⁵so *variant of* SOL
¹soak \'sōk\ *verb* [Middle English *soken,* from Old English *socian;* akin to Old English *sūcan* to suck] (before 12th century)
intransitive verb
1 : to lie immersed in liquid (as water) **:** become saturated by or as if by immersion
2 a : to enter or pass through something by or as if by pores or interstices **:** PERMEATE **b :** to penetrate or affect the mind or feelings — usually used with *in* or *into*
3 : to drink alcoholic beverages intemperately
transitive verb
1 : to permeate so as to wet, soften, or fill thoroughly
2 : to place in a surrounding element (as liquid) to wet or permeate thoroughly
3 : to extract by or as if by steeping ⟨*soak* the dirt out⟩

4 a : to draw in by or as if by suction or absorption ⟨*soaked* up the sunshine⟩ **b :** to intoxicate (oneself) by drinking alcoholic beverages
5 : to cause to pay an exorbitant amount ☆
— **soak·er** *noun*
²soak *noun* (15th century)
1 a : the act or process of soaking **:** the state of being soaked **b :** that (as liquid) in which something is soaked
2 : DRUNKARD
3 *slang* **:** ²PAWN 2
¹so–and–so \'sō-ən-ˌsō\ *noun, plural* **so-and–sos** *or* **so–and–so's** \-ˌsōz\ (1596)
1 : an unnamed or unspecified person, thing, or action
2 : BASTARD 3
²so–and–so *adverb* (1631)
1 : to an unspecified amount or degree
2 : in an unspecified manner or fashion
¹soap \'sōp\ *noun* [Middle English *sope,* from Old English *sāpe;* akin to Old High German *seifa* soap] (before 12th century)
1 a : a cleansing and emulsifying agent made usually by action of alkali on fat or fatty acids and consisting essentially of sodium or potassium salts of such acids **b :** a salt of a fatty acid and a metal
2 : SOAP OPERA
²soap *transitive verb* (1585)
1 : to rub soap over or into
2 : FLATTER
soap·bark \'sōp-ˌbärk\ *noun* (1861)
: a Chilean tree (*Quillaja saponaria*) of the rose family with glossy leaves and terminal white flowers; *also* **:** its saponin-rich bark used in cleaning and in emulsifying oils
soap·ber·ry \-ˌber-ē\ *noun* (1693)
: any of a genus (*Sapindus*) of the family Sapindaceae, the soapberry family) of chiefly tropical woody plants; *also* **:** the fruit of a soapberry and especially of a tree (*S. saponaria*) that is saponin-rich and used as a soap substitute
soap·box \-ˌbäks\ *noun* (1907)
: an improvised platform used by a self-appointed, spontaneous, or informal orator; *broadly* **:** something that provides an outlet for delivering opinions
— **soapbox** *adjective*
soap bubble *noun* (1800)
: a hollow iridescent globe formed by blowing a film of soapsuds (as from a pipe)
soap·er \'sō-pər\ *noun* (1946)
: SOAP OPERA
soap opera *noun* [from its sponsorship by soap manufacturers] (1939)
1 a : a serial drama performed originally on a daytime radio or television program and chiefly characterized by tangled interpersonal situations and melodramatic or sentimental treatment **b :** a series of real-life events resembling a soap opera
2 : the melodrama and sentimentality characteristic of a soap opera ⟨even cops need a little *soap opera* in their lives —Joseph Wambaugh⟩; *also* **:** something (as a novel) having such qualities
soap plant *noun* (1844)
: a plant having a part (as a root or fruit) that may be used in place of soap; *especially* **:** a California plant (*Chlorogalum pomeridianum*) of the lily family
soap·stone \'sōp-ˌstōn\ *noun* (circa 1681)
: a soft stone having a soapy feel and composed essentially of talc, chlorite, and often some magnetite
soap·suds \-ˌsədz\ *noun plural* (1611)
: SUDS 1
soap·wort \-ˌwərt, -ˌwȯrt\ *noun* (1548)
: BOUNCING BET
soapy \'sō-pē\ *adjective* **soap·i·er; -est** (1610)
1 : smeared with soap **:** LATHERED
2 : containing or combined with soap or saponin

3 a : resembling or having the qualities of soap; *especially* **:** being smooth and slippery **b :** UNCTUOUS, SUAVE
4 : of, relating to, or having the characteristics of soap opera
— **soap·i·ly** \-pə-lē\ *adverb*
— **soap·i·ness** \-pē-nəs\ *noun*
¹soar \'sōr, 'sȯr\ *intransitive verb* [Middle English *soren,* from Middle French *essorer,* from (assumed) Vulgar Latin *exaurare,* from Latin *ex- + aura* air — more at AURA] (14th century)
1 a : to fly aloft or about **b** (1) **:** to sail or hover in the air often at a great height **:** GLIDE (2) *of a glider* **:** to fly without engine power and without loss of altitude
2 : to rise or increase dramatically (as in position, value, or price)
3 : to ascend to a higher or more exalted level
4 : to rise to majestic stature
— **soar·er** *noun*
²soar *noun* (1596)
1 : the range, distance, or height attained in soaring
2 : the act of soaring **:** upward flight
soar·ing *noun* (15th century)
: the act or process of soaring; *specifically* **:** the act or sport of flying a heavier-than-air craft without power by utilizing ascending air currents
Soa·ve \'swä-(ˌ)vā\ *noun* [*Soave,* village near Verona, Italy] (1935)

☆ SYNONYMS
Soak, saturate, drench, steep, impregnate mean to permeate or be permeated with a liquid. SOAK implies usually prolonged immersion as for softening or cleansing ⟨*soak* the garment in soapy water⟩. SATURATE implies a resulting effect of complete absorption until no more liquid can be held ⟨a *saturated* sponge⟩. DRENCH implies a thorough wetting by something that pours down or is poured ⟨clothes *drenched* by a cloudburst⟩. STEEP suggests either the extraction of an essence (as of tea leaves) by the liquid or the imparting of a quality (as a color) to the thing immersed ⟨*steep* the tea for five minutes⟩. IMPREGNATE implies a thorough interpenetration of one thing by another ⟨a cake strongly *impregnated* with brandy⟩.

▫ USAGE
¹so The intensive use of the adverb *so* (sense 2b) is widely condemned in college handbooks but is nonetheless standard ⟨why is American television *so* shallow? —Anthony Lewis⟩ ⟨the cephalopod eye is an example of a remarkable evolutionary parallel because it is *so* like the eye of a vertebrate —Sarah F. Robbins⟩ ⟨the kind of sterile over-ingenuity which afflicts *so* many academic efforts —*Times Literary Supplement*⟩. There is no stigma attached to its use in negative contexts and when qualified by a dependent clause ⟨not *so* long ago⟩ ⟨was *so* good in mathematics that he began to consider engineering —*Current Biography*⟩. The denotation in these uses is, of course, slightly different (see sense 2a).

²so Although occasionally condemned, use of the conjunction *so* to introduce clauses of result (sense 1a) and purpose (sense 1b) is standard. In sense 1b *so that* is more common in formal contexts than *so* alone.

\ə\ abut \ᵊ\ kitten \ər\ further \a\ ash \ā\ ace
\ä\ mop, mar \aù\ out \ch\ chin \e\ bet \ē\ easy
\g\ go \i\ hit \ī\ ice \j\ job \ŋ\ sing \ō\ go
\ȯ\ law \ȯi\ boy \th\ thin \t͟h\ the \ü\ loot \ù\ foot
\y\ yet \zh\ vision *see also* Guide to Pronunciation

: a dry white Italian wine

¹sob \'säb\ *verb* **sobbed; sob·bing** [Middle English *sobben*] (13th century)
intransitive verb
1 a : to catch the breath audibly in a spasmodic contraction of the throat **b :** to cry or weep with convulsive catching of the breath
2 : to make a sound like that of a sob or sobbing
transitive verb
1 : to bring (as oneself) to a specified state by sobbing ⟨*sobbed* himself to sleep⟩
2 : to utter with sobs ⟨*sobbed* out her grief⟩

²sob *noun* (14th century)
1 : an act of sobbing
2 : a sound like that of a sob

SOB \,es-,ō-'bē\ *noun* [*s*on *o*f a *b*itch] (1918)
: BASTARD 3, SON OF A BITCH

¹so·ber \'sō-bər\ *adjective* **so·ber·er** \-bər-ər\; **so·ber·est** \-b(ə-)rəst\ [Middle English *sobre*, from Middle French, from Latin *sobrius*; akin to Latin *ebrius* drunk] (14th century)
1 a : sparing in the use of food and drink : ABSTEMIOUS **b :** not addicted to intoxicating drink **c :** not drunk
2 : marked by sedate or gravely or earnestly thoughtful character or demeanor
3 : UNHURRIED, CALM
4 : marked by temperance, moderation, or seriousness
5 : subdued in tone or color
6 : showing no excessive or extreme qualities of fancy, emotion, or prejudice
synonym see SERIOUS
— **so·ber·ly** \-bər-lē\ *adverb*
— **so·ber·ness** *noun*

²sober *verb* **so·bered; so·ber·ing** \-b(ə-)riŋ\ (14th century)
transitive verb
: to make sober
intransitive verb
: to become sober — usually used with *up*

so·ber·ing *adjective* (1816)
: tending to make one thoughtful or sober

so·ber·ize \'sō-bə-,rīz\ *transitive verb* **-ized; -iz·ing** (1706)
archaic : to make sober

so·ber·sid·ed \,sō-bər-'sī-dəd\ *adjective* (1847)
: solemn or serious in nature or appearance
— **so·ber·sid·ed·ness** \-nəs\ *noun*

so·ber·sides \'sō-bər-,sīdz\ *noun plural but singular or plural in construction* (1705)
: a sobersided person

so·bri·ety \sə-'brī-ə-tē, sō-\ *noun* [Middle English *sobrietie*, from Middle French *sobrieté*, from Latin *sobrietat-, sobrietas*, from *sobrius*] (15th century)
: the quality or state of being sober

so·bri·quet \'sō-bri-,kā, -,ket, ,sō-bri-'\ *noun* [French] (1646)
: a descriptive name or epithet : NICKNAME

sob sister *noun* (1912)
1 : a journalist who specializes in writing or editing sob stories or other material of a sentimental type
2 : a sentimental and often impractical person usually engaged in good works

sob story *noun* (1913)
: a sentimental story or account intended chiefly to evoke sympathy or sadness

so·cage \'sä-kij, 'sō-\ *also* **soc·cage** \'sä-\ *noun* [Middle English, from *soc* soke] (14th century)
: a tenure of land by agricultural service fixed in amount and kind or by payment of money rent only and not burdened with any military service
— **so·cag·er** \-ki-jər\ *noun*

so—called \'sō-'kȯld\ *adjective* (15th century)
1 : commonly named : popularly so termed ⟨the *so-called* pocket veto⟩
2 : falsely or improperly so named ⟨deceived by a *so-called* friend⟩

soc·cer \'sä-kər\ *noun* [by shortening & alteration from *association football*] (1889)
: a game played on a field between two teams of 11 players each with the object to propel a round ball into the opponent's goal by kicking or by hitting it with any part of the body except the hands and arms — called also *association football* ◇

so·cia·bil·i·ty \,sō-shə-'bi-lə-tē\ *noun, plural* **-ties** (15th century)
: the quality or state of being sociable; *also* : the act or an instance of being sociable

¹so·cia·ble \'sō-shə-bəl\ *adjective* [Middle French or Latin; Middle French, from Latin *sociabilis*, from *sociare* to join, associate, from *socius*] (1553)
1 : inclined by nature to companionship with others of the same species : SOCIAL
2 a : inclined to seek or enjoy companionship **b :** marked by or conducive to friendliness or pleasant social relations
synonym see GRACIOUS
— **so·cia·ble·ness** *noun*
— **so·cia·bly** \-blē\ *adverb*

²sociable *noun* (1750)
: an informal social gathering frequently involving a special activity or interest

¹so·cial \'sō-shəl\ *adjective* [Middle English, from Latin *socialis*, from *socius* companion, ally, associate; akin to Old English *secg* man, companion, Latin *sequi* to follow — more at SUE] (14th century)
1 : involving allies or confederates ⟨the *Social* War between the Athenians and their allies⟩
2 a : marked by or passed in pleasant companionship with one's friends or associates ⟨leads a very full *social* life⟩ **b :** SOCIABLE **c :** of, relating to, or designed for sociability ⟨a *social* club⟩
3 : of or relating to human society, the interaction of the individual and the group, or the welfare of human beings as members of society ⟨*social* institutions⟩
4 a : tending to form cooperative and interdependent relationships with others of one's kind : GREGARIOUS **b :** living and breeding in more or less organized communities ⟨*social* insects⟩ **c :** *of a plant* : tending to grow in groups or masses so as to form a pure stand
5 a : of, relating to, or based on rank or status in a particular society ⟨a member of our *social* set⟩ **b :** of, relating to, or characteristic of the upper classes **c :** FORMAL

²social *noun* (1870)
: SOCIABLE

social climber *noun* (1924)
: one who attempts to gain a higher social position or acceptance in fashionable society
— **social climbing** *noun*

social contract *noun* (circa 1850)
: an actual or hypothetical agreement among individuals forming an organized society or between the community and the ruler that defines and limits the rights and duties of each

social Darwinism *noun* (1887)
: an extension of Darwinism to social phenomena; *specifically* : a theory in sociology: sociocultural advance is the product of intergroup conflict and competition and the socially elite classes (as those possessing wealth and power) possess biological superiority in the struggle for existence
— **social Darwinist** *noun or adjective*

social democracy *noun* (1888)
: a political movement advocating a gradual and peaceful transition from capitalism to socialism by democratic means
— **social democrat** *noun*
— **social democratic** *adjective*

social disease *noun* (1891)
1 : VENEREAL DISEASE
2 : a disease (as tuberculosis) whose incidence is directly related to social and economic factors

social drinker *noun* (circa 1949)

: a person who drinks alcoholic beverages in moderation at social gatherings especially as distinguished from one who drinks habitually or to excess

social engineering *noun* (1925)
: management of human beings in accordance with their place and function in society : applied social science
— **social engineer** *noun*

social gospel *noun* (1890)
1 : the application of Christian principles to social problems
2 *S&G capitalized* **:** a movement in American Protestant Christianity especially in the first part of the 20th century to bring the social order into conformity with Christian principles

social insurance *noun* (1909)
: protection of the individual against economic hazards (as unemployment, old age, or disability) in which the government participates or enforces the participation of employers and affected individuals

so·cial·ise *British variant of* SOCIALIZE

so·cial·ism \'sō-shə-,li-zəm\ *noun* (1837)
1 : any of various economic and political theories advocating collective or governmental ownership and administration of the means of production and distribution of goods
2 a : a system of society or group living in which there is no private property **b :** a system or condition of society in which the means of production are owned and controlled by the state
3 : a stage of society in Marxist theory transitional between capitalism and communism and distinguished by unequal distribution of goods and pay according to work done

so·cial·ist \'sō-sh(ə-)list\ *noun* (1827)
1 : one who advocates or practices socialism
2 *capitalized* **:** a member of a party or political group advocating socialism
— **socialist** *adjective, often capitalized*
— **so·cial·is·tic** \,sō-shə-'lis-tik\ *adjective*
— **so·cial·is·ti·cal·ly** \-ti-k(ə-)lē\ *adverb*

socialist realism *noun* (1934)
: a Marxist aesthetic theory calling for the didactic use of literature, art, and music to develop social consciousness in an evolving socialist state
— **socialist realist** *noun or adjective*

so·cial·ite \'sō-shə-,līt\ *noun* (1928)
: a socially prominent person

◇ **WORD HISTORY**
soccer At University College, Oxford, in 1875, it became fashionable among students to create slang versions of everyday words or phrases by clipping them to a single syllable and adding the empty suffix *-er*. Allegedly this linguistic fad originated at Rugby, one of England's exclusive private boys schools (called by tradition "public schools"). Whether this is true or not, *footer* for *football* is attested at Harrow, another private school, in 1863—the earliest of these clipped words to see print. Most examples, such as *fresher* "freshman," *brekker* "breakfast," *tosher* "student unattached to a college," and *ekker* "exercise" are unfamiliar to North Americans, and many more have proved ephemeral even in Britain. However, one *-er* coinage has become extraordinarily successful in the U.S.: the word *soccer*, clipped from *association* (or *assoc.*) football, the game played according to the rules of the Football Association founded in England in 1863. *Football* now denotes only the game of soccer in most of the English-speaking world and has been borrowed into many other languages around the world. But in the U.S. a different kind of kicking game claimed the word, and *soccer* has been adopted as the name for what Americans still tend to think of as an imported sport.

so·ci·al·i·ty \ˌsō-shē-'a-lə-tē\ *noun, plural* **-ties** (circa 1649)
1 a : SOCIABILITY **b :** an instance of social intercourse or sociability
2 : the tendency to associate in or form social groups

so·cial·ize \'sō-shə-ˌlīz\ *verb* **-ized; -iz·ing** (1828)
transitive verb
1 : to make social; *especially* **:** to fit or train for a social environment
2 a : to constitute on a socialistic basis ⟨*socialize* industry⟩ **b :** to adapt to social needs or uses ⟨*socialize* science⟩
3 : to organize group participation in ⟨*socialize* a recitation⟩
intransitive verb
: to participate actively in a social group
— **so·cial·i·za·tion** \ˌsō-sh(ə-)lə-'zā-shən\ *noun*
— **so·cial·iz·er** \'sō-shə-ˌlī-zər\ *noun*

socialized medicine *noun* (1938)
: medical and hospital services for the members of a class or population administered by an organized group (as a state agency) and paid for from funds obtained usually by assessments, philanthropy, or taxation

so·cial·ly \'sō-sh(ə-)lē\ *adverb* (circa 1763)
1 : in a social manner
2 : with respect to society
3 : by or through society

so·cial–mind·ed \ˌsō-shəl-'mīn-dəd\ *adjective* (1927)
: having an interest in society; *specifically* **:** actively interested in social welfare or the well-being of society as a whole

social psychology *noun* (1891)
: the study of the manner in which the personality, attitudes, motivations, and behavior of the individual influence and are influenced by social groups
— **social psychologist** *noun*

social science *noun* (1811)
1 : a branch of science that deals with the institutions and functioning of human society and with the interpersonal relationships of individuals as members of society
2 : a science (as economics or political science) dealing with a particular phase or aspect of human society
— **social scientist** *noun*

social secretary *noun* (1903)
: a personal secretary employed to handle social correspondence and appointments

social security *noun* (1908)
1 : the principle or practice or a program of public provision (as through social insurance or assistance) for the economic security and social welfare of the individual and his or her family; *especially, often both Ss capitalized* **:** a U.S. government program established in 1935 to include old-age and survivors insurance, contributions to state unemployment insurance, and old-age assistance
2 : money paid out through a social security program ⟨began collecting *social security*⟩

social service *noun* (1851)
: an activity designed to promote social well-being; *specifically* **:** organized philanthropic assistance of the sick, destitute, or unfortunate **:** WELFARE WORK

social studies *noun plural* (1926)
: a part of a school or college curriculum concerned with the study of social relationships and the functioning of society and usually made up of courses in history, government, economics, civics, sociology, geography, and anthropology

social welfare *noun* (1917)
: organized public or private social services for the assistance of disadvantaged groups; *specifically* **:** SOCIAL WORK

social work *noun* (1890)
: any of various professional activities or methods concretely concerned with providing social services and especially with the investi-

gation, treatment, and material aid of the economically underprivileged and socially maladjusted
— **social worker** *noun*

so·ci·e·tal \sə-'sī-ə-t°l\ *adjective* (1898)
: of or relating to society **:** SOCIAL ⟨*societal* forces⟩
— **so·ci·e·tal·ly** \-t°l-ē\ *adverb*

¹**so·ci·e·ty** \sə-'sī-ə-tē\ *noun, plural* **-ties** [Middle French *societé,* from Latin *societat-, societas,* from *socius* companion — more at SOCIAL] (1531)
1 : companionship or association with one's fellows **:** friendly or intimate intercourse **:** COMPANY
2 : a voluntary association of individuals for common ends; *especially* **:** an organized group working together or periodically meeting because of common interests, beliefs, or profession
3 a : an enduring and cooperating social group whose members have developed organized patterns of relationships through interaction with one another **b :** a community, nation, or broad grouping of people having common traditions, institutions, and collective activities and interests
4 a : a part of a community that is a unit distinguishable by particular aims or standards of living or conduct **:** a social circle or a group of social circles having a clearly marked identity ⟨move in polite *society*⟩ ⟨literary *society*⟩ **b :** a part of the community that sets itself apart as a leisure class and that regards itself as the arbiter of fashion and manners
5 a : a natural group of plants usually of a single species or habit within an association **b :** the progeny of a pair of insects when constituting a social unit (as a hive of bees); *broadly* **:** an interdependent system of organisms or biological units

²**society** *adjective* (1693)
: of, relating to, or characteristic of fashionable society

So·cin·i·an \sə-'si-nē-ən, sō-\ *noun* [New Latin *socinianus,* from Faustus *Socinus*] (1645)
: an adherent of a 16th and 17th century theological movement professing belief in God and adherence to the Christian Scriptures but denying the divinity of Christ and consequently denying the Trinity
— **Socinian** *adjective*
— **So·cin·i·an·ism** \-nē-ə-ˌni-zəm\ *noun*

socio- *combining form* [French, from Latin *socius* companion]
1 : social ⟨*socio*gram⟩
2 : social and ⟨*socio*political⟩

so·cio·bi·ol·o·gy \ˌsō-sē-ō-bī-'ä-lə-jē, ˌsō-shē-\ *noun* (1946)
: the comparative study of social organization in animals including humans especially with regard to its genetic basis and evolutionary history
— **so·cio·bio·log·i·cal** \-ˌbī-ə-'lä-ji-kəl\ *adjective*
— **so·cio·bi·ol·o·gist** \-bī-'ä-lə-jist\ *noun*

so·cio·cul·tur·al \-'kəlch-rəl, -'kəl-chə-\ *adjective* (1928)
: of, relating to, or involving a combination of social and cultural factors
— **so·cio·cul·tur·al·ly** \-rə-lē\ *adverb*

so·cio·eco·nom·ic \-ˌe-kə-'nä-mik, -ˌē-kə-\ *adjective* (1883)
: of, relating to, or involving a combination of social and economic factors
— **so·cio·eco·nom·i·cal·ly** \-mi-k(ə-)lē\ *adverb*

so·cio·gram \'sō-sē-ə-ˌgram, 'sō-shē-\ *noun* (1933)
: a sociometric chart plotting the structure of interpersonal relations in a group situation

so·cio·his·tor·i·cal \ˌsō-sē-ō-his-'tòr-i-kəl, ˌsō-shē-, -'tär-\ *adjective* (1949)
: of, relating to, or involving social history or a combination of social and historical factors

so·cio·lin·guist \-'liŋ-gwist\ *noun* (1960)

: a linguist specializing in sociolinguistics

so·cio·lin·guis·tic \-liŋ-'gwis-tik\ *adjective* (1949)
1 : of or relating to the social aspects of language
2 : of or relating to sociolinguistics

so·cio·lin·guis·tics \-tiks\ *noun plural but singular in construction* (1938)
: the study of linguistic behavior as determined by sociocultural factors

so·ci·ol·o·gese \ˌsō-sē-ˌä-lə-'jēz, ˌsō-shē-, -'jēs\ *noun* [*sociology* + ²*-ese*] (1952)
: a style of writing held to be characteristic of sociologists

so·cio·log·i·cal \ˌsō-sē-ə-'lä-ji-kəl, ˌsō-sh(ē-)ə-\ *also* **so·cio·log·ic** \-jik\ *adjective* (1843)
1 : of or relating to sociology or to the methodological approach of sociology
2 : oriented or directed toward social needs and problems
— **so·cio·log·i·cal·ly** \-ji-k(ə-)lē\ *adverb*

so·ci·ol·o·gy \ˌsō-sē-'ä-lə-jē, ˌsō-shē-\ *noun* [French *sociologie,* from *socio-* + *-logie* -logy] (1843)
1 : the science of society, social institutions, and social relationships; *specifically* **:** the systematic study of the development, structure, interaction, and collective behavior of organized groups of human beings
2 : the scientific analysis of a social institution as a functioning whole and as it relates to the rest of society
3 : SYNECOLOGY
— **so·ci·ol·o·gist** \-jist\ *noun*

so·ci·om·e·try \-'ä-mə-trē\ *noun* [International Scientific Vocabulary] (1908)
: the study and measurement of interpersonal relationships in a group of people
— **so·cio·met·ric** \ˌsō-sē-ə-'me-trik, ˌsō-shē-\ *adjective*

so·cio·path \'sō-sē-ə-ˌpath, 'sō-sh(ē-)ə-\ *noun* (1930)
: PSYCHOPATH

so·cio·path·ic \ˌsō-sē-ə-'pa-thik, ˌsō-sh(ē-)ə-\ *adjective* (1930)
: of, relating to, or characterized by asocial or antisocial behavior or a psychopathic personality

so·cio·po·lit·i·cal \ˌsō-sē-ō-pə-'li-ti-kəl, ˌsō-shē-\ *adjective* (1884)
: of, relating to, or involving a combination of social and political factors

so·cio·psy·cho·log·i·cal \-ˌsī-kə-'lä-ji-kəl\ *adjective* (1899)
1 : of, relating to, or involving a combination of social and psychological factors
2 : of or relating to social psychology

so·cio·re·li·gious \-ri-'li-jəs\ *adjective* (1871)
: involving a combination of social and religious factors

so·cio·sex·u·al \-'sek-sh(ə-)wəl, -'sek-shəl\ *adjective* (1932)
: of or relating to the interpersonal aspects of sexuality

¹**sock** \'säk\ *noun, plural* **socks** [Middle English *socke,* from Old English *socc,* from Latin *soccus*] (before 12th century)
1 *archaic* **:** a low shoe or slipper
2 *also plural* **sox** \'säks\ **:** a knitted or woven covering for the foot usually extending above the ankle and sometimes to the knee
3 a : a shoe worn by actors in Greek and Roman comedy **b :** comic drama
— **sock·less** *adjective*

²**sock** *verb* [origin unknown] (circa 1700)
transitive verb
: to hit, strike, or apply forcefully ⟨*sock* a home run⟩ ⟨an area *socked* by a blizzard⟩

intransitive verb
: to deliver a blow : HIT
— **sock it to** *slang* : to subject to or as if to a vigorous assault ⟨they may let you off the first time . . . but the second time they'll *sock it to* you —James Jones⟩

³sock *noun* (circa 1700)
: a vigorous or violent blow; *also* : ²PUNCH 3

sock away *transitive verb* [from the practice of concealing savings in the toe of a sock] (circa 1942)
: to put away (money) as savings or investment

sock·dol·a·ger *or* **sock·dol·o·ger** \säk-'dä-li-jər\ *noun* [origin unknown] (circa 1830)
1 : something that settles a matter : a decisive blow or answer : FINISHER
2 : something outstanding or exceptional

¹sock·et \'sä-kət\ *noun* [Middle English *soket*, from Anglo-French, diminutive of Old French *soc* plowshare, of Celtic origin; akin to Middle Irish *soc* plowshare, snout; akin to Old English *sugu* sow — more at SOW] (15th century)
: an opening or hollow that forms a holder for something ⟨an electric bulb *socket*⟩ ⟨the eye *socket*⟩

²socket *transitive verb* (1533)
: to provide with or support in or by a socket

socket wrench *noun* (circa 1890)
: a wrench usually in the form of a bar and removable socket made to fit a bolt or nut

sock·eye \'säk-,ī\ *noun* [by folk etymology from Northern Straits (Salishan language of southern Vancouver Island and nearby islands) *sə́qəy̓*] (1869)
: a small but commercially important Pacific salmon (*Oncorhynchus nerka*) that ascends rivers chiefly from the Columbia northward to spawn in late summer or fall — called also *red salmon*

socket wrenches

sock in *transitive verb* [(wind) sock] (1944)
1 : to close to takeoffs or landings by aircraft ⟨an airport *socked in* by fog⟩
2 : to restrict from flying

socko \'sä-(,)kō\ *adjective* [²sock] (1938)
: strikingly impressive, effective, or successful : OUTSTANDING

so·cle \'sō-kəl, 'sä-\ *noun* [French, from Italian *zoccolo* sock, socle, from Latin *socculus*, diminutive of *soccus* sock] (circa 1704)
: a projecting usually molded member at the foot of a wall or pier or beneath the base of a column, pedestal, or superstructure

¹So·crat·ic \sə-'kra-tik, sō-\ *adjective* (1628)
: of or relating to Socrates, his followers, or his philosophical method of systematic doubt and questioning of another to elicit a clear expression of a truth supposed to be implicitly known by all rational beings
— **So·crat·i·cal·ly** \-ti-k(ə-)lē\ *adverb*

²Socratic *noun* (1678)
: a follower of Socrates

Socratic irony *noun* (circa 1871)
: IRONY 1

¹sod \'säd\ *noun* [Middle English, from Middle Dutch or Middle Low German *sode;* akin to Old Frisian *sātha* sod] (15th century)
1 : TURF 1; *also* : the grass- and forb-covered surface of the ground
2 : one's native land

²sod *transitive verb* **sod·ded; sod·ding** (1653)
: to cover with sod or turfs

³sod *noun* [short for *sodomite*] (1818)
chiefly British : BUGGER ⟨if I ever find the *sod* I'll kill him —John Le Carré⟩ ⟨he's not a bad little *sod* taken by and large —Noel Coward⟩

⁴sod *transitive verb* (1904)
chiefly British : DAMN 2

so·da \'sō-də\ *noun* [Italian, from Arabic *suwwād*, any of several saltworts from the ashes of which sodium carbonate is obtained] (1558)
1 a : SODIUM CARBONATE **b** : SODIUM BICARBONATE **c** : SODIUM — used in combination ⟨*soda* alum⟩
2 a : SODA WATER 2a **b** : SODA POP **c** : a sweet drink consisting of soda water, flavoring, and often ice cream
3 : the faro card that shows faceup in the dealing box before play begins

soda ash *noun* (1839)
: commercial anhydrous sodium carbonate

soda biscuit *noun* (1830)
1 : a biscuit leavened with baking soda and sour milk or buttermilk
2 : SODA CRACKER

soda bread *noun* (1850)
: a quick bread made especially with buttermilk and leavened with baking soda

soda cracker *noun* (1830)
: a cracker leavened with bicarbonate of soda and cream of tartar

soda fountain *noun* (1824)
1 : an apparatus with delivery tube and faucets for drawing soda water
2 : the equipment and counter for the preparation and serving of sodas, sundaes, and ice cream

soda jerk \-,jərk\ *noun* (1922)
: a person who dispenses carbonated drinks and ice cream at a soda fountain — called also *soda jerker*

soda lime *noun* (1862)
: a mixture of sodium hydroxide and slaked lime used especially to absorb moisture and gases

so·da·list \'sō-dᵊl-ist, sō-'da-list\ *noun* (1794)
: a member of a sodality

so·da·lite \'sō-dᵊl-,īt\ *noun* [soda] (1810)
: a transparent to translucent mineral that consists of a silicate of sodium and aluminum with some chlorine, has a vitreous or greasy luster, and is found in various igneous rocks

so·dal·i·ty \sō-'da-lə-tē\ *noun, plural* **-ties** [Latin *sodalitat-, sodalitas* comradeship, club, from *sodalis* comrade — more at SIB] (1600)
1 : BROTHERHOOD, COMMUNITY
2 : an organized society or fellowship; *specifically* : a devotional or charitable association of Roman Catholic laity

soda pop *noun* (1863)
: a beverage consisting of soda water, flavoring, and a sweet syrup

soda water *noun* (1802)
1 : a weak solution of sodium bicarbonate with some acid added to cause effervescence
2 a : a beverage consisting of water highly charged with carbon dioxide **b** : SODA POP

sod·bust·er \'säd-,bəs-tər\ *noun* (circa 1918)
: one (as a farmer or a plow) that breaks the sod

¹sod·den \'sä-dᵊn\ *adjective* [Middle English *soden*, from past participle of *sethen* to seethe] (1589)
1 a : dull or expressionless especially from continued indulgence in alcoholic beverages ⟨*sodden* features⟩ **b** : TORPID, SLUGGISH ⟨*sodden* minds⟩
2 a : heavy with or as if with moisture or water ⟨the *sodden* ground⟩ **b** : heavy or doughy because of imperfect cooking ⟨*sodden* biscuits⟩
— **sod·den·ly** *adverb*
— **sod·den·ness** \-dᵊn-(n)əs\ *noun*

²sodden *verb* **sod·dened; sod·den·ing** \'säd-niŋ, 'sä-dᵊn-iŋ\ (1812)
transitive verb
: to make sodden
intransitive verb
: to become soaked or saturated

so·dic \'sō-dik\ *adjective* (1859)
: of, relating to, or containing sodium

so·di·um \'sō-dē-əm\ *noun* [New Latin, from English *soda*] (1807)

: a silver white soft waxy ductile element of the alkali metal group that occurs abundantly in nature in combined form and is very active chemically — see ELEMENT table

sodium azide *noun* (circa 1937)
: a poisonous crystalline salt NaN_3 used especially to make lead azide

sodium benzoate *noun* (circa 1900)
: a crystalline or granular salt $C_7H_5O_2Na$ used chiefly as a food preservative

sodium bicarbonate *noun* (1885)
: a white crystalline weakly alkaline salt $NaHCO_3$ used especially in baking powders, fire extinguishers, and medicine — called also *baking soda, bicarbonate of soda*

sodium bo·ro·hy·dride \-,bȯr-ə-'hī-,drīd, -,bȯr-\ *noun* [*sodium* + *boron* + *hydride*] (1946)
: a crystalline compound $NaBH_4$ used in various industrial applications and as a reducing agent in organic chemistry

sodium carbonate *noun* (1868)
: a sodium salt of carbonic acid used especially in making soaps and chemicals, in water softening, in cleaning and bleaching, and in photography: as **a** : a hygroscopic crystalline anhydrous strongly alkaline salt Na_2CO_3 **b** : WASHING SODA

sodium chlorate *noun* (1885)
: a colorless crystalline salt $NaClO_3$ used especially as an oxidizing agent and weed killer

sodium chloride *noun* (1868)
: an ionic crystalline chemical compound consisting of equal numbers of sodium and chlorine atoms : SALT 1a

sodium citrate *noun* (1919)
: a crystalline salt $Na_3C_6H_5O_7$ used chiefly as a buffering agent, as an emulsifier, as an alkalizer and cathartic in pharmaceuticals, and as a blood anticoagulant

sodium cyanide *noun* (1885)
: a white deliquescent poisonous salt $NaCN$ used especially in electroplating, in fumigating, and in treating steel

sodium dichromate *noun* (circa 1903)
: a red crystalline salt $Na_2Cr_2O_7$ used especially in tanning leather, in cleaning metals, and as an oxidizing agent

sodium fluoride *noun* (circa 1903)
: a poisonous crystalline salt NaF that is used in trace amounts in the fluoridation of water, in metallurgy, as a flux, and as a pesticide

sodium fluo·ro·ac·e·tate \-,flu̇r-ō-'a-sə-,tāt, -,flȯr-, -,flōr-\ *noun* (1945)
: a poisonous powdery compound $C_2H_2FNaO_2$ — compare 1080

sodium hydroxide *noun* (1885)
: a white brittle solid $NaOH$ that is a strong caustic base used especially in making soap, rayon, and paper

sodium hypochlorite *noun* (1885)
: an unstable salt $NaOCl$ produced usually in aqueous solution and used as a bleaching and disinfecting agent

sodium meta·sil·i·cate \-,me-tə-'si-lə-,kāt, -'si-li-kət\ *noun* (circa 1926)
: a toxic corrosive crystalline salt Na_2SiO_3 used especially as a detergent or as a substitute for phosphates in detergent formulations

sodium nitrate *noun* (1885)
: a deliquescent crystalline salt $NaNO_3$ used as a fertilizer and an oxidizing agent and in curing meat

sodium nitrite *noun* (circa 1903)
: a salt $NaNO_2$ used especially in dye manufacture and as a meat preservative

sodium pump *noun* (1951)
: a molecular mechanism by which sodium ions are actively transported across a cell membrane; *especially* : the one by which the appropriate internal and external concentrations of sodium and potassium ions are maintained in a nerve fiber and which involves the active transport of sodium ions outward with movement of potassium ions to the interior

sodium salicylate *noun* (circa 1904)

: a crystalline salt NaC$_7$H$_5$O$_3$ that has a sweetish saline taste and is used chiefly as an analgesic, antipyretic, and antirheumatic

sodium sulfate *noun* (1885)
: a bitter salt Na$_2$SO$_4$ used especially in detergents, in the manufacture of wood pulp and rayon, in dyeing and finishing textiles, and in its hydrated form as a cathartic — compare GLAUBER'S SALT

sodium thiosulfate *noun* (1885)
: a hygroscopic crystalline salt Na$_2$S$_2$O$_3$ used especially as a photographic fixing agent and a reducing or bleaching agent — called also *hypo*

so·di·um tri·poly·phos·phate \-,trī-,pä-li-'fäs-,fāt\ *noun* (1945)
: a crystalline salt Na$_5$P$_3$O$_{10}$ that is used as a food additive and as a component in some detergents and is suspected of contributing to water pollution

sodium–vapor lamp *noun* (1936)
: an electric lamp that contains sodium vapor and electrodes between which a luminous discharge takes place and that is used especially for lighting highways

sod off *intransitive verb* [4sod] (1960)
British : SCRAM — usually used as a command

Sod·om \'sä-dəm\ *noun* [*Sodom*, ancient city destroyed by God for its wickedness in Genesis 19] (1598)
: a place notorious for vice or corruption

sod·om·ist \'sä-də-mist\ *noun* (1891)
: SODOMITE

sod·om·ite \-,mīt\ *noun* (14th century)
: one who practices sodomy

sod·om·ize \-,mīz\ *transitive verb* **-ized; -iz·ing** (1868)
: to perform sodomy on

sod·omy \'sä-də-mē\ *noun* [Middle English, from Old French *sodomie*, from Late Latin *Sodoma* Sodom; from the homosexual proclivities of the men of the city in Genesis 19:1–11] (13th century)
1 : copulation with a member of the same sex or with an animal
2 : noncoital and especially anal or oral copulation with a member of the opposite sex
— **sod·om·it·ic** \,sä-də-'mi-tik\ *or* **sod·om·it·i·cal** \-ti-kəl\ *adjective*

so·ev·er \sō-'e-vər\ *adverb* [*-soever* (as in *howsoever*)] (12th century)
1 : to any possible or known extent — used after an adjective preceded by *how* or a superlative preceded by *the* ⟨how fair *soever* she may be⟩ ⟨the most selfish *soever* in this world⟩
2 : of any or every kind that may be specified — used after a noun modified especially by *any, no,* or *what* ⟨gives no information *soever*⟩

so·fa \'sō-fə\ *noun* [Arabic *ṣuffah* long bench] (1717)
: a long upholstered seat usually with arms and a back and often convertible into a bed

sofa bed *noun* (1816)
: a sofa that can be made to serve as a bed by lowering its hinged upholstered back to horizontal position or by pulling out a concealed mattress

so·far \'sō-,fär\ *noun* [*so*und *f*ixing *a*nd *r*anging] (1946)
: a system for locating an underwater explosion at sea by triangulation based on the reception of the sound by three widely separated stations

so far as *conjunction* (1565)
: INSOFAR AS

sof·fit \'sä-fət\ *noun* [French *soffite*, from Italian *soffitto*, from (assumed) Vulgar Latin *suffictus*, past participle of Latin *suffigere* to fasten underneath — more at SUFFIX] (1592)
: the underside of a part or member of a building (as of an overhang or staircase); *especially*
: the intrados of an arch

1**soft** \'sȯft\ *adjective* [Middle English, from Old English *sōfte*, alteration of *sēfte;* akin to Old High German *semfti* soft] (before 12th century)
1 a : pleasing or agreeable to the senses : bringing ease, comfort, or quiet ⟨the *soft* influences of home⟩ **b** : having a bland or mellow rather than a sharp or acid taste **c** (1) : not bright or glaring : SUBDUED (2) : having or producing little contrast or a relatively short range of tones ⟨a *soft* photographic print⟩ **d** : quiet in pitch or volume **e** *of the eyes* : having a liquid or gentle appearance **f** : smooth or delicate in texture, grain, or fiber ⟨*soft* cashmere⟩ ⟨*soft* fur⟩ **g** (1) : balmy, mild, or clement in weather or temperature (2) : moving or falling with slight force or impact : not violent ⟨*soft* breezes⟩
2 : demanding little work or effort : EASY ⟨a *soft* job⟩
3 a : sounding as in *ace* and *gem* respectively — used of *c* and *g* or their sound **b** *of a consonant* : VOICED **c** : constituting a vowel before which there is a \y\ sound or a \y\-like modification of a consonant or constituting a consonant in whose articulation there is a \y\-like modification or which is followed by a \y\ sound (as in Russian)
4 *archaic* : moving in a leisurely manner
5 : rising gradually ⟨a *soft* slope⟩
6 : having curved or rounded outline : not harsh or jagged ⟨*soft* hills against the horizon⟩
7 : marked by a gentleness, kindness, or tenderness: as **a** (1) : not harsh or onerous in character ⟨a policy of *soft* competition⟩ (2) : based on negotiation, conciliation, or flexibility rather than on force, threats, or intransigence ⟨took a *soft* line during the crisis⟩ (3) : tending to take a soft line — usually used with *on* ⟨*soft* on dictators⟩ ⟨*soft* on law and order⟩ **b** : tending to ingratiate or disarm : ENGAGING, KIND ⟨a *soft* answer turns away wrath —Proverbs 15:1 (Revised Standard Version)⟩ **c** : marked by mildness : UNASSUMING, LOW-KEY
8 a : emotionally suggestible or responsive : IMPRESSIONABLE **b** : unduly susceptible to influence : COMPLIANT **c** : lacking firmness or strength of character : FEEBLE, UNMANLY **d** : amorously attracted or emotionally involved — used with *on* ⟨has been *soft* on her for years⟩
9 a : lacking robust strength, stamina, or endurance especially because of living in ease or luxury ⟨grown *soft* and indolent⟩ **b** : weak or deficient mentally ⟨*soft* in the head⟩
10 a : yielding to physical pressure **b** : permitting someone or something to sink in — used of wet ground **c** (1) : of a consistency that may be shaped or molded (2) : capable of being spread **d** : easily magnetized and demagnetized **e** : lacking relatively or comparatively in hardness ⟨*soft* iron⟩
11 : deficient in or free from substances (as calcium and magnesium salts) that prevent lathering of soap ⟨*soft* water⟩
12 : having relatively low energy ⟨*soft* X rays⟩
13 *of news* : relatively less serious or significant
14 : occurring at such a speed and under such circumstances as to avoid destructive impact ⟨*soft* landing of a spacecraft on the moon⟩
15 : not protected against enemy attack ⟨a *soft* aboveground launching site⟩ ⟨*soft* targets⟩
16 : BIODEGRADABLE ⟨a *soft* detergent⟩ ⟨*soft* pesticides⟩
17 *of a drug* : considered less detrimental than a hard narcotic
18 : easily polarized — used of acids and bases
19 a *of currency* : not readily convertible **b** *of a loan* : not secured by collateral
20 a : being low due to sluggish market conditions ⟨*soft* prices⟩ **b** : SLUGGISH, SLOW ⟨a *soft* market⟩

21 : not firmly committed ⟨*soft* unreliable political support⟩
22 : SOFT-CORE ⟨*soft* porn⟩
23 a : being or based on interpretive or speculative data ⟨*soft* evidence⟩ **b** : utilizing or based on soft data ⟨*soft* science⟩
24 : being or using renewable sources of energy (as solar radiation, wind, or tides) ⟨*soft* technologies⟩
— **soft·ish** \'sȯf-tish\ *adjective*
— **soft·ly** \'sȯf(t)-lē\ *adverb*
— **soft·ness** \'sȯf(t)-nəs\ *noun*

2**soft** *adverb* (before 12th century)
: in a soft or gentle manner : SOFTLY

3**soft** *noun* (15th century)
: a soft object, material, or part ⟨the *soft* of the thumb⟩

soft·back \'sȯf(t)-,bak\ *adjective* (1958)
: SOFTCOVER
— **softback** *noun*

soft·ball \-,bȯl\ *noun* (1926)
: baseball played on a small diamond with a ball that is larger than a baseball and that is pitched underhand; *also* : the ball used in this game
— **soft·ball·er** \-,bȯ-lər\ *noun*

soft-boiled \-'bȯi(ə)ld\ *adjective* (circa 1902)
1 *of an egg* : boiled to a soft consistency
2 : SENTIMENTAL

soft·bound \-,baùnd\ *adjective* (1953)
: SOFTCOVER

soft chancre *noun* (1859)
: CHANCROID

soft coal *noun* (1789)
: BITUMINOUS COAL

soft–coated wheaten terrier *noun* (1948)
: any of a breed of compact medium-sized terriers developed in Ireland and having a soft abundant lightly fawn coat

soft–core \'sȯf(t)-'kōr, -'kȯr\ *adjective* [1*soft* + hard-*core*] (1966)
of pornography : containing descriptions or scenes of sex acts that are less explicit than hard-core material

soft·cov·er \-,kə-vər\ *adjective* (1952)
: bound in flexible covers : not bound in hard covers; *specifically* : PAPERBACK ⟨*softcover* books⟩
— **softcover** *noun*

soft drink *noun* (1880)
: a usually carbonated nonalcoholic beverage; *especially* : SODA POP

soft·en \'sȯ-fən\ *verb* **soft·ened; soft·en·ing** \'sȯ-fə-niŋ, 'sȯf-niŋ\ (14th century)
transitive verb
1 : to make soft or softer
2 a : to weaken the military resistance or the morale of especially by harassment (as preliminary bombardment) — often used with *up* **b** : to impair the strength or resistance of — often used with *up* ⟨*soften* up a sales prospect⟩
intransitive verb
: to become soft or softer
— **soft·en·er** \'sȯ-fə-nər, 'sȯf-nər\ *noun*

soft–fo·cus \'sȯf(t)-'fō-kəs\ *adjective* (1916)
1 *of a photographic image* : having unsharp outlines
2 *of a lens* : producing an image having unsharp outlines

soft goods *noun plural* (1894)
: goods that are not durable — used especially of textile products

soft hail *noun* (1894)
: GRAUPEL

soft·head \'sȯft-,hed\ *noun* (1650)
: a silly or feebleminded person

soft·head·ed \-,he-dəd\ *adjective* (1667)
: having or indicative of a weak, unrealistic, or uncritical mind
— **soft·head·ed·ly** *adverb*

\ə\ abut \ᵊ\ kitten \ər\ further \a\ ash \ā\ ace \ä\ mop, mar \aù\ out \ch\ chin \e\ bet \ē\ easy \g\ go \i\ hit \ī\ ice \j\ job \ŋ\ sing \ō\ go \ȯ\ law \ȯi\ boy \th\ thin \th\ the \ü\ loot \ù\ foot \y\ yet \zh\ vision *see also* Guide to Pronunciation

— **soft·head·ed·ness** *noun*

soft·heart·ed \-,här-təd\ *adjective* (1593)
: emotionally responsive : SYMPATHETIC
— **soft·heart·ed·ly** *adverb*
— **soft·heart·ed·ness** *noun*

soft–land \-'land\ *verb* [back-formation from *soft landing*] (1960)
transitive verb
: to cause to make a soft landing on a celestial body (as the moon)
intransitive verb
: to make a soft landing
— **soft–lander** *noun*

soft–line \-'līn\ *adjective* (1949)
: advocating or involving a conciliatory or flexible course of action
— **soft–lin·er** \-'lī-nər\ *noun*

soft palate *noun* (circa 1811)
: the fold at the back of the hard palate that partially separates the mouth and pharynx

soft–ped·al \'sóf(t)-'pe-dᵊl\ *transitive verb* (1925)
1 : PLAY DOWN, DE-EMPHASIZE ⟨*soft-pedal* the issue⟩
2 : to use the soft pedal in playing

soft pedal *noun* (1854)
1 : a foot pedal on a piano that reduces the volume of sound
2 : something that muffles, deadens, or reduces effect

soft rock *noun* (1967)
: rock music that is less driving and gentler sounding than hard rock

soft rot *noun* (1901)
: a mushy, watery, or slimy decay of plants or their parts caused by bacteria or fungi

soft sell *noun* (1954)
: the use of suggestion or gentle persuasion in selling rather than aggressive pressure — compare HARD SELL

soft–shell \'sóf(t)-,shel\ *noun* (1771)
: any of a family (Trionychidae) of aquatic turtles that have sharp claws and mandibles and a flat shell covered with soft leathery skin instead of with horny plates — called also *soft-shelled turtle*

softshell

soft–shell \'sóf(t)-,shel\ *or* **soft–shelled** \-'sheld\ *adjective* (1805)
: having a soft or fragile shell especially as a result of recent shedding ⟨*soft-shell* crabs⟩

soft–shell clam *noun* (1796)
: an elongated clam (*Mya arenaria*) of the east coast of North America that has a thin friable shell and long siphons and is used especially for steaming — called also *soft-shelled clam, steamer*

soft–shoe \'sóf(t)-,shü\ *adjective* (1920)
: of or relating to tap dancing done in soft-soled shoes without metal taps

soft–soap \'sóf(t)-'sōp\ *transitive verb* (1840)
: to soothe or persuade with flattery or blarney
— **soft–soap·er** \-,sō-pər\ *noun*

soft soap *noun* (1634)
1 : a semifluid soap made especially from potassium hydroxide
2 : FLATTERY

soft–spo·ken \-'spō-kən\ *adjective* (1609)
: having a mild or gentle voice; *also* : SUAVE

soft spot *noun* (1845)
1 : a sentimental weakness ⟨has a *soft spot* for him⟩
2 : a vulnerable point ⟨a *soft spot* in the defense system⟩

soft touch *noun* (1939)
: one who is easily imposed on or taken advantage of

soft·ware \'sóft-,war, -,wer\ *noun* (1960)
: something used or associated with and usually contrasted with hardware: as **a** : the entire set of programs, procedures, and related documentation associated with a system and especially a computer system; *specifically* : computer programs **b** : materials for use with audiovisual equipment

soft wheat *noun* (1812)
: a wheat with soft starchy kernels high in starch but usually low in gluten

soft·wood \'sóft-,wùd\ *noun* (1832)
1 : the wood of a coniferous tree (as a fir or pine) whether hard or soft as distinguished from that of an angiospermous tree
2 : a tree that yields softwood

softwood *adjective* (1905)
: having or made of softwood

soft–wood·ed \'sóft-,wù-dəd\ *adjective* (1827)
1 : having soft wood that is easy to work or finish
2 : SOFTWOOD

softy *or* **soft·ie** \'sóf-tē\ *noun, plural* **soft·ies** [¹*soft*] (1863)
1 : a weak or foolish person
2 : a softhearted or sentimental person

Sog·di·an \'säg-dē-ən\ *noun* [Latin *Sogdiani*, plural, from Greek *Sogdianoi*, from Old Persian *Suguda* Sogdiana] (1553)
1 : a native or inhabitant of Sogdiana
2 : an Iranian language of the Sogdians — see INDO-EUROPEAN LANGUAGES table
— **Sogdian** *adjective*

sog·gy \'sä-gē, 'só-\ *adjective* **sog·gi·er; -est** [English dialect *sog* to soak] (1599)
1 : saturated or heavy with water or moisture: as **a** : WATERLOGGED, SOAKED ⟨a *soggy* lawn⟩ **b** : heavy or doughy because of imperfect cooking ⟨*soggy* bread⟩
2 : heavily dull : SPIRITLESS ⟨*soggy* prose⟩
— **sog·gi·ly** \'sä-gə-lē, 'só-\ *adverb*
— **sog·gi·ness** \'sä-gē-nəs, 'só-\ *noun*

soi–di·sant \,swä-dē-'zäⁿ\ *adjective* [French, literally, saying oneself] (1752)
: SELF-STYLED, SO-CALLED — usually used disparagingly ⟨a *soi-disant* artist⟩

soi·gné *or* **soi·gnée** \swän-'yā\ *adjective* [French, from past participle of *soigner* to take care of] (1821)
1 : WELL-GROOMED, SLEEK
2 : elegantly maintained or designed ⟨a *soigné* restaurant⟩ ⟨a *soigné* black dress⟩

soil \'sói(ə)l\ *verb* [Middle English, from Old French *souillier* to wallow, soil, from *soil* abyss, pigpen, probably from Latin *solium* chair, bathtub; akin to Latin *sedēre* to sit — more at SIT] (13th century)
transitive verb
1 : to stain or defile morally : CORRUPT, POLLUTE
2 : to make unclean especially superficially : DIRTY
3 : to blacken or besmirch (as a person's reputation) by word or deed
intransitive verb
: to become soiled or dirty

soil *noun* (1501)
1 a : SOILAGE, STAIN ⟨protect a dress from *soil*⟩ **b** : moral defilement : CORRUPTION
2 : something that spoils or pollutes: as **a** : REFUSE **b** : SEWAGE **c** : DUNG, EXCREMENT

soil *noun* [Middle English, from Anglo-French, probably from Latin *solium* chair] (14th century)
1 : firm land : EARTH
2 a : the upper layer of earth that may be dug or plowed and in which plants grow **b** : the superficial unconsolidated and usually weathered part of the mantle of a planet and especially of the earth
3 : COUNTRY, LAND ⟨our native *soil*⟩
4 : the agricultural life or calling
5 : a medium in which something takes hold and develops

soil *transitive verb* [origin unknown] (1605)
: to feed (livestock) in the barn or an enclosure with fresh grass or green food; *also* : to purge (livestock) by feeding on green food

soil·age \'sói-lij\ *noun* [¹*soil*] (1926)
: the act of soiling : the condition of being soiled

soilage *noun* [⁴*soil*] (1928)
: green crops for feeding confined animals

soil bank *noun* (1955)
: acreage retired from crop cultivation and planted with soil-building plants under a plan sponsored by the U.S. government that provides subsidies to farmers for the retired land

soil·borne \'sóil-,bórn, -,bórn\ *adjective* (1944)
: transmitted by or in soil ⟨*soilborne* fungi⟩ ⟨*soilborne* diseases⟩

soil·less \'sói(ə)l-ləs\ *adjective* (1938)
: having, containing, or utilizing no soil ⟨*soilless* agriculture⟩

soil pipe *noun* (1833)
: a pipe for carrying off wastes from toilets

soil science *noun* (1915)
: a science dealing with soils — called also *pedology*
— **soil scientist** *noun*

soil series *noun* (1905)
: a group of soils with similar profiles developed from similar parent materials under comparable climatic and vegetational conditions

soil·ure \'sói-yər\ *noun* [Middle English, from Old French *soilleure*, from *souillier* to soil] (13th century)
1 : the act of soiling : the condition of being soiled
2 : STAIN, SMUDGE

soi·ree *or* **soi·rée** \swä-'rā\ *noun* [French *soirée* evening period, evening party, from Middle French, from *soir* evening, from Latin *sero* at a late hour, from *serus* late; akin to Old Irish *sír* long, lasting and perhaps to Old English *sīth* late — more at SINCE] (1802)
: a party or reception held in the evening

soi·xante–neuf \swä-säⁿt-nœf\ *noun* [French] (1888)
: SIXTY-NINE 2

so·journ \'sō-,jərn, sō-'\ *noun* [Middle English *sojorn*, from Old French, from *sojorner*] (13th century)
: a temporary stay ⟨a *sojourn* in the country⟩

sojourn *intransitive verb* [Middle English *sojornen*, from Old French *sojorner*, from (assumed) Vulgar Latin *subdiurnare*, from Latin *sub* under, during + Late Latin *diurnum* day — more at UP, JOURNEY] (14th century)
: to stay as a temporary resident : STOP ⟨*sojourned* for a month at a resort⟩
— **so·journ·er** *noun*

soke \'sōk\ *noun* [Middle English *soc, soke*, from Old English *soka*, from Medieval Latin *soca*, from Old English *sōcn* inquiry, jurisdiction; akin to Old English *sēcan* to seek] (12th century)
1 : the right in Anglo-Saxon and early English law to hold court and administer justice with the franchise to receive certain fees or fines arising from it : jurisdiction over a territory or over people
2 : the district included in a soke jurisdiction or franchise

soke·man \'sōk-mən\ *noun* (1579)
: a man who is under the soke of another

sol \'sól\ *also* **so** \'sō\ *noun* [Medieval Latin *sol;* from the syllable sung to this note in a medieval hymn to Saint John the Baptist] (14th century)
: the 5th tone of the diatonic scale in solmization

sol \'säl, 'sól\ *noun* [Middle French — more at SOU] (1583)
: an old French coin equal to 12 deniers; *also* : a corresponding unit of value

sol \'säl, 'sól\ *noun, plural* **so·les** \'sō-(,)lās\ [American Spanish, from Spanish, sun, from Latin] (circa 1883)

: the basic monetary unit of Peru before 1985 and since 1990 — see MONEY table

⁴sol \'säl, 'sȯl\ *noun* [-sol (as in *hydrosol*), from *solution*] (1899)
: a fluid colloidal system; *especially* : one in which the continuous phase is a liquid

Sol \'säl\ *noun* [Middle English, from Latin]
1 : the Roman god of the sun — compare HELIOS
2 : SUN

sola *plural of* SOLUM

¹so·lace \'sä-ləs *also* 'sō-\ *transitive verb* **so·laced; so·lac·ing** (13th century)
1 : to give solace to : CONSOLE
2 a : to make cheerful **b** : AMUSE
3 : ALLAY, SOOTHE ⟨*solace* grief⟩
— **so·lace·ment** \-mənt\ *noun*
— **so·lac·er** *noun*

²solace *noun* [Middle English *solas,* from Old French, from Latin *solacium,* from *solari* to console] (14th century)
1 : alleviation of grief or anxiety
2 : a source of relief or consolation

so·la·na·ceous \ˌsō-lə-'nā-shəs\ *adjective* [New Latin *Solanaceae,* family name, from *Solanum*] (1804)
: of or relating to the nightshade family of plants

so·la·nine *also* **so·la·nin** \'sō-lə-ˌnēn, -nən\ *noun* [French *solanine,* from Latin *solanum*] (1838)
: a bitter poisonous crystalline alkaloid $C_{45}H_{73}NO_{15}$ from several plants (as some potatoes or tomatoes) of the nightshade family

so·la·num \sō-'lā-nəm, -'lä-, -'la-\ *noun* [New Latin, from Latin, nightshade] (circa 1652)
: any of a genus (*Solanum*) chiefly of herbs and shrubs of the nightshade family that have often prickly-veined leaves, cymose white, purple, or yellow flowers, and a fruit that is a berry

so·lar \'sō-lər, -ˌlär\ *adjective* [Middle English, from Latin *solaris,* from *sol* sun; akin to Old English & Old Norse *sōl* sun, Lithuanian *saulė,* Greek *hēlios*] (15th century)
1 : of, derived from, or relating to the sun especially as affecting the earth
2 : measured by the earth's course in relation to the sun ⟨*solar* time⟩ ⟨*solar* year⟩; *also* : relating to or reckoned by solar time
3 a : produced or operated by the action of the sun's light or heat ⟨*solar* energy⟩ ⟨*solar* cooker⟩ **b** : utilizing the sun's rays especially to produce heat or electricity ⟨a *solar* house⟩; *also* : of or relating to such utilization ⟨*solar* design⟩ ⟨*solar* subsidies⟩

solar battery *noun* (1954)
: an array of solar cells

solar cell *noun* (1955)
: a photovoltaic cell (as one including a junction between two types of silicon semiconductors) that is able to convert light into electrical energy and is used as a power source

solar collector *noun* (1955)
: any of various devices for the absorption of solar radiation for the heating of water or buildings or the production of electricity

solar constant *noun* (1869)
: the quantity of radiant solar energy received at the outer layer of the earth's atmosphere that has a mean value of 1370 watts per square meter

solar day *noun* (1764)
: the interval between transits of the apparent or mean sun across the meridian at any place

solar eclipse *noun* (circa 1890)
: an eclipse of the sun by the moon — see ECLIPSE illustration

solar flare *noun* (1938)
: a sudden temporary outburst of energy from a small area of the sun's surface — called also *flare*

so·lar·i·um \sō-'lar-ē-əm, sə-, -'ler-\ *noun, plural* **-ia** \-ē-ə\ *also* **-ums** [Latin, porch exposed to the sun, from *sol*] (circa 1823)
: a glass-enclosed porch or room; *also* : a room (as in a hospital) used especially for sunbathing or therapeutic exposure to light

so·lar·i·za·tion \ˌsō-lə-rə-'zā-shən\ *noun* (1853)
1 : a reversal of gradation in a photographic image obtained by intense or continued exposure
2 : an act or process of solarizing

so·lar·ize \'sō-lə-ˌrīz\ *transitive verb* **-ized; -iz·ing** (1853)
1 a : to affect by the action of the sun's rays **b** : to expose to sunlight
2 : to subject (photographic materials) to solarization

solar panel *noun* (1961)
: a battery of solar cells (as in a spacecraft)

so·lar plexus \'sō-lər-\ *noun* [from the radiating nerve fibers] (1771)
1 : a nerve plexus in the abdomen that is situated behind the stomach and in front of the aorta and the crura of the diaphragm and contains several ganglia distributing nerve fibers to the viscera
2 : the pit of the stomach

solar pond *noun* (1961)
: a pool of salt water heated by the sun and used either as a direct source of heat or to provide power for an electric generator

solar sail *noun* (1958)
: a propulsive device for a spacecraft that consists of a flat material (as aluminized plastic) designed to receive thrust from solar radiation pressure

solar system *noun* (circa 1704)
: the sun together with the group of celestial bodies that are held by its attraction and revolve around it; *also* : a similar system centered on another star

solar wind *noun* (1958)
: plasma continuously ejected from the sun's surface into and through interplanetary space

so·la·tion \sä-'lā-shən, sò-\ *noun* (1915)
: the process of changing to a sol

so·la·ti·um \sō-'lā-shē-əm\ *noun, plural* **-tia** \-shē-ə\ [Late Latin *solacium, solatium,* from Latin, solace] (1817)
: a compensation (as money) given as solace for suffering, loss, or injured feelings

sold *past and past participle of* SELL

sol·dan \'säl-dən, 'sōl-\ *noun* [Middle English, from Old French, from Arabic *sulṭān*] (14th century)
archaic : SULTAN; *especially* : the sultan of Egypt

¹sol·der \'sä-dər, 'sò-, *British also* 'säl-dər, 'sōl-\ *noun* [Middle English *soudure,* from Middle French, from *souder* to solder, from Latin *solidare* to make solid, from *solidus* solid] (14th century)
1 : a metal or metallic alloy used when melted to join metallic surfaces; *especially* : an alloy of lead and tin so used
2 : something that unites

²solder *verb* **sol·dered; sol·der·ing** \-d(ə-)riŋ\ (15th century)
transitive verb
1 : to unite or make whole by solder
2 : to bring into or restore to firm union ⟨a friendship *soldered* by common interests⟩
intransitive verb
1 : to use solder
2 : to become united or repaired by or as if by solder
— **sol·der·abil·i·ty** \ˌsä-də-rə-'bi-lə-tē, ˌsò-\ *noun*
— **sol·der·er** \'sä-dər-ər, 'sò-\ *noun*

soldering iron *noun* (1688)
: a pointed or wedge-shaped device that is usually electrically heated and that is used for soldering

¹sol·dier \'sōl-jər\ *noun* [Middle English *soudier,* from Middle French *soulde* pay, from Late Latin *solidus* solidus] (14th century)
1 a : one engaged in military service and especially in the army **b** : an enlisted man or woman **c** : a skilled warrior
2 : a militant leader, follower, or worker
3 a : one of a caste of wingless sterile termites usually differing from workers in larger size and head and long jaws **b** : one of a type of worker ants distinguished by exceptionally large head and jaws
4 \'sō-jər, 'sōl-\ : one who shirks work
— **sol·dier·ly** \-lē\ *adjective or adverb*
— **sol·dier·ship** \-ˌship\ *noun*

²soldier *intransitive verb* **sol·diered; sol·dier·ing** \'sō-jə-riŋ, 'sōlj-riŋ\ (1647)
1 a : to serve as a soldier **b** : to behave in a soldierly manner **c** : to push doggedly forward — usually used with *on* ⟨*soldiered* on to the end⟩
2 : to make a pretense of working while really loafing

soldiering *noun* (1643)
: the life, service, or practice of one who soldiers

soldier of fortune (1661)
: one who follows a military career wherever there is promise of profit, adventure, or pleasure

soldiers' home *noun* (1860)
: an institution maintained (as by the federal or a state government) for the care and relief of military veterans

soldier's medal *noun* (circa 1930)
: a U.S. military decoration awarded for heroism not involving combat

sol·diery \'sōl-jə-rē, 'sōlj-rē\ *noun* (circa 1570)
1 a : a body of soldiers **b** : SOLDIERS, MILITARY
2 : the profession or technique of soldiering

sol·do \'sòl-(ˌ)dō\ *noun, plural* **sol·di** \-(ˌ)dē\ [Italian, from Late Latin *solidus* solidus] (1599)
: an old Italian coin worth five centesimi

sold–out \'sōld-'aùt\ *adjective* (1907)
: having all available tickets or accommodations sold completely and especially in advance

¹sole \'sōl\ *noun* [Middle English, from Middle French, from Latin *solea* sandal, a flatfish] (13th century)
: any of various flatfishes (family Soleidae) having a small mouth, small or rudimentary fins, and small eyes placed close together and including superior food fishes (as the European Dover sole); *also* : any of various mostly market flatfishes (as lemon sole) of other families (as Pleuronectidae)

²sole *noun* [Middle English, from Middle French, from Latin *solea* sandal; akin to Latin *solum* base, ground, soil] (14th century)
1 a : the undersurface of a foot **b** : the part of an item of footwear on which the sole rests and upon which the wearer treads
2 : the usually flat or flattened bottom or lower part of something or the base on which something rests
— **soled** \'sōld\ *adjective*

³sole *transitive verb* **soled; sol·ing** (1570)
1 : to furnish with a sole ⟨*sole* a shoe⟩
2 : to place the sole of (a golf club) on the ground

⁴sole *adjective* [Middle English, alone, from Middle French *seul,* from Latin *solus*] (14th century)
1 : not married — used chiefly of women
2 *archaic* : having no companion : SOLITARY
3 a : having no sharer **b** : being the only one ⟨she was her mother's *sole* support⟩
4 : functioning independently and without assistance or interference ⟨let conscience be the *sole* judge⟩

5 : belonging exclusively or otherwise limited to one usually specified individual, unit, or group
— **sole·ness** \'sōl-nəs\ *noun*

sol·e·cism \'sä-lə-ˌsi-zəm, 'sō-\ *noun* [Latin *soloecismus,* from Greek *soloikismos,* from *soloikos* speaking incorrectly, literally, inhabitant of Soloi, from *Soloi,* city in ancient Cilicia where a substandard form of Attic was spoken] (circa 1555)
1 : an ungrammatical combination of words in a sentence; *also* **:** a minor blunder in speech
2 : something deviating from the proper, normal, or accepted order
3 : a breach of etiquette or decorum
— **so·le·cis·tic** \ˌsä-lə-'sis-tik, ˌsō-\ *adjective*

sole·ly \'sō(l)-lē\ *adverb* (15th century)
1 : without another **:** SINGLY ⟨went *solely* on her way⟩
2 : to the exclusion of all else ⟨done *solely* for money⟩

sol·emn \'sä-ləm\ *adjective* [Middle English *solemne,* from Middle French, from Latin *sollemnis* regularly appointed, solemn] (14th century)
1 : marked by the invocation of a religious sanction ⟨a *solemn* oath⟩
2 : marked by the observance of established form or ceremony; *specifically* **:** celebrated with full liturgical ceremony
3 a : awe-inspiring **:** SUBLIME **b :** marked by grave sedateness and earnest sobriety **c :** SOMBER, GLOOMY
synonym see SERIOUS
— **sol·emn·ly** *adverb*
— **sol·emn·ness** *noun*

so·lem·ni·fy \sə-'lem-nə-ˌfī\ *transitive verb* **-fied; -fy·ing** (1780)
: to make solemn

so·lem·ni·ty \sə-'lem-nə-tē\ *noun, plural* **-ties** (14th century)
1 : formal or ceremonious observance of an occasion or event
2 : a solemn event or occasion
3 : a solemn condition or quality ⟨the *solemnity* of his words⟩

sol·em·nize \'sä-ləm-ˌnīz\ *verb* **-nized; -niz·ing** (14th century)
transitive verb
1 : to observe or honor with solemnity
2 : to perform with pomp or ceremony; *especially* **:** to celebrate (a marriage) with religious rites
3 : to make solemn **:** DIGNIFY
intransitive verb
: to speak or act with solemnity
— **sol·em·ni·za·tion** \ˌsä-ləm-nə-'zā-shən\ *noun*

solemn mass *noun* (15th century)
: a mass marked by the use of incense and by the presence of a deacon and a subdeacon in attendance on the celebrant

solemn vow *noun* (14th century)
: an absolute and irrevocable public vow taken by a religious in the Roman Catholic Church under which ownership of property by the individual is prohibited and marriage is invalid under canon law

so·le·noid \'sō-lə-ˌnȯid, 'sä-\ *noun* [French *solénoïde,* from Greek *sōlēnoeidēs* pipe-shaped, from Greek *sōlēn* pipe] (1827)
: a coil of wire usually in cylindrical form that when carrying a current acts like a magnet so that a movable core is drawn into the coil when a current flows and that is used especially as a switch or control for a mechanical device (as a valve)
— **so·le·noi·dal** \ˌsō-lə-'nȯi-dᵊl, ˌsä-\ *adjective*

sole·plate \'sōl-ˌplāt\ *noun* (1741)
1 : the lower plate of a studded partition on which the bases of the studs butt
2 : the undersurface of a flatiron

soles *plural of* SOL

so·le·us \'sō-lē-əs\ *noun, plural* **so·lei** \-lē-ˌī\ [New Latin, from Latin *solea* sandal — more at SOLE] (1676)
: a broad flat muscle of the calf of the leg lying immediately below the gastrocnemius

¹sol–fa \ˌsōl-'fä, 'sōl-ˌ\ (circa 1529)
intransitive verb
: to sing the sol-fa syllables
transitive verb
: to sing (as a melody) to sol-fa syllables

²sol–fa *noun* (1548)
1 : SOL-FA SYLLABLES
2 : SOLMIZATION; *also* **:** an exercise thus sung
3 : TONIC SOL-FA
— **sol–fa·ist** \-'fä(-i)st, -'fä-ˌist\ *noun*

sol–fa syllables *noun plural* (1913)
: the syllables *do, re, mi, fa, sol, la, ti,* used in singing the tones of the scale

sol·fa·ta·ra \ˌsōl-fə-'tär-ə\ *noun* [Italian, sulfur mine, from *solfo* sulfur, from Latin *sulfur*] (1777)
: a volcanic area or vent that yields only hot vapors and sulfurous gases

sol·fège \säl-'fezh\ *noun* [French, from Italian *solfeggio*] (circa 1903)
1 : the application of the sol-fa syllables to a musical scale or to a melody
2 : a singing exercise especially using sol-fa syllables; *also* **:** practice in sight-reading vocal music using the sol-fa syllables

sol·feg·gio \säl-'fe-j(ē-ˌ)ō\ *noun* [Italian, from *sol-fa*] (1774)
: SOLFÈGE

sol–gel \'säl-ˌjel, 'sōl-\ *adjective* (1915)
: involving alternation between sol and gel states

soli *plural of* SOLO

so·lic·it \sə-'li-sət\ *verb* [Middle English, to disturb, take charge of, from Middle French *solliciter,* from Latin *sollicitare* to disturb, from *sollicitus* anxious, from *sollus* whole (from Oscan; akin to Greek *holos* whole) + *citus,* past participle of *ciēre* to move — more at SAFE, -KINESIS] (15th century)
transitive verb
1 a : to make petition to **:** ENTREAT **b :** to approach with a request or plea
2 : to urge (as one's cause) strongly
3 a : to entice or lure especially into evil **b :** to proposition (someone) especially as or in the character of a prostitute
4 : to try to obtain by usually urgent requests or pleas
intransitive verb
1 : to make solicitation **:** IMPORTUNE
2 *of a prostitute* **:** to offer to have sexual relations with someone for money
synonym see ASK

so·lic·i·tant \sə-'li-sə-tənt\ *noun* (circa 1812)
: one who solicits

so·lic·i·ta·tion \sə-ˌli-sə-'tā-shən\ *noun* (circa 1520)
1 : the practice or act or an instance of soliciting; *especially* **:** ENTREATY, IMPORTUNITY
2 : a moving or drawing force **:** INCITEMENT, ALLUREMENT

so·lic·i·tor \sə-'li-sə-tər, -'lis-tər\ *noun* (15th century)
1 : one that solicits; *especially* **:** an agent that solicits (as contributions to charity)
2 : a British lawyer who advises clients, represents them in the lower courts, and prepares cases for barristers to try in higher courts
3 : the chief law officer of a municipality, county, or government department
— **so·lic·i·tor·ship** \-ˌship\ *noun*

solicitor general *noun, plural* **solicitors general** (1647)
: a law officer appointed primarily to assist an attorney general

so·lic·i·tous \sə-'li-sə-təs, -'lis-təs\ *adjective* [Latin *sollicitus*] (1563)
1 : manifesting or expressing solicitude ⟨a *solicitous* inquiry about his health⟩
2 : full of concern or fears **:** APPREHENSIVE ⟨*solicitous* about the future⟩

3 : meticulously careful ⟨*solicitous* in matters of dress⟩
4 : full of desire **:** EAGER
— **so·lic·i·tous·ly** *adverb*
— **so·lic·i·tous·ness** *noun*

so·lic·i·tude \sə-'li-sə-ˌtüd, -ˌtyüd\ *noun* (15th century)
1 a : the state of being solicitous **:** ANXIETY **b :** attentive care and protectiveness; *also* **:** an attitude of solicitous concern or attention
2 : a cause of care or concern — usually used in plural

¹sol·id \'sä-ləd\ *adjective* [Middle English *solide,* from Middle French, from Latin *solidus;* akin to Greek *holos* whole — more at SAFE] (14th century)
1 a : being without an internal cavity ⟨a *solid* ball of rubber⟩ **b** (1) **:** printed with minimum space between lines (2) **:** joined without a hyphen ⟨a *solid* compound⟩ **c :** not interrupted by a break or opening ⟨a *solid* wall⟩
2 : having, involving, or dealing with three dimensions or with solids ⟨*solid* configuration⟩
3 a : of uniformly close and coherent texture **:** not loose or spongy **:** COMPACT **b :** possessing or characterized by the properties of a solid **:** neither gaseous nor liquid
4 : of good substantial quality or kind ⟨*solid* comfort⟩: as **a :** SOUND ⟨*solid* reasons⟩ **b :** made firmly and well ⟨*solid* furniture⟩
5 a : having no break or interruption ⟨waited three *solid* hours⟩ **b :** UNANIMOUS ⟨had the *solid* support of the party⟩ **c :** intimately friendly or associated ⟨*solid* with the boss⟩
6 a : PRUDENT; *also* **:** well-established financially **b :** serious in purpose or character
7 : of one substance or character: as **a :** entirely of one metal or containing the minimum of alloy necessary to impart hardness ⟨*solid* gold⟩ **b :** of a single color
— **sol·id·ly** *adverb*
— **sol·id·ness** *noun*

²solid *noun* (15th century)
1 : a geometrical figure or element (as a cube or sphere) having three dimensions — see VOLUME table
2 a : a substance that does not flow perceptibly under moderate stress, has a definite capacity for resisting forces (as compression or tension) which tend to deform it, and under ordinary conditions retains a definite size and shape **b :** the part of a solution or suspension that when freed from solvent or suspending medium has the qualities of a solid — usually used in plural ⟨milk *solids*⟩
3 : something that is solid: as **a :** a solid color **b :** a compound word whose members are joined together without a hyphen

³solid *adverb* (1651)
: in a solid manner; *also* **:** UNANIMOUSLY

sol·i·da·go \ˌsä-lə-'dā-(ˌ)gō, -'dä-\ *noun, plural* **-gos** [New Latin, from Medieval Latin *soldago,* an herb reputed to heal wounds, from *soldare* to make whole, from Latin *solidare,* from *solidus* solid] (circa 1771)
: any of a genus (*Solidago*) of chiefly North American composite herbs including the typical goldenrods

solid angle *noun* (circa 1704)
: the three-dimensional angular spread at the vertex of a cone measured by the area intercepted by the cone on a unit sphere whose center is the vertex of the cone

sol·i·da·rism \'sä-lə-də-ˌri-zəm\ *noun* (1906)
: SOLIDARITY
— **sol·i·da·rist** \-rist\ *noun*
— **sol·i·da·ris·tic** \ˌsä-lə-də-'ris-tik\ *adjective*

sol·i·dar·i·ty \ˌsä-lə-'dar-ə-tē\ *noun* [French *solidarité,* from *solidaire* characterized by solidarity, from Latin *solidum* whole sum, from neuter of *solidus* solid] (1841)
: unity (as of a group or class) that produces or is based on community of interests, objectives, and standards

solid geometry *noun* (1733)

: a branch of geometry that deals with figures of three-dimensional space

so·lid·i·fy \sə-'li-də-ˌfī\ *verb* **-fied; -fy·ing** (1799)
transitive verb
1 : to make solid, compact, or hard
2 : to make secure, substantial, or firmly fixed ⟨factors that *solidify* public opinion⟩
intransitive verb
: to become solid, compact, or hard
— **so·lid·i·fi·ca·tion** \-ˌli-də-fə-'kā-shən\ *noun*

so·lid·i·ty \sə-'li-də-tē\ *noun, plural* **-ties** (14th century)
1 : the quality or state of being solid
2 : something solid

sol·id–look·ing \ˌsä-ləd-'lu̇k-iŋ\ *adjective* (1840)
: giving an impression of solid worth or substance ⟨*solid-looking* citizens⟩

solid of revolution (1816)
: a mathematical solid conceived as formed by the revolution of a plane figure about an axis in its plane

solid–state *adjective* (circa 1951)
1 : relating to the properties, structure, or reactivity of solid material; *especially* **:** relating to the arrangement or behavior of ions, molecules, nucleons, electrons, and holes in the crystals of a substance (as a semiconductor) or to the effect of crystal imperfections on the properties of a solid substance ⟨*solid-state* physics⟩
2 a : utilizing the electric, magnetic, or optical properties of solid materials ⟨*solid-state* circuitry⟩ **b :** using semiconductor devices rather than electron tubes ⟨a *solid-state* stereo system⟩

sol·i·dus \'sä-lə-dəs\ *noun, plural* **-i·di** \-lə-ˌdī, -ˌdē\ [Middle English, from Late Latin, from Latin, solid] (14th century)
1 : an ancient Roman gold coin introduced by Constantine and used to the fall of the Byzantine Empire
2 [Medieval Latin, shilling, from Late Latin; from its use as a symbol for shillings] **:** DIAGONAL 3

so·li·fluc·tion \'sō-lə-ˌflək-shən\ *noun* [Latin *solum* soil + *-i-* + *fluction-, fluctio* act of flowing, from *fluere* to flow — more at FLUID] (1906)
: the slow creeping of saturated fragmental material (as soil) down a slope that usually occurs in regions of perennial frost

so·lil·o·quist \sə-'li-lə-kwist\ *noun* (1804)
: one who soliloquizes

so·lil·o·quise British variant of SOLILOQUIZE

so·lil·o·quize \-ˌkwīz\ *intransitive verb* **-quized; -quiz·ing** (1759)
: to utter a soliloquy : talk to oneself
— **so·lil·o·quiz·er** *noun*

so·lil·o·quy \sə-'li-lə-kwē\ *noun, plural* **-quies** [Late Latin *soliloquium,* from Latin *solus* alone + *loqui* to speak] (circa 1613)
1 : the act of talking to oneself
2 : a dramatic monologue that gives the illusion of being a series of unspoken reflections

so·lip·sism \'sō-ləp-ˌsi-zəm, 'sä-\ *noun* [Latin *solus* alone + *ipse* self] (1874)
: a theory holding that the self can know nothing but its own modifications and that the self is the only existent thing
— **so·lip·sist** \'sō-ləp-sist, 'sä-ləp-, sə-'lip-\ *noun*
— **so·lip·sis·tic** \ˌsō-ləp-'sis-tik, ˌsä-\ *adjective*
— **so·lip·sis·ti·cal·ly** \-ti-k(ə-)lē\ *adverb*

sol·i·taire \'sä-lə-ˌtar, -ˌter\ *noun* [French, from *solitaire,* adjective, solitary, from Latin *solitarius*] (circa 1727)
1 : a single gem (as a diamond) set alone
2 : any of various card games that can be played by one person

¹sol·i·tary \'sä-lə-ˌter-ē\ *adjective* [Middle English, from Latin *solitarius,* from *solitas* aloneness, from *solus* alone] (14th century)

1 a : being, living, or going alone or without companions **b :** saddened by isolation
2 : UNFREQUENTED, DESOLATE
3 a : taken, passed, or performed without companions ⟨a *solitary* ramble⟩ **b :** keeping a prisoner apart from others ⟨*solitary* confinement⟩
4 : being at once single and isolated ⟨a *solitary* example⟩
5 a : occurring singly and not as part of a group or cluster ⟨flowers terminal and *solitary*⟩ **b :** not gregarious, colonial, social, or compound ⟨*solitary* bees⟩
synonym see ALONE
— **sol·i·tar·i·ly** \ˌsä-lə-'ter-ə-lē\ *adverb*
— **sol·i·tar·i·ness** \'sä-lə-ˌter-ē-nəs\ *noun*

²solitary *noun, plural* **-tar·ies** (15th century)
1 : one who lives or seeks to live a solitary life : RECLUSE
2 : solitary confinement in prison

sol·i·ton \'sä-lə-ˌtän\ *noun* [*solit*ary + ²-*on*] (1965)
: a solitary wave (as in a gaseous plasma) that propagates with little loss of energy and retains its shape and speed after colliding with another such wave

sol·i·tude \'sä-lə-ˌtüd, -ˌtyüd\ *noun* [Middle English, from Middle French, from Latin *solitudin-, solitudo,* from *solus*] (14th century)
1 : the quality or state of being alone or remote from society : SECLUSION
2 : a lonely place (as a desert) ☆

sol·i·tu·di·nar·i·an \ˌsä-lə-ˌtü-d°n-'er-ē-ən, -ˌtyü-\ *noun* [Latin *solitudin-, solitudo* + English *-arian*] (1691)
: RECLUSE

sol·ler·et \ˌsä-lə-'ret\ *noun* [French] (1826)
: a flexible steel shoe forming part of a medieval suit of armor — see ARMOR illustration

sol·mi·za·tion \ˌsäl-mə-'zā-shən\ *noun* [French *solmisation,* from *solmiser* to sol-fa, from *sol* (from Medieval Latin) + *mi* (from Medieval Latin) + *-iser* -ize] (1730)
: the act, practice, or system of using syllables to denote the tones of a musical scale

¹so·lo \'sō-(ˌ)lō\ *noun, plural* **solos** [Italian, from *solo* alone, from Latin *solus*] (1695)
1 *or plural* **so·li** \'sō-(ˌ)lē\ **a :** a musical composition for a single voice or instrument with or without accompaniment **b :** the featured part of a concerto or similar work
2 : a performance in which the performer has no partner or associate
3 : any of several card games in which a player elects to play without a partner against the other players

²solo *adverb* (1712)
: without a companion : ALONE ⟨fly *solo*⟩

³solo *adjective* (1774)
: of, relating to, or being a solo ⟨a *solo* performance⟩

⁴solo *intransitive verb* **so·loed; so·lo·ing** \-(ˌ)lō-iŋ, -lə-wiŋ\ (1886)
: to perform by oneself; *especially* **:** to fly an airplane without one's instructor on board

so·lo·ist \'sō-lə-wist, -(ˌ)lō-ist\ *noun* (1864)
: one who performs a solo

Sol·o·mon \'sä-lə-mən\ *noun* [Late Latin, from Hebrew *Shĕlōmōh*]
: a son of David and 10th century B.C. king of Israel proverbial for his wisdom

Sol·o·mon·ic \ˌsä-lə-'mä-nik\ *adjective* (1857)
: marked by notable wisdom, reasonableness, or discretion especially under trying circumstances

Solomon's seal *noun* (1543)
1 : any of a genus (*Polygonatum*) of perennial herbs of the lily family with tubular flowers and gnarled rhizomes — called also *Solomonseal*
2 : an emblem consisting of two interlaced triangles forming a 6-pointed star and formerly used as an amulet especially against fever — compare HEXAGRAM

so·lon \'sō-lən, -ˌlän\ *noun* [Solon] (1625)
1 : a wise and skillful lawgiver

2 : a member of a legislative body

sol·on·chak \ˌsä-lən-'chak\ *noun* [Russian, salt marsh] (1925)
: any of a group of intrazonal strongly saline usually pale soils found especially in poorly drained arid or semiarid areas

sol·o·netz \ˌsä-lə-'nets\ *noun* [Russian *solonets* salt not extracted by decoction] (1924)
: any of a group of intrazonal dark hard alkaline soils evolved by leaching and alkalizing from solonchak
— **sol·o·netz·ic** \-'net-sik\ *adjective*

so long \sō-'lȯŋ, sə-\ *interjection* [origin unknown] (circa 1861)
— used to express farewell

so long as *conjunction* (14th century)
1 : during and up to the end of the time that : WHILE
2 : provided that

sol·stice \'säl-stəs, 'sōl-, 'sȯl-\ *noun* [Middle English, from Old French, from Latin *solstitium,* from *sol* sun + *-stit-, -stes* standing; akin to Latin *stare* to stand — more at SOLAR, STAND] (13th century)
1 : either of the two points on the ecliptic at which its distance from the celestial equator is greatest and which is reached by the sun each year about June 22d and December 22d
2 : the time of the sun's passing a solstice which occurs about June 22d to begin summer in the northern hemisphere and about December 22d to begin winter in the northern hemisphere

sol·sti·tial \säl-'sti-shəl, sōl-, sȯl-\ *adjective* [Middle English *solsticial,* from Old French & Latin; Old French, from Latin *solstitialis,* from *solstitium*] (14th century)
1 : of, relating to, or characteristic of a solstice and especially the summer solstice
2 : happening or appearing at or associated with a solstice

sol·u·bi·lise British variant of SOLUBILIZE

sol·u·bil·i·ty \ˌsäl-yə-'bi-lə-tē\ *noun* (1661)
1 : the quality or state of being soluble
2 : the amount of a substance that will dissolve in a given amount of another substance

sol·u·bi·lize \'säl-yə-bə-ˌlīz\ *transitive verb* **-lized; -liz·ing** (circa 1926)
: to make soluble or increase the solubility of
— **sol·u·bi·li·za·tion** \ˌsäl-yə-bə-lə-'zā-shən\ *noun*

sol·u·ble \'säl-yə-bəl\ *adjective* [Middle English, from Middle French, capable of being loosened or dissolved, from Late Latin *solubilis,* from Latin *solvere* to loosen, dissolve — more at SOLVE] (15th century)
1 : susceptible of being dissolved in or as if in a liquid and especially water
2 : subject to being solved or explained ⟨*soluble* questions⟩

so·lum \'sō-ləm\ *noun, plural* **so·la** \-lə\ *or* **solums** [New Latin, from Latin, ground, soil] (1928)

\ə\ **abut** \ᵊ\ **kitten** \ər\ **further** \a\ **ash** \ā\ **ace**
\ä\ **mop, mar** \au̇\ **out** \ch\ **chin** \e\ **bet** \ē\ **easy**
\g\ **go** \i\ **hit** \ī\ **ice** \j\ **job** \ŋ\ **sing** \ō\ **go**
\ȯ\ **law** \ȯi\ **boy** \th\ **thin** \t͟h\ **the** \ü\ **loot** \u̇\ **foot**
\y\ **yet** \zh\ **vision** *see also* Guide to Pronunciation

: the altered layer of soil above the parent material that includes the A and B horizons

so·lus \'sō-ləs\ *adverb or adjective* [Latin] (1599)
: ALONE — often used in stage directions

sol·ute \'säl-,yüt\ *noun* [Latin *solutus*, past participle of *solvere*] (1893)
: a dissolved substance

so·lu·tion \sə-'lü-shən\ *noun* [Middle English, from Middle French, from Latin *solution-, solutio,* from *solvere* to loosen, solve] (14th century)
1 a : an action or process of solving a problem **b** : an answer to a problem : EXPLANATION; *specifically* : a set of values of the variables that satisfies an equation
2 a : an act or the process by which a solid, liquid, or gaseous substance is homogeneously mixed with a liquid or sometimes a gas or solid **b** : a homogeneous mixture formed by this process; *especially* : a single-phase liquid system **c** : the condition of being dissolved
3 : a bringing or coming to an end or into a state of discontinuity

solution set *noun* (1959)
: the set of values that satisfy an equation; *also* : TRUTH SET

So·lu·tre·an \sə-'lü-trē-ən\ *adjective* [Solutré, village in France] (1888)
: of or relating to an upper Paleolithic culture characterized by leaf-shaped finely flaked stone implements

solv·able \'säl-və-bəl, 'sol-\ *adjective* (circa 1676)
: susceptible of solution or of being solved, resolved, or explained
— **solv·abil·i·ty** \,säl-və-'bi-lə-tē, ,sol-\ *noun*

¹sol·vate \'säl-,vāt, 'sol-\ *noun* [*solvent* + ¹*-ate*] (1904)
: an aggregate that consists of a solute ion or molecule with one or more solvent molecules; *also* : a substance (as a hydrate) containing such ions

²solvate *transitive verb* **sol·vat·ed; sol·vat·ing** (1909)
: to make part of a solvate
— **sol·va·tion** \säl-'vā-shən, sol-\ *noun*

Sol·vay process \'säl-,vā-\ *noun* [Ernest Solvay (died 1922) Belgian chemist] (1884)
: a process for making soda from common salt by passing carbon dioxide into ammoniacal brine resulting in precipitation of sodium bicarbonate which is then calcined to carbonate

solve \'sälv, 'solv\ *verb* **solved; solv·ing** [Middle English, to loosen, from Latin *solvere* to loosen, solve, dissolve, from *sed-, se-* apart + *luere* to release — more at SECEDE, LOSE] (circa 1533)
transitive verb
1 : to find a solution, explanation, or answer for ⟨*solve* a problem⟩ ⟨*solved* the crime⟩
2 : to pay (as a debt) in full
intransitive verb
: to solve something ⟨substitute the known values of the constants and *solve* for *x*⟩
— **solv·er** *noun*

sol·ven·cy \'säl-vən(t)-sē, 'sol-\ *noun* (circa 1727)
: the quality or state of being solvent

¹sol·vent \-vənt\ *adjective* [Latin *solvent-, solvens,* present participle of *solvere* to dissolve, pay] (1630)
1 : able to pay all legal debts
2 : that dissolves or can dissolve ⟨*solvent* action of water⟩
— **sol·vent·ly** *adverb*

²solvent *noun* (1671)
1 : a usually liquid substance capable of dissolving or dispersing one or more other substances
2 : something that provides a solution
3 : something that eliminates or attenuates something especially unwanted
— **sol·vent·less** \-ləs\ *adjective*

sol·vol·y·sis \säl-'vä-lə-səs, sol-\ *noun* [New Latin, from English *solv*ent + New Latin *-o-* + *-lysis*] (1916)
: a chemical reaction (as hydrolysis) of a solvent and solute that results in the formation of new compounds
— **sol·vo·lyt·ic** \,säl-və-'li-tik, ,sol-\ *adjective*

¹so·ma \'sō-mə\ *noun* [Sanskrit; akin to Avestan *haoma,* a Zoroastrian ritual drink, Sanskrit *sunoti* he presses out] (1827)
: an intoxicating plant juice probably from a leafless vine (*Sarcostemma intermedium*) of the milkweed family used in ancient India as an offering to the gods and as a drink of immortality by worshipers in Vedic ritual and worshiped as a Vedic god

²soma *noun, plural* **so·ma·ta** \'sō-mə-tə\ *or* **somas** [New Latin *somat-, soma,* from Greek *sōmat-, sōma* body] (circa 1885)
1 : the body of an organism
2 : all of an organism except the germ cells
3 : CELL BODY

So·ma·li \sō-'mä-lē, sə-\ *noun, plural* **Somali** *or* **Somalis** (1814)
1 : a member of a people of Somaliland
2 : the Cushitic language of the Somali

so many *adjective* (1533)
1 : constituting an unspecified number ⟨read *so many* chapters each night⟩
2 : constituting a group or pack ⟨behaved like *so many* animals⟩

somat- *or* **somato-** *combining form* [New Latin, from Greek *sōmat-, sōmato-,* from *sōmat-, sōma* body]
: body ⟨*somato*logy⟩

so·mat·ic \sō-'ma-tik, sə-\ *adjective* [Greek *sōmatikos,* from *sōmat-, sōma*] (circa 1775)
1 : of, relating to, or affecting the body especially as distinguished from the germ plasm or the psyche
2 : of or relating to the wall of the body : PARIETAL
— **so·mat·i·cal·ly** \-ti-k(ə-)lē\ *adverb*

somatic cell *noun* (1888)
: one of the cells of the body that compose the tissues, organs, and parts of that individual other than the germ cells

so·ma·tol·o·gy \,sō-mə-'tä-lə-jē\ *noun* [New Latin *somatologia,* from *somat-* + *-logia* -logy] (circa 1878)
: a branch of anthropology primarily concerned with the comparative study of human evolution, variation, and classification especially through measurement and observation
— **so·ma·to·log·i·cal** \,sō-mə-t°l-'ä-ji-kəl, sō-,ma-\ *adjective*

so·ma·to·me·din \,sō-mə-tō-'mē-d°n, sō-,ma-tə-\ *noun* [*somat-* + inter*med*iary + ¹*-in*] (1971)
: any of several endogenous peptides produced especially in the liver that are dependent on and probably mediate growth hormone activity (as in sulfate uptake by epiphyseal cartilage)

so·ma·to·pleure \sō-'ma-tə-,plùr\ *noun* [New Latin *somatopleura,* from *somat-* + Greek *pleura* side] (1874)
: a complex fold of tissue in the embryo of a craniate vertebrate consisting of an outer layer of mesoderm together with the ectoderm that sheathes it and giving rise to the amnion and chorion

so·ma·to·sen·so·ry \sō-,ma-tə-'sen(t)s-rē, -'sen(t)-sə-rē\ *adjective* (1952)
: of, relating to, or being sensory activity having its origin elsewhere than in the special sense organs (as eyes and ears) and conveying information about the state of the body proper and its immediate environment

so·ma·to·stat·in \sō-,ma-tə-'sta-t°n\ *noun* [*somat-* + Latin *status* (past participle of *sistere* to halt, cause to stand) + English ¹*-in*; akin to Latin *stare* to stand — more at STAND] (1973)

: a polypeptide neurohormone that is found especially in the hypothalamus and inhibits the secretion of several other hormones (as growth hormone, insulin, and gastrin)

so·ma·to·tro·pic hormone \-'trō-pik-\ *noun* [*somat-* + *-tropic*] (1938)
: GROWTH HORMONE 1

so·ma·to·tro·pin \-'trō-pən\ *also* **so·ma·to·tro·phin** \-fən\ *noun* [*somatotropic* + ¹*-in*] (1941)
: GROWTH HORMONE 1

so·ma·to·type \sō-'ma-tə-,tīp\ *noun* (1940)
: body type : PHYSIQUE

som·ber *or* **som·bre** \'säm-bər\ *adjective* [French *sombre*] (1760)
1 : so shaded as to be dark and gloomy
2 a : of a serious mien : GRAVE **b** : of a dismal or depressing character : MELANCHOLY **c** : conveying gloomy suggestions or ideas
3 : of a dull or heavy cast or shade : dark colored
— **som·ber·ly** *adverb*
— **som·ber·ness** *noun*

som·bre·ro \səm-'brer-(,)ō, säm-\ *noun, plural* **-ros** [Spanish, from *sombra* shade] (1599)
: a high-crowned hat of felt or straw with a very wide brim worn especially in the Southwest and Mexico

sombrero

som·brous \'säm-brəs\ *adjective* [French *sombre*] (1730)
archaic : SOMBER

¹some \'səm, *for* 2 *without stress*\ *adjective* [Middle English *som,* adjective & pronoun, from Old English *sum*; akin to Old High German *sum* some, Greek *hamē* somehow, *homos* same — more at SAME] (before 12th century)
1 : being an unknown, undetermined, or unspecified unit or thing ⟨*some* person knocked⟩
2 a : being one, a part, or an unspecified number of something (as a class or group) named or implied ⟨*some* gems are hard⟩ **b** : being of an unspecified amount or number ⟨give me *some* water⟩ ⟨have *some* apples⟩
3 : REMARKABLE, STRIKING ⟨that was *some* party⟩
4 : being at least one — used to indicate that a logical proposition is asserted only of a subclass or certain members of the class denoted by the term which it modifies

²some \'səm\ *pronoun, singular or plural in construction* (before 12th century)
1 : one indeterminate quantity, portion, or number as distinguished from the rest
2 : an indefinite additional amount ⟨ran a mile and then *some*⟩

³some \'səm, ,səm\ *adverb* (before 12th century)
1 : ABOUT ⟨*some* 80 houses⟩ ⟨twenty-*some* people⟩
2 a : in some degree : SOMEWHAT ⟨felt *some* better⟩ **b** : to some degree or extent : a little ⟨the cut bled *some*⟩ ⟨I need to work on it *some* more⟩ **c** — used as a mild intensive ⟨that's going *some*⟩ □

¹-some *adjective suffix* [Middle English *-som,* from Old English *-sum*; akin to Old High German *-sam* -some, Old English *sum* some]
: characterized by a (specified) thing, quality, state, or action ⟨awe*some*⟩ ⟨burden*some*⟩ ⟨cuddle*some*⟩

²-some *noun suffix* [Middle English (northern dialect) *-sum,* from Middle English *sum,* pronoun, one, some]
: group of (so many) members and especially persons ⟨four*some*⟩

³-some *noun combining form* [New Latin *-somat-, -soma,* from Greek *sōmat-, sōma*]
1 : body ⟨chromo*some*⟩
2 : chromosome ⟨mono*some*⟩

¹some·body \'səm-(,)bə-dē, -,bä-\ *pronoun* (14th century)

: one or some person of unspecified or indefinite identity ⟨*somebody* will come in⟩ □
²somebody *noun* (circa 1566)
: a person of position or importance
some·day \'səm-ˌdā\ *adverb* (14th century)
: at some future time
some·deal \'səm-ˌdēl\ *adverb* (before 12th century)
archaic : SOMEWHAT
some·how \'səm-ˌhaů\ *adverb* (1664)
: in one way or another not known or designated : by some means
some·one \-(ˌ)wən\ *pronoun* (14th century)
: some person : SOMEBODY
usage see SOMEBODY
some·place \-ˌplās\ *adverb* (1880)
: SOMEWHERE
som·er·sault \'sə-mər-ˌsȯlt\ *noun* [Middle French *sombresaut* leap, ultimately from Latin *super* over + *saltus* leap, from *salire* to jump — more at OVER, SALLY] (circa 1530)
: a leap or roll in which a person turns forward or backward in a complete revolution bringing the feet over the head and finally landing on the feet; *also* : a falling or tumbling head over heels
— **somersault** *intransitive verb*
som·er·set \-ˌset\ *noun or intransitive verb* [by alteration] (1591)
: SOMERSAULT
¹some·thing \'səm(p)-thiŋ, *especially in rapid speech or for 2* 'səm-p³m\ *pronoun* (before 12th century)
1 : some indeterminate or unspecified thing
2 : a person or thing of consequence
3 : one having more or less the character, qualities, or nature of something different ⟨is *something* of a bore⟩
— **something else** : something or someone special or extraordinary
²something *adverb* (13th century)
1 : in some degree : SOMEWHAT
2 — used as an intensive giving adverbial force to an adjective ⟨swears *something* awful⟩
¹some·time \'səm-ˌtīm\ *adverb* (14th century)
1 *archaic* : in the past : FORMERLY
2 *archaic* : once in a while : OCCASIONALLY
3 : at some time in the future ⟨I'll do it *sometime*⟩
4 : at some not specified or definitely known point of time ⟨*sometime* last night⟩
²sometime *adjective* (14th century)
1 : having been formerly : FORMER, LATE
2 : being so occasionally or in only some respects ⟨a *sometime* . . . father who appears and disappears —Evelyn Shelby⟩
¹some·times \'səm-ˌtīmz *also* (ˌ)səm-'\ *adverb* (14th century)
: at times : now and then : OCCASIONALLY
²sometimes *adjective* (1593)
: SOMETIME
some·way \'səm-ˌwā\ *also* **some·ways** \-ˌwāz\ *adverb* (15th century)
: SOMEHOW
¹some·what \-ˌ(h)wät, -ˌ(h)wət, (ˌ)səm-'\ *pronoun* (13th century)
: SOMETHING
²somewhat *adverb* (13th century)
: in some degree or measure : SLIGHTLY
some·when \'səm-ˌ(h)wen\ *adverb* (1833)
: SOMETIME
¹some·where \-ˌ(h)wer, -ˌ(h)war, -(ˌ)(h)wər\ *adverb* (13th century)
1 : in, at, from, or to a place unknown or unspecified ⟨mentions it *somewhere*⟩
2 : to a place symbolizing positive accomplishment or progress ⟨now we're getting *somewhere*⟩
3 : in the vicinity of : APPROXIMATELY ⟨*somewhere* about nine o'clock⟩
²somewhere *noun* (1647)
: an undetermined or unnamed place
some·wheres \-ˌ(h)werz, -ˌ(h)warz, -(ˌ)(h)wərz\ *adverb* (1815)
: SOMEWHERE
some·whith·er \-ˌ(h)wi-thər\ *adverb* (1530)

archaic : to some place : SOMEWHERE
-somic *adjective combining form* [International Scientific Vocabulary ³-*some* + -*ic*]
: having or being a chromosome complement of which one or more but not all members exhibit (such) a degree of reduplication of chromosomes or genomes ⟨mono*somic*⟩
so·mite \'sō-ˌmīt\ *noun* [International Scientific Vocabulary, from Greek *sōma* body] (1869)
: one of the longitudinal series of segments into which the body of many animals (as articulate animals and vertebrates) is divided
: METAMERE
som·me·lier \ˌsə-məl-'yā\ *noun, plural* **sommeliers** \-'yā(z)\ [French, from Middle French, court official charged with transportation of supplies, pack animal driver, from Old Provençal *saumalier* pack animal driver, from *sauma* pack animal, load of a pack animal, from Late Latin *sagma* packsaddle — more at SUMPTER] (1829)
: a waiter in a restaurant who has charge of wines and their service : a wine steward
somnambul- *combining form* [New Latin, from *somnambulus* somnambulist, from Latin *somnus* sleep + -*ambulus* (as in *funambulus* funambulist) — more at SOMNOLENT]
: somnambulism : somnambulist ⟨*somnambulant*⟩
som·nam·bu·lant \säm-'nam-byə-lənt\ *adjective* (1866)
: walking or addicted to walking while asleep
som·nam·bu·late \-ˌlāt\ *intransitive verb* **-lat·ed; -lat·ing** (1833)
: to walk when asleep
— **som·nam·bu·la·tion** \(ˌ)säm-ˌnam-byə-'lā-shən\ *noun*
som·nam·bu·lism \säm-'nam-byə-ˌli-zəm\ *noun* (1797)
1 : an abnormal condition of sleep in which motor acts (as walking) are performed
2 : actions characteristic of somnambulism
— **som·nam·bu·list** \-list\ *noun*
— **som·nam·bu·lis·tic** \(ˌ)säm-ˌnam-byə-'lis-tik\ *adjective*
— **som·nam·bu·lis·ti·cal·ly** \-ti-k(ə-)lē\ *adverb*
som·ni·fa·cient \ˌsäm-nə-'fā-shənt\ *adjective* [Latin *somnus* sleep + English -*facient*] (circa 1890)
: HYPNOTIC 1
— **somnifacient** *noun*
som·nif·er·ous \säm-'ni-f(ə-)rəs\ *adjective* [Latin *somnifer* somniferous, from *somnus* + -*fer* -ferous] (1602)
: SOPORIFIC
som·no·lence \'säm-nə-lən(t)s\ *noun* (14th century)
: the quality or state of being drowsy : SLEEPINESS
som·no·lent \-lənt\ *adjective* [Middle English *sompnolent*, from Middle French, from Latin *somnolentus*, from *somnus* sleep; akin to Old English *swefn* sleep, Greek *hypnos*] (15th century)
1 : of a kind likely to induce sleep ⟨a *somnolent* sermon⟩
2 a : inclined to or heavy with sleep : DROWSY **b** : SLEEPY 2 ⟨*somnolent* rivers⟩
— **som·no·lent·ly** *adverb*
¹so much *adverb* (13th century)
: by the amount indicated or suggested ⟨if they lose their way, *so much* the better for us⟩
²so much *pronoun* (14th century)
1 : something (as an amount or price) unspecified or undetermined ⟨charge *so much* a mile⟩
2 : all that can be or is to be said or done ⟨*so much* for the history of the case⟩
³so much *adjective* (1557)
— used as an intensive ⟨the house burned like *so much* paper⟩ ⟨sounded like *so much* nonsense⟩
so much as *adverb* (15th century)
: EVEN 3d

son \'sən\ *noun* [Middle English *sone*, from Old English *sunu*; akin to Old High German *sun* son, Greek *hyios*] (before 12th century)
1 a : a male offspring especially of human beings **b** : a male adopted child **c** : a male descendant
2 *capitalized* : the second person of the Trinity
3 : a person closely associated with or deriving from a formative agent (as a nation, school, or race)
— **son·hood** \-ˌhůd\ *noun*
son- *or* **sono-** *combining form* [Latin *sonus* sound]
: sound ⟨*sonic*⟩ ⟨*sonogram*⟩
so·nant \'sō-nənt\ *adjective* [Latin *sonant-, sonans*, present participle of *sonare* to sound — more at SOUND] (1846)
1 : VOICED 2
2 : SYLLABIC 1a
— **sonant** *noun*
so·nar \'sō-ˌnär\ *noun* [*so*und *na*vigation *r*anging] (1945)

\ə\ abut \ᵊ\ kitten \ər\ further \a\ ash \ā\ ace
\ä\ mop, mar \aů\ out \ch\ chin \e\ bet \ē\ easy
\g\ go \i\ hit \ī\ ice \j\ job \ŋ\ sing \ō\ go
\ȯ\ law \ȯi\ boy \th\ thin \th\ the \ü\ loot \ů\ foot
\y\ yet \zh\ vision *see also* Guide to Pronunciation

: a method or device for detecting and locating objects especially underwater by means of sound waves sent out to be reflected by the objects; *also* : a device for detecting the presence of a vessel (as a submarine) by the sound it emits in water ◇

so·na·ta \sə-'nä-tə\ *noun* [Italian, from *sonare* to sound, from Latin] (1694)
: an instrumental musical composition typically of three or four movements in contrasting forms and keys

sonata form *noun* (1873)
: a musical form that consists basically of an exposition, a development, and a recapitulation and that is used especially for the first movement of a sonata

son·a·ti·na \ˌsä-nə-'tē-nə\ *noun* [Italian, diminutive of *sonata*] (circa 1801)
: a short usually simplified sonata

sonde \'sänd\ *noun* [French, literally, sounding line — more at SOUND] (1901)
: any of various devices for testing physical conditions (as at high altitudes, below the earth's surface, or inside the body)

sone \'sōn\ *noun* [International Scientific Vocabulary, from Latin *sonus* sound — more at SOUND] (1948)
: a subjective unit of loudness for an average listener equal to the loudness of a 1000-hertz sound that has an intensity 40 decibels above the listener's own threshold of hearing

son et lu·mière \ˌsō-(n)ā-lüm-'yer\ *noun* [French, literally, sound and light] (1957)
: an outdoor spectacle at an historic site consisting of recorded narration with light and sound effects

song \'sȯŋ\ *noun* [Middle English, from Old English *sang*; akin to Old English *singan* to sing] (before 12th century)
1 : the act or art of singing
2 : poetical composition
3 a : a short musical composition of words and music **b** : a collection of such compositions
4 : a distinctive or characteristic sound or series of sounds (as of a bird or insect)
5 a : a melody for a lyric poem or ballad **b** : a poem easily set to music
6 a : a habitual or characteristic manner **b** : a violent, abusive, or noisy reaction ⟨put up quite a *song*⟩
7 : a small amount ⟨sold for a *song*⟩
— **song·like** \-ˌlīk\ *adjective*

song and dance *noun* (1872)
1 : a theatrical performance (as a vaudeville performance) combining singing and dancing
2 : a long and often familiar statement or explanation that is usually not true or pertinent

song·bird \'sȯŋ-ˌbərd\ *noun* (1774)
1 a : a bird that utters a succession of musical tones **b** : an oscine bird
2 : a female singer

song·book \-ˌbu̇k\ *noun* (before 12th century)
: a collection of songs; *specifically* : a book containing vocal music (as hymns)

song cycle *noun* (1899)
: a group of related songs designed to form a musical entity

song·fest \'sȯŋ-ˌfest\ *noun* (circa 1912)
: an informal session of group singing of popular or folk songs

song·ful \-fəl\ *adjective* (14th century)
: given to or suggestive of singing : MELODIOUS
— **song·ful·ly** \-fə-lē\ *adverb*
— **song·ful·ness** *noun*

song·less \-ləs\ *adjective* (circa 1805)
: lacking in, incapable of, or not given to song
— **song·less·ly** *adverb*

Song of Sol·o·mon \-'sä-lə-mən\ [from the opening verse: "The song of songs, which is Solomon's"]
: a collection of love poems forming a book in the Protestant canon of the Old Testament — see BIBLE table

Song of Songs [translation of Hebrew *shīr hashshīrīm*]
: a collection of love poems forming a book in the canonical Jewish Scriptures and in the Roman Catholic canon of the Old Testament and corresponding to the Song of Solomon in the Protestant canon of the Old Testament — see BIBLE table

song·smith \'sȯŋ-ˌsmith\ *noun* (1795)
: a composer of songs

song sparrow *noun* (1810)
: a common North American sparrow (*Melospiza melodia*) that is brownish above and white below with brownish streaks on the breast and that is noted for it melodious song

song·ster \'sȯŋ(k)-stər\ *noun* (14th century)
1 : one that sings with skill
2 : SONGBOOK

song·stress \'sȯŋ(k)-strəs\ *noun* (1703)
: a female singer

song thrush *noun* (1668)
: an Old World thrush (*Turdus philomelos*) that is largely brown above with brown-spotted white underparts — called also *mavis*, *throstle*

song·writ·er \'sȯŋ-ˌrī-tər\ *noun* (1821)
: a person who composes words or music or both especially for popular songs
— **song·writ·ing** \-ˌrī-tiŋ\ *noun*

son·ic \'sä-nik\ *adjective* (1923)
1 : utilizing, produced by, or relating to sound waves ⟨*sonic* altimeter⟩; *broadly* : of or involving sound ⟨*sonic* pollution⟩
2 : having a frequency within the audibility range of the human ear — used of waves and vibrations
3 : of, relating to, or being the speed of sound in air or about 761 miles per hour (1224 kilometers per hour) at sea level at 59°F (15°C)
4 : capable of uttering sounds
— **son·i·cal·ly** \-ni-k(ə-)lē\ *adverb*

son·i·cate \'sä-nə-ˌkāt\ *transitive verb* **-cat·ed; -cat·ing** [*sonic* + ⁴-*ate*] (1960)
: to disrupt (as bacteria) by treatment with high-frequency sound waves
— **son·i·ca·tion** \ˌsä-nə-'kā-shən\ *noun*

sonic barrier *noun* (1946)
: SOUND BARRIER

sonic boom *noun* (1952)
: a sound resembling an explosion produced when a shock wave formed at the nose of an aircraft traveling at supersonic speed reaches the ground — called also *sonic bang*

son–in–law \'sən-ən-ˌlȯ\ *noun, plural* **sons–in–law** (14th century)
: the husband of one's daughter

son·less \'sən-ləs\ *adjective* (14th century)
: not possessing or never having had a son

son·ly \-lē\ *adjective* (15th century)
: FILIAL

son·net \'sä-nət\ *noun* [Italian *sonetto*, from Old Provençal *sonet* little song, from *son* sound, song, from Latin *sonus* sound] (1557)
: a fixed verse form of Italian origin consisting of fourteen lines that are typically five-foot iambics rhyming according to a prescribed scheme; *also* : a poem in this pattern

son·ne·teer \ˌsä-nə-'tir\ *noun* (1665)
1 : a composer of sonnets
2 : a minor or insignificant poet
— **son·ne·teer·ing** \-iŋ\ *noun*

sonnet sequence *noun* (1881)
: a series of sonnets often having a unifying theme

son·ny \'sə-nē\ *noun* (1850)
: a young boy — usually used in address

so·no·buoy \'sä-nə-ˌbȯi, -ˌbü-ē\ *noun* (1945)
: a buoy equipped for detecting underwater sounds and transmitting them by radio

son of a bitch \ˌsən-ə-'bich *also* 'səm-ˌbich; *as an interjection* ˌsən-ə-və-'bich\ *noun, plural* **sons of bitch·es** \ˌsən-zə-'bi-chəz\ (1671)
: BASTARD 3 — sometimes considered vulgar; sometimes used interjectionally to express surprise or disappointment

son of a gun \'sən-ə-və-ˌgən; *as an interjection* ˌsən-ə-və-'gən\ *noun, plural* **sons of guns** (1708)
— usually used as a mild or euphemistic alternative to *son of a bitch*; sometimes used interjectionally to express surprise or disappointment

son of God (14th century)
1 *often S capitalized* : a superhuman or divine being (as an angel)
2 *S capitalized* : MESSIAH 1
3 : a person established in the love of God by divine promise

son of man (14th century)
1 : a human being
2 *often S capitalized* : God's messiah destined to preside over the final judgment of mankind

sono·gram \'sä-nə-ˌgram\ *noun* (1956)
: an image produced by ultrasound

so·nog·ra·phy \sō-'nä-grə-fē\ *noun* (1977)
: ULTRASOUND 2

so·nor·i·ty \sə-'nȯr-ə-tē, -'när-\ *noun, plural* **-ties** (circa 1623)
1 : the quality or state of being sonorous : RESONANCE
2 : a sonorous tone or speech

so·no·rous \sə-'nȯr-əs, -'nȯr-; 'sä-nə-rəs\ *adjective* [Latin *sonorus*; akin to Latin *sonus* sound] (1611)
1 : producing sound (as when struck)
2 : full or loud in sound
3 : imposing or impressive in effect or style
4 : having a high or an indicated degree of sonority ⟨*sonorous* sounds such as \ä\ and \ȯ\⟩
— **so·no·rous·ly** *adverb*
— **so·no·rous·ness** *noun*

son·ship \'sən-ˌship\ *noun* (1587)
: the relationship of son to father

sonsy *or* **sons·ie** \'sän(t)-sē\ *adjective* [Scots *sons* health] (1725)
chiefly dialect : BUXOM, COMELY

soon \'sün, *especially New England* 'su̇n\ *adverb* [Middle English *soone*, from Old English *sōna*; akin to Old High German *sān* immediately] (before 12th century)
1 a *obsolete* : at once : IMMEDIATELY **b** : before long : without undue time lapse ⟨*soon* after sunrise⟩
2 : in a prompt manner : SPEEDILY ⟨as *soon* as possible⟩ ⟨the *sooner* the better⟩
3 *archaic* : before the usual time

◇ WORD HISTORY
sonar The shadowy history of acronymic words such as *sonar* that have grown out of secret government projects sets many pitfalls for the etymologist. When F.V. ("Ted") Hunt, the director of the Harvard Underwater Sound Laboratory, coined *sonar*, most likely in 1942, he applied it to a specific piece of scanning equipment rather than the general technique of active echolocation, perhaps having in mind the words *sonic*, *azimuth*, and *range*. Years later Hunt recalled only that he intended it as a phonetic analogue to *radar* (radio detection and ranging), and that *sonar* had a more pleasing sound than *sodar*. The interpretation of *sonar* as sound *navigation* and *ranging* was promulgated by the U.S. Navy only after the fact. *Asdic*, the British counterpart to *sonar* but developed decades earlier, also has an involved history. When Winston Churchill uttered what had long been a top secret term in the House of Commons in 1939, the British Admiralty said that *asdic* stood for Allied Submarine Detection Investigation Committee, allegedly formed during World War I. But no such committee ever existed. First noted as *asdics* in a now declassified report of 1918, the word appears to have been coined from *Anti-Submarine Division*, an Admiralty department, with *-ics* extracted from *supersonics*.

4 : in agreement with one's choice or preference **:** WILLINGLY ⟨I'd just as *soon* walk as drive⟩

soon·er \'sü-nər\ *noun* [*sooner*, comparative of *soon*] (1890)
1 : a person settling on land in the early West before its official opening to settlement in order to gain the prior claim allowed by law to the first settler after official opening
2 *capitalized* **:** a native or resident of Oklahoma — used as a nickname

sooner or later *adverb* (1577)
: at some uncertain future time **:** SOMETIME

¹**soot** \'sut, 'sət, 'süt\ *noun* [Middle English, from Old English *sōt;* akin to Old Irish *suide* soot, Old English *sittan* to sit] (before 12th century)
: a black substance formed by combustion or separated from fuel during combustion, rising in fine particles, and adhering to the sides of the chimney or pipe conveying the smoke; *especially* **:** the fine powder consisting chiefly of carbon that colors smoke

²**soot** *transitive verb* (1602)
: to coat or cover with soot

¹**sooth** \'süth\ *adjective* [Middle English, from Old English *sōth;* akin to Old High German *sand* true, Latin *esse* to be] (before 12th century)
1 *archaic* **:** TRUE
2 *archaic* **:** SOFT, SWEET

²**sooth** *noun* (before 12th century)
1 : TRUTH, REALITY
2 *obsolete* **:** BLANDISHMENT

soothe \'süth\ *verb* **soothed; sooth·ing** [Middle English *sothen* to verify, from Old English *sōthian,* from *sōth*] (1697)
transitive verb
1 : to please by or as if by attention or concern **:** PLACATE
2 : RELIEVE, ALLEVIATE
3 : to bring comfort, solace, or reassurance to
intransitive verb
: to bring peace, composure, or quietude
— **sooth·er** *noun*

sooth·fast \'süth-,fast\ *adjective* (before 12th century)
1 *archaic* **:** TRUE
2 *archaic* **:** TRUTHFUL

sooth·ing \'sü-thin\ *adjective* (1749)
: tending to soothe; *also* **:** having a sedative effect ⟨*soothing* syrup⟩
— **sooth·ing·ly** \-thin-lē\ *adverb*
— **sooth·ing·ness** *noun*

sooth·ly \'süth-lē\ *adverb* (before 12th century)
archaic **:** in truth **:** TRULY

sooth·say·er \-,sā-ər, -,se(-ə)r\ *noun* (14th century)
: a person who predicts the future by magical, intuitive, or more rational means **:** PROGNOSTICATOR

sooth·say·ing \-,sā-in\ *noun* (15th century)
1 : the act of foretelling events
2 : PREDICTION, PROPHECY
— **sooth·say** \-,sā\ *intransitive verb*

sooty \'su-tē, 'sə-, 'sü-\ *adjective* **soot·i·er; -est** (13th century)
1 a : of, relating to, or producing soot **b :** soiled with soot
2 : of the color of soot
— **soot·i·ly** \-t°l-ē\ *adverb*
— **soot·i·ness** \-tē-nəs\ *noun*

sooty mold *noun* (1901)
: a dark growth of fungus mycelium growing in insect honeydew on plants; *also* **:** a fungus producing such growth

sooty tern *noun* (1785)
: a widely distributed tern (*Sterna fuscata*) of tropical oceans that is blackish above and white below — called also *wideawake*

¹**sop** \'säp\ *noun* [Middle English *soppe,* from Old English *soppe;* akin to Old English *sūpan* to swallow — more at SUP] (before 12th century)

1 *chiefly dialect* **:** a piece of food dipped or steeped in a liquid
2 : a conciliatory or propitiatory bribe, gift, or gesture

²**sop** *transitive verb* **sopped; sop·ping** (circa 1529)
1 a : to steep or dip in or as if in liquid **b :** to wet thoroughly **:** SOAK
2 : MOP A
3 : to give a bribe or conciliatory gift to

so·pai·pil·la \,sō-pī-'pē-yə, -'pēl-yə\ *or* **so·pa·pil·la** \,sō-pə-\ *noun* [American Spanish *sopaipilla,* diminutive of Spanish *sopaipa* fritter soaked in honey, from *sopa* food soaked in milk, of Germanic origin; akin to Old English *sūpan* to swallow] (circa 1940)
: a square of deep-fried dough often sweetened and eaten as dessert

soph·ism \'sä-,fi-zəm\ *noun* (15th century)
1 : an argument apparently correct in form but actually invalid; *especially* **:** such an argument used to deceive
2 : SOPHISTRY 1

soph·ist \'sä-fist\ *noun* [Latin *sophista,* from Greek *sophistēs,* literally, expert, wise man, from *sophizesthai* to become wise, deceive, from *sophos* clever, wise] (1542)
1 *capitalized* **:** any of a class of ancient Greek teachers of rhetoric, philosophy, and the art of successful living prominent about the middle of the 5th century B.C. for their adroit subtle and allegedly often specious reasoning
2 : PHILOSOPHER, THINKER
3 : a captious or fallacious reasoner

so·phis·tic \sä-'fis-tik, sə-\ *or* **so·phis·ti·cal** \-ti-kəl\ *adjective* (15th century)
1 : of or relating to sophists, sophistry, or the ancient Sophists ⟨*sophistic* rhetoric⟩ ⟨*sophistic* subtleties⟩
2 : plausible but fallacious ⟨*sophistic* reasoning⟩
— **so·phis·ti·cal·ly** \-ti-k(ə-)lē\ *adverb*

¹**so·phis·ti·cate** \sə-'fis-tə-,kāt\ *transitive verb* **-cat·ed; -cat·ing** [Middle English, from Medieval Latin *sophisticatus,* past participle of *sophisticare,* from Latin *sophisticus* sophistic, from Greek *sophistikos,* from *sophistēs* sophist] (15th century)
1 : to alter deceptively; *especially* **:** ADULTERATE
2 : to deprive of genuineness, naturalness, or simplicity; *especially* **:** to deprive of naïveté and make worldly-wise **:** DISILLUSION
3 : to make complicated or complex

²**so·phis·ti·cate** \-ti-kət, -tə-,kāt\ *noun* (1923)
: a sophisticated person

so·phis·ti·cat·ed \-tə-,kā-təd\ *adjective* [Medieval Latin *sophisticatus*] (1601)
1 : not in a natural, pure, or original state **:** ADULTERATED ⟨a *sophisticated* oil⟩
2 : deprived of native or original simplicity: as **a :** highly complicated or developed **:** COMPLEX ⟨*sophisticated* electronic devices⟩ **b :** having a refined knowledge of the ways of the world cultivated especially through wide experience ⟨a *sophisticated* lady⟩
3 : devoid of grossness: as **a :** finely experienced and aware ⟨a *sophisticated* columnist⟩ **b :** intellectually appealing ⟨a *sophisticated* novel⟩ ☆
— **so·phis·ti·cat·ed·ly** *adverb*

so·phis·ti·ca·tion \sə-,fis-tə-'kā-shən\ *noun* (15th century)
1 a : the use of sophistry **:** sophistic reasoning **b :** SOPHISM, QUIBBLE
2 : the process of making impure or weak **:** ADULTERATION
3 : the process or result of becoming cultured, knowledgeable, or disillusioned; *especially* **:** CULTIVATION, URBANITY
4 : the process or result of becoming more complex, developed, or subtle

soph·ist·ry \'sä-fə-strē\ *noun* (14th century)
1 : subtly deceptive reasoning or argumentation

2 : SOPHISM 1

soph·o·more \'säf-,mōr, -,mor *also* 'säf- *or* 'sä-fə- *or* 'so-fə-\ *noun* [perhaps from Greek *sophos* wise + *mōros* foolish] (1688)
: a student in the second year at college or a 4-year secondary school

soph·o·mor·ic \,säf-'mōr-ik, -'mor-, -'mär- *also* ,säf- *or* ,sä-fə- *or* ,so-fə-\ *adjective* (1813)
1 : conceited and overconfident of knowledge but poorly informed and immature
2 : of, relating to, or characteristic of a sophomore ⟨a *sophomoric* prank⟩

So·pho·ni·as \,sä-fə-'nī-əs, ,sō-\ *noun* [Late Latin, from Greek, from Hebrew *Sĕphanyāh*] **:** ZEPHANIAH

so·phy \'sō-fē\ *noun* [Persian *Safī*] (1534)
archaic **:** a sovereign of Persia

-sophy *noun combining form* [Middle English *-sophie,* from Old French, from Latin *-sophia,* from Greek, from *sophia* wisdom, from *sophos*]
: knowledge **:** wisdom **:** science ⟨anthropo*sophy*⟩

so·pite \sō-'pīt\ *transitive verb* **so·pit·ed; so·pit·ing** [Latin *sopitus,* past participle of *sopire* to put to sleep; akin to Latin *sopor* deep sleep] (1542)
1 : to put to sleep **:** LULL
2 *archaic* **:** to put an end to (as a claim) **:** SETTLE

sop·o·rif·er·ous \,sä-pə-'ri-f(ə-)rəs\ *adjective* [Latin *soporifer* soporiferous, from *sopor* + *-fer* -ferous] (1590)
: SOPORIFIC
— **sop·o·rif·er·ous·ness** *noun*

¹**sop·o·rif·ic** \-'ri-fik\ *adjective* [probably from French *soporifique,* from Latin *sopor* deep sleep; akin to Latin *somnus* sleep — more at SOMNOLENT] (1665)
1 a : causing or tending to cause sleep **b :** tending to dull awareness or alertness
2 : of, relating to, or marked by sleepiness or lethargy

²**soporific** *noun* (circa 1727)
: a soporific agent; *specifically* **:** HYPNOTIC 1

sop·ping \'sä-pin\ *adjective* (1877)
: wet through **:** SOAKING

sop·py \'sä-pē\ *adjective* **sop·pi·er; -est** (1823)
1 a : soaked through **:** SATURATED **b :** very wet
2 : SENTIMENTAL, MAWKISH
— **sop·pi·ness** \-nəs\ *noun*

so·pra·ni·no \,sō-prə-'nē-(,)nō, ,sä-\ *noun, plural* **-nos** [Italian, diminutive of *soprano*] (1905)
: a musical instrument (as a recorder or saxophone) higher in pitch than the soprano

¹**so·pra·no** \sə-'pra-(,)nō, -'prä-\ *adjective* [Italian, adjective & noun, from *sopra* above, from Latin *supra* — more at SUPRA-] (1730)
: relating to or having the range or part of a soprano

☆ SYNONYMS
Sophisticated, worldly-wise, blasé mean experienced in the ways of the world. SOPHISTICATED often implies refinement, urbanity, cleverness, and cultivation ⟨guests at her salon were usually rich and *sophisticated*⟩. WORLDLY-WISE suggests a close and practical knowledge of the affairs and manners of society and an inclination toward materialism ⟨a *worldly-wise* woman with a philosophy of personal independence⟩. BLASÉ implies a lack of responsiveness to common joys as a result of a real or affected surfeit of experience and cultivation ⟨*blasé* travelers who claimed to have been everywhere⟩.

²soprano *noun, plural* **-nos** (1738)
1 : the highest singing voice of women, boys, or castrati; *also* **:** a person having this voice
2 : the highest voice part in a 4-part chorus
3 : a member of a family of instruments having the highest range

so·ra \'sōr-ə, 'sȯr-\ *noun* [origin unknown] (1705)
: a small short-billed North American rail (*Porzana carolina*) common in marshes

sorb \'sȯrb\ *transitive verb* [back-formation from *absorb* & *adsorb*] (1909)
: to take up and hold by either adsorption or absorption
— **sorb·abil·i·ty** \,sȯr-bə-'bi-lə-tē\ *noun*
— **sorb·able** \'sȯr-bə-bəl\ *adjective*

Sorb \'sȯrb\ *noun* [German *Sorbe*, from Sorbian *serbje*] (1843)
1 : WEND
2 : WENDISH
— **Sor·bi·an** \'sȯr-bē-ən\ *adjective or noun*

sor·bate \'sȯr-,bāt, 'sȯr-bət\ *noun* (circa 1823)
: a salt or ester of sorbic acid — compare POTASSIUM SORBATE

sor·bent \'sȯr-bənt\ *noun* [Latin *sorbent-, sorbens*, present participle of *sorbēre* to suck up — more at ABSORB] (circa 1856)
: a substance that sorbs

sor·bet \'sȯr-'bā *also* 'sȯr-bət\ *noun* [Middle French, from Old Italian *sorbetto*, from Turkish *şerbet* — more at SHERBET] (1864)
: a fruit-flavored ice served as a dessert or between courses as a palate refresher

sor·bic acid \'sȯr-bik-\ *noun* [*sorb* fruit of the service or related trees, from French *sorbe*, from Latin *sorbum*] (1815)
: a crystalline acid $C_6H_8O_2$ obtained from the unripe fruits of the mountain ash or synthesized and used especially as a fungicide and food preservative

sor·bi·tol \'sȯr-bə-,tȯl, -,tōl\ *noun* [*sorb* fruit of the service or related trees + *-itol*] (1895)
: a faintly sweet alcohol $C_6H_{14}O_6$ that occurs in some fruits, is made synthetically, and is used especially as a humectant and softener and in making ascorbic acid

sor·cer·er \'sȯr-sə-rər, 'sȯrs-rər\ *noun* (15th century)
: a person who practices sorcery **:** WIZARD

sor·cer·ess \-rəs\ *noun* (14th century)
: a woman who is a sorcerer

sor·cer·ous \-rəs\ *adjective* (1546)
: of or relating to sorcery **:** MAGICAL

sor·cery \-rē\ *noun* [Middle English *sorcerie*, from Middle French, from *sorcier* sorcerer, from (assumed) Vulgar Latin *sortiarius*, from Latin *sort-, sors* chance, lot — more at SERIES] (14th century)
1 : the use of power gained from the assistance or control of evil spirits especially for divining **:** NECROMANCY
2 : MAGIC 2a

sor·did \'sȯr-dəd\ *adjective* [Latin *sordidus*, from *sordes* dirt — more at SWART] (1609)
1 : marked by baseness or grossness **:** VILE ⟨*sordid* motives⟩
2 a : DIRTY, FILTHY **b :** WRETCHED, SQUALID
3 : meanly avaricious **:** COVETOUS
4 : of a dull or muddy color
synonym see MEAN
— **sor·did·ly** *adverb*
— **sor·did·ness** *noun*

sor·di·no \sȯr-'dē-(,)nō\ *noun, plural* **-di·ni** \-(,)nē\ [Italian, from *sordo* silent, from Latin *surdus*] (circa 1801)
: MUTE 3

¹sore \'sōr, 'sȯr\ *adjective* **sor·er; sor·est** [Middle English *sor*, from Old English *sār*; akin to Old High German *sēr* sore and probably to Old Irish *saeth* distress] (before 12th century)
1 a : causing pain or distress **b :** painfully sensitive **:** TENDER ⟨*sore* muscles⟩ **c :** hurt or inflamed so as to be or seem painful ⟨*sore* runny eyes⟩ ⟨a dog limping on a *sore* leg⟩

2 : attended by difficulties, hardship, or exertion
3 : ANGRY, IRKED ⟨a *sore* loser⟩
— **sore·ness** *noun*

²sore *noun* (before 12th century)
1 : a localized sore spot on the body; *especially* **:** one (as an ulcer) with the tissues ruptured or abraded and usually with infection
2 : a source of pain or vexation **:** AFFLICTION

³sore *adverb* (before 12th century)
: SORELY

sore·head \'sōr-,hed, 'sȯr-\ *noun* (1848)
: a person easily angered or disgruntled
— **sorehead** *or* **sore·head·ed** \-'he-dəd\ *adjective*

sore·ly \'sōr-lē, 'sȯr-\ *adverb* (before 12th century)
1 : in a sore manner **:** PAINFULLY
2 : VERY, EXTREMELY ⟨*sorely* needed changes⟩

sore throat *noun* (1686)
: pain in the throat due to inflammation of the fauces and pharynx

sor·ghum \'sȯr-gəm\ *noun* [New Latin, from Italian *sorgo*, from (assumed) Vulgar Latin *Syricum* (*granum*), literally, Syrian grain] (1597)
1 : any of an economically important genus (*Sorghum*) of Old World tropical grasses similar to Indian corn in habit but with the spikelets in pairs on a hairy rachis; *especially* **:** any of various cultivars (as grain sorghum or sorgo) derived from a wild form (*S. bicolor* synonym *S. vulgare*)
2 : syrup from the juice of a sorgo that resembles cane syrup
3 : something cloyingly sentimental

sor·go \'sȯr-(,)gō\ *noun* [Italian] (circa 1760)
: a sorghum cultivated primarily for the sweet juice in its stems from which sugar and syrup are made but also used for fodder and silage — called also *sweet sorghum*

sorghum 1

so·ri·tes \sə-'rī-(,)tēz\ *noun, plural* **sorites** [Latin, from Greek *sōritēs*, from *sōros* heap] (1551)
: an argument consisting of propositions so arranged that the predicate of any one forms the subject of the next and the conclusion unites the subject of the first proposition with the predicate of the last

So·rop·ti·mist \sə-'räp-tə-mist, sȯ-\ *noun* [*Soroptimist* (Club)] (1924)
: a member of a service club composed of professional women and women business executives

so·ro·ral \sə-'rōr-əl, -'rȯr-\ *adjective* [Latin *soror* sister — more at SISTER] (1858)
: of, relating to, or characteristic of a sister **:** SISTERLY

so·ro·rate \sə-'rōr-ət, -'rȯr-\ *noun* [Latin *soror*] (1910)
: the marriage of one man to two or more sisters usually successively and after the first wife has been found to be barren or after her death

so·ror·i·ty \sə-'rȯr-ə-tē, -'rär-\ *noun, plural* **-ties** [Medieval Latin *sororitas* sisterhood, from Latin *soror* sister] (1900)
: a club of women; *specifically* **:** a women's student organization (as at a college) that is formed chiefly for social purposes and has a name consisting of Greek letters

sorp·tion \'sȯrp-shən\ *noun* [back-formation from *absorption* & *adsorption*] (1909)
: the process of sorbing **:** the state of being sorbed
— **sorp·tive** \'sȯrp-tiv\ *adjective*

¹sor·rel \'sȯr-əl\ *noun* [Middle English *sorelle*, from Middle French *sorel*, noun & adjective, from *sor* reddish brown] (15th century)

1 : a sorrel-colored animal; *especially* **:** a light bright chestnut horse often with white mane and tail — compare ¹CHESTNUT 4, ²BAY 1
2 : a brownish orange to light brown

²sorrel *noun* [Middle English *sorel*, from Middle French *surele*, from Old French *sur* sour, of Germanic origin; akin to Old High German *sūr* sour — more at SOUR] (15th century)
: any of various plants or plant parts with sour juice: as **a :** any of various docks (as *Rumex acetosa* and *R. acetosella*); *also* **:** the leaves used as a potherb **b :** WOOD SORREL

sorrel tree *noun* (1687)
: SOURWOOD

¹sor·row \'sär-(,)ō, 'sȯr-\ *noun* [Middle English *sorow*, from Old English *sorg*; akin to Old High German *sorga* sorrow] (before 12th century)
1 a : deep distress, sadness, or regret especially for the loss of someone or something loved **b :** resultant unhappy or unpleasant state ⟨to his *sorrow* he lost his temper⟩
2 : a cause of grief or sadness
3 : a display of grief or sadness ☆

²sorrow *intransitive verb* (before 12th century)
: to feel or express sorrow
— **sor·row·er** \'sär-ə-wər, 'sȯr-\ *noun*

sor·row·ful \-ō-fəl, -ə-fəl\ *adjective* (before 12th century)
1 : full of or marked by sorrow
2 : expressive of or inducing sorrow
— **sor·row·ful·ly** \-f(ə-)lē\ *adverb*
— **sor·row·ful·ness** \-fəl-nəs\ *noun*

sor·ry \'sär-ē, 'sȯr-\ *adjective* **sor·ri·er; -est** [Middle English *sory*, from Old English *sārig*, from *sār* sore] (before 12th century)
1 : feeling sorrow, regret, or penitence
2 : MOURNFUL, SAD
3 : inspiring sorrow, pity, scorn, or ridicule
synonym see CONTEMPTIBLE
— **sor·ri·ly** \-ə-lē\ *adverb*
— **sor·ri·ness** \-ē-nəs\ *noun*

¹sort \'sȯrt\ *noun* [Middle English, from Middle French *sorte*, probably from Medieval Latin *sort-, sors*, from Latin, chance, lot — more at SERIES] (14th century)
1 a : a group set up on the basis of any characteristic in common **:** CLASS, KIND **b :** an instance of a kind ⟨a *sort* of black Paul Bunyan, towering 6'10"—Jack Olsen⟩ **c :** PERSON, INDIVIDUAL ⟨he's not a bad *sort*⟩
2 *archaic* **:** GROUP, COMPANY
3 a : method or manner of acting **:** WAY, MANNER **b :** CHARACTER, NATURE ⟨people of an evil *sort*⟩
4 a : a letter or character that is one element of a font **b :** a character or piece of type that is not part of a regular font
5 : an instance of sorting ⟨a numeric *sort* of a data file⟩
synonym see TYPE
— **after a sort :** in a rough or haphazard way
— **of sorts** *or* **of a sort :** of an inconsequential or mediocre quality ⟨a poet *of sorts*⟩

— out of sorts 1 : somewhat ill **2**
: GROUCHY, IRRITABLE
²**sort** (14th century)
transitive verb
1 a : to put in a certain place or rank according to kind, class, or nature ⟨*sort* apples⟩ ⟨*sort* mail⟩ **b** : to arrange according to characteristics : CLASSIFY ⟨*sort* out colors⟩
2 *chiefly Scottish* : to put to rights : put in order
3 a : to examine in order to clarify ⟨*sorting* out his problems⟩ **b** : to free of confusion : CLARIFY ⟨waited until things *sorted* themselves out⟩
intransitive verb
1 : to join or associate with others especially of the same kind ⟨*sort* with thieves⟩
2 : SUIT, AGREE
— **sort·able** \'sȯr-tə-bəl\ *adjective*
— **sort·er** *noun*
sor·tie \'sȯr-tē, sȯr-'tē\ *noun* [French, from Middle French, from *sortir* to escape] (1778)
1 : a sudden issuing of troops from a defensive position against the enemy
2 : one mission or attack by a single plane
3 : FORAY, RAID
— **sortie** *intransitive verb*
sor·ti·lege \'sȯr-tᵊl-ij, -ˌej\ *noun* [Middle English, from Medieval Latin *sortilegium*, from Latin *sortilegus* foretelling, from *sort-*, *sors* lot + *-i- + legere* to gather — more at LEGEND] (14th century)
1 : divination by lots
2 : SORCERY
sor·ti·tion \sȯr-'ti-shən\ *noun* [Latin *sortition-*, *sortitio*, from *sortiri* to cast or draw lots, from *sort-*, *sors* lot] (1597)
: the act or an instance of casting lots
sort of \'sȯr-dəv, -dər\ *adverb* (1790)
: to a moderate degree : RATHER
so·rus \'sōr-əs, 'sȯr-\ *noun, plural* **so·ri** \'sōr-ˌī, 'sȯr-, -ˌē\ [New Latin, from Greek *sōros* heap] (1832)
: a cluster of plant reproductive bodies: as **a** : one of the dots on the underside of a fertile fern frond consisting of a cluster of sporangia **b** : a mass of spores bursting through the epidermis of the host plant of a parasitic fungus **c** : a cluster of gemmae on the thallus of a lichen
SOS \ˌes-(ˌ)ō-'es\ *noun* (1910)
1 : an internationally recognized signal of distress in radio code · · · − − − · · · used especially by ships calling for help
2 : a call or request for help or rescue
¹**so-so** \'sō-'sō\ *adverb* (circa 1530)
: moderately well : TOLERABLY, PASSABLY
²**so-so** *adjective* (1542)
: neither very good nor very bad : MIDDLING
¹**sos·te·nu·to** \ˌsōs-tə-'nü-(ˌ)tō, ˌsȯs-\ *adjective or adverb* [Italian, from past participle of *sostenere* to sustain, from Latin *sustinēre*] (circa 1724)
: sustained to or beyond the note's full value — used as a direction in music
²**sostenuto** *noun* (1757)
: a movement or passage whose notes are markedly prolonged
sot \'sät\ *noun* [Middle English, fool, from Old English *sott*] (1592)
: a habitual drunkard
so·te·ri·ol·o·gy \sō-ˌtir-ē-'ä-lə-jē\ *noun* [Greek *sōtērion* salvation (from *sōtēr* savior, preserver) + English *-logy* — more at CREOSOTE] (circa 1774)
: theology dealing with salvation especially as effected by Jesus Christ
— **so·te·ri·o·log·i·cal** \-ē-ə-'lä-ji-kəl\ *adjective*
so that *conjunction* (before 12th century)
: THAT 2a(1)
So·tho \'sō-(ˌ)tō\ *noun* (1928)
1 : any one of the Sotho languages and especially Sesotho

2 : a group of closely related Bantu languages of Lesotho, Botswana, and northern South Africa
so·tol \'sō-ˌtōl\ *noun* [American Spanish, from Nahuatl *zōtōlin* palm tree] (1881)
: any of several plants (genus *Dasylirion*) of the agave family of the southwestern U.S. and Mexico that resemble a yucca
sot·tish \'sä-tish\ *adjective* (1583)
: resembling a sot : DRUNKEN; *also* : DOLTISH, STUPID
— **sot·tish·ly** *adverb*
— **sot·tish·ness** *noun*
sot·to vo·ce \ˌsä-tō-'vō-chē\ *adverb or adjective* [Italian *sottovoce*, literally, under the voice] (1737)
1 : under the breath : in an undertone; *also* : in a private manner
2 : very softly — used as a direction in music
sou \'sü\ *noun, plural* **sous** \'süz\ [French, from Old French *sol*, from Late Latin *solidus* solidus] (1814)
1 : ²SOL
2 : a 5-centime piece
sou·bise \sü-'bēz\ *noun* [French, from Charles de Rohan, Prince de *Soubise* (died 1787) French nobleman] (1822)
: a garnish or white sauce containing onions or onion purée
sou·brette \sü-'bret\ *noun* [French, from Provençal *soubreto*, feminine of *soubret* coy, from *soubra* to surmount, exceed, from Latin *superare* — more at INSUPERABLE] (1753)
1 a : a coquettish maid or frivolous young woman in comedies **b** : an actress who plays such a part
2 : a soprano who sings supporting roles in comic opera
sou·bri·quet \'sō-, ˌsō-, 'sü-, ˌsü-\ *variant of* SOBRIQUET
sou·chong \'sü-ˌchȯŋ, -ˌshȯŋ\ *noun* [of Chinese origin; akin to Chinese (Beijing) *xiǎozhǒng*, literally, small sort] (1760)
: a tea made from the larger leaves of the shoot
¹**souf·flé** \sü-'flā, 'sü-\ *noun* [French, from *soufflé*, past participle of *souffler* to blow, puff up, from Latin *sufflare*, from *sub-* + *flare* to blow — more at BLOW] (1813)
: a dish that is made from a sauce, egg yolks, beaten egg whites, and a flavoring or purée (as of seafood, fruit, or vegetables) and baked until puffed up
²**soufflé** *or* **souf·fléed** \-'flād, -ˌflād\ *adjective* (1888)
: puffed up by or in cooking
sough \'saù, 'səf\ *intransitive verb* [Middle English *swoughen*, from Old English *swōgan*; akin to Gothic *gaswogjan* to groan, Lithuanian *svagéti* to sound] (before 13th century)
: to make a moaning or sighing sound
— **sough** *noun*
sought *past and past participle of* SEEK
souk \'sük\ *noun* [Arabic *sūq* market] (1826)
: a marketplace in northern Africa or the Middle East; *also* : a stall in such a marketplace
¹**soul** \'sōl\ *noun* [Middle English *soule*, from Old English *sāwol*; akin to Old High German *sēula* soul] (before 12th century)
1 : the immaterial essence, animating principle, or actuating cause of an individual life
2 a : the spiritual principle embodied in human beings, all rational and spiritual beings, or the universe **b** *capitalized, Christian Science* : GOD 1b
3 : a person's total self
4 a : an active or essential part **b** : a moving spirit : LEADER
5 a : the moral and emotional nature of human beings **b** : the quality that arouses emotion and sentiment **c** : spiritual or moral force : FERVOR
6 : PERSON
7 : EXEMPLIFICATION, PERSONIFICATION ⟨she is the *soul* of integrity⟩
8 a : a strong positive feeling (as of intense sensitivity and emotional fervor) conveyed especially by black American performers **b** : NEGRITUDE **c** : SOUL MUSIC **d** : SOUL FOOD **e** : SOUL BROTHER
²**soul** *adjective* (1958)
1 : of, relating to, or characteristic of black Americans or their culture
2 : designed for or controlled by blacks ⟨*soul* radio stations⟩
soul brother *noun* (1959)
: a black male
souled \'sōld\ *adjective* (15th century)
: having a soul : possessing soul and feeling — usually used in combination ⟨whole-*souled* repentance⟩
soul food *noun* (1964)
: food (as chitterlings, ham hocks, and collard greens) traditionally eaten by southern black Americans
soul·ful \'sōl-fəl\ *adjective* (1860)
: full of or expressing feeling or emotion
— **soul·ful·ly** \-fə-lē\ *adverb*
— **soul·ful·ness** *noun*
soul kiss *noun* (circa 1948)
: FRENCH KISS
soul·less \'sōl-ləs\ *adjective* (15th century)
: having no soul or no greatness or warmth of mind or feeling
— **soul·less·ly** *adverb*
— **soul·less·ness** *noun*
soul mate *noun* (1822)
: a person temperamentally suited to another
soul music *noun* (1961)
: music that originated in black American gospel singing, is closely related to rhythm and blues, and is characterized by intensity of feeling and earthiness
soul–search·ing \'sōl-ˌsər-chiŋ\ *noun* (1924)
: examination of one's conscience especially with regard to motives and values
¹**sound** \'saùnd\ *adjective* [Middle English, from Old English *gesund*; akin to Old High German *gisunt* healthy] (13th century)
1 a : free from injury or disease : exhibiting normal health **b** : free from flaw, defect, or decay ⟨*sound* timber⟩
2 : SOLID, FIRM; *also* : STABLE
3 a : free from error, fallacy, or misapprehension ⟨*sound* reasoning⟩ **b** : exhibiting or based on thorough knowledge and experience ⟨*sound* scholarship⟩ **c** : legally valid ⟨a *sound* title⟩ **d** : logically valid and having true premises **e** : agreeing with accepted views : ORTHODOX
4 a : THOROUGH **b** : deep and undisturbed ⟨a *sound* sleep⟩ **c** : HARD, SEVERE ⟨a *sound* whipping⟩
5 : showing good judgment or sense
synonym see HEALTHY, VALID
— **sound·ly** \'saùn(d)-lē\ *adverb*
— **sound·ness** \'saùn(d)-nəs\ *noun*
²**sound** *adverb* (14th century)
: to the full extent : THOROUGHLY ⟨*sound* asleep⟩
³**sound** *noun* [Middle English *soun*, from Old French *son*, from Latin *sonus*, from *sonare* to sound; akin to Old English *swinn* melody, Sanskrit *svanati* it sounds] (13th century)
1 a : a particular auditory impression : TONE **b** : the sensation perceived by the sense of hearing **c** : mechanical radiant energy that is transmitted by longitudinal pressure waves in a material medium (as air) and is the objective cause of hearing
2 a : a speech sound ⟨a peculiar *r-sound*⟩ **b** : value in terms of speech sounds ⟨*-cher* of *teacher* and *-ture* of *creature* have the same *sound*⟩
3 *archaic* : RUMOR, FAME
4 a : meaningless noise **b** *obsolete* : MEANING **c** : the impression conveyed : IMPORT
5 : hearing distance : EARSHOT

\ə\ **abut** \ᵊ\ **kitten** \ər\ **further** \a\ **ash** \ā\ **ace** \ä\ **mop, mar** \aù\ **out** \ch\ **chin** \e\ **bet** \ē\ **easy** \g\ **go** \i\ **hit** \ī\ **ice** \j\ **job** \ŋ\ **sing** \ō\ **go** \ȯ\ **law** \ȯi\ **boy** \th\ **thin** \th̲\ **the** \ü\ **loot** \ù\ **foot** \y\ **yet** \zh\ **vision** *see also* Guide to Pronunciation

6 : recorded auditory material

7 : a particular musical style characteristic of an individual, a group, or an area ⟨the Nashville *sound*⟩

⁴**sound** (13th century)
transitive verb
1 a : to cause to sound ⟨*sound* a trumpet⟩ **b :** PRONOUNCE 3a
2 : to put into words **:** VOICE
3 a : to make known **:** PROCLAIM **b :** to order, signal, or indicate by a sound ⟨*sound* the alarm⟩
4 : to examine by causing to emit sounds ⟨*sound* the lungs⟩
5 *chiefly British* **:** to convey the impression of **:** sound like ⟨that *sounds* a logical use of resources —*Economist*⟩
intransitive verb
1 a : to make a sound **b :** RESOUND **c :** to give a summons by sound ⟨the bugle *sounds* to battle⟩
2 : to make or convey an impression especially when heard ⟨it *sounds* good to me⟩ ⟨you *sound* just like your mother⟩
— **sound·able** \'saún-də-bəl\ *adjective*

⁵**sound** *noun* [Middle English, from Old English *sund* swimming, sea & Old Norse *sund* swimming, strait; akin to Old English *swimman* to swim] (14th century)
1 a : a long broad inlet of the ocean generally parallel to the coast **b :** a long passage of water connecting two larger bodies (as a sea with the ocean) or separating a mainland and an island
2 : the air bladder of a fish

⁶**sound** *verb* [Middle English, from Middle French *sonder*, from *sonde* sounding line, probably of Germanic origin; akin to Old English *sundlīne* sounding line, *sund* sea] (15th century)
transitive verb
1 : to measure the depth of **:** FATHOM
2 : to try to find out the views or intentions of **:** PROBE — often used with *out*
3 : to explore or examine (a body cavity) with a sound
intransitive verb
1 a : to ascertain the depth of water especially with a sounding line **b :** to look into or investigate the possibility ⟨sent commissioners . . . to *sound* for peace —Thomas Jefferson⟩
2 : to dive down suddenly — used of a fish or whale

⁷**sound** *noun* [French *sonde*, from Middle French, literally, sounding line] (1739)
: an elongated instrument for exploring or sounding body cavities

sound·alike \'saún-də-,līk\ *noun* (1970)
: one that sounds like another

sound–and–light show *noun* (1967)
: SON ET LUMIÈRE

sound barrier *noun* (1939)
: a sudden large increase in aerodynamic drag that occurs as the speed of an aircraft approaches the speed of sound

sound bite *noun* (1972)
: a brief recorded statement (as by a public figure) broadcast especially on a television news program; *also* **:** a brief catchy comment suitable for use as a sound bite

sound·board \'saún(d)-,bōrd, -,bȯrd\ *noun* (1504)
1 : a thin resonant board (as the belly of a violin) so placed in an instrument as to reinforce its tones by sympathetic vibration — see VIOLIN illustration
2 : SOUNDING BOARD 1a

sound bow *noun* (1688)
: the thick part of a bell against which the clapper strikes

sound box *noun* (circa 1875)
1 : a device in an early phonograph for producing sound from a record by using the vibration of a needle to move a diaphragm

2 : a hollow chamber in a musical instrument for increasing its sonority

sound effects *noun plural* (1909)
: effects that are imitative of sounds called for in the script of a dramatic production (as a radio show) and that enhance the production's illusion of reality

sound·er \'saún-dər\ *noun* (1575)
: one that sounds; *specifically* **:** a device for making soundings

sound hole *noun* (1611)
: an opening in the top surface of a stringed instrument (as a violin) to enhance vibration and resonance — see VIOLIN illustration

¹**sound·ing** \'saún-diŋ\ *adjective* (14th century)
1 : RESONANT, SONOROUS
2 a : POMPOUS **b :** IMPOSING
— **sound·ing·ly** \-diŋ-lē\ *adverb*

²**sounding** *noun* (15th century)
1 a : measurement of depth especially with a sounding line **b :** the depth so ascertained **c** *plural* **:** a place or part of a body of water where a hand sounding line will reach bottom
2 : measurement of atmospheric conditions at various heights
3 : a probe, test, or sampling of opinion or intention

sounding board *noun* (1729)
1 a : a structure behind or over a pulpit, rostrum, or platform to give distinctness and sonority to sound **b :** a device or agency that helps propagate opinions or utterances **c :** a person or group on whom one tries out an idea or opinion as a means of evaluating it
2 : SOUNDBOARD 1

sounding line *noun* (14th century)
: a line or wire weighted at one end for sounding

sounding rocket *noun* (circa 1945)
: a rocket used to obtain information concerning atmospheric conditions at various altitudes

¹**sound·less** \'saún(d)-ləs\ *adjective* [⁶*sound*] (1586)
: incapable of being sounded **:** UNFATHOMABLE

²**soundless** *adjective* [³*sound*] (1601)
: making no sound **:** SILENT
— **sound·less·ly** *adverb*

sound·man \'saún(d)-,man\ *noun* (1929)
: a person who controls the volume and tone of sound picked up by a microphone (as in a recording studio or on a motion-picture set) for recording

sound off *intransitive verb* (1909)
1 : to play three chords before and after marching up and down a line of troops during a ceremonial parade or formal guard mount
2 : to count cadence while marching
3 a : to speak up in a loud voice **b :** to voice one's opinions freely and vigorously

sound pressure *noun* (1893)
: the difference between the actual pressure at any point in the field of a sound wave at any instant and the average pressure at that point

¹**sound·proof** \'saún(d)-,prüf\ *adjective* (circa 1878)
: impervious to sound

²**soundproof** *transitive verb* (1919)
: to insulate so as to obstruct the passage of sound

sound·stage \'saún(d)-,stāj\ *noun* (1931)
: the part of a motion-picture studio in which a production is filmed

sound track *noun* (circa 1929)
1 : the area on a motion-picture film or television videotape that carries the sound record
2 : the sound recorded on a sound track; *especially* **:** the music on a sound track

sound truck *noun* (1936)
: a truck equipped with a loudspeaker

sound wave *noun* (1848)
1 : ³SOUND 1a
2 *plural* **:** longitudinal pressure waves in any material medium regardless of whether they

constitute audible sound ⟨earthquake waves and ultrasonic waves are sometimes called *sound waves*⟩

soup \'süp\ *noun* [Middle English *soupe*, from Middle French, sop, soup, of Germanic origin; akin to Old Norse *soppa* soup, Old English *sopp* sop — more at SUP] (14th century)
1 : a liquid food especially with a meat, fish, or vegetable stock as a base and often containing pieces of solid food
2 : something (as a heavy fog or nitroglycerine) having or suggesting the consistency or nutrient qualities of soup
3 : an unfortunate predicament

soup·çon \süp-'sōⁿ, 'süp-,sän\ *noun* [French, literally, suspicion, from (assumed) Vulgar Latin *suspection-, suspectio*, from Latin *suspicere* to suspect — more at SUSPECT] (1766)
: a little bit **:** TRACE

soup du jour \,süp-də-'zhür\ *noun* [part translation of French *soupe du jour* soup of the day] (circa 1945)
: a soup that is offered by a restaurant on a particular day

soup kitchen *noun* (1839)
: an establishment dispensing minimum dietary essentials (as soup and bread) to the needy

soup·spoon \'süp-,spün\ *noun* (1705)
: a spoon with a large or rounded bowl for eating soup

soup up *transitive verb* [*soup* (drug injected into a racehorse to improve its performance)] (circa 1933)
: to increase the power or efficiency of ⟨*soup up* an engine⟩

soupy \'sü-pē\ *adjective* **soup·i·er; -est** (1869)
1 : having the consistency of soup
2 : densely foggy or cloudy
3 : overly sentimental

¹**sour** \'saú(-ə)r\ *adjective* [Middle English, from Old English *sūr*; akin to Old High German *sūr* sour, Lithuanian *sūrus* salty] (before 12th century)
1 : causing or characterized by the one of the four basic taste sensations that is produced chiefly by acids ⟨*sour* pickles⟩ — compare BITTER, SALT, SWEET
2 a (1) **:** having the acid taste or smell of or as if of fermentation **:** TURNED ⟨*sour* milk⟩ (2) **:** of or relating to fermentation **b :** smelling or tasting of decay **:** RANCID, ROTTEN ⟨*sour* breath⟩ **c** (1) **:** BAD, WRONG ⟨a project gone *sour*⟩ (2) **:** HOSTILE, DISENCHANTED ⟨went *sour* on Marxism⟩
3 a : UNPLEASANT, DISTASTEFUL **b :** CROSS, SULLEN **c :** not up to the usual, expected, or standard quality or pitch
4 : acid in reaction — used especially of soil
5 : containing malodorous sulfur compounds — used especially of petroleum products
— **sour·ish** \'saú(-ə)r-ish\ *adjective*
— **sour·ly** *adverb*
— **sour·ness** *noun*

²**sour** *noun* (before 12th century)
1 a : something sour **b :** the primary taste sensation produced by acid stimuli
2 : a cocktail consisting of a liquor (as whiskey), lemon or lime juice, sugar, and sometimes ice

³**sour** (14th century)
intransitive verb
: to become sour
transitive verb
: to make sour

sour ball *noun* (circa 1909)
: a spherical hard candy having a tart flavor

¹**source** \'sōrs, 'sȯrs\ *noun* [Middle English *sours*, from Middle French *sors, sourse*, from Old French, from past participle of *sourdre* to rise, spring forth, from Latin *surgere* — more at SURGE] (14th century)

1 a : a generative force **:** CAUSE **b** (1) **:** a point of origin or procurement **:** BEGINNING (2) **:** one that initiates **:** AUTHOR; *also* **:** PROTOTYPE, MODEL (3) **:** one that supplies information **2 a :** the point of origin of a stream of water **:** FOUNTAINHEAD **b** *archaic* **:** SPRING, FOUNT **3 :** a firsthand document or primary reference work **4 :** an electrode in a field-effect transistor that supplies the charge carriers for current flow — compare DRAIN, GATE

synonym see ORIGIN

— **source·less** \-ləs\ *adjective*

²source *transitive verb* **sourced; sourc·ing** (1957) **1 :** to specify the source of (as quoted material) **2 :** to obtain from a source 〈metals *sourced* from abroad〉

³source *adjective* (1959) **:** of, relating to, or being a computer program in its original programming language 〈*source* listing〉 〈*source* code〉

source·book \-,bůk\ *noun* (1899) **:** a fundamental document or record (as of history, literature, art, or religion) on which subsequent writings, compositions, opinions, beliefs, or practices are based; *also* **:** a collection of such documents

source language *noun* (1953) **:** a language which is to be translated into another language — compare TARGET LANGUAGE

sour cherry *noun* (circa 1884) **:** a widely cultivated cherry (*Prunus cerasus*) that has a round crown and bright red to almost black soft-fleshed acid fruits; *also* **:** the fruit

sour cream *noun* (1855) **:** a soured cream product produced by the action of lactobacilli

sour·dough \'saù(-ə)r-,dō, *1 is also* -'dō\ *noun* (14th century) **1 :** a leaven consisting of dough in which fermentation is active **2** [from the use of sourdough for making bread in prospectors' camps] **:** a veteran inhabitant and especially an old-time prospector of Alaska or northwestern Canada

sour grapes *noun plural* [from the fable ascribed to Aesop of the fox who after finding himself unable to reach some grapes he had desired disparaged them as sour] (1760) **:** disparagement of something that has proven unattainable

sour gum *noun* (1785) **:** BLACK GUM

sour mash *noun* (1885) **:** grain mash for brewing or distilling whose initial acidity has been adjusted to optimum condition for yeast fermentation by mash from a previous run

sour orange *noun* (1748) **:** a citrus tree (*Citrus aurantium*) that is used especially as a stock in grafting citrus; *also* **:** its bitter fruit

sour·puss \'saù(-ə)r-,půs\ *noun* [²*puss*] (1937) **:** GROUCH, KILLJOY

sour·sop \'saù(-ə)r-,säp\ *noun* (1667) **:** a small tropical American tree (*Annona muricata*) of the custard-apple family that has spicy odoriferous leaves; *also* **:** its large edible fruit that has fleshy spines and a slightly acid fibrous pulp

sour·wood \-,wůd\ *noun* (1709) **:** a small U.S. tree (*Oxydendrum arboreum*) of the heath family with white flowers and sour-tasting leaves

sous \'sü\ *adjective* [French, preposition, literally, under, from Latin *subtus*, adverb, below, under; akin to Latin *sub* under — more at UP] (1687) **:** being an assistant — used chiefly in titles 〈a *sous*-chef〉

sou·sa·phone \'sü-zə-,fōn, -sə-\ *noun* [John Philip *Sousa*] (1925) **:** a large circular tuba that has a flared adjustable bell — compare HELICON

¹souse \'saùs\ *verb* **soused; sous·ing** [Middle English, from Middle French *souz, souce* pickling solution, of Germanic origin; akin to Old High German *sulza* brine, Old English *sealt* salt] (14th century) *transitive verb* **1 :** PICKLE **2 a :** to plunge in liquid **:** IMMERSE **b :** DRENCH, SATURATE **3 :** to make drunk **:** INEBRIATE *intransitive verb* **:** to become immersed or drenched

²souse *noun* (14th century) **1 :** something pickled; *especially* **:** seasoned and chopped pork trimmings, fish, or shellfish **2 :** an act of sousing **:** WETTING **3 a :** a habitual drunkard **b :** a drinking spree **:** BINGE

³souse *verb* **soused; sous·ing** [Middle English *souce*, noun, start of a bird's flight, alteration of *sours*, from Middle French *sourse* source — more at SOURCE] (1583) *intransitive verb archaic* **:** to swoop down **:** PLUNGE *transitive verb archaic* **:** to swoop down on

sou·tache \sü-'tash\ *noun* [French, from Hungarian *sujtás*] (circa 1856) **:** a narrow braid with herringbone pattern used as trimming

sou·tane \sü-'tän, -'tan\ *noun* [French, from Italian *sottana*, literally, undergarment, from feminine of *sottano* being underneath, from Medieval Latin *subtanus*, from Latin *subtus* underneath — more at SOUS] (1838) **:** CASSOCK

sou·ter \'sü-tər\ *noun* [Middle English, from Old English *sūtere*, from Latin *sutor*, from *su-ere* to sew — more at SEW] (before 12th century) *chiefly Scottish* **:** SHOEMAKER

¹south \'saùth\ *adverb* [Middle English, from Old English *sūth;* akin to Old High German *sund-* south and probably to Old English *sunne* sun] (before 12th century) **1 :** to, toward, or in the south **2 :** into a state of decline or ruin 〈causes the sluggish economy to go *south* —G. F. Will〉

²south *adjective* (12th century) **1 :** situated toward or at the south 〈the *south* entrance〉 **2 :** coming from the south 〈a *south* wind〉

³south *noun* (13th century) **1 a :** the direction of the south terrestrial pole **:** the direction to the right of one facing east **b :** the compass point directly opposite to north **2** *capitalized* **:** regions or countries lying to the south of a specified or implied point of orientation; *especially* **:** the southeastern part of the U.S. **3 :** the right side of a church looking toward the altar from the nave **4** *often capitalized* **a :** the one of four positions at 90-degree intervals that lies to the south or at the bottom of a diagram **b :** a person (as a bridge player) occupying this position in the course of a specified activity; *specifically* **:** the declarer in bridge **5** *often capitalized* **:** the developing nations of the world **:** THIRD WORLD 3 — compare NORTH 2b

South African *noun* (1806)

: a native or inhabitant of the Republic of South Africa; *especially* **:** AFRIKANER
— **South African** *adjective*

south·bound \'saùth-,baùnd\ *adjective* (1885) **:** traveling or heading south

south by east (circa 1771) **:** a compass point that is one point east of due south **:** S11°15′E

south by west (circa 1743) **:** a compass point that is one point west of due south **:** S11°15′W

South Dev·on \-'de-vən\ *noun* [*Devon*, England] (1897) **:** any of a breed of large red dual-purpose cattle of English origin

South·down \'saùth-,daùn\ *noun* [*South Downs*, England] (1787) **:** any of a breed of small medium-wooled hornless sheep of English origin

¹south·east \saù-'thēst, *nautical* saù-'ēst\ *adverb* (before 12th century) **:** to, toward, or in the southeast

²southeast *noun* (14th century) **1 a :** the general direction between south and east **b :** the point midway between the south and east compass points **2** *capitalized* **:** regions or countries lying to the southeast of a specified or implied point of orientation

³southeast *adjective* (14th century) **1 :** coming from the southeast 〈a *southeast* wind〉 **2 :** situated toward or at the southeast 〈the *southeast* corner〉

southeast by east (circa 1771) **:** a compass point that is one point east of due southeast **:** S56°15′E

southeast by south (1682) **:** a compass point that is one point south of due southeast **:** S33°45′E

south·east·er \saù-'thē-stər, saù-'ē-\ *noun* (1797) **1 :** a strong southeast wind **2 :** a storm with southeast winds

south·east·er·ly \-stər-lē\ *adverb or adjective* [²*southeast* + -*erly* (as in *easterly*)] (1708) **1 :** from the southeast **2 :** toward the southeast

south·east·ern \-stərn\ *adjective* [²*southeast* + -*ern* (as in *eastern*)] (1577) **1** *often capitalized* **:** of, relating to, or characteristic of a region conventionally designated southeast **2 :** lying toward or coming from the southeast — **south·east·ern·most** \-,mōst\ *adjective*

South·east·ern·er \-stə(r)-nər\ *noun* (1919) **:** a native or inhabitant of the Southeast; *especially* **:** a native or resident of the southeastern part of the U.S.

¹south·east·ward \saù-'thēs-twərd, saù-'ēs-\ *adverb or adjective* (1528) **:** toward the southeast — **south·east·wards** \-twərdz\ *adverb*

²southeastward *noun* (1555) **:** SOUTHEAST

¹south·er·ly \'sə-thər-lē\ *adjective or adverb* [³*south* + -*erly* (as in *easterly*)] (1551) **1 :** situated toward or belonging to the south 〈the *southerly* shore of the lake〉 **2 :** coming from the south 〈a *southerly* wind〉

²southerly *noun, plural* -**lies** (1943) **:** a wind from the south

south·ern \'sə-thərn\ *adjective* [Middle English *southern, southren*, from Old English *sūtherne;* akin to Old High German *sundrōni* southern, Old English *sūth* south] (before 12th century) **1** *capitalized* **:** of, relating to, or characteristic of a region conventionally designated South

2 a : lying toward the south **b :** coming from the south ⟨a *southern* breeze⟩
— **south·ern·most** \-,mōst\ *adjective*
— **south·ern·ness** \-thərn-nəs\ *noun, often capitalized*
Southern *noun* (1935)
: the dialect of English spoken in most of the Chesapeake Bay area, the coastal plain and the greater part of the upland plateau in Virginia, North Carolina, South Carolina, and Georgia, and the Gulf states at least as far west as the valley of the Brazos in Texas and sometimes taken to include the south Midland area
Southern blot *noun* [Edwin M. *Southern* 20th century British biologist] (1981)
: a blot consisting of a nitrocellulose sheet containing spots of DNA for identification by a suitable molecular probe — compare WESTERN BLOT
— **Southern blotting** *noun*
southern corn rootworm *noun* (1918)
: SPOTTED CUCUMBER BEETLE
Southern Cross *noun*
: four bright stars in the southern hemisphere, situated as if at the extremities of a Latin cross; *also* **:** the constellation of which these four stars are the brightest
Southern Crown *noun*
: CORONA AUSTRALIS
Southern English *noun* (14th century)
1 : the English spoken especially by cultivated people native to or educated in the South of England
2 : SOUTHERN
South·ern·er \'sə-thə(r)-nər\ *noun* (1828)
: a native or inhabitant of the South; *especially* **:** a native or resident of the southern part of the U.S.
southern hemisphere *noun, often S&H capitalized* (circa 1771)
: the part of the earth that lies south of the equator
South·ern·ism \'sə-thər,ni-zəm\ *noun* (1861)
1 : an attitude or trait characteristic of the South or Southerners especially in the U.S.
2 : a locution or pronunciation characteristic of the southern U.S.
southern lights *noun plural* (1775)
: AURORA AUSTRALIS
south·ern·wood \'sə-thərn-,wůd\ *noun* (before 12th century)
: a shrubby fragrant European wormwood (*Artemisia abrotanum*) with bitter foliage
south·ing \'saů-thiŋ, -thiŋ\ *noun* (1669)
1 : difference in latitude to the south from the last preceding point of reckoning
2 : southerly progress
south·land \'saůth-,land, -lənd\ *noun, often capitalized* (before 12th century)
: land in the south **:** the south of a country
south·paw \-,pó\ *noun* (1891)
: LEFT-HANDER; *especially* **:** a left-handed baseball pitcher ◇
— **southpaw** *adjective*
south pole *noun* (14th century)
1 a *often S&P capitalized* **:** the southernmost point of the earth **b :** the zenith of the heavens as viewed from the south terrestrial pole
2 *of a magnet* **:** the pole that points toward the south
¹South·ron \'səth-rən\ *adjective* [Middle English (Scots)] (15th century)
chiefly Scottish **:** SOUTHERN; *specifically* **:** ENGLISH
²Southron *noun* (15th century)
: SOUTHERNER: as **a** *chiefly Scottish* **:** ENGLISHMAN **b** *chiefly Southern* **:** a native or inhabitant of the southern U.S.
south–seek·ing pole *noun* (circa 1922)
: SOUTH POLE 2
south–southeast *noun* (15th century)
: a compass point that is two points east of due south **:** S22°30′E
south–southwest *noun* (1513)
: a compass point that is two points west of due south **:** S22°30′W

¹south·ward \'saůth-wərd\ *adverb or adjective* (before 12th century)
: toward the south
— **south·wards** \-wərdz\ *adverb*
²southward *noun* (14th century)
: southward direction or part ⟨sail to the *southward*⟩
¹south·west \saůth-'west, *nautical* saů-'west\ *adverb* (before 12th century)
: to, toward, or in the southwest
²southwest *noun* (12th century)
1 a : the general direction between south and west **b :** the point midway between the south and west compass points
2 *capitalized* **:** regions or countries lying to the southwest of a specified or implied point of orientation
³southwest *adjective* (14th century)
1 : coming from the southwest ⟨a *southwest* wind⟩
2 : situated toward or at the southwest ⟨the *southwest* corner⟩
southwest by south (1725)
: a compass point that is one point south of due southwest **:** S33°45′W
southwest by west (circa 1771)
: a compass point that is one point west of due southwest **:** S56°15′W
south·west·er \saů(th)-'wes-tər\ *noun* (1833)
1 : a strong southwest wind
2 : a storm with southwest winds
south·west·er·ly \-tər-lē\ *adverb or adjective* [²*southwest* + *-erly* (as in *westerly*)] (1708)
1 : from the southwest
2 : toward the southwest
south·west·ern \-tərn\ *adjective* [Middle English, from Old English *sūth-westerne*, from *sūth* south + *westerne* western] (before 12th century)
1 : lying toward or coming from the southwest
2 *often capitalized* **:** of, relating to, or characteristic of a region conventionally designated Southwest
— **south·west·ern·most** \-,mōst\ *adjective*
southwestern corn borer *noun* (1943)
: a pyralid moth (*Diatraea grandiosella*) whose larva causes serious damage especially to corn crops by boring in the stalks
South·west·ern·er \saů(th)-'wes-tə(r)-nər\ *noun* (1860)
: a native or inhabitant of the Southwest; *especially* **:** a native or resident of the southwestern U.S.
¹south·west·ward \saů(th)-'wes-twərd\ *adverb or adjective* (1548)
: toward the southwest
— **south·west·wards** \-twərdz\ *adverb*
²southwestward *noun* (1775)
: SOUTHWEST
sou·ve·nir \'sü-və-,nir, ,sü-və-'\ *noun* [French, literally, act of remembering, from Middle French, from (*se*) *souvenir* to remember, from Latin *subvenire* to come up, come to mind — more at SUBVENTION] (1782)
: something that serves as a reminder **:** MEMENTO
souvenir sheet *noun* (1940)
: a block or set of postage stamps or a single stamp printed on a single sheet of paper often without gum or perforations and with margins containing lettering or design that identifies some notable event being commemorated
sou·vla·kia \süv-'lä-kē-ə\ *or* **sou·vla·ki** \-'lä-kē\ *noun* [New Greek *soublakia*, plural of *soublaki*, from diminutive of *soubla* skewer, from Middle Greek, from Latin *subula* awl, from *suere* to sew — more at SEW] (1950)
: SHISH KEBAB
sou'·west·er \saů-'wes-tər\ *noun* (1837)
1 : a long oilskin coat worn especially at sea during stormy weather
2 : a waterproof hat with wide slanting brim longer in back than in front

¹sov·er·eign *also* **sov·ran** \'sä-v(ə-)rən, -vərn *also* 'sə-\ *noun* [Middle English *soverain*, from Old French, from *soverain*, adjective] (13th century)
1 a : one possessing or held to possess sovereignty **b :** one that exercises supreme authority within a limited sphere **c :** an acknowledged leader **:** ARBITER
2 : any of various gold coins of the United Kingdom
²sovereign *also* **sovran** *adjective* [Middle English *soverain*, from Middle French, from Old French, from (assumed) Vulgar Latin *superanus*, from Latin *super* over, above — more at OVER] (14th century)
1 a : superlative in quality **:** EXCELLENT **b :** of the most exalted kind **:** SUPREME ⟨*sovereign* virtue⟩ **c :** having generalized curative powers ⟨a *sovereign* remedy⟩ **d :** of an unqualified nature **:** UNMITIGATED ⟨*sovereign* contempt⟩ **e :** having undisputed ascendancy **:** PARAMOUNT
2 a : possessed of supreme power ⟨*sovereign* ruler⟩ **b :** unlimited in extent **:** ABSOLUTE **c :** enjoying autonomy **:** INDEPENDENT ⟨*sovereign* state⟩
3 : relating to, characteristic of, or befitting a sovereign
synonym see FREE
— **sov·er·eign·ly** *adverb*
sov·er·eign·ty *also* **sov·ran·ty** \-tē\ *noun, plural* **-ties** [Middle English *soverainte*, from Middle French *souveraineté*, from Old French, from *soverain*] (14th century)
1 *obsolete* **:** supreme excellence or an example of it
2 a : supreme power especially over a body politic **b :** freedom from external control **:** AUTONOMY **c :** controlling influence
3 : one that is sovereign; *especially* **:** an autonomous state
so·vi·et \'sō-vē-,et, 'sä-, -vē-ət\ *noun* [Russian *sovet* council, soviet] (1917)
1 : an elected governmental council in a Communist country
2 *plural, capitalized* **a :** BOLSHEVIKS **b :** the people and especially the political and military leaders of the U.S.S.R.
— **soviet** *adjective, often capitalized*
— **so·vi·et·ism** \-vē-ə-,ti-zəm\ *noun, often capitalized*
so·vi·et·ize \'sō-vē-ə,e,-tīz, 'sä-, -vē-ə-\ *transitive verb* **-ized; -iz·ing** *often capitalized* (1919)
1 : to bring under Soviet control

2 : large or magnificent in scale **:** EXPANSIVE ⟨a more *spacious* and stimulating existence than the farm could offer —H. L. Mencken⟩ ☆
— **spa·cious·ly** *adverb*
— **spa·cious·ness** *noun*

spack·le \'spa-kəl\ *transitive verb* **spack·led; spack·ling** \-k(ə-)liŋ\ [Spackle] (1940)
: to apply Spackle paste to
Spackle *trademark*
— used for a powder mixed with water to form a paste and used as a filler for cracks in a surface before painting

¹spade \'spād\ *noun* [Middle English, from Old English *spadu;* akin to Greek *spathē* blade of a sword or oar] (before 12th century)
1 : a digging implement adapted for being pushed into the ground with the foot
2 : a spade-shaped instrument
— **spade·ful** \-ˌful\ *noun*
— **call a spade a spade 1 :** to call a thing by its right name however coarse **2 :** to speak frankly

²spade *verb* **spad·ed; spad·ing** (1647)
transitive verb
: to dig up or out or shape with or as if with a spade
intransitive verb
: to use a spade
— **spad·er** *noun*

³spade *noun* [Italian *spada* or Spanish *espada* broadsword; both from Latin *spatha,* from Greek *spathē* blade] (1598)
1 a : a black figure that resembles a stylized spearhead on each playing card of one of the four suits; *also* **:** a card marked with this figure **b** *plural but singular or plural in construction* **:** the suit comprising cards marked spades
2 : BLACK 4 — usually taken to be offensive
— **in spades :** to an unusually great degree **:** in the extreme

spade beard *noun* [¹spade] (1598)
1 : an oblong beard with square ends
2 : a beard rounded off at the top and pointed at the bottom
— **spade–beard·ed** \'spād-'bir-dəd\ *adjective*

spade·fish \'spād-ˌfish\ *noun* (1704)
: a deep-bodied bony fish (*Chaetodipterus faber* of the family Ephippidae) that resembles the angelfishes and is found in the warmer parts of the western Atlantic

spade·foot toad \'spād-ˌfut-\ *noun* (1867)
: any of a family (Pelobatidae) of burrowing toads having the inner bone of the tarsus edged with a strong horny sheath with which they dig

spade·work \-ˌwərk\ *noun* (1778)
1 : work done with a spade
2 : the hard plain preliminary drudgery in an undertaking

spa·dille \spə-'dil, -'dē\ *noun* [French, from Spanish *espadilla,* diminutive of *espada* broadsword, spade (in cards) — more at SPADE] (1728)
: the highest trump in various card games (as ombre)

spa·dix \'spā-diks\ *noun, plural* **spa·di·ces** \'spā-də-ˌsēz\ [New Latin *spadic-, spadix,* from Latin, frond torn from a palm tree, from Greek *spadik-, spadix,* from *span* to draw, pull] (circa 1760)
: a floral spike with a fleshy or succulent axis usually enclosed in a spathe

spae \'spā\ *transitive verb* **spaed; spae·ing** [Middle English *span,* from Old Norse *spā;* akin to Old High German *spehōn* to watch, spy — more at SPY] (14th century)
chiefly Scottish **:** FORETELL

1 spadix

spaetz·le \'shpet-slə, -sˑl, -slē *also* 'shpät-\ *noun, plural* **spaetzle** *or* **spaetzles** [German, from German *Spätzle,* from German dialect, diminutive of *Spatz* sparrow, dumpling] (1933)
: a small dumpling cooked by running batter through a colander into boiling water

spa·ghet·ti \spə-'ge-tē\ *noun* [Italian, from plural of *spaghetto,* diminutive of *spago* cord, string, from Late Latin *spacus*] (1888)
1 : pasta made in thin solid strings
2 : insulating tubing typically of varnished cloth or of plastic for covering bare wire or holding insulated wires together
— **spa·ghet·ti·like** \-ˌlīk\ *adjective*

spa·ghet·ti·ni \ˌspə-ˌge-'tē-nē\ *noun* [Italian, diminutive of *spaghetti*] (1923)
: a pasta thinner than spaghetti but thicker than vermicelli

spaghetti squash *noun* (1975)
: an oval winter squash with flesh that once cooked is similar in texture to spaghetti

spaghetti western *noun, often W capitalized* (1969)
: a western motion picture produced in Italy

spa·hi \'spä-ˌhē\ *noun* [Middle French, from Turkish *sipahi,* from Persian *sipāhī* cavalryman] (1562)
1 : one of a former corps of irregular Turkish cavalry
2 : one of a former corps of Algerian native cavalry in the French army

spake \'spāk\ *archaic past of* SPEAK

¹spall \'spȯl\ *noun* [Middle English *spalle*] (15th century)
: a small fragment or chip especially of stone

²spall (1758)
transitive verb
: to break up or reduce by or as if by chipping with a hammer
intransitive verb
1 : to break off chips, scales, or slabs **:** EXFOLIATE
2 : to undergo spallation
— **spall·able** \'spȯ-lə-bəl\ *adjective*

spall·ation \spȯ-'lā-shən\ *noun* (1947)
1 : a nuclear reaction in which light particles are ejected as the result of bombardment (as by high-energy protons)
2 : the process of spalling

spal·peen \spal-'pēn, spȯl-\ *noun* [Irish *spailpín* seasonal laborer, rascal] (1815)
chiefly Irish **:** RASCAL

¹span \'span\ *archaic past of* SPIN

²span *noun* [Middle English, from Old English *spann;* akin to Old High German *spanna* span, Middle Dutch *spannen* to stretch, hitch up] (before 12th century)
1 : the distance from the end of the thumb to the end of the little finger of a spread hand; *also* **:** an English unit of length equal to 9 inches (22.9 centimeters)
2 : an extent, stretch, reach, or spread between two limits: as **a :** a limited space (as of time); *especially* **:** an individual's lifetime **b :** the spread or extent between abutments or supports (as of a bridge); *also* **:** a portion thus supported **c :** the maximum distance laterally from tip to tip of an airplane

³span *transitive verb* **spanned; span·ning** (1560)
1 a : to measure by or as if by the hand with fingers and thumb extended **b :** MEASURE
2 a : to extend across ⟨a career that *spanned* four decades⟩ **b :** to form an arch over ⟨a small bridge *spanned* the pond⟩ **c :** to place or construct a span over
3 : to be capable of expressing any element of under given operations ⟨a set of vectors that *spans* a vector space⟩

⁴span *noun* [Dutch, from Middle Dutch, from *spannen* to hitch up] (1769)
: a pair of animals (as mules) usually matched in appearance and action and driven together

spa·na·ko·pi·ta *also* **spa·no·ko·pi·ta** \ˌspä-nə-'kō-pē-tə, -pi-tə\ *noun* [New Greek

spanakopēta, from *spanaki* spinach + *pēta, pita* pie] (1950)
: a traditional Greek pie of spinach, feta cheese, and seasonings baked in phyllo

span·dex \'span-ˌdeks\ *noun* [anagram of *expands*] (1959)
: any of various elastic textile fibers made chiefly of polyurethane; *also* **:** clothing made of this material

span·drel *also* **span·dril** \'span-drəl\ *noun* [Middle English *spandrell,* from Anglo-French *spaundre,* from Old French *espandre* to spread out — more at SPAWN] (15th century)
1 : the sometimes ornamented space between the right or left exterior curve of an arch and an enclosing right angle
2 : the triangular space beneath the string of a stair

spang \'span\ *adverb* [Scots *spang* to leap, cast, bang] (1843)
1 : to a complete degree
2 : in an exact or direct manner **:** SQUARELY

¹span·gle \'span-gəl\ *noun* [Middle English *spangel,* diminutive of *spang* shiny ornament, probably of Scandinavian origin; akin to Old Norse *spǫng* spangle; akin to Old English *spang* buckle, Middle Dutch *spannen* to stretch] (15th century)
1 : a small plate of shining metal or plastic used for ornamentation especially on clothing
2 : a small glittering object or particle

²spangle *verb* **span·gled; span·gling** \'span-g(ə-)liŋ\ (1598)
transitive verb
: to set or sprinkle with or as if with spangles
intransitive verb
: to glitter as if covered with spangles **:** SPARKLE

Span·glish \'span-glish, -lish\ *noun* [blend of *Spanish* and *English*] (1965)
: Spanish marked by numerous borrowings from English; *broadly* **:** any of various combinations of Spanish and English

Span·iard \'span-yərd\ *noun* [Middle English *Spaignard,* from Middle French *Espaignart,* from *Espaigne* Spain, from Latin *Hispania*] (15th century)
: a native or inhabitant of Spain

span·iel \'span-yəl *also* 'spa-nᵊl\ *noun* [Middle English *spaniell,* from Middle French *espaignol,* literally, Spaniard, from (assumed) Vulgar Latin *Hispaniolus,* from Latin *Hispania* Spain] (14th century)
1 : a member of any of several breeds of small or medium-sized mostly short-legged dogs usually having long wavy hair, feathered legs and tail, and large drooping ears
2 : a fawning servile person

Span·ish \'spa-nish\ *noun* [*Spanish,* adjective, from Middle English *Spainish,* from *Spain*] (15th century)
1 : the Romance language of the largest part of Spain and of the countries colonized by Spaniards
2 *plural in construction* **:** the people of Spain
— **Spanish** *adjective*
— **Span·ish·ness** *noun*

Spanish American *noun* (1811)

1 : a resident of the U.S. whose native language is Spanish and whose culture is of Spanish origin
2 : a native or inhabitant of one of the countries of America in which Spanish is the national language
— **Spanish–American** *adjective*

Spanish bayonet *noun* (1843)
: any of several yuccas; *especially* : one (*Yucca aloifolia*) with a short trunk and rigid spine-tipped leaves

Spanish chestnut *noun* (1699)
: MARRON

Spanish fly *noun* (1634)
1 : a green blister beetle (*Lytta vesicatoria*) of southern Europe
2 : CANTHARIS 2

Spanish mackerel *noun* (1666)
: a large scombroid food and game fish (*Scomberomorus maculatus*) that is bluish above with oval brown spots on the sides and is found off the American Atlantic coast from Cape Ann to Brazil

Spanish moss *noun* (1823)
: an epiphytic plant (*Tillandsia usneoides*) of the pineapple family forming pendent tufts of grayish green filaments on trees from the southern U.S. to Argentina

Spanish moss

Spanish needles *noun plural but singular or plural in construction* (1743)
: any of several bur marigolds; *especially* : an annual (*Bidens bipinnata*) of North America and Asia having yellow flowers and dissected leaves

Spanish omelet *noun* (circa 1886)
: an omelet served with a sauce containing chopped green pepper, onion, and tomato

Spanish rice *noun* (1928)
: rice cooked with onions, green pepper, and tomatoes

¹**spank** \'spaŋk\ *transitive verb* [imitative] (circa 1727)
: to strike especially on the buttocks with the open hand
— **spank** *noun*

²**spank** *intransitive verb* [back-formation from *spanking*] (circa 1810)
: to move quickly, dashingly, or spiritedly ⟨*spanking* along in his new car⟩

span·ker \'spaŋ-kər\ *noun* [origin unknown] (1794)
1 : the fore-and-aft sail on the mast nearest the stern of a square-rigged ship
2 : the sail on the sternmost mast in a schooner of four or more masts

¹**spank·ing** \'spaŋ-kiŋ\ *adjective* [origin unknown] (1666)
1 : remarkable of its kind
2 : being fresh and strong : BRISK

²**spanking** *adverb* (1886)
: VERY ⟨a *spanking* clean floor⟩ ⟨*spanking* new⟩

span·ner \'spa-nər\ *noun* [German, instrument for winding springs, from *spannen* to stretch; akin to Middle Dutch *spannen* to stretch — more at SPAN] (circa 1790)
1 *chiefly British* : WRENCH
2 : a wrench that has a hole, projection, or hook at one or both ends of the head for engaging with a corresponding device on the object that is to be turned

spanner 2

span–new \'span-'nü, -'nyü\ *adjective* [Middle English, part translation of Old Norse *spānnȳr*, from *spānn* chip of wood + *nȳr* new] (14th century)

: BRAND-NEW

span·worm \'span-ˌwərm\ *noun* [³*span*] (1820)
: LOOPER 1

¹**spar** \'spär\ *noun* [Middle English *sparre*; akin to Old English *spere* spear — more at SPEAR] (14th century)
1 : a stout pole
2 a : a stout rounded wood or metal piece (as a mast, boom, gaff, or yard) used to support rigging **b** : any of the main longitudinal members of the wing of an airplane that carry the ribs

²**spar** *intransitive verb* **sparred; spar·ring** [probably alteration of ²*spur*] (1537)
1 a : BOX; *especially* : to gesture without landing a blow to draw one's opponent or create an opening **b** : to engage in a practice or exhibition bout of boxing
2 : SKIRMISH, WRANGLE
3 : to strike or fight with feet or spurs in the manner of a gamecock

³**spar** *noun* (1814)
1 : a movement of offense or defense in boxing
2 : a sparring match or session

⁴**spar** *noun* [Low German; akin to Old English *spærstān* gypsum, *spæren* of plaster] (1581)
: any of various nonmetallic usually cleavable and lustrous minerals

SPAR \'spär\ *noun* [Semper *Paratus*, motto of the U.S. Coast Guard, from New Latin, always ready] (1942)
: a member of the women's reserve of the U.S. Coast Guard

¹**spare** \'spar, 'sper\ *verb* **spared; spar·ing** [Middle English, from Old English *sparian*; akin to Old High German *sparōn* to spare, Old English *spær*, adjective, scant] (before 12th century)
transitive verb
1 : to forbear to destroy, punish, or harm
2 : to refrain from attacking or reprimanding with necessary or salutary severity
3 : to relieve of the necessity of doing or undergoing something ⟨*spare* yourself the trouble⟩
4 : to refrain from : AVOID ⟨*spared* no expense⟩
5 : to use or dispense frugally — used chiefly in the negative ⟨don't *spare* the syrup⟩
6 a : to give up as not strictly needed ⟨do you have any cash to *spare*⟩ **b** : to have left over or as margin ⟨time to *spare*⟩
intransitive verb
1 : to be frugal
2 : to refrain from doing harm : be lenient
— **spare·able** \-ə-bəl\ *adjective*
— **spar·er** *noun*

²**spare** *adjective* **spar·er; spar·est** [Middle English, from Old English *spær* sparing, scant; akin to Old High German *spar* spare] (14th century)
1 : not being used; *especially* : held for emergency use ⟨a *spare* tire⟩
2 : being over and above what is needed : SUPERFLUOUS ⟨*spare* time⟩
3 : not liberal or profuse : SPARING ⟨a *spare* prose style⟩
4 : healthily lean
5 : not abundant or plentiful
synonym see LEAN, MEAGER
— **spare·ly** *adverb*
— **spare·ness** *noun*

³**spare** *noun* (1642)
1 a : a spare tire **b** : a duplicate (as a key or a machine part) kept in reserve
2 : the knocking down of all 10 pins with the first 2 balls in a frame in bowling

spare·ribs \'spar-ˌ(r)ibz, 'sper-, -əbz\ *noun plural* [by folk etymology from Low German *ribbesper* pickled pork ribs roasted on a spit, from Middle Low German, from *ribbe* rib + *sper* spear, spit] (1596)
: a cut of pork ribs separated from the bacon strip

sparge \'spärj\ *transitive verb* **sparged; sparg·ing** [probably from Middle French *espargier*, from Latin *spargere* to scatter] (1785)
1 : SPRINKLE, BESPATTER; *especially* : SPRAY
2 : to agitate (a liquid) by means of compressed air or gas entering through a pipe
— **sparge** *noun*
— **sparg·er** *noun*

spar·ing \'spar-iŋ, 'sper-\ *adjective* (14th century)
1 : marked by or practicing careful restraint (as in the use of resources)
2 : MEAGER, BARE ⟨the map is *sparing* of information⟩ ☆
— **spar·ing·ly** \-iŋ-lē\ *adverb*

¹**spark** \'spärk\ *noun* [Middle English *sparke*, from Old English *spearca*; akin to Middle Dutch *sparke* spark and perhaps to Latin *spargere* to scatter] (before 12th century)
1 a : a small particle of a burning substance thrown out by a body in combustion or remaining when combustion is nearly completed **b** : a hot glowing particle struck from a larger mass; *especially* : one heated by friction
2 a : a luminous disruptive electrical discharge of very short duration between two conductors separated by a gas (as air) **b** : the discharge in a spark plug **c** : the mechanism controlling the discharge in a spark plug
3 : SPARKLE, FLASH
4 : something that sets off a sudden force ⟨provided the *spark* that helped the team to rally⟩
5 : a latent particle capable of growth or developing : GERM ⟨still retains a *spark* of decency⟩
6 *plural but singular in construction* : a radio operator on a ship

²**spark** (13th century)
intransitive verb
1 a : to throw out sparks **b** : to flash or fall like sparks
2 : to produce sparks; *specifically* : to have the electric ignition working
3 : to respond with enthusiasm
transitive verb
1 : to set off in a burst of activity : ACTIVATE ⟨the question *sparked* a lively discussion⟩ — often used with *off*
2 : to stir to activity : INCITE ⟨*sparked* her team to victory⟩
— **spark·er** *noun*

³**spark** *noun* [perhaps of Scandinavian origin; akin to Old Norse *sparkr* sprightly] (circa 1600)
1 : a foppish young man
2 : LOVER, BEAU
— **spark·ish** \'spär-kish\ *adjective*

⁴**spark** *verb* (1787)
: WOO, COURT
— **spark·er** *noun*

spark chamber *noun* (1961)
: a device usually used to detect the path of a high-energy particle that consists of a series of

\ə\ **abut** \ᵊ\ **kitten** \ər\ **further** \a\ **ash** \ā\ **ace**
\ä\ **mop, mar** \aù\ **out** \ch\ **chin** \e\ **bet** \ē\ **easy**
\g\ **go** \i\ **hit** \ī\ **ice** \j\ **job** \ŋ\ **sing** \ō\ **go**
\ò\ **law** \òi\ **boy** \th\ **thin** \t͟h\ **the** \ü\ **loot** \ù\ **foot**
\y\ **yet** \zh\ **vision** *see also* Guide to Pronunciation

charged metal plates or wires separated by a gas (as neon) in which observable electric discharges follow the path of the particle

spark coil *noun* (1896)
: an induction coil for producing the spark for an internal combustion engine

spark gap *noun* (1889)
: a space between two high-potential terminals (as of an induction coil) through which pass discharges of electricity; *also* : a device having a spark gap

sparking plug *noun* (1902)
British : SPARK PLUG

¹**spar·kle** \ˈspär-kəl\ *verb* **spar·kled; spar·kling** \-k(ə-)liŋ\ [Middle English, frequentative of *sparken* to spark] (13th century)
intransitive verb
1 a : to throw out sparks **b** : to give off or reflect bright moving points of light **c** : to perform brilliantly
2 : EFFERVESCE ⟨wine that *sparkles*⟩
3 : to become lively or animated ⟨the dialogue *sparkles* with wit⟩ ⟨eyes *sparkling* with anger⟩
transitive verb
: to cause to glitter or shine
synonym see FLASH
— **spar·kly** \-k(ə-)lē\ *adjective*

²**sparkle** *noun* [Middle English, diminutive of *sparke*] (14th century)
1 : a little spark : SCINTILLATION
2 : the quality of sparkling
3 a : ANIMATION, LIVELINESS **b** : the quality or state of being effervescent

spar·kler \ˈspär-klər\ *noun* (1713)
: one that sparkles: as **a** : DIAMOND **b** : a firework that throws off brilliant sparks on burning **c** : SPARKLING WINE

sparkling wine *noun* (1697)
: an effervescent table wine

spark plug *noun* (1903)
1 : a part that fits into the cylinder head of an internal combustion engine and carries two electrodes separated by an air gap across which the current from the ignition system discharges to form the spark for combustion
2 : one that initiates or gives impetus to an undertaking
— **spark·plug** \ˈspärk-ˌpləg\ *transitive verb*

sparky \ˈspär-kē\ *adjective* **spark·i·er; -est** (circa 1865)
: marked by animation : LIVELY
— **spark·i·ly** \-kə-lē\ *adverb*

spar·row \ˈspar-(ˌ)ō\ *noun* [Middle English *sparowe*, from Old English *spearwa*; akin to Old High German *sparo* sparrow] (before 12th century)
1 : any of a genus (*Passer* of the family Ploceidae) of small chiefly brownish or grayish Old World oscine songbirds that include some which have been widely introduced; *especially* : HOUSE SPARROW
2 : any of various finches (as the song sparrow or tree sparrow) resembling the true sparrows
— **spar·row-like** \-ō-ˌlīk, -ə-ˌlīk\ *adjective*

sparrow hawk *noun* (15th century)
: any of various small hawks: as **a** : an Old World accipiter (*Accipiter nisus*) that is dark gray to blackish above with the female having a grayish brown barred underside and the male having a chestnut barred underside **b** : KESTREL b

sparse \ˈspärs\ *adjective* **spars·er; spars·est** [Latin *sparsus* spread out, from past participle of *spargere* to scatter — more at SPARK] (1753)
: of few and scattered elements; *especially* : not thickly grown or settled
synonym see MEAGER

sparrow hawk

— **sparse·ly** *adverb*
— **sparse·ness** *noun*
— **spar·si·ty** \ˈspär-sə-tē, -stē\ *noun*

Spar·ta·cist \ˈspär-tə-sist\ *noun* [German *Spartakist*, from *Spartakusbund*, literally, league of Spartakus, a revolutionary organization, from *Spartakus*, pen name of Karl Liebknecht, its cofounder] (1919)
: a member of a revolutionary political group organized in Germany in 1918 and advocating extreme socialistic doctrines

¹**Spar·tan** \ˈspär-t³n\ *noun* (15th century)
1 : a native or inhabitant of ancient Sparta
2 : a person of great courage and self-discipline
— **Spar·tan·ism** \-ˌi-zəm\ *noun*

²**Spartan** *adjective* (1582)
1 : of or relating to Sparta in ancient Greece
2 a *often not capitalized* : marked by strict self-discipline or self-denial ⟨a *Spartan* athlete⟩ **b** *often not capitalized* : marked by simplicity, frugality, or avoidance of luxury and comfort ⟨a *Spartan* room⟩ **c** : LACONIC **d** : undaunted by pain or danger
— **Spar·tan·ly** *adverb*

spar·te·ine \ˈspär-tē-ən, ˈspär-ˌtēn\ *noun* [Latin *spartum* esparto, broom + International Scientific Vocabulary *-eine* — more at ESPARTO] (1851)
: a liquid alkaloid $C_{15}H_{26}N_2$ extracted from the Scotch broom and used in medicine in the form of its sulfate

spar varnish *noun* [¹*spar*] (circa 1909)
: an exterior waterproof varnish

spasm \ˈspa-zəm\ *noun* [Middle English *spasme*, from Middle French, from Latin *spasmus*, from Greek *spasmos*, from *span* to draw, pull] (14th century)
1 : an involuntary and abnormal muscular contraction
2 : a sudden violent and temporary effort or emotion ⟨a *spasm* of creativity⟩

spas·mod·ic \spaz-ˈmä-dik\ *adjective* [New Latin *spasmodicus*, from Greek *spasmōdēs*, from *spasmos*] (1681)
1 a : relating to or affected or characterized by spasm **b** : resembling a spasm especially in sudden violence ⟨a *spasmodic* jerk⟩
2 : acting or proceeding fitfully : INTERMITTENT
3 : subject to outbursts of emotional excitement : EXCITABLE
synonym see FITFUL
— **spas·mod·i·cal·ly** \-di-k(ə-)lē\ *adverb*

spas·mo·lyt·ic \ˌspaz-mə-ˈli-tik\ *adjective* [International Scientific Vocabulary *spasmo-* (from Greek *spasmos* spasm) + *-lytic*] (circa 1935)
: tending or having the power to relieve spasms or convulsions
— **spasmolytic** *noun*

¹**spas·tic** \ˈspas-tik\ *adjective* [Latin *spasticus*, from Greek *spastikos* drawing in, from *span*] (1753)
1 : of, relating to, characterized by, or affected with spasm ⟨a *spastic* colon⟩ ⟨a *spastic* patient⟩
2 : SPASMODIC 2 ⟨a *spastic* influx of data⟩
— **spas·ti·cal·ly** \-ti-k(ə-)lē\ *adverb*

²**spastic** *noun* (1896)
: one suffering from spastic paralysis

spas·tic·i·ty \spa-ˈsti-sə-tē\ *noun* (circa 1827)
: a spastic state or condition; *especially* : muscular hypertonicity with increased tendon reflexes

spastic paralysis *noun* (1879)
: paralysis with tonic spasm of the affected muscles and with increased tendon reflexes
— compare CEREBRAL PALSY

¹**spat** \ˈspat\ *past and past participle of* SPIT

²**spat** *noun, plural* **spat** *or* **spats** [origin unknown] (1667)
: a young bivalve (as an oyster)

³**spat** *noun* [short for *spatterdash* legging] (circa 1802)
: a cloth or leather gaiter covering the instep and ankle

⁴**spat** *noun* [origin unknown] (1804)
1 : a brief petty quarrel or angry outburst
2 *chiefly dialect* : SLAP
3 : a sound like that of rain falling in large drops

⁵**spat** *verb* **spat·ted; spat·ting** (circa 1832)
transitive verb
chiefly dialect : SLAP
intransitive verb
1 : to quarrel pettily or briefly
2 : to strike with a sound like that of rain falling in large drops

spate \ˈspāt\ *noun* [Middle English] (15th century)
1 : FRESHET, FLOOD
2 a : a large number or amount ⟨a *spate* of books on gardening⟩ **b** : a sudden or strong outburst : RUSH ⟨a *spate* of anger⟩

spathe \ˈspāth\ *noun* [New Latin *spatha*, from Latin, broadsword — more at SPADE] (1785)
: a sheathing bract or pair of bracts partly enclosing an inflorescence and especially a spadix on the same axis ⟨the *spathe* of the calla lily⟩

spath·u·late \ˈspath-yə-lət\ *adjective* [Late Latin *spathula, spatula*] (1821)
: SPATULATE ⟨*spathulate* petals of a flower⟩

spa·tial \ˈspā-shəl\ *adjective* [Latin *spatium* space] (1847)
: relating to, occupying, or having the character of space
— **spa·ti·al·i·ty** \ˌspā-shē-ˈa-lə-tē\ *noun*
— **spa·tial·ly** \ˈspā-sh(ə-)lē\ *adverb*

spatial summation *noun* (1968)
: sensory summation that involves stimulation of several spatially separated neurons at the same time

spa·tio·tem·po·ral \ˌspā-shē-ō-ˈtem-p(ə-)rəl\ *adjective* [Latin *spatium* + *tempor-, tempus* time] (1900)
1 : having both spatial and temporal qualities
2 : of or relating to space-time
— **spa·tio·tem·po·ral·ly** \-p(ə-)rə-lē\ *adverb*

¹**spat·ter** \ˈspa-tər\ *verb* [akin to Flemish *spetteren* to spatter] (1600)
intransitive verb
: to spurt forth in scattered drops ⟨blood *spattering* everywhere⟩
transitive verb
1 : to splash with or as if with a liquid; *also* : to soil in this way ⟨his coat was *spattered* with mud⟩
2 : to scatter by or as if by splashing ⟨*spatter* water⟩
3 : to cover with or as if with splashes or spots
4 : to injure by aspersion : DEFAME ⟨*spattered* my reputation⟩

²**spatter** *noun* (1797)
1 a : the act or process of spattering : the state of being spattered **b** : the noise of spattering
2 a : a drop or splash spattered on something or a spot or stain due to spattering **b** : a small amount or number : SPRINKLE ⟨a *spatter* of applause⟩

spat·ter·dock \ˈspa-tər-ˌdäk\ *noun* (1813)
: a common yellow North American water lily (*Nuphar advena*); *also* : a congeneric plant

spat·u·la \ˈspa-chə-lə, ˈspach-lə\ *noun* [Late Latin, spoon, spatula — more at EPAULET] (1525)
: a flat thin usually metal implement used especially for spreading or mixing soft substances, scooping, or lifting

spat·u·late \ˈspa-chə-lət\ *adjective* (1760)
: shaped like a spatula ⟨a *spatulate* leaf⟩ ⟨*spatulate* spines of a caterpillar⟩ ⟨a *spatulate* tool⟩
— see LEAF illustration

spätz·le *variant of* SPAETZLE

spav·in \ˈspa-vən\ *noun* [Middle English *spavayne*, from Middle French *espavain*] (15th century)
: SWELLING; *especially* : a bony enlargement of the hock of a horse associated with strain

spav·ined \-vənd\ *adjective* (15th century)
1 : affected with spavin

2 : old and decrepit **:** OVER-THE-HILL

¹spawn \'spȯn, 'spän\ *verb* [Middle English, from Anglo-French *espaundre*, from Old French *espandre* to spread out, expand, from Latin *expandere*] (15th century)
intransitive verb
1 : to deposit spawn
2 : to produce young especially in large numbers
transitive verb
1 a : to produce or deposit (eggs) — used of an aquatic animal **b :** to induce (fish) to spawn **c :** to plant with mushroom spawn
2 : BRING FORTH, GENERATE
— **spawn·er** *noun*

²spawn *noun* (15th century)
1 : the eggs of aquatic animals (as fishes or oysters) that lay many small eggs
2 : PRODUCT, OFFSPRING; *also* **:** numerous issue
3 : the seed, germ, or source of something
4 : mycelium especially prepared (as in bricks) for propagating mushrooms

spay \'spā, *nonstandard* 'spād\ *transitive verb* **spayed** \'spād, *nonstandard* 'spā-dəd\; **spay·ing** \'spā-iŋ, *nonstandard* 'spā-diŋ\ [Middle English, from Middle French *espeer* to cut with a sword, from Old French, from *espee* sword, from Latin *spatha* sword — more at SPADE] (15th century)
: to remove the ovaries of (a female animal)

spaz \'spaz\ *noun, plural* **spaz·zes** [by shortening & alteration from *spastic*] (1965)
slang **:** one who is inept **:** KLUTZ

speak \'spēk\ *verb* **spoke** \'spōk\; **spo·ken** \'spō-kən\; **speak·ing** [Middle English *speken*, from Old English *sprecan, specan*; akin to Old High German *sprehhan* to speak, Greek *spharageisthai* to crackle] (before 12th century)
intransitive verb
1 a : to utter words or articulate sounds with the ordinary voice **:** TALK (1) **:** to express thoughts, opinions, or feelings orally (2) **:** to extend a greeting (3) **:** to be on speaking terms (still were not *speaking* after the dispute) **c** (1) **:** to express oneself before a group (2) **:** to address one's remarks (*speak* to the issue)
2 a : to make a written statement (his diaries . . . *spoke* . . . of his entrancement with death —Sy Kahn) **b :** to use such an expression — often used in the phrase *so to speak* (was at the enemy's gates, so to *speak* —C. S. Forester) **c :** to serve as spokesman (*spoke* for the whole group)
3 a : to express feelings by other than verbal means (actions *speak* louder than words) **b :** SIGNAL **c :** to be interesting or attractive **:** APPEAL (great music . . . *speaks* directly to the emotions —A. N. Whitehead)
4 : to make a request **:** ASK (*spoke* for the remaining piece of pie)
5 : to make a characteristic or natural sound (all at once the thunder *spoke* —George Meredith)
6 a : TESTIFY **b :** to be indicative or suggestive (his gold . . . *spoke* of riches in the land —Julian Dana)
transitive verb
1 a (1) **:** to utter with the speaking voice **:** PRONOUNCE (2) **:** to give a recitation of **:** DECLAIM **b :** to express orally **:** DECLARE (free to *speak* their minds) **c :** ADDRESS, ACCOST; *especially* **:** HAIL
2 : to make known in writing **:** STATE
3 : to use or be able to use in speaking (*speaks* Spanish)
4 : to indicate by other than verbal means
5 *archaic* **:** DESCRIBE, DEPICT
— **speak·able** \'spē-kə-bəl\ *adjective*
— **to speak of :** worthy of mention or notice — usually used in negative constructions
-speak \-,spēk\ *noun combining form* [*newspeak*]
— used to form especially nonce words denoting a particular kind of jargon (architect*speak*) (California*speak*)

speak·easy \'spēk-,ē-zē\ *noun, plural* **-easies** (1889)
: a place where alcoholic beverages are illegally sold; *specifically* **:** such a place during the period of prohibition in the U.S.

speak·er \'spē-kər\ *noun* (14th century)
1 a : one that speaks; *especially* **:** one who uses a language (native *speakers* of French) **b :** one who makes a public speech **c :** one who acts as a spokesman
2 : the presiding officer of a deliberative assembly (*Speaker* of the House of Representatives)
3 : LOUDSPEAKER
— **speak·er·ship** \-,ship\ *noun*

speak·er·phone \'spē-kər-,fōn\ *noun* (1955)
: a combination microphone and loudspeaker device for two-way communication by telephone lines

speak·ing \'spē-kiŋ\ *adjective* (13th century)
1 a : that speaks **:** capable of speech **b :** having a population that speaks a specified language — usually used in combination (English-*speaking* countries) **c :** that involves talking or giving speeches (a *speaking* role) (a *speaking* tour)
2 : highly significant or expressive **:** ELOQUENT
3 : resembling a living being or a real object

speaking tube *noun* (1833)
: a pipe through which conversation may be conducted (as between different parts of a building)

speak-out \'spēk-,aut\ *noun* (1968)
: an event in which people publicly share their experiences of or views on an issue

speak out *intransitive verb* (1530)
1 : to speak loud enough to be heard
2 : to speak boldly **:** express an opinion frankly (*spoke out* on the issues)

speak up *intransitive verb* (1705)
1 : to express an opinion freely (*speak up* for truth and justice —Clive Bell)
2 : to speak loudly and distinctly

spean \'spēn\ *transitive verb* [Middle Dutch *spenen*] (1595)
chiefly Scottish **:** WEAN

¹spear \'spir\ *noun* [Middle English *spere*, from Old English; akin to Old High German *sper* spear, Latin *sparus* hunting spear] (before 12th century)
1 : a thrusting or throwing weapon with long shaft and sharp head or blade
2 : a sharp-pointed instrument with barbs used in spearing fish
3 : SPEARMAN

²spear (15th century)
transitive verb
1 : to pierce, strike, or take with or as if with a spear (*spear* salmon) (*speared* a chop from the platter)
2 : to catch (as a baseball) with a sudden thrust of the arm
intransitive verb
: to thrust at or wound something with or as if with a spear
— **spear·er** *noun*

³spear *adjective* (1861)
: PATERNAL, MALE (the *spear* side of the family) — compare DISTAFF

⁴spear *intransitive verb* [⁵*spear*] (1573)
of a plant **:** to thrust a spear upward

⁵spear *noun* [alteration of ¹*spire*] (1647)
: a usually young blade, shoot, or sprout (as of grass)

spear–car·ri·er \'spir-,kar-ē-ər\ *noun* (1953)
1 a : a member of an opera chorus **b :** a bit actor in a play
2 : a person whose actions are of little significance or value in an event or organization

¹spear·fish \-,fish\ *noun* (circa 1882)
: any of several billfishes (genus *Tetrapturus*) having the anterior part of the first dorsal fin about as high as the body is deep

²spearfish *intransitive verb* (circa 1949)
: to fish with a spear

spear·gun \'spir-,gən\ *noun* (1951)
: a gun that shoots a spear and is used in spearfishing

¹spear·head \-,hed\ *noun* (14th century)
1 : the sharp-pointed head of a spear
2 : a leading element, force, or influence in an undertaking or development

²spearhead *transitive verb* (1937)
: to serve as leader or leading element of

spear·man \'spir-mən\ *noun* (14th century)
: one armed with a spear

spear·mint \-,mint, -mənt\ *noun* (1562)
: a common mint (*Mentha spicata*) grown for flavoring and especially for its aromatic oil

spear–throw·er \-,thrō(-ə)r\ *noun* (1871)
: ATLATL

spear·wort \-,wərt, -,wȯrt\ *noun* (14th century)
: any of several buttercups (especially *Ranunculus flammula*) with spear-shaped leaves

spearmint

spec \'spek\ *transitive verb* **specced** *or* **spec'd** \'spekt\; **spec·cing** [²*specs*] (1965)
: to write specifications for

¹spe·cial \'spe-shəl\ *adjective* [Middle English, from Old French or Latin; Old French *especial*, from Latin *specialis* individual, particular, from *species* species] (13th century)
1 : distinguished by some unusual quality; *especially* **:** being in some way superior (our *special* blend)
2 : held in particular esteem (a *special* friend)
3 a : readily distinguishable from others of the same category **:** UNIQUE (they set it apart as a *special* day of thanksgiving) **b :** of, relating to, or constituting a species **:** SPECIFIC
4 : being other than the usual **:** ADDITIONAL, EXTRA
5 : designed for a particular purpose or occasion ☆
— **spe·cial·ness** *noun*

²special *noun* (1866)
1 : one that is used for a special service or occasion (caught the commuter *special* to work)
2 : something (as a television program) that is not part of a regular series

special assessment *noun* (1875)
: a specific tax levied on private property to meet the cost of public improvements that enhance the value of the property

special delivery *noun* (1886)
: expedited messenger delivery of mail matter for an extra fee

special district *noun* (1950)
: a political subdivision of a state established to provide a single public service (as water supply or sanitation) within a specific geographical area

☆ **SYNONYMS**
Special, especial, specific, particular, individual mean of or relating to one thing or class. SPECIAL stresses having a quality, character, identity, or use of its own (*special* ingredients). ESPECIAL may add implications of preeminence or preference (a matter of *especial* importance). SPECIFIC implies a quality or character distinguishing a kind or a species (children with *specific* nutritional needs). PARTICULAR stresses the distinctness of something as an individual (a ballet step of *particular* difficulty). INDIVIDUAL implies unequivocal reference to one of a class or group (valued each *individual* opinion).

\ə\ abut \ᵊ\ kitten \ər\ further \a\ ash \ā\ ace \ä\ mop, mar \au̇\ out \ch\ chin \e\ bet \ē\ easy \g\ go \i\ hit \ī\ ice \j\ job \ŋ\ sing \ō\ go \ȯ\ law \ȯi\ boy \th\ thin \t͟h\ the \ü\ loot \u̇\ foot \y\ yet \zh\ vision *see also* Guide to Pronunciation

special drawing rights *noun* (1967)
: a means of exchange used by governments to settle their international indebtedness

special education *noun* (1921)
: classes for students (as the handicapped) with special educational needs

special effects *noun plural* (1937)
: visual or sound effects introduced into a motion picture or a taped television production

Special Forces *noun plural* (1962)
: a branch of the army composed of soldiers specially trained in guerrilla warfare

special handling *noun* (1928)
: the handling of parcel-post or fourth-class mail as first-class but not as special-delivery matter for an extra fee

special interest *noun* (1910)
: a person or group seeking to influence legislative or government policy to further often narrowly defined interests; *especially* : LOBBY

spe·cial·i·sa·tion, spe·cial·ise, specialised *British variant of* SPECIALIZATION, SPECIALIZE, SPECIALIZED

spe·cial·ism \'spe-shə-ˌli-zəm\ *noun* (1856)
1 : specialization in an occupation or branch of learning
2 : a field of specialization : SPECIALTY

spe·cial·ist \'spe-sh(ə-)list\ *noun* (1856)
1 : one who specializes in a particular occupation, practice, or branch of learning
2 : any of four enlisted ranks in the army corresponding to the grades of corporal through sergeant first class
— **specialist** *or* **spe·cial·is·tic** \ˌspe-shə-'lis-tik\ *adjective*

spe·ci·al·i·ty \ˌspe-shē-'a-lə-tē\ *noun, plural* **-ties** (15th century)
1 : a special mark or quality
2 : a special object or class of objects
3 a : a special aptitude or skill **b** : SPECIALTY 3

spe·cial·i·za·tion \ˌspe-sh(ə-)lə-'zā-shən\ *noun* (1843)
1 : a making or becoming specialized
2 a : structural adaptation of a body part or of an organism for life in a particular environment **b** : a body part or an organism adapted by specialization

spe·cial·ize \'spe-shə-ˌlīz\ *verb* **-ized; -izing** (1613)
transitive verb
1 : to make particular mention of : PARTICULARIZE
2 : to apply or direct to a specific end or use ⟨*specialized* their study⟩
intransitive verb
1 : to concentrate one's efforts in a special activity, field, or practice
2 : to undergo specialization; *especially* : to change adaptively

specialized *adjective* (1853)
1 : characterized by or exhibiting biological specialization; *especially* : highly differentiated especially in a particular direction or for a particular end
2 : designed or fitted for one particular purpose or occupation ⟨*specialized* personnel⟩

spe·cial·ly \'spe-sh(ə-)lē\ *adverb* (14th century)
1 : in a special manner ⟨treated her friends *specially*⟩
2 a : for a special purpose ⟨dresses made *specially* for the occasion⟩ ⟨wines *specially* selected to match each course⟩ **b** : in particular : SPECIFICALLY ⟨made *specially* for you⟩
3 : ESPECIALLY 2 ⟨makes a *specially* fine curry⟩ ⟨was *specially* pleased with the gift⟩

special pleading *noun* (1684)
1 : the allegation of special or new matter to offset the effect of matter pleaded by the opposite side and admitted, as distinguished from a direct denial of the matter pleaded
2 : misleading argument that presents one point or phase as if it covered the entire question at issue

special relativity *noun* (1941)
: RELATIVITY 3a

special theory of relativity (1920)
: RELATIVITY 3a

spe·cial·ty \'spe-shəl-tē\ *noun, plural* **-ties** [Middle English *specialte*, from Middle French *especialté*, from Late Latin *specialitat-, specialitas,* from Latin *specialis* special] (15th century)
1 : a distinctive mark or quality
2 a : a special object or class of objects: as (1) : a legal agreement embodied in a sealed instrument (2) : a product of a special kind or of special excellence ⟨fried chicken is my *specialty*⟩ **b** : the state of being special, distinctive, or peculiar
3 : something in which one specializes

spe·ci·a·tion \ˌspē-shē-'ā-shən, -sē-\ *noun* (1906)
: the process of biological species formation
— **spe·ci·ate** \'spē-shē-ˌāt, -sē-\ *intransitive verb*
— **spe·ci·a·tion·al** \ˌspē-shē-'ā-shnəl, -sē-, -shə-nᵊl\ *adjective*

¹spe·cie \'spē-shē, -sē\ *noun* [from *in specie,* from Latin, in kind] (1617)
: money in coin
— **in specie** : in the same or like form or kind ⟨ready to return insult *in specie*⟩; *also* : in coin

²specie *noun* [back-formation from *species* (taken as a plural)] (1711)
nonstandard : SPECIES

¹spe·cies \'spē-(ˌ)shēz, -(ˌ)sēz\ *noun, plural* **species** [Middle English, from Latin, appearance, kind, species, from *specere* to look — more at SPY] (14th century)
1 a : KIND, SORT **b** : a class of individuals having common attributes and designated by a common name; *specifically* : a logical division of a genus or more comprehensive class **c** : the human race : human beings — often used with *the* ⟨survival of the *species* in the nuclear age⟩ **d** (1) : a category of biological classification ranking immediately below the genus or subgenus, comprising related organisms or populations potentially capable of interbreeding, and being designated by a binomial that consists of the name of a genus followed by a Latin or latinized uncapitalized noun or adjective agreeing grammatically with the genus name (2) : an individual or kind belonging to a biological species **e** : a particular kind of atomic nucleus, atom, molecule, or ion
2 : the consecrated eucharistic elements of the Roman Catholic or Eastern Orthodox Eucharist
3 a : a mental image; *also* : a sensible object **b** : an object of thought correlative with a natural object
word history see SPICE

²species *adjective* (1899)
: belonging to a biological species as distinguished from a horticultural variety ⟨a *species* rose⟩

spe·cies·ism \'spē-shē-ˌzi-zəm, -sē-\ *noun* (1973)
1 : prejudice or discrimination based on species; *especially* : discrimination against animals
2 : the assumption of human superiority on which speciesism is based

¹spe·cif·ic \spi-'si-fik\ *adjective* [Late Latin *specificus,* from Latin *species*] (circa 1631)
1 a : constituting or falling into a specifiable category **b** : sharing or being those properties of something that allow it to be referred to a particular category
2 a : restricted to a particular individual, situation, relation, or effect ⟨a disease *specific* to horses⟩ **b** : exerting a distinctive influence (as on a body part or a disease) ⟨*specific* antibodies⟩
3 : free from ambiguity : ACCURATE ⟨a *specific* statement of faith⟩
4 : of, relating to, or constituting a species and especially a biologic species

5 a : being any of various arbitrary physical constants and especially one relating a quantitative attribute to unit mass, volume, or area **b** : imposed at a fixed rate per unit (as of weight or count) ⟨*specific* import duties⟩ — compare AD VALOREM
synonym see SPECIAL, EXPLICIT
— **spe·cif·i·cal·ly** \-fi-k(ə-)lē\ *adverb*

²specific *noun* (1661)
1 a : something peculiarly adapted to a purpose or use **b** : a drug or remedy having a specific mitigating effect on a disease
2 a : a characteristic quality or trait **b** : DETAILS, PARTICULARS — usually used in plural ⟨haggling over the legal and financial *specifics* of independence —*Time*⟩ **c** *plural* : SPECIFICATION 2a

spec·i·fi·ca·tion \ˌspe-sə-fə-'kā-shən, ˌspes-fə-\ *noun* (1633)
1 : the act or process of specifying
2 a : a detailed precise presentation of something or of a plan or proposal for something — usually used in plural **b** : a statement of legal particulars (as of charges or of contract terms); *also* : a single item of such statement **c** : a written description of an invention for which a patent is sought

specific epithet *noun* (1906)
: the Latin or latinized noun or adjective that follows the genus name in a taxonomic binomial

specific gravity *noun* (1666)
: the ratio of the density of a substance to the density of some substance (as pure water) taken as a standard when both densities are obtained by weighing in air

specific heat *noun* (1832)
: the heat in calories required to raise the temperature of one gram of a substance one degree Celsius

specific impulse *noun* (1947)
: the thrust produced per unit rate of consumption of the propellant that is usually expressed in pounds of thrust per pound of propellant used per second and that is a measure of the efficiency of a rocket engine

spec·i·fic·i·ty \ˌspe-sə-'fi-sə-tē\ *noun* (1876)
: the quality or condition of being specific: as **a** : the condition of being peculiar to a particular individual or group of organisms ⟨host *specificity* of a parasite⟩ **b** : the condition of participating in or catalyzing only one or a few chemical reactions ⟨the *specificity* of an enzyme⟩

specific performance *noun* (circa 1876)
1 : the performance of a legal contract strictly or substantially according to its terms
2 : an equitable remedy enjoining specific performance

spec·i·fy \'spe-sə-ˌfī\ *transitive verb* **-fied; -fy·ing** [Middle English *specifien,* from Middle French *specifier,* from Late Latin *specificare,* from *specificus*] (14th century)
1 : to name or state explicitly or in detail
2 : to include as an item in a specification
— **spec·i·fi·able** \ˌspe-sə-'fī-ə-bəl\ *adjective*
— **spec·i·fi·er** \'spe-sə-ˌfī(-ə)r\ *noun*

spec·i·men \'spes-mən, 'spe-sə-\ *noun* [Latin, from *specere* to look at, look — more at SPY] (1610)
1 a : an individual, item, or part considered typical of a group, class, or whole **b** : a portion or quantity of material for use in testing, examination, or study ⟨a urine *specimen*⟩
2 a : something that obviously belongs to a particular category but is noticed by reason of an individual distinguishing characteristic **b** : PERSON, INDIVIDUAL ⟨he's a tough *specimen*⟩
3 : a plant grown for exhibition or in the open to display its full development ⟨*specimen* trees⟩ ⟨*specimen* plantings⟩
synonym see INSTANCE

spe·ci·os·i·ty \ˌspē-shē-'ä-sə-tē\ *noun* (1608)
: the quality or state of being specious : SPECIOUSNESS

spe·cious \'spē-shəs\ *adjective* [Middle English, visually pleasing, from Latin *speciosus* beautiful, plausible, from *species*] (1513)
1 *obsolete* : SHOWY
2 : having deceptive attraction or allure
3 : having a false look of truth or genuineness : SOPHISTIC
— **spe·cious·ly** *adverb*
— **spe·cious·ness** *noun*

¹speck \'spek\ *noun* [Middle English *specke*, from Old English *specca*] (before 12th century)
1 : a small discoloration or spot especially from stain or decay
2 : a very small amount : BIT
3 : something marked or marred with specks
— **specked** \'spekt\ *adjective*

²speck *transitive verb* (1580)
: to produce specks on or in

¹speck·le \'spe-kəl\ *noun* [Middle English; akin to Old English *specca*] (15th century)
: a little speck (as of color)

²speckle *transitive verb* **speck·led; speck·ling** \-k(ə-)liŋ\ (circa 1570)
1 : to mark with speckles
2 : to be distributed in or on like speckles

speckled perch *noun* (1877)
: BLACK CRAPPIE

speckled trout *noun* (1805)
1 : BROOK TROUT
2 : SPOTTED SEA TROUT

speckle interferometry *noun* (1970)
: a technique for generating a clear composite image of a celestial object blurred by atmospheric turbulence in which a large number of short-exposure photographs are mathematically correlated by a computer

¹specs \'speks\ *noun plural* [contraction of *spectacles*] (1807)
: GLASSES

²specs *noun plural* [by contraction] (1942)
: SPECIFICATIONS

spec·ta·cle \'spek-ti-kəl *also* -ti-kəl\ *noun* [Middle English, from Middle French, from Latin *spectaculum*, from *spectare* to watch, frequentative of *specere* to look, look at — more at SPY] (14th century)
1 a : something exhibited to view as unusual, notable, or entertaining; *especially* : an eye-catching or dramatic public display **b** : an object of curiosity or contempt ⟨made a *spectacle* of herself⟩
2 *plural* : GLASSES
3 : something (as natural markings on an animal) suggesting a pair of glasses

spec·ta·cled \-kəld\ *adjective* (1607)
1 : having or wearing spectacles
2 : having markings suggesting a pair of spectacles ⟨a *spectacled* alligator⟩

¹spec·tac·u·lar \spek-'ta-kyə-lər, spək-\ *adjective* [Latin *spectaculum*] (1682)
: of, relating to, or being a spectacle : STRIKING, SENSATIONAL ⟨a *spectacular* display of fireworks⟩
— **spec·tac·u·lar·ly** *adverb*

²spectacular *noun* (1890)
: something that is spectacular; *especially* : an elaborate film, television, or theatrical production

spec·tate \'spek-ˌtāt\ *intransitive verb* **spec·tat·ed; spec·tat·ing** [back-formation from *spectator*] (1858)
: to be present as a spectator (as at a sports event)

spec·ta·tor \'spek-ˌtā-tər, spek-'\ *noun* [Latin, from *spectare* to watch] (circa 1586)
1 : one who looks on or watches
2 : a woman's pump usually having contrasting colors with a perforated design at the toe and sometimes heel
— **spectator** *adjective*
— **spec·ta·tor·i·al** \ˌspek-tə-'tōr-ē-əl, -'tor-\ *adjective*
— **spec·ta·tor·ship** \'spek-ˌtā-tər-ˌship, spek-'\ *noun*

spec·ter *or* **spec·tre** \'spek-tər\ *noun* [French *spectre*, from Latin *spectrum* appearance, specter, from *specere* to look, look at — more at SPY] (1605)
1 : a visible disembodied spirit : GHOST
2 : something that haunts or perturbs the mind : PHANTASM ⟨the *specter* of hunger⟩

spec·ti·no·my·cin \ˌspek-tə-nō-'mī-sᵊn\ *noun* [*spect-* (from New Latin *spectabilis*, specific epithet of *Streptomyces spectabilis*) + actinomycin] (1964)
: a white crystalline broad-spectrum antibiotic $C_{14}H_{24}N_2O_7$ produced by a bacterium (*Streptomyces spectabilis*) that is used clinically especially in the form of its hydrochloride to treat gonorrhea

spec·tral \'spek-trəl\ *adjective* (1815)
1 : of, relating to, or suggesting a specter : GHOSTLY
2 : of, relating to, or made by a spectrum
— **spec·tral·ly** \'spek-trə-lē\ *adverb*

spectral line *noun* (1866)
: one of a series of linear images of the narrow slit of a spectrograph or similar instrument corresponding to a component of the spectrum of the radiation emitted by a particular source

spectro- *combining form* [New Latin *spectrum*]
: spectrum ⟨*spectro*scope⟩

spec·tro·flu·o·rom·e·ter \'spek-(ˌ)trō-ˌflü-'rä-mə-tər, -flō-, -flō-\ *also* **spec·tro·flu·o·rim·e·ter** \-'ri-\ *noun* (1957)
: a device for measuring and recording fluorescence spectra
— **spec·tro·flu·o·ro·met·ric** \-ˌflür-ə-'me-trik, -ˌflo-, -ˌflō-\ *adjective*
— **spec·tro·flu·o·rom·e·try** \-flü-'rä-mə-trē, -ˌflo-, -ˌflō-\ *noun*

spec·tro·gram \'spek-t(r)ə-ˌgram\ *noun* [International Scientific Vocabulary] (1892)
: a photograph or diagram of a spectrum

spec·tro·graph \-ˌgraf\ *noun* [International Scientific Vocabulary] (1884)
: an instrument for dispersing radiation (as electromagnetic radiation or sound waves) into a spectrum and photographing or mapping the spectrum
— **spec·tro·graph·ic** \ˌspek-t(r)ə-'gra-fik\ *adjective*
— **spec·tro·graph·i·cal·ly** \-fi-k(ə-)lē\ *adverb*
— **spec·trog·ra·phy** \spek-'trä-grə-fē\ *noun*

spec·tro·he·lio·gram \ˌspek-trō-'hē-lē-ə-ˌgram\ *noun* (1905)
: a photograph of the sun that is made by monochromatic light and shows the sun's faculae and prominences

spec·tro·he·lio·graph \-ˌgraf\ *noun* [International Scientific Vocabulary] (1892)
: an apparatus for making spectroheliograms
— **spec·tro·he·li·og·ra·phy** \-ˌhē-lē-'ä-grə-fē\ *noun*

spec·tro·he·lio·scope \-'hē-lē-ə-ˌskōp\ *noun* [International Scientific Vocabulary] (1906)
1 : SPECTROHELIOGRAPH
2 : an instrument similar to a spectroheliograph used for visual as distinguished from photographic observations

spec·trom·e·ter \spek-'trä-mə-tər\ *noun* [International Scientific Vocabulary] (1874)
1 : an instrument used for measuring wavelengths of light spectra
2 : any of various analytical instruments in which an emission (as of particles or radiation) is dispersed according to some property (as mass or energy) of the emission and the amount of dispersion is measured ⟨nuclear magnetic resonance *spectrometer*⟩
— **spec·tro·met·ric** \ˌspek-trə-'me-trik\ *adjective*
— **spec·trom·e·try** \spek-'trä-mə-trē\ *noun*

spec·tro·pho·tom·e·ter \ˌspek-trō-fə-'tä-mə-tər\ *noun* [International Scientific Vocabulary] (1881)
: a photometer for measuring the relative intensities of the light in different parts of a spectrum
— **spec·tro·pho·to·met·ric** \-trə-ˌfō-tə-'me-trik\ *also* **spec·tro·pho·to·met·ri·cal** \-tri-kəl\ *adjective*
— **spec·tro·pho·to·met·ri·cal·ly** \-tri-k(ə-)lē\ *adverb*
— **spec·tro·pho·tom·e·try** \ˌspek-(ˌ)trō-fə-'tä-mə-trē\ *noun*

spec·tro·scope \'spek-trə-ˌskōp\ *noun* [International Scientific Vocabulary] (1861)
: an instrument for forming and examining spectra especially in the visible region of the electromagnetic spectrum
— **spec·tro·scop·ic** \ˌspek-trə-'skä-pik\ *adjective*
— **spec·tro·scop·i·cal·ly** \-pi-k(ə-)lē\ *adverb*
— **spec·tros·co·pist** \spek-'träs-kə-pist\ *noun*

spec·tros·co·py \spek-'träs-kə-pē\ *noun* (1870)
1 : the production and investigation of spectra
2 : the process or technique of using a spectroscope or spectrometer

spec·trum \'spek-trəm\ *noun, plural* **spec·tra** \-trə\ *or* **spectrums** [New Latin, from Latin, appearance — more at SPECTER] (1671)
1 a : a continuum of color formed when a beam of white light is dispersed (as by passage through a prism) so that its component wavelengths are arranged in order **b** : any of various continua that resemble a spectrum in consisting of an ordered arrangement by a particular characteristic (as frequency or energy): as (1) : ELECTROMAGNETIC SPECTRUM (2) : RADIO SPECTRUM (3) : the range of frequencies of sound waves (4) : MASS SPECTRUM **c** : the representation (as a plot) of a spectrum
2 a : a continuous sequence or range ⟨a wide *spectrum* of interests⟩ **b** : kinds of organisms associated with a particular situation (as an environment) or susceptible to an agent (as an antibiotic)

spec·u·lar \'spe-kyə-lər\ *adjective* [Latin *specularis* of a mirror, from *speculum*] (1661)
: of, relating to, or having the qualities of a mirror
— **spec·u·lar·i·ty** \ˌspe-kyə-'lar-ə-tē\ *noun*
— **spec·u·lar·ly** \'spe-kyə-lər-lē\ *adverb*

spec·u·late \'spe-kyə-ˌlāt\ *verb* **-lat·ed; -lat·ing** [Latin *speculatus*, past participle of *speculari* to spy out, examine, from *specula* watchtower, from *specere* to look, look at — more at SPY] (1599)
intransitive verb
1 a : to meditate on or ponder a subject : REFLECT **b** : to review something idly or casually and often inconclusively
2 : to assume a business risk in hope of gain; *especially* : to buy or sell in expectation of profiting from market fluctuations
transitive verb
1 : to take to be true on the basis of insufficient evidence : THEORIZE ⟨*speculated* that a virus caused the disease⟩
2 : to be curious or doubtful about : WONDER ⟨*speculates* whether it will rain all vacation⟩
synonym see THINK
— **spec·u·la·tor** \-ˌlā-tər\ *noun*

spec·u·la·tion \ˌspe-kyə-'lā-shən\ *noun* (14th century)
: an act or instance of speculating: as **a** : assumption of unusual business risk in hopes of

obtaining commensurate gain **b** : a transaction involving such speculation

spec·u·la·tive \'spe-kyə-lə-tiv, -,lā-\ *adjective* (14th century)
1 : involving, based on, or constituting intellectual speculation; *also* : theoretical rather than demonstrable ⟨*speculative* knowledge⟩
2 : marked by questioning curiosity ⟨gave him a *speculative* glance⟩
3 : of, relating to, or being a financial speculation ⟨*speculative* stocks⟩ ⟨*speculative* venture⟩
— **spec·u·la·tive·ly** *adverb*

spec·u·lum \'spe-kyə-ləm\ *noun, plural* **-la** \-lə\ *also* **-lums** [Middle English, from Latin, mirror, from *specere*] (15th century)
1 : an instrument inserted into a body passage for inspection or medication
2 : a drawing or table showing the relative positions of all the planets (as in an astrological nativity)
3 : a patch of color on the secondaries of most ducks and some other birds

speech \'spēch\ *noun* [Middle English *speche*, from Old English *sprǣc*, *spǣc*; akin to Old English *sprecan* to speak — more at SPEAK] (before 12th century)
1 a : the communication or expression of thoughts in spoken words **b** : exchange of spoken words : CONVERSATION
2 a : something that is spoken : UTTERANCE **b** : a usually public discourse : ADDRESS
3 a : LANGUAGE, DIALECT **b** : an individual manner or style of speaking
4 : the power of expressing or communicating thoughts by speaking

speech community *noun* (1894)
: a group of people sharing characteristic patterns of vocabulary, grammar, and pronunciation

speech form *noun* (1863)
: LINGUISTIC FORM

speech·i·fy \'spē-chə-,fī\ *intransitive verb* **-ified; -ify·ing** (1723)
: to make a speech

speech·less \'spēch-ləs\ *adjective* (before 12th century)
1 : unable to speak : DUMB
2 : not speaking : SILENT
3 : not capable of being expressed in words
— **speech·less·ly** *adverb*
— **speech·less·ness** *noun*

speech·writ·er \-,rī-tər\ *noun* (1834)
: a person who writes speeches (as for a politician)

¹speed \'spēd\ *noun* [Middle English *spede*, from Old English *spēd*; akin to Old High German *spuot* prosperity, speed, Old English *spōwan* to succeed, Latin *spes* hope, Latin *spēti* to be in time] (before 12th century)
1 *archaic* : prosperity in an undertaking : SUCCESS
2 a : the act or state of moving swiftly : SWIFTNESS **b** : rate of motion: as (1) : VELOCITY 1, 3a (2) : the magnitude of a velocity irrespective of direction **c** : IMPETUS
3 : swiftness or rate of performance or action
4 a : the sensitivity of a photographic film, plate, or paper expressed numerically **b** : the light-gathering power of a lens or optical system **c** : the time during which a camera shutter is open
5 : a transmission gear in automotive vehicles or bicycles — usually used in combination ⟨a ten-*speed* bicycle⟩
6 : someone or something that appeals to one's taste
7 : METHAMPHETAMINE; *also* : a related stimulant drug and especially an amphetamine
synonym see HASTE
— **speed·ster** \'spēd-stər\ *noun*
— **at speed** *chiefly British* : FAST, RAPIDLY
— **up to speed** : operating at full effectiveness or potential

²speed *verb* **sped** \'sped\ *or* **speed·ed; speed·ing** (before 12th century)
intransitive verb

1 a *archaic* : to prosper in an undertaking **b** *archaic* : GET ALONG, FARE
2 a : to make haste ⟨*sped* to her bedside⟩ **b** : to go or drive at excessive or illegal speed
3 : to move, work, or take place faster : ACCELERATE ⟨the heart *speeds* up⟩
transitive verb
1 a *archaic* : to cause or help to prosper : AID **b** : to further the success of
2 a : to cause to move quickly : HASTEN **b** : to wish Godspeed to **c** : to increase the speed of : ACCELERATE
3 : to send out ⟨*speed* an arrow⟩
— **speed·er** *noun*

¹speed·ball \'spēd-,bȯl\ *noun* (1905)
1 *slang* : a dose of cocaine mixed with heroin or morphine or an amphetamine and usually taken by injection
2 a : a game which resembles soccer but in which a ball caught in the air may be passed with the hands and in which a score is made by kicking or heading the ball between the goalposts or by a successful forward pass over the goal line
3 : one that is outstandingly fast

²speedball *intransitive verb* (1970)
slang : to take a speedball especially by injection

speed·boat \-,bōt\ *noun* (1911)
: a fast launch or motorboat
— **speed·boat·ing** \-,bō-tiŋ\ *noun*

speed bump *noun* (1972)
: a low raised ridge across a roadway (as in a parking lot) to limit vehicle speed

speed freak *noun* (1967)
: one who habitually misuses amphetamines and especially methamphetamine

speed limit *noun* (1902)
: the maximum or minimum speed permitted by law in a given area under specified circumstances

speedo \'spē-(,)dō\ *noun, plural* **speed·os** [by shortening] (1934)
chiefly British : SPEEDOMETER

speed of light *noun* (1823)
: a fundamental physical constant that is the speed at which electromagnetic radiation propagates in a vacuum and that has a value fixed by international convention of 299,792,458 meters per second — symbol c

speed·om·e·ter \spi-'dä-mə-tər\ *noun* (1903)
1 : an instrument for indicating speed : TACHOMETER
2 : an instrument for indicating distance traversed as well as speed of travel; *also* : ODOMETER

speed–read·ing \'spēd-,rē-diŋ\ *noun* (1962)
: a method of reading rapidly by skimming
— **speed–read** *transitive verb*

speed shop *noun* (1953)
: a shop that sells custom automotive equipment especially to hot-rodders

speed skating *noun* (1885)
: the sport of racing on skates
— **speed skater** *noun*

speed trap *noun* (1925)
: a stretch of road policed by often concealed officers or devices (as radar) so as to catch speeders

speed-up \'spēd-,əp\ *noun* (1921)
1 : ACCELERATION
2 : an employer's demand for accelerated output without increased pay

speed·way \'spēd-,wā\ *noun* (1894)
1 : a public road on which fast driving is allowed; *specifically* : EXPRESSWAY
2 : a racecourse for automobiles or motorcycles
3 : a sprint race for motorcycles

speed·well \'spēd-,wel\ *noun* (1578)
: a perennial European herb (*Veronica officinalis*) of the snapdragon family that is naturalized in North America and has small bluish flowers in axillary racemes; *also* : any plant of the same genus

speedy \'spē-dē\ *adjective* **speed·i·er; -est** (14th century)
: marked by swiftness of motion or action; *also* : PROMPT 2
synonym see FAST
— **speed·i·ly** \'spē-d°l-ē\ *adverb*
— **speed·i·ness** \'spē-dē-nəs\ *noun*

speel \'spē(ə)l\ *verb* [origin unknown] (1513)
chiefly Scottish : CLIMB

speer *or* **speir** \'spir\ *verb* [Middle English (Scots) *speren*, from Old English *spyrian* to seek after; akin to Old English *spor* spoor] (before 13th century)
chiefly Scottish : ASK, INQUIRE

spe·le·ol·o·gy \,spē-lē-'ä-lə-jē, ,spe-\ *noun* [Latin *speleum* cave (from Greek *spēlaion*) + International Scientific Vocabulary *-o-* + *-logy* — more at SPELUNKER] (1895)
: the scientific study or exploration of caves
— **spe·le·o·log·i·cal** \,spē-lē-ə-'lä-ji-kəl, ,spe-\ *adjective*
— **spe·le·ol·o·gist** \,spē-lē-'ä-lə-jist, ,spe-\ *noun*

¹spell \'spel\ *verb* **spelled** \'speld, 'spelt\; **spell·ing** [Middle English, from Middle French *espeller*, of Germanic origin; akin to Old English *spell* talk] (14th century)
transitive verb
1 : to read slowly and with difficulty — often used with *out*
2 : to find out by study : come to understand — often used with *out* ⟨it requires some pains to *spell* out those decorations —F. J. Mather⟩
3 a (1) : to name the letters of in order; *also* : to write or print the letters of in order (2) : to write or print the letters of in a particular way ⟨you can *spell* it either way⟩ ⟨I *spelled* it wrong⟩ **b** : to make up (a word) ⟨what word do these letters *spell*⟩ **c** : WRITE 1b ⟨catnip is *spelled* as one word⟩
4 : to add up to : MEAN ⟨crop failure was likely to *spell* stark famine —Stringfellow Barr⟩
intransitive verb
: to form words with letters ⟨teach children to *spell*⟩; *also* : to spell words in a certain way ⟨*spells* the way he speaks⟩

²spell *noun* [Middle English, talk, tale, from Old English; akin to Old High German *spel* talk, tale] (1579)
1 a : a spoken word or form of words held to have magic power : INCANTATION **b** : a state of enchantment
2 : a strong compelling influence or attraction

³spell \'spel\ *transitive verb* **spelled** \'speld\; **spell·ing** (circa 1623)
: to put under a spell

⁴spell *noun* [probably alteration of Middle English *spale* substitute, from Old English *spala*] (1593)
1 a *archaic* : a shift of workers **b** : one's turn at work
2 a : a period spent in a job or occupation **b** *chiefly Australian* : a period of rest from work, activity, or use
3 a : an indeterminate period of time ⟨waited a *spell* before advancing⟩; *also* : a continuous period of time ⟨did a *spell* in prison⟩ **b** : a stretch of a specified type of weather
4 : a period of bodily or mental distress or disorder ⟨a *spell* of coughing⟩ ⟨fainting *spells*⟩

⁵spell *verb* **spelled** \'speld\; **spell·ing** [Middle English *spelen*, from Old English *spelian*; akin to Old English *spala* substitute] (1595)
transitive verb
1 : to take the place of for a time : RELIEVE ⟨he and the other assistant . . . *spelled* each other —Mary McCarthy⟩
2 : REST
intransitive verb
1 : to work in turns
2 *chiefly Australian* : to rest from work or activity for a time

spell·bind \'spel-,bīnd\ *transitive verb* **-bound** \-,baund\; **-bind·ing** [back-formation from *spellbound*] (1808)

: to bind or hold by or as if by a spell or charm **:** FASCINATE

spell·bind·er \-ˌbīn-dər\ *noun* (1888)
: a speaker of compelling eloquence; *also*
: one that compels attention

spell·bind·ing \-ˌbīn-diŋ\ *adjective* (circa 1934)
: holding the attention as if by a spell
— **spell·bind·ing·ly** \-diŋ-lē\ *adverb*

spell·bound \-ˌbau̇nd\ *adjective* (1799)
: held by or as if by a spell

spell·er \'spe-lər\ *noun* (15th century)
1 : a person who spells words especially in a certain way ⟨a poor *speller*⟩
2 : a book with exercises for teaching spelling

spell·ing \'spe-liŋ\ *noun* (15th century)
1 : the forming of words from letters according to accepted usage **:** ORTHOGRAPHY
2 a : a sequence of letters composing a word **b :** the way in which a word is spelled

spelling bee *noun* (1872)
: a spelling contest in which contestants are eliminated as soon as they misspell a word

spelling pronunciation *noun* (1901)
: a pronunciation of a word based on its spelling alone

spell out *transitive verb* (1940)
1 : to make plain ⟨*spelled out* the orders in detail⟩
2 : to write or print in letters and in full ⟨numbers are to be *spelled out*⟩

¹spelt \'spelt\ *noun* [Middle English, from Old English, from Late Latin *spelta*, of Germanic origin; perhaps akin to Middle High German *spelte* split piece of wood, Old High German *spaltan* to split — more at SPLIT] (before 12th century)
: a wheat (*Triticum aestivum spelta*) with lax spikes and spikelets containing two light red kernels

²spelt \'spelt\ *chiefly British past and past participle of* SPELL

spel·ter \'spel-tər\ *noun* [probably alteration of Middle Dutch *speauter*] (1661)
: ZINC; *especially* **:** zinc cast in slabs for commercial use

spe·lunk·er \spi-'ləŋ-kər, 'spē-ˌ\ *noun* [Latin *spelunca* cave, from Greek *spēlynx*; akin to Greek *spēlaion* cave] (1944)
: one who makes a hobby of exploring and studying caves

spe·lunk·ing \-kiŋ\ *noun* (1944)
: the hobby or practice of exploring caves

spence \'spen(t)s\ *noun* [Middle English, from Middle French *despense*, from Medieval Latin *dispensa*, from Latin, feminine of *dispensus*, past participle of *dispendere* to weigh out — more at DISPENSE] (14th century)
chiefly dialect British **:** PANTRY

¹spen·cer \'spen(t)-sər\ *noun* [George John, 2d earl *Spencer* (died 1834) English politician] (1795)
: a short waist-length jacket

²spencer *noun* [probably from the name *Spencer*] (1840)
: a trysail abaft the foremast or mainmast

Spen·ce·ri·an \spen-'sir-ē-ən\ *adjective* [Platt R. *Spencer* (died 1864) American calligrapher] (1863)
: of or relating to a form of slanting handwriting

Spen·ce·ri·an·ism \spen-'sir-ē-ə-ˌni-zəm\ *noun* (1881)
: the synthetic philosophy of Herbert Spencer that has as its central idea the mechanistic evolution of the cosmos from relative simplicity to relative complexity

spend \'spend\ *verb* **spent** \'spent\; **spending** [Middle English, from Old English & Old French; Old English *spendan*, from Latin *expendere* to expend; Old French *despendre*, from Latin *dispendere* to weigh out — more at DISPENSE] (13th century)
transitive verb
1 : to use up or pay out **:** EXPEND

2 a : EXHAUST, WEAR OUT ⟨the hurricane gradually *spent* itself⟩ **b :** to consume wastefully **:** SQUANDER ⟨the waters are not ours to *spend* —J. R. Ellis⟩
3 : to cause or permit to elapse **:** PASS ⟨*spend* the night⟩
4 : GIVE UP, SACRIFICE
intransitive verb
1 : to expend or waste wealth or strength
2 : to become expended or consumed
3 : to have an orgasm
— **spend·able** \'spen-də-bəl\ *adjective*
— **spend·er** *noun*

spending money *noun* (15th century)
: POCKET MONEY

spend·thrift \'spen(d)-ˌthrift\ *noun* (1601)
: a person who spends improvidently or wastefully
— **spendthrift** *adjective*

Spen·gle·ri·an \ˌshpeŋ-'glir-ē-ən, ˌspeŋ-, -'lir-\ *adjective* (1922)
: of or relating to the theory of world history developed by Oswald Spengler which holds that all major cultures undergo similar cyclical developments from birth to maturity to decay
— **Spenglerian** *noun*

Spen·se·ri·an stanza \spen-'sir-ē-ən-\ *noun* [Edmund *Spenser*] (1817)
: a stanza consisting of eight verses of iambic pentameter and an alexandrine with a rhyme scheme *ababbcbcc*

spent \'spent\ *adjective* [Middle English, from past participle of *spenden* to spend] (15th century)
1 a : used up **:** CONSUMED **b :** exhausted of active or required components or qualities often for a particular purpose ⟨*spent* nuclear fuel⟩
2 : drained of energy or effectiveness **:** EXHAUSTED
3 : exhausted of spawn or sperm ⟨a *spent* salmon⟩

sperm \'spərm\ *noun, plural* **sperm** *or* **sperms** [Middle English, from Middle French *esperme*, from Late Latin *spermat-, sperma*, from Greek, literally, seed, from *speirein* to sow; probably akin to Armenian *p'aratem* I dispense] (14th century)
1 a : the male fecundating fluid **:** SEMEN **b :** a male gamete
2 : a product (as spermaceti or oil) of the sperm whale

sperm- *or* **spermo-** *or* **sperma-** *or* **spermi-** *combining form* [Greek *sperm-, spermo-*, from *sperma*]
: seed **:** germ **:** sperm ⟨*sperma*theca⟩ ⟨*spermi*cide⟩

sper·ma·ce·ti \ˌspər-mə-'sē-tē, -'se-\ *noun* [Middle English *sperma cete*, from Medieval Latin *sperma ceti* whale sperm] (15th century)
: a waxy solid obtained from the oil of cetaceans and especially sperm whales and used in ointments, cosmetics, and candles

sper·ma·go·ni·um \ˌspər-mə-'gō-nē-əm\ *noun, plural* **-nia** \-nē-ə\ [New Latin] (1861)
: a flask-shaped or depressed receptacle in which spermatia are produced in some fungi and lichens

sper·ma·ry \'spər-mə-rē, 'spərm-rē\ *noun, plural* **-ries** [New Latin *spermarium*, from Greek *sperma*] (circa 1859)
: an organ in which male gametes are developed

spermat- *or* **spermato-** *combining form* [Middle French, from Late Latin, from Greek, from *spermat-, sperma*]
: seed **:** spermatozoon ⟨*spermat*id⟩ ⟨*spermato*cyte⟩

sper·ma·the·ca \ˌspər-mə-'thē-kə\ *noun* [New Latin] (1826)
: a sac for sperm storage in the female reproductive tract of various lower animals and especially insects

sper·mat·ic \ˌspər-'ma-tik\ *adjective* (15th century)
1 : relating to sperm or a spermary
2 : resembling, carrying, or full of sperm

spermatic cord *noun* (1797)
: a cord that suspends the testis within the scrotum and contains the vas deferens and vessels and nerves of the testis

sper·ma·tid \'spər-mə-təd\ *noun* (1889)
: one of the haploid cells that are formed by division of the secondary spermatocytes and that differentiate into spermatozoa

sper·ma·ti·um \(ˌ)spər-'mā-sh(ē-)əm\ *noun, plural* **-tia** \-sh(ē-)ə\ [New Latin, from Greek *spermation*, diminutive of *spermat-, sperma*] (1856)
: a nonmotile cell functioning as a male gamete in some lower plants (as red algae)
— **sper·ma·tial** \-sh(ē-)əl\ *adjective*

sper·mato·cyte \(ˌ)spər-'ma-tə-ˌsīt\ *noun* (1886)
: a cell giving rise to sperm cells; *especially* **:** a cell that is derived from a spermatogonium and ultimately gives rise to four haploid spermatids

sper·mato·gen·e·sis \(ˌ)spər-ˌma-tə-'je-nə-səs\ *noun* [New Latin] (1881)
: the process of male gamete formation including formation of a primary spermatocyte from a spermatogonium, meiotic division of the spermatocyte, and transformation of the four resulting spermatids into spermatozoa
— **sper·mato·gen·ic** \-'je-nik\ *adjective*

sper·mato·go·ni·um \-ˈgō-nē-əm\ *noun, plural* **-nia** \-nē-ə\ [New Latin] (1861)
: a primitive male germ cell
— **sper·mato·go·ni·al** \-nē-əl\ *adjective*

sper·mato·phore \(ˌ)spər-'ma-tə-ˌfōr, -ˌfȯr\ *noun* [International Scientific Vocabulary] (circa 1849)
: a capsule, packet, or mass enclosing spermatozoa extruded by the male and conveyed to the female in the insemination of various lower animals (as insects)

sper·mato·phyte \-ˌfīt\ *noun* [ultimately from New Latin *spermat-* + Greek *phyton* plant — more at PHYT-] (1897)
: any of a group (Spermatophyta) of higher plants comprising those that produce seeds and including the gymnosperms and angiosperms
— **sper·mato·phyt·ic** \-ˌma-tə-'fi-tik\ *adjective*

sper·mato·zo·an \(ˌ)spər-ˌma-tə-'zō-ən, ˌspər-mə-tə-\ *noun* (circa 1900)
: SPERMATOZOON
— **spermatozoan** *adjective*

sper·ma·to·zo·id \-'zō-id\ *noun* [International Scientific Vocabulary, from New Latin *spermatozoon*] (1857)
: a male gamete of a plant motile by anterior cilia and usually produced in an antheridium

sper·ma·to·zo·on \-'zō-ˌän, -'zō-ən\ *noun, plural* **-zoa** \-'zō-ə\ [New Latin] (circa 1839)
1 : a motile male gamete of an animal usually with rounded or elongate head and a long posterior flagellum
2 : SPERMATOZOID
— **sper·ma·to·zo·al** \-'zō-əl\ *adjective*

sperm cell *noun* (1851)
: a male gamete **:** a male germ cell

sper·mi·cide \'spər-mə-ˌsīd\ *noun* (1929)
: a preparation or substance (as nonoxynol-9) used to kill sperm
— **sper·mi·cid·al** \ˌspər-mə-'sī-dəl\ *adjective*

sper·mio·gen·e·sis \ˌspər-mē-ō-'je-nə-səs\ *noun* [New Latin, from *spermium* spermatozoon + *-o-* + Latin *genesis*] (1916)
: SPERMATOGENESIS; *specifically* **:** transformation of a spermatid into a spermatozoon

sperm nucleus *noun* (1887)

\ə\ **abut** \ᵊ\ **kitten** \ər\ **further** \a\ **ash** \ā\ **ace**
\ä\ **mop, mar** \au̇\ **out** \ch\ **chin** \e\ **bet** \ē\ **easy**
\g\ **go** \i\ **hit** \ī\ **ice** \j\ **job** \ŋ\ **sing** \ō\ **go**
\ȯ\ **law** \ȯi\ **boy** \th\ **thin** \ṯẖ\ **the** \ü\ **loot** \u̇\ **foot**
\y\ **yet** \zh\ **vision** *see also* Guide to Pronunciation

: either of two nuclei that derive from the generative nucleus of a pollen grain and function in the fertilization of a seed plant

sperm oil *noun* (1839)
: a pale yellow oil from the sperm whale

sper·mo·phile \'spər-mə-ˌfīl\ *noun* [ultimately from Greek *sperma* seed + *philos* loving] (1824)
: GROUND SQUIRREL

sperm whale \'spərm-\ *noun* [short for *spermaceti whale*] (1834)
: a large toothed whale (*Physeter macrocephalus* synonym *P. catodon*) with a large closed cavity in the head containing a fluid mixture of spermaceti and oil

sperm whale

-spermy *noun combining form* [Greek *sperma* seed, sperm]
: state of exhibiting or resulting from (such) a fertilization ⟨agamo*spermy*⟩

sper·ry·lite \'sper-i-ˌlīt\ *noun* [Francis L. *Sperry*, 19th century Canadian chemist + English *-lite*] (1889)
: a mineral consisting of an arsenide of platinum that is found near Sudbury, Ontario, and occurs in grains and minute isometric crystals of a bluish white color

spes·sar·tite \'spe-sər-ˌtīt\ *or* **spes·sar·tine** \-ˌtēn\ *noun* [French, from *Spessart* mountain range, Germany] (1868)
: a manganese aluminum garnet usually containing other elements (as iron and magnesium) in minor amounts

¹spew \'spyü\ *verb* [Middle English, from Old English *spīwan;* akin to Old High German *spī-wan* to spit, Latin *spuere,* Greek *ptyein*] (before 12th century)
intransitive verb
1 : VOMIT
2 : to come forth in a flood or gush
3 : to ooze out as if under pressure : EXUDE
transitive verb
1 : VOMIT
2 : to send or cast forth with vigor or violence or in great quantity — often used with *out*
— **spew·er** *noun*

²spew *noun* (15th century)
1 : matter that is vomited : VOMIT
2 : material that exudes or is extruded

sphag·nous \'sfag-nəs\ *adjective* (circa 1828)
: of, relating to, or abounding in sphagnum

sphag·num \'sfag-nəm\ *noun* [New Latin, from Latin *sphagnos,* a moss, from Greek] (1741)
1 : any of an order (Sphagnales, containing a single genus *Sphagnum*) of atypical mosses that grow only in wet acid areas where their remains become compacted with other plant debris to form peat
2 : a mass of sphagnum plants

sphal·er·ite \'sfa-lə-ˌrīt\ *noun* [German *Sphalerit,* from Greek *sphaleros* deceitful, from *sphallein* to cause to fall; from its often being mistaken for galena — more at SPILL] (circa 1868)
: a widely distributed ore of zinc composed essentially of zinc sulfide

S phase *noun* [synthesis] (1945)
: the period in the cell cycle during which DNA replication takes place — compare G₁ PHASE, G₂ PHASE, M PHASE

sphene \'sfēn\ *noun* [French *sphène,* from Greek *sphēn* wedge] (1815)
: a mineral that is a silicate of calcium and titanium and often contains other elements

sphen·odon \'sfē-nə-ˌdän, 'sfe-\ *noun* [New Latin, genus name, from Greek *sphēn* wedge + *odōn, odous* tooth — more at TOOTH] (1878)
: TUATARA

— **sphen·odont** \-ˌdänt\ *adjective*

¹sphe·noid \'sfē-ˌnȯid\ *or* **sphe·noi·dal** \sfi-'nȯi-dᵊl\ *adjective* [New Latin *sphenoides,* from Greek *sphēnoeidēs* wedge-shaped, from *sphēn* wedge] (1732)
1 : of, relating to, or being a winged compound bone of the base of the cranium
2 *usually* sphenoidal : having a wedged shape

²sphenoid *noun* (1828)
: a sphenoid bone

sphe·nop·sid \sfi-'näp-səd\ *noun* [ultimately from Greek *sphēn* wedge + New Latin *-opsis*] (1957)
: any of a class (Sphenopsida or Sphenophyta) of the tracheophytes characterized by jointed ribbed stems, small leaves usually in whorls at distinct stem nodes, and sporangia in sporangiophores and made up of the equisetums and extinct related forms

spher- *or* **sphero-** *also* **sphaer-** *or* **sphaero-** *combining form* [Latin *sphaer-,* from Greek *sphair-, sphairo-,* from *sphaira* sphere]
: sphere ⟨*spher*ule⟩ ⟨*sphero*meter⟩

spher·al \'sfir-əl\ *adjective* (1545)
1 : SPHERICAL
2 : of or relating to the spheres of ancient astronomy

¹sphere \'sfir\ *noun* [Middle English *spere* globe, celestial sphere, from Middle French *espere,* from Latin *sphaera,* from Greek *sphaira,* literally, ball; perhaps akin to Greek *spairein* to quiver — more at SPURN] (14th century)
1 a (1) : the apparent surface of the heavens of which half forms the dome of the visible sky (2) : any of the concentric and eccentric revolving spherical transparent shells in which according to ancient astronomy stars, sun, planets, and moon are set **b** : a globe depicting such a sphere; *broadly* : GLOBE a
2 a : a globular body : BALL **b** : PLANET, STAR **c** (1) : a solid that is bounded by a surface consisting of all points at a given distance from a point constituting its center — see VOLUME table (2) : the bounding surface of a sphere
3 : natural, normal, or proper place; *especially* : social order or rank
4 a *obsolete* : ORBIT **b** : an area or range over or within which someone or something acts, exists, or has influence or significance
— **spher·ic** \'sfir-ik, 'sfer-\ *adjective, archaic*
— **sphe·ric·i·ty** \sfir-'i-sə-tē\ *noun*

²sphere *transitive verb* **sphered; sphering** (1607)
1 : to place in a sphere or among the spheres : ENSPHERE
2 : to form into a sphere

sphere of influence (1885)
: a territorial area within which the political influence or the interests of one nation are held to be more or less paramount

spher·i·cal \'sfir-i-kəl, 'sfer-\ *adjective* (15th century)
1 : having the form of a sphere or of one of its segments
2 : relating to or dealing with a sphere or its properties
— **spher·i·cal·ly** \-k(ə-)lē\ *adverb*

spherical aberration *noun* (1868)
: aberration that is caused by the spherical form of a lens or mirror and that gives different foci for central and marginal rays

spherical angle *noun* (1678)
: the angle between two intersecting arcs of great circles of a sphere measured by the plane angle formed by the tangents to the arcs at the point of intersection

spherical coordinate *noun* (circa 1864)

: one of three coordinates that are used to locate a point in space and that comprise the radius of the sphere on which the point lies in a system of concentric spheres, the angle formed by the point, the center, and a given axis of the sphere, and the angle between the plane of the first angle and a reference plane through the given axis of the sphere

spherical geometry *noun* (1728)
: the geometry of figures on a sphere

spherical polygon *noun* (circa 1825)
: a figure analogous to a plane polygon that is formed on a sphere by arcs of great circles

spherical triangle *noun* (1585)
: a spherical polygon of three sides

spherical trigonometry *noun* (1728)
: trigonometry applied to spherical triangles and polygons

spher·oid \'sfir-ˌȯid, 'sfer-\ *noun* (1570)
: a figure resembling a sphere; *also* : an object of approximately spherical shape
— **sphe·roi·dal** \sfi-'rȯi-dᵊl\ *also* **spher·oid** *adjective*
— **sphe·roi·dal·ly** \-dᵊl-ē\ *adverb*

sphe·rom·e·ter \sfir-'ä-mə-tər\ *noun* [International Scientific Vocabulary] (circa 1828)
: an instrument for measuring the curvature of a surface

sphe·ro·plast \'sfir-ə-ˌplast, 'sfer-\ *noun* (circa 1920)
: a bacterium or yeast cell that is modified by nutritional or environmental factors or by artificial means (as the use of a lysozyme) and that is characterized by partial loss of the cell wall and by increased osmotic sensitivity

spher·ule \'sfir-ü(ə)l, 'sfer-, -ˌyü(ə)l\ *noun* (1665)
: a little sphere or spherical body

spher·u·lite \'sfir-yə-ˌlīt, 'sfer-, -ə-ˌlīt\ *noun* (1823)
: a usually spherical crystalline body of radiating crystal fibers often found in vitreous volcanic rocks
— **spher·u·lit·ic** \ˌsfir-yə-'li-tik, ˌsfer-, -ə-ˌli-\ *adjective*

sphery \'sfir-ē\ *adjective* (1590)
1 : of, relating to, or suggestive of the celestial bodies
2 : ROUND, SPHERICAL

sphinc·ter \'sfiŋ(k)-tər\ *noun* [Late Latin, from Greek *sphinktēr,* literally, band, from *sphingein* to bind tight] (1578)
: an annular muscle surrounding and able to contract or close a bodily opening
— **sphinc·ter·ic** \ˌsfiŋ(k)-'ter-ik\ *adjective*

sphin·gid \'sfin-jəd\ *noun* [ultimately from Greek *sphing-, sphinx* sphinx] (circa 1909)
: HAWKMOTH

sphin·go·sine \'sfiŋ-gə-ˌsēn\ *noun* [Greek *sphingos* (genitive of *sphinx*) + English ²*-ine;* from riddles it posed to its first investigators] (1884)
: a long-chain unsaturated amino alcohol $C_{18}H_{37}O_2N$ found especially in nervous tissue and cell membranes

sphinx \'sfiŋ(k)s\ *noun, plural* **sphinx·es** *or* **sphin·ges** \'sfin-ˌjēz\ [Latin, from Greek *Sphinx, Sphix*]
1 a *capitalized* : a winged female monster in Greek mythology having a woman's head and a lion's body and noted for killing anyone unable to answer its riddle **b** : an enigmatic or mysterious person
2 : an ancient Egyptian image in the form of a recumbent lion having a man's head, a ram's head, or a hawk's head
3 : HAWKMOTH
— **sphinx·like** \-ˌlīk\ *adjective*

sphyg·mo·graph \'sfig-mə-ˌgraf\ *noun* [Greek *sphygmos* pulse + International Scientific Vocabulary *-graph*] (circa 1859)
: an instrument that records graphically the movements or character of the pulse

sphyg·mo·ma·nom·e·ter \ˌsfig-mō-mə-'nä-mə-tər\ *noun* [Greek *sphygmos* pulse (from

sphyzein to throb) + International Scientific Vocabulary *manometer*] (circa 1891)
: an instrument for measuring blood pressure and especially arterial blood pressure
— **sphyg·mo·ma·nom·e·try** \-mə-'nä-mə-trē\ *noun*

spi·ca \'spī-kə\ *noun, plural* **spi·cae** \-ˌkē\ *or* **spicas** [Latin, ear of grain — more at SPINE] (circa 1731)
: a bandage that is applied in successive V-shaped crossings and is used to immobilize a limb especially at a joint

Spi·ca \'spī-kə\ *noun* [Latin, literally, ear of grain]
: a star of the first magnitude in the constellation Virgo

spi·cate \'spī-ˌkāt\ *adjective* [Latin *spicatus*, past participle of *spicare* to arrange in the shape of heads of grain, from *spica*] (1668)
: arranged in the form of a spike ⟨a *spicate* inflorescence⟩

¹spic·ca·to \spi-'kä-(ˌ)tō\ *adjective* [Italian, past participle of *spiccare* to detach, pick off] (circa 1724)
: performed with a slight lifting of the bow after each note — used as a direction in music

²spiccato *noun, plural* **-tos** (circa 1903)
: a spiccato technique, performance, or passage

¹spice \'spīs\ *noun* [Middle English, from Old French *espice*, from Late Latin *species* spices, from Latin, species, from *specere* to look — more at SPY] (13th century)
1 : any of various aromatic vegetable products (as pepper or nutmeg) used to season or flavor foods
2 a *archaic* **:** a small portion, quantity, or admixture **:** DASH **b :** something that gives zest or relish ⟨variety's the very *spice* of life —William Cowper⟩
3 : a pungent or fragrant odor **:** PERFUME ◇
— **spice·less** \-ləs\ *adjective*

²spice *transitive verb* **spiced; spic·ing** (14th century)
1 : to season with spices
2 : to add zest or relish to ⟨cynicism *spiced* with humor —J. W. Dawson⟩ — often used with *up*

spice·bush \'spīs-ˌbu̇sh\ *noun* (1770)
: an aromatic shrub (*Lindera benzoin*) of the laurel family that bears dense clusters of small yellow flowers followed by scarlet or yellow berries

spic·ery \'spī-sə-rē, 'spīs-rē\ *noun, plural* **-er·ies** (13th century)
1 : SPICES
2 *archaic* **:** a repository of spices
3 : a spicy quality

spick *or* **spic** *or* **spik** \'spik\ *noun* [by shortening & alteration from *spiggoty*, of unknown origin] (1916)
: SPANISH AMERICAN — usually taken to be offensive

spick–and–span *or* **spic–and–span** \ˌspik-ən(d)-'span, ˌspik-ᵊn-\ *adjective* [short for *spick-and-span-new*, from obsolete English *spick* spike + English *and* + *span-new* brand-new] (1665)
1 : FRESH, BRAND-NEW
2 : spotlessly clean

spic·ule \'spi-(ˌ)kyü(ə)l\ *noun* [New Latin *spicula* & Latin *spiculum*; New Latin *spicula*, alteration of Latin *spiculum* head of a spear or arrow, diminutive of *spicum, spica* ear of grain] (1785)
1 : a slender pointed usually hard body; *especially* **:** one of the minute calcareous or siliceous bodies that support the tissue of various invertebrates (as a sponge)
2 : a spikelike short-lived prominence appearing close to the chromosphere of the solar atmosphere
— **spic·u·lar** \'spi-kyə-lər\ *adjective*
— **spic·u·la·tion** \ˌspi-kyə-'lā-shən\ *noun*

spicy \'spī-sē\ *adjective* **spic·i·er; -est** (1562)

1 : having the quality, flavor, or fragrance of spice
2 : producing or abounding in spices
3 : LIVELY, SPIRITED
4 : PIQUANT, RACY; *especially* **:** somewhat scandalous or salacious ⟨*spicy* gossip⟩
— **spic·i·ly** \-sə-lē\ *adverb*
— **spic·i·ness** \-sē-nəs\ *noun*

spi·der \'spī-dər\ *noun* [Middle English *spyder*, alteration of *spithre*; akin to Old English *spin-nan* to spin] (15th century)
1 : any of an order (Araneae synonym Araneida) of arachnids having the abdomen usually unsegmented and constricted at the base, chelicerae modified into poison fangs, and two or more pairs of abdominal spinnerets for spinning threads of silk used in making cocoons for their eggs, nests for themselves, or webs to catch prey
2 : a cast-iron frying pan originally made with short feet to stand among coals on the hearth
3 : any of various devices consisting of a frame or skeleton with radiating arms or members
— **spi·der·ish** \-də-rish\ *adjective*
— **spi·der·like** \-dər-ˌlīk\ *adjective*

spider crab *noun* (circa 1710)
: any of a family (Majidae) of crabs with extremely long legs and nearly triangular bodies which they often cover with kelp

spider mite *noun* (1870)
: any of several small web-spinning mites (family Tetranychidae) that attack forage and crop plants — called also *red spider*

spider monkey *noun* (1764)
: any of a genus (*Ateles*) of New World monkeys with long slender limbs, the thumb absent or rudimentary, and a very long prehensile tail

spider plant *noun* (1944)
: a widely grown houseplant (*Chlorophytum comosum* variety *variegatum*) of the lily family having long narrow green leaves usually striped with white or ivory and producing white flowers and tufts of plantlets on long hanging stems

spi·der·web \'spī-dər-ˌweb\ *noun* (circa 1649)
1 : the network of silken thread spun by most spiders and used as a resting place and as a trap for small prey
2 : something that resembles or suggests a spiderweb

spi·der·wort \-ˌwərt, -ˌwȯrt\ *noun* (1629)
: any of a genus (*Tradescantia* of the family Commelinaceae, the spiderwort family) of American monocotyledonous plants with ephemeral often blue or violet flowers

spi·dery \'spī-də-rē\ *adjective* (1837)
1 a : resembling a spider in form or manner **b :** resembling a spiderweb; *especially* **:** composed of fine threads or lines in a weblike arrangement ⟨*spidery* lace⟩
2 : infested with spiders

spie·gel·ei·sen \'spē-gə-ˌlī-zᵊn\ *also* **spie·gel** \'spē-gəl\ *noun* [German *Spiegeleisen*, from *Spiegel* mirror + *Eisen* iron] (1868)
: a composition of iron that contains 15 to 30 percent manganese and 4.5 to 6.5 percent carbon

¹spiel \'spē(ə)l\ *verb* [German *spielen* to play, from Old High German *spilōn*; akin to Old English *spilian* to revel] (1870)
intransitive verb
1 : to play music
2 : to talk volubly or extravagantly
transitive verb
: to utter, express, or describe volubly or extravagantly
— **spiel·er** \'spē-lər\ *noun*

²spiel *noun* (1896)
: a voluble line of often extravagant talk **:** PITCH

¹spi·er \'spī(-ə)r\ *noun* (13th century)
: SPY

²spier \'spir\ *chiefly Scottish variant of* SPEER

spiff \'spif\ *verb* [English dialect spiff *dandified*] (1877)
: SPRUCE — usually used with *up* ⟨*spiff* up your wardrobe⟩
— **spiffed–up** \'spift-'əp\ *adjective*

spiffy \'spi-fē\ *adjective* **spiff·i·er; -est** (1853)
: fine looking **:** SMART ⟨a *spiffy* sports jacket⟩
— **spiff·i·ly** \-fə-lē\ *adverb*
— **spiff·i·ness** \-fē-nəs\ *noun*

spig·ot \'spi-gət, -kət\ *noun* [Middle English] (14th century)
1 a : SPILE 2 **b :** the plug of a faucet or cock **c :** FAUCET
2 : something resembling a spigot especially in regulating availability or flow (as of money)

¹spike \'spīk\ *noun* [Middle English, probably from Middle Dutch; akin to Middle High German *spīcher* spike] (13th century)
1 : a very large nail
2 a : one of a row of pointed irons placed (as on the top of a wall) to prevent passage **b** (1) **:** one of several metal projections set in the sole and heel of a shoe to improve traction (2) *plural* **:** a pair of shoes having spikes attached to the soles or soles and heels **c :** SPINDLE 1e
3 : something resembling a spike: as **a :** a young mackerel not over six inches (15.2 centimeters) long **b :** an unbranched antler of a young deer
4 *plural* **:** shoes with spike heels
5 : the act or an instance of spiking (as in volleyball)
6 a : a pointed element in a graph or tracing **b :** an unusually high and sharply defined maximum (as of amplitude in a wave train)
7 *slang* **:** HYPODERMIC NEEDLE
8 : a momentary sharp increase and fall in the record of an electric potential; *also* **:** ACTION POTENTIAL
9 : an abrupt sharp increase in prices or rates
— **spike·like** \-ˌlīk\ *adjective*

²spike *transitive verb* **spiked; spik·ing** (1624)
1 : to fasten or furnish with spikes

\ə\ **abut** \ᵊ\ **kitten** \ər\ **further** \a\ **ash** \ā\ **ace**
\ä\ **mop, mar** \au̇\ **out** \ch\ **chin** \e\ **bet** \ē\ **easy**
\g\ **go** \i\ **hit** \ī\ **ice** \j\ **job** \ŋ\ **sing** \ō\ **go**
\ȯ\ **law** \ȯi\ **boy** \th\ **thin** \th\ **the** \ü\ **loot** \u̇\ **foot**
\y\ **yet** \zh\ **vision** *see also* Guide to Pronunciation

2 a : to disable (a muzzle-loading cannon) temporarily by driving a spike into the vent **b :** to suppress or block completely ⟨*spiked* the rumor⟩
3 a : to pierce or impale with or on a spike **b :** to reject (as a story) for publication or broadcast for editorial reasons
4 a : to add an alcoholic beverage to (a drink) **b :** to add something highly reactive (as a radioactive tracer) to **c :** to add vitality, zest, or spice to : LIVEN ⟨*spiked* the speech with humor⟩ ⟨*spike* the broth with peppers⟩
5 : to drive (as a volleyball) sharply downward with a hard blow; *also* : to throw down sharply ⟨*spiked* the ball in the end zone⟩
6 : to undergo a sudden sharp increase in (temperature or fever) ⟨the patient *spiked* a fever of 103°⟩
— **spik·er** *noun*

³spike *noun* [Middle English *spik*, from Latin *spica* — more at SPINE] (14th century)
1 : an ear of grain
2 : an elongated inflorescence similar to a raceme but having the flowers sessile on the main axis — see INFLORESCENCE illustration
spiked \ˈspīkt, ˈspī-kəd\ *adjective* (1601)
1 : having an inflorescence that is a spike
2 : having a sharp projecting point

spike heel *noun* (1926)
: a very high tapering heel used on women's shoes

spike lavender \ˈspīk-\ *noun* [alteration of English dialect *spick* lavender] (1607)
: a European mint (*Lavandula latifolia*) related to true lavender

spike·let \ˈspī-klət\ *noun* (1851)
: a small or secondary spike; *specifically* : one of the small few-flowered bracted spikes that make up the compound inflorescence of a grass or sedge

spike·nard \ˈspīk-ˌnärd\ *noun* [Middle English, from Middle French or Medieval Latin; Middle French *spicanarde*, from Medieval Latin *spica nardi*, literally, spike of nard] (14th century)
1 a : a fragrant ointment of the ancients **b :** a Himalayan aromatic plant (*Nardostachys jatamansi*) of the valerian family from which spikenard is believed to have been derived
2 : an American herb (*Aralia racemosa*) of the ginseng family with aromatic root and panicled umbels

spike–tooth harrow \ˈspīk-ˈtüth-\ *noun* (1926)
: a harrow with straight steel teeth set in horizontal bars

spiky *also* **spikey** \ˈspī-kē\ *adjective* **spik·i·er; -est** (1720)
1 : of, relating to, or characterized by spikes
2 : sharply irritating or acerbic (as in temper or manner)
3 [from the alleged harshness of such views] *British* **:** strongly favoring Anglo-Catholic teaching or practice
— **spik·i·ly** \-kə-lē\ *adverb*
— **spik·i·ness** \-kē-nəs\ *noun*

¹spile \ˈspī(ə)l\ *noun* [probably from Dutch *spijl* stake] (1513)
1 : ¹PILE 1
2 : a small plug used to stop the vent of a cask **:** BUNG
3 : a spout inserted in a tree to draw off sap

²spile *transitive verb* **spiled; spil·ing** (1691)
1 : to plug with a spile
2 : to supply with a spile

¹spill \ˈspil\ *verb* **spilled** \ˈspild, ˈspilt\ *also* **spilt** \ˈspilt\; **spill·ing** [Middle English, from Old English *spillan*; akin to Old English *spildan* to destroy and perhaps to Latin *spolium* animal skin, Greek *sphallein* to cause to fall] (before 12th century)
transitive verb
1 a *archaic* **:** KILL, DESTROY **b :** to cause (blood) to flow

2 : to cause or allow especially accidentally or unintentionally to fall, flow, or run out so as to be lost or wasted
3 a : to relieve (a sail) from the pressure of the wind so as to reef or furl it **b :** to relieve the pressure of (wind) on a sail by coming about or by adjusting the sail with lines
4 : to throw off or out ⟨a horse *spilled* him⟩
5 : to let out **:** DIVULGE ⟨*spill* a secret⟩
intransitive verb
1 a : to flow, run, or fall out, over, or off and become wasted, scattered, or lost **b :** to cause or allow something to spill
2 : to spread profusely or beyond bounds ⟨crowds *spilled* into the streets⟩
3 : to fall from one's place (as on a horse)
— **spill·able** \ˈspi-lə-bəl\ *adjective*
— **spill·er** *noun*
— **spill the beans :** to divulge secret or hidden information

²spill *noun* (circa 1845)
1 : the act or an instance of spilling; *especially* **:** a fall from a horse or vehicle or an erect position
2 : something spilled

³spill *noun* [Middle English *spille*] (14th century)
1 : a wooden splinter
2 : a slender piece: as **a :** a metallic rod or pin **b** (1) **:** a small roll or twist of paper or slip of wood for lighting a fire (2) **:** a roll or cone of paper serving as a container **c :** a peg or pin for plugging a hole **:** SPILE

spill·age \ˈspi-lij\ *noun* (1924)
1 : the act or process of spilling
2 : the quantity that spills **:** material lost or scattered by spilling

spil·li·kin \ˈspi-li-kən\ *noun* [probably alteration of obsolete Dutch *spelleken* small peg] (1734)
1 : JACKSTRAW 2
2 *plural* **:** JACKSTRAW 1

spill·over \ˈspil-ˌō-vər\ *noun, often attributive* (1920)
1 : the act or an instance of spilling over
2 : a quantity that spills over
3 : an extension of something especially when due to an excess

spill·way \-ˌwā\ *noun* (1889)
: a passage for surplus water to run over or around an obstruction (as a dam)

spilth \ˈspilth\ *noun* (1607)
1 : the act or an instance of spilling
2 a : something spilled **b :** REFUSE, RUBBISH

¹spin \ˈspin\ *verb* **spun** \ˈspən\; **spin·ning** [Middle English *spinnen*, from Old English *spinnan*; akin to Old High German *spinnan* to spin and perhaps to Lithuanian *spęsti* to set (a trap)] (before 12th century)
intransitive verb
1 : to draw out and twist fiber into yarn or thread
2 : to form a thread by extruding a viscous rapidly hardening fluid — used especially of a spider or insect
3 a : to revolve rapidly **:** GYRATE **b :** to feel as if in a whirl **:** REEL ⟨my head is *spinning*⟩
4 : to move swiftly especially on or as if on wheels or in a vehicle
5 : to fish with spinning bait **:** TROLL
6 a *of an airplane* **:** to fall in a spin **b :** to plunge helplessly and out of control
transitive verb
1 a : to draw out and twist into yarns or threads **b :** to produce by drawing out and twisting a fibrous material
2 : to form (as a web or cocoon) by spinning
3 a : to stretch out or extend (as a story) lengthily **:** PROTRACT — usually used with *out* **b :** to evolve, express, or fabricate by processes of mind or imagination ⟨*spin* a yarn⟩
4 : to cause to whirl **:** impart spin to ⟨*spin* a top⟩
5 : to shape into threadlike form in manufacture; *also* **:** to manufacture by a whirling process

²spin *noun* (1831)
1 a : the act of spinning or twirling something; *also* **:** an instance of spinning or of spinning something ⟨doing axels and *spins*⟩ ⟨an assortment of *spins* and lobs⟩ **b :** the whirling motion imparted (as to a ball or top) by spinning **c :** an excursion or ride in a vehicle especially on wheels ⟨go for a *spin*⟩
2 a : an aerial maneuver or flight condition consisting of a combination of roll and yaw with the longitudinal axis of the airplane inclined steeply downward **b :** a plunging descent or downward spiral **c :** a state of mental confusion ⟨in a *spin*⟩
3 a : a quantum characteristic of an elementary particle that is visualized as the rotation of the particle on its axis and that is responsible for measurable angular momentum and magnetic moment **b :** the angular momentum associated with such rotation whose magnitude is quantized and which may assume either of two possible directions; *also* **:** the angular momentum of a system of such particles derived from the spins and orbital motions of the particles
4 : a special point of view, emphasis, or interpretation ⟨put the most favorable *spin* on the findings⟩
— **spin·less** \ˈspin-ləs\ *adjective*

spi·na bi·fi·da \ˌspī-nə-ˈbi-fə-də\ *noun* [New Latin, literally, spine split in two] (1720)
: a congenital cleft of the vertebral column with hernial protrusion of the meninges and sometimes the spinal cord

spin·ach \ˈspi-nich\ *noun* [Middle English *spynache*, from Middle French *espinache, espinage*, from Old Spanish *espinaca*, from Arabic *isfānākh*, from Persian] (15th century)
1 : an Asian herb (*Spinacia oleracea*) of the goosefoot family cultivated for its edible leaves which form in a dense basal rosette
2 a : something unwanted, pretentious, or spurious **b :** an untidy overgrowth
— **spin·ach·like** \-nich-ˌlīk\ *adjective*
— **spin·achy** \-ni-chē\ *adjective*

¹spi·nal \ˈspī-nᵊl\ *adjective* (1578)
1 : of, relating to, or situated near the backbone
2 a : of, relating to, or affecting the spinal cord ⟨*spinal* reflexes⟩ **b :** having the spinal cord functionally isolated (as by surgical section) from the brain ⟨experiments on *spinal* animals⟩
3 : of, relating to, or resembling a spine

²spinal *noun* (1944)
: a spinal anesthetic

spinal canal *noun* (1845)
: VERTEBRAL CANAL

spinal column *noun* (1836)
: the axial skeleton of the trunk and tail of a vertebrate consisting of an articulated series of vertebrae and protecting the spinal cord — called also *backbone*

spinal cord *noun* (1836)
: the cord of nervous tissue that extends from the brain lengthwise along the back in the vertebral canal, gives off the pairs of spinal nerves, carries impulses to and from the brain, and serves as a center for initiating and coordinating many reflex acts — see BRAIN illustration

spinal ganglion *noun* (circa 1860)
: a ganglion on the dorsal root of each spinal nerve that is one of a series of ganglia lodging cell bodies of sensory neurons

spi·nal·ly \ˈspī-nᵊl-ē\ *adverb* (1885)
: with respect to or along the spine

spinal nerve *noun* (circa 1793)
: any of the paired nerves which leave the spinal cord of a craniate vertebrate, supply muscles of the trunk and limbs, and connect with the nerves of the sympathetic nervous system, which arise by a short motor ventral root and a short sensory dorsal root, and of which there are 31 pairs in humans classified according to the part of the spinal cord from which they

arise into 8 cervical pairs, 12 thoracic pairs, 5 lumbar pairs, 5 sacral pairs, and one coccygeal pair

¹spin·dle \'spin-dᵊl\ *noun* [Middle English *spindel*, from Old English *spinel*; akin to Old English *spinnan* to spin] (12th century)
1 a : a round stick with tapered ends used to form and twist the yarn in hand spinning **b :** the long slender pin by which the thread is twisted in a spinning wheel **c :** any of various rods or pins holding a bobbin in a textile machine (as a spinning frame) **d :** the pin in a loom shuttle **e :** a device usually consisting of a long upright pin in a base on which papers can be stuck for filing — called also *spindle file*
2 : something shaped like a spindle: as **a :** a spindle-shaped network of chiefly microtubular fibers along which the chromosomes are distributed during mitosis and meiosis **b : MUSCLE SPINDLE**
3 a : the bar or shaft usually of square section that carries the knobs and actuates the latch or bolt of a lock **b (1) :** a turned often decorative piece (as in a baluster) **(2) : NEWEL c (1) :** a revolving piece especially when thinner than a shaft **(2) :** a horizontal or vertical axle revolving on pin or pivot ends **d :** the part of an axle on which a vehicle wheel turns

²spindle *verb* **spin·dled; spin·dling** \'spin(d)-liŋ, 'spin-dᵊl-iŋ\ (1577)
intransitive verb
1 : to shoot or grow into a long slender stalk
2 : to grow to stalk or stem rather than to flower or fruit
transitive verb
1 : to impale, thrust, or perforate on the spike of a spindle file
2 : to make or equip (as a piece of furniture) with spindles
— **spin·dler** \'spin(d)-lər, 'spin-dᵊl-ər\ *noun*

spindle cell *noun* (1878)
: a fusiform cell (as in some tumors)

spin·dle–legged \'spin-dᵊl-,(l)e-gəd *also* -,(l)ā- *or* -,(l)egd\ *adjective* (1710)
: having long slender legs

spin·dle–shanked \-,shaŋ(k)t\ *adjective* (circa 1600)
: SPINDLE-LEGGED

spindle tree *noun* (1548)
: any of various often evergreen shrubs, small trees, or vines (genus *Euonymus*) of the staff-tree family

spin·dling \'spin(d)-liŋ, -lən; 'spin-dᵊl-iŋ, -ən\ *adjective* (1750)
: SPINDLY

spin·dly \'spin(d)-lē, 'spin-dᵊl-ē\ *adjective* **spin·dli·er; -est** (1651)
1 : of a disproportionately tall or long and thin appearance that often suggests physical weakness ⟨*spindly* legs⟩
2 : frail or flimsy in appearance or structure

spin doctor *noun* (1984)
: a person (as a political aide) responsible for ensuring that others interpret an event from a particular point of view

spin·drift \'spin-,drift\ *noun* [alteration of Scots *speendrift*, from *speen* to drive before a strong wind + English *drift*] (1823)
1 : sea spray; *especially* **:** spray blown from waves during a gale
2 : fine wind-borne snow or sand

spine \'spīn\ *noun* [Middle English, thorn, spinal column, from Latin *spina*; perhaps akin to Latin *spica* ear of grain] (15th century)
1 a : SPINAL COLUMN b : something resembling a spinal column or constituting a central axis or chief support **c :** the part of a book to which the pages are attached and on the cover of which usually appear the title and author's and publisher's names
2 : a stiff pointed plant process; *especially* **:** one that is a modified leaf or leaf part
3 a : a sharp rigid process on an animal: as **a : SPICULE b :** a stiff unsegmented fin ray of a fish **c :** a pointed prominence on a bone

— **spined** \'spīnd\ *adjective*
— **spine–like** \-,līk\ *adjective*

spine–chill·ing \-,chi-liŋ\ *adjective* (1946)
: alarmingly or eerily frightening

spi·nel *or* **spi·nelle** \spə-'nel\ *noun* [Italian *spinella*, diminutive of *spina* thorn, from Latin] (1528)
1 : a hard crystalline mineral consisting of an oxide of magnesium and aluminum that varies from colorless to ruby-red to black and is used as a gem
2 : any of a group of minerals that are essentially oxides of magnesium, ferrous iron, zinc, or manganese

spine·less \'spīn-ləs\ *adjective* (1827)
1 : free from spines, thorns, or prickles
2 a : having no spinal column **: INVERTEBRATE**
b : lacking strength of character
— **spine·less·ly** *adverb*
— **spine·less·ness** *noun*

spin·et \'spi-nət *also* spi-'net\ *noun* [Italian *spinetta*, perhaps from diminutive of *spina* thorn, from Latin; from the manner of plucking its strings] (1664)
1 : an early harpsichord having a single keyboard and only one string for each note
2 a : a compactly built small upright piano **b :** a small electronic organ

spin fishing *noun* (1950)
: SPINNING

spi·ni·fex \'spī-nə-,feks\ *noun* [New Latin, from Latin *spina* + *facere* to make — more at DO] (1846)
: any of several Australian grasses (genera *Spinifex* and *Triodia*) with spiny seeds or stiff sharp leaves

spin·na·ker \'spi-ni-kər\ *noun* [origin unknown] (1866)
: a large triangular sail set on a long light pole and used when running before the wind

spin·ner \'spi-nər\ *noun* (13th century)
1 : one that spins
2 : a fisherman's lure consisting of a spoon, blade, or set of wings that revolves when drawn through the water
3 : a conical sheet metal fairing that is attached to an airplane propeller boss and revolves with it
4 : a movable arrow that is spun on its dial to indicate the number or kind of moves a player may make in a board game

spin·ner·et \,spi-nə-'ret\ *noun* (1826)
1 : an organ (as of a spider or caterpillar) for producing threads of silk from the secretion of silk glands
2 *or* **spin·ner·ette :** a small metal plate, thimble, or cap with fine holes through which a chemical solution (as of cellulose) is forced in the spinning of man-made filaments (as of rayon or nylon)

spin·ney \'spi-nē\ *noun, plural* **spinneys** [Middle French *espinaye* thorny thicket, from *espine* thorn, from Latin *spina*] (1597)
chiefly British **:** a small wood with undergrowth

spin·ning \'spi-niŋ\ *noun* (1855)
: a method of fishing in which a lure is cast by use of a light flexible rod, a spinning reel, and a light line

spinning frame *noun* (1825)
: a machine that draws, twists, and winds yarn

spinning jen·ny \-,je-nē\ *noun* [*Jenny*, nickname for *Jane*] (1783)
: an early multiple-spindle machine for spinning wool or cotton

spinning reel *noun* (1950)
: a fishing reel with a nonmoving spool on which the line is wound by means of a revolving arm which can be disengaged to allow the line to spiral freely off the spool during casting

spinning rod *noun* (1870)
: a light flexible fishing rod used with a spinning reel

spinning wheel *noun* (15th century)

: a small domestic hand-driven or foot-driven machine for spinning yarn or thread

spin–off \'spin-,of\ *noun* (1950)
1 : the distribution by a business to its stockholders of particular assets and especially of stock of another company; *also* **:** the new company created by such a distribution
2 : a collateral or derived product or effect **: BY-PRODUCT;** *also* **:** a number of such products ⟨the *spin-off* from the space program⟩
3 : something that is imitative or derivative of an earlier work; *especially* **:** a television show starring a character popular in a secondary role of an earlier show

spin off (1950)
transitive verb
: to establish or produce as a spin-off ⟨the company *spun off* its computer division⟩ ⟨*spin off* a new TV series⟩
intransitive verb
: to establish or become a spin-off

spin·or \'spi-nər, -,nȯr\ *noun* [International Scientific Vocabulary *spin* + *-or* (as in *vector*)] (1931)
: a vector whose components are complex numbers in a two-dimensional or four-dimensional space and which is used especially in the mathematics of the theory of relativity

spi·nose \'spī-,nōs\ *adjective* (1660)
: SPINY 1 ⟨a fly with black *spinose* legs⟩
— **spi·nos·i·ty** \spī-'nä-sə-tē\ *noun*

spi·nous \'spī-nəs\ *adjective* (15th century)
1 : SPINY 1, 3 ⟨*spinous* appendages⟩ ⟨a *spinous* larva⟩
2 : difficult or unpleasant to handle or meet **: THORNY**

spin·out \'spin-,aut\ *noun* (1955)
: a rotational skid by an automobile that usually causes it to leave the roadway

spin out *intransitive verb* (1951)
: to make a rotational skid in an automobile

Spi·no·zism \spi-'nō-,zi-zəm\ *noun* (1728)
: the philosophy of Baruch Spinoza who taught that reality is one substance with an infinite number of attributes of which only thought and extension are capable of being apprehended by the human mind
— **Spi·no·zist** \-zist\ *noun*
— **Spi·no·zis·tic** \,spi-nō-'zis-tik\ *adjective*

spin·ster \'spin(t)-stər\ *noun* (14th century)
1 : a woman whose occupation is to spin
2 a *archaic* **:** an unmarried woman of gentle family **b :** an unmarried woman and especially one past the common age for marrying
3 : a woman who seems unlikely to marry ◇
— **spin·ster·hood** \-,hud\ *noun*
— **spin·ster·ish** \-st(ə-)rish\ *adjective*
— **spin·ster·ly** *adjective*

◇ WORD HISTORY
spinster Before the industrial revolution spinning was a humble but all-important task generally carried out in the home. When the word *spinster* appeared in 14th century English, it meant a person of either sex who spun, especially as a regular occupation. Since spinning was traditionally regarded as women's work, *spinster* gradually came to be applied exclusively to women spinners. By the 17th century the word had also become an established legal designation for an unmarried woman. Not until the 18th century did *spinster* refer to a single woman who, according to the mores of her time, is regarded as having passed the usual or desirable age for marrying.

\ə\ abut \ᵊ\ kitten \ər\ further \a\ ash \ā\ ace
\ä\ mop, mar \au̇\ out \ch\ chin \e\ bet \ē\ easy
\g\ go \i\ hit \ī\ ice \j\ job \ŋ\ sing \ō\ go
\ȯ\ law \ȯi\ boy \th\ thin \th\ the \ü\ loot \u̇\ foot
\y\ yet \zh\ vision *see also* Guide to Pronunciation

spin·thar·i·scope \spin-'thar-ə-,skōp\ *noun* [Greek *spintharis* spark + English *-scope*] (1903)
: an instrument for visual detection of alpha particles that consists of a fluorescent screen and a magnifying lens system

spin the bottle *noun* (1955)
: a kissing game in which one has as a partner the person a bottle points to when it stops spinning

spin·to \'spēn-(,)tō, 'spin-\ *noun, plural* **spin·tos** [Italian, literally, pushed, from past participle of *spingere* to push, from (assumed) Vulgar Latin *expingere*, from Latin *ex-* + *pangere* to fasten — more at PACT] (1944)
: a singing voice having both lyric and dramatic qualities
— **spinto** *adjective*

spi·nule \'spī-(,)nyü(ə)l\ *noun* [Latin *spinula*, diminutive of *spina* thorn — more at SPINE] (1752)
: a minute spine
— **spi·nu·lose** \'spī-nyə-,lōs\ *adjective*

spiny \'spī-nē\ *adjective* **spin·i·er; -est** (1586)
1 : covered or armed with spines; *broadly* : bearing spines, prickles, or thorns
2 : abounding with difficulties, obstacles, or annoyances : THORNY ⟨*spiny* problems⟩
3 : slender and pointed like a spine
— **spin·i·ness** *noun*

spiny anteater *noun* (1827)
: ECHIDNA

spiny–head·ed worm \'spī-nē-,he-dəd-\ *noun* (1946)
: any of a small phylum (Acanthocephala) of unsegmented parasitic worms that have a proboscis bearing hooks by which attachment is made to the intestinal wall of the host

spiny lobster *noun* (1819)
: any of several edible crustaceans (family Palinuridae and especially genus *Panulirus*) distinguished from the true lobsters by the simple unenlarged first pair of legs and claws and the spiny carapace

spi·ra·cle \'spir-i-kəl, 'spī-ri-\ *noun* [Middle English, from Latin *spiraculum*, from *spirare* to breathe] (15th century)
1 : a breathing hole : VENT
2 : a breathing orifice: as **a** : BLOWHOLE 2 **b** : an external tracheal aperture of a terrestrial arthropod that in an insect is usually one of a series of small apertures located along each side of the thorax and abdomen — see INSECT illustration
— **spi·rac·u·lar** \spə-'ra-kyə-lər, spī-\ *adjective*

¹spi·ral \'spī-rəl\ *adjective* [Medieval Latin *spiralis*, from Latin *spira* coil — more at SPIRE] (1551)
1 **a** : winding around a center or pole and gradually receding from or approaching it ⟨the *spiral* curve of a watch spring⟩ **b** : HELICAL **c** : SPIRAL-BOUND ⟨a *spiral* notebook⟩
2 : of or relating to the advancement to higher levels through a series of cyclical movements
— **spi·ral·ly** \-rə-lē\ *adverb*

²spiral *noun* (1656)
1 **a** : the path of a point in a plane moving around a central point while continuously receding from or approaching it **b** : a three-dimensional curve (as a helix) with one or more turns about an axis
2 : a single turn or coil in a spiral object
3 **a** : something having a spiral form **b** (1) : a spiral flight (2) : a kick or pass in which a football rotates on its long axis while moving through the air
4 : a continuously spreading and accelerating increase or decrease ⟨wage *spirals*⟩

³spiral *verb* **-raled** *or* **-ralled; -ral·ing** *or* **-ral·ling** (1834)
intransitive verb
: to go and especially to rise or fall in a spiral course ⟨costs *spiraled* upward⟩
transitive verb

1 : to form into a spiral
2 : to cause to spiral

spiral binding *noun* (1944)
: a book or notebook binding in which a continuous spiral wire or plastic strip is passed through holes along one edge

spi·ral–bound \'spī-rəl-,baund\ *adjective* (1941)
: having a spiral binding

spiral cleavage *noun* (1892)
: holoblastic cleavage that is typical of protostomes and that is characterized by arrangement of the blastomeres of each upper tier over the cell junctions of the next lower tier so that the blastomeres spiral around the pole to pole axis of the embryo — compare RADIAL CLEAVAGE

spiral galaxy *noun* (1913)
: a galaxy exhibiting a central nucleus or barred structure from which extend concentrations of matter forming curved arms — called also *spiral nebula*

spiral of Ar·chi·me·des \-,är-kə-'mē-dēz\ [*Archimedes*] (circa 1856)
: a plane curve that is generated by a point moving away from or toward a fixed point at a constant rate while the radius vector from the fixed point rotates at a constant rate and that has the equation $\rho = a\theta$ in polar coordinates

spiral spring *noun* (1690)
: a spring consisting of a wire coiled usually in a flat spiral or in a helix

spi·rant \'spī-rənt\ *noun* [International Scientific Vocabulary, from Latin *spirant-, spirans*, present participle of *spirare* to breathe] (1862)
: a consonant (as \f\, \s\, \sh\) uttered with friction of the breath against some part of the oral passage : FRICATIVE
— **spirant** *adjective*

¹spire \'spīr\ *noun* [Middle English, from Old English *spīr*; akin to Middle Dutch *spier* blade of grass] (before 12th century)
1 : a slender tapering blade or stalk (as of grass)
2 : the upper tapering part of something (as a tree or antler) : PINNACLE
3 **a** : a tapering roof or analogous pyramidal construction surmounting a tower **b** : STEEPLE

²spire *intransitive verb* **spired; spir·ing** (14th century)
: to rise like a spire

³spire *noun* [Latin *spira* coil, from Greek *speira*; perhaps akin to Greek *sparton* rope, esparto] (1545)
1 **a** : SPIRAL **b** : COIL
2 : the inner or upper part of a spiral gastropod shell consisting of all the whorls except the whorl in contact with the body

⁴spire *intransitive verb* **spired; spir·ing** (1591)
: to rise in or as if in a spiral

spi·rea *or* **spi·raea** \spī-'rē-ə\ *noun* [New Latin *Spiraea*, from Latin, a plant, from Greek *speiraia*] (1669)
1 : any of a genus (*Spiraea*) of shrubs of the rose family with small perfect usually white or pink flowers in dense racemes, corymbs, cymes, or panicles
2 : any of several garden plants resembling spireas; *especially* : a shrub (*Astilbe japonica*) of the saxifrage family

spired \'spīrd\ *adjective* (1610)
1 : having a spire ⟨a *spired* church⟩
2 : tapering usually to a sharp point ⟨*spired* cedars⟩

spi·ril·lum \spī-'ri-ləm\ *noun, plural* **-ril·la** \-'ri-lə\ [New Latin, from diminutive of Latin *spira* coil] (circa 1875)
: any of a genus (*Spirillum*) of long curved bacteria having tufts of flagella; *broadly* : a spiral filamentous bacterium (as a spirochete)

¹spir·it \'spir-ət\ *noun* [Middle English, from Old French or Latin; Old French, from Latin *spiritus*, literally, breath, from *spirare* to blow, breathe] (13th century)

1 : an animating or vital principle held to give life to physical organisms
2 : a supernatural being or essence: as **a** *capitalized* : HOLY SPIRIT **b** : SOUL 2a **c** : an often malevolent being that is bodiless but can become visible; *specifically* : GHOST 2 **d** : a malevolent being that enters and possesses a human being
3 : temper or disposition of mind or outlook especially when vigorous or animated ⟨in high *spirits*⟩
4 : the immaterial intelligent or sentient part of a person
5 **a** : the activating or essential principle influencing a person ⟨acted in a *spirit* of helpfulness⟩ **b** : an inclination, impulse, or tendency of a specified kind : MOOD
6 **a** : a special attitude or frame of mind ⟨the money-making *spirit* was for a time driven back —J. A. Froude⟩ **b** : the feeling, quality, or disposition characterizing something ⟨undertaken in a *spirit* of fun⟩
7 : a lively or brisk quality in a person or a person's actions
8 : a person having a character or disposition of a specified nature
9 : a mental disposition characterized by firmness or assertiveness ⟨denied the charge with *spirit*⟩
10 **a** : DISTILLATE 1: as (1) : the liquid containing ethyl alcohol and water that is distilled from an alcoholic liquid or mash — often used in plural (2) : any of various volatile liquids obtained by distillation or cracking (as of petroleum, shale, or wood) — often used in plural **b** : a usually volatile organic solvent (as an alcohol, ester, or hydrocarbon)
11 **a** : prevailing tone or tendency ⟨*spirit* of the age⟩ **b** : general intent or real meaning ⟨*spirit* of the law⟩
12 : an alcoholic solution of a volatile substance ⟨*spirit* of camphor⟩
13 : enthusiastic loyalty ⟨school *spirit*⟩
14 *capitalized, Christian Science* : GOD 1b
synonym see COURAGE

²spirit *transitive verb* (1608)
1 : to infuse with spirit; *especially* : ANIMATE ⟨hope and apprehension of feasibleness *spirits* all industry —John Goodman⟩
2 : to carry off usually secretly or mysteriously ⟨was hustled into a . . . motorcar and *spirited* off to the country —W. L. Shirer⟩

spir·it·ed \'spir-ə-təd\ *adjective* (1592)
: full of energy, animation, or courage ⟨a *spirited* discussion⟩
— **spir·it·ed·ly** *adverb*
— **spir·it·ed·ness** *noun*

spirit gum *noun* (1886)
: a solution (as of gum arabic in ether) used especially for attaching false hair to the skin

spir·it·ism \'spir-ə-,ti-zəm\ *noun* (1856)
: SPIRITUALISM 2a
— **spir·it·ist** \-tist\ *noun*
— **spir·it·is·tic** \,spir-ə-'tis-tik\ *adjective*

spir·it·less \'spir-ət-ləs\ *adjective* (1597)
: lacking animation, cheerfulness, or courage
— **spir·it·less·ly** *adverb*
— **spir·it·less·ness** *noun*

spirit level *noun* (1768)
: LEVEL 1

spirit of hartshorn (circa 1684)
: AMMONIA WATER

spirit of wine (1753)
: ALCOHOL 1c

spir·i·to·so \,spir-ə-'tō-(,)sō, -(,)zō\ *adjective* [Italian, from *spirito* spirit, from Latin *spiritus*] (circa 1724)
: ANIMATED — used as a direction in music

spir·it·ous \'spir-ə-təs\ *adjective* (1605)
1 *archaic* : PURE, REFINED
2 : SPIRITUOUS

spirit rapping *noun* (1852)
: communication by raps held to be from the spirits of the dead

spirits of hartshorn (circa 1909)
: AMMONIA WATER

spirits of turpentine (circa 1792)
: TURPENTINE 2a
spirits of wine (1710)
: rectified spirit : ALCOHOL 1c
¹**spir·i·tu·al** \'spir-i-chə-wəl, -ich-əl, -ich-wəl\ *adjective* [Middle English, from Middle French & Late Latin; Middle French *spirituel,* from Late Latin *spiritualis,* from Latin, of breathing, of wind, from *spiritus*] (14th century)
1 : of, relating to, consisting of, or affecting the spirit : INCORPOREAL ⟨man's *spiritual* needs⟩
2 a : of or relating to sacred matters ⟨*spiritual* songs⟩ **b** : ecclesiastical rather than lay or temporal ⟨*spiritual* authority⟩ ⟨lords *spiritual*⟩
3 : concerned with religious values
4 : related or joined in spirit ⟨our *spiritual* home⟩ ⟨his *spiritual* heir⟩
5 a : of or relating to supernatural beings or phenomena **b** : of, relating to, or involving spiritualism : SPIRITUALISTIC
— **spir·i·tu·al·ly** *adverb*
— **spir·i·tu·al·ness** *noun*
²**spiritual** *noun* (1582)
1 *plural* : things of a spiritual, ecclesiastical, or religious nature
2 : a religious song usually of a deeply emotional character that was developed especially among blacks in the southern U.S.
3 *capitalized* : any of a party of 13th and 14th century Franciscans advocating strict observance of a rule of poverty for their order
spiritual bouquet *noun* (1926)
: a card notifying the recipient of a number of devotional acts performed by a Roman Catholic on behalf of a person on special occasions (as name days or anniversaries) or for the soul of someone recently deceased especially as an expression of sympathy
spir·i·tu·al·ism \'spir-i-chə-wə-,li-zəm, -i-chə-,li-, -ich-wə-,li-\ *noun* (1796)
1 : the view that spirit is a prime element of reality
2 a : a belief that spirits of the dead communicate with the living usually through a medium **b** *capitalized* : a movement comprising religious organizations emphasizing spiritualism
— **spir·i·tu·al·ist** \-list\ *noun, often capitalized*
— **spir·i·tu·al·is·tic** \,spir-i-chə-wə-'lis-tik, -i-chə-'lis-, -ich-wə-'lis-\ *adjective*
spir·i·tu·al·i·ty \,spir-i-chə-'wa-lə-tē\ *noun, plural* **-ties** (15th century)
1 : something that in ecclesiastical law belongs to the church or to a cleric as such
2 : CLERGY
3 : sensitivity or attachment to religious values
4 : the quality or state of being spiritual
spir·i·tu·al·ize \'spir-i-chə-wə-,līz, -i-chə-,līz, -ich-wə-,līz\ *transitive verb* **-ized; -iz·ing** (1631)
1 : to make spiritual; *especially* : to purify from the corrupting influences of the world
2 : to give a spiritual meaning to or understand in a spiritual sense
— **spir·i·tu·al·i·za·tion** \,spir-i-chə-wə-lə-'zā-shən, -i-chə-lə-, -ich-wə-lə-\ *noun*
spir·i·tu·al·ty \'spir-i-chə-wəl-tē, -i-chəl-tē, -ich-wəl-tē\ *noun* [Middle English *spiritualte,* from Middle French *spiritualté,* from Medieval Latin *spiritualitat-, spiritualitas,* from Late Latin *spiritualis* spiritual] (14th century)
1 : SPIRITUALITY 1
2 : CLERGY
spir·i·tu·el *or* **spir·i·tu·elle** \,spir-i-chə-'wel, spē-rē-tw⁽ʸ⁾el\ *adjective* [*spirituel* from French, literally, spiritual; *spirituelle* from French, feminine of *spirituel*] (1673)
: having or marked by a refined and especially sprightly or witty nature
spir·i·tu·ous \'spir-i-chə-wəs, -ich-wəs\ *adjective* [probably from French *spiritueux,* from Latin *spiritus* spirit] (1681)
: containing or impregnated with alcohol obtained by distillation ⟨*spirituous* liquors⟩
spirit varnish *noun* (1850)
: a varnish in which a volatile liquid (as alcohol) is the solvent
spirit writing *noun* (1864)
: automatic writing held to be produced under the influence of spirits
spi·ro·chet·al \,spī-rə-'kē-t°l\ *adjective* (1915)
: caused by spirochetes
spi·ro·chete *also* **spi·ro·chaete** \'spī-rə-,kēt\ *noun* [New Latin *Spirochaeta,* genus of bacteria, from Latin *spira* coil + Greek *chaitē* long hair — more at SPIRE] (circa 1877)
: any of an order (Spirochaetales) of slender spirally undulating bacteria including those causing syphilis and relapsing fever
spi·ro·chet·osis \,spī-rə-,kē-'tō-səs\ *noun, plural* **-oses** \-,sēz\ [New Latin] (1906)
: infection with or a disease caused by spirochetes
spi·ro·gy·ra \,spī-rə-'jī-rə\ *noun* [New Latin, from Latin *spira* + Greek *gyros* ring, circle] (1875)
: any of a genus (Spirogyra) of freshwater green algae with spiral chloroplasts
spi·rom·e·ter \spī-'rä-mə-tər\ *noun* [International Scientific Vocabulary *spiro-* (from Latin *spirare* to breathe) + *-meter*] (1846)
: an instrument for measuring the air entering and leaving the lungs
— **spi·ro·met·ric** \,spī-rə-'me-trik\ *adjective*
— **spi·rom·e·try** \spī-'rä-mə-trē\ *noun*
spirt *variant of* SPURT
spiry \'spīr-ē\ *adjective* (1602)
: resembling a spire; *especially* : being tall, slender, and tapering ⟨*spiry* trees⟩
¹**spit** \'spit\ *noun* [Middle English, from Old English *spitu;* akin to Old High German *spiz* spit, *spizzi* pointed] (before 12th century)
1 : a slender pointed rod for holding meat over a fire
2 : a small point of land especially of sand or gravel running into a body of water
²**spit** *transitive verb* **spit·ted; spit·ting** (13th century)
: to fix on or as if on a spit : IMPALE
³**spit** *verb also* **spat** \'spat\ **spit·ting** [Middle English *spitten,* from Old English *spittan;* akin to Middle High German *spiutzen* to spit] (before 12th century)
transitive verb
1 a : to eject (as saliva) from the mouth : EXPECTORATE **b** (1) : to express (unpleasant or malicious feelings) by or as if by spitting (2) : to utter with a spitting sound or scornful expression ⟨*spat* out his words⟩ **c** : to emit as if by spitting; *especially* : to emit (precipitation) in driving particles or in flurries ⟨*spit* rain⟩
2 : to set to burning ⟨*spit* a fuse⟩
intransitive verb
1 a (1) : to eject saliva as an expression of aversion or contempt (2) : to exhibit contempt **b** : to eject matter (as saliva) from the mouth : EXPECTORATE
2 : to rain or snow slightly or in flurries
3 : to make a noise suggesting expectoration : SPUTTER
— **spit it out** : to say what is in the mind without further delay
⁴**spit** *noun* (14th century)
1 a (1) : SPITTLE, SALIVA (2) : the act or an instance of spitting **b** (1) : a frothy secretion exuded by spittlebugs (2) : SPITTLEBUG
2 : perfect likeness
3 : a sprinkle of rain or flurry of snow
spit·al \'spi-t°l\ *noun* [Middle English *spitel,* modification of Medieval Latin *hospitale* — more at HOSPITAL] (14th century)
archaic : LAZARETTO, HOSPITAL
spit and polish *noun* [from the practice of polishing objects such as shoes by spitting on them and then rubbing them with a cloth] (1895)
: extreme attention to cleanliness, orderliness, smartness of appearance, and ceremony often at the expense of operational efficiency
— **spit–and–polish** *adjective*
spit·ball \'spit-,bȯl\ *noun* (1846)
1 : paper chewed and rolled into a ball to be thrown or shot as a missile
2 : a baseball pitch delivered after the ball has been moistened with saliva or sweat
spit curl *noun* [probably from its being sometimes plastered down with saliva] (1831)
: a spiral curl that is usually plastered on the forehead, temple, or cheek
¹**spite** \'spīt\ *noun* [Middle English, short for *despite*] (14th century)
1 : petty ill will or hatred with the disposition to irritate, annoy, or thwart
2 : an instance of spite
synonym see MALICE
— **in spite of** : in defiance or contempt of : without being prevented by
²**spite** *transitive verb* **spit·ed; spit·ing** (circa 1555)
1 a : ANNOY, OFFEND **b** : to fill with spite
2 : to treat maliciously (as by shaming or thwarting)
spite·ful \'spīt-fəl\ *adjective* (15th century)
: filled with or showing spite : MALICIOUS
— **spite·ful·ly** \-fə-lē\ *adverb*
— **spite·ful·ness** *noun*
spit·fire \'spit-,fīr\ *noun* (1680)
: a quick-tempered or highly emotional person
¹**spit·ter** \'spi-tər\ *noun* (14th century)
: one that spits
²**spitter** *noun* (1908)
: SPITBALL 2
spitting cobra *noun* (1910)
: either of two African cobras (*Naja nigricollis* and *Hemachatus haemachatus*) that in defense typically eject their venom toward the victim without striking
spitting image *noun* [alteration of *spit and image*] (1901)
: IMAGE 3b
spit·tle \'spi-t°l\ *noun* [Middle English *spetil,* from Old English *spætl;* akin to Old English *spittan* to spit] (before 12th century)
1 : SALIVA
2 : ⁴SPIT 1b(1)
spit·tle·bug \-,bəg\ *noun* (1882)
: any of a family (Cercopidae) of leaping homopterous insects whose larvae secrete froth — called also *froghopper*
spittle insect *noun* (1891)
: SPITTLEBUG
spit·toon \spi-'tün, spə-\ *noun* [⁴*spit* + *-oon* (as in *balloon*)] (1823)
: a receptacle for spit — called also *cuspidor*
spit up *verb* (1779)
: REGURGITATE, VOMIT
spitz \'spits\ *noun* [German, from *spitz* pointed, from Old High German *spizzi;* from the shape of its ears and muzzle — more at SPIT] (1842)
: a member of any of several breeds of stocky heavy-coated dogs of northern origin with erect ears and usually a heavily furred tail carried over the back

spitz

spiv \'spiv\ *noun* [alteration of English dialect *spiff* flashy dresser, from *spiff* dandified] (circa 1934)
1 *British* : one who lives by his wits without regular employment

2 *British* : SLACKER

splanch·nic \'splaŋk-nik\ *adjective* [New Latin *splanchnicus*, from Greek *splanchnikos*, from *splanchna*, plural, viscera; akin to Greek *splēn* spleen] (1681)
: of or relating to the viscera : VISCERAL

¹splash \'splash\ *verb* [alteration of *plash*] (circa 1727)
transitive verb
1 a (1) : to dash a liquid or thinly viscous substance upon or against (2) : to soil or stain with splashed liquid **b** : to mark or overlay with patches of contrasting color or texture **c** : to display prominently
2 a : to cause (a liquid or thinly viscous substance) to spatter about especially with force **b** : to scatter in the manner of a splashed liquid
intransitive verb
1 a : to strike and dash about a liquid or semi-liquid substance **b** : to move in or into a liquid or semiliquid substance and cause it to splash
2 a (1) : to become spattered about (2) : to spread or scatter in the manner of splashed liquid **b** : to fall, strike, or move with a splashing sound ⟨a brook *splashing* over rocks⟩
— **splash·er** *noun*
²splash *noun* (1736)
1 a (1) : splashed liquid or semiliquid substance; *also* : impounded water released suddenly (2) : a spot or daub from or as if from splashed liquid ⟨a mud *splash* on the fender⟩ **b** : a colored patch
2 a : the action of splashing **b** : a short plunge
3 : a sound produced by or as if by a liquid falling, moving, being hurled, or oscillating
4 a : a vivid impression created especially by ostentatious activity or appearance **b** : ostentatious display
5 : a small amount : SPRINKLING

splash·board \'splash-,bōrd, -,bȯrd\ *noun* (1826)
1 : DASHBOARD 1
2 : a panel to protect against splashes

splash·down \'splash-,daün\ *noun* (1959)
: the landing of a manned spacecraft in the ocean
— **splash down** *intransitive verb*

splash guard *noun* (1926)
: a flap suspended behind a rear wheel to prevent tire splash from muddying windshields of following vehicles

splashy \'spla-shē\ *adjective* **splash·i·er; -est** (1856)
1 : that can be easily splashed about
2 : moving or being moved with a splash or splashing sounds
3 : tending to or exhibiting ostentatious display
4 : consisting of, being, or covered with colored splashes
— **splash·i·ly** \'spla-shə-lē\ *adverb*
— **splash·i·ness** \'spla-shē-nəs\ *noun*

¹splat \'splat\ *noun* [obsolete *splat* to spread flat] (1833)
: a single flat thin often ornamental member of a back of a chair

²splat *noun* [imitative] (1897)
: a splattering or slapping sound

¹splat·ter \'spla-tər\ *verb* [probably blend of *splash* and *spatter*] (1785)
transitive verb
: SPATTER
intransitive verb
: to scatter or fall in or as if in drops

²splatter *noun* (1819)
: SPATTER, SPLASH

¹splay \'splā\ *verb* [Middle English, short for *displayen* — more at DISPLAY] (15th century)
transitive verb
1 : to cause to spread outward
2 : to make oblique : BEVEL
intransitive verb
1 : to extend apart or outward especially in an awkward manner
2 : SLOPE, SLANT

²splay *noun* (circa 1508)

1 : a slope or bevel especially of the sides of a door or window
2 : SPREAD, EXPANSION

³splay *adjective* (1767)
1 : turned outward ⟨*splay* knees⟩
2 : AWKWARD, UNGAINLY

splay·foot \'splā-,fút\ *noun* (1548)
: a foot abnormally flattened and spread out; *specifically* : FLATFOOT
— **splay·foot·ed** \-,fú-təd\ *adjective*

spleen \'splēn\ *noun* [Middle English *splen*, from Middle French or Latin; Middle French *esplen*, from Latin *splen*, from Greek *splēn*; akin to Latin *lien* spleen, Sanskrit *plīhan*] (14th century)
1 : a highly vascular ductless organ that is located in the left abdominal region near the stomach or intestine of most vertebrates and is concerned with final destruction of red blood cells, filtration and storage of blood, and production of lymphocytes
2 *obsolete* : the seat of emotions or passions
3 *archaic* : MELANCHOLY
4 : feelings of anger or ill will often suppressed
5 *obsolete* : a sudden impulse or whim : CAPRICE
synonym see MALICE

spleen·ful \-fəl\ *adjective* (1588)
: full of or affected with spleen : SPLENETIC

spleen·wort \-,wərt, -,wȯrt\ *noun* [from the belief in its power to cure disorders of the spleen] (1578)
: any of a large genus (*Asplenium*) of chiefly evergreen ferns having linear or oblong sori

spleeny \'splē-nē\ *adjective* (1604)
1 : full of or displaying spleen
2 *New England* : peevish and irritable with hypochondriac inclinations

splen- *or* **spleno-** *combining form* [Latin, from Greek *splēn-*, *splēno-*, from *splēn*]
: spleen ⟨*splen*ectomy⟩ ⟨*spleno*megaly⟩

splen·dent \'splen-dənt\ *adjective* [Middle English, from Late Latin *splendent-*, *splendens*, from Latin, present participle of *splendēre*] (15th century)
1 : SHINING, GLOSSY ⟨*splendent* luster⟩
2 : ILLUSTRIOUS, BRILLIANT ⟨*splendent* genius⟩

splen·did \'splen-dəd\ *adjective* [Latin *splendidus*, from *splendēre* to shine; perhaps akin to Middle Irish *lainn* bright] (1634)
1 : possessing or displaying splendor: as **a** : SHINING, BRILLIANT **b** : marked by showy magnificence
2 : ILLUSTRIOUS, GRAND
3 a : EXCELLENT ⟨a *splendid* opportunity⟩ **b** : being out of the ordinary : SINGULAR ☆
— **splen·did·ly** *adverb*
— **splen·did·ness** *noun*

splen·dif·er·ous \splen-'di-f(ə-)rəs\ *adjective* [*splendor* + *-i-* + *-ferous*] (1843)
: extraordinarily or showily impressive
— **splen·dif·er·ous·ly** *adverb*
— **splen·dif·er·ous·ness** *noun*

splen·dor \'splen-dər\ *noun* [Middle English *splendure*, from Anglo-French *splendur*, from Latin *splendor*, from *splendēre*] (15th century)
1 a : great brightness or luster : BRILLIANCY **b** : MAGNIFICENCE, POMP
2 : something splendid
— **splen·dor·ous** *also* **splen·drous** \-d(ə-)rəs\ *adjective*

splen·dour \-dər\ *chiefly British variant of* SPLENDOR

sple·nec·to·my \spli-'nek-tə-mē\ *noun*, *plural* **-mies** [International Scientific Vocabulary] (circa 1859)
: surgical removal of the spleen
— **sple·nec·to·mize** \-,mīz\ *transitive verb*

sple·net·ic \spli-'ne-tik, *archaic* 'sple-nə-(,)tik\ *adjective* [Late Latin *spleneticus*, from Latin *splen* spleen] (1697)
1 *archaic* : given to melancholy
2 : marked by bad temper, malevolence, or spite

— **splenetic** *noun*
— **sple·net·i·cal·ly** \spli-'ne-ti-k(ə-)lē\ *adverb*

splen·ic \'sple-nik\ *adjective* [Latin *splenicus*, from Greek *splēnikos*, from *splēn* spleen] (1619)
: of, relating to, or located in the spleen ⟨*splenic* blood flow⟩

sple·ni·us \'splē-nē-əs\ *noun*, *plural* **-nii** \-nē-,ī\ [New Latin, from Latin *splenium* plaster, compress, from Greek *splēnion*, from *splēn*] (1732)
: either of two flat oblique muscles on each side of the back of the neck and upper thoracic region

spleno·meg·a·ly \,sple-nō-'me-gə-lē\ *noun*, *plural* **-lies** [International Scientific Vocabulary] (circa 1900)
: enlargement of the spleen

spleu·chan \'splü-kən, 'splyü-\ *noun* [Scottish Gaelic *spliùcan* & Irish *spliúchán*] (1785)
Scottish & Irish : a pouch especially for tobacco or money

¹splice \'splīs\ *transitive verb* **spliced; splic·ing** [obsolete Dutch *splissen*; akin to Middle Dutch *splitten* to split] (circa 1525)
1 a : to unite (as two ropes) by interweaving the strands **b** : to unite (as lengths of magnetic tape) by lapping two ends together or by applying a piece that laps upon two ends and making fast
2 : to unite, link, or insert as if by splicing
3 : to combine (genetic material) from either the same organism or different organisms ⟨use enzymes to cut and *splice* genes⟩
— **splic·er** *noun*

²splice *noun* (1627)
1 : a joining or joint made by splicing something
2 : MARRIAGE, WEDDING

splice 1

spliff \'splif\ *noun* [origin unknown] (1936)
: JOINT 4

spline \'splīn\ *noun* [origin unknown] (1756)
1 : a thin wood or metal strip used in building construction
2 : a key that is fixed to one of two connected mechanical parts and fits into a keyway in the other; *also* : a keyway for such a key
3 : a function that is defined on an interval, is used to approximate a given function, and is composed of pieces of simple functions defined on subintervals and joined at their endpoints with a suitable degree of smoothness

¹splint \'splint\ *also* **splent** *noun* [Middle English, from Middle Low German *splinte*, *splente*; probably akin to Middle Dutch *splitten* to split] (14th century)
1 : a small plate or strip of metal used in making armor

☆ SYNONYMS
Splendid, resplendent, gorgeous, glorious, sublime, superb mean extraordinarily or transcendently impressive. SPLENDID implies outshining the usual or customary ⟨the wedding was a *splendid* occasion⟩. RESPLENDENT suggests a glowing or blazing splendor ⟨*resplendent* in her jewelry⟩. GORGEOUS implies a rich splendor especially in display of color ⟨a *gorgeous* red dress⟩. GLORIOUS suggests radiance that heightens beauty or distinction ⟨a *glorious* sunset⟩. SUBLIME implies an exaltation or elevation almost beyond human comprehension ⟨a vision of *sublime* beauty⟩. SUPERB suggests a magnificence or excellence reaching the highest conceivable degree ⟨her singing was *superb*⟩.

2 a : a thin strip of wood suitable for interweaving (as into baskets) **b :** SPLINTER **c :** material or a device used to protect and immobilize a body part (as a broken arm)
3 : a bony enlargement on the upper part of the cannon bone of a horse usually on the inside of the leg

²**splint** *transitive verb* (15th century)
1 : to support and immobilize (as a broken bone) with a splint
2 : to brace with or as if with splints

splint bone *noun* (1704)
: one of the slender rudimentary metacarpal or metatarsal bones on either side of the cannon bone in the limbs of the horse and related animals

¹**splin·ter** \'splin-tər\ *noun* [Middle English, from Middle Dutch; akin to Middle Low German *splinte* splint] (14th century)
1 a : a thin piece split or broken off lengthwise **:** SLIVER **b :** a small needlelike particle
2 : a group or faction broken away from a parent body
— **splinter** *adjective*
— **splin·tery** \'splin-tə-rē, -trē\ *adjective*

²**splinter** *verb* **splin·tered; splin·ter·ing** \'splin-tə-riŋ, -triŋ\ (1582)
transitive verb
1 : to split or rend into long thin pieces **:** SHIVER
2 : to split into fragments, parts, or factions
intransitive verb
: to become splintered

¹**split** \'split\ *verb* **split; split·ting** [Dutch *splitten*, from Middle Dutch; akin to Middle High German *splīzen* to split and probably to Old High German *spaltan* to split] (1593)
transitive verb
1 a : to divide lengthwise usually along a grain or seam or by layers **b :** to affect as if by cleaving or forcing apart ⟨the river *splits* the town in two⟩
2 a (1) **:** to tear or rend apart **:** BURST (2) **:** to subject (an atom or atomic nucleus) to artificial disintegration by fission **b :** to affect as if by breaking up or tearing apart **:** SHATTER ⟨a roar that *split* the air⟩
3 : to divide into parts or portions: as **a :** to divide between persons **:** SHARE **b :** to divide into factions, parties, or groups **c :** to mark (a ballot) or cast or register (a vote) so as to vote for candidates of different parties **d** (1) **:** to divide or break down (a chemical compound) into constituents ⟨*split* a fat into glycerol and fatty acids⟩ (2) **:** to remove by such separation ⟨*split* off carbon dioxide⟩ **e :** to divide (stock) by issuing a larger number of shares to existing shareholders usually without increase in total par value
4 : to separate (the parts of a whole) by interposing something ⟨*split* an infinitive⟩
5 : LEAVE ⟨*split* the party⟩ ⟨*split* town⟩
intransitive verb
1 a : to become split lengthwise or into layers **b :** to break apart **:** BURST
2 a : to become divided up or separated off ⟨*split* into factions⟩ **b :** to sever relations or connections **c :** LEAVE; *especially* **:** to leave without delay
3 *British* **:** to betray confidence **:** act as an informer — usually used with *on*
4 : to apportion shares
synonym see TEAR
— **split hairs :** to make oversubtle or trivial distinctions
— **split one's sides :** to laugh heartily

²**split** *noun* (1597)
1 a : a narrow break made by or as if by splitting **b :** an arrangement of bowling pins left standing with space for pins between them
2 : a piece split off or made thin by splitting
3 a : a division into or between divergent or antagonistic elements or forces **b :** a faction formed in this way

4 a : the act or process of splitting (as the stock of a corporation) **b :** the act of lowering oneself to the floor or leaping into the air with legs extended at right angles to the trunk
5 : a product of division by or as if by splitting
6 : a wine bottle holding one quarter the usual amount or about .1875 liters (6 to 6.5 ounces); *also* **:** the quantity held by a split
7 : an ice cream sundae served over slices of fruit (as banana)
8 : the recorded time at or for a specific part of a race

³**split** *adjective* (1648)
1 : DIVIDED, FRACTURED
2 : prepared for use by splitting ⟨*split* bamboo⟩ ⟨*split* hides⟩
3 : HETEROZYGOUS — used especially by breeders of cage birds sometimes with *for*
4 : widely spaced

split–brain \'split-'brān\ *adjective* (1958)
: having the optic chiasma and corpus callosum severed ⟨behavior in *split-brain* animals⟩

split decision *noun* (1952)
: a decision in a boxing match reflecting a division of opinion among the referee and judges

split end *noun* (1955)
: an offensive football end who lines up usually several yards to the side of the formation

split–fingered fastball \'split-'fiŋ-gərd-\ *noun* (1979)
: a fast baseball pitch thrown with the ball gripped as for a forkball

split infinitive *noun* (1897)
: an infinitive with *to* having a modifier between the *to* and the verbal (as in "to really start") □

split–lev·el \'split-'le-vəl\ *adjective* (1946)
: divided vertically so that the floor level of rooms in one part is approximately midway between the levels of two successive stories in an adjoining part ⟨a *split-level* house⟩
— **split–lev·el** \-,le-vəl\ *noun*

split pea *noun* (1736)
: a dried hulled pea in which the cotyledons usually split apart

split personality *noun* (1927)
: SCHIZOPHRENIA; *also* **:** MULTIPLE PERSONALITY

split rail *noun* (1826)
: a fence rail split from a log

split screen *noun* (1944)
: a film or video technique in which the frame is divided into discrete nonoverlapping images; *also* **:** the visual composition based on this technique

split second *noun* (1912)
: a fractional part of a second **:** FLASH

split shift *noun* (1943)
: a shift of working hours divided into two or more working periods at times (as morning and evening) separated by more than normal periods of time off (as for lunch or rest)

split·ter \'spli-tər\ *noun* (1648)
1 : one that splits
2 : one who classifies organisms into numerous named groups based on relatively minor variations or characters — compare LUMPER
3 : SPLIT-FINGERED FASTBALL

split ticket *noun* (1836)
: a ballot cast by a voter who votes for candidates of more than one party

split·ting \'spli-tiŋ\ *adjective* (1593)
: that splits or causes to split: as **a :** causing a piercing sensation ⟨a *splitting* headache⟩ **b :** very fast or quick **c :** SIDESPLITTING ⟨a *splitting* laugh⟩

splore \'splōr, 'splȯr\ *noun* [origin unknown] (1785)
1 *Scottish* **:** FROLIC, CAROUSAL
2 *Scottish* **:** COMMOTION

¹**splotch** \'spläch\ *noun* [perhaps blend of *spot* and *blotch*] (1601)
: SPOT, BLOTCH
— **splotchy** \'splä-chē\ *adjective*

²**splotch** *transitive verb* (1654)

: to mark with a splotch **:** cover with splotches

¹**splurge** \'splərj\ *noun* [perhaps blend of *splash* and *surge*] (1830)
: an ostentatious effort, display, or expenditure

²**splurge** *verb* **splurged; splurg·ing** (1843)
intransitive verb
1 : to make a splurge
2 : to indulge oneself extravagantly — often used with *on* ⟨*splurge* on a new dress⟩
transitive verb
: to spend extravagantly or ostentatiously

¹**splut·ter** \'splə-tər\ *noun* [probably alteration of *sputter*] (1677)
1 : a confused noise (as of hasty speaking)
2 : a splashing or sputtering sound

²**splutter** (1818)
intransitive verb
1 : to make a noise as if spitting
2 : to speak hastily and confusedly
transitive verb
: to utter hastily or confusedly **:** STAMMER
— **splut·ter·er** \'splə-tər-ər\ *noun*

splut·tery \'splə-tə-rē\ *adjective* (1866)
: marked by spluttering

Spode \'spōd\ *noun* (1869)
: ceramic ware (as bone china, stone china, or Parian ware) made at the works established by Josiah Spode in 1770 at Stoke in Staffordshire, England

spod·u·mene \'spä-jə-,mēn\ *noun* [probably from French *spodumène*, from German *Spodumen*, from Greek *spodoumenos*, present participle of *spodousthai* to be burnt to ashes, from *spodos* ashes] (1893)
: a white to yellowish, purplish, or emerald-green monoclinic mineral that is a silicate of lithium and aluminum and occurs in prismatic crystals often of great size

¹**spoil** \'spȯi(ə)l\ *noun* [Middle English *spoile*, from Middle French *espoille*, from Latin *spolia*, plural of *spolium* animal skin — more at SPILL] (14th century)
1 a : plunder taken from an enemy in war or a victim in robbery **:** LOOT **b :** public offices made the property of a successful party — usually used in plural **c :** something valuable or desirable gained through special effort or opportunism or in return for a favor — usually used in plural
2 a : SPOLIATION, PLUNDERING **b :** the act of damaging **:** HARM, IMPAIRMENT
3 : an object of plundering **:** PREY
4 : earth and rock excavated or dredged

\ə\ abut \ə\ kitten \ər\ further \a\ ash \ā\ ace \ä\ mop, mar \aù\ out \ch\ chin \e\ bet \ē\ easy \g\ go \i\ hit \ī\ ice \j\ job \ŋ\ sing \ō\ go \ȯ\ law \ȯi\ boy \th\ thin \th\ the \ü\ loot \ù\ foot \y\ yet \zh\ vision *see also* Guide to Pronunciation

5 : an object damaged or flawed in the making
☆
²spoil *verb* **spoiled** \'spói(ə)ld, 'spói(ə)lt\ *also* **spoilt** \'spói(ə)lt\; **spoil·ing** [Middle English, from Middle French *espoillier*, from Latin *spoliare*, from *spolium*] (14th century)
transitive verb
1 a *archaic* : DESPOIL, STRIP **b** : PILLAGE, ROB
2 *archaic* : to seize by force
3 a : to damage seriously : RUIN **b** : to impair the quality or effect of ⟨a quarrel *spoiled* the celebration⟩
4 a : to impair the disposition or character of by overindulgence or excessive praise **b** : to pamper excessively : CODDLE
intransitive verb
1 : to practice plunder and robbery
2 : to lose valuable or useful qualities usually as a result of decay
3 : to have an eager desire ⟨*spoiling* for a fight⟩
synonym see DECAY, INDULGE
— **spoil·able** \'spói-lə-bəl\ *adjective*
spoil·age \'spói-lij\ *noun* (1597)
1 : the act or process of spoiling; *especially* : the process of decay in foodstuffs
2 : something spoiled or wasted
3 : loss by spoilage
spoil·er \'spói-lər\ *noun* (15th century)
1 a : one that spoils **b** : one (as a political candidate) having little or no chance of winning but capable of depriving a rival of success
2 a : a long narrow plate along the upper surface of an airplane wing that may be raised for reducing lift and increasing drag — see AIRPLANE illustration **b** : an air deflector on an automobile to reduce the tendency to lift off the road at high speeds
spoils·man \'spói(ə)lz-mən\ *noun* (1846)
: one who serves a party for a share of the spoils; *also* : one who sanctions such practice
spoil·sport \'spói(ə)l-ˌspōrt, -ˌspórt\ *noun* (1821)
: one who spoils the sport or pleasure of others
spoils system *noun* (1838)
: a practice of regarding public offices and their emoluments as plunder to be distributed to members of the victorious party
¹spoke \'spōk\ *past & archaic past participle of* SPEAK
²spoke *noun* [Middle English, from Old English *spāca;* akin to Middle Dutch *spike* spike — more at SPIKE] (before 12th century)
1 a : any of the small radiating bars inserted in the hub of a wheel to support the rim **b** : something resembling the spoke of a wheel
2 : any of the projecting handles of a steering wheel of a boat
³spoke *transitive verb* **spoked; spok·ing** (before 12th century)
: to furnish with or as if with spokes
spo·ken \'spō-kən\ *adjective* [past participle of *speak*] (1595)
1 : delivered by word of mouth : ORAL
2 : characterized by speaking in (such) a manner — used in combination ⟨soft-*spoken*⟩ ⟨plain*spoken*⟩
spoke·shave \'spōk-ˌshāv\ *noun* [²*spoke*] (1510)
: a drawknife or small transverse plane with end handles for planing convex or concave surfaces
spokes·man \'spōks-mən\ *noun* [probably irregular from *spoke*, obsolete past participle of *speak*] (1537)
: a person who speaks as the representative of another or others often in a professional capacity
— **spokes·man·ship** \-ˌship\ *noun*
spokes·peo·ple \-ˌpē-pəl\ *noun plural* (1972)
: people serving as spokesmen or spokeswomen
spokes·per·son \-ˌpər-sᵊn\ *noun* (1972)
: SPOKESMAN
spokes·wom·an \-ˌwu̇-mən\ *noun* (1654)

: a woman who speaks as the representative of another or others often in a professional capacity
spo·li·ate \'spō-lē-ˌāt\ *transitive verb* **-at·ed; -at·ing** [Latin *spoliatus,* past participle of *spoliare*] (circa 1727)
: DESPOIL
— **spo·li·a·tor** \-ˌā-tər\ *noun*
spo·li·a·tion \ˌspō-lē-'ā-shən\ *noun* [Middle English, from Latin *spoliation-, spoliatio,* from *spoliare* to plunder — more at SPOIL] (15th century)
1 a : the act of plundering **b** : the state of having been plundered especially in war
2 : the act of injuring especially beyond reclaim
spon·dee \'spän-ˌdē\ *noun* [Middle English *sponde,* from Middle French or Latin; Middle French *spondee,* from Latin *spondeum,* from Greek *spondeios,* from *spondeios* of a libation, from *spondē* libation, from *spendein* to make a libation; from its use in music accompanying libations — more at SPOUSE] (14th century)
: a metrical foot consisting of two long or stressed syllables
— **spon·da·ic** \spän-'dā-ik\ *adjective or noun*
spon·dy·li·tis \ˌspän-də-'lī-təs\ *noun* [New Latin, from Greek *sphondylos, spondylos* vertebra] (circa 1849)
: inflammation of the vertebrae
¹sponge \'spənj\ *noun* [Middle English, from Old English, from Latin *spongia,* from Greek] (before 12th century)
1 a (1) : an elastic porous mass of interlacing horny fibers that forms the internal skeleton of various marine animals (phylum Porifera) and is able when wetted to absorb water (2) : a piece of sponge (as for scrubbing and cleaning) (3) : a porous rubber or cellulose product used similarly to a sponge **b** : any of a phylum (Porifera) of aquatic chiefly marine lower invertebrate animals that are essentially double-walled cell colonies that are permanently attached as adults
2 : a pad (as of folded gauze) used in surgery and medicine (as to remove discharge or apply medication)
3 : one who lives on others : SPONGER
4 a : raised dough (as for yeast bread) **b** : a whipped dessert usually containing whites of eggs or gelatin **c** : a metal (as platinum) obtained in porous form usually by reduction without fusion ⟨titanium *sponge*⟩ **d** : the egg mass of a crab
5 : an absorbent contraceptive device that is impregnated with spermicide and inserted into the vagina before sexual intercourse to cover the cervix
synonym see PARASITE
²sponge *verb* **sponged; spong·ing** (14th century)
transitive verb
1 : to cleanse, wipe, or moisten with or as if with a sponge
2 : to erase or destroy with or as if with a sponge — often used with *out*
3 : to get by sponging on another
4 : to absorb with or as if with or in the manner of a sponge
intransitive verb
1 : to absorb, soak up, or imbibe like a sponge
2 : to get something from or live on another by imposing on hospitality or good nature
3 : to dive or dredge for sponges
— **spong·er** *noun*
sponge cake *noun* (1805)
: a light cake made without shortening
sponge cloth *noun* (1862)
: any of various soft porous fabrics especially in a loose honeycomb weave
sponge rubber *noun* (1886)
: cellular rubber resembling a natural sponge in structure used especially for cushions, vibration dampeners, weather stripping, and gaskets

sponge·ware \'spənj-ˌwar, -ˌwer\ *noun* (1943)
: a typically 19th century earthenware with background color spattered or dabbed (as with a sponge) and usually a freehand central design
spon·gin \'spän-jən\ *noun* [German, from Latin *spongia* sponge] (circa 1868)
: a scleroprotein that is the chief constituent of flexible fibers in sponge skeletons
spongy \'spän-jē\ *adjective* **spong·i·er; -est** (14th century)
1 : resembling a sponge: **a** : soft and full of cavities ⟨*spongy* ice⟩ **b** : elastic, porous, and absorbent
2 a : not firm or solid **b** : being in the form of a metallic sponge ⟨*spongy* iron⟩
3 : moist and soft like a sponge full of water ⟨a *spongy* moor⟩
— **spong·i·ness** *noun*
spongy parenchyma *noun* (1884)
: a spongy layer of irregular chlorophyll-bearing cells interspersed with air spaces that fills the interior part of a leaf below the palisade layer — called also *spongy layer, spongy tissue*
spon·son \'spän(t)-sən\ *noun* [perhaps by shortening & alteration from *expansion*] (1835)
1 a : a projection (as a gun platform) from the side of a ship or a tank **b** : an air chamber along a canoe to increase stability and buoyancy
2 : a light air-filled structure or a winglike part protruding from the hull of a seaplane to steady it on water
¹spon·sor \'spän(t)-sər\ *noun* [Late Latin, from Latin, guarantor, surety, from *spondēre* to promise — more at SPOUSE] (1651)
1 : one who presents a candidate for baptism or confirmation and undertakes responsibility for the person's religious education or spiritual welfare
2 : one who assumes responsibility for some other person or thing
3 : a person or an organization that pays for or plans and carries out a project or activity; *especially* : one that pays the cost of a radio or television program usually in return for advertising time during its course
— **spon·so·ri·al** \spän-'sōr-ē-əl, -'sór-\ *adjective*
— **spon·sor·ship** \'spän(t)-sər-ˌship\ *noun*
²sponsor *transitive verb* **spon·sored; spon·sor·ing** \'spän(t)s-(ə-)riŋ\ (1884)
: to be or stand sponsor for
spon·ta·ne·i·ty \ˌspän-tə-'nē-ə-tē, -'nā-; -'tᵊn-ē-, -'ā-\ *noun* (1651)
1 : the quality or state of being spontaneous
2 : voluntary or undetermined action or movement; *also* : its source
spon·ta·ne·ous \spän-'tā-nē-əs\ *adjective* [Late Latin *spontaneus,* from Latin *sponte* of one's free will, voluntarily] (1656)
1 : proceeding from natural feeling or native tendency without external constraint

☆ **SYNONYMS**
Spoil, plunder, booty, prize, loot mean something taken from another by force or craft. SPOIL, more commonly SPOILS, applies to what belongs by right or custom to the victor in war or political contest ⟨the *spoils* of political victory⟩. PLUNDER applies to what is taken not only in war but in robbery, banditry, grafting, or swindling ⟨a bootlegger's *plunder*⟩. BOOTY implies plunder to be shared among confederates ⟨thieves dividing up their *booty*⟩. PRIZE applies to spoils captured on the high seas or territorial waters of the enemy ⟨the wartime right of seizing *prizes* at sea⟩. LOOT applies especially to what is taken from victims of a catastrophe ⟨picked through the ruins for *loot*⟩.

2 : arising from a momentary impulse
3 : controlled and directed internally **:** SELF-ACTING ⟨*spontaneous* movement characteristic of living things⟩
4 : produced without being planted or without human labor **:** INDIGENOUS
5 : developing without apparent external influence, force, cause, or treatment
6 : not apparently contrived or manipulated **:** NATURAL ☆
— **spon·ta·ne·ous·ly** *adverb*
— **spon·ta·ne·ous·ness** *noun*

spontaneous combustion *noun* (1795)
: self-ignition of combustible material through chemical action (as oxidation) of its constituents — called also *spontaneous ignition*

spontaneous generation *noun* (1665)
: ABIOGENESIS

spontaneous recovery *noun* (1943)
: reappearance of an extinguished conditioned response without positive reinforcement

spon·toon \spän-ˈtün\ *noun* [French *sponton*, from Italian *spuntone*, from *punta* sharp point, from (assumed) Vulgar Latin *puncta* — more at POINT] (1598)
: a short pike formerly borne by subordinate officers of infantry

¹spoof \ˈspüf\ *transitive verb* [*Spoof*, a hoaxing game invented by Arthur Roberts (died 1933) English comedian] (1889)
1 : DECEIVE, HOAX
2 : to make good-natured fun of
²spoof *noun* (1889)
1 : HOAX, DECEPTION
2 : a light humorous parody
— **spoof·ery** \ˈspü-f(ə-)rē\ *noun*
— **spoofy** \ˈspü-fē\ *adjective*

¹spook \ˈspük\ *noun* [Dutch; akin to Middle Low German *spōk* ghost] (1801)
1 : GHOST, SPECTER
2 : an undercover agent **:** SPY
— **spook·ish** \ˈspü-kish\ *adjective*
²spook (1883)
transitive verb
1 : HAUNT 3
2 : to make frightened or frantic **:** SCARE; *especially* **:** to startle into violent activity (as stampeding)
intransitive verb
: to become spooked ⟨cattle *spooking* at shadows⟩
spook·ery \ˈspü-k(ə-)rē\ *noun, plural* **-er·ies** (1893)
: the quality of being spooky; *also* **:** something (as a story) that involves spooks
spooky \ˈspü-kē\ *adjective* **spook·i·er; -est** (1854)
1 : relating to, resembling, or suggesting spooks
2 : NERVOUS, SKITTISH ⟨a *spooky* horse⟩
— **spook·i·ly** \-kə-lē\ *adverb*
— **spook·i·ness** \-kē-nəs\ *noun*

¹spool \ˈspül\ *noun* [Middle English *spole*, from Middle French or Middle Dutch; Middle French *espole*, from Middle Dutch *spoele*; akin to Old High German *spuola* spool] (14th century)
1 : a cylindrical device which has a rim or ridge at each end and an axial hole for a pin or spindle and on which material (as thread, wire, or tape) is wound
2 : material or the amount of material wound on a spool
²spool (1603)
transitive verb
1 : to wind on a spool
2 : WIND ⟨*spool* the thread off the bobbin⟩
intransitive verb
1 : to wind itself on a spool
2 : WIND

¹spoon \ˈspün\ *noun* [Middle English, from Old English *spōn* splinter, chip; akin to Old High German *spān* splinter, chip] (14th century)

1 : an eating or cooking implement consisting of a small shallow bowl with a relatively long handle
2 : something (as a tool or fishing lure) that resembles a spoon in shape
²spoon (1715)
transitive verb
: to take up and usually transfer in a spoon
intransitive verb
[perhaps from the Welsh custom of an engaged man's presenting his fiancée with an elaborately carved wooden spoon] **:** to make love by caressing, kissing, and talking amorously **:** NECK

spoon·bill \ˈspün-ˌbil\ *noun* (circa 1678)
1 : any of several wading birds (family Threskiornithidae) related to the ibises that have an expanded bill that is flattened and rounded at the tip
2 : any of several broad-billed ducks (as the shoveler)

spoonbill cat *noun* (circa 1882)
: a paddlefish (*Polyodon spathula*)

spoon–billed \ˈspün-ˌbild\ *adjective* (1668)
: having the bill or snout expanded and spatulate at the end

spoon bread *noun* (1916)
: soft bread made of cornmeal mixed with milk, eggs, and shortening and served with a spoon

spoo·ner·ism \ˈspü-nə-ˌri-zəm\ *noun* [William A. *Spooner* (died 1930) English clergyman & educator] (1900)
: a transposition of usually initial sounds of two or more words (as in *tons of soil* for *sons of toil*) ◆

spoon–feed \ˈspün-ˌfēd\ *transitive verb* **-fed** \-ˌfed\; **-feed·ing** (1615)
1 : to feed by means of a spoon
2 a : to present (information) so completely as to preclude independent thought ⟨*spoon-feed* material to students⟩ **b :** to present information to in this manner

spoon·ful \ˈspün-ˌful\ *noun, plural* **spoon·fuls** \-ˌfülz\ *also* **spoons·ful** \ˈspünz-ˌful\ (14th century)
: as much as a spoon will hold; *specifically* **:** TEASPOONFUL
usage see ²-FUL

spoony *or* **spoon·ey** \ˈspü-nē\ *adjective* **spoon·i·er; -est** [English slang *spoon* simpleton] (circa 1812)
1 : SILLY, FOOLISH; *especially* **:** unduly sentimental
2 : being sentimentally in love

¹spoor \ˈspur, ˈspōr, ˈspȯr\ *noun, plural* **spoor** *or* **spoors** [Afrikaans, from Dutch; akin to Old English *spor* footprint, spoor, *spurnan* to kick — more at SPURN] (1823)
1 : a track, a trail, a scent, or droppings especially of a wild animal
2 : a trace by which the progress of someone or something may be followed
²spoor (1850)
transitive verb
: to track by a spoor
intransitive verb
: to track something by its spoor

spor- *or* **spori-** *or* **sporo-** *combining form* [New Latin *spora*]
: seed **:** spore ⟨*sporo*cyst⟩ ⟨*spor*angium⟩ ⟨*spori*cidal⟩

spo·rad·ic \spə-ˈra-dik\ *adjective* [Medieval Latin *sporadicus*, from Greek *sporadikos*, from *sporadēn* here and there, from *sporad-*, *sporas* scattered; akin to Greek *speirein* to sow — more at SPERM] (circa 1689)
: occurring occasionally, singly, or in scattered instances
synonym see INFREQUENT
— **spo·rad·i·cal·ly** \-di-k(ə-)lē\ *adverb*

sporadic E layer *noun* (1949)
: a layer of ionization occurring irregularly within the E region of the ionosphere

spo·ran·gio·phore \spə-ˈran-jē-ə-ˌfōr, -ˌfȯr\ *noun* (1875)

: a stalk or similar structure bearing sporangia
spo·ran·gi·um \spə-ˈran-jē-əm\ *noun, plural* **-gia** \-jē-ə\ [New Latin, from *spor-* + Greek *angeion* vessel — more at ANGI-] (1821)
: a structure within which spores are produced
— **spo·ran·gial** \-jē-əl\ *adjective*

¹spore \ˈspōr, ˈspȯr\ *noun* [New Latin *spora* seed, spore, from Greek, act of sowing, seed, from *speirein* to sow — more at SPERM] (1836)
: a primitive usually unicellular often environmentally resistant dormant or reproductive body produced by plants and some microorganisms and capable of development into a new individual either directly or after fusion with another spore
— **spored** \ˈspōrd, ˈspȯrd\ *adjective*
²spore *intransitive verb* **spored; spor·ing** (1903)
: to produce or reproduce by spores

spore case *noun* (1836)
: a case containing spores **:** SPORANGIUM

spo·ri·cid·al \ˌspōr-ə-ˈsī-dᵊl, ˌspȯr-\ *adjective* (1939)
: tending to kill spores
— **spo·ri·cide** \ˈspōr-ə-ˌsīd, ˈspȯr-\ *noun*

spo·ro·carp \ˈspōr-ə-ˌkärp, ˈspȯr-\ *noun* [International Scientific Vocabulary] (1849)
: a structure (as in red algae, fungi, or mosses) in or on which spores are produced

spo·ro·cyst \-ˌsist\ *noun* [International Scientific Vocabulary] (1861)
1 : a case or cyst secreted by some sporozoans preliminary to sporogony; *also* **:** a sporozoan encysted in such a case

\ə\ abut \ᵊ\ kitten \ər\ further \a\ ash \ā\ ace
\ä\ mop, mar \au̇\ out \ch\ chin \e\ bet \ē\ easy
\g\ go \i\ hit \ī\ ice \j\ job \ŋ\ sing \ō\ go
\ȯ\ law \ȯi\ boy \th\ thin \t͟h\ the \ü\ loot \u̇\ foot
\y\ yet \zh\ vision *see also* Guide to Pronunciation

2 : a saccular body that is the first asexual reproductive form of a digenetic trematode, develops from a miracidium, and buds off cells from its inner surface which develop into rediae

spo·ro·gen·e·sis \ˌspōr-ə-'je-nə-səs, ˌspȯr-\ *noun* [New Latin] (circa 1890)
1 : reproduction by spores
2 : spore formation
— **spo·rog·e·nous** \spə-'rä-jə-nəs, spȯ-\ *also* **spo·ro·gen·ic** \ˌspōr-ə-'je-nik, ˌspȯr-\ *adjective*

spo·ro·go·ni·um \ˌspōr-ə-'gō-nē-əm, ˌspȯr-\ *noun, plural* **-nia** \-nē-ə\ [New Latin, from *spor-* + *-gonium* (as in *archegonium*)] (1875)
: the sporophyte of a moss or liverwort consisting typically of a stalk bearing a spore-producing capsule which remains permanently attached to the gametophyte

spo·rog·o·ny \spə-'rä-gə-nē, spȯ-\ *noun* [International Scientific Vocabulary] (1888)
: reproduction by spores; *specifically* : formation of spores typically containing sporozoites that is characteristic of some sporozoans and that results from the encystment and subsequent division of a zygote
— **spo·ro·gon·ic** \ˌspōr-ə-'gä-nik, ˌspȯr-\ *adjective*

spo·ro·phore \'spōr-ə-ˌfōr, 'spȯr-ə-ˌfȯr\ *noun* [International Scientific Vocabulary] (1849)
: the spore-producing organ of a fungus or slime mold

spo·ro·phyll \-ˌfil\ *noun* [International Scientific Vocabulary] (1888)
: a spore-bearing and usually greatly modified leaf

spo·ro·phyte \-ˌfīt\ *noun* [International Scientific Vocabulary] (1886)
: the individual or generation of a plant exhibiting alternation of generations that bears asexual spores — compare GAMETOPHYTE
— **spo·ro·phyt·ic** \ˌspōr-ə-'fi-tik, ˌspȯr-\ *adjective*

spo·ro·pol·len·in \ˌspōr-ə-'pä-lə-nən, ˌspȯr-\ *noun* [International Scientific Vocabulary *spor-* + *pollen* + *¹-in*] (1931)
: a relatively chemically inert polymer that makes up the outer layer of pollen grains and some spores

spo·ro·tri·cho·sis \spə-ˌrä-tri-'kō-səs; ˌspōr-ə-tri-, ˌspȯr-\ *noun* [New Latin, from *Sporotrich-*, *Sporothrix*, genus name, from *spor-* + Greek *trich-*, *thrix* hair] (1908)
: infection with or disease caused by a fungus (*Sporothrix schenckii*) that is characterized by nodules and abscesses in the superficial lymph nodes, skin, and subcutaneous tissues and that is usually transmitted by entry of the fungus through a skin abrasion or wound

-sporous *adjective combining form* [New Latin *spora* spore]
: having (such or so many) spores ⟨homo*sporous*⟩

spo·ro·zo·an \ˌspōr-ə-'zō-ən, ˌspȯr-\ *noun* [New Latin *Sporozoa*, from *spor-* + *-zoa*] (1888)
: any of a large class (Sporozoa) of strictly parasitic protozoans that have a complicated life cycle usually involving both asexual and sexual generations often in different hosts and include important pathogens (as malaria parasites and babesias)
— **sporozoan** *adjective*

spo·ro·zo·ite \-'zō-ˌīt\ *noun* [New Latin *Sporozoa* + International Scientific Vocabulary *-ite*] (1888)
: a usually motile infective form of some sporozoans that is a product of sporogony and initiates an asexual cycle in the new host

spor·ran \'spȯr-ən, 'spär-\ *noun* [Scottish Gaelic *sporan* purse] (1752)
: a pouch usually of skin with the hair or fur on that is worn in front of the kilt with Scots Highland dress

¹sport \'spōrt, 'spȯrt\ *verb* [Middle English, to divert, disport, short for *disporten*] (15th century)
intransitive verb
1 a : to amuse oneself : FROLIC ⟨lambs *sporting* in the meadow⟩ **b** : to engage in a sport
2 a : to mock or ridicule something **b** : to speak or act in jest : TRIFLE
3 [²*sport*] : to deviate or vary abruptly from type (as by bud variation) : MUTATE
transitive verb
1 : to display or wear usually ostentatiously : BOAST
2 [²*sport*] : to put forth as a sport or bud variation

²sport *noun* (15th century)
1 a : a source of diversion : RECREATION **b** : sexual play **c** (1) : physical activity engaged in for pleasure (2) : a particular activity (as an athletic game) so engaged in
2 a : PLEASANTRY, JEST **b** : often mean-spirited jesting : MOCKERY, DERISION
3 a : something tossed or driven about in or as if in play **b** : LAUGHINGSTOCK
4 a : SPORTSMAN **b** : a person considered with respect to living up to the ideals of sportsmanship ⟨a good *sport*⟩ ⟨a poor *sport*⟩ **c** : a companionable person
5 : an individual exhibiting a sudden deviation from type beyond the normal limits of individual variation usually as a result of mutation especially of somatic tissue
synonym see FUN

³sport *or* **sports** *adjective* (1582)
: of, relating to, or suitable for sports; *especially* : styled in a manner suitable for casual or informal wear ⟨*sport* coats⟩

sport fish *noun* (1944)
: a fish important for the sport it affords anglers

sport·fish·er·man \'spōrt-ˌfi-shər-mən, 'spȯrt-\ *noun* (1954)
: a motorboat equipped for sportfishing

sport·fish·ing \-ˌfi-shiŋ\ *noun* (1910)
: fishing done with a rod and reel for sport or recreation

sport·ful \-fəl\ *adjective* (15th century)
1 a : productive of sport or amusement : ENTERTAINING, DIVERTING **b** : PLAYFUL, FROLICSOME
2 : done in sport
— **sport·ful·ly** \-fə-lē\ *adverb*
— **sport·ful·ness** *noun*

spor·tif \'spōr-tif, 'spȯr-\ *adjective* [French, sporting, of sports, from *sport* sport, from English] (1920)
: SPORTY

sport·ing \'spōr-tiŋ, 'spȯr-\ *adjective* (1799)
1 a : of, relating to, used, or suitable for sport **b** : marked by or calling for sportsmanship **c** : involving such risk as a sports contender may expect to take or encounter ⟨a *sporting* chance⟩
2 : of or relating to dissipation and especially gambling
3 : tending to mutate freely
— **sport·ing·ly** \-tiŋ-lē\ *adverb*

sporting house *noun* (1894)
: BORDELLO

sport·ive \'spōr-tiv, 'spȯr-\ *adjective* (1590)
1 a : FROLICSOME, PLAYFUL **b** : ARDENT, WANTON
2 : of or relating to sports and especially field sports
— **sport·ive·ly** *adverb*
— **sport·ive·ness** *noun*

sports car *noun* (1928)
: a low small usually 2-passenger automobile designed for quick response, easy maneuverability, and high-speed driving

1 sporran

sports·cast \'spōrts-ˌkast, 'spȯrts-\ *noun* [*sport* + broad*cast*] (1941)
: a radio or television broadcast of a sports event or of information about sports
— **sports·cast·er** \-ˌkas-tər\ *noun*

sports·man \'spōrts-mən, 'spȯrts-\ *noun* (circa 1707)
1 : a person who engages in sports (as in hunting or fishing)
2 : a person who shows sportsmanship
— **sports·man·like** \-ˌlīk\ *adjective*
— **sports·man·ly** \-lē\ *adjective*

sports·man·ship \-ˌship\ *noun* (1745)
: conduct (as fairness, respect for one's opponent, and graciousness in winning or losing) becoming to one participating in a sport

sports·wear \'spōrts-ˌwar, 'spȯrts-, -ˌwer\ *noun* (1912)
: clothing suitable for recreation; *broadly* : clothing designed for casual or informal wear

sports·wom·an \-ˌwu̇-mən\ *noun* (1754)
: a woman who engages in sports

sports·writ·er \'spōrts-ˌrī-tər, 'spȯrts-\ *noun* (1927)
: one who writes about sports especially for a newspaper
— **sports·writ·ing** \-tiŋ\ *noun*

sporty \'spōr-tē, 'spȯr-\ *adjective* **sport·i·er; -est** (1889)
1 : of, relating to, or typical of sports, sportsmen, sportswomen, or sportswear ⟨a *sporty* life⟩ ⟨clothes of a *sporty* cut⟩
2 *of an automobile* : resembling a sports car in styling or performance
— **sport·i·ly** \'spōr-tᵊl-ē, 'spȯr-\ *adverb*
— **sport·i·ness** \'spōr-tē-nəs, 'spȯr-\ *noun*

spor·u·late \'spōr-yə-ˌlāt, 'spȯr-, -ə-ˌlāt\ *intransitive verb* **-lat·ed; -lat·ing** [back-formation from *sporulation*] (circa 1891)
: to undergo sporulation

spor·u·la·tion \ˌspōr-yə-'lā-shən, ˌspȯr-, -ə-'lā-\ *noun* [International Scientific Vocabulary, from New Latin *sporula*, diminutive of *spora* spore] (1876)
: the formation of spores; *especially* : division into many small spores (as after encystment)
— **spor·u·la·tive** \'spōr-yə-ˌlā-tiv, 'spȯr-, -ə-, -ˌlā-\ *adjective*

-spory *noun combining form* [*-spor*ous + ²*-y*]
: quality or state of having (such) spores ⟨homo*spory*⟩

¹spot \'spät\ *noun* [Middle English; akin to Middle Dutch *spotte* stain, speck, Old Norse *spotti* small piece] (13th century)
1 : a taint on character or reputation : FAULT ⟨the only *spot* on the family name⟩
2 a : a small area visibly different (as in color, finish, or material) from the surrounding area **b** (1) : an area marred or marked (as by dirt) (2) : a circumscribed surface lesion of disease (as measles) or decay ⟨*spots* of rot⟩ ⟨rust *spots* on a leaf⟩ **c** : a conventionalized design used on playing cards to distinguish the suits and indicate values
3 : an object having a specified number of spots or a specified numeral on its surface
4 : a small quantity or amount : BIT
5 a : a particular place, area, or part **b** : a small extent of space
6 *plural usually* **spot** : a small croaker (*Leiostomus xanthurus*) of the Atlantic coast with a black spot behind the opercula
7 a : a particular position (as in an organization or a hierarchy) **b** : a place or appearance on an entertainment program
8 : SPOTLIGHT
9 : a position usually of difficulty or embarrassment
10 : a brief announcement or advertisement broadcast between scheduled radio or television programs
11 : a brief segment or report on a broadcast especially of news

— on the spot 1 : at once : IMMEDIATELY **2 :** at the place of action **3 a :** in a responsible or accountable position **b :** in a difficult or trying situation

²**spot** *verb* **spot·ted; spot·ting** (14th century)
transitive verb
1 : to stain the character or reputation of : DISGRACE
2 : to mark in or with a spot : STAIN
3 : to locate or identify by a spot
4 a : to single out : IDENTIFY; *especially* : to note as a known criminal or a suspicious person **b :** DETECT, NOTICE ⟨*spot* a mistake⟩ **c** (1) : to locate accurately ⟨*spot* an enemy position⟩ (2) : to cause to strike accurately ⟨*spot* the battery's fire⟩
5 a : to lie at intervals in or over : STUD **b :** to place at intervals or in a desired spot ⟨*spot* field telephones⟩ **c :** to fix in or as if in the beam of a spotlight **d :** to schedule in a particular spot or at a particular time
6 : to remove a spot from
7 : to allow as a handicap
intransitive verb
1 : to become stained or discolored in spots
2 : to cause a spot
3 : to act as a spotter; *especially* : to locate targets
4 : to experience abnormal and sporadic bleeding in small amounts from the uterus
— spot·ta·ble \'spä-tə-bəl\ *adjective*

³**spot** *adjective* (1881)
1 a : being, originating, or done on the spot or in or for a particular spot ⟨*spot* coverage of the news⟩ **b :** available for immediate delivery after sale ⟨*spot* commodities⟩ **c** (1) : paid out upon delivery ⟨*spot* cash⟩ (2) : involving immediate cash payment ⟨*spot* transaction⟩ **d** (1) : broadcast between scheduled programs ⟨*spot* announcements⟩ (2) : originating in a local station for a national advertiser **e :** performing occasionally when needed ⟨chance of making the . . . varsity as a *spot* starter and relief pitcher⟩ —*N. Y. Times*⟩
2 : made at random or restricted to a few places or instances ⟨a *spot* check⟩; *also* : selected at random or as a sample

spot–check \'spät-,chek\ (1943)
transitive verb
: to sample or investigate quickly or at random
intransitive verb
: to make a spot check

spot·less \'spät-ləs\ *adjective* (14th century)
: having no spot: **a :** free from impurity : IMMACULATE ⟨*spotless* kitchens⟩ **b :** PURE, UNBLEMISHED ⟨*spotless* reputation⟩
— spot·less·ly *adverb*
— spot·less·ness *noun*

¹**spot·light** \'spät-,līt\ *noun* (1904)
1 a : a projected spot of light used to illuminate brilliantly a person, object, or group on a stage **b :** conspicuous public notice ⟨held the political *spotlight*⟩
2 a : a light designed to direct a narrow intense beam of light on a small area **b :** something that illuminates brilliantly

²**spotlight** *transitive verb* **-light·ed** *or* **-lit; -light·ing** (1922)
: to illuminate with or as if with a spotlight

spot pass *noun* (1948)
: a pass (as in football or basketball) made to a predetermined spot on the field or court rather than directly to a player

spot·ted \'spä-təd\ *adjective* (13th century)
1 : marked with spots
2 : being sullied : TARNISHED
3 : characterized by the appearance of spots

spotted alfalfa aphid *noun* (1958)
: a highly destructive Old World aphid (*Therioaphis maculata*) that is established in the U.S. in warmer areas and causes yellowing and stunting of affected plants

spotted cucumber beetle *noun* (1923)
: a rather slender greenish yellow beetle (*Diabrotica undecimpunctata howardi*) that feeds

as an adult on various ornamental and crop plants and is a vector of wilt disease especially of cucumbers and melons

spotted fever *noun* (1650)
: any of various eruptive fevers: as **a :** TYPHUS **b :** ROCKY MOUNTAIN SPOTTED FEVER

spotted owl *noun* (1910)
: a rare large dark brown dark-eyed owl (*Strix occidentalis*) that has barred and spotted underparts and is found in humid old growth forests and thickly wooded canyons from British Columbia to southern California and central Mexico

spotted salamander *noun* (1922)
: a common salamander (*Ambystoma maculatum*) of eastern North America with glossy black skin spotted with yellow or orange on the back

spotted sea trout *noun* (1902)
: a weakfish (*Cynoscion nebulosus*) that is a valuable food and sport fish of the southern Atlantic and Gulf coasts of the U.S. — called also *sea trout, speckled trout, spotted weakfish*

spotted turtle *noun* (circa 1909)
: a freshwater turtle (*Clemmys guttata*) of the eastern U.S. that has a blackish carapace with round yellow spots

spot·ter \'spä-tər\ *noun* (1611)
1 : one that makes or applies a spot (as for identification)
2 : one that looks or keeps watch: as **a :** one that locates enemy targets **b :** a civilian who watches for approaching airplanes
3 : one that removes spots
4 : one that places something on or in a desired spot

spot test *noun* (1922)
1 : a test limited to a few key or sample points or a relatively small percentage of random spots
2 : a test conducted on the spot to yield immediate results

spot·ty \'spä-tē\ *adjective* **spot·ti·er; -est** (14th century)
1 : marked with spots : SPOTTED
2 : lacking uniformity especially in quality ⟨the performance was *spotty*⟩; *also* : irregularly or sparsely distributed ⟨*spotty* attendance⟩ ⟨*spotty* data⟩
— spot·ti·ly \'spä-t°l-ē\ *adverb*
— spot·ti·ness \'spä-tē-nəs\ *noun*

spou·sal \'spaů-zəl, -səl\ *noun* [Middle English *spousaille*, from Middle French *espousailles* espousal] (14th century)
: NUPTIALS — usually used in plural

¹**spouse** \'spaůs *also* 'spaůz\ *noun* [Middle English, from Old French *espous* (masculine) & *espouse* (feminine), from Latin *sponsus* betrothed man, groom & *sponsa* betrothed woman, bride, both from *sponsus*, past participle of *spondēre* to promise, betroth; akin to Greek *spendein* to pour a libation, Hittite *šipant-*] (13th century)
: married person : HUSBAND, WIFE
— spou·sal \'spaů-zəl, -səl\ *adjective*

²**spouse** \'spaůs, 'spaůz\ *transitive verb* **spoused; spous·ing** (13th century)
archaic : WED

¹**spout** \'spaůt\ *verb* [Middle English; akin to Middle Dutch *spoiten* to spout, Old English *spīwan* to spew] (14th century)
transitive verb
1 : to eject (as liquid) in a stream ⟨wells *spouting* oil⟩
2 a : to speak or utter readily, volubly, and at length **b :** to speak or utter in a pompous or oratorical manner : DECLAIM
intransitive verb
1 : to issue with force or in a jet : SPURT
2 : to eject material (as liquid) in a jet
3 : DECLAIM
— spout·er *noun*

²**spout** *noun* (14th century)

1 : a pipe or conductor through which a liquid is discharged or conveyed in a stream: as **a :** a pipe for carrying rainwater from a roof **b :** a projecting tube or lip from which a liquid (as water) issues
2 : a discharge or jet of liquid from or as if from a pipe; *especially* : WATERSPOUT
3 *archaic* : PAWNSHOP
— spout·ed \'spaů-təd\ *adjective*

sprach·ge·fühl \'shpräk-gə-,fŭ̄l\ *noun* [German, from *Sprache* language + *Gefühl* feeling] (1894)
1 : the character of a language
2 : an intuitive sense of what is linguistically appropriate

sprad·dle \'spra-d°l\ *verb* **sprad·dled; sprad·dling** \'sprad-liŋ, 'spra-d°l-iŋ\ [perhaps blend of *straddle* and *sprawl*] (1632)
intransitive verb
1 : SPRAWL
2 : to go or walk with a straddling gait : STRADDLE
transitive verb
1 : SPRAWL
2 : to spread (the legs) in walking : STRADDLE

sprag \'sprag\ *noun* [origin unknown] (1878)
: a pointed stake or steel bar let down from a halted vehicle (as a wagon) to prevent it from rolling

¹**sprain** \'sprān\ *noun* [origin unknown] (1601)
1 : a sudden or violent twist or wrench of a joint with stretching or tearing of ligaments
2 : a sprained condition

²**sprain** *transitive verb* (1622)
: to injure by a sudden or severe twist

¹**sprang** \'spraŋ\ *past of* SPRING

²**sprang** *noun* [probably from Norwegian, a kind of embroidery] (1951)
: a weaving technique in which threads or cords are intertwined and twisted over another to form an openwork mesh

sprat \'sprat\ *noun* [alteration of Middle English *sprot*, from Old English *sprott*] (1537)
1 a : a small European herring (*Sprattus sprattus*) related to the common herring — called also *brisling* **b :** a small or young herring or similar fish (as an anchovy)
2 : a young, small, or insignificant person

sprawl \'sprȯl\ *verb* [Middle English, from Old English *sprēawlian*] (before 12th century)
intransitive verb
1 a *archaic* : to lie thrashing or tossing about **b :** to creep or clamber awkwardly
2 : to lie or sit with arms and legs spread out
3 : to spread or develop irregularly
transitive verb
: to cause to spread out carelessly or awkwardly
— sprawl *noun*

¹**spray** \'sprā\ *noun* [Middle English] (13th century)
1 : a usually flowering branch or shoot
2 : a decorative flat arrangement of flowers and foliage (as on a coffin)
3 : something (as a jeweled pin) resembling a spray

²**spray** *noun* [obsolete English *spray* to sprinkle, from Middle Dutch *sprayen*] (1621)
1 : water flying in small drops or particles blown from waves or thrown up by a waterfall
2 a : a jet of vapor or finely divided liquid **b :** a device (as an atomizer or sprayer) by which a spray is dispersed or applied **c** (1) : an application of a spray or by spraying (2) : a substance (as paint) so applied

³**spray** (1829)
transitive verb
1 : to disperse or apply as a spray
2 : to project spray on or into
intransitive verb

1 : to break up into spray
2 : to disperse or apply a spray
3 : to emit a stream or spray of urine ⟨a cat may *spray* to mark its territory⟩
— **spray·er** *noun*

spray can *noun* (1958)
: a pressurized container from which aerosols are dispensed

spray gun *noun* (1920)
: an apparatus resembling a gun for applying a substance (as paint or insecticide) in the form of a spray

¹**spread** \'spred\ *verb* **spread; spread·ing** [Middle English *spreden*, from Old English *-sprædan*; akin to Old High German *spreiten* to spread] (13th century)
transitive verb
1 a : to open or expand over a larger area ⟨*spread* out the map⟩ **b :** to stretch out **:** EXTEND ⟨*spread* its wings for flight⟩
2 a : to distribute over an area ⟨*spread* fertilizer⟩ **b :** to distribute over a period or among a group ⟨*spread* the work over a few weeks⟩ **c :** to apply on a surface ⟨*spread* butter on bread⟩ **d** (1) **:** to cover or overlay something with ⟨*spread* the cloth on the table⟩ (2) *archaic* **:** to cover completely **e** (1) **:** to prepare or furnish for dining **:** SET ⟨*spread* the table⟩ (2) **:** SERVE ⟨*spread* the afternoon tea⟩
3 a : to make widely known ⟨*spread* the news⟩ **b :** to extend the range or incidence of ⟨*spread* a disease⟩ **c :** DIFFUSE, EMIT ⟨flowers *spreading* their fragrance⟩
4 : to push apart by weight or force
intransitive verb
1 a : to become dispersed, distributed, or scattered **b :** to become known or disseminated ⟨panic *spread* rapidly⟩
2 : to grow in length or breadth **:** EXPAND
3 : to move apart (as from pressure or weight) **:** SEPARATE
— **spread·abil·i·ty** \,spre-də-'bi-lə-tē\ *noun*
— **spread·able** \'spre-də-bəl\ *adjective*

²**spread** *noun* (1626)
1 a : the act or process of spreading **b :** extent of spreading
2 : something spread out: as **a :** a surface area **:** EXPANSE **b** *West* (1) **:** RANCH (2) **:** a herd of animals **c** (1) **:** a prominent display in a periodical (2) **:** two facing pages (as of a newspaper) usually with matter running across the fold; *also* **:** the matter occupying these pages
3 : something spread on or over a surface: as **a :** a food to be spread (as on bread or crackers) ⟨a cheese *spread*⟩ **b :** a sumptuous meal **:** FEAST **c :** a cloth cover for a table or bed
4 : distance between two points **:** GAP
5 : a commodities market transaction in which a participant hedges with simultaneous long and short options in different commodities or different delivery dates in the same commodity

¹**spread–ea·gle** \'spred-,ē-gəl\ *verb* **-ea·gled; -ea·gling** \-,ē-g(ə-)liŋ\ (1826)
intransitive verb
1 : to execute a spread eagle (as in skating)
2 : to stand or move with arms and legs stretched out **:** SPRAWL
transitive verb
1 : to stretch out into the position of a spread eagle
2 : to spread over

²**spread–eagle** *adjective* [from the spread eagle on the Great Seal of the U.S.] (1858)
: marked by bombast and boastful exaggeration especially of the greatness of the U.S. ⟨*spread-eagle* oratory⟩

spread eagle *noun* (1570)
1 : a representation of an eagle with wings raised and legs extended
2 : something resembling or suggestive of a spread eagle; *specifically* **:** a skating figure executed with the skates heel to heel in a straight line

spread·er \'spre-dər\ *noun* (15th century)

: one that spreads: as **a :** an implement for scattering material **b :** a small knife for spreading butter **c :** a device (as a bar) holding two linear elements (as lines, guys, rails) apart and usually taut

spread formation *noun* (circa 1949)
: an offensive football formation in which the pass receivers are spread out across the field

spreading factor *noun* (1932)
: HYALURONIDASE

spread·sheet \'spred-,shēt\ *noun* (1982)
: an accounting program for a computer; *also* **:** the ledger layout modeled by such a program

spree \'sprē\ *noun* [origin unknown] (1804)
: an unrestrained indulgence in or outburst of an activity ⟨went on a buying *spree*⟩; *especially* **:** BINGE, CAROUSAL

sprent \'sprent\ *adjective* [Middle English *spreynt*, from past participle of *sprengen* to sprinkle] (14th century)
archaic **:** sprinkled over

sprier *comparative of* SPRY
spriest *superlative of* SPRY

¹**sprig** \'sprig\ *noun* [Middle English *sprigge*] (14th century)
1 a : a small shoot **:** TWIG ⟨a *sprig* of parsley⟩ **b :** a small division of grass used for propagation
2 a : HEIR **b :** YOUTH **c :** a small specimen
3 : an ornament resembling a sprig, stemmed flower, or leaf
4 : a small headless nail **:** BRAD

²**sprig** *transitive verb* **sprigged; sprig·ging** (1713)
1 : to drive sprigs or brads into
2 : to mark or adorn with the representation of plant sprigs
3 : to propagate (a grass) by means of stolons or small divisions

spright·ful \'sprīt-fəl\ *adjective* [obsolete *spright*] (1595)
archaic **:** full of life or spirit **:** SPRIGHTLY
— **spright·ful·ly** \-fə-lē\ *adverb*
— **spright·ful·ness** *noun*

spright·ly \-lē\ *adjective* **spright·li·er; -est** [obsolete *spright* (sprite), alteration of *sprite*] (1596)
: marked by a gay lightness and vivacity **:** SPIRITED
synonym see LIVELY
— **spright·li·ness** *noun*
— **sprightly** *adverb*

¹**spring** \'spriŋ\ *verb* **sprang** \'spraŋ\ *or* **sprung** \'sprəŋ\; **sprung; spring·ing** \'spriŋ-iŋ\ [Middle English, from Old English *springan*; akin to Old High German *springan* to jump and perhaps to Greek *sperchesthai* to hasten] (before 12th century)
intransitive verb
1 a (1) **:** DART, SHOOT (2) **:** to be resilient or elastic; *also* **:** to move by elastic force ⟨the lid *sprang* shut⟩ **b :** to become warped
2 : to issue with speed and force or as a stream
3 a : to grow as a plant **b :** to issue by birth or descent **c :** to come into being **:** ARISE ⟨towns *sprang* up across the plains⟩ **d** *archaic* **:** DAWN **e :** to begin to blow — used with *up* ⟨a breeze quickly *sprang* up⟩
4 a : to make a leap or series of leaps **b :** to leap or jump up suddenly
5 : to stretch out in height **:** RISE
6 : PAY — used with *for* ⟨I'll *spring* for the drinks⟩
transitive verb
1 : to cause to spring
2 a : to undergo or bring about the splitting or cracking of ⟨wind *sprang* the mast⟩ **b :** to undergo the opening of (a leak)
3 a : to cause to operate suddenly ⟨*spring* a trap⟩ **b :** to apply or insert by bending **c :** to bend by force
4 : to leap over
5 : to produce or disclose suddenly or unexpectedly
6 : to make lame

7 : to release or cause to be released from confinement or custody ☆

²**spring** *noun, often attributive* (before 12th century)
1 a : a source of supply; *especially* **:** a source of water issuing from the ground **b :** an ultimate source especially of action or motion
2 : SPRING TIDE
3 : a time or season of growth or development; *specifically* **:** the season between winter and summer comprising in the northern hemisphere usually the months of March, April, and May or as reckoned astronomically extending from the March equinox to the June solstice
4 : an elastic body or device that recovers its original shape when released after being distorted
5 a : the act or an instance of leaping up or forward **:** BOUND **b** (1) **:** capacity for springing **:** RESILIENCE (2) **:** ENERGY, BOUNCE
6 : the point or plane at which an arch or vault curve springs from its impost
— **spring·like** \-,līk\ *adjective*

³**spring** *transitive verb* **sprung** \'sprəŋ\; **spring·ing** \'spriŋ-iŋ\ (1884)
: to fit with springs

spring·ald \'spriŋ-əld\ *or* **spring·al** \-əl\ *noun* [probably from Middle English, a kind of catapult, from Middle French *espringale*] (1501)
: a young man **:** STRIPLING

spring beauty *noun* (1821)
: any of a genus (*Claytonia*) of herbs of the purslane family; *especially* **:** one (*C. virginica*) that sends up in early spring a 2-leaved stem bearing delicate pink flowers

spring·board \'spriŋ-,bōrd, -,bȯrd\ *noun* (1799)
1 : a flexible board usually secured at one end and used for gymnastic stunts or diving
2 : a point of departure **:** JUMPING-OFF PLACE

spring·bok \'spriŋ-,bäk\ *noun, plural* **spring·bok** *or* **springboks** [Afrikaans, from *spring* to jump + *bok* male goat] (1775)
: a swift and graceful southern African gazelle (*Antidorcas marsupialis*) noted for its habit of springing lightly and suddenly into the air

spring bolt *noun* (1634)
: a bolt retracted by pressure and shot by a spring when the pressure is released

spring chicken *noun* (1879)
: a young person ⟨is no *spring chicken*⟩

spring·clean·ing
\'spriŋ-ˈklē-niŋ\ *noun*
[²*spring*] (1857)
: the act or process of doing a thorough cleaning of a place

springe \'sprinj\ *noun* [Middle English *sprenge, springe;* akin to Old English *springan* to spring] (13th century)
1 : a noose fastened to an elastic body to catch small game
2 : SNARE, TRAP

springbok

spring·er \'spriŋ-ər\ *noun* (1611)
1 : a stone or other solid laid at the impost of an arch — see ARCH illustration
2 : one that springs
3 : SPRINGER SPANIEL
4 : a cow nearly ready to calve

springer spaniel *noun* (1885)
: a medium-sized sporting dog of either of two breeds that is often used for finding and flushing small game: **a** : ENGLISH SPRINGER SPANIEL **b** : WELSH SPRINGER SPANIEL

spring fever *noun* (1843)
: a lazy or restless feeling often associated with the onset of spring

Spring·field rifle \'spriŋ-ˌfēld-\ *noun* [*Springfield*, Mass.] (1888)
: a .30 caliber bolt-action rifle used by U.S. troops especially in World War I

spring·form pan \'spriŋ-ˌfȯrm-\ *noun* (1927)
: a pan or mold with an upright detachable rim fastened to the bottom of the pan with a clamp or spring

spring·head \'spriŋ-ˌhed\ *noun* (1561)
: FOUNTAINHEAD

spring·house \-ˌhau̇s\ *noun* (1755)
: a small building situated over a spring and used for cool storage (as of dairy products or meat)

spring·ing \'spriŋ-iŋ\ *noun* (1590)
1 : SPRING 5
2 : a point where an arch rises from its support

spring–load \'spriŋ-ˈlōd\ *transitive verb* (1944)
: to load or secure by means of spring tension or compression

spring peeper *noun* (1906)
: a small brown tree frog (*Hyla crucifer*) of the eastern U.S. and Canada that has a shrill piping call and breeds in ponds and streams in the spring

spring peeper

spring roll *noun* (1943)
: EGG ROLL; *also* : any of various similar appetizers in oriental cuisine

spring·tail \'spriŋ-ˌtāl\ *noun* (circa 1797)
: any of an order (Collembola) of small primitive wingless insects usually with a forked structure on the fourth or fifth abdominal segment that is used for jumping — called also *collembolan*

spring·tide \-ˌtīd\ *noun* (1530)
: SPRINGTIME

spring tide *noun* (1548)
: a tide of greater-than-average range around the times of new and full moon

spring·time \'spriŋ-ˌtīm\ *noun* (15th century)
1 : the season of spring
2 : YOUTH 1a
3 : an early or flourishing stage of development

spring wagon *noun* (1794)
: a light farm wagon equipped with springs

spring·wa·ter \'spriŋ-ˌwȯ-tər, -ˌwä-\ *noun* (15th century)
: water from a spring

spring·wood \-ˌwu̇d\ *noun* (1884)
: the softer more porous portion of an annual ring of wood that develops early in the growing season — compare SUMMERWOOD

springy \'spriŋ-ē\ *adjective* **spring·i·er; -est** (1641)
1 : having an elastic quality : RESILIENT
2 : having or showing a lively and energetic movement (walks with a *springy* step)
synonym see ELASTIC
— **spring·i·ly** \'spriŋ-ə-lē\ *adverb*
— **spring·i·ness** \'spriŋ-ē-nəs\ *noun*

¹sprin·kle \'spriŋ-kəl\ *verb* **sprin·kled; sprin·kling** \-k(ə-)liŋ\ [Middle English *sprenklen, sprinclen;* akin to Middle High German *spreckel, sprenkel* spot] (14th century)
transitive verb
1 : to scatter in drops or particles
2 a : to scatter over **b** : to scatter at intervals in or among : DOT (*sprinkled* the speech with quips) **c** : to wet lightly
intransitive verb
1 : to scatter a liquid in fine drops
2 : to rain lightly in scattered drops
— **sprin·kler** \-k(ə-)lər\ *noun*

²sprinkle *noun* (1641)
1 : the act or an instance of sprinkling; *especially* : a light rain
2 : SPRINKLING
3 *plural* : small particles of candy used as a topping (as on ice cream) : JIMMIES

sprin·klered \'spriŋ-klərd\ *adjective* (1927)
: having a sprinkler system

sprinkler system *noun* (circa 1909)
: a system for protecting a building against fire by means of overhead pipes which convey an extinguishing fluid (as water) to heat-activated outlets

sprin·kling \'spriŋ-kliŋ\ *noun* (1594)
1 : a limited quantity or amount : MODICUM
2 : a small quantity falling in scattered drops or particles
3 : a small number distributed at random : SCATTERING

¹sprint \'sprint\ *intransitive verb* [of Scandinavian origin; akin to Swedish dialect *sprinta* to jump, hop; akin to Old High German *sprinzan* to jump up] (circa 1864)
: to run or go at top speed especially for a short distance
— **sprint·er** *noun*

²sprint *noun* (circa 1865)
1 : the act or an instance of sprinting
2 a : DASH 6b **b** : a burst of speed

sprint car *noun* (circa 1965)
: a rugged racing automobile that is midway in size between midget racers and ordinary racers, has about the same horsepower as the larger racers, and is usually raced on a dirt track

sprit \'sprit\ *noun* [Middle English *spret, sprit,* from Old English *sprēot* pole, spear; akin to Old English *-sprūtan* to sprout] (14th century)
: a spar that crosses a fore-and-aft sail diagonally

sprite \'sprīt\ *noun* [Middle English *sprit,* from Middle French *esprit,* from Latin *spiritus* spirit — more at SPIRIT] (14th century)
1 a *archaic* : SOUL **b** : a disembodied spirit : GHOST
2 a : ELF, FAIRY **b** : an elfish person

sprit·sail \'sprit-ˌsāl, -səl\ *noun* (15th century)
1 : a sail extended by a sprit
2 : a sail formerly set on a yard beneath the bowsprit

spritz \'sprits, 'shprits\ *verb* [German *spritzen* to squirt, spray] (1902)
transitive verb
: SPRAY
intransitive verb
: to disperse or apply a spray
— **spritz** *noun*

spritz·er \'sprit-sər, 'shprit-\ *noun* [German, from *spritzen*] (1945)
: a beverage of usually white wine and soda water

sprock·et \'sprä-kət\ *noun* [origin unknown] (1750)
1 : a toothed wheel whose teeth engage the links of a chain
2 : a cylinder with teeth around the circumference at either end that project through perforations in something (as motion-picture film) to move it through a mechanism (as a projector)

¹sprout \'sprau̇t\ *verb* [Middle English *spruten,* from Old English *-sprūtan;* akin to Old High German *spriozan* to sprout, Lithuanian *sprausti* to squeeze, thrust] (13th century)
intransitive verb
1 : to grow, spring up, or come forth as or as if a sprout
2 : to send out new growth
transitive verb
: to send forth or up : cause to develop : GROW

²sprout *noun* (13th century)
1 a : SHOOT 1a; *especially* : a young shoot (as from a seed or root) **b** *plural* (1) *chiefly British* : BRUSSELS SPROUT 2 (2) : edible sprouts especially from recently germinated seeds (as of alfalfa or mung beans)
2 : something resembling a sprout: as **a** : a young person **b** : SCION

sprouting broccoli *noun* (1852)
: BROCCOLI 2a(2)

¹spruce \'sprüs\ *verb* **spruced; spruc·ing** (1594)
transitive verb
: to make spruce — often used with *up*
intransitive verb
: to make oneself spruce (*spruce* up a bit)

²spruce *adjective* **spruc·er; spruc·est** [perhaps from obsolete English *Spruce leather* leather imported from Prussia] (1599)
: neat or smart in appearance : TRIM
— **spruce·ly** *adverb*
— **spruce·ness** *noun*

³spruce *noun* [obsolete *Spruce* Prussia, from Middle English, alteration of *Pruce,* from Old French] (1670)
1 a : any of a genus (*Picea*) of evergreen trees of the pine family with a conical head of dense foliage and soft light wood **b** : any of several coniferous trees (as Douglas fir) of similar habit
2 : the wood of a spruce ◊

spruce beer *noun* (1500)

◊ WORD HISTORY

spruce Between the 14th and 17th centuries Prussia was called *Pruce* or *Spruce* in English, and hence *Spruce* was used attributively to characterize goods imported from Prussia, as *spruce canvas, spruce iron,* and *spruce leather.* Perhaps the most important of these Prussian products was a tall, straight conifer, called the *spruce tree* or *spruce,* that was especially desirable for use as the mast of a ship. By the middle of the 17th century *Spruce* as a name for the country had largely been supplanted by *Prussia.* By that time, however, *spruce* had become well established as the name for the tree. The particular species (*Picea abies*) that was originally called *spruce* is not limited to Prussia. Another of its native countries gave it its present common name, *Norway spruce,* which is something of an etymological paradox. *Spruce* is now the common name applied to any member of the genus *Picea.*

: a beverage flavored with spruce; *especially*
: one made from spruce twigs and leaves boiled with molasses or sugar and fermented with yeast

spruce budworm *noun* (1884)
: a tortricid moth (*Choristoneura fumiferana*) whose larva feeds on evergreen trees (as spruce and balsam fir) in the northern U.S. and Canada

spruce pine *noun* (1684)
: an American tree (as some pines and spruces or the common eastern hemlock) of the pine family with light, soft, or weak wood

sprucy \'sprü-sē\ *adjective* **spruc·i·er; -est** (1774)
: SPRUCE

¹sprue \'sprü\ *noun* [origin unknown] (1880)
1 : the hole through which metal or plastic is poured into the gate and thence into a mold
2 : the waste piece cast in a sprue

²sprue *noun* [Dutch *spruw*; akin to Middle Low German *sprüwe*, a kind of tumor] (1888)
1 : CELIAC DISEASE
2 : a disease of tropical regions that is of unknown cause and is characterized by fatty diarrhea and malabsorption of nutrients — called also *tropical sprue*

sprung *past and past participle of* SPRING

sprung rhythm *noun* (1877)
: a poetic rhythm designed to approximate the natural rhythm of speech and characterized by the frequent juxtaposition of single accented syllables and the occurrence of mixed types of feet

spry \'sprī\ *adjective* **spri·er** *or* **spry·er** \'sprī(-ə)r\; **spri·est** *or* **spry·est** \'sprī-əst\ [perhaps of Scandinavian origin; akin to Swedish dialect *sprygg* spry] (1746)
: NIMBLE 1 ⟨a *spry* 75-year-old⟩
— **spry·ly** *adverb*
— **spry·ness** *noun*

¹spud \'spəd\ *verb* **spud·ded; spud·ding** (1652)
transitive verb
1 : to dig with a spud
2 : to begin to drill (an oil well)
intransitive verb
: to use a spud

²spud *noun* [Middle English *spudde* dagger] (1667)
1 : a tool or device (as for digging, lifting, or cutting) having the characteristics of a spade and a chisel
2 : POTATO

¹spume \'spyüm\ *noun* [Middle English, from Middle French, from Latin *spuma* — more at FOAM] (14th century)
: frothy matter on liquids : FOAM, SCUM
— **spu·mous** \'spyü-məs\ *adjective*
— **spumy** \-mē\ *adjective*

²spume *intransitive verb* **spumed; spuming** (14th century)
: FROTH, FOAM

spu·mo·ni *or* **spu·mo·ne** \spu̇-'mō-nē\ *noun* [Italian *spumone*, augmentative of *spuma* foam, from Latin] (1924)
: ice cream in layers of different colors, flavors, and textures often with candied fruits and nuts

spun *past and past participle of* SPIN

spun·bond·ed \'spən-ˌbän-dəd\ *adjective* (1961)
: of or relating to a nonwoven polymeric material that resembles cloth or fabric

spun glass *noun* (1779)
1 : blown glass that has slender threads of glass incorporated in it
2 : FIBERGLASS

¹spunk \'spəŋk\ *noun* [Scottish Gaelic *spong* sponge, tinder, from Latin *spongia* sponge] (1582)
1 a : a woody tinder : PUNK **b** : any of various fungi used to make tinder
2 : METTLE, PLUCK
3 : SPIRIT, LIVELINESS

²spunk *intransitive verb* (1840)

dialect : to show spirit — usually used with *up*

spunk·ie \'spəŋ-kē\ *noun* (1727)
Scottish : IGNIS FATUUS 1

spunky \'spəŋ-kē\ *adjective* **spunk·i·er; -est** (1786)
: full of spunk : SPIRITED
— **spunk·i·ly** \-kə-lē\ *adverb*
— **spunk·i·ness** \-kē-nəs\ *noun*

spun sugar *noun* (1846)
: sugar boiled to long threads and gathered up and shaped or heaped on a stick as a candy

spun yarn *noun* (14th century)
1 : a textile yarn spun from staple-length fiber
2 : a small rope or stuff formed of two or more rope yarns loosely twisted and used for seizings especially on board ship

¹spur \'spər\ *noun* [Middle English *spure*, from Old English *spura*; akin to Old English *spurnan* to kick — more at SPURN] (before 12th century)
1 a : a pointed device secured to a rider's heel and used to urge on the horse **b** *plural* [from the acquisition of spurs by a person achieving knighthood] : recognition and reward for achievement ⟨won his academic *spurs* as the holder of a chair in a university —James Mountford⟩
2 a : a goad to action : STIMULUS
3 : something projecting like or suggesting a spur: as **a** : a projecting root or branch of a tree, shrub, or vine **b** (1) : a stiff sharp spine (as on the wings or legs of a bird or insect); *especially* : one on a cock's leg (2) : a gaff for a gamecock **c** : a hollow projecting appendage of a corolla or calyx (as in larkspur or columbine) **d** : a bony outgrowth (as on the heel of the foot) **e** : CLIMBING IRON
4 a : an angular projection, offshoot, or branch extending out beyond or away from a main body or formation; *especially* : a ridge or lesser elevation that extends laterally from a mountain or mountain range **b** : a railroad track that branches off from a main line
5 : a reinforcing buttress of masonry in a fortification
synonym see MOTIVE
— **on the spur of the moment** : on impulse : SUDDENLY

²spur *verb* **spurred; spur·ring** (13th century)
transitive verb
1 : to urge (a horse) on with spurs
2 : to incite to action or accelerated growth or development : STIMULATE
3 : to put spurs on
intransitive verb
: to spur one's horse on

spurge \'spərj\ *noun* [Middle English, from Middle French, purge, spurge, from *espurgier* to purge, from Latin *expurgare* — more at EXPURGATE] (14th century)
: any of a genus (*Euphorbia* of the family Euphorbiaceae, the spurge family) of chiefly herbs and shrubs with a bitter milky juice

spur gear *noun* (1823)
: a gear wheel with radial teeth parallel to its axis — called also *spur wheel*

spurge laurel *noun* (1597)
: a low Eurasian shrub (*Daphne laureola*) with oblong evergreen leaves and axillary racemes of yellowish flowers

spur gear

spu·ri·ous \'spyu̇r-ē-əs\ *adjective* [Late Latin & Latin; Late Latin *spurius* false, from Latin, of illegitimate birth, from *spurius*, noun, bastard] (1598)
1 : of illegitimate birth : BASTARD
2 : outwardly similar or corresponding to something without having its genuine qualities : FALSE
3 a : of falsified or erroneously attributed origin : FORGED **b** : of a deceitful nature or quality
— **spu·ri·ous·ly** *adverb*
— **spu·ri·ous·ness** *noun*

¹spurn \'spərn\ *verb* [Middle English, from Old English *spurnan*; akin to Old High German *spurnan* to kick, Latin *spernere* to spurn, Greek *spairein* to quiver] (before 12th century)
intransitive verb
1 *obsolete* **a** : STUMBLE **b** : KICK
2 *archaic* : to reject something disdainfully
transitive verb
1 : to tread sharply or heavily upon : TRAMPLE
2 : to reject with disdain or contempt : SCORN
synonym see DECLINE
— **spurn·er** *noun*

²spurn *noun* (14th century)
1 a : KICK **b** *obsolete* : STUMBLE
2 a : disdainful rejection **b** : contemptuous treatment

spur-of-the-moment *adjective* (1948)
: occurring or developing without premeditation : hastily extemporized ⟨a *spur-of-the-moment* decision⟩

spurred \'spərd\ *adjective* (15th century)
1 : wearing spurs
2 : having one or more spurs ⟨a *spurred* violet⟩

spur·rey *or* **spur·ry** \'spər-ē, 'spə-rē\ *noun*, *plural* **spurreys** *or* **spurries** [Dutch *spurrie*, from Medieval Latin *spergula*] (1577)
: a small white-flowered European weed (*Spergula arvensis*) of the pink family with whorled filiform leaves; *also* : any of several related and similar herbs

¹spurt \'spərt\ *verb* [perhaps akin to Middle High German *spürzen* to spit, Old English *-sprūtan* to sprout — more at SPROUT] (1570)
intransitive verb
: to gush forth : SPOUT
transitive verb
: to expel in a stream or jet : SQUIRT

²spurt *noun* (circa 1775)
: a sudden gush : JET

³spurt *noun* [origin unknown] (circa 1591)
1 : a short period of time : MOMENT
2 a : a sudden brief burst of effort or activity **b** : a sharp or sudden increase in business activity

⁴spurt *intransitive verb* (1664)
: to make a spurt

spur·tle \'spər-t²l\ *noun* [origin unknown] (1756)
chiefly Scottish : a wooden stick for stirring porridge

sput·nik \'spu̇t-nik, 'spət-, 'spüt-\ *noun* [Russian, literally, traveling companion, from *s, so* with + *put'* path] (1957)
: SATELLITE 2b

¹sput·ter \'spə-tər\ *verb* [akin to Dutch *sputteren* to sputter] (1598)
transitive verb
1 : to spit or squirt from the mouth with explosive sounds
2 : to utter hastily or explosively in confusion or excitement
3 : to dislodge (atoms) from the surface of a material by collision with high energy particles; *also* : to deposit (a metallic film) by such a process
intransitive verb
1 : to spit or squirt particles of food or saliva noisily from the mouth
2 : to speak explosively or confusedly in anger or excitement
3 : to make explosive popping sounds
— **sput·ter·er** *noun*

²sputter *noun* (1673)
1 : confused and excited speech or discussion
2 : the act or sound of sputtering

spu·tum \'spyü-təm, 'spü-\ *noun, plural* **spu·ta** \-tə\ [Latin, from neuter of *sputus*, past participle of *spuere* to spit — more at SPEW] (circa 1693)
: expectorated matter made up of saliva and often discharges from the respiratory passages

¹**spy** \'spī\ *verb* **spied; spy·ing** [Middle English *spien,* from Old French *espier,* of Germanic origin; akin to Old High German *spehōn* to spy; akin to Latin *specere* to look, look at, Greek *skeptesthai* & *skopein* to watch, look at, consider] (13th century)
transitive verb
1 : to watch secretly usually for hostile purposes
2 : to catch sight of **:** SEE
3 : to search or look for intensively
intransitive verb
1 : to observe or search for something **:** LOOK
2 : to watch secretly as a spy
²**spy** *noun, plural* **spies** (13th century)
1 : one that spies: **a :** one who keeps secret watch on a person or thing to obtain information **b :** a person employed by one nation to secretly convey classified information of strategic importance to another nation; *also* **:** a person who conveys the trade secrets of one company to another
2 : an act of spying
spy·glass \'spī-,glas\ *noun* (1706)
: a small telescope
spy·mas·ter \'spī-,mas-tər\ *noun* (1938)
: the head of a ring of spies **:** a director of intelligence
squab \'skwäb\ *noun, plural* **squabs** [probably of Scandinavian origin; akin to Swedish dialect *skvabb* anything soft and thick] (1664)
1 a : COUCH **b :** a cushion for a chair or couch
2 *or plural* **squab :** a fledgling bird; *specifically* **:** a fledgling pigeon about four weeks old
3 : a short fat person
— **squab** *adjective*
¹**squab·ble** \'skwä-bəl\ *noun* [probably of Scandinavian origin; akin to Swedish dialect *skvabbel* dispute] (1602)
: a noisy altercation or quarrel usually over trifles
²**squabble** *intransitive verb* **squab·bled; squab·bling** \-b(ə-)liŋ\ (1604)
: to quarrel noisily and usually over trifles
— **squab·bler** \-b(ə-)lər\ *noun*
¹**squad** \'skwäd\ *noun* [Middle French *esquade,* from Old Spanish & Old Italian; Old Spanish *escuadra* & Old Italian *squadra,* ultimately from (assumed) Vulgar Latin *exquadrare* to make square — more at SQUARE] (1649)
1 : a small organized group of military personnel; *especially* **:** a tactical unit that can be easily directed in the field
2 : a small group engaged in a common effort or occupation
²**squad** *transitive verb* **squad·ded; squad·ding** (circa 1802)
: to arrange in squads
squad car *noun* (1938)
: a police automobile connected by a two-way radio with headquarters — called also *cruiser, prowl car*
squad·ron \'skwä-drən\ *noun* [Italian *squadrone,* augmentative of *squadra* squad, from Old Italian] (1562)
: a unit of military organization: **a :** a cavalry unit higher than a troop and lower than a regiment **b :** a naval unit consisting of two or more divisions and sometimes additional vessels **c** (1) **:** a unit of the U.S. Air Force higher than a flight and lower than a group (2) **:** a military flight formation
squadron leader *noun* (1919)
: a commissioned officer in the British air force who ranks with a major in the army
squad room *noun* (1943)
1 : a room in a barracks used to billet soldiers
2 : a room in a police station where members of the force assemble
squa·lene \'skwä-,lēn\ *noun* [International Scientific Vocabulary, from Latin *squalus,* a sea fish — more at WHALE] (1916)
: an acyclic hydrocarbon $C_{30}H_{50}$ that is widely distributed in nature (as a major component of

sebum and in shark-liver oils) and is a precursor of sterols (as cholesterol)
squal·id \'skwä-ləd\ *adjective* [Latin *squalidus* rough, dirty, from *squalēre* to be covered with scales or dirt, from *squalus* dirty; perhaps akin to *squama* scale] (1596)
1 : marked by filthiness and degradation from neglect or poverty
2 : SORDID
synonym see DIRTY
— **squal·id·ly** *adverb*
— **squal·id·ness** *noun*
¹**squall** \'skwȯl\ *verb* [probably of Scandinavian origin; akin to Old Norse *skval* useless chatter] (circa 1631)
intransitive verb
: to cry out raucously **:** SCREAM
transitive verb
: to utter in a strident voice
— **squall·er** *noun*
²**squall** *noun* (1709)
: a raucous cry
³**squall** *noun* [probably of Scandinavian origin; akin to Swedish *skval* rushing water] (1699)
1 : a sudden violent wind often with rain or snow
2 : a short-lived commotion
⁴**squall** *intransitive verb* (circa 1890)
: to blow a squall
squally \'skwȯ-lē\ *adjective* **squall·i·er; -est** (1719)
1 : marked by squalls
2 : GUSTY
squa·lor \'skwä-lər *also* 'skwā- *or* 'skwȯ-\ *noun* [Latin, from *squalēre*] (1621)
: the quality or state of being squalid
squa·ma \'skwä-mə, 'skwä-\ *noun, plural* **squa·mae** \'skwä-,mē, 'skwä-,mī\ [Latin] (circa 1706)
: SCALE; *also* **:** a structure resembling a scale
squa·mate \-,māt\ *adjective* (1826)
: SCALY ⟨*squamate* reptiles⟩
squa·ma·tion \skwə-'mā-shən\ *noun* (1881)
1 : the state of being scaly
2 : the arrangement of scales on an animal
¹**squa·mo·sal** \skwə-'mō-səl, -zəl\ *noun* (1848)
: a squamosal bone
²**squamosal** *adjective* (circa 1852)
1 : SQUAMOUS
2 : of, relating to, or being a bone of the skull of many vertebrates corresponding to the squamous portion of the temporal bone of most mammals including humans
squa·mous \'skwä-məs *also* 'skwä-\ *adjective* [Middle English, from Latin *squamosus,* from *squama* scale] (15th century)
1 a : covered with or consisting of scales **:** SCALY **b :** of, relating to, or being a stratified epithelium that consists at least in its outer layers of small scalelike cells
2 : of, relating to, or being the anterior upper portion of the temporal bone of most mammals including humans
squamous cell *noun* (circa 1947)
: a cell of or derived from squamous epithelium
squa·mu·lose \'skwä-myə-,lōs, 'skwä-\ *adjective* [Latin *squamula,* diminutive of *squama*] (1846)
: being or having a thallus made up of small leafy lobes ⟨a *squamulose* lichen⟩
¹**squan·der** \'skwän-dər\ *verb* **squan·dered; squan·der·ing** \-d(ə-)riŋ\ [origin unknown] (1536)
transitive verb
1 : to spend extravagantly or foolishly **:** DISSIPATE
2 : to cause to disperse **:** SCATTER
3 : to lose (as an advantage or opportunity) through negligence or inaction
intransitive verb
: DISPERSE, SCATTER
— **squan·der·er** \-dər-ər\ *noun*
²**squander** *noun* (1709)

: an act of squandering
¹**square** \'skwar, 'skwer\ *noun* [Middle English, from Middle French *esquarre,* from (assumed) Vulgar Latin *exquadra,* from *exquadrare* to square, from Latin *ex-* + *quadrare* to square — more at QUADRATE] (13th century)
1 : an instrument having at least one right angle and two straight edges used especially to lay out or test right angles
2 : a rectangle with all four sides equal
3 : any of the quadrilateral spaces marked out on a board for playing games
4 : the product of a number multiplied by itself
5 a : an open place or area formed at the meeting of two or more streets **b :** BLOCK 6a
6 : a solid object or piece approximating a cube or having a square as its largest face
7 : an unopened cotton flower with its enclosing bracts
8 : a person who is conventional or conservative in taste or way of life
— **on the square 1 :** at right angles **2 :** in a fair open manner **:** HONESTLY
— **out of square :** not at an exact right angle
²**square** *adjective* **squar·er; squar·est** (14th century)
1 a : having four equal sides and four right angles **b :** forming a right angle ⟨*square* corner⟩ **c :** having a square base ⟨a *square* pyramid⟩
2 : raised to the second power
3 a : being approximately a cube ⟨*square* cabinet⟩ **b :** having a shape that is broad for the height and rectangular rather than curving in outline ⟨*square* shoulders⟩ ⟨a *square,* thick, hard-working man —Maria Edgeworth⟩ **c :** rectangular and equilateral in section ⟨*square* tower⟩
4 a : being or converted to a unit of area equal in measure to a square each side of which measures one unit of a specified unit of length ⟨a *square* foot⟩ — see METRIC SYSTEM table, WEIGHT table **b :** being of a specified length in each of two equal dimensions ⟨10 feet *square*⟩
5 a : exactly adjusted **:** precisely constructed or aligned **b :** JUST, FAIR ⟨a *square* deal⟩ ⟨*square* in all his dealings⟩ **c :** leaving no balance **:** SETTLED **d :** EVEN, TIED **e :** SUBSTANTIAL, SATISFYING ⟨*square* meal⟩ **f :** being unsophisticated, conservative, or conventional
6 : set at right angles with the mast and keel — used of the yards of a square-rigged ship
— **square·ness** *noun*
³**square** *verb* **squared; squar·ing** (14th century)
transitive verb
1 a : to make square or rectangular ⟨*square* a building stone⟩ **b :** to test for deviation from a right angle, straight line, or plane surface
2 : to bring approximately to a right angle ⟨*squared* his shoulders⟩
3 a : to multiply (a number) by itself **:** raise to the second power **b :** to find a square equal in area to ⟨*square* a circle⟩
4 : to regulate or adjust by or to some standard or principle ⟨*square* our actions by the opinions of others —John Milton⟩
5 a : BALANCE, SETTLE ⟨*square* an account⟩ **b :** to even the score of
6 : to mark off into squares
7 a : to set right **:** bring into agreement **b :** BRIBE, FIX
intransitive verb
1 : to agree precisely **:** CORRESPOND ⟨your actions should *square* with your words⟩
2 : to settle matters; *especially* **:** to pay the bill
— **squar·er** *noun*
⁴**square** *adverb* (circa 1582)

1 : in a straightforward or honest manner
2 a : so as to face or be face to face **b :** at right angles
3 : with nothing intervening **:** DIRECTLY ⟨ran *square* into it⟩
4 : in a firm manner ⟨looked her *square* in the eye⟩
5 : in a square shape

square away (1849)
intransitive verb
1 : to square the yards so as to sail before the wind
2 : to put everything in order or in readiness
3 : to take up a fighting stance
transitive verb
: to put in order or in readiness

square bracket *noun* (circa 1888)
: BRACKET 3a

square dance *noun* (1870)
: a dance for four couples who form the sides of a square
— **square–dance** *intransitive verb*
— **square dancer** *noun*
— **square dancing** *noun*

square knot *noun* (circa 1867)
: a knot made of two reverse half-knots and typically used to join the ends of two cords — see KNOT illustration

square·ly \'skwar-lē, 'skwer-\ *adverb* (1564)
1 : in a straightforward or honest manner ⟨we must *squarely* face the issue⟩
2 a : EXACTLY, PRECISELY ⟨*squarely* in the middle⟩ **b :** so as to make solid contact ⟨hit the ball *squarely*⟩ ⟨feet *squarely* planted⟩
3 : in a square form or manner **:** so as to be square ⟨a *squarely* cut dress⟩
4 : in a plain or unequivocal manner ⟨the responsibility lies *squarely* with us⟩ ⟨align ourselves *squarely* with our allies⟩

square matrix *noun* (1858)
: a mathematical matrix with the same number of rows and columns

square measure *noun* (1728)
: a unit or system of units for measuring area — see METRIC SYSTEM table, WEIGHT table

square off *intransitive verb* (1837)
: to take a fighting stance **:** prepare to fight; *also* **:** FIGHT

square of opposition (1864)
: a square figure on which may be demonstrated the logical relationships of contraries, contradictories, subcontraries, and subalterns and superalterns

square one *noun* [from the use of numbered squares in some board games] (1960)
: the initial stage or starting point ⟨the failure set us back to *square one*⟩

square rig *noun* (circa 1875)
: a sailing-ship rig in which the principal sails are extended on yards fastened to the masts horizontally and at their center

square–rigged \'skwar-'rigd, 'skwer-\ *adjective* (1769)
: having or equipped with a square rig

square–rig·ger \-,ri·gər\ *noun* (1855)
: a square-rigged craft

square root *noun* (1557)
: a factor of a number that when squared gives the number ⟨the *square root* of 9 is ±3⟩

square sail \'skwar-,sāl, 'skwer-, -səl\ *noun* (1600)
: a 4-sided sail extended on a yard suspended at the middle from a mast

square-rigger

square shooter *noun* (circa 1914)
: a just or honest person

square–shoul·dered \'skwar-'shōl-dərd, 'skwer-\ *adjective* (1825)
: having shoulders of a rectangular outline that are straight across the back

square–toed \-'tōd\ *adjective* (1785)
1 : having a toe that is square
2 : OLD-FASHIONED, CONSERVATIVE

square wave *noun* (1932)
: the rectangular waveform of a quantity that varies periodically and abruptly from one to the other of two uniform values

squar·ish \'skwar-ish, 'skwer-\ *adjective* (1742)
: somewhat square in form or appearance
— **squar·ish·ly** *adverb*
— **squar·ish·ness** *noun*

¹squash \'skwäsh, 'skwȯsh\ *verb* [Middle French *esquasser*, from (assumed) Vulgar Latin *exquassare*, from Latin *ex-* + *quassare* to shake — more at QUASH] (1565)
transitive verb
1 : to press or beat into a pulp or a flat mass **:** CRUSH
2 : PUT DOWN, SUPPRESS ⟨*squash* a revolt⟩
intransitive verb
1 : to flatten out under pressure or impact
2 : to proceed with a splashing or squelching sound
3 : SQUEEZE, PRESS
— **squash·er** *noun*

²squash *noun* (1590)
1 *obsolete* **:** something soft and easily crushed; *specifically* **:** an unripe pod of peas
2 : the sudden fall of a heavy soft body or the sound of such a fall
3 : a squelching sound made by walking on oozy ground or in water-soaked boots
4 : a crushed mass
5 *British* **:** sweetened citrus fruit juice often served with added soda water
6 : a singles or doubles game played in a 4-wall court with a long-handled racket and a rubber ball that can be hit off any number of walls

³squash *adverb* (1766)
: with a squash or a squashing sound

⁴squash *noun, plural* **squash·es** *or* **squash** [by shortening & alteration from earlier *isquoutersquash*, from Narraganset *askútasquash*] (1634)
: any of various fruits of plants (genus *Cucurbita*) of the gourd family widely cultivated as vegetables; *also* **:** a plant and especially a vine that bears squashes — compare SUMMER SQUASH, WINTER SQUASH

squash bug *noun* (circa 1846)
: a large black American bug (*Anasa tristis* of the family Coreidae) injurious to plants of the gourd family

squash racquets *noun plural but singular in construction* (1886)
: SQUASH 6

squash tennis *noun* (1901)
: a singles racket game resembling squash played with an inflated ball the size of a tennis ball

squashy \'skwä-shē, 'skwȯ-\ *adjective* **squash·i·er; -est** (1698)
1 : easily squashed **:** very soft ⟨*squashy* cushions⟩
2 : softly wet **:** BOGGY
3 : soft because overripe ⟨*squashy* melons⟩
— **squash·i·ly** \-shə-lē\ *adverb*
— **squash·i·ness** \-shē-nəs\ *noun*

¹squat \'skwät\ *verb* **squat·ted; squat·ting** [Middle English *squatten*, from Middle French *esquatir*, from *es-* ex- (from Latin *ex-*) + *quatir* to press, from (assumed) Vulgar Latin *coactire* to press together, from Latin *coactus*, past participle of *cogere* to drive together — more at COGENT] (15th century)
transitive verb
1 : to cause (oneself) to crouch or sit on the ground
2 : to occupy as a squatter
intransitive verb
1 : to crouch close to the ground as if to escape observation ⟨a hare *squatting* in the grass⟩

2 : to assume or maintain a position in which the body is supported on the feet and the knees are bent so that the buttocks rest on or near the heels
3 : to be or become a squatter

²squat *adjective* **squat·ter; squat·test** (15th century)
1 : sitting with the haunches close above the heels
2 a : low to the ground **b :** marked by disproportionate shortness or thickness
— **squat·ly** *adverb*
— **squat·ness** *noun*

³squat *noun* (1580)
1 a : the act of squatting **b :** the posture of one that squats
2 a : a place where one squats **b :** the lair of a small animal ⟨*squat* of a hare⟩
3 : a lift in weight lifting in which the lifter performs a knee bend while holding a barbell on the shoulders; *also* **:** a competitive event involving this lift
4 *chiefly British* **:** an empty house or building that is occupied by squatters
5 *slang* **:** DIDDLY-SQUAT

¹squat·ter \'skwä-tər\ *intransitive verb* [imitative] (1785)
: to go along through or as if through water

²squatter *noun* (1788)
: one that squats: as **a :** one that settles on property without right or title or payment of rent **b :** one that settles on public land under government regulation with the purpose of acquiring title

squatter sovereignty *noun* (1854)
: POPULAR SOVEREIGNTY 2

squat·ty \'skwä-tē\ *adjective* **squat·ti·er; -est** (1881)
1 : low to the ground
2 : DUMPY, THICKSET

squaw \'skwȯ\ *noun* [Massachuset *squa, ussqua* woman] (1634)
1 : an American Indian woman
2 : WOMAN, WIFE — usually used disparagingly

squaw·fish \-,fish\ *noun* (1881)
: any of several large cyprinid fishes (genus *Ptychocheilus*) of western North America

¹squawk \'skwȯk\ *intransitive verb* [probably blend of *squall* and *squeak*] (1821)
1 : to utter a harsh abrupt scream
2 : to complain or protest loudly or vehemently
— **squawk·er** *noun*

²squawk *noun* (1850)
1 : a harsh abrupt scream
2 : a noisy complaint

squawk box *noun* (1945)
: an intercom speaker

squaw man *noun* (1866)
: a white man married to an Indian woman and usually living as one of her tribe

squaw·root \'skwȯ-,rüt, -,rut\ *noun* (circa 1848)
: a North American scaly herb (*Conopholis americana*) of the broomrape family parasitic on oak and hemlock roots

¹squeak \'skwēk\ *verb* [Middle English *squeken*] (14th century)
intransitive verb
1 : to utter or make a short shrill cry or noise
2 : SQUEAL 2a
3 : to pass, succeed, or win by a narrow margin ⟨just *squeaked* by in the election⟩
transitive verb
: to utter in a shrill piping tone

²squeak *noun* (1700)
1 : a sharp shrill cry or sound
2 : ESCAPE ⟨a close *squeak*⟩
— **squeaky** \'skwē-kē\ *adjective*

squeak·er \'skwē-kər\ *noun* (1671)
1 : one that squeaks
2 : a contest (as a game or an election) won by a small margin

squeaky–clean *adjective* (1968)
1 : completely clean ⟨*squeaky-clean* hair⟩

2 : completely free from moral taint of any kind ⟨a *squeaky-clean* reputation⟩

¹**squeal** \'skwē(ə)l\ *verb* [Middle English *squelen*] (14th century)
intransitive verb
1 : to make a shrill cry or noise
2 a : to turn informer **b :** COMPLAIN, PROTEST
transitive verb
1 : to utter or express with or as if with a squeal
2 : to cause to make a loud shrill noise ⟨*squealing* the tires⟩
— **squeal·er** *noun*
²**squeal** *noun* (1747)
: a shrill sharp cry or noise
squea·mish \'skwē-mish\ *adjective* [Middle English *squaymisch*, modification of Anglo-French *escoymous*] (15th century)
1 a : easily nauseated **:** QUEASY **b :** affected with nausea
2 a : excessively fastidious or scrupulous in conduct or belief **b :** easily offended or disgusted
— **squea·mish·ly** *adverb*
— **squea·mish·ness** *noun*
¹**squee·gee** \'skwē-,jē\ *noun* [origin unknown] (1844)
: a blade of leather or rubber set on a handle and used for spreading, pushing, or wiping liquid material on, across, or off a surface (as a window); *also* **:** a smaller similar device or a small rubber roller with handle used by a photographer or lithographer
²**squeegee** *transitive verb* **squee·geed; squee·gee·ing** (1883)
: to smooth, wipe, or treat with a squeegee
¹**squeeze** \'skwēz\ *verb* **squeezed; squeez·ing** [alteration of obsolete English *quease*, from Middle English *queysen*, from Old English *cwȳsan*; akin to Icelandic *kveisa* stomach cramps] (circa 1601)
transitive verb
1 a : to exert pressure especially on opposite sides of **:** COMPRESS **b :** to extract or emit under pressure **c :** to force or thrust by compression
2 a (1) **:** to get by extortion (2) **:** to deprive by extortion **b :** to cause economic hardship to **c :** to reduce the amount of ⟨*squeezes* profits⟩
3 : to crowd into a limited space
4 : to gain or win by a narrow margin
5 : to force (another player) to discard in bridge so as to unguard a suit
6 : to score by means of a squeeze play
intransitive verb
1 : to give way before pressure
2 : to exert pressure; *also* **:** to practice extortion or oppression
3 : to force one's way ⟨*squeeze* through a door⟩
4 : to pass, win, or get by narrowly
— **squeez·abil·i·ty** \,skwē-zə-'bi-lə-tē\ *noun*
— **squeez·able** \'skwē-zə-bəl\ *adjective*
— **squeez·er** *noun*
²**squeeze** *noun* (1611)
1 a : an act or instance of squeezing **:** COMPRESSION **b :** HANDCLASP; *also* **:** EMBRACE
2 a : a quantity squeezed out from something ⟨a *squeeze* of lemon⟩ **b :** a group crowded together **:** CROWD
3 : a profit taken by a middleman on goods or transactions
4 : a financial pressure caused by narrowing margins or by shortages
5 : a forced discard in bridge
6 : SQUEEZE PLAY
7 *slang* **:** MAIN SQUEEZE
squeeze bottle *noun* (1950)
: a bottle of flexible plastic that dispenses its contents when it is squeezed
squeeze off *verb* (circa 1949)
transitive verb
: to fire (a round) by squeezing the trigger
intransitive verb
: to fire a weapon by squeezing the trigger
squeeze play *noun* (1905)

1 a : a baseball play in which a runner on third base starts for home plate as the ball is being pitched and the batter attempts to bunt to give the runner a chance to score
2 : the exertion of pressure in order to extort a concession or gain a goal
¹**squelch** \'skwelch\ *verb* [origin unknown] (1624)
transitive verb
1 a : to fall or stamp on so as to crush **b** (1) **:** to completely suppress **:** QUELL (2) **:** SILENCE
2 : to emit or move with a sucking sound
intransitive verb
1 : to emit a sucking sound
2 : to splash through water, slush, or mire
— **squelch·er** *noun*
²**squelch** *noun* (1895)
1 : a sound of or as if of semiliquid matter under suction ⟨the *squelch* of mud⟩
2 : the act of suppressing; *especially* **:** a retort that silences an opponent
— **squelchy** *adjective*
sque·teague \skwi-'tēg\ *noun, plural* **squeteague** [of Algonquian origin; akin to Mohegan *cheegut* weakfish] (1803)
: any of several weakfishes (especially *Cynoscion regalis*)
¹**squib** \'skwib\ *noun* [origin unknown] (circa 1525)
1 a : a short humorous or satiric writing or speech **b :** a short news item; *especially* **:** FILLER
2 a : a small firecracker **b :** a broken firecracker in which the powder burns with a fizz
3 : a small electric or pyrotechnic device used to ignite a charge
²**squib** *verb* **squibbed; squib·bing** (circa 1580)
intransitive verb
1 : to speak, write, or publish squibs
2 : to fire a squib
transitive verb
1 a : to utter in an offhand manner **b :** to make squibs against **:** LAMPOON
2 : to shoot off **:** FIRE
3 : to kick (a football) just far enough on a kickoff to be legally recoverable by the kicking team
squib kick *noun* (circa 1956)
: ONSIDE KICK
¹**squid** \'skwid\ *noun, plural* **squid** *or* **squids** [origin unknown] (1613)
: any of an order (Teuthoidea) of cephalopods having eight short arms and two usually longer tentacles, a long tapered body, a caudal fin on each side, and usually a slender internal chitinous support
²**squid** *intransitive verb* **squid·ded; squid·ding** (circa 1859)
: to fish with or for squid
SQUID \'skwid\ *noun* [superconducting *quantum interference device*] (1967)
: an instrument for detecting and measuring very weak magnetic fields
squiffed \'skwift\ *or* **squif·fy** \'skwi-fē\ *adjective* [origin unknown] (circa 1855)
: INTOXICATED, DRUNK
¹**squig·gle** \'skwi-gəl\ *verb* **squig·gled; squig·gling** \-g(ə-)liŋ\ [blend of *squirm* and *wriggle*] (circa 1816)
intransitive verb
1 : SQUIRM, WRIGGLE
2 : to write or paint hastily **:** SCRIBBLE
transitive verb
1 : SCRIBBLE
2 : to form or cause to form in squiggles
²**squiggle** *noun* (1900)
: a short wavy twist or line **:** CURLICUE; *especially* **:** an illegible scrawl
— **squig·gly** \-g(ə-)lē\ *adjective*
squil·gee \'skwē-,jē, 'skwil-,jē\ *variant of* SQUEEGEE
squill \'skwil\ *noun* [Middle English, from Latin *squilla, scilla*, from Greek *skilla*] (14th century)

1 a : a Mediterranean bulbous herb (*Urginea maritima*) of the lily family — called also *sea onion*; compare RED SQUILL **1 b** (1) **:** the dried sliced bulb scales of a squill used as an expectorant, cardiac stimulant, and diuretic (2) **:** RED SQUILL 2
2 : SCILLA
squil·la \'skwi-lə\ *noun, plural* **squillas** *or* **squil·lae** \'skwi-,lē, -,lī\ [New Latin, from Latin, shrimp, crayfish] (1658)
: any of various stomatopod crustaceans (especially genus *Squilla*) that burrow in mud or beneath stones in shallow water along the seashore
¹**squinch** \'skwinch\ *verb* [probably blend of *squint* and *pinch*] (1835)
transitive verb
1 : to screw up (the eyes or face) **:** SQUINT
2 a : to make more compact **b :** to cause to crouch down or draw together
intransitive verb
1 : FLINCH
2 : to crouch down or draw together
3 : SQUINT
²**squinch** *noun* [alteration of earlier *scunch* back part of the side of an opening] (circa 1840)
: a support (as an arch, lintel, or corbeling) carried across the corner of a room under a superimposed mass
¹**squin·ny** \'skwi-nē\ *verb* **squin·nied; squin·ny·ing** [probably from obsolete English *squin* asquint, from Middle English *skuin*] (1605)
: SQUINT
²**squinny** *noun* (circa 1881)
: SQUINT
— **squinny** *adjective*
¹**squint** \'skwint\ *adjective* [Middle English *asquint*] (1579)
1 *of an eye* **:** looking or tending to look obliquely or askance (as with envy or disdain)
2 *of the eyes* **:** not having the visual axes parallel **:** CROSSED
²**squint** (1599)
intransitive verb
1 a : to have an indirect bearing, reference, or aim **b :** to deviate from a true line
2 a : to look in a squint-eyed manner **b :** to be cross-eyed **c :** to look or peer with eyes partly closed
transitive verb
: to cause (an eye) to squint
— **squint·er** *noun*
— **squint·ing·ly** \'skwin-tiŋ-lē\ *adverb*
³**squint** *noun* (circa 1652)
1 : STRABISMUS
2 : an instance of squinting
3 : HAGIOSCOPE
— **squinty** \'skwin-tē\ *adjective*
squint—eyed \'skwint-,īd\ *adjective* (1589)
1 : having eyes that squint; *specifically* **:** affected with cross-eye
2 : looking askance (as in envy)
squinting modifier *noun* (1924)
: a modifier (as *often* in "getting dressed often is a nuisance") so placed in a sentence that it can be interpreted as modifying either what precedes or what follows
¹**squire** \'skwīr\ *noun* [Middle English *squier*, from Old French *esquier* — more at ESQUIRE] (13th century)
1 : a shield bearer or armor bearer of a knight
2 a : a male attendant especially on a great personage **b :** a man who devotedly attends a lady **:** GALLANT
3 a : a member of the British gentry ranking below a knight and above a gentleman **b :** an owner of a country estate; *especially* **:** the

\ə\ abut \ᵊ\ kitten \ər\ further \a\ ash \ā\ ace
\ä\ mop, mar \aů\ out \ch\ chin \e\ bet \ē\ easy
\g\ go \i\ hit \ī\ ice \j\ job \ŋ\ sing \ō\ go
\ȯ\ law \ȯi\ boy \th\ thin \t͟h\ the \ü\ loot \ů\ foot
\y\ yet \zh\ vision *see also* Guide to Pronunciation

principal landowner in a village or district **c**
(1) **:** JUSTICE OF THE PEACE (2) **:** LAWYER (3)
: JUDGE
— **squir·ish** \'skwīr-ish\ *adjective*
²**squire** *transitive verb* **squired; squir·ing**
(14th century)
: to attend as a squire **:** ESCORT
squire·ar·chy *also* **squir·ar·chy** \'skwīr-
,är-kē\ *noun, plural* **-chies** (1796)
: the class of landed gentry or landed propri-
etors
squirm \'skwərm\ *intransitive verb* [origin un-
known] (circa 1691)
: to twist about like a worm **:** FIDGET
— **squirm** *noun*
— **squirmy** \'skwər-mē\ *adjective*
¹**squir·rel** \'skwər(-ə)l, 'skwə-rəl, *chiefly Brit-
ish* 'skwir-əl\ *noun, plural* **squirrels** *also*
squirrel [Middle English *squirel*, from Mid-
dle French *esquireul*, from (assumed) Vulgar
Latin *scuriolus*, diminutive of *scurius*, alter-
ation of Latin *sciurus*, from Greek *skiouros*,
probably from *skia* shadow + *oura* tail —
more at SHINE, ASS] (14th century)
1 : any of various small or medium-sized ro-
dents (family Sciuridae, the squirrel family):
as **a :** any of numerous New or Old World ar-
boreal forms having a long bushy tail and
strong hind legs **b :** GROUND SQUIRREL
2 : the fur of a squirrel ◇
²**squirrel** *transitive verb* **-reled** *or* **-relled;
-rel·ing** *or* **-rel·ling** [from the squirrel's hab-
it of storing up gathered nuts and seeds for
winter use] (1925)
: to store up for future use — often used with
away
squirrel cage *noun* (1821)
1 : a cage for a small animal (as a squirrel)
that contains a rotatable cylinder for exercis-
ing
2 : something resembling the working of a
squirrel cage in repetitiveness or endlessness
squirrel corn *noun* (1843)
: a North American herb (*Dicentra canaden-
sis*) of the fumitory family with much-divided
leaves and a scapose raceme of cream-colored
flowers
squir·rel·ly \'skwər(-ə)-lē, 'skwə-rə-\ *adjective*
(1928)
: NUTTY 3
squirrel monkey *noun* (1773)
: a small soft-haired South American monkey
(*Saimiri sciureus*) that has a long tail not used
for grasping and is colored chiefly yellowish
gray with a white face and black muzzle
squirrel rifle *noun* [from its being suitable
only for small game] (1834)
: a small-caliber rifle — called also *squirrel
gun*
¹**squirt** \'skwərt\ *verb* [Middle English; akin to
Low German *swirtjen* to squirt] (15th century)
intransitive verb
: to come forth in a sudden rapid stream from
a narrow opening **:** SPURT
transitive verb
: to cause to squirt
— **squirt·er** *noun*
²**squirt** *noun* (15th century)
1 a : an instrument (as a syringe) for squirting
a liquid **b :** a small quick stream **:** JET **c :** the
action or an instance of squirting
2 a : an impudent youngster **b :** KID
squirt gun *noun* (1803)
: WATER PISTOL
squirting cucumber *noun* (1802)
: a Mediterranean plant (*Ecballium elaterium*)
of the gourd family with oblong fruit that
bursts from the peduncle when ripe and forc-
ibly ejects the seeds
squish \'skwish\ *verb* [alteration of *squash*]
(circa 1647)
transitive verb
1 : SQUASH
2 : SQUELCH, SUCK

intransitive verb
: SQUELCH, SUCK ⟨their wet tennis shoes
squished —Frank Noel⟩
— **squish** *noun*
squishy \'skwi-shē\ *adjective* **squish·i·er;
-est** (circa 1847)
: being soft, yielding, and damp
— **squish·i·ness** *noun*
squoosh \'skwush, 'skwüsh\ *verb* [by alter-
ation] (1942)
: SQUASH
squush \'skwəsh\ *verb* [by alteration] (1837)
: SQUASH
Sra·nan \'srä-nən\ *noun* [Sranan, short for
Sranan Tongo, literally, Suriname tongue]
(1953)
: an English-based creole widely spoken in
Suriname
sri \'srē, 'shrē\ *noun* [Sanskrit *śrī*, literally,
beauty, majesty; akin to Greek *kreiōn* ruler,
master] (1799)
— used as a conventional title of respect
when addressing or speaking of a distin-
guished Indian
sRNA \'es-,är-,en-'ā\ *noun* [soluble *RNA*]
(1957)
: TRANSFER RNA
SRO \,es-(,)är-'ō\ *noun* [single-room *occupan-
cy*] (1941)
: a house, apartment building, or residential
hotel in which low-income or welfare tenants
live in single rooms
SS \'es-'es\ *noun* [German, abbreviation for
Schutzstaffel, literally, protection echelon]
(1932)
: a unit of Nazis created to serve as bodyguard
to Hitler and later expanded to take charge of
intelligence, central security, policing action,
and the mass extermination of those they con-
sidered inferior or undesirable
SST \,es-,es-'tē\ *noun* [*supersonic transport*]
(1961)
: SUPERSONIC TRANSPORT
¹**-st** — see -EST
²**-st** *symbol*
— used after the figure 1 to indicate the ordi-
nal number *first* ⟨1*st*⟩ ⟨91*st*⟩
¹**stab** \'stab\ *noun* [Middle English *stabbe*]
(15th century)
1 : a wound produced by a pointed weapon
2 a : a thrust of a pointed weapon **b :** a jerky
thrust
3 : EFFORT, TRY
²**stab** *verb* **stabbed; stab·bing** (1530)
transitive verb
1 : to wound or pierce by the thrust of a point-
ed weapon
2 : THRUST, DRIVE
intransitive verb
: to thrust or give a wound with or as if with a
pointed weapon
— **stab·ber** *noun*
¹**sta·bile** \'stā-,bīl, -,bil\ *adjective* [Latin *stabi-
lis* — more at STABLE] (1896)
: STATIONARY, STABLE
²**sta·bile** \-,bēl\ *noun* [probably from French,
from Latin *stabilis*, adjective] (1937)
: an abstract sculpture or construction similar
in appearance to a mobile but made to be sta-
tionary
sta·bil·i·ty \stə-'bi-lə-tē\ *noun, plural* **-ties**
(14th century)
1 : the quality, state, or degree of being stable:
as **a :** the strength to stand or endure **:** FIRM-
NESS **b :** the property of a body that causes it
when disturbed from a condition of equilibri-
um or steady motion to develop forces or mo-
ments that restore the original condition **c :** re-
sistance to chemical change or to physical
disintegration
2 : residence for life in one monastery
sta·bi·lize \'stā-bə-,līz\ *verb* **-lized; -liz·ing**
(1861)
transitive verb
1 : to make stable, steadfast, or firm

2 : to hold steady: as **a :** to maintain the sta-
bility of (as an airplane) by means of a stabi-
lizer **b :** to limit fluctuations of (as prices) **c**
: to establish a minimum price for
intransitive verb
: to become stable, firm, or steadfast
— **sta·bi·li·za·tion** \,stā-bə-lə-'zā-shən\
noun
sta·bi·liz·er \'stā-bə-,lī-zər\ *noun* (circa 1909)
: one that stabilizes something: as **a :** a sub-
stance added to another substance (as an ex-
plosive or plastic) or to a system (as an emul-
sion) to prevent or retard an unwanted
alteration of physical state **b :** a gyroscope de-
vice to keep ships steady in a heavy sea **c :** an
airfoil providing stability for an airplane; *spe-
cifically* **:** the fixed horizontal member of the
tail assembly — see AIRPLANE illustration
¹**sta·ble** \'stā-bəl\ *noun* [Middle English, from
Old French *estable*, from Latin *stabulum*, from
stare to stand — more at STAND] (13th centu-
ry)
1 : a building in which domestic animals are
sheltered and fed; *especially* **:** such a building
having stalls or compartments ⟨horse *stable*⟩
2 a : the racehorses of one owner **b :** a group
of athletes (as boxers) or performers under one
management **c :** the racing cars of one owner
d : GROUP, COLLECTION
— **sta·ble·man** \-mən, -,man\ *noun*
²**stable** *verb* **sta·bled; sta·bling** \-b(ə-)liŋ\
(14th century)
transitive verb
: to put or keep in a stable
intransitive verb
: to dwell in or as if in a stable
³**stable** *adjective* **sta·bler** \-b(ə-)lər\; **sta-
blest** \-b(ə-)ləst\ [Middle English, from Mid-
dle French *estable*, from Latin *stabilis*, from
stare to stand] (13th century)
1 a : firmly established **:** FIXED, STEADFAST **b**
: not changing or fluctuating **:** UNVARYING **c**
: PERMANENT, ENDURING
2 a : steady in purpose **:** firm in resolution **b**
: not subject to insecurity or emotional illness
: SANE, RATIONAL ⟨a *stable* personality⟩
3 a (1) **:** placed so as to resist forces tending to
cause motion or change of motion (2) **:** de-
signed so as to develop forces that restore the
original condition when disturbed from a con-
dition of equilibrium or steady motion **b** (1)
: not readily altering in chemical makeup or
physical state ⟨*stable* emulsions⟩ (2) **:** not
spontaneously radioactive
synonym see LASTING
— **sta·ble·ness** \-bəl-nəs\ *noun*
— **sta·bly** \-b(ə-)lē\ *adverb*
stable fly *noun* (1862)
: a biting dipteran fly (*Stomoxys calcitrans*)
that resembles the common housefly and is
abundant about stables

◇ WORD HISTORY
squirrel The ultimate source of English
squirrel is Greek *skiouros*, a word first attest-
ed in the early centuries A.D. whose literal
meaning is probably "shadow-tailed." This
name would appear to come from the
Greeks' observation that when the animal
sits upright with its bushy tail behind its back,
it looks as if it could be shading itself from
the sun. The Greek word entered Latin as
sciurus, which underwent a variety of permu-
tations in the spoken Latin of the Roman
provinces. One outcome is presumed to be a
diminutive form *scuriolus*, which developed
into Old French *escuireul*. This was eventual-
ly borrowed into Middle English as *squirel* or
squerel. The Old English word for "squirrel"
was *ācwern*, with a Germanic and Indo-
European pedigree; *ācwern* passed as *oc-
querne* or *aquerne* into early Middle English,
but no trace of the word is found after the
13th century.

sta·ble·mate \'stā-bəl-ˌmāt\ *noun* (1926)
1 : an animal stabled with another
2 : a member of a stable
sta·bler \-b(ə-)lər\ *noun* (15th century)
: one who keeps a stable
sta·bling \-b(ə-)liŋ\ *noun* (15th century)
: accommodation for animals in a building; *also* : the building for this
stab·lish \'sta-blish\ *verb* [Middle English, short for *establissen*] (14th century)
archaic : ESTABLISH
— **stab·lish·ment** \-mənt\ *noun, archaic*
stac·ca·to \stə-'kä-(ˌ)tō\ *adjective* [Italian, from past participle of *staccare* to detach, from *s-* ex- (from Latin *ex-*) + at*taccare* to attack, attach, perhaps from Old French *es-tachier* — more at ATTACH] (circa 1724)
1 a : cut short or apart in performing : DISCON-NECTED ⟨*staccato* notes⟩ **b** : marked by short clear-cut playing or singing of tones or chords ⟨a *staccato* style⟩
2 : ABRUPT, DISJOINTED
— **staccato** *adverb*
— **staccato** *noun*
staccato mark *noun* (circa 1903)
: a pointed vertical stroke or a dot placed over or under a musical note to be produced stacca-to
¹stack \'stak\ *noun* [Middle English *stak,* from Old Norse *stakkr;* akin to Russian *stog* stack and probably to Old English *staca* stake] (14th century)
1 : a large usually conical pile (as of hay, straw, or grain in the sheaf) left standing in the field for storage
2 a : an orderly pile or heap **b** : a large quantity or number
3 : an English unit of measure especially for firewood that is equal to 108 cubic feet
4 a : a number of flues embodied in one structure rising above a roof **b** : a vertical pipe (as to carry off smoke) **c** : the exhaust pipe of an internal combustion engine
5 : a structure of bookshelves for compact storage of books — usually used in plural
6 : a pile of chips sold to or won by a poker player
7 a : a memory or a section of memory in a computer for temporary storage in which the last item stored is the first retrieved; *also* : a data structure that simulates a stack ⟨a push-down *stack*⟩ **b** : a computer memory consisting of arrays of memory elements stacked one on top of another
²stack (14th century)
transitive verb
1 a : to arrange in a stack : PILE **b** : to pile in or on ⟨*stacked* the table with books⟩ ⟨*stack* the dishwasher⟩
2 a : to arrange secretly for cheating ⟨*stack* a deck of cards⟩ **b** : to arrange or fix so as to make a particular result likely ⟨the odds are *stacked* against us⟩ ⟨will *stack* juries to suit themselves —Patrice Horn⟩
3 a : to assign (an airplane) by radio to a particular altitude and position within a group circling before landing **b** : to put into a waiting line ⟨another dozen rigs are *stacked* up and waiting —P. H. Hutchins, Jr.⟩
4 : COMPARE — used with *against* ⟨such a crime is nothing when *stacked* against a murder —Pete Censky⟩
intransitive verb
: to form a stack
— **stack·er** *noun*
stack·able \'sta-kə-bəl\ *adjective* (1958)
: easily arranged in a stack
stacked \'stakt\ *adjective* (1942)
of a woman : being shapely and having large breasts
stack up *intransitive verb* (1896)
1 : to add up : TOTAL
2 : MEASURE UP, COMPARE — usually used with *against*
stac·te \'stak-tē\ *noun* [Middle English *stacten,* from Latin *stacte,* from Greek *staktē,*

from feminine of *staktos* oozing out in drops, from *stazein* to drip] (1535)
: a sweet spice used by the ancient Jews in preparing incense
stad·dle \'sta-dᵊl\ *noun* [Middle English *stathel* base, support, bottom of a stack, from Old English *statho* base; akin to Old High German *stān* to stand — more at STAND] (15th century)
: a base (as of piling) for a stack of hay or straw
stade \'stād\ *noun* [Middle French *estade,* from Latin *stadium*] (1537)
: STADIUM 1a
sta·dia \'stā-dē-ə\ *noun* [Italian, probably from Latin, plural of *stadium*] (1865)
: a surveying method for determination of distances and differences of elevation by means of a telescopic instrument having two horizontal lines through which the marks on a graduated rod are observed; *also* : the instrument or rod
sta·di·um \'stā-dē-əm\ *noun, plural* **-dia** \-dē-ə\ *or* **-di·ums** [Middle English, from Latin, from Greek *stadion*] (14th century)
1 a : any of various ancient Greek units of length ranging in value from 607 to 738 feet (about 185 to 225 meters) **b** : an ancient Roman unit of length equal to 607 feet (185 meters)
2 a : a course for footraces in ancient Greece originally one stadium in length **b** : a tiered structure with seats for spectators surrounding an ancient Greek running track **c** : a large usually unroofed building with tiers of seats for spectators at sports events
3 [New Latin, from Latin] : a stage in a life history; *especially* : one between successive molts
stadt·hold·er \'stat-ˌhōl-dər\ *noun* [part translation of Dutch *stadhouder,* from *stad* place + *houder* holder] (1668)
1 : a viceroy in a province of the Netherlands
2 : a chief executive officer of the provinces that formed a union leading to establishment of the Netherlands
— **stadt·hold·er·ate** \-də-rət\ *noun*
— **stadt·hold·er·ship** \-dər-ˌship\ *noun*
¹staff \'staf\ *noun, plural* **staffs** \'stafs, 'stavz\ *or* **staves** \'stavz, 'stāvz\ [Middle English *staf,* from Old English *stæf;* akin to Old High German *stab* staff, Sanskrit *stabhnāti* he supports] (before 12th century)
1 a : a long stick carried in the hand for support in walking **b** : a supporting rod: as (1) *archaic* : SHAFT 1a(1) (2) : a crosspiece in a ladder or chair : RUNG (3) : FLAGSTAFF (4) : a pivoted arbor **c** : CLUB, CUDGEL
2 a : CROSIER **b** : a rod carried as a symbol of office or authority
3 : the horizontal lines with their spaces on which music is written — called also *stave*
4 : any of various graduated sticks or rules used for measuring : ROD
5 *plural* **staffs a** : the officers chiefly responsible for the internal operations of an institution or business **b** : a group of officers appointed to assist a civil executive or commanding officer **c** : military or naval officers not eligible for operational command **d** : the personnel who assist a director in carrying out an assigned task **e** *plural* **staff** : a member of a staff
— **staff** *adjective*
²staff *transitive verb* (1859)
1 : to supply with a staff or with workers
2 : to serve as a staff member of
³staff *noun* [probably from German *staffieren* to trim] (1892)
: a building material having a plaster of Paris base and used in exterior wall coverings of temporary buildings
staff·er \'sta-fər\ *noun* (1941)
: a member of a staff (as of a newspaper)
staff officer *noun* (1777)
: a commissioned officer assigned to a military commander's staff — compare LINE OFFICER

staff of life (1638)
: a staple of diet; *especially* : BREAD
Staf·ford·shire bull terrier \'sta-fərd-ˌshir, -shər-\ *noun* [*Staffordshire,* England] (1901)
: any of a breed of compact muscular terriers that have a short stiff glossy coat

Staffordshire bull terrier

staff sergeant *noun* (1851)
: a noncommissioned officer ranking in the army above a sergeant and below a platoon sergeant or sergeant first class, in the air force above a sergeant and below a technical sergeant, and in the marine corps above a sergeant and below a gunnery sergeant
staff sergeant major *noun* (1967)
: a noncommissioned officer in the army ranking above a master sergeant
staff tree *noun* (circa 1633)
: any of a genus (*Celastrus* of the family Celastraceae, the staff-tree family) of mostly twining shrubby plants including the common bittersweet
¹stag \'stag\ *noun, plural* **stags** [Middle English *stagge,* from Old English *stagga;* akin to Old Norse andar*steggi* drake] (12th century)
1 *or plural* **stag** : an adult male red deer; *also* : the male of various other deer (especially genus *Cervus*)
2 *chiefly Scottish* : a young horse; *especially* : a young unbroken stallion
3 : a male animal castrated after maturity — compare STEER 1
4 : a young adult male domestic fowl
5 a : a social gathering of men only **b** : one who attends a dance or party without a companion
²stag *verb* **stagged; stag·ging** [*stag* (informer)] (circa 1823)
transitive verb
British : to spy on
intransitive verb
: to attend a dance or party without a companion
³stag *adjective* (1843)
1 a : restricted to men ⟨a *stag* party⟩ **b** : intended or suitable for a gathering of men only; *especially* : PORNOGRAPHIC ⟨*stag* movies⟩
2 : unaccompanied by someone of the opposite sex ⟨*stag* women⟩
— **stag** *adverb*

◇ WORD HISTORY
stadium In ancient Greece a *stadion* was a unit of measurement equal to about 185 meters. One of the most important events in the ancient Olympic Games was a footrace exactly one *stadion* long. The course on which the race was run, including artificial embankments around the sides to accommodate spectators, also became known as a *stadion.* The Romans borrowed the word as *stadium.* When *stadium* first appeared in English-language contexts, in the 14th century, it was with reference to the Greco-Roman unit of measurement or to the racecourse at Olympia or one modeled after it. Over time *stadium* has come to be used of variously sized arenas surrounded by tiered seating and used for a variety of athletic contests.

stag beetle *noun* (1681)
: any of a family (Lucanidae) of mostly large lamellicorn beetles having males with long and often branched mandibles suggesting the antlers of a stag

¹**stage** \'stāj\ *noun* [Middle English, from Middle French *estage*, from (assumed) Vulgar Latin *staticum*, from Latin *stare* to stand — more at STAND] (14th century)
1 a : one of a series of positions or stations one above the other **:** STEP **b :** the height of the surface of a river above an arbitrary zero point ⟨flood *stage*⟩
2 a (1) **:** a raised platform (2) **:** the part of a theater on which the acting takes place and which often includes the wings (3) **:** the acting profession **:** the theater as an occupation or activity (4) **:** SOUNDSTAGE **b :** a center of attention or scene of action
3 a : a scaffold for workmen **b :** the small platform of a microscope on which an object is placed for examination
4 a : a place of rest formerly provided for those traveling by stagecoach **:** STATION **b :** the distance between two stopping places on a road **c :** STAGECOACH
5 a : a period or step in a progress, activity, or development; *especially* **:** one of the distinguishable periods of growth and development of a plant or animal ⟨the larval *stage* of an insect⟩ **b :** one passing through a (specified) stage
6 : an element or part of an electronic device (as an amplifier)
7 : one of two or more sections of a rocket that have their own fuel and engine
— **stage·ful** \-ˌfu̇l\ *noun*
— **stage·like** \-ˌlīk\ *adjective*
— **on the stage :** in or into the acting profession

²**stage** *transitive verb* **staged; stag·ing** (1879)
1 : to produce (as a play) on a stage
2 : to produce or cause to happen for public view or public effect ⟨*stage* a track meet⟩ ⟨*stage* a hunger strike⟩
— **stage·able** \'stā-jə-bəl\ *adjective*

³**stage** *adjective* (1824)
: intended to represent a type or stereotype ⟨a *stage* Irishman⟩ ⟨a *stage* French accent⟩

stage business *noun* (1825)
: BUSINESS 6

stage·coach \'stāj-ˌkōch\ *noun* (1658)
: a horse-drawn passenger and mail coach running on a regular schedule between established stops

stage·craft \-ˌkraft\ *noun* (1882)
: the effective management of theatrical devices or techniques

stage direction *noun* (1790)
: a description (as of a character or setting) or direction (as to indicate stage business) provided in the text of a play

stage director *noun* (1782)
1 : DIRECTOR c
2 : STAGE MANAGER

stage fright *noun* (1878)
: nervousness felt at appearing before an audience

stage·hand \'stāj-ˌhand\ *noun* (circa 1902)
: a stage worker who handles scenery, properties, or lights

stage left *noun* (1931)
: the left part of a stage from the viewpoint of one who faces the audience

stage–man·age \-ˌma-nij\ *transitive verb* [back-formation from *stage manager*] (1879)
1 a : to arrange or exhibit so as to achieve a desired effect **b :** to arrange or direct from behind the scenes
2 : to act as stage manager for
— **stage management** *noun*

stage manager *noun* (1805)
: one who supervises the physical aspects of a stage production, assists the director during rehearsals, and is in charge of the stage during a performance

stag·er \'stā-jər\ *noun* (1570)
: an experienced person **:** VETERAN

stage right *noun* (1931)
: the right part of a stage from the viewpoint of one who faces the audience

stage set *noun* (1861)
: scenery and properties designed and arranged for a particular scene in a play

stage·struck \'stāj-ˌstrək\ *adjective* (1813)
: fascinated by the stage; *especially* **:** having an ardent desire to become an actor

stage whisper *noun* (circa 1865)
1 : a loud whisper by an actor that is audible to the spectators but is supposed for dramatic effect not to be heard by one or more of the actors
2 : an audible whisper
— **stage–whisper** *verb*

stag·fla·tion \ˌstag-'flā-shən\ *noun* [blend of *stagnation* and *inflation*] (1965)
: persistent inflation combined with stagnant consumer demand and relatively high unemployment
— **stag·fla·tion·ary** \-shə-ˌner-ē\ *adjective*

¹**stag·ger** \'sta-gər\ *verb* **stag·gered; stag·ger·ing** \-g(ə-)riŋ\ [alteration of earlier *stacker*, from Middle English *stakeren*, from Old Norse *stakra*, frequentative of *staka* to push; perhaps akin to Old English *staca* stake — more at STAKE] (15th century)
intransitive verb
1 a : to reel from side to side **:** TOTTER **b :** to move on unsteadily
2 : to waver in purpose or action **:** HESITATE
3 : to rock violently ⟨the ship *staggered*⟩
transitive verb
1 : to cause to doubt or hesitate **:** PERPLEX
2 : to cause to reel or totter
3 : to arrange in any of various zigzags, alternations, or overlappings of position or time ⟨*stagger* work shifts⟩ ⟨*stagger* teeth on a cutter⟩
— **stag·ger·er** \-gər-ər\ *noun*

²**stagger** *noun* (1577)
1 *plural but singular or plural in construction* **:** an abnormal condition of domestic mammals and birds associated with damage to the central nervous system and marked by incoordination and a reeling unsteady gait
2 : a reeling or unsteady gait or stance
3 : an arrangement in which the leading edge of the upper wing of a biplane is advanced over that of the lower

³**stagger** *adjective* (1875)
: marked by an alternating or overlapping pattern

stag·ger·bush \'sta-gər-ˌbu̇sh\ *noun* (1847)
: a shrubby heath (*Lyonia mariana*) of the eastern U.S. that is poisonous to livestock

staggering *adjective* (1530)
: so great as to cause one to stagger **:** ASTONISHING, OVERWHELMING ⟨a *staggering* feat⟩ ⟨*staggering* medical bills⟩
— **stag·ger·ing·ly** \'sta-g(ə-)riŋ-lē\ *adverb*

stag·gery \'sta-g(ə-)rē\ *adjective* (1778)
: UNSTEADY

stag·gy \'sta-gē\ *adjective* (1918)
: having the appearance of a mature male — used of female or castrated male domestic animals

stag·horn coral \'stag-ˌhȯrn-\ *noun* (1884)
: any of several large branching corals (genus *Acropora* and especially *A. cervicornis*) that somewhat resemble antlers

staghorn sumac *noun* (circa 1868)
: a sumac (*Rhus typhina*) of eastern North America that is a shrub or small tree with velvety-pubescent branches and flower stalks, leaves turning brilliant red in fall, and dense panicles of greenish yellow flowers followed by hairy crimson fruits

stag·hound \'stag-ˌhȧund\ *noun* (1707)
: a hound formerly used in hunting the stag and other large animals; *specifically* **:** a large heavy hound resembling the English foxhound

staghorn sumac

stag·ing \'stā-jiŋ\ *noun* (14th century)
1 : SCAFFOLDING
2 a : the business of running stagecoaches **b :** the act of journeying in stagecoaches
3 : the putting of a play on the stage
4 a : the moving of troops or matériel forward in several stages **b :** the assembling of troops or matériel in transit in a particular place

staging area *noun* (1943)
: an area in which participants in a new operation or mission are assembled and readied

Stag·i·rite \'sta-jə-ˌrīt\ *noun* [Greek *Stagiritēs*, from *Stagira*, city in ancient Macedonia] (circa 1620)
: a native or resident of Stagira ⟨Aristotle the *Stagirite*⟩

stag·nant \'stag-nənt\ *adjective* (1666)
1 a : not flowing in a current or stream ⟨*stagnant* water⟩ **b :** STALE ⟨long disuse had made the air *stagnant* and foul —Bram Stoker⟩
2 : not advancing or developing
— **stag·nan·cy** \-nən(t)-sē\ *noun*
— **stag·nant·ly** *adverb*

stag·nate \'stag-ˌnāt\ *intransitive verb* **stag·nat·ed; stag·nat·ing** [Latin *stagnatus*, past participle of *stagnare*, from *stagnum* body of standing water] (1669)
: to become or remain stagnant
— **stag·na·tion** \stag-'nā-shən\ *noun*

stagy \'stā-jē\ *or* **stag·ey** *adjective* **stag·i·er; -est** (1860)
: of or characteristic of the stage; *especially* **:** marked by pretense or artificiality **:** THEATRICAL
— **stag·i·ly** \-jə-lē\ *adverb*
— **stag·i·ness** \-jē-nəs\ *noun*

¹**staid** \'stād\ *adjective* [from past participle of ³*stay*] (1557)
: marked by settled sedateness and often prim self-restraint **:** SOBER, GRAVE
synonym see SERIOUS
— **staid·ly** *adverb*
— **staid·ness** *noun*

²**staid** *past and past participle of* STAY

¹**stain** \'stān\ *verb* [Middle English *steynen*, partly from Middle French *desteindre* to discolor & partly of Scandinavian origin; akin to Old Norse *steina* to paint — more at DISTAIN] (14th century)
transitive verb
1 : to suffuse with color
2 : DISCOLOR, SOIL
3 a : to taint with guilt, vice, or corruption **b :** to bring reproach on
4 : to color (as wood, glass, or cloth) by processes affecting chemically or otherwise the material itself
intransitive verb
: to receive a stain
— **stain·able** \'stā-nə-bəl\ *adjective*
— **stain·er** \'stā-nər\ *noun*

²**stain** *noun* (1583)
1 a : a soiled or discolored spot **b :** a natural spot of color contrasting with the ground
2 : a taint of guilt **:** STIGMA
3 a : a preparation (as of dye or pigment) used in staining; *especially* **:** one capable of penetrating the pores of wood **b :** a dye or mixture of dyes used in microscopy to make visible minute and transparent structures, to differentiate tissue elements, or to produce specific chemical reactions
— **stain-proof** \-ˌprüf\ *adjective*

stain·abil·i·ty \,stā-nə-'bi-lə-tē\ noun (1890)
: the capacity of cells and cell parts to stain specifically and consistently with particular dyes and stains

stained glass noun (1791)
: glass colored or stained (as by fusing metallic oxides into it) for decorative applications (as in windows)

¹**stain·less** \'stān-ləs\ adjective (1586)
1 a : free from stain or stigma **b :** highly resistant to stain or corrosion
2 : made from materials resistant to stain
— **stain·less·ly** adverb

²**stainless** noun (1945)
: tableware made of stainless steel

stainless steel noun (1920)
: an alloy of steel with chromium and sometimes another element (as nickel or molybdenum) that is practically immune to rusting and ordinary corrosion

stair \'star, 'ster\ noun [Middle English steir, from Old English stæger; akin to Old English & Old High German stīgan to rise, Greek steichein to walk] (before 12th century)
1 : a series of steps or flights of steps for passing from one level to another — often used in plural but singular or plural in construction ⟨a narrow private stairs —Lewis Mumford⟩
2 : a single step of a stairway

stair·case \-,kās\ noun (1624)
1 : the structure containing a stairway
2 : a flight of stairs with the supporting framework, casing, and balusters

stair·way \-,wā\ noun (1767)
: one or more flights of stairs usually with landings to pass from one level to another

stair·well \-,wel\ noun (1920)
: a vertical shaft in which stairs are located

¹**stake** \'stāk\ noun [Middle English, from Old English staca; akin to Middle Low German stake stake and perhaps to Latin tignum beam] (before 12th century)
1 : a pointed piece of wood or other material driven or to be driven into the ground as a marker or support
2 a : a post to which a person is bound for execution by burning **b :** execution by burning at a stake
3 a : something that is staked for gain or loss **b :** the prize in a contest **c :** an interest or share in an undertaking (as a commercial venture)
4 : a Mormon territorial jurisdiction comprising a group of wards
5 : an upright stick at the side or end of a vehicle to retain the load
6 : GRUBSTAKE
— **at stake :** at issue **:** in jeopardy

²**stake** transitive verb **staked; stak·ing** (14th century)
1 : to mark the limits of by or as if by stakes
2 : to tether to a stake
3 : BET, WAGER
4 : to fasten up or support (as plants) with stakes
5 : to back financially
6 : GRUBSTAKE
— **stake a claim :** to assert a title or right to something by or as if by placing stakes to satisfy a legal requirement

stake body noun (1907)
: an open motortruck body consisting of a platform with stakes inserted along the outside edges to retain a load

stake·hold·er \'stāk-,hōl-dər\ noun (1708)
: a person entrusted with the stakes of bettors

stake·out \'stā-,kaut\ noun (circa 1942)
: a surveillance maintained by the police of an area or a person suspected of criminal activity

stake out transitive verb (1951)
1 : to assign (as a police officer) to an area usually to conduct a surveillance
2 : to maintain a stakeout of

stake race noun (1896)

: a horse race in which the prize offered is made up at least in part of money (as entry fees) put up by the owners of the horses entered

stake truck noun (1907)
: a truck having a stake body

Sta·kha·nov·ite \stə-'kä-nə-,vīt\ noun [translation of Russian stakhanovets, from Alexei G. Stakhanov (died 1977) Russian miner] (1935)
: a Soviet industrial worker awarded recognition and special privileges for output beyond production norms
— **Sta·kha·nov·ism** \-,vi-zəm\ noun

sta·lac·tite \stə-'lak-,tīt also 'sta-lək-\ noun [New Latin stalactites, from Greek stalaktos dripping, from stalassein to let drip] (1677)
: a deposit of calcium carbonate (as calcite) resembling an icicle hanging from the roof or sides of a cavern
— **sta·lac·tit·ic** \,sta-(,)lak-'ti-tik, stə-,\ adjective

sta·lag \'stä-,läg\ noun [German, short for Stammlager base camp, from Stamm base + Lager camp] (1940)
: a German prison camp for noncommissioned officers or enlisted men; broadly : PRISON CAMP 2

sta·lag·mite \stə-'lag-,mīt also 'sta-ləg-\ noun [New Latin stalagmites, from Greek stalagma drop or stalagmos dripping, from stalassein to let drip] (1681)
: a deposit of calcium carbonate like an inverted stalactite formed on the floor of a cave by the drip of calcareous water
— **sta·lag·mit·ic** \,sta-(,)lag-'mi-tik, stə-\ adjective

stalactite and stalagmite

¹**stale** \'stā(ə)l\ adjective **stal·er; stal·est** [Middle English, aged (of ale), not fresh; akin to Middle Dutch stel stale] (15th century)
1 : tasteless or unpalatable from age
2 : tedious from familiarity
3 : impaired in legal force or effect by reason of being allowed to rest without timely use, action, or demand ⟨a stale affidavit⟩ ⟨a stale debt⟩
4 : impaired in vigor or effectiveness
— **stale·ly** \'stā(ə)l-lē\ adverb
— **stale·ness** noun

²**stale** verb **staled; stal·ing** (1599)
transitive verb
1 : to make stale
2 archaic : to make common : CHEAPEN
intransitive verb
: to become stale

³**stale** intransitive verb **staled; stal·ing** [Middle English; akin to Middle Low German stallen to urinate, stal urine of horses] (15th century)
: URINATE — used chiefly of camels and horses

⁴**stale** noun (1548)
: urine of a domestic animal (as a horse)

¹**stale·mate** \'stā(ə)l-,māt\ noun [obsolete English stale stalemate + English ¹mate] (1765)
1 : a drawing position in chess in which only the king can move and although not in check can move only into check
2 : a drawn contest : DEADLOCK; also : the state of being stalemated

²**stalemate** transitive verb (1765)
: to bring into a stalemate

Sta·lin·ism \'stä-lə-,ni-zəm, 'sta-\ noun (1927)
: the political, economic, and social principles and policies associated with Stalin; especially : the theory and practice of communism developed by Stalin from Marxism-Leninism and marked especially by rigid authoritarianism,

widespread use of terror, and often emphasis on Russian nationalism
— **Sta·lin·ist** \-nist\ noun or adjective
— **Sta·lin·ize** \-,nīz\ transitive verb
— **Sta·lin·oid** \-,nôid\ noun or adjective

¹**stalk** \'stök\ noun [Middle English stalke; akin to Old English stela stalk, support] (14th century)
1 : a slender upright object or supporting or connecting part; especially : PEDUNCLE ⟨the stalk of a crinoid⟩
2 a : the main stem of an herbaceous plant often with its dependent parts **b :** a part of a plant (as a petiole, stipe, or peduncle) that supports another
— **stalked** \'stökt\ adjective
— **stalk·less** \'stö-kləs\ adjective
— **stalky** \'stö-kē\ adjective

²**stalk** verb [Middle English, from Old English bestealcian; akin to Old English stelan to steal — more at STEAL] (14th century)
intransitive verb
1 : to pursue quarry or prey stealthily
2 : to walk stiffly or haughtily
transitive verb
1 : to pursue by stalking
2 : to go through (an area) in search of prey or quarry ⟨stalk the woods for deer⟩
— **stalk·er** noun

³**stalk** noun (14th century)
1 : the act of stalking
2 : a stalking gait

stalk·ing-horse \'stö-kiŋ-,hörs\ noun (1519)
1 : a horse or a figure like a horse behind which a hunter stalks game
2 : something used to mask a purpose
3 : a candidate put forward to divide the opposition or to conceal someone's real candidacy

¹**stall** \'stöl\ noun [Middle English, from Old English steall; akin to Old High German stal place, stall and perhaps to Latin locus (Old Latin stlocus) place] (before 12th century)
1 a : a compartment for a domestic animal in a stable or barn **b :** a space marked off for parking a motor vehicle
2 a : a seat in the chancel of a church with back and sides wholly or partly enclosed **b :** a church pew **c** chiefly British : a front orchestra seat in a theater — usually used in plural
3 : a booth, stand, or counter at which articles are displayed for sale
4 : a protective sheath for a finger or toe
5 : a small compartment ⟨a shower stall⟩

²**stall** (14th century)
transitive verb
1 : to put into or keep in a stall
2 obsolete : to install in office
3 a : to bring to a standstill : BLOCK; especially : MIRE **b :** to cause (an engine) to stop usually inadvertently **c :** to cause (an aircraft or airfoil) to go into a stall
intransitive verb
1 : to come to a standstill (as from mired wheels or engine failure)
2 : to experience a stall in flying

³**stall** noun (1916)
: the condition of an airfoil or aircraft in which excessive angle of attack causes disruption of airflow with attendant loss of lift

⁴**stall** noun [alteration of stale lure] (1903)
: a ruse to deceive or delay

⁵**stall** (1903)
intransitive verb
: to play for time : DELAY
transitive verb
: to hold off, divert, or delay by evasion or deception

stall-feed \'stöl-,fēd\ transitive verb **-fed** \-,fed\; **-feed·ing** (1554)

: to feed in a stall especially so as to fatten ⟨*stall-feed* an ox⟩

stall·hold·er \-ˌhōl-dər\ *noun* (1881)
chiefly British : one who manages a stall at which articles are sold

stal·lion \'stal-yən\ *noun* [Middle English *stalion*, from Middle French *estalon*, of Germanic origin; akin to Old High German *stal* stall] (14th century)
: an uncastrated male horse : a male horse kept for breeding; *also* : a male animal (as a dog or a sheep) kept primarily as a stud

¹stal·wart \'stȯl-wərt\ *adjective* [Middle English, alteration of *stalworth*, from Old English *stælwierthe* serviceable] (15th century)
: marked by outstanding strength and vigor of body, mind, or spirit ⟨*stalwart* common sense⟩
synonym see STRONG
— **stal·wart·ly** *adverb*
— **stal·wart·ness** *noun*

²stalwart *noun* (15th century)
1 : a stalwart person
2 : an unwavering partisan

stal·worth \'stȯl-(ˌ)wərth\ *archaic variant of* STALWART

sta·men \'stā-mən\ *noun, plural* **stamens** *also* **sta·mi·na** \'stā-mə-nə, -ˌstä-\ [Latin, warp, thread, from *stare* to stand — more at STAND] (1668)
: a microsporophyll of a seed plant; *specifically* : the pollen-producing male organ of a flower that consists of an anther and a filament — see FLOWER illustration

stamin- *combining form* [Latin *stamin-, stamen*]
: stamen ⟨*stamin*odium⟩

stam·i·na \'sta-mə-nə\ *noun* [Latin, plural of *stamen* warp, thread of life spun by the Fates] (1726)
: STAYING POWER, ENDURANCE ◇

sta·mi·nate \'stā-mə-nət, -ˌstä-, -ˌnāt\ *adjective* (circa 1850)
1 : having or producing stamens
2 *of a diclinous flower* : having stamens but no pistils

sta·mi·no·di·um \ˌstā-mə-ˈnō-dē-əm, ˌsta-\ *noun, plural* **-dia** \-dē-ə\ [New Latin, from *stamin-* + *-odium* thing resembling, from Greek *-ōdēs* like] (circa 1821)
: an abortive or sterile stamen

stam·mel \'sta-məl\ *noun* [probably from *stamin* a woolen fabric] (1530)
1 *obsolete* : a coarse woolen clothing fabric usually dyed red and used sometimes for undershirts of penitents
2 *archaic* : the bright red color of stammel

stam·mer \'sta-mər\ *verb* **stam·mered; stam·mer·ing** \'sta-mə-riŋ, 'stam-riŋ\ [Middle English *stameren*, from Old English *stamerian*; akin to Old High German *stamalōn* to stammer, Old Norse *stemma* to hinder, damn up — more at STEM] (before 12th century)
intransitive verb
: to make involuntary stops and repetitions in speaking : HALT — compare STUTTER
transitive verb
: to utter with involuntary stops or repetitions
— **stammer** *noun*
— **stam·mer·er** \-mər-ər\ *noun*

¹stamp \'stamp; *verb transitive & verb intransitive are also* 'stämp *or* 'stȯmp\ *verb* [Middle English; akin to Old High German *stampfōn* to stamp and perhaps to Greek *stembein* to shake up] (13th century)
transitive verb
1 : to pound or crush with a pestle or a heavy instrument
2 a (1) : to strike or beat forcibly with the bottom of the foot (2) : to bring down (the foot) forcibly **b** : to extinguish or destroy by or as if by stamping with the foot — usually used with *out* ⟨*stamp* out cancer⟩
3 a : IMPRESS, IMPRINT ⟨*stamp* "paid" on the bill⟩ **b** : to attach a stamp to

4 : to cut out, bend, or form with a stamp or die
5 a : to provide with a distinctive character ⟨*stamped* with a dreary, institutionalized look —Bernard Taper⟩ **b** : CHARACTERIZE
intransitive verb
1 : POUND 1
2 : to strike or thrust the foot forcibly or noisily downward

²stamp *noun* (15th century)
1 : a device or instrument for stamping
2 : the impression or mark made by stamping or imprinting
3 a : a distinctive character, indication, or mark **b** : a lasting imprint
4 : the act of stamping
5 : a stamped or printed paper affixed in evidence that a tax has been paid; *also* : POSTAGE STAMP
— **stamp·less** *adjective*

¹stam·pede \(ˌ)stam-ˈpēd\ *noun* [American Spanish *estampida*, from Spanish, crash, from *estampar* to stamp, of Germanic origin; akin to Old High German *stampfōn* to stamp] (1828)
1 : a wild headlong rush or flight of frightened animals
2 : a mass movement of people at a common impulse
3 : an extended festival combining a rodeo with exhibitions, contests, and social events

²stampede *verb* **stam·ped·ed; stam·ped·ing** (1838)
transitive verb
1 : to cause to run away in headlong panic
2 : to cause (as a group of people) to act on sudden or rash impulse
intransitive verb
1 : to flee headlong in panic
2 : to act on mass impulse
— **stam·ped·er** *noun*

stamp·er \'stam-pər, 'stäm-, 'stȯm-; *compare* ¹STAMP\ *noun* (14th century)
: one that stamps: as **a** : a worker who performs an industrial stamping operation **b** : an implement for pounding or stamping **c** : any of various stamping machines

stamping ground \'stam-piŋ, 'stäm-, 'stȯm-\ *noun* (1786)
: a favorite or habitual resort; *also* : familiar territory

stamp·ing mill \'stam-piŋ-\ *noun* (1552)
: STAMP MILL

stamp mill \'stamp-\ *noun* (1749)
: a mill in which ore is crushed with stamps; *also* : a machine for stamping ore

stamp tax *noun* (1797)
: a tax collected by means of a stamp purchased and affixed (as to a deck of playing cards); *specifically* : such a tax on a document (as a deed or promissory note) — called also **stamp duty**

stance \'stan(t)s\ *noun* [Middle French *estance* position, posture, stay, from (assumed) Vulgar Latin *stantia*, from Latin *stant-, stans*, present participle of *stare* to stand] (14th century)
1 *chiefly Scottish* **a** : STATION **b** : SITE
2 a : a way of standing or being placed : POSTURE **b** : intellectual or emotional attitude ⟨took an antiwar *stance*⟩
3 a : the position of the feet of a golfer or batter preparatory to making a swing **b** : the position of both body and feet from which an athlete starts or operates

¹stanch \'stȯnch, 'stänch, 'stanch\ *transitive verb* [Middle English *staunchen*, from Middle French *estancher*, perhaps from (assumed) Vulgar Latin *stanticare*, from Latin *stant-, stans*, present participle] (14th century)
1 : to check or stop the flowing of ⟨*stanched* her tears⟩; *also* : to stop the flow of blood from (a wound)
2 *archaic* : ALLAY, EXTINGUISH

3 a : to stop or check in its course ⟨trying to *stanch* the crime wave⟩ **b** : to make watertight : stop up
— **stanch·er** *noun*

²stanch *variant of* STAUNCH

stan·chion \'stan-chən\ *noun* [Middle English *stanchon*, from Middle French *estanchon*, from Old French, diminutive of *estance* stay, prop] (15th century)
1 : an upright bar, post, or support (as for a roof)
2 : a device that fits loosely around the neck of an animal (as a cow) and limits forward and backward motion (as in a stall)
— **stan·chioned** \-chənd\ *adjective*

¹stand \'stand\ *verb* **stood** \'stud\; **standing** [Middle English, from Old English *standan*; akin to Old High German *stantan, stān* to stand, Latin *stare*, Greek *histanai* to cause to stand, set, *histasthai* to stand, be standing] (before 12th century)
intransitive verb
1 a : to support oneself on the feet in an erect position **b** : to be a specified height when fully erect ⟨*stands* six feet two⟩ **c** : to rise to an erect position
2 a : to take up or maintain a specified position or posture ⟨*stand* aside⟩ ⟨can you *stand* on your head⟩ **b** : to maintain one's position ⟨*stand* firm⟩
3 : to be in a particular state or situation ⟨*stands* accused⟩
4 : to hold a course at sea
5 *obsolete* : HESITATE
6 a : to have or maintain a relative position in or as if in a graded scale ⟨*stands* first in the class⟩ **b** : to be in a position to gain or lose because of an action taken or a commitment made ⟨*stands* to make quite a profit⟩
7 *chiefly British* : to be a candidate : RUN
8 a : to rest or remain upright on a base or lower end ⟨a clock *stood* on the mantle⟩ **b** : to occupy a place or location ⟨the house *stands* on a knoll⟩
9 a : to remain stationary or inactive ⟨the car *stood* in the garage for a week⟩ **b** : to gather slowly and remain ⟨tears *standing* in her eyes⟩
10 : AGREE, ACCORD — used chiefly in the expression *it stands to reason*
11 a : to exist in a definite written or printed form ⟨copy a passage exactly as it *stands*⟩ **b** : to remain valid or efficacious (the order given last week still *stands*)
12 *of a male animal* : to be available as a sire — used especially of horses
transitive verb

1 a : to endure or undergo successfully ⟨this book will *stand* the test of time⟩ **b :** to tolerate without flinching **:** bear courageously ⟨*stands* pain well⟩ **c :** to endure the presence or personality of ⟨can't *stand* the boss⟩ **d :** to derive benefit or enjoyment from ⟨you look like you could *stand* a drink⟩ **2 :** to remain firm in the face of ⟨*stand* a siege⟩ **3 :** to submit to ⟨*stand* trial⟩ **4 a :** to perform the duty of ⟨*stand* guard⟩ **b :** to participate in (a military formation) **5 :** to pay the cost of (a treat) **:** pay for ⟨I'll *stand* you a dinner⟩ ⟨*stand* drinks⟩ **6 :** to cause to stand **:** set upright **7 :** to make available for breeding ⟨*stand* a stallion⟩
synonym see BEAR
— stand·er *noun*
— stand a chance : to have a chance
— stand for 1 : to be a symbol for **:** REPRESENT **2 :** to put up with **:** PERMIT
— stand on 1 : to depend on **2 :** to insist on ⟨never *stands on* ceremony⟩
— stand one's ground : to maintain one's position
— stand on one's own feet : to think or act independently
— stand treat : to pay the cost of food, drink, or entertainment for others in a group
²stand *noun* (1592)
1 : an act of stopping or staying in one place
2 a : a halt for defense or resistance **b :** an often defensive effort of some duration or degree of success ⟨a goal-line *stand*⟩ **c** (1) **:** a stop made to give a performance ⟨a 6-game *stand* at home⟩ (2) **:** a town where such a stop is made
3 a : a place or post where one stands **b :** a strongly or aggressively held position especially on a debatable issue
4 a : the place taken by a witness for testifying in court **b** *plural* (1) **:** a section of the tiered seats for spectators of a sport or spectacle (2) **:** the occupants of such seats **c :** a raised platform (as for a speaker) serving as a point of vantage
5 a : a small often open-air structure for a small retail business ⟨a vegetable *stand*⟩ ⟨a hot dog *stand*⟩ **b :** a site fit for business opportunity
6 : a place where a passenger vehicle stops or parks ⟨a taxi *stand*⟩
7 : HIVE 2
8 : a frame on or in which something may be placed for support
9 : a group of plants growing in a continuous area
10 : a standing posture
stand–alone \ˈstan-də-ˈlōn\ *adjective* (1966)
: SELF-CONTAINED; *especially* **:** operating or capable of operating independently of a computer system ⟨a *stand-alone* word processor⟩
¹stan·dard \ˈstan-dərd\ *noun* [Middle English, from Old French *estandard* rallying point, standard, of Germanic origin; akin to Old English *standan* to stand and to Old English *ord* point — more at ODD] (12th century)
1 : a conspicuous object (such as a banner) formerly carried at the top of a pole and used to mark a rallying point especially in battle or to serve as an emblem
2 a : a long narrow tapering flag that is personal to an individual or corporation and bears heraldic devices **b :** the personal flag of the head of a state or of a member of a royal family **c :** an organization flag carried by a mounted or motorized military unit **d :** BANNER
3 : something established by authority, custom, or general consent as a model or example **:** CRITERION
4 : something set up and established by authority as a rule for the measure of quantity, weight, extent, value, or quality

5 a : the fineness and legally fixed weight of the metal used in coins **b :** the basis of value in a monetary system
6 : a structure built for or serving as a base or support
7 a : a shrub or herb grown with an erect main stem so that it forms or resembles a tree **b :** a fruit tree grafted on a stock that does not induce dwarfing
8 a : the large odd upper petal of a papilionaceous flower (as the pea) **b :** one of the three inner usually erect and incurved petals of an iris
9 : a musical composition (as a song) that has become a part of the standard repertoire ☆
— stan·dard·less *adjective*
²standard *adjective* (1622)
1 a : constituting or conforming to a standard especially as established by law or custom ⟨*standard* weight⟩ **b :** sound and usable but not of top quality ⟨*standard* beef⟩
2 a : regularly and widely used, available, or supplied ⟨*standard* automobile equipment⟩ **b :** well-established and very familiar ⟨the *standard* opera⟩
3 : having recognized and permanent value ⟨a *standard* reference work⟩
4 : substantially uniform and well established by usage in the speech and writing of the educated and widely recognized as acceptable ⟨*standard* pronunciation is subject to regional variations⟩
— stan·dard·ly *adverb*
stan·dard–bear·er \ˈstan-dərd-ˌbar-ər, -ˌber-\ *noun* (15th century)
1 : one that bears a standard or banner
2 : the leader of an organization, movement, or party
stan·dard·bred \-ˌbred\ *noun, often capitalized* (1921)
: any of a breed of trotting and pacing horses developed in the U.S., noted for speed and stamina, and used especially in harness racing

standardbred

standard can·dle *noun* (1879)
: CANDELA
standard deviation *noun* (1894)
1 : a measure of the dispersion of a frequency distribution that is the square root of the arithmetic mean of the squares of the deviation of each of the class frequencies from the arithmetic mean of the frequency distribution; *also* **:** a similar quantity found by dividing by one less than the number of squares in the sum of squares instead of taking the arithmetic mean
2 : a parameter that indicates the way in which a probability function or a probability density function is centered around its mean and that is equal to the square root of the moment in which the deviation from the mean is squared
Standard English *noun* (1836)
: the English that with respect to spelling, grammar, pronunciation, and vocabulary is substantially uniform though not devoid of regional differences, that is well established by usage in the formal and informal speech and writing of the educated, and that is widely recognized as acceptable wherever English is spoken and understood
standard error *noun* (1897)
: the standard deviation of the probability function or probability density function of a random variable and especially of a statistic; *specifically* **:** the standard error of the mean of a sample from a population with a normal distribution that is equal to the standard deviation of the normal distribution divided by the square root of the sample size

standard gauge *noun* (1871)
: a railroad gauge of 4 feet 8½ inches
stan·dard·ise *British variant of* STANDARDIZE
stan·dard·ize \ˈstan-dər-ˌdīz\ *transitive verb* **-ized; -iz·ing** (1873)
1 : to compare with a standard
2 : to bring into conformity with a standard
— stan·dard·i·za·tion \ˌstan-dər-də-ˈzā-shən\ *noun*
standard of living (1902)
1 : the necessities, comforts, and luxuries enjoyed or aspired to by an individual or group
2 : a minimum of necessities, comforts, or luxuries held essential to maintaining a person or group in customary or proper status or circumstances
standard operating procedure *noun* (1952)
: established or prescribed methods to be followed routinely for the performance of designated operations or in designated situations — called also *standing operating procedure*
standard position *noun* (1950)
: the position of an angle with its vertex at the origin of a rectangular-coordinate system and its initial side coinciding with the positive x-axis
standard schnauzer *noun* (circa 1934)
: any of a breed of medium-sized schnauzers that attain a height at the highest point of the shoulder blades of 18 to 20 inches (46 to 51 centimeters) and have a pepper-and-salt or black coat
standard score *noun* (1928)
: an individual test score expressed as the deviation from the mean score of the group in units of standard deviation
standard time *noun* (1879)
: the time of a region or country that is established by law or general usage as civil time; *specifically* **:** the mean solar time of a meridian that is a multiple of 15 arbitrarily applied to a local area or to one of the 24 time zones and designated as a number of hours earlier or later than Greenwich time
stand·away \ˈstan-də-ˌwā\ *adjective* (1948)
: standing out from the body ⟨a *standaway* skirt⟩
¹stand·by \ˈstan(d)-ˌbī\ *noun, plural* **stand·bys** \-ˌbīz\ (1796)
1 a : one to be relied on especially in emergencies **b :** a favorite or reliable choice or resource
2 : one that is held in reserve ready for use **:** SUBSTITUTE

☆ **SYNONYMS**
Standard, criterion, gauge, yardstick, touchstone mean a means of determining what a thing should be. STANDARD applies to any definite rule, principle, or measure established by authority ⟨*standards* of behavior⟩. CRITERION may apply to anything used as a test of quality whether formulated as a rule or principle or not ⟨questioned the critic's *criteria* for excellence⟩. GAUGE applies to a means of testing a particular dimension (as thickness, depth, diameter) or figuratively a particular quality or aspect ⟨polls as a *gauge* of voter dissatisfaction⟩. YARDSTICK is an informal substitute for CRITERION that suggests quantity more often than quality ⟨housing construction as a *yardstick* of economic growth⟩. TOUCHSTONE suggests a simple test of the authenticity or value of something intangible ⟨fine service is one *touchstone* of a first-class restaurant⟩.

\ə\ abut \ᵊ\ kitten \ər\ further \a\ ash \ā\ ace
\ä\ mop, mar \aů\ out \ch\ chin \e\ bet \ē\ easy
\g\ go \i\ hit \ī\ ice \j\ job \ŋ\ sing \ō\ go
\ȯ\ law \ȯi\ boy \th\ thin \t͟h\ the \ü\ loot \ů\ foot
\y\ yet \zh\ vision *see also* Guide to Pronunciation

— **on standby** : ready or available for immediate action or use

²**standby** *adjective* (1882)
1 : held near at hand and ready for use ⟨a *standby* power plant⟩ ⟨*standby* equipment⟩
2 : relating to the act or condition of standing by ⟨*standby* duty⟩ ⟨*standby* period⟩
3 : of, relating to, or traveling by an airline service in which the passenger must wait for an available unreserved seat ⟨*standby* passengers⟩ ⟨a *standby* ticket⟩

³**standby** *adverb* (1971)
: on a standby basis ⟨fly *standby*⟩

stand by (13th century)
intransitive verb
1 : to be present; *also* : to remain apart or aloof
2 : to be or to get ready to act
transitive verb
: to remain loyal or faithful to : DEFEND

stand–down \'stan(d)-ˌdau̇n\ *noun* (circa 1919)
: a relaxation of status of a military unit or force from an alert or operational posture

stand down *intransitive verb* (1681)
1 : to leave the witness stand
2 *chiefly British* **a** : to go off duty **b** : to withdraw from a contest or from a position of leadership

stand·ee \stan-'dē\ *noun* (1856)
: one who occupies standing room

stand–in \'stan-ˌdin\ *noun* (circa 1928)
1 : someone employed to occupy an actor's place while lights and camera are readied
2 : SUBSTITUTE

stand in *intransitive verb* (1904)
: to act as a stand-in
— **stand in with** : to be in a specially favored position with

¹**stand·ing** \'stan-diŋ\ *adjective* (14th century)
1 a : not yet cut or harvested ⟨*standing* timber⟩ ⟨*standing* grain⟩ **b** : upright on the feet or base : ERECT ⟨the *standing* audience⟩
2 a : not being used or operated ⟨a *standing* factory⟩ **b** : not flowing : STAGNANT ⟨*standing* water⟩
3 a : remaining at the same level, degree, or amount for an indeterminate period ⟨a *standing* offer⟩ **b** : continuing in existence or use indefinitely
4 : established by law or custom
5 : not movable
6 : done from a standing position ⟨a *standing* jump⟩ ⟨a *standing* ovation⟩

²**standing** *noun* (15th century)
1 a : a place to stand in : LOCATION **b** : a position from which one may assert or enforce legal rights and duties
2 a : length of service or experience especially as determining rank, pay, or privilege **b** : position or condition in society or in a profession; *especially* : good reputation **c** : position relative to a standard of achievement or to achievements of competitors
3 : maintenance of position or condition : DURATION ⟨a custom of long *standing*⟩

standing army *noun* (1603)
: a permanent army of paid soldiers

standing committee *noun* (circa 1636)
: a permanent committee especially of a legislative body

standing crop *noun* (1861)
: the total amount or number of living things or of one kind of living thing (as an uncut farm crop, the fish in a pond, or organisms in an ecosystem) in a particular situation at any given time

standing O \-'ō\ *noun* [ovation] (1975)
: a standing ovation

standing order *noun* (1737)
: an instruction or prescribed procedure in force permanently or until changed or canceled; *especially* : any of the rules for the guidance and government of parliamentary procedure which endure through successive sessions until vacated or repealed

standing room *noun* (1603)
: space for standing; *especially* : accommodation available for spectators or passengers after all seats are filled

standing wave *noun* (1896)
: a single-frequency mode of vibration of a body or physical system in which the amplitude varies from place to place, is constantly zero at fixed points, and has maxima at other points

stan·dish \'stan-dish\ *noun* [Middle English *standyshe*] (14th century)
: a stand for writing materials : INKSTAND

¹**stand–off** \'stan-ˌdȯf\ *adjective* (1837)
1 : STANDOFFISH
2 : used for holding something at a distance from a surface ⟨a *standoff* insulator⟩

²**standoff** *noun* (1843)
1 a : TIE, DEADLOCK ⟨the two teams played to a *standoff*⟩ **b** : a counterbalancing effect
2 : the act of standing off

stand off (1601)
intransitive verb
1 : to stay at a distance from something
2 : to sail away from the shore
transitive verb
1 : to keep from advancing : REPEL
2 : PUT OFF, STALL

stand·off·ish \stan-'dȯ-fish\ *adjective* (1860)
: somewhat cold and reserved
— **stand·off·ish·ly** *adverb*
— **stand·off·ish·ness** *noun*

stand oil *noun* (1908)
: a thickened drying oil; *especially* : linseed oil heated to about 600° F (315° C)

stand·out \'stan-ˌdau̇t\ *noun, often attributive* (1928)
: one that is prominent or conspicuous especially because of excellence

stand out *intransitive verb* (15th century)
1 a : to appear as if in relief : PROJECT **b** : to be prominent or conspicuous
2 : to steer away from shore
3 : to be stubborn in resolution or resistance

stand·pat \'stan(d)-'pat\ *adjective* (1904)
: stubbornly conservative : resisting or opposing change

stand pat *intransitive verb* [⁴*pat*] (1882)
1 : to play one's hand as dealt in draw poker without drawing
2 : to oppose or resist change
— **stand·pat·ter** \'stan(d)-ˌpa-tər, -'pa-tər\ *noun*
— **stand·pat·tism** \-ˌpa-ˌti-zəm\ *noun*

stand·pipe \'stan(d)-ˌpīp\ *noun* (circa 1850)
: a high vertical pipe or reservoir that is used to secure a uniform pressure in a water-supply system

stand·point \-ˌpȯint\ *noun* (1829)
: a position from which objects or principles are viewed and according to which they are compared and judged

stand·still \-ˌstil\ *noun* (1702)
: a state characterized by absence of motion or of progress : STOP

¹**stand–up** \'stan-ˌdəp\ *adjective* (1812)
1 a : ERECT, UPRIGHT **b** : stiffened to stay upright without folding over ⟨a *stand-up* collar⟩
2 : performed in, performing in, or requiring a standing position ⟨a *stand-up* bar⟩; *especially* : of, relating to, performing, or being a monologue of jokes, gags, or satirical comments delivered usually while standing alone on a stage or in front of a camera ⟨*stand-up* comedy⟩ ⟨a *stand-up* comedian⟩

²**stand–up** *noun* (1971)
: stand-up comedy

stand up (before 12th century)
intransitive verb
1 : to rise to a standing position
2 : to remain sound and intact under stress, attack, or close scrutiny
transitive verb
: to fail to keep an appointment with
— **stand up for** : to defend against attack or criticism

— **stand up to 1** : to meet fairly and fully
2 : to face boldly
— **stand up with** : to be best man or maid of honor for at a wedding ceremony

stand–up–per \'stan-'də-pər\ *noun* (1973)
: a television news report or interview by an on-camera reporter standing usually at the scene of an occurrence

stane \'stān\ *Scottish variant of* STONE

Stan·ford–Bi·net test \ˌstan-fərd-bi-'nā-\ *noun* [*Stanford* University + Alfred *Binet* (died 1911) French psychologist] (1918)
: an intelligence test prepared at Stanford University as a revision of the Binet-Simon scale and commonly used with children — called also *Stanford-Binet*

¹**stang** \'staŋ\ *transitive verb* [Middle English, from Old Norse *stanga* to prick; akin to Old Norse *stinga* to sting] (14th century)
chiefly Scottish : STING

²**stang** *noun* (1513)
chiefly Scottish : PANG

³**stang** *variant of* SATANG

stan·hope \'sta-nəp\ *noun* [Fitzroy *Stanhope* (died 1864) British clergyman] (1825)
: a gig, buggy, or phaeton typically having a high seat and closed back

sta·nine \'stā-ˌnīn\ *noun* [*sta*ndard (score) + *nine*] (1944)
: any of the nine classes into which a set of normalized standard scores arranged according to rank in educational testing are divided, which include the bottom 4% and the top 4% of the scores in the first and ninth classes and the middle 20% in the fifth, and which have a standard deviation of 2 and a mean of 5

Sta·ni·slav·ski method \ˌsta-nə-'slaf-ski-, -'slav-\ *noun* [Konstantin *Stanislavsky*] (1941)
: a technique in acting by which an actor strives to empathize with the character being portrayed so as to effect a realistic interpretation

¹**stank** \'staŋk\ *past of* STINK

²**stank** *noun* [Middle English, from Middle French *estanc*, from *estancher* to dam up, stanch — more at STANCH] (14th century)
1 *dialect British* **a** : POND, POOL **b** : a ditch containing water
2 *British* : a small dam : WEIR

stan·na·ry \'sta-nə-rē\ *noun, plural* **-ries** [Middle English *stannarie*, from Medieval Latin *stannaria* tin mine, from Late Latin *stannum* tin] (15th century)
: any of the regions in England containing establishments for the working of tin — usually used in plural

stan·nic \'sta-nik\ *adjective* [probably from French *stannique*, from Late Latin *stannum* tin, from Latin *stagnum*, an alloy of silver and lead] (1790)
: of, relating to, or containing tin especially with a valence of four

stan·nite \'sta-ˌnīt\ *noun* [Late Latin *stannum*] (1868)
: a mineral that is a steel-gray or iron-black sulfide of copper, iron, and tin with a metallic luster and occurs in granular masses

stan·nous \'sta-nəs\ *adjective* [International Scientific Vocabulary, from Late Latin *stannum*] (1849)
: of, relating to, or containing tin especially with a valence of two

stan·za \'stan-zə\ *noun* [Italian, stay, abode, room, stanza, from (assumed) Vulgar Latin *stantia* stay — more at STANCE] (1588)
: a division of a poem consisting of a series of lines arranged together in a usually recurring pattern of meter and rhyme : STROPHE
— **stan·za·ic** \stan-'zā-ik\ *adjective*

sta·pe·dec·to·my \ˌstā-pi-'dek-tə-mē\ *noun, plural* **-mies** [International Scientific Vocabulary, from New Latin *staped-, stapes*] (1894)
: surgical removal and prosthetic replacement of part or all of the stapes to relieve deafness

sta·pe·di·al \stā-'pē-dē-əl, stə-\ adjective (circa 1859)
: of, relating to, or located near the stapes

sta·pe·lia \stə-'pēl-yə\ noun [New Latin, from J. B. van Stapel (died 1636) Dutch botanist] (circa 1785)
: any of a genus (Stapelia) of African perennial herbs of the milkweed family with succulent typically leafless toothed stems like cactus joints and showy but usually putrid-smelling flowers

sta·pes \'stā-(,)pēz\ noun, plural **stapes** or **sta·pe·des** \'stā-pə-,dēz\ [New Latin staped-, stapes, from Medieval Latin, stirrup, alteration of Late Latin stapia] (1670)
: the innermost ossicle of the ear of mammals — called also stirrup; see EAR illustration

staph \'staf\ noun (circa 1933)
: STAPHYLOCOCCUS

staph·y·li·nid \sta-fə-'lī-nəd\ noun [New Latin Staphylinidae, ultimately from Greek staphylē bunch of grapes] (circa 1891)
: ROVE BEETLE
— **staphylinid** adjective

staph·y·lo·coc·cal \sta-f(ə-)lō-'kä-kəl\ also **staph·y·lo·coc·cic** \-'kä-kik, -'käk-sik\ adjective (1900)
: of, relating to, caused by, or being a staphylococcus

staph·y·lo·coc·cus \-'kä-kəs\ noun, plural **-coc·ci** \-'kä-,kī, -(,)kē-; -'käk-,sī, -(,)sē\ [New Latin, from Greek staphylē bunch of grapes + New Latin -coccus] (1887)
: any of various nonmotile gram-positive spherical bacteria (especially genus Staphylococcus) that occur singly, in pairs or tetrads, or in irregular clusters and include pathogens which infect skin and mucous membranes

¹sta·ple \'stā-pəl\ noun [Middle English stapel post, staple, from Old English stapol post; akin to Middle Dutch stapel step, heap, emporium, Old English steppan to step] (13th century)
1 : a U-shaped metal loop both ends of which are driven into a surface to hold the hook, hasp, or bolt of a lock, secure a rope, or fix a wire in place
2 : a small U-shaped wire both ends of which are driven through layers of thin and easily penetrable material (as paper) and usually clinched to hold the layers together

²staple transitive verb **sta·pled; sta·pling** \-p(ə-)liŋ\ (14th century)
: to provide with or secure by staples

³staple noun [Middle English, from Middle French estaple, from Middle Dutch stapel emporium] (14th century)
1 : a town used as a center for the sale or exportation of commodities in bulk
2 : a place of supply : SOURCE
3 : a chief commodity or production of a place
4 a : a commodity for which the demand is constant b : something having widespread and constant use or appeal c : the sustaining or principal element : SUBSTANCE
5 : RAW MATERIAL
6 a : textile fiber (as wool and rayon) of relatively short length that when spun and twisted forms a yarn rather than a filament b : the length of a piece of such textile fiber

⁴staple adjective (1615)
1 : used, needed, or enjoyed constantly usually by many individuals
2 : produced regularly or in large quantities ⟨staple crops such as wheat and rice⟩
3 : PRINCIPAL, CHIEF

¹sta·pler \'stā-p(ə-)lər\ noun (circa 1513)
: one that deals in staple goods or in staple fiber

²stapler noun (circa 1909)
: one that inserts staples; especially : a small usually hand-operated device for inserting wire staples

¹star \'stär\ noun, often attributive [Middle English sterre, from Old English steorra; akin to Old High German sterno star, Latin stella, Greek astēr, astron] (before 12th century)
1 a : a natural luminous body visible in the sky especially at night b : a self-luminous gaseous celestial body of great mass which produces energy by means of nuclear fusion reactions, whose shape is usually spheroidal, and whose size may be as small as the earth or larger than the earth's orbit
2 a (1) : a planet or a configuration of the planets that is held in astrology to influence one's destiny or fortune — usually used in plural (2) : a waxing or waning fortune or fame ⟨her star was rising⟩ b obsolete : DESTINY
3 a : a conventional figure with five or more points that represents a star; especially : ASTERISK b : an other star-shaped ornament or medal worn as a badge of honor, authority, or rank or as the insignia of an order c : one of a group of conventional stars used to place something in a scale of value
4 : something resembling a star ⟨was hit on the head and saw stars⟩
5 a : the principal member of a theatrical or operatic company who usually plays the chief roles b : a highly publicized theatrical or motion-picture performer c : an outstandingly talented performer ⟨a track star⟩ d : a person who is preeminent in a particular field
— **star·less** \-ləs\ adjective
— **star·like** \-,līk\ adjective

²star verb **starred; star·ring** (1718)
transitive verb
1 : to sprinkle or adorn with stars
2 a : to mark with a star as being preeminent b : to mark with an asterisk
3 : to advertise or display prominently : FEATURE ⟨the movie stars a famous stage personality⟩
intransitive verb
1 : to play the most prominent or important role
2 : to perform outstandingly

³star adjective (1832)
1 : of, relating to, or being a star ⟨received star billing⟩
2 : of outstanding excellence : PREEMINENT ⟨a star athlete⟩

star apple noun (1683)
: a tropical American tree (Chrysophyllum cainito) of the sapodilla family grown in warm regions for ornament or fruit; also : its usually green to purple apple-shaped edible fruit

¹star·board \'stär-bərd\ noun [Middle English sterbord, from Old English stēorbord, from stēor- steering oar + bord ship's side — more at STEER, BOARD] (before 12th century)
: the right side of a ship or aircraft looking forward — compare PORT ◇

²starboard adjective (15th century)
: of, relating to, or situated to starboard

³starboard transitive verb (1598)
: to turn or put (a helm or rudder) to the right

¹starch \'stärch\ transitive verb [Middle English sterchen, probably from (assumed) Old English stercan to stiffen; akin to Old English stearc stiff — more at STARK] (15th century)
: to stiffen with or as if with starch

²starch noun (15th century)
1 : a white odorless tasteless granular or powdery complex carbohydrate $(C_6H_{10}O_5)_x$ that has the chief storage form of carbohydrate in plants, is an important foodstuff, and is used also in adhesives and sizes, in laundering, and in pharmacy and medicine
2 : a stiff formal manner : FORMALITY
3 : resolute vigor

star–cham·ber \'stär-'chām-bər\ adjective [Star Chamber, a court existing in England from the 15th century until 1641] (1800)
: characterized by secrecy and often being irresponsibly arbitrary and oppressive

starchy \'stär-chē\ adjective **starch·i·er; -est** (1802)
1 : containing, consisting of, or resembling starch

2 : consisting of or marked by formality or stiffness
— **starch·i·ly** \-chə-lē\ adverb
— **starch·i·ness** \-chē-nəs\ noun

star–crossed \'stär-,krȯst\ adjective (1592)
: not favored by the stars : ILL-FATED ⟨a pair of star-crossed lovers take their life —Shakespeare⟩

star·dom \'stär-dəm\ noun (1865)
: the status or position of a star

star·dust \'stär-,dəst\ noun (1927)
: a feeling or impression of romance, magic, or ethereality

¹stare \'star, 'ster\ verb **stared; star·ing** [Middle English, from Old English starian; akin to Old High German starēn to stare, Greek stereos solid, Lithuanian starinti to stiffen] (before 12th century)
intransitive verb
1 : to look fixedly often with wide-open eyes
2 : to show oneself conspicuously ⟨the error stared from the page⟩
3 of hair : to stand on end : BRISTLE; also : to appear rough and lusterless
transitive verb
1 : to have an effect on by staring
2 : to look at with a searching or earnest gaze
— **star·er** noun
— **stare one in the face** : to be undeniably and forcefully evident or apparent

²stare noun (15th century)
: the act or an instance of staring ⟨a blank stare⟩

sta·re de·ci·sis \,ster-ē-di-'sī-səs, ,star-, ,stär-\ noun [Latin, to stand by decided matters] (1782)
: a doctrine or policy of following rules or principles laid down in previous judicial decisions unless they contravene the ordinary principles of justice

stare down transitive verb (1925)
: to cause to waver or submit by or as if by staring

sta·rets \'stär-əts, -yəts\ noun, plural **star·tsy** \'stärt-sē\ [Russian, from staryĭ old — more at STOUR] (1917)
: a spiritual director or religious teacher in the Eastern Orthodox Church; specifically : a spiritual adviser who is not necessarily a priest,

◇ WORD HISTORY
starboard Appearances to the contrary notwithstanding, the star- in starboard has nothing to do with the stars. The word starboard descends from Old English stēorbord, a compound of stēor "steering oar, rudder" and bord "side of a ship." Early Germanic craft such as those used by the Angles and Saxons who invaded Britain were steered by means of a long oar attached to the right of the ship; the right side was hence the "steering side." Stēor is related to the Modern English verb steer. Bord is the ancestor of Modern English board, though the sense "side of a ship" is now rare outside of compounds such as overboard. Starboard used to be contrasted with larboard, in Middle English laddebord, the first element of which has never been identified with certainty. English-speaking navies replaced larboard in the 19th century with port, first attested in the verb phrase to port the helm (turn the ship to the left) in the 16th century. Port, too, is a nautical mystery, since there is no sure connection between the left side of a ship and port meaning "harbor" or "gate."

who is recognized for his piety, and who is turned to by monks or laymen for spiritual guidance

star facet *noun* (1751)
: one of the eight small triangular facets which abut on the table in the bezel of a brilliant

star·fish \'stär-ˌfish\ *noun* (1538)
: any of a class (Asteroidea) of echinoderms having a body of usually five radially disposed arms about a central disk and feeding largely on mollusks (as oysters) — called also *sea star*

star·flow·er \-ˌflaú-(-ə)r\ *noun* (1629)
: any of several plants having star-shaped pentamerous flowers; *especially* : any of a genus (*Trientalis*, especially *T. borealis*) of perennial herbs of the primrose family

star fruit *noun* (1974)
: CARAMBOLA 1

star·gaze \-ˌgāz\ *intransitive verb* [back-formation from *stargazer*] (1626)
1 : to gaze at stars
2 : to gaze raptly or contemplatively

star·gaz·er \-ˌgā-zər\ *noun* (1560)
1 : one who gazes at the stars: as **a** : ASTROLOGER **b** : ASTRONOMER
2 : any of various marine bony fishes (families Uranoscopidae and Dactyloscopidae) with the eyes on top of a blocky or conical head

star·gaz·ing \-ˌgā-ziŋ\ *noun* (1576)
1 : the act or practice of a stargazer
2 a : absorption in chimerical or impractical ideas : WOOLGATHERING **b** : the quality or state of being absentminded

star grass *noun* (1687)
: any of various grassy plants with stellate flowers or arrangement of leaves: as **a** : any of a genus (*Hypoxis*) of herbs of the amaryllis family **b** : either of two colicroots (*Aletris farinosa* and *A. aurea*)

¹stark \'stärk\ *adjective* [Middle English, stiff, strong, from Old English *stearc;* akin to Old High German *starc* strong, Lithuanian *starinti* to stiffen — more at STARE] (before 12th century)
1 a : rigid in or as if in death **b** : rigidly conforming (as to a pattern or doctrine) : ABSOLUTE ⟨*stark* discipline⟩
2 *archaic* : STRONG, ROBUST
3 : UTTER, SHEER ⟨*stark* nonsense⟩
4 a : BARREN, DESOLATE **b** (1) : having few or no ornaments : BARE ⟨a *stark* white room⟩ (2) : HARSH, BLUNT ⟨the *stark* realities of death⟩
5 : sharply delineated ⟨a *stark* contrast⟩
— **stark·ly** *adverb*
— **stark·ness** *noun*

²stark *adverb* (13th century)
1 : in a stark manner
2 : to an absolute or complete degree : WHOLLY ⟨*stark* naked⟩ ⟨*stark* mad⟩

stark·ers \'stär-kərz\ *adjective* [alteration of ¹*stark*] (circa 1923)
chiefly British : completely unclothed : NAKED
word history SEE NUTS

star·let \'stär-lət\ *noun* (1920)
: a young movie actress being coached and publicized for starring roles

star·light \-ˌlīt\ *noun* (14th century)
: the light given by the stars

star·ling \'stär-liŋ\ *noun* [Middle English, from Old English *stærlinc,* from *stær* starling + *-ling, -linc* -ling; akin to Old High German *stara* starling, Latin *sturnus*] (before 12th century)
: any of a family (Sturnidae, especially genus *Sturnus*) of usually dark gregarious oscine birds; *especially* : a dark brown or in summer glossy greenish black European bird (*S. vulgaris*) naturalized nearly worldwide and often considered a pest

star·lit \'stär-ˌlit\ *adjective* (circa 1835)
: lighted by the stars

star-nosed mole \'stär-ˌnōz(d)-\ *noun* (1826)

: a common black long-tailed semi-aquatic mole (*Condylura cristata*) of the northeastern U.S. and adjacent Canada that has a series of pink fleshy projections surrounding the nostrils

star-nosed mole

star–of–Beth·le·hem \-'beth-li-ˌhem, -lē-(h)əm\ *noun* (1573)
: any of various Old World bulbous herbs (genus *Ornithogalum*) of the lily family with basal leaves resembling grass; *especially* : one (*O. umbellatum*) with white flowers that is naturalized in the eastern U.S.

star of Bethlehem
: a star which according to Christian tradition guided the Magi to the infant Jesus in Bethlehem

Star of Da·vid \-'dā-vəd\ (circa 1936)
: MAGEN DAVID

star route *noun* [so called from the asterisk used to designate such routes in postal publications] (1880)
: a mail-delivery route in a rural or thinly populated area served by a private carrier under contract who takes mail from one post office to another or from a railroad station to a post office and usually also delivers mail to private mailboxes along the route

star·ry \'stär-ē\ *adjective* **star·ri·er; -est** (14th century)
1 a : adorned with stars; *especially* : STAR-STUDDED **b** : of, relating to, or consisting of stars : STELLAR **c** : shining like stars : SPARKLING **d** : having parts arranged like the rays of a star : STELLATE
2 : as high as or seemingly as high as the stars ⟨*starry* speculations⟩
3 : STARRY-EYED

star·ry–eyed \'stär-ē-ˌīd\ *adjective* (1904)
: regarding an object or a prospect in an overly favorable light; *specifically* : characterized by dreamy, impracticable, or utopian thinking : VISIONARY

Stars and Bars *noun plural but singular in construction* (1861)
: the first flag of the Confederate States of America having three bars of red, white, and red respectively and a blue union with white stars in a circle representing the seceded states

Stars and Stripes *noun plural but singular in construction* (1777)
: the flag of the United States having 13 alternately red and white horizontal stripes and a blue union with white stars representing the states

star sapphire *noun* (circa 1817)
: a sapphire that when cut with a convex surface and polished exhibits asterism

star shell *noun* (circa 1876)
1 : a shell that on bursting releases a shower of brilliant stars and is used for signaling
2 : a shell with an illuminating projectile

star·ship \'stär-ˌship\ *noun* (1934)
: a spacecraft designed for interstellar travel

star–span·gled \'stär-ˌspaŋ-gəld\ *adjective* (1591)
: STAR-STUDDED

star·struck \-ˌstrək\ *adjective* (1968)
: particularly taken with celebrities (as movie stars)

star–stud·ded \'stär-ˌstə-dəd\ *adjective* (1955)
: abounding in or covered with stars ⟨a *star-studded* cast⟩ ⟨a *star-studded* uniform⟩

star system *noun* (1902)
: the practice of casting famous performers in principal roles (as in motion pictures or the theater) especially in order to capitalize on their popular appeal

¹start \'stärt\ *verb* [Middle English *sterten;* akin to Middle High German *sterzen* to stand up stiffly, move quickly] (14th century)
intransitive verb
1 a : to move suddenly and violently : SPRING ⟨*started* angrily to his feet⟩ **b** : to react with a sudden brief involuntary movement ⟨*started* when a shot rang out⟩
2 a : to issue with sudden force ⟨blood *starting* from the wound⟩ **b** : to come into being, activity, or operation ⟨when does the movie *start*⟩ ⟨the rain *started* up again⟩
3 : to protrude or seem to protrude ⟨eyes *starting* from their sockets⟩
4 : to become loosened or forced out of place ⟨one of the planks has *started*⟩
5 a : to begin a course or journey ⟨*started* toward the door⟩ ⟨just *starting* out⟩ **b** : to range from a specified initial point ⟨the rates *start* at $10⟩
6 : to begin an activity or undertaking; *especially* : to begin work
7 : to be a participant in a game or contest; *especially* : to be in the starting lineup
transitive verb
1 : to cause to leave a place of concealment : FLUSH ⟨*start* a rabbit⟩
2 *archaic* : STARTLE, ALARM
3 : to bring up for consideration or discussion
4 : to bring into being ⟨*start* a rumor⟩
5 : to cause to become loosened or displaced
6 : to begin the use of ⟨*start* a fresh loaf of bread⟩
7 a : to cause to move, act, or operate ⟨*start* the motor⟩ **b** : to cause to enter a game or contest; *especially* : to put in the starting lineup **c** : to care for or train during the early stages of growth and development ⟨*started* plants⟩ ⟨a well-*started* coonhound⟩
8 : to do or experience the first stages or actions of ⟨*started* studying music at the age of five⟩
synonym see BEGIN
— **start something** *also* **start anything** : to make trouble ⟨always trying to *start something*⟩ ⟨don't *start anything*⟩
— **to start with 1** : at the beginning : INITIALLY **2** : in any event

²start *noun* (14th century)
1 a : a sudden involuntary bodily movement or reaction ⟨woke with a *start*⟩ **b** : a brief and sudden action or movement **c** : a sudden capricious impulse or outburst
2 : a beginning of movement, activity, or development ⟨a false *start*⟩ ⟨housing *starts*⟩
3 : HEAD START
4 : a place of beginning
5 : the act or an instance of being a competitor in a race or a member of a starting lineup in a game ⟨undefeated in six *starts* —*Current Biography*⟩

start·er \'stär-tər\ *noun* (1622)
1 : a person who initiates or sets going: as **a** : an official who gives the signal to begin a race **b** : one who dispatches vehicles
2 a : one that engages in a competition; *especially* : a member of a starting lineup **b** : one that begins to engage in an activity or process
3 : one that causes something to begin operating: as **a** : a device for starting an engine; *especially* : an electric motor used to start an internal combustion engine **b** : material containing microorganisms used to induce a desired fermentation
4 : something that is the beginning of a process, activity, or series; *especially* : APPETIZER
— **for starters** : to begin with

star thistle *noun* (1578)
1 : a widely naturalized spiny European knapweed (*Centaurea calcitrapa*) with purple flowers — called also *caltrops*
2 : any of various knapweeds related to the star thistle

starting block *noun* (1937)
: a device that consists of two blocks mounted on either side of an adjustable frame which is usually anchored to the ground and that provides a runner with a rigid surface against which to brace the feet at the start of a race

starting gate *noun* (1898) **starting block**
1 : a mechanically operated barrier used as a starting device for a race
2 : a barrier that when knocked aside by a competitor (as a skier) starts an electronic timing device

¹**star·tle** \'stär-t°l\ *verb* **star·tled; star·tling** \'stärt-liŋ, 'stär-t°l-iŋ\ [Middle English *stertlen*, frequentative of *sterten* to start] (1530)
intransitive verb
: to move or jump suddenly (as in surprise or alarm) ⟨the baby *startles* easily⟩
transitive verb
: to frighten or surprise suddenly and usually not seriously
— **star·tle·ment** \-mənt\ *noun*
²**startle** *noun* (1714)
: a sudden mild shock (as of surprise or alarm)
star·tling *adjective* (1714)
: causing momentary fright, surprise, or astonishment
— **star·tling·ly** \'stärt-liŋ-lē, 'stär-t°l-iŋ-\ *adverb*
start-up \'stärt-,əp\ *noun, often attributive* (1845)
1 : the act or an instance of setting in operation or motion
2 : a fledgling business enterprise
star turn *noun* (1898)
chiefly British : the featured skit or number in a theatrical production; *broadly* : the most widely publicized person or item in a group
star·va·tion \stär-'vā-shən\ *noun* (1778)
1 : the act or an instance of starving
2 : the state of being starved
starvation wages *noun* (1898)
: wages insufficient to provide the ordinary necessities of life
starve \'stärv\ *verb* **starved; starv·ing** [Middle English *sterven* to die, starve, from Old English *steorfan* to die; akin to Old High German *sterban* to die, Lithuanian *starinti* to stiffen — more at STARE] (15th century)
intransitive verb
1 a : to perish from lack of food **b** : to suffer extreme hunger
2 a *archaic* : to die of cold **b** *British* : to suffer greatly from cold
3 : to suffer or perish from deprivation ⟨*starved* for affection⟩
transitive verb
1 a : to kill with hunger **b** : to deprive of nourishment **c** : to cause to capitulate by or as if by depriving of nourishment
2 : to destroy by or cause to suffer from deprivation
3 *archaic* : to kill with cold
¹**starve·ling** \'stärv-liŋ\ *noun* (1546)
: one that is thin from or as if from lack of food
²**starveling** *adjective* (1597)
: being a starveling; *also* : marked by poverty or inadequacy ⟨*starveling* wages⟩
¹**stash** \'stash\ *transitive verb* [origin unknown] (1785)
: to store in a usually secret place for future use — often used with *away*
²**stash** *noun* (circa 1914)
1 : hiding place : CACHE

2 : something stored or hidden away ⟨a *stash* of narcotics⟩
sta·sis \'stā-səs, 'sta-\ *noun, plural* **sta·ses** \'stā-,sēz, 'sta-\ [New Latin, from Greek, act or condition of standing, stopping, from *histasthai* to stand — more at STAND] (1745)
1 : a slowing or stoppage of the normal flow of a bodily fluid or semifluid: as **a** : slowing of the current of circulating blood **b** : reduced motility of the intestines with retention of feces
2 : a state of static balance or equilibrium : STAGNATION
-stasis *noun combining form, plural* **-stases** [New Latin, from Greek *stasis*]
1 : stoppage : slowing ⟨hemo*stasis*⟩ ⟨bacterio*stasis*⟩
2 : stable state ⟨homeo*stasis*⟩
stat \'stat\ *noun* (circa 1961)
: STATISTIC
-stat *noun combining form* [New Latin *-stata*, from Greek *-statēs* one that stops or steadies, from *histanai* to cause to stand — more at STAND]
1 : stabilizing agent or device ⟨thermo*stat*⟩
2 : instrument for reflecting (something specified) constantly in one direction ⟨helio*stat*⟩
3 : agent causing inhibition of growth without destruction ⟨bacterio*stat*⟩
sta·tant \'stā-t°nt\ *adjective* [Latin *status*, past participle + English *-ant*] (circa 1500)
: standing in profile with all feet on the ground — used of a heraldic animal
¹**state** \'stāt\ *noun, often attributive* [Middle English *stat*, from Old French & Latin; Old French *estat*, from Latin *status*, from *stare* to stand — more at STAND] (13th century)
1 a : mode or condition of being ⟨a *state* of readiness⟩ **b** (1) : condition of mind or temperament ⟨in a highly nervous *state*⟩ (2) : a condition of abnormal tension or excitement
2 a : a condition or stage in the physical being of something ⟨insects in the larval *state*⟩ ⟨the gaseous *state* of water⟩ **b** : any of various conditions characterized by definite quantities (as of energy, angular momentum, or magnetic moment) in which an atomic system may exist
3 a : social position; *especially* : high rank **b** (1) : elaborate or luxurious style of living (2) : formal dignity : POMP — usually used with *in*
4 a : a body of persons constituting a special class in a society : ESTATE 3 **b** *plural* : the members or representatives of the governing classes assembled in a legislative body **c** *obsolete* : a person of high rank (as a noble)
5 a : a politically organized body of people usually occupying a definite territory; *especially* : one that is sovereign **b** : the political organization of such a body of people **c** : a government or politically organized society having a particular character ⟨a police *state*⟩ ⟨the welfare *state*⟩
6 : the operations or concerns of the government of a country
7 a : one of the constituent units of a nation having a federal government ⟨the fifty *states*⟩ **b** *plural, capitalized* : The United States of America
8 : the territory of a state
²**state** *transitive verb* **stat·ed; stat·ing** (1647)
1 : to set by regulation or authority
2 : to express the particulars of especially in words : REPORT; *broadly* : to express in words
— **stat·able** *or* **state·able** \'stā-tə-bəl\ *adjective*
state aid *noun* (1856)
: public monies appropriated by a state government for the partial support or improvement of a public local institution
state bank *noun* (1815)
1 : CENTRAL BANK
2 : a bank chartered by and operating under the laws of a state of the U.S.
state bird *noun* (1910)

: a bird selected (as by the legislature) as an emblem of a state of the U.S.
state capitalism *noun* (1903)
: an economic system in which private capitalism is modified by a varying degree of government ownership and control
state church *noun, often S&C capitalized* (1726)
: ESTABLISHED CHURCH
state college *noun* (1831)
: a college that is financially supported by a state government, often specializes in a branch of technical or professional education, and often forms part of the state university
state·craft \'stāt-,kraft\ *noun* (1642)
: the art of conducting state affairs
stat·ed \'stā-təd\ *adjective* (circa 1641)
1 : FIXED, REGULAR ⟨the president shall, at *stated* times, receive . . . a compensation —*U.S. Constitution*⟩
2 : set down explicitly : DECLARED ⟨our *stated* intention⟩
— **stat·ed·ly** *adverb*
stated clerk *noun* (circa 1909)
: an executive officer of a Presbyterian general assembly, synod, or presbytery ranking below the moderator
state flower *noun* (1898)
: a flowering plant selected (as by the legislature) as an emblem of a state of the U.S.
state·hood \'stāt-,hu̇d\ *noun* (1868)
: the condition of being a state; *especially* : the status of being one of the states of the U.S.
state·house \-,hau̇s\ *noun* (1638)
: the building in which a state legislature sits
state·less \-ləs\ *adjective* (1609)
1 : having no state
2 : lacking the status of a national ⟨a *stateless* refugee⟩
— **state·less·ness** *noun*
state·ly \-lē\ *adjective* **state·li·er; -est** (15th century)
1 a : marked by lofty or imposing dignity **b** : HAUGHTY, UNAPPROACHABLE
2 : impressive in size or proportions
synonym SEE GRAND
— **state·li·ness** *noun*
— **stately** *adverb*
state·ment \'stāt-mənt\ *noun* (circa 1775)
1 : something stated: as **a** : a single declaration or remark : ASSERTION **b** : a report of facts or opinions
2 : the act or process of stating or presenting orally or on paper
3 : PROPOSITION 2a
4 : the presentation of a theme in a musical composition
5 : a summary of a financial account showing the balance due
6 : an opinion, comment, or message conveyed indirectly usually by nonverbal means ⟨monuments are *statements* in form and space —O. B. Hardison, Jr.⟩
7 : an instruction in a computer program
state of the art (1910)
: the level of development (as of a device, procedure, process, technique, or science) reached at any particular time usually as a result of modern methods
— **state-of-the-art** *adjective*
state of war (1880)
1 a : a state of actual armed hostilities regardless of a formal declaration of war **b** : a legal state created and ended by official declaration regardless of actual armed hostilities and usually characterized by operation of the rules of war
2 : the period of time during which a state of war is in effect

sta·ter \'stā-tər, stä-'ter\ *noun* [Middle English, from Late Latin *statēr*, from Greek *statēr*, literally, a unit of weight, from *histanai* to cause to stand, weigh — more at STAND] (14th century)
: an ancient gold or silver coin of the Greek city-states

state·room \'stāt-,rüm, -,rum\ *noun* (1660)
1 : CABIN 1a(1)
2 : a private room on a railroad car with one or more berths and a toilet

state's attorney *noun* (1809)
: a legal officer (as a district attorney) appointed or elected to represent a state in court proceedings within a district — called also *state attorney*

state's evidence *noun, often S capitalized* (1827)
: a participant in a crime or an accomplice who gives evidence for the prosecution especially in return for a reduced sentence; *also* : the evidence given — used chiefly in the phrase *turn state's evidence*

States General *noun plural* (1585)
1 : the assembly of the three orders of clergy, nobility, and third estate in France before the Revolution
2 : the legislature of the Netherlands from the 15th century to 1796

¹state·side \'stāt-,sīd\ *adjective, often capitalized* [(United) States + side] (1944)
: being in, going to, coming from, or characteristic of the 48 conterminous states of the U.S. ⟨transferred from Europe to *stateside* duty⟩

²stateside *adverb, often capitalized* (1945)
: in or to the continental U.S.

states·man \'stāts-mən\ *noun* (1592)
1 : one versed in the principles or art of government; *especially* : one actively engaged in conducting the business of a government or in shaping its policies
2 : one who exercises political leadership wisely and without narrow partisanship
— **states·man·like** \-,līk\ *adjective*
— **states·man·ly** \-lē\ *adjective*
— **states·man·ship** \-,ship\ *noun*

state socialism *noun* (1879)
: an economic system with limited socialist characteristics introduced by usually gradual political action

states' right·er \'stāts-'rī-tər\ *noun* (1945)
: one who advocates strict interpretation of the U.S. constitutional guarantee of states' rights

states' rights *noun plural* (1858)
: all rights not vested by the Constitution of the U.S. in the federal government nor forbidden by it to the separate states

state tree *noun* (1917)
: a tree selected (as by the legislature) as an emblem of a state of the U.S.

state university *noun* (1831)
: a university maintained and administered by one of the states of the U.S. as part of the state public educational system

¹state·wide \'stāt-'wīd\ *adjective* (1911)
: affecting or extending throughout all parts of a state

²statewide *adverb* (circa 1934)
: throughout the state

¹stat·ic \'sta-tik\ *adjective* [New Latin *staticus*, from Greek *statikos* causing to stand, skilled in weighing, from *histanai* to cause to stand, weigh — more at STAND] (1638)
1 : exerting force by reason of weight alone without motion
2 : of or relating to bodies at rest or forces in equilibrium
3 : showing little change ⟨a *static* population⟩
4 a : characterized by a lack of movement, animation, or progression **b :** producing an effect of repose or quiescence ⟨a *static* design⟩
5 a : standing or fixed in one place : STATIONARY **b** *of water* : stored in a tank but not under pressure

6 : of, relating to, or producing stationary charges of electricity : ELECTROSTATIC
7 : of, relating to, or caused by radio static
— **stat·i·cal** \-ti-kəl\ *adjective*
— **stat·i·cal·ly** \-ti-k(ə-)lē\ *adverb*

²static *noun* [*static electricity*] (1913)
1 : noise produced in a radio or television receiver by atmospheric or various natural or man-made electrical disturbances; *also* : the electrical disturbances producing this noise
2 : heated opposition or criticism
— **stat·icky** \'sta-ti-kē\ *adjective*

-static *adjective combining form* [New Latin *-staticus*, from *staticus*]
1 : of or relating to a position or state ⟨ortho*static*⟩
2 : inhibiting the growth of ⟨fungi*static*⟩

stat·i·ce \'sta-tə-(,)sē\ *noun* [New Latin, genus of herbs, from Latin, an astringent plant, from Greek *statikē*, from feminine of *statikos* causing to stand, astringent] (1745)
: SEA LAVENDER

static electricity *noun* (1876)
: electricity that consists of isolated motionless charges (as those produced by friction)

static line *noun* (1930)
: a cord attached to a parachute pack and to an airplane to open the parachute after a jumper clears the plane

stat·ics \'sta-tiks\ *noun plural but singular or plural in construction* (1837)
: mechanics dealing with the relations of forces that produce equilibrium among material bodies

static tube *noun* (1923)
: a tube used for indicating static as distinct from impact pressure in a stream of fluid

¹sta·tion \'stā-shən\ *noun* [Middle English *stacioun*, from Middle French *station*, from Latin *station-, statio*, from *stare* to stand — more at STAND] (14th century)
1 a : the place or position in which something or someone stands or is assigned to stand or remain **b :** any of the places in a manufacturing operation at which one part of the work is done **c :** equipment used usually by one person for performing a particular job
2 : the act or manner of standing : POSTURE
3 : a stopping place: as **a** (1) : a regular stopping place in a transportation route (2) : the building connected with such a stopping place : DEPOT 3 **b :** one of the stations of the cross
4 a : a post or sphere of duty or occupation **b :** a stock farm or ranch especially of Australia or New Zealand
5 : STANDING, RANK ⟨a woman of high *station*⟩
6 : a place for specialized observation and study of scientific phenomena ⟨a seismological *station*⟩ ⟨a marine biological *station*⟩
7 : a place established to provide a public service: as **a** (1) : FIRE STATION (2) : POLICE STATION **b :** a branch post office
8 : SERVICE STATION 1
9 a : a complete assemblage of radio or television equipment for transmitting or receiving **b :** the place in which such a station is located

²station *transitive verb* **sta·tioned; sta·tion·ing** \'stā-sh(ə-)niŋ\ (1748)
: to assign to or set in a station or position : POST

sta·tion·al \'stā-shnəl, -shə-nᵊl\ *adjective* (1902)
: of, relating to, or being a mass formerly celebrated by the pope at designated churches in Rome on appointed holy days

sta·tion·ary \'stā-shə-,ner-ē\ *adjective* (1626)
1 : fixed in a station, course, or mode : IMMOBILE
2 : unchanging in condition

stationary bicycle *noun* (1962)
: an exercise apparatus that can be pedaled like a bicycle — called also *stationary bike*

stationary front *noun* (circa 1940)
: the boundary between two air masses neither of which is replacing the other

stationary wave *noun* (1856)

: STANDING WAVE

station break *noun* (1937)
: a pause in a radio or television broadcast for announcement of the identity of the network or station; *also* : an announcement or advertisement during this pause

sta·tio·ner \'stā-sh(ə-)nər\ *noun* [Middle English *staciouner*, from Medieval Latin *stationarius*, from *station-, statio* shop, from Latin, station] (14th century)
1 *archaic* **a :** BOOKSELLER **b :** PUBLISHER
2 : one that sells stationery

sta·tio·nery \'stā-shə-,ner-ē\ *noun* [*stationer*] (circa 1688)
1 : materials (as paper, pens, and ink) for writing or typing
2 : letter paper usually accompanied with matching envelopes

station house *noun* (1833)
: a house at a post or station; *especially* : POLICE STATION

sta·tion·mas·ter \'stā-shən-,mas-tər\ *noun* (1856)
: an official in charge of the operation of a railroad station

stations of the cross *often S&C capitalized* (circa 1890)
1 : a series of usually 14 images or pictures especially in a church that represent the stages of Christ's passion and death
2 : a devotion involving commemorative meditation before the stations of the cross

station wagon *noun* (1904)
: an automobile that has a passenger compartment which extends to the back of the vehicle, that has no trunk, that has one or more rear seats which can be folded down to make space for light cargo, and that has a tailgate or liftgate

stat·ism \'stā-,ti-zəm\ *noun* (1880)
: concentration of economic controls and planning in the hands of a highly centralized government

stat·ist \'stā-tist\ *noun* (1946)
: an advocate of statism
— **statist** *adjective*

sta·tis·tic \stə-'tis-tik\ *noun* [singular of *statistics*] (1880)
1 : a single term or datum in a collection of statistics
2 a : a quantity (as the mean of a sample) that is computed from a sample; *specifically* : ESTIMATE 3b **b :** a random variable that takes on the possible values of a statistic

sta·tis·ti·cal \-ti-kəl\ *adjective* (1787)
: of, relating to, based on, or employing the principles of statistics
— **sta·tis·ti·cal·ly** \-k(ə-)lē\ *adverb*

statistical mechanics *noun plural but usually singular in construction* (1885)
: a branch of mechanics dealing with the application of the principles of statistics to the mechanics of a system consisting of a large number of parts having motions that differ by small steps over a large range

stat·is·ti·cian \,sta-tə-'sti-shən\ *noun* (1825)
: one versed in or engaged in compiling statistics

sta·tis·tics \stə-'tis-tiks\ *noun plural but singular or plural in construction* [German *Statistik* study of political facts and figures, from New Latin *statisticus* of politics, from Latin *status* state] (1770)
1 : a branch of mathematics dealing with the collection, analysis, interpretation, and presentation of masses of numerical data
2 : a collection of quantitative data

sta·tive \'stā-tiv\ *adjective* (1874)
: expressing a state, condition, or relation — compare ACTIVE 3b

stato- *combining form* [International Scientific Vocabulary, from Greek *statos* stationary, from *histasthai* to stand — more at STAND]
1 : resting ⟨*stato*blast⟩
2 : equilibrium ⟨*stato*cyst⟩

stato·blast \'sta-tə-ˌblast\ *noun* [International Scientific Vocabulary] (1855)
1 : a bud in a freshwater bryozoan that overwinters in a chitinous envelope and develops into a new individual in spring
2 : GEMMULE b

stato·cyst \-ˌsist\ *noun* [International Scientific Vocabulary] (1902)
: an organ of equilibrium occurring especially among invertebrate animals and consisting usually of a fluid-filled vesicle in which are suspended statoliths

stato·lith \'sta-tᵊl-ˌith\ *noun* [International Scientific Vocabulary] (1900)
1 : any of the usually calcareous bodies suspended in a statocyst
2 : any of various starch grains or other solid bodies in the plant cytoplasm that are held to be responsible by changes in their position for changes in orientation of a part or organ

sta·tor \'stā-tər\ *noun* [New Latin, from Latin, one that stands, from *stare* to stand — more at STAND] (1902)
: a stationary part in a machine in or about which a rotor revolves

stato·scope \'sta-tə-ˌskōp\ *noun* [International Scientific Vocabulary] (circa 1900)
: a sensitive aneroid barometer for recording small changes in atmospheric pressure; *especially* **:** one used for indicating small changes in the altitude of an aircraft

¹stat·u·ary \'sta-chə-ˌwer-ē\ *noun, plural* **-aries** (1542)
1 : SCULPTOR
2 a : the art of making statues **b :** a collection of statues **:** STATUES

²statuary *adjective* (1627)
: of, relating to, or suitable for statues

stat·ue \'sta-(ˌ)chü\ *noun* [Middle English, from Middle French, from Latin *statua*, from *statuere* to set up — more at STATUTE] (14th century)
: a three-dimensional representation usually of a person, animal, or mythical being that is produced by sculpturing, modeling, or casting

Statue of Liberty (circa 1900)
1 : a large copper statue of a woman holding a torch aloft in her right hand located on Liberty Island in New York harbor
2 : a trick played in football in which the ball-carrier takes the ball from the raised hand of a teammate who is faking a pass

stat·u·esque \ˌsta-chə-'wesk\ *adjective* (1834)
: resembling a statue especially in dignity, shapeliness, or stillness; *especially* **:** tall and shapely
— stat·u·esque·ly *adverb*

stat·u·ette \ˌsta-chə-'wet\ *noun* (1843)
: a small statue

stat·ure \'sta-chər\ *noun* [Middle English, from Middle French, from Latin *statura*, from *status*, past participle of *stare* to stand — more at STAND] (14th century)
1 : natural height (as of a person) in an upright position
2 : quality or status gained by growth, development, or achievement

sta·tus \'stā-təs, 'sta-\ *noun, plural* **statuses** *often attributive* [Latin — more at STATE] (1791)
1 : the condition of a person or thing in the eyes of the law
2 a : position or rank in relation to others ⟨the *status* of a father⟩ **b :** relative rank in a hierarchy of prestige; *especially* **:** high prestige
3 : state of affairs

status offender *noun* (circa 1976)
: a young offender (as a runaway or a truant) who is under the jurisdiction of a court for repeated offenses that are not crimes

status quo \-'kwō\ *noun* [Latin, state in which] (1833)
: the existing state of affairs ⟨seeks to preserve the *status quo*⟩

status quo an·te \-'an-tē\ *noun* [Latin, state in which previously] (1877)
: the state of affairs that existed previously

sta·tusy \'stā-tə-sē, 'sta-\ *adjective* (1962)
: having, showing, or conferring prestige

stat·ut·able \'sta-chə-tə-bəl, 'sta-ˌchü-\ *adjective* (1636)
: made, regulated, or imposed by or in conformity to statute **:** STATUTORY ⟨*statutable* tonnage⟩

stat·ute \'sta-(ˌ)chüt, -chət\ *noun* [Middle English, from Old French *statut*, from Late Latin *statutum* law, regulation, from Latin, neuter of *statutus*, past participle of *statuere* to set up, station, from *status* position, state] (14th century)
1 : a law enacted by the legislative branch of a government
2 : an act of a corporation or of its founder intended as a permanent rule
3 : an international instrument setting up an agency and regulating its scope or authority
synonym see LAW

statute book *noun* (1593)
: the whole body of legislation of a given jurisdiction whether or not published as a whole — usually used in plural

statute mile *noun* (1862)
: MILE 1a

statute of limitations (1768)
: a statute assigning a certain time after which rights cannot be enforced by legal action or offenses cannot be punished

stat·u·to·ry \'sta-chə-ˌtōr-ē, -ˌtȯr-\ *adjective* (1766)
1 : of or relating to statutes
2 : enacted, created, or regulated by statute ⟨a *statutory* age limit⟩
— stat·u·to·ri·ly \ˌsta-chə-'tōr-ə-lē, -'tȯr-\ *adverb*

statutory rape *noun* (1898)
: sexual intercourse with a person who is below the statutory age of consent

¹staunch \'stȯnch, 'stänch\ *variant of* STANCH

²staunch *adjective* [Middle English, from Middle French *estanche*, feminine of *estanc*, from Old French, from *estancher* to stanch — more at STANCH] (15th century)
1 a : WATERTIGHT, SOUND **b :** strongly built **:** SUBSTANTIAL
2 : steadfast in loyalty or principle
synonym see FAITHFUL
— staunch·ly *adverb*
— staunch·ness *noun*

stau·ro·lite \'stȯr-ə-ˌlīt\ *noun* [French, from Greek *stauros* cross + French *-lite* — more at STEER] (circa 1815)
: a mineral consisting of a basic silicate of iron and aluminum in prismatic orthorhombic crystals often twinned so as to resemble a cross
— stau·ro·lit·ic \ˌstȯr-ə-'li-tik\ *adjective*

¹stave \'stāv\ *noun* [Middle English, back-formation from *staves*, plural of *staf* staff] (13th century)
1 : ¹STAFF 1, 2
2 : any of the narrow strips of wood or narrow iron plates placed edge to edge to form the sides, covering, or lining of a vessel (as a barrel) or structure
3 : STANZA
4 : ¹STAFF 3

²stave *verb* **staved** *or* **stove** \'stōv\; **staving** (circa 1595)
transitive verb
1 : to break in the staves of (a cask)
2 : to smash a hole in ⟨*stove* in the boat⟩; *also* **:** to crush or break inward ⟨*staved* in several ribs⟩
3 : to drive or thrust away
intransitive verb
1 *archaic* **:** to become stove in — used of a boat or ship
2 : to walk or move rapidly

stave off *transitive verb* (1624)
1 : to fend off ⟨*staving off* creditors⟩

2 : to ward off (as something adverse) **:** FORESTALL ⟨trying to *stave off* disaster⟩

staves *plural of* STAFF

staves·acre \'stāv-ˌzā-kər\ *noun* [by folk etymology from Middle English *staphisagre*, from Medieval Latin *staphis agria*, from Greek, literally, wild raisin] (15th century)
: a Eurasian delphinium (*Delphinium staphisagria*); *also* **:** its violently emetic and cathartic seeds

¹stay \'stā\ *noun* [Middle English, from Old English *stæg*; akin to Old Norse *stag* stay, Old English *stēle* steel] (before 12th century)
1 : a large strong rope usually of wire used to support a mast
2 : ¹GUY

²stay (1627)
transitive verb
1 : to secure upright with or as if with stays
2 : to incline (a mast) forward, aft, or to one side by the stays
intransitive verb
: to go about **:** TACK

³stay *verb* **stayed** \'stād\ *also* **staid** \'stād\; **staying** [Middle English, from Middle French *ester* to stand, stay, from Latin *stare* — more at STAND] (15th century)
intransitive verb
1 : to stop going forward **:** PAUSE
2 : to stop doing something **:** CEASE
3 : to continue in a place or condition **:** REMAIN ⟨*stayed* up all night⟩ ⟨went for a short vacation but *stayed* on for weeks⟩ ⟨*stay* put till I come back⟩
4 : to stand firm
5 : to take up residence **:** LODGE
6 : to keep even in a contest or rivalry ⟨*stay* with the leaders⟩
7 : to call a poker bet without raising
8 *obsolete* **:** to be in waiting or attendance
transitive verb
1 : to wait for **:** AWAIT
2 : to stick or remain with (as a race or trial of endurance) to the end — usually used in the phrase *stay the course*
3 : to remain during ⟨*stayed* the whole time⟩
4 a : to stop or delay the proceeding or advance of by or as if by interposing an obstacle **:** HALT ⟨*stay* an execution⟩ **b :** to check the course of (as a disease) **c :** ALLAY, PACIFY ⟨*stayed* tempers⟩ **d :** to quiet the hunger of temporarily
synonym see DEFER

⁴stay *noun* (1536)
1 a : the action of halting **:** the state of being stopped **b :** a stopping or suspension of procedure or execution by judicial or executive order
2 *obsolete* **:** SELF-CONTROL, MODERATION
3 : a residence or sojourn in a place
4 : capacity for endurance

⁵stay *noun* [Middle French *estaie*, of Germanic origin; akin to Old High German *stān* to stand — more at STAND] (1515)
1 : one that serves as a prop **:** SUPPORT
2 : a corset stiffened with bones — usually used in plural

⁶stay *transitive verb* (1548)
1 : to provide physical or moral support for **:** SUSTAIN
2 : to fix on something as a foundation

stay–at–home \'stā-ət-ˌhōm\ *adjective* (1806)
: remaining habitually in one's residence, locality, or country
— stay–at–home *noun*

stay·er \'stā-ər\ *noun* (circa 1580)
: one that stays; *especially* **:** one that upholds or supports

staying power *noun* (1859)
: capacity for endurance **:** STAMINA

stay·sail \'stā-,sāl, -səl\ *noun* (1669)
: a fore-and-aft sail hoisted on a stay — see SAIL illustration

STD \,es-(,)tē-'dē\ *noun* [*sexually transmitted disease*] (1976)
: any of various diseases transmitted by direct sexual contact that include the classic venereal diseases (as syphilis, gonorrhea, and chancroid) and other diseases (as hepatitis A, hepatitis B, giardiasis, and AIDS) that are often or sometimes contracted by other than sexual means

¹**stead** \'sted\ *noun* [Middle English *stede*, from Old English; akin to Old High German *stat* place, Old English *standan* to stand — more at STAND] (before 12th century)
1 *obsolete* : LOCALITY, PLACE
2 : ADVANTAGE — used chiefly in the phrase *to stand one in good stead*
3 : the office, place, or function ordinarily occupied or carried out by someone or something else ⟨acted in his brother's *stead*⟩

²**stead** *transitive verb* (13th century)
: to be of avail to : HELP

stead·fast \'sted-,fast *also* -fəst\ *adjective* [Middle English *stedefast*, from Old English *stedefæst*, from *stede* + *fæst* fixed, fast] (before 12th century)
1 a : firmly fixed in place : IMMOVABLE **b** : not subject to change ⟨the *steadfast* doctrine of original sin —Ellen Glasgow⟩
2 : firm in belief, determination, or adherence : LOYAL
synonym see FAITHFUL
— **stead·fast·ly** *adverb*
— **stead·fast·ness** \-,fas(t)-nəs, -fəs(t)-\ *noun*

stead·ing \'ste-d³n, 'stē-, -diŋ\ *noun* [Middle English *steding*, from *stede* place, farm] (15th century)
1 : a small farm
2 *chiefly Scottish* : the service buildings or area of a farm

¹**steady** \'ste-dē\ *adjective* **steadi·er; -est** [Middle English *stedy*, from *stede*] (14th century)
1 a : direct or sure in movement : UNFALTERING **b** : firm in position : FIXED **c** : keeping nearly upright in a seaway ⟨a *steady* ship⟩
2 : showing little variation or fluctuation : STABLE, UNIFORM ⟨a *steady* breeze⟩ ⟨*steady* prices⟩
3 a : not easily disturbed or upset ⟨*steady* nerves⟩ **b** (1) : constant in feeling, principle, purpose, or attachment (2) : DEPENDABLE **c** : not given to dissipation : SOBER ☆
— **steadi·ly** \'ste-d³l-ē\ *adverb*
— **steadi·ness** \'ste-dē-nəs\ *noun*

²**steady** *verb* **stead·ied; steady·ing** (1530)
transitive verb
: to make or keep steady
intransitive verb
: to become steady
— **steadi·er** *noun*

³**steady** *adverb* (circa 1605)
1 : in a steady manner : STEADILY
2 : on the course set — used as a direction to the helmsman of a ship

⁴**steady** *noun, plural* **stead·ies** (1792)
: one that is steady; *specifically* : a boyfriend or girlfriend with whom one goes steady

steady state *noun* (1885)
: a state or condition of a system or process (as one of the energy states of an atom) that does not change in time; *broadly* : a condition that changes only negligibly over a specified time

steady state theory *noun* (1948)
: a theory in astronomy: the universe has always existed and has always been expanding with hydrogen being created continuously — compare BIG BANG THEORY

steak \'stāk\ *noun* [Middle English *steke*, from Old Norse *steik*; akin to Old Norse *steikja* to roast on a stake, *stik* stick, stake — more at STICK] (15th century)
1 a : a slice of meat cut from a fleshy part of a beef carcass **b** : a similar slice of a specified meat other than beef ⟨ham *steak*⟩ **c** : a cross-section slice of a large fish ⟨swordfish *steak*⟩
2 : ground beef prepared for cooking or for serving in the manner of a steak ⟨hamburger *steak*⟩

steak house *noun* (1762)
: a restaurant whose specialty is beefsteak

steak knife *noun* (1895)
: a table knife with a sharp often serrated blade

steak tar·tare \-tär-'tär\ *noun* [French *tartare* Tartar] (1911)
: highly seasoned ground beef eaten raw

¹**steal** \'stē(ə)l\ *verb* **stole** \'stōl\; **sto·len** \'stō-lən\; **steal·ing** [Middle English *stelen*, from Old English *stelan*; akin to Old High German *stelan* to steal] (before 12th century)
intransitive verb
1 : to take the property of another wrongfully and especially as an habitual or regular practice
2 : to come or go secretly, unobtrusively, gradually, or unexpectedly
3 : to steal or attempt to steal a base
transitive verb
1 a : to take or appropriate without right or leave and with intent to keep or make use of wrongfully ⟨*stole* a car⟩ **b** : to take away by force or unjust means ⟨they've *stolen* our liberty⟩ **c** : to take surreptitiously or without permission ⟨*steal* a kiss⟩ **d** : to appropriate to oneself or beyond one's proper share : make oneself the focus of ⟨*steal* the show⟩
2 a : to move, convey, or introduce secretly : SMUGGLE **b** : to accomplish in a concealed or unobserved manner ⟨*steal* a visit⟩
3 a : to seize, gain, or win by trickery, skill, or daring ⟨a basketball player adept at *stealing* the ball⟩ ⟨*stole* the election⟩ **b** *of a base runner* : to reach (a base) safely solely by running and usually catching the opposing team off guard ☆
— **steal·able** \'stē-lə-bəl\ *adjective*
— **steal·er** *noun*
— **steal a march on** : to gain an advantage on unobserved
— **steal one's thunder** : to grab attention from another especially by anticipating an idea, plan, or presentation; *also* : to claim credit for another's idea

²**steal** *noun* (circa 1825)
1 : the act or an instance of stealing
2 : a fraudulent or questionable political deal
3 : BARGAIN 2 ⟨it's a *steal* at that price⟩

stealth \'stelth\ *noun* [Middle English *stelthe*; akin to Old English *stelan* to steal] (13th century)
1 a *archaic* : THEFT **b** *obsolete* : something stolen
2 : the act or action of proceeding furtively, secretly, or imperceptibly ⟨the state moves by *stealth* to gather information —Nat Hentoff⟩
3 : the state of being furtive or unobtrusive
4 : an aircraft-design characteristic consisting of oblique angular construction and avoidance of vertical surfaces that is intended to produce a very weak radar return

stealthy \'stel-thē\ *adjective* **stealth·i·er; -est** (1605)
1 : slow, deliberate, and secret in action or character
2 : intended to escape observation : FURTIVE
synonym see SECRET
— **stealth·i·ly** \-thə-lē\ *adverb*
— **stealth·i·ness** \-thē-nəs\ *noun*

¹**steam** \'stēm\ *noun* [Middle English *stem*, from Old English *stēam*; akin to Dutch *stoom* steam] (before 12th century)
1 : a vapor arising from a heated substance

2 a : the invisible vapor into which water is converted when heated to the boiling point **b** : the mist formed by the condensation on cooling of water vapor
3 a : water vapor kept under pressure so as to supply energy for heating, cooking, or mechanical work; *also* : the power so generated **b** : active force : POWER, MOMENTUM ⟨got there under his own *steam*⟩ ⟨sales began to pick up *steam*⟩; *also* : normal force ⟨at full *steam*⟩ **c** : pent-up emotional tension ⟨needed to let off a little *steam*⟩
4 a : STEAMER 2a **b** : travel by or a trip in a steamer

²**steam** (15th century)
transitive verb
1 : to give out as fumes : EXHALE
2 : to apply steam to; *especially* : to expose to the action of steam (as for softening or cooking)
intransitive verb
1 : to rise or pass off as vapor
2 : to give off steam or vapor
3 a : to move or travel by the agency of steam **b** : to move or proceed with energy or force
4 : to be angry : BOIL ⟨*steaming* over the insult⟩

steam·boat \'stēm-,bōt\ *noun* (1785)
: a boat driven by steam power; *specifically* : a shallow-draft vessel used on inland waterways

steamboat Gothic *noun* [from its use in homes of retired steamboat captains in imitation of the style of river steamboats] (1941)
: an elaborately ornamented architectural style used in homes built in the middle 19th century in the Ohio and Mississippi river valleys

steam boiler *noun* (1805)
: a boiler for producing steam

steam chest *noun* (1797)
: the chamber from which steam is distributed to a cylinder of a steam engine

steamed \'stēmd\ *adjective* (1802)
1 : cooked by steam
2 : ANGRY 1 — often used with *up*

steam engine *noun* (1751)
: an engine driven or worked by steam; *specifically* : a reciprocating engine having a piston driven in a closed cylinder by steam

steam·er \'stē-mər\ *noun* (1814)
1 : a vessel in which articles are subjected to steam
2 a : a ship propelled by steam **b** : an engine, machine, or vehicle operated or propelled by steam
3 : one that steams
4 : SOFT-SHELL CLAM

steamer rug *noun* (1890)

☆ SYNONYMS

Steady, even, equable mean not varying throughout a course or extent. STEADY implies lack of fluctuation or interruption of movement ⟨*steady* progress⟩. EVEN suggests a lack of variation in quality or character ⟨an *even* distribution⟩. EQUABLE implies lack of extremes or of sudden sharp changes ⟨maintain an *equable* temper⟩.

Steal, pilfer, filch, purloin mean to take from another without right or without detection. STEAL may apply to any surreptitious taking of something and differs from the other terms by commonly applying to intangibles as well as material things ⟨*steal* jewels⟩ ⟨*stole* a look at the gifts⟩. PILFER implies stealing repeatedly in small amounts ⟨*pilfered* from his employer⟩. FILCH adds a suggestion of snatching quickly and surreptitiously ⟨*filched* an apple from the tray⟩. PURLOIN stresses removing or carrying off for one's own use or purposes ⟨printed a *purloined* document⟩.

: a warm covering for the lap and feet especially of a person sitting on a ship's deck

steamer trunk *noun* (1886)
: a trunk suitable for use in a stateroom of a steamer; *especially* : a shallow trunk that may be stowed beneath a berth

steam·fit·ter \'stēm-ˌfi-tər\ *noun* (circa 1890)
: one that installs or repairs equipment (as steam pipes) for heating, ventilating, or refrigerating systems
— steam fitting *noun*

steam iron *noun* (circa 1943)
: a pressing iron with a compartment holding water that is converted to steam by the iron's heat and emitted through the soleplate onto the fabric being pressed

¹**steam·roll·er** \'stēm-ˌrō-lər\ *noun* (1866)
1 : a steam-driven road roller; *broadly* : ROAD ROLLER
2 : a crushing force especially when ruthlessly applied to overcome opposition

²**steamroller** *or* **steam·roll** \-ˌrōl\ (1879) *transitive verb*
1 : to overwhelm usually by greatly superior force ⟨*steamroller* the opposition⟩
2 : to bring or advance by overwhelming force or pressure ⟨*steamrollered* the bill through the legislature⟩
intransitive verb
: to move or proceed with irresistible force

steam·ship \'stēm-ˌship\ *noun* (1790)
: STEAMER 2a

steamship round *noun* (1964)
: a large beef roast consisting of the whole round with rump and heel

steam shovel *noun* (1879)
: a power shovel operated by steam; *broadly* : POWER SHOVEL

steam table *noun* (1861)
: a table having openings to hold containers of cooked food over steam or hot water circulating beneath them

steam turbine *noun* (1900)
: a turbine that is driven by the pressure of steam discharged at high velocity against the turbine vanes

steam up *transitive verb* (1860)
: to make angry or excited : AROUSE

steamy \'stē-mē\ *adjective* **steam·i·er; -est** (1644)
1 : consisting of, characterized by, or full of steam
2 : intensely or uncomfortably hot: as **a** : hot and humid ⟨a *steamy* afternoon⟩ **b** : sensually hot ⟨a *steamy* love scene⟩
— steam·i·ly \-mə-lē\ *adverb*
— steam·i·ness \-mē-nəs\ *noun*

ste·ap·sin \stē-'ap-sən\ *noun* [Greek *stear* hard fat + English *-psin* (as in *pepsin*)] (1896)
: the lipase in pancreatic juice

stea·rate \'stē-ə-ˌrāt, 'sti-(ə)r-ˌāt\ *noun* (1841)
: a salt or ester of stearic acid

stea·ric acid \stē-'ar-ik-, 'sti(ə)r-ik-\ *noun* (1831)
: a white crystalline fatty acid $C_{18}H_{36}O_2$ obtained by saponifying tallow or other hard fats containing stearin; *also* : a commercial mixture of stearic and palmitic acids

stea·rin \'stē-ə-rən, 'stir-ən\ *noun* [French *stéarine*, from Greek *stear*] (1817)
: an ester of glycerol and stearic acid

ste·a·tite \'stē-ə-ˌtīt\ *noun* [Latin *steatitis*, a precious stone, from Greek, from *steat-, stear*] (1758)
1 : a massive talc having a grayish green or brown color : SOAPSTONE
2 : an electrically insulating porcelain composed largely of steatite
— ste·a·tit·ic \ˌstē-ə-'ti-tik\ *adjective*

steato- *combining form* [Greek, from *steat-, stear*; perhaps akin to Sanskrit *styāyate* it hardens]
: fat ⟨*steato*rrhea⟩

ste·a·to·py·gia \ˌstē-a-tə-'pi-j(ē-)ə, -'pī-\ *noun* [New Latin, from *steat-, stear* + Greek *pygē* buttocks] (1879)

: an excessive development of fat on the buttocks that occurs especially among women of the Hottentots and some black peoples
— ste·a·to·py·gous \-gəs\ *or* **ste·a·to·py·gic** \ˌstē-ə-'tä-pə-jik, -tə-'pī-jik\ *adjective*

ste·at·or·rhea \(ˌ)stē-ˌa-tə-'rē-ə\ *noun* [New Latin] (circa 1859)
: an excess of fat in the stools

stedfast *variant of* STEADFAST

steed \'stēd\ *noun* [Middle English *stede*, from Old English *stēda* stallion; akin to Old English *stōd* stud — more at STUD] (before 12th century)
: HORSE; *especially* : a spirited horse (as for war)

steek \'stēk\ *verb* [Middle English *steken* to pierce, fix, enclose; akin to Old English *stician* to pierce — more at STICK] (13th century)
chiefly Scottish : SHUT, CLOSE

¹**steel** \'stē(ə)l\ *noun* [Middle English *stele*, from Old English *stȳle, stēle*; akin to Old High German *stahal* steel and perhaps to Sanskrit *stakati* he resists] (before 12th century)
1 : commercial iron that contains carbon in any amount up to about 1.7 percent as an essential alloying constituent, is malleable when under suitable conditions, and is distinguished from cast iron by its malleability and lower carbon content
2 : an instrument or implement of or characteristically of steel: as **a** : a thrusting or cutting weapon **b** : an instrument (as a fluted round rod with a handle) for sharpening knives **c** : a piece of steel for striking sparks from flint
3 : a quality (as hardness of mind or spirit) that suggests steel ⟨nerves of *steel*⟩
4 a : the steel manufacturing industry **b** *plural* : shares of stock in steel companies

²**steel** *transitive verb* (13th century)
1 : to overlay, point, or edge with steel
2 a : to cause to resemble steel (as in looks or hardness) **b** : to fill with resolution or determination

³**steel** *adjective* (13th century)
1 : made of steel
2 : of or relating to the production of steel
3 : resembling steel

steel band *noun* (1949)
: a band of steel drums

steel blue *noun* (1817)
1 : a grayish blue
2 : any of the blue colors assumed by steel at various temperatures in tempering

steel drum *noun* (1952)
: a musical instrument originally developed in Trinidad that is played by hammering raised and tuned portions of the bottom of an oil drum

steel engraving *noun* (1824)
1 : the art or process of engraving on steel
2 : an impression taken from an engraved steel plate

steel guitar *noun* (1925)
1 : HAWAIIAN GUITAR
2 : PEDAL STEEL
— steel guitarist *noun*

steel·head \'stē(ə)l-ˌhed\ *noun, plural* **steelhead** *also* **steelheads** (circa 1882)
: an anadromous rainbow trout

steel·ie *also* **steely** \'stē-lē\ *noun, plural* **steel·ies** (1922)
: a steel playing marble

steel·mak·er \'stē(ə)l-ˌmā-kər\ *noun* (1839)
: a manufacturer of steel
— steel·mak·ing \-kiŋ\ *noun*

steel–trap \'stē(ə)l-'trap\ *adjective* (1945)
: QUICK, INCISIVE ⟨a *steel-trap* mind⟩

steel wool *noun* (1896)
: an abrasive material composed of long fine steel shavings and used especially for scouring and burnishing

steel·work \'stē(ə)l-ˌwərk\ *noun* (1681)
1 : work in steel

2 *plural but singular or plural in construction*
: an establishment where steel is made

steel·work·er \-ˌwər-kər\ *noun* (1884)
: one who works in steel and especially in the manufacturing of it

steely \'stē-lē\ *adjective* **steel·i·er; -est** (1509)
1 : resembling or suggesting steel (as in hardness, color, strength, or coldness) ⟨*steely* determination⟩ ⟨*steely* blue⟩
2 : made of steel
— steel·i·ness *noun*

steel·yard \'stē(ə)l-ˌyärd, 'stil-yərd\ *noun* [probably from ³*steel* + ⁴*yard* (rod)] (1639)
: a balance in which an object to be weighed is suspended from the shorter arm of a lever and the weight determined by moving a counterpoise along a graduated scale on the longer arm until equilibrium is attained

steelyard

steen·bok \'stēn-ˌbäk, 'stän-\ *or* **stein·bok** \'stīn-, 'stän-\ *noun* [Afrikaans *steenbok;* akin to Old English *stānbucca* ibex, *stān* stone, *bucca* buck] (1775)
: a small slender antelope (*Raphicerus campestris*) with long legs that inhabits chiefly grasslands of eastern and southern Africa

¹**steep** \'stēp\ *adjective* [Middle English *stepe*, from Old English *stēap* high, steep, deep; akin to Middle High German *stief* steep] (before 12th century)
1 : LOFTY, HIGH — used chiefly of a sea
2 : making a large angle with the plane of the horizon
3 a : mounting or falling precipitously ⟨the stairs were very *steep*⟩ **b** : being or characterized by a rapid and intensive decline or increase
4 : extremely or excessively high ⟨*steep* prices⟩ ☆
— steep·ish \'stē-pish\ *adjective*
— steep·ly *adverb*
— steep·ness *noun*

²**steep** *noun* (1555)
: a precipitous place

³**steep** *verb* [Middle English *stepen;* akin to Swedish *stöpa* to steep] (14th century)
transitive verb
1 : to soak in a liquid at a temperature under the boiling point (as for softening, bleaching, or extracting an essence)
2 : to cover with or plunge into a liquid (as in bathing, rinsing, or soaking)
3 : to saturate with or subject thoroughly to (some strong or pervading influence) ⟨practices *steeped* in tradition⟩

☆ **SYNONYMS**
Steep, abrupt, precipitous, sheer mean having an incline approaching the perpendicular. STEEP implies such sharpness of pitch that ascent or descent is very difficult ⟨a *steep* hill⟩ ⟨a *steep* dive⟩. ABRUPT implies a sharper pitch and a sudden break in the level ⟨a beach with an *abrupt* drop-off⟩. PRECIPITOUS applies to an incline approaching the vertical ⟨the river winds through a *precipitous* gorge⟩. SHEER suggests an unbroken perpendicular expanse ⟨*sheer* cliffs that daunted the climbers⟩.

\ə\ abut \ᵊ\ kitten \ər\ **further** \a\ ash \ā\ **ace**
\ä\ mop, mar \au̇\ **out** \ch\ **chin** \e\ bet \ē\ **easy**
\g\ **go** \i\ hit \ī\ **ice** \j\ **job** \ŋ\ **sing** \ō\ **go**
\ȯ\ **law** \ȯi\ **boy** \th\ **thin** \t̲h̲\ **the** \ü\ **loot** \u̇\ **foot**
\y\ **yet** \zh\ **vision** *see also* Guide to Pronunciation

intransitive verb
: to undergo the process of soaking in a liquid
synonym see SOAK
— **steep·er** *noun*
⁴steep *noun* (15th century)
1 : the state or process of being steeped
2 : a bath or solution in which something is steeped
steep·en \'stē-pən, -pᵊm\ *verb* **steep·ened; steep·en·ing** \'stē-pə-niŋ, 'stēp-niŋ\ (1847)
intransitive verb
: to become steeper
transitive verb
: to make steeper
stee·ple \'stē-pəl\ *noun* [Middle English *stepel,* from Old English *stēpel* tower; akin to Old English *stēap* steep] (before 12th century)
: a tall structure usually having a small spire at the top and surmounting a church tower; *broadly* **:** a whole church tower
— **stee·pled** \-pəld\ *adjective*
stee·ple·bush \'stē-pəl-,bush\ *noun* (circa 1818)
: HARDHACK
stee·ple·chase \-,chās\ *noun* [from the use of church steeples as landmarks to guide the riders] (1793)
1 a : a horse race across country **b :** a horse race over a closed course with obstacles (as hedges and walls)
2 : a footrace of usually 3000 meters over hurdles and a water jump
— **stee·ple·chas·er** \-,chā-sər\ *noun*
— **stee·ple·chas·ing** \-siŋ\ *noun*
stee·ple·jack \-,jak\ *noun* (1881)
: one whose work is building smokestacks, towers, or steeples or climbing up the outside of such structures to paint and make repairs
¹steer \'stir\ *noun* [Middle English, from Old English *stēor* young ox; akin to Old High German *stior* young ox] (before 12th century)
1 : a male bovine animal castrated before sexual maturity — compare STAG 3
2 : an ox less than four years old
²steer *verb* [Middle English *steren,* from Old English *stīeran;* akin to Old English *stēor-* steering oar, Greek *stauros* stake, cross, *stylos* pillar, Sanskrit *sthavira, sthūra* stout, thick] (12th century)
transitive verb
1 : to control the course of **:** DIRECT; *especially* **:** to guide by mechanical means (as a rudder)
2 : to set and hold to (a course)
intransitive verb
1 : to direct the course (as of a ship or automobile)
2 : to pursue a course of action
3 : to be subject to guidance or direction ⟨an automobile that *steers* well⟩
synonym see GUIDE
— **steer·able** \'stir-ə-bəl\ *adjective*
— **steer·er** *noun*
— **steer clear :** to keep entirely away — often used with *of* ⟨trying to *steer clear* of controversy⟩
³steer *noun* (1894)
: a hint as to procedure **:** TIP
⁴steer *dialect British variant of* STIR
steer·age \'stir-ij\ *noun* (15th century)
1 : the act or practice of steering; *broadly* **:** DIRECTION
2 [from its originally being located near the rudder] **:** a section of inferior accommodations in a passenger ship for passengers paying the lowest fares
steer·age·way \-,wā\ *noun* (1769)
: a rate of motion sufficient to make a ship or boat respond to movements of the rudder
steering column *noun* (1903)
: the column that encloses the connections to the steering gear of a vehicle (as an automobile)
steering committee *noun* (1887)
: a managing or directing committee; *specifically* **:** a committee that determines the order

in which business will be taken up in a U.S. legislative body
steering gear *noun* (1869)
: a mechanism by which something is steered
steering wheel *noun* (1750)
: a handwheel by means of which one steers
steers·man \'stirz-mən\ *noun* (before 12th century)
: one who steers **:** HELMSMAN
¹steeve \'stēv\ *transitive verb* **steeved; steev·ing** [Middle English *steven,* probably from Spanish *estibar* or Portuguese *estivar* to pack tightly, from Latin *stipare* to press together — more at STIFF] (15th century)
archaic **:** to stow especially in a ship's hold
²steeve *verb* **steeved; steev·ing** [origin unknown] (circa 1644)
intransitive verb
of a bowsprit **:** to incline upward at an angle with the horizon or the line of the keel
transitive verb
: to set (a bowsprit) at an upward inclination
stego·saur \'ste-gə-,sȯr\ *noun* [New Latin *Stegosauria,* from *Stegosaurus*] (1901)
: any of a suborder (Stegosauria) of quadrupedal ornithischian dinosaurs with strongly developed dorsal plates and spikes
stego·sau·rus \,ste-gə-'sȯr-əs\ *noun* [New Latin, from Greek *stegos* roof + *sauros* lizard — more at THATCH] (1892)
: any of a genus (*Stegosaurus*) of stegosaurs known from the Upper Jurassic rocks especially of Colorado and Wyoming
stein \'stīn\ *noun* [probably from German *Steingut* stoneware, from *Stein* stone + *Gut* goods] (1855)
: a large mug (as of earthenware) used especially for beer; *also* **:** the quantity of beer that a stein holds
ste·la \'stē-lə\ *or* **ste·le** \'stē-lē\ *noun, plural* **ste·lae** \-(,)lē\ [Latin & Greek; Latin *stela,* from Greek *stēlē;* akin to Old High German *stollo* pillar, Greek *stellein* to set up] (1776)
: a usually carved or inscribed stone slab or pillar used for commemorative purposes
ste·lar \'stē-lər, -,lär\ *adjective* (1901)
: of, relating to, or constituting a stele
stele \'stē(ə)l, 'stē-lē\ *noun* [New Latin, from Greek *stēlē* stela, pillar] (1895)
: the usually cylindrical central vascular portion of the axis of a vascular plant
stel·la \'ste-lə\ *noun* [Latin, star; from the star on the reverse] (1879)
: an experimental international coin based on the metric system that was issued by the U.S. in 1879 and 1880 and was worth about four dollars
stel·lar \'ste-lər\ *adjective* [Late Latin *stellaris,* from Latin *stella* star — more at STAR] (circa 1656)
1 a : of or relating to the stars **:** ASTRAL **b :** composed of stars
2 : of or relating to a theatrical or film star ⟨*stellar* names⟩
3 a : PRINCIPAL, LEADING ⟨a *stellar* role⟩ **b :** OUTSTANDING ⟨a *stellar* student⟩ ⟨a *stellar* performance⟩
stellar wind *noun* (1965)
: plasma continuously ejected from a star's surface into surrounding space
stel·late \'ste-,lāt\ *adjective* [Latin *stella*] (1661)
: resembling a star (as in shape) ⟨a *stellate* leaf⟩
Stel·ler's jay \'ste-lərz, 'shte-\ *noun* [Georg W. *Steller* (died 1746) German naturalist] (1828)
: a jay (*Cyanocitta stelleri*) of western North America with a high crest and black and dark blue plumage
Steller's sea cow *noun* (1814)
: an extinct very large aquatic sirenian (*Hydrodamalis gigas*) formerly common near the Asian coast of the Bering Sea
¹stem \'stem\ *noun* [Middle English *stem,* from Old English *stefn, stemn* stem of a plant or ship;

akin to Old High German *stam* plant stem and probably to Greek *stamnos* wine jar, *histanai* to set — more at STAND] (before 12th century)
1 a : the main trunk of a plant; *specifically* **:** a primary plant axis that develops buds and shoots instead of roots **b :** a plant part (as a branch, petiole, or stipe) that supports another (as a leaf or fruit) **c :** the complete fruiting stalk of a banana plant with its bananas
2 a : the main upright member at the bow of a ship **b :** the bow or prow of a ship — compare STERN
3 : a line of ancestry **:** STOCK; *especially* **:** a fundamental line from which others have arisen
4 : the part of an inflected word that remains unchanged except by phonetic changes or variations throughout an inflection
5 : something held to resemble a plant stem: as **a :** a main or heavy stroke of a letter **b :** the short perpendicular line extending from the head of a musical note **c :** the part of a tobacco pipe from the bowl outward **d :** the cylindrical support of a piece of stemware (as a goblet) **e :** a shaft of a watch used for winding
— **from stem to stern :** THROUGHOUT, THOROUGHLY
²stem *transitive verb* **stemmed; stemming** [Middle English (Scots) *stemmen* to keep a course, from ¹*stem* (of a ship)] (1593)
1 : to make headway against (as an adverse tide, current, or wind)
2 : to check or go counter to (something adverse)
— **stem·mer** *noun*
³stem *verb* **stemmed; stem·ming** [¹*stem* (of a plant)] (1724)
transitive verb
1 : to remove the stem from
2 : to make stems for (as artificial flowers)
intransitive verb
: to occur or develop as a consequence **:** have or trace an origin ⟨her success *stems* from hard work⟩
synonym see SPRING
— **stem·mer** *noun*
⁴stem *verb* **stemmed; stem·ming** [Middle English *stemmen* to dam up, from Old Norse *stemma;* akin to Middle High German *stemmen* to dam up and probably to Lithuanian *stumti* to shove] (14th century)
transitive verb
1 a : to stop or dam up (as a river) **b :** to stop or check by or as if by damming; *especially* **:** STANCH ⟨*stem* a flow of blood⟩
2 : to turn (a ski) in stemming
intransitive verb
1 : to restrain or check oneself; *also* **:** to become checked or stanched
2 : to slide the heel of one ski or of both skis outward usually in making or preparing to make a turn
⁵stem *noun* (circa 1700)
1 : CHECK, DAM
2 : an act or instance of stemming on skis
stem cell *noun* (1885)
: an unspecialized cell that gives rise to differentiated cells ⟨hematopoietic *stem cells* in bone marrow⟩
stem christie *noun, often C capitalized* (1936)
: a turn in skiing begun by stemming a ski and completed by bringing the skis parallel into a christie
stem·less \'stem-ləs\ *adjective* (1796)
: having no stem **:** ACAULESCENT
stem·ma \'ste-mə\ *noun, plural* **stem·ma·ta** \-mə-tə\ [Latin, wreath, pedigree (from the wreaths placed on ancestral images), from Greek, wreath, from *stephein* to crown, enwreathe] (1826)
1 : a simple eye present in some insects
2 : a scroll (as among the ancient Romans) containing a genealogical list

3 : a tree showing the relationships of the manuscripts of a literary work
— **stem·mat·ic** \ste-'ma-tik, stə-\ *adjective*
stemmed \'stemd\ *adjective* (1576)
: having a stem — usually used in combination ⟨long-*stemmed* roses⟩
stem·my \'ste-mē\ *adjective* **stem·mi·er; -est** (1863)
: abounding in stems
stem rust *noun* (1899)
1 : a rust attacking the stem of a plant; *especially* **:** a destructive disease especially of wheat caused by a rust fungus (*Puccinia graminis*) which produces reddish brown lesions in the uredospore stage and black lesions in the teliospore stage and has any of several plants of the barberry family as an intermediate host
2 : the fungus causing stem rust
stem turn *noun* (1922)
: a skiing turn executed by stemming an outside ski
stem·ware \'stem-,war, -,wer\ *noun* (1926)
: glass hollowware mounted on a stem
stem–wind·er \-,wīn-dər\ *noun* (1875)
1 : a stem-winding watch
2 [from the superiority of the stem-winding watch over the older key-wound watch] **:** one that is first-rate of its kind; *especially* **:** a stirring speech
stem–wind·ing \-diŋ\ *adjective* (1867)
: wound by an inside mechanism turned by the knurled knob at the outside end of the stem ⟨a *stem-winding* watch⟩
Sten \'sten\ *noun* [R. V. Sheppard, 20th century English army officer + H. J. Turpin, 20th century English civil servant + *E*ngland] (1942)
: a light simple 9-millimeter British submachine gun
sten- *or* **steno-** *combining form* [Greek, from *stenos*]
: close **:** narrow **:** little ⟨*steno*bathic⟩
stench \'stench\ *noun* [Middle English, from Old English *stenc*; akin to Old English *stincan* to emit a smell — more at STINK] (before 12th century)
: STINK
— **stench·ful** \-fəl\ *adjective*
— **stenchy** \-chē\ *adjective*
¹sten·cil \'sten(t)-səl\ *noun* [Middle English *stanselen* to ornament with sparkling colors, from Middle French *estanceler*, from *estancele* spark, from (assumed) Vulgar Latin *stincilla*, alteration of Latin *scintilla*] (1707)
1 : an impervious material (as a sheet of paper, thin wax, or woven fabric) perforated with lettering or a design through which a substance (as ink, paint, or metallic powder) is forced onto a surface to be printed
2 : something (as a pattern, design, or print) that is produced by means of a stencil
3 : a printing process that uses a stencil
²stencil *transitive verb* **sten·ciled** *or* **sten·cilled; sten·cil·ing** *or* **sten·cil·ling** \-s(ə-)liŋ\ (circa 1828)
1 : to mark or paint with a stencil
2 : to produce by stencil
— **sten·cil·er** *or* **sten·cil·ler** \-s(ə-)lər\ *noun*
steno \'ste-(,)nō\ *noun, plural* **sten·os** (1913)
1 : STENOGRAPHER
2 : STENOGRAPHY
steno·bath·ic \,ste-nə-'ba-thik\ *adjective* [*sten-* + Greek *bathos* depth] (1902)
of a pelagic organism **:** living within narrow limits of depth
ste·nog·ra·pher \stə-'nä-grə-fər\ *noun* (1809)
1 : a writer of shorthand
2 : a person employed chiefly to take and transcribe dictation
ste·nog·ra·phy \-fē\ *noun* (1602)
1 : the art or process of writing in shorthand
2 : shorthand especially written from dictation or oral discourse
3 : the making of shorthand notes and subsequent transcription of them

— **steno·graph·ic** \,ste-nə-'gra-fik\ *adjective*
— **steno·graph·i·cal·ly** \-fi-k(ə-)lē\ *adverb*
steno·ha·line \,ste-nō-'hā-,līn, -'ha-,līn\ *adjective* [International Scientific Vocabulary *sten-* + Greek *halinos* of salt, from *hals* salt — more at SALT] (circa 1920)
of an aquatic organism **:** unable to withstand wide variation in salinity of the surrounding water
ste·nosed \stə-'nōzd, -'nōst\ *adjective* [from past participle of *stenose* to affect with stenosis] (1897)
: affected with stenosis
ste·no·sis \stə-'nō-səs\ *noun, plural* **-no·ses** \-,sēz\ [New Latin, from Greek *stenōsis* act of narrowing, from *stenoun* to narrow, from *stenos* narrow] (circa 1860)
: a narrowing or constriction of the diameter of a bodily passage or orifice
— **ste·not·ic** \-'nä-tik\ *adjective*
steno·ther·mal \,ste-nə-'thər-məl\ *adjective* (1881)
: capable of surviving over only a narrow range of temperatures ⟨*stenothermal* fish⟩
— **steno·therm** \'ste-nə-,thərm\ *noun*
steno·top·ic \,ste-nə-'tä-pik\ *adjective* [probably from German *stenotop* stenotopic, from *sten-* + Greek *topos* place] (1945)
: having a narrow range of adaptability to changes in environmental conditions
steno·type \'ste-nə-,tīp\ *noun* [*steno-* (as in *stenography*) + *type*] (1922)
: a small machine somewhat like a typewriter used to record speech by means of phonograms
— **stenotype** *transitive verb*
— **steno·typ·ist** \-,tī-pist\ *noun*
— **ste·no·ty·py** \-,tī-pē\ *noun*
sten·tor \'sten-,tȯr, -tər\ *noun* [Latin, from Greek *Stentōr* Stentor, a Greek herald in the Trojan War noted for his loud voice] (1609)
1 : a person having a loud voice
2 : any of a widely distributed genus (*Stentor*) of ciliate protozoans having a trumpet-shaped body with the mouth at the broad end and with the narrow end often attached to the substrate
sten·to·ri·an \sten-'tōr-ē-ən, -'tȯr-\ *adjective* (1605)
: extremely loud
synonym see LOUD
¹step \'step\ *noun* [Middle English, from Old English *stæpe*; akin to Old High German *stapfo* step, *stampfōn* to stamp] (before 12th century)
1 : a rest for the foot in ascending or descending: as **a :** one of a series of structures consisting of a riser and a tread **b :** a ladder rung
2 a (1) **:** an advance or movement made by raising the foot and bringing it down elsewhere (2) **:** a combination of foot or foot and body movements constituting a unit or a repeated pattern ⟨a dance *step*⟩ (3) **:** manner of walking **:** STRIDE **b :** FOOTPRINT 1 **c :** the sound of a footstep ⟨heard *steps* in the hall⟩
3 a : the space passed over in one step **b :** a short distance ⟨just a *step* away from the bank⟩ **c :** the height of one stair
4 *plural* **:** COURSE, WAY ⟨directed his *steps* toward the river⟩
5 a : a degree, grade, or rank in a scale **b :** a stage in a process ⟨was guided through every *step* of my career⟩
6 : a frame on a ship designed to receive an upright shaft; *especially* **:** a block supporting the heel of a mast
7 : an action, proceeding, or measure often occurring as one in a series ⟨taking *steps* to improve the situation⟩
8 : a steplike offset or part usually occurring in a series
9 : an interval in a musical scale
— **step·like** \-,līk\ *adjective*
— **stepped** \'stept\ *adjective*

— **in step 1 :** with each foot moving to the same time as the corresponding foot of others or in time to music **2 :** in harmony or agreement
— **out of step :** not in step ⟨*out of step* with the times⟩
²step *verb* **stepped; step·ping** (before 12th century)
intransitive verb
1 a : to move by raising the foot and bringing it down elsewhere or by moving each foot in succession **b :** DANCE
2 a : to go on foot **:** WALK **b** *obsolete* **:** ADVANCE, PROCEED **c :** to be on one's way **:** LEAVE — often used with *along* **d :** to move briskly ⟨kept us *stepping*⟩
3 : to press down with the foot ⟨*step* on the brake⟩
4 : to come as if at a single step ⟨*stepped* into a good job⟩
transitive verb
1 : to take by moving the feet in succession ⟨*step* three paces⟩
2 a : to move (the foot) in any direction **:** SET ⟨the first man to *step* foot on the moon⟩ **b :** to traverse on foot
3 : to go through the steps of **:** PERFORM ⟨*step* a minuet⟩
4 : to make erect by fixing the lower end in a step ⟨*step* the mast⟩
5 : to measure by steps ⟨*step* off 50 yards⟩
6 a : to provide with steps **b :** to make steps in ⟨*step* a key⟩
7 : to construct or arrange in or as if in steps ⟨craggy peaks with terraces *stepped* up the sides —*Time*⟩
— **step on it :** to increase one's speed **:** hurry up
step- *combining form* [Middle English, from Old English *stēop-*; akin to Old High German *stiof-* step-, Old English *astēpan* to deprive, bereave]
: related by virtue of a remarriage (as of a parent) and not by blood ⟨*step*parent⟩ ⟨*step*sister⟩
step·broth·er \'step-,brə-thər\ *noun* (15th century)
: a son of one's stepparent by a former marriage
step–by–step \,step-bī-'step\ *adjective or adverb* (1701)
: marked by successive degrees usually of limited extent **:** GRADUAL
step·child \'step-,chīld\ *noun* (before 12th century)
1 : a child of one's wife or husband by a former marriage
2 : one that fails to receive proper care or attention ⟨is no longer a *stepchild* in the family of nations —F. R. Smith⟩
step dance *noun* (1887)
: a dance in which steps are emphasized rather than gesture or posture
step·daugh·ter \'step-,dȯ-tər\ *noun* (before 12th century)
: a daughter of one's wife or husband by a former marriage
step–down \'step-,daun\ *noun* (1922)
: a decrease or reduction in size or amount ⟨a *step-down* in dosage⟩
step down (1890)
intransitive verb
: RETIRE, RESIGN
transitive verb
1 : to lower (a voltage) by means of a transformer
2 : to decrease or reduce especially by one or more steps
— **step–down** \'step-,daun\ *adjective*
step·fam·i·ly \'step-,fam-lē, -,fa-mə-\ *noun* (1966)

\ə\ abut \ᵊ\ kitten \ər\ further \a\ ash \ā\ ace \ä\ mop, mar \au̇\ out \ch\ chin \e\ bet \ē\ easy \g\ go \i\ hit \ī\ ice \j\ job \ŋ\ sing \ō\ go \ȯ\ law \ȯi\ boy \th\ thin \t̲h̲\ the \ü\ loot \u̇\ foot \y\ yet \zh\ vision *see also* Guide to Pronunciation

: a family in which there is a stepparent

step·fa·ther \'step-ˌfä-thər\ *noun* (before 12th century)
: the husband of one's mother by a subsequent marriage

step function *noun* (circa 1929)
: a mathematical function of a single real variable that remains constant within each of a series of adjacent intervals but changes in value from one interval to the next

steph·a·no·tis \ˌste-fə-'nō-təs\ *noun* [New Latin, from Greek *stephanōtis* fit for a crown, from *stephanos* crown, from *stephein* to crown] (1843)
: any of a genus (*Stephanotis* and especially *S. floribunda*) of Old World tropical woody vines of the milkweed family with fragrant white flowers the corolla of which has a cylindrical dilated tube and spreading limb

stephanotis

step–in \'step-ˌin\ *noun* (1921)
: an article of clothing put on by being stepped into: as **a** : a shoe resembling but usually having a higher vamp than a pump and concealed elastic to adjust the fit **b** : short panties for women — usually used in plural
— **step–in** *adjective*

step in *intransitive verb* (15th century)
1 : to intervene in an affair or dispute
2 : to make a brief informal visit

step·lad·der \'step-ˌla-dər\ *noun* (1751)
: a ladder that has broad flat steps and two pairs of legs connected by a hinge at the top and that opens at the bottom to become freestanding

step·moth·er \-ˌmə-thər\ *noun* (before 12th century)
: the wife of one's father by a subsequent marriage

step out *intransitive verb* (circa 1533)
1 : to go away from a place usually for a short distance and for a short time
2 : to go or march at a vigorous or increased pace
3 : DIE
4 : to lead an active social life
5 : to be unfaithful — usually used with *on*

step·par·ent \'step-ˌpar-ənt, -ˌper-\ *noun* (circa 1890)
: the spouse of one's mother or father by a subsequent marriage

step·par·ent·ing *noun* (1979)
: the raising of a child by a stepparent

steppe \'step\ *noun* [Russian *step'*] (1671)
1 : one of the vast usually level and treeless tracts in southeastern Europe or Asia
2 : arid land with xerophilous vegetation found usually in regions of extreme temperature range and loess soil

stepped–up \'ste-pər\ *adjective* (1902)
: increased in intensity : ACCELERATED, INTENSIFIED ⟨*stepped-up* security⟩

step·per \'ste-pər\ *noun* (1835)
: one (as a fast horse or a dancer) that steps

stepper motor *noun* (1961)
: a motor whose driveshaft rotates in small steps rather than continuously — called also *stepping motor*

step·ping–stone \'ste-piŋ-ˌstōn\ *noun* (14th century)
1 : a stone on which to step (as in crossing a stream)
2 : a means of progress or advancement

step·sis·ter \'step-ˌsis-tər\ *noun* (15th century)
: a daughter of one's stepparent by a former marriage

step·son \-ˌsən\ *noun* (before 12th century)
: a son of one's husband or wife by a former marriage

step stool *noun* (1946)
: a stool with one or two steps that often fold away beneath the seat

step turn *noun* (1941)
: a skiing turn executed in a downhill traverse by lifting the upper ski from the ground, placing it in the desired direction, weighting it, and bringing the other ski parallel

step–up \'step-ˌəp\ *noun* (1922)
: an increase or advance in size or amount

step up (1902)
transitive verb
1 : to increase (a voltage) by means of a transformer
2 : to increase, augment, or advance especially by one or more steps ⟨*step up* production⟩
intransitive verb
1 : to come forward
2 : to undergo an increase ⟨business is *stepping up*⟩
3 : to receive a promotion
— **step–up** \'step-ˌəp\ *adjective*

step·wise \-ˌwīz\ *adjective* (1902)
1 : marked by or proceeding in steps
2 : moving by step to adjacent musical tones

-ster *noun combining form* [Middle English, from Old English *-estre* female agent; akin to Middle Dutch *-ster*]
1 : one that does or handles or operates ⟨spin*ster*⟩ ⟨tap*ster*⟩ ⟨team*ster*⟩
2 : one that makes or uses ⟨song*ster*⟩ ⟨pun*ster*⟩
3 : one that is associated with or participates in ⟨game*ster*⟩ ⟨gang*ster*⟩
4 : one that is ⟨young*ster*⟩

ster·co·ra·ceous \ˌstər-kə-'rā-shəs\ *adjective* [Latin *stercor-, stercus* excrement] (1731)
: relating to, being, or containing feces

ster·cu·lia gum \ˌstər-'k(y)ü-lē-ə-\ *noun* [New Latin *Sterculia,* genus of trees] (circa 1943)
: KARAYA GUM

stere- *or* **stereo-** *combining form* [New Latin, from Greek, from *stereos* solid — more at STARE]
1 : solid : solid body ⟨*stereo*gram⟩
2 a : stereoscopic ⟨*stereo*opsis⟩ **b** : having or dealing with three dimensions of space ⟨*stereo*chemistry⟩

¹ste·reo \'ster-ē-ˌō, 'stir-\ *noun, plural* **ste·re·os** (circa 1823)
1 : STEREOTYPE
2 [by shortening] **a** : stereophonic reproduction **b** : a stereophonic sound system

²stereo *adjective* (1876)
1 a : STEREOSCOPIC **b** : produced by or as if by means of a stereotype
2 : STEREOPHONIC

ste·reo·chem·is·try \ˌster-ē-ō-'ke-mə-strē, ˌstir-\ *noun* [International Scientific Vocabulary] (1890)
1 : a branch of chemistry that deals with the spatial arrangement of atoms and groups in molecules
2 : the spatial arrangement of atoms and groups in a compound and its relation to the properties of the compound
— **ste·reo·chem·i·cal** \-'ke-mi-kəl\ *adjective*

ste·reo·gram \'ster-ē-ə-ˌgram, 'stir-\ *noun* [International Scientific Vocabulary] (1868)
1 : a diagram or picture representing objects with an impression of solidity or relief
2 : STEREOGRAPH

ste·reo·graph \-ˌgraf\ *noun* [International Scientific Vocabulary] (1859)
: a pair of stereoscopic pictures or a picture composed of two superposed stereoscopic images that gives a three-dimensional effect when viewed with a stereoscope or special spectacles
— **stereograph** *transitive verb*

ste·reo·graph·ic \ˌster-ē-ə-'gra-fik\ *adjective* (1704)
: of, relating to, or being a delineation of the form of a solid body (as the earth) on a plane ⟨*stereographic* projection⟩

— ste·re·og·ra·phy \ˌster-ē-'ä-grə-fē\ *noun*

ste·reo·iso·mer \ˌster-ē-ō-'ī-sə-mər, ˌstir-\ *noun* [International Scientific Vocabulary] (1894)
: any of a group of isomers in which atoms are linked in the same order but differ in their spatial arrangement
— **ste·reo·iso·mer·ic** \-ˌī-sə-'mer-ik\ *adjective*
— **ste·reo·isom·er·ism** \-ī-'sä-mə-ˌri-zəm\ *noun*

ste·re·ol·o·gy \ˌster-ē-'ä-lə-jē, ˌstir-\ *noun* [International Scientific Vocabulary] (1963)
: a branch of science concerned with inferring the three-dimensional properties of objects or matter ordinarily observed two-dimensionally
— **ste·reo·log·i·cal** \-ē-ə-'lä-ji-kəl\ *adjective*
— **ste·reo·log·i·cal·ly** \-ji-k(ə-)lē\ *adverb*

ste·reo·mi·cro·scope \-'mī-krə-ˌskōp\ *noun* (1948)
: a microscope having a set of optics for each eye to make an object appear in three dimensions
— **ste·reo·mi·cro·scop·ic** \-ˌmī-krə-'skä-pik\ *adjective*
— **ste·reo·mi·cro·scop·i·cal·ly** \-pi-k(ə-)lē\ *adverb*

ste·reo·phon·ic \ˌster-ē-ə-'fä-nik, ˌstir-\ *adjective* [International Scientific Vocabulary] (1927)
: of, relating to, or constituting sound reproduction involving the use of separated microphones and two transmission channels to achieve the sound separation of a live hearing
— **ste·reo·phon·i·cal·ly** \-ni-k(ə-)lē\ *adverb*
— **ste·reo·pho·ny** \ˌster-ē-'ä-fə-nē, ˌstir-; 'ster-ē-ə-ˌfō-nē, 'stir\ *noun*

ste·reo·pho·tog·ra·phy \ˌster-ē-ō-fə-'tä-grə-fē, ˌstir-\ *noun* [International Scientific Vocabulary] (1903)
: stereoscopic photography
— **ste·reo·pho·to·graph·ic** \-ˌfō-tə-'gra-fik\ *adjective*

ste·re·op·sis \ˌster-ē-'äp-səs, ˌstir-\ *noun* [New Latin, from *stere-* + Greek *opsis* vision, appearance — more at OPTIC] (circa 1911)
: stereoscopic vision

ste·re·op·ti·con \-'äp-ti-kən\ *noun* [New Latin, from *stere-* + Greek *optikon,* neuter of *optikos* optic] (1863)
1 : a projector for transparent slides often made double so as to produce dissolving views
2 : STEREOSCOPE

ste·reo·reg·u·lar \ˌster-ē-ō-'re-gyə-lər, ˌstir-\ *adjective* (1958)
: of, relating to, or involving stereochemical regularity in the repeating units of a polymeric structure
— **ste·reo·reg·u·lar·i·ty** \-ˌre-gyə-'lar-ə-tē\ *noun*

ste·reo·scope \'ster-ē-ə-ˌskōp, 'stir-\ *noun* (1838)
: an optical instrument with two eyeglasses for helping the observer to combine the images of two pictures taken from points of view a little way apart and thus to get the effect of solidity or depth

ste·reo·scop·ic \ˌster-ē-ə-'skä-pik, ˌstir-\ *adjective* (1855)
1 : of or relating to stereoscopy or the stereoscope
2 : characterized by stereoscopy ⟨*stereoscopic* vision⟩
— **ste·reo·scop·i·cal·ly** \-pi-k(ə-)lē\ *adverb*

ste·re·os·co·py \ˌster-ē-'äs-kə-pē, ˌstir-; 'ster-ē-ə-ˌskō-pē, 'stir-\ *noun* [International Scientific Vocabulary] (circa 1859)
1 : a science that deals with stereoscopic effects and methods
2 : the seeing of objects in three dimensions

ste·reo·spe·cif·ic \,ster-ē-ō-spi-'si-fik, ,stir-\ *adjective* (1949)
: being, produced by, or involved in a stereochemically specific process ⟨many enzymes act as *stereospecific* catalysts⟩ ⟨*stereospecific* plastics⟩
— **ste·reo·spe·cif·i·cal·ly** \-fi-k(ə-)lē\ *adverb*
— **ste·reo·spec·i·fic·i·ty** \-,spe-sə-'fi-sə-tē\ *noun*

ste·reo·tac·tic \,ster-ē-ə-'tak-tik, ,stir-\ *adjective* (1950)
: STEREOTAXIC

ste·reo·tax·ic \,ster-ē-ə-'tak-sik, ,stir-\ *adjective* [New Latin *stereotaxis* stereotaxic technique, from *stere-* + *-taxis*] (1908)
: of, relating to, or being a technique or apparatus used in neurological research or surgery for directing the tip of a delicate instrument (as a needle or an electrode) in three planes in attempting to reach a specific locus in the brain
— **ste·reo·tax·i·cal·ly** \-si-k(ə-)lē\ *adverb*

¹ste·reo·type \'ster-ē-ə-,tīp, 'stir-\ *transitive verb* (1804)
1 : to make a stereotype from
2 a : to repeat without variation : make hackneyed **b** : to develop a mental stereotype about
— **ste·reo·typ·er** *noun*

²stereotype *noun* [French *stéréotype*, from *stéré-* stere- + *type*] (1817)
1 : a plate cast from a printing surface
2 : something conforming to a fixed or general pattern; *especially* : a standardized mental picture that is held in common by members of a group and that represents an oversimplified opinion, prejudiced attitude, or uncritical judgment
word history see CLICHÉ
— **ste·reo·typ·i·cal** \,ster-ē-ə-'ti-pi-kəl\ *also* **ste·reo·typ·ic** \-pik\ *adjective*
— **ste·reo·typ·i·cal·ly** \-pi-k(ə-)lē\ *adverb*

ste·reo·typed *adjective* (1849)
: lacking originality or individuality
synonym see TRITE

ste·reo·ty·py \'ster-ē-ə-,tī-pē, 'stir-\ *noun, plural* **-pies** (circa 1889)
: frequent almost mechanical repetition of the same posture, movement, or form of speech (as in schizophrenia)

ste·ric \'ster-ik, 'stir-\ *adjective* [International Scientific Vocabulary *stere-* + *¹-ic*] (1898)
: relating to or involving the arrangement of atoms in space : SPATIAL
— **ste·ri·cal·ly** \'ster-i-k(ə-)lē, 'stir-\ *adverb*

ste·rig·ma \stə-'rig-mə\ *noun, plural* **-ma·ta** \-mə-tə\ *also* **-mas** [New Latin, from Greek *stērigma* support, from *stērizein* to prop; perhaps akin to Greek *stereos* solid — more at STARE] (circa 1866)
: one of the slender stalks at the top of the basidium of some fungi from the tips of which the basidiospores are formed; *broadly* : a stalk or filament that bears conidia or spermatia

ster·il·ant \'ster-ə-lənt\ *noun* (1941)
: a sterilizing agent

ster·ile \'ster-əl, *chiefly British* -,īl\ *adjective* [Middle English *steryle*, from Latin *sterilis*; akin to Gothic *stairo* barren animal, Sanskrit *starī* sterile cow] (15th century)
1 a : failing to bear or incapable of producing fruit or spores **b** : failing to produce or incapable of producing offspring ⟨a *sterile* hybrid⟩ **c** : incapable of germinating ⟨*sterile* spores⟩ **d** *of a flower* : neither perfect nor pistillate
2 a : unproductive of vegetation ⟨a *sterile* arid region⟩ **b** : free from living organisms and especially microorganisms **c** : lacking in stimulating emotional or intellectual quality : LIFELESS ⟨a *sterile* work of art⟩
— **ster·ile·ly** \-ə(l)-lē\ *adverb*
— **ste·ril·i·ty** \stə-'ri-lə-tē\ *noun*

ster·il·ize \'ster-ə-,līz\ *transitive verb* **-ized; -iz·ing** (1695)

: to make sterile: as **a** : to cause (land) to become unfruitful **b** (1) : to deprive of the power of reproducing (2) : to make incapable of germination **c** : to make powerless or useless usually by restraining from a normal function, relation, or participation **d** : to free from living microorganisms
— **ster·il·i·za·tion** \,ster-ə-lə-'zā-shən\ *noun*
— **ster·il·iz·er** \'ster-ə-,lī-zər\ *noun*

¹ster·ling \'stər-liŋ\ *noun* [Middle English, silver penny, probably from (assumed) Old English *steorling*, from Old English *steorra* star + *¹-ling* — more at STAR] (14th century)
1 : British money
2 : sterling silver or articles of it

²sterling *adjective* (15th century)
1 a : of, relating to, or calculated in terms of British sterling **b** : payable in sterling
2 a *of silver* : having a fixed standard of purity usually defined legally as represented by an alloy of 925 parts of silver with 75 parts of copper **b** : made of sterling silver
3 : conforming to the highest standard ⟨*sterling* character⟩
— **ster·ling·ly** \-liŋ-lē\ *adverb*
— **ster·ling·ness** *noun*

sterling area *noun* (1932)
: a former group of countries with currencies tied to the British pound sterling

¹stern \'stərn\ *adjective* [Middle English *sterne*, from Old English *styrne*; akin to Old English *starian* to stare — more at STARE] (before 12th century)
1 a : having a definite hardness or severity of nature or manner : AUSTERE **b** : expressive of severe displeasure : HARSH
2 : forbidding or gloomy in appearance
3 : INEXORABLE ⟨*stern* necessity⟩
4 : STURDY, STOUT ⟨a *stern* resolve⟩
synonym see SEVERE
— **stern·ly** *adverb*
— **stern·ness** \'stərn-nəs\ *noun*

²stern *noun* [Middle English, rudder, probably of Scandinavian origin; akin to Old Norse *stjōrn* act of steering; akin to Old English *stīeran* to steer — more at STEER] (14th century)
1 : the rear end of a boat
2 : a hinder or rear part : the last or latter part

ster·nal \'stər-n°l\ *adjective* (1756)
: of or relating to the sternum

stern chase *noun* [²*stern*] (1627)
: a chase in which a pursuing ship follows in the path of another

stern chaser *noun* (1815)
: a gun so placed as to be able to fire astern at a pursuing ship

stern·fore·most \'stərn-'fōr-,mōst, -'fòr-\ *adverb* (1840)
: with the stern in advance : BACKWARD

ster·nite \'stər-,nīt\ *noun* [International Scientific Vocabulary, from Greek *sternon* chest] (1868)
: the ventral part or shield of a somite of an arthropod; *especially* : the chitinous plate that forms the ventral surface of an abdominal or occasionally a thoracic segment of an insect

stern·most \'stərn-,mōst\ *adjective* (1622)
: farthest astern

ster·no·cos·tal \,stər-nō-'käs-t°l\ *adjective* [New Latin *stern*um + English *-o-* + *costal*] (1785)
: of, relating to, or situated between the sternum and ribs

stern·post \'stərn-,pōst\ *noun* (15th century)
: the principal member at the stern of a ship extending from keel to deck

stern sheets *noun plural* (15th century)
: the space in the stern of an open boat not occupied by the thwarts

ster·num \'stər-nəm\ *noun, plural* **sternums** *or* **ster·na** \-nə\ [New Latin, from Greek *sternon* chest, breastbone; akin to Old High German *stirna* forehead, Latin *sternere* to spread out — more at STREW] (1667)

: a compound ventral bone or cartilage of most vertebrates other than fishes that connects the ribs or the shoulder girdle or both and in humans consists of the manubrium, gladiolus, and xiphoid process — called also *breastbone*

ster·nu·ta·tion \,stər-nyə-'tā-shən\ *noun* [Middle English *sternutacion*, from Latin *sternutation-, sternutatio*, from *sternutare* to sneeze, frequentative of *sternuere* to sneeze; akin to Greek *ptarnysthai* to sneeze] (15th century)
: the act, fact, or noise of sneezing

ster·nu·ta·tor \'stər-nyə-,tā-tər\ *noun* (1922)
: an agent that induces sneezing and often lacrimation and vomiting

stern·ward \'stərn-wərd\ *or* **stern·wards** \-wərdz\ *adverb* (1832)
: AFT

stern·way \'stərn-,wā\ *noun* (1769)
: movement of a ship backward or with stern foremost

stern–wheel·er \-'hwē-lər, -'wē-\ *noun* (1855)
: a steamboat driven by a single paddle wheel at the stern

ste·roid \'stir-,óid *also* 'ster-\ *noun* [International Scientific Vocabulary *ster*ol + *-oid*] (1926)
: any of numerous compounds containing a 17-carbon 4-ring system and including the sterols and various hormones and glycosides
— **steroid** *or* **ste·roi·dal** \stə-'rói-d°l\ *adjective*

ste·roido·gen·e·sis \stə-,rói-də-'je-nə-səs, ,stir-,óid- *also* ,ster-\ *noun* [New Latin] (1951)
: synthesis of steroids
— **ste·roido·gen·ic** \-'je-nik\ *adjective*

ste·rol \'stir-,ól, 'ster-, -,ōl\ *noun* [International Scientific Vocabulary, from *-sterol* (as in *cho-lesterol*)] (1913)
: any of various solid steroid alcohols (as cholesterol) widely distributed in animal and plant lipids

-sterone *combining form* [*ster*ol + *-one*]
: steroid hormone ⟨andro*sterone*⟩

ster·tor \'stər-tər, -,tòr\ *noun* [New Latin, from Latin *stertere* to snore; akin to *sternuere* to sneeze] (1804)
: the act or fact of producing a snoring sound : SNORING

ster·to·rous \'stər-tə-rəs\ *adjective* (1802)
: characterized by a harsh snoring or gasping sound
— **ster·to·rous·ly** *adverb*

stet \'stet\ *transitive verb* **stet·ted; stet·ting** [Latin, let it stand, from *stare* to stand — more at STAND] (1755)
: to direct retention of (a word or passage previously ordered to be deleted or omitted from a manuscript or printer's proof) by annotating usually with the word *stet*

stetho·scope \'ste-thə-,skōp *also* -thə-\ *noun* [French *stéthoscope*, from Greek *stēthos* chest + French *-scope*] (1820)
: an instrument used to detect and study sounds produced in the body
— **stetho·scop·ic** \,ste-thə-'skä-pik *also* -thə-\ *adjective*

Stet·son \'stet-sən\ *trademark*
— used for a broad-brimmed high-crowned felt hat

¹ste·ve·dore \'stē-və-,dōr, -,dòr *also* 'stēv-,\ *noun* [Spanish *estibador*, from *estibar* to pack, from Latin *stipare* to press together — more at STIFF] (1788)
: one who works at or is responsible for loading and unloading ships in port

²stevedore *verb* **-dored; -dor·ing** (1862)
transitive verb

\ə\ abut	\°\ kitten	\ər\ further	\a\ ash \ā\ ace
\ä\ mop, mar	\aù\ out	\ch\ chin	\e\ bet \ē\ easy
\g\ go	\i\ hit	\ī\ ice	\j\ job \ŋ\ sing
\ō\ law	\òi\ boy	\th\ thin	\t͟h\ the \ü\ loot \ù\ foot
\y\ yet	\zh\ vision		*see also* Guide to Pronunciation

: to handle (cargo) as a stevedore; *also* **:** to load or unload the cargo of (a ship) in port
intransitive verb
: to work as a stevedore

stevedore knot *noun* (circa 1863)
: a stopper knot similar to a figure eight knot but with one or more extra turns — called also *stevedore's knot; see* KNOT illustration

Ste·ven·graph \'stē-vən-ˌgraf\ *or* **Ste·vens·graph** \-vənz-\ *noun* [Thomas *Stevens,* 19th century American weaver] (1879)
: a woven silk picture

¹stew \'stü, 'styü\ *noun* [Middle English *stewe* heated room for a steam bath, from Middle French *estuve,* from (assumed) Vulgar Latin *extufa* — more at STOVE] (13th century)
1 *obsolete* **:** a utensil used for boiling
2 : a hot bath
3 a : WHOREHOUSE **b :** a district of bordellos — usually used in plural
4 a : fish or meat usually with vegetables prepared by stewing **b** (1) **:** a heterogeneous mixture (2) **:** a state of heat and congestion
5 : a state of excitement, worry, or confusion

²stew (14th century)
transitive verb
: to boil slowly or with simmering heat
intransitive verb
1 : to become cooked by stewing
2 : to swelter especially from confinement in a hot or stuffy atmosphere
3 : to be in a state of suppressed agitation, worry, or resentment

³stew *noun* [short for *stewardess*] (1970)
: FLIGHT ATTENDANT

¹stew·ard \'stü-ərd, 'styü-; 'st(y)u̇(-ə)rd\ *noun* [Middle English, from Old English *stīweard,* from *stī, stig* hall, sty + *weard* ward — more at STY, WARD] (before 12th century)
1 : one employed in a large household or estate to manage domestic concerns (as the supervision of servants, collection of rents, and keeping of accounts)
2 : SHOP STEWARD
3 : a fiscal agent
4 a : an employee on a ship, airplane, bus, or train who manages the provisioning of food and attends passengers **b :** one appointed to supervise the provision and distribution of food and drink in an institution
5 : one who actively directs affairs **:** MANAGER ◇

²steward (1621)
transitive verb
: to act as a steward for **:** MANAGE
intransitive verb
: to perform the duties of a steward

stew·ard·ess \'stü-ər-dəs, 'styü-; 'st(y)u̇(-ə)r-dəs\ *noun* (1631)
: a woman who performs the duties of a steward; *especially* **:** one who attends passengers (as on an airplane)
usage see -ESS

stew·ard·ship \'stü-ərd-ˌship, 'styü-; 'st(y)u̇(-ə)rd-\ *noun* (15th century)
1 : the office, duties, and obligations of a steward
2 : the conducting, supervising, or managing of something; *especially* **:** the careful and responsible management of something entrusted to one's care ⟨*stewardship* of our natural resources⟩

stewed *adjective* (circa 1737)
: DRUNK 1a

stew·pan \'stü-ˌpan, 'styü-\ *noun* (1651)
: a pan used for stewing

stib·nite \'stib-ˌnīt\ *noun* [alteration of obsolete English *stibine* stibnite, from French, from Latin *stibium* antimony, from Greek *stibi,* from Egyptian *sṭm*] (circa 1854)
: a mineral that consists of the trisulfide of antimony and occurs in orthorhombic lead-gray crystals of metallic luster or in massive form

sticho·myth·ia \ˌsti-kə-'mi-thē-ə\ *also* **sti·chom·y·thy** \sti-'kä-mə-thē\ *noun* [Greek *stichomythia,* from *stichomythein* to speak dia-

logue in alternate lines, from *stichos* row, verse + *mythos* speech, myth; akin to Greek *steichein* to walk, go — more at STAIR] (1861)
: dialogue especially of altercation or dispute delivered by two actors in alternating lines (as in classical Greek drama)
— **sticho·myth·ic** \ˌsti-kə-'mi-thik\ *adjective*

¹stick \'stik\ *noun* [Middle English *stik,* from Old English *sticca;* akin to Old Norse *stik* stick, Old English *stician* to stick] (before 12th century)
1 : a woody piece or part of a tree or shrub: as **a :** a usually dry or dead severed shoot, twig, or slender branch **b :** a cut or broken branch or piece of wood gathered for fuel or construction material
2 a : a long slender piece of wood or metal: as (1) **:** a club or staff used as a weapon (2) **:** WALKING STICK **b :** an implement used for striking or propelling an object in a game **c :** something used to force compliance **d :** a baton symbolizing an office or dignity; *also* **:** a person entitled to bear such a baton
3 : a piece of the materials composing something (as a building)
4 a : any of various implements resembling a stick in shape, origin, or use: as (1) **:** COMPOSING STICK (2) **:** an airplane lever operating the elevators and ailerons (3) **:** the gearshift lever of an automobile **b :** STICKFUL
5 : something prepared (as by cutting, molding, or rolling) in a relatively long and slender often cylindrical form ⟨a *stick* of candy⟩ ⟨a *stick* of butter⟩
6 a : PERSON, CHAP **b :** a dull, inert, stiff, or spiritless person
7 *plural* **:** remote usually rural districts regarded especially as backward, dull, or unsophisticated **:** BOONDOCKS
8 : an herbaceous stalk resembling a woody stick ⟨celery *sticks*⟩
9 : ¹MAST 1; *also* **:** ¹YARD 4
10 : a piece of furniture
11 a : a number of bombs arranged for release from a bombing plane in a series across a target **b :** a number of parachutists dropping together
12 *slang* **:** a marijuana cigarette
13 a : punishment or the threat of punishment used to force compliance or cooperation ⟨choosing between the carrot and the *stick*⟩ **b** *British* **:** CRITICISM, ABUSE
— **stick·like** \-ˌlīk\ *adjective*

²stick *transitive verb* (1573)
1 : to arrange (lumber) in stacks
2 : to provide a stick as a support for

³stick *verb* **stuck** \'stək\; **stick·ing** [Middle English *stikken,* from Old English *stician;* akin to Old High German *sticken* to prick, Latin *instigare* to urge on, goad, Greek *stizein* to tattoo] (before 12th century)
transitive verb
1 a : to pierce with something pointed **:** STAB **b :** to kill by piercing
2 : to push or thrust so as or as if to pierce
3 a : to fasten by thrusting in **b :** IMPALE **c :** PUSH, THRUST
4 : to put or set in a specified place or position
5 : to furnish with things fastened on by or as if by piercing
6 : to attach by or as if by causing to adhere to a surface
7 a : to compel to pay especially by trickery ⟨got *stuck* with the bar bill⟩ **b :** OVERCHARGE

stick 2b: *a* lacrosse, *b* ice hockey, *c* field hockey

8 a : to halt the movement or action of **b :** BAFFLE, STUMP
9 a : CHEAT, DEFRAUD **b :** to saddle with something disadvantageous or disagreeable ⟨is still *stuck* with that lousy car⟩
intransitive verb
1 : to hold to something firmly by or as if by adhesion: **a :** to become fixed in place by means of a pointed end **b :** to become fast by or as if by miring or by gluing or plastering ⟨*stuck* in the mud⟩
2 a : to remain in a place, situation, or environment **b :** to hold fast or adhere resolutely **:** CLING **c :** to remain effective **d :** to keep close in a chase or competition
3 : to become blocked, wedged, or jammed
4 a : BALK, SCRUPLE **b :** to find oneself baffled **c :** to be unable to proceed
5 : PROJECT, PROTRUDE ☆
— **stick in one's craw :** to irritate, nag at, or obsess one
— **stick it to :** to treat harshly or unfairly
— **stick one's neck out :** to make oneself vulnerable by taking a risk
— **stick to one's guns :** to maintain one's position especially in face of opposition
— **stuck on :** infatuated with

⁴stick *noun* (1633)
1 : a thrust with a pointed instrument **:** STAB
2 a : DELAY, STOP **b :** IMPEDIMENT
3 : adhesive quality or substance

stick around *intransitive verb* (circa 1912)
: to stay or wait about **:** LINGER

stick·ball \'stik-ˌbȯl\ *noun* (1934)
: baseball adapted for play in streets or small areas and using a broomstick and a lightweight ball

stick·er \'sti-kər\ *noun* (15th century)
1 : one that pierces with a point
2 a : one that adheres or causes adhesion **b :** a slip of paper with adhesive back that can be fastened to a surface

sticker price *noun* (1969)
: a manufacturer's suggested retail price that is printed on a sticker and affixed to a new automobile

☆ **SYNONYMS**
Stick, adhere, cohere, cling, cleave mean to become closely attached. STICK implies attachment by affixing or by being glued together (couldn't get the label to *stick*). ADHERE is often interchangeable with *stick* but sometimes implies a growing together ⟨antibodies *adhering* to a virus⟩. COHERE suggests a sticking together of parts so that they form a unified mass ⟨eggs will make the mixture *cohere*⟩. CLING implies attachment by hanging on with arms or tendrils ⟨*clinging* to a capsized boat⟩. CLEAVE stresses strength of attachment ⟨the wet shirt *cleaved* to his back⟩.

◇ **WORD HISTORY**
steward The Old English word *stig* or *stī* meant "sty or pen" (for hogs) and "hall" (for people). We have no evidence, however, that *stigweard* or *stīweard,* a compound of *stig* or *stī* with *weard* "keeper, guard," ever referred to a keeper of pigs or pigsties. It meant rather the keeper of the hall, the supervisor of the household's domestic concerns, and thus an official of importance. One important concern of a medieval English hall or household was the dispensing, as well as the husbanding, of wealth, both of which were the responsibility of the steward. Even today the English sovereign has a Lord Steward of the Household, who is a peer and a member of the Privy Council, although his real power is now, unlike formerly, restricted to the royal household.

stick figure *noun* (1949)
1 : a drawing showing the head of a human being or animal as a circle and all other parts as straight lines
2 : a fictional character lacking depth and believability

stick·ful \'stik-ˌfúl\ *noun* (1683)
: as much set type as fills a composing stick

stick·han·dle \'stik-ˌhan-dᵊl\ *intransitive verb* (1929)
: to maneuver a puck (as in hockey) or a ball (as in lacrosse) with a stick
— **stick·han·dler** \-ˌhan(d)-lər, -ˌhan-dᵊl-ər\ *noun*

sticking plaster *noun* (1655)
chiefly British **:** an adhesive plaster especially for closing superficial wounds

sticking point *noun* (1946)
: an item (as in negotiations) resulting or likely to result in an impasse

stick insect *noun* (1854)
: any of various usually wingless insects (especially family Phasmatidae) with a long cylindrical body resembling a stick

stick–in–the–mud \'stik-ən-thə-ˌməd\ *noun* (1733)
: one who is slow, old-fashioned, or unprogressive; *especially* **:** an old fogy

stick·it \'sti-kət\ *adjective* [Scots, from past participle of English ³*stick*] (1787)
1 *Scottish* **:** UNFINISHED
2 *chiefly Scottish* **:** having failed especially in an intended profession

stick·le \'sti-kəl\ *intransitive verb* **stick·led; stick·ling** \-k(ə-)liŋ\ [alteration of Middle English *stightlen,* frequentative of *stighten* to arrange, from Old English *stihtan;* akin to Old Norse *stētta* to found, support] (1642)
1 : to contend especially stubbornly and usually on insufficient grounds
2 : to feel scruples **:** SCRUPLE

stick·le·back \'sti-kəl-ˌbak\ *noun* [Middle English *stykylbak,* from Old English *sticel* goad + Middle English *bak* back; akin to Old English *stician* to stick] (15th century)
: any of a family (Gasterosteidae) of small scaleless bony fishes having two or more free spines in front of the dorsal fin and including marine, anadromous, and freshwater forms

stick·ler \'sti-k(ə-)lər\ *noun* (1644)
1 : one who insists on exactness or completeness in the observance of something ⟨a *stickler* for the rules⟩
2 : something that baffles or puzzles **:** POSER, STICKER

stick·man \'stik-ˌman, -mən\ *noun* (circa 1931)
: one who handles a stick: as **a :** one who supervises the play at a dice table, calls the decisions, and retrieves the dice **b :** a player in any of various games (as hockey or lacrosse) played with a stick

stick out (1567)
intransitive verb
1 a : to jut out **:** PROJECT **b :** to be prominent or conspicuous
2 : to be persistent (as in a demand or an opinion)
transitive verb
: ENDURE, LAST — often used with *it* ⟨*stuck it out* to the end⟩

stick·pin \'stik-ˌpin\ *noun* (1895)
: an ornamental pin; *especially* **:** one worn in a necktie

stick·seed \-ˌsēd\ *noun* (1843)
: any of various weedy herbs (genera *Lappula* and *Hackelia*) of the borage family with bristly adhesive fruit

stick shift *noun* (1959)
: a manually operated gearshift for a motor vehicle usually mounted on the floor

stick·tight \'stik-ˌtīt\ *noun* (circa 1884)
: BUR MARIGOLD

stick–to–it·ive·ness \stik-'tü-ə-tiv-nəs\ *noun* [from the phrase *stick to it*] (1867)
: dogged perseverance **:** TENACITY

stick·um \'sti-kəm\ *noun* [³*stick* + -*um* (probably alteration of *'em* them)] (circa 1909)
: a substance that adheres or causes adhesion

stick·up \'stik-ˌəp\ *noun* (1904)
: a robbery at gunpoint **:** HOLDUP

stick up (15th century)
intransitive verb
: to stand upright or on end **:** PROTRUDE
transitive verb
: to rob at gunpoint
— **stick up for :** to speak or act in defense of **:** SUPPORT

stick·weed \'stik-ˌwēd\ *noun* (1743)
: any of several plants (as a beggar's-lice) with adhesive seeds

stick·work \-ˌwərk\ *noun* (1903)
: the use of one's stick in offensive and defensive techniques (as in hockey)

sticky \'sti-kē\ *adjective* **stick·i·er; -est** (circa 1735)
1 a : ADHESIVE **b** (1) **:** VISCOUS, GLUEY (2) **:** coated with a sticky substance
2 : HUMID, MUGGY; *also* **:** CLAMMY
3 : tending to stick
4 a : DISAGREEABLE, UNPLEASANT **b :** AWKWARD, STIFF **c :** DIFFICULT, PROBLEMATIC
5 : excessively sentimental **:** CLOYING
— **stick·i·ly** \'sti-kə-lē\ *adverb*
— **stick·i·ness** \'sti-kē-nəs\ *noun*

sticky wicket *noun* (1926)
: a difficult or delicate problem or situation

stic·tion \'stik-shən\ *noun* [*static* + fr*iction*] (1946)
: the force required to cause one body in contact with another to begin to move

¹**stiff** \'stif\ *adjective* [Middle English *stif,* from Old English *stíf;* akin to Middle Dutch *stijf* stiff, Latin *stipare* to press together, Greek *steibein* to tread on] (before 12th century)
1 a : not easily bent **:** RIGID **b :** lacking in suppleness or responsiveness ⟨*stiff* muscles⟩ **c :** impeded in movement — used of a mechanism **d :** DRUNK 1a
2 a : FIRM, RESOLUTE **b :** STUBBORN, UNYIELDING **c :** PROUD **d** (1) **:** marked by reserve or decorum (2) **:** lacking in ease or grace **:** STILTED
3 : hard fought **:** PUGNACIOUS, SHARP
4 a (1) **:** exerting great force ⟨a *stiff* wind⟩ (2) **:** FORCEFUL, VIGOROUS **b :** POTENT ⟨a *stiff* dose⟩
5 : of a dense or glutinous consistency **:** THICK
6 a : HARSH, SEVERE ⟨a *stiff* penalty⟩ **b :** ARDUOUS, RUGGED ⟨*stiff* terrain⟩
7 : not easily heeled over by an external force (as the wind) ⟨a *stiff* ship⟩
8 : EXPENSIVE, STEEP ⟨paid a *stiff* price⟩ ☆
— **stiff·ish** \'sti-fish\ *adjective*
— **stiff·ly** *adverb*
— **stiff·ness** *noun*

²**stiff** *adverb* (13th century)
1 : in a stiff manner **:** STIFFLY
2 : to an extreme degree **:** SEVERELY ⟨scared *stiff*⟩ ⟨bored *stiff*⟩

³**stiff** *noun* (circa 1859)
1 : CORPSE
2 a : TRAMP, BUM **b :** HAND, LABORER **c :** PERSON ⟨a lucky *stiff*⟩
3 : FLOP, FAILURE

⁴**stiff** *transitive verb* (1950)
1 a : to refuse to pay or tip ⟨*stiffed* the doctor for the fee⟩ ⟨*stiffed* the waiter⟩ **b :** CHEAT ⟨*stiffed* him in a business deal⟩ **c :** STICK 7a ⟨*stiffed* us with the bar bill⟩
2 : SNUB 3 ⟨*stiffed* sportswriters after the game⟩

stiff–arm \'stif-ˌärm\ *verb or noun* (1909)
: STRAIGHT-ARM

stiff·en \'sti-fən\ *verb* **stiff·ened; stiff·en·ing** \'sti-fə-niŋ, 'stif-niŋ\ (15th century)
transitive verb
: to make stiff or stiffer
intransitive verb
: to become stiff or stiffer
— **stiff·en·er** \'sti-fə-nər, 'stif-nər\ *noun*

stiff–necked \'stif-'nekt\ *adjective* (1526)
1 : HAUGHTY, STUBBORN
2 : STILTED

stiff upper lip *noun* [from the phrase *keep a stiff upper lip*] (1815)
: a steady and determined attitude or manner in the face of trouble
— **stiff–upper–lip** *adjective*

¹**sti·fle** \'stī-fəl\ *noun* [Middle English] (14th century)
: the joint next above the hock in the hind leg of a quadruped (as a horse or dog) corresponding to the human knee — see HORSE illustration

²**stifle** *verb* **sti·fled; sti·fling** \-f(ə-)liŋ\ [alteration of Middle English *stuflen*] (1513)
transitive verb
1 a : to kill by depriving of oxygen **:** SUFFOCATE **b** (1) **:** SMOTHER (2) **:** MUFFLE
2 a : to cut off (as the voice or breath) **:** REPRESS ⟨*stifled* our anger⟩ **b :** to withhold from circulation or expression **:** REPRESS ⟨*stifled* our anger⟩ **c :** DETER, DISCOURAGE
intransitive verb
: to become suffocated by or as if by lack of oxygen **:** SMOTHER
— **sti·fler** \-f(ə-)lər\ *noun*
— **sti·fling·ly** \-f(ə-)liŋ-lē\ *adverb*

stig·ma \'stig-mə\ *noun, plural* **stig·ma·ta** \stig-'mä-tə, 'stig-mə-tə\ *or* **stig·mas** [Latin *stigmat-, stigma* mark, brand, from Greek, from *stizein* to tattoo — more at STICK] (circa 1593)
1 a *archaic* **:** a scar left by a hot iron **:** BRAND **b :** a mark of shame or discredit **:** STAIN **c :** an identifying mark or characteristic; *specifically* **:** a specific diagnostic sign of a disease
2 a *stigmata plural* **:** bodily marks or pains resembling the wounds of the crucified Christ and sometimes accompanying religious ecstasy **b :** PETECHIA
3 a : a small spot, scar, or opening on a plant or animal **b :** the usually apical part of the pistil of a flower which receives the pollen grains and on which they germinate — see FLOWER illustration ◇
— **stig·mal** \'stig-məl\ *adjective*

stig·mas·ter·ol \stig-'mas-tə-,ról, -,röl\ *noun* [New Latin Physo*stigma* (genus including the Calabar bean) + International Scientific Vocabulary *sterol*] (1907)
: a crystalline sterol $C_{29}H_{48}O$ obtained especially from the oils of Calabar beans and soybeans

¹**stig·mat·ic** \stig-'ma-tik\ *noun* (1594)
: one marked with stigmata

²**stigmatic** *adjective* (1607)
1 : having or conveying a social stigma
2 : of or relating to supernatural stigmata
3 : ANASTIGMATIC — used especially of a bundle of light rays intersecting at a single point
— **stig·mat·i·cal·ly** \-ti-k(ə-)lē\ *adverb*

stig·ma·tist \'stig-mə-tist, stig-'mä-\ *noun* (1607)
: STIGMATIC

stig·ma·tize \'stig-mə-,tīz\ *transitive verb* **-tized; -tiz·ing** (1585)
1 a *archaic* : BRAND **b** : to describe or identify in opprobrious terms
2 : to mark with stigmata
— **stig·ma·ti·za·tion** \,stig-mə-tə-'zā-shən\ *noun*

stil·bene \'stil-,bēn\ *noun* [International Scientific Vocabulary, from Greek *stilbein* to glitter] (circa 1868)
: an aromatic hydrocarbon $C_{14}H_{12}$ used as a phosphor and in making dyes; *also* : a compound derived from stilbene

stil·bes·trol \stil-'bes-,tról, -,tröl\ *noun* [*stilbene* + *estr*us + *¹-ol*] (1938)
1 : a crystalline synthetic derivative $C_{14}H_{12}O_2$ of stilbene that differs from the related diethylstilbestrol in lack of the ethyl groups and in possession of but slight estrogenic activity
2 : DIETHYLSTILBESTROL

stil·bite \'stil-,bīt\ *noun* [French, from Greek *stilbein*] (1815)
: a mineral consisting of a hydrous silicate of aluminum, calcium, and sodium and often occurring in sheaflike aggregations of crystals

¹**stile** \'stī(ə)l\ *noun* [Middle English, from Old English *stigel;* akin to Old English *stǣger* stair — more at STAIR] (before 12th century)
: a step or set of steps for passing over a fence or wall; *also* : TURNSTILE

²**stile** *noun* [probably from Dutch *stijl* post] (1678)
: one of the vertical members in a frame or panel into which the secondary members are fitted

sti·let·to \stə-'le-(,)tō\ *noun, plural* **-tos** *or* **-toes** [Italian, diminutive of *stilo* stylus, dagger, from Latin *stilus* stylus — more at STYLE] (1611)
1 : a slender dagger with a blade thick in proportion to its breadth
2 : a pointed instrument for piercing holes for eyelets or embroidery
3 : STILETTO HEEL

stiletto heel *noun* (1953)
: a high thin heel on women's shoes that is narrower than a spike heel

¹**still** \'stil\ *adjective* [Middle English *stille,* from Old English; akin to Old High German *stilli* still and perhaps to Old English *steall* stall — more at STALL] (before 12th century)
1 a : devoid of or abstaining from motion **b** *archaic* : SEDENTARY **c** : not effervescent ⟨*still* wine⟩ **d** (1) : of, relating to, or being a static photograph as contrasted with a motion picture (2) : designed for taking still photographs ⟨a *still* camera⟩ (3) : engaged in taking still photographs ⟨a *still* photographer⟩
2 a : uttering no sound : QUIET **b** : SUBDUED, MUTED
3 a : CALM, TRANQUIL **b** : free from noise or turbulence
— **still·ness** *noun*

²**still** (before 12th century)
intransitive verb
: to become motionless or silent : QUIET
transitive verb

1 a : ALLAY, CALM **b** : to put an end to : SETTLE
2 a : to arrest the motion of
3 : SILENCE

³**still** *adverb* (before 12th century)
1 : without motion ⟨sit *still*⟩
2 *archaic* **a** : ALWAYS, CONTINUALLY **b** : in a progressive manner : INCREASINGLY
3 — used as a function word to indicate the continuance of an action or condition ⟨*still* lives there⟩ ⟨drink it while it's *still* hot⟩
4 : in spite of that : NEVERTHELESS ⟨those who take the greatest care *still* make mistakes⟩
5 a : EVEN 2c ⟨a *still* more difficult problem⟩ **b** : YET 1a

⁴**still** *noun* (13th century)
1 : QUIET, SILENCE
2 : a static photograph; *specifically* : a photograph of actors or scenes of a motion picture for publicity or documentary purposes

⁵**still** *verb* [Middle English *stillen,* short for *distillen* to distill] (13th century)
: DISTILL

⁶**still** *noun* (1533)
1 : DISTILLERY
2 : apparatus used in distillation comprising either the chamber in which the vaporization is carried out or the entire equipment

still alarm *noun* (1875)
: a fire alarm transmitted (as by telephone call) without sounding the signal apparatus

still and all *adverb* (1829)
: NEVERTHELESS, STILL

still·birth \'stil-,bərth, -'bərth\ *noun* (1785)
: the birth of a dead fetus

still·born \-'bórn\ *adjective* (1593)
1 : dead at birth
2 : failing from the start : ABORTIVE ⟨a *still-born* venture⟩
— **still-born** \-,bórn\ *noun*

still–hunt \-,hənt\ (1858)
intransitive verb
: to ambush or stalk a quarry; *especially* : to pursue game noiselessly usually without a dog
transitive verb
: to lie in wait for : approach by stealth

still hunt *noun* (1828)
: a quiet pursuing or ambushing of game

still life *noun, plural* **still lifes** (1695)
1 : a picture consisting predominantly of inanimate objects
2 : the category of graphic arts concerned with inanimate subject matter

still·man \'stil-mən\ *noun* (circa 1864)
: one who owns or operates a still

still·room \'stil-,rüm, -,rùm\ *noun* [⁶*still*] (circa 1710)
British : a room connected with the kitchen where liqueurs, preserves, and cakes are kept and beverages (as tea) are prepared

still water *noun* (1832)
: a part of a stream where no current is visible

¹**stil·ly** \'stil-lē\ *adverb* (before 12th century)
: in a calm manner : QUIETLY

²**stilly** \'sti-lē\ *adjective* [⁴*still* + *-y*] (1776)
: STILL, QUIET

¹**stilt** \'stilt\ *noun* [Middle English *stilte;* akin to Old High German *stelza* stilt] (15th century)
1 a : one of two poles each with a rest or strap for the foot used to elevate the wearer above the ground in walking **b** : a pile or post serving as one of the supports of a structure above ground or water level
2 *plural also* **stilt** : any of various notably long-legged 3-toed shorebirds (genera *Himantopus* and *Cladorhynchus*) that are related to the avocets, frequent inland ponds and marshes, and nest in small colonies

²**stilt** *transitive verb* (1649)
: to raise on or as if on stilts

stilt·ed \'stil-təd\ *adjective* (1820)
1 a : POMPOUS, LOFTY **b** : FORMAL, STIFF
2 : having the curve beginning at some distance above the impost ⟨a *stilted* arch⟩
— **stilt·ed·ly** *adverb*
— **stilt·ed·ness** *noun*

Stil·ton \'stil-t°n\ *noun* [*Stilton,* Huntingdonshire, England] (1826)
: a blue-veined cheese with wrinkled rind made of whole cows' milk enriched with cream

stime \'stīm\ *noun* [Middle English (northern dialect)] (14th century)
chiefly Scottish & Irish : GLIMMER; *also* : GLIMPSE

stim·u·lant \'stim-yə-lənt\ *noun* (circa 1728)
1 : an agent (as a drug) that produces a temporary increase of the functional activity or efficiency of an organism or any of its parts
2 : STIMULUS
3 : an alcoholic beverage — not used technically
— **stimulant** *adjective*

stim·u·late \-,lāt\ *verb* **-lat·ed; -lat·ing** [Latin *stimulatus,* past participle of *stimulare,* from *stimulus* goad; perhaps akin to Latin *stilus* stem, stylus — more at STYLE] (1619)
transitive verb
1 : to excite to activity or growth or to greater activity : ANIMATE, AROUSE
2 a : to function as a physiological stimulus to **b** : to arouse or affect by a stimulant (as a drug)
intransitive verb
: to act as a stimulant or stimulus
synonym see PROVOKE
— **stim·u·la·tion** \,stim-yə-'lā-shən\ *noun*
— **stim·u·la·tive** \'stim-yə-,lā-tiv\ *adjective*
— **stim·u·la·tor** \-,lā-tər\ *noun*
— **stim·u·la·to·ry** \-lə-,tōr-ē, -,tòr-\ *adjective*

stim·u·lus \'stim-yə-ləs\ *noun, plural* **-li** \-,lī, -,lē\ [Latin] (1684)
: something that rouses or incites to activity: as **a** : INCENTIVE **b** : STIMULANT 1 **c** : an agent (as an environmental change) that directly influences the activity of a living organism or one of its parts (as by exciting a sensory organ or evoking muscular contraction or glandular secretion)

¹**sting** \'stiŋ\ *verb* **stung** \'stəŋ\; **sting·ing** \'stiŋ-iŋ\ [Middle English, from Old English *stingan;* akin to Old Norse *stinga* to sting and probably to Greek *stachys* spike of grain, *stochos* target, aim] (before 12th century)
transitive verb
1 : to prick painfully: as **a** : to pierce or wound with a poisonous or irritating process **b** : to affect with sharp quick pain or smart ⟨hail *stung* their faces⟩
2 : to cause to suffer acutely ⟨*stung* with remorse⟩
3 : OVERCHARGE, CHEAT
intransitive verb
1 : to wound one with or as if with a sting
2 : to feel a keen burning pain or smart; *also* : to cause such pain
— **sting·ing·ly** \-iŋ-lē\ *adverb*

²**sting** *noun* (before 12th century)
1 a : the act of stinging; *specifically* : the thrust of a stinger into the flesh **b** : a wound or pain caused by or as if by stinging
2 : STINGER 2
3 : a sharp or stinging element, force, or quality
4 : an elaborate confidence game; *specifically* : such a game worked by undercover police in order to trap criminals

sting·a·ree \'stiŋ-ə-rē *also* 'stiŋ-rē\ *noun* [by alteration] (1836)
: STINGRAY

sting·er \'stiŋ-ər\ *noun* (circa 1552)
1 : one that stings; *specifically* : a sharp blow or remark
2 : a sharp organ (as of a bee, scorpion, or stingray) that is usually connected with a poison gland or otherwise adapted to wound by piercing and injecting a poison
3 : a cocktail usually consisting of brandy and white crème de menthe

stinging nettle *noun* (1525)

: NETTLE 1; *especially* : one (*Urtica dioica*) established in North America that has broad coarsely toothed leaves

sting·less \'stiŋ-ləs\ *adjective* (1554)
: having no sting or stinger

sting·ray \-ˌrā\ *noun* (1624)
: any of numerous rays (as of the family Dasyatidae) with one or more large sharp barbed dorsal spines near the base of the whiplike tail capable of inflicting severe wounds

stin·gy \'stin-jē\ *adjective* **stin·gi·er; -est** [perhaps from (assumed) English dialect *stinge*, noun, sting; akin to Old English *stingan* to sting] (1659)
1 : not generous or liberal : sparing or scant in giving or spending
2 : meanly scanty or small ☆
— **stin·gi·ly** \-jə-lē\ *adverb*
— **stin·gi·ness** \-jē-nəs\ *noun*

¹stink \'stiŋk\ *intransitive verb* **stank** \'staŋk\ *or* **stunk** \'stəŋk\; **stunk; stink·ing** [Middle English, from Old English *stincan*; akin to Old High German *stinkan* to emit a smell] (before 12th century)
1 : to emit a strong offensive odor
2 : to be offensive; *also* : to be in bad repute
3 : to possess something to an offensive degree ⟨*stinking* with wealth⟩
4 : to be extremely bad in quality
— **stinky** \'stiŋ-kē\ *adjective*

²stink *noun* (13th century)
1 : a strong offensive odor : STENCH
2 : a public outcry against something

stink·ard \'stiŋ-kərd\ *noun* (circa 1600)
: a mean or contemptible person

stink bomb *noun* (1915)
: a small bomb charged usually with chemicals that gives off a foul odor on bursting

stink·bug \'stiŋk-ˌbəg\ *noun* (1877)
: any of various hemipterous bugs (especially family Pentatomidae) that emit a disagreeable odor

stink·er \'stiŋ-kər\ *noun* (1607)
1 a : one that stinks **b** : an offensive or contemptible person **c** : something of very poor quality
2 : any of several large petrels that have an offensive odor
3 *slang* : something extremely difficult ⟨the examination was a real *stinker*⟩

stink·horn \'stiŋk-ˌhȯrn\ *noun* (1724)
: any of various fetid basidiomycetous fungi (order Phallales, especially *Phallus impudicus*) having spores dispersed by insects

¹stink·ing *adjective* (before 12th century)
1 : strong and offensive to the sense of smell
2 *slang* : offensively drunk
synonym see MALODOROUS
— **stink·ing·ly** \'stiŋ-kiŋ-lē\ *adverb*

²stinking *adverb* (1887)
: to an extreme degree ⟨got *stinking* drunk⟩

stinking smut *noun* (circa 1891)
: ⁴BUNT

stink·pot \'stiŋk-ˌpät\ *noun* (1669)
1 : an earthen jar filled with fetid material and formerly sometimes thrown as a stink bomb on an enemy's deck
2 : MUSK TURTLE
3 : STINKER 1
4 *slang* : MOTORBOAT

stink up *transitive verb* (1941)
: to cause to stink or be filled with a stench

stink·weed \'stiŋk-ˌwēd\ *noun* (1753)
: any of various strong-scented or fetid plants; *especially* : PENNYCRESS

stink·wood \-ˌwu̇d\ *noun* (1731)

1 : any of several trees with a wood of unpleasant odor; *especially* : a southern African tree (*Ocotea bullata*) of the laurel family yielding a valued cabinet wood
2 : the wood of a stinkwood

¹stint \'stint\ *verb* [Middle English, from Old English *styntan* to blunt, dull; akin to Old Norse *stuttr* scant] (13th century)
intransitive verb
1 *archaic* : STOP, DESIST
2 : to be sparing or frugal
transitive verb
1 *archaic* : to put an end to : STOP
2 a : to restrain within certain limits : CONFINE
b : to restrict with respect to a share or allowance
3 : to assign a task to (a person)
— **stint·er** *noun*

²stint *noun* (circa 1530)
1 a : a definite quantity of work assigned **b** : a period of time spent at a particular activity ⟨served a brief *stint* as a waiter⟩
2 : RESTRAINT, LIMITATION
synonym see TASK

³stint *noun, plural* **stints** *also* **stint** [Middle English *stynte*] (15th century)
: any of several small sandpipers

stipe \'stīp\ *noun* [New Latin *stipes*, from Latin, tree trunk; akin to Latin *stipare* to press together — more at STIFF] (1785)
: a usually short plant stalk: as **a** : the stem supporting the cap of a fungus **b** : a part that is similar to a stipe and connects the holdfast and blade of a frondose alga **c** : the petiole of a fern frond **d** : a prolongation of the receptacle beneath the ovary of a seed plant
— **stiped** \'stīpt\ *adjective*

sti·pend \'stī-ˌpend, -pənd\ *noun* [Middle English, alteration of *stipendy*, from Latin *stipendium*, from *stip-, stips* gift + *pendere* to weigh, pay] (15th century)
: a fixed sum of money paid periodically for services or to defray expenses

¹sti·pen·di·ary \stī-'pen-dē-ˌer-ē\ *noun, plural* **-ar·ies** (15th century)
: one who receives a stipend

²stipendiary *adjective* (circa 1545)
1 : receiving or compensated by wages or salary ⟨a *stipendiary* curate⟩
2 : of or relating to a stipend

sti·pes \'stī-ˌpēz\ *noun, plural* **stip·i·tes** \'sti-pə-ˌtēz\ [New Latin *stipit-, stipes*, from Latin, tree trunk] (1760)
: PEDUNCLE; *especially* : the second basal segment of a maxilla of an insect or crustacean

¹stip·ple \'sti-pəl\ *transitive verb* **stip·pled; stip·pling** \-p(ə-)liŋ\ [Dutch *stippelen* to spot, dot] (circa 1762)
1 : to engrave by means of dots and flicks
2 a : to make by small short touches (as of paint or ink) that together produce an even or softly graded shadow **b** : to apply (as paint) by repeated small touches
3 : SPECKLE, FLECK
— **stip·pler** \-p(ə-)lər\ *noun*

²stipple *noun* (1837)
: production of gradation of light and shade in graphic art by stippling small points, larger dots, or longer strokes; *also* : an effect produced in this way

stip·u·lar \'sti-pyə-lər\ *adjective* (1793)
: of, resembling, or provided with stipules ⟨*stipular* glands⟩

¹stip·u·late \'sti-pyə-ˌlāt\ *verb* **-lat·ed; -lat·ing** [Latin *stipulatus*, past participle of *stipulari* to demand some term in an agreement] (circa 1624)
intransitive verb
1 : to make an agreement or covenant to do or forbear something : CONTRACT
2 : to demand an express term in an agreement — used with *for*
transitive verb
1 : to specify as a condition or requirement of an agreement or offer
2 : to give a guarantee of

— **stip·u·la·tor** \-ˌlā-tər\ *noun*

²stip·u·late \'sti-pyə-lət\ *adjective* [New Latin *stipula*] (1776)
: having stipules

stip·u·la·tion \ˌsti-pyə-'lā-shən\ *noun* (circa 1552)
1 : an act of stipulating
2 : something stipulated; *especially* : a condition, requirement, or item specified in a legal instrument
— **stip·u·la·to·ry** \'sti-pyə-lə-ˌtōr-ē, -ˌtȯr-\ *adjective*

stip·ule \'sti-(ˌ)pyü(ə)l\ *noun* [New Latin *stipula*, from Latin, stalk; akin to Latin *stipes* tree trunk] (1793)
: either of a pair of appendages borne at the base of the leaf in many plants

¹stir \'stər\ *verb* **stirred; stir·ring** [Middle English, from Old English *styrian*; akin to Old High German *stōren* to scatter] (before 12th century)
transitive verb
1 a : to cause an especially slight movement or change of position of **b** : to disturb the quiet of : AGITATE
2 a : to disturb the relative position of the particles or parts of especially by a continued circular movement **b** : to mix by or as if by stirring
3 : BESTIR, EXERT
4 : to bring into notice or debate : RAISE
5 a : to rouse to activity : evoke strong feelings in **b** : to call forth (as a memory) : EVOKE
c : PROVOKE
intransitive verb
1 a : to make a slight movement **b** : to begin to move (as in rousing)
2 : to begin to be active
3 : to be active or busy
4 : to pass an implement through a substance with a circular movement
5 : to be able to be stirred
— **stir·rer** *noun*

²stir *noun* (14th century)
1 a : a state of disturbance, agitation, or brisk activity **b** : widespread notice and discussion : IMPRESSION ⟨the book caused quite a *stir*⟩
2 : a slight movement
3 : a stirring movement

³stir *noun* [origin unknown] (1851)
slang : PRISON

stir·about \'stər-ə-ˌbau̇t\ *noun* (1682)
: a porridge of Irish origin consisting of oatmeal or cornmeal boiled in water or milk and stirred

stir–cra·zy \'stər-'krā-zē\ *adjective* [³*stir*] (circa 1908)

☆ **SYNONYMS**
Stingy, close, niggardly, parsimonious, penurious, miserly mean being unwilling or showing unwillingness to share with others. STINGY implies a marked lack of generosity ⟨a *stingy* child, not given to sharing⟩. CLOSE suggests keeping a tight grip on one's money and possessions ⟨folks who are very *close* when charity calls⟩. NIGGARDLY implies giving or spending the very smallest amount possible ⟨the *niggardly* amount budgeted for the town library⟩. PARSIMONIOUS suggests a frugality so extreme as to lead to stinginess ⟨a *parsimonious* life-style notably lacking in luxuries⟩. PENURIOUS implies niggardliness that gives an appearance of actual poverty ⟨the *penurious* eccentric bequeathed a fortune⟩. MISERLY suggests a sordid avariciousness and a morbid pleasure in hoarding ⟨a *miserly* couple devoid of social conscience⟩.

\ə\ abut \ᵊ\ kitten \ər\ further \a\ ash \ā\ ace
\ä\ mop, mar \au̇\ out \ch\ chin \e\ bet \ē\ easy
\g\ go \i\ hit \ī\ ice \j\ job \ŋ\ sing \ō\ go
\ȯ\ law \ȯi\ boy \th\ thin \t͟h\ the \ü\ loot \u̇\ foot
\y\ yet \zh\ vision *see also* Guide to Pronunciation

slang **:** distraught because of prolonged confinement

¹stir–fry \-'frī\ *transitive verb* (1958)
: to fry quickly over high heat in a lightly oiled pan (as a wok) while stirring continuously

²stir–fry \-ˌfrī\ *noun* (1959)
: a dish of something stir-fried

stirk \'stərk\ *noun* [Middle English, from Old English *stirc;* akin to Middle Low German *sterke* young cow and perhaps to Gothic *stairo* sterile animal — more at STERILE] (before 12th century)
British **:** a young bull or cow especially between one and two years old

Stir-ling engine \'stər-liŋ-\ *noun* [Robert *Stirling* (died 1878) Scottish engineer] (1896)
: an external combustion engine having an enclosed working fluid (as helium) that is alternately compressed and expanded to operate a piston

Stir-ling's formula \'stər-liŋz-\ *noun* [James *Stirling* (died 1770) Scottish mathematician] (1926)
: a formula

$$\sqrt{2\pi n}\, n^n e^{-n}$$

that approximates the value of the factorial of a very large number *n*

stirp \'stərp\ *noun* [Latin *stirp-, stirps*] (1502)
: a line descending from a common ancestor
: STOCK, LINEAGE

stirps \'stirps, 'stərps\ *noun, plural* **stir-pes** \'stir-ˌpās, 'stər-(ˌ)pēz\ [Latin, literally, stem, stock] (1681)
1 : a branch of a family; *also* **:** the person from whom it is descended
2 a : a group of animals equivalent to a superfamily **b :** a race or fixed variety of plants

stir-ring \'stər-iŋ\ *adjective* (before 12th century)
1 : ACTIVE, BUSTLING
2 : ROUSING, INSPIRING ⟨a *stirring* speech⟩

stir-rup \'stər-əp *also* 'stir-əp *or* 'stə-rəp\ *noun* [Middle English *stirop,* from Old English *stigrāp,* from *stig-* (akin to Old High German *stīgan* to go up) + *rāp* rope — more at STAIR, ROPE] (before 12th century)
1 : either of a pair of small light frames or rings for receiving the foot of a rider that are attached by a strap to a saddle and used to aid in mounting and as a support while riding
2 : a piece resembling a stirrup (as a support or clamp in carpentry and machinery)
3 : a rope secured to a yard and attached to a thimble in its lower end for supporting a footrope
4 : STAPES

stirrup cup *noun* (1681)
1 : a small serving of drink (as wine) taken by a rider about to depart; *also* **:** the vessel in which it is served
2 : a farewell cup

stirrup leather *noun* (14th century)
: the looped strap suspending a stirrup

stirrup pump *noun* (1939)
: a portable hand pump held in position by a foot bracket and used for throwing a jet or spray of liquid

¹stitch \'stich\ *noun* [Middle English *stiche,* from Old English *stice;* akin to Old English *stician* to stick] (before 12th century)
1 : a local sharp and sudden pain especially in the side
2 a : one in-and-out movement of a threaded needle in sewing, embroidering, or suturing **b :** a portion of thread left in the material or suture left in the tissue after one stitch
3 : a least part especially of clothing
4 : a single loop of thread or yarn around an implement (as a knitting needle or crochet hook)
5 : a stitch or series of stitches formed in a particular way ⟨a basting *stitch*⟩

— in stitches : in a state of uncontrollable laughter

²stitch (13th century)
transitive verb
1 a : to fasten, join, or close with or as if with stitches **b :** to make, mend, or decorate with or as if with stitches
2 : to unite by means of staples
intransitive verb
: SEW

— stitch-er *noun*

stitch-ery \'stich-rē, 'sti-chə-\ *noun* (1607)
: NEEDLEWORK

stitch-wort \'stich-ˌwərt, -ˌwȯrt\ *noun* (13th century)
: any of several chickweeds (genus *Stellaria*)

stithy \'sti-thē, -thē\ *noun, plural* **stith-ies** [Middle English, from Old Norse *stethi;* akin to Old English *stede* stead] (13th century)
1 *archaic* **:** ANVIL
2 *archaic* **:** SMITHY 1

sti-ver \'stī-vər\ *noun* [Dutch *stuiver*] (1502)
1 : a unit of value and coin of the Netherlands equal to ¹⁄₂₀ gulden
2 : something of little value

stoa \'stō-ə\ *noun* [Greek; akin to Greek *stylos* pillar — more at STEER] (1603)
: an ancient Greek portico usually walled at the back with a front colonnade designed to afford a sheltered promenade

stoat \'stōt\ *noun, plural* **stoats** *also* **stoat** [Middle English *stote*] (15th century)
: the common Holarctic ermine (*Mustela erminea*) especially in its brown summer coat

stob \'stäb\ *noun* [Middle English, stump; akin to Middle English *stubb* stub] (15th century)
chiefly dialect **:** STAKE, POST

stoc-ca-do \stə-'kä-(ˌ)dō\ *noun, plural* **-dos** [Italian *stoccata*] (1582)
archaic **:** a thrust with a rapier

sto-chas-tic \stə-'kas-tik, stō-\ *adjective* [Greek *stochastikos* skillful in aiming, from *stochazesthai* to aim at, guess at, from *stochos* target, aim, guess — more at STING] (1923)
1 : RANDOM; *specifically* **:** involving a random variable ⟨a *stochastic* process⟩
2 : involving chance or probability **:** PROBABILISTIC ⟨a *stochastic* model of radiation-induced mutation⟩

— sto-chas-ti-cal-ly \-ti-k(ə-)lē\ *adverb*

¹stock \'stäk\ *noun* [Middle English *stok,* from Old English *stocc;* akin to Old High German *stoc* stick] (before 12th century)
1 a *archaic* **:** STUMP **b** *archaic* **:** a log or block of wood **c** (1) *archaic* **:** something without life or consciousness (2) **:** a dull, stupid, or lifeless person
2 : a supporting framework or structure: as **a** *plural* **:** the frame or timbers holding a ship during construction **b** *plural* **:** a device for publicly punishing offenders consisting of a wooden frame with holes in which the feet or feet and hands can be locked **c** (1) **:** the wooden part by which a shoulder arm is held during firing (2) **:** the butt of an implement (as a whip or fishing rod) (3) **:** BITSTOCK, BRACE **d :** a long beam on a field gun forming the third support point in firing
3 a : the main stem of a plant **:** TRUNK **b** (1) **:** a plant or plant part united with a scion in grafting and supplying mostly underground parts to a graft (2) **:** a plant from which slips or cuttings are taken
4 : the crosspiece of an anchor — see ANCHOR illustration
5 a : the original (as a person, race, or language) from which others derive **:** SOURCE **b** (1) **:** the descendants of one individual **:** FAMILY, LINEAGE (2) **:** a compound organism — compare CLONE **c :** an infraspecific group usually having unity of descent **d** (1) **:** a related group of languages (2) **:** a language family
6 a (1) **:** the equipment, materials, or supplies of an establishment (2) **:** LIVESTOCK **b :** a store or supply accumulated; *especially* **:** the inventory of goods of a merchant or manufacturer

7 a *archaic* **:** a supply of capital **:** FUNDS; *especially* **:** money or capital invested or available for investment or trading **b** (1) **:** the part of a tally formerly given to the creditor in a transaction (2) **:** a debt or fund due (as from a government) for money loaned at interest; *also, British* **:** capital or a debt or fund bearing interest in perpetuity and not ordinarily redeemable as to principal **c** (1) **:** the proprietorship element in a corporation usually divided into shares and represented by transferable certificates (2) **:** a portion of such stock of one or more companies (3) **:** STOCK CERTIFICATE
8 : any of a genus (Matthiola) of Old World herbs or subshrubs of the mustard family with racemes of usually sweet-scented flowers
9 : a wide band or scarf worn about the neck especially by some clergymen
10 a : liquid in which meat, fish, or vegetables have been simmered that is used as a basis for soup, gravy, or sauce **b** (1) **:** raw material from which something is manufactured (2) **:** paper used for printing **c :** the portion of a pack of cards not distributed to the players at the beginning of a game
11 a (1) **:** an estimate or evaluation of something ⟨take *stock* of the situation⟩ (2) **:** the estimation in which someone or something is held ⟨his *stock* with the electorate remains high —*Newsweek*⟩ **b :** confidence or faith placed in someone or something ⟨put little *stock* in his testimony⟩
12 : the production and presentation of plays by a stock company
13 : STOCK CAR 1

— in stock : on hand **:** in the store and ready for delivery

— out of stock : having no more on hand **:** completely sold out

²stock (15th century)
transitive verb
1 : to make (a domestic animal) pregnant
2 : to fit to or with a stock
3 : to provide with stock or a stock **:** SUPPLY ⟨*stock* a stream with trout⟩
4 : to procure or keep a stock of
5 : to graze (livestock) on land
intransitive verb
1 : to send out new shoots
2 : to put in stock or supplies ⟨*stock* up on canned goods⟩

³stock *adjective* (1625)
1 a : kept regularly in stock ⟨comes in *stock* sizes⟩ ⟨a *stock* model⟩ **b :** commonly used or brought forward **:** STANDARD ⟨the *stock* answer⟩
2 a : kept for breeding purposes **:** BROOD ⟨a *stock* mare⟩ **b :** devoted to the breeding and rearing of livestock ⟨a *stock* farm⟩ **c :** used or intended for livestock ⟨a *stock* train⟩ **d :** used in herding livestock ⟨a *stock* horse⟩ ⟨a *stock* dog⟩
3 : of or relating to a stock company
4 : employed in handling, checking, or taking care of the stock of merchandise on hand ⟨a *stock* clerk⟩

¹stock-ade \stä-'kād\ *noun* [Spanish *estacada,* from *estaca* stake, pale, of Germanic origin; akin to Old English *staca* stake] (1614)
1 : a line of stout posts set firmly to form a defense
2 a : an enclosure or pen made with posts and stakes **b :** an enclosure in which prisoners are kept

²stockade *transitive verb* **stock-ad-ed; stock-ad-ing** (1677)
: to fortify or surround with a stockade

stockade fence (1985)
: a solid fence of half-round boards pointed at the top

stock-breed-er \'stäk-ˌbrē-dər\ *noun* (1815)
: a person engaged in the breeding and care of livestock for the market, for show purposes, or for racing

stock-bro-ker \-ˌbrō-kər\ *noun* (circa 1706)

: a broker who executes orders to buy and sell securities and often also acts as a security dealer
— **stock·bro·ker·age** \-k(ə-)rij\ *noun*
— **stock·brok·ing** \-,brō-kiŋ\ *noun*

stock car *noun* (1858)
1 : a latticed railroad boxcar for carrying live-stock
2 : a racing car having the basic chassis of a commercially produced assembly-line model

stock certificate *noun* (1863)
: an instrument evidencing ownership of one or more shares of the capital stock of a corporation

stock company *noun* (1827)
1 : a corporation or joint-stock company of which the capital is represented by stock
2 : a theatrical company attached to a repertory theater; *especially* : one without outstanding stars

stock dividend *noun* (circa 1902)
1 : the payment by a corporation of a dividend in the form of shares usually of its own stock without change in par value — compare STOCK SPLIT
2 : the stock distributed in a stock dividend

stock·er \'stä-kər\ *noun* (1881)
1 : a young animal (as a steer or heifer) suitable for being fed and fattened for market
2 : an animal (as a heifer) suitable for use in a breeding establishment
3 : STOCK CAR 2

stock exchange *noun* (1773)
1 : a place where security trading is conducted on an organized system
2 : an association of people organized to provide an auction market among themselves for the purchase and sale of securities

stock·fish \-,fish\ *noun* [Middle English *stok-fish,* from Middle Dutch *stocvisch,* from *stoc* stick + *visch* fish] (13th century)
: fish (as cod, haddock, or hake) dried hard in the open air without salt

stock·hold·er \'stäk-,hōl-dər\ *noun* (circa 1776)
: an owner of corporate stock

stock·i·nette *or* **stock·i·net** \,stä-kə-'net\ *noun* [alteration of earlier *stocking net*] (1784)
: a soft elastic usually cotton fabric used especially for bandages and infants' wear

stock·ing \'stä-kiŋ\ *noun* [obsolete *stock* to cover with a stocking] (1583)
1 a : a usually knit close-fitting covering for the foot and leg **b** : SOCK
2 : something resembling a stocking; *especially* : a ring of distinctive color on the lower part of the leg of an animal
— **stock·inged** \-kiŋd\ *adjective*
— **in one's stocking feet** : having on stockings but no shoes

stocking cap *noun* (circa 1897)
: a long knitted cone-shaped cap with a tassel or pom-pom worn especially for winter sports or play

stocking stuffer *noun* (1948)
: a small gift suitable for placing in a Christmas stocking

stock–in–trade \,stäk-ən-'trād, 'stäk-ən-,\ *noun* (circa 1771)
1 : the equipment, merchandise, or materials necessary to or used in a trade or business
2 : something that resembles the standard equipment of a tradesman or business ⟨humor was her *stock-in-trade* as a writer⟩

stock·ish \'stä-kish\ *adjective* (1596)
: like a stock : STUPID

stock·ist \'stä-kist\ *noun* (1910)
British : one (as a retailer) that stocks goods

stock·job·ber \'stäk-,jä-bər\ *noun* (circa 1626)
: one who deals in stocks: as **a** : a member of the London Stock Exchange who deals speculatively with brokers or other jobbers and usually specializes in one class of securities — called also *jobber* **b** : STOCKBROKER — usually used disparagingly

stock·job·bing \-,jä-biŋ\ *noun* (1692)
: speculative exchange dealings

stock·keep·er \'stäk-,kē-pər\ *noun* (circa 1786)
1 : one (as a herdsman or shepherd) having the charge or care of livestock
2 : one that keeps and records stock (as in a warehouse) : one that keeps an inventory of goods on hand, shipped, or received

stock·man \-mən, -,man\ *noun* (1806)
: one occupied as an owner or worker in the raising of livestock (as cattle or sheep)

stock market *noun* (1809)
1 : STOCK EXCHANGE 1
2 a : a market for particular stocks **b** : the market for stocks throughout a country

stock option *noun* (1945)
1 : an option contract involving stock
2 : a right granted by a corporation to officers or employees as a form of compensation that allows purchase of corporate stock at a fixed price at a specified time with reimbursement derived from the difference between purchase and market prices

¹stock·pile \'stäk-,pīl\ *noun* (1872)
: a storage pile: as **a** : a reserve supply of something essential accumulated within a country for use during a shortage **b** : a gradually accumulated reserve of something ⟨avert *stockpiles* of unsold cars —Bert Pierce⟩

²stockpile *transitive verb* (1921)
1 : to place or store in or on a stockpile
2 : to accumulate a stockpile of ⟨*stockpile* war materials in Europe —A. O. Wolfers⟩
— **stock·pil·er** *noun*

stock·pot \'stäk-,pät\ *noun* (1853)
1 : a pot in which soup stock is prepared
2 : an abundant supply : REPOSITORY

stock·room \-,rüm, -,rùm\ *noun* (1825)
: a storage place for supplies or goods used in a business

stock saddle *noun* (1886)
: WESTERN SADDLE

stock split *noun* (1950)
: a division of corporate stock by the issuance to existing shareholders of a specified number of new shares with a corresponding lowering of par value for each outstanding share — compare STOCK DIVIDEND

stock–still \'stäk-'stil\ *adjective* (15th century)
: very still : MOTIONLESS ⟨stood *stock-still*⟩

stock·tak·ing \'stäk-,tā-kiŋ\ *noun* (circa 1858)
1 : INVENTORY 3
2 : the action of estimating a situation at a given moment

stocky \'stä-kē\ *adjective* **stock·i·er; -est** (1622)
: compact, sturdy, and relatively thick in build
— **stock·i·ly** \'stä-kə-lē\ *adverb*
— **stock·i·ness** \'stä-kē-nəs\ *noun*

stock·yard \'stäk-,yärd\ *noun* (1802)
: a yard for stock; *specifically* : one in which transient cattle, sheep, swine, or horses are kept temporarily for slaughter, market, or shipping

¹stodge \'stäj\ *transitive verb* **stodged; stodg·ing** [origin unknown] (1674)
British : to stuff full especially with food

²stodge *noun* (1825)
British : something or someone stodgy

stodgy \'stä-jē\ *adjective* **stodg·i·er; -est** (1858)
1 : having a rich filling quality : HEAVY ⟨*stodgy* bread⟩
2 : moving in a slow plodding way especially as a result of physical bulkiness
3 : BORING, DULL ⟨on a peaceful rather *stodgy* Sunday boat trip —Edna Ferber⟩
4 : extremely old-fashioned : HIDEBOUND ⟨received a pompously Victorian letter from his *stodgy* father —E. S. Montagu⟩
5 a : DRAB **b** : DOWDY
— **stodg·i·ly** \'stä-jə-lē\ *adverb*
— **stodg·i·ness** \'stä-jē-nəs\ *noun*

sto·gie *or* **sto·gy** \'stō-gē\ *noun, plural* **sto·gies** [*Conestoga,* Pa.] (1853)
1 : a stout coarse shoe : BROGAN
2 : an inexpensive slender cylindrical cigar; *broadly* : CIGAR

¹sto·ic \'stō-ik\ *noun* [Middle English, from Latin *stoicus,* from Greek *stōïkos,* literally, of the portico, from *Stoa (Poikilē)* the Painted Portico, portico at Athens where Zeno taught] (14th century)
1 *capitalized* : a member of a school of philosophy founded by Zeno of Citium about 300 B.C. holding that the wise man should be free from passion, unmoved by joy or grief, and submissive to natural law
2 : one apparently or professedly indifferent to pleasure or pain ◇

²stoic *or* **sto·i·cal** \-i-kəl\ *adjective* (15th century)
1 *capitalized* : of, relating to, or resembling the Stoics or their doctrines ⟨*Stoic* logic⟩
2 : not affected by or showing passion or feeling; *especially* : firmly restraining response to pain or distress ⟨a *stoic* indifference to cold⟩
synonym see IMPASSIVE
— **sto·i·cal·ly** \-i-k(ə-)lē\ *adverb*

stoi·chio·met·ric \,stòi-kē-ō-'me-trik\ *adjective* (1892)
: of, relating to, used in, or marked by stoichiometry
— **stoi·chio·met·ri·cal·ly** \-tri-k(ə-)lē\ *adverb*

stoi·chi·om·e·try \,stòi-kē-'ä-mə-trē\ *noun* [Greek *stoicheion* element (from *stoichos* row) + English *-metry*; akin to Greek *steichein* to walk, go — more at STAIR] (1807)
1 : a branch of chemistry that deals with the application of the laws of definite proportions and of the conservation of mass and energy to chemical activity
2 a : the quantitative relationship between constituents in a chemical substance **b** : the quantitative relationship between two or more substances especially in processes involving physical or chemical change

sto·i·cism \'stō-ə-,si-zəm\ *noun* (1626)
1 *capitalized* : the philosophy of the Stoics
2 : indifference to pleasure or pain : IMPASSIVENESS

◇ **WORD HISTORY**
stoic In Athens about the year 300 B.C. the philosopher Zeno began to teach a radically new doctrine that was to spread its influence throughout the Greco-Roman world for at least the next five hundred years. He gave lectures at a public hall adjacent to the agora (marketplace) called the *Stoa Poikilē* ("Painted Colonnade"). In later years Zeno's philosophical school itself became known as the *Stoa,* and the derivative adjective *stōïkos,* literally, "of the colonnade," was used to refer to the school. Basically what he taught was that happiness and well-being do not depend on material things or on one's situation in life, but on one's reasoning faculty. Through reason, one can emulate the calm and order of the universe by learning to accept events with a stern and tranquil mind. Zeno's Greek followers elaborated and systematized his teachings, which were later adopted and popularized by the Roman Stoics Seneca, Epictetus, and Marcus Aurelius. Greek *stōïkos* became *stoicus* in Latin, and by the 14th century had found a place in English. By the 16th century the word was also being used as a common noun for "one apparently or professedly indifferent to pleasure or pain."

stoke \'stōk\ *verb* **stoked; stok·ing** [Dutch *stoken;* akin to Middle Dutch *stuken* to push] (1683)
transitive verb
1 : to poke or stir up (as a fire) **:** supply with fuel
2 : to feed abundantly
intransitive verb
: to stir up or tend a fire (as in a furnace) **:** supply a furnace with fuel
stoked \'stōkt\ *adjective* (1965)
slang **:** being in an enthusiastic or exhilarated state
stoke·hold \'stōk-,hōld\ *noun* (1887)
: the boiler room of a ship
stok·er \'stō-kər\ *noun* (1660)
1 : one employed to tend a furnace and supply it with fuel; *specifically* **:** one that tends a marine steam boiler
2 : a machine for feeding a fire
Stokes' aster \'stōks-\ *noun* [Jonathan *Stokes* (died 1831) English botanist] (circa 1890)
: a perennial composite herb (*Stokesia laevis*) of the southern U.S. often grown for its large showy heads of usually blue flowers — called also *sto·ke·sia* \stō-'kē-zh(ē-)ə, -zē-ə\
¹stole \'stōl\ *past of* STEAL
²stole *noun* [Middle English, from Old English, from Latin *stola*, from Greek *stolē* equipment, robe, from *stellein* to set up, make ready] (before 12th century)
1 : a long loose garment **:** ROBE
2 : an ecclesiastical vestment consisting of a long usually silk band worn traditionally around the neck by bishops and priests and over the left shoulder by deacons
3 : a long wide scarf or similar covering worn by women usually across the shoulders
stolen *past participle of* STEAL
stol·id \'stä-ləd\ *adjective* [Latin *stolidus* dull, stupid] (circa 1600)
: having or expressing little or no sensibility **:** UNEMOTIONAL
synonym *see* IMPASSIVE
— **sto·lid·i·ty** \stä-'li-də-tē, stə-\ *noun*
— **stol·id·ly** \'stä-ləd-lē\ *adverb*
stol·len \'shtō-lən, 'shtō-, 'shtə-, *or with* s *for* sh\ *noun, plural* **stollen** *or* **stollens** [German, literally, post, support, from Old High German *stollo* — more at STELA] (1906)
: a sweet yeast bread of German origin containing fruit and nuts
sto·lon \'stō-lən, -,län\ *noun* [New Latin *stolon-, stolo*, from Latin, branch, sucker; akin to Old English *stela* stalk, Armenian *steln* branch] (1601)
1 a : a horizontal branch from the base of a plant that produces new plants from buds at its tip or nodes (as in the strawberry) — called also *runner* **b :** a hypha (as of rhizopus) produced on the surface and connecting a group of conidiophores

s stolon 1a

2 : an extension of the body wall (as of a hydrozoan or bryozoan) that develops buds giving rise to new zooids which usually remain united by the stolon
sto·lon·if·er·ous \,stō-lə-'ni-f(ə-)rəs\ *adjective* (circa 1777)
: bearing or developing stolons
sto·ma \'stō-mə\ *noun, plural* **sto·ma·ta** \-mə-tə\ *also* **stomas** [New Latin, from Greek *stomat-, stoma* mouth] (circa 1684)
1 : any of various small simple bodily openings especially in a lower animal
2 : one of the minute openings in the epidermis of a plant organ (as a leaf) through which gaseous interchange takes place; *also* **:** the opening with its associated cellular structures

3 : an artificial permanent opening especially in the abdominal wall made in surgical procedures
¹stom·ach \'stə-mək, -mik\ *noun* [Middle English *stomak*, from Middle French *estomac*, from Latin *stomachus* gullet, esophagus, stomach, from Greek *stomachos*, from *stoma* mouth; akin to Middle Breton *staffn* mouth, Avestan *staman-*] (14th century)
1 a (1) **:** a dilatation of the alimentary canal of a vertebrate communicating anteriorly with the esophagus and posteriorly with the duodenum (2) **:** one of the compartments of a ruminant stomach ⟨the *abomasum* is the fourth *stomach* of a ruminant⟩ **b :** a cavity in an invertebrate animal that is analogous to a stomach **c :** the part of the body that contains the stomach **:** BELLY, ABDOMEN
2 a : desire for food caused by hunger **:** APPETITE **b :** INCLINATION, DESIRE ⟨had no *stomach* for an argument⟩; *also* **:** COURAGE, GUTS
3 *obsolete* **a :** SPIRIT, VALOR **b :** PRIDE **c :** SPLEEN, RESENTMENT
²stomach *transitive verb* (1523)
1 *archaic* **:** to take offense at
2 : to bear without overt reaction or resentment **:** put up with ⟨couldn't *stomach* office politics⟩
stom·ach·ache \-,āk\ *noun* (1763)
: pain in or in the region of the stomach
stom·ach·er \'stə-mi-kər, -chər\ *noun* (15th century)
: the center front section of a waist or underwaist or a usually heavily embroidered or jeweled separate piece for the center front of a bodice worn by men and women in the 15th and 16th centuries and later by women only
¹sto·mach·ic \stə-'ma-kik\ *adjective* (circa 1656)
: of or relating to the stomach ⟨*stomachic* vessels⟩
²stomachic *noun* (1735)
: a stimulant or tonic for the stomach
stom·achy \'stə-mə-kē, -mi-\ *adjective* (circa 1825)
1 *dialect British* **:** IRASCIBLE, IRRITABLE
2 : having a large stomach
sto·mal \'stō-məl\ *adjective* (circa 1941)
: of, relating to, or situated near a surgical stoma ⟨a *stomal* ulcer⟩
stomat- *or* **stomato-** *combining form* [New Latin, from Greek, from *stomat-, stoma*]
: mouth ⟨*stomatitis*⟩
sto·ma·tal \'stō-mə-t°l\ *adjective* (1861)
: of, relating to, or constituting plant stomata ⟨*stomatal* openings⟩ ⟨*stomatal* transpiration⟩
sto·mate \'stō-,māt\ *noun* [irregular from New Latin *stomat-, stoma*] (1835)
: STOMA 2
sto·ma·ti·tis \,stō-mə-'tī-təs\ *noun, plural* **-tit·i·des** \-'ti-tə-,dēz\ *or* **-ti·tis·es** \-'tī-tə-səz\ [New Latin] (1859)
: any of numerous inflammatory diseases of the mouth
sto·ma·to·pod \stō-'ma-tə-,päd\ *noun* [New Latin *Stomatopoda*, from *stomat-* + Greek *pod-, pous* foot — more at FOOT] (1877)
: any of an order (Stomatopoda) of marine crustaceans (as a squilla) that have gills on the abdominal appendages
— **stomatopod** *adjective*
sto·mo·de·um *or* **sto·mo·dae·um** \,stō-mə-'dē-əm\ *noun, plural* **-dea** \-'dē-ə\ *or* **-daea** \-'dē-ə\ *also* **-deums** *or* **-daeums** [New Latin, from Greek *stoma* mouth + *hodaion*, neuter of *hodaios* being on the way, from *hodos* way] (1876)
: the embryonic anterior ectodermal part of the alimentary canal or tract
— **sto·mo·de·al** *or* **sto·mo·dae·al** \-'dē-əl\ *adjective*
¹stomp \'stämp, 'stömp\ *verb* [by alteration] (1803)
: STAMP 1, 2
²stomp *noun* (circa 1899)
1 : STAMP 4

2 : a jazz dance marked by heavy stamping
stomping ground *noun* (1854)
: STAMPING GROUND
-stomy *noun combining form* [International Scientific Vocabulary, from Greek *stoma* mouth, opening]
: surgical operation establishing a usually permanent opening into (such) a part ⟨enterostomy⟩
¹stone \'stōn\ *noun* [Middle English, from Old English *stān;* akin to Old High German *stein* stone, Old Church Slavonic *stěna* wall, and perhaps to Sanskrit *styāyate* it hardens — more at STEATO-] (before 12th century)
1 : a concretion of earthy or mineral matter: **a** (1) **:** such a concretion of indeterminate size or shape (2) **:** ROCK **b :** a piece of rock for a specified function: as (1) **:** a building block (2) **:** a paving block (3) **:** a precious stone **:** GEM (4) **:** GRAVESTONE (5) **:** GRINDSTONE (6) **:** WHETSTONE (7) **:** a surface upon which a drawing, text, or design to be lithographed is drawn or transferred
2 : something resembling a small stone: as **a :** CALCULUS 3a **b :** the hard central portion of a drupaceous fruit (as a peach) **c :** a hard stony seed (as of a date)
3 *plural usually* **stone :** any of various units of weight; *especially* **:** an official British unit equal to 14 pounds (6.3 kilograms)
4 a : CURLING STONE **b :** a round playing piece used in various games (as backgammon or go)
5 : a stand or table with a smooth flat top on which to impose or set type
²stone *transitive verb* **stoned; ston·ing** (13th century)
1 : to hurl stones at; *especially* **:** to kill by pelting with stones
2 *archaic* **:** to make hard or insensitive to feeling
3 : to face, pave, or fortify with stones
4 : to remove the stones or seeds of (a fruit)
5 a : to rub, scour, or polish with a stone **b :** to sharpen with a whetstone
— **ston·er** *noun*
³stone *adverb* (13th century)
: ENTIRELY, UTTERLY — used as an intensive; often used in combination ⟨*stone*-broke⟩ ⟨*stone*-cold soup⟩ ⟨*stone*-dead⟩
⁴stone *adjective* (14th century)
1 : of, relating to, or made of stone
2 : ABSOLUTE, UTTER ⟨pure *stone* craziness —Edwin Shrake⟩
Stone Age *noun* (1864)
: the first known period of prehistoric human culture characterized by the use of stone tools
stone–blind \'stōn-'blīnd\ *adjective* (14th century)
: totally blind
stone·boat \-,bōt\ *noun* (1859)
: a flat sledge or drag for transporting heavy articles (as stones)
stone canal *noun* (1887)
: a tube in many echinoderms that contains calcareous deposits and leads from the madreporite to the ring of the water-vascular system surrounding the mouth
stone cell *noun* (1875)
: SCLEREID
stone·chat \-,chat\ *noun* [²chat] (circa 1783)
: an Old World oscine songbird (*Saxicola torquata*) related to the thrushes; *also* **:** any of various related birds (genus *Saxicola*)
stone china *noun* (1823)
: a hard dense opaque feldspathic pottery developed in England; *broadly* **:** IRONSTONE CHINA
stone–cold \'stōn-'kōld\ *adverb* (1592)
: ABSOLUTELY ⟨*stone-cold* sober⟩
stone crab *noun* (1709)
: a large brownish edible crab (*Menippe mercenaria*) found on the southern coast of the U.S. and in the Caribbean area
stone·crop \'stōn-,kräp\ *noun* (before 12th century)

1 : SEDUM; *especially* **:** an Old World creeping evergreen sedum (*Sedum acre*) with pungent fleshy leaves and yellow flowers
2 : any of various plants of the orpine family related to the sedums
stone·cut·ter \-ˌkə-tər\ *noun* (1540)
1 : one that cuts, carves, or dresses stone
2 : a machine for dressing stone
— **stone·cut·ting** \-ˌkə-tiŋ\ *noun*
stoned \'stōnd\ *adjective* (1952)
1 : DRUNK 1a
2 : being under the influence of a drug (as marijuana) taken especially for pleasure **:** HIGH
stone–deaf \-'def\ *adjective* (1837)
: totally deaf
stone–faced \-ˌfāst\ *adjective* (1932)
: showing no emotion **:** EXPRESSIONLESS
stone·fish \'stōn-ˌfish\ *noun* (1896)
: any of several small spiny venomous scorpion fishes (especially genus *Synanceja*) common about coral reefs of the tropical Indo-Pacific

stonefish

stone fly *noun* (15th century)
: any of an order (Plecoptera) of insects with an aquatic carnivorous nymph having gills and an adult having long antennae, two pairs of membranous wings, and usually long cerci
stone fruit *noun* (circa 1534)
: a fruit with a stony endocarp **:** DRUPE
stone–ground \'stōn-'graȯnd\ *adjective* (1905)
: ground in a buhrstone mill ⟨*stone-ground* flour⟩
stone·ma·son \'stōn-ˌmā-sᵊn\ *noun* (1758)
: a mason who builds with stone
— **stone·ma·son·ry** \-rē\ *noun*
stone roller *noun* (1878)
1 : HOG SUCKER
2 : a common cyprinid fish (*Campostoma anomalum*) found especially in clear streams of the central U.S.
stone's throw *noun* (1581)
: a short distance ⟨lives within a *stone's throw* of town⟩
stone·wall \'stōn-ˌwȯl\ (1880)
intransitive verb
1 *chiefly British* **:** to engage in obstructive parliamentary debate or delaying tactics
2 : to be uncooperative, obstructive, or evasive
transitive verb
: to refuse to comply or cooperate with
— **stone·wall·er** *noun*
stone wall *noun* (before 12th century)
1 : a fence made of stones; *especially* **:** one built of rough stones without mortar to enclose a field
2 : an immovable block or obstruction (as in public affairs)
stone·ware \-ˌwar, -ˌwer\ *noun* (1683)
: a strong opaque ceramic ware that is high-fired, well vitrified, and nonporous
stone·washed \-ˌwȯsht, -ˌwäsht *also* -ˌwȯrsht *or* -ˌwärsht\ *adjective* (1982)
: subjected to a washing process during manufacture that includes the use of abrasive stones especially to create a softer fabric ⟨*stone-washed* denim jeans⟩
stone·work \-ˌwərk\ *noun* (before 12th century)
1 : a structure or part built of stone **:** MASONRY
2 : the shaping, preparation, or setting of stone
stone·wort \-ˌwərt, -ˌwȯrt\ *noun* (1816)
: any of various freshwater green algae (order Charales) that have a thallus differentiated into rhizoids and stems with whorls of branchlets and that are often encrusted with calcareous deposits
stony *also* **ston·ey** \'stō-nē\ *adjective* **ston·i·er; -est** (before 12th century)

1 : abounding in or having the nature of stone **:** ROCKY
2 a : insensitive to pity or human feeling **:** OBDURATE **b :** manifesting no movement or reaction **:** DUMB, EXPRESSIONLESS **c :** fearfully gripping **:** PETRIFYING
3 *archaic* **:** consisting of or made of stones
4 *British* **:** stone-broke
— **ston·i·ly** \'stō-nᵊl-ē\ *adverb*
— **ston·i·ness** \'stō-nē-nəs\ *noun*
stony–heart·ed \'stō-nē-ˌhär-təd\ *adjective* (1569)
: UNFEELING, CRUEL
stood *past and past participle of* STAND
¹stooge \'stüj\ *noun* [origin unknown] (1913)
1 a : one who plays a subordinate or compliant role to a principal **b :** PUPPET 3
2 : STRAIGHT MAN
3 : STOOL PIGEON
²stooge *intransitive verb* **stooged; stoog·ing** (1939)
: to act as a stooge ⟨congressmen who *stooge* for the oil and mineral interests —*New Republic*⟩
stook \'stük, 'stu̇k\ *noun* [Middle English *stouk;* akin to Old English *stocc* stock — more at STOCK] (15th century)
chiefly British **:** ¹SHOCK
— **stook** *transitive verb, chiefly British*
¹stool \'stül\ *noun* [Middle English, from Old English *stōl;* akin to Old High German *stuol* chair, Old Church Slavonic *stolŭ* seat, throne] (before 12th century)
1 a : a seat usually without back or arms supported by three or four legs or by a central pedestal **b :** a low bench or portable support for the feet or knees **:** FOOTSTOOL
2 : a seat used as a symbol of office or authority; *also* **:** the rank, dignity, office, or rule of a chieftain
3 a : a seat used while defecating or urinating **b :** a discharge of fecal matter
4 a : a stump or group of stumps of a tree especially when producing suckers **b :** a plant crown from which shoots grow out **c :** a shoot or growth from a stool
5 : STOOL PIGEON
²stool *intransitive verb* (1770)
: to throw out shoots in the manner of a stool
stool·ie \'stü-lē\ *noun* (1924)
: STOOL PIGEON 2
stool pigeon *noun* [probably from the early practice of fastening the decoy bird to a stool] (1836)
1 : a pigeon used as a decoy to draw others within a net
2 : a person acting as a decoy or informer; *especially* **:** a spy sent into a group to report (as to the police) on its activities
¹stoop \'stüp\ *verb* [Middle English *stoupen,* from Old English *stūpian;* akin to Old English *stēap* steep, deep — more at STEEP] (before 12th century)
intransitive verb
1 a : to bend the body or a part of the body forward and downward sometimes simultaneously bending the knees **b :** to stand or walk with a forward inclination of the head, body, or shoulders
2 : YIELD, SUBMIT
3 a : to descend from a superior rank, dignity, or status **b :** to lower oneself morally
4 a *archaic* **:** to move down from a height **:** ALIGHT **b :** to fly or dive down swiftly usually to attack prey
transitive verb
1 : DEBASE, DEGRADE
2 : to bend (a part of the body) forward and downward
²stoop *noun* (1571)
1 a : an act of bending the body forward **b :** a temporary or habitual forward bend of the back and shoulders
2 : the descent of a bird especially on its prey
3 : a lowering of oneself

³stoop *noun* [Dutch *stoep;* akin to Old English *stæpe* step — more at STEP] (1755)
: a porch, platform, entrance stairway, or small veranda at a house door
stoop·ball \'stüp-ˌbȯl\ *noun* (1941)
: a variation of baseball in which a player throws a ball against a stoop or building and runs to base while other players attempt to retrieve the rebound and put the runner out
stoop labor *noun* (1949)
: the hard labor done or required to plant, cultivate, and harvest a crop and especially a crop of vegetables
¹stop \'stäp\ *verb* **stopped; stop·ping** [Middle English *stoppen,* from Old English *-stoppian,* from (assumed) Vulgar Latin *stuppare* to stop with tow, from Latin *stuppa* tow, from Greek *styppē*] (13th century)
transitive verb
1 a : to close by filling or obstructing **b :** to hinder or prevent the passage of **c :** to get in the way of **:** be wounded or killed by ⟨easy to *stop* a bullet along a lonely . . . road —Harvey Fergusson⟩
2 a : to close up or block off (an opening) **:** PLUG **b :** to make impassable **:** CHOKE, OBSTRUCT **c :** to cover over or fill in (a hole or crevice)
3 a : to cause to give up or change a course of action **b :** to keep from carrying out a proposed action **:** RESTRAIN, PREVENT
4 a : to cause to cease **:** CHECK, SUPPRESS **b :** DISCONTINUE
5 a : to deduct or withhold (a sum due) **b :** to instruct one's bank to refuse (payment) or refuse payment of (as a check)
6 a : to arrest the progress or motion of **:** cause to halt ⟨*stopped* the car⟩ **b :** PARRY **c :** to check by means of a weapon **:** BRING DOWN, KILL **d :** to beat in a boxing match by a knockout; *broadly* **:** DEFEAT **e :** BAFFLE, NONPLUS
7 : to change the pitch of (as a violin string) by pressing with the finger or (as a wind instrument) by closing one or more finger holes or by thrusting the hand or a mute into the bell
8 : to hold an honor card and enough protecting cards to be able to block (a bridge suit) before an opponent can run many tricks
intransitive verb
1 a : to cease activity or operation **b :** to come to an end especially suddenly **:** CLOSE, FINISH
2 a : to cease to move on **:** HALT **b :** PAUSE, HESITATE
3 a : to break one's journey **:** STAY **b** *chiefly British* **:** REMAIN **c :** to make a brief call **:** drop in
4 : to become choked **:** CLOG ☆

— **stop·pa·ble** \'stä-pə-bəl\ *adjective*
²**stop** *noun* (15th century)
1 a : CESSATION, END **b :** a pause or breaking off in speech
2 a (1) **:** a graduated set of organ pipes of similar design and tone quality (2) **:** a corresponding set of vibrators or reeds of a reed organ (3) **:** STOP KNOB — often used figuratively in phrases like *pull out all the stops* to suggest holding nothing back **b :** a means of regulating the pitch of a musical instrument
3 a : something that impedes, obstructs, or brings to a halt **:** IMPEDIMENT, OBSTACLE **b :** the aperture of a camera lens; *also* **:** a marking of a series (as of f-numbers) on a camera for indicating settings of the diaphragm **c :** a drain plug **:** STOPPER
4 : a device for arresting or limiting motion
5 : the act of stopping **:** the state of being stopped **:** CHECK
6 a : a halt in a journey **:** STAY ⟨made a brief *stop* to refuel⟩ **b :** a stopping place ⟨a bus *stop*⟩
7 a *chiefly British* **:** any of several punctuation marks **b** — used in telegrams and cables to indicate a period **c :** a pause or break in a verse that marks the end of a grammatical unit
8 a : an order stopping payment (as of a check or note) by a bank **:** STOP ORDER
9 : a consonant characterized by complete closure of the breath passage in the course of articulation — compare CONTINUANT
10 : a depression in the face of an animal at the junction of forehead and muzzle
³**stop** *adjective* (1594)
: serving to stop **:** designed to stop ⟨*stop* line⟩ ⟨*stop* signal⟩
stop–and–go \,stäp-ən-'gō, -°m-, *attributively* -,gō\ *adjective* (1925)
: of, relating to, or involving frequent stops; *especially* **:** controlled or regulated by traffic lights ⟨*stop-and-go* driving⟩
stop bath *noun* (1898)
: an acid bath used to check photographic development of a negative or print
stop·cock \'stäp-,käk\ *noun* (1584)
: a cock for stopping or regulating flow (as through a pipe)
stop down *transitive verb* (circa 1891)
: to reduce the effective aperture of (a lens) by means of a diaphragm
stope \'stōp\ *noun* [probably from Low German *stope*, literally, step; akin to Old English *stæpe* step — more at STEP] (1747)
: a usually steplike excavation underground for the removal of ore that is formed as the ore is mined in successive layers
stop·gap \'stäp-,gap\ *noun, often attributive* (1684)
: something that serves as a temporary expedient **:** MAKESHIFT ⟨*stopgap* measures⟩
synonym see RESOURCE
stop knob *noun* (1887)
: one of the handles by which an organist draws or shuts off a particular stop
stop·light \'stäp-,līt\ *noun* (1926)
1 : a light on the rear of a motor vehicle that is illuminated when the driver presses the brake pedal
2 : TRAFFIC SIGNAL
stop order *noun* (circa 1891)
: an order to a broker to buy or sell respectively at the market when the price of a security advances or declines to a designated level
stop out *intransitive verb* [after *drop out*] (1973)
: to withdraw temporarily from enrollment at a college or university
— **stop-out** \'stäp-,aut\ *noun*
stop·over \'stäp-,ō-vər\ *noun* (1885)
1 : a stop at an intermediate point in one's journey
2 : a stopping place on a journey
stop·page \'stä-pij\ *noun* (15th century)
: the act of stopping **:** the state of being stopped **:** HALT, OBSTRUCTION
stop payment *noun* (circa 1919)

: a depositor's order to a bank to refuse to honor a specified check drawn by him or her
¹**stop·per** \'stä-pər\ *noun* (15th century)
1 : one that brings to a halt or causes to stop operating or functioning **:** CHECK: as **a :** a playing card that will stop the running of a suit **b :** a baseball pitcher depended on to win important games or to stop a losing streak; *also* **:** an effective relief pitcher
2 : one that closes, shuts, or fills up; *specifically* **:** something (as a bung or cork) used to plug an opening
²**stopper** *transitive verb* **stop·pered; stop·per·ing** \-p(ə-)riŋ\ (circa 1769)
: to close or secure with or as if with a stopper
stopper knot *noun* (1860)
: a knot used to prevent a rope from passing through a hole or opening
¹**stop·ple** \'stä-pəl\ *noun* [Middle English *stoppell*, from *stoppen* to stop] (14th century)
: something that closes an aperture **:** STOPPER, PLUG
²**stopple** *transitive verb* **stop·pled; stop·pling** \-p(ə-)liŋ\ (1795)
: STOPPER
stop·watch \'stäp-,wäch\ *noun* (1737)
: a watch with a hand or a digital display that can be started and stopped at will for exact timing (as of a race)
stor·age \'stōr-ij, 'stȯr-\ *noun* (circa 1613)
1 a : space or a place for storing **b :** an amount stored **c :** MEMORY 4
2 a : the act of storing **:** the state of being stored; *especially* **:** the safekeeping of goods in a depository (as a warehouse) **b :** the price charged for keeping goods in a storehouse
3 : the production by means of electric energy of chemical reactions that when allowed to reverse themselves generate electricity again without serious loss
storage battery *noun* (1881)
: a cell or connected group of cells that converts chemical energy into electrical energy by reversible chemical reactions and that may be recharged by passing a current through it in the direction opposite to that of its discharge — called also *storage cell*
sto·rax \'stōr-,aks, 'stȯr-\ *noun* [Middle English, from Late Latin, alteration of Latin *styrax*, from Greek] (14th century)
1 a : a fragrant balsam obtained from the bark of an Asian tree (*Liquidambar orientalis*) of the witch-hazel family that is used as an expectorant and sometimes in perfumery — called also *Levant storax* **b :** a balsam from the sweet gum that is similar to storax
2 : any of a genus (*Styrax* of the family Styracaceae, the storax family) of trees or shrubs with usually hairy leaves and white flowers in drooping racemes — compare BENZOIN
¹**store** \'stōr, 'stȯr\ *transitive verb* **stored; stor·ing** [Middle English, from Old French *estorer* to construct, restore, store, from Latin *instaurare* to renew, restore] (13th century)
1 : LAY AWAY, ACCUMULATE ⟨*store* vegetables for winter use⟩ ⟨an organism that absorbs and *stores* DDT⟩
2 : FURNISH, SUPPLY; *especially* **:** to stock against a future time ⟨*store* a ship with provisions⟩
3 : to place or leave in a location (as a warehouse, library, or computer memory) for preservation or later use or disposal
4 : to provide storage room for **:** HOLD ⟨elevators for *storing* surplus wheat⟩
— **stor·able** \'stōr-ə-bəl, 'stȯr-\ *adjective*
²**store** *noun* (13th century)
1 a : something that is stored or kept for future use **b** *plural* **:** articles (as of food) accumulated for some specific object and drawn upon as needed **:** STOCK, SUPPLIES **c :** something that is accumulated **d :** a source from which things may be drawn as needed **:** a reserve fund

2 : STORAGE — usually used with *in* ⟨when placing eggs in *store* —*Dublin Sunday Independent*⟩
3 : VALUE, IMPORTANCE ⟨set great *store* by a partner's opinion⟩
4 : a large quantity, supply, or number **:** ABUNDANCE
5 a : STOREHOUSE, WAREHOUSE **b** *chiefly British* **:** MEMORY 4
6 : a business establishment where usually diversified goods are kept for retail sale ⟨grocery *store*⟩ — compare SHOP
— **in store :** in readiness **:** in preparation ⟨there's a surprise *in store* for you⟩
³**store** *adjective* (1602)
1 *or* **stores :** of, relating to, kept in, or used for a store
2 : purchased from a store as opposed to being natural or homemade **:** MANUFACTURED, READY-MADE ⟨*store* clothes⟩ ⟨*store* bread⟩
store–bought \'stōr-,bȯt, 'stȯr-\ *adjective* (1905)
: STORE 2
store cheese *noun* [from its being a staple article stocked in grocery stores] (1863)
: CHEDDAR
¹**store·front** \'stōr-,frənt, 'stȯr-\ *noun* (1880)
1 : the front side of a store or store building facing a street
2 : a building, room, or suite of rooms having a storefront
²**storefront** *adjective* (1937)
1 : of, relating to, or characteristic of a storefront church ⟨a *storefront* evangelist⟩
2 : occupying a room or suite of rooms in a store building at street level and immediately behind a storefront ⟨a *storefront* school⟩
3 : of, relating to, or being outreach professional services ⟨*storefront* lawyers⟩ ⟨a *storefront* clinic⟩
storefront church *noun* (1937)
: a city church that utilizes storefront quarters as a meeting place
store·house \'stōr-,haus, 'stȯr-\ *noun* (14th century)
1 : a building for storing goods (as provisions) **:** MAGAZINE, WAREHOUSE
2 : an abundant supply or source **:** REPOSITORY
store·keep·er \-,kē-pər\ *noun* (1618)
1 : one that has charge of supplies (as military stores)
2 : one that operates a retail store
store·room \-,rüm, -,rum\ *noun* (1746)
1 : a room or space for the storing of goods or supplies
2 : STOREHOUSE 2
store·ship \-,ship\ *noun* (1693)
: a ship used to carry supplies
store·wide \-'wīd\ *adjective* (circa 1937)
: including all or most merchandise in a store ⟨a *storewide* sale⟩
¹**sto·ried** \'stōr-ēd, 'stȯr-\ *adjective* (14th century)
1 : decorated with designs representing scenes from story or history ⟨a *storied* tapestry⟩
2 : having an interesting history **:** celebrated in story or history ⟨a *storied* institution⟩
²**storied** *or* **sto·reyed** \'stōr-ēd, 'stȯr-\ *adjective* (1624)
: having stories — used in combination ⟨a two-*storied* house⟩
stork \'stȯrk\ *noun* [Middle English, from Old English *storc*; akin to Old High German *storah* stork and probably to Old English *stearc* stiff — more at STARK] (before 12th century)
: any of various large mostly Old World wading birds (family Ciconiidae) that have long stout bills and are related to the ibises and herons
storks·bill \'stȯrks-,bil\ *noun* (1562)
: any of several plants of the geranium family with elongate beaked fruits: **a :** PELARGONIUM **b :** ALFILARIA; *also* **:** any of several related plants (genus *Erodium*)
¹**storm** \'stȯrm\ *noun, often attributive* [Middle English, from Old English; akin to Old

High German *sturm* storm, Old English *styrian* to stir) (before 12th century)
1 a : a disturbance of the atmosphere marked by wind and usually by rain, snow, hail, sleet, or thunder and lightning **b :** a heavy fall of rain, snow, or hail **c** (1) : wind having a speed of 64 to 72 miles (103 to 116 kilometers) per hour (2) **:** WHOLE GALE — see BEAUFORT SCALE table **d :** a serious disturbance of any element of nature
2 : a disturbed or agitated state **:** a sudden or violent commotion
3 : a heavy discharge of objects (as missiles)
4 : a tumultuous outburst
5 a : PAROXYSM, CRISIS **b :** a sudden heavy influx or onset
6 : a violent assault on a defended position
7 *plural* **:** STORM WINDOW
— **by storm :** by or as if by employing a bold swift frontal movement especially with the intent of defeating or winning over quickly ⟨took the literary world *by storm*⟩
— **up a storm :** in a remarkable or energetic fashion — used as an intensifier ⟨dancing *up a storm*⟩ ⟨can write *up a storm*⟩
²**storm** (15th century)
intransitive verb
1 a : to blow with violence **b :** to rain, hail, snow, or sleet vigorously
2 : to attack by storm ⟨*stormed* ashore at zero hour⟩
3 : to be in or to exhibit a violent passion **:** RAGE ⟨*storming* at the unusual delay⟩
4 : to rush about or move impetuously, violently, or angrily ⟨the mob *stormed* through the streets⟩
transitive verb
: to attack, take, or win over by storm ⟨*storm* a fort⟩
synonym see ATTACK
storm and stress *noun, often both Ss capitalized* (1855)
: STURM UND DRANG
storm·bound \'storm-'baund\ *adjective* (1830)
: cut off from outside communication by a storm or its effects **:** stopped or delayed by storms
storm cellar *noun* (circa 1902)
: a cellar or covered excavation designed for protection from dangerous windstorms (as tornadoes)
storm door *noun* (1878)
: an additional door placed outside an ordinary outside door for protection against severe weather
storm petrel *noun* (circa 1833)
: any of various small petrels (family Hydrobatidae); *especially* **:** a small sooty black white-marked petrel (*Hydrobates pelagicus*) frequenting the north Atlantic and Mediterranean
storm trooper *noun* (1933)
1 : a member of a private Nazi army notorious for aggressiveness, violence, and brutality
2 : one that resembles a Nazi storm trooper
storm window *noun* (circa 1888)

stork

storm petrel

: a sash placed outside an ordinary window as a protection against severe weather — called also *storm sash*
stormy \'stor-mē\ *adjective* **storm·i·er; -est** (12th century)
1 : relating to, characterized by, or indicative of a storm ⟨a *stormy* day⟩ ⟨a *stormy* autumn⟩
2 : marked by turmoil or fury ⟨a *stormy* life⟩ ⟨a *stormy* conference⟩
— **storm·i·ly** \'stor-mə-lē\ *adverb*
— **storm·i·ness** \-mē-nəs\ *noun*
stormy petrel *noun* (circa 1776)
1 : STORM PETREL
2 a : one fond of strife **b :** a harbinger of trouble
¹**sto·ry** \'stōr-ē, 'stor-\ *noun, plural* **stories** [Middle English *storie*, from Old French *estorie*, from Latin *historia* — more at HISTORY] (13th century)
1 *archaic* **:** HISTORY 1, 3
2 a : an account of incidents or events **b :** a statement regarding the facts pertinent to a situation in question **c :** ANECDOTE; *especially* **:** an amusing one
3 a : a fictional narrative shorter than a novel; *specifically* **:** SHORT STORY **b :** the intrigue or plot of a narrative or dramatic work
4 : a widely circulated rumor
5 : LIE, FALSEHOOD
6 : LEGEND, ROMANCE
7 : a news article or broadcast
8 : MATTER, SITUATION
²**story** *transitive verb* **sto·ried; sto·ry·ing** (15th century)
1 *archaic* **:** to narrate or describe in story
2 : to adorn with a story or a scene from history
³**story** also **sto·rey** \'stōr-ē, 'stor-ē\ *noun, plural* **stories** also **storeys** [Middle English *storie*, from Medieval Latin *historia* picture, story of a building, from Latin, history, tale; probably from pictures adorning the windows of medieval buildings] (14th century)
1 a : the space in a building between two adjacent floor levels or between a floor and the roof **b :** a set of rooms in such a space **c :** a unit of measure equal to the height of the story of a building ⟨one *story* high⟩
2 : a horizontal division of a building's exterior or not necessarily corresponding exactly with the stories within
sto·ry·board \-,bōrd, -,bord\ *noun* (1942)
: a panel or series of panels on which a set of sketches is arranged depicting consecutively the important changes of scene and action in a series of shots (as for a film, television show, or commercial)
— **storyboard** *transitive verb*
¹**sto·ry·book** \-,buk\ *noun* (1711)
: a book of stories ⟨*storybooks* for children⟩
²**storybook** *adjective* (1844)
: FAIRY-TALE
story line *noun* (1941)
: the plot of a story or drama
sto·ry·tell·er \'stōr-ē-,te-lər, 'stor-\ *noun* (1709)
: a teller of stories: as **a :** a relater of anecdotes **b :** a reciter of tales (as in a children's library) **c :** LIAR, FIBBER **d :** a writer of stories
— **sto·ry·tell·ing** *noun*
stoss \'stäs, 'stos, 'stōs, 'shtōs\ *adjective* [German *stoss-*, from *stossen* to push, from Old High German *stōzen*; akin to Gothic *stautan* to strike — more at CONTUSION] (1878)
: facing toward the direction from which an overriding glacier impinges ⟨the *stoss* slope of a hill⟩
sto·tin·ka \stō-'tiŋ-kə, stə-\ *noun, plural* **-tin·ki** \-kē\ [Bulgarian] (circa 1892)
— see *lev* at MONEY table
stound \'staund, 'stünd\ *noun* [Middle English, from Old English *stund*; akin to Old High German *stunta* time, hour] (before 12th century)
archaic **:** TIME, WHILE

stoup \'stüp\ *noun* [Middle English *stowp*, probably of Scandinavian origin; akin to Old Norse *staup* cup] (14th century)
1 a : a beverage container (as a glass or tankard) **b :** FLAGON
2 : a basin for holy water at the entrance of a church
¹**stour** \'stür\ *adjective* [Middle English *stor*, from Old English *stōr*; akin to Old High German *stuori* large, Russian *staryĭ* old, Old English *standan* to stand] (before 12th century)
1 *chiefly Scottish* **:** STRONG, HARDY
2 *chiefly Scottish* **:** STERN, HARSH
²**stour** *noun* [Middle English, from Middle French *estour*, of Germanic origin; akin to Old High German *sturm* storm, battle — more at STORM] (14th century)
1 a *archaic* **:** BATTLE, CONFLICT **b** *dialect British* **:** TUMULT, UPROAR
2 *chiefly Scottish* **:** DUST, POWDER
¹**stout** \'staut\ *adjective* [Middle English, from Middle French *estout*, of Germanic origin; akin to Old High German *stolz* proud; perhaps akin to Old High German *stelza* stilt — more at STILT] (14th century)
1 : strong of character: as **a :** BRAVE, BOLD **b :** FIRM, DETERMINED; *also* **:** OBSTINATE, UNCOMPROMISING
2 : physically or materially strong: **a :** STURDY, VIGOROUS **b :** STAUNCH, ENDURING **c :** sturdily constructed **:** SUBSTANTIAL
3 : FORCEFUL ⟨a *stout* attack⟩; *also* **:** VIOLENT ⟨a *stout* wind⟩
4 : bulky in body **:** FAT
synonym see STRONG
— **stout·ish** \'stau-tish\ *adjective*
— **stout·ly** *adverb*
— **stout·ness** *noun*
²**stout** *noun* (1677)
1 : a very dark full-bodied ale with a distinctive malty flavor
2 a : a fat person **b :** a clothing size designed for the large figure
stout·en \'stau-tᵊn\ *verb* **stout·ened; stout·en·ing** \'stau-tiŋ, 'stau-tᵊn-iŋ\ (1834)
transitive verb
: to make stout ⟨*stouten* a resolve⟩
intransitive verb
: to become stout
stout·heart·ed \'staut-,här-təd\ *adjective* (1552)
: having a stout heart or spirit: **a :** COURAGEOUS **b :** STUBBORN
— **stout·heart·ed·ly** *adverb*
— **stout·heart·ed·ness** *noun*
¹**stove** \'stōv\ *noun* [Middle English, heated room, steam room, from Middle Dutch or Middle Low German, from (assumed) Vulgar Latin *extufa*, ultimately from Latin *ex-* + Greek *typhein* to smoke — more at DEAF] (1591)
1 a : a portable or fixed apparatus that burns fuel or uses electricity to provide heat (as for cooking or heating) **b :** a device that generates heat for special purposes (as for heating tools or heating air for a hot blast) **c :** KILN
2 *chiefly British* **:** a hothouse especially for the cultivation of tropical exotics; *broadly* **:** GREENHOUSE
²**stove** *past and past participle of* STAVE
stove·pipe \'stōv-,pīp\ *noun* (1699)
1 : pipe of large diameter usually of sheet steel used as a stove chimney or to connect a stove with a flue
2 : SILK HAT
sto·ver \'stō-vər\ *noun* [Middle English, modification of Anglo-French *estovers* necessary supplies, from Old French *estoveir* to be necessary, ultimately from Latin *est opus* there is need] (14th century)

\ə\ abut \ᵊ\ kitten \ər\ further \a\ ash \ā\ ace
\ä\ mop, mar \au\ out \ch\ chin \e\ bet \ē\ easy
\g\ go \i\ hit \ī\ ice \j\ job \ŋ\ go
\ō\ law \òi\ boy \th\ thin \th\ the \ü\ loot \u\ foot
\y\ yet \zh\ vision *see also* Guide to Pronunciation

1 *chiefly dialect English* : FODDER
2 : mature cured stalks of grain with the ears removed that are used as feed for livestock
stow \'stō\ *transitive verb* [Middle English, to place, from *stowe* place, from Old English *stōw*; akin to Old Frisian *stō* place, Greek *stylos* pillar — more at STEER] (14th century)
1 : HOUSE, LODGE
2 a : to put away for future use : STORE **b** *obsolete* : to lock up for safekeeping : CONFINE
3 a : to dispose in an orderly fashion : ARRANGE, PACK **b** : LOAD
4 *slang* : to put aside : STOP
5 a *archaic* : CROWD **b** : to eat or drink up : CONSUME — usually used with *away* ⟨*stowed* away a huge dinner⟩
stow·age \-ij\ *noun* (14th century)
1 a : an act or process of stowing **b** : goods in storage or to be stowed
2 a : storage capacity **b** : a place or receptacle for storage
3 : the state of being stored
stow·away \'stō-ə-,wā\ *noun* (1850)
: one that stows away
stow away *intransitive verb* (1879)
: to secrete oneself aboard a vehicle as a means of obtaining transportation
STP \,es-,tē-'pē\ *noun* [probably from *STP*, a trademark for a motor fuel additive] (1967)
: a psychedelic drug chemically related to mescaline and amphetamine
stra·bis·mus \stra-'biz-məs\ *noun* [New Latin, from Greek *strabismos* condition of squinting, from *strabizein* to squint, from *strabos* squint-eyed; akin to Greek *strephein* to twist] (circa 1684)
: inability of one eye to attain binocular vision with the other because of imbalance of the muscles of the eyeball — called also *squint*
— **stra·bis·mic** \-mik\ *adjective*
¹**strad·dle** \'stra-d°l\ *verb* **strad·dled;** **strad·dling** \'strad-liŋ, 'stra-d°l-iŋ\ [irregular from *stride*] (1565)
intransitive verb
1 : to stand, sit, or walk with the legs wide apart; *especially* : to sit astride
2 : to spread out irregularly : SPRAWL
3 : to favor or seem to favor two apparently opposite sides
4 : to execute a commodities market spread
transitive verb
1 : to stand, sit, or be astride of ⟨*straddle* a horse⟩
2 : to be noncommittal in regard to ⟨*straddle* an issue⟩
— **strad·dler** \'strad-lər, 'stra-d°l-ər\ *noun*
— **straddle the fence** : to be in a position of neutrality or indecision
²**straddle** *noun* (1611)
1 : the act or position of one who straddles
2 : a noncommittal or equivocal position
3 : SPREAD 5
Stra·di·va·ri \,stra-də-'vär-ē, -'var-, -'ver-\ *noun* (circa 1903)
: STRADIVARIUS
Strad·i·var·i·us \,stra-də-'var-ē-əs, -'ver-\ *noun, plural* **-var·ii** \-ē-,ī\ [Latinized form of *Stradivari*] (1833)
: a stringed instrument (as a violin) made by Antonio Stradivari of Cremona
strafe \'strāf, *especially British* 'sträf\ *transitive verb* **strafed; straf·ing** [German *Gott strafe England* God punish England, German propaganda slogan during World War I] (1915)
: to rake (as ground troops) with fire at close range and especially with machine-gun fire from low-flying aircraft
— **strafe** *noun*
— **straf·er** *noun*
¹**strag·gle** \'stra-gəl\ *intransitive verb* **straggled; strag·gling** \-g(ə-)liŋ\ [Middle English *straglen*] (15th century)
1 : to wander from the direct course or way : ROVE, STRAY

2 : to trail off from others of its kind ⟨little cabins *straggling* off into the woods⟩
— **strag·gler** \-g(ə-)lər\ *noun*
²**straggle** *noun* (1865)
: a straggling group (as of persons or objects)
strag·gly \'stra-g(ə-)lē\ *adjective* **strag·gli·er; -est** (1862)
: spread out or scattered irregularly ⟨a *straggly* beard⟩
¹**straight** \'strāt\ *adjective* [Middle English *streght, straight*, from past participle of *strecchen* to stretch — more at STRETCH] (14th century)
1 a : free from curves, bends, angles, or irregularities ⟨*straight* hair⟩ ⟨*straight* timber⟩ **b** : generated by a point moving continuously in the same direction and expressed by a linear equation ⟨a *straight* line⟩ ⟨the *straight* segment of a curve⟩
2 a : lying along or holding to a direct or proper course or method ⟨a *straight* thinker⟩ **b** : CANDID, FRANK ⟨a *straight* answer⟩ **c** : coming directly from a trustworthy source ⟨a *straight* tip on the horses⟩ **d** (1) : having the elements in an order ⟨the *straight* sequence of events⟩ (2) : CONSECUTIVE ⟨12 *straight* days⟩ **e** : having the cylinders arranged in a single straight line ⟨a *straight* 8-cylinder engine⟩ **f** : PLUMB, VERTICAL ⟨the picture isn't quite *straight*⟩
3 a : exhibiting honesty and fairness ⟨*straight* dealing⟩ **b** : properly ordered or arranged ⟨set the kitchen *straight*⟩ ⟨set us *straight* on that issue⟩; *also* : CORRECT ⟨get the facts *straight*⟩ **c** : free from extraneous matter : UNMIXED ⟨*straight* whiskey⟩ **d** : marked by no exceptions or deviations in support of a principle or party ⟨votes a *straight* Democratic ticket⟩ **e** : having a fixed price for each regardless of the number sold **f** : not deviating from an indicated pattern ⟨writes *straight* humor⟩ ⟨a *straight*-A student⟩ **g** (1) : exhibiting no deviation from what is established or accepted as usual, normal, or proper : CONVENTIONAL; *also* : SQUARE 5f (2) : not using or under the influence of drugs or alcohol **h** : HETEROSEXUAL
4 : being the only form of remuneration ⟨on *straight* commission⟩
— **straight·ish** \'strā-tish\ *adjective*
— **straight·ly** *adverb*
— **straight·ness** *noun*
²**straight** *adverb* (14th century)
: in a straight manner
³**straight** *transitive verb* (15th century)
chiefly Scottish : STRAIGHTEN
⁴**straight** *noun* (1645)
1 : something that is straight: as **a** : a straight line or arrangement **b** : STRAIGHTAWAY; *especially* : HOMESTRETCH **c** : a true or honest report or course
2 a : a sequence (as of shots, strokes, or moves) resulting in a perfect score in a game or contest **b** : first place at the finish of a horse race : WIN
3 : a poker hand containing five cards in sequence but not of the same suit — see POKER illustration
4 : a person who adheres to conventional attitudes and mores
straight–ahead \'strāt-ə-'hed\ *adjective* (1836)
: relating to or being music performed in an unembellished manner typical of a given idiom or performer; *broadly* : STRAIGHTFORWARD
straight and narrow *noun* [probably alteration of *strait and narrow*; from the admonition of Matthew 7:14 (Authorized Version), "strait is the gate and narrow is the way which leadeth unto life"] (1930)
: the way of propriety and rectitude — used with *the*
straight angle *noun* (1601)
: an angle whose sides lie in opposite directions from the vertex in the same straight line and which equals two right angles
straight–arm \'strāt-,ärm\ *noun* (1903)

: an act or instance of warding off a football tackler with the arm fully extended from the shoulder, elbow locked, and the palm of the hand placed firmly against any part of his body — called also *stiff-arm*
— **straight–arm** *verb*
straight–arrow \-'ar-(,)ō\ *adjective* [from the expression *straight as an arrow*] (circa 1969)
: rigidly proper and conventional
¹**straight·away** \,strāt-ə-'wā\ *adverb* (1662)
: without hesitation or delay
²**straight·away** \'strāt-ə-,wā\ *adjective* (1874)
1 : proceeding in a straight line : continuous in direction
2 : IMMEDIATE
³**straight·away** \'strā-tə-,wā\ *noun* (1878)
: a straight course: as **a** : the straight part of a closed racecourse : STRETCH **b** : a straight and unimpeded stretch of road or way
straight·bred \'strāt-'bred\ *adjective* (1898)
: produced by breeding a single breed, strain, or type ⟨*straightbred* cattle⟩
— **straight·bred** \-,bred\ *noun*
straight chain *noun* (1890)
: an open chain of atoms having no side chains — usually hyphenated when used attributively
straight·edge \'strāt-,ej\ *noun* (1812)
: a bar or piece of material (as of wood, metal, or plastic) with a straight edge for testing straight lines and surfaces or drawing straight lines
straight·en \'strā-t°n\ *verb* **straight·ened; straight·en·ing** \'strāt-niŋ, 'strā-t°n-iŋ\ (1542)
transitive verb
: to make straight — usually used with *up* or *out*
intransitive verb
: to become straight — usually used with *up* or *out*
word history see STRAITEN
— **straight·en·er** \'strāt-nər, 'strā-t°n-ər\ *noun*
straight face *noun* (circa 1890)
: a face giving no evidence of emotion and especially of merriment
— **straight–faced** \'strāt-'fāst\ *adjective*
— **straight–faced·ly** \-'fā-səd-lē, -'fāst-lē\ *adverb*
straight flush *noun* (1864)
: a poker hand containing five cards of the same suit in sequence — see POKER illustration
¹**straight·for·ward** \,strāt-'fòr-wərd, 'strāt-,\ *adjective* (1806)
1 a : free from evasiveness or obscurity : EXACT, CANDID ⟨a *straightforward* account⟩ **b** : CLEAR-CUT, PRECISE
2 : proceeding in a straight course or manner : DIRECT, UNDEVIATING
— **straight·for·ward·ly** *adverb*
— **straight·for·ward·ness** *noun*
²**straightforward** *also* **straight·for·wards** \-wərdz\ *adverb* (1809)
: in a straightforward manner
straight–line \'strāt-'līn\ *adjective* (1843)
1 : being a mechanical linkage or equivalent device designed to produce or copy motion in a straight line
2 : having the principal parts arranged in a straight line
3 : marked by a uniform spread and especially in equal segments over a given term ⟨*straight-line* amortization⟩ ⟨*straight-line* depreciation⟩
4 : occurring, measured, or made in or along a straight line ⟨*straight-line* motion⟩ ⟨*straight-line* extrapolation⟩
straight man *noun* (1923)
: a member of a comedy team who feeds lines to his partner who in turn replies with usually humorous quips
straight off *adverb* (1873)
: at once : IMMEDIATELY
straight–out \'strāt-'aut\ *adjective* (1848)

1 : FORTHRIGHT, BLUNT ⟨gave him a *straight-out* answer⟩
2 : OUTRIGHT, THOROUGHGOING
— straight–out *adverb*
straight poker *noun* (1864)
: poker in which the players bet on the five cards dealt to them and then have a showdown without drawing — compare DRAW POKER, STUD POKER
straight razor *noun* (1938)
: a razor with a rigid steel cutting blade hinged to a case that forms a handle when the razor is open for use
straight·way \'strāt-'wā, -,wā\ *adverb* (15th century)
1 : in a direct course **:** DIRECTLY ⟨fell *straightway* down the stairs⟩
2 : RIGHT AWAY, IMMEDIATELY, STRAIGHTAWAY ⟨*straightway* the clouds began to part⟩
¹strain \'strān\ *noun* [Middle English *streen* progeny, lineage, from Old English *strēon* gain, acquisition; akin to Old High German gi*striuni* gain, Latin *struere* to heap up — more at STREW] (13th century)
1 a : LINEAGE, ANCESTRY **b :** a group of presumed common ancestry with clear-cut physiological but usually not morphological distinctions ⟨a high-yielding *strain* of winter wheat⟩; *broadly* **:** a specified infraspecific group (as a stock, line, or ecotype) **c :** KIND, SORT ⟨discussions of a lofty *strain*⟩
2 a : inherited or inherent character, quality, or disposition ⟨a *strain* of madness in the family⟩ **b :** TRACE, STREAK ⟨a *strain* of fanaticism⟩
3 a : TUNE, AIR **b :** a passage of verbal or musical expression **c :** a stream or outburst of forceful or impassioned speech
4 : the tenor, pervading note, burden, or tone of an utterance or of a course of action or conduct **b :** MOOD, TEMPER
²strain *verb* [Middle English, from Middle French *estraindre*, from Latin *stringere* to bind or draw tight, press together; akin to Greek *strang-, stranx* drop squeezed out, *strangalē* halter] (14th century)
transitive verb
1 a : to draw tight **:** cause to fit firmly ⟨*strain* the bandage over the wound⟩ **b :** to stretch to maximum extension and tautness ⟨*strain* a canvas over a frame⟩
2 a : to exert (as oneself) to the utmost **b :** to injure by overuse, misuse, or excessive pressure ⟨*strained* his back⟩ **c :** to cause a change of form or size in (a body) by application of external force
3 : to squeeze or clasp tightly: as **a :** HUG **b :** to compress painfully **:** CONSTRICT
4 a : to cause to pass through a strainer **:** FILTER **b :** to remove by straining ⟨*strain* lumps out of the gravy⟩
5 : to stretch beyond a proper limit ⟨that story *strains* my credulity⟩
6 *obsolete* **:** to squeeze out **:** EXTORT
intransitive verb
1 a : to make violent efforts **:** STRIVE ⟨has to *strain* to reach the high notes⟩ **b :** to pull against resistance ⟨a dog *straining* at its leash⟩ **c :** to contract the muscles forcefully in attempting to defecate — often used in the phrase *strain at stool*
2 : to pass through or as if through a strainer ⟨the liquid *strains* readily⟩
3 : to make great difficulty or resistance **:** BALK
word history see STRAITEN
— strain a point : to go beyond a usual, accepted, or proper limit or rule
³strain *noun* (1558)
1 : an act of straining or the condition of being strained: as **a :** bodily injury from excessive tension, effort, or use ⟨heart *strain*⟩; *especially* **:** one resulting from a wrench or twist and involving undue stretching of muscles or ligaments ⟨back *strain*⟩ **b :** excessive or difficult exertion or labor **c :** excessive physical or mental tension; *also* **:** a force, influence, or

factor causing such tension ⟨her responsibilities were a constant *strain*⟩ **d :** deformation of a material body under the action of applied forces
2 : an unusual reach, degree, or intensity **:** PITCH
3 *archaic* **:** a strained interpretation of something said or written
strained \'strānd\ *adjective* (circa 1542)
1 : done or produced with excessive effort
2 : pushed by antagonism near to open conflict ⟨*strained* relations⟩
strain·er \'strā-nər\ *noun* (14th century)
: one that strains: as **a :** a device (as a sieve) to retain solid pieces while a liquid passes through **b :** any of various devices for stretching or tightening something
strain gauge *noun* (1910)
: EXTENSOMETER
¹strait \'strāt\ *adjective* [Middle English, from Old French *estreit*, from Latin *strictus* strait, strict, from past participle of *stringere*] (13th century)
1 *archaic* **:** STRICT, RIGOROUS
2 *archaic* **a :** NARROW **b :** limited in space or time **c :** closely fitting **:** CONSTRICTED, TIGHT
3 a : causing distress **:** DIFFICULT **b :** limited as to means or resources
— strait·ly *adverb*
— strait·ness *noun*
²strait *adverb* (13th century)
obsolete **:** in a close or tight manner
³strait *noun* (14th century)
1 a *archaic* **:** a narrow space or passage **b :** a comparatively narrow passageway connecting two large bodies of water — often used in plural but singular in construction **c :** ISTHMUS
2 : a situation of perplexity or distress — often used in plural ⟨in dire *straits*⟩
synonym see JUNCTURE
strait·en \'strā-t°n\ *transitive verb* **strait·ened**; **strait·en·ing** \'strāt-niŋ, 'strā-t°n-iŋ\ (circa 1552)
1 a : to make strait or narrow **b :** to hem in **:** CONFINE
2 *archaic* **:** to restrict in freedom or scope **:** HAMPER
3 : to subject to distress, privation, or deficiency ⟨in *straitened* circumstances⟩ ◇
¹strait·jack·et *also* **straight·jack·et** \'strāt-,ja-kət\ *noun* (1814)
1 : a cover or overgarment of strong material (as canvas) used to bind the body and especially the arms closely in restraining a violent prisoner or patient
2 : something that restricts or confines like a straitjacket
²straitjacket *also* **straightjacket** *transitive verb* (1863)
: to confine in or as if in a straitjacket
strait-laced *or* **straight-laced** \'strāt-'lāst\ *adjective* (1554)
1 : excessively strict in manners, morals, or opinion
2 : wearing or having a bodice or stays tightly laced
— strait-laced·ly \-'lā-səd-lē, -'lāst-lē\ *adverb*
— strait-laced·ness \-'lās(t)-nəs, -'lā-səd-nəs\ *noun*
Straits dollar \'strāts-\ *noun* [*Straits* Settlements, former British crown colony] (1908)
: a dollar formerly issued by British Malaya and used in much of southern and eastern Asia and the East Indies
strake \'strāk\ *noun* [Middle English; akin to Old English *streccan* to stretch — more at STRETCH] (14th century)
1 : a continuous band of hull planking or plates on a ship; *also* **:** the width of such a band
2 : STREAK, STRIPE
stra·mash \strə-'mash\ *noun* [origin unknown] (1803)
1 *chiefly Scottish* **:** DISTURBANCE, RACKET

2 *chiefly Scottish* **:** CRASH, SMASHUP
stra·mo·ni·um \strə-'mō-nē-əm\ *noun* [New Latin] (1663)
1 : the dried leaves of the jimsonweed or of a related plant (genus *Datura*) that contain toxic alkaloids (as atropine) and are used in medicine similarly to belladonna
2 : JIMSONWEED
¹strand \'strand\ *noun* [Middle English, from Old English; akin to Old Norse *strǫnd* shore] (before 12th century)
: the land bordering a body of water **:** SHORE, BEACH
²strand (1621)
transitive verb
1 : to run, drive, or cause to drift onto a strand **:** run aground
2 : to leave in a strange or an unfavorable place especially without funds or means to depart
3 : to leave (a base runner) on base at the end of an inning in baseball
intransitive verb
: to become stranded
³strand *noun* [Middle English *stronde, strande*] (13th century)
1 *Scottish & dialect English* **:** STREAM
2 *Scottish & dialect English* **:** SEA
⁴strand *noun* [Middle English *strond*] (15th century)
1 a : fibers or filaments twisted, plaited, or laid parallel to form a unit for further twisting or plaiting into yarn, thread, rope, or cordage **b :** one of the wires twisted together or laid parallel to form a wire rope or cable **c :** something (as a molecular chain) resembling a strand
2 : an element (as a yarn or thread) of a woven or plaited material
3 : an elongated or twisted and plaited body resembling a rope ⟨a *strand* of pearls⟩
4 : one of the elements interwoven in a complex whole
⁵strand *transitive verb* (1841)
1 : to break a strand of (a rope) accidentally
2 a : to form (as a rope) from strands **b :** to play out, twist, or arrange in a strand
strand·ed \'stran-dəd\ *adjective* (1875)
: having a strand or strands especially of a specified kind or number — usually used in combination ⟨the double-*stranded* molecule of DNA⟩
— strand·ed·ness *noun*
strand·line \'stran(d)-,līn\ *noun* (1903)
: SHORELINE; *especially* **:** a shoreline above the present water level
strange \'strānj\ *adjective* **strang·er**; **strang·est** [Middle English, from Old

French *estrange*, from Latin *extraneus*, literally, external, from *extra* outside — more at EXTRA-] (13th century)
1 a *archaic* **:** of, relating to, or characteristic of another country **:** FOREIGN **b :** not native to or naturally belonging in a place **:** of external origin, kind, or character
2 a : not before known, heard, or seen **:** UNFAMILIAR **b :** exciting wonder or awe **:** EXTRAORDINARY
3 a : discouraging familiarities **:** RESERVED, DISTANT **b :** ILL AT EASE
4 : UNACCUSTOMED 2 ⟨she was *strange* to his ways⟩
5 : having the quantum characteristic of strangeness ⟨*strange* quark⟩ ⟨*strange* particle⟩
☆
— **strange·ly** *adverb*
strange·ness \'strānj-nəs\ *noun* (14th century)
1 : the quality or state of being strange
2 : a quantum characteristic of subatomic particles that accounts for the relatively long lifetime of certain particles, is conserved in interactions involving electromagnetism or the strong force, and has a value of zero for most known particles
¹**strang·er** \'strān-jər\ *noun* [Middle English, from Middle French *estrangier* foreign, foreigner, from *estrange*] (14th century)
1 : one who is strange: as **a** (1) **:** FOREIGNER (2) **:** a resident alien **b :** one in the house of another as a guest, visitor, or intruder **c :** a person or thing that is unknown or with whom one is unacquainted **d :** one who does not belong to or is kept from the activities of a group **e :** one not privy or party to an act, contract, or title **:** one that interferes without right
2 : one ignorant of or unacquainted with someone or something
²**stranger** *adjective* (15th century)
: of, relating to, or being a stranger **:** FOREIGN
³**stranger** *transitive verb* (1605)
obsolete **:** ESTRANGE, ALIENATE
strange woman *noun* [from the expression frequently used in Proverbs (Authorized Version)] (1535)
: PROSTITUTE
stran·gle \'straŋ-gəl\ *verb* **stran·gled; stran·gling** \-g(ə-)liŋ\ [Middle English, from Middle French *estrangler*, from Latin *strangulare*, from Greek *strangalan*, from *strangalē* halter — more at STRAIN] (14th century)
transitive verb
1 a : to choke to death by compressing the throat with something (as a hand or rope) **:** THROTTLE **b :** to obstruct seriously or fatally the normal breathing of **c :** STIFLE
2 : to suppress or hinder the rise, expression, or growth of
intransitive verb
1 : to become strangled
2 : to die from or as if from interference with breathing
— **stran·gler** \-g(ə-)lər\ *noun*
stran·gle·hold \'straŋ-gəl-,hōld\ *noun* (1893)
1 : an illegal wrestling hold by which one's opponent is choked
2 : a force or influence that chokes or suppresses freedom of movement or expression
strangler fig *noun* (1933)
: any of various vines and trees especially of the mulberry family (as *Ficus aurea* of the southeastern U.S.) and Saint-John's-wort family (as *Clusia rosea* of tropical America) that start as epiphytes but send down roots to the ground around the host tree
stran·gles \'straŋ-gəlz\ *noun plural but singular or plural in construction* [plural of obsolete *strangle* act of strangling] (circa 1706)
: an infectious febrile disease of horses caused by a bacterium (*Streptococcus equi*) and marked by inflammation and congestion of mucous membranes

stran·gu·late \'straŋ-gyə-,lāt\ *verb* **-lat·ed; -lat·ing** [Latin *strangulatus*, past participle of *strangulare*] (1665)
transitive verb
: STRANGLE, CONSTRICT
intransitive verb
: to become constricted so as to stop circulation ⟨the hernia will *strangulate*⟩
stran·gu·la·tion \,straŋ-gyə-'lā-shən\ *noun* (1542)
1 : the action or process of strangling or strangulating
2 : the state of being strangled or strangulated; *especially* **:** excessive or pathological constriction or compression of a bodily tube (as a blood vessel or a loop of intestine) that interrupts its ability to act as a passage
stran·gu·ry \'straŋ-gyə-rē, -,gyur-ē\ *noun, plural* **-ries** [Middle English, from Latin *stranguria*, from Greek *strangouria*, from *strang-, stranx* drop squeezed out + *ourein* to urinate, from *ouron* urine — more at STRAIN, URINE] (14th century)
: a slow and painful spasmodic discharge of urine drop by drop
¹**strap** \'strap\ *noun* [alteration of *strop*, from Middle English, band or loop of leather or rope, from Old English, thong for securing an oar, from Latin *struppus* band, strap, from Greek *strophos* twisted band, from *strephein* to twist] (1601)
1 a : a narrow usually flat strip or thong of a flexible material and especially leather used for securing, holding together, or wrapping **b :** something made of a strap forming a loop ⟨a boot *strap*⟩ **c :** a strip of leather used for flogging **d :** STROP
2 : a band, plate, or loop of metal for binding objects together or for clamping an object in position
3 : a shoe fastened with a usually buckled strap
4 *Irish* **:** TROLLOP 2
²**strap** *transitive verb* **strapped; strapping** (1711)
1 a (1) **:** to secure with or attach by means of a strap (2) **:** to support (as a sprained joint) with overlapping strips of adhesive plaster **b :** BIND, CONSTRICT
2 : to beat or punish with a strap
3 : STROP
4 : to cause to suffer from an extreme scarcity ⟨is often *strapped* for cash⟩
strap·hang·er \'strap-,haŋ-ər\ *noun* (1905)
: a standing passenger in a subway, streetcar, bus, or train who clings for support to one of the short straps or similar devices placed along the aisle
— **strap·hang** \-,haŋ\ *intransitive verb*
strap·less \-ləs\ *adjective* (1846)
: having no strap; *specifically* **:** made or worn without shoulder straps ⟨a *strapless* evening gown⟩
— **strapless** *noun*
strap·pa·do \stra-'pā-(,)dō, -'pä-\ *noun* [modification of Italian *strappata*, literally, sharp pull] (1560)
: a punishment or torture in which the subject is hoisted by rope and allowed to fall its full length; *also* **:** a machine used to inflict this torture
strap·per \'stra-pər\ *noun* (1675)
: one that is unusually large or robust
¹**strap·ping** \'stra-piŋ\ *adjective* (1657)
: having a vigorously sturdy constitution
²**strapping** *noun* (1818)
1 : material for a strap
2 : STRAPS
strass \'stras\ *noun* [French *stras, strass*] (1820)
: PASTE 3
strat·a·gem \'stra-tə-jəm, -,jem\ *noun* [Italian *stratagemma*, from Latin *strategema*, from Greek *stratēgēma*, from *stratēgein* to be a general, maneuver, from *stratēgos* general, from *stratos* camp, army (akin to Latin *stra-*

tus, past participle, spread out) + *agein* to lead — more at STRATUM, AGENT] (15th century)
1 : an artifice or trick in war for deceiving and outwitting the enemy **b :** a cleverly contrived trick or scheme for gaining an end
2 : skill in ruses or trickery
synonym see TRICK
stra·te·gic \strə-'tē-jik\ *adjective* (1825)
1 : of, relating to, or marked by strategy ⟨a *strategic* retreat⟩
2 a : necessary to or important in the initiation, conduct, or completion of a strategic plan **b :** required for the conduct of war and not available in adequate quantities domestically ⟨*strategic* materials⟩ **c :** of great importance within an integrated whole or to a planned effect ⟨emphasized *strategic* points⟩
3 : designed or trained to strike an enemy at the sources of his military, economic, or political power ⟨a *strategic* bomber⟩
— **stra·te·gi·cal** \-ji-kəl\ *adjective*
— **stra·te·gi·cal·ly** \-ji-k(ə-)lē\ *adverb*
strat·e·gist \'stra-tə-jist\ *noun* (1838)
: one skilled in strategy
strat·e·gize \-,jīz\ *intransitive verb* **-gized; -giz·ing** (1921)
: to devise a strategy or course of action
strat·e·gy \-jē\ *noun, plural* **-gies** [Greek *stratēgia* generalship, from *stratēgos*] (1810)
1 (1) **:** the science and art of employing the political, economic, psychological, and military forces of a nation or group of nations to afford the maximum support to adopted policies in peace or war (2) **:** the science and art of military command exercised to meet the enemy in combat under advantageous conditions **b :** a variety of or instance of the use of strategy
2 a : a careful plan or method **:** a clever stratagem **b :** the art of devising or employing plans or stratagems toward a goal
3 : an adaptation or complex of adaptations (as of behavior, metabolism, or structure) that serves or appears to serve an important function in achieving evolutionary success ⟨foraging *strategies* of insects⟩
strath \'strath\ *noun* [Scottish Gaelic *srath*] (1540)
: a flat wide river valley or the low-lying grassland along it
strath·spey \,strath-'spā\ *noun, plural* **strathspeys** [*Strath Spey*, district of Scotland] (circa 1653)

☆ SYNONYMS
Strange, singular, unique, peculiar, eccentric, erratic, odd, queer, quaint, outlandish mean departing from what is ordinary, usual, or to be expected. STRANGE stresses unfamiliarity and may apply to the foreign, the unnatural, the unaccountable ⟨a journey filled with *strange* sights⟩. SINGULAR suggests individuality or puzzling strangeness ⟨a *singular* feeling of impending disaster⟩. UNIQUE implies singularity and the fact of being without a known parallel ⟨a career *unique* in the annals of science⟩. PECULIAR implies a marked distinctiveness ⟨the *peculiar* status of America's first lady⟩. ECCENTRIC suggests a wide divergence from the usual or normal especially in behavior ⟨the *eccentric* eating habits of preschoolers⟩. ERRATIC stresses a capricious and unpredictable wandering or deviating ⟨a friend's suddenly *erratic* behavior⟩. ODD applies to a departure from the regular or expected ⟨an *odd* sense of humor⟩. QUEER suggests a dubious sometimes sinister oddness ⟨*queer* happenings offering no ready explanation⟩. QUAINT suggests an old-fashioned but pleasant oddness ⟨a *quaint* fishing village⟩. OUTLANDISH applies to what is uncouth, bizarre, or barbaric ⟨the *outlandish* getups of heavy metal bands⟩.

: a Scottish dance that is similar to but slower than the reel; *also* : the music for this dance

strati- *combining form* [New Latin *stratum*] : stratum ⟨*stratiform*⟩

strat·i·fi·ca·tion \,stra-tə-fə-ˈkā-shən\ *noun* (circa 1617)
1 a : the act or process of stratifying **b** : the state of being stratified
2 : a stratified formation

strat·i·fi·ca·tion·al grammar \,stra-tə-fə-ˈkā-shnəl-, -shə-nᵊl-\ *noun* (1962)
: a grammar based on the theory that language consists of a series of hierarchically related strata linked together by representational rules

stratified charge engine *noun* (1962)
: an internal-combustion engine in whose cylinders the combustion of fuel in a layer of rich fuel-air mixture promotes ignition in a greater volume of lean mixture

strat·i·form \ˈstra-tə-ˌfȯrm\ *adjective* (1805)
: having a stratified formation

strat·i·fy \ˈstra-tə-ˌfī\ *verb* **-fied; -fy·ing** [New Latin *stratificare*, from *stratum* + Latin *-ificare* -ify] (1661)
transitive verb
1 : to form, deposit, or arrange in strata
2 a : to divide or arrange into classes, castes, or social strata **b** : to divide into a series of graded statuses
intransitive verb
: to become arranged in strata

strati·graph·ic \,stra-tə-ˈgra-fik\ *adjective* (1877)
: of, relating to, or determined by stratigraphy

stra·tig·ra·phy \strə-ˈti-grə-fē\ *noun* [International Scientific Vocabulary] (1865)
1 : geology that deals with the origin, composition, distribution, and succession of strata
2 : the arrangement of strata

strato- *combining form* [New Latin *stratus*] : stratus and ⟨*strato*cumulus⟩

stra·toc·ra·cy \strə-ˈtä-krə-sē\ *noun, plural* **-cies** [Greek *stratos* army — more at STRAT-AGEM] (1652)
: a military government

stra·to·cu·mu·lus \,strā-tō-ˈkyü-myə-ləs, ,stra-\ *noun* [New Latin] (circa 1891)
: stratified cumulus consisting of large balls or rolls of dark cloud which often cover the whole sky especially in winter — see CLOUD illustration

strato·sphere \ˈstra-tə-ˌsfir\ *noun* [French *stratosphère*, from New Latin *stratum* + *-o-* + French *sphère* sphere, from Latin *sphaera*] (1909)
1 : the part of the earth's atmosphere which extends from about 7 miles (11 kilometers) above the surface to about 31 miles (50 kilometers) and in which temperature increases gradually to about 32° F (0° C) and clouds rarely form
2 : a very high or the highest region on or as if on a graded scale ⟨construction costs in the *stratosphere*⟩ ⟨the celebrity *stratosphere*⟩
— **strato·spher·ic** \,stra-tə-ˈsfir-ik, -ˈsfer-\ *adjective*

stra·to·vol·ca·no \,stra-tō-väl-ˈkā-(ˌ)nō, ,strā-, -vȯl-\ *noun* [New Latin *stratum* + English *-o-* + *volcano*] (1937)
: a volcano composed of explosively erupted cinders and ash with occasional lava flows

stra·tum \ˈstrā-təm, ˈstra-\ *noun, plural* **stra·ta** \ˈstrā-tə, ˈstra-\ [New Latin, from Latin, spread, bed, from neuter of *stratus*, past participle of *sternere* to spread out — more at STREW] (1599)
1 : a bed or layer artificially made
2 a : a sheetlike mass of sedimentary rock or earth of one kind lying between beds of other kinds **b** : a region of the sea or atmosphere that is analogous to a stratum of the earth **c** : a layer of tissue ⟨deep *stratum* of the skin⟩ **d** : a layer in which archaeological material (as artifacts, skeletons, and dwelling remains) is found on excavation
3 a : a part of a historical or sociological series representing a period or a stage of devel-

opment **b** : a socioeconomic level of society comprising persons of the same or similar status especially with regard to education or culture
4 : one of a series of layers, levels, or gradations in an ordered system ⟨*strata* of thought⟩
5 : a statistical subpopulation ▢

stra·tus \ˈstrā-təs, ˈstra-\ *noun, plural* **stra·ti** \ˈstrā-ˌtī, ˈstra-\ [New Latin, from Latin, past participle of *sternere*] (circa 1803)
: a cloud form extending over a large area at altitudes of usually 2000 to 7000 feet (600 to 2100 meters) — see CLOUD illustration

stra·vage *or* **stra·vaig** \strə-ˈvāg\ *intransitive verb* [probably by shortening & alteration from *extravagate*] (1773)
chiefly Scottish : ROAM

¹straw \ˈstrȯ\ *noun* [Middle English, from Old English *strēaw*; akin to Old High German *strō* straw, Old English *strewian* to strew] (before 12th century)
1 a : stalks of grain after threshing; *broadly* : dry stalky plant residue used like grain straw (as for bedding or packing) **b** : a natural or artificial heavy fiber used for weaving, plaiting, or braiding
2 : a dry coarse stem especially of a cereal grass
3 a (1) : something of small worth or significance (2) : something too insubstantial to provide support or help in a desperate situation ⟨clutching at *straws*⟩ **b** : CHAFF 2
4 a : something (as a hat) made of straw **b** : a tube (as of paper, plastic, or glass) for sucking up a beverage
— **strawy** \ˈstrȯ-ē\ *adjective*
— **straw in the wind** : a slight fact that is an indication of a coming event

²straw *adjective* (15th century)
1 : made of straw ⟨a *straw* rug⟩
2 : of, relating to, or used for straw ⟨a *straw* barn⟩
3 : of the color of straw ⟨*straw* hair⟩
4 : of little or no value : WORTHLESS
5 : of, relating to, resembling, or being a straw man
6 : of, relating to, or concerned with the discovery of preferences by means of a straw vote

straw·ber·ry \ˈstrȯ-ˌber-ē, -b(ə-)rē\ *noun, often attributive* [Middle English, from Old English *strēawberige*, from *strēaw* straw + *berige* berry; perhaps from the appearance of the achenes on the surface] (before 12th century)
: the juicy edible usually red fruit of any of several low-growing temperate herbs (genus *Fragaria*) of the rose family that is technically an enlarged pulpy receptacle bearing numerous achenes; *also* : a plant whose fruits are strawberries

strawberry bush *noun* (circa 1856)
1 : a shrubby North American spindle tree (*Euonymus americanus*) with crimson pods and seeds with a scarlet aril
2 : ²WAHOO

strawberry mark *noun* (1847)
: a tumor of the skin filled with small blood vessels and appearing usually as a red and elevated birthmark

strawberry roan *noun* (1955)
: a roan horse with a light red ground color

strawberry shrub *noun* (circa 1890)
: any of a genus (*Calycanthus* of the family Calycanthaceae, the strawberry-shrub family) of shrubs with fragrant brownish red flowers

strawberry tomato *noun* (circa 1847)

: GROUND-CHERRY; *especially* : a stout hairy annual herb (*Physalis pruinosa*) of eastern North America with sweet globular yellow fruits

strawberry tree *noun* (15th century)
: a small European evergreen tree (*Arbutus unedo*) of the heath family with racemose white flowers and fruits like strawberries

straw boss *noun* (1894)
1 : an assistant to a foreman in charge of supervising and expediting the work of a small gang of workers
2 : a member of a group of workers who supervises the work of the others in addition to doing his or her own job

straw·flow·er \ˈstrȯ-ˌflau̇(-ə)r\ *noun* (circa 1922)
: any of several everlasting flowers; *especially* : an Australian perennial composite herb (*Helichrysum bracteatum*) that is widely cultivated for its heads of chaffy brightly colored long-keeping flowers

straw·hat \ˌstrȯ-ˈhat\ *adjective* [from the former fashion of wearing straw hats in summer] (1935)
: of, relating to, or being summer theater

straw man *noun* (1896)
1 : a weak or imaginary opposition (as an argument or adversary) set up only to be easily confuted
2 : a person set up to serve as a cover for a usually questionable transaction

straw vote *noun* (1866)
: an unofficial vote taken (as at a chance gathering) to indicate the relative strength of opposing candidates or issues — called also *straw poll*

straw wine *noun* (1824)
: a sweet wine produced by partially drying the grapes on beds of straw prior to vinification

straw yellow *noun* (circa 1796)
: a pale yellow

¹stray \ˈstrā\ *noun* [Middle English, from Old French *estraié*, past participle of *estraier*] (13th century)
1 a : a domestic animal that is wandering at large or is lost **b** : a person or thing that strays
2 [Middle English, from *straien* to stray] *archaic* : the act of going astray

²stray *intransitive verb* [Middle English *straien*, from Middle French *estraier*, from (assumed) Vulgar Latin *extravagare*, from Latin *extra-* outside + *vagari* to wander — more at EXTRA-] (14th century)
: WANDER: as **a** : to wander from company, restraint, or proper limits **b** : to roam about without fixed direction or purpose **c** : to move in a winding course : MEANDER **d** : to move without conscious or intentional effort ⟨eyes *straying* absently around the room⟩ **e** : to become distracted from an argument or chain of

▢ USAGE
stratum The plural *strata* has occasionally been used as a singular since the 18th century and is sometimes given the plural *stratas* (there was a *strata* of Paris which mere criticism of books fails to get hold of —Ezra Pound) ⟨a Roman burial ground suggests *stratas* of corruption and decay —Connie Fletcher, *Booklist*). Current evidence shows senses 2, 3b, and 4 so used, with 3b the most common. Singular *strata* is persistent but not frequent. It may someday establish itself as a singular like *agenda,* but its current status is something less than established.

thought ⟨*strayed* from the point⟩ **f :** to wander accidentally from a fixed or chosen route **g :** ERR, SIN

— **stray·er** *noun*

³**stray** *adjective* (1607)
1 : having strayed or escaped from a proper or intended place ⟨a *stray* cow⟩ ⟨hit by a *stray* bullet⟩ ⟨fixed a few *stray* hairs⟩
2 : occurring at random or sporadically ⟨a few *stray* thoughts⟩
3 : not serving any useful purpose **:** UNWANTED ⟨*stray* light⟩

¹**streak** \'strēk\ *noun* [Middle English *streke,* from Old English *strica;* akin to Old High German *strich* line, Latin *striga* row — more at STRIKE] (before 12th century)
1 : a line or mark of a different color or texture from the ground **:** STRIPE
2 a : the color of the fine powder of a mineral obtained by scratching or rubbing against a hard white surface and constituting an important distinguishing character **b :** inoculum implanted in a line on a solid medium **c :** any of several virus diseases of plants (as the potato, tomato, or raspberry) resembling mosaic but usually producing at least some linear markings
3 a : a narrow band of light **b :** a lightning bolt
4 a : a slight admixture **:** TRACE ⟨had a mean *streak* in him⟩ **b :** a brief run (as of luck) **c :** a consecutive series ⟨was on a winning *streak*⟩
5 : a narrow layer (as of ore)
6 : an act or instance of streaking

²**streak** (1595)
transitive verb
: to make streaks on or in ⟨tears *streaking* her face⟩
intransitive verb
1 : to move swiftly **:** RUSH ⟨a jet *streaking* across the sky⟩
2 : to have a streak (as of winning or outstanding performances)
3 : to run naked through a public place
— **streak·er** *noun*

streak camera *noun* (1959)
: a camera for recording very fast or short-lived phenomena (as fluorescence or shock waves)

streaked \'strēkt, 'strē-kəd\ *adjective* (1596)
1 : marked with stripes or linear discolorations
2 : physically or mentally disturbed **:** UPSET

streak·ing \'strē-kiŋ\ *noun* (circa 1964)
: the lightening (as by chemicals) of a few long strands of hair to produce a streaked effect

streaky \'strē-kē\ *adjective* **streak·i·er; -est** (1745)
1 : marked with streaks ⟨*streaky* bacon⟩
2 : APPREHENSIVE ⟨nervous and *streaky*⟩
3 : apt to vary (as in effectiveness) **:** UNRELIABLE
— **streak·i·ness** *noun*

¹**stream** \'strēm\ *noun* [Middle English *streme,* from Old English *strēam;* akin to Old High German *stroum* stream, Greek *rhein* to flow] (before 12th century)
1 : a body of running water (as a river or brook) flowing on the earth; *also* **:** any body of flowing fluid (as water or gas)
2 a : a steady succession (as of words or events) ⟨kept up an endless *stream* of chatter⟩ **b :** a constantly renewed supply **c :** a continuous moving procession ⟨a *stream* of traffic⟩
3 : an unbroken flow (as of gas or particles of matter)
4 : a ray of light
5 a : a prevailing attitude or group ⟨has always run against the *stream* of current fashion⟩ **b :** a dominant influence or line of development
6 *British* **:** TRACK 3c

²**stream** (13th century)
intransitive verb

1 a : to flow in or as if in a stream **b :** to leave a bright trail ⟨a meteor *streamed* through the sky⟩
2 a : to exude a bodily fluid profusely ⟨her eyes were *streaming*⟩ **b :** to become wet with a discharge of bodily fluid ⟨*streaming* with perspiration⟩
3 : to trail out at full length ⟨her hair *streaming* back as she ran⟩
4 : to pour in large numbers ⟨complaints came *streaming* in⟩
transitive verb
1 : to emit freely or in a stream ⟨his eyes *streamed* tears⟩
2 : to display (as a flag) by waving

stream·bed \'strēm-,bed\ *noun* (1857)
: the channel occupied or formerly occupied by a stream

stream·er \'strē-mər\ *noun* (13th century)
1 a : a flag that streams in the wind; *especially* **:** PENNANT **b :** any long narrow wavy strip resembling or suggesting a banner floating in the wind **c :** BANNER 2
2 a : a long extension of the solar corona visible only during a total solar eclipse **b** *plural* **:** AURORA BOREALIS

stream·ing \'strē-miŋ\ *noun* (14th century)
1 : an act or instance of flowing; *specifically* **:** CYCLOSIS
2 *British* **:** TRACKING

stream·let \'strēm-lət\ *noun* (circa 1552)
: a small stream

¹**stream·line** \'strēm-,līn\ *noun* (1868)
1 : the path of a particle in a fluid relative to a solid body past which the fluid is moving in smooth flow without turbulence
2 a : a contour designed to minimize resistance to motion through a fluid (as air) **b :** a smooth or flowing line designed as if for decreasing air resistance

²**streamline** *transitive verb* (1913)
1 : to design or construct with a streamline
2 : to bring up to date **:** MODERNIZE
3 a : to put in order **:** ORGANIZE **b :** to make simpler or more efficient

stream·lined \-,līnd\ *adjective* (1913)
1 a : contoured to reduce resistance to motion through a fluid (as air) **b :** stripped of nonessentials **:** COMPACT **c :** effectively integrated **:** ORGANIZED
2 : having flowing lines
3 : brought up to date **:** MODERNIZED
4 : of or relating to streamline flow

streamline flow *noun* (circa 1918)
: an uninterrupted flow (as of air) past a solid body in which the direction at every point remains unchanged with the passage of time

stream·lin·er \'strēm-,lī-nər\ *noun* (1934)
: one that is streamlined; *especially* **:** a streamlined train

stream of consciousness (1855)
1 : the continuous unedited chronological flow of conscious experience through the mind
2 : INTERIOR MONOLOGUE

stream·side \'strēm-,sīd\ *noun* (1844)
: the land bordering on a stream

streek \'strēk\ *transitive verb* [Middle English (northern dialect) *streken;* akin to Old English *streccan* to stretch] (13th century)
1 *chiefly Scottish* **:** STRETCH, EXTEND
2 *chiefly Scottish* **:** to lay out (a dead body)

¹**streel** \'strē(ə)l\ *intransitive verb* [Irish *straoill-, sraoill-* to tear apart, trail, trudge, from Old Irish *sroiglid* he scourges, from *sroigell* scourge, from Latin *flagellum* — more at FLAGELLATE] (1805)
1 *chiefly Irish* **:** to saunter idly and aimlessly
2 *chiefly Irish* **:** to trail or float in the manner of a streamer

²**streel** *noun* [Irish *straoill, sraoill,* from *straoill-,* verb] (1842)
chiefly Irish **:** an untidy slovenly person

¹**street** \'strēt\ *noun* [Middle English *strete,* from Old English *strǣt,* from Late Latin *strata*

paved road, from Latin, feminine of *stratus,* past participle — more at STRATUM] (before 12th century)
1 a : a thoroughfare especially in a city, town, or village that is wider than an alley or lane and that usually includes sidewalks **b :** the part of a street reserved for vehicles **c :** a thoroughfare with abutting property ⟨lives on a fashionable *street*⟩
2 : the people occupying property on a street ⟨the whole *street* knew about the accident⟩
3 : a promising line of development or a channeling of effort
4 *capitalized* **:** a district (as Wall Street or Fleet Street) identified with a particular profession
5 : an environment (as in a depressed neighborhood or section of a city) of prostitution, poverty, dereliction, or crime
— **on the street** *or* **in the street 1 :** idle, homeless, or out of a job **2 :** out of prison **:** at liberty
— **up one's street** *or* **down one's street :** suited to one's abilities or taste

²**street** *adjective* (15th century)
: of or relating to the streets: as **a :** adjoining or giving access to a street ⟨the *street* door⟩ **b :** carried on or taking place in the street ⟨*street* fighting⟩ **c :** living or working on the streets ⟨a *street* peddler⟩ ⟨*street* people⟩ **d :** located in, used for, or serving as a guide to the streets ⟨a *street* map⟩ **e :** performing in or heard on the street ⟨a *street* band⟩ **f** (1) **:** suitable for wear or use on the street ⟨*street* clothes⟩ (2) **:** not touching the ground — used of a woman's dress in lengths reaching the knee, calf, or ankle **g :** of or relating to the street environment ⟨*street* drugs⟩

street arab \-'ar-əb, -'ā-,rab\ *noun, often A capitalized* (1859)
: a homeless vagabond and especially an outcast boy or girl in the streets of a city **:** GAMIN

street·car \'strēt-,kär\ *noun* (1862)
: a vehicle on rails used primarily for transporting passengers and typically operating on city streets

street·light \-,līt\ *noun* (1906)
: a light usually mounted on a pole and constituting one of a series spaced at intervals along a public street or highway — called also *streetlamp*

street railway *noun* (1861)
: a line operating streetcars or buses

streets \'strēts\ *adverb* (1898)
chiefly British **:** by a considerable margin ⟨a nice woman, *streets* above these other callers —Katherine Mansfield⟩

street·scape \'strēt-,skāp\ *noun* (1924)
1 : the appearance or view of a street
2 : a work of art depicting a view of a street
word history see LANDSCAPE

street–smart \-,smärt\ *adjective* (1974)
: STREETWISE

street smarts *noun plural* (1972)
: the quality of being streetwise

street theater *noun* (1967)
: drama dealing with controversial social and political issues that is usually performed outdoors

street virus *noun* (circa 1911)
: a naturally occurring rabies virus as distinguished from virus attenuated in the laboratory

street·walk·er \'strēt-,wò-kər\ *noun* (1592)
: PROSTITUTE; *especially* **:** one who solicits in the streets — compare CALL GIRL
— **street·walk·ing** \-kiŋ\ *noun*

street·wise \-,wīz\ *adjective* (1965)
: possessing the skills and attitudes necessary to survive in an often violent urban environment

strength \'streŋ(k)th, 'stren(t)th\ *noun, plural* **strengths** \'streŋ(k)ths, 'stren(t)ths, 'streŋks\ [Middle English *strengthe,* from Old English *strengthu;* akin to Old High German *strengi* strong — more at STRONG] (before 12th century)

1 : the quality or state of being strong **:** capacity for exertion or endurance
2 : power to resist force **:** SOLIDITY, TOUGHNESS
3 : power of resisting attack **:** IMPREGNABILITY
4 a : legal, logical, or moral force **b :** a strong attribute or inherent asset ⟨the *strengths* and the weaknesses of the book are evident⟩
5 a : degree of potency of effect or of concentration **b :** intensity of light, color, sound, or odor **c :** vigor of expression
6 : force as measured in numbers **:** effective numbers of any body or organization ⟨an army at full *strength*⟩
7 : one regarded as embodying or affording force or firmness **:** SUPPORT
8 : maintenance of or a rising tendency in a price level **:** firmness of prices
9 : BASIS — used in the phrase *on the strength of*
synonym SEE POWER
— from strength to strength : vigorously forward **:** from one high point to the next
strength·en \'streŋ(k)-thən, 'stren(t)-\ *verb*
strength·ened; strength·en·ing \'streŋ(k)th-niŋ, 'stren(t)th-; 'streŋ(k)-thə-, 'stren(t)-\ (15th century)
transitive verb
: to make stronger
intransitive verb
: to become stronger
— strength·en·er \'streŋ(k)th-nər, 'stren(t)th-; 'streŋ(k)-thə-, 'stren(t)-\ *noun*
stren·u·ous \'stren-yə-wəs\ *adjective* [Latin *strenuus*] (1599)
1 a : vigorously active **:** ENERGETIC **b :** FERVENT, ZEALOUS
2 : marked by or calling for energy or stamina **:** ARDUOUS
synonym SEE VIGOROUS
— stren·u·os·i·ty \,stren-yə-'wä-sə-tē\ *noun*
— stren·u·ous·ly \'stren-yə-wəs-lē\ *adverb*
— stren·u·ous·ness *noun*
strep \'strep\ *noun, often attributive* (1927)
: STREPTOCOCCUS
strep throat *noun* (circa 1927)
: an inflammatory sore throat caused by hemolytic streptococci and marked by fever, prostration, and toxemia — called also *septic sore throat*
strepto- *combining form* [New Latin, from Greek, from *streptos* twisted, from *strephein* to twist]
1 : twisted **:** twisted chain ⟨*strepto*coccus⟩
2 : streptococcus ⟨*strepto*kinase⟩
strep·to·ba·cil·lus \,strep-tō-bə-'si-ləs\ *noun* [New Latin] (1897)
: any of a genus (*Streptobacillus*) of nonmotile gram-negative rod-shaped bacteria in which the individual cells are often joined in a chain; *especially* **:** one (*S. moniliformis*) that is the causative agent of one form of rat-bite fever
strep·to·coc·cal \,strep-tə-'kä-kəl\ *also* **strep·to·coc·cic** \-'kä-kik, -'käk-sik\ *adjective* (1877)
: of, relating to, caused by, or being streptococci ⟨a *streptococcal* sore throat⟩ ⟨*streptococcal* organisms⟩
strep·to·coc·cus \-'kä-kəs\ *noun, plural* **-coc·ci** \-'kä-,kī, -(,)kē; -'käk-,sī, -(,)sē\ [New Latin] (1877)
: any of a genus (*Streptococcus*) of spherical or ovoid chiefly nonmotile and parasitic gram-positive bacteria that divide only in one plane, occur in pairs or chains, and include important pathogens of humans and domestic animals; *broadly* **:** a coccus occurring in chains
strep·to·ki·nase \,strep-tō-'kī-,nās, -,nāz\ *noun* (1944)
: a proteolytic enzyme from hemolytic streptococci active in promoting dissolution of blood clots
strep·to·ly·sin \,strep-tə-'lī-s⁰n\ *noun* (1904)
: an antigenic hemolysin produced by streptococci

strep·to·my·ces \-'mī-,sēz\ *noun, plural* **streptomyces** [New Latin, from *strepto-* + Greek *mykēs* fungus — more at MYC-] (1951)
: any of a genus (*Streptomyces*) of mostly soil streptomycetes including some that form antibiotics as by-products of their metabolism
strep·to·my·cete \-'mī-,sēt, -,mī-'sēt\ *noun* [New Latin *Streptomycet-, Streptomyces,* genus name] (1948)
: any of a family (Streptomycetaceae) of actinomycetes (as a streptomyces) that form vegetative mycelia which rarely break up into bacillary forms, have conidia borne on sporophores, and are typically aerobic soil saprophytes but include a few parasites of plants and animals
strep·to·my·cin \-'mī-s⁰n\ *noun* (1944)
: an antibiotic organic base $C_{21}H_{39}N_7O_{12}$ produced by a soil actinomycete (*Streptomyces griseus*), active against many bacteria, and used especially in the treatment of infections (as tuberculosis) by gram-negative bacteria
strep·to·thri·cin \-'thrī-s⁰n, -'thri-\ *noun* [New Latin *Streptothric-, Streptothrix,* genus of bacteria, from *strepto-* + Greek *trich-, thrix* hair] (1926)
: any of a group of related basic antibiotics produced by a soil actinomycete (*Streptomyces lavendulae*) and active against bacteria and to some degree against fungi
¹**stress** \'stres\ *noun* [Middle English *stresse* stress, distress, short for *destresse* — more at DISTRESS] (14th century)
1 : constraining force or influence: as **a :** a force exerted when one body or body part presses on, pulls on, pushes against, or tends to compress or twist another body or body part; *especially* **:** the intensity of this mutual force commonly expressed in pounds per square inch **b :** the deformation caused in a body by such a force **c :** a physical, chemical, or emotional factor that causes bodily or mental tension and may be a factor in disease causation **d :** a state resulting from a stress; *especially* **:** one of bodily or mental tension resulting from factors that tend to alter an existent equilibrium **e :** STRAIN, PRESSURE ⟨the environment is under *stress* to the point of collapse —Joseph Shoben⟩
2 : EMPHASIS, WEIGHT ⟨lay *stress* on a point⟩
3 *archaic* **:** intense effort or exertion
4 : intensity of utterance given to a speech sound, syllable, or word producing relative loudness
5 a : relative force or prominence of sound in verse **b :** a syllable having relative force or prominence
6 : ACCENT 6a
²**stress** *transitive verb* (1545)
1 : to subject to physical or psychological stress
2 : to subject to phonetic stress **:** ACCENT
3 : to lay stress on **:** EMPHASIZE
stressed-out \'strest-'aut\ *adjective* (1983)
: suffering from high levels of physical or especially psychological stress
stress fracture *noun* (1952)
: a usually hairline fracture of a bone that has been subjected to repeated stress
stress·ful \'stres-fəl\ *adjective* (1853)
: full of or tending to induce stress
— stress·ful·ly \-fə-lē\ *adverb*
stress·less \-ləs\ *adjective* (1885)
: having no stress; *specifically* **:** having no accent ⟨a *stressless* syllable⟩
— stress·less·ness *noun*
stress mark *noun* (1888)
: a mark used with (as before, after, or over) a written syllable in the respelling of a word to show that this syllable is to be stressed when spoken **:** ACCENT MARK
stress·or \'stre-sər, -,sòr\ *noun* (1950)
: a stimulus that causes stress
stress test *noun* (1975)

: an electrocardiographic test of heart function before, during, and after a controlled period of increasingly strenuous exercise (as on a treadmill)
¹**stretch** \'strech\ *verb* [Middle English *strecchen,* from Old English *streccan;* akin to Old High German *strecchan* to stretch, Old English *stræc* firm, severe] (before 12th century)
transitive verb
1 : to extend (as one's limbs or body) in a reclining position
2 : to reach out **:** EXTEND ⟨*stretched* out her arms⟩
3 : to extend in length ⟨*stretched* his neck to see what was going on⟩
4 : to fell with or as if with a blow
5 : to cause the limbs of (a person) to be pulled especially in torture
6 : to draw up (one's body) from a cramped, stooping, or relaxed position
7 : to pull taut ⟨canvas *stretched* on a frame⟩
8 a : to enlarge or distend especially by force **b :** to extend or expand as if by physical force ⟨*stretch* one's mind with a good book⟩ **c :** STRAIN ⟨*stretched* his already thin patience⟩
9 : to cause to reach or continue (as from one point to another or across a space) ⟨*stretch* a wire between two posts⟩
10 a : to amplify or enlarge beyond natural or proper limits ⟨the rules can be *stretched* this once⟩ **b :** to expand (as by improvisation) to fulfill a larger function ⟨*stretching* a dollar⟩
11 : to extend (a hit) to an extra base usually by fast or daring running ⟨*stretch* a single into a double⟩
intransitive verb
1 a : to become extended in length or breadth or both **:** SPREAD ⟨broad plains *stretching* to the sea⟩ **b :** to extend over a continuous period
2 : to become extended without breaking
3 a : to extend one's body or limbs **b :** to lie down at full length
— stretch·abil·i·ty \,stre-chə-'bi-lə-tē\ *noun*
— stretch·able \'stre-chə-bəl\ *adjective*
— stretchy \-chē\ *adjective*
— stretch a point : to go beyond what is strictly warranted in making a claim or concession
— stretch one's legs 1 : to extend the legs **2 :** to take a walk in order to relieve stiffness caused by prolonged sitting
²**stretch** *noun* (1541)
1 a : an exercise of something (as the understanding or the imagination) beyond ordinary or normal limits **b :** an extension of the scope or application of something ⟨a *stretch* of language⟩
2 : the extent to which something may be stretched
3 : the act of stretching **:** the state of being stretched
4 a : an extent in length or area ⟨a *stretch* of woods⟩ **b :** a continuous period of time ⟨can write for eight hours at a *stretch*⟩
5 : a walk to relieve fatigue
6 : a term of imprisonment
7 a : either of the straight sides of a racecourse; *especially* **:** HOMESTRETCH **b :** a final stage
8 : the capacity for being stretched **:** ELASTICITY
9 : STRETCH LIMO
³**stretch** *adjective* (1954)
: easily stretched **:** ELASTIC ⟨a *stretch* wig⟩
stretch·er \'stre-chər\ *noun* (15th century)
1 a : one that stretches; *especially* **:** a device or machine for stretching or expanding something **b :** an exaggerated story **:** a tall tale

\ə\ abut \ᵊ\ kitten \ər\ further \a\ ash \ā\ ace
\ä\ mop, mar \aú\ out \ch\ chin \e\ bet \ē\ easy
\g\ go \i\ hit \ī\ ice \j\ job \ŋ\ sing \ō\ go
\ò\ law \òi\ boy \th\ thin \t̶h̶\ the \ü\ loot \ú\ foot
\y\ yet \zh\ vision *see also* Guide to Pronunciation

2 a : a brick or stone laid with its length parallel to the face of the wall **b :** a timber or rod used especially when horizontal as a tie in framed work
3 : a device for carrying a sick, injured, or dead person
4 : a rod or bar extending between two legs of a chair or table

stretch limo *noun* (1971)
: a long limousine that is luxuriously furnished (as with a TV or bar) — called also *stretch limousine*

stretch marks *noun plural* (1956)
: striae on the skin (as of the hips, abdomen, and breasts) from excessive stretching and rupture of elastic fibers especially due to pregnancy or obesity

stretch–out \'strech-ˌau̇t\ *noun* (1930)
1 : a system of industrial operation in which workers are required to do extra work with slight or with no additional pay
2 : the act of stretching out **:** the state of being stretched out
3 : an economizing measure that spreads a limited quantity over a larger field than originally intended: as **a :** a slackening of production schedules so that a quantity of goods will be produced over a longer period than initially planned **b :** a restructuring of a loan repayment schedule over an extended period of time

stretch receptor *noun* (1936)
: MUSCLE SPINDLE

stretch runner *noun* (1922)
: a racehorse that makes a strong bid in the homestretch

stret·to \'stre-(ˌ)tō\ *also* **stret·ta** \-tə\ *noun, plural* **stret·ti** \-(ˌ)tē\ *or* **strettos** [*stretto* from Italian, from *stretto* narrow, close, from Latin *strictus*, past participle, *stretta* from Italian, from feminine of *stretto* — more at STRICT] (circa 1740)
1 a : the overlapping of answer with subject in a musical fugue **b :** the part of a fugue characterized by this overlapping
2 : a concluding passage performed in a quicker tempo

streu·sel \'strü-səl, -zəl, 'strȯi-, 'shtrȯi-\ *noun* [German, literally, something strewn, from Middle High German *strousel*, from *strouwen* to strew, from Old High German *strewen*] (1909)
: a crumbly mixture of fat, sugar, and flour and sometimes nuts and spices that is used as topping or filling for cake

strew \'strü\ *transitive verb* **strewed; strewed** *or* **strewn** \'strün\; **strew·ing** [Middle English *strewen, strowen,* from Old English *strewian, strēowian;* akin to Old High German *strewen* to strew, Latin *struere* to heap up, *sternere* to spread out, Greek *stornynai*] (before 12th century)
1 : to spread by scattering
2 : to cover by or as if by scattering something ⟨*strewing* the highways with litter⟩
3 : to become dispersed over as if scattered
4 : to spread abroad : DISSEMINATE

strew·ment \'strü-mənt\ *noun* (1602)
archaic **:** something (as flowers) strewed or designed for strewing

stria \'strī-ə\ *noun, plural* **stri·ae** \'strī-ˌē\ [Latin, furrow, channel — more at STRIKE] (1563)
1 : STRIATION 2
2 : a stripe or line (as in the skin) distinguished from the surrounding area by color, texture, or elevation — compare STRETCH MARKS

¹stri·ate \'strī-ət, -ˌāt\ *adjective* (1670)
: STRIATED

²stri·ate \-ˌāt\ *transitive verb* **stri·at·ed; stri·at·ing** (1709)
: to mark with striations or striae

stri·at·ed \'strī-ˌā-təd\ *adjective* (1646)
1 : marked with striations or striae
2 : of, relating to, or being striated muscle

striated muscle *noun* (1866)

: muscle tissue that is marked by transverse dark and light bands, that is made up of elongated multinuclear fibers, and that includes skeletal muscle, cardiac muscle, and most muscle of arthropods — compare SMOOTH MUSCLE, VOLUNTARY MUSCLE

stri·a·tion \strī-'ā-shən\ *noun* (circa 1847)
1 a : the fact or state of being striated **b :** arrangement of striations or striae
2 : a minute groove, scratch, or channel especially when one of a parallel series
3 : any of the alternate dark and light cross bands of a myofibril of striated muscle

strick \'strik\ *noun* [Middle English *stric, strik,* probably of Low German or Dutch origin; akin to Middle Low German *strik* rope, Middle Dutch *stric*] (14th century)
: a bunch of hackled flax, jute, or hemp

strick·en \'stri-kən\ *adjective* [Middle English *striken,* from past participle of *striken* to strike] (14th century)
1 a : afflicted or overwhelmed by or as if by disease, misfortune, or sorrow **b :** made incapable or unfit
2 : hit or wounded by or as if by a missile

strick·le \'stri-kəl\ *noun* [Middle English *strikell* a piece of wood for leveling a measure of grain; akin to Old English *strīcan* to stroke — more at STRIKE] (1688)
: a foundry tool for smoothing the surface of a core or mold
— **strickle** *transitive verb*

strict \'strikt\ *adjective* [Middle English *stricte,* from Latin *strictus,* from past participle of *stringere* to bind tight — more at STRAIN] (15th century)
1 *archaic* **a :** TIGHT, CLOSE; *also* **:** INTIMATE **b :** NARROW
2 a : stringent in requirement or control ⟨under *strict* orders⟩ **b :** severe in discipline ⟨a *strict* teacher⟩
3 a : inflexibly maintained or adhered to ⟨*strict* secrecy⟩ **b :** rigorously conforming to principle or a norm or condition
4 : EXACT, PRECISE ⟨in the *strict* sense of the word⟩
5 : of narrow erect habit of growth ⟨a *strict* inflorescence⟩
synonym see RIGID
— **strict·ly** \'strik(t)-lē\ *adverb*
— **strict·ness** \-nəs\ *noun*

strict liability *noun* (1896)
: liability imposed without regard to fault

stric·ture \'strik-chər\ *noun* [Middle English, from Late Latin *strictura,* from Latin *strictus,* past participle] (14th century)
1 a : an abnormal narrowing of a bodily passage; *also* **:** the narrowed part **b :** a constriction of the breath passage in the production of a speech sound
2 : something that closely restrains or limits **:** RESTRICTION ⟨moral *strictures*⟩
3 : an adverse criticism **:** CENSURE

¹stride \'strīd\ *verb* **strode** \'strōd\; **strid·den** \'stri-dᵊn\; **strid·ing** \'strī-diŋ\ [Middle English, from Old English *strīdan;* akin to Middle Low German *striden* to straddle, Old High German *strītan* to quarrel] (before 12th century)
intransitive verb
1 : to stand astride
2 : to move with or as if with long steps
3 : to take a very long step
transitive verb
1 : BESTRIDE, STRADDLE
2 : to step over
3 : to move over or along with or as if with long measured steps
— **strid·er** \'strī-dər\ *noun*

²stride *noun* (before 12th century)
1 a : a cycle of locomotor movements (as of a horse) completed when the feet regain the initial relative positions; *also* **:** the distance traversed in a stride **b :** the most effective natural pace **:** maximum competence or capability — often used in the phrase *hit one's stride*

2 : a long step
3 : an act of striding
4 : a stage of progress **:** ADVANCE
5 : a manner of striding
6 : STRIDE PIANO
— **in stride 1 :** without interference with regular activities **2 :** without emotional reaction ⟨took the news *in stride*⟩

stri·dence \'strī-dᵊn(t)s\ *noun* (1890)
: STRIDENCY

stri·den·cy \'strī-dᵊn(t)-sē\ *noun* (1865)
: the quality or state of being strident

stri·dent \'strī-dᵊnt\ *adjective* [Latin *strident-, stridens,* present participle of *stridere, strīdere* to make a harsh noise] (circa 1656)
: characterized by harsh, insistent, and discordant sound ⟨a *strident* voice⟩; *also* **:** commanding attention by a loud or obtrusive quality ⟨*strident* slogans⟩
synonym see LOUD, VOCIFEROUS
— **stri·dent·ly** *adverb*

stride piano *noun* [from *stride bass* left hand part consisting of large skips] (1952)
: a style of jazz piano playing in which the right hand plays the melody while the left hand alternates between a single note and a chord played an octave or more higher

stri·dor \'strī-dər, -ˌdȯr\ *noun* [Latin, from *stridere, strīdere*] (1632)
1 : a harsh, shrill, or creaking noise
2 : a harsh vibrating sound heard during respiration in cases of obstruction of the air passages

strid·u·late \'stri-jə-ˌlāt\ *intransitive verb* **-lat·ed; -lat·ing** [back-formation from *stridulation,* from French, high-pitched sound, from Latin *stridulus* shrill] (1838)
: to make a shrill creaking noise by rubbing together special bodily structures — used especially of male insects (as crickets or grasshoppers)
— **strid·u·la·tion** \ˌstri-jə-'lā-shən\ *noun*
— **strid·u·la·to·ry** \'stri-jə-lə-ˌtȯr-ē, -ˌtȯr-\ *adjective*

strid·u·lous \'stri-jə-ləs\ *adjective* [Latin *stridulus,* from *stridere, strīdere*] (1611)
: making a shrill creaking sound
— **strid·u·lous·ly** *adverb*

strife \'strīf\ *noun* [Middle English *strif,* from Old French *estrif,* probably from *estriver* to struggle — more at STRIVE] (13th century)
1 a : bitter sometimes violent conflict or dissension ⟨political *strife*⟩ **b :** an act of contention **:** FIGHT, STRUGGLE
2 : exertion or contention for superiority
3 *archaic* **:** earnest endeavor
synonym see DISCORD
— **strife·less** \'strī-fləs\ *adjective*

strig·il \'stri-jəl\ *noun* [Latin *strigilis;* akin to Latin *stringere* to touch lightly] (1581)
: an instrument used by ancient Greeks and Romans for scraping moisture off the skin after bathing or exercising

stri·gose \'strī-ˌgōs\ *adjective* [New Latin *strigosus,* from *striga* row of bristles, from Latin, furrow] (1793)
: having appressed bristles or scales ⟨a *strigose* leaf⟩

¹strike \'strīk\ *verb* **struck** \'strək\; **struck** *also* **strick·en** \'stri-kən\; **strik·ing** \'strī-kiŋ\ [Middle English, from Old English *strīcan* to stroke, go; akin to Old High German *strīhhan* to stroke, Latin *stringere* to touch lightly, *striga, stria* furrow] (before 12th century)
intransitive verb
1 : to take a course **:** GO ⟨*struck* off through the brush⟩
2 a : to aim and usually deliver a blow, stroke, or thrust (as with the hand, a weapon, or a

strigil

tool〉 **b :** to arrive with detrimental effect 〈disaster *struck*〉 **c :** to attempt to undermine or harm something as if by a blow 〈*struck* at . . . cherished notions —R. P. Warren〉
3 : to come into contact forcefully 〈two ships *struck* in mid channel〉
4 : to delete something
5 : to lower a flag usually in surrender
6 a : to become indicated by a clock, bell, or chime 〈the hour had just *struck*〉 **b :** to make known the time by sounding 〈the clock *struck* as they entered〉
7 : PIERCE, PENETRATE 〈the wind seemed to *strike* through our clothes〉
8 a : to engage in battle **b :** to make a military attack
9 : to become ignited
10 : to discover something 〈*struck* on a new plan of attack〉
11 a : to pull on a fishing rod in order to set the hook **b** *of a fish* **:** to seize the bait
12 : DART, SHOOT
13 a *of a plant cutting* **:** to take root **b** *of a seed* **:** GERMINATE
14 : to make an impression
15 : to stop work in order to force an employer to comply with demands
16 : to make a beginning 〈the need to *strike* vigorously for success〉
17 : to thrust oneself forward 〈he *struck* into the midst of the argument〉
18 : to work diligently **:** STRIVE
transitive verb
1 a : to strike at **:** HIT **b :** to drive or remove by or as if by a blow **c :** to attack or seize with a sharp blow (as of fangs or claws) 〈*struck* by a snake〉 **d :** INFLICT 〈*strike* a blow〉 **e :** to produce or as if by a blow or stroke 〈Moses *struck* water from the rock〉 **f :** to separate by a sharp blow 〈*strike* off flints〉
2 a : to haul down **:** LOWER 〈*strike* the sails〉 **b :** to dismantle and take away **c :** to strike the tents of (a camp)
3 : to afflict suddenly 〈*stricken* by a heart attack〉
4 a : to engage in (a battle) **:** FIGHT **b :** to make a military attack on
5 : DELETE, CANCEL 〈*strike* the last paragraph〉
6 a : to penetrate painfully **:** PIERCE **b :** to cause to penetrate **c :** to send down or out 〈trees *struck* roots deep into the soil〉
7 a : to level (as a measure of grain) by scraping off what is above the rim **b :** to smooth or form with a strickle
8 : to indicate by sounding
9 a (1) **:** to bring into forceful contact (2) **:** to shake (hands) in confirming an agreement (3) **:** to thrust suddenly **b :** to come into contact or collision with **c** *of light* **:** to fall on **d** *of a sound* **:** to become audible to
10 a : to affect with a mental or emotional state or a strong emotion 〈*struck* with horror at the sight〉 **b :** to affect a person with (a strong emotion) 〈words that *struck* fear in the listeners〉 **c :** to cause to become by or as if by a sudden blow 〈*struck* him dead〉
11 a : to produce by stamping **b** (1) **:** to produce (as fire) by or as if by striking (2) **:** to cause to ignite by friction
12 : to make and ratify the terms of 〈*strike* a bargain〉
13 a : to play or produce by stroking keys or strings 〈*struck* a series of chords on the piano〉 **b :** to produce as if by playing an instrument 〈his voice *struck* a note of concern〉
14 a : to hook (a fish) by a sharp pull on the line **b** *of a fish* **:** to snatch at (a bait)
15 a : to occur to 〈the answer *struck* me suddenly〉 **b :** to appear to especially as a revelation or as remarkable **:** IMPRESS
16 : BEWITCH
17 : to arrive at by or as if by computation 〈*strike* a balance〉
18 a : to come to **:** ATTAIN **b :** to come upon **:** DISCOVER 〈*strike* gold〉

19 : to engage in a strike against (an employer)
20 : TAKE ON, ASSUME 〈*strike* a pose〉
21 a : to place (a plant cutting) in a medium for growth and rooting **b :** to so propagate (a plant)
22 : to make one's way along
23 : to cause (an arc) to form (as between electrodes of an arc lamp)
24 *of an insect* **:** to oviposit on or in
synonym see AFFECT
— strike it rich : to become rich usually suddenly
²strike *noun* (15th century)
1 : STRICKLE
2 : an act or instance of striking
3 a : a work stoppage by a body of workers to enforce compliance with demands made on an employer **b :** a temporary stoppage of activities in protest against an act or condition
4 : the direction of the line of intersection of a horizontal plane with an uptilted geological stratum
5 a : a pull on a fishing rod to strike a fish **b :** a pull on a line by a fish in striking
6 : a stroke of good luck; *especially* **:** a discovery of a valuable mineral deposit
7 a : a pitched ball that is in the strike zone or is swung at and is not hit fair **b :** a perfectly thrown ball or pass
8 : DISADVANTAGE, HANDICAP
9 : an act or instance of knocking down all the bowling pins with the first bowl
10 : establishment of roots and plant growth
11 : cutaneous myiasis (as of sheep)
12 a : a military attack; *especially* **:** an air attack on a single objective **b :** a group of airplanes taking part in such an attack
strike-bound \'strīk-,baund\ *adjective* (1943) **:** subjected to a strike
strike-break-er \-,brā-kər\ *noun* (1904) **:** a person hired to replace a striking worker
strike-break-ing \-kiŋ\ *noun* (1905) **:** action designed to break up a strike
strike force *noun* (1968) **:** a team of federal agents assigned to investigate organized crime in a specific area
strike off *transitive verb* (1821)
1 : to produce in an effortless manner
2 : to depict clearly and exactly
strike-out \'strīk-,aut\ *noun* (1887) **:** an out in baseball resulting from a batter's being charged with three strikes
strike out (1712)
intransitive verb
1 : to enter upon a course of action
2 : to set out vigorously
3 : to make an out in baseball by a strikeout
4 : to finish bowling a string with consecutive strikes; *specifically* **:** to bowl three strikes in the last frame
5 : FAIL 2c
transitive verb
of a baseball pitcher **:** to retire (as a batter) by a strikeout
strike-over \'strīk-,ō-vər\ *noun* (1938) **:** an act or instance of striking a typewriter character on a spot occupied by another character
strik-er \'strī-kər\ *noun* (1581)
1 : one that strikes: as **a :** a player in any of several games who is striking or attempting to strike a ball **b :** the hammer of the striking mechanism of a clock or watch **c :** a blacksmith's helper who swings the sledgehammer **d :** a worker on strike
2 : a junior enlisted man in the U.S. Navy who has declared an occupational specialty
strike up (circa 1562)
intransitive verb
: to begin to sing or play or to be sung or played
transitive verb
1 : to cause to begin singing or playing 〈*strike* up the band〉
2 : to cause to begin 〈*strike* up a conversation〉

strike zone *noun* (1948) **:** the area over home plate through which a pitched baseball must pass to be called a strike
strik-ing \'strī-kiŋ\ *adjective* (1752) **:** attracting attention or notice through unusual or conspicuous qualities 〈a place of *striking* beauty〉
synonym see NOTICEABLE
— strik-ing-ly \-kiŋ-lē\ *adverb*
striking distance *noun* (1751) **:** a distance from which something can be easily reached or attained 〈almost within *striking distance* of their goal〉
striking price *noun* (1961) **:** an agreed-upon price at which an option contract can be exercised — called also *strike price*
¹string \'striŋ\ *noun* [Middle English, from Old English *streng;* akin to Old High German *strang* rope, Latin *stringere* to bind tight — more at STRAIN] (before 12th century)
1 : a small cord used to bind, fasten, or tie
2 a *archaic* **:** a cord (as a tendon or ligament) of an animal body **b :** a plant fiber (as a leaf vein)
3 : the gut, wire, or nylon cord of a musical instrument **b** *plural* (1) **:** the stringed instruments of an orchestra (2) **:** the players of such instruments
4 a : a group of objects threaded on a string 〈a *string* of fish〉 〈a *string* of pearls〉 **b** (1) **:** a series of things arranged in or as if in a line 〈a *string* of cars〉 〈a *string* of names〉 (2) **:** a sequence of like items (as bits, characters, or words) **c :** a group of business properties scattered geographically 〈a *string* of newspapers〉 **d :** the animals and especially horses belonging to or used by one individual
5 a : a means of recourse **:** EXPEDIENT **b :** a group of players ranked according to skill or proficiency
6 : SUCCESSION 3a 〈a *string* of successes〉
7 a : one of the inclined sides of a stair supporting the treads and risers **b :** STRINGCOURSE
8 a : BALKLINE 1 **b :** the action of lagging for break in billiards
9 : LINE 13
10 *plural* **a :** contingent conditions or obligations **b :** CONTROL, DOMINATION
11 : a scanty bikini — called also *string bikini*
12 : a hypothetical one-dimensional object that is infinitely thin but has a length of 10^{-33} centimeters, that vibrates as it moves through space, and whose mode of vibration manifests itself as a subatomic particle
— string-less \'striŋ-ləs\ *adjective*
— on the string : subject to one's influences
²string *verb* **strung** \'strəŋ\; **string-ing** \'striŋ-iŋ\ (15th century)
transitive verb
1 a : to equip with strings **b :** to tune the strings of
2 : to make tense **:** key up
3 a : to thread on or as if on a string **b :** to thread with objects **c :** to tie, hang, or fasten with string **d :** to put together (as words or ideas) like objects threaded on a string
4 : to hang by the neck — used with *up*
5 : to remove the strings of 〈*string* beans〉
6 a : to extend or stretch like a string 〈*string* wires from tree to tree〉 **b :** to set out in a line or series — often used with *out*
7 : FOOL, HOAX 〈cowboys *stringing* tenderfeet with tall tales —Carl Van Doren〉 — often used with *along*
intransitive verb
1 : to move, progress, or lie in a string
2 : to form into strings

3 : LAG 3

³string *adjective* (1712)
: of or relating to stringed musical instruments 〈the *string* section〉

string along (1914)
transitive verb
: to keep waiting
intransitive verb
: GO ALONG, AGREE

string bass *noun* (circa 1927)
: DOUBLE BASS

string bean (1759)
1 a : a bean of one of the older varieties of kidney bean that have stringy fibers on the lines of separation of the pods; *broadly*
: SNAP BEAN
2 : a very tall thin person

string·course \-ˌkȯrs, -ˌkȯrs\ *noun* (1825)
: a horizontal band (as of bricks) in a building forming a part of the design

stringed \'striŋd\ *adjective* (before 12th century)
1 : having strings 〈*stringed* instruments〉
2 : produced by strings

strin·gen·cy \'strin-jən(t)-sē\ *noun* (1844)
: the quality or state of being stringent

strin·gen·do \strin-'jen-(ˌ)dō\ *adverb* [Italian, verbal of *stringere* to press, from Latin, to bind tight — more at STRAIN] (1853)
: with quickening of tempo (as to a climax) — used as a direction in music

strin·gent \'strin-jənt\ *adjective* [Latin *stringent-, stringens*, present participle of *stringere*] (1736)
1 : TIGHT, CONSTRICTED
2 : marked by rigor, strictness, or severity especially with regard to rule or standard
3 : marked by money scarcity and credit strictness
synonym see RIGID
— **strin·gent·ly** *adverb*

string·er \'striŋ-ər\ *noun* (14th century)
1 : one that strings
2 : a string, wire, or chain often with snaps on which fish are strung by a fisherman
3 : a narrow vein or irregular filament of mineral traversing a rock mass of different material
4 a : a long horizontal timber to connect uprights in a frame or to support a floor **b** : STRING 7a **c** : a tie in a truss
5 a : a longitudinal member extending from bent to bent of a railroad bridge and carrying the track **b** : a longitudinal member (as in an airplane fuselage or wing) to reinforce the skin
6 a : a news correspondent who is paid space rates **b** : a reporter who works for a publication or news agency on a part-time basis; *broadly* : CORRESPONDENT
7 : one estimated to be of specified excellence or efficiency — used in combination 〈first-*stringer*〉 〈second-*stringer*〉

string·halt \'striŋ-ˌhȯlt\ *noun* (circa 1534)
: a condition of lameness in a horse's hind legs caused by muscular spasms
— **string·halt·ed** \-ˌhȯl-təd\ *adjective*

string·ing \'striŋ-iŋ\ *noun* (1812)
1 : lines of inlay in furniture decoration
2 : the material with which a racket is strung

string line *noun* (1867)
: BALKLINE 1

string·piece \'striŋ-ˌpēs\ *noun* (1769)
: the heavy squared timber lying along the top of the piles forming a dock front or timber pier

string quartet *noun* (1875)
1 : a composition for string quartet
2 : a quartet of performers on stringed instruments usually including a first and second violin, a viola, and a cello

string tie *noun* (1895)

string bean 1

: a narrow necktie

stringy \'striŋ-ē\ *adjective* **string·i·er; -est** (1669)
1 a : containing, consisting of, or resembling fibrous matter or string 〈*stringy* hair〉 **b** : lean and sinewy in build : WIRY
2 : capable of being drawn out to form a string : ROPY 〈a *stringy* precipitate〉
— **string·i·ness** *noun*

stringy·bark \'striŋ-ē-ˌbärk\ *noun* (1799)
1 : any of several Australian eucalypti with fibrous inner bark
2 : the bark of a stringybark

¹strip \'strip\ *verb* **stripped** \'stript\ *also* **stript; strip·ping** [Middle English *strippen*, from Old English *-strīepan*; akin to Old High German *stroufen* to strip] (13th century)
transitive verb
1 a : to remove clothing, covering, or surface matter from **b** : to deprive of possessions **c** : to divest of honors, privileges, or functions
2 a : to remove extraneous or superficial matter from 〈a prose style *stripped* to the bones〉 **b** : to remove furniture, equipment, or accessories from 〈*strip* a ship for action〉
3 : to make bare or clear (as by cutting or grazing)
4 : to finish a milking of by pressing the last available milk from the teats 〈*strip* a cow〉
5 a : to remove cured leaves from the stalks of (tobacco) **b** : to remove the midrib from (tobacco leaves)
6 : to tear or damage the thread of (a separable part or fitting)
7 : to separate (components) from a mixture or solution
8 : to press eggs or milt out of (a fish)
intransitive verb
1 a : to take off clothes **b** : to perform a striptease
2 : PEEL 1
— **strip·pa·ble** \'stri-pə-bəl\ *adjective*

²strip *noun* [Middle English, perhaps from Middle Low German *strippe* strap] (15th century)
1 a : a long narrow piece of a material **b** : a long narrow area of land or water
2 : AIRSTRIP
3 : a commercially developed area especially along a highway
4 : COMIC STRIP
5 : STRIPTEASE

strip–chart recorder \'strip-ˌchärt-\ *noun* (1950)
: a device used for the continuous graphic recording of time-dependent data
— **strip–chart recording** *noun*

strip–crop·ping \'strip-ˌkrä-piŋ\ *noun* (1936)
: the growing of a cultivated crop (as corn) in strips alternating with strips of a sod-forming crop (as hay) arranged to follow an approximate contour of the land and minimize erosion
— **strip–crop** \'strip-ˌkräp\ *verb*

¹stripe \'strīp\ *noun* [Middle English; akin to Middle Dutch *stripe* strip, stripe] (15th century)
: a stroke or blow with a rod or lash

²stripe *transitive verb* **striped** \'strīpt\; **strip·ing** [probably from Middle Dutch; akin to Middle High German *strīfe* stripe] (15th century)
: to make stripes on or variegate with stripes

³stripe *noun* (1626)
1 a : a line or long narrow section differing in color or texture from parts adjoining **b** (1) : a textile design consisting of lines or bands against a plain background (2) : a fabric with a striped design
2 : a narrow strip of braid or embroidery usually in the shape of a bar, arc, or chevron that is worn (as on the sleeve of a military uniform) to indicate rank or length of service
3 : a distinct variety or sort : TYPE 〈persons of the same political *stripe*〉
— **stripe·less** \'strī-pləs\ *adjective*

striped \'strīpt, 'strī-pəd\ *adjective* (1616)

: having stripes or streaks

striped bass *noun* (1818)
: a large anadromous food and sport fish (*Morone saxatilis* of the family Percichthyidae) that occurs along the Atlantic coast of the U.S. and has been introduced along the Pacific coast — called also *rockfish*

striped skunk *noun* (1882)
: a common North American skunk (*Mephitis mephitis*) usually with white on the top of the head that extends posteriorly in two narrowly separated stripes

strip·er \'strī-pər\ *noun* (1937)
: STRIPED BASS

strip·ing \'strī-piŋ\ *noun* (1677)
1 a : the stripes marked or painted on something **b** : a design of stripes
2 : the act or process of marking with stripes

strip·ling \'stri-pliŋ\ *noun* [Middle English] (14th century)
: YOUTH 2a

strip mine *noun* (1926)
: a mine that is worked from the earth's surface by the stripping of overburden; *especially* : a coal mine situated along the outcrop of a flat dipping bed
— **strip–mine** *verb*
— **strip miner** *noun*

stripped–down \'strip(t)-'daŭn\ *adjective* (1928)
: lacking any extra features : SIMPLE 2b

strip·per \'stri-pər\ *noun* (1581)
1 : one that strips
2 : STRIPTEASER
3 : a machine that separates a desired part of an agricultural crop
4 : an oil well that produces 10 barrels or less per day

strip poker *noun* (1919)
: a poker game in which players pay their losses by removing articles of clothing

strip search *noun* (1947)
: a search for something concealed on a person made after removal of the person's clothing
— **strip–search** *verb*

strip·tease \'strip-ˌtēz\ *noun* (1936)
: a burlesque act in which a performer removes clothing piece by piece

strip·teas·er \-ˌtē-zər\ *noun* (1930)
: one who performs a striptease

stripy \'strī-pē\ *adjective* **strip·i·er; -est** (1513)
: marked by stripes or streaks

strive \'strīv\ *intransitive verb* **strove** \'strōv\ *also* **strived** \'strīvd\; **striv·en** \'stri-vən\ *or* **strived; striv·ing** \'strī-viŋ\ [Middle English, from Old French *estriver*, of Germanic origin; akin to Middle High German *streben* to endeavor] (13th century)
1 : to devote serious effort or energy : ENDEAVOR
2 : to struggle in opposition : CONTEND
synonym see ATTEMPT
— **striv·er** \'strī-vər\ *noun*

strobe \'strōb\ *noun* [by shortening & alteration] (1942)
1 : STROBOSCOPE
2 : a device that utilizes a flashtube for high-speed illumination (as in photography)
3 : STROBOTRON

strobe light *noun* (1947)
: STROBE

stro·bi·la \strō-'bī-lə, 'strō-bə-\ *noun, plural* **-lae** \-(ˌ)lē\ [New Latin, from Greek *strobilē* plug of lint shaped like a pinecone, from *strobilos* pinecone] (1864)
: a linear series of similar animal structures (as the proglottids of a tapeworm) produced by budding

stro·bi·la·tion \ˌstrō-bə-'lā-shən\ *noun* [New Latin *strobila*] (1878)

: asexual reproduction (as in various coelenterates and tapeworms) by transverse division of the body into segments which develop into separate individuals, zooids, or proglottids

stro·bi·lus \strō-'bī-ləs, 'strō-bə-\ *noun, plural* **-li** \-,lī\ [New Latin, from Late Latin, pinecone, from Greek *strobilos* twisted object, top, pinecone, from *strobos* action of whirling; akin to *strephein* to twist] (circa 1753)
1 : an aggregation of sporophylls resembling a cone (as in the club mosses and horsetails)
2 : the cone of a gymnosperm

stro·bo·scope \'strō-bə-,skōp\ *noun* [Greek *strobos* whirling + International Scientific Vocabulary *-scope*] (1896)
: an instrument for determining the speed of cyclic motion (as rotation or vibration) that causes the motion to appear slowed or stopped: as **a :** a revolving disk with holes around the edge through which an object is viewed **b :** a device that uses a flashtube to intermittently illuminate a moving object **c :** a cardboard disk with marks to be viewed under intermittent light

stro·bo·scop·ic \,strō-bə-'skä-pik\ *adjective* (circa 1846)
: of, utilizing, or relating to a stroboscope or a strobe
— **stro·bo·scop·i·cal·ly** \-pi-k(ə-)lē\ *adverb*

stro·bo·tron \'strō-bə-,trän\ *noun* [*strobo-scope* + *-tron*] (1937)
: a gas-filled electron tube used especially as a source of bright flashes of light for a stroboscope

strode *past of* STRIDE

¹stroke \'strōk\ *transitive verb* **stroked; strok·ing** [Middle English, from Old English *strācian*; akin to Old High German *strīhhan* to stroke — more at STRIKE] (before 12th century)
1 : to rub gently in one direction; *also* **:** CARESS
2 : to flatter or pay attention to in a manner designed to reassure or persuade
— **strok·er** *noun*

²stroke *noun* [Middle English; akin to Old English *strīcan* to stroke — more at STRIKE] (13th century)
1 : the act of striking; *especially* **:** a blow with a weapon or implement
2 : a single unbroken movement; *especially* **:** one of a series of repeated or to-and-fro movements
3 a : a controlled swing intended to hit a ball or shuttlecock; *also* **:** a striking of the ball **b :** such a stroke charged to a player as a unit of scoring in golf
4 a : a sudden action or process producing an impact ⟨*stroke* of lightning⟩ **b :** an unexpected result ⟨*stroke* of luck⟩
5 : sudden diminution or loss of consciousness, sensation, and voluntary motion caused by rupture or obstruction (as by a clot) of an artery of the brain — called also *apoplexy*
6 a : one of a series of propelling beats or movements against a resisting medium ⟨a *stroke* of the oar⟩ **b :** a rower who sets the pace for a crew
7 a : a vigorous or energetic effort ⟨a *stroke* of genius⟩ **b :** a delicate or clever touch in a narrative, description, or construction
8 : HEARTBEAT
9 : the movement or the distance of the movement in either direction of a mechanical part (as a piston) having a reciprocating motion
10 : the sound of a bell being struck ⟨at the *stroke* of twelve⟩
11 : [¹*stroke*] **:** an act of stroking or caressing
12 a : a mark or dash made by a single movement of an implement **b :** one of the lines of a letter of the alphabet

³stroke *verb* **stroked; strok·ing** (1597)
transitive verb

1 a : to mark with a short line ⟨*stroke* the *t*'s⟩
b : to cancel by drawing a line through ⟨*stroked* out his name⟩
2 : to set the stroke for (a rowing crew); *also* **:** to set the stroke for the crew of (a rowing boat)
3 : HIT; *especially* **:** to propel (a ball) with a controlled swinging blow
intransitive verb
1 : to execute a stroke
2 : to row at a certain number of strokes a minute

stroke play *noun* (1905)
: golf competition scored by total number of strokes

stroll \'strōl\ *verb* [probably from German dialect *strollen*] (1680)
intransitive verb
1 : to walk in a leisurely or idle manner **:** RAMBLE
2 : to go from place to place in search of work or profit ⟨*strolling* players⟩ ⟨*strolling* musicians⟩
transitive verb
: to walk at leisure along or about
— **stroll** *noun*

stroll·er \'strō-lər\ *noun* (1608)
1 a : an itinerant actor **b :** VAGRANT, TRAMP
2 : one that strolls
3 : a collapsible carriage designed as a chair in which a small child may be pushed

stro·ma \'strō-mə\ *noun, plural* **stro·ma·ta** \-mə-tə\ [New Latin *stromat-, stroma*, from Latin, bed covering, from Greek *strōmat-, strōma*, from *stornynai* to spread out — more at STREW] (1832)
1 a : a compact mass of fungal hyphae producing perithecia or pycnidia **b :** the colorless proteinaceous matrix of a chloroplast in which the chlorophyll-containing lamellae are embedded
2 a : the supporting framework of an animal organ typically consisting of connective tissue **b :** the spongy protoplasmic framework of some cells (as a red blood cell)
— **stro·mal** \-məl\ *adjective*

stro·mat·o·lite \strō-'ma-t²l-,īt\ *noun* [Latin *stromat-, stroma* bed covering + English *-o-* + *-lite*] (1930)
: a laminated sedimentary fossil formed from layers of blue-green algae
— **stro·mat·o·lit·ic** \-,ma-t²l-'i-tik\ *adjective*

strong \'strȯŋ\ *adjective* **stron·ger** \'strȯŋ-gər *also* -ər\; **stron·gest** \'strȯŋ-gəst *also* -əst\ [Middle English, from Old English *strang; also* akin to Old High German *strengi* strong, Latin *stringere* to bind tight — more at STRAIN] (before 12th century)
1 : having or marked by great physical power
2 : having moral or intellectual power
3 : having great resources (as of wealth or talent)
4 : of a specified number ⟨an army ten thousand *strong*⟩
5 a : striking or superior of its kind ⟨a *strong* resemblance⟩ **b :** effective or efficient especially in a specified direction ⟨*strong* on watching other people work —A. Alvarez⟩
6 : FORCEFUL, COGENT ⟨*strong* evidence⟩ ⟨*strong* talk⟩
7 : not mild or weak **:** EXTREME, INTENSE: as **a :** rich in some active agent ⟨*strong* beer⟩ **b :** *of a color* **:** high in chroma **c :** ionizing freely in solution ⟨*strong* acids and bases⟩ **d :** magnifying by refracting greatly ⟨*strong* lens⟩
8 *obsolete* **:** FLAGRANT
9 : moving with rapidity or force ⟨*strong* wind⟩
10 : ARDENT, ZEALOUS ⟨a *strong* supporter⟩
11 a : not easily injured or disturbed **:** SOLID **b :** not easily subdued or taken ⟨a *strong* fort⟩
12 : well established **:** FIRM ⟨*strong* beliefs⟩
13 : not easily upset or nauseated ⟨a *strong* stomach⟩

14 : having an offensive or intense odor or flavor **:** RANK
15 : tending to steady or higher prices ⟨a *strong* market⟩
16 : of, relating to, or being a verb that is inflected by a change in the root vowel (as *strive, strove, striven*) rather than by regular affixation ☆
— **strong** *adverb*
— **strong·ish** \'strȯŋ-ish\ *adjective*
— **strong·ly** \'strȯŋ-lē\ *adverb*

strong anthropic principle *noun* (1985)
: ANTHROPIC PRINCIPLE b

¹strong–arm \'strȯŋ-'ärm\ *adjective* (1897)
: having or using undue force

²strong–arm *transitive verb* (1903)
1 a : to use force on **:** ASSAULT **b :** BULLY, INTIMIDATE
2 : to rob by force

strong·box \'strȯŋ-,bäks\ *noun* (1684)
: a strongly made chest or case for money or valuables

strong breeze *noun* (1867)
: wind having a speed of 25 to 31 miles (40 to 50 kilometers) per hour — see BEAUFORT SCALE table

strong drink *noun* (14th century)
: intoxicating liquor

strong force *noun* (1969)
: a fundamental physical force that acts on hadrons and is responsible for the binding together of protons and neutrons in the atomic nucleus and for processes of particle creation in high-energy collisions and that is the strongest known fundamental physical force but acts only over distances comparable to those between nucleons in an atomic nucleus — called also *strong interaction, strong nuclear force*; compare ELECTROMAGNETISM 2a, GRAVITY 3a(2), WEAK FORCE

strong gale *noun* (circa 1867)
: wind having a speed of 47 to 54 miles (76 to 87 kilometers) per hour — see BEAUFORT SCALE table

strong·hold \'strȯŋ-,hōld\ *noun* (15th century)
1 : a fortified place
2 a : a place of security or survival ⟨one of the last *strongholds* of the ancient Gaelic language —George Holmes⟩ **b :** a place dominated by a particular group or marked by a particular characteristic ⟨a Republican *stronghold*⟩ ⟨*strongholds* of snobbery —Lionel Trilling⟩

strong·man \'strȯŋ-,man\ *noun* (1859)
: one who leads or controls by force of will and character or by military methods

strong–mind·ed \'strȯŋ-'mīn-dəd\ *adjective* (1791)

☆ **SYNONYMS**
Strong, stout, sturdy, stalwart, tough, tenacious mean showing power to resist or to endure. STRONG may imply power derived from muscular vigor, large size, structural soundness, intellectual or spiritual resources ⟨*strong* arms⟩ ⟨the defense has a *strong* case⟩. STOUT suggests an ability to endure stress, pain, or hard use without giving way ⟨*stout* hiking boots⟩. STURDY implies strength derived from vigorous growth, determination of spirit, solidity of construction ⟨a *sturdy* table⟩ ⟨people of *sturdy* independence⟩. STALWART suggests an unshakable dependability ⟨*stalwart* environmentalists⟩. TOUGH implies great firmness and resiliency ⟨a *tough* political opponent⟩. TENACIOUS suggests strength in seizing, retaining, clinging to, or holding together ⟨*tenacious* farmers clinging to an age-old way of life⟩.

: having a vigorous mind; *especially* : marked by independence of thought and judgment
— **strong–mind·ed·ly** *adverb*
— **strong–mind·ed·ness** *noun*
strong room *noun* (1761)
: a room for money or valuables specially constructed to be fireproof and burglarproof
strong safety *noun* (1970)
: a safety in football who plays opposite the strong side of an offensive formation
strong side *noun* (circa 1951)
: the side of a football formation having the greater number of players; *specifically* : the side on which the tight end plays
strong suit *noun* (1857)
1 : a long suit containing high cards
2 : something in which one excels : FORTE ⟨details of legislation have never been my *strong suit* —Tip O'Neill⟩
stron·gyle \'strän-ˌjīl, -jəl\ *noun* [New Latin *Strongylus*, genus of worms, from Greek *strongylos* round, compact; akin to Greek *stranx* drop squeezed out — more at STRAIN] (1847)
: any of various nematode worms (family Strongylidae) related to the hookworms and parasitic especially in the alimentary tract and tissues of horses
stron·gy·loi·di·a·sis \ˌsträn-jə-ˌlȯi-'dī-ə-səs\ *also* **stron·gy·loi·do·sis** \-'dō-səs\ *noun* [New Latin, from *Strongyloides*, genus name, from *Strongylus*] (1905)
: infestation with or disease caused by any of a genus (*Strongyloides*) of strongyles that sometimes parasitize the intestines of vertebrates including humans
stron·tian·ite \'strän(t)-shə-ˌnīt\ *noun* (1794)
: a mineral consisting of a carbonate of strontium and occurring in various forms and colors
stron·tium \'strän(t)-sh(ē-)əm, 'strän-tē-əm\ *noun* [New Latin, from *strontia* strontium oxide, from obsolete English *strontian*, from *Strontian*, village in Scotland] (1808)
: a soft malleable ductile metallic element of the alkaline-earth group occurring only in combination and used especially in color TV tubes, in crimson fireworks, and in the production of some ferrites — see ELEMENT table
strontium 90 *noun* (1952)
: a heavy radioactive isotope of strontium of mass number 90 that has a half-life of 29 years and that is present in the fallout from nuclear explosions and is hazardous because like calcium it can be assimilated in biological processes and deposited in the bones of human beings and animals — called also *radiostrontium*
¹strop \'sträp\ *noun* [Middle English — more at STRAP] (before 12th century)
: STRAP: **a** : a short rope with its ends spliced to form a circle **b** : a usually leather band for sharpening a razor
²strop *transitive verb* **stropped; stropping** (1841)
: to sharpen (a razor) on a strop
stro·phan·thin \strō-'fan(t)-thən\ *noun* [International Scientific Vocabulary, from New Latin *Strophanthus*, from Greek *strophos* twisted band (from *strephein* to twist) + *anthos* flower — more at ANTHOLOGY] (1873)
: any of several glycosides (as ouabain) or mixtures of glycosides from African plants (genera *Strophanthus* and *Acokanthera*) of the dogbane family; *especially* : a bitter toxic glycoside $C_{36}H_{54}O_{14}$ from a woody vine (*Strophanthus kombé*) used similarly to digitalis
stro·phe \'strō-(ˌ)fē\ *noun* [Greek *strophē*, literally, act of turning, from *strephein* to turn, twist] (1603)
1 a : a rhythmic system composed of two or more lines repeated as a unit; *especially* : such a unit recurring in a series of strophic units **b** : STANZA
2 a : the movement of the classical Greek chorus while turning from one side to the oth-

er of the orchestra **b** : the part of a Greek choral ode sung during the strophe of the dance
stro·phic \'strō-fik, 'strä-\ *adjective* (1848)
1 : relating to, containing, or consisting of strophes
2 *of a song* : using the same music for successive stanzas — compare THROUGH-COMPOSED
strop·py \'strä-pē\ *adjective* [perhaps by shortening & alteration from *obstreperous*] (1951)
British : TOUCHY, BELLIGERENT
stroud \'straůd\ *noun* [probably from *Stroud*, town in England] (1683)
1 *also* **stroud·ing** \'straů-diŋ\ : a coarse woolen cloth formerly used in trade with North American Indians
2 : a blanket or garment of stroud
strove *past & chiefly dialect past participle of* STRIVE
strow \'strō\ *transitive verb* **strowed; strown** \'strōn\ *or* **strowed; strow·ing** [Middle English — more at STREW] (14th century)
archaic : SCATTER
stroy *verb* [Middle English *stroyen*, short for *destroyen*] (13th century)
obsolete : DESTROY
¹struck \'strək\ *past and past participle of* STRIKE
²struck *adjective* (1894)
: closed by or subjected to a labor strike ⟨a *struck* factory⟩ ⟨a *struck* employer⟩
struc·tur·al \'strək-chə-rəl, 'strək-shrəl\ *adjective* (1835)
1 : of or relating to the physical makeup of a plant or animal body
2 a : of, relating to, or affecting structure ⟨*structural* stability⟩ **b** : used in building structures ⟨*structural* clay⟩ **c** : involved in or caused by structure especially of the economy ⟨*structural* unemployment⟩
3 : of, relating to, or resulting from the effects of folding or faulting of the earth's crust : TECTONIC
4 : concerned with or relating to structure rather than history or comparison ⟨*structural* linguistics⟩
— **struc·tur·al·ly** *adverb*
structural formula *noun* (1872)
: an expanded molecular formula showing the arrangement within the molecule of atoms and of bonds
structural gene *noun* (1959)
: a gene that codes for the amino acid sequence of a protein (as an enzyme) or for a ribosomal RNA or transfer RNA
struc·tur·al·ism \'strək-chə-rə-ˌli-zəm, 'strək-shrə-\ *noun* (1907)
1 : psychology concerned especially with resolution of the mind into structural elements
2 : structural linguistics
3 : an anthropological movement associated especially with Claude Lévi-Strauss that seeks to analyze social relationships in terms of highly abstract relational structures often expressed in a logical symbolism
4 : a method of analysis (as of a literary text or a political system) that is related to cultural anthropology and that focuses on recurring patterns of thought and behavior
— **struc·tur·al·ist** \-list\ *noun or adjective*
structural isomer *noun* (1926)
: one of two or more compounds that contain the same number and kinds of atoms but that differ significantly in their geometric arrangement
struc·tur·al·ize \'strək-chə-rə-ˌlīz, 'strək-shrə-ˌlīz\ *transitive verb* **-ized; -iz·ing** (circa 1931)
: to organize or incorporate into a structure
— **struc·tur·al·i·za·tion** \ˌstrək-chə-rə-lə-'zā-shən, ˌstrək-shrə-\ *noun*
structural steel *noun* (1895)
1 : rolled steel in structural shapes
2 : steel suitable for structural shapes
struc·tur·a·tion \ˌstrək-chə-'rā-shən, -shə-'rä-\ *noun* (1925)

: the interrelation of parts in an organized whole
¹struc·ture \'strək-chər\ *noun* [Middle English, from Latin *structura*, from *structus*, past participle of *struere* to heap up, build — more at STREW] (15th century)
1 : the action of building : CONSTRUCTION
2 a : something (as a building) that is constructed **b** : something arranged in a definite pattern of organization ⟨a rigid totalitarian *structure* —J. L. Hess⟩ ⟨leaves and other plant *structures*⟩
3 : manner of construction : MAKEUP ⟨Gothic in *structure*⟩
4 a : the arrangement of particles or parts in a substance or body ⟨soil *structure*⟩ ⟨molecular *structure*⟩ **b** : organization of parts as dominated by the general character of the whole ⟨economic *structure*⟩ ⟨personality *structure*⟩
5 : the aggregate of elements of an entity in their relationships to each other
— **struc·ture·less** \-ləs\ *adjective*
— **struc·ture·less·ness** \-nəs\ *noun*
²structure *transitive verb* **struc·tured; struc·tur·ing** \'strək-chə-riŋ, 'strək-shriŋ\ (circa 1693)
1 : to form into or according to a structure
2 : CONSTRUCT
struc·tured *adjective* (1966)
: of, relating to, or being a method of computer programming in which each step of the solution to a problem is contained in a separate subprogram
stru·del \'strü-dᵊl, 'shtrü-\ *noun* [German, literally, whirlpool] (circa 1893)
: a pastry made from a thin sheet of dough rolled up with filling and baked ⟨apple *strudel*⟩
¹strug·gle \'strə-gəl\ *intransitive verb* **struggled; strug·gling** \-g(ə-)liŋ\ [Middle English *struglen*] (14th century)
1 : to make strenuous or violent efforts against opposition : CONTEND
2 : to proceed with difficulty or with great effort ⟨*struggled* through the high grass⟩ ⟨*struggling* to make a living⟩
— **strug·gler** \-g(ə-)lər\ *noun*
²struggle *noun* (1692)
1 : CONTEST, STRIFE ⟨armed *struggle*⟩ ⟨a power *struggle*⟩
2 : a violent effort or exertion : an act of strongly motivated striving
struggle for existence (1832)
: the automatic competition (as for food, space, or light) of members of a natural population that tends to eliminate less efficient individuals and thereby increase the chance of the more efficient to pass on inherited adaptive traits
¹strum \'strəm\ *verb* **strummed; strumming** [imitative] (1777)
transitive verb
1 a : to brush the fingers over the strings of (a musical instrument) in playing ⟨*strum* a guitar⟩; *also* : ³THRUM 1 **b** : to play (music) on a stringed instrument ⟨*strum* a tune⟩
2 : to cause to sound vibrantly ⟨winds *strummed* the rigging —H. A. Chippendale⟩
intransitive verb
1 : to strum a stringed instrument
2 : to sound vibrantly
— **strum·mer** *noun*
²strum *noun* (circa 1793)
: an act, instance, or sound of strumming
stru·ma \'strü-mə\ *noun, plural* **stru·mae** \-(ˌ)mē, -ˌmī\ *or* **strumas** [Latin, swelling of the lymph glands] (1565)
: GOITER
strum·pet \'strəm-pət\ *noun* [Middle English] (14th century)
: PROSTITUTE 1a
strung \'strəŋ\ *past and past participle of* STRING
strung out *adjective* (circa 1959)
1 : physically debilitated (as from long-term drug addiction)

2 : addicted to a drug
3 : intoxicated or stupefied from drug use
strunt \'strənt\ *intransitive verb* [by alteration] (1786) *Scottish* : STRUT
¹strut \'strət\ *verb* **strut·ted; strut·ting** [Middle English *strouten*, from Old English *strūtian* to exert oneself; akin to Middle High German *strozzen* to be swollen] (13th century) *intransitive verb*
1 : to become turgid : SWELL
2 a : to walk with a proud gait **b** : to walk with a pompous and affected air
transitive verb
: to parade (as clothes) with a show of pride
— **strut·ter** *noun*
— **strut one's stuff** : to display one's best work : SHOW OFF
²strut *noun* (1587)
1 : a structural piece designed to resist pressure in the direction of its length
2 : a pompous step or walk
3 : arrogant behavior : SWAGGER
³strut *transitive verb* **strut·ted; strut·ting** (circa 1828)
: to provide, stiffen, support, or hold apart with or as if with a strut
stru·thi·ous \'strü-thē-əs, -thē-\ *adjective* [Late Latin *struthio* ostrich, irregular from Greek *strouthos*] (1773)
: of or relating to the ostriches and related birds
strych·nine \'strik-ˌnīn, -nən, -ˌnēn\ *noun* [French, from New Latin *Strychnos*, from Latin, nightshade, from Greek] (1819)
: a bitter poisonous alkaloid $C_{21}H_{22}N_2O_2$ that is obtained from nux vomica and related plants (genus *Strychnos*) and is used as a poison (as for rodents) and medicinally as a stimulant to the central nervous system
Stu·art \'stü-ərt, 'styü-; 'st(y)ü(-ə)rt\ *adjective* [Robert *Stewart* (Robert II of Scotland) (died 1390)] (1873)
: of or relating to the Scottish royal house to which belonged the rulers of Scotland from 1371 to 1603 and of Great Britain from 1603 to 1649 and from 1660 to 1714
— **Stuart** *noun*
¹stub \'stəb\ *noun* [Middle English *stubb*, from Old English *stybb*; akin to Old Norse *stūfr* stump, Greek *stypos* stem, *typtein* to beat — more at TYPE] (before 12th century)
1 a : STUMP 2 **b** : a short piece remaining on a stem or trunk where a branch has been lost
2 : something made or worn to a short or blunt shape; *especially* : a pen with a short blunt nib
3 : a short blunt part left after a larger part has been broken off or used up ⟨pencil *stub*⟩
4 : something cut short or stunted
5 a : a small part of a leaf (as of a checkbook) attached to the backbone for memoranda of the contents of the part torn away **b** : the part of a ticket returned to the user
²stub *transitive verb* **stubbed; stub·bing** (15th century)
1 a : to grub up by the roots **b** : to clear (land) by grubbing out rooted growth **c** : to hew or cut down (a tree) close to the ground
2 : to extinguish (as a cigarette) by crushing
3 : to strike (one's foot or toe) against an object
stub·ble \'stə-bəl\ *noun, often attributive* [Middle English *stuble*, from Old French *estuble*, from Latin *stupula* stalk, straw, alteration of *stipula* — more at STIPULE] (14th century)
1 : the basal part of herbaceous plants and especially cereal grasses remaining attached to the soil after harvest
2 : a rough surface or growth resembling stubble; *especially* : a short growth of beard
— **stub·bled** \-bəld\ *adjective*
— **stub·bly** \-b(ə-)lē\ *adjective*
stubble mulch *noun* (1942)

: a lightly tilled mulch of plant residue used to prevent erosion, conserve moisture, and add organic matter to the soil
stub·born \'stə-bərn\ *adjective* [Middle English *stuborn*] (14th century)
1 a (1) : unreasonably or perversely unyielding **: MULISH** (2) : justifiably unyielding : RESOLUTE **b** : suggestive or typical of a strong stubborn nature ⟨a *stubborn* jaw⟩
2 : performed or carried on in an unyielding, obstinate, or persistent manner ⟨*stubborn* effort⟩
3 : difficult to handle, manage, or treat ⟨a *stubborn* cold⟩
4 : LASTING ⟨*stubborn* facts⟩
synonym see OBSTINATE
— **stub·born·ly** *adverb*
— **stub·born·ness** \-bər(n)-nəs\ *noun*
stub·by \'stə-bē\ *adjective* **stub·bi·er; -est** (15th century)
1 : abounding with stubs
2 a : resembling a stub : being short and thick ⟨*stubby* fingers⟩ **b** : being short and thickset : SQUAT **c** : being short, broad, or blunt (as from use or wear)
stuc·co \'stə-(ˌ)kō\ *noun, plural* **stuccos** *or* **stuccoes** [Italian, of Germanic origin; akin to Old High German *stucki* piece, crust, Old English *stocc* stock — more at STOCK] (1598)
1 a : a fine plaster used in decoration and ornamentation (as of interior walls) **b** : a material usually made of portland cement, sand, and a small percentage of lime and applied in a plastic state to form a hard covering for exterior walls
2 : STUCCOWORK
— **stuc·coed** \-(ˌ)kōd\ *adjective*
stuc·co·work \'stə-kō-ˌwərk\ *noun* (1686)
: work done in stucco
stuck *past and past participle of* STICK
stuck-up \'stək-'əp\ *adjective* (1829)
: superciliously self-important : CONCEITED
¹stud \'stəd\ *noun, often attributive* [Middle English *stod*, from Old English *stōd*; akin to Old Church Slavonic *stado* flock and probably to Old High German *stān* to stand — more at STAND] (before 12th century)
1 a : a group of animals and especially horses kept primarily for breeding **b** : a place (as a farm) where a stud is kept
2 : STUDHORSE; *broadly* : a male animal kept for breeding
3 a : a young man : GUY; *especially* : one who is virile and promiscuous **b** : a tough person **c** : HUNK 2
— **at stud** : for breeding as a stud ⟨retired racehorses *at stud*⟩
²stud *noun* [Middle English *stode*, from Old English *studu*; akin to Middle High German *stud* prop, Old English *stōw* place — more at STOW] (before 12th century)
1 a : one of the smaller uprights in the framing of the walls of a building to which sheathing, paneling, or laths are fastened : SCANTLING **b** : height from floor to ceiling
2 a : a boss, rivet, or nail with a large head used (as on a shield or belt) for ornament or protection **b** : a solid button with a shank or eye on the back inserted (as through an eyelet in a garment) as a fastener or ornament **c** : a small often round earring made for a pierced ear
3 a : any of various infixed pieces (as a rod or pin) projecting from a machine and serving chiefly as a support or axis **b** : one of the metal cleats inserted in a snow tire to increase traction
³stud *transitive verb* **stud·ded; stud·ding** (circa 1506)
1 : to furnish (as a building or wall) with studs
2 : to adorn, cover, or protect with studs
3 : to set, mark, or decorate conspicuously often at intervals ⟨a sky *studded* with stars⟩ ⟨a career *studded* with honors⟩
stud-book \'stəd-ˌbùk\ *noun* (1803)

: an official record (as in a book) of the pedigree of purebred animals (as horses or dogs)
stud·ding \'stə-diŋ\ *noun* (1588)
: the studs of a building or wall
stud·ding sail \'stə-diŋ-ˌsāl, 'stən(t)-səl\ *noun* [origin unknown] (1549)
: a light sail set at the side of a principal square sail of a ship in free winds
stu·dent \'stü-d°nt, 'styü-, *chiefly Southern* -d°nt\ *noun, often attributive* [Middle English, from Latin *student-, studens*, from present participle of *studēre* to study — more at STUDY] (14th century)
1 : SCHOLAR, LEARNER; *especially* : one who attends a school
2 : one who studies : an attentive and systematic observer
student body *noun* (1906)
: the students at an educational institution
student government *noun* (1948)
: the organization and management of student life by various student organizations
student lamp *noun* (1873)
: a desk reading lamp with a tubular shaft, one or two arms for a shaded light, and originally an oil reservoir
stu·dent·ship \'stü-d°nt-ˌship, 'styü-, -d°nt-\ *noun* (circa 1782)
1 *British* : a grant for university study
2 : the state of being a student
stu·dent's t distribution \'stü-d°n(t)s-, -d°n(t)s-\ *noun, often S capitalized* [*Student*, pen name of W. S. Gossett (died 1937) British statistician] (1929)
: T DISTRIBUTION
Student's t-test *noun* (1935)
: T-TEST
student teacher *noun* (1909)
: a student who is engaged in practice teaching
student teaching *noun* (1929)
: PRACTICE TEACHING
student union *noun* (1949)
: a building on a college campus that is devoted to student activities and that usually contains lounges, auditoriums, offices, and game rooms
stud·horse \'stəd-ˌhòrs\ *noun* (before 12th century)
: a stallion kept especially for breeding
stud·ied \'stə-dēd\ *adjective* (15th century)
1 : carefully considered or prepared : THOUGHTFUL
2 : KNOWLEDGEABLE, LEARNED
3 : produced or marked by conscious design or premeditation : CALCULATED ⟨*studied* indifference⟩
— **stud·ied·ly** *adverb*
— **stud·ied·ness** *noun*
stu·dio \'stü-dē-(ˌ)ō, 'styü-\ *noun, plural* **-dios** [Italian, literally, study, from Latin *studium*] (1819)
1 a : the working place of a painter, sculptor, or photographer **b** : a place for the study of an art (as dancing, singing, or acting)
2 : a place where motion pictures are made
3 : a place maintained and equipped for the transmission of radio or television programs
4 : a place where audio recordings are made
5 : STUDIO APARTMENT
studio apartment *noun* (1903)
: a small apartment consisting typically of a main room, kitchenette, and bathroom
studio couch *noun* (1931)
: an upholstered usually backless couch that can be made to serve as a double bed by sliding from underneath it the frame of a single cot

\ə\ **abut** \°\ **kitten** \ər\ **further** \a\ **ash** \ā\ **ace**
\ä\ **mop, mar** \aù\ **out** \ch\ **chin** \e\ **bet** \ē\ **easy**
\g\ **go** \i\ **hit** \ī\ **ice** \j\ **job** \ŋ\ **sing** \ō\ **go**
\ò\ **law** \òi\ **boy** \th\ **thin** \th\ **the** \ü\ **loot** \ù\ **foot**
\y\ **yet** \zh\ **vision** *see also* Guide to Pronunciation

stu·di·ous \'stü-dē-əs, 'styü-\ *adjective* (14th century)
1 : assiduous in the pursuit of learning
2 a : of, relating to, or concerned with study **b** : favorable to study ⟨a *studious* environment⟩
3 a : diligent or earnest in intent ⟨made a *studious* effort⟩ **b** : marked by or suggesting purposefulness or diligence ⟨a *studious* expression on his face⟩ **c** : deliberately or consciously planned ⟨spoke with a *studious* accent⟩
— **stu·di·ous·ly** *adverb*
— **stu·di·ous·ness** *noun*

stud·ly \'stəd-lē\ *adjective* [¹*stud*] (1972) *slang* : HUNKY

stud poker *noun* [¹*stud*] (1864)
: poker in which each player is dealt the first card facedown and the other four cards faceup with a round of betting taking place after each of the last four rounds of dealing

¹study \'stə-dē\ *noun, plural* **stud·ies** [Middle English *studie*, from Old French *estudie*, from Latin *studium*, from *studēre* to devote oneself, study; probably akin to Latin *tundere* to beat — more at CONTUSION] (14th century)
1 : a state of contemplation : REVERIE
2 a : application of the mental faculties to the acquisition of knowledge ⟨years of *study*⟩ **b** : such application in a particular field or to a specific subject ⟨the *study* of Latin⟩ **c** : careful or extended consideration ⟨the proposal is under *study*⟩ **d** (1) : a careful examination or analysis of a phenomenon, development, or question (2) : the published report of such a study
3 : a building or room devoted to study or literary pursuits
4 : PURPOSE, INTENT
5 a : a branch or department of learning : SUBJECT **b** : the activity or work of a student ⟨returning to her *studies* after vacation⟩ **c** : an object of study or deliberation ⟨every gesture a careful *study* —Marcia Davenport⟩ **d** : something attracting close attention or examination
6 : a person who learns or memorizes something (as a part in a play) — usually used with a qualifying adjective ⟨he's a fast *study*⟩
7 : a literary or artistic production intended as a preliminary outline, an experimental interpretation, or an exploratory analysis of specific features or characteristics
8 : a musical composition for the practice of a point of technique

²study *verb* **stud·ied; study·ing** (14th century)
intransitive verb
1 a : to engage in study **b** : to undertake formal study of a subject
2 *dialect* : MEDITATE, REFLECT
3 : ENDEAVOR, TRY
transitive verb
1 : to read in detail especially with the intention of learning
2 : to engage in the study of ⟨*study* biology⟩
3 : PLOT, DESIGN
4 : to consider attentively or in detail
synonym see CONSIDER
— **studi·er** \'stə-dē-ər\ *noun*

study hall *noun* (1846)
1 : a room in a school set aside for study
2 : a period in a student's day set aside for study and homework

¹stuff \'stəf\ *noun* [Middle English, from Middle French *estoffe*, from Old French, from *estoffer* to equip, stock, of Germanic origin; akin to Old High German *stopfōn* to stop up, from (assumed) Vulgar Latin *stuppare* — more at STOP] (14th century)
1 : materials, supplies, or equipment used in various activities: as **a** *obsolete* : military baggage **b** : PERSONAL PROPERTY
2 : material to be manufactured, wrought, or used in construction ⟨clear half-inch pine *stuff* —Emily Holt⟩

3 : a finished textile suitable for clothing; *especially* : wool or worsted material
4 a : literary or artistic production **b** : writing, discourse, talk, or ideas of little value : TRASH
5 a : an unspecified material substance or aggregate of matter ⟨volcanic rock is curious *stuff*⟩ **b** : something (as a drug or food) consumed or introduced into the body by humans **c** : a matter to be considered ⟨the truth was heady *stuff*⟩ ⟨long-term policy *stuff*⟩ **d** : a group or scattering of miscellaneous objects or articles ⟨pick that *stuff* up off the floor⟩; *also* : nonphysical miscellaneous material
6 a : fundamental material : SUBSTANCE ⟨*stuff* of greatness⟩ **b** : subject matter ⟨a teacher who knows her *stuff*⟩
7 : special knowledge or capability ⟨showing their *stuff*⟩
8 a : spin imparted to a thrown or hit ball to make it curve or change course **b** : the movement of a baseball pitch out of its apparent line of flight ⟨the liveliness of a pitch ⟨greatest pitcher of my time . . . had tremendous *stuff* —Ted Williams⟩
9 : DUNK SHOT
— **stuff·less** *adjective*

²stuff *transitive verb* (15th century)
1 a : to fill by packing things in : CRAM ⟨the boy *stuffed* his pockets with candy⟩ **b** : to fill to satiety : SURFEIT ⟨*stuffed* themselves with turkey⟩ **c** : to prepare (meat or vegetables) by filling or lining with a stuffing **d** : to fill (as a cushion) with a soft material **e** : to fill out the skin of (an animal) for mounting
2 a : to fill by intellectual effort ⟨*stuffing* their heads with facts⟩ **b** : to pack full of something immaterial ⟨a book *stuffed* with information⟩
3 : to fill or block up (as nasal passages)
4 a : to cause to enter or fill : THRUST ⟨*stuffed* a lot of clothing into a laundry bag⟩ **b** : to put (as a ball or puck) into a goal forcefully from close range
5 — used in the imperative to express contempt ⟨if they didn't like it, *stuff* 'em —Eric Clapton⟩; often used in the phrases *stuff it* and *get stuffed*
6 : to stop abruptly in a football game ⟨*stuff* the run⟩

stuffed shirt *noun* (1913)
: a smug, conceited, and usually pompous person often with an inflexibly conservative or reactionary attitude

stuff·er \'stə-fər\ *noun* (1611)
1 : one that stuffs
2 : an enclosure (as a leaflet) inserted in an envelope in addition to a bill, statement, or notice
3 : a series of extra threads or yarn running lengthwise in a fabric to add weight and bulk and to form a backing especially for carpets

stuff·ing \'stə-fiŋ\ *noun* (15th century)
: material used to stuff; *especially* : a seasoned mixture used to stuff food (as meat, vegetables, or eggs)

stuffing box *noun* (1798)
: a device that prevents leakage along a moving part (as a connecting rod) passing through a hole in a vessel (as a cylinder) containing steam, water, or oil and that consists of a box or chamber made by enlarging the hole and a gland to compress the contained packing

stuffy \'stə-fē\ *adjective* **stuff·i·er; -est** (1813)
1 : lacking in vitality or interest : STODGY, DULL
2 : ILL-NATURED, ILL-HUMORED
3 a : oppressive to the breathing : CLOSE **b** : stuffed up ⟨a *stuffy* nose⟩
4 : narrowly inflexible in standards of conduct : SELF-RIGHTEOUS
— **stuff·i·ly** \'stə-fə-lē\ *adverb*
— **stuff·i·ness** \'stə-fē-nəs\ *noun*

stul·ti·fy \'stəl-tə-ˌfī\ *transitive verb* **-fied;**

-fy·ing [Late Latin *stultificare* to make foolish, from Latin *stultus* foolish; akin to Latin *stolidus* stolid] (1766)
1 : to allege or prove to be of unsound mind and hence not responsible
2 : to cause to appear or be stupid, foolish, or absurdly illogical
3 a : to impair, invalidate, or make ineffective : NEGATE **b** : to have a dulling or inhibiting effect on
— **stul·ti·fi·ca·tion** \ˌstəl-tə-fə-'kā-shən\ *noun*

¹stum·ble \'stəm-bəl\ *verb* **stum·bled; stum·bling** \-b(ə-)liŋ\ [Middle English, probably of Scandinavian origin; akin to Norwegian dialect *stumle* to stumble; akin to Old Norse *stemma* to hinder — more at STEM] (14th century)
intransitive verb
1 a : to fall into sin or waywardness **b** : to make an error : BLUNDER **c** : to come to an obstacle to belief
2 : to trip in walking or running
3 a : to walk unsteadily or clumsily **b** : to speak or act in a hesitant or faltering manner
4 a : to come unexpectedly or by chance ⟨*stumble* onto the truth⟩ **b** : to fall or move carelessly
transitive verb
1 : to cause to stumble : TRIP
2 : BEWILDER, CONFOUND
— **stum·bler** \-b(ə-)lər\ *noun*
— **stum·bling·ly** \-b(ə-)liŋ-lē\ *adverb*

²stumble *noun* (1547)
: an act or instance of stumbling

stum·ble·bum \'stəm-bəl-ˌbəm\ *noun* (1932)
: a clumsy or inept person; *especially* : an inept boxer

stum·bling block \'stəm-bliŋ-\ *noun* (1588)
1 : an obstacle to progress
2 : an impediment to belief or understanding : PERPLEXITY

¹stump \'stəmp\ *noun* [Middle English *stumpe*; akin to Old High German *stumpf* stump and perhaps to Middle English *stampen* to stamp] (14th century)
1 a : the basal portion of a bodily part remaining after the rest is removed **b** : a rudimentary or vestigial bodily part
2 : the part of a plant and especially a tree remaining attached to the root after the trunk is cut
3 : a remaining part : STUB
4 : one of the pointed rods stuck in the ground to form a cricket wicket
5 : a place or occasion for public speaking (as for a cause or candidate); *also* : the circuit followed by a maker of such speeches — used especially in the phrase *on the stump*

²stump (1596)
transitive verb
1 : to reduce to a stump : TRIM
2 a : DARE, CHALLENGE **b** : to frustrate the progress or efforts of : BAFFLE
3 : to clear (land) of stumps
4 : to travel over (a region) making political speeches or supporting a cause
5 a : to walk over heavily or clumsily **b** : STUB 3
intransitive verb
1 : to walk heavily or clumsily
2 : to go about making political speeches or supporting a cause
— **stump·er** *noun*

³stump *noun* [French or Flemish; French *estompe*, from Flemish *stomp*, literally, stub, from Middle Dutch; akin to Old High German *stumpf* stump] (1778)
: a short thick roll of leather, felt, or paper usually pointed at both ends and used for shading or blending a drawing in crayon, pencil, charcoal, pastel, or chalk

⁴stump *transitive verb* (1807)
: to tone or treat (a drawing) with a stump

stump·age \'stəm-pij\ *noun* (1835)
1 : the value of standing timber
2 : uncut marketable timber; *also* : the right to cut it

stump-tailed macaque \'stəmp-'tāl(d)-\ *noun* (1938)
: a dark reddish brown naked-faced short-tailed macaque (*Macaca arctoides* synonym *M. speciosa*) that is found in eastern Asia — called also *stump-tailed monkey*

stump work *noun* (1904)
: embroidery with intricate padded designs or scenes in high relief popular especially in the 17th century

stumpy \'stəm-pē\ *adjective* (1600)
1 : being short and thick : STUBBY
2 : full of stumps

¹**stun** \'stən\ *transitive verb* **stunned; stun-ning** [Middle English, modification of Middle French *estoner* — more at ASTONISH] (14th century)
1 : to make senseless, groggy, or dizzy by or as if by a blow : DAZE
2 : to shock with noise
3 : to overcome especially with paralyzing astonishment or disbelief

²**stun** *noun* (1727)
: the effect of something that stuns : SHOCK

stung *past and past participle of* STING

stun gun *noun* (1967)
: a weapon designed to stun or immobilize (as by electric shock) rather than kill or injure the one affected

stunk *past and past participle of* STINK

stun·ner \'stə-nər\ *noun* (1829)
: one that stuns or is stunning

stun·ning \'stə-niŋ\ *adjective* (1667)
1 : causing astonishment or disbelief
2 : strikingly impressive especially in beauty or excellence
— **stun·ning·ly** \-niŋ-lē\ *adverb*

¹**stunt** \'stənt\ *transitive verb* [English dialect *stunt* stubborn, stunted, abrupt, probably of Scandinavian origin; akin to Old Norse *stuttr* scant — more at STINT] (1659)
: to hinder the normal growth, development, or progress of
— **stunt·ed·ness** *noun*

²**stunt** *noun* (1725)
1 : one (as an animal) that is stunted
2 : a check in growth
3 : a plant disease in which dwarfing occurs

³**stunt** *noun* [origin unknown] (1878)
1 : an unusual or difficult feat requiring great skill or daring; *especially* : one performed or undertaken chiefly to gain attention or publicity
2 : a shifting or switching of the positions by defensive players at the line of scrimmage in football to disrupt the opponent's blocking efforts

⁴**stunt** *intransitive verb* (1917)
: to perform or engage in a stunt

stunt·man \'stənt-,man\ *noun* (1927)
: a man who performs stunts; *especially* : one who doubles for an actor during the filming of stunts and dangerous scenes

stunt·wom·an \-,wu̇-mən\ *noun* (1948)
: a woman who doubles for an actress during the filming of stunts and dangerous scenes

stu·pa \'stü-pə\ *noun* [Sanskrit *stūpa*] (1876)
: a usually dome-shaped structure (as a mound) serving as a Buddhist shrine

¹**stupe** \'stüp, 'styüp\ *noun* [Middle English, from Latin *stuppa* coarse part of flax, tow, from Greek *styppē*] (14th century)
: a hot wet often medicated cloth applied externally (as to stimulate circulation)

stupa

²**stupe** *noun* [short for *stupid*] (1762)
: a stupid person : DOLT

stu·pe·fac·tion \,stü-pə-'fak-shən, ,styü-\ *noun* [Middle English *stupefaccioun*, from Medieval Latin *stupefaction-, stupefactio*, from Latin *stupefacere*] (15th century)
: the act of stupefying : the state of being stupefied

stu·pe·fy \'stü-pə-,fī, 'styü-\ *transitive verb* **-fied; -fy·ing** [Middle English *stupifien*, from Middle French *stupefier*, modification of Latin *stupefacere*, from *stupēre* to be astonished + *facere* to make, do — more at DO] (15th century)
1 : to make stupid, groggy, or insensible
2 : ASTONISH, ASTOUND
— **stu·pe·fy·ing·ly** \-iŋ-lē\ *adverb*

stu·pen·dous \stu̇-'pen-dəs, styü-\ *adjective* [Latin *stupendus*, gerundive of *stupēre*] (1666)
1 : causing astonishment or wonder : AWESOME, MARVELOUS
2 : of amazing size or greatness : TREMENDOUS
synonym see MONSTROUS
— **stu·pen·dous·ly** *adverb*
— **stu·pen·dous·ness** *noun*

¹**stu·pid** \'stü-pəd, 'styü-\ *adjective* [Middle French *stupide*, from Latin *stupidus*, from *stupēre* to be numb, be astonished — more at TYPE] (1541)
1 a : slow of mind : OBTUSE **b** : given to unintelligent decisions or acts : acting in an unintelligent or careless manner **c** : lacking intelligence or reason : BRUTISH
2 : dulled in feeling or sensation : TORPID ⟨still *stupid* from the sedative⟩
3 : marked by or resulting from unreasoned thinking or acting : SENSELESS
4 a : lacking interest or point **b** : VEXATIOUS, EXASPERATING ⟨this *stupid* flashlight won't work⟩ ☆
— **stu·pid·ly** *adverb*
— **stu·pid·ness** *noun*

²**stupid** *noun* (1712)
: a stupid person

stu·pid·i·ty \stu̇-'pi-də-tē, styü-\ *noun, plural* **-ties** (1541)
1 : the quality or state of being stupid
2 : a stupid idea or act

stu·por \'stü-pər, 'styü-\ *noun* [Middle English, from Latin, from *stupēre*] (14th century)
1 : a condition of greatly dulled or completely suspended sense or sensibility ⟨drunken *stupor*⟩
2 : a state of extreme apathy or torpor resulting often from stress or shock : DAZE
synonym see LETHARGY

stu·por·ous \'stü-p(ə-)rəs, 'styü-\ *adjective* (1892)
: marked or affected by or as if by stupor

stur·dy \'stər-dē\ *adjective* **stur·di·er; -est** [Middle English, brave, stubborn, from Middle French *estourdi*, from past participle of *estourdir* to stun, from (assumed) Vulgar Latin *exturdire*, from Latin *ex-* + (assumed) Vulgar Latin *turdus* simpleton, from Latin, thrush — more at THRUSH] (14th century)
1 a : firmly built or constituted : STOUT **b** : HARDY **c** : sound in design or execution : SUBSTANTIAL
2 a : marked by or reflecting physical strength or vigor **b** : FIRM, RESOLUTE **c** : RUGGED, STABLE
synonym see STRONG
— **stur·di·ly** \'stər-d°l-ē\ *adverb*
— **stur·di·ness** \'stər-dē-nəs\ *noun*

stur·geon \'stər-jən\ *noun* [Middle English, from Middle French *estourjon*, of Germanic origin; akin to Old English *styria* sturgeon] (13th century)
: any of a family (Acipenseridae) of usually large elongate anadromous or freshwater bony fishes which are widely distributed in the north temperate zone and whose roe is made into caviar

Sturm und Drang \,shtu̇rm-u̇nt-'dräŋ, ,stu̇r-, -ənt-\ *noun* [German, literally, storm and stress, from *Sturm und Drang* (1776), drama by Friedrich von Klinger (died 1831) German novelist and dramatist] (1845)
1 : a late 18th century German literary movement characterized by works containing rousing action and high emotionalism that often deal with the individual's revolt against society
2 : TURMOIL

sturt \'stərt\ *noun* [Middle English, contention, alteration of *strut*; akin to Old English *strūtian* to exert oneself — more at STRUT] (14th century)
chiefly Scottish : CONTENTION

¹**stut·ter** \'stə-tər\ *verb* [frequentative of English dialect *stut* to stutter, from Middle English *stutten*; akin to Dutch *stotteren* to stutter, Gothic *stautan* to strike — more at CONTUSION] (circa 1570)
intransitive verb
1 : to speak with involuntary disruption or blocking of speech (as by spasmodic repetition or prolongation of vocal sounds)
2 : to move or act in a halting or spasmodic

☆ **SYNONYMS**
Stupid, dull, dense, crass, dumb mean lacking in power to absorb ideas or impressions. STUPID implies a slow-witted or dazed state of mind that may be either congenital or temporary ⟨*stupid* students just keeping the seats warm⟩ ⟨*stupid* with drink⟩. DULL suggests a slow or sluggish mind such as results from disease, depression, or shock ⟨monotonous work that leaves the mind *dull*⟩. DENSE implies a thickheaded imperviousness to ideas ⟨too *dense* to take a hint⟩. CRASS suggests a grossness of mind precluding discrimination or delicacy ⟨a *crass*, materialistic people⟩. DUMB applies to an exasperating obtuseness or lack of comprehension ⟨too *dumb* to figure out what's going on⟩.

◇ **WORD HISTORY**
sturdy The usual modern meanings of *sturdy*, such as "firmly constituted" or "marked by physical strength or vigor," lie at the end of a long historical trail. Though these senses were already present in the English of Chaucer, Middle English also shows a wide range of other meanings now obsolete, such as "bold, valiant," "violent, furious," "severe, harsh," and "refractory, obstinate." (The latter sense long survived in the collocation *sturdy beggar*, referring to someone who lived by begging but who was able-bodied and hard to manage.) The source of *sturdy* was Old French *estourdi*, the past participle of *estourdir* "to stun, daze, befuddle." Though *estourdi* usually meant "dazed, stunned," it also is attested in the senses "giddy" or "foolish," and the association of giddiness with recklessness and recklessness with valor presumably led to the Middle English meaning "bold, valiant." Old French *estourdir*, in turn, most likely developed from an unattested spoken Latin verb *exturdire*, a derivative of Latin *turdus* "thrush." The thrush in folk belief was considered giddy or foolish, perhaps from the notion that it gorged itself on overripe and hence slightly alcoholic grapes until it became dizzy.

\ə\ **abut** \ᵊ\ **kitten** \ər\ **further** \a\ **ash** \ā\ **ace**
\ä\ **mop, mar** \au̇\ **out** \ch\ **chin** \e\ **bet** \ē\ **easy**
\g\ **go** \i\ **hit** \ī\ **ice** \j\ **job** \ŋ\ **sing** \ō\ **go**
\ȯ\ **law** \ȯi\ **boy** \th\ **thin** \t͟h\ **the** \ü\ **loot** \u̇\ **foot**
\y\ **yet** \zh\ **vision** *see also* Guide to Pronunciation

manner ⟨the old jalopy bucks and *stutters* uphill —William Cleary⟩
transitive verb
: to say, speak, or sound with or as if with a stutter
— **stut·ter·er** \-tər-ər\ *noun*

²**stutter** *noun* (circa 1847)
1 : an act or instance of stuttering
2 : a speech disorder involving stuttering accompanied by fear and anxiety

¹**sty** \'stī\ *noun, plural* **sties** *also* **styes** [Middle English, from Old English *stig;* akin to Old Norse *-stī* sty] (before 12th century)
1 : a pen or enclosed housing for swine
2 : an unkempt filthy place ⟨this house is a sty⟩

²**sty** *verb* **stied** *or* **styed; sty·ing** (before 12th century)
transitive verb
: to lodge or keep in a sty
intransitive verb
: to live in a sty

³**sty** *or* **stye** \'stī\ *noun, plural* **sties** *or* **styes** [short for obsolete English *styan,* from (assumed) Middle English, alteration of Old English *stīgend,* from *stīgan* to go up, rise — more at STAIR] (1617)
: an inflamed swelling of a sebaceous gland at the margin of an eyelid

sty·gian \'sti-j(ē-)ən\ *adjective, often capitalized* [Latin *stygius,* from Greek *stygios,* from *Styg-, Styx* Styx] (1566)
1 : of or relating to the river Styx
2 : extremely dark, gloomy, or forbidding

styl- *or* **styli-** *or* **stylo-** *combining form* [Latin *stilus* spike, stem — more at STYLE]
: style ⟨*stylo*podium⟩ ⟨*stylog*raphy⟩

sty·lar \'stī-lər, -,lär\ *adjective* [¹*style*] (circa 1928)
: of or relating to the style of a plant ovary

¹**style** \'stī(ə)l\ *noun* [Middle English *stile, style,* from Latin *stilus* spike, stem, stylus, style of writing; perhaps akin to Latin *instigare* to goad — more at STICK] (14th century)
1 : DESIGNATION, TITLE
2 a : a distinctive manner of expression (as in writing or speech) ⟨writes with more attention to *style* than to content⟩ ⟨the flowery *style* of 18th century prose⟩ **b** : a distinctive manner or custom of behaving or conducting oneself ⟨the formal *style* of the court⟩ ⟨his *style* is abrasive⟩; *also* : a particular mode of living ⟨in high *style*⟩ **c** : a particular manner or technique by which something is done, created, or performed ⟨a unique *style* of horseback riding⟩ ⟨the classical *style* of dance⟩
3 a : STYLUS **b** : GNOMON 1b **c** : a filiform prolongation of a plant ovary bearing a stigma at its apex — see FLOWER illustration **d** : a slender elongated process (as a bristle) on an animal
4 : a distinctive quality, form, or type of something ⟨a new dress *style*⟩ ⟨the Greek *style* of architecture⟩
5 a : the state of being popular : FASHION ⟨clothes that are always in *style*⟩ **b** : fashionable elegance **c** : beauty, grace, or ease of manner or technique ⟨an awkward moment she handled with *style*⟩
6 : a convention with respect to spelling, punctuation, capitalization, and typographic arrangement and display followed in writing or printing
synonym SEE FASHION
— **style·less** \'stī(ə)l-ləs\ *adjective*
— **style·less·ness** *noun*

²**style** *transitive verb* **styled; styl·ing** (circa 1580)
1 : to call or designate by an identifying term : NAME
2 a : to give a particular style to **b** : to design, make, or arrange in accord with the prevailing mode

— **styl·er** *noun*
-style *adjective or adverb combining form*
: being in the style of ⟨a Beaujolais-*style* wine⟩

style·book *noun* (1708)
: a book explaining, describing, or illustrating a prevailing, accepted, or authorized style

sty·let \'stī-'let, 'stī-lət\ *noun* [French, from Middle French *stilet* stiletto, from Old Italian *stiletto* — more at STILETTO] (1697)
1 a : a slender surgical probe **b** : a thin wire inserted into a catheter to maintain rigidity or into a hollow needle to maintain patency **c** : a pointed instrument (as for graving)
2 : a relatively rigid elongated organ or appendage (as a piercing mouthpart) of an animal
3 : STILETTO

sty·li·form \'stī-lə-,form\ *adjective* [New Latin *stiliformis,* from Latin *stilus* + *-formis* -form] (1578)
: resembling a style : bristle-shaped ⟨a *styliform* copulatory organ⟩

styl·ing \'stī-liŋ\ *noun* (1928)
: the way in which something is styled

styl·ise *British variant of* STYLIZE

styl·ish \'stī-lish\ *adjective* (1785)
: having style; *specifically* : conforming to current fashion
— **styl·ish·ly** *adverb*
— **styl·ish·ness** *noun*

styl·ist \'stī-list\ *noun* (1795)
1 a : a master or model of style; *especially* : a writer or speaker who is eminent in matters of style **b** : one (as a writer or singer) noted for a distinctive style
2 a : one who develops, designs, or advises on styles **b** : HAIRSTYLIST

sty·lis·tic \stī-'lis-tik\ *adjective* (1860)
: of or relating especially to literary or artistic style
— **sty·lis·ti·cal·ly** \-ti-k(ə-)lē\ *adverb*

sty·lis·tics \stī-'lis-tiks\ *noun plural but singular or plural in construction* (circa 1883)
1 : an aspect of literary study that emphasizes the analysis of various elements of style (as metaphor and diction)
2 : the study of the devices in a language that produce expressive value

sty·lite \'stī-,līt\ *noun* [Late Greek *stylitēs,* from Greek *stylos* pillar — more at STEER] (circa 1638)
: a Christian ascetic living atop a pillar
— **sty·lit·ic** \stī-'li-tik\ *adjective*

styl·ize \'stī-(ə)-,līz\ *transitive verb* **styl·ized; styl·iz·ing** (1898)
: to conform to a conventional style; *specifically* : to represent or design according to a style or stylistic pattern rather than according to nature or tradition
— **styl·i·za·tion** \,stī-lə-'zā-shən\ *noun*

sty·lo·bate \'stī-lə-,bāt\ *noun* [Latin *stylobates,* from Greek, *stylobatēs,* from *stylos* pillar + *bainein* to walk, go — more at COME] (1694)
: a continuous flat coping or pavement supporting a row of architectural columns

sty·log·ra·phy \stī-'lä-grə-fē\ *noun* (circa 1840)
: a mode of writing or tracing lines by means of a style or similar instrument

sty·loid \'stī-(ə)-,loid\ *adjective* (1709)
: resembling a style : STYLIFORM — used especially of slender pointed skeletal processes (as on the ulna)

sty·lo·po·di·um \,stī-lə-'pō-dē-əm\ *noun, plural* **-dia** \-dē-ə\ [New Latin, from *styl-* + Greek *podion* small foot, base — more at PEW] (circa 1832)
: a disk-shaped or conical expansion at the base of the style in plants of the carrot family

sty·lus \'stī-ləs\ *noun, plural* **sty·li** \'stī-(ə)-,lī\ *also* **sty·lus·es** \'stī-lə-səz\ [Latin *stylus, stilus* spike, stylus — more at STYLE] (1807)

: an instrument for writing, marking, or incising: as **a** : an instrument used by the ancients in writing on clay or waxed tablets **b** : a hard-pointed pen-shaped instrument for marking on stencils used in a reproducing machine **c** (1) : NEEDLE 3c (2) : a cutting tool used to produce an original record groove during disc recording **d** : a pen-shaped pointing device used for entering positional information (as from a graphics tablet) into a computer

sty·mie \'stī-mē\ *transitive verb* **sty·mied; sty·mie·ing** [Scots *stimie, stymie* to obstruct a golf shot by interposition of the opponent's ball] (1902)
: to present an obstacle to : stand in the way of

styp·tic \'stip-tik\ *adjective* [Middle English *stiptik,* from Latin *stypticus,* from Greek *styptikos,* from *styphein* to contract] (14th century)
: tending to contract or bind : ASTRINGENT; *especially* : tending to check bleeding
— **styptic** *noun*

styptic pencil *noun* (1908)
: a stick of a medicated styptic substance for use especially in shaving to stop the bleeding from small cuts

sty·rax \'stī-,raks\ *noun* [Latin — more at STORAX] (1558)
: STORAX

sty·rene \'stī-,rēn\ *noun* [International Scientific Vocabulary, from Latin *styrax*] (1885)
: a fragrant liquid unsaturated hydrocarbon C_8H_8 used chiefly in making synthetic rubber, resins, and plastics and in improving drying oils; *also* : any of various synthetic plastics made from styrene by polymerization or copolymerization

Sty·ro·foam \'stī-rə-,fōm\ *trademark*
— used for an expanded rigid polystyrene plastic

Styx \'stiks\ *noun* [Latin *Styg-, Styx,* from Greek]
: the principal river of the underworld in Greek mythology

su·able \'sü-ə-bəl\ *adjective* (circa 1623)
: liable to be sued in court
— **su·abil·i·ty** \,sü-ə-'bi-lə-tē\ *noun*
— **su·ably** \-blē\ *adverb*

sua·sion \'swā-zhən\ *noun* [Middle English, from Latin *suasion-, suasio,* from *suadēre* to urge, persuade — more at SWEET] (14th century)
: the act of influencing or persuading
— **sua·sive** \'swā-siv, -ziv\ *adjective*
— **sua·sive·ly** *adverb*
— **sua·sive·ness** *noun*

suave \'swäv\ *adjective* **suav·er; -est** [Middle French, pleasant, sweet, from Latin *suavis* — more at SWEET] (1847)
1 : smoothly though often superficially gracious and sophisticated
2 : smooth in texture, performance, or style ☆
— **suave·ly** *adverb*
— **suave·ness** *noun*

☆ **SYNONYMS**
Suave, urbane, diplomatic, bland, smooth, politic mean pleasantly tactful and well-mannered. SUAVE suggests a specific ability to deal with others easily and without friction ⟨a *suave* public relations coordinator⟩. URBANE implies high cultivation and poise coming from wide social experience ⟨an *urbane* traveler⟩. DIPLOMATIC stresses an ability to deal with ticklish situations tactfully ⟨a *diplomatic* negotiator⟩. BLAND emphasizes mildness of manner and absence of irritating qualities ⟨a *bland* master of ceremonies⟩. SMOOTH suggests often a deliberately assumed suavity ⟨a *smooth* salesman⟩. POLITIC implies shrewd as well as tactful and suave handling of people ⟨a cunningly *politic* manager⟩.

— **sua·vi·ty** \'swä-və-tē\ *noun*

¹**sub** \'səb\ *noun* (1830)
: SUBSTITUTE

²**sub** *verb* **subbed; sub·bing** (1853)
intransitive verb
: to act as a substitute
transitive verb
1 *British* : to read and edit as a copy editor
: SUBEDIT
2 : SUBCONTRACT 1

³**sub** *noun* (1916)
: SUBMARINE

sub- *prefix* [Middle English, from Latin, under, below, secretly, from below, up, near, from *sub* under, close to — more at UP]
1 : under : beneath : below ⟨*subsoil*⟩ ⟨*subaqueous*⟩
2 a : subordinate : secondary : next lower than or inferior to ⟨*substation*⟩ ⟨*subeditor*⟩ **b** : subordinate portion of : subdivision of ⟨*subcommittee*⟩ ⟨*subspecies*⟩ **c** : with repetition (as of a process) so as to form, stress, or deal with subordinate parts or relations ⟨*sublet*⟩ ⟨*subcontract*⟩
3 : less than completely, perfectly, or normally : somewhat ⟨*subacute*⟩ ⟨*subclinical*⟩
4 a : almost : nearly ⟨*suberect*⟩ **b** : falling nearly in the category of and often adjoining : bordering on ⟨*subarctic*⟩

sub·ad·o·les·cent
sub·agen·cy
sub·agent
sub·al·lo·ca·tion
sub·ar·ea
sub·au·di·ble
sub·av·er·age
sub·base·ment
sub·ba·sin
sub·block
sub·branch
sub·caste
sub·cat·e·go·ri·za·tion
sub·cat·e·go·rize
sub·cat·e·go·ry
sub·ceil·ing
sub·cel·lar
sub·chap·ter
sub·chief
sub·clan
sub·clus·ter
sub·code
sub·col·lec·tion
sub·col·lege
sub·col·le·giate
sub·col·o·ny
sub·com·mis·sion
sub·com·po·nent
sub·cor·date
sub·co·ri·a·ceous
sub·coun·ty
sub·cult
sub·cu·ra·tive
sub·dean
sub·de·ci·sion
sub·de·part·ment
sub·de·vel·op·ment
sub·di·a·lect
sub·di·rec·tor
sub·dis·ci·pline
sub·dis·trict
sub·econ·o·my
sub·erect
sub·file
sub·frame
sub·gen·er·a·tion
sub·genre
sub·goal
sub·gov·ern·ment
sub·hu·mid
sub·in·dus·try
sub·in·hib·i·to·ry

sub·lan·guage
sub·lev·el
sub·li·brar·i·an
sub·li·cense
sub·lit·er·a·cy
sub·lit·er·ate
sub·lot
sub·man·ag·er
sub·mar·ket
sub·max·i·mal
sub·menu
sub·min·i·mal
sub·min·is·ter
sub·na·tion·al
sub·net·work
sub·niche
sub·op·ti·mal
sub·op·ti·mi·za·tion
sub·op·ti·mize
sub·op·ti·mum
sub·or·bic·u·lar
sub·or·ga·ni·za·tion
sub·pan·el
sub·par
sub·para·graph
sub·par·al·lel
sub·part
sub·pe·ri·od
sub·phase
sub·pri·mate
sub·pro·cess
sub·prod·uct
sub·proj·ect
sub·pro·le·tar·i·at
sub·ra·tio·nal
sub·sat·u·rat·ed
sub·sat·u·ra·tion
sub·scale
sub·science
sub·sea
sub·sec·re·tary
sub·sec·tor
sub·seg·ment
sub·sei·zure
sub·sense
sub·sen·tence
sub·se·ries
sub·site
sub·skill
sub·so·ci·ety
sub·spe·cial·ist
sub·spe·cial·ize
sub·spe·cial·ty

sub·state
sub·sys·tem
sub·task
sub·tax·on
sub·test
sub·theme
sub·ther·a·peu·tic
sub·top·ic
sub·trea·sury
sub·trend
sub·tribe

sub·type
sub·unit
sub·va·ri·ety
sub·vas·sal
sub·vis·i·ble
sub·vi·su·al
sub·world
sub·writ·er
sub·ze·ro
sub·zone

sub·ac·id \,səb-'a-səd\ *adjective* [Latin *subacidus,* from *sub-* + *acidus* acid] (1765)
: somewhat acrimonious : CUTTING ⟨*subacid* comments⟩
— **sub·ac·id·ly** *adverb*
— **sub·ac·id·ness** *noun*

sub·acute \-ə-'kyüt\ *adjective* (1822)
1 : having a tapered but not sharply pointed form ⟨*subacute* leaves⟩
2 a : falling between acute and chronic in character especially when closer to acute ⟨*subacute* endocarditis⟩ **b** : less marked in severity or duration than a corresponding acute state ⟨*subacute* pain⟩
— **sub·acute·ly** *adverb*

subacute sclerosing pan·en·ceph·a·li·tis \-,pan-in-,se-fə-'lī-təs\ *noun* [*panencephalitis* from New Latin, from *pan-* + *encephalitis*] (1950)
: a central nervous system disease of children and young adults caused by infection of the brain by measles virus or a closely related virus and marked by intellectual deterioration, convulsions, and paralysis

sub·adult \,səb-ə-'dəlt\ ,səb-'a-,dəlt\ *noun* (1923)
: an individual that has passed through the juvenile period but not yet attained typical adult characteristics
— **subadult** *adjective*

sub·aer·i·al \-'ar-ē-əl, -'er-; -ā-'ir-ē-əl\ *adjective* (1833)
: situated, formed, or occurring on or immediately adjacent to the surface of the earth ⟨*subaerial* erosion⟩ ⟨*subaerial* roots⟩
— **sub·aer·i·al·ly** \-ē-ə-lē\ *adverb*

su·bah·dar *or* **su·ba·dar** \,sü-bə-'där\ *noun* [Persian *sūbadār*] (1698)
1 : a governor of a province
2 : the chief Indian officer of a company of Indian troops in the British army of India

sub·al·pine \,səb-'al-,pīn\ *adjective* (circa 1656)
1 : of or relating to the region about the foot and lower slopes of the Alps
2 : of, relating to, or inhabiting high upland slopes and especially the zone just below the timberline

¹**sub·al·tern** \sə-'bòl-tərn, *especially British* 'sə-bəl-tərn\ *adjective* [Late Latin *subalternus,* from Latin *sub-* + *alternus* alternate, from *alter* other (of two) — more at ALTER] (1570)
1 : particular with reference to a related universal proposition ⟨"some S is P" is a *subaltern* proposition to "all S is P"⟩
2 : SUBORDINATE

²**subaltern** *noun* (1605)
1 : a person holding a subordinate position; *specifically* : a junior officer (as in the British army)
2 : a particular proposition that follows immediately from a universal

sub·ant·arc·tic \,səb-ant-'ärk-tik, -'är-tik\ *adjective* (1875)
: of, relating to, characteristic of, or being a region just outside the antarctic circle

sub·api·cal \-'ā-pi-kəl *also* -'a-\ *adjective* (1846)
: situated below or near an apex

sub·aquat·ic \-ə-'kwä-tik, -'kwa-\ *adjective* [International Scientific Vocabulary] (1844)

: somewhat aquatic ⟨a marginal *subaquatic* flora⟩

sub·aque·ous \-'ā-kwē-əs, -'a-\ *adjective* (1677)
: existing, formed, or taking place in or under water

sub·arach·noid \-ə-'rak-,nòid\ *also* **sub·arach·noid·al** \-rak-'nòi-d³l\ *adjective* (1843)
: of, relating to, occurring, or situated under the arachnoid membrane ⟨*subarachnoid* hemorrhage⟩

sub·arc·tic \-'ärk-tik, -'är-tik\ *adjective* [International Scientific Vocabulary] (1854)
: of, relating to, characteristic of, or being regions immediately outside of the arctic circle or regions similar to these in climate or conditions of life
— **subarctic** *noun*

sub·as·sem·bly \-ə-'sem-blē\ *noun* (1919)
: an assembled unit designed to be incorporated with other units in a finished product

sub·at·mo·spher·ic \-,at-mə-'sfir-ik, -'sfer-\ *adjective* (1941)
: less or lower than that of the atmosphere ⟨*subatmospheric* pressure⟩

sub·atom·ic \-ə-'tä-mik\ *adjective* (1903)
1 : of or relating to the inside of the atom
2 : of, relating to, or being particles smaller than atoms

sub·au·di·tion \-ò-'di-shən\ *noun* [Late Latin *subaudition-, subauditio,* from *subaudire* to understand, from Latin *sub-* + *audire* to hear — more at AUDIBLE] (1798)
: the act of understanding or supplying something not expressed : a reading between the lines

sub·base \'səb-,bās\ *noun* (1826)
: underlying support placed below what is normally construed as a base: as **a** : the lowest member horizontally of an architectural base or of a baseboard or pedestal **b** : pervious fill (as crushed stone) placed under a roadbed

sub·bi·tu·mi·nous \,səb-bə-'tü-mə-nəs, -bī-, -'tyü-\ *adjective* (1908)
: of, relating to, or being coal of lower rank than bituminous coal but higher than lignite

sub·cab·i·net \-'kab-nit, -'ka-bə-\ *adjective* (1954)
: of, relating to, or being a high administrative position in the U.S. government that ranks below the cabinet level

sub·cap·su·lar \-'kap-sə-lər\ *adjective* (1889)
: situated or occurring beneath or within a capsule ⟨*subcapsular* cataracts⟩

sub·cel·lu·lar \-'sel-yə-lər\ *adjective* (1948)
: of less than cellular scope or level of organization ⟨*subcellular* particles⟩ ⟨*subcellular* studies⟩

sub·cen·ter \-'sen-tər\ *noun* (circa 1925)
: a secondary center; *especially* : a center (as for shopping) located outside the main business area of a city

sub·cen·tral \-trəl\ *adjective* (1822)
1 : nearly but not quite central
2 : located under a center
— **sub·cen·tral·ly** \-trə-lē\ *adverb*

sub·chas·er \'səb-,chā-sər\ *noun* (circa 1918)
: a small maneuverable patrol or escort vessel used for antisubmarine warfare

sub·class \'səb-,klas\ *noun* (1819)
: a primary division of a class: as **a** : a category in biological classification ranking below a class and above an order **b** : SUBSET

sub·clas·si·fi·ca·tion \,səb-,kla-sə-fə-'kā-shən\ *noun* (1873)
1 : a primary division of a classification

2 : arrangement into or assignment to subclassifications

— **sub·clas·si·fy** \-'kla-sə-ˌfī\ *transitive verb*

¹**sub·cla·vi·an** \-'klā-vē-ən\ *adjective* [New Latin *subclavius,* from *sub-* + *clavicula* clavicle] (1646)
: of, relating to, being, or performed on a part (as an artery, vein, or nerve) located under the clavicle ⟨*subclavian* angioplasty⟩

²**subclavian** *noun* (1719)
: a subclavian part (as an artery, vein, or nerve)

subclavian artery *noun* (1688)
: the proximal part of the main artery of the arm or forelimb

subclavian vein *noun* (1770)
: the proximal part of the main vein of the arm or forelimb

sub·cli·max \ˌsəb-'klī-ˌmaks\ *noun* (1916)
: a stage or community in an ecological succession immediately preceding a climax; *especially* **:** one held in relative stability throughout edaphic or biotic influences or by fire

sub·clin·i·cal \-'kli-ni-kəl\ *adjective* (circa 1935)
: not detectable or producing effects that are not detectable by the usual clinical tests ⟨a *subclinical* infection⟩ ⟨*subclinical* cancer⟩
— **sub·clin·i·cal·ly** \-k(ə-)lē\ *adverb*

sub·com·mit·tee \'səb-kə-ˌmi-tē, ˌsəb-kə-'\ *noun* (circa 1607)
: a subdivision of a committee usually organized for a specific purpose

sub·com·mu·ni·ty \ˌsəb-kə-'myü-nə-tē\ *noun* (1966)
: a distinct grouping within a community

sub·com·pact \'səb-'käm-ˌpakt\ *noun* (1967)
: an automobile smaller than a compact

¹**sub·con·scious** \ˌsəb-'kän(t)-shəs, 'səb-\ *adjective* (circa 1834)
: existing in the mind but not immediately available to consciousness ⟨a *subconscious* motive⟩
— **sub·con·scious·ly** *adverb*
— **sub·con·scious·ness** *noun*

²**subconscious** *noun* (1886)
: the mental activities just below the threshold of consciousness

sub·con·ti·nent \ˌsəb-'kän-tⁿn-ənt, -'känt-nənt\ *noun* (1863)
: a large landmass smaller than a continent; *especially* **:** a major subdivision of a continent ⟨the Indian *subcontinent*⟩
— **sub·con·ti·nen·tal** \ˌsəb-ˌkän-tⁿn-'en-tⁿl\ *adjective*

¹**sub·con·tract** \ˌsəb-'kän-ˌtrakt\ *noun* (1817)
: a contract between a party to an original contract and a third party; *especially* **:** one to provide all or a specified part of the work or materials required in the original contract

²**sub·con·tract** \ˌsəb-'kän-ˌtrakt, ˌsəb-kən-'\ (1842)
intransitive verb
: to let out or undertake work under a subcontract
transitive verb
1 : to engage a third party to perform under a subcontract all or part of (work included in an original contract) — sometimes used with *out*
2 : to undertake (work) under a subcontract

sub·con·trac·tor \ˌsəb-'kän-ˌtrak-tər, ˌsəb-kən-'\ *noun* (1842)
: an individual or business firm contracting to perform part or all of another's contract

sub·con·tra·oc·tave \ˌsəb-ˌkän-trə-'äk-tiv, -təv, -ˌtāv\ *noun* (circa 1901)
: the musical octave that begins on the fourth C below middle C — see PITCH illustration

sub·con·trary \ˌsəb-'kän-ˌtrer-ē\ *noun* (1685)
: a proposition so related to another that though both may be true they cannot both be false

— **subcontrary** *adjective*

sub·cool \-'kül\ *transitive verb* (1916)
: SUPERCOOL

sub·cor·ti·cal \-'kȯr-ti-kəl\ *adjective* (1887)
: of, relating to, involving, or being nerve centers below the cerebral cortex ⟨*subcortical* lesions⟩

sub·crit·i·cal \-'kri-ti-kəl\ *adjective* (1930)
1 : less or lower than critical in respect to a specified factor
2 a : of insufficient size to sustain a chain reaction ⟨a *subcritical* mass of fissionable material⟩ **b :** designed for use with fissionable material of subcritical mass ⟨a *subcritical* reactor⟩

sub·crust·al \-'krəs-tⁿl\ *adjective* (1897)
: situated or occurring below a crust and especially the crust of the earth

sub·cul·ture \'səb-ˌkəl-chər\ *noun* (1886)
1 a : a culture (as of bacteria) derived from another culture **b :** an act or instance of producing a subculture
2 : an ethnic, regional, economic, or social group exhibiting characteristic patterns of behavior sufficient to distinguish it from others within an embracing culture or society ⟨a criminal *subculture*⟩
— **sub·cul·tur·al** \-'kəlch-rəl, -'kəl-chə-\ *adjective*
— **sub·cul·tur·al·ly** *adverb*
— **subculture** *transitive verb*

sub·cu·ta·ne·ous \ˌsəb-kyü-'tā-nē-əs\ *adjective* [Late Latin *subcutaneus,* from Latin *sub-* + *cutis* skin — more at HIDE] (1651)
: being, living, used, or made under the skin ⟨*subcutaneous* parasites⟩
— **sub·cu·ta·ne·ous·ly** *adverb*

sub·cu·tis \ˌsəb-'kyü-təs\ *noun* [New Latin, from Late Latin, beneath the skin, from Latin *sub-* + *cutis*] (1900)
: the deeper part of the dermis

sub·dea·con \-'dē-kən\ *noun* [Middle English *subdecon,* from Late Latin *subdiaconus,* from Latin *sub-* + Late Latin *diaconus* deacon — more at DEACON] (14th century)
: a cleric ranking below a deacon: as **a :** a cleric in the lowest of the former major orders of the Roman Catholic Church **b :** an Eastern Orthodox or Armenian cleric in minor orders **c :** a clergyman performing the liturgical duties of a subdeacon

sub·deb \'səb-ˌdeb\ *noun* (1917)
: SUBDEBUTANTE

sub·deb·u·tante \ˌsəb-'de-byü-ˌtänt\ *noun* (1919)
: a young girl who is about to become a debutante; *broadly* **:** a girl in her middle teens

sub·der·mal \-'dər-məl\ *adjective* (1887)
: SUBCUTANEOUS
— **sub·der·mal·ly** \-mə-lē\ *adverb*

sub·di·vide \ˌsəb-də-'vīd, 'səb-də-ˌ\ *verb* [Middle English, from Late Latin *subdividere,* from Latin *sub-* + *dividere* to divide] (15th century)
transitive verb
1 : to divide the parts of into more parts
2 : to divide into several parts; *especially* **:** to divide (a tract of land) into building lots
intransitive verb
: to separate or become separated into subdivisions
— **sub·di·vid·able** \-'vī-də-bəl, -ˌvī-\ *adjective*
— **sub·di·vid·er** *noun*

sub·di·vi·sion \'səb-də-ˌvi-zhən\ *noun* (15th century)
1 : an act or instance of subdividing
2 : something produced by subdividing; *especially* **:** a tract of land surveyed and divided into lots for purposes of sale
3 : a category in botanical classification ranking below a division and above a class

sub·dom·i·nant \ˌsəb-'däm-nənt, -'dä-mə-\ *noun* (1793)

1 : the fourth tone of a diatonic scale
2 : something partly but incompletely dominant; *especially* **:** an ecologically important life form subordinate in influence to the dominants of a community
— **subdominant** *adjective*

sub·duc·tion \(ˌ)səb-'dək-shən\ *noun* [Late Latin *subduction-, subductio* withdrawal, from Latin *subducere* to withdraw, from *sub-* + *ducere* to draw — more at TOW] (1970)
: the action or process of the edge of one crustal plate descending below the edge of another
— **sub·duct** \(ˌ)səb-'dəkt\ *verb*

sub·due \səb-'dü, -'dyü\ *transitive verb* **subdued; sub·du·ing** [Middle English *sodewen, subduen* (influenced in form and meaning by Latin *subdere* to subject), from Middle French *soduire* to seduce (influenced in meaning by Latin *seducere* to seduce, from Latin *subducere*] (14th century)
1 : to conquer and bring into subjection **:** VANQUISH
2 : to bring under control especially by an exertion of the will **:** CURB ⟨*subdued* my foolish fears⟩
3 : to bring under cultivation
4 : to reduce the intensity or degree of **:** tone down
synonym see CONQUER
— **sub·du·er** *noun*

sub·dued \-'düd, -'dyüd\ *adjective* (1591)
: lacking in vitality, intensity, or strength ⟨*subdued* colors⟩
— **sub·dued·ly** \-'dü(-ə)d-lē, -'dyü(-ə)d-\ *adverb*

sub·dur·al \ˌsəb-'dur-əl, -'dyur-; 'səb-ˌ\ *adjective* [*sub-* + *dura (mater)*] (1875)
: situated or occurring beneath the dura mater or between the dura mater and the arachnoid membrane ⟨*subdural* space⟩ ⟨*subdural* hematomas⟩

sub·ed·i·tor \-'e-də-tər\ *noun* (1835)
chiefly British **:** COPY EDITOR
— **sub·ed·it** \-'e-dət\ *transitive verb, chiefly British*
— **sub·ed·i·to·ri·al** \ˌsəb-ˌe-də-'tȯr-ē-əl, -tȯr-\ *adjective, chiefly British*

sub·em·ployed \ˌsəb-im-'plȯid\ *adjective* (1967)
: UNDEREMPLOYED

sub·em·ploy·ment \-'plȯi-mənt\ *noun* (1967)
: a condition of inadequate employment in a labor force including unemployment and underemployment

sub·en·try \'səb-ˌen-trē\ *noun* (circa 1891)
: an entry (as in a catalog or an account) made under a more general entry

sub·epi·der·mal \ˌsəb-ˌe-pə-'dər-məl\ *adjective* (1853)
: lying beneath or constituting the innermost part of the epidermis

su·ber·in \'sü-bə-rən\ *noun* [French *subérine,* from Latin *suber* cork tree, cork] (1830)
: a complex fatty substance found especially in the cell walls of cork

su·ber·i·za·tion \ˌsü-bə-rə-'zā-shən\ *noun* (1882)
: conversion of the cell walls into corky tissue by infiltration with suberin
— **su·ber·ized** \'sü-bə-ˌrīzd\ *adjective*

sub·fam·i·ly \'səb-ˌfam-lē, -ˌfa-mə-\ *noun* [International Scientific Vocabulary] (1833)
1 : a category in biological classification ranking below a family and above a genus
2 : a subgroup of languages within a language family

sub·field \-ˌfēld\ *noun* (circa 1949)
1 : a subset of a mathematical field that is itself a field
2 : a subdivision of a field (as of study)

sub·floor \-ˌflȯr, -ˌflȯr\ *noun* (1893)

: a rough floor laid as a base for a finished floor

sub·fos·sil \-,fä-səl\ *adjective* [International Scientific Vocabulary] (1832)
: of less than typical fossil age but partially fossilized
— **subfossil** *noun*

sub·freez·ing \-'frē-ziŋ\ *adjective* (1949)
: being or marked by temperature below the freezing point (as of water) ⟨*subfreezing* weather⟩

sub·fusc \(,)səb-'fəsk, 'səb-,\ *adjective* [Latin *subfuscus* brownish, dusky, from *sub-* + *fuscus* dark brown — more at DUSK] (1710)
chiefly British : DRAB, DUSKY

sub·ge·nus \'səb-,jē-nəs\ *noun* [New Latin] (1813)
: a category in biological classification ranking below a genus and above a species

sub·gla·cial \,səb-'glā-shəl\ *adjective* (1820)
: of or relating to the bottom of a glacier or the area immediately underlying a glacier
— **sub·gla·cial·ly** \-shə-lē\ *adverb*

sub·grade \'səb-,grād\ *noun* (1898)
: a surface of earth or rock leveled off to receive a foundation (as of a road)

sub·graph \'səb-,graf\ *noun* (1963)
: a graph all of whose points and lines are contained in a larger graph

sub·group \-,grüp\ *noun* (1845)
1 : a subordinate group whose members usually share some common differential quality
2 : a subset of a mathematical group that is itself a group

sub·gum \'səb-'gəm\ *noun* [Chinese (Guangdong) *sahp-gám*, literally, assorted, mixed] (1938)
: a dish of Chinese origin prepared with a mixture of vegetables (as peppers, water chestnuts, and mushrooms)

sub·head \-,hed\ *noun* (1673)
1 : a heading of a subdivision (as in an outline)
2 : a subordinate caption, title, or headline

sub·head·ing \-,he-diŋ\ *noun* (1889)
: SUBHEAD

¹sub·hu·man \,səb-'hyü-mən, -'yü-\ *adjective* (1793)
: less than human: as **a** : failing to attain the level (as of morality or intelligence) associated with normal human beings **b** : unsuitable to or unfit for human beings ⟨*subhuman* living conditions⟩ **c** : of or relating to an infrahuman taxonomic group ⟨the *subhuman* primates⟩

²subhuman *noun* (1937)
: a subhuman being

sub·in·dex \,səb-'in-,deks\ *noun* (1923)
: an index to a division of a main classification

sub·in·feu·da·tion \,səb-,in-fyü-'dā-shən\ *noun* [*sub-* + *infeudation* enfeoffment] (circa 1730)
: the subdivision of a feudal estate by a vassal who in turn becomes feudal lord over his tenants
— **sub·in·feu·date** *transitive verb*

sub·in·ter·val \,səb-'in-tər-vəl\ *noun* (1927)
: an interval that is a subdivision or a subset of an interval

sub·ir·ri·ga·tion \-,ir-ə-'gā-shən\ *noun* (1880)
: irrigation below the surface (as by a periodic rise of the water table or by a system of underground porous pipes)
— **sub·ir·ri·gate** \-'ir-ə-,gāt\ *transitive verb*

su·bi·to \'sü-bi-,tō\ *adverb* [Italian, from Latin, suddenly, from *subitus* sudden — more at SUDDEN] (circa 1724)
: IMMEDIATELY, SUDDENLY — used as a direction in music

sub·ja·cen·cy \,səb-'jā-sᵊn(t)-sē\ *noun* (circa 1891)
: the quality or state of being subjacent

sub·ja·cent \-sᵊnt\ *adjective* [Latin *subjacent-, subjacens*, present participle of *sub-*

jacēre to lie under, from *sub-* + *jacēre* to lie — more at ADJACENT] (1597)
: lying under or below; *also* : lower than though not directly below ⟨hills and *subjacent* valleys⟩
— **sub·ja·cent·ly** *adverb*

¹sub·ject \'səb-jikt, -(,)jekt\ *noun* [Middle English, from Middle French, from Latin *subjectus* one under authority & *subjectum* subject of a proposition, from masculine & neuter respectively of *subjectus*, past participle of *subicere* to subject, literally, to throw under, from *sub-* + *jacere* to throw — more at JET] (14th century)
1 : one that is placed under authority or control: as **a** : VASSAL **b** (1) : one subject to a monarch and governed by the monarch's law (2) : one who lives in the territory of, enjoys the protection of, and owes allegiance to a sovereign power or state
2 a : that of which a quality, attribute, or relation may be affirmed or in which it may inhere **b** : SUBSTRATUM; *especially* : material or essential substance **c** : the mind, ego, or agent of whatever sort that sustains or assumes the form of thought or consciousness
3 a : a department of knowledge or learning **b** : MOTIVE, CAUSE **c** (1) : one that is acted on ⟨the helpless *subject* of their cruelty⟩ (2) : an individual whose reactions or responses are studied (3) : a dead body for anatomical study and dissection **d** (1) : something concerning which something is said or done ⟨the *subject* of the essay⟩ (2) : something represented or indicated in a work of art **e** (1) : the term of a logical proposition that denotes the entity of which something is affirmed or denied; *also* : the entity denoted (2) : a word or word group denoting that of which something is predicated **f** : the principal melodic phrase on which a musical composition or movement is based
synonym see CITIZEN
— **sub·ject·less** \-ləs\ *adjective*

²subject *adjective* (14th century)
1 : owing obedience or allegiance to the power or dominion of another
2 a : suffering a particular liability or exposure ⟨*subject* to temptation⟩ **b** : having a tendency or inclination : PRONE ⟨*subject* to colds⟩
3 : contingent on or under the influence of some later action ⟨the plan is *subject* to discussion⟩
synonym see LIABLE

³sub·ject \səb-'jekt, 'səb-,jekt\ *transitive verb* (14th century)
1 a : to bring under control or dominion : SUBJUGATE **b** : to make (as oneself) amenable to the discipline and control of a superior
2 : to make liable : PREDISPOSE
3 : to cause or force to undergo or endure (something unpleasant, inconvenient, or trying) ⟨was *subjected* to constant verbal abuse⟩
— **sub·jec·tion** \səb-'jek-shən\ *noun*

¹sub·jec·tive \(,)səb-'jek-tiv\ *adjective* (15th century)
1 : of, relating to, or constituting a subject: as **a** *obsolete* : of, relating to, or characteristic of one that is a subject especially in lack of freedom of action or in submissiveness **b** : being or relating to a grammatical subject; *especially* : NOMINATIVE
2 : of or relating to the essential being of that which has substance, qualities, attributes, or relations
3 a : characteristic of or belonging to reality as perceived rather than as independent of mind : PHENOMENAL — compare OBJECTIVE 1b **b** : relating to or being experience or knowledge as conditioned by personal mental characteristics or states
4 a (1) : peculiar to a particular individual : PERSONAL ⟨*subjective* judgments⟩ (2) : modified or affected by personal views, experience,

or background ⟨a *subjective* account of the incident⟩ **b** : arising from conditions within the brain or sense organs and not directly caused by external stimuli ⟨*subjective* sensations⟩ **c** : arising out of or identified by means of one's perception of one's own states and processes ⟨a *subjective* symptom of disease⟩ — compare OBJECTIVE 1c
5 : lacking in reality or substance : ILLUSORY
— **sub·jec·tive·ly** *adverb*
— **sub·jec·tive·ness** *noun*
— **sub·jec·tiv·i·ty** \-,jek-'ti-və-tē\ *noun*

²subjective *noun* (1817)
: something that is subjective; *also* : NOMINATIVE

subjective complement *noun* (1923)
: a grammatical complement relating to the subject of an intransitive verb (as *sick* in "he had fallen sick")

sub·jec·tiv·ise *British variant of* SUBJECTIVIZE

sub·jec·tiv·ism \(,)səb-'jek-ti-,vi-zəm\ *noun* (circa 1857)
1 a : a theory that limits knowledge to subjective experience **b** : a theory that stresses the subjective elements in experience
2 a : a doctrine that the supreme good is the realization of a subjective experience or feeling (as pleasure) **b** : a doctrine that individual feeling or apprehension is the ultimate criterion of the good and the right
— **sub·jec·tiv·ist** \-vist\ *noun*
— **sub·jec·tiv·is·tic** \-,jek-ti-'vis-tik\ *adjective*

sub·jec·tiv·ize \-ti-,vīz\ *transitive verb* **-ized; -iz·ing** (1868)
: to make subjective
— **sub·jec·tiv·i·za·tion** \-,jek-ti-və-'zā-shən\ *noun*

subject matter *noun* (1598)
: matter presented for consideration in discussion, thought, or study

sub·join \(,)səb-'join\ *transitive verb* [Middle French *subjoindre*, from Latin *subjungere* to join beneath, add, from *sub-* + *jungere* to join — more at YOKE] (1573)
: ANNEX, APPEND ⟨*subjoined* a statement of expenses to her report⟩

sub ju·di·ce \,sūb-'yü-di-,kā, 'səb-'jü-də-(,)sē\ *adverb* [Latin] (1613)
: before a judge or court : not yet judicially decided

sub·ju·gate \'səb-ji-,gāt\ *transitive verb* **-gat·ed; -gat·ing** [Middle English, from Latin *subjugatus*, past participle of *subjugare*, from *sub-* + *jugum* yoke — more at YOKE] (15th century)
1 : to bring under control and governance as a subject : CONQUER
2 : to make submissive : SUBDUE
— **sub·ju·ga·tion** \,səb-ji-'gā-shən\ *noun*
— **sub·ju·ga·tor** \'səb-ji-,gā-tər\ *noun*

sub·junc·tion \(,)səb-'jəŋ(k)-shən\ *noun* (1633)
1 : an act of subjoining or the state of being subjoined
2 : something subjoined

¹sub·junc·tive \səb-'jəŋ(k)-tiv\ *adjective* [Late Latin *subjunctivus*, from Latin *subjunctus*, past participle of *subjungere* to join beneath, subordinate] (1530)
: of, relating to, or constituting a verb form or set of verb forms that represents a denoted act or state not as fact but as contingent or possible or viewed emotionally (as with doubt or desire) ⟨the *subjunctive* mood⟩

²subjunctive *noun* (1622)
1 : the subjunctive mood of a language

\ə\ abut \ᵊ\ kitten \ər\ further \a\ ash \ā\ ace
\ä\ mop, mar \aù\ out \ch\ chin \e\ bet \ē\ easy
\g\ go \i\ hit \ī\ ice \j\ job \ŋ\ sing \ō\ go
\ò\ law \òi\ boy \th\ thin \th\ the \ü\ loot \ù\ foot
\y\ yet \zh\ vision *see also* Guide to Pronunciation

2 : a form of verb or verbal in the subjective mood ☐

sub·king·dom \'səb-ˌkiŋ-dəm\ *noun* (1825)
: a category in biological classification ranking below a kingdom and above a phylum

sub·late \sə-'blāt\ *transitive verb* **sub·lat·ed; sub·lat·ing** [Latin *sublatus* (past participle of *tollere* to take away, lift up), from *sub-* up + *latus,* past participle of *ferre* to carry — more at SUB-, TOLERATE, BEAR] (1838)
1 : NEGATE, DENY
2 : to negate or eliminate (as an element in a dialectic process) but preserve as a partial element in a synthesis
— **sub·la·tion** \-'blā-shən\ *noun*

¹sub·lease \'səb-ˌlēs, -ˌlēs\ *noun* (1826)
: a lease by a tenant or lessee of part or all of leased premises to another person but with the original tenant retaining some right or interest under the original lease

²sublease *transitive verb* (circa 1843)
: to make or obtain a sublease of

¹sub·let \'səb-'let\ *verb* **-let; -let·ting** (1766)
transitive verb
1 : SUBLEASE
2 : SUBCONTRACT 1
intransitive verb
: to lease or rent all or part of a leased or rented property

²sub·let \-ˌlet\ *noun* (1906)
: property and especially housing obtained by or available through a sublease

sub·le·thal \ˌsəb-'lē-thəl\ *adjective* (1895)
: less than but usually only slightly less than lethal ⟨a *sublethal* dose⟩
— **sub·le·thal·ly** \-thə-lē\ *adverb*

sub·lieu·ten·ant \ˌsəb-lü-'te-nənt, *British* -le(f)-'ten-\ *noun* (1804)
: a commissioned officer in the British navy ranking immediately below lieutenant

¹sub·li·mate \'sə-blə-ˌmāt\ *transitive verb* **-mat·ed; -mat·ing** [Middle English, from Medieval Latin *sublimatus,* past participle of *sublimare*] (15th century)
1 a : SUBLIME 1 **b** *archaic* **:** to improve or refine as if by subliming
2 : to divert the expression of (an instinctual desire or impulse) from its primitive form to one that is considered more socially or culturally acceptable
— **sub·li·ma·tion** \ˌsə-blə-'mā-shən\ *noun*

²sub·li·mate \'sə-blə-ˌmāt, -mət\ *noun* (circa 1626)
: a chemical product obtained by sublimation

¹sub·lime \sə-'blīm\ *verb* **sub·limed; sub·lim·ing** [Middle English, from Middle French *sublimer,* from Medieval Latin *sublimare* to refine, sublime, from Latin, to elevate, from *sublimis*] (14th century)
transitive verb
1 : to cause to pass directly from the solid to the vapor state and condense back to solid form
2 [French *sublimer,* from Latin *sublimare*] **a** (1) **:** to elevate or exalt especially in dignity or honor (2) **:** to render finer (as in purity or excellence) **b :** to convert (something inferior) into something of higher worth
intransitive verb
: to pass directly from the solid to the vapor state
— **sub·lim·able** \-'blī-mə-bəl\ *adjective*
— **sub·lim·er** *noun*

²sublime *adjective* **sub·lim·er; -est** [Latin *sublimis,* literally, high, elevated] (1586)
1 a : lofty, grand, or exalted in thought, expression, or manner **b :** of outstanding spiritual, intellectual, or moral worth **c :** tending to inspire awe usually because of elevated quality (as of beauty, nobility, or grandeur) or transcendent excellence
2 a *archaic* **:** high in place **b** *obsolete* **:** lofty of mien **:** HAUGHTY **c** *capitalized* **:** SUPREME — used in a style of address **d :** COMPLETE, UTTER ⟨*sublime* ignorance⟩
synonym see SPLENDID

— **sub·lime·ly** *adverb*
— **sub·lime·ness** *noun*

sub·lim·i·nal \(ˌ)sə-'bli-mə-nᵊl\ *adjective* [*sub-* + Latin *limin-, limen* threshold] (1886)
1 : inadequate to produce a sensation or a perception
2 : existing or functioning below the threshold of consciousness ⟨the *subliminal* mind⟩ ⟨*subliminal* advertising⟩
— **sub·lim·i·nal·ly** *adverb*

sub·lim·i·ty \sə-'bli-mə-tē\ *noun, plural* **-ties** (15th century)
1 : the quality or state of being sublime
2 : something sublime or exalted

sub·line \'səb-ˌlīn\ *noun* (1942)
: an inbred or selectively cultured line (as of cells) within a strain

sub·lin·gual \ˌsəb-'liŋ-gwəl, -gyə-wəl\ *adjective* [New Latin *sublingualis,* from Latin *sub-* + *lingua* tongue — more at TONGUE] (1661)
: situated or administered under the tongue ⟨*sublingual* tablets⟩ ⟨*sublingual* glands⟩

sub·lit·er·ary \-'li-tə-ˌrer-ē\ *adjective* (1936)
: relating to or being subliterature

sub·lit·er·a·ture \-'li-tə-rə-ˌchùr, -'li-trə-ˌchùr, -'li-tə(r)-ˌchùr, -chər, -ˌtyùr, -ˌtùr\ *noun* (1952)
: popular writing (as mystery or adventure stories) considered inferior to standard literature

¹sub·lit·to·ral \-'li-tə-rəl; ˌsəb-ˌli-tə-'ral, -'räl\ *adjective* (1846)
1 : situated, occurring, or formed on the aquatic side of a shoreline or littoral zone
2 : constituting the sublittoral

²sublittoral *noun* (circa 1935)
: the deeper part of the littoral portion of a body of water: **a :** the region in a lake between the deepest-growing rooted vegetation and the part of the lake below the thermocline **b :** the region in an ocean between the lowest point exposed by a low tide and the margin of the continental shelf

sub·lu·na·ry \ˌsəb-'lü-nə-rē, 'səb-lù-ˌner-ē\ *also* **sub·lu·nar** \ˌsəb-'lü-nər *also* -ˌnär\ *adjective* [modification of Late Latin *sublunaris,* from Latin *sub-* + *luna* moon — more at LUNAR] (1592)
: of, relating to, or characteristic of the terrestrial world ⟨dull *sublunary* lovers —John Donne⟩

sub·lux·a·tion \ˌsə-ˌblək-'sā-shən\ *noun* (circa 1688)
: partial dislocation (as of one of the bones in a joint)

sub·ma·chine gun \ˌsəb-mə-'shēn-ˌgən\ *noun* (1920)
: a portable automatic firearm that uses pistol-type ammunition and is fired from the shoulder or hip

¹sub·man·dib·u·lar \ˌsəb-man-'di-byə-lər\ *adjective* (1875)
1 : of, relating to, situated in, or performed in the region below the lower jaw
2 : of, relating to, or associated with the salivary glands inside of and near the lower edge of the mandible on each side

²submandibular *noun* (1974)
: a submandibular part (as an artery or bone)

sub·mar·gin·al \ˌsəb-'märj-nəl, -'mär-jə-nᵊl\ *adjective* (1829)
1 : adjacent to a margin or a marginal part or structure ⟨*submarginal* spots on an insect wing⟩
2 : falling below a necessary minimum ⟨*submarginal* economic conditions⟩

¹sub·ma·rine \'səb-mə-ˌrēn, ˌsəb-mə-'\ *adjective* (1648)
: UNDERWATER; *especially* **:** UNDERSEA ⟨*submarine* plants⟩ ⟨*submarine* minerals⟩

²submarine *noun* (1703)
1 : something that functions or operates underwater; *specifically* **:** a naval vessel designed to operate underwater
2 : a large sandwich on a long split roll with any of a variety of fillings (as meatballs or cold cuts, cheese, lettuce, and tomato) —

called also *grinder, hero, hoagie, Italian sandwich, poor boy, sub, torpedo*

³submarine *verb* **-rined; -rin·ing** (1914)
transitive verb
: to attack by or as if by a submarine **:** attack from beneath
intransitive verb
: to dive or slide under something

sub·ma·ri·ner \ˌsəb-mə-'rē-nər, -'mar-ə-nər\ *noun* (1914)
: a member of a submarine crew

sub·max·il·lary \ˌsəb-'mak-sə-ˌler-ē, 'səb-, *chiefly British* ˌsəb-mak-'si-lə-rē\ *adjective or noun* (1787)
: SUBMANDIBULAR

sub·me·di·ant \ˌsəb-'mē-dē-ənt\ *noun* (1806)
: the sixth tone of a diatonic scale

sub·merge \səb-'mərj\ *verb* **sub·merged; sub·merg·ing** [Latin *submergere,* from *sub-* + *mergere* to plunge — more at MERGE] (1611)
transitive verb
1 : to put under water

2 : to cover or overflow with water
3 : to make obscure or subordinate : SUPPRESS ⟨personal lives *submerged* by professional responsibilities⟩
intransitive verb
: to go under water
— **sub·mer·gence** \-'mər-jən(t)s\ *noun*
— **sub·merg·ible** \-'mər-jə-bəl\ *adjective*
submerged *adjective* (1799)
1 : covered with water
2 : SUBMERSED b
3 : sunk in poverty and misery ⟨the *submerged* masses⟩ ⟨the *submerged* tenth of the population⟩
4 : HIDDEN, SUPPRESSED ⟨*submerged* emotions⟩
sub·merse \səb-'mərs\ *transitive verb* **submersed; sub·mers·ing** [Latin *submersus*, past participle of *submergere*] (1837)
: SUBMERGE
— **sub·mer·sion** \-'mər-zhən, -shən\ *noun*
submersed *adjective* (circa 1727)
: SUBMERGED: as **a** : covered with water **b** : growing or adapted to grow underwater ⟨*submersed* weeds⟩
¹sub·mers·ible \səb-'mər-sə-bəl\ *adjective* (1866)
: capable of being submerged
²submersible *noun* (1900)
: something that is submersible; *especially* : a usually small underwater craft used especially for deep-sea research
sub·meta·cen·tric \səb-,me-tə-'sen-trik\ *adjective* (1962)
: having the centromere situated so that one chromosome is somewhat shorter than the other
— **submetacentric** *noun*
sub·mi·cro·gram \səb-'mī-krə-,gram\ *adjective* (1946)
: relating to or having a mass of less than one microgram ⟨*submicrogram* quantities of a chemical⟩
sub·mi·cron \-,krän\ *adjective* (1948)
1 : being less than a micron in a (specified) measurement and especially in diameter ⟨a *submicron* particle⟩
2 : having or consisting of submicron particles ⟨a *submicron* metal powder⟩
sub·mi·cro·scop·ic \,səb-,mī-krə-'skä-pik\ *adjective* [International Scientific Vocabulary] (1912)
1 : too small to be seen in an ordinary light microscope
2 : of, relating to, or dealing with the very minute ⟨the *submicroscopic* world⟩
— **sub·mi·cro·scop·i·cal·ly** \-pi-k(ə-)lē\ *adverb*
sub·mil·li·me·ter \,səb-'mi-lə-,mē-tər\ *adjective* (1955)
: being less than a millimeter in diameter or wavelength ⟨a *submillimeter* particle⟩ ⟨a *submillimeter* radio wave⟩
sub·min·i·a·ture \,səb-'mi-nē-ə-,chůr, -'mi-ni-,chůr, -'min-yə-, -,chər, -,tyůr, -,tůr\ *adjective* [International Scientific Vocabulary] (1947)
: very small — used especially of a very compact assembly of electronic equipment
sub·miss \səb-'mis\ *adjective* [Latin *submissus*, from past participle of *submittere*] (1570) *archaic* : SUBMISSIVE, HUMBLE
sub·mis·sion \səb-'mi-shən\ *noun* [Middle English, from Middle French, from Latin *submission-, submissio* act of lowering, from *submittere*] (14th century)
1 a : a legal agreement to submit to the decision of arbitrators **b** : an act of submitting something (as for consideration or inspection); *also* : something submitted (as a manuscript)
2 : the condition of being submissive, humble, or compliant
3 : an act of submitting to the authority or control of another
sub·mis·sive \-'mi-siv\ *adjective* (circa 1586)
: submitting to others
— **sub·mis·sive·ly** *adverb*

— **sub·mis·sive·ness** *noun*
sub·mit \səb-'mit\ *verb* **sub·mit·ted; sub·mit·ting** [Middle English *submitten*, from Latin *submittere* to lower, submit, from *sub-* + *mittere* to send] (14th century)
transitive verb
1 a : to yield to governance or authority **b** : to subject to a condition, treatment, or operation ⟨the metal was *submitted* to analysis⟩
2 : to present or propose to another for review, consideration, or decision ⟨*submit* a question to the court⟩ ⟨*submit* a bid on a contract⟩ ⟨*submit* a report⟩; *also* : to deliver formally ⟨*submitted* my resignation⟩
3 : to put forward as an opinion or contention ⟨we *submit* that the charge is not proved⟩
intransitive verb
1 a : to yield oneself to the authority or will of another : SURRENDER **b** : to permit oneself to be subjected to something ⟨had to *submit* to surgery⟩
2 : to defer to or consent to abide by the opinion or authority of another
synonym see YIELD
sub·mit·tal \-'mi-t°l\ *noun*
sub·mi·to·chon·dri·al \,səb-,mī-tə-'kän-drē-əl\ *adjective* (1963)
: relating to, composed of, or being parts and especially fragments of mitochondria ⟨*submitochondrial* membranes⟩ ⟨*submitochondrial* particles⟩
sub·mu·co·sa \,səb-myü-'kō-zə\ *noun* [New Latin] (1885)
: a supporting layer of loose connective tissue directly under a mucous membrane
— **sub·mu·co·sal** \-zəl\ *adjective*
sub·mul·ti·ple \-'məl-tə-pəl\ *noun* (1758)
: an exact divisor of a number ⟨8 is a *submultiple* of 72⟩
sub·mu·ni·tion \(,)səb-myü-'ni-shən\ *noun* (1975)
: any of a group of smaller weapons carried as a warhead by a missile or projectile and expelled as the carrier approaches its target
sub·nor·mal \-'nȯr-məl\ *adjective* [International Scientific Vocabulary] (circa 1890)
1 : lower or smaller than normal
2 : having less of something and especially of intelligence than is normal
— **sub·nor·mal·i·ty** \,səb-nȯr-'ma-lə-tē\ *noun*
— **sub·nor·mal·ly** \,səb-'nȯr-mə-lē\ *adverb*
sub·nu·cle·ar \,səb-'nü-klē-ər, -'nyü-, -;kyə-lər\ *adjective* (1937)
: of, relating to, or being a particle smaller than the atomic nucleus
sub·oce·an·ic \,səb-,ō-shē-'a-nik\ *adjective* (1858)
: situated, taking place, or formed beneath the ocean or its bottom ⟨*suboceanic* oil resources⟩
sub·or·bit·al \,səb-'ȯr-bə-t°l\ *adjective* (circa 1827)
1 : situated beneath the eye or the orbit of the eye
2 : being or involving less than one orbit (as of the earth or moon) ⟨a spacecraft's *suborbital* flight⟩; *also* : intended for suborbital flight ⟨a *suborbital* rocket⟩
sub·or·der \'səb-,ȯr-dər\ *noun* (1826)
: a subdivision of an order ⟨a soil *suborder*⟩; *especially* : a taxonomic category ranking between an order and a family
¹sub·or·di·nate \sə-'bȯr-d°n-ət, -'bȯrd-nət\ *adjective* [Middle English *subordinat*, from Medieval Latin *subordinatus*, past participle of *subordinare* to subordinate, from *sub-* + *ordinare* to order — more at ORDAIN] (15th century)
1 : placed in or occupying a lower class, rank, or position : INFERIOR
2 : submissive to or controlled by authority
3 a : of, relating to, or constituting a clause that functions as a noun, adjective, or adverb **b** : SUBORDINATING
— **sub·or·di·nate·ly** *adverb*
— **sub·or·di·nate·ness** *noun*

²subordinate *noun* (1640)
: one that is subordinate
³sub·or·di·nate \sə-'bȯr-d°n-,āt\ *transitive verb* **-nat·ed; -nat·ing** [Medieval Latin *subordinatus*] (1597)
1 : to make subject or subservient
2 : to treat as of less value or importance ⟨stylist . . . whose crystalline prose *subordinates* content to form —Susan Heath⟩
— **sub·or·di·na·tion** \-,bȯr-d°n-'ā-shən\ *noun*
— **sub·or·di·na·tive** \-'bȯr-d°n-,ā-tiv\ *adjective*
subordinating *adjective* (1857)
: introducing and linking a subordinate clause to a main clause ⟨*subordinating* conjunction⟩
sub·or·di·na·tor \-,ā-tər\ *noun* (1959)
: one that subordinates; *especially* : a subordinating conjunction
sub·orn \sə-'bȯrn\ *transitive verb* [Middle French *suborner*, from Latin *subornare*, from *sub-* secretly + *ornare* to furnish, equip — more at ORNATE] (1534)
1 : to induce secretly to do an unlawful thing
2 : to induce to commit perjury; *also* : to obtain (perjured testimony) from a witness
— **sub·or·na·tion** \,sə-,bȯr-'nā-shən\ *noun*
— **sub·orn·er** *noun*
sub·phy·lum \'səb-,fī-ləm\ *noun* [New Latin] (circa 1934)
: a category in biological classification ranking below a phylum and above a class
sub·plot \'səb-,plät\ *noun* (1916)
1 : a subordinate plot in fiction or drama
2 : a subdivision of an experimental plot of land
¹sub·poe·na \sə-'pē-nə, ÷-nē\ *noun* [Middle English *suppena*, from Latin *sub poena* under penalty] (15th century)
: a writ commanding a person designated in it to appear in court under a penalty for failure
²subpoena *transitive verb* **-naed; -na·ing** (1640)
: to serve or summon with a writ of subpoena
subpoena ad tes·ti·fi·can·dum \-,ad-,tes-tə-fi-'kan-dəm\ *noun* [New Latin, under penalty to give testimony] (circa 1769)
: a writ commanding a person to appear in court to testify as a witness
subpoena du·ces te·cum \-,dü-səs-'tē-kəm\ *noun* [New Latin, under penalty you shall bring with you] (1768)
: a writ commanding a person to produce in court certain designated documents or evidence
sub·po·lar \,səb-'pō-lər\ *adjective* (1826)
: SUBANTARCTIC, SUBARCTIC
sub·pop·u·la·tion \'səb-,pä-pyə-'lā-shən\ *noun* (1944)
: an identifiable fraction or subdivision of a population
sub·po·tent \,səb-'pō-t°nt\ *adjective* (circa 1909)
: less potent than normal ⟨*subpotent* drugs⟩
— **sub·po·ten·cy** \-'pō-t°n(t)-sē\ *noun*
sub·prin·ci·pal \-'prin(t)-s(ə-)pəl, -sə-bəl\ *noun* (1597)
1 : an assistant principal (as of a school)
2 : a secondary or bracing rafter
sub·prob·lem \'səb-,prä-bləm\ *noun* (1906)
: a problem that is contingent on or forms a part of another more inclusive problem
sub·pro·fes·sion·al \,səb-prə-'fesh-nəl, -'fe-shə-n°l\ *adjective* (1941)
: functioning or qualified to function below the professional level but distinctly above the clerical or labor level and usually under the supervision of a professionally trained person
— **subprofessional** *noun*

sub·pro·gram \'səb-ˌprō-ˌgram, -grəm\ *noun* (1947)
: a semi-independent portion of a program (as for a computer)

sub·re·gion \'səb-ˌrē-jən\ *noun* [International Scientific Vocabulary] (1864)
1 : a subdivision of a region
2 : one of the primary divisions of a biogeographic region
— **sub·re·gion·al** \-ˌrēj-nəl, -ˌrē-jə-nᵊl\ *adjective*

sub·rep·tion \(ˌ)səb-'rep-shən\ *noun* [Late Latin *subreption-, subreptio*, from Latin, act of stealing, from *subripere, surripere* to take away secretly — more at SURREPTITIOUS] (1600)
: a deliberate misrepresentation; *also* : an inference drawn from it
— **sub·rep·ti·tious** \ˌsəb-ˌrep-'ti-shəs\ *adjective*
— **sub·rep·ti·tious·ly** *adverb*

sub·ring \'səb-ˌriŋ\ *noun* (1937)
: a subset of a mathematical ring which is itself a ring

sub·ro·gate \'sə-brō-ˌgāt\ *transitive verb* **-gat·ed; -gat·ing** [Middle English, from Latin *subrogatus*, past participle of *subrogare, surrogare* — more at SURROGATE] (15th century)
: to put in the place of another; *especially* : to substitute (as a second creditor) for another with regard to a legal right or claim

sub·ro·ga·tion \ˌsə-brō-'gā-shən\ *noun* (15th century)
: the act of subrogating; *specifically* : the assumption by a third party (as a second creditor or an insurance company) of another's legal right to collect a debt or damages

sub·rosa *adjective* (1923)
: SECRETIVE, PRIVATE

sub rosa \ˌsəb-'rō-zə\ *adverb* [New Latin, literally, under the rose; from the ancient association of roses with secrecy] (1654)
: in confidence : SECRETLY

sub·rou·tine \'səb-(ˌ)rü-ˌtēn\ *noun* [International Scientific Vocabulary] (circa 1946)
: a subordinate routine; *specifically* : a sequence of computer instructions for performing a specified task that can be used repeatedly

sub-Sa·ha·ran \ˌsəb-sə-'har-ən, -'her-, -'här-\ *adjective* (1955)
: of, relating to, or being the part of Africa south of the Sahara

¹**sub·sam·ple** \'səb-ˌsam-pəl, ˌsəb-'sam-\ *transitive verb* (circa 1899)
: to draw samples from (a previously selected group or population) : sample a sample of

²**subsample** *noun* (circa 1899)
: a sample or specimen obtained by subsampling

sub·sat·el·lite \ˌsəb-'sa-tᵊl-ˌīt\ *noun* (1956)
: an object carried into orbit in and subsequently released from a satellite or spacecraft

sub·scribe \səb-'skrīb\ *verb* **sub·scribed; sub·scrib·ing** [Middle English, from Latin *subscribere*, literally, to write beneath, from *sub- + scribere* to write — more at SCRIBE] (15th century)
transitive verb
1 : to write (one's name) underneath : SIGN
2 a : to sign (as a document) with one's own hand in token of consent or obligation **b** : to attest by signing **c** : to pledge (a gift or contribution) by writing one's name with the amount
3 : to assent to : SUPPORT
intransitive verb
1 : to sign one's name to a document
2 a : to give consent or approval to something written by signing ⟨unwilling to *subscribe* to the agreement⟩ **b** : to set one's name to a paper in token of promise to give something (as a sum of money); *also* : to give something in accordance with such a promise **c** : to enter one's name for a publication or service; *also*

: to receive a periodical or service regularly on order **d** : to agree to purchase and pay for securities especially of a new offering ⟨*subscribed* for 1000 shares⟩
3 : to feel favorably disposed ⟨I *subscribe* to your sentiments⟩
synonym see ASSENT
— **sub·scrib·er** *noun*

sub·script \'səb-ˌskript\ *noun* [Latin *subscriptus*, past participle of *subscribere*] (1895)
: a distinguishing symbol (as a letter or numeral) written immediately below or below and to the right or left of another character
— **subscript** *adjective*

sub·scrip·tion \səb-'skrip-shən\ *noun* [Middle English *subscripcioun* signature, from Latin *subscription-, subscriptio*, from *subscribere*] (15th century)
1 a : the act of signing one's name (as in attesting or witnessing a document) **b** : the acceptance (as of ecclesiastical articles of faith) attested by the signing of one's name
2 : something that is subscribed: as **a** : an autograph signature; *also* : a paper to which a signature is attached **b** : a sum subscribed or pledged
3 : an arrangement for providing, receiving, or making use of something of a continuing or periodic nature on a prepayment plan: as **a** : a purchase by prepayment for a certain number of issues (as of a periodical) **b** : application to purchase securities of a new issue **c** : a method of offering or presenting a series of public performances **d** *British* : membership dues

subscription TV *noun* (1953)
: pay-TV that broadcasts programs directly over the air to customers provided with a special receiver — called also subscription television; compare PAY-CABLE, PAY-TV

sub·sec·tion \'səb-ˌsek-shən\ *noun* (1621)
1 : a subdivision or a subordinate division of a section
2 : a subordinate part or branch

¹**sub·se·quence** \'səb-sə-ˌkwen(t)s, -si-kwən(t)s\ *noun* (circa 1500)
: the quality or state of being subsequent; *also* : a subsequent event

²**sub·se·quence** \'səb-ˌsē-kwən(t)s, -ˌkwen(t)s\ *noun* (1908)
: a mathematical sequence that is part of another sequence

sub·se·quent \'səb-si-kwənt, -sə-ˌkwent\ *adjective* [Middle English, from Latin *subsequent-, subsequens*, present participle of *subsequi* to follow close, from *sub- near + sequi* to follow — more at SUB-, SUE] (15th century)
: following in time, order, or place
— **subsequent** *noun*
— **sub·se·quent·ly** \-ˌkwent-lē, -kwənt-\ *adverb*

subsequent to *preposition* (1647)
: at a time later or more recent than : SINCE

sub·serve \(ˌ)səb-'sərv\ *transitive verb* [Latin *subservire* to serve, be subservient, from *sub- + servire* to serve] (1661)
1 : to promote the welfare or purposes of
2 : to serve as an instrument or means in carrying out

sub·ser·vi·ence \səb-'sər-vē-ən(t)s\ *noun* (circa 1676)
1 : a subservient or subordinate place or function
2 : obsequious servility

sub·ser·vi·en·cy \-ən(t)-sē\ *noun* (1651)
: SUBSERVIENCE

sub·ser·vi·ent \-ənt\ *adjective* [Latin *subservient-, subserviens*, present participle of *subservire*] (1632)
1 : serving to promote some end
2 : useful in an inferior capacity : SUBORDINATE
3 : obsequiously submissive : TRUCKLING ☆
— **sub·ser·vi·ent·ly** *adverb*

sub·set \'səb-ˌset\ *noun* (1902)

: a set each of whose elements is an element of an inclusive set

sub·shrub \-ˌshrəb, *especially Southern* -ˌsrəb\ *noun* (1851)
: a perennial plant having woody stems except for the terminal part of the new growth which is killed back annually; *also* : a low shrub

sub·side \səb-'sīd\ *intransitive verb* **sub·sid·ed; sub·sid·ing** [Latin *subsidere*, from *sub- + sidere* to sit down, sink; akin to Latin *sedēre* to sit — more at SIT] (1607)
1 : to sink or fall to the bottom : SETTLE
2 : to tend downward : DESCEND; *especially* : to flatten out so as to form a depression
3 : to let oneself settle down : SINK ⟨*subsided* into a chair⟩
4 : to become quiet or less ⟨as the fever *subsides*⟩ ⟨my anger *subsided*⟩
synonym see ABATE
— **sub·si·dence** \səb-'sī-dᵊn(t)s, 'səb-sə-dən(t)s\ *noun*

sub·sid·i·ar·i·ty \ˌsəb-ˌsi-də-'er-ə-tē, səb-ˌsi-\ *noun* (1936)
1 : the quality or state of being subsidiary
2 : a principle in social organization: functions which subordinate or local organizations perform effectively belong more properly to them than to a dominant central organization

¹**sub·sid·i·ary** \səb-'si-dē-ˌer-ē, -'si-də-rē\ *adjective* [Latin *subsidiarius*, from *subsidium* reserve troops] (1543)
1 a : furnishing aid or support : AUXILIARY ⟨*subsidiary* details⟩ **b** : of secondary importance ⟨a *subsidiary* stream⟩
2 : of, relating to, or constituting a subsidy ⟨a *subsidiary* payment to an ally⟩
— **sub·sid·i·ari·ly** \-ˌsi-dē-'er-ə-lē\ *adverb*

²**subsidiary** *noun, plural* **-ar·ies** (1603)
: one that is subsidiary; *especially* : a company wholly controlled by another

sub·si·dise *British variant of* SUBSIDIZE

sub·si·dize \'səb-sə-ˌdīz, -zə-\ *transitive verb* **-dized; -diz·ing** (1795)
: to furnish with a subsidy: as **a** : to purchase the assistance of by payment of a subsidy **b** : to aid or promote (as a private enterprise) with public money ⟨*subsidize* soybean farmers⟩ ⟨*subsidize* public transportation⟩
— **sub·si·di·za·tion** \ˌsəb-sə-də-'zā-shən, -zə-\ *noun*
— **sub·si·diz·er** *noun*

sub·si·dy \'səb-sə-dē, -zə-\ *noun, plural* **-dies** [Middle English, from Latin *subsidium* reserve troops, support, assistance, from *sub- near + sedēre* to sit — more at SUB-, SIT] (14th century)
: a grant or gift of money: as **a** : a sum of money formerly granted by the British Parliament to the crown and raised by special taxation **b** : money granted by one state to another **c** : a grant by a government to a private person or company to assist an enterprise deemed advantageous to the public

sub·sist \səb-'sist\ *verb* [Late Latin *subsistere* to exist, from Latin, to come to a halt, remain, from *sub- + sistere* to come to a stand; akin to Latin *stare* to stand — more at STAND] (1549)

☆ **SYNONYMS**
Subservient, servile, slavish, obsequious mean showing or characterized by extreme compliance or abject obedience. SUBSERVIENT implies the cringing manner of one very conscious of a subordinate position ⟨domestic help was expected to be properly *subservient*⟩. SERVILE suggests the mean or fawning behavior of a slave ⟨a political boss and his entourage of *servile* hangers-on⟩. SLAVISH suggests abject or debased servility ⟨the *slavish* status of migrant farm workers⟩. OBSEQUIOUS implies fawning or sycophantic compliance and exaggerated deference of manner ⟨waiters who are *obsequious* in the presence of celebrities⟩.

intransitive verb
1 a : to have existence **:** BE **b :** PERSIST, CONTINUE
2 : to have or acquire the necessities of life (as food and clothing); *especially* **:** to nourish oneself ⟨*subsisting* on roots, berries and grubs⟩
3 a : to hold true **b :** to be logically conceivable as the subject of true statements
transitive verb
: to support with provisions

sub·sis·tence \səb-'sis-tən(t)s\ *noun* [Middle English, from Late Latin *subsistentia,* from *subsistent-, subsistens,* present participle of *subsistere*] (15th century)
1 a (1) **:** real being **:** EXISTENCE (2) **:** the condition of remaining in existence **:** CONTINUATION, PERSISTENCE **b :** an essential characteristic quality of something that exists **c :** the character possessed by whatever is logically conceivable
2 : means of subsisting: as **a :** the minimum (as of food and shelter) necessary to support life **b :** a source or means of obtaining the necessities of life
— **sub·sis·tent** \-tənt\ *adjective*

subsistence farming *noun* (1939)
1 : farming or a system of farming that provides all or almost all the goods required by the farm family usually without any significant surplus for sale
2 : farming or a system of farming that produces a minimum and often inadequate return to the farmer — called also *subsistence agriculture*
— **subsistence farmer** *noun*

sub·so·cial \ˌsəb-'sō-shəl\ *adjective* (circa 1909)
: incompletely social; *especially* **:** tending to associate gregariously but lacking fixed or complex social organization ⟨*subsocial* insects⟩

¹sub·soil \'səb-ˌsȯil\ *noun* (1799)
: the stratum of weathered material that underlies the surface soil

²subsoil *transitive verb* (1840)
: to turn, break, or stir the subsoil of
— **sub·soil·er** *noun*

sub·so·lar point \ˌsəb-'sō-lər-\ *noun* (circa 1908)
: the point on the surface of the earth or a planet at which the sun is at the zenith

sub·son·ic \ˌsəb-'sä-nik\ *adjective* [International Scientific Vocabulary] (1937)
1 : of, relating to, or being a speed less than that of sound in air
2 : moving, capable of moving, or utilizing air currents moving at a subsonic speed
3 : INFRASONIC 1
— **sub·son·i·cal·ly** \-ni-k(ə-)lē\ *adverb*

sub·space \'səb-ˌspās\ *noun* (1927)
: a subset of a space; *especially* **:** one that has the essential properties (as those of a vector space or topological space) of the including space

sub spe·cie ae·ter·ni·ta·tis \ˌsu̇b-'spe-kē-ˌā-ˌī-ˌter-nə-'tä-təs\ *adverb* [New Latin, literally, under the aspect of eternity] (1895)
: in its essential or universal form or nature

sub·spe·cies \'səb-ˌspē-shēz, -sēz\ *noun* [New Latin] (1699)
: a subdivision of a species: as **a :** a category in biological classification that ranks immediately below a species and designates a population of a particular geographical region genetically distinguishable from other such populations of the same species and capable of interbreeding successfully with them where its range overlaps theirs **b :** a named subdivision (as a race or variety) of a taxonomic species **c :** SUBGROUP 1 ⟨*subspecies* of economy fares —Michael DiPaola⟩
— **sub·spe·cif·ic** \ˌsəb-spi-'si-fik\ *adjective*

sub·stage \'səb-ˌstāj\ *noun* (1888)
: an attachment to a microscope by means of which accessories (as mirrors, diaphragms, or condensers) are held in place beneath the stage of the instrument

sub·stance \'səb-stən(t)s\ *noun* [Middle English, from Middle French, from Latin *substantia,* from *substant-, substans,* present participle of *substare* to stand under, from *sub-* + *stare* to stand — more at STAND] (14th century)
1 a : essential nature **:** ESSENCE **b :** a fundamental or characteristic part or quality **c** *Christian Science* **:** GOD 1b
2 a : ultimate reality that underlies all outward manifestations and change **b :** practical importance **:** MEANING, USEFULNESS ⟨the . . . bill—which will be without *substance* in the sense that it will authorize nothing more than a set of ideas —Richard Reeves⟩
3 a : physical material from which something is made or which has discrete existence **b :** matter of particular or definite chemical constitution **c :** something (as drugs or alcoholic beverages) deemed harmful and usually subject to legal restriction ⟨possession of a controlled *substance*⟩ ⟨has a *substance* problem⟩
4 : material possessions **:** PROPERTY ⟨a family of *substance*⟩
— **sub·stance·less** \-ləs\ *adjective*
— **in substance :** in respect to essentials **:** FUNDAMENTALLY

substance abuse *noun* (1982)
: excessive use of a drug (as alcohol, narcotics, or cocaine) **:** use of a drug without medical justification
— **substance abuser** *noun*

substance P *noun* (1934)
: a neuropeptide that consists of 11 amino-acid residues, that is widely distributed in the brain, spinal cord, and peripheral nervous system, and that acts across nerve synapses to produce prolonged postsynaptic excitation

sub·stan·dard \ˌsəb-'stan-dərd\ *adjective* (1897)
: deviating from or falling short of a standard or norm: as **a :** of a quality lower than that prescribed by law **b :** conforming to a pattern of linguistic usage existing within a speech community but not that of the prestige group in that community **c :** constituting a greater than normal risk to an insurer

sub·stan·tial \səb-'stan(t)-shəl\ *adjective* (14th century)
1 a : consisting of or relating to substance **b :** not imaginary or illusory **:** REAL, TRUE **c :** IMPORTANT, ESSENTIAL
2 : ample to satisfy and nourish **:** FULL ⟨a *substantial* meal⟩
3 a : possessed of means **:** WELL-TO-DO **b :** considerable in quantity **:** significantly great ⟨earned a *substantial* wage⟩
4 : firmly constructed **:** STURDY
5 : being largely but not wholly that which is specified ⟨a *substantial* lie⟩
— **substantial** *noun*
— **sub·stan·ti·al·i·ty** \-ˌstan(t)-shē-'a-lə-tē\ *noun*
— **sub·stan·tial·ly** \-'stan(t)-sh(ə-)lē\ *adverb*
— **sub·stan·tial·ness** \-'stan(t)-shəl-nəs\ *noun*

sub·stan·tia ni·gra \səb-ˌstan(t)-shē-ə-'nī-grə, -'ni-\ *noun, plural* **sub·stan·ti·ae ni·grae** \-chē-ˌē-'nī-(ˌ)grē, -'ni-\ [New Latin, literally, black substance] (1882)
: a layer of deeply pigmented gray matter situated in the midbrain and containing the cell bodies of a tract of dopamine-producing nerve cells whose secretion tends to be deficient in Parkinson's disease

sub·stan·ti·ate \səb-'stan(t)-shē-ˌāt\ *transitive verb* **-at·ed; -at·ing** (1657)
1 : to give substance or form to **:** EMBODY
2 : to establish by proof or competent evidence **:** VERIFY ⟨*substantiate* a charge⟩
synonym see CONFIRM
— **sub·stan·ti·a·tion** \-ˌstan(t)-shē-'ā-shən\ *noun*

— sub·stan·ti·a·tive \-'stan(t)-shē-ˌā-tiv\ *adjective*

sub·stan·ti·val \ˌsəb-stən-'tī-vəl\ *adjective* (circa 1832)
: of, relating to, or serving as a substantive
— **sub·stan·ti·val·ly** \-və-lē\ *adverb*

¹sub·stan·tive \'səb-stən-tiv\ *noun* [Middle English *substantif,* from Middle French, from *substantif,* adjective, having or expressing substance, from Late Latin *substantivus*] (14th century)
: NOUN; *broadly* **:** a word or word group functioning syntactically as a noun
— **sub·stan·tiv·ize** \-ti-ˌvīz\ *transitive verb*

²sub·stan·tive \'səb-stən-tiv; 2c & 3 *also* səb-'stan-tiv\ *adjective* [Middle English, from Late Latin *substantivus* having substance, from *substantia*] (14th century)
1 : being a totally independent entity
2 a : real rather than apparent **:** FIRM; *also* **:** PERMANENT, ENDURING **b :** belonging to the substance of a thing **:** ESSENTIAL **c :** expressing existence ⟨the *substantive* verb is the verb *to be*⟩ **d :** requiring or involving no mordant ⟨a *substantive* dyeing process⟩
3 a : having the nature or function of a grammatical substantive ⟨a *substantive* phrase⟩ **b :** relating to or having the character of a noun or pronominal term in logic
4 : considerable in amount or numbers **:** SUBSTANTIAL
5 : creating and defining rights and duties ⟨*substantive* law⟩ — compare PROCEDURAL
6 : having substance **:** involving matters of major or practical importance to all concerned ⟨*substantive* discussions among world leaders⟩
— **sub·stan·tive·ly** *adverb*
— **sub·stan·tive·ness** *noun*

substantive due process *noun* (1954)
: DUE PROCESS 2

substantive right *noun* (1939)
: a right (as of life, liberty, property, or reputation) held to exist for its own sake and to constitute part of the normal legal order of society

sub·sta·tion \'səb-ˌstā-shən\ *noun* (1881)
: a subordinate or subsidiary station: as **a :** a branch post office **b :** a subsidiary station in which electric current is transformed **c :** a police station serving a particular area

sub·stit·u·ent \səb-'sti-chə-wənt, -'stich-wənt\ *noun* [Latin *substituent-, substituens,* present participle of *substituere*] (circa 1896)
: an atom or group that replaces another atom or group in a molecule
— **substituent** *adjective*

sub·sti·tut·able \'səb-stə-ˌtü-tə-bəl, -ˌtyü-\ *adjective* (1805)
: capable of being substituted
— **sub·sti·tut·abil·i·ty** \ˌsəb-stə-ˌtü-tə-'bi-lə-tē, -ˌtyü-\ *noun*

¹sub·sti·tute \'səb-stə-ˌtüt, -ˌtyüt\ *noun* [Middle English, from Latin *substitutus,* past participle of *substituere* to put in place of, from *sub-* + *statuere* to set up, place — more at STATUTE] (15th century)
: a person or thing that takes the place or function of another
— **substitute** *adjective*

²substitute *verb* **-tut·ed; -tut·ing** (1588)
transitive verb
1 a : to put or use in the place of another **b :** to introduce (an atom or group) as a substituent; *also* **:** to alter (as a compound) by introduction of a substituent ⟨a *substituted* benzene ring⟩
2 : to take the place of **:** REPLACE
intransitive verb
: to serve as a substitute

sub·sti·tu·tion \ˌsəb-stə-'tü-shən, -'tyü-\ *noun*

\ə\ abut \ᵊ\ kitten \ər\ further \a\ ash \ā\ ace
\ä\ mop, mar \au̇\ out \ch\ chin \e\ bet \ē\ easy
\g\ go \i\ hit \ī\ ice \j\ job \ŋ\ sing \ō\ go
\ȯ\ law \ȯi\ boy \th\ thin \t͟h\ the \ü\ loot \u̇\ foot
\y\ yet \zh\ vision *see also* Guide to Pronunciation

[Middle English *substitucion*, from Middle French *substitution*, from Late Latin *substitution-*, *substitutio*, from *substituere*] (14th century)

1 a : the act, process, or result of substituting one thing for another **b :** replacement of one mathematical entity by another of equal value **2 :** one that is substituted for another
— **sub·sti·tu·tion·al** \-shnəl, -shə-n°l\ *adjective*
— **sub·sti·tu·tion·al·ly** *adverb*
— **sub·sti·tu·tion·ary** \-shə-ˌner-ē\ *adjective*

substitution cipher *noun* (1936)
: a cipher in which the letters of the plaintext are systematically replaced by substitute letters — compare TRANSPOSITION CIPHER

sub·sti·tu·tive \'səb-stə-ˌtü-tiv, -ˌtyü-\ *adjective* (1668)
: serving or suitable as a substitute
— **sub·sti·tu·tive·ly** *adverb*

sub·strate \'səb-ˌstrāt\ *noun* [Medieval Latin *substratum*] (1807)
1 : SUBSTRATUM
2 : the base on which an organism lives ⟨the soil is the *substrate* of most seed plants⟩
3 : a substance acted upon (as by an enzyme)

sub·stra·tum \'səb-ˌstrā-təm, -ˌstra-, ˌsəb-'\ *noun, plural* **-stra·ta** \-tə\ [Medieval Latin, from Latin, neuter of *substratus*, past participle of *substernere* to spread under, from *sub-* + *sternere* to spread — more at STREW] (1631)
: an underlying support **:** FOUNDATION: as **a :** a substance that is a permanent subject of qualities or phenomena **b :** the material of which something is made and from which it derives its special qualities **c :** a layer beneath the surface soil; *specifically* **:** SUBSOIL **d :** SUBSTRATE 2

sub·struc·ture \'səb-ˌstrək-chər\ *noun* (1726)
: an underlying or supporting part of a structure
— **sub·struc·tur·al** \-chə-rəl, -shrəl\ *adjective*

sub·sume \səb-'süm\ *transitive verb* **sub·sumed; sub·sum·ing** [New Latin *subsumere*, from Latin *sub-* + *sumere* to take up — more at CONSUME] (1825)
: to include or place within something larger or more comprehensive **:** encompass as a subordinate or component element ⟨red, green, and yellow are *subsumed* under the term "color"⟩
— **sub·sum·able** \-'sü-mə-bəl\ *adjective*

sub·sump·tion \səb-'səm(p)-shən\ *noun* [New Latin *subsumption-*, *subsumptio*, from *subsumere*] (1651)
: the act or process of subsuming

¹sub·sur·face \'səb-ˌsər-fəs\ *noun* (1778)
: earth material (as rock) near but not exposed at the surface of the ground

²sub·sur·face \ˌsəb-'sər-fəs\ *adjective* (1875)
: of, relating to, or being something located beneath a surface and especially underground

sub·teen \'səb-ˌtēn\ *noun* (1951)
: a preadolescent child

sub·tem·per·ate \ˌsəb-'tem-p(ə-)rət\ *adjective* (1852)
: of or occurring in the colder parts of the temperate zones

sub·ten·an·cy \-'te-nən(t)-sē\ *noun* (circa 1861)
: the state of being a subtenant

sub·ten·ant \-'te-nənt\ *noun* (15th century)
: one who rents from a tenant

sub·tend \səb-'tend\ *transitive verb* [Latin *subtendere* to stretch beneath, from *sub-* + *tendere* to stretch — more at THIN] (1570)
1 a : to be opposite to and extend from one side to the other of ⟨a hypotenuse *subtends* a right angle⟩ **b :** to fix the angular extent of with respect to a fixed point or object taken as the vertex ⟨the angle *subtended* at the eye by an object of given width and a fixed distance away⟩ ⟨a central angle *subtended* by an arc⟩ **c**

: to determine the measure of by marking off the endpoints of ⟨a chord *subtends* an arc⟩
2 a : to underlie so as to include **b :** to occupy an adjacent and usually lower position to and often so as to embrace or enclose ⟨a bract that *subtends* a flower⟩

sub·ter·fuge \'səb-tər-ˌfyüj\ *noun* [Late Latin *subterfugium*, from Latin *subterfugere* to escape, evade, from *subter-* secretly (from *subter* underneath; akin to Latin *sub* under) + *fugere* to flee — more at UP, FUGITIVE] (1573)
1 : deception by artifice or stratagem in order to conceal, escape, or evade
2 : a deceptive device or stratagem
synonym see DECEPTION

sub·ter·mi·nal \ˌsəb-'tərm-nəl, -'tər-mə-n°l\ *adjective* (1828)
: situated or occurring near but not precisely at an end ⟨a *subterminal* band of color on the tail feathers⟩

sub·ter·ra·nean \ˌsəb-tə-'rā-nē-ən, -nyən\ *also* **sub·ter·ra·neous** \-nē-əs, -nyəs\ *adjective* [Latin *subterraneus*, from *sub-* + *terra* earth — more at THIRST] (1603)
1 : being, lying, or operating under the surface of the earth
2 : existing or working in secret **:** HIDDEN
— **sub·ter·ra·nean·ly** *also* **sub·ter·ra·neous·ly** *adverb*

sub·text \'səb-ˌtekst\ *noun* (1950)
: the implicit or metaphorical meaning (as of a literary text)
— **sub·tex·tu·al** \ˌsəb-'teks-chə-wəl, -chəl\ *adjective*

sub·thresh·old \ˌsəb-'thre-ˌshōld, -'thresh-ˌhōld\ *adjective* (1942)
: inadequate to produce a response ⟨*subthreshold* dosage⟩ ⟨a *subthreshold* stimulus⟩

sub·tile \'sə-t°l, ˌsə-t°l\ *adjective* **sub·til·er** \'sət-lər, 'sə-t°l-ər; 'sə-tə-lər\; **sub·til·est** \'sət-ləst, 'sə-t°l-əst; 'sə-tə-ləst\ [Middle English, from Latin *subtilis*] (14th century)
1 : SUBTLE, ELUSIVE ⟨a *subtile* aroma⟩
2 a : CUNNING, CRAFTY **b :** SAGACIOUS, DISCERNING
— **sub·tile·ly** \'sət-lē, 'sə-t°l-(l)ē; 'sə-tə-lē\ *adverb*
— **sub·tile·ness** \'sət-°l-nəs, 'sə-t°l-\ *noun*

sub·til·i·sin \ˌsəb-'ti-lə-sən\ *noun* [New Latin *subtilis*, specific epithet of *Bacillus subtilis*, species to which *Bacillus amyloliquefaciens* was once thought to belong] (1953)
: an extracellular protease produced by a soil bacillus (*Bacillus amyloliquefaciens*)

sub·til·ize \'sə-t°l-ˌīz, ˌsəb-tə-ˌlīz\ *verb* **-ized; -iz·ing** (1592)
intransitive verb
: to act or think subtly
transitive verb
: to make subtle
— **sub·til·i·za·tion** \ˌsə-t°l-ə-'zā-shən, ˌsəb-tə-lə-\ *noun*

sub·til·ty \'sə-t°l-tē, 'səb-t°l-\ *noun, plural* **-ties** (14th century)
: SUBTLETY

¹sub·ti·tle \'səb-ˌtī-t°l\ *noun* (1825)
1 : a secondary or explanatory title
2 : a printed statement or fragment of dialogue appearing on the screen between the scenes of a silent motion picture or appearing as a translation at the bottom of the screen during the scenes of a motion picture or television show in a foreign language

²subtitle *transitive verb* (1891)
: to give a subtitle to

sub·tle \'sə-t°l\ *adjective* **sub·tler** \'sət-lər, 'sə-t°l-ər\; **sub·tlest** \'sət-ləst, 'sə-t°l-əst\ [Middle English *sutil*, *sotil*, from Middle French *soutil*, from Latin *subtilis*, literally, finely textured, from *sub-* + *tela* cloth on a loom; akin to Latin *texere* to weave — more at TECHNICAL] (14th century)
1 a : DELICATE, ELUSIVE ⟨a *subtle* fragrance⟩ **b :** difficult to understand or perceive **:** OBSCURE ⟨*subtle* differences in sound⟩
2 a : PERCEPTIVE, REFINED ⟨a writer's sharp and

subtle moral sense⟩ **b :** having or marked by keen insight and ability to penetrate deeply and thoroughly ⟨a *subtle* scholar⟩
3 a : highly skillful **:** EXPERT ⟨a *subtle* craftsman⟩ **b :** cunningly made or contrived **:** INGENIOUS
4 : ARTFUL, CRAFTY ⟨a *subtle* rogue⟩
5 : operating insidiously ⟨*subtle* poisons⟩
— **sub·tle·ness** \'sə-t°l-nəs\ *noun*
— **sub·tly** \'sət-lē, 'sə-t°l-(l)ē\ *adverb*

sub·tle·ty \'sə-t°l-tē\ *noun, plural* **-ties** [Middle English *sutilte*, from Middle French *sutilté*, from Latin *subtilitat-*, *subtilitas*, from *subtilis*] (14th century)
1 : the quality or state of being subtle
2 : something subtle

sub·ton·ic \ˌsəb-'tä-nik\ *noun* [from its being a half tone below the upper tonic] (circa 1854)
: LEADING TONE

¹sub·to·tal \'səb-ˌtō-t°l\ *noun* (1906)
: the sum of part of a series of figures

²sub·to·tal \ˌsəb-'tō-t°l\ *adjective* (1908)
: somewhat less than complete **:** nearly total ⟨*subtotal* thyroidectomy⟩
— **sub·to·tal·ly** *adverb*

sub·tract \səb-'trakt\ *verb* [Latin *subtractus*, past participle of *subtrahere* to draw from beneath, withdraw, from *sub-* + *trahere* to draw] (1557)
transitive verb
: to take away by or as if by deducting ⟨*subtract* 5 from 9⟩ ⟨*subtract* funds from the project⟩
intransitive verb
: to perform a subtraction
— **sub·tract·er** *noun*

sub·trac·tion \səb-'trak-shən\ *noun* [Middle English *subtraccion*, from Late Latin *subtraction-*, *subtractio*, from Latin *subtrahere*] (15th century)
: an act, operation, or instance of subtracting: as **a :** the withdrawing or withholding of a right to which an individual is entitled **b :** the operation of deducting one number from another

sub·trac·tive \-'trak-tiv\ *adjective* (1690)
1 : tending to subtract
2 : constituting or involving subtraction

sub·tra·hend \'səb-trə-ˌhend\ *noun* [Latin *subtrahendus*, gerundive of *subtrahere*] (1674)
: a number that is to be subtracted from a minuend

sub·trop·i·cal \ˌsəb-'trä-pi-kəl\ *also* **sub·trop·ic** \-'pik\ *adjective* [International Scientific Vocabulary] (1842)
: of, relating to, or being the regions bordering on the tropical zone ⟨*subtropical* environment⟩ ⟨*subtropical* grasses⟩

sub·trop·ics \-piks\ *noun plural* (1886)
: subtropical regions

su·bu·late \'sü-byə-lət, 'sə-, -ˌlāt\ *adjective* [New Latin *subulatus*, from Latin *subula* awl, from *suere* to sew — more at SEW] (circa 1760)
: linear and tapering to a fine point ⟨a *subulate* leaf⟩

sub·um·brel·la \ˌsəb-(ˌ)əm-'bre-lə\ *noun* (1878)
: the concave undersurface of a jellyfish

sub·urb \'sə-ˌbərb\ *noun* [Middle English, from Latin *suburbium*, from *sub-* near + *urbs* city — more at SUB-] (14th century)
1 a : an outlying part of a city or town **b :** a smaller community adjacent to or within commuting distance of a city **c** *plural* **:** the residential area on the outskirts of a city or large town
2 *plural* **:** the near vicinity **:** ENVIRONS
— **sub·ur·ban** \sə-'bər-bən\ *adjective or noun*
— **sub·ur·ban·ite** \-bə-ˌnīt\ *noun*

sub·ur·ban·ise *British variant of* SUBURBANIZE

sub·ur·ban·ize \sə-'bər-bə-ˌnīz\ *transitive verb* **-ized; -iz·ing** (1893)

: to make suburban : give a suburban character to
— **sub·ur·ban·i·za·tion** \-ˌbər-bə-nə-'zā-shən\ *noun*
sub·ur·bia \sə-'bər-bē-ə\ *noun* [New Latin, from English *suburb*] (1895)
1 : the suburbs of a city
2 : people who live in the suburbs
3 : suburban life
sub·ven·tion \səb-'ven(t)-shən\ *noun* [Middle English *subvencion,* from Old French & Late Latin; Old French *subvención,* from Late Latin *subvention-, subventio* assistance, from Latin *subvenire* to come up, come to the rescue, from *sub-* up + *venire* to come — more at SUB-, COME] (15th century)
: the provision of assistance or financial support: as **a** : ENDOWMENT **b** : a subsidy from a government or foundation
— **sub·ven·tion·ary** \-shə-ˌner-ē\ *adjective*
sub·ver·sion \səb-'vər-zhən, -shən\ *noun* [Middle English, from Middle French, from Late Latin *subversion-, subversio,* from Latin *subvertere*] (14th century)
1 : the act of subverting : the state of being subverted; *especially* : a systematic attempt to overthrow or undermine a government or political system by persons working secretly from within
2 *obsolete* : a cause of overthrow or destruction
— **sub·ver·sion·ary** \-zhə-ˌner-ē, -shə-\ *adjective*
— **sub·ver·sive** \-'vər-siv, -ziv\ *adjective or noun*
— **sub·ver·sive·ly** *adverb*
— **sub·ver·sive·ness** *noun*
sub·vert \səb-'vərt\ *transitive verb* [Middle English, from Middle French *subvertir,* from Latin *subvertere,* literally, to turn from beneath, from *sub-* + *vertere* to turn — more at WORTH] (14th century)
1 : to overturn or overthrow from the foundation : RUIN
2 : to pervert or corrupt by an undermining of morals, allegiance, or faith
— **sub·vert·er** *noun*
sub·vi·ral \ˌsəb-'vī-rəl\ *adjective* (1963)
: relating to, being, or caused by a piece or a structural part (as a protein) of a virus ⟨*subviral* infection⟩
sub·vo·cal \-'vō-kəl\ *adjective* (1924)
: characterized by the occurrence in the mind of words in speech order with or without inaudible articulation of the speech organs
— **sub·vo·cal·ly** \-kə-lē\ *adverb*
sub·vo·cal·i·za·tion \ˌsəb-ˌvō-kə-lə-'zā-shən\ *noun* (1947)
: the act or process of inaudibly articulating speech with the speech organs
— **sub·vo·cal·ize** \ˌsəb-'vō-kə-ˌlīz\ *verb*
sub·way \'səb-ˌwā\ *noun* (1825)
: an underground way: as **a** : a passage under a street (as for pedestrians, power cables, or water or gas mains) **b** : a usually electric underground railway **c** : UNDERPASS
— **subway** *intransitive verb*
suc·ce·da·ne·um \ˌsək-sə-'dā-nē-əm\ *noun, plural* **-ne·ums** *or* **-nea** \-nē-ə\ [New Latin, from Latin, neuter of *succedaneus* substituted, from *succedere* to follow after] (1641)
: SUBSTITUTE
— **suc·ce·da·ne·ous** \-nē-əs\ *adjective*
suc·ce·dent \sək-'sē-dᵊnt\ *adjective* [Middle English, from Latin *succedent-, succedens,* present participle of *succedere*] (15th century)
: coming next : SUCCEEDING, SUBSEQUENT
suc·ceed \sək-'sēd\ *verb* [Middle English *succeden,* from Latin *succedere* to go up, follow after, succeed, from *sub-* near + *cedere* to go — more at SUB-] (14th century)
intransitive verb
1 a : to come next after another in office or position or in possession of an estate; *especially* : to inherit sovereignty, rank, or title **b** : to follow after another in order

2 a : to turn out well **b** : to attain a desired object or end
3 *obsolete* : to pass to a person by inheritance
transitive verb
1 : to follow in sequence and especially immediately
2 : to come after as heir or successor
synonym see FOLLOW
— **suc·ceed·er** *noun*
suc·cès de scan·dale \sək-ˌsā-də-skäⁿ-'däl, (ˌ)sük-\ *noun* [French, literally, success of scandal] (1896)
: something (as a work of art) that wins popularity or notoriety because of its scandalous nature; *also* : the reception accorded such a piece
suc·cès d'es·time \-ˌdes-'tēm\ *noun* [French, literally, success of esteem] (1859)
: something (as a work of art) that wins critical respect but not popular success; *also* : the reception accorded such a piece
suc·cès fou \-'fü\ *noun* [French, literally, mad success] (1878)
: an extraordinary success
suc·cess \sək-'ses\ *noun* [Latin *successus,* from *succedere*] (1537)
1 *obsolete* : OUTCOME, RESULT
2 a : degree or measure of succeeding **b** : favorable or desired outcome; *also* : the attainment of wealth, favor, or eminence
3 : one that succeeds
suc·cess·ful \-fəl\ *adjective* (1588)
1 : resulting or terminating in success
2 : gaining or having gained success
— **suc·cess·ful·ly** \-fə-lē\ *adverb*
— **suc·cess·ful·ness** *noun*
suc·ces·sion \sək-'se-shən\ *noun* [Middle English, from Middle French or Latin; Middle French, from Latin *succession-, successio,* from *succedere*] (14th century)
1 a : the order in which or the conditions under which one person after another succeeds to a property, dignity, title, or throne **b** : the right of a person or line to succeed **c** : the line having such a right
2 a : the act or process of following in order : SEQUENCE **b** (1) : the act or process of one person's taking the place of another in the enjoyment of or liability for rights or duties or both (2) : the act or process of a person's becoming beneficially entitled to a property or property interest of a deceased person **c** : the continuance of corporate personality **d** : unidirectional change in the composition of an ecosystem as the available competing organisms and especially the plants respond to and modify the environment
3 a : a number of persons or things that follow each other in sequence **b** : a group, type, or series that succeeds or displaces another
— **suc·ces·sion·al** \-'sesh-nəl, -'se-shə-nᵊl\ *adjective*
— **suc·ces·sion·al·ly** *adverb*
succession duty *noun* (1853)
chiefly British : INHERITANCE TAX
suc·ces·sive \sək-'se-siv\ *adjective* (15th century)
1 : following in order : following each other without interruption
2 : characterized by or produced in succession
— **suc·ces·sive·ly** *adverb*
— **suc·ces·sive·ness** *noun*
suc·ces·sor \sək-'se-sər\ *noun* [Middle English *successour,* from Old French, from Latin *successor,* from *succedere*] (14th century)
: one that follows; *especially* : one who succeeds to a throne, title, estate, or office
suc·ci·nate \'sək-sə-ˌnāt\ *noun* (1790)
: a salt or ester of succinic acid
succinate dehydrogenase *noun* (1962)
: an iron-containing flavoprotein enzyme that catalyzes often reversibly the dehydrogenation of succinic acid to fumaric acid in the Krebs cycle and that is widely distributed especially in animal tissues, bacteria, and yeast — called also *succinic dehydrogenase*

suc·cinct \(ˌ)sək-'si(ŋ)kt, sə-'si(ŋ)kt\ *adjective* [Middle English, from Latin *succinctus,* past participle of *succingere* to gird from below, tuck up, from *sub-* + *cingere* to gird — more at CINCTURE] (15th century)
1 *archaic* **a** : being girded **b** : close-fitting
2 : marked by compact precise expression without wasted words
synonym see CONCISE
— **suc·cinct·ly** \-'si(ŋ)kt-lē, -'siŋ-klē\ *adverb*
— **suc·cinct·ness** \-'siŋt-nəs, -'siŋk-nəs\ *noun*
suc·cin·ic acid \(ˌ)sək-si-nik-\ *noun* [French *succinique,* from Latin *succinum* amber] (circa 1790)
: a crystalline dicarboxylic acid $C_4H_6O_4$ found widely in nature and active in energy-yielding metabolic reactions
suc·ci·nyl \'sək-sə-nᵊl, -ˌnil\ *noun* [International Scientific Vocabulary] (circa 1868)
: either of two groups of succinic acid: **a** : a bivalent group $OCCH_2CH_2CO$ **b** : a univalent group $HOOCCH_2CH_2CO$
suc·ci·nyl·cho·line \ˌsək-sə-nᵊl-'kō-ˌlēn, -ˌnil-\ *noun* (1950)
: a basic compound that is used intravenously chiefly in the form of a hydrated chloride $C_{14}H_{30}Cl_2N_2O_4 \cdot 2H_2O$ as a muscle relaxant in surgery
¹suc·cor \'sə-kər\ *noun* [Middle English *succur,* from earlier *sucurs,* taken as plural, from Old French *sucors,* from Medieval Latin *sucursus,* from Latin *succurrere* to run up, run to help, from *sub-* up + *currere* to run — more at CAR] (13th century)
1 : RELIEF; *also* : AID, HELP
2 : something that furnishes relief
²succor *transitive verb* **suc·cored; suc·cor·ing** \'sə-k(ə-)riŋ\ (13th century)
: to go to the aid of : RELIEVE
— **suc·cor·er** \'sə-kər-ər\ *noun*
suc·co·ry \'sə-k(ə-)rē\ *noun* [alteration of Middle English *cicoree*] (1533)
: CHICORY
suc·co·tash \'sə-kə-ˌtash\ *noun* [Narraganset *msíckquatash* boiled corn kernels] (1751)
: lima or shell beans and green corn cooked together
suc·cour \'sə-kər\ *chiefly British variant of* SUCCOR
suc·cu·ba \'sə-kyə-bə\ *noun, plural* **-bae** \-ˌbē, -ˌbī\ [Latin, paramour] (1559)
: SUCCUBUS
suc·cu·bus \-bəs\ *noun, plural* **-bi** \-ˌbī, -ˌbē\ [Middle English, from Medieval Latin, alteration of Latin *succuba* paramour, from *succubare* to lie under, from *sub-* + *cubare* to lie, recline] (14th century)
: a demon assuming female form to have sexual intercourse with men in their sleep — compare INCUBUS
suc·cu·lence \'sə-kyə-lən(t)s\ *noun* (1787)
1 : the state of being succulent
2 : succulent feed ⟨wild game subsisting on *succulence*⟩
¹suc·cu·lent \-lənt\ *adjective* [Latin *suculentus,* from *sucus* juice, sap; perhaps akin to Latin *sugere* to suck — more at SUCK] (1601)
1 a : full of juice : JUICY **b** : moist and tasty : TOOTHSOME **c** *of a plant* : having fleshy tissues that conserve moisture
2 : rich in interest
— **suc·cu·lent·ly** *adverb*
²succulent *noun* (1825)
: a succulent plant (as a cactus)
suc·cumb \sə-'kəm\ *intransitive verb* [French & Latin; French *succomber,* from Latin *succumbere,* from *sub-* + *-cumbere* to lie down; akin to Latin *cubare* to lie] (1604)

\ə\ abut \ᵊ\ kitten \ər\ further \a\ ash \ā\ ace
\ä\ mop, mar \au̇\ out \ch\ chin \e\ bet \ē\ easy
\g\ go \i\ hit \ī\ ice \j\ job \ŋ\ sing \ō\ go
\ȯ\ law \ȯi\ boy \th\ thin \t̲h̲\ the \ü\ loot \u̇\ foot
\y\ yet \zh\ vision *see also* Guide to Pronunciation

1 : to yield to superior strength or force or overpowering appeal or desire
2 : to be brought to an end (as death) by the effect of destructive or disruptive forces — more at YIELD

¹such \'səch, 'sich\ *adjective* [Middle English, from Old English *swilc*; akin to Old High German *sulīh* such, Old English *swā* so, *gelīk* like — more at SO, LIKE] (before 12th century)
1 a : of a kind or character to be indicated or suggested ⟨a bag *such* as a doctor carries⟩ **b :** having a quality to a degree to be indicated ⟨his excitement was *such* that he shouted⟩
2 : of the character, quality, or extent previously indicated or implied ⟨in the past few years many *such* women have shifted to full-time jobs⟩
3 : of so extreme a degree or quality ⟨never heard *such* a hubbub⟩
4 : of the same class, type, or sort ⟨other *such* clinics throughout the state⟩
5 : not specified

²such *pronoun* (before 12th century)
1 : such a person or thing
2 : someone or something stated, implied, or exemplified ⟨*such* was the result⟩
3 : someone or something similar **:** similar persons or things ⟨tin and glass and *such*⟩ □
— as such : intrinsically considered **:** in itself ⟨*as such* the gift was worth little⟩

³such *adverb* (before 12th century)
1 a : to such a degree **:** SO ⟨*such* tall buildings⟩ ⟨*such* a fine person⟩ **b :** VERY, ESPECIALLY ⟨hasn't been in *such* good spirits lately⟩
2 : in such a way ⟨related *such* that each excludes the other⟩

¹such and such *adjective* (13th century)
: not named or specified

²such and such *pronoun* (15th century)
: something not specified

¹such·like \'səch-ˌlīk\ *adjective* (15th century)
: of like kind **:** SIMILAR

²suchlike *pronoun* (15th century)
: SUCH 3

¹suck \'sək\ *verb* [Middle English *suken*, from Old English *sūcan*; akin to Old High German *sūgan* to suck, Latin *sugere*] (before 12th century)
transitive verb
1 a : to draw (as liquid) into the mouth through a suction force produced by movements of the lips and tongue ⟨*sucked* milk from his mother's breast⟩ **b :** to draw something from or consume by such movements ⟨*suck* an orange⟩ ⟨*suck* a lollipop⟩ **c :** to apply the mouth to in order to or as if to suck out a liquid ⟨*sucked* his burned finger⟩
2 a : to draw by or as if by suction ⟨when a receding wave *sucks* the sand from under your feet —Kenneth Brower⟩ ⟨inadvertently *sucked* into the . . . intrigue —Martin Levin⟩ **b :** to take in and consume by or as if by suction ⟨a vacuum cleaner *sucking* up dirt⟩ ⟨*suck* up a few beers⟩ ⟨opponents say that malls *suck* the life out of downtown areas —Michael Knight⟩
intransitive verb
1 : to draw something in by or as if by exerting a suction force; *especially* **:** to draw milk from a breast or udder with the mouth
2 : to make a sound or motion associated with or caused by suction ⟨his pipe *sucked* wetly⟩ ⟨flanks *sucked* in and out, the long nose resting on his paws —Virginia Woolf⟩
3 : to act in an obsequious manner ⟨when they want votes . . . the candidates come *sucking* around —W. G. Hardy⟩ ⟨*sucked* up to the boss⟩
4 *slang* **:** to be objectionable or inadequate ⟨our lifestyle *sucks* —*Playboy*⟩ ⟨people who went said it *sucked* —H. S. Thompson⟩

²suck *noun* (13th century)
1 : a sucking movement or force
2 : the act of sucking

¹suck·er \'sə-kər\ *noun* (14th century)
1 a : one that sucks especially a breast or udder **:** SUCKLING **b :** a device for creating or reg-

ulating suction ⟨as a piston or valve in a pump⟩ **c :** a pipe or tube through which something is drawn by suction **d** (1) **:** an organ in various animals for adhering or holding (2) **:** a mouth (as of a leech) adapted for sucking or adhering
2 : a shoot from the roots or lower part of the stem of a plant
3 : any of numerous chiefly North American freshwater bony fishes (family Catostomidae) closely related to the carps but distinguished from them especially by the structure of the mouth which usually has thick soft lips
4 : LOLLIPOP 1
5 a : a person easily cheated or deceived **b :** a person irresistibly attracted by something specified ⟨a *sucker* for ghost stories⟩ **c** — used as generalized term of reference ⟨see if you can get that *sucker* working again⟩

²sucker *verb* **suck·ered; suck·er·ing** \'sə-k(ə-)riŋ\ (circa 1661)
transitive verb
1 : to remove suckers from ⟨*sucker* tobacco⟩
2 : HOODWINK
intransitive verb
: to send out suckers

sucker punch *transitive verb* (1964)
: to punch (a person) suddenly without warning and often without apparent provocation
— sucker punch *noun*

suck in *transitive verb* (1840)
1 : DUPE, HOODWINK
2 : to contract, flatten, and tighten (the abdomen) especially by inhaling deeply

suck·ing *adjective* (before 12th century)
: not yet weaned; *broadly* **:** very young

sucking louse *noun* (circa 1907)
: any of an order (Anoplura) of wingless insects comprising the true lice with mouthparts adapted to sucking body fluids

suck·le \'sə-kəl\ *verb* **suck·led; suck·ling** \-k(ə-)liŋ\ [Middle English *suklen*, probably back-formation from *suklyng*] (14th century)
transitive verb
1 a : to give milk to from the breast or udder ⟨a mother *suckling* her child⟩ **b :** to nurture as if by giving milk from the breast ⟨was *suckled* on pulp magazines⟩
2 : to draw milk from the breast or udder of ⟨lambs *suckling* the ewes⟩
intransitive verb
: to draw milk from the breast or udder

suck·ling \'sə-kliŋ\ *noun* [Middle English *suklyng*, from *suken* to suck] (13th century)
: a young unweaned animal

su·crase \'sü-ˌkrās, -ˌkrāz\ *noun* [International Scientific Vocabulary, from French *sucre* sugar, from Middle French — more at SUGAR] (circa 1900)
: INVERTASE

su·cre \'sü-(ˌ)krā\ *noun* [Spanish, from Antonio José de *Sucre*] (1886)
— see MONEY table

su·crose \'sü-ˌkrōs, -ˌkrōz\ *noun* [International Scientific Vocabulary, from French *sucre* sugar] (1857)
: a sweet crystalline dextrorotatory disaccharide sugar $C_{12}H_{22}O_{11}$ that occurs naturally in most plants and is obtained commercially especially from sugarcane or sugar beets

¹suc·tion \'sək-shən\ *noun* [Late Latin *suction-, suctio*, from Latin *sugere* to suck — more at SUCK] (1626)
1 : the act or process of sucking
2 a : the act or process of exerting a force upon a solid, liquid, or gaseous body by reason of reduced air pressure over part of its surface **b :** force so exerted
3 : a device (as a pipe or fitting) used in a machine that operates by suction
— suc·tion·al \-shə-nᵊl, -shnəl\ *adjective*

²suction *transitive verb* (1954)
: to remove (as from a body cavity or passage) by suction

suction cup *noun* (1942)

: a cup-shaped device in which a partial vacuum can be produced when applied to a surface

suction pump *noun* (1825)
: a common pump in which the liquid to be raised is pushed by atmospheric pressure into the partial vacuum under a retreating valved piston on the upstroke and reflux is prevented by a check valve in the pipe

suction stop *noun* (1887)
: a voice stop in the formation of which air behind the articulation is rarefied with consequent inrush of air when articulation is broken

suc·to·ri·al \ˌsək-'tōr-ē-əl, -'tȯr-\ *adjective* [New Latin *suctorius*, from Latin *sugere*] (1833)
: adapted for sucking; *especially* **:** serving to draw up fluid or to adhere by suction ⟨*suctorial* mouths⟩

suc·to·ri·an \-ē-ən\ *noun* [New Latin *Suctoria*, from neuter plural of *suctorius* suctorial] (circa 1842)
: any of a class or subclass (Suctoria) of complex protozoans which are ciliated only early in development and in which the mature form is fixed to the substrate, lacks locomotor organelles or a mouth, and obtains food through specialized suctorial tentacles

Su·dan grass \sü-'dan-, -'dän-\ *noun* [the *Sudan*, region in Africa] (1911)
: a vigorous tall-growing annual sorghum grass (*Sorghum bicolor sudanese*) widely grown for hay and fodder

Su·dan·ic \sü-'da-nik\ *noun* [the *Sudan* region] (1912)
: a group of languages neither Bantu nor Afro-Asiatic spoken in central and western Africa that were formerly considered a residual category and are now divided among the Niger-Congo and other families
— Sudanic *adjective*

su·da·to·ri·um \ˌsü-də-'tōr-ē-əm, -'tȯr-\ *noun* [Latin, from *sudare* to sweat — more at SWEAT] (circa 1757)
: a sweat room in a bath

su·da·to·ry \'sü-də-ˌtōr-ē, -ˌtȯr-\ *noun, plural* **-ries** (1615)
: SUDATORIUM

sudd \'səd\ *noun* [Arabic, literally, obstruction] (1874)
: floating vegetable matter that forms obstructive masses especially in the upper White Nile

¹sud·den \'sə-dᵊn\ *adjective* [Middle English *sodain*, from Middle French, from Latin *subitaneus*, from *subitus* sudden, from past participle of *subire* to come up, from *sub-* up + *ire* to go — more at SUB-, ISSUE] (14th century)
1 a : happening or coming unexpectedly ⟨a *sudden* shower⟩ **b :** changing angle or character all at once
2 : marked by or manifesting abruptness or haste
3 : made or brought about in a short time **:** PROMPT
synonym see PRECIPITATE
— sud·den·ly *adverb*
— sud·den·ness \'sə-dᵊn-(n)əs\ *noun*

²sudden *noun* (1559)
obsolete **:** an unexpected occurrence **:** EMERGENCY
— all of a sudden *or* **on a sudden**
: sooner than was expected **:** at once

sudden death *noun* (14th century)
1 : unexpected death that is instantaneous or occurs within minutes from any cause other than violence ⟨*sudden death* following coronary occlusion⟩

□ USAGE

such For reasons that are hard to understand, commentators on usage disapprove of *such* used as a pronoun. Dictionaries, however, recognize it as standard; all of the citations upon which our definitions of this word are based are clearly standard.

2 : extra play to break a tie in a sports contest in which the first to go ahead wins

sudden infant death syndrome *noun* (1970)
: death of an apparently healthy infant usually before one year of age that is of unknown cause and occurs especially during sleep — called also *crib death;* abbreviation *SIDS*

su·do·rif·er·ous \ˌsü-də-'ri-f(ə-)rəs\ *adjective* [Late Latin *sudorifer,* from Latin *sudor* sweat (from *sudare* to sweat) + *-ifer* -iferous — more at SWEAT] (1597)
: producing or conveying sweat ⟨*sudoriferous* glands⟩ ⟨a *sudoriferous* duct⟩

su·do·rif·ic \-'ri-fik\ *adjective* [New Latin *sudorificus,* from Latin *sudor*] (1626)
: causing or inducing sweat : DIAPHORETIC ⟨*sudorific* herbs⟩
— **sudorific** *noun*

Su·dra \'sü-drə, 'shü-\ *noun* [Sanskrit *śūdra*] (1630)
: a Hindu of a lower caste traditionally assigned to menial occupations
— **Sudra** *adjective*

¹suds \'sədz\ *noun plural but singular or plural in construction* [probably from Middle Dutch *sudse* marsh; akin to Old English *sēothan* to seethe — more at SEETHE] (1581)
1 : water impregnated with soap or a synthetic detergent compound and worked up into froth; *also* : the lather or froth on such water
2 a : FOAM, FROTH **b** : BEER
— **suds·less** \-ləs\ *adjective*

²suds (1834)
transitive verb
: to wash in suds
intransitive verb
: to form suds

suds·er \'səd-zər\ *noun* (1967)
: SOAP OPERA

sudsy \'səd-zē\ *adjective* **suds·i·er; -est** (1866)
1 : full of suds : FROTHY, FOAMY
2 : SOAPY 4

sue \'sü\ *verb* **sued; su·ing** [Middle English, from Middle French *suivre,* from (assumed) Vulgar Latin *sequere,* from Latin *sequi* to follow, come or go after; akin to Greek *hepesthai* to follow, Sanskrit *sacate* he accompanies] (14th century)
transitive verb
1 *obsolete* : to make petition to or for
2 *archaic* : to pay court or suit to : WOO
3 a : to seek justice or right from (a person) by legal process; *specifically* : to bring an action against **b** : to proceed with and follow up (a legal action) to proper termination
intransitive verb
1 : to make a request or application : PLEAD — usually used with *for* or *to*
2 : to pay court : WOO
3 : to take legal proceedings in court
— **su·er** *noun*

¹suede *or* **suède** \'swād\ *noun* [French *gants de Suède* Swedish gloves] (1884)
1 : leather with a napped surface
2 : a fabric finished with a nap to simulate suede

²suede *verb* **sued·ed; sued·ing** (1921)
transitive verb
: to give a suede finish or nap to (a fabric or leather)
intransitive verb
: to give cloth or leather a suede finish

su·et \'sü-ət\ *noun* [Middle English *sewet,* from (assumed) Anglo-French, diminutive of Anglo-French *sue,* from Latin *sebum* tallow] (14th century)
: the hard fat about the kidneys and loins in beef and mutton that yields tallow

suf·fer \'sə-fər\ *verb* **suf·fered; suf·fer·ing** \-f(ə-)riŋ\ [Middle English *suffren,* from Old French *souffrir,* from (assumed) Vulgar Latin *sufferire,* from Latin *sufferre,* from *sub-* up + *ferre* to bear — more at SUB-, BEAR] (13th century)
transitive verb
1 a : to submit to or be forced to endure ⟨*suffer* martyrdom⟩ **b** : to feel keenly : labor under ⟨*suffer* thirst⟩
2 : UNDERGO, EXPERIENCE
3 : to put up with especially as inevitable or unavoidable
4 : to allow especially by reason of indifference ⟨the eagle *suffers* little birds to sing —Shakespeare⟩
intransitive verb
1 : to endure death, pain, or distress
2 : to sustain loss or damage
3 : to be subject to disability or handicap
synonym see BEAR
— **suf·fer·able** \'sə-f(ə-)rə-bəl\ *adjective*
— **suf·fer·able·ness** *noun*
— **suf·fer·ably** \-blē\ *adverb*
— **suf·fer·er** \'sə-fər-ər\ *noun*

suf·fer·ance \'sə-f(ə-)rən(t)s\ *noun* (14th century)
1 : patient endurance : LONG-SUFFERING
2 : PAIN, MISERY
3 : consent or sanction implied by a lack of interference or failure to enforce a prohibition
4 : power or ability to withstand : ENDURANCE

suffering *noun* (14th century)
1 : the state or experience of one that suffers
2 : PAIN
synonym see DISTRESS

suf·fice \sə-'fīs *also* -'fīz\ *verb* **suf·ficed; suf·fic·ing** [Middle English, from Middle French *suffis-,* stem of *suffire,* from Latin *sufficere* to provide, be adequate, from *sub-* + *facere* to make, do — more at DO] (14th century)
intransitive verb
1 : to meet or satisfy a need : be sufficient ⟨a brief note will *suffice*⟩ — often used with an impersonal *it* ⟨*suffice* it to say that they are dedicated, serious personalities —Cheryl Aldridge⟩
2 : to be competent or capable
transitive verb
: to be enough for
— **suf·fic·er** *noun*

suf·fi·cien·cy \sə-'fi-shən(t)-sē\ *noun* (15th century)
1 : sufficient means to meet one's needs : COMPETENCY; *also* : a modest but adequate scale of living
2 : the quality or state of being sufficient : ADEQUACY

suf·fi·cient \sə-'fi-shənt\ *adjective* [Middle English, from Latin *sufficient-, sufficiens,* from present participle of *sufficere*] (14th century)
1 a : enough to meet the needs of a situation or a proposed end ⟨*sufficient* provisions for a month⟩ **b** : being a sufficient condition
2 *archaic* : QUALIFIED, COMPETENT ☆
— **suf·fi·cient·ly** *adverb*

sufficient condition *noun* (1914)
1 : a proposition whose truth assures the truth of another proposition
2 : a state of affairs whose existence assures the existence of another state of affairs

¹suf·fix \'sə-fiks\ *noun* [New Latin *suffixum,* from Latin, neuter of *suffixus,* past participle of *suffigere* to fasten underneath, from *sub-* + *figere* to fasten — more at FIX] (1778)
: an affix occurring at the end of a word, base, or phrase — compare PREFIX
— **suf·fix·al** \'sə-fik-səl, (ˌ)sə-'fik-səl\ *adjective*

²suf·fix \'sə-fiks, (ˌ)sə-'fiks\ *transitive verb* (1778)
: to attach as a suffix
— **suf·fix·a·tion** \ˌsə-fik-'sā-shən\ *noun*

suf·fo·cate \'sə-fə-ˌkāt\ *verb* **-cat·ed; -cat·ing** [Middle English, from Latin *suffocatus,* past participle of *suffocare* to choke, stifle, from *sub-* + *fauces* throat] (15th century)
transitive verb
1 a : to stop the respiration of (as by strangling or asphyxiation) **b** : to deprive of oxygen **c** : to make uncomfortable by want of cool fresh air
2 : to impede or stop the development of
intransitive verb
1 : to become suffocated: **a** : to die from being unable to breathe **b** : to be uncomfortable through lack of air
2 : to become checked in development
— **suf·fo·cat·ing·ly** \-ˌkā-tiŋ-lē\ *adverb*
— **suf·fo·ca·tion** \ˌsə-fə-'kā-shən\ *noun*
— **suf·fo·ca·tive** \'sə-fə-ˌkā-tiv\ *adjective*

Suf·folk \'sə-fək, -ˌfȯk\ *noun* [*Suffolk,* England] (1831)
1 : any of a breed of chestnut-colored draft horses of English origin — called also *Suffolk punch*
2 : any of a breed of large hornless black-faced sheep of English origin raised chiefly for mutton

¹suf·fra·gan \'sə-fri-gən, -jən\ *noun* [Middle English, from Middle French, from Medieval Latin *suffraganeus,* from *suffragium* support, prayer] (14th century)
1 : a diocesan bishop (as in the Roman Catholic Church and the Church of England) subordinate to a metropolitan
2 : an Anglican or Episcopal bishop assisting a diocesan bishop and not having the right of succession

²suffragan *adjective* (15th century)
1 : of or being a suffragan
2 : subordinate to a metropolitan or archiepiscopal see

suf·frage \'sə-frij, *sometimes* -fə-rij\ *noun* [in sense 1, from Middle English, from Middle French, from Medieval Latin *suffragium,* from Latin, vote, political support, from *suffragari* to support with one's vote; in other senses, from Latin *suffragium*] (14th century)
1 : a short intercessory prayer usually in a series
2 : a vote given in deciding a controverted question or in the choice of a person for an office or trust
3 : the right of voting : FRANCHISE; *also* : the exercise of such right

suf·frag·ette \ˌsə-fri-'jet\ *noun* (1906)
: a woman who advocates suffrage for women

suf·frag·ist \'sə-fri-jist\ *noun* (1822)
: one who advocates extension of suffrage especially to women

suf·fuse \sə-'fyüz\ *transitive verb* **suf·fused; suf·fus·ing** [Latin *suffusus,* past participle of *suffundere,* literally, to pour beneath, from *sub-* + *fundere* to pour — more at FOUND] (1590)
: to spread over or through in the manner of fluid or light : FLUSH, FILL
synonym see INFUSE
— **suf·fu·sion** \-'fyü-zhən\ *noun*
— **suf·fu·sive** \-'fyü-siv, -ziv\ *adjective*

Su·fi \'sü-(ˌ)fē\ *noun* [Arabic *ṣūfīy,* perhaps from *ṣūf* wool] (1653)

☆ SYNONYMS
Sufficient, enough, adequate, competent mean being what is necessary or desirable. SUFFICIENT suggests a close meeting of a need ⟨*sufficient* savings⟩. ENOUGH is less exact in suggestion than SUFFICIENT ⟨do you have *enough* food?⟩. ADEQUATE may imply barely meeting a requirement ⟨the service was *adequate*⟩. COMPETENT suggests measuring up to all requirements without question or being adequately adapted to an end ⟨had no *competent* notion of what was going on⟩.

\ə\ abut \ᵊ\ kitten \ər\ further \a\ ash \ā\ ace
\ä\ mop, mar \au̇\ out \ch\ chin \e\ bet \ē\ easy
\g\ go \i\ hit \ī\ ice \j\ job \ŋ\ sing \ō\ go
\ȯ\ law \ȯi\ boy \th\ thin \t͟h\ the \ü\ loot \u̇\ foot
\y\ yet \zh\ vision *see also* Guide to Pronunciation

: a Muslim mystic
— **Sufi** *adjective*
— **Su·fic** \-fik\ *adjective*
— **Su·fism** \-ˌfi-zəm\ *noun*

¹sug·ar \'shu̇-gər\ *noun* [Middle English *sugre, sucre,* from Middle French *sucre,* from Medieval Latin *zuccarum,* from Old Italian *zucchero,* from Arabic *sukkar,* from Persian *shakar,* from Sanskrit *śarkarā;* akin to Sanskrit *śarkara* pebble — more at CROCODILE] (14th century)
1 a : a sweet crystallizable material that consists wholly or essentially of sucrose, is colorless or white when pure tending to brown when less refined, is obtained commercially from sugarcane or sugar beet and less extensively from sorghum, maples, and palms, and is important as a source of dietary carbohydrate and as a sweetener and preservative of other foods **b :** any of various water-soluble compounds that vary widely in sweetness and include the oligosaccharides (as sucrose) **2 :** a unit (as a spoonful, cube, or lump) of sugar **3 :** a sugar bowl
— **sug·ar·less** \-ləs\ *adjective*

²sugar *verb* **sug·ared; sug·ar·ing** \'shu̇-g(ə-)riŋ\ (15th century)
transitive verb
1 : to make palatable or attractive : SWEETEN **2 :** to sprinkle or mix with sugar
intransitive verb
1 : to form or be converted into sugar **2 :** to become granular : GRANULATE **3 :** to make maple syrup or maple sugar

sugar apple *noun* (1738)
: a tropical American tree (*Annona squamosa*) of the custard apple family; *also :* its edible sweet pulpy fruit with thick green scaly rind and shining black seeds

sugar beet *noun* (1817)
: a white-rooted beet grown for the sugar in its roots

sug·ar·ber·ry \'shu̇-gər-ˌber-ē\ *noun* (circa 1818)
: any of several hackberries (especially *Celtis laevigata* and *C. occidentalis*) with sweet edible fruits

sugar bush *noun* (1823)
: a woods in which sugar maples predominate

sug·ar·cane \'shu̇-gər-ˌkān\ *noun* (15th century)
: a stout tall perennial grass (*Saccharum officinarum*) that has a large terminal panicle and is widely grown in warm regions as a source of sugar

sugarcane

sug·ar·coat \'shu̇-gər-ˌkōt\ *transitive verb* [back-formation from *sugarcoated*] (1870)
1 : to coat with sugar **2 :** to make superficially attractive or palatable ⟨tried to *sugarcoat* an unpleasant truth⟩

sugar daddy *noun* (1926)
1 : a well-to-do usually older man who supports or spends lavishly on a mistress or girlfriend **2 :** a generous benefactor of a cause

sug·ar·house \'shu̇-gər-ˌhau̇s\ *noun* (1600)
: a building where sugar is made or refined; *specifically :* one where maple sap is boiled and maple syrup and maple sugar are made

sugaring off *noun* (1836)
1 : the act or process of converting maple syrup into sugar **2 :** a party held at the time of sugaring off

sug·ar·loaf \'shu̇-gər-ˌlōf\ *noun* (15th century)
1 : refined sugar molded into a cone **2 :** a hill or mountain shaped like a sugarloaf
— **sugar–loaf** *adjective*

sugar maple *noun* (1731)
1 : a maple (*Acer saccharum*) of eastern North America with 3- to 5-lobed leaves, hard close-grained wood much used for cabinetwork, and sap that is the chief source of maple syrup and maple sugar — called also *rock maple, hard maple* **2 :** any of several maples (especially *Acer nigrum* and *A. grandidentatum*) sometimes considered subspecies of the sugar maple

sugar off *intransitive verb* (1836)
1 : to complete the process of boiling down the syrup in making maple sugar until it is thick enough to crystallize **2 :** to approach or reach the state of granulation

sugar orchard *noun* (1833)
chiefly New England : SUGAR BUSH

sugar pea *noun* (1707)
: SNOW PEA

sugar pine *noun* (1846)
: a very tall pine (*Pinus lambertiana*) found from Oregon to Baja California and having needles in clusters of five, cones up to 18 inches (46 cm) long, and soft reddish brown wood; *also :* its wood

sug·ar·plum \'shu̇-gər-ˌpləm\ *noun* (circa 1668)
: a small candy in the shape of a ball or disk : SWEETMEAT

sugar snap pea *noun* (1979)
: SNAP PEA

sug·ary \'shu̇-g(ə-)rē\ *adjective* (1591)
1 a : exaggeratedly sweet : HONEYED ⟨his *sugary* deprecating voice —D. H. Lawrence⟩ **b :** cloyingly sweet : SENTIMENTAL **2 :** containing, resembling, or tasting of sugar

sug·gest \səg-'jest, sə-'jest\ *transitive verb* [Latin *suggestus,* past participle of *suggerere* to pile up, furnish, suggest, from *sub-* + *gerere* to carry] (1526)
1 a *obsolete :* to seek to influence : SEDUCE **b :** to call forth : EVOKE **c :** to mention or imply as a possibility ⟨*suggested* that he might bring his family⟩ **d :** to propose as desirable or fitting ⟨*suggest* a stroll⟩ **e :** to offer for consideration or as a hypothesis ⟨*suggest* a solution to a problem⟩ **2 a :** to call to mind by thought or association ⟨the explosion . . . *suggested* sabotage —F. L. Paxson⟩ **b :** to serve as a motive or inspiration for ⟨a play *suggested* by a historic incident⟩ ☆
— **sug·gest·er** *noun*

sug·gest·ible \səg-'jes-tə-bəl, sə-'jes-\ *adjective* (1890)
: easily influenced by suggestion
— **sug·gest·ibil·i·ty** \-ˌjes-tə-'bi-lə-tē\ *noun*

sug·ges·tion \səg-'jes-chən, sə-'jes-, -'jesh-\ *noun* (14th century)
1 a : the act or process of suggesting **b :** something suggested **2 a :** the process by which a physical or mental state is influenced by a thought or idea ⟨the power of *suggestion*⟩ **b :** the process by which one thought leads to another especially through association of ideas **3 :** a slight indication : TRACE ⟨a *suggestion* of a smile⟩

sug·ges·tive \səg-'jes-tiv, sə-'jes-\ *adjective* (1631)
1 a : giving a suggestion : INDICATIVE ⟨*suggestive* of a past era⟩ **b :** full of suggestions : stimulating thought ⟨provided a *suggestive* . . . commentary on the era —Lloyd Morris⟩ **c :** stirring mental associations : EVOCATIVE **2 :** suggesting or tending to suggest something improper or indecent : RISQUÉ
— **sug·ges·tive·ly** *adverb*
— **sug·ges·tive·ness** *noun*

sui·cid·al \ˌsü-ə-'sī-dᵊl\ *adjective* (1777)
1 a : dangerous especially to life **b :** destructive to one's own interests **2 :** relating to or of the nature of suicide **3 :** marked by an impulse to commit suicide
— **sui·cid·al·ly** *adverb*

¹sui·cide \'sü-ə-ˌsīd\ *noun* [Latin *sui* (genitive) of oneself + English *-cide;* akin to Old English & Old High German *sīn* his, Latin *suus* one's own, *sed, se* without, Sanskrit *sva* oneself, one's own] (1643)
1 a : the act or an instance of taking one's own life voluntarily and intentionally especially by a person of years of discretion and of sound mind **b :** ruin of one's own interests ⟨political *suicide*⟩ **2 :** one that commits or attempts suicide

²suicide *verb* **sui·cid·ed; sui·cid·ing** (1841)
intransitive verb
: to commit suicide
transitive verb
: to put (oneself) to death

suicide squad *noun* [from the fact that kickoffs are more dangerous than other plays] (circa 1966)
: a special squad used on kickoffs in football

suicide squeeze *noun* (1955)
: a squeeze play in which the runner runs all out at the pitch without knowing whether the batter will contact the ball

sui ge·ner·is \ˌsü-ˌī-'je-nə-rəs; ˌsü-ē-'je-, -'ge-\ *adjective* [Latin, of its own kind] (1787)
: constituting a class alone : UNIQUE, PECULIAR

sui ju·ris \ˌsü-ˌī-'ju̇r-əs, ˌsü-ē-'yu̇r-\ *adjective* [Latin, of one's own right] (1675)
: having full legal rights or capacity

su·int \'sü-ənt, 'swint\ *noun* [French, from Middle French, from *suer* to sweat, from Latin *sudare* — more at SWEAT] (1791)
: dried perspiration of sheep deposited in the wool and rich in potassium salts

¹suit \'süt\ *noun* [Middle English *siute* act of following, retinue, sequence, set, from Old French, act of following, retinue, from (assumed) Vulgar Latin *sequita,* from feminine of *sequitus,* past participle of *sequere* to follow — more at SUE] (14th century)
1 *archaic :* SUITE 1 **2 a :** recourse or appeal to a feudal superior for justice or redress **b :** an action or process in a court for the recovery of a right or claim **3 :** an act or instance of suing or seeking by entreaty : APPEAL; *specifically :* COURTSHIP **4 :** SUITE 2 — used chiefly of armor, sails, and counters in games **5 :** a set of garments: as **a :** an outer costume of two or more pieces **b :** a costume to be worn for a special purpose or under particular conditions ⟨gym *suit*⟩ **6 a :** all the playing cards in a pack bearing the same symbol **b :** all the dominoes bearing the same number **c :** all the cards or counters in a particular suit held by one player ⟨a 5-card *suit*⟩ **d :** the suit led ⟨follow *suit*⟩ **7** *slang :* a business executive — usually used in plural

☆ **SYNONYMS**
Suggest, imply, hint, intimate, insinuate mean to convey an idea indirectly. SUGGEST may stress putting into the mind by association of ideas, awakening of a desire, or initiating a train of thought ⟨a film title that *suggests* its subject matter⟩. IMPLY is close to SUGGEST but may indicate a more definite or logical relation of the unexpressed idea to the expressed ⟨measures *implying* that bankruptcy was imminent⟩. HINT implies the use of slight or remote suggestion with a minimum of overt statement ⟨*hinted* that she might have a job lined up⟩. INTIMATE stresses delicacy of suggestion without connoting any lack of candor ⟨*intimates* that there is more to the situation than meets the eye⟩. INSINUATE applies to the conveying of a usually unpleasant idea in a sly underhanded manner ⟨*insinuated* that there were shady dealings⟩.

²suit (14th century)
transitive verb
1 a : to be becoming to **b** : to be proper for : BEFIT
2 : to outfit with clothes : DRESS
3 : ACCOMMODATE, ADAPT ⟨*suit* the action to the word⟩
4 : to meet the needs or desires of : PLEASE ⟨*suits* me fine⟩
intransitive verb
1 : to be in accordance : AGREE ⟨the position *suits* with your abilities⟩
2 : to be appropriate or satisfactory ⟨these prices don't *suit*⟩
3 : to put on specially required clothing (as a uniform or protective garb) — usually used with *up*

suit·able \'sü-tə-bəl\ *adjective* (1582)
1 *obsolete* : SIMILAR, MATCHING
2 a : adapted to a use or purpose **b** : satisfying propriety : PROPER **c** : ABLE, QUALIFIED
synonym see FIT
— **suit·abil·i·ty** \ˌsü-tə-'bi-lə-tē\ *noun*
— **suit·able·ness** *noun*
— **suit·ably** \-blē\ *adverb*

suit·case \'süt-ˌkās\ *noun* (1897)
: a bag or case carried by hand and designed to hold a traveler's clothing and personal articles

suite \'swēt, *2d is also* 'süt\ *noun* [French, alteration of Old French *siute* — more at SUIT] (1673)
1 : RETINUE; *especially* : the personal staff accompanying a ruler, diplomat, or dignitary on official business
2 : a group of things forming a unit or constituting a collection : SET: as **a** : a group of rooms occupied as a unit **b** (1) : a 17th and 18th century instrumental musical form consisting of a series of dances in the same or related keys (2) : a modern instrumental composition in several movements of different character (3) : a long orchestral concert arrangement in suite form of material drawn from a longer work (as a ballet) **c** : a collection of minerals or rocks having some characteristic in common (as type or origin) **d** : a set of matched furniture

suit·er \'sü-tər\ *noun* (1952)
: a suitcase for holding a specified number of suits — usually used in combination ⟨a two-*suiter*⟩

suit·ing \'sü-tiŋ\ *noun* (1883)
1 : fabric for suits
2 : a suit of clothes

suit·or \'sü-tər\ *noun* [Middle English, follower, pleader, from Anglo-French, from Latin *secutor* follower, from *sequi* to follow — more at SUE] (15th century)
1 : one that petitions or entreats
2 : a party to a suit at law
3 : one who courts a woman or seeks to marry her
4 : one who seeks to take over a business

su·ki·ya·ki \ˌskē-'yä-kē, ˌsü-kē-', ˌsü-\ *noun* [Japanese, from *suki-* slice + *yaki* broil] (1920)
: a dish consisting of thin slices of meat, bean curd, and vegetables cooked in soy sauce and sugar

suk·kah \'sù-kə\ *noun* [Hebrew *sukkāh*] (1875)
: a booth or shelter with a roof of branches and leaves that is used especially for meals during the Sukkoth

Suk·koth *or* **Suk·kot** \'sù-kəs, -ˌkōt, -ˌkōth, -ˌkōs\ *noun* [Hebrew *sukkōth*, plural of *sukkāh*] (1882)
: a Jewish harvest festival beginning on the 15th of Tishri and commemorating the temporary shelters used by the Jews during their wandering in the wilderness

sul·cate \'səl-ˌkāt\ *adjective* [Latin *sulcatus*, past participle of *sulcare* to furrow, from *sulcus*] (1760)
: scored with usually longitudinal furrows ⟨a *sulcate* seedpod⟩

sul·cus \'səl-kəs\ *noun, plural* **sul·ci** \-ˌkī, -ˌkē, -ˌsī\ [Latin; akin to Old English *sulh* plow, Greek *holkos* furrow, *helkein* to pull] (1662)
: FURROW, GROOVE; *especially* : a shallow furrow on the surface of the brain separating adjacent convolutions

sulf- *or* **sulfo-** *combining form* [French *sulf-*, *sulfo-*, from Latin *sulfur*]
: sulfur : containing sulfur ⟨*sulf*ide⟩

sul·fa \'səl-fə\ *adjective* [short for *sulfanilamide*] (1940)
1 : related chemically to sulfanilamide
2 : of, relating to, or containing sulfa drugs

sul·fa·di·a·zine \ˌsəl-fə-'dī-ə-ˌzēn\ *noun* [*sulfa* + *diazine* ($C_4H_4N_2$)] (1940)
: a sulfa drug $C_{10}H_{10}N_4O_2S$ that is used especially in the treatment of meningitis, pneumonia, and intestinal infections

sulfa drug *noun* (1940)
: any of various synthetic organic bacteria-inhibiting drugs that are sulfonamides closely related chemically to sulfanilamide

sul·fa·nil·amide \ˌsəl-fə-'ni-lə-ˌmīd, -ˌməd\ *noun* [*sulfanilic* + *amide*] (1937)
: a crystalline sulfonamide $C_6H_8N_2O_2S$ that is the amide of sulfanilic acid and the parent compound of most of the sulfa drugs

sul·fa·nil·ic acid \ˌsəl-fə-'ni-lik-\ *noun* [International Scientific Vocabulary *sulf-* + *anil*ine + *-ic*] (1856)
: a crystalline acid $C_6H_7NO_3S$ obtained from aniline

sul·fa·tase \'səl-fə-ˌtās, -ˌtāz\ *noun* [¹*sulfate*] (1924)
: any of various esterases that accelerate the hydrolysis of sulfuric esters and that are found in animal tissues and in microorganisms

¹sul·fate \'səl-ˌfāt\ *noun* [French, from Latin *sulfur*] (1790)
1 : a salt or ester of sulfuric acid
2 : a bivalent group or anion SO_4 characteristic of sulfuric acid and the sulfates

²sulfate *transitive verb* **sul·fat·ed; sul·fat·ing** (1802)
: to treat or combine with sulfuric acid or a sulfate

sulf·hy·dryl \ˌsəlf-'(h)ī-drəl\ *noun* [International Scientific Vocabulary] (circa 1901)
: THIOL 2 — used chiefly in molecular biology

sul·fide \'səl-ˌfīd\ *noun* (1836)
1 : any of various organic compounds characterized by a sulfur atom attached to two carbon atoms
2 : a binary compound (as CuS) of sulfur usually with a more electropositive element or group : a salt of hydrogen sulfide

sul·fin·py·ra·zone \ˌsəl-fən-'pī-rə-ˌzōn\ *noun* [*sulf*inic acid (RSO₂H) + *pyr-* + *azole* + *-one*] (1958)
: a uricosuric drug $C_{23}H_{20}N_2O_3S$ used in long-term treatment of chronic gout

sul·fite \'səl-ˌfīt\ *noun* [French *sulfite*, alteration of *sulfate*] (1790)
: a salt or ester of sulfurous acid
— **sul·fit·ic** \ˌsəl-'fi-tik\ *adjective*

sulfon- *combining form* [International Scientific Vocabulary *sulfonic*]
: sulfonic ⟨*sulfon*amide⟩

sul·fon·amide \ˌsəl-'fä-nə-ˌmīd, -məd; -'fō-nə-ˌmīd\ *noun* (1881)
: any of various amides (as sulfanilamide) of a sulfonic acid; *also* : SULFA DRUG

¹sul·fo·nate \'səl-fə-ˌnāt\ *noun* (1876)
: a salt or ester of a sulfonic acid

²sulfonate *transitive verb* **-nat·ed; -nat·ing** (1882)
: to introduce the SO_3H group into; *broadly* : to treat (an organic substance) with sulfuric acid
— **sul·fo·na·tion** \ˌsəl-fə-'nā-shən\ *noun*

sul·fone \'səl-ˌfōn\ *noun* (1872)
: any of various compounds containing the sulfonyl group with its sulfur atom having two bonds with carbon

sul·fon·ic \ˌsəl-'fä-nik, -'fō-\ *adjective* (circa 1891)
: of, relating to, being, or derived from the univalent acid group SO_3H

sulfonic acid *noun* (1873)
: any of numerous acids that contain the SO_3H group and may be derived from sulfuric acid by replacement of a hydroxyl group by either an inorganic anion or a univalent organic group

sul·fo·ni·um \ˌsəl-'fō-nē-əm\ *noun* [New Latin, from *sulf-* + *-onium*] (1885)
: a univalent group or cation SH_3 or derivative SR_3

sul·fo·nyl \'səl-fə-ˌnil\ *noun* (1920)
: the bivalent group SO_2

sul·fo·nyl·urea \ˌsəl-fə-ˌnil-'yùr-ē-ə\ *noun* [New Latin, from International Scientific Vocabulary *sulfonyl* + New Latin *urea*] (1956)
: any of several hypoglycemic compounds related to the sulfonamides and used in the oral treatment of diabetes

sulf·ox·ide \ˌsəl-'fäk-ˌsīd\ *noun* [International Scientific Vocabulary] (circa 1894)
: any of a class of organic compounds characterized by an SO group with its sulfur atom having two bonds with carbon

sul·fur *also* **sul·phur** \'səl-fər\ *noun* [Middle English *sulphur* brimstone, from Latin *sulpur, sulphur, sulfur*] (14th century)
1 : a nonmetallic element that occurs either free or combined especially in sulfides and sulfates, is a constituent of proteins, exists in several allotropic forms including yellow orthorhombic crystals, resembles oxygen chemically but is less active and more acidic, and is used especially in the chemical and paper industries, in rubber vulcanization, and in medicine for treating skin diseases — see ELEMENT table
2 : something (as scathing language) that suggests sulfur □
— **sul·fury** *or* **sul·phury** \-ē\ *adjective*

sulfur bacterium *noun* (1891)
: any of various bacteria (especially genus *Thiobacillus*) capable of metabolizing sulfur compounds

sulfur dioxide *noun* (1869)
: a heavy pungent toxic gas SO_2 that is easily condensed to a colorless liquid, is used especially in making sulfuric acid, in bleaching, as a preservative, and as a refrigerant, and is a major air pollutant especially in industrial areas

sul·fu·ric \ˌsəl-'fyùr-ik\ *adjective* (1790)
: of, relating to, or containing sulfur especially with a higher valence than sulfurous compounds ⟨*sulfuric* esters⟩

sulfuric acid *or* **sul·phu·ric acid** \ˌsəl-'fyùr-ik-\ *noun* (1790)
: a heavy corrosive oily dibasic strong acid H_2SO_4 that is colorless when pure and is a vigorous oxidizing and dehydrating agent
usage see SULFUR

sul·fu·rize \'səl-fə-ˌrīz, -fyə-\ *transitive verb* **-rized; -riz·ing** (1794)
: to treat with sulfur or a sulfur compound

sul·fu·rous *also* **sul·phu·rous** \'səl-fə-rəs,

\ə\ abut \ᵊ\ kitten \ər\ **further** \a\ ash \ā\ ace
\ä\ mop, mar \aù\ out \ch\ chin \e\ bet \ē\ easy
\g\ go \i\ hit \ī\ ice \j\ job \ŋ\ sing \ō\ go
\ò\ law \òi\ boy \th\ thin \t͟h\ the \ü\ loot \ù\ foot
\y\ yet \zh\ vision *see also* Guide to Pronunciation

-fyə- *also especially for 1b* ,səl-'fyür-əs\ *adjective* (15th century)
1 a : of, relating to, or containing sulfur especially with a lower valence than sulfuric compounds ⟨*sulfurous* esters⟩ **b :** resembling or emanating from sulfur and especially burning sulfur
2 a : of, relating to, or dealing with the fire of hell **:** INFERNAL **b :** SCATHING, VIRULENT ⟨*sulfurous* denunciations⟩ **c :** PROFANE, BLASPHEMOUS ⟨*sulfurous* language⟩
usage see SULFUR
— **sul·fu·rous·ly** *adverb*
— **sul·fu·rous·ness** *noun*

sulfurous acid *noun* (1790)
: a weak unstable dibasic acid H₂SO₃ known in solution and through its salts and used as a reducing and bleaching agent

sul·fu·ryl \'səl-fə-,ril, -fyə-\ *noun* [International Scientific Vocabulary] (1867)
: SULFONYL — used especially in names of inorganic compounds

¹sulk \'səlk\ *intransitive verb* [back-formation from *sulky*] (1781)
: to be moodily silent

²sulk *noun* (1804)
1 : the state of one sulking — often used in plural ⟨had a case of the *sulks*⟩
2 : a sulky mood or spell ⟨in a *sulk*⟩

¹sulky \'səl-kē\ *adjective* [probably alteration of obsolete *sulke* sluggish] (1744)
1 a : sulking or given to spells of sulking **b :** relating to or indicating a sulk ⟨a *sulky* expression⟩
2 [²*sulky*] **:** having wheels and usually a seat for the driver ⟨a *sulky* plow⟩
synonym see SULLEN
— **sulk·i·ly** \-kə-lē\ *adverb*
— **sulk·i·ness** \-kē-nəs\ *noun*

²sulky *noun, plural* **sulkies** [probably from ¹*sulky*; from its having room for only one person] (1756)
: a light 2-wheeled vehicle (as for harness racing) having a seat for the driver only and usually no body

sul·lage \'sə-lij\ *noun* [probably from Middle French *soiller, souiller* to soil — more at SOIL] (1553)
: REFUSE, SEWAGE

sul·len \'sə-lən\ *adjective* [Middle English *solain* solitary, probably from (assumed) Anglo-French *solein*, alteration of Old French *soltain*, from Late Latin *solitaneus* private, ultimately from Latin *solus* alone] (14th century)
1 a : gloomily or resentfully silent or repressed **b :** suggesting a sullen state **:** LOWERING
2 : dull or somber in sound or color
3 : DISMAL, GLOOMY
4 : moving sluggishly ☆
— **sul·len·ly** *adverb*
— **sul·len·ness** \'sə-lə(n)-nəs\ *noun*

¹sul·ly \'sə-lē\ *transitive verb* **sul·lied; sul·ly·ing** [Middle English *sollyen*, probably from Middle French *soiller* to soil] (15th century)
: to make soiled or tarnished **:** DEFILE

²sully *noun, plural* **sullies** (1602)
archaic **:** SOIL, STAIN

sulph- *or* **sulpho-** *chiefly British variant of* SULF-

sul·phate, sul·phide *chiefly British variant of* SULFATE, SULFIDE

sulphur butterfly *noun* (1879)
: any of numerous butterflies (especially *Colias* and related genera of the family Pieridae) having the wings usually yellow or orange with a black border — called also *sulphur*

sul·phu·re·ous *adjective* (circa 1552)
: SULFUROUS

sul·phu·rise *British variant of* SULFURIZE

sulphur yellow *noun* (1816)
: a brilliant greenish yellow

Sul·pi·cian \,səl-'pi-shən\ *noun* [French *sulpicien*, from Compagnie de Saint-Sulpice Society of Saint Sulpice] (1786)

: a member of the Society of Priests of Saint Sulpice founded by Jean Jacques Olier in Paris, France, in 1642 and dedicated to the teaching of seminarians

sul·tan \'səl-t°n\ *noun* [Middle French, from Arabic *sulṭān*] (1555)
: a king or sovereign especially of a Muslim state
— **sul·tan·ic** \,səl-'ta-nik\ *adjective*

sul·ta·na \(,)səl-'ta-nə\ *noun* [Italian, feminine of *sultano* sultan, from Arabic *sulṭān*] (1585)
1 : a female member of a sultan's family; *especially* **:** a sultan's wife
2 a : a pale yellow seedless grape grown for raisins and wine **b :** the raisin of a sultana

sul·tan·ate \'səl-t°n-,āt\ *noun* (1822)
1 : a state or country governed by a sultan
2 : the office, dignity, or power of a sultan

sul·tan·ess \'səl-t°n-əs\ *noun* (1611)
archaic **:** SULTANA 1

sul·try \'səl-trē\ *adjective* **sul·tri·er; -est** [obsolete English *sulter* to swelter, alteration of English *swelter*] (1594)
1 a : very hot and humid **:** SWELTERING ⟨a *sultry* day⟩ **b :** burning hot **:** TORRID
2 a : hot with passion or anger **b :** exciting or capable of exciting strong sexual desire ⟨*sultry* glances⟩
— **sul·tri·ly** \-trə-lē\ *adverb*
— **sul·tri·ness** \-trē-nəs\ *noun*

¹sum \'səm\ *noun* [Middle English *summe*, from Old French, from Latin *summa*, from feminine of *summus* highest; akin to Latin *super* over — more at OVER] (14th century)
1 : an indefinite or specified amount of money
2 : the whole amount **:** AGGREGATE
3 : the utmost degree **:** SUMMIT ⟨reached the *sum* of human happiness⟩
4 a : a summary of the chief points or thoughts **:** SUMMATION ⟨the *sum* of this criticism follows —C. W. Hendel⟩ **b :** GIST ⟨the *sum* and substance of an argument⟩
5 a (1) **:** the result of adding numbers ⟨*sum* of 5 and 7 is 12⟩ (2) **:** the limit of the sum of the first *n* terms of an infinite series as *n* increases indefinitely **b :** numbers to be added; *broadly* **:** a problem in arithmetic **c** (1) **:** DISJUNCTION 2 (2) **:** UNION 2d
— **sum·ma·bil·i·ty** \,sə-mə-'bi-lə-tē\ *noun*
— **sum·ma·ble** \'sə-mə-bəl\ *adjective*
— **in sum :** in short **:** BRIEFLY

²sum *verb* **summed; sum·ming** (14th century)
transitive verb
1 : to calculate the sum of **:** TOTAL
2 : SUMMARIZE
intransitive verb
: to reach a sum **:** AMOUNT

su·mac *also* **su·mach** \'shü-,mak, 'sü-\ *noun* [Middle English *sumac*, from Middle French, from Arabic *summāq*] (14th century)
1 : a material used in tanning and dyeing that consists of dried powdered leaves and flowers of various sumacs
2 : any of a genus (*Rhus*) of trees, shrubs, and woody vines of the cashew family that have pinnately compound leaves turning to brilliant colors in the autumn, dioecious flowers, spikes or loose clusters of red or whitish berries, and in some cases foliage poisonous to the touch — compare POISON IVY, POISON OAK

Su·me·ri·an \sü-'mer-ē-ən, -'mir-\ *noun* (1878)
1 : a native of Sumer
2 : the language of the Sumerians that has no known linguistic affinities
— **Sumerian** *adjective*

Su·me·rol·o·gy \,sü-mə-'rä-lə-jē\ *noun* (1897)
: the study of Sumerian culture, language, and history
— **Su·me·rol·o·gist** \-jist\ *noun*

sum·ma \'sù-mə, 'sü-, 'sə-\ *noun, plural* **sum·mae** \'sü-,mī, 'sü-, -,mā; 'sə-,mē, -,mī\ [Medieval Latin *summa*, from Latin, sum] (1725)

: a comprehensive treatise; *especially* **:** one by a scholastic philosopher

sum·ma cum lau·de \,sù-mə-(,)kùm-'laù-də, ,sü-, -'laù-de; ,sə-mə-,kəm-'lô-dē\ *adverb or adjective* [Latin, with highest praise] (1900)
: with highest distinction ⟨graduated *summa cum laude*⟩ — compare CUM LAUDE, MAGNA CUM LAUDE

sum·mand \'sə-,mand, ,sə-'mand\ *noun* [Medieval Latin *summandus*, gerund of *summare* to sum, from *summa*] (1893)
: a term in a summation **:** ADDEND

sum·ma·rise *British variant of* SUMMARIZE

sum·ma·ri·za·tion \,sə-mə-rə-'zā-shən, ,səm-rə-\ *noun* (1865)
1 : the act of summarizing
2 : SUMMARY

sum·ma·rize \'sə-mə-,rīz\ *verb* **-rized; -riz·ing** (1871)
transitive verb
: to tell in or reduce to a summary
intransitive verb
: to make a summary
— **sum·ma·riz·able** \,sə-mə-'rī-zə-bəl\ *adjective*
— **sum·ma·riz·er** *noun*

¹sum·ma·ry \'sə-mə-rē *also* 'sə-,mə-rē or -,mer-ē\ *adjective* [Middle English, from Medieval Latin *summarius*, from Latin *summa* sum] (15th century)
1 : COMPREHENSIVE; *especially* **:** covering the main points succinctly
2 a : done without delay or formality **:** quickly executed ⟨a *summary* dismissal⟩ **b :** of, relating to, or using a summary proceeding ⟨a *summary* trial⟩
synonym see CONCISE
— **sum·mar·i·ly** \(,)sə-'mer-ə-lē\ *adverb*

²sum·ma·ry \'sə-mə-rē *also* 'səm-rē\ *noun, plural* **-ries** (1509)
: an abstract, abridgment, or compendium especially of a preceding discourse

sum·mate \'sə-,māt\ *verb* **sum·mat·ed; sum·mat·ing** [back-formation from *summation*] (1900)
transitive verb
: to add together **:** SUM UP
intransitive verb
: to form a sum or cumulative effect

sum·ma·tion \(,)sə-'mā-shən\ *noun* (1760)
1 : the act or process of forming a sum **:** ADDITION
2 : SUM, TOTAL
3 : cumulative action or effect; *especially* **:** the process by which a sequence of stimuli that are individually inadequate to produce a response are cumulatively able to induce a nerve impulse

☆ **SYNONYMS**
Sullen, glum, morose, surly, sulky, crabbed, saturnine, gloomy mean showing a forbidding or disagreeable mood. SULLEN implies a silent ill humor and a refusal to be sociable ⟨remained *sullen* amid the festivities⟩. GLUM suggests a silent dispiritedness ⟨a *glum* candidate left to ponder a stunning defeat⟩. MOROSE adds to GLUM an element of bitterness or misanthropy ⟨*morose* job seekers who are inured to rejection⟩. SURLY implies gruffness and sullenness of speech or manner ⟨a typical *surly* teenager⟩. SULKY suggests childish resentment expressed in peevish sullenness ⟨grew *sulky* after every spat⟩. CRABBED applies to a forbidding morose harshness of manner ⟨the school's notoriously *crabbed* headmaster⟩. SATURNINE describes a heavy forbidding aspect or suggests a bitter disposition ⟨a *saturnine* cynic always finding fault⟩. GLOOMY implies a depression in mood making for seeming sullenness or glumness ⟨a *gloomy* mood ushered in by bad news⟩.

4 : a final part of an argument reviewing points made and expressing conclusions
— **sum·ma·tion·al** \-shnəl, -shə-nᵊl\ *adjective*

sum·ma·tive \'sə-mə-tiv, -ˌmā-\ *adjective* (1881)
: ADDITIVE, CUMULATIVE

¹**sum·mer** \'sə-mər\ *noun* [Middle English *sumer*, from Old English *sumor*; akin to Old High German & Old Norse *sumer* summer, Sanskrit *samā* year, season] (before 12th century)
1 : the season between spring and autumn comprising in the northern hemisphere usually the months of June, July, and August or as reckoned astronomically extending from the June solstice to the September equinox
2 : the warmer half of the year
3 : YEAR ⟨a girl of seventeen *summers*⟩
4 : a period of maturing powers
— **sum·mer·like** \-ˌlīk\ *adjective*

²**summer** *adjective* (14th century)
1 : of, relating to, or suitable for summer ⟨*summer* vacation⟩ ⟨a *summer* home⟩
2 : sown in the spring and harvested in the same year as sown ⟨*summer* wheat⟩ — compare WINTER

³**summer** *verb* **sum·mered; sum·mer·ing** \'sə-mə-riŋ, 'səm-riŋ\ (15th century)
intransitive verb
: to pass the summer
transitive verb
: to keep or carry through the summer; *especially* : to provide (as cattle or sheep) with pasture during the summer

summer cypress *noun* (1767)
: a densely branched Eurasian herb (*Kochia scoparia*) of the goosefoot family grown for its foliage which turns red in autumn

sum·mer·house \'sə-mər-ˌhaus\ *noun* (before 12th century)
1 : a country house for summer residence
2 : a covered structure in a garden or park designed to provide a shady resting place in summer

summer kitchen *noun* (1874)
: a small building or shed that is usually adjacent to a house and is used as a kitchen in warm weather

sum·mer·long \-ˌlȯŋ, -'lȯŋ\ *adjective* (1960)
: lasting through the summer

sum·mers \'sə-mərz\ *adverb* (1907)
: during the summers ⟨worked *summers* as a waiter⟩

sum·mer·sault *variant of* SOMERSAULT

summer savory *noun* (circa 1573)
: an annual European mint (*Satureja hortensis*) used in cookery — compare WINTER SAVORY

summer school *noun* (1860)
: a school or school session conducted in summer enabling students to accelerate progress toward a degree, to make up credits lost through absence or failure, or to round out professional education

summer squash *noun* (1815)
: any of various garden squashes derived from a variety (*Cucurbita pepo* variety *melopepo*) and used as a vegetable while immature and before hardening of the seeds and rind

summer stock *noun* (1927)
: theatrical productions of stock companies presented during the summer

summer theater *noun* (1801)
: a theater that presents several different plays or musicals during the summer

sum·mer·time \'sə-mər-ˌtīm\ *noun* (14th century)
: the summer season or a period like summer

summer time *noun* (1916)
chiefly British : DAYLIGHT SAVING TIME

sum·mer·wood \'sə-mər-ˌwud\ *noun* (1902)
: the harder less porous portion of an annual ring of wood that develops late in the growing season — compare SPRINGWOOD

sum·mery \'sə-mə-rē, 'səm-rē\ *adjective* (1824)

: of, resembling, or fit for summer

sum·ming–up \ˌsə-miŋ-'əp\ *noun, plural* **sum·mings–up** \-miŋz-\ (1790)
: the act or statement of one who sums up

¹**sum·mit** \'sə-mət\ *noun* [Middle English *somete*, from Middle French, from Old French, diminutive of *sum* top, from Latin *summum*, neuter of *summus* highest — more at SUM] (15th century)
1 : TOP, APEX; *especially* : the highest point : PEAK
2 : the topmost level attainable ⟨the *summit* of human fame⟩
3 a : the highest level of officials; *especially* : the diplomatic level of heads of government **b :** a conference of highest-level officials (as heads of government) ⟨an economic *summit*⟩
☆

²**summit** *intransitive verb* (1972)
: to participate in a summit conference

sum·mit·eer \ˌsə-mə-'tir\ *noun* (1957)
: one who takes part in a summit

sum·mit·ry \'sə-mə-trē\ *noun* (1958)
: the use of a summit conference for international negotiation

sum·mon \'sə-mən\ *transitive verb* **sum·moned; sum·mon·ing** \'sə-mə-niŋ, 'səm-niŋ\ [Middle English *somonen*, from Old French *somondre*, from (assumed) Vulgar Latin *summonere*, alteration of Latin *summonēre* to remind secretly, from *sub-* secretly + *monēre* to warn — more at SUB-, MIND] (13th century)
1 : to issue a call to convene : CONVOKE
2 : to command by service of a summons to appear in court
3 : to call upon for specified action
4 : to bid to come : send for ⟨*summon* a physician⟩
5 : to call forth : EVOKE — often used with *up*
☆
— **sum·mon·able** \'sə-mə-nə-bəl\ *adjective*
— **sum·mon·er** \'sə-mə-nər, 'səm-nər\ *noun*

¹**sum·mons** \'sə-mənz\ *noun, plural* **sum·mons·es** [Middle English *somouns*, from Old French *somonse*, from past participle of *somondre*] (13th century)
1 : the act of summoning; *especially* : a call by authority to appear at a place named or to attend to a duty
2 : a warning or citation to appear in court: as **a :** a written notification to be served on a person as a warning to appear in court at a day specified to answer to the plaintiff **b :** a subpoena to appear as a witness
3 : something (as a call) that summons

²**summons** *transitive verb* (1683)
: SUMMON 2

sum·mum bo·num \ˌsu̇-məm-'bō-nəm, ˌsü-, sə-\ *noun* [Latin] (1563)
: the supreme good from which all others are derived

su·mo \'sü-(ˌ)mō\ *noun* [Japanese *sumō*] (1880)
: a Japanese form of wrestling in which a contestant loses if he is forced out of the ring or if any part of his body except the soles of his feet touches the ground

sump \'səmp\ *noun* [Middle English *sompe* swamp — more at SWAMP] (1653)
1 : a pit or reservoir serving as a drain or receptacle for liquids: as **a :** CESSPOOL **b :** a pit at the lowest point in a circulating or drainage system (as the oil-circulating system of an internal combustion engine) **c** *chiefly British* : OIL PAN
2 *British* : CRANKCASE
3 [German *Sumpf*, literally, marsh, from Middle High German — more at SWAMP] **a :** the lowest part of a mine shaft into which water drains **b :** an excavation ahead of regular work in driving a mine tunnel or sinking a mine shaft
4 : something resembling a sump : SINK 2

sump pump *noun* (circa 1899)
: a pump (as in a basement) to remove accumulations of liquid from a sump pit

sump·ter \'səm(p)-tər\ *noun* [Middle English, short for *sumpter horse*, from *sumpter* driver of a packhorse, from Middle French *sometier*, from (assumed) Vulgar Latin *sagmatarius*, from Late Latin *sagmat-*, *sagma* packsaddle, from Greek; akin to Greek *sattein* to pack, stuff] (15th century)
: a pack animal

sump·tu·ary \'səm(p)-chə-ˌwer-ē\ *adjective* [Latin *sumptuarius*, from *sumptus* expense, from *sumere* to take, spend — more at CONSUME] (1600)
1 : relating to personal expenditures and especially to prevent extravagance and luxury ⟨conservative *sumptuary* tastes —John Cheever⟩
2 : designed to regulate extravagant expenditures or habits especially on moral or religious grounds ⟨*sumptuary* laws⟩ ⟨*sumptuary* tax⟩

sump·tu·ous \'səm(p)(t)-shə-wəs, -shəs, -shwəs\ *adjective* [Middle English, from Middle French *sumptueux*, from Latin *sumptuosus*, from *sumptus*] (15th century)
: extremely costly, rich, luxurious, or magnificent ⟨*sumptuous* banquets⟩ ⟨a *sumptuous* residence⟩; *also* : MAGNIFICENT 4
— **sump·tu·ous·ly** *adverb*
— **sump·tu·ous·ness** *noun*

sum total *noun* (14th century)
1 : a total arrived at through the counting of sums
2 : total result : TOTALITY

sum–up \'səm-ˌəp\ *noun* (1894)
: SUMMARY

☆ **SYNONYMS**
Summit, peak, pinnacle, climax, apex, acme, culmination mean the highest point attained or attainable. SUMMIT implies the topmost level attainable ⟨at the *summit* of the Victorian social scene⟩. PEAK suggests the highest among other high points ⟨an artist working at the *peak* of her powers⟩. PINNACLE suggests a dizzying and often insecure height ⟨the *pinnacle* of worldly success⟩. CLIMAX implies the highest point in an ascending series ⟨the war was the *climax* to a series of hostile actions⟩. APEX implies the point where all ascending lines converge ⟨the *apex* of Dutch culture⟩. ACME implies a level of quality representing the perfection of a thing ⟨a statue that was once deemed the *acme* of beauty⟩. CULMINATION suggests the outcome of a growth or development representing an attained objective ⟨the *culmination* of years of effort⟩.

Summon, call, cite, convoke, convene, muster mean to demand the presence of. SUMMON implies the exercise of authority ⟨was *summoned* to answer charges⟩. CALL may be used less formally for SUMMON ⟨*called* the legislature into special session⟩. CITE implies a summoning to court usually to answer a charge ⟨*cited* for drunken driving⟩. CONVOKE implies a summons to assemble for deliberative or legislative purposes ⟨*convoked* a Vatican council⟩. CONVENE is somewhat less formal than CONVOKE ⟨*convened* the students⟩. MUSTER suggests a calling up of a number of things that form a group in order that they may be exhibited, displayed, or utilized as a whole ⟨*mustered* the troops⟩.

\ə\ **abut** \ᵊ\ **kitten** \ər\ **further** \a\ **ash** \ā\ **ace**
\ä\ **mop, mar** \au̇\ **out** \ch\ **chin** \e\ **bet** \ē\ **easy**
\g\ **go** \i\ **hit** \ī\ **ice** \j\ **job** \ŋ\ **sing** \ō\ **go**
\ȯ\ **law** \ȯi\ **boy** \th\ **thin** \t͟h\ **the** \ü\ **loot** \u̇\ **foot**
\y\ **yet** \zh\ **vision** *see also* Guide to Pronunciation

sum up (15th century)
transitive verb
1 : to be the sum of : bring to a total ⟨10 victories *summed up* his record⟩
2 a : to present or show succinctly : SUMMARIZE ⟨*sum up* the evidence presented⟩ **b** : to assess and then describe briefly : size up
intransitive verb
: to present a summary or recapitulation

¹sun \'sən\ *noun* [Middle English *sunne,* from Old English; akin to Old High German *sunna* sun, Latin *sol* — more at SOLAR] (before 12th century)
1 a *often capitalized* : the luminous celestial body around which the earth and other planets revolve, from which they receive heat and light, and which has a mean distance from earth of 93,000,000 miles (150,000,000 kilometers), a linear diameter of 864,000 miles (1,390,000 kilometers), a mass 332,000 times greater than earth, and a mean density about one fourth that of earth **b** : a celestial body like the sun
2 : the heat or light radiated from the sun
3 : one resembling the sun (as in warmth or brilliance)
4 : the rising or setting of the sun ⟨from *sun* to *sun*⟩
5 : GLORY, SPLENDOR
— **in the sun** : in the public eye
— **under the sun** : in the world : on earth
²sun *verb* **sunned; sun·ning** (15th century)
transitive verb
: to expose to or as if to the rays of the sun
intransitive verb
: to sun oneself

sun·baked \'sən-,bākt\ *adjective* (1628)
1 : heated, parched, or compacted especially by excessive sunlight
2 : baked by exposure to sunshine

sun·bath \'sən-,bath, -,båth\ *noun* (1866)
: an exposure to sunlight or a sunlamp

sun·bathe \-,bāth\ *intransitive verb* [back-formation from *sunbather*] (1600)
: to take a sunbath
— **sun·bath·er** \-,bā-<u>th</u>ər\ *noun*

sun·beam \-,bēm\ *noun* (before 12th century)
: a ray of sunlight

sun bear *noun* (1842)
: a small forest-dwelling bear (*Ursus malayanus* synonym *Helarctos malayanus*) that is found from Myanmar to Borneo and has short glossy black fur with a lighter muzzle and often an orange or white breast mark

sun·bird \-,bərd\ *noun* (1826)
: any of numerous small brilliantly colored oscine birds (family Nectariniidae) of the tropical Old World somewhat resembling hummingbirds

sun·block \-,bläk\ *noun* (1972)
: a preparation designed to block out more of the sun's rays than a sunscreen; *also* : its active ingredient (as para-aminobenzoic acid)

sun·bon·net \-,bä-nət\ *noun* (1824)
: a woman's bonnet with a wide brim framing the face and usually having a ruffle at the back to protect the neck from the sun

sun·bow \-,bō\ *noun* (1816)
: an arch resembling a rainbow made by the sun shining through vapor or mist

sunbonnet

¹sun·burn \-,bərn\ *verb* **-burned** \-,bərnd\ *or* **-burnt** \-,bərnt\; **-burn·ing** [back-formation from *sunburned,* from *sun* + *burned*] (1530)
transitive verb
: to burn or discolor by the sun
intransitive verb
: to become sunburned

²sunburn *noun* (1652)
: inflammation of the skin caused by overexposure to sunlight

sun·burst \'sən-,bərst\ *noun, often attributive* (1816)
1 : a flash of sunlight especially through a break in clouds
2 a : a jeweled brooch representing a sun surrounded by rays **b** : a design in the form of rays diverging from a central point

sun·choke \-,chōk\ *noun* (1980)
: JERUSALEM ARTICHOKE

sun·dae \'sən-dē, -,(,)dā\ *noun* [probably alteration of *Sunday*] (1897)
: ice cream served with topping (as crushed fruit, syrup, nuts, or whipped cream)

sun dance *noun, often S&D capitalized* (1849)
: a solo or group solstice rite of American Indians

¹Sun·day \'sən-dē, -,(,)dā\ *noun* [Middle English, from Old English *sunnandæg* (akin to Old High German *sunnūntag*), from *sunne* sun + *dæg* day] (before 12th century)
: the first day of the week : the Christian analogue of the Jewish Sabbath
— **Sun·days** \-dēz, -,(,)dāz\ *adverb*

²Sunday *adjective* (14th century)
1 : of, relating to, or associated with Sunday
2 [from the practice of wearing one's best clothes on Sunday to attend church] : BEST ⟨*Sunday* suit⟩
3 : AMATEUR ⟨*Sunday* painters⟩

Sun·day–go–to–meet·ing \'sən-dē-,gō-tə-'mē-tiŋ\ *adjective* (1831)
: appropriate for Sunday churchgoing

Sunday punch *noun* (1929)
1 : a powerful or devastating blow; *especially* : a knockout punch
2 : something capable of delivering a powerful or devastating blow to the opposition ⟨saving his *Sunday punch* for the end of the campaign —*Newsweek*⟩

Sunday school *noun* (1783)
: a school held on Sunday for religious education; *also* : the teachers and pupils of such a school

sun·deck \'sən-,dek\ *noun* (1897)
1 : the usually upper deck of a ship that is exposed to the most sun
2 : a roof, deck, or terrace for sunning

sun·der \'sən-dər\ *verb* **sun·dered; sun·der·ing** \-d(ə-)riŋ\ [Middle English, from Old English ge*sundrian, syndrian;* akin to Old High German *suntarōn* to sunder, Old English *sundor* apart, Latin *sine* without, Sanskrit *sanutar* away] (before 12th century)
transitive verb
: to break apart or in two : separate by or as if by violence or by intervening time or space
intransitive verb
: to become parted, disunited, or severed
synonym see SEPARATE

sun·dew \'sən-(,)dü, -(,)dyü\ *noun* (1578)
: any of a genus (*Drosera* of the family Droseraceae, the sundew family) of bog-inhabiting insectivorous herbs having viscid glands on the leaves

sun·di·al \-,dī(-ə)l\ *noun* (1599)
: an instrument to show the time of day by the shadow of a gnomon on a usually horizontal plate or on a cylindrical surface

sun disk *noun* (1877)
: an ancient Near Eastern symbol consisting of a disk with conventionalized

sun disk

wings emblematic of the sun-god (as Ra in Egypt)

sun dog *noun* (1635)
1 : PARHELION
2 : a small nearly round halo on the parhelic circle most frequently just outside the halo of 22 degrees

sun·down \'sən-,daun\ *noun* (1620)
: SUNSET 2

sun·down·er \-,daú-nər\ *noun* (1868)
1 [from his habit of arriving at a place where he hopes to obtain food and lodging too late to do any work] *Australian* : HOBO, TRAMP
2 *chiefly British* : a drink taken at sundown

sun·dress \-,dres\ *noun* (1942)
: a dress with an abbreviated bodice usually exposing the shoulders, arms, and back

sun·dries \'sən-drēz\ *noun plural* [¹*sundry*] (1755)
: miscellaneous small articles, details, or items

sun·drops \'sən-,dräps\ *noun plural but singular or plural in construction* (1784)
: any of several day-flowering herbs (genus *Oenothera*) of the evening-primrose family

¹sun·dry \'sən-drē\ *adjective* [Middle English, different for each, from Old English *syndrig,* from *sundor* apart — more at SUNDER] (13th century)
: MISCELLANEOUS, VARIOUS ⟨*sundry* articles⟩

²sundry *pronoun, plural in construction* (15th century)
: an indeterminate number ⟨recommended for reading by all and *sundry* —Edward Huberman⟩

sun·fish \-,fish\ *noun* (1629)
1 : OCEAN SUNFISH
2 : any of numerous American freshwater bony fishes (family Centrarchidae, especially genus *Lepomis*) usually with a deep compressed body and metallic luster

Sunfish *trademark*
— used for a light sailboat that has one sail and is designed for use by no more than two people

sun·flow·er \-,flaú-(-ə)r\ *noun* (1597)
: any of a genus (*Helianthus*) of New World composite plants with large yellow-rayed flower heads bearing edible seeds that yield an edible oil

sung \'səŋ\ *past and past participle of* SING

Sung \'sùŋ\ *noun* [Chinese (Beijing) *Sòng*] (1673)
: a Chinese dynasty dated A.D. 960–1280 and marked by cultural refinement and achievements in philosophy, literature, and art
— **Sung** *adjective*

sun·glass \'sən-,glas\ *noun* (1804)
1 : a convex lens for converging the sun's rays
2 *plural* : glasses to protect the eyes from the sun

sung mass *noun* (1931)
: HIGH MASS

sun god *noun, often capitalized* (1592)
: a god that represents or personifies the sun in various religions

sun goddess *noun, often capitalized* (1861)
: a goddess that represents or personifies the sun in various religions

sun–grebe \'sən-,grēb\ *noun* (circa 1889)
: any of a small family (Heliornithidae) of African, Asian, and American tropical birds related to the rails

¹sunk \'səŋk\ *past and past participle of* SINK
²sunk *adjective* (1719)
1 : depressed in spirits
2 : DONE FOR, RUINED

sunk·en \'səŋ-kən\ *adjective* [Middle English *sonkyn,* past participle of *sinken* to sink] (14th century)
1 : SUBMERGED; *especially* : lying at the bottom of a body of water
2 a : HOLLOW, RECESSED ⟨*sunken* cheeks⟩ **b** : lying in a depression ⟨a *sunken* garden⟩ **c** : settled below the normal level **d** : constructed below the normal floor level ⟨a *sunken* living room⟩

sunk fence *noun* (circa 1771)
: a ditch with a retaining wall used to divide lands without defacing a landscape — called also *ha-ha*

sun·lamp \'sən-,lamp\ *noun* (1885)
: an electric lamp designed to emit radiation of wavelengths from ultraviolet to infrared

sun·less \-ləs\ *adjective* (1589)
: lacking sunshine : DARK, CHEERLESS

sun·light \-ˌlīt\ *noun* (13th century)
: the light of the sun : SUNSHINE

sun·lit \-ˌlit\ *adjective* (1822)
: lighted by or as if by the sun

sunn \'sən\ *noun* [Hindi *san,* from Sanskrit *śana*] (1774)
: an East Indian leguminous plant (*Crotalaria juncea*) with slender branches, simple leaves, and yellow flowers; *also* : its valuable fiber resembling hemp that is lighter and stronger than jute

sun·na *also* **sun·nah** \'sù(n)-ˌnə, 'sə(n)-\ *noun, often capitalized* [Arabic *sunnah*] (1728)
: the body of Islamic custom and practice based on Muhammad's words and deeds

sunn hemp *noun* (1849)
: SUNN

Sun·ni \'sù(n)-ˌnē\ *noun* [Arabic *sunnīy,* from *sunnah*] (1595)
1 : the Muslims of the branch of Islam that adheres to the orthodox tradition and acknowledges the first four caliphs as rightful successors of Muhammad — compare SHIA
2 : a Sunni Muslim
— **Sunni** *adjective*

Sun·nism \'sù(n)-ˌni-zəm\ *noun* (1892)
: the religious system or distinctive tenets of the Sunni

Sun·nite \-ˌnīt\ *noun* (1718)
: SUNNI 2
— **Sun·nite** \'sù(n)-ˌnīt\ *adjective*

sun·ny \'sə-nē\ *adjective* **sun·ni·er; -est** (14th century)
1 : marked by brilliant sunlight : full of sunshine
2 : CHEERFUL, OPTIMISTIC ⟨a *sunny* disposition⟩
3 : exposed to, brightened, or warmed by the sun ⟨a *sunny* room⟩
— **sun·ni·ly** \'sə-nᵊl-ē\ *adverb*
— **sun·ni·ness** \'sə-nē-nəs\ *noun*

sun·ny–side up \ˌsə-nē-ˌsīd-'əp\ *adjective* (circa 1901)
of an egg : fried on one side only

sun·porch \-ˌpōrch, -ˌpòrch\ *noun* (1918)
: a screened-in or glassed-in porch with a sunny exposure

sun·rise \'sən-ˌrīz\ *noun* (15th century)
1 : the apparent rising of the sun above the horizon; *also* : the accompanying atmospheric effects
2 : the time when the upper limb of the sun appears above the horizon as a result of the diurnal rotation of the earth

sun·roof \-ˌrüf, -ˌrùf\ *noun* (1952)
: a panel in an automobile roof that can be opened

sun·room \-ˌrüm, -ˌrùm\ *noun* (1917)
: a glass-enclosed porch or living room with a sunny exposure — called also *sun parlor*

sun·scald \-ˌskòld\ *noun* (1855)
: an injury of woody plants (as fruit or forest trees) characterized by localized death of the tissues and sometimes by cankers and caused when it occurs in the summer by the combined action of both the heat and light of the sun and in the winter by the combined action of sun and low temperature to produce freezing of bark and underlying tissues

sun·screen \-ˌskrēn\ *noun* (1738)
: a screen to protect against sun; *especially* : a substance (as para-aminobenzoic acid) used in suntan preparations to protect the skin from excessive ultraviolet radiation
— **sun·screen·ing** *adjective*

sun·seek·er \-ˌsē-kər\ *noun* (1954)
: a person who travels to an area of warmth and sun especially in winter

¹sun·set \-ˌset\ *noun* (14th century)
1 : the apparent descent of the sun below the horizon; *also* : the accompanying atmospheric effects

2 : the time when the upper limb of the sun disappears below the horizon as a result of the diurnal rotation of the earth
3 : a period of decline; *especially* : old age

²sunset *adjective* (1976)
: stipulating the periodic review of government agencies and programs in order to continue their existence ⟨*sunset* law⟩

sun·shade \'sən-ˌshād\ *noun* (1842)
: something used as a protection from the sun's rays: as **a** : PARASOL **b** : AWNING

¹sun·shine \-ˌshīn\ *noun* (13th century)
1 a : the sun's light or direct rays **b** : the warmth and light given by the sun's rays **c** : a spot or surface on which the sun's light shines
2 : something (as a person, condition, or influence) that radiates warmth, cheer, or happiness
— **sun·shiny** \-ˌshī-nē\ *adjective*

²sunshine *adjective* (1972)
: forbidding or restricting closed meetings of legislative or executive bodies and sometimes providing for public access to records ⟨*sunshine* law⟩

sun·spot \-ˌspät\ *noun* (1868)
: any of the dark spots that appear from time to time on the sun's surface and are usually visible only through a telescope

sun·stroke \-ˌstrōk\ *noun* (1851)
: heatstroke caused by direct exposure to the sun

sun·struck \-ˌstrək\ *adjective* (1794)
: affected or touched by the sun

sun·suit \-ˌsüt\ *noun* (1929)
: an outfit worn usually for sunbathing and play

sun·tan \-ˌtan\ *noun* (1904)
1 : a browning of the skin from exposure to the rays of the sun
2 *plural* : a tan-colored summer uniform
— **sun·tanned** \-ˌtand\ *adjective*

sun·up \-ˌəp\ *noun* (1712)
: SUNRISE

¹sun·ward \'sən-wərd\ *or* **sun·wards** \-wərdz\ *adverb* (1611)
: toward the sun

²sunward *adjective* (1769)
: facing the sun

sun·wise \'sən-ˌwīz\ *adverb* (circa 1864)
: CLOCKWISE

¹sup \'səp\ *verb* **supped; sup·ping** [Middle English *suppen,* from Old English *sūpan, suppan;* akin to Old High German *sūfan* to drink, sip, Old English *sopp* sop] (before 12th century)
transitive verb
: to take or drink in swallows or gulps
intransitive verb
chiefly dialect : to take food and especially liquid food into the mouth a little at a time

²sup *noun* (circa 1570)
: a mouthful especially of liquor or broth : SIP; *also* : a small quantity of liquid ⟨pour me just a *sup* of tea⟩

³sup *intransitive verb* **supped; sup·ping** [Middle English *soupen, suppen,* from Old French *souper,* from *soupe* sop, soup — more at SOUP] (14th century)
1 : to eat the evening meal
2 : to make one's supper — used with *on* or *off* ⟨*sup* on roast beef⟩

¹su·per \'sü-pər\ *adjective* [*super-*] (1837)
1 a — used as a generalized term of approval ⟨a *super* cook⟩ **b** : of high grade or quality
2 : very large or powerful ⟨a *super* atomic bomb⟩
3 : exhibiting the characteristics of its type to an extreme or excessive degree ⟨*super* secrecy⟩

²super *noun* (1838)
1 [by shortening] **a** : SUPERNUMERARY; *especially* : a supernumerary actor **b** : SUPERINTENDENT, SUPERVISOR; *especially* : the superintendent of an apartment building
2 [short for obsolete *superhive*] : a removable upper story of a beehive

3 [¹*super*] : a superfine grade or extra large size
4 [origin unknown] : a thin loosely woven open-meshed starched cotton fabric used especially for reinforcing books

³super *adverb* [*super-*] (1946)
1 : VERY, EXTREMELY ⟨a *super* fast car⟩
2 : to an excessive degree

super- *prefix* [Latin, over, above, in addition, from *super* over, above, on top of — more at OVER]
1 a (1) : over and above : higher in quantity, quality, or degree than : more than ⟨*super*human⟩ (2) : in addition : extra ⟨*super*tax⟩ **b** (1) : exceeding or so as to exceed a norm ⟨*super*heat⟩ (2) : in or to an extreme or excessive degree or intensity ⟨*super*subtle⟩ **c** : surpassing all or most others of its kind ⟨*super*highway⟩
2 a : situated or placed above, on, or at the top of ⟨*super*lunary⟩; *specifically* : situated on the dorsal side of **b** : next above or higher ⟨*super*tonic⟩
3 : having the (specified) ingredient present in a large or unusually large proportion ⟨*super*phosphate⟩
4 : constituting a more inclusive category than that specified ⟨*super*family⟩
5 : superior in status, title, or position ⟨*super*power⟩

su·per·ab·sor·bent	su·per·em·i·nent
su·per·achiev·er	su·per·em·i·nent·ly
su·per·ac·tiv·i·ty	su·per·ex·pen·sive
su·per·ad·di·tion	su·per·ex·press
su·per·ad·min·is·tra·tor	su·per·fan
su·per·agent	su·per·farm
su·per·am·bi·tious	su·per·fast
su·per·ath·lete	su·per·firm
su·per·bad	su·per·flack
su·per·bank	su·per·fund
su·per·bil·lion·aire	su·per·good
su·per·bitch	su·per·gov·ern·ment
su·per·board	su·per·growth
su·per·bomb	su·per·hard·en
su·per·bomb·er	su·per·heavy
su·per·bright	su·per·her·o·ine
su·per·bu·reau·crat	su·per·hit
su·per·cab·i·net	su·per·hot
su·per·car	su·per·hype
su·per·car·ri·er	su·per·in·su·lat·ed
su·per·cau·tious	su·per·in·tel·lec·tu·al
su·per·cen·ter	su·per·in·tel·li·gence
su·per·chic	su·per·in·tel·li·gent
su·per·church	su·per·in·ten·si·ty
su·per·civ·i·li·za·tion	su·per·jock
su·per·civ·i·lized	su·per·jum·bo
su·per·clean	su·per·large
su·per·club	su·per·law·yer
su·per·co·los·sal	su·per·light
su·per·com·fort·able	su·per·lob·by·ist
su·per·com·pet·i·tive	su·per·loy·al·ist
su·per·con·fi·dent	su·per·lux·u·ri·ous
su·per·con·glom·er·ate	su·per·lux·u·ry
su·per·con·ser·va·tive	su·per·ma·cho
su·per·con·ve·nient	su·per·ma·jor·i·ty
su·per·cop	su·per·male
su·per·cor·po·ra·tion	su·per·mas·cu·line
su·per·crim·i·nal	su·per·mas·sive
su·per·cute	su·per·mil·i·tant
su·per·de·luxe	su·per·mil·lion·aire
su·per·dip·lo·mat	su·per·mind
su·per·ef·fec·tive	su·per·min·is·ter
su·per·ef·fi·cien·cy	su·per·mod·el
su·per·ef·fi·cient	su·per·mod·ern
su·per·ego·ist	su·per·mom
su·per·elite	su·per·na·tion
su·per·em·i·nence	su·per·na·tion·al
	su·per·nu·tri·tion
	su·per·or·gan·ic
	su·per·or·gasm

su·per·pa·tri·ot
su·per·pa·tri·ot·ic
su·per·pa·tri·o·tism
su·per·per·son
su·per·per·son·al
su·per·phe·nom·e·non
su·per·pimp
su·per·plane
su·per·play·er
su·per·po·lite
su·per·port
su·per·pow·er·ful
su·per·pre·mi·um
su·per·pro
su·per·prof·it
su·per·qual·i·ty
su·per·real
su·per·race
su·per·re·al·ism
su·per·re·gion·al
su·per·rich
su·per·road
su·per·ro·man·tic
su·per·ro·man·ti·cism
su·per·safe
su·per·sale
su·per·sales·man
su·per·scale
su·per·school
su·per·scout
su·per·se·cre·cy
su·per·se·cret
su·per·sell
su·per·sell·er
su·per·sex·u·al·i·ty
su·per·sharp
su·per·show
su·per·sing·er
su·per·size
su·per·sized

su·per·sleuth
su·per·slick
su·per·smart
su·per·smooth
su·per·soft
su·per·so·phis·ti·cat·ed
su·per·spe·cial
su·per·spe·cial·ist
su·per·spe·cial·i·za·tion
su·per·spe·cial·ized
su·per·spec·ta·cle
su·per·spec·tac·u·lar
su·per·spec·u·la·tion
su·per·spy
su·per·state
su·per·sta·tion
su·per·stim·u·late
su·per·stock
su·per·stra·tum
su·per·strength
su·per·strike
su·per·strong
su·per·stud
su·per·sub·tle
su·per·sub·tle·ty
su·per·sur·geon
su·per·sweet
su·per·tank·er
su·per·ter·rif·ic
su·per·thick
su·per·thin
su·per·thril·ler
su·per·tight
su·per·vir·ile
su·per·vir·tu·o·so
su·per·wave
su·per·weap·on
su·per·wide
su·per·wife

su·per·a·ble \'sü-p(ə-)rə-bəl\ *adjective* [Latin *superabilis,* from *superare* to surmount — more at INSUPERABLE] (1629)
: capable of being overcome or conquered
— **su·per·a·ble·ness** *noun*
— **su·per·a·bly** \-blē\ *adverb*

su·per·abound \,sü-pər-ə-'baùnd\ *intransitive verb* [Middle English, from Late Latin *superabundare,* from Latin *super-* + *abundare* to abound] (14th century)
: to abound or prevail in greater measure or to excess

su·per·abun·dant \-'bən-dənt\ *adjective* [Middle English, from Late Latin *superabundant-, superabundans,* from present participle of *superabundare*] (15th century)
: more than ample : EXCESSIVE
— **su·per·abun·dance** \-dən(t)s\ *noun*
— **su·per·abun·dant·ly** *adverb*

su·per·add \,sü-pər-'ad\ *transitive verb* [Middle English, from Latin *superaddere,* from *super-* + *addere* to add] (15th century)
: to add especially in a way that compounds an effect ⟨the loss of his job was *superadded* to the loss of his house⟩

su·per·agen·cy \'sü-pər-,ā-jən(t)-sē\ *noun* (1943)
: a large complex governmental agency especially when set up to supervise other agencies

su·per·al·loy \'sü-pər-'a-,lòi, -ə-'lòi\ *noun* (1948)
: any of various high-strength often complex alloys resistant to high temperature

su·per·al·tern \,sü-pər-'òl-tərn\ *noun* [*super-* + sub*altern*] (1921)
: a universal proposition in traditional logic that is a ground for the immediate inference of a corresponding subaltern

su·per·an·nu·ate \,sü-pər-'an-yə-,wāt\ *verb* **-at·ed; -at·ing** [back-formation from *superannuated*] (1649)
transitive verb

1 : to make, declare, or prove obsolete or out-of-date
2 : to retire and pension because of age or infirmity
intransitive verb
1 : to become retired
2 : to become antiquated
— **su·per·an·nu·a·tion** \-,an-yə-'wā-shən\ *noun*

superannuated *adjective* [Medieval Latin *superannuatus,* past participle of *superannuari* to be too old, from Latin *super-* + *annus* year — more at ANNUAL] (1740)
: incapacitated or disqualified for active duty by advanced age

su·perb \sü-'pərb\ *adjective* [Latin *superbus* excellent, proud, from *super* above + *-bus* (akin to Old English *bēon* to be) — more at OVER, BE] (1549)
: marked to the highest degree by grandeur, excellence, brilliance, or competence
synonym see SPLENDID
— **su·perb·ly** *adverb*
— **su·perb·ness** *noun*

Su·per·ball \'sü-pər-,bòl\ *trademark*
— used for a toy rubber ball with a high bounce

su·per·block \-,bläk\ *noun* (1928)
: a very large commercial or residential block barred to through traffic, crossed by pedestrian walks and sometimes access roads, and often spotted with grassed malls

Super Bowl *noun* [from the *Super Bowl,* annual championship game of the National Football League] (1969)
: a contest or event that is the most important or prestigious of its kind ⟨the 2,500-mile, 24-day *Super Bowl* of bicycle racing —John Krakauer⟩

¹su·per·cal·en·der \'sü-pər-,ka-lən-dər\ *transitive verb* (1888)
: to process (paper) in a supercalender

²supercalender *noun* (1894)
: a stack of highly polished calender rolls used to give an extra finish to paper

su·per·car·go \,sü-pər-'kär-(,)gō, 'sü-pər-,\ *noun* [Spanish *sobrecargo,* from *sobre-* over (from Latin *super-*) + *cargo* cargo] (1697)
: an officer on a merchant ship in charge of the commercial concerns of the voyage

supercede *variant of* SUPERSEDE

su·per·charge \'sü-pər-,chärj\ *transitive verb* (1876)
1 : to charge greatly or excessively (as with vigor or tension)
2 : to supply a charge to the intake of (as an engine) at a pressure higher than that of the surrounding atmosphere
3 : PRESSURIZE 1
— **supercharge** *noun*

su·per·charg·er \-,chär-jər\ *noun* (1921)
: a device (as a blower or compressor) for pressurizing the cabin of an airplane or for increasing the volume air charge of an internal combustion engine over that which would normally be drawn in through the pumping action of the pistons

su·per·cil·i·ary \,sü-pər-'si-lē-,er-ē\ *adjective* [New Latin *superciliaris,* from Latin *supercilium*] (1732)
: of, relating to, or adjoining the eyebrow : SUPRAORBITAL

su·per·cil·ious \-'si-lē-əs, -'sil-yəs\ *adjective* [Latin *superciliosus,* from *supercilium* eyebrow, haughtiness, from *super-* + *-cilium* eyelid (akin to *celare* to hide) — more at HELL] (1598)
: coolly and patronizingly haughty ◇
synonym see PROUD
— **su·per·cil·ious·ly** *adverb*
— **su·per·cil·ious·ness** *noun*

su·per·city \'sü-pər-,si-tē\ *noun* (1925)
: MEGALOPOLIS

su·per·class \-,klas\ *noun* (circa 1891)

: a category in biological classification ranking below a phylum or division and above a class

su·per·clu·ster \'sü-pər-,kləs-tər\ *noun* (1926)
: a group of gravitationally associated clusters of galaxies

su·per·coil \-,kòi(ə)l\ *noun* (1965)
: SUPERHELIX
— **supercoil** *verb*

su·per·col·lid·er \-kə-,lī-dər\ *noun* (1984)
: a very large collider capable of accelerating particles to very high energies

su·per·com·put·er \-kəm-,pyü-tər\ *noun* (1968)
: a large very fast mainframe used especially for scientific computations

su·per·con·duct \,sü-pər-kən-'dəkt\ *intransitive verb* (1952)
: to exhibit superconductivity
— **su·per·con·duc·tive** \-'dək-tiv\ *adjective*
— **su·per·con·duc·tiv·i·ty** \-,kän-,dək-'ti-və-tē, -kən-\ *noun* (1913)
: a complete disappearance of electrical resistance in a substance especially at very low temperatures
— **su·per·con·duc·tor** \-kən-'dək-tər\ *noun*

su·per·con·ti·nent \'sü-pər-,kän-t°n-ənt, -,känt-nənt\ *noun* (1960)
: a former large continent from which other continents are held to have broken off and drifted away

su·per·cool \,sü-pər-'kül\ (1906)
transitive verb
: to cool below the freezing point without solidification or crystallization
intransitive verb
: to become supercooled

su·per·crit·i·cal \-'kri-ti-kəl\ *adjective* (1934)
: being or having a temperature above a critical temperature ⟨*supercritical* fluid⟩

su·per·cur·rent \'sü-pər-,kər-ənt, -,kə-rənt\ *noun* (1940)
: a current of electricity flowing in a superconductor

su·per–du·per \'sü-pər-,dü-pər\ *adjective* [reduplication of ¹*super*] (1940)
: of the greatest excellence, size, effectiveness, or impressiveness

su·per·ego \,sü-pər-'ē-(,)gō *also* -'e-(,)gō\ *noun* [New Latin, translation of German *Über-ich,* from *über* over + *ich* I] (1919)
: the one of the three divisions of the psyche in psychoanalytic theory that is only partly conscious, represents internalization of parental conscience and the rules of society, and functions to reward and punish through a system of moral attitudes, conscience, and a sense of guilt — compare EGO, ID

su·per·el·e·vate \-'e-lə-,vāt\ *transitive verb* (circa 1945)
: BANK 1c

su·per·el·e·va·tion \-,e-lə-'vā-shən\ *noun* (1889)

◇ WORD HISTORY
supercilious Anyone who has ever been on the receiving end of disapprovingly raised eyebrows will have no trouble understanding the etymology of *supercilious.* The Latin word for "eyebrow" was *supercilium,* formed from *super-* "above, over" and *cilium* "eyelid." The raising of the eyebrows to express an attitude of haughty disdain was evidently as well-known in ancient times as it is now, inasmuch as Latin *supercilium* was also used figuratively to mean "haughtiness, disdainful superiority." The derivative adjective in Latin was *superciliosus,* which was adopted in English as *supercilious* in the 16th century.

1 : the vertical distance between the heights of inner and outer edges of highway pavement or railroad rails
2 : additional elevation

su·per·er·o·ga·tion \,sü-pə-,rer-ə-'gā-shən\ *noun* [Medieval Latin *supererogation-, supererogatio,* from *supererogare* to perform beyond the call of duty, from Late Latin, to expend in addition, from Latin *super-* + *erogare* to expend public funds after asking the consent of the people, from *e-* + *rogare* to ask — more at RIGHT] (1526)
: the act of performing more than is required by duty, obligation, or need

su·per·er·og·a·to·ry \,sü-pə-ri-'rä-gə-,tōr-ē, -,tòr-\ *adjective* (1593)
1 : observed or performed to an extent not enjoined or required
2 : exceeding what is needed : SUPERFLUOUS

su·per·fam·i·ly \'sü-pər-,fam-lē, -'fa-mə-\ *noun* (circa 1890)
: a category of biological classification ranking below an order and above a family

su·per·fat·ted \-,fa-təd\ *adjective* (1891)
: containing extra oil or fat ⟨*superfatted* soap⟩

su·per·fe·cun·da·tion \,sü-pər-,fe-kən-'dā-shən, -,fē-\ *noun* (circa 1855)
1 : successive fertilization of two or more ova from the same ovulation especially by different sires
2 : fertilization at one time of a number of ova excessive for the species

su·per·fe·ta·tion \-,fē-'tā-shən\ *noun* [Medieval Latin *superfetation-, superfetatio,* from Latin *superfetare* to conceive while already pregnant, from *super-* + *fetus* act of bearing young, offspring — more at FETUS] (1603)
: a progressive accumulation or accretion reaching an extreme or excessive degree

su·per·fi·cial \,sü-pər-'fi-shəl\ *adjective* [Middle English, from Late Latin *superficialis,* from Latin *superficies*] (15th century)
1 a (1) : of or relating to a surface (2) : lying on, not penetrating below, or affecting only the surface ⟨*superficial* wounds⟩ **b** *British, of a unit of measure* : SQUARE ⟨*superficial* foot⟩
2 a : concerned only with the obvious or apparent : SHALLOW **b** : lying on the surface : EXTERNAL **c** : presenting only an appearance without substance or significance ☆
— **su·per·fi·cial·ly** \-'fi-sh(ə-)lē\ *adverb*

superficial fascia *noun* (1876)
: the thin layer of loose fatty connective tissue underlying the skin and binding it to the parts beneath — called also *hypodermis*

su·per·fi·ci·al·i·ty \,sü-pər-,fi-shē-'a-lə-tē\ *noun, plural* **-ties** (1530)
1 : the quality or state of being superficial
2 : something superficial

su·per·fi·cies \-'fi-(,)shēz, -shē-,ēz\ *noun, plural* **superficies** [Latin, surface, from *super-* + *facies* face, aspect — more at FACE] (1530)
1 : a surface of a body or a region of space
2 : the external aspects or appearance of a thing

su·per·fine \,sü-pər-'fīn\ *adjective* (1575)
1 : overly refined or nice
2 : of extremely fine size or texture ⟨*superfine* toothbrush bristles⟩ ⟨*superfine* sugar⟩
3 : of high quality or grade — used especially of merchandise

su·per·fix \'sü-pər-,fiks\ *noun* [*super-* + *-fix* (as in *prefix*)] (circa 1948)
: a morpheme consisting of a pattern of stress, intonation, or juncture features that are associated with the syllables of a word or phrase (as the distinctive stress patterns of the noun *subject* and the verb *subject*)

su·per·flu·id \,sü-pər-'flü-əd\ *noun* (1938)
: an unusual state of matter noted only in liquid helium cooled to near absolute zero and characterized by apparently frictionless flow (as through fine holes)
— **superfluid** *adjective*
— **su·per·flu·id·i·ty** \-,flü-'i-də-tē\ *noun*

su·per·flu·i·ty \,sü-pər-'flü-ə-tē\ *noun, plural* **-ties** [Middle English *superfluitee,* from Middle French *superfluité,* from Late Latin *superfluitat-, superfluitas,* from Latin *superfluus*] (14th century)
1 a : EXCESS, OVERSUPPLY **b** : something unnecessary or superfluous
2 : immoderate and especially luxurious living, habits, or desires

su·per·flu·ous \su̇-'pər-flü-əs\ *adjective* [Middle English, from Latin *superfluus,* literally, running over, from *superfluere* to overflow, from *super-* + *fluere* to flow — more at FLUID] (15th century)
1 a : exceeding what is sufficient or necessary **b** : not needed : UNNECESSARY
2 *obsolete* : marked by wastefulness : EXTRAVAGANT
— **su·per·flu·ous·ly** *adverb*
— **su·per·flu·ous·ness** *noun*

su·per·gene \'sü-pər-,jēn\ *noun* (circa 1949)
: a group of linked genes acting as an allelic unit especially when due to the suppression of crossing-over

su·per·gi·ant \-,jī-ənt\ *noun* (1926)
: something that is extremely large; *especially* : a star of very great intrinsic luminosity and enormous size
— **supergiant** *adjective*

su·per·glue *noun* (1946)
: a very strong glue; *specifically* : a glue whose chief ingredient is a cyanoacrylate that becomes adhesive through polymerization rather than evaporation of a solvent

su·per·graph·ics \-,gra-fiks\ *noun plural but singular or plural in construction* (1969)
: billboard-sized graphic shapes usually of bright color and simple design

su·per·grav·i·ty \,sü-pər-'gra-və-tē\ *noun* (1976)
: any of various theories in physics that are based on supersymmetry and attempt to unify general relativity and quantum theory and that state that the principle transmitter of gravity is the graviton

su·per·group \'sü-pər-,grüp\ *noun* (1968)
: a rock group made up of prominent former members of other rock groups; *also* : an extremely successful rock group

¹su·per·heat \,sü-pər-'hēt\ *transitive verb* (1859)
1 : to heat (a vapor not in contact with its own liquid) so as to cause to remain free from suspended liquid droplets ⟨*superheated* steam⟩
2 : to heat (a liquid) above the boiling point without converting into vapor
— **su·per·heat·er** *noun*

²su·per·heat \'sü-pər-,hēt, ,sü-pər-'\ *noun* (1884)
: the extra heat imparted to a vapor in superheating it from a dry and saturated condition; *also* : the corresponding rise of temperature

su·per·heat·ed \-,hē-təd, -'hē-\ *adjective* (1857)
: very hot; *also* : exceedingly emotional or intense

su·per·hea·vy·weight \,sü-pər-'he-vē-,wāt\ *noun* (1971)
: an athlete (as an Olympic weightlifter, boxer, or wrestler) who competes in the heaviest class or division

su·per·he·lix \'sü-pər-,hē-liks\ *noun* (1964)
: a helix (as of DNA) which has its axis arranged in a helical coil
— **su·per·he·li·cal** \,sü-pər-'he-li-kəl, -'hē-\ *adjective*

su·per·hero \-,hir-(,)ō, -,hē-(,)rō\ *noun* (1917)
: a fictional hero having extraordinary or superhuman powers; *also* : an exceptionally skillful or successful person

su·per·het·ero·dyne \,sü-pər-'he-tə-rə-,dīn, -'he-trə-\ *adjective* [*supersonic* + *heterodyne*] (1922)
: used in or being a radio receiver in which an incoming signal is mixed with a locally generated frequency to produce an ultrasonic signal

at a fixed frequency that is then rectified, amplified, and rectified again to reproduce the sound
— **superheterodyne** *noun*

su·per·high frequency \'sü-pər-,hī-\ *noun* (circa 1945)
: a radio frequency in the next to the highest range of the radio spectrum — see RADIO FREQUENCY table

su·per·high·way \,sü-pər-'hī-,wā, 'sü-pər-,\ *noun* (1925)
: a multilane highway (as an expressway or turnpike) designed for high-speed traffic

su·per·hu·man \,sü-pər-'hyü-mən, -'yü-\ *adjective* (1633)
1 : being above the human : DIVINE ⟨*superhuman* beings⟩
2 : exceeding normal human power, size, or capability : HERCULEAN ⟨a *superhuman* effort⟩; *also* : having such power, size, or capability
— **su·per·hu·man·i·ty** \-hyü-'ma-nə-tē, -yü-\ *noun*
— **su·per·hu·man·ly** \-'hyü-mən-lē, -'yü-\ *adverb*
— **su·per·hu·man·ness** \-mən-nəs\ *noun*

su·per·im·pose \,sü-pər-im-'pōz\ *transitive verb* (1794)
: to place or lay over or above something ⟨*superimposed* images⟩ ⟨*superimposed* a formula on the stories⟩
— **su·per·im·pos·able** \-'pō-zə-bəl\ *adjective*
— **su·per·im·po·si·tion** \-,im-pə-'zi-shən\ *noun*

su·per·in·cum·bent \-in-'kəm-bənt\ *adjective* [Latin *superincumbent-, superincumbens,* present participle of *superincumbere* to lie on top of, from *super-* + *incumbere* to lie down on — more at INCUMBENT] (1664)
: lying or resting and usually exerting pressure on something else
— **su·per·in·cum·bent·ly** *adverb*

su·per·in·di·vid·u·al \,sü-pər-,in-də-'vij-wəl, -'vi-jə-wəl, -'vi-jəl\ *adjective* (1916)
: of, relating to, or being an organism, entity, or complex of more than individual complexity or nature

su·per·in·duce \-in-'düs, -'dyüs\ *transitive verb* [Latin *superinducere,* from *super-* + *inducere* to lead in — more at INDUCE] (circa 1555)
1 : to introduce as an addition over or above something already existing
2 : BRING ON, INDUCE
— **su·per·in·duc·tion** \-'dək-shən\ *noun*

su·per·in·fec·tion \-in-'fek-shən\ *noun* (circa 1922)
: reinfection or a second infection with a microbial agent (as a bacterium, fungus, or virus)
— **su·per·in·fect** \-'fekt\ *transitive verb*

su·per·in·tend \,sü-p(ə-)rin-'tend, ,sü-pərn-\ *transitive verb* [Late Latin *superintendere,*

☆ SYNONYMS
Superficial, shallow, cursory mean lacking in depth or solidity. SUPERFICIAL implies a concern only with surface aspects or obvious features ⟨a *superficial* analysis of the problem⟩. SHALLOW is more generally derogatory in implying lack of depth in knowledge, reasoning, emotions, or character ⟨a light, *shallow,* and frivolous review⟩. CURSORY suggests a lack of thoroughness or a neglect of details ⟨gave the letter only a *cursory* reading⟩.

from Latin *super-* + *intendere* to stretch out, direct — more at INTEND] (circa 1615)
: to have or exercise the charge and oversight of : DIRECT

su·per·in·ten·dence \-'ten-dən(t)s\ *noun* (1603)
: the act or function of superintending or directing : SUPERVISION

su·per·in·ten·den·cy \-dən(t)-sē\ *noun, plural* **-cies** (1598)
: the office, post, or jurisdiction of a superintendent; *also* : SUPERINTENDENCE

su·per·in·ten·dent \-dənt\ *noun* [Medieval Latin *superintendent-, superintendens*, from Late Latin, present participle of *superintendere*] (1554)
: one who has executive oversight and charge
— **superintendent** *adjective*

¹**su·pe·ri·or** \su̇-'pir-ē-ər\ *adjective* [Middle English, from Middle French *superieur*, from Latin *superior*, comparative of *superus* upper, from *super* over, above — more at OVER] (14th century)
1 : situated higher up : UPPER
2 : of higher rank, quality, or importance
3 : courageously or serenely indifferent (as to something painful or disheartening)
4 a : greater in quantity or numbers ⟨escaped by *superior* speed⟩ **b** : excellent of its kind : BETTER ⟨her *superior* memory⟩
5 : being a superscript
6 a *of an animal structure* : situated above or anterior or dorsal to another and especially a corresponding part ⟨a *superior* artery⟩ **b** *of a plant structure* : situated above or near the top of another part: as (1) *of a calyx* : attached to and apparently arising from the ovary (2) *of an ovary* : free from the calyx or other floral envelope
7 : more comprehensive ⟨a genus is *superior* to a species⟩
8 : affecting or assuming an air of superiority : SUPERCILIOUS
— **su·pe·ri·or·ly** *adverb*

²**superior** *noun* (15th century)
1 : one who is above another in rank, station, or office; *especially* : the head of a religious house or order
2 : one that surpasses another in quality or merit
3 : SUPERSCRIPT

superior conjunction *noun* (1833)
: a conjunction in which the primary of an orbiting celestial body is aligned between the celestial body and an observer

superior court *noun* (1686)
1 : a court of general jurisdiction intermediate between the inferior courts (as a justice of the peace court) and the higher appellate courts
2 : a court with juries having original jurisdiction

superior general *noun, plural* **superiors general** (1775)
: the superior of a religious order or congregation

su·pe·ri·or·i·ty \su̇-,pir-ē-'ȯr-ə-tē, -,sü-, -'är-\ *noun, plural* **-ties** (15th century)
: the quality or state of being superior; *also* : a superior characteristic

superiority complex *noun* (circa 1924)
: an exaggerated opinion of oneself

superior planet *noun* (1583)
: a planet whose orbit lies outside that of the earth

superior vena cava *noun* (1901)
: the branch of the vena cava of a vertebrate that brings blood back from the head and anterior part of the body to the heart

su·per·ja·cent \,sü-pər-'jā-sᵊnt\ *adjective* [Latin *superjacent-, superjacens*, present participle of *superjacēre* to lie over or upon, from *super-* + *jacēre* to lie; akin to Latin *jacere* to throw — more at JET] (1610)
: lying above or upon : OVERLYING ⟨*superjacent* rocks⟩

su·per·jet \'sü-pər-,jet\ *noun* (1958)
: a very large jet airplane

¹**su·per·la·tive** \su̇-'pər-lə-tiv\ *adjective* [Middle English *superlatif*, from Middle French, from Late Latin *superlativus*, from Latin *superlatus* (past participle of *superferre* to carry over, raise high), from *super-* + *latus*, past participle of *ferre* to carry — more at TOLERATE, BEAR] (14th century)
1 : of, relating to, or constituting the degree of grammatical comparison that denotes an extreme or unsurpassed level or extent
2 a : surpassing all others : SUPREME **b** : of very high quality : EXCELLENT
3 : EXCESSIVE, EXAGGERATED
— **su·per·la·tive·ly** *adverb*
— **su·per·la·tive·ness** *noun*

²**superlative** *noun* (15th century)
1 a : the superlative degree of comparison in a language **b** : a superlative form of an adjective or adverb
2 : the superlative or utmost degree of something : ACME
3 : a superlative person or thing
4 : an admiring sometimes exaggerated expression especially of praise □

su·per·lin·er \'sü-pər-,lī-nər\ *noun* (1919)
: a fast luxurious passenger liner of great size

su·per·lu·na·ry \,sü-pər-'lü-nə-rē\ *or* **su·per·lu·nar** \-nər, -,när\ *adjective* [Latin *super-* + *luna* moon — more at LUNAR] (1614)
archaic : being above the moon : CELESTIAL

su·per·man \'sü-pər-,man\ *noun* [translation of German *Übermensch*, from *über* over, super- + *Mensch* man] (1903)
1 : a superior man that according to Nietzsche has learned to forgo fleeting pleasures and attain happiness and dominance through the exercise of creative power
2 : a person of extraordinary or superhuman power or achievements

su·per·mar·ket \-,mär-kət\ *noun, often attributive* (1933)
1 : a self-service retail market selling especially foods and household merchandise
2 : something resembling a supermarket especially in the variety or volume of its goods or services

su·per·mi·cro \-,mī-(,)krō\ *noun* (1982)
: a very fast and powerful microcomputer

su·per·mini·com·put·er \-'mi-nē-kəm-,pyü-tər\ *noun* (1980)
: a very fast and powerful minicomputer — called also *supermini*

su·per·nal \su̇-'pər-nᵊl\ *adjective* [Middle English, from Middle French, from Latin *supernus*, from *super* over, above — more at OVER] (15th century)
1 a : being or coming from on high **b** : HEAVENLY, ETHEREAL ⟨*supernal* melodies⟩ **c** : superlatively good ⟨*supernal* trumpet playing⟩
2 : located in or belonging to the sky
— **su·per·nal·ly** \-nᵊl-ē\ *adverb*

su·per·na·tant \,sü-pər-'nā-tᵊnt\ *noun* [Latin *supernatant-, supernatans*, present participle of *supernatare* to float, from *super-* + *natare* to swim — more at NATANT] (1922)
: the usually clear liquid overlying material deposited by settling, precipitation, or centrifugation
— **supernatant** *adjective*

su·per·nat·u·ral \,sü-pər-'na-chə-rəl, -'nach-rəl\ *adjective* [Medieval Latin *supernaturalis*, from Latin *super-* + *natura* nature] (15th century)
1 : of or relating to an order of existence beyond the visible observable universe; *especially* : of or relating to God or a god, demigod, spirit, or devil
2 a : departing from what is usual or normal especially so as to appear to transcend the laws of nature **b** : attributed to an invisible agent (as a ghost or spirit)
— **supernatural** *noun*
— **su·per·nat·u·ral·ly** \-'na-chər-ə-lē, -'nach-rə-, -'na-chər-lē\ *adverb*
— **su·per·nat·u·ral·ness** *noun*

su·per·nat·u·ral·ism \,sü-pər-'na-chə-rə-,li-zəm, -'nach-rə-\ *noun* (1799)
1 : the quality or state of being supernatural
2 : belief in a supernatural power and order of existence
— **su·per·nat·u·ral·ist** \-list\ *noun or adjective*
— **su·per·nat·u·ral·is·tic** \-,na-chə-rə-'lis-tik, -,nach-rə-\ *adjective*

su·per·na·ture \'sü-pər-,nā-chər\ *noun* [back-formation from *supernatural*] (1844)
: the realm of the supernatural

su·per·nor·mal \,sü-pər-'nȯr-məl\ *adjective* (1868)
1 : exceeding the normal or average
2 : being beyond normal human powers : PARANORMAL
— **su·per·nor·mal·i·ty** \-nȯr-'ma-lə-tē\ *noun*
— **su·per·nor·mal·ly** \-'nȯr-mə-lē\ *adverb*

su·per·no·va \,sü-pər-'nō-və\ *noun* [New Latin] (1926)
1 : the explosion of a very large star in which the star may reach a maximum intrinsic luminosity one billion times that of the sun
2 : one that explodes into prominence or popularity; *also* : SUPERSTAR

¹**su·per·nu·mer·ary** \,sü-pər-'nü-mə-,rer-ē, -'nyü-, -mə-rē; -'n(y)üm-rē\ *adjective* [Late Latin *supernumerarius*, from Latin *super-* + *numerus* number] (1605)
1 a : exceeding the usual, stated, or prescribed number ⟨a *supernumerary* tooth⟩ **b** : not enumerated among the regular components of a group and especially of a military organization
2 : exceeding what is necessary, required, or desired
3 : more numerous

²**supernumerary** *noun, plural* **-ar·ies** (1639)
1 : a supernumerary person or thing
2 : an actor employed to play a walk-on

su·per·or·der \'sü-pər-,ȯr-dər\ *noun* (circa 1890)
: a category of biological classification ranking below a class and above an order

su·per·or·di·nate \,sü-pər-'ȯrd-nət, -'ȯr-dᵊn-ət, -'ȯr-dᵊn-,āt\ *adjective* [*super-* + *subordinate*] (1620)
: superior in rank, class, or status

□ USAGE
superlative "Miss Fletcher and I were very thick, but I am the thinnest of the two," wrote Jane Austen in 1796, unmindful of having committed one of the newest improprieties of the grammarians, using the superlative of two. Just how this subject became a staple of handbooks and schoolbooks for two centuries is not entirely clear, for two of the earliest and most widely copied commentators found it a trivial matter. However, one man's preference became another man's rule soon enough, and we can still find warnings against using the superlative of two in present-day handbooks for student writers. Jane Austen's little joke is perfectly understandable even though she used the superlative, and it does not become any more understandable (or any funnier) if the comparative is substituted for the superlative. Thus the rule serves no useful purpose. Nor has it reflected real usage accurately; examples of the superlative used by two abound in literature from Shakespeare to the present. When a rule serves no purpose other than to divide those who observe it from those who don't, it has little authority.

su·per·or·gan·ism \-'ȯr-gə-,ni-zəm\ *noun* (circa 1899)
: an organized society (as of a social insect) that functions as an organic whole

su·per·ovu·la·tion \-,äv-yə-'lā-shən, -,ōv-\ *noun* (1927)
: production of exceptional numbers of ova at one time
— **su·per·ovu·late** \-'äv-yə-,lāt, -'ōv-\ *verb*

su·per·ox·ide \-'äk-,sīd\ *noun* (circa 1847)
: the univalent anion O^-_2 or a compound containing it ⟨potassium *superoxide* KO_2⟩

superoxide dis·mut·ase \-dis-'myü-,tās, -,tāz\ *noun* [*dismutation* (simultaneous oxidation and reduction) + *-ase*] (1969)
: a metal-containing enzyme that reduces potentially harmful free radicals of oxygen formed during normal metabolic cell processes to oxygen and hydrogen peroxide

su·per·par·a·sit·ism \,sü-pər-'par-ə-,sī-,ti-zəm, -sə-\ *noun* (circa 1899)
: parasitization of a host by more than one parasitic individual usually of one kind — used especially of parasitic insects

su·per·phos·phate \,sü-pər-'fäs-,fāt\ *noun* (1797)
1 : an acid phosphate
2 : a soluble mixture of phosphates used as fertilizer and made from insoluble mineral phosphates by treatment with sulfuric acid

su·per·phys·i·cal \-'fi-zi-kəl\ *adjective* (circa 1603)
: being above or beyond the physical world or explanation on physical principles

su·per·plas·tic \-'plas-tik\ *adjective* (1947)
1 : capable of plastic deformation under low stress at an elevated temperature — used of metals and alloys
2 : of or relating to superplastic materials ⟨*superplastic* forming⟩
— **su·per·plas·tic·i·ty** \-pla-'sti-sə-tē\ *noun*

su·per·pose \,sü-pər-'pōz\ *transitive verb* **-posed; -pos·ing** [probably from French *superposer*, back-formation from *superposition*, from Late Latin *superposition-, superpositio*, from Latin *superponere* to superpose, from *super-* + *ponere* to place — more at POSITION] (1823)
1 : to place or lay over or above whether in or not in contact : SUPERIMPOSE
2 : to !ay (as a geometric figure) upon another so as to make all like parts coincide
— **su·per·pos·able** \-'pō-zə-bəl\ *adjective*
— **su·per·po·si·tion** \-pə-'zi-shən\ *noun*

su·per·posed \-'pōzd\ *adjective* (1823)
: situated vertically over another layer or part

su·per·pow·er \'sü-,pər-,paù(-ə)r\ *noun* (1922)
1 : excessive or superior power
2 a : an extremely powerful nation; *specifically* : one of a very few dominant states in an era when the world is divided politically into these states and their satellites **b** : an international governing body able to enforce its will upon the most powerful states
— **su·per·pow·ered** \-,paù(-ə)rd\ *adjective*

su·per·sat·u·rate \,sü-pər-'sa-chə-,rāt\ *transitive verb* (1788)
: to add to (a solution) beyond saturation

su·per·sat·u·rat·ed *adjective* (1854)
: containing an amount of a substance greater than that required for saturation as a result of having been cooled from a higher temperature to a temperature below that at which saturation occurs ⟨a *supersaturated* solution⟩ ⟨air *supersaturated* with water vapor⟩

su·per·sat·u·ra·tion \-,sa-chə-'rā-shən\ *noun* (1836)
: the state of being supersaturated

su·per·scribe \'sü-pər-,skrīb, ,sü-pər-\ *transitive verb* **-scribed; -scrib·ing** [Middle English, from Latin *superscribere*, from *super-* + *scribere* to write — more at SCRIBE] (15th century)
1 : to write (as a name or address) on the outside or cover of : ADDRESS
2 : to write or engrave on the top or outside

su·per·script \'sü-pər-,skript\ *noun* [Latin *superscriptus*, past participle of *superscribere*] (1901)
: a distinguishing symbol (as a numeral or letter) written immediately above or above and to the right or left of another character
— **superscript** *adjective*

su·per·scrip·tion \,sü-pər-'skrip-shən\ *noun* [Middle English, from Middle French, from Late Latin *superscription-, superscriptio*, from Latin *superscribere*] (14th century)
1 : something written or engraved on the surface of, outside, or above something else : INSCRIPTION; *also* : ADDRESS
2 : the act of superscribing

su·per·sede \,sü-pər-'sēd\ *transitive verb* **-sed·ed; -sed·ing** [Middle English *superceden*, from Middle French *superseder* to refrain from, from Latin *supersedēre* to be superior to, refrain from, from *super-* + *sedēre* to sit — more at SIT] (15th century)
1 a : to cause to be set aside **b** : to force out of use as inferior
2 : to take the place, room, or position of
3 : to displace in favor of another : SUPPLANT
synonym see REPLACE
— **su·per·sed·er** *noun*

su·per·se·de·as \-'sē-dē-əs\ *noun, plural* **su·persedeas** [Middle English, from Latin, you shall refrain, from *supersedēre*] (14th century)
1 : a common-law writ commanding a stay of legal proceedings that is issued under various conditions and especially to stay an officer from proceeding under another writ
2 : an order staying proceedings of an inferior court

su·per·se·dure \-'sē-jər\ *noun* (1788)
: the act or process of superseding; *especially* : the replacement of an old or inferior queen bee by a young or superior queen

su·per·sen·si·ble \,sü-pər-'sen(t)-sə-bəl\ *adjective* (1798)
: being above or beyond that which is apparent to the senses : SPIRITUAL

su·per·sen·si·tive \-'sen(t)-sə-tiv, -'sen(t)-stiv\ *adjective* (1839)
: HYPERSENSITIVE ⟨a *supersensitive* palate⟩
— **su·per·sen·si·tive·ly** *adverb*
— **su·per·sen·si·tiv·i·ty** \-,sen(t)-sə-'ti-və-tē\ *noun*

su·per·sen·so·ry \-'sen(t)-sə-rē, -'sen(t)s-rē\ *adjective* (1883)
: SUPERSENSIBLE

su·per·ser·vice·able \-'sər-və-sə-bəl\ *adjective* (1605)
: offering unwanted services : OFFICIOUS

su·per·ses·sion \,sü-pər-'se-shən\ *noun* [Medieval Latin *supersession-, supersessio*, from Latin *supersedēre*] (1790)
: the act of superseding : the state of being superseded

¹su·per·son·ic \-'sä-nik\ *adjective* [Latin *super-* + *sonus* sound — more at SOUND] (1919)
1 : ULTRASONIC
2 : of, being, or relating to speeds from one to five times the speed of sound in air — compare SONIC
3 : moving, capable of moving, or utilizing air currents moving at supersonic speed
4 : relating to supersonic airplanes or missiles ⟨the *supersonic* age⟩
— **su·per·son·i·cal·ly** \-ni-k(ə-)lē\ *adverb*

²supersonic *noun* (circa 1924)
1 : a supersonic wave or frequency
2 : a supersonic airplane

su·per·son·ics \,sü-pər-'sä-niks\ *noun plural but singular in construction* (1925)
: the science of supersonic phenomena

supersonic transport *noun* (1961)
: a supersonic transport airplane

su·per·star \'sü-pər-,stär\ *noun* (1924)
1 : a star (as in sports or the movies) who is considered extremely talented, has great public appeal, and can usually command a high salary
2 : one that is very prominent or is a prime attraction
— **su·per·star·dom** \-dəm\ *noun*

su·per·sti·tion \,sü-pər-'sti-shən\ *noun* [Middle English *supersticion*, from Middle French, from Latin *superstition-, superstitio*, from *superstit-, superstes* standing over (as witness or survivor), from *super-* + *stare* to stand — more at STAND] (13th century)
1 a : a belief or practice resulting from ignorance, fear of the unknown, trust in magic or chance, or a false conception of causation **b** : an irrational abject attitude of mind toward the supernatural, nature, or God resulting from superstition
2 : a notion maintained despite evidence to the contrary

su·per·sti·tious \-'sti-shəs\ *adjective* [Middle English *supersticious*, from Middle French *supersticieux*, from Latin *superstitiosus*, from *superstitio*] (14th century)
: of, relating to, or swayed by superstition
— **su·per·sti·tious·ly** *adverb*

su·per·store \'sü-pər-,stȯr, -,stȯr\ *noun* (1943)
: a very large store offering a wide variety of merchandise for sale

su·per·string \-,striŋ\ *noun* (1983)
: a hypothetical string obeying the rules of supersymmetry whose vibrations manifest themselves as particles existing in ten dimensions of which only four are evident

su·per·struc·ture \-,strək-chər\ *noun* (1641)
1 a : an entity, concept, or complex based on a more fundamental one **b** : social institutions (as the law or politics) that are in Marxist theory erected upon the economic base
2 : a structure built as a vertical extension of something else: as **a** : all of a building above the basement **b** : the structural part of a ship above the main deck
— **su·per·struc·tur·al** \,sü-pər-'strək-chə-rəl, -'strək-shrəl\ *adjective*

su·per·sub·stan·tial \,sü-pər-səb-'stan(t)-shəl\ *adjective* [Late Latin *supersubstantialis*, from Latin *super-* + *substantia* substance] (1534)
: being above material substance : of a transcending substance

su·per·sym·me·try \-'si-mə-trē\ *noun* (1974)
: the correspondence between fermions and bosons of identical mass that is postulated to have existed during the opening moments of the big bang and that relates gravity to the other forces of nature
— **su·per·sym·met·ric** \-sə-'me-trik\ *adjective*

su·per·sys·tem \'sü-pər-,sis-təm\ *noun* (circa 1928)
: a system that is made up of systems

su·per·tax \-,taks\ *noun* (1906)
: SURTAX

su·per·ton·ic \,sü-pər-'tä-nik\ *noun* (1806)
: the second tone of a diatonic scale

su·per·vene \,sü-pər-'vēn\ *intransitive verb* **-vened; -ven·ing** [Latin *supervenire*, from *super-* + *venire* to come — more at COME] (circa 1648)

: to follow or result as an additional, adventitious, or unlooked-for development

synonym see FOLLOW

— **su·per·ven·tion** \-'ven(t)-shən\ *noun*

su·per·ve·nient \-'vē-nyənt\ *adjective* [Latin *supervenient-, superveniens,* present participle of *supervenire*] (1594)
: coming or occurring as something additional, extraneous, or unexpected

su·per·vise \'sü-pər-ˌvīz\ *transitive verb* **-vised; -vis·ing** [Medieval Latin *supervisus,* past participle of *supervidēre,* from Latin *super-* + *vidēre* to see — more at WIT] (1588)
: SUPERINTEND, OVERSEE

su·per·vi·sion \ˌsü-pər-'vi-zhən\ *noun* (1640)
: the action, process, or occupation of supervising; *especially* : a critical watching and directing (as of activities or a course of action)

su·per·vi·sor \'sü-pər-ˌvī-zər\ *noun* (15th century)
: one that supervises; *especially* : an administrative officer in charge of a business, government, or school unit or operation

— **su·per·vi·so·ry** \ˌsü-pər-'vī-zə-rē, -'vīz-rē\ *adjective*

su·per·wom·an \'sü-pər-ˌwu̇-mən\ *noun* (1906)
: an exceptional woman; *especially* : a woman who succeeds in having a career and raising a family

su·pi·nate \'sü-pə-ˌnāt\ *verb* **-nat·ed; -nat·ing** [Latin *supinatus,* past participle of *supinare* to lay backward or on the back, from *supinus*] (1831)
transitive verb
: to cause to undergo supination
intransitive verb
: to undergo supination

su·pi·na·tion \ˌsü-pə-'nā-shən\ *noun* (1666)
1 : rotation of the forearm and hand so that the palm faces forward or upward and the radius lies parallel to the ulna; *also* : a corresponding movement of the foot and leg
2 : the position resulting from supination

su·pi·na·tor \'sü-pə-ˌnā-tər\ *noun* [New Latin, from Latin *supinare*] (1615)
: a muscle that produces the motion of supination

¹**su·pine** \'sü-ˌpīn\ *noun* [Middle English *supyn,* from Late Latin *supinum,* from Latin, neuter of *supinus,* adjective] (15th century)
1 : a Latin verbal noun having an accusative of purpose in *-um* and an ablative of specification in *-u*
2 : an English infinitive with *to*

²**su·pine** \su̇-'pīn, attributive also 'sü-ˌpīn\ *adjective* [Middle English *supyne,* from Latin *supinus;* akin to Latin *sub* under, up to — more at UP] (15th century)
1 a : lying on the back or with the face upward **b** : marked by supination
2 : exhibiting indolent or apathetic inertia or passivity; *especially* : mentally or morally slack
3 *archaic* : leaning or sloping backward

synonym see PRONE, INACTIVE
usage see PRONE

— **su·pine·ly** \su̇-'pīn-lē\ *adverb*
— **su·pine·ness** \-'pīn-nəs\ *noun*

sup·per \'sə-pər\ *noun* [Middle English, from Old French *souper,* from *souper* to sup — more at SUP] (13th century)
1 a : the evening meal especially when dinner is taken at midday **b** : a social affair featuring a supper; *especially* : an evening social especially for raising funds ⟨a church *supper*⟩
2 : the food served as a supper ⟨eat your *supper*⟩
3 : a light meal served late in the evening

supper club *noun* (1925)
: NIGHTCLUB

sup·plant \sə-'plant\ *transitive verb* [Middle English, from Middle French *supplanter,* from Latin *supplantare* to overthrow by tripping up,

from *sub-* + *planta* sole of the foot — more at PLACE] (14th century)
1 : to supersede (another) especially by force or treachery
2 a (1) *obsolete* : UPROOT (2) : to eradicate and supply a substitute for ⟨efforts to *supplant* the vernacular⟩ **b** : to take the place of and serve as a substitute for especially by reason of superior excellence or power

synonym see REPLACE

— **sup·plan·ta·tion** \ˌ(ˌ)sə-ˌplan-'tā-shən\ *noun*
— **sup·plant·er** \sə-'plan-tər\ *noun*

¹**sup·ple** \'sə-pəl *also* 'sü-\ *adjective* **sup·pler** \-p(ə-)lər\; **sup·plest** \-p(ə-)ləst\ [Middle English *souple,* from Middle French, from Latin *supplic-, supplex* entreating for mercy, suppliant, perhaps from *sub-* + *-plic-* (akin to *plicare* to fold) — more at PLY] (14th century)
1 a : compliant often to the point of obsequiousness **b** : readily adaptable or responsive to new situations
2 a : capable of being bent or folded without creases, cracks, or breaks : PLIANT ⟨*supple* leather⟩ **b** : able to perform bending or twisting movements with ease and grace : LIMBER ⟨*supple* legs of a dancer⟩ **c** : easy and fluent without stiffness or awkwardness ⟨sang with a lively, *supple* voice —Douglas Watt⟩

synonym see ELASTIC

— **sup·ple·ly** \-pə(l)-lē\ *or* **sup·ply** \-p(ə-)lē\ *adverb*
— **sup·ple·ness** \-pəl-nəs\ *noun*

²**supple** *verb* **sup·pled; sup·pling** \-p(ə-)liŋ\ (14th century)
transitive verb
1 : to make pacific or complaisant ⟨*supple* the tempers of your race —Laurence Sterne⟩
2 : to alleviate with a salve
3 : to make flexible or pliant
intransitive verb
: to become soft and pliant

sup·ple·jack \'sə-pəl-ˌjak *also* 'sü-\ *noun* (circa 1725)
: any of various woody climbers having tough pliant stems; *especially* : a southern U.S. vine (*Berchemia scandens*) of the buckthorn family

¹**sup·ple·ment** \'sə-plə-mənt\ *noun* [Middle English, from Latin *supplementum,* from *supplēre* to fill up, complete — more at SUPPLY] (14th century)
1 : something that completes or makes an addition ⟨dietary *supplements*⟩
2 : a part added to or issued as a continuation of a book or periodical to correct errors or make additions
3 : an angle or arc that when added to a given angle or arc equals 180°

²**sup·ple·ment** \'sə-plə-ˌment\ *transitive verb* (1829)
: to add or serve as a supplement to ⟨does odd jobs to *supplement* his income⟩

— **sup·ple·men·ta·tion** \ˌsə-plə-ˌmen-'tā-shən, -mən-\ *noun*
— **sup·ple·ment·er** \'sə-plə-ˌmen-tər\ *noun*

sup·ple·men·tal \ˌsə-plə-'men-t°l\ *adjective* (1605)
1 : serving to supplement
2 : NONSCHEDULED ⟨a *supplemental* airline⟩
— **supplemental** *noun*

sup·ple·men·ta·ry \ˌsə-plə-'men-tə-rē, -'men-trē\ *adjective* (1667)
1 : added or serving as a supplement : ADDITIONAL ⟨*supplementary* reading⟩
2 : being or relating to a supplement or a supplementary angle

supplementary angle *noun* (circa 1924)
: one of two angles or arcs whose sum is 180° — usually used in plural

sup·ple·tion \sə-'plē-shən\ *noun* [Medieval Latin *suppletion-, suppletio* act of supplementing, from Latin *supplēre*] (1914)

: the occurrence of phonemically unrelated allomorphs of the same morpheme (as *went* as the past tense of *go* or *better* as the comparative form of *good*)

— **sup·ple·tive** \sə-'plē-tiv, 'sə-plə-\ *adjective*

sup·ple·to·ry \sə-'plē-tə-rē; 'sə-plə-ˌtōr-ē, -ˌtòr-\ *adjective* [Latin *supplēre*] (1628)
: supplying deficiencies : SUPPLEMENTARY

sup·pli·ance \'sə-plē-ən(t)s\ *noun* (circa 1611)
: ENTREATY, SUPPLICATION

¹**sup·pli·ant** \-ənt\ *noun* [Middle English, from Middle French, from present participle of *supplier* to supplicate, from Latin *supplicare*] (15th century)
: one who supplicates

²**suppliant** *adjective* [Middle French, present participle] (circa 1586)
1 : humbly imploring : ENTREATING ⟨a *suppliant* sinner seeking forgiveness —O. J. Baab⟩
2 : expressing supplication ⟨uplifted to the heavens . . . *suppliant* arms —William Styron⟩

— **sup·pli·ant·ly** *adverb*

¹**sup·pli·cant** \'sə-pli-kənt\ *adjective* (1597)
: SUPPLIANT

²**supplicant** *noun* (1597)
: SUPPLIANT

sup·pli·cate \'sə-plə-ˌkāt\ *verb* **-cat·ed; -cat·ing** [Middle English, from Latin *supplicatus,* past participle of *supplicare,* from *supplic-, supplex* suppliant — more at SUPPLE] (15th century)
intransitive verb
: to make a humble entreaty; *especially* : to pray to God
transitive verb
1 : to ask humbly and earnestly of
2 : to ask for earnestly and humbly

synonym see BEG

— **sup·pli·ca·tion** \ˌsə-plə-'kā-shən\ *noun*

sup·pli·ca·to·ry \'sə-pli-kə-ˌtōr-ē, -ˌtòr-\ *adjective* (15th century)
: expressing supplication : SUPPLIANT ⟨a *supplicatory* prayer⟩

¹**sup·ply** \sə-'plī\ *verb* **sup·plied; sup·ply·ing** [Middle English *supplien,* from Middle French *soupleier,* from Latin *supplēre* to fill up, supplement, supply, from *sub-* up + *plēre* to fill — more at SUB-, FULL] (14th century)
transitive verb
1 : to add as a supplement
2 a : to provide for : SATISFY ⟨laws by which the material wants of man are *supplied* —Bulletin of Bates College⟩ **b** : to make available for use : PROVIDE ⟨*supplied* the necessary funds⟩ **c** : to satisfy the needs or wishes of **d** : to furnish (organs, tissues, or cells) with a vital element (as blood or nerve fibers)
3 : to substitute for another in; *specifically* : to serve as a supply in (a church or pulpit)
intransitive verb
: to serve as a supply or substitute

— **sup·pli·er** \-'plī(-ə)r\ *noun*

²**supply** *noun, plural* **supplies** (15th century)
1 *obsolete* : ASSISTANCE, SUCCOR
2 a *obsolete* : REINFORCEMENTS — often used in plural **b** : a clergyman filling a vacant pulpit temporarily **c** : the quantity or amount (as of a commodity) needed or available ⟨beer was in short *supply* in that hot weather —Nevil Shute⟩ **d** : PROVISIONS, STORES — usually used in plural
3 : the act or process of filling a want or need ⟨engaged in the *supply* of raw materials to industry⟩
4 : the quantities of goods or services offered for sale at a particular time or at one price
5 : something that maintains or constitutes a supply

sup·ply–side \sə-'plī-ˌsīd\ *adjective* (1976)
: of, relating to, or being an economic theory that reduction of tax rates encourages more

earnings, savings, and investment and thereby expands economic activity and the total taxable national income
— **sup·ply–sid·er** \-'sī-dər\ *noun*

¹**sup·port** \sə-'pōrt, -'pȯrt\ *transitive verb* [Middle English, from Middle French *supporter,* from Late Latin *supportare,* from Latin, to carry, from *sub-* + *portare* to carry — more at FARE] (14th century)
1 : to endure bravely or quietly **:** BEAR
2 a (1) **:** to promote the interests or cause of (2) **:** to uphold or defend as valid or right **:** ADVOCATE (3) **:** to argue or vote for **b** (1) **:** ASSIST, HELP (2) **:** to act with ⟨a star actor⟩ (3) **:** to bid in bridge so as to show support for **c :** to provide with substantiation **:** CORROBORATE ⟨*support* an alibi⟩
3 a : to pay the costs of **:** MAINTAIN **b :** to provide a basis for the existence or subsistence of ⟨the island could probably *support* three —A. B. C. Whipple⟩
4 a : to hold up or serve as a foundation or prop for **b :** to maintain (a price) at a desired level by purchases or loans; *also :* to maintain the price of by purchases or loans
5 : to keep from fainting, yielding, or losing courage **:** COMFORT
6 : to keep (something) going ☆
— **sup·port·abil·i·ty** \sə-ˌpȯr-tə-'bi-lə-tē, -ˌpȯr-\ *noun*
— **sup·port·able** \-'pȯr-tə-bəl, -'pȯr-\ *adjective*
— **sup·port·ive** \-'pōr-tiv, -'pȯr-\ *adjective*
— **sup·port·ive·ness** \-nəs\ *noun*

²**support** *noun* (14th century)
1 : the act or process of supporting **:** the condition of being supported
2 : one that supports
3 : sufficient strength in a suit bid by one's partner in bridge to justify raising the suit

sup·port·er *noun* (15th century)
: one that supports or acts as a support: as **a :** ADHERENT, PARTISAN **b :** one of two figures (as of men or animals) placed one on each side of an escutcheon and exterior to it **c :** GARTER 1 **d :** ATHLETIC SUPPORTER

support group *noun* (1969)
: a group of people with common experiences and concerns who provide emotional and moral support for one another

support hose *noun* (1963)
: elastic stockings

support level *noun* (1953)
: a price level on a declining market at which a security resists further decline due to increased attractiveness to traders and investors — called also *support area*

support system *noun* (1980)
: a network of people who provide an individual with practical or emotional support

sup·pos·able \sə-'pō-zə-bəl\ *adjective* (1643)
: capable of being supposed **:** CONCEIVABLE
— **sup·pos·ably** \-blē\ *adverb*

sup·pos·al \-'pō-zəl\ *noun* (14th century)
1 : the act or process of supposing
2 : something supposed **:** HYPOTHESIS, SUPPOSITION

sup·pose \sə-'pōz, oftenest after "*I*" 'spōz\ *verb* **sup·posed; sup·pos·ing** [Middle English, from Middle French *supposer,* from Medieval Latin *supponere* (perfect indicative *supposui*), from Latin, to put under, substitute, from *sub-* + *ponere* to put — more at POSITION] (14th century)
transitive verb
1 a : to lay down tentatively as a hypothesis, assumption, or proposal ⟨*suppose* a fire broke out⟩ ⟨*suppose* you bring the salad⟩ **b** (1) **:** to hold as an opinion **:** BELIEVE ⟨they *supposed* they were early⟩ (2) **:** to think probable or in keeping with the facts ⟨seems reasonable to *suppose* that he would profit⟩
2 a : CONCEIVE, IMAGINE **b :** to have a suspicion of

3 : PRESUPPOSE
intransitive verb
: CONJECTURE, OPINE

sup·posed \sə-'pōzd; *1b & 2a usually* -'pō-zəd, *3 & 4 often* -'pōst\ *adjective* (1566)
1 a : PRETENDED ⟨twelve hours are *supposed* to elapse between Acts I and II —A. S. Sullivan⟩ **b :** ALLEGED ⟨trusted my *supposed* friends⟩
2 a : held as an opinion **:** BELIEVED; *also :* mistakenly believed **:** IMAGINED ⟨the sight which makes *supposed* terror true —Shakespeare⟩ **b :** considered probable or certain **:** EXPECTED ⟨it was not *supposed* that everybody could master the technical aspects —J. C. Murray⟩ **c :** UNDERSTOOD ⟨you will be *supposed* to refer to my grandaunt —G. B. Shaw⟩
3 : made or fashioned by intent or design ⟨what's that button *supposed* to do⟩
4 a : required by or as if by authority ⟨soldiers are *supposed* to obey their commanding officers⟩ **b :** given permission **:** PERMITTED ⟨was not *supposed* to have visitors⟩
— **sup·pos·ed·ly** \-'pō-zəd-lē *also* -'pōzd-lē\ *adverb*

sup·pos·ing \sə-'pō-ziŋ\ *conjunction* (circa 1843)
: if by way of hypothesis **:** on the assumption that

sup·po·si·tion \ˌsə-pə-'zi-shən\ *noun* [Middle English, from Late Latin *supposition-, suppositio,* from Latin, act of placing beneath, from *supponere*] (15th century)
1 : something that is supposed **:** HYPOTHESIS
2 : the act of supposing
— **sup·po·si·tion·al** \-'zish-nəl, -'zi-shə-nᵊl\ *adjective*

sup·po·si·tious \-'zi-shəs\ *adjective* [by contraction] (1624)
: SUPPOSITITIOUS

sup·pos·i·ti·tious \sə-ˌpä-zə-'ti-shəs\ *adjective* [Latin *supposititius,* from *suppositus,* past participle of *supponere* to substitute] (1611)
1 a : fraudulently substituted **:** SPURIOUS **b** *of a child* (1) **:** falsely presented as a genuine heir (2) **:** ILLEGITIMATE
2 [influenced in meaning by *supposition*] **a :** IMAGINARY **b :** of the nature of or based on a supposition **:** HYPOTHETICAL
— **sup·pos·i·ti·tious·ly** *adverb*

sup·pos·i·to·ry \sə-'pä-zə-ˌtōr-ē, -ˌtȯr-\ *noun, plural* **-ries** [Middle English, from Medieval Latin *suppositorium,* from Late Latin, neuter of *suppositorius* placed beneath, from Latin *supponere* to put under] (14th century)
: a solid but readily meltable cone or cylinder of usually medicated material for insertion into a bodily passage or cavity (as the rectum)

sup·press \sə-'pres\ *transitive verb* [Middle English, from Latin *suppressus,* past participle of *supprimere,* from *sub-* + *premere* to press — more at PRESS] (14th century)
1 : to put down by authority or force **:** SUBDUE
2 : to keep from public knowledge: as **a :** to keep secret **b :** to stop or prohibit the publication or revelation of
3 a : to exclude from consciousness **b :** to keep from giving vent to **:** CHECK
4 *obsolete* **:** to press down
5 a : to restrain from a usual course or action **:** ARREST ⟨*suppress* a cough⟩ **b :** to inhibit the growth or development of **:** STUNT
6 : to inhibit the genetic expression of ⟨*suppress* a mutation⟩
— **sup·press·ibil·i·ty** \-ˌpre-sə-'bi-lə-tē\ *noun*
— **sup·press·ible** \-'pre-sə-bəl\ *adjective*
— **sup·pres·sive** \-'pre-siv\ *adjective*
— **sup·pres·sive·ness** \-nəs\ *noun*

sup·pres·sant \sə-'pre-sᵊnt\ *noun* (1942)
: an agent (as a drug) that tends to suppress or reduce in intensity rather than eliminate something (as appetite)

sup·pres·sion \sə-'pre-shən\ *noun* (15th century)

1 : an act or instance of suppressing **:** the state of being suppressed
2 : the conscious intentional exclusion from consciousness of a thought or feeling

sup·pres·sor \-'pre-sər\ *noun* (1560)
: one that suppresses; *especially :* a mutant gene that suppresses the expression of another nonallelic mutant gene when both are present

suppressor T cell *noun* (1972)
: a T cell that suppresses the immune response of B cells and other T cells to an antigen — called also *suppressor cell*

sup·pu·rate \'sə-pyə-ˌrāt\ *intransitive verb* **-rat·ed; -rat·ing** [Latin *suppuratus,* past participle of *suppurare,* from *sub-* + *pur-, pus* pus — more at FOUL] (1656)
: to form or discharge pus
— **sup·pu·ra·tion** \ˌsə-pyə-'rā-shən\ *noun*
— **sup·pu·ra·tive** \'sə-pyə-rə-tiv, -ˌrā-; 'sə-prə-tiv\ *adjective*

su·pra \'sü-prə, -ˌprä\ *adverb* [Latin] (1526)
: earlier in this writing **:** ABOVE

supra- *prefix* [Latin, from *supra* above, beyond, earlier; akin to Latin *super* over — more at OVER]
1 : SUPER- 2a ⟨*supra*orbital⟩
2 : transcending ⟨*supra*molecular⟩

su·pra·lim·i·nal \ˌsü-prə-'li-mə-nᵊl, -ˌprä-\ *adjective* [*supra-* + Latin *limin-, limen* threshold] (1892)
1 : existing above the threshold of consciousness
2 : adequate to evoke a response or induce a sensation ⟨*supraliminal* stimulus⟩

su·pra·mo·lec·u·lar \-mə-'le-kyə-lər\ *adjective* (circa 1909)
: more complex than a molecule; *also :* composed of many molecules

su·pra·na·tion·al \-'nash-nəl, -'na-shə-nᵊl\ *adjective* (1908)
: transcending national boundaries, authority, or interests ⟨a *supranational* authority, regulating ocean usage —N. H. Jacoby⟩
— **su·pra·na·tion·al·ism** \-'nash-nə-ˌli-zəm, -'na-shə-nᵊl-ˌi-\ *noun*
— **su·pra·na·tion·al·ist** \-list, -ist\ *noun*
— **su·pra·na·tion·al·i·ty** \-ˌna-shə-'na-lə-tē\ *noun*

su·pra·op·tic \-'äp-tik\ *adjective* (1921)
: situated above the optic chiasma; *also :* being a small nucleus of closely packed neurons overlying the optic chiasma and intimately connected with the neurohypophysis

su·pra·or·bit·al \-'ȯr-bə-tᵊl\ *adjective* [New Latin *supraorbitalis,* from Latin *supra-* + Medieval Latin *orbita* orbit] (1828)
: situated or occurring above the orbit of the eye

☆ **SYNONYMS**
Support, uphold, advocate, back, champion mean to favor actively one that meets opposition. SUPPORT is least explicit about the nature of the assistance given ⟨*supports* waterfront development⟩. UPHOLD implies extended support given to something attacked ⟨*upheld* the legitimacy of the military action⟩. ADVOCATE stresses urging or pleading ⟨*advocated* prison reform⟩. BACK suggests supporting by lending assistance to one failing or falling ⟨refusing to *back* the call for sanctions⟩. CHAMPION suggests publicly defending one unjustly attacked or too weak to advocate his or her own cause ⟨*championed* the rights of children⟩.

\ə\ abut \ᵊ\ kitten \ər\ **further** \a\ ash \ā\ ace
\ä\ mop, mar \au̇\ **out** \ch\ **chin** \e\ bet \ē\ **easy**
\g\ go \i\ hit \ī\ ice \j\ job \ŋ\ sing \ō\ go
\ȯ\ law \ȯi\ boy \th\ **thin** \t͟h\ **the** \ü\ **loot** \u̇\ **foot**
\y\ yet \zh\ vision *see also* Guide to Pronunciation

su·pra·ra·tio·nal \-'rash-nəl, -'ra-shə-n°l\ *adjective* (1894)
: transcending the rational **:** based on or involving factors not to be comprehended by reason alone ⟨the stars inspire *suprarational* dreams —R. J. Dubos⟩

¹**su·pra·re·nal** \-'rē-n°l\ *adjective* [New Latin *suprarenalis*, from Latin *supra-* + *renes* kidneys] (1828)
: situated above or anterior to the kidneys

²**suprarenal** *noun* (1841)
: a suprarenal part; *especially* **:** ADRENAL GLAND

suprarenal gland *noun* (1876)
: ADRENAL GLAND

su·pra·seg·men·tal \,sü-prə-seg-'men-t°l, -,prä-\ *adjective* (1941)
: of or relating to significant features (as stress, pitch, or juncture) that occur simultaneously with vowels and consonants in an utterance

sup·ra·ven·tric·u·lar \-ven-'tri-kyə-lər, -vən-\ *adjective* (1951)
: relating to or being a rhythmic abnormality of the heart caused by impulses originating above the ventricles ⟨*supraventricular* tachycardia⟩

su·pra·vi·tal \-'vī-t°l\ *adjective* [International Scientific Vocabulary] (1919)
: constituting or relating to the staining of living tissues or cells surviving after removal from a living body by dyes that penetrate living substance but induce more or less rapid degenerative changes — compare INTRAVITAL 2
— **su·pra·vi·tal·ly** \-t°l-ē\ *adverb*

su·prem·a·cist \sə-'pre-mə-sist, sü-\ *noun* (1949)
1 : an advocate or adherent of group supremacy
2 : WHITE SUPREMACIST

su·prem·a·cy \sə-'pre-mə-sē, sü- *also* -'prē-\ *noun, plural* **-cies** [*supreme* + *-acy* (as in *primacy*)] (1537)
: the quality or state of being supreme; *also*
: supreme authority or power

su·prem·a·tism \-mə-,ti-zəm\ *noun, often capitalized* [Russian *suprematizm*, from French *suprématie* supremacy + Russian *-izm* -ism] (1933)
: an early 20th-century art movement in Russia producing abstract works featuring flat geometric forms
— **su·prem·a·tist** \-tist\ *adjective or noun, often capitalized*

su·preme \sə-'prēm, sü-\ *adjective* [Latin *supremus*, superlative of *superus* upper — more at SUPERIOR] (circa 1533)
1 : highest in rank or authority ⟨the *supreme* commander⟩
2 : highest in degree or quality ⟨*supreme* endurance in war and in labour —R. W. Emerson⟩
3 : ULTIMATE, FINAL ⟨the *supreme* sacrifice⟩
— **su·preme·ly** *adverb*
— **su·preme·ness** *noun*

Supreme Being *noun* (1699)
: GOD 1

supreme court *noun, often S&C capitalized* (1709)
1 : the highest judicial tribunal in a political unit (as a nation or state)
2 : a court of original jurisdiction in New York state subordinate to a final court of appeals

Supreme Soviet *noun* (1936)
: the highest legislative body of a nation (as Russia or the former Soviet Union)

su·pre·mo \sə-'prē-(,)mō, sü-\ *noun, plural* **-mos** [Spanish & Italian, from *supremo*, adjective, supreme, from Latin *supremus*] (1937)
British **:** one who is highest in rank or authority

suq \'sük\ *variant of* SOUK

sur- *prefix* [Middle English, from Old French, from Latin *super-*]
1 : over **:** SUPER- ⟨*surprint*⟩ ⟨*sur*tax⟩
2 : above **:** up ⟨*surbase*⟩

su·ra \'sùr-ə\ *noun* [Arabic *sūrah*, literally, row] (1661)
: a chapter of the Koran

su·rah \'sùr-ə\ *noun* [probably alteration of *surat*, a cotton produced in Surat, India] (1873)
: a soft twilled fabric of silk or rayon

sur·base \'sər-,bās\ *noun* (1678)
: a molding just above the base of a wall, pedestal, or podium

¹**sur·cease** \(,)sər-'sēs, 'sər-,\ *verb* **surceased; sur·ceas·ing** [Middle English *sursesen, surcesen*, from Middle French *sursis*, past participle of *surseoir*, from Latin *supersedēre* — more at SUPERSEDE] (15th century)
intransitive verb
: to desist from action; *also* **:** to come to an end **:** CEASE
transitive verb
: to put an end to **:** DISCONTINUE

²**sur·cease** \'sər-,sēs, (,)sər-'\ *noun* (1586)
: CESSATION; *especially* **:** a temporary respite or end ⟨to borrow from my books *surcease* of sorrow —E. A. Poe⟩

¹**sur·charge** \'sər-,chärj\ *transitive verb* [Middle English, from Middle French *surchargier*, from *sur-* + *chargier* to charge, from Old French — more at CHARGE] (15th century)
1 a : OVERCHARGE **b :** to charge an extra fee **c :** to show an omission in (an account) for which credit ought to have been given
2 *British* **:** OVERSTOCK
3 : to fill or load to excess ⟨the atmosphere . . . was *surcharged* with war hysteria —H. A. Chippendale⟩
4 a : to mark a surcharge on (a stamp) **b :** OVERPRINT ⟨*surcharge* a banknote⟩

²**surcharge** *noun* (15th century)
1 a : an additional tax, cost, or impost **b :** an extra fare ⟨a sleeping car *surcharge*⟩ **c :** an instance of surcharging an account
2 : an excessive load or burden
3 : the action of surcharging **:** the state of being surcharged
4 a (1) **:** an overprint on a stamp; *specifically* **:** one that alters the denomination (2) **:** a stamp bearing such an overprint **b :** an overprint on a currency note

sur·cin·gle \'sər-,siŋ-gəl\ *noun* [Middle English *sursengle*, from Middle French *surcengle*, from *sur-* + *cengle* girdle, from Latin *cingulum* — more at CINGULUM] (14th century)
1 : a belt, band, or girth passing around the body of a horse to bind a saddle or pack fast to the horse's back
2 *archaic* **:** the cincture of a cassock

sur·coat \'sər-,kōt\ *noun* [Middle English *surcote*, from Middle French, from *sur-* + *cote* coat] (13th century)
: an outer coat or cloak; *specifically* **:** a tunic worn over armor

¹**surd** \'sərd\ *adjective* [Latin *surdus* deaf, silent, stupid] (1551)
1 : lacking sense **:** IRRATIONAL ⟨the *surd* mystery and the strange forces of existence —D. C. Williams⟩
2 : VOICELESS — used of speech sounds

²**surd** *noun* (1557)
1 a : an irrational root (as $\sqrt{3}$) **b :** IRRATIONAL NUMBER
2 : a surd speech sound

¹**sure** \'shùr, *especially Southern* 'shōr\ *adjective* **sur·er; sur·est** [Middle English, from Middle French *sur*, from Latin *securus* secure] (13th century)
1 *obsolete* **:** safe from danger or harm
2 : firmly established **:** STEADFAST ⟨a *sure* hold⟩
3 : RELIABLE, TRUSTWORTHY

4 : marked by or given to feelings of confident certainty ⟨I'm *sure* I'm right⟩
5 : admitting of no doubt **:** INDISPUTABLE ⟨spoke from *sure* knowledge⟩
6 a : bound to happen **:** INEVITABLE ⟨*sure* disaster⟩ **b :** BOUND, DESTINED ⟨is *sure* to win⟩
7 : careful to remember, attend to, or find out something ⟨be *sure* to lock the door⟩ ☆
— **sure·ness** *noun*
— **for sure :** without doubt or question **:** CERTAINLY
— **to be sure :** it must be acknowledged **:** ADMITTEDLY

²**sure** *adverb* (14th century)
: SURELY □

sure–enough \'shùr-ə-'nəf\ *adjective* (circa 1846)
: ACTUAL, GENUINE, REAL

sure enough *adverb* (circa 1545)
: as one might expect **:** CERTAINLY

sure·fire \'shùr-'fīr\ *adjective* (circa 1909)
: certain to get successful or expected results ⟨a *surefire* recipe⟩

sure·foot·ed \-'fù-təd\ *adjective* (1633)
: not liable to stumble, fall, or err
— **sure·foot·ed·ly** *adverb*
— **sure·foot·ed·ness** *noun*

sure–hand·ed \-'han-dəd\ *adjective* (1930)
: proficient and confident in performance especially using the hands
— **sure–hand·ed·ness** *noun*

sure·ly \'shùr-lē, *especially Southern* 'shōr-\ *adverb* (14th century)

1 : in a sure manner: **a** *archaic* : without danger or risk of injury or loss : SAFELY **b** (1) : with assurance : CONFIDENTLY ⟨answered quickly and *surely*⟩ (2) : without doubt : CERTAINLY ⟨they will *surely* be heard from in the future —R. J. Lifton⟩
2 : INDEED, REALLY — often used as an intensive ⟨you *surely* don't believe that⟩
usage see ²SURE

sure thing *noun* (1836)
: one that is certain to succeed : a sure bet

sure·ty \'shůr(-ə)-tē\ *noun, plural* **-ties** [Middle English *surte*, from Middle French *surté*, from Latin *securitat-, securitas* security, from *securus*] (14th century)
1 : the state of being sure: as **a** : sure knowledge : CERTAINTY **b** : confidence in manner or behavior : ASSURANCE
2 a : a formal engagement (as a pledge) given for the fulfillment of an undertaking : GUARANTEE **b** : ground of confidence or security
3 : one who has become legally liable for the debt, default, or failure in duty of another
— **sure·ty·ship** \-,ship\ *noun*

surety bond *noun* (1911)
: a bond guaranteeing performance of a contract or obligation

¹surf \'sərf\ *noun* [origin unknown] (1685)
1 : the swell of the sea that breaks upon the shore
2 : the foam, splash, and sound of breaking waves

²surf *intransitive verb* (1926)
: to ride the surf (as on a surfboard)
— **surf·er** *noun*

¹sur·face \'sər-fəs\ *noun* [French, from *sur-* + *face* face, from Old French — more at FACE] (circa 1604)
1 : the exterior or upper boundary of an object or body
2 : a plane or curved two-dimensional locus of points (as the boundary of a three-dimensional region) ⟨plane *surface*⟩ ⟨*surface* of a sphere⟩
3 a : the external or superficial aspect of something **b** : an external part or layer
— **on the surface** : to all outward appearances

²surface *adjective* (1664)
1 a : of, located on, or designed for use at the surface of something **b** : situated, transported, or employed on the surface of the earth ⟨*surface* mail⟩ ⟨*surface* vehicles⟩
2 : appearing to be such on the surface only : SUPERFICIAL ⟨*surface* friendships⟩

³surface *verb* **sur·faced; sur·fac·ing** (1778)
transitive verb
1 : to give a surface to: as **a** : to plane or make smooth **b** : to apply the surface layer to ⟨*surface* a highway⟩
2 : to bring to the surface
intransitive verb
1 : to work on or at the surface
2 : to come to the surface
3 : to come into public view : SHOW UP
— **sur·fac·er** *noun*

surface–active *adjective* (1920)
: altering the properties and especially lowering the tension at the surface of contact between phases ⟨soaps and wetting agents are typical *surface-active* substances⟩

surface of revolution *noun* (1840)
: a surface formed by the revolution of a plane curve about a line in its plane

sur·face–rip·ened \'sər-fəs-,rī-pənd, -,rī-p°md\ *adjective* (1945)
of cheese : ripened by the action of microorganisms (as molds) on the surface

surface structure *noun* (1964)
: a formal representation of the phonetic form of a sentence; *also* : the structure which such a representation describes

surface tension *noun* (1876)
: the attractive force exerted upon the surface molecules of a liquid by the molecules beneath that draw the surface molecules

into the bulk of the liquid and makes the liquid assume the shape having the least surface area

surface–to–air *adjective* (1949)
: launched from the ground against a target in the air

surfacing *noun* (1882)
: material forming or used to form a surface

sur·fac·tant \(,)sər-'fak-tənt, 'sər-,\ *noun* [*surface-active* + *-ant*] (1950)
: a surface-active substance (as a detergent)
— **surfactant** *adjective*

surf and turf *noun* (1973)
: seafood and steak served as a single course

surf·bird \'sərf-,bərd\ *noun* (1839)
: a shorebird (*Aphriza virgata*) of the Pacific coasts of America that has a black-tipped white tail

surf·board \-,bōrd, -,bòrd\ *noun* (circa 1826)
: a long narrow buoyant board (as of lightweight wood or fiberglass-covered foam) used in the sport of surfing
— **surfboard** *intransitive verb*
— **surf·board·er** *noun*

surf·boat \-,bōt\ *noun* (1847)
: a boat for use in heavy surf

surf casting *noun* (1928)
: a method of fishing in which artificial or natural bait is cast into the open ocean or in a bay where waves break on a beach
— **surf caster** *noun*

surf clam *noun* (1884)
: any of various typically rather large surf-dwelling edible clams (family Mactridae); *especially* : a common clam (*Spisula solidissima*) of the Atlantic coast chiefly from Nova Scotia to South Carolina

¹sur·feit \'sər-fət\ *noun* [Middle English *surfait*, from Middle French, from *surfaire* to overdo, from *sur-* + *faire* to do, from Latin *facere* — more at DO] (14th century)
1 : an overabundant supply : EXCESS
2 : an intemperate or immoderate indulgence in something (as food or drink)
3 : disgust caused by excess

²surfeit (14th century)
transitive verb
: to feed, supply, or give to surfeit
intransitive verb
archaic : to indulge to satiety in a gratification (as indulgence of the appetite or senses)
synonym see SATIATE
— **sur·feit·er** *noun*

surf fish *noun* (1882)
: SURFPERCH

sur·fi·cial \,sər-'fi-shəl\ *adjective* [*surface* + *-icial* (as in *superficial*)] (1892)
: of or relating to a surface ⟨*surficial* geologic processes⟩

surf·ing \'sər-fiŋ\ *noun* (1926)
: the sport of riding the surf especially on a surfboard

surf·perch \'sərf-,pərch\ *noun* (1885)
: any of a family (Embiotocidae) of small or medium-sized viviparous bony fishes chiefly of shallow water along the Pacific coast of North America that resemble the perches

¹surge \'sərj\ *verb* **surged; surg·ing** [Middle French *sourge-*, stem of *sourdre* to rise, surge, from Latin *surgere* to go straight up, rise, from *sub-* up + *regere* to lead straight — more at SUB-, RIGHT] (1511)
intransitive verb
1 : to rise and fall actively : TOSS ⟨a ship *surging* in heavy seas⟩
2 : to rise and move in waves or billows : SWELL
3 : to slip around a windlass, capstan, or bitts — used especially of a rope
4 : to rise suddenly to an excessive or abnormal value ⟨the stock market *surgeed* to a record high⟩
5 : to move with a surge or in surges ⟨felt the blood *surging* into his face —Harry Hervey⟩
transitive verb

: to let go or slacken gradually (as a rope)

²surge *noun* (1520)
1 : a swelling, rolling, or sweeping forward like that of a wave or series of waves ⟨a *surge* of interest⟩
2 a : a large wave or billow : SWELL **b** (1) : a series of such swells or billows (2) : the resulting elevation of water level
3 : the tapered part of a windlass barrel or a capstan
4 a : a movement (as a slipping or slackening) of a rope or cable **b** : a sudden jerk or strain caused by such a movement
5 : a transient sudden rise of current or voltage in an electrical circuit

sur·geon \'sər-jən\ *noun* [Middle English *surgien*, from Anglo-French, from Old French *cirurgien*, from *cirurgie* surgery] (14th century)
: a medical specialist who practices surgery

sur·geon·fish \-,fish\ *noun* (1871)
: any of a family (Acanthuridae) of tropical bony fishes that have toxic flesh and typically a movable spine on each side of the body near the base of the tail capable of inflicting a painful wound

surgeon general *noun, plural* **surgeons general** (1706)
: the chief medical officer of a branch of the armed services or of a public health service

surgeon's knot *noun* (1733)
: any of several knots used in tying ligatures or surgical stitches; *especially* : a reef knot in which the first knot has two turns — see KNOT illustration

sur·gery \'sərj-rē, 'sər-jə-\ *noun, plural* **-ger·ies** [Middle English *surgerie*, from Middle French *cirurgie, surgerie*, from Latin *chirurgia*, from Greek *cheirourgia*, from *cheirourgos* surgeon, from *cheirourgos* doing by hand, from *cheir* hand + *ergon* work — more at CHIR-, WORK] (14th century)
1 : a branch of medicine concerned with diseases and conditions requiring or amenable to operative or manual procedures
2 : alterations made as if by surgery ⟨literary *surgery*⟩
3 a *British* : a physician's or dentist's office **b** : a room or area where surgery is performed
4 a : the work done by a surgeon **b** : OPERATION

sur·gi·cal \'sər-ji-kəl\ *adjective* [*surgeon* + *-ical*] (1770)
1 a : of or relating to surgeons or surgery ⟨*surgical* skills⟩ **b** : used in or in connection with surgery **c** : characteristic of or resembling surgery or a surgeon especially in control or incisiveness ⟨*surgical* precision⟩
2 : following or resulting from surgery ⟨*surgical* fevers⟩
— **sur·gi·cal·ly** \-k(ə-)lē\ *adverb*

su·ri·mi \sů-'rē-mē\ *noun* [Japanese, chopped meat or fish] (1976)
: a fish product made from inexpensive whitefish and often processed to resemble more expensive seafood (as crabmeat)

sur·jec·tion \(,)sər-'jek-shən\ *noun* [probably from *sur-* + *-jection* (as in *projection*)] (1964)
: a mathematical function that is an onto mapping — compare BIJECTION, INJECTION 3

sur·jec·tive \-'jek-tiv\ *adjective* (1964)
: ONTO ⟨a set of *surjective* functions⟩

sur·ly \'sər-lē\ *adjective* **sur·li·er; -est** [alteration of Middle English *sirly* lordly, imperious, from *sir*] (circa 1572)
1 *obsolete* : ARROGANT, IMPERIOUS
2 : irritably sullen and churlish in mood or manner : CRABBED

3 : menacing or threatening in appearance ⟨*surly* weather⟩ ◇
synonym see SULLEN
— **sur·li·ly** \-lə-lē\ *adverb*
— **sur·li·ness** \-lē-nəs\ *noun*
— **surly** *adverb*

¹sur·mise \sər-ˈmīz, ˈsər-\ *noun* (1569)
: a thought or idea based on scanty evidence
: CONJECTURE

²sur·mise \sər-ˈmīz\ *transitive verb* **sur·mised; sur·mis·ing** [Middle English, to accuse, from Middle French *surmis*, past participle of *surmetre*, from Latin *supermittere* to throw on, from *super-* + *mittere* to send] (1700)
: to imagine or infer on slight grounds

sur·mount \sər-ˈmaủnt\ *transitive verb* [Middle English, from Middle French *surmonter*, from *sur-* + *monter* to mount] (14th century)
1 *obsolete* : to surpass in quality or attainment : EXCEL
2 : to prevail over : OVERCOME ⟨*surmount* an obstacle⟩
3 : to get to the top of : CLIMB
4 : to stand or lie at the top of
— **sur·mount·able** \-ˈmaủn-tə-bəl\ *adjective*

¹sur·name \ˈsər-ˌnām\ *noun* (14th century)
1 : an added name derived from occupation or other circumstance : NICKNAME 1
2 : the name borne in common by members of a family

²surname *transitive verb* (15th century)
: to give a surname to

sur·pass \sər-ˈpas\ *transitive verb* [Middle French *surpasser*, from *sur-* + *passer* to pass] (1555)
1 : to become better, greater, or stronger than : EXCEED
2 : to go beyond : OVERSTEP
3 : to transcend the reach, capacity, or powers of
synonym see EXCEED
— **sur·pass·able** \-ˈpa-sə-bəl\ *adjective*

sur·pass·ing *adjective* (circa 1580)
: greatly exceeding others : of a very high degree
— **sur·pass·ing·ly** \-ˈpa-siŋ-lē\ *adverb*

¹sur·plice \ˈsər-pləs\ *noun* [Middle English *surplis*, from Old French *surpliz*, from Medieval Latin *superpellicium*, from *super-* + *pellicium* coat of skins, from Latin, neuter of *pellicius* made of skins, from *pellis* skin — more at FELL] (13th century)
: a loose white outer ecclesiastical vestment usually of knee length with large open sleeves

²surplice *adjective* (1845)
: having a diagonally overlapping neckline or closing ⟨a *surplice* collar⟩ ⟨*surplice* sweaters⟩

sur·plus \ˈsər-(ˌ)pləs\ *noun* [Middle English, from Middle French, from Medieval Latin *superplus*, from Latin *super-* + *plus* more — more at PLUS] (14th century)
1 a : the amount that remains when use or need is satisfied **b** : an excess of receipts over disbursements
2 : the excess of a corporation's net worth over the par or stated value of its capital stock
— **surplus** *adjective*

sur·plus·age \-(ˌ)plə-sij\ *noun* (15th century)
1 : SURPLUS 1a
2 a : excessive or nonessential matter **b** : matter introduced in legal pleading which is not necessary or relevant to the case

surplus value *noun* (1887)
: the difference in Marxist theory between the value of work done or of commodities produced by labor and the usually subsistence wages paid by the employer

sur·print \ˈsər-ˌprint\ *transitive verb or noun* (1917)
: OVERPRINT

sur·pris·al \sə(r)-ˈprī-zəl\ *noun* (1591)
: the action of surprising : the state of being surprised

¹sur·prise *also* **sur·prize** \sə(r)-ˈprīz\ *noun* [Middle English, from Middle French, from feminine of *surpris*, past participle of *surprendre* to take over, surprise, from *sur-* + *prendre* to take — more at PRIZE] (15th century)
1 a : an attack made without warning **b** : a taking unawares
2 : something that surprises
3 : the state of being surprised : ASTONISHMENT

²surprise *also* **surprize** *verb* **sur·prised; sur·pris·ing** (15th century)
transitive verb
1 : to attack unexpectedly; *also* : to capture by an unexpected attack
2 a : to take unawares **b** : to detect or elicit by a taking unawares
3 : to strike with wonder or amazement especially because unexpected
intransitive verb
: to cause astonishment or surprise ⟨her success didn't *surprise*⟩ ☆
— **sur·pris·er** *noun*

sur·pris·ing *adjective* (1645)
: of a nature that excites surprise

sur·pris·ing·ly \sə(r)-ˈprī-ziŋ-lē\ *adverb* (1661)
1 : in a surprising manner : to a surprising degree ⟨a *surprisingly* fast runner⟩
2 : it is surprising that ⟨*surprisingly*, voter turnout was high⟩

sur·ra \ˈsủr-ə\ *noun* [Marathi *sūra* wheezing sound] (1883)
: a severe Old World febrile and hemorrhagic disease of domestic animals that is caused by a flagellate protozoan (*Trypanosoma evansi*) and is transmitted by biting insects

sur·re·al \sə-ˈrē(-ə)l, -ˈri-əl *also* -ˈrā-əl\ *adjective* [back-formation from *surrealism*] (1937)
1 : having the intense irrational reality of a dream
2 : SURREALISTIC
— **sur·re·al·ly** *adverb*

sur·re·al·ism \sə-ˈrē-ə-ˌli-zəm, -ˈri- *also* -ˈrā-\ *noun* [French *surréalisme*, from *sur-* + *réalisme* realism] (1925)
: the principles, ideals, or practice of producing fantastic or incongruous imagery or effects in art, literature, film, or theater by means of unnatural juxtapositions and combinations
— **sur·re·al·ist** \-list\ *noun or adjective*

sur·re·al·is·tic \-ˌrē-ə-ˈlis-tik, -ˌri- *also* -ˌrā-\ *adjective* (1925)
1 : of or relating to surrealism
2 : having a strange dreamlike atmosphere or quality like that of a surrealist painting
— **sur·re·al·is·ti·cal·ly** \-ti-k(ə-)lē\ *adverb*

sur·re·but·ter \ˌsər-(r)i-ˈbə-tər\ *noun* (circa 1601)
: the reply in common law pleading of a plaintiff to a defendant's rebutter

sur·re·join·der \-(r)i-ˈjoin-dər\ *noun* (circa 1543)
: the reply in common law pleading of a plaintiff to a defendant's rejoinder

¹sur·ren·der \sə-ˈren-dər\ *verb* **-dered; -der·ing** \-d(ə-)riŋ\ [Middle English, from Middle French *surrendre*, from *sur-* + *rendre* to give back, yield — more at RENDER] (15th century)
transitive verb
1 a : to yield to the power, control, or possession of another upon compulsion or demand ⟨*surrendered* the fort⟩ **b** : to give up completely or agree to forgo especially in favor of another
2 a : to give (oneself) up into the power of another especially as a prisoner **b** : to give (oneself) over to something (as an influence)
intransitive verb
: to give oneself up into the power of another : YIELD
synonym see RELINQUISH

²surrender *noun* (15th century)
1 a : the action of yielding one's person or giving up the possession of something espe-

cially into the power of another **b** : the relinquishment by a patentee of rights or claims under a patent **c** : the delivery of a principal into lawful custody by bail — called also *surrender by bail* **d** : the voluntary cancellation of the legal liability of an insurance company by the insured and beneficiary for a consideration **e** : the delivery of a fugitive from justice by one government to another
2 : an instance of surrendering

sur·rep·ti·tious \ˌsər-əp-ˈti-shəs, ˌsə-rəp-, sə-ˌrep-\ *adjective* [Middle English, from Latin *surrepticius*, from *surreptus*, past participle of *surripere* to snatch secretly, from *sub-* + *rapere* to seize — more at RAPID] (15th century)
1 : done, made, or acquired by stealth : CLANDESTINE
2 : acting or doing something clandestinely : STEALTHY
synonym see SECRET
— **sur·rep·ti·tious·ly** *adverb*

sur·rey \ˈsər-ē, ˈsə-rē\ *noun, plural* **surreys** [Surrey, England] (circa 1891)
: a four-wheel two-seated horse-drawn pleasure carriage

sur·ro·ga·cy \ˈsər-ə-gə-sē\ *noun* (1984)
: the practice of serving as a surrogate mother

¹sur·ro·gate \ˈsər-ə-ˌgāt, ˈsə-rə-\ *transitive verb* **-gat·ed; -gat·ing** [Latin *surrogatus*, past participle of *surrogare* to choose in place of another, substitute, from *sub-* + *rogare* to ask — more at RIGHT] (1533)
: to put in the place of another: **a** : to appoint as successor, deputy, or substitute for oneself **b** : SUBSTITUTE

²sur·ro·gate \-ˌgāt, -gət\ *noun, often attributive* (1603)
1 a : one appointed to act in place of another : DEPUTY **b** : a local judicial officer in some states (as New York) who has jurisdiction over the probate of wills, the settlement of estates, and the appointment and supervision of guardians
2 : one that serves as a substitute
3 : SURROGATE MOTHER

surrogate mother *noun* (1978)
: a woman who becomes pregnant usually by artificial insemination or surgical implantation of a fertilized egg for the purpose of carrying the fetus to term for another woman

☆ SYNONYMS
Surprise, astonish, astound, amaze, flabbergast mean to impress forcibly through unexpectedness. SURPRISE stresses causing an effect through being unexpected at a particular time or place rather than by being essentially unusual or novel ⟨*surprised* to find them at home⟩. ASTONISH implies surprising so greatly as to seem incredible ⟨a discovery that *astonished* the world⟩. ASTOUND stresses the shock of astonishment ⟨too *astounded* to respond⟩. AMAZE suggests an effect of bewilderment ⟨*amazed* by the immense size of the place⟩. FLABBERGAST may suggest thorough astonishment and bewilderment or dismay ⟨*flabbergasted* by his angry refusal⟩.

◇ WORD HISTORY
surly To the highborn an association between good manners and aristocratic birth might seem obvious and inescapable, but the fact that the two do not inevitably go together is evidenced by the word *surly*. In Middle English the word was spelled *sirly*, thus making clearer its connection to *sir*, the traditional title of respect. *Sirly* had much the same meaning as *lordly* has today, that is, "proud, haughty." Although its meaning has evolved into "sullen," *surly* still refers to a disposition that is less than noble.

— **surrogate motherhood** *noun*

¹sur·round \sə-'raund\ *transitive verb* [Middle English, to overflow, from Middle French *suronder,* from Late Latin *superundare,* from Latin *super-* + *unda* wave; influenced in meaning by ⁵*round* — more at WATER] (circa 1616)
1 a (1) : to enclose on all sides : ENVELOP ⟨the crowd *surrounded* her⟩ (2) : to enclose so as to cut off communication or retreat : INVEST **b** : to form or be a member of the entourage of ⟨flatterers who *surround* the king⟩ **c** : to constitute part of the environment of ⟨*surrounded* by poverty⟩ **d** : to extend around the margin or edge of : ENCIRCLE ⟨a wall *surrounds* the old city⟩
2 : to cause to be surrounded by something ⟨*surrounded* himself with friends⟩
²surround *noun* (1825)
: something (as a border or ambient environment) that surrounds ⟨from urban centre to rural *surround* —Emrys Jones⟩
sur·round·ings \sə-'raun-diŋz\ *noun plural* (1861)
: the circumstances, conditions, or objects by which one is surrounded : ENVIRONMENT
sur·roy·al \'sər-ˌroi(-ə)l\ *noun* [Middle English *surryal,* from *sur-* + *ryall* royal antler] (15th century)
: one of the terminal tines above the royal antler of a large deer (as a stag) usually grown by four years of age
sur·sum cor·da \ˌsur-səm-'kor-də, -ˌdä\ *noun* [Late Latin, (lift) up (your) hearts; from the opening words] (1537)
1 *often S&C capitalized* : a versicle that in traditional eucharistic liturgies exhorts the faithful to enthusiastic worship
2 : something inspiriting
sur·tax \'sər-ˌtaks\ *noun* (1881)
1 : an extra tax or charge
2 : a graduated income tax in addition to the normal income tax imposed on the amount by which one's net income exceeds a specified sum
sur·tout \(ˌ)sər-'tü, 'sər-ˌ\ *noun* [French, from *sur* over (from Latin *super*) + *tout* all, from Latin *totus* whole — more at OVER] (1686)
: a man's long close-fitting overcoat
sur·veil \sər-'vā(ə)l\ *transitive verb* **sur·veilled; sur·veil·ling** [back-formation from *surveillance*] (1949)
: to subject to surveillance
sur·veil·lance \sər-'vā-lən(t)s *also* -'vāl-yən(t)s *or* -'vā-ən(t)s\ *noun* [French, from *surveiller* to watch over, from *sur-* + *veiller* to watch, from Latin *vigilare,* from *vigil* watchful — more at VIGIL] (1802)
: close watch kept over someone or something (as by a detective); *also* : SUPERVISION
sur·veil·lant \-'vā-lənt *also* -'vāl-yənt *or* -'vā-ənt\ *noun* (1819)
: one that exercises surveillance
¹sur·vey \sər-'vā, 'sər-ˌ\ *verb* **sur·veyed; sur·vey·ing** [Middle English, from Middle French *surveeir* to look over, from *sur-* + *veeir* to see — more at VIEW] (15th century)
transitive verb
1 a : to examine as to condition, situation, or value : APPRAISE **b** : to query (someone) in order to collect data for the analysis of some aspect of a group or area
2 : to determine and delineate the form, extent, and position of (as a tract of land) by taking linear and angular measurements and by applying the principles of geometry and trigonometry
3 : to view or consider comprehensively
4 : INSPECT, SCRUTINIZE ⟨he *surveyed* us in a lordly way —Alan Harrington⟩
intransitive verb
: to make a survey
²sur·vey \'sər-ˌvā, sər-'\ *noun, plural* **sur·veys** (1548)
1 : the act or an instance of surveying: as **a** : a broad treatment of a subject **b** : POLL 5a

2 : something that is surveyed
survey course \'sər-ˌvā-\ *noun* (1916)
: a course treating briefly the chief topics of a broad field of knowledge
sur·vey·ing \sər-'vā-iŋ\ *noun* (1682)
: a branch of applied mathematics that teaches the art of determining the area of any portion of the earth's surface, the lengths and directions of the bounding lines, and the contour of the surface and of accurately delineating the whole on paper
sur·vey·or \sər-'vā-ər\ *noun* (15th century)
: one that surveys; *especially* : one whose occupation is surveying land
sur·viv·able \sər-'vī-və-bəl\ *adjective* (1955)
: resulting in or permitting survival
— **sur·viv·abil·i·ty** \-ˌvī-və-'bi-lə-tē\ *noun*
sur·viv·al \sər-'vī-vəl\ *noun, often attributive* (1598)
1 a : a living or continuing longer than another person or thing **b** : the continuation of life or existence ⟨problems of *survival* in arctic conditions⟩
2 : one that survives
sur·viv·al·ist \-və-list\ *noun* (1970)
: one who views survival as a primary objective; *especially* : one who has prepared to survive in the anarchy of an anticipated breakdown of society
— **survivalist** *adjective*
survival of the fittest (1864)
: NATURAL SELECTION
sur·viv·ance \sər-'vī-vən(t)s\ *noun* (circa 1623)
: SURVIVAL
sur·vive \sər-'vīv\ *verb* **sur·vived; sur·viv·ing** [Middle English, from Middle French *survivre* to outlive, from Latin *supervivere,* from *super-* + *vivere* to live — more at QUICK] (15th century)
intransitive verb
1 : to remain alive or in existence : live on
2 : to continue to function or prosper
transitive verb
1 : to remain alive after the death of ⟨he is *survived* by his wife⟩
2 : to continue to exist or live after ⟨*survived* the earthquake⟩
3 : to continue to function or prosper despite : WITHSTAND
— **sur·vi·vor** \-'vī-vər\ *noun*
sur·viv·er \-'vī-vər\ *noun* (1602)
archaic : one that survives : SURVIVOR
sur·vi·vor·ship \-'vī-vər-ˌship\ *noun* (circa 1625)
1 : the legal right of the survivor of persons having joint interests in property to take the interest of the person who has died
2 : the state of being a survivor
3 : the probability of surviving to a particular age; *also* : the number or proportion of survivors (as of an age group)
Su·san B. An·tho·ny Day \'sü-z°n-ˌbē-'an(t)-thə-nē-\ *noun* (circa 1951)
: February 15 observed to commemorate the birth of Susan B. Anthony
sus·cep·ti·bil·i·ty \sə-ˌsep-tə-'bi-lə-tē\ *noun, plural* **-ties** (1644)
1 : the quality or state of being susceptible; *especially* : lack of ability to resist some extraneous agent (as a pathogen or drug) : SENSITIVITY
2 a : a susceptible temperament or constitution **b** *plural* : FEELINGS, SENSIBILITIES
3 a : the ratio of the magnetization in a substance to the corresponding magnetizing force **b** : the ratio of the electric polarization to the electric intensity in a polarized dielectric
sus·cep·ti·ble \sə-'sep-tə-bəl\ *adjective* [Late Latin *susceptibilis,* from Latin *susceptus,* past participle of *suscipere* to take up, admit, from *sub-, sus-* up + *capere* to take — more at SUB-, HEAVE] (1605)
1 : capable of submitting to an action, process, or operation ⟨a theory *susceptible* to proof⟩

2 : open, subject, or unresistant to some stimulus, influence, or agency
3 : IMPRESSIONABLE, RESPONSIVE
synonym see LIABLE
— **sus·cep·ti·ble·ness** *noun*
— **sus·cep·ti·bly** \-blē\ *adverb*
sus·cep·tive \-tiv\ *adjective* (15th century)
1 : RECEPTIVE
2 : SUSCEPTIBLE
— **sus·cep·tive·ness** *noun*
— **sus·cep·tiv·i·ty** \sə-ˌsep-'ti-və-tē\ *noun*
su·shi \'sü-shē *also* 'su-\ *noun* [Japanese] (1893)
: cold rice dressed with vinegar, formed into any of various shapes, and garnished especially with bits of raw fish or shellfish
su·slik \'sü-slik\ *noun* [Russian] (1774)
1 : any of several rather large short-tailed ground squirrels (genus *Citellus*) of eastern Europe or northern Asia
2 : the mottled grayish black fur of a suslik
¹sus·pect \'səs-ˌpekt, sə-'spekt\ *adjective* [Middle English, from Middle French, from Latin *suspectus,* from past participle of *suspicere*] (14th century)
1 : regarded or deserving to be regarded with suspicion : SUSPECTED ⟨investigates *suspect* employees⟩
2 : DOUBTFUL, QUESTIONABLE ⟨whose skills are *suspect* —Peter Vecsey⟩
²sus·pect \'səs-ˌpekt\ *noun* (1591)
: one who is suspected; *especially* : one suspected of a crime
³sus·pect \sə-'spekt\ *verb* [Middle English, from Latin *suspectare,* frequentative of *suspicere* to look up at, regard with awe, suspect, from *sub-, sus-* up, secretly + *specere* to look at — more at SUB-, SPY] (15th century)
transitive verb
1 : to imagine (one) to be guilty or culpable on slight evidence or without proof ⟨*suspect* him of giving false information⟩
2 : to have doubts of : DISTRUST
3 : to imagine to exist or be true, likely, or probable
intransitive verb
: to imagine something to be true or likely
sus·pend \sə-'spend\ *verb* [Middle English, from Old French *suspendre* to hang up, interrupt, from Latin *suspendere,* from *sub-, sus-* up + *pendere* to cause to hang, weigh] (14th century)
transitive verb
1 : to debar temporarily from a privilege, office, or function ⟨*suspend* a student from school⟩
2 a : to cause to stop temporarily ⟨*suspend* bus service⟩ **b** : to set aside or make temporarily inoperative ⟨*suspend* the rules⟩
3 : to defer to a later time on specified conditions ⟨*suspend* sentence⟩
4 : to hold in an undetermined or undecided state awaiting further information ⟨*suspend* judgment⟩ ⟨*suspend* disbelief⟩
5 a : HANG; *especially* : to hang so as to be free on all sides except at the point of support ⟨*suspend* a ball by a thread⟩ **b** : to keep from falling or sinking by some invisible support (as buoyancy) ⟨dust *suspended* in the air⟩
6 a : to keep fixed or lost (as in wonder or contemplation) **b** : to keep waiting in suspense or indecision
7 : to hold (a musical note) over into the following chord
intransitive verb
1 : to cease operation temporarily
2 : to stop payment or fail to meet obligations
3 : HANG
synonym see DEFER

\ə\ abut \ᵊ\ kitten \ər\ **further** \a\ ash \ā\ ace
\ä\ mop, mar \au̇\ **out** \ch\ **chin** \e\ bet \ē\ **easy**
\g\ go \i\ **hit** \ī\ ice \j\ **job** \ŋ\ **sing**
\ō\ law \oi\ **boy** \th\ **thin** \t͟h\ **the** \ü\ **loot** \u̇\ **foot**
\y\ yet \zh\ vision *see also* Guide to Pronunciation

suspended animation *noun* (1795)
: temporary suspension of the vital functions (as in persons nearly drowned)
sus·pend·er \sə-'spen-dər\ *noun* (1524)
1 : one that suspends
2 a : a device by which something may be suspended: as **a** : one of two supporting bands worn across the shoulders to support trousers, skirt, or belt — usually used in plural and often with *pair* **b** *British* : a fastener attached to a garment or garter to hold up a stocking or sock; *also* : a device consisting of garter and fastener
— **sus·pend·ered** \-dərd\ *adjective*
sus·pense \sə-'spen(t)s\ *noun* [Middle English, from Middle French, from *suspendre*] (15th century)
1 : the state of being suspended : SUSPENSION
2 a : mental uncertainty : ANXIETY **b** : pleasant excitement as to a decision or outcome ⟨a novel of *suspense*⟩
3 : the state or character of being undecided or doubtful : INDECISIVENESS
— **sus·pense·ful** \-fəl\ *adjective*
— **sus·pense·ful·ly** \-fə-lē\ *adverb*
— **sus·pense·ful·ness** \-fəl-nəs\ *noun*
— **sus·pense·less** \-ləs\ *adjective*
suspense account *noun* (1869)
: an account for the temporary entry of charges or credits or especially of doubtful accounts receivable pending determination of their ultimate disposition
sus·pens·er \sə-'spen(t)-sər\ *noun* (circa 1960)
: a suspenseful film
sus·pen·sion \sə-'spen(t)-shən\ *noun* [Middle English *suspensyon*, from Middle French *suspension*, from Late Latin *suspension-, suspensio*, from Latin *suspendere*] (15th century)
1 : the act of suspending : the state or period of being suspended: as **a** : temporary removal from office or privileges **b** : temporary withholding (as of belief or decision) **c** : temporary abrogation of a law or rule **d** (1) : the holding over of one or more musical tones of a chord into the following chord producing a momentary discord and suspending the concord which the ear expects; *specifically* : such a dissonance which resolves downward — compare ANTICIPATION, RETARDATION (2) : the tone thus held over **e** : stoppage of payment of business obligations : FAILURE — used especially of a business or a bank **f** : a rhetorical device whereby the principal idea is deferred to the end of a sentence or longer unit
2 a : the act of hanging : the state of being hung **b** (1) : the state of a substance when its particles are mixed with but undissolved in a fluid or solid (2) : a substance in this state (3) : a system consisting of a solid dispersed in a solid, liquid, or gas usually in particles of larger than colloidal size — compare EMULSION
3 : something suspended
4 a : a device by which something (as a magnetic needle) is suspended **b** : the system of devices (as springs) supporting the upper part of a vehicle on the axles **c** : the act, process, or manner in which the pendulum of a timepiece is suspended
suspension bridge *noun* (1821)
: a bridge that has its roadway suspended from two or more cables usually passing over towers and securely anchored at the ends — see BRIDGE illustration
suspension points *noun plural* (1919)
: usually three spaced periods used to show the omission of a word or word group from a written context
sus·pen·sive \sə-'spen(t)-siv\ *adjective* (15th century)
1 : stopping temporarily : SUSPENDING ⟨a *suspensive* veto⟩
2 : characterized by suspense, suspended judgment, or indecisiveness
3 : characterized by suspension
— **sus·pen·sive·ly** *adverb*

sus·pen·sor \sə-'spen(t)-sər\ *noun* [New Latin, from Latin *suspendere*] (1832)
: a suspending part or structure: as **a** : a group or chain of cells that is produced from the zygote of a heterosporous plant and serves to push the embryo which arises at its extremity deeper into the embryo sac and into contact with the food supply of the megaspore **b** : either of a pair of gametangia-bearing hyphal outgrowths in fungi (order Mucorales) that extend from two sexually compatible hyphae and support the resulting zygospore
¹sus·pen·so·ry \sə-'spen(t)-sə-rē, -'spen(t)s-rē\ *adjective* (15th century)
1 : held in suspension; *also* : fitted or serving to suspend
2 : temporarily leaving undetermined : SUSPENSIVE 1
²suspensory *noun, plural* -ries (15th century)
: something that suspends or holds up; *especially* : a fabric supporter for the scrotum
suspensory ligament *noun* (1831)
: a ligament or fibrous membrane suspending an organ or part; *especially* : a ringlike fibrous membrane connecting the ciliary body and the lens of the eye and holding the lens in place — see EYE illustration
¹sus·pi·cion \sə-'spi-shən\ *noun* [Middle English, from Latin *suspicion-, suspicio*, from *suspicere* to suspect — more at SUSPECT] (14th century)
1 a : the act or an instance of suspecting something wrong without proof or on slight evidence : MISTRUST **b** : a state of mental uneasiness and uncertainty : DOUBT
2 : a barely detectable amount : TRACE ⟨just a *suspicion* of garlic⟩
synonym see UNCERTAINTY
²suspicion *transitive verb* **sus·pi·cioned; sus·pi·cion·ing** \-'spi-sh(ə-)niŋ\ (circa 1637)
chiefly dialect : SUSPECT
sus·pi·cious \sə-'spi-shəs\ *adjective* (14th century)
1 : tending to arouse suspicion : QUESTIONABLE
2 : disposed to suspect : DISTRUSTFUL ⟨*suspicious* of strangers⟩
3 : expressing or indicative of suspicion ⟨a *suspicious* glance⟩
— **sus·pi·cious·ly** *adverb*
— **sus·pi·cious·ness** *noun*
sus·pi·ra·tion \səs-pə-'rā-shən\ *noun* (15th century)
: a long deep breath : SIGH
sus·pire \sə-'spīr\ *intransitive verb* **suspired; sus·pir·ing** [Middle English, from Latin *suspirare*, from *sub-* + *spirare* to breathe] (15th century)
: to draw a long deep breath : SIGH
suss \'səs\ *transitive verb* [by shortening & alteration from *suspect*] (1966)
1 *chiefly British* : to inspect or investigate so as to gain more knowledge — usually used with *out*
2 *chiefly British* : FIGURE OUT — usually used with *out*
Sus·sex spaniel \'sə-siks-, -,seks-\ *noun* [Sussex, England] (1856)
: any of a breed of short-legged short-necked long-bodied spaniels of English origin with a flat or slightly wavy golden liver-colored coat
sus·tain \sə-'stān\ *transitive verb* [Middle English *sustenen*, from Old French *sustenir*, from Latin *sustinēre* to hold up, sustain, from *sub-, sus-* up + *tenēre* to hold — more at SUB-, THIN] (13th century)
1 : to give support or relief to
2 : to supply with sustenance : NOURISH
3 : KEEP UP, PROLONG
4 : to support the weight of : PROP; *also* : to carry or withstand (a weight or pressure)
5 : to buoy up ⟨*sustained* by hope⟩
6 a : to bear up under **b** : SUFFER, UNDERGO ⟨*sustained* heavy losses⟩
7 a : to support as true, legal, or just **b** : to al-

low or admit as valid ⟨the court *sustained* the motion⟩
8 : to support by adequate proof : CONFIRM ⟨testimony that *sustains* our contention⟩ □
— **sus·tained·ly** \-'stā-nəd-lē, -'stānd-lē\ *adverb*
— **sus·tain·er** *noun*
sus·tain·able \sə-'stā-nə-bəl\ *adjective* (circa 1727)
1 : capable of being sustained
2 a : of, relating to, or being a method of harvesting or using a resource so that the resource is not depleted or permanently damaged ⟨*sustainable* techniques⟩ ⟨*sustainable* agriculture⟩ **b** : of or relating to a lifestyle involving the use of sustainable methods ⟨*sustainable* society⟩
— **sus·tain·abil·i·ty** \-,stā-nə-'bi-lə-tē\ *noun*
sustained yield *noun* (circa 1905)
: production of a biological resource (as timber or fish) under management procedures which insure replacement of the part harvested by regrowth or reproduction before another harvest occurs
— **sustained–yield** *adjective*
sus·tain·ing *adjective* (1605)
1 : serving to sustain
2 : aiding in the support of an organization through a special fee ⟨a *sustaining* member⟩
sus·te·nance \'səs-tə-nən(t)s\ *noun* [Middle English, from Old French, from *sustenir*] (14th century)
1 a : means of support, maintenance, or subsistence : LIVING **b** : FOOD, PROVISIONS; *also* : NOURISHMENT
2 a : the act of sustaining : the state of being sustained **b** : a supplying or being supplied with the necessaries of life
3 : something that gives support, endurance, or strength
sus·ten·tac·u·lar cell \,səs-tən-'ta-kyə-lər-, -,ten-\ *noun* [New Latin *sustentaculum* supporting part, from Latin, prop, from *sustentare*] (1901)
: a supporting epithelial cell (as a Sertoli cell or a cell of the olfactory epithelium) that lacks a specialized function (as nerve-impulse conduction)
sus·ten·ta·tion \-'tā-shən\ *noun* [Middle English, from Middle French, from Latin *sustentation-, sustentatio* act of holding up, from *sustentare* to hold up, frequentative of *sustinēre* to sustain] (14th century)
1 : the act of sustaining : the state of being sustained: as **a** : MAINTENANCE, UPKEEP **b** : PRESERVATION, CONSERVATION **c** : maintenance of life, growth, or morale **d** : provision with sustenance

□ USAGE
sustain Sense 6b of *sustain* has been around since the 1400s and has been given without stigma in dictionaries at least since Johnson's of 1755, yet a few commentators have found fault with it. The earliest of these was evidently offended by the frequency with which the word was used in English newspapers in the 1860s. More recent commentators content themselves with finding something vaguely pretentious about the use; a few call it formal, which is odd, since it is commonly found in journalistic surroundings ⟨the company *sustained* operating losses totalling more than $30 million —Richard A. Lester *(New Republic)*⟩ ⟨from injuries *sustained* before and during arrest —E. J. Kahn, Jr. *(New Yorker)*⟩ and especially in sportswriting ⟨in a 1983 game against the Eagles, he *sustained* a concussion —Jill Lieber *(Sports Illustrated)*⟩. It has also been considered a bit of a cliché ⟨is man ever hurt in a motor smash? No. He *sustains* an injury —Flann O'Brien⟩ but is nonetheless standard.

2 : something that sustains **:** SUPPORT
— **sus·ten·ta·tive** \'səs-tən-ˌtā-tiv, sə-'sten-tə-tiv\ *adjective*
Su·su \'sü-(ˌ)sü\ *noun, plural* **Susu** or **Susus** (1786)
1 : a member of a West African people of Mali, Guinea, and the area along the northern border of Sierra Leone
2 : the Mande language of the Susu people
su·sur·ra·tion \ˌsü-sə-'rā-shən\ *noun* (14th century)
: a whispering sound **:** MURMUR
su·sur·rous \sù-'sər-əs, -'sə-rəs\ *adjective* (1859)
: full of whispering sounds
su·sur·rus \sù-'sər-əs, -'sə-rəs\ *noun* [Latin, hum, whisper — more at SWARM] (1826)
: a whispering or rustling sound
— **su·sur·rant** \-'sər-ənt, -'sə-rənt\ *adjective*
sut·ler \'sət-lər\ *noun* [obsolete Dutch *soeteler*, from Low German *suteler* sloppy worker, camp cook] (1599)
: a civilian provisioner to an army post often with a shop on the post
su·tra \'sü-trə\ *noun* [Sanskrit *sūtra* precept, literally, thread; akin to Latin *suere* to sew — more at SEW] (1801)
1 : a precept summarizing Vedic teaching; *also* **:** a collection of these precepts
2 : a discourse of the Buddha
sut·tee \(ˌ)sə-'tē, 'sə-ˌtē\ *noun* [Sanskrit *satī* wife who performs suttee, literally, devoted woman, from feminine of *sat* true, good; akin to Old English *sōth* true — more at SOOTH] (1786)
: the act or custom of a Hindu widow willingly being cremated on the funeral pyre of her husband as an indication of her devotion to him; *also* **:** a woman cremated in this way
¹su·ture \'sü-chər\ *noun* [Middle French & Latin; Middle French, from Latin *sutura* seam, suture, from *sutus*, past participle of *suere* to sew — more at SEW] (1541)
1 a : a strand or fiber used to sew parts of the living body; *also* **:** a stitch made with a suture **b :** the act or process of sewing with sutures
2 a : a uniting of parts **b :** the seam or seamlike line along which two things or parts are sewed or united
3 a : the line of union in an immovable articulation (as between the bones of the skull); *also* **:** such an articulation **b :** a furrow at the junction of adjacent bodily parts; *especially* **:** a line of dehiscence (as on a fruit)
— **su·tur·al** \'sü-chə-rəl, 'süch-rəl\ *adjective*
— **su·tur·al·ly** \-rə-lē\ *adverb*
²suture *transitive verb* **su·tured; su·tur·ing** \'sü-chə-riŋ, 'süch-riŋ\ (1777)
: to unite, close, or secure with sutures ⟨*suture* a wound⟩
su·ze·rain \'sü-zə-rən, -ˌrän; 'süz-rən\ *noun* [French, from (assumed) Middle French *suserain*, from Middle French *sus* up (from Latin *sursum*, from *sub-* up + *versum* -ward, from neuter of *versus*, past participle of *vertere* to turn) + *-erain* (as in *soverain* sovereign) — more at SUB-, WORTH] (1823)
1 : a superior feudal lord to whom fealty is due **:** OVERLORD
2 : a dominant state controlling the foreign relations of a vassal state but allowing it sovereign authority in its internal affairs
su·zer·ain·ty \-tē\ *noun* [French *suzeraineté*, from Middle French *suserenete*, from (assumed) Middle French *suserain*] (1823)
: the dominion of a suzerain **:** OVERLORDSHIP
sved·berg \'sved-ˌbərg, 'sfed-, -ˌber-ē\ *noun* [The *Svedberg*] (1939)
: a unit of time amounting to 10^{-13} second that is used to measure the sedimentation velocity of a colloidal solution (as of a protein) in an ultracentrifuge and to determine molecular weight by substitution in an equation — called also *svedberg unit*
svelte \'svelt, 'sfelt\ *adjective* [French, from

Italian *svelto*, from past participle of *svellere* to pluck out, modification of Latin *evellere*, from *e-* + *vellere* to pluck — more at VULNERABLE] (circa 1817)
1 a : SLENDER, LITHE **b :** having clean lines **:** SLEEK
2 : URBANE, SUAVE
— **svelte·ly** *adverb*
— **svelte·ness** *noun*
Sven·ga·li \sven-'gä-lē, sfen-\ *noun* [*Svengali*, maleficent hypnotist in the novel *Trilby* (1894) by George du Maurier] (1919)
: one who attempts usually with evil intentions to persuade or force another to do his bidding
¹swab \'swäb\ *noun* [probably from obsolete Dutch *swabbe*; akin to Low German *swabber* mop] (1653)
1 a : MOP; *especially* **:** a yarn mop **b** (1) **:** a wad of absorbent material usually wound around one end of a small stick and used for applying medication or for removing material from an area (2) **:** a specimen taken with a swab **c :** a sponge or cloth patch attached to a long handle and used to clean the bore of a firearm
2 a : a useless or contemptible person **b :** SAILOR, GOB
²swab *transitive verb* **swabbed; swab·bing** [back-formation from *swabber*] (1719)
1 : to clean with or as if with a swab
2 : to apply medication to with a swab ⟨*swabbed* the wound with iodine⟩
swab·ber \'swä-bər\ *noun* [akin to Low German *swabber* mop, Middle English *swabben* to sway] (1592)
1 : one that swabs
2 : SWAB 2a
swab·bie *also* **swab·by** \'swä-bē\ *noun, plural* **swabbies** (1944)
slang **:** SWAB 2b
swad·dle \'swä-dᵊl\ *transitive verb* **swad·dled; swad·dling** \'swäd-liŋ, 'swä-dᵊl-iŋ\ [Middle English *swadelen, swathelen*, probably alteration of *swedelen, swethelen*, from *swethel* swaddling band, from Old English; akin to Old English *swathian* to swathe] (14th century)
1 a : to wrap (an infant) with swaddling clothes **b :** ENVELOP, SWATHE ⟨*swaddled* ourselves in sleeping bags⟩
2 : RESTRAIN, RESTRICT ⟨marriage . . . *swaddled* him in a domesticity he came to loathe —Nina Auerbach⟩
swaddling clothes *noun plural* (1535)
1 : narrow strips of cloth wrapped around an infant to restrict movement
2 : limitations or restrictions imposed on the immature or inexperienced
¹swag \'swag\ *verb* **swagged; swag·ging** [probably of Scandinavian origin; akin to Old Norse *sveggja* to cause to sway; akin to Old High German *swingan* to swing] (1530)
intransitive verb
1 : SWAY, LURCH
2 : SAG
transitive verb
1 : to adorn with swags
2 : to arrange (as drapery) in swags
²swag *noun* (1660)
1 : SWAY
2 a : something (as a decoration) hanging in a curve between two points **:** FESTOON **b :** a suspended cluster (as of evergreen branches)
3 a : goods acquired by unlawful means **:** LOOT **b :** SPOILS, PROFITS
4 : a depression in the earth
5 *chiefly Australian* **:** a pack of personal belongings
¹swage \'swāj, 'swej\ *noun* [Middle English, ornamental border, from Middle French *souage*] (circa 1812)
: a tool used by metalworkers for shaping their work by holding it on the work or the work on it and striking it with a hammer or sledge
²swage *transitive verb* **swaged; swag·ing** (1831)

: to shape by or as if by means of a swage
swage block *noun* (1843)
: a perforated cast-iron or steel block with grooved sides that is used in heading bolts and swaging bars by hand
¹swag·ger \'swa-gər\ *verb* **swag·gered; swag·ger·ing** \-g(ə-)riŋ\ [probably from *¹swag + -er* (as in *chatter*)] (1590)
intransitive verb
1 : to conduct oneself in an arrogant or superciliously pompous manner; *especially* **:** to walk with an air of overbearing self-confidence
2 : BOAST, BRAG
transitive verb
: to force by argument or threat **:** BULLY
— **swag·ger·er** \-gər-ər\ *noun*
— **swag·ger·ing·ly** \-g(ə-)riŋ-lē\ *adverb*
²swagger *noun* (1725)
1 a : an act or instance of swaggering **b :** arrogant or conceitedly self-assured behavior **c :** ostentatious display or bravado
2 : a self-confident outlook **:** COCKINESS
³swagger *adjective* (1879)
: marked by elegance or showiness **:** POSH
swagger stick *noun* (1887)
: a short light stick usually covered with leather and tipped with metal at each end and intended for carrying in the hand (as by military officers)
swag·gie \'swa-gē\ *noun* [by shortening & alteration] (1891)
chiefly Australian **:** SWAGMAN
swag·man \'swag-mən\ *noun* (1851)
chiefly Australian **:** DRIFTER; *especially* **:** one who carries a swag when traveling
Swa·hi·li \swä-'hē-lē\ *noun, plural* **Swahili** or **Swahilis** [Arabic *sawāḥil*, plural of *sāḥil* coast] (1814)
1 : a member of a Bantu-speaking people of Zanzibar and the adjacent coast
2 : a Bantu language that is a trade and governmental language over much of East Africa and in the Congo region
swain \'swān\ *noun* [Middle English *swein* boy, servant, from Old Norse *sveinn*; akin to Old English *swān* swain, Latin *suus* one's own — more at SUICIDE] (14th century)
1 : RUSTIC, PEASANT; *specifically* **:** SHEPHERD
2 : a male admirer or suitor
— **swain·ish** \'swä-nish\ *adjective*
— **swain·ish·ness** *noun*
Swain·son's hawk \'swän(t)-sənz-\ *noun* [William *Swainson* (died 1855) English naturalist] (1895)
: a buteo (*Buteo swainsonii*) chiefly of western North America and South America having pointed wings and usually a dark breast
swale \'swā(ə)l\ *noun* [origin unknown] (1584)
: a low-lying or depressed and often wet stretch of land; *also* **:** a shallow depression on a golf fairway or green
¹swal·low \'swä-(ˌ)lō\ *noun* [Middle English *swalowe*, from Old English *swealwe*; akin to Old High German *swalawa* swallow] (before 12th century)
1 : any of numerous small widely distributed oscine birds (family Hirundinidae) that have a short bill, long pointed wings, and often a deeply forked tail and that feed on insects caught on the wing
2 : any of several swifts that superficially resemble swallows

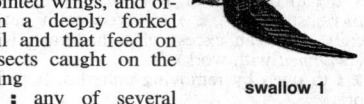

swallow 1

²swallow *verb* [Middle English *swalowen,* from Old English *swelgan;* akin to Old High German *swelgan* to swallow] (before 12th century)
transitive verb
1 : to take through the mouth and esophagus into the stomach
2 : to envelop or take in as if by swallowing **:** ABSORB
3 : to accept without question, protest, or resentment ⟨*swallow* an insult⟩ ⟨a hard story to *swallow*⟩
4 : TAKE BACK, RETRACT ⟨had to *swallow* my words⟩
5 : to keep from expressing or showing **:** REPRESS ⟨*swallowed* my anger⟩
6 : to utter (as words) indistinctly
intransitive verb
1 : to receive something into the body through the mouth and esophagus
2 : to perform the action characteristic of swallowing something especially under emotional stress
— **swal·low·able** \'swä-lō-ə-bəl\ *adjective*
— **swal·low·er** \'swä-lə-wər\ *noun*
³swallow *noun* (14th century)
1 : the passage connecting the mouth to the stomach
2 : a capacity for swallowing
3 a : an act of swallowing **b :** an amount that can be swallowed at one time
4 : an aperture in a block on a ship between the sheave and frame through which the rope reeves
swal·low·tail \'swä-lō-ˌtāl, -lə-\ *noun* (1703)
1 : a deeply forked and tapering tail (as of a swallow)
2 : TAILCOAT
3 : any of various large butterflies (family Papilionidae and especially genus *Papilio*) with each hind wing usually having an elongated process

swallowtail 3

— **swal·low–tailed** \-ˌtāld\ *adjective*
swam *past of* SWIM
swa·mi \'swä-mē\ *noun* [Hindi *svāmī,* from Sanskrit *svāmin* owner, lord, from *sva* one's own — more at SUICIDE] (1895)
1 : a Hindu ascetic or religious teacher; *specifically* **:** a senior member of a religious order — used as a title
2 : one that resembles or emulates a swami **:** PUNDIT, SEER
¹swamp \'swämp, 'swómp\ *noun* [perhaps alteration of Middle English *sompe,* from Middle Dutch *somp* morass; akin to Middle High German *sumpf* marsh, Greek *somphos* spongy] (1624)
1 : a wetland often partially or intermittently covered with water; *especially* **:** one dominated by woody vegetation
2 : a tract of swamp
3 : a difficult or troublesome situation or subject
— **swamp** *adjective*
²swamp (1784)
transitive verb
1 a : to fill with or as if with water **:** INUNDATE, SUBMERGE **b :** to overwhelm numerically or by an excess of something **:** FLOOD ⟨*swamped* with work⟩
2 : to open by removing underbrush and debris
intransitive verb
: to become submerged
swamp buggy *noun* (1941)
: a vehicle designed to travel over swampy terrain; *especially* **:** a four-wheel motor vehicle with oversize tires
swamp·er \'swäm-pər, 'swóm-\ *noun* (1775)

1 a : an inhabitant of swamps or lowlands **b :** one familiar with swampy terrain
2 : a general assistant **:** HANDYMAN, HELPER
swamp·land \'swämp-ˌland, 'swómp-\ *noun* (1662)
: SWAMP 1
swampy \'swäm-pē, 'swóm-\ *adjective* **swamp·i·er; -est** (1649)
: consisting of, suggestive of, or resembling swamp **:** MARSHY
— **swamp·i·ness** *noun*
¹swan \'swän\ *noun, plural* **swans** [Middle English, from Old English; akin to Middle High German *swan* and perhaps to Latin *sonus* sound — more at SOUND] (before 12th century)
1 *plural also* **swan :** any of various large heavy-bodied long-necked mostly pure white aquatic birds (family Anatidae and especially genus *Cygnus*) that are related to but larger than the geese
2 : one that resembles or is likened to a swan
3 *capitalized* **:** the constellation Cygnus
²swan *intransitive verb* **swanned; swan·ning** (1942)
: to wander aimlessly or idly **:** DALLY
³swan *intransitive verb* **swanned; swan·ning** [perhaps euphemism for *swear*] (1784)
dialect **:** DECLARE, SWEAR
swan boat *noun* (1953)
: a small boat usually for children or sightseers pedaled by an operator who sits aft in a large model of a swan
swan dive *noun* (1898)
: a front dive executed with the head back, back arched, and arms spread sideways and then brought together above the head to form a straight line with the body as the diver enters the water
¹swank \'swaŋk\ *adjective* [Middle Low German or Middle Dutch *swanc* supple; akin to Old High German *swingan* to swing] (1773)
Scottish **:** full of life or energy **:** ACTIVE
²swank *intransitive verb* [perhaps akin to Middle High German *swanken* to sway; akin to Middle Dutch *swanc* supple] (circa 1809)
: SHOW OFF, SWAGGER; *also* **:** BOAST 1
³swank *or* **swanky** \'swaŋ-kē\ *adjective* **swank·er** *or* **swank·i·er; -est** (circa 1842)
1 : characterized by showy display **:** OSTENTATIOUS ⟨a *swank* limousine⟩
2 : fashionably elegant **:** SMART ⟨a *swank* restaurant⟩
— **swank·i·ly** \-kə-lē\ *adverb*
— **swank·i·ness** \-kē-nəs\ *noun*
⁴swank *noun* (circa 1854)
1 : arrogance or ostentation of dress or manner **:** PRETENTIOUSNESS, SWAGGER
2 : ELEGANCE, FASHIONABLENESS
swan·nery \'swä-nə-rē, 'swän-rē\ *noun, plural* **-ner·ies** (1754)
: a place where swans are bred or kept
swans·down \'swänz-ˌdaún\ *noun* (1606)
1 : the soft downy feathers of the swan often used as trimming on articles of dress
2 : a heavy cotton flannel that has a thick nap on the face and is made with sateen weave
swan·skin \'swän-ˌskin\ *noun* (1610)
1 : the skin of a swan with the down or feathers on it
2 : fabric resembling flannel and having a soft nap or surface
swan song *noun* (1831)
1 : a song of great sweetness said to be sung by a dying swan
2 : a farewell appearance or final act or pronouncement
¹swap \'swäp\ *verb* **swapped; swap·ping** [Middle English *swappen* to strike; from the practice of striking hands in closing a business deal] (14th century)
transitive verb
1 a : to give in trade **:** BARTER **b :** EXCHANGE 2

2 : to take turns in telling ⟨*swap* stories⟩
intransitive verb
: to make an exchange
— **swap·per** *noun*
²swap *noun* (1625)
: an act, instance, or process of exchanging one thing for another
swap meet *noun* (1965)
: a gathering for the sale or barter of usually secondhand objects
swa·raj \swə-'räj\ *noun* [Hindi *svarāj,* from Sanskrit *sva* own + Hindi *rāj* rule — more at SUICIDE, RAJ] (1908)
: national or local self-government in India
— **swa·raj·ist** \-'rä-jist\ *noun*
sward \'swórd\ *noun* [Middle English, from Old English *sweard, swearth* skin, rind; akin to Middle High German *swart* skin, hide] (15th century)
1 : a portion of ground covered with grass
2 : the grassy surface of land
— **sward·ed** \'swór-dəd\ *adjective*
swarf \'swórf\ *noun* [of Scandinavian origin; akin to Old Norse *svarf* file dust; akin to Old English *sweorfan* to file away — more at SWERVE] (1587)
: material (as metallic particles and abrasive fragments) removed by a cutting or grinding tool
¹swarm \'swórm\ *noun* [Middle English, from Old English *swearm;* akin to Old High German *swaram* swarm and probably to Latin *susurrus* hum] (before 12th century)
1 a (1) **:** a great number of honeybees emigrating together from a hive in company with a queen to start a new colony elsewhere (2) **:** a colony of honeybees settled in a hive **b :** an aggregation of free-floating or free-swimming unicellular organisms — usually used of zoospores
2 a : a large number of animate or inanimate things massed together and usually in motion **:** THRONG ⟨*swarms* of sightseers⟩ ⟨a *swarm* of locusts⟩ ⟨a *swarm* of meteors⟩ **b :** a number of similar geological features or phenomena close together in space or time ⟨a *swarm* of dikes⟩ ⟨an earthquake *swarm*⟩
²swarm (14th century)
intransitive verb
1 : to form and depart from a hive in a swarm
2 a : to move or assemble in a crowd **:** THRONG **b :** to hover about in the manner of a bee in a swarm
3 : to contain a swarm **:** TEEM
transitive verb
1 : to fill with a swarm
2 : to beset or surround in a swarm ⟨players *swarming* the quarterback⟩
— **swarm·er** *noun*
³swarm *verb* [origin unknown] (14th century)
intransitive verb
: to climb with the hands and feet; *specifically* **:** SHIN ⟨*swarm* up a pole⟩
transitive verb
: to climb up **:** MOUNT
swarm spore *noun* (1859)
: any of various minute motile sexual or asexual spores; *especially* **:** ZOOSPORE
swart \'swórt\ *adjective* [Middle English, from Old English *sweart;* akin to Old High German *swarz* black, Latin *sordes* dirt] (before 12th century)
1 a : SWARTHY **b** *archaic* **:** producing a swarthy complexion
2 : BANEFUL, MALIGNANT
— **swart·ness** *noun*
swar·thy \'swór-thē, -thē\ *adjective* **swar·thi·er; -est** [alteration of obsolete *swarty,* from *swart*] (1587)
: of a dark color, complexion, or cast
— **swar·thi·ness** *noun*
¹swash \'swäsh, 'swósh\ *verb* [probably imitative] (1556)
intransitive verb
1 : BLUSTER, SWAGGER
2 : to make violent noisy movements

3 : to move with a splashing sound
transitive verb
: to cause to splash
²**swash** *noun* (1593)
1 : SWAGGER
2 : a narrow channel of water lying within a sandbank or between a sandbank and the shore
3 : a dashing of water against or on something; *especially* **:** the rush of water up a beach from a breaking wave
³**swash** *noun* [obsolete English *swash* slanting] (1683)
: an extended flourish on a printed character
⁴**swash** *adjective* (1683)
: having one or more swashes ⟨*swash* capitals⟩
swash·buck·le \'swäsh-,bə-kəl, 'swȯsh-\ *intransitive verb* **-led; -ling** \-,bə-k(ə-)liŋ\ [back-formation from *swashbuckler*] (1897)
: to act the part of a swashbuckler
swash·buck·ler \-,bə-klər\ *noun* [¹*swash* + *buckler*] (1560)
1 : a swaggering or daring soldier or adventurer
2 : a novel or drama dealing with a swashbuckler
swash·buck·ling \-,bə-k(ə-)liŋ\ *adjective* [*swashbuckler*] (circa 1693)
1 : acting in the manner of a swashbuckler
2 : characteristic of, marked by, or done by swashbucklers
swash·er \'swä-shər, 'swȯ-\ *noun* (1589)
: SWASHBUCKLER
swas·ti·ka \'swäs-ti-kə *also* swä-'stē-\ *noun* [Sanskrit *svastika*, from *svasti* well-being, from *su-* well + *as-* to be; akin to Sanskrit *asti* he is, Old English *is;* from its being regarded as a good luck symbol] (1871)
1 : a symbol or ornament in the form of a Greek cross with the ends of the arms extended at right angles all in the same rotary direction
2 : a swastika used as a symbol of anti-Semitism or of Nazism
¹**swat** \'swät\ *transitive verb* **swat·ted; swat·ting** [English dialect, to squat, alteration of English *squat*] (circa 1796)
: to hit with a sharp slapping blow usually with an instrument (as a bat or swatter)
²**swat** *noun* (circa 1800)
1 : a powerful or crushing blow
2 : a long hit in baseball; *especially* **:** HOME RUN
swatch \'swäch\ *noun* [origin unknown] (1647)
1 a : a sample piece (as of fabric) or a collection of samples **b :** a characteristic specimen
2 : PATCH
3 : a small collection
4 : SWATH 2
swath \'swäth, 'swȯth\ *or* **swathe** \'swäth, 'swȯth, 'swäth\ *noun* [Middle English, from Old English *swæth* footstep, trace; akin to Middle High German *swade* swath] (14th century)
1 a : a row of cut grain or grass left by a scythe or mowing machine **b :** the sweep of a scythe or a machine in mowing or the path cut in one course
2 : a long broad strip or belt
3 : a stroke of or as if of a scythe
4 : a space devastated as if by a scythe
¹**swathe** \'swäth, 'swȯth, 'swäth\ *or* **swath** \'swäth, 'swäth, 'swȯth, 'swȯth\ *noun* [Middle English, from (assumed) Old English *swæth;* akin to Old English *swathian* to swathe] (before 12th century)
1 : a band used in swathing
2 : an enveloping medium
²**swathe** \'swäth, 'swȯth, 'swäth\ *transitive verb* **swathed; swath·ing** [Middle English, from Old English *swathian*] (12th century)
1 : to bind, wrap, or swaddle with or as if with a bandage
2 : ENVELOP

swath·er \'swä-thər, -thər\ *noun* (circa 1875)
: a harvesting machine that cuts and windrows grain and seed crops; *also* **:** a mower attachment that windrows the swath
swathing clothes *noun plural* [Middle English] (14th century)
obsolete **:** SWADDLING CLOTHES
swats \'swäts\ *noun plural* [probably from Old English *swātan*, plural, beer] (1508)
Scottish **:** DRINK; *especially* **:** new ale
swat·ter \'swä-tər\ *noun* (1912)
: one that swats; *especially* **:** FLYSWATTER
S wave *noun* [*s*econdary] (1937)
: a wave (as from an earthquake) in which the propagated disturbance is a shear in an elastic medium (as the earth) — compare PRESSURE WAVE
¹**sway** \'swā\ *noun* (14th century)
1 : the action or an instance of swaying or of being swayed **:** an oscillating, fluctuating, or sweeping motion
2 : an inclination or deflection caused by or as if by swaying
3 a : a controlling influence **b :** sovereign power **:** DOMINION **c :** the ability to exercise influence or authority **:** DOMINANCE
synonym see POWER
²**sway** *verb* [alteration of earlier *swey* to fall, swoon, from Middle English *sweyen*, probably of Scandinavian origin; akin to Old Norse *sveigja* to sway; akin to Lithuanian *svaigti* to become dizzy] (circa 1500)
intransitive verb
1 a : to swing slowly and rhythmically back and forth from a base or pivot **b :** to move gently from an upright to a leaning position
2 : to hold sway **:** act as ruler or governor
3 : to fluctuate or veer between one point, position, or opinion and another
transitive verb
1 a : to cause to sway **:** set to swinging, rocking, or oscillating **b :** to cause to bend downward to one side **c :** to cause to turn aside **:** DEFLECT, DIVERT
2 *archaic* **a :** WIELD **b :** GOVERN, RULE
3 a : to cause to vacillate **b :** to exert a guiding or controlling influence on
4 : to hoist in place ⟨*sway* up a mast⟩
synonym see SWING, AFFECT
— **sway·er** *noun*
sway-backed \'swā-,bakt\ *also* **sway·back** \-,bak\ *adjective* (1680)
: having an abnormally hollow or sagging back ⟨a *swaybacked* mare⟩
— **sway·back** *noun*
sway bar *noun* (1949)
: a bar that torsionally couples the right and left front-wheel suspensions of an automobile to reduce roll and sway
Swa·zi \'swä-zē\ *noun, plural* **Swazi** *or* **Swazis** (1878)
1 : a member of a Bantu people of southeastern Africa
2 : a Bantu language of the Swazi people
¹**swear** \'swar, 'swer\ *verb* **swore** \'swōr, 'swȯr\; **sworn** \'swōrn, 'swȯrn\; **swear·ing** [Middle English *sweren*, from Old English *swerian;* akin to Old High German *swerien* to swear and perhaps to Old Church Slavonic *svarŭ* quarrel] (before 12th century)
transitive verb
1 : to utter or take solemnly (an oath)
2 a : to assert as true or promise under oath ⟨a *sworn* affidavit⟩ **b :** to assert or promise emphatically or earnestly ⟨*swore* to uphold the Constitution⟩
3 a : to put to an oath **:** administer an oath to **b :** to bind by an oath ⟨*swore* them to secrecy⟩
4 *obsolete* **:** to invoke the name of (a sacred being) in an oath
5 : to bring into a specified state by swearing ⟨*swore* his life away⟩
intransitive verb
1 : to take an oath

2 : to use profane or obscene language **:** CURSE
— **swear·er** *noun*
— **swear by :** to place great confidence in
— **swear for :** to give assurance for **:** GUARANTEE
— **swear off :** to vow to abstain from **:** RENOUNCE ⟨*swear off* smoking⟩
²**swear** *noun* (14th century)
: OATH, SWEARWORD
swear in *transitive verb* (1536)
: to induct into office by administration of an oath
swear out *transitive verb* (1895)
: to procure (a warrant for arrest) by making a sworn accusation
swear·word \'swar-,wərd, 'swer-\ *noun* (1883)
: a profane or obscene oath or word
¹**sweat** \'swet\ *verb* **sweat** *or* **sweat·ed; sweat·ing** [Middle English *sweten*, from Old English *swǣtan*, from *swāt* sweat; akin to Old High German *sweiz* sweat, Latin *sudare* to sweat, Greek *hidrōs* sweat] (before 12th century)
intransitive verb
1 a : to excrete moisture in visible quantities through the openings of the sweat glands **:** PERSPIRE **b :** to labor or exert oneself so as to cause perspiration
2 a : to emit or exude moisture ⟨cheese *sweats* in ripening⟩ **b :** to gather surface moisture in beads as a result of condensation ⟨stones *sweat* at night⟩ **c (1) :** FERMENT **(2) :** PUTREFY
3 : to undergo anxiety or mental or emotional distress
4 : to become exuded through pores or a porous surface **:** OOZE
transitive verb
1 : to emit or seem to emit from pores **:** EXUDE
2 : to manipulate or produce by hard work or drudgery
3 : to get rid of or lose (weight) by or as if by sweating or being sweated
4 : to make wet with perspiration
5 a : to cause to excrete moisture from the skin **b :** to drive hard **:** OVERWORK **c :** to exact work from at low wages and under unfair or unhealthful conditions **d** *slang* **:** to give the third degree to
6 : to cause to exude or lose moisture; *especially* **:** to subject (as tobacco leaves) to fermentation
7 a : to extract something valuable from by unfair or dishonest means **:** FLEECE **b :** to remove particles of metal from (a coin) by abrasion
8 a : to heat (as solder) so as to melt and cause to run especially between surfaces to unite them; *also* **:** to unite by such means ⟨*sweat* a pipe joint⟩ **b :** to heat so as to extract an easily fusible constituent ⟨*sweat* bismuth ore⟩ **c :** to sauté in a covered vessel until natural juices are exuded
9 : to worry about ⟨doesn't *sweat* the small stuff —Barry McDermott⟩
— **sweat blood :** to work or worry intensely ⟨in preparing speeches *sweats blood* in his own way —Stewart Cockburn⟩
²**sweat** *noun* (13th century)
1 : hard work **:** DRUDGERY
2 : the fluid excreted from the sweat glands of the skin **:** PERSPIRATION
3 : moisture issuing from or gathering in drops on a surface
4 a : the condition of one sweating or sweated **b :** a spell of sweating
5 : a state of anxiety or impatience
6 *plural* **a :** SWEAT SUIT **b :** SWEATPANTS
— **no sweat** *slang* **:** with little or no difficulty **:** EASILY; *also* **:** EASY — often used interjectionally

\ə\ abut \ᵊ\ kitten \ər\ further \a\ ash \ā\ ace
\ä\ mop, mar \aú\ out \ch\ chin \e\ bet \ē\ easy
\g\ go \i\ hit \ī\ ice \j\ job \ŋ\ sing \ō\ go
\ȯ\ law \ȯi\ boy \th\ thin \t͟h\ the \ü\ loot \ú\ foot
\y\ yet \zh\ vision *see also* Guide to Pronunciation

sweat·band \'swet-,band\ *noun* (1891)
1 : a usually leather band lining the inner edge of a hat or cap to prevent sweat damage
2 : a band of material worn around the head or wrist to absorb sweat
sweat bee *noun* (1894)
: any of various small black or brownish bees (family Halictidae) that are attracted to perspiration
sweat·box \-,bäks\ *noun* (1864)
1 : a place in which one is made to sweat; *especially* **:** a narrow box or cell in which a prisoner is placed for punishment
2 : a device for sweating something (as hides in tanning or dried figs)
sweat·ed \'swe-təd\ *adjective* (1882)
: of, subjected to, or produced under sweatshop conditions ⟨*sweated* labor⟩ ⟨*sweated* goods⟩
sweat equity *noun* (1966)
: equity in a property resulting from labor invested in improvements that increase its value; *also* **:** the labor so invested
sweat·er \'swe-tər\ *noun* (15th century)
1 : one that sweats or causes sweating
2 : a knitted or crocheted jacket or pullover
sweat·er·dress \-,dres\ *noun* (1952)
: a knitted or crocheted dress
sweater girl *noun* (1940)
: a woman with a shapely bust
sweat·er–vest \'swe-tər-,vest\ *noun* (1952)
: a sleeveless pullover or buttoned sweater
sweat gland *noun* (1845)
: a simple tubular gland of the skin that secretes perspiration, is widely distributed in nearly all parts of the human skin, and consists typically of an epithelial tube extending spirally from a minute pore on the surface of the skin into the dermis or subcutaneous tissues where it ends in a convoluted tuft
sweat lodge *noun* (1850)
: a hut, lodge, or cavern heated by steam from water poured on hot stones and used especially by American Indians for ritual or therapeutic sweating
sweat out *transitive verb* (1589)
1 : to work one's way painfully through or to
2 : to endure or wait through the course of
sweat·pants \'swet-,pan(t)s\ *noun plural* (1925)
: pants having a drawstring or elastic waist and elastic cuffs at the ankle that are worn especially by athletes in warming up
sweat·shirt \-,shərt\ *noun* (1925)
: a loose collarless pullover usually of heavy cotton jersey
sweat·shop \-,shäp\ *noun* (1892)
: a shop or factory in which workers are employed for long hours at low wages and under unhealthy conditions
sweat suit *noun* (1930)
: a suit worn usually for exercise that consists of a sweatshirt and sweatpants
sweat test *noun* (1978)
: a test for cystic fibrosis that involves measuring the subject's sweat for abnormally high sodium chloride content
sweaty \'swe-tē\ *adjective* **sweat·i·er; -est** (14th century)
1 : causing sweat ⟨a *sweaty* day⟩ ⟨*sweaty* work⟩
2 : wet or stained with or smelling of sweat
— **sweat·i·ly** \'swe-tᵊl-ē\ *adverb*
— **sweat·i·ness** \'swe-tē-nəs\ *noun*
swede \'swēd\ *noun* [Low German or obsolete Dutch] (1589)
1 *capitalized* **a :** a native or inhabitant of Sweden **b :** a person of Swedish descent
2 *chiefly British* **:** RUTABAGA
Swe·den·bor·gian \,swē-d°n-'bȯr-j(ē-)ən, -'bȯr-gē-ən\ *adjective* (1807)
: of or relating to the teachings of Emanuel Swedenborg or the Church of the New Jerusalem based on his teachings
— **Swedenborgian** *noun*

— **Swe·den·bor·gian·ism** \-j(ē-)ə-,ni-zəm, -gē-ə-\ *noun*
Swed·ish \'swē-dish\ *noun* (1605)
1 : the North Germanic language spoken in Sweden and a part of Finland
2 *plural in construction* **:** the people of Sweden
— **Swedish** *adjective*
Swedish massage *noun* (1911)
: massage involving a system of active and passive exercise of muscles and joints
¹sweep \'swēp\ *verb* **swept** \'swept\; **sweep·ing** [Middle English *swepen*; akin to Old English *swāpan* to sweep, Old High German *sweifen* to wander] (14th century)
transitive verb
1 a : to remove from a surface with or as if with a broom or brush ⟨*swept* the crumbs from the table⟩ **b :** to destroy completely — WIPE OUT — usually used with *away* ⟨everything she cherished, might be *swept* away overnight —Louis Bromfield⟩ **c :** to remove or take with a single continuous forceful action ⟨*swept* the books off the desk⟩ **d :** to remove from sight or consideration ⟨the problem can't be *swept* under the rug⟩ **e :** to drive or carry along with irresistible force ⟨a wave of protest that *swept* the opposition into office⟩
2 a : to clean with or as if with a broom or brush **b :** to clear by repeated and forcible action **c :** to move across or along swiftly, violently, or overwhelmingly ⟨fire *swept* the business district —American Guide Series: Maryland⟩ **d :** to win an overwhelming victory in or on ⟨*sweep* the elections⟩ **e :** to win all the games or contests of ⟨*sweep* a double-header⟩ ⟨*sweep* a series⟩
3 : to touch in passing with a swift continuous movement
4 : to trace or describe the locus or extent of (as a line, circle, or angle)
5 : to cover the entire range of ⟨his eyes *swept* the horizon⟩
intransitive verb
1 a : to clean a surface with or as if with a broom **b :** to move swiftly, forcefully, or devastatingly ⟨the wind *swept* through the treetops⟩
2 : to go with stately or sweeping movements ⟨proudly *swept* into the room⟩
3 : to move or extend in a wide curve or range
— **sweep one off one's feet :** to gain immediate and unquestioning support, approval, or acceptance by a person
— **sweep the board** *or* **sweep the table 1 :** to win all the bets on the table **2 :** to win everything **:** beat all competitors
²sweep *noun* (1548)
1 : something that sweeps or works with a sweeping motion: as **a :** a long pole or timber pivoted on a tall post and used to raise and lower a bucket in a well **b :** a triangular cultivator

sweep 1a

blade that cuts off weeds under the soil surface **c :** a windmill sail
2 a : an instance of sweeping; *especially* **:** a clearing out or away with or as if with a broom **b :** the removal from the table in one play in casino of all the cards by pairing or combining **c :** an overwhelming victory **d :** a winning of all the contests or prizes in a competition **e :** a wide-ranging search of an area (as by police)
3 a : a movement of great range and force **b :** a curving or circular course or line **c :** the compass of a sweeping movement **:** SCOPE **d**

: a broad unbroken area or extent **e :** an end run in football in which one or more linemen pull back and run interference for the ballcarrier
4 : CHIMNEY SWEEP
5 : SWEEPSTAKES
6 : obliquity with respect to a reference line ⟨*sweep* of an airplane wing⟩; *especially* **:** SWEEPBACK
7 *plural* **:** a television ratings period during which surveys are taken to determine advertising rates
synonym SEE RANGE
sweep·back \'swēp-,bak\ *noun* (1914)
: the backward slant of an airplane wing in which the outer portion of the wing is downstream from the inner portion
sweep·er \'swē-pər\ *noun* (15th century)
1 : one that sweeps
2 : a lone back in soccer who plays between the line of the defenders and the goal
sweep hand *noun* (1943)
: SWEEP-SECOND HAND
¹sweep·ing *noun* (14th century)
1 : the act or action of one that sweeps ⟨gave the room a good *sweeping*⟩
2 *plural* **:** things collected by sweeping **:** REFUSE
²sweep·ing *adjective* (1610)
1 a : moving or extending in a wide curve or over a wide area **b :** having a curving line or form
2 a : EXTENSIVE ⟨*sweeping* reforms⟩ **b :** marked by wholesale and indiscriminate inclusion ⟨*sweeping* generalities⟩
— **sweep·ing·ly** \'swē-piŋ-lē\ *adverb*
— **sweep·ing·ness** *noun*
sweep–sec·ond hand \'swēp-,se-kənd-, -kənt-\ *noun* (circa 1940)
: a hand marking seconds on a timepiece mounted concentrically with the other hands and read from the same dial as the minute hand
sweep·stakes \-,stāks\ *noun plural but singular or plural in construction, also* **sweep–stake** \-,stāk\ [Middle English *swepestake* one who wins all the stakes in a game, from *swepen* to sweep + *stake*] (1785)
1 a : a race or contest in which the entire prize may be awarded to the winner; *specifically* **:** STAKE RACE **b :** CONTEST, COMPETITION
2 : any of various lotteries
sweepy \'swē-pē\ *adjective* **sweep·i·er; -est** (1697)
: sweeping in motion, line, or force
¹sweet \'swēt\ *adjective* [Middle English *swete*, from Old English *swēte*; akin to Old High German *suozi* sweet, Latin *suadēre* to urge, *suavis* sweet, Greek *hēdys*] (before 12th century)
1 a (1) : pleasing to the taste **(2) :** being or inducing the one of the four basic taste sensations that is typically induced by disaccharides and is mediated especially by receptors in taste buds at the front of the tongue — compare BITTER, SALT, SOUR **b (1)** *of a beverage* **:** containing a sweetening ingredient **:** not dry **(2)** *of wine* **:** retaining a portion of natural sugar
2 a : pleasing to the mind or feelings **:** AGREEABLE, GRATIFYING — often used as a generalized term of approval ⟨how *sweet* it is⟩ **b :** marked by gentle good humor or kindliness **c :** FRAGRANT **d (1) :** delicately pleasing to the ear or eye **(2) :** played in a straightforward melodic style ⟨*sweet* jazz⟩ **e :** SACCHARINE, CLOYING
3 : much loved **:** DEAR
4 a : not sour, rancid, decaying, or stale **:** WHOLESOME ⟨*sweet* milk⟩ **b :** not salt or salted **:** FRESH ⟨*sweet* butter⟩ **c** *of land* **:** free from excessive acidity **d :** free from noxious gases and odors **e :** free from excess of acid, sulfur, or corrosive salts ⟨*sweet* crude oil⟩

5 : SKILLFUL, PROFICIENT ⟨a *sweet* golf swing⟩
6 — used as an intensive ⟨take your own *sweet* time⟩
— **sweet·ly** *adverb*
— **sweet·ness** *noun*
— **sweet on :** having a crush on
²**sweet** *adverb* (13th century)
: in a sweet manner
³**sweet** *noun* (14th century)
1 : something that is sweet to the taste: as **a** **:** a food (as a candy or preserve) having a high sugar content ⟨fill up on *sweets*⟩ **b** *British* **:** DESSERT **c** *British* **:** HARD CANDY
2 : a sweet taste sensation
3 : a pleasant or gratifying experience, possession, or state
4 : DARLING, SWEETHEART
5 a *archaic* **:** FRAGRANCE **b** *plural, archaic* **:** things having a sweet smell
sweet alyssum *noun* (1822)
: a widely cultivated perennial European herb (*Lobularia maritima*) of the mustard family having narrow leaves and clusters of small fragrant usually white or pink flowers
sweet–and–sour \ˌswē-tᵊn-ˈsau̇(ə)r\ *adjective* (1928)
: seasoned with a sauce containing sugar and vinegar or lemon juice ⟨*sweet-and-sour* shrimp⟩
sweet basil *noun* (circa 1647)
: a basil (*Ocimum basilicum*) with whitish or purple flowers that includes several cultivars (as bush basil)
sweet bay *noun* (1716)
1 : LAUREL 1
2 : a magnolia (*Magnolia virginiana*) of the eastern U.S. that has fragrant white flowers and leaves with glaucous undersides
sweet birch *noun* (1785)
: a common birch (*Betula lenta*) of the eastern U.S. that has spicy brown bark when young, hard dark-colored wood, and a volatile oil in its bark resembling wintergreen — called also *black birch*
sweet·bread \ˈswēt-ˌbred\ *noun* (1565)
: the thymus or pancreas of a young animal (as a calf) used for food
sweet·bri·er *also* **sweet·bri·ar** \-ˌbrī-(ə)r\ *noun* (1538)
: an Old World rose (especially *Rosa eglanteria*) with stout recurved prickles and white to deep rosy pink single flowers — called also *eglantine*
sweet cherry *noun* (circa 1901)
: a white-flowered Eurasian cherry (*Prunus avium*) widely grown for its large sweet-flavored fruits; *also* **:** its fruit
sweet chocolate *noun* (1897)
: chocolate that contains added sugar
sweet cic·e·ly \-ˈsi-s(ə-)lē\ *noun* [*cicely* from Latin *seselis,* from Greek] (1668)
: any of a genus (*Osmorhiza*) of American and eastern Asian herbs of the carrot family that typically have thick fleshy roots and grow in moist woodlands
sweet clover *noun* (1868)
: any of a genus (*Melilotus*) of Old World legumes that have trifoliolate leaves and are widely grown for soil improvement or hay
sweet corn *noun* (1646)
: an Indian corn (especially *Zea mays rugosa*) with kernels containing a high percentage of sugar and adapted for table use when the kernels are unripe
sweet·en \ˈswēt-ᵊn\ *verb* **sweet·ened; sweet·en·ing** \ˈswēt-niŋ, ˈswē-t°n-iŋ\ (circa 1552)
transitive verb
1 : to make sweet
2 : to soften the mood or attitude of
3 : to make less painful or trying
4 : to free from a harmful or undesirable quality or substance; *especially* **:** to remove sulfur compounds from ⟨*sweeten* natural gas⟩

5 : to make more valuable or attractive: as **a** **:** to increase (a pot not won on the previous deal) by anteing prior to another deal **b** **:** to place additional securities as collateral for (a loan)
intransitive verb
: to become sweet
— **sweet·en·er** \ˈswēt-nər, ˈswē-t°n-ər\ *noun*
sweetening *noun* (1819)
: something that sweetens
sweet fern *noun* (1654)
: a small North American shrub (*Comptonia peregrina*) of the wax-myrtle family with aromatic leaves
sweet flag *noun* (1784)
: a perennial marsh herb (*Acorus calamus*) of the arum family with long narrow leaves and an aromatic rootstock — called also *calamus*
sweet gum *noun* (1700)
1 : a North American tree (*Liquidambar styraciflua*) of the witch-hazel family with palmately lobed leaves, corky branches, and hard wood
2 : heartwood of the sweet gum or reddish brown lumber sawed from it
¹**sweet·heart** \ˈswēt-ˌhärt\ *noun* (14th century)
1 : DARLING
2 : one who is loved
3 : a generally likable person
4 : a remarkable one of its kind
²**sweetheart** *adjective* (1942)
: of or relating to an agreement between an employer and a labor union official arranged privately for their benefit usually at the expense of the workers ⟨a *sweetheart* contract⟩; *broadly* **:** arranged in private for the benefit of a few at the expense of many ⟨a *sweetheart* deal⟩
sweetheart neckline *noun* (1941)
: a neckline for women's clothing that is high in back and low in front where it is scalloped to resemble the top of a heart
sweet·ie \ˈswē-tē\ *noun* (1705)
1 *plural, British* **:** SWEET 1a
2 : SWEETHEART
sweetie pie *noun* (1928)
: SWEETHEART
sweet·ing \ˈswē-tiŋ\ *noun* (13th century)
1 *archaic* **:** SWEETHEART
2 : a sweet apple
sweet·ish \-tish\ *adjective* (1580)
1 : somewhat sweet
2 : unpleasantly sweet
— **sweet·ish·ly** *adverb*
sweet marjoram *noun* (1565)
: a perennial marjoram (*Origanum majorana* synonym *Majorana hortensis*) with dense spikelike flower clusters
sweet·meat \ˈswēt-ˌmēt\ *noun* (14th century)
: a food rich in sugar: as **a** **:** a candied or crystallized fruit **b** **:** CANDY, CONFECTION
sweetness and light *noun* (1704)
1 : a harmonious combination of beauty and enlightenment viewed as a hallmark of culture
2 a : amiable reasonableness of disposition ⟨they were all *sweetness and light*⟩ **b** **:** an untroubled or harmonious state or condition ⟨but all was not *sweetness and light*⟩
sweet orange *noun* (1538)
1 a : an orange (*Citrus sinensis*) that is probably native to southeastern Asia, has a fruit with a pithy central axis, and is the source of the widely cultivated oranges of commerce **b** **:** a cultivated orange derived from the sweet orange and usually having fruit with a relatively thin skin and sweet juicy edible pulp
2 : the fruit of a sweet orange

sweet pea *noun* (1732)
1 : a widely cultivated Italian legume (*Lathyrus odoratus*) having slender usually climbing stems, ovate leaves, and large fragrant flowers
2 : the flower of a sweet pea
sweet pepper *noun* (1814)
: a large mild thick-walled capsicum fruit; *also* **:** a pepper plant bearing this fruit
sweet potato *noun* (1750)
1 : a tropical vine (*Ipomoea batatas*) related to the morning glory with variously shaped leaves and purplish flowers; *also* **:** its large thick sweet and nutritious tuberous root that is cooked and eaten as a vegetable — compare YAM 2
2 : OCARINA
sweet·shop \ˈswēt-ˌshäp\ *noun* (1879)
chiefly British **:** a candy store
sweet·sop \-ˌsäp\ *noun* (1696)
: SUGAR APPLE
sweet sorghum *noun* (1867)
: SORGO
sweet spot *noun* (circa 1949)
: the area around the center of mass of a bat, racket, or head of a club that is the most effective part with which to hit a ball
sweet·talk \ˈswēt-ˌtȯk\ *verb* (1928)
transitive verb
: CAJOLE, COAX
intransitive verb
: to use flattery
sweet talk *noun* (1926)
: FLATTERY
sweet tooth *noun* (14th century)
: a craving or fondness for sweet food
sweet wil·liam \ˌswēt-ˈwil-yəm\ *noun, often W capitalized* [from the name *William*] (1573)
: a widely cultivated Old World pink (*Dianthus barbatus*) with small white to deep red or purple flowers often showily spotted, banded, or mottled and borne in flat bracteate heads on erect stalks

sweet william

¹**swell** \ˈswel\ *verb* **swelled; swelled** *or* **swol·len** \ˈswō-lən\; **swell·ing** [Middle English, from Old English *swellan*; akin to Old High German *swellan* to swell] (before 12th century)
intransitive verb
1 a : to expand (as in size, volume, or numbers) gradually beyond a normal or original limit ⟨the population *swelled*⟩ **b** **:** to become distended or puffed up ⟨her ankle is badly *swollen*⟩ **c** **:** to form a bulge or rounded elevation
2 a : to become filled with pride and arrogance **b** **:** to behave or speak in a pompous, blustering, or self-important manner **c** **:** to play the swell
3 : to become distended with emotion
transitive verb
1 : to affect with a powerful or expansive emotion
2 : to increase the size, number, or intensity of
synonym see EXPAND
²**swell** *noun* (1606)
1 : a long often massive and crestless wave or succession of waves often continuing beyond or after its cause (as a gale)
2 a : the condition of being protuberant **b** **:** a rounded elevation
3 a : the act or process of swelling **b** (1) **:** a gradual increase and decrease of the loudness of a musical sound; *also* **:** a sign indicating a swell (2) **:** a device used in an organ for governing loudness

4 a *archaic* : an impressive, pompous, or fashionable air or display **b** : a person dressed in the height of fashion **c** : a person of high social position or outstanding competence

³**swell** *adjective* (1785)
1 a : STYLISH **b** : socially prominent
2 : EXCELLENT — used as a generalized term of enthusiasm

swell box *noun* (circa 1801)
: a chamber in an organ containing a set of pipes and having shutters that open or shut to regulate the volume of tone

swelled head *noun* (1891)
: an exaggerated opinion of oneself : SELF-CONCEIT
— **swelled–head·ed** \'sweld-,he-dəd\ *adjective*
— **swelled–head·ed·ness** *noun*

swell·fish \'swel-,fish\ *noun* (1807)
: PUFFER 2a

swell–front \'swel-,frənt\ *adjective* (1914)
: BOWFRONT 1

swell–head \-,hed\ *noun* (1845)
: one who has a swelled head
— **swell·head·ed** \-,he-dəd\ *adjective*
— **swell·head·ed·ness** *noun*

swell·ing \'swe-liŋ\ *noun* (before 12th century)
1 : something that is swollen; *specifically* : an abnormal bodily protuberance or localized enlargement
2 : the condition of being swollen

¹**swel·ter** \'swel-tər\ *verb* **swel·tered; swel·ter·ing** \-t(ə-)riŋ\ [Middle English *sweltren*, frequentative of *swelten* to die, be overcome by heat, from Old English *sweltan* to die; akin to Gothic *swiltan* to die] (14th century)
intransitive verb
1 : to suffer, sweat, or be faint from heat
2 : to become exceedingly hot ⟨in summer, the place *swelters*⟩
transitive verb
1 : to oppress with heat
2 *archaic* : EXUDE ⟨*sweltered* venom —Shakespeare⟩

²**swelter** *noun* (1851)
1 : a state of oppressive heat
2 : WELTER
3 : an excited or overwrought state of mind : SWEAT ⟨in a *swelter*⟩

swel·ter·ing *adjective* (1586)
: oppressively hot
— **swel·ter·ing·ly** \-t(ə-)riŋ-lē\ *adverb*

swept \'swept\ *adjective* [*swept*, past participle of *sweep*] (1903)
: slanted backward

swept–back \'swep(t)-'bak\ *adjective* (1914)
: possessing sweepback

swerve \'swərv\ *verb* **swerved; swerv·ing** [Middle English, from Old English *sweorfan* to wipe, file away; akin to Old High German *swerban* to wipe off, Welsh *chwerfu* to whirl] (14th century)
intransitive verb
: to turn aside abruptly from a straight line or course : DEVIATE
transitive verb
: to cause to turn aside or deviate ☆
— **swerve** *noun*

swev·en \'swe-vən\ *noun* [Middle English, from Old English *swefn* sleep, dream, vision — more at SOMNOLENT] (before 12th century)
archaic : DREAM, VISION

swid·den \'swi-dᵊn\ *noun, often attributive* [English dialect, burned clearing, probably from Old Norse *svithinn*, past participle of *svitha* to burn, singe] (circa 1868)
: a temporary agricultural plot produced by cutting back and burning off vegetative cover

¹**swift** \'swift\ *adjective* [Middle English, from Old English; akin to Old English *swīfan* to revolve — more at SWIVEL] (before 12th century)
1 : moving or capable of moving with great speed

2 : occurring suddenly or within a very short time
3 : quick to respond : READY
synonym see FAST

²**swift** *adverb* (14th century)
: SWIFTLY ⟨*swift*-flowing⟩

³**swift** *noun* (15th century)
1 : any of several lizards (especially of the genus *Sceloporus*) that run swiftly
2 : a reel for winding yarn or thread
3 : any of numerous small plainly colored birds (family Apodidae) that are related to the hummingbirds but superficially much resemble swallows

swift fox *noun* (1869)
: a small fox (*Vulpes velox*) with large ears that occurs on the plains of western North America

swift·let \'swif(t)-lət\ *noun* (circa 1890)
: any of various cave-dwelling swifts (genus *Collocalia*) of Asia including one (*C. unicolor*) that produces the nest used in bird's nest soup

swift·ly *adverb* (before 12th century)
: in a swift manner : with speed : QUICKLY

swift·ness \'swif(t)-nəs\ *noun* (before 12th century)
1 : the quality or state of being swift : CELERITY
2 : the fact of being swift

¹**swig** \'swig\ *noun* [origin unknown] (circa 1623)
: a quantity drunk at one time

²**swig** *verb* **swigged; swig·ging** (circa 1650)
transitive verb
: to drink in long drafts ⟨*swig* cider⟩
intransitive verb
: to take a swig : DRINK
— **swig·ger** *noun*

¹**swill** \'swil\ *verb* [Middle English *swilen*, from Old English *swillan*] (before 12th century)
transitive verb
1 : WASH, DRENCH
2 : to drink great drafts of : GUZZLE
3 : to feed (as a pig) with swill
intransitive verb
1 : to drink or eat freely, greedily, or to excess
2 : SWASH
— **swill·er** *noun*

²**swill** *noun* (1553)
1 : something suggestive of slop or garbage : REFUSE
2 a : a semiliquid food for animals (as swine) composed of edible refuse mixed with water or skimmed or sour milk **b** : GARBAGE

¹**swim** \'swim\ *verb* **swam** \'swam\; **swum** \'swəm\; **swim·ming** [Middle English *swimmen*, from Old English *swimman*; akin to Old High German *swimman* to swim] (before 12th century)
intransitive verb
1 a : to propel oneself in water by natural means (as movements of the limbs, fins, or tail) **b** : to play in the water (as at a beach or swimming pool)
2 : to move with a motion like that of swimming : GLIDE ⟨a cloud *swam* slowly across the moon⟩
3 a : to float on a liquid : not sink **b** : to surmount difficulties : not go under ⟨sink or *swim*, live or die, survive or perish —Daniel Webster⟩
4 : to become immersed in or flooded with or as if with a liquid ⟨potatoes *swimming* in gravy⟩
5 : to have a floating or reeling appearance or sensation
transitive verb
1 a : to cross by propelling oneself through water ⟨*swim* a stream⟩ **b** : to execute in swimming
2 : to cause to swim or float
— **swim·mer** *noun*

²**swim** *noun* (1599)

1 : a smooth gliding motion
2 : an act or period of swimming
3 : a temporary dizziness or unconsciousness
4 a : an area frequented by fish **b** : the main current of activity ⟨in the *swim*⟩

³**swim** *adjective* (1924)
: of, relating to, or used in or for swimming ⟨a *swim* meet⟩

swim bladder *noun* (1837)
: the air bladder of a fish

swim fin *noun* (1947)
: FLIPPER 1b

swim·ma·ble \'swi-mə-bəl\ *adjective* (1852)
: that can be swum

swim·mer·et \,swi-mə-'ret, 'swi-mə-,\ *noun* (1840)
: one of a series of small unspecialized appendages under the abdomen of many crustaceans that are best developed in some decapods (as a lobster) and usually function in locomotion or reproduction

swimmer's itch *noun* (1928)
: a severe urticarial reaction to the presence in the skin of larval schistosomes that are not normally human parasites

¹**swimming** *adjective* (before 12th century)
1 [present participle of *swim*] : that swims ⟨a *swimming* bird⟩
2 [gerund of *swim*] : adapted to or used in or for swimming

²**swimming** *noun* (14th century)
: the act, art, or sport of one that swims and dives

swim·ming·ly \'swi-miŋ-lē\ *adverb* (1622)
: very well : SPLENDIDLY

swimming pool *noun* (1899)
: a pool suitable for swimming; *especially* : a tank (as of concrete or plastic) made for swimming

swim·my \'swi-mē\ *adjective* **swim·mi·er; -est** (1836)
1 : verging on, causing, or affected by dizziness or giddiness
2 *of vision* : UNSTEADY, BLURRED
— **swim·mi·ly** \'swi-mə-lē\ *adverb*

swim·suit \'swim-,süt\ *noun* (1926)
: a suit for swimming or bathing

swim·wear \-,war, -,wer\ *noun* (1935)
: clothing suitable for wear while swimming or bathing

¹**swin·dle** \'swin-dᵊl\ *verb* **swin·dled; swin·dling** \'swin(d)-liŋ, 'swin-dᵊl-iŋ\ [back-formation from *swindler*, from German *Schwindler* giddy person, from *schwindeln* to be dizzy, from Old High German *swintilōn*, frequentative of *swintan* to diminish, vanish; akin to Old English *swindan* to vanish] (circa 1782)
intransitive verb
: to obtain money or property by fraud or deceit
transitive verb

☆ SYNONYMS
Swerve, veer, deviate, depart, digress, diverge mean to turn aside from a straight course. SWERVE may suggest a physical, mental, or moral turning away from a given course, often with abruptness ⟨*swerved* to avoid hitting the dog⟩. VEER implies a major change in direction ⟨at that point the path *veers* to the right⟩. DEVIATE implies a turning from a customary or prescribed course ⟨never *deviated* from her daily routine⟩. DEPART suggests a deviation from a traditional or conventional course or type ⟨occasionally *departs* from his own guidelines⟩. DIGRESS applies to a departing from the subject of one's discourse ⟨a professor prone to *digress*⟩. DIVERGE may equal DEPART but usually suggests a branching of a main path into two or more leading in different directions ⟨after school their paths *diverged*⟩.

: to take money or property from by fraud or deceit ◇
***synonym* see** CHEAT
— **swin·dler** \ˈswin(d)-lər, ˈswin-dᵊl-ər\ *noun*

²swindle *noun* (1833)
: an act or instance of swindling : FRAUD

swine \ˈswīn\ *noun, plural* **swine** [Middle English, from Old English *swīn;* akin to Old High German *swīn* swine, Latin *sus* — more at SOW] (before 12th century)
1 : any of various stout-bodied short-legged omnivorous mammals (family Suidae) with a thick bristly skin and a long mobile snout; *especially* **:** a domesticated member of the species (*Sus scrofa*) that includes the European wild boar
2 : a contemptible person

swine·herd \-ˌhərd\ *noun* (before 12th century)
: one who tends swine

¹swing \ˈswiŋ\ *verb* **swung** \ˈswəŋ\; **swing·ing** \ˈswiŋ-iŋ\ [Middle English, to beat, fling, hurl, rush, from Old English *swingan* to beat, fling oneself, rush; akin to Old High German *swingan* to fling, rush] (13th century)
transitive verb
1 a : to cause to move vigorously through a wide arc or circle ⟨*swing* an ax⟩ **b :** to cause to sway to and fro **c** (1) **:** to cause to turn on an axis (2) **:** to cause to face or move in another direction ⟨*swing* the car into a side road⟩
2 : to suspend so as to permit swaying or turning
3 : to convey by suspension ⟨cranes *swinging* cargo into the ship's hold⟩
4 a (1) **:** to influence decisively ⟨*swing* a lot of votes⟩ (2) **:** to bring around by influence **b :** to handle successfully **:** MANAGE ⟨wasn't able to *swing* a new car on his income⟩ ⟨*swing* a deal⟩
5 : to play or sing (as a melody) in the style of swing music
intransitive verb
1 : to move freely to and fro especially in suspension from an overhead support
2 a : to die by hanging **b :** to hang freely from a support
3 : to move in or describe a circle or arc: **a :** to turn on a hinge or pivot **b :** to turn in place **c :** to convey oneself by grasping a fixed support ⟨*swing* aboard the train⟩
4 a : to have a steady pulsing rhythm **b :** to play or sing with a lively compelling rhythm; *specifically* **:** to play swing music
5 : to shift or fluctuate from one condition, form, position, or object of attention or favor to another ⟨*swing* constantly from optimism to pessimism and back —Sinclair Lewis⟩
6 a : to move along rhythmically **b :** to start up in a smooth vigorous manner ⟨ready to *swing* into action⟩
7 : to hit or aim at something with a sweeping arm movement
8 a : to be lively and up-to-date **b :** to engage freely in sex ☆ ☆

²swing *noun* (14th century)
1 : an act or instance of swinging **:** swinging movement: as **a** (1) **:** a stroke or blow delivered with a sweeping arm movement ⟨a batter with a powerful *swing*⟩ (2) **:** a sweeping or rhythmic movement of the body or a bodily part (3) **:** a dance figure in which two dancers revolve with joined arms or hands (4) **:** jazz dancing in moderate tempo with a lilting syncopation **b** (1) **:** the regular movement of a freely suspended object (as a pendulum) along an arc and back (2) **:** back and forth sweep ⟨the *swing* of the tides⟩ **c** (1) **:** steady pulsing rhythm (as in poetry or music) (2) **:** a steady vigorous movement characterizing an activity or creative work **d** (1) **:** a trend toward a high or low point in a fluctuating cycle (as of business activity) (2) **:** an often periodic shift from one condition, form, position, or object of attention or favor to another

2 a : liberty of action **b** (1) **:** the driving power of something swung or hurled (2) **:** steady vigorous advance **:** driving speed ⟨a train approaching at full *swing*⟩
3 : the progression of an activity, process, or phase of existence ⟨the work is in full *swing*⟩
4 : the arc or range through which something swings
5 : something that swings freely from or on a support; *especially* **:** a seat suspended by a rope or chains for swinging to and fro on for pleasure
6 a : a curving course or outline **b :** a course from and back to a point **:** a circular tour
7 : jazz played usually by a large dance band and characterized by a steady lively rhythm, simple harmony, and a basic melody often submerged in improvisation
8 : a short pass in football thrown to a back running to the outside

³swing *adjective* (1934)
1 : of or relating to musical swing ⟨a *swing* band⟩ ⟨*swing* music⟩
2 : that may swing often decisively either way on an issue or in an election ⟨*swing* voters⟩ ⟨a *swing* state⟩

¹swinge \ˈswinj\ *transitive verb* **swinged; swinge·ing** [Middle English *swengen* to shake, from Old English *swengan;* akin to Old English *swingan*] (12th century)
chiefly dialect **:** BEAT, SCOURGE

²swinge *transitive verb* **swinged; swinge·ing** [alteration of *singe*] (1590)
dialect **:** SINGE, SCORCH

¹swinge·ing *also* **swing·ing** \ˈswin-jiŋ\ *adjective* [from present participle of ¹*swinge*] (circa 1590)
chiefly British **:** very large, high, or severe ⟨*swingeing* fines⟩ ⟨*swingeing* taxes⟩

²swingeing *or* **swinging** *adverb* (1690)
chiefly British **:** VERY, SUPERLATIVELY

¹swing·er \ˈswiŋ-ər\ *noun* (1543)
: one that swings: as **a :** a lively up-to-date person who indulges in what is considered fashionable **b :** one who engages freely in sex

²swing·er \ˈswin-jər\ *noun* [¹*swinge*] (1599)
: WHOPPER 1

swing·ing \ˈswiŋ-iŋ\ *adjective* [present participle of ¹*swing*] (1956)
: being lively and up-to-date; *also* **:** abounding in swingers and swinging entertainment ⟨a *swinging* coffeehouse⟩

¹swing·ing·ly \ˈswin-jiŋ-lē\ *adverb* (1672)
chiefly British **:** VERY, EXTREMELY

²swing·ing·ly \ˈswiŋ-iŋ-lē\ *adverb* (1882)
: in a swinging manner **:** with a swinging movement

swin·gle·tree \ˈswiŋ-gəl-ˌ(ˌ)trē\ *noun* [Middle English *swyngyll tre,* from *swyngyll* rod for beating flax (from Middle Dutch *swengel*) + *tre* tree] (15th century)
: WHIFFLETREE

swing·man \ˈswiŋ-ˌman, -mən\ *noun* (1965)
: a player capable of playing effectively in two different positions and especially of playing both guard and forward on a basketball team

swing shift *noun* (1940)
1 : the work shift between the day and night shifts (as from 4 P.M. to midnight)
2 : a group of workers in a factory operating seven days a week that work as needed to permit the regular shift workers to have one or more free days per week

swingy \ˈswiŋ-ē\ *adjective* **swing·i·er; -est** (1915)
: marked by swing

swin·ish \ˈswī-nish\ *adjective* (13th century)
: of, suggesting, or characteristic of swine **:** BEASTLY
— **swin·ish·ly** *adverb*
— **swin·ish·ness** *noun*

¹swink \ˈswiŋk\ *intransitive verb* [Middle English, from Old English *swincan;* akin to Old High German *swingan* to rush — more at SWING] (before 12th century)
archaic **:** TOIL, SLAVE

²swink *noun* (12th century)
archaic **:** LABOR, DRUDGERY

¹swipe \ˈswīp\ *noun* [probably alteration of *sweep*] (1739)
1 : a strong sweeping blow
2 : a sharp often critical remark ⟨took a parting *swipe* at management⟩

²swipe *verb* **swiped; swip·ing** (circa 1825)
intransitive verb
: to strike or move with a sweeping motion
transitive verb
1 : to strike or wipe with a sweeping motion
2 : STEAL, PILFER

swipes \ˈswīps\ *noun plural* [origin unknown] (circa 1796)
British **:** poor, thin, or spoiled beer; *also* **:** BEER

¹swirl \ˈswər(-ə)l\ *verb* [Middle English] (14th century)

☆ **SYNONYMS**
Swing, wave, flourish, brandish, thrash mean to wield or cause to move to and fro or up and down. SWING implies regular or uniform movement ⟨*swing* the rope back and forth⟩. WAVE usually implies smooth or continuous motion ⟨*waving* the flag⟩. FLOURISH suggests vigorous, ostentatious, graceful movement ⟨*flourished* the winning lottery ticket⟩. BRANDISH implies threatening or menacing motion ⟨*brandishing* a knife⟩. THRASH suggests vigorous, abrupt, violent movement ⟨an infant *thrashing* his arms about⟩.

Swing, sway, oscillate, vibrate, fluctuate, waver, undulate mean to move from one direction to its opposite. SWING implies a movement of something attached at one end or one side ⟨the door suddenly *swung* open⟩. SWAY implies a slow swinging or teetering movement ⟨trees *swaying* in the breeze⟩. OSCILLATE stresses a usually regular alternation of direction ⟨an *oscillating* fan⟩. VIBRATE suggests the rapid oscillation of an elastic body under stress or impact ⟨the *vibrating* strings of a piano⟩. FLUCTUATE suggests constant irregular changes of level, intensity, or value ⟨*fluctuating* interest rates⟩. WAVER stresses irregular motion suggestive of reeling or tottering ⟨the exhausted runner *wavered* before collapsing⟩. UNDULATE suggests a gentle wavelike motion ⟨an *undulating* sea of grass⟩.

◇ **WORD HISTORY**
swindle One would hardly think that someone whose head is whirling could be convincing enough to perpetrate a swindle. However, the original meaning of the German noun *Schwindler* was "giddy person." In the same way that *giddy* has been extended in English to describe someone who is frivolous or foolish, *Schwindler* was extended to individuals given to habitual flights of fancy. The Germans applied the word as well to a fantastic schemer, then to a participant in shaky business deals, and finally to a cheat. The word *Schwindler* is a derivative of the verb *schwindeln,* first used to mean "to be dizzy" and then "to cheat." *Swindler* appeared first in English in the second half of the 18th century, and *swindle* was created from it by removal of the suffix. At first they were slang terms associated with the criminal underworld, but they soon became standard.

\ə\ **abut** \ᵊ\ **kitten** \ər\ **further** \a\ **ash** \ā\ **ace**
\ä\ **mop, mar** \au̇\ **out** \ch\ **chin** \e\ **bet** \ē\ **easy**
\g\ **go** \i\ **hit** \ī\ **ice** \j\ **job** \ŋ\ **sing** \ō\ **go**
\ȯ\ **law** \ȯi\ **boy** \th\ **thin** \t͟h\ **the** \ü\ **loot** \u̇\ **foot**
\y\ **yet** \zh\ **vision** *see also* Guide to Pronunciation

intransitive verb
1 a : to move with an eddying or whirling motion **b :** to pass in whirling confusion
2 : to have a twist or convolution
transitive verb
: to cause to swirl
— **swirl·ing·ly** \'swər-liŋ-lē\ *adverb*
²**swirl** *noun* (15th century)
1 a : a whirling mass or motion : EDDY **b** : whirling confusion ⟨a *swirl* of events⟩
2 : a twisting shape, mark, or pattern
3 : an act or instance of swirling
swirly \'swər-lē\ *adjective* **swirl·i·er; -est** (1785)
1 *Scottish* : KNOTTED, TWISTED
2 : that swirls : SWIRLING ⟨the *swirly* water of the rapids⟩
¹**swish** \'swish\ *verb* [imitative] (1756)
intransitive verb
: to move, pass, swing, or whirl with the sound of a swish
transitive verb
1 : to move, cut, or strike with a swish ⟨the horse *swished* its tail⟩
2 : to make (a basketball shot) so that the ball falls through the rim without touching it ⟨*swished* a three-point jumper⟩
— **swish·er** *noun*
— **swish·ing·ly** \'swi-shiŋ-lē\ *adverb*
²**swish** *noun* (1820)
1 a : a prolonged hissing sound (as of a whip cutting the air) **b :** a light sweeping or brushing sound (as of a full silk skirt in motion)
2 : a swishing movement
3 : an effeminate homosexual — usually used disparagingly
³**swish** *adjective* [origin unknown] (1879)
: SMART, FASHIONABLE
swishy \'swi-shē\ *adjective* **swish·i·er; -est** (1828)
1 : producing a swishing sound
2 : characterized by effeminate behavior
¹**Swiss** \'swis\ *noun* [Middle French *Suisse*, from Middle High German *Swīzer*, from *Swīz* Switzerland] (1515)
1 *plural* **Swiss a :** a native or inhabitant of Switzerland **b :** one that is of Swiss descent
2 *often not capitalized* : any of various fine sheer fabrics of cotton originally made in Switzerland; *especially* : DOTTED SWISS
3 : SWISS CHEESE
²**Swiss** *adjective* (1530)
: of, relating to, or characteristic of Switzerland or the Swiss
Swiss chard *noun* (1832)
: a beet (*Beta vulgaris cicla*) having large leaves and succulent stalks often cooked as a vegetable — called also *chard*
Swiss cheese *noun* (1822)
: a hard cheese characterized by elastic texture, mild nutlike flavor, and large holes that form during ripening
Swiss steak *noun* (1924)
: a slice of steak pounded with flour and braised usually with vegetables and seasonings
¹**switch** \'swich\ *noun* [perhaps from Middle Dutch *swijch* twig] (1592)
1 : a slender flexible whip, rod, or twig ⟨a riding *switch*⟩
2 : an act of switching: as **a :** a blow with a switch **b :** a shift from one to another **c :** a change from the usual
3 : a tuft of long hairs at the end of the tail of an animal (as a cow) — see COW illustration
4 a : a device made usually of two movable rails and necessary connections and designed to turn a locomotive or train from one track to another **b :** a railroad siding
5 : a device for making, breaking, or changing the connections in an electrical circuit
6 : a heavy strand of hair used in addition to a person's own hair for some coiffures
²**switch** (circa 1611)
transitive verb
1 : to strike or beat with or as if with a switch

2 : WHISK, LASH ⟨a cat *switching* its tail⟩
3 a (1) **:** to turn from one railroad track to another **:** SHUNT (2) **:** to move (cars) to different positions on the same track within terminal areas **b :** to make a shift in or exchange of ⟨*switch* seats⟩
4 a : to shift to another electrical circuit by means of a switch **b :** to operate an electrical switch so as to turn (as a light) off or on
intransitive verb
1 : to lash from side to side
2 : to make a shift or exchange
— **switch·able** \'swi-chə-bəl\ *adjective*
— **switch·er** *noun*
¹**switch·back** \'swich-ˌbak\ *noun* (1863)
: a zigzag road, trail, or section of railroad tracks for climbing a steep hill
²**switchback** *adjective* (1887)
: resembling a switchback (as in taking a zigzag course) ⟨a *switchback* career⟩
³**switchback** *intransitive verb* (1903)
: to follow a zigzag course especially in ascending or descending
switch·blade \-ˌblād\ *noun* (1932)
: a pocketknife having the blade spring-operated so that pressure on a release catch causes it to fly open — called also *switch-blade knife*
switch·board \-ˌbōrd, -ˌbȯrd\ *noun* (1873)
: an apparatus (as in a telephone exchange) consisting of a panel on which are mounted electric switches so arranged that a number of circuits may be connected, combined, and controlled
switch engine *noun* (1867)
: a railroad engine used in switching cars
switch·er·oo \ˌswi-chə-'rü\ *noun, plural* **-oos** [alteration of *switch*] (1933)
slang : a surprising variation : REVERSAL
switch·grass \'swich-ˌgras\ *noun* (1840)
: a panic grass (*Panicum virgatum*) of the western U.S. that is used for hay
switch–hit \-'hit\ *intransitive verb* **-hit; -hit·ting** [back-formation from *switch-hitter*] (1938)
: to bat right-handed against a left-hander and left-handed against a right-hander in baseball
switch–hit·ter \-'hi-tər\ *noun* (1948)
1 : a baseball player who switch-hits
2 *slang* : BISEXUAL
switch knife *noun* (1950)
: SWITCHBLADE
switch·man \'swich-mən\ *noun* (1843)
: one who attends a switch (as in a railroad yard)
switch·yard \-ˌyärd\ *noun* (1943)
: a usually enclosed area for the switching facilities of a power station
swith \'swith\ *adverb* [Middle English, strongly, quickly, from Old English *swīthe* strongly, from *swīth* strong; akin to Gothic *swinths* strong, Old English *gesund* sound — more at SOUND] (13th century)
chiefly dialect : INSTANTLY, QUICKLY
swith·er \'swi-thər\ *intransitive verb* [origin unknown] (1501)
dialect chiefly British : DOUBT, WAVER
— **swither** *noun, dialect chiefly British*
Swit·zer \'swit-sər\ *noun* [Middle High German *Swīzer*] (1549)
: SWISS
¹**swiv·el** \'swi-vəl\ *noun, often attributive* [Middle English; akin to Old English *swīfan* to revolve, Old High German *swebōn* to roll, heave] (14th century)
: a device joining two parts so that one or both can pivot freely (as on a bolt or pin)
²**swivel** *verb* **-eled** *or* **-elled; -el·ing** *or* **-el·ling** \'swi-və-liŋ, 'swiv-liŋ\ (1794)
transitive verb
: to turn on or as if on a swivel ⟨*swiveled* his eyes in various directions⟩
intransitive verb
: to swing or turn on or as if on a swivel
swivel chair *noun* (1860)
: a chair that swivels on its base

swiv·el–hipped \'swi-vəl-ˌhipt\ *adjective* (1947)
: moving with or characterized by movement with a twisting motion of the hips
swiv·et \'swi-vət\ *noun* [origin unknown] (circa 1892)
: a state of extreme agitation
¹**swiz·zle** \'swi-zəl\ *noun* [origin unknown] (1813)
: an iced whiskey sour churned with a swizzle stick until the glass or pitcher becomes frosted
²**swizzle** *verb* **swiz·zled; swiz·zling** \'swi-zə-liŋ, 'swiz-liŋ\ (circa 1847)
intransitive verb
: to drink especially to excess : GUZZLE
transitive verb
: to mix or stir with or as if with a swizzle stick
— **swiz·zler** \'swi-zə-lər, 'swiz-lər\ *noun*
swizzle stick *noun* (1879)
: a stick used to stir mixed drinks
swob *archaic variant of* SWAB
swollen *past participle of* SWELL
¹**swoon** \'swün\ *intransitive verb* [Middle English *swounen*] (13th century)
1 a : FAINT **b :** to become enraptured ⟨*swooning* with joy⟩
2 : DROOP, FADE
— **swoon·er** *noun*
— **swoon·ing·ly** \'swü-niŋ-lē\ *adverb*
²**swoon** *noun* (13th century)
1 a : a partial or total loss of consciousness **b** : a state of bewilderment or ecstasy : DAZE, RAPTURE
2 : a state of suspended animation : TORPOR
¹**swoop** \'swüp\ *verb* [alteration of Middle English *swopen* to sweep, from Old English *swāpan* — more at SWEEP] (1566)
intransitive verb
: to move with a sweep ⟨the eagle *swooped* down on its prey⟩
transitive verb
: to gain or carry off in or as in a swoop — usually used with *up*
— **swoop·er** *noun*
²**swoop** *noun* (1605)
: an act or instance of swooping
swoop-stake \'swüp-ˌstāk\ *adverb* [from alteration of *sweepstake*] (1602)
obsolete : in an indiscriminate manner
¹**swoosh** \'swüsh, 'swu̇sh\ *verb* [imitative] (1867)
intransitive verb
1 : to make or move with a rushing sound ⟨a car *swooshed* by⟩
2 : GUSH, SWIRL
transitive verb
: to discharge or transport with a rushing sound
²**swoosh** *noun* (1885)
: an act or instance of swooshing
swop *chiefly British variant of* SWAP
sword \'sȯrd, 'sȯrd\ *noun, often attributive* [Middle English, from Old English *sweord*; akin to Old High German *swert* sword] (before 12th century)
1 : a weapon (as a cutlass or rapier) with a long blade for cutting or thrusting that is often used as a symbol of honor or authority
2 a : an agency or instrument of destruction or combat **b :** the use of force ⟨the pen is mightier than the *sword* —E. G. Bulwer-Lytton⟩
3 : coercive power
4 : something that resembles a sword
— **sword·like** \-ˌlīk\ *adjective*
— **at swords' points :** mutually antagonistic : ready to fight
sword cane *noun* (1837)
: a cane in which a sword blade is concealed
sword dance *noun* (1604)
1 : a dance performed by men in a circle holding a sword in the right hand and grasping the tip of a neighbor's sword in the left hand
2 : a dance performed over or around swords
— **sword dancer** *noun*

sword fern *noun* (circa 1829)
: any of several ferns with long narrow more or less sword-shaped fronds: as **a** : a tropical fern (*Nephrolepis exaltata*) from which the Boston fern has been developed **b** : a fern (*Polystichum munitum*) of western North America with a large fleshy rhizome

sword·fish \'sōrd-,fish, 'sȯrd-\ *noun* (15th century)
: a very large oceanic bony fish (*Xiphias gladius* of the family Xiphiidae) that has a long swordlike beak formed by the bones of the upper jaw and is an important food and game fish

swordfish

sword grass *noun* (1598)
: any of various grasses or sedges having leaves with a sharp or toothed edge

sword knot *noun* (1694)
: an ornamental cord or tassel tied to the hilt of a sword

sword of Dam·o·cles \-'da-mə-,klēz\ *often S capitalized* (1820)
: an impending disaster

sword·play \'sōrd-,plā, 'sȯrd-\ *noun* (1627)
1 : the art or skill of wielding a sword especially in fencing
2 : an exhibition of swordplay
— **sword·play·er** *noun*

swords·man \'sōrdz-mən, 'sȯrdz-\ *noun* (circa 1680)
1 : one skilled in swordplay; *especially* : a saber fencer
2 *archaic* : a soldier armed with a sword

swords·man·ship \-,ship\ *noun* (circa 1852)
: SWORDPLAY

sword·tail \'sōrd-,tāl, 'sȯrd-\ *noun* (circa 1928)
: a small brightly marked Central American live-bearer (*Xiphophorus helleri* of the family Poeciliidae) often kept in tropical aquariums and bred in many colors

swore *past of* SWEAR

sworn *past participle of* SWEAR

¹swot \'swät\ *noun* [English dialect, sweat, from Middle English *swot*, from Old English *swāt* — more at SWEAT] (1850)
British : GRIND 2b

²swot *intransitive verb* **swot·ted; swot·ting** (circa 1860)
British : GRIND 4

¹swound \'swaund, 'swünd\ *noun* [Middle English, alteration of *swoun* swoon, from *swounen* to swoon] (15th century)
archaic : SWOON 1a

²swound *intransitive verb* (1530)
archaic : SWOON

swum *past participle of* SWIM

swung *past and past participle of* SWING

swung dash *noun* (1951)
: a character ~ used in printing to conserve space by representing part or all of a previously spelled-out word

syb·a·rite \'si-bə-,rīt\ *noun* (circa 1555)
1 [from the notorious luxury of the Sybarites] : VOLUPTUARY, SENSUALIST
2 *capitalized* : a native or resident of the ancient city of Sybaris
— **syb·a·rit·ic** \,si-bə-'ri-tik\ *adjective*
— **syb·a·rit·i·cal·ly** \-ti-k(ə-)lē\ *adverb*
— **syb·a·rit·ism** \'si-bə-,rī-,tī-zəm\ *noun*

syc·a·mine \'si-kə-,mīn, -mən\ *noun* [Latin *sycaminus*, from Greek *sykaminos*, of Semitic

origin; akin to Hebrew *shiqmāh* mulberry tree, sycamore] (1526)
: a tree of the Bible that is usually considered a mulberry (*Morus nigra*)

syc·a·more \'si-kə-,mōr, -,mȯr\ *noun* [Middle English *sicamour*, from Middle French *sicamor*, from Latin *sycomorus*, from Greek *sykomoros*, probably modification of a Semitic word akin to Hebrew *shiqmāh* sycamore] (14th century)
1 *also* **syc·o·more** \-kə-,\ : a fig tree (*Ficus sycomorus*) of Africa and the Middle East that is the sycamore of Scripture and has sweet and edible fruit similar but inferior to the common fig
2 : a Eurasian maple (*Acer pseudoplatanus*) with long racemes of showy yellowish green flowers that is widely planted as a shade tree
3 : ²PLANE; *especially* : a very large spreading tree (*Platanus occidentalis*) of eastern and central North America with 3- to 5-lobed broadly ovate leaves

syce \'sīs\ *noun* [Hindi *sāīs*, from Arabic *sā'is*] (1653)
: an attendant (as a groom) especially in India

sy·cee \'sī-,sē\ *noun* [Chinese (Guangdong) *sai-sì*, literally, fine silk] (1711)
: silver money made in the form of ingots and formerly used in China

sy·co·ni·um \sī-'kō-nē-əm\ *noun, plural* **-nia** \-nē-ə\ [New Latin, from Greek *sykon* fig + New Latin *-ium*] (circa 1856)
: the multiple fleshy fruit of a fig in which the ovaries are borne within an enlarged succulent concave or hollow receptacle

sy·co·phan·cy \'si-kə-fən(t)-sē *also* 'sī- & -,fan(t)-sē\ *noun* (1672)
: obsequious flattery; *also* : the character or behavior of a sycophant

sy·co·phant \-fənt *also* -,fant\ *noun* [Latin *sycophanta* slanderer, swindler, from Greek *sykophantēs* slanderer, from *sykon* fig + *phainein* to show — more at FANCY] (1575)
: a servile self-seeking flatterer
synonym see PARASITE
— **sycophant** *adjective*

sy·co·phan·tic \,si-kə-'fan-tik *also* ,sī-\ *adjective* (1676)
: of, relating to, or characteristic of a sycophant : FAWNING, OBSEQUIOUS
— **sy·co·phan·ti·cal·ly** \-'fan-ti-k(ə-)lē\ *adverb*

sy·co·phant·ish \,si-kə-'fan-tish *also* ,sī-\ *adjective* (1794)
: SYCOPHANTIC
— **sy·co·phant·ish·ly** *adverb*

sy·co·phant·ism \'si-kə-fən-,ti-zəm *also* 'sī- & -,fan-\ *noun* (1821)
: SYCOPHANCY

sy·co·phant·ly \-lē\ *adverb* (1672)
: in a sycophantic manner

sy·co·sis \sī-'kō-səs\ *noun* [New Latin, from Greek *sykōsis*, from *sykon* fig] (circa 1827)
: a chronic inflammatory disorder of the hair follicles marked by papules, pustules, and tubercles with crusting

sy·e·nite \'sī-ə-,nīt\ *noun* [Latin *Syenites* (*lapis*) stone of Syene, from *Syene*, ancient city in Egypt] (circa 1796)
: an igneous rock composed chiefly of feldspar
— **sy·e·nit·ic** \,sī-ə-'ni-tik\ *adjective*

sy·li \'sē-lē\ *noun, plural* **sylis** [Susu *sílí*, literally, elephant] (1974)
: the monetary unit of Guinea from 1972 to 1986

syl·la·bary \'si-lə-,ber-ē\ *noun, plural* **-bar·ies** [New Latin *syllabarium*, from Latin *syllaba* syllable] (1586)
: a table or listing of syllables; *specifically* : a series or set of written characters each one of which is used to represent a syllable

¹syl·lab·ic \sə-'la-bik\ *adjective* [Late Latin *syllabicus*, from Greek *syllabikos*, from *syllabē* syllable] (1728)
1 : constituting a syllable or the nucleus of a

syllable: **a** : not accompanied in the same syllable by a vowel 〈a *syllabic* consonant〉 **b** : having vowel quality more prominent than that of another vowel in the syllable 〈the first vowel of a falling diphthong, as \o̍\ in \oi\, is *syllabic*〉
2 : of, relating to, or denoting syllables 〈*syllabic* accent〉
3 : characterized by distinct enunciation or separation of syllables
4 : of, relating to, or constituting a type of verse distinguished primarily by count of syllables rather than by rhythmical arrangement of accents or quantities
— **syl·lab·i·cal·ly** \-bi-k(ə-)lē\ *adverb*

²syllabic *noun* (1880)
: a syllabic character or sound

syl·lab·i·cate \sə-'la-bə-,kāt\ *transitive verb* **-cat·ed; -cat·ing** (circa 1654)
: SYLLABIFY

syl·lab·i·ca·tion \sə-,la-bə-'kā-shən\ *noun* (15th century)
: the act, process, or method of forming or dividing words into syllables

syl·la·bic·i·ty \,si-lə-'bi-sə-tē\ *noun* (1933)
: the state of being or the power of forming a syllable

syl·lab·i·fi·ca·tion \sə-,la-bə-fə-'kā-shən\ *noun* (1838)
: SYLLABICATION

syl·lab·i·fy \sə-'la-bə-,fī\ *transitive verb* **-fied; -fy·ing** [Latin *syllaba* syllable] (circa 1859)
: to form or divide into syllables

¹syl·la·ble \'si-lə-bəl\ *noun* [Middle English, from Middle French *sillabe*, from Latin *syllaba*, from Greek *syllabē*, from *syllambanein* to gather together, from *syn-* + *lambanein* to take — more at LATCH] (14th century)
1 : a unit of spoken language that is next bigger than a speech sound and consists of one or more vowel sounds alone or of a syllabic consonant alone or of either with one or more consonant sounds preceding or following
2 : one or more letters (as *syl*, *la*, and *ble*) in a word (as *syl·la·ble*) usually set off from the rest of the word by a centered dot or a hyphen and roughly corresponding to the syllables of spoken language and treated as helps to pronunciation or as guides to placing hyphens at the end of a line
3 : the smallest conceivable expression or unit of something : JOT
4 : SOL-FA SYLLABLES

²syllable *transitive verb* **syl·la·bled; syl·la·bling** \-b(ə-)liŋ\ (15th century)
1 : to give a number or arrangement of syllables to (a word or verse)
2 : to express or utter in or as if in syllables

syl·la·bub \'si-lə-,bəb\ *noun* [origin unknown] (circa 1537)
1 : a drink made by curdling milk or cream with an acid beverage (as wine or cider)
2 : a sweetened drink or topping made of milk or cream beaten with wine or liquor and sometimes further thickened with gelatin and served as a dessert

syl·la·bus \-bəs\ *noun, plural* **-bi** \-,bī, -,bē\ *or* **-bus·es** [Late Latin, alteration of Latin *sillybus* label for a book, from Greek *sillybos*] (circa 1656)
1 : a summary outline of a discourse, treatise, or course of study or of examination requirements
2 : HEADNOTE 2

syl·lep·sis \sə-'lep-səs\ *noun, plural* **-lep·ses** \-,sēz\ [Latin, from Greek *syllēpsis*, from *syllambanein*] (circa 1550)
1 : the use of a word to modify or govern syntactically two or sometimes more words with only one of which it formally agrees in gender, number, or case

\ə\ abut \ᵊ\ kitten \ər\ further \a\ ash \ā\ ace
\ä\ mop, mar \au̇\ out \ch\ chin \e\ bet \ē\ easy
\g\ go \i\ hit \ī\ ice \j\ job \ŋ\ sing \ō\ go
\ȯ\ law \ȯi\ boy \th\ thin \t͟h\ the \ü\ loot \u̇\ foot
\y\ yet \zh\ vision *see also* Guide to Pronunciation

2 : the use of a word in the same grammatical relation to two adjacent words in the context with one literal and the other metaphorical in sense
— **syl·lep·tic** \-'lep-tik\ *adjective*

syl·lo·gism \'si-lə-,ji-zəm\ *noun* [Middle English *silogisme*, from Middle French, from Latin *syllogismus*, from Greek *syllogismos*, from *syllogizesthai* to syllogize, from *syn-* + *logizesthai* to calculate, from *logos* reckoning, word — more at LEGEND] (14th century)
1 : a deductive scheme of a formal argument consisting of a major and a minor premise and a conclusion (as in "every virtue is laudable; kindness is a virtue; therefore kindness is laudable")
2 : a subtle, specious, or crafty argument
3 : deductive reasoning
— **syl·lo·gis·tic** \,si-lə-'jis-tik\ *adjective*
— **syl·lo·gis·ti·cal·ly** \-ti-k(ə-)lē\ *adverb*

syl·lo·gist \'si-lə-jist\ *noun* (1799)
: one who applies or is skilled in syllogistic reasoning

syl·lo·gize \'si-lə-,jīz\ *verb* **-gized; -giz·ing** [Middle English *sylogysen*, from Late Latin *syllogizare*, from Greek *syllogizesthai*] (15th century)
intransitive verb
: to reason by means of syllogisms
transitive verb
: to deduce by syllogism ⟨*syllogizes* moral laws⟩

sylph \'silf\ *noun* [New Latin *sylphus*] (1657)
1 : an elemental being in the theory of Paracelsus that inhabits air
2 : a slender graceful woman or girl
— **sylph·like** \'sil-,flīk\ *adjective*

sylph·id \'sil-fəd\ *noun* (1680)
: a young or diminutive sylph

sylva, sylviculture *variant of* SILVA, SILVICULTURE

¹syl·van \'sil-vən\ *noun* (1565)
: one that frequents groves or woods

²sylvan *adjective* [Medieval Latin *silvanus*, *sylvanus*, from Latin *silva*, *sylva* wood] (circa 1583)
1 a : living or located in the woods or forest **b** : of, relating to, or characteristic of the woods or forest
2 a : made, shaped, or formed of woods or trees **b** : abounding in woods, groves, or trees : WOODED

syl·va·nite \'sil-və-,nīt\ *noun* [French *sylvanite*, from New Latin *sylvanium* tellurium, from *Transylvania*, region in Romania] (1796)
: a mineral that is a gold silver telluride and often occurs in crystals resembling written characters

syl·vat·ic \sil-'va-tik\ *adjective* [Latin *silvaticus* of the woods, wild — more at SAVAGE] (1661)
1 : SYLVAN ⟨*sylvatic* rodents⟩
2 : occurring in or affecting wild animals ⟨*sylvatic* diseases⟩

syl·vite \'sil-,vīt\ *also* **syl·vine** \-,vēn\ *noun* [alteration of *sylvine*, from French, from New Latin *sal digestivus Sylvii* digestive salt of Sylvius, from *Sylvius* latinized name of Jacques Dubois (died 1555) French physician] (1868)
: a mineral that is a natural potassium chloride and occurs in colorless cubes or crystalline masses

sym- — *see* SYN-

sym·bi·ont \'sim-bē-,änt\ *noun* [probably from German, modification of Greek *symbiount-*, *symbiōn*, present participle of *symbioun*] (1887)
: an organism living in symbiosis; *especially* : the smaller member of a symbiotic pair

sym·bi·o·sis \,sim-bē-'ō-səs, -,bī-\ *noun, plural* **-bi·o·ses** \-,sēz\ [New Latin, from German *Symbiose*, from Greek *symbiōsis* state of living together, from *symbioun* to live together, from *symbios* living together, from *syn-* + *bios* life — more at QUICK] (1622)

1 : the living together in more or less intimate association or close union of two dissimilar organisms
2 : the intimate living together of two dissimilar organisms in a mutually beneficial relationship; *especially* : MUTUALISM
3 : a cooperative relationship (as between two persons or groups) ⟨the *symbiosis* . . . between the resident population and the immigrants —John Geipel⟩
— **sym·bi·ot·ic** \-'ä-tik\ *adjective*
— **sym·bi·ot·i·cal·ly** \-ti-k(ə-)lē\ *adverb*

sym·bi·ote \'sim-bē-,ōt, -,bī-\ *noun* [French, from Greek *symbiōtēs* companion, from *symbioun* to live together] (circa 1909)
: SYMBIONT

¹sym·bol \'sim-bəl\ *noun* [in sense 1, from Late Latin *symbolum*, from Late Greek *symbolon*, from Greek, token, sign; in other senses from Latin *symbolum* token, sign, symbol, from Greek *symbolon*, literally, token of identity verified by comparing its other half, from *symballein* to throw together, compare, from *syn-* + *ballein* to throw — more at DEVIL] (15th century)
1 : an authoritative summary of faith or doctrine : CREED
2 : something that stands for or suggests something else by reason of relationship, association, convention, or accidental resemblance; *especially* : a visible sign of something invisible ⟨the lion is a *symbol* of courage⟩
3 : an arbitrary or conventional sign used in writing or printing relating to a particular field to represent operations, quantities, elements, relations, or qualities
4 : an object or act representing something in the unconscious mind that has been repressed ⟨phallic *symbols*⟩
5 : an act, sound, or object having cultural significance and the capacity to excite or objectify a response

²symbol *verb* **-boled** *or* **-bolled; -bol·ing** *or* **-bol·ling** (1832)
: SYMBOLIZE

sym·bol·ic \sim-'bä-lik\ *also* **sym·bol·i·cal** \-li-kəl\ *adjective* (1610)
1 a : using, employing, or exhibiting a symbol
b : consisting of or proceeding by means of symbols
2 : of, relating to, or constituting a symbol
3 : characterized by or terminating in symbols ⟨*symbolic* thinking⟩
4 : characterized by symbolism ⟨a *symbolic* dance⟩
— **sym·bol·i·cal·ly** \-li-k(ə-)lē\ *adverb*

symbolic logic *noun* (1856)
: a science of developing and representing logical principles by means of a formalized system consisting of primitive symbols, combinations of these symbols, axioms, and rules of inference

sym·bol·ise *British variant of* SYMBOLIZE

sym·bol·ism \'sim-bə-,li-zəm\ *noun* (1654)
1 : the art or practice of using symbols especially by investing things with a symbolic meaning or by expressing the invisible or intangible by means of visible or sensuous representations: as **a** : artistic imitation or invention that is a method of revealing or suggesting immaterial, ideal, or otherwise intangible truth or states **b** : the use of conventional or traditional signs in the representation of divine beings and spirits
2 : a system of symbols or representations

sym·bol·ist \'sim-bə-list\ *noun* (1812)
1 : one who employs symbols or symbolism
2 : one skilled in the interpretation or explication of symbols
3 : one of a group of writers and artists in France after 1880 reacting against realism, concerning themselves with general truths instead of actualities, exalting the metaphysical and the mysterious, and aiming to unify and blend the arts and the functions of the senses
— **symbolist** *adjective*

sym·bol·is·tic \,sim-bə-'lis-tik\ *adjective* (circa 1864)
: SYMBOLIC

sym·bol·i·za·tion \,sim-bə-lə-'zā-shən\ *noun* (1603)
1 : an act or instance of symbolizing
2 : the human capacity to develop a system of meaningful symbols

sym·bol·ize \'sim-bə-,līz\ *verb* **-ized; -iz·ing** (1603)
transitive verb
1 : to serve as a symbol of
2 : to represent, express, or identify by a symbol
intransitive verb
: to use symbols or symbolism
— **sym·bol·iz·er** *noun*

sym·bol·o·gy \sim-'bä-lə-jē\ *noun, plural* **-gies** [*symbol* + *-logy*] (1840)
1 : the art of expression by symbols
2 : the study or interpretation of symbols
3 : a system of symbols

sym·met·al·lism \(,)si(m)-'me-t²l-,i-zəm\ *noun* [*syn-* + *-metallism* (as in *bimetallism*)] (circa 1895)
: a system of coinage in which the unit of currency consists of a particular weight of an alloy of two or more metals

sym·met·ri·cal \sə-'me-tri-kəl\ *or* **sym·met·ric** \-trik\ *adjective* (1751)
1 : having, involving, or exhibiting symmetry
2 : having corresponding points whose connecting lines are bisected by a given point or perpendicularly bisected by a given line or plane ⟨*symmetrical* curves⟩
3 *symmetric* : being such that the terms or variables may be interchanged without altering the value, character, or truth ⟨*symmetric* equations⟩ ⟨R is a *symmetric* relation if *aRb* implies *bRa*⟩
4 a : capable of division by a longitudinal plane into similar halves ⟨*symmetrical* plant parts⟩ **b** : having the same number of members in each whorl of floral leaves ⟨*symmetrical* flowers⟩
5 : affecting corresponding parts simultaneously and similarly ⟨*symmetrical* rash⟩
6 : exhibiting symmetry in a structural formula; *especially* : being a derivative with groups substituted symmetrically in the molecule
— **sym·met·ri·cal·ly** \-tri-k(ə-)lē\ *adverb*
— **sym·met·ri·cal·ness** \-kəl-nəs\ *noun*

symmetric group *noun* (1897)
: a permutation group that is composed of all of the permutations of *n* things

symmetric matrix *noun* (circa 1949)
: a matrix that is its own transpose

sym·me·trize \'si-mə-,trīz\ *transitive verb* **-trized; -triz·ing** (1796)
: to make symmetrical
— **sym·me·tri·za·tion** \,si-mə-trə-'zā-shən\ *noun*

sym·me·try \'si-mə-trē\ *noun, plural* **-tries** [Latin *symmetria*, from Greek, from *symmetros* symmetrical, from *syn-* + *metron* measure — more at MEASURE] (1541)
1 : balanced proportions; *also* : beauty of form arising from balanced proportions
2 : the property of being symmetrical; *especially* : correspondence in size, shape, and relative position of parts on opposite sides of a dividing line or median plane or about a center or axis — compare BILATERAL SYMMETRY, RADIAL SYMMETRY
3 : a rigid motion of a geometric figure that determines a one-to-one mapping onto itself
4 : the property of remaining invariant under certain changes (as of orientation in space, of the sign of the electric charge, of parity, or of the direction of time flow) — used of physical phenomena and of equations describing them

sympath- *or* **sympatho-** *combining form* [International Scientific Vocabulary, from *sympathetic*]
: sympathetic nerve ⟨*sympatho*lytic⟩

sym·pa·thec·to·my \ˌsim-pə-'thek-tə-mē\ *noun, plural* **-mies** [International Scientific Vocabulary] (1900)
: surgical interruption of sympathetic nerve pathways
— **sym·pa·thec·to·mized** \-ˌmīzd\ *adjective*

¹**sym·pa·thet·ic** \ˌsim-pə-'the-tik\ *adjective* [New Latin *sympatheticus,* from Latin *sympathia* sympathy] (1644)
1 : existing or operating through an affinity, interdependence, or mutual association
2 a : not discordant or antagonistic b : appropriate to one's mood, inclinations, or disposition c : marked by kindly or pleased appreciation
3 : given to, marked by, or arising from sympathy, compassion, friendliness, and sensitivity to others' emotions ⟨a *sympathetic* gesture⟩
4 : favorably inclined : APPROVING ⟨not *sympathetic* to the idea⟩
5 a : showing empathy b : arousing sympathy or compassion ⟨a *sympathetic* role in the play⟩
6 a : of or relating to the sympathetic nervous system b : mediated by or acting on the sympathetic nerves
7 : relating to musical tones produced by sympathetic vibration or to strings so tuned as to sound by sympathetic vibration
— **sym·pa·thet·i·cal·ly** \-ti-k(ə-)lē\ *adverb*

²**sympathetic** *noun* (1808)
: a sympathetic structure; *especially* : SYMPATHETIC NERVOUS SYSTEM

sympathetic magic *noun* (1905)
: magic based on the assumption that a person or thing can be supernaturally affected through its name or an object representing it

sympathetic nervous system *noun* (circa 1891)
: the part of the autonomic nervous system that contains chiefly adrenergic fibers and tends to depress secretion, decrease the tone and contractility of smooth muscle, and increase heart rate — compare PARASYMPATHETIC NERVOUS SYSTEM

sympathetic strike *noun* (1895)
: SYMPATHY STRIKE

sympathetic vibration *noun* (1898)
: a vibration produced in one body by the vibrations of exactly the same period in a neighboring body

sym·pa·thin \'sim-pə-thən\ *noun* [International Scientific Vocabulary] (1931)
: a substance (as norepinephrine) that is secreted by sympathetic nerve endings and acts as a chemical mediator

sym·pa·thise *chiefly British variant of* SYMPATHIZE

sym·pa·thize \'sim-pə-ˌthīz\ *intransitive verb* **-thized; -thiz·ing** (1591)
1 : to be in keeping, accord, or harmony
2 : to react or respond in sympathy
3 : to share in suffering or grief : COMMISERATE ⟨*sympathize* with a friend in trouble⟩; *also* : to express such sympathy
4 : to be in sympathy intellectually ⟨*sympathize* with a proposal⟩
— **sym·pa·thiz·er** *noun*

sym·pa·tho·lyt·ic \ˌsim-pə-thō-'li-tik\ *adjective* [International Scientific Vocabulary] (1943)
: tending to oppose the physiological results of sympathetic nervous activity or of sympathomimetic drugs
— **sympatholytic** *noun*

sym·pa·tho·mi·met·ic \-mə-'me-tik, -(ˌ)mī-\ *adjective* [International Scientific Vocabulary] (1910)
: simulating sympathetic nervous action in physiological effect
— **sympathomimetic** *noun*

sym·pa·thy \'sim-pə-thē\ *noun, plural* **-thies** [Latin *sympathia,* from Greek *sympatheia,* from *sympathēs* having common feelings, sympathetic, from *syn-* + *pathos* feelings, emotion, experience — more at PATHOS] (1579)
1 a : an affinity, association, or relationship between persons or things wherein whatever affects one similarly affects the other b : mutual or parallel susceptibility or a condition brought about by it c : unity or harmony in action or effect
2 a : inclination to think or feel alike : emotional or intellectual accord b : feeling of loyalty : tendency to favor or support ⟨republican *sympathies*⟩
3 a : the act or capacity of entering into or sharing the feelings or interests of another b : the feeling or mental state brought about by such sensitivity ⟨have *sympathy* for the poor⟩
4 : the correlation existing between bodies capable of communicating their vibrational energy to one another through some medium
synonym see ATTRACTION, PITY

sympathy strike *noun* (1912)
: a strike in which the strikers have no direct grievance against their own employer but attempt to support or aid usually another group of workers on strike

sym·pat·ric \sim-'pa-trik\ *adjective* [*syn-* + Greek *patra* fatherland, from *patēr* father — more at FATHER] (circa 1904)
: occurring in the same area; *specifically* : occupying the same range without loss of identity from interbreeding ⟨*sympatric* species⟩ — compare ALLOPATRIC
— **sym·pat·ri·cal·ly** \-tri-k(ə-)lē\ *adverb*
— **sym·pat·ry** \'sim-ˌpa-trē\ *noun*

sym·pet·al·ous \(ˌ)sim-'pe-t°l-əs\ *adjective* (circa 1877)
: GAMOPETALOUS
— **sym·pet·aly** \-t°l-ē, 'sim-ˌ\ *noun*

sym·phon·ic \sim-'fä-nik\ *adjective* (1856)
1 : HARMONIOUS, SYMPHONIOUS
2 : relating to or having the form or character of a symphony ⟨*symphonic* music⟩
3 : suggestive of a symphony especially in form, interweaving of themes, or harmonious arrangement ⟨a *symphonic* drama⟩
— **sym·phon·i·cal·ly** \-ni-k(ə-)lē\ *adverb*

symphonic poem *noun* (1873)
: an extended programmatic composition for symphony orchestra usually freer in form than a symphony

sym·pho·ni·ous \sim-'fō-nē-əs\ *adjective* (1652)
: agreeing especially in sound : HARMONIOUS
— **sym·pho·ni·ous·ly** *adverb*

sym·pho·nist \'sim(p)-fə-nist\ *noun* (1767)
1 : a member of a symphony orchestra
2 : a composer of symphonies

sym·pho·ny \-nē\ *noun, plural* **-nies** [Middle English *symphonie,* from Middle French, from Latin *symphonia,* from Greek *symphōnia,* from *symphōnos* concordant in sound, from *syn-* + *phōnē* voice, sound — more at BAN] (15th century)
1 : consonance of sounds
2 a : RITORNELLO 1 b : SINFONIA 1 c (1) : a usually long and complex sonata for symphony orchestra (2) : a musical composition (as for organ) resembling such a symphony in complexity or variety
3 : consonance or harmony of color (as in a painting)
4 a : SYMPHONY ORCHESTRA b : a symphony orchestra concert
5 : something that in its harmonious complexity or variety suggests a symphonic composition

symphony orchestra *noun* (circa 1881)
: a large orchestra of winds, strings, and percussion that plays symphonic works

sym·phy·se·al \ˌsim(p)-fə-'sē-əl\ *also* **sym·phys·i·al** \sim-'fi-zē-əl\ *adjective* [Greek *symphyse-, symphysis* symphysis] (circa 1836)
: of, relating to, or constituting a symphysis

sym·phy·sis \'sim(p)-fə-səs\ *noun, plural* **-phy·ses** \-ˌsēz\ [New Latin, from Greek, state of growing together, from *symphyesthai* to grow together, from *syn-* + *phyein* to make grow, bring forth — more at BE] (circa 1578)
1 : an immovable or more or less movable articulation of various bones in the median plane of the body
2 : an articulation in which the bony surfaces are connected by pads of fibrous cartilage without a synovial membrane

sym·po·di·al \sim-'pō-dē-əl\ *adjective* [New Latin *sympodium* apparent main axis formed from secondary axes, from Greek *syn-* + *podion* base — more at -PODIUM] (1875)
: having or involving the formation of an apparent main axis from successive secondary axes ⟨*sympodial* branching of a cyme⟩

sym·po·si·arch \sim-'pō-zē-ˌärk\ *noun* [Greek *symposiarchos,* from *symposion* symposium + *-archos* -arch] (1603)
: one who presides over a symposium

sym·po·si·ast \-zē-ˌast, -əst\ *noun* [Greek *symposiazein* to take part in a symposium, from *symposion*] (circa 1656)
: a contributor to a symposium

sym·po·sium \sim-'pō-zē-əm *also* -zh(ē-)əm\ *noun, plural* **-sia** \-zē-ə, -zh(ē-)ə\ *or* **-siums** [Latin, from Greek *symposion,* from *sympinein* to drink together, from *syn-* + *pinein* to drink — more at POTABLE] (1711)
1 a : a convivial party (as after a banquet in ancient Greece) with music and conversation b : a social gathering at which there is free interchange of ideas
2 a : a formal meeting at which several specialists deliver short addresses on a topic or on related topics — compare COLLOQUIUM b : a collection of opinions on a subject; *especially* : one published by a periodical c : DISCUSSION

symp·tom \'sim(p)-təm\ *noun* [Late Latin *symptomat-, symptoma,* from Greek *symptōmat-, symptōma* happening, attribute, symptom, from *sympiptein* to happen, from *syn-* + *piptein* to fall — more at FEATHER] (1541)
1 a : subjective evidence of disease or physical disturbance; *broadly* : something that indicates the presence of bodily disorder b : an evident reaction by a plant to a pathogen

◇ WORD HISTORY
symposium In ancient Greece the evening meal was often followed by a drinking party, attended only by men, that usually featured songs, games, and performances by hired entertainers. This party was called in Greek *symposion,* a derivative of *sympotēs* "drinking companion," itself formed from the prefix *syn-* "together" and *po-,* a variant stem of the verb *pinein* "to drink." For Greeks with somewhat loftier aspirations, the drinking became subordinate to the entertainment, which at its most exalted might take the form of philosophical discussion. The Platonic dialogue known as the *Symposium* is one example of a Greek literary genre that used conversation at a drinking party as a frame for extended treatment of a serious topic—in the case of Plato's work, love and beauty. The Greek word has been borrowed into English via Latin, but the *symposion* as philosophical discussion has influenced the modern use of English *symposium* more than actual Greek practice, and the stuffy academic connotations the word now has could hardly be further from the riotous excess more typical of the ancient *symposion.*

\ə\ abut \ə\ kitten \ər\ further \a\ ash \ā\ ace
\ä\ mop, mar \aù\ out \ch\ chin \e\ bet \ē\ easy
\g\ go \i\ hit \ī\ ice \j\ job \ŋ\ sing \ō\ go
\ò\ law \òi\ boy \th\ thin \t͟h\ the \ü\ loot \ù\ foot
\y\ yet \zh\ vision *see also* Guide to Pronunciation

2 a : something that indicates the existence of something else ⟨*symptoms* of the time⟩ **b :** a slight indication **:** TRACE
synonym see SIGN
— **symp·tom·less** \-ləs\ *adjective*
symp·tom·at·ic \ˌsim(p)-tə-'ma-tik\ *adjective* (1698)
1 a : being a symptom of a disease **b :** having the characteristics of a particular disease but arising from another cause
2 : concerned with or affecting symptoms
3 : CHARACTERISTIC, INDICATIVE ⟨his behavior was *symptomatic* of his character⟩
— **symp·tom·at·i·cal·ly** \-ti-k(ə-)lē\ *adverb*
symp·tom·a·tol·o·gy \ˌsim(p)-tə-mə-'tä-lə-jē\ *noun* (1798)
1 : the symptom complex of a disease
2 : a branch of medical science concerned with symptoms of diseases
— **symp·tom·at·o·log·i·cal** \-ˌma-t°l-'ä-ji-kəl\ *or* **symp·tom·at·o·log·ic** \-'ä-jik\ *adjective*
— **symp·tom·at·o·log·i·cal·ly** \-ji-k(ə-)lē\ *adverb*
syn- *or* **sym-** *prefix* [Middle English, from Old French, from Latin, from Greek, from *syn* with, together with]
1 : with **:** along with **:** together ⟨*syn*clinal⟩ ⟨*sym*petalous⟩
2 : at the same time ⟨*syn*esthesia⟩
syn·ae·re·sis *variant of* SYNERESIS
syn·aes·the·sia *variant of* SYNESTHESIA
syn·aes·the·sis \ˌsi-nəs-'thē-səs\ *noun* [Greek *synaisthēsis* joint perception, from *synaisthanesthai* to perceive simultaneously, from *syn-* + *aisthanesthai* to perceive — more at AUDIBLE] (1922)
: harmony of different or opposing impulses produced by a work of art
syn·a·gogue *or* **syn·a·gog** \'si-nə-ˌgäg\ *noun* [Middle English *synagoge*, from Old French, from Late Latin *synagoga*, from Greek *synagōgē* assembly, synagogue, from *synagein* to bring together, from *syn-* + *agein* to lead — more at AGENT] (13th century)
1 : a Jewish congregation
2 : the house of worship and communal center of a Jewish congregation
— **syn·a·gog·al** \ˌsi-nə-'gä-gəl\ *adjective*
syn·a·loe·pha *or* **syn·a·le·pha** \ˌsi-nə-'lē-fə\ *noun* [New Latin, from Greek *synaloiphē*, from *synaleiphein* to clog up, coalesce, unite two syllables into one, from *syn-* + *aleiphein* to anoint — more at ALIPHATIC] (1540)
: the reduction to one syllable of two vowels of adjacent syllables (as in *th' army* for *the army*)
¹**syn·apse** \'si-ˌnaps, sə-'naps\ *noun* [New Latin *synapsis*, from Greek, juncture, from *synaptein* to fasten together, from *syn-* + *haptein* to fasten] (1899)
: the point at which a nervous impulse passes from one neuron to another
²**synapse** *intransitive verb* **syn·apsed; syn·aps·ing** (1910)
1 : to form a synapse
2 : to come together in synapsis
syn·ap·sid \sə-'nap-səd\ *noun* [New Latin *Synapsida*, from Greek *syn-* + *apsid-, apsis* arch, vault — more at APSIS] (1956)
: any of a subclass (Synapsida) of extinct reptiles existing during the Pennsylvanian, Permian, and Jurassic, having a single pair of lateral temporal openings in the skull, and usually held to be ancestral to mammals
— **synapsid** *adjective*
syn·ap·sis \sə-'nap-səs\ *noun, plural* **-ap·ses** \-ˌsēz\ [New Latin] (circa 1892)
: the association of homologous chromosomes that is characteristic of the first meiotic prophase
syn·ap·tic \sə-'nap-tik\ *adjective* [New Latin *synapsis*] (1895)
1 : of or relating to a synapsis
2 : of or relating to a synapse

— **syn·ap·ti·cal·ly** \-ti-k(ə-)lē\ *adverb*
syn·ap·to·ne·mal complex \sə-ˌnap-tə-'nē-məl-\ *noun* [*synaptic* + *-o-* or *-i-* + Greek *nēma* thread — more at NEMAT-] (1958)
: a complex tripartite protein structure that spans the region between synapsed chromosomes in meiotic prophase — called also *syn·ap·ti·ne·mal complex* \sə-ˌnap-tə-'nē-məl-\
syn·ap·to·some \sə-'nap-tə-ˌsōm\ *noun* [*synaptic* + *-o-* + ³*-some*] (1964)
: a nerve ending that is isolated from homogenized nerve tissue
— **syn·ap·to·som·al** \-ˌnap-tə-'sō-məl\ *adjective*
syn·ar·thro·di·al \ˌsin-är-'thrō-dē-əl\ *adjective* [New Latin *synarthrodia* synarthrosis] (1830)
: of, relating to, or being a synarthrosis
syn·ar·thro·sis \-'thrō-səs\ *noun, plural* **-thro·ses** \-ˌsēz\ [Greek *synarthrōsis*, from *syn-* + *arthrōsis* arthrosis] (1578)
: an immovable articulation in which the bones are united by intervening fibrous connective tissues
¹**sync** *also* **synch** \'siŋk\ *transitive verb* **synced** *also* **synched** \'siŋ(k)t\; **sync·ing** *also* **synch·ing** \'siŋ-kiŋ\ (1929)
: SYNCHRONIZE
²**sync** *also* **synch** *noun* (1937)
: SYNCHRONIZATION, SYNCHRONISM
— **sync** *adjective*
syn·car·pous \(ˌ)sin-'kär-pəs\ *adjective* (circa 1830)
: having the carpels of the gynoecium united in a compound ovary
— **syn·car·py** \'sin-ˌkär-pē\ *noun*
syn·cat·e·go·re·mat·ic \ˌsin-ˌka-tə-ˌgȯr-ə-'ma-tik, -ˌgȯr-ē-\ *adjective* [Late Latin *syncategoremat-, syncategorema* syncategorematic term, from Greek *synkatēgorēma*, from *synkatēgorein* to predicate jointly, from *syn-* + *katēgorein* to predicate — more at CATEGORY] (1827)
: forming a meaningful expression only in conjunction with a denotative expression (as a content word) ⟨logical operators and function words are *syncategorematic*⟩
— **syn·cat·e·gor·e·mat·i·cal·ly** \-ti-k(ə-)lē\ *adverb*
¹**syn·chro** \'siŋ-(ˌ)krō, 'sin-\ *noun, plural* **syn·chros** [*synchronous*] (1943)
: SELSYN
²**synchro** *adjective* [*synchro-*] (1947)
: adapted to synchronization
synchro- *combining form* [*synchronized & synchronous*]
: synchronized **:** synchronous ⟨*synchro*mesh⟩
syn·chro·cy·clo·tron \ˌsin-(ˌ)krō-'sī-klə-ˌträn, ˌsin-\ *noun* (1947)
: a modified cyclotron that achieves greater energies for the charged particles by compensating for the variation in mass that the particles experience with increasing velocity
syn·chro·mesh \'siŋ-krō-ˌmesh, 'sin-\ *adjective* (1928)
: designed for effecting synchronized shifting of gears
— **synchromesh** *noun*
syn·chro·nal \'siŋ-krə-n°l, 'sin-\ *adjective* (1660)
: SYNCHRONOUS
syn·chro·ne·ity \ˌsiŋ-krə-'nē-ə-tē, ˌsin-, -'nā-\ *noun* [*synchronous* + *-eity* (as in *spontaneity*)] (circa 1909)
: the state of being synchronous
syn·chron·ic \sin-'krä-nik, siŋ-\ *adjective* (1833)
1 : SYNCHRONOUS
2 a : DESCRIPTIVE 4 ⟨*synchronic* linguistics⟩ **b :** concerned with events existing in a limited time period and ignoring historical antecedents
— **syn·chron·i·cal** \-ni-kəl\ *adjective*
— **syn·chron·i·cal·ly** \-ni-k(ə-)lē\ *adverb*
syn·chro·nic·i·ty \ˌsiŋ-krə-'ni-sə-tē, ˌsin-\ *noun* (circa 1889)

1 : the quality or fact of being synchronous
2 : the coincidental occurrence of events and especially psychic events (as similar thoughts in widely separated persons or a mental image of an unexpected event before it happens) that seem related but are not explained by conventional mechanisms of causality — used especially in the psychology of C. G. Jung
syn·chro·ni·sa·tion, syn·chro·nise *British variant of* SYNCHRONIZATION, SYNCHRONIZE
syn·chro·nism \'siŋ-krə-ˌni-zəm, 'sin-\ *noun* (1588)
1 : the quality or state of being synchronous **:** SIMULTANEOUSNESS
2 : chronological arrangement of historical events and personages so as to indicate coincidence or coexistence; *also* **:** a table showing such concurrences
— **syn·chro·nis·tic** \ˌsiŋ-krə-'nis-tik, ˌsin-\ *adjective*
syn·chro·ni·za·tion \ˌsiŋ-krə-nə-'zā-shən, ˌsin-\ *noun* (1828)
1 : the act or result of synchronizing
2 : the state of being synchronous
syn·chro·nize \'siŋ-krə-ˌnīz, 'sin-\ *verb* **-nized; -niz·ing** (circa 1624)
intransitive verb
: to happen at the same time
transitive verb
1 : to represent or arrange (events) to indicate coincidence or coexistence
2 : to make synchronous in operation
3 : to make (motion picture sound) exactly simultaneous with the action
— **syn·chro·niz·er** *noun*
synchronized swimming *noun* (1950)
: swimming in which the movements of one or more swimmers are synchronized with a musical accompaniment so as to form changing patterns
syn·chro·nous \'siŋ-krə-nəs, 'sin-\ *adjective* [Late Latin *synchronos*, from Greek, from *syn-* + *chronos* time] (1669)
1 : happening, existing, or arising at precisely the same time
2 : recurring or operating at exactly the same periods
3 : involving or indicating synchronism
4 a : having the same period; *also* **:** having the same period and phase **b :** GEOSTATIONARY
5 : of, used in, or being digital communication (as between computers) in which a common timing signal is established that dictates when individual bits can be transmitted, in which characters are not individually delimited, and which allows for very high rates of data transfer
synonym see CONTEMPORARY
— **syn·chro·nous·ly** *adverb*
— **syn·chro·nous·ness** *noun*
synchronous motor *noun* (1897)
: an electric motor having a speed strictly proportional to the frequency of the operating current
syn·chro·ny \'siŋ-krə-nē, 'sin-\ *noun, plural* **-nies** (1848)
: synchronistic occurrence, arrangement, or treatment
syn·chro·scope \-ˌskōp\ *noun* (1907)
: any of several devices for showing whether two associated machines or moving parts are operating in synchronism with each other
syn·chro·tron \'siŋ-krə-ˌträn, 'sin-\ *noun* (1945)
1 : an apparatus for imparting very high speeds to charged particles by means of a combination of a high-frequency electric field and a low-frequency magnetic field
2 : SYNCHROTRON RADIATION
synchrotron radiation *noun* [from its having been first observed in a synchrotron] (1956)
: radiation emitted by high-energy charged relativistic particles (as electrons) when they are accelerated by a magnetic field (as in a nebula)

syn·cli·nal \(,)sin-'klī-nᵊl\ *adjective* [Greek *syn-* + *klinein* to lean — more at LEAN] (1833)
1 : inclined down from opposite directions so as to meet
2 : having or relating to a folded rock structure in which the sides dip toward a common line or plane

syn·cline \'sin-,klīn\ *noun* [back-formation from *synclinal*] (1873)
: a trough of stratified rock in which the beds dip toward each other from either side — compare ANTICLINE

cross section of strata showing syncline

syn·co·pate \'siŋ-kə-,pāt, 'sin-\ *transitive verb* **-pat·ed; -pat·ing** (1605)
1 a : to shorten or produce by syncope ⟨*syncopate* suppose to *s'pose*⟩ **b :** to cut short : CLIP, ABBREVIATE
2 : to modify or affect (musical rhythm) by syncopation
— **syn·co·pa·tor** \-,pā-tər\ *noun*

syncopated *adjective* (1665)
1 : cut short : ABBREVIATED
2 : marked by or exhibiting syncopation ⟨*syncopated* rhythm⟩

syn·co·pa·tion \,siŋ-kə-'pā-shən, ,sin-\ *noun* (1597)
1 : a temporary displacement of the regular metrical accent in music caused typically by stressing the weak beat
2 : a syncopated rhythm, passage, or dance step
— **syn·co·pa·tive** \'siŋ-kə-,pā-tiv, 'sin-\ *adjective*

syn·co·pe \'siŋ-kə-(,)pē, 'sin-\ *noun* [Late Latin, from Greek *synkopē*, literally, cutting short, from *synkoptein* to cut short, from *syn-* + *koptein* to cut — more at CAPON] (circa 1550)
1 : loss of consciousness resulting from insufficient blood flow to the brain : FAINT
2 : the loss of one or more sounds or letters in the interior of a word (as in *fo'c'sle* for *forecastle*)
— **syn·co·pal** \-kə-pəl\ *adjective*

syn·cret·ic \sin-'kre-tik, siŋ-\ *adjective* (1840)
: characterized or brought about by syncretism : SYNCRETISTIC

syn·cre·tise *British variant of* SYNCRETIZE

syn·cre·tism \'siŋ-krə-,ti-zəm, 'sin-\ *noun* [New Latin *syncretismus*, from Greek *synkrētismos* federation of Cretan cities, from *syn-* + *Krēt-, Krēs* Cretan] (1618)
1 : the combination of different forms of belief or practice
2 : the fusion of two or more originally different inflectional forms
— **syn·cre·tist** \-tist\ *noun or adjective*
— **syn·cre·tis·tic** \,siŋ-krə-'tis-tik, ,sin-\ *adjective*

syn·cre·tize \'siŋ-krə-,tīz, 'sin-\ *transitive verb* **-tized; -tiz·ing** (circa 1891)
: to attempt to unite and harmonize especially without critical examination or logical unity

syn·cy·tium \sin-'si-sh(ē-)əm\ *noun, plural* **-tia** \-sh(ē-)ə\ [New Latin, from *syn-* + *cyt-*] (1877)
1 : a multinucleate mass of protoplasm (as in the plasmodium of a slime mold) resulting from fusion of cells
2 : COENOCYTE 1
— **syn·cy·tial** \-'si-sh(ē-)əl\ *adjective*

syn·dac·ty·lism \(,)sin-'dak-tə-,li-zəm\ *noun* (1889)
: SYNDACTYLY

syn·dac·ty·ly \-lē\ *noun* [New Latin *syndactylia*, from *syn-* + Greek *daktylos* finger] (1864)
: a union of two or more digits that is normal in some animals (as various marsupials) and

occurs as a human hereditary disorder marked by webbing of two or more fingers or toes

syn·des·mo·sis \,sin-,dez-'mō-səs, -,des-\ *noun, plural* **-mo·ses** \-,sēz\ [New Latin, from Greek *syndesmos* fastening, ligament, from *syndein*] (1726)
: an articulation in which the contiguous surfaces of the bones are rough and are bound together by a ligament

syn·det·ic \sin-'de-tik\ *adjective* [Greek *syndetikos*, from *syndein* to bind together — more at ASYNDETON] (1621)
: CONNECTIVE, CONNECTING ⟨*syndetic* pronoun⟩; *also* : marked by a conjunctive ⟨*syndetic* relative clause⟩
— **syn·det·i·cal·ly** \-ti-k(ə-)lē\ *adverb*

syn·dic \'sin-dik\ *noun* [French, from Late Latin *syndicus* representative of a corporation, from Greek *syndikos* assistant at law, advocate, representative of a state, from *syn-* + *dikē* judgment, case at law — more at DICTION] (1601)
1 : a municipal magistrate in some countries
2 : an agent of a university or corporation

syn·di·cal \-di-kəl\ *adjective* (1864)
1 : of or relating to a syndic or to a committee that assumes the powers of a syndic
2 : of or relating to syndicalism

syn·di·cal·ism \'sin-di-kə-,li-zəm\ *noun* [French *syndicalisme*, from *chambre syndicale* trade union] (1907)
1 : a revolutionary doctrine by which workers seize control of the economy and the government by direct means (as a general strike)
2 : a system of economic organization in which industries are owned and managed by the workers
3 : a theory of government based on functional rather than territorial representation
— **syn·di·cal·ist** \-list\ *adjective or noun*

¹syn·di·cate \'sin-di-kət\ *noun* [French *syndicat*, from *syndic*] (1624)
1 a : a council or body of syndics **b :** the office or jurisdiction of a syndic
2 : an association of persons officially authorized to undertake a duty or negotiate business
3 a : a group of persons or concerns who combine to carry out a particular transaction **b :** CARTEL 2 **c :** a loose association of racketeers in control of organized crime
4 : a business concern that sells materials for publication in a number of newspapers or periodicals simultaneously
5 : a group of newspapers under one management

²syn·di·cate \'sin-də-,kāt\ *verb* **-cat·ed; -cat·ing** (1882)
transitive verb
1 : to subject to or manage as a syndicate
2 a : to sell (as a cartoon) to a syndicate or for publication in many newspapers or periodicals at once **b :** to sell (as a series of television programs) directly to local stations
intransitive verb
: to unite to form a syndicate
— **syn·di·ca·tion** \,sin-də-'kā-shən\ *noun*
— **syn·di·ca·tor** \'sin-də-,kā-tər\ *noun*

syn·drome \'sin-,drōm *also* -drəm\ *noun* [New Latin, from Greek *syndromē* combination, syndrome, from *syn-* + *dramein* to run — more at DROMEDARY] (1541)
1 : a group of signs and symptoms that occur together and characterize a particular abnormality
2 : a set of concurrent things (as emotions or actions) that usually form an identifiable pattern

¹syne \'sīn\ *adverb* [Middle English (northern), probably from Old Norse *sīthan;* akin to Old English *siththan* since — more at SINCE] (14th century)
chiefly Scottish : since then : AGO

²syne *conjunction or preposition* (14th century)
Scottish : SINCE

syn·ec·do·che \sə-'nek-də-(,)kē\ *noun* [Latin, from Greek *synekdochē*, from *syn-* + *ekdochē* sense, interpretation, from *ekdechesthai* to receive, understand, from *ex* from + *dechesthai* to receive; akin to Greek *dokein* to seem good — more at EX-, DECENT] (15th century)
: a figure of speech by which a part is put for the whole (as *fifty sail* for *fifty ships*), the whole for a part (as *society* for *high society*), the species for the genus (as *cutthroat* for *assassin*), the genus for the species (as *a creature* for *a man*), or the name of the material for the thing made (as *boards* for *stage*)
— **syn·ec·doch·ic** \,si-,nek-'dä-kik\ *adjective*
— **syn·ec·doch·i·cal** \-'dä-ki-kəl\ *adjective*
— **syn·ec·doch·i·cal·ly** \-ki-k(ə-)lē\ *adverb*

syn·ecol·o·gy \,si-ni-'kä-lə-jē, ,si-ne-\ *noun* [German *Synökologie*, from *syn-* syn- + *Ökologie* ecology] (1910)
: a branch of ecology that deals with the structure, development, and distribution of ecological communities
— **syn·eco·log·i·cal** \,si-,nē-kə-'lä-ji-kəl, ,si-,ne-\ *adjective*

syn·er·e·sis \sə-'ner-ə-səs, -'nir-, *especially for 2* ,si-nə-'rē-\ *noun* [Late Latin *synaeresis*, from Greek *synairesis*, from *synairein* to contract, from *syn-* + *hairein* to take] (circa 1577)
1 : SYNIZESIS
2 : the separation of liquid from a gel caused by contraction

syn·er·get·ic \,si-nər-'je-tik\ *adjective* [Greek *synergētikos*, from *synergein* to work with, cooperate, from *synergos* working together, from *syn-* + *ergon* work — more at WORK] (circa 1836)
: SYNERGIC

syn·er·gic \sə-'nər-jik\ *adjective* (circa 1859)
: working together : COOPERATING
— **syn·er·gi·cal·ly** \-ji-k(ə-)lē\ *adverb*

syn·er·gid \sə-'nər-jəd, 'si-nər-\ *noun* [New Latin *synergida*, from Greek *synergos* working together] (1898)
: one of two small cells lying near the micropyle of the embryo sac of an angiosperm

syn·er·gism \'si-nər-,ji-zəm\ *noun* [New Latin *synergismus*, from Greek *synergos*] (1910)
: interaction of discrete agencies (as industrial firms), agents (as drugs), or conditions such that the total effect is greater than the sum of the individual effects

syn·er·gist \-jist\ *noun* (1876)
: something (as a chemical or a muscle) that enhances the effectiveness of an active agent; *broadly* : either member of a synergistic pair

syn·er·gis·tic \,si-nər-'jis-tik\ *adjective* (circa 1847)
1 : having the capacity to act in synergism ⟨*synergistic* drugs⟩
2 : of, relating to, or resembling synergism ⟨a *synergistic* reaction⟩
— **syn·er·gis·ti·cal·ly** \-ti-k(ə-)lē\ *adverb*

syn·er·gy \'si-nər-jē\ *noun* [New Latin *synergia*, from Greek *synergos* working together] (1660)
: SYNERGISM; *broadly* : combined action or operation

syn·e·sis \'si-nə-səs\ *noun* [New Latin, from Greek, understanding, sense, from *synienai* to bring together, understand, from *syn-* + *hienai* to send — more at JET] (circa 1891)
: a grammatical construction in which agreement or reference is according to sense rather than strict syntax (as *anyone* and *them* in "if anyone calls, tell them I am out")

syn·es·the·sia \ˌsi-nəs-ˈthē-zh(ē-)ə\ *noun* [New Latin, from *syn-* + *-esthesia* (as in *anesthesia*)] (circa 1891)
: a concomitant sensation; *especially* : a subjective sensation or image of a sense (as of color) other than the one (as of sound) being stimulated
— **syn·es·thet·ic** \-ˈthe-tik\ *adjective*

syn·fu·el \ˈsin-ˌfyü(-ə)l\ *noun* [synthetic + fuel] (1976)
: a liquid or gaseous fuel derived especially from a fossil fuel that is a solid (as coal) or part of a solid (as tar sand or oil shale)

syn·ga·my \ˈsiŋ-gə-mē\ *noun* [International Scientific Vocabulary] (1904)
: sexual reproduction by union of gametes

syn·gas \ˈsin-ˌgas\ *noun* (1975)
: SYNTHESIS GAS

syn·ge·ne·ic \ˌsin-jə-ˈnē-ik\ *adjective* [*syn-* + *-geneic* (as in *isogeneic*)] (1961)
: genetically identical or similar especially with respect to antigens or immunological reactions ⟨*syngeneic* tumor cells⟩ ⟨grafts between *syngeneic* mice⟩ — compare ALLOGENEIC, XENOGENEIC

syn·i·ze·sis \ˌsi-nə-ˈzē-səs\ *noun* [Late Latin, from Greek *synizēsis,* from *synizein* to sit down together, collapse, blend, from *syn-* + *hizein* to sit down; akin to Latin *sidere* to sit down — more at SUBSIDE] (1846)
: contraction of two syllables into one by uniting in pronunciation two adjacent vowels

syn·kary·on \sin-ˈkar-ē-ˌän, -ē-ən\ *noun* [New Latin, from Greek *syn-* + *karyon* nut — more at CAREEN] (1905)
: a cell nucleus formed by the fusion of two preexisting nuclei

syn·od \ˈsi-nəd *also* -ˌäd\ *noun* [Middle English *sinod,* from Late Latin *synodus,* from Late Greek *synodos,* from Greek, meeting, assembly, from *syn-* + *hodos* way, journey] (14th century)
1 : an ecclesiastical governing or advisory council: as **a** : the governing assembly of an Episcopal province **b** : a Presbyterian governing body ranking between the presbytery and the general assembly **c** : a regional or national organization of Lutheran congregations
2 : the ecclesiastical district governed by a synod
— **syn·od·al** \ˈsi-nə-dᵊl, -ˌnä-; sə-ˈnä-dᵊl\ *adjective*

syn·od·ic \sə-ˈnä-dik\ *or* **syn·od·i·cal** \-di-kəl\ *adjective* (1561)
1 : of or relating to a synod : SYNODAL
2 *usually* **synodic** [Greek *synodikos,* from *synodos* meeting, conjunction] : relating to conjunction; *especially* : relating to the period between two successive conjunctions of the same celestial bodies (as the moon and the sun)

synodic month *noun* (1654)
: a lunar month

syn·o·nym \ˈsi-nə-ˌnim\ *noun* [Middle English *sinonyme,* from Latin *synonymum,* from Greek *synōnymon,* from neuter of *synōnymos* synonymous, from *syn-* + *onyma* name — more at NAME] (15th century)
1 : one of two or more words or expressions of the same language that have the same or nearly the same meaning in some or all senses
2 : a symbolic or figurative name : METONYM
3 : a taxonomic name rejected as being incorrectly applied or incorrect in form — compare HOMONYM
— **syn·o·nym·ic** \ˌsi-nə-ˈni-mik\ *also* **syn·o·nym·i·cal** \-mi-kəl\ *adjective*
— **syn·o·nym·i·ty** \-ˈni-mə-tē\ *noun*

syn·on·y·mist \sə-ˈnä-nə-mist\ *noun* (circa 1753)
: one who lists, studies, or discriminates synonyms

syn·on·y·mize \-ˌmīz\ *transitive verb* **-mized; -miz·ing** (circa 1595)

1 a : to give or analyze the synonyms of (a word) **b** : to provide (as a dictionary) with synonymies
2 : to demonstrate (a taxonomic name) to be a synonym

syn·on·y·mous \-məs\ *adjective* (1610)
1 : having the character of a synonym; *also* : alike in meaning or significance
2 : having the same connotations, implications, or reference ⟨to runners, Boston is *synonymous* with marathon —*Runners World*⟩
— **syn·on·y·mous·ly** *adverb*

syn·on·y·my \-mē\ *noun, plural* **-mies** (1683)
1 a : a list or collection of synonyms often defined and discriminated from each other **b** : the study or discrimination of synonyms
2 : the scientific names that have been used in different publications to designate a taxonomic group (as a species); *also* : a list of these
3 : the quality or state of being synonymous

syn·op·sis \sə-ˈnäp-səs\ *noun, plural* **-op·ses** \-ˌsēz\ [Late Latin, from Greek, literally, comprehensive view, from *synopsesthai* to be going to see together, from *syn-* + *opsesthai* to be going to see — more at OPTIC] (1611)
1 : a condensed statement or outline (as of a narrative or treatise) : ABSTRACT
2 : the abbreviated conjugation of a verb in one person only

syn·op·size \-ˌsīz\ *transitive verb* **-sized; -siz·ing** (1882)
1 : EPITOMIZE
2 : to make a synopsis of (as a novel)

syn·op·tic \sə-ˈnäp-tik\ *also* **syn·op·ti·cal** \-ti-kəl\ *adjective* [Greek *synoptikos,* from *synopsesthai*] (1763)
1 : affording a general view of a whole
2 : manifesting or characterized by comprehensiveness or breadth of view
3 : presenting or taking the same or common view; *specifically, often capitalized* : of or relating to the first three Gospels of the New Testament
4 : relating to or displaying conditions (as of the atmosphere or weather) as they exist simultaneously over a broad area
— **syn·op·ti·cal·ly** \-ti-k(ə-)lē\ *adverb*

syn·os·to·sis \ˌsi-ˌnäs-ˈtō-səs\ *noun, plural* **-to·ses** \-ˌsēz\ [New Latin] (circa 1848)
: union of two or more separate bones to form a single bone

sy·no·via \sə-ˈnō-vē-ə, sī-\ *noun* [New Latin] (1726)
: a transparent viscid lubricating fluid secreted by a membrane of an articulation, bursa, or tendon sheath

sy·no·vi·al \-vē-əl\ *adjective* (1756)
: of, relating to, secreting, or being synovia ⟨*synovial* membranes⟩ ⟨*synovial* fluid⟩

sy·no·vi·tis \ˌsī-nə-ˈvī-təs\ *noun* (circa 1836)
: inflammation of a synovial membrane

syn·tac·tic \sin-ˈtak-tik\ *or* **syn·tac·ti·cal** \-ti-kəl\ *adjective* [New Latin *syntacticus,* from Greek *syntaktikos* arranging together, from *syntassein*] (1577)
: of, relating to, or according to the rules of syntax or syntactics
— **syn·tac·ti·cal·ly** \-ti-k(ə-)lē\ *adverb*

syn·tac·tics \-tiks\ *noun plural but singular or plural in construction* (1937)
: a branch of semiotic that deals with the formal relations between signs or expressions in abstraction from their signification and their interpreters

syn·tag·ma \sin-ˈtag-mə\ *noun, plural* **-mas** *or* **-ma·ta** \-mə-tə\ [Greek, from *syntassein*] (1937)
: a syntactic element
— **syn·tag·mat·ic** \ˌsin-ˌtag-ˈma-tik\ *adjective*

syn·tax \ˈsin-ˌtaks\ *noun* [French or Late Latin; French *syntaxe,* from Late Latin *syntaxis,* from Greek, from *syntassein* to arrange together, from *syn-* + *tassein* to arrange] (1574)
1 a : the way in which linguistic elements (as

words) are put together to form constituents (as phrases or clauses) **b** : the part of grammar dealing with this
2 : a connected or orderly system : harmonious arrangement of parts or elements
3 : syntactics especially as dealing with the formal properties of languages or calculi

synth \ˈsin(t)th\ *noun, often attributive* (1976)
: SYNTHESIZER 2

syn·the·sis \ˈsin(t)-thə-səs\ *noun, plural* **-the·ses** \-ˌsēz\ [Greek, from *syntithenai* to put together, from *syn-* + *tithenai* to put, place — more at DO] (1589)
1 a : the composition or combination of parts or elements so as to form a whole **b** : the production of a substance by the union of chemical elements, groups, or simpler compounds or by the degradation of a complex compound **c** : the combining of often diverse conceptions into a coherent whole; *also* : the complex so formed
2 a : deductive reasoning **b** : the dialectic combination of thesis and antithesis into a higher stage of truth
3 : the frequent and systematic use of inflected forms as a characteristic device of a language
— **syn·the·sist** \-sist\ *noun*

synthesis gas *noun* (circa 1941)
: a mixture of carbon monoxide and hydrogen used especially in chemical synthesis

syn·the·size \-ˌsīz\ *verb* **-sized; -siz·ing** (1830)
transitive verb
1 : to combine or produce by synthesis
2 : to make a synthesis of
intransitive verb
: to make a synthesis

syn·the·siz·er \-ˌsī-zər\ *noun* (1869)
1 : one that synthesizes ⟨an expert *synthesizer* of diverse views⟩
2 : a usually computerized electronic apparatus for the production and control of sound (as for producing music)

syn·the·tase \ˈsin-thə-ˌtās, -ˌtāz\ *noun* [*synthetic* + *-ase*] (1947)
: an enzyme that catalyzes the linking together of two molecules usually using the energy derived from the concurrent splitting off of a pyrophosphate group from a triphosphate (as ATP) — called also *ligase*

¹syn·thet·ic \sin-ˈthe-tik\ *adjective* [Greek *synthetikos* of composition, component, from *syntithenai* to put together] (1697)
1 : relating to or involving synthesis : not analytic
2 : attributing to a subject something determined by observation rather than analysis of the nature of the subject and not resulting in self-contradiction if negated — compare ANALYTIC
3 : characterized by frequent and systematic use of inflected forms to express grammatical relationships
4 a (1) : of, relating to, or produced by chemical or biochemical synthesis; *especially* : produced artificially ⟨*synthetic* drugs⟩ ⟨*synthetic* silk⟩ (2) : of or relating to a synfuel **b** : devised, arranged, or fabricated for special situations to imitate or replace usual realities **c** : FACTITIOUS, BOGUS
— **syn·thet·i·cal·ly** \-ti-k(ə-)lē\ *adverb*

²synthetic *noun* (1946)
: something resulting from synthesis rather than occurring naturally; *especially* : a product (as a drug or plastic) of chemical synthesis

synthetic division *noun* (1904)
: a simplified method for dividing a polynomial by another polynomial of the first degree by writing down only the coefficients of the several powers of the variable and changing the sign of the constant term in the divisor so as to replace the usual subtractions by additions

synthetic geometry *noun* (1889)
: elementary euclidean geometry or projective geometry as distinguished from analytic geometry

synthetic resin *noun* (1907)
: RESIN 2
syph \'sif\ *noun* (circa 1914)
slang **:** SYPHILIS
syph·i·lis \'si-f(ə-)ləs\ *noun* [New Latin, from *Syphilus*, hero of the poem *Syphilis sive Morbus Gallicus* (*Syphilis or the French disease*) (1530) by Girolamo Fracastoro (died 1553) Italian poet, physician, and astronomer] (1718)
: a chronic contagious usually venereal and often congenital disease caused by a spirochete (*Treponema pallidum*) and if left untreated producing chancres, rashes, and systemic lesions in a clinical course with three stages continued over many years — compare PRIMARY SYPHILIS, SECONDARY SYPHILIS, TERTIARY SYPHILIS ◇
— **syph·i·lit·ic** \,si-fə-'li-tik\ *adjective or noun*
sy·phon *variant of* SIPHON
Sy·rette \sə-'ret\ *trademark*
— used for a small collapsible tube fitted with a hypodermic needle for injecting a single dose of a medicinal agent
Syr·i·ac \'sir-ē-,ak\ *noun* [Latin *syriacus* Syrian, from Greek *syriakos*, from *Syria*, ancient country in Asia] (1605)
1 : a literary language based on an eastern Aramaic dialect and used as the literary and liturgical language by several eastern Christian churches
2 : Aramaic spoken by Christian communities
— **Syriac** *adjective*
Syr·i·an hamster \'sir-ē-ən-\ *noun* [*Syria*, Asia] (circa 1949)
: GOLDEN HAMSTER
sy·rin·ga \sə-'riŋ-gə\ *noun* [New Latin, genus name, from Greek *syring-, syrinx* panpipe] (1664)
: MOCK ORANGE 1
¹sy·ringe \sə-'rinj *also* 'sir-inj\ *noun* [Middle English *syring*, from Medieval Latin *syringa*, from Late Latin, injection, from Greek *syring-, syrinx* panpipe, tube] (14th century)
: a device used to inject fluids into or withdraw them from something (as the body or its cavities): as **a :** a device that consists of a nozzle of varying length and a compressible rubber bulb and is used for injection or irrigation **b :** an instrument (as for the injection of medicine or the withdrawal of bodily fluids) that consists of a hollow barrel fitted with a plunger and a hollow needle **c :** a gravity device consisting of a reservoir fitted with a long rubber tube ending with an exchangeable nozzle that is used for irrigation of the vagina or bowel
²syringe *transitive verb* **sy·ringed; sy·ring·ing** (1610)
: to irrigate or spray with or as if with a syringe
sy·rin·go·my·e·lia \sə-,riŋ-gō-mī-'ē-lē-ə\ *noun* [New Latin, from Greek *syring-, syrinx* tube, fistula + New Latin *myel-* + *-ia*] (1897)
: a chronic progressive disease of the spinal cord associated with sensory disturbances, muscle atrophy, and spasticity
— **sy·rin·go·my·el·ic** \-'e-lik\ *adjective*
syr·inx \'sir-iŋ(k)s\ *noun, plural* **sy·rin·ges** \sə-'rin-,gēz, -'rin-,jēz\ *or* **syr·inx·es** (1606)
1 [Late Latin, from Greek] **:** PANPIPE
2 [New Latin, from Greek] **:** the vocal organ of birds that is a special modification of the lower part of the trachea or of the bronchi or of both
syr·phid fly \'sər-fəd-, 'sir-\ *noun* [New Latin *Syrphidae*, from *Syrphus*, genus of flies, from Greek *syrphos* gnat] (circa 1891)
: any of a family (Syrphidae) of dipteran flies which frequent flowers and some of whose larvae prey on plant lice — called also *syrphid*

— **syrphid** *adjective*
syr·up \'sər-əp, 'sir-əp, 'sə-rəp\ *noun* [Middle English *sirup*, from Middle French *sirop*, from Medieval Latin *syrupus*, from Arabic *sharāb*] (14th century)
1 a : a thick sticky solution of sugar and water often flavored or medicated **b :** the concentrated juice of a fruit or plant
2 : cloying sweetness or sentimentality
— **syr·upy** *adjective*
sys·op \'sis-(,)äp\ *noun* [*system op*erator] (1983)
: the administrator of a computer bulletin board
sys·tal·tic \sis-'tól-tik, -'tal-\ *adjective* [Late Latin *systalticus*, from Greek *systaltikos*, from *systellein* to contract — more at SYSTOLE] (1676)
: marked by regular contraction and dilatation **:** PULSING
sys·tem \'sis-təm\ *noun* [Late Latin *systemat-, systema*, from Greek *systēmat-, systēma*, from *synistanai* to combine, from *syn-* + *histanai* to cause to stand — more at STAND] (1603)
1 : a regularly interacting or interdependent group of items forming a unified whole ⟨a number *system*⟩: as **a** (1) **:** a group of interacting bodies under the influence of related forces ⟨a gravitational *system*⟩ (2) **:** an assemblage of substances that is in or tends to equilibrium ⟨a thermodynamic *system*⟩ **b** (1) **:** a group of body organs that together perform one or more vital functions ⟨the digestive *system*⟩ (2) **:** the body considered as a functional unit **c :** a group of related natural objects or forces ⟨a river *system*⟩ **d :** a group of devices or artificial objects or an organization forming a network especially for distributing something or serving a common purpose ⟨a telephone *system*⟩ ⟨a heating *system*⟩ ⟨a highway *system*⟩ ⟨a data processing *system*⟩ **e :** a major division of rocks usually larger than a series and including all formed during a period or era **f :** a form of social, economic, or political organization or practice ⟨the capitalist *system*⟩
2 : an organized set of doctrines, ideas, or principles usually intended to explain the arrangement or working of a systematic whole ⟨the Newtonian *system* of mechanics⟩
3 a : an organized or established procedure ⟨the touch *system* of typing⟩ **b :** a manner of classifying, symbolizing, or schematizing ⟨a taxonomic *system*⟩ ⟨the decimal *system*⟩
4 : harmonious arrangement or pattern **:** ORDER ⟨bring *system* out of confusion —Ellen Glasgow⟩
5 : an organized society or social situation regarded as stultifying **:** ESTABLISHMENT 2 — usually used with *the*
synonym see METHOD
— **sys·tem·less** \-ləs\ *adjective*
sys·tem·at·ic \,sis-tə-'ma-tik\ *adjective* [Late Latin *systematicus*, from Greek *systēmatikos*, from *systēmat-, systēma*] (circa 1680)
1 : relating to or consisting of a system
2 : presented or formulated as a coherent body of ideas or principles ⟨*systematic* thought⟩
3 a : methodical in procedure or plan ⟨a *systematic* approach⟩ ⟨a *systematic* scholar⟩ **b :** marked by thoroughness and regularity ⟨*systematic* efforts⟩
4 : of, relating to, or concerned with classification; *specifically* **:** TAXONOMIC
— **sys·tem·at·i·cal·ly** \-ti-k(ə-)lē\ *adverb*
— **sys·tem·at·ic·ness** \-tik-nəs\ *noun*
systematic error *noun* (1891)
: an error that is not determined by chance but is introduced by an inaccuracy (as of observation or measurement) inherent in the system
sys·tem·at·ics \,sis-tə-'ma-tiks\ *noun plural but singular in construction* (1888)
1 : the science of classification
2 a : a system of classification **b :** the classifi-

cation and study of organisms with regard to their natural relationships **:** TAXONOMY
systematic theology *noun* (1836)
: a branch of theology concerned with summarizing the doctrinal traditions of a religion (as Christianity) especially with a view to relating the traditions convincingly to the religion's present-day setting
sys·tem·a·tise *British variant of* SYSTEMATIZE
sys·tem·a·tism \'sis-tə-mə-,ti-zəm, sis-'te-mə-\ *noun* (1846)
: the practice of forming intellectual systems
sys·tem·a·tist \'sis-tə-mə-tist, sis-'te-mə-\ *noun* (1700)
1 : a maker or follower of a system
2 : a specialist in taxonomy **:** TAXONOMIST
sys·tem·a·tize \'sis-tə-mə-,tīz\ *transitive verb* **-tized; -tiz·ing** (circa 1767)
: to arrange in accord with a definite plan or scheme **:** order systematically ⟨the need to *systematize* their work⟩
synonym see ORDER
— **sys·tem·a·ti·za·tion** \,sis-tə-mə-tə-'zā-shən, sis-,te-mə-\ *noun*
— **sys·tem·a·tiz·er** *noun*
¹sys·tem·ic \sis-'te-mik\ *adjective* (1803)
: of, relating to, or common to a system: as **a :** affecting the body generally **b :** supplying those parts of the body that receive blood through the aorta rather than through the pulmonary artery **c :** of, relating to, or being a pesticide that as used is harmless to the plant or higher animal but when absorbed into its sap or bloodstream makes the entire organism toxic to pests (as an insect or fungus)
— **sys·tem·i·cal·ly** \-mi-k(ə-)lē\ *adverb*
²systemic *noun* (1951)
: a systemic pesticide
systemic lupus er·y·the·ma·to·sus \-,er-ə-,thē-mə-'tō-səs\ *noun* (1951)
: an inflammatory connective tissue disease of unknown cause that occurs chiefly in women, is characterized especially by fever, skin rash, and arthritis, often by acute hemolytic anemia, by small hemorrhages in the skin and mucous membranes, by inflammation of the pericardium, and in serious cases by involvement of the kidneys and central nervous system
sys·tem·ize \'sis-tə-,mīz\ *transitive verb* **-ized; -iz·ing** (1778)
: SYSTEMATIZE

◇ WORD HISTORY
syphilis In 1530 the Italian physician and poet Girolamo Fracastoro (circa 1478–1553) published a medical poem entitled *Syphilis, sive morbus Gallicus* ("Syphilis or the French Disease"). The "hero" of the poem is an unfortunate swineherd named Syphilus, whose name in Greek literally means "swine lover." The poem is actually a mythological tale that purports to tell how the disease first came into being. In the course of the poem Syphilus offends the sun god; for his punishment he becomes the first person to be afflicted with the fearsome contagion. In a way the poem also serves as a kind of digest of all that was then known about the disease. It discusses the venereal nature of syphilis and its symptoms and stages. Fracastoro's title gave us our name for the disease, but his work is also notable for contributing to the time-honored tradition of blaming the disease on some other country than one's own.

\ə\ abut \ə'\ kitten \ər\ further \a\ ash \ā\ ace \ä\ mop, mar \au̇\ out \ch\ chin \e\ bet \ē\ easy \g\ go \i\ hit \ī\ ice \j\ job \ŋ\ sing \ō\ go \ȯ\ law \ȯi\ boy \th\ thin \t͟h\ this \ü\ loot \u̇\ foot \y\ yet \zh\ vision *see also* Guide to Pronunciation

— **sys·tem·i·za·tion** \ˌsis-tə-mə-ˈzā-shən\ *noun*

systems analysis *noun* (1950)
: the act, process, or profession of studying an activity (as a procedure, a business, or a physiological function) typically by mathematical means in order to define its goals or purposes and to discover operations and procedures for accomplishing them most efficiently
— **systems analyst** *noun*

sys·to·le \ˈsis-tə-(ˌ)lē\ *noun* [Greek *systolē*, from *systellein* to contract, from *syn-* + *stellein* to send] (1578)
: a rhythmically recurrent contraction; *especially* : the contraction of the heart by which the blood is forced onward and the circulation kept up
— **sys·tol·ic** \sis-ˈtä-lik\ *adjective*

syz·y·gy \ˈsi-zə-jē\ *noun, plural* **-gies** [Late Latin *syzygia* conjunction, from Greek, from *syzygos* yoked together, from *syn-* + *zygon* yoke — more at YOKE] (circa 1847)
: the nearly straight-line configuration of three celestial bodies (as the sun, moon, and earth during a solar or lunar eclipse) in a gravitational system

Szech·uan *or* **Szech·wan** \ˈsech-ˌwän, ˈsesh-\ *adjective* [*Szechwan* or *Szechuan* (Sichuan), province in China] (1956)
: of, relating to, or being a style of Chinese cooking that is spicy, oily, and especially peppery

T

T *is the twentieth letter of the English alphabet. It came through Etruscan and Latin from the Greek* tau, *which itself was taken from Phoenician* tāw. *In modern English,* t *usually represents an alveolar stop, that is, a consonant produced by touching the tongue against the upper gum ridge (or alveolus) so as to stop the air flow through the mouth. In many other languages it is dental, or pronounced by pressing the tongue against the teeth. Unlike the otherwise identical sound of* d, *it is voiceless, that is, pronounced without vibration of the vocal cords. With* i *it often represents the sound of* sh, *as in* nation *and* palatial; *before* u *it often represents the sound of* ch, *as in* nature *and* mutual. *With* h *it forms the digraph* th, *which has two sounds, one voiceless, as in* thin, *the other voiced, as in* then. *T is frequently silent before syllabic* n, *as in* chasten *and* soften. *Small* t *came into being when medieval scribes began forming the miniaturized variant of the letter with two pen strokes, thus allowing the vertical stroke to emerge above the letter's crossbar.*

t \'tē\ *noun, plural* **t's** *or* **ts** \'tēz\ *often capitalized, often attributive* (before 12th century)
1 a : the 20th letter of the English alphabet **b :** a graphic representation of this letter **c :** a speech counterpart of orthographic *t*
2 : a graphic device for reproducing the letter *t*
3 : one designated *t* especially as the 20th in order or class
4 : something shaped like the letter T
5 : T FORMATION
6 : TECHNICAL FOUL
— **to a T** [short for *to a tittle*] **:** to perfection

't \t\ *pronoun*
: IT ⟨my country, 'tis of thee —S. F. Smith⟩

ta \'tä\ *noun* [baby talk] (1772)
British **:** THANKS

Taal \'täl\ *noun* [Afrikaans, from Dutch, language; akin to Old English *talu* talk — more at TALE] (1896)
: AFRIKAANS — usually used with *the*

¹tab \'tab\ *noun, often attributive* [origin unknown] (1607)
1 a : a short projecting device: as (1) **:** a small flap or loop by which something may be grasped or pulled (2) **:** a projection from a card used as an aid in filing **b :** a small insert, addition, or remnant **c :** APPENDAGE, EXTENSION; *especially* **:** one of a series of small pendants forming a decorative border or edge of a garment **d :** a small auxiliary airfoil hinged to a control surface (as a trailing edge) to help stabilize an airplane in flight — see AIRPLANE illustration
2 [partly short for ¹*table*; partly from sense 1] **a :** close surveillance ⟨keep *tabs* on trends⟩ **b :** a creditor's statement **:** BILL, CHECK **c :** COST ⟨the *tab* for the new program⟩
3 [by shortening] **a :** TABLOID **b :** TABLET
4 [short for *tabulator*] **:** a device (as on a typewriter) for arranging data in columns

²tab *transitive verb* **tabbed; tab·bing** (1872)
1 : to furnish or ornament with tabs
2 : to single out **:** DESIGNATE
3 : TABULATE

ta·ba·nid \tə-'bā-nəd, -'ba-\ *noun* [ultimately from Latin *tabanus* horsefly] (circa 1891)
: HORSEFLY

tab·ard \'ta-bərd *also* -,bärd\ *noun* [Middle English, from Middle French *tabart*] (14th century)
: a short loose-fitting sleeveless or short-sleeved coat or cape: as **a :** a tunic worn by a knight over his armor and emblazoned with his arms **b :** a herald's official cape or coat emblazoned with his lord's arms **c :** a woman's sleeveless outer garment often with side slits

Ta·bas·co \tə-'bas-(,)kō\ *trademark*
— used for a pungent condiment sauce made from hot peppers

tab·bou·leh \tə-'bü-lə, -,lē\ *noun* [Arabic *tab-būla*] (1955)
: a salad of Lebanese origin consisting chiefly of cracked wheat, tomatoes, parsley, mint, onions, lemon juice, and olive oil

¹tab·by \'ta-bē\ *noun, plural* **tabbies** [French *tabis,* from Medieval Latin *attabi,* from Arabic *'attābī,* from Al-*'Attābīya,* quarter in Baghdad] (1638)
1 a : *archaic* **:** a plain silk taffeta especially with moiré finish **b :** a plain-woven fabric
2 [²*tabby*] **a :** a domestic cat with a striped and mottled coat **b :** a domestic cat; *especially* **:** a female cat ◇

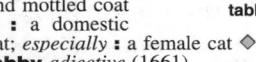

tabby 2a

²tabby *adjective* (1661)
1 : of, relating to, or made of tabby
2 : striped and mottled with darker color **:** BRINDLED ⟨a *tabby* cat⟩

³tabby *noun* [Gullah *tabi,* ultimately from Spanish *tapia* adobe wall] (1775)
: a cement made of lime, sand or gravel, and oyster shells and used chiefly along the coast of Georgia and South Carolina in the 17th and 18th centuries

¹tab·er·na·cle \'ta-bər-,na-kəl\ *noun* [Middle English, from Old French, from Late Latin *tabernaculum,* from Latin, tent, from *taberna* hut] (13th century)
1 a : *often capitalized* **:** a tent sanctuary used by the Israelites during the Exodus **b :** *archaic* **:** a dwelling place **c :** *archaic* **:** a temporary shelter **:** TENT
2 : a receptacle for the consecrated elements of the Eucharist; *especially* **:** an ornamental locked box used for reserving the Communion hosts
3 : a house of worship; *specifically* **:** a large building or tent used for evangelistic services
— **tab·er·nac·u·lar** \,ta-bər-'na-kyə-lər\ *adjective*

²tabernacle *intransitive verb* **tab·er·na·cled; tab·er·na·cling** \-,na-k(ə-)liŋ\ (1653)
: to take up temporary residence; *especially* **:** to inhabit a physical body

ta·bes \'tā-(,)bēz\ *noun, plural* **tabes** [Latin, wasting disease, decay, from *tabēre* to decay — more at THAW] (1651)
: wasting accompanying a chronic disease

— **ta·bet·ic** \tə-'be-tik\ *adjective or noun*

tabes dor·sa·lis \-dór-'sa-ləs, -'sä-, -'sä-\ *noun* [New Latin, dorsal tabes] (circa 1681)
: a syphilitic disorder of the nervous system marked by wasting, pain, lack of coordination of voluntary movements and reflexes, and disorders of sensation, nutrition, and vision — called also *locomotor ataxia*

ta·bla \'tä-blə\ *noun* [Hindi *tablā,* from Arabic *ṭabla*] (1865)
: a pair of small different-sized hand drums used especially in music of India

tabla

tab·la·ture \'ta-blə-,chùr, -chər, -,tyùr, -,tùr\ *noun* [Middle French, from Medieval Latin *tabulatus* tablet, from Latin *tabula*] (1574)
: an instrumental notation indicating the string, fret, key, or finger to be used instead of the tone to be sounded

¹ta·ble \'tā-bəl\ *noun, often attributive* [Middle English, from Old English *tabule* & Old French *table*; both from Latin *tabula* board, tablet, list] (before 12th century)
1 : TABLET 1a
2 a *plural* **:** BACKGAMMON **b :** one of the two leaves of a backgammon board or either half of a leaf
3 a : a piece of furniture consisting of a smooth flat slab fixed on legs **b** (1) **:** a supply or source of food (2) **:** an act or instance of assembling to eat **:** MEAL ⟨sit down to *table*⟩ **c** (1) **:** a group of people assembled at or as if at a table (2) **:** a legislative or negotiating session ⟨the bargaining *table*⟩
4 : STRINGCOURSE
5 a : a systematic arrangement of data usually in rows and columns for ready reference **b :** a condensed enumeration **:** LIST ⟨a *table* of contents⟩
6 : something that resembles a table especially in having a plane surface: as **a :** the upper flat surface of a cut precious stone **b** (1) **:** TABLELAND (2) **:** a horizontal stratum ⟨water *table*⟩
— **under the table 1 :** into a stupor ⟨can drink you *under the table*⟩ **2 :** in a covert manner ⟨took money *under the table*⟩

²table *transitive verb* **ta·bled; ta·bling** \-b(ə-)liŋ\ (15th century)
1 : to enter in a table
2 a *British* **:** to place on the agenda **b :** to remove (as a parliamentary motion) from consideration indefinitely **c :** to put on a table

³table *adjective* (1547)

◇ **WORD HISTORY**

tabby A silk cloth with a moiré or wavy pattern was once made in a quarter of the city of Baghdad, now the capital of the modern nation of Iraq. In Arabic the cloth was known as '*attābī,* from *Al-'Attābīya,* the name of its place of origin. The name for the cloth passed into Medieval Latin as *attabi* and then into French as *tabis.* When the word was borrowed into English as *tabby* in the 17th century, it was solely with reference to a plain-woven silk cloth with a moiré pattern. Before long, however, people noted a resemblance between the cloth's pattern and the striped or mottled markings on the coats of their domestic cats. *Tabby* has been the standard name for this type of cat ever since.

\ə\ abut \ᵊ\ kitten \ər\ further \a\ ash \ā\ ace
\ä\ mop, mar \au̇\ out \ch\ chin \e\ bet \ē\ easy
\g\ go \i\ hit \ī\ ice \j\ job \ŋ\ sing \ō\ go
\ȯ\ law \ȯi\ boy \th\ thin \th̲\ the \ü\ loot \u̇\ foot
\y\ yet \zh\ vision *see also* Guide to Pronunciation

1 : suitable for a table or for use at a table ⟨a *table* lamp⟩
2 : suitable for serving at a table ⟨*table* grapes⟩
3 : proper for conduct at a table ⟨*table* manners⟩

tab·leau \'ta-ˌblō, ta-'blō\ *noun, plural* **tableaux** \-ˌblōz, -'blōz\ *also* **tableaus** [French, from Middle French *tablel*, diminutive of *table*, from Old French] (1699)
1 : a graphic description or representation : PICTURE ⟨winsome *tableaus* of old-fashioned literary days —J. D. Hart⟩
2 : a striking or artistic grouping
3 [short for *tableau vivant* (from French, literally, living picture)] : a depiction of a scene usually presented on a stage by silent and motionless costumed participants

tableau curtain *noun* (1881)
: a stage curtain that opens in the center and has its sections drawn upward as well as to the side

ta·ble·cloth \'tā-bəl-ˌklȯth\ *noun* (15th century)
: a covering spread over a dining table before the tableware is set

ta·ble d'hôte \ˌtä-bəl-'dōt, ˌta-\ *noun* [French, literally, host's table] (1617)
1 : a meal served to all guests at a stated hour and fixed price
2 : a complete meal of several courses offered at a fixed price

ta·ble·ful \'tā-bəl-ˌfu̇l\ *noun* (1535)
: as much or as many as a table can hold or accommodate

ta·ble–hop \'tā-bəl-ˌhäp\ *intransitive verb* (1942)
: to move from table to table (as in a restaurant) in order to chat with friends
— **ta·ble–hop·per** *noun*

ta·ble·land \-bə(l)-ˌland\ *noun* (1697)
: a broad level elevated area : PLATEAU

table linen *noun* (1629)
: linen (as tablecloths and napkins) for the table

ta·ble·mate \'tā-bəl-ˌmāt\ *noun* (1624)
: a dining companion

table of organization (circa 1918)
: a table listing the number and duties of personnel and the major items of equipment authorized for a military unit

table salt *noun* (1878)
: salt suitable for use at the table and in cooking

ta·ble·spoon \'tā-bəl-ˌspün\ *noun* (1763)
1 : a large spoon used for serving
2 : a unit of measure used especially in cookery equal to ½ fluid ounce (15 milliliters)

ta·ble·spoon·ful \ˌtā-bəl-'spün-ˌfu̇l, 'tā-bəl-ˌ\ *noun, plural* **tablespoonfuls** \-ˌfu̇lz\ *also* **ta·ble·spoons·ful** \-'spünz-ˌfu̇l, -ˌspünz-\ (1772)
1 : enough to fill a tablespoon
2 : TABLESPOON 2

table sugar *noun* (1958)
: SUGAR 1a; *especially* : granulated white sugar

tab·let \'ta-blət\ *noun* [Middle English *tablett*, from Middle French *tablete*, diminutive of *table* table] (14th century)
1 a : a flat slab or plaque suited for or bearing an inscription **b** : a thin slab or one of a set of portable sheets used for writing **c** : PAD 4
2 a : a compressed or molded block of a solid material **b** : a small mass of medicated material ⟨an aspirin *tablet*⟩
3 : GRAPHICS TABLET

table talk *noun* (1569)
: informal conversation at or as if at a dining table; *especially* : the social talk of a celebrity recorded for publication

table tennis *noun* (1901)
: a game resembling tennis that is played on a tabletop with wooden paddles and a small hollow plastic ball

ta·ble·top \'tā-bəl-ˌtäp\ *noun* (1807)
1 : the top of a table

2 : a photograph of small objects or a miniature scene arranged on a table
— **table·top** *adjective*

ta·ble·ware \-ˌwar, -ˌwer\ *noun* (1832)
: utensils (as of china, glass, or silver) for table use

table wine *noun* (circa 1827)
: an unfortified wine averaging 12 percent alcohol by volume and usually suitable for serving with food

¹tab·loid \'ta-ˌblȯid\ *adjective* [from *Tabloid*, a trademark] (1901)
1 : compressed or condensed into small scope ⟨*tabloid* criticism⟩
2 : of, relating to, or characteristic of tabloids; *especially* : featuring stories of violence, crime, or scandal presented in a sensational manner

²tabloid *noun* (1906)
1 : DIGEST, SUMMARY
2 : a newspaper that is about half the page size of an ordinary newspaper and that contains news in condensed form and much photographic matter

¹ta·boo *also* **ta·bu** \tə-'bü, ta-\ *adjective* [Tongan *tabu*] (1777)
1 : forbidden to profane use or contact because of what are held to be dangerous supernatural powers
2 a : banned on grounds of morality or taste ⟨the subject is *taboo*⟩ **b** : banned as constituting a risk ⟨the area beyond is *taboo*, still alive with explosives —Robert Leckie⟩

²taboo *also* **tabu** *noun, plural* **taboos** *also* **tabus** (1777)
1 : a prohibition against touching, saying, or doing something for fear of immediate harm from a supernatural force
2 : a prohibition imposed by social custom or as a protective measure
3 : belief in taboos

³taboo *also* **tabu** *transitive verb* (1777)
1 : to set apart as taboo especially by marking with a ritualistic symbol
2 : to avoid or ban as taboo

ta·bor *also* **ta·bour** \'tā-bər\ *noun* [Middle English, from Old French] (14th century)
: a small drum with one head of soft calfskin used to accompany a pipe or fife played by the same person

ta·bor·er *also* **ta·bour·er** \-bər-ər\ *noun* (15th century)
: one that plays on the tabor

tab·o·ret *or* **tab·ou·ret** \ˌta-bə-'ret, -'rā\ *noun* [French *tabouret*, literally, small drum, from Middle French, diminutive of *tabor, tabour* drum] (1630)
1 : a cylindrical seat or stool without arms or back
2 : a small portable stand or cabinet

tabor

ta·bou·li *variant of* TABBOULEH

Ta·briz \tə-'brēz\ *noun, plural* **Tabriz** [*Tabriz*, Iran] (1904)
: a Persian rug usually having a cotton warp, firm wool pile, and a medallion pattern

tab·u·lar \'ta-byə-lər\ *adjective* [Latin *tabularis* of boards, from *tabula* board, tablet] (circa 1656)
1 : having a flat surface : LAMINAR ⟨a *tabular* crystal⟩
2 a : of, relating to, or arranged in a table; *specifically* : set up in rows and columns **b** : computed by means of a table

ta·bu·la ra·sa \ˌta-byə-lə-'rä-zə, -sə\ *noun, plural* **ta·bu·lae ra·sae** \-ˌlī-'rä-ˌzī, -ˌsī\ [Latin, smoothed or erased tablet] (1607)
1 : the mind in its hypothetical primary blank or empty state before receiving outside impressions
2 : something existing in its original pristine state

tab·u·late \'ta-byə-ˌlāt\ *transitive verb* **-lat·ed; -lat·ing** [Latin *tabula* tablet] (1734)

1 : to put into tabular form
2 : to count, record, or list systematically
— **tab·u·la·tion** \ˌta-byə-'lā-shən\ *noun*
— **tab·u·la·tor** \'ta-byə-ˌlā-tər\ *noun*

ta·bun \'tä-ˌbu̇n\ *noun* [German] (1948)
: a liquid organophosphate $C_5H_{11}N_2O_2P$ that acts as a nerve gas

tac·a·ma·hac \'ta-kə-mə-ˌhak\ *noun* [Spanish *tacamahaca*, from Nahuatl *tecamac*] (1739)
: BALSAM POPLAR

TACAN \'ta-ˌkan\ *noun, often attributive* [*tac*tical *air* *n*avigation] (1955)
: a system of navigation that uses ultrahigh frequency signals to determine the distance and bearing of an aircraft from a transmitting station

ta·cet \'tä-ˌket; 'tā-sət, 'ta-sət\ [Latin, literally, (it) is silent, from *tacēre* to be silent — more at TACIT] (circa 1724)
— used as a direction in music to indicate that an instrument is not to play during a movement or long section

tach \'tak\ *noun* (circa 1930)
: TACHOMETER

tach·i·nid \'ta-kə-nəd, -ˌnid\ *noun* [New Latin *Tachinidae*, from *Tachina*, genus of flies, from Greek *tachinos* fleet, from *tachys* swift] (1888)
: any of a family (Tachinidae) of bristly usually grayish or black dipteran flies whose parasitic larvae are often used in the biological control of insect pests
— **tachinid** *adjective*

tach·ism \'ta-ˌshi-zəm\ *noun, often capitalized* [French *tachisme*, from *tache* stain, spot, blob, from Middle French *teche, tache*, of Germanic origin; akin to Old Saxon *tēkan* sign, Old High German *zeihhan* — more at TOKEN] (1955)
: ACTION PAINTING
— **tach·ist** \'ta-shist\ *also* **ta·chiste** \ta-'shēst\ *adjective or noun, often capitalized*

ta·chis·to·scope \tə-'kis-tə-ˌskōp, ta-\ *noun* [Greek *tachistos* (superlative of *tachys* swift) + International Scientific Vocabulary *-scope*] (circa 1890)
: an apparatus for the brief exposure of visual stimuli that is used in the study of learning, attention, and perception
— **ta·chis·to·scop·ic** \-ˌkis-tə-'skä-pik\ *adjective*
— **ta·chis·to·scop·i·cal·ly** \-pi-k(ə-)lē\ *adverb*

ta·chom·e·ter \ta-'kä-mə-tər, tə-\ *noun* [Greek *tachos* speed + English *-meter*] (1810)
: a device for indicating speed of rotation

tachy- *combining form* [Greek, from *tachys*]
: rapid : accelerated ⟨*tachy*cardia⟩

tachy·ar·rhyth·mia \ˌta-kē-ā-'rith-mē-ə\ *noun* [New Latin] (1926)
: arrhythmia characterized by a rapid irregular heartbeat

tachy·car·dia \ˌta-ki-'kär-dē-ə\ *noun* [New Latin] (1889)
: relatively rapid heart action whether physiological (as after exercise) or pathological — compare BRADYCARDIA

tachy·on \'ta-kē-ˌän\ *noun* [*tachy*- + ²*-on*] (1967)
: a hypothetical particle held to travel only faster than light

tac·it \'ta-sət\ *adjective* [French or Latin; French *tacite*, from Latin *tacitus* silent, from past participle of *tacēre* to be silent; akin to Old High German *dagēn* to be silent] (circa 1604)
1 : expressed or carried on without words or speech
2 a : implied or indicated but not actually expressed ⟨*tacit* consent⟩ **b** (1) : arising without express contract or agreement (2) : arising by operation of law ⟨*tacit* mortgage⟩
— **tac·it·ly** *adverb*
— **tac·it·ness** *noun*

tac·i·turn \'ta-sə-,tərn\ *adjective* [French or Latin; French *taciturne*, from Latin *taciturnus*, from *tacitus*] (1771)
: temperamentally disinclined to talk
synonym see SILENT
— **tac·i·tur·ni·ty** \,ta-sə-'tər-nə-tē\ *noun*

¹tack \'tak\ *verb* [Middle English *takken*, from *tak*] (14th century)
transitive verb
1 : ATTACH; *especially* : to fasten or affix with tacks
2 : to join in a slight or hasty manner
3 a : to add as a supplement **b** : to add (a rider) to a parliamentary bill
4 : to change the direction of (a sailing ship) when sailing close-hauled by turning the bow to the wind and shifting the sails so as to fall off on the other side at about the same angle as before
intransitive verb
1 a : to tack a sailing ship **b** *of a ship* : to change to an opposite tack by turning the bow to the wind **c** : to follow a course against the wind by a series of tacks
2 a : to follow a zigzag course **b** : to modify one's policy or attitude abruptly
— **tack·er** *noun*

²tack *noun* [Middle English *tak* something that attaches; akin to Middle Dutch *tac* sharp point] (1574)
1 : a small short sharp-pointed nail usually having a broad flat head
2 a : the direction of a ship with respect to the trim of her sails ⟨starboard *tack*⟩ **b** : the run of a sailing ship on one tack **c** : a change when close-hauled from the starboard to the port tack or vice versa **d** : a zigzag movement on land **e** : a course or method of action; *especially* : one sharply divergent from that previously followed
3 : any of various usually temporary stitches
4 : the lower forward corner of a fore-and-aft sail
5 : a sticky or adhesive quality or condition

³tack *noun* [origin unknown] (1841)
: HARDTACK 1

⁴tack *noun* [perhaps short for *tackle*] (1924)
: stable gear; *especially* : articles of harness (as saddle and bridle) for use on a saddle horse

tack·board \'tak-,bōrd, -,bȯrd\ *noun* (circa 1927)
: a board (as of cork) for tacking up notices and display materials

tack claw *noun* (circa 1876)
: a small hand tool for removing tacks

tack·i·fy \'ta-kə-,fī\ *transitive verb* **-fied; -fy·ing** (1942)
: to make (as a resin adhesive) tacky or more tacky
— **tack·i·fi·er** \-,fī(-ə)r\ *noun*

tack·i·ly \'ta-kə-lē\ *adverb* (1903)
: in a tacky manner : so as to be tacky

tack·i·ness \'ta-kē-nəs\ *noun* (1883)
: the quality or state of being tacky

¹tack·le \'ta-kəl, *nautical often* 'tā-\ *noun* [Middle English *takel*; akin to Middle Dutch *takel* ship's rigging] (13th century)
1 : a set of the equipment used in a particular activity : GEAR ⟨fishing *tackle*⟩
2 a : a ship's rigging **b** : an assemblage of ropes and pulleys arranged to gain mechanical advantage for hoisting and pulling
3 a : the act or an instance of tackling **b** (1) : either of two offensive football players positioned on each side of the center and between guard and end (2) : either of two football players positioned on the inside of a defensive line

²tackle *verb* **tack·led; tack·ling** \-k(ə-)liŋ\ (1714)
transitive verb
1 : to attach or secure with or as if with tackle

2 a : to seize, take hold of, or grapple with especially with the intention of stopping or subduing **b** : to seize and throw down or stop (an opposing player with the ball) in football
3 : to set about dealing with ⟨*tackle* the problem⟩
intransitive verb
: to tackle an opposing player in football
— **tack·ler** \-k(ə-)lər\ *noun*

tack·ling \'ta-kliŋ, *nautical often* 'tā-\ *noun* (15th century)
: TACKLE, GEAR

¹tacky \'ta-kē\ *adjective* **tack·i·er; -est** [²*tack*] (1788)
: somewhat sticky to the touch ⟨*tacky* varnish⟩; *also* : characterized by tack : ADHESIVE

²tacky *adjective* **tack·i·er; -est** [*tacky* a low-class person] (1862)
1 a : characterized by lack of good breeding **b** : COMMON ⟨couldn't run around downtown . . . in a bikini, which was *tacky* —Cyra McFadden⟩ **b** : SHABBY, SEEDY ⟨a *tacky* town whose citrus groves were blighted by smoke —Bryce Nelson⟩
2 : not having or exhibiting good taste ⟨hopelessly *tacky* bric-a-brac —T. C. Boyle⟩: as **a** : marked by lack of style : DOWDY **b** : marked by cheap showiness : GAUDY

ta·co \'tä-(,)kō\ *noun, plural* **tacos** \-(,)kōz\ [Mexican Spanish] (1934)
: a usually fried tortilla that is folded or rolled and stuffed with a mixture (as of seasoned meat, cheese, and lettuce)

tac·o·nite \'ta-kə-,nīt\ *noun* [*Taconic* Range, mountains in U.S.] (1892)
: a flintlike rock high enough in iron content to constitute a low-grade iron ore

tact \'takt\ *noun* [French, sense of touch, from Latin *tactus*, from *tangere* to touch — more at TANGENT] (1797)
1 : sensitive mental or aesthetic perception ⟨converted the novel into a play with remarkable skill and *tact*⟩
2 : a keen sense of what to do or say in order to maintain good relations with others or avoid offense ☆

tact·ful \'takt-fəl\ *adjective* (1864)
: having or showing tact
— **tact·ful·ly** \-fə-lē\ *adverb*
— **tact·ful·ness** *noun*

¹tac·tic \'tak-tik\ *noun* [New Latin *tactica*, from Greek *taktikē*, from feminine of *taktikos*] (1640)
1 : a device for accomplishing an end
2 : a method of employing forces in combat

²tactic *adjective* [New Latin *tacticus*, from Greek *taktikos*] (1871)
: of or relating to arrangement or order

-tactic *adjective combining form* [Greek *taktikos*]
1 : of, relating to, or having (such) an arrangement or pattern ⟨para*tactic*⟩
2 : showing orientation or movement directed by a (specified) force or agent ⟨geo*tactic*⟩

tac·ti·cal \'tak-ti-kəl\ *adjective* (1570)
1 : of or relating to combat tactics: as **a** (1) : of or occurring at the battlefront ⟨*tactical* defense⟩ ⟨*tactical* first strike⟩ (2) : using or being weapons or forces employed at the battlefront ⟨*tactical* missiles⟩ **b** *of an air force* : of, relating to, or designed for air attack in close support of friendly ground forces
2 a : of or relating to tactics: as (1) : of or relating to small-scale actions serving a larger purpose (2) : made or carried out with only a limited or immediate end in view **b** : adroit in planning or maneuvering to accomplish a purpose
— **tac·ti·cal·ly** \-k(ə-)lē\ *adverb*

tac·ti·cian \tak-'ti-shən\ *noun* (1798)
: one versed in tactics

tac·tics \'tak-tiks\ *noun plural but singular or*

plural in construction [New Latin *tactica*, plural, from Greek *taktika*, from neuter plural of *taktikos* of order, of tactics, fit for arranging, from *tassein* to arrange, place in battle formation] (1626)
1 a : the science and art of disposing and maneuvering forces in combat **b** : the art or skill of employing available means to accomplish an end
2 : a system or mode of procedure
3 : the study of the grammatical relations within a language including morphology and syntax

tac·tile \'tak-t⁹l, -,tīl\ *adjective* [French or Latin; French, from Latin *tactilis*, from *tangere* to touch — more at TANGENT] (1615)
1 : perceptible by touch : TANGIBLE
2 : of or relating to the sense of touch
— **tac·tile·ly** \-tə-lē, -,tīl-lē\ *adverb*

tactile corpuscle *noun* (1873)
: an end organ of touch

tac·til·i·ty \tak-'ti-lə-tē\ *noun* (1659)
1 : the capability of being felt or touched
2 : responsiveness to stimulation of the sense of touch

tac·tion \'tak-shən\ *noun* [Latin *taction-, tactio*, from *tangere*] (circa 1623)
: TOUCH

tact·less \'takt-ləs\ *adjective* (circa 1847)
: marked by lack of tact
— **tact·less·ly** *adverb*
— **tact·less·ness** *noun*

tac·tu·al \'tak-chə-wəl, -chəl\ *adjective* [Latin *tactus* sense of touch — more at TACT] (1642)
: TACTILE 2
— **tac·tu·al·ly** *adverb*

tad \'tad\ *noun* [probably from English dialect, toad, from Middle English *tode* — more at TOAD] (circa 1877)
1 : a small child; *especially* : BOY
2 : a small or insignificant amount or degree : BIT ⟨might give him some water and a *tad* to eat —C. T. Walker⟩
— **a tad** : SOMEWHAT, RATHER ⟨looked *a tad* bigger than me —Larry Hodgson⟩

tad·pole \'tad-,pōl\ *noun* [Middle English *taddepol*, from *tode* toad + *polle* head] (15th century)
: a larval amphibian; *specifically* : a frog or toad larva that has a rounded body with a long tail bordered by fins and external gills soon replaced by

tadpole

tackle 2b

internal gills and that undergoes a metamorphosis to the adult

Ta·dzhik *variant of* TAJIK

tae·di·um vi·tae \,tē-dē-əm-'vī-,tē, ,tī-dē-əm-'wē-,tī\ *noun* [Latin] (1759)
: weariness or loathing of life

tae kwon do \'tī-'kwän-'dō\ *noun, often T&K&D capitalized* [Korean *t'aekwŏndo,* from *t'ae-* to trample + *kwŏn* fist + *to* way] (1967)
: a Korean martial art resembling karate

tael \'tā(ə)l\ *noun* [Portuguese, from Malay *tahil*] (1588)
1 : any of various Chinese units of value based on the value of a tael weight of silver
2 : any of various units of weight of eastern Asia

tae·nia \'tē-nē-ə\ *noun, plural* **-ni·ae** \-nē-,ī, -,ē\ *or* **-nias** [Latin, ribbon, fillet, from Greek *tainia;* akin to Greek *teinein* to stretch — more at THIN] (1563)
1 : a band on a Doric order separating the frieze from the architrave
2 : TAPEWORM
3 : an ancient Greek fillet
4 [New Latin, from Latin, fillet, band] : a band of nervous tissue or muscle

tae·ni·a·sis \tē-'nī-ə-səs\ *noun* [New Latin, from Latin *taenia* tapeworm] (circa 1890)
: infestation with or disease caused by tapeworms

taf·fe·ta \'ta-fə-tə\ *noun* [Middle English, from Middle French *taffetas,* from Old Italian *taffettà,* from Turkish *tafta,* from Persian *tāftah* woven] (14th century)
: a crisp plain-woven lustrous fabric of various fibers used especially for women's clothing

taf·fe·tized \'ta-fə-,tīzd\ *adjective* (1949)
of cloth : having a crisp finish

taf·frail \'taf-,rāl, -rəl\ *noun* [modification of Dutch *tafereel,* from Middle Dutch, panel, from Old French *tablel* — more at TABLEAU] (circa 1704)
1 : the upper part of the stern of a wooden ship
2 : a rail around the stern of a ship

taf·fy \'ta-fē\ *noun, plural* **taffies** [origin unknown] (circa 1817)
1 : a boiled candy usually of molasses or brown sugar that is pulled until porous and light-colored
2 : insincere flattery

¹tag \'tag\ *noun* [Middle English *tagge,* probably of Scandinavian origin; akin to Swedish *tagg* barb] (15th century)
1 : a loose hanging piece of cloth : TATTER
2 : a metal or plastic binding on an end of a shoelace
3 : a piece of hanging or attached material; *specifically* : a loop, knot, or tassel on a garment
4 a : a brief quotation used for rhetorical emphasis or sentientious effect **b** : a recurrent or characteristic verbal expression **c** : TAG LINE 1
5 a : a cardboard, plastic, or metal marker used for identification or classification ⟨license *tags*⟩ **b** : a descriptive or identifying epithet **c** : something used for identification or location : FLAG **d** : LABEL 3d **e** : PRICE TAG
6 : a detached fragmentary piece : BIT

²tag *verb* **tagged; tag·ging** (15th century)
transitive verb
1 : to provide or mark with or as if with a tag: as **a** : to supply with an identifying marker or price ⟨*tagged* every item in the store⟩ ⟨was *tagged* at $4.95⟩ **b** : to provide with a name or epithet : LABEL, BRAND ⟨*tagged* him a has-been⟩ **c** : to put a ticket on (a motor vehicle) for a traffic violation
2 : to attach as an addition : APPEND
3 : to follow closely and persistently
4 : to hold to account; *especially* : to charge with violating the law ⟨was *tagged* for . . . assault —Burt Woolis⟩
5 : LABEL 2

intransitive verb
: to keep close ⟨*tagging* at their heels —Corey Ford⟩

³tag *noun* [origin unknown] (1738)
1 : a game in which the player who is it chases others and tries to touch one of them who then becomes it
2 : an act or instance of tagging a runner in baseball

⁴tag *transitive verb* **tagged; tag·ging** (1878)
1 a : to touch in or as if in a game of tag **b** : to put out (a runner) in baseball by a touch with the ball or the gloved hand containing the ball
2 : to hit solidly
3 : to choose usually for a special purpose : SELECT
4 : to make a hit or run off (a pitcher) in baseball

Ta·ga·log \tə-'gä-,lóg\ *noun, plural* **Tagalog** *or* **Tagalogs** [Tagalog] (circa 1808)
1 : a member of a people of central Luzon
2 : an Austronesian language of the Tagalog people — compare PILIPINO

tag·along \'ta-gə-,lóŋ\ *noun* (1935)
: one that persistently and often annoyingly follows the lead of another

tag along *intransitive verb* (1900)
: to follow another's lead especially in going from one place to another

tag·board \'tag-,bórd, -,bòrd\ *noun* (1904)
: strong cardboard used especially for making shipping tags

tag end *noun* (1807)
1 : the last part
2 : a miscellaneous or random bit

ta·glia·tel·le \,täl-yä-'te-(,)lā\ *noun* [Italian, from *tagliare* to cut, from Late Latin *taliare* — more at TAILOR] (1899)
: FETTUCCINE

tag line *noun* (1926)
1 : a final line (as in a play or joke); *especially* : one that serves to clarify a point or create a dramatic effect
2 : a reiterated phrase identified with an individual, group, or product : SLOGAN

tag question *noun* (1933)
: a question (as *isn't it* in "it's fine, isn't it?") added to a statement or command (as to gain the assent of or challenge the person addressed); *also* : a sentence ending in a tag question

tag, rag, and bobtail *or* **tagrag and bobtail** \,tag-,rag-ən-'bäb-,tāl, -,rag-ᵊŋ-\ *noun* (1645)
: RABBLE

tag sale *noun* [from the price tag on each item] (1955)
: GARAGE SALE

tag team *noun* [⁴tag] (1952)
: a team of two or more professional wrestlers who spell each other during a match

tag up *intransitive verb* (1942)
: to touch a base before running in baseball after a fly ball is caught

ta·hi·ni \tə-'hē-nē, tä-\ *noun* [Arabic dialect *ṭaḥīna,* from *ṭaḥana* to grind] (1950)
: a smooth paste of sesame seeds

Ta·hi·tian \tə-'hē-shən\ *noun* (1825)
1 : a native or inhabitant of Tahiti
2 : the Polynesian language of the Tahitians
— **Tahitian** *adjective*

tahr \'tär\ *noun* [Nepali *thār*] (1835)
: any of a genus (*Hemitragus*) of wild Asian goats; *especially* : one (*H. jemlahicus*) of the Himalayas having a reddish brown to dark brown coat and a long shaggy mane

tah·sil \tä-'sē(ə)l\ *noun* [Urdu *taḥṣīl,* from Arabic, collection of revenue] (1846)
: a district administration or revenue subdivision in India

Tai \'tī\ *noun, plural* **Tai** (1693)
: a widespread group of peoples in southeast Asia associated ethnically with valley paddy-rice culture

tai chi chuan *or* **t'ai chi ch'uan** \'tī-'jē-chü-'än, 'tī-'chē-\ *noun, often T and both Cs capitalized* [Chinese (Beijing) *tàijíquán,* from *tàijí* the Absolute in Chinese cosmology + *quán* fist, boxing] (1954)
: an ancient Chinese discipline of meditative movements practiced as a system of exercises — called also *tai chi, t'ai chi*

tai·ga \'tī-gə\ *noun* [Russian *taĭga*] (1888)
: a moist subarctic forest dominated by conifers (as spruce and fir) that begins where the tundra ends

¹tail \'tā(ə)l\ *noun, often attributive* [Middle English, from Old English *tægel;* akin to Old High German *zagal* tail, Middle Irish *dúal* lock of hair] (before 12th century)
1 : the rear end or a process or prolongation of the rear end of the body of an animal
2 : something resembling an animal's tail in shape or position: as **a** : the luminous train of a comet **b** : the rear part of an airplane consisting usually of horizontal and vertical stabilizing surfaces with attached control surfaces
3 : RETINUE
4 *plural* **a** : TAILCOAT **b** : full evening dress for men
5 a : BUTTOCKS, BUTT **b** : a female sexual partner — usually considered vulgar
6 : the back, last, lower, or inferior part of something
7 : TAILING 1 — usually used in plural
8 : the reverse of a coin — usually used in plural ⟨*tails,* I win⟩
9 : one (as a detective) who follows or keeps watch on someone
10 : the blank space at the bottom of a page
11 : a location immediately or not far behind ⟨had a posse on his *tail*⟩
— **tailed** \'tā(ə)ld\ *adjective*
— **tail·less** \'tā(ə)l-ləs\ *adjective*
— **tail·like** \-,līk\ *adjective*

²tail (1523)
transitive verb
1 : to connect end to end
2 a : to remove the tail of (an animal) : DOCK **b** : to remove the stem or bottom part of ⟨topping and *tailing* gooseberries⟩
3 a : to make or furnish with a tail **b** : to follow or be drawn behind like a tail
4 : to follow for purposes of surveillance
intransitive verb
1 : to form or move in a straggling line
2 : to grow progressively smaller, fainter, or more scattered : ABATE — usually used with *off* ⟨productivity is *tailing* off —Tom Nicholson⟩
3 : to swing or lie with the stern in a named direction — used of a ship at anchor
4 : ²TAG
— **tail·er** *noun*

³tail *noun* [Middle English, from Middle French, from Old French, from *taillier*] (14th century)
: ENTAIL 1a

⁴tail *adjective* [Middle English *taille,* from Anglo-French *taylé,* from Old French *taillié,* past participle of *taillier* to cut, limit — more at TAILOR] (15th century)
: limited as to tenure : ENTAILED

tail·back \'tā(ə)l-,bak\ *noun* (1930)
: the offensive football back farthest from the line of scrimmage

tail·board \-,bórd, -,bòrd\ *noun* (1805)
chiefly British : TAILGATE 1

tail·bone \-,bōn\ *noun* (circa 1577)
1 : a caudal vertebra
2 : COCCYX

tail·coat \-,kōt\ *noun* (1847)
: a coat with tails; *especially* : a man's full-dress coat with two long tapering skirts at the back
— **tail·coat·ed** \-,kō-təd\ *adjective*

tail covert *noun* (1815)
: one of the coverts of the tail quills

tail end *noun* (14th century)

1 : BUTTOCKS, RUMP
2 : the hindmost end
3 : the concluding period ⟨the *tail end* of the session⟩
tail·end·er \'tā(ə)l-,en-dər\ *noun* (1885)
: one positioned at the end or in last place ⟨the *tailenders* in a race⟩
tail fin *noun* (1681)
1 : the terminal fin of a fish or cetacean
2 : FIN 2b
¹**tail·gate** \'tā(ə)l-,gāt\ *noun* (1868)
1 : a board or gate at the rear of a vehicle that can be removed or let down (as for loading)
2 [from the custom of seating trombonists at the rear of trucks carrying jazz bands in parades] **:** a jazz trombone style marked by much use of slides to and from long sustained tones
²**tailgate** *verb* **tail·gat·ed; tail·gat·ing** (1949)
intransitive verb
1 : to drive dangerously close behind another vehicle
2 : to hold a tailgate picnic
transitive verb
: to drive dangerously close behind
— **tail·gat·er** *noun*
³**tailgate** *adjective* (1965)
: relating to or being a picnic set up on the tailgate especially of a station wagon
tail·ing \'tā-liŋ\ *noun* (1764)
1 : residue separated in the preparation of various products (as grain or ores) — usually used in plural
2 : the part of a projecting stone or brick inserted in a wall
taille \'tä-yə, 'tī-, 'tā(ə)l\ *noun* [Middle French, from Old French, from *taillier* to cut, tax] (circa 1533)
: a tax formerly levied by a French king or seigneur on his subjects or on lands held of him
tail·light \'tā(ə)l-,līt\ *noun* (1844)
: a usually red warning light mounted at the rear of a vehicle — called also *taillamp*
¹**tai·lor** \'tā-lər\ *noun* [Middle English *taillour*, from Old French *tailleur*, from *taillier* to cut, from Late Latin *taliare*, from Latin *talea* twig, cutting] (14th century)
: a person whose occupation is making or altering outer garments
²**tailor** (1719)
intransitive verb
: to do the work of a tailor
transitive verb
1 a : to make or fashion as the work of a tailor **b :** to make or adapt to suit a special need or purpose
2 : to fit with clothes
3 : to style with trim straight lines and finished handwork
tai·lor·bird \'tā-lər-,bərd\ *noun* (1769)
: any of a genus (*Orthotomus* of the family Sylviidae) of chiefly Asian warblers that stitch leaves together to support and hide their nests
tai·lored \'tā-lərd\ *adjective* (1862)
1 : fashioned or fitted to resemble a tailor's work
2 : CUSTOM-MADE
3 : having the look of one fitted by a custom tailor
tai·lor·ing \'tā-lə-riŋ\ *noun* (1662)
1 a : the business or occupation of a tailor **b :** the work or workmanship of a tailor
2 : the making or adapting of something to suit a particular purpose
¹**tai·lor–made** \,tā-lər-'mād\ *adjective* (1832)
1 : made by a tailor or with a tailor's care and style
2 : made or fitted especially to a particular use or purpose
3 : factory made rather than hand-rolled ⟨*tailor-made* cigarettes⟩
²**tailor–made** *noun* (1892)

: one that is tailor-made; *specifically* **:** a woman's garment styled for a trim fit and with stiff straight lines
tail·piece \'tā(ə)l-,pēs\ *noun* (1601)
1 : a piece added at the end
2 : a device from which the strings of a stringed instrument are stretched to the pegs — see VIOLIN illustration
3 : an ornament placed below the text matter of a page
tail·pipe \-,pīp\ *noun* (1922)
: an outlet by which the exhaust gases are removed from an engine (as of an automobile or jet aircraft)
tail·plane \-,plān\ *noun* (1909)
: the horizontal tail surfaces of an airplane including the stabilizer and the elevator
tail·race \'tā(ə)l-,rās\ *noun* (1776)
: a race for conveying water away from a point of industrial application (as a waterwheel or turbine) — compare HEADRACE
tail·slide \-,slīd\ *noun* (1916)
: an aerobatic maneuver in which an aircraft that has been pulled into a steep climb stalls and then loses altitude by dropping backward
tail·spin \-,spin\ *noun* (circa 1917)
1 : SPIN 2a
2 : a mental or emotional letdown or collapse
3 : a sustained and usually severe decline or downturn ⟨stock prices in a *tailspin*⟩
tail·wa·ter \-,wò-tər, -,wä-\ *noun* (1759)
1 : water below a dam or waterpower development
2 : excess surface water draining especially from a field under cultivation
tail·wind \-,wind\ *noun* (1897)
: a wind having the same general direction as a course of movement (as of an aircraft)
Tai·no \'tī-(,)nō\ *noun, plural* **Taino** or **Tainos** [Spanish] (circa 1895)
1 : a member of an aboriginal Arawakan people of the Greater Antilles and the Bahamas
2 : the extinct language of the Taino people
¹**taint** \'tānt\ *verb* [Middle English *tainten* to color & *taynten* to attaint; Middle English *tainten*, from Anglo-French *teinter*, from Middle French *teint*, past participle of *teindre*, from Latin *tingere*; Middle English *taynten*, from Middle French *ataint*, past participle of *ataindre* — more at TINGE, ATTAIN] (1573)
transitive verb
1 : to contaminate morally **:** CORRUPT ⟨scholarship *tainted* by envy⟩
2 : to affect with putrefaction **:** SPOIL
3 : to touch or affect slightly with something bad ⟨persons *tainted* with prejudice⟩
intransitive verb
1 *obsolete* **:** to become weak
2 : to become affected with putrefaction **:** SPOIL
synonym see CONTAMINATE
²**taint** *noun* (1601)
: a contaminating mark or influence
— **taint·less** \-ləs\ *adjective*
'**tain't** \'tānt\ (1818)
: it ain't
¹**tai·pan** \'tī-,pan, 'tī-'pän\ *noun* [Chinese (Guangdong) *daaih-bāan*, from *daaih* big + *bāan* class] (1834)
: a powerful businessman and especially formerly a foreigner living and operating in Hong Kong or China
²**tai·pan** \'tī-,pan\ *noun* [Wik Munkan (Australian aboriginal language of northern Queensland) *dhayban*] (1933)
: an exceedingly venomous elapid snake (*Oxyuranus scutellatus*) of northern Australia and New Guinea
Ta·jik \tä-'jik, tə-, -'jēk\ *noun* (1815)
1 : a member of a Persian-speaking ethnic group living in Tajikistan, Afghanistan, and adjacent areas of central Asia
2 : the form of Persian spoken by the Tajiks
ta·ka \'tä-kə, -(,)kä\ *noun* [Bengali *ṭākā* rupee, taka, from Sanskrit *ṭaṅka* stamped coin] (1972)

— see MONEY table
ta·ka·he \tä-kä-(,)hä\ *noun* [Maori] (1851)
: a flightless bird (*Notornis mantelli* synonym *Porphyrio mantelli*) of New Zealand that is related to the gallinules
¹**take** \'tāk\ *verb* **took** \'tùk\; **tak·en** \'tā-kən\; **tak·ing** [Middle English, from Old English *tacan*, from Old Norse *taka*; akin to Middle Dutch *taken* to take] (before 12th century)
transitive verb
1 : to get into one's hands or into one's possession, power, or control: as **a :** to seize or capture physically ⟨*took* them as prisoners⟩ **b :** to get possession of (as fish or game) by killing or capturing **c** (1) **:** to move against (as an opponent's piece in chess) and remove from play (2) **:** to win in a card game ⟨able to *take* 12 tricks⟩ **d :** to acquire by eminent domain
2 : GRASP, GRIP ⟨*take* the ax by the handle⟩
3 a : to catch or attack through the effect of a sudden force or influence ⟨*taken* with a fit of laughing⟩ ⟨*taken* ill⟩ **b :** to catch or come upon in a particular situation or action ⟨was *taken* unawares⟩ **c :** to gain the approval or liking of **:** CAPTIVATE, DELIGHT ⟨was quite *taken* with her at their first meeting⟩
4 a : to receive into one's body (as by swallowing, drinking, or inhaling) ⟨*take* a pill⟩ **b :** to expose oneself to (as sun or air) for pleasure or physical benefit **c :** to partake of **:** EAT ⟨*takes* dinner about seven⟩
5 a : to bring or receive into a relation or connection ⟨*takes* just four students a year⟩ ⟨it's time he *took* a wife⟩ **b :** to copulate with
6 : to transfer into one's own keeping: **a :** APPROPRIATE **b :** to obtain or secure for use (as by lease, subscription, or purchase) ⟨*take* a cottage for the summer⟩ ⟨I'll *take* the red one⟩ ⟨*took* an ad in the paper⟩
7 a : ASSUME ⟨gods often *took* the likeness of a human being⟩ ⟨when the college *took* its present form⟩ **b** (1) **:** to enter into or undertake the duties of ⟨*take* a job⟩ ⟨*take* office⟩ ⟨*took* command of the fleet⟩ (2) **:** to move onto or into **:** move into position on ⟨the home team *took* the field⟩ **c** (1) **:** to bind oneself by ⟨*take* the oath of office⟩ (2) **:** to make (a decision) especially with finality or authority **d :** to impose upon oneself ⟨*take* the trouble to do good work⟩ **e** (1) **:** to adopt as one's own ⟨*take* a stand on the issue⟩ ⟨*take* an interest⟩ (2) **:** to align or ally oneself with ⟨mother *took* his side⟩ **f :** to assume as if rightfully one's own or as if granted ⟨*take* the credit⟩ **g :** to have or assume as a proper part of or accompaniment to itself ⟨transitive verbs *take* an object⟩
8 a : to secure by winning in competition ⟨*took* first place⟩ **b :** DEFEAT
9 : to pick out **:** CHOOSE, SELECT
10 : to adopt, choose, or avail oneself of for use: as **a :** to have recourse to as an instrument for doing something ⟨*take* a scythe to the weeds⟩ **b :** to use as a means of transportation or progression ⟨*take* the bus⟩ **c :** to have recourse to for safety or refuge ⟨*take* shelter⟩ **d :** to go along, into, or through ⟨*took* a different route⟩ **e** (1) **:** to proceed to occupy ⟨*take* a seat in the rear⟩ (2) **:** to use up (as space or time) ⟨*takes* a long time to dry⟩ (3) **:** NEED, REQUIRE ⟨*takes* a size nine shoe⟩ ⟨it *takes* two to start a fight⟩
11 a : to obtain by deriving from a source **:** DRAW ⟨*takes* its title from the name of the hero⟩ **b** (1) **:** to obtain as the result of a special procedure **:** ASCERTAIN ⟨*take* the temperature⟩ ⟨*take* a census⟩ (2) **:** to get in or as if in writing ⟨*take* notes⟩ ⟨*take* an inventory⟩ (3) **:** to get by drawing or painting or by photography ⟨*take* a

snapshot⟩ (4) **:** to get by transference from one surface to another ⟨*take* a proof⟩ ⟨*take* finger-prints⟩ **12 :** to receive or accept whether willingly or reluctantly ⟨*take* a bribe⟩ ⟨will you *take* this call⟩ ⟨*take* a bet⟩: as **a** (1) **:** to submit to **:** ENDURE ⟨*take* a cut in pay⟩ (2) **:** WITHSTAND ⟨it will *take* a lot of punishment⟩ (3) **:** SUFFER ⟨*took* a direct hit⟩ **b** (1) **:** to accept as true **:** BELIEVE ⟨I'll *take* your word for it⟩ (2) **:** FOLLOW ⟨*take* my advice⟩ (3) **:** to accept with the mind in a specified way ⟨*took* the news hard⟩ **c :** to indulge in and enjoy ⟨was *taking* his ease on the porch⟩ **d :** to receive or accept as a return (as in payment, compensation, or reparation) **e :** to accept in a usually professional relationship — often used with *on* ⟨agreed to *take* him on as a client⟩ **f :** to refrain from hitting at (a pitched ball) **13 a** (1) **:** to let in **:** ADMIT ⟨the boat was *taking* water fast⟩ (2) **:** ACCOMMODATE ⟨the suitcase wouldn't *take* another thing⟩ **b :** to be affected injuriously by (as a disease) **:** CONTRACT ⟨*take* cold⟩; *also* **:** to be seized by ⟨*take* a fit⟩ ⟨*take* fright⟩ **c :** to absorb or become impregnated with (as dye); *also* **:** to be effectively treated by ⟨a surface that *takes* a fine polish⟩ **14 a :** APPREHEND, UNDERSTAND ⟨how should I *take* your remark⟩ **b :** CONSIDER, SUPPOSE ⟨I *take* it you're not going⟩ **c :** RECKON, ACCEPT ⟨*taking* a stride at 30 inches⟩ **d :** FEEL, EXPERIENCE ⟨*take* pleasure⟩ ⟨*take* an instant dislike to someone⟩ ⟨*take* offense⟩ **15 :** to lead, carry, or cause to go along to another place ⟨this bus will *take* you into town⟩ ⟨*took* an umbrella with her⟩ **16 a :** REMOVE ⟨*take* eggs from a nest⟩ **b** (1) **:** to put an end to (life) (2) **:** to remove by death ⟨was *taken* in his prime⟩ **c :** SUBTRACT ⟨*take* two from four⟩ **d :** EXACT ⟨the weather *took* its toll⟩ **17 a :** to undertake and make, do, or perform ⟨*take* a walk⟩ ⟨*take* aim⟩ ⟨*take* legal action⟩ ⟨*take* a test⟩ ⟨*take* a look⟩ **b :** to participate in ⟨*take* a meeting⟩ **18 a :** to deal with ⟨*take* first things first⟩ **b :** to consider or view in a particular relation ⟨*taken* together, the details were significant⟩; *especially* **:** to consider as an example ⟨*take* style, for instance⟩ **c** (1) **:** to apply oneself to the study of ⟨*take* music lessons⟩ ⟨*take* French⟩ (2) **:** to study for especially successfully ⟨*taking* a degree in engineering⟩ ⟨*took* holy orders⟩ **19 :** to obtain money from especially fraudulently ⟨*took* me for all I had⟩ **20 :** to pass or attempt to pass through, along, or over ⟨*took* the curve too fast⟩

intransitive verb
1 : to obtain possession: as **a :** CAPTURE **b :** to receive property under law as one's own **2 :** to lay hold **:** CATCH, HOLD **3 :** to establish a take especially by uniting or growing ⟨90 percent of the grafts *take*⟩ **4 a :** to betake oneself **:** set out **:** GO ⟨*take* after a purse snatcher⟩ **b** *chiefly dialect* — used as an intensifier or redundantly with a following verb ⟨*took* and swung at the ball⟩ **5 a :** to take effect **:** ACT, OPERATE ⟨hoped the lesson he taught would *take*⟩ **b :** to show the natural or intended effect ⟨dry fuel *takes* readily⟩ **6 :** CHARM, CAPTIVATE ⟨a *taking* smile⟩ **7 :** DETRACT **8 :** to be seized or attacked in a specified way **:** BECOME ⟨*took* sick⟩
usage see BRING ☆
— **tak·er** *noun*
— **take a back seat :** to have or assume a secondary position or status
— **take a bath :** to suffer a heavy financial loss
— **take account of :** to take into account
— **take advantage of 1 :** to use to advantage **:** profit by **2 :** to impose on **:** EXPLOIT
— **take after :** to resemble in features, build, character, or disposition

— **take apart 1 :** to disconnect the pieces of **:** DISASSEMBLE **2 :** to treat roughly or harshly **:** tear into
— **take a powder :** to leave hurriedly
— **take care :** to be careful or watchful **:** exercise caution or prudence
— **take care of :** to attend to or provide for the needs, operation, or treatment of
— **take charge :** to assume care, custody, command, or control
— **take effect 1 :** to become operative **2 :** to be effective
— **take exception :** OBJECT ⟨*took* exception to the remark⟩
— **take five** *or* **take ten :** to take a break especially from work
— **take for :** to suppose to be; *especially* **:** to suppose mistakenly to be
— **take for granted 1 :** to assume as true, real, or expected **2 :** to value too lightly
— **take heart :** to gain courage or confidence
— **take hold 1 :** GRASP, GRIP, SEIZE **2 :** to become attached or established **:** take effect
— **take into account :** to make allowance for
— **take in vain :** to use (a name) profanely or without proper respect
— **take issue :** DISAGREE
— **take it on the chin :** to suffer from the results of a situation
— **take kindly to :** to show an inclination to accept or approve
— **take notice of :** to observe or treat with special attention
— **take one's time :** to be leisurely about doing something
— **take part :** JOIN, PARTICIPATE, SHARE
— **take place :** HAPPEN, OCCUR
— **take root 1 :** to become rooted **2 :** to become fixed or established
— **take shape :** to assume a definite or distinctive form
— **take stock :** to make an assessment
— **take the cake :** to carry off the prize **:** rank first
— **take the count 1** *of a boxer* **:** to be counted out **2 :** to go down in defeat
— **take the floor :** to rise (as in a meeting or a legislative assembly) to make a formal address
— **take to 1 :** to go to or into ⟨*take to* the woods⟩ **2 :** to apply or devote oneself to (as a practice, habit, or occupation) ⟨*take to* begging⟩ **3 :** to adapt oneself to **:** respond to ⟨*takes to* water like a duck⟩ **4 :** to conceive a liking for
— **take to task :** to call to account for a shortcoming **:** CRITICIZE
— **take turns :** ALTERNATE

²**take** *noun* (1654)
1 : something that is taken: **a :** the amount of money received **:** PROCEEDS, RECEIPTS, INCOME **b :** SHARE, CUT ⟨wanted a bigger *take*⟩ **c :** the number or quantity (as of animals, fish, or pelts) taken at one time **:** CATCH, HAUL **d :** a section or installment done as a unit or at one time **e** (1) **:** a scene filmed or televised at one time without stopping the camera (2) **:** a sound recording made during a single recording period; *especially* **:** a trial recording **2 :** an act or the action of taking: as **a :** the action of killing, capturing, or catching (as game or fish) **b** (1) **:** the uninterrupted photographing or televising of a scene (2) **:** the making of a sound recording **3 a :** a local or systemic reaction indicative of successful vaccination (as against smallpox) **b :** a successful union (as of a graft) **4 :** a visible response or reaction (as to something unexpected) ⟨a delayed *take*⟩ **5 :** a distinct or personal point of view, outlook, or assessment ⟨was asked for her *take* on recent developments⟩; *also* **:** a distinct treatment or variation ⟨a new *take* on an old style⟩
— **on the take :** illegally paid for favors

take–away \'tāk-ə-,wā\ *adjective* (1964) *British* **:** TAKE-OUT
— **take–away** *noun*
take back *transitive verb* (1775) **:** to make a retraction of **:** WITHDRAW
take–charge \'tāk-'chärj\ *adjective* (1954) **:** having the qualities of a forceful leader ⟨a *take-charge* executive⟩
¹**take·down** \'tāk-,daůn\ *noun* (1893) **1 :** the action or an act of taking down **2 :** something (as a rifle) having takedown construction
²**take·down** \'tāk-'daůn\ *adjective* (1907) **:** constructed so as to be readily taken apart ⟨a *takedown* rifle⟩
take down (15th century) *transitive verb* **1 :** to lower without removing ⟨*took down* his pants⟩ **2 a :** to pull to pieces ⟨*take down* a building⟩ **b :** DISASSEMBLE ⟨*take* a rifle *down*⟩ **3 :** to lower the spirit or vanity of **4 a :** to write down **b :** to record by mechanical means
intransitive verb **:** to become seized or attacked especially by illness
take–home pay \'tāk-,hōm-\ *noun* (1943) **:** income remaining from salary or wages after deductions (as for income-tax withholding)
take–in \'tā-,kin\ *noun* (1778) **:** an act of taking in especially by deceiving
take in *transitive verb* (circa 1515) **1 :** to draw into a smaller compass ⟨*take in* the slack of a line⟩: **a :** FURL **b :** to make (a garment) smaller by enlarging seams or tucks **2 a :** to receive as a guest or boarder **b :** to give shelter to **c :** to take to a police station as a prisoner **3 :** to receive as payment or proceeds **4 :** to receive (work) into one's house to be done for pay ⟨*take in* washing⟩ **5 :** to encompass within its limits **6 a :** to include in an itinerary **b :** ATTEND ⟨*take in* a movie⟩ **7 :** to receive into the mind **:** PERCEIVE **8 :** DECEIVE, DUPE
taken *past participle of* TAKE
take·off \'tā-,kȯf\ *noun* (1846) **1 :** an imitation especially in the way of caricature **2 a :** a spot at which one takes off **b :** a starting point **:** point of departure **3 a :** a rise or leap from a surface in making a jump or flight or an ascent in an aircraft or in the launching of a rocket **b :** an action of starting out **c :** a rapid rise in activity, growth, or popularity ⟨an economic *takeoff*⟩ **4 :** an action of removing something **5 :** a mechanism for transmission of the power of an engine or vehicle to operate some other mechanism

take off (14th century)
transitive verb
1 : REMOVE 〈*take* your shoes *off*〉
2 a : RELEASE 〈*take* the brake *off*〉 **b** : DISCONTINUE, WITHDRAW 〈*took off* the morning train〉 **c** : to take or allow as a discount : DEDUCT 〈*took* 10 percent *off*〉 **d** : to spend (a period of time) away from a usual occupation or activity 〈*took* two weeks *off*〉
3 *slang* : ROB
intransitive verb
1 : to take away : DETRACT
2 a : to start off or away : SET OUT, DEPART **b** (1) : to branch off (as from a main stream or stem) (2) : to take a point of origin **c** : to begin a leap or spring **d** : to leave the surface : begin flight **e** : to embark on rapid activity, development, or growth **f** : to spring into wide use or popularity
take on (15th century)
transitive verb
1 a : to begin to perform or deal with : UNDERTAKE 〈*took on* new responsibilities〉 **b** : to contend with as an opponent 〈*took on* the neighborhood bully〉
2 : ENGAGE, HIRE
3 a : to assume or acquire as or as if one's own 〈the city's plaza *takes on* a carnival air —W. T. LeViness〉 **b** : to have as a mathematical domain or range 〈what values does the function *take on*〉
intransitive verb
: to show one's feelings especially of grief or anger in a demonstrative way 〈they cried and *took on* something terrible —Bob Hope〉
take-out \'tā-ˌkau̇t\ *noun* (circa 1917)
1 : the action or an act of taking out
2 a : something taken out or prepared to be taken out **b** (1) : an article (as in a newspaper) printed on consecutive pages so as to be conveniently removed (2) : an intensive study or report
3 : CARRYOUT 1
take-out \'tā-ˌkau̇t\ *adjective* (1965)
: of, relating to, selling, or being food not to be consumed on the premises 〈*take-out* counter〉 〈a *take-out* supper〉
take out (13th century)
transitive verb
1 a (1) : DEDUCT, DEDUCT, SEPARATE (2) : EXCLUDE, OMIT (3) : WITHDRAW, WITHHOLD **b** : to find release for : VENT 〈*take out* their resentments on one another —J. W. Aldridge〉 **c** (1) : ELIMINATE (2) : KILL, DESTROY (3) : KNOCK OUT
2 : to take as an equivalent in another form 〈*took* the debt *out* in trade〉
3 a : to obtain from the proper authority 〈*take out* a charter〉 **b** : to arrange for (insurance)
4 : to overcall (a bridge partner) in a different suit
intransitive verb
: to start on a course : SET OUT
— **take it out on** : to expend anger, vexation, or frustration in harassment of
take-out double \'tā-ˌkau̇t-\ *noun* (circa 1944)
: a double made in bridge to convey information to and request a bid from one's partner
take-over \'tā-ˌkō-vər\ *noun* (circa 1917)
: the action or an act of taking over
take over (1884)
transitive verb
: to assume control or possession of or responsibility for 〈military leaders *took over* the government〉
intransitive verb
1 : to assume control or possession
2 : to become dominant
take–up \'tā-ˌkəp\ *noun* (1838)
: the action of taking up
take up (14th century)
transitive verb
1 : PICK UP, LIFT
2 a : to begin to occupy (land) **b** : to gather from a number of sources 〈*took up* a collection〉

3 a : to accept or adopt for the purpose of assisting 〈*took up* the life of a farmer〉 〈*took up* Irish citizenship〉 **c** : to absorb or incorporate into itself 〈plants *taking up* nutrients〉
4 a : to enter upon (as a business, hobby, or subject of study) 〈*take up* skiing〉 〈*took up* the trumpet〉 〈had *taken up* Marxism〉 **b** : to proceed to consider or deal with 〈*take up* one problem at a time〉
5 : to establish oneself in 〈*took up* residence in town〉
6 : to occupy entirely or exclusively : fill up 〈the meeting was *taken up* with old business〉
7 : to make tighter or shorter 〈*take up* the slack〉
8 : to respond favorably to (as a person offering a bet, challenge, or proposal) 〈*took* me *up* on it〉
9 : to begin again or take over from another 〈we must *take* the good work *up* again〉
intransitive verb
1 : to make a beginning where another has left off
2 : to become shortened : draw together : SHRINK
— **take up the cudgels** : to engage vigorously in a defense or dispute
— **take up with 1** : to become interested or absorbed in **2** : to begin to associate or consort with
ta·kin \'tä-ˌkēn\ *noun* [Mishmi (Tibeto-Burman language of northeast India)] (1850)
: a large heavily built ruminant (*Budorcas taxicolor*) of Tibet and adjacent areas of Asia that is related to the goats but in some respects resembles the antelopes

takin

tak·ings \'tā-kiŋz\ *noun plural* (1632)
chiefly British : receipts especially of money
¹ta·la \'tä-lə\ *noun* [Sanskrit *tāla*, literally, hand-clapping] (1891)
: one of the ancient traditional rhythmic patterns of Indian music — compare RAGA
²ta·la \'tä-lə, -(ˌ)lä\ *noun, plural* **tala** [Samoan, from English *dollar*] (1967)
— see MONEY table
Tal·bot \'tȯl-bət, 'tal-\ *noun* [probably from *Talbot*, name of a Norman family in England] (1562)
: a large heavy mostly white hound with pendulous ears and drooping flews held to be ancestral to the bloodhound
talc \'talk\ *noun* [Middle French *talc* mica, from Medieval Latin *talk*, from Arabic *ṭalq*] (1610)
1 : a very soft mineral that is a basic silicate of magnesium, has a soapy feel, and is used especially in making talcum powder
2 : TALCUM POWDER
— **talc·ose** \'tal-ˌkōs\ *adjective*
tal·cum powder \'tal-kəm-\ *noun* [Medieval Latin *talcum* mica, alteration of earlier *talk*] (circa 1890)
1 : powdered talc
2 : a toilet powder composed of perfumed talc or talc and a mild antiseptic
tale \'tā(ə)l\ *noun* [Middle English, from Old English *talu*; akin to Old Norse *tala* talk] (before 12th century)
1 *obsolete* : DISCOURSE, TALK
2 a : a series of events or facts told or presented : ACCOUNT **b** (1) : a report of a private or confidential matter 〈dead men tell no *tales*〉 (2) : a libelous report or piece of gossip
3 a : a usually imaginative narrative of an event : STORY **b** : an intentionally untrue report : FALSEHOOD 〈always preferred the *tale* to the truth —Sir Winston Churchill〉
4 a : COUNT, TALLY **b** : TOTAL

tale-bear·er \-ˌbar-ər, -ˌber-\ *noun* (15th century)
: one that spreads gossip or rumors; *also* : TATTLETALE
— **tale-bear·ing** \-iŋ\ *adjective or noun*
tal·ent \'ta-lənt\ *noun* [Middle English, from Old English *talente*, from Latin *talenta*, plural of *talentum* unit of weight or money, from Greek *talanton* pan of a scale, weight; akin to Greek *tlēnai* to bear; in senses 2–5, from the parable of the talents in Matthew 25:14–30 — more at TOLERATE] (before 12th century)
1 a : any of several ancient units of weight **b** : a unit of value equal to the value of a talent of gold or silver
2 *archaic* : a characteristic feature, aptitude, or disposition of a person or animal
3 : the natural endowments of a person
4 a : a special often creative or artistic aptitude **b** : general intelligence or mental power : ABILITY
5 : a person of talent or a group of persons of talent in a field or activity ◇
synonym see GIFT
— **tal·ent·ed** \-lən-təd\ *adjective*
— **tal·ent·less** \-lənt-ləs\ *adjective*
talent scout *noun* (1936)
: a person engaged in discovering and recruiting people of talent for a specialized field or activity
talent show *noun* (1953)
: a show consisting of a series of individual performances (as singing) by amateurs who may be selected for special recognition as performing talent
ta·ler \'tä-lər\ *noun* [German — more at DOLLAR] (circa 1905)
: any of numerous silver coins issued by various German states from the 15th to the 19th centuries
tales·man \'tā(ə)lz-mən, 'tā-lēz-\ *noun* [Middle English *tales* talesmen, from Medieval Latin *tales de circumstantibus* such (persons) of the bystanders; from the wording of the writ summoning them] (1679)
1 : a person added to a jury usually from among bystanders to make up a deficiency in the available number of jurors
2 : a member of a large pool of persons called for jury duty from which jurors are selected

◇ **WORD HISTORY**
talent The ancient Greek word *talanton*, originally denoting the pan of a scale, was also applied to a unit of weight and then a monetary unit. Borrowed into English through Latin as *talent*, the word has developed several figurative meanings based on its use in the New Testament parable of the talents (Matthew 25:14–30). In the parable a master gives money to his servants: five talents to one, two talents to another, and finally a single talent to a third. The first two doubled their capital, and the master was pleased. The third servant, however, buried his talent in the earth for fear of losing it. This made the master very angry since he expected his servant at least to have invested his talent with bankers so that it would gain interest. The master then took back the one talent and gave it to the servant who had ten. Traditionally the talent has been taken as a metaphor for a God-given endowment that if not used would be lost. The English word *talent* has had this metaphorical sense since the 15th century, and several centuries later it gave rise to the extended meaning "mental ability or aptitude."

tale–tell·er \'tā(ə)l-ˌte-lər\ *noun* (14th century)
1 : one who tells tales or stories
2 : TALEBEARER
— **tale–tell·ing** \-ˌte-liŋ\ *adjective or noun*
tali *plural of* TALUS
tali·pes \'ta-lə-ˌpēz\ *noun* [New Latin, from Latin *talus* ankle + *pes* foot — more at FOOT] (circa 1841)
: CLUBFOOT
tal·is·man \'ta-ləs-mən, -ləz-\ *noun, plural* **-mans** [French *talisman* or Spanish *talismán* or Italian *talismano*; all from Arabic *tilsam*, from Middle Greek *telesma*, from Greek, consecration, from *telein* to initiate into the mysteries, complete, from *telos* end — more at TELOS] (1638)
1 : an object held to act as a charm to avert evil and bring good fortune
2 : something producing apparently magical or miraculous effects
— **tal·is·man·ic** \ˌta-ləs-'ma-nik, -ləz-\ *adjective*
— **tal·is·man·i·cal·ly** \-ni-k(ə-)lē\ *adverb*
¹talk \'tȯk\ *verb* [Middle English; akin to Old English *talu* tale] (13th century)
transitive verb
1 : to deliver or express in speech : UTTER
2 : to make the subject of conversation or discourse : DISCUSS ⟨*talk* business⟩
3 : to influence, affect, or cause by talking ⟨*talked* them into going⟩
4 : to use (a language) for conversing or communicating : SPEAK
intransitive verb
1 a : to express or exchange ideas by means of spoken words **b** : to convey information or communicate in any way (as with signs or sounds) ⟨can make a trumpet *talk*⟩
2 : to use speech : SPEAK
3 a : to speak idly : PRATE **b** : GOSSIP **c** : to reveal secret or confidential information
4 : to give a talk : LECTURE
— **talk·er** *noun*
— **talk back** : to answer impertinently
— **talk sense** : to voice rational, logical, or sensible thoughts
— **talk through one's hat** : to voice irrational, illogical, or erroneous ideas
— **talk turkey** : to speak frankly or bluntly
²talk *noun* (15th century)
1 : the act or an instance of talking : SPEECH
2 : a way of speaking : LANGUAGE
3 : pointless or fruitless discussion : VERBIAGE
4 : a formal discussion, negotiation, or exchange of views — often used in plural
5 a : MENTION, REPORT **b** : RUMOR, GOSSIP
6 : the topic of interested comment, conversation, or gossip ⟨it's the *talk* of the town⟩
7 a : ADDRESS, LECTURE **b** : written analysis or discussion presented in an informal or conversational manner
8 : communicative sounds or signs resembling or functioning as talk ⟨bird *talk*⟩
talk·a·thon \'tȯ-kə-ˌthän\ *noun* (1934)
: a long session of discussion or speechmaking
talk·a·tive \'tȯ-kə-tiv\ *adjective* (15th century)
: given to talking; *also* : full of talk ☆
— **talk·a·tive·ly** *adverb*
— **talk·a·tive·ness** *noun*
talk down (1901)
intransitive verb
: to speak in a condescending or oversimplified fashion
transitive verb
: to disparage or belittle by talking
talk·ie \'tȯ-kē\ *noun* (1913)
: a motion picture with a synchronized sound track
talking book *noun* (1932)
: a phonograph or tape recording of a reading of a book or magazine designed chiefly for the use of the blind
talking head *noun* (1968)

: the televised head and shoulders shot of a person talking; *also* : a television personality who appears in such shots
talking machine *noun* (1890)
: an early phonograph
talking point *noun* (circa 1914)
: something that lends support to an argument; *also* : a subject of discussion
talk·ing–to \'tȯ-kiŋ-ˌtü\ *noun* (1884)
: REPRIMAND, LECTURE
talk out *transitive verb* (1954)
: to clarify or settle by oral discussion
talk over *transitive verb* (1734)
: to review or consider in conversation : DISCUSS
talk radio *noun* (1972)
: radio programming consisting of call-in shows
talk show *noun* (1965)
: a radio or television program in which usually well-known persons engage in discussions or are interviewed
talk up (1722)
transitive verb
: to discuss favorably : ADVOCATE, PROMOTE
intransitive verb
: to speak up plainly or directly
talky \'tȯ-kē\ *adjective* **talk·i·er; -est** (1815)
1 : TALKATIVE
2 : containing too much talk
— **talk·i·ness** \-nəs\ *noun*
tall \'tȯl\ *adjective* [Middle English, probably from Old English *getæl* quick, ready; akin to Old High German *gizal* quick] (15th century)
1 *obsolete* : BRAVE, COURAGEOUS
2 a : high in stature **b** : of a specified height ⟨five feet *tall*⟩
3 a : of considerable height ⟨*tall* trees⟩ **b** : long from bottom to top ⟨a *tall* book⟩ **c** : of a higher growing variety or species of plant
4 a : large or formidable in amount, extent, or degree ⟨a *tall* order to fill⟩ **b** : POMPOUS, HIGH-FLOWN ⟨*tall* talk about the vast mysteries of life —W. A. White⟩ **c** : highly exaggerated : INCREDIBLE, IMPROBABLE ⟨a *tall* story⟩
synonym see HIGH
— **tall** *adverb*
— **tall·ish** \'tȯ-lish\ *adjective*
— **tall·ness** \'tȯl-nəs\ *noun*
tal·lage \'ta-lij\ *noun* [Middle English *taillage, tallage*, from Old French *taillage*, from *taillier* to cut, limit, tax — more at TAILOR] (14th century)
: an impost or due levied by a lord upon his tenants
tall·boy \'tȯl-ˌbȯi\ *noun* (1769)
1 a : HIGHBOY **b** : a double chest of drawers usually with the upper section slightly smaller than the lower
2 *British* : CLOTHESPRESS
tall fescue *noun* (circa 1762)
: a European fescue (*Festuca elatior*) with erect smooth stems 3 to 4 feet (about 1 meter) high that has been introduced into North America — called also *tall fescue grass*; compare FESCUE FOOT
tall·grass prairie \'tȯl-ˌgras-\ *noun* (1920)
: PRAIRIE 2a
tal·lith \'tä-ləs, 'ta-, -lət, -ləth\ *or* **tal·lis** \-ləs\ *noun* [Hebrew *ṭallīth* cover, cloak] (1613)
: a shawl with fringed corners worn over the head or shoulders by Jewish men especially during morning prayers
tall oil \'täl-, 'tȯl-\ *noun* [part translation of German *Tallöl*, part translation of Swedish *tallolja*, from *tall* pine + *olja* oil] (circa 1926)
: a resinous by-product from the manufacture of chemical wood pulp used especially in making soaps, coatings, and oils

¹tal·low \'ta-(ˌ)lō\ *noun* [Middle English *talgh, talow*; akin to Middle Dutch *talch* tallow] (14th century)
: the white nearly tasteless solid rendered fat of cattle and sheep used chiefly in soap, candles, and lubricants
— **tal·lowy** \'ta-lə-wē\ *adjective*
²tallow *transitive verb* (15th century)
: to grease or smear with tallow
tall ship *noun* (circa 1548)
: a sailing vessel with at least two masts; *especially* : SQUARE-RIGGER
¹tal·ly \'ta-lē\ *noun, plural* **tallies** [Middle English *talye*, from Medieval Latin *talea, tallia*, from Latin *talea* twig, cutting] (15th century)
1 : a device (as a notched rod or mechanical counter) for visibly recording or accounting especially business transactions
2 a : a recorded reckoning or account (as of items or charges) ⟨keep a daily *tally* of accidents⟩ **b** : a score or point made (as in a game)
3 a : a part that corresponds to an opposite or companion member : COMPLEMENT **b** : a state of correspondence or agreement
²tally *verb* **tal·lied; tal·ly·ing** (15th century)
transitive verb
1 a : to record on or as if on a tally : TABULATE **b** : to list or check off (as a cargo) by items **c** : to register (as a score) in a contest
2 : to make a count of : RECKON
3 : to cause to correspond
intransitive verb
1 a : to make a tally by or as if by tabulating **b** : to register a point in a contest : SCORE
2 : CORRESPOND, MATCH
tal·ly-ho \ˌta-lē-'hō\ *noun, plural* **-hos** [probably from French *taïaut*, a cry used to excite hounds in deer hunting] (1772)
1 : a call of a huntsman at sight of the fox
2 [*Tally-ho*, name of a coach formerly plying between London and Birmingham] : a four-in-hand coach
tal·ly·man \'ta-lē-mən, -ˌman\ *noun* (1654)
1 *British* : one who sells goods on the installment plan
2 : one who tallies, checks, or keeps an account or record (as of receipt of goods)
Tal·mud \'täl-ˌmud, 'tal-məd\ *noun* [Late Hebrew *talmūdh*, literally, instruction] (1532)
: the authoritative body of Jewish tradition comprising the Mishnah and Gemara
— **Tal·mu·dic** \tal-'mü-dik, -'myü-, -'mə-; täl-'mu-\ *adjective*
— **tal·mud·ism** \'täl-ˌmu-ˌdi-zəm, 'tal-, -mə-\ *noun, often capitalized*
Tal·mud·ist \'täl-ˌmu-dist, 'tal-, -mə-\ *noun* (1569)
: a specialist in Talmudic studies
tal·on \'ta-lən\ *noun* [Middle English, from Middle French, heel, spur, from (assumed) Vulgar Latin *talon-, talo*, from Latin *talus* ankle, anklebone] (15th century)
1 a : the claw of an animal and especially of a bird of prey **b** : a finger or hand of a human being
2 : a part or object shaped like or suggestive of a heel or claw: as **a** : an ogee molding **b** : the shoulder of the bolt of a lock on which the key acts to shoot the bolt

tallith

3 a : cards laid aside in a pile in solitaire **b** : STOCK 10c
— **tal·oned** \-lənd\ *adjective*

¹ta·lus \'tā-ləs, 'tä-\ *noun* [French, from Latin *talutium* slope indicating presence of gold under the soil] (1645)
1 : a slope formed especially by an accumulation of rock debris
2 : rock debris at the base of a cliff

²ta·lus \'tā-ləs\ *noun, plural* **ta·li** \'tā-,lī\ [New Latin, from Latin] (circa 1693)
1 : the human tarsal bone that bears the weight of the body and that together with the tibia and fibula forms the ankle joint
2 : the entire ankle

tam \'tam\ *noun* (1895)
: TAM-O'-SHANTER

ta·ma·le \tə-'mä-lē\ *noun* [Mexican Spanish *tamales*, plural of *tamal* tamale, from Nahuatl *tamalli* steamed cornmeal dough] (1854)
: ground meat seasoned usually with chili, rolled in cornmeal dough, wrapped in corn husks, and steamed

ta·man·dua \tə-'man-də-wə, -,man-də-'wä\ *noun* [Portuguese *tamanduá*, from Tupi] (1834)
: either of two arboreal anteaters (*Tamandua mexicana* and *T. tetradactyla*) of Central and South America having a nearly hairless tail

tam·a·rack \'ta-mə-,rak, 'tam-rak\ *noun* [origin unknown] (1805)
1 : any of several American larches; *especially* **:** a larch (*Larix laricina*) of northern North America that inhabits usually moist or wet areas
2 : the wood of a tamarack

tam·a·rau \,ta-mə-'raù\ *noun* [Tagalog *tamaráw*] (1898)
: a small dark sturdily built buffalo (*Bubalus mindorensis*) native to Mindoro

ta·ma·ri \tə-'mär-ē\ *noun* [Japanese] (1965)
: an aged soy sauce prepared with little or no added wheat

tam·a·ril·lo \,ta-mə-'ri-(,)lō\ *noun* [alteration of *tomatillo*] (1966)
: the reddish edible fruit of an arborescent shrub (*Cyphomandra betacea*) of the nightshade family that is native to South America but is grown commercially elsewhere; *also* **:** the shrub itself

tam·a·rin \'ta-mə-rən, -,ran\ *noun* [French, from Carib] (1780)
: any of numerous small chiefly South American monkeys (genera *Saguinus* and *Leontopithecus*) that are related to the marmosets and have silky fur, a long tail, and lower canine teeth that are longer than the incisors

tam·a·rind \'ta-mə-rənd, -,rind\ *noun* [Spanish & Portuguese *tamarindo*, from Arabic *tamr hindī*, literally, Indian date] (1533)
: a tropical Old World leguminous tree (*Tamarindus indica*) with hard yellowish wood, pinnate leaves, and red-striped yellow flowers; *also* **:** its fruit which has an acid pulp often used for preserves or in a cooling laxative drink

tam·a·risk \'ta-mə-,risk\ *noun* [Middle English *tamarisc*, from Late Latin *tamariscus*, from Latin *tamaric-, tamarix*] (14th century)
: any of a genus (*Tamarix* of the family Tamaricaceae, the tamarisk family) of chiefly Old World desert shrubs and trees having tiny narrow leaves and masses of minute flowers with five stamens and a one-celled ovary

tam·ba·la \täm-'bä-lə\ *noun, plural* **-la** *or* **-las** [Nyanja (Bantu language of Malawi), literally, cockerel] (1970)
— see *kwacha* at MONEY table

¹tam·bour \'tam-,bùr, tam-'\ *noun* [Middle French, drum, from Arabic *ṭanbūr*, modification of Persian *ṭabīr*] (15th century)
1 : ¹DRUM 1
2 a : an embroidery frame; *especially* **:** a set of two interlocking hoops between which cloth is stretched before stitching **b :** embroidery made on a tambour frame

3 : a shallow metallic cup or drum with a thin elastic membrane supporting a writing lever used to transmit and register slight motions (as arterial pulsations)
4 : a rolling top or front (as of a rolltop desk) of narrow strips of wood glued on canvas

²tambour (1774)
transitive verb
: to embroider (cloth) with tambour
intransitive verb
: to work at a tambour frame
— **tam·bour·er** *noun*

tam·bou·ra *or* **tam·bu·ra** \tam-'bùr-ə\ *noun* [Persian *ṭambūra*] (1585)
: an Asian musical instrument resembling a lute in construction but without frets and used to produce a drone accompaniment to singing

tam·bou·rine \,tam-bə-'rēn\ *noun* [Middle French *tambourin*, diminutive of *tambour*] (1579)
: a small drum; *especially* **:** a shallow one-headed drum with loose metallic disks at the sides played especially by shaking or striking with the hand

tambourine

¹tame \'tām\ *adjective* **tam·er; tam·est** [Middle English, from Old English *tam;* akin to Old High German *zam* tame, Latin *domare* to tame, Greek *damnanai*] (before 12th century)
1 : reduced from a state of native wildness especially so as to be tractable and useful to humans **:** DOMESTICATED ⟨*tame* animals⟩
2 : made docile and submissive **:** SUBDUED
3 : lacking spirit, zest, interest, or the capacity to excite **:** INSIPID ⟨a *tame* campaign⟩
— **tame·ly** *adverb*
— **tame·ness** *noun*

²tame *verb* **tamed; tam·ing** (14th century)
transitive verb
1 a : to reduce from a wild to a domestic state **b :** to subject to cultivation **c :** to bring under control **:** HARNESS
2 : to deprive of spirit **:** HUMBLE, SUBDUE ⟨the once revolutionary . . . party, long since *tamed* —*Times Literary Supplement*⟩
3 : to tone down **:** SOFTEN ⟨*tamed* the language in the play⟩
intransitive verb
: to become tame
— **tam·able** *or* **tame·able** \'tā-mə-bəl\ *adjective*
— **tam·er** *noun*

tame·less \'tām-ləs\ *adjective* (circa 1598)
: not tamed or not capable of being tamed

Tam·il \'ta-məl, 'tä-\ *noun* (1734)
1 : a Dravidian language of Tamil Nadu state, India, and of northern and eastern Sri Lanka
2 : a Tamil-speaking person or a descendant of Tamil-speaking ancestors

Tam·ma·ny \'ta-mə-nē\ *adjective* [*Tammany Hall*, headquarters of the Tammany Society, political organization in New York City] (1872)
: of, relating to, or constituting a group or organization exercising or seeking municipal political control by methods often associated with corruption and bossism
— **Tam·ma·ny·ism** \-,i-zəm\ *noun*

Tam·muz \'tä-,mùz\ *noun* [Hebrew *Tammūz*] (1614)
: the 10th month of the civil year or the 4th month of the ecclesiastical year in the Jewish calendar — see MONTH table

Tam o' Shan·ter (1772)
1 \,ta-mə-'shan-tər\ **:** the hero of Burns's poem *Tam o' Shanter*
2 *usually* **tam-o'-shanter** \'ta-mə-,\ **:** a woolen cap of Scottish origin with a tight headband, wide flat circular crown, and usually a pompon in the center

ta·mox·i·fen \tə-'mäk-sə-,fen\ *noun* [perhaps from *trans-* + *amine* + *oxi-* (alteration of *oxy*) + *-fen* (alteration of *phenyl*)] (1972)

: an estrogen antagonist $C_{26}H_{29}NO$ used especially to treat postmenopausal breast cancer

¹tamp \'tamp\ *transitive verb* [probably back-formation from obsolete *tampion, tampin* plug, from Middle English, from Middle French *tapon, tampon*, from (assumed) Old French *taper* to plug, of Germanic origin; akin to Old English *tæppa* tap] (1834)
1 : to drive in or down by a succession of light or medium blows ⟨*tamp* wet concrete⟩
2 : to put a check on **:** REDUCE, LESSEN
— **tamp·er** *noun*

²tamp *noun* (1920)
: a tool for tamping

tam·per \'tam-pər\ *intransitive verb* **tam·pered; tam·per·ing** \-p(ə-)riŋ\ [probably from Middle French *temperer* to temper, mix, meddle — more at TEMPER] (1567)
1 : to carry on underhand or improper negotiations (as by bribery)
2 a : to interfere so as to weaken or change for the worse — used with *with* **b :** to try foolish or dangerous experiments — used with *with*
— **tam·per·er** \-pər-ər\ *noun*
— **tam·per-proof** \'tam-pər-,prüf\ *adjective*

tam·pi·on \'tam-pē-ən, 'täm-\ *noun* [obsolete *tampion, tampin* plug — more at TAMP] (circa 1625)
: a wooden plug or a metal or canvas cover for the muzzle of a gun

¹tam·pon \'tam-,pän\ *noun* [French, literally, plug, from Middle French — more at TAMP] (1848)
: a plug (as of cotton) introduced into a body cavity usually to absorb secretions (as from menstruation) or to arrest hemorrhaging

²tampon *transitive verb* (1860)
: to plug with a tampon

tam–tam \'täm-,tam, 'täm-,täm\ *noun* [Hindi *ṭamṭam*] (1782)
1 : TOM-TOM
2 : GONG; *especially* **:** one of a tuned set in a gamelan orchestra

Tam·worth \'tam-(,)wərth\ *noun* [Tamworth, borough in Staffordshire, England] (1860)
: any of a breed of large long-bodied red swine developed in England especially for the production of bacon

¹tan \'tan\ *verb* **tanned; tan·ning** [Middle English *tannen*, from Middle French *tanner*, from Medieval Latin *tannare*, from *tanum, tannum* tanbark] (14th century)
transitive verb
1 a : to convert (hide) into leather by treatment with an infusion of tannin-rich bark or other agent of similar effect **b :** to convert (protein) to leather or a similar substance
2 : to make (skin) tan especially by exposure to the sun
3 : THRASH, WHIP
intransitive verb
: to get or become tanned

²tan *adjective* **tan·ner; tan·nest** (1586)
1 : of, relating to, or used for tan or tanning
2 : of the color tan

³tan *noun* [French, tanbark, from Old French, from Medieval Latin *tanum*] (1674)
1 : a tanning material or its active agent (as tannin)
2 : a brown color imparted to the skin by exposure to the sun or wind
3 : a light yellowish brown
4 *plural* **:** tan-colored articles of clothing

tan·a·ger \'ta-ni-jər\ *noun* [New Latin *tanagra*, from Portuguese *tangará*, from Tupi] (1688)
: any of numerous chiefly tropical American oscine birds (family Thraupidae) that are often

\ə\ abut \ᵊ\ kitten \ər\ further \a\ ash \ā\ ace
\ä\ mop, mar \aù\ out \ch\ chin \e\ bet \ē\ easy
\g\ go \i\ hit \ī\ ice \j\ job \ŋ\ sing \ō\ go
\ȯ\ law \ȯi\ boy \th\ thin \th\ the \ü\ loot \ù\ foot
\y\ yet \zh\ vision *see also* Guide to Pronunciation

brightly colored and usually unmusical and inhabit mostly woodlands

tan·bark \'tan-,bärk\ *noun* (1799)
1 : a bark rich in tannin bruised or cut into small pieces and used in tanning
2 : a surface (as a circus ring) covered with spent tanbark

¹tan·dem \'tan-dəm\ *noun* [Latin, at last, at length (taken to mean "lengthwise"), from *tam* so; akin to Old English *thæt* that] (circa 1785)
1 a (1) : a 2-seated carriage drawn by horses harnessed one before the other (2) : a team so harnessed **b** : TANDEM BICYCLE **c** : a vehicle (as a motortruck) having close-coupled pairs of axles
2 : a group of two or more arranged one behind the other or used or acting in conjunction
◇
— **in tandem 1** : in a tandem arrangement **2** : in partnership or conjunction

²tandem *adverb* (circa 1795)
: one after or behind another ⟨ride *tandem*⟩

³tandem *adjective* (1801)
1 : consisting of things or having parts arranged one behind the other
2 : working or occurring in conjunction with each other

tandem bicycle *noun* (circa 1890)
: a bicycle for usually two persons sitting tandem

tan·door \tän-'dur\ *noun* [Hindi *tandūr, tannūr*, from Persian *tanūr*, from Arabic *tannūr*] (1840)
: a cylindrical clay oven in which food is cooked over charcoal

tan·doori \tän-'dur-ē\ *adjective* [Hindi *tandūrī*, from *tandūr*] (circa 1968)
: cooked in a tandoor ⟨*tandoori* chicken⟩
— **tandoori** *noun*

¹tang \'taŋ\ *noun* [Middle English, of Scandinavian origin; akin to Old Norse *tangi* point of land, tang] (15th century)
1 : a projecting shank, prong, fang, or tongue (as on a knife, file, or sword) to connect with the handle
2 a : a sharp distinctive often lingering flavor **b** : a pungent odor **c** : something having the effect of a tang (as in stimulation of the senses)
3 a : a faint suggestion : TRACE **b** : a distinguishing characteristic that sets apart or gives a special individuality
— **tanged** \'taŋd\ *adjective*

²tang *transitive verb* (1566)
1 : to furnish with a tang
2 : to affect with a tang

³tang *verb* [imitative] (1556)
: CLANG, RING

⁴tang *noun* (circa 1625)
: a sharp twanging sound

Tang *or* **T'ang** \'täŋ\ *noun* [Chinese (Beijing) *Táng*] (1669)
: a Chinese dynasty dated A.D. 618–907 and marked by wide contacts with other cultures and by the development of printing and the flourishing of poetry and art

tan·ge·lo \'tan-jə-,lō\ *noun, plural* **-los** [*tangerine + pomelo*] (1904)
: the fruit of a hybrid (*Citrus tangelo*) between a tangerine or mandarin orange and a grapefruit; *also* : the tree

tan·gen·cy \'tan-jən(t)-sē\ *noun* (1819)
: the quality or state of being tangent

¹tan·gent \-jənt\ *adjective* [Latin *tangent-, tangens*, present participle of *tangere* to touch; perhaps akin to Old English *thaccian* to touch gently, stroke] (1594)
1 a : meeting a curve or surface in a single point if a sufficiently small interval is considered ⟨straight line *tangent* to a curve⟩ **b** (1) : having a common tangent line at a point ⟨*tangent* curves⟩ (2) : having a common tangent plane at a point ⟨*tangent* surfaces⟩
2 : diverging from an original purpose or course : IRRELEVANT ⟨*tangent* remarks⟩

²tangent *noun* [New Latin *tangent-, tangens*, from *linea tangens* tangent line] (1594)
1 a : the trigonometric function that for an acute angle is the ratio between the leg opposite to the angle when it is considered part of a right triangle and the leg adjacent **b** : a trigonometric function that is equal to the sine divided by the cosine for all real numbers θ for which the cosine is not equal to zero and is exactly equal to the tangent of an angle of measure θ in radians
2 : a line that is tangent; *specifically* : a straight line that is the limiting position of a secant of a curve through a fixed point and a variable point on the curve as the variable point approaches the fixed point — see CIRCLE illustration
3 : an abrupt change of course : DIGRESSION ⟨the speaker went off on a *tangent*⟩
4 : a small upright flat-ended metal pin at the inner end of a clavichord key that strikes the string to produce the tone

tan·gen·tial \tan-'jen(t)-shəl\ *adjective* (1630)
1 : of, relating to, or of the nature of a tangent
2 : acting along or lying in a tangent ⟨*tangential* forces⟩
3 a : DIVERGENT, DIGRESSIVE **b** : touching lightly : INCIDENTAL, PERIPHERAL ⟨*tangential* involvement⟩
— **tan·gen·tial·ly** \-'jen(t)-sh(ə-)lē\ *adverb*

tangent plane *noun* (1856)
: the plane through a point of a surface that contains the tangent lines to all the curves on the surface through the same point

tan·ger·ine \'tan-jə-,rēn, ,tan-jə-'\ *noun* [French *Tanger* Tangier, Morocco] (1842)
1 a : any of various mandarins that have usually deep orange skin and pulp; *broadly* : MANDARIN 3b **b** : a tree producing tangerines
2 : a moderate to strong reddish orange

¹tan·gi·ble \'tan-jə-bəl\ *adjective* [Late Latin *tangibilis*, from Latin *tangere* to touch] (1589)
1 a : capable of being perceived especially by the sense of touch : PALPABLE **b** : substantially real : MATERIAL
2 : capable of being precisely identified or realized by the mind ⟨her grief was *tangible*⟩
3 : capable of being appraised at an actual or approximate value ⟨*tangible* assets⟩
synonym see PERCEPTIBLE
— **tan·gi·bil·i·ty** \,tan-jə-'bi-lə-tē\ *noun*
— **tan·gi·ble·ness** \'tan-jə-bəl-nəs\ *noun*
— **tan·gi·bly** \-blē\ *adverb*

²tangible *noun* (1890)
: something tangible; *especially* : a tangible asset

¹tan·gle \'taŋ-gəl\ *verb* **tan·gled; tan·gling** \-g(ə-)liŋ\ [Middle English *tangilen*, probably of Scandinavian origin; akin to Swedish dialect *taggla* to tangle] (14th century)
transitive verb
1 : to involve so as to hamper, obstruct, or embarrass
2 : to seize and hold in or as if in a snare : ENTRAP
3 : to unite or knit together in intricate confusion
intransitive verb
1 : to interact in a contentious or conflicting way
2 : to become entangled

²tangle *noun* (1615)
1 : a tangled twisted mass : SNARL
2 a : a complicated or confused state or condition **b** : a state of perplexity or complete bewilderment
3 : a serious altercation : DISPUTE

³tangle *noun* [of Scandinavian origin; akin to Old Norse *thongull* tangle, *thang* kelp] (1536)
: a large seaweed

tan·gled \'taŋ-gəld\ *adjective* (1590)
1 : existing in or giving the appearance of a state of utter disorder
2 : very involved : exceedingly complex

tan·gle·ment \-gəl-mənt\ *noun* (1831)
: ENTANGLEMENT

tan·gly \'taŋ-g(ə-)lē\ *adjective* (1813)
: full of tangles or knots : INTRICATE

¹tan·go \'taŋ-(,)gō\ *noun, plural* **tangos** [American Spanish] (1913)
: a ballroom dance of Latin-American origin in ¾ time with a basic pattern of step-step-step-step-close and characterized by long pauses and stylized body positions; *also* : the music for this dance

²tango *intransitive verb* (1913)
: to dance the tango

Tan·go (1952)
— a communications code word for the letter *t*

tan·gram \'taŋ-grəm, 'tan-\ *noun* [perhaps from Chinese (Beijing) *táng* Chinese + English *-gram*] (circa 1864)
: a Chinese puzzle made by cutting a square of thin material into five triangles, a square, and a rhomboid which are capable of being recombined in many different figures

tangy \'taŋ-ē\ *adjective*
tang·i·er; -est (1875)
: having or suggestive of a tang

tangram

¹tank \'taŋk\ *noun* [Portuguese *tanque*, alteration of *estanque*, from *estancar* to stanch, perhaps from (assumed) Vulgar Latin *stanticare* — more at STANCH] (circa 1616)
1 *dialect* : POND, POOL; *especially* : one built as a water supply
2 : a usually large receptacle for holding, transporting, or storing liquids (as water or fuel)
3 : an enclosed heavily armed and armored combat vehicle that moves on tracks
4 : a prison cell or enclosure used especially for receiving prisoners
5 : TANK TOP
— **tank·ful** \-,ful\ *noun*
— **tank·like** \-,līk\ *adjective*

²tank (1863)
transitive verb
1 : to place, store, or treat in a tank
2 : to make no effort to win : lose intentionally ⟨*tanked* the match⟩
intransitive verb
: to lose intentionally : give up in competition

tan·ka \'tän-kə\ *noun* [Japanese] (circa 1877)
: an unrhymed Japanese verse form of five lines containing 5, 7, 5, 7, and 7 syllables respectively; *also* : a poem in this form — compare HAIKU

tank·age \'taŋ-kij\ *noun* (1866)
1 a : the aggregate of tanks required for a purpose **b** : the capacity or contents of a tank

◇ WORD HISTORY

tandem When a pair of horses pulls a carriage, the two are usually harnessed side by side. But there is a type of two-wheeled, two-seated carriage that is drawn by two horses harnessed one after the other. This carriage, a *tandem*, apparently owes its name to a rather contorted Latin-English pun. The Latin word *tandem* means "at length, at last, finally." We do not know the identity of the punster who first suggested that horses arranged lengthwise should be thought of as "at length" and the carriage called a *tandem*, but the individual need not have been a scholar. The Latin word is not a rare one and would have been known to any student of the language. First attested in a slang dictionary published in 1785, *tandem* in the course of the 19th century came to be used in a general way of any arrangement of things or of people one behind the other.

2 : dried animal residues usually freed from the fat and gelatin and used as fertilizer and feedstuff

3 : the act or process of putting or storing in tanks

tan·kard \'taŋ-kərd\ *noun* [Middle English] (15th century)
: a tall one-handled drinking vessel; *especially* : a silver or pewter mug with a lid

tank destroyer *noun* (1941)
: a highly mobile lightly armored vehicle usually on a half-track or a tank chassis and mounting a cannon

tanked \'taŋ(k)t\ *adjective* (1893)
slang : DRUNK 1a — often used with *up*

tankard

tank·er \'taŋ-kər\ *noun* (1900)
1 a : a cargo ship fitted with tanks for carrying liquid in bulk **b** : a vehicle on which a tank is mounted to carry fluids; *also* : a cargo airplane for transporting fuel
2 : a member of a military tank crew

tank suit *noun* (1940)
: a one-piece bathing suit with usually wide shoulder straps

tank top *noun* (1950)
: a sleeveless collarless shirt with usually wide shoulder straps and no front opening

tank town *noun* [from the fact that formerly trains stopped at such towns only to take on water] (1906)
: a small town

tan·nage \'ta-nij\ *noun* (1662)
: the act, process, or result of tanning

tan·nate \'ta-,nāt\ *noun* [French, from *tannin*] (1802)
: a compound of a tannin

¹tan·ner \'ta-nər\ *noun* (before 12th century)
1 : one that tans hides
2 : one who acquires or seeks to acquire a suntan

²tanner *noun* [origin unknown] (circa 1811)
British : SIXPENCE

tanner crab *noun* [probably from New Latin *tanneri*, specific epithet of *Chionoecetes tanneri*, from Zera L. *Tanner* (died 1906) American naval officer] (1947)
: any of several spider crabs (genus *Chionoecetes*); *especially* : SNOW CRAB

tan·nery \'ta-nə-rē, 'tan-rē\ *noun, plural* **-ner·ies** (1736)
: a place where tanning is carried on

tan·nic \'ta-nik\ *adjective* [French *tannique*, from *tannin*] (circa 1859)
1 : of, resembling, or derived from tan or a tannin
2 *of wine* : containing an abundance of tannins : markedly astringent

tannic acid *noun* (1836)
: TANNIN 1

tan·nin \'ta-nən\ *noun* [French, from *tanner* to tan] (1802)
1 : any of various soluble astringent complex phenolic substances of plant origin used especially in tanning, dyeing, the making of ink, and in medicine
2 : a substance that has a tanning effect

tan·ning \'ta-niŋ\ *noun* (15th century)
1 : the art or process by which a skin is tanned
2 : a browning of the skin especially by exposure to sun
3 : a sound spanking
4 : a natural darkening and hardening of the cuticle of an insect immediately after molting

tan·nish \'ta-nish\ *adjective* (1935)
: somewhat tan

tan oak *noun* (circa 1925)
: a U.S. Pacific coast evergreen tree (*Lithocarpus densiflora*) of the beech family that has erect staminate catkins and is rich in tannins

Ta·no·an \tə-'nō-ən, 'tä-nə-wən\ *noun* [*Tano*, a group of former pueblos in New Mexico] (1891)
: a family of American Indian languages spoken in New Mexico and Arizona
— **Tanoan** *adjective*

tan·sy \'tan-zē\ *noun, plural* **tansies** [Middle English *tanesey*, from Middle French *tanesie*, from Medieval Latin *athanasia*, from Greek, immortality, from *athanatos* immortal, from *a-* + *thanatos* death — more at THANATOS] (15th century)
: a common aromatic Old World composite herb (*Tanacetum vulgare*) that is naturalized in North America and has bitter-tasting finely divided leaves; *broadly* : a plant of the same genus

tansy ragwort *noun* (circa 1900)
: an Old World yellow-flowered senecio (*Senecio jacobaea*) that is naturalized in North America and is toxic to livestock

tan·ta·late \'tan-tᵊl-,āt\ *noun* (1849)
: a salt containing tantalum in combination with oxygen

tan·ta·lise *British variant of* TANTALIZE

tan·ta·lite \'tan-tᵊl-,īt\ *noun* (1805)
: a mineral consisting of a heavy dark lustrous oxide of tantalum and usually other metals (as iron or manganese)

tan·ta·lize \'tan-tᵊl-,īz\ *verb* **-lized; -liz·ing** [*Tantalus*] (1597)
transitive verb
: to tease or torment by or as if by presenting something desirable to the view but continually keeping it out of reach
intransitive verb
: to cause one to be tantalized
— **tan·ta·liz·er** *noun*

tantalizing *adjective* (circa 1683)
: possessing a quality that arouses or stimulates desire or interest; *also* : mockingly or teasingly out of reach
— **tan·ta·liz·ing·ly** \-,ī-ziŋ-lē\ *adverb*

tan·ta·lum \'tan-tᵊl-əm\ *noun* [New Latin, from Latin *Tantalus*; from its inability to absorb acid] (1802)
: a hard ductile gray-white acid-resisting metallic element of the vanadium family found combined in rare minerals (as tantalite and columbite) — see ELEMENT table

Tan·ta·lus \'tan-tᵊl-əs\ *noun* [Latin, from Greek *Tantalos*]
1 : a legendary king of Lydia condemned to stand up to the chin in a pool of water in Hades and beneath fruit-laden boughs only to have the water or fruit recede at each attempt to drink or eat
2 *not capitalized* : a locked cellarette with contents visible but not obtainable without a key

tan·ta·mount \'tan-tə-,maùnt\ *adjective* [obsolete *tantamount*, noun, equivalent, from Anglo-French *tant amunter* to amount to as much] (1641)
: equivalent in value, significance, or effect

tan·ta·ra \tan-'tar-ə, -'tär-\ *noun* [Latin *taratantara*, of imitative origin] (1584)
: the blare of a trumpet or horn

¹tan·tivy \tan-'ti-vē\ *adverb* [origin unknown] (1641)
: at a gallop

²tantivy *noun, plural* **-tiv·ies** (circa 1658)
1 : a rapid gallop or ride
2 : TANTARA

tan·tra \'tən-trə, 'tän-, 'tan-\ *noun, often capitalized* [Sanskrit, literally, warp, from *tanoti* he stretches, weaves; akin to Greek *teinein* to stretch — more at THIN] (1799)
: one of the later Hindu or Buddhist scriptures dealing especially with techniques and rituals including meditative and sexual practices; *also* : the rituals or practices outlined in the tantra
— **tan·tric** \-trik\ *adjective, often capitalized*
— **Tan·trism** \-,tri-zəm\ *noun*
— **Tan·trist** \-trist\ *noun*

tan·trum \'tan-trəm\ *noun* [origin unknown] (1714)
: a fit of bad temper

ta·nu·ki \tä-'nü-kē\ *noun* [Japanese, raccoon dog] (circa 1929)
: the fur of a raccoon dog; *also* : RACCOON DOG

tan·yard \'tan-,yärd\ *noun* (1666)
: the section or part of a tannery housing tanning vats

tan·za·nite \'tan-zə-,nīt\ *noun* [*Tanzania*, Africa] (1968)
: a mineral that is a deep blue variety of zoisite and is used as a gemstone

Tao \'daù, 'taù\ *noun* [Chinese (Beijing) *dào*, literally, way] (1736)
1 a : the unconditional and unknowable source and guiding principle of all reality as conceived by Taoists **b** : the process of nature by which all things change and which is to be followed for a life of harmony
2 *often not capitalized* : the path of virtuous conduct as conceived by Confucians
3 *often not capitalized* : the art or skill of doing something in harmony with the essential nature of the thing ⟨the *tao* of archery⟩

Tao·ism \-,i-zəm\ *noun* [*Tao*] (1838)
1 : a Chinese mystical philosophy traditionally founded by Lao-tzu in the 6th century B.C. that teaches conformity to the Tao by unassertive action and simplicity
2 : a religion developed from Taoist philosophy and folk and Buddhist religion and concerned with obtaining long life and good fortune often by magical means
— **Tao·ist** \-ist\ *adjective or noun*
— **Tao·is·tic** \daù-'is-tik, taù-\ *adjective*

¹tap \'tap\ *noun* [Middle English *tappe*, from Old English *tæppa*; akin to Old High German *zapho* tap] (before 12th century)
1 a : a plug for a hole (as in a cask) : SPIGOT **b** : a device consisting of a spout and valve attached to the end of a pipe to control the flow of a fluid : FAUCET
2 a : a liquor drawn through a tap **b** : the procedure of removing fluid (as from a body cavity)
3 : a tool for forming an internal screw thread
4 : an intermediate point in an electric circuit where a connection may be made
5 : WIRETAP
— **on tap 1** : ready to be drawn from a large container (as a cask or keg) ⟨ale *on tap*⟩ **2** : broached or furnished with a tap **3** : on hand : AVAILABLE ⟨services instantly *on tap* —Hugh Dwan⟩ **4** : coming up ⟨other matches *on tap* —H. W. Wind⟩

²tap *transitive verb* **tapped; tap·ping** (15th century)
1 : to let out or cause to flow by piercing or by drawing a plug from the containing vessel ⟨*tap* wine from a cask⟩
2 a : to pierce so as to let out or draw off a fluid ⟨*tap* maple trees⟩ **b** : to draw out, from, or upon ⟨*tap* new sources of revenue⟩
3 a : to cut in on (a telephone or telegraph wire) to get information **b** : to cut in (an electrical circuit) on another circuit
4 : to form an internal screw thread in by means of a tap
5 : to get money from as a loan or gift
6 : to connect (a street gas or water main) with a local supply
— **tap·per** *noun*
— **tap into** : to make a usually advantageous connection with ⟨clothing that . . . *taps into* the currents of popular culture —John Duka⟩

³tap *verb* **tapped; tap·ping** [Middle English *tappen*, from Middle French *taper* to strike with the flat of the hand, of Germanic origin; akin to Middle High German *tāpe* paw, blow dealt with the paw] (13th century)
transitive verb

\ə\ **abut** \ᵊ\ **kitten** \ər\ **further** \a\ **ash** \ā\ **ace** \ä\ **mop, mar** \aù\ **out** \ch\ **chin** \e\ **bet** \ē\ **easy** \g\ **go** \i\ **hit** \ī\ **ice** \j\ **job** \ŋ\ **sing** \ō\ **go** \ò\ **law** \òi\ **boy** \th\ **thin** \t͟h\ **the** \ü\ **loot** \ù\ **foot** \y\ **yet** \zh\ **vision** *see also* Guide to Pronunciation

1 : to strike lightly especially with a slight sound
2 : to give a light blow with ⟨*tap* a pencil on the table⟩
3 : to bring about by repeated light blows ⟨*tap* out a story on the typewriter⟩
4 : to repair by putting a tap on
5 : SELECT, DESIGNATE ⟨was *tapped* for police commissioner⟩; *specifically* **:** to elect to membership (as in a fraternity)
intransitive verb
1 : to strike a light audible blow **:** RAP
2 : to walk with light audible steps
3 : TAP-DANCE
— **tap·per** *noun*
⁴tap *noun* (14th century)
1 a : a light usually audible blow; *also* **:** its sound **b :** one of several usually rapid drumbeats on a snare drum
2 : HALF SOLE
3 : a small metal plate for the sole or heel of a shoe
4 : TAP DANCE 1
5 : FLAP 7
¹ta·pa \'tä-pə, 'ta-\ *noun* [Marquesan & Tahitian] (1823)
: a coarse cloth made in the Pacific islands from the pounded bark especially of the paper mulberry and usually decorated with geometric patterns
²tapa *noun* [Spanish, literally, cover, lid, probably of Germanic origin; akin to Old English *tæppa* tap] (1953)
: an hors d'oeuvre served with drinks in Spanish bars — usually used in plural
tap dance *noun* (1928)
1 : a step dance tapped out audibly by means of shoes with hard soles or soles and heels to which taps have been added
2 : something suggesting a tap dance; *especially* **:** an action or discourse intended to rationalize or distract ⟨does a clever *tap dance* to explain —Campbell Geeslin⟩
— **tap–dance** *intransitive verb*
— **tap dancer** *noun*
— **tap dancing** *noun*
¹tape \'tāp\ *noun* [Middle English, from Old English *tæppe*] (before 12th century)
1 : a narrow woven fabric
2 : a string or ribbon stretched breast-high above the finish line of a race
3 : a narrow flexible strip or band: as **a :** ADHESIVE TAPE **b :** MAGNETIC TAPE
4 : TAPE RECORDING
²tape *verb* **taped; tap·ing** (1609)
transitive verb
1 : to fasten, tie, bind, cover, or support with tape
2 : to record on tape and especially magnetic tape ⟨*tape* an interview⟩
intransitive verb
: to record something on tape and especially magnetic tape
³tape *adjective* (1947)
1 : recorded on tape ⟨*tape* music⟩
2 : intended for use with recording (as magnetic) tape ⟨a *tape* cartridge⟩
tape deck *noun* (1949)
: a device used to play back and often to record on magnetic tape that usually has to be connected to an audio system
tape grass *noun* (circa 1818)
: any of several submerged aquatic monocotyledonous plants (genus *Vallisneria* of the family Hydrocharitaceae) with long ribbonlike leaves — called also *eelgrass, wild celery*
tape measure *noun* (1845)
: a narrow strip (as of a limp cloth or steel tape) marked off in units (as in inches or centimeters) for measuring
¹ta·per \'tā-pər\ *noun* [Middle English, from Old English *tapor* candle, wick, perhaps modification of Latin *papyrus* papyrus] (before 12th century)
1 a : a slender candle **b :** a long waxed wick used especially for lighting candles, lamps,

pipes, or fires **c :** a feeble light
2 a : a tapering form or figure **b :** gradual diminution of thickness, diameter, or width in an elongated object **c :** a gradual decrease
²taper *adjective* (15th century)
1 : progressively narrowed toward one end
2 : furnished with or adjusted to a scale **:** GRADUATED ⟨*taper* freight rates⟩
³taper *verb* **ta·pered; ta·per·ing** \'tā-p(ə-)riŋ\ (1610)
intransitive verb
1 : to become progressively smaller toward one end
2 : to diminish gradually
transitive verb
: to cause to taper
⁴tap·er \'tā-pər\ *noun* [¹*tape*] (circa 1920)
: one that applies or dispenses tape
tape–re·cord \ˌtā-pri-'kȯrd, 'tā-pri-ˌ\ *transitive verb* [back-formation from *tape recording*] (1950)
: to make a recording of on magnetic tape
tape recorder *noun* (1932)
: a device for recording on and playing back magnetic tape
tape recording *noun* (1940)
: magnetic recording on magnetic tape; *also*
: a recording made by this process
ta·per·er \'tā-pər-ər\ *noun* (15th century)
: one who bears a taper in a religious procession
taper off *verb* (1848)
: TAPER ⟨business growth had *tapered off* seriously while the unemployment rate had climbed —*Current Biography*⟩
ta·per·stick \'tā-pər-ˌstik\ *noun* (1546)
: a candlestick that holds tapers
tap·es·tried \'ta-pə-strēd\ *adjective* (1769)
1 : covered or decorated with or as if with tapestry
2 : woven or depicted in tapestry
tap·es·try \'ta-pə-strē\ *noun, plural* **-tries** [Middle English *tapistry*, modification of Middle French *tapisserie*, from *tapisser* to carpet, cover with tapestry, from Old French *tapis* carpet, from Greek *tapēt-, tapēs* rug, carpet] (15th century)
1 a : a heavy handwoven reversible textile used for hangings, curtains, and upholstery and characterized by complicated pictorial designs **b :** a nonreversible imitation of tapestry used chiefly for upholstery **c :** embroidery on canvas resembling woven tapestry ⟨needlepoint *tapestry*⟩
2 : something resembling tapestry (as in complexity or richness of design)
tapestry carpet *noun* (1852)
: a carpet in which the designs are printed in colors on the threads before the fabric is woven
ta·pe·tum \tə-'pē-təm\ *noun, plural* **ta·pe·ta** \-'pē-tə\ [New Latin, from Latin *tapete* carpet, tapestry, from Greek *tapēt-, tapēs* rug, carpet] (1713)
1 : any of various membranous layers or areas especially of the choroid coat and retina of the eye
2 : a layer of nutritive cells that invests the sporogenous tissue in the sporangium of higher plants
tape·worm \'tāp-ˌwərm\ *noun* [from its shape] (1752)
: any of a class (Cestoda) of platyhelminthic worms parasitic especially in the intestines of vertebrates — called also *cestode*
tap·hole \'tap-ˌhōl\ *noun* (1594)
: a hole for a tap; *specifically* **:** a hole at or near the bottom of a furnace or ladle through which molten metal, matte, or slag can be tapped
ta·phon·o·my \tə-'fä-nə-mē, ta-\ *noun* [Greek *taphē* burial + English *-nomy*] (1940)
: the study of the processes (as burial, decay, and preservation) that affect animal and plant remains as they become fossilized
— **taph·o·nom·ic** \ˌta-fə-'nä-mik\ *adjective*

— **ta·phon·o·mist** \tə-'fä-nə-mist, ta-\ *noun*
tap–in \'tap-ˌin\ *noun* (1948)
1 : TIP-IN
2 : a short putt in golf
tap·i·o·ca \ˌta-pē-'ō-kə\ *noun* [Spanish & Portuguese, from Tupi *tipióka*] (1707)
1 : a usually granular preparation of cassava starch used especially in puddings and as a thickening in liquid food; *also* **:** a dish (as pudding) containing tapioca
2 : CASSAVA
ta·pir \'tā-pər *also* 'tā-ˌpir *or* tə-'pir\ *noun, plural* **tapir** *or* **tapirs** [Portuguese *tapira*, from Tupi *tapiíra*] (1774)
: any of a genus (*Tapirus*) of chiefly nocturnal perissodactyl ungulates of tropical America and Myanmar to Sumatra that have the snout and upper lip prolonged into a short flexible proboscis

tapir

ta·pis \'ta-pē, ta-'pē\ *noun* [Middle English, from Middle French — more at TAPESTRY] (15th century)
archaic **:** a small tapestry used for hangings and floor and table coverings
— **on the tapis :** under consideration
tap–off \'tap-ˌȯf\ *noun* (circa 1932)
: ²TIP-OFF
tap out *intransitive verb* (1939)
: to run out of money by betting
tap pants *noun plural* (1977)
: a loose-fitting woman's undergarment of a style similar to shorts formerly worn for tap dancing
tapped out *adjective* (1950)
: out of money **:** BROKE
tap·pet \'ta-pət\ *noun* [irregular from ³*tap*] (1745)
: a lever or projection moved by some other piece (as a cam) or intended to tap or touch something else to cause a particular motion
tapping *noun* (1597)
: the act, process, or means by which something is tapped
tap·pit hen \'ta-pət-\ *noun* [Scots *tappit*, alteration of English *topped*] (1721)
Scottish **:** a drinking vessel with a knob on the lid
tap·room \'tap-ˌrüm, -ˌrùm\ *noun* (1807)
: BARROOM
tap·root \-ˌrüt, -ˌrùt\ *noun* [¹*tap*] (1601)
1 : a primary root that grows vertically downward and gives off small lateral roots
2 : the central element or position in a line of growth or development
taps \'taps\ *noun plural but singular or plural in construction* [probably alteration of earlier *taptoo* tattoo — more at TATTOO] (1824)
: the last bugle call at night blown as a signal that lights are to be put out; *also* **:** a similar call blown at military funerals and memorial services
tap·sal–tee·rie \ˌtap-səl-'tē-rē\ *adverb* [by alteration] (1784)
Scottish **:** TOPSY-TURVY
tap·ster \'tap-stər\ *noun* (before 12th century)
: BARTENDER
tap water *noun* (1881)
: water as it comes from a tap (as in a home)
¹tar \'tär\ *noun* [Middle English *terr, tarr*, from Old English *teoru*; akin to Old English *trēow* tree — more at TREE] (before 12th century)
1 a : a dark brown or black bituminous usually odorous viscous liquid obtained by destructive distillation of organic material (as wood, coal, or peat) **b :** a substance in some respects resembling tar; *especially* **:** a condensable residue present in smoke from burning tobacco

that contains combustion by-products (as resins, acids, phenols, and essential oils)
2 [short for *tarpaulin*] **:** SAILOR

²**tar** *transitive verb* **tarred; tar·ring** (13th century)
1 : to cover with tar
2 : to defile as if with tar ⟨least *tarred* by the scandal —*Newsweek*⟩
— **tar and feather :** to smear (a person) with tar and cover with feathers as a punishment or indignity
— **tar with the same brush :** to mark or stain with the same fault or characteristic

³**tar** *or* **tarre** \'tär\ *transitive verb* **tarred; tar·ring; tars** *or* **tarres** [Middle English *terren, tarren,* from Old English *tyrwan*] (before 12th century)
: to urge to action — usually used with *on*

tar·a·did·dle *or* **tar·ra·did·dle** \'tar-ə-'did-°l, 'tar-ə-,\ *noun* [origin unknown] (circa 1796)
1 : FIB
2 : pretentious nonsense

Tar·a·hu·ma·ra \,tar-ə-hü-'mär-ə\ *noun, plural* **Tarahumara** *or* **Tarahumaras** [Spanish] (1874)
1 : a member of an American Indian people living in the state of Chihuahua, Mexico
2 : the Uto-Aztecan language of the Tarahumara people

tar·an·tel·la \,tar-ən-'te-lə\ *noun* [Italian, from *Taranto,* Italy] (1782)
: a lively folk dance of southern Italy in ⅜ time

tar·an·tism \'tar-ən-,ti-zəm\ *noun* [New Latin *tarantismus,* from *Taranto,* Italy] (circa 1656)
: a dancing mania or malady of late medieval Europe

ta·ran·tu·la \tə-'ran-chə-lə, -tə-lə; -'ranch-lə, -'rant-\ *noun, plural* **ta·ran·tu·las** *also* **ta·ran·tu·lae** \-,lē\ [Medieval Latin, from Old Italian *tarantola,* from *Taranto*] (1561)
1 : a European wolf spider (*Lycosa tarentula*) popularly held to be the cause of tarantism
2 : any of a family (Theraphosidae) of large hairy American spiders that are typically rather sluggish and capable of biting sharply though most forms are not significantly poisonous to humans

Ta·ras·can \tə-'ras-kən, -'räs-\ *noun* [Spanish *tarasco*] (1922)
1 : a member of an American Indian people of the state of Michoacán, Mexico
2 : the language of the Tarascan people

tar baby *noun* [from the tar baby that trapped Brer Rabbit in an Uncle Remus story by Joel Chandler Harris] (1924)
: something from which it is nearly impossible to extricate oneself

tar·boosh *also* **tar·bush** \tär-'büsh, 'tär-,\ *noun* [Arabic *ṭarbūsh*] (1702)
: a red hat similar to the fez worn especially by Muslim men

tar·di·grade \'tär-də-,grād\ *noun* [ultimately from Latin *tardigradus* slow-moving, from *tardus* slow + *gradi* to step, go — more at GRADE] (1860)
: any of a phylum (Tardigrada) of microscopic arthropods with four pairs of stout legs that live usually in water or damp moss — called also *water bear*

tar·di·ly \'tär-d°l-ē\ *adverb* (1597)
1 : at a slow pace
2 : LATE

tar·dive dyskinesia \'tär-div-\ *noun* [*tardive* tending toward late development (from French, feminine of *tardif,* from Middle French) + *dyskinesia*] (1964)
: a central nervous system disorder characterized by twitching of the face and tongue and involuntary motor movements of the trunk and limbs and occurring especially as a side effect of prolonged use of antipsychotic drugs (as phenothiazine)

tar·do \'tär-(,)dō\ *adjective* [Italian, from Latin *tardus*] (circa 1843)

: SLOW — used as a direction in music

¹**tar·dy** \'tär-dē\ *adjective* **tar·di·er; -est** [alteration of earlier *tardif,* from Middle French, from (assumed) Vulgar Latin *tardivus,* from Latin *tardus*] (15th century)
1 : moving slowly **:** SLUGGISH
2 : delayed beyond the expected or proper time **:** LATE
— **tar·di·ness** \'tär-dē-nəs\ *noun*

²**tardy** *noun, plural* **tardies** (1960)
: an instance of being tardy (as to a class)

¹**tare** \'tar, 'ter\ *noun* [Middle English; probably akin to Middle Dutch *tarwe* wheat] (14th century)
1 a : the seed of a vetch **b :** any of several vetches (especially *Vicia sativa* and *V. hirsuta*)
2 : a weed of grainfields usually held to be the darnel
3 *plural* **:** an undesirable element

²**tare** *noun* [Middle English, from Middle French, from Old Italian *tara,* from Arabic *ṭarḥa,* literally, that which is removed] (15th century)
1 : a deduction from the gross weight of a substance and its container made in allowance for the weight of the container; *also* **:** the weight of the container
2 : COUNTERWEIGHT

³**tare** *transitive verb* **tared; tar·ing** (1812)
: to ascertain or mark the tare of; *especially* **:** to weigh so as to determine the tare

targe \'tärj\ *noun* [Middle English, from Old French] (14th century)
: a light shield used especially by the Scots

¹**tar·get** \'tär-gət\ *noun, often attributive* [Middle English, from Middle French *targette,* diminutive of *targe* light shield, of Germanic origin; akin to Old Norse *targa* shield] (15th century)
1 : a small round shield
2 a : a mark to shoot at **b :** a target marked by shots fired at it **c :** something or someone fired at or marked for attack **d :** a goal to be achieved
3 a : an object of ridicule or criticism **b :** something or someone to be affected by an action or development
4 a : a railroad day signal that is attached to a switch stand and indicates whether the switch is open or closed **b :** a sliding sight on a surveyor's leveling rod
5 a : the metallic surface (as of platinum or tungsten) upon which the stream of electrons within an X-ray tube is focused and from which the X rays are emitted **b :** a body, surface, or material bombarded with nuclear particles or electrons; *especially* **:** fluorescent material on which desired visual effects are produced in electronic devices (as in radar) ◆
— **off target :** not valid **:** INACCURATE
— **on target :** precisely correct or valid especially in interpreting or addressing a problem or vital issue

²**target** *transitive verb* (1837)
1 : to make a target of; *especially* **:** to set as a goal
2 : to direct or use toward a target

tar·get·able \'tär-gə-tə-bəl\ *adjective* (1964)
: capable of being aimed at a target ⟨missiles with *targetable* warheads⟩

target date *noun* (1945)
: the date set for an event or for the completion of a project, goal, or quota

target language *noun* (1953)
1 : a language into which another language is to be translated — compare SOURCE LANGUAGE
2 : a language other than one's native language that is being learned

Tar·gum \'tär-,güm, -,güm\ *noun* [Late Hebrew *targūm,* from Aramaic, translation] (1587)
: an Aramaic translation or paraphrase of a portion of the Old Testament

Tar·heel \'tär-,hēl\ *noun* (1864)

: a native or resident of North Carolina — used as a nickname

¹**tar·iff** \'tar-əf\ *noun* [Italian *tariffa,* from Arabic *ta'rīf* notification] (1592)
1 a : a schedule of duties imposed by a government on imported or in some countries exported goods **b :** a duty or rate of duty imposed in such a schedule
2 : a schedule of rates or charges of a business or a public utility
3 : PRICE, CHARGE

²**tariff** *transitive verb* (circa 1828)
: to subject to a tariff

tar·la·tan \'tär-lə-t°n\ *noun* [French *tarlatane*] (circa 1741)
: a sheer cotton fabric in open plain weave usually heavily sized for stiffness

tar·mac \'tär-,mak\ *noun* [from *Tarmac,* a trademark] (1919)
: a tarmacadam road, apron, or runway
Tarmac *trademark*
— used for a bituminous binder for roads

tar·mac·ad·am \,tär-mə-'ka-dəm\ *noun* (1882)
1 : a pavement constructed by spraying or pouring a tar binder over layers of crushed stone and then rolling
2 : a material of tar and aggregates mixed in a plant and shaped on the roadway

tarn \'tärn\ *noun* [Middle English *tarne,* of Scandinavian origin; akin to Old Norse *tjǫrn* small lake] (14th century)
: a small steep-banked mountain lake or pool

tar·na·tion \tär-'nā-shən\ *noun* [alteration of *darnation,* euphemism for *damnation*] (1790)
: DAMNATION — often used as an interjection or intensive; often used with *in* ⟨*tarnation* strike me —James Joyce⟩ ⟨where in *tarnation* you from? —Jessamyn West⟩

¹**tar·nish** \'tär-nish\ *verb* [Middle French *terniss-,* stem of *ternir,* probably of Germanic origin; akin to Old High German *ternen* to hide] (1598)
transitive verb
1 : to dull or destroy the luster of by or as if by air, dust, or dirt **:** SOIL, STAIN
2 a : to detract from the good quality of **:** VITIATE ⟨his fine dreams now slightly *tarnished*⟩ **b :** to bring disgrace on **:** SULLY
intransitive verb
: to become tarnished
— **tar·nish·able** \-ni-shə-bəl\ *adjective*

²**tarnish** *noun* (1713)
: something that tarnishes; *especially* **:** a film of chemically altered material on the surface of a metal (as silver)

tarnished plant bug *noun* (circa 1890)

◇ WORD HISTORY
target Old French *targe,* a name for a small leather-covered shield carried by a foot soldier, is probably of Frankish origin and hence akin to Old Norse *targa* "round shield." *Targe* and its diminutive form *targette* were both borrowed into Middle English. Our pronunciation of the modern word *target* with \g\ rather than \j\, as well as occasional Middle English variants such as *targatte,* shows the influence of forms with a "hard *g*" such as Middle French *targuete* or late Old Provençal *targueta.* Not until the later 18th century was *target* used with reference to something to be aimed at, originally a shieldlike object used in archery practice. During the 19th century the word acquired the general sense "a mark to shoot at," either literal or figurative.

\ə\ abut \°\ kitten \ər\ further \a\ ash \ā\ ace
\ä\ mop, mar \aú\ out \ch\ chin \e\ bet \ē\ easy
\g\ go \i\ hit \ī\ ice \j\ job \ŋ\ sing
\ō\ law \ói\ boy \th\ thin \t͟h\ the \ü\ loot \ú\ foot
\y\ yet \zh\ vision *see also* Guide to Pronunciation

: a common hemipterous bug (*Lygus lineolaris*) of eastern North America that causes injury to plants by sucking sap from buds, leaves, and fruits and that carries plant diseases

ta·ro \'tär-(,)ō, 'tar-, 'ter-\ *noun, plural* **taros** [Tahitian & Maori] (1769)
: a plant (*Colocasia esculenta*) of the arum family grown throughout the tropics for its edible starchy tuberous rootstocks and in temperate regions for ornament; *also* : its rootstock

tar·ok \'tar-,äk\ *noun* [Italian *tarocchi* tarots] (1739)
: an old card game popular in central Europe and played with a pack containing 40, 52, or 56 cards equivalent to modern playing cards plus the 22 tarots

tar·ot \'tar-(,)ō\ *noun* [Middle French, from Italian *tarocchi* (plural)] (circa 1623)
: any of a set of usually 78 playing cards including 22 pictorial cards used for fortune-telling; *also* : the 22 pictorial cards serving as trumps in tarok

tarp \'tärp\ *noun* (1906)
: TARPAULIN

tar paper *noun* (1891)
: a heavy paper coated or impregnated with tar for use especially in building

tar·pau·lin \tär-'pò-lən, 'tär-pə-; ÷tär-'pōl-yən\ *noun* [probably from ¹*tar* + *-palling, -pauling* (from *pall*)] (1605)
1 : a piece of material (as durable plastic) used for protecting exposed objects or areas
2 : SAILOR

tar pit *noun* (1839)
: an area in which natural bitumens collect and are exposed at the earth's surface and which tends to trap animals and preserve their hard parts (as bones or teeth)

tar·pon \'tär-pən\ *noun, plural* **tarpon** *or* **tarpons** [origin unknown] (1685)
: a large silvery elongate anadromous bony fish (*Megalops atlanticus* of the family Elopidae) that occurs especially in the Gulf of Mexico, Caribbean, and warm coastal waters of the Atlantic, reaches a length of about six feet (two meters), and is often caught for sport

tar·ra·gon \'tar-ə-gən\ *noun* [Middle French *targon*, from Medieval Latin *tarchon*, from Arabic *ṭarkhūn*] (1538)
: a small widely cultivated perennial artemisia (*Artemisia dracunculus*) having pungent narrow usually entire leaves; *also* : its leaves used as a flavoring

tarre *variant of* TAR

tar·ri·ance \'tar-ē-ən(t)s\ *noun* (15th century)
: the act or an instance of tarrying

¹tar·ry \'tar-ē\ *intransitive verb* **tar·ried; tar·ry·ing** [Middle English *tarien*] (14th century)
1 a : to delay or be tardy in acting or doing **b** : to linger in expectation : WAIT
2 : to abide or stay in or at a place

²tarry *noun, plural* **tarries** (14th century)
: STAY, SOJOURN

³tar·ry \'tär-ē\ *adjective* (1552)
: of, resembling, or covered with tar

¹tar·sal \'tär-səl\ *adjective* (1817)
1 : of or relating to the tarsus
2 : being or relating to plates of dense connective tissue that serve to stiffen the eyelids

²tarsal *noun* (1881)
: a tarsal part (as a bone or cartilage)

tar sand *noun* (1899)
: a natural impregnation of sand or sandstone with petroleum from which the lighter portions have escaped

tar·si·er \'tär-sē-ər, -sē-,ā\ *noun* [French, from *tarse* tarsus, from New Latin *tarsus*] (1774)
: any of a family (Tarsiidae) of small chiefly nocturnal and arboreal carnivorous primates of the Malay Archipelago that have large round eyes, long legs, and a long nearly hairless tail

tar·so·meta·tar·sus \'tär-(,)sō-'me-tə-,tär-səs\ *noun* [New Latin, from *tarsus* + *-o-* + *metatarsus*] (1854)

: the large compound bone of the tarsus of a bird; *also* : the segment of the limb it supports

tar·sus \'tär-səs\ *noun, plural* **tar·si** \-,sī, -,sē\ [New Latin, from Greek *tarsos* wickerwork mat, flat of the foot, ankle, edge of the eyelid; akin to Greek *tersesthai* to become dry — more at THIRST] (1676)
1 : the part of the foot of a vertebrate between the metatarsus and the leg; *also* : the small bones that support this part of the limb
2 : the tarsal plate of the eyelid
3 : the distal part of the limb of an arthropod
4 : TARSOMETATARSUS

¹tart \'tärt\ *adjective* [Middle English, from Old English *teart* sharp, severe; akin to Middle High German *traz* spite] (14th century)
1 : agreeably sharp or acid to the taste
2 : marked by a biting, acrimonious, or cutting quality
— **tart·ish** \'tär-tish\ *adjective*
— **tart·ly** *adverb*
— **tart·ness** *noun*

²tart *noun* [Middle English *tarte*, from Middle French] (15th century)
1 : a dish baked in a pastry shell : PIE: as **a** : a small pie or pastry shell without a top containing jelly, custard, or fruit **b** : a small pie made of pastry folded over a filling
2 : PROSTITUTE

tar·tan \'tär-t°n\ *noun* [probably from Middle French *tiretaine* linsey-woolsey] (circa 1500)
1 : a plaid textile design of Scottish origin consisting of stripes of varying width and color usually patterned to designate a distinctive clan
2 a : a twilled woolen fabric with tartan design **b** : a fabric with tartan design
3 : a garment of tartan design

¹tar·tar \'tär-tər\ *noun* [Middle English, from Medieval Latin *tartarum*] (14th century)
1 : a substance consisting essentially of cream of tartar that is derived from the juice of grapes and deposited in wine casks together with yeast and other suspended matters as a pale or dark reddish crust or sediment; *especially* : a recrystallized product yielding cream of tartar on further purification
2 : an incrustation on the teeth consisting of salivary secretion, food residue, and various salts (as calcium carbonate)

²tartar *noun* [Middle English *Tartre*, from Middle French *Tartare*, probably from Medieval Latin *Tartarus*, modification of Persian *Tātār* — more at TATAR] (14th century)
1 *capitalized* : a native or inhabitant of Tatary
2 *capitalized* : TATAR 2
3 *often capitalized* : a person of irritable or violent temper
4 : one that proves to be unexpectedly formidable
— **Tartar** *adjective*
— **Tar·tar·i·an** \tär-'tar-ē-ən, -'ter-\ *adjective*

Tar·tar·e·an \tär-'tar-ē-ən, -'ter-\ *adjective* [Latin *tartareus*, from Greek *tartareios*, from *Tartaros* Tartarus] (circa 1623)
: of, relating to, or resembling Tartarus : INFERNAL

tartar emetic *noun* (1704)
: a poisonous efflorescent crystalline salt $KSbOC_4H_4O_6 \cdot \frac{1}{2}H_2O$ of sweetish metallic taste that is used in dyeing as a mordant and in medicine especially in the treatment of amebiasis

tar·tar·ic acid \(,)tär-'tar-ik-\ *noun* (1810)
: a strong dicarboxylic acid $C_4H_6O_6$ of plant origin that occurs in three optically isomeric forms, is usually obtained from tartar, and is used especially in food and medicines, in photography, and in making salts and esters

tar·tar sauce *or* **tar·tare sauce** \'tär-tər-\ *noun* [French *sauce tartare*] (1855)
: a sauce made principally of mayonnaise and chopped pickles

Tar·ta·rus \'tär-tə-rəs\ *noun* [Latin, from Greek *Tartaros*]

: a section of Hades reserved for punishment of the wicked

tart·let \'tärt-lət\ *noun* (15th century)
: a small tart

tar·trate \'tär-,trāt\ *noun* [International Scientific Vocabulary, from French *tartre* tartar, from Medieval Latin *tartarum*] (1794)
: a salt or ester of tartaric acid

Tar·tuffe \,tär-'tüf, -'tüf\ *noun* [French *Tartufe*]
: a religious hypocrite and protagonist in Molière's play *Tartuffe*

tart up *transitive verb* (1938)
: DRESS UP, FANCY UP ⟨*tarted up* pubs and restaurants for the spenders —Arnold Ehrlich⟩

tarty \'tär-(,)tē\ *adjective* [²*tart*] (1918)
: resembling or suggestive of a prostitute (as in clothing or manner)

¹task \'task\ *noun* [Middle English *taske*, from Old North French *tasque*, from Medieval Latin *tasca* tax or service imposed by a feudal superior, from *taxare* to tax] (14th century)
1 a : a usually assigned piece of work often to be finished within a certain time **b** : something hard or unpleasant that has to be done **c** : DUTY, FUNCTION
2 : subjection to adverse criticism : REPRIMAND — used in the expressions *to take, call,* or *bring to task* ☆

²task *transitive verb* (15th century)
1 *obsolete* : to impose a tax on
2 : to assign a task to
3 : to oppress with great labor ⟨*tasks* his mind with petty details⟩

task force *noun* (1941)
: a temporary grouping under one leader for the purpose of accomplishing a definite objective

task·mas·ter \'task-,mas-tər\ *noun* (1530)
: one that imposes a task or burdens another with labor

task·mis·tress \-,mis-trəs\ *noun* (1603)
: a woman who is a taskmaster

Tas·ma·nian devil \(,)taz-'mā-nē-ən-, -nyən-\ *noun* (1867)
: a powerful heavily built carnivorous terrestrial Tasmanian marsupial (*Sarcophilus harrisii*) that is about the size of a badger and has a chiefly black coat marked with white on the chest

Tasmanian wolf *noun* (circa 1890)
: a somewhat doglike carnivorous marsupial (*Thylacinus cynocephalus*) that formerly inhabited Tasmania but is now considered extinct — called also *Tasmanian tiger*

tasse \'tas\ *noun* [perhaps from Middle French *tasse* purse, pouch] (circa 1548)
: one of a series of overlapping metal plates in a suit of armor that form a short skirt over the body below the waist — see ARMOR illustration

☆ SYNONYMS
Task, duty, job, chore, stint, assignment mean a piece of work to be done. TASK implies work imposed by a person in authority or an employer or by circumstance ⟨charged with a variety of *tasks*⟩. DUTY implies an obligation to perform or responsibility for performance ⟨the *duties* of a lifeguard⟩. JOB applies to a piece of work voluntarily performed; it may sometimes suggest difficulty or importance ⟨the *job* of turning the company around⟩. CHORE implies a minor routine activity necessary for maintaining a household or farm ⟨every child was assigned *chores*⟩. STINT implies a carefully allotted or measured quantity of assigned work or service ⟨a two-month *stint* as a reporter⟩. ASSIGNMENT implies a definite limited task assigned by one in authority ⟨a reporter's *assignment*⟩.

¹tas·sel \'ta-səl, *oftenest of corn* 'tä-, 'tȯ-\ *noun* [Middle English, clasp, tassel, from Middle French, from (assumed) Vulgar Latin *tassellus*, alteration of Latin *taxillus* small die; akin to Latin *talus* anklebone, die] (14th century)
1 : a dangling ornament made by laying parallel a bunch of cords or threads of even length and fastening them at one end
2 : something resembling a tassel; *especially* : the terminal male inflorescence of some plants and especially Indian corn

tassel 1

²tassel *verb* **-seled** *or* **-selled;** **-sel·ing** *or* **-sel·ling** \-s(ə-)liŋ\ (14th century)
transitive verb
: to adorn with tassels
intransitive verb
: to put forth tassel inflorescences

¹taste \'tāst\ *verb* **tast·ed; tast·ing** [Middle English, to touch, test, taste, from Middle French *taster*, from (assumed) Vulgar Latin *taxitare*, frequentative of Latin *taxare* to touch, feel — more at TAX] (14th century)
transitive verb
1 : to become acquainted with by experience ⟨has *tasted* the frustration of defeat⟩
2 : to ascertain the flavor of by taking a little into the mouth
3 : to eat or drink especially in small quantities
4 : to perceive or recognize as if by the sense of taste
5 *archaic* : APPRECIATE, ENJOY
intransitive verb
1 : to eat or drink a little
2 : to test the flavor of something by taking a small part into the mouth
3 : to have perception, experience, or enjoyment : PARTAKE — often used with *of*
4 : to have a specific flavor ⟨the apple *tastes* sour⟩

²taste *noun* (14th century)
1 *obsolete* : TEST
2 a *obsolete* : the act of tasting **b** : a small amount tasted **c** : a small amount : BIT; *especially* : a sample of experience ⟨first *taste* of success⟩
3 : the one of the special senses that perceives and distinguishes the sweet, sour, bitter, or salty quality of a dissolved substance and is mediated by taste buds on the tongue
4 : the objective sweet, sour, bitter, or salty quality of a dissolved substance as perceived by the sense of taste
5 a : a sensation obtained from a substance in the mouth that is typically produced by the stimulation of the sense of taste combined with those of touch and smell : FLAVOR **b** : the distinctive quality of an experience ⟨that gruesome scene left a bad *taste* in my mouth⟩
6 : individual preference : INCLINATION
7 a : critical judgment, discernment, or appreciation **b** : manner or aesthetic quality indicative of such discernment or appreciation
taste bud *noun* (1879)
: an end organ mediating the sensation of taste and lying chiefly in the epithelium of the tongue
taste·ful \'tāst-fəl\ *adjective* (1611)
1 : TASTY 1a
2 : having, exhibiting, or conforming to good taste
— **taste·ful·ly** \-fə-lē\ *adverb*
— **taste·ful·ness** *noun*
taste·less \'tāst-ləs\ *adjective* (1603)
1 a : having no taste : INSIPID ⟨*tasteless* vegetables⟩ **b** : arousing no interest : DULL ⟨the tale comes to a flat and *tasteless* end —R. C. Carpenter⟩
2 : not having or exhibiting good taste
— **taste·less·ly** *adverb*
— **taste·less·ness** *noun*
taste·mak·er \-,mā-kər\ *noun* (1954)

: one who sets the standards of what is currently popular or fashionable
tast·er \'tā-stər\ *noun* (15th century)
1 : one that tastes: as **a** : one that tests (as tea) for quality by tasting **b** : a person who is able to taste the chemical phenylthiocarbamide
2 : a device for tasting or sampling
tasty \'tā-stē\ *adjective* **tast·i·er; -est** (1617)
1 a : having a marked and appetizing flavor **b** : strikingly attractive or interesting ⟨a *tasty* bit of gossip⟩
2 : TASTEFUL
synonym see PALATABLE
— **tast·i·ly** \-stə-lē\ *adverb*
— **tast·i·ness** \-stē-nəs\ *noun*
tat \'tat\ *verb* **tat·ted; tat·ting** [back-formation from *tatting*] (1882)
intransitive verb
: to work at tatting
transitive verb
: to make by tatting
ta·ta·mi \tä-'tä-mē, ta-\ *noun, plural* **-mi** *or* **-mis** [Japanese] (1614)
: straw matting used as a floor covering in a Japanese home
Ta·tar \'tä-tər\ *noun* [Persian *Tātār*, of Turkic origin; akin to Turkish *Tatar* Tatar] (1811)
1 : a member of any of a group of Turkic peoples found mainly in the Tatar Republic of Russia and parts of Siberia and central Asia
2 : any of the Turkic languages spoken by the Tatar peoples
ta·ter \'tā-tər\ *noun* [by shortening & alteration] (1759)
dialect : POTATO
¹tat·ter \'ta-tər\ (14th century)
transitive verb
: to make ragged
intransitive verb
: to become ragged
²tatter *noun* [Middle English, of Scandinavian origin; akin to Old Norse *tǫturr* tatter; akin to Old English *tætteca*, Old High German *zotta* matted hair, tuft] (15th century)
1 : a part torn and left hanging : SHRED
2 *plural* : tattered clothing : RAGS
¹tat·ter·de·ma·lion \,ta-tər-di-'māl-yən, -'mal-, -'ma-lē-ən\ *noun* [origin unknown] (1611)
: a person dressed in ragged clothing : RAGA-MUFFIN
²tatterdemalion *adjective* (1614)
1 a : ragged or disreputable in appearance **b** : being in a decayed state or condition : DILAPIDATED
2 : BEGGARLY, DISREPUTABLE
tat·tered \'ta-tərd\ *adjective* (14th century)
1 : wearing ragged clothes ⟨a *tattered* barefoot boy⟩
2 : torn into shreds : RAGGED ⟨a *tattered* flag⟩
3 a : broken down : DILAPIDATED ⟨decaying houses along *tattered* paved streets —P. B. Martin⟩ **b** : being in a shattered condition : DISRUPTED ⟨led their *tattered* party to victory⟩
tat·ter·sall \'ta-tər-,sȯl, -səl\ *noun* [*Tattersall's* horse market, London, England] (1891)
1 : a pattern of colored lines forming squares of solid background
2 : a fabric woven or printed in a tattersall pattern
tat·tie \'ta-tē\ *noun* [by shortening & alteration] (1788)
Scottish : POTATO
tat·ting \'ta-tiŋ\ *noun* [origin unknown] (1842)
1 : a delicate handmade lace formed usually by looping and knotting with a single cotton thread and a small shuttle

tatting 1

2 : the act or process of making tatting
¹tat·tle \'ta-t³l\ *noun* (circa 1529)
1 : idle talk : CHATTER
2 : GOSSIP

²tattle *verb* **tat·tled; tat·tling** \'tat-liŋ, 'ta-t³l-iŋ\ [Middle Dutch *tatelen*; akin to Middle English *tateren* to tattle] (1547)
intransitive verb
1 : CHATTER, PRATE
2 : to tell secrets : BLAB
transitive verb
: to utter or disclose in gossip or chatter
tat·tler \'tat-lər, 'ta-t³l-ər\ *noun* (1550)
1 : TATTLETALE
2 : any of various slender long-legged shorebirds (as the willet, yellowlegs, and redshank) with a loud and frequent call
tat·tle·tale \'ta-t³l-,tāl\ *noun* (1888)
: one that tattles : INFORMER
¹tat·too \ta-'tü\ *noun, plural* **tattoos** [alteration of earlier *taptoo*, from Dutch *taptoe*, from the phrase *tap toe!* taps shut!] (circa 1627)
1 : a rapid rhythmic rapping
2 a : a call sounded shortly before taps as notice to go to quarters **b** : outdoor military exercise given by troops as evening entertainment
²tattoo (1780)
transitive verb
: to beat or rap rhythmically on : drum on
intransitive verb
: to give a series of rhythmic taps
³tattoo *transitive verb* [Tahitian *tatau*, noun, tattoo] (1769)
1 : to mark or color (the skin) with tattoos
2 : to mark the skin with (a tattoo) ⟨*tattooed* a flag on his chest⟩
— **tat·too·er** *noun*
— **tat·too·ist** \-'tü-ist\ *noun*
⁴tattoo *noun, plural* **tattoos** (1777)
1 : the act of tattooing : the fact of being tattooed
2 : an indelible mark or figure fixed upon the body by insertion of pigment under the skin or by production of scars
tat·ty \'ta-tē\ *adjective* **tat·ti·er; -est** [perhaps akin to Old English *tætteca* rag — more at TATTER] (1513)
: rather worn, frayed, or dilapidated : SHABBY
— **tat·ti·ness** \-nəs\ *noun*
tau \'taú, 'tȯ\ *noun* [Middle English *taw*, from Latin *tau*, from Greek, of Semitic origin; akin to Hebrew *tāw* taw] (14th century)
1 : the 19th letter of the Greek alphabet — see ALPHABET table
2 : a short-lived elementary particle of the lepton family that exists in positive and negative charge states and has a mass about 3500 times heavier than an electron — called also *tau particle*
tau cross *noun* (15th century)
: a T-shaped cross sometimes having expanded ends and foot — see CROSS illustration
taught *past and past participle of* TEACH
¹taunt \'tȯnt, 'tänt\ *noun* (circa 1529)
: a sarcastic challenge or insult
²taunt *transitive verb* [perhaps from Middle French *tenter* to try, tempt — more at TEMPT] (1539)
: to reproach or challenge in a mocking or insulting manner : jeer at
synonym SEE RIDICULE
— **taunt·er** *noun*
— **taunt·ing·ly** \'tȯn-tiŋ-lē, 'tän-\ *adverb*
taupe \'tōp\ *noun* [French, literally, mole, from Latin *talpa*] (circa 1909)
: a brownish gray
Tau·re·an \'tȯr-ē-ən\ *noun* (1911)
: TAURUS 2b
¹tau·rine \'tȯ-,rīn\ *adjective* [Latin *taurinus*, from Greek *tauros* bull; akin to Greek *tauros* bull, Middle Irish *tarb*] (1613)
: of or relating to a bull : BOVINE

²tau·rine \'tȯ-ˌrēn\ *noun* [International Scientific Vocabulary, from Latin *taurus;* from its having been discovered in ox bile] (1845) : a colorless crystalline cysteine derivative $C_2H_7NO_3S$ of neutral reaction found in the juices of muscle especially in invertebrates, nerve tissue, and bile

tau·ro·cho·lic acid \ˌtȯr-ə-ˈkō-lik-, -ˈkä-\ *noun* [Latin *taurus* + International Scientific Vocabulary -*o*- + *cholic* (*acid*)] (1857) : a deliquescent acid $C_{26}H_{45}NO_7S$ occurring as the sodium salt in the bile of the ox, humans, and various carnivores

Tau·rus \'tȯr-əs\ *noun* [Middle English, from Latin (genitive *Tauri*), literally, bull] **1** : a zodiacal constellation that contains the Pleiades and Hyades and is represented pictorially by a bull's forequarters **2 a** : the 2d sign of the zodiac in astrology **b** : one born under the sign of Taurus — see ZODIAC table

¹taut \'tȯt\ *adjective* [Middle English *tought*] (14th century) **1 a** : having no give or slack : tightly drawn **b** : HIGH-STRUNG, TENSE ⟨*taut* nerves⟩ **2 a** : kept in proper order or condition ⟨a *taut* ship⟩ **b** (1) : not loose or flabby (2) : marked by economy of structure and detail ⟨a *taut* story⟩ — **taut·ly** *adverb* — **taut·ness** *noun*

²taut *transitive verb* [origin unknown] (1721) *Scottish* : MAT, TANGLE

taut- *or* **tauto-** *combining form* [Late Latin, from Greek, from *tauto* the same, contraction of *to auto*] : same ⟨*tauto*merism⟩ ⟨*tauto*nym⟩

taut·en \'tȯt-ᵊn\ *verb* **taut·ened; taut·en·ing** \'tȯt-niŋ, 'tȯt-ᵊn-iŋ\ (circa 1814) *transitive verb* : to make taut *intransitive verb* : to become taut

tau·tog \'tȯ-ˌtȯg, -ˌtäg, tȯ-ˈ\ *noun* [Narraganset *tautaûog,* plural] (1643) : an edible fish (*Tautoga onitis*) of the wrasse family found along the Atlantic coast of the U.S. and adjacent Canada — called also *blackfish*

tau·to·log·i·cal \ˌtȯ-tᵊl-ˈä-ji-kəl\ *adjective* (1620) : TAUTOLOGOUS — **tau·to·log·i·cal·ly** \-k(ə-)lē\ *adverb*

tau·tol·o·gous \tȯ-ˈtä-lə-gəs\ *adjective* [Greek *tautologos,* from *taut-* + *legein* to say — more at LEGEND] (1714) **1** : involving or containing rhetorical tautology : REDUNDANT **2** : true by virtue of its logical form alone — **tau·tol·o·gous·ly** *adverb*

tau·tol·o·gy \tȯ-ˈtä-lə-jē\ *noun, plural* **-gies** [Late Latin *tautologia,* from Greek, from *tautologos*] (1574) **1 a** : needless repetition of an idea, statement, or word **b** : an instance of tautology **2** : a tautologous statement

tau·to·mer \'tȯ-tə-mər\ *noun* [International Scientific Vocabulary, from *tautomeric*] (1903) : any of the forms of a tautomeric compound

tau·to·mer·ic \ˌtȯ-tə-ˈmer-ik\ *adjective* [International Scientific Vocabulary] (circa 1890) : of, relating to, or marked by tautomerism

tau·tom·er·ism \tȯ-ˈtä-mə-ˌri-zəm\ *noun* (circa 1890) : isomerism in which the isomers change into one another with great ease so that they ordinarily exist together in equilibrium

taut·o·nym \'tȯ-tə-ˌnim\ *noun* (1899) : a taxonomic binomial in which the generic name and specific epithet are alike and which is common in zoology especially to designate a typical form but is forbidden to botany under the International Code of Botanical Nomenclature

— **tau·ton·y·my** \tȯ-ˈtä-nə-mē\ *noun*

tav·ern \'ta-vərn\ *noun* [Middle English *taverne,* from Old French, from Latin *taberna* hut, shop] (14th century) **1** : an establishment where alcoholic beverages are sold to be drunk on the premises **2** : INN

ta·ver·na \tä-ˈver-nə\ *noun* [New Greek *taberna,* probably from Late Greek, drinking establishment, from Latin *taberna*] (1914) : a café in Greece

tav·ern·er \'tav-ə(r)-nər\ *noun* (14th century) : one who keeps a tavern

¹taw \'tȯ\ *transitive verb* [Middle English, to prepare for use, from Old English *tawian;* akin to Old High German *zawjan* to hasten, Gothic *taujan* to do, make] (before 12th century) : to dress (skins) usually by a dry process (as with alum or salt)

²taw \'täf, 'tȯf, 'täv, 'tȯv\ *noun* [Hebrew *tāw,* literally, mark, cross] (1701) : the 23d letter of the Hebrew alphabet — see ALPHABET table

³taw *noun* [origin unknown] (1709) **1 a** : a marble used as a shooter **b** : RINGTAW **2** : the line from which players shoot at marbles **3** : a square-dance partner

⁴taw *intransitive verb* (1863) : to shoot a marble

¹taw·dry \'tȯ-drē, 'tä-\ *adjective* **taw·dri·er; -est** [*tawdry lace* a tie of lace for the neck, from *Saint Audrey* (Saint Etheldreda) (died 679) queen of Northumbria] (1676) : cheap and gaudy in appearance or quality; *also* : IGNOBLE

synonym see GAUDY — **taw·dri·ly** \-drə-lē\ *adverb* — **taw·dri·ness** \-drē-nəs\ *noun*

²tawdry *noun* (circa 1680) : cheap showy finery

¹taw·ny \'tȯ-nē, 'tä-nē\ *adjective* **taw·ni·er; -est** [Middle English, from Middle French *tanné,* past participle of *tanner* to tan] (14th century) **1** : of the color tawny **2** : of a warm sandy color like that of well-tanned skin ⟨the lion's *tawny* coat⟩ — **taw·ni·ness** *noun*

²tawny *noun, plural* **tawnies** (15th century) : a brownish orange to light brown color

taw·pie \'tȯ-pē\ *noun* [of Scandinavian origin; akin to Norwegian *tåpe* simpleton] (1728) *chiefly Scottish* : a foolish or awkward young person

tawse *also* **taws** \'tȯz\ *noun plural but singular or plural in construction* [probably from plural of obsolete *taw* tawed leather] (circa 1585) *British* : a leather strap slit into strips at the end and used especially for disciplining children

¹tax \'taks\ *transitive verb* [Middle English, to estimate, assess, tax, from Old French *taxer,* from Medieval Latin *taxare,* from Latin, to feel, estimate, censure, frequentative of *tangere* to touch — more at TANGENT] (14th century) **1** : to assess or determine judicially the amount of (costs in a court action) **2** : to levy a tax on **3** *obsolete* : to enter (a name) in a list ⟨there went out a decree . . . that all the world should be *taxed* —Luke 2:1 (Authorized Version)⟩ **4** : CHARGE, ACCUSE ⟨*taxed* him with neglect of duty⟩; *also* : CENSURE **5** : to make onerous and rigorous demands on ⟨the job *taxed* her strength⟩ — **tax·able** \'tak-sə-bəl\ *adjective* — **tax·er** *noun*

²tax *noun, often attributive* (14th century) **1 a** : a charge usually of money imposed by authority on persons or property for public purposes **b** : a sum levied on members of an organization to defray expenses **2** : a heavy demand

tax- *or* **taxo-** *also* **taxi-** *combining form* [Greek *taxi-,* from *taxis*] : arrangement ⟨*taxe*me⟩ ⟨*taxi*dermy⟩

taxa *plural of* TAXON

tax·a·tion \tak-ˈsā-shən\ *noun* (14th century) **1** : the action of taxing; *especially* : the imposition of taxes **2** : revenue obtained from taxes **3** : the amount assessed as a tax

tax base *noun* (circa 1943) : the wealth (as real estate or income) within a jurisdiction that is liable to taxation

tax·eme \'tak-ˌsēm\ *noun* [*tax-*] (1933) : a minimum grammatical feature of selection, order, stress, pitch, or phonetic modification — **tax·e·mic** \tak-ˈsē-mik\ *adjective*

tax-ex·empt \ˌtaks-ig-ˈzem(p)t\ *adjective* (1923) **1** : exempted from a tax **2** : bearing interest that is free from federal or state income tax

¹taxi \'tak-sē\ *noun, plural* **tax·is** \-sēz\ *also* **tax·ies** (circa 1907) : TAXICAB; *also* : a similarly operated boat or aircraft ◇

²taxi *verb* **tax·ied; taxi·ing** *or* **taxy·ing; tax·is** *or* **tax·ies** (1916) *intransitive verb* **1 a** *of an aircraft* : to go at low speed along the surface of the ground or water **b** : to operate an aircraft on the ground under its own power **2** : to ride in a taxicab *transitive verb* **1** : to transport by or as if by taxi **2** : to cause (an aircraft) to taxi

taxi·cab \'tak-sē-ˌkab\ *noun* [*taximeter cab*] (circa 1907) : an automobile that carries passengers for a fare usually determined by the distance traveled

taxi dancer *noun* (circa 1927) : a girl employed by a dance hall, café, or cabaret to dance with patrons who pay a certain amount for each dance

taxi·der·my \'tak-sə-ˌdər-mē\ *noun* [*tax-* + *derm-* + *²-y*] (1820)

◇ WORD HISTORY

taxi *Taxi* in the sense "an automobile that carries passengers for a fare usually determined by distance" is shortened from *taxicab,* itself shortened from *taximeter cab.* The taximeter is the mechanical device in a taxi that is activated when the ride starts and automatically shows the fare due at the end of the ride. Meters of this kind were first used in 19th century Germany under the name *Taxameter,* attached to horsedrawn vehicles for hire. *Taxameter* was made up irregularly in terms of the rules of Greco-Latin word formation from *Taxe* "fee, tax," Latinized to *taxa* (which happens to be the original Medieval Latin form from which *Taxe* was ultimately borrowed), and *-meter,* which as in English is used in names of measuring instruments. (The regular outcome would have been *Taxometer.*) The word soon showed up in French as *taxamètre* and in English as *taxameter,* but both languages then altered the internal *-a-* to *-i-,* yielding French *taximètre* and English *taximeter.* Though these forms violate no rules of the classical languages, they assume a nonexistent connection with Greek *taxis* "arrangement." Etymological confusion notwithstanding, *taxi* has become an international word, finding its way into languages as diverse as Arabic (*taksi*) and Japanese (*takushī*).

: the art of preparing, stuffing, and mounting the skins of animals and especially vertebrates
— **taxi·der·mic** \,tak-sə-'dər-mik\ *adjective*
— **taxi·der·mist** \'tak-sə-,dər-mist\ *noun*

taxi·man \'tak-sē-mən\ *noun* (1909)
chiefly British : the operator of a taxi

taxi·me·ter \'tak-sē-,mē-tər\ *noun* [French *taximètre*, modification of German *Taxameter*, from Medieval Latin *taxa* tax, charge (from *taxare* to tax) + German *-meter*] (1894)
: an instrument for use in a hired vehicle (as a taxicab) for automatically showing the fare due
word history see TAXI

tax·ing \'tak-siŋ\ *adjective* (1841)
: ONEROUS, WEARING ⟨a *taxing* operatic role⟩
— **tax·ing·ly** \-siŋ-lē\ *adverb*

tax·is \'tak-səs\ *noun, plural* **tax·es** \-,sēz\ [Greek, literally, arrangement, order, from *tassein* to arrange] (1758)
1 : reflex translational or orientational movement by a freely motile and usually simple organism in relation to a source of stimulation (as a light or a temperature or chemical gradient)
2 : a reflex reaction involving a taxis

-taxis *noun combining form, plural* **-taxes** [New Latin, from Greek, from *taxis*]
1 : arrangement : ordering ⟨thermo*taxis*⟩
2 : physiological taxis ⟨chemo*taxis*⟩

taxi stand *noun* (1922)
: a place where taxis may park while awaiting hire

taxi·way \'tak-sē-,wā\ *noun* (circa 1933)
: a usually paved strip for taxiing (as from the terminal to a runway) at an airport

tax·on \'tak-,sän\ *noun, plural* **taxa** \-sə\ *also* **tax·ons** [New Latin, from International Scientific Vocabulary *taxonomy*] (1929)
1 : a taxonomic group or entity
2 : the name applied to a taxonomic group in a formal system of nomenclature

tax·on·o·my \tak-'sä-nə-mē\ *noun* [French *taxonomie*, from *tax-* + *-nomie* -nomy] (circa 1828)
1 : the study of the general principles of scientific classification : SYSTEMATICS
2 : CLASSIFICATION; *especially* : orderly classification of plants and animals according to their presumed natural relationships
— **tax·o·nom·ic** \,tak-sə-'nä-mik\ *adjective*
— **tax·o·nom·i·cal·ly** \-mi-k(ə-)lē\ *adverb*
— **tax·on·o·mist** \tak-'sä-nə-mist\ *noun*

tax·pay·er \'taks-,pā-ər\ *noun* (1816)
: one that pays or is liable for a tax

tax·pay·ing \-,pā-iŋ\ *adjective* (1832)
: of, relating to, or subject to the paying of a tax

tax selling *noun* (1963)
: concerted selling of securities late in the year to establish gains and losses for income-tax purposes

tax shelter *noun* (1952)
: a strategy, investment, or tax code provision that reduces tax liability
— **tax–shel·tered** \'taks-,shel-tərd\ *adjective*

tax stamp *noun* (circa 1929)
: a stamp marked on or affixed to a taxable item as evidence that the tax has been paid

tax·us \'tak-səs\ *noun, plural* **tax·us** \-səs\ [New Latin, genus comprising the yews, from Latin, yew] (circa 1945)
: YEW 1a

-taxy *noun combining form* [Greek *-taxia*, from *taktos*, verbal of *tassein* to arrange]
: -TAXIS (epi*taxy*)

Tay·lor's series \'tā-lərz-\ *noun* [Brook *Taylor* (died 1731) English mathematician] (1842)
: a power series that gives the expansion of a function $f(x)$ in the neighborhood of a point a provided that in the neighborhood the function is continuous, all its derivatives exist, and the series converges to the function in which case it has the form

$$f(x) = f(a) + \frac{f^{[1]}(a)}{1!}(x-a) + \frac{f^{[2]}(a)}{2!}(x-a)^2 + \ldots$$
$$+ \frac{f^{[n]}(a)}{n!}(x-a)^n + \ldots$$

where $f^{[n]}(a)$ is the derivative of nth order of $f(x)$ evaluated at a — called also *Taylor series*

Tay–Sachs disease \'tā-'saks-\ *noun* [Warren *Tay* (died 1927) British physician & Bernard P. *Sachs* (died 1944) American neurologist] (1907)
: a hereditary disorder of lipid metabolism typically affecting individuals of eastern European Jewish ancestry that is characterized by the accumulation of lipids especially in nervous tissue due to a deficiency of hexosaminidase and causes death in early childhood — called also *Tay-Sachs*

taz·za \'tät-sə\ *noun* [Italian, cup, from Arabic *ṭassah*] (1824)
: a shallow cup or vase on a pedestal

TB \,tē-'bē\ *noun* [*TB* (abbreviation for *tubercle bacillus*)] (1912)
: TUBERCULOSIS

T-ball \'tē-,bȯl\ *noun* [²*tee*] (1976)
: baseball modified for youngsters in which the ball is batted from a tee rather than being pitched

T–bar \'tē-,bär\ *noun* (1948)
: a ski lift having a series of T-shaped bars each of which pulls two skiers — called also *T-bar lift*

T–bill \'tē-,bil\ *noun* [Treasury] (1973)
: a U.S. treasury note

T–bone \'tē-,bōn\ *noun* (circa 1916)
: a small steak from the thin end of the short loin containing a T-shaped bone and a small piece of tenderloin; *also* : this bone — see BEEF illustration

TCDD \,tē-(,)sē-(,)dē-'dē\ *noun* [tetra- + chlor- + *di*benzo- (containing two benzene rings) + *di*oxin] (1971)
: a carcinogenic dioxin $C_{12}H_4O_2Cl_4$ found especially as a contaminant in 2,4,5-T

T cell *noun* [*t*hymus-derived *cell*] (1970)
: any of several lymphocytes (as a helper T cell) that differentiate in the thymus, possess highly specific cell-surface antigen receptors, and include some that initiation or suppression of cell-mediated and humoral immunity (as by the regulation of T and B cell maturation and proliferation) and others that lyse antigen-bearing cells — called also *T lymphocyte*; compare B CELL

tchotch·ke \'chäch-kə, 'tsäts-\ *noun* [Yiddish *tshatshke* trinket, from obsolete Polish *czaczko*] (1971)
: KNICKKNACK, TRINKET

t distribution *noun* (circa 1957)
: a probability density function that is used especially in testing hypotheses concerning means of normal distributions whose standard deviations are unknown and that is the distribution of a random variable

$$t = \frac{u\sqrt{n}}{v}$$

where u and v are themselves independent random variables and u has a normal distribution with mean 0 and a standard deviation of 1 and v^2 has a chi-square distribution with n degrees of freedom — called also *student's t distribution*

tea \'tē\ *noun* [Chinese (Xiamen) *t'e*] (circa 1655)
1 a : a shrub (*Camellia sinensis* of the family Theaceae, the tea family) cultivated especially in China, Japan, and the East Indies **b** : the leaves, leaf buds, and internodes of the tea plant prepared and cured for the market, classed according to method of manufacture into one set of types (as green tea, black tea, or oolong), and graded according to leaf size into another (as orange pekoe, pekoe, or souchong)
2 : an aromatic beverage prepared from tea leaves by infusion with boiling water
3 : any of various plants somewhat resembling tea in properties; *also* : an infusion of their leaves used medicinally or as a beverage
4 a : refreshments usually including tea with sandwiches, crackers, or cookies served in late afternoon **b** : a reception at which tea is served
5 *slang* : MARIJUANA
— **tea·like** \-,līk\ *adjective*

tea bag *noun* (1935)
: a bag usually of filter paper holding enough tea for an individual serving

tea ball *noun* (1895)
: a perforated metal ball that holds tea leaves and is used in brewing tea in a pot or cup

tea·ber·ry \'tē-,ber-ē\ *noun* [from the use of its leaves as a substitute for tea] (1818)
: CHECKERBERRY

tea caddy *noun* (1790)
: CADDY

tea cake *noun* (1824)
1 : a small flat cake usually made with raisins
2 : COOKIE

tea cart *noun* (1817)
: TEA WAGON

teach \'tēch\ *verb* **taught** \'tȯt\; **teach·ing** [Middle English *techen* to show, instruct, from Old English *tǣcan*; akin to Old English *tācn* sign — more at TOKEN] (before 12th century)
transitive verb
1 a : to cause to know something ⟨*taught* them a trade⟩ **b** : to cause to know how ⟨is *teaching* me to drive⟩ **c** : to accustom to some action or attitude ⟨*teach* students to think for themselves⟩ **d** : to cause to know the disagreeable consequences of some action ⟨I'll *teach* you to come home late⟩
2 : to guide the studies of
3 : to impart the knowledge of ⟨*teach* algebra⟩
4 a : to instruct by precept, example, or experience **b** : to make known and accepted ⟨experience *teaches* us our limitations⟩
5 : to conduct instruction regularly in ⟨*teach* school⟩
intransitive verb
: to provide instruction : act as a teacher ☆
usage see LEARN

teach·able \'tē-chə-bəl\ *adjective* (15th century)
1 a : capable of being taught **b** : apt and willing to learn
2 : favorable to teaching
— **teach·able·ness** *noun*
— **teach·ably** \-blē\ *adverb*

☆ **SYNONYMS**
Teach, instruct, educate, train, discipline, school mean to cause to acquire knowledge or skill. TEACH applies to any manner of imparting information or skill so that others may learn ⟨*taught* us a lot about our planet⟩. INSTRUCT suggests methodical or formal teaching ⟨*instructs* raw recruits in military drill⟩. EDUCATE implies development of the mind ⟨more things than formal schooling serve to *educate* a person⟩. TRAIN stresses instruction and drill with a specific end in view ⟨*trained* foreign pilots to operate the new aircraft⟩. DISCIPLINE implies training in habits of order and precision ⟨a *disciplined* mind⟩. SCHOOL implies training or disciplining especially in what is hard to master ⟨*schooled* the horse in five gaits⟩.

\ə\ **abut** \ə\ **kitten** \ər\ **further** \a\ **ash** \ā\ **ace**
\ä\ **mop, mar** \au̇\ **out** \ch\ **chin** \e\ **bet** \ē\ **easy**
\g\ **go** \i\ **hit** \ī\ **ice** \j\ **job** \ŋ\ **sing** \ō\ **go**
\ȯ\ **law** \ȯi\ **boy** \th\ **thin** \t͟h\ **the** \ü\ **loot** \u̇\ **foot**
\y\ **yet** \zh\ **vision** *see also* Guide to Pronunciation

teach·er \'tē-chər\ *noun* (14th century)
1 : one that teaches; *especially* : one whose occupation is to instruct
2 : a Mormon ranking above a deacon in the Aaronic priesthood

teach·er·ly \-lē\ *adjective* (circa 1683)
: resembling, characteristic of, or befitting a teacher

teachers college *noun* (circa 1911)
: a college for the training of teachers usually offering a full 4-year course and granting a bachelor's degree

teacher's pet *noun* (1914)
1 : a pupil who has won his teacher's special favor
2 : one who has ingratiated himself with an authority

teach–in \'tēch-,in\ *noun* (1965)
: an extended meeting usually held on a college campus for lectures, debates, and discussions to raise awareness of or express a position on a social or political issue

¹teaching *noun* (13th century)
1 : the act, practice, or profession of a teacher
2 : something taught; *especially* : DOCTRINE ⟨the *teachings* of Confucius⟩

²teaching *adjective* (1642)
: of, relating to, used for, or engaged in teaching ⟨a *teaching* aid⟩ ⟨the *teaching* profession⟩ ⟨a *teaching* assistant⟩

teaching hospital *noun* (circa 1951)
: a hospital that is affiliated with a medical school and provides means for medical education

tea·cup \'tē-,kəp\ *noun* (1700)
: a small cup usually with a handle used with a saucer for hot beverages
— **teacupful** *noun*

tea dance *noun* (1885)
: a dance held in the late afternoon

tea garden *noun* (1802)
1 : a public garden where tea and light refreshments are served
2 : a tea plantation

tea gown *noun* (1878)
: a semiformal gown of fine materials in graceful flowing lines worn especially for afternoon entertaining at home

tea·house \'tē-,haüs\ *noun* (1689)
: a public house or restaurant where tea and light refreshments are sold

teak \'tēk\ *noun* [Portuguese *teca*, from Malayalam *tēkka*] (1698)
1 : a tall East Indian timber tree (*Tectona grandis*) of the vervain family
2 : the hard yellowish brown wood of teak used especially for furniture and shipbuilding

tea·ket·tle \'tē-,ke-t³l\ *noun* (1705)
: a covered kettle with a handle and spout for boiling water

teak·wood \'tēk-,wüd\ *noun* (1783)
: TEAK 2

teal \'tē(ə)l\ *noun, plural* **teal** *or* **teals** [Middle English *tele*; akin to Middle Dutch *teling* teal] (14th century)
1 : any of various widely distributed small short-necked dabblers (genus *Anas*) — compare GREEN-WINGED TEAL
2 : TEAL BLUE

teal blue *noun* (1938)
: a dark greenish blue

teal 1

¹team \'tēm\ *noun* [Middle English *teme*, from Old English *tēam* offspring, lineage, group of draft animals; akin to Old High German *zoum* rein, Old English *tēon* to draw, pull — more at TOW] (before 12th century)
1 a : two or more draft animals harnessed to the same vehicle or implement; *also* : these with their harness and attached vehicle **b** : a draft animal often with harness and vehicle
2 *obsolete* : LINEAGE, RACE

3 : a group of animals: as **a** : a brood especially of young pigs or ducks **b** : a matched group of animals for exhibition
4 : a number of persons associated together in work or activity: as **a** : a group on one side (as in football or a debate) **b** : CREW, GANG

²team (1552)
transitive verb
1 : to yoke or join in a team; *also* : to put together in a coordinated ensemble
2 : to convey or haul with a team
intransitive verb
1 : to drive a team or motortruck
2 : to form a team or association : COLLABORATE ⟨*teamed* up to write a book⟩

³team *adjective* (1886)
: of or performed by a team ⟨a *team* effort⟩; *also* : marked by devotion to teamwork rather than individual achievement ⟨a *team* player⟩

team foul *noun* (1966)
: one of a designated number of personal fouls the players on a basketball team may commit during a given period of play before the opposing team begins receiving bonus free throws

team handball *noun* (1970)
: a game developed from soccer which is played between two teams of seven players each and in which the ball is thrown, caught, and dribbled with the hands

team·mate \'tēm-,māt\ *noun* (1915)
: a fellow member of a team

team·ster \'tēm(p)-stər\ *noun* (1777)
: one who drives a team or motortruck especially as an occupation

team·work \'tēm-,wərk\ *noun* (circa 1828)
: work done by several associates with each doing a part but all subordinating personal prominence to the efficiency of the whole

tea party *noun* (1778)
1 : an afternoon social gathering at which tea is served
2 [from the Boston Tea Party, name applied to the occasion in 1773 when a shipment of tea was thrown into Boston harbor in protest against the tax on imports] : an exciting disturbance or proceeding

tea·pot \'tē-,pät\ *noun* (1705)
: a vessel with a spout and a handle in which tea is brewed and from which it is served

tea·poy \'tē-,pöi\ *noun* [Hindi *tipāī*] (1828)
1 : a 3-legged ornamental stand
2 [influenced by *tea*] : a stand or table containing a tea chest or caddy and used for supporting a tea set; *also* : TEA CADDY

¹tear \'tir\ *noun* [Middle English, from Old English *tæhher, tēar*; akin to Old High German *zahar* tear, Greek *dakry*] (before 12th century)
1 a : a drop of clear saline fluid secreted by the lacrimal gland and diffused between the eye and eyelids to moisten the parts and facilitate their motion **b** *plural* : a secretion of profuse tears that overflow the eyelids and dampen the face
2 : a transparent drop of fluid or hardened fluid matter (as resin)
3 *plural* : an act of weeping or grieving ⟨broke into *tears*⟩
— **tear·less** *adjective*

²tear *intransitive verb* (before 12th century)
: to fill with tears : shed tears ⟨eyes *tearing* in the November wind —Saul Bellow⟩

³tear \'tar, 'ter\ *verb* **tore** \'tōr, 'tòr\; **torn** \'tōrn, 'tòrn\; **tear·ing** [Middle English *teren*, from Old English *teran*; akin to Old High German *zeran* to destroy, Greek *derein* to skin, Sanskrit *dṛṇāti* he bursts, tears] (before 12th century)
transitive verb
1 a : to separate parts of or pull apart by force : REND **b** : to wound by or as if by tearing : LACERATE ⟨*tear* the skin⟩
2 : to divide or disrupt by the pull of contrary forces ⟨a mind *torn* with doubts⟩

3 a : to remove by force : WRENCH — often used with *off* ⟨*tear* a cover off a box⟩ **b** : to remove as if by wrenching ⟨*tear* your thoughts away from the scene⟩
4 : to make or effect by or as if by tearing ⟨*tear* a hole in the wall⟩
intransitive verb
1 : to separate on being pulled : REND ⟨this cloth *tears* easily⟩
2 a : to move or act with violence, haste, or force ⟨went *tearing* down the street⟩ **b** : to smash or penetrate something with violent force ⟨the bullet *tore* through his leg⟩ ☆
— **tear·able** \'tar-ə-bəl, 'ter-\ *adjective*
— **tear·er** *noun*
— **tear at** : to cause anguish to : DISTRESS ⟨her grief *tore at* his heart⟩
— **tear into** : to attack without restraint or caution
— **tear it** : to cause frustration, defeat, or an end to plans or hopes ⟨that *tears it*⟩
— **tear one's hair** : to pull one's hair as an expression of grief, rage, frustration, desperation, or anxiety

⁴tear \'tar, 'ter\ *noun* (1611)
1 a : damage from being torn; *especially* : a hole or flaw made by tearing **b** : the act of tearing
2 a : a tearing pace : HURRY **b** : SPREE ⟨go on a *tear*⟩ **c** : a run of unusual success ⟨the team was on a *tear*⟩

tear·away \'tar-ə-,wā, 'ter-\ *noun* (1950)
British : a rebellious and unruly or reckless young person

tear away *transitive verb* (circa 1699)
: to remove (as oneself) reluctantly

tear·down \'tar-,daün, 'ter-\ *noun* (1926)
: the act or process of disassembling

tear down *transitive verb* (1614)
1 a : to cause to decompose or disintegrate **b** : VILIFY, DENIGRATE
2 : to take apart : DISASSEMBLE

tear·drop \'tir-,dräp\ *noun* (1789)
1 : ¹TEAR 1a
2 : something shaped like a dropping tear; *specifically* : a pendent gem (as on an earring)

tear·ful \'tir-fəl\ *adjective* (circa 1586)
1 : flowing with or accompanied by tears ⟨*tearful* entreaties⟩
2 : causing tears : TEARY
— **tear·ful·ly** \-fə-lē\ *adverb*
— **tear·ful·ness** *noun*

tear·gas \-,gas\ *transitive verb* (1946)
: to use tear gas on

tear gas *noun* (1917)
: a solid, liquid, or gaseous substance that on dispersion in the atmosphere blinds the eyes with tears and is used chiefly in dispelling mobs

tear·ing \'tar-iŋ, 'ter-\ *adjective* (1606)
1 : causing continued or repeated pain or distress
2 : HASTY, VIOLENT
3 *chiefly British* : SPLENDID

tear·jerk·er \'tir-,jər-kər\ *noun* (1912)

☆ SYNONYMS
Tear, rip, rend, split, cleave, rive mean to separate forcibly. TEAR implies pulling apart by force and leaving jagged edges ⟨*tear* up the letter⟩. RIP implies a pulling apart in one rapid uninterrupted motion often along a line or joint ⟨*ripped* the shirt on a nail⟩. REND implies very violent or ruthless severing or sundering ⟨an angry mob *rent* the prisoner's clothes⟩. SPLIT implies a cutting or breaking apart in a continuous, straight, and usually lengthwise direction or in the direction of grain or layers ⟨*split* logs for firewood⟩. CLEAVE implies very forceful splitting or cutting with a blow ⟨a bolt of lightning *cleaved* the giant oak⟩. RIVE occurs most often in figurative use ⟨a political party *riven* by conflict⟩.

: an extravagantly pathetic story, song, play, film, or broadcast
— **tear–jerk·ing** \-kiŋ\ *adjective*
tea-room \'tē-,rüm, -,ṙüm\ *noun* (1778)
: a small restaurant or café with service and decor designed primarily for a female clientele
tea rose *noun* (1850)
: a garden bush rose (*Rosa odorata*) of Chinese origin that includes several cultivars and is valued especially for its abundant large usually tea-scented blossoms — compare HYBRID TEA ROSE
tear sheet *noun* (circa 1924)
: a sheet torn from a publication
tear·stain \'tir-,stān\ *noun* (1922)
: a spot or streak left by tears
— **tear·stained** \-,stānd\ *adjective*
tear up *transitive verb* (1699)
: to damage, remove, or effect an opening in ⟨*tore up* the street to lay a new water main⟩
teary \'tir-ē\ *adjective* **tear·i·er; -est** (14th century)
1 a : wet or stained with tears : TEARFUL **b** : consisting of tears or drops resembling tears
2 : causing tears : PATHETIC ⟨a *teary* story⟩
¹tease \'tēz\ *transitive verb* **teased; teas·ing** [Middle English *tesen*, from Old English *tǣsan;* akin to Old High German *zeisan* to tease] (before 12th century)
1 a : to disentangle and lay parallel by combing or carding ⟨*tease* wool⟩ **b :** TEASEL
2 : to tear in pieces; *especially* : to shred (a tissue or specimen) for microscopic examination
3 a : to disturb or annoy by persistent irritating or provoking especially in a petty or mischievous way **b :** to annoy with petty persistent requests : PESTER; *also* : to obtain by repeated coaxing **c :** to persuade to acquiesce especially by persistent small efforts : COAX **d** : to manipulate or influence as if by teasing
4 : to comb (hair) by taking hold of a strand and pushing the short hairs toward the scalp with the comb
5 : to tantalize especially by arousing desire or curiosity without intending to satisfy it
synonym see WORRY
— **teas·ing·ly** \'tē-ziŋ-lē\ *adverb*
²tease *noun* (1693)
1 : the act of teasing : the state of being teased
2 : one that teases
¹tea·sel \'tē-zəl\ *noun* [Middle English *tesel*, from Old English *tǣsel;* akin to Old English *tǣsan* to tease] (before 12th century)
1 a : an Old World prickly herb (*Dipsacus fullonum* of the family Dipsacaceae, the teasel family) with flower heads that are covered with stiff hooked bracts and are used in the woolen industry — called also *fuller's teasel* **b :** a plant of the same genus as the teasel
2 a : a flower head of the fuller's teasel used when dried to raise a nap on woolen cloth **b** : a wire substitute for the teasel

teasel 1a

²teasel *transitive verb* **tea·seled** *or* **tea·selled; tea·sel·ing** *or* **tea·sel·ling** \'tēz-liŋ, 'tē-zə-\ (1543)
: to nap (cloth) with teasels
tease out *transitive verb* (1828)
: to obtain by or as if by disentangling or freeing with a pointed instrument
teas·er \'tē-zər\ *noun* (1659)
1 : one that teases
2 : an advertising or promotional device intended to arouse interest or curiosity especially in something to follow
tea service *noun* (1809)
: TEA SET
tea set *noun* (1849)
: a matching set of metalware or china (as a teapot, sugar bowl, creamer, and often plates, cups, and saucers) for serving tea and sometimes coffee at table

tea shop *noun* (1856)
chiefly British : a small restaurant or café
: TEAROOM
tea·spoon \'tē-,spün, -'spün\ *noun* (1686)
1 : a small spoon that is used especially for eating soft foods and stirring beverages and that holds one third of a tablespoon
2 : a unit of measure especially in cookery equal to ⅙ fluid ounces or ⅓ tablespoon (5 milliliters)
tea·spoon·ful \-,fül\ *noun, plural* **tea-spoonfuls** \-,fülz\ *also* **tea·spoons·ful** \-,spünz-,fül, -'spünz-\ (1731)
1 : as much as a teaspoon can hold
2 : TEASPOON 2
usage see ²-FUL
teat \'tit, 'tēt\ *noun* [Middle English *tete*, from Old French, of Germanic origin; akin to Old English *tit* teat, Middle High German *zitze*] (13th century)
1 : the protuberance through which milk is drawn from an udder or breast : NIPPLE
2 : a small projection or a nib (as on a mechanical part)
— **teat·ed** \'ti-təd, 'tē-\ *adjective*
tea table *noun* (1688)
: a table used or spread for tea; *specifically* : a small table for serving afternoon tea
tea·time \'tē-,tīm\ *noun* (1741)
: the customary time for tea : late afternoon or early evening
tea towel *noun* (1871)
: a cloth for drying dishes
tea tray *noun* (1773)
: a tray that accommodates a tea set
tea wagon *noun* (1921)
: a small table on wheels used in serving tea
Te·bet \tä-'vät, -'vāth, 'tä-,ves\ *noun* [Hebrew *Ṭēbhēth*] (14th century)
: the 4th month of the civil year or the 10th month of the ecclesiastical year in the Jewish calendar — see MONTH table
teched \'techt\ *adjective* [alteration of *touched*] (1921)
: mentally unbalanced
tech·ie \'te-kē\ *noun* [by shortening & alteration] (1982)
: TECHNICIAN 1
tech·ne·tium \tek-'nē-sh(ē-)əm\ *noun* [New Latin, from Greek *technētos* artificial, from *technasthai* to devise by art, from *technē*] (circa 1946)
: a metallic element obtained by bombarding molybdenum with deuterons or neutrons and in the fission of uranium — see ELEMENT table
tech·ne·tron·ic \,tek-nə-'trä-nik\ *adjective* [*technological* + *electronic*] (1967)
: shaped or influenced by the changes wrought by advances in technology and communications ⟨our modern *technetronic* society⟩
tech·nic \'tek-nik, *for 1 also* tek-'nēk\ *noun* (1855)
1 : TECHNIQUE 1
2 *plural but singular or plural in construction* : TECHNOLOGY 1a
tech·ni·cal \'tek-ni-kəl\ *adjective* [Greek *technikos* of art, skillful, from *technē* art, craft, skill; akin to Greek *tektōn* builder, carpenter, Latin *texere* to weave, Sanskrit *takṣati* he fashions] (1617)
1 a : having special and usually practical knowledge especially of a mechanical or scientific subject ⟨a *technical* consultant⟩ **b** : marked by or characteristic of specialization ⟨*technical* language⟩
2 a : of or relating to a particular subject **b** : of or relating to a practical subject organized on scientific principles ⟨a *technical* school⟩ **c** : TECHNOLOGICAL 1
3 a : based on or marked by a strict or legal interpretation **b :** LEGAL 6
4 : of or relating to technique
5 : of, relating to, or produced by ordinary commercial processes without being subjected to special purification ⟨*technical* sulfuric acid⟩

6 : relating to or caused by the functioning of the market as a discrete mechanism not influenced by macroeconomic factors ⟨*technical* rally⟩ ⟨*technical* analysis⟩
— **tech·ni·cal·ly** \-k(ə-)lē\ *adverb*
technical foul *noun* (circa 1929)
: a foul (as in basketball) that involves no physical contact with an opponent and that usually is incurred by unsportsmanlike conduct — called also *technical*; compare PERSONAL FOUL
tech·ni·cal·i·ty \,tek-nə-'ka-lə-tē\ *noun, plural* **-ties** (1814)
1 : something technical; *especially* : a detail meaningful only to a specialist ⟨a legal *technicality*⟩
2 : the quality or state of being technical
tech·ni·cal·ize \'tek-ni-kə-,līz\ *transitive verb* **-ized; -iz·ing** (1852)
: to give a technical slant to
— **tech·ni·cal·i·za·tion** \,tek-ni-kə-lə-'zā-shən\ *noun*
technical knockout *noun* (1921)
: the termination of a boxing match when a boxer is unable or is declared by the referee to be unable (as because of injuries) to continue the fight
technical sergeant *noun* (circa 1956)
: a noncommissioned officer in the air force ranking above a staff sergeant and below a master sergeant
tech·ni·cian \tek-'ni-shən\ *noun* (1833)
1 : a specialist in the technical details of a subject or occupation ⟨a computer *technician*⟩
2 : one who has acquired the technique of an art or other area of specialization ⟨a superb *technician* and a musician of integrity —Irving Kolodin⟩
Tech·ni·col·or \'tek-ni-,kə-lər\ *trademark*
— used for a process of color cinematography
tech·nique \tek-'nēk\ *noun* [French, from *technique* technical, from Greek *technikos*] (1817)
1 : the manner in which technical details are treated (as by a writer) or basic physical movements are used (as by a dancer); *also* : ability to treat such details or use such movements ⟨good piano *technique*⟩
2 a : a body of technical methods (as in a craft or in scientific research) **b :** a method of accomplishing a desired aim
techno- *combining form* [*technology*]
: technical : technological ⟨*techno*cracy⟩
tech·no·bab·ble \'tek-nə-,ba-bəl\ *noun* (1981)
: technical jargon
tech·noc·ra·cy \tek-'nä-krə-sē\ *noun* (circa 1919)
1 : government by technicians; *specifically* : management of society by technical experts
tech·no·crat \'tek-nə-,krat\ *noun* (1932)
1 : an adherent of technocracy
2 : a technical expert; *especially* : one exercising managerial authority
tech·no·crat·ic \,tek-nə-'kra-tik\ *adjective* (1932)
: of, relating to, or suggestive of a technocrat or a technocracy
tech·no·log·i·cal \,tek-nə-'lä-ji-kəl\ *also* **tech·no·log·ic** \-'lä-jik\ *adjective* (1800)
1 : of, relating to, or characterized by technology ⟨*technological* advances⟩
2 : resulting from improvements in technical processes that increase productivity of machines and eliminates manual operations or operations done by older machines ⟨*technological* unemployment⟩
— **tech·no·log·i·cal·ly** \-ji-k(ə-)lē\ *adverb*
tech·nol·o·gize \tek-'nä-lə-,jīz\ *transitive verb* **-gized; -giz·ing** (1954)

\ə\ abut \ᵊ\ kitten \ər\ further \a\ ash \ā\ ace
\ä\ mop, mar \aú\ out \ch\ chin \e\ bet \ē\ easy
\g\ go \i\ hit \ī\ ice \j\ job \ŋ\ sing \ō\ go
\ȯ\ law \ȯi\ boy \th\ thin \t͟h\ the \ü\ loot \ú\ foot
\y\ yet \zh\ vision *see also* Guide to Pronunciation

: to affect or alter by technology

tech·nol·o·gy \-jē\ *noun, plural* **-gies** [Greek *technologia* systematic treatment of an art, from *technē* art, skill + *-o-* + *-logia* -logy] (1859)
1 a : the practical application of knowledge especially in a particular area : ENGINEERING 2 〈medical *technology*〉 **b :** a capability given by the practical application of knowledge 〈a car's fuel-saving *technology*〉
2 : a manner of accomplishing a task especially using technical processes, methods, or knowledge 〈new *technologies* for information storage〉
3 : the specialized aspects of a particular field of endeavor 〈educational *technology*〉
— **tech·nol·o·gist** \-jist\ *noun*
tech·no·phile \'tek-nə-ˌfīl\ *noun* (1968)
: an enthusiast of technology
tech·no·pho·bia \ˌtek-nə-'fō-bē-ə\ *noun* (1965)
: fear or dislike of advanced technology or complex devices and especially computers
— **tech·no·phobe** \'tek-nə-ˌfōb\ *noun*
— **tech·no·pho·bic** \ˌtek-nə-'fō-bik\ *adjective*
tech·no·pop \'tek-(ˌ)nō-ˌpäp\ *noun* (1980)
: pop music featuring extensive use of synthesizers
tech·no·struc·ture \'tek-nō-ˌstrək-chər\ *noun* (1967)
: the network of professionally skilled managers (as scientists, engineers, and administrators) that tends to control the economy both within and beyond individual corporate groups
tech·no·thrill·er \'tek-nō-ˌthri-lər, -nə-\ *noun* (1989)
: a thriller whose plot relies on modern technology
tec·ton·ic \tek-'tä-nik\ *adjective* [Late Latin *tectonicus,* from Greek *tektonikos* of a builder, from *tektōn* builder — more at TECHNICAL] (1894)
: of or relating to tectonics
— **tec·ton·i·cal·ly** \-ni-k(ə-)lē\ *adverb*
tec·ton·ics \-niks\ *noun plural but singular or plural in construction* (1899)
1 : geological structural features as a whole
2 a : a branch of geology concerned with the structure of the crust of a planet (as earth) or moon and especially with the formation of folds and faults in it **b :** DIASTROPHISM
tec·to·nism \'tek-tə-ˌni-zəm\ *noun* [International Scientific Vocabulary] (1948)
: DIASTROPHISM
tec·tum \'tek-təm\ *noun, plural* **tec·ta** \-tə\ [New Latin, from Latin, roof, dwelling, from neuter of *tectus,* past participle of *tegere* to cover — more at THATCH] (circa 1905)
: a bodily structure resembling or serving as a roof; *especially* : the dorsal part of the midbrain
— **tec·tal** \'tek-t'l\ *adjective*
ted \'ted\ *transitive verb* **ted·ded; ted·ding** [(assumed) Middle English *tedden,* probably from Old Norse *tethja* to manure; akin to Old Norse *tath* spread dung, Old High German *zetten* to spread] (15th century)
: to spread or turn from the swath and scatter (as new-mown grass) for drying
ted·der \'te-dər\ *noun* (15th century)
: one that teds; *specifically* : a machine for stirring and spreading hay to hasten drying and curing
ted·dy \'te-dē\ *noun, plural* **teddies** [origin unknown] (1924)
: CHEMISE 1
ted·dy bear \'te-dē-ˌ\ *noun* [*Teddy,* nickname of Theodore Roosevelt; from a cartoon depicting the president sparing the life of a bear cub while hunting] (1906)
: a stuffed toy bear
teddy boy *noun* [*Teddy,* nickname for Edward] (1954)
: a young British hoodlum affecting Edwardian dress

Te De·um \ˌtā-'dā-əm, ˌtē-'dē-\ *noun, plural* **Te Deums** [Middle English, from Late Latin *te deum laudamus* thee, God, we praise; from the opening words of the hymn] (before 12th century)
: a liturgical Christian hymn of praise to God
te·dious \'tē-dē-əs, 'tē-jəs\ *adjective* [Middle English, from Late Latin *taediosus,* from Latin *taedium*] (15th century)
: tiresome because of length or dullness : BORING 〈a *tedious* public ceremony〉
— **te·dious·ly** *adverb*
— **te·dious·ness** *noun*
te·di·um \'tē-dē-əm\ *noun* [Latin *taedium* disgust, irksomeness, from *taedēre* to disgust, weary] (1662)
1 : the quality or state of being tedious : TEDIOUSNESS; *also* : BOREDOM
2 : a tedious period of time 〈long *tediums* of strained anxiety —H. G. Wells〉
¹tee \'tē\ *noun* [Middle English] (15th century)
1 : the letter *t*
2 : something shaped like a capital T
3 : a mark aimed at in various games (as curling)
— **to a tee** : EXACTLY, PRECISELY
²tee *noun* [origin unknown] (1673)
1 a : a small mound or a peg on which a golf ball is placed before being struck at the beginning of play on a hole **b :** a device for holding a football in position for kicking
2 : the area from which a golf ball is struck at the beginning of play on a hole
³tee *transitive verb* **teed; tee·ing** (1673)
: to place (a ball) on a tee — often used with *up*
teed off *adjective* [probably from *tee off* (on)] (1951)
: ANGRY, ANNOYED
¹teem \'tēm\ *verb* [Middle English *temen,* from Old English *tīman, tǣman;* akin to Old English *tēam* offspring — more at TEAM] (before 12th century)
transitive verb
archaic : BRING FORTH : give birth to : PRODUCE
intransitive verb
1 *obsolete* : to become pregnant : CONCEIVE
2 a : to become filled to overflowing : ABOUND **b :** to be present in large quantity
— **teem·ing·ly** \'tē-miŋ-lē\ *adverb*
— **teem·ing·ness** *noun*
²teem *transitive verb* [Middle English *temen,* from Old Norse *tæma;* akin to Old English *tōm* empty] (14th century)
: EMPTY, POUR 〈*teem* molten metal into a mold〉
¹teen \'tēn\ *noun* [Middle English *tene,* from Old English *tēona* injury, grief; akin to Old Norse *tjōn* loss, damage] (14th century)
archaic : MISERY, AFFLICTION
²teen *noun* (1818)
: TEENAGER
— **teen** *adjective*
teen·age \'tē-ˌnāj\ *or* **teen·aged** \-ˌnājd\ *adjective* (1921)
: of, being, or relating to people in their teens
— **teen·ag·er** \-ˌnā-jər\ *noun*
teen·er \'tē-nər\ *noun* (1894)
: a teenage person
teens \'tēnz\ *noun plural* [-*teen* (as in *thirteen*)] (1604)
: the numbers 13 to 19 inclusive; *specifically* : the years 13 to 19 in a lifetime or century
teen·sy \'tēn(t)-sē\ *adjective* **teen·si·er; -est** [baby-talk alteration of *teeny*] (1899)
: TINY
teen·sy–ween·sy \ˌtēn(t)-sē-'wēn(t)-sē\ *adjective* [baby-talk alteration of *teeny-weeny*] (circa 1906)
: TINY
tee·ny \'tē-nē\ *adjective* **tee·ni·er; -est** [by alteration] (1825)
: TINY
teeny·bop \'tē-nē-ˌbäp\ *adjective* [back-formation from *teenybopper*] (1967)
: of, relating to, or being a teenybopper

teeny·bop·per \-ˌbä-pər\ *noun* [*teeny* teenager + *-bopper,* perhaps from ⁴*bop*] (1966)
1 : a teenage girl
2 : a young teenager who is enthusiastically devoted to pop music and to current fads
tee·ny–wee·ny \ˌtē-nē-'wē-nē\ *adjective* [*teeny* + *weeny*] (circa 1879)
: TINY
tee off *intransitive verb* (1895)
1 : to drive from a tee
2 : BEGIN, START
3 : to hit hard
4 : to make an angry denunciation — often used with *on*
tee·pee *variant of* TEPEE
tee shirt *variant of* T-SHIRT
¹tee·ter \'tē-tər\ *intransitive verb* [Middle English *titeren* to totter, reel; akin to Old High German *zittarōn* to shiver] (1844)
1 a : to move unsteadily : WOBBLE **b :** WAVER, VACILLATE 〈*teetered* on the brink of bankruptcy〉
2 : SEESAW
²teeter *noun* (1863)
: SEESAW
tee·ter·board \-ˌbōrd, -ˌbȯrd\ *noun* (1855)
1 : SEESAW 2b
2 : a board placed on a raised support so that a person standing on one end of the board is thrown into the air if another jumps on the opposite end
tee·ter–tot·ter \'tē-tər-ˌtä-tər\ *noun* (circa 1905)
: SEESAW 2b
teeth *plural of* TOOTH
teethe \'tēth\ *intransitive verb* **teethed; teeth·ing** [back-formation from *teething*] (15th century)
: to cut one's teeth : grow teeth
teeth·er \'tē-thər\ *noun* (1946)
: an object (as a teething ring) designed for a baby to bite on during teething
teeth·ing \'tē-thiŋ\ *noun* [*teeth*] (1732)
1 : the first growth of teeth
2 : the phenomena accompanying growth of teeth through the gums
teething ring *noun* (1872)
: a usually rubber or plastic ring for a teething infant to bite on
teeth·ridge \'tēth-ˌrij\ *noun* (1928)
: the inner surface of the gums of the upper front teeth
tee·to·tal \'tē-'tō-t'l, -ˌtō-\ *adjective* [total + *total* (abstinence)] (1834)
1 : of, relating to, or practicing teetotalism
2 : TOTAL, COMPLETE
— **tee·to·tal·ly** \-t'l-ē\ *adverb*
tee·to·tal·er *or* **tee·to·tal·ler** \-'tō-t'l-ər\ *noun* (1834)
: one who practices or advocates teetotalism
tee·to·tal·ism \-t'l-ˌi-zəm\ *noun* (1834)
: the principle or practice of complete abstinence from alcoholic drinks
— **tee·to·tal·ist** \-t'l-ist\ *noun*
tee·to·tum \'tē-ˌtō-təm\ *noun* [¹*tee* + Latin *totum* all, from neuter of *totus* whole; from the letter *T* inscribed on one side as an abbreviation of *totum* (take) all] (1720)
: a small top usually inscribed with letters and used in put-and-take
teff \'tef\ *noun* [Amharic *ṭef*] (1790)
: an economically important African cereal grass (*Eragrostis tef* synonym *E. abyssinica*) that is grown for its grain which yields a white flour and as a forage and hay crop
te·fil·lin \tē-'fi-lən *also* -ləm\ *noun plural but sometimes singular in construction* [Late Hebrew *tĕphīlīn,* from Aramaic, attachments] (1613)
: the phylacteries worn by Jews
Tef·lon \'te-ˌflän\ *trademark*
— used for synthetic fluorine-containing resins used especially for molding articles and for coatings to prevent sticking (as of food in cookware)

teg·men \'teg-mən\ *noun, plural* **teg·mi·na** \-mə-nə\ [New Latin *tegmin-, tegmen*, from Latin, covering, from *tegere* to cover — more at THATCH] (1807)
: a superficial layer or cover usually of a plant or animal part

teg·men·tal \teg-'men-t⁰l\ *adjective* (circa 1890)
: of, relating to, or associated with an integument or a tegmentum

teg·men·tum \teg-'men-təm\ *noun, plural* **-men·ta** \-'men-tə\ [New Latin, from Latin *tegumentum, tegmentum*, covering, from *tegere*] (1832)
: an anatomical covering **:** TEGMEN; *especially* **:** the part of the ventral midbrain above the substantia nigra formed of longitudinal white fibers with arched transverse fibers and gray matter

teg·u·ment \'te-gyə-mənt\ *noun* [Middle English, from Latin *tegumentum*] (15th century)
: INTEGUMENT

te·iid \'tē-əd, 'tī-\ *noun* [New Latin *Teiidae*, from *Teius*, genus of lizards, from Portuguese *teiu*, a lizard, from Tupi *tejú*] (1956)
: any of a family (Teiidae) of mostly tropical American lizards (as the race runner) with a flat elongate scaly forked tongue
— **teiid** *adjective*

tek·tite \'tek-,tīt\ *noun* [International Scientific Vocabulary, from Greek *tēktos* molten, from *tēkein* to melt — more at THAW] (1909)
: a glassy body of probably meteoritic origin and of rounded but indefinite shape
— **tek·tit·ic** \tek-'ti-tik\ *adjective*

tel- *or* **telo-** *combining form* [International Scientific Vocabulary, from Greek *telos* — more at TELOS]
: end ⟨*tel*angiectasia⟩

tel·a·mon \'te-lə-,män\ *noun, plural* **tel·a·mo·nes** \,te-lə-'mō-(,)nēz\ [Latin, from Greek *telamōn* bearer, supporter; akin to Greek *tlēnai* to bear — more at TOLERATE] (circa 1706)
: ATLAS 5

tel·an·gi·ec·ta·sia \te-,lan-jē-,ek-'tā-zh(ē-)ə, ,tē-, tə-\ *or* **tel·an·gi·ec·ta·sis** \-'ek-tə-səs\ *noun, plural* **-ta·sias** *or* **-ta·ses** \-tə-,sēz\ [New Latin, from *tel-* + *angi-* + *ectasia, ectasis* (as in *atelectasis*)] (1831)
: an abnormal dilatation of capillary vessels and arterioles that often forms an angioma
— **tel·an·gi·ec·tat·ic** \-,ek-'ta-tik\ *adjective*

tele \'te-lē\ *noun* (1936)
British **:** TELEVISION

tele- *or* **tel-** *combining form* [New Latin, from Greek *tēle-, tēl-*, from *tēle* far off — more at PALE-]
1 : distant **:** at a distance **:** over a distance ⟨*tele*gram⟩
2 a : telegraph ⟨*tele*typewriter⟩ **b :** television ⟨*tele*cast⟩ **c :** telecommunication ⟨*tele*marketing⟩

tele·cast \'te-li-,kast\ *verb* **-cast** *also* **-cast·ed; -cast·ing** [*tele-* + broad*cast*] (1937)
transitive verb
: to broadcast by television
intransitive verb
: to broadcast a television program
— **telecast** *noun*
— **tele·cast·er** *noun*

tele·com·mu·ni·ca·tion \,te-li-kə-,myü-nə-'kā-shən\ *noun* [International Scientific Vocabulary] (1932)
1 : communication at a distance (as by telephone)
2 : a science that deals with telecommunication — usually used in plural

tele·com·mute \'te-li-kə-,myüt\ *intransitive verb* (1974)
: to work at home by the use of an electronic linkup with a central office
— **tele·com·mut·er** *noun*

tele·con·fer·enc·ing \'te-li-,kän-f(ə-)rən(t)-siŋ, -fərn(t)-\ *noun* (1974)

: the holding of a conference among people remote from one another by means of telecommunication devices (as telephones or computer terminals)
— **tele·con·fer·ence** \-f(ə-)rən(t)s, -fərn(t)s\ *noun*

Tele·copi·er \'te-lə-,kä-pē-ər\ *trademark*
— used for transmitting and receiving equipment for producing facsimile copies of documents

tele·course \'te-li-,kōrs, -,kȯrs\ *noun* (1950)
: a course of study conducted over television; *especially* **:** such a course taken at home for academic credit

tele·fac·sim·i·le \,te-li-fak-'si-mə-(,)lē\ *noun* (1952)
: FACSIMILE 2

tele·film \'te-li-,film\ *noun* (1939)
: a motion picture made to be telecast

tele·gen·ic \,te-lə-'je-nik, -'jē-\ *adjective* (1939)
: well-suited to the medium of television; *especially* **:** having an appearance and manner that are markedly attractive to television viewers

¹tele·gram \'te-lə-,gram, *Southern also* -grəm\ *noun* (circa 1852)
: a telegraphic dispatch

²tele·gram \-,gram\ *transitive verb* **-grammed; -gram·ming** (1864)
: TELEGRAPH

¹tele·graph \-,graf\ *noun* [French *télégraphe*, from *télé-* tele- (from Greek *tēle-*) + *-graphe* -graph] (1794)
1 : an apparatus for communication at a distance by coded signals; *especially* **:** an apparatus, system, or process for communication at a distance by electric transmission over wire
2 : TELEGRAM

²telegraph *transitive verb* (1805)
1 a : to send or communicate by or as if by telegraph **b :** to send a telegram to **c :** to send by means of a telegraphic order ⟨*telegraph* flowers to a sick friend⟩
2 : to make known by signs especially unknowingly and in advance ⟨*telegraph* a punch⟩
— **tele·gra·pher** \tə-'le-grə-fər\ *noun*
— **tele·gra·phist** \-fist\ *noun*

tele·graph·ese \,te-lə-gra-'fēz, -'fēs\ *noun* (1885)
: language characterized by the terseness and ellipses that are common in telegrams

tele·graph·ic \,te-lə-'gra-fik\ *adjective* (1794)
1 : of or relating to the telegraph
2 : CONCISE, TERSE
— **tele·graph·i·cal·ly** \-fi-k(ə-)lē\ *adverb*

te·leg·ra·phy \tə-'le-grə-fē\ *noun* (1795)
: the use or operation of a telegraph apparatus or system for communication

tele·ki·ne·sis \,te-li-kə-'nē-səs, -kī-\ *noun* [New Latin] (1890)
: the production of motion in objects (as by a spiritualistic medium) without contact or other physical means
— **tele·ki·net·ic** \-'ne-tik\ *adjective*
— **tele·ki·net·i·cal·ly** \-ti-k(ə-)lē\ *adverb*

Te·lem·a·chus \tə-'le-mə-kəs\ *noun* [Latin, from Greek *Tēlemachos*]
: the son of Odysseus and Penelope who contrives with his father to slay his mother's suitors

tel·e·mark \'te-lə-,märk\ *noun, often capitalized* [Norwegian, from *Telemark*, region in Norway] (1904)
: a turn in skiing in which the outside ski is advanced considerably ahead of the other ski and then turned inward at a steadily widening angle until the turn is completed

tele·mar·ket·ing \,te-lə-'mär-kə-tiŋ\ *noun* (1980)
: the marketing of goods or services by telephone
— **tele·mar·ket·er** \-tər\ *noun*

¹tele·me·ter \'te-lə-,mē-tər\ *noun* [International Scientific Vocabulary] (1860)

1 : an instrument for measuring the distance of an object from an observer
2 : an electrical apparatus for measuring a quantity (as pressure, speed, or temperature), transmitting the result especially by radio to a distant station, and there indicating or recording the quantity measured

²telemeter (1925)
transitive verb
: to transmit (as the measurement of a quantity) by telemeter
intransitive verb
: to telemeter the measurement of a quantity

te·lem·e·try \tə-'le-mə-trē\ *noun* (1885)
1 : the science or process of telemetering data
2 : data transmitted by telemetry
3 : BIOTELEMETRY
— **tele·met·ric** \,te-lə-'me-trik\ *adjective*
— **tele·met·ri·cal·ly** \-tri-k(ə-)lē\ *adverb*

tel·en·ceph·a·lon \,te-len-'se-fə-,län, -lən\ *noun* [New Latin] (1897)
: the anterior subdivision of the embryonic forebrain or the corresponding part of the adult forebrain that includes the cerebral hemispheres and associated structures
— **tel·en·ce·phal·ic** \-,len(t)-sə-'fa-lik\ *adjective*

tel·e·o·log·i·cal \,te-lē-ə-'lä-ji-kəl, ,tē-\ *also* **tel·e·o·log·ic** \-'lä-jik\ *adjective* (1798)
: exhibiting or relating to design or purpose especially in nature
— **tel·e·o·log·i·cal·ly** \-ji-k(ə-)lē\ *adverb*

tel·e·ol·o·gy \,te-lē-'ä-lə-jē, ,tē-\ *noun* [New Latin *teleologia*, from Greek *tele-, telos* end, purpose + *-logia* -logy — more at WHEEL] (1740)
1 a : the study of evidences of design in nature **b :** a doctrine (as in vitalism) that ends are immanent in nature **c :** a doctrine explaining phenomena by final causes
2 : the fact or character attributed to nature or natural processes of being directed toward an end or shaped by a purpose
3 : the use of design or purpose as an explanation of natural phenomena
— **tel·e·ol·o·gist** \-jist\ *noun*

tel·e·on·o·my \,te-lē-'ä-nə-mē, ,tē-\ *noun* [*teleo-* (as in *teleology*) + *-nomy*] (1958)
: the quality of apparent purposefulness in living organisms that derives from their evolutionary adaptation
— **tel·e·o·nom·ic** \,te-lē-ə-'nä-mik, ,tē-\ *adjective*

tel·e·ost \'te-lē-,äst, 'tē-\ *noun* [ultimately from Greek *teleios* complete, perfect (from *telos* end) + *osteon* bone — more at OSSEOUS] (1862)
: BONY FISH
— **teleost** *adjective*
— **tel·e·os·te·an** \,te-lē-'äs-tē-ən, ,tē-\ *adjective*

tele·path \'te-lə-,path\ *noun* (1904)
: one who is able to communicate by telepathy

te·lep·a·thy \tə-'le-pə-thē\ *noun* (1882)
: communication from one mind to another by extrasensory means
— **tele·path·ic** \,te-lə-'pa-thik\ *adjective*
— **tele·path·i·cal·ly** \-thi-k(ə-)lē\ *adverb*

¹tele·phone \'te-lə-,fōn\ *noun, often attributive* (1849)
: an instrument for reproducing sounds at a distance; *specifically* **:** one in which sound is converted into electrical impulses for transmission by wire

²telephone *verb* **-phoned; -phon·ing** (1877)
transitive verb
1 : to speak to or attempt to reach by telephone
2 : to send by telephone

intransitive verb
: to communicate by telephone
— **tele·phon·er** *noun*
telephone book *noun* (1915)
: a book listing the names, addresses, and telephone numbers of telephone customers
telephone booth *noun* (circa 1895)
: an enclosure within which one may stand or sit while making a telephone call
telephone box *noun* (1904)
British : a public telephone booth
telephone directory *noun* (1907)
: TELEPHONE BOOK
telephone number *noun* (1885)
: a number assigned to a telephone line for a specific location that is used to call that location
telephone tag *noun* (1980)
: telephoning back and forth by parties trying to reach each other without success
tele·phon·ic \,te-lə-'fä-nik\ *adjective* (1877)
: of, relating to, or conveyed by a telephone
— **tele·phon·i·cal·ly** \-ni-k(ə-)lē\ *adverb*
tele·pho·nist \tə-'le-fə-nist, 'te-lə-,fō-nist\ *noun* (1880)
British : a telephone switchboard operator
tele·pho·ny \tə-'le-fə-nē *also* 'te-lə-,fō-\ *noun* (1835)
: the use or operation of an apparatus for transmission of sounds between widely removed points with or without connecting wires
¹**tele·pho·to** \,te-lə-'fō-(,)tō\ *adjective* (circa 1895)
: being a camera lens system designed to give a large image of a distant object; *also* : relating to or being photography in which a telephoto lens is used
²**telephoto** *noun, plural* **-tos** (1904)
1 : a telephoto lens
2 : a photograph taken with a camera having a telephoto lens
Telephoto *trademark*
— used for an apparatus for transmitting photographs electrically or for a photograph so transmitted
tele·pho·tog·ra·phy \-fə-'tä-grə-fē\ *noun* [International Scientific Vocabulary] (1892)
: the photography of distant objects (as by a camera provided with a telephoto lens)
tele·play \'te-li-,plā\ *noun* (1952)
: a play written for television
tele·port \'te-lə-,pōrt, -,pȯrt\ *transitive verb* [back-formation from *teleportation*] (1947)
: to transfer by teleportation
tele·por·ta·tion \,te-lə-,pōr-'tā-shən, -,pȯr-, -pər-\ *noun* [*tele-* + trans*portation*] (1931)
: the act or process of moving an object or person by psychokinesis
tele·print·er \'te-lə-,prin-tər\ *noun* (1929)
: a device capable of producing hard copy from signals received over a communications circuit; *especially* : TELETYPEWRITER
tele·pro·cess·ing \-'prä-,se-siŋ, -'prō-, -sə-siŋ\ *noun* (1962)
: computer processing via remote terminals
Tele·Promp·Ter \'te-lə-,präm(p)-tər\ *trademark*
— used for a device for unrolling a magnified script in front of a speaker on television
¹**tele·scope** \'te-lə-,skōp\ *noun, often attributive* [New Latin *telescopium*, from Greek *tēleskopos* farseeing, from *tēle-* tele- + *skopos* watcher; akin to Greek *skopein* to look — more at SPY] (1648)
1 : a usually tubular optical instrument for viewing distant objects by means of the refraction of light rays through a lens or the reflection of light rays by a concave mirror — compare REFLECTOR, REFRACTOR
2 : any of various tubular magnifying optical instruments
3 : RADIO TELESCOPE
²**telescope** *verb* **-scoped; -scop·ing** (1867)
intransitive verb

1 : to become forced together lengthwise with one part entering another as the result of collision
2 : to slide or pass one within another like the cylindrical sections of a collapsible hand telescope
3 : to become compressed or condensed
transitive verb
1 : to cause to telescope
2 : COMPRESS, CONDENSE ⟨the book arbitrarily *telescopes* time and space, and as arbitrarily extends them —Phoebe Adams⟩
tele·scop·ic \,te-lə-'skä-pik\ *adjective* (1705)
1 a : of, relating to, or performed with a telescope **b** : suitable for seeing or magnifying distant objects
2 : seen or discoverable only by a telescope ⟨*telescopic* stars⟩
3 : able to discern objects at a distance
4 : having parts that telescope
— **tele·scop·i·cal·ly** \-pi-k(ə-)lē\ *adverb*
tel·e·sis \'te-lə-səs\ *noun, plural* **-e·ses** \-,sēz\ [New Latin, from Greek, fulfillment, from *telein* to complete, from *telos* end — more at TELOS] (1896)
: progress that is intelligently planned and directed : the attainment of desired ends by the application of intelligent human effort to the means
tele·text \'te-lə-,tekst\ *noun* (1974)
: a system for broadcasting text over an unused portion of a television signal and displaying it on a decoder-equipped television set — compare VIDEOTEX
tele·thon \'te-lə-,thän\ *noun* [*tele-* + *-thon*] (1949)
: a long television program usually to solicit funds especially for a charity
Tele·type \'te-lə-,tīp\ *trademark*
— used for a teletypewriter
Tele·type·set·ter \,te-lə-'tīp-,se-tər\ *trademark*
— used for a telegraphic apparatus for the automatic operation of a keyboard typesetting machine
tele·type·writ·er \-,rī-tər\ *noun* (1903)
: a printing device resembling a typewriter that is used to send and receive telephonic signals
te·leu·to·spore \tə-'lü-tə-,spōr, -,spȯr\ *noun* [Greek *teleutē* end (akin to Greek *telos* end) + International Scientific Vocabulary *spore* — more at TELOS] (1874)
: TELIOSPORE
tel·evan·ge·list \,te-li-'van-jə-list\ *noun* (1973)
: an evangelist who conducts regularly televised religious programs
— **tel·evan·ge·lism** \-,li-zəm\ *noun*
tele·view \'te-li-,vyü\ *intransitive verb* (1935)
: to observe or watch by means of a television receiver
— **tele·view·er** *noun*
tele·vise \'te-lə-,vīz\ *verb* **-vised; -vis·ing** [back-formation from *television*] (1927)
transitive verb
: to broadcast (as a baseball game) by television
intransitive verb
: to broadcast by television
tele·vi·sion \'te-lə-,vi-zhən *especially British* ,te-lə-'\ *noun, often attributive* [French *télévision*, from *télé-* tele- + *vision* vision] (1907)
1 : an electronic system of transmitting transient images of fixed or moving objects together with sound over a wire or through space by apparatus that converts light and sound into electrical waves and reconverts them into visible light rays and audible sound
2 : a television receiving set
3 a : the television broadcasting industry **b** : television as a medium of communication
television tube *noun* (1937)
: PICTURE TUBE
tele·vi·su·al \,te-lə-'vi-zhə-wəl, -zhəl; -'vizh-wəl\ *adjective* (1926)

chiefly British : of, relating to, or suitable for broadcast by television
¹**tel·ex** \'te-,leks\ *noun* [*teleprinter* + *exchange*] (1932)
1 : a communication service involving teletypewriters connected by wire through automatic exchanges; *also* : a teletypewriter used in telex
2 : a message sent by telex
²**telex** *transitive verb* (1960)
1 : to send (as a message) by telex
2 : to communicate with by telex
te·lic \'te-lik, 'tē-\ *adjective* [Greek *telikos*, from *telos* end — more at TELOS] (1889)
: tending toward an end
— **te·li·cal·ly** \-li-k(ə-)lē\ *adverb*
te·lio·spore \'tē-lē-ə-,spōr, -,spȯr\ *noun* [Greek *teleios* complete (from *telos* end) + English *spore*] (1905)
: a chlamydospore that is the final stage in the life cycle of a rust fungus and that after nuclear fusion gives rise to the basidium
te·li·um \'tē-lē-əm\ *noun, plural* **te·lia** \-lē-ə\ [New Latin, from Greek *teleios* complete] (circa 1905)
: a teliospore-producing sorus or pustule on the host plant of a rust fungus
— **te·li·al** \'tē-lē-əl\ *adjective*
¹**tell** \'tel\ *verb* **told** \'tōld\; **tell·ing** [Middle English, from Old English *tellan;* akin to Old High German *zellen* to count, tell, Old English *talu* tale] (before 12th century)
transitive verb
1 : COUNT, ENUMERATE
2 a : to relate in detail : NARRATE **b** : to give utterance to : SAY ⟨who dares think one thing, and another *tell* —Alexander Pope⟩
3 a : to make known : DIVULGE, REVEAL **b** : to express in words ⟨she never *told* her love —Shakespeare⟩
4 a : to report to : INFORM **b** : to assure emphatically ⟨they did not do it, I *tell* you⟩
5 : ORDER, DIRECT ⟨*told* me to wait⟩
6 : to find out by observing : RECOGNIZE ⟨you can *tell* it's a masterpiece⟩
intransitive verb
1 : to give an account
2 : to act as an informer — often used with *on* ⟨I'll get even with you if you ever *tell* on me —*Inside Detective*⟩
3 : to have a marked effect
4 : to serve as evidence or indication
synonym see REVEAL
²**tell** *noun* [Arabic *tall*] (1864)
: HILL, MOUND; *specifically* : an ancient mound in the Middle East composed of remains of successive settlements
tell–all \'tel-'ȯl\ *noun* (1954)
: a written account (as a biography) that contains revealing and often scandalous information
— **tell–all** *adjective*
tell·er \'te-lər\ *noun* (14th century)
1 : one that relates or communicates ⟨a *teller* of stories⟩
2 : one that reckons or counts: as **a** : one appointed to count votes **b** : a member of a bank's staff concerned with the direct handling of money received or paid out
tell·ing \'te-liŋ\ *adjective* (1851)
: carrying great weight and producing a marked effect : EFFECTIVE, EXPRESSIVE ⟨the most *telling* evidence⟩
synonym see VALID
— **tell·ing·ly** \-liŋ-lē\ *adverb*
tell off *transitive verb* (1804)
1 : to number and set apart; *especially* : to assign to a special duty ⟨*told off* a detail and put them to opening a trench —J. F. Dobie⟩
2 : REPRIMAND, EXCORIATE ⟨*told* him *off* for his arrogance⟩
tell·tale \'tel-,tāl\ *noun* (circa 1548)
1 a : TALEBEARER, INFORMER **b** : an outward sign : INDICATION

2 : a device for indicating or recording something: as **a** : a wind-direction indicator often in the form of a ribbon **b** : a strip of metal on the front wall of a racquets or squash court above which the ball must be hit
— **telltale** *adjective*

tellur- *or* **telluro-** *combining form* [Latin *tellur-, tellus* — more at THILL]
1 : earth 〈*tellur*ic〉
2 [New Latin *tellurium*] : tellurium 〈*tellur*ide〉

tel·lu·ric \tə-'lur-ik, te-\ *adjective* (1836)
1 : of or relating to the earth : TERRESTRIAL
2 : being or relating to a usually natural electric current flowing near the earth's surface

tel·lu·ride \'tel-yə-ˌrīd\ *noun* [International Scientific Vocabulary] (1849)
: a binary compound of tellurium with a more electropositive element or group

tel·lu·ri·um \tə-'lur-ē-əm, te-\ *noun* [New Latin, from Latin *tellur-, tellus* earth] (1800)
: a semimetallic element related to selenium and sulfur that occurs in a silvery white brittle crystalline form of metallic luster, in a dark amorphous form, or combined with metals and that is used especially in alloys — see ELEMENT table

tel·lu·rom·e·ter \ˌtel-yə-'rä-mə-tər\ *noun* (1957)
: a device that measures distance by means of microwaves

tel·ly \'te-lē\ *noun, plural* **tellys** *also* **tellies** [by shortening & alteration] (1939)
chiefly British : TELEVISION

telo- — see TEL-

telo·cen·tric \ˌte-lə-'sen-trik, ˌtē-\ *adjective* [International Scientific Vocabulary *tel-* + *centromere* + *-ic*] (1939)
: having the centromere terminally situated so that there is only one chromosomal arm 〈a *telocentric* chromosome〉
— **telocentric** *noun*

te·lome \'tē-ˌlōm\ *noun* [International Scientific Vocabulary *tel-* + *-ome*] (1935)
: a hypothetical plant structure in a theory of the evolution of leaves and sporophylls in vascular plants that consists of one of the vegetative or reproductive terminal branchlets of a dichotomously branched axis

telo·mere \'te-lə-ˌmir, 'tē-\ *noun* [International Scientific Vocabulary] (1940)
: the natural end of a eukaryotic chromosome

telo·phase \'te-lə-ˌfāz, 'tē-\ *noun* [International Scientific Vocabulary] (1895)
1 : the final stage of mitosis and of the second division of meiosis in which the spindle disappears and the nuclear envelope reforms around each set of chromosomes
2 : the final stage in the first division of meiosis that may be missing in some organisms and is characterized by the gathering at opposite poles of the cell of half the original number of chromosomes including one from each homologous pair

te·los \'te-ˌläs, 'tē-\ *noun* [Greek; probably akin to Greek *tellein* to accomplish, *tlēnai* to bear — more at TOLERATE] (1904)
: an ultimate end

telo·tax·is \ˌte-lə-'tak-səs, ˌtē-\ *noun* [New Latin] (1934)
: a taxis in which an organism orients itself in respect to a stimulus (as a light source) as though that were the only stimulus acting on it

tel·son \'tel-sən\ *noun* [New Latin, from Greek, end of a plowed field; perhaps akin to Greek *telos* end] (1855)
: the terminal segment of the body of an arthropod or segmented worm; *especially* : that of a crustacean forming the middle lobe of the tail

Tel·u·gu \'te-lə-ˌgü\ *noun, plural* **Telugu** *or* **Telugus** (1789)
1 : a member of the largest group of people in Andhra Pradesh, India
2 : the Dravidian language of the Telugu people

tem·blor \'tem-blər; 'tem-ˌblȯr, -ˌblōr, tem-'\ *noun* [Spanish, literally, trembling, from *temblar* to tremble, from Medieval Latin *tremulare* — more at TREMBLE] (1876)
: EARTHQUAKE

tem·er·ar·i·ous \ˌte-mə-'rer-ē-əs, -'rar-\ *adjective* [Latin *temerarius*, from *temere*] (1532)
: marked by temerity : rashly or presumptuously daring
— **tem·er·ar·i·ous·ly** *adverb*
— **tem·er·ar·i·ous·ness** *noun*

te·mer·i·ty \tə-'mer-ə-tē\ *noun, plural* **-ties** [Middle English *temeryte*, from Latin *temeritas*, from *temere* blindly, recklessly; akin to Old High German *demar* darkness, Latin *tenebrae*, Sanskrit *tamas*] (15th century)
1 : unreasonable or foolhardy contempt of danger or opposition : RASHNESS, RECKLESSNESS
2 : an act or instance of temerity ☆

¹temp \'temp\ *noun* (1886)
1 : TEMPERATURE 2a, c
2 : a temporary worker

²temp *intransitive verb* (1973)
: to work as a temp

tem·peh \'tem-ˌpā\ *noun* [Javanese *témpé*] (1961)
: an Asian food prepared by fermenting soybeans with a rhizopus

¹tem·per \'tem-pər\ *transitive verb* **tempered; tem·per·ing** \-p(ə-)riŋ\ [Middle English, from Old English & Old French; Old English *temprian* & Old French *temprer*, from Latin *temperare* to moderate, mix, temper; probably akin to Latin *tempor-, tempus* time] (before 12th century)
1 : to dilute, qualify, or soften by the addition or influence of something else : MODERATE 〈*temper* justice with mercy〉
2 *archaic* **a** : to exercise control over : GOVERN, RESTRAIN **b** : to cause to be well disposed : MOLLIFY 〈*tempered* and reconciled them both —Richard Steele〉
3 : to bring to a suitable state by mixing in or adding a usually liquid ingredient: as **a** : to mix (clay) with water or a modifier (as grog) and knead to a uniform texture **b** : to mix oil with (colors) in making paint ready for use
4 a (1) : to soften (as hardened steel or cast iron) by reheating at a lower temperature (2) : to harden (as steel) by reheating and cooling in oil **b** : to anneal or toughen (glass) by a process of gradually heating and cooling
5 : to make stronger and more resilient through hardship : TOUGHEN 〈troops *tempered* in battle〉
6 a : to put in tune with something : ATTUNE **b** : to adjust the pitch of (a note, chord, or instrument) to a temperament
— **tem·per·able** \-p(ə-)rə-bəl\ *adjective*
— **tem·per·er** \-pər-ər\ *noun*

²temper *noun* (14th century)
1 a *archaic* : a suitable proportion or balance of qualities : a middle state between extremes : MEAN, MEDIUM 〈virtue is . . . a just *temper* between propensities —T. B. Macaulay〉 **b** *archaic* : CHARACTER, QUALITY 〈the *temper* of the land you design to sow —John Mortimer〉 **c** : characteristic tone : TREND, TENDENCY 〈the *temper* of the times〉 **d** : high quality of mind or spirit : COURAGE, METTLE
2 a : the state of a substance with respect to certain desired qualities (as hardness, elasticity, or workability); *especially* : the degree of hardness or resiliency given steel by tempering **b** : the feel and relative solidity of leather
3 a : a characteristic cast of mind or state of feeling : DISPOSITION **b** : calmness of mind : COMPOSURE, EQUANIMITY **c** : state of feeling or frame of mind at a particular time usually dominated by a single strong emotion **d** : heat of mind or emotion : proneness to anger : PASSION
4 : a substance (as a metal) added to or mixed with something else (as another metal) to

modify the properties of the latter
synonym see DISPOSITION

tem·pera \'tem-pə-rə\ *noun* [Italian *tempera*, literally, temper, from *temperare* to temper, from Latin] (1832)
1 : a process of painting in which an albuminous or colloidal medium (as egg yolk) is employed as a vehicle instead of oil; *also* : a painting done in tempera
2 : POSTER COLOR

tem·per·a·ment \'tem-p(ə-)rə-mənt, -pər-mənt\ *noun* [Middle English, from Latin *temperamentum*, from *temperare* to mix, temper] (15th century)
1 *obsolete* **a** : constitution of a substance, body, or organism with respect to the mixture or balance of its elements, qualities, or parts : MAKEUP **b** : COMPLEXION 1
2 *obsolete* **a** : CLIMATE **b** : TEMPERATURE 2
3 a : the peculiar or distinguishing mental or physical character determined by the relative proportions of the humors according to medieval physiology **b** : characteristic or habitual inclination or mode of emotional response 〈a nervous *temperament*〉 **c** : extremely high sensibility; *especially* : excessive sensitiveness or irritability
4 a : the act or process of tempering or modifying : ADJUSTMENT, COMPROMISE **b** : middle course : MEAN
5 : the process of slightly modifying the musical intervals of the pure scale to produce a set of 12 equally spaced tones to the octave which enables a keyboard instrument to play in all keys
synonym see DISPOSITION

tem·per·a·men·tal \ˌtem-p(ə-)rə-'men-tᵊl, ˌtem-pər-'\ *adjective* (1646)
1 : of, relating to, or arising from temperament : CONSTITUTIONAL 〈*temperamental* peculiarities〉
2 a : marked by excessive sensitivity and impulsive changes of mood 〈a *temperamental* child〉 **b** : unpredictable in behavior or performance
— **tem·per·a·men·tal·ly** \-tᵊl-ē\ *adverb*

tem·per·ance \'tem-p(ə-)rən(t)s, -pərn(t)s\ *noun* [Middle English, from Latin *temperantia*, from *temperant-, temperans*, present participle of *temperare* to moderate, be moderate] (14th century)
1 : moderation in action, thought, or feeling : RESTRAINT
2 a : habitual moderation in the indulgence of the appetites or passions **b** : moderation in or abstinence from the use of intoxicating drink

☆ **SYNONYMS**
Temerity, audacity, hardihood, effrontery, nerve, cheek, gall, chutzpah mean conspicuous or flagrant boldness. TEMERITY suggests boldness arising from rashness and contempt of danger 〈had the *temerity* to refuse〉. AUDACITY implies a disregard of restraints commonly imposed by convention or prudence 〈an entrepreneur with *audacity* and vision〉. HARDIHOOD suggests firmness in daring and defiance 〈admired for her *hardihood*〉. EFFRONTERY implies shameless, insolent disregard of propriety or courtesy 〈outraged at his *effrontery*〉. NERVE, CHEEK, GALL, and CHUTZPAH are informal equivalents for EFFRONTERY 〈the *nerve* of that guy〉 〈has the *cheek* to call herself a singer〉 〈had the *gall* to demand proof〉 〈the *chutzpah* needed for a career in show business〉.

tem·per·ate \'tem-p(ə-)rət\ *adjective* [Middle English *temperat*, from Latin *temperatus*, from past participle of *temperare*] (14th century)
1 : marked by moderation: as **a :** keeping or held within limits **:** not extreme or excessive **:** MILD **b :** moderate in indulgence of appetite or desire **c :** moderate in the use of intoxicating liquors **d :** marked by an absence or avoidance of extravagance, violence, or extreme partisanship **:** RESTRAINED
2 a : having a moderate climate **b :** found in or associated with a moderate climate ⟨*temperate* insects⟩
3 : existing as a prophage in infected cells and rarely causing lysis ⟨*temperate* bacteriophages⟩
— **tem·per·ate·ly** *adverb*
— **tem·per·ate·ness** *noun*
temperate rain forest *noun* (circa 1930)
: woodland of a usually rather mild climatic area within the temperate zone that receives heavy rainfall, usually includes numerous kinds of trees, and is distinguished from a tropical rain forest by the presence of a dominant tree
temperate zone *noun, often T&Z capitalized* (1551)
: the area or region between the tropic of Cancer and the arctic circle or between the tropic of Capricorn and the antarctic circle
tem·per·a·ture \'tem-pə(r)-,chúr, -p(ə-)rə-, -chər, -,tyùr, -,tùr\ *noun* [Latin *temperatura* mixture, moderation, from *temperatus*, past participle of *temperare*] (1533)
1 *archaic* **a :** COMPLEXION 1 **b :** TEMPERAMENT 3b
2 a : degree of hotness or coldness measured on a definite scale — compare THERMOMETER **b :** the degree of heat that is natural to the body of a living being **c :** abnormally high body heat **d :** relative state of emotional warmth ⟨aware of a change in the *temperature* of our friendship —Christopher Isherwood⟩
temperature inversion *noun* (1921)
: INVERSION 6
tem·pered \'tem-pərd\ *adjective* (14th century)
1 a : having the elements mixed in satisfying proportions **:** TEMPERATE **b :** qualified, lessened, or diluted by the mixture or influence of an additional ingredient **:** MODERATED ⟨a pale gleam of *tempered* sunlight fell through the leaves —W. H. Hudson (died 1922)⟩
2 : treated by tempering; *especially, of glass* **:** treated so as to impart increased strength and the property of shattering into pellets when broken
3 : having a specified temper — used in combination ⟨short-*tempered*⟩
4 : conforming to adjustment by temperament — used of a musical interval, intonation, semitone, or scale
¹tem·pest \'tem-pəst\ *noun* [Middle English, from Old French *tempeste*, from (assumed) Vulgar Latin *tempesta*, alteration of Latin *tempestas* season, weather, storm, from *tempus* time] (13th century)
1 : a violent storm
2 : TUMULT, UPROAR
²tempest *transitive verb* (14th century)
: to raise a tempest in or around
tem·pes·tu·ous \tem-'pes-chə-wəs, -'pesh-\ *adjective* [Late Latin *tempestuosus*, from Old Latin *tempestus* season, weather, storm, from *tempus*] (1509)
: of, relating to, or resembling a tempest **:** TURBULENT, STORMY ⟨*tempestuous* weather⟩ ⟨a *tempestuous* relationship⟩
— **tem·pes·tu·ous·ly** *adverb*
— **tem·pes·tu·ous·ness** *noun*
Tem·plar \'tem-plər\ *noun* [Middle English *templer*, from Old French *templier*, from Medieval Latin *templarius*, from Latin *templum* temple] (13th century)

1 : a knight of a religious military order established in the early 12th century in Jerusalem for the protection of pilgrims and the Holy Sepulcher
2 *not capitalized* **:** a barrister or student of law in London
3 : KNIGHT TEMPLAR 2
tem·plate *also* **tem·plet** \'tem-plət\ *noun* [probably from French *templet*, diminutive of *temple*, part of a loom, probably from Latin *templum*] (1677)
1 : a short piece or block placed horizontally in a wall under a beam to distribute its weight or pressure (as over a door)
2 a (1) **:** a gauge, pattern, or mold (as a thin plate or board) used as a guide to the form of a piece being made (2) **:** a molecule (as of DNA) that serves as a pattern for the generation of another macromolecule (as messenger RNA) **b :** OVERLAY C
3 : something that establishes or serves as a pattern
¹tem·ple \'tem-pəl\ *noun* [Middle English, from Old English & Old French; Old English *tempel* & Old French *temple*, both from Latin *templum* space marked out for observation of auguries, temple, small timber; probably akin to Greek *temenos* sacred precinct, *temnein* to cut — more at TOME] (before 12th century)
1 : an edifice for religious exercises: as **a** *often capitalized* **:** one of three successive national sanctuaries in ancient Jerusalem **b :** a building for Mormon sacred ordinances **c :** a Reform or Conservative synagogue
2 : a local lodge of any of various fraternal orders; *also* **:** the building housing it
3 : a place devoted to a special purpose
— **tem·pled** \-pəld\ *adjective*
²temple *noun* [Middle English, from Middle French, from (assumed) Vulgar Latin *tempula*, alteration of Latin *tempora* (plural) temples] (14th century)
1 : the flattened space on each side of the forehead of some mammals including humans
2 : one of the side supports of a pair of glasses jointed to the bows and passing on each side of the head
tem·po \'tem-(,)pō\ *noun, plural* **tem·pi** \-(,)pē\ *or* **tempos** [Italian, literally, time, from Latin *tempus*] (circa 1724)
1 : the rate of speed of a musical piece or passage indicated by one of a series of directions (as largo, presto, or allegro) and often by an exact metronome marking
2 : rate of motion or activity **:** PACE
¹tem·po·ral \'tem-p(ə-)rəl\ *adjective* [Middle English, from Latin *temporalis*, from *tempor-, tempus* time] (14th century)
1 a : of or relating to time as opposed to eternity **b :** of or relating to earthly life **c :** lay or secular rather than clerical or sacred **:** CIVIL ⟨lords *temporal*⟩
2 : of or relating to grammatical tense or a distinction of time
3 a : of or relating to time as distinguished from space **b :** of or relating to the sequence of time or to a particular time **:** CHRONOLOGICAL
— **tem·po·ral·ly** *adverb*
²temporal *noun* [Middle French, from *temporal*, *adjective*] (1541)
: a temporal part (as a bone or muscle)
³temporal *adjective* [Middle French, from Late Latin *temporalis*, from Latin *tempora* temples] (1597)
: of or relating to the temples or the sides of the skull behind the orbits
temporal bone *noun* (1771)
: a compound bone of the side of the skull of some mammals including humans
tem·po·ral·i·ty \,tem-pə-'ra-lə-tē\ *noun, plural* **-ties** (14th century)
1 a : civil or political as distinguished from spiritual or ecclesiastical power or authority **b :** an ecclesiastical property or revenue — often used in plural

2 : the quality or state of being temporal
tem·po·ral·ize \'tem-p(ə-)rə-,līz\ *transitive verb* **-ized; -iz·ing** (1828)
1 : SECULARIZE
2 : to place or define in time relations
temporal lobe *noun* (circa 1891)
: a large lobe of each cerebral hemisphere that is situated in front of the occipital lobe and contains a sensory area associated with the organ of hearing
temporal summation *noun* (1950)
: sensory summation that involves the addition of single stimuli over a short period of time
tem·po·rar·i·ly \,tem-pə-'rer-ə-lē\ *adverb* (1534)
: during a limited time
¹tem·po·rary \'tem-pə-,rer-ē\ *adjective* [Latin *temporarius*, from *tempor-, tempus* time] (circa 1564)
: lasting for a limited time
— **tem·po·rar·i·ness** *noun*
²temporary *noun, plural* **-rar·ies** (1848)
: one serving for a limited time ⟨adding several *temporaries* as typists during the summer⟩
temporary duty *noun* (1945)
: temporary military service away from one's permanent duty station
tem·po·rise *British variant of* TEMPORIZE
tem·po·rize \'tem-pə-,rīz\ *intransitive verb* **-rized; -riz·ing** [Middle French *temporiser*, from Medieval Latin *temporizare* to pass the time, from Latin *tempor-, tempus*] (1579)
1 : to act to suit the time or occasion **:** yield to current or dominant opinion **:** COMPROMISE
2 : to draw out discussions or negotiations so as to gain time ⟨you'd have to *temporize* until you found out how she wanted to be advised —Mary Austin⟩
— **tem·po·ri·za·tion** \,tem-pə-rə-'zā-shən\ *noun*
— **tem·po·riz·er** *noun*
tem·po·ro·man·dib·u·lar \'tem-pə-rō-man-'di-byə-lər\ *adjective* [³*temporal* + *-o-* + *mandibular*] (1889)
: of, relating to, being, or affecting the joint between the temporal bone and the mandible ⟨*temporomandibular* dysfunction⟩
tempt \'tem(p)t\ *transitive verb* [Middle English, from Old French *tempter, tenter*, from Latin *temptare, tentare* to feel, try] (13th century)
1 : to entice to do wrong by promise of pleasure or gain
2 a *obsolete* **:** to make trial of **:** TEST **b :** to try presumptuously **:** PROVOKE **c :** to risk the dangers of
3 a : to induce to do something **b :** to cause to be strongly inclined ⟨was *tempted* to call it quits⟩
synonym see LURE
— **tempt·able** \'tem(p)-tə-bəl\ *adjective*
temp·ta·tion \tem(p)-'tā-shən\ *noun* (13th century)
1 : the act of tempting or the state of being tempted especially to evil **:** ENTICEMENT
2 : something tempting **:** a cause or occasion of enticement
tempt·er \'tem(p)-tər\ *noun* (14th century)
: one that tempts or entices
tempt·ing *adjective* (1596)
: having an appeal **:** ENTICING ⟨a *tempting* offer⟩
— **tempt·ing·ly** \-tiŋ-lē\ *adverb*
tempt·ress \'tem(p)-trəs\ *noun* (1594)
: a woman who tempts or entices
tem·pu·ra \'tem-pə-rə, -,rä; tem-'pùr-ə\ *noun* [Japanese *tenpura*] (1920)
: seafood or vegetables dipped in batter and fried in deep fat
ten \'ten\ *noun* [Middle English, from Old English *tīene*, from *tīen*, adjective, ten; akin to Old High German *zehan* ten, Latin *decem*, Greek *deka*] (before 12th century)
1 — see NUMBER table
2 : the 10th in a set or series ⟨wears a *ten*⟩
3 : something having 10 units or members

4 : a 10-dollar bill
— **ten** *adjective*
— **ten** *pronoun, plural in construction*

ten·a·ble \'te-nə-bəl\ *adjective* [Middle French, from Old French, from *tenir* to hold, from Latin *tenēre* — more at THIN] (1579)
: capable of being held, maintained, or defended : DEFENSIBLE, REASONABLE
— **ten·a·bil·i·ty** \,te-nə-'bi-lə-tē\ *noun*
— **ten·a·ble·ness** *noun*
— **ten·a·bly** \'te-nə-blē\ *adverb*

ten·ace \'te-,nās, te-'nās, 'te-nəs\ *noun* [modification of Spanish *tenaza*, literally, forceps, probably from Latin *tenacia*, neuter plural of *tenax*] (1655)
: a combination of two high or relatively high cards (as ace and queen) of the same suit in one hand with one ranking two degrees below the other

te·na·cious \tə-'nā-shəs\ *adjective* [Latin *tenac-, tenax* tending to hold fast, from *tenēre* to hold] (1607)
1 a : not easily pulled apart : COHESIVE, TOUGH ⟨a *tenacious* metal⟩ **b :** tending to adhere or cling especially to another substance : STICKY ⟨*tenacious* burs⟩ ⟨*tenacious* clay⟩
2 a : persistent in maintaining or adhering to something valued or habitual ⟨a man very *tenacious* of his rights⟩ **b :** RETENTIVE ⟨a *tenacious* memory⟩
synonym see STRONG
— **te·na·cious·ly** *adverb*
— **te·na·cious·ness** *noun*

te·nac·i·ty \tə-'na-sə-tē\ *noun* (1526)
: the quality or state of being tenacious
synonym see COURAGE

te·nac·u·lum \tə-'na-kyə-ləm\ *noun, plural* **-la** \-lə\ *or* **-lums** [New Latin, from Late Latin, instrument for holding, from Latin *tenēre*] (circa 1693)
1 : a slender sharp-pointed hook attached to a handle and used mainly in surgery for seizing and holding parts (as arteries)
2 : an adhesive animal structure

ten·an·cy \'te-nən(t)-sē\ *noun, plural* **-cies** (1590)
: a holding of an estate or a mode of holding an estate : the temporary possession or occupancy of something (as a house) that belongs to another; *also* : the period of a tenant's occupancy or possession

¹ten·ant \'te-nənt\ *noun* [Middle English, from Middle French, from present participle of *tenir* to hold] (14th century)
1 a : one who holds or possesses real estate or sometimes personal property (as an annuity) by any kind of right **b :** one who has the occupation or temporary possession of lands or tenements of another; *specifically* : one who rents or leases (as a house) from a landlord
2 : OCCUPANT, DWELLER
— **ten·ant·less** \-ləs\ *adjective*

²tenant *transitive verb* (1634)
: to hold or occupy as a tenant : INHABIT
— **ten·ant·able** \-nən-tə-bəl\ *adjective*

tenant farmer *noun* (1748)
: a farmer who works land owned by another and pays rent either in cash or in shares of produce

ten·ant·ry \'te-nən-trē\ *noun, plural* **-ries** (14th century)
1 : TENANCY
2 : a body of tenants

ten–cent store \'ten-'sent-\ *noun* (1901)
: FIVE-AND-TEN

tench \'tench\ *noun, plural* **tench** *or* **tench·es** [Middle English, from Middle French *tenche*, from Late Latin *tinca*] (14th century)
: a cyprinid fish (*Tinca tinca*) native to Eurasia but introduced in the U.S. and noted for its ability to survive outside water

Ten Commandments *noun plural* (13th century)
: the ethical commandments of God given according to biblical accounts to Moses by voice and by writing on stone tablets on Mount Sinai

¹tend \'tend\ *verb* [Middle English, short for *attenden* to attend] (14th century)
intransitive verb
1 *archaic* : LISTEN
2 : to pay attention : apply oneself ⟨*tend* to your own affairs⟩
3 : to act as an attendant : SERVE
4 *obsolete* : AWAIT
transitive verb
1 *archaic* : to attend as a servant
2 a : to apply oneself to the care of : watch over **b :** to have or take charge of as a caretaker or overseer **c :** CULTIVATE, FOSTER **d :** to manage the operations of : MIND ⟨*tend* the store⟩
3 : to stand by (as a rope) in readiness to prevent mischance (as fouling)

²tend *intransitive verb* [Middle English, from Middle French *tendre* to stretch, from Latin *tendere* — more at THIN] (14th century)
1 : to move, direct, or develop one's course in a particular direction ⟨cannot tell where society is *tending*⟩
2 : to exhibit an inclination or tendency : CONDUCE ⟨*tends* to be optimistic⟩

ten·dance \'ten-dən(t)s\ *noun* [short for *attendance*] (1573)
1 : watchful care
2 *archaic* : persons in attendance : RETINUE

ten·den·cious *chiefly British variant of* TENDENTIOUS

ten·den·cy \'ten-dən(t)-sē\ *noun, plural* **-cies** [Medieval Latin *tendentia*, from Latin *tendent-, tendens*, present participle of *tendere*] (1628)
1 a : direction or approach toward a place, object, effect, or limit **b :** a proneness to a particular kind of thought or action
2 a : the purposeful trend of something written or said : AIM **b :** deliberate but indirect advocacy ☆

ten·den·tious \ten-'den(t)-shəs\ *adjective* (1900)
: marked by a tendency in favor of a particular point of view : BIASED
— **ten·den·tious·ly** *adverb*
— **ten·den·tious·ness** *noun*

¹ten·der \'ten-dər\ *adjective* [Middle English, from Old French *tendre*, from Latin *tener*; perhaps akin to Latin *tenuis* thin, slight — more at THIN] (13th century)
1 a : having a soft or yielding texture : easily broken, cut, or damaged : DELICATE, FRAGILE ⟨*tender* feet⟩ **b :** easily chewed : SUCCULENT
2 a : physically weak : not able to endure hardship **b :** IMMATURE, YOUNG ⟨children of *tender* years⟩ **c :** incapable of resisting cold : not hardy
3 : marked by, responding to, or expressing the softer emotions : FOND, LOVING ⟨a *tender* lover⟩
4 a : showing care : CONSIDERATE, SOLICITOUS ⟨*tender* regard⟩ **b :** highly susceptible to impressions or emotions : IMPRESSIONABLE ⟨a *tender* conscience⟩
5 a : appropriate or conducive to a delicate or sensitive constitution or character : GENTLE, MILD ⟨*tender* breeding⟩ ⟨*tender* irony⟩ **b :** delicate or soft in quality or tone ⟨never before heard the piano sound so *tender* —Elva S. Daniels⟩
6 *obsolete* : DEAR, PRECIOUS
7 a : sensitive to touch or palpation ⟨the bruise was still *tender*⟩ **b :** sensitive to injury or insult : TOUCHY ⟨*tender* pride⟩ **c :** demanding careful and sensitive handling ⟨a *tender* situation⟩ **d** *of a ship* : ⁵CRANK
— **ten·der·ly** *adverb*
— **ten·der·ness** *noun*

²tender *verb* **ten·dered; ten·der·ing** \-d(ə-)riŋ\ (14th century)
transitive verb

1 : to make tender : SOFTEN, WEAKEN
2 *archaic* : to regard or treat with tenderness
intransitive verb
: to become tender

³tender *verb* **ten·dered; ten·der·ing** \-d(ə-)riŋ\ [Middle French *tendre* to stretch, stretch out, offer — more at TEND] (1535)
transitive verb
1 : to make a tender of
2 : to present for acceptance : OFFER ⟨*tendered* my resignation⟩
intransitive verb
: to make a bid or tender ⟨*tender* for a building contract⟩ ⟨*tendered* for 6% of the stock⟩

⁴tender *noun, often attributive* (circa 1543)
1 : an unconditional offer of money or service in satisfaction of a debt or obligation made to save a penalty or forfeiture for nonpayment or nonperformance
2 : an offer or proposal made for acceptance: as **a :** an offer of a bid for a contract **b :** a public expression of willingness to buy not less than a specified number of shares of a stock at a fixed price from stockholders usually in an attempt to gain control of the issuing company
3 : something that may be offered in payment; *specifically* : MONEY

⁵tender *noun* [¹*tender*] (1596)
obsolete : CONSIDERATION, REGARD

⁶tend·er \'ten-dər\ *noun* (1675)
: one that tends: as **a** (1) : a ship employed to attend other ships (as to supply provisions) (2) : a boat for communication between shore and a larger ship (3) : a warship that provides logistic support **b :** a car attached to a steam locomotive for carrying a supply of fuel and water

ten·der·foot \'ten-dər-,fut\ *noun, plural* **ten·der·feet** \-,fēt\ *also* **ten·der·foots** \-,futs\ (1849)
1 : a newcomer in a comparatively rough or newly settled region; *especially* : one not hardened to frontier or outdoor life
2 : an inexperienced beginner : NOVICE ⟨a political *tenderfoot*⟩

ten·der·heart·ed \'ten-dər-,här-təd\ *adjective* (15th century)
: easily moved to love, pity, or sorrow : COMPASSIONATE, IMPRESSIONABLE
— **ten·der·heart·ed·ly** *adverb*
— **ten·der·heart·ed·ness** *noun*

ten·der·ize \'ten-də-,rīz\ *transitive verb* **-ized; -iz·ing** (1930)
: to make (meat or meat products) tender by applying a process or substance that breaks down connective tissue
— **ten·der·i·za·tion** \,ten-d(ə-)rə-'zā-shən\ *noun*

— **ten·der·iz·er** \'ten-də-,rī-zər\ *noun*

ten·der·loin \'ten-dər-,lòin\ *noun* (circa 1828)
1 : a strip of tender meat consisting of a large internal muscle of the loin on each side of the vertebral column
2 [from its making possible a luxurious diet for a corrupt police officer] : a district of a city largely devoted to vice

ten·der–mind·ed \'ten-dər-,mīn-dəd\ *adjective* (1605)
: marked by idealism, optimism, and dogmatism

ten·der·om·e·ter \,ten-də-'rä-mə-tər\ *noun* (1938)
: a device for determining the maturity and tenderness of samples of fruits and vegetables

ten·di·ni·tis *or* **ten·don·itis** \,ten-də-'nī-təs\ *noun* [tendinitis from New Latin, from *tendin, tendo* + *-itis*; tendonitis from *tendon* + *-itis*] (circa 1900)
: inflammation of a tendon

ten·di·nous \'ten-də-nəs\ *adjective* [New Latin *tendinosus*, from *tendin-, tendo* tendon, alteration of Medieval Latin *tendon-, tendo*] (1658)
1 : consisting of tendons : SINEWY ⟨*tendinous* tissue⟩
2 : of, relating to, or resembling a tendon

ten·don \'ten-dən\ *noun* [Medieval Latin *tendon-, tendo*, from Latin *tendere* to stretch — more at THIN] (1541)
: a tough cord or band of dense white fibrous connective tissue that unites a muscle with some other part (as a bone) and transmits the force which the muscle exerts

tendon of Achil·les \-ə-'ki-lēz\ (circa 1885)
: ACHILLES TENDON

ten·dresse \tä⁼-dres\ *noun* [Middle English, from Middle French, from *tendre* tender] (14th century)
: FONDNESS

ten·dril \'ten-drəl\ *noun* [probably modification of Middle French *tendron, tendrum* bud, cartilage, from (assumed) Vulgar Latin *tenerumen*, from Latin *tener* tender — more at TENDER] (1538)
1 : a leaf, stipule, or stem modified into a slender spirally coiling sensitive organ serving to attach a climbing plant to its support
2 : something suggestive of a tendril ⟨*hair hanging in tendrils*⟩ ⟨*creeping tendrils of fog*⟩
— **ten·driled** *or* **ten·drilled** \-drəld\ *adjective*
— **ten·dril·ous** \-drə-ləs\ *adjective*

tendril 1

¹**-tene** *adjective combining form* [French *-tène*, from Latin *taenia* ribbon, band — more at TAENIA]
: having (such or so many) chromosomal filaments ⟨poly*tene*⟩ ⟨pachy*tene*⟩

²**-tene** *noun combining form*
: stage of meiotic prophase characterized by (such) chromosomal filaments ⟨diplo*tene*⟩ ⟨pachy*tene*⟩

Ten·e·brae \'te-nə-,brā, -,brī, -,brē\ *noun plural but singular or plural in construction* [Medieval Latin, from Latin, darkness — more at TEMERITY] (1651)
: a church service observed during the final part of Holy Week commemorating the sufferings and death of Christ

ten·e·brif·ic \,te-nə-'bri-fik\ *adjective* [Latin *tenebrae* darkness] (1785)
1 : GLOOMY
2 : causing gloom or darkness

te·ne·bri·o·nid \tə-'ne-brē-ə-nəd, ,te-nə-'brī-ə-nəd\ *noun* [New Latin *Tenebrionidae*, from *Tenebrion-, Tenebrio*, type genus, from Latin, one that shuns the light, from *tenebrae* darkness — more at TEMERITY] (1902)
: any of a family (Tenebrionidae) of firm-bodied mostly dark-colored vegetable-feeding beetles which often have vestigial and functionless wings and whose larvae are usually hard cylindrical worms (as a mealworm) — called also *darkling beetle*
— **tenebrionid** *adjective*

te·neb·ri·ous \tə-'ne-brē-əs\ *adjective* [by alteration] (1594)
: TENEBROUS

ten·e·brism \'te-nə-,bri-zəm\ *noun, often capitalized* [Latin *tenebrae* darkness] (1954)
: a style of painting especially associated with the Italian painter Caravaggio and his followers in which most of the figures are engulfed in shadow but some are dramatically illuminated by a concentrated beam of light usually from an identifiable source
— **ten·e·brist** \-brist\ *noun or adjective, often capitalized*

ten·e·brous \'te-nə-brəs\ *adjective* [Middle English, from Middle French *tenebreus*, from Latin *tenebrosus*, from *tenebrae*] (15th century)
1 : shut off from the light : DARK, MURKY
2 : hard to understand : OBSCURE
3 : causing gloom

1080 *also* **ten–eighty** \(,)ten-'ā-tē\ *noun* [from its laboratory serial number] (1945)
: a poisonous preparation of sodium fluoroacetate used as a rodenticide and pesticide

ten·e·ment \'te-nə-mənt\ *noun* [Middle English, from Middle French, from Medieval Latin *tenementum*, from Latin *tenēre* to hold — more at THIN] (14th century)
1 : any of various forms of corporeal property (as land) or incorporeal property that is held by one person from another
2 : DWELLING
3 a : a house used as a dwelling : RESIDENCE **b** : APARTMENT, FLAT **c** : TENEMENT HOUSE

tenement house *noun* (1858)
: APARTMENT HOUSE; *especially* : one meeting minimum standards of sanitation, safety, and comfort and usually located in a city

te·nes·mus \tə-'nez-məs\ *noun* [Latin, from Greek *teinesmos*, from *teinein* to stretch, strain — more at THIN] (1527)
: a distressing but ineffectual urge to evacuate the rectum or bladder

te·net \'te-nət *also* 'tē-nət\ *noun* [Latin, he holds, from *tenēre* to hold] (circa 1600)
: a principle, belief, or doctrine generally held to be true; *especially* : one held in common by members of an organization, movement, or profession

ten·fold \'ten-,fōld, -'fōld\ *adjective* (before 12th century)
1 : being 10 times as great or as many
2 : having 10 units or members
— **ten·fold** \-'fōld\ *adverb*

ten–gallon hat *noun* (1927)
: COWBOY HAT

te·nia, te·ni·a·sis *variant of* TAENIA, TAENIASIS

ten·ner \'te-nər\ *noun* (1845)
1 : a 10-pound note
2 : a 10-dollar bill

Ten·nes·see walking horse \'te-nə-,sē-\ *noun* [*Tennessee*, state of U.S.] (1938)
: any of an American breed of large easy-gaited saddle horses largely of standardbred and Morgan ancestry — called also *Tennessee walker*

ten·nies \'te-nēz\ *noun plural* [by shortening & alteration] (1951)
: TENNIS SHOES, SNEAKERS

Tennessee walking horse

ten·nis \'te-nəs\ *noun, often attributive* [Middle English *tenetz, tenys*, probably from Anglo-French *tenetz*, 2d person plural imperative of *tenir* to hold — more at TENABLE] (15th century)
1 : COURT TENNIS
2 : an indoor or outdoor game that is played with rackets and a light elastic ball by two players or pairs of players on a level court (as of clay or grass) divided by a low net

tennis elbow *noun* (1883)
: inflammation and pain over the outer side of the elbow usually resulting from excessive strain on and twisting of the forearm

tennis shoe *noun* (1886)
: a lightweight usually low-cut sneaker

ten·nist \'te-nist\ *noun* [blend of *tennis* and *-ist*] (1932)
: a tennis player

¹**ten·on** \'te-nən\ *noun* [Middle English, from Middle French, from *tenir* to hold — more at TENABLE] (15th century)
: a projecting member in a piece of wood or other material for insertion into a mortise to make a joint — see DOVETAIL illustration

²**tenon** *transitive verb* (1596)
1 : to unite by a tenon
2 : to cut or fit for insertion in a mortise

¹**ten·or** \'te-nər\ *noun* [Middle English, from Middle French, from Latin *tenor* uninterrupted course, from *tenēre* to hold — more at THIN] (14th century)
1 a : the drift of something spoken or written : PURPORT **b** : an exact copy of a writing : TRANSCRIPT **c** : the concept, object, or person meant in a metaphor
2 a : the melodic line usually forming the cantus firmus in medieval music **b** : the voice part next to the lowest in a 4-part chorus **c** : the highest natural adult male singing voice; *also* : a person having this voice **d** : a member of a family of instruments having a range next lower than that of the alto
3 : a continuance in a course, movement, or activity
4 : habitual condition : CHARACTER
synonym *see* TENDENCY

²**tenor** *adjective* (1522)
: relating to or having the range or part of a tenor

ten·or·ist \'te-nə-rist\ *noun* (1865)
: one who sings tenor or plays a tenor instrument

te·no·syn·o·vi·tis \,te-nō-,si-nə-'vī-təs, ,tē-\ *noun* [New Latin, from Greek *tenōn* tendon (akin to Greek *teinein* to stretch) + New Latin *synovitis* — more at THIN] (circa 1860)
: inflammation of a tendon sheath

ten·our \'te-nər\ *chiefly British variant of* TENOR

ten·pen·ny \'ten-'pe-nē, *British* -pə-nē\ *adjective* (1592)
: amounting to, worth, or costing 10 pennies

tenpenny nail *noun* [from its original price per hundred] (15th century)
: a nail three inches (7.6 centimeters) long

ten·pin \'ten-,pin\ *noun* (1807)
1 : a bottle-shaped bowling pin 15 inches high
2 *plural but singular in construction* : a bowling game using 10 tenpins and a large ball 27 inches in circumference and allowing each player to bowl 2 balls in each of 10 frames

ten·pound·er \'ten-'paùn-dər\ *noun* (1699)
: LADYFISH 2

ten·rec \'ten-,rek\ *noun* [French, from Malagasy *tàndraka*] (1785)
: any of numerous small often spiny mammalian insectivores (family Tenrecidae) chiefly of Madagascar

¹**tense** \'ten(t)s\ *noun* [Middle English *tens* time, tense, from Middle French, from Latin *tempus*] (14th century)
1 : a distinction of form in a verb to express distinctions of time or duration of the action or state it denotes
2 a : a set of inflectional forms of a verb that express distinctions of time **b** : an inflectional form of a verb expressing a specific time distinction

²**tense** *adjective* **tens·er; tens·est** [Latin *tensus*, from past participle of *tendere* to stretch — more at THIN] (1670)
1 : stretched tight : made taut : RIGID
2 a : feeling or showing nervous tension **b** : marked by strain or suspense
3 : produced with the muscles involved in a relatively tense state ⟨the vowels \ē\ and \ü\ in contrast with the vowels \i\ and \u̇\ are *tense*⟩
— **tense·ly** *adverb*
— **tense·ness** *noun*

³**tense** *verb* **tensed; tens·ing** (1676)
transitive verb
: to make tense
intransitive verb
: to become tense

ten·sile \'ten(t)-səl *also* 'ten-ˌsīl\ *adjective* [New Latin *tensilis*, from Latin *tensus*, past participle] (1626)
1 : capable of tension : DUCTILE
2 : of, relating to, or involving tension ⟨*tensile* stress⟩
— **ten·sil·i·ty** \ten-'si-lə-tē\ *noun*

tensile strength *noun* (circa 1864)
: the greatest longitudinal stress a substance can bear without tearing apart

ten·si·om·e·ter \ˌten(t)-sē-'ä-mə-tər\ *noun* [*tension*] (1912)
1 : a device for measuring tension (as of structural material)
2 : an instrument for determining the moisture content of soil
3 : an instrument for measuring the surface tension of liquids
— **ten·sio·met·ric** \-sē-ō-'me-trik\ *adjective*
— **ten·si·om·e·try** \-sē-'ä-mə-trē\ *noun*

¹**ten·sion** \'ten(t)-shən\ *noun* [Middle French or Latin; Middle French, from Latin *tension-, tensio*, from *tendere*] (1533)
1 a : the act or action of stretching or the condition or degree of being stretched to stiffness : TAUTNESS **b** : STRESS 1b
2 a : either of two balancing forces causing or tending to cause extension **b** : the stress resulting from the elongation of an elastic body
3 a : inner striving, unrest, or imbalance often with physiological indication of emotion **b** : a state of latent hostility or opposition between individuals or groups **c** : a balance maintained in an artistic work between opposing forces or elements
4 : a device to produce a desired tension (as in a loom)
— **ten·sion·al** \'ten(t)-sh(ə-)nəl\ *adjective*
— **ten·sion·less** \'ten(t)-shən-ləs\ *adjective*

²**tension** *transitive verb* **ten·sioned; ten·sion·ing** \'ten(t)-sh(ə-)niŋ\ (1891)
: to subject to tension; *especially* : to tighten to a desired or appropriate degree
— **ten·sion·er** \-sh(ə-)nər\ *noun*

ten·si·ty \'ten(t)-sə-tē\ *noun, plural* **-ties** (circa 1658)
: the quality or state of being tense : TENSENESS

ten·sive \'ten(t)-siv\ *adjective* (1702)
: of, relating to, or causing tension

ten·sor \'ten(t)-sər, 'ten-ˌsȯr\ *noun* [New Latin, from Latin *tendere*] (circa 1704)
1 : a muscle that stretches a part
2 : a generalized vector with more than three components each of which is a function of the coordinates of an arbitrary point in space of an appropriate number of dimensions

ten–speed \'ten-ˌspēd\ *noun* (1971)
: a bicycle with 10 gear combinations

tens place \'tenz-\ *noun* (1937)
: the place two to the left of the decimal point in a number expressed in the Arabic system of writing numbers

ten–strike \'ten-ˌstrīk\ *noun* (1840)
1 : a strike in tenpins
2 : a highly successful stroke or achievement

¹**tent** \'tent\ *noun* [Middle English *tente*, from Old French *tente*, feminine of *ten-*

tus, past participle of *tendere* to stretch — more at THIN] (14th century)
1 : a collapsible shelter of fabric (as nylon or canvas) stretched and sustained by poles and used for camping outdoors or as a temporary building
2 : DWELLING
3 a : something that resembles a tent or that serves as a shelter; *especially* : a canopy or enclosure placed over the head and shoulders to retain vapors or oxygen during medical administration **b** : the web of a tent caterpillar
— **tent·less** \'tent-ləs\ *adjective*
— **tent·like** \-ˌlīk\ *adjective*

²**tent** (1607)
intransitive verb
1 : to reside for the time being : LODGE
2 : to live in a tent
transitive verb
1 : to cover with or as if with a tent
2 : to lodge in tents

³**tent** *transitive verb* [Middle English, from *tent* attention, short for *attent*, from Old French *attente*, from *atendre* to attend] (14th century)
chiefly Scottish : to attend to

ten·ta·cle \'ten-ti-kəl\ *noun* [New Latin *tentaculum*, from Latin *tentare* to feel, touch — more at TEMPT] (1762)
1 : any of various elongate flexible usually tactile or prehensile processes borne by animals and especially invertebrates chiefly on the head or about the mouth
2 a : something that resembles a tentacle especially in or as if in grasping or feeling out **b** : a sensitive hair or emergence on a plant (as the sundew)
— **ten·ta·cled** \-kəld\ *adjective*

ten·tac·u·lar \ten-'ta-kyə-lər\ *adjective* [New Latin *tentaculum*] (1828)
1 : of, relating to, or resembling tentacles
2 : equipped with tentacles

tent·age \'ten-tij\ *noun* (1603)
: a collection of tents : tent equipment

ten·ta·tive \'ten-tə-tiv\ *adjective* [Medieval Latin *tentativus*, from Latin *tentatus*, past participle of *tentare, temptare* to feel, try] (1626)
1 : not fully worked out or developed ⟨*tentative* plans⟩
2 : HESITANT, UNCERTAIN ⟨a *tentative* smile⟩
— **tentative** *noun*
— **ten·ta·tive·ly** *adverb*
— **ten·ta·tive·ness** *noun*

tent caterpillar *noun* (1854)
: any of several destructive gregarious caterpillars (genus *Malacosoma* and especially *M. americanum* of the family Lasiocampidae) that construct large silken webs on trees

tent·ed \'ten-təd\ *adjective* (1604)
1 : covered with a tent or tents
2 : shaped like a tent

¹**ten·ter** \'ten-tər\ *noun* [Middle English *teyntur, tentowre*] (14th century)
1 : a frame or endless track with hooks or clips along two sides that is used for drying and stretching cloth
2 *archaic* : TENTERHOOK

²**tenter** *noun* (1846)
: one who lives in or occupies a tent

ten·ter·hook \'ten-tər-ˌhu̇k\ *noun* (15th century)
: a sharp hooked nail used especially for fastening cloth on a tenter
— **on tenterhooks** : in a state of uneasiness, strain, or suspense

tenth \'ten(t)th\ *noun, plural* **tenths** \'ten(t)s, 'ten(t)ths\ (15th century)
1 — see NUMBER table
2 a : a musical interval embracing an octave and a third **b** : the tone at this interval
— **tenth** *adjective or adverb*

tenth–rate \'tenth-'rāt\ *adjective* (1834)
: of the lowest character or quality

tent stitch *noun* (1639)

: a short stitch slanting to the right that is used in embroidery to form even lines of solid background

tenty *also* **tent·ie** \'ten-tē\ *adjective* [³*tent*] (circa 1555)
Scottish : ATTENTIVE, WATCHFUL

te·nu·is \'ten-yə-wəs\ *noun, plural* **-u·es** \-yə-ˌwēz, -ˌwās\ [Medieval Latin, from Latin, thin, slight] (1650)
: an unaspirated voiceless stop

te·nu·ity \te-'nü-ə-tē, tə-, -'nyü-\ *noun* [Latin *tenuitas*, from *tenuis* thin, tenuous] (circa 1536)
1 : lack of substance or strength
2 : lack of thickness : SLENDERNESS, THINNESS
3 : lack of density : rarefied quality or state

ten·u·ous \'ten-yə-wəs\ *adjective* [Latin *tenuis* thin, slight, tenuous — more at THIN] (1597)
1 : not dense ⟨a *tenuous* fluid⟩
2 : not thick : SLENDER ⟨a *tenuous* rope⟩
3 a : having little substance or strength : FLIMSY, WEAK ⟨*tenuous* influences⟩ **b** : SHAKY 2a ⟨*tenuous* reasons⟩ ⟨on grounds that were *tenuous*⟩
synonym see THIN
— **ten·u·ous·ly** *adverb*
— **ten·u·ous·ness** *noun*

ten·ure \'ten-yər *also* -ˌyu̇r\ *noun* [Middle English, from Middle French *teneüre, tenure*, from Medieval Latin *tenitura*, from (assumed) Vulgar Latin *tenitus*, past participle of Latin *tenēre* to hold — more at THIN] (15th century)
1 : the act, right, manner, or term of holding something (as a landed property, a position, or an office); *especially* : a status granted after a trial period to a teacher that gives protection from summary dismissal
2 : GRASP, HOLD
— **ten·ur·able** \-ə-bəl\ *adjective*
— **te·nur·ial** \te-'nyu̇r-ē-əl\ *adjective*
— **te·nur·ial·ly** \-ə-lē\ *adverb*

ten·ured \'ten-yərd\ *adjective* (1965)
: having tenure ⟨*tenured* faculty members⟩

ten·ure–track \'ten-yər-ˌtrak *also* -ˌyu̇r-\ *adjective* (1976)
: relating to or being a teaching position that may lead to a grant of tenure

te·nu·to \tā-'nü-(ˌ)tō\ *adverb or adjective* [Italian, from past participle of *tenere* to hold, from Latin *tenēre*] (1762)
: in a manner so as to hold a tone or chord to its full value — used as a direction in music

te·o·cal·li \ˌtē-ə-'ka-lē, ˌtā-ə-'kä-\ *noun* [Nahuatl *teōcalli*, from *teōtl* god + *calli* house] (1613)
: an ancient temple of Mexico or Central America usually built upon the summit of a truncated pyramidal mound; *also* : the mound itself

te·o·sin·te \ˌtā-ō-'sin-tē\ *noun* [Mexican Spanish, from Nahuatl *teōcintli*, from *teōtl* god + *cintli* dried ears of maize] (circa 1877)
: a tall annual grass (*Zea mexicana* synonym *Euchlaena mexicana*) of Mexico and Central America that is closely related to and sometimes considered ancestral to maize

te·pa \'tē-pə\ *noun* [*tri-* + *ethylene* + *phosphor-* + *amide*] (1953)
: a soluble crystalline compound $C_6H_{12}N_3OP$ that is used especially as a chemical sterilizing agent of insects, a palliative in some kinds of cancer, and in finishing and flame-proofing textiles

te·pa·ry bean \'te-pə-rē-\ *noun* [origin unknown] (1912)
: an annual twining bean (*Phaseolus acutifolius* variety *latifolius*) that is native to the

\ə\ abut \ᵊ\ kitten \ər\ further \a\ ash \ā\ ace
\ä\ mop, mar \au̇\ out \ch\ chin \e\ bet \ē\ easy
\g\ go \i\ hit \ī\ ice \j\ job \ŋ\ sing \ō\ go
\ȯ\ law \ȯi\ boy \th\ thin \th\ the \ü\ loot \u̇\ foot
\y\ yet \zh\ vision *see also* Guide to Pronunciation

southwestern U.S. and Mexico and is cultivated for its roundish white, yellow, brown, or bluish black edible seeds; *also* : the seed

te·pee \'tē-(,)pē\ *noun* [Dakota *tʰípi,* from *tʰi-* to dwell] (1743)
: a conical tent usually consisting of skins and used especially by American Indians of the Plains

teph·ra \'te-frə\ *noun* [New Latin, from Greek, ashes; akin to Sanskrit *dahati* it burns — more at FOMENT] (1944)
: solid material ejected into the air during a volcanic eruption; *especially* : ²ASH 2b

tepee

tep·id \'te-pəd\ *adjective* [Middle English *teped,* from Latin *tepidus,* from *tepēre* to be moderately warm; akin to Sanskrit *tapati* it heats, Old Irish *tess* heat] (14th century)
1 : moderately warm : LUKEWARM ⟨a *tepid* bath⟩
2 a : lacking in passion, force, or zest ⟨a *tepid* joke⟩ **b** : marked by an absence of enthusiasm or conviction ⟨a *tepid* interest⟩
— **te·pid·i·ty** \te-'pi-də-tē, te-\ *noun*
— **tep·id·ly** \'te-pəd-lē\ *adverb*
— **tep·id·ness** *noun*

TEPP \,tē-(,)ē-(,)pē-'pē\ *noun* [tetra- + ethyl + pyrophosphate] (1948)
: a mobile hygroscopic corrosive liquid organophosphate $C_8H_{20}O_7P_2$ that is a powerful anticholinesterase and is used especially as an insecticide

te·qui·la \tə-'kē-lə, tā-\ *noun* [Spanish, from *Tequila,* town in Jalisco state, Mexico] (1849)
: a Mexican liquor distilled from pulque

tequila sunrise *noun* (1965)
: a cocktail consisting of tequila, orange juice, and grenadine

ter- *combining form* [Latin, from *ter;* akin to Greek & Sanskrit *tris* three times, Latin *tres* three — more at THREE]
: three times : threefold : three ⟨*tercentenary*⟩

tera- *combining form* [International Scientific Vocabulary, from Greek *terat-, teras* monster]
: trillion ⟨*terawatt*⟩

te·rai \tə-'rī\ *noun* [*Tarai,* lowland belt of India] (1888)
: a wide-brimmed double felt sun hat worn especially in subtropical regions

ter·aph \'ter-əf\ *noun, plural* **ter·a·phim** \'ter-ə-,fim\ [Hebrew *tĕrāphīm* (plural in form but singular in meaning)] (14th century)
: an image of a Semitic household god

terat- *or* **terato-** *combining form* [Greek, from *terat-, teras* marvel, portent, monster]
: developmental malformation ⟨*teratogenic*⟩

te·rato·car·ci·no·ma \,ter-ə-tō-,kär-sᵊn-'ō-mə\ *noun* (1946)
: a malignant teratoma; *especially* : one involving germinal cells of the testis

te·rato·gen \tə-'ra-tə-jən\ *noun* (1959)
: a teratogenic agent

ter·a·to·gen·e·sis \,ter-ə-tə-'je-nə-səs\ *noun* [New Latin] (1901)
: production of developmental malformations

ter·a·to·gen·ic \-'je-nik\ *adjective* (1879)
: of, relating to, or causing developmental malformations ⟨*teratogenic* substances⟩ ⟨*teratogenic* effects⟩
— **ter·a·to·ge·nic·i·ty** \-jə-'ni-sə-tē\ *noun*

ter·a·to·log·i·cal \,ter-ə-tᵊl-'ä-ji-kəl\ *or* **ter·a·to·log·ic** \-jik\ *adjective* (1857)
1 : abnormal in growth or structure
2 : of or relating to teratology

ter·a·tol·o·gy \,ter-ə-'tä-lə-jē\ *noun* (circa 1842)
: the study of malformations or serious deviations from the normal type in organisms
— **ter·a·tol·o·gist** \-jist\ *noun*

ter·a·to·ma \,ter-ə-'tō-mə\ *noun* [New Latin] (1879)
: a tumor made up of a heterogeneous mixture of tissues

tera·watt \'ter-ə-,wät\ *noun* (1970)
: a unit of power equal to one trillion watts

ter·bi·um \'tər-bē-əm\ *noun* [New Latin, from *Ytterby,* Sweden] (1843)
: a usually trivalent metallic element of the rare-earth group — see ELEMENT table

terce \'tərs\ *noun, often capitalized* [Middle English, third, terce — more at TIERCE] (14th century)
: the third of the canonical hours

ter·cel \'tər-səl\ *variant of* TIERCEL

ter·cen·te·na·ry \,tər-(,)sen-'te-nə-rē, (,)tər-'sen-tᵊn-,er-ē\ *noun, plural* **-ries** (1855)
: a 300th anniversary or its celebration
— **tercentenary** *adjective*

ter·cen·ten·ni·al \,tər-(,)sen-'te-nē-əl\ *adjective or noun* (1872)
: TERCENTENARY

ter·cet \'tər-sət\ *noun* [Italian *terzetto,* from diminutive of *terzo* third, from Latin *tertius* — more at THIRD] (1598)
: a unit or group of three lines of verse: **a** : one of the 3-line stanzas in terza rima **b** : one of the two groups of three lines forming the sestet in an Italian sonnet

ter·e·binth \'ter-ə-,bin(t)th\ *noun* [Middle English *terebynt,* from Middle French *terebinthe,* from Latin *terebinthus* — more at TURPENTINE] (14th century)
: a small European tree (*Pistacia terebinthus*) of the cashew family yielding turpentine

te·re·do \tə-'rē-(,)dō, -'rā-\ *noun, plural* **teredos** *or* **te·red·i·nes** \-'re-dᵊn-,ēz\ [Middle English, from Latin *teredin-, teredo,* from Greek *terēdōn;* akin to Greek *tetrainein* to bore — more at THROW] (14th century)
: SHIPWORM

tere·phthal·ate \,ter-ə(f)-'tha-,lāt\ *noun* (1868)
: a salt or ester of terephthalic acid; *especially* : a dimethyl-ester that is a major starting material for polyester fibers and coatings

tere·phthal·ic acid \,ter-ə(f)-'tha-lik-\ *noun* [International Scientific Vocabulary *terebene,* mixture of terpenes from distilled turpentine + *phthalic acid*] (1857)
: a *p*-dicarboxylic acid $C_8H_6O_4$ that is obtained especially by oxidation of xylene and is used chiefly in the synthesis of polyesters

te·rete \tə-'rēt, te-\ *adjective* [Latin *teret-, teres* well turned, rounded; akin to Latin *terere* to rub — more at THROW] (circa 1619)
: approximately cylindrical but usually tapering at both ends ⟨a *terete* seedpod⟩

Te·reus \'tir-,yüs, 'tē-,rüs\ *noun* [Latin, from Greek *Tēreus*]
: the husband of Procne who rapes his sister-in-law Philomela

ter·gite \'tər-,gīt\ *noun* [New Latin *tergum*] (1885)
: the dorsal plate or dorsal portion of the covering of a metameric segment of an arthropod; *especially* : one on the abdomen

ter·gi·ver·sate \'tər-jə-vər-,sāt; ,tər-'ji-vər-,sāt, -'gi-; ,tər-jə-'vər\ *intransitive verb* **-sat·ed; -sat·ing** [Latin *tergiversatus,* past participle of *tergiversari* to show reluctance, from *tergum* back + *versare* to turn, frequentative of *vertere* to turn — more at WORTH] (1654)
: to engage in tergiversation
— **ter·gi·ver·sa·tor** \-,sā-tər\ *noun*

ter·gi·ver·sa·tion \,tər-,ji-vər-'sā-shən, -,gi-; ,tər-ji-(,)vər-\ *noun* (1570)
1 : evasion of straightforward action or clear-cut statement : EQUIVOCATION
2 : desertion of a cause, position, party, or faith

ter·gum \'tər-gəm\ *noun, plural* **ter·ga** \-gə\ [New Latin, from Latin, back] (circa 1826)
: the dorsal part or plate of a segment of an arthropod : TERGITE, NOTUM
— **ter·gal** \-gəl\ *adjective*

ter·i·ya·ki \,ter-ē-'yä-kē\ *noun* [Japanese, from *teri* glaze + *yaki* broil] (1962)
: a Japanese dish of meat or fish that is grilled or broiled after being soaked in a seasoned soy sauce marinade

¹term \'tərm\ *noun* [Middle English *terme* boundary, end, from Old French, from Latin *terminus;* akin to Greek *termōn* boundary, end, Sanskrit *tarman* top of a post] (13th century)
1 a : END, TERMINATION; *also* : a point in time assigned to something (as a payment) **b** : the time at which a pregnancy of normal length terminates ⟨had her baby at full *term*⟩
2 a : a limited or definite extent of time; *especially* : the time for which something lasts : DURATION, TENURE ⟨*term* of office⟩ ⟨lost money in the short *term*⟩ **b** : the whole period for which an estate is granted; *also* : the estate or interest held by one for a term **c** : the time during which a court is in session
3 *plural* : provisions that determine the nature and scope of an agreement : CONDITIONS ⟨*terms* of sale⟩ ⟨liberal credit *terms*⟩
4 a : a word or expression that has a precise meaning in some uses or is peculiar to a science, art, profession, or subject ⟨legal *terms*⟩ **b** *plural* : expression of a specified kind ⟨described in glowing *terms*⟩
5 a : a unitary or compound expression connected with another by a plus or minus sign **b** : an element of a fraction or proportion or of a series or sequence
6 *plural* **a** : mutual relationship : FOOTING ⟨on good *terms*⟩ **b** : AGREEMENT, CONCORD ⟨come to *terms*⟩
7 : any of the three substantive elements of a syllogism
8 : a quadrangular pillar often tapering downward and adorned on the top with the figure of a head or the upper part of the body
9 : division in a school year during which instruction is regularly given to students
— **in terms of** : with respect to or in relation to ⟨thinks of everything *in terms of* money⟩
— **on one's own terms** : in accordance with one's wishes : in one's own way ⟨prefers to live *on his own terms*⟩

²term *transitive verb* (circa 1557)
: to apply a term to : CALL, NAME

¹ter·ma·gant \'tər-mə-gənt\ *noun* [Middle English]
1 *capitalized* : a deity erroneously ascribed to Islam by medieval European Christians and represented in early English drama as a violent character
2 : an overbearing or nagging woman : SHREW

²termagant *adjective* (1596)
: OVERBEARING, SHREWISH

term·er \'tər-mər\ *noun* (1634)
: a person serving for a specified term (as in a political office or in prison) ⟨a first *termer*⟩

ter·mi·na·ble \'tər-mə-nə-bəl, 'tərm-nə-\ *adjective* [Middle English, from *terminen* to terminate, from Middle French *terminer,* from Latin *terminare*] (15th century)
: capable of being terminated
— **ter·mi·na·ble·ness** *noun*
— **ter·mi·na·bly** \-blē\ *adverb*

¹ter·mi·nal \'tərm-nəl, 'tər-mə-nᵊl\ *adjective* [Latin *terminalis,* from *terminus*] (1744)
1 a : of or relating to an end, extremity, boundary, or terminus ⟨a *terminal* pillar⟩ **b** : growing at the end of a branch or stem ⟨a *terminal* bud⟩
2 a : of, relating to, or occurring in a term or each term ⟨*terminal* payments⟩ **b** : leading ultimately to death ⟨*terminal* cancer⟩ **c** : approaching or close to death : being in the final stages of a fatal disease ⟨a *terminal* patient⟩ **d** : extremely or hopelessly severe ⟨*terminal* boredom⟩
3 a : occurring at or constituting the end of a period or series : CONCLUDING ⟨the *terminal*

moments of life⟩ **b :** not intended as preparation for further academic work ⟨a *terminal* curriculum⟩
synonym see LAST
— **ter·mi·nal·ly** *adverb*

²**terminal** *noun* (1831)
1 : a part that forms the end **:** EXTREMITY, TERMINATION
2 : a terminating usually ornamental detail **:** FINIAL
3 : a device attached to the end of a wire or cable or to an electrical apparatus for convenience in making connections
4 a : either end of a carrier line having facilities for the handling of freight and passengers **b :** a freight or passenger station that is central to a considerable area or serves as a junction at any point with other lines **c :** a town or city at the end of a carrier line **:** TERMINUS
5 : a combination of a keyboard and output device (as a video display unit) by which data can be entered into or output from a computer or electronic communications system

terminal leave *noun* (1944)
: a final leave consisting of accumulated unused leave granted to a member of the armed forces just prior to separation or discharge from service

terminal side *noun* (1927)
: a straight line that has been rotated around a point on another line to form an angle measured in a clockwise or counterclockwise direction — compare INITIAL SIDE

¹**ter·mi·nate** \'tər-mə-nət\ *adjective* [Middle English, from Latin *terminatus*, past participle of *terminare*, from *terminus*] (15th century)
: coming to an end or capable of ending

²**ter·mi·nate** \-ˌnāt\ *verb* **-nat·ed; -nat·ing** (1610)
intransitive verb
1 : to extend only to a limit (as a point or line); *especially* **:** to reach a terminus
2 : to form an ending
3 : to come to an end in time
transitive verb
1 a : to bring to an end **:** CLOSE ⟨*terminate* a marriage by divorce⟩ ⟨*terminate* a transmission line⟩ **b :** to form the conclusion of ⟨review questions *terminate* each chapter⟩ **c :** to discontinue the employment of ⟨workers *terminated* because of slow business⟩
2 : to serve as an ending, limit, or boundary of
synonym see CLOSE

terminating decimal *noun* (circa 1909)
: a decimal which can be expressed in a finite number of figures or for which all figures to the right of some place are zero — compare REPEATING DECIMAL

ter·mi·na·tion \ˌtər-mə-'nā-shən\ *noun* (circa 1500)
1 : end in time or existence **:** CONCLUSION ⟨the *termination* of life⟩
2 : the last part of a word; *especially* **:** an inflectional ending
3 : the act of terminating
4 : a limit in space or extent **:** BOUND
5 : OUTCOME, RESULT
— **ter·mi·na·tion·al** \-shnəl, -shə-n°l\ *adjective*

ter·mi·na·tive \'tər-mə-ˌnā-tiv\ *adjective* (15th century)
: tending or serving to terminate **:** ENDING
— **ter·mi·na·tive·ly** *adverb*

ter·mi·na·tor \-ˌnā-tər\ *noun* (1770)
1 : the dividing line between the illuminated and the unilluminated part of the moon's or a planet's disk
2 : one that terminates

ter·mi·nol·o·gy \ˌtər-mə-'nä-lə-jē\ *noun, plural* **-gies** [Medieval Latin *terminus* term, expression (from Latin, boundary, limit) + English *-o-* + *-logy*] (1801)
1 : the technical or special terms used in a business, art, science, or special subject
2 : nomenclature as a field of study

— **ter·mi·no·log·i·cal** \-mə-n°l-'ä-ji-kəl\ *adjective*
— **ter·mi·no·log·i·cal·ly** \-ji-k(ə-)lē\ *adverb*

term insurance *noun* (1897)
: insurance for a specified period that provides for no payment to the insured except on losses during the period and that becomes void upon its expiration

ter·mi·nus \'tər-mə-nəs\ *noun, plural* **-ni** \-ˌnī, -ˌnē\ *or* **-nus·es** [Latin, boundary, end — more at TERM] (circa 1617)
1 : a final goal **:** a finishing point
2 : a post or stone marking a boundary
3 : either end of a transportation line or travel route; *also* **:** the station, town, or city at such a place **:** TERMINAL
4 : an extreme point or element **:** TIP ⟨the *terminus* of a glacier⟩

terminus ad quem \-ˌäd-'kwem\ *noun* [New Latin, literally, limit to which] (circa 1555)
1 : a goal, object, or course of action **:** DESTINATION, PURPOSE
2 : a final limiting point in time

terminus a quo \-ˌä-'kwō\ *noun* [New Latin, literally, limit from which] (circa 1555)
1 : a point of origin
2 : a first limiting point in time

ter·mi·tar·i·um \ˌtər-mə-'ter-ē-əm, -ˌmī-\ *noun, plural* **-ia** \-ē-ə\ [New Latin] (1863)
: a termites' nest

ter·mi·tary \'tər-mə-ˌter-ē, -ˌmī-ˌter-ē\ *noun, plural* **-tar·ies** (1826)
: TERMITARIUM

ter·mite \'tər-ˌmīt\ *noun* [New Latin *Termit-, Termes*, genus of termites, from Late Latin, a worm that eats wood, alteration of Latin *tarmit-, tarmes*; akin to Greek *tetrainein* to bore — more at THROW] (1781)
: any of numerous pale-colored soft-bodied social insects (order Isoptera) that live in colonies consisting usually of winged sexual forms, wingless sterile workers, and soldiers, feed on wood, and include some which are very destructive to wooden structures and trees — called also *white ant*

term·less \'tərm-ləs\ *adjective* (circa 1541)
1 : having no term or end **:** BOUNDLESS, UNENDING
2 : UNCONDITIONED, UNCONDITIONAL

term paper *noun* (1926)
: a major written assignment in a school or college course representative of a student's achievement during a term

tern \'tərn\ *noun* [of Scandinavian origin; akin to Danish *terne* tern] (1678)
: any of various chiefly marine birds (subfamily Sterninae of the family Laridae and especially genus *Sterna*) that differ from the related gulls in usually smaller size, a more slender build, a sharply pointed bill, narrower wings, and an often forked tail

ter·na·ry \'tər-nə-rē\ *adjective* [Middle English, from Latin *ternarius*, from *terni* three each; akin to Latin *tres* three — more at THREE] (15th century)
1 a : of, relating to, or proceeding by threes **b :** having three elements, parts, or divisions **:** THREEFOLD **c :** arranged in threes ⟨*ternary* petals⟩
2 : using three as the base ⟨a *ternary* logarithm⟩
3 a : being or consisting of an alloy of three elements **b :** of, relating to, or containing three different elements, atoms, radicals, or groups ⟨sulfuric acid is a *ternary* acid⟩
4 : third in order or rank

ter·nate \'tər-ˌnāt, -nət\ *adjective* [New Latin *ternatus*, from Medieval Latin, past participle of *ternare* to treble, from Latin *terni*] (1760)
: arranged in threes or in subdivisions so arranged ⟨a *ternate* leaf⟩
— **ter·nate·ly** *adverb*

terne \'tərn\ *noun* [terneplate] (1891)

1 : an alloy of lead and tin typically in a ratio of four to one that is used as a coating in producing terneplate
2 : TERNEPLATE

terne·plate \-ˌplāt\ *noun* [probably from French *terne* dull (from Middle French, from *ternir* to tarnish) + English *plate*] (circa 1858)
: sheet iron or steel coated with an alloy of about four parts lead to one part tin

ter·pene \'tər-ˌpēn\ *noun* [International Scientific Vocabulary *terp-* (from German *Terpentin* turpentine, from Medieval Latin *terbentina*) + *-ene* — more at TURPENTINE] (1873)
: any of various isomeric hydrocarbons $C_{10}H_{16}$ found present in essential oils (as from conifers) and used especially as solvents and in organic synthesis; *broadly* **:** any of numerous hydrocarbons $(C_5H_8)_n$ found especially in essential oils, resins, and balsams
— **ter·pene·less** \-ləs\ *adjective*
— **ter·pe·noid** \-ˌtər-pə-ˌnóid, ˌtər-'pē-\ *adjective* or *noun*

ter·pin·e·ol \ˌtər-'pi-nē-ˌól, -ˌōl\ *noun* [International Scientific Vocabulary, from *terpine* $(C_{10}H_{18}(OH)_2)$] (1894)
: any of three fragrant isomeric alcohols $C_{10}H_{17}OH$ found in essential oils or made artificially and used especially in perfume or as solvents

ter·poly·mer \ˌtər-'pä-lə-mər\ *noun* (1947)
: a polymer (as a complex resin) that results from copolymerization of three discrete monomers

Terp·sich·o·re \ˌtərp-'si-kə-(ˌ)rē\ *noun* [Latin, from Greek *Terpsichorē*]
: the Greek Muse of dancing and choral song

terp·si·cho·re·an \ˌtərp-(ˌ)si-kə-'rē-ən; -sə-'kór-ē-, -'kór-\ *adjective* (1825)
: of or relating to dancing

ter·ra \'ter-ə\ *noun, plural* **ter·rae** \-(ˌ)ē, -ˌī\ [New Latin, from Latin, land] (1946)
: any of the relatively light-colored highland areas on the surface of the moon or a planet

¹**ter·race** \'ter-əs\ *noun* [Middle French, pile of earth, platform, terrace, from Old Provençal *terrassa*, from *terra* earth, from Latin, earth, land; akin to Latin *torrēre* to parch — more at THIRST] (1515)
1 a : a colonnaded porch or promenade **b :** a flat roof or open platform **c :** a relatively level paved or planted area adjoining a building
2 a : a raised embankment with the top leveled **b :** one of usually a series of horizontal ridges made in a hillside to increase cultivatable land, conserve moisture, or minimize erosion
3 : a level ordinarily narrow plain usually with steep front bordering a river, lake, or sea; *also* **:** a similar undersea feature
4 a : a row of houses or apartments on raised ground or a sloping site **b :** a group of row houses **c :** a strip of park in the middle of a street often planted with trees or shrubs **d :** STREET
5 : a section of a British soccer stadium set aside for standing spectators

²**terrace** *transitive verb* **ter·raced; ter·rac·ing** (1615)
1 : to provide (as a building or hillside) with a terrace
2 : to make into a terrace

ter·ra-cot·ta \ˌter-ə-'kä-tə\ *noun, often attributive* [Italian *terra cotta*, literally, baked earth] (1722)
1 : a glazed or unglazed fired clay used especially for statuettes and vases and architectural purposes (as roofing, facing, and relief ornamentation)
2 : a brownish orange

terra fir·ma \-'fər-mə *also* -'fir-\ *noun* [New Latin, literally, solid land] (1693)
: dry land : solid ground

ter·rain \tə-'rān *also* te-\ *noun* [French, land, ground, from (assumed) Vulgar Latin *terranum,* alteration of Latin *terrenum,* from neuter of *terrenus* of earth — more at TERRENE] (1766)
1 a (1) : a geographical area (2) : a piece of land : GROUND **b** : the physical features of a tract of land
2 : TERRANE 1
3 a : a field of knowledge or interest : TERRITORY **b** : ENVIRONMENT, MILIEU

ter·ra in·cog·ni·ta \'ter-ə-,in-'käg-'nē-tə, -in-'käg-nə-tə\ *noun, plural* **ter·rae in·cog·ni·tae** \'ter-ī-,in,-käg-nē-,tī, -in-'käg-nə-,tī\ [Latin] (1616)
: unknown territory : an unexplored country or field of knowledge

Ter·ra·my·cin \,ter-ə-'mī-s⁰n\ *trademark*
— used for oxytetracycline

ter·rane \tə-'rān, te-\ *noun* [alteration of *terrain*] (1864)
1 : the area or surface over which a particular rock or group of rocks is prevalent
2 : TERRAIN 1a

ter·ra·pin \'ter-ə-pən, 'tar-\ *noun* [of Algonquian origin; akin to Delaware (dialect of New York) *tó'lpe'w,* a kind of turtle] (1613)
: any of various aquatic turtles (family Emydidae); *especially* : DIAMOND-BACK TERRAPIN

terrapin

terr·aque·ous \te-'rä-kwē-əs, tə-, -'ra-\ *adjective* [Latin *terra* land + English *aqueous*] (circa 1658)
: consisting of land and water

ter·rar·i·um \tə-'rar-ē-əm, -'rer-\ *noun, plural* **-ia** \-ē-ə\ *or* **-i·ums** [New Latin, from Latin *terra* + *-arium* (as in *vivarium*)] (1890)
: a usually transparent enclosure for keeping or raising plants or usually small animals (as turtles) indoors

ter·raz·zo \tə-'ra-(,)zō, -'rät-(,)sō\ *noun* [Italian, literally, terrace, perhaps from Old Provençal *terrassa*] (1897)
: a mosaic flooring consisting of small pieces of marble or granite set in mortar and given a high polish

¹ter·rene \te-'rēn, tə-; 'ter-,ēn\ *adjective* [Middle English, from Latin *terrenus* of earth, from *terra* earth] (14th century)
: MUNDANE, EARTHLY

²terrene *noun* (1667)
: a land area : EARTH, TERRAIN

ter·re·plein \'ter-ə-,plān\ *noun* [Middle French, from Old Italian *terrapieno,* from Medieval Latin *terraplenum,* from *terra plenus* filled with earth] (1591)
: the level space behind a parapet of a rampart where guns are mounted

ter·res·tri·al \tə-'res-t(r)ē-əl; -'res-chəl, -'resh-\ *adjective* [Middle English, from Latin *terrestris,* from *terra* earth — more at TERRACE] (15th century)
1 a : of or relating to the earth or its inhabitants 〈*terrestrial* magnetism〉 **b** : mundane in scope or character : PROSAIC
2 a : of or relating to land as distinct from air or water 〈*terrestrial* transportation〉 **b** (1) : living on or in or growing from land 〈*terrestrial* plants〉 (2) : of or relating to terrestrial organisms 〈*terrestrial* habits〉
3 : belonging to the class of planets that are like the earth (as in density and silicate composition) 〈the *terrestrial* planets Mercury, Venus, and Mars〉
— **terrestrial** *noun*
— **ter·res·tri·al·ly** *adverb*

ter·ret \'ter-ət\ *noun* [Middle English *turette,* alteration of *toret,* from Middle French, from Old French, diminutive of *tour* circuit, ring — more at TURN] (15th century)
: one of the rings on the top of a harness pad through which the reins pass

ter·ri·ble \'ter-ə-bəl\ *adjective* [Middle English, from Middle French, from Latin *terribilis,* from *terrēre* to frighten — more at TERROR] (15th century)
1 a : exciting extreme alarm or intense fear : TERRIFYING **b** : formidable in nature : AWESOME 〈a *terrible* responsibility〉 **c** : DIFFICULT 〈in a *terrible* bind〉
2 : EXTREME, GREAT 〈a *terrible* disappointment〉
3 : extremely bad: as **a** : strongly repulsive : OBNOXIOUS 〈a *terrible* smell〉 **b** : notably unattractive or objectionable **c** : of very poor quality 〈a *terrible* movie〉
— **ter·ri·ble·ness** *noun*
— **ter·ri·bly** \-blē\ *adverb*

ter·ric·o·lous \te-'ri-kə-ləs, tə-\ *adjective* [Latin *terricola* earth dweller, from *terra* earth + *colere* to inhabit — more at WHEEL] (circa 1836)
: living on or in the ground

ter·ri·er \'ter-ē-ər\ *noun* [Middle English, from Middle French (*chien*) *terrier,* literally, earth dog, from *terrier* of earth, from Medieval Latin *terrarius,* from Latin *terra*] (15th century)
: any of various usually small dogs originally used by hunters to dig for small furred game and engage the quarry underground or drive it out

ter·rif·ic \tə-'ri-fik\ *adjective* [Latin *terrificus,* from *terrēre* to frighten] (1667)
1 a : very bad : FRIGHTFUL **b** : exciting or fit to excite fear or awe
2 : EXTRAORDINARY 〈*terrific* speed〉
3 : unusually fine : MAGNIFICENT 〈*terrific* weather〉
— **ter·rif·i·cal·ly** \-fi-k(ə-)lē\ *adverb*

ter·ri·fy \'ter-ə-,fī\ *transitive verb* **-fied; -fy·ing** [Latin *terrificare,* from *terrificus*] (1575)
1 a : to drive or impel by menacing : SCARE : DETER, INTIMIDATE
2 : to fill with terror

ter·ri·fy·ing \-,fī-in\ *adjective* (circa 1586)
1 : causing terror or apprehension
2 : of a formidable nature
— **ter·ri·fy·ing·ly** \-in-lē\ *adverb*

ter·rig·e·nous \te-'ri-jə-nəs, tə-\ *adjective* [Latin *terrigena* earthborn, from *terra* earth + *gignere* to beget — more at KIN] (1882)
: being or relating to oceanic sediment derived directly from the destruction of rocks on the earth's surface

ter·rine \tə-'rēn, ter-'ēn\ *noun* [French — more at TUREEN] (circa 1706)
1 a : TUREEN **b** : a usually earthenware dish in which foods are cooked and served
2 : a mixture of chopped meat, fish, or vegetables cooked and served in a terrine

¹ter·ri·to·ri·al \,ter-ə-'tōr-ē-əl, -'tȯr-\ *adjective* (1625)
1 a : NEARBY, LOCAL **b** : serving outlying areas : REGIONAL
2 a : of or relating to a territory 〈*territorial* government〉 **b** : of or relating to or organized chiefly for home defense 〈a *territorial* army〉 **c** : of or relating to private property
3 a : of or relating to an assigned or preempted area 〈*territorial* commanders〉 **b** : exhibiting territoriality 〈*territorial* birds〉
— **ter·ri·to·ri·al·ly** \-ē-ə-lē\ *adverb*

²territorial *noun* (1907)
: a member of a territorial military unit

territorial court *noun* (1857)
: a court in a U.S. territory that has jurisdiction over local and federal cases

ter·ri·to·ri·al·ism \,ter-ə-'tōr-ē-ə-,li-zəm, -'tȯr-\ *noun* (1881)
1 : LANDLORDISM
2 : the principle established in 1555 requiring the inhabitants of a territory of the Holy Roman Empire to conform to the religion of their ruler or to emigrate
— **ter·ri·to·ri·al·ist** \-list\ *noun*

ter·ri·to·ri·al·i·ty \-,tōr-ē-'a-lə-tē, -,tȯr-\ *noun* (1894)
1 : territorial status
2 a : persistent attachment to a specific territory **b** : the pattern of behavior associated with the defense of a territory

ter·ri·to·ri·al·ize \-'tōr-ē-ə-,līz, -'tȯr-\ *transitive verb* **-ized; -iz·ing** (1818)
: to organize on a territorial basis
— **ter·ri·to·ri·al·i·za·tion** \-,tōr-ē-ə-lə-'zā-shən, -,tȯr-\ *noun*

territorial waters *noun plural* (1841)
: the waters under the sovereign jurisdiction of a nation or state including both marginal sea and inland waters

ter·ri·to·ry \'ter-ə-,tōr-ē, -,tȯr-\ *noun, plural* **-ries** [Middle English, from Latin *territorium,* literally, land around a town, from *terra* land — more at TERRACE] (15th century)
1 a : a geographical area belonging to or under the jurisdiction of a governmental authority **b** : an administrative subdivision of a country **c** : a part of the U.S. not included within any state but organized with a separate legislature **d** : a geographical area (as a colonial possession) dependent on an external government but having some degree of autonomy
2 a : an indeterminate geographical area **b** : a field of knowledge or interest
3 a : an assigned area; *especially* : one in which a sales representative or distributor operates **b** : an area often including a nesting or denning site and a variable foraging range that is occupied and defended by an animal or group of animals
— **go with the territory** *or* **come with the territory** : to be a natural or unavoidable aspect or accompaniment of a particular situation, position, or field 〈criticism *goes with the territory* in this job〉

ter·ror \'ter-ər\ *noun* [Middle English, from Middle French *terreur,* from Latin *terror,* from *terrēre* to frighten; akin to Greek *trein* to be afraid, flee, *tremein* to tremble — more at TREMBLE] (14th century)
1 : a state of intense fear
2 a : one that inspires fear : SCOURGE **b** : a frightening aspect 〈the *terrors* of invasion〉 **c** : a cause of anxiety : WORRY **d** : an appalling person or thing; *especially* : BRAT
3 : REIGN OF TERROR
4 : violence (as bombing) committed by groups in order to intimidate a population or government into granting their demands 〈insurrection and revolutionary *terror*〉
synonym see FEAR
— **ter·ror·less** \-ləs\ *adjective*

ter·ror·ise *chiefly British variant of* TERRORIZE

ter·ror·ism \'ter-ər-,i-zəm\ *noun* (1795)
: the systematic use of terror especially as a means of coercion
— **ter·ror·ist** \-ər-ist\ *adjective or noun*
— **ter·ror·is·tic** \,ter-ər-'is-tik\ *adjective*

ter·ror·ize \'ter-ər-,īz\ *transitive verb* **-ized; -iz·ing** (1823)
1 : to fill with terror or anxiety : SCARE
2 : to coerce by threat or violence
— **ter·ror·i·za·tion** \,ter-ər-ə-'zā-shən\ *noun*

ter·ry \'ter-ē\ *noun, plural* **terries** [perhaps modification of French *tiré,* past participle of *tirer* to draw] (1784)
1 : the loop forming the pile in uncut pile fabrics
2 : an absorbent fabric with such loops — called also *terry cloth*

terse \'tərs\ *adjective* **ters·er; ters·est** [Latin *tersus* clean, neat, from past participle of *tergēre* to wipe off] (1601)
1 : smoothly elegant : POLISHED
2 : devoid of superfluity 〈a *terse* summary〉; *also* : SHORT, BRUSQUE 〈dismissed me with a *terse* "no"〉
synonym see CONCISE
— **terse·ly** *adverb*
— **terse·ness** *noun*

¹ter·tian \'tər-shən\ *adjective* [Middle English *tercian,* from Latin *tertianus,* literally, of the third, from *tertius* third — more at THIRD] (14th century)
: recurring at approximately 48-hour intervals — used of malaria

²tertian *noun* (14th century)
: a tertian fever (as vivax malaria)

¹ter·tia·ry \'tər-shē-,er-ē, -shə-rē\ *noun, plural* **-ries** (circa 1550)
1 [Medieval Latin *tertiarius,* from Latin, of a third] : a member of a monastic third order especially of lay people
2 *capitalized* : the Tertiary period or system of rocks

²tertiary *adjective* [Latin *tertiarius* of or containing a third, from *tertius* third] (circa 1656)
1 a : of third rank, importance, or value **b** *chiefly British* : of, relating to, or being higher education **c** : of, relating to, or constituting the third strongest of the three or four degrees of stress recognized by most linguists (as the stress of the third syllable of *basketball team*)
2 *capitalized* : of, relating to, or being the first period of the Cenozoic era or the corresponding system of rocks marked by the formation of high mountains (as the Alps, Caucasus, and Himalayas) and the dominance of mammals on land — see GEOLOGIC TIME table
3 a : involving or resulting from the substitution of three atoms or groups ⟨a *tertiary* salt⟩ ⟨*tertiary* amine⟩ **b** : being or containing a carbon atom having bonds to three other carbon atoms ⟨an acid containing a *tertiary* carbon⟩ ⟨*tertiary* alcohols⟩
4 : occurring in or being a third stage: as **a** : being or relating to the recovery of oil and gas from old wells by means of the underground application of heat and chemicals **b** : being or relating to the purification of wastewater by removal of fine particles, nitrates, and phosphates

tertiary color *noun* (circa 1864)
1 : a color produced by mixing two secondary colors
2 : a color produced by an equal mixture of a primary color with a secondary color adjacent to it on the color wheel

tertiary syphilis *noun* (1875)
: the third stage of syphilis that develops after the disappearance of the secondary symptoms and is marked by ulcers in and gummas under the skin and commonly by involvement of the skeletal, cardiovascular, and nervous systems

ter·ti·um quid \,tər-shē-əm-'kwid, ,tər-tē-\ *noun* [Late Latin, literally, third something; from its failing to fit into a dichotomy] (circa 1724)
1 : a middle course or an intermediate component ⟨where there are two systems of law and two orders of courts, there must . . . be some *tertium quid* to deal with conflicts of law and jurisdiction —Ernest Baker⟩
2 : a third party of ambiguous status ⟨there was a man and his wife and a *tertium quid* —Rudyard Kipling⟩

ter·va·lent \,tər-'vā-lənt, 'tər-\ *adjective* (circa 1903)
: TRIVALENT

ter·za ri·ma \,tert-sə-'rē-mə\ *noun* [Italian, literally, third rhyme] (1819)
: a verse form consisting of tercets usually in iambic pentameter in English poetry with an interlaced rhyme scheme (as *aba, bcb, cdc*)

tes·la \'tes-lə\ *noun* [Nikola *Tesla*] (1958)
: a unit of magnetic flux density in the meter-kilogram-second system equivalent to one weber per square meter

tes·sel·late \'te-sə-,lāt\ *transitive verb* **-lat·ed; -lat·ing** [Late Latin *tessellatus,* past participle of *tessellare* to pave with tesserae, from Latin *tessella,* diminutive of *tessera*] (1789)
: to form into or adorn with mosaic

tes·sel·lat·ed \-,lā-təd\ *adjective* (1695)
: having a checkered appearance

tes·sel·la·tion \,te-sə-'lā-shən\ *noun* (1660)
1 : MOSAIC; *especially* : a covering of an infinite geometric plane without gaps or overlaps by congruent plane figures of one type or a few types
2 : an act of tessellating : the state of being tessellated

tes·sera \'te-sə-rə\ *noun, plural* **-ser·ae** \-,rē, -,rī\ [Latin, probably ultimately from Greek *tessares* four; from its having four corners — more at FOUR] (circa 1656)
1 : a small tablet (as of wood, bone, or ivory) used by the ancient Romans as a ticket, tally, voucher, or means of identification
2 : a small piece (as of marble, glass, or tile) used in mosaic work

tes·ser·act \'te-sə-,rakt\ *noun* [Greek *tessares* four + *aktis* ray — more at ACTIN-] (1888)
: the four-dimensional analogue of a cube

tes·si·tu·ra \,te-sə-'tür-ə\ *noun* [Italian, literally, texture, from Latin *textura*] (circa 1891)
: the general range of a melody or voice part; *specifically* : the part of the register in which most of the tones of a melody or voice part lie

¹test \'test\ *noun* [Middle English, vessel in which metals were assayed, cupel, from Middle French, from Latin *testum* earthen vessel; akin to Latin *testa* earthen pot, shell] (14th century)
1 a *chiefly British* : CUPEL **b** (1) : a critical examination, observation, or evaluation : TRIAL; *specifically* : the procedure of submitting a statement to such conditions or operations as will lead to its proof or disproof or to its acceptance or rejection ⟨a *test* of a statistical hypothesis⟩ (2) : a basis for evaluation : CRITERION **c** : an ordeal or oath required as proof of conformity with a set of beliefs
2 a : a means of testing: as (1) : a procedure, reaction, or reagent used to identify or characterize a substance or constituent (2) : something (as a series of questions or exercises) for measuring the skill, knowledge, intelligence, capacities, or aptitudes of an individual or group **b** : a positive result in such a test
3 : a result or value determined by testing
4 : TEST MATCH ◇

²test (1689)
transitive verb
1 : to put to test or proof : TRY
2 : to require a doctrinal oath of
intransitive verb
1 a : to undergo a test **b** : to be assigned a standing or evaluation on the basis of tests ⟨*tested* positive for cocaine⟩ ⟨the cake *tested* done⟩
2 : to apply a test as a means of analysis or diagnosis — used with *for* ⟨*test* for mechanical aptitude⟩
— **test·abil·i·ty** \,tes-tə-'bi-lə-tē\ *noun*
— **test·able** \'tes-tə-bəl\ *adjective*
— **test the waters** *also* **test the water** : to make a preliminary test or survey (as of reaction or interest) before embarking on a course of action

³test *noun* [Latin *testa* shell] (circa 1842)
: an external hard or firm covering (as a shell) of many invertebrates (as a foraminifer or a mollusk)

tes·ta \'tes-tə\ *noun, plural* **tes·tae** \-,tē, -,tī\ [New Latin, from Latin, shell] (1796)
: the hard external coating or integument of a seed

tes·ta·ceous \tes-'tā-shəs\ *adjective* [Latin *testaceus,* from *testa* shell, earthen pot, brick] (1646)
1 : having a shell ⟨a *testaceous* protozoan⟩
2 : of any of the several light colors of bricks

tes·ta·cy \'tes-tə-sē\ *noun, plural* **-cies** (circa 1864)
: the state of being testate

tes·ta·ment \'tes-tə-mənt\ *noun* [Middle English, from Late Latin & Latin; Late Latin *testamentum* covenant with God, holy scripture, from Latin, last will, from *testari* to be a witness, call to witness, make a will, from *testis* witness; akin to Latin *tres* three & to Latin

stare to stand; from the witness's standing by as a third party in a litigation — more at THREE, STAND] (14th century)
1 a *archaic* : a covenant between God and the human race **b** *capitalized* : either of two main divisions of the Bible
2 a : a tangible proof or tribute **b** : an expression of conviction : CREDO
3 a : an act by which a person determines the disposition of his or her property after death **b** : WILL
— **tes·ta·men·ta·ry** \,tes-tə-'men-tə-rē, -'men-trē\ *adjective*

tes·tate \'tes-,tāt, -tət\ *adjective* [Middle English, from Latin *testatus,* past participle of *testari* to make a will] (15th century)
: having left a valid will ⟨she died *testate*⟩

tes·ta·tor \'tes-,tā-tər, tes-'\ *noun* [Middle English *testatour,* from Anglo-French, from Late Latin *testator,* from *testari*] (15th century)
: a person who dies leaving a will or testament in force

tes·ta·trix \'tes-,tā-triks, tes-'\ *noun* [Late Latin, feminine of *testator*] (1591)
: a female testator

test ban *noun* (1958)
: a self-imposed partial or complete ban on the testing of nuclear weapons that is mutually agreed to by countries possessing such weapons

test bed *noun* (1914)
: a vehicle (as an airplane) used for testing new equipment (as engines or weapons systems)

test case *noun* (1894)
1 : a representative case whose outcome is likely to serve as a precedent
2 : a proceeding brought by agreement or on an understanding of the parties to obtain a decision as to the constitutionality of a statute

test·cross \'tes(t)-,kròs\ *noun* (1934)
: a genetic cross between a homozygous recessive individual and a corresponding suspected heterozygote to determine the genotype of the latter
— **testcross** *transitive verb*

test–drive \'tes(t)-,drīv\ *transitive verb* **-drove** \-,drōv\; **-driv·en** \-,dri-vən\; **-driv·ing** \-,drī-vin\ (1950)

◇ **WORD HISTORY**
test Latin *testu* or *testum* was a generally used word for an earthenware pot. In the Middle Ages its descendant in Old French, *test,* denoted a specific type of vessel that was used in the assaying of precious metals, namely, a cupel. The cupel or test is a shallow, porous cup. When impure silver or gold is heated in it, the impurities are absorbed in the porous material, leaving a relatively pure button of silver or gold. As the name for a cupel, *test* was borrowed into later Middle English as *test* or *teste.* By about 1600 it was being used figuratively: *to put to the test* or *to bring to the test* was to make trial of something, to determine its quality or genuineness, as a precious metal might be tried in a cupel. The sense "trial, critical examination" soon became the most common meaning of *test.* French *têt,* the modern outcome of Old French *test,* has retained only its limited reference to an assayer's cupel; but Latin *testa* "earthenware jar, shard, shell," a feminine noun closely related to *testu,* went off in a quite different figurative direction, developing in French into *tête,* the usual word for "head."

\ə\ **abut** \ᵊ\ **kitten** \ər\ **further** \a\ **ash** \ā\ **ace** \ä\ **mop, mar** \aù\ **out** \ch\ **chin** \e\ **bet** \ē\ **easy** \g\ **go** \i\ **hit** \ī\ **ice** \j\ **job** \ŋ\ **sing** \ō\ **go** \ò\ **law** \òi\ **boy** \th\ **thin** \ṯẖ\ **the** \ü\ **loot** \ù\ **foot** \y\ **yet** \zh\ **vision** *see also* Guide to Pronunciation

: to drive (a motor vehicle) in order to evaluate performance
— **test–drive** *noun*

test·ed \'tes-təd\ *adjective* (1748)
: subjected to or qualified through testing — often used in combination ⟨time-*tested* principles⟩

test·ee \tes-'tē\ *noun* (1930)
: one who takes an examination

¹**tes·ter** \'tēs-tər, 'tes-\ *noun* [Middle English, from Middle French *testiere* headpiece, head covering, from *teste* head, from Late Latin *testa* skull, from Latin, shell] (14th century)
: the canopy over a bed, pulpit, or altar

²**tes·ter** \'tes-tər\ *noun* [modification of Middle French *testart*, from *teston*] (1546)
: TESTON a

³**test·er** \'tes-tər\ *noun* (1661)
: one that tests or is used for testing

test–fly \-,flī\ *transitive verb* -**flew** \-,flü\; -**flown** \-,flōn\; -**fly·ing** (1936)
: to subject to a flight test ⟨*test-fly* an experimental plane⟩

tes·ti·cle \'tes-ti-kəl\ *noun* [Middle English *testicle*, from Latin *testiculus*, diminutive of *testis*] (15th century)
: TESTIS; *especially* : one of a higher mammal usually with its enclosing structures
— **tes·tic·u·lar** \tes-'ti-kyə-lər\ *adjective*

tes·ti·fy \'tes-tə-,fī\ *verb* -**fied**; -**fy·ing** [Middle English *testifien*, from Latin *testificari*, from *testis* witness] (14th century)
intransitive verb
1 a : to make a statement based on personal knowledge or belief **b** : to serve as evidence or proof
2 : to express a personal conviction
3 : to make a solemn declaration under oath for the purpose of establishing a fact (as in a court)
transitive verb
1 a : to bear witness to : ATTEST **b** : to serve as evidence of : PROVE
2 *archaic* **a** : to make known (a personal conviction) **b** : to give evidence of : SHOW
3 : to declare under oath before a tribunal or officially constituted public body
— **tes·ti·fi·er** \-,fī(-ə)r\ *noun*

¹**tes·ti·mo·ni·al** \,tes-tə-'mō-nē-əl, -nyəl\ *adjective* (15th century)
1 : of, relating to, or constituting testimony
2 : expressive of appreciation or esteem ⟨a *testimonial* dinner⟩

²**testimonial** *noun* (15th century)
1 : EVIDENCE, TESTIMONY
2 a : a statement testifying to benefits received **b** : a character reference : letter of recommendation
3 : an expression of appreciation : TRIBUTE

tes·ti·mo·ny \'tes-tə-,mō-nē\ *noun, plural* -**nies** [Middle English, from Late Latin & Latin; Late Latin *testimonium* Decalogue, from Latin, evidence, witness, from *testis* witness — more at TESTAMENT] (14th century)
1 a (1) : the tablets inscribed with the Mosaic law (2) : the ark containing the tablets **b** : a divine decree attested in the Scriptures
2 a : firsthand authentication of a fact : EVIDENCE **b** : an outward sign **c** : a solemn declaration usually made orally by a witness under oath in response to interrogation by a lawyer or authorized public official
3 a : an open acknowledgment **b** : a public profession of religious experience

test·ing *adjective* (1878)
: requiring maximum effort or ability ⟨a most difficult and *testing* problem —Ernest Bevin⟩

tes·tis \'tes-təs\ *noun, plural* **tes·tes** \'tes-,tēz\ [Latin, witness, testis] (circa 1704)
: a typically paired male reproductive gland that produces sperm and that in most mammals is contained within the scrotum at sexual maturity

test–mar·ket \'tes(t)-,mär-kət\ *transitive verb* (1953)

: to subject (a product) to trial in a limited market

test match *noun* (1862)
1 : any of a series of championship cricket matches played between teams representing Australia and England
2 : a championship game or series (as of cricket) played between teams representing different countries

tes·ton \'tes-,tän\ *or* **tes·toon** \tes-'tün\ *noun* [Middle French, from Old Italian *testone*, augmentative of *testa* head, from Late Latin, skull — more at TESTER] (1536)
: any of several old European coins: as **a** : a shilling of Henry VIII of England decreasing in value to ninepence and then to sixpence in Shakespeare's time **b** : a French silver coin of the 16th century worth between 10 and 14½ sous

tes·tos·ter·one \te-'stäs-tə-,rōn\ *noun* [*testis* + -*o*- + *sterone*] (1935)
: a hormone that is a hydroxy steroid ketone $C_{19}H_{28}O_2$ produced especially by the testes or made synthetically and that is responsible for inducing and maintaining male secondary sex characters

test pattern *noun* (circa 1946)
: a fixed picture broadcast by a television station to assist viewers in adjusting their receivers

test pilot *noun* (1917)
: a pilot who specializes in putting new or experimental airplanes through maneuvers designed to test them (as for strength) by producing strains in excess of normal

test–tube *adjective* (1935)
: produced by fertilization in laboratory apparatus and implantation in the uterus, by fertilization and growth in laboratory apparatus, or sometimes by artificial insemination ⟨*test-tube* babies⟩

test tube *noun* (1846)
: a plain or lipped tube usually of thin glass closed at one end and used especially in chemistry and biology

tes·tu·do \tes-'tü-(,)dō, -'tyü-\ *noun, plural* -**dos** [Latin *testudin-, testudo*, literally, tortoise, tortoise shell; akin to Latin *testa* shell] (1609)
: a cover of overlapping shields or a shed wheeled up to a wall used by the ancient Romans to protect an attacking force

tes·ty \'tes-tē\ *adjective* **tes·ti·er; -est** [Middle English *testif*, from Anglo-French, headstrong, from Old French *teste* head — more at TESTER] (1526)
1 : easily annoyed : IRRITABLE
2 : marked by impatience or ill humor ⟨*testy* remarks⟩
— **tes·ti·ly** \-tə-lē\ *adverb*
— **tes·ti·ness** \-tē-nəs\ *noun*

Tet \'tet\ *noun* [Vietnamese *tết*] (1885)
: the Vietnamese New Year observed for three days beginning at the first new moon after January 20

tet·a·nal \'te-t⁵n-əl\ *adjective* (1939)
: of, relating to, or derived from tetanus ⟨*tetanal* toxin⟩

te·tan·ic \te-'ta-nik\ *adjective* (circa 1727)
: of, relating to, being, or tending to produce tetany or tetanus
— **te·tan·i·cal·ly** \-ni-k(ə-)lē\ *adverb*

tet·a·nize \'te-t⁵n-,īz\ *transitive verb* -**nized; -niz·ing** (1849)
: to induce tetanus in ⟨*tetanize* a muscle⟩
— **tet·a·ni·za·tion** \,te-t⁵n-ə-'zā-shən, ,tet-nə-\ *noun*

tet·a·nus \'te-t⁵n-əs, 'tet-nəs\ *noun* [Middle English, from Latin, from Greek *tetanos*, from *tetanos* stretched, rigid; akin to Greek *teinein* to stretch — more at THIN] (14th century)
1 a : an acute infectious disease characterized by tonic spasm of voluntary muscles especially of the jaw and caused by the specific toxin of a bacterium (*Clostridium tetani*) which is usually introduced through a wound — com-

pare LOCKJAW **b** : the bacterium that causes tetanus
2 : prolonged contraction of a muscle resulting from rapidly repeated motor impulses

tet·a·ny \'te-t⁵n-ē, 'tet-nē\ *noun* [International Scientific Vocabulary, from Latin *tetanus*] (circa 1885)
: a condition of physiologic calcium imbalance marked by tonic spasm of muscles and often associated with deficient parathyroid secretion

te·tar·to·he·dral \te-,tär-tə-'hē-drəl\ *adjective* [Greek *tetartos* fourth; akin to Greek *tettares* four — more at FOUR] (circa 1858)
of a crystal : having one fourth the number of planes required by complete symmetry — compare HEMIHEDRAL, HOLOHEDRAL

tetched *variant of* TECHED

tetchy \'te-chē\ *adjective* **tetch·i·er; -est** [perhaps from obsolete *tetch* habit] (1592)
: irritably or peevishly sensitive : TOUCHY ⟨the *tetchy* manner of two women living in the same house —Elizabeth Taylor (died 1975)⟩
— **tetch·i·ly** \-chə-lē\ *adverb*
— **tetch·i·ness** \-chē-nəs\ *noun*

¹**tête–à–tête** \,tet-ə-'tet, ,tät-ə-'tät, 2 is also 'tēt-ə-,tēt\ *noun* [French, literally, head to head] (1697)
1 : a private conversation between two persons
2 : a short piece of furniture (as a sofa) intended to seat two persons especially facing each other

²**tête–à–tête** \,tet-ə-'tet, ,tät-ə-'tät\ *adverb* (1700)
: in private

³**tête–à–tête** \,tet-ə-,tet, ,tät-ə-,tät\ *adjective* (1728)
: FACE-TO-FACE, PRIVATE

tête–bêche \'tet-'besh\ *adjective* [French, noun, pair of inverted stamps, from *tête* head + -*bêche*, alteration of Middle French *bechevet* head against foot] (circa 1913)
: of or relating to a pair of stamps inverted in relation to one another either through a printing error or intentionally

teth \'tāt, 'tāth, 'tās\ *noun* [Hebrew *tēth*] (circa 1823)
: the 9th letter of the Hebrew alphabet — see ALPHABET table

¹**teth·er** \'te-thər\ *noun* [Middle English *tethir*, probably of Scandinavian origin; akin to Old Norse *tjōthr* tether; akin to Old High German *zeotar* pole of a wagon] (14th century)
1 : something (as a rope or chain) by which an animal is fastened so that it can range only within a set radius
2 : the limit of one's strength or resources ⟨at the end of my *tether*⟩

²**tether** *transitive verb* **teth·ered; teth·er·ing** \-th(ə-)riŋ\ (15th century)
: to fasten or restrain by or as if by a tether

teth·er·ball \'te-thər-,bol\ *noun* (circa 1900)
: a game played with a ball suspended by a string from an upright pole in which the object for each contestant is to wrap the string around the pole by striking the ball in a direction opposite to that of the other contestant; *also* : the ball used in this game

Te·thys \'tē-thəs\ *noun* [Latin, from Greek *Tēthys*]
: a Titaness and wife of Oceanus

tet·ra \'te-trə\ *noun* [by shortening from New Latin *Tetragonopterus*, former genus name, from Late Latin *tetragonum* quadrangle + Greek *pteron* wing — more at TETRAGONAL, FEATHER] (1931)
: any of numerous small often brightly colored South American characin fishes often bred in tropical aquariums

tetra- *or* **tetr-** *combining form* [Middle English, from Latin, from Greek; akin to Greek *tettares* four — more at FOUR]
1 : four : having four : having four parts ⟨*tetravalent*⟩

2 : containing four atoms or groups (of a specified kind) ⟨*tetrachloride*⟩

tet·ra·caine \'te-trə-ˌkān\ *noun* [*tetra-* + *-caine*] (circa 1935)
: a crystalline basic ester $C_{15}H_{24}N_2O_2$ that is closely related chemically to procaine and is used chiefly in the form of its hydrochloride as a local anesthetic

tet·ra·chlo·ride \ˌte-trə-'klōr-ˌīd, -'klȯr-\ *noun* (1866)
: a chloride containing four atoms of chlorine

tet·ra·chord \'te-trə-ˌkȯrd\ *noun* [Greek *tetrachordon*, from neuter of *tetrachordos* of four strings, from *tetra-* + *chordē* string — more at YARN] (1603)
: a diatonic series of four tones with an interval of a perfect fourth between the first and last

tet·ra·cy·cline \ˌte-trə-'sī-ˌklēn\ *noun* [International Scientific Vocabulary *tetracyclic* having four fused hydrocarbon rings + ²-*ine*] (1952)
: a yellow crystalline broad-spectrum antibiotic $C_{22}H_{24}N_2O_8$ produced by streptomyces or synthetically

tet·rad \'te-ˌtrad\ *noun* [Greek *tetrad-, tetras,* from *tetra-*] (1653)
: a group or arrangement of four: as **a :** a group of four cells produced by the successive divisions of a mother cell ⟨a *tetrad* of spores⟩ **b :** a group of four synapsed chromatids that become visibly evident in the pachytene stage of meiotic prophase
— **te·trad·ic** \te-'tra-dik\ *adjective*

tet·ra·drachm \'te-trə-ˌdram\ *noun* [Greek *tetradrachmon,* from *tetra-* + *drachmē* drachma] (circa 1580)
: an ancient Greek silver coin worth four drachmas

tet·ra·dy·na·mous \ˌte-trə-'dī-nə-məs\ *adjective* [International Scientific Vocabulary *tetra-* + Greek *dynamis* power — more at DYNAMIC] (1830)
: having six stamens four of which are longer than the others ⟨*tetradynamous* plants of the mustard family⟩

tet·ra·eth·yl lead \ˌte-trə-ˌe-thəl-'led\ *noun* (1923)
: a heavy oily poisonous liquid $Pb(C_2H_5)_4$ used as an antiknock agent

tet·ra·flu·o·ride \ˌte-trə-'flȯr-ˌīd, -'flu̇r-\ *noun* (circa 1909)
: a fluoride containing four atoms of fluorine

te·trag·o·nal \te-'tra-gə-nᵊl\ *adjective* [Late Latin *tetragonalis* having four angles and four sides, from *tetragonum* quadrangle, from Greek *tetragōnon,* from neuter of *tetragōnos* tetragonal, from *tetra-* + *gōnia* angle — more at -GON] (1868)
: of, relating to, or characteristic of the tetragonal system
— **te·trag·o·nal·ly** \-nᵊl-ē\ *adverb*

tetragonal system *noun* (1879)
: a crystal system characterized by three axes at right angles of which only the two lateral axes are equal

tet·ra·gram·ma·ton \ˌte-trə-'gra-mə-ˌtän\ *noun* [Middle English, from Greek, from neuter of *tetragrammatos* having four letters, from *tetra-* + *grammat-, gramma* letter — more at GRAM] (15th century)
: the four Hebrew letters usually transliterated YHWH or JHVH that form a biblical proper name of God — compare YAHWEH

tet·ra·he·dral \ˌte-trə-'hē-drəl\ *adjective* (1794)
1 : being a polyhedral angle with four faces
2 : relating to, forming, or having the form of a tetrahedron
— **tet·ra·he·dral·ly** \-drə-lē\ *adverb*

tet·ra·he·drite \-ˌdrīt\ *noun* [German *Tetraëdrit,* from Late Greek *tetraedros* having four faces] (1868)
: a fine-grained gray mineral that consists of a sulfide of copper, iron, and antimony, often

contains other elements (as silver), and occurs in tetrahedral crystals or in massive form

tet·ra·he·dron \ˌte-trə-'hē-drən\ *noun, plural* **-drons** *or* **-dra** \-drə\ [New Latin, from Late Greek *tetraedron,* neuter of *tetraedros* having four faces, from Greek *tetra-* + *hedra* seat, face — more at SIT] (1570)
: a polyhedron that has four faces

tetrahedron

tet·ra·hy·dro·can·nab·i·nol \-ˌhī-drə-kə-'na-bə-ˌnȯl, -ˌnōl\ *noun* [*tetrahydro-* (combined with four atoms of hydrogen) + *cannabin-* + ¹-*ol*] (1940)
: THC

tet·ra·hy·dro·fu·ran \-'fyu̇r-ˌan, -fyu̇-'ran\ *noun* [*tetrahydro-* + *furan*] (circa 1943)
: a flammable liquid heterocyclic ether C_4H_8O that is derived from furan and used as a solvent and as an intermediate in organic synthesis

tet·ra·hy·me·na \ˌte-trə-'hī-mə-nə\ *noun* [New Latin, from *tetra-* + Greek *hymēn* membrane] (1962)
: any of a genus (*Tetrahymena*) of ciliate protozoans

te·tral·o·gy \te-'trä-lə-jē, -'tra-\ *noun, plural* **-gies** [Greek *tetralogia,* from *tetra-* + *-logia* -logy] (1656)
1 : a group of four dramatic pieces presented consecutively on the Attic stage at the Dionysiac festival
2 : a series of four connected works (as operas or novels)

tet·ra·mer \'te-trə-mər\ *noun* (1929)
: a molecule (as an enzyme or a polymer) that consists of four structural subunits (as peptide chains or condensed monomers)
— **tet·ra·mer·ic** \ˌte-trə-'mer-ik\ *adjective*

te·tram·er·ous \te-'tra-mə-rəs\ *adjective* [New Latin *tetramerus,* from Greek *tetramerēs,* from *tetra-* + *meros* part — more at MERIT] (1826)
: having or characterized by the presence of four parts or of parts arranged in sets or multiples of four ⟨*tetramerous* flowers⟩

te·tram·e·ter \te-'tra-mə-tər\ *noun* [Greek *tetrametron,* from neuter of *tetrametros* having four measures, from *tetra-* + *metron* measure — more at MEASURE] (1612)
: a line of verse consisting either of four dipodies (as in classical iambic, trochaic, and anapestic verse) or four metrical feet (as in modern English verse)

tet·ra·meth·yl·lead \ˌte-trə-ˌme-thəl-'led\ *noun* (1964)
: a volatile poisonous liquid $Pb(CH_3)_4$ used as an antiknock agent

¹tet·ra·ploid \'te-trə-ˌplȯid\ *adjective* [International Scientific Vocabulary] (1912)
: having or being a chromosome number four times the monoploid number ⟨a *tetraploid* cell⟩
— **tet·ra·ploi·dy** \-ˌplȯi-dē\ *noun*

²tetraploid *noun* (1921)
: a tetraploid individual

tet·ra·pod \'te-trə-ˌpäd\ *noun* [New Latin *tetrapodus,* from Greek *tetrapod-, tetrapous* four-footed, from *tetra-* + *pod-, pous* foot — more at FOOT] (circa 1891)
: a vertebrate (as a frog, bird, or cat) with two pairs of limbs

tet·ra·pyr·role \ˌte-trə-'pir-ˌōl\ *noun* (circa 1928)
: a chemical group consisting of four pyrrole rings joined either in a straight chain or in a ring (as in chlorophyll)

te·trarch \'te-ˌträrk, 'tē-\ *noun* [Middle English, from Latin *tetrarcha,* from Greek *tetrarchēs,* from *tetra-* + *-archēs* -arch] (14th century)
1 : a governor of the fourth part of a province
2 : a subordinate prince
— **te·trar·chic** \te-'trär-kik, tē-\ *adjective*

te·trar·chy \'te-ˌträr-kē, 'tē-\ *noun, plural* **-chies** (circa 1630)
: government by four persons ruling jointly

tet·ra·spore \'te-trə-ˌspȯr, -ˌspȯr\ *noun* [International Scientific Vocabulary] (1857)
: one of the haploid asexual spores developed meiotically in the red algae usually in groups of four
— **tet·ra·spor·ic** \ˌte-trə-'spȯr-ik, -'spȯr-\ *adjective*

tet·ra·va·lent \ˌte-trə-'vā-lənt\ *adjective* [International Scientific Vocabulary] (1868)
: having a valence of four

te·traz·zi·ni \ˌte-trə-'zē-nē\ *adjective, often capitalized* [Luisa *Tetrazzini* (died 1940) Italian opera singer] (1951)
: prepared with pasta and a white sauce seasoned with sherry and served au gratin ⟨chicken *tetrazzini*⟩

tet·ra·zo·li·um \ˌte-trə-'zō-lē-əm\ *noun* [New Latin, from International Scientific Vocabulary *tetrazole* (CH_2N_4)] (1895)
: a univalent cation or group CH_3N_4 that is analogous to ammonium; *also* : any of several of its derivatives used especially as electron acceptors to test for metabolic activity in living cells

tet·rode \'te-ˌtrōd\ *noun* (1902)
: a vacuum tube with a cathode, an anode, a control grid, and an additional grid or other electrode

tet·ro·do·tox·in \te-ˌtrō-də-'täk-sən\ *noun* [International Scientific Vocabulary *tetrodo-* (from New Latin *Tetrodon,* genus of tropical marine fishes) + *toxin*] (1911)
: a neurotoxin $C_{11}H_{17}N_3O_8$ found especially in puffer fish that blocks nerve conduction by suppressing permeability of the nerve fiber to sodium ions

te·trox·ide \te-'träk-ˌsīd\ *noun* [International Scientific Vocabulary] (1866)
: a compound of an element or group with four atoms of oxygen

tet·ryl \'te-trəl\ *noun* [International Scientific Vocabulary] (1909)
: a pale yellow crystalline explosive $C_7H_5N_5O_8$ used especially as a detonator

tet·ter \'te-tər\ *noun* [Middle English *teter,* from Old English; akin to Old High German *zittaroh* tetter, Sanskrit *dadru* leprosy, *dr̥ṇāti* he tears — more at TEAR] (before 12th century)
: any of various vesicular skin diseases (as ringworm, eczema, and herpes)

Teu·ton \'tü-tᵊn, 'tyü-\ *noun* [Latin *Teutoni,* plural] (circa 1741)
1 : a member of an ancient probably Germanic or Celtic people
2 : a member of a people speaking a language of the Germanic branch of the Indo-European language family; *especially* : GERMAN

¹Teu·ton·ic \tü-'tä-nik, tyü-\ *noun* (1612)
: GERMANIC

²Teutonic *adjective* (1618)
: of, relating to, or characteristic of the Teutons
— **Teu·ton·i·cal·ly** \-ni-k(ə-)lē\ *adverb*

Teu·ton·ism \'tü-tᵊn-ˌi-zəm, 'tyü-\ *noun* (1854)
: GERMANISM

Teu·ton·ist \-ist\ *noun* (1882)
: GERMANIST

teu·ton·ize \-ˌīz\ *transitive verb* **-ized; -iz·ing** *often capitalized* (1845)
: GERMANIZE

tex·as \'tek-səs, -siz\ *noun* [*Texas,* state of U.S.; from the naming of cabins on Mississippi steamboats after states, the officers' cabins being the largest] (1857)

: a structure on the awning deck of a steamer that contains the officers' cabins and has the pilothouse in front or on top

Texas fever *noun* (1866)
: an infectious disease of cattle transmitted by the cattle tick and caused by a protozoan (*Babesia bigemina*) that multiplies in the blood and destroys the red blood cells

Texas Independence Day *noun* (circa 1928)
: March 2 observed as the anniversary of the declaration of independence of Texas from Mexico in 1836 and also as the birthday of Sam Houston

Texas leaguer *noun* [*Texas League*, a baseball minor league] (1905)
: a fly in baseball that falls too far out to be caught by an infielder and too close in to be caught by an outfielder

Texas longhorn *noun* (1908)
1 : LONGHORN 1a
2 : any of a breed of relatively small cattle developed in the U.S. from descendants of the original longhorns and typically having a 40 inch (one meter) horn spread and a highly variable color pattern

Texas Ranger *noun* (1846)
: a member of a formerly mounted police force in Texas

Tex–Mex \'teks-ˌmeks\ *adjective* [*Tex*as + *Mex*ico] (1949)
: of, relating to, or being the Mexican-American culture or cuisine existing or originating in especially southern Texas ⟨*Tex-Mex* cooking⟩ ⟨*Tex-Mex* music⟩

text \'tekst\ *noun* [Middle English, from Middle French *texte*, from Medieval Latin *textus*, from Latin, texture, context, from *texere* to weave — more at TECHNICAL] (14th century)
1 a (1) **:** the original words and form of a written or printed work (2) **:** an edited or emended copy of an original work **b :** a work containing such text
2 a : the main body of printed or written matter on a page **b :** the principal part of a book exclusive of front and back matter **c :** the printed score of a musical composition
3 a (1) **:** a verse or passage of Scripture chosen especially for the subject of a sermon or for authoritative support (as for a doctrine) (2) **:** a passage from an authoritative source providing an introduction or basis (as for a speech) **b :** a source of information or authority
4 : THEME, TOPIC
5 a : the words of something (as a poem) set to music **b :** matter chiefly in the form of words that is treated as data for processing by computerized equipment ⟨a *text*-editing typewriter⟩
6 : a type suitable for printing running text
7 : TEXTBOOK
8 a : something written or spoken considered as an object to be examined, explicated, or deconstructed **b :** something likened to a text ⟨the surfaces of daily life are *texts* to be explicated —Michiko Kakutani⟩ ⟨he ceased to be a teacher as he became a *text* —D. J. Boorstin⟩

¹text·book \'teks(t)-ˌbuk\ *noun* (1779)
: a book used in the study of a subject: as **a :** one containing a presentation of the principles of a subject **b :** a literary work relevant to the study of a subject

²textbook *adjective* (1905)
: of, suggesting, or suitable to a textbook; *especially* **:** CLASSIC ⟨a *textbook* example of bureaucratic waste⟩

text·book·ish \-ˌbu-kish\ *adjective* (1914)
: of, relating to, or having the characteristics of a textbook ⟨the style is heavy and *textbookish* —*Nation*⟩

text edition *noun* (1895)
: an edition of a book prepared for use especially in schools and colleges — compare TRADE EDITION

tex·tile \'tek-ˌstīl, 'teks-t�ᵊl\ *noun* [Latin, from neuter of *textilis* woven, from *texere*] (1626)
1 : CLOTH 1a; *especially* **:** a woven or knit cloth
2 : a fiber, filament, or yarn used in making cloth

tex·tu·al \'teks-chə-wəl, -chəl\ *adjective* [Middle English, from Medieval Latin *textus* text] (15th century)
: of, relating to, or based on a text
— **tex·tu·al·ly** *adverb*

textual critic *noun* (1938)
: a practitioner of textual criticism

textual criticism *noun* (1859)
1 : the study of a literary work that aims to establish the original text
2 : a critical study of literature emphasizing a close reading and analysis of the text

¹tex·tu·ary \'teks-chə-ˌwer-ē\ *noun, plural* **-ar·ies** [Medieval Latin *textus*] (1608)
: one who is well informed in the Bible or in biblical scholarship

²textuary *adjective* (1646)
: TEXTUAL

¹tex·ture \'teks-chər\ *noun* [Latin *textura*, from *textus*, past participle of *texere* to weave — more at TECHNICAL] (1578)
1 a : something composed of closely interwoven elements; *specifically* **:** a woven cloth **b :** the structure formed by the threads of a fabric
2 a : essential part **:** SUBSTANCE **b :** identifying quality **:** CHARACTER
3 a : the disposition or manner of union of the particles of a body or substance **b :** the visual or tactile surface characteristics and appearance of something ⟨the *texture* of an oil painting⟩
4 a : a composite of the elements of prose or poetry ⟨all these words . . . meet violently to form a *texture* impressive and exciting —John Berryman⟩ **b :** a pattern of musical sound created by tones or lines played or sung together
5 a : basic scheme or structure **b :** overall structure
— **tex·tur·al** \-chə-rəl\ *adjective*
— **tex·tur·al·ly** \-rə-lē\ *adverb*
— **tex·tured** \-chərd\ *adjective*
— **tex·ture·less** \-chər-ləs\ *adjective*

²texture *transitive verb* **tex·tured; tex·tur·ing** (1694)
: to give a particular texture to

tex·tur·ize \'teks-chə-ˌrīz\ *transitive verb* **-ized; -iz·ing** (circa 1950)
: TEXTURE ⟨*texturize* a polyester yarn⟩

tex·tus re·cep·tus \ˌtek-stəs-ri-'sep-təs\ *noun* [New Latin, literally, received text] (1856)
: the generally accepted text of a literary work (as the Greek New Testament)

T formation *noun* (1930)
: an offensive football formation in which the fullback lines up behind the center and quarterback with one halfback stationed on each side of the fullback

T4 cell \ˌtē-'fȯr-, -'fȯr-\ *noun* [*T cell* + *CD4*] (1983)
: any of the T cells (as a helper T cell) that bear the CD4 molecular marker and become severely depleted in AIDS — called also *T4 lymphocyte*

T–group \'tē-ˌgrüp\ *noun* [*training group*] (1950)
: a group of people under the leadership of a trainer who seek to develop self-awareness and sensitivity to others by verbalizing feelings uninhibitedly at group sessions — compare ENCOUNTER GROUP

¹-th — see -ETH

²-th *or* **-eth** *adjective suffix* [Middle English *-the, -te*, from Old English *-tha, -ta*; akin to Old High German *-do* -th, Latin *-tus*, Greek *-tos*, Sanskrit *-tha*]
— used in forming ordinal numbers ⟨hundred*th*⟩ ⟨forti*eth*⟩

³-th *noun suffix* [Middle English, from Old English; akin to Old High German *-ida*, suffix forming abstract nouns, Latin *-ta*, Greek *-tē*, Sanskrit *-tā*]
1 : act or process ⟨spil*th*⟩
2 : state or condition ⟨dear*th*⟩

⁴-th *symbol* [²*-th*]
— used with the figures 4, 5, 6, 7, 8, 9, and 0 and related Roman numerals to indicate an ordinal number ⟨25*th*⟩ ⟨50*th* wedding anniversary⟩ ⟨XXV*th* Olympiad⟩

¹Thai \'tī\ *noun, plural* **Thai** *or* **Thais** (1808)
1 : a family of languages including Thai and Shan spoken in southeast Asia and China
2 a : a native or inhabitant of Thailand **b :** one who is descended from a Thai
3 : the official language of Thailand

²Thai *adjective* (1808)
: of or relating to Thailand, its people, or their language or culture

thal·a·mus \'tha-lə-məs\ *noun, plural* **-mi** \-ˌmī, -ˌmē\ [New Latin, from Greek *thalamos* chamber] (1756)
: the largest subdivision of the diencephalon that consists chiefly of an ovoid mass of nuclei in each lateral wall of the third ventricle and functions in the integration of sensory information — see BRAIN illustration
— **tha·lam·ic** \thə-'la-mik\ *adjective*

thal·as·sae·mia *chiefly British variant of* THALASSEMIA

thal·as·se·mia \ˌtha-lə-'sē-mē-ə\ *noun* [New Latin, from Greek *thalassa* sea + New Latin *-emia*] (1932)
: any of a group of inherited disorders of hemoglobin synthesis affecting the globin chain that are characterized usually by mild to severe hemolytic anemia, are caused by a series of allelic genes, and tend to occur especially in individuals of Mediterranean, black, or southeast Asian ancestry; *especially* **:** COOLEY'S ANEMIA
— **thal·as·se·mic** \-mik\ *adjective or noun*

thalassemia major *noun* [New Latin, greater thalassemia] (1944)
: COOLEY'S ANEMIA

thalassemia minor *noun* [New Latin, lesser thalassemia] (1944)
: a mild form of thalassemia associated with the heterozygous condition for the gene involved

tha·las·sic \thə-'la-sik\ *adjective* [French *thalassique*, from Greek *thalassa* sea] (1883)
: of, relating to, or situated or developed about inland seas ⟨*thalassic* civilizations of the Aegean⟩

thal·as·soc·ra·cy \ˌtha-lə-'sä-krə-sē\ *noun* [Greek *thalassokratia*, from *thalassa* + *-kratia* -cracy] (1846)
: maritime supremacy

tha·las·so·crat \thə-'la-sə-ˌkrat\ *noun* (1846)
: one who has maritime supremacy

tha·ler \'tä-lər\ *variant of* TALER

Tha·lia \thə-'lī-ə\ *noun* [Latin, from Greek *Thaleia*]
1 : the Greek Muse of comedy
2 : one of the three Graces

tha·lid·o·mide \thə-'li-də-ˌmīd, -məd\ *noun* [ph*thal*ic acid + *-id-* (from *imide*) + *-o-* + *imide*] (1958)
: a sedative and hypnotic drug $C_{13}H_{10}N_2O_4$ that has been the cause of malformation of infants born to mothers using it during pregnancy

thal·li·um \'tha-lē-əm\ *noun* [New Latin, from Greek *thallos* green shoot; from the bright green line in its spectrum] (1861)
: a sparsely but widely distributed poisonous metallic element that resembles lead in physical properties and is used chiefly in the form of compounds in photoelectric cells or as a pesticide — see ELEMENT table

thal·loid \'tha-ˌlȯid\ *adjective* (1857)
: of, relating to, resembling, or consisting of a thallus ⟨*thalloid* liverworts⟩

thal·lo·phyte \'tha-lə-ˌfīt\ *noun* [ultimately from Greek *thallos* + *phyton* plant — more at PHYT-] (1854)
: any of a primary division (Thallophyta) of the plant kingdom comprising plants with single-celled sex organs or with many-celled sex organs of which all cells give rise to gametes, including the algae, fungi, and lichens, and usually held to be a heterogeneous assemblage
— **thal·lo·phyt·ic** \ˌtha-lə-'fi-tik\ *adjective*

thal·lus \'tha-ləs\ *noun, plural* **thal·li** \'tha-ˌlī, -ˌlē\ *or* **thal·lus·es** [New Latin, from Greek *thallos,* from *thallein* to sprout; akin to Armenian *dalar* green, fresh, Albanian *dal* I come forth] (1829)
: a plant body that is characteristic of thallophytes, lacks differentiation into distinct members (as stem, leaves, and roots), and does not grow from an apical point

¹than \thən, 'than\ *conjunction* [Middle English *than, then* then, than — more at THEN] (before 12th century)
1 a : used as a function word to indicate the second member or the member taken as the point of departure in a comparison expressive of inequality; used with comparative adjectives and comparative adverbs ⟨older *than* I am⟩ ⟨easier said *than* done⟩ **b** — used as a function word to indicate difference of kind, manner, or identity; used especially with some adjectives and adverbs that express diversity ⟨anywhere else *than* at home⟩
2 : rather than — usually used only after *prefer, preferable,* and *preferably*
3 : other than
4 : WHEN — used especially after *scarcely* and *hardly*

²than *preposition* (1560)
: in comparison with ⟨you are older *than* me⟩
◻

than·a·tol·o·gy \ˌtha-nə-'tä-lə-jē\ *noun* [Greek *thanatos* + English *-logy*] (circa 1842)
: the description or study of the phenomena of death and of psychological mechanisms for coping with them
— **than·a·to·log·i·cal** \ˌtha-nə-tᵊl-'ä-ji-kəl\ *adjective*
— **than·a·tol·o·gist** \-ə-'tä-lə-jist\ *noun*

Than·a·tos \'tha-nə-ˌtäs\ *noun* [Greek, death; akin to Sanskrit *adhvanīt* it vanished] (1935)
: DEATH INSTINCT

thane \'thān\ *noun* [Middle English *theyn,* from Old English *thegn;* akin to Old High German *thegan* thane and perhaps to Greek *tiktein* to bear, beget] (before 12th century)
1 : a free retainer of an Anglo-Saxon lord; *especially* : one resembling a feudal baron by holding lands of and performing military service for the king
2 : a Scottish feudal lord
— **thane·ship** \-ˌship\ *noun*

thank \'thaŋk\ *transitive verb* [Middle English, from Old English *thancian;* akin to Old English *thanc* gratitude — more at THANKS] (before 12th century)
1 : to express gratitude to ⟨*thanked* her for the present⟩ — used in the phrase *thank you* usually without a subject to politely express gratitude ⟨*thank* you for your consideration⟩; used in such phrases as *thank God, thank goodness* usually without a subject to express gratitude or more often only the speaker's or writer's pleasure or satisfaction in something
2 : to hold responsible ⟨had only himself to *thank* for his loss⟩
— **thank·er** *noun*

thank·ful \'thaŋk-fəl\ *adjective* (before 12th century)
1 : conscious of benefit received ⟨for what we are about to receive make us truly *thankful*⟩
2 : expressive of thanks ⟨*thankful* service⟩
3 : well pleased : GLAD ⟨was *thankful* that it didn't rain⟩
— **thank·ful·ness** *noun*

thank·ful·ly \-f(ə-)lē\ *adverb* (before 12th century)
1 : in a thankful manner ⟨spoke *thankfully*⟩
2 : as makes one thankful ⟨graceless stadiums . . . *thankfully* going out of fashion —R. G. Echevarría⟩ ⟨*thankfully*, those opinions are advanced with graceful prose —Ken Auletta⟩

thank·less \'thaŋ-kləs\ *adjective* (1536)
1 : not expressing or feeling gratitude : UNGRATEFUL ⟨how sharper than a serpent's tooth it is to have a *thankless* child —Shakespeare⟩
2 : not likely to obtain thanks : UNAPPRECIATED ⟨a *thankless* task⟩
— **thank·less·ly** *adverb*
— **thank·less·ness** *noun*

thanks \'thaŋ(k)s\ *noun plural* [plural of Middle English *thank,* from Old English *thanc* thought, gratitude; akin to Old High German *dank* gratitude, Latin *tongēre* to know] (before 12th century)
1 : kindly or grateful thoughts : GRATITUDE
2 : an expression of gratitude ⟨return *thanks* before the meal⟩ — often used in an utterance containing no verb and serving as a courteous and somewhat informal expression of gratitude ⟨many *thanks*⟩
— **no thanks to** : not as a result of any benefit conferred by ⟨he feels better now, *no thanks to* you⟩
— **thanks to** : with the help of : owing to ⟨arrived early, *thanks to* good weather⟩

thanks·giv·ing \thaŋ(k)s-'gi-viŋ *also* 'thaŋ(k)s-ˌ\ *noun* (1533)
1 : the act of giving thanks
2 : a prayer expressing gratitude
3 a : a public acknowledgment or celebration of divine goodness **b** *capitalized* : THANKSGIVING DAY

Thanksgiving Day *noun* (1674)
: a day appointed for giving thanks for divine goodness: as **a** : the fourth Thursday in November observed as a legal holiday in the U.S. **b** : the second Monday in October observed as a legal holiday in Canada

thank·wor·thy \'thaŋk-ˌkwər-thē\ *adjective* (14th century)
: worthy of thanks or gratitude : MERITORIOUS

thank-you \'thaŋk-ˌkyü\ *noun* [from the phrase *thank you* used in expressing gratitude] (1792)
: a polite expression of one's gratitude

thank-you-ma'am \'thaŋk-yü-ˌmam, -(y)ē-\ *noun* [probably from its causing a nodding of the head] (1849)
: a bump or depression in a road; *especially* : a ridge or hollow made across a road on a hillside to cause water to run off

¹that \'that, thət\ *pronoun, plural* **those** \'thōz\ [Middle English, from Old English *thæt,* neuter demonstrative pronoun & definite article; akin to Old High German *daz,* neuter demonstrative pronoun & definite article, Greek *to,* Latin i*stud,* neuter demonstrative pronoun] (before 12th century)
1 a : the person, thing, or idea indicated, mentioned, or understood from the situation ⟨*that* is my father⟩ **b** : the time, action, or event specified ⟨after *that* I went to bed⟩ **c** : the kind or thing specified as follows ⟨the purest water is *that* produced by distillation⟩ **d** : one or a group of the indicated kind ⟨*that's* a cat — quick and agile⟩
2 a : the one farther away or less immediately under observation or discussion ⟨*those* are maples and these are elms⟩ **b** : the former one
3 a — used as a function word after *and* to indicate emphatic repetition of the idea expressed by a previous word or phrase ⟨he was helpful, and *that* to an unusual degree⟩ **b** — used as a function word immediately before or after a word group consisting of a verbal auxiliary or a form of the verb *be* preceded by *there* or a personal pronoun subject to indicate emphatic repetition of the idea expressed by a previous verb or predicate noun or predicate adjective ⟨is she capable? She is *that*⟩

4 a : the one : the thing : the kind : SOMETHING, ANYTHING ⟨the truth of *that* which is true⟩ ⟨the senses are *that* whereby we experience the world⟩ ⟨what's *that* you say⟩ **b** *plural* : some persons ⟨*those* who think the time has come⟩
— **all that** : everything of the kind indicated ⟨tact, discretion, and *all that*⟩
— **at that 1** : in spite of what has been said or implied **2** : in addition : ²BESIDES

²that \that, 'that\ *conjunction* (before 12th century)
1 a (1) — used as a function word to introduce a noun clause that is usually the subject or object of a verb or a predicate nominative ⟨said *that* he was afraid⟩ (2) — used as a function word to introduce a subordinate clause that is anticipated by the expletive *it* occurring as subject of the verb ⟨it is unlikely *that* he'll be in⟩ (3) — used as a function word to introduce a subordinate clause that is joined as complement to a noun or adjective ⟨we are certain *that* this is true⟩ ⟨the fact *that* you are here⟩ (4) — used as a function word to introduce a subordinate clause modifying an adverb or adverbial expression ⟨will go anywhere *that* he is invited⟩ **b** — used as a function word to introduce an exclamatory clause expressing a strong emotion especially of surprise, sorrow, or indignation ⟨*that* it should come to this!⟩
2 a (1) — used as a function word to introduce a subordinate clause expressing purpose or desired result ⟨cutting down expenses *that* her son might inherit an unencumbered estate —W. B. Yeats⟩ (2) — used as a function word to introduce a subordinate clause expressing a reason or cause ⟨rejoice *that* you are lightened of a load —Robert Browning⟩ (3) — used as a function word to introduce a subordinate clause expressing consequence, result, or effect ⟨are of sufficient importance *that* they cannot be neglected —Hannah Wormington⟩ **b** — used as a function word to introduce an exclamatory clause expressing a wish ⟨oh, *that* he would come⟩
3 — used as a function word after a subordinating conjunction without modifying its

\ə\ **abut** \ᵊ\ **kitten** \ər\ **further** \a\ **ash** \ā\ **ace**
\ä\ **mop, mar** \aú\ **out** \ch\ **chin** \e\ **bet** \ē\ **easy**
\g\ **go** \i\ **hit** \ī\ **ice** \j\ **job** \ŋ\ **sing** \ō\ **go**
\ò\ **law** \òi\ **boy** \th\ **thin** \t̲h̲\ **the** \ü\ **loot** \ú\ **foot**
\y\ **yet** \zh\ **vision** *see also* Guide to Pronunciation

meaning ⟨if *that* thy bent of love be honorable —Shakespeare⟩

³**that** *adjective, plural* **those** (13th century)
1 a : being the person, thing, or idea specified, mentioned, or understood **b :** being the one specified — usually used for emphasis ⟨*that* rarity among leaders⟩ ⟨*that* brother of yours⟩ **c :** so great a : SUCH
2 : the farther away or less immediately under observation or discussion ⟨this chair or *that* one⟩

⁴**that** \thət, 'that\ *pronoun* [Middle English, from Old English *thæt*, neuter relative pronoun, from *thæt*, neuter demonstrative pronoun] (before 12th century)
1 — used as a function word to introduce a restrictive relative clause and to serve as a substitute within that clause for the substantive modified by the clause ⟨the house *that* Jack built⟩ ⟨I'll make a ghost of him *that* lets me —Shakespeare⟩
2 a : at which : in which : on which : by which : with which : to which ⟨each year *that* the lectures are given⟩ **b :** according to what : to the extent of what — used after a negative ⟨has never been here *that* I know of⟩
3 a *archaic* **:** that which **b** *obsolete* **:** the person who ☐ ☐

⁵**that** \that\ *adverb* (15th century)
1 : to such an extent ⟨a nail about *that* long⟩
2 : VERY, EXTREMELY — usually used with the negative ⟨did not take the festival *that* seriously —Eric Goldman⟩

that·a·way \'tha-də-,wā\ *adverb* [alteration of *that way*] (1839)
: in that direction

¹**thatch** \'thach\ *transitive verb* [Middle English *thecchen*, from Old English *theccan* to cover; akin to Old High German *decchen* to cover, Latin *tegere*, Greek *stegein* to cover, *stegos* roof, Sanskrit *sthagati* he covers] (14th century)
: to cover with or as if with thatch
— **thatch·er** *noun*

²**thatch** *noun* (14th century)
1 a : a plant material (as straw) used as a sheltering cover especially of a house **b :** a sheltering cover (as a house roof) made of such material **c :** a mat of undecomposed plant material (as grass clippings) accumulated next to the soil in a grassy area (as a lawn)
2 : something likened to the thatch of a house; *especially* **:** the hair of one's head

thau·ma·turge \'thȯ-mə-,tərj\ *noun* [French, from New Latin *thaumaturgus*, from Greek *thaumatourgos* working miracles, from *thaumat-, thauma* miracle + *ergon* work — more at THEATER, WORK] (1715)
: THAUMATURGIST

thau·ma·tur·gic \,thȯ-mə-'tər-jik\ *adjective* (1680)
1 : performing miracles
2 : of, relating to, or dependent on thaumaturgy

thau·ma·tur·gist \'thȯ-mə-,tər-jist\ *noun* (1829)
: a performer of miracles; *especially* **:** MAGICIAN

thau·ma·tur·gy \-jē\ *noun* (circa 1727)
: the performance of miracles; *specifically* **:** MAGIC

¹**thaw** \'thȯ\ *verb* [Middle English, from Old English *thawian*; akin to Old High German *douwen* to thaw, Greek *tēkein* to melt, Latin *tabēre* to waste away] (before 12th century)
transitive verb
: to cause to thaw
intransitive verb
1 a : to go from a frozen to a liquid state **:** MELT **b :** to become free of the effect (as stiffness, numbness, or hardness) of cold as a result of exposure to warmth
2 : to be warm enough to melt ice and snow — used with *it* in reference to the weather
3 : to abandon aloofness, reserve, or hostility **:** UNBEND

4 : to become mobile, active, or susceptible to change

²**thaw** *noun* (15th century)
1 : the action, fact, or process of thawing
2 : a period of weather warm enough to thaw ice ⟨the January *thaw*⟩
3 : the action or process of becoming less aloof, less hostile, or more genial ⟨a *thaw* in international relations⟩

THC \,tē-(,)āch-'sē\ *noun* [tetrahydrocannabinol] (1967)
: a physiologically active chemical $C_{21}H_{30}O_2$ from hemp plant resin that is the chief intoxicant in marijuana — called also *tetrahydrocannabinol*

¹**the** \before consonants usually thə, before vowels usually thē, before vowels also thə; for emphasis before titles and names or to suggest uniqueness often 'thē\ *definite article* [Middle English, from Old English *thē*, masculine demonstrative pronoun & definite article, alteration (influenced by oblique cases — as *thæs*, genitive — & neuter, *thæt*) of *sē*; akin to Greek *ho*, masculine demonstrative pronoun & definite article — more at THAT] (before 12th century)
1 a — used as a function word to indicate that a following noun or noun equivalent is definite or has been previously specified by context or by circumstance ⟨put *the* cat out⟩ **b** — used as a function word to indicate that a following noun or noun equivalent is a unique or a particular member of its class ⟨the President⟩ ⟨*the* Lord⟩ **c** — used as a function word before nouns that designate natural phenomena or points of the compass ⟨*the* night is cold⟩ **d** — used as a function word before a noun denoting time to indicate reference to what is present or immediate or is under consideration ⟨in *the* future⟩ **e** — used as a function word before names of some parts of the body or of the clothing as an equivalent of a possessive adjective ⟨how's *the* arm today⟩ **f** — used as a function word before the name of a branch of human endeavor or proficiency ⟨*the* law⟩ **g** — used as a function word in prepositional phrases to indicate that the noun in the phrase serves as a basis for computation ⟨sold by *the* dozen⟩ **h** — used as a function word before a proper name (as of a ship or a well-known building) ⟨*the* Mayflower⟩ **i** — used as a function word before the plural form of a numeral that is a multiple of ten to denote a particular decade of a century or of a person's life ⟨life in *the* twenties⟩ **j** — used as a function word before the name of a commodity or any familiar appurtenance of daily life to indicate reference to the individual thing, part, or supply thought of as at hand ⟨talked on *the* telephone⟩ **k** — used as a function word to designate one of a class as the best, most typical, best known, or most worth singling out ⟨this is *the* life⟩ ⟨*the* Pill⟩; sometimes used before a personal name to denote the most prominent bearer of that name
2 a (1) — used as a function word with a noun modified by an adjective or by an attributive noun to limit the application of the modified noun to that specified by the adjective or by the attributive noun ⟨*the* right answer⟩ ⟨Peter *the* Great⟩ (2) — used as a function word before an absolute adjective or an ordinal number ⟨nothing but *the* best⟩ ⟨due on *the* first⟩ **b** (1) — used as a function word before a noun to limit its application to that specified by a succeeding element in the sentence ⟨*the* poet Wordsworth⟩ ⟨*the* days of our youth⟩ ⟨didn't have *the* time to write⟩ (2) — used as a function word after a person's name to indicate a characteristic trait or notorious activity specified by the succeeding noun ⟨Jack *the* Ripper⟩
3 a — used as a function word before a singular noun to indicate that the noun is to be understood generically ⟨*the* dog is a domestic

animal⟩ **b** — used as a function word before a singular substantivized adjective to indicate an abstract idea ⟨an essay on *the* sublime⟩
4 — used as a function word before a noun or a substantivized adjective to indicate reference to a group as a whole ⟨*the* elite⟩

²**the** *adverb* [Middle English, from Old English *thȳ* by that, instrumental of *thæt* that] (before 12th century)
1 : than before : than otherwise — used before a comparative ⟨none *the* wiser for attending⟩
2 a : to what extent ⟨*the* sooner the better⟩ **b :** to that extent ⟨the sooner *the* better⟩
3 : beyond all others ⟨likes this *the* best⟩

³**the** *preposition* [¹*the*] (15th century)
: PER 2 ⟨a dollar *the* dozen⟩

the- *or* **theo-** *combining form* [Middle English *theo-*, from Latin, from Greek *the-, theo-*, from *theos*]
: god **:** God ⟨*theism*⟩ ⟨*theo*centric⟩

¹**the·a·ter** *or* **the·a·tre** \'thē-ə-tər, 'thi-ə-, *oftenest in Southern* 'thē-,ā- *also* thē-'ā-\ *noun* [Middle English *theatre*, from Middle French, from Latin *theatrum*, from Greek *theatron*, from *theasthai* to view, from *thea* act of seeing; akin to Greek *thauma* miracle] (14th century)
1 a : an outdoor structure for dramatic performances or spectacles in ancient Greece and Rome **b :** a building for dramatic performances **c :** a building or area for showing motion pictures
2 : a place or sphere of enactment of usually significant events or action ⟨the *theater* of public life⟩
3 a : a place rising by steps or gradations ⟨a woody *theater* of stateliest view —John Milton⟩ **b :** a room often with rising tiers of seats for assemblies (as for lectures or surgical demonstrations)
4 a : dramatic literature **:** PLAYS **b :** dramatic representation as an art or profession **:** DRAMA
5 a : dramatic or theatrical quality or effectiveness **b :** SPECTACLE 1a

²**theater** *adjective* (1977)
: of, relating to, or appropriate for use in a theater of operations ⟨*theater* nuclear weapons⟩

the·ater·go·er \'thē-ə-tər-,gō-(ə)r\ *noun* (1870)
: a person who frequently goes to the theater
— **the·ater·go·ing** \-,gō-iŋ, -gȯ(-)iŋ\ *noun or adjective*

theater–in–the–round *noun, plural* **theaters–in–the–round** (1948)
: a theater in which the stage is located in the center of the auditorium — called also *arena theater*

theater of operations (circa 1879)

☐ USAGE
that *That, which, who:* In current usage *that* refers to persons or things, *which* chiefly to things and rarely to subhuman entities, *who* chiefly to persons and sometimes to animals. The notion that *that* should not be used to refer to persons is without foundation; such use is entirely standard. Because *that* has no genitive form or construction, *of which* or *whose* must be substituted for it in contexts that call for the genitive. See in addition WHOSE.

that *That, which:* Although some handbooks say otherwise, *that* and *which* are both regularly used to introduce restrictive clauses in edited prose. *Which* is also used to introduce nonrestrictive clauses. *That* was formerly used to introduce nonrestrictive clauses; such use is virtually nonexistent in present-day edited prose, though it may occasionally be found in poetry.

: the part of a theater of war in which active combat operations are conducted

theater of the absurd (1961)
: theater that seeks to represent the absurdity of human existence in a meaningless universe by bizarre or fantastic means

theater of war (circa 1890)
: the entire land, sea, and air area that is or may become involved directly in war operations

The·a·tine \ˈthē-ə-ˌtīn, -ˌtēn\ *noun* [New Latin *Theatinus*, from Latin *Teatinus* inhabitant of Chieti, from *Teate* Chieti, Italy] (circa 1598)
: a priest of the Order of Clerks Regular founded in 1524 in Italy by Saint Cajetan and Gian Pietro Caraffa to reform Catholic morality and combat Lutheranism
— **Theatine** *adjective*

¹**the·at·ri·cal** \thē-ˈa-tri-kəl\ *also* **the·at·ric** \-trik\ *adjective* (1558)
1 : of or relating to the theater or the presentation of plays ⟨a *theatrical* costume⟩
2 : marked by pretense or artificiality of emotion
3 a : HISTRIONIC ⟨a *theatrical* gesture⟩ **b** : marked by extravagant display or exhibitionism
synonym see DRAMATIC
— **the·at·ri·cal·ism** \-kə-ˌli-zəm\ *noun*
— **the·at·ri·cal·i·ty** \-ˌa-trə-ˈka-lə-tē\ *noun*
— **the·at·ri·cal·ly** \-ˈa-tri-k(ə-)lē\ *adverb*

²**theatrical** *noun* (circa 1683)
1 *plural* **a** : the performance of plays **b** : DRAMATICS
2 *British* : a professional actor
3 *plural* : showy or extravagant gestures

the·at·ri·cal·ize \thē-ˈa-tri-kə-ˌlīz\ *transitive verb* **-ized; -iz·ing** (1778)
1 : to adapt to the theater : DRAMATIZE
2 : to display in showy fashion
— **the·at·ri·cal·i·za·tion** \-ˌa-tri-kə-lə-ˈzā-shən\ *noun*

the·at·rics \thē-ˈa-triks\ *noun plural* (1807)
1 : THEATRICAL 1
2 : staged or contrived effects

the·be \ˈthā-(ˌ)bā\ *noun, plural* **thebe** [Tswana, literally, shield] (1967)
— see *pula* at MONEY table

the·ca \ˈthē-kə\ *noun, plural* **the·cae** \ˈthē-ˌsē, -ˌkē\ [New Latin, from Greek *thēkē* case — more at TICK] (circa 1666)
: an enveloping sheath or case of an animal or animal part
— **the·cal** \ˈthē-kəl\ *adjective*

-thecium *noun combining form, plural* **-thecia** [New Latin, from Greek *thēkion*, diminutive of *thēkē* case]
: small containing structure ⟨endo*thecium*⟩

¹**the·co·dont** \ˈthē-kə-ˌdänt\ *adjective* [International Scientific Vocabulary *thec-* (from New Latin *theca*) + *-odont*] (1840)
: having the teeth inserted in sockets

²**thecodont** *noun* (1840)
: any of an order (Thecodontia) of Triassic diapsid thecodont reptiles that were presumably on the common ancestral line of the dinosaurs, birds, and crocodiles

thé dan·sant \tā-däⁿ-ˈsäⁿ\ *noun, plural* **thés dansants** *same*\ [French] (circa 1845)
: TEA DANCE

thee \ˈthē\ *pronoun, archaic objective case of* THOU
1 a — used especially in ecclesiastical or literary language and by Friends especially among themselves in contexts where the objective case form would be expected **b** — used by Friends especially among themselves in contexts where the subjective case form would be expected
2 : THYSELF
word history see YOU

thee·lin \ˈthē(-ə)-lən\ *noun* [irregular from Greek *thēlys* female; akin to Greek *thēlē* nipple — more at FEMININE] (1930)
: ESTRONE

theft \ˈtheft\ *noun* [Middle English *thiefthe*, from Old English *thīefth*; akin to Old English *thēof* thief] (before 12th century)
1 a : the act of stealing; *specifically* : the felonious taking and removing of personal property with intent to deprive the rightful owner of it **b** : an unlawful taking (as by embezzlement or burglary) of property
2 *obsolete* : something stolen
3 : a stolen base in baseball

thegn \ˈthān\ *noun* [Old English — more at THANE] (1848)
: THANE 1

thegn·ly \-lē\ *adjective* (1876)
: of, relating to, or befitting a thegn

their \thər, ˈther, ˈthar\ *adjective* [Middle English, from *their*, pronoun, from Old Norse *theirra*, genitive plural demonstrative & personal pronoun; akin to Old English *thæt* that] (13th century)
1 : of or relating to them or themselves especially as possessors, agents, or objects of an action ⟨*their* furniture⟩ ⟨*their* verses⟩ ⟨*their* being seen⟩
2 : his or her : HIS, HER, ITS — used with an indefinite third person singular antecedent ⟨anyone in *their* senses —W. H. Auden⟩
usage see ANYBODY, EVERYBODY, NOBODY, SOMEBODY, THEY

theirs \ˈtherz, ˈtharz\ *pronoun, singular or plural in construction* (14th century)
1 : that which belongs to them — used without a following noun as a pronoun equivalent in meaning to the adjective *their*
2 : his or hers : HIS, HERS — used with an indefinite third person singular antecedent ⟨I will do my part if everybody else will do *theirs*⟩

their·selves \thər-ˈselvz, (ˌ)ther-, (ˌ)thar-, *Southern also* -ˈsevz\ *pronoun plural* (14th century)
chiefly dialect : THEMSELVES

the·ism \ˈthē-ˌi-zəm\ *noun* (1678)
: belief in the existence of a god or gods; *specifically* : belief in the existence of one God viewed as the creative source of man and the world who transcends yet is immanent in the world
— **the·ist** \-ist\ *noun or adjective*
— **the·is·tic** \thē-ˈis-tik\ *also* **the·is·ti·cal** \-ti-kəl\ *adjective*
— **the·is·ti·cal·ly** \-ti-k(ə-)lē\ *adverb*

T–help·er cell \ˈtē-ˈhel-pər-\ *noun* (1980)
: HELPER T CELL

¹**them** \(th)əm, ˈthem, *after* p, b, v, f, *also* ᵊm\ *pronoun, objective case of* THEY
usage see ANYBODY, EVERYBODY, NOBODY, SOMEBODY

²**them** \ˈthem\ *adjective* (1594)
nonstandard : THOSE — used chiefly in the speech of less educated people and in the familiar speech of educated people especially when they are being humorous

the·mat·ic \thi-ˈma-tik\ *adjective* [Greek *thematikos*, from *themat-, thema* theme] (1861)
1 a : of or relating to the stem of a word **b** *of a vowel* : being the last part of a word stem before an inflectional ending
2 : of, relating to, or constituting a theme
— **the·mat·i·cal·ly** \-ti-k(ə-)lē\ *adverb*

thematic apperception test *noun* (1941)
: a projective technique that is widely used in clinical psychology to make personality, psychodynamic, and diagnostic assessments based on the subject's verbal responses to a series of black and white pictures

theme \ˈthēm\ *noun* [Middle English *teme, theme*, from Middle French & Latin; Middle French *teme*, from Latin *thema*, from Greek, literally, something laid down, from *tithenai* to place — more at DO] (14th century)
1 a : a subject or topic of discourse or of artistic representation **b** : a specific and distinctive quality, characteristic, or concern ⟨the campaign has lacked a *theme*⟩

2 : STEM 4
3 : a written exercise : COMPOSITION ⟨a research *theme*⟩
4 : a melodic subject of a musical composition or movement
— **themed** \ˈthēmd\ *adjective*

theme park *noun* (1960)
: an amusement park in which the structures and settings are based on a central theme

theme song *noun* (1929)
1 : a melody recurring so often in a musical play that it characterizes the production or one of its characters
2 : a song used as a signature

them·selves \thəm-ˈselvz, them-\ *pronoun plural* (14th century)
1 a : those identical ones that are they — compare THEY 1a; used reflexively, for emphasis, or in absolute constructions ⟨nations that govern *themselves*⟩ ⟨they *themselves* were present⟩ ⟨*themselves* busy, they disliked idleness in others⟩ **b** : himself or herself : HIMSELF, HERSELF — used with an indefinite third person singular antecedent ⟨nobody can call *themselves* oppressed —Leonard Wibberley⟩
2 : their normal, healthy, or sane condition ⟨were *themselves* again after a night's rest⟩
usage see THEY

¹**then** \ˈthen\ *adverb* [Middle English *than, then* then, than, from Old English *thonne, thænne*; akin to Old High German *denne* then, than, Old English *thæt* that] (before 12th century)
1 : at that time
2 a : soon after that : next in order of time ⟨walked to the door, *then* turned⟩ **b** : following next after in order of position, narration, or enumeration : being next in a series ⟨first came the clowns, *then* came the elephants⟩ **c** : in addition : BESIDES ⟨*then* there is the interest to be paid⟩
3 a (1) : in that case ⟨take it, *then*, if you want it so much⟩ (2) — used after *but* to qualify or offset a preceding statement ⟨she lost the race, but *then* she never really expected to win⟩ **b** : according to that : as may be inferred ⟨your mind is made up, *then*⟩ **c** : as it appears : by way of summing up ⟨the cause of the accident, *then*, is established⟩ **d** : as a necessary consequence ⟨if the angles are equal, *then* the complements are equal⟩
— **and then some** : with much more in addition ⟨would require all his strength *and then some*⟩

²**then** *noun* (14th century)
: that time ⟨since *then*, he's been more cautious⟩

³**then** *adjective* (1584)
: existing or acting at or belonging to the time mentioned ⟨the *then* secretary of state⟩

then and there *adverb* (15th century)
: on the spot : IMMEDIATELY ⟨wanted the money right *then and there*⟩

the·nar \ˈthē-ˌnär, -nər\ *adjective* [New Latin, palm of the hand, from Greek; akin to Old High German *tenar* palm of the hand] (circa 1857)
: of, relating to, involving, or constituting the ball of the thumb or the intrinsic musculature of the thumb ⟨*thenar* muscles⟩

thence \ˈthen(t)s *also* ˈthen(t)s\ *adverb* [Middle English *thannes*, from *thanne* from that place, from Old English *thanon*; akin to Old High German *thanan* from that place, Old English *thænne* then — more at THEN] (14th century)
1 : from that place
2 *archaic* : from that time : THENCEFORTH
3 : from that fact or circumstance : THEREFROM
— **from thence** : from that place

\ə\ **abut** \ᵊ\ **kitten** \ər\ **further** \a\ **ash** \ā\ **ace**
\ä\ **mop, mar** \au̇\ **out** \ch\ **chin** \e\ **bet** \ē\ **easy**
\g\ **go** \i\ **hit** \ī\ **ice** \j\ **job** \ŋ\ **sing** \ō\ **go**
\ȯ\ **law** \ȯi\ **boy** \th\ **thin** \t͟h\ **the** \ü\ **loot** \u̇\ **foot**
\y\ **yet** \zh\ **vision** *see also* Guide to Pronunciation

thence·forth \-ˌfōrth, -ˌförth\ *adverb* (14th century)
: from that time forward
thence·for·ward \then(t)s-ˈför-wərd *also* then(t)s-\ *also* **thence·for·wards** \-wərdz\ *adverb* (15th century)
: onward from that place or time
theo- — see THE-
theo·bro·mine \ˌthē-ə-ˈbrō-ˌmēn, -mən\ *noun* [New Latin *Theobroma,* genus that includes the cacao, from *the-* + Greek *brōma* food, from *bibrōskein* to devour — more at VORACIOUS] (1842)
: a bitter alkaloid $C_7H_8N_4O_2$ closely related to caffeine that occurs especially in cacao beans and has stimulant and diuretic properties
theo·cen·tric \-ˈsen-trik\ *adjective* (1886)
: having God as the central interest and ultimate concern ⟨a *theocentric* culture⟩
— **theo·cen·tric·i·ty** \-ˌsen-ˈtri-sə-tē\ *noun*
— **theo·cen·trism** \-ˈsen-ˌtri-zəm\ *noun*
theo·oc·ra·cy \thē-ˈä-krə-sē\ *noun, plural* **-cies** [Greek *theokratia,* from *the-* + *-kratia* -cracy] (1622)
1 : government of a state by immediate divine guidance or by officials who are regarded as divinely guided
2 : a state governed by a theocracy
theo·crat \ˈthē-ə-ˌkrat\ *noun* (1827)
1 : one who rules in or lives under a theocratic form of government
2 : one who favors a theocratic form of government
theo·crat·ic \ˌthē-ə-ˈkra-tik *also* **theo·crat·i·cal** \-ti-kəl\ *adjective* (1690)
: of, relating to, or being a theocracy
— **theo·crat·i·cal·ly** \-ti-k(ə-)lē\ *adverb*
theo·di·cy \thē-ˈä-də-sē\ *noun, plural* **-cies** [modification of French *théodicée,* from *théo-* the- (from Latin *theo-*) + Greek *dikē* judgment, right — more at DICTION] (1797)
: defense of God's goodness and omnipotence in view of the existence of evil
the·od·o·lite \thē-ˈä-d°l-ˌīt\ *noun* [New Latin *theodelitus*] (1571)
: a surveyor's instrument for measuring horizontal and usually also vertical angles
the·og·o·ny \thē-ˈä-gə-nē\ *noun, plural* **-nies** [Greek *theogonia,* from *the-* + *-gonia* -gony] (1612)
: an account of the origin and descent of the gods
— **theo·gon·ic** \ˌthē-ə-ˈgä-nik\ *adjective*
theo·lo·gian \ˌthē-ə-ˈlō-jən\ *noun* (15th century)
: a specialist in theology
theo·log·i·cal \-ˈlä-ji-kəl\ *also* **theo·log·ic** \-jik\ *adjective* (15th century)
1 : of or relating to theology
2 : preparing for a religious vocation ⟨a *theological* student⟩
— **theo·log·i·cal·ly** \-ji-k(ə-)lē\ *adverb*
theological virtue *noun* (1526)
: one of the three spiritual graces faith, hope, and charity drawing the soul to God according to scholastic theology
the·ol·o·gise *British variant of* THEOLOGIZE
the·ol·o·gize \thē-ˈä-lə-ˌjīz\ *verb* **-gized; -giz·ing** (1649)
transitive verb
: to make theological : give a religious significance to
intransitive verb
: to theorize theologically
— **the·ol·o·giz·er** *noun*
theo·logue *also* **theo·log** \ˈthē-ə-ˌlög, -ˌläg\ *noun* [Latin *theologus* theologian, from Greek *theologos,* from *the-* + *legein* to speak — more at LEGEND] (1663)
: a theological student or specialist
the·ol·o·gy \thē-ˈä-lə-jē\ *noun, plural* **-gies** [Middle English *theologie,* from Latin *theologia,* from Greek, from *the-* + *-logia* -logy] (14th century)

1 : the study of religious faith, practice, and experience; *especially* : the study of God and of God's relation to the world
2 a : a theological theory or system ⟨Thomist *theology*⟩ ⟨a *theology* of atonement⟩ **b** : a distinctive body of theological opinion ⟨Catholic *theology*⟩
3 : a usually 4-year course of specialized religious training in a Roman Catholic major seminary
the·on·o·mous \thē-ˈä-nə-məs\ *adjective* [*the-* + *-nomous* (as in *autonomous*\)] (1947)
: governed by God : subject to God's authority
the·on·o·my \-mē\ *noun* [German *theonomie,* from *theo-* the- (from Latin) + *-nomie* -nomy] (1890)
: the state of being theonomous : government by God
the·oph·a·ny \thē-ˈä-fə-nē\ *noun, plural* **-nies** [Medieval Latin *theophania,* from Late Greek *theophaneia,* from Greek *the-* + *-phaneia* (as in *epiphaneia* appearance) — more at EPIPHANY] (circa 1633)
: a visible manifestation of a deity
— **theo·phan·ic** \ˌthē-ə-ˈfa-nik\ *adjective*
the·oph·yl·line \thē-ˈä-fə-lən\ *noun* [International Scientific Vocabulary *theo-* (from New Latin *thea* tea) + *phyll-* + ²*-ine*] (circa 1894)
: a feebly basic bitter crystalline compound $C_7H_8N_4O_2$ from tea leaves that is isomeric with theobromine and is used in medicine especially as a bronchodilator
the·or·bo \thē-ˈör-(ˌ)bō\ *noun, plural* **-bos** [modification of Italian *tiorba, teorba*] (1605)
: a stringed instrument of the 17th century resembling a large lute but having an extra set of long bass strings
the·o·rem \ˈthē-ə-rəm, ˈthi(-ə)r-əm\ *noun* [Late Latin *theorema,* from Greek *theōrēma,* from *theōrein* to look at, from *theōros* spectator, from *thea* act of seeing — more at THEATER] (1551)
1 : a formula, proposition, or statement in mathematics or logic deduced or to be deduced from other formulas or propositions
2 : an idea accepted or proposed as a demonstrable truth often as a part of a general theory : PROPOSITION ⟨the *theorem* that the best defense is offense⟩
3 : STENCIL
4 : a painting produced especially on velvet by the use of stencils for each color
— **the·o·rem·at·ic** \ˌthē-ə-rə-ˈma-tik, ˌthi(-ə)r-ə-\ *adjective*
the·o·ret·i·cal \ˌthē-ə-ˈre-ti-kəl, ˌthi(-ə)r-ˈe-\ *also* **the·o·ret·ic** \-tik\ *adjective* [Late Latin *theoreticus,* from Greek *theōrētikos,* from *theōrein* to look at] (1601)
1 a : relating to or having the character of theory : ABSTRACT **b** : confined to theory or speculation often in contrast to practical applications : SPECULATIVE ⟨*theoretical* physics⟩
2 : given to or skilled in theorizing ⟨a brilliant *theoretical* physicist⟩
3 : existing only in theory : HYPOTHETICAL ⟨gave as an example a *theoretical* situation⟩
the·o·ret·i·cal·ly \-ti-k(ə-)lē\ *adverb* (1701)
1 : in a theoretical way
2 : according to an ideal or assumed set of facts or principles : in theory
the·o·re·ti·cian \ˌthē-ə-rə-ˈti-shən, -re-; ˌthi(-ə)r-ə-\ *noun* (1886)
: THEORIST
the·o·rise *British variant of* THEORIZE
the·o·rist \ˈthē-ə-rist, ˈthi(-ə)r-ist\ *noun* (1646)
: a person who theorizes
the·o·rize \ˈthē-ə-ˌrīz\ *verb* **-rized; -riz·ing** (1638)
intransitive verb
: to form a theory : SPECULATE
transitive verb
1 : to form a theory about

2 : to propose as a theory
— **the·o·ri·za·tion** \ˌthē-ə-rə-ˈzā-shən, ˌthi(-ə)r-ə-\ *noun*
— **the·o·riz·er** *noun*
the·o·ry \ˈthē-ə-rē, ˈthi(-ə)r-ē\ *noun, plural* **-ries** [Late Latin *theoria,* from Greek *theōria,* from *theōrein*] (1592)
1 : the analysis of a set of facts in their relation to one another
2 : abstract thought : SPECULATION
3 : the general or abstract principles of a body of fact, a science, or an art ⟨music *theory*⟩
4 a : a belief, policy, or procedure proposed or followed as the basis of action ⟨her method is based on the *theory* that all children want to learn⟩ **b** : an ideal or hypothetical set of facts, principles, or circumstances — often used in the phrase *in theory* ⟨in *theory,* we have always advocated freedom for all⟩
5 : a plausible or scientifically acceptable general principle or body of principles offered to explain phenomena ⟨wave *theory* of light⟩
6 a : a hypothesis assumed for the sake of argument or investigation **b** : an unproved assumption : CONJECTURE **c** : a body of theorems presenting a concise systematic view of a subject ⟨*theory* of equations⟩
synonym see HYPOTHESIS
theory of games (1951)
: GAME THEORY
theory of numbers (1811)
: NUMBER THEORY
the·os·o·phist \thē-ˈä-sə-fist\ *noun* (1656)
1 : an adherent of theosophy
2 *capitalized* : a member of a theosophical society
the·os·o·phy \-fē\ *noun* [Medieval Latin *theosophia,* from Late Greek, from Greek *the-* + *sophia* wisdom — more at -SOPHY] (1650)
1 : teaching about God and the world based on mystical insight
2 *often capitalized* : the teachings of a modern movement originating in the U.S. in 1875 and following chiefly Buddhist and Brahmanic theories especially of pantheistic evolution and reincarnation
— **theo·soph·i·cal** \ˌthē-ə-ˈsä-fi-kəl\ *adjective*
— **theo·soph·i·cal·ly** \-k(ə-)lē\ *adverb*
Theo·to·kos \ˌthē-ə-ˈtō-(ˌ)kōs, ˌthā-, -kəs\ *noun* [Late Greek, from Greek *the-* + *tokos* childbirth; akin to Greek *tiktein* to beget — more at THANE]
: VIRGIN MARY
ther·a·peu·sis \ˌther-ə-ˈpyü-səs\ *noun* [New Latin, from Greek, treatment, from *therapeuein*] (circa 1857)
: THERAPEUTICS
ther·a·peu·tic \-ˈpyü-tik\ *adjective* [Greek *therapeutikos,* from *therapeuein* to attend, treat, from *theraps* attendant] (1646)
1 : of or relating to the treatment of disease or disorders by remedial agents or methods ⟨a *therapeutic* rather than a diagnostic specialty⟩
2 : providing or assisting in a cure : CURATIVE, MEDICINAL ⟨*therapeutic* diets⟩ ⟨a *therapeutic* investigation of government waste⟩
— **ther·a·peu·ti·cal·ly** \-ti-k(ə-)lē\ *adverb*
therapeutic index *noun* (1926)
: a measure of the relative desirability of a drug for the attaining of a particular medical end that is usually expressed as the ratio of the largest dose producing no toxic symptoms to the smallest dose routinely producing cures
ther·a·peu·tics \ˌther-ə-ˈpyü-tiks\ *noun plural but singular or plural in construction* (1671)
: a branch of medical science dealing with the application of remedies to diseases
ther·a·pist \ˈther-ə-pist\ *noun* (1886)
: one specializing in therapy; *especially* : a person trained in methods of treatment and rehabilitation other than the use of drugs or surgery ⟨a speech *therapist*⟩
ther·ap·sid \thə-ˈrap-səd\ *noun* [New Latin *Therapsida,* from *ther-* mammal (from Greek

theorbo

thēr wild animal) + *apsid-, apsis* arch, vault — more at FIERCE, APSIS] (1912)
: any of an order (Therapsida) of Permian and Triassic reptiles that are considered ancestors of the mammals
— **therapsid** *adjective*

ther·a·py \'ther-ə-pē\ *noun, plural* **-pies** [New Latin *therapia,* from Greek *therapeia,* from *therapeuein*] (circa 1846)
: therapeutic treatment especially of bodily, mental, or behavioral disorder

Ther·a·va·da \,ther-ə-'vä-də\ *noun* [Pali *theravāda,* literally, doctrine of the elders] (1882)
: a conservative branch of Buddhism comprising sects chiefly in Sri Lanka, Myanmar, Thailand, Laos, and Cambodia and adhering to the original Pali scriptures alone and to the nontheistic ideal of nirvana for a limited select number — compare MAHAYANA

¹there \'thar, 'ther\ *adverb* [Middle English, from Old English *thǣr;* akin to Old High German *dār* there, Old English *thæt* that] (before 12th century)
1 : in or at that place ⟨stand over *there*⟩ — often used interjectionally
2 : to or into that place : THITHER ⟨went *there* after church⟩
3 : at that point or stage ⟨stop right *there* before you say something you'll regret⟩
4 : in that matter, respect, or relation ⟨*there* is where I disagree with you⟩
5 — used interjectionally to express satisfaction, approval, encouragement or sympathy, or defiance ⟨*there,* it's finished⟩

²there \'thar, 'ther, *1 is also* thər\ *pronoun* (before 12th century)
1 : used as a function word to introduce a sentence or clause ⟨*there* shall come a time⟩
2 : used as an indefinite substitute for a name ⟨hi *there*⟩

³there *same as* ¹\ *noun* (1588)
1 : that place or position ⟨there is no here and no *there* . . . in pure space —James Ward⟩
2 : that point ⟨you take it from *there*⟩

⁴there *same as* ¹\ *adjective* (1590)
1 — used for emphasis especially after a demonstrative pronoun or a noun modified by a demonstrative adjective ⟨those men *there* can tell you⟩
2 *nonstandard* — used for emphasis after a demonstrative adjective but before the noun modified ⟨I bet I cussed that *there* blamed mule five hundred times —Elizabeth M. Roberts⟩
3 : capable of being relied on for support or aid ⟨she is always *there* for him⟩
4 : fully conscious, rational, or aware ⟨not all *there*⟩

there·abouts *also* **there·about** \,thar-ə-'baút(s), 'thar-ə-,, ,ther-ə-'baút(s), 'ther-ə-,\ *adverb* (before 12th century)
1 : near that place or time
2 : near that number, degree, or quantity ⟨a boy of 18 or *thereabouts*⟩

there·af·ter \tha-'raf-tər, the-\ *adverb* (before 12th century)
1 : after that
2 *archaic* : according to that : ACCORDINGLY

there·at \-'rat\ *adverb* (before 12th century)
1 : at that place
2 : at that occurrence

there·by \thar-'bī, ther-, 'thar-,, 'ther-,\ *adverb* (before 12th century)
1 : by that : by that means ⟨*thereby* lost her chance to win⟩
2 : connected with or with reference to that ⟨*thereby* hangs a tale —Shakespeare⟩

there·for \thar-'fôr, ther-\ *adverb* (12th century)
: for or in return for that ⟨ordered a change and gave his reasons *therefor*⟩

there·fore \'thar-,fôr, 'ther-, -,fôr\ *adverb* (14th century)
1 a : for that reason : CONSEQUENTLY **b** : because of that **c** : on that ground

2 : to that end
there·from \thar-'frəm, ther-, -'främ\ *adverb* (13th century)
: from that or it

there·in \tha-'rin, the-\ *adverb* (before 12th century)
1 : in or into that place, time, or thing
2 : in that particular or respect ⟨*therein* lies the problem⟩

there·in·af·ter \,thar-in-'af-tər, ,ther-\ *adverb* (1818)
: in the following part of that matter (as writing, document, or speech)

there·in·to \tha-'rin-(,)tü, the-\ *adverb* (14th century)
archaic : into that or it

the·re·min \'ther-ə-mən\ *noun* [Lev Theremin (born 1896) Russian engineer & inventor] (1927)
: a purely melodic electronic musical instrument typically played by moving a hand between two projecting electrodes

there·of \tha-'rəv, -'räv, the-\ *adverb* (before 12th century)
1 : of that or it
2 : from that cause or particular : THEREFROM

there·on \-'rön, -'rän\ *adverb* (before 12th century)
1 : on that ⟨a text with a commentary *thereon*⟩
2 *archaic* : THEREUPON

there·to \thar-'tü, ther-\ *adverb* (before 12th century)
: to that ⟨a text and the notes *thereto*⟩

there·to·fore \'thar-tə-,fōr, 'ther-, -,fôr; ,thar-tə-', ,ther-\ *adverb* (14th century)
: up to that time ⟨a *theretofore* unknown author⟩

there·un·der \tha-'rən-dər, the-\ *adverb* (before 12th century)
: under that

there·un·to \-'rən-(,)tü; ,thar-ən-'tü, ,ther-\ *adverb* (14th century)
archaic : THERETO

there·up·on \'thar-ə-,pön, 'ther-, -,pän; ,thar-ə-', ,ther-\ *adverb* (13th century)
1 : on that matter
2 : THEREFORE
3 : immediately after that

there·with \thar-'with, ther-, -'with\ *adverb* (before 12th century)
1 : with that
2 *archaic* : THEREUPON, FORTHWITH

there·with·al \'thar-wi-,thôl, 'ther-, -thôl\ *adverb* (14th century)
1 *archaic* : BESIDES
2 : THEREWITH

the·ri·ac \'thir-ē-,ak\ *noun* [New Latin *theriaca*] (1568)
1 : THERIACA
2 : CURE-ALL

the·ri·a·ca \thi-'rī-ə-kə\ *noun* [New Latin, from Latin, antidote against poison — more at TREACLE] (1562)
: a mixture of many drugs and honey formerly held to be an antidote to poison
— **the·ri·a·cal** \-kəl\ *adjective*

the·rio·mor·phic \,thir-ē-ō-'mör-fik\ *adjective* [Greek *thēriomorphos,* from *thērion* beast + *morphē* form — more at TREACLE] (1882)
: having an animal form ⟨*theriomorphic* gods⟩

therm \'thərm\ *noun* [Greek *thermē* heat, from *thermos* hot; akin to Latin *formus* warm, Sanskrit *gharma* heat] (1888)
: a unit used to measure quantity of heat that equals 100,000 British thermal units

therm- *or* **thermo-** *combining form* [Greek, from *thermē*]
1 : heat ⟨*thermo*stat⟩
2 : thermoelectric ⟨*thermo*pile⟩

-therm *noun combining form* [Greek *thermē* heat]
: animal having a (specified) body temperature ⟨ecto*therm*⟩

¹ther·mal \'thər-məl\ *adjective* [Greek *thermē*] (1756)

1 [Latin *thermae* public baths, from Greek *thermai,* plural of *thermē*] : of, relating to, or marked by the presence of hot springs ⟨*thermal* waters⟩
2 a : of, relating to, or caused by heat ⟨*thermal* stress⟩ ⟨*thermal* insulation⟩ **b** : being or involving a state of matter dependent upon temperature ⟨*thermal* conductivity⟩ ⟨*thermal* agitation of molecular structure⟩
3 : designed (as with insulating air spaces) to prevent the dissipation of body heat ⟨*thermal* underwear⟩
4 : having energies of the order of those due to thermal agitation ⟨*thermal* neutrons⟩
— **ther·mal·ly** \-mə-lē\ *adverb*

²thermal *noun* (1933)
: a rising body of warm air

ther·mal·ize \'thər-mə-,līz\ *transitive verb* **-ized; -iz·ing** (1948)
: to change the effective speed of (a particle) to a thermal value ⟨*thermalize* a neutron⟩
— **ther·mal·i·za·tion** \,thər-mə-lə-'zā-shən\ *noun*

thermal pollution *noun* (1966)
: the discharge of heated liquid (as wastewater from a factory) into natural waters at a temperature harmful to the environment

thermal printer *noun* (1966)
: a dot matrix printer (as for a computer) in which heat is applied to the pins of the matrix to form dots on usually heat-sensitive paper

ther·mic \'thər-mik\ *adjective* (1842)
: ¹THERMAL 2 ⟨*thermic* energy⟩
— **ther·mi·cal·ly** \-mi-k(ə-)lē\ *adverb*

therm·ion·ic \,thər-(,)mī-'ä-nik\ *adjective* [*thermion* charged particle from an incandescent source, from *therm-* + *ion*] (1909)
: relating to, using, or being the emission of charged particles (as electrons) by an incandescent material

therm·ion·ics \,thər-(,)mī-'ä-niks\ *noun plural but singular in construction* (1909)
: physics dealing with thermionic phenomena

therm·is·tor \'thər-,mis-tər\ *noun* [*therm*al re*sistor*] (1940)
: an electrical resistor making use of a semiconductor whose resistance varies sharply in a known manner with the temperature

Ther·mit \'thər-mət, -,mīt\ *trademark*
— used for thermite

ther·mite \'thər-,mīt\ *noun* [*therm-* + ¹*-ite*] (1900)
: a mixutre of aluminum powder and a metal oxide (as iron oxide) that when ignited evolves a great deal of heat and is used in welding and in incendiary bombs

ther·mo·chem·is·try \,thər-mō-'ke-mə-strē\ *noun* (1844)
: a branch of chemistry that deals with the interrelation of heat with chemical reaction or physical change of state
— **ther·mo·chem·i·cal** \-'ke-mi-kəl\ *adjective*
— **ther·mo·chem·ist** \-'ke-mist\ *noun*

ther·mo·cline \'thər-mə-,klīn\ *noun* (1898)
: the region in a thermally stratified body of water which separates warmer oxygen-rich surface water from cold oxygen-poor deep water and in which temperature decreases rapidly with depth

ther·mo·cou·ple \'thər-mə-,kə-pəl\ *noun* (1890)
: a device for measuring temperature in which a pair of wires of dissimilar metals (as copper and iron) are joined and the free ends of the wires are connected to an instrument (as a voltmeter) that measures the difference in potential created at the junction of the two metals

ther·mo·du·ric \ˌthər-mō-ˈdu̇r-ik, -ˈdyu̇r-\ *adjective* [*therm-* + Latin *durare* to last — more at DURING] (1927)
: able to survive high temperatures; *specifically* : able to survive pasteurization — used of microorganisms

ther·mo·dy·nam·ic \ˌthər-mō-dī-ˈna-mik, -də-\ *also* **ther·mo·dy·nam·i·cal** \-mi-kəl\ *adjective* (1849)
1 : of or relating to thermodynamics
2 : being or relating to a system of atoms, molecules, colloidal particles, or larger bodies considered as an isolated group in the study of thermodynamic processes
— **ther·mo·dy·nam·i·cal·ly** \-mi-k(ə-)lē\ *adverb*

ther·mo·dy·nam·ics \-miks\ *noun plural but singular or plural in construction* (1854)
1 : physics that deals with the mechanical action or relations of heat
2 : thermodynamic processes and phenomena
— **ther·mo·dy·nam·i·cist** \-ˈna-mə-sist\ *noun*

ther·mo·elec·tric \ˌthər-mō-i-ˈlek-trik\ *adjective* (1823)
: of, relating to, or dependent on phenomena that involve relations between the temperature and the electrical condition in a metal or in contacting metals

ther·mo·elec·tric·i·ty \ˌthər-mō-i-ˌlek-ˈtri-sə-tē, -ˈtris-tē\ *noun* (1823)
: electricity produced by the direct action of heat (as by the unequal heating of a circuit composed of two dissimilar metals)

ther·mo·el·e·ment \-ˈe-lə-mənt\ *noun* (circa 1888)
: a device for measuring small currents consisting of a wire heating element and a thermocouple in electrical contact with it

ther·mo·form \ˈthər-mə-ˌfȯrm\ *transitive verb* (1956)
: to give a final shape to (as a plastic) with the aid of heat and usually pressure
— **ther·mo·form·able** \-ˌfȯr-mə-bəl\ *adjective*

ther·mo·gram \-ˌgram\ *noun* (1883)
1 : the record made by a thermograph
2 : a photographic record made by thermography

ther·mo·graph \-ˌgraf\ *noun* [International Scientific Vocabulary] (1843)
1 : THERMOGRAM
2 : a self-recording thermometer
3 : the apparatus used in thermography

ther·mog·ra·phy \(ˌ)thər-ˈmä-grə-fē\ *noun* (1840)
1 : a process of writing or printing involving the use of heat; *especially* : a raised-printing process in which matter printed by letterpress is dusted with powder and heated to make the lettering rise
2 : a technique for detecting and measuring variations in the heat emitted by various regions of the body and transforming them into visible signals that can be recorded photographically (as for diagnosing abnormal or diseased underlying conditions); *also* : a similar technique used elsewhere (as on buildings)
— **ther·mo·graph·ic** \ˌthər-mə-ˈgra-fik\ *adjective*
— **ther·mo·graph·i·cal·ly** \-fi-k(ə-)lē\ *adverb*

ther·mo·ha·line \ˌthər-mō-ˈhā-ˌlīn, -ˈha-\ *adjective* [*therm-* + Greek *hal-*, *hals* salt — more at SALT] (1942)
: involving or dependent upon the conjoint effect of temperature and salinity ⟨*thermohaline* circulation in the eastern Pacific⟩

ther·mo·junc·tion \-ˈjən(k)-shən\ *noun* (1889)
: a junction of two dissimilar conductors used to produce a thermoelectric current

ther·mo·la·bile \-ˈlā-ˌbīl, -bəl\ *adjective* [International Scientific Vocabulary] (1904)
: unstable when heated; *specifically* : subject to loss of characteristic properties on being

heated to or above 55°C ⟨many immune bodies, enzymes, and vitamins are *thermolabile*⟩
— **ther·mo·la·bil·i·ty** \-lā-ˈbi-lə-tē\ *noun*

ther·mo·lu·mi·nes·cence \-ˌlü-mə-ˈne-sᵊn(t)s\ *noun* [International Scientific Vocabulary] (1897)
1 : phosphorescence developed in a previously excited substance upon gentle heating
2 : the determination of the age of old material (as pottery) by the amount of thermoluminescence it produces — called also *thermoluminescence dating*
— **ther·mo·lu·mi·nes·cent** \-sᵊnt\ *adjective*

ther·mo·mag·net·ic \-mag-ˈne-tik\ *adjective* (1823)
: of or relating to the effects of heat upon the magnetic properties of substances or to the effects of a magnetic field upon thermal conduction

ther·mom·e·ter \thə(r)-ˈmä-mə-tər\ *noun* [French *thermomètre*, from Greek *thermē* heat + French *-o-* + *-mètre* -meter — more at THERM] (1633)
: an instrument for determining temperature consisting typically of a glass bulb attached to a fine tube of glass with a numbered scale and containing a liquid (as mercury or colored alcohol) that is sealed in and rises and falls with changes of temperature
— **ther·mo·met·ric** \ˌthər-mə-ˈme-trik\ *adjective*
— **ther·mo·met·ri·cal·ly** \-tri-k(ə-)lē\ *adverb*

ther·mom·e·try \thə(r)-ˈmä-mə-trē\ *noun* [International Scientific Vocabulary] (1858)
: the measurement of temperature

ther·mo·nu·cle·ar \ˌthər-mō-ˈnü-klē-ər, -ˈnyü-, ÷-ˈn(y)ü-kyə-lər\ *adjective* [International Scientific Vocabulary] (1938)
1 : of or relating to the transformations in the nucleus of atoms of low atomic weight (as hydrogen) that require a very high temperature for their inception (as in the hydrogen bomb or in the sun) ⟨*thermonuclear* reaction⟩ ⟨*thermonuclear* weapon⟩
2 : of, utilizing, or relating to a thermonuclear bomb ⟨*thermonuclear* war⟩ ⟨*thermonuclear* attack⟩

ther·mo·pe·ri·od·ic·i·ty \-ˌpir-ē-ə-ˈdi-sə-tē\ *noun* (1944)
: THERMOPERIODISM

ther·mo·pe·ri·od·ism \ˌthər-mō-ˈpir-ē-ə-ˌdi-zəm\ *noun* (1937)
: the sum of the responses of an organism and especially a plant to appropriately fluctuating temperatures

ther·mo·phil·ic \ˌthər-mə-ˈfi-lik\ *also* **ther·moph·i·lous** \(ˌ)thər-ˈmä-fə-ləs\ *or* **ther·mo·phile** \ˈthər-mə-ˌfīl\ *adjective* (1894)
: of, relating to, or being an organism growing at a high temperature ⟨*thermophilic* fermentation⟩ ⟨*thermophilic* bacteria⟩
— **thermophile** *noun*

ther·mo·pile \ˈthər-mə-ˌpīl\ *noun* [⁴*pile*] (1849)
: an apparatus that consists of a number of thermocouples combined so as to multiply the effect and is used for generating electric currents or for determining intensities of radiation

ther·mo·plas·tic \ˌthər-mə-ˈplas-tik\ *adjective* (1883)
: capable of softening or fusing when heated and of hardening again when cooled ⟨*thermoplastic* synthetic resins⟩ — compare THERMOSETTING
— **thermoplastic** *noun*
— **ther·mo·plas·tic·i·ty** \-ˌpla-ˈsti-sə-tē\ *noun*

ther·mo·re·cep·tor \ˌthər-mō-ri-ˈsep-tər\ *noun* (1937)
: a sensory end organ that is stimulated by heat or cold

ther·mo·reg·u·la·tion \-ˌre-gyə-ˈlā-shən\ *noun* [International Scientific Vocabulary] (1927)

: the maintenance or regulation of temperature; *specifically* : the maintenance of a particular temperature of the living body
— **ther·mo·reg·u·late** \-ˈre-gyə-ˌlāt\ *verb*

ther·mo·reg·u·la·tor \-ˈre-gyə-ˌlā-tər\ *noun* [International Scientific Vocabulary] (1875)
: a device (as a thermostat) for the regulation of temperature

ther·mo·reg·u·la·to·ry \-ˈre-gyə-lə-ˌtōr-ē, -ˌtȯr-\ *adjective* (1941)
: tending to maintain a body at a particular temperature whatever its environmental temperature ⟨*thermoregulatory* adjustments⟩

ther·mo·rem·a·nent \-ˈre-mə-nənt\ *adjective* (1951)
: being or relating to magnetic remanence (as in a rock cooled from a molten state or in a baked clay object containing magnetic minerals) that indicates the strength and direction of the earth's magnetic field at a former time
— **ther·mo·rem·a·nence** \-nən(t)s\ *noun*

ther·mos \ˈthər-məs\ *noun* [from *Thermos*, a trademark] (1907)
: a container (as a bottle or jar) with a vacuum between an inner and outer wall used to keep material and especially liquids either hot or cold for considerable periods

ther·mo·scope \ˈthər-mə-ˌskōp\ *noun* [New Latin *thermoscopium*, from *therm-* + *-scopium* -scope] (1804)
: an instrument for indicating changes of temperature by accompanying changes in volume (as of a gas)

ther·mo·set \ˈthər-mō-ˌset\ *noun* (1947)
: a thermosetting resin or plastic

ther·mo·set·ting \-ˌse-tiŋ\ *adjective* (circa 1931)
: capable of becoming permanently rigid when heated or cured ⟨a *thermosetting* resin⟩ — compare THERMOPLASTIC

ther·mo·sphere \ˈthər-mə-ˌsfir\ *noun* [International Scientific Vocabulary] (1950)
: the part of the earth's atmosphere that begins at about 50 miles (80 kilometers) above the earth's surface, extends to outer space, and is characterized by steadily increasing temperature with height
— **ther·mo·spher·ic** \ˌthər-mə-ˈsfir-ik, -ˈsfer-\ *adjective*

ther·mo·sta·ble \ˌthər-mō-ˈstā-bəl\ *adjective* (1904)
: stable when heated; *specifically* : retaining characteristic properties on being moderately heated ⟨a *thermostable* bacterial protease⟩
— **ther·mo·sta·bil·i·ty** \-stə-ˈbi-lə-tē\ *noun*

¹**ther·mo·stat** \ˈthər-mə-ˌstat\ *noun* (1831)
: an automatic device for regulating temperature (as by controlling the supply of gas or electricity to a heating apparatus); *also* : a similar device for actuating fire alarms or for controlling automatic sprinklers
— **ther·mo·stat·ic** \ˌthər-mə-ˈsta-tik\ *adjective*
— **ther·mo·stat·i·cal·ly** \-ti-k(ə-)lē\ *adverb*

²**thermostat** *transitive verb* **-stat·ed** \-ˌsta-təd\ *also* **-stat·ted; -stat·ing** *also* **-stat·ting** (1924)
: to provide with or control the temperature of by a thermostat

ther·mo·tac·tic \ˌthər-mə-ˈtak-tik\ *adjective* (1839)
: of, relating to, or exhibiting thermotaxis

ther·mo·tax·is \-ˈtak-səs\ *noun* [New Latin] (circa 1891)
1 : the regulation of body temperature
2 : a taxis in which a temperature gradient constitutes the directive factor

ther·mo·trop·ic \-ˈträ-pik\ *adjective* [International Scientific Vocabulary] (1885)
: of, relating to, or exhibiting thermotropism

ther·mot·ro·pism \(ˌ)thər-ˈmä-trə-ˌpi-zəm\ *noun* [International Scientific Vocabulary] (circa 1890)

: a tropism in which a temperature gradient determines the orientation

-thermy *noun combining form* [New Latin *-thermia*, from Greek *thermē* heat — more at THERM]
1 : state of heat ⟨endo*thermy*⟩
2 : generation of heat ⟨dia*thermy*⟩

the·ro·pod \'thir-ə-,päd\ *noun* [New Latin *Theropoda*, from Greek *thēr* wild animal + *pod-, pous* foot — more at FIERCE, FOOT] (circa 1891)
: any of a suborder (Theropoda) of carnivorous bipedal saurischian dinosaurs (as a tyrannosaur or allosaurus) usually having small forelimbs

Ther·si·tes \(,)thər-'sī-(,)tēz\ *noun* [Latin, from Greek *Thersitēs*]
: a Greek warrior at Troy known as a carping critic and slain by Achilles for mocking him

the·sau·rus \thi-'sȯr-əs\ *noun, plural* **-sau·ri** \-'sȯr-,ī, -,ē\ *or* **-sau·rus·es** \-'sȯr-ə-səz\ [New Latin, from Latin, treasure, collection, from Greek *thēsauros*] (circa 1823)
1 : TREASURY, STOREHOUSE
2 a : a book of words or of information about a particular field or set of concepts; *especially* : a book of words and their synonyms **b** : a list of subject headings or descriptors usually with a cross-reference system for use in the organization of a collection of documents for reference and retrieval
— **the·sau·ral** \-'sȯr-əl\ *adjective*

these *plural of* THIS

The·seus \'thē-,süs, -sē-əs\ *noun* [Latin, from Greek *Thēseus*]
: a king of Athens in Greek mythology who kills Procrustes and the Minotaur before defeating the Amazons and marrying their queen

the·sis \'thē-səs, *British especially for 1* 'thesis\ *noun, plural* **the·ses** \'thē-,sēz\ [in sense 1, Middle English, from Late Latin & Greek; Late Latin, lowering of the voice, from Greek, downbeat, more important part of a foot, literally, act of laying down; in other senses, Latin, from Greek, literally, act of laying down, from *tithenai* to put, lay down — more at DO] (14th century)
1 a (1) : the unstressed part of a poetic foot especially in accentual verse (2) : the longer part of a poetic foot especially in quantitative verse **b** : the accented part of a musical measure : DOWNBEAT — compare ARSIS
2 a : a position or proposition that a person (as a candidate for scholastic honors) advances and offers to maintain by argument **b** : a proposition to be proved or one advanced without proof : HYPOTHESIS
3 : the first and least adequate stage of dialectic — compare SYNTHESIS
4 : a dissertation embodying results of original research and especially substantiating a specific view; *especially* : one written by a candidate for an academic degree

¹thes·pi·an \'thes-pē-ən\ *adjective* (1675)
1 *capitalized* : of or relating to Thespis
2 *often capitalized* [from the tradition that Thespis was the originator of the actor's role] : relating to the drama : DRAMATIC

²thespian *noun* (1827)
: ACTOR

Thes·sa·lo·nians \,the-sə-'lō-nyənz, -nē-ənz\ *noun plural but singular in construction* [*Thessalonian* inhabitant of ancient Thessalonica, irregular from *Thessalonica*]
: either of two letters written by Saint Paul to the Christians of Thessalonica and included as books in the New Testament — see BIBLE table

the·ta \'thā-tə, *chiefly British* 'thē-tə\ *noun* [Greek *thēta*, of Semitic origin; akin to Hebrew *tēth* teth] (1603)
1 : the 8th letter of the Greek alphabet — see ALPHABET table
2 : THETA RHYTHM

theta rhythm *noun* (1944)
: a relatively high amplitude brain wave pattern between approximately 4 and 9 hertz that is characteristic especially of the hippocampus but occurs in many regions of the brain including the cortex — called also *theta wave*

thet·ic \'the-tik, 'thē-\ *adjective* [Greek *thetikos* of a proposition, from *tithenai* to lay down — more at DO] (1815)
: constituting or beginning with a poetic thesis ⟨a *thetic* syllable⟩
— **thet·i·cal·ly** \-ti-k(ə-)lē\ *adverb*

The·tis \'thē-təs\ *noun* [Latin, from Greek]
: a sea goddess who marries Peleus and becomes the mother of Achilles

the·ur·gist \'thē-(,)ər-jist\ *noun* (1652)
: WONDER-WORKER, MAGICIAN

the·ur·gy \'thē-(,)ər-jē\ *noun* [Late Latin *theurgia*, from Late Greek *theourgia*, from *theourgos* miracle worker, from Greek *the-* + *ergon* work — more at WORK] (1569)
: the art or technique of compelling or persuading a god or beneficent or supernatural power to do or refrain from doing something
— **the·ur·gic** \thē-'ər-jik\ *or* **the·ur·gi·cal** \-ji-kəl\ *adjective*

thew \'thü, 'thyü\ *noun* [Middle English, personal quality, virtue, from Old English *thēaw*; akin to Old High German *thau* custom] (15th century)
1 a : muscular power or development **b** : STRENGTH, VITALITY
2 : MUSCLE, SINEW — usually used in plural

they \'thā\ *pronoun, plural in construction* [Middle English, from Old Norse *their*, masculine plural demonstrative & personal pronoun; akin to Old English *thæt* that] (13th century)
1 a : those ones — used as third person pronoun serving as the plural of *he, she,* or *it* or referring to a group of two or more individuals not all of the same sex ⟨*they* dance well⟩ **b** : ¹HE 2 — often used with an indefinite third person singular antecedent ⟨everyone knew where *they* stood —E. L. Doctorow⟩ ⟨nobody has to go to school if *they* don't want to — N. Y. Times⟩
2 : PEOPLE 2 — used in a generic sense ⟨as lazy as *they* come⟩ □ □

they'd \'thād\ (1676)
: they had : they would

they'll \'thā(ə)l, thel\ (1607)
: they will : they shall

they're \thər, 'ther\ (circa 1594)
: they are

they've \'thāv\ (1611)
: they have

thi- *or* **thio-** *combining form* [International Scientific Vocabulary, from Greek *thei-, theio-* sulfur, from *theion*]
: containing sulfur ⟨*thia*mine⟩ ⟨*thio*cyanate⟩

thia·ben·da·zole \,thī-ə-'ben-də-,zōl\ *noun* [*thiazole* + *benz-* + *imid*e + *azole*] (1961)
: a drug $C_{10}H_7N_3S$ used in the control of parasitic nematode worms, in the treatment of fungus infections, and as an agricultural fungicide

thi·ami·nase \thī-'a-mə-,nās, 'thī-ə-mə-, -,nāz\ *noun* [International Scientific Vocabulary] (1938)
: an enzyme that catalyzes the breakdown of thiamine

thi·a·mine \'thī-ə-mən, -,mēn\ *also* **thi·a·min** \-mən\ *noun* [*thiamine* alteration of *thiamin*, from *thi-* + *-amin* (as in *vitamin*)] (1937)
: a vitamin $(C_{12}H_{17}N_4OS)Cl$ of the B complex that is essential to normal metabolism and nerve function and is widespread in plants and animals — called also *vitamin B₁*

thi·a·zide \'thī-ə-,zīd, -zəd\ *noun* [*thi-* + *diaz*ine + *diox*ide] (1959)
: any of a group of drugs used as oral diuretics especially in the control of high blood pressure

thi·a·zine \'thī-ə-,zēn\ *noun* [International Scientific Vocabulary] (1900)
: any of various compounds that are characterized by a ring composed of four carbon atoms, one sulfur atom, and one nitrogen atom and

include some important as dyes and others as tranquilizers — compare PHENOTHIAZINE

thi·a·zole \'thī-ə-,zōl\ *noun* [International Scientific Vocabulary] (1888)
1 : a colorless basic liquid C_3H_3NS consisting of a 5-membered ring and having an odor like pyridine
2 : any of various thiazole derivatives including some used in medicine and others important as chemical accelerators

¹thick \'thik\ *adjective* [Middle English *thikke*, from Old English *thicce*; akin to Old High German *dicki* thick, Old Irish *tiug*] (before 12th century)
1 a : having or being of relatively great depth or extent from one surface to its opposite ⟨a *thick* plank⟩ **b** : heavily built : THICKSET
2 a : close-packed with units or individuals ⟨the air was *thick* with snow⟩ **b** : occurring in large numbers : NUMEROUS **c** : viscous in consistency ⟨*thick* syrup⟩ **d** : SULTRY, STUFFY **e** : marked by haze, fog, or mist ⟨*thick* weather⟩ **f** : impenetrable to the eye : PROFOUND ⟨*thick* darkness⟩ **g** : extremely intense ⟨*thick* silence⟩
3 : measuring in thickness ⟨12 inches *thick*⟩
4 a : imperfectly articulated : INDISTINCT ⟨*thick* speech⟩ **b** : plainly apparent : DECIDED ⟨a *thick* French accent⟩ **c** : producing inarticulate speech ⟨a *thick* tongue⟩
5 : OBTUSE, STUPID
6 : associated on close terms : INTIMATE ⟨was quite *thick* with his pastor⟩
7 : exceeding bounds of propriety or fitness : EXCESSIVE ⟨called it a bit *thick* to be fired without warning⟩
— **thick·ish** \'thi-kish\ *adjective*
— **thick·ly** *adverb*

□ USAGE

they *They* used as an indefinite subject (sense 2) is sometimes objected to on the grounds that it does not have an antecedent. Not every pronoun requires an antecedent, however. The indefinite *they* is used in all varieties of contexts and is standard.

they *They, their, them, themselves:* English lacks a common-gender third person singular pronoun that can be used to refer to indefinite pronouns (as *everyone, anyone, someone*). Writers and speakers have supplied this lack by using the plural pronouns ⟨and every one to rest *themselves* betake —Shakespeare⟩ ⟨I would have everybody marry if *they* can do it properly —Jane Austen⟩ ⟨it is too hideous for anyone in *their* senses to buy —W. H. Auden⟩. The plural pronouns have also been put to use as pronouns of indefinite number to refer to singular nouns that stand for many persons ⟨'tis meet that some more audience than a mother, since nature makes *them* partial, should o'erhear the speech —Shakespeare⟩ ⟨a person can't help *their* birth —W. M. Thackeray⟩ ⟨no man goes to battle to be killed. — But *they* do get killed —G. B. Shaw⟩. The use of *they, their, them,* and *themselves* as pronouns of indefinite gender and indefinite number is well established in speech and writing, even in literary and formal contexts. This gives you the option of using the plural pronouns where you think they sound best, and of using the singular pronouns (as *he, she, he or she,* and their inflected forms) where you think they sound best. See in addition ANYBODY, EVERYBODY, HE, NOBODY, SOMEBODY.

\ə\ abut \ᵊ\ kitten \ər\ **further** \a\ ash \ā\ ace \ä\ mop, mar \au̇\ out \ch\ chin \e\ bet \ē\ easy \g\ go \i\ hit \ī\ ice \j\ job \ŋ\ sing \ō\ go \ȯ\ law \ȯi\ boy \th\ thin \th\ the \ü\ loot \u̇\ foot \y\ yet \zh\ vision *see also* Guide to Pronunciation

²thick *adverb* (before 12th century)
: in a thick manner : THICKLY
³thick *noun* (13th century)
1 : the most crowded or active part ⟨in the *thick* of the battle⟩
2 : the part of greatest thickness ⟨the *thick* of the thumb⟩
thick and thin *noun* (14th century)
: every difficulty and obstacle — used especially in the phrase *through thick and thin*
thick·en \'thi-kən\ *verb* **thick·ened; thick·en·ing** \'thik-niŋ, 'thi-kə-\ (15th century)
transitive verb
1 a : to make thick, dense, or viscous in consistency ⟨*thicken* gravy with flour⟩ **b** : to make close or compact
2 : to increase the depth or diameter of
3 : to make inarticulate : BLUR ⟨alcohol *thickened* his speech⟩
intransitive verb
1 a : to become dense ⟨the mist *thickened*⟩ **b** : to become concentrated in numbers, mass, or frequency
2 : to grow blurred or obscure
3 : to grow broader or bulkier
4 : to grow complicated or keen ⟨the plot *thickens*⟩
— **thick·en·er** \'thik-nər, 'thi-kə-\ *noun*
thickening *noun* (circa 1580)
1 : the act of making or becoming thick
2 : a thickened part or place
3 : something used to thicken
thick·et \'thi-kət\ *noun* [(assumed) Middle English *thikket,* from Old English *thiccet,* from *thicce* thick] (before 12th century)
1 : a dense growth of shrubbery or small trees : COPPICE
2 : something resembling a thicket in density or impenetrability : TANGLE
— **thick·ety** \-kə-tē\ *adjective*
thick·et·ed \'thi-kə-təd\ *adjective* (circa 1624)
: dotted or covered with thickets
thick·head \'thik-,hed\ *noun* (1824)
: a stupid person : BLOCKHEAD
thick·head·ed \-,he-dəd\ *adjective* (1707)
1 : having a thick head
2 : sluggish and obtuse of mind
thick·ness \-nəs\ *noun* (before 12th century)
1 : the smallest of three dimensions ⟨length, width, and *thickness*⟩
2 : the quality or state of being thick
3 a : viscous consistency ⟨boiled to the *thickness* of honey⟩ **b** : the condition of being smoky, foul, or foggy
4 : the thick part of something
5 : CONCENTRATION, DENSITY
6 : STUPIDITY, DULLNESS
7 : LAYER, PLY, SHEET ⟨a single *thickness* of canvas⟩
thick·set \-,set\ *adjective* (14th century)
1 : closely placed; *also* : growing thickly ⟨a *thickset* wood⟩
2 : having a thick body : BURLY
thick–skinned \-,skind\ *adjective* (1545)
1 : having a thick skin : PACHYDERMATOUS
2 a : CALLOUS, INSENSITIVE **b** : impervious to criticism
thick–wit·ted \-,wi-təd\ *adjective* (1634)
: dull or slow of mind : STUPID
thief \'thēf\ *noun, plural* **thieves** \'thēvz\ [Middle English *theef,* from Old English *thēof;* akin to Old High German *diob* thief] (before 12th century)
: one that steals especially stealthily or secretly; *also* : one who commits theft or larceny
thieve \'thēv\ *verb* **thieved; thiev·ing** (before 12th century)
: STEAL, ROB
thiev·ery \'thēv-rē, 'thē-və-\ *noun, plural* **-er·ies** (1568)
: the act or practice or an instance of stealing : THEFT
thiev·ish \'thē-vish\ *adjective* (1538)
1 : given to stealing
2 : of, relating to, or characteristic of a thief

— **thiev·ish·ly** *adverb*
— **thiev·ish·ness** *noun*
thigh \'thī\ *noun* [Middle English, from Old English *thēoh;* akin to Old High German *dioh* thigh, Lithuanian *taukai,* plural, fat] (before 12th century)
1 a : the proximal segment of the vertebrate hind limb extending from the hip to the knee and supported by a single large bone **b** : the segment of the leg immediately distal to the thigh in a bird or in a quadruped in which the true thigh is obscured **c** : the femur of an insect
2 : something resembling or covering a thigh
— **thighed** \'thīd\ *adjective*
thigh·bone \'thī-,bōn\ *noun* (15th century)
: FEMUR 1
thig·mo·tax·is \,thig-mə-'tak-səs\ *noun* [New Latin, from Greek *thigma* touch (from *thinganein* to touch) + New Latin *-taxis;* akin to Latin *fingere* to shape — more at DOUGH] (1903)
: a taxis in which contact especially with a solid body is the directive factor
thig·mot·ro·pism \thig-'mä-trə-,pi-zəm\ *noun* [Greek *thigma* + International Scientific Vocabulary *-o-* + *-tropism*] (circa 1900)
: a tropism in which contact especially with a solid or a rigid surface is the orienting factor
thill \'thil\ *noun* [Middle English *thille,* perhaps from Old English, plank; akin to Old English *thel* board, Old High German *dili,* and probably to Latin *tellus* earth] (14th century)
: a shaft of a vehicle
thim·ble \'thim-bəl\ *noun* [Middle English *thymbyl,* probably alteration of Old English *thȳmel* covering for the thumb, from *thūma* thumb] (15th century)
1 : a pitted cap or cover worn on the finger to push the needle in sewing
2 a : a grooved ring of thin metal used to fit in a spliced loop in a rope as protection from chafing **b** : a lining (as of metal) for an opening (as in a roof or wall) through which a stovepipe or chimney passes
thim·ble·ber·ry \-,ber-ē\ *noun* (1788)
: any of several American raspberries or blackberries (especially *Rubus occidentalis, R. parviflorus,* and *R. odoratus*) having thimble-shaped fruit
thim·ble·ful \-,fùl\ *noun* (1607)
1 : as much as a thimble will hold
2 : a very small quantity
¹thim·ble·rig \-,rig\ *noun* (1826)
1 : a swindling trick in which a small ball or pea is quickly shifted from under one to another of three small cups to fool the spectator guessing its location
2 : one who manipulates the cup in thimblerig : THIMBLERIGGER
²thimblerig *transitive verb* (1839)
1 : to cheat by trickery
2 : to swindle by thimblerig
— **thim·ble·rig·ger** *noun*
thim·ble·weed \'thim-bəl-,wēd\ *noun* (1833)
: any of various anemones (as *Anemone virginiana* and *A. cylindrica*)
thi·mer·o·sal \thī-'mer-ə-,sal\ *noun* [probably from *thi-* + *mer*cury + *-o-* + *sal*icylate] (1949)
: a crystalline organic mercurial antiseptic $C_9H_9HgNaO_2S$ used especially for its antifungal and bacteriostatic properties
¹thin \'thin\ *adjective* **thin·ner; thin·nest** [Middle English *thinne,* from Old English *thynne;* akin to Old High German *dunni* thin, Latin *tenuis* thin, *tenēre* to hold, *tendere* to stretch, Greek *teinein*] (before 12th century)
1 a : having little extent from one surface to its opposite ⟨*thin* paper⟩ **b** : measuring little in cross section or diameter ⟨*thin* rope⟩
2 : not dense in arrangement or distribution ⟨*thin* hair⟩
3 : not well fleshed : LEAN

4 a : more fluid or rarefied than normal ⟨*thin* air⟩ **b** : having less than the usual number : SCANTY ⟨*thin* attendance⟩ **c** : few in number : SCARCE **d** : scantily supplied **e** : characterized by a paucity of bids or offerings ⟨a *thin* market⟩
5 a : lacking substance or strength ⟨*thin* broth⟩ ⟨a *thin* plot⟩ **b** *of a soil* : INFERTILE, POOR
6 a : FLIMSY, UNCONVINCING ⟨a *thin* disguise⟩ **b** : disappointingly poor or hard ⟨had a *thin* time of it⟩
7 : somewhat feeble, shrill, and lacking in resonance ⟨a *thin* voice⟩
8 : lacking in intensity or brilliance ⟨*thin* light⟩
9 : lacking sufficient photographic density or contrast ☆
— **thin·ly** *adverb*
— **thin·ness** \'thin-nəs\ *noun*
— **thin·nish** \'thi-nish\ *adjective*
²thin *verb* **thinned; thin·ning** (before 12th century)
transitive verb
: to make thin or thinner: **a** : to reduce in thickness or depth : ATTENUATE **b** : to make less dense or viscous **c** : DILUTE, WEAKEN **d** : to cause to lose flesh ⟨*thinned* by weeks of privation⟩ **e** : to reduce in number or bulk
intransitive verb
1 : to become thin or thinner
2 : to become weak
³thin *adverb* **thin·ner; thin·nest** (13th century)
: in a thin manner : THINLY — used especially in combinations ⟨*thin*-clad⟩ ⟨*thin*-flowing⟩
¹thine \'thīn\ *adjective* [Middle English *thin,* from Old English *thīn*] (before 12th century)
archaic : THY — used especially before a word beginning with a vowel or *h*
²thine *pronoun, singular or plural in construction* [Middle English *thin,* from Old English *thīn,* from *thīn* thy — more at THY] (before 12th century)
archaic : that which belongs to thee — used without a following noun as a pronoun equivalent in meaning to the adjective *thy;* used especially in ecclesiastical or literary language and still surviving in the speech of Friends especially among themselves
thin film *noun* (1944)
: a very thin layer of a substance on a supporting material; *especially* : a coating (as of a semiconductor) that is deposited in a layer one atom or one molecule thick
thing \'thiŋ\ *noun* [Middle English, from Old English, thing, assembly; akin to Old High German *ding* thing, assembly, Gothic *theihs* time] (before 12th century)
1 a : a matter of concern : AFFAIR ⟨many *things* to do⟩ **b** *plural* : state of affairs in general or within a specified or implied sphere ⟨*things* are improving⟩ **c** : a particular state of affairs : SITUATION ⟨look at this *thing* another way⟩ **d** : EVENT, CIRCUMSTANCE ⟨that shooting was a terrible *thing*⟩

2 a : DEED, ACT, ACCOMPLISHMENT ⟨do great *things*⟩ **b :** a product of work or activity ⟨likes to build *things*⟩ **c :** the aim of effort or activity ⟨the *thing* is to get well⟩
3 a : a separate and distinct individual quality, fact, idea, or usually entity **b :** the concrete entity as distinguished from its appearances **c :** a spatial entity **d :** an inanimate object distinguished from a living being
4 a *plural* **:** POSSESSIONS, EFFECTS ⟨pack your *things*⟩ **b :** whatever may be possessed or owned or be the object of a right **c :** an article of clothing ⟨not a *thing* to wear⟩ **d** *plural* **:** equipment or utensils especially for a particular purpose ⟨bring the tea *things*⟩
5 : an object or entity not precisely designated or capable of being designated ⟨use this *thing*⟩
6 a : DETAIL, POINT ⟨checks every little *thing*⟩ **b :** a material or substance of a specified kind ⟨avoid fatty *things*⟩
7 a : a spoken or written observation or point **b :** IDEA, NOTION ⟨says the first *thing* he thinks of⟩ **c :** a piece of news or information ⟨couldn't get a *thing* out of him⟩
8 : INDIVIDUAL ⟨not a living *thing* in sight⟩
9 : the proper or fashionable way of behaving, talking, or dressing — used with *the*
10 a : a mild obsession or phobia ⟨has a *thing* about driving⟩; *also* **:** the object of such an obsession or phobia **b :** something (as an activity) that makes a strong appeal to the individual **:** FORTE, SPECIALTY ⟨letting students do their own *thing* —*Newsweek*⟩ ⟨I think travelling is very much a novelist's *thing* —Philip Larkin⟩
◇

thing·am·a·bob \ˈthiŋ-ə-mə-ˌbäb\ *noun* (1832)
: THINGAMAJIG
thing·am·a·jig *or* **thing·um·a·jig** \ˈthiŋ-ə-mə-ˌjig\ *noun* [alteration of earlier *thingum*, from *thing*] (1828)
: something that is hard to classify or whose name is unknown or forgotten
thing–in–itself *noun, plural* **things–in–themselves** [translation of German *Ding an sich*] (1798)
: NOUMENON
thing·ness \ˈthiŋ-nəs\ *noun* (1896)
: the quality or state of objective existence or reality
thing·um·my \ˈthiŋ-ə-mē\ *noun, plural* **-mies** [alteration of earlier *thingum*] (1796)
: THINGAMAJIG
¹think \ˈthiŋk\ *verb* **thought** \ˈthȯt\; **thinking** [Middle English *thenken*, from Old English *thencan*; akin to Old High German *denken* to think, Latin *tongēre* to know — more at THANKS] (before 12th century)
transitive verb
1 : to form or have in the mind
2 : to have as an intention ⟨*thought* to return early⟩
3 a : to have as an opinion ⟨*think* it's so⟩ **b :** to regard as **:** CONSIDER ⟨*think* the rule unfair⟩
4 a : to reflect on **:** PONDER ⟨*think* the matter over⟩ **b :** to determine by reflecting ⟨*think* what to do next⟩
5 : to call to mind **:** REMEMBER ⟨he never *thinks* to ask how we do⟩
6 : to devise by thinking — usually used with *up* ⟨*thought* up a plan to escape⟩
7 : to have as an expectation **:** ANTICIPATE ⟨we didn't *think* we'd have any trouble⟩
8 a : to center one's thoughts on ⟨talks and *thinks* business⟩ **b :** to form a mental picture of
9 : to subject to the processes of logical thought ⟨*think* things out⟩
intransitive verb
1 a : to exercise the powers of judgment, conception, or inference **:** REASON **b :** to have in the mind or call to mind a thought
2 a : to have the mind engaged in reflection **:** MEDITATE **b :** to consider the suitability ⟨*thought* of her for president⟩

3 : to have a view or opinion ⟨*thinks* of himself as a poet⟩
4 : to have concern — usually used with *of* ⟨a man must *think* first of his family⟩
5 : to consider something likely **:** SUSPECT ⟨may happen sooner than you *think*⟩ ☆ ☆
— **think·er** *noun*
— **think better of :** to reconsider and make a wiser decision
— **think much of :** to view with satisfaction — APPROVE — usually used in negative constructions ⟨I didn't *think much of* the new car⟩
²think *noun* (1834)
: an act of thinking ⟨has another *think* coming⟩
³think *adjective* (1906)
: relating to, requiring, or stimulating thinking
think·able \ˈthiŋ-kə-bəl\ *adjective* (1854)
1 : capable of being comprehended or reasoned about ⟨the ultimate nature of Deity is scarcely *thinkable*⟩
2 : conceivably possible
— **think·able·ness** *noun*
— **think·ably** \-blē\ *adverb*
¹thinking *noun* (14th century)
1 : the action of using one's mind to produce thoughts
2 a : OPINION, JUDGMENT ⟨I'd like to know your *thinking* on this⟩ **b :** thought that is characteristic (as of a period, group, or person) ⟨the current student *thinking* on fraternities⟩
²thinking *adjective* (1681)
: marked by use of the intellect **:** RATIONAL ⟨*thinking* citizens⟩
— **think·ing·ly** \ˈthiŋ-kiŋ-lē\ *adverb*
— **think·ing·ness** *noun*
thinking cap *noun* (1874)
: a state or mood in which one thinks — usually used in the phrase *put one's thinking cap on*
think piece *noun* (1941)
: a piece of writing meant to be thought-provoking and speculative that consists chiefly of background material and personal opinion and analysis
think tank *noun* (1959)
: an institute, corporation, or group organized for interdisciplinary research (as in technological and social problems) — called also *think factory*
thin–layer chromatography *noun* (1957)
: chromatography in which the stationary phase is an absorbent medium (as alumina or silica gel) arranged as a thin layer on a rigid support (as a glass plate)
thin·ner \ˈthin-nər\ *noun* (1832)
: one that thins; *specifically* **:** a volatile liquid (as turpentine) used especially to thin paint
thin–skinned \ˈthin-ˌskind\ *adjective* (1598)
1 : having a thin skin or rind
2 : unduly susceptible to criticism or insult **:** TOUCHY
thio- — see THI-
thio acid \ˈthī-ō-\ *noun* [International Scientific Vocabulary, from *thi-*] (circa 1891)
: an acid in which oxygen is partly or wholly replaced by sulfur
thio·cy·a·nate \ˌthī-ō-ˈsī-ə-ˌnāt, -nət\ *noun* [International Scientific Vocabulary] (1877)
: a compound that consists of the chemical group SCN bonded by the sulfur atom to a group or an atom other than a hydrogen atom
thi·ol \ˈthī-ˌȯl, -ˌōl\ *noun* [International Scientific Vocabulary *thi-* + *¹-ol*] (circa 1890)
1 : any of various compounds having the general formula RSH which are analogous to alcohols but in which sulfur replaces the oxygen of the hydroxyl group and which have disagreeable odors
2 : the functional group — SH characteristic of thiols
— **thi·o·lic** \thī-ˈō-lik\ *adjective*
thion- *combining form* [International Scientific Vocabulary, from Greek *theion*]
: sulfur ⟨*methionine*⟩

◇ WORD HISTORY
thing Old English *thing* and its cognates in other early Germanic languages meant "assembly, court." This meaning has long fallen into disuse in English, German, and Dutch, but the Scandinavian languages preserve it, notably in the names of national legislatures, such as the *Althing* ("general assembly") in Iceland and the *Storting* ("big assembly") in Norway. The passage of Old English *thing* from "assembly" to a meaning as nebulous as "thing" seems peculiar, but is actually fairly straightforward given some intermediary steps. The sequence runs from "assembly, court" to "matter before an assembly, case before a court" to the more general "matter, affair, concern" and finally to "thing" in its many and varied modern applications. Parallel shifts of meaning can be found in the histories of English *sake* and its German cognate *Sache* "thing, affair," both of whose antecedents meant "action at law," and French *chose* "thing," from Latin *causa* "legal case." Before it meant "assembly" the common Germanic word represented by Old English *thing* most likely meant simply "something fixed, fixed time" (hence, "meeting at a fixed time"). A hint of this earlier meaning is given by the cognate word *theihs* "time, occasion" in Gothic, the oldest fully attested Germanic language.

thio·pen·tal \ˌthī-ō-ˈpen-ˌtal, -ˌtȯl\ *noun* [*thi-* + *pento*barbi*tal*] (1947)
: a barbiturate $C_{11}H_{18}N_2O_2S$ used in the form of its sodium salt especially as an intravenous anesthetic — compare PENTOTHAL

thio·phene \ˈthī-ə-ˌfēn\ *noun* [International Scientific Vocabulary *thi-* + *phene* benzene] (1883)
: a heterocyclic liquid C_4H_4S from coal tar that resembles benzene

thio·rid·a·zine \ˌthī-ə-ˈri-də-ˌzēn, -zən\ *noun* [*thi-* + piperi*dine* + phenothia*zine*] (1959)
: a phenothiazine tranquilizer used as the hydrochloride $C_{21}H_{26}N_2S_2 \cdot HCl$ for relief of anxiety states and in the treatment of schizophrenia

thio·sul·fate \-ˈsəl-ˌfāt\ *noun* [International Scientific Vocabulary] (1873)
: a salt containing the anion $S_2O_3{}^{2-}$

thio·te·pa \ˌthī-ə-ˈtē-pə\ *noun* (1953)
: a sulfur analogue of tepa $C_6H_{12}N_3PS$ that is used especially as an antineoplastic agent

thio·ura·cil \ˌthī-ō-ˈyu̇r-ə-ˌsil\ *noun* [International Scientific Vocabulary] (1905)
: a bitter crystalline compound $C_4H_4N_2OS$ that depresses the function of the thyroid gland

thio·urea \-yu̇-ˈrē-ə\ *noun* [New Latin] (1894)
: a colorless crystalline bitter compound $CS(NH_2)_2$ analogous to and resembling urea that is used especially as a photographic and organic chemical reagent; *also* : a substituted derivative of this compound

thir \ˈthər, ˈthi(ə)r, ˈthu̇r\ *pronoun or adjective* [Middle English (northern), perhaps irregular from Middle English *this*] (14th century)
dialect British : THESE

thi·ram \ˈthī-ˌram\ *noun* [probably by alteration from *thiuram* the chemical group NH_2CS] (1949)
: a compound $C_6H_{12}N_2S_4$ used as a fungicide and seed disinfectant

¹third \ˈthərd\ *adjective* [Middle English *thridde, thirde,* from Old English *thridda, thirdda;* akin to Latin *tertius* third, Greek *tritos, treis* three — more at THREE] (before 12th century)
1 a : being next after the second in place or time 〈the *third* taxi in line〉 **b :** ranking next after the second of a grade or degree in authority or precedence 〈*third* mate〉 **c :** being the forward speed or gear next higher than second especially in a motor vehicle
2 a : being one of three equal parts into which something is divisible **b :** being the last in each group of three in a series 〈take out every *third* card〉
— **third** *or* **third·ly** *adverb*

²third *noun* (14th century)
1 : one of three equal parts of something
2 a — see NUMBER table **b :** one that is next after second in rank, position, authority, or precedence 〈the *third* in line〉
3 a : the musical interval embracing three diatonic degrees **b :** a tone at this interval; *specifically* **:** MEDIANT **c :** the harmonic combination of two tones a third apart
4 *plural* : merchandise whose quality falls below the manufacturer's standard for seconds
5 : THIRD BASE
6 : the third forward gear or speed especially of a motor vehicle

third base *noun* (1845)
1 : the base that must be touched third by a base runner in baseball
2 : the player position for defending the area around third base
— **third baseman** *noun*

third–class *adjective* (1839)
: of or relating to a class, rank, or grade next below the second
— **third–class** *adverb*

third class *noun* (1844)
1 : the third and usually next below second class in a classification
2 : the least expensive class of accommodations (as on a passenger ship)

3 a : a class of U.S. mail comprising printed matter exclusive of regularly issued periodicals and merchandise less than 16 ounces (454 grams) in weight that is not sealed against inspection **b :** a similar class of Canadian mail with different weight limits

third degree *noun* (1900)
: the subjection of a prisoner to mental or physical torture to extract a confession

third–degree burn *noun* (1930)
: a severe burn characterized by destruction of the skin through its deeper layers and possibly into underlying tissues, loss of fluid, and sometimes shock

third dimension *noun* (1858)
1 : THICKNESS, DEPTH; *also* : a dimension that adds the effect of solidity to a two-dimensional system
2 : a quality that confers reality or lifelikeness 〈night sounds that stick in the mind and give a *third dimension* to the memory —Adie Suehsdorf〉
— **third–dimensional** *adjective*

third estate *noun, often T&E capitalized* (1604)
: the third of the traditional political orders; *specifically* : the commons

third force *noun* [translation of French *troisième force*] (1936)
: a grouping (as of political parties or international powers) intermediate between two opposing political forces

third·hand \ˈthərd-ˈhand\ *adjective* (1599)
1 : received from or through two intermediaries 〈*thirdhand* information〉
2 a : acquired after being used by two previous owners **b :** dealing in thirdhand merchandise

third house *noun* (1849)
: a legislative lobby

third market *noun* (1964)
: the over-the-counter market in listed securities

third order *noun, often T&O capitalized* (1629)
1 : an organization composed of lay people living in secular society under a religious rule and directed by a religious order
2 : a congregation especially of teaching or nursing sisters affiliated with a religious order

third party *noun* (1801)
1 a : a major political party operating over a limited period of time in addition to two other major parties in a nation or state normally characterized by a two-party system **b :** MINOR PARTY
2 : a person other than the principals 〈a *third party* to a divorce proceeding〉

third person *noun* (circa 1586)
1 a : a set of linguistic forms (as verb forms, pronouns, and inflectional affixes) referring to one that is neither the speaker or writer of the utterance in which they occur nor the one to whom that utterance is addressed **b :** a linguistic form belonging to such a set
2 : reference of a linguistic form to one that is neither the speaker or writer of the utterance in which it occurs nor the one to whom that utterance is addressed

third rail *noun* (1890)
: a metal rail through which electric current is led to the motors of an electric vehicle (as a subway car)

third–rate \ˈthərd-ˈrāt\ *adjective* (1814)
: of third quality or value; *specifically* : worse than second-rate
— **third–rat·er** \-ˈrā-tər\ *noun*

third reading *noun* (circa 1571)
: the final stage of the consideration of a legislative bill before a vote on its final disposition

third–stream *adjective* (1962)
: of, relating to, or being music that incorporates elements of classical music and jazz

third ventricle *noun* (circa 1860)

: the median unpaired ventricle of the brain bounded by parts of the telencephalon and diencephalon

third world *noun, often T&W capitalized* [translation of French *tiers monde*] (1963)
1 : a group of nations especially in Africa and Asia not aligned with either the Communist or the non-Communist blocs
2 : an aggregate of minority groups within a larger predominant culture
3 : the aggregate of the underdeveloped nations of the world
— **third world·er** \-ˈwər(-ə)l-dər\ *noun, often T&W capitalized*

¹thirl \ˈthər(-ə)l\ *noun* [Middle English, from Old English *thyrel,* from *thurh* through — more at THROUGH] (before 12th century)
dialect : HOLE, PERFORATION, OPENING

²thirl *transitive verb* (before 12th century)
dialect British : PIERCE, PERFORATE

¹thirst \ˈthərst\ *noun* [Middle English, from Old English *thurst;* akin to Old High German *durst* thirst, Latin *torrēre* to dry, parch, Greek *tersesthai* to become dry] (before 12th century)
1 a : a sensation of dryness in the mouth and throat associated with a desire for liquids; *also* : the bodily condition (as of dehydration) that induces this sensation **b :** a desire or need to drink
2 : an ardent desire : CRAVING, LONGING

²thirst *intransitive verb* (before 12th century)
1 : to feel thirsty : suffer thirst
2 : to crave vehemently and urgently
synonym see LONG
— **thirst·er** *noun*

thirst·i·ly \ˈthər-stə-lē\ *adverb* (1549)
: with or on account of thirst

thirsty \ˈthər-stē\ *adjective* **thirst·i·er; -est** (before 12th century)
1 a : feeling thirst **b :** deficient in moisture : PARCHED 〈*thirsty* land〉 **c :** highly absorbent 〈*thirsty* towels〉
2 : having a strong desire : AVID 〈*thirsty* for knowledge〉
— **thirst·i·ness** \-stē-nəs\ *noun*

thir·teen \ˌthər(t)-ˈtēn, ˈthər(t)-\ *noun* [Middle English *thrittene,* from *thrittene,* adjective, from Old English *thrēotīene;* akin to Old English *tīen* ten — more at TEN] (14th century)
— see NUMBER table
— **thirteen** *adjective*
— **thirteen** *pronoun, plural in construction*
— **thir·teenth** \-ˈtēn(t)th, -ˌtēn(t)th\ *adjective or noun*

thir·ty \ˈthər-tē\ *noun, plural* **thirties** [Middle English *thritty,* from *thritti,* adjective, from Old English *thrītig,* from *thrītig* group of 30, from *thrīe* three + *-tig* group of ten; akin to Old English *tīen* ten] (before 12th century)
1 — see NUMBER table
2 *plural* : the numbers 30 to 39; *specifically* : the years 30 to 39 in a lifetime or century
3 : a sign of completion : END — usually written 30 〈wrote *thirty* on the last page of the story〉
4 : the second point scored by a side in a game of tennis
— **thir·ti·eth** \-tē-əth\ *adjective or noun*
— **thirty** *adjective*
— **thirty** *pronoun, plural in construction*
— **thir·ty·ish** \-ish\ *adjective*

thir·ty–eight \ˌthər-tē-ˈāt\ *noun* (circa 1934)
1 — see NUMBER table
2 : a handgun nominally of .38 caliber — usually written .38
— **thirty–eight** *adjective*
— **thirty–eight** *pronoun, plural in construction*

thir·ty–sec·ond note \-ˈse-kən(d)-ˌnōt, -kən(t)-\ *noun* (circa 1890)
: a musical note with the time value of $1/32$ of a whole note — see NOTE illustration

thirty–second rest *noun* (circa 1903)
: a musical rest corresponding in time value to a thirty-second note

thir·ty–thir·ty \,thər-tē-'thər-tē\ *noun* (1929)
: a rifle that fires a .30 caliber cartridge having a 30 grain powder charge — usually written .30–30

thir·ty–three \,thər-tē-'thrē\ *noun* (1902)
1 — see NUMBER table
2 : a microgroove phonograph record designed to be played at 33⅓ revolutions per minute — usually written 33
— **thirty–three** *adjective*
— **thirty–three** *pronoun, plural in construction*

thir·ty–two \-'tü\ *noun* (1904)
1 — see NUMBER table
2 : a .32 caliber handgun — usually written .32
— **thirty–two** *adjective*
— **thirty–two** *pronoun, plural in construction*

thir·ty–two·mo \-(,)mō\ *noun, plural* **-mos** (circa 1841)
: the size of a piece of paper cut 32 from a sheet; *also* : a book, a page, or paper of this size

¹**this** \'this, thəs\ *pronoun, plural* **these** \'thēz\ [Middle English, pronoun & adjective, from Old English *thes* (masculine), *this* (neuter); akin to Old High German *dese* this, Old English *thæt* that] (before 12th century)
1 a (1) : the person, thing, or idea that is present or near in place, time, or thought or that has just been mentioned ⟨*these* are my hands⟩ (2) : what is stated in the following phrase, clause, or discourse ⟨I can only say *this*: it wasn't here yesterday⟩ **b** : this time or place ⟨expected to return before *this*⟩
2 a : the one nearer or more immediately under observation or discussion ⟨*this* is iron and that is tin⟩ **b** : the one more recently referred to

²**this** *adjective, plural* **these** (before 12th century)
1 a : being the person, thing, or idea that is present or near in place, time, or thought or that has just been mentioned ⟨*this* book is mine⟩ ⟨early *this* morning⟩ **b** : constituting the immediately following part of the present discourse **c** : constituting the immediate past or future ⟨friends all *these* years⟩ **d** : being one not previously mentioned — used especially in narrative to give a sense of immediacy or vividness ⟨then *this* guy runs in⟩
2 : being the nearer at hand or more immediately under observation or discussion ⟨*this* car or that one⟩

³**this** \'this\ *adverb* (15th century)
: to the degree or extent indicated by something in the immediate context or situation ⟨didn't expect to wait *this* long⟩

This·be \'thiz-bē\ *noun* [Latin, from Greek *Thisbē*]
: a legendary young woman of Babylon who dies for love of Pyramus

this·tle \'thi-səl\ *noun* [Middle English *thistel*, from Old English; akin to Old High German *distill* thistle] (before 12th century)
: any of various prickly composite plants (especially genera *Carduus, Cirsium,* and *Onopordum*) with often showy heads of mostly tubular flowers; *also* : any of various other prickly plants
— **this·tly** \'this-(ə-)lē\ *adjective*

this·tle·down \'thi-səl-,daůn\ *noun* (1561)
: the typically plumose pappus from the ripe flower head of a thistle

thistle

thistle tube *noun* (circa 1891)
: a funnel tube usually of glass with a bulging top and flaring mouth

this–world·li·ness \'this-'wərld-lē-nəs\ *noun* (1887)
: interest in, concern with, or devotion to things of this world especially as opposed to a future stage of existence (as after death)

this–world·ly \-lē\ *adjective* (1883)
: characterized by or manifesting this-worldliness

¹**thith·er** \'thi-thər *also* 'thi-\ *adverb* [Middle English, from Old English *thider;* akin to Old Norse *thathra* there, Old English *thæt* that] (before 12th century)
: to that place : THERE

²**thither** *adjective* (1830)
: being on the other and farther side : more remote

thith·er·to \-,tü; ,thi-thər-', ,thi-\ *adverb* (15th century)
: until that time

thith·er·ward \'thi-thər-wərd, 'thi-\ *also* **thith·er·wards** \-wərdz\ *adverb* (before 12th century)
: toward that place : THITHER

thix·ot·ro·py \thik-'sä-trə-pē\ *noun* [International Scientific Vocabulary *thixo-* (from Greek *thixis* act of touching, from *thinganein* to touch) + *-tropy* — more at THIGMOTAXIS] (1927)
: the property of various gels of becoming fluid when disturbed (as by shaking)
— **thixo·tro·pic** \,thik-sə-'trō-pik, -'trä-\ *adjective*

tho *variant of* THOUGH

¹**thole** \'thōl\ *verb* **tholed; thol·ing** [Middle English, from Old English *tholian* — more at TOLERATE] (before 12th century)
chiefly dialect : ENDURE

²**thole** *noun* [Middle English *tholle,* from Old English *thol;* akin to Old Norse *thollr* fir tree, peg, Greek *tylos* knob, callus] (before 12th century)
1 : either of a pair of pins set in the gunwale of a boat to hold an oar in place
2 : PEG, PIN

tho·lei·ite \'tō-lə-,īt, 'thō-\ *noun* [German *Tholeiit,* from *Tholey,* village in Saarland, Germany + German *-it -ite*] (1866)
: a basaltic rock that is rich in aluminum and low in potassium, is found typically in the ocean floor, and is probably derived from the earth's mantle
— **tho·lei·it·ic** \,tō-lə-'i-tik, ,thō-\ *adjective*

thole·pin \'thōl-,pin\ *noun* (1598)
: THOLE 1

Thom·as \'tä-məs\ *noun* [Greek *Thōmas,* from Hebrew *t'ōm* twin]
: an apostle who demanded proof of Christ's resurrection

Thom·as Jef·fer·son's Birthday \'tä-məs-'je-fər-sənz-\ *noun* (circa 1928)
: April 13 observed as a legal holiday in Alabama

Tho·mism \'tō-,mi-zəm\ *noun* [New Latin *Thomista* Thomist, from Saint *Thomas* Aquinas] (circa 1731)
: the scholastic philosophical and theological system of Saint Thomas Aquinas
— **Tho·mist** \-mist\ *noun or adjective*
— **Tho·mis·tic** \tō-'mis-tik\ *adjective*

Thomp·son submachine gun \'täm(p)-sən-\ *noun* [John T. *Thompson* (died 1940) American army officer] (1920)
: a .45 caliber submachine gun with a drum or stick magazine, a pistol grip, and a detachable buttstock

Thom·son's gazelle \'täm(p)-sənz-\ *noun* [Joseph *Thomson* (died 1895) Scottish explorer] (1897)
: a small gazelle (*Gazella thomsoni*) of eastern Africa that is tan above and white below with a broad black stripe on each side

thong \'thȯŋ\ *noun* [Middle English, from Old English *thwong;* akin Old Norse *thvengr* thong] (before 12th century)
1 : a strip especially of leather or hide
2 : a sandal held on the foot by a thong fitting between the toes and connected to a strap across the top or around the sides of the foot

— **thonged** \'thȯŋd\ *adjective*

Thor \'thȯr\ *noun* [Old Norse *Thōrr*]
: the Norse god of thunder, weather, and crops

tho·rac·ic \thə-'ra-sik\ *adjective* (circa 1658)
: of, relating to, located within, or involving the thorax
— **tho·rac·i·cal·ly** \-si-k(ə-)lē\ *adverb*

thoracic duct *noun* (circa 1741)
: the main trunk of the system of lymphatic vessels that lies along the front of the spinal column and opens into the left subclavian vein

tho·ra·cot·o·my \,thȯr-ə-'kä-tə-mē, ,thȯr-\ *noun, plural* **-mies** [Latin *thorac-, thorax* + International Scientific Vocabulary *-tomy*] (circa 1857)
: surgical incision of the chest wall

tho·rax \'thȯr-,aks, 'thȯr-\ *noun, plural* **tho·rax·es** *or* **tho·ra·ces** \'thȯr-ə-,sēz, 'thȯr-\ [Middle English, from Latin *thorac-, thorax* breastplate, thorax, from Greek *thōrak-, thōrax*] (15th century)
1 : the part of the mammalian body between the neck and the abdomen; *also* : its cavity in which the heart and lungs lie
2 : the middle of the three chief divisions of the body of an insect; *also* : the corresponding part of a crustacean or an arachnid

Tho·ra·zine \'thȯr-ə-,zēn, 'thȯr-\ *trademark*
— used for chlorpromazine

tho·ria \'thȯr-ē-ə, 'thȯr-\ *noun* [New Latin, from *thorium* + *-a*] (circa 1841)
: a powdery white oxide of thorium ThO_2 used especially as a catalyst and in crucibles and refractories and optical glass

tho·ri·a·nite \'thȯr-ē-ə-,nīt\ *noun* [irregular from *thoria*] (1904)
: a strongly radioactive mineral that is an oxide of thorium and often contains rare-earth metals

tho·rite \'thȯr-,īt, 'thȯr-\ *noun* [Swedish *thorit,* from New Latin *thorium*] (1832)
: a rare mineral that is a brown to black or sometimes orange-yellow silicate of thorium resembling zircon

tho·ri·um \'thȯr-ē-əm, 'thȯr-\ *noun* [New Latin, from Old Norse *Thōrr* Thor] (1832)
: a radioactive metallic element that occurs combined in minerals and is usually associated with rare earths — see ELEMENT table

thorn \'thȯrn\ *noun, often attributive* [Middle English, from Old English; akin to Old High German *dorn* thorn, Sanskrit *tṛṇa* grass, blade of grass] (before 12th century)
1 : a woody plant bearing sharp impeding processes (as briers, prickles, or spines); *especially* : HAWTHORN
2 a : a sharp rigid process on a plant; *specifically* : a short, indurated, sharp-pointed, and leafless modified branch **b** : any of various sharp spinose structures on an animal
3 : the runic letter þ used in Old English, Middle English, and Icelandic to represent either of the fricatives \th\ or \th\
4 : something that causes distress or irritation — often used in the phrase *thorn in one's side*
— **thorned** \'thȯrnd\ *adjective*
— **thorn·less** \'thȯrn-ləs\ *adjective*
— **thorn·like** \-,līk\ *adjective*

thorn apple *noun* (1578)
1 : JIMSONWEED; *also* : any plant of the same genus
2 : the fruit of a hawthorn; *also* : HAWTHORN

thorn·back \'thȯrn-,bak\ *noun* (14th century)
: any of various rays having spines on the back

thorn·bush \-,bůsh\ *noun* (1535)
1 : any of various spiny or thorny shrubs or small trees
2 : a low growth of thorny shrubs especially of dry tropical regions

thorny \'thȯr-nē\ *adjective* **thorn·i·er; -est** (before 12th century)
1 : full of thorns
2 : full of difficulties or controversial points : TICKLISH ⟨a *thorny* problem⟩
— **thorn·i·ness** *noun*

thoro *nonstandard variant of* THOROUGH

¹thor·ough \'thər-(,)ō, *sometimes* 'thȯr-; 'thə-(,)rō\ *preposition* [Middle English *thorow*, from Old English *thurh, thuruh*, preposition & adverb] (before 12th century)
archaic : THROUGH

²thorough *adverb* (before 12th century)
archaic : THROUGH

³thorough *adjective* (15th century)
1 : carried through to completion : EXHAUSTIVE ⟨a *thorough* search⟩
2 a : marked by full detail ⟨a *thorough* description⟩ **b** : careful about detail : PAINSTAKING ⟨a *thorough* scholar⟩ **c** : complete in all respects ⟨*thorough* pleasure⟩ **d** : having full mastery (as of an art) ⟨a *thorough* musician⟩
3 : passing through
— **thor·ough·ly** *adverb*
— **thor·ough·ness** *noun*

thor·ough·bass \'thər-ə-,bās, 'thə-rə-\ *noun* (1662)
: CONTINUO

thor·ough·brace \-,brās\ *noun* (1837)
: any of several leather straps supporting the body of a carriage and serving as springs

¹thor·ough·bred \-,bred\ *adjective* (1701)
1 : thoroughly trained or skilled
2 : bred from the best blood through a long line : PUREBRED ⟨*thoroughbred* dogs⟩
3 a *capitalized* : of, relating to, or being a member of the Thoroughbred breed of horses **b** : having characteristics resembling those of a Thoroughbred

²thoroughbred *noun* (1842)
1 *capitalized* : any of an English breed of light speedy horses kept chiefly for racing that originated from crosses between English mares of uncertain ancestry and Arabian stallions
2 : a purebred or pedigreed animal
3 : one that has characteristics resembling those of a Thoroughbred

Thoroughbred

thor·ough·fare \-,far, -,fer\ *noun* (14th century)
1 : a way or place for passage: as **a** : a street open at both ends **b** : a main road
2 a : PASSAGE, TRANSIT **b** : the conditions necessary for passing through

thor·ough·go·ing \,thər-ə-'gō-iŋ, ,thə-rə-, -'gó(-)iŋ\ *adjective* (1800)
: marked by thoroughness or zeal : THOROUGH, COMPLETE

thor·ough–paced \-'pāst\ *adjective* (1646)
1 : THOROUGH, COMPLETE
2 : thoroughly trained : ACCOMPLISHED

thor·ough·pin \'thər-ə-,pin, 'thə-rə-\ *noun* (1789)
: a synovial swelling just above the hock of a horse on both sides of the leg and slightly anterior to the hamstring tendon that is often associated with lameness

thor·ough·wort \-,wərt, -,wȯrt\ *noun* (1814)
: BONESET

thorp \'thȯrp\ *noun* [Middle English, from Old English, perhaps from Old Norse; akin to Old High German *dorf* village, Latin *trabs* beam, roof] (before 12th century)
archaic : VILLAGE, HAMLET

those [Middle English, from *those* these, from Old English *thās*, plural of *thes* this — more at THIS] *plural of* THAT

¹thou \'thau\ *pronoun* [Middle English, from Old English *thū*; akin to Old High German *dū* thou, Latin *tu*, Greek *sy*] (before 12th century)
archaic : the one addressed ⟨*thou* shalt have no other gods before me —Exodus 20:3 (Authorized Version)⟩ — used especially in ecclesiastical or literary language and by Friends as the universal form of address to one person; compare THEE, THINE, THY, YE, YOU
word history *see* YOU

²thou *transitive verb* (15th century)
: to address as *thou*

³thou \'thau\ *noun, plural* **thou** [short for *thousand*] (1867)
: a thousand of something (as dollars)

¹though \'thō\ *conjunction* [Middle English, adverb & conjunction, of Scandinavian origin; akin to Old Norse *thō* nevertheless; akin to Old English *thēah* nevertheless, Old High German *doh*] (before 12th century)
1 : in spite of the fact that : WHILE ⟨*though* they know the war is lost, they continue to fight —Bruce Bliven (died 1977)⟩
2 : in spite of the possibility that : even if ⟨*though* I may fail, I will try⟩

²though *adverb* (13th century)
: HOWEVER, NEVERTHELESS ⟨It's hard work. I enjoy it *though*⟩

¹thought \'thȯt\ *past and past participle of* THINK

²thought *noun* [Middle English, from Old English *thōht*; akin to Old English *thencan* to think — more at THINK] (before 12th century)
1 a : the action or process of thinking : COGITATION **b** : serious consideration : REGARD **c** *archaic* : RECOLLECTION, REMEMBRANCE
2 a : reasoning power **b** : the power to imagine : CONCEPTION
3 : something that is thought: as **a** : an individual act or product of thinking **b** : a developed intention or plan ⟨had no *thought* of leaving home⟩ **c** : something (as an opinion or belief) in the mind ⟨he spoke his *thoughts* freely⟩ **d** : the intellectual product or the organized views and principles of a period, place, group, or individual ⟨contemporary Western *thought*⟩
synonym *see* IDEA
— **a thought** : a little : SOMEWHAT ⟨a *thought* too much vinegar in the dressing⟩

thought experiment *noun* (1945)
: GEDANKENEXPERIMENT

thought·ful \'thȯt-fəl\ *adjective* (13th century)
1 a : absorbed in thought : MEDITATIVE **b** : characterized by careful reasoned thinking
2 a : having thoughts : HEEDFUL ⟨became *thoughtful* about religion⟩ **b** : given to or chosen or made with heedful anticipation of the needs and wants of others
— **thought·ful·ly** \-fə-lē\ *adverb*
— **thought·ful·ness** *noun*

thought·less \-ləs\ *adjective* (1592)
1 a : insufficiently alert : CARELESS **b** : RECKLESS, RASH
2 : devoid of thought : INSENSATE
3 : lacking concern for others : INCONSIDERATE
— **thought·less·ly** *adverb*
— **thought·less·ness** *noun*

thought–out \-'aut\ *adjective* (1870)
: produced or arrived at through mental effort and especially through careful and thorough consideration

thought·way \-,wā\ *noun* (circa 1944)
: a way of thinking that is characteristic of a particular group, time, or culture

thou·sand \'thau-z°n(d)\ *noun, plural* **thousands** *or* **thousand** [Middle English, from Old English *thūsend*; akin to Old High German *dūsunt* thousand, Lithuanian *tūkstantis*, and probably to Sanskrit *tavas* strong, Latin *tumēre* to swell — more at THUMB] (before 12th century)
1 — see NUMBER table
2 : a very large number ⟨*thousands* of ants⟩
— **thousand** *adjective*

— **thou·sand·fold** \-z°n(d)-,fōld\ *adjective or adverb*
— **thou·sandth** \-z°n(t)th\ *adjective or noun*

Thousand Island dressing *noun* [*Thousand Islands*, islands in the Saint Lawrence River] (1924)
: mayonnaise with chili sauce and seasonings (as chopped pimientos, green peppers, and onion)

thousand–leg·ger \,thau-z°n(d)-'le-gər, -'lā-\ *noun* (1914)
: MILLIPEDE

thousands place *noun* (1937)
: the place four to the left of the decimal point in a number expressed in the Arabic system of writing numbers

Thra·cian \'thrā-shən\ *noun* (1569)
1 : a native or inhabitant of Thrace
2 : the Indo-European language of the ancient Thracians — see INDO-EUROPEAN LANGUAGES table
— **Thracian** *adjective*

¹thrall \'thrȯl\ *noun* [Middle English *thral*, from Old English *thræl*, from Old Norse *thræll*] (before 12th century)
1 a : a servant slave : BONDMAN; *also* : SERF **b** : a person in moral or mental servitude
2 a : a state of servitude or submission ⟨in *thrall* to his emotions⟩ **b** : a state of complete absorption ⟨mountains could hold me in *thrall* with a subtle attraction of their own —Elyne Mitchell⟩
— **thrall** *adjective*
— **thrall·dom** *or* **thral·dom** \'thrȯl-dəm\ *noun*

²thrall *transitive verb* (13th century)
archaic : ENTHRALL, ENSLAVE

¹thrash \'thrash\ *verb* [alteration of *thresh*] (1588)
transitive verb
1 : to separate the seeds of from the husks and straw by beating : THRESH 1
2 a : to beat soundly with or as if with a stick or whip : FLOG **b** : to defeat decisively or severely ⟨*thrashed* the visiting team⟩
3 : to swing, beat, or strike in the manner of a rapidly moving flail ⟨*thrashing* his arms⟩
4 a : to go over again and again ⟨*thrash* the matter over inconclusively⟩ **b** : to hammer out : FORGE ⟨*thrash* out a plan⟩
intransitive verb
1 : THRESH 1
2 : to deal blows or strokes like one using a flail or whip
3 : to move or stir about violently : toss about ⟨*thrash* in bed with a fever⟩
synonym *see* SWING

²thrash *noun* (1840)
: an act of thrashing

¹thrash·er \'thra-shər\ *noun* (1632)
: one that thrashes or threshes

²thrasher *noun* [perhaps alteration of dialect *thresher* thrush] (circa 1814)
: any of various American oscine birds (family Mimidae and especially genus *Toxostoma*) related to the mockingbird that resemble thrushes but have a curved bill and long tail

thra·son·i·cal \thrā-'sä-ni-kəl, thrə-\ *adjective* [Latin *Thrason-, Thraso* Thraso, braggart soldier in the comedy *Eunuchus* by Terence] (1564)
: of, relating to, resembling, or characteristic of Thraso : BRAGGING, BOASTFUL
— **thra·son·i·cal·ly** \-k(ə-)lē\ *adverb*

¹thraw \'thrä\ *verb* [Middle English — more at THROW] (before 12th century)
transitive verb
1 *chiefly Scottish* : to cause to twist or turn
2 *chiefly Scottish* : CROSS, THWART
intransitive verb
1 *chiefly Scottish* : TWIST, TURN
2 *chiefly Scottish* : to be in disagreement

²thraw *noun* (circa 1585)
1 *chiefly Scottish* : TWIST, TURN

2 *chiefly Scottish* : ill humor

thra·wart \'thrȯ-wərt\ *adjective* [Middle English (Scots), alteration of Middle English *fraward, froward* froward] (15th century)
1 *chiefly Scottish* : STUBBORN
2 *Scottish* : CROOKED

thrawn \'thrȯn\ *adjective* [Middle English (Scots) *thrawin*, from past participle of Middle English *thrawen* to twist] (15th century)
chiefly Scottish : lacking in pleasing or attractive qualities: as **a** : PERVERSE, RECALCITRANT **b** : CROOKED, MISSHAPEN
— **thrawn·ly** *adverb, chiefly Scottish*

¹**thread** \'thred\ *noun* [Middle English *thred*, from Old English *thrǣd*; akin to Old High German *drāt* wire, Old English *thrāwan* to cause to twist or turn — more at THROW] (before 12th century)
1 a : a filament, a group of filaments twisted together, or a filamentous length formed by spinning and twisting short textile fibers into a continuous strand **b** : a piece of thread
2 a : any of various natural filaments ⟨the *threads* of a spiderweb⟩ **b** : a slender stream (as of water) **c** : a streak of light or color **d** : a projecting helical rib (as in a fitting or on a pipe) by which parts can be screwed together : SCREW THREAD
3 : something continuous or drawn out: as **a** : a train of thought **b** : a continuing element ⟨a *thread* of melancholy marked all his writing⟩
4 : a tenuous or feeble support
5 *plural* : CLOTHING
— **thread·less** \-ləs\ *adjective*
— **thread·like** \-,līk\ *adjective*

²**thread** (14th century)
transitive verb
1 a : to pass a thread through the eye of (a needle) **b** : to arrange a thread, yarn, or lead-in piece in working position for use in (a machine)
2 a (1) : to pass something through in the manner of a thread ⟨*thread* a pipe with wire⟩ (2) : to pass (as a tape, line, or film) into or through something ⟨*threaded* a fresh film into the camera⟩ **b** : to make one's way through or between ⟨*threading* narrow alleys⟩; *also* : to make (one's way) usually cautiously through a hazardous situation
3 : to put together on or as if on a thread : STRING ⟨*thread* beads⟩
4 : to interweave with or as if with threads : INTERSPERSE ⟨dark hair *threaded* with silver⟩
5 : to form a screw thread on or in
intransitive verb
1 : to make one's way
2 : to form a thread
— **thread·er** *noun*

thread·bare \'thred-,bar, -,ber\ *adjective* (14th century)
1 : having the nap worn off so that the thread shows : SHABBY
2 : exhausted of interest or freshness
synonym see TRITE
— **thread·bare·ness** *noun*

thread·fin \-,fin\ *noun* (circa 1890)
: any of various bony fishes (family Polynemidae and especially genus *Polydactylus*) having filamentous rays on the lower part of the pectoral fin

thread·worm \-,wərm\ *noun* (1802)
: a long slender nematode worm

thready \'thre-dē\ *adjective* (1597)
1 : consisting of or bearing fibers or filaments ⟨a *thready* bark⟩
2 a : resembling a thread : FILAMENTOUS **b** : tending to form or draw out into strands : ROPY
3 : lacking in fullness, body, or vigor : THIN ⟨a *thready* voice⟩
— **thread·i·ness** *noun*

threap \'thrēp\ *transitive verb* [Middle English *threpen*, from Old English *thrēapian*] (before 12th century)
1 *chiefly Scottish* : SCOLD, CHIDE
2 *chiefly Scottish* : to maintain persistently

¹**threat** \'thret\ *noun* [Middle English *thret* coercion, threat, from Old English *thrēat* coercion; akin to Middle High German *drōz* annoyance, Latin *trudere* to push, thrust] (before 12th century)
1 : an expression of intention to inflict evil, injury, or damage
2 : one that threatens
3 : an indication of something impending ⟨the sky held a *threat* of rain⟩

²**threat** *verb* (before 12th century)
archaic : THREATEN

threat·en \'thre-t°n\ *verb* **threat·ened**; **threat·en·ing** \'thret-niŋ, 'thre-t°n-iŋ\ (13th century)
transitive verb
1 : to utter threats against
2 a : to give signs or warning of : PORTEND ⟨the clouds *threatened* rain⟩ **b** : to hang over dangerously : MENACE
3 : to announce as intended or possible ⟨the workers *threatened* a strike⟩
intransitive verb
1 : to utter threats
2 : to portend evil
— **threat·en·er** \'thret-nər, 'thre-t°n-ər\ *noun*
— **threat·en·ing·ly** \'thret-niŋ-lē, 'thre-t°n-iŋ-\ *adverb*

threatened *adjective* (1960)
: having an uncertain chance of continued survival ⟨a *threatened* species of owls⟩; *specifically* : likely to become an endangered species

three \'thrē\ *noun* [Middle English, from *three*, adjective, from Old English *thrīe* (masculine), *thrēo* (feminine & neuter); akin to Old High German *drī* three, Latin *tres*, Greek *treis*] (before 12th century)
1 — see NUMBER table
2 : the third in a set or series ⟨the *three* of hearts⟩
3 : something having three units or members
— **three** *adjective*
— **three** *pronoun, plural in construction*

three–bag·ger \-'ba-gər\ *noun* (1881)
: TRIPLE

three–ball \-,bȯl\ *adjective* (circa 1890)
: relating to or being a golf match in which three players compete against one another with each playing a single ball

three–card monte \'thrē-'kärd-\ *noun* (1854)
: a gambling game in which the dealer shows three cards, shuffles them, places them face down, and invites spectators to bet they can identify the location of a particular card

three–col·or \'thrē-'kə-lər\ *adjective* (1893)
: being or relating to a printing or photographic process wherein three primary colors are used to reproduce all the colors of the subject

3–D \'thrē-'dē\ *noun* [*D*, abbreviation of *dimensional*] (1951)
: the three-dimensional form; *also* : an image or a picture produced in it
— **3–D** *adjective*

three–deck·er \'thrē-'de-kər\ *noun* (1795)
1 : a wooden warship carrying guns on three decks
2 : TRIPLE-DECKER

three–dimensional *adjective* (circa 1891)
1 : of or relating to three dimensions
2 : giving the illusion of depth or varying distances — used of an image or a pictorial representation especially when this illusion is enhanced by stereoscopic means
3 : describing or being described in well-rounded completeness ⟨a *three-dimensional* analysis of multiple historical processes —L. L. Snyder⟩
4 : true to life : LIFELIKE

three·fold \'thrē-,fōld, -'fōld\ *adjective* (before 12th century)
1 : having three units or members : TRIPLE
2 : being three times as great or as many
— **three·fold** \-'fōld\ *adverb*

three–gait·ed \-'gā-təd\ *adjective* (1948)
of a horse : trained to use the walk, trot, and canter

three–hand·ed \-'han-dəd\ *adjective* (1719)
: played by three players ⟨*three-handed* bridge⟩

Three Hours *noun* (circa 1891)
: a service of devotion between noon and three o'clock on Good Friday

three–legged \'thrē-'legd, -'lāgd; -'le-gəd, -'lā-\ *adjective* (1596)
: having three legs ⟨a *three-legged* stool⟩

three–legged race *noun* (1903)
: a race between pairs of competitors with each pair having their adjacent legs bound together

three–line octave *noun* (circa 1931)
: the musical octave that begins on the second C above middle C — see PITCH illustration

three–mile limit *noun* (circa 1891)
: the limit of the marginal sea of three miles included in the territorial waters of a state

three of a kind (circa 1897)
: three cards of the same rank in one hand — see POKER illustration

three·pence \'thre-pən(t)s, 'thri-, 'thrə-, *US* also 'thrē-pen(t)s\ *noun* (1589)
1 *plural* **threepence** *or* **three·penc·es** : a coin worth threepence
2 : the sum of three British pennies

three·pen·ny \'thre-p(ə-)nē, 'thri-, 'thrə-, *US* also 'thrē-,pe-nē\ *adjective* (15th century)
1 : costing or worth threepence
2 : POOR

three–phase *adjective* (circa 1900)
: of, relating to, or operating by means of a combination of three circuits energized by alternating electromotive forces that differ in phase by one third of a cycle

three–piece *adjective* (circa 1909)
: consisting of or made in three pieces ⟨a *three-piece* suit⟩

three–point landing *noun* (1918)
: an airplane landing in which the two main wheels of the landing gear and the tail wheel or skid or nose wheel touch the ground simultaneously

three–quarter *adjective* (1677)
: extending to three-quarters of the normal full length ⟨a *three-quarter* sleeve⟩

three–quarter–bound *adjective* (circa 1951)
of a book : bound like a half-bound book but having the material on the spine extended to cover about one third of the boards
— **three–quarter binding** *noun*

three–ring circus *noun* (1904)
1 : a circus with simultaneous performances in three rings
2 : something wild, confusing, engrossing, or entertaining

three R's *noun plural* [from the facetiously used phrase *reading, 'riting, and 'rithmetic*] (1828)
1 : the fundamentals taught in elementary school; *especially* : reading, writing, and arithmetic
2 : the fundamental skills in a field of endeavor

three·score \'thrē-'skȯr, -'skór\ *adjective* (14th century)
: being three times twenty : SIXTY

three·some \'thrē-səm\ *noun* (14th century)
1 : a group of three persons or things : TRIO
2 : a golf match in which one person plays his ball against the ball of two others playing each stroke alternately

\ə\ abut \ᵊ\ kitten \ər\ further \a\ ash \ā\ ace \ä\ mop, mar \aù\ out \ch\ chin \e\ bet \ē\ easy \g\ go \i\ hit \ī\ ice \j\ job \ŋ\ sing \ō\ go \ȯ\ law \ȯi\ boy \th\ thin \ṯh\ the \ü\ loot \ù\ foot \y\ yet \zh\ vision *see also* Guide to Pronunciation

three–spined stickleback \ˈthrē-ˈspīn(d)-\ *noun* (1769)
: a stickle-back (*Gasterosteus aculeatus*) chiefly of fresh and brackish waters that typically has three dorsal spines

three-spined stickleback

three–toed sloth \ˌthrē-ˈtōd-\ *noun* (1879)
: any of a genus (*Bradypus*) of sloths having three clawed digits on each foot and nine vertebrae in the neck — compare TWO-TOED SLOTH

three–wheel·er \-ˌhwē-lər, -ˌwē-\ *noun* (1886)
: any of various vehicles having three wheels

thre·node \ˈthrē-ˌnōd, ˈthre-\ *noun* (1858)
: THRENODY
— **thre·nod·ic** \thri-ˈnä-dik\ *adjective*
— **thren·o·dist** \ˈthre-nə-dist\ *noun*

thren·o·dy \ˈthre-nə-dē\ *noun, plural* **-dies** [Greek *thrēnōidia,* from *thrēnos* dirge + *aeidein* to sing — more at DRONE, ODE] (1634)
: a song of lamentation for the dead : ELEGY

thre·o·nine \ˈthrē-ə-ˌnēn\ *noun* [probably from *threonic acid* (C$_4$H$_8$O$_5$)] (1936)
: a colorless crystalline essential amino acid C$_4$H$_9$NO$_3$

thresh \ˈthrash, ˈthresh\ *verb* [Middle English *threshen,* from Old English *threscan;* akin to Old High German *dreskan* to thresh] (before 12th century)
transitive verb
1 : to separate seed from (a harvested plant) mechanically; *also* : to separate (seed) in this way
2 : THRASH 4
3 : to strike repeatedly
intransitive verb
1 : to thresh grain
2 : THRASH 2, 3

thresh·er *noun* (14th century)
1 : one that threshes; *especially* : THRESHING MACHINE
2 : THRESHER SHARK

thresher shark *noun* (1888)
: a large nearly cosmopolitan shark (*Alopias vulpinus*) having a greatly elongated curved upper lobe of its tail with which it is said to thresh the water to round up the fish on which it feeds — see SHARK illustration

threshing machine *noun* (1775)
: a machine for separating grain crops into grain or seeds and straw

thresh·old \ˈthresh-ˌhōld, ˈthre-ˌshōld\ *noun* [Middle English *thresshold,* from Old English *threscwald;* akin to Old Norse *threskjǫldr* threshold, Old English *threscan* to thresh] (before 12th century)
1 : the plank, stone, or piece of timber that lies under a door : SILL
2 a : GATE, DOOR **b** (1) : END, BOUNDARY; *specifically* : the end of a runway (2) : the place or point of entering or beginning : OUTSET ⟨on the *threshold* of a new age⟩
3 a : the point at which a physiological or psychological effect begins to be produced **b** : a level, point, or value above which something is true or will take place and below which it is not or will not

threw *past of* THROW

thrice \ˈthrīs\ *adverb* [Middle English *thrie, thries,* from Old English *thriga;* akin to Old Frisian *thria* three times, Old English *thrīe* three] (13th century)
1 : three times
2 a : in a threefold manner or degree **b** : to a high degree

thrift \ˈthrift\ *noun* [Middle English, from Old Norse, prosperity, from *thrīfask* to thrive] (13th century)
1 : healthy and vigorous growth
2 : careful management especially of money

3 *chiefly Scottish* : gainful occupation
4 : any of a genus (*Armeria*) of the plumbago family of perennial evergreen acaulescent herbs; *especially* : a scapose herb (*A. maritima*) with pink or white flower heads
5 : a savings bank or savings and loan association — called also *thrift institution*

thrift·less \ˈthrift-ləs\ *adjective* (1568)
1 : lacking usefulness or worth
2 : careless, wasteful, or incompetent in handling money or resources : IMPROVIDENT
— **thrift·less·ly** *adverb*
— **thrift·less·ness** *noun*

thrift shop *noun* (1944)
: a shop that sells secondhand articles and especially clothes and is often run for charitable purposes

thrifty \ˈthrif-tē\ *adjective* **thrift·i·er; -est** (15th century)
1 : thriving by industry and frugality : PROSPEROUS
2 : growing vigorously
3 : given to or marked by economy and good management
synonym see SPARING
— **thrift·i·ly** \-tə-lē\ *adverb*
— **thrift·i·ness** *noun*

thrill \ˈthril\ *verb* [Middle English *thirlen, thrillen* to pierce, from Old English *thyrlian,* from *thyrel* hole, from *thurh* through — more at THROUGH] (1592)
transitive verb
1 a : to cause to experience a sudden sharp feeling of excitement **b** : to cause to have a shivering or tingling sensation
2 : to cause to vibrate or tremble perceptibly
intransitive verb
1 : to move or pass so as to cause a sudden wave of emotion
2 : to become thrilled: **a** : to experience a sudden sharp excitement **b** : TINGLE, THROB
3 : TREMBLE, VIBRATE ◆
— **thrill** *noun*
— **thrill·ing·ly** \ˈthri-liŋ-lē\ *adverb*

thril·ler \ˈthri-lər\ *noun* (1889)
: one that thrills; *especially* : a work of fiction or drama designed to hold the interest by the use of a high degree of intrigue, adventure, or suspense

thrips \ˈthrips\ *noun, plural* **thrips** [Latin, woodworm, from Greek] (1795)
: any of an order (Thysanoptera) of small to minute sucking insects most of which feed often destructively on plant juices

thrive \ˈthrīv\ *intransitive verb* **throve** \ˈthrōv\ *or* **thrived; thriv·en** \ˈthri-vən\ *also* **thrived; thriv·ing** \ˈthrī-viŋ\ [Middle English, from Old Norse *thrīfask,* probably reflexive of *thrīfa* to grasp] (13th century)
1 : to grow vigorously : FLOURISH
2 : to gain in wealth or possessions : PROSPER
3 : to progress toward or realize a goal
— **thriv·er** \ˈthrī-vər\ *noun*

thriving *adjective* (1607)
: characterized by success or prosperity
— **thriv·ing·ly** \ˈthrī-viŋ-lē\ *adverb*

thro \ˈthrü\ *preposition* (15th century)
archaic : THROUGH

¹throat \ˈthrōt\ *noun* [Middle English *throte,* from Old English; akin to Old High German *drozza* throat] (before 12th century)
1 (1) : the part of the neck in front of the spinal column (2) : the passage through the neck to the stomach and lungs **b** (1) : VOICE (2) : the seat of the voice
2 : something resembling the throat especially in being an entrance, a passageway, a constriction, or a narrowed part: as **a** : the orifice of a tubular organ especially of a plant **b** : the opening in the vamp of a shoe at the instep **c** : the part of a tennis racket that connects the head with the shaft
3 : the curved part of an anchor's arm where it joins the shank — see ANCHOR illustration
— **at each other's throats** : in open and aggressive conflict

²throat *transitive verb* (circa 1611)
1 : to utter in the throat : MUTTER
2 : to sing or enunciate in a throaty voice

throat·ed \ˈthrō-təd\ *adjective* (circa 1530)
: having a throat especially of a specified kind — usually used in combination ⟨white-throated⟩

throat·latch \ˈthrōt-ˌlach\ *noun* (1794)
1 : a strap of a bridle or halter passing under a horse's throat
2 : the part of a horse's throat around which the throatlatch passes — see HORSE illustration

throaty \ˈthrō-tē\ *adjective* **throat·i·er; -est** (circa 1645)
1 : uttered or produced from low in the throat ⟨a *throaty* voice⟩
2 : heavy, thick, and deep as if from the throat ⟨*throaty* notes of a horn⟩
— **throat·i·ly** \ˈthrō-tᵊl-ē\ *adverb*
— **throat·i·ness** \ˈthrō-tē-nəs\ *noun*

¹throb \ˈthräb\ *intransitive verb* **throbbed; throb·bing** [Middle English *throbben*] (14th century)
1 : to pulsate or pound with abnormal force or rapidity
2 : to beat or vibrate rhythmically
— **throb·ber** *noun*

²throb *noun* (1579)
: BEAT, PULSE

throe \ˈthrō\ *noun* [Middle English *thrawe, throwe,* from Old English *thrawu, thrēa* threat, pang; akin to Old High German *drawa* threat] (13th century)
1 : PANG, SPASM ⟨death *throes*⟩ ⟨*throes* of childbirth⟩
2 *plural* : a hard or painful struggle ⟨the *throes* of revolutionary social change —M. D. Geismar⟩

thromb- *or* **thrombo-** *combining form* [Greek *thrombos* clot]
: blood clot : clotting of blood ⟨*thromb*in⟩ ⟨*thrombo*plastic⟩

throm·bin \ˈthräm-bən\ *noun* [International Scientific Vocabulary] (1898)
: a proteolytic enzyme that is formed from prothrombin and facilitates the clotting of blood by catalyzing conversion of fibrinogen to fibrin

throm·bo·cyte \-bə-ˌsīt\ *noun* [International Scientific Vocabulary] (1893)
: BLOOD PLATELET; *also* : an invertebrate cell with similar function
— **throm·bo·cyt·ic** \ˌthräm-bə-ˈsi-tik\ *adjective*

throm·bo·cy·to·pe·nia \ˌthräm-bə-ˌsī-tə-ˈpē-nē-ə, -nyə\ *noun* [New Latin, from International Scientific Vocabulary *thrombocyte* + New Latin *-o-* + *-penia*] (1923)
: persistent decrease in the number of blood platelets that is often associated with hemorrhagic conditions
— **throm·bo·cy·to·pe·nic** \-nik\ *adjective*

◇ WORD HISTORY
thrill In the 14th century a person who was *thrilled* might not live long enough to tell anyone about it, because the Middle English verb *thrillen,* an altered form of *thirlen* with the first vowel and *r* transposed, meant "to pierce, stab, penetrate," as with a sword or spear. The older form *thirlen* continued Old English *thyrlian,* a verbal derivative of *thyrel* "hole." (The word *thyrel* also enters into Old English *nosthyrl,* literally, "nose hole," the ancestor of Modern English *nostril.*) In early Modern English a connection was made between the physical sensation of being pierced and the experience of being strongly moved by some emotion, so that *thrill* came to mean "to cause (someone) to feel excited." The old literal sense of the word has become obsolete, and "to be thrilled" now usually denotes a quite positive feeling.

throm·bo·em·bo·lism \,thräm-bō-'em-bə-,li-zəm\ *noun* (1907)
: the blocking of a blood vessel by a particle that has broken away from a blood clot at its site of formation
— **throm·bo·em·bol·ic** \-em-'bä-lik\ *adjective*

throm·bo·ki·nase \,thräm-bō-'kī-,nās, -,nāz\ *noun* [International Scientific Vocabulary] (1908)
: THROMBOPLASTIN

throm·bo·lyt·ic \,thräm-bə-'li-tik\ *adjective* (1929)
: destroying or breaking up a thrombus ⟨a *thrombolytic* agent⟩ ⟨*thrombolytic* therapy⟩

throm·bo·phle·bi·tis \,thräm-bō-fli-'bī-təs\ *noun* [New Latin] (circa 1890)
: inflammation of a vein with formation of a thrombus

throm·bo·plas·tic \-'plas-tik\ *adjective* [International Scientific Vocabulary] (1911)
: initiating or accelerating the clotting of blood

throm·bo·plas·tin \-'plas-tən\ *noun* [International Scientific Vocabulary, from *thrombo-plastic*] (1911)
: a complex enzyme found especially in blood platelets that functions in the conversion of prothrombin into thrombin in the clotting of blood

throm·bo·sis \thräm-'bō-səs, thrəm-\ *noun, plural* **-bo·ses** \-,sēz\ [New Latin, from Greek *thrombōsis* clotting, from *thromboust-hai* to become clotted, from *thrombos* clot] (1866)
: the formation or presence of a blood clot within a blood vessel
— **throm·bot·ic** \-'bä-tik\ *adjective*

throm·box·ane \thräm-'bäk-,sān\ *noun* [*thromb-* + *ox-* + *-ane*] (1975)
: any of several substances that are formed from endoperoxides, cause constriction of vascular and bronchial smooth muscle, and promote blood coagulation

throm·bus \'thräm-bəs\ *noun, plural* **throm·bi** \-,bī, -,bē\ [New Latin, from Greek *thrombos* clot] (circa 1693)
: a clot of blood formed within a blood vessel and remaining attached to its place of origin — compare EMBOLUS

¹**throne** \'thrōn\ *noun* [Middle English *trone, throne,* from Old French *trone,* from Latin *thronus,* from Greek *thronos* — more at FIRM] (13th century)
1 a : the chair of state of a sovereign or high dignitary ⟨as a bishop⟩ **b :** the seat of a deity
2 : royal power and dignity : SOVEREIGNTY
3 *plural* : an order of angels — see CELESTIAL HIERARCHY

²**throne** *verb* **throned; thron·ing** (14th century)
transitive verb
1 : to seat on a throne
2 : to invest with kingly rank or power
intransitive verb
1 : to sit on a throne
2 : to hold kingly power

throne room *noun* (1864)
: a formal audience room containing the throne of a sovereign

¹**throng** \'thrôn\ *noun* [Middle English *thrang, throng,* from Old English *thrang, gethrang;* akin to Old English *thringan* to press, crowd, Old High German *dringan,* Lithuanian *trenkti* to jolt] (before 12th century)
1 a : a multitude of assembled persons **b :** a large number : HOST
2 a : a crowding together of many persons **b :** PRESSURE ⟨this *throng* of business —S. R. Crockett⟩
synonym see CROWD

²**throng** *verb* **thronged; throng·ing** \'thrôn-iŋ\ (1534)
transitive verb
1 : to crowd upon : PRESS
2 : to crowd into : PACK ⟨shoppers *thronging* the streets⟩

intransitive verb
: to crowd together in great numbers

thros·tle \'thrä-səl\ *noun* [Middle English, from Old English — more at THRUSH] (before 12th century)
: ¹THRUSH 1; *specifically* : SONG THRUSH

¹**throt·tle** \'thrä-t³l\ *verb* **throt·tled; throt·tling** \'thrät-liŋ, 'thrä-t³l-iŋ\ [Middle English *throtlen,* from *throte* throat] (15th century)
transitive verb
1 a (1) : to compress the throat of : CHOKE (2) : to kill by such action **b :** to prevent or check expression or activity of : SUPPRESS
2 a : to decrease the flow of (as steam or fuel to an engine) by a valve **b :** to regulate and especially to reduce the speed of (as an engine) by such means **c :** to vary the thrust of (a rocket engine) during flight
intransitive verb
: to throttle something (as an engine) — usually used with *back* or *down* ⟨the pilot *throttled* back⟩
— **throt·tler** \'thrät-lər, 'thrä-t³l-ər\ *noun*

²**throttle** *noun* [perhaps from (assumed) Middle English, diminutive of Middle English *throte* throat] (circa 1547)
1 a : THROAT 1a **b :** TRACHEA 1
2 a : a valve for regulating the supply of a fluid (as steam) to an engine; *especially* : the valve controlling the volume of vaporized fuel charge delivered to the cylinders of an internal combustion engine **b :** the lever controlling this valve **c :** the condition of being throttled
— **at full throttle :** at full speed

throt·tle·able \'thrä-t³l-ə-bəl\ *adjective* (1960)
: capable of having the thrust varied — used of a rocket engine

throt·tle·hold \'thrä-t³l-,hōld\ *noun* (1935)
: a vicious, strangling, or stultifying control

¹**through** \'thrü\ *preposition* [Middle English *thurh, thruh, through,* from Old English *thurh;* akin to Old High German *durh* through, Latin *trans* across, beyond, Sanskrit *tarati* he crosses over] (before 12th century)
1 a (1) — used as a function word to indicate movement into at one side or point and out at another and especially the opposite side of ⟨drove a nail *through* the board⟩ (2) : by way of ⟨left *through* the door⟩ (3) — used as a function word to indicate passage from one end or boundary to another ⟨a highway *through* the forest⟩ ⟨a road *through* the desert⟩ (4) : without stopping for : PAST ⟨drove *through* a red light⟩ **b** — used as a function word to indicate passage into and out of a treatment, handling, or process ⟨the matter has already passed *through* her hands⟩
2 — used as a function word to indicate means, agency, or intermediacy: as **a :** by means of : by the agency of **b :** because of ⟨failed *through* ignorance⟩ **c :** by common descent from or relationship with ⟨related *through* their grandfather⟩
3 a : over the whole surface or extent of : THROUGHOUT ⟨homes scattered *through* the valley⟩ **b** — used as a function word to indicate movement within a large expanse ⟨flew *through* the air⟩ **c** — used as a function word to indicate exposure to a specified set of conditions ⟨put him *through* hell⟩
4 — used as a function word to indicate a period of time: as **a :** during the entire period of ⟨all *through* her life⟩ **b :** from the beginning to the end of ⟨the tower stood *through* the earthquake⟩ **c :** to and including ⟨Monday *through* Friday⟩
5 a — used as a function word to indicate completion or exhaustion ⟨got *through* the book⟩ ⟨went *through* the money in a year⟩ **b** — used as a function word to indicate acceptance or approval especially by an official body ⟨got the bill *through* the legislature⟩

²**through** \'thrü\ *adverb* (before 12th century)
1 : from one end or side to the other

2 a : from beginning to end **b :** to completion, conclusion, or accomplishment ⟨see it *through*⟩
3 : to the core : COMPLETELY ⟨soaked *through*⟩
4 : into the open : OUT ⟨break *through*⟩

³**through** \'thrü\ *adjective* (1523)
1 a : extending from one surface to another ⟨a *through* mortise⟩ **b :** admitting free or continuous passage : DIRECT ⟨a *through* road⟩
2 a (1) : going from point of origin to destination without change or reshipment ⟨a *through* train⟩ (2) : of or relating to such movement ⟨a *through* ticket⟩ **b :** initiated at and destined for points outside a local zone ⟨*through* traffic⟩
3 a : arrived at completion or accomplishment ⟨is *through* with the job⟩ **b :** WASHED-UP, FINISHED

through and through *adverb* (15th century)
: in every way : THOROUGHLY

through–com·posed \,thrü-kəm-'pōzd\ *adjective* [translation of German *durchkomponiert*] (1884)
of a song : having new music provided for each stanza — compare STROPHIC

through·ith·er *or* **through·oth·er** \'thrü-(ə-)thər\ *adverb* [¹*through* + *other*] (1596)
chiefly Scottish : in confusion : PROMISCUOUSLY

through·ly \'thrü-lē\ *adverb* (15th century)
archaic : in a thorough manner

¹**through·out** \thrü-'aüt\ *adverb* (13th century)
1 : in or to every part : EVERYWHERE ⟨of one color *throughout*⟩
2 : during the whole time or action : from beginning to end ⟨remained loyal *throughout*⟩

²**throughout** *preposition* (13th century)
1 : all the way from one end to the other of : in or to every part of ⟨cities *throughout* the United States⟩
2 : during the whole course or period of ⟨troubled her *throughout* her life⟩

through·put \'thrü-,püt\ *noun* (circa 1915)
: OUTPUT, PRODUCTION ⟨the *throughput* of a computer⟩

through street *noun* (1930)
: a street on which the through movement of traffic is given preference

throve *past of* THRIVE

¹**throw** \'thrō\ *verb* **threw** \'thrü\; **thrown** \'thrōn\; **throw·ing** [Middle English *thrawen, throwen* to cause to twist, throw, from Old English *thrāwan* to cause to twist or turn; akin to Old High German *drāen* to turn, Latin *terere* to rub, Greek *tribein* to rub, *tetrainein* to bore, pierce] (14th century)
transitive verb
1 a : to propel through the air by a forward motion of the hand and arm ⟨*throw* a baseball⟩ **b :** to propel through the air in any manner ⟨a rifle that can *throw* a bullet a mile⟩
2 a : to cause to fall ⟨*threw* his opponent⟩ **b :** to cause to fall off : UNSEAT ⟨the horse *threw* its rider⟩ **c :** to get the better of : OVERCOME ⟨the problem didn't *throw* her⟩
3 a : to fling (oneself) precipitately ⟨*threw* herself down on the sofa⟩ **b :** to drive or impel violently : DASH ⟨the ship was *thrown* on a reef⟩
4 a (1) : to put in a particular position or condition ⟨*threw* her arms around him⟩ (2) : to put on or off hastily or carelessly ⟨*threw* on a coat⟩ **b :** to bring to bear : EXERT ⟨*threw* all his efforts into the boy's defense⟩ **c :** BUILD, CONSTRUCT ⟨*threw* a pontoon bridge over the river⟩
5 : to form or shape on a potter's wheel
6 : to deliver (a blow) in or as if in boxing
7 : to twist two or more filaments of into a thread or yarn

\ə\ abut \ˀ\ kitten \ər\ further \a\ ash \ā\ ace
\ä\ mop, mar \aü\ out \ch\ chin \e\ bet \ē\ easy
\g\ go \i\ hit \ī\ ice \j\ job \ŋ\ sing \ō\ go
\ö\ law \öi\ boy \th\ thin \th\ the \ü\ loot \ü\ foot
\y\ yet \zh\ vision *see also* Guide to Pronunciation

8 a : to make a cast of (dice or a specified number on dice) **b :** ROLL 1a ⟨*throw* a bowling ball⟩
9 : to give up : ABANDON
10 : to send forth : PROJECT ⟨the setting sun *threw* long shadows⟩
11 : to make (oneself) dependent : commit (oneself) for help, support, or protection ⟨*threw* himself on the mercy of the court⟩
12 : to indulge in : give way to ⟨*threw* a temper tantrum⟩
13 : to bring forth : give birth to : SIRE, PRODUCE ⟨*throws* a good crop⟩ ⟨*threw* large litters⟩
14 : to lose intentionally ⟨*throw* a game⟩
15 : to move (a lever) so as to connect or disconnect parts of a clutch or switch; *also* : to make or break (a connection) with a lever
16 : to give by way of entertainment ⟨*throw* a party⟩
intransitive verb
: CAST, HURL ☆
— **throw·er** \'thrō(-ə)r\ *noun*
— **throw one's weight around** *or* **throw one's weight about :** to exercise influence or authority especially in an excessive degree or in an objectionable manner
— **throw together 1 :** to put together in a hurried and usually careless manner ⟨a bookshelf hastily *thrown together*⟩ **2 :** to bring into casual association ⟨different kinds of people are *thrown together* —Richard Sennett⟩
²throw *noun* (1530)
1 a : an act of throwing, hurling, or flinging **b** (1) : an act of throwing dice (2) : the number thrown with a cast of dice **c :** a method of throwing an opponent in wrestling or judo
2 : the distance a missile may be thrown or light rays may be projected
3 : an undertaking involving chance or danger : RISK, VENTURE
4 : the amount of vertical displacement produced by a geological fault
5 a : the extreme movement given to a pivoted or reciprocating piece by a cam, crank, or eccentric : STROKE **b :** the length of the radius of a crank or the virtual crank radius of an eccentric or cam
6 a : a light coverlet (as for a bed) **b :** a woman's scarf or light wrap
— **a throw :** for each one : APIECE ⟨copies are to be sold at $5 *a throw* —Harvey Breit⟩
¹throw·away \'thrō-ə-,wā\ *noun* (1903)
1 : one that is or is designed to be thrown away: as **a :** a free handbill or circular **b :** a line of dialogue (as in a play) de-emphasized by casual delivery; *especially* : a joke or witticism delivered casually
2 : something made or done without care or interest
²throwaway *adjective* (1928)
1 : designed to be thrown away : DISPOSABLE ⟨*throwaway* containers⟩
2 : written or spoken (as in a play) in a low-key or unemphatic manner ⟨*throwaway* lines⟩
3 : NONCHALANT, CASUAL
throw away *transitive verb* (1530)
1 a : to get rid of as worthless or unnecessary **b :** DISCARD 2b
2 a : to use in a foolish or wasteful manner : SQUANDER **b :** to fail to take advantage of : WASTE
3 : to make (as a line in a play) unemphatic by casual delivery
throw·back \'thrō-,bak\ *noun* (1888)
1 a : reversion to an earlier type or phase : ATAVISM **b :** an instance or product of atavistic reversion
2 : one that is suggestive of or suited to an earlier time or style ⟨his manners were a *throwback* to a more polite era⟩
throw back (1840)
transitive verb
1 : to delay the progress or advance of : CHECK
2 : to cause to rely : make dependent ⟨they are *thrown back* upon . . . native intelligence —Michael Novak⟩

3 : REFLECT
intransitive verb
: to revert to an earlier type or phase
throw down *transitive verb* (14th century)
1 : to cause to fall : OVERTHROW
2 : PRECIPITATE
3 : to cast off : DISCARD
throw-in \'thrō-,in\ *noun* (1881)
: an act or instance of throwing a ball in: as **a** : a throw made from the touchline in soccer to put the ball back in play after it has gone into touch **b :** a throw from an outfielder to the infield in baseball **c :** an inbounds pass in basketball
throw in (1678)
transitive verb
1 : to add as a gratuity or supplement
2 : to introduce or interject in the course of something : CONTRIBUTE ⟨they *throw in* some . . . sound effects on several songs —Tom Phillips⟩
3 : DISTRIBUTE 3b
4 : ENGAGE ⟨*throw in* the clutch⟩
intransitive verb
: to enter into association or partnership : JOIN ⟨agrees to *throw in* with a crooked ex-cop —*Newsweek*⟩
— **throw in the towel** *also* **throw in the sponge :** to abandon a struggle or contest : acknowledge defeat : GIVE UP
throw off (1618)
transitive verb
1 a : to free oneself from : get rid of ⟨*threw off* his inhibitions⟩ **b :** to cast off often in a hurried or vigorous manner : ABANDON ⟨*threw off* all restraint⟩ **c :** DISTRACT, DIVERT ⟨dogs *thrown off* by a false scent⟩
2 : EMIT, GIVE OFF ⟨stacks *throwing off* plumes of smoke⟩
3 : to produce in an offhand manner : execute with speed or facility ⟨some little . . . tune that the composer had *thrown off* —James Hilton⟩
4 a : to cause to depart from an expected or desired course ⟨mistakes *threw* his calculations *off* a bit⟩ **b :** to cause to make a mistake : MISLEAD
intransitive verb
1 : to begin hunting
2 : to make derogatory comments
throw out *transitive verb* (1526)
1 a : to remove from a place, office, or employment usually in a sudden or unexpected manner **b :** to get rid of as worthless or unnecessary
2 : to give expression to : UTTER ⟨*threw out* a remark . . . that utterly confounded him —Jean Stafford⟩
3 : to dismiss from acceptance or consideration : REJECT ⟨the testimony was *thrown out*⟩
4 : to make visible or manifest : DISPLAY ⟨the signal was *thrown out* for the . . . fleet to prepare for action —Archibald Duncan⟩
5 : to leave behind : OUTDISTANCE
6 : to give forth from within : EMIT
7 a : to send out **b :** to cause to project : EXTEND
8 : CONFUSE, DISCONCERT ⟨automobiles in line blocking the road . . . *threw* the whole schedule *out* —F. D. Roosevelt⟩
9 : to cause to stand out : make prominent
10 : to make a throw that enables a teammate to put out (a base runner)
throw over *transitive verb* (1835)
1 : to forsake despite bonds of attachment or duty
2 : to refuse to accept : REJECT
throw pillow *noun* (1956)
: a small pillow used especially as a decorative accessory
throw rug *noun* (1928)
: SCATTER RUG
throw·ster \'thrō-stər\ *noun* (15th century)
: one who throws textile filaments
throw up (15th century)
transitive verb

1 : to raise quickly
2 : GIVE UP, QUIT ⟨the urge . . . to *throw up* all intellectual work —Norman Mailer⟩
3 : to build hurriedly ⟨new houses *thrown up* almost overnight⟩
4 : VOMIT
5 : to bring forth : PRODUCE
6 : to make distinct especially by contrast : cause to stand out
7 : to mention repeatedly by way of reproach
intransitive verb
: VOMIT
— **throw up one's hands :** to admit defeat ⟨in the end *throws up his hands* in despair —Frank Conroy⟩
throw weight *noun* (1969)
: the maximum payload of an ICBM
thru *variant of* THROUGH
¹thrum \'thrəm\ *noun* [Middle English, from Old English *-thrum* (in *tungethrum* ligament of the tongue); akin to Old High German *drum* fragment] (14th century)
1 a (1) : a fringe of warp threads left on the loom after the cloth has been removed (2) : one of these warp threads **b :** a tuft or short piece of rope yarn used in thrumming canvas — usually used in plural **c :** BIT, PARTICLE
2 : a hair, fiber, or threadlike leaf on a plant; *also* : a tuft or fringe of such structures
— **thrum** *adjective*
²thrum *transitive verb* **thrummed; thrumming** (15th century)
1 : to furnish with thrums : FRINGE
2 : to insert short pieces of rope yarn or spun yarn in (a piece of canvas) to make a rough surface or a mat which can be wrapped about rigging to prevent chafing
³thrum *verb* **thrummed; thrum·ming** [imitative] (1592)
intransitive verb
1 : to play or pluck a stringed instrument idly : STRUM
2 : to sound with a monotonous hum
transitive verb
1 : to play (as a stringed instrument) in an idle or relaxed manner
2 : to recite tiresomely or monotonously
⁴thrum *noun* (1798)
: the monotonous sound of thrumming
¹thrush \'thrəsh\ *noun* [Middle English *thrusche*, from Old English *thrysce*; akin to Old English *throstle* thrush, Old High German *droscala*, Latin *turdus*] (before 12th century)
1 : any of numerous small or medium-sized oscine birds (families Turdidae and Muscicapidae) which are mostly of a plain color often with spotted underparts and many of which are excellent singers
2 : a bird held to resemble a thrush
²thrush *noun* [probably of Scandinavian origin; akin to Danish & Norwegian *trøske* thrush] (1665)

☆ **SYNONYMS**
Throw, cast, toss, fling, hurl, pitch, sling mean to cause to move swiftly through space by a propulsive movement or a propelling force. THROW is general and interchangeable with the other terms but may specifically imply a distinctive motion with bent arm (can *throw* a fastball and a curve). CAST usually implies lightness in the thing thrown and sometimes a scattering (*cast* it to the winds). TOSS suggests a light or careless or aimless throwing and may imply an upward motion (*tossed* the coat on the bed). FLING stresses a violent throwing (*flung* the ring back in his face). HURL implies power as in throwing a massive weight (*hurled* himself at the intruder). PITCH suggests throwing carefully at a target (*pitch* horseshoes). SLING stresses either the use of whirling momentum in throwing or directness of aim (*slung* the bag over his shoulder).

1 : a disease that is caused by a fungus (*Candida albicans*), occurs especially in infants and children, and is marked by white patches in the oral cavity; *broadly* : CANDIDIASIS ⟨vaginal *thrush*⟩
2 : a suppurative disorder of the feet in various animals (as a horse)

¹thrust \'thrəst\ *verb* **thrust; thrust·ing** [Middle English *thrusten, thristen,* from Old Norse *thrȳsta;* probably akin to Old Norse *thrjōta* to tire, Old English *thrēat* coercion — more at THREAT] (13th century)
transitive verb
1 : to push or drive with force : SHOVE
2 : to cause to enter or pierce something by or as if by pushing ⟨*thrust* a dagger into his heart⟩
3 : EXTEND, SPREAD
4 : STAB, PIERCE
5 a : to put (as an unwilling person) forcibly into a course of action or position ⟨was *thrust* into the job⟩ **b :** to introduce often improperly into a position : INTERPOLATE
6 : to press, force, or impose the acceptance of upon someone ⟨*thrust* new responsibilities upon her⟩
intransitive verb
1 a : to force an entrance or passage **b :** to push forward : press onward **c :** to push upward : PROJECT
2 : to make a thrust, stab, or lunge with or as if with a pointed weapon ⟨*thrust* at them with a knife⟩

²thrust *noun* (circa 1586)
1 a : a push or lunge with a pointed weapon **b** (1) **:** a verbal attack (2) **:** a military assault
2 a : a strong continued pressure **b :** the sideways force or pressure of one part of a structure against another part (as of an arch against an abutment) **c :** the force produced by a propeller or by a jet or rocket engine that drives a vehicle (as an aircraft) forward **d :** a nearly horizontal geological fault
3 a : a forward or upward push **b :** a movement (as by a group of people) in a specified direction
4 a : salient or essential element or meaning **b :** principal concern or objective

thrust·er *also* **thrust·or** \'thrəs-tər\ *noun* (1597)
: one that thrusts; *especially* : an engine (as a jet engine) that develops thrust by expelling a jet of fluid or a stream of particles

thrust·ful \'thrəst-fəl\ *adjective* (1909)
British : characterized by thrust : AGGRESSIVE ⟨*thrustful* young man on the make —*Current Literature*⟩

thrust stage *noun* [*thrust,* past participle of ¹*thrust*] (1965)
: a stage that projects beyond the proscenium so that the audience sits around the projection; *also* : a forestage that is extended into the auditorium to increase the stage area

thru·way \'thrü-ˌwā\ *noun* (1930)
: EXPRESSWAY

¹thud \'thəd\ *noun* [imitative] (1787)
1 : BLOW
2 : a dull sound : THUMP

²thud *intransitive verb* **thud·ded; thud·ding** (1796)
: to move or strike so as to make a thud

thug \'thəg\ *noun* [Hindi *ṭhag,* literally, thief] (1810)
: a brutal ruffian or assassin : GANGSTER, KILLER ◇
— **thug·gery** \'thə-g(ə-)rē\ *noun*
— **thug·gish** \'thə-gish\ *adjective*

thu·ja \'thü-jə, 'thyü-\ *noun* [New Latin *Thuja,* from Medieval Latin *thuia,* a cedar, from Greek *thyia,* from *thyein* to sacrifice — more at THYME] (circa 1760)
: any of a genus (*Thuja*) of evergreen shrubs and trees (as an arborvitae) of the cypress family having scalelike closely imbricated or compressed leaves

¹Thu·le \'thü-lē, 'thyü-\ *noun* [Middle English *Tyle,* from Old English, from Latin *Thule, Thyle,* from Greek *Thoulē, Thylē*] (before 12th century)
: the northernmost part of the habitable ancient world

²Thu·le \'tü-lē\ *adjective* [*Thule,* Greenland] (1925)
: of, relating to, or being the culture existing in the arctic lands from Alaska to Greenland from about 500 A.D. to 1400 A.D.

thu·li·um \'thü-lē-əm, 'thyü-\ *noun* [New Latin, from Latin *Thule*] (1879)
: a trivalent metallic element of the rare-earth group — see ELEMENT table

¹thumb \'thəm\ *noun* [Middle English *thoume, thoumbe,* from Old English *thūma;* akin to Old High German *thūmo* thumb, Latin *tumēre* to swell] (before 12th century)
1 : the short thick digit of the human hand that is analogous in position to the big toe and differs from the other fingers in having only two phalanges, allowing greater freedom of movement, and being opposable to each of them; *also* : a corresponding digit in lower animals
2 : the part of a glove or mitten that covers the thumb
3 : a convex molding : OVOLO
— **all thumbs :** extremely awkward or clumsy
— **under one's thumb** *or* **under the thumb :** under control : in a state of subservience ⟨her father did not have her that much *under his thumb* —Hamilton Basso⟩

²thumb (circa 1647)
transitive verb
1 a : to leaf through (pages) with the thumb **:** TURN **b :** to soil or wear by or as if by repeated thumbing ⟨a badly *thumbed* book⟩
2 : to request or obtain (a ride) in a passing automobile by signaling with the thumb
intransitive verb
1 : to turn over pages ⟨*thumb* through a book⟩
2 : to travel by thumbing rides : HITCHHIKE ⟨*thumbed* across the country⟩
— **thumb one's nose 1 :** to place the thumb at one's nose and extend the fingers as a gesture of scorn or defiance **2 :** to express disdain or defiance ⟨*thumb their nose* at opulence —*Sales Management*⟩

thumb·hole \'thəm-ˌhōl\ *noun* (1859)
1 : an opening in which to insert the thumb
2 : a hole in a wind musical instrument opened or closed by the thumb

thumb index *noun* (1903)
: a series of notches cut in the fore edge of a book to facilitate reference

¹thumb·nail \'thəm-ˌnāl, -'nā(ə)l\ *noun* (1604)
: the nail of the thumb

²thumbnail *adjective* (1852)
: CONCISE, BRIEF ⟨a *thumbnail* sketch⟩

thumb piano *noun* (1949)
: MBIRA

thumb·print \'thəm-ˌprint\ *noun* (1900)
: an impression made by the thumb; *especially* : a print made by the inside of the first joint

thumb·screw \-ˌskrü\ *noun* (1794)
1 : a screw having a flat-sided or knurled head so that it may be turned by the thumb and forefinger
2 : an instrument of torture for compressing the thumb by a screw

thumbs–down \'thəmz-ˈdaủn\ *noun* (1889)
: an instance or gesture of rejection, disapproval, or condemnation

thumbscrew 1

thumbs–up \-'əp\ *noun* (circa 1917)
: an instance or gesture of approval or encouragement

¹thumb·tack \'thəm-ˌtak\ *noun* (1884)
: a tack with a broad flat head for pressing into a surface with the thumb

²thumbtack *transitive verb* (1914)

: to fasten with a thumbtack

thumb·wheel \'thəm-ˌhwēl, -ˌwēl\ *noun* (1903)
: a control for various devices consisting of a partially exposed wheel that can be turned by moving the exposed edge with a finger

¹thump \'thəmp\ *verb* [imitative] (1548)
transitive verb
1 : to strike or beat with or as if with something thick or heavy so as to cause a dull sound
2 : POUND, KNOCK
3 : WHIP, THRASH
4 : to produce (music) mechanically or in a mechanical manner — usually used with *out* ⟨*thumped* out a tune on the piano⟩
intransitive verb
1 a : to inflict a thump **b :** to make or move with a thumping sound
2 : to make a vigorous endorsement ⟨got a couple of . . . senators to *thump* for him —*N.Y. Herald Tribune*⟩
— **thump·er** *noun*

²thump *noun* (1552)
: a blow or knock with or as if with something blunt or heavy; *also* : the sound made by such a blow

thump·ing *adjective* [*thumping,* present participle of ¹*thump*] (1576)
: impressively large, great, or excellent ⟨a *thumping* majority⟩

¹thun·der \'thən-dər\ *noun* [Middle English *thoner, thunder,* from Old English *thunor;* akin to Old High German *thonar* thunder, Latin *tonare* to thunder] (before 12th century)
1 : the sound that follows a flash of lightning and is caused by sudden expansion of the air in the path of the electrical discharge
2 : a loud utterance or threat
3 : BANG, RUMBLE ⟨the *thunder* of big guns⟩

²thunder *verb* **thun·dered; thun·der·ing** \-d(ə-)riŋ\ (before 12th century)
intransitive verb

\ə\ abut \ᵊ\ kitten \ər\ further \a\ ash \ā\ ace
\ä\ mop, mar \aủ\ out \ch\ chin \e\ bet \ē\ easy
\g\ go \i\ hit \ī\ ice \j\ job \ŋ\ sing \ō\ go
\ȯ\ law \ȯi\ boy \th\ thin \th\ the \ü\ loot \ủ\ foot
\y\ yet \zh\ vision *see also* Guide to Pronunciation

1 a : to produce thunder — usually used impersonally ⟨it *thundered*⟩ **b** : to give forth a sound that resembles thunder ⟨horses *thundered* down the road⟩
2 : ROAR, SHOUT
transitive verb
1 : to utter loudly : ROAR
2 : to strike with a sound likened to thunder
— **thun·der·er** \-dər-ər\ *noun*

thun·der·bird \'thən-dər-ˌbərd\ *noun* (1871)
: a bird that causes lightning and thunder in American Indian myth

thun·der·bolt \-ˌbōlt\ *noun* (15th century)
1 a : a single discharge of lightning with the accompanying thunder **b** : an imaginary elongated mass cast as a missile to earth in the lightning flash
2 a : a person or thing that resembles lightning in suddenness, effectiveness, or destructive power **b** : a vehement threat or censure

thun·der·clap \-ˌklap\ *noun* (14th century)
1 : a clap of thunder
2 : something sharp, loud, or sudden like a clap of thunder

thun·der·cloud \-ˌklau̇d\ *noun* (1697)
: a cloud charged with electricity and producing lightning and thunder

thunder egg *noun* (1941)
: chalcedony in rounded concretionary nodules

thun·der·head \-ˌhed\ *noun* (1853)
: a rounded mass of cumulus cloud often appearing before a thunderstorm

thun·der·ing *adjective* [*thundering*, present participle of ²*thunder*] (1543)
: awesomely great, intense, or unusual
— **thun·der·ing·ly** \-d(ə-)riṇ-lē\ *adverb*

thunder lizard *noun* [translation of New Latin *Brontosaurus*] (1960)
: BRONTOSAURUS

thun·der·ous \'thən-d(ə-)rəs\ *adjective* (1582)
1 a : producing thunder **b** : making or accompanied by a noise like thunder ⟨*thunderous* applause⟩
2 : THUNDERING
— **thun·der·ous·ly** *adverb*

thun·der·show·er \-ˌshau̇(-ə)r\ *noun* (1699)
: a shower accompanied by lightning and thunder

thun·der·stone \-ˌstōn\ *noun* (1598)
1 *archaic* : THUNDERBOLT 1b
2 : any of various stones (as a meteorite or an ancient artifact) that are the probable source of the imaginary thunderbolt

thun·der·storm \-ˌstȯrm\ *noun* (1652)
: a storm accompanied by lightning and thunder

thun·der·strike \-ˌstrīk\ *transitive verb* **-struck** \-ˌstrək\; **-struck** *also* **-strick·en** \-ˌstri-kən\; **-strik·ing** \-ˌstrī-kiṇ\ (circa 1586)
1 : to strike dumb : ASTONISH ⟨was *thunderstruck* at the news⟩
2 *archaic* : to strike by or as if by lightning

thun·der·stroke \-ˌstrōk\ *noun* (1587)
: a stroke of or as if of lightning with the attendant thunder

¹**thunk** \'thəṇk\ *dialect past and past participle of* THINK

²**thunk** *noun* [imitative] (1947)
: a flat hollow sound

thu·ri·ble \'thu̇r-ə-bəl, 'thyu̇r-, 'thər-\ *noun* [Middle English *turrible*, from Middle French *thurible*, from Latin *thuribulum*, from *thur-*, *thus* incense, from Greek *thyos* incense, sacrifice, from *thyein* to sacrifice — more at THYME] (15th century)
: CENSER

thu·ri·fer \-ə-fər\ *noun* [New Latin, from Latin *thurifer*, adjective, incense-bearing, from *thur-*, *thus* + *-ifer* -iferous] (1853)
: one who carries a censer in a liturgical service

Thu·rin·ger \'thu̇r-ən-jər, 'thyu̇r-\ *noun* [German *Thüringerwurst*, from *Thüringer* Thuringian + *Wurst* sausage] (circa 1923)
: a mildly seasoned fresh or smoked sausage

Thu·rin·gian \thu̇-'rin-j(ē-)ən, thyu̇r-\ *noun* (1618)
1 : a member of an ancient Germanic people whose kingdom was overthrown by the Franks in the 6th century
2 : a native or inhabitant of Thuringia
— **Thuringian** *adjective*

thurl \'thər(-ə)l\ *noun* [perhaps from English dialect, *gaunt*]
: the hip joint in cattle — see COW illustration

Thurs·day \'thərz-dē, -ˌdā\ *noun* [Middle English, from Old English *thursdæg*, from Old Norse *thōrsdagr*; akin to Old English *thunresdæg* Thursday, Old Norse *Thōrr* Thor, Old English *thunor* thunder — more at THUNDER] (before 12th century)
: the fifth day of the week
— **Thurs·days** \-dēz, -ˌdāz\ *adverb*

thus \'thəs\ *adverb* [Middle English, from Old English; akin to Old Saxon *thus* thus] (before 12th century)
1 : in this or that manner or way
2 : to this degree or extent : SO
3 : because of this or that : HENCE, CONSEQUENTLY
4 : as an example

thus·ly \-lē\ *adverb* (1865)
: in this manner : THUS □

¹**thwack** \'thwak\ *transitive verb* [imitative] (circa 1530)
: to strike with or as if with something flat or heavy : WHACK

²**thwack** *noun* (1587)
: a heavy blow : WHACK; *also* : the sound of or as if of such a blow

¹**thwart** \'thwȯrt\ *transitive verb* [Middle English *thwerten*, from *thwert*, adverb] (13th century)
1 a : to run counter to so as to effectively oppose or baffle : CONTRAVENE **b** : to oppose successfully : defeat the hopes or aspirations of
2 : to pass through or across
synonym see FRUSTRATE
— **thwart·er** *noun*

²**thwart** \'thwȯrt, nautical often 'thȯrt\ *adverb* [Middle English *thwert*, from Old Norse *thvert*, from neuter of *thverr* transverse, oblique; akin to Old High German *dwerah* transverse, oblique] (14th century)
: ATHWART

³**thwart** *adjective* (15th century)
: situated or placed across something else : TRANSVERSE
— **thwart·ly** *adverb*

⁴**thwart** *noun* [alteration of obsolete *thought*, *thoft*, from Middle English *thoft*, from Old English *thofte*; akin to Old High German *dofta* rower's seat] (circa 1736)
: a rower's seat extending athwart a boat

thwart·wise \-ˌwīz\ *adverb or adjective* (1589)
: CROSSWISE

thy \'thī\ *adjective* [Middle English *thin*, *thy*, from Old English *thīn*, genitive of *thū* thou — more at THOU] (12th century)
archaic : of or relating to thee or thyself especially as possessor or agent or as object of an action — used especially in ecclesiastical or literary language and sometimes by Friends especially among themselves

Thy·es·te·an \thī-'es-tē-ən\ *adjective* [*Thyestes*, brother of Atreus who unwittingly ate the flesh of his children] (1667)
: of or relating to the eating of human flesh : CANNIBAL

thy·la·cine \'thī-lə-ˌsīn\ *noun* [New Latin *Thylacinus*, genus of marsupials, from Greek *thylakos* sack, pouch] (1838)
: TASMANIAN WOLF

thy·la·koid \'thī-lə-ˌkȯid\ *noun* [International Scientific Vocabulary *thylak-* (from Greek *thylakos* sack) + *-oid*] (1966)
: any of the membranous disks of lamellae within plant chloroplasts that are composed of protein and lipid and are the sites of the photochemical reactions of photosynthesis

thym- *or* **thymo-** *combining form* [New Latin *thymus*]
: thymus ⟨*thymic*⟩ ⟨*thymocyte*⟩

thyme \'tīm *also* 'thīm\ *noun* [Middle English, from Middle French *thym*, from Latin *thymum*, from Greek *thymon*, probably from *thyein* to make a burnt offering, sacrifice; akin to Latin *fumus* smoke — more at FUME] (14th century)
1 : any of a genus (*Thymus*) of Eurasian mints with small pungent aromatic leaves; *especially* : a garden herb (*T. vulgaris*)
2 : thyme leaves used as a seasoning

thy·mec·to·my \thī-'mek-tə-mē\ *noun, plural* **-mies** (circa 1905)
: excision of the thymus
— **thy·mec·to·mize** \-ˌmīz\ *transitive verb*

-thymia *noun combining form* [New Latin, from Greek, from *thymos* mind]
: condition of mind and will ⟨cyclo*thymia*⟩

thy·mic \'thī-mik\ *adjective* (circa 1656)
: of or relating to the thymus

thy·mi·dine \'thī-mə-ˌdēn\ *noun* [*thymine* + *-idine*] (1912)
: a nucleoside $C_{10}H_{14}N_2O_5$ that is composed of thymine and deoxyribose and occurs as a structural part of DNA

thy·mine \'thī-ˌmēn\ *noun* [International Scientific Vocabulary, from New Latin *thymus*] (1894)
: a pyrimidine base $C_5H_6N_2O_2$ that is one of the four bases coding genetic information in the polynucleotide chain of DNA — compare ADENINE, CYTOSINE, GUANINE, URACIL

thy·mo·cyte \'thī-mə-ˌsīt\ *noun* [International Scientific Vocabulary] (circa 1923)
: a cell of the thymus; *especially* : a thymic lymphocyte

thy·mol \'thī-ˌmȯl, -ˌmōl\ *noun* [International Scientific Vocabulary, from Latin *thymum* thyme] (1857)
: a crystalline phenol $C_{10}H_{14}O$ of aromatic odor and antiseptic properties found especially in thyme oil or made synthetically and used chiefly as a fungicide and preservative

thy·mo·sin \'thī-mə-sən\ *noun* [Greek *thymos* thymus + English ¹*-in*] (1966)
: a mixture of polypeptides isolated from the thymus; *also* : any of these

thy·mus \'thī-məs\ *noun* [New Latin, from Greek *thymos* warty excrescence, thymus] (circa 1693)

: a glandular structure of largely lymphoid tissue that functions especially in the development of the body's immune system, is present in the young of most vertebrates typically in the upper anterior chest or at the base of the neck, and tends to atrophy in the adult

thy·my or **thym·ey** \'tī-mē also 'thī-\ adjective (1727)
: abounding in or fragrant with thyme

thyr- or **thyro-** combining form [thyroid]
: thyroid ⟨thyrotoxicosis⟩ ⟨thyroxine⟩

thy·ra·tron \'thī-rə-ˌträn\ noun [from Thyratron, a trademark] (1929)
: a gas-filled hot-cathode electron tube in which the grid controls only the start of a continuous current thus giving the tube a trigger effect

thy·ris·tor \thī-'ris-tər\ noun [thyratron + transistor] (1958)
: any of several semiconductor devices that act as switches, rectifiers, or voltage regulators

thy·ro·cal·ci·to·nin \ˌthī-rō-ˌkal-sə-'tō-nən\ noun (1963)
: CALCITONIN

thy·ro·glob·u·lin \-'glä-byə-lən\ noun [International Scientific Vocabulary] (circa 1905)
: an iodine-containing protein of the thyroid gland that is the precursor of thyroxine and triiodothyronine

¹thy·roid \'thī-ˌröid\ also **thy·roi·dal** \thī-'röi-dᵊl\ adjective [New Latin thyroides, from Greek thyreoeidēs shield-shaped, thyroid, from thyreos shield shaped like a door, from thyra door — more at DOOR] (circa 1741)
1 a : of, relating to, or being a large bilobed endocrine gland of craniate vertebrates lying at the base of the neck and producing especially the hormones thyroxine and triiodothyronine **b :** suggestive of a disordered thyroid ⟨a thyroid personality⟩
2 : of, relating to, or being the chief cartilage of the larynx

²thyroid noun (1840)
1 : a thyroid gland or cartilage; also : a part (as an artery or nerve) associated with either of these
2 : a preparation of mammalian thyroid gland used in treating thyroid disorders

thy·roid·ec·to·my \ˌthī-ˌröi-'dek-tə-mē, ˌthī-rə-\ noun, plural **-mies** (1889)
: surgical removal of thyroid gland tissue
— **thy·roid·ec·to·mized** \-ˌmīzd\ adjective

thy·roid·itis \ˌthī-ˌröi-'dī-təs, ˌthī-rə-\ noun [New Latin] (circa 1885)
: inflammation of the thyroid gland

thyroid–stimulating hormone noun (1941)
: THYROTROPIN

thy·ro·tox·i·co·sis \ˌthī-rō-ˌtäk-sə-'kō-səs\ noun [New Latin] (circa 1911)
: HYPERTHYROIDISM

thy·ro·tro·pic \ˌthī-rə-'trō-pik, -'trä-\ also **thy·ro·tro·phic** \-'trō-fik\ adjective (circa 1923)
: exerting or characterized by a direct influence on the secretory activity of the thyroid gland ⟨thyrotropic functions⟩

thy·ro·tro·pin \ˌthī-rə-'trō-pən\ also **thy·ro·tro·phin** \-fən\ noun [thyrotropic, thyrotrophic] (1939)
: a hormone secreted by the anterior pituitary that stimulates the thyroid gland — called also thyroid-stimulating hormone, thyrotropic hormone

thyrotropin–releasing hormone noun (1968)
: a tripeptide hormone synthesized in the hypothalamus that stimulates secretion of thyrotropin by the anterior lobe of the pituitary gland — called also thyrotropin-releasing factor

thy·rox·ine or **thy·rox·in** \thī-'räk-ˌsēn, -sən\ noun [International Scientific Vocabulary] (1918)

: an iodine-containing hormone $C_{15}H_{11}I_4NO_4$ that is an amino acid produced by the thyroid gland as a product of the cleavage of thyroglobulin, increases metabolic rate, and is used to treat thyroid disorders

thyrse \'thərs\ noun [New Latin thyrsus, from Latin, thyrsus] (1744)
: an inflorescence (as in the lilac and horse chestnut) in which the main axis is racemose and the secondary and later axes are cymose

thyr·sus \'thər-səs\ noun, plural **thyr·si** \-ˌsī, -ˌsē\ [Latin, from Greek thyrsos] (1591)
: a staff surmounted by a pinecone or by a bunch of vine or ivy leaves with grapes or berries that is carried by Bacchus and by satyrs and others engaging in bacchic rites

thy·sa·nu·ran \ˌthī-sə-'nür-ən, -'nyür-\ noun [ultimately from Greek thysanos tassel + oura tail — more at ASS] (1835)
: BRISTLETAIL
— **thysanuran** adjective

thy·self \thī-'self\ pronoun (before 12th century)
archaic : YOURSELF — used especially in ecclesiastical or literary language and sometimes by Friends especially among themselves

¹ti \'tē\ noun [Tahitian, Marquesan, Samoan, & Maori] (1832)
: any of several Asian and Pacific trees or shrubs (genus Cordyline) of the agave family with leaves in terminal tufts

²ti noun [alteration of si] (1839)
: the seventh tone of the diatonic scale in solmization

ti·ara \tē-'ar-ə, -'er-, -'är-\ noun [Latin, royal Persian headdress, from Greek] (1616)
1 : a 3-tiered crown worn by the pope
2 : a decorative jeweled or flowered headband or semicircle for formal wear by women

tiara 2

Ti·bet·an \tə-'be-tᵊn\ noun (1747)
1 a : a member of the predominant people of Tibet and adjacent areas of Asia **b :** a native or inhabitant of Tibet
2 : the Tibeto-Burman language of the Tibetan people
— **Tibetan** adjective

Tibetan terrier noun (1905)
: any of a breed of terriers resembling Old English sheepdogs but having a curled well-feathered tail

Ti·beto–Bur·man \tə-ˌbe-tō-'bər-mən\ noun (1901)
1 : a language family that includes Tibetan, Burmese, and related languages of southern and eastern Asia
2 : a member of a people speaking a Tibeto-Burman language

Tibetan terrier

tib·ia \'ti-bē-ə\ noun, plural **-i·ae** \-bē-ˌē, -bē-ˌī\ also **-i·as** [Latin] (circa 1706)
1 : the inner and usually larger of the two bones of the vertebrate hind limb between the knee and ankle
2 : the fourth joint of the leg of an insect between the femur and tarsus
— **tib·i·al** \-bē-əl\ adjective

tib·io·fib·u·la \ˌti-bē-ō-'fi-byə-lə\ noun [New Latin] (circa 1909)
: a bone especially in frogs and toads that is formed by fusion of the tibia and fibula

tic \'tik\ noun [French] (circa 1834)
1 : local and habitual spasmodic motion of particular muscles especially of the face
: TWITCHING

2 : a frequent usually unconscious quirk of behavior or speech ⟨"you know" is a verbal tic⟩

ti·cal \ti-'käl, 'ti-kəl\ noun, plural **ticals** or **ti·cal** [Thai, from Portuguese, from Malay tikal, a monetary unit] (1662)
: BAHT

tic dou·lou·reux \ˌtik-ˌdü-lə-'rü, -'rə(r)\ noun [French, painful twitch] (1800)
: TRIGEMINAL NEURALGIA

¹tick \'tik\ noun [Middle English tyke, teke; akin to Middle High German zeche tick, Armenian tiz] (14th century)
1 : any of a superfamily (Ixodoidea of the order Acarina) of bloodsucking arachnids that are larger than the related mites, attach themselves to warm-blooded vertebrates to feed, and include important vectors of infectious diseases
2 : any of various usually wingless parasitic dipteran flies — compare SHEEP KED

¹tick 1

²tick noun [Middle English tike, probably from Middle Dutch (akin to Old High German ziahha tick), from Latin theca cover, from Greek thēkē case; akin to Greek tithenai to place — more at DO] (15th century)
1 : the fabric case of a mattress, pillow, or bolster; also : a mattress consisting of a tick and its filling
2 : TICKING

³tick noun [Middle English tek pat, light stroke; akin to Middle High German zic light push] (1680)
1 a : a light rhythmic audible tap or beat; also : a series of such ticks **b** chiefly British : the time taken by the tick of a clock : MOMENT
2 : a small spot or mark; especially : one used to direct attention to something, to check an item on a list, or to represent a point on a scale

⁴tick (1721)
intransitive verb
1 : to make the sound of a tick or a series of ticks
2 : to operate as a functioning mechanism : RUN ⟨tried to understand what made him tick⟩ ⟨the motor was ticking over quietly⟩
transitive verb
1 : to mark with a written tick : CHECK — usually used with off ⟨ticked off each item in the list⟩
2 : to mark, count, or announce by or as if by ticking beats ⟨a meter ticking off the cab fare⟩
3 : to touch with a momentary glancing blow ⟨ticked the ball⟩

⁵tick noun [short for ¹ticket] (1642)
chiefly British : CREDIT, TRUST; also : a credit account

tick–borne \'tik-ˌbörn, -ˌbȯrn\ adjective (1921)
: capable of being transmitted by the bites of ticks ⟨tick-borne encephalitis⟩

¹ticked \'tikt\ adjective (circa 1688)
1 : marked with ticks : FLECKED
2 : having or made of hair banded with two or more colors ⟨a ticked cat⟩ ⟨a ticked coat⟩

²ticked adjective [tick off] (circa 1959)
: ANGRY, UPSET

tick·er \'ti-kər\ noun (1828)
: something that ticks or produces a ticking sound: as **a :** WATCH **b :** a telegraphic receiving instrument that automatically prints off information (as stock quotations or news) on a paper ribbon **c** slang : HEART

ticker tape noun (1902)
: the paper ribbon on which a telegraphic ticker prints off its information

¹**tick·et** \'ti-kət\ *noun* [Middle French *etiquet,* *estiquette* notice attached to something, from *estiquier* to attach, from Middle Dutch *steken* to stick; akin to Old High German *sticken* to prick — more at STICK] (1529)
1 a : a document that serves as a certificate, license, or permit; *especially* **:** a mariner's or airman's certificate **b :** TAG, LABEL
2 a : a certificate or token showing that a fare or admission fee has been paid **b :** a means of access or passage ⟨education is the *ticket* to a good job⟩
3 : a list of candidates for nomination or election **:** SLATE
4 : the correct or desirable thing ⟨cooperation, that's the *ticket* —K. E. Trombley⟩
5 : a slip or card recording a transaction or undertaking or giving instructions ⟨a savings deposit *ticket*⟩
6 : a summons or warning issued to a traffic-law violator
— **tick·et·less** \-ləs\ *adjective*

²**ticket** *transitive verb* (1611)
1 : to attach a ticket to **:** LABEL; *also* **:** DESIGNATE
2 : to furnish or serve with a ticket ⟨*ticketed* for illegal parking⟩

ticket agency *noun* (1923)
: an agency selling transportation or theater and entertainment tickets

ticket agent *noun* (1861)
: one who sells transportation or theater and entertainment tickets

ticket office *noun* (circa 1667)
: an office of a transportation company, theatrical or entertainment enterprise, or ticket agency where tickets are sold and reservations made

tick·et-of-leave \,ti-kət-ə(v)-'lēv\ *noun, plural* **tickets-of-leave** (1732)
: a license or permit formerly given in the United Kingdom and the Commonwealth to a convict under imprisonment to go at large and to get work subject to certain specific conditions

tick fever *noun* (circa 1897)
1 : TEXAS FEVER
2 : a febrile disease (as Rocky Mountain spotted fever) transmitted by the bites of ticks

¹**tick·ing** \'ti-kiŋ\ *noun* [²*tick*] (1649)
: a strong linen or cotton fabric used in upholstering and as a covering for a mattress or pillow

²**ticking** *noun* [³*tick*] (1885)
: ticked marking on a bird or mammal or on individual hairs

¹**tick·le** \'ti-kəl\ *verb* **tick·led; tick·ling** \-k(ə-)liŋ\ [Middle English *tikelen;* akin to Old English *tinclian* to tickle] (14th century)
transitive verb
1 a : to excite or stir up agreeably **:** PLEASE ⟨music . . . does more than *tickle* our sense of rhythm —Edward Sapir⟩ **b :** to provoke to laughter or merriment **:** AMUSE ⟨were *tickled* by the clown's antics⟩
2 : to touch (as a body part) lightly so as to excite the surface nerves and cause uneasiness, laughter, or spasmodic movements
intransitive verb
1 : to have a tingling or prickling sensation ⟨my back *tickles*⟩
2 : to excite the surface nerves to prickle

²**tickle** *noun* (1801)
1 : the act of tickling
2 : a tickling sensation
3 : something that tickles

tick·ler \'ti-k(ə-)lər\ *noun* (1680)
1 : a person or device that tickles
2 : a device for jogging the memory; *specifically* **:** a file that serves as a reminder and is arranged to bring matters to timely attention

tick·lish \'ti-k(ə-)lish\ *adjective* (1581)
1 a : TOUCHY, OVERSENSITIVE ⟨*ticklish* about his baldness⟩ **b :** easily overturned ⟨a canoe is a *ticklish* craft⟩

2 : requiring delicate handling ⟨a *ticklish* subject⟩
3 : sensitive to tickling
— **tick·lish·ly** *adverb*
— **tick·lish·ness** *noun*

tick off *transitive verb* [⁴*tick*] (circa 1919)
1 : REPRIMAND, REBUKE ⟨his father *ticked* him *off* for his impudence⟩
2 : to make angry or indignant ⟨the cancellation really *ticked* me *off*⟩

tick·seed \'tik-,sēd\ *noun* [¹*tick*] (circa 1562) **:** COREOPSIS

tick·tack *or* **tic·tac** \'tik-,tak\ *noun* [reduplication of *tick*] (1549)
1 : a ticking or tapping beat like that of a clock or watch
2 : a contrivance used by children to tap on a window from a distance

tick·tack·toe *also* **tic-tac-toe** \,tik-,tak-'tō\ *noun* [*tic-tac-toe,* former game in which players with eyes shut brought a pencil down on a slate marked with numbers and scored the number hit] (circa 1866)
: a game in which two players alternately put Xs and Os in compartments of a figure formed by two vertical lines crossing two horizontal lines and each tries to get a row of three Xs or three Os before the opponent does

tick·tock \'tik-,täk, -,täk\ *noun* [imitative] (1848)
: the ticking sound of a clock

tick trefoil *noun* [¹*tick*] (1857)
: any of various leguminous plants (genus *Desmodium*) with trifoliolate leaves and rough sticky loments

¹**ticky-tacky** \,ti-kē-'ta-kē\ *also* **ticky-tack** \-'tak\ *noun, plural* **ticky-tackies** *also* **ticky-tacks** [reduplication of *tacky*] (1962)
: sleazy or shoddy material used especially in the construction of look-alike tract houses; *also* **:** something built of ticky-tacky

²**ticky-tacky** *also* **ticky-tack** *adjective* (1964)
1 : of an uninspired or monotonous sameness
2 : TACKY
3 : built of ticky-tacky

tid·al \'tī-d²l\ *adjective* (1807)
1 a : of, relating to, caused by, or having tides ⟨*tidal* cycles⟩ ⟨*tidal* erosion⟩ **b :** periodically rising and falling or flowing and ebbing ⟨*tidal* waters⟩
2 : dependent (as to the time of arrival or departure) upon the state of the tide ⟨a *tidal* steamer⟩
— **tid·al·ly** \-d²l-ē\ *adverb*

tidal wave *noun* (1830)
1 a : an unusually high sea wave that sometimes follows an earthquake **b :** an unusual rise of water alongshore due to strong winds
2 : something overwhelming especially in quantity or volume ⟨a *tidal wave* of tourists⟩

tid·bit \'tid-,bit\ *noun* [perhaps from *tit-* (as in *titmouse*) + *bit*] (circa 1640)
1 : a choice morsel of food
2 : a choice or pleasing bit (as of information)

tid·dle·dy-winks \'ti-d²l-dē-,wiŋ(k)s\ *or* **tid·dly-winks** \'ti-d²l-ē-, 'tid-lē-\ *noun plural but singular in construction* [probably from English dialect *tiddly* little, alteration of *little*] (1898)
: a game whose object is to snap small disks from a flat surface into a small container

tid·dler \'ti-d²l-ər, 'tid-lər\ *noun* [probably from English dialect *tiddly* little] (1885)
British **:** a small fish (as a stickleback or minnow)

tid·dly \'ti-d²l-ē, 'tid-lē\ *adjective* [*tiddly* an alcoholic drink, probably from English dialect *tiddly*] (1905)
chiefly British **:** slightly drunk

¹**tide** \'tīd\ *noun* [Middle English, time, from Old English *tīd;* akin to Old High German *zīt* time and perhaps to Greek *daiesthai* to divide] (before 12th century)

1 a *obsolete* **:** a space of time **:** PERIOD **b :** a fit or opportune time **:** OPPORTUNITY **c :** an ecclesiastical anniversary or festival; *also* **:** its season — usually used in combination ⟨Eastertide⟩
2 a (1) **:** the alternate rising and falling of the surface of the ocean and of water bodies (as gulfs and bays) connected with the ocean that occurs usually twice a day and is caused by the gravitational attraction of the sun and moon occurring unequally on different parts of the earth (2) **:** a less marked rising and falling of an inland body of water (3) **:** a periodic movement in the earth's crust caused by the same forces that produce ocean tides (4) **:** a tidal distortion on one celestial body caused by the gravitational attraction of another (5) **:** one of the tidal movements of the atmosphere resembling those of the ocean and produced by gravitation or diurnal temperature changes **b :** FLOOD TIDE 1
3 a : something that fluctuates like the tides of the sea ⟨the *tide* of public opinion⟩ **b :** a surging movement of a group ⟨a *tide* of opportunists⟩
4 a : a flowing stream **:** CURRENT **b :** the waters of the ocean **c :** the overflow of a flooding stream
— **tide·less** \-ləs\ *adjective*

²**tide** *verb* **tid·ed; tid·ing** (1593)
intransitive verb
: to flow as or in a tide **:** SURGE
transitive verb
: to cause to float with or as if with the tide

³**tide** *intransitive verb* **tid·ed; tid·ing** [Middle English, from Old English *tīdan;* akin to Middle Dutch *tiden* to go, come, Old English *tīd* time] (before 12th century)
archaic **:** BETIDE, BEFALL

tide·land \'tīd-,land, -lənd\ *noun* (1802)
1 : land overflowed during flood tide
2 : land underlying the ocean and lying beyond the low-water limit of the tide but being within the territorial waters of a nation — often used in plural

tide·mark \-,märk\ *noun* (1799)
1 a : a high-water or sometimes low-water mark left by tidal water or a flood **b :** a mark placed to indicate this point
2 : the point to which something has attained or below which it has receded ⟨the *tidemark* of tolerance has risen —*New Republic*⟩

tide over *transitive verb* [²*tide*] (1821)
: to enable to surmount or endure a difficulty ⟨money to *tide* us *over* the emergency⟩

tide table *noun* (1594)
: a table that indicates the height of the tide at one place at different times of day throughout one year

tide·wa·ter \-,wȯ-tər, -,wä-\ *noun* (1772)
1 : water overflowing land at flood tide; *also* **:** water affected by the ebb and flow of the tide
2 : low-lying coastal land

tide·way \-,wā\ *noun* (1798)
: a channel in which the tide runs

tid·ing \'tī-diŋ\ *noun* [Middle English, from Old English *tīdung,* from *tīdan* to betide] (12th century)
: a piece of news — usually used in plural ⟨good *tidings*⟩

¹**ti·dy** \'tī-dē\ *adjective* **ti·di·er; -est** [Middle English, timely, in good condition, from *tide* time] (13th century)
1 : properly filled out **:** PLUMP
2 : adequately satisfactory **:** ACCEPTABLE, FAIR ⟨a *tidy* solution to their problem⟩
3 a : neat and orderly in appearance or habits **:** well ordered and cared for **b :** METHODICAL, PRECISE ⟨a *tidy* mind⟩
4 : LARGE, SUBSTANTIAL ⟨a *tidy* profit⟩
— **ti·di·ly** \'tī-d²l-ē\ *adverb*
— **ti·di·ness** \'tī-dē-nəs\ *noun*

²**tidy** *verb* **ti·died; ti·dy·ing** (1821)
transitive verb
: to put in order ⟨*tidy* up a room⟩

intransitive verb
: to make things tidy ⟨*tidying* up after supper⟩
— **ti·di·er** *noun*
³tidy *noun, plural* **tidies** (circa 1828)
1 : a usually compartmentalized receptacle for various small objects
2 : a piece of fancywork used to protect the back, arms, or headrest of a chair or sofa from wear or soil
ti·dy·tips \'tī-dē-ˌtips\ *noun plural but singular or plural in construction* (1888)
: an annual California composite herb (*Layia platyglossa*) having yellow-rayed flower heads often tipped with white
¹tie \'tī\ *noun* [Middle English *teg, tye,* from Old English *tēag;* akin to Old Norse *taug* rope, Old English *tēon* to pull — more at TOW] (before 12th century)
1 a : a line, ribbon, or cord used for fastening, uniting, or drawing something closed; *especially* **:** SHOELACE **b** (1) **:** a structural element (as a rod or angle iron) holding two pieces together **:** a tension member in a construction (2) **:** any of the transverse supports to which railroad rails are fastened to keep them in line
2 : something that serves as a connecting link: as **a :** a moral or legal obligation to someone or something typically constituting a restraining power, influence, or duty **b :** a bond of kinship or affection
3 : a curved line that joins two musical notes of the same pitch to denote a single tone sustained through the time value of the two
4 a : an equality in number (as of votes or scores) **b :** equality in a contest; *also* **:** a contest that ends in a draw
5 : a method or style of tying or knotting
6 : something that is knotted or is to be knotted when worn: as **a :** NECKTIE **b :** a low laced shoe **:** OXFORD
— **tie·less** \-ləs\ *adjective*
²tie *verb* **tied; ty·ing** \'tī-iŋ\ *or* **tie·ing** (before 12th century)
transitive verb
1 a : to fasten, attach, or close by means of a tie **b :** to form a knot or bow in ⟨*tie* your scarf⟩ **c :** to make by tying constituent elements ⟨*tied* a wreath⟩ ⟨*tie* a fishing fly⟩
2 a : to place or establish in relationship **:** CONNECT **b :** to unite in marriage **c :** to unite (musical notes) by a tie **d :** to join (power systems) electrically
3 : to restrain from independence or freedom of action or choice **:** constrain by or as if by authority, influence, agreement, or obligation
4 a (1) **:** to make or have an equal score with in a contest (2) **:** to equalize (the score) in a game or contest (3) **:** to equalize the score of (a game) **b :** to provide or offer something equal to **:** EQUAL
intransitive verb
: to make a tie: as **a :** to make a bond or connection **b :** to make an equal score **c :** to become attached **d :** to close by means of a tie
— **tie into :** to attack with vigor
— **tie one on** *slang* **:** to get drunk
— **tie the knot :** to perform a marriage ceremony; *also* **:** to get married
tie–and–dye \'tī-ən-ˌdī\ *noun* (1928)
: TIE-DYEING
tie·back \'tī-ˌbak\ *noun* (1926)
1 : a decorative strip or device of cloth, cord, or metal for draping a curtain to the side of a window
2 : a curtain with a tieback — usually used in plural
tie·break·er \'tī-ˌbrā-kər\ *noun* (circa 1932)
: a contest used to select a winner from among contestants with tied scores at the end of a previous contest
tied cottage *noun* (1899)
British **:** a cottage or house owned by an employer (as a farmer) and reserved for occupancy by an employee
tie–down \-ˌdaún\ *noun* (circa 1942)

: a fitting or a system of lines and fittings used to secure something (as an aircraft or cargo)
tie–dye \'tī-ˌdī\ *noun* (circa 1939)
1 : TIE-DYEING
2 : a tie-dyed garment or fabric
tie–dyed *adjective* (1904)
: having patterns produced by tie-dyeing ⟨*tie-dyed* shirts⟩
tie–dye·ing *noun* (1904)
: a hand method of producing patterns in textiles by tying portions of the fabric or yarn so that they will not absorb the dye
tie–in \'tī-ˌin\ *noun* (1925)
1 : something that ties in, relates, or connects especially in a promotional campaign
2 : a book that inspired or was inspired by a motion picture or television program
tie in (1793)
transitive verb
: to bring into connection with something relevant: as **a :** to make the final connection of ⟨*tied in* the new branch pipeline⟩ **b :** to coordinate in such a manner as to produce balance and unity ⟨the illustrations were *tied in* with the text⟩ **c :** to use as a tie-in especially in advertising
intransitive verb
: to become tied in
tie–line \'tī-ˌlīn\ *noun* (1923)
: a telephone line that directly connects two or more private branch exchanges
tie·mann·ite \'tē-mə-ˌnīt\ *noun* [German *Tiemannit,* from W. *Tiemann* (died 1899) German scientist] (1868)
: a mineral that consists of mercuric selenide and occurs in dark gray or nearly black masses of metallic luster
tie·pin \'tī-ˌpin\ *noun* (1780)
: an ornamental straight pin that has usually a sheath for the point and is used to hold the ends of a necktie in place
¹tier \'tir\ *noun* [Middle French *tire* rank, from Old French — more at ATTIRE] (1569)
1 a : a row, rank, or layer of articles; *especially* **:** one of two or more rows, levels, or ranks arranged one above another **b :** a group of political or geographical divisions that form a row across the map ⟨the southern *tier* of states⟩
2 : CLASS, CATEGORY
²tier (circa 1889)
transitive verb
: to place or arrange in tiers
intransitive verb
: to rise in tiers
³ti·er \'tī(-ə)r\ *noun* (1633)
: one that ties
¹tierce \'tirs\ *variant of* TERCE
²tierce *noun* [Middle English *terce, tierce,* from Middle French, from feminine of *terz,* adjective, third, from Latin *tertius* — more at THIRD] (15th century)
1 *obsolete* **:** THIRD 2
2 : a sequence of three playing cards of the same suit
tier·cel \'tir-səl\ *noun* [Middle English *tercel,* from Middle French, from (assumed) Vulgar Latin *tertiolus,* from diminutive of Latin *tertius* third] (14th century)
: a male hawk
tiered \'tird\ *adjective* (1807)
: having or arranged in tiers, rows, or layers — often used in combination ⟨triple-*tiered*⟩
tie–rod \'tī-ˌräd\ *noun* (1839)
: a rod (as of steel) used as a connecting member or brace
tie silk *noun* (circa 1915)
: a silk fabric of firm resilient pliable texture used for neckties and for blouses and accessories
tie tack *or* **tie tac** \-ˌtak\ *noun* (1954)
: an ornamental pin with a receiving button or clasp that is used to attach the two parts of a necktie together or to attach a necktie to a shirt
tie–up \'tī-ˌəp\ *noun* (1851)

1 a : a cow stable; *also* **:** a space for a single cow in a stable **b :** a mooring place for a boat
2 : a slowdown or stoppage of traffic, business, or operation (as by a mechanical breakdown)
3 : CONNECTION, ASSOCIATION ⟨helpful financial *tie-ups*⟩
tie up (1530)
transitive verb
1 : to attach, fasten, or bind securely; *also* **:** to wrap up and fasten
2 a : to connect closely **:** JOIN ⟨*tie up* the loose ends⟩ **b :** to cause to be linked so as to depend on or relate to something
3 a : to place or invest in such a manner as to make unavailable for other purposes ⟨their money was *tied up* in stocks⟩ **b :** to restrain from normal movement, operation, or progress ⟨traffic was *tied up* for miles⟩
4 a : to keep busy ⟨was *tied up* in conference all day⟩ **b :** to preempt the use of ⟨*tied up* the phone for an hour⟩
intransitive verb
1 : DOCK ⟨the ferry *ties up* at the south slip⟩
2 : to assume a definite relationship ⟨this *ties up* with what I told you before⟩
¹tiff \'tif\ *intransitive verb* [origin unknown] (1700)
: to have a petty quarrel
²tiff *noun* (1754)
: a petty quarrel
tif·fa·ny \'ti-fə-nē\ *noun, plural* **-nies** [perhaps from obsolete French *tiphanie* Epiphany, from Late Latin *theophania,* from Late Greek, ultimately from Greek *theos* god + *phainein* to show] (1601)
1 : a sheer silk gauze formerly used for clothing and trimmings
2 : a plain-woven open-mesh cotton fabric (as cheesecloth)
Tif·fa·ny \'ti-fə-nē\ *adjective* (1936)
: being glass or an article of glass made by or in the manner of Louis C. Tiffany; *especially* **:** made of pieces of stained glass ⟨a *Tiffany*-style lamp⟩ ⟨a *Tiffany* window⟩
tif·fin \'ti-fən\ *noun* [probably alteration of *tiffing,* gerund of obsolete English *tiff* to eat between meals] (1800)
chiefly British **:** a light midday meal **:** LUNCHEON
ti·ger \'tī-gər\ *noun, plural* **tigers** [Middle English *tigre,* from Old English *tiger* & Old French *tigre,* both from Latin *tigris,* from Greek, probably of Iranian origin; akin to Avestan *tighra-* pointed; akin to Greek *stizein* to tattoo — more at STICK] (before 12th century)
1 *plural also* **ti·ger a :** a large Asian carnivorous mammal (*Panthera tigris*) of the cat family having a usually tawny coat transversely striped with black **b**

tiger 1a

: any of several large wildcats (as the jaguar or cougar) **c :** a domestic cat with striped pattern **d** *Australian* **:** TASMANIAN WOLF
2 a : a fierce, daring, or aggressive person or quality ⟨aroused the *tiger* in him⟩ ⟨a *tiger* for work⟩ **b :** one (as a situation) that is formidable or impossible to control ⟨how the *tiger* of inflation can be tamed —J. A. Davenport⟩ — often used in the phrases *ride a tiger* and *have a tiger by the tail*
3 *British* **:** a groom in livery
— **ti·ger·ish** \-g(ə-)rish\ *adjective*
— **ti·ger·ish·ly** *adverb*

— **ti·ger·ish·ness** *noun*
— **ti·ger·like** \-gər-ˌlīk\ *adjective*
tiger beetle *noun* (1826)
: any of numerous active carnivorous beetles (family Cicindelidae) having larvae that tunnel in the soil
tiger cat *noun* (1699)
1 : any of various wildcats (as the serval, ocelot, or margay) of moderate size and variegated coloration
2 : a striped or sometimes blotched tabby cat
ti·ger·eye \'tī-gər-ˌī\ *or* **ti·ger's–eye** \-gərz-\ *noun* (circa 1891)
: a usually yellowish to grayish brown chatoyant stone that is much used for ornament and is a silicified crocidolite
tiger lily *noun* (1824)
: a common Asian garden lily (*Lilium lancifolium* synonym *L. tigrinum*) having nodding orange-colored flowers densely spotted with black; *also* : any of various lilies with similar flowers

tiger lily

tiger maple *noun* (1952)
: maple lumber having a distinct irregularly striped pattern and much used for furniture
tiger moth *noun* (1816)
: any of a family (Arctiidae) of stout-bodied moths usually with broad striped or spotted wings
tiger salamander *noun* (circa 1909)
: a large widely distributed North American salamander (*Ambystoma tigrinum*) that is variably colored with contrasting blotches, spots, or bars
tiger shark *noun* (circa 1785)
: a large gray or brown stocky-bodied requiem shark (*Galeocerdo cuvieri*) that is nearly cosmopolitan especially in warm seas and can be dangerous to humans — see SHARK illustration
tiger shrimp *noun* (1979)
: a large shrimp (*Penaeus monodon*) of the Indian and Pacific oceans that is often farmed and widely sold as food
tiger swallowtail *noun* (circa 1890)
: a large widely distributed swallowtail (*Papilio glaucus*) of eastern North America that in the male is largely yellow with black margins and black stripes on the wings and in the female is usually similarly marked in the north but is very often all or mostly black in the south; *also* : any of several closely related black and yellow swallowtails (as *P. rutulus* of western North America)
¹**tight** \'tīt\ *adjective* [alteration of earlier *thight* close set, dense, of Scandinavian origin; akin to Old Norse *thēttr* tight; akin to Middle High German *dīhte* thick, Sanskrit *tanakti* it causes to coagulate] (1507)
1 a : so close in structure as to prevent passage or escape (as of liquid, gas, or light) ⟨a *tight* ship⟩ ⟨a *tight* seal⟩ — compare LIGHTPROOF, WATERTIGHT **b** : fitting very close to the body ⟨*tight* jeans⟩; *also* : too snug ⟨*tight* shoes⟩ **c** (1) : closely packed : very full ⟨a *tight* bale of hay⟩ (2) : barely allowing time for completion ⟨a *tight* schedule⟩ ⟨*tight* deadlines⟩ **d** : having elements close together ⟨a *tight* formation⟩ ⟨*tight* line of type⟩ **e** : allowing little or no room for free motion or movement ⟨a *tight* connection⟩ ⟨a *tight* crawl space⟩; *also* : having a small radius ⟨a *tight* turn⟩
2 a : strongly fixed or held : SECURE ⟨a *tight* jar lid⟩ ⟨a *tight* grip on the ladder⟩ **b** (1) : not slack or loose : TAUT ⟨kept the reins *tight*⟩ ⟨a *tight* knot⟩ ⟨a *tight* drumhead⟩; *also* : marked by firmness and muscle tone ⟨a *tight* stomach⟩

(2) : marked by unusual tension (as in the face or body) ⟨lips *tight* with anger⟩ ⟨a family *tight* with fear⟩
3 *chiefly dialect* **a** : CAPABLE, COMPETENT **b** : having a graceful or shapely form : COMELY
4 a : difficult to cope with ⟨in a *tight* spot financially⟩ **b** : relatively difficult to obtain ⟨money is *tight* just now⟩; *also* : characterized by such difficulty ⟨a *tight* job market⟩ **c** : not liberal in giving : STINGY ⟨*tight* with a penny⟩
5 : characterized by little difference in the relative positions of contestants with respect to final outcome : CLOSE ⟨a *tight* race for mayor⟩
6 : somewhat drunk
7 a : characterized by firmness or strictness in control or application or in attention to details ⟨*tight* zoning codes⟩ ⟨*tight* security⟩ ⟨ran a *tight* newsroom⟩ ⟨keeps a *tight* hand on her investments⟩ **b** : marked by control or discipline in expression or style : having little or no extraneous matter ⟨*tight* writing⟩ **c** : characterized by a polished style and precise arrangements in music performance
8 : having a close personal or working relationship : INTIMATE ⟨in *tight* with the boss⟩
9 : being such that the subject fills the frame ⟨filming a *tight* close-up⟩
— **tight·ly** *adverb*
— **tight·ness** *noun*
²**tight** *adverb* (1680)
1 : FAST, TIGHTLY, FIRMLY ⟨the door was shut *tight*⟩
2 : in a sound manner : SOUNDLY ⟨sleep *tight*⟩
tight·en \'tī-tᵊn\ *verb* **tight·ened; tight·en·ing** \'tīt-niŋ, 'tī-tᵊn-iŋ\ (circa 1727)
transitive verb
: to make tight or tighter
intransitive verb
: to become tight or tighter
— **tight·en·er** \'tīt-nər, 'tī-tᵊn-ər\ *noun*
— **tighten one's belt** : to practice strict economy
tight end *noun* (1962)
: an offensive football end who lines up within two yards of the tackle
tight·fist·ed \'tīt-'fis-təd\ *adjective* (1844)
: reluctant to part with money
— **tight·fist·ed·ness** \-nəs\ *noun*
tight–knit \-'nit\ *adjective* (1946)
: closely integrated and bound in love or friendship ⟨a *tight-knit* family⟩
tight–lipped \-'lipt\ *adjective* (1876)
1 : having the lips closed tight (as in determination)
2 : reluctant to speak : TACITURN
tight–mouthed \-'mauthd, -'mautht\ *adjective* (1926)
: CLOSEMOUTHED
tight·rope \'tīt-ˌrōp\ *noun* (1801)
1 : a rope or wire stretched taut for acrobats to perform on
2 : a dangerously precarious situation — usually used in the phrase *walk a tightrope*
tights \'tīts\ *noun plural* (circa 1837)
: a skintight garment covering the body from the neck down or from the waist down; *also, British* : PANTY HOSE
tight·wad \'tīt-ˌwäd\ *noun* (1906)
: a close or miserly person
tight–wire \-ˌwīr\ *noun* (1928)
: a tightrope made of wire
ti·glon \'tī-glən\ *noun* [*tiger* + *lion*] (1942)
: a hybrid between a male tiger and a female lion
ti·gon \'tī-gən\ *noun* [*tiger* + *lion*] (1926)
: TIGLON
Ti·gre \'ti-(ˌ)grā, 'tē-; tē-'\ *noun* (1878)
: a Semitic language of northern Ethiopia
ti·gress \'tī-grəs\ *noun* (1611)
: a female tiger; *also* : a tigerish woman
Ti·gri·nya \tə-'grē-nyə\ *noun* (1878)
: a Semitic language of northern Ethiopia
tike *variant of* TYKE

ti·ki \'tē-kē\ *noun* [Maori & Marquesan, from *Tiki*, first man or creator of first man] (1777)
: a wood or stone image of a Polynesian supernatural power
til \'til\ *noun* [Hindi, from Sanskrit *tila*] (1840)
: SESAME
'til *or* **till** \'til\ *variant of* ¹TILL 2, ²TILL
ti·la·pia \tə-'lä-pē-ə, -'lā-\ *noun* [New Latin, genus name] (1849)
: any of a genus (*Tilapia*) of African freshwater cichlid fishes often raised for food
til·bury \'til-ˌber-ē, -b(ə-)rē\ *noun, plural* **-buries** [*Tilbury*, 19th century English coach builder] (1814)
: a light 2-wheeled carriage
til·de \'til-də\ *noun* [Spanish, from Medieval Latin *titulus* tittle] (circa 1864)
1 : a mark ˜ placed especially over the letter *n* (as in Spanish *señor* sir) to denote the sound \nʸ\ or over vowels (as in Portuguese *irmã* sister) to indicate nasality
2 : the mark ˜ used to indicate negation in logic and the geometric relation "is similar to" in mathematics
¹**tile** \'tī(ə)l\ *noun, often attributive* [Middle English, from Old English *tigele*, from Latin *tegula* tile; akin to Latin *tegere* to cover — more at THATCH] (before 12th century)
1 *plural* **tiles** *or* **tile a** : a flat or curved piece of fired clay, stone, or concrete used especially for roofs, floors, or walls and often for ornamental work **b** : a hollow or a semicircular and open earthenware or concrete piece used in constructing a drain **c** : a hollow building unit made of fired clay or of shale or gypsum
2 : TILING
3 : HAT; *especially* : a high silk hat
4 : a thin piece of resilient material (as cork, linoleum, or rubber) used especially for covering floors or walls
5 : a thin piece resembling a ceramic tile that usually bears a mark or letter and is used as a playing piece in a board game (as mah-jongg)
— **on the tiles** *British* : engaged in late-night carousing
²**tile** *transitive verb* **tiled; til·ing** (14th century)
1 : to cover with tiles
2 : to install drainage tile in
— **til·er** *noun*
tile·fish \'tī(ə)l-ˌfish\ *noun* [*tile*- modification of New Latin *Lopholatilus*] (1881)
: any of various marine bony fishes (family Malacanthidae) used as food; *especially* : a large fish (*Lopholatilus chamaeleonticeps*) of deep waters of the Atlantic and Gulf of Mexico with a fleshy appendage on the head and yellow spots on the upper body and some of its fins
til·ing \'tī-liŋ\ *noun* (15th century)
1 : the action or work of one who tiles
2 a : TILES **b** : a surface of tiles
¹**till** \tᵊl, təl, 'til\ *preposition* [Middle English, from Old English *til;* akin to Old Norse *til* to, till, Old English *til* good] (before 12th century)
1 *chiefly Scottish* : TO
2 : UNTIL
²**till** *conjunction* (12th century)
: UNTIL
³**till** \'til\ *transitive verb* [Middle English *tilien, tillen,* from Old English *tilian;* akin to Old English *til* good, suitable, Old High German *zil* goal] (13th century)
: to work by plowing, sowing, and raising crops : CULTIVATE
— **till·able** \'ti-lə-bəl\ *adjective*
⁴**till** \'til\ *noun* [Anglo-French *tylle*] (15th century)
1 a : a box, drawer, or tray in a receptacle (as a cabinet or chest) used especially for valuables **b** : a money drawer in a store or bank; *also* : CASH REGISTER

2 a : the money contained in a till **b :** a supply of especially ready money

⁵till \'til\ *noun* [origin unknown] (1842)
: unstratified glacial drift consisting of clay, sand, gravel, and boulders intermingled

till·age \'ti-lij\ *noun* (15th century)
1 : the operation of tilling land
2 : cultivated land

til·land·sia \tə-'lan(d)-zē-ə\ *noun* [New Latin, from Elias *Tillands* (died 1693) Finnish botanist] (1759)
: any of a large genus (*Tillandsia*) of chiefly epiphytic plants of the pineapple family native to tropical and subtropical America

¹til·ler \'ti-lər\ *noun* [from (assumed) Middle English, from Old English *telgor, telgra* twig, shoot; akin to Old High German *zelga* twig, Old Irish *dlongaid* he splits] (before 12th century)
: STALK, SPROUT; *especially* : one from the base of a plant or from the axils of its lower leaves

²til·ler *intransitive verb* **til·lered; til·ler·ing** \'ti-lə-riŋ, 'til-riŋ\ (1677)
of a plant : to put forth tillers

³till·er \'ti-lər\ *noun* (13th century)
: one that tills : CULTIVATOR

⁴til·ler \'ti-lər\ *noun* [Middle English *tiler* stock of a crossbow, from Middle French *telier*, literally, beam of a loom, from Medieval Latin *telarium*, from Latin *tela* web — more at TOIL] (circa 1625)
: a lever used to turn the rudder of a boat from side to side; *broadly* : a device or system that plays a part in steering something

til·ler·man \'ti-lər-mən\ *noun* (circa 1934)
: one in charge of a tiller : STEERSMAN

Til·sit \'til-sət\ *also* **Til·sit·er** \-sə-tər\ *noun* [German *Tilsiter*, from *Tilsit* (now Sovetsk, Russia) (circa 1932)
: a semisoft porous light yellow cheese with a flavor that ranges from mild to sharp

¹tilt \'tilt\ *noun* [Middle English *teld, telte* tent, canopy, from Old English *teld*; akin to Old High German *zelt* tent] (15th century)
: a canopy for a wagon, boat, or stall

²tilt *transitive verb* (15th century)
: to cover or provide with a tilt

³tilt *noun* [⁴*tilt*] (1511)
1 a : a contest on horseback in which two combatants charging with lances or similar weapons try to unhorse each other : JOUST **b :** a tournament of tilts
2 a : DISPUTE, CONTENTION **b :** SPEED — used in the phrase *full tilt*
3 a : the act of tilting : the state or position of being tilted **b :** a sloping surface **c :** SLANT, BIAS ⟨a *tilt* toward military involvement⟩
4 : any of various contests resembling or suggesting tilting with lances
— **tilt** *adjective*

⁴tilt *verb* [Middle English *tulten, tilten* to cause to fall; akin to Swedish *tulta* to waddle] (1594)
transitive verb
1 : to cause to have an inclination
2 a : to point or thrust in or as if in a tilt ⟨*tilt* a lance⟩ **b :** to charge against ⟨*tilt* an adversary⟩
intransitive verb
1 a : to move or shift so as to lean or incline : SLANT **b :** to incline, tend, or become drawn toward an opinion, course of action, or one side of a controversy
2 a : to engage in a combat with lances : JOUST **b :** to make an impetuous attack ⟨*tilt* at social evils⟩
— **tilt·able** \'til-tə-bəl\ *adjective*
— **tilt·er** *noun*

tilth \'tilth\ *noun* [Middle English, from Old English, from *tilian* to till] (before 12th century)
1 : cultivated land : TILLAGE
2 : the state of aggregation of a soil especially in relation to its suitability for crop growth

tilt·me·ter \'tilt-,mē-tər\ *noun* (1932)
: an instrument to measure the tilting of the earth's surface

tilt–ro·tor \-,rō-tər\ *noun* (1980)
: an aircraft that has rotors at the end of each wing which can be oriented vertically for vertical takeoffs and landings, horizontally for forward flight, or to any position in between

tilt·yard \'tilt-,yärd\ *noun* (1528)
: a yard or place for tilting contests

tim·bal \'tim-bəl\ *noun* [French *timbale*, from Middle French, alteration of *tamballe*, modification of Old Spanish *atabal*, from Arabic *aṭ-ṭablative* the drum] (1680)
: KETTLEDRUM

tim·bale \'tim-bəl; tim-'bäl, tam-\ *noun* [French, literally, kettledrum] (1824)
1 : a creamy mixture (as of meat or vegetables) baked in a mold; *also* : the mold in which it is baked
2 : a small pastry shell filled with a cooked timbale mixture

¹tim·ber \'tim-bər\ *noun* [Middle English, from Old English, building, wood; akin to Old High German *zimbar* wood, room, Greek *demein* to build, *domos* course of stones or bricks] (before 12th century)
1 a : growing trees or their wood **b** — used interjectionally to warn of a falling tree
2 : wood suitable for building or for carpentry
3 : MATERIAL, STUFF; *especially* : personal qualification for a particular position or status
4 a : a large squared or dressed piece of wood ready for use or forming part of a structure **b** *British* : LUMBER 2a **c :** a curving frame branching outward from the keel of a ship and bending upward in a vertical direction that is usually composed of several pieces united : RIB
— **timber** *adjective*

²timber *transitive verb* **tim·bered; tim·ber·ing** \-b(ə-)riŋ\ (before 12th century)
: to frame, cover, or support with timbers

tim·ber·doo·dle \,tim-bər-'dü-d°l\ *noun* [¹*timber* + *doodle* cock] (1856)
: the American woodcock

tim·bered \'tim-bərd\ *adjective* (15th century)
1 : having walls framed by exposed timbers
2 : having a specified structure or constitution
3 : covered with growing timber : WOODED

tim·ber·head \'tim-bər-,hed\ *noun* (1794)
1 : the top end of a ship's timber used above the gunwale (as for belaying ropes)
2 : a bollard bolted to the deck where the end of a timber would come

timber hitch *noun* (circa 1815)
: a knot used to secure a line to a log or spar — see KNOT illustration

tim·ber·ing \'tim-b(ə-)riŋ\ *noun* (15th century)
: a set or arrangement of timbers

tim·ber·land \-bər-,land\ *noun* (1654)
: wooded land especially with marketable timber

tim·ber·line \-,līn\ *noun* (1867)
: the upper limit of arboreal growth in mountains or high latitudes — called also *tree line*

tim·ber·man \-mən\ *noun* (1889)
: LUMBERMAN

timber rattlesnake *noun* (1895)
: a widely distributed rattlesnake (*Crotalus horridus*) of the eastern U.S.

timber wolf *noun* (1860)
: GRAY WOLF

tim·ber·work \'tim-bər-,wərk\ *noun* (14th century)
: timber construction

tim·bre *also* **tim·ber** \'tam-bər, 'tim-; 'tam-(br°)\ *noun* [French, from Middle French, bell struck by a hammer, from Old French, drum, from Middle Greek *tymbanon* kettledrum, from Greek *tympanon* — more at TYMPANUM] (1849)

: the quality given to a sound by its overtones: as **a :** the resonance by which the ear recognizes and identifies a voiced speech sound **b :** the quality of tone distinctive of a particular singing voice or musical instrument
— **tim·bral** \'tam-brəl, 'tim-\ *adjective*

tim·brel \'tim-brəl\ *noun* [diminutive of obsolete English *timbre* tambourine, from Middle English, from Old French, drum] (circa 1520)
: a small hand drum or tambourine
— **tim·brelled** \-brəld\ *adjective*

¹time \'tīm\ *noun* [Middle English, from Old English *tīma*; akin to Old Norse *tīmiles* time, Old English *tīd* — more at TIDE] (before 12th century)
1 a : the measured or measurable period during which an action, process, or condition exists or continues : DURATION **b :** a nonspatial continuum that is measured in terms of events which succeed one another from past through present to future **c :** LEISURE ⟨*time* for reading⟩
2 : the point or period when something occurs : OCCASION
3 a : an appointed, fixed, or customary moment or hour for something to happen, begin, or end ⟨arrived ahead of *time*⟩ **b :** an opportune or suitable moment ⟨decided it was *time* to retire⟩ — often used in the phrase *about time* ⟨about *time* for a change⟩
4 a : an historical period : AGE **b :** a division of geologic chronology **c :** conditions at present or at some specified period — usually used in plural ⟨*times* are hard⟩ ⟨move with the *times*⟩ **d :** the present time ⟨issues of the *time*⟩
5 a : LIFETIME **b :** a period of apprenticeship **c** : a term of military service **d :** a prison sentence
6 : SEASON ⟨very hot for this *time* of year⟩
7 a : rate of speed : TEMPO **b :** the grouping of the beats of music : RHYTHM
8 a : a moment, hour, day, or year as indicated by a clock or calendar ⟨what *time* is it⟩ **b :** any of various systems (as sidereal or solar) of reckoning time
9 a : one of a series of recurring instances or repeated actions ⟨you've been told many *times*⟩ **b** *plural* **(1) :** added or accumulated quantities or instances ⟨five *times* greater⟩ **(2) :** equal fractional parts of which an indicated number equal a comparatively greater quantity ⟨seven *times* smaller⟩ ⟨three *times* closer⟩ **c :** TURN ⟨three *times* at bat⟩
10 : finite as contrasted with infinite duration
11 : a person's experience during a specified period or on a particular occasion ⟨a good *time*⟩ ⟨a hard *time*⟩
12 a : the hours or days required to be occupied by one's work ⟨make up *time*⟩ ⟨on company *time*⟩ **b :** an hourly pay rate ⟨straight *time*⟩ **c :** wages paid at discharge or resignation ⟨pick up your *time* and get out⟩
13 a : the playing time of a game **b :** TIME-OUT
14 : a period during which something is used or available for use ⟨computer *time*⟩
— **at the same time** : NEVERTHELESS, YET ⟨slick and *at the same time* strangely unprofessional —Gerald Weaks⟩
— **at times** : at intervals : OCCASIONALLY
— **for the time being** : for the present
— **from time to time** : once in a while : OCCASIONALLY
— **in no time** : very quickly or soon
— **in time 1 :** sufficiently early **2 :** EVENTUALLY **3 :** in correct tempo ⟨learn to play *in time*⟩
— **on time 1 a :** at the appointed time **b** : on schedule **2 :** on the installment plan
— **time and again** : FREQUENTLY, REPEATEDLY

²**time** *verb* **timed; tim·ing** (14th century)
transitive verb
1 a : to arrange or set the time of **:** SCHEDULE **b :** to regulate (a watch) to keep correct time **2 :** to set the tempo, speed, or duration of ⟨*timed* his leap perfectly —Neil Amdur⟩ **3 :** to cause to keep time with something **4 :** to determine or record the time, duration, or rate of ⟨*time* a horse⟩ **5 :** to dispose (as a mechanical part) so that an action occurs at a desired instant or in a desired way
intransitive verb
: to keep or beat time

³**time** *adjective* (circa 1711)
1 a : of or relating to time **b :** recording time **2 :** timed to ignite or explode at a specific moment ⟨a *time* bomb⟩ **3 a :** payable on a specified future day or a certain length of time after presentation for acceptance ⟨a *time* draft⟩ ⟨*time* deposits⟩ **b :** based on installment payments ⟨a *time* sale⟩

time and a half *noun* (1888)
: payment for work (as overtime or holiday work) at one and a half times the worker's regular wage rate

time bomb *noun* (1893)
1 : a bomb so made as to explode at a predetermined time **2 :** something with a potentially dangerous or detrimental delayed reaction

time capsule *noun* (1938)
1 : a container holding historical records or objects representative of current culture that is deposited (as in a cornerstone) for preservation until discovery by some future age **2 :** something resembling a time capsule ⟨sunken vessels are archaeological *time capsules* —Philip Trupp⟩

time card *noun* (circa 1891)
: a card used with a time clock to record an employee's starting and quitting times each day or on each job

time chart *noun* (circa 1830)
1 : a chart showing the standard times in various parts of the world with reference to a specified time at a specified place **2 :** TIME LINE 1

time clock *noun* (1887)
: a clock that stamps starting and quitting times on an employee's time card

time–con·sum·ing \ˈtīm-kən-ˈsü-miŋ\ *adjective* (1890)
1 : using or taking up a great deal of time ⟨*time-consuming* chores⟩ **2 :** wasteful of time ⟨*time-consuming* tactics⟩

timed \ˈtīmd\ *adjective* (circa 1760)
1 : made to occur at or in a set time ⟨a *timed* explosion⟩ **2 :** done or taking place at a time of a specified sort ⟨an ill-*timed* arrival⟩

time dilation *noun* (1934)
: a slowing of time in accordance with the theory of relativity that occurs in a system in motion relative to an outside observer and that becomes apparent especially as the speed of the system approaches that of light — called also *time dilatation*

timed–re·lease \ˈtīmd-ri-ˈlēs\ *or* **time–re·lease** \ˈtīm-\ *adjective* (1966)
: consisting of or containing a drug that is released in small amounts over time (as by dissolution of a coating) usually in the gastrointestinal tract ⟨*timed-release* capsules⟩

time exposure *noun* (1893)
: exposure of a photographic film for a definite time usually of more than one half second; *also* **:** a photograph taken by such exposure

time frame *noun* (1964)
: a period of time especially with respect to some action or project

time–hon·ored \ˈtīm-ˌä-nərd\ *adjective* (1593)
: honored because of age or long usage ⟨*time-honored* traditions⟩

time immemorial *noun* (1602)
1 : a time antedating a period legally fixed as the basis for a custom or right **2 :** time so long past as to be indefinite in history or tradition — called also *time out of mind*

time·keep·er \ˈtīm-ˌkē-pər\ *noun* (1686)
1 : TIMEPIECE **2 :** a clerk who keeps records of the time worked by employees **3 :** a person appointed to mark and announce the time in an athletic game or contest
— **time·keep·ing** \-piŋ\ *noun*

time killer *noun* (1751)
1 : a person with free time **2 :** something that passes the time **:** DIVERSION

time lag *noun* (1892)
: an interval of time between two related phenomena (as a cause and its effect)

time–lapse \ˈtīm-ˌlaps\ *adjective* (1927)
: of, relating to, or constituting a motion picture made so that when projected a slow action (as the opening of a flower bud) appears to be speeded up

time·less \ˈtīm-ləs\ *adjective* (circa 1560)
1 *archaic* **:** PREMATURE, UNTIMELY **2 a :** having no beginning or end **:** ETERNAL **b :** not restricted to a particular time or date ⟨the *timeless* themes of love, solitude, joy, and nature —*Writer*⟩ **3 :** not affected by time **:** AGELESS
— **time·less·ly** *adverb*
— **time·less·ness** *noun*

time line *noun* (1951)
1 : a table listing important events for successive years within a particular historical period **2** *usually* **time·line** \ˈtīm-ˌlīn\ **:** a schedule of events and procedures **:** TIMETABLE 2

time lock *noun* (circa 1891)
: a lock controlled by clockwork to prevent its being opened before a set time

¹**time·ly** \ˈtīm-lē\ *adverb* (before 12th century)
1 *archaic* **:** EARLY, SOON **2 :** in time **:** OPPORTUNELY ⟨the question was not . . . *timely* raised in the state court —W. O. Douglas⟩

²**timely** *adjective* **time·li·er; -est** (13th century)
1 : coming early or at the right time **:** OPPORTUNE **2 :** appropriate or adapted to the times or the occasion ⟨a *timely* book⟩
— **time·li·ness** *noun*

time machine *noun* (1895)
: a hypothetical device that permits travel into the past and future

time–of–flight \ˈtīm-ə(v)-ˈflīt\ *adjective* (1945)
: of, relating to, being, or done with an instrument (as a mass spectrometer) that separates particles (as ions) according to the time required for them to traverse a tube of a certain length

time·ous \ˈtī-məs\ *adjective* (circa 1520)
chiefly British **:** TIMELY
— **time·ous·ly** *adverb*

time–out \ˈtīm-ˈaut\ *noun* (1926)
: a brief suspension of activity **:** BREAK; *especially* **:** a suspension of play in an athletic game

time out of mind (15th century)
: TIME IMMEMORIAL 2

time·piece \ˈtīm-ˌpēs\ *noun* (1765)
: a device (as a clock or watch) to measure or show progress of time; *especially* **:** one that does not chime

time·pleas·er \-ˌplē-zər\ *noun* (1601)
obsolete **:** TIMESERVER

tim·er \ˈtī-mər\ *noun* (1841)
: one that times: as **a :** TIMEPIECE; *especially* **:** a stopwatch for timing races **b :** TIMEKEEPER **c :** a device (as a clock) that indicates by a sound the end of an interval of time or that starts or stops a device at predetermined times

time reversal *noun* (1955)
: a formal operation in mathematical physics that reverses the order in which a sequence of events occurs

times \ˈtīmz\ *preposition* (14th century)
: multiplied by ⟨two *times* two is four⟩

time·sav·ing \ˈtīm-ˌsā-viŋ\ *adjective* (1865)
: intended or serving to expedite something ⟨*timesaving* kitchen appliances⟩
— **time·sav·er** \-ˌsā-vər\ *noun*

time·scale \-ˌskā(ə)l\ *noun* (1890)
: an arrangement of events used as a measure of the relative or absolute duration or antiquity of a period of history or geologic or cosmic time

time series *noun* (1919)
: a set of data collected sequentially usually at fixed intervals of time

time·serv·er \-ˌsər-vər\ *noun* (1584)
: a person whose behavior is adjusted to the pattern of the times or to please superiors **:** TEMPORIZER

¹**time·serv·ing** \-viŋ\ *noun* (1621)
: the behavior or practice of a timeserver

²**timeserving** *adjective* (1630)
: marked by or revealing a lack of independence or integrity ⟨a mean, *timeserving* little man, grovelling odiously before the wealthy people —Peter Forster⟩

time·shar·ing \ˈtīm-ˌsher-iŋ, -ˌshar-\ *noun* (1953)
1 : simultaneous use of a central computer by many users at remote locations **2** *or* **time–share** \-ˌsher, -ˌshar\ **:** joint ownership or rental of a vacation lodging (as a condominium) by several persons with each occupying the premises in turn for short periods
— **time–share** *transitive verb*

time sheet *noun* (circa 1909)
1 : a sheet for recording the time of arrival and departure of workers and for recording the amount of time spent on each job **2 :** a sheet for summarizing hours worked by each worker during a pay period

time signature *noun* (1875)
: a sign used in music to indicate meter and usually written as a fraction with the bottom number indicating the kind of note used as a unit of time and the top number indicating the number of units in each measure

times sign *noun* (1948)
: the symbol × used to indicate multiplication

time stamp *noun* (1892)
: a device for recording the date and time of day that letters or papers are received or sent out
— **time–stamp** *transitive verb*

time·ta·ble \ˈtīm-ˌtā-bəl\ *noun* (1838)
1 : a table of departure and arrival times of trains, buses, or airplanes **2 a :** a schedule showing a planned order or sequence **b :** PROGRAM 3
— **time–table** *transitive verb*

time–test·ed \-ˌtes-təd\ *adjective* (1930)
: having effectiveness that has been proved over a long period of time ⟨*time-tested* methods⟩

time trial *noun* (circa 1949)
: a competitive event (as in auto racing) in which individuals are successively timed over a set course or distance

time warp *noun* (1954)
: an anomaly, discontinuity, or suspension held to occur in the progress of time

time·work \ˈtīm-ˌwərk\ *noun* (1829)
: work paid for at a standard rate for the hour or the day
— **time·work·er** \-ˌwər-kər\ *noun*

time·worn \-ˌwōrn, -ˌwȯrn\ *adjective* (1729)
1 : worn or impaired by time ⟨*timeworn* mansions⟩ **2 a :** AGE-OLD, ANCIENT ⟨*timeworn* procedures⟩ **b :** HACKNEYED, STALE ⟨a *timeworn* joke⟩

time zone *noun* (1892)
: a geographical region within which the same standard time is used

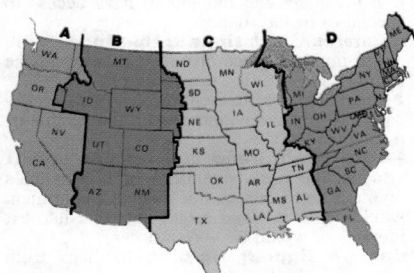

time zones in the conterminous United States:
A Pacific time, *B* mountain time, *C* central time, *D* eastern time

tim·id \'ti-məd\ *adjective* [Latin *timidus,* from *timēre* to fear] (1549)
1 : lacking in courage or self-confidence ⟨a *timid* person⟩
2 : lacking in boldness or determination ⟨a *timid* policy⟩
— **ti·mid·i·ty** \tə-'mi-də-tē\ *noun*
— **tim·id·ly** \'ti-məd-lē\ *adverb*
— **tim·id·ness** *noun*

tim·ing \'tī-miŋ\ *noun* (1597)
1 : selection or the ability to select for maximum effect of the precise moment for beginning or doing something ⟨haven't got my *timing* down⟩
2 : observation and recording (as by a stopwatch) of the elapsed time of an act, action, or process

ti·moc·ra·cy \tī-'mä-krə-sē\ *noun* [Middle French *tymocracie,* from Medieval Latin *timocratia,* from Greek *timokratia,* from *timē* price, value, honor + *-kratia* -cracy; akin to Greek *tiein* to honor, Sanskrit *cāyati* he respects] (1586)
1 : government in which a certain amount of property is necessary for office
2 : government in which love of honor is the ruling principle
— **ti·mo·crat·ic** \tī-mə-'kra-tik\ *or* **ti·mo·crat·i·cal** \-ti-kəl\ *adjective*

ti·mo·lol \'tī-mə-,lōl, -,lȯl\ *noun* [*tim-* (of unknown origin) + *-olol* (as in *propranolol*)] (1973)
: a beta-blocker $C_{13}H_{24}N_4O_3S$ used in the form of its maleate salt to treat glaucoma and to reduce the risk of second heart attacks

tim·o·rous \'ti-mə-rəs, 'tim-rəs\ *adjective* [Middle English, from Middle French *timoureus,* from Medieval Latin *timorosus,* from Latin *timor* fear, from *timēre* to fear] (15th century)
1 : of a timid disposition : FEARFUL
2 : expressing or suggesting timidity ⟨proceed with doubtful and *timorous* steps —Edward Gibbon⟩
— **tim·o·rous·ly** *adverb*
— **tim·o·rous·ness** *noun*

Tim·o·thy \'ti-mə-thē\ *noun* [probably after *Timothy* Hanson, 18th century American farmer said to have introduced it from New England to the southern states] (1747)
: a European grass (*Phleum pratense*) that has long cylindrical spikes and is widely grown for hay

Tim·o·thy \'ti-mə-thē\ *noun* [Latin *Timotheus,* from Greek *Timotheos*]
1 : a disciple of the apostle Paul
2 : either of two letters written with regard to pastoral care in the early Church and included as books in the New Testament — see BIBLE table

tim·pa·ni \'tim-pə-nē\ *noun plural but singular or plural in construction* [Italian, plural of *timpano* kettledrum, from Latin *tympanum* drum — more at TYMPANUM] (circa 1854)

: a set of two or more kettledrums played by one performer in an orchestra or band

tim·pa·nist \-nist\ *noun* (1906)
: one who plays the timpani

¹tin \'tin\ *noun* [Middle English, from Old English; akin to Old High German *zin* tin] (before 12th century)
1 : a soft faintly bluish white lustrous low-melting crystalline metallic element that is malleable and ductile at ordinary temperatures and that is used as a protective coating, in tinfoil, and in soft solders and alloys — see ELEMENT table
2 a : a box, can, pan, vessel, or a sheet made of tinplate; *broadly* : such a container of any metal (as aluminum) **b** : a metal container and its contents ⟨a *tin* of tomatoes⟩
— **tin** *adjective*
— **tin·ful** \-,fúl\ *noun*

²tin *transitive verb* **tinned; tin·ning** (14th century)
1 : to cover or plate with tin or a tin alloy
2 : to put up or pack in tins : CAN

tin·a·mou \'ti-nə-,mü\ *noun* [French, from Carib *tinamu*] (circa 1783)
: any of a family (Tinamidae) of South and Central American game birds that have a deeply keeled sternum and a rudimentary tail and that produce eggs with a surface resembling enamel

tin can *noun* (1770)
1 : a can made of tinplate; *broadly* : CAN 1c
2 *slang* : DESTROYER 2

¹tinct \'tiŋ(k)t\ *adjective* [Latin *tinctus,* past participle] (1579)
: COLORED, TINGED

²tinct *noun* (1602)
: TINCTURE, TINGE

tinc·to·ri·al \tiŋ(k)-'tȯr-ē-əl, -'tȯr-\ *adjective* [Latin *tinctorius,* from *tingere* to tinge] (1655)
: of or relating to colors or to dyeing or staining; *also* : imparting color
— **tinc·to·ri·al·ly** \-ē-ə-lē\ *adverb*

¹tinc·ture \'tiŋ(k)-chər\ *noun* [Middle English, from Latin *tinctura* act of dyeing, from *tinctus,* past participle of *tingere* to tinge] (14th century)
1 a *archaic* : a substance that colors, dyes, or stains **b** : COLOR, TINT
2 a : a characteristic quality : CAST **b** : a slight admixture : TRACE
3 *obsolete* : an active principle or extract
4 : a heraldic metal, color, or fur
5 : a solution of a medicinal substance in an alcoholic menstruum

²tincture *transitive verb* **tinc·tured; tinc·tur·ing** \'tiŋ(k)-chə-riŋ, -shriŋ\ (1616)
1 : to tint or stain with a color : TINGE
2 a : to infuse or instill with a property or entity : IMPREGNATE **b** : to imbue with a quality : AFFECT ⟨writing *tinctured* with wit and wisdom⟩

tin·der \'tin-dər\ *noun* [Middle English, from Old English *tynder;* akin to Old High German *zuntra* tinder, Old English *tendan* to kindle] (before 12th century)
1 : a very flammable substance adaptable for use as kindling
2 : something that serves to incite or inflame

tin·der·box \'tin-dər-,bäks\ *noun* (1530)
1 a : a metal box for holding tinder and usually a flint and steel for striking a spark **b** : a highly inflammable object or place
2 : a potentially explosive place or situation

¹tine \'tīn\ *noun* [Middle English *tind,* from Old English; akin to Old High German *zint* point, tine] (before 12th century)
1 : a slender pointed projecting part : PRONG
2 : a pointed branch of an antler
— **tined** \'tīnd\ *adjective*

²tine *verb* **tined** \'tīnd\ *or* **tint** \'tint\; **tin·ing** \'tī-niŋ\ [Middle English, of Scandinavian origin; akin to Old Norse *týna* to lose, destroy, *tjōn* injury, loss — more at TEEN] (13th century)

transitive verb
dialect British : LOSE
intransitive verb
dialect British : to become lost

tin·ea \'ti-nē-ə\ *noun* [Middle English, from Medieval Latin, from Latin, worm, moth] (14th century)
: any of several fungal diseases of the skin; *especially* : RINGWORM
— **tin·e·al** \-nē-əl\ *adjective*

tinea cru·ris \-'krúr-əs\ *noun* [New Latin, literally, tinea of the leg] (circa 1923)
: a fungal infection involving especially the groin and perineum

tin ear *noun* (1935)
: a deafened or insensitive ear

tin·foil \'tin-,fȯil\ *noun* (15th century)
: a paper-thin metal sheeting usually of aluminum or tin-lead alloy

ting *noun* [*ting,* verb, from Middle English *tingen,* of imitative origin] (1602)
: a high-pitched sound like that made by a light stroke on a crystal goblet
— **ting** *intransitive verb*

¹tinge \'tinj\ *transitive verb* **tinged; tinge·ing** *or* **ting·ing** \'tin-jiŋ\ [Middle English, from Latin *tingere* to dip, moisten, tinge; akin to Greek *tengein* to moisten and probably to Old High German *dunkōn* to dip] (15th century)
1 a : to color with a slight shade or stain : TINT
b : to affect or modify with a slight odor or taste
2 : to affect or modify in character

²tinge *noun* (1752)
1 : a slight staining or suffusing shade or color
2 : an affective or modifying property or influence : TOUCH

tin·gle \'tiŋ-gəl\ *intransitive verb* **tin·gled; tin·gling** \-g(ə-)liŋ\ [Middle English, alteration of *tinklen* to tinkle, tingle] (14th century)
1 a : to feel a ringing, stinging, prickling, or thrilling sensation **b** : to cause such a sensation
2 : TINKLE
— **tingle** *noun*
— **tin·gling·ly** \-g(ə-)liŋ-lē\ *adverb*
— **tin·gly** \-g(ə-)lē\ *adjective*

tin hat *noun* (1903)
: a metal helmet

tin·horn \'tin-,hȯrn\ *noun* (1885)
: one (as a gambler) who pretends to have money, ability, or influence

¹tin·ker \'tiŋ-kər\ *noun* [Middle English *tinkere*] (14th century)
1 a : a usually itinerant mender of household utensils **b** : an unskillful mender : BUNGLER
2 *chiefly Irish* : GYPSY

²tinker *verb* **tin·kered; tin·ker·ing** \-k(ə-)riŋ\ (1592)
intransitive verb
: to work in the manner of a tinker; *especially*
: to repair, adjust, or work with something in an unskilled or experimental manner : FIDDLE
transitive verb
: to repair, adjust, or experiment with
— **tin·ker·er** \-kər-ər\ *noun*

tinker's damn *also* **tinker's dam** \-'dam\ *noun* [probably from the tinkers' reputation for blasphemy] (1839)
: a minimum amount or degree (as of care) ⟨didn't give a *tinker's damn* about poetry —James Blish⟩

Tin·ker·toy \'tiŋ-kər-,tȯi\ *trademark*
— used for a construction toy of fitting parts

¹tin·kle \'tiŋ-kəl\ *verb* **tin·kled; tin·kling** \-k(ə-)liŋ\ [Middle English, frequentative of *tinken* to tinkle, of imitative origin] (15th century)
intransitive verb

1 : to make or emit a tinkle or a sound suggestive of a tinkle
2 : URINATE
transitive verb
1 : to sound or make known (the time) by a tinkle
2 a : to cause to make a tinkle **b :** to produce by tinkling ⟨*tinkle* a tune⟩
²**tinkle** *noun* (1725)
1 : a jingling effect in verse or prose
2 : a series of short high ringing or clinking sounds
tin·kly \ˈtiŋ-k(ə-)lē\ *adjective* (1892)
: that tinkles : TINKLING
tin liz·zie \-ˈli-zē\ *noun* [from *Tin Lizzie*, nickname for the Model T Ford automobile] (1915)
: a small inexpensive early automobile
tin·ner \ˈti-nər\ *noun* (1512)
1 : a tin miner
2 : TINSMITH
tin·ni·tus \ˈti-nə-təs, tə-ˈnī-təs\ *noun* [Latin, ringing, tinnitus, from *tinnire* to ring, of imitative origin] (1843)
: a sensation of noise (as a ringing or roaring) that is caused by a bodily condition (as a disturbance of the auditory nerve or wax in the ear) and can usually be heard only by the one affected
tin·ny \ˈti-nē\ *adjective* **tin·ni·er; -est** (1552)
1 : of, abounding in, or yielding tin
2 a : resembling tin **b :** LIGHT, CHEAP
3 : thin in tone ⟨a *tinny* voice⟩
— **tin·ni·ly** \ˈti-nᵊl-ē\ *adverb*
— **tin·ni·ness** \ˈti-nē-nəs\ *noun*
Tin Pan Alley *noun* (1908)
: a district that is a center for composers and publishers of popular music; *also* : the body of such composers and publishers
tin·plate \ˈtin-ˌplāt\ *noun* (1677)
: thin sheet iron or steel coated with tin
tin–plate *transitive verb* (1890)
: to plate or coat (as a metal sheet) with tin
tin–pot \ˈtin-ˈpät\ *adjective* (1838)
: SMALL-TIME
¹**tin·sel** \ˈtin(t)-səl *also* ˈtin-zəl\ *noun* [Middle French *estincelle, estancele, etincelle* spark, glitter, spangle — more at STENCIL] (1538)
1 : a thread, strip, or sheet of metal, paper, or plastic used to produce a glittering and sparkling appearance in fabrics, yarns, or decorations
2 : something superficially attractive or glamorous but of little real worth ⟨disfigured by no gaudy *tinsel* of rhetoric or declamation —Thomas Jefferson⟩
²**tinsel** *adjective* (1575)
1 : made of or covered with tinsel
2 a : cheaply gaudy : TAWDRY **b :** SPECIOUS ⟨*tinsel* promises⟩
³**tinsel** *transitive verb* **tin·seled** *or* **tin·selled; tin·sel·ing** *or* **tin·sel·ling** \ˈtin(t)-s(ə-)liŋ *also* ˈtin-zə-liŋ\ (1594)
1 : to interweave, overlay, or adorn with or as if with tinsel
2 : to impart a specious brightness to
tin·sel·ly \ˈtin(t)-s(ə-)lē *also* ˈtin-zə-lē\ *adjective* (1811)
: TINSEL
tin·smith \ˈtin-ˌsmith\ *noun* (1812)
: a worker who makes or repairs things of sheet metal (as tinplate)
— **tin·smith·ing** \-ˌsmi-thiŋ\ *noun*
tin·stone \ˈtin-ˌstōn\ *noun* (1602)
: CASSITERITE
¹**tint** \ˈtint\ *noun* [alteration of earlier *tinct*, from Latin *tinctus* act of dyeing, from *tingere* to tinge] (1717)
1 a : a usually slight or pale coloration : HUE **b :** any of various lighter or darker shades of a color : TINGE
2 : a variation of a color produced by adding white to it and characterized by a low saturation with relatively high lightness
3 : a usually slight modifying quality or characteristic : TOUCH

4 : a shaded effect in engraving produced by fine parallel lines close together
5 : a panel of light color serving as background
6 : dye for the hair
— **tint·er** *noun*
²**tint** *transitive verb* (1791)
: to impart or apply a tint to : COLOR
tint·ing *noun* (circa 1841)
1 : the act or process of one that tints
2 : the engraved or colored tint produced by tinting
tin·tin·nab·u·lary \ˌtin-tə-ˈna-byə-ˌler-ē\ *adjective* [Latin *tintinnabulum* bell] (1787)
: of, relating to, or characterized by bells or their sounds
tin·tin·nab·u·la·tion \ˌtin-tə-ˌna-byə-ˈlā-shən\ *noun* [Latin *tintinnabulum* bell, from *tintinnare* to ring, jingle, from *tinnire*] (1831)
1 : the ringing or sounding of bells
2 : a jingling or tinkling sound as if of bells
tint·less \ˈtint-ləs\ *adjective* (1789)
archaic **:** having no tints : lacking color
tin·type \-ˌtīp\ *noun* (1864)
: FERROTYPE 1
tin·ware \ˈtin-ˌwar, -ˌwer\ *noun* (1758)
: articles and especially utensils made of tinplate
tin·work \-ˌwərk\ *noun* (circa 1934)
: work in tin
ti·ny \ˈtī-nē\ *adjective* **ti·ni·er; -est** [alteration of Middle English *tine*] (1598)
: very small or diminutive : MINUTE
synonym see SMALL
— **ti·ni·ly** \ˈtī-nᵊl-ē\ *adverb*
— **ti·ni·ness** \ˈtī-nē-nəs\ *noun*
¹**tip** \ˈtip\ *verb* **tipped; tip·ping** [Middle English] (14th century)
transitive verb
1 : OVERTURN, UPSET — usually used with *over*
2 a : CANT, TILT **b :** to raise and tilt forward in salute ⟨*tipped* his hat⟩
intransitive verb
1 : to become tipped : TOPPLE
2 : LEAN, SLANT
— **tip the scales 1 :** to register weight ⟨*tips the scales* at 285 pounds⟩ **2 :** to shift the balance of power or influence ⟨*tipped the scales* in favor of a declaration of war —S. F. Bemis⟩
²**tip** *noun* (1673)
1 : the act or an instance of tipping : TILT
2 *chiefly British* **:** a place for depositing something (as rubbish) by dumping
³**tip** *transitive verb* **tipped; tip·ping** [Middle English *tipped* having a tip, from ⁴*tip*] (14th century)
1 a : to furnish with a tip **b** (1) **:** to cover or adorn the tip of (2) **:** to blend (furs) for improved appearance by brushing the tips of the hair with dye
2 : to affix (an insert) in a book — often used with *in*
3 : to remove the ends of ⟨*tip* raspberries⟩
⁴**tip** *noun* [Middle English; akin to Middle High German *zipf* tip, Old English *tæppa* tap — more at TAP] (15th century)
1 : the usually pointed end of something
2 : a small piece or part serving as an end, cap, or point
— **tipped** \ˈtipt\ *adjective*
— **on the tip of one's tongue 1 :** about to be uttered ⟨it was *on the tip of my tongue* to tell him exactly what I thought⟩ **2 :** just eluding recall
⁵**tip** *noun* [Middle English *tippe*; akin to Low German *tippen* to tap] (15th century)
: a light touch or blow
⁶**tip** *verb* **tipped; tip·ping** (1567)
transitive verb
1 : to strike lightly : TAP
2 : to give (a baseball) a glancing blow
intransitive verb
: TIPTOE
⁷**tip** *noun* [origin unknown] (1567)

1 : a piece of advice or expert or authoritative information
2 : a piece of advance or confidential information given by one thought to have access to special or inside sources
⁸**tip** *transitive verb* **tipped; tip·ping** (1883)
1 : to impart a piece of information or advice about or to — often used with *off*
2 *chiefly British* **:** to mention as a likely candidate, prospective winner, or profitable investment : TOUT 4
— **tip one's hand** *also* **tip one's mitt**
: to declare one's intentions or reveal one's opinions or resources ⟨the Justice Department wouldn't *tip its hand* by saying what its next move . . . would be —*Newsweek*⟩
⁹**tip** *verb* **tipped; tip·ping** [perhaps from ⁶*tip*] (circa 1610)
transitive verb
1 : GIVE, PRESENT
2 : to give a gratuity to
intransitive verb
: to bestow a gratuity
¹⁰**tip** *noun* (1755)
: a gift or a sum of money tendered for a service performed or anticipated : GRATUITY
tip·cart \ˈtip-ˌkärt\ *noun* (circa 1877)
: a cart whose body can be tipped on the frame to empty its contents
tip·cat \-ˌkat\ *noun* [⁶*tip*] (1676)
: a game in which one player using a bat strikes lightly a tapered wooden peg and as it flies up strikes it again to drive it as far as possible while fielders try to recover it; *also* : the peg used in this game
ti·pi \ˈtē-(ˌ)pē\ *variant of* TEPEE
tip–in \ˈtip-ˌin\ *noun* [⁶*tip*] (1948)
: a goal in basketball made by deflecting a rebound into the basket with the fingertips
¹**tip–off** \ˈtip-ˌof\ *noun* [⁸*tip*] (1901)
1 : WARNING, TIP
2 : a telltale sign
²**tip–off** *noun* [⁶*tip*] (1922)
: the act or an instance of putting the ball in play in basketball by a jump ball
tip of the iceberg [from an iceberg being mostly submerged] (1969)
: the earliest, most obvious, or most superficial manifestation of some phenomenon
tip·per \ˈti-pər\ *noun* (1819)
: one that tips
tip·pet \ˈti-pət\ *noun* [Middle English *tipet*] (14th century)
1 : a long hanging end of cloth attached to a sleeve, cap, or hood
2 : a shoulder cape of fur or cloth often with hanging ends
3 : a long black scarf worn over the robe by Anglican clergymen during morning and evening prayer
¹**tip·ple** \ˈti-pəl\ *verb* **tip·pled; tip·pling** \-p(ə-)liŋ\ [back-formation from obsolete *tippler* barkeeper] (1560)
intransitive verb
: to drink liquor especially by habit or to excess
transitive verb
: to drink (liquor) especially continuously in small amounts
— **tip·pler** \-p(ə-)lər\ *noun*
²**tipple** *noun* (1581)
: DRINK 1, 2
³**tipple** *noun* [English dialect *tipple* to tip over, frequentative of English ¹*tip*] (1880)
1 : a place where or an apparatus by which cars (as for coal) are loaded or emptied
2 : a coal-screening plant
tip·py \ˈti-pē\ *adjective* **tip·pi·er; -est** (1886)
: liable to tip ⟨a *tippy* boat⟩
tip·staff \ˈtip-ˌstaf\ *noun, plural* **tip·staves** \-ˌstavz, -ˌstāvz\ [obsolete *tipstaff* staff tipped with metal] (1535)
: an officer (as a constable or bailiff) who bears a staff
tip·ster \ˈtip-stər\ *noun* (1862)

: one who gives or sells tips especially for gambling or speculation

tip·sy \'tip-sē\ *adjective* **tip·si·er; -est** [¹*tip* + *-sy* (as in *tricksy*)] (1577)
1 : unsteady, staggering, or foolish from the effects of liquor : FUDDLED
2 : UNSTEADY, ASKEW ⟨a *tipsy* angle⟩
— **tip·si·ly** \-sə-lē\ *adverb*
— **tip·si·ness** \-sē-nəs\ *noun*

¹**tip·toe** \'tip-,tō, -'tō\ *noun* (14th century)
: the position of being balanced on the balls of the feet and toes with the heels raised — usually used with *on*; *also* : the ends of the toes
— **on tiptoe** : ALERT, AROUSED ⟨the contest of skill that puts one *on tiptoe* to win —*Deerfield (Wisconsin) Independent*⟩

²**tiptoe** *adverb* (1592)
: on or as if on tiptoe

³**tiptoe** *adjective* (1593)
1 : standing or walking on or as if on tiptoe
2 : CAUTIOUS, STEALTHY

⁴**tiptoe** *intransitive verb* **tip·toed; tip·toe·ing** (circa 1661)
1 : to stand or raise oneself on tiptoe
2 : to walk or proceed quietly or cautiously on or as if on tiptoe

¹**tip-top** \'tip-'täp, -,täp\ *noun* [⁴*tip* + *top*] (1702)
: the highest point

²**tip-top** *adjective* (1722)
: EXCELLENT, FIRST-RATE ⟨*tip-top* working conditions⟩

³**tip-top** *adverb* (1882)
: very well

ti·rade \'tī-,rād *also* ti-'\ *noun* [French, shot, tirade, from Middle French, from Old Italian *tirata*, from *tirare* to draw, shoot] (1802)
: a protracted speech usually marked by intemperate, vituperative, or harshly censorious language

tir·a·mi·su \,tir-ə-'mē-(,)sü, -'mi-; -mē-'sü\ *noun* [Italian *tiramisù*, from *tirami su*!, literally, pull me up!] (1982)
: a dessert made with ladyfingers, mascarpone, chocolate, and espresso

¹**tire** \'tīr\ *verb* **tired; tir·ing** [Middle English *tyren*, from Old English *tēorian, tȳrian*] (before 12th century)
intransitive verb
: to become weary
transitive verb
1 : to exhaust or greatly decrease the physical strength of : FATIGUE
2 : to wear out the patience of : BORE ☆

²**tire** *noun* [Middle English, short for *attire*] (14th century)
1 *obsolete* : ATTIRE
2 *archaic* : a woman's headband or hair ornament

³**tire** *transitive verb* **tired; tir·ing** (14th century)
1 *obsolete* : ATTIRE
2 *archaic* : to adorn (the hair) with an ornament

⁴**tire** *noun, often attributive* [Middle English, probably from ²*tire*] (15th century)
1 : a metal hoop forming the tread of a wheel
2 : a rubber cushion that fits around a wheel (as of an automobile) and usually contains compressed air

tired \'tīrd\ *adjective* (15th century)
1 : drained of strength and energy : fatigued often to the point of exhaustion
2 : obviously worn by hard use : RUN-DOWN
3 : TRITE, HACKNEYED
— **tired·ly** *adverb*
— **tired·ness** *noun*

tire·less \'tīr-ləs\ *adjective* (1591)
: seemingly incapable of tiring : INDEFATIGABLE
— **tire·less·ly** *adverb*
— **tire·less·ness** *noun*

Ti·re·si·as \tī-'rē-sē-əs, -zē-\ *noun* [Latin, from Greek *Teiresias*]

: a blind seer of Thebes who in one Greek myth is changed into a woman for several years and then changed back to a man

tire·some \'tīr-səm\ *adjective* (circa 1520)
: WEARISOME, TEDIOUS
— **tire·some·ly** *adverb*
— **tire·some·ness** *noun*

tir·ing-house \'tī-riŋ-,haús\ *noun* [³*tire*] (1590)
: a section of a theater reserved for the actors and used especially for dressing for stage entrances

tir·ing-room \-,rüm, -,rúm\ *noun* [³*tire*] (1623)
: a dressing room especially in a theater

tirl \'tərl\ *verb* [alteration of ¹*trill*] (circa 1550)
intransitive verb
chiefly Scottish : to make a rattling sound (as with a door latch)
transitive verb
chiefly Scottish : TWIRL

tiro *chiefly British variant of* TYRO

'**tis** \'tiz, (,)tiz, təz\ [contraction] (15th century)
: it is

ti·sane \ti-'zan, -'zän\ *noun* [Middle English, from Middle French, from Latin *ptisana*, from Greek *ptisanē*, literally, crushed barley, from *ptissein* to crush — more at PESTLE] (14th century)
: an infusion (as of dried herbs) used as a beverage or for medicinal effects

Tish·ah–b'Ab \'ti-shə-,bäv, -,bȯv\ *noun* [Hebrew *tish'āh bĕ Ābh* ninth in Ab] (circa 1902)
: a Jewish holiday observed with fasting on the 9th of Ab in commemoration of the destruction of the temples at Jerusalem

Tish·ri \'tish-rē\ *noun* [Hebrew *tishrī*] (circa 1771)
: the 1st month of the civil year or the 7th month of the ecclesiastical year in the Jewish calendar — see MONTH table

tis·sue \'ti-(,)shü, *chiefly British* 'tis-(,)yü\ *noun* [Middle English *tissu*, a rich fabric, from Old French *tissu*, from past participle of *tistre* to weave, from Latin *texere* — more at TECHNICAL] (1563)
1 a : a fine lightweight often sheer fabric **b** : MESH, NETWORK, WEB ⟨a *tissue* of lies⟩
2 : a piece of soft absorbent tissue paper used especially as a handkerchief or for removing cosmetics
3 : an aggregate of cells usually of a particular kind together with their intercellular substance that form one of the structural materials of a plant or an animal
— **tis·su·ey** \'ti-shə-wē\ *adjective*

tissue culture *noun* (1912)
: the process or technique of making body tissue grow in a culture medium outside the organism; *also* : a culture of tissue (as epithelium)

tissue fluid *noun* (1900)
: a fluid that permeates the spaces between individual cells, that is in osmotic contact with the blood and lymph, and that serves in interstitial transport of nutrients and waste

tissue paper *noun* (1777)
: a thin gauzy paper used especially for protecting something (as by covering or wrapping)

tissue plasminogen activator *noun* (1981)
: a clot-dissolving enzyme with an affinity for fibrin that is produced naturally in blood vessel linings and is used in a genetically engineered form to prevent damage to heart muscle following a heart attack — abbreviation *TPA*

tis·su·lar \'ti-shə-lər\ *adjective* [*tissue* + *-lar* (as in *cellular*)] (circa 1935)
: of, relating to, or affecting organismic tissue ⟨*tissular* grafts⟩ ⟨*tissular* lesions⟩

'**tit** \'tit\ *noun* [Middle English, from Old English — more at TEAT] (before 12th century)
1 : TEAT

2 : BREAST — usually used in plural; usually considered vulgar

²**tit** *noun* (circa 1706)
: TITMOUSE; *broadly* : any of various small plump often long-tailed birds

ti·tan \'tī-t°n\ *noun* [Greek] (circa 1741)
1 *capitalized* : any of a family of giants born of Uranus and Gaea and ruling the earth until overthrown by the Olympian gods
2 : one that is gigantic in size or power : one that stands out for greatness of achievement

titan- *or* **titani-** *combining form* [New Latin *titanium*]
: titanium ⟨*titanate*⟩

ti·ta·nate \'tī-t°n-,āt\ *noun* (1839)
1 : any of various multiple oxides of titanium dioxide with other metallic oxides
2 : a titanium ester of the general formula $Ti(OR)_4$

ti·tan·ess \'tī-t°n-əs\ *noun, often capitalized* (1596)
: a female titan

ti·ta·nia \tī-'tā-nē-ə, tə-, -'tān-yə *also* -'ta-nē-ə *or* -'tan-yə\ *noun* [New Latin] (1922)
: TITANIUM DIOXIDE

Ti·ta·nia \tə-'tā-nyə, -'tän-; tī-'tān-\ *noun*
: the wife of Oberon and queen of the fairies in Shakespeare's *A Midsummer Night's Dream*

ti·tan·ic \tī-'ta-nik *also* tə-\ *adjective* [Greek *titanikos* of the Titans] (1709)
: having great magnitude, force, or power : COLOSSAL
— **ti·tan·i·cal·ly** \-ni-k(ə-)lē\ *adverb*

ti·ta·nif·er·ous \,tī-t°n-'i-f(ə-)rəs\ *adjective* (circa 1828)
: containing or yielding titanium ⟨*titaniferous* minerals⟩

ti·tan·ism \'tī-t°n-,i-zəm\ *noun, often capitalized* [from the Titans' rebellion against their father Uranus] (1867)
: defiance of and revolt against social or artistic conventions

ti·ta·ni·um \tī-'tā-nē-əm, tə- *also* -'ta-nē-əm, -'tan-yəm\ *noun* [New Latin, from Greek *Titan*] (circa 1796)
: a silvery gray light strong metallic element found combined in ilmenite and rutile and used especially in alloys (as steel) and combined in refractory materials and in coatings — see ELEMENT table

titanium dioxide *noun* (1877)
: an oxide TiO_2 of titanium that occurs in rutile, anatase, or ilmenite and is used especially as a pigment

titanium white *noun* (1920)
: TITANIUM DIOXIDE; *also* : a brilliant white lead-free pigment consisting of titanium dioxide often together with barium sulfate and zinc oxide

tit·bit \'tit-,bit\ *variant of* TIDBIT

☆ SYNONYMS
Tire, weary, fatigue, exhaust, jade, fag mean to make or become unable or unwilling to continue. TIRE implies a draining of one's strength or patience ⟨the long ride *tired* us out⟩. WEARY stresses tiring until one is unable to endure more of the same thing ⟨*wearied* of the constant arguing⟩. FATIGUE suggests causing great lassitude through excessive strain or undue effort ⟨*fatigued* by the day's chores⟩. EXHAUST implies complete draining of strength by hard exertion ⟨shoveling snow *exhausted* him⟩. JADE suggests the loss of all freshness and eagerness ⟨*jaded* by overindulgence⟩. FAG implies a drooping with fatigue ⟨shoppers all *fagged* out by the Christmas rush⟩.

\ə\ abut \ᵊ\ kitten \ər\ further \a\ ash \ā\ ace \ä\ mop, mar \au̇\ out \ch\ chin \e\ bet \ē\ easy \g\ go \i\ hit \ī\ ice \j\ job \ŋ\ sing \ō\ go \ȯ\ law \ȯi\ boy \th\ thin \th\ the \ü\ loot \u̇\ foot \y\ yet \zh\ vision *see also* Guide to Pronunciation

ti·ter \'tī-tər\ *noun* [French *titre* title, proportion of gold or silver in a coin, from Old French *title* inscription, title] (1888)
: the strength of a solution or the concentration of a substance (as an antibody) in solution as determined by titration

tit·fer \'tit-fər\ *noun* [by shortening & alteration from *tit for tat*, rhyming slang for *hat*] (circa 1930)
British : HAT

tit for tat \,tit-fər-'tat\ [alteration of earlier *tip for tap*, from *tip* (blow) + *for* + *tap*] (1556)
: an equivalent given in return (as for an injury) : retaliation in kind
— **tit–for–tat** *adjective*

tith·able \'tī-thə-bəl\ *adjective* (15th century)
: subject or liable to payment of tithes

¹**tithe** \'tīth\ *verb* **tithed; tith·ing** [Middle English, from Old English *teogothian,* from *teogotha* tenth] (before 12th century)
transitive verb
1 : to pay or give a tenth part of especially for the support of the church
2 : to levy a tithe on
intransitive verb
: to give a tenth of one's income as a tithe

²**tithe** *noun* [Middle English, from Old English *teogotha* tenth; akin to Middle Low German *tegede* tenth, Old English *tīen* ten — more at TEN] (before 12th century)
1 : a tenth part of something paid as a voluntary contribution or as a tax especially for the support of a religious establishment
2 : the obligation represented by individual tithes
3 : TENTH; *broadly* : a small part
4 : a small tax or levy

tith·er \'tī-thər\ *noun* (14th century)
1 : one that pays tithes
2 : one that collects or advocates the payment of tithes

tith·ing \'tī-thiŋ\ *noun* [Middle English, from Old English *tēothung,* from *teogothian, tēothian* to tithe, take one tenth] (before 12th century)
: a small administrative division preserved in parts of England apparently originally made up of ten men with their families

ti·tho·nia \tə-'thō-nyə, tī-, -nē-ə\ *noun* [New Latin, probably from Latin *Tithonia,* poetical name of Aurora] (1940)
: any of a genus (*Tithonia*) of tall composite herbs or shrubs of Mexico and Central America that have flower heads resembling sunflowers and that are sometimes grown as ornamentals

¹**ti·ti** \'tī-,tī\ *noun* [origin unknown] (1827)
1 : a tree (*Cliftonia monophylla* of the family Cyrillaceae) of the southeastern U.S. with leathery leaves and racemes of fragrant white flowers
2 : LEATHERWOOD 2

²**ti·ti** \ti-'tē\ *noun* [American Spanish *tití*] (1832)
: any of a genus (*Callicebus*) of small South American monkeys having long thick variably colored fur and a tail that is not prehensile

ti·tian \'ti-shən\ *adjective, often capitalized* [*Titian* (Tiziano Vecellio)] (1896)
: of a brownish orange color

tit·il·late \'ti-t°l-,āt\ *verb* **-lat·ed; -lat·ing** [Latin *titillatus,* past participle of *titillare*] (1620)
transitive verb
1 : to excite pleasurably : arouse by stimulation
2 : TICKLE

titi

intransitive verb
: to act as a stimulant to pleasurable excitement
— **tit·il·la·tion** \,ti-t°l-'ā-shən\ *noun*
— **tit·il·la·tive** \'ti-t°l-,ā-tiv\ *adjective*

tit·il·lat·ing \'ti-t°l-,ā-tiŋ\ *adjective* (circa 1714)
: pleasantly stimulating or exciting ⟨*titillating* reading⟩; *also* : EROTIC
— **tit·il·lat·ing·ly** \-tiŋ-lē\ *adverb*

tit·i·vate *or* **tit·ti·vate** \'ti-tə-,vāt\ *verb* **-vat·ed; -vat·ing** [perhaps from ¹*tidy* + reno*vate*] (1824)
transitive verb
: to make smart or spruce
intransitive verb
: SMARTEN, SPRUCE
— **tit·i·va·tion** \,ti-tə-'vā-shən\ *noun*

tit·lark \'tit-,lärk\ *noun* [*tit-* (as in *titmouse*) + *lark*] (1688)
: PIPIT

¹**ti·tle** \'tī-t°l\ *noun* [Middle English, from Middle French, from Latin *titulus* inscription, title] (14th century)
1 a *obsolete* : INSCRIPTION **b** : written material introduced into a motion picture or television program to give credits, explain an action, or represent dialogue — usually used in plural
2 a : all the elements constituting legal ownership **b** : a legally just cause of exclusive possession **c** : the instrument (as a deed) that is evidence of a right
3 a : something that justifies or substantiates a claim **b** : an alleged or recognized right
4 a : a descriptive or general heading (as of a chapter in a book) **b** : the heading which names an act or statute **c** : the heading of a legal action or proceeding
5 a : the distinguishing name of a written, printed, or filmed production **b** : a similar distinguishing name of a musical composition or a work of art
6 : a descriptive name : APPELLATION
7 : a division of an instrument, book, or bill; *especially* : one larger than a section or article
8 a : an appellation of dignity, honor, distinction, or preeminence attached to a person or family by virtue of rank, office, precedent, privilege, attainment, or lands **b** : a person holding a title especially of nobility
9 : a written work as distinguished from a particular copy ⟨published 25 *titles* last year⟩
10 : CHAMPIONSHIP 1 ⟨won the batting *title*⟩

²**title** *transitive verb* **ti·tled; ti·tling** \'tīt-liŋ, 'tī-t°l-iŋ\ (14th century)
1 : to provide a title for
2 : to designate or call by a title : TERM, STYLE

³**title** *adjective* (1886)
: of or relating to a title: as **a** : having the same name as the title of a production ⟨did the *title* role in *Hamlet*⟩ **b** : having the same title as or providing the title for the collection or production of which it forms a part ⟨the *title* song⟩ **c** : of, relating to, or involving a championship ⟨a *title* match⟩ **d** : of, relating to, or used with the titles that introduce a motion picture or television program ⟨*title* music⟩

ti·tled \'tī-t°ld\ *adjective* (1593)
: having a title especially of nobility

title deed *noun* (circa 1768)
: the deed constituting the evidence of a person's legal ownership

ti·tle·hold·er \'tī-t°l-,hōl-dər\ *noun* (1904)
: one that holds a title; *specifically* : CHAMPION

title page *noun* (1594)
: a page of a book bearing the title and usually the names of the author and publisher and the place and sometimes date of publication

ti·tlist \'tī-t°l-ist, 'tīt-list\ *noun* (1924)
: TITLEHOLDER

tit·mouse \'tit-,maủs\ *noun, plural* **tit·mice** \-,mīs\ [by folk etymology from Middle English *titmose,* from (assumed) Middle English *tit* any small object or creature + Middle English *mose* titmouse, from Old English *māse;*

akin to Old High German *meisa* titmouse] (14th century)
: any of numerous small widely distributed insectivorous oscine birds (family Paridae and especially genus *Parus*) that are related to the chickadees and have small bills and relatively long tails

Ti·to·ism \'tē-(,)tō-,i-zəm\ *noun* (1949)
: the political, economic, and social policies associated with Tito; *specifically* : nationalistic policies and practices followed by a communist state or group independently of and often in opposition to the U.S.S.R.
— **Ti·to·ist** \-,ō-ist\ *noun or adjective*

ti·trant \'tī-trənt\ *noun* (1939)
: a substance (as a reagent solution of precisely known concentration) that is added in titration

ti·trate \'tī-,trāt\ *verb* **ti·trat·ed; ti·trat·ing** [*titer*] (circa 1859)
transitive verb
: to subject to titration
intransitive verb
: to perform titration
— **ti·trat·able** \-,trā-tə-bəl\ *adjective*
— **ti·tra·tor** \-,trā-tər\ *noun*

ti·tra·tion \tī-'trā-shən\ *noun* (circa 1859)
: a method or the process of determining the concentration of a dissolved substance in terms of the smallest amount of a reagent of known concentration required to bring about a given effect in reaction with a known volume of the test solution

ti·tre \'tī-tər\ *variant of* TITER

ti·tri·met·ric \,tī-trə-'me-trik\ *adjective* [*titration* + *-i-* + *-metric*] (1902)
: employing or determined by titration

tit–tat–toe \,ti-,ta(t)-'tō\ *variant of* TICKTACK-TOE

tit·ter \'ti-tər\ *intransitive verb* [imitative] (circa 1619)
: to laugh in a nervous, affected, or partly suppressed manner : GIGGLE, SNICKER
— **titter** *noun*

tit·tie \'ti-tē\ *noun* [probably baby talk alteration of *sister*] (circa 1700)
chiefly Scottish : SISTER

tit·tle \'ti-t°l\ *noun* [Middle English *titel,* from Medieval Latin *titulus,* from Latin, title] (14th century)
1 : a point or small sign used as a diacritical mark in writing or printing
2 : a very small part

tit·tle–tat·tle \'ti-t°l-,ta-t°l\ *noun* [reduplication of ¹*tattle*] (circa 1529)
: GOSSIP, PRATTLE
— **tittle–tattle** *intransitive verb*

¹**tit·tup** \'ti-təp\ *noun* [imitative of the sound of a horse's hooves] (1703)
: lively, gay, or restless behavior

²**tittup** *intransitive verb* **-tupped** *or* **-tuped; -tup·ping** *or* **-tup·ing** (1785)
: to move in a lively manner often with an exaggerated or affected action

¹**tit·u·lar** \'ti-chə-lər, 'tich-lər\ *adjective* [Latin *titulus* title] (1611)
1 a : existing in title only; *especially* : bearing a title derived from a defunct ecclesiastical jurisdiction (as an episcopal see) ⟨a *titular* bishop⟩ **b** : having the title and usually the honors belonging to an office or dignity without the duties, functions, or responsibilities ⟨the *titular* head of a political party⟩
2 : bearing a title : TITLED
3 : of, relating to, or constituting a title ⟨the *titular* hero of the play⟩
— **tit·u·lar·ly** *adverb*

²**titular** *noun* (1613)
: a person holding a title

Ti·tus \'tī-təs\ *noun* [Late Latin, from Greek *Titos*]
1 : an early Christian convert who assisted Paul in his missionary work

2 : a letter written on the subject of pastoral care in the early Church and included as a book in the New Testament — see BIBLE table

Tiu \'tē-(,)ü\ *noun* [Old English *Tīw* — more at DEITY]
: an ancient Germanic god of war identified with Tyr

tiz·zy \'ti-zē\ *noun, plural* **tizzies** [origin unknown] (1935)
: a highly excited and distracted state of mind

TKO \,tē-,kā-'ō\ *noun* [technical *k*nockout] (1941)
: TECHNICAL KNOCKOUT

Tlin·git \'tliŋ-kət, -gət *also* 'kliŋ-\ *noun, plural* **Tlingit** *or* **Tlingits** (1865)
1 : a member of a group of American Indian peoples of the islands and coast of southern Alaska
2 : the language of the Tlingit peoples
— **Tlingit** *adjective*

T lymphocyte *noun* [*t*hymus-derived] (1972)
: T CELL

T–man \'tē-,man\ *noun* [*T*reasury *man*] (1937)
: a special agent of the U.S. Treasury Department

tme·sis \(tə-)'mē-səs\ *noun* [Late Latin, from Greek *tmēsis* act of cutting, from *temnein* to cut — more at TOME] (1550)
: separation of parts of a compound word by the intervention of one or more words (as *what place soever* for *whatsoever place*)

TNT \,tē-(,)en-'tē\ *noun* [*tr*i*n*i*t*rotoluene] (1915)
: a flammable toxic compound $C_7H_5N_3O_6$ used as a high explosive and in chemical synthesis

¹**to** \tə, tü, 'tü\ *preposition* [Middle English, from Old English *tō*; akin to Old High German *zuo* to, Latin *donec* as long as, until] (before 12th century)
1 a — used as a function word to indicate movement or an action or condition suggestive of movement toward a place, person, or thing reached ⟨drove *to* the city⟩ ⟨went back *to* the original idea⟩ **b** — used as a function word to indicate direction ⟨a mile *to* the south⟩ ⟨turned his back *to* the door⟩ ⟨a tendency *to* silliness⟩ **c** — used as a function word to indicate contact or proximity ⟨applied polish *to* the table⟩ ⟨put her hand *to* her heart⟩ **d** (1) — used as a function word to indicate the place or point that is the far limit ⟨100 miles *to* the nearest town⟩ (2) — used as a function word to indicate the limit of extent ⟨stripped *to* the waist⟩ **e** — used as a function word to indicate relative position ⟨perpendicular *to* the floor⟩
2 a — used as a function word to indicate purpose, intention, tendency, result, or end ⟨came *to* our aid⟩ ⟨drink *to* his health⟩ **b** — used as a function word to indicate the result of an action or a process ⟨broken all *to* pieces⟩ ⟨go *to* seed⟩ ⟨*to* their surprise, the train left on time⟩
3 — used as a function word to indicate position or relation in time: as **a** : BEFORE ⟨five minutes *to* five⟩ **b** : TILL ⟨from eight *to* five⟩ ⟨up *to* now⟩
4 — used as a function word to indicate addition, attachment, connection, belonging, possession, accompaniment, or response ⟨the key *to* the door⟩ ⟨danced *to* live music⟩ ⟨comes *to* her call⟩
5 — used as a function word (1) to indicate the extent or degree (as of completeness or accuracy) ⟨loyal *to* a man⟩ ⟨generous *to* a fault⟩ or the extent and result (as of an action or a condition) ⟨beaten *to* death⟩ (2) to indicate the last or an intermediate point of a series ⟨moderate *to* cool temperatures⟩
6 a — used as a function word (1) to indicate a relation to one that serves as a standard ⟨inferior *to* her earlier works⟩ (2) to indicate similarity, correspondence, dissimilarity, or proportion ⟨compared him *to* a god⟩ **b** — used as a function word to indicate agreement or conformity ⟨add salt *to* taste⟩ ⟨*to* my knowledge⟩

c — used as a function word to indicate a proportion in terms of numbers or quantities ⟨400 *to* the box⟩ ⟨odds of ten *to* one⟩
7 a — used as a function word (1) to indicate the application of an adjective or a noun ⟨agreeable *to* everyone⟩ ⟨attitude *to* friends⟩ ⟨title *to* the property⟩ (2) to indicate the relation of a verb to its complement or to a complementary element ⟨refers us *to* the traditions⟩ (3) to indicate the receiver of an action or the one for which something is done or exists ⟨spoke *to* his mother⟩ ⟨gives a dollar *to* the man⟩ and often used with a reflexive pronoun to indicate exclusiveness (as of possession) or separateness ⟨had the house *to* themselves⟩ ⟨thought *to* herself⟩ **b** — used as a function word to indicate agency ⟨falls *to* his opponent's blows⟩
8 — used as a function word to indicate that the following verb is an infinitive ⟨wants *to* go⟩ and often used by itself at the end of a clause in place of an infinitive suggested by the preceding context ⟨knows more than she seems *to*⟩

²**to** \'tü\ *adverb* (before 12th century)
1 a — used as a function word to indicate direction toward ⟨feathers wrong end *to*⟩ ⟨run *to* and fro⟩ **b** : close to the wind ⟨the gale having gone over, we came *to* —R. H. Dana⟩
2 a : into contact especially with the frame — used of a door or a window ⟨the door snapped *to*⟩ **b** — used as a function word to indicate physical application or attachment ⟨he . . . hath set *to* his seal —John 3:33 (Authorized Version)⟩
3 — used as a function word to indicate application or attention ⟨will stand *to* —Shakespeare⟩
4 : to a state of consciousness or awareness ⟨brings her *to* with smelling salts⟩
5 : at hand : BY ⟨get *to* see 'em close *to* —Richard Llewellyn⟩

toad \'tōd\ *noun* [Middle English *tode*, from Old English *tāde*, *tādige*] (before 12th century)
1 : any of numerous anuran amphibians (especially family Bufonidae) that as compared with the related frogs are generally more terrestrial in habit though returning to water to lay their eggs, squatter and shorter in build and with weaker hind limbs, and rough, dry, and warty rather than smooth and moist of skin
2 : a contemptible person or thing

toad 1

toad·eat·er \-,ē-tər\ *noun* (circa 1572)
archaic : TOADY

toad·fish \-,fish\ *noun* (1704)
: any of a family (Batrachoididae) of chiefly marine bony fishes with jugular pelvic fins, a large thick head, a wide mouth, and usually scaleless slimy skin

toad·flax \-,flaks\ *noun* (1578)
: BUTTER-AND-EGGS; *also* : any of several related plants (especially genus *Linaria*) of the snapdragon family

toad·stone \-,stōn\ *noun* (1558)
: a stone or similar object held to have formed in the head or body of a toad and formerly often worn as a charm or antidote to poison

toad·stool \-,stül\ *noun* (14th century)
: a fungus having an umbrella-shaped pileus : MUSHROOM; *especially* : a poisonous or inedible one as distinguished from an edible mushroom

¹**toady** \'tō-dē\ *noun, plural* **toad·ies** [by shortening & alteration from *toadeater*] (1826)
: one who flatters in the hope of gaining favors : SYCOPHANT
synonym see PARASITE

²**toady** *intransitive verb* **toad·ied; toady·ing** (circa 1859)
: to behave as a toady : engage in sycophancy
synonym see FAWN
— **toady·ism** \-ē-,i-zəm\ *noun*

¹**to–and–fro** \,tü-ən-'frō\ *adjective* (1749)
: forward and backward ⟨*to-and-fro* motion⟩

²**to–and–fro** *noun* (1847)
: activity involving alternating movement in opposite directions ⟨the busy *to-and-fro* of the holiday shoppers⟩

to and fro *adverb* (14th century)
: from one place to another

¹**toast** \'tōst\ *verb* [Middle English *tosten*, from Middle French *toster*, from Late Latin *tostare* to roast, from Latin *tostus*, past participle of *torrēre* to dry, parch — more at THIRST] (14th century)
transitive verb
1 : to warm thoroughly
2 : to make (as bread) crisp, hot, and brown by heat
intransitive verb
: to become toasted; *especially* : to warm thoroughly

²**toast** *noun* (15th century)
1 a : sliced bread browned on both sides by heat **b** : food prepared with toasted bread
2 [from the use of pieces of spiced toast to flavor drinks] **a** : someone or something in honor of which persons usually drink **b** : one that is highly admired ⟨she's the *toast* of society⟩
3 [³*toast*] : an act of proposing or of drinking in honor of a toast
4 : a rhyming narrative poem existing in oral tradition among black Americans

³**toast** *transitive verb* (1640)
: to propose or drink to as a toast

toast·er \'tō-stər\ *noun* (1582)
: one that toasts; *especially* : an electrical appliance for toasting

toaster oven *noun* (1961)
: a portable electrical appliance that can function as an oven or a toaster

toast·mas·ter \'tōs(t)-,mas-tər\ *noun* (1749)
: one who presides at a banquet and introduces the after-dinner speakers

toast·mis·tress \-,mis-trəs\ *noun* (1921)
: a woman who acts as toastmaster

toasty \'tō-stē\ *adjective* **toast·i·er; -est** (1953)
: pleasantly or comfortably warm ⟨felt snug and *toasty* by the fire⟩

to·bac·co \tə-'ba-(,)kō\ *noun, plural* **-cos** [Spanish *tabaco*, probably from Taino, roll of tobacco leaves] (circa 1565)
1 : any of a genus (*Nicotiana*) of chiefly American plants of the nightshade family with viscid foliage and tubular flowers; *especially* : a tall erect annual tropical American herb (*N. tabacum*) cultivated for its leaves
2 : the leaves of cultivated tobacco prepared for use in smoking or chewing or as snuff
3 : manufactured products of tobacco (as cigars or cigarettes); *also* : smoking as a practice ⟨has sworn off *tobacco*⟩

tobacco 1

tobacco budworm *noun* (1918)
: a noctuid moth (*Heliothis virescens* synonym *Helicoverpa virescens*) whose small rusty often green-striped caterpillar feeds on buds and young leaves especially of tobacco and cotton

tobacco hornworm *noun* (circa 1909)
: a hawkmoth (*Manduca sexta*) whose large usually green larva is a hornworm that feeds on plants of the nightshade family

tobacco juice *noun* (1833)
: saliva colored brown by tobacco or snuff
tobacco mosaic *noun* (1914)
: any of a complex of virus diseases of plants of the nightshade family and especially of tobacco
to·bac·co·nist \tə-'ba-kə-nist\ *noun* [irregular from *tobacco* + *-ist*] (1657)
: a dealer in tobacco especially at retail
tobacco road *noun, often T&R capitalized* [from *Tobacco Road,* novel (1932) by Erskine Caldwell and play (1933) by Jack Kirkland (died 1969) American playwright] (1937)
: a squalid poverty-stricken rural area or community
to–be \tə-'bē\ *adjective* (circa 1600)
: that is to be : FUTURE — usually used postpositively and often in combination ⟨a bride-to-be⟩
To·bi·as \tə-'bī-əs\ *noun* [Greek *Tobias*]
1 : a Jewish hero who with divine aid marries his kinswoman Sarah in spite of a jealous evil spirit and restores his father Tobit's sight
2 : TOBIT 2
To·bit \'tō-bət\ *noun* [Greek *Tōbit*]
1 : the elderly father of Tobias
2 : a book of Scripture included in the Roman Catholic canon of the Old Testament and in the Protestant Apocrypha — see BIBLE table
¹**to·bog·gan** \tə-'bä-gən\ *noun* [Canadian French *tobogan,* of Algonquian origin; akin to Micmac *tobâgun* drag made of skin] (circa 1820)
1 : a long flat-bottomed light sled made usually of thin boards curved up at one end with usually low handrails at the sides

toboggan 1

2 : a downward course or a sharp decline
²**toboggan** *intransitive verb* (1846)
1 : to coast on or as if on a toboggan
2 : to decline suddenly and sharply
— **to·bog·gan·er** *noun*
— **to·bog·gan·ist** \-gə-nist\ *noun*
to·bog·gan·ing *noun* (1849)
: the act, art, or sport of riding a toboggan
to·by jug \'tō-bē-\ *noun, often capitalized* [*Toby,* nickname from the name *Tobias*] (1840)
: a small jug, pitcher, or mug shaped somewhat like a stout man with a cocked hat for the brim — called also *toby*
toc·ca·ta \tə-'kä-tə\ *noun* [Italian, from *toccare* to touch, from (assumed) Vulgar Latin — more at TOUCH] (circa 1724)
: a musical composition usually for organ or harpsichord in a free style and characterized by full chords, rapid runs, and high harmonies
To·char·i·an \tō-'kar-ē-ən, -'ker-, -'kär-\ *noun* [Greek *Tocharoi*] (circa 1926)
1 a : a language of central Asia known from documents from the sixth to eighth centuries A.D. **b** : a branch of the Indo-European language family containing Tocharian — see INDO-EUROPEAN LANGUAGES table
2 : a member of a people of presumably European origin dwelling in central Asia during the first millennium of the Christian era
Tocharian A *noun* (1926)
: the eastern dialect of Tocharian — see INDO-EUROPEAN LANGUAGES table
Tocharian B *noun* (1926)
: the western dialect of Tocharian — see INDO-EUROPEAN LANGUAGES table
toch·er \'tä-kər\ *noun* [Middle English (Scots) *tochir,* from Scottish Gaelic *tochar*] (15th century)
chiefly Scottish : DOWRY 2, 3
to·coph·er·ol \tō-'kä-fə-,rȯl, -,rōl\ *noun* [International Scientific Vocabulary, ultimately from Greek *tokos* childbirth, offspring (akin to Greek *tiktein* to beget) + *pherein* to carry, bear — more at THANE, BEAR] (1936)

: any of several fat-soluble oily phenolic compounds with varying degrees of antioxidant vitamin E activity; *especially* : one $C_{29}H_{50}O_2$ of high vitamin E potency obtained from germ oils or by synthesis
toc·sin \'täk-sən\ *noun* [Middle French *toquassen,* from Old Provençal *tocasenh,* from *tocar* to touch, ring a bell (from assumed Vulgar Latin *toccare*) + *senh* sign, bell, from Medieval Latin & Latin *signum;* Medieval Latin, bell, from Late Latin, ringing of a bell, from Latin, mark, sign — more at TOUCH, SIGN] (1586)
1 : an alarm bell or the ringing of it
2 : a warning signal
¹**tod** \'täd\ *noun* [Middle English] (12th century)
chiefly Scottish : FOX
²**tod** *noun* [Middle English *todd, todde;* probably akin to Old High German *zotta* tuft of hair] (15th century)
1 *archaic* : any of various units of weight for wool; *especially* : one equal to 28 pounds (13 kilograms)
2 *British* : a bushy clump (as of ivy)
¹**to·day** \tə-'dā\ *adverb* (before 12th century)
1 : on or for this day
2 : at the present time
²**today** *noun* (1535)
: the present day, time, or age ⟨*today's* youth⟩
³**today** *adjective* (1966)
: of or characteristic of today : NOW
tod·dle \'tä-d°l\ *intransitive verb* **tod·dled; tod·dling** \'täd-liŋ, 'tä-d°l-iŋ\ [origin unknown] (circa 1600)
1 : to walk with short tottering steps in the manner of a young child
2 : to take a stroll : SAUNTER
— **toddle** *noun*
tod·dler \'täd-lər, 'tä-d°l-ər\ *noun* (1793)
: one that toddles; *especially* : a young child
— **tod·dler·hood** \-,hu̇d\ *noun*
tod·dy \'tä-dē\ *noun, plural* **toddies** [Hindi *tāṛī* juice of the palmyra palm, from *tāṛ* palmyra palm, from Sanskrit *tāla*] (circa 1610)
1 : the fresh or fermented sap of various chiefly East Indian palms
2 : a usually hot drink consisting of liquor (as rum), water, sugar, and spices
to–do \tə-'dü\ *noun, plural* **to–dos** \-'düz\ (circa 1576)
: BUSTLE, STIR, FUSS
¹**toe** \'tō\ *noun* [Middle English *to,* from Old English *tā;* akin to Old High German *zēha* toe] (before 12th century)
1 a (1) : one of the terminal members of a vertebrate's foot (2) : the fore end of a foot or hoof **b** : a terminal segment of a limb of an invertebrate **c** : the forepart of something worn on the foot ⟨the *toe* of a boot⟩
2 : a part that by its position or form is felt to resemble a toe ⟨the *toe* of Italy⟩: as **a** : a lateral projection at one end or between the ends of a piece (as a rod or bolt) **b** : the lowest part (as of an embankment, dam, or cliff)
3 : TOE DANCE
— **toe·less** \-ləs\ *adjective*
— **on one's toes** : ALERT 1
— **toe to toe** : facing one another
²**toe** *verb* **toed; toe·ing** (1607)
transitive verb
1 : to furnish with a toe ⟨*toe* a sock⟩
2 : to touch, reach, or drive with the toe ⟨*toe* a football⟩
3 : to drive (as a nail) obliquely; *also* : to clinch or fasten by or with nails or rods so driven
intransitive verb
1 : TIPTOE
2 : to stand, walk, or be placed so that the toes assume an indicated position or direction ⟨*toe* in⟩
— **toe the line** *or* **toe the mark** : to conform rigorously to a rule or standard

toea \'tȯi-ə\ *noun, plural* **toea** [Hiri Motu (pidgin of Papua New Guinea based on Motu, an Austronesian language), a kind of shell] (1975)
— see *kina* at MONEY table
toe cap *noun* (1797)
: a piece of leather covering the toe of a shoe and reinforcing or decorating it
toed \'tōd\ *adjective* [¹*toe*] (1611)
1 : having a toe or toes especially of a specified kind or number — usually used in combination ⟨five-*toed*⟩ ⟨round-*toed* shoes⟩
2 [from past participle of ²*toe*] : driven obliquely ⟨a *toed* nail⟩; *also* : secured by diagonal or oblique nailing
toe dance *noun* (1898)
: a dance executed on the tips of the toes by means of a ballet slipper with a reinforced toe
— **toe–dance** *intransitive verb*
— **toe dancer** *noun*
— **toe dancing** *noun*
toe·hold \'tō-,hōld\ *noun* (1880)
1 a : a hold or place of support for the toes (as in climbing) **b** (1) : a means of progressing (as in surmounting barriers) (2) : a slight footing ⟨used his money to get a *toehold,* then a foothold, then a near stranglehold on the political economy —R. W. Armstrong⟩
2 : a wrestling hold in which the aggressor bends or twists his opponent's foot
toe–in \'tō-,in\ *noun* (1928)
1 : CAMBER 3
2 : adjustment of the front wheels of an automotive vehicle so that they are closer together at the front than at the back
¹**toe·nail** \'tō-,nāl, -'nā(ə)l\ *noun* (1841)
: a nail of a toe
²**toenail** *transitive verb* (1900)
: to fasten by toed nails : TOE
toe–piece \'tō-,pēs\ *noun* (1879)
: a piece designed to form a toe (as of a shoe) or cover the toes of the foot
toe–plate \-,plāt\ *noun* (1894)
: a tab attached to the toe of a shoe (as to prevent wear due to heavy use)
toe–to–toe *adjective or adverb* (circa 1942)
: slugging it out at or as if at close range ⟨a *toe-to-toe* confrontation over the new policy⟩
toff \'täf\ *noun* [probably alteration of *tuft* titled college student] (1851)
chiefly British : DANDY, SWELL
tof·fee *or* **tof·fy** \'tȯ-fē, 'tä-\ *noun, plural* **toffees** *or* **toffies** [alteration of *taffy*] (circa 1825)
: candy of brittle but tender texture made by boiling sugar and butter together
tof·fee–nosed \-,nōzd\ *adjective* (circa 1925)
chiefly British : STUCK-UP
toft \'tȯft, 'täft\ *noun* [Middle English, from Old English, from Old Norse *topt;* probably akin to Greek *dapedon* floor, *demein* to build, *pedon* ground — more at TIMBER, PED] (before 12th century)
British : a site for a dwelling and its outbuildings; *also* : an entire holding comprising a homestead and additional land
to·fu \'tō-(,)fü\ *noun* [Japanese *tōfu*] (1771)
: BEAN CURD
tog \'täg, 'tȯg\ *transitive verb* **togged; tog·ging** [*togs*] (circa 1785)
: to dress especially in fine clothing — usually used with *up* or *out*
to·ga \'tō-gə\ *noun* [Latin; akin to Latin *tegere* to cover — more at THATCH] (1600)
: the loose outer garment worn in public by citizens of ancient Rome; *also* : a similar loose wrap or a professional, official, or academic gown

toga

— **to·gaed** \-gəd\ *adjective*

to·ga vi·ri·lis \ˌtō-gə-və-ˈrē-ləs, -ˈri-\ *noun,* plural **to·gae vi·ri·les** \ˈtō-ˌgī-və-ˈrē-ˌlās, -ˈri-\ [Latin, men's toga] (1600)
: the white toga of manhood assumed by boys of ancient Rome at age 15

¹**to·geth·er** \tə-ˈge-thər\ *adverb* [Middle English *togedere,* from Old English *togædere,* from *tō* to + *gædere* together; akin to Middle High German *gater* together, Old English *ga·derian* to gather] (before 12th century)
1 a : in or into one place, mass, collection, or group ⟨the men get *together* every Thursday for poker⟩ **b :** in a body : as a group ⟨students and faculty *together* presented the petition⟩
2 a : in or into contact ⟨as connection, collision, or union⟩ ⟨mix these ingredients *together*⟩ **b :** in or into association or relationship ⟨colors that go well *together*⟩ ⟨went to school *together*⟩
3 a : at one time : SIMULTANEOUSLY ⟨events that happened *together*⟩ **b :** in succession : without intermission ⟨was depressed for days *together*⟩
4 a : by combined action : JOINTLY ⟨*together* we forced the door⟩ **b :** in or into agreement or harmony ⟨the soloist and the orchestra weren't quite *together*⟩ **c :** in or into a unified or coherent structure or an integrated whole ⟨can't even put a simple sentence *together*⟩ ⟨pull yourself *together*⟩
5 a : with each other — used as an intensive after certain verbs ⟨join *together*⟩ ⟨add *together*⟩ **b :** as a unit : in the aggregate ⟨these arguments taken *together* make a convincing case⟩ **c :** considered as a whole : counted or summed up ⟨all *together,* there were 21 entries⟩
— **to·geth·er·ness** *noun*
— **together with :** in addition to : in association with

²**together** *adjective* (1963)
1 : appropriately prepared, organized, or balanced
2 : composed in mind or manner : SELF-POSSESSED ⟨a warm, sensitive, reasonably *together* girl —*East Village Other*⟩

Tog·gen·burg \ˈtä-gən-ˌbərg\ *noun* [*Toggenburg,* district in northeastern Switzerland] (1886)
: any of a breed of brown hornless dairy goats of Swiss origin with white stripes on the face

tog·gery \ˈtä-g(ə-)rē, ˈtȯ-\ *noun* [*togs*] (circa 1811)
: CLOTHING

¹**tog·gle** \ˈtä-gəl\ *noun* [origin unknown] (circa 1775)
1 : a piece or device for holding or securing: as **a :** a pin inserted in a nautical knot to make it more secure or easier to slip **b :** a crosspiece attached to the end of or to a loop in something ⟨as a chain, rope, line, strap, or belt⟩ usually to prevent slipping, to serve in twisting or tightening, or to hold something attached
2 : a device consisting of two bars jointed together end to end but not in line so that when a force is applied to the joint tending to straighten it pressure will be exerted on the parts adjacent or fixed to the outer ends of the bars; *also* : a device with a joint using a toggle

²**toggle** *transitive verb* **tog·gled; tog·gling** \-g(ə-)liŋ\ (1836)
1 : to fasten with or as if with a toggle
2 : to furnish with a toggle

toggle bolt *noun* (1906)
: a bolt that has a nut with wings which close for passage through a small hole and spring open after passing through the hole to keep the bolt from slipping back through

toggle switch *noun* (circa 1924)
: an electric switch operated by pushing a projecting lever through a small arc

togs \ˈtägz, ˈtȯgz\ *noun plural* [plural of English slang *tog* coat, short for obsolete English cant *togeman, togman*] (1779)
: CLOTHING; *especially* : a set of clothes and accessories for a specified use ⟨riding *togs*⟩

togue \ˈtōg\ *noun* [Canadian French] (1839)
: LAKE TROUT

¹**toil** \ˈtȯi(ə)l\ *noun* [Middle English *toile,* from Anglo-French *toyl,* from Old French *toeil* battle, confusion, from *toeillier*] (14th century)
1 *archaic* **a :** STRUGGLE, BATTLE **b :** laborious effort
2 : long strenuous fatiguing labor
synonym see WORK
— **toil·ful** \-fəl\ *adjective*
— **toil·ful·ly** \-fə-lē\ *adverb*

²**toil** *verb* [Middle English, to argue, struggle, from Anglo-French *toiller,* from Old French *toeillier* to stir, disturb, dispute, from Latin *tudiculare* to crush, grind, from *tudicula* machine for crushing olives, from *tudes* hammer; akin to Latin *tundere* to beat — more at CONTUSION] (14th century)
intransitive verb
1 : to work hard and long : LABOR
2 : to proceed with laborious effort : PLOD ⟨*toiling* wearily up the hill⟩
transitive verb
1 *archaic* : OVERWORK
2 *archaic* : to get or accomplish with great effort
— **toil·er** \ˈtȯi-lər\ *noun*

³**toil** *noun* [Middle French *toile* cloth, net, from Latin *tela* cloth on a loom — more at SUBTLE] (circa 1529)
1 : a net to trap game
2 : something by which one is held fast or inextricably involved : SNARE, TRAP — usually used in plural ⟨caught in the *toils* of the law⟩

toile \ˈtwäl\ *noun* [French, cloth, linen, from Middle French] (1794)
1 : any of many plain or simple twill weave fabrics; *especially* : LINEN
2 : a mock-up model of a garment

toile de Jouy \ˌtwäl-də-ˈzhwē\ *noun* [French, literally, cloth of Jouy, from *Jouy-en-Josas,* France] (circa 1920)
: an 18th century French scenic pattern usually printed on cotton, linen, or silk in one color on a light ground; *broadly* : a similar printed fabric

¹**toi·let** \ˈtȯi-lət\ *noun* [Middle French *toilette* cloth put over the shoulders while dressing the hair or shaving, diminutive of *toile* cloth] (circa 1695)
1 *archaic* : DRESSING TABLE
2 : the act or process of dressing and grooming oneself
3 a (1) : BATHROOM, LAVATORY 2 (2) : PRIVY **b :** a fixture that consists usually of a water-flushed bowl and seat and is used for defecation and urination
4 : cleansing in preparation for or in association with a medical or surgical procedure ⟨a pharyngeal *toilet*⟩ ◇

²**toilet** (1840)
intransitive verb
1 : to dress and groom oneself
2 : to use the toilet — usually used of a child
transitive verb
1 : DRESS, GARB
2 : to help ⟨as a child or sick person⟩ use the toilet

toilet paper *noun* (1884)
: a thin sanitary absorbent paper for bathroom use chiefly after defecation and urination

toilet powder *noun* (1840)
: a fine powder usually with soothing or antiseptic ingredients for sprinkling or rubbing ⟨as after bathing⟩ over the skin

toi·let·ry \ˈtȯi-lə-trē\ *noun, plural* **-ries** (1892)
: an article or preparation ⟨as toothpaste, shaving cream, or cologne⟩ used in making one's toilet — usually used in plural

toilet soap *noun* (1839)
: a mild soap that is often perfumed and colored and stabilized with preservatives

toi·lette \twä-ˈlet\ *noun* [French, from Middle French] (1681)
1 : TOILET 2

2 a : formal or fashionable attire or style of dressing **b :** a particular costume or outfit
word history see TOILET

toilet training *noun* (1940)
: the process of training a child to control bladder and bowel movements and to use the toilet
— **toilet train** *transitive verb*

toilet water *noun* (1855)
: a perfumed liquid containing a high percentage of alcohol for use in or after a bath or as a skin freshener

toil·some \-səm\ *adjective* (1581)
: marked by or full of toil or fatigue : LABORIOUS
— **toil·some·ly** *adverb*
— **toil·some·ness** *noun*

toil·worn \-ˌwȯrn, -ˌwȯrn\ *adjective* (1751)
: showing the effects of or worn out with toil ⟨*toilworn* hands⟩

to-ing and fro-ing \ˈtü-iŋ-ən(d)-ˈfrō-iŋ\ *noun, plural* **to-ings and fro-ings** [*to and fro*] (1847)
: a passing back and forth

to·ka·mak *also* **to·ko·mak** \ˈtō-kə-ˌmak, ˈtä-\ *noun* [Russian, from *toroidal'naya kamera s aksial'nym magnitnym polem* ⟨toroidal chamber with an axial magnetic field⟩] (1965)
: a toroidal device for producing controlled nuclear fusion that involves the confining and heating of a gaseous plasma by means of an electric current and magnetic field

To·kay \tō-ˈkā\ *noun* (1710)
1 : a naturally sweet wine from the area around Tokaj, Hungary
2 : a blend of Angelica, port, and sherry made in California

toke \ˈtōk\ *noun* [American Spanish *toque,* from Spanish, touch, test, from *tocar* to touch, from Vulgar Latin *toccare* — more at TOUCH] (1968)
slang : a puff on a marijuana cigarette or pipe
— **toke** *intransitive verb, slang*

¹**to·ken** \ˈtō-kən\ *noun* [Middle English, from Old English *tācen, tācn* sign, token; akin to Old High German *zeihhan* sign, Greek *deiknynai* to show — more at DICTION] (before 12th century)
1 : an outward sign or expression ⟨his tears were *tokens* of his grief⟩

\ə\ **abut** \ᵊ\ **kitten** \ər\ **further** \a\ **ash** \ā\ **ace**
\ä\ **mop, mar** \au̇\ **out** \ch\ **chin** \e\ **bet** \ē\ **easy**
\g\ **go** \i\ **hit** \ī\ **ice** \j\ **job** \ŋ\ **sing** \ō\ **go**
\ȯ\ **law** \ȯi\ **boy** \th\ **thin** \t͟h\ **the** \ü\ **loot** \u̇\ **foot**
\y\ **yet** \zh\ **vision** *see also* Guide to Pronunciation

2 a : SYMBOL, EMBLEM ⟨a white flag is a *token* of surrender⟩ **b :** an instance of a linguistic expression
3 : a distinguishing feature **:** CHARACTERISTIC
4 a : SOUVENIR, KEEPSAKE **b :** a small part representing the whole **:** INDICATION ⟨this is only a *token* of what we hope to accomplish⟩ **c :** something given or shown as a guarantee (as of authority, right, or identity)
5 a : a piece resembling a coin issued as money by some person or body other than a de jure government **b :** a piece resembling a coin issued for use (as for fare on a bus) by a particular group on specified terms
6 : a member of a group (as a minority) that is included within a larger group through tokenism; *especially* **:** a token employee
synonym see SIGN
— by the same token : for the same reason

²**token** *adjective* (1547)
1 : done or given as a token especially in partial fulfillment of an obligation or engagement ⟨a *token* payment⟩
2 a : representing no more than a symbolic effort **:** MINIMAL, PERFUNCTORY ⟨*token* resistance⟩ ⟨*token* integration⟩ **b :** serving or intended to show absence of discrimination ⟨a *token* female employee⟩

to·ken·ism \'tō-kə-ˌni-zəm\ *noun* (1961)
: the policy or practice of making only a symbolic effort (as to desegregate)

token money *noun* (1889)
: money of regular government issue (as paper currency or coins) having a greater face value than intrinsic value

To·khar·i·an *variant of* TOCHARIAN

to·ko·no·ma \ˌtō-kə-'nō-mə\ *noun* [Japanese] (1871)
: a niche or alcove in the wall of a Japanese house for the display of a decorative object

Tok Pis·in \'tòk-'pi-zən, -sən\ *noun* [Tok Pisin, literally, pidgin talk] (1974)
: an English-based creole that is a national language of Papua New Guinea

tol- *or* **tolu-** *combining form* [International Scientific Vocabulary, from *toluene*]
: toluene ⟨*tolyl*⟩

to·la \'tō-lə, tō-'lä\ *noun* [Hindi *tolā*, from Sanskrit *tulā* weight; akin to Latin *tollere* to lift up] (1614)
: a unit of weight of India equal to 180 grains troy or 0.4114 ounce (11.7 grams)

tol·booth \'tō(l)-ˌbüth, 'täl-, 'tòl-\ *noun* [Middle English *tolbothe, tollbothe* tollbooth, town hall, jail] (15th century)
1 *Scottish* **:** a town or market hall
2 *Scottish* **:** JAIL, PRISON

tol·bu·ta·mide \täl-'byü-tə-ˌmīd\ *noun* [*tol-* + *butyric* + *amide*] (1956)
: a sulfonylurea $C_{12}H_{18}N_2O_3S$ used in the treatment of diabetes

told *past and past participle of* TELL

tole \'tōl\ *noun, often attributive* [French *tôle*, from Middle French dialect *taule*, from Latin *tabula* board, tablet] (1927)
: sheet metal and especially tinplate for use in domestic and ornamental wares in which it is usually japanned or painted and often elaborately decorated; *also* **:** objects made of tole

To·le·do \tə-'lē-(ˌ)dō\ *noun, plural* **-dos** (1596)
: a finely tempered sword of a kind made in Toledo, Spain

tol·er·a·ble \'tä-lə-rə-bəl, 'täl-rə-; 'tä-lər-bəl\ *adjective* (15th century)
1 : capable of being borne or endured ⟨*tolerable* pain⟩
2 : moderately good or agreeable **:** PASSABLE ⟨a *tolerable* singing voice⟩
— tol·er·a·bil·i·ty \ˌtä-lə-rə-'bi-lə-tē, ˌtäl-rə-\ *noun*
— tol·er·a·bly \'tä-lə-rə-blē, 'täl-rə-; 'tä-lər-blē\ *adverb*

tol·er·ance \'tä-lə-rən(t)s, 'täl-rən(t)s\ *noun* (15th century)

1 : capacity to endure pain or hardship **:** ENDURANCE, FORTITUDE, STAMINA
2 a : sympathy or indulgence for beliefs or practices differing from or conflicting with one's own **b :** the act of allowing something **:** TOLERATION
3 : the allowable deviation from a standard; *especially* **:** the range of variation permitted in maintaining a specified dimension in machining a piece
4 a (1) **:** the capacity of the body to endure or become less responsive to a substance (as a drug) or a physiological insult with repeated use or exposure ⟨immunological *tolerance* to a virus⟩ ⟨an addict's increasing *tolerance* for a drug⟩ (2) **:** relative capacity of an organism to grow or thrive when subjected to an unfavorable environmental factor **b :** the maximum amount of a pesticide residue that may lawfully remain on or in food

tol·er·ant \-rənt\ *adjective* (1784)
1 : inclined to tolerate; *especially* **:** marked by forbearance or endurance
2 : exhibiting tolerance (as for a drug or an environmental factor)
— tol·er·ant·ly *adverb*

tol·er·ate \'tä-lə-ˌrāt\ *transitive verb* **-at·ed; -at·ing** [Latin *toleratus,* past participle of *tolerare* to endure, put up with; akin to Old English *tholian* to bear, Latin *tollere* to lift up, *latus* carried (suppletive past participle of *ferre*), Greek *tlēnai* to bear] (1531)
1 : to exhibit physiological tolerance for (as a drug)
2 a : to suffer to be or to be done without prohibition, hindrance, or contradiction **b :** to put up with
synonym see BEAR
— tol·er·a·tive \-ˌrā-tiv\ *adjective*
— tol·er·a·tor \-ˌrā-tər\ *noun*

tol·er·a·tion \ˌtä-lə-'rā-shən\ *noun* (1531)
1 a : the act or practice of tolerating something **b :** a government policy of permitting forms of religious belief and worship not officially established
2 : TOLERANCE 4a(1)

tol·i·dine \'tä-lə-ˌdēn\ *noun* [International Scientific Vocabulary *tol-* + *-idine*] (1879)
: any of several isomeric aromatic diamines $C_{14}H_{16}N_2$ that are homologues of benzidine and used especially as dye intermediates

¹**toll** \'tōl\ *noun* [Middle English, from Old English, from (assumed) Vulgar Latin *tolonium,* alteration of Late Latin *telonium* customhouse, from Greek *tolōnion,* from *telōnēs* collector of tolls, from *telos* tax, toll; perhaps akin to Greek *tlēnai* to bear] (before 12th century)
1 : a tax or fee paid for some liberty or privilege (as of passing over a highway or bridge)
2 : compensation for services rendered: as **a :** a charge for transportation **b :** a charge for a long-distance telephone call
3 : a grievous or ruinous price ⟨inflation has taken its *toll*⟩; *especially* **:** cost in life or health ⟨the death *toll* from the hurricane⟩

²**toll** (14th century)
intransitive verb
: to take or levy toll
transitive verb
1 a : to exact part of as a toll **b :** to take as toll
2 : to exact a toll from (someone)

³**toll** *or* **tole** \'tōl\ *transitive verb* **tolled** *or* **toled; toll·ing** *or* **tol·ing** [Middle English *tollen, tolen;* akin to Old English for*tyllan* to seduce] (13th century)
1 : ALLURE, ENTICE
2 a : to entice (game) to approach **b :** to attract (fish) with scattered bait **c :** to lead or attract (domestic animals) to a desired point

⁴**toll** *verb* [Middle English, perhaps from *tollen* to entice] (15th century)
transitive verb
1 : to sound (a bell) by pulling the rope
2 a : to give signal or announcement of ⟨the clock *tolled* each hour⟩ **b :** to announce by tolling ⟨church bells *tolled* the death of the

bishop⟩ **c :** to call to or from a place or occasion ⟨bells *tolled* the congregation to church⟩
intransitive verb
: to sound with slow measured strokes ⟨the bell *tolls* solemnly⟩

⁵**toll** *noun* (15th century)
: the sound of a tolling bell

toll·booth \'tōl-ˌbüth\ *noun* [Middle English *tolbothe, tollbothe* tollbooth, town hall, jail, from *tol, toll* toll + *bothe* booth] (14th century)
: a booth (as on a highway or bridge) where tolls are paid

toll call *noun* (1928)
: a long-distance telephone call at charges above a local rate

toll·gate \'tōl-ˌgāt\ *noun* (1773)
: a point where the driver of a vehicle must pay a toll

toll·house \-ˌhaus\ *noun* (15th century)
: a house or booth where tolls are taken

Toll House *trademark*
— used for cookies containing chocolate morsels

toll·way \-ˌwā\ *noun* (1949)
: TURNPIKE 2a(1)

Tol·tec \'tōl-ˌtek, 'täl-\ *noun* [Spanish *tolteca,* from Nahuatl *tōltēcah,* plural of *tōltēcatl,* literally, person from *Tōllān* (now Tula de Allende, Mexico)] (1787)
: a member of a people that dominated central and southern Mexico prior to the Aztecs
— Tol·tec·an \-ən\ *adjective*

tol·u·ene \'täl-yə-ˌwēn\ *noun* [French *toluène,* from *tolu* balsam from the tropical American tree *Myroxylon balsamum,* from Spanish *tolú,* from Santiago de *Tolú,* Colombia] (1871)
: a liquid aromatic hydrocarbon C_7H_8 that resembles benzene but is less volatile, flammable, and toxic and is used as a solvent, in organic synthesis, and as an antiknock agent for gasoline

to·lu·i·dine \tə-'lü-ə-ˌdēn\ *noun* [International Scientific Vocabulary] (1850)
: any of three isomeric amino derivatives of toluene C_7H_9N that are analogous to aniline and are used as dye intermediates

toluidine blue (1898)
: a basic thiazine dye that is related to methylene blue and is used as a biological stain

tol·u·ol \'täl-yə-ˌwòl, -ˌwōl\ *noun* (circa 1848)
: toluene especially of commercial grade

tol·yl \'tä-ləl\ *noun* [International Scientific Vocabulary] (circa 1868)
: any of three univalent groups $CH_3C_6H_4$ derived from toluene

tom \'täm\ *noun* [*Tom,* nickname for *Thomas*] (1762)
1 : the male of various animals: as **a :** TOMCAT **b :** a male turkey
2 *capitalized* **:** UNCLE TOM 2

¹**tom·a·hawk** \'tä-mi-ˌhòk\ *noun* [Virginia Algonquian *tomahack*] (circa 1612)
: a light ax used as a missile and as a hand weapon especially by North American Indians

²**tomahawk** *transitive verb* (circa 1650)
: to cut, strike, or kill with a tomahawk

to·mal·ley \tə-'ma-lē; 'tä-mə-lē, -mə-lē\ *noun, plural* **-leys** [Carib *tumali* sauce of lobster livers] (circa 1666)
: the liver of the lobster

Tom and Jer·ry \ˌtäm-ən(d)-'jer-ē\ *noun* [Corinthian *Tom & Jerry* Hawthorne, characters in *Life in London* (1821) by Pierce Egan (died 1849) English sportswriter] (1845)
: a hot drink that is a combination of a toddy and an eggnog

to·ma·til·lo \ˌtō-mə-'tē-(ˌ)yō, -'tēl-(ˌ)yō\ *noun, plural* **-los** [Spanish, diminutive of *tomate*] (circa 1913)
: the small round pale green or yellow or purplish edible viscid fruit of a Mexican ground-cherry (*Physalis ixocarpa*); *also* **:** the plant

to·ma·to \tə-'mā-(ˌ)tō; *chiefly British, eastern New England, northeastern Virginia, and sometimes elsewhere in cultivated speech*

-'mȧ- *or* -'mä-; *chiefly Northern* -'ma-\ *noun*, *plural* **-toes** [alteration of earlier *tomate*, from Spanish, from Nahuatl *tomatl*] (1604)
1 : the usually large rounded typically red or yellow pulpy berry of a tomato
2 : any of a genus (*Lycopersicon*) of South American herbs of the nightshade family; *especially* **:** one (*L. lycopersicum* synonym *L. esculentum*) that is more or less perennial in its native habitat but is widely cultivated as an annual for its edible fruit □
to·ma·to·ey \-tə-wē\ *adjective* (1972)
1 : of, relating to, or characteristic of a tomato
2 : richly flavored with tomatoes
tomato fruitworm *noun* (circa 1891)
: CORN EARWORM
tomato hornworm *noun* (1921)
: a hawkmoth (*Manduca quinquemaculata*) whose larva is a hornworm feeding on plants of the nightshade family and especially tobacco and tomato
¹tomb \'tüm\ *noun* [Middle English *tombe*, from Anglo-French *tumbe*, from Late Latin *tumba* sepulchral mound, from Greek *tymbos*; perhaps akin to Latin *tumēre* to be swollen — more at THUMB] (13th century)
1 a : an excavation in which a corpse is buried **:** GRAVE **b :** a place of interment
2 : a house, chamber, or vault for the dead
3 : a building or structure resembling a tomb (as in appearance)
— **tomb·less** \-ləs\ *adjective*
²tomb *transitive verb* (14th century)
: BURY, ENTOMB
tom·bac \'täm-,bak\ *noun* [French, from Dutch *tombak*, from Malay *těmbaga* copper] (1602)
: an alloy essentially of copper and zinc and sometimes tin or arsenic that is used especially for cheap jewelry and gilding
tom·bo·lo \'töm-bə-,lö, 'täm-\ *noun*, *plural* **-los** [Italian, from Latin *tumulus* mound, tumulus] (1899)
: a sand or gravel bar connecting an island with the mainland or another island
tom·boy \'täm-,bȯi\ *noun* (1592)
: a girl who behaves in a manner usually considered boyish **:** HOYDEN
— **tom·boy·ish** \-ish\ *adjective*
— **tom·boy·ish·ness** *noun*
tomb·stone \'tüm-,stön\ *noun* (1565)
: GRAVESTONE
tom·cat \'täm-,kat\ *noun* (1789)
: a male domestic cat
tom·cod \-,käd\ *noun* (1722)
: either of two small fishes (*Microgadus tomcod* of the Atlantic and *M. proximus* of the Pacific) of the cod family
Tom Col·lins \'täm-'kä-lənz\ *noun* [from the name *Tom Collins*] (circa 1909)
: a collins with a base of gin
Tom, Dick, and Har·ry \,täm-,dik-ən(d)-'har-ē\ *noun*, *plural* **Toms, Dicks, and Harrys** (1815)
: the common man **:** ANYONE — often used with *every* ⟨helps every *Tom, Dick, and Harry* in need⟩
tome \'töm\ *noun* [Middle French or Latin; Middle French, from Latin *tomus*, from Greek *tomos* section, roll of papyrus, tome, from *temnein* to cut; akin to Middle Irish *tamnaid* he lops, Polish *ciąć* to cut, and perhaps to Latin *tondēre* to shear] (1519)
1 : a volume forming part of a larger work
2 : BOOK; *especially* **:** a large or scholarly book
-tome *noun combining form* [Greek *tomos*]
1 : part **:** segment ⟨myo*tome*⟩
2 : cutting instrument ⟨micro*tome*⟩
to·men·tose \tö-'men-,tös, 'tö-mən-\ *adjective* [New Latin *tomentosus*, from *tomentum*] (1698)
: covered with densely matted hairs ⟨a *tomentose* leaf⟩
to·men·tum \tö-'men-təm\ *noun*, *plural* **-ta** \-tə\ [New Latin, from Latin, cushion stuffing] (1699)

: pubescence composed of densely matted woolly hairs
¹tom·fool \'täm-'fül\ *noun* (circa 1709)
: a great fool **:** BLOCKHEAD
²tomfool *adjective* (1819)
: extremely foolish, stupid, or doltish
tom·fool·ery \,täm-'fül-rē, -'fü-lə-\ *noun* (1812)
: playful or foolish behavior
Tom·my \'tä-mē\ *noun*, *plural* **Tommies** [*Thomas* Atkins, name used as model in official army forms] (1892)
: a British soldier
Tommy At·kins \-'at-kənz\ *noun* (1883)
: TOMMY
tom·my–gun \'tä-mē-,gən\ *transitive verb* (1942)
: to shoot with a tommy gun
tommy gun *noun* [by shortening & alteration] (1929)
: THOMPSON SUBMACHINE GUN; *broadly* **:** SUBMACHINE GUN
tom·my·rot \'tä-mē-,rät\ *noun* [English dialect *tommy* fool + English *rot*] (1884)
: utter foolishness or nonsense
to·mo·gram \'tö-mə-,gram\ *noun* (1936)
: a roentgenogram made by tomography
to·mog·ra·phy \tö-'mä-grə-fē\ *noun* [Greek *tomos* section + International Scientific Vocabulary *-graphy* — more at TOME] (1935)
: a method of producing a three-dimensional image of the internal structures of a solid object (as the human body or the earth) by the observation and recording of the differences in the effects on the passage of waves of energy impinging on those structures — compare COMPUTED TOMOGRAPHY
— **to·mo·graph·ic** \,tö-mə-'gra-fik\ *adjective*
¹to·mor·row \tə-'mär-(,)ö, -'mȯr-\ *adverb* [Middle English *to morgen*, from Old English *tō morgen*, from *tō* to + *morgen* morrow, morning — more at MORN] (13th century)
: on or for the day after today ⟨will do it *tomorrow*⟩
²tomorrow *noun* (14th century)
1 : the day after the present ⟨the court will recess until *tomorrow*⟩
2 : FUTURE 1a ⟨the world of *tomorrow*⟩
tom·pi·on \'täm-pē-ən\ *noun* variant of TAMPION
Tom Thumb \'täm-'thəm\ *noun*
1 : a legendary English dwarf
2 : a dwarf type, race, or individual
tom·tit \'täm-,tit, ,täm-\ *noun* [probably short for *tomtitmouse*, from the name *Tom* + *titmouse*] (1700)
: any of various small active birds
tom–tom \'täm-,täm, 'təm-,təm\ *noun* [Hindi *ṭamṭam*] (1693)
1 : a usually long and narrow small-headed drum commonly beaten with the hands
2 : a monotonous beating, rhythm, or rhythmical sound
-tomy *noun combining form* [New Latin *-tomia*, from Greek, from *-tomos* that cuts, from *temnein* to cut — more at TOME]
: incision **:** section ⟨laparo*tomy*⟩
¹ton \'tən\ *noun*, *plural* **tons** *also* **ton** [Middle English *tunne* unit of weight or capacity — more at TUN] (14th century)
1 a : a unit of internal capacity for ships equal to 100 cubic feet — called also *register ton* **b :** a unit approximately equal to the volume of a long ton weight of seawater used in reckoning the displacement of ships and equal to 35 cubic feet **c :** a unit of volume for cargo freight usually reckoned at 40 cubic feet — called also *measurement ton*
2 : any of various units of weight: **a** — see WEIGHT table **b :** METRIC TON
3 : a great quantity **:** LOT — often used in plural ⟨ate *tons* of hamburgers⟩ ⟨has *tons* of money⟩
²ton \'tö*ⁿ*\ *noun* [French, literally, tone, from Latin *tonus*] (1765)
1 : the prevailing fashion **:** VOGUE

2 : the quality or state of being smart or fashionable
ton·al \'tö-n°l\ *adjective* (1776)
1 : of or relating to tone, tonality, or tonicity
2 : having tonality
— **ton·al·ly** \-n°l-ē\ *adverb*
to·nal·i·ty \tö-'na-lə-tē\ *noun*, *plural* **-ties** (1838)
1 : tonal quality
2 a : KEY 7 **b :** the organization of all the tones and harmonies of a piece of music in relation to a tonic
3 : the arrangement or interrelation of the tones of a work of visual art
ton·do \'tän-(,)dö\ *noun*, *plural* **ton·di** \-(,)dē\ [Italian, from *tondo* round, short for *rotondo*, from Latin *rotundus* — more at ROTUND] (1890)
1 : a circular painting
2 : a sculptured medallion
¹tone \'tön\ *noun* [Middle English, from Latin *tonus* tension, tone, from Greek *tonos*, literally, act of stretching; akin to Greek *teinein* to stretch — more at THIN] (14th century)
1 : vocal or musical sound of a specific quality ⟨spoke in low *tones*⟩ ⟨masculine *tones*⟩; *especially* **:** musical sound with respect to timbre and manner of expression
2 a : a sound of definite pitch and vibration **b :** WHOLE STEP
3 : accent or inflection expressive of a mood or emotion
4 : the pitch of a word often used to express differences of meaning
5 : a particular pitch or change of pitch constituting an element in the intonation of a phrase or sentence ⟨high *tone*⟩ ⟨low *tone*⟩ ⟨mid *tone*⟩ ⟨low-rising *tone*⟩ ⟨falling *tone*⟩
6 : style or manner of expression in speaking or writing ⟨seemed wise to adopt a conciliatory *tone*⟩
7 a (1) : color quality or value **(2) :** a tint or shade of color **b :** the color that appreciably modifies a hue or white or black ⟨gray walls of greenish *tone*⟩
8 : the effect in painting of light and shade together with color
9 a : the state of a living body or of any of its organs or parts in which the functions are

\ə\ abut	\°\ kitten	\ər\ further \a\ ash \ā\ ace
\ä\ mop, mar	\au̇\ out	\ch\ chin \e\ bet \ē\ easy
\g\ go	\i\ hit	\ī\ ice \j\ job \ŋ\ sing \ö\ go
\ȯ\ law	\ȯi\ boy	\th\ thin \th\ the \ü\ loot \u̇\ foot
\y\ yet	\zh\ vision	*see also* Guide to Pronunciation

healthy and performed with due vigor **b :** normal tension or responsiveness to stimuli; *specifically* **:** muscular tonus
10 a : healthy elasticity **:** RESILIENCY **b :** general character, quality, or trend ⟨a city's upbeat *tone*⟩ **c :** frame of mind **:** MOOD
²tone *verb* **toned; ton·ing** (1660)
transitive verb
1 : INTONE
2 : to give a particular intonation or inflection to
3 a : to impart tone to **:** STRENGTHEN ⟨medicine to *tone* up the system⟩ **b :** to soften or reduce in intensity, color, appearance, or sound **:** MELLOW — often used with *down* **c :** to change the normal silver image of (as a photographic print) into a colored image
intransitive verb
1 : to assume a pleasing color quality or tint
2 : to blend or harmonize in color
tone·arm \'tōn-,ärm\ *noun* (1913)
: the movable part of a phonograph or record player that carries the pickup and permits the needle to follow the record groove
tone color *noun* (1881)
: TIMBRE
toned \'tōnd\ *adjective* (15th century)
1 : having tone or a specified tone **:** characterized or distinguished by a tone
2 *of paper* **:** having a slight tint
tone-deaf \'tōn-,def\ *adjective* (1894)
: relatively insensitive to differences in musical pitch
— **tone deafness** *noun*
tone language *noun* (circa 1909)
: a language (as Chinese or Zulu) in which variations in tone distinguish words or phrases of different meaning that otherwise would sound alike
tone·less \'tōn-ləs\ *adjective* (1773)
: lacking in tone, modulation, or expression
— **tone·less·ly** *adverb*
— **tone·less·ness** *noun*
to·neme \'tō-,nēm\ *noun* (1923)
: an intonation phoneme in a tone language
— **to·ne·mic** \tō-'nē-mik\ *adjective*
tone poem *noun* (1902)
: SYMPHONIC POEM
— **tone poet** *noun*
ton·er \'tō-nər\ *noun* (1888)
: one that tones or is a source of tones: as **a :** a solution used to impart color to a silver photographic image **b :** a substance used to develop a latent xerographic image **c :** a liquid cosmetic for cleansing the skin and contracting the pores
tone row *noun* (1936)
: the chosen sequence of tones that serves as the basis for a work of serial music; *specifically* **:** TWELVE-TONE ROW
to·net·ic \tō-'ne-tik\ *adjective* (1922)
1 : relating to linguistic tones or to tone languages
2 : of or relating to intonation ⟨*tonetic* notation⟩
— **to·net·i·cal·ly** \-ti-k(ə-)lē\ *adverb*
to·net·ics \-tiks\ *noun plural but singular in construction* (1921)
: the use or study of linguistic tones
to·nette \tō-'net\ *noun* [¹*tone* + *-ette*] (1939)
: a simple fipple flute with a range somewhat larger than an octave that is often used in elementary music education
ton·ey *variant of* TONY
¹tong \'täŋ, 'tòŋ\ *noun* [Chinese (Guangdong) *tòhng*, literally, hall] (1883)
: a secret society or fraternal organization especially of Chinese in the U.S. formerly notorious for gang warfare
²tong *verb* [*tongs*] (1901)
transitive verb
: to take, gather, hold, or handle with tongs ⟨*tong* oysters⟩
intransitive verb
: to use tongs especially in taking or gathering something

— **tong·er** \'täŋ-ər, 'tòŋ-\ *noun*
ton·ga \'täŋ-gə\ *noun* [Hindi *tāṅgā*] (1874)
: a light 2-wheeled vehicle for two or four persons drawn by one horse and common in India
Ton·gan \'täŋ-gən *also* -ən\ *noun* (1853)
1 : a member of a Polynesian people of Tonga
2 : the Polynesian language of the Tongans
— **Tongan** *adjective*
tongs \'täŋz, 'tòŋz\ *noun plural but singular or plural in construction* [Middle English *tonges*, plural of *tonge*, from Old English *tang*; akin to Old High German *zanga* tongs and perhaps to Greek *daknein* to bite] (before 12th century)
: any of numerous grasping devices consisting commonly of two pieces joined at one end by a pivot or hinged like scissors
¹tongue \'təŋ\ *noun* [Middle English *tunge*, from Old English; akin to Old High German *zunga* tongue, Latin *lingua*] (before 12th century)
1 a : a fleshy movable process of the floor of the mouths of most vertebrates that bears sensory end organs and small glands and functions especially in taking and swallowing food and in humans as a speech organ **b :** a part of various invertebrate animals that is analogous to the tongue
2 : the flesh of a tongue (as of the ox or sheep) used as food
3 : the power of communication through speech
4 a : LANGUAGE; *especially* **:** a spoken language **b :** manner or quality of utterance with respect to tone or sound, the sense of what is expressed, or the intention of the speaker ⟨she has a clever *tongue*⟩ ⟨a sharp *tongue*⟩ **c :** ecstatic usually unintelligible utterance accompanying religious excitation — usually used in plural **d :** the cry of or as if of a hound pursuing or in sight of game — used especially in the phrase *to give tongue*
5 : a tapering flame ⟨*tongues* of fire⟩
6 : a long narrow strip of land projecting into a body of water
7 : something resembling an animal's tongue in being elongated and fastened at one end only: as **a :** a movable pin in a buckle **b :** a metal ball suspended inside a bell so as to strike against the sides as the bell is swung **c :** the pole of a vehicle **d :** the flap under the lacing or buckles of a shoe at the throat of the vamp
8 a : the rib on one edge of a board that fits into a corresponding groove in an edge of another board to make a flush joint **b :** FEATHER 4
— **tongue·like** \-,līk\ *adjective*
²tongue *verb* **tongued; tongu·ing** \'təŋ-iŋ\ (14th century)
transitive verb
1 *archaic* **:** SCOLD
2 : to touch or lick with or as if with the tongue
3 a : to cut a tongue on ⟨*tongue* a board⟩ **b :** to join (as boards) by means of a tongue and groove ⟨*tongue* flooring together⟩
4 : to articulate (notes) by tonguing
intransitive verb
1 : to project in a tongue
2 : to articulate notes on a wind instrument by successively interrupting the stream of wind with the action of the tongue
tongue and groove *noun* (circa 1876)
: a joint made by a tongue on one edge of a board fitting into a corresponding groove on the edge of another board
— **tongue–and–groove** *adjective*
tongued \'təŋd\ *adjective* (14th century)
: having a tongue especially of a specified kind — often used in combination ⟨sharp⸗ *tongued*⟩
tongue–in–cheek *adjective* (1933)
: characterized by insincerity, irony, or whimsical exaggeration
tongue in cheek *adverb* (circa 1934)
: with insincerity, irony, or whimsical exaggeration

tongue–lash \'təŋ-,lash\ *verb* [back-formation from *tongue-lashing*] (1881)
: CHIDE, SCOLD
— **tongue–lash·ing** *noun*
tongue·less \'təŋ-ləs\ *adjective* (14th century)
1 : having no tongue
2 : lacking power of speech **:** MUTE
¹tongue–tie \'təŋ-,tī\ *transitive verb* [back-formation from *tongue-tied*] (1555)
: to deprive of speech or the power of distinct articulation
²tongue–tie *noun* (circa 1852)
: limited mobility of the tongue due to shortness of its frenulum
tongue–tied \'təŋ-,tīd\ *adjective* (1529)
1 : unable or disinclined to speak freely (as from shyness)
2 : affected with tongue-tie
tongue twister *noun* (1904)
: a word, phrase, or sentence difficult to articulate because of a succession of similar consonantal sounds (as in "twin-screw steel cruiser")
-tonia *noun combining form* [New Latin, from *tonus*]
: condition or degree of tonus ⟨myo*tonia*⟩
¹ton·ic \'tä-nik\ *adjective* [Greek *tonikos*, from *tonos* tension, tone] (1649)
1 a : characterized by tonus ⟨*tonic* contraction of muscle⟩; *also* **:** marked by prolonged muscular contraction ⟨*tonic* convulsions⟩ **b :** producing or adapted to produce healthy muscular condition and reaction of organs (as muscles)
2 a : increasing or restoring physical or mental tone **:** REFRESHING **b :** yielding a tonic substance
3 : relating to or based on the first tone of a scale ⟨*tonic* harmony⟩
4 *of a syllable* **:** bearing a principal stress or accent
5 : of or relating to speech tones or to languages using them to distinguish words otherwise identical
— **ton·i·cal·ly** \'tä-ni-k(ə-)lē\ *adverb*
²tonic *noun* (1799)
1 a : an agent (as a drug) that increases body tone **b :** one that invigorates, restores, refreshes, or stimulates ⟨a day in the country was a *tonic* for him⟩ **c :** a liquid preparation for the scalp or hair **d** *chiefly New England* **:** a carbonated flavored beverage **e :** TONIC WATER
2 : the first tone of a diatonic scale **:** KEYNOTE
3 : a voiced sound
tonic accent *noun* (1867)
1 : relative phonetic prominence (as from greater stress or higher pitch) of a spoken syllable or word
2 : accent depending on pitch rather than stress
to·nic·i·ty \tō-'ni-sə-tē\ *noun* (1824)
1 : the property of possessing tone; *especially* **:** healthy vigor of body or mind
2 : muscular tonus
tonic sol–fa *noun* (1852)
: a system of solmization based on key relationships that replaces the normal notation with sol-fa syllables or their initials
tonic water *noun* (1926)
: a carbonated beverage flavored with a small amount of quinine, lemon, and lime
¹to·night \tə-'nīt\ *adverb* (before 12th century)
: on this present night or the night following this present day ⟨will do it *tonight*⟩
²tonight *noun* (14th century)
: the present night or the night following this present day
ton·ka bean \'täŋ-kə-\ *noun* [probably from Tupi *tonka*] (1796)
: the coumarin-containing seed of any of several tropical American leguminous trees (genus *Dipteryx*) that is used in perfumes and as an artificial vanilla flavoring; *also* **:** a tree bearing tonka beans
ton·nage \'tə-nij\ *noun* [in sense 1, from Middle English, from Middle French, from *tonne*

tun; in other senses, from ¹*ton* — more at TUNNEL] (15th century)
1 : a duty formerly levied on every tun of wine imported into England
2 a : a duty or impost on vessels based on cargo capacity **b :** a duty on goods per ton transported
3 : ships in terms of the total number of tons registered or carried of or of their carrying capacity
4 a : the cubical content of a merchant ship in units of 100 cubic feet **b :** the displacement of a warship
5 a : total weight in tons shipped, carried, or produced **b :** impressively large amount or weight

tonne \ˈtən\ *noun* [French, from *tonne* tun, from Old French — more at TUNNEL] (1877)
: METRIC TON

ton·neau \ˈtä-ˌnō, tə-ˈnō\ *noun, plural* **ton·neaus** [French, literally, tun, from Old French *tonel* — more at TUNNEL] (1901)
1 : the rear seating compartment of an automobile; *also* **:** the entire seating compartment
2 : a shape of watch case or dial resembling a barrel in profile

ton·ner \ˈtə-nər\ *noun* (1851)
: an object (as a ship) having a specified tonnage — used in combination ⟨a thousand-*tonner*⟩

to·nom·e·ter \tō-ˈnä-mə-tər\ *noun* [Greek *tonos* tone + English *-meter*] (1725)
1 : an instrument or device for determining the exact pitch or the vibration rate of tones
2 : an instrument for measuring tension or pressure and especially intraocular pressure
— to·nom·e·try \tō-ˈnä-mə-trē\ *noun*

to·no·plast \ˈtō-nə-ˌplast\ *noun* [International Scientific Vocabulary *tono-* (from Greek *tonos* tension) + *-plast* — more at TONE] (circa 1888)
: a semipermeable membrane surrounding a plant-cell vacuole

ton·sil \ˈtän(t)-səl\ *noun* [Latin *tonsillae*, plural, tonsils] (1601)
1 : either of a pair of prominent masses of lymphoid tissue that lie one on each side of the throat between the anterior and posterior pillars of the fauces
2 : any of various masses of lymphoid tissue that are similar to tonsils
— ton·sil·lar \ˈtän(t)-s(ə-)lər\ *adjective*

tonsill- *combining form* [Latin *tonsillae*]
: tonsil ⟨*tonsill*ectomy⟩

ton·sil·lec·to·my \ˌtän(t)-sə-ˈlek-tə-mē\ *noun, plural* **-mies** (1899)
: the surgical removal of the tonsils

ton·sil·li·tis \-ˈlī-təs\ *noun* [New Latin] (1801)
: inflammation of the tonsils

ton·so·ri·al \tän-ˈsōr-ē-əl, -ˈsòr-\ *adjective* [Latin *tonsorius*, from *tondēre*] (1813)
: of or relating to a barber or the work of a barber

¹ton·sure \ˈtän(t)-shər\ *noun* [Middle English, from Medieval Latin *tonsura*, from Latin, act of shearing, from *tonsus*, past participle of *tondēre* to shear — more at TOME] (14th century)
1 : the Roman Catholic or Eastern rite of admission to the clerical state by the clipping or shaving of a portion of the head
2 : the shaven crown or patch worn by monks and other clerics
3 : a bald spot resembling a tonsure

²tonsure *transitive verb* **ton·sured; ton·sur·ing** \ˈtän(t)-sh(ə-)riŋ\ (1706)
: to shave the head of; *especially* **:** to confer the tonsure upon

ton·tine \ˈtän-ˌtēn, tän-ˈ\ *noun* [French, from Lorenzo *Tonti* (died 1695) Italian banker] (1765)
: a joint financial arrangement whereby the participants usually contribute equally to a prize that is awarded entirely to the participant who survives all the others

to·nus \ˈtō-nəs\ *noun* [New Latin, from Latin, tension, tone] (1876)
: TONE 9a; *especially* **:** a state of partial contraction characteristic of normal muscle

tony \ˈtō-nē\ *adjective* **ton·i·er; -est** (1877)
: marked by an aristocratic or high-toned manner or style ⟨*tony* private schools⟩

To·ny \ˈtō-nē\ *noun, plural* **Tonys** [*Tony*, nickname of Antoinette Perry (died 1946) American actress & producer] (1947)
: a medallion awarded annually by a professional organization for notable achievement in the theater

too \ˈtü\ *adverb* [Middle English, from Old English *tō* to, too — more at TO] (before 12th century)
1 : BESIDES, ALSO ⟨sell the house and furniture *too*⟩
2 a : to an excessive degree **:** EXCESSIVELY ⟨*too* large a house for us⟩ **b :** to such a degree as to be regrettable ⟨this time he has gone *too* far⟩ **c :** VERY ⟨didn't seem *too* interested⟩
3 : SO 2d ("I didn't do it." "You did *too*.")

took *past of* TAKE

¹tool \ˈtül\ *noun* [Middle English, from Old English *tōl*; akin to Old English *tawian* to prepare for use — more at TAW] (before 12th century)
1 a : a handheld device that aids in accomplishing a task **b** (1) **:** the cutting or shaping part in a machine or machine tool (2) **:** a machine for shaping metal **:** MACHINE TOOL
2 a : something (as an instrument or apparatus) used in performing an operation or necessary in the practice of a vocation or profession ⟨a scholar's books are his *tools*⟩ **b :** a means to an end ⟨a book's cover can be a marketing *tool*⟩ **c :** PENIS — often considered vulgar
3 : one that is used or manipulated by another
4 *plural* **:** natural ability ⟨has all the *tools*⟩
synonym see IMPLEMENT

²tool (1812)
transitive verb
1 a : to cause (a vehicle) to go **:** DRIVE **b :** to convey in a vehicle
2 : to shape, form, or finish with a tool; *especially* **:** to letter or ornament (as leather or gold) by means of hand tools
3 : to equip (as a plant or industry) with tools, machines, and instruments for production
intransitive verb
1 : DRIVE, RIDE
2 : to equip a plant or industry with the means (as machines, machine tools, and instruments) of production — often used with *up*

³tool *noun* (1881)
: a design (as on the binding of a book) made by tooling

tool·box \ˈtül-ˌbäks\ *noun* (1832)
: a chest for tools

tool·hold·er \-ˌhōl-dər\ *noun* (circa 1876)
: a short steel bar having a shank at one end by which it is clamped to a machine and a clamp at the other end to hold small interchangeable cutting bits

tool·house \-ˌhaùs\ *noun* (1818)
: TOOLSHED

tool·mak·er \ˈtül-ˌmā-kər\ *noun* (1844)
: one that makes tools; *especially* **:** a machinist who specializes in the construction, repair, maintenance, and calibration of the tools, jigs, fixtures, and instruments of a machine shop

tool·mak·ing \-kiŋ\ *noun* (1893)
: the action, process, or art of making tools; *also* **:** the trade of a toolmaker

tool·room \ˈtül-ˌrüm, -ˌrùm\ *noun* (1878)
: a room where tools are kept; *especially* **:** a room in a machine shop in which tools are made, stored, and issued for use by workers

tool·shed \-ˌshed\ *noun* (1840)
: an outbuilding for storing tools

tools of ignorance [from the notion that a smart athlete would not play such a grueling position] (1939)
: a baseball catcher's equipment

tool subject *noun* (1925)
: a subject studied to gain competence in a skill used in other subjects

toom \ˈtüm\ *adjective* [Middle English, from Old English *tōm* — more at TEEM] (before 12th century)
chiefly Scottish **:** EMPTY

toon \ˈtün\ *noun* [Hindi *tūn*, from Sanskrit *tunna*] (1810)
: a southeast Asian and Australian tree (*Cedrela toona*) of the mahogany family with fragrant dark red wood and flowers that yield a dye; *also* **:** its wood

¹toot \ˈtüt\ *verb* [probably imitative] (circa 1510)
intransitive verb
1 a : to sound a short blast ⟨the horn *tooted*⟩ **b :** to sound a note or call suggesting the short blast of a wind instrument
2 : to blow or sound an instrument (as a horn) especially so as to produce short blasts
transitive verb
: to cause to sound ⟨*toot* a whistle⟩
— toot·er *noun*

²toot *noun* (1641)
: a short blast (as on a horn); *also* **:** a sound resembling such a blast

³toot *noun* [Scots *toot* to drink heavily] (circa 1790)
: a drinking bout **:** SPREE

tooth \ˈtüth\ *noun, plural* **teeth** \ˈtēth\ [Middle English, from Old English *tōth;* akin to Old High German *zand* tooth, Latin *dent-, dens*, Greek *odont-, odous*] (before 12th century)
1 a : one of the hard bony appendages that are borne on the jaws or in many of the lower vertebrates on other bones in the walls of the mouth or pharynx and serve especially for the prehension and mastication of food and as weapons of offense and defense **b :** any of various usually hard and sharp processes especially about the mouth of an invertebrate
2 : TASTE, LIKING
3 : a projection resembling or

tooth 1a: *A* outside of a molar: *1* crown, *2* neck, *3* roots; *B* cross section of a molar: *1* enamel, *2* dentin, *3* pulp, *4* cementum, *5* gum; *C* dentition of adult human, upper; *D* dentition of adult human, lower: *1* incisors, *2* canines, *3* bicuspids, *4* molars

suggesting the tooth of an animal in shape, arrangement, or action ⟨a saw *tooth*⟩: as **a :** any of the regular projections on the circumference or sometimes the face of a wheel that engage with corresponding projections on another wheel especially to transmit force **:** COG **b :** a small sharp-pointed marginal lobe or process on a plant
4 a : something that injures, tortures, devours, or destroys **b** *plural* **:** effective means of enforcement
5 : a roughness of surface produced by mechanical or artificial means
— tooth·like \ˈtüth-ˌlīk\ *adjective*
— in the teeth of 1 : in or into direct contact or collision with ⟨found themselves sailing *in the teeth of* a hurricane —*Current Biography*⟩ **2 :** in direct opposition to ⟨rule had . . . been imposed by conquest *in the teeth of* obstinate resistance —A. J. Toynbee⟩

— to the teeth : FULLY, COMPLETELY ⟨armed *to the teeth*⟩
tooth·ache \'tüth-,āk\ *noun* (14th century)
: pain in or about a tooth
tooth and nail *adverb* (1550)
: with every available means : ALL OUT ⟨fight *tooth and nail*⟩
tooth·brush \'tüth-,brəsh\ *noun* (1690)
: a brush for cleaning the teeth
tooth·brush·ing *noun* (1920)
: the action of using a toothbrush to clean teeth
toothed \'tütht, *uncompounded also* 'tü-thəd\ *adjective* (14th century)
: having teeth especially of a specified kind or number — often used in combination ⟨buck-*toothed*⟩
toothed whale \'tütht-, 'tü-thəd-\ *noun* (1843)
: any of a suborder (Odontoceti) of cetaceans (as a dolphin, porpoise, or killer whale) bearing usually numerous simple conical teeth — compare BALEEN WHALE
tooth fairy *noun* (1962)
: a fairy believed by children to leave money while they sleep in exchange for a tooth that has come out
tooth·less \'tüth-ləs\ *adjective* (14th century)
1 : having no teeth
2 a : lacking in sharpness or bite ⟨spoke in *toothless* generalities —Arthur Hepner⟩ **b :** lacking in means of enforcement or coercion : INEFFECTUAL
tooth·paste \-,pāst\ *noun* (1832)
: a paste for cleaning the teeth
tooth·pick \-,pik\ *noun* (15th century)
: a pointed instrument (as a slender tapering piece of wood) for removing food particles lodged between the teeth
tooth powder *noun* (1542)
: a powder for cleaning the teeth
tooth shell *noun* (circa 1711)
: any of a class (Scaphopoda) of burrowing marine mollusks with a tapering tubular shell; *also* : this shell
tooth·some \'tüth-səm\ *adjective* (1551)
1 a : AGREEABLE, ATTRACTIVE **b :** sexually attractive ⟨a *toothsome* blonde⟩
2 : of palatable flavor and pleasing texture : DELICIOUS ⟨crisp *toothsome* fried chicken⟩
synonym see PALATABLE
— tooth·some·ly *adverb*
— tooth·some·ness *noun*
tooth·wort \-,wərt, -,wȯrt\ *noun* (1597)
1 : a European parasitic plant (*Lathraea squamaria*) of the broomrape family having a rootstock covered with tooth-shaped scales
2 : any of various cresses (genus *Dentaria*) including several cultivated for their showy flowers
toothy \'tü-thē\ *adjective* **tooth·i·er; -est** (1530)
1 : having or showing prominent teeth ⟨*toothy* grin⟩
2 : TOOTHSOME 2
— tooth·i·ly \-thə-lē\ *adverb*
too·tle \'tü-t°l\ *verb* **too·tled; too·tling** \'tüt-liŋ, 'tü-t°l-iŋ\ [frequentative of ¹*toot*] (1820)
intransitive verb
1 : to toot gently, repeatedly, or continuously
2 : to drive or move along in a leisurely manner
transitive verb
: to toot continuously on
— tootle *noun*
— too·tler \'tüt-lər, 'tü-t°l-ər\ *noun*
too-too \'tü-'tü\ *adjective* (1881)
1 : going beyond the bounds of convention, good taste, or common sense : EXTREME
2 : LA-DI-DA
toot·sie \'tùt-sē\ *noun* [origin unknown] (1905)
1 : DEAR, SWEETHEART
2 : PROSTITUTE

toot·sy *also* **toot·sie** \'tùt-sē\ *noun, plural* **tootsies** [baby-talk alteration of *foot*] (1854)
: FOOT
¹top \'täp\ *noun* [Middle English, from Old English; akin to Old High German *zopf* tip, tuft of hair] (before 12th century)
1 a (1) : the highest point, level, or part of something : SUMMIT, CROWN (2) : the head or top of the head — used especially in the phrase *top to toe* (3) : the head of a plant and especially one with edible roots ⟨beet *tops*⟩ (4) : a garment worn on the upper body **b** (1) : the highest or uppermost region or part (2) : the upper end, edge, or surface
2 : a fitted, integral, or attached part or unit serving as an upper piece, lid, or covering
3 a : a platform surrounding the head of a lower mast that serves to spread the topmast rigging, strengthen the mast, and furnish a standing place for men aloft **b :** a comparable part of the superstructure; *especially* : such a part on a warship used as a fire-control station or antiaircraft gun platform
4 a : the highest degree or pitch conceivable or attained : ACME, PINNACLE **b :** the loudest or highest range of a sound
5 a : the part that is nearest in space or time to the source or beginning **b :** the first half of an inning in baseball
6 a (1) : the highest position (as in rank or achievement) (2) : a person or thing at the top **b** *plural* : aces and kings in a hand or the three highest honors in a suit
7 : the choicest part : CREAM, PICK
8 : a forward spin given to a ball (as in golf or billiards) by striking it on or near the top or above the center; *also* : the stroke so given
— topped \'täpt\ *adjective*
— off the top of one's head : in an impromptu manner ⟨sat down and wrote the . . . story *off the top of his head* —Jerome Beatty, Jr.⟩
— on top of 1 a : in control of ⟨acted like a man *on top of* his job —*Newsweek*⟩ **b :** informed about ⟨tried to keep *on top of* new developments⟩ **2 :** in sudden and unexpected proximity to ⟨the deadline was *on top of* them⟩ **3 :** in addition to
— on top of the world : in a position of eminent success, happiness, or fame
— over the top : beyond the bounds of what is expected, usual, normal, or appropriate
²top *verb* **topped; top·ping** (1509)
transitive verb
1 : to remove or cut the top of: as **a :** to shorten or remove the top of (a plant) : PINCH 1b **b :** to remove the most volatile parts from (as crude petroleum)
2 a : to cover with a top or on the top : provide, form, or serve as a top for **b :** to supply with a decorative or protective finish or final touch **c :** to resupply or refill to capacity — usually used with *off* ⟨*topped* off the tank⟩ **d :** to complete the basic structure of (as a high-rise building) by putting on a cap or uppermost section — usually used with *out* or *off* **e :** to bring to an end or climax — usually used with *off* (the event was *topped* off with a relay race —Paula Rodenas⟩
3 a : to be or become higher than : OVERTOP ⟨*tops* the previous record⟩ **b :** to be superior to : EXCEL, SURPASS **c :** to gain ascendancy over : DOMINATE
4 a : to rise to, reach, or be at the top of **b :** to go over the top of : CLEAR, SURMOUNT
5 : to strike (a ball) above the center thereby imparting topspin
intransitive verb
1 : to make an end, finish, or conclusion
2 : to reach a summit or crest — usually used with *off* or *out*
³top *adjective* (1593)
1 : of, relating to, or being at the top : UPPERMOST
2 : CHIEF, LEADING ⟨one of the world's *top* journalists⟩

3 : of the highest quality, amount, or degree ⟨*top* value⟩ ⟨*top* form⟩
4 : having a quantum characteristic whose existence was postulated on the basis of the discovery of the bottom quark ⟨*top* quark⟩
⁴top *noun* [Middle English, from Old English, plaything] (14th century)
: a commonly cylindrical or conoidal device that has a tapering usually steel-shod point on which it is made to spin and that is used especially as a toy
top- *or* **topo-** *combining form* [Middle English, from Late Latin, from Greek, from *topos*]
: place : locality ⟨*topo*logy⟩ ⟨*topo*nymy⟩
to·paz \'tō-,paz\ *noun* [Middle English *topace*, from Old French, from Latin *topazus*, from Greek *topazos*] (13th century)
1 a : a mineral that is essentially a silicate of aluminum and usually occurs in orthorhombic translucent or transparent crystals or in white translucent masses **b :** a usually yellow to brownish yellow transparent mineral topaz used as a gem **c :** a yellow sapphire **d :** a yellow quartz
2 : either of two large brilliantly colored South American hummingbirds (*Topaza pella* and *T. pyra*)
top banana *noun* [from a burlesque routine involving three comedians in which the one that gets the punch line also gets a banana] (1952)
: the leading comedian in a burlesque show; *broadly* : KINGPIN 2
top billing *noun* (1945)
1 : prominent emphasis, featuring, or advertising
2 : the position at the top of a theatrical bill usually featuring the star's name
top boot *noun* (1768)
: a high boot often with light-colored leather bands around the upper part
top·coat \'täp-,kōt\ *noun* (1804)
1 : a lightweight overcoat
2 : OVERCOAT 2
top·cross \-,krȯs\ *noun* (1890)
: a cross between a superior or purebred male and inferior female stock to improve the average quality of the progeny; *also* : the product of such a cross
top dog *noun* (1900)
: a person or group in a position of authority especially through victory in a hard-fought competition
top dollar *noun* (1970)
: the highest amount being paid for a commodity or service ⟨willing to pay *top dollar* to get them —Dean Failey⟩
top–down \'täp-'daùn\ *adjective* [from the phrase *from the top down*] (1941)
1 : controlled, directed, or instituted from the top level ⟨a *top-down* corporate structure⟩
2 : proceeding by breaking large general aspects (as of a problem) into smaller more detailed constituents : working from the general to the specific ⟨*top-down* programming⟩ ⟨*top-down* design⟩
top drawer *noun* (1905)
: the highest level of society, authority, or excellence
— top–draw·er \-'drȯ(-ə)r\ *adjective*
top–dress \'täp-,dres\ *transitive verb* (1733)
: to apply material to (as land or a road) without working it in; *especially* : to scatter fertilizer over (land)
top·dress·ing \-,dre-siŋ\ *noun* (1744)
: a material applied to top-dress soil
¹tope \'tōp\ *intransitive verb* **toped; top·ing** [obsolete English *tope*, interjection used to wish good health before drinking] (1667)
: to drink liquor to excess
²tope *noun* [origin unknown] (1686)
: a small cosmopolitan shark (*Galeorhinus galeus*) with a liver very rich in vitamin A
³tope *noun* [perhaps from Panjabi *ṭop* hat] (1815)

: STUPA

to·pee or **to·pi** \tō-'pē, 'tō-(,)pē\ noun [Hindi ṭopī] (1835)
: a lightweight helmet-shaped hat made of pith or cork

top·er \'tō-pər\ noun (1673)
: one that topes; especially : DRUNKARD

top–flight \'täp-'flīt\ adjective (1931)
: of, relating to, or being the highest level of achievement, excellence, or eminence
— **top flight** noun

¹Top 40 noun plural (1966)
: the forty best-selling phonograph records for a given period

²Top 40 adjective (1966)
: constituting, playing, listing, or relating to the Top 40 ⟨Top 40 hits⟩ ⟨Top 40 stations⟩ ⟨Top 40 charts⟩

top·ful or **top·full** \'täp-'fùl\ adjective (1553)
: BRIMFUL

¹top·gal·lant \(,)täp-'ga-lənt, tə-'ga-\ adjective [¹top + ²gallant] (1514)
: of, relating to, or being a part next above the topmast and below the royal mast ⟨topgallant sails⟩ ⟨the topgallant mast⟩

²topgallant noun (1581)
1 archaic : the topmost point : SUMMIT ⟨the high topgallant of my joy —Shakespeare⟩
2 : a topgallant mast or sail

top gun noun (1976)
: one who is at the top (as in ability, rank, or prestige)

top–ham·per \'täp-'ham-pər\ noun (1791)
1 : matter or weight (as spars or rigging) in the upper part of a ship
2 : unnecessary cumbersome matter

top hat noun (1881)
: a tall-crowned hat usually of beaver or silk

top–heavy \'täp-,he-vē\ adjective (circa 1533)
1 : having the top part too heavy for the lower part
2 : having too high a proportion of administrators ⟨a top-heavy bureaucracy⟩
3 : oversupplied with one element at the expense of others : lacking balance ⟨a novel top-heavy with description⟩

To·phet \'tō-fət\ noun [Middle English, shrine south of ancient Jerusalem where human sacrifices were performed to Moloch in Jeremiah 7:31, Gehenna, from Late Latin Topheth, from Hebrew tōpheth] (14th century)
: HELL, GEHENNA

top–hole \'täp-'hōl\ adjective (1908)
chiefly British : EXCELLENT, FIRST-CLASS

to·phus \'tō-fəs\ noun, plural **to·phi** \'tō-,fī, -,fē\ [Latin, tufa] (1607)
: a deposit of urates in tissues (as cartilage) characteristic of gout

to·pi \'tō-pē\ noun, plural **topi** or **topis** [perhaps from Swahili] (1894)
: a sub-Saharan antelope (Damaliscis lunatus synonym D. korrigum) having a glossy reddish brown coat with purplish black and yellowish markings

¹to·pi·ary \'tō-pē-,er-ē\ adjective [Latin topiarius, from topia ornamental gardening, irregular from Greek topos place] (1592)
: of, relating to, or being the practice or art of training, cutting, and trimming trees or shrubs into odd or ornamental shapes; also : characterized by such work

²topiary noun, plural **-ar·ies** (1908)
1 : topiary art or gardening; also : a topiary garden
2 a : a plant shaped by topiary art **b** : topiary plants

top·ic \'tä-pik\ noun [Latin Topica Topics (work by Aristotle), from Greek Topika, from topika, neuter plural of topikos of a place, of a topos, from topos place, topos] (1603)
1 a : one of the general forms of argument employed in probable reasoning **b** : ARGUMENT, REASON
2 a : a heading in an outlined argument or exposition **b** : the subject of a discourse or of a section of a discourse

top·i·cal \-pi-kəl\ adjective (1588)
1 : designed for or involving local application and action (as on the body) ⟨a topical anesthetic⟩ ⟨a topical remedy⟩
2 a : of, relating to, or arranged by topics ⟨set down in topical form⟩ **b** : referring to the topics of the day or place : of local or temporary interest ⟨a topical novel⟩ ⟨topical references⟩
— **top·i·cal·ly** \-k(ə-)lē\ adverb

top·i·cal·i·ty \,tä-pə-'ka-lə-tē\ noun, plural **-ties** (1904)
1 : the quality or state of being topical
2 : an item of topical interest

topic sentence noun (1885)
: a sentence that states the main thought of a paragraph or of a larger unit of discourse and is usually placed at or near the beginning

top·kick \'täp-,kik\ noun (1918)
: FIRST SERGEANT 1

top·knot \-,nät\ noun (circa 1688)
1 : an ornament (as a knot of ribbons or a pompom) forming a headdress or worn as part of a coiffure
2 : a crest of feathers or tuft of hair on the top of the head

top·less \-ləs\ adjective (1589)
1 archaic : so high as to reach up beyond sight ⟨and burnt the topless towers of Ilium —Christopher Marlowe⟩
2 : being without a top
3 a : wearing no clothing on the upper body **b** : featuring topless waitresses or entertainers ⟨topless bars⟩ **c** : being a place where topless women are permitted ⟨a topless beach⟩
— **top·less·ness** \-nəs\ noun

top·line \-,līn\ noun (circa 1909)
: the outline of the top of the body of an animal (as a dog or horse)

top·lofty \'täp-,lòf-tē\ also **top·loft·i·cal** \täp-'lòf-ti-kəl\ adjective [probably from the phrase top loft] (1823)
: very superior in air or attitude
— **top·loft·i·ly** \täp-'lòf-tə-lē\ adverb
— **top·loft·i·ness** \täp-'lòf-tē-nəs\ noun

top·mast \'täp-,mast, -məst\ noun (15th century)
: the mast that is next above the lower mast and is topmost in a fore-and-aft rig

top milk noun (1891)
: the upper layer of milk in a container enriched by whatever cream has risen

top·min·now \'täp-,mi-(,)nō\ noun (1884)
: any of several live-bearers (family Poeciliidae) or killifish (family Cyprinodontidae)

top·most \'täp-,mōst\ adjective (1697)
: highest of all : UPPERMOST

top–notch \-'näch\ adjective (1900)
: of the highest quality : FIRST-RATE
— **top·notch·er** \-'nä-chər\ noun

to·po·cen·tric \,tä-pə-'sen-trik, ,tō-\ adjective (circa 1942)
: relating to, measured from, or as if observed from a particular point on the earth's surface : having or relating to such a point as origin ⟨topocentric coordinates⟩ — compare GEOCENTRIC

to·pog·ra·pher \tə-'pä-grə-fər\ noun (1603)
: one skilled in topography

to·po·graph·ic \,tä-pə-'gra-fik, ,tō-\ adjective (1632)
: of, relating to, or concerned with topography ⟨topographic maps⟩

to·po·graph·i·cal \-fi-kəl\ adjective (circa 1576)
1 : TOPOGRAPHIC
2 : of, relating to, or concerned with the artistic representation of a particular locality ⟨a topographical poem⟩ ⟨topographical painting⟩
— **to·po·graph·i·cal·ly** \-k(ə-)lē\ adverb

to·pog·ra·phy \tə-'pä-grə-fē\ noun [Middle English topographie, from Greek, from topographia, from Greek, from topographein to describe a place, from topos place + graphein to write — more at CARVE] (15th century)
1 a : the art or practice of graphic delineation in detail usually on maps or charts of natural

and man-made features of a place or region especially in a way to show their relative positions and elevations **b** : topographical surveying
2 a : the configuration of a surface including its relief and the position of its natural and man-made features **b** : the physical or natural features of an object or entity and their structural relationships

to·po·log·i·cal \,tä-pə-'lä-ji-kəl\ adjective (1715)
1 : of or relating to topology
2 : being or involving properties unaltered under a homeomorphism ⟨continuity and connectedness are topological properties⟩
— **to·po·log·i·cal·ly** \-k(ə-)lē\ adverb

topological group noun (1946)
: a mathematical group which is also a topological space, whose multiplicative operation is continuous such that given any neighborhood of a product there exist neighborhoods of the elements composing the product with the property that any pair of elements representing each of these neighborhoods form a product belonging to the given neighborhood, and whose operation of taking inverses is continuous such that for any neighborhood of the inverse of an element there exists a neighborhood of the element itself in which every element has its inverse in the other neighborhood

topologically equivalent adjective (1915)
: related by a homeomorphism

topological space noun (1926)
: a set with a collection of subsets satisfying the conditions that both the empty set and the set itself belong to the collection, the union of any number of the subsets is also an element of the collection, and the intersection of any finite number of the subsets is an element of the collection

topological transformation noun (1946)
: HOMEOMORPHISM

to·pol·o·gy \tə-'pä-lə-jē, tä-\ noun, plural **-gies** [International Scientific Vocabulary] (1850)
1 : topographic study of a particular place; specifically : the history of a region as indicated by its topography
2 a (1) : a branch of mathematics concerned with those properties of geometric configurations (as point sets) which are unaltered by elastic deformations (as a stretching or a twisting) that are homeomorphisms (2) : the set of all open subsets of a topological space **b** : CONFIGURATION ⟨topology of a molecule⟩ ⟨topology of a magnetic field⟩
— **to·pol·o·gist** \-jist\ noun

top·o·nym \'tä-pə-,nim, 'tō-\ noun [International Scientific Vocabulary, back-formation from toponymy] (1899)
: PLACE-NAME

top·o·nym·ic \,tä-pə-'ni-mik, ,tō-\ adjective (1896)
: of or relating to toponyms or toponymy
— **top·o·nym·i·cal** \-mi-kəl\ adjective

to·pon·y·my \tə-'pä-nə-mē, tō-\ noun [International Scientific Vocabulary, from top- + Greek onyma, onoma name — more at NAME] (1876)
: the place-names of a region or language or especially the etymological study of them
— **to·pon·y·mist** \-mist\ noun

to·pos \'tō-,päs, 'tä-\ noun, plural **to·poi** \-,pòi\ [Greek, short for koinos topos, literally, common place] (1936)
: a traditional or conventional literary or rhetorical theme or topic

top·per \'tä-pər\ noun (1688)
1 : one that puts on or takes off tops

2 : one that is at or on the top
3 a : SILK HAT **b** : OPERA HAT
4 : something (as a joke) that caps everything preceding
5 : a woman's usually short and loose-fitting lightweight outer coat

¹**top·ping** \'tä-piŋ\ noun (14th century)
1 : something that forms a top; especially : a garnish (as a sauce, bread crumbs, or whipped cream) placed on top of a food for flavor or decoration
2 : the action of one that tops
3 : something removed by topping

²**topping** adjective (circa 1685)
1 : highest in rank or eminence
2 New England : PROUD, ARROGANT
3 chiefly British : EXCELLENT

top·ple \'tä-pəl\ verb **top·pled; top·pling** \-p(ə-)liŋ\ [frequentative of ²top] (1590)
intransitive verb
: to fall from or as if from being top-heavy
transitive verb
1 : to cause to topple
2 a : OVERTHROW **2 b** : DEFEAT 3

top round noun (1903)
: meat from the inner part of a round of beef

¹**tops** \'täps\ adjective [plural of ¹top] (1935)
: topmost in quality, ability, popularity, or importance — used predicatively ⟨is tops in his field⟩

²**tops** adverb (1956)
: at the very most ⟨will cost $50, tops⟩

top·sail \'täp-,sāl, -səl\ also **top·s'l** \-səl\ noun (14th century)
1 : the sail next above the lowermost sail on a mast in a square-rigged ship
2 : the sail set above and sometimes on the gaff in a fore-and-aft rigged ship

top secret adjective (1944)
1 : protected by a high degree of secrecy ⟨a top secret weapon⟩ ⟨a top secret meeting⟩
2 a : containing or being information whose unauthorized disclosure could result in exceptionally grave danger to the nation ⟨top secret messages⟩ — compare CONFIDENTIAL, SECRET **b** : of or relating to top secret documents ⟨a top secret clearance⟩

top sergeant noun (1898)
: FIRST SERGEANT 1

top–shelf \'täp-'shelf\ adjective (circa 1892)
: of the best quality

¹**top·side** \'täp-'sīd\ noun (1815)
1 plural : the top portion of the outer surface of a ship on each side above the waterline
2 : the highest level of authority
3 : the upper portion of the ionosphere

²**topside** adverb or adjective (1873)
1 : to or on the top or surface
2 : in a position of authority
3 : on deck

Top–Sid·er \'täp-,sī-dər\ trademark
— used for a low casual shoe having a rubber sole

top·soil \'täp-,soil\ noun (1836)
: surface soil usually including the organic layer in which plants have most of their roots and which the farmer turns over in plowing

top·spin \-,spin\ noun [¹top] (1902)
: a rotary motion imparted to a ball that causes it to rotate forward in the direction it is traveling

top·stitch \'täp-,stich\ transitive verb (1934)
: to make a line of stitching on the outside of (a garment) close to a seam

top·sy–tur·vi·ness \,täp-sē-'tər-vē-nəs\ noun (1842)
: the quality or state of being topsy-turvy

¹**top·sy–tur·vy** \,täp-sē-'tər-vē\ adverb [probably ultimately from tops (plural of ¹top) + obsolete English terve to turn upside down] (1528)
1 : in utter confusion or disorder
2 : with the top or head downward : UPSIDE DOWN

²**topsy–turvy** adjective (1612)
: turned topsy-turvy : totally disordered

— **top·sy–tur·vi·ly** \-'tər-və-lē\ adverb
— **top·sy–tur·vy·dom** \-vē-dəm\ noun

³**topsy–turvy** noun (1655)
: TOPSY-TURVINESS

top up (1937)
transitive verb
British : to make up to the full quantity, capacity, or amount
intransitive verb
British : to replenish a supply
— **top–up** \'täp-,əp\ noun, British

top–work \'täp-,wərk\ transitive verb (1882)
: to graft scions of another variety on the main branches of (as fruit trees) usually to obtain more desirable fruit

toque \'tōk\ noun [Middle French, soft hat with a narrow brim worn especially in the 16th century, from Old Spanish toca headdress] (1505)
1 : a woman's small hat without a brim made in any of various soft close-fitting shapes
2 : TUQUE
3 : a tall brimless hat worn by a chef — called also toque blanche

tor \'tòr\ noun [Middle English, from Old English torr] (before 12th century)
: a high craggy hill

To·rah \'tōr-ə, 'tòr-; 'tòi-rə\ noun [Hebrew tōrāh] (1577)
1 : the five books of Moses constituting the Pentateuch
2 : the body of wisdom and law contained in Jewish Scripture and other sacred literature and oral tradition
3 : a leather or parchment scroll of the Pentateuch used in a synagogue for liturgical purposes

¹**torch** \'tòrch\ noun, often attributive [Middle English torche, from Old French, bundle of twisted straw or tow, torch, from (assumed) Vulgar Latin torca; akin to Latin torquēre to twist — more at TORTURE] (14th century)
1 : a burning stick of resinous wood or twist of tow used to give light and usually carried in the hand : FLAMBEAU
2 : something (as tradition, wisdom, or knowledge) likened to a torch as giving light or guidance
3 : any of various portable devices for emitting an unusually hot flame — compare BLOWTORCH
4 chiefly British : FLASHLIGHT 2
5 : INCENDIARY 1a

²**torch** transitive verb (1901)
: to set fire to with or as if with a torch

torch·bear·er \-,bar-ər, -,ber-\ noun (1538)
1 : one that carries a torch
2 : someone in the forefront of a campaign, crusade, or movement

tor·chère \,tòr-'sher\ noun [French, from torche torch] (1904)
1 : a tall ornamental stand for a candlestick or candelabra
2 : an electric floor lamp giving indirect light

torch·light \-,līt\ noun (15th century)
1 : light given by torches
2 : TORCH

tor·chon \'tòr-,shän\ noun [French, duster, from Old French, bundle of twisted straw, from torche] (1865)
: a coarse bobbin or machine-made lace made with fan-shaped designs forming a scalloped edge

torch singer noun (circa 1932)
: a singer of torch songs

torch song noun [from the phrase to carry a torch for (to be in love)] (1930)
: a popular sentimental song of unrequited love

torch·wood \'tòrch-,wùd\ noun (1833)
1 : any of a genus (Amyris) of tropical American trees and shrubs of the rue family with hard heavy fragrant resinous streaky yellowish brown wood
2 : the wood of a torchwood

torchy \'tòr-chē\ adjective **torch·i·er; -est** (1941)
: of, relating to, or characteristic of a torch song or torch singer

tore past of TEAR

to·re·a·dor \'tòr-ē-ə-,dòr, 'tòr-, 'tär-\ noun [Spanish, from torear to fight bulls, from toro bull, from Latin taurus — more at TAURINE] (1618)
: TORERO, BULLFIGHTER

to·re·ro \tə-'rer-(,)ō\ noun, plural **-ros** [Spanish, from Latin taurarius bullfighter, from Latin taurus bull] (1728)
: a matador or a member of the attending cuadrilla

to·reu·tics \tə-'rü-tiks\ noun plural but singular in construction [toreutic, adjective, from Greek toreutikos, from toreuein to bore through, chase, from toreus boring tool; akin to Greek tetrainein to bore — more at THROW] (1847)
: the art or process of working in metal especially by embossing or chasing
— **to·reu·tic** \-'rü-tik\ adjective

tori plural of TORUS

to·ric \'tōr-ik, 'tòr-\ adjective (circa 1898)
: of, relating to, or shaped like a torus or segment of a torus ⟨a toric lens⟩

to·rii \'tōr-ē-,ē, 'tòr-\ noun, plural **torii** [Japanese] (1727)
: a Japanese gateway of light construction commonly built at the approach to a Shinto shrine

¹**tor·ment** \'tòr-,ment\ noun [Middle English, from Old French, from Latin tormentum torture; akin to torquēre to twist — more at TORTURE] (14th century)
1 : the infliction of torture (as by rack or wheel)
2 : extreme pain or anguish of body or mind : AGONY
3 : a source of vexation or pain

²**tor·ment** \tòr-'ment, 'tòr-,\ transitive verb (14th century)
1 : to cause severe usually persistent or recurrent distress of body or mind to ⟨cattle tormented by flies⟩
2 : DISTORT, TWIST
synonym see AFFLICT

tor·men·til \'tòr-mən-,til\ noun [Middle English turmentill, from Medieval Latin tormentilla, from Latin tormentum; from its use in allaying pain] (15th century)
: a yellow-flowered Eurasian cinquefoil (Potentilla erecta synonym P. tormentilla) with a root sometimes used in tanning and dyeing

tor·men·tor also **tor·ment·er** \tòr-'men-tər, 'tòr-,\ noun (14th century)
1 : one that torments
2 : a fixed curtain or flat on each side of a theater stage that prevents the audience from seeing into the wings

torn past participle of TEAR

tor·na·dic \tòr-'nā-dik, -'na-\ adjective (1884)
: relating to, characteristic of, or constituting a tornado

tor·na·do \tòr-'nā-(,)dō\ noun, plural **-does** or **-dos** [modification of Spanish tronada thunderstorm, from tronar to thunder, from Latin tonare — more at THUNDER] (1556)
1 archaic : a tropical thunderstorm
2 a : a squall accompanying a thunderstorm in Africa **b** : a violent destructive whirling wind accompanied by a funnel-shaped cloud that progresses in a narrow path over the land
3 : a violent windstorm : WHIRLWIND

tor·nil·lo \tòr-'nē-(,)yō, -'ni-(,)lō\ noun, plural **-los** [Spanish, literally, small lathe, screw, diminutive of torno lathe, from Latin tornus — more at TURN] (circa 1844)
: SCREWBEAN 1

to·roid \'tōr-,òid, 'tòr-\ noun [New Latin torus] (circa 1900)
1 : a surface generated by a plane closed curve rotated about a line that lies in the same plane as the curve but does not intersect it

2 : a body whose surface has the form of a toroid

to·roi·dal \tȯ-'rȯi-dᵊl\ adjective (circa 1889)
: of, relating to, or shaped like a torus or toroid : doughnut-shaped ⟨a toroidal resistance coil⟩
— **to·roi·dal·ly** \-dᵊl-ē\ adverb

¹tor·pe·do \tȯr-'pē-(,)dō\ noun, plural **-does** [Latin, literally, stiffness, numbness, from torpēre to be sluggish or numb — more at TORPID] (circa 1520)
1 : ELECTRIC RAY
2 : a weapon for destroying ships by rupturing their hulls below the waterline: as **a** : a marine mine **b** : a thin cylindrical self-propelled underwater projectile
3 : a small firework that explodes when thrown against a hard object
4 : a professional gunman or assassin
5 : SUBMARINE 2 ◇

²torpedo transitive verb **tor·pe·doed; tor·pe·do·ing** \-'pē-də-wiŋ\ (circa 1879)
1 : to hit or sink (a ship) with a naval torpedo : strike or destroy by torpedo
2 : to destroy or nullify altogether : WRECK ⟨torpedo a plan⟩

torpedo boat noun (1810)
: a boat designed for launching torpedoes; specifically : a small very fast boat with one or more torpedo tubes

torpedo bomber noun (1930)
: a military airplane designed to carry torpedoes — called also torpedo plane

torpedo tube noun (circa 1891)
: a tube from which torpedoes are fired

tor·pid \'tȯr-pəd\ adjective [Latin torpidus, from torpēre to be sluggish or numb; akin to Lithuanian tirpti to become numb] (1613)
1 a : having lost motion or the power of exertion or feeling : DORMANT, NUMB **b** : sluggish in functioning or acting ⟨a torpid frog⟩ ⟨a torpid mind⟩
2 : lacking in energy or vigor : APATHETIC, DULL
— **tor·pid·i·ty** \tȯr-'pi-də-tē\ noun

tor·por \'tȯr-pər\ noun [Latin, from torpēre] (1607)
1 : APATHY, DULLNESS
2 : a state of mental and motor inactivity with partial or total insensibility : extreme sluggishness or stagnation of function
synonym see LETHARGY

¹torque \'tȯrk\ noun [French, from Latin torques, from torquēre to twist — more at TORTURE] (1695)
: a usually metal collar or neck chain worn by the ancient Gauls, Germans, and Britons

²torque noun [Latin torquēre to twist] (circa 1884)
1 : a force that produces or tends to produce rotation or torsion ⟨an automobile engine delivers torque to the drive shaft⟩; also : a measure of the effectiveness of such a force that consists of the product of the force and the perpendicular distance from the line of action of the force to the axis of rotation
2 : a turning or twisting force

³torque transitive verb **torqued; torqu·ing** (1959)
: to impart torque to : cause to twist (as about an axis)
— **torqu·er** noun

torque converter noun (1927)
: a device for transmitting and amplifying torque especially by hydraulic means

torr \'tȯr\ noun, plural **torr** [Evangelista Torricelli] (1949)
: a unit of pressure equal to 1/760 of an atmosphere (about 133.3 pascals)

¹tor·rent \'tȯr-ənt, 'tär-\ noun [Middle French, from Latin torrent-, torrens, from torrent-, torrens, adjective, burning, seething, rushing, from present participle of torrēre to parch, burn — more at THIRST] (1582)
1 : a tumultuous outpouring : RUSH

2 : a violent stream of a liquid (as water or lava)
3 : a channel of a mountain stream

²torrent adjective (1667)
: TORRENTIAL

tor·ren·tial \tȯ-'ren(t)-shəl, tə-\ adjective (1849)
1 a : relating to or having the character of a torrent ⟨torrential rains⟩ **b** : caused by or resulting from action of rapid streams ⟨torrential gravel⟩
2 : resembling a torrent in violence or rapidity of flow
— **tor·ren·tial·ly** \-'ren(t)-sh(ə-)lē\ adverb

tor·rid \'tȯr-əd, 'tär-\ adjective [Latin torridus, from torrēre] (1545)
1 a : parched with heat especially of the sun : HOT ⟨torrid sands⟩ **b** : giving off intense heat : SCORCHING
2 : ARDENT, PASSIONATE ⟨torrid love letters⟩
— **tor·rid·i·ty** \tȯ-'ri-də-tē\ noun
— **tor·rid·ly** \'tȯr-əd-lē, 'tär-\ adverb
— **tor·rid·ness** noun

torrid zone noun, often T&Z capitalized (1586)
: the region of the earth between the tropic of Cancer and the tropic of Capricorn

tor·sade \tȯr-'säd, -'sad\ noun [French, from obsolete French tors twisted, from (assumed) Vulgar Latin torsus, alteration of Latin tortus, past participle of torquēre to twist] (1882)
: a twisted cord or ribbon used especially as a hat ornament

tor·sion \'tȯr-shən\ noun [Late Latin torsion-, torsio twisting, alteration of Latin tortio, from torquēre to twist] (1543)
1 : the twisting or wrenching of a body by the exertion of forces tending to turn one end or part about a longitudinal axis while the other is held fast or turned in the opposite direction; also : the state of being twisted
2 : the twisting of a bodily organ or part on its own axis
3 : the reactive torque that an elastic solid exerts by reason of being under torsion
— **tor·sion·al** \'tȯr-shnəl, -shə-nᵊl\ adjective
— **tor·sion·al·ly** adverb

torsion bar noun (1948)
: a long metal element in an automobile suspension that has one end held rigidly to the frame end and the other twisted and connected to the axle and that acts as a spring

tor·so \'tȯr-(,)sō\ noun, plural **torsos** or **tor·si** \'tȯr-,sē\ [Italian, literally, stalk, from Latin thyrsus stalk, thyrsus] (1722)
1 : a sculptured representation of the trunk of a human body
2 : something (as a piece of writing) that is mutilated or left unfinished
3 : the human trunk

tort \'tȯrt\ noun [Middle English, injury, from Middle French, from Medieval Latin tortum, from Latin, neuter of tortus twisted, from past participle of torquēre] (1586)
: a wrongful act other than a breach of contract for which relief may be obtained in the form of damages or an injunction

torte \'tȯrt-ə, 'tȯrt\ noun, plural **tor·ten** \'tȯr-tᵊn\ or **tortes** [German, probably from Italian torta cake, from Late Latin, round loaf of bread] (1555)
: a cake made with many eggs and often grated nuts or dry bread crumbs and usually covered with a rich frosting

tor·tel·li·ni \,tȯr-tᵊl-'ē-nē\ noun [Italian, plural of tortellino pasta round, diminutive of tortello, from torta cake] (circa 1911)
: pasta cut in rounds, folded around a filling (as of meat or cheese), formed into rings, and boiled

tor·ti·col·lis \,tȯr-tə-'kä-ləs\ noun [New Latin, from Latin tortus twisted + -i- + collum neck — more at COLLAR] (circa 1811)

: a twisting of the neck to one side that results in abnormal carriage of the head and is usually caused by muscle spasms — called also wryneck

tor·ti·lla \tȯr-'tē-yə\ noun [American Spanish, from Spanish, diminutive of torta cake, from Late Latin, round loaf of bread] (circa 1699)
: a round thin cake of unleavened cornmeal or wheat flour bread usually eaten hot with a topping or filling (as of ground meat or cheese)

tor·tious \'tȯr-shəs\ adjective (1544)
: implying or involving tort
— **tor·tious·ly** adverb

tor·toise \'tȯr-təs\ noun [Middle English tortu, tortuce, from Middle French tortue — more at TURTLE] (14th century)
1 : any of a family (Testudinidae) of terrestrial turtles; broadly : TURTLE
2 : someone or something regarded as slow or laggard

tortoise beetle noun (circa 1711)
: any of various chrysomelid beetles (subfamily Cassidinae) with leaf-eating larvae

¹tor·toise·shell \'tȯr-tə-,shel, -əsh-,shel\ noun (1632)
1 : the mottled horny substance of the shell of some turtles (as the hawksbill turtle) used in inlaying and in making various ornamental articles
2 : any of several showy nymphalid butterflies (genus Nymphalis)

²tortoiseshell adjective (1651)
1 : made of or resembling tortoiseshell especially in mottled brown and yellow coloring
2 : of, relating to, or being a color pattern of the domestic cat consisting of patches of black, orange, and cream

tor·to·ni \tȯr-'tō-nē\ noun [probably from Tortoni 19th century Italian restaurateur in Paris] (1922)
: ice cream made of heavy cream often with minced almonds and chopped maraschino cherries and often flavored with rum

tor·tri·cid \'tȯr-trə-səd\ noun [New Latin Tortricidae, from Tortric-, Tortrix] (circa 1891)

◇ **WORD HISTORY**

torpedo In 1776, David Bushnell, a Connecticut native and supporter of the American cause in the Revolutionary War, devised and built a wooden submarine with a detachable powder magazine that was to be hooked to an enemy ship and set to explode after the submarine had steered clear. According to later accounts, Bushnell dubbed his magazine, with a mixture of learning and whimsy, with the Latin word torpedo "electric ray," a fish that delivers an electric shock. The following year Bushnell experimented with floating mines—powder kegs set off by a spring-released flintlock—but neither his submarine nor his mines succeeded in damaging a British ship. Both of Bushnell's innovations were taken up in the early 1800s by the American inventor Robert Fulton, who also employed torpedo as the name for a "submarine bomb." Though Fulton's schemes came to naught as well, torpedo became fixed as the term for a naval mine. This situation changed in the late 1860s, when the British engineer Robert Whitehead perfected the cylindrical, self-propelled underwater projectile to which the word torpedo soon referred exclusively. Bushnell's crude experiments bore awful fruit in World War I, when submarine-launched torpedoes sank hundreds of ships and changed the character of warfare.

\ə\ abut \ᵊ\ kitten \ər\ further \a\ ash \ā\ ace
\ä\ mop, mar \aů\ out \ch\ chin \e\ bet \ē\ easy
\g\ go \i\ hit \ī\ ice \j\ job \ŋ\ sing \ō\ go
\ȯ\ law \ȯi\ boy \th\ thin \th\ the \ü\ loot \ů\ foot
\y\ yet \zh\ vision see also Guide to Pronunciation

: any of a family (Tortricidae) of small stout-bodied moths many of whose larvae feed in fruits
— **tor·tricid** adjective

tor·trix \'tòr-triks\ noun [New Latin Tortric-, Tortrix, genus of moths, from Latin tortus, past participle of torquēre to twist; from the habit of twisting or rolling leaves to make a nest] (circa 1797)
: a tortricid moth

tor·tu·os·i·ty \,tòr-chə-'wä-sə-tē\ noun, plural **-ties** (1603)
1 : the quality or state of being tortuous
2 : something winding or twisted : BEND

tor·tu·ous \'tòrch-wəs, 'tòr-chə-\ adjective [Middle English, from Middle French tor-tueux, from Latin tortuosus, from tortus twist, from torquēre to twist] (15th century)
1 : marked by repeated twists, bends, or turns : WINDING 〈a tortuous path〉
2 a : marked by devious or indirect tactics : CROOKED, TRICKY 〈a tortuous conspiracy〉 **b** : CIRCUITOUS, INVOLVED 〈the tortuous jargon of legal forms〉
— **tor·tu·ous·ly** adverb
— **tor·tu·ous·ness** noun

¹tor·ture \'tòr-chər\ noun [French, from Late Latin tortura, from Latin tortus, past participle of torquēre to twist; probably akin to Old High German drāhsil turner, Greek atraktos spindle] (1540)
1 a : anguish of body or mind : AGONY **b** : something that causes agony or pain
2 : the infliction of intense pain (as from burning, crushing, or wounding) to punish, coerce, or afford sadistic pleasure
3 : distortion or overrefinement of a meaning or an argument : STRAINING

²torture transitive verb **tor·tured; tor·tur·ing** \'tòrch-riŋ, 'tòr-chə-\ (1588)
1 : to cause intense suffering to : TORMENT
2 : to punish or coerce by inflicting excruciating pain
3 : to twist or wrench out of shape : DISTORT, WARP
synonym see AFFLICT
— **tor·tur·er** \'tòr-chər-ər\ noun

tor·tur·ous \'tòrch-rəs, 'tòr-chə-\ adjective (15th century)
1 a : causing torture 〈torturous inquisitions〉 **b** : very unpleasant or painful 〈a torturous day〉 〈torturous self-doubts〉
2 : painfully difficult or slow 〈the torturous course of the negotiations〉
— **tor·tur·ous·ly** adverb

tor·u·la \'tòr-yə-lə, 'tär-, -ə-lə\ noun, plural **-lae** \-,lē, -,lī\ also **-las** [New Latin, from Latin torus protuberance] (1861)
: any of various fungi and especially yeasts that lack sexual spores, do not produce alcoholic fermentations, and are typically acid formers — called also torula yeast

to·rus \'tòr-əs, 'tòr-\ noun, plural **to·ri** \'tòr-,ī, 'tòr-, -,ē\ [New Latin, from Latin, protuberance, bulge, torus molding] (1563)
1 : a large molding of convex profile commonly occurring as the lowest molding in the base of a column — see BASE illustration
2 : the thickening of a membrane closing a wood-cell pit (as of gymnosperm tracheids) having the secondary cell wall arched over the pit cavity
3 : a doughnut-shaped surface generated by a circle rotated about an axis in its plane that does not intersect the circle; broadly : TOROID
4 : a smooth rounded anatomical protuberance (as a bony ridge on the skull)

To·ry \'tòr-ē, 'tòr-\ noun, plural **Tories** [Irish tóraidhe outlaw, robber, from Middle Irish tóir pursuit] (1646)
1 : a dispossessed Irishman subsisting as an outlaw chiefly in the 17th century
2 obsolete : BANDIT, OUTLAW
3 a : a member or supporter of a major British political group of the 18th and early 19th centuries favoring at first the Stuarts and later

royal authority and the established church and seeking to preserve the traditional political structure and defeat parliamentary reform — compare WHIG **b** : CONSERVATIVE 1b
4 : an American upholding the cause of the British Crown against the supporters of colonial independence during the American Revolution : LOYALIST
5 often not capitalized : an extreme conservative especially in political and economic principles
— **Tory** adjective

Tory Democracy noun (1879)
: a political philosophy advocating preservation of established institutions and traditional principles combined with political democracy and a social and economic program designed to benefit the common man

To·ry·ism \'tòr-ē-,i-zəm, 'tòr-\ noun (1682)
1 : the principles and practices of or associated with Tories
2 : the British Tory party or its members

tosh \'täsh\ noun [origin unknown] (1528)
: sheer nonsense : BOSH, TWADDLE

¹toss \'tòs, 'täs\ verb [probably of Scandinavian origin; akin to Swedish dialect tossa to spread, scatter] (1506)
transitive verb
1 a : to fling or heave continuously about, to and fro, or up and down 〈a ship tossed by waves〉 **b** : BANDY 2b, c, d **c** : to mix lightly until well coated with a dressing or until the elements are thoroughly combined 〈toss a salad〉
2 : to make uneasy : stir up : DISTURB
3 a : to throw with a quick, light, or careless motion or with a sudden jerk 〈toss a ball around〉 **b** : to throw up in the air 〈tossed by a bull〉 **c** : MATCH 5a **d** : to send as if by throwing 〈tossed in jail〉 〈tossed out of the game〉 **e** : to get rid of : THROW AWAY
4 a : to fling or lift with a sudden motion 〈tosses her head angrily〉 **b** : to tilt suddenly so as to empty by drinking 〈tossed his glass〉; also : to consume by drinking 〈toss down a drink〉
5 : to accomplish, provide, or produce readily or easily 〈toss off a few verses〉
6 : THROW 16 〈toss a party〉
7 : VOMIT 1 — often used in the phrase toss one's cookies
intransitive verb
1 a : to move restlessly or turbulently; especially : to twist and turn repeatedly 〈tossed sleeplessly all night〉 **b** : to move with a quick or spirited gesture
2 : to decide an issue by flipping a coin
synonym see THROW
— **toss·er** noun

²toss noun (1634)
1 : the state or fact of being tossed
2 : an act or instance of tossing: as **a** : an abrupt tilting or upward fling **b** : a deciding by chance and especially by flipping a coin **c** : THROW, PITCH

toss·pot \-,pät\ noun (1568)
: DRUNKARD, SOT

toss-up \-,əp\ noun (1812)
1 : TOSS 2b
2 : an even chance
3 : something that offers no clear basis for choice

tos·ta·da \tō-'stä-də\ also **tos·ta·do** \-(,)dō\ noun [Mexican Spanish tostada, from Spanish, feminine of tostado, past participle of tostar to toast, roast, from Late Latin tostare — more at TOAST] (1939)
: a tortilla fried in deep fat

¹tot \'tät\ noun [origin unknown] (1725)
1 : a small child : TODDLER
2 : a small drink or allowance of liquor : SHOT

²tot verb **tot·ted; tot·ting** [tot., abbreviation of total] (circa 1772)
transitive verb
: to add together : TOTAL — usually used with up 〈tots up the score〉

intransitive verb
: ADD

¹to·tal \'tōt-ᵊl\ adjective [Middle English, from Middle French, from Medieval Latin totalis, from Latin totus whole, entire] (15th century)
1 : comprising or constituting a whole : ENTIRE 〈the total amount〉
2 : ABSOLUTE, UTTER 〈a total failure〉
3 : involving a complete and unified effort especially to achieve a desired effect 〈total war〉 〈total theater〉
synonym see WHOLE

²total noun (1557)
1 : a product of addition : SUM
2 : an entire quantity : AMOUNT

³total adverb (1601)
: TOTALLY

⁴total transitive verb **to·taled** or **to·talled; to·tal·ing** or **to·tal·ling** (1716)
1 : to add up : COMPUTE
2 : to amount to : NUMBER
3 : to make a total wreck of : DEMOLISH 〈totaled the car〉

total depravity noun (1794)
: a state of corruption due to original sin held in Calvinism to infect every part of man's nature and to make the natural man unable to know or obey God

total eclipse noun (1671)
: an eclipse in which one celestial body is completely obscured by the shadow or body of another

to·tal·ism \'tōt-ᵊl-,i-zəm\ noun (1941)
: TOTALITARIANISM
— **to·tal·is·tic** \,tōt-ᵊl-'is-tik\ adjective

¹to·tal·i·tar·i·an \(,)tō-,ta-lə-'ter-ē-ən\ adjective [Italian totalitario, from totalità totality] (1926)
1 a : of or relating to centralized control by an autocratic leader or hierarchy : AUTHORITARIAN, DICTATORIAL; especially : DESPOTIC **b** : of or relating to a political regime based on subordination of the individual to the state and strict control of all aspects of the life and productive capacity of the nation especially by coercive measures (as censorship and terrorism)
2 a : advocating or characteristic of totalitarianism **b** : completely regulated by the state especially as an aid to national mobilization in an emergency **c** : exercising autocratic powers : tending toward monopoly

²totalitarian noun (circa 1934)
: an advocate or practitioner of totalitarianism

to·tal·i·tar·i·an·ism \(,)tō-,ta-lə-'ter-ē-ə-,ni-zəm\ noun (1926)
1 : centralized control by an autocratic authority
2 : the political concept that the citizen should be totally subject to an absolute state authority

to·tal·i·tar·i·an·ize \-,nīz\ transitive verb **-ized; -iz·ing** (1935)
: to make totalitarian 〈a society totalitarianized by the military-industrial complex —W. F. Buckley (born 1925)〉

to·tal·i·ty \tō-'ta-lə-tē\ noun, plural **-ties** (1598)
1 : an aggregate amount : SUM, WHOLE
2 a : the quality or state of being total : WHOLENESS **b** : the phase of an eclipse during which it is total : state of total eclipse

to·tal·iza·tor or **to·tal·isa·tor** \'tō-tᵊl-ə-,zā-tər\ noun (1879)
: PARI-MUTUEL 2

to·tal·ize \'tō-tᵊl-,īz\ transitive verb **-ized; -iz·ing** (1818)
1 : to add up : TOTAL
2 : to express as a whole

to·tal·iz·er \-,ī-zər\ noun (1887)
: one that totalizes: as **a** : PARI-MUTUEL 2 **b** : a device (as a meter) that records a remaining total (as of fuel)

to·tal·ly \'tō-tᵊl-ē\ adverb (1509)
: in a total manner : to a total or complete degree : WHOLLY, ENTIRELY

total recall noun (1926)

: the faculty of remembering with complete clarity and in complete detail

¹tote \'tōt\ *transitive verb* **tot·ed; tot·ing** [perhaps from an English-based creole; akin to Gullah & Krio *tot* to carry] (1677)
1 : to carry by hand **:** bear on the person **:** LUG, PACK
2 : HAUL, CONVEY ◇
— **tot·er** \'tō-tər\ *noun*
²tote *noun* (circa 1772)
1 : BURDEN, LOAD
2 : TOTE BAG
³tote *transitive verb* **tot·ed; tot·ing** [English dialect *tote*, noun, total] (1888)
: ADD, TOTAL — usually used with *up* ⟨*toted* up his accomplishments —G. P. Morrill⟩
⁴tote *noun* [short for *totalizator*] (1891)
: PARI-MUTUEL 2
tote bag *noun* (1900)
: a large 2-handled open-topped bag (as of canvas)
tote board *noun* [⁴*tote*] (circa 1949)
: an electrically operated board (as at a race-track) on which pertinent information (as betting odds and race results) is posted
to·tem \'tō-təm\ *noun* [Ojibwa *oto'te'man* his totem] (circa 1776)
1 a : an object (as an animal or plant) serving as the emblem of a family or clan and often as a reminder of its ancestry; *also* **:** a usually carved or painted representation of such an object **b :** a family or clan identified by a common totemic object
2 : something that serves as an emblem or revered symbol
to·tem·ic \tō-'te-mik\ *adjective* (1846)
1 : of, relating to, suggestive of, or characteristic of a totem or totemism ⟨a *totemic* animal⟩
2 : based on or practicing totemism ⟨*totemic* clan structure⟩
to·tem·ism \'tō-tə-,mi-zəm\ *noun* (1791)
1 : belief in kinship with or a mystical relationship between a group or an individual and a totem
2 : a system of social organization based on totemic affiliations
to·tem·is·tic \,tō-tə-'mis-tik\ *adjective* (1873)
: TOTEMIC
totem pole *noun* (1897)
1 : a pole or pillar carved and painted with a series of totemic symbols representing family lineage and often mythical or historical incidents and erected before the houses of Indian tribes of the northwest coast of North America
2 : an order of rank **:** HIERARCHY
toth·er *or* **t'oth·er** \'tə-thər\ *pronoun or adjective* [Middle English *tother*, alteration (resulting from misdivision of *thet other* the other, from *thet the*— from Old English *thæt* — + *other*) of *other* — more at THAT] (13th century)
chiefly dialect **:** the other

totem pole
1

to·ti·po·ten·cy \tō-'ti-pə-tən(t)-sē, ,tō-tə-'pō-t⁵n-\ *noun* (1909)
: ability to generate or regenerate a whole organism from a part
to·ti·po·tent \-tənt, -'t⁵nt\ *adjective* [Latin *totus* whole, entire + English -*i*- + *potent*] (circa 1899)
: capable of developing into a complete organism or differentiating into any of its cells or tissues ⟨*totipotent* blastomeres⟩
¹tot·ter \'tä-tər\ *intransitive verb* [Middle English *toteren*] (15th century)
1 a : to tremble or rock as if about to fall **:** SWAY **b :** to become unstable **:** threaten to collapse
2 : to move unsteadily **:** STAGGER, WOBBLE
²totter *noun* (1747)
: an unsteady gait **:** WOBBLE
tot·ter·ing *adjective* (1534)
1 a : being in an unstable condition ⟨a *tottering* building⟩ **b :** walking unsteadily

2 : lacking firmness or stability **:** INSECURE ⟨a *tottering* regime⟩
— **tot·ter·ing·ly** \-tə-riŋ-lē\ *adverb*
tot·tery \'tä-tə-rē\ *adjective* (circa 1755)
: of an infirm or precarious nature
Toua·reg *variant of* TUAREG
tou·can \'tü-,kan, -,kän, tü-'\ *noun* [French, from Portuguese *tucano*, from Tupi *tukána*] (1568)
: any of a family (Ramphastidae) of fruit-eating birds of tropical America with brilliant coloring and a very large but light and thin-walled beak
¹touch \'təch\ *verb* [Middle English, from Old French *tuchier*, from (assumed) Vulgar Latin *toccare* to knock, strike a bell, touch, probably of imitative origin] (14th century)
transitive verb
1 : to bring a bodily part into contact with especially so as to perceive through the tactile sense **:** handle or feel gently usually with the intent to understand or appreciate ⟨loved to *touch* the soft silk⟩
2 : to strike or push lightly especially with the hand or foot or an implement
3 : to lay hands upon (one afflicted with scrofula) with intent to heal
4 *archaic* **a :** to play on (a stringed instrument) **b :** to perform (a melody) by playing or singing
5 a : to take into the hands or mouth ⟨never *touches* alcohol⟩ **b :** to put hands upon in any way or degree ⟨don't *touch* anything before the police come⟩; *especially* **:** to commit violence upon ⟨swears he never *touched* the child⟩
6 : to deal with **:** become involved with ⟨a sticky situation and I wouldn't *touch* it with a 10-foot pole⟩
7 : to induce to give or lend ⟨*touched* him for ten dollars⟩
8 : to cause to be briefly in contact or conjunction with something ⟨*touched* her spurs to the horse⟩ ⟨*touched* his hand to his hat⟩
9 a (1) **:** to meet without overlapping or penetrating **:** ADJOIN (2) **:** to get to **:** REACH ⟨the speedometer needle *touched* 80⟩ **b :** to be tangent to **c :** to rival in quality or value ⟨nothing can *touch* that cloth for durability⟩
10 : to speak or tell of especially in passing ⟨barely *touched* the incident in the speech⟩
11 a : to relate to **:** CONCERN **b :** to have an influence on **:** AFFECT
12 a : to leave a mark or impression on ⟨few reagents will *touch* gold⟩; *also* **:** TINGE **b :** to harm slightly by or as if by contact **:** TAINT, BLEMISH ⟨fruit *touched* by frost⟩ **c :** to give a delicate tint, line, or expression to ⟨a smile *touched* her lips⟩
13 : to draw or delineate with light strokes
14 a : to hurt the feelings of **:** WOUND **b :** to move to sympathetic feeling
intransitive verb
1 a : to feel something with a body part (as the hand or foot) **b :** to lay hand or finger on a person to cure disease (as scrofula)
2 : to be in contact
3 : to come close **:** VERGE ⟨your actions *touch* on treason⟩
4 : to have a bearing **:** RELATE — used with *on* or *upon*
5 a : to make a brief or incidental stop on shore during a trip by water ⟨*touched* at several ports⟩ **b :** to treat a topic in a brief or casual manner — used with *on* or *upon* ⟨*touched* upon many points⟩
synonym see AFFECT
— **touch·able** \'tə-chə-bəl\ *adjective*
— **touch·er** *noun*
— **touch base :** to come in contact or communication ⟨coming in from the cold to *touch base* with civilization —Carla Hunt⟩
²touch *noun* (14th century)
1 : a light stroke, tap, or push
2 : the act or fact of touching

3 : the special sense by which pressure or traction exerted on the skin or mucous membrane is perceived
4 : mental or moral sensitiveness, responsiveness, or tact ⟨has a wonderful *touch* with children⟩
5 : a specified sensation that arises in response to stimulation of the tactile receptors **:** FEEL ⟨the velvety *touch* of velour⟩
6 a : the act of rubbing gold or silver on a touchstone to test its quality **b :** TEST, TRIAL — used chiefly in the phrase *put to the touch*
7 a : a visible effect **:** MARK ⟨a *touch* of the tropical sun⟩ **b :** WEAKNESS, DEFECT
8 : something slight of its kind: as **a :** a light attack ⟨a *touch* of fever⟩ **b :** a small quantity or indication **:** HINT ⟨a *touch* of spring in the air⟩ **c :** a transient emotion ⟨a momentary *touch* of compunction⟩ **d :** a near approach **:** CLOSE CALL ⟨beaten in the championships by a mere *touch*⟩
9 a *archaic* **:** the playing of an instrument (as a lute or piano) with the fingers; *also* **:** musical notes or strains so produced **b :** particular action of a keyboard with reference to the resistance of its keys to pressure ⟨piano with a stiff *touch*⟩
10 : control of the hands: as **a :** a manner or method of touching or striking especially the keys of a keyboard instrument **b :** ability to control the distance something (as a ball) is propelled ⟨developed his putting *touch*⟩
11 : a set of changes in change ringing that is less than a peal
12 a : an effective and subtle detail ⟨applies the finishing *touches* to the story⟩ **b :** distinctive and often effective manner or method ⟨the *touch* of a master⟩ **c :** a characteristic or distinguishing trait or quality
13 *slang* **:** an act of soliciting or getting a gift or loan
14 : the state or fact of being in contact or communication or of having awareness ⟨lost *touch* with her cousin⟩ ⟨let's keep in *touch*⟩ ⟨out of *touch* with modern times⟩

15 : the area outside of the touchlines in soccer or outside of and including the touchlines in rugby

— **a touch :** SOMEWHAT, RATHER ⟨aimed *a touch* too low and missed⟩

touch–and–go \ˌtəch-ən(d)-ˈgō\ *noun* (1953)
: an airplane landing followed immediately by application of power and a takeoff and usually executed as one of a series for practice at landings

touch and go *adjective* (1815)
: unpredictable as to outcome **:** UNCERTAIN ⟨it was *touch and go* there for a while⟩

touch·back \ˈtəch-ˌbak\ *noun* (circa 1890)
: a situation in football in which the ball is down behind the goal line after a kick or intercepted forward pass after which it is put in play by the team defending the goal on its own 20-yard line — compare SAFETY

touch·down \ˈtəch-ˌdaun\ *noun* (1876)
1 : the act of touching a football to the ground behind an opponent's goal; *specifically* **:** the act of scoring six points in American football by being lawfully in possession of the ball on, above, or behind an opponent's goal line when the ball is declared dead
2 : the act or moment of touching down (as with an airplane or spacecraft)

touch down (1864)
transitive verb
: to place (the ball in rugby) by hand on the ground on or over an opponent's goal line in scoring a try or behind one's own goal line as a defensive measure
intransitive verb
: to reach the ground **:** LAND

tou·ché \tü-ˈshā\ *interjection* [French, from past participle of *toucher* to touch, from Old French *tuchier*] (1904)
— used to acknowledge a hit in fencing or the success or appropriateness of an argument, an accusation, or a witty point

touched \ˈtəcht\ *adjective* (14th century)
1 : emotionally stirred (as with gratitude)
2 : slightly unbalanced mentally

touch football *noun* (1933)
: football played informally and chiefly characterized by the substitution of touching for tackling

touch·hole \ˈtəch-ˌhōl\ *noun* (1501)
: the vent in muzzle-loading guns through which the charge is ignited

¹touch·ing *preposition* (14th century)
: in reference to **:** CONCERNING

²touching *adjective* (1601)
: capable of arousing emotions of tenderness or compassion
synonym see MOVING
— **touch·ing·ly** \ˈtə-chiŋ-lē\ *adverb*

touch·line \ˈtəch-ˌlīn\ *noun* (1868)
: either of the lines that bound the long sides of the field of play in rugby and soccer

touch·mark \-ˌmärk\ *noun* (1904)
: an identifying maker's mark impressed on pewter

touch–me–not \ˈtəch-mē-ˌnät\ *noun* [from the bursting of the ripe pods and scattering of their seeds when touched] (1659)
: either of two North American impatiens growing in moist areas: as **a :** one (*Impatiens capensis*) typically having crimson-spotted orange flowers **b :** one (*I. pallida*) having yellow to white flowers sometimes spotted with brownish red

touch off *transitive verb* (circa 1765)
1 : to describe or characterize with precision
2 a : to cause to explode by or as if by touching with fire **b :** to provoke or initiate with sudden intensity ⟨the verdict *touched off* local riots⟩

touch pad *noun* (1979)
: a keypad for an electronic device (as a microwave oven) that consists of a flat surface divided into several differently marked areas which are touched to choose options

touch screen *noun* (1974)

: a display screen on which the user selects options (as from a menu) by touching the screen

touch·stone \ˈtəch-ˌstōn\ *noun* (1530)
1 : a black siliceous stone related to flint and formerly used to test the purity of gold and silver by the streak left on the stone when rubbed by the metal
2 : a test or criterion for determining the quality or genuineness of a thing
3 : a fundamental or quintessential part or feature
synonym see STANDARD

touch system *noun* (1918)
: a method of typing that assigns a particular finger to each key and makes it possible to type without looking at the keyboard

Touch–Tone \ˈtəch-ˌtōn, -ˌtōn\ *trademark*
— used for a telephone having push buttons that produce tones corresponding to numbers

touch–type \ˈtəch-ˌtīp\ *intransitive verb* (1943)
: to type by the touch system
— **touch typist** *noun*

touch–up \ˈtəch-ˌəp\ *noun* (1885)
: an act or instance of touching up

touch up *transitive verb* (1715)
1 : to improve or perfect by small additional strokes or alterations **:** fix the minor and usually visible defects or damages of
2 : to stimulate by or as if by a flick of a whip

touch·wood \ˈtəch-ˌwud\ *noun* (1579)
: ³PUNK

touchy \ˈtə-chē\ *adjective* **touch·i·er; -est** (1605)
1 : marked by readiness to take offense on slight provocation
2 a : *of a body part* **:** acutely sensitive or irritable **b :** *of a chemical* **:** highly explosive or inflammable
3 : calling for tact, care, or caution in treatment ⟨a *touchy* subject⟩
— **touch·i·ly** \ˈtə-chə-lē\ *adverb*
— **touch·i·ness** \ˈtə-chē-nəs\ *noun*

touchy–feely \ˌtə-chē-ˈfē-lē\ *adjective* (1968)
: characterized by or encouraging interpersonal touching especially in the free expression of emotions ⟨*touchy-feely* therapy⟩; *also* **:** openly or excessively emotional and personal ⟨*touchy-feely* management⟩

¹tough \ˈtəf\ *adjective* [Middle English, from Old English *tōh*; akin to Old High German *zāhi* tough] (before 12th century)
1 a : strong or firm in texture but flexible and not brittle **b :** not easily chewed
2 : GLUTINOUS, STICKY
3 : characterized by severity or uncompromising determination
4 : capable of enduring strain, hardship, or severe labor
5 : very hard to influence **:** STUBBORN
6 : difficult to accomplish, resolve, endure, or deal with ⟨a *tough* question⟩ ⟨*tough* luck⟩
7 : stubbornly fought ⟨a *tough* contest⟩
8 : UNRULY, ROWDYISH
9 : marked by absence of softness or sentimentality
synonym see STRONG
— **tough·ly** *adverb*
— **tough·ness** *noun*

²tough *adverb* (14th century)
: in a tough manner ⟨talks *tough* and insensitively —A. E. Stevenson (died 1965)⟩

³tough *transitive verb* (1830)
: to bear unflinchingly **:** ENDURE — usually used with *out* especially in the phrase *tough it out*

⁴tough *noun* (1866)
: a tough person **:** ROWDY

tough·en \ˈtə-fən\ *verb* **tough·ened; tough·en·ing** \ˈtə-fə-niŋ, ˈtəf-niŋ\ (1582)
transitive verb
: to make tough
intransitive verb
: to become tough

tough·ie *also* **toughy** \ˈtə-fē\ *noun, plural* **tough·ies** (1921)
: one that is tough: as **a :** a loud rough rowdy person **b :** a difficult problem or question

tough–mind·ed \ˈtəf-ˌmīn-dəd\ *adjective* (1909)
: realistic or unsentimental in temper or outlook
— **tough–mind·ed·ness** *noun*

tou·pee \tü-ˈpā\ *noun* [French *toupet* forelock, from Old French, diminutive of *top, toup,* of Germanic origin; akin to Old High German *zopf* tuft of hair — more at TOP] (1728)
1 : a curl or lock of hair made into a topknot on a periwig or natural coiffure; *also* **:** a periwig with such a topknot
2 : a wig or section of hair worn to cover a bald spot

¹tour \ˈtur, *1 is also* ˈtaur\ *noun* [Middle English, from Middle French, from Old French *tourn, tour* lathe, circuit, turn — more at TURN] (14th century)
1 a : one's turn in an orderly schedule **:** SHIFT **b :** a period during which an individual or unit is on a specific duty or at one place ⟨a *tour* of duty⟩
2 a : a journey for business, pleasure, or education often involving a series of stops and ending at the starting point; *also* **:** something resembling such a tour ⟨a *tour* of the history of philosophy⟩ **b :** a brief turn **:** ROUND **c :** a series of professional tournaments (as in golf or tennis)

²tour (1789)
intransitive verb
: to make a tour
transitive verb
1 : to make a tour of
2 : to present (as a theatrical production) on a tour

tou·ra·co \ˈtur-ə-ˌkō\ *noun, plural* **-cos** [origin unknown] (circa 1743)
: any of a family (Musophagidae) of African birds that are related to the cuckoos and have a long tail, a short stout often colored bill, and red wing feathers

tour·bil·lion \tur-ˈbil-yən\ *or* **tour·bil·lon** \tur-bē-yōⁿ\ *noun* [Middle English, from Middle French *tourbillon,* from Latin *turbin-, turbo* — more at TURBINE] (15th century)
1 : WHIRLWIND
2 : a vortex especially of a whirlwind or whirlpool

tour de force \ˌtur-də-ˈfōrs, -ˈfors\ *noun, plural* **tours de force** *same*\ [French] (1802)
: a feat of strength, skill, or ingenuity

tour·er \ˈtur-ər\ *noun* (1926)
1 : TOURING CAR
2 : one that tours

Tou·rette's syndrome \tü-ˈrets-\ *noun* [Georges Gille de la *Tourette* (died 1904) French physician] (1970)
: a rare disease characterized by involuntary tics and by uncontrollable verbalization involving especially echolalia and the use of obscene language — called also *Tou·rette syndrome* \-ˈret\-

tour·ing \ˈtur-iŋ\ *noun* (1794)
1 : participation in a tour
2 : cross-country skiing for pleasure

touring car *noun* (1903)
: an automobile suitable for distance driving: as **a :** a vintage automobile with two cross seats, usually four doors, and a folding top **:** PHAETON 2 **b :** a modern usually 2-door sedan as distinguished from a sports car

touring car a

tour·ism \ˈtur-ˌi-zəm\ *noun* (1811)
1 : the practice of traveling for recreation
2 : the guidance or management of tourists

3 a : the promotion or encouragement of touring **b :** the accommodation of tourists

tour·ist \'túr-ist\ *noun* (1780)
1 : one that makes a tour for pleasure or culture
2 : TOURIST CLASS
— **tourist** *adjective or adverb*

tourist card *noun* (1948)
: a citizenship identity card issued to a tourist usually for a stated period of time in lieu of a passport or a visa

tourist class *noun* (1935)
: economy accommodations (as on a ship)

tourist court *noun* (1937)
: MOTEL

tour·is·tic \túr-'is-tik\ *adjective* (1848)
: of or relating to a tour, tourism, or tourists
— **tour·is·ti·cal·ly** \-ti-k(ə-)lē\ *adverb*

tourist trap *noun* (1939)
: a place that attracts and exploits tourists

tour·isty \'túr-əs-tē\ *adjective* (1906)
: of or relating to tourists: as **a :** patronized by tourists **b :** of a type appealing to tourists

tour·ma·line \'túr-mə-lən, -,lēn\ *noun* [Sinhalese *toramalli* carnelian] (1759)
: a mineral of variable color that consists of a complex borosilicate and makes a striking gem when transparent and cut

tour·na·ment \'túr-nə-mənt *also* 'tər- *or* 'tòr-\ *noun* [Middle English *tornement*, from Old French *torneiement*, from *torneier*] (14th century)
1 a : a knightly sport of the middle ages between mounted combatants armed with blunted lances or swords and divided into two parties contesting for a prize or favor bestowed by the lady of the tournament **b :** the whole series of knightly sports, jousts, and tilts occurring at one time and place
2 : a series of games or contests that make up a single unit of competition (as on the professional golf tour), the championship play-offs of a league or conference, or an invitational event

tour·ne·dos \,túr-nə-'dō\ *noun, plural* **tour·ne·dos** \-'dō(z)\ [French, from *tourner* to turn + *dos* back] (1877)
: a small fillet of beef usually cut from the tip of the tenderloin

¹tour·ney \'túr-nē, 'tər- *also* 'tòr-\ *intransitive verb* **tour·neyed; tour·ney·ing** [Middle English, from Middle French *torneier*, from Old French, from *torn, tourn* lathe, circuit] (14th century)
: to perform in a tournament

²tourney *noun, plural* **tourneys** (14th century)
: TOURNAMENT

tour·ni·quet \'túr-ni-kət, 'tər-\ *noun* [French, turnstile, tourniquet, from *tourner* to turn, from Old French — more at TURN] (1695)
: a device (as a bandage twisted tight with a stick) to check bleeding or blood flow

¹touse \'taúz\ *transitive verb* **toused; tous·ing** [Middle English *-tousen;* akin to Old High German *zirzūsōn* to pull to pieces] (1598)
: RUMPLE, TOUSLE

²touse *noun* (1795)
: a noisy disturbance

¹tou·sle \'taú-zəl, -səl\ *transitive verb* **tou·sled; tou·sling** \'taúz-liŋ, 'taús-; 'taú-zə-, -sə-\ [Middle English *touselen*, frequentative of *-tousen*] (15th century)
: DISHEVEL, RUMPLE

²tou·sle \'taú-zəl, *1 is also* 'tü-\ *noun* (1788)
1 *Scottish* **:** rough dalliance **:** TUSSLE
2 : a tangled mass (as of hair)

¹tout \'taút, *in sense 4 also* 'tüt\ *verb* [Middle English *tuten* to peep; probably akin to Old English *tōtian* to stick out, Norwegian *tyte*] (circa 1700)
transitive verb
1 : to spy on **:** WATCH

2 a *British* **:** to spy out information about (as a racing stable or horse) **b :** to give a tip or solicit bets on (a racehorse)
3 : to solicit, peddle, or persuade importunately ⟨not meant to *tout* you off the movie —Russell Baker⟩
4 : to praise or publicize loudly or extravagantly ⟨*touted* as the . . . most elaborate suburban shopping development —*Wall Street Journal*⟩
intransitive verb
1 : to solicit patronage
2 a *chiefly British* **:** to spy on racehorses in training to gain information for betting **b :** to give a tip or solicit bets on a racehorse

²tout *noun* (1853)
: one who touts: as **a :** one who solicits patronage **b** *chiefly British* **:** one who spies out racing information for betting purposes **c :** one who gives tips or solicits bets on a racehorse

tout·er \'taú-tər\ *noun* (circa 1754)
: one that touts

to·va·rich *or* **to·va·rish** \tə-'vär-ish, -ich\ *noun* [Russian *tovarishch*] (circa 1917)
: COMRADE

¹tow \'tō\ *verb* [Middle English, from Old English *togian;* akin to Old English *tēon* to draw, pull, Old High German *ziohan* to draw, pull, Latin *ducere* to draw, lead] (before 12th century)
transitive verb
: to draw or pull along behind **:** HAUL
intransitive verb
: to move in tow ⟨trailers that *tow* behind the family auto —Bob Munger⟩

²tow *noun* (1600)
1 : a rope or chain for towing
2 a : the act or an instance of towing **b :** the fact or state of being towed
3 a : something towed (as a boat or car) **b :** a group of barges lashed together and usually pushed
4 a : something (as a tugboat) that tows **b :** SKI TOW

— **in tow 1 :** under guidance or protection ⟨taken *in tow* by a friendly native⟩ **2 :** in the position of a dependent or devoted follower or admirer

³tow *noun* [Middle English, from Old English *tow-* spinning; akin to Old Norse *tō* tuft of wool for spinning, Old English *tawian* to prepare for use — more at TAW] (14th century)
1 : short or broken fiber (as of flax, hemp, or synthetic material) that is used especially for yarn, twine, or stuffing
2 a : yarn or cloth made of tow **b :** a loose essentially untwisted strand of synthetic fibers

⁴tow *noun* [Middle English (Scots), probably from Old English *toh-* (in *tohlīne* towline); akin to Old English *togian* to tow] (15th century)
chiefly Scottish & dialect English **:** ROPE

tow·age \'tō-ij\ *noun* (14th century)
1 : the act of towing
2 : a charge for towing

¹to·ward \'tō(-ə)rd, 'tò(-ə)rd\ *adjective* [Middle English *toward*, from Old English *tōweard* facing, imminent, from *tō*, preposition, to + *-weard* -ward] (before 12th century)
1 *also* **to·wards** \'tō(-ə)rdz, 'tò(-ə)rdz\ [Middle English *towardes*, from Old English *tōweardes*, preposition, toward, from *tōweard*, adjective] **a :** coming soon **:** IMMINENT **b :** happening at the moment **:** AFOOT
2 a *obsolete* **:** quick to learn **:** APT **b :** PROPITIOUS, FAVORING ⟨a *toward* breeze⟩

²to·ward *or* **to·wards** \'tō(-ə)rd(z), 'tò(-ə)rd(z), tə-'wòrd(z), 'twòrd(z), 'twōrd(z)\ *preposition* (before 12th century)
1 : in the direction of ⟨driving *toward* town⟩
2 a : along a course leading to ⟨a long stride *toward* disarmament⟩ **b :** in relation to ⟨an attitude *toward* life⟩

3 a : at a point in the direction of **:** NEAR ⟨a cottage somewhere up *toward* the lake⟩ **b :** in such a position as to be in the direction of ⟨your back was *toward* me⟩
4 : not long before ⟨*toward* the end of the afternoon⟩
5 a : in the way of help or assistance in ⟨did all he could *toward* raising campaign funds⟩ **b :** for the partial payment of ⟨proceeds go *toward* the establishment of a scholarship⟩

to·ward·li·ness \'tōrd-lē-nəs, 'tòrd-\ *noun* (1566)
archaic **:** the quality or state of being toward or towardly

to·ward·ly \'tō(-ə)rd-lē, 'tò(-ə)rd-\ *adjective* (1513)
archaic
1 : PLEASANT, AFFABLE
2 : FAVORABLE, PROPITIOUS
3 : developing favorably **:** PROMISING
— **towardly** *adverb*

tow·boat \'tō-,bōt\ *noun* (1815)
1 : TUGBOAT
2 : a compact shallow-draft boat with a squared bow designed and fitted for pushing tows of barges on inland waterways

¹tow·el \'taú-(ə)l\ *noun* [Middle English *towaille*, from Old French *toaille*, of Germanic origin; akin to Old High German *dwahila* towel; akin to Old High German *dwahan* to wash] (13th century)
: an absorbent cloth or paper for wiping or drying

²towel *verb* **-eled** *or* **-elled; -el·ing** *or* **-el·ling** (circa 1839)
transitive verb
: to rub or dry (as the body) with a towel
intransitive verb
: to use a towel to dry oneself

tow·el·ette \,taú-(ə-)'let\ *noun* (1902)
: a small usually premoistened piece of material used for personal cleansing (as of the hands)

tow·el·ing *or* **tow·el·ling** \'taú-(ə-)liŋ\ *noun* (1583)
: a cotton or linen fabric often used for making towels

¹tow·er \'taú-(ə)r\ *noun* [Middle English *tour, tor*, from Old English *torr* & Old French *tor, tur*, both from Latin *turris*, from Greek *tyrris, tyrsis*] (before 12th century)
1 : a building or structure typically higher than its diameter and high relative to its surroundings that may stand apart (as a campanile), or be attached (as a church belfry) to a larger structure, and that may be fully walled in or of skeleton framework (as an observation or transmission tower)
2 : a towering citadel **:** FORTRESS
3 : one that provides support or protection **:** BULWARK ⟨a *tower* of strength⟩
— **tow·ered** \'taú(-ə)rd\ *adjective*
— **tow·er·like** \'taú(-ə)r-,līk\ *adjective*

²tower *intransitive verb* (1582)
1 : to reach or rise to a great height
2 : to exhibit superior qualities **:** SURPASS ⟨her intellect *towered* over the others⟩

tower block *noun* (1966)
chiefly British **:** a tall building (as a high-rise apartment building)

tower house *noun* (1687)
: a medieval fortified castle (as in Scotland)

tow·er·ing *adjective* (1592)
1 : impressively high or great **:** IMPOSING ⟨*towering* pines⟩
2 : reaching a high point of intensity **:** OVERWHELMING ⟨a *towering* rage⟩
3 : going beyond proper bounds **:** EXCESSIVE ⟨*towering* ambitions⟩
— **tow·er·ing·ly** \'taú(-ə)r-iŋ-lē\ *adverb*

Tower of Babel (circa 1887)
: BABEL 2

tow·head \'tō-,hed\ *noun* (1829)
1 : a low alluvial island or shoal in a river
: SANDBAR
2 : a head of hair resembling tow especially in being flaxen or tousled; *also* : a person having such a head of hair
— **tow·head·ed** \-,he-dəd\ *adjective*

to·whee \tō-,hē, 'tō-(,)ē, tō-'hē\ *noun* [imitative] (circa 1729)
1 : a common finch (*Pipilo erythrophthalmus*) of eastern North America having the male black, white, and rufous — called also *chewink*
2 : any of the North American finches belonging to the same genus (*Pipilo*) as the towhee

to wit \tə-'wit\ *adverb* [Middle English *to witen*, literally, to know — more at WIT] (14th century)
: that is to say : NAMELY

tow·line \'tō-,līn\ *noun* (1719)
: TOWROPE

tow·mond \'tō-,mänd\ *noun* [Middle English *towlmonyth*, from Old English *twelf mōnath*, from *twelf* twelve + *mōnath* month] (15th century)
Scottish : YEAR, TWELVEMONTH

town \'taůn\ *noun* [Middle English, from Old English *tūn* enclosure, village, town; akin to Old High German *zūn* enclosure, Old Irish *dún* fortress] (before 12th century)
1 *dialect English* : a cluster or aggregation of houses recognized as a distinct place with a place-name : HAMLET
2 a : a compactly settled area as distinguished from surrounding rural territory **b** : a compactly settled area usually larger than a village but smaller than a city **c** : a large densely populated urban area : CITY **d** : an English village having a periodic fair or market
3 : a neighboring city, capital city, or metropolis
4 : the city or urban life as contrasted with the country
5 : the inhabitants of a city or town
6 : a New England territorial and political unit usually containing both rural and unincorporated urban areas under a single town government; *also* : a New England community governed by a town meeting
7 : a group of prairie dog burrows
— **town** *adjective*
— **on the town** : in usually carefree pursuit of entertainment or amusement (as city nightlife) especially as a relief from routine

town car *noun* (1907)
: a 4-door automobile with a usually open driver's compartment and a separate enclosed passenger compartment

town clerk *noun* (14th century)
: a public officer charged with recording the official proceedings and vital statistics of a town

town crier *noun* (1602)
: a town officer who makes public proclamations

town·ee \taů-'nē\ *noun* (1897)
chiefly British : TOWNIE

town hall *noun* (15th century)
: a public building used for town-government offices and meetings

town house *noun* (1803)
1 : a house in town; *specifically* : the city residence of one having a countryseat or having a chief residence elsewhere ⟨stayed at their *town house* during the social season⟩
2 : a usually single-family house of two or sometimes three stories that is usually connected to a similar house by a common sidewall; *also* : ROW HOUSE

town·ie *or* **towny** \'taů-nē\ *noun, plural* **townies** (1852)
: TOWNSMAN; *especially* : a permanent inhabitant of a town as distinguished from a member of another group (as the academic community)

town·let \'taůn-lət\ *noun* (circa 1552)
: a very small town

town manager *noun* (1922)
: an official appointed to direct the administration of a town government

town meeting *noun* (1636)
: a meeting of inhabitants or taxpayers constituting the legislative authority of a town

town·scape \-,skāp\ *noun* (1880)
1 : a representation of an urban scene
2 : a town or city viewed as a scene

towns·folk \'taůnz-,fōk\ *noun plural* (1737)
: TOWNSPEOPLE

town·ship \'taůn-,ship\ *noun* (15th century)
1 : an ancient unit of administration in England identical in area with or a division of a parish
2 a : TOWN 6 **b** : a unit of local government in some northeastern and north central states usually having a chief administrative officer or board **c** : an unorganized subdivision of the county in Maine, New Hampshire, and Vermont **d** : an electoral and administrative district of the county in the southern U.S.
3 : a division of territory in surveys of U.S. public land containing 36 sections or 36 square miles
4 : an area in the Republic of South Africa segregated for occupation by persons of non-European descent

towns·man \'taůnz-mən\ *noun* (before 12th century)
1 a : a native or resident of a town or city **b** : an urban or urbane person
2 : a fellow citizen of a town

towns·peo·ple \-,pē-pəl\ *noun plural* (1648)
1 : the inhabitants of a town or city : TOWNSMEN
2 : town-dwelling or town-bred persons

towns·wom·an \-,wů-mən\ *noun* (1684)
1 : a woman who is a native or resident of a town or city
2 : a woman born or residing in the same town or city as another

tow·path \'tō-,path, -,påth\ *noun* (1788)
: a path (as along a canal) traveled especially by draft animals towing boats — called also *towing path*

tow·rope \-,rōp\ *noun* (1743)
: a line used in towing something (as a boat)

tow sack \'tō-'sak\ *noun* [³tow] (1926)
Midland & Southern : GUNNYSACK

tow truck *noun* (1944)
: a truck with winches and hoist mechanisms for freeing stuck vehicles and towing wrecked or disabled vehicles

tox- *or* **toxi-** *or* **toxo-** *combining form* [Late Latin, from Latin *toxicum* poison]
: poisonous : poison ⟨*toxemia*⟩

tox·a·phene \'täk-sə-,fēn\ *noun* [from *Toxaphene*, a trademark] (1947)
: an insecticide with the approximate empirical formula $C_{10}H_{10}Cl_8$ that is a complex mixture of chlorinated compounds

tox·e·mia \täk-'sē-mē-ə\ *noun* [New Latin] (circa 1860)
: an abnormal condition associated with the presence of toxic substances in the blood
— **tox·e·mic** \-mik\ *adjective*

¹tox·ic \'täk-sik\ *adjective* [Late Latin *toxicus*, from Latin *toxicum* poison, from Greek *toxikon* arrow poison, from neuter of *toxikos* of a bow, from *toxon* bow, arrow] (1664)
1 : of, relating to, or caused by a poison or toxin
2 : affected by a poison or toxin ⟨*toxic* pregnant women⟩
3 : POISONOUS
— **tox·ic·i·ty** \täk-'si-sə-tē\ *noun*

²toxic *noun* (1890)
: a toxic substance

toxic- *or* **toxico-** *combining form* [New Latin, from Latin *toxicum*]
: poison ⟨*toxicology*⟩

tox·i·cant \'täk-si-kənt\ *noun* [Medieval Latin *toxicant-, toxicans*, present participle of *toxicare* to poison, from Latin *toxicum*] (circa 1882)
: a toxic agent; *especially* : PESTICIDE

tox·i·co·log·i·cal \,täk-si-kə-'lä-ji-kəl\ *or* **tox·i·co·log·ic** \-jik\ *adjective* (1839)
: of or relating to toxicology or toxins
— **tox·i·co·log·i·cal·ly** \-ji-k(ə-)lē\ *adverb*

tox·i·col·o·gy \-'kä-lə-jē\ *noun* (circa 1799)
: a science that deals with poisons and their effect and with the problems involved (as clinical, industrial, or legal)
— **tox·i·col·o·gist** \-jist\ *noun*

tox·i·co·sis \,täk-sə-'kō-səs\ *noun, plural* **-co·ses** \-,sēz\ [New Latin] (circa 1857)
: a pathological condition caused by the action of a poison or toxin

toxic shock syndrome *noun* (1978)
: an acute disease that is characterized by fever, diarrhea, nausea, diffuse erythema, and shock, that is associated especially with the presence of a bacterium (*Staphylococcus aureus*), and that occurs especially in menstruating females using tampons — called also *toxic shock*

toxi·gen·ic \,täk-sə-'je-nik\ *adjective* (circa 1923)
: producing toxin ⟨*toxigenic* bacteria and fungi⟩
— **toxi·ge·nic·i·ty** \,täk-si-jə-'ni-sə-tē\ *noun*

tox·in \'täk-sən\ *noun* [International Scientific Vocabulary] (1886)
: a poisonous substance that is a specific product of the metabolic activities of a living organism and is usually very unstable, notably toxic when introduced into the tissues, and typically capable of inducing antibody formation

tox·in-an·ti·tox·in \'täk-sən-'an-ti-,täk-sən\ *noun* (1904)
: a mixture of toxin and antitoxin used especially formerly in immunizing against a disease (as diphtheria) for which they are specific

tox·oid \'täk-,sȯid\ *noun* [International Scientific Vocabulary] (circa 1894)
: a toxin of a pathogenic organism treated so as to destroy its toxicity but leave it capable of inducing the formation of antibodies on injection

tox·oph·i·lite \täk-'sä-fə-,līt\ *noun* [Greek *toxon* bow, arrow + *philos* dear, loving] (1794)
: a person fond of or expert at archery
— **toxophilite** *adjective*
— **tox·oph·i·ly** \-lē\ *noun*

toxo·plas·ma \,täk-sə-'plaz-mə\ *noun* [New Latin] (1926)
: any of a genus (*Toxoplasma*) of sporozoans that are typically serious pathogens of vertebrates
— **toxo·plas·mic** \-mik\ *adjective*

toxo·plas·mo·sis \-,plaz-'mō-səs\ *noun, plural* **-mo·ses** \-,sēz\ [New Latin] (1926)
: infection of humans, other mammals, or birds with disease caused by a toxoplasma (*Toxoplasma gondii*) that invades the tissues and may seriously damage the central nervous system especially of infants

¹toy \'tȯi\ *noun* [Middle English *toye*] (15th century)
1 *obsolete* **a** : flirtatious or seductive behavior **b** : PASTIME; *also* : a sportive or amusing act : ANTIC
2 a : something (as a preoccupation) that is paltry or trifling **b** : a literary or musical trifle or diversion **c** : TRINKET, BAUBLE
3 : something for a child to play with
4 : something diminutive; *especially* : a diminutive animal (as of a small breed or variety)
5 : something that can be toyed with
6 *Scottish* : a headdress of linen or woolen hanging down over the shoulders and formerly worn by old women of the lower classes

— **toy·like** \-ˌlīk\ *adjective*

²**toy** *intransitive verb* (circa 1529)
1 : to act or deal with something lightly or without vigor or purpose
2 : to engage in flirtation
3 : to amuse oneself as if with a toy : PLAY
synonym see TRIFLE
— **toy·er** \ˈtȯi-ər\ *noun*

³**toy** *adjective* (1801)
1 : resembling a toy especially in diminutive size
2 : designed or made for use as a toy ⟨a *toy* stove⟩

toy Man·ches·ter terrier \-ˈman-ˌches-tər-, -chə-stər-\ *noun* (1935)
: any of a breed of toy dogs developed from the Manchester terrier that have erect ears of moderate size and weigh not more than 12 pounds (5.4 kilograms) — called also *toy Manchester*

toy Manchester terrier

toy·on \ˈtȯi-ˌän\ *noun* [American Spanish *tollon*] (1848)
: a chiefly Californian ornamental evergreen shrub (*Heteromeles arbutifolia*) of the rose family having white flowers succeeded by persistent usually bright red berries

toy poodle *noun* (1935)
: any of a breed of toy dogs developed from the standard poodle that are not more than 10 inches (25 centimeters) high at the withers

TPN \ˌtē-ˌpē-ˈen\ *noun* [*tri*phospho*p*yridine *n*ucleotide] (1938)
: NADP

tra·be·at·ed \ˈtrā-bē-ˌā-təd\ *also* **tra·be·ate** \-ˌāt\ *adjective* [Latin *trabs, trabes* beam — more at THORP] (1843)
: designed or constructed with horizontal beams or lintels
— **tra·be·a·tion** \ˌtrā-bē-ˈā-shən\ *noun*

tra·bec·u·la \trə-ˈbe-kyə-lə\ *noun, plural* **-lae** \-ˌlē, -ˌlī\ *also* **-las** [New Latin, from Latin, little beam, diminutive of *trabs, trabes* beam] (circa 1866)
1 : a small bar, rod, bundle of fibers, or septal membrane in the framework of a body organ or part
2 : a fold, ridge, or bar projecting into or extending from a plant part; *especially* : a row of cells bridging an intercellular space
— **tra·bec·u·lar** \-lər\ *adjective*
— **tra·bec·u·late** \-lət\ *adjective*

¹**trace** \ˈtrās\ *noun* [Middle English, from Middle French, from *tracier* to trace] (14th century)
1 *archaic* : a course or path that one follows
2 a : a mark or line left by something that has passed; *also* : FOOTPRINT **b** : a path, trail, or road made by the passage of animals, people, or vehicles
3 a : a sign or evidence of some past thing : VESTIGE **b** : ENGRAM
4 : something (as a line) traced or drawn: as **a** : the marking made by a recording instrument (as a seismograph or kymograph) **b** : the ground plan of a military installation or position either on a map or on the ground
5 a : the intersection of a line or plane with a plane **b** : the usually bright line or spot that moves across the screen of a cathode-ray tube; *also* : the path taken by such a line or spot
6 a : a minute and often barely detectable amount or indication ⟨a *trace* of a smile⟩ **b** : an amount of a chemical constituent not always quantitatively determinable because of minuteness ☆
— **trace·less** \-ləs\ *adjective*

²**trace** *verb* **traced; trac·ing** [Middle English, from Middle French *tracier*, from (assumed) Vulgar Latin *tractiare* to drag, from Latin *tractus*, past participle of *trahere* to pull] (14th century)
transitive verb
1 a : DELINEATE, SKETCH **b** : to form (as letters or figures) carefully or painstakingly **c** : to copy (as a drawing) by following the lines or letters as seen through a transparent superimposed sheet **d** : to impress or imprint (as a design or pattern) with a tracer **e** : to record a tracing of in the form of a curved, wavy, or broken line ⟨*trace* the heart action⟩ **f** : to adorn with linear ornamentation (as tracery or chasing)
2 *archaic* : to travel over : TRAVERSE
3 a : to follow the footprints, track, or trail of **b** : to follow or study out in detail or step by step ⟨*trace* the history of the labor movement⟩ **c** : to discover by going backward over the evidence step by step ⟨*trace* your ancestry⟩ **d** : to discover signs, evidence, or remains of
4 : to lay out the trace of (a military installation)
intransitive verb
1 : to make one's way; *especially* : to follow a track or trail
2 : to be traceable historically
— **trace·abil·i·ty** \ˌtrā-sə-ˈbi-lə-tē\ *noun*
— **trace·able** \ˈtrā-sə-bəl\ *adjective*

³**trace** *noun* [Middle English *trais*, plural, traces, from Middle French, plural of *trait* pull, draft, trace — more at TRAIT] (14th century)
1 : either of two straps, chains, or lines of a harness for attaching a draft animal to something (as a vehicle) to be drawn
2 : LEADER 1e(2)
3 : one or more vascular bundles supplying a leaf or twig
4 : a connecting bar or rod pivoted at each end to another piece and used for transmitting motion

trace element *noun* (1932)
: a chemical element present in minute quantities; *especially* : one used by organisms and held essential to their physiology

trac·er \ˈtrā-sər\ *noun* (circa 1552)
1 : one that traces, tracks down, or searches out: as **a** : a person who traces missing persons or property and especially goods lost in transit **b** : an inquiry sent out in tracing a shipment lost in transit
2 : one who traces designs, patterns, or markings
3 : a device (as a stylus) used in tracing
4 a : ammunition containing a chemical composition to mark the flight of projectiles by a trail of smoke or fire **b** : a substance used to trace the course of a chemical or biological process; *especially* : LABEL 3d

trac·ery \ˈtrā-sə-rē, ˈtrās-rē\ *noun, plural* **-er·ies** (1669)
1 : architectural ornamental work with branching lines; *especially* : decorative openwork in the head of a Gothic window
2 : a decorative interlacing of lines suggestive of Gothic tracery
— **trac·er·ied** \-rēd\ *adjective*

tracery 1

trache- or tracheo- *combining form* [New Latin, from Medieval Latin *trachea*]
1 : trachea ⟨*trache*itis⟩ ⟨*tracheo*tomy⟩
2 : tracheal and ⟨*tracheo*bronchial⟩

tra·chea \ˈtrā-kē-ə\ *noun, plural* **-che·ae** \-kē-ˌē, -kē-ˌī\ *also* **-che·as** [Middle English, from Medieval Latin, from Late Latin *trachia*, from Greek *tracheia* (*artēria*) rough (artery), from feminine of *trachys* rough] (14th century)
1 : the main trunk of the system of tubes by which air passes to and from the lungs in vertebrates
2 [New Latin, from Medieval Latin] : VESSEL 3b; *also* : one of its constituent cellular elements
3 [New Latin] : one of the air-conveying tubules forming the respiratory system of most insects and many other arthropods
— **tra·che·al** \-kē-əl\ *adjective*

tra·che·ary \ˈtrā-kē-ˌer-ē\ *adjective* (1885)
: of, relating to, or being plant tracheae ⟨*tracheary* elements⟩

tra·che·ate \-kē-ˌāt, -ət\ *or* **tra·che·at·ed** \-ˌā-təd\ *adjective* (1877)
: having tracheae as breathing organs

tra·cheid \ˈtrā-kē-əd, -ˌkēd\ *noun* [International Scientific Vocabulary] (1875)
: a long tubular pitted cell that is peculiar to xylem, functions in conduction and support, and has tapering closed ends and thickened lignified walls

tra·che·i·tis \ˌtrā-kē-ˈī-təs\ *noun* [New Latin] (1859)
: inflammation of the trachea

tra·cheo·bron·chi·al \ˌtrā-kē-ō-ˈbräŋ-kē-əl\ *adjective* (1896)
: of or relating to both trachea and bronchi ⟨*tracheobronchial* lesions⟩

tra·che·ole \ˈtrā-kē-ˌōl\ *noun* [New Latin *tracheola*, diminutive of *trachea*] (1901)
: one of the minute delicate endings of a branched trachea of an insect
— **tra·cheo·lar** \ˈtrā-ˈkē-ə-lər\ *adjective*

tra·cheo·phyte \ˈtrā-kē-ə-ˌfīt\ *noun* [New Latin *Tracheophyta*, from *trache-* + Greek *phyton* plant; akin to Greek *phyein* to bring forth — more at BE] (1937)
: any of a division (Tracheophyta) comprising green plants (as ferns and seed plants) with a vascular system that contains tracheids or tracheary elements

tra·che·os·to·my \ˌtrā-kē-ˈäs-tə-mē\ *noun, plural* **-mies** (circa 1923)
: the surgical formation of an opening into the trachea through the neck especially to allow the passage of air

tra·che·ot·o·my \ˌtrā-kē-ˈä-tə-mē\ *noun, plural* **-mies** (circa 1726)
: the surgical operation of cutting into the trachea especially through the skin

tra·cho·ma \trə-ˈkō-mə\ *noun* [New Latin, from Greek *trachōma*, from *trachys* rough] (circa 1693)
: a chronic contagious bacterial conjunctivitis marked by inflammatory granulations on the conjunctival surfaces, caused by a chlamydia (*Chlamydia trachomatis*), and commonly resulting in blindness if left untreated

tra·chyte \ˈtra-ˌkīt, ˈtrā-\ *noun* [French, from Greek *trachys* rough] (1821)
: a usually light-colored volcanic rock consisting chiefly of potash feldspar

☆ **SYNONYMS**
Trace, vestige, track mean a perceptible sign made by something that has passed. TRACE may suggest any line, mark, or discernible effect ⟨a snowfield pockmarked with the *traces* of caribou⟩. VESTIGE applies to a tangible reminder such as a fragment or remnant of what is past and gone ⟨boulders that are *vestiges* of the last ice age⟩. TRACK implies a continuous line that can be followed ⟨the fossilized *tracks* of dinosaurs⟩.

\ə\ abut \ᵊ\ kitten \ər\ further \a\ ash \ā\ ace
\ä\ mop, mar \au̇\ out \ch\ chin \e\ bet \ē\ easy
\g\ go \i\ hit \ī\ ice \j\ job \ŋ\ sing \ō\ go
\ȯ\ law \ȯi\ boy \th\ thin \th\ the \ü\ loot \u̇\ foot
\y\ yet \zh\ vision see also Guide to Pronunciation

tra·chyt·ic \trə-'ki-tik\ *adjective* (1827)
: of or relating to a texture of igneous rocks in which lath-shaped feldspar crystals are in almost parallel lines

trac·ing \'trā-siŋ\ *noun* (15th century)
1 : the act of one that traces
2 : something that is traced: as **a** : a copy made on a superimposed transparent sheet **b** : a graphic record made by an instrument (as a seismograph) that registers some movement

tracing paper *noun* (1824)
: a semitransparent paper for tracing drawings; *also* : a thin paper containing a clothing pattern to be transferred to fabric (as through carbon paper) by tracing

tracing wheel *noun* (circa 1891)
: a usually toothed wheel with a handle that is used on tracing paper to trace a pattern

¹track \'trak\ *noun* [Middle English *trak*, from Middle French *trac*, perhaps of Germanic origin; akin to Middle Dutch *tracken*, *trecken* to pull, haul — more at TREK] (15th century)
1 a : detectable evidence (as the wake of a ship, a line of footprints, or a wheel rut) that something has passed **b** : a path made by repeated footfalls : TRAIL **c** : a course laid out especially for racing **d** : the parallel rails of a railroad **e** (1) : one of a series of parallel or concentric paths along which material (as music or information) is recorded (as on a phonograph record or magnetic tape) (2) : a group of grooves on a phonograph record containing recorded sound (3) : material recorded especially on a track **f** : a usually metal way (as a groove) serving as a guide (as for a movable lighting fixture)
2 : a footprint whether recent or fossil ⟨the huge *track* of a dinosaur⟩
3 a : the course along which something moves **b** : a way of life, conduct, or action **c** : one of several curricula of study to which students are assigned according to their needs or levels of ability **d** : the projection on the earth's surface of the path along which something (as a missile or an airplane) has flown
4 a : a sequence of events : a train of ideas : SUCCESSION **b** : an awareness of a fact, progression, or condition ⟨keep *track* of the costs⟩ ⟨lose *track* of the time⟩
5 a : the width of a wheeled vehicle from wheel to wheel and usually from the outside of the rims **b** : the tread of an automobile tire **c** : either of two endless metal belts on which a tracklaying vehicle travels
6 : track-and-field sports; *especially* : those performed on a running track
synonym see TRACE
— **track·less** \'trak-ləs\ *adjective*
— **in one's tracks** : where one stands or is at the moment : on the spot ⟨was stopped *in his tracks*⟩

²track (1565)
transitive verb
1 a : to follow the tracks or traces of : TRAIL **b** : to search for by following evidence until found ⟨*track* down the source⟩
2 a : to follow by vestiges : TRACE **b** : to observe or plot the moving path of (as a spacecraft or missile) instrumentally
3 : to travel over : TRAVERSE ⟨*track* a desert⟩
4 a : to make tracks upon **b** : to carry (as mud) on the feet and deposit
5 : to keep track of (as a trend) : FOLLOW
intransitive verb
1 : TRAVEL ⟨comet *tracks* eastward⟩
2 a *of a phonograph needle* : to follow the groove undulations of a recording **b** *of a pair of wheels* (1) : to maintain a constant distance apart on the straightaway (2) : to fit a track or rails **c** *of a rear wheel of a vehicle* : to follow accurately the corresponding fore wheel on a straightaway
3 : to leave tracks (as on a floor)
— **track·er** *noun*

track·age \'tra-kij\ *noun* (1880)
1 : lines of railway track
2 a : a right to use the tracks of another railroad line **b** : the charge for such right

track–and–field \,trak-ən(d)-'fē(ə)ld\ *adjective* (1905)
: of, relating to, or being any of various competitive athletic events (as running, jumping, and weight throwing) performed on a running track and on the adjacent field

track·ball \'trak-,bȯl\ *noun* (1967)
: a ball that is mounted usually in a computer console so as to be only partially exposed and is rotated to control the movement of a cursor on a display

tracked \'trakt\ *adjective* (1926)
1 : traveling on endless metal belts instead of wheels
2 : moving along a rail ⟨a *tracked* air-cushion vehicle⟩

track·ing \'tra-kiŋ\ *noun* (circa 1929)
: the assigning of students to a curricular track

tracking shot *noun* (circa 1940)
: a scene photographed from a moving dolly

track·lay·er \'trak-,lā-ər, -,le(-ə)r\ *noun* (circa 1861)
1 : a worker engaged in tracklaying
2 : a tracklaying vehicle

¹track·lay·ing \-,lā-iŋ\ *noun* (1857)
: the laying of tracks on a railway line

²tracklaying *adjective* (1884)
: of, relating to, or being a vehicle that travels on two or more endless usually metal belts

trackless trolley *noun* (1921)
: TROLLEYBUS

track lighting *noun* (1972)
: adjustable lamps mounted along an electrified metal track

track·man \'trak-mən, -,man\ *noun* (1922)
: a runner on a track team

track record *noun* [¹track (track-and-field sports)] (1952)
: a record of past performance often taken as an indicator of likely future performance

track·side \'trak-,sīd\ *adjective* (1886)
: of, relating to, or situated in the area immediately adjacent to a track
— **trackside** *noun*

track·suit \'trak-,süt\ *noun* (1922)
: a suit of clothing consisting usually of a jacket and pants that is often worn by athletes when working out

track·walk·er \-,wȯ-kər\ *noun* (1872)
: a worker employed to walk over and inspect a section of railroad tracks

track·way \-,wā\ *noun* (1818)
1 : a beaten or trodden path
2 : a series of fossil footprints of a dinosaur

¹tract \'trakt\ *noun, often capitalized* [Middle English *tracte*, from Medieval Latin *tractus*, from Latin, action of drawing, extension; perhaps from its being sung without a break by one voice] (14th century)
: verses of Scripture (as from the Psalms) used between the gradual and the Gospel at some masses (as during penitential seasons)

²tract *noun* [Middle English *tracte*, from Latin *tractus* action of drawing, extension, from *trahere* to pull, draw] (15th century)
1 : extent or lapse of time
2 : an area either large or small: as **a** : an indefinite stretch of land **b** : a defined area of land
3 a : a system of body parts or organs that act together to perform some function ⟨the digestive *tract*⟩ **b** : a bundle of nerve fibers having a common origin, termination, and function

³tract *noun* [Middle English, treatise, modification of Latin *tractatus* tractate] (1760)
: a pamphlet or leaflet of political or religious propaganda; *also* : a piece of writing that is suggestive of such a tract

trac·ta·ble \'trak-tə-bəl\ *adjective* [Latin *tractabilis*, from *tractare* to handle, treat] (1502)
1 : capable of being easily led, taught, or controlled : DOCILE ⟨a *tractable* horse⟩
2 : easily handled, managed, or wrought : MALLEABLE
synonym see OBEDIENT
— **trac·ta·bil·i·ty** \,trak-tə-'bi-lə-tē\ *noun*
— **trac·ta·ble·ness** \'trak-tə-bəl-nəs\ *noun*
— **trac·ta·bly** \-blē\ *adverb*

Trac·tar·i·an \trak-'ter-ē-ən\ *noun* [from *Tracts for the Times*, series of pamphlets expounding the Oxford movement] (circa 1839)
: a promoter or supporter of the Oxford movement

Trac·tar·i·an·ism \-ē-ə-,ni-zəm\ *noun* (1840)
: a system of High Church principles set forth in a series of tracts at Oxford (1833–41)

trac·tate \'trak-,tāt\ *noun* [Latin *tractatus*, from *tractare* to draw out, handle, treat — more at TREAT] (15th century)
: TREATISE, DISSERTATION

tract house *noun* (1956)
: any of many similarly designed houses built on a tract of land

trac·tion \'trak-shən\ *noun* [Medieval Latin *traction-, tractio*, from Latin *trahere*] (1615)
1 : the act of drawing : the state of being drawn; *also* : the force exerted in drawing
2 : the drawing of a vehicle by motive power; *also* : the motive power employed
3 a : the adhesive friction of a body on a surface on which it moves ⟨the *traction* of a wheel on a rail⟩ **b** : a pulling force exerted on a skeletal structure (as in a fracture) by means of a special device ⟨a *traction* splint⟩; *also* : a state of tension created by such a pulling force ⟨a leg in *traction*⟩
— **trac·tion·al** \-shnəl, -shə-nºl\ *adjective*

trac·tive \'trak-tiv\ *adjective* [Latin *tractus*, past participle] (1615)
1 : serving to draw
2 : of or relating to traction : TRACTIONAL

trac·tor \'trak-tər\ *noun* [New Latin, from Latin *trahere*] (1900)
1 a : a 4-wheeled or tracklaying automotive vehicle used especially for drawing farm equipment **b** : a smaller 2-wheeled apparatus controlled through handlebars by a walking operator **c** : ³TRUCK 3f
2 : an airplane having the propeller forward of the main supporting surfaces

trad \'trad\ *adjective* (1958)
chiefly British : TRADITIONAL

¹trade \'trād\ *noun* [Middle English, from Middle Low German; akin to Old High German *trata* track, course, Old English *tredan* to tread] (14th century)
1 a *obsolete* : a path traversed : WAY **b** *archaic* : a track or trail left by a person or animal : TREAD 1
2 : a customary course of action : PRACTICE ⟨thy sin's not accidental, but a *trade* —Shakespeare⟩
3 a : the business or work in which one engages regularly : OCCUPATION **b** : an occupation requiring manual or mechanical skill : CRAFT **c** : the persons engaged in an occupation, business, or industry
4 a *obsolete* : dealings between persons or groups **b** (1) : the business of buying and selling or bartering commodities : COMMERCE 2 : BUSINESS, MARKET ⟨novelties for the tourist *trade*⟩ ⟨did a good *trade* in small appliances⟩
5 a : an act or instance of trading : TRANSACTION; *also* : an exchange of property usually without use of money **b** : a firm's customers : CLIENTELE **c** : the group of firms engaged in a business or industry
6 : TRADE WIND — usually used in plural
7 : a publication intended for persons in the entertainment business — usually used in plural
synonym see BUSINESS

²trade *verb* **trad·ed; trad·ing** (1553)
intransitive verb
1 *obsolete* : to have dealings : NEGOTIATE
2 a : to engage in the exchange, purchase, or sale of goods **b** : to make one's purchases : SHOP ⟨*trades* at his store⟩
3 : to give one thing in exchange for another
4 : SELL 3
transitive verb
1 *archaic* : to do business with
2 a : to give in exchange for another commodity : BARTER; *also* : to make an exchange of ⟨*traded* places⟩ **b** : to engage in frequent buying and selling of (as stocks or commodities) usually in search of quick profits
— **trad·able** *also* **trade·able** \'trā-də-bəl\ *adjective*
— **trade on** : to take often unscrupulous advantage of : EXPLOIT ⟨*traded on* their influence . . . in securing special favors —T. C. Pease⟩

³trade *adjective* (1633)
1 : of, relating to, or used in trade
2 a : intended for or limited to persons in a business or industry ⟨a *trade* publication⟩ ⟨*trade* sales⟩ **b** : serving others in the same business rather than the ultimate user or consumer ⟨a *trade* printing house⟩
3 *also* **trades** : of, composed of, or representing the trades or trade unions ⟨a *trade* committee⟩
4 : of a larger softcover format than mass-market paperbacks and usually sold only in bookstores ⟨*trade* paperbacks⟩; *also* : of or relating to the publishing of such books

trade acceptance *noun* (1916)
: a time draft or bill of exchange for the amount of a specific purchase drawn by the seller on the buyer, bearing the buyer's acceptance, and often noting the place of payment (as a bank)

trade agreement *noun* (circa 1921)
1 : an international agreement on conditions of trade in goods and services
2 : an agreement resulting from collective bargaining

trade book *noun* (circa 1945)
1 : a book intended for general readership
2 : TRADE EDITION

trade·craft \'trād-,kraft\ *noun* (1961)
: the techniques and procedures of espionage

trade discount *noun* (1901)
: a deduction from the list price of goods allowed by a manufacturer or wholesaler to a retailer

trade dollar *noun* (1873)
: a U.S. silver dollar weighing 420 grains .900 fine issued 1873–85 for use in oriental trade

trade down *intransitive verb* (1942)
1 : to trade something in (as an automobile) for something less expensive or valuable of its kind
2 : to stock or purchase lower-priced items : ECONOMIZE

trade edition *noun* (1930)
: an edition of a book intended for general distribution — compare TEXT EDITION

trade–in \'trād-,in\ *noun* (1917)
: an item of merchandise (as an automobile or refrigerator) taken as payment or part payment for a purchase

trade in *transitive verb* (1923)
1 : to turn in as payment or part payment for a purchase or bill ⟨*trade* the old car *in* on a new one⟩
2 : EXCHANGE 2

trade language *noun* (1662)
: a restructured language (as a lingua franca or pidgin) used especially in commercial communication

trade–last \'trād-,last\ *noun* (1891)
: a complimentary remark by a third person that a hearer offers to repeat to the person complimented if he or she will first report a compliment made about the hearer

¹trade·mark \-,märk\ *noun* (1838)
1 : a device (as a word) pointing distinctly to the origin or ownership of merchandise to which it is applied and legally reserved to the exclusive use of the owner as maker or seller
2 : a distinguishing characteristic or feature firmly associated with a person or thing ⟨derringers . . . became almost a *trademark* of gamblers —Elmer Keith⟩ ⟨wearing his *trademark* bow tie and derby hat⟩

²trademark *transitive verb* (1906)
: to secure trademark rights for : register the trademark of

¹trade name *noun* (1861)
1 a : the name used for an article among traders **b** : an arbitrarily adopted name that is given by a manufacturer or merchant to an article or service to distinguish it as produced or sold by him and that may be used and protected as a trademark
2 : the name or style under which a concern does business

²trade name *transitive verb* (1945)
: to designate with a trade name

trade–off \'trād-,óf\ *noun* (1961)
1 : a balancing of factors all of which are not attainable at the same time ⟨the education versus experience *trade-off* which governs personnel practices —H. S. White⟩
2 : a giving up of one thing in return for another : EXCHANGE
— **trade off** *transitive verb*

trad·er \'trā-dər\ *noun* (1585)
1 : a person whose business is buying and selling or barter: as **a** : MERCHANT **b** : a person who buys and sells (as stocks or commodities futures) in search of short-term profits
2 : a ship engaged in the coastal or foreign trade

trade route *noun* (1876)
1 : a route followed by traders (as in caravans)
2 : one of the sea-lanes ordinarily used by merchant ships

trad·es·can·tia \,tra-də-'skan(t)-sh(ē-)ə\ *noun* [New Latin, genus name, from John Tradescant (died 1638) English traveler & gardener] (circa 1909)
: SPIDERWORT

trade school *noun* (1889)
: a secondary school teaching the skilled trades

trade secret *noun* (1895)
: a formula, process, or device used in a business that is not published or divulged and that thereby gives an advantage over competitors

trades·man \'trādz-mən\ *noun* (1597)
1 : a worker in a skilled trade : CRAFTSMAN
2 : one who runs a retail store : SHOPKEEPER

trades·peo·ple \-,pē-pəl\ *noun plural* (1728)
: people engaged in trade

trade union *also* **trades union** *noun* (1835)
: LABOR UNION
— **trade unionism** *noun*
— **trade unionist** *noun*

trade up *intransitive verb* (1926)
1 : to trade something in (as an automobile) for something more expensive or valuable of its kind
2 : to stock or purchase higher-priced items

trade wind *noun* (1650)
: a wind blowing almost constantly in one direction; *especially* : a wind blowing almost continually toward the equator from the northeast in the belt between the northern horse latitudes and the doldrums and from the southeast in the belt between the southern horse latitudes and the doldrums — usually used in plural

trading post *noun* (1796)
1 : a station of a trader or trading company established in a sparsely settled region where trade in products of local origin (as furs) is carried on

2 : ⁶POST 3b

trading stamp *noun* (1897)
: a printed stamp of value given as a premium to a retail customer to be redeemed in merchandise when accumulated in numbers

tra·di·tion \trə-'di-shən\ *noun* [Middle English *tradicioun*, from Middle French & Latin; Middle French *tradition*, from Latin *tradition-*, *traditio* action of handing over, tradition — more at TREASON] (14th century)
1 : an inherited, established, or customary pattern of thought, action, or behavior (as a religious practice or a social custom)
2 : the handing down of information, beliefs, and customs by word of mouth or by example from one generation to another without written instruction
3 : cultural continuity in social attitudes, customs, and institutions
4 : characteristic manner, method, or style
word history see TREASON
— **tra·di·tion·al** \-'dish-nəl, -'di-shə-nºl\ *adjective*
— **tra·di·tion·al·ly** *adverb*
— **tra·di·tion·less** \-'di-shən-ləs\ *adjective*

tra·di·tion·al·ism \trə-'dish-nə-,li-zəm, -'di-shə-nºl-,i-\ *noun* (circa 1859)
1 : adherence to the doctrines or practices of a tradition
2 : the beliefs of those opposed to modernism, liberalism, or radicalism
— **tra·di·tion·al·ist** \-list, -ist\ *noun or adjective*
— **tra·di·tion·al·is·tic** \-,dish-nə-'lis-tik, -,di-shə-nºl-'is-\ *adjective*

tra·di·tion·al·ize \trə-'dish-nə-,līz, -'di-shə-nºl-,īz\ *transitive verb* **-ized; -iz·ing** (1882)
: to make traditional : imbue with traditions or traditionalism

tra·di·tion·ary \trə-'di-shə-,ner-ē\ *adjective* (1661)
: TRADITIONAL

tra·duce \trə-'düs, -'dyüs\ *transitive verb* **tra·duced; tra·duc·ing** [Latin *traducere* to lead across, transfer, degrade, from *tra-*, *trans-* trans- + *ducere* to lead — more at TOW] (1592)
1 : to expose to shame or blame by means of falsehood and misrepresentation
2 : VIOLATE, BETRAY ⟨*traduce* a principle of law⟩
synonym see MALIGN
— **tra·duce·ment** \-mənt\ *noun*
— **tra·duc·er** *noun*

¹traf·fic \'tra-fik\ *noun, often attributive* [Middle French *trafique*, from Old Italian *traffico*, from *trafficare* to trade] (1506)
1 a : import and export trade **b** : the business of bartering or buying and selling **c** : illegal or disreputable usually commercial activity ⟨the drug *traffic*⟩
2 a : communication or dealings especially between individuals or groups **b** : EXCHANGE ⟨a lively *traffic* in ideas —F. L. Allen⟩
3 *archaic* : WARES, GOODS
4 a : the movement (as of vehicles or pedestrians) through an area or along a route **b** : the vehicles, pedestrians, ships, or planes moving along a route **c** : the information or signals transmitted over a communications system : MESSAGES
5 a : the passengers or cargo carried by a transportation system **b** : the business of transporting passengers or freight
6 : the volume of customers visiting a business establishment
synonym see BUSINESS
— **the traffic will bear** : existing conditions will allow or permit ⟨charge what *the traffic will bear*⟩

²traffic *verb* **traf·ficked; traf·fick·ing** (1540)
intransitive verb
: to carry on traffic
transitive verb
1 : to travel over ⟨heavily *trafficked* highways⟩
2 : TRADE, BARTER
— **traf·fick·er** *noun*

traf·fic·abil·i·ty \ˌtra-fi-kə-'bi-lə-tē\ *noun* (1899)
: the quality of a terrain that permits passage (as of vehicles and troops)
— **traf·fic·able** \'tra-fi-kə-bəl\ *adjective*

traffic circle *noun* (1942)
: ROTARY 2

traffic cone *noun* (1953)
: a conical marker used on a road or highway (as for indicating an area under repair)

traffic court *noun* (1919)
: a minor court for disposition of petty prosecutions for violations of statutes, ordinances, and local regulations governing the use of highways and motor vehicles

traffic engineering *noun* (1931)
: engineering dealing with the design of streets and control of traffic
— **traffic engineer** *noun*

traffic island *noun* (1931)
: ISLAND 2a

traffic light *noun* (1912)
: an electrically operated visual signal (as a system of colored lights) for controlling traffic

traffic manager *noun* (1862)
1 : a supervisor of the traffic functions of a commercial or industrial organization
2 : the director of a large telegraph office

traffic signal *noun* (1917)
: a signal (as a traffic light) for controlling traffic

trag·a·canth \'tra-jə-ˌkan(t)th, 'tra-gə-, -kən(t)th; *also* 'tra-jə-ˌsan(t)th\ *noun* [Middle French *tragacanthe*, from Latin *tragacantha*, from Greek *tragakantha*, from *tragos* goat + *akantha* thorn] (1573)
: a gum obtained from various Asian or East European leguminous plants (genus *Astragalus* and especially *A. gummifer*) that swells in water and is used chiefly as an emulsifying, suspending, or thickening agent

tra·ge·di·an \trə-'jē-dē-ən\ *noun* [Middle English *tragedien*, from Middle French, from *tragedie*] (14th century)
1 : a writer of tragedies
2 : an actor specializing in tragic roles

tra·ge·di·enne \trə-ˌjē-dē-'en\ *noun* [French *tragédienne*, from Middle French, from *tragedie*] (1851)
: an actress who plays tragic roles

trag·e·dy \'tra-jə-dē\ *noun, plural* **-dies** [Middle English *tragedie*, from Middle French, from Latin *tragoedia*, from Greek *tragōidia*, from *tragos* goat (akin to Greek *trōgein* to gnaw) + *aeidein* to sing — more at TROGLODYTE, ODE] (14th century)
1 a : a medieval narrative poem or tale typically describing the downfall of a great man **b** : a serious drama typically describing a conflict between the protagonist and a superior force (as destiny) and having a sorrowful or disastrous conclusion that excites pity or terror **c** : the literary genre of tragic dramas
2 a : a disastrous event : CALAMITY **b** : MISFORTUNE
3 : tragic quality or element

trag·ic \'tra-jik\ *also* **trag·i·cal** \-ji-kəl\ *adjective* [Middle English, from Latin *tragicus*, from Greek *tragikos*, irregular from *tragōidia* tragedy] (15th century)
1 : of, marked by, or expressive of tragedy ⟨the *tragic* significance of the atomic bomb —H. S. Truman⟩
2 a : dealing with or treated in tragedy ⟨the *tragic* hero⟩ **b** : appropriate to or typical of tragedy

3 a : regrettably serious or unpleasant : DEPLORABLE, LAMENTABLE ⟨a *tragic* mistake⟩ **b** : marked by a sense of tragedy
— **trag·i·cal·ly** \-ji-k(ə-)lē\ *adverb*

tragic flaw *noun* (1913)
: a flaw in character that brings about the downfall of the hero of a tragedy

tragic irony *noun* (1833)
: IRONY 3b

tragi·com·e·dy \ˌtra-ji-'kä-mə-dē\ *noun* [Middle French *tragicomedie*, from Old Italian *tragicomedia*, from Old Spanish, from Latin *tragicomoedia*, from *tragicus* + *comoedia* comedy] (circa 1580)
: a drama or a situation blending tragic and comic elements
— **tragi·com·ic** \-'kä-mik\ *also* **tragi·com·i·cal** \-mi-kəl\ *adjective*

tra·gus \'trā-gəs\ *noun, plural* **tra·gi** \-ˌgī, -ˌjī\ [New Latin, from Greek *tragos*, a part of the ear, literally, goat] (circa 1693)
: the prominence in front of the external opening of the ear

¹trail \'trā(ə)l\ *verb* [Middle English, from Middle French *trailler* to tow, from (assumed) Vulgar Latin *tragulare*, from Latin *tragula* sledge, dragnet; akin to Latin *trahere* to pull] (14th century)
intransitive verb
1 a : to hang down so as to drag along or sweep the ground **b** : to extend over a surface in a loose or straggling manner ⟨a vine that *trails* over the ground⟩ **c** : to grow to such length as to droop over toward the ground ⟨*trailing* branches of a weeping birch⟩
2 a : to walk or proceed draggingly, heavily, or wearily : PLOD, TRUDGE **b** : to lag behind : do poorly in relation to others
3 : to move, flow, or extend slowly in thin streams ⟨smoke *trailing* from chimneys⟩
4 a : to extend in an erratic or uneven course or line : STRAGGLE **b** : DWINDLE ⟨voice *trailing* off⟩
5 : to follow a trail : track game
transitive verb
1 a : to draw or drag loosely along a surface : allow to sweep the ground **b** : HAUL, TOW
2 a : to drag (as a limb or the body) heavily or wearily **b** : to carry or bring along as an addition, burden, or encumbrance **c** : to draw along in one's wake
3 a : to follow upon the scent or trace of : TRACK **b** : to follow in the footsteps of : PURSUE **c** : to follow along behind **d** : to lag behind (as a competitor)
synonym see CHASE

²trail *noun* (14th century)
1 : something that trails or is trailed: as **a** : a trailing plant **b** : the train of a gown **c** : a trailing arrangement (as of flowers) **d** : the part of a gun carriage that rests on the ground when the piece is unlimbered
2 a : something that follows or moves along as if being drawn along : TRAIN ⟨a *trail* of admirers⟩ **b** (1) : the streak produced by a meteor (2) : a continuous line produced photographically by permitting the image of a celestial body (as a star) to move over the plate **c** : a chain of consequences : AFTERMATH ⟨the . . . movement left a *trail* of bitterness and prejudice behind it —Paul Blanshard⟩
3 a : a trace or mark left by something that has passed or been drawn along : SCENT, TRACK ⟨a *trail* of blood⟩ **b** (1) : a track made by passage especially through a wilderness (2) : a marked or established path or route especially through a forest or mountainous region **c** : a course followed or to be followed ⟨hit the campaign *trail*⟩
— **trail·less** \'trā(ə)l-ləs\ *adjective*

trail bike *noun* (1966)
: a small motorcycle designed for off-road use

trail·blaz·er \'trā(ə)l-ˌblā-zər\ *noun* (1908)
1 : one that blazes a trail to guide others
: PATHFINDER

2 : PIONEER 2 ⟨a *trailblazer* in astrophysics⟩

trail·blaz·ing \-ziŋ\ *adjective* (1951)
: making or pointing a new way ⟨*trailblazing* legislation⟩

trail·break·er \-ˌbrā-kər\ *noun* (1925)
: TRAILBLAZER

¹trail·er \'trā-lər\ *noun* (1590)
1 : one that trails
2 : a trailing plant
3 : a nonautomotive vehicle designed to be hauled by road: as **a** : a vehicle for transporting something ⟨a boat *trailer*⟩; *especially* : SEMITRAILER **b** : a vehicle designed to serve wherever parked as a temporary dwelling or place of business **c** : MOBILE HOME
4 a : PREVIEW 2 **b** : a short blank strip of film attached to the end of a reel

²trailer (1938)
intransitive verb
1 : to live or travel in or with a trailer
2 : to be transportable by trailer ⟨a light boat that *trailers* easily⟩
transitive verb
: to transport (as a boat) by means of a trailer
— **trail·er·able** \-lə-rə-bəl\ *adjective*
— **trail·er·ing** *noun*

trail·er·ist \-lə-rist\ *noun* (1950)
1 : a person traveling or vacationing with a trailer
2 : TRAILERITE 1

trail·er·ite \-ˌrīt\ *noun* (1936)
1 : a person living in a mobile home
2 : TRAILERIST 1

trailer park *noun* (1942)
: an area equipped to accommodate mobile homes — called also *trailer camp, trailer court*

trail·head \'trāl-ˌhed\ *noun* (1948)
: the point at which a trail begins

trailing arbutus *noun* (1785)
: ARBUTUS 2

trailing edge *noun* (1909)
: the rearmost edge of an object that moves and especially of an airfoil

trail mix *noun* (1979)
: a mixture of seeds, nuts, and dried fruits eaten as a snack especially by hikers

trail·side \'trāl-ˌsīd\ *adjective* (1923)
: of, relating to, or situated in the area immediately adjacent to a trail

¹train \'trān\ *noun* [Middle English *traine*, from Middle French, from Old French, from *traïr* to betray, from Latin *tradere* — more at TRAITOR] (14th century)
obsolete : SCHEME, TRICK

²train *noun* [Middle English, from Middle French, from Old French, from *trainer* to draw, drag] (15th century)
1 : a part of a gown that trails behind the wearer
2 a : RETINUE, SUITE **b** : a moving file of persons, vehicles, or animals
3 : the vehicles, personnel, and sometimes animals that furnish supply, maintenance, and evacuation services to a combat unit
4 a : order of occurrence leading to some result — often used in the phrase *in train* ⟨this humiliating process had been in *train* for decades —Paul Fussell⟩ **b** : an orderly succession ⟨a *train* of thought⟩ **c** : accompanying or resultant circumstances : AFTERMATH ⟨consequences the discovery will bring in its *train*⟩
5 : a line of combustible material laid to lead fire to a charge
6 : a series of moving mechanical parts (as gears) that transmit and modify motion
7 a : a connected line of railroad cars with or without a locomotive **b** : an automotive tractor with one or more trailer units
8 : a series of parts or elements that together constitute a system for producing a result and

especially for carrying on a process (as of manufacture) automatically ◇
— **train·ful** \'trān-,fùl\ *noun*
³**train** *verb* [Middle English, from Middle French *trainer*, from Old French, from (assumed) Vulgar Latin *traginare*; akin to Latin *trahere* to draw] (15th century)
transitive verb
1 : TRAIL, DRAG
2 : to direct the growth of (a plant) usually by bending, pruning, and tying
3 a : to form by instruction, discipline, or drill **b :** to teach so as to make fit, qualified, or proficient
4 : to make prepared (as by exercise) for a test of skill
5 : to aim at an object or objective **:** DIRECT ⟨*trained* his camera on the deer⟩ ⟨*training* every effort toward success⟩
intransitive verb
1 : to undergo instruction, discipline, or drill
2 : to go by train
synonym see TEACH
— **train·abil·i·ty** \,trā-nə-'bi-lə-tē\ *noun*
— **train·able** \'trā-nə-bəl\ *adjective*
train·band \'trān-,band\ *noun* [alteration of *trained* band] (1630)
: a 17th or 18th century militia company in England or America
train·bear·er \'trān-,bar-ər, -,ber-\ *noun* (1722)
: an attendant who holds up (as on a ceremonial occasion) the train of a robe or gown
train case *noun* (1948)
: a small boxlike piece of luggage used especially for toilet articles
train dispatcher *noun* (1857)
: a railroad employee who directs the movement of trains within a division and coordinates their movement from one division to another
train·ee \trā-'nē\ *noun* (1841)
: one that is being trained especially for a job
— **train·ee·ship** \-'nē-,ship\ *noun*
train·er \'trā-nər\ *noun* (1598)
1 : one that trains
2 : one (as a machine or vehicle) used in training
3 : a person who treats the ailments and minor injuries of the members of an athletic team
train·ing *noun* (1548)
1 a : the act, process, or method of one that trains **b :** the skill, knowledge, or experience acquired by one that trains
2 : the state of being trained
training college *noun* (circa 1829)
British **:** TEACHERS COLLEGE
training school *noun* (1829)
1 : a school preparing students for a particular occupation
2 : a correctional institution for the custody and reeducation of juvenile delinquents
training table *noun* (1893)
: a table where athletes under a training regimen eat meals planned to help in their conditioning
training wheels *noun plural* (1964)
: a pair of small wheels connected to the rear axle of a bicycle to help a beginning bicyclist maintain balance
train·load \'trān-,lōd\ *noun* (1876)
: the full freight or passenger capacity of a railroad train; *also* **:** a load that fills a train
train·man \'trān-mən, -,man\ *noun* (1877)
: a member of a train crew supervised by a conductor
train oil \'trān-\ *noun* [obsolete *train* train oil, from Middle English *trane*, from Middle Dutch *trane* or Middle Low German *trān*; akin to Old High German *trahan* tear] (circa 1553)
: oil from a marine animal (as a whale)
traipse \'trāps\ *verb* **traipsed; traips·ing** [origin unknown] (1647)
intransitive verb

: to go on foot **:** WALK ⟨*traipsed* over to the restaurant⟩ ⟨children *traipsing* at her heels⟩; *also* **:** to walk or travel about without apparent plan but with or without a purpose ⟨a week *traipsing* through the Ozarks⟩ ⟨*traipsing* from office to office⟩
transitive verb
: TRAMP, WALK
synonym see WANDER
— **traipse** *noun*
trait \'trāt, *British usually* 'trā\ *noun* [Middle French, literally, act of drawing, from Latin *tractus* — more at TRACT] (1589)
1 a : a stroke of or as if of a pencil **b :** TOUCH, TRACE
2 a : a distinguishing quality (as of personal character) **:** PECULIARITY **b :** an inherited characteristic
trai·tor \'trā-tər\ *noun* [Middle English *traitre*, from Old French, from Latin *traditor*, from *tradere* to hand over, deliver, betray, from *trans-, tra-* trans- + *dare* to give — more at DATE] (13th century)
1 : one who betrays another's trust or is false to an obligation or duty
2 : one who commits treason
word history see TREASON
trai·tor·ous \'trā-tə-rəs, 'trā-trəs\ *adjective* (14th century)
1 : guilty or capable of treason
2 : constituting treason ⟨*traitorous* activities⟩
synonym see FAITHLESS
— **trai·tor·ous·ly** *adverb*
trai·tress \'trā-trəs\ *or* **trai·tor·ess** \'trā-tə-rəs, 'trā-trəs\ *noun* (14th century)
: a female traitor
tra·ject \trə-'jekt\ *transitive verb* [Latin *trajectus*, past participle of *traicere*] (1657)
: TRANSMIT
— **tra·jec·tion** \-'jek-shən\ *noun*
tra·jec·to·ry \trə-'jek-t(ə-)rē\ *noun, plural* **-ries** [New Latin *trajectoria*, from feminine of *trajectorius* of passing, from Latin *traicere* to cause to cross, cross, from *trans-, tra-* trans- + *jacere* to throw — more at JET] (1696)
1 : the curve that a body (as a planet or comet in its orbit or a rocket) describes in space
2 : a path, progression, or line of development resembling a physical trajectory
Tra·keh·ner \tra-'kā-nər\ *noun* [German, from *Trakehnen*, site of the Prussian royal stud in East Prussia] (1926)
: any of a breed of large powerful saddle horses that originated in East Prussia and excel in dressage and jumping
¹**tram** \'tram\ *noun* [English dialect, shaft of a wheelbarrow, probably from Low German *traam*, literally, beam] (circa 1517)
1 : any of various vehicles: as **a :** a boxlike wagon running on rails (as in a mine) **b** *chiefly British* **:** STREETCAR **c :** a carrier that travels on an overhead cable or rails
2 *plural, chiefly British* **:** a streetcar line
²**tram** *transitive verb* **trammed; tram·ming** (1874)
: to haul in a tram or over a tramway
tram·car \'tram-,kär\ *noun* (1873)
1 *chiefly British* **:** STREETCAR
2 : TRAM 1a
tram·line \-,līn\ *noun* (1886)
British **:** a streetcar line
¹**tram·mel** \'tra-məl\ *noun* [Middle English *tramayle*, a kind of net, from Middle French *tremail*, from Late Latin *tremaculum*, from Latin *tres* three + *macula* mesh, spot — more at THREE] (15th century)
1 : a net for catching birds or fish; *especially* **:** one having three layers with the middle one finer-meshed and slack so that fish passing through carry some of the center net through the coarser opposite net and are trapped
2 : an adjustable pothook for a fireplace crane
3 : a shackle used for making a horse amble
4 : something impeding activity, progress, or freedom **:** RESTRAINT — usually used in plural

5 a : an instrument for drawing ellipses **b :** a compass for drawing large circles that consists of a beam with two sliding parts — usually used in plural **c :** any of various gauges used for aligning or adjusting machine parts
²**trammel** *transitive verb* **-meled** *or* **-melled** *or* **-mel·ing** *or* **-mel·ling** \'tra-mə-liŋ, 'tram-liŋ\ (1605)
1 : to catch or hold in or as if in a net **:** ENMESH
2 : to prevent or impede the free play of **:** CONFINE
synonym see HAMPER
¹**tra·mon·tane** \trə-'män-,tān, ,tra-mən-'\ *noun* (1593)
: one dwelling in a tramontane region; *broadly* **:** FOREIGNER
²**tramontane** *adjective* [Italian *tramontano*, from Latin *transmontanus*, from *trans-* + *mont-, mons* mountain — more at MOUNT] (1596)
1 : TRANSALPINE
2 : lying on or coming from the other side of a mountain range
¹**tramp** \'tramp, *verb intransitive 1 & verb transitive 1 are also* 'trämp, 'trömp\ *verb* [Middle English; akin to Middle Low German *trampen* to stamp] (14th century)
intransitive verb
1 : to walk, tread, or step especially heavily
2 a : to travel about on foot **:** HIKE **b :** to journey as a tramp
transitive verb
1 : to tread on forcibly and repeatedly
2 : to travel or wander through or over on foot ⟨have *tramped* all the woods on their property⟩
— **tramp·er** *noun*
²**tramp** \'tramp, *3, 4 are also* 'trämp, 'trömp\ *noun* (1664)
1 a : a foot traveler **b :** a begging or thieving vagrant **c :** a woman of loose morals; *specifically* **:** PROSTITUTE
2 : a walking trip **:** HIKE
3 : the succession of sounds made by the beating of feet on a surface (as a road, pavement, or floor)
4 : an iron plate to protect the sole of a shoe

◇ **WORD HISTORY**
train The word *train* in the sense "a connected series of railroad cars" has given rise to words with the same meaning in a number of European languages, though sometimes in a rather roundabout way. Railways and trains with their associated vocabulary were British inventions, spreading from Britain to the continent. In English, *train* in its railway sense was shortened from phrases such as *train of carriages* or *train of wagons*, with *train* used in its long-established sense "a set of objects linked in succession." French had given English the word centuries before and now borrowed this particular meaning back. *Train* is first noted in French with the sense "series of railroad cars" in 1829, about five years after the meaning first appeared in English. Spanish and Italian borrowed the French or English word directly as, respectively, *tren* and *treno*. In central Europe, however, a different kind of borrowing took place. Because French *train* is a transparent derivative of the verb *trainer* "to pull, drag," German translated *train* with the noun *Zug*, which functions as a derivative of the verb *ziehen* "to pull, draw"—appropriate enough since a locomotive pulls a series of cars.

\ə\ **abut** \ᵊ\ **kitten** \ər\ **further** \a\ **ash** \ā\ **ace** \ä\ **mop, mar** \aù\ **out** \ch\ **chin** \e\ **bet** \ē\ **easy** \g\ **go** \i\ **hit** \ī\ **ice** \j\ **job** \ŋ\ **sing** \ō\ **go** \ò\ **law** \òi\ **boy** \th\ **thin** \th̲\ **the** \ü\ **loot** \ù\ **foot** \y\ **yet** \zh\ **vision** *see also* Guide to Pronunciation

5 : a ship not making regular trips but taking cargo when and where it offers and to any port — called also *tramp steamer*

³**tramp** \'tramp\ *adjective* (1873)
: having no fixed abode, connection, or destination ⟨a *tramp* dog⟩

tramp art *noun* (1974)
: a style of wood carving flourishing in the U.S. from about 1875 to 1930 that is characterized by ornate layered whittling often of cigar boxes or fruit crates; *also* : an object carved in this style

tram·ple \'tram-pəl\ *verb* **tram·pled; tram·pling** \-p(ə-)liŋ\ [Middle English, frequentative of *trampen* to tramp] (14th century)
intransitive verb
1 : TRAMP; *especially* : to tread heavily so as to bruise, crush, or injure
2 : to inflict injury or destruction especially contemptuously or ruthlessly — usually used with *on, over,* or *upon* ⟨*trampling* on the rights of others⟩
transitive verb
: to crush, injure, or destroy by or as if by treading
— **trample** *noun*
— **tram·pler** \-p(ə-)lər\ *noun*

tram·po·line \,tram-pə-'lēn, 'tram-pə-,\ *noun* [Italian *trampolino* springboard, from *trampoli* stilts, of Germanic origin; akin to Middle Low German *trampen* to stamp] (1928)
: a resilient sheet or web (as of nylon) supported by springs in a metal frame and used as a springboard and landing area in tumbling
— **tram·po·lin·er** \-'lē-nər, -,lē-\ *noun*
— **tram·po·lin·ist** \-nist\ *noun*

tram·po·lin·ing *noun* (1949)
: the sport of jumping and tumbling on a trampoline

tram·way \'tram-,wā\ *noun* (1825)
1 a : a railway for trams **b** *British* : a streetcar line
2 : an overhead cable for trams

¹**trance** \'tran(t)s\ *noun* [Middle English, from Middle French *transe,* from *transir* to pass away, swoon, from Latin *transire* to pass, pass away — more at TRANSIENT] (14th century)
1 : a state of partly suspended animation or inability to function
2 : a somnolent state (as of deep hypnosis)
3 : a state of profound abstraction or absorption
— **trance·like** \-,līk\ *adjective*

²**trance** *transitive verb* **tranced; tranc·ing** (circa 1598)
: ENTRANCE, ENRAPTURE

tranche \'träⁿsh\ *noun* [French, literally, slice, from Old French, from *trenchier, trancher* to cut — more at TRENCH] (1930)
: a bond series issued for sale in a foreign country

tran·gam \'traŋ-gəm\ *noun* [origin unknown] (circa 1658)
archaic : TRINKET, GIMCRACK

tran·quil \'traŋ-kwəl, 'tran-\ *adjective* [Latin *tranquillus*] (1604)
1 a : free from agitation of mind or spirit ⟨a *tranquil* self-assurance⟩ **b** : free from disturbance or turmoil ⟨a *tranquil* scene⟩
2 : unvarying in aspect : STEADY, STABLE
synonym see CALM
— **tran·quil·ly** \-kwə-lē\ *adverb*
— **tran·quil·ness** *noun*

tran·quil·ize *also* **tran·quil·lize** \'traŋ-kwə-,līz, 'tran-\ *verb* **-ized** *also* **-lized; -iz·ing** *also* **-liz·ing** (1623)
transitive verb
: to make tranquil or calm : PACIFY; *especially* : to relieve of mental tension and anxiety by means of drugs
intransitive verb
1 : to become tranquil : RELAX 1
2 : to make one tranquil

tran·quil·iz·er *also* **tran·quil·liz·er** \-,līzər\ *noun* (1800)
1 : one that tranquilizes

2 : a drug used to reduce mental disturbance (as anxiety and tension)

tran·quil·li·ty *or* **tran·quil·i·ty** \tran-'kwi-lə-tē, traŋ-\ *noun* (14th century)
: the quality or state of being tranquil

trans \'tran(t)s, 'tranz\ *adjective* (1892)
: characterized by having certain groups of atoms on opposite sides of the longitudinal axis of a double bond or of the plane of a ring in a molecule

trans- *prefix* [Latin *trans-, tra-* across, beyond, through, so as to change, from *trans* across, beyond — more at THROUGH]
1 : on or to the other side of : across : beyond ⟨*trans*atlantic⟩
2 a : beyond (a specified chemical element) in the periodic table ⟨*trans*uranium⟩ **b** *usually italic* : trans ⟨*trans*-dichloro-ethylene⟩ — compare CIS- 2
3 : through ⟨*trans*cutaneous⟩
4 : so or such as to change or transfer ⟨*trans*literate⟩ ⟨*trans*location⟩ ⟨*trans*amination⟩ ⟨*trans*ship⟩

trans·act \tran-'zakt, tran(t)-'sakt\ *verb* [Latin *transactus,* past participle of *transigere* to drive through, complete, transact, from *trans-* + *agere* to drive, do — more at AGENT] (circa 1585)
intransitive verb
: to carry on business
transitive verb
1 : to carry to completion ⟨*transact* a sale⟩
2 : to carry on the operation or management of : DO ⟨*transact* business⟩
— **trans·ac·tor** \-'zak-tər, -'sak-tər\ *noun*

trans·ac·ti·nide \tran(t)-'sak-tə-,nīd, tran-'zak-\ *adjective* (1969)
: of, relating to, or being actual or hypothetical elements with atomic weights higher than those of the actinide series ⟨*transactinide* chemistry⟩

trans·ac·tion \tran-'zak-shən, tran(t)-'sak-\ *noun* (1647)
1 a : something transacted; *especially* : an exchange or transfer of goods, services, or funds ⟨electronic *transactions*⟩ **b** *plural* : the often published record of the meeting of a society or association
2 a : an act, process, or instance of transacting **b** : a communicative action or activity involving two parties or things that reciprocally affect or influence each other
— **trans·ac·tion·al** \-shnəl, -shə-nᵊl\ *adjective*

transactional analysis *noun* (1961)
: a system of psychotherapy involving analysis of individual episodes of social interaction for insight that will aid communication

trans·al·pine \tran(t)s-'al-,pīn, tranz-\ *adjective* [Latin *transalpinus,* from *trans-* + *Alpes* the Alps] (1590)
: situated on the north side of the Alps ⟨*Transalpine* Gaul⟩ — compare CISALPINE

trans·am·i·nase \tran(t)s-'a-mə-,nās, tranz-, -,nāz\ *noun* (1940)
: an enzyme promoting transamination — called also *aminotransferase*

trans·am·i·na·tion \,tran(t)s-,a-mə-'nā-shən, ,tranz-\ *noun* (1939)
: a reversible oxidation-reduction reaction in which an amino group is transferred typically from an alpha-amino acid to the carbonyl carbon atom of an alpha-keto acid

trans·at·lan·tic \,tran(t)s-ət-'lan-tik, ,tranz-\ *adjective* (1779)
1 a : crossing or extending across the Atlantic Ocean ⟨a *transatlantic* cable⟩ **b** : relating to or involving crossing the Atlantic Ocean ⟨*transatlantic* air fares⟩
2 a : situated or originating from beyond the Atlantic Ocean **b** : of, relating to, or involving countries on both sides of the Atlantic Ocean and especially the U.S. and Great Britain ⟨*transatlantic* cooperation⟩

trans·ax·le \tran(t)s-'ak-səl, tranz-\ *noun* [*transmission* + *axle*] (1958)

: a unit that consists of a combination of transmission and front axle used in front-wheel-drive automobiles

trans·ceiv·er \tran(t)-'sē-vər\ *noun* [*transmitter* + re*ceiver*] (1934)
: a radio transmitter-receiver that uses many of the same components for both transmission and reception

tran·scend \tran(t)-'send\ *verb* [Middle English, from Latin *transcendere* to climb across, transcend, from *trans-* + *scandere* to climb — more at SCAN] (14th century)
transitive verb
1 a : to rise above or go beyond the limits of **b** : to triumph over the negative or restrictive aspects of : OVERCOME **c** : to be prior to, beyond, and above (the universe or material existence)
2 : to outstrip or outdo in some attribute, quality, or power
intransitive verb
: to rise above or extend notably beyond ordinary limits
synonym see EXCEED

tran·scen·dence \-'sen-dən(t)s\ *noun* (1601)
: the quality or state of being transcendent

tran·scen·den·cy \-dən(t)-sē\ *noun* (1615)
: TRANSCENDENCE

tran·scen·dent \-dənt\ *adjective* [Latin *transcendent-, transcendens,* present participle of *transcendere*] (1598)
1 a : exceeding usual limits : SURPASSING **b** : extending or lying beyond the limits of ordinary experience **c** *in Kantian philosophy* : being beyond the limits of all possible experience and knowledge
2 : being beyond comprehension
3 : transcending the universe or material existence
— **tran·scen·dent·ly** *adverb*

tran·scen·den·tal \,tran(t)-,sen-'den-tᵊl, -sən-\ *adjective* (1624)
1 a : TRANSCENDENT 1b **b** : SUPERNATURAL **c** : ABSTRUSE, ABSTRACT **d** : of or relating to transcendentalism
2 a : incapable of being the root of an algebraic equation with rational coefficients ⟨π is a *transcendental* number⟩ **b** : being, involving, or representing a function (as sin x, log x, e^x) that cannot be expressed by a finite number of algebraic operations ⟨*transcendental* curves⟩
3 *in Kantian philosophy* **a** : of or relating to experience as determined by the mind's make-up **b** : transcending experience but not human knowledge
4 : TRANSCENDENT 1a
— **tran·scen·den·tal·ly** \-tᵊl-ē\ *adverb*

tran·scen·den·tal·ism \-tᵊl-,i-zəm\ *noun* (1803)
1 : a philosophy that emphasizes the a priori conditions of knowledge and experience or the unknowable character of ultimate reality or that emphasizes the transcendent as the fundamental reality
2 : a philosophy that asserts the primacy of the spiritual and transcendental over the material and empirical
3 : the quality or state of being transcendental; *especially* : visionary idealism
— **tran·scen·den·tal·ist** \-tᵊl-ist\ *adjective or noun*

transcendental meditation *noun* (1966)
: a technique of meditation in which a mantra is chanted in order to foster calm, creativity, and spiritual well-being

trans·con·ti·nen·tal \,tran(t)s-,kän-tᵊn-'en-tᵊl, ,tranz-\ *adjective* (1853)
: extending or going across a continent ⟨a *transcontinental* railroad⟩

tran·scribe \tran(t)-'skrīb\ *transitive verb* **tran·scribed; tran·scrib·ing** [Latin *transcribere,* from *trans-* + *scribere* to write — more at SCRIBE] (1552)

1 a : to make a written copy of **b :** to make a copy of (dictated or recorded matter) in longhand or on a machine (as a typewriter) **c :** to paraphrase or summarize in writing **d :** WRITE DOWN, RECORD **2 a :** to represent (speech sounds) by means of phonetic symbols **b :** TRANSLATE 2a **c :** to transfer (data) from one recording form to another **d :** to record (as on magnetic tape) for later broadcast **3 :** to make a musical transcription of **4 :** to cause (as DNA) to undergo genetic transcription — **tran·scrib·er** *noun*

tran·script \'tran(t)-ˌskript\ *noun* [Middle English, from Medieval Latin *transcriptum*, from Latin, neuter of *transcriptus*, past participle of *transcribere*] (14th century) **1 a :** a written, printed, or typed copy; *especially :* a usually typewritten copy of dictated or recorded material **b :** an official or legal and often published copy ⟨a court reporter's *transcript*⟩; *especially :* an official copy of a student's educational record **2 :** a representation (as of experience) in an art form **3 :** a sequence of RNA produced by transcription from a DNA template

tran·scrip·tase \tran-'skrip-ˌtās, -ˌtāz\ *noun* [*transcription* + *-ase*] (1963) **:** RNA POLYMERASE; *also :* REVERSE TRANSCRIPTASE

tran·scrip·tion \tran(t)-'skrip-shən\ *noun* (1598) **1 :** an act, process, or instance of transcribing **2 :** COPY, TRANSCRIPT: as **a :** an arrangement of a musical composition for some instrument or voice other than the original **b :** a recording (as on magnetic tape) made especially for use in radiobroadcasting **3 :** the process of constructing a messenger RNA molecule using a DNA molecule as a template with resulting transfer of genetic information to the messenger RNA — compare TRANSLATION 2, REVERSE TRANSCRIPTION — **tran·scrip·tion·al** \-shnəl, -shə-nᵊl\ *adjective* — **tran·scrip·tion·al·ly** *adverb*

tran·scrip·tion·ist \-shə-nist\ *noun* (1963) **:** one that transcribes; *especially :* a typist who transcribes dictated medical reports

trans·cul·tur·al \tran(t)s-'kəl-chə-rəl, tranz-, -'kəlch-rəl\ *adjective* (1951) **:** involving, encompassing, or extending across two or more cultures ⟨*transcultural* problems⟩

trans·cu·ta·ne·ous \ˌtran(t)s-kyu̇-'tā-nē-əs\ *adjective* (circa 1941) **:** passing, entering, or made by penetration through the skin ⟨*transcutaneous* infection⟩ ⟨*transcutaneous* inoculation⟩

trans·der·mal \tran(t)s-'dər-məl, tranz-\ *adjective* (1944) **:** relating to, being, or supplying a medication in a form for absorption through the skin into the bloodstream ⟨*transdermal* drug delivery⟩ ⟨*transdermal* nitroglycerin⟩ ⟨*transdermal* nicotine patch⟩

trans·dis·ci·plin·ary \-'di-sə-plə-ˌner-ē\ *adjective* (1948) **:** INTERDISCIPLINARY

trans·duce \tran(t)s-'düs, tranz-, -'dyüs\ *transitive verb* **trans·duced; trans·duc·ing** [Latin *transducere* to lead across, transfer, from *trans-* + *ducere* to lead — more at TOW] (1947) **1 :** to convert (as energy or a message) into another form ⟨essentially sense organs *transduce* physical energy into a nervous signal⟩ **2 :** to bring about the transfer of (as a gene) from one microorganism to another by means of a viral agent

trans·duc·er \-'dü-sər, -'dyü-\ *noun* (1924) **:** a device that is actuated by power from one system and supplies power usually in another form to a second system ⟨a loudspeaker is a

transducer that transforms electrical signals into sound energy⟩

trans·duc·tion \-'dək-shən\ *noun* [Latin *transducere*] (1947) **:** the action or process of transducing; *especially :* the transfer of genetic determinants from one microorganism to another by a viral agent (as a bacteriophage) — **trans·duc·tant** \-tənt\ *noun* — **trans·duc·tion·al** \-shnəl, -shə-nᵊl\ *adjective*

¹**tran·sect** \tran(t)-'sekt\ *transitive verb* [*trans-* + inter*sect*] (1634) **:** to cut transversely — **trans·sec·tion** \-'sek-shən\ *noun*

²**tran·sect** \'tran(t)-ˌsekt\ *noun* (1905) **:** a sample area (as of vegetation) usually in the form of a long continuous strip

tran·sept \'tran(t)-ˌsept\ *noun* [New Latin *transeptum*, from Latin *trans-* + *septum*, *saeptum* enclosure, wall] (circa 1542) **:** the part of a cruciform church that crosses at right angles to the greatest length between the nave and the apse or choir; *also :* either of the projecting ends of a transept — **tran·sep·tal** \tran(t)-'sep-tᵊl\ *adjective*

trans·fec·tion \tran(t)s-'fek-shən, tranz-\ *noun* [*trans-* + in*fection*] (1964) **:** infection of a cell with isolated viral nucleic acid followed by production of the complete virus in the cell; *also :* the incorporation of exogenous DNA into a cell — **trans·fect** \-'fekt\ *transitive verb*

¹**trans·fer** \tran(t)s-'fər, 'tran(t)s-ˌ\ *verb* **trans·ferred; trans·fer·ring** [Middle English *transferren*, from Latin *transferre*, from *trans-* + *ferre* to carry — more at BEAR] (14th century) *transitive verb* **1 a :** to convey from one person, place, or situation to another **:** TRANSPORT **b :** to cause to pass from one to another **:** TRANSMIT **c :** TRANSFORM, CHANGE **2 :** to make over the possession or control of **:** CONVEY **3 :** to print or otherwise copy from one surface to another by contact *intransitive verb* **1 :** to move to a different place, region, or situation; *especially :* to withdraw from one educational institution to enroll at another **2 :** to change from one vehicle or transportation line to another — **trans·fer·abil·i·ty** \(ˌ)tran(t)s-ˌfər-ə-'bi-lə-tē\ *noun* — **trans·fer·able** *also* **trans·fer·ra·ble** \tran(t)s-'fər-ə-bəl\ *adjective* — **trans·fer·al** \-əl\ *noun* — **trans·fer·rer** \-ər\ *noun*

²**trans·fer** \'tran(t)s-ˌfər\ *noun* (1674) **1 a :** conveyance of right, title, or interest in real or personal property from one person to another **b :** removal or acquisition of property by mere delivery with intent to transfer title **2 a :** an act, process, or instance of transferring **:** TRANSFERENCE 2 **b :** the carryover or generalization of learned responses from one type of situation to another **3 :** one that transfers or is transferred; *especially :* a graphic image transferred by contact from one surface to another **4 :** a place where a transfer is made (as of trains to ferries or as where one form of power is changed to another) **5 :** a ticket entitling a passenger on a public conveyance to continue the trip on another route

trans·fer·ase \'tran(t)s-(ˌ)fər-ˌās, -ˌāz\ *noun* (1948) **:** an enzyme that promotes transfer of a group from one molecule to another

trans·fer·ee \ˌtran(t)s-(ˌ)fər-'ē\ *noun* (circa 1736) **1 :** a person to whom a conveyance is made **2 :** one who is transferred

trans·fer·ence \tran(t)s-'fər-ən(t)s, 'tran(t)s-(ˌ)\ *noun* (1681) **1 :** an act, process, or instance of transferring **:** CONVEYANCE, TRANSFER **2 :** the redirection of feelings and desires and especially of those unconsciously retained from childhood toward a new object (as a psychoanalyst conducting therapy) — **trans·fer·en·tial** \ˌtran(t)s-fə-'ren(t)-shəl\ *adjective*

transfer factor *noun* (1956) **:** a substance that is produced and secreted by a lymphocyte functioning in cell-mediated immunity and that upon incorporation into a lymphocyte which has not been sensitized confers on it the same immunological specificity as the sensitized cell

trans·fer·or \ˌtran(t)s-(ˌ)fər-'ȯr\ *noun* (1875) **:** one that conveys a title, right, or property

transfer payment *noun* (circa 1945) **1 :** a public expenditure made for a purpose (as unemployment compensation) other than procuring goods or services — usually used in plural **2** *plural :* money (as welfare payments) that is received by individuals and that is neither compensation for goods or services currently supplied nor income from investments

trans·fer·rin \tran(t)s-'fer-ən\ *noun* [*trans-* + Latin *ferrum* iron] (1947) **:** a beta globulin in blood plasma capable of combining with ferric ions and transporting iron in the body

transfer RNA *noun* (1961) **:** a relatively small RNA that transfers a particular amino acid to a growing polypeptide chain at the ribosomal site of protein synthesis during translation — compare MESSENGER RNA

trans·fig·u·ra·tion \(ˌ)tran(t)s-ˌfi-gyə-'rā-shən, -gə-\ *noun* (14th century) **1 a :** a change in form or appearance **:** METAMORPHOSIS **b :** an exalting, glorifying, or spiritual change **2** *capitalized :* August 6 observed as a Christian feast in commemoration of the transfiguration of Christ on a mountaintop in the presence of three disciples

trans·fig·ure \tran(t)s-'fi-gyər, *especially British* -'fi-gər\ *transitive verb* **-ured; -ur·ing** [Middle English, from Latin *transfigurare*, from *trans-* + *figurare* to shape, fashion, from *figura* figure] (14th century) **:** to give a new and typically exalted or spiritual appearance to **:** transform outwardly and usually for the better **synonym** see TRANSFORM

trans·fi·nite \(ˌ)tran(t)s-'fī-ˌnīt\ *adjective* [German *transfinit*, from *trans-* (from Latin) + *finit*, from Latin *finitus*] (1902) **1 :** going beyond or surpassing any finite number, group, or magnitude **2 :** being or relating to cardinal and ordinal numbers of sets with an infinite number of elements

trans·fix \tran(t)s-'fiks\ *transitive verb* [Latin *transfixus*, past participle of *transfigere*, from *trans-* + *figere* to fasten, pierce — more at FIX] (1590) **1 :** to pierce through with or as if with a pointed weapon **:** IMPALE **2 :** to hold motionless by or as if by piercing — **trans·fix·ion** \-'fik-shən\ *noun*

¹**trans·form** \tran(t)s-'fȯrm\ *verb* [Middle English, from Latin *transformare*, from *trans-* + *formare* to form, from *forma* form] (14th century) *transitive verb* **1 a :** to change in composition or structure **b :** to change the outward form or appearance of

c : to change in character or condition : CONVERT **2** : to subject to mathematical transformation **3** : to cause (a cell) to undergo genetic transformation *intransitive verb* : to become transformed : CHANGE ☆ — **trans·form·able** \-'fȯr-mə-bəl\ *adjective* — **trans·for·ma·tive** \-'fȯr-mə-tiv\ *adjective*

²**trans·form** \'tran(t)s-ˌfȯrm\ *noun* (1853) **1** : a mathematical element obtained from another by transformation **2** : TRANSFORMATION 3a(1), (2) **3** : a linguistic structure (as a sentence) produced by means of a transformation 〈"the duckling is killed by the farmer" is a *transform* of "the farmer kills the duckling"〉

trans·for·ma·tion \ˌtran(t)s-fər-'mā-shən, -fȯr-\ *noun* (15th century) **1** : an act, process, or instance of transforming or being transformed **2** : false hair worn especially by a woman to replace or supplement natural hair **3 a** (1) : the operation of changing (as by rotation or mapping) one configuration or expression into another in accordance with a mathematical rule; *especially* : a change of variables or coordinates in which a function of new variables or coordinates is substituted for each original variable or coordinate (2) : the formula that effects a transformation **b** : FUNCTION 5a **c** : an operation that converts (as by insertion, deletion, or permutation) one grammatical string (as a sentence) into another; *also* : a formal statement of such an operation **4 a** : genetic modification of a bacterium by incorporation of free DNA from another ruptured bacterial cell — compare TRANSDUCTION **b** : genetic modification of a cell by the uptake and incorporation of exogenous DNA

trans·for·ma·tion·al \-shnəl, -shə-n°l\ *adjective* (1894) : of, relating to, characterized by, or concerned with transformation and especially linguistic transformation — **trans·for·ma·tion·al·ly** *adverb*

transformational grammar *noun* (1961) : a grammar that generates the deep structures of a language and converts these to the surface structures by means of transformations

trans·for·ma·tion·al·ist \ˌtran(t)s-fər-'mā-shnə-list, -shə-n°l-ist\ *noun* (1964) : an exponent of transformational grammar

trans·form·er \tran(t)s-'fȯr-mər\ *noun* (1596) : one that transforms; *specifically* : a device employing the principle of mutual induction to convert variations of current in a primary circuit into variations of voltage and current in a secondary circuit

trans·fuse \tran(t)s-'fyüz\ *transitive verb* **trans·fused; trans·fus·ing** [Middle English, from Latin *transfusus*, past participle of *transfundere*, from *trans-* + *fundere* to pour — more at FOUND] (15th century) **1 a** : to cause to pass from one to another : TRANSMIT **b** : to diffuse into or through : PERMEATE 〈sunlight *transfuses* the bay〉 **2 a** : to transfer (as blood) into a vein of a person or animal **b** : to subject (a patient) to transfusion — **trans·fus·ible** *or* **trans·fus·able** \-'fyü-zə-bəl\ *adjective*

trans·fu·sion \tran(t)s-'fyü-zhən\ *noun* (1578) **1** : an act, process, or instance of transfusing; *especially* : the process of transfusing fluid into a vein or artery **2** : something transfused — **trans·fu·sion·al** \-'fyüzh-nəl, -'fyü-zhə-n°l\ *adjective*

trans·gen·ic \ˌtran(t)s-'je-nik\ *adjective* (1982) : having chromosomes into which one or more heterologous genes have been incorporated either artificially or naturally 〈*transgenic* mice〉

trans·gress \tran(t)s-'gres, tranz-\ *verb* [Middle French *transgresser*, from Latin *transgressus*, past participle of *transgredi* to step beyond or across, from *trans-* + *gradi* to step — more at GRADE] (1526) *transitive verb* **1** : to go beyond limits set or prescribed by : VIOLATE 〈*transgress* divine law〉 **2** : to pass beyond or go over (a limit or boundary) *intransitive verb* **1** : to violate a command or law : SIN **2** : to go beyond a boundary or limit — **trans·gres·sive** \-'gre-siv\ *adjective* — **trans·gres·sor** \-'gre-sər\ *noun*

trans·gres·sion \-'gre-shən\ *noun* (15th century) : an act, process, or instance of transgressing: as **a** : infringement or violation of a law, command, or duty **b** : the spread of the sea over land areas and the consequent unconformable deposit of sediments on older rocks

tran·ship *variant of* TRANSSHIP

trans·his·tor·i·cal \ˌtran(t)s-(h)is-'tȯr-i-kəl, ˌtranz-, -'tär-\ *adjective* (1909) : transcending historical bounds

trans·hu·mance \ˌtran(t)s-'hyü-mən(t)s, tranz-, -'yü-\ *noun* [French, from *transhumer* to practice transhumance, from Spanish *trashumar*, from *tras-* trans- (from Latin *trans-*) + Latin *humus* earth — more at HUMBLE] (circa 1901) : seasonal movement of livestock and especially sheep between mountain and lowland pastures either under the care of herders or in company with the owners — **trans·hu·mant** \-mənt\ *adjective or noun*

tran·sience \'tran(t)-sh(ē-)ən(t)s; 'tran-zē-ən(t)s, 'tran(t)-sē-; 'tran-zhən(t)s, -jən(t)s\ *noun* (1745) : the quality or state of being transient

tran·sien·cy \-sh(ē-)ən(t)-sē, -zē-ən(t)-, -sē-ən(t)-; -zhən(t)-sē, -jən(t)-\ *noun* (1652) : TRANSIENCE

¹**tran·sient** \-sh(ē-)ənt, -zē-ənt, -sē-; -zhənt, -jənt\ *adjective* [Latin *transeunt-, transiens*, present participle of *transire* to go across, pass, from *trans-* + *ire* to go — more at ISSUE] (1599) **1 a** : passing especially quickly into and out of existence : TRANSITORY **b** : passing through or by a place with only a brief stay or sojourn **2** : affecting something or producing results beyond itself ☆ — **tran·sient·ly** *adverb*

²**transient** *noun* (1652) **1** : one that is transient: as **a** : a transient guest **b** : a person traveling about usually in search of work **2 a** : a temporary oscillation that occurs in a circuit because of a sudden change of voltage or of load **b** : a transient current or voltage

transient ischemic attack *noun* (1966) : a brief episode of cerebral ischemia that is usually characterized by temporary blurring of vision, slurring of speech, numbness, paralysis, or syncope and that is often predictive of more serious cerebral accidents — abbreviation TIA

trans·il·lu·mi·nate \ˌtran(t)s-ə-'lü-mə-ˌnāt, ˌtranz-\ *transitive verb* : to cause light to pass through; *especially* : to pass light through (a body part) for medical examination — **trans·il·lu·mi·na·tion** \-ˌlü-mə-'nā-shən\ *noun* — **trans·il·lu·mi·na·tor** \-'lü-mə-ˌnā-tər\ *noun*

tran·sis·tor \tran-'zis-tər, tran(t)-'sis-\ *noun* [*transfer* + *resistor;* from its transferring an electrical signal across a resistor] (1948) **1** : a solid-state electronic device that is used to control the flow of electricity in electronic equipment and consists of a small block of a semiconductor (as germanium) with at least three electrodes **2** : a transistorized radio

tran·sis·tor·ise *British variant of* TRANSISTORIZE

tran·sis·tor·ize \-tə-ˌrīz\ *transitive verb* **-ized; -iz·ing** (circa 1952) : to equip (a device) with transistors — **tran·sis·tor·i·za·tion** \-ˌzis-tə-rə-'zā-shən\ *noun*

¹**tran·sit** \'tran(t)-sət, 'tran-zət\ *noun* [Middle English *transite*, from Latin *transitus*, from *transire* to go across, pass] (15th century) **1 a** : an act, process, or instance of passing through or over : PASSAGE **b** : CHANGE, TRANSITION **c** (1) : conveyance of persons or things from one place to another (2) : usually local transportation especially of people by public conveyance; *also* : vehicles or a system engaged in such transportation **2 a** : passage of a celestial body over the meridian of a place or through the field of a telescope **b** : passage of a smaller body (as Venus) across the disk of a larger (as the sun) **3** : a theodolite with the telescope mounted so that it can be transited

²**transit** (15th century) *intransitive verb* : to make a transit *transitive verb* **1 a** : to pass over or through : TRAVERSE **b** : to cause to pass over or through **2** : to pass across (a meridian, a celestial body, or the field of view of a telescope) **3** : to turn (a telescope) over about the horizontal transverse axis in surveying

☆ **SYNONYMS**
Transform, metamorphose, transmute, convert, transmogrify, transfigure mean to change a thing into a different thing. TRANSFORM implies a major change in form, nature, or function 〈*transformed* a small company into a corporate giant〉. METAMORPHOSE suggests an abrupt or startling change induced by or as if by magic or a supernatural power 〈awkward girls *metamorphosed* into graceful ballerinas〉. TRANSMUTE implies transforming into a higher element or thing 〈attempted to *transmute* lead into gold〉. CONVERT implies a change fitting something for a new or different use or function 〈*converted* the study into a nursery〉. TRANSMOGRIFY suggests a strange or preposterous metamorphosis 〈a story in which a frog is *transmogrified* into a prince〉. TRANSFIGURE implies a change that exalts or glorifies 〈joy *transfigured* her face〉.

Transient, transitory, ephemeral, momentary, fugitive, fleeting, evanescent mean lasting or staying only a short time. TRANSIENT applies to what is actually short in its duration or stay 〈a hotel catering primarily to *transient* guests〉. TRANSITORY applies to what is by its nature or essence bound to change, pass, or come to an end 〈fame in the movies is *transitory*〉. EPHEMERAL implies striking brevity of life or duration 〈many slang words are *ephemeral*〉. MOMENTARY suggests coming and going quickly and therefore being merely a brief interruption of a more enduring state 〈my feelings of guilt were only *momentary*〉. FUGITIVE and FLEETING imply passing so quickly as to make apprehending difficult 〈let a *fugitive* smile flit across his face〉 〈*fleeting* moments of joy〉. EVANESCENT suggests a quick vanishing and an airy or fragile quality 〈the story is lost in translation〉.

tran·si·tion \tran(t)-'si-shən, tran-'zi-, *chiefly British* tran(t)-'si-zhən\ *noun* [Latin *transition-, transitio,* from *transire*] (1551) **1 a :** passage from one state, stage, subject, or place to another **:** CHANGE **b :** a movement, development, or evolution from one form, stage, or style to another **2 a :** a musical modulation **b :** a musical passage leading from one section of a piece to another **3 :** an abrupt change in energy state or level (as of an atomic nucleus or a molecule) usually accompanied by loss or gain of a single quantum of energy — **tran·si·tion·al** \-'sish-nəl, -'sizh-, -'zish-; -'si-shə-n°l, -'zi-, -zhə-\ *adjective* — **tran·si·tion·al·ly** *adverb*

transition metal *noun* [from their being transitional between the more highly electropositive and the less highly electropositive elements] (1940) **:** any of various metallic elements (as chromium, iron, and nickel) that have valence electrons in two shells instead of only one — called also *transition element*

tran·si·tive \'tran(t)-sə-tiv, 'tran-zə-; 'tran(t)s-tiv\ *adjective* [Late Latin *transitivus,* from Latin *transitus,* past participle of *transire*] (1590) **1 :** characterized by having or containing a direct object ⟨a *transitive* verb⟩ ⟨a *transitive* construction⟩ **2 :** being or relating to a relation with the property that if the relation holds between a first element and a second and between the second element and a third, it holds between the first and third elements ⟨equality is a *transitive* relation⟩ **3 :** of, relating to, or characterized by transition — **tran·si·tive·ly** *adverb* — **tran·si·tive·ness** *noun* — **tran·si·tiv·i·ty** \,tran(t)-sə-'ti-və-tē, ,tran-zə-\ *noun*

tran·si·to·ry \'tran(t)-sə-,tōr-ē, 'tran-zə-, -,tòr-\ *adjective* [Middle English *transitorie,* from Middle French *transitoire,* from Late Latin *transitorius,* from Latin, of or allowing passage, from *transire*] (14th century) **1 :** tending to pass away **:** not persistent **2 :** of brief duration **:** TEMPORARY ⟨the *transitory* nature of earthly joy⟩ **synonym** see TRANSIENT — **tran·si·to·ri·ly** \,tran(t)-sə-'tōr-ə-lē, ,tran-zə-, -'tòr-\ *adverb* — **tran·si·to·ri·ness** \'tran(t)-sə-,tōr-ē-nəs, 'tran-zə-, -,tòr-\ *noun*

trans·late \tran(t)s-'lāt, tranz-; 'tran(t)s-,lāt, 'tranz-\ *verb* **trans·lat·ed; trans·lat·ing** [Middle English, from Latin *translatus* (past participle of *transferre* to transfer, translate), from *trans-* + *latus,* past participle of *ferre* to carry — more at TOLERATE, BEAR] (14th century) *transitive verb* **1 a :** to bear, remove, or change from one place, state, form, or appearance to another **:** TRANSFER, TRANSFORM ⟨a country boy *translated* to the city⟩ ⟨*translate* ideas into action⟩ **b :** to convey to heaven or to a nontemporal condition without death **c :** to transfer (a bishop) from one see to another **2 a :** to turn into one's own or another language **b :** to transfer or turn from one set of symbols into another **:** TRANSCRIBE **c** (1) **:** to express in different terms and especially different words **:** PARAPHRASE (2) **:** to express in more comprehensible terms **:** EXPLAIN, INTERPRET **3 :** ENRAPTURE **4 :** to subject to mathematical translation **5 :** to subject (as genetic information) to translation in protein synthesis *intransitive verb*

1 : to practice translation or make a translation; *also* **:** to admit of or be adaptable to translation ⟨a word that doesn't *translate* easily⟩ **2 :** to undergo a translation **3 :** LEAD, RESULT — usually used with *into* ⟨tax cuts *translate* into bigger savings⟩ — **trans·lat·abil·i·ty** \(,)tran(t)s-,lā-tə-'bi-lə-tē, (,)tranz-\ *noun* — **trans·lat·able** \tran(t)s-'lā-tə-bəl, tranz-\ *adjective* — **trans·la·tor** \-'lā-tər\ *noun*

trans·la·tion \tran(t)s-'lā-shən, tranz-\ *noun* (14th century) **1 :** an act, process, or instance of translating: as **a :** a rendering from one language into another; *also* **:** the product of such a rendering **b :** a change to a different substance, form, or appearance **:** CONVERSION **c** (1) **:** a transformation of coordinates in which the new axes are parallel to the old ones (2) **:** uniform motion of a body in a straight line **2 :** the process of forming a protein molecule at a ribosomal site of protein synthesis from information contained in messenger RNA — compare TRANSCRIPTION 3 — **trans·la·tion·al** \-shnəl, -shə-n°l\ *adjective*

trans·la·tive \-'lā-tiv\ *adjective* (circa 1682) **1 :** of, relating to, or involving removal or transference from one person or place to another **2 :** of, relating to, or serving to translate from one language or system into another

trans·la·to·ry \'tran(t)s-lə-,tōr-ē, 'tranz-, -,tòr-; tran(t)s-'lā-tə-rē, tranz-\ *adjective* (1849) **:** of, relating to, or involving uniform motion in one direction

trans·lit·er·ate \tran(t)s-'li-tə-,rāt, tranz-\ *transitive verb* **-at·ed; -at·ing** [*trans-* + Latin *littera* letter] (1861) **:** to represent or spell in the characters of another alphabet — **trans·lit·er·a·tion** \(,)tran(t)s-,li-tə-'rā-shən, (,)tranz-\ *noun*

trans·lo·ca·tion \,tran(t)s-lō-'kā-shən, ,tranz-\ *noun* (1624) **:** a change of location **:** DISPLACEMENT: as **a :** the conduction of soluble material (as metabolic products) from one part of a plant to another **b :** transfer of part of a chromosome to a different position especially on a nonhomologous chromosome; *especially* **:** the exchange of parts between nonhomologous chromosomes — **trans·lo·cate** \'trans(t)s-lō-,kāt, 'tranz-, (,)tran(t)s-', (,)tranz-'\ *verb*

trans·lu·cence \tran(t)s-'lü-s°n(t)s, tranz-\ *noun* (1755) **:** the quality or state of being translucent

trans·lu·cen·cy \-s°n(t)-sē\ *noun, plural* **-cies** (circa 1610) **1 :** TRANSLUCENCE **2 :** something that is translucent

trans·lu·cent \-s°nt\ *adjective* [Latin *translucent-, translucens,* present participle of *translucēre* to shine through, from *trans-* + *lucēre* to shine — more at LIGHT] (1607) **1 :** permitting the passage of light: **a :** CLEAR, TRANSPARENT ⟨*translucent* water⟩ **b :** transmitting and diffusing light so that objects beyond cannot be seen clearly **2 :** free from disguise or falseness ⟨his *translucent* patriotism —*Newsweek*⟩ **synonym** see CLEAR — **trans·lu·cent·ly** *adverb*

trans·ma·rine \,tran(t)s-mə-'rēn, ,tranz-\ *adjective* [Latin *transmarinus,* from *trans-* + *mare* sea — more at MARINE] (1583) **1 :** being or coming from beyond or across the sea ⟨a *transmarine* people⟩ **2 :** passing over or extending across the sea

trans·mem·brane \(,)tran(t)s-'mem-,brān, (,)tranz-\ *adjective* (1944) **:** taking place or existing across a membrane ⟨a *transmembrane* potential⟩

trans·mi·grate \(,)tran(t)s-'mī-,grāt, (,)tranz-, 'tran(t)s-,, 'tranz-,\ *verb* [Latin *transmigratus,* past participle of *transmigrare* to migrate to another place, from *trans-* + *migrare* to migrate] (circa 1559) *transitive verb* **:** to cause to go from one state of existence or place to another *intransitive verb* **1** *of the soul* **:** to pass at death from one body or being to another **2 :** MIGRATE — **trans·mi·gra·tion** \,tran(t)s-mī-'grā-shən, ,tranz-\ *noun* — **trans·mi·gra·tor** \(,)tran(t)s-'mī-,grā-tər, (,)tranz-, 'tran(t)s-,, 'tranz-,\ *noun* — **trans·mi·gra·to·ry** \tran(t)s-'mī-grə-,tōr-ē, -,tòr-\ *adjective*

trans·mis·si·ble \tran(t)s-'mi-sə-bəl, tranz-\ *adjective* (1644) **:** capable of being transmitted ⟨*transmissible* diseases⟩ — **trans·mis·si·bil·i·ty** \(,)tran(t)s-,mi-sə-'bi-lə-tē, (,)tranz-\ *noun*

trans·mis·sion \tran(t)s-'mi-shən, tranz-\ *noun* [Latin *transmission-, transmissio,* from *transmittere* to transmit] (1611) **1 :** an act, process, or instance of transmitting ⟨*transmission* of a nerve impulse across a synapse⟩ **2 :** the passage of radio waves in the space between transmitting and receiving stations; *also* **:** the act or process of transmitting by radio or television **3 :** an assembly of parts including the speed-changing gears and the propeller shaft by which the power is transmitted from an automobile engine to a live axle; *also* **:** the speed-changing gears in such an assembly **4 :** something that is transmitted **:** MESSAGE — **trans·mis·sive** \-'mi-siv\ *adjective* — **trans·mis·siv·i·ty** \,tran(t)s-(,)mi-'si-və-tē, tranz-\ *noun*

trans·mis·som·e·ter \,tran(t)s-(,)mi-'sä-mə-tər, ,tranz-\ *noun* (circa 1931) **:** an instrument for measuring the transmission of light through a fluid (as the atmosphere)

trans·mit \tran(t)s-'mit, tranz-\ *verb* **trans·mit·ted; trans·mit·ting** [Middle English *transmitten,* from Latin *transmittere,* from *trans-* + *mittere* to send] (15th century) *transitive verb* **1 a :** to send or convey from one person or place to another **:** FORWARD **b :** to cause or allow to spread: as (1) **:** to convey by or as if by inheritance or heredity **:** HAND DOWN (2) **:** to convey (infection) abroad or to another **2 a** (1) **:** to cause (as light or force) to pass or be conveyed through space or a medium (2) **:** to admit the passage of **:** CONDUCT ⟨glass *transmits* light⟩ **b :** to send out (a signal) either by radio waves or over a wire *intransitive verb* **:** to send out a signal either by radio waves or over a wire — **trans·mit·ta·ble** \-'mi-tə-bəl\ *adjective* — **trans·mit·tal** \-'mi-t°l\ *noun*

trans·mit·tance \-'mi-t°n(t)s\ *noun* (circa 1855) **1 :** TRANSMISSION **2 :** the fraction of radiant energy that having entered a layer of absorbing matter reaches its farther boundary

trans·mit·ter \tran(t)s-'mi-tər, tranz-; 'tran(t)s-,, 'tranz-\ *noun* (1727) **:** one that transmits: as **a :** an apparatus for transmitting radio or television signals **b :** NEUROTRANSMITTER

trans·mog·ri·fy \tran(t)s-'mä-grə-,fī, tranz-\ *verb* **-fied; -fy·ing** [origin unknown] (1656)

\ə\ abut \°\ kitten \ər\ further \a\ ash \ā\ ace \ä\ mop, mar \aù\ out \ch\ chin \e\ bet \ē\ easy \g\ go \i\ hit \ī\ ice \j\ job \ŋ\ sing \ō\ go \ò\ law \òi\ boy \th\ thin \th\ the \ü\ loot \ù\ foot \y\ yet \zh\ vision *see also* Guide to Pronunciation

transitive verb
: to change or alter greatly and often with grotesque or humorous effect
intransitive verb
: to become transmogrified
synonym SEE TRANSFORM
— **trans·mog·ri·fi·ca·tion** \(ˌ)tran(t)s-ˌmä-grə-fə-ˈkā-shən, (ˌ)tranz-\ *noun*

trans·mon·tane \(ˌ)tran(t)s-ˈmän-ˌtān, (ˌ)tranz-; ˌtran(t)s-(ˌ)män-ˌ, ˌtranz-\ *adjective* [Latin *transmontanus*] (1727)
: TRAMONTANE

trans·moun·tain \ˌtran(t)s-ˈmaùn-t°n, ˌtranz-\ *adjective* (1929)
: crossing or extending over or through a mountain ⟨a *transmountain* road⟩ ⟨a *transmountain* tunnel⟩

trans·mu·ta·tion \ˌtran(t)s-myù-ˈtā-shən, ˌtranz-\ *noun* [Middle English *transmutacioun*, from Middle French or Latin; Middle French *transmutation*, from Latin *transmutation-*, *transmutatio*, from *transmutare*] (14th century)
: an act or instance of transmuting or being transmuted: as **a :** the conversion of base metals into gold or silver **b :** the conversion of one element or nuclide into another either naturally or artificially
— **trans·mu·ta·tive** \tran(t)s-ˈmyü-tə-tiv, tranz-\ *adjective*

trans·mute \tran(t)s-ˈmyüt, tranz-\ *verb*
trans·mut·ed; trans·mut·ing [Middle English, from Latin *transmutare*, from *trans-* + *mutare* to change — more at MUTABLE] (15th century)
transitive verb
1 : to change or alter in form, appearance, or nature and especially to a higher form
2 : to subject (as an element) to transmutation
intransitive verb
: to undergo transmutation
synonym SEE TRANSFORM
— **trans·mut·able** \-ˈmyü-tə-bəl\ *adjective*

trans·na·tion·al \(ˌ)tran(t)s-ˈnash-nəl, (ˌ)tranz-, -ˈna-shə-n°l\ *adjective* (1921)
: extending or going beyond national boundaries ⟨*transnational* corporations⟩
— **trans·na·tion·al·ism** \-ˈnash-nə-ˌli-zəm, -ˈna-shə-n°l-ˌi-zəm\ *noun*

trans·nat·u·ral \-ˈna-chə-rəl, -ˈnach-rəl\ *adjective* (1569)
: being above or beyond nature

trans·oce·an·ic \ˌtran(t)s-ˌō-shē-ˈa-nik, ˌtranz-\ *adjective* (1827)
1 : lying or dwelling beyond the ocean
2 : crossing or extending across the ocean ⟨a *transoceanic* telephone cable⟩

tran·som \ˈtran(t)-səm\ *noun* [Middle English *traunsom*, *transyn*, probably alteration of *traversayn*, from Middle French *traversin*, from *traverse* traverse] (15th century)
1 : a transverse piece in a structure **:** CROSSPIECE: as **a :** LINTEL **b :** a horizontal crossbar in a window, over a door, or between a door and a window or fanlight above it **c :** the horizontal bar or member of a cross or gallows **d :** any of several transverse timbers or beams secured to the sternpost of a boat; *also* **:** the planking forming the stern of a square-ended boat

T: transom 1b

2 : a window above a door or other window built on and commonly hinged to a transom
— **over the transom :** without solicitation or prior arrangement ⟨the manuscript arrived *over the transom*⟩

tran·son·ic *also* **trans·son·ic** \tran(t)s-ˈsä-nik, tran-ˈsä-\ *adjective* [*trans-* + *supersonic*] (1945)
1 : being or relating to speeds near that of sound in air or about 741 miles (1185 kilome-

ters) per hour at sea level and especially to speeds slightly below the speed of sound at which the speed of airflow varies from subsonic to supersonic at different points along the surface of a body in motion relative to the surrounding air
2 : moving, capable of moving, or utilizing air currents moving at a transonic speed

trans·pa·cif·ic \ˌtran(t)s-pə-ˈsi-fik\ *adjective* (1891)
1 a : crossing or extending across the Pacific Ocean ⟨*transpacific* airlines⟩ **b :** relating to or involving crossing the Pacific Ocean ⟨*transpacific* airfares⟩
2 a : situated or occurring beyond the Pacific Ocean **b :** of, relating to, or involving countries on both sides of the Pacific Ocean ⟨the *transpacific* economy⟩

trans·par·ence \tran(t)s-ˈpar-ən(t)s, -ˈper-\ *noun* (1594)
: TRANSPARENCY 1

trans·par·en·cy \-ən(t)-sē\ *noun, plural* **-cies** (1615)
1 : the quality or state of being transparent
2 : something transparent; *especially* **:** a picture (as on film) viewed by light shining through it or by projection

trans·par·ent \-ənt\ *adjective* [Middle English, from Medieval Latin *transparent-*, *transparens*, present participle of *transparēre* to show through, from Latin *trans-* + *parēre* to show oneself] (15th century)
1 a (1) **:** having the property of transmitting light without appreciable scattering so that bodies lying beyond are seen clearly **:** PELLUCID (2) **:** allowing the passage of a specified form of radiation (as X rays or ultraviolet light) **b :** fine or sheer enough to be seen through **:** DIAPHANOUS
2 a : free from pretense or deceit **:** FRANK **b :** easily detected or seen through **:** OBVIOUS **c :** readily understood
synonym SEE CLEAR
— **trans·par·ent·ly** *adverb*
— **trans·par·ent·ness** *noun*

trans·par·ent·ize \-ən-ˌtīz\ *transitive verb* **-ized; -iz·ing** (1925)
: to make transparent or more nearly transparent ⟨*transparentize* tracing paper⟩

trans·per·son·al \(ˌ)tran(t)s-ˈpərs-nəl, -ˈpər-sə-n°l\ *adjective* (circa 1906)
1 : extending or going beyond the personal or individual
2 : of, relating to, or being psychology concerned especially with esoteric mental experience (as mysticism and altered states of consciousness) beyond the usual limits of ego and personality

tran·spic·u·ous \tran(t)s-ˈpi-kyə-wəs\ *adjective* [New Latin *transpicuus*, from Latin *transpicere* to look through, from *trans-* + *specere* to look, see — more at SPY] (1638)
: clearly seen through or understood

trans·pierce \tran(t)s-ˈpirs\ *transitive verb* [Middle French *transpercer*, from Old French, from *trans-* (from Latin) + *percer* to pierce] (1592)
: to pierce through **:** PENETRATE

tran·spi·ra·tion \ˌtran(t)s-pə-ˈrā-shən\ *noun* (1551)
: the act or process or an instance of transpiring; *especially* **:** the passage of watery vapor from a living body through a membrane or pores
— **tran·spi·ra·tion·al** \-shnəl, -shə-n°l\ *adjective*

tran·spire \tran(t)-ˈspīr\ *verb* **tran·spired; tran·spir·ing** [Middle French *transpirer*, from Latin *trans-* + *spirare* to breathe] (1597)
transitive verb
: to pass off or give passage to (a fluid) through pores or interstices; *especially* **:** to excrete (as water) in the form of a vapor through a living membrane (as the skin)
intransitive verb

1 : to give off vaporous material; *specifically* **:** to give off or exude watery vapor especially from the surfaces of leaves
2 : to pass in the form of a vapor from a living body
3 a : to be revealed **:** come to light **b :** to become known or apparent **:** DEVELOP
4 : to take place **:** GO ON, OCCUR □

trans·pla·cen·tal \ˌtran(t)s-plə-ˈsen-t°l\ *adjective* [International Scientific Vocabulary] (circa 1929)
: passing through or occurring by way of the placenta ⟨*transplacental* immunization⟩
— **trans·pla·cen·tal·ly** \-t°l-ē\ *adverb*

¹trans·plant \tran(t)s-ˈplant\ *verb* [Middle English *transplaunten*, from Late Latin *transplantare*, from Latin *trans-* + *plantare* to plant] (15th century)
transitive verb
1 : to lift and reset (a plant) in another soil or situation
2 : to remove from one place or context and settle or introduce elsewhere **:** RELOCATE
3 : to transfer (an organ or tissue) from one part or individual to another
intransitive verb
: to admit of being transplanted
— **trans·plant·abil·i·ty** \ˌtran(t)s-ˌplan-tə-ˈbi-lə-tē\ *noun*
— **trans·plant·able** \tran(t)s-ˈplan-tə-bəl\ *adjective*
— **trans·plan·ta·tion** \ˌtran(t)s-ˌplan-ˈtā-shən\ *noun*
— **trans·plant·er** \tran(t)s-ˈplan-tər\ *noun*

²trans·plant \ˈtran(t)s-ˌplant\ *noun* (1756)
1 : a person or thing that is transplanted
2 : the act or process of transplanting

trans·po·lar \(ˌ)tran(t)s-ˈpō-lər\ *adjective* (1850)
: crossing or extending across either of the polar regions

tran·spon·der \tran(t)-ˈspän-dər\ *noun* [*transmitter* + re*sponder*] (circa 1944)
: a radio or radar set that upon receiving a designated signal emits a radio signal of its own and that is used especially for the detection, identification, and location of objects

trans·pon·tine \tran(t)s-ˈpän-ˌtīn\ *adjective* [*trans-* + Latin *pont-*, *pons* bridge — more at FIND] (1844)
1 : situated on the farther side of a bridge
2 *British* **:** situated on the south side of the Thames

¹trans·port \tran(t)s-ˈpōrt, -ˈpòrt, ˈtran(t)s-ˌ\ *transitive verb* [Middle English, from Middle French or Latin; Middle French *transporter*, from Latin *transportare*, from *trans-* + *portare* to carry — more at FARE] (14th century)

1 : to transfer or convey from one place to another ⟨*transporting* ions across a living membrane⟩
2 : to carry away with strong and often intensely pleasant emotion
3 : to send to a penal colony overseas
synonym see BANISH
— **trans·port·abil·i·ty** \(,)tran(t)s-,pōr-tə-'bi-lə-tē, -,pȯr-\ *noun*
— **trans·port·able** \tran(t)s-'pōr-tə-bəl, -'pȯr-\ *adjective*
²**trans·port** \'tran(t)s-,pōrt, -,pȯrt\ *noun* (1611)
1 : an act or process of transporting : TRANSPORTATION
2 : strong or intensely pleasurable emotion ⟨*transports* of joy⟩
3 a : a ship for carrying soldiers or military equipment **b** : a vehicle (as a truck or airplane) used to transport persons or goods **c** : TRANSPORTATION 3
4 : a transported convict
5 : a mechanism for moving magnetic tape past a recording head
synonym see ECSTASY
trans·por·ta·tion \,tran(t)s-pər-'tā-shən\ *noun* (1540)
1 : an act, process, or instance of transporting or being transported
2 : banishment to a penal colony
3 a : means of conveyance or travel from one place to another **b** : public conveyance of passengers or goods especially as a commercial enterprise
— **trans·por·ta·tion·al** \-shnəl, -shə-n°l\ *adjective*
transport café \-ka-'fā, -'kaf\ *noun* (1938)
British : a roadside restaurant frequented chiefly by truck drivers
trans·port·er \tran(t)s-'pōr-tər, -'pȯr-, 'tran(t)s-,\ *noun* (1535)
: one that transports; *especially* : a vehicle for transporting large or heavy loads
transposable element *noun* (1979)
: a segment of genetic material that is capable of changing its location in the genome or in some bacteria of undergoing transfer between an extrachromosomal plasmid and a chromosome
¹**trans·pose** \tran(t)s-'pōz\ *transitive verb* **trans·posed; trans·pos·ing** [Middle English, from Middle French *transposer*, from Latin *transponere* (perfect indicative *transposui*) to change the position of, from *trans-* + *ponere* to put, place — more at POSITION] (14th century)
1 : to change in form or nature : TRANSFORM
2 : to render into another language, style, or manner of expression : TRANSLATE
3 : to transfer from one place or period to another : SHIFT
4 : to change the relative place or normal order of : alter the sequence of ⟨*transpose* letters to change the spelling⟩
5 : to write or perform (a musical composition) in a different key
6 : to bring (a term) from one side of an algebraic equation to the other with change of sign
synonym see REVERSE
— **trans·pos·able** \-'pō-zə-bəl\ *adjective*
²**trans·pose** \'tran(t)s-,pōz\ *noun* (1937)
: a matrix formed from another matrix by interchanging the rows and columns
trans·po·si·tion \,tran(t)s-pə-'zi-shən\ *noun* [Medieval Latin *transposition-, transpositio*, from Latin *transponere* to transpose] (1538)
1 : an act, process, or instance of transposing or being transposed
2 a : the transfer of any term of an equation from one side over to the other side with a corresponding change of the sign **b** : a mathematical permutation or interchange of two letters or symbols
— **trans·po·si·tion·al** \-'zish-nəl, -'zi-shə-n°l\ *adjective*

transposition cipher *noun* (1939)
: a cipher in which the letters of the plaintext are systematically rearranged into another sequence — compare SUBSTITUTION CIPHER
trans·po·son \tran(t)s-'pō-zän\ *noun* [*transpose* + ²*-on*] (1974)
: a transposable element especially when it contains genetic material controlling functions other than those related to its relocation
trans·sex·u·al \(,)tran(t)s-'sek-sh(ə-)wəl, -shəl\ *noun* (1957)
: a person with a psychological urge to belong to the opposite sex that may be carried to the point of undergoing surgery to modify the sex organs to mimic the opposite sex
— **trans·sex·u·al·ism** \-sh(ə-)wə-,li-zəm, -shə-,li-\ *noun*
— **trans·sex·u·al·i·ty** \-,sek-shə-'wa-lə-tē\ *noun*
trans·shape \tran(sh)-'shāp, tran(t)s-\ *transitive verb* (1575)
archaic : to change into another shape : TRANSFORM
trans·ship \tran(sh)-'ship, tran(t)s-\ (1792) *transitive verb*
: to transfer for further transportation from one ship or conveyance to another
intransitive verb
: to change from one ship or conveyance to another
— **trans·ship·ment** \-mənt\ *noun*
trans·tho·rac·ic \,tran(t)s-thə-'ra-sik\ *adjective* (1905)
: done or made by way of the thoracic cavity
— **trans·tho·rac·i·cal·ly** \-si-k(ə-)lē\ *adverb*
tran·sub·stan·tial \,tran(t)-səb-'stan(t)-shəl\ *adjective* (1567)
: changed or capable of being changed from one substance to another
tran·sub·stan·ti·ate \,tran(t)-səb-'stan(t)-shē-,āt\ *verb* **-at·ed; -at·ing** [Medieval Latin *transubstantiatus*, past participle of *transubstantiare*, from Latin *trans-* + *substantia* substance] (1533)
transitive verb
1 : to change into another substance : TRANSMUTE
2 : to effect transubstantiation in (sacramental bread and wine)
intransitive verb
: to undergo transubstantiation
tran·sub·stan·ti·a·tion \-,stan(t)-shē-'ā-shən\ *noun* (14th century)
1 : an act or instance of transubstantiating or being transubstantiated
2 : the miraculous change by which according to Roman Catholic and Eastern Orthodox dogma the eucharistic elements at their consecration become the body and blood of Christ while keeping only the appearances of bread and wine
tran·su·date \'tran(t)-sü-,dāt, -syü-; 'tran-zü-, -zyü-\ *noun* (1876)
: a transuded substance
tran·su·da·tion \,tran(t)-sü-'dā-shən, -syü-; ,tran-zü-, -zyü-\ *noun* (1617)
1 : the act or process of transuding or being transuded
2 : TRANSUDATE
tran·sude \tran(t)-'süd, -'syüd; tran-'züd, -'zyüd\ *verb* **tran·sud·ed; tran·sud·ing** [New Latin *transudare*, from Latin *trans-* + *sudare* to sweat — more at SWEAT] (1664)
intransitive verb
: to pass through a membrane or permeable substance : EXUDE
transitive verb
: to permit passage of
¹**trans·ura·nic** \,tran(t)-syü-'ra-nik, -shə-, -'rā-; ,tran-zyü-, -zhə-\ *or* **trans·ura·ni·um** \-'rā-nē-əm\ *adjective* (1935)
: of, relating to, or being an element with an atomic number greater than that of uranium

²**transuranic** *noun* (1950)
: a transuranic element
trans·val·u·ate \(,)tran(t)s-'val-yə-,wāt, (,)tranz-\ *transitive verb* **-at·ed; -at·ing** [back-formation from *transvaluation*] (1912)
: TRANSVALUE
trans·val·u·a·tion \,tran(t)s-,val-yə-'wā-shən, ,tranz-\ *noun* (1898)
: the act or process of transvaluing
trans·val·ue \(,)tran(t)s-'val-(,)yü, (,)tranz-\ *transitive verb* **-val·ued; -valu·ing** (1911)
: to reevaluate especially on a basis that repudiates accepted standards
trans·ver·sal \tran(t)s-'vər-səl, tranz-\ *noun* [*transversal*, adjective, transverse, from Middle English, from Medieval Latin *transversalis*, from Latin *transversus*] (circa 1847)
: a line that intersects a system of lines
¹**trans·verse** \tran(t)s-'vərs, tranz-, 'tran(t)s-, 'tranz-,\ *adjective* [Latin *transversus*, from *trans-* + *-versus* (as in *adversus* adverse)] (1621)
1 : acting, lying, or being across : set crosswise
2 : made at right angles to the anterior-posterior axis of the body ⟨a *transverse* section⟩
— **trans·verse·ly** *adverb*
²**trans·verse** \'tran(t)s-,vərs, 'tranz-\ *noun* (circa 1633)
: something (as a piece, section, or part) that is transverse
transverse colon *noun* (circa 1860)
: the middle portion of the colon that extends across the abdominal cavity
transverse process *noun* (1696)
: a lateral process of a vertebra
transverse wave *noun* (1922)
: a wave in which the vibrating element moves in a direction perpendicular to the direction of advance of the wave
trans·ves·tite \tran(t)s-'ves-,tīt, tranz-\ *noun* [German *Transvestit*, from Latin *trans-* + *vestire* to clothe — more at VEST] (circa 1922)
: a person and especially a male who adopts the dress and often the behavior typical of the opposite sex especially for purposes of emotional or sexual gratification
— **trans·ves·tism** \-'ves-,ti-zəm\ *noun*
— **transvestite** *adjective*
¹**trap** \'trap\ *noun* [Middle English, from Old English *treppe* & Old French *trape* (of Germanic origin); akin to Middle Dutch *trappe* trap, stair, Old English *treppan* to tread] (before 12th century)
1 : a device for taking game or other animals; *especially* : one that holds by springing shut suddenly
2 a : something by which one is caught or stopped unawares; *also* : a position or situation from which it is difficult or impossible to escape **b** : a football play in which a defensive player is allowed to cross the line of scrimmage and then is blocked from the side while the ballcarrier advances through the spot vacated by the defensive player
3 a : a device for hurling clay pigeons into the air **b** : SAND TRAP **c** : a piece of leather or section of interwoven leather straps between the thumb and forefinger of a baseball glove that forms an extension of the pocket
4 *slang* : MOUTH
5 : a light usually one-horse carriage with springs
6 : any of various devices for preventing passage of something often while allowing other matter to proceed; *especially* : a device for

drains or sewers consisting of a bend or partitioned chamber in which the liquid forms a seal to prevent the passage of sewer gas
7 *plural* : a group of percussion instruments (as a bass drum, snare drums, and cymbals) used especially in a dance or jazz band
8 : an arrangement of rock strata that favors the accumulation of oil and gas
9 *plural* [*speed trap*] : a measured stretch of a course over which electronic timing devices measure the speed of a vehicle (as a racing car or dragster)

²**trap** *verb* **trapped; trap·ping** (14th century)
transitive verb
1 a : to catch or take in or as if in a trap : ENTRAP **b** : to place in a restricted position : CONFINE ⟨*trapped* in the burning wreck⟩
2 : to provide or set (a place) with traps
3 a : STOP, HOLD ⟨these mountains *trap* rains and fogs generated over the ocean —*American Guide Series: California*⟩ **b** : to separate out (as water from steam)
4 a : to catch (as a baseball) immediately after a bounce **b** : to block out (a defensive football player) by means of a trap
intransitive verb
: to engage in trapping animals (as for furs)
synonym see CATCH
— **trap·per** *noun*

³**trap** *transitive verb* **trapped; trap·ping** [Middle English *trappen*, from *trappe* cloth, perhaps modification of Middle French *drap* — more at DRAB] (14th century)
: to adorn with or as if with trappings

⁴**trap** *noun* [Swedish *trapp*, from *trappa* stair, from Middle Low German *trappe*; akin to Middle Dutch *trappe* stair] (1794)
: TRAPROCK

trap·door \'trap-ˌdōr, -ˌdȯr\ *noun* (14th century)
: a lifting or sliding door covering an opening (as in a roof, ceiling, or floor)

trap–door spider *noun* (1826)
: any of various often large burrowing spiders (especially family Ctenizidae) that construct a tubular subterranean silk-lined nest topped with a hinged lid

trap-door spider

tra·peze \tra-ˈpēz *also* trə-\ *noun* [French *trapèze*, from New Latin *trapezium*] (1861)
: a gymnastic or acrobatic apparatus consisting of a short horizontal bar suspended by two parallel ropes

tra·pez·ist \-ˈpē-zist\ *noun* (1875)
: a performer on the trapeze — called also *trapeze artist*

tra·pe·zi·um \trə-ˈpē-zē-əm, tra-\ *noun, plural* **-zi·ums** *or* **-zia** \-zē-ə\ [New Latin, from Greek *trapezion*, literally, small table, diminutive of *trapeza* table, from *tra-* four (akin to *tettares* four) + *peza* foot; akin to Greek *pod-, pous* foot — more at FOUR, FOOT] (1570)
1 a : a quadrilateral having no two sides parallel **b** *British* : TRAPEZOID 1b
2 : a bone in the wrist at the base of the thumb

tra·pe·zi·us \-zē-əs\ *noun* [New Latin, from *trapezium*; from the pair on the back forming together the figure of a trapezium] (circa 1704)
: a large flat triangular superficial muscle of each side of the upper back

tra·pe·zo·he·dron \trə-ˌpē-zō-ˈhē-drən, ˌtra-pə-\ *noun, plural* **-drons** *or* **-dra** \-drə\ [New Latin, from *trapezium* + -o- + -*hedron*] (1822)

: a crystalline form whose faces are trapeziums

trap·e·zoid \'tra-pə-ˌzȯid\ *noun* [New Latin *trapezoides*, from Greek *trapezoeidēs* trapezium-shaped, from *trapeza* table] (circa 1706)
1 a *British* : TRAPEZIUM 1a
b : a quadrilateral having only two sides parallel
2 : a bone in the wrist at the base of the forefinger
— **trap·e·zoi·dal** \ˌtra-pə-ˈzȯi-dᵊl\ *adjective*

trapezoid 1b

trap·line \'trap-ˌlīn\ *noun* (1920)
: a line or series of traps; *also* : the route along which such a line of traps is set

trap·ping \'tra-piŋ\ *noun* [Middle English, from gerund of *trappen* to adorn] (14th century)
1 : CAPARISON 1 — usually used in plural
2 *plural* : outward decoration or dress : ornamental equipment; *also* : outward signs ⟨conventional men with all the *trappings* . . . of banality —Robert Plank⟩

Trap·pist \'tra-pist\ *noun* [French *trappiste*, from La *Trappe*, France] (1814)
: a member of a reformed branch of the Roman Catholic Cistercian Order established by the Abbot de Rancé in 1664 at the monastery of La Trappe in Normandy
— **Trappist** *adjective*

trap·rock \'trap-ˌräk\ *noun* [⁴*trap*] (1813)
: any of various dark-colored fine-grained igneous rocks (as basalt) used especially in road making

traps \'traps\ *noun plural* [Middle English *trappe* cloth — more at TRAP] (1813)
: personal belongings : LUGGAGE

trap·shoot·er \'trap-ˌshü-tər\ *noun* (1875)
: a person who engages in trapshooting

trap·shoot·ing \-ˌshü-tiŋ\ *noun* (1875)
: shooting at clay pigeons sprung from a trap into the air away from the shooter

tra·pun·to \trə-ˈpün-(ˌ)tō, -ˈpün-\ *noun, plural* **-tos** [Italian, from past participle of *trapungere* to embroider, from *tra-* across (from Latin *trans-*) + *pungere* to prick, from Latin — more at TRANS-, PUNGENT] (circa 1924)
: a decorative quilted design in high relief worked through at least two layers of cloth by outlining the design in running stitch and padding it from the underside

¹**trash** \'trash\ *noun* [of Scandinavian origin; akin to Norwegian *trask* trash; akin to Old Norse *tros* fallen leaves and twigs, Old English *trus*] (circa 1518)
1 : something worth little or nothing: as **a** : JUNK, RUBBISH **b** (1) : empty talk : NONSENSE (2) : inferior or worthless writing or artistic matter; *also* : such material intended purely for entertainment
2 : something in a crumbled or broken condition or mass; *especially* : debris from pruning or processing plant material
3 : a worthless person; *also* : such persons as a group : RIFFRAFF

²**trash** (circa 1859)
transitive verb
1 : VANDALIZE, DESTROY
2 : ATTACK, ASSAULT
3 : SPOIL, RUIN ⟨*trashing* the environment⟩
4 : to subject to criticism or invective; *especially* : to disparage strongly ⟨a film *trashed* by the critics⟩
5 : THROW AWAY 1 ⟨standards of reality and truth were *trashed* —Edwin Diamond⟩
intransitive verb
: to trash something or someone

trash fish *noun* (1944)
1 : ROUGH FISH
2 : any of various sea fishes that have no market value as human food but are sometimes processed for use in animal feed, fertilizers, and paints

trash·man \'trash-ˌman, -mən\ *noun* (1951)
: a worker who collects and hauls away trash

trashy \'tra-shē\ *adjective* **trash·i·er; -est** (circa 1620)
: resembling or containing trash : of inferior quality
— **trash·i·ness** *noun*

trat·to·ria \ˌträ-tə-ˈrē-ə\ *noun, plural* **-ri·as** *or* **-rie** \-ˈrē-ˌā\ [Italian, from *trattore* restaurateur, from French *traiteur*, from *traiter* to treat, from Old French *traitier* — more at TREAT] (1832)
: RESTAURANT; *specifically* : a usually small modest Italian restaurant
word history see RESTAURANT

trau·ma \'traú-mə, 'trȯ-\ *noun, plural* **trau·mas** *or* **trau·ma·ta** \-mə-tə\ [Greek *traumat-, trauma* wound, alteration of *trōma*; akin to Greek *titrōskein* to wound, *tetrainein* to pierce — more at THROW] (circa 1693)
1 a : an injury (as a wound) to living tissue caused by an extrinsic agent ⟨surgical *trauma*⟩
b : a disordered psychic or behavioral state resulting from mental or emotional stress or physical injury
2 : an agent, force, or mechanism that causes trauma
— **trau·mat·ic** \trə-ˈma-tik, trȯ-, traú-\ *adjective*
— **trau·mat·i·cal·ly** \-ti-k(ə-)lē\ *adverb*

trau·ma·tise *British variant of* TRAUMATIZE

trau·ma·tism \'traú-mə-ˌti-zəm, 'trȯ-\ *noun* (1857)
: the development or occurrence of trauma; *also* : TRAUMA

trau·ma·tize \-ˌtīz\ *transitive verb* **-tized; -tiz·ing** (1903)
: to inflict a trauma upon
— **trau·ma·ti·za·tion** \ˌtraú-mə-tə-ˈzā-shən, ˌtrȯ-\ *noun*

¹**tra·vail** \trə-ˈvā(ə)l, 'tra-ˌvāl\ *noun* [Middle English, from Old French, from *travaillier* to torture, labor, from (assumed) Vulgar Latin *trepaliare* to torture, from Late Latin *trepalium* instrument of torture, from Latin *tripalis* having three stakes, from *tri-* + *palus* stake — more at POLE] (13th century)
1 a : work especially of a painful or laborious nature : TOIL **b** : a physical or mental exertion or piece of work : TASK, EFFORT **c** : AGONY, TORMENT
2 : LABOR, PARTURITION
synonym see WORK
word history see TRAVEL

²**travail** *same as* ¹; *in prayer-book communion service usually* 'tra-ˌvāl\ *intransitive verb* [Middle English, from Old French *travaillier*] (13th century)
1 : to labor hard : TOIL
2 : LABOR 3

¹**trav·el** \'tra-vəl\ *verb* **-eled** *or* **-elled; -el·ing** *or* **-el·ling** \'tra-və-liŋ, 'trav-liŋ\ [Middle English *travailen* to labor, journey, from Old French *travaillier* to labor] (14th century)
intransitive verb
1 a : to go on or as if on a trip or tour : JOURNEY **b** (1) : to go as if by traveling : PASS ⟨the news *traveled* fast⟩ (2) : ASSOCIATE ⟨*travels* with a sophisticated crowd⟩ **c** : to go from place to place as a sales representative or business agent
2 a : to move or undergo transmission from one place to another ⟨goods *traveling* by plane⟩ **b** : to move in a given direction or path or through a given distance ⟨the stylus *travels* in a groove⟩ **c** : to move rapidly ⟨a car that can really *travel*⟩
3 : to walk or run with a basketball in violation of the rules
transitive verb
1 a : to journey through or over **b** : to follow (a course or path) as if by traveling
2 : to traverse (a specified distance)

3 : to cover (a place or region) as a commercial traveler ◇
— **travel light :** to travel with a minimum of equipment or baggage
²travel *noun* (14th century)
1 a : the act of traveling **:** PASSAGE **b :** a journey especially to a distant or unfamiliar place **:** TOUR, TRIP — often used in plural
2 *plural* **:** an account of one's travels
3 : the number traveling **:** TRAFFIC
4 a : MOVEMENT, PROGRESSION ⟨the *travel* of satellites around the earth⟩ **b :** the motion of a piece of machinery; *especially* **:** reciprocating motion
travel agency *noun* (1927)
: an agency engaged in selling and arranging personal transportation and accommodations for travelers — called also *travel bureau*
travel agent *noun* (1925)
: a person engaged in selling and arranging transportation, tours, or trips for travelers
trav·eled *or* **trav·elled** \'tra-vəld\ *adjective* (15th century)
1 : experienced in travel ⟨a widely *traveled* journalist⟩
2 : used by travelers ⟨a well-*traveled* highway⟩
trav·el·er *or* **trav·el·ler** \'tra-və-lər, 'trav-lər\ *noun* (14th century)
1 : one that travels: as **a :** one that goes on a trip or journey **b :** TRAVELING SALESMAN
2 a : an iron ring sliding along a rope, bar, or rod of a ship **b :** a rod on the deck on which such a ring slides
3 : any of various devices for handling something that is being transported laterally
traveler's check *noun* (1891)
: a draft purchased from a bank or express company and signed by the purchaser at the time of purchase and again at the time of cashing as a precaution against forgery
trav·el·ing *or* **trav·el·ling** \'tra-və-liŋ, 'trav-liŋ\ *adjective* (14th century)
1 : that travels ⟨a *traveling* opera company⟩ ⟨a *traveling* executive⟩
2 : carried, used by, or accompanying a traveler ⟨a *traveling* alarm clock⟩ ⟨a *traveling* companion⟩
traveling bag *noun* (1838)
: SUITCASE
traveling case *noun* (1744)
: a usually rigid and box-shaped suitcase
traveling fellowship *noun* (1789)
: a fellowship whose terms permit or direct the holder to travel or go abroad for study or research
traveling salesman *noun* (1885)
: a traveling representative of a business concern who solicits orders usually in an assigned territory
trav·el·ogue *or* **trav·el·og** \'tra-və-,lòg, -,läg\ *noun* [*travel* + *-logue*] (1903)
1 : a talk or lecture on travel usually accompanied by a film or slides
2 : a narrated motion picture about travel
3 : a piece of writing about travel
travel trailer *noun* (1961)
: a trailer drawn especially by a passenger automobile and equipped for use (as while traveling) as a dwelling
tra·vers·al \trə-'vər-səl *also* tra-' *or* 'tra-,\ *noun* (1897)
: the act or an instance of traversing
¹tra·verse \'tra-vərs *also* -,vərs, *especially for* 6 & 8 *also* trə-' *or* tra-'\ *noun* [Middle English *travers*, from Middle French *traverse*, from *traverser* to cross, from Late Latin *transversare*, from Latin *transversus* transverse — more at TRANSVERSE] (14th century)
1 : something that crosses or lies across
2 : OBSTACLE, ADVERSITY
3 : a formal denial of a matter of fact alleged by the opposite party in a legal pleading

4 a : a compartment or recess formed by a partition, curtain, or screen **b :** a gallery or loft of communication from side to side in a large building
5 : a route or way across or over: as **a :** a zigzag course of a sailing ship with contrary winds **b :** a curving or zigzag way up a steep grade **c :** the course followed in traversing
6 : the act or an instance of traversing **:** CROSSING
7 : a protective projecting wall or bank of earth in a trench
8 a : a lateral movement (as of the saddle of a lathe carriage); *also* **:** a device for imparting such movement **b :** the lateral movement of a gun about a pivot or on a carriage to change direction of fire
9 : a line surveyed across a plot of ground
²tra·verse \trə-'vərs *also* tra-' *or* 'tra-,\ *verb* **tra·versed; tra·vers·ing** (14th century)
transitive verb
1 a : to go against or act in opposition to **:** OPPOSE, THWART **b :** to deny (as an allegation of fact or an indictment) formally at law
2 a : to go or travel across or over **b :** to move or pass along or through ⟨light rays *traversing* a crystal⟩
3 : to make a study of **:** EXAMINE
4 : to lie or extend across **:** CROSS ⟨the bridge *traverses* a brook⟩
5 a : to move to and fro over or along **b :** to ascend, descend, or cross (a slope or gap) at an angle **c :** to move (a gun) to right or left on a pivot
6 : to make or carry out a survey of by using traverses
intransitive verb
1 : to move back and forth or from side to side
2 : to move or turn laterally **:** SWIVEL
3 a : to climb at an angle or in a zigzag course **b :** to ski across rather than straight down a hill
4 : to make a survey by using traverses
— **tra·vers·able** \-'vər-sə-bəl, -(,)vər-\ *adjective*
— **tra·vers·er** *noun*
³tra·verse \'tra-(,)vərs, trə-', tra-'\ *adjective* (15th century)
: lying across **:** TRANSVERSE
trav·erse jury \'trav-ərs-\ *noun* (1823)
: PETIT JURY
traverse rod *noun* (1948)
: a metal rod or track with a pulley mechanism for drawing curtains
trav·er·tine \'tra-vər-,tēn, -tən\ *noun* [French *travertin*, from Italian *travertino, trevertino*, from Latin *tiburtinus*, adjective, of travertine, literally, of Tibur (Tivoli)] (1797)
: a mineral consisting of a massive usually layered calcium carbonate (as aragonite or calcite) formed by deposition from spring waters or especially from hot springs
¹trav·es·ty \'tra-və-stē\ *transitive verb* **-tied; -ty·ing** (1673)
: to make a travesty of **:** PARODY
²travesty *noun, plural* **-ties** [obsolete English *travesty*, disguised, parodied, from French *travesti*, past participle of *travestir* to disguise, from Italian *travestire*, from *tra-* across (from Latin *trans-*) + *vestire* to dress, from Latin — more at VEST] (1674)
1 : a burlesque translation or literary or artistic imitation usually grotesquely incongruous in style, treatment, or subject matter
2 : a debased, distorted, or grossly inferior imitation ⟨a *travesty* of justice⟩
synonym see CARICATURE
tra·vois \trə-'vòi, 'tra-,vòi\ *noun, plural* **tra·vois** *also* **tra·voises** \-'vòiz, -,vòiz\ [American French *travail*, from Canadian French, shaft of a cart, from Middle French *traveil* catafalque, prop, from Late Latin *trepalium* instrument of torture — more at TRAVAIL] (1847)

: a simple vehicle used by Plains Indians consisting of two trailing poles serving as shafts and bearing a platform or net for the load

travois

¹trawl \'tròl\ *verb* [probably from obsolete Dutch *tragelen*] (1561)
intransitive verb
1 : to fish with a trawl
2 : TROLL 2
transitive verb
: to catch (fish) with a trawl
²trawl *noun* (1759)
1 : a large conical net dragged along the sea bottom in gathering fish or other marine life
2 : SETLINE
trawl·er \'trò-lər\ *noun* (1630)
1 : a person who fishes by trawling
2 : a boat used in trawling
trawl·er·man \-mən\ *noun* (1633)
: a fisherman who trawls or one who mans a trawler
tray \'trā\ *noun* [Middle English, from Old English *trīg, trēg*; akin to Old Swedish *trø* wooden grain measure and probably to Old English *trēow* tree — more at TREE] (before 12th century)
: an open receptacle with a flat bottom and a low rim for holding, carrying, or exhibiting articles
— **tray·ful** \-,fùl\ *noun*
treach·er·ous \'tre-chə-rəs, 'trech-rəs\ *adjective* (14th century)
1 : characterized by or manifesting treachery **:** PERFIDIOUS
2 a : likely to betray trust **:** UNRELIABLE ⟨a *treacherous* memory⟩ **b :** providing insecure footing or support ⟨*treacherous* quicksand⟩ **c :** marked by hidden dangers, hazards, or perils
synonym see FAITHLESS
— **treach·er·ous·ly** *adverb*
— **treach·er·ous·ness** *noun*
treach·ery \-rē\ *noun, plural* **-eries** [Middle English *trecherie*, from Old French, from *trechier, trichier* to deceive, from (assumed) Vulgar Latin *triccare* — more at TRICK] (13th century)

◇ WORD HISTORY
travel For many of us in the U.S. travel is usually for pleasure and work is not very taxing physically, so that we are unlikely to associate travel with hard labor, and labor with torture. However, travel, labor, and torture are all bound up in the history of the word *travel*. The ultimate source of both *travel* and *travail* is an unattested spoken Latin verb *trepaliare* "to torture," a derivative of Late Latin *trepalium*, a name for an instrument of torture. *Trepaliare* developed into Old French *travaillier*, which meant "to torture, torment" and intransitively "to suffer, labor." Middle English borrowed the Old French verb as well as its noun derivative *travail*, and Modern English *travail* preserves the original sense "torment." But the difficulties of getting from place to place in the Middle Ages, when any journey was a wearisome effort and a pilgrimage to a distant religious shrine a real act of devotion, led medieval Englishmen to apply *travailen* "to labor" to the act of making a trip. Shift in stress and a weakening of the vowel in the second syllable eventually led to a distinction between *travail* and *travel*.

\ə\ abut \ᵊ\ kitten \ər\ further \a\ ash \ā\ ace
\ä\ mop, mar \aù\ out \ch\ chin \e\ bet \ē\ easy
\g\ go \i\ hit \ī\ ice \j\ job \ŋ\ sing \ō\ go
\ò\ law \òi\ boy \th\ thin \t͟h\ the \ü\ loot \ù\ foot
\y\ yet \zh\ vision *see also* Guide to Pronunciation

1 : violation of allegiance or of faith and confidence **:** TREASON
2 : an act of perfidy or treason

trea·cle \\'trē-kəl\\ *noun* [Middle English *triacle*, from Middle French, from Latin *theriaca*, from Greek *thēriakē* antidote against a poisonous bite, from feminine of *thēriakos* of a wild animal, from *thērion* wild animal, diminutive of *thēr* wild animal — more at FIERCE] (14th century)
1 : a medicinal compound formerly in wide use as a remedy against poison
2 *chiefly British* **a :** MOLASSES **b :** a blend of molasses, invert sugar, and corn syrup used as syrup at the table — called also *golden syrup*
3 : something (as a tone of voice) heavily sweet and cloying

trea·cly \\-k(ə-)lē\\ *adjective* (1733)
: resembling treacle (as in quality or appearance) ⟨*treacly* sentimentality⟩

¹tread \\'tred\\ *verb* **trod** \\'träd\\ *also* **tread·ed; trod·den** \\'trä-dᵊn\\ *or* **trod; tread·ing** [Middle English *treden*, from Old English *tredan*; akin to Old High German *tretan* to tread] (before 12th century)
transitive verb
1 a : to step or walk on or over **b :** to walk along **:** FOLLOW
2 a : to beat or press with the feet **:** TRAMPLE **b :** to subdue or repress as if by trampling **:** CRUSH
3 : to copulate with — used of a male bird
4 a : to form by treading **:** BEAT ⟨*tread* a path⟩ **b :** to execute by stepping or dancing ⟨*tread* a measure⟩
intransitive verb
1 : to move on foot **:** WALK
2 a : to set foot **b :** to put one's foot **:** STEP
3 : COPULATE
— **tread·er** *noun*
— **tread on one's toes :** to give offense (as by encroaching on one's rights or feelings)
— **tread water :** to keep the body nearly upright in the water and the head above water by a treading motion of the feet usually aided by the hands

²tread *noun* (13th century)
1 : a mark (as a footprint or the imprint of a tire) made by or as if by treading
2 a (1) **:** the action of treading (2) **:** an act or instance of treading **:** STEP **b :** manner of stepping **c :** the sound of treading
3 a : the part of a shoe or boot sole that touches the ground; *also* **:** the pattern on the bottom of a sole **b** (1) **:** the part of a wheel or tire that makes contact with a road or rail (2) **:** the pattern of ridges or grooves made or cut in the face of a tire
4 : the distance between the points of contact with the ground of the two front wheels or the two rear wheels of a vehicle
5 a : the upper horizontal part of a step **b :** the width of such a tread
— **tread·less** \\-ləs\\ *adjective*

¹trea·dle \\'tre-dᵊl\\ *noun* [Middle English *tredel* step of a stair, from Old English, from *tredan*] (15th century)
: a swiveling or lever device pressed by the foot to drive a machine

²treadle *verb* **trea·dled; trea·dling** \\'tred-liŋ, 'tre-dᵊl-iŋ\\ (1891)
intransitive verb
: to operate a treadle
transitive verb
: to operate (as a machine) by a treadle

tread·mill \\'tred-,mil\\ *noun* (1822)
1 a : a mill worked by persons treading on steps on the periphery of a wide wheel having a horizontal axis and used formerly in prison punishment **b :** a mill worked by an animal treading an endless belt **c :** a device having an endless belt on which an individual walks or runs in place for exercise or physiological testing
2 : a wearisome or monotonous routine resembling continued activity on a treadmill

trea·son \\'trē-zᵊn\\ *noun* [Middle English *tresoun*, from Old French *traison*, from Latin *tradition-, traditio* act of handing over, from *tradere* to hand over, betray — more at TRAITOR] (13th century)
1 : the betrayal of a trust **:** TREACHERY
2 : the offense of attempting by overt acts to overthrow the government of the state to which the offender owes allegiance or to kill or personally injure the sovereign or the sovereign's family ◇

trea·son·able \\'trēz-nə-bəl, 'trē-zᵊn-ə-bəl\\ *adjective* (14th century)
: relating to, consisting of, or involving treason
— **trea·son·ably** \\-blē\\ *adverb*

trea·son·ous \\'trēz-nəs, 'trē-zᵊn-əs\\ *adjective* (1593)
: TREASONABLE

trea·sur·able \\'tre-zhə-rə-bəl, 'trā-; 'trezh-rə-, 'trāzh-rə-\\ *adjective* (1607)
: worthy of being treasured **:** PRECIOUS

¹trea·sure \\'tre-zhər, 'trā-\\ *noun* [Middle English *tresor*, from Old French, from Latin *thesaurus* — more at THESAURUS] (12th century)
1 a (1) **:** wealth (as money, jewels, or precious metals) stored up or hoarded ⟨buried *treasure*⟩ (2) **:** wealth of any kind or in any form **:** RICHES **b :** a store of money in reserve
2 : something of great worth or value; *also* **:** a person esteemed as rare or precious
3 : a collection of precious things

²treasure *transitive verb* **trea·sured; trea·sur·ing** \\-zh(ə-)riŋ\\ (14th century)
1 : to collect and store up (something of value) for future use **:** HOARD
2 : to hold or keep as precious **:** CHERISH, PRIZE ⟨she *treasured* those memories⟩
synonym see APPRECIATE

trea·sure–house \\'tre-zhər-,haus, 'trā-\\ *noun* (15th century)
1 : a building where treasure is kept **:** TREASURY
2 : a place or source (as a collection) where many things of value can be found

trea·sur·er \\'tre-zhə-rər, 'trā-; 'trezh-rər, 'trāzh-\\ *noun* (14th century)
1 : a guardian of a collection of treasures **:** CURATOR
2 : an officer entrusted with the receipt, care, and disbursement of funds: as **a :** a governmental officer charged with receiving, keeping, and disbursing public revenues **b :** the executive financial officer of a club, society, or business corporation
— **trea·sur·er·ship** \\-,ship\\ *noun*

treasure trove \\-,trōv\\ *noun* [Anglo-French *tresor trové*, literally, found treasure] (1523)
1 : treasure that anyone finds; *specifically* **:** gold or silver in the form of money, plate, or bullion which is found hidden and whose ownership is not known
2 : a valuable discovery, resource, or collection

trea·sury \\'tre-zh(ə-)rē, 'trā-\\ *noun, plural* **-sur·ies** [Middle English *tresorie*, from Old French, from *tresor* treasure] (14th century)
1 a : a place in which stores of wealth are kept **b :** the place of deposit and disbursement of collected funds; *especially* **:** one where public revenues are deposited, kept, and disbursed **c :** funds kept in such a depository
2 *obsolete* **:** TREASURE
3 *capitalized* **a :** a governmental department in charge of finances and especially the collection, management, and expenditure of public revenues **b :** the building in which the business of such a governmental department is transacted
4 *capitalized* **:** a government security (as a note or bill) issued by the Treasury
5 : a repository for treasures ⟨a *treasury* of poems⟩

treasury note *noun* (1890)

1 : a currency note issued by the U.S. Treasury in payment for silver bullion purchased under the Sherman Silver Purchase Act of 1890
2 : a U.S. government bond usually with a maturity of not less than one year or more than seven years

treasury of merits (1884)
: the superabundant satisfaction of Christ for human sins and the excess of merit of the saints which according to Roman Catholic theology is effective for salvation of others and is available for dispensation through indulgences

treasury stock *noun* (1903)
: issued stock reacquired by a corporation and held as an asset

¹treat \\'trēt\\ *verb* [Middle English *treten*, from Old French *traitier*, from Latin *tractare* to drag about, handle, deal with, frequentative of *trahere* to drag, pull] (14th century)
intransitive verb
1 : to discuss terms of accommodation or settlement **:** NEGOTIATE
2 : to deal with a matter especially in writing **:** DISCOURSE — usually used with *of* ⟨a book *treating* of conservation⟩
3 : to pay another's expenses (as for a meal or drink) especially as a compliment or as an expression of regard or friendship
transitive verb
1 a : to deal with in speech or writing **:** EXPOUND **b :** to present or represent artistically **c :** to deal with **:** HANDLE ⟨food is plentiful and *treated* with imagination —Cecil Beaton⟩
2 a : to bear oneself toward **:** USE ⟨*treat* a horse cruelly⟩ **b :** to regard and deal with in a specified manner — usually used with *as*
3 a : to provide with free food, drink, or entertainment **b :** to provide with enjoyment or gratification
4 : to care for or deal with medically or surgically ⟨*treat* a disease⟩
5 : to act upon with some agent especially to improve or alter ⟨*treat* a metal with acid⟩
— **treat·er** *noun*

²treat *noun* (1651)
1 : an entertainment given without expense to those invited
2 : an especially unexpected source of joy, delight, or amusement

treat·able \\'trē-tə-bəl\\ *adjective* (14th century)
: capable of being treated **:** yielding or responsive to treatment ⟨a *treatable* disease⟩
— **treat·abil·i·ty** \\,trē-tə-'bi-lə-tē\\ *noun*

trea·tise \\'trē-təs *also* -təz\\ *noun* [Middle English *tretis*, from Anglo-French *tretiz*, from Old French *traitier* to treat] (14th century)

1 : a systematic exposition or argument in writing including a methodical discussion of the facts and principles involved and conclusions reached ⟨a *treatise* on higher education⟩ **2** *obsolete* **:** ACCOUNT, TALE

treat·ment \'trēt-mənt\ *noun* (circa 1560) **1 a :** the act or manner or an instance of treating someone or something **:** HANDLING, USAGE **b :** the techniques or actions customarily applied in a specified situation **2 a :** a substance or technique used in treating **b :** an experimental condition

trea·ty \'trēt-ē\ *noun, plural* **treaties** [Middle English *tretee*, from Middle French *traité*, from Medieval Latin *tractatus*, from Latin, handling, treatment, from *tractare* to treat, handle] (14th century) **1 :** the action of treating and especially of negotiating **2 a :** an agreement or arrangement made by negotiation: (1) **:** PRIVATE TREATY (2) **:** a contract in writing between two or more political authorities (as states or sovereigns) formally signed by representatives duly authorized and usually ratified by the lawmaking authority of the state **b :** a document in which such a contract is set down

treaty port *noun* (1863) **:** any of numerous ports and inland cities in China, Japan, and Korea formerly open by treaty to foreign commerce

¹tre·ble \'tre-bəl\ *noun* [Middle English, perhaps from Middle French, trio, from *treble,* adjective] (14th century) **1 a :** the highest voice part in harmonic music **:** SOPRANO **b :** one that performs a treble part; *also* **:** a member of a family of instruments having the highest range **c :** a high-pitched or shrill voice, tone, or sound **d :** the upper half of the whole vocal or instrumental tonal range — compare BASS **e :** the higher portion of the audio frequency range in sound recording and broadcasting **2 :** something treble in construction, uses, amount, number, or value

²treble *adjective* [Middle English, from Middle French, from Latin *triplus* — more at TRIPLE] (14th century) **1 a :** having three parts or uses **:** THREEFOLD **b :** triple in number or amount **2 a :** relating to or having the range or part of a treble **:** HIGH-PITCHED, SHRILL **c :** of, relating to, or having the range of treble in sound recording and broadcasting ⟨*treble* frequencies⟩ — **tre·bly** \'tre-b(ə-)lē\ *adverb*

³treble *verb* **tre·bled; tre·bling** \'tre-b(ə-)liŋ\ (14th century) *transitive verb* **:** to increase threefold *intransitive verb* **1 :** to sing treble **2 :** to grow to three times the size, amount, or number

treble clef *noun* [¹*treble;* from its use for the notation of treble parts] (circa 1854) **1 :** a clef that places G above middle C on the second line of the staff **2 :** TREBLE STAFF

treble staff *noun* (circa 1854) **:** the musical staff carrying the treble clef

treb·u·chet \,tre-byə-'shet, -bə-, -'chet\ *or* **treb·uc·ket** \,tre-bə-'ket\ *noun* [Middle English *trebochet,* from Middle French *trebuchet*] (15th century) **:** a medieval military engine for hurling heavy missiles (as rocks)

tre·cen·to \trā-'chen-(,)tō\ *noun* [Italian, literally, three hundred, from Latin *tres* three + *centum* hundred — more at THREE, HUNDRED] (1841) **:** the 14th century; *specifically* **:** the 14th century in Italian literature and art

tre·de·cil·lion \,trē-di-'sil-yən\ *noun, often attributive* [Latin *tredecim* thirteen (from *tres*

three + *decem* ten) + English *-illion* (as in *million*) — more at THREE, TEN] (circa 1934) — see NUMBER table

¹tree \'trē\ *noun* [Middle English, from Old English *trēow;* akin to Old Norse *trē* tree, Greek *drys,* Sanskrit *dāru* wood] (before 12th century) **1 a :** a woody perennial plant having a single usually elongate main stem generally with few or no branches on its lower part **b :** a shrub or herb of arborescent form ⟨rose *trees*⟩ ⟨a banana *tree*⟩ **2 a** (1) **:** a piece of wood (as a post or pole) usually adapted to a particular use or forming part of a structure or implement (2) *archaic* **:** the cross on which Jesus was crucified **b** *archaic* **:** GALLOWS **3 :** something in the form of or resembling a tree: as **a :** a diagram or graph that branches usually from a simple stem without forming loops or polygons ⟨genealogical *tree*⟩ **b :** a much-branched system of channels especially in an animal body ⟨the vascular *tree*⟩ **4 :** SADDLETREE — **tree·less** \-ləs\ *adjective* — **tree·like** \-,līk\ *adjective*

²tree *transitive verb* **treed; tree·ing** (1575) **1 a :** to drive to or up a tree ⟨*treed* by a bull⟩ ⟨dogs *treeing* game⟩ **b :** to put into a position of extreme disadvantage **:** CORNER; *especially* **:** to bring to bay **2 :** to furnish or fit (as a shoe) with a tree

treed \'trēd\ *adjective* (1860) **:** planted or grown with trees **:** WOODED

tree ear *noun* (1967) **:** any of several brown ear-shaped basidiomycetous fungi (genus *Auricularia*); *especially* **:** one (*A. polytricha*) used especially in Chinese cooking

tree farm *noun* (1941) **:** an area of forest land managed to ensure continuous commercial production

tree fern *noun* (1832) **:** any of various ferns (especially families Cyatheaceae and Marattiaceae) of arborescent habit with a woody stem

tree frog *noun* (1738) **:** any of numerous small anuran amphibians (especially family Hylidae) of usually arboreal habits that typically have adhesive suckers on the toes

tree·hop·per \'trē-,hä-pər\ *noun* (circa 1839) **:** any of a family (Membracidae) of small leaping homopterous insects that feed on the sap especially of shrubs and trees

tree house *noun* (circa 1899) **:** a structure (as a playhouse) built among the branches of a tree

tree line *noun* (1893) **:** TIMBERLINE

treen \'trēn\ *noun, singular or plural in construction* [*treen* wooden, from Middle English, from Old English *trēowen,* from *treow* tree, wood] (1927) **:** small woodenware — called also *treenware*

tree·nail *also* **tre·nail** \'trə-n°l\ *noun* (13th century) **:** a wooden peg made usually of dry compressed timber so as to swell in its hole when moistened

tree of heaven (1845) **:** a Chinese ailanthus (*Ailanthus altissima* synonym *A. glandulosa*) that has foliage similar to that of the sumacs, has ill-scented staminate flowers, and is grown as a shade and ornamental tree

tree of life (1880) **:** a conventionalized and often ornate representation of a tree used as a decorative motif

tree peony *noun* (circa 1891) **:** a shrubby Chinese peony (*Paeonia suffruticosa*) that has large showy flowers and is the source of many horticultural varieties

tree ring *noun* (1919) **:** ANNUAL RING

tree shrew *noun* (circa 1893) **:** any of an order (Scandentia) of arboreal insectivorous mammals of southeastern Asia often classified as true insectivores or sometimes as primitive primates

tree shrew

tree sparrow *noun* (circa 1770) **1 :** a European sparrow (*Passer montanus*) that has a black spot on the ear coverts **2 :** a North American sparrow (*Spizella arborea*) that has a single dark spot on the breast and breeds in northern North America and winters in the U.S.

tree surgeon *noun* (1908) **:** a specialist in tree surgery — compare ARBORIST

tree surgery *noun* (1902) **:** operative treatment of diseased trees especially for control of decay; *broadly* **:** practices forming part of the professional care of specimen or shade trees

tree swallow *noun* (1873) **:** an American swallow (*Tachycineta bicolor* synonym *Iridoprocne bicolor*) with iridescent greenish blue upperparts and white underparts

tree toad *noun* (1778) **:** TREE FROG

tree tomato *noun* (circa 1881) **:** TAMARILLO

tree-top \'trē-,täp\ *noun* (1530) **1 :** the topmost part of a tree **2** *plural* **:** the height or line marked by the tops of a group of trees

tre·foil \'trē-,fȯil, 'trē-\ *noun* [Middle English, from Middle French *trefeuil,* from Latin *trifolium,* from *tri-* + *folium* leaf — more at BLADE] (15th century) **1 a :** CLOVER; *broadly* **:** any of several trifoliolate leguminous herbs **b :** a trifoliolate leaf **2 :** an ornament or symbol in the form of a stylized trifoliolate leaf

trefoil 2

tre·ha·lose \tri-'hä-,lōs, -,lōz\ *noun* [International Scientific Vocabulary *trehala* (a sweet substance constituting the pupal covering of a beetle) + ²-*ose*] (1862) **:** a crystalline disaccharide $C_{12}H_{22}O_{11}$ stored instead of starch by many fungi and found in the blood of many insects

treil·lage \tre-'yäzh\ *noun* [French, from Middle French, from *treille* vine arbor, from Latin *trichila*] (1698) **:** latticework for vines **:** TRELLIS 1

¹trek \'trek\ *intransitive verb* **trekked; trek·king** [Afrikaans, from Dutch *trecken* to pull, haul, migrate; akin to Old High German *trechan* to pull] (1821) **1** *chiefly South African* **a :** to travel by ox wagon **b :** to migrate by ox wagon or in a train of such **2 :** to make one's way arduously; *broadly* **:** to go on a journey — **trek·ker** *noun*

²trek *noun* [Afrikaans, from Dutch *treck* pull, haul, from *trecken*] (1835) **1** *chiefly South African* **:** a journey by ox wagon; *especially* **:** an organized migration by a group of settlers

2 : a trip or movement especially when involving difficulties or complex organization

¹trel·lis \'tre-ləs\ noun [Middle English trelis, from Middle French treliz fabric of coarse weave, trellis, from (assumed) Vulgar Latin trilicius woven with triple thread, from Latin tri- + licium thread] (15th century)
1 : a frame of latticework used as a screen or as a support for climbing plants
2 : a construction (as a summerhouse) chiefly of latticework
3 : an arrangement that forms or gives the effect of a lattice ⟨a trellis of interlacing streams⟩
— **trel·lised** \'tre-ləst\ adjective

²trellis transitive verb (15th century)
1 : to provide with a trellis; especially **:** to train (as a vine) on a trellis
2 : to cross or interlace on or through **:** INTERWEAVE

trel·lis·work \'tre-ləs-,wərk\ noun (1712)
: LATTICEWORK

trem·a·tode \'tre-mə-,tōd\ noun [ultimately from Greek trēmatōdēs pierced with holes, from trēmat-, trēma hole, from tetrainein to bore — more at THROW] (circa 1859)
: any of a class (Trematoda) of parasitic platyhelminthic flatworms including the flukes
— **trematode** adjective

¹trem·ble \'trem-bəl\ intransitive verb **trem·bled; trem·bling** \-b(ə-)liŋ\ [Middle English, from Middle French trembler, from Medieval Latin tremulare, from Latin tremulus tremulous, from tremere to tremble; akin to Greek tremein to tremble] (14th century)
1 : to shake involuntarily (as with fear or cold) **:** SHIVER
2 : to move, sound, pass, or come to pass as if shaken or tremulous ⟨the building trembled from the blast⟩
3 : to be affected with fear or doubt ⟨tremble for the safety of another⟩
— **trem·bler** \-b(ə-)lər\ noun

²tremble noun (1609)
1 : an act or instance of trembling; especially **:** a fit or spell of involuntary shaking or quivering
2 : plural but singular in construction **:** severe poisoning of livestock and especially cattle by a toxic alcohol present in a snakeroot (Eupatorium rugosum) and rayless goldenrod that is characterized by muscular tremors, weakness, and constipation

trem·bly \'trem-b(ə-)lē\ adjective (1848)
: marked by trembling

tre·men·dous \tri-'men-dəs\ adjective [Latin tremendus, from gerundive of tremere] (1632)
1 : being such as may excite trembling or arouse dread, awe, or terror
2 a : notable by reason of extreme size, power, greatness, or excellence — often used as a generalized term of approval **b :** unusually large **:** HUGE
synonym see MONSTROUS
— **tre·men·dous·ly** adverb
— **tre·men·dous·ness** noun

trem·o·lite \'tre-mə-,līt\ noun [French trémolite, from Tremola, valley in Switzerland] (1799)
: a white or gray mineral of the amphibole group that is a silicate of calcium and magnesium
— **trem·o·lit·ic** \,tre-mə-'li-tik\ adjective

trem·o·lo \'tre-mə-,lō\ noun, plural -los [Italian, from tremolo tremulous, from Latin tremulus] (circa 1801)
1 a : the rapid reiteration of a musical tone or of alternating tones to produce a tremulous effect **b :** vocal vibrato especially when prominent or excessive
2 : a mechanical device in an organ for causing a tremulous effect

trem·or \'tre-mər\ noun [Middle English tremour terror, from Middle French, from Latin tremor trembling, from tremere] (1615)

1 : a trembling or shaking usually from physical weakness, emotional stress, or disease
2 : a quivering or vibratory motion; especially **:** a discrete small movement following or preceding a major seismic event
3 a : a feeling of uncertainty or insecurity **b :** a cause of such a feeling

trem·u·lant \'trem-yə-lənt\ adjective [Medieval Latin tremulant-, tremulans, present participle of tremulare — more at TREMBLE] (1837)
: TREMULOUS, TREMBLING

trem·u·lous \-ləs\ adjective [Latin tremulus — more at TREMBLE] (1611)
1 : characterized by or affected with trembling or tremors
2 : affected with timidity **:** TIMOROUS
3 : such as is or might be caused by nervousness or shakiness ⟨a tremulous smile⟩ ⟨tremulous handwriting⟩
4 : exceedingly sensitive **:** easily shaken or disordered
— **trem·u·lous·ly** adverb
— **trem·u·lous·ness** noun

¹trench \'trench\ noun [Middle English trenche track cut through a wood, from Middle French, act of cutting, from trenchier to cut, probably from (assumed) Vulgar Latin trinicare to cut in three, from Latin trini three each — more at TRINE] (15th century)
1 a : a long cut in the ground **:** DITCH; especially **:** one used for military defense often with the excavated dirt thrown up in front **b** plural **:** a place, position, or level at which an activity is carried on in a manner likened to trench warfare — often used in the phrase in the trenches
2 : a long, narrow, and usually steep-sided depression in the ocean floor — compare TROUGH
3 : TRENCH COAT

²trench (15th century)
transitive verb
1 : to make a cut in **:** CARVE
2 a : to protect with or as if with a trench **b** **:** to cut a trench in **:** DITCH
intransitive verb
1 a : ENTRENCH, ENCROACH ⟨trenching on other domains which were more vital —Sir Winston Churchill⟩ **b :** to come close **:** VERGE
2 : to dig a trench

tren·chan·cy \'tren-chən(t)-sē\ noun (1866)
: the quality or state of being trenchant

tren·chant \-chənt\ adjective [Middle English, from Middle French, present participle of trenchier] (14th century)
1 : KEEN, SHARP
2 : vigorously effective and articulate ⟨a trenchant analysis⟩; also **:** CAUSTIC ⟨trenchant remarks⟩
3 a : sharply perceptive **:** PENETRATING **b** **:** CLEAR-CUT, DISTINCT ⟨the trenchant divisions between right and wrong —Edith Wharton⟩
— **tren·chant·ly** adverb

trench coat noun (1916)
1 : a waterproof overcoat with a removable lining designed for wear in trenches
2 : a usually double-breasted raincoat with deep pockets, wide belt, and often straps on the shoulders

trenched \'trencht\ adjective (1541)
1 : furrowed or drained by trenches
2 : provided with protective trenches

¹tren·cher \'tren-chər\ noun [Middle English, from Middle French trencheoir, from trenchier to cut] (14th century)
: a wooden platter for serving food

²trencher adjective (15th century)
1 : of or relating to a trencher or to meals
2 archaic **:** having the nature of a parasite **:** SYCOPHANTIC

³trench·er \'tren-chər\ noun [²trench] (circa 1864)
: one that digs trenches; specifically **:** a usually self-propelled excavating machine typically

employing a bucket conveyor and used to dig trenches especially for pipelines and cables

tren·cher·man \'tren-chər-mən\ noun (1590)
1 : a hearty eater
2 archaic **:** HANGER-ON, SPONGER

trench fever noun (1915)
: a disease that is marked by fever and pain in muscles, bones, and joints and that is caused by a bacterium (Rochalimaea quintana) transmitted by the human body louse (Pediculus humanus)

trench foot noun (1915)
: a painful foot disorder resembling frostbite and resulting from exposure to cold and wet

trench mouth noun (1918)
1 : VINCENT'S ANGINA
2 : VINCENT'S INFECTION

trench warfare noun (1917)
: warfare in which the opposing forces attack and counterattack from a relatively permanent system of trenches protected by barbed-wire entanglements

¹trend \'trend\ intransitive verb [Middle English, to turn, revolve, from Old English trendan; akin to Middle High German trendel disk, spinning top] (1598)
1 a : to extend in a general direction **:** follow a general course ⟨mountain ranges trending north and south⟩ **b :** to veer in a new direction **:** BEND ⟨coastline that trends westward⟩
2 a : to show a tendency **:** INCLINE ⟨prices trending upward⟩ **b :** to become deflected **:** SHIFT ⟨opinions trending toward conservatism⟩

²trend noun (1777)
1 : a line of general direction or movement ⟨the trend of the coast turned toward the west⟩
2 a : a prevailing tendency or inclination **:** DRIFT **b :** a general movement **:** SWING ⟨the trend toward suburban living⟩ **c :** a current style or preference **:** VOGUE ⟨new fashion trends⟩ **d :** a line of development **:** APPROACH
3 : the general movement in the course of time of a statistically detectable change; also **:** a statistical curve reflecting such a change
synonym see TENDENCY

trend·set·ter \'tren(d)-,se-tər\ noun (1960)
: one that sets a trend

trend·set·ting \-,se-tiŋ\ adjective (1960)
: that sets a trend ⟨a trendsetting fashion look⟩

trendy \'tren-dē\ adjective **trend·i·er; -est** (1962)
1 : very fashionable **:** UP-TO-DATE ⟨he's a trendy dresser —Sunday Mirror⟩
2 : marked by ephemeral, superficial, or faddish appeal or taste ⟨a newspaper of trendy triviality —J.H. Plumb⟩
— **trend·i·ly** \-də-lē\ adverb
— **trend·i·ness** \-dē-nəs\ noun
— **trendy** \-dē\ noun

¹tre·pan \tri-'pan\ transitive verb **tre·panned; tre·pan·ning** [Middle English, from trepane trephine] (15th century)
1 : to use a trephine on (the skull)
2 : to remove a disk or cylindrical core (as from metal for testing)
— **trep·a·na·tion** \,tre-pə-'nā-shən\ noun

²tre·pan \tri-'pan, tri-'pan\ noun [Middle English trepane trephine, from Medieval Latin trepanum, from Greek trypanon auger, from trypan to bore] (circa 1477)
: a heavy tool used in boring mine shafts

³tre·pan \tri-'pan\ noun [origin unknown] (1641)
1 archaic **:** TRICKSTER
2 archaic **:** a deceptive device **:** SNARE

⁴tre·pan \tri-'pan\ transitive verb **tre·panned; tre·pan·ning** (circa 1656)
archaic **:** ENTRAP, LURE

tre·pang \tri-'paŋ, 'trē-\ noun [Malay tĕripang] (1783)
: any of several large sea cucumbers (especially genera Actinopyga and Holothuria) that are taken mostly in the southwestern Pacific and

are boiled, dried, and used especially by the Chinese for making soup — called also *bêche-de-mer*

treph·i·na·tion \,tre-fə-'nā-shən\ *noun* (1874)
: an act or instance of perforating the skull with a surgical instrument

tre·phine \'trē-,fīn\ *noun* [French *tréphine*, from obsolete English *trefine, trafine*, from Latin *tres fines* three ends, from *tres* three + *fines*, plural of *finis* end — more at THREE] (1628)
: a surgical instrument for cutting out circular sections (as of bone or corneal tissue)
— **trephine** *transitive verb*

trep·id \'tre-pəd\ *adjective* [Latin *trepidus*] (1650)
: TIMOROUS, FEARFUL

trep·i·dant \'tre-pə-dənt\ *adjective* [Latin *trepidant-, trepidans*, present participle of *trepidare*] (1892)
: TIMID, TREMBLING

trep·i·da·tion \,tre-pə-'dā-shən\ *noun* [Latin *trepidation-, trepidatio*, from *trepidare* to tremble, from *trepidus* agitated; probably akin to Old English *thrafian* to urge, push, Greek *trapein* to press grapes] (1605)
1 *archaic* : a tremulous motion : TREMOR
2 : timorous uncertain agitation : APPREHENSION
synonym see FEAR

trep·o·ne·ma \,tre-pə-'nē-mə\ *noun, plural* **-ma·ta** \-mə-tə\ *or* **-mas** [New Latin *Treponemat-, Treponema*, from Greek *trepein* to turn + *nēma* thread, from *nēn* to spin — more at NEEDLE] (circa 1908)
: any of a genus (*Treponema*) of spirochetes that are pathogenic in humans and other warm-blooded animals and include organisms causing syphilis and yaws
— **trep·o·ne·mal** \-məl\ *adjective*

trep·o·ne·ma·to·sis \-,nē-mə-'tō-səs, -,ne-\ *noun, plural* **-to·ses** \-,sēz\ [New Latin] (1927)
: infection with or disease caused by treponemata

trep·o·neme \'tre-pə-,nēm\ *noun* (1919)
: TREPONEMA

¹tres·pass \'tres-pəs, -,pas\ *noun* [Middle English *trespas*, from Old French, crossing, trespass, from *trespasser* to go across] (14th century)
1 a : a violation of moral or social ethics : TRANSGRESSION; *especially* : SIN **b** : an unwarranted infringement
2 a : an unlawful act committed on the person, property, or rights of another; *especially* : a wrongful entry on real property **b** : the legal action for injuries resulting from trespass

²trespass \-,pas *also* -pəs\ *verb* [Middle English, from Middle French *trespasser*, from Old French, literally, to go across, from *tres* across (from Latin *trans*) + *passer* to pass — more at THROUGH, PASS] (14th century)
intransitive verb
1 a : ERR, SIN **b** : to make an unwarranted or uninvited incursion
2 : to commit a trespass; *especially* : to enter unlawfully upon the land of another
transitive verb
: VIOLATE ⟨*trespass* the bounds of good taste⟩
☆
— **tres·pass·er** *noun*

tress \'tres\ *noun* [Middle English *tresse*, from Middle French *trece*] (14th century)
1 : a long lock of hair; *especially* : the long unbound hair of a woman — usually used in plural
2 *archaic* : a plait of hair : BRAID

tressed \'trest\ *adjective* (14th century)
1 *obsolete* : being braided : PLAITED
2 : having tresses — usually used in combination ⟨golden-*tressed*⟩

tres·tle *also* **tres·sel** \'tre-səl\ *noun* [Middle English *trestel*, from Middle French, from (assumed) Vulgar Latin *transtellum*, from Latin *transtillum*, diminutive of *tran-*

strum traverse beam, from *translation* across — more at THROUGH] (14th century)
1 : HORSE 2b
2 : a braced frame serving as a support
3 : a braced framework of timbers, piles, or steelwork for carrying a road or railroad over a depression

trestle table *noun* (circa 1891)
: a table supported on trestles

tres·tle·work \-,wərk\ *noun* (1848)
: a system of connected trestles supporting a structure (as a railroad bridge)

tre·tin·o·in \tre-'ti-nə-win\ *noun* [perhaps from *trans-* + *retinoic acid*] (1980)
: RETINOIC ACID

trews \'trüz\ *noun plural* [Scottish Gaelic *triubhas*] (circa 1568)
1 *chiefly British* : ³PANT 1; *especially* : tight-fitting trousers usually of tartan
2 : close-cut tartan shorts worn under the kilt in Highland dress

trey \'trā\ *noun, plural* **treys** [Middle English *treye, treis*, from Middle French *treie, treis*, from Latin *tres* three] (14th century)
1 : the side of a die or domino that has three spots
2 : a card numbered three or having three main pips

tri- *combining form* [Middle English, from Latin (from *tri-, tres*) & Greek, from *tri-, treis* — more at THREE]
1 : three : having three elements or parts ⟨*tri*graph⟩
2 : into three ⟨*tri*sect⟩
3 a : thrice ⟨*tri*weekly⟩ **b** : every third ⟨*tri*monthly⟩

tri·able \'trī-ə-bəl\ *adjective* (15th century)
: liable or subject to judicial or quasi-judicial examination or trial

tri·ac·e·tate \(,)trī-'a-sə-,tāt\ *noun* [International Scientific Vocabulary] (1885)
1 : an acetate containing three CH_3COO- groups
2 : a textile fiber or fabric consisting of cellulose that is completely or almost completely acetylated

tri·ad \'trī-,ad *also* -əd\ *noun* [Latin *triad-, trias*, from Greek, from *treis* three] (1546)
1 : a union or group of three : TRINITY
2 : a chord of three tones consisting of a root with its third and fifth and constituting the harmonic basis of tonal music
— **tri·ad·ic** \trī-'a-dik\ *adjective*
— **tri·ad·i·cal·ly** \-di-k(ə-)lē\ *adverb*

tri·age \trē-'äzh, 'trē-,\ *noun* [French, sorting, sifting, from *trier* to sort, from Old French — more at TRY] (1918)
: the sorting of and allocation of treatment to patients and especially battle and disaster victims according to a system of priorities designed to maximize the number of survivors; *broadly* : the assigning of priority order to projects on the basis of where funds and resources can be best used or are most needed
— **triage** *transitive verb*

¹tri·al \'trī(-ə)l\ *noun* [Anglo-French, from *trier* to try] (15th century)
1 a : the action or process of trying or putting to the proof : TEST **b** : a preliminary contest (as in a sport)
2 : the formal examination before a competent tribunal of the matter in issue in a civil or criminal cause in order to determine such issue
3 : a test of faith, patience, or stamina through subjection to suffering or temptation; *broadly* : a source of vexation or annoyance
4 a : a tryout or experiment to test quality, value, or usefulness **b** : one of a number of repetitions of an experiment
5 : ATTEMPT

²trial *adjective* (1555)
1 : of, relating to, or used in a trial
2 : made or done as a test or experiment
3 : used or tried out in a test or experiment

trial and error *noun* (1806)

: a finding out of the best way to reach a desired result or a correct solution by trying out one or more ways or means and by noting and eliminating errors or causes of failure; *also* : the trying of one thing or another until something succeeds

trial balance *noun* (1838)
: a list of the debit and credit balances of accounts in a double-entry ledger at a given date prepared primarily to test their equality

trial balloon *noun* (1935)
: a project or scheme tentatively announced in order to test public opinion

trial court *noun* (1890)
: the court before which issues of fact and law are first determined as distinguished from an appellate court

trial examiner *noun* (1949)
: a person appointed to hold hearings and to investigate and report facts sometimes with recommendations to an administrative or quasi-judicial agency or tribunal

trial horse *noun* (1901)
: one set up as an opponent for a champion in trial competitions or workouts

trial jury *noun* (1884)
: a jury impaneled to try a cause : PETIT JURY

trial lawyer *noun* (circa 1914)
: a lawyer who engages chiefly in the trial of cases before courts of original jurisdiction

tri·a·logue \'trī-ə-,lȯg, -,läg\ *noun* [*tri-* + *-alogue* (as in *dialogue*)] (1532)
: a scene, discourse, or colloquy in which three persons share

trial run *noun* (1903)
: a testing exercise : EXPERIMENT

tri·am·cin·o·lone \,trī-,am-'si-nº-l-,ōn\ *noun* [*tri-* + *-amcin-* (alteration of *American Cyanimid Company*) + ¹-*ol* + -*one*] (1957)
: a glucocorticoid drug $C_{21}H_{27}FO_6$ used especially in treating psoriasis and allergic skin and respiratory disorders

tri·an·gle \'trī-,aŋ-gəl\ *noun* [Middle English, from Latin *triangulum*, from neuter of *triangulus* triangular, from *tri-* + *angulus* angle] (14th century)
1 : a polygon having three sides — compare SPHERICAL TRIANGLE
2 a : a percussion instrument consisting of a rod of steel bent into the form of a triangle open at one angle and sounded by striking with a small metal rod **b** : a drafting instrument consisting of a thin flat right-angled

triangle 1: *1* equilateral, *2* acute, *3* obtuse, *4* scalene, *5* isosceles, *6* right triangle

triangle of wood or plastic with acute angles of 45 degrees or of 30 degrees and 60 degrees **3** : a situation in which one member of a couple is involved in a love affair with a third person

triangle inequality *noun* [from its application to the distances between three points in a coordinate system] (1941)
: an inequality stating that the absolute value of a sum is less than or equal to the sum of the absolute values of the terms

tri·an·gu·lar \trī-'aŋ-gyə-lər\ *adjective* [Late Latin *triangularis,* from Latin *triangulum*] (1541)
1 a : of, relating to, or having the form of a triangle ⟨a *triangular* plot of land⟩ **b** : having a triangular base or principal surface ⟨a *triangular* table⟩ ⟨a *triangular* pyramid⟩
2 a (1) : of, relating to, or involving three elements ⟨a *triangular* agreement⟩ (2) *of a military group* : based primarily on three units **b** : of or relating to a love triangle
— **tri·an·gu·lar·i·ty** \(,)trī-,aŋ-gyə-'lar-ə-tē\ *noun*
— **tri·an·gu·lar·ly** \trī-'aŋ-gyə-lər-lē\ *adverb*

triangular number *noun* (1796)
: any of the numbers (as 1, 3, 6, 10, 15) that represent the number of dots in the figures formed starting with one dot and adding rows one after another to form triangles each row of which has one more dot than the one before and are of the general form

$$\frac{n(n + 1)}{2}$$ where n = 1, 2, 3, . . .

¹tri·an·gu·late \trī-'aŋ-gyə-lət\ *adjective* [Medieval Latin *triangulatus,* past participle of *triangulare* to make triangles, from Latin *triangulum*] (1766)
: consisting of or marked with triangles

²tri·an·gu·late \-,lāt\ *transitive verb* **-lat·ed; -lat·ing** (1833)
1 : to survey, map, or determine by triangulation
2 a : to divide into triangles **b** : to give triangular form to

tri·an·gu·la·tion \(,)trī-,aŋ-gyə-'lā-shən\ *noun* (1818)
: the measurement of the elements necessary to determine the network of triangles into which any part of the earth's surface is divided in surveying; *broadly* : any similar trigonometric operation for finding a position or location by means of bearings from two fixed points a known distance apart

tri·ar·chy \'trī-,är-kē\ *noun, plural* **-chies** [Greek *triarchia,* from *tri-* + *-archia* -archy] (circa 1656)
1 : government by three persons : TRIUMVIRATE
2 : a country under three rulers

Tri·as·sic \trī-'a-sik\ *adjective* [International Scientific Vocabulary, from Latin *trias* triad; from the three subdivisions of the European Triassic — more at TRIAD] (1841)
: of, relating to, or being the earliest period of the Mesozoic era or the corresponding system of rocks marked by the first appearance of the dinosaurs — see GEOLOGIC TIME table
— **Triassic** *noun*

tri·ath·lete \trī-'ath-,lēt, ÷'a-thə-\ *noun* (1982)
: an athlete who competes in a triathlon

tri·ath·lon \trī-'ath-lən, -,län, ÷-'a-thə-\ *noun* [*tri-* + *-athlon* (as in dec*athlon*)] (1978)
: an athletic contest that is a long-distance race consisting of three phases (as swimming, bicycling, and running)

tri·atom·ic \,trī-ə-'tä-mik\ *adjective* [International Scientific Vocabulary] (1862)
: having three atoms in the molecule ⟨ozone is *triatomic* oxygen⟩

tri·ax·i·al \(,)trī-'ak-sē-əl\ *adjective* [International Scientific Vocabulary] (1886)

: having or involving three axes
— **tri·ax·i·al·i·ty** \-,ak-sē-'a-lə-tē\ *noun*

tri·azine \'trī-ə-,zēn, trī-'a-,zēn\ *noun* [International Scientific Vocabulary] (1894)
: any of three compounds $C_3H_3N_3$ containing a ring composed of three carbon and three nitrogen atoms; *also* : any of various derivatives of these including several used as herbicides

trib·al \'trī-bəl\ *adjective* (1632)
: of, relating to, or characteristic of a tribe ⟨*tribal* customs⟩
— **trib·al·ly** \-bə-lē\ *adverb*

trib·al·ism \-bə-,li-zəm\ *noun* (1886)
1 : tribal consciousness and loyalty; *especially* : exaltation of the tribe above other groups
2 : strong in-group loyalty

tri·ba·sic \(,)trī-'bā-sik\ *adjective* (1837)
: having three replaceable hydrogen atoms — used of acids

tribe \'trīb\ *noun* [Middle English, from Latin *tribus,* a division of the Roman people, tribe] (13th century)
1 a : a social group comprising numerous families, clans, or generations together with slaves, dependents, or adopted strangers **b** : a political division of the Roman people originally representing one of the three original tribes of ancient Rome **c** : PHYLE
2 : a group of persons having a common character, occupation, or interest
3 : a category of taxonomic classification ranking below a subfamily; *also* : a natural group irrespective of taxonomic rank ⟨the cat *tribe*⟩ ⟨rose *tribe*⟩

tribes·man \'trībz-mən\ *noun* (1798)
: a member of a tribe

tribes·peo·ple \-,pē-pəl\ *noun plural* (1888)
: members of a tribe

tribo- *combining form* [French, from Greek *tribein* to rub; probably akin to Latin *terere* to rub — more at THROW]
: friction ⟨*tribo*luminescence⟩

tri·bo·elec·tric·i·ty \,trī-bō-i-,lek-'tri-sə-tē, ,tri-, -'tris-tē\ *noun* (circa 1917)
: a charge of electricity generated by friction (as by rubbing glass with silk)
— **tri·bo·elec·tric** \-'lek-trik\ *adjective*

tri·bol·o·gy \trī-'bä-lə-jē, tri-\ *noun* (1966)
: a study that deals with the design, friction, wear, and lubrication of interacting surfaces in relative motion (as in bearings or gears)
— **tri·bo·log·i·cal** \,trī-bə-'lä-ji-kəl, ,tri-\ *adjective*
— **tri·bol·o·gist** \trī-'bä-lə-jist, tri-\ *noun*

tri·bo·lu·mi·nes·cence \,trī-bō-,lü-mə-'ne-s°n(t)s, ,tri-\ *noun* [International Scientific Vocabulary] (1889)
: luminescence due to friction
— **tri·bo·lu·mi·nes·cent** \-s°nt\ *adjective*

tri·brach \'trī-,brak\ *noun* [Latin *tribrachys,* from Greek, having three short syllables, from *tri-* + *brachys* short — more at BRIEF] (1589)
: a metrical foot of three short syllables of which two belong to the thesis and one to the arsis
— **tri·brach·ic** \trī-'bra-kik\ *adjective*

trib·u·late \'tri-byə-,lāt\ *transitive verb* **-lat·ed; -lat·ing** [Late Latin *tribulatus,* past participle of *tribulare*] (circa 1637)
: to cause to endure tribulation

trib·u·la·tion \,tri-byə-'lā-shən\ *noun* [Middle English *tribulacion,* from Old French, from Latin *tribulation-, tribulatio,* from *tribulare* to press, oppress, from *tribulum* drag used in threshing, from *terere* to rub — more at THROW] (13th century)
: distress or suffering resulting from oppression or persecution; *also* : a trying experience

tri·bu·nal \trī-'byü-n°l, tri-\ *noun* [Latin, platform for magistrates, from *tribunus* tribune] (1526)
1 : ²TRIBUNE
2 : a court or forum of justice
3 : something that decides or determines ⟨the *tribunal* of public opinion⟩

tri·bu·nate \'tri-byə-,nāt, trī-'byü-nət\ *noun* (1546)
: the office, function, or term of office of a tribune

¹tri·bune \'tri-,byün, tri-\ *noun* [Middle English, from Latin *tribunus,* from *tribus* tribe] (14th century)
1 : a Roman official under the monarchy and the republic with the power of protecting the plebeian citizen from arbitrary action by the patrician magistrates
2 : an unofficial defender of the rights of the individual
— **tri·bune·ship** \-,ship\ *noun*

²tribune *noun* [French, from Italian *tribuna,* from Latin *tribunal*] (circa 1771)
: a dais or platform from which an assembly is addressed

¹trib·u·tary \'tri-byə-,ter-ē\ *adjective* (14th century)
1 : paying tribute to another to acknowledge submission, to obtain protection, or to purchase peace : SUBJECT
2 : paid or owed as tribute
3 : channeling material or supplies into something more inclusive : CONTRIBUTORY

²tributary *noun, plural* **-tar·ies** (15th century)
1 : a ruler or state that pays tribute to a conqueror
2 : a stream feeding a larger stream or a lake

trib·ute \'tri-(,)byüt, -byət\ *noun* [Middle English *tribut,* from Latin *tributum,* from neuter of *tributus,* past participle of *tribuere* to allot, bestow, grant, pay, from *tribus* tribe] (14th century)
1 a : a payment by one ruler or nation to another in acknowledgment of submission or as the price of protection; *also* : the tax levied for such a payment **b** (1) : an excessive tax, rental, or tariff imposed by a government, sovereign, lord, or landlord (2) : an exorbitant charge levied by a person or group having the power of coercion **c** : the liability to pay tribute
2 a : something given or contributed voluntarily as due or deserved; *especially* : a gift or service showing respect, gratitude, or affection ⟨floral *tribute*⟩ **b** : something (as material evidence or a formal attestation) that indicates the worth, virtue, or effectiveness of the one in question ⟨the product is a *tribute* to their ingenuity⟩
synonym see ENCOMIUM

tri·car·box·yl·ic \,trī-,kär-,bäk-'si-lik\ *adjective* (1894)
: containing three carboxyl groups in the molecule ⟨*tricarboxylic* acid⟩

tricarboxylic acid cycle *noun* (1945)
: KREBS CYCLE

¹trice \'trīs\ *transitive verb* **triced; tric·ing** [Middle English *trisen, tricen* to pull, trice, from Middle Dutch *trisen* to hoist, from *trise* windlass] (15th century)
: to haul up or in and lash or secure (as a sail) with a small rope

²trice *noun* [Middle English *trise,* literally, pull, from *trisen*] (15th century)
: a brief space of time : INSTANT — used chiefly in the phrase *in a trice*

tri·ceps \'trī-,seps\ *noun, plural* **triceps** [New Latin *tricipit-, triceps,* from Latin, three-headed, from *tri-* + *capit-, caput* head — more at HEAD] (circa 1704)
: a muscle that arises from three heads; *especially* : the great extensor muscle along the back of the upper arm

tri·cer·a·tops \(,)trī-'ser-ə-,täps\ *noun, plural* **-tops** *also* **-tops·es** \-,täp-səz\ [New Latin, from *tri-* + Greek *kerat-, keras* horn + *ōps* face — more at HORN, EYE] (1892)
: any of a genus (*Triceratops*) of large herbivorous Cretaceous dinosaurs with three horns, a bony hood or crest on the neck, and hoofed toes

-trices *plural of* -TRIX

trich- *or* **tricho-** *combining form* [New Latin, from Greek, from *trich-*, *thrix* hair]
: hair : filament ⟨*trichogyne*⟩

tri·chi·a·sis \trī-'kī-ə-səs\ *noun* [Late Latin, from Greek, from *trich-* + *-iasis*] (1661)
: a turning inward of the eyelashes often causing irritation of the eyeball

tri·chi·na \tri-'kī-nə\ *noun, plural* **-nae** \-(,)nē\ *also* **-nas** [New Latin, from Greek *trichinos* made of hair, from *trich-*, *thrix* hair] (1857)
: a small slender nematode worm (*Trichinella spiralis*) that in the larval state is parasitic in the voluntary muscles of flesh-eating mammals (as humans and swine)
— **tri·chi·nal** \-nᵊl\ *adjective*

trich·i·nize \'tri-kə-ˌnīz\ *transitive verb* **-nized; -niz·ing** (1864)
: to infest with trichinae ⟨*trichinized* pork⟩

trich·i·no·sis \ˌtri-kə-'nō-səs\ *noun* [New Latin] (1866)
: infestation with or disease caused by trichinae and marked especially by muscular pain, dyspnea, fever, and edema

tri·chi·nous \'tri-kə-nəs, tri-'kī-\ *adjective* [International Scientific Vocabulary] (1857)
1 : infested with trichinae ⟨*trichinous* meat⟩
2 : of, relating to, or involving trichinae or trichinosis ⟨*trichinous* infection⟩

tri·chlor·fon *also* **tri·chlor·phon** \(,)trī-'klȯr-ˌfän, -'klȯr-\ *noun* [*tri-* + *chlor-* + *-fon* (irregular from *phosphonate* — a salt derived from phosphine)] (1960)
: a crystalline compound $C_4H_8Cl_3O_4P$ used especially as an insecticide

tri·chlo·ro·ace·tic acid \ˌtrī-ˌklȯr-ō-ə-'sē-tik-, -ˌklȯr-\ *noun* [International Scientific Vocabulary] (1885)
: a strong vesicant pungent acid $C_2Cl_3HO_2$ used in weed control and in medicine as a caustic and astringent

tri·chlo·ro·eth·y·lene \-'e-thə-ˌlēn\ *noun* (circa 1919)
: a nonflammable liquid C_2HCl_3 used especially as a solvent and in dry cleaning and for the removal of grease from metal

tricho·cyst \'tri-kə-ˌsist\ *noun* (1859)
: any of the minute lassoing or stinging organelles of protozoans and especially of many ciliates

tricho·gyne \-ˌjīn, -ˌgīn\ *noun* [International Scientific Vocabulary] (circa 1875)
: a slender terminal prolongation of the ascogonium of a fungus or lichen that may serve as a fertilization tube; *also* : a similar reproductive structure in a red alga

tri·chol·o·gist \tri-'kä-lə-jist\ *noun* (1887)
: a person who cares for and dresses hair : HAIRDRESSER
— **tri·chol·o·gy** \-jē\ *noun*

tri·chome \'tri-ˌkōm, 'trī-\ *noun* [German *Trichom*, from Greek *trichōma* growth of hair, from *trichoun* to cover with hair, from *trich-*, *thrix* hair] (1875)
: a filamentous outgrowth; *especially* : an epidermal hair structure on a plant

tricho·mo·na·cide \ˌtri-kə-'mō-nə-ˌsīd\ *noun* [*trichomonad* + *-cide*] (1949)
: an agent used to destroy trichomonads
— **tricho·mo·na·cid·al** \-ˌmō-nə-'sī-dᵊl\ *adjective*

tricho·mo·nad \ˌtri-kə-'mō-ˌnad, -nəd\ *noun* [New Latin *Trichomonad-, Trichomonas*, from *trich-* + Late Latin *monad-, monas* monad] (1861)
: any of a genus (*Trichomonas*) of flagellated protozoans parasitic in many animals
— **trichomonad** *or* **tricho·mo·nal** \-'mō-nᵊl\ *adjective*

tricho·mo·ni·a·sis \ˌtri-kə-mə-'nī-ə-səs\ *noun, plural* **-a·ses** \-ˌsēz\ [New Latin, from *Trichomonas* + *-iasis*] (1915)
: infection with or disease caused by trichomonads: as **a** : a human sexually transmitted disease occurring especially as vaginitis with a persistent discharge and caused by a

trichomonad (*Trichomonas vaginalis*) that may also invade the male urethra and bladder **b** : a venereal disease of domestic cattle marked by abortion and sterility **c** : one or more diseases of various birds resembling blackhead — called also *roup*

tri·chop·ter·an \trī-'käp-tə-rən\ *noun* [ultimately from Greek *trich-*, *thrix* hair + *pteron* wing — more at FEATHER] (circa 1842)
: CADDIS FLY
— **trichopteran** *adjective*

tricho·the·cene \ˌtri-kə-'thē-ˌsēn\ *noun* [New Latin *Trichothecium* (from *trich-* + *-thecium*) + English *-ene*] (1971)
: any of several mycotoxins that are produced by imperfect fungi (genera *Fusarium* and *Trichothecium*) and that include some contaminants of livestock feed and some held to be found in yellow rain

tri·chot·o·mous \trī-'kä-tə-məs\ *adjective* [Late Greek *trichotomein* to trisect, from Greek *tricha* in three (akin to *treis* three) + *-tomein* (akin to *temnein* to cut) — more at THREE, TOME] (1800)
: divided or dividing into three parts or into threes ⟨*trichotomous* branching⟩
— **tri·chot·o·mous·ly** *adverb*

tri·chot·o·my \-mē\ *noun, plural* **-mies** (1610)
: division into three parts, elements, or classes

tri·chro·mat \'trī-krō-ˌmat, (,)trī-'\ *noun* [back-formation from *trichromatic*] (1929)
: a person with trichromatism

tri·chro·mat·ic \ˌtrī-krō-'ma-tik\ *adjective* (circa 1890)
1 : of, relating to, or consisting of three colors ⟨*trichromatic* light⟩
2 a : relating to or being the theory that human color vision involves three types of retinal sensory receptors **b** : characterized by trichromatism ⟨*trichromatic* vision⟩

tri·chro·ma·tism \(,)trī-'krō-mə-ˌti-zəm\ *noun* (circa 1895)
: color vision based on the perception of three primary colors and especially red, green, and blue

¹trick \'trik\ *noun* [Middle English *trik*, from Old North French *trique*, from *trikier* to deceive, cheat, from (assumed) Vulgar Latin *triccare*, alteration of Latin *tricari* to behave evasively, shuffle, from *tricae* complications, trifles] (15th century)
1 a : a crafty procedure or practice meant to deceive or defraud **b** : a mischievous act : PRANK **c** : an indiscreet or childish action **d** : a deceptive, dexterous, or ingenious feat; *especially* : one designed to puzzle or amuse ⟨a juggler's *tricks*⟩
2 a : a habitual peculiarity of behavior or manner ⟨a horse with the *trick* of shying⟩ **b** : a characteristic and identifying feature ⟨a *trick* of speech⟩ **c** : a delusive appearance especially when caused by art or legerdemain : an optical illusion ⟨a mere *trick* of the light⟩
3 a : a quick or artful way of getting a result : KNACK **b** : a technical device (as of an art or craft) ⟨the *tricks* of stage technique⟩
4 : the cards played in one round of a card game often used as a scoring unit
5 a : a turn of duty at the helm usually lasting for two hours **b** : SHIFT 4b(1) **c** : a trip taken as part of one's employment **d** : a sexual act performed by a prostitute; *also* : JOHN 2
6 : an attractive child or woman ⟨a cute little *trick*⟩ ☆

²trick *transitive verb* (circa 1500)
1 : to dress or adorn fancifully or ornately : ORNAMENT ⟨*tricked* out in a gaudy uniform⟩
2 : to deceive by cunning or artifice : CHEAT
synonym see DUPE

³trick *adjective* (circa 1530)
1 : TRIG
2 a : of or relating to or involving tricks or trickery ⟨*trick* photography⟩ ⟨*trick* dice⟩ **b** : skilled in or used for tricks ⟨a *trick* horse⟩

3 a : somewhat defective and unreliable ⟨a *trick* lock⟩ **b** : inclined to give way unexpectedly ⟨a *trick* knee⟩

trick·er \'tri-kər\ *noun* (circa 1553)
: one that tricks : TRICKSTER

trick·ery \'tri-k(ə-)rē\ *noun* (1800)
: the practice of crafty underhanded ingenuity to deceive or cheat
synonym see DECEPTION

trick·ish \'tri-kish\ *adjective* (1705)
: given to or characterized by tricks or trickery : TRICKY
— **trick·ish·ly** *adverb*
— **trick·ish·ness** *noun*

¹trick·le \'tri-kəl\ *intransitive verb* **trick·led; trick·ling** \-k(ə-)liŋ\ [Middle English, of imitative origin] (14th century)
1 a : to issue or fall in drops **b** : to flow in a thin gentle stream
2 a : to move or go one by one or little by little **b** : to dissipate slowly ⟨his enthusiasm *trickled* away⟩

²trickle *noun* (1580)
: a thin, slow, or intermittent stream or movement

trickle–down *adjective* (1944)
1 : relating to or working on the principle of trickle-down theory
2 : relating to or being an effect caused gradually by remote or indirect influences

trickle–down theory *noun* (1954)
: a theory that financial benefits given to big business will in turn pass down to smaller businesses and consumers

trick or treat *noun* (circa 1941)
: a children's Halloween practice of asking for treats from door to door under threat of playing tricks on householders who refuse
— **trick–or–treat** *intransitive verb*
— **trick–or–treater** *noun*

trick·ster \'trik-stər\ *noun* (1711)
: one who tricks: as **a** : a dishonest person who defrauds others by trickery **b** : a person (as a stage magician) skilled in the use of tricks and illusion **c** : a deceptive character appearing in various forms in the folklore of many cultures

tricksy \'trik-sē\ *adjective* **tricks·i·er; -est** [*tricks*, plural of *trick*] (1552)
1 *archaic* : smartly attired : SPRUCE
2 : full of tricks : PRANKISH
3 a *archaic* : having the craftiness of a trickster **b** : difficult to cope with or handle : TRYING ⟨a *tricksy* job⟩
— **tricks·i·ness** *noun*

☆ **SYNONYMS**
Trick, ruse, stratagem, maneuver, artifice, wile, feint mean an indirect means to gain an end. TRICK may imply deception, roguishness, illusion, and either an evil or harmless end ⟨the *tricks* of the trade⟩. RUSE stresses an attempt to mislead by a false impression ⟨the *ruses* of smugglers⟩. STRATAGEM implies a ruse used to entrap, outwit, circumvent, or surprise an opponent or enemy ⟨the *stratagem*-filled game⟩. MANEUVER suggests adroit and skillful avoidance of difficulty ⟨last-minute *maneuvers* to avert bankruptcy⟩. ARTIFICE implies ingenious contrivance or invention ⟨the clever *artifices* of the stage⟩. WILE suggests an attempt to entrap or deceive with false allurements ⟨used all of his *wiles* to ingratiate himself⟩. FEINT implies a diversion or distraction of attention away from one's real intent ⟨a *feint* toward the enemy's left flank⟩.

\ə\ abut \ᵊ\ kitten \ər\ further \a\ ash \ā\ ace
\ä\ mop, mar \aù\ out \ch\ chin \e\ bet \ē\ easy
\g\ go \i\ hit \ī\ ice \j\ job \ŋ\ sing \ō\ go
\ȯ\ law \ȯi\ boy \th\ thin \t͟h\ the \ü\ loot \ù\ foot
\y\ yet \zh\ vision *see also* Guide to Pronunciation

tricky \'tri-kē\ *adjective* **trick·i·er; -est** (1786)
1 : inclined to or marked by trickery
2 a : giving a deceptive impression of easiness, simplicity, or order **: TICKLISH** ⟨a *tricky* path through the swamp⟩ **b :** TRICK 3
3 : requiring skill, knack, or caution (as in doing or handling) **: DIFFICULT;** *also* **: INGENIOUS** ⟨a *tricky* rhythm⟩
synonym see SLY
— **trick·i·ly** \'tri-kə-lē\ *adverb*
— **trick·i·ness** \'tri-kē-nəs\ *noun*
tri·clad \'trī-ˌklad\ *noun* [New Latin *Tricladida*, from *tri-* + Greek *klados* branch — more at CLAD-] (1888)
: any of an order (Tricladida) of turbellarian flatworms (as a planarian) that have the intestine composed of a median anterior division and two lateral posterior divisions with side branches
— **triclad** *adjective*
tri·clin·ic \(ˌ)trī-'kli-nik\ *adjective* [International Scientific Vocabulary] (1854)
: having three unequal axes intersecting at oblique angles — used especially of a crystal
tri·clin·i·um \trī-'kli-nē-əm\ *noun, plural* **-ia** \-nē-ə\ [Latin, from Greek *triklinion*, from *tri-* + *klinein* to lean, recline — more at LEAN] (1646)
1 : a couch extending round three sides of a table used by the ancient Romans for reclining at meals
2 : a dining room furnished with a triclinium
tric·o·lette \ˌtri-kə-'let\ *noun* [*tricot* + *-lette* (as in *flannelette*)] (1919)
: a usually silk or rayon knitted fabric used especially for women's clothing
¹tri·col·or \'trī-ˌkə-lər *also* 'trē-, especially British* 'tri-kə-lər\ *adjective* [French *tricolore*, from Late Latin *tricolor*, from Latin *tri-* + *color* color] (1795)
1 a *or* **tri·col·ored** \'trī-'kə-lərd\ **:** having, using, or marked with three colors **b** *of a dog* **:** having a coat of black, tan, and white
2 : of, relating to, or characteristic of a tricolor or a nation whose flag is a tricolor; *especially* **: FRENCH**
²tricolor *noun* (1797)
1 : a flag of three colors arranged in equal horizontal or vertical bands ⟨the French *tricolor*⟩
2 : a tricolor animal; *especially* **:** a tricolor dog
tri·corn \'trī-ˌkȯrn\ *adjective* [Latin *tricornis*] (circa 1844)
: having three horns or corners
tri·corne *or* **tri·corn** \'trī-ˌkȯrn\ *noun* [French *tricorne*, from *tricorne* three-cornered, from Latin *tricornis*, from *tri-* + *cornu* horn — more at HORN] (1876)
: COCKED HAT 1
tri·cor·nered \'trī-'kȯ(r)-nərd\ *adjective* (1819)
: having three corners
tri·cot \'trē-(ˌ)kō, 'trī-kət\ *noun* [French, from *tricoter* to knit, from Middle French, to agitate, hop, ultimately from Old French *estriquier* to stroke, from Germanic origin; akin to Old English *strīcan* to stroke — more at STRIKE] (1872)
1 : a plain warp-knitted fabric (as of nylon, wool, rayon, silk, or cotton) with a close inelastic knit and used especially in clothing (as underwear)
2 : a twilled clothing fabric of wool with fine warp ribs or of wool and cotton with fine weft ribs
tri·co·tine \ˌtri-kə-'tēn, ˌtrē-\ *noun* [French, from *tricot*] (circa 1899)
: a sturdy suiting woven of tightly twisted yarns in a double twill
tric·trac \'trik-ˌtrak\ *noun* [French, of imitative origin] (1687)
: an old form of backgammon played with pegs

¹tri·cus·pid \(ˌ)trī-'kəs-pəd\ *adjective* [Latin *tricuspid-, tricuspis*, from *tri-* + *cuspid-, cuspis* point] (1834)
: having three cusps ⟨a *tricuspid* molar⟩
²tricuspid *noun* (circa 1860)
: a tricuspid anatomical structure; *especially* **:** a tooth having three cusps
tricuspid valve *noun* (1670)
: a valve of three flaps that prevents reflux of blood from the right ventricle to the right atrium
tri·cy·cle \'trī-sə-kəl, -ˌsi-kəl\ *noun* [French, from *tri-* + Greek *kyklos* wheel — more at WHEEL] (1868)
: a 3-wheeled vehicle propelled by pedals or a motor
tri·cy·clic \(ˌ)trī-'sī-klik, -'si-klik\ *adjective* [*tri-* + *cyclic*] (1891)
: being a chemical with three usually fused rings in the molecular structure and especially a tricyclic antidepressant
tricyclic antidepressant *noun* (1966)
: any of a group of antidepressant drugs (as imipramine, amitriptyline, desipramine, and nortriptyline) that potentiate the action of catecholamines and do not inhibit the action of monoamine oxidase — called also *tricyclic*
¹tri·dent \'trī-d°nt\ *adjective* [Latin *trident-, tridens*] (1589)
: having three teeth, processes, or points
²trident *noun* [Latin *trident-, tridens,* from *trident-, tridens* having three teeth, from *tri-* + *dent-, dens* tooth — more at TOOTH] (1599)
1 : a 3-pronged spear serving in classical mythology as the attribute of a sea god (as Neptune)
2 : a 3-pronged spear (as for fishing)
Tri·den·tine \trī-'den-ˌtīn, -ˌtēn; 'trī-d°n-, 'tri-\ *adjective* [New Latin *Tridentinus*, from Latin *Tridentum* Trent, Italy] (1561)
: of or relating to the Roman Catholic Church council held at Trent from 1545 to 1563
tri·di·men·sion·al \ˌtrī-də-'mench-nəl, -ˌdī-, -'men(t)-shə-n°l\ *adjective* [International Scientific Vocabulary] (1858)
: of, relating to, or concerned with three dimensions ⟨*tridimensional* space⟩
— **tri·di·men·sion·al·i·ty** \-ˌmen(t)-shə-'na-lə-tē\ *noun*
trid·u·um \'tri-jə-wəm, 'tri-dyə-\ *noun* [Latin, space of three days, from *tri-* + *-duum* (akin to *dies* day) — more at DEITY] (1873)
: a period of three days of prayer usually preceding a Roman Catholic feast
tried \'trīd\ *adjective* [Middle English, from past participle of *trien* to try, test] (15th century)
1 : found good, faithful, or trustworthy through experience or testing ⟨a *tried* recipe⟩
2 : subjected to trials or distress ⟨a kind but much-*tried* father⟩
tried–and–true *adjective* (1935)
: proved good, desirable, or feasible **:** shown or known to be worthy ⟨a *tried-and-true* sales technique⟩
tri·ene \'trī-ˌēn\ *noun* (1917)
: a chemical compound containing three double bonds
tri·en·ni·al \(ˌ)trī-'e-nē-əl\ *adjective* (1562)
1 : occurring or being done every three years ⟨the *triennial* convention⟩
2 : consisting of or lasting for three years ⟨a *triennial* contract⟩
— **triennial** *noun*
— **tri·en·ni·al·ly** \-nē-ə-lē\ *adverb*
tri·en·ni·um \trī-'e-nē-əm\ *noun, plural* **-ni·ums** *or* **-nia** \-nē-ə\ [Latin, from *tri-* + *annus* year — more at ANNUAL] (1847)
: a period of three years
tri·er \'trī-(ə)r\ *noun* (14th century)
1 : someone or something that tries
2 : an implement (as a tapered hollow tube) used in obtaining samples of bulk material for examination and testing
tri·er·arch \'trī-(ə)-ˌrärk\ *noun* [Latin *trierarchus*, from Greek *trierarchos*, from *trierēs* tri-

reme (from *tri-* + *-ērēs* — akin to Latin *remus* oar) + *-archos* -arch — more at ROW] (circa 1656)
1 : the commander of a trireme
2 : an Athenian citizen who had to fit out a trireme for the public service
tri·er·ar·chy \-ˌrär-kē\ *noun* (1837)
: the ancient Athenian plan whereby individual citizens furnished and maintained triremes as a civic duty
tri·eth·yl \(ˌ)trī-'e-thəl\ *adjective* [International Scientific Vocabulary] (1858)
: containing three ethyl groups in the molecule
tri·fec·ta \trī-'fek-tə, 'trī-ˌ\ *noun* [*tri-* + *perfecta*] (1974)
: a variation of the perfecta in which a bettor wins by selecting the first three finishers of a race in the correct order of finish
tri·fid \'trī-ˌfid, -fəd\ *adjective* [Latin *trifidus* split into three, from *tri-* + *findere* to split — more at BITE] (1753)
: being deeply and narrowly cleft into three teeth, processes, or points ⟨a spoon with a *trifid* top⟩
¹tri·fle \'trī-fəl\ *noun* [Middle English *trufle, trifle,* from Old French *trufe, trufle* mockery] (13th century)
1 : something of little value, substance, or importance
2 : a dessert of many varieties typically including plain or sponge cake, sherry, rum, or brandy, jam or jelly, fruit, custard, and whipped cream
— **a trifle :** to some small degree **: SLIGHTLY** ⟨a *trifle* annoyed⟩
²trifle *verb* **tri·fled; tri·fling** \-f(ə-)liŋ\ [Middle English *truflen, triflen,* from Old French *trufer, trufler* to mock, trick] (14th century)
intransitive verb
1 a : to talk in a jesting or mocking manner or with intent to delude or mislead **b :** to treat someone or something as unimportant
2 : to handle something idly
transitive verb
: to spend or waste in trifling or on trifles ☆
— **tri·fler** \-f(ə-)lər\ *noun*
tri·fling \'trī-fliŋ\ *adjective* (1535)
: lacking in significance or solid worth: as **a : FRIVOLOUS** ⟨*trifling* talk⟩ **b :** TRIVIAL ⟨a *trifling* gift⟩ **c** *chiefly dialect* **:** LAZY, SHIFTLESS ⟨a *trifling* fellow⟩
tri·flu·o·per·a·zine \ˌtrī-ˌflü-ō-'per-ə-ˌzēn, -zən\ *noun* [*tri-* + *fluor-* + *piperazine*] (circa 1957)
: a phenothiazine tranquilizer $C_{21}H_{24}F_3N_3S$ used to treat psychotic conditions and especially schizophrenia
tri·flu·ra·lin \trī-'flùr-ə-lən\ *noun* [*tri-* + *fluor-* + *aniline*] (circa 1961)
: an herbicide $C_{13}H_{16}F_3N_3O_4$ used in the control of weeds
¹tri·fo·cal \(ˌ)trī-'fō-kəl\ *adjective* (1826)
: having three focal lengths
²trifocal *noun* (1899)
1 *plural* **:** eyeglasses with trifocal lenses
2 : a trifocal glass or lens

Trifle, toy, dally, flirt, coquet mean to deal with or act toward without serious purpose. TRIFLE may imply playfulness, unconcern, indulgent contempt ⟨to *trifle* with a lover's feelings⟩. TOY implies acting without full attention or serious exertion of one's powers ⟨a political novice *toying* with great issues⟩. DALLY suggests indulging in thoughts or plans merely as an amusement ⟨*dallying* with the idea of building a boat someday⟩. FLIRT implies an interest or attention that soon passes to another object ⟨*flirted* with one fashionable ism after another⟩. COQUET implies attracting interest or admiration without serious intention ⟨companies that *coquet* with environmentalism solely for public relations⟩.

tri·fo·li·ate \(ˌ)trī-ˈfō-lē-ə̇t\ *adjective* [*tri-* + Latin *folium* leaf — more at BLADE] (1753)
1 : having three leaves ⟨a *trifoliate* plant⟩
2 : TRIFOLIOLATE

trifoliate orange *noun* (circa 1900)
: a Chinese citrus (*Poncirus trifoliata*) with trifoliolate leaves that is widely grown for ornament and especially as a stock for budding oranges

tri·fo·li·o·late \(ˌ)trī-ˈfō-lē-ə-ˌlāt\ *adjective* [International Scientific Vocabulary *tri-* + Late Latin *foliolum* leaflet, diminutive of Latin *folium* leaf] (circa 1828)
: having three leaflets ⟨a *trifoliolate* leaf⟩ — see LEAF illustration

tri·fo·li·um \trī-ˈfō-lē-əm\ *noun* [New Latin, from Latin, trefoil — more at TREFOIL] (1541)
: CLOVER 1

tri·fo·ri·um \trī-ˈfōr-ē-əm, -ˈfȯr-\ *noun, plural* **-ria** \-ē-ə\ [Medieval Latin] (1703)
: a gallery forming an upper story to the aisle of a church and typically an arcaded story between the nave arches and clerestory

tri·form \ˈtrī-ˌfȯrm\ *adjective* [Middle English *triforme*, from Latin *triformis*, from *tri-* + *forma* form] (15th century)
: having a triple form or nature

tri·fur·cate \(ˌ)trī-ˈfər-kət, -ˌkāt; ˈtrī-(ˌ)fər-ˌkāt\ *adjective* [Latin *trifurcus*, from *tri-* + *furca* fork] (circa 1831)
: having three branches or forks **:** TRICHOTOMOUS
— **tri·fur·cate** \ˈtrī-(ˌ)fər-ˌkāt, trī-ˈfər-\ *intransitive verb*
— **tri·fur·ca·tion** \ˌtrī-(ˌ)fər-ˈkā-shən\ *noun*

¹trig \ˈtrig\ *adjective* [Middle English, trusty, nimble, of Scandinavian origin; akin to Old Norse *tryggr* faithful; akin to Old English *trēowe* faithful — more at TRUE] (1513)
1 : stylishly or jauntily trim
2 : extremely precise **:** PRIM
3 *dialect chiefly British* **:** FIRM, VIGOROUS

²trig *noun* [by shortening] (circa 1895)
: TRIGONOMETRY

tri·gem·i·nal \trī-ˈje-mə-nᵊl\ *adjective* [New Latin *trigeminus* trigeminal nerve, from Latin, threefold, from *tri-* + *geminus* twin] (1872)
: of or relating to the trigeminal nerve

trigeminal nerve *noun* (1830)
: either of a pair of large mixed nerves that are the 5th cranial nerves and supply motor and sensory fibers mostly to the face — called also *trigeminal*

trigeminal neuralgia *noun* (1874)
: an intense paroxysmal neuralgia involving one or more branches of the trigeminal nerve

¹trig·ger \ˈtri-gər\ *noun* [alteration of earlier *tricker*, from Dutch *trekker*, from Middle Dutch *trecker* one that pulls, from *trecken* to pull — more at TREK] (1621)
1 a : a piece (as a lever) connected with a catch or detent as a means of releasing it; *especially* **:** the part of the action moved by the finger to fire a gun **b :** a similar movable part by which a mechanism is actuated ⟨*trigger* of a spray gun⟩
2 : something that acts like a mechanical trigger in initiating a process or reaction
— **trigger** *adjective*
— **trig·gered** \-gərd\ *adjective*

²trigger *verb* **trig·gered; trig·ger·ing** \ˈtri-g(ə-)riŋ\ (1916)
transitive verb
1 a : to release or activate by means of a trigger; *especially* **:** to fire by pulling a mechanical trigger ⟨*trigger* a rifle⟩ **b :** to cause the explosion of ⟨*trigger* a missile with a proximity fuze⟩
2 : to initiate, actuate, or set off by a trigger ⟨an indiscreet remark that *triggered* a fight⟩ ⟨a stimulus that *triggered* a reflex⟩
intransitive verb
: to release a mechanical trigger

trig·ger·fish \ˈtri-gər-ˌfish\ *noun* (1849)
: any of various deep-bodied bony fishes (family Balistidae, especially genus *Balistes*) of warm seas having an anterior dorsal fin with two or three stout erectile spines

triggerfish

trig·ger–hap·py \-ˌha-pē\ *adjective* (1943)
1 : irresponsible in the use of firearms; *especially* **:** inclined to shoot before clearly identifying the target
2 a : inclined to be irresponsible in matters that might precipitate war **b :** aggressively belligerent in attitude

trig·ger·man \-mən, -ˌman\ *noun* (circa 1930)
: a gunman who shoots the victim (as in a gangland murder)

tri·glyc·er·ide \(ˌ)trī-ˈgli-sə-ˌrīd\ *noun* [International Scientific Vocabulary] (circa 1860)
: an ester formed from glycerol by reacting all three of its alcohol hydroxy groups with fatty acids

tri·glyph \ˈtrī-ˌglif\ *noun* [Latin *triglyphus*, from Greek *triglyphos*, from *tri-* + *glyphein* to carve — more at CLEAVE] (1563)
: a slightly projecting rectangular tablet in a Doric frieze with two vertical channels of V section and two corresponding chamfers or half channels on the vertical sides
— **tri·glyph·ic** \trī-ˈgli-fik\ *or* **tri·glyph·i·cal** \-fi-kəl\ *adjective*

tri·gon \ˈtrī-ˌgän\ *noun* [Latin *trigonum*, from Greek *trigōnon*, from neuter of *trigōnos* triangular, from *tri-* + *gōnia* angle — more at -GON] (1563)
: TRIPLICITY 1

tri·go·nal \ˈtrī-ˈgō-nᵊl\ *adjective* (1878)
: of, relating to, or being the division of the hexagonal crystal system or the forms belonging to it characterized by a vertical axis of threefold symmetry
— **tri·go·nal·ly** \-nᵊl-ē\ *adverb*

trig·o·no·met·ric \ˌtri-gə-nə-ˈme-trik\ *also* **trig·o·no·met·ri·cal** \-tri-kəl\ *adjective* (1690)
: of, relating to, or being in accordance with trigonometry
— **trig·o·no·met·ri·cal·ly** \-tri-k(ə-)lē\ *adverb*

trigonometric function *noun* (1909)
1 : a function (as the sine, cosine, tangent, cotangent, secant, or cosecant) of an arc or angle most simply expressed in terms of the ratios of pairs of sides of a right-angled triangle — called also *circular function*
2 : the inverse (as the arcsine, arccosine, or arctangent) of a trigonometric function

trig·o·nom·e·try \ˌtri-gə-ˈnä-mə-trē\ *noun* [New Latin *trigonometria*, from Greek *trigōnon* + *-metria* -metry] (1614)
: the study of the properties of triangles and trigonometric functions and of their applications

tri·gram \ˈtrī-ˌgram\ *noun* (1606)
1 : TRIGRAPH 2
2 : any of the eight possible combinations of three whole or broken lines used especially in Chinese divination

tri·graph \ˈtrī-ˌgraf\ *noun* (circa 1836)
1 : three letters spelling a single consonant, vowel, or diphthong ⟨*eau* of *beau* is a *trigraph*⟩
2 : a cluster of three successive letters ⟨*the*, *ion*, and *ing* are high frequency *trigraphs*⟩
— **tri·graph·ic** \(ˌ)trī-ˈgra-fik\ *adjective*

tri·halo·meth·ane \ˌtrī-ˌha-lə-ˈme-ˌthān, *British usually* -ˈmē-\ *noun* (1969)
: any of various derivatives CHX_3 of methane (as chloroform) that have three halogen atoms per molecule and are formed especially during the chlorination of drinking water

tri·he·dral \-ˈhē-drəl\ *adjective* (1789)
1 : having three faces ⟨*trihedral* angle⟩
2 : of or relating to a trihedral angle
— **trihedral** *noun*

tri·hy·brid \-ˈhī-brəd\ *noun* (1903)
: an individual or strain that is heterozygous for three pairs of genes
— **trihybrid** *adjective*

tri·hy·droxy \ˌtrī-hī-ˈdräk-sē, -hə-\ *adjective* [International Scientific Vocabulary] (1903)
: containing three hydroxyl groups in the molecule

tri·io·do·thy·ro·nine \ˌtrī-ˌī-ə-dō-ˈthī-rə-ˌnēn\ *noun* [*tri-* + *iod-* + *thyronine* (an amino acid of which thyroxine is a derivative)] (1952)
: an iodine-containing hormone $C_{15}H_{12}I_3NO_4$ that is an amino acid derived from thyroxine

tri·jet \ˈtrī-ˌjet\ *noun* (1967)
: an aircraft powered with three jet engines

trike \ˈtrīk\ *noun* [by shortening & alteration] (1884)
: TRICYCLE

tri·lat·er·al \(ˌ)trī-ˈla-tə-rəl, -ˈla-trəl\ *adjective* [Latin *trilaterus*, from *tri-* + *later-, latus* side] (1660)
: having three sides or parties ⟨*trilateral* business ventures⟩ ⟨*trilateral* discussions⟩

tril·by \ˈtril-bē\ *noun, plural* **trilbies** [from the fact that such a hat was worn in the London stage version of the novel *Trilby* (1894) by George du Maurier] (1897)
chiefly British **:** a soft felt hat with indented crown

tri·lin·e·ar \(ˌ)trī-ˈli-nē-ər\ *adjective* (1715)
: of, relating to, or involving three lines ⟨*trilinear* coordinates⟩

tri·lin·gual \-ˈliŋ-gwəl *also* -ˈliŋ-gyə-wəl\ *adjective* (1834)
: consisting of, having, or expressed in three languages; *also* **:** familiar with or able to use three languages
— **tri·lin·gual·ly** *adverb*

¹tri·lit·er·al \-ˈli-t(ə-)rəl\ *adjective* [*tri-* + Latin *littera* letter] (1751)
: consisting of three letters and especially of three consonants ⟨*triliteral* roots in Semitic languages⟩
— **tri·lit·er·al·ism** \-t(ə-)rə-ˌli-zəm\ *noun*

²triliteral *noun* (circa 1828)
: a root or word that is triliteral

¹trill \ˈtril\ *verb* [Middle English, probably of Scandinavian origin; akin to Swedish *trilla* to roll; akin to Middle Dutch *trillen* to vibrate] (14th century)
intransitive verb
1 : to flow in a small stream or in drops **:** TRICKLE
2 : TWIRL, REVOLVE
transitive verb
: to cause to flow in a small stream

²trill *noun* [Italian *trillo* probably of imitative origin] (1649)
1 a : the alternation of two musical tones a diatonic second apart — called also *shake* **b :** VIBRATO **c :** a rapid reiteration of the same tone especially on a percussion instrument
2 : a sound resembling a musical trill **:** WARBLE
3 a : the rapid vibration of one speech organ against another (as of the tip of the tongue against the teethridge) **b :** a speech sound made by a trill

³trill (circa 1667)
intransitive verb
: to play or sing with a trill **:** QUAVER
transitive verb
: to utter as or with or as if with a trill ⟨*trill* the *r*⟩
— **trill·er** *noun*

tril·lion \ˈtri(l)-yən\ *noun* [French, from *tri-* + *-illion* (as in *million*)] (circa 1690)

1 — see NUMBER table
2 : a very large number
— **trillion** *adjective*
— **tril·lionth** \-yən(t)th\ *adjective or noun*
tril·li·um \'tri-lē-əm\ *noun* [New Latin, from Swedish *trilling* triplet; from its three leaves] (circa 1760)
: any of a genus (*Trillium*) of herbs of the lily family with an erect stem bearing a whorl of three leaves and a large solitary typically spring-blooming flower

trillium

tri·lo·bate \(,)trī-'lō-,bāt\ *adjective* (1785)
: TRILOBED
tri·lobed \'trī-'lōbd\ *adjective* (1826)
: having three lobes ⟨a *trilobed* leaf⟩
tri·lo·bite \'trī-lə-,bīt\ *noun* [ultimately from Greek *trilobos* three-lobed, from *tri-* + *lobos* lobe] (1832)
: any of numerous extinct Paleozoic marine arthropods (group Trilobita) having the segments of the body divided by furrows on the dorsal surface into three lobes
tril·o·gy \'tri-lə-jē\ *noun*, *plural* **-gies** [Greek *trilogia*, from *tri-* + *-logia* -logy] (circa 1661)
: a series of three dramas or literary works or sometimes three musical compositions that are closely related and develop a single theme

trilobite

¹trim \'trim\ *verb* **trimmed; trim·ming** [probably from (assumed) Middle English *trimmen* to prepare, put in order, from Old English *trymian, tryman* to strengthen, arrange, from *trum* strong, firm; probably akin to Old English *trēo* tree, wood — more at TREE] (circa 1521)
transitive verb
1 : to embellish with or as if with ribbons, lace, or ornaments ⟨*trim* the Christmas tree⟩ ⟨the coat was *trimmed* with fur⟩
2 a : to administer a beating to : THRASH **b** : DEFEAT ⟨*trimmed* me at chess⟩
3 a : to make trim and neat especially by cutting or clipping ⟨*trim* the hedges⟩ **b** : to free of excess or extraneous matter by or as if by cutting ⟨*trim* a budget⟩ ⟨*trim* down the inventory⟩ **c** : to remove by or as if by cutting ⟨*trimmed* thousands from federal payrolls —*Grit*⟩
4 a (1) : to cause (as a ship) to assume a desirable position in the water by arrangement of ballast, cargo, or passengers (2) : to adjust (as an airplane or submarine) for horizontal movement or for motion upward or downward **b** : to adjust (as cargo or a sail) to a desired position
5 : to adjust (as one's opinions) for reasons of expediency — often used in the phrase *trim one's sails*
intransitive verb
1 a : to maintain neutrality between opposing parties or to favor each equally **b** : to change one's views for reasons of expediency
2 : to assume or cause a boat to assume a desired position in the water ⟨a boat that *trims* badly⟩
— **trim one's sails** : to adjust oneself or one's actions to prevailing conditions
²trim *adjective* **trim·mer; trim·mest** (circa 1521)
1 *obsolete* : EXCELLENT, FINE
2 : ready for service or use; *also* : in good physical condition ⟨keeps *trim* by jogging⟩
3 : exhibiting neatness, good order, or compactness of line or structure ⟨*trim* houses⟩
— **trim·ly** *adverb*
— **trim·ness** *noun*

³trim *adverb* (1529)
: in a trim manner : TRIMLY — used chiefly in combination ⟨the *trim*-cut forest vistas —W. M. Thackeray⟩
⁴trim *noun* (1590)
1 : suitable or excellent condition ⟨tries to keep in *trim*⟩
2 a : one's clothing or appearance **b** : material used for ornament or trimming **c** : the lighter woodwork in the finish of a building especially around openings **d** : the interior furnishings of an automobile
3 a : the position of a ship or boat especially with reference to the horizontal; *also* : the difference between the draft of a ship forward and that aft **b** : the relation between the plane of a sail and the direction of the ship **c** : the buoyancy status of a submarine **d** : the attitude of a lighter-than-air craft relative to a fore-and-aft horizontal plane **e** : the attitude with respect to wind axes at which an airplane will continue in level flight with free controls
4 : something that is trimmed off or cut out
5 : a haircut that neatens a previous haircut
tri·ma·ran \'trī-mə-,ran, ,trī-mə-'-\ *noun* [*tri-* + cata*maran*] (1949)
: a fast pleasure sailboat with three hulls side by side
tri·mer \'trī-mər\ *noun* [International Scientific Vocabulary] (circa 1930)
: a polymer formed from three molecules of a monomer
— **tri·mer·ic** \trī-'mer-ik\ *adjective*
trim·er·ous \'tri-mə-rəs\ *adjective* [New Latin *trimerus*, from Greek *tri-* + *meros* part — more at MERIT] (1826)
: having the parts in threes — used of a flower and often written *3-merous*
tri·mes·ter \(,)trī-'mes-tər, 'trī-,\ *noun* [French *trimestre*, from Latin *trimestris* of three months, from *tri-* + *mensis* month — more at MOON] (1821)
1 : a period of three or about three months; *especially* : any of three periods of approximately three months each into which a human pregnancy is divided
2 : one of three terms into which the academic year is sometimes divided
trim·e·ter \'tri-mə-tər\ *noun* [Latin *trimetrus*, from Greek *trimetros* having three measures, from *tri-* + *metron* measure — more at MEASURE] (1567)
: a line of verse consisting of three dipodies or three metrical feet
tri·meth·o·prim \trī-'me-thə-,prim\ *noun* [*tri-* + *meth-* + *-prim* (by shortening & alteration from *pyrimidine*)] (1964)
: a synthetic antibacterial and antimalarial drug $C_{14}H_{18}N_4O_3$ often used with a sulfa drug
tri·met·ro·gon \trī-'me-trə-,gän\ *noun* [*tri-* + Greek *metron* measure + English *-gon*] (1943)
: a system of aerial mapping involving the use of sets of one vertical and two oblique aerial photographs taken simultaneously over the area being mapped
trim·mer \'tri-mər\ *noun* (1555)
1 a (1) : one that trims articles (2) : one that stows coal or freight on a ship so as to distribute the weight properly **b** : an instrument or machine with which trimming is done **c** : a circuit element (as a capacitor) used to tune a circuit to a desired frequency
2 : a beam that receives the end of a header in floor framing
3 : a person who modifies a policy, position, or opinion especially out of expediency
trim·ming *noun* (circa 1518)
1 : DEFEAT, BEATING
2 : the act of one who trims
3 a : a decorative accessory or additional item ⟨*trimmings* for a hat⟩ **b** : an additional garnishing ⟨turkey and all the *trimmings*⟩
tri·month·ly \(,)trī-'mən(t)th-lē\ *adjective* (1856)
: occurring every three months

tri·mor·phic \(,)trī-'mȯr-fik\ *adjective* [Greek *trimorphos* having three forms, from *tri-* + *-morphous* -morphous] (1866)
: occurring in or having three distinct forms
tri·mo·tor \'trī-,mō-tər, -'mō-\ *noun* (1923)
: an airplane powered by three engines
trim size *noun* (circa 1929)
: the actual size (as of a book page) after excess material required in production has been cut off
Tri·mur·ti \tri-'mur-tē\ *noun* [Sanskrit *-trimūrti*, from *trimūrti* having three forms, from *tri-* + *mūrti* body, form] (1810)
: the great triad of Hindu gods comprising Brahma, Vishnu, and Siva
tri·nal \'trī-nᵊl\ *adjective* [Late Latin *trinalis*, from Latin *trini* three each] (1590)
: THREEFOLD
¹trine \'trīn\ *adjective* [Middle English, from Middle French *trin*, from Latin *trinus*, from *trini* three each; akin to Latin *tres* three — more at THREE] (14th century)
1 : THREEFOLD, TRIPLE
2 : of, relating to, or being the favorable astrological aspect of two celestial bodies 120 degrees apart
²trine *noun* (1552)
1 : a group of three : TRIAD
2 : the trine astrological aspect of two celestial bodies
trine immersion *noun* (1637)
: the practice of immersing a candidate for baptism three times in the names of the members of the Trinity
trin·i·tar·i·an \,tri-nə-'ter-ē-ən\ *adjective* (1628)
1 *capitalized* : of or relating to the Trinity, the doctrine of the Trinity, or adherents to that doctrine
2 : having three parts or aspects : THREEFOLD
Trinitarian *noun* (1628)
1 : a member of a religious teaching and nursing order for men founded in France in 1198 by John of Matha and Philip of Valois
2 : one who subscribes to the doctrine of the Trinity
— **Trin·i·tar·i·an·ism** \-ē-ə-,ni-zəm\ *noun*
tri·ni·tro·tol·u·ene \,trī-,nī-trō-'täl-yə-,wēn\ *noun* [International Scientific Vocabulary] (circa 1900)
: TNT
Trin·i·ty \'tri-nə-tē\ *noun* [Middle English *trinite*, from Old French *trinité*, from Late Latin *trinitat-*, *trinitas* state of being threefold, from Latin *trinus* threefold] (13th century)
1 : the unity of Father, Son, and Holy Spirit as three persons in one Godhead according to Christian dogma
2 *not capitalized* : a group of three closely related persons or things
3 : the Sunday after Whitsunday observed as a feast in honor of the Trinity
Trin·i·ty·tide \-,tīd\ *noun* (1511)
: the season of the church year between Trinity Sunday and Advent
¹trin·ket \'triŋ-kət\ *noun* [origin unknown] (circa 1533)
1 : a small ornament (as a jewel or ring)
2 : a small article of equipment
3 : a thing of little value : TRIFLE
²trinket *intransitive verb* [perhaps from ¹*trinket*] (1646)
: to deal clandestinely : INTRIGUE
— **trin·ket·er** *noun*
trin·ket·ry \-kə-trē\ *noun* (1810)
: small items of personal ornament
trin·oc·u·lar \(,)trī-'nä-kyə-lər\ *adjective* [*tri-* + b*inocular*] (1960)
: relating to or being a binocular microscope equipped with a lens for photographic recording during direct visual observation
¹tri·no·mi·al \trī-'nō-mē-əl\ *noun* [*tri-* + *-nomial* (as in *binomial*)] (1674)
1 : a polynomial of three terms
2 : a biological taxonomic name of three terms of which the first designates the genus, the

second the species, and the third the subspecies or variety

²trinomial *adjective* (circa 1704)
1 : consisting of three mathematical terms
2 : of, relating to, or being a biological trinomial

tri·nu·cle·o·tide \(ˌ)trī-'nü-klē-ə-ˌtīd, -'nyü-\ *noun* (1918)
: a nucleotide consisting of three mononucleotides in combination : CODON

trio \'trē-(ˌ)ō\ *noun, plural* **tri·os** [French, from Italian, from *tri-* (from Latin)] (circa 1724)
1 a : a musical composition for three voice parts or three instruments **b** : the secondary or episodic division of a minuet or scherzo, a march, or of various dance forms
2 : the performers of a musical or dance trio
3 : a group or set of three

tri·ode \'trī-ˌōd\ *noun* (1922)
: an electron tube with an anode, a cathode, and a controlling grid

tri·ol \'trī-ˌol, -ˌōl\ *noun* (1936)
: a chemical compound containing three hydroxyl groups

tri·o·let \'trē-ə-lət, 'trī-\ *noun* [French, from Middle French, literally, clover leaf, clover, ultimately from Greek *triphyllon,* from *tri-* tri- + *phyllon* leaf — more at BLADE] (1651)
: a poem or stanza of eight lines in which the first line is repeated as the fourth and seventh and the second line as the eighth with a rhyme scheme of *ABaAabAB*

tri·ose \'trī-ˌōs, -ˌōz\ *noun* [International Scientific Vocabulary] (1894)
: either of two simple sugars $C_3H_6O_3$ containing three carbon atoms

tri·ox·ide \(ˌ)trī-'äk-ˌsīd\ *noun* [International Scientific Vocabulary] (circa 1868)
: an oxide containing three atoms of oxygen

¹trip \'trip\ *verb* **tripped; trip·ping** [Middle English *trippen,* from Middle French *triper,* of Germanic origin; akin to Old English *treppan* to tread — more at TRAP] (14th century)
intransitive verb
1 a : to dance, skip, or caper with light quick steps **b** : to walk with light quick steps
2 : to catch the foot against something so as to stumble
3 : to make a mistake or false step (as in morality or accuracy)
4 : to stumble in articulation when speaking
5 : to make a journey
6 : to run past the pallet of an escapement without previously locking — used of a tooth of the escapement wheel of a watch
7 a : to actuate a mechanism **b** : to become operative
8 : to get high on a psychedelic drug (as LSD) : TURN ON — often used with *out*
transitive verb
1 a : to cause to stumble — often used with *up* **b** : to cause to fail : OBSTRUCT — often used with *up*
2 : to detect in a misstep, fault, or blunder; *also* : EXPOSE — usually used with *up*
3 *archaic* : to perform (as a dance) lightly or nimbly
4 : to raise (an anchor) from the bottom so as to hang free
5 a : to pull (a yard) into a perpendicular position for lowering **b** : to hoist (a topmast) far enough to enable the fid to be withdrawn preparatory to housing or lowering
6 : to release or operate (a mechanism) especially by releasing a catch or detent
— trip the light fantastic : DANCE

²trip *noun* (15th century)
1 : a stroke or catch by which a wrestler is made to lose footing
2 a : VOYAGE, JOURNEY **b** : a single round or tour on a business errand
3 : ERROR, MISSTEP
4 : a quick light step
5 : a faltering step caused by stumbling

6 a : the action of tripping mechanically **b** (1) : a device for tripping a mechanism (as a catch or detent) (2) : TUP 2
7 : an intense visionary experience undergone by a person who has taken a psychedelic drug (as LSD)
8 : absorption in or obsession with an interest, attitude, or state of mind ⟨a guilt *trip*⟩ ⟨on a nostalgia *trip*⟩
9 : SCENE, LIFESTYLE

tri·pack \'trī-ˌpak\ *noun* (1911)
: a combination of three superposed films or emulsions each sensitive to a different primary color for simultaneous exposure in one camera

tri·par·tite \(ˌ)trī-'pär-ˌtīt\ *adjective* [Middle English, from Latin *tripartitus,* from *tri-* + *partitus* divided — more at PARTITE] (15th century)
1 : divided into or composed of three parts
2 : having three corresponding parts or copies
3 : made between or involving three parties ⟨a *tripartite* treaty⟩

tripe \'trīp\ *noun* [Middle English, from Middle French] (14th century)
1 : stomach tissue of a ruminant and especially of the ox used as food
2 : something poor, worthless, or offensive

¹trip–ham·mer \'trip-ˌha-mər\ *noun* (1781)
: a massive power hammer having a head that is tripped and allowed to fall by cam or lever action

²trip–hammer *adjective* (circa 1864)
: suggesting a trip-hammer in loud pounding or persistent action

tri·phe·nyl·meth·ane \ˌtrī-ˌfe-n²l-'me-ˌthān, -ˌfē-\ *noun* [International Scientific Vocabulary] (circa 1885)
: a crystalline hydrocarbon $CH(C_6H_5)_3$ that is the parent compound of many dyes

tri·phos·phate \(ˌ)trī-'fäs-ˌfāt\ *noun* (circa 1826)
: a salt or acid that contains three phosphate groups — compare ATP, GTP

tri·phos·pho·pyr·i·dine nucleotide \ˌtrī-ˌfäs-fō-'pir-ə-ˌdēn-\ *noun* (1937)
: NADP

triph·thong \'trif-ˌthȯŋ, 'trip-\ *noun* [*tri-* + *-phthong* (as in *diphthong*)] (circa 1599)
1 : a phonological unit consisting of three successive vocalic sounds in one syllable
2 : TRIGRAPH
— triph·thon·gal \trif-'thȯŋ-gəl, trip-, -əl\ *adjective*

tri·pin·nate \(ˌ)trī-'pi-ˌnāt\ *adjective* (circa 1760)
: bipinnate with each division pinnate
— tri·pin·nate·ly *adverb*

tri·plane \'trī-ˌplān\ *noun* (1909)
: an airplane with three main supporting surfaces superposed

¹tri·ple \'tri-pəl\ *verb* **tri·pled; tri·pling** \-p(ə-)liŋ\ [Middle English, from Late Latin *triplare,* from Latin *triplus,* adjective] (14th century)
transitive verb
1 : to make three times as great or as many
2 a : to score (a base runner) by a triple **b** : to bring about the scoring of (a run) by a triple
intransitive verb
1 : to become three times as great or as numerous
2 : to make a triple in baseball

²triple *noun* [Middle English, from Latin *triplus,* adjective] (15th century)
1 a : a triple sum, quantity, or number **b** : a combination, group, or series of three
2 : a base hit that allows the batter to reach third base safely
3 : TRIFECTA

³triple *adjective* [Middle French or Latin; Middle French, from Latin *triplus,* from *tri-* + *-plus* multiplied by — more at -FOLD] (1550)
1 : being three times as great or as many
2 : having three units or members

3 : having a threefold relation or character ⟨worked as a double or even *triple* agent —*Time*⟩
4 : three times repeated : TREBLE
5 : marked by three beats per musical measure ⟨*triple* meter⟩
6 a : having units of three components ⟨*triple* feet⟩ **b** *of rhyme* : involving correspondence of three syllables (as in *unfortunate-importunate*)

triple bond *noun* (1889)
: a chemical bond in which three pairs of electrons are shared by two atoms in a molecule — compare DOUBLE BOND, SINGLE BOND

triple counterpoint *noun* (circa 1869)
: three-part musical counterpoint so written that any part may be transposed above or below any other

Triple Crown *noun* (circa 1897)
1 : an unofficial title in horse racing representing the championship achieved by a horse that wins the three classic races for a designated category
2 : the unofficial title signifying the achievement of a baseball player who at the end of a season leads the league in batting average, home runs, and runs batted in

tri·ple–deck·er \ˌtri-pəl-'de-kər\ *noun, often attributive* (1938)
: something having three basic components or levels: as **a** : TRILOGY **b** : a sandwich consisting of three pieces of bread and two layers of filling **c** : a 3-story dwelling with an apartment on each floor

tri·ple–head·er \-'he-dər\ *noun* (circa 1949)
: a program consisting of three consecutive games, contests, or events

triple jump *noun* (1964)
: a jump for distance in track-and-field athletics usually from a running start and combining a hop, a stride, and a jump in succession
— triple jumper *noun*

triple play *noun* (1869)
: a play in baseball by which three players are put out

triple point *noun* (1872)
: the condition of temperature and pressure under which the gaseous, liquid, and solid phases of a substance can exist in equilibrium

triple sec \-'sek\ *noun* [from *Triple Sec,* a trademark] (1943)
: a colorless orange-flavored liqueur

tri·ple–space \ˌtri-pəl-'spās\ (circa 1939)
transitive verb
: to type (text) leaving two blank lines between lines of copy
intransitive verb
: to type on every third line

trip·let \'tri-plət\ *noun* [²*triple*] (1656)
1 : a unit of three lines of verse
2 a : a combination, set, or group of three **b** : a group of three elementary particles (as positive, negative, and neutral pions) with different charge states but otherwise similar properties **c** : an atom or molecule with an even number of electrons that have a net magnetic moment **d** : CODON
3 : one of three children or offspring born at one birth
4 : a group of three musical notes or tones performed in the time of two of the same value

tri·ple–tail \'tri-pəl-ˌtāl\ *noun* (circa 1803)
: a large marine bony fish (*Lobotes surinamensis* of the family Lobotidae) of warm and tropical waters that has long dorsal and anal fins which extend backward and together with the caudal fin appear like a 3-lobed tail

triple threat *noun* (1924)
1 : a football player adept at running, kicking, and passing

\ə\ **abut** \ᵊ\ **kitten** \ər\ **further** \a\ **ash** \ā\ **ace**
\ä\ **mop, mar** \aù\ **out** \ch\ **chin** \e\ **bet** \ē\ **easy**
\g\ **go** \i\ **hit** \ī\ **ice** \j\ **job** \ŋ\ **sing** \ō\ **go**
\ȯ\ **law** \ȯi\ **boy** \th\ **thin** \th\ **the** \ü\ **loot** \ù\ **foot**
\y\ **yet** \zh\ **vision** *see also* Guide to Pronunciation

2 : a person adept in three different fields of activity
— **triple–threat** *adjective*
tri·ple–tongue \,tri-pəl-'təη\ *intransitive verb* (1879)
: to articulate the notes of triplets in fast tempo on a wind instrument by using the tongue positions especially for *t, k, t* for the notes of each successive triplet
¹**tri·plex** \'trī-,pleks, 'trī-\ *noun* (1601)
: something (as an apartment) that is triplex
²**triplex** *adjective* [Latin, from *tri-* + *-plex* -fold — more at -FOLD] (1655)
1 : THREEFOLD, TRIPLE ⟨*triplex* windows⟩
2 : having three apartments, floors, or sections ⟨*triplex* buildings⟩ ⟨*triplex* apartments⟩ ⟨a *triplex* theater⟩
¹**trip·li·cate** \'tri-pli-kət\ *adjective* [Middle English, from Latin *triplicatus*, past participle of *triplicare* to triple, from *triplic-, triplex* threefold] (15th century)
: consisting of or existing in three corresponding or identical parts or examples ⟨*triplicate* invoices⟩
²**trip·li·cate** \-plə-,kāt\ *transitive verb* **-cat·ed; -cat·ing** (circa 1623)
1 : to make triple or threefold
2 : to prepare in triplicate
— **trip·li·ca·tion** \,tri-plə-'kā-shən\ *noun*
³**trip·li·cate** \-pli-kət\ *noun* (1810)
: three copies all alike — used with *in* ⟨typed in *triplicate*⟩
tri·plic·i·ty \tri-'pli-sə-tē, trī-\ *noun, plural* **-ties** [Middle English *triplicite*, from Late Latin *triplicitas* condition of being threefold, from Latin *triplic-, triplex*] (14th century)
1 : one of the groups of three signs each distant 120 degrees from the other two into which the signs of the zodiac are divided — called also *trigon*
2 : the quality or state of being triple or threefold
trip·lo·blas·tic \,tri-plō-'blas-tik\ *adjective* [Latin *triplus* + English *-o-* + *-blastic*] (circa 1888)
: having three primary germ layers
trip·loid \'tri-,plòid\ *adjective* [International Scientific Vocabulary, from Latin *triplus* triple] (1911)
: having or being a chromosome number three times the monoploid number
— **trip·loid** *noun*
— **trip·loi·dy** \-,plòi-dē\ *noun*
tri·ply \'tri-p(ə-)lē\ *adverb* (1660)
: in a triple degree, amount, or manner
tri·pod \'trī-,päd\ *noun* [Latin *tripod-, tripus*, from Greek *tripod-, tripous*, from *tripod-, tripous*, adjective, three-footed, from *tri-* + *pod-, pous* foot — more at FOOT] (1603)
1 : a vessel (as a cauldron) resting on three legs
2 : a stool, table, or altar with three legs
3 : a three-legged stand (as for a camera)
— **tripod** *or* **tri·po·dal** \'trī-pə-dºl, 'trī-,pä-\ *adjective*
trip·o·li \'tri-pə-lē\ *noun* [French, from *Tripoli*, region of Africa] (circa 1601)
1 : an earth consisting of very friable soft schistose deposits of silica and including diatomite and kieselguhr
2 : an earth consisting of friable dustlike silica not of diatomaceous origin
tri·pos \'trī-,päs\ *noun* [modification of Latin *tripus*] (1589)
1 *archaic* : TRIPOD
2 [from the three-legged stool occupied by a participant in a disputation at the degree ceremonies] : a final honors examination at Cambridge university originally in mathematics
trip·per \'tri-pər\ *noun* (1813)
1 *chiefly British* : one that takes a trip — TOURIST
2 : a tripping device (as for operating a railroad signal)
trip·ping·ly \'tri-piη-lē\ *adverb* (1590)

: in a nimble or lively manner ⟨the new name . . . may not roll *trippingly* off the tongue —Paul B. Carroll⟩
trip·py \'tri-pē\ *adjective* (1968)
: of, relating to, or suggesting a trip on psychedelic drugs or the culture associated with such drugs
trip·tych \'trip-(,)tik\ *noun* [Greek *triptychos* having three folds, from *tri-* + *ptychē* fold] (1731)
1 : an ancient Roman writing tablet with three waxed leaves hinged together
2 a : a picture (as an altarpiece) or carving in three panels side by side **b** : something composed or presented in three parts or sections; *especially* : TRILOGY
trip wire *noun* (1916)
1 : a low-placed concealed wire used especially in warfare to trip an enemy or trespasser and usually to trigger an alarm or explosive device when moved
2 : something (as a small military force) intended to function like a trip wire (as to set a larger military force in motion)
tri·que·trous \trī-'kwē-trəs, -'kwe-\ *adjective* [Latin *triquetrus* three-cornered, from *tri-* + *-quetrus*; probably akin to Old High German *waz* sharp — more at WHET] (circa 1879)
: having three acute angles ⟨*triquetrous* stems⟩
tri·ra·di·ate \(,)trī-'rā-dē-ət, -dē-,āt\ *adjective* (1846)
: having three rays or radiating branches ⟨a *triradiate* sponge spicule⟩
tri·reme \'trī-,rēm\ *noun* [Latin *triremis*, from *tri-* + *remus* oar — more at ROW] (1601)
: an ancient galley having three banks of oars
tri·sac·cha·ride \(,)trī-'sa-kə-,rīd\ *noun* [International Scientific Vocabulary] (circa 1899)
: a sugar that yields on complete hydrolysis three monosaccharide molecules
tri·sect \'trī-,sekt, trī-'\ *transitive verb* [*tri-* + inter*sect*] (1695)
: to divide into three usually equal parts
— **tri·sec·tion** \'trī-,sek-shən, trī-'\ *noun*
— **tri·sec·tor** \'trī-,sek-tər, trī-'\ *noun*
tri·shaw \'trī-,shò\ *noun* [*tri-* + rick*shaw*] (1946)
: PEDICAB
tris·kai·deka·pho·bia \,tris-,kī-,de-kə-'fō-bē-ə, ,tris-kə-\ *noun* [New Latin, from Greek *treiskaideka* thirteen (from *treis* three + *kai* and + *deka* ten) + New Latin *phobia* — more at THREE, TEN] (circa 1911)
: fear of the number 13
tri·skel·i·on \trī-'ske-lē-ən, tri-\ *or* **tri·skele** \'trī-,skēl, 'trī-\ *noun* [*triskelion* from New Latin, from Greek *triskelēs* three-legged, from *tri-* + *skelos* leg; *triskele* from Greek *triskelēs* — more at ISOSCELES] (1857)
: a figure composed of three usually curved or bent branches radiating from a center
tris·mus \'triz-məs\ *noun* [New Latin, from Greek *trismos* gnashing (of teeth), from *trizein* to squeak, gnash; akin to Latin *stridēre* to creak — more at STRIDENT] (circa 1693)
: spasm of the muscles of mastication — LOCKJAW

triskelion

tris·oc·ta·he·dron \,tri-,säk-tə-'hē-drən\ *noun* [Greek *tris* thrice + English *octahedron* — more at TER-] (circa 1847)
: a solid (as a crystal) having 24 congruent faces meeting on the edges of a regular octahedron
tri·so·di·um phosphate \,trī-'sō-dē-əm-\ *noun* (1923)
: a crystalline compound Na_3PO_4 that is used especially in cleaning compositions
tri·so·my \'trī-,sō-mē\ *noun, plural* **-mies** [*tri-* + ³*-some* + ²*-y*] (1930)

: the condition (as in Down's syndrome) of having one or a few chromosomes triploid in an otherwise diploid set
— **tri·so·mic** \(,)trī-'sō-mik\ *adjective or noun*
Tris·tan \'tris-tən, -,tän, -,tan\ *noun*
: TRISTRAM
tri·state \'trī-'stāt, -,stāt\ *adjective* (1900)
: of, relating to, or consisting of three adjoining states ⟨the *tristate* area⟩
triste \'trēst\ *adjective* [French, from Latin *tristis*] (1756)
: SAD, MOURNFUL; *also* : WISTFUL
tri·stea·rin \(,)trī-'stē-ə-rən, -'sti(-ə)r-ən\ *noun* [International Scientific Vocabulary] (circa 1856)
: the crystallizable triglyceride $C_{57}H_{110}O_6$ of stearic acid that is found especially in hard fats
tris·te·za \tri-'stā-zə\ *noun* [Portuguese, literally, sadness, from Latin *tristitia*, from *tristis* sad] (circa 1902)
: a highly infectious virus disease of citrus trees grafted on sour orange rootstocks that is characterized by rotting of the rootlets and eventually causes the death of the trees
trist·ful \'trist-fəl\ *adjective* [Middle English *trist* sad, from Middle French *triste*] (15th century)
: SAD, MELANCHOLY
— **trist·ful·ly** \-fə-lē\ *adverb*
— **trist·ful·ness** *noun*
tri·stim·u·lus \(,)trī-'stim-yə-ləs\ *adjective* (1933)
: of or relating to values giving the amounts of the three colored lights red, green, and blue that when combined additively produce a match for the color being considered
Tris·tram \'tris-trəm\ *noun* [Middle English *Tristrem*, from Anglo-French *Tristan*, from Old Welsh *Trystan*]
: the lover of Isolde of Ireland and husband of Isolde of Brittany in medieval legend
tri·sub·sti·tut·ed \'trī-'səb-stə-,tü-təd, -,tyü-\ *adjective* (circa 1899)
: having three substituent atoms or groups in the molecule
tri·sul·fide \-'səl-,fīd\ *noun* (1866)
: a compound of an element or radical with three atoms of sulfur
tri·syl·lab·ic \,trī-sə-'la-bik\ *adjective* [Latin *trisyllabus*, from Greek *trisyllabos*, from *tri-* + *syllabē* syllable] (1637)
: having three syllables ⟨a *trisyllabic* word⟩
tri·syl·la·ble \'trī-,si-lə-bəl, (,)trī-'\ *noun* (1589)
: a word of three syllables
trite \'trīt\ *adjective* **trit·er; trit·est** [Latin *tritus*, from past participle of *terere* to rub, wear away — more at THROW] (1548)
: hackneyed or boring from much use : not fresh or original ☆
— **trite·ly** *adverb*
— **trite·ness** *noun*
tri·the·ism \'trī-thē-,i-zəm\ *noun* (1678)

☆ SYNONYMS
Trite, hackneyed, stereotyped, threadbare mean lacking the freshness that evokes attention or interest. TRITE applies to a once effective phrase or idea spoiled from long familiarity ⟨"you win some, you lose some" is a *trite* expression⟩. HACKNEYED stresses being worn out by overuse so as to become dull and meaningless ⟨all of the metaphors and images in the poem are *hackneyed*⟩. STEREOTYPED implies falling invariably into the same pattern or form ⟨views of minorities that are *stereotyped* and out-of-date⟩. THREADBARE applies to what has been used until its possibilities of interest have been totally exhausted ⟨a mystery novel with a *threadbare* plot⟩.

: the doctrine that the Father, Son, and Holy Spirit are three distinct Gods
— **tri·the·ist** \-\(.)thē-ist\ *noun or adjective*
— **tri·the·is·tic** \.trī-thē-'is-tik\ *or* **tri·the·is·ti·cal** \-'is-ti-kəl\ *adjective*

tri·thing \'trī-thin\ *noun* [Middle English, alteration of (assumed) Old English *thrithing, thriding*] (13th century)
archaic : ³RIDING 1

tri·ti·at·ed \'tri-tē-.ā-təd, 'tri-shē-\ *adjective* (1953)
: containing and especially labeled with tritium

trit·i·ca·le \.tri-tə-'kā-lē\ *noun* [New Latin, blend of *Triticum*, genus of wheat, and *Secale*, genus of rye] (1952)
: an amphidiploid hybrid between wheat and rye that has a high yield and rich protein content

tri·ti·um \'tri-tē-əm, 'tri-shē-\ *noun* [New Latin, from Greek *tritos* third — more at THIRD] (1933)
: a radioactive isotope of hydrogen with atoms of three times the mass of ordinary light hydrogen atoms

trit·o·ma \'tri-tə-mə\ *noun* [New Latin, genus name, from Greek *tritomos* thrice cut, from *tri-* + *temnein* to cut; from their trimerous flowers — more at TOME] (1804)
: any of a genus (*Kniphofia*) of African herbs of the lily family that are often grown for their spikes of showy red or yellow flowers

¹tri·ton \'trī-t³n\ *noun* [Latin, from Greek *Tritōn*]
1 *capitalized* : a son of Poseidon described as a demigod of the sea with the lower part of his body like that of a fish
2 [New Latin, genus name, from Latin *Triton*] : any of various large marine gastropod mollusks (especially family Ranellidae) with a heavy elongated conical shell; *also* : the shell

²tri·ton \'trī-.tän\ *noun* [*tritium* + ²*-on*] (1934)
: the nucleus of tritium

tri·tone \'trī-.tōn\ *noun* [Greek *tritonon*, from *tri-* + *tonos* tone] (1609)
: a musical interval of three whole steps

¹trit·u·rate \'tri-chə-.rāt\ *transitive verb* **-rat·ed; -rat·ing** [Late Latin *trituratus*, past participle of *triturare* to thresh, from Latin *tritura* act of rubbing, threshing, from *tritus*, past participle — more at TRITE] (circa 1755)
1 : CRUSH, GRIND
2 : to pulverize and comminute thoroughly by rubbing or grinding
— **trit·u·ra·ble** \'tri-chə-rə-bəl\ *adjective*
— **trit·u·ra·tor** \-.rā-tər\ *noun*

²trit·u·rate \-rət\ *noun* (circa 1891)
: a triturated substance : TRITURATION 2

trit·u·ra·tion \.tri-chə-'rā-shən\ *noun* (1646)
1 : the act or process of triturating : the state of being triturated : COMMINUTION
2 : a triturated medicinal powder made by triturating a substance with a diluent

¹tri·umph \'trī-əm(p)f\ *noun, plural* **tri·umphs** \-əm(p)fs, -əm(p)s\ [Middle English *triumphe*, from Middle French, from Latin *triumphus*] (14th century)
1 : a ceremony attending the entering of Rome by a general who had won a decisive victory over a foreign enemy — compare OVATION 1
2 : the joy or exultation of victory or success
3 a : a victory or conquest by or as if by military force **b** : a notable success
— **tri·um·phal** \trī-'əm(p)-fəl\ *adjective*

²triumph *intransitive verb* (1508)
1 : to obtain victory : PREVAIL
2 a : to receive the honor of a triumph **b** : to celebrate a triumph or success boastfully or exultingly

tri·um·phal·ism \trī-'əm(p)-fə-.li-zəm\ *noun* (1964)
: the doctrine, attitude, or belief that one religious creed is superior to all others
— **tri·um·phal·ist** \-fə-list\ *noun or adjective*

tri·um·phant \trī-'əm(p)-fənt\ *adjective* (15th century)
1 : VICTORIOUS, CONQUERING
2 *archaic* : of or relating to a triumph
3 : rejoicing for or celebrating victory
4 : notably successful
— **tri·um·phant·ly** *adverb*

tri·um·vir \trī-'əm-vər\ *noun, plural* **-virs** *also* **-vi·ri** \-və-.rī, -.rē\ [Latin, back-formation from *triumviri*, plural, commission of three men, from *trium virum* of three men] (circa 1580)
: one of a commission or ruling body of three

tri·um·vi·rate \-və-rət\ *noun* (1584)
1 : a body of triumvirs
2 : the office or government of triumvirs
3 : a group or association of three

¹tri·une \'trī-.yün\ *noun, often capitalized* [Latin *tri-* + *unus* one — more at ONE] (1605)
: TRINITY 1

²triune *adjective* (1635)
: three in one: **a** *often capitalized* : of or relating to the Trinity ⟨the *triune* God⟩ **b** : consisting of three parts, members, or aspects

tri·va·lent \(.)trī-'vā-lənt\ *adjective* [International Scientific Vocabulary] (1868)
1 : having a chemical valence of three
2 : reacting immunologically with three different combining sites (as of antigens or antibodies) ⟨*trivalent* oral polio vaccine⟩

triv·et \'tri-vət\ *noun* [Middle English *trevet*, from Old English *trefet*, probably modification of Late Latin *triped-, tripes*, from Latin, three-footed, from *tri-* + *ped-, pes* foot — more at FOOT] (before 12th century)
1 : a three-legged stand : TRIPOD
2 : a usually metal stand with short feet for use under a hot dish at table

triv·ia \'tri-vē-ə\ *noun plural but singular or plural in construction* [(assumed) New Latin, back-formation from Latin *trivialis*] (1920)
: unimportant matters : trivial facts or details; *also, singular in construction* : a quizzing game involving obscure facts

triv·i·al \'tri-vē-əl\ *adjective* [Latin *trivialis* found everywhere, commonplace, from *trivium* crossroads, from *tri-* + *via* way — more at WAY] (1589)
1 : COMMONPLACE, ORDINARY
2 a : of little worth or importance **b** : relating to or being the mathematically simplest case; *specifically* : characterized by having all variables equal to zero ⟨a *trivial* solution to a linear equation⟩
3 : SPECIFIC 4 ◇
— **triv·i·al·ist** \-ə-list\ *noun*
— **triv·i·al·ly** \-ə-lē\ *adverb*

triv·i·al·ise *British variant of* TRIVIALIZE

triv·i·al·i·ty \.tri-vē-'a-lə-tē\ *noun, plural* **-ties** (1598)
1 : the quality or state of being trivial
2 : something trivial : TRIFLE

triv·i·al·ize \'tri-vē-ə-.līz\ *transitive verb* **-ized; -iz·ing** (1846)
: to make trivial : reduce to triviality
— **triv·i·al·i·za·tion** \.tri-vē-ə-lə-'zā-shən\ *noun*

trivial name *noun* (1759)
1 : SPECIFIC EPITHET
2 : a common or vernacular name of an organism or chemical

triv·i·um \'tri-vē-əm\ *noun, plural* **triv·ia** \-vē-ə\ [Medieval Latin, from Latin, meeting of three ways, crossroads] (1804)
: a group of studies consisting of grammar, rhetoric, and logic and forming the lower division of the seven liberal arts in medieval universities — compare QUADRIVIUM

¹tri·week·ly \(.)trī-'wē-klē\ *adjective* (1832)
1 : occurring or appearing three times a week
2 : occurring or appearing every three weeks
— **triweekly** *adverb*

²triweekly *noun, plural* **-lies** (1851)
: a triweekly publication

-trix *noun suffix, plural* **-trices** *or* **-trixes** [Middle English, from Latin, feminine of *-tor*, suffix denoting an agent]
1 : female that does or is associated with a (specified) thing ⟨avia*trix*⟩
2 : geometric line, point, or surface ⟨genera*trix*⟩

tRNA \.tē-.är-.en-'ā, 'tē-.är-.en-.ā\ *noun* (1962)
: TRANSFER RNA

tro·car *also* **tro·char** \'trō-.kär\ *noun* [French *trocart*, from *trois* three (from Latin *tres*) + *carre* side of a sword blade, from *carrer* to make square, from Latin *quadrare* — more at THREE, QUADRATE] (circa 1706)
: a sharp-pointed surgical instrument fitted with a cannula and used especially to insert the cannula into a body cavity as a drainage outlet

tro·cha·ic \trō-'kā-ik\ *adjective* [Middle French *trochaïque*, from Latin *trochaicus*, from Greek *trochaikos*, from *trochaios* trochee] (1589)
: of, relating to, or consisting of trochees
— **trochaic** *noun*

tro·chan·ter \trō-'kan-tər\ *noun* [Greek *trochantēr*; akin to Greek *trechein* to run] (1615)
1 : a rough prominence at the upper part of the femur of many vertebrates
2 : the second segment counting from the base of the leg of an insect
— **tro·chan·ter·al** \-tə-rəl\ *adjective*
— **tro·chan·ter·ic** \.trō-kən-'ter-ik, -.kan-\ *adjective*

tro·che \'trō-kē, *British usually* 'trōsh\ *noun* [alteration of earlier *trochisk*, from Late Latin *trochiscus*, from Greek *trochiskos*, from diminutive of *trochos* wheel] (1597)
: a usually circular medicinal tablet or lozenge for slow dissolution in the mouth; *especially* : one used as a demulcent

tro·chee \'trō-(.)kē\ *noun* [probably from Middle French *trochée*, from Latin *trochaeus*, from Greek *trochaios*, from *trochaios* running, from *trochē* run, course, from *trechein* to run; akin to Greek *trochos* wheel, Old Irish *droch*] (1589)
: a metrical foot consisting of one long syllable followed by one short syllable or of one stressed syllable followed by one unstressed syllable (as in *apple*)

◇ WORD HISTORY
trivial The ancient Romans used the adjective *trivialis* to refer to what is commonplace or ordinary. Literally meaning "pertaining to a crossroads," *trivialis* is a derivative of *trivium*, which was compounded from *tri-* "three" and *via* "way, road." Thus *trivium* might be rendered literally as "a place where three roads meet." The extended sense of *trivialis* rested on the belief that things found at such a public place as a crossroads, where all the world may pass by, are generally common things. The notion that people often stop where roads meet to pass the time of day with inconsequential talk may also have influenced the development of this sense. This is the source for the modern senses of *trivial* such as "commonplace" or "of little importance." It was not until the 1920s that the word *trivia* began being used for "unimportant matters." Its form is just like that of the plural of Latin *trivium*, but its meaning is dependent on Modern English senses of *trivial*.

\ə\ abut \ᵊ\ kitten \ər\ further \a\ ash \ā\ ace \ä\ mop, mar \aú\ out \ch\ chin \e\ bet \ē\ easy \g\ go \i\ hit \ī\ ice \j\ job \n\ sing \ō\ go \ó\ law \ói\ boy \th\ thin \th\ the \ü\ loot \ú\ foot \y\ yet \zh\ vision *see also* Guide to Pronunciation

troch·lea \'trä-klē-ə\ *noun* [New Latin, from Latin, block of pulleys, from Greek *trochileia*, from *trochilos* sheave, from *trochos* wheel] (circa 1693)
: an anatomical structure that is held to resemble a pulley; *especially* : the articular surface on the medial condyle of the humerus that articulates with the ulna

troch·le·ar \-ər\ *adjective* (circa 1681)
1 : of, relating to, or being a trochlea
2 : of, relating to, or being a trochlear nerve

trochlear nerve *noun* (circa 1893)
: either of the 4th pair of cranial nerves that supply some of the eye muscles with motor fibers — called also *trochlear*

tro·choid \'trō-,kȯid, 'trä-,kȯid\ *noun* [Greek *trochoeidēs* like a wheel, from *trochos* wheel] (circa 1704)
: the curve generated by a point on the radius of a circle or the radius extended as the circle rolls on a fixed straight line
— **tro·choi·dal** \trō-'kȯi-d³l, trä-\ *adjective*

trocho·phore \'trä-kə-,fōr, -,fȯr\ *noun* [ultimately from Greek *trochos* wheel + *pherein* to carry — more at BEAR] (1892)
: a free-swimming ciliate larva occurring in several invertebrate groups (as the polychaete worms and mollusks)

trod *past and past participle of* TREAD

trodden *past participle of* TREAD

trof·fer \'trä-fər, 'trȯ-\ *noun* [blend of *trough* and *coffer*] (1942)
: an inverted trough serving as a support and reflector usually for a fluorescent lighting unit

trog·lo·dyte \'trä-glə-,dīt\ *noun* [Latin *troglodytae*, plural, from Greek *trōglodytai*, from *trōglē* hole, cave (akin to Greek *trōgein* to gnaw, Armenian *aracem* I lead to pasture, graze) + *dyein* to enter] (1558)
1 : a member of a primitive people dwelling in caves
2 : a person resembling a troglodyte (as in reclusive habits or outmoded or reactionary attitudes)
— **trog·lo·dyt·ic** \,trä-glə-'di-tik\ *adjective*

tro·gon \'trō-,gän\ *noun* [New Latin, genus name, from Greek *trōgōn*, present participle of *trōgein* to gnaw] (1792)
: any of numerous nonpasserine tropical birds (family Trogonidae) with brilliant often iridescent plumage

troi·ka \'trȯi-kə\ *noun* [Russian *troĭka*, from *troe* three; akin to Old English *thrīe* three] (1842)
1 : a Russian vehicle drawn by three horses abreast; *also* : a team for such a vehicle
2 : a group of three; *especially* : an administrative or ruling body of three

troi·lite \'trō-ə-,līt, 'trȯi-,līt\ *noun* [German *Troilit*, from Domenico *Troili*, 18th century Italian scientist + German *-it* -ite] (circa 1868)
: a mineral that is a variety of pyrrhotite and that is widely but sparsely distributed (as on earth, in meteorites, and in lunar soil samples)

Troi·lus \'trȯi-ləs, 'trō-ə-ləs\ *noun* [Middle English, from Latin, from Greek *Trōilos*]
: a son of Priam who in medieval legend loved Cressida and lost her to Diomedes

¹Tro·jan \'trō-jən\ *noun* [Middle English, from Latin *trojanus* of Troy, from *Troia, Troja* Troy, from Greek *Trōïa*] (14th century)
1 : a native or inhabitant of Troy
2 : one who shows qualities (as pluck, endurance, or determined energy) attributed to the defenders of ancient Troy
3 : a gay, irresponsible, or disreputable companion

²Trojan *adjective* (14th century)
1 : of, relating to, or resembling ancient Troy or its inhabitants
2 : of, relating to, or constituting a Trojan horse

Trojan horse *noun* [from the large hollow wooden horse filled with Greek soldiers and introduced within the walls of Troy by a stratagem] (1837)

1 : someone or something intended to defeat or subvert from within
2 : a seemingly useful computer program that contains concealed instructions which when activated perform an illicit or malicious action (as destroying data files); *also* : the concealed instructions of such a program — compare VIRUS

Trojan War *noun*
: a 10-year war between the Greeks and Trojans brought on by the abduction of Helen by Paris and ended with the destruction of Troy

¹troll \'trōl\ *verb* [Middle English] (15th century)
transitive verb
1 : to cause to move round and round : ROLL
2 a : to sing the parts of (as a round or catch) in succession **b** : to sing loudly **c** : to celebrate in song
3 a : to fish for by trolling **b** : to fish by trolling in ⟨*troll* lakes⟩ **c** : to pull through the water in trolling ⟨*troll* a lure⟩
intransitive verb
1 : to move around : RAMBLE
2 : to fish by trailing a lure or baited hook from a moving boat
3 : to sing or play in a jovial manner
4 : to speak rapidly
— **troll·er** *noun*

²troll *noun* (1869)
: a lure or a line with its lure and hook used in trolling

³troll *noun* [Norwegian *troll* & Danish *trold*, from Old Norse *troll* giant, demon; probably akin to Middle High German *trolle* lout] (1616)
: a dwarf or giant in Scandinavian folklore inhabiting caves or hills

¹trol·ley *also* **trol·ly** \'trä-lē\ *noun, plural* **trolleys** *also* **trollies** [probably from ¹*troll*] (1823)
1 *dialect English* : a cart of any of various kinds
2 a : a device that carries electric current from an overhead wire to an electrically driven vehicle **b** : a streetcar powered electrically through a trolley — called also *trolley car*
3 : a wheeled carriage running on an overhead rail or track
4 *chiefly British* : a cart or wheeled stand used for conveying something (as food or books)

²trolley *also* **trolly** *verb* **trol·leyed** *also* **trol·lied; trol·ley·ing** *also* **trol·ly·ing** (1882)
transitive verb
: to convey by a trolley
intransitive verb
: to ride on a trolley

trol·ley·bus \'trä-lē-,bəs\ *noun* (1921)
: a bus powered electrically from two overhead wires

trol·lop \'trä-ləp\ *noun* [perhaps irregular from *trull*] (1621)
: a vulgar or disreputable woman; *especially* : one who engages in sex promiscuously or for money

Trombe wall \'trȯmb-, 'trämb-, 'trō^n b-\ *noun* [Félix *Trombe* 20th century French designer] (1978)
: a masonry wall that is usually separated from the outdoors by a glass wall and is designed to absorb solar heat and release it into the interior of a building

trom·bone \träm-'bōn, (,)trəm-', 'träm-,\ *noun* [Italian, augmentative of *tromba* trumpet, of Germanic origin; akin to Old High German *trumba, trumpa* trumpet] (circa 1724)
: a brass instrument consisting of a long cylindrical metal tube with two turns and having a movable slide or valves for varying the tone and a usual range one octave lower than that of the trumpet
— **trom·bon·ist** \-'bō-nist, -,bō-\ *noun*

trombone

trom·mel \'trä-məl\ *noun* [German, drum, from Middle High German *trummel*, diminutive of *trumme* drum — more at DRUM] (circa 1877)
: a usually cylindrical or conical revolving screen used especially for screening or sizing rock, ore, or coal

tromp \'trämp, 'trȯmp\ *verb* [by alteration] (1883)
intransitive verb
1 : TRAMP 1 ⟨a lot of knocking on doors, *tromping* from room to room —Sara Davidson⟩
2 : to step hard : STAMP ⟨*tromped* on the brake⟩
transitive verb
1 : TRAMP
2 : STAMP ⟨*tromps* the accelerator to the floor —Jim Becker⟩
3 a : to give a physical beating to **b** : to defeat decisively

trompe l'oeil \(,)trȯmp-'ləi, trō^n p-lˈœi\ *noun, often attributive* [French *trompe-l'œil*, literally, deceive the eye] (1889)
1 : a style of painting in which objects are depicted with photographically realistic detail; *also* : the use of similar technique in interior decorating
2 : a trompe l'oeil painting or effect

-tron *noun suffix* [Greek, suffix denoting an instrument; akin to Old English *-thor*, suffix denoting an instrument, Latin *-trum*]
1 : vacuum tube ⟨magne*tron*⟩
2 : device for the manipulation of subatomic particles ⟨cyclo*tron*⟩

tro·na \'trō-nə\ *noun* [Swedish, probably from Arabic *natrūn* natron — more at NATRON] (1799)
: a gray-white or yellowish white monoclinic mineral consisting of a hydrous acid sodium carbonate

¹troop \'trüp\ *noun* [Middle French *trope, troupe* company, herd, of Germanic origin; akin to Old English *thorp, throp* village — more at THORP] (1545)
1 a : a group of soldiers **b** : a cavalry unit corresponding to an infantry company **c** *plural* : ARMED FORCES, SOLDIERS
2 : a collection of people or things : CREW 2
3 : a flock of mammals or birds
4 : the basic organizational unit of Boy Scouts or Girl Scouts under an adult leader

²troop *intransitive verb* (1565)
1 : to move or gather in crowds
2 : to go one's way : WALK
3 : to spend time together : ASSOCIATE
4 : to move in large numbers

troop·er \'trü-pər\ *noun* (1640)
1 a (1) : an enlisted cavalryman (2) : the horse of a cavalryman **b** : PARATROOPER **c** : SOLDIER
2 a : a mounted police officer **b** : a state police officer
3 : TROUPER 2

troop·ship \'trüp-,ship\ *noun* (1862)
: a ship for carrying troops : TRANSPORT

trop- *or* **tropo-** *combining form* [International Scientific Vocabulary, from Greek *tropos*]
1 : turn : turning : change ⟨*tropo*sphere⟩
2 : tropism ⟨*tropic*⟩

trope \'trōp\ *noun* [Latin *tropus*, from Greek *tropos* turn, way, manner, style, trope, from *trepein* to turn] (1533)
1 : the use of a word or expression in a figurative sense : FIGURE OF SPEECH
2 : a phrase or verse added as an embellishment or interpolation to the sung parts of the Mass in the medieval period

troph- *or* **tropho-** *combining form* [French, from Greek, from *trophē* nourishment]
: nutritive ⟨*tropho*blast⟩

troph·al·lax·is \ˌtrō-fə-'lak-səs\ *noun* [New Latin, from *troph-* + Greek *allaxis* exchange, from *allassein* to change, exchange, from *allos* other — more at ELSE] (1918) : exchange of food (as from special glands) between social insects (as ants or termites)

tro·phic \'trō-fik\ *adjective* [French *trophique*, from Greek *trophikos*, from *trophē* nourishment, from *trephein* to nourish] (1873) **1** : of or relating to nutrition : NUTRITIONAL ⟨*trophic* disorders⟩ **2** : ³TROPIC

— **tro·phi·cal·ly** \-fi-k(ə-)lē\ *adverb*

-trophic *adjective combining form* [New Latin *-trophia* -trophy] **1 a** : of, relating to, or characterized by (such) nutrition ⟨ecto*trophic*⟩ **b** : requiring or utilizing (such) a kind of nutrition ⟨hetero*trophic*⟩ **2** : -TROPIC 2 ⟨gonado*trophic*⟩

trophic level (1942) : one of the hierarchical strata of a food web characterized by organisms which are the same number of steps removed from the primary producers

tro·pho·blast \'trō-fə-ˌblast\ *noun* [International Scientific Vocabulary] (1889) : a thin layer of ectoderm that forms the wall of many mammalian blastulas and functions in the nutrition and implantation of the embryo

— **tro·pho·blas·tic** \ˌtrō-fə-'blas-tik\ *adjective*

tro·pho·zo·ite \ˌtrō-fə-'zō-ˌīt\ *noun* [*troph-* + *zo-* + ¹*-ite*] (circa 1909) : a protozoan of a vegetative form as distinguished from one of a reproductive or resting form

tro·phy \'trō-fē\ *noun, plural* **trophies** [Middle French *trophee*, from Latin *tropaeum, trophaeum*, from Greek *tropaion*, from neuter of *tropaios* of a turning, of a rout, from *tropē* turn, rout, from *trepein* to turn] (15th century) **1** : something gained or given in victory or conquest especially when preserved or mounted as a memorial **2 a** : a memorial of an ancient Greek or Roman victory raised on the field of battle or in case of a naval victory on the nearest land **b** : a representation of such a memorial (as on a medal); *also* : an architectural ornament representing a group of military weapons **3** : a game animal or fish suitable for mounting as a trophy — usually used attributively

◇ — **trophy** *transitive verb*

-trophy *noun combining form* [New Latin *-trophia*, from Greek, from *-trophos* nourishing, from *trephein*] : nutrition : nurture : growth ⟨dys*trophy*⟩

¹trop·ic \'trä-pik\ *noun* [Middle English *tropik*, from Latin *tropicus* of the solstice, from Greek *tropikos*, from *tropē* turn] (1527) **1** : either of the two parallels of terrestrial latitude at a distance of about 23½ degrees north or south of the equator where the sun is directly overhead when it reaches its most northerly or southerly point in the sky — compare TROPIC OF CANCER, TROPIC OF CAPRICORN **2** *plural, often capitalized* : the region lying between the tropics

²tropic *adjective* (1551) : of, relating to, or occurring in the tropics : TROPICAL

³tro·pic \'trō-pik\ *adjective* [trop-] (1903) **1** : of, relating to, or characteristic of tropism or of a tropism **2** *of a hormone* : influencing the activity of a specified gland

-tropic *adjective combining form* [French *-tropique*, from Greek *-tropos* -tropous] **1** : turning, changing, or tending to turn or change in a (specified) manner or in response to a (specified) stimulus ⟨geo*tropic*⟩ **2** : attracted to or acting upon (something specified) ⟨neuro*tropic*⟩

trop·i·cal \for 1 'trä-pi-kəl, for 2 'trō- also 'trä-\ *adjective* (1527)

1 a : of, relating to, occurring in, or suitable for use in the tropics **b** : of, being, or characteristic of a region or climate that is frost-free with temperatures high enough to support year-round plant growth given sufficient moisture ⟨*tropical* Florida⟩ **2** [Latin *tropicus*, from Greek *tropikos*, from *tropos* trope] : FIGURATIVE 2

— **trop·i·cal·ly** \-pi-k(ə-)lē\ *adverb*

tropical aquarium *noun* (circa 1948) : an aquarium kept at a uniform warmth and used especially for tropical fish

tropical cyclone *noun* (1920) : a cyclone in the tropics characterized by winds rotating at the rate of 74 miles (119 kilometers) an hour or more

tropical fish *noun* (1931) : any of various small usually showy fishes of tropical origin often kept in the tropical aquarium

trop·i·cal·ize \'trä-pi-kə-ˌlīz\ *transitive verb* **-ized; -iz·ing** (1885) **1** : to make tropical (as in character, conditions, or appearance) **2** : to fit or adapt for use in a tropical climate especially by measures designed to combat the effects of fungi and moisture

tropical oil *noun* (1988) : any of several oils (as coconut oil and palm oil) that are high in saturated fatty acids

tropical rain forest *noun* (1926) : RAIN FOREST 1

tropical sprue *noun* (circa 1955) : SPRUE 2

tropical storm *noun* (circa 1945) : a tropical cyclone with strong winds of less than hurricane intensity

tropic bird *noun* (circa 1681) : any of a genus (*Phaethon* of the family Phaethontidae) of web-footed birds that are related to the pelicans, are found chiefly in tropical seas often far from land, and have mostly white satiny plumage marked with a little black, a greatly elongated central pair of tail feathers, and a bright-colored bill

tropic bird

tropic of Cancer [from the sign of the zodiac which its celestial projection intersects] (1555) : the parallel of latitude that is approximately 23½ degrees north of the equator and that is the northernmost latitude reached by the overhead sun

tropic of Capricorn [from the sign of the zodiac which its celestial projection intersects] (1545) : the parallel of latitude that is approximately 23½ degrees south of the equator and that is the southernmost latitude reached by the overhead sun

-tropin *or* **-trophin** *noun combining form* [-*tropin*, alteration of -*trophin*, from -*trophic* + ¹*-in*] : hormone ⟨gonado*tropin*⟩ ⟨somato*tropin*⟩

tro·pism \'trō-ˌpi-zəm\ *noun* [International Scientific Vocabulary -*tropism*] (1899) **1 a** : involuntary orientation by an organism or one of its parts that involves turning or curving by movement or by differential growth and is a positive or negative response to a source of stimulation **b** : a reflex reaction involving a tropism **2** : an innate tendency to react in a definite manner to stimuli; *broadly* : a natural inclination : PROPENSITY

— **tro·pis·tic** \trō-'pis-tik\ *adjective*

-tropism *noun combining form* [International Scientific Vocabulary, from *trop-*] : tropism ⟨helio*tropism*⟩

tropo- — see TROP-

tro·po·col·la·gen \ˌträ-pə-'kä-lə-jən, ˌtrō-\ *noun* (1954) : a subunit of collagen fibrils consisting of three polypeptide strands arranged in a helix

tro·po·log·i·cal \ˌtrō-pə-'lä-ji-kəl, ˌträ-\ *also* **tro·po·log·ic** \-jik\ *adjective* (14th century) **1** : of, relating to, or involving biblical interpretation stressing moral metaphor; *also* : MORAL **2** : characterized or varied by tropes : FIGURATIVE

— **tro·po·log·i·cal·ly** \-ji-k(ə-)lē\ *adverb*

tropo·my·o·sin \ˌträ-pə-'mī-ə-sən, ˌtrō-\ *noun* (1946) : a protein of muscle that forms a complex with troponin regulating the interaction of actin and myosin in muscular contraction

tro·po·nin \'trō-pə-nən, 'trä-, -ˌnin\ *noun* [by shortening & alteration from *tropomyosin*] (1966) : a protein of muscle that together with tropomyosin forms a regulatory protein complex controlling the interaction of actin and myosin and that when combined with calcium ions permits muscular contraction

tro·po·pause \'trō-pə-ˌpóz, 'trä-\ *noun* [International Scientific Vocabulary *tropo*sphere + *pause*] (1918) : the region at the top of the troposphere; *also* : a comparable layer of a celestial body

tro·po·sphere \'trō-pə-ˌsfir, 'trä-\ *noun* [International Scientific Vocabulary] (1909) : the lowest densest part of the earth's atmosphere in which most weather changes occur and temperature generally decreases rapidly with altitude and which extends from the surface to the bottom of the stratosphere

— **tro·po·spher·ic** \ˌtrō-pə-'sfir-ik, ˌträ-, -'sfer-\ *adjective*

tro·po·tax·is \ˌtrō-pə-'tak-səs, ˌträ-\ *noun* [New Latin] (1934) : a taxis in which an organism orients itself by the simultaneous comparison of stimuli of different intensity acting on separate end organs

-tropous *adjective combining form* [Greek *-tropos*, from *trepein* to turn] : turning or curving in (such) a way : exhibiting (such) a tropism ⟨ana*tropous*⟩

-tropy *noun combining form* [French *-tropie*, from Greek *-tropia*, from *-tropos*] **1** : condition of exhibiting (such) a behavior ⟨allo*tropy*⟩

◇ WORD HISTORY

trophy After a military victory, the ancient Greeks had a custom of hanging captured enemy arms and armor from a stake or tree somewhere on the battlefield, ideally at the spot where the enemy had first turned in retreat. The Greek name for such a memorial was *tropaion*, from the neuter form of the adjective *tropaios* "of or relating to a turn or rout," a derivative of *tropē* "turn, rout." Eventually *tropaion* was applied to much more elaborate and permanent victory memorials of stone or bronze, ones not necessarily erected on the actual battlefield. From Hellenistic Greece the ancient Romans took the custom as well as the word, which was Latinized as *tropaeum*, later *trophaeum*. English borrowed the word via French as *trophe* in the 16th century. From its original classical reference, the meaning of *trophy* has been generalized to apply to anything that could be displayed as a reminder of success, whether in war, sports, or life.

\ə\ abut \ᵊ\ kitten \ər\ further \a\ ash \ā\ ace
\ä\ mop, mar \aú\ out \ch\ chin \e\ bet \ē\ easy
\g\ go \i\ hit \ī\ ice \j\ job \ŋ\ sing \ō\ go
\ó\ law \ói\ boy \th\ thin \t͟h\ the \ü\ loot \ú\ foot
\y\ yet \zh\ vision *see also* Guide to Pronunciation

2 : change in a (specified) way or in response to a (specified) stimulus ⟨thix*otropy*⟩

¹trot \'trät\ *noun* [Middle English, from Middle French, from *troter* to trot, of Germanic origin; akin to Old High German *trottōn* to tread, Old English *tredan*] (14th century) **1 a** (1) : a moderately fast gait of a quadruped (as a horse) in which the legs move in diagonal pairs (2) : a jogging gait of a human that falls between a walk and a run **b** : a ride on horseback **2** : an old woman **3** : a literal translation of a foreign text **4** *plural* : DIARRHEA

²trot *verb* **trot·ted; trot·ting** (14th century) *intransitive verb* **1** : to ride, drive, or proceed at a trot ⟨the fox *trotted* over the knoll⟩ **2** : to proceed briskly : HURRY *transitive verb* **1** : to cause to go at a trot **2** : to traverse at a trot

³trot *noun* (1883) : TROTLINE; *also* : one of the short lines with hooks that are attached to it at intervals

¹troth \'träth, 'trȯth, 'trōth, *or with* th\ *noun* [Middle English *trouth*, from Old English *trēowth* — more at TRUTH] (13th century) **1** : loyal or pledged faithfulness : FIDELITY **2** : one's pledged word; *also* : BETROTHAL

²troth *transitive verb* (15th century) : PLEDGE, BETROTH

¹troth·plight \'träth-ˌplīt, 'trȯth-, 'trōth-\ *transitive verb* (15th century) : BETROTH

²trothplight *noun* (1513) : BETROTHAL

trot·line \'trät-ˌlīn\ *noun* [probably from ²*trot*] (1826) : SETLINE; *especially* : a comparatively short setline used near shore or along streams

trot out *transitive verb* (1838) **1** : to lead out and show the paces of (as a horse) **2** : to bring forward for display ⟨always *trots out* some new excuse⟩

Trots·ky·ism \'trät-skē-ˌi-zəm, 'trȯt-\ *noun* (1925) : the political, economic, and social principles advocated by Trotsky; *especially* : the theory and practice of communism developed by or associated with Trotsky and usually including adherence to the concept of worldwide revolution as opposed to socialism in one country
— **Trots·ky·ist** \-skē-ist\ *noun or adjective*
— **Trots·ky·ite** \-skē-ˌīt\ *noun or adjective*

trot·ter \'trä-tər\ *noun* (14th century) **1** : one that trots; *specifically* : a standardbred horse trained for harness racing **2** : a pig's foot used as food

trou·ba·dour \'trü-bə-ˌdȯr, -ˌdȯr, -ˌdu̇r\ *noun* [French, from Old Provençal *trobador,* from *trobar* to compose, probably from (assumed) Vulgar Latin *tropare,* from Latin *tropus* trope] (circa 1741) : one of a class of lyric poets and poet-musicians often of knightly rank who flourished from the 11th to the end of the 13th century chiefly in the south of France and the north of Italy and whose major theme was courtly love — compare TROUVÈRE

¹trou·ble \'trə-bəl\ *verb* **trou·bled; trou·bling** \'trə-b(ə-)liŋ\ [Middle English, from Old French *tourbler, troubler,* from (assumed) Vulgar Latin *turbulare,* from *turbulus* agitated, alteration of Latin *turbulentus* — more at TURBULENT] (13th century) *transitive verb* **1 a** : to agitate mentally or spiritually : WORRY, DISTURB **b** (1) *archaic* : MISTREAT, OPPRESS (2) : to produce physical disorder in : AFFLICT ⟨*troubled* by a cold⟩ **c** : to put to exertion or inconvenience **2** : to put into confused motion ⟨the wind *troubled* the sea⟩ *intransitive verb*

1 : to become mentally agitated : WORRY ⟨refused to *trouble* over trifles⟩ **2** : to make an effort : be at pains ⟨did not *trouble* to come⟩
— **trou·bler** \-b(ə-)lər\ *noun*

²trouble *noun* (13th century) **1** : the quality or state of being troubled especially mentally **2** : public unrest or disturbance ⟨there's *trouble* brewing downtown⟩ **3** : an instance of trouble ⟨used to disguise her frustrations and despair by making light of her troubles —*Current Biography*⟩ **4** : a state or condition of distress, annoyance, or difficulty ⟨in *trouble* with the law⟩ ⟨heading for *trouble*⟩ ⟨got into financial *trouble*⟩: as **a** : a condition of physical distress or ill health : AILMENT ⟨back *trouble*⟩ ⟨heart *trouble*⟩ **b** : a condition of mechanical malfunction ⟨engine *trouble*⟩ **c** : a condition of doing something badly or only with great difficulty ⟨has *trouble* reading⟩ ⟨has *trouble* breathing⟩ **d** : pregnancy out of wedlock ⟨got a girl in *trouble*⟩ **5** : an effort made : PAINS ⟨took the *trouble* to do it right⟩ **6 a** : a cause of distress, annoyance, or inconvenience ⟨don't mean to be any *trouble*⟩ ⟨what's the *trouble*?⟩ **b** : a negative feature : DRAWBACK ⟨the *trouble* with you is you're too honest⟩ ⟨the main *trouble* with electronic systems is the overreliance on them —John Perham⟩ **c** : the unhappy or sad fact ⟨the *trouble* is, I need the money⟩

trou·bled \'trə-bəld\ *adjective* (14th century) **1 a** : CONCERNED, WORRIED ⟨*troubled* feelings about the decision⟩ **b** : emotionally or mentally disturbed ⟨a home for *troubled* children⟩ **2** : characterized by or indicative of trouble ⟨our *troubled* cities⟩ ⟨a gray and *troubled* sky⟩

trou·ble·mak·er \'trə-bəl-ˌmā-kər\ *noun* (circa 1914) : a person who consciously or unconsciously causes trouble
— **trou·ble·mak·ing** \-kiŋ\ *adjective or noun*

trou·ble·shoot \-ˌshüt\ *verb* **-shot** \-ˌshät\; **-shoot·ing** [back-formation from *troubleshooter*] (1918) *intransitive verb* : to operate or serve as a troubleshooter ⟨is *troubleshooting* for an electronics firm⟩ *transitive verb* : to investigate or deal with in the role of troubleshooter ⟨*troubleshoots* TV receivers⟩

trou·ble·shoot·er \-ˌshü-tər\ *noun* (1905) **1** : a skilled worker employed to locate trouble and make repairs in machinery and technical equipment **2** : an expert in resolving diplomatic or political disputes : a mediator of disputes that are at an impasse **3** : a person skilled at solving or anticipating problems or difficulties

trou·ble·some \-səm\ *adjective* (1542) **1** : DIFFICULT, BURDENSOME **2** : giving trouble or anxiety : VEXATIOUS
— **trou·ble·some·ly** *adverb*
— **trou·ble·some·ness** *noun*

trou·blous \'trə-b(ə-)ləs\ *adjective* (15th century) **1** : full of trouble : STORMY ⟨these *troublous* times⟩ **2** : causing trouble : TROUBLESOME ⟨inflation is a *troublous* matter⟩
— **trou·blous·ly** *adverb*
— **trou·blous·ness** *noun*

trough \'trȯf, 'trȯth, *by bakers often* 'trō\ *noun, plural* **troughs** \'trȯfs, 'trȯvz, 'trȯths, 'trȯ(th)z; 'trōz\ [Middle English, from Old English *trog;* akin to Old High German *trog* trough, Old English *trēow* tree, wood — more at TREE] (before 12th century) **1 a** : a long shallow often V-shaped receptacle for the drinking water or feed of domestic animals **b** : any of various domestic or industrial containers

2 a : a conduit, drain, or channel for water; *especially* : a gutter along the eaves of a building **b** : a long and narrow or shallow channel or depression (as between waves or hills); *especially* : a long but shallow depression in the bed of the sea — compare TRENCH **3** : the minimum point of a complete cycle of a periodic function: as **a** : an elongated area of low barometric pressure **b** : the low point in a business cycle

trounce \'trau̇n(t)s\ *transitive verb* **trounced; trounc·ing** [origin unknown] (1868) : to thrash or punish severely; *especially* : to defeat decisively

¹troupe \'trüp\ *noun* [French, from Middle French — more at TROOP] (1825) : COMPANY, TROOP; *especially* : a group of theatrical performers

²troupe *intransitive verb* **trouped; troup·ing** (1900) : to travel in a troupe; *also* : to perform as a member of a theatrical troupe

troup·er \'trü-pər\ *noun* (1890) **1** : a member of a troupe; *especially* : ACTOR **2** : a person who deals with and persists through difficulty or hardship without complaint ⟨you're a real *trouper* to wait so long⟩

trou·pi·al \'trü-pē-əl\ *noun* [French *troupiale,* from *troupe;* from its living in flocks] (1825) : a large showy oriole (*Icterus icterus*) of Central and South America; *also* : any of various related birds (family Icteridae)

¹trou·ser \'trau̇-zər\ *noun* [alteration of earlier *trouse,* from Scottish Gaelic *triubhas*] (1613) : ³PANT 1 — usually used in plural

²trouser *adjective* (circa 1771) **1** : of, relating to, or designed for trousers ⟨*trouser* pockets⟩ **2** : of or relating to a male dramatic role played by a woman

trouser suit *noun* (1939) *chiefly British* : PANTSUIT

trous·seau \'trü-ˌsō, trü-'\ *noun, plural* **trous·seaux** \-ˌsōz, -'sōz\ *or* **trous·seaus** [French, from Old French, diminutive of *trousse* bundle, from *trousser* to truss] (1833) : the personal possessions of a bride usually including clothes, accessories, and household linens and wares

trout \'trau̇t\ *noun, plural* **trout** *also* **trouts** [Middle English, from Old English *trūht,* from Late Latin *trocta, tructa,* a fish with sharp teeth, from Greek *trōktēs,* literally, gnawer, from *trōgein* to gnaw — more at TROGLODYTE] (before 12th century) **1** : any of various salmonid food and sport fishes that are mostly smaller than the typical salmons and are anadromous or restricted to cool clear fresh waters: **a** : any of various Old or New World fishes (genera *Salmo* and *Oncorhynchus*) — compare BROWN TROUT, RAINBOW TROUT **b** : ¹CHAR **2** : any of various fishes (as the largemouth bass) held to resemble the true trouts

trout lily *noun* [probably from its speckled leaves] (circa 1898) : DOGTOOTH VIOLET

trout–perch \'trau̇t-ˌpərch\ *noun* (1883) : a small freshwater fish (*Percopsis omiscomaycus* of the family Percopsidae) chiefly of northern North America having a scaleless head and large eyes

trouty \'trau̇-tē\ *adjective* **trout·i·er; -est** (1676) : containing or likely to contain abundant trout

trou·vère \trü-'ver\ *noun* [French, from Old French *troveor, troverre,* from *trover* to compose, find, from (assumed) Vulgar Latin *tropare* — more at TROUBADOUR] (1795) : one of a school of poets who flourished from the 11th to the 14th centuries and who composed mostly narrative works (as chansons de geste and fabliaux) — compare TROUBADOUR

trove \'trōv\ *noun* [short for *treasure trove*] (1888)
1 : DISCOVERY, FIND
2 : a valuable collection : TREASURE; *also* : HAUL, COLLECTION

tro·ver \'trō-vər\ *noun* [Middle French *trover* to find, from Old French] (1594)
: a common law action to recover the value of goods wrongfully converted to another's own use

trow \'trō\ *verb* [Middle English, from Old English *trēowan;* akin to Old English *trēowe* faithful, true — more at TRUE] (before 12th century)
1 *obsolete* : BELIEVE
2 *archaic* : THINK

¹**trow·el** \'traú(-ə)l\ *noun* [Middle English *truel,* from Middle French *truelle,* from Late Latin *truella,* from Latin *trulla* ladle] (14th century)
: any of various hand tools used to apply, spread, shape, or smooth loose or plastic material; *also* : a scoop-shaped or flat-bladed garden tool for taking up and setting small plants

trowel: *1* gardener's, *2* plasterer's, *3* bricklayer's

²**trowel** *transitive verb* **-eled** *or* **-elled; -el·ing** *or* **-el·ling** (circa 1670)
: to smooth, mix, or apply with or as if with a trowel
— **trow·el·er** *noun*

troy \'troi\ *adjective* [Middle English *troye,* from *Troyes,* France] (15th century)
: expressed in troy weight

troy weight *noun* (15th century)
: a series of units of weight based on a pound of 12 ounces and an ounce of 480 grains — see WEIGHT table

tru·an·cy \'trü-ən(t)-sē\ *noun, plural* **-cies** (1784)
: an act or instance of playing truant : the state of being truant

¹**tru·ant** \'trü-ənt\ *noun* [Middle English, vagabond, idler, from Old French, vagrant, of Celtic origin; akin to Old Irish *trógán* wretch, *trúag* wretched] (15th century)
: one who shirks duty; *especially* : one who stays out of school without permission

²**truant** *adjective* (1561)
1 : shirking responsibility
2 : being, resembling, or characteristic of a truant

³**truant** *intransitive verb* (1580)
: to idle away time especially while playing truant

truant officer *noun* (1872)
: ATTENDANCE OFFICER

tru·ant·ry \'trü-ən-trē\ *noun, plural* **-ries** (15th century)
: TRUANCY

¹**truce** \'trüs\ *noun* [Middle English *trewes,* plural of *trewe* agreement, from Old English *trēow* fidelity; akin to Old English *trēowe* faithful — more at TRUE] (13th century)
1 : a suspension of fighting especially of considerable duration by agreement of opposing forces : ARMISTICE, CEASE-FIRE
2 : a respite especially from a disagreeable or painful state or action

²**truce** *verb* **truced; truc·ing** (1569)
intransitive verb
: to make a truce
transitive verb
: to end with a truce

¹**truck** \'trək\ *verb* [Middle English *trukken,* from Old French *troquer*] (13th century)
transitive verb
1 : to give in exchange : SWAP
2 : to barter or dispose of by barter
intransitive verb
1 : to exchange commodities : BARTER
2 : to negotiate or traffic especially in an underhanded way : have dealings

²**truck** *noun* (1553)
1 : BARTER
2 : commodities appropriate for barter or for small trade
3 : close association or connection ⟨will have no *truck* with crooks⟩
4 : payment of wages in goods instead of cash
5 : vegetables grown for market
6 : heterogeneous small articles often of little value; *also* : RUBBISH

³**truck** *noun* [probably back-formation from *truckle* small wheel — more at TRUCKLE BED] (1611)
1 : a small wheel; *specifically* : a small strong wheel for a gun carriage
2 : a small wooden cap at the top of a flagstaff or masthead usually having holes for reeving flag or signal halyards
3 : a wheeled vehicle for moving heavy articles: as **a** : a strong horse-drawn or automotive vehicle for hauling **b** : a small barrow consisting of a rectangular frame having at one end a pair of handles and at the other end a pair of small heavy wheels and a projecting edge to slide under a load — called also *hand truck* **c** : a small heavy rectangular frame supported on four wheels for moving heavy objects **d** : a small flat-topped car pushed or pulled by hand **e** : a shelved stand mounted on casters **f** : an automotive vehicle with a short chassis equipped with a swivel for attaching a trailer and used especially for the highway hauling of freight; *also* : a truck with attached trailer
4 a *British* : an open railroad freight car **b** : a swiveling carriage consisting of a frame with one or more pairs of wheels and springs to carry and guide one end (as of a railroad car) in turning sharp curves
— **truck·ful** \-,fül\ *noun*

⁴**truck** (1748)
transitive verb
: to load or transport on a truck
intransitive verb
1 : to transport goods by truck
2 : to be employed in driving a truck
3 : to roll along especially in an easy untroubled way

truck·age \'trə-kij\ *noun* (1830)
1 : conveyance by truck
2 : money paid for conveyance by a truck

¹**truck·er** \'trə-kər\ *noun* [¹*truck*] (1598)
1 : one that barters
2 *Scottish* : PEDDLER

²**trucker** *noun* [⁴*truck*] (1878)
1 : one whose business is transporting goods by truck
2 : a truck driver

truck farm *noun* [²*truck*] (1866)
: a farm devoted to the production of vegetables for the market
— **truck farmer** *noun*

truck·ing *noun* (1809)
: the process or business of transporting goods on trucks

truck·le \'trə-kəl\ *intransitive verb* **truck·led; truck·ling** \-k(ə-)liŋ\ [from the lower position of the truckle bed] (1667)
: to act in a subservient manner : SUBMIT
synonym see FAWN
— **truck·ler** \-k(ə-)lər\ *noun*

truckle bed *noun* [*truckle* small wheel, pulley, from Middle English *trocle,* from Latin *trochlea* block of pulleys — more at TROCHLEA] (15th century)
: TRUNDLE BED

truck·line \'trək-,līn\ *noun* (1924)
: a transportation line using trucks

truck·load \-'lōd, -,lōd\ *noun* (1862)
1 : a load or amount that fills or could fill a truck
2 : the minimum weight required for shipping at truckload rates

truck·man \-mən\ *noun* (1787)
1 : ²TRUCKER
2 : a member of a fire department unit that operates a hook and ladder truck

truck·mas·ter \-,mas-tər\ *noun* (1637)
archaic : an officer in charge of trade with Indians especially among the early settlers

truck stop *noun* (circa 1951)
: a facility especially for truckers that is usually by a highway and that includes a diner, fuel pumps, and a garage

truck system *noun* (1830)
: the system of paying wages in goods instead of cash

tru·cu·lence \'trə-kyə-lən(t)s *also* 'trü-\ *noun* (circa 1727)
: the quality or state of being truculent

tru·cu·len·cy \-lən(t)-sē\ *noun* (1569)
: TRUCULENCE

tru·cu·lent \-lənt\ *adjective* [Latin *truculentus,* from *truc-, trux* savage; perhaps akin to Middle Irish *trú* doomed person] (circa 1540)
1 : feeling or displaying ferocity : CRUEL, SAVAGE
2 : DEADLY, DESTRUCTIVE
3 : scathingly harsh : VITRIOLIC
4 : aggressively self-assertive : BELLIGERENT
— **tru·cu·lent·ly** *adverb*

¹**trudge** \'trəj\ *verb* **trudged; trudg·ing** [origin unknown] (1547)
intransitive verb
: to walk or march steadily and usually laboriously ⟨*trudged* through deep snow⟩
transitive verb
: to trudge along or over
— **trudg·er** *noun*

²**trudge** *noun* (1835)
: a long tiring walk : TRAMP

trud·gen stroke \'trə-jən-\ *noun* [John Trudgen (died 1902) English swimmer] (1893)
: a swimming stroke consisting of alternating overarm strokes and a scissors kick

¹**true** \'trü\ *adjective* **tru·er; tru·est** [Middle English *trewe,* from Old English *trēowe* faithful; akin to Old High German *gitriuwi* faithful, Old Irish *derb* sure, and probably to Sanskrit *dāruṇa* hard, *dāru* wood — more at TREE] (before 12th century)
1 a : STEADFAST, LOYAL **b** : HONEST, JUST **c** *archaic* : TRUTHFUL
2 a (1) : being in accordance with the actual state of affairs ⟨*true* description⟩ (2) : conformable to an essential reality (3) : fully realized or fulfilled ⟨dreams come *true*⟩ **b** : IDEAL, ESSENTIAL **c** : being that which is the case rather than what is manifest or assumed ⟨the *true* dimension of the problem⟩ **d** : CONSISTENT ⟨*true* to character⟩
3 a : properly so called ⟨*true* love⟩ ⟨the *true* faith⟩ ⟨the *true* stomach of ruminant mammals⟩ **b** (1) : possessing the basic characters of and belonging to the same natural group as ⟨a whale is a *true* but not a typical mammal⟩ (2) : TYPICAL ⟨the *true* cats⟩
4 : LEGITIMATE, RIGHTFUL ⟨our *true* and lawful king⟩
5 a : that is fitted or formed or that functions accurately **b** : conformable to a standard or pattern : ACCURATE
6 : determined with reference to the earth's axis rather than the magnetic poles ⟨*true* north⟩
7 : logically necessary
8 : NARROW, STRICT ⟨in the *truest* sense⟩
9 : corrected for error
— **true·ness** *noun*

²**true** *adverb* (14th century)
1 : in accordance with fact or reality
2 a : without deviation ⟨the bullet flew straight and *true*⟩ **b** : without variation from type ⟨breed *true*⟩

³**true** *noun* (1812)
1 : TRUTH, REALITY — usually used with *the*

\ə\ **abut** \ᵊ\ **kitten** \ər\ **further** \a\ **ash** \ā\ **ace**
\ä\ **mop, mar** \aú\ **out** \ch\ **chin** \e\ **bet** \ē\ **easy**
\g\ **go** \i\ **hit** \ī\ **ice** \j\ **job** \ŋ\ **sing** \ō\ **go**
\ò\ **law** \òi\ **boy** \th\ **thin** \th\ **the** \ü\ **loot** \ú\ **foot**
\y\ **yet** \zh\ **vision** *see also* Guide to Pronunciation

2 : the quality or state of being accurate (as in alignment or adjustment) — used in the phrases *in true* and *out of true*

⁴true *transitive verb* **trued; tru·ing** *also* **tru·ing** (1841)
: to make level, square, balanced, or concentric **:** bring or restore to a desired mechanical accuracy or form ⟨*true* up a board⟩ ⟨*true* up an engine cylinder⟩

true believer *noun* (circa 1820)
1 : one who professes absolute belief in something
2 : a zealous supporter of a particular cause

true bill *noun* (1769)
: a bill of indictment endorsed by a grand jury as warranting prosecution of the accused

true–blue *adjective* (1674)
1 : marked by unswerving loyalty (as to a party)
2 : GENUINE ⟨a *true-blue* romantic⟩

true blue *noun* [from the association of blue with constancy] (1762)
: one who is true-blue

true·born \'trü-,bòrn\ *adjective* (1591)
: genuinely such by birth ⟨a *trueborn* Englishman —Shakespeare⟩

true bug *noun* (1895)
: BUG 1c

true–false test \'trü-,fòls-\ *noun* (1924)
: a test consisting of a series of statements to be marked as true or false

true·heart·ed \-'här-təd\ *adjective* (15th century)
: FAITHFUL, LOYAL
— **true·heart·ed·ness** *noun*

true–life \'trü-'līf\ *adjective* (1926)
: true to life ⟨a *true-life* story⟩

true·love \'trü-,ləv\ *noun* (14th century)
: one truly beloved or loving **:** SWEETHEART

true lover's knot *noun* (1615)
: a complicated ornamental knot not readily untied and symbolic of mutual love — called also *truelove knot;* see KNOT illustration

true·pen·ny \'trü-,pe-nē\ *noun* (1595)
: an honest or trusty person

true rib *noun* (1741)
: any of the ribs having costal cartilages connected directly with the sternum and in humans constituting the first seven pairs

true seal *noun* (1923)
: HAIR SEAL

truf·fle \'trə-fəl, 'trü-\ *noun* [modification of Middle French *truffe,* from Old Provençal *trufa,* from (assumed) Vulgar Latin *tufera;* akin to Latin *tuber* swelling, truffle — more at TUBER] (1591)
1 : the usually dark and rugose edible subterranean fruiting body of several European ascomycetous fungi (especially genus *Tuber*); *also* **:** one of these fungi
2 : a candy made of chocolate, butter, sugar, and sometimes liqueur shaped into balls and often coated with cocoa

truf·fled \-fəld\ *adjective* (1837)
: cooked, stuffed, or garnished with truffles

trug \'trəg\ *noun* [origin unknown] (circa 1864) *chiefly British* **:** a shallow rectangular gardening basket

tru·ism \'trü-,i-zəm\ *noun* (1708)
: an undoubted or self-evident truth; *especially* **:** one too obvious for mention
— **tru·is·tic** \trü-'is-tik\ *adjective*

trull \'trəl\ *noun* [German *Trulle,* from Middle High German; akin to Middle High German *trolle* lout — more at TROLL] (1519)
: PROSTITUTE, STRUMPET

tru·ly \'trü-lē\ *adverb* (13th century)
1 a : INDEED — often used as an intensive ⟨*truly,* she is fair⟩ or interjectionally to express astonishment or doubt **b :** without feigning, falsity, or inaccuracy in truth or fact
2 : in all sincerity **:** SINCERELY — often used with *yours* as a complimentary close
3 : in agreement with fact **:** TRUTHFULLY
4 : with exactness of construction or operation
5 : in a proper or suitable manner

¹trump \'trəmp\ *noun* [Middle English *trompe,* from Old French, of Germanic origin; akin to Old High German *trumba, trumpa* trumpet] (14th century)
1 a : TRUMPET **b** *chiefly Scottish* **:** JEW'S HARP
2 : a sound of or as if of trumpeting ⟨the *trump* of doom⟩

²trump *noun* [alteration of ¹*triumph*] (1529)
1 a : a card of a suit any of whose cards will win over a card that is not of this suit **b :** the suit whose cards are trumps for a particular hand — often used in plural
2 : a decisive overriding factor or final resource
3 : a dependable and exemplary person

³trump (1586)
transitive verb
1 : to get the better of **:** OUTDO
2 : to play a trump on (a card or trick) when another suit was led
intransitive verb
: to play a trump when another suit was led

trump card *noun* (1822)
: ²TRUMP 1a, 2

trumped–up \'trəm(p)t-'əp\ *adjective* (1728)
: fraudulently concocted **:** SPURIOUS ⟨*trumped-up* charges⟩

trum·pery \'trəm-p(ə-)rē\ *noun* [Middle English *tromperie* deceit, from Middle French, from *tromper* to deceive] (15th century)
1 a : worthless nonsense **b :** trivial or useless articles **:** JUNK ⟨a wagon loaded with household *trumpery* —Washington Irving⟩
2 *archaic* **:** tawdry finery
— **trumpery** *adjective*

¹trum·pet \'trəm-pət\ *noun* [Middle English *trompette,* from Middle French, from Old French *trompe* trump] (14th century)
1 a : a wind instrument consisting of a conical or cylindrical usually metal tube, a cup-shaped mouthpiece, and a flared

trumpet 1a

bell; *specifically* **:** a valved brass instrument having a cylindrical tube with two turns and a usual range from F sharp below middle C upward for 2½ octaves **b :** a musical instrument (as a cornet) resembling a trumpet
2 : a trumpet player
3 : something that resembles a trumpet or its tonal quality: as **a :** a funnel-shaped instrument (as a megaphone) for collecting, directing, or intensifying sound **b** (1) **:** a stentorian voice (2) **:** a penetrating cry (as of an elephant)
— **trum·pet·like** *adjective*

²trumpet (1530)
intransitive verb
1 : to blow a trumpet
2 : to make a sound suggestive of that of a trumpet
transitive verb
: to sound or proclaim on or as if on a trumpet

trumpet creeper *noun* (1818)
: a North American woody vine (*Campsis radicans* of the family Bignoniaceae, the trumpet-creeper family) having pinnate leaves and large typically red trumpet-shaped flowers

trum·pet·er \'trəm-pə-tər\ *noun* (15th century)
1 a : a trumpet player; *specifically* **:** one that gives signals with a trumpet **b :** one that praises or advocates **:** EULOGIST, SPOKESMAN

trumpet creeper

2 a : any of a genus (*Psophia* of the family Psophiidae) of several large gregarious long-legged long-necked South American birds related to the cranes **b :** any of an Asian breed of pigeons with a rounded crest and heavily feathered feet

trumpeter swan *noun* (1834)
: a rare pure white North American wild swan (*Cygnus buccinator*) that is noted for its sonorous voice and is sometimes considered a subspecies (*C. cygnus buccinator*) of the whooper swan

trumpet flower *noun* (circa 1731)
1 : any of various plants (as a trumpet creeper or a datura) with trumpet-shaped flowers
2 : the flower of a trumpet flower

trumpet honeysuckle *noun* (1731)
: a North American honeysuckle (*Lonicera sempervirens*) with coral-red or orange flowers having a trumpet-shaped corolla

trumpet vine *noun* (1709)
: TRUMPET CREEPER

trump up *transitive verb* (1695)
1 : to concoct especially with intent to deceive **:** FABRICATE, INVENT
2 *archaic* **:** to cite as support for an action or claim

¹trun·cate \'trəŋ-,kāt, 'trən-\ *adjective* [Latin *truncatus,* past participle of *truncare* to shorten, from *truncus* trunk] (1716)
: having the end square or even ⟨the *truncate* leaves of the tulip tree⟩

²truncate *transitive verb* **trun·cat·ed; trun·cat·ing** (circa 1727)
1 : to shorten by or as if by cutting off
2 : to replace (an edge or corner of a crystal) by a plane
— **trun·ca·tion** \trəŋ-'kā-shən, trən-\ *noun*

trun·cat·ed \-,kā-təd\ *adjective* (circa 1704)
1 : having the apex replaced by a plane section and especially by one parallel to the base ⟨*truncated* cone⟩
2 a : cut short **:** CURTAILED **b :** lacking an expected or normal element (as a syllable) at the beginning or end **:** CATALECTIC

¹trun·cheon \'trən-chən\ *noun* [Middle English *tronchoun,* from Middle French *tronchon,* from (assumed) Vulgar Latin *truncion-, truncio,* from Latin *truncus* trunk] (14th century)
1 : a shattered spear or lance
2 a *obsolete* **:** CLUB, BLUDGEON **b :** BATON 2 **c :** a police officer's billy club

²truncheon *transitive verb* (1597)
archaic **:** to beat with a truncheon

¹trun·dle \'trən-dºl\ *verb* **trun·dled; trun·dling** \'trən(d)-liŋ, 'trən-dºl-iŋ\ [²*trundle*] (1598)
transitive verb
1 a : to propel by causing to rotate **:** ROLL **b** *archaic* **:** to cause to revolve **:** SPIN
2 : to transport in or as if in a wheeled vehicle **:** HAUL, WHEEL
intransitive verb
1 : to progress by revolving
2 : to move on or as if on wheels **:** ROLL
— **trun·dler** \'trən(d)-lər, 'trən-dºl-ər\ *noun*

²trundle *noun* [from *trundle* small wheel, alteration of earlier *trendle,* from Middle English, circle, ring, wheel, from Old English *trendel;* akin to Old English *trendan* to revolve — more at TREND] (1851)
1 : TRUNDLE BED
2 : the motion or sound of something rolling
3 : a round or oval wooden tub

trundle bed *noun* (1542)
: a low bed usually on casters that can be rolled or slid under a higher bed when not in use — called also *truckle bed*

trun·dle–tail \'trən-dºl-,tāl\ *noun* (15th century)
archaic **:** a curly-tailed dog

trunk \'trəŋk\ *noun* [Middle English *tronke* box, trunk, from Middle French *tronc,* from Latin *truncus* trunk, torso] (15th century)
1 a : the main stem of a tree apart from limbs and roots — called also *bole* **b** (1) **:** the human or animal body apart from the head and appendages **:** TORSO (2) **:** the thorax of an insect **c :** the central part of anything; *specifically* **:** the shaft of a column or pilaster

2 a (1) : a large rigid piece of luggage used usually for transporting clothing and personal effects (2) : the luggage compartment of an automobile **b** (1) : a superstructure over a ship's hatches usually level with the poop deck (2) : the part of the cabin of a boat projecting above the deck (3) : the housing for a centerboard or rudder
3 : PROBOSCIS; *especially* : the long muscular proboscis of the elephant
4 *plural* : men's shorts worn chiefly for sports
5 a : a usually major channel or passage (as a chute or shaft) **b** : a circuit between two telephone exchanges for making connections between subscribers; *broadly* : a usually electronic path over which information is transmitted (as between computer memories)
6 a : the principal channel of a tributary system ⟨an arterial *trunk*⟩ ⟨*trunk* of a river⟩ **b** : TRUNK LINE
— **trunk·ful** \'trəŋk-ˌfu̇l\ *noun*
trunked \'trəŋ(k)t\ *adjective* (1640)
: having a trunk especially of a specified kind — usually used in combination ⟨a gray-*trunked* tree⟩
trunk·fish \'trəŋk-ˌfish\ *noun* (circa 1804)
: any of numerous small often bright-colored bony fishes (family Ostraciidae) of tropical seas with the body and head enclosed in a bony carapace
trunk hose \'trəŋk-\ *noun plural* [probably from obsolete English *trunk* to truncate] (1637)
: short full breeches reaching about halfway down the thigh that were worn chiefly in the late 16th and early 17th centuries
trunk line *noun* (1843)
1 : a transportation system (as an airline, railroad, or highway) handling long-distance through traffic
2 a : a main supply channel (as for gas or oil) **b** : TRUNK 5b
trun·nel \'trə-nᵊl\ *variant of* TREENAIL
trun·nion \'trən-yən\ *noun* [French *trognon* core, stump] (circa 1625)
: a pin or pivot on which something can be rotated or tilted; *especially* : either of two opposite gudgeons on which a cannon is swiveled
¹truss \'trəs\ *transitive verb* [Middle English, from Old French *trousser, tourser* to bundle, pack, from (assumed) Vulgar Latin *torsare*, from *torsus* twisted — more at TORSADE] (13th century)
1 a : to secure tightly : BIND **b** : to arrange for cooking by binding close the wings or legs of (a fowl)
2 : to support, strengthen, or stiffen by or as if by a truss
— **truss·er** *noun*
²truss *noun* (13th century)
1 : an iron band around a lower mast with an attachment by which a yard is secured to the mast
2 a : BRACKET 1 **b** : an assemblage of members (as beams) forming a rigid framework
3 : a device worn to reduce a hernia by pressure
4 : a compact flower or fruit cluster
truss bridge *noun* (1840)
: a bridge supported mainly by trusses — see BRIDGE illustration
truss·ing \'trə-siŋ\ *noun* (1840)
1 : the members forming a truss
2 : the trusses and framework of a structure
¹trust \'trəst\ *noun* [Middle English, probably of Scandinavian origin; akin to Old Norse *traust* trust; akin to Old English *trēowe* faithful — more at TRUE] (13th century)
1 a : assured reliance on the character, ability, strength, or truth of someone or something **b** : one in which confidence is placed
2 a : dependence on something future or contingent : HOPE **b** : reliance on future payment for property (as merchandise) delivered : CREDIT

3 a : a property interest held by one person for the benefit of another **b** : a combination of firms or corporations formed by a legal agreement; *especially* : one that reduces or threatens to reduce competition
4 *archaic* : TRUSTWORTHINESS
5 a (1) : a charge or duty imposed in faith or confidence or as a condition of some relationship (2) : something committed or entrusted to one to be used or cared for in the interest of another **b** : responsible charge or office **c** : CARE, CUSTODY ⟨the child committed to her *trust*⟩
— **in trust** : in the care or possession of a trustee
²trust (13th century)
intransitive verb
1 a : to place confidence : DEPEND ⟨*trust* in God⟩ ⟨*trust* to luck⟩ **b** : to be confident : HOPE
2 : to sell or deliver on credit
transitive verb
1 a : to commit or place in one's care or keeping : ENTRUST **b** : to permit to stay or go or to do something without fear or misgiving
2 a : to rely on the truthfulness or accuracy of : BELIEVE **b** : to place confidence in : rely on **c** : to hope or expect confidently
3 : to extend credit to
— **trust·abil·i·ty** \ˌtrəs-tə-'bi-lə-tē\ *noun*
— **trust·able** \'trəs-tə-bəl\ *adjective*
— **trust·er** *noun*
— **trust·ing·ly** \'trəs-tiŋ-lē\ *adverb*
— **trust·ing·ness** *noun*
trust-bust·er \'trəs(t)-ˌbəs-tər\ *noun* (1903)
: one who seeks to break up business trusts; *specifically* : a federal official who prosecutes trusts under the antitrust laws
— **trust–bust·ing** \-tiŋ\ *noun*
trust company *noun* (1834)
: an incorporated trustee; *broadly* : a corporation that functions as a corporate and personal trustee and usually also engages in the normal activities of a commercial bank
¹trust·ee \ˌtrəs-'tē\ *noun* (1647)
1 a : one to whom something is entrusted **b** : a country charged with the supervision of a trust territory
2 a : a natural or legal person to whom property is legally committed to be administered for the benefit of a beneficiary (as a person or a charitable organization) **b** : one (as a corporate director) occupying a position of trust and performing functions comparable to those of a trustee
²trustee *verb* **trust·eed; trust·ee·ing** (1818)
transitive verb
: to commit to the care of a trustee
intransitive verb
: to serve as trustee
trust·ee·ship \ˌtrəs-'tē-ˌship\ *noun* (circa 1736)
1 : the office or function of a trustee
2 : supervisory control by one or more countries over a trust territory
trust·ful \'trəst-fəl\ *adjective* (1834)
: full of trust : CONFIDING
— **trust·ful·ly** \-fə-lē\ *adverb*
— **trust·ful·ness** *noun*
trust fund *noun* (1780)
: property (as money or securities) settled or held in trust
trust·less \'trəst-ləs\ *adjective* (circa 1530)
1 : not deserving of trust : FAITHLESS
2 : DISTRUSTFUL
trust territory *noun* (1945)
: a non-self-governing territory placed under an administrative authority by the Trusteeship Council of the United Nations
trust·wor·thy \'trəst-ˌwər-the̅\ *adjective* (1829)
: worthy of confidence : DEPENDABLE
— **trust·wor·thi·ly** \-thə-lē\ *adverb*
— **trust·wor·thi·ness** *noun*
¹trusty \'trəs-tē\ *adjective* **trust·i·er; -est** (14th century)

: TRUSTWORTHY, DEPENDABLE
— **trust·i·ness** *noun*
²trusty \'trəs-tē *also* ˌtrəs-'tē\ *noun, plural* **trust·ies** (1573)
: a trusty or trusted person; *specifically* : a convict considered trustworthy and allowed special privileges
truth \'trüth\ *noun, plural* **truths** \'trüthz, 'trüths\ [Middle English *trewthe*, from Old English *trēowth* fidelity; akin to Old English *trēowe* faithful — more at TRUE] (before 12th century)
1 a *archaic* : FIDELITY, CONSTANCY **b** : sincerity in action, character, and utterance
2 a (1) : the state of being the case : FACT (2) : the body of real things, events, and facts : ACTUALITY (3) *often capitalized* : a transcendent fundamental or spiritual reality **b** : a judgment, proposition, or idea that is true or accepted as true ⟨*truths* of thermodynamics⟩ **c** : the body of true statements and propositions
3 a : the property (as of a statement) of being in accord with fact or reality **b** *chiefly British* : TRUE 2 **c** : fidelity to an original or to a standard
4 *capitalized, Christian Science* : GOD
— **in truth** : in accordance with fact : ACTUALLY
truth·ful \'trüth-fəl\ *adjective* (1596)
: telling or disposed to tell the truth
— **truth·ful·ly** \-fə-lē\ *adverb*
— **truth·ful·ness** *noun*
truth serum *noun* (1925)
: a hypnotic or anesthetic held to induce a subject under questioning to talk freely
truth set *noun* (1940)
: a mathematical or logical set containing all the elements that make a given statement of relationships true when substituted in it ⟨the equation $x + 7 = 10$ has as its *truth set* the single number 3⟩
truth table *noun* (1921)
: a table that shows the truth-value of a compound statement for every truth-value of its component statements; *also* : a similar table (as for a computer logic circuit) showing the value of the output for each value of each input

TRUTH TABLE

a statement	a statement	not p denial	p and q conjunction	p or q (inclusive) inclusive disjunction	p or q (exclusive) exclusive disjunction	if p then q conditional	p if and only if q biconditional
p	q	$\sim p$	$p \cdot q$	$p \lor q$		$p \supset q$	$p \equiv q$
T	T	F	T	T	F	T	T
T	F	F	F	T	T	F	F
F	T	T	F	T	T	T	F
F	F	T	F	F	F	T	T

T = true F = false

truth–value *noun* (1903)
: the truth or falsity of a proposition or statement
¹try \'trī\ *verb* **tried; try·ing** [Middle English *trien*, from Anglo-French *trier*, from Old French, to pick out, sift, probably from Late

Latin *tritare* to grind, frequentative of Latin *terere* to rub — more at THROW] (14th century)
transitive verb
1 a : to examine or investigate judicially **b** (1) **:** to conduct the trial of (2) **:** to participate as counsel in the judicial examination of
2 a : to put to test or trial ⟨*try* one's luck⟩ — often used with *out* **b :** to subject to something (as undue strain or excessive hardship or provocation) that tests the powers of endurance **c :** DEMONSTRATE, PROVE
3 a *obsolete* **:** PURIFY, REFINE **b :** to melt down and procure in a pure state **:** RENDER ⟨*try* out whale oil from blubber⟩
4 : to fit or finish with accuracy
5 : to make an attempt at — often used with an infinitive
intransitive verb
: to make an attempt □
synonym see AFFLICT, ATTEMPT
— try one's hand : to attempt something for the first time
²**try** *noun, plural* **tries** (1607)
1 : an experimental trial **:** ATTEMPT
2 : a play in rugby that is similar to a touchdown in football, scores usually four points, and entitles the scoring side to attempt a placekick at the goal for additional points; *also* **:** the score made on a try
try for point (1929)
: an attempt made after scoring a touchdown in football to score one or two additional points by kicking the ball over the crossbar or again carrying it into the opponents' end zone
try·ing \'trī-iŋ\ *adjective* (1718)
: severely straining the powers of endurance
— try·ing·ly \-iŋ-lē\ *adverb*
try on *transitive verb* (1693)
1 : to put on (a garment) in order to test the fit
2 : to use or test experimentally
— try–on \'trī-ˌȯn, -ˌän\ *noun*
try·out \'trī-ˌau̇t\ *noun* (1903)
: an experimental performance or demonstration: as **a :** a test of the ability (as of an athlete or actor) to fill a part or meet standards **b :** a performance of a play prior to its official opening to determine response and discover weaknesses
try out *intransitive verb* (1909)
: to compete for a position especially on an athletic team or for a part in a play
try·pano·some \tri-'pa-nə-ˌsōm\ *noun* [New Latin *Trypanosoma*, from Greek *trypanon* auger + New Latin -*soma* -some — more at TREPAN] (1903)
: any of a genus (*Trypanosoma*) of parasitic flagellate protozoans that infest the blood of various vertebrates including humans, are usually transmitted by the bite of an insect, and include some that cause serious disease (as sleeping sickness)
try·pano·so·mi·a·sis \tri-ˌpa-nə-sə-'mī-ə-səs\ *noun, plural* -**a·ses** \-ˌsēz\ [New Latin] (1902)
: infection with or disease caused by trypanosomes
try-pot \'trī-ˌpät\ *noun* (1795)
: a metallic pot used on a whaler or on shore to render whale oil from blubber
tryp·sin \'trip-sən\ *noun* [perhaps from Greek *tryein* to wear down + English pe*psin;* akin to Latin *terere* to rub — more at THROW] (1876)
: a proteolytic enzyme from pancreatic juice active in an alkaline medium — compare CHYMOTRYPSIN
tryp·sin·o·gen \trip-'si-nə-jən\ *noun* [International Scientific Vocabulary] (circa 1890)
: the inactive substance released by the pancreas into the duodenum to form trypsin
trypt·amine \'trip-tə-ˌmēn\ *noun* [*trypt*ophan + *amine*] (1929)
: a crystalline amine $C_{10}H_{12}N_2$ derived from tryptophan
tryp·tic \'trip-tik\ *adjective* [International Scientific Vocabulary, from *trypsin*] (1888)

: of, relating to, or produced by trypsin or its action
tryp·to·phan \'trip-tə-ˌfan\ *also* **tryp·to·phane** \-ˌfān\ *noun* [International Scientific Vocabulary *tryp*tic + -*o*- + -*phane*] (1890)
: a crystalline essential amino acid $C_{11}H_{12}N_2O_2$ that is widely distributed in proteins
try·sail \'trī-ˌsāl, -səl\ *noun* [obsolete *at try* lying to] (1769)
: a fore-and-aft sail bent to a gaff and hoisted on a lower mast or a small mast close abaft
try square *noun* (circa 1877)
: an instrument consisting of two straightedges fixed at right angles to each other and used for laying off right angles and testing whether work is square
¹**tryst** \'trist, *especially British* 'trīst\ *noun* [Middle English, from Middle French *triste* watch post, probably of Scandinavian origin; akin to Old Norse *traust* trust] (14th century)
1 : an agreement (as between lovers) to meet
2 : an appointed meeting or meeting place
²**tryst** *intransitive verb* (14th century)
: to make or keep a tryst
— tryst·er \'tris-tər, 'trīs-\ *noun*
try·works \'trī-ˌwərks\ *noun plural* (1792)
: a brick furnace in which try-pots are placed; *also* **:** the furnace with the pots
tsa·de \'(t)sä-də, -dē\ *variant of* SADHE
tsar \'zär, '(t)sär\ *variant of* CZAR
tset·se fly \'(t)set-sē-, 'tet-, '(t)sēt-, 'tēt-\ *noun* [Afrikaans, from Tswana *tsètsè* fly] (1865)
: any of several dipteran flies (genus *Glossina*) that occur in Africa south of the Sahara and include vectors of human and animal trypanosomes — called also *tsetse;* compare SLEEPING SICKNESS
Tshi \'chwē, chə-'wē, 'twē, 'chē\ *variant of* TWI
Tshi·lu·ba \chi-'lü-bə\ *noun* (circa 1961)
: a Bantu language used as a lingua franca in southeastern Zaire
T–shirt \'tē-ˌshərt\ *noun* (1920)
: a collarless short-sleeved or sleeveless usually cotton undershirt; *also* **:** an outer shirt of similar design
— T–shirt·ed *adjective*
T square *noun* (1785)
: a ruler with a crosspiece or head at one end used in making parallel lines
tsu·na·mi \(t)su̇-'nä-mē\ *noun, plural* **tsuna·mis** *also* **tsunami** [Japanese, from *tsu* harbor + *nami* wave] (1897)
: a great sea wave produced by submarine earth movement or volcanic eruption **:** TIDAL WAVE
— tsu·na·mic \-mik\ *adjective*
tsu·tsu·ga·mu·shi disease \ˌ(t)süt-sə-gə-'mü-shē-, ˌtüt-\ *noun* [Japanese *tsutsugamushi* scrub typhus mite, from *tsutsuga* sickness + *mushi* insect] (1906)
: an acute febrile bacterial disease that is caused by a rickettsia (*Rickettsia tsutsugamushi*) transmitted by mite larvae, resembles louse-borne typhus, and is widespread in the western Pacific area — called also *scrub typhus, tsutsugamushi*
Tswa·na \'(t)swä-nə\ *noun, plural* **Tswana** *or* **Tswanas** (1937)
1 : the language of the Tswana people
2 : a member of a Bantu-speaking people of Botswana and the Republic of South Africa
t–test \'tē-ˌtest\ *noun* (1932)
: a statistical test involving confidence limits for the random variable t of a t distribution and used especially in testing hypotheses about means of normal distributions when the standard deviations are unknown
T₃ *also* **T–3** \'tē-'thrē\ *noun* [*T*, abbreviation for *thyronine* + *3*, number of iodine atoms attached to the thyronine nucleus] (1956)
: TRIIODOTHYRONINE
Tua·reg \'twä-ˌreg\ *noun, plural* **Tuareg** *or* **Tuaregs** [Arabic *Tawāriq*] (1821)
: a member of a nomadic people of the central and western Sahara and along the middle Niger from Tombouctou to Nigeria

tu·a·ta·ra \ˌtü-ə-'tär-ə\ *noun* [Maori *tuatàra*] (1890)
: a large spiny quadrupedal reptile (*Sphenodon punctatum*) of islands off the coast of New Zealand that has a vestigial third eye in the mid-

tuatara

dle of the forehead representing the pineal gland and that is the only surviving rhynchocephalian
¹**tub** \'təb\ *noun* [Middle English *tubbe*, from Middle Dutch; akin to Middle Low German *tubbe* tub] (14th century)
1 a : a wide low vessel originally formed with wooden staves, round bottom, and hoops **b :** a small round container in which a product is sold ⟨a *tub* of oleo⟩
2 : an old or slow boat
3 : BATHTUB; *also* **:** BATH
4 : the amount that a tub will hold
— tub·ful \-ˌfu̇l\ *noun*
— tub·like \-ˌlīk\ *adjective*
²**tub** *verb* **tubbed; tub·bing** (1610)
transitive verb
1 : to wash or bathe in a tub
2 : to put or store in a tub
intransitive verb
1 : BATHE
2 : to undergo washing
— tub·ba·ble \'tə-bə-bəl\ *adjective*
— tub·ber *noun*
tu·ba \'tü-bə, 'tyü-\ *noun* [Italian, from Latin, trumpet] (1852)
: a large low-pitched brass instrument usually oval in shape and having a conical tube, a cup-shaped mouthpiece, and a usual range an octave lower than that of the euphonium
— tu·ba·ist \-bə-(i)st\ *or* **tub·ist** \-bist\ *noun*
tub·al \'tü-bəl, 'tyü-\ *adjective* (circa 1736)

tuba

: of, relating to, or involving a tube and especially a fallopian tube ⟨*tubal* infection⟩

tubal ligation *noun* (1948)
: ligation of the fallopian tubes to prevent passage of ova from the ovaries to the uterus used as a method of female sterilization

tub·by \ˈtə-bē\ *adjective* **tub·bi·er; -est** (circa 1807)
1 : sounding dull and without proper resonance or freedom of sound ⟨a *tubby* violin⟩
2 : PUDGY, FAT

tube \ˈtüb, ˈtyüb\ *noun* [French, from Latin *tubus*; akin to Latin *tuba* trumpet] (1651)
1 : any of various usually cylindrical structures or devices: as **a** : a hollow elongated cylinder; *especially* : one to convey fluids **b** : a soft tubular container whose contents (as toothpaste) can be removed by squeezing **c** (1) : TUNNEL (2) *British* : SUBWAY b **d** : the basically cylindrical section between the mouthpiece and bell that is the fundamental part of a wind instrument
2 a : a slender channel within a plant or animal body : DUCT — compare FALLOPIAN TUBE **b** : the narrow basal portion of a gamopetalous corolla or a calyx with united sepals
3 : INNER TUBE
4 a : ELECTRON TUBE; *especially* : VACUUM TUBE **b** : CATHODE-RAY TUBE; *especially* : a television picture tube **c** : TELEVISION
5 : an article of clothing shaped like a tube ⟨*tube* top⟩ ⟨*tube* socks⟩
— **tubed** \ˈtübd, ˈtyübd\ *adjective*
— **tube·like** \ˈtüb-ˌlīk, ˈtyüb-\ *adjective*
— **down the tube** *or* **down the tubes** : into a state of collapse, deterioration, or ruin

tube foot *noun* (1888)
: one of the small flexible tubular processes of most echinoderms that are extensions of the water-vascular system and are used especially in locomotion and grasping

tube·less \ˈtü-bləs, ˈtyü-\ *adjective* (1855)
: lacking a tube; *specifically* : being a pneumatic tire that does not depend on an inner tube for airtightness

tube nucleus *noun* (1939)
: the one of the two nuclei formed by mitotic division of a microspore during the formation of a pollen grain that is held to control subsequent growth of the pollen tube and that does not divide again — compare GENERATIVE NUCLEUS

tube pan *noun* (1926)
: a round cake pan having a hollow tube in the center

tu·ber \ˈtü-bər, ˈtyü-\ *noun* [Latin, swelling, truffle; perhaps akin to Latin *tumēre* to swell — more at THUMB] (1668)
1 a : a short fleshy usually underground stem bearing minute scale leaves each of which bears a bud in its axil and is potentially able to produce a new plant — compare BULB, CORM **b** : a fleshy root or rhizome resembling a tuber
2 : an anatomical prominence : TUBEROSITY

tu·ber·cle \ˈtü-bər-kəl, ˈtyü-\ *noun* [Latin *tuberculum*, diminutive of *tuber*] (1578)
1 : a small knobby prominence or excrescence especially on a plant or animal : NODULE: as **a** : a protuberance near the head of a rib that articulates with the transverse process of a vertebra **b** : any of several prominences in the central nervous system **c** : NODULE b
2 : a small abnormal discrete lump in the substance of an organ or in the skin; *especially* : the specific lesion of tuberculosis

tubercle bacillus *noun* (circa 1890)
: a bacterium (*Mycobacterium tuberculosis*) that is a major cause of tuberculosis

tubercul- *combining form* [New Latin, from Latin *tuberculum*]
1 : tubercle ⟨*tubercular*⟩
2 : tubercle bacillus ⟨*tubercu*lin⟩
3 : tuberculosis ⟨*tubercu*loid⟩

¹tu·ber·cu·lar \tü-ˈbər-kyə-lər, tyü-\ *adjective* (1799)

1 a : of, relating to, or affected with tuberculosis : TUBERCULOUS **b** : caused by the tubercle bacillus ⟨*tubercular* meningitis⟩
2 : characterized by lesions that are or resemble tubercles ⟨*tubercular* leprosy⟩
3 : relating to, resembling, or constituting a tubercle : TUBERCULATED

²tubercular *noun* (1925)
: a person with tuberculosis

tu·ber·cu·lat·ed \tü-ˈbər-kyə-ˌlā-təd, tyü-\ *also* **tu·ber·cu·late** \-lət\ *adjective* (1771)
: having tubercles : characterized by or beset with tubercles

tu·ber·cu·lin \tü-ˈbər-kyə-lən, tyü-\ *noun* [International Scientific Vocabulary] (circa 1890)
: a sterile liquid containing the growth products of or specific substances extracted from the tubercle bacillus and used in the diagnosis of tuberculosis especially in children and cattle

tuberculin test *noun* (circa 1900)
: a test for hypersensitivity to tuberculin as an indication of past or present tubercular infection

tu·ber·cu·loid \tü-ˈbər-kyə-ˌloid, tyü-\ *adjective* [International Scientific Vocabulary] (circa 1923)
: resembling tuberculosis especially in the presence of tubercles ⟨*tuberculoid* leprosy⟩

tu·ber·cu·lo·sis \tü-ˌbər-kyə-ˈlō-səs, tyü-\ *noun, plural* **-lo·ses** \-ˌsēz\ [New Latin] (1860)
: a highly variable communicable disease of humans and some other vertebrates caused by the tubercle bacillus and rarely in the U.S. by a related mycobacterium (*Mycobacterium bovis*) and characterized by toxic symptoms or allergic manifestations which in humans primarily affect the lungs

tu·ber·cu·lous \tü-ˈbər-kyə-ləs, tyü-\ *adjective* (1891)
1 : constituting or affected with tuberculosis ⟨a *tuberculous* process⟩
2 : caused by or resulting from the presence or products of the tubercle bacillus ⟨*tuberculous* peritonitis⟩

tube·rose \ˈtü-ˌbrōz, ˈtyü-, *also* -bə-ˌrōz, -bə-ˌrōs\ *noun* [New Latin *tuberosa*, specific epithet, from Latin, feminine of *tuberosus* tuberous, from *tuber* tuber] (1664)
: a Mexican bulbous herb (*Polianthes tuberosa*) of the agave family cultivated for its spike of fragrant white single or double flowers

tu·ber·os·i·ty \ˌtü-bə-ˈrä-sə-tē, ˌtyü-\ *noun, plural* **-ties** (1611)
: a rounded prominence; *especially* : a large prominence on a bone usually serving for the attachment of muscles or ligaments

tu·ber·ous \ˈtü-b(ə-)rəs, ˈtyü-\ *adjective* (1650)
1 : consisting of, bearing, or resembling a tuber
2 : of, relating to, or being a plant tuber or tuberous root of a plant

tuberous root *noun* (circa 1668)
: a thick fleshy storage root like a tuber but lacking buds or scale leaves
— **tuberous–rooted** *adjective*

tube worm *noun* (circa 1819)
: a worm that lives in a tube: as **a** : any of various polychaetes or oligochaetes **b** : a pogonophoran and especially an extremely large one that is found near deep-ocean hydrothermal vents

tu·bi·fex \ˈtü-bə-ˌfeks, ˈtyü-\ *noun* [New Latin *Tubific-, Tubifex,* from Latin *tubus* tube + *facere* to make — more at DO] (1948)
: any of a genus (*Tubifex*) of slender reddish oligochaete worms that live in tubes in fresh or brackish water and are widely used as food for aquarium fish

tu·bi·fi·cid \tü-ˈbi-fə-səd, tyü-; ˌt(y)ü-bə-ˈfi-səd\ *noun* [New Latin *Tubificidae,* from *Tubific-, Tubifex*] (1950)

: any of a family (Tubificidae) of aquatic oligochaetes including the tubifex worms
— **tubificid** *adjective*

tub·ing \ˈtü-biŋ, ˈtyü-\ *noun* (1845)
1 : material in the form of a tube; *also* : a length or piece of tube
2 : a series or system of tubes

tu·bo·cu·ra·rine \ˌtü-bō-kyù-ˈrär-ən, ˌtyü-, -ˌēn\ *noun* [International Scientific Vocabulary *tubo-* (from Latin *tubus* tube) + *curare* + *-ine*; from its being shipped in sections of hollow bamboo] (1898)
: a toxic alkaloid or its crystalline hydrated hydrochloride salt $C_{37}H_{42}Cl_2N_2O_6 \cdot 5H_2O$ that is obtained chiefly from the bark and stems of a South American vine (*Chondrodendron tomentosum* of the family Menispermaceae) and in its dextrorotatory form constitutes the chief active constituent of curare and is used especially as a skeletal muscle relaxant

tub–thump·er \ˈtəb-ˌthəm-pər\ *noun* (1662)
: a vociferous supporter (as of a cause)
— **tub–thump** \-ˌthəmp\ *verb*

tu·bu·lar \ˈtü-byə-lər, ˈtyü-\ *adjective* (1673)
1 a : having the form of or consisting of a tube ⟨a *tubular* calyx⟩ **b** : made or provided with tubes
2 : of, relating to, or sounding as if produced through tubes

tu·bule \ˈtü-(ˌ)byü(ə)l, ˈtyü-\ *noun* [Latin *tubulus*, diminutive of *tubus*] (1677)
: a small tube; *especially* : a slender elongated anatomical channel

tu·bu·lin \ˈtü-byə-lən, ˈtyü-\ *noun* [*tubule* + ¹*-in*] (1968)
: a globular protein that polymerizes to form microtubules

tu·chun \ˈdü-ˈjün, -ˈjēn\ *noun* [Chinese (Beijing) *dūjūn*] (1917)
1 : a Chinese military governor (as of a province)
2 : a Chinese warlord

¹tuck \ˈtək\ *verb* [Middle English *tuken* to pull up sharply, scold, from Old English *tūcian* to ill-treat; akin to Old High German *zuhhen* to jerk, Old English *togian* to pull — more at TOW] (15th century)
transitive verb
1 a : to pull up into a fold **b** : to make a tuck in
2 : to put into a snug often concealing or isolating place ⟨cottage *tucked* away in the hill⟩
3 a : to push in the loose end of so as to hold tightly ⟨*tuck* in your shirt⟩ **b** : to cover by tucking in bedclothes — usually used with *in*
4 : EAT — usually used with *away* or *in* ⟨*tucked* away a big lunch⟩
5 : to put into a tuck position
intransitive verb
1 : to draw together into tucks or folds
2 : to eat or drink heartily — usually used with *into* ⟨*tucked* into their beer and pretzels⟩
3 : to fit snugly

²tuck *noun* (1532)
1 : a fold stitched into cloth to shorten, decorate, or control fullness
2 : the part of a vessel where the ends of the lower planks meet under the stern
3 a : an act or instance of tucking **b** : something tucked or to be tucked in
4 a : a body position (as in diving) in which the knees are bent, the thighs drawn tightly to the chest, and the hands clasped around the shins **b** : a skiing position in which the skier squats forward and holds the ski poles under the arms and parallel to the ground
5 : a cosmetic surgical operation for the removal of excess skin or fat from a body part ⟨a tummy *tuck*⟩

\ə\ **abut** \ᵊ\ **kitten** \ər\ **further** \a\ **ash** \ā\ **ace**
\ä\ **mop, mar** \au\ **out** \ch\ **chin** \e\ **bet** \ē\ **easy**
\g\ **go** \i\ **hit** \ī\ **ice** \j\ **job** \ŋ\ **sing** \ō\ **go**
\o\̇ **law** \oi\ **boy** \th\ **thin** \t̷h\ **the** \ü\ **loot** \u\̇ **foot**
\y\ **yet** \zh\ **vision** *see also* Guide to Pronunciation

³tuck *noun* [Middle English (Scots) *tuicke* beat, stroke] (15th century)
: a sound of or as if of a drumbeat

⁴tuck *noun* [Middle French *estoc,* from Old French, tree trunk, sword point, of Germanic origin; akin to Old English *stocc* stump of a tree — more at STOCK] (1508)
archaic : RAPIER

⁵tuck *noun* [probably from ²*tuck*] (1878)
: VIGOR, ENERGY ⟨seemed to kind of take the *tuck* all out of me —Mark Twain⟩

tuck·a·hoe \'tə-kə-ˌhō\ *noun* [Virginia Algonquian *tockawhoughe*] (1612)
1 : either of two arums (*Peltandra virginica* and *Orontium aquaticum*) of the U.S. with rootstocks used as food by American Indians
2 : the large edible sclerotium of a subterranean fungus (*Poria cocos*)

¹tuck·er \'tə-kər\ *noun* (1688)
1 : a piece of lace or cloth in the neckline of a dress
2 : one that tucks
3 *chiefly Australian* : FOOD

²tucker *transitive verb* **tuck·ered; tuck·er·ing** \'tə-k(ə-)riŋ\ [obsolete English *tuck* to reproach + *-er* (as in ¹*batter*)] (1833)
: EXHAUST — often used with *out*

tuck·er–bag \'tə-kər-ˌbag\ *noun* (1885)
chiefly Australian : a bag used especially by travelers in the bush to hold food

tuck·et \'tə-kət\ *noun* [probably from obsolete English *tuk* to beat the drum, sound the trumpet] (1593)
: a fanfare on a trumpet

tuck–point \'tək-ˌpȯint\ *transitive verb* (1881)
: to finish (the mortar joints between bricks or stones) with a narrow ridge of putty or fine lime mortar

tuckshop \-ˌshäp\ *noun* [British *tuck* food, confectionery] (1857)
British : a confectioner's shop : CONFECTIONERY

Tu·dor \'tü-dər, 'tyü-\ *adjective* [Henry *Tudor* (Henry VII of England)] (1779)
1 : of or relating to the English royal house that ruled from 1485 to 1603
2 : of, relating to, or characteristic of the Tudor period
— **Tudor** *noun*

Tudor arch *noun* (1815)
: a low elliptical 3-, 4-, or 5-centered arch; *especially* : a 4-centered pointed arch — see ARCH illustration

Tues·day \'tüz-dē, 'tyüz-, -(ˌ)dā\ *noun* [Middle English *tiwesday,* from Old English *tīwesdæg* (akin to Old High German *zīostag* Tuesday), from Old English *Tīw* Tiu + *dæg* day — more at DEITY] (before 12th century)
: the third day of the week
— **Tues·days** \-dēz, -(ˌ)dāz\ *adverb*

tu·fa \'tü-fə, 'tyü-\ *noun* [Italian *tufo,* from Latin *tofus*] (1770)
1 : TUFF
2 : a porous rock formed as a deposit from springs or streams
— **tu·fa·ceous** \tü-'fā-shəs, tyü-\ *adjective*

tuff \'təf\ *noun* [Middle French *tuf,* from Old Italian *tufo*] (1815)
: a rock composed of the finer kinds of volcanic detritus usually fused together by heat
— **tuff·a·ceous** \ˌtə-'fā-shəs\ *adjective*

tuf·fet \'tə-fət\ *noun* [alteration of ¹*tuft*] (1553)
1 : TUFT 1a
2 : a low seat

¹tuft \'təft\ *noun* [Middle English, modification of Middle French *tufe*] (14th century)
1 a : a small cluster of elongated flexible outgrowths attached or close together at the base and free at the opposite ends; *especially* : a growing bunch of grasses or close-set plants **b** : a bunch of soft fluffy threads cut off short and used as ornament
2 : CLUMP, CLUSTER
3 : MOUND

4 : any of the projections of yarns drawn through a fabric or making up a fabric so as to produce a surface of raised loops or cut pile
— **tuft·ed** \'təf-təd\ *adjective*
— **tufty** \'təf-tē\ *adjective*

²tuft (1535)
transitive verb
1 a : to provide or adorn with a tuft **b** : to make (a fabric) or with tufts
2 : to make (as a mattress) firm by stitching at intervals and sewing on tufts
intransitive verb
: to form into or grow in tufts
— **tuft·er** *noun*

¹tug \'təg\ *verb* **tugged; tug·ging** [Middle English *tuggen;* akin to Old English *togian* to pull — more at TOW] (14th century)
intransitive verb
1 : to pull hard
2 : to struggle in opposition : CONTEND
3 : to exert oneself laboriously : LABOR
transitive verb
1 : to pull or strain hard at
2 a : to move by pulling hard : HAUL **b** : to carry with difficulty : LUG
3 : to tow with a tugboat
— **tug·ger** *noun*

²tug *noun* (15th century)
1 a : ³TRACE 1 **b** : a short leather strap or loop **c** : a rope or chain used for pulling
2 a : an act or instance of tugging : PULL **b** : a strong pulling force
3 a : a straining effort **b** : a struggle between two people or opposite forces
4 : TUGBOAT

tug·boat \'təg-ˌbōt\ *noun* (1830)
: a strongly built powerful boat used for towing and pushing — called also *towboat*

tug–of–war \ˌtəg-ə(v)-'wȯr\ *noun, plural* **tugs–of–war** (1677)
1 : a struggle for supremacy or control usually involving two antagonists
2 : a contest in which two teams pull against each other at opposite ends of a rope with the object of pulling the middle of the rope over a mark on the ground

tu·grik *or* **tu·ghrik** \'tü-grik\ *noun* [Mongolian *tögrig,* literally, circle, wheel] (1927)
— see MONEY table

tuille \'twē(ə)l\ *noun* [Middle English *toile,* from Middle French *tuille* tile, from Latin *tegula* — more at TILE] (15th century)
: one of the hinged plates before the thigh in plate armor — see ARMOR illustration

tu·ition \tə-'wi-shən, tyü-\ *noun* [Middle English *tuicioun* protection, from Old French *tuicion,* from Latin *tuition-, tuitio,* from *tueri* to look at, look after] (15th century)
1 *archaic* : CUSTODY, GUARDIANSHIP
2 : the act or profession of teaching : INSTRUCTION ⟨pursued his studies under private *tuition*⟩
3 : the price of or payment for instruction
— **tu·ition·al** \-'wish-nəl, -'wi-shə-n°l\ *adjective*

tu·la·re·mia \ˌtü-lə-'rē-mē-ə, ˌtyü-\ *noun* [New Latin, from *Tulare* County, Calif.] (1921)
: an infectious disease especially of wild rabbits, rodents, humans, and some domestic animals that is caused by a bacterium (*Francisella tularensis*), is transmitted especially by the bites of insects, and in humans is marked by symptoms (as fever) of toxemia
— **tu·la·re·mic** \-mik\ *adjective*

tu·le \'tü-lē\ *noun* [Spanish, from Nahuatl *tōllin*] (1837)
: either of two large New World bulrushes (*Scirpus californicus* and *S. acutus*)

tu·lip \'tü-ləp, 'tyü-\ *noun* [New Latin *tulipa,* from Turkish *tülbent* turban — more at TURBAN] (1578)
: any of a genus (*Tulipa*) of Eurasian bulbous herbs of the lily family that have linear or broadly lanceolate leaves and are widely grown for their showy flowers; *also* : the flower or bulb of a tulip ◆

tulip tree *noun* (1705)
1 : a tall North American timber tree (*Liriodendron tulipifera*) of the magnolia family having large greenish yellow tulip-shaped flowers and soft white wood used especially for cabinetwork and woodenware — called also *tulip poplar, yellow poplar*
2 : any of various trees other than the tulip tree with tulip-shaped flowers

tu·lip·wood \'tü-ləp-ˌwud, 'tyü-\ *noun* (1843)
1 : wood of the North American tulip tree
2 a : any of several showily striped or variegated woods; *especially* : the rose-colored wood of a Brazilian tree (*Physocalymma scaberimum* of the family Lythraceae) that is much used by cabinetmakers for inlaying **b** : a tree that yields tulipwood

tulle \'tül\ *noun* [French, from *Tulle,* France] (circa 1818)
: a sheer often stiffened silk, rayon, or nylon net used chiefly for veils or ballet costumes

¹tum·ble \'təm-bəl\ *verb* **tum·bled; tum·bling** \-b(ə-)liŋ\ [Middle English, frequentative of *tumben* to dance, from Old English *tumbian;* akin to Old High German *tūmōn* to reel] (14th century)
intransitive verb
1 a : to fall suddenly and helplessly **b** : to suffer a sudden downfall, overthrow, or defeat **c** : to decline suddenly and sharply (as in price) : DROP ⟨the stock market *tumbled*⟩ **d** : to fall into ruin : COLLAPSE
2 a : to perform gymnastic feats in tumbling **b** : to turn end over end in falling or flight
3 : to roll over and over, to and fro, or end over end : TOSS
4 : to issue forth hurriedly and confusedly
5 : to come by chance : STUMBLE
6 : to come to understand : CATCH ON ⟨didn't *tumble* to the seriousness of the problem⟩
transitive verb
1 : to cause to tumble (as by pushing or toppling)
2 a : to throw together in a confused mass **b** : RUMPLE, DISORDER
3 : to whirl in a tumbling barrel

²tumble *noun* (1634)
1 a : a disordered mass of objects or material **b** : a disorderly state
2 : an act or instance of tumbling

tum·ble·bug \'təm-bəl-ˌbəg\ *noun* (1805)

◇ WORD HISTORY
tulip Although the tulip is often associated with Holland, where it has been cultivated diligently, the Dutch and other Western European peoples originally introduced the plant from Turkey in the later 16th century. The first known reference to the flower is in the Latin letters of Augier Ghislain de Busbecq, the Holy Roman Empire's ambassador to the Turkish court, who, while traveling to Constantinople in 1554 alludes to the "huge abundance of flowers . . . narcissi, hyacinths, and those which the Turks call *tulipan.*" Busbecq appears to have heard the 16th century word corresponding to Modern Turkish *tülbent* "muslin, gauzy fabric." That word was once also applied to turbans wound from such fabric, which Busbecq's interpreter may have compared to the tulip. (*Tülbent* in the sense "turban" had earlier been borrowed into Romance languages and is the ultimate source of English *turban.*) It is not known for certain how Busbecq's word lost its *n* and became *tulipa*—the form on which modern English *tulip* is based—though *tulpe* and *tulipa* appear in an early Dutch dictionary, and the Dutch word may have influenced other languages. Curiously, the Turks both in Busbecq's time and today employ an entirely different word for the tulip, *lâle.*

: any of various scarabaeid beetles (especially genera *Scarabaeus, Canthon, Copris,* or *Phanaeus*) that roll dung into small balls, bury them in the ground, and lay eggs in them

tum·ble·down \ˈtəm-bəl-ˈdaùn\ *adjective* (1818)

: DILAPIDATED, RAMSHACKLE ⟨a *tumbledown* house at the edge of town —Sherwood Anderson⟩

tumble dry *transitive verb* (1962)

: to dry (as clothes) by tumbling in a dryer
— **tumble dryer** *noun*
— **tumble drying** *noun*

tum·bler \ˈtəm-blər\ *noun* (14th century)

1 : one that tumbles: as **a** : one that performs tumbling feats : ACROBAT **b** : any of various domestic pigeons that tumble or somersault backward in flight or on the ground **2** : a drinking glass without foot or stem and originally with pointed or convex base **3 a** : a movable obstruction in a lock (as a lever, latch, wheel, slide, or pin) that must be adjusted to a particular position (as by a key) before the bolt can be thrown **b** : a piece on which the mainspring acts in a gun's lock **4** : a device or mechanism for tumbling (as a revolving cage in which clothes are dried) **5** : a worker that operates a tumbler
— **tum·bler·ful** \-ˌfùl\ *noun*

tum·ble·weed \ˈtəm-bəl-ˌwēd\ *noun* (1887)

: a plant (as Russian thistle or any of several amaranths) that breaks away from its roots in the autumn and is driven about by the wind as a light rolling mass

¹tum·bling \ˈtəm-b(ə-)liŋ\ *noun* (1604)

: the skill, practice, or sport of executing gymnastic feats (as somersaults and handsprings) without the use of apparatus

²tumbling *adjective* (circa 1916)

: tipped or slanted out of the vertical — used especially of a cattle brand

tumbling barrel *noun* (circa 1890)

: a revolving cask in which objects or materials undergo a process (as drying or polishing) by being whirled about

tumbling verse *noun* (1585)

: an early modern English type of verse having four stresses but no prevailing type of foot and no regular number of syllables

tum·brel *or* **tum·bril** \ˈtəm-brəl\ *noun* [Middle English *tombrel,* from Old French *tumberel* tipcart, from *tomber* to tumble, of Germanic origin; akin to Old High German *tūmōn* to reel — more at TUMBLE] (15th century)

1 : a farm tipcart **2** : a vehicle carrying condemned persons (as political prisoners during the French Revolution) to a place of execution

tu·me·fac·tion \ˌtü-mə-ˈfak-shən, ˌtyü-\ *noun* [Middle French, from Latin *tumefacere* to cause to swell, from *tumēre* to swell + *facere* to make, do — more at THUMB, DO] (1597)

1 : an action or process of swelling or becoming tumorous **2** : SWELLING

tu·mes·cence \tü-ˈme-s³n(t)s, tyü-\ *noun* (1859)

: the quality or state of being tumescent; *especially* : readiness for sexual activity marked especially by vascular congestion of the sex organs

tu·mes·cent \-s³nt\ *adjective* [Latin *tumescent-, tumescens,* present participle of *tumescere* to swell up, inchoative of *tumēre* to swell] (1882)

: somewhat swollen ⟨*tumescent* tissue⟩

tu·mid \ˈtü-məd, ˈtyü-\ *adjective* [Latin *tumidus,* from *tumēre*] (1541)

1 : marked by swelling : SWOLLEN, ENLARGED ⟨a badly infected *tumid* leg⟩ **2** : PROTUBERANT, BULGING ⟨sails *tumid* in the breeze⟩ **3** : BOMBASTIC, TURGID

tum·my \ˈtə-mē\ *noun, plural* **tummies** [baby-talk alteration of *stomach*] (1867)

: STOMACH 1c

tu·mor \ˈtü-mər, ˈtyü-\ *noun* [Latin *tumor,* from *tumēre*] (1597)

1 : a swollen or distended part **2** : an abnormal benign or malignant mass of tissue that is not inflammatory, arises without obvious cause from cells of preexistent tissue, and possesses no physiologic function
— **tu·mor·al** \-mə-rəl\ *adjective*
— **tu·mor·like** \-mər-ˌlīk\ *adjective*

tu·mor·i·gen·ic \ˌtü-mə-rə-ˈje-nik, ˌtyü-\ *adjective* (1941)

: producing or tending to produce tumors; *also* : CARCINOGENIC
— **tu·mor·i·gen·e·sis** \-ˈje-nə-səs\ *noun*
— **tu·mor·i·ge·nic·i·ty** \-jə-ˌni-sə-tē\ *noun*

tumor necrosis factor *noun* (1975)

: a protein that is produced by monocytes and macrophages in response especially to endotoxins and that activates leukocytes and has antitumor activity

tu·mor·ous \ˈtü-mə-rəs, ˈtyü-; ˈtüm-rəs, ˈtyüm-\ *adjective* (1547)

: of, relating to, or resembling a tumor

tu·mour \ˈtyü-mər\ *chiefly British variant of* TUMOR

¹tump \ˈtəmp\ *noun* [origin unknown] (1589)

1 *chiefly dialect English* : MOUND, HUMMOCK **2** : a clump of vegetation

²tump *verb* [perhaps akin to British dialect *tumpoke* to fall head over heels] (1967)
intransitive verb
chiefly Southern : to tip or turn over especially accidentally — usually used with *over* ⟨sooner or later everybody *tumps* over. Nothing to worry about if you don't get caught under the canoe —Don Kennard⟩
transitive verb
chiefly Southern : to cause to tip over : OVERTURN, UPSET — usually used with *over*

tump·line \ˈtəm-ˌplīn\ *noun* [*tump,* of Algonquian origin; akin to Eastern Abenaki *mádûmbí* pack strap] (1796)

: a sling formed by a strap slung over the forehead or chest and used for carrying or helping to support a pack on the back or in hauling loads

tu·mult \ˈtü-ˌməlt, ˈtyü- *also* ˈtə-\ *noun* [Middle English *tumulte,* from Middle French, from Latin *tumultus;* perhaps akin to Sanskrit *tumula* noisy] (15th century)

1 a : disorderly agitation or milling about of a crowd usually with uproar and confusion of voices : COMMOTION **b** : a turbulent uprising : RIOT **2** : HUBBUB, DIN **3 a** : violent agitation of mind or feelings **b** : a violent outburst

tu·mul·tu·ary \tù-ˈməl-chə-ˌwer-ē, tyù-, tə-\ *adjective* (1590)

: attended or marked by tumult, riot, lawlessness, confusion, or impetuosity

tu·mul·tu·ous \tù-ˈməl-chə-wəs, tyù-, tə-, -chəs; -ˈməlch-wəs\ *adjective* (circa 1548)

1 : marked by tumult **2** : tending or disposed to cause or incite a tumult **3** : marked by violent or overwhelming turbulence or upheaval
— **tu·mul·tu·ous·ly** *adverb*
— **tu·mul·tu·ous·ness** *noun*

tu·mu·lus \ˈtü-myə-ləs, ˈtyü-, ˈtə-\ *noun, plural* **-li** \-ˌlī, -ˌlē\ [Latin; akin to Latin *tumēre* to swell — more at THUMB] (1686)

: an artificial hillock or mound (as over a grave); *especially* : an ancient grave : BARROW

tun \ˈtən\ *noun* [Middle English *tunne,* from Old English, from Medieval Latin *tunna*] (before 12th century)

1 : a large cask especially for wine **2** : any of various units of liquid capacity; *especially* : one equal to 252 gallons

¹tu·na \ˈtü-nə\ *noun* [Spanish, from Taino] (circa 1555)

1 : any of various flat-jointed prickly pears (genus *Opuntia*); *especially* : one (*O. tuna*) of tropical America **2** : the edible fruit of a tuna

²tu·na \ˈtü-nə, ˈtyü-\ *noun, plural* **tuna** *or* **tunas** [American Spanish, alteration of Spanish *atún,* modification of Arabic *tūn,* from Latin *thunnus,* from Greek *thynnos*] (1881)

1 : any of numerous large vigorous scombroid food and sport fishes (as an albacore or a bluefin tuna) **2** : the flesh of a tuna especially when canned for use as food — called also *tuna fish*

tun·able \ˈtü-nə-bəl, ˈtyü-\ *adjective* (circa 1500)

1 *archaic* **a** : TUNEFUL **b** : sounding in tune : CONCORDANT **2** : capable of being tuned
— **tun·abil·i·ty** \ˌtü-nə-ˈbi-lə-tē, ˌtyü-\ *noun*
— **tun·able·ness** \ˈtü-nə-bəl-nəs, ˈtyü-\ *noun*
— **tun·ably** \-blē\ *adverb*

tun·dish \ˈtən-ˌdish\ *noun* [Middle English, funnel for filling a tun] (14th century)

1 : FUNNEL 1a **2** : a reservoir in the top part of a mold into which molten metal is poured

tun·dra \ˈtən-drə *also* ˈtùn-\ *noun* [Russian, of Lappish origin; akin to Kola Lappish *tundar* hill] (circa 1841)

: a level or rolling treeless plain that is characteristic of arctic and subarctic regions, consists of black mucky soil with a permanently frozen subsoil, and has a dominant vegetation of mosses, lichens, herbs, and dwarf shrubs; *also* : a similar region confined to mountainous areas above timberline

¹tune \ˈtün, ˈtyün\ *noun* [Middle English, alteration of *tone*] (14th century)

1 a *archaic* : quality of sound : TONE **b** : manner of utterance : INTONATION; *specifically* : phonetic modulation **2 a** : a succession of pleasing musical tones : MELODY **b** : a dominant theme **3** : correct musical pitch or consonance — used chiefly in the phrases *in tune* and *out of tune* **4 a** *archaic* : a frame of mind : MOOD **b** : AGREEMENT, HARMONY ⟨in *tune* with the times⟩ **c** : general attitude : APPROACH ⟨changed his *tune* when the going got rough⟩ **5** : AMOUNT, EXTENT ⟨custom-made to the *tune* of $40 to $50 apiece —*American Fabrics*⟩

²tune *verb* **tuned; tun·ing** (15th century)
transitive verb
1 : to adjust in musical pitch or cause to be in tune ⟨*tuned* her guitar⟩ **2 a** : to bring into harmony : ATTUNE **b** : to adjust for precise functioning — often used with *up* ⟨*tune* up an engine⟩ **c** : to make more precise, intense, or effective **3** : to adjust with respect to resonance at a particular frequency: as **a** : to adjust (a radio or television receiver) to respond to waves of a particular frequency — often used with *in* **b** : to establish radio contact with ⟨*tune* in a directional beacon⟩ **4** : to adjust the frequency of the output of (a device) to a chosen frequency or range of frequencies; *also* : to alter the frequency of (radiation)
intransitive verb
1 : to become attuned **2** : to adjust a radio or television receiver to respond to waves of a particular frequency

tuned–in \ˈtünd-ˈin, ˈtyünd-\ *adjective* (1963)

: TURNED-ON

tune·ful \ˈtün-fəl, ˈtyün-\ *adjective* (1591)

: MELODIOUS, MUSICAL
— **tune·ful·ly** \-fə-lē\ *adverb*
— **tune·ful·ness** *noun*

tune in (1913)
transitive verb
: to listen to or view a broadcast of ⟨*tuned in* the weather report⟩
intransitive verb
: to listen to or view a broadcast ⟨*tune in* next week for the conclusion⟩
tune·less \'tün-ləs, 'tyün-\ *adjective* (1591)
1 : not tuneful
2 : not producing music
— **tune·less·ly** *adverb*
tune out (1910)
transitive verb
: to become unresponsive to : IGNORE
intransitive verb
: to dissociate oneself from what is happening or one's surroundings
tun·er \'tü-nər, 'tyü-\ *noun* (circa 1801)
1 : one that tunes ⟨a piano *tuner*⟩
2 : something used for tuning; *specifically* : the part of a receiving set that converts radio signals into audio or video signals
tune·smith \'tün-ˌsmith, 'tyün-\ *noun* (1926)
: a composer especially of popular songs
tune–up \-ˌəp\ *noun* (1933)
1 : a general adjustment to insure operation at peak efficiency
2 : a preliminary trial : WARM-UP
tung \'təŋ\ *noun* (1914)
: TUNG TREE
tung oil *noun* [part translation of Chinese (Beijing) *tóngyóu*] (1881)
: a pale yellow pungent drying oil obtained from the seeds of tung trees and used chiefly in quick-drying varnishes and paints and as a waterproofing agent
tung·state \'təŋ-ˌstāt\ *noun* (1800)
: a salt or ester of a tungstic acid and especially of H_2WO_4
tung·sten \'təŋ-stən\ *noun* [Swedish, from *tung* heavy + *sten* stone] (1796)
: a gray-white heavy high-melting ductile hard polyvalent metallic element that resembles chromium and molybdenum in many of its properties and is used especially for electrical purposes and in hardening alloys (as steel) — called also *wolfram*; see ELEMENT table
tung·stic acid \'təŋ-stik-\ *noun* [*tungsten*] (1796)
: a yellow crystalline powder WO_3 that is the trioxide of tungsten; *also* : an acid (as H_2WO_4) derived from this
tung tree *noun* [Chinese (Beijing) *tóng*] (1895)
: any of several trees (genus *Aleurites*) of the spurge family whose seeds yield tung oil; *especially* : an Asian tree (*A. fordii*) widely grown in warm regions
Tun·gus \ˈtu̇ŋ-ˈgüz, tən-\ *noun, plural* **Tungus** or **Tun·gus·es** [Russian] (1674)
1 : a member of an indigenous people of central and southeastern Siberia
2 : the Tungusic language of the Tungus people
Tun·gu·sic \-'gü-zik\ *noun* (circa 1867)
: a family of Altaic languages spoken in Manchuria and northward
— **Tungusic** *adjective*
tu·nic \'tü-nik, 'tyü-\ *noun* [Latin *tunica*, of Semitic origin; akin to Hebrew *kuttōneth* coat] (circa 1609)
1 a : a simple slip-on garment made with or without sleeves and usually knee-length or longer, belted at the waist, and worn as an under or outer garment by men and women of ancient Greece and Rome **b** : SURCOAT
2 : an enclosing or covering membrane or tissue ⟨the *tunic* of a seed⟩
3 : a long usually plain close-fitting jacket with high collar worn especially as part of a uniform
4 : TUNICLE
5 a : a short overskirt **b** : a hip-length or long-er blouse or jacket

tu·ni·ca \'tü-ni-kə, 'tyü-\ *noun, plural* **tu·ni·cae** \-nə-ˌkē, -ˌkī, -ˌsē\ [Latin, tunic, membrane] (circa 1828)
: an enveloping membrane or layer of body tissue
¹**tu·ni·cate** \'tü-ni-kət, 'tyü-, -nə-ˌkāt\ *also* **tu·ni·cat·ed** \-nə-ˌkā-təd\ *adjective* [Latin *tunicatus*, from *tunica*] (circa 1623)
1 a : having or covered with a tunic or tunica
b : having, arranged in, or made up of concentric layers ⟨a *tunicate* bulb⟩
2 : of or relating to the tunicates
²**tu·ni·cate** \-ni-kət, -nə-ˌkāt\ *noun* [New Latin Tunicata, from neuter plural of Latin *tunicatus*] (1889)
: any of a subphylum (Urochordata synonym Tunicata) of marine chordate animals that have a thick secreted covering layer, a greatly reduced nervous system, a heart able to reverse the direction of blood flow, and only in the larval stage a notochord
tu·ni·cle \'tü-ni-kəl, 'tyü-\ *noun* [Middle English, from Latin *tunicula*, diminutive of *tunica*] (15th century)
: a short vestment worn by a subdeacon over the alb during mass and by a bishop under the dalmatic at pontifical ceremonies
tuning fork *noun* (1799)
: a 2-pronged metal implement that gives a fixed tone when struck and is useful for tuning musical instruments and ascertaining standard pitch
tuning pipe *noun* (1897)
: PITCH PIPE; *specifically* : one of a set of pitch pipes used especially for tuning stringed musical instruments
¹**tun·nel** \'tə-nᵊl\ *noun* [Middle English *tonel* tube-shaped net, from Middle French, tun, from Old French, from *tonne* tun, from Medieval Latin *tunna*] (1548)
1 : a hollow conduit or recess : TUBE, WELL
2 a : a covered passageway; *specifically* : a horizontal passageway through or under an obstruction **b** : a subterranean gallery (as in a mine) **c** : BURROW
— **tun·nel·like** \-nᵊl-ˌ(l)īk\ *adjective*
²**tunnel** *verb* **-neled** or **-nelled; -nel·ing** or **-nel·ling** \'tən-liŋ, 'tə-nᵊl-iŋ\ (1795)
intransitive verb
1 : to make or use a tunnel
2 *physics* : to pass through a potential barrier ⟨electrons *tunneling* through an insulator between semiconductors⟩
transitive verb
: to make a tunnel or similar opening through or under; *also* : to make (one's way) by or as if by making a tunnel
— **tun·nel·er** \'tən-lər, 'tə-nᵊl-ər\ *noun*
tunnel vision *noun* (circa 1942)
1 : constriction of the visual field resulting in loss of peripheral vision
2 : extreme narrowness of viewpoint : NARROWMINDEDNESS; *also* : single-minded concentration on one objective
— **tun·nel·vi·sioned** \-'vi-zhənd\ *adjective*
tun·ny \'tə-nē\ *noun, plural* **tunnies** *also* **tunny** [modification of Middle French *thon* or Old Italian *tonno*; both from Old Provençal *ton*, from Latin *thunnus* — more at TUNA] (circa 1530)
: TUNA
¹**tup** \'təp\ *noun* [Middle English *tupe*] (14th century)
1 *chiefly British* : RAM 1a
2 : a heavy metal body (as the weight of a pendulum)
²**tup** *transitive verb* **tupped; tup·ping** (1604)
chiefly British : to copulate with (a ewe)
tu·pe·lo \'tü-pə-ˌlō, 'tyü-\ *noun, plural* **-los** [perhaps from Creek *ito opilwa* swamp tree] (circa 1730)
1 : any of a genus (*Nyssa* of the family Nyssaceae) of North American and Asian deciduous trees that have simple alternate leaves,

small greenish dioecious stalked flowers, and a rounded drupe; *especially* : BLACK GUM
2 : the pale soft wood of a tupelo
Tu·pi \tü-'pē, 'tü-(ˌ)\ *noun, plural* **Tupi** or **Tu·pis** (1842)
1 : the language of the Tupi people
2 : a member of a group of Tupi-Guaranian peoples of Brazil living especially in the Amazon valley
Tu·pi·an \tü-'pē-ən, 'tü-(ˌ)\ *adjective* (1902)
: of, relating to, or constituting the Tupi or other Tupi-Guaranian peoples or their languages
Tu·pi–Gua·ra·ni \tü-ˌpē-gwär-ə-'nē, 'tü-(ˌ)pē-\ *noun* (1850)
1 : a member of a group of South American Indian peoples spread over an area from eastern Brazil to the Peruvian Andes and from the Guianas to Uruguay
2 : TUPI-GUARANIAN
Tu·pi–Gua·ra·ni·an \-'nē-ən\ *noun* (circa 1902)
: a language family widely distributed in tropical South America
-tu·ple \ˌtə-pəl, ˌtü-\ *noun combining form* [quin*tuple*, sex*tuple*]
: set of (so many) elements — usually used of sets with ordered elements ⟨the ordered 2-*tuple* (a, b)⟩
tup·pence *variant of* TWOPENCE
tuque \'tük, 'tyük\ *noun* [Canadian French, from French *toque* — more at TOQUE] (1871)
: a warm knitted usually pointed stocking cap
tu quo·que \'tü-'kwō-kwē, 'tyü-, -'kō-\ *noun* [Latin, you too] (1614)
: a retort charging an adversary with being or doing what he criticizes in others
tu·ra·co \'tu̇r-ə-(ˌ)kō\ *noun, plural* **-cos** [origin unknown] (1743)
: any of a family (Musophagidae) of African birds that are related to the cuckoos and have a long tail, a short stout often colored bill, and red wing feathers
Tu·ra·ni·an \tu̇-'rä-nē-ən, tyü-, -'rä-\ *noun* [Persian *Tūrān* Turkestan, the region north of the Amu Darya] (circa 1777)
1 : a member of any of various peoples speaking Ural-Altaic languages
2 : URAL-ALTAIC
— **Turanian** *adjective*
tur·ban \'tər-bən\ *noun* [Middle French *turbant*, from Italian *turbante*, from Turkish *tülbent*, from Persian *dulband*] (1588)
1 : a headdress worn chiefly in countries of the eastern Mediterranean and southern Asia especially by Muslims and made of a cap around which is wound a long cloth
2 : a headdress resembling a turban; *specifically* : a woman's close-fitting hat without a brim
3 : a rolled stuffed fillet of fish ⟨*turban* of sole⟩
word history see TULIP
— **tur·baned** *or* **tur·banned** \-bənd\ *adjective*

turban 1

tur·bel·lar·i·an \ˌtər-bə-'ler-ē-ən, -'lar-\ *noun* [ultimately from Latin *turbellae* (plural) bustle, stir, diminutive of *turba* confusion, crowd; from the tiny eddies created in water by the cilia] (1883)
: any of a class (Turbellaria) of mostly aquatic and free-living flatworms (as a planarian)
— **turbellarian** *adjective*
tur·bid \'tər-bəd\ *adjective* [Latin *turbidus* confused, turbid, from *turba* confusion, crowd, probably from Greek *tyrbē* confusion] (1626)
1 a : thick or opaque with or as if with roiled sediment ⟨a *turbid* stream⟩ **b** : heavy with smoke or mist
2 a : deficient in clarity or purity : FOUL, MUDDY ⟨*turbid* depths of degradation and misery —C. I. Glicksberg⟩ **b** : characterized by or producing obscurity (as of mind or emotions) ⟨an emotionally *turbid* response⟩

— **tur·bid·i·ty** \ˌtər-ˈbi-də-tē\ *noun*
— **tur·bid·ly** \ˈtər-bəd-lē\ *adverb*
— **tur·bid·ness** *noun*

tur·bi·dim·e·ter \ˌtər-bə-ˈdi-mə-tər\ *noun* [International Scientific Vocabulary *turbidi*ty + *-meter*] (1905)
1 : an instrument for measuring and comparing the turbidity of liquids by viewing light through them and determining how much light is cut off
2 : NEPHELOMETER
— **tur·bi·di·met·ric** \ˌtər-bə-də-ˈme-trik, ˌtər-ˌbi-də-\ *adjective*
— **tur·bi·di·met·ri·cal·ly** \-tri-k(ə-)lē\ *adverb*
— **tur·bi·dim·e·try** \ˌtər-bə-ˈdi-mə-trē\ *noun*

tur·bi·dite \ˈtər-bə-ˌdīt\ *noun* [*turbidi*ty current (a current flowing down a slope and spreading out on the ocean floor) + ¹*-ite*] (1957)
: a sedimentary deposit consisting of material that has moved down the steep slope at the edge of a continental shelf; *also* : a rock formed from this deposit

¹**tur·bi·nate** \ˈtər-bə-nət, -ˌnāt\ *also* **tur·bi·nat·ed** \-ˌnā-təd\ *adjective* [Latin *turbinatus*, from *turbin-, turbo*] (1661)
1 : shaped like a top or an inverted cone ⟨*turbinate* seed capsule⟩
2 : relating to or being a turbinate

²**turbinate** *noun* (circa 1803)
: one of usually several thin plicated membrane-covered bony or cartilaginous plates on the walls of the nasal chambers

tur·bine \ˈtər-bən, -ˌbīn\ *noun* [French, from Latin *turbin-, turbo* top, whirlwind, whirl, from *turba* confusion — more at TURBID] (1842)
: a rotary engine actuated by the reaction or impulse or both of a current of fluid (as water, steam, or air) subject to pressure and usually made with a series of curved vanes on a central rotating spindle

tur·bo \ˈtər-ˌbō\ *noun, plural* **turbos** [*turbo-*] (1904)
1 : TURBINE
2 [by shortening] : TURBOCHARGER

turbo- *combining form* [*turbine*]
1 : coupled directly to a driving turbine ⟨*turbo*fan⟩
2 : consisting of or incorporating a turbine ⟨*turbo*jet engine⟩

tur·bo·car \ˈtər-bō-ˌkär\ *noun* (1950)
: an automotive vehicle propelled by a gas turbine

tur·bo·charged \-ˌchärjd\ *adjective* (1945)
: equipped with a turbocharger

tur·bo·charg·er \-ˌchär-jər\ *noun* (1934)
: a centrifugal blower driven by exhaust gas turbines and used to supercharge an engine

tur·bo·elec·tric \ˌtər-bō-ə-ˈlek-trik\ *adjective* (1904)
: using or being a turbine generator that produces electricity usually for motive power

tur·bo·fan \ˈtər-bō-ˌfan\ *noun* (1911)
1 : a fan that is directly connected to and driven by a turbine and is used to supply air for cooling, ventilation, or combustion
2 : a jet engine having a turbofan

tur·bo·gen·er·a·tor \ˌtər-bō-ˈje-nə-ˌrā-tər\ *noun* (1898)
: an electric generator driven by a turbine

tur·bo·jet \-ˌjet\ *noun* (1945)
1 : an airplane powered by turbojet engines
2 : TURBOJET ENGINE

turbojet engine *noun* (1944)
: a jet engine in which a turbine drives a compressor that supplies air to a burner and hot gases from the burner drive the turbine before being discharged rearward

tur·bo·ma·chin·ery \ˌtər-bō-mə-ˈshēn-rē, -ˈshē-nə-\ *noun* (1948)
: machinery consisting of, incorporating, or constituting a turbine

tur·bo·prop \ˈtər-bō-ˌpräp\ *noun* (1945)
1 : TURBOPROP ENGINE

2 : an airplane powered by turboprop engines

turboprop engine *noun* (1947)
: a jet engine designed to produce thrust principally by means of a propeller driven by a turbine with additional thrust usually obtained by the rearward discharge of hot exhaust gases

tur·bo·shaft \ˈtər-bō-ˌshaft\ *noun* (1958)
: a gas turbine engine that is similar in operation to a turboprop engine but instead of being used to power a propeller is used through a transmission system for powering other devices (as helicopter rotors and pumps)

tur·bot \ˈtər-bət\ *noun, plural* **turbot** *also* **turbots** [Middle English, from Old French *tourbot*] (14th century)
1 : a large European flatfish (*Psetta maxima*) that is a popular food fish and has a brownish upper surface marked with scattered tubercles and a white undersurface
2 : any of various flatfishes resembling the turbot

tur·bu·lence \ˈtər-byə-lən(t)s\ *noun* (1598)
: the quality or state of being turbulent: as **a** : wild commotion **b** : irregular atmospheric motion especially when characterized by up-and-down currents **c** : departure in a fluid from a smooth flow

tur·bu·len·cy \-lən(t)-sē\ *noun, plural* **-cies** (1607)
archaic : TURBULENCE

tur·bu·lent \-lənt\ *adjective* [Latin *turbulentus*, from *turba* confusion, crowd — more at TURBID] (1538)
1 : causing unrest, violence, or disturbance
2 a : characterized by agitation or tumult : TEMPESTUOUS **b** : exhibiting physical turbulence
— **tur·bu·lent·ly** *adverb*

turbulent flow *noun* (1895)
: a fluid flow in which the velocity at a given point varies erratically in magnitude and direction — compare LAMINAR FLOW

Tur·co- *or* **Tur·ko-** \ˈtər-(ˌ)kō\ *combining form* [*Turco-* from Medieval Latin *Turcus* Turk; *Turko-* from *Turk*]
1 : Turkic : Turkish : Turk ⟨*Turco*phil⟩
2 : Turkish and ⟨*Turco*-Greek⟩

turd \ˈtərd\ *noun* [Middle English *tord, turd,* from Old English *tord;* akin to Middle Dutch *tort* dung and probably to Old English *teran* to tear — more at TEAR] (before 12th century)
1 : a piece of excrement — sometimes considered vulgar
2 : a contemptible person — usually considered vulgar

tu·reen \tə-ˈrēn, tyù-\ *noun* [French *terrine,* from Middle French, from feminine of *terrin* of earth, from (assumed) Vulgar Latin *terrinus,* from Latin *terra* earth — more at TERRACE] (circa 1706)
1 : a deep and usually covered bowl from which foods (as soup) are served
2 : CASSEROLE 1

¹**turf** \ˈtərf\ *noun, plural* **turfs** \ˈtərfs\ *also* **turves** \ˈtərvz\ [Middle English, from Old English; akin to Old High German *zurba* turf, Sanskrit *darbha* tuft of grass] (before 12th century)
1 a : the upper stratum of soil bound by grass and plant roots into a thick mat; *also* : a piece of this **b** : an artificial substitute for this (as on a playing field)
2 a : PEAT 2 **b** : a piece of peat dried for fuel
3 a : a track or course for horse racing **b** : the sport or business of horse racing
4 a : territory considered by a teenage gang to be under its control **b** : TERRITORY 2 ⟨have to play two of the last three games on hostile *turf* —Joe Klein⟩ ⟨points toward the biographer's *turf,* not the critic's —Hugh Kenner⟩; *also* : a sphere of activity or influence ⟨people who could hurt him on his own foreign-policy *turf* —Wall Street Journal⟩
— **turfy** \ˈtər-fē\ *adjective*

²**turf** *transitive verb* (15th century)
1 : to cover with turf

2 *chiefly British* : to eject forcibly : KICK — usually used with *out*

turf accountant *noun* (1915)
British : BOOKMAKER 2

turf·man \ˈtərf-mən\ *noun* (1818)
: a devotee of horse racing; *especially* : a person who owns and races horses

turf·ski \-ˌskē\ *noun* (1967)
: a short ski with rollers on the bottom that can be used to ski down a grassy slope
— **turf·ski·ing** *noun*

tur·ges·cent \ˌtər-ˈje-sᵊnt\ *adjective* [Latin *turgescent-, turgescens,* present participle of *turgescere* to swell, inchoative of *turgēre* to be swollen] (circa 1727)
: becoming turgid, distended, or inflated : SWELLING
— **tur·ges·cence** \-sᵊn(t)s\ *noun*

tur·gid \ˈtər-jəd\ *adjective* [Latin *turgidus,* from *turgēre* to be swollen] (1620)
1 : being in a state of distension : SWOLLEN, TUMID ⟨*turgid* limbs⟩; *especially* : exhibiting turgor
2 : excessively embellished in style or language : BOMBASTIC, POMPOUS
— **tur·gid·i·ty** \ˌtər-ˈji-də-tē\ *noun*
— **tur·gid·ly** \ˈtər-jəd-lē\ *adverb*
— **tur·gid·ness** *noun*

tur·gor \ˈtər-gər, -ˌgòr\ *noun* [Late Latin, turgidity, swelling, from Latin *turgēre*] (1876)
: the normal state of turgidity and tension in living cells; *especially* : the distension of the protoplasmic layer and wall of a plant cell by the fluid contents

Tu·ring machine \ˈtùr-iŋ-, ˈtyùr-\ *noun* [A. M. *Turing* (died 1954) English mathematician] (1937)
: a hypothetical computing machine that has an unlimited amount of information storage

tu·ris·ta \tù-ˈrē-stə\ *noun* [Spanish, tourist] (1962)
: intestinal sickness and diarrhea commonly affecting a tourist in a foreign country; *especially* : MONTEZUMA'S REVENGE

Turk \ˈtərk\ *noun* [Middle English, from Middle French or Turkish; Middle French *Turc,* from Medieval Latin or Turkish; Medieval Latin *Turcus,* from Turkish *Türk*] (14th century)
1 : a member of any of numerous Asian peoples speaking Turkic languages who live in a region extending from the Balkans to eastern Siberia and western China
2 : a native or inhabitant of Turkey
3 *archaic* : one who is cruel or tyrannical
4 : MUSLIM; *specifically* : a Muslim subject of the Turkish sultan
5 : a Turkish horse; *specifically* : a Turkish strain of Arab and crossbred horses
6 *often not capitalized* : a usually young dynamic person eager for change; *especially* : YOUNG TURK

tur·key \ˈtər-kē\ *noun, plural* **turkeys** [*Turkey,* country in western Asia and southeastern Europe; from confusion with the guinea fowl, supposed to be imported from Turkish territory] (1555)
1 *plural also* **turkey** : a large North American gallinaceous bird (*Meleagris gallopavo*) that is domesticated in most parts of the world
2 : FAILURE, FLOP; *especially* : a theatrical production that has failed

turkey 1

3 : three successive strikes in bowling
4 : a stupid, foolish, or inept person

tur·key–cock \'tər-kē-,käk\ *noun* (1578)
 1 : GOBBLER
 2 : a strutting pompous person

turkey oak *noun* (1709)
 : a small oak (*Quercus laevis* synonym *Q. catesbaei*) of the southeastern U.S.; *also* : a Eurasian oak (*Q. cerris*)

Tur·key red \'tər-kē-\ *noun* [*Turkey*] (1789)
 : a brilliant durable red produced on cotton by means of alizarin in connection with an aluminum mordant and fatty matter

tur·key shoot \'tər-kē-\ *noun* (1845)
 : a marksmanship contest using a moving target with a turkey offered as a prize

turkey trot *noun* (1908)
 : a ragtime dance danced with the feet well apart and with a characteristic rise on the ball of the foot followed by a drop upon the heel

turkey vulture *noun* (1823)
 : an American vulture (*Cathartes aura*) with a red head and whitish bill — called also *turkey buzzard*

Turk·ic \'tər-kik\ *adjective* (1859)
 1 a : of, relating to, or constituting a family of Altaic languages including Turkish **b** : of or relating to the peoples speaking Turkic
 2 : TURKISH 1
 — **Turkic** *noun*

¹**Turk·ish** \'tər-kish\ *adjective* (1545)
 1 : of, relating to, or characteristic of Turkey, the Turks, or Turkish
 2 : TURKIC 1a

²**Turkish** *noun* (1677)
 : the Turkic language of the Republic of Turkey

Turkish bath *noun* (1644)
 : a bath in which the bather passes through a series of steam rooms of increasing temperature and then receives a rubdown, massage, and cold shower

Turkish coffee *noun* (1854)
 : a sweetened decoction of pulverized coffee

Turkish delight *noun* (1877)
 : a jellylike or gummy confection usually cut in cubes and dusted with sugar — called also *Turkish paste*

Turkish towel *noun* (1862)
 : a towel made of cotton terry cloth

Turk·ism \'tər-,ki-zəm\ *noun* (1595)
 : the customs, beliefs, institutions, and principles of the Turks

Tur·ko·man *or* **Tur·co·man** \'tər-kə-mən\ *noun, plural* **Turkomans** *or* **Turcomans** [Medieval Latin *Turcomannus,* from Persian *Turkmān,* from *turkmān* resembling a Turk, from *Turk*] (circa 1520)
 : a member of a Turkic-speaking traditionally nomadic people living chiefly in Turkmenistan, Afghanistan, and Iran
 — **Turkoman** *or* **Turcoman** *adjective*

Turk's head *noun* (1833)
 : a turban-shaped knot worked on a rope with a piece of small line — see KNOT illustration

tur·mer·ic \'tər-mə-rik *also* 'tü-mə- *or* 'tyü-\ *noun* [modification of Middle French *terre merite* saffron, from Medieval Latin *terra merita,* literally, deserving or deserved earth] (1545)
 1 : an East Indian perennial herb (*Curcuma domestica* synonym *C. longa*) of the ginger family with a large aromatic yellow rhizome
 2 : the cleaned, boiled, dried, and usually pulverized rhizome of the turmeric plant used as a coloring agent, a flavoring, or a stimulant
 3 : a yellow to reddish brown dyestuff obtained from turmeric

tur·moil \'tər-,moil\ *noun* [origin unknown] (1526)
 : a state or condition of extreme confusion, agitation, or commotion

¹**turn** \'tərn\ *verb* [Middle English; partly from Old English *tyrnan* & *turnian* to turn, from Medieval Latin *tornare,* from Latin, to turn on a lathe, from *tornus* lathe, from Greek *tornos;* partly from Old French *torner, tourner* to turn, from Medieval Latin *tornare;* akin to Latin *terere* to rub — more at THROW] (before 12th century)

transitive verb
1 a : to cause to move around an axis or a center : make rotate or revolve ⟨*turn* a wheel⟩ ⟨*turn* a crank⟩ **b** (1) : to cause to move around so as to effect a desired end (as of locking, opening, or shutting) ⟨*turned* the knob till the door opened⟩ (2) : to affect or alter the functioning of (as a mechanical device) by such movement ⟨*turned* the oven to a higher temperature⟩ **c** : to execute or perform by rotating or revolving ⟨*turn* handsprings⟩ **d** : to twist out of line or shape : WRENCH ⟨had *turned* his ankle⟩
2 a (1) : to cause to change position by moving through an arc of a circle ⟨*turned* her chair to the fire⟩ (2) : to cause to move around a center so as to show another side of ⟨*turn* the page⟩ (3) : to cause (as a scale) to move so as to register weight **b** : to revolve mentally : think over : PONDER
3 a : to reverse the sides or surfaces of : INVERT ⟨*turn* pancakes⟩ ⟨*turn* the shirt inside out⟩: as (1) : to dig or plow so as to bring the lower soil to the surface (2) : to make (as a garment) over by reversing the material and resewing ⟨*turn* a collar⟩ (3) : to invert feet up and face down (as a character, rule, or slug) in setting type **b** : to reverse or upset the order or disposition of ⟨everything was *turned* topsyturvy⟩ **c** : to disturb or upset the mental balance of : DERANGE, UNSETTLE ⟨a mind *turned* by grief⟩ **d** : to set in another especially contrary direction
4 a : to bend or change the course of : DIVERT **b** : to cause to retreat ⟨used fire hoses to *turn* the mob⟩ **c** : to alter the drift, tendency, or expected result of **d** : to bend a course around or about : ROUND ⟨*turned* the corner at full speed⟩
5 a (1) : to direct or point (as the face) in a specified way or direction (2) : to present by a change in direction or position ⟨*turning* his back to his guests⟩ **b** : to bring to bear (as by aiming, pointing, or focusing) : TRAIN ⟨*turned* the light into the dark doorway⟩ ⟨*turned* a questioning eye toward her⟩ **c** : to direct (as the attention or mind) toward or away from something **d** : to direct the employment of : APPLY, DEVOTE ⟨*turned* his skills to the service of mankind⟩ **e** (1) : to cause to rebound or recoil ⟨*turns* their argument against them⟩ (2) : to make antagonistic : PREJUDICE ⟨*turn* a child against its mother⟩ **f** (1) : to cause to go in a particular direction ⟨*turned* our steps homeward⟩ (2) : DRIVE, SEND ⟨*turn* cows to pasture⟩ (3) : to convey or direct into or out of a receptacle by inverting
6 a (1) : to make acid or sour (2) : to change the color of (as foliage) **b** (1) : CONVERT, TRANSFORM ⟨*turn* defeat into victory⟩ (2) : TRANSLATE, PARAPHRASE **c** : to cause to become of a specified nature or appearance ⟨*turned* him into a frog⟩ ⟨illness *turned* her hair white⟩ **d** : to exchange for something else ⟨*turn* coins into paper money⟩ **e** : to cause to defect to another side
7 a : to shape especially in a rounded form by applying a cutting tool while revolving in a lathe **b** : to give a rounded form to by any means ⟨*turn* the heel of a sock⟩ **c** : to shape or mold artistically, gracefully, or neatly ⟨a well *turned* phrase⟩
8 : to make a fold, bend, or curve in: **a** : to form by bending ⟨*turn* a lead pipe⟩ **b** : to cause (the edge of a blade) to bend back or over : BLUNT, DULL
9 a : to keep (as money or goods) moving; *specifically* : to dispose of (a stock) to make room for another **b** : to gain in the course of business ⟨*turning* a quick profit⟩ **c** : to make use of ⟨*turned* her education to advantage⟩ **d** : to carry to completion ⟨*turned* a double play⟩
10 : to engage in (an act of prostitution) ⟨*turn* tricks⟩

intransitive verb
1 a : to move around on an axis or through an arc of a circle : ROTATE **b** : to become giddy or dizzy : SPIN ⟨heights always made his head *turn*⟩ **c** (1) : to have as a decisive factor : HINGE ⟨the argument *turns* on a point of logic⟩ ⟨the outcome of the game *turned* on an interception⟩ (2) : to have a center (as of interest) in something specified
2 a : to direct one's course **b** (1) : to reverse a course or direction (2) : to have a reactive usually adverse effect : RECOIL **c** : to take a different course or direction ⟨*turned* toward home⟩ ⟨the main road *turns* sharply to the right⟩
3 a : to change position so as to face another way **b** : to face toward or away from someone or something **c** : to change one's attitude or reverse one's course of action to one of opposition or hostility ⟨felt the world had *turned* against him⟩ **d** : to make a sudden violent assault especially without evident cause ⟨dogs *turning* on their owners⟩
4 a : to direct one's attention or thoughts to or away from someone or something **b** (1) : to change one's religion (2) : to go over to another side or party : DEFECT **c** : to have recourse : REFER, RESORT ⟨*turned* to a friend for help⟩ ⟨*turned* to his notes for the exact figures⟩ **d** : to direct one's efforts or interests : devote or apply oneself ⟨*turned* to the study of the law⟩
5 a : to become changed, altered, or transformed: as (1) *archaic* : to become different (2) : to change color ⟨the leaves have *turned*⟩ (3) : to become sour, rancid, or tainted ⟨the milk had *turned*⟩ (4) : to be variable or inconstant (5) : to become mentally unbalanced : become deranged **b** (1) : to pass from one state to another : CHANGE ⟨water had *turned* to ice⟩ (2) : BECOME, GROW ⟨his hair had *turned* gray⟩ ⟨the weather *turned* bad⟩ ⟨just *turned* twenty⟩ (3) : to become someone or something specified by change from another state : change into ⟨*turn* pro⟩ ⟨doctors *turned* authors⟩
6 : to become curved or bent (as from pressure); *especially* : to become blunted by bending ⟨edge of the knife had *turned*⟩
7 : to operate a lathe
8 *of merchandise* : to be stocked and disposed of : change hands
 — **turn·able** \'tər-nə-bəl\ *adjective*
 — **turn a blind eye** : to refuse to see : to be oblivious ⟨might *turn a blind eye* to the use of violence —Arthur Krock⟩
 — **turn a deaf ear** : to refuse to listen
 — **turn a hair** : to give a sign of distress or disturbance ⟨did not *turn a hair* when told of the savage murder —*Times Literary Supplement*⟩
 — **turn color 1** : to become of a different color **2 a** : BLUSH, FLUSH **b** : to grow pale
 — **turn loose 1 a** : to set free ⟨*turned loose* the captured animal⟩ **b** : to free from all restraints ⟨*turned* them *loose* with a pile of theme paper to write whatever they liked —Elizabeth P. Schafer⟩ **2** : to fire off : DISCHARGE **3** : to open fire
 — **turn one's back on 1** : REJECT, DENY ⟨would be *turning one's back on* history —Pius Walsh⟩ **2** : FORSAKE ⟨*turned his back on* his obligations⟩
 — **turn one's hand** *or* **turn a hand** : to set to work : apply oneself
 — **turn one's head** : to cause to become infatuated or conceited ⟨success had not *turned his head*⟩
 — **turn one's stomach** : to disgust completely : SICKEN, NAUSEATE ⟨the foul smell *turned his stomach*⟩
 — **turn tail** : to turn away so as to flee ⟨*turned tail* and ran⟩
 — **turn the other cheek** : to respond to injury or unkindness with patience : forgo retaliation

— **turn the tables** : to bring about a reversal of the relative conditions or fortunes of two contending parties

— **turn the trick** : to bring about the desired result or effect

— **turn turtle** : CAPSIZE, OVERTURN

²**turn** *noun* [Middle English; partly from Old French *tourn, tour* lathe, circuit, turn (partly from Latin *tornus* lathe; partly from Old French *torner, tourner* to turn); partly from Middle English *turnen* to turn] (13th century)

1 a : the action or an act of turning about a center or axis : REVOLUTION, ROTATION **b** : any of various rotating or pivoting movements in dancing or gymnastics

2 a : the action or an act of giving or taking a different direction : change of course or posture ⟨illegal left *turn*⟩: as (1) : a drill maneuver in which troops in mass formation change direction without preserving alignment (2) : any of various shifts of direction in skiing (3) : an interruption of a curve in figure skating **b** : DEFLECTION, DEVIATION **c** : the action or an act of turning so as to face in the opposite direction : reversal of posture or course ⟨an *about turn*⟩ ⟨*turn* of the tide⟩ **d** : a change effected by turning over to another side ⟨*turn* of the cards⟩ **e** : a place at which something turns, turns off, or turns back : BEND, CURVE

3 : a short trip out and back or round about ⟨took a *turn* through the park⟩

4 : an act or deed affecting another especially when incidental or unexpected ⟨one good *turn* deserves another⟩

5 a : a period of action or activity : GO, SPELL **b** : a place, time, or opportunity accorded an individual or unit of a series in simple succession or in a scheduled order ⟨waiting her *turn* in line⟩ **c** : a period or tour of duty : SHIFT **d** : a short act or piece (as for a variety show); *also* : PERFORMANCE 3 **e** (1) : an event in any gambling game after which bets are settled (2) : the order of the last three cards in faro — used in the phrase *call the turn*

6 : something that revolves around a center: as **a** (1) : LATHE (2) : a catch or latch for a cupboard or cabinet door operated by turning a handle **b** : a musical ornament consisting of a group of four or more notes that wind about the principal note by including the notes next above and next below

7 : a special purpose or requirement — used chiefly in the phrase *serve one's turn*

8 a : an act of changing : ALTERATION, MODIFICATION ⟨a nasty *turn* in the weather⟩ **b** : a change in tendency, trend, or drift ⟨hoped for a *turn* in his luck⟩ ⟨a *turn* for the better⟩ **c** : the beginning of a new period of time ⟨the *turn* of the century⟩

9 a : distinctive quality or character **b** (1) : a skillful fashioning of language or arrangement of words (2) : a particular form of expression or peculiarity of phrasing **c** : the shape or mold in which something is fashioned : CAST

10 a : the state or manner of being coiled or twisted **b** : a single round (as of rope passed about an object or of wire wound on a core)

11 : natural or special ability or aptitude : BENT, INCLINATION ⟨a *turn* for logic⟩ ⟨an optimistic *turn* of mind⟩

12 : a special twist, construction, or interpretation ⟨gave the old yarn a new *turn*⟩

13 a : a disordering spell or attack (as of illness, faintness, or dizziness) **b** : a nervous start or shock

14 a : a complete transaction involving a purchase and sale of securities; *also* : a profit from such a transaction **b** : TURNOVER 7b

15 : something turned or to be turned: as **a** : a character or slug inverted in setting type **b** : a piece of type placed bottom up

— **at every turn** : on every occasion : CONTINUALLY ⟨they opposed her *at every turn*⟩

— **by turns 1** : one after another in regular succession **2** : VARIOUSLY, ALTERNATELY ⟨a book that is *by turns* pedantic, delightful, and infuriating⟩

— **in turn** : in due order of succession

— **on the turn** : at the point of turning ⟨tide is *on the turn*⟩

— **out of turn 1** : not in due order of succession ⟨play *out of turn*⟩ **2** : at a wrong time or place and usually imprudently ⟨talking *out of turn*⟩

— **to a turn** : to perfection

turn·about \'tər-nə-ˌbaůt\ *noun* (1789)

1 : MERRY-GO-ROUND

2 a : a change or reversal of direction, trend, policy, role, or character **b** : a changing from one allegiance to another **c** : TURNCOAT, RENEGADE **d** : an act or instance of retaliating ⟨*turnabout* is fair play⟩

turn·around \-ˌraůnd\ *noun* (1926)

1 a : the process of readying a vehicle for departure after its arrival especially without any intervening delays; *also* : the time spent in this process **b** : the action of receiving, processing, and returning something

2 : a space permitting the turning around of a vehicle

3 : TURNABOUT 2a, b

turn around (1949)

intransitive verb

1 : to act in an abrupt, different, or surprising manner — used with *and* ⟨after three years he just *turned around* and left school⟩

2 : to become changed for the better

transitive verb

: to change for the better ⟨*turned* her life *around*⟩

turn away (13th century)

transitive verb

1 : DEFLECT, AVERT

2 a : to send away : REJECT, DISMISS **b** : REPEL **c** : to refuse admittance or acceptance to

intransitive verb

: to start to go away : DEPART

turn back (1535)

intransitive verb

1 a : to go in the reverse direction **b** : to stop going forward

2 : to refer to an earlier time or place

transitive verb

1 : to drive back or away

2 : to stop the advance of

3 : to fold back

4 : GIVE BACK, RETURN

— **turn back the clock** : to revert to or remind of a condition existing in the past

turn·buck·le \'tərn-ˌbə-kəl\ *noun* (circa 1877)

: a device that usually consists of a link with screw threads at both ends, that is turned to bring the ends closer together, and that is used for tightening a rod or stay

turnbuckles

turn·coat \-ˌkōt\ *noun* (1557)

: one who switches to an opposing side or party; *specifically* : TRAITOR

¹**turn·down** \'tərn-'daůn\ *adjective* (1840)

: capable of being turned down; *especially* : worn turned down ⟨*turndown* collar⟩

²**turn·down** \'tərn-ˌdaůn\ *noun* (1849)

1 : something turned down; *also* : an instance of turning something (as a bed sheet) down ⟨hotel *turndown* service⟩

2 : REJECTION

3 : DOWNTURN

turn down (1601)

transitive verb

1 : to fold or double down

2 : to turn (a card) face downward

3 : to reduce the height or intensity of by turning a control ⟨*turn down* the radio⟩

4 : to decline to accept : REJECT ⟨*turned down* the offer⟩

intransitive verb

: to be capable of being folded or doubled down ⟨the collar *turns down*⟩

turned–on \'tərnd-'ȯn, -'än\ *adjective* (1966)

: keenly aware of and responsive to what is new and fashionable : HIP

¹**turn·er** \'tər-nər\ *noun* (15th century)

: one that turns or is used for turning ⟨a pancake *turner*⟩; *especially* : a person who forms articles with a lathe

²**tur·ner** \'tər-nər, 'tůr-\ *noun* [German, from *turnen* to perform gymnastic exercises, from Old High German *turnēn* to turn, from Medieval Latin *tornare* — more at TURN] (1854)

: a member of a turnverein : GYMNAST

Tur·ner's syndrome \'tər-nərz-\ *noun* [Henry Hubert *Turner* (died 1970) American physician] (1942)

: a genetically determined condition that is associated with the presence of only one complete X chromosome and no Y chromosome and that is characterized by a female phenotype with underdeveloped and infertile ovaries

turn·ery \'tər-nə-rē\ *noun, plural* **-er·ies** (1644)

: the work, products, or shop of a turner

turn–in \'tər-ˌnin\ *noun* (1902)

: something that turns in or is turned in

turn in (1535)

intransitive verb

1 : to make an entrance by turning from a road or path

2 : to go to bed ⟨*turned in* early⟩

transitive verb

1 : to deliver up : HAND OVER ⟨*turned in* his badge and quit⟩

2 a : to inform on : BETRAY **b** : to deliver to an authority ⟨urged the wanted man to *turn* himself *in*⟩

3 : to acquit oneself of : PUT ON, PRODUCE ⟨*turned in* a good performance⟩

turn·ing *noun* (14th century)

1 : the act or course of one that turns

2 : a place of a change in direction

3 a : a forming by use of a lathe; *broadly* : TURNERY **b** *plural* : waste produced in turning

turning chisel *noun* (circa 1877)

: a chisel used for shaping or finishing work in a lathe

turning point *noun* (1851)

: a point at which a significant change occurs

tur·nip \'tər-nəp\ *noun* [probably from ¹*turn* + *neep*; from the well-rounded root] (1533)

1 a : either of two biennial herbs of the mustard family with thick edible roots: (1) : one (*Brassica rapa rapifera*) with usually flattened roots and leaves that are cooked as a vegetable (2) : RUTABAGA **b** : the root of a turnip

2 : a large pocket watch

¹**turn·key** \'tərn-ˌkē\ *noun, plural* **turnkeys** (1654)

: one who has charge of a prison's keys

²**turnkey** *adjective* (1927)

: built, supplied, or installed complete and ready to operate ⟨a *turnkey* nuclear plant⟩ ⟨a *turnkey* computer system⟩; *also* : of or relating to a turnkey building or installation ⟨a *turnkey* contract⟩ ⟨*turnkey* vendors⟩

turn·off \'tər-ˌnȯf\ *noun* (circa 1852)

1 : a turning off

2 : a place where one turns off; *especially* : EXIT 4

3 : one that causes loss of interest or enthusiasm ⟨the music was a *turnoff*⟩

turn off (1564)

transitive verb

1 a : DISMISS, DISCHARGE **b :** to dispose of : SELL
2 : DEFLECT, EVADE
3 : PRODUCE, ACCOMPLISH
4 : to stop the flow of or shut off by or as if by turning a control ⟨*turn* the water *off*⟩
5 : HANG 1b
6 a : to remove (material) by the process of turning **b :** to shape or produce by turning
7 : to cause to lose interest : BORE ⟨economics *turns* me *off*⟩; *also :* to evoke a negative feeling in
intransitive verb
1 : to deviate from a straight course or from a main road ⟨*turn off* into a side road⟩
2 a *British :* to turn bad : SPOIL **b :** to change to a specified state : BECOME
3 : to lose interest : WITHDRAW

turn on (1833)
transitive verb
1 : to activate or cause to flow, operate, or function by or as if by turning a control ⟨*turn* the water *on* full⟩ ⟨*turn on* the power⟩
2 a : to cause to undergo an intense often visionary experience by taking a drug; *broadly :* to cause to get high **b :** to move pleasurably ⟨rock music *turns* her *on*⟩; *also :* to excite sexually **c :** to cause to gain knowledge or appreciation of something specified ⟨*turned* her *on* to ballet⟩
intransitive verb
: to become turned on
— **turn-on** \'tər-ˌnȯn, -ˌnän\ *noun*

turn-out \'tər-ˌnau̇t\ *noun* (1688)
1 : an act of turning out
2 *chiefly British* **a :** STRIKE 3a **b :** STRIKER 1d
3 : the number of people who participate in or attend an event ⟨a heavy voter *turnout*⟩
4 a : a place where something (as a road) turns out or branches off **b :** a space adjacent to a highway in which vehicles may park or pull into to enable others to pass **c :** a railroad siding
5 : a clearing out and cleaning
6 a : a coach or carriage together with the horses, harness, and attendants **b :** EQUIPMENT, RIG **c :** manner of dress : GETUP
7 : net quantity of produce yielded

turn out (1546)
transitive verb
1 a : EXPEL, EVICT **b :** to put (as a horse) to pasture
2 a : to turn inside out ⟨*turning out* his pockets⟩ **b :** to empty the contents of especially for cleaning or rearranging; *also :* CLEAN
3 : to produce often rapidly or regularly by or as if by machine ⟨a writer *turning out* stories⟩
4 : to equip, dress, or finish in a careful or elaborate way
5 : to put out by turning a switch ⟨*turn out* the lights⟩
6 : to call (as the guard or a company) out from rest or shelter and into formation
intransitive verb
1 a : to come or go out from home in or as if in answer to a summons ⟨voters *turned out* in droves⟩ **b :** to get out of bed
2 a : to prove to be in the result or end ⟨the play *turned out* to be a flop⟩ ⟨it *turned out* that we were both wrong⟩ **b :** to become in maturity ⟨nobody thought he'd *turn out* like this⟩ **c :** END ⟨stories that *turn out* happily⟩

¹turn-over \'tər-ˌnō-vər\ *noun* (14th century)
1 : an act or result of turning over : UPSET
2 : a turning from one side, place, or direction to its opposite : SHIFT, REVERSAL
3 : a reorganization with a view to a shift in personnel : SHAKE-UP
4 : something that is turned over
5 : a filled pastry made by folding half of the crust over the other half
6 : the amount of business done; *especially :* the volume of shares traded on a stock exchange

7 a : movement (as of goods or people) into, through, and out of a place **b :** a cycle of purchase, sale, and replacement of a stock of goods; *also :* the ratio of sales for a stated period to average inventory **c :** the number of persons hired within a period to replace those leaving or dropped from a workforce; *also :* the ratio of this number to the number in the average force maintained
8 : the act or an instance of a team's losing possession of a ball through error or a minor violation of the rules (as in basketball or football)

²turnover *adjective* (circa 1849)
: capable of being turned over

turn over (14th century)
transitive verb
1 a : to turn from an upright position : OVERTURN **b :** ROTATE ⟨*turn over* a stiff valve with a wrench⟩; *also :* to cause (an internal combustion engine) to begin firing
2 : to search (as clothes or papers) by lifting or moving one by one
3 : to read or examine (as a book) slowly or idly
4 : DELIVER, SURRENDER ⟨I'm *turning* the job *over* to you⟩; *also :* to lose possession of ⟨*turned* the ball *over* three times⟩
5 a : to receive and dispose of (a stock of merchandise) **b :** to do business to the amount of ⟨*turning over* $1000 a week⟩
intransitive verb
1 : UPSET, CAPSIZE
2 a : ROTATE **b** *of an engine :* to have crankshaft rotation especially by external means (as by a starter) ⟨the engine *turned over* but didn't start⟩
3 a *of one's stomach :* to heave with nausea **b** *of one's heart :* to seem to leap or lurch convulsively with sudden fright
— **turn over a new leaf :** to make a change for the better especially in one's way of living

turn·pike \'tərn-ˌpīk\ *noun* [Middle English *turnepike* revolving frame bearing spikes and serving as a barrier, from *turnen* to turn + *pike*] (1533)
1 : TOLLGATE
2 a (1) **:** a road (as an expressway) for the use of which tolls are collected (2) **:** a road formerly maintained as a turnpike **b :** a main road; *especially :* a paved highway with crowned surface

turn·sole \'tərn-ˌsōl\ *noun* [Middle English *turnesole*, from Middle French *tournesol*, from Old Italian *tornasole*, from *tornare* to turn (from Medieval Latin) + *sole* sun, from Latin *sol* — more at TURN, SOLAR] (14th century)
1 : a European herb (*Chrozophora tinctoria*) of the spurge family with juice that is turned blue by ammonia; *also :* a purple dye obtained from it
2 : HELIOTROPE 1

turn·spit \-ˌspit\ *noun* (1570)
1 a : one that turns a spit; *specifically :* a small dog formerly used in a treadmill to turn a spit **b :** a roasting jack
2 : a rotatable spit

turn·stile \-ˌstīl\ *noun* (1643)
: a post with arms pivoted on the top set in a passageway so that persons can pass through only on foot one by one

turn·stone \-ˌstōn\ *noun* [from a habit of turning over stones to find food] (circa 1674)
: either of two shorebirds (genus *Arenaria*) that resemble the related plovers and sandpipers: **a :** a bird (*A. interpres*) of worldwide distribution that has black and chestnut upperparts and a black breast **b :** a North American bird (*A. melanocephala*) with black upperparts and breast

turn·ta·ble \-ˌtā-bəl\ *noun* (1835)

: a revolvable platform: as **a** **:** a platform with a track for turning wheeled vehicles **b** **:** LAZY SUSAN **c :** a rotating platform that carries a phonograph record

turn to *intransitive verb* (1813)
: to apply oneself to work : act vigorously

¹turn-up \'tər-ˌnəp\ *adjective* (1685)
1 : turned up ⟨a *turnup* nose⟩
2 : made or fitted to be turned up ⟨a *turnup* collar⟩

²turn-up \'tər-ˌnəp\ *noun* (1688)
: something that is turned up

turn up (1563)
transitive verb
1 : FIND, DISCOVER
2 : to raise or increase by or as if by turning a control ⟨*turn up* the volume on the radio⟩
3 *British* **a :** to look up (as a word or fact) in a book **b :** to refer to or consult (a book)
4 : to turn (a card) face upward
intransitive verb
1 : to appear or come to light unexpectedly or after being lost ⟨new evidence has *turned up*⟩
2 a (1) **:** to turn out to be ⟨he *turned up* missing at roll call⟩ (2) **:** APPEAR 4 ⟨her name is always *turning up* in the newspapers⟩ **b :** to arrive or show up at an appointed or expected time or place ⟨*turned up* half an hour late⟩
3 : to happen or occur unexpectedly ⟨something always *turned up* to prevent their meeting⟩
4 *of a ship :* TACK 1b
— **turn up one's nose :** to show scorn or disdain

turn·ver·ein \'tərn-və-ˌrīn, 'tu̇rn-\ *noun* [German, from *turnen* to perform gymnastic exercises + *Verein* club] (1852)
: an athletic club

tu·ro·phile \'tu̇r-ə-ˌfīl, 'tyu̇r-\ *noun* [irregular from Greek *tyros* cheese + English *-phile* — more at BUTTER] (1938)
: a connoisseur of cheese : a cheese fancier

¹tur·pen·tine \'tər-pən-ˌtīn, -tər-ˌp⁰m-\ *noun* [Middle English *terbentyne, turpentyne*, from Middle French & Medieval Latin; Middle French *terbentina, tourbentine*, from Medieval Latin *terbentina*, from Latin *terebinthina*, feminine of *terebinthinus* of terebinth, from *terebinthus* terebinth, from Greek *terebinthos*] (14th century)
1 a : a yellow to brown semifluid oleoresin obtained as an exudate from the terebinth **b :** an oleoresin obtained from various conifers (as some pines and firs)
2 a : an essential oil obtained from turpentines by distillation and used especially as a solvent and thinner — called also *gum turpentine* **b :** a similar oil obtained by distillation or carbonization of pinewood — called also *wood turpentine*

²turpentine *transitive verb* **-tined; -tin·ing** (1759)
1 : to apply turpentine to
2 : to extract turpentine from; *especially :* to tap (pine trees) in order to obtain turpentine

tur·pi·tude \'tər-pə-ˌtüd, -ˌtyüd\ *noun* [Middle French, from Latin *turpitudo*, from *turpis* vile, base] (15th century)
: inherent baseness : DEPRAVITY ⟨moral *turpitude*⟩; *also :* a base act

turps \'tərps\ *noun plural but singular in construction* [by shortening & alteration] (circa 1823)
: TURPENTINE

tur·quoise *also* **tur·quois** \'tər-ˌkȯiz, -ˌkwȯiz\ *noun* [Middle English *turkeis, turcas*, from Middle French *turquoyse*, from feminine of *turquoys* Turkish, from Old French, from *Turc* Turk] (14th century)

turnstone

1 : a mineral that is a blue, bluish green, or greenish gray hydrous basic phosphate of copper and aluminum, takes a high polish, and is valued as a gem when skyblue
2 : a light greenish blue

turquoise blue *noun* (1799)
: a light greenish blue that is paler and slightly bluer than average turquoise

turquoise green *noun* (1886)
: a light bluish green

tur·ret \'tər-ət, 'tə-rət, 'tùr-ət\ *noun* [Middle English *touret*, from Middle French *torete, tourete*, from Old French, diminutive of *tor, tur* tower — more at TOWER] (14th century)
1 : a little tower; *specifically* **:** an ornamental structure at an angle of a larger structure
2 a : a pivoted and revolvable holder in a machine tool **b :** a device (as on a microscope or a television camera) holding several lenses
3 a : a tall building usually moved on wheels and formerly used for carrying soldiers and equipment for breaching or scaling a wall **b** (1) **:** a gunner's fixed or movable enclosure in an airplane (2) **:** a revolving armored structure on a warship that protects one or more guns mounted within it (3) **:** a similar upper structure usually for one gun on a tank

tur·ret·ed \'tər-ə-təd, 'tə-rə-, 'tùr-ə-\ *adjective* (1550)
: furnished with or as if with turrets

¹tur·tle \'tər-t°l\ *noun* [Middle English, from Old English *turtla*, from Latin *turtur*] (before 12th century)
archaic **:** TURTLEDOVE

²turtle *noun, plural* **turtles** *also* **turtle** *often attributive* [modification of French *tortue*, from Late Latin *tartaruca*, feminine of *tartaruchus* of Tartarus, from Greek *tartarouchos*, from *Tartaros* Tartarus] (1657)
: any of an order (Testudines) of terrestrial, freshwater, and marine reptiles that have a toothless horny beak and a shell of bony dermal plates usually covered with horny shields enclosing the trunk and into which the head, limbs, and tail usually may be withdrawn ◇

³turtle *noun* (1952)
: TURTLENECK

tur·tle·back \'tər-t°l-,bak\ *noun* (1881)
: a raised convex surface
— **turtleback** *or* **tur·tle·backed** \-,bakt\ *adjective*

tur·tle·dove \-,dəv\ *noun* (14th century)
: any of several small wild pigeons (genus *Streptopelia* and especially *S. turtur*) noted for plaintive cooing

tur·tle·head \-,hed\ *noun* (1857)
: any of a genus (*Chelone*) of perennial herbs of the snapdragon family with spikes of showy white or purple flowers

tur·tle·neck \-,nek\ *noun* (1897)
1 : a high close-fitting turnover collar used especially for sweaters
2 : a sweater with a turtleneck
— **tur·tle·necked** \-,nekt\ *adjective*

tur·tling \'tərt-liŋ, 'tər-t°l-iŋ\ *noun* (1726)
: the action or process of catching turtles

turves *plural of* TURF

¹Tus·can \'təs-kən\ *adjective* [Latin *tuscanus* Etruscan, from *Tusci* Etruscans] (1563)
1 : of or relating to one of the five classical orders of architecture that is of Roman origin and plain in style
2 : of, relating to, or characteristic of Tuscany, the Tuscans, or Tuscan

²Tuscan *noun* (1568)
1 a : the Italian language as spoken in Tuscany **b :** the standard literary dialect of Italian
2 : a native or inhabitant of Tuscany

Tus·ca·ro·ra \,təs-kə-'rōr-ə, -'ròr-\ *noun, plural* **Tuscarora** *or* **Tuscaroras** [Tuscarora *skarò⸱r⸱ʔ*] (1650)
1 : a member of an American Indian people originally of North Carolina and later of New York and Ontario
2 : the Iroquoian language of the Tuscarora people

tu·sche \'tüsh, 'tü-shə\ *noun* [German, from *tuschen* to lay on color, from French *toucher*, literally, to touch, from Old French *tuchier* — more at TOUCH] (1885)
: a black liquid used in lithography for drawing and painting and in etching and the silkscreen process as a resist

¹tush \'təsh\ *noun* [Middle English *tusch*, from Old English *tūsc*; akin to Old Frisian *tusk* tooth, Old English *tōth* tooth] (before 12th century)
: a long pointed tooth; *especially* **:** a horse's canine

²tush *interjection* [Middle English *tussch*] (15th century)
— used to express disdain or reproach

³tush \'tùsh\ *noun* [perhaps modification of Yiddish *tokhes*, from Hebrew *taḥath* under, beneath] (1962)
slang **:** BUTTOCKS

¹tusk \'təsk\ *noun* [Middle English, alteration of *tux*, from Old English *tūx*; akin to Old English *tūsc* tush] (before 12th century)
1 : an elongated greatly enlarged tooth (as of an elephant or walrus) that projects when the mouth is closed and serves for digging food or as a weapon; *broadly* **:** a long protruding tooth
2 : one of the small projections on a tusk tenon
— **tusked** \'təskt\ *adjective*
— **tusk·like** \'təsk-,līk\ *adjective*

²tusk *transitive verb* (1629)
: to dig up with a tusk; *also* **:** to gash with a tusk

tusk·er \'təs-kər\ *noun* (1859)
: an animal with tusks; *especially* **:** a male elephant with two normally developed tusks

tusk tenon *noun* (circa 1825)
: a tenon strengthened by one or more smaller tenons underneath forming a steplike outline

tus·sah \'tə-sə, -,sò\ *or* **tus·sore** \-,sōr, -,sòr\ *noun* [Hindi *tasar*] (1590)
: silk or silk fabric from the brownish fiber produced by larvae of some saturniid moths (as *Antheraea paphia*)

tus·sive \'tə-siv\ *adjective* [Latin *tussis* cough] (circa 1857)
: of, relating to, or involved in coughing

¹tus·sle \'tə-səl\ *noun* (1629)
1 : a physical contest or struggle **:** SCUFFLE
2 : an intense argument, controversy, or struggle

²tussle *intransitive verb* **tus·sled; tus·sling** \-s(ə-)liŋ\ [Middle English *tussillen*, frequentative of Middle English *-tusen, -tousen* to tousle — more at TOUSE] (1638)
: to struggle roughly **:** SCUFFLE

tus·sock \'tə-sək\ *noun* [origin unknown] (1580)
: a compact tuft especially of grass or sedge; *also* **:** an area of raised solid ground in a marsh or bog that is bound together by roots of low vegetation
— **tus·socky** \-sə-kē\ *adjective*

tussock grass *noun* (1842)
: a grass or sedge that typically grows in tussocks

tussock moth *noun* (1826)
: any of numerous dull-colored moths (family Lymantriidae) that usually have wingless females and larvae with long tufts of hair

tut \ə t-sound made by suction rather than explosion; often read as 'tət\ *interjection* (circa 1529)
— used to express disapproval or disbelief

tu·tee \tü-'tē, tyü-\ *noun* [*tutor* + *-ee*] (circa 1927)
: one who is being tutored

tu·te·lage \'tü-t°l-ij, 'tyü-\ *noun* [Latin *tutela* protection, guardian (from *tutari* to protect, frequentative of *tueri* to look at, guard) + English *-age*] (1605)
1 a : an act or process of serving as guardian or protector **:** GUARDIANSHIP **b :** hegemony over a foreign territory **:** TRUSTEESHIP 2
2 : the state of being under a guardian or tutor

3 a : instruction especially of an individual **b :** a guiding influence

tu·te·lar \'tü-t°l-ər, 'tyü-, -,är\ *adjective or noun* (1600)
: TUTELARY

¹tu·te·lary \'tü-t°l-,er-ē, 'tyü-\ *adjective* (1611)
1 : having the guardianship of a person or a thing ⟨a *tutelary* goddess⟩
2 : of or relating to a guardian

²tutelary *noun, plural* **-lar·ies** (1652)
: a tutelary power (as a deity)

¹tu·tor \'tü-tər, 'tyü-\ *noun* [Middle English, from Middle French & Latin; Middle French *tuteur*, from Latin *tutor*, from *tueri*] (14th century)
: a person charged with the instruction and guidance of another: as **a :** a private teacher **b :** a teacher in a British university who gives individual instruction to undergraduates

²tutor (1592)
transitive verb
1 : to have the guardianship, tutelage, or care of
2 : to teach or guide usually individually in a special subject or for a particular purpose **:** COACH
intransitive verb
1 : to do the work of a tutor
2 : to receive instruction especially privately

tu·tor·age \'tü-tə-rij, 'tyü-\ *noun* (1617)
: the function or work of a tutor

tu·tor·ess \'tü-tə-rəs, 'tyü-\ *noun* (1614)
: a woman or girl who is a tutor

¹tu·to·ri·al \tü-'tōr-ē-əl, tyü-, -'tòr-\ *adjective* (1822)
: of, relating to, or involving a tutor

²tutorial *noun* (1923)
1 : a class conducted by a tutor for one student or a small number of students
2 : a paper, book, film, or computer program that provides practical information about a specific subject

tu·tor·ship \'tü-tər-,ship, 'tyü-\ *noun* (1581)
1 : the office, function, or work of a tutor
2 : TUTELAGE 3

tu·toy·er \,tü-twä-yā\ *transitive verb* [French, to address with the familiar pronoun *tu* thou,

◇ **WORD HISTORY**

turtle The word *turtle* appears to have developed in 17th century nautical English out of an earlier word *tortu*, or its French source *tortue*, from which English *tortoise* is also derived. French *tortue* as a name for this animal, like Spanish *tortuga* and Italian *tartaruga*, ultimately descends from Late Latin *tartarucha* (or a similar collocation), literally, "infernal beast" or "beast of the nether regions." Such a humble and generally inoffensive animal hardly seems to deserve this epithet, but in early Christian literature and art the turtle, thought because of its lowness to the ground to wallow in mud and filth, was taken as a symbol of heresy and evil. A mosaic of the late 3rd century A.D. in Aquileia, northern Italy, depicts a turtle partly withdrawn into its shell aggressively confronted by a rooster, symbolic of goodness. Both rooster and turtle are emblems of light and darkness were taken from the pre-Christian cult of Mithras popular in the Roman empire. This demonic characterization of the animal was pervasive enough to affect everyday speech, and the Romance descendants of *tartarucha* largely ousted the descendants of the classical Latin word for "turtle," *testudo*.

\ə\ abut \°\ kitten \ər\ further \a\ ash \ā\ ace
\ä\ mop, mar \aù\ out \ch\ chin \e\ bet \ē\ easy
\g\ go \i\ hit \ī\ ice \j\ job \ŋ\ sing \ō\ go
\ò\ law \òi\ boy \th\ thin \th̲\ the \ü\ loot \ù\ foot
\y\ yet \zh\ vision *see also* Guide to Pronunciation

from Middle French, from *tu* thou (from Latin) + *toi* thee, from Latin *te* (accusative of *tu*) — more at THOU] (1697)
: to address familiarly

Tut·si \'tü-sē, 'tüt-\ *noun, plural* **Tutsi** *or* **Tutsis** (1950)
: a member of a Nilotic people of Rwanda and Burundi

¹**tut·ti** \'tü-tē, 'tù-; 'tü,tē, 'tù-\ *adjective or adverb* [Italian, masculine plural of *tutto* all, from (assumed) Vulgar Latin *tottus,* alteration of Latin *totus*] (circa 1724)
: with all voices or instruments performing together — used as a direction in music

²**tutti** *noun* (1816)
: a passage or section performed by all the performers

tut·ti–frut·ti \,tü-ti-'frü-tē, ,tù-\ *noun* [Italian *tutti frutti* all fruits] (1834)
: a confection or ice cream containing chopped usually candied fruits

¹**tut–tut** *two t-sounds made by suction rather than explosion; often read as* 'tət-'tət\ *interjection* (1591)
: TUT

²**tut–tut** \'tət-'tət\ *intransitive verb* **tut–tut·ted; tut–tut·ting** (1873)
: to express disapproval or disbelief by or as if by uttering tut ⟨the civilian press corps *tut-tutted* over the officers' equivocation, ignorance and bigotry —M. B. Duberman⟩

tu·tu \'tü-(,)tü\ *noun* [French, from (baby talk) *tutu* backside] (1913)
: a short projecting skirt worn by a ballerina

tu–whit tu–whoo \tə-,(h)wit-tə-'(h)wü\ *noun* [imitative] (1588)
: the cry of an owl

tux \'təks\ *noun* (1922)
: TUXEDO

tux·e·do \,tək-'sē-(,)dō\ *noun, plural* **-dos** *or* **-does** [Tuxedo Park, N.Y.] (1889)
1 : a single-breasted or double-breasted usually black or blackish blue jacket
2 : semiformal evening clothes for men
— **tux·e·doed** \-(,)dōd\ *adjective*

tutu

tu·yere \twē-'er\ *noun* [French *tuyère,* from Middle French, from *tuyau* pipe] (1781)
: a nozzle through which an air blast is delivered to a forge or blast furnace

TV \'tē-'vē\ *noun* [television] (1947)
: TELEVISION

TV dinner *noun* [from its saving the television viewer from having to interrupt viewing to prepare and serve a meal] (1954)
: a quick-frozen packaged dinner (as of meat, potatoes, and a vegetable) that requires only heating before it is served

twa \'twȧ\ *or* **twae** \'twȧ, 'twē\ *Scottish variant of* TWO

¹**twad·dle** \'twä-d⁾l\ *noun* [probably alteration of English dialect *twattle* idle talk] (1782)
1 : silly idle talk : DRIVEL
2 : one that twaddles : TWADDLER

²**twaddle** *verb* **twad·dled; twad·dling** \'twäd-liŋ, 'twä-d⁾l-iŋ\ (1826)
: PRATE, BABBLE
— **twad·dler** \'twäd-lər, 'twä-d⁾l-ər\ *noun*

¹**twain** \'twān\ *adjective* [Middle English, from Old English *twēgen* — more at TWO] (before 12th century)
archaic : TWO

²**twain** *pronoun* (before 12th century)
: TWO; *especially* : two fathoms ⟨mark *twain*⟩

³**twain** *noun* (14th century)
1 : TWO
2 : COUPLE, PAIR

¹**twang** \'twaŋ\ *noun* [imitative] (circa 1553)
1 : a harsh quick ringing sound like that of a plucked banjo string
2 a : nasal speech or resonance b : the charac-

teristic speech of a region, locality, or group of people
3 a : an act of plucking b : PANG, TWINGE
— **twangy** \'twaŋ-ē\ *adjective*

²**twang** *verb* **twanged; twang·ing** \'twaŋ-iŋ\ (1567)
intransitive verb
1 : to sound with a twang ⟨the couch *twanged* when he sat down⟩
2 : to speak or sound with a nasal intonation
3 : to throb or twitch with pain or tension
transitive verb
1 : to cause to sound with a twang
2 : to utter or pronounce with a nasal twang
3 : to pluck the string of
— **twang·er** *noun*

³**twang** *noun* [alteration of *tang*] (1611)
1 : a persisting flavor, taste, or odor : TANG
2 : SUGGESTION, TRACE

'**twas** \'twəz, 'twäz\ [by contraction] (1588)
: it was

twat \'twät\ *noun* [origin unknown] (1656)
: VULVA — usually considered vulgar

tway-blade \'twā-,blād\ *noun* [English dialect *tway* two] (1578)
: any of various orchids (genera *Listera* and *Liparis*) often having two leaves

¹**tweak** \'twēk\ *verb* [probably alteration of Middle English *twikken* to pull sharply, from Old English *twiccian* to pluck — more at TWITCH] (1601)
transitive verb
1 : to pinch and pull with a sudden jerk and twist : TWITCH ⟨*tweaked* a bud from the stem⟩
2 : to pinch (a person or a body part) lightly or playfully ⟨*tweaked* the baby's ear affectionately⟩
3 : to make small adjustments in or to ⟨*tweak* the controls⟩; *especially* : FINE-TUNE
intransitive verb
: PULL 1a, PLUCK

²**tweak** *noun* (1609)
: an act of tweaking : PINCH

twee \'twē\ *adjective* [baby-talk alteration of *sweet*] (1905)
chiefly British : affectedly or excessively dainty, delicate, cute, or quaint ⟨such a theme might sound *twee* or corny —*Times Literary Supplement*⟩

tweed \'twēd\ *noun* [probably short for Scots *tweedling, twidling* twilled cloth] (1841)
1 : a rough woolen fabric made usually in twill weaves and used especially for suits and coats
2 *plural* : tweed clothing; *specifically* : a tweed suit

Twee·dle·dum and Twee·dle·dee \,twē-d⁾l-'dəm-ən(d)-,twē-d⁾l-'dē\ *noun* [English *tweedle* to chirp + *dum* (imitative of a low musical note) & *dee* (imitative of a high musical note)] (1725)
: two individuals or groups that are practically indistinguishable

tweedy \'twē-dē\ *adjective* **tweed·i·er; -est** (1912)
1 : of or resembling tweed
2 a : given to wearing tweeds b : informal or suggestive of the outdoors in taste or habits
— **tweed·i·ness** *noun*

tween \'twēn\ *preposition* [Middle English *twene,* short for *betwene*] (14th century)
: BETWEEN

tweet \'twēt\ *noun* [imitative] (1845)
: a chirping note
— **tweet** *intransitive verb*

tweet·er \'twē-tər\ *noun* (1934)
: a small loudspeaker responsive only to the higher acoustic frequencies and reproducing sounds of high pitch — compare WOOFER

tweeze \'twēz\ *transitive verb* **tweezed; tweez·ing** [back-formation from *tweezers*] (1932)
: to pluck, remove, or handle with tweezers

twee·zer \'twē-zər\ *noun* (1904)
: TWEEZERS

twee·zers \-zərz\ *noun plural but singular or*

plural in construction [obsolete English *tweeze,* noun, *etui,* short for obsolete English *etweese,* from plural of obsolete English *etwee,* from French *étui*] (1654)
: any of various small metal instruments that are usually held between the thumb and forefinger, are used for plucking, holding, or manipulating, and consist of two legs joined at one end

Twelfth Day *noun* [from its being the 12th day after Christmas] (before 12th century)
: EPIPHANY 1

Twelfth Night *noun* (before 12th century)
: the evening or sometimes the eve of Epiphany

twelve \'twelv\ *noun* [Middle English, from Old English *twelf;* akin to Old High German *zwelif* twelve, Old English *twā* two, *-leofan* (as in *endleofan* eleven) — more at TWO, ELEVEN] (before 12th century)
1 — see NUMBER table
2 *capitalized* a : the twelve original disciples of Jesus b : the books of the Minor Prophets in the Jewish Scriptures
3 : the 12th in a set or series
4 : something having 12 units or members
5 *plural* : TWELVEMO
— **twelfth** \'twelf(t)th\ *adjective or noun*
— **twelve** *adjective*
— **twelve** *pronoun, plural in construction*

twelve·mo \'twelv-(,)mō\ *noun, plural* **-mos** (1819)
: the size of a piece of paper cut 12 from a sheet; *also* : a book, a page, or paper of this size

twelve·month \-,mən(t)th\ *noun* (13th century)
: YEAR

twelve–tone \-'tōn\ *adjective* (1926)
: of, relating to, or being serial music utilizing the 12 chromatic tones

twelve–tone row *noun* (1941)
: the 12 chromatic tones of the octave placed in a chosen fixed order and constituting with some permitted permutations and derivations the melodic and harmonic material of a serial musical piece

twen·ty \'twen-tē, 'twən-\ *noun, plural* **twenties** [Middle English, from *twenty,* adjective, from Old English *twēntig,* noun, group of 20, from *twēn-* (akin to Old English *twā* two) + *-tig* group of 10; akin to Old English *tīen* ten — more at TWO, TEN] (15th century)
1 — see NUMBER table
2 *plural* : the numbers 20 to 29; *specifically* : the years 20 to 29 in a lifetime or century
3 : a 20-dollar bill
— **twen·ti·eth** \-tē-əth\ *adjective or noun*
— **twenty** *adjective*
— **twenty** *pronoun, plural in construction*

twen·ty–four–mo \,twen-tē-'fȯr-(,)mō, ,twən-, -'fȯr-\ *noun, plural* **-mos** (circa 1841)
: the size of a piece of paper cut 24 from a sheet; *also* : a book, a page, or paper of this size

twen·ty–one \,twen-tē-'wən, ,twən-\ *noun* (1611)
1 — see NUMBER table
2 [translation of French *vingt-et-un*] : BLACKJACK
— **twenty–one** *adjective*
— **twenty–one** *pronoun, plural in construction*

twen·ty–twen·ty *or* **20/20** \-'twen-tē, -'twən-\ *adjective* [from the testing of vision by reading letters at a distance of 20 feet] (1875)
of the human eye : meeting a standard of normal visual acuity ⟨*twenty-twenty* vision⟩

twen·ty–two \-'tü\ *noun* (1526)
1 — see NUMBER table
2 : a .22-caliber firearm; *especially* : one firing rimfire cartridges — usually written .22
— **twenty–two** *adjective*
— **twenty–two** *pronoun, plural in construction*

'twere \'twər\ [by contraction] (1588)
: it were

twerp \'twərp\ *noun* [origin unknown] (circa 1923)
: a silly, insignificant, or contemptible person

Twi \'chwē, chə-'wē, 'twē, 'chē\ *noun* (1874)
1 : a dialect of Akan
2 : a literary language based on the Twi dialect and used by the Akan-speaking peoples (as the Ashanti)

twi- \'twī\ *prefix* [Middle English, from Old English; akin to Old High German *zwi-* twi-, Latin *bi-*, Greek *di-*, Old English *twā* two]
: two : double : doubly : twice ⟨*twi*-headed⟩

twice \'twīs\ *adverb* [Middle English *twiges, twies,* from Old English *twiga*; akin to Old English *twi-*] (12th century)
1 : on two occasions ⟨*twice* absent⟩
2 : two times : in doubled quantity or degree ⟨*twice* two is four⟩ ⟨*twice* as much⟩

twice–born \-'bȯrn\ *adjective* (15th century)
1 : born a second time
2 : having undergone a definite experience of fundamental moral and spiritual renewal : REGENERATE
3 : of or forming one of the three upper Hindu caste groups in which boys undergo an initiation symbolizing spiritual birth

twice–laid \-'lād\ *adjective* (circa 1593)
: made from the ends of rope and strands of used rope ⟨*twice-laid* rope⟩

twice–told \-'tōld\ *adjective* (1595)
: well known from repeated telling — used chiefly in the phrase *a twice-told tale*

'twid-dle \'twi-dᵊl\ *verb* **twid-dled; twid-dling** \'twid-liŋ, 'twi-dᵊl-iŋ\ [origin unknown] (circa 1540)
intransitive verb
1 : to play negligently with something : FIDDLE
2 : to turn or jounce lightly ⟨*twiddles* round and round in the water —J. B. S. Haldane⟩
transitive verb
: to rotate lightly or idly ⟨*twiddled* his cigar —James Lord⟩
— **twiddle one's thumbs** : to spend time idly : do nothing

²twiddle *noun* (1774)
: TURN, TWIST

¹twig \'twig\ *noun* [Middle English *twigge,* from Old English; akin to Old High German *zwīg* twig, Old English *twā* two] (before 12th century)
1 : a small shoot or branch usually without its leaves
2 : a minute branch of a nerve or artery
— **twigged** \'twigd\ *adjective*
— **twig-gy** \'twi-gē\ *adjective*

²twig *verb* **twigged; twig-ging** [perhaps from Irish & Scottish Gaelic *tuig-* understand] (1764)
transitive verb
1 : NOTICE, OBSERVE
2 : to understand the meaning of : COMPREHEND
intransitive verb
: to gain a grasp : UNDERSTAND ⟨*twigged* instinctively about things —H. E. Bates⟩

³twig *noun* [origin unknown] (circa 1811)
British : FASHION, STYLE

twi-light \'twī-,līt\ *noun, often attributive* (15th century)
1 : the light from the sky between full night and sunrise or between sunset and full night produced by diffusion of sunlight through the atmosphere and its dust
2 a : an intermediate state that is not clearly defined ⟨lived in the *twilight* of neutrality —*Newsweek*⟩ **b** : a period of decline ⟨the *twilight* of a great career⟩

twilight glow *noun* (1819)
: airglow seen at twilight

Twilight of the Gods
: RAGNAROK

twilight zone *noun* (1909)
1 a : TWILIGHT 2a **b** : an area just beyond ordinary legal and ethical limits

2 : a world of fantasy, illusion, or unreality

twi-lit \'twī-,lit\ *adjective* [*twilight* + *lit*] (1869)
: lighted by or as if by twilight

twill \'twil\ *noun* [Middle English *twyll, twylle,* from Old English *twilic* having a double thread, part translation of Latin *bilic-, bilix,* from *bi-* + *licium* thread] (14th century)
1 : a fabric with a twill weave
2 : a textile weave in which the filling threads pass over one and under two or more warp threads to give an appearance of diagonal lines

twilled \'twild\ *adjective* (15th century)
: made with a twill weave

twill-ing \'twi-liŋ\ *noun* (circa 1859)
: twilled fabric; *also* : the process of making it

¹twin \'twin\ *noun* [Middle English, from *twin* twofold] (14th century)
1 a : either of two offspring produced at a birth **b** *plural, capitalized* : GEMINI
2 : one of two persons or things closely related to or resembling each other
3 : a compound crystal composed of two adjoining crystals or parts of crystals of the same kind that share a common plane of atoms
— **twin-ship** \-,ship\ *noun*

²twin *verb* **twinned; twin-ning** (14th century)
transitive verb
1 : to bring together in close association : COUPLE
2 : DUPLICATE, MATCH
intransitive verb
1 : to bring forth twins
2 : to grow as a twin crystal

³twin *adjective* [Middle English, twofold, double, from Old English *twinn*; akin to Old Norse *tvinnr* two by two, Old English *twā* two] (1590)
1 : born with one other or as a pair at one birth ⟨*twin* brother⟩ ⟨*twin* girls⟩
2 a : made up of two similar, related, or connected members or parts : DOUBLE **b** : paired in a close or necessary relationship : MATCHING **c** : having or consisting of two identical units **d** : being one of a pair

twin bed *noun* (1919)
: one of a pair of matching single beds

twin-ber-ry \'twin-,ber-ē\ *noun* [from the occurrence of the berries in pairs] (1821)
1 : a shrubby North American honeysuckle (*Lonicera involucrata*) with yellowish involucrate flowers
2 : PARTRIDGEBERRY

twin bill *noun* (circa 1939)
: DOUBLEHEADER

twin-born \'twin-'bȯrn\ *adjective* (1598)
: born at the same birth

twin double *noun* (1960)
: a system of betting (as on horse races) in which the bettor must pick the winners of four stipulated races in order to win — compare DAILY DOUBLE

¹twine \'twīn\ *noun* [Middle English *twin,* from Old English *twīn*; akin to Middle Dutch *twijn* twine, Old English *twā* two] (before 12th century)
1 : a strong string of two or more strands twisted together
2 : a twined or interlaced part or object
3 : an act of twining, interlacing, or embracing
— **twiny** \'twī-nē\ *adjective*

²twine *verb* **twined; twin-ing** (13th century)
transitive verb
1 a : to twist together **b** : to form by twisting : WEAVE
2 a : INTERLACE ⟨the girl *twined* her hands —John Buchan⟩ **b** : to cause to encircle or enfold something **c** : to cause to be encircled
intransitive verb
1 : to coil about a support
2 : to stretch or move in a sinuous manner : MEANDER ⟨the river *twines* through the valley⟩
— **twin-er** *noun*

³twine *verb* **twined; twin-ing** [alteration of

Scots *twin,* from Middle English *twinnen,* from *twin* double] (1722)
transitive verb
chiefly Scottish : to cause (one) to lose possession : DEPRIVE ⟨*twined* him of his nose —J. C. Ransom⟩
intransitive verb
chiefly Scottish : PART ⟨you and me must *twine* —R. L. Stevenson⟩

twin-flow-er \'twin-,flaů(-ə)r\ *noun* (circa 1818)
: a low prostrate subshrub (*Linnaea borealis*) of the honeysuckle family that is found in cool regions of the northern hemisphere and has fragrant usually pink flowers

¹twinge \'twinj\ *verb* **twinged; twing-ing** \'twin-jiŋ\ *or* **twinge-ing** [Middle English *twengen,* from Old English *twengan*; akin to Old High German *zwengen* to pinch] (before 12th century)
transitive verb
1 *dialect* : PLUCK, TWEAK
2 : to affect with a sharp pain or pang
intransitive verb
: to feel a sudden sharp local pain

²twinge *noun* (1608)
1 : a sudden sharp stab of pain
2 : a moral or emotional pang ⟨a *twinge* of conscience⟩

twi–night \'twī-,nīt\ *adjective* [*twilight* + *night*] (1946)
: of, relating to, or being a baseball doubleheader in which the first game is played in the late afternoon and the second continues into the evening

¹twin-kle \'twin-kəl\ *verb* **twin-kled; twin-kling** \-k(ə-)liŋ\ [Middle English, from Old English *twinclian*; akin to Middle High German *zwinken* to blink] (before 12th century)
intransitive verb
1 : to shine with a flickering or sparkling light : SCINTILLATE
2 a : to flutter the eyelids **b** : to appear bright especially with merriment ⟨his eyes *twinkled*⟩
3 : to flutter or flit rapidly
transitive verb
1 : to cause to shine with fluctuating light
2 : to flicker or flirt rapidly ⟨*twinkled* the straight, red-lacquered toes —Glenway Wescott⟩
— **twin-kler** \-k(ə-)lər\ *noun*

²twinkle *noun* (1548)
1 : a wink of the eyelids
2 : the instant's duration of a wink : TWINKLING
3 : an intermittent radiance : FLICKER, SPARKLE
4 : a rapid flashing motion : FLIT
— **twin-kly** \-k(ə-)lē\ *adjective*

twin-kling \'twin-kliŋ\ *noun* (14th century)
: the time required for a wink : INSTANT ⟨the kettle will boil in a *twinkling* —Punch⟩

twin-set \'twin-'set\ *noun* (1937)
: a combination of a matching pullover and cardigan worn together

twin–size \'twin-'sīz\ *adjective* [*twin bed*] (1926)
: having the dimensions 39 inches by 75 inches or about 99 centimeters by 191 centimeters) — used of a bed; compare FULL-SIZE, KING-SIZE, QUEEN-SIZE

¹twirl \'twər(-ə)l\ *verb* [perhaps of Scandinavian origin; akin to Norwegian dialect *tvirla* to twirl; akin to Old High German *dweran* to stir] (1598)
intransitive verb
1 : to revolve rapidly
2 : to pitch in a baseball game
transitive verb
1 : to cause to rotate rapidly
2 : PITCH 2a

— **twirl·er** \'twər-lər\ *noun*

²**twirl** *noun* (1598)
1 : an act of twirling
2 : COIL, WHORL
— **twirl·y** \'twər-lē\ *adjective*

twirp *variant of* TWERP

¹**twist** \'twist\ *verb* [Middle English, from Old English *-twist* rope; akin to Middle Dutch *twist* quarrel, twine, Old English *twā* two] (15th century)
transitive verb
1 a : to unite by winding ⟨*twisting* strands together⟩ **b** : to make by twisting strands together ⟨*twist* thread from yarn⟩ **c** : to mingle by interlacing
2 : TWINE, COIL
3 a : to wring or wrench so as to dislocate or distort; *especially* : SPRAIN ⟨*twisted* my ankle⟩ **b** : to alter the meaning of : DISTORT, PERVERT ⟨*twisted* the facts⟩ **c** : CONTORT ⟨*twisted* his face into a grin⟩ **d** : to pull off, turn, or break by torsion **e** : to cause to move with a churning motion **f** : to form into a spiral shape **g** : to cause to take on moral, mental, or emotional deformity **h** : to make (one's way) in a winding or devious manner to a destination or objective
intransitive verb
1 : to follow a winding course : SNAKE
2 a : to turn or change shape under torsion **b** : to assume a spiral shape **c** : SQUIRM, WRITHE **d** : to dance the twist
3 *of a ball* : to rotate while taking a curving path or direction
4 : TURN 3a ⟨*twisted* around to see behind him⟩
— **twist one's arm** : to bring strong pressure to bear on one

²**twist** *noun* (1555)
1 : something formed by twisting or winding: as **a** : a thread, yarn, or cord formed by twisting two or more strands together **b** : a strong tightly twisted sewing silk **c** : a baked piece of twisted dough **d** : tobacco leaves twisted into a thick roll **e** : a strip of citrus peel used to flavor a drink
2 a : an act of twisting : the state of being twisted **b** : a dance performed with strenuous gyrations especially of the hips **c** : the spin given the ball in any of various games **d** : a spiral turn or curve **e** (1) : torque or torsional stress applied to a body (as a rod or shaft) (2) : torsional strain (3) : the angle through which a thing is twisted
3 a : a turning off a straight course **b** : ECCENTRICITY, IDIOSYNCRASY **c** : a distortion of meaning or sense
4 a : an unexpected turn or development ⟨weird *twists* of fate —W. L. Shirer⟩ **b** : a clever device : TRICK ⟨questions demanding special *twists* of thinking —*New Yorker*⟩ **c** : a variant approach or method : GIMMICK ⟨a kind of *twist* on the old triangle theme —Dave Fedo⟩
5 : a front or back dive in which the diver twists sideways a half or full turn before entering the water
— **twisty** \'twis-tē\ *adjective*

twist drill *noun* (circa 1875)
: a drill having deep helical grooves extending from the point to the smooth portion of the shank

twist·ed \'twis-təd\ *adjective* (circa 1890)
: mentally or emotionally unsound or disturbed : SICK

twist·er \'twis-tər\ *noun* (1579)
1 : one that twists; *especially* : a ball with a forward and spinning motion
2 : a tornado, waterspout, or dust devil in which the rotatory ascending movement of a column of air is especially apparent

twist·ing \'twis-tiŋ\ *noun* (circa 1905)
: the use of misrepresentation or trickery to get someone to lapse a life insurance policy and buy another usually in another company

¹**twit** \'twit\ *noun* (1528)
1 : an act of twitting : TAUNT

2 : a silly annoying person : FOOL

²**twit** *transitive verb* **twit·ted; twit·ting** [Middle English *atwiten* to reproach, from Old English *ætwītan*, from *æt* at + *wītan* to reproach; akin to Old High German *wīzan* to punish, Old English *witan* to know] (1530)
1 : to subject to light ridicule or reproach : RALLY
2 : to make fun of as a fault

¹**twitch** \'twich\ *verb* [Middle English *twicchen*; akin to Old English *twiccian* to pluck, Old High German *gizwickan* to pinch] (14th century)
transitive verb
: to move or pull with a sudden motion : JERK
intransitive verb
1 : PULL 1a, PLUCK ⟨*twitched* at my sleeve⟩
2 : to move jerkily : QUIVER
— **twitch·er** *noun*

²**twitch** *noun* (1523)
1 : an act of twitching; *especially* : a short sudden pull or jerk
2 : a physical or mental pang
3 : a loop of rope or strap that is tightened over a horse's lip as a restraining device
4 a : a short spastic contraction of the muscle fibers **b** : a slight jerk of a body part
— **twitch·i·ly** \'twi-chə-lē\ *adverb*
— **twitchy** \'twi-chē\ *adjective*

³**twitch** *noun* [alteration of *quitch*] (1598)
: QUACK GRASS

¹**twit·ter** \'twi-tər\ *verb* [Middle English *twiteren*; akin to Old High German *zwizzirōn* to twitter] (14th century)
intransitive verb
1 : to utter successive chirping noises
2 a : to talk in a chattering fashion **b** : GIGGLE, TITTER
3 : to tremble with agitation : FLUTTER
transitive verb
1 : to utter in chirps or twitters ⟨the robin *twittered* its morning song⟩
2 : to shake rapidly back and forth : FLUTTER

²**twitter** *noun* (1678)
1 : a trembling agitation : QUIVER
2 : a small tremulous intermittent sound (as of birds)
3 a : a light chattering **b** : a light silly laugh : GIGGLE
— **twit·tery** \'twi-tə-rē\ *adjective*

twixt \'twikst\ *or* **'twixt** *preposition* [Middle English *twix*, short for *betwix, betwixt*] (14th century)
: BETWEEN

¹**two** \'tü\ *adjective* [Middle English *twa, two*, from Old English *twā* (feminine & neuter); akin to Old English *twēgen* two (masculine), *tū* (neuter), Old High German *zwēne*, Latin *duo*, Greek *dyo*] (before 12th century)
1 : being one more than one in number
2 : being the second — used postpositively ⟨section *two* of the instructions⟩

²**two** *pronoun, plural in construction* (before 12th century)
1 : two countable individuals not specified ⟨only *two* were found⟩
2 : a small approximate number of indicated things ⟨only a shot or *two* were fired⟩

³**two** *noun, plural* **twos** (circa 1585)
1 — see NUMBER table
2 : the second in a set or series ⟨the *two* of spades⟩
3 : a 2-dollar bill
4 : something having two units or members

two–bag·ger \-'ba-gər\ *noun* (1880)
: DOUBLE 1b

two–bit \'tü-'bit\ *adjective* (1802)
1 : of the value of two bits
2 : cheap or trivial of its kind : PETTY, SMALL-TIME

two bits *noun plural but singular or plural in construction* (1730)
1 : the value of a quarter of a dollar
2 : something of small worth or importance

¹**two–by–four** \ˌtü-bī-'fȯr, -'fȯr\ *noun* (1884)
: a piece of lumber approximately 2 by 4 inch-

es as sawed and usually 1⅝ by 3⅝ inches if dressed

²**two–by–four** *adjective* (1897)
1 : measuring two units (as inches) by four
2 : small or petty of its kind ⟨this house and its *two-by-four* garden —Philip Barry⟩

two cents *noun* (1947)
1 : a sum or object of very small value : practically nothing ⟨said angrily that for *two cents* he'd punch your nose⟩
2 *or* **two cents worth** : an opinion offered on a topic under discussion ⟨each speaker . . . is getting in his *two cents worth* —Dwight Macdonald⟩

two–cycle *adjective* (1902)
of an internal combustion engine : having a 2-stroke cycle

two–dimensional *adjective* (1883)
1 : having two dimensions
2 : lacking depth of characterization ⟨*two-dimensional* characters⟩
— **two–dimensionality** *noun*

two–edged sword \'tü-'ejd-, -'e-jəd-\ *noun* (1526)
: DOUBLE-EDGED SWORD

two–faced \'tü-'fāst\ *adjective* (1609)
1 : DOUBLE-DEALING, FALSE
2 : having two faces
— **two–faced·ness** \-'fāst-nəs, -'fā-səd-nəs\ *noun*

two–fer \'tü-fər\ *noun* [alteration of *two for one*] (1890)
1 : a cheap item of merchandise; *especially* : a cigar selling at two for a nickel
2 : a free coupon entitling the bearer to purchase two tickets to a specified theatrical production for the price of one
3 : two articles available for the price of one or about the price of one

two–fist·ed \-'fis-təd\ *adjective* (1774)
: marked by vigorous often virile energy : HARD-HITTING

two·fold \'tü-ˌfōld, -'fōld\ *adjective* (1559)
1 : having two parts or aspects
2 : being twice as great or as many
— **twofold** \-'fōld\ *adverb*

2,4–D \ˌtü-ˌfȯr-'dē, -ˌfȯr-\ *noun* [*di-*] (circa 1945)
: a white crystalline irritant compound $C_8H_6Cl_2O_3$ used especially as a weed killer

2,4,5–T \-ˌfiv-'tē\ *noun* [*tri-*] (1946)
: an irritant compound $C_8H_5Cl_3O_3$ used especially as an herbicide and defoliant

two–hand·ed \'tü-'han-dəd\ *adjective* (15th century)
1 : used with both hands ⟨a *two-handed* sword⟩
2 : requiring two persons ⟨a *two-handed* saw⟩
3 *archaic* : STOUT, STRONG
4 a : having two hands **b** : efficient with either hand

two–line octave *noun* (circa 1931)
: the musical octave that begins on the first C above middle C — see PITCH illustration

two–party *adjective* (1925)
: characterized by two major political parties of comparable strength

two·pence \'tə-pən(t)s, US also 'tü-ˌpen(t)s\ *noun* (15th century)
1 : the sum of two British pennies
2 *plural* **twopence** *or* **two·pen·ces** : a coin worth twopence

two·pen·ny \'təp-nē, 'tə-pə-, US also 'tü-ˌpe-nē\ *adjective* (1532)
: costing or worth twopence

two–phase *adjective* (circa 1896)
: DIPHASIC

¹**two–piece** \'tü-'pēs\ *adjective* (1910)
: forming a clothing ensemble with matching top and bottom parts

²**two–piece** \'tü-ˌpēs\ *noun* (1930)
: a garment (as a bathing suit) that is two-piece

two–piec·er \'tü-'pē-sər\ *noun* (1943)
: TWO-PIECE

two–ply \-'plī\ *adjective* (circa 1847)

1 : consisting of two thicknesses
2 a : woven with two sets of warp thread and two of filling ⟨a *two-ply* carpet⟩ **b** : consisting of two strands ⟨*two-ply* yarn⟩
two-sid·ed \-'sī-dəd\ *adjective* (1884)
: having two sides : BILATERAL
two·some \'tü-səm\ *noun* (14th century)
1 : a group of two persons or things : COUPLE
2 : a golf singles match
two-spot·ted spider mite \'tü-'spä-təd-\ *noun* (1947)
: a widely distributed mite (*Tetranychus urticae*) that feeds on soft plant parts and is a serious pest in greenhouses and gardens
two-step \'tü-,step\ *noun* (1895)
1 : a ballroom dance in ²⁄₄ or ⁴⁄₄ time having a basic pattern of step-close-step
2 : a piece of music for the two-step
— two-step *intransitive verb*
two-suit·er \-'sü-tər\ *noun* (1948)
: a man's suitcase designed to hold two suits and accessories
two-tailed \'tü-'tāl(d)\ *also* **two-tail** \-'tā(ə)l\ *adjective* (1945)
: being a statistical test for which the critical region consists of all values of the test statistic greater than a given value plus the values less than another given value — compare ONE-TAILED
two-time \'tü-,tīm\ *transitive verb* (1924)
1 : DOUBLE-CROSS
2 : to betray (a spouse or lover) by secret lovemaking with another
— two-tim·er *noun*
two-toed sloth \'tü-'tōd-\ *noun* (1781)
: any of a genus (*Choloepus*) of sloths having two clawed digits on each forefoot, three clawed digits on each hind foot, and usually six or seven vertebrae in the neck — compare THREE-TOED SLOTH
two-tone \'tü-'tōn\ *adjective* (1906)
: colored in two colors or in two shades of one color ⟨*two-tone* shoes⟩
two-toned \'tü-'tōnd\ *adjective* (1897)
: TWO-TONE
two-way *adjective* (1571)
1 : being a cock or valve that will connect a pipe or channel with either of two others
2 : moving or allowing movement in either direction ⟨a *two-way* bridge⟩
3 a : involving or allowing an exchange between two individuals or groups ⟨there must be good *two-way* communication —Jerrold Orne⟩; *especially* : designed for both sending and receiving messages ⟨*two-way* radio⟩ **b** : involving mutual responsibility or reciprocal relationships ⟨political alliance is a *two-way* thing —T. H. White (died 1986)⟩
4 : involving two participants ⟨a *two-way* race⟩
5 : usable in either of two manners ⟨a *two-way* lamp⟩
two-way street *noun* (1948)
: a situation or relationship requiring give-and-take ⟨marriage is a *two-way street*⟩
two-wheel·er \-'hwē-lər, -'wē-\ *noun* (1861)
: a 2-wheeled vehicle (as a bicycle)
two-winged fly \'tü-'wiŋ(d)-\ *noun* (1753)
: ⁴FLY 2a
-ty *noun suffix* [Middle English *-te*, from Old French *-té*, from Latin *-tat-, -tas* — more at -ITY]
: quality : condition : degree ⟨apriori*ty*⟩
ty·coon \tī-'kün\ *noun* [Japanese *taikun*] (1857)
1 : SHOGUN
2 a : a top leader (as in politics) **b** : a businessman of exceptional wealth and power : MAGNATE ◇
ty·er \'tī(-ə)r\ *variant of* ³TIER
tying *present participle of* TIE
tyke \'tīk\ *noun* [Middle English *tyke*, from Old Norse *tīk* bitch; akin to Middle Low German *tīke* bitch] (15th century)
1 : DOG; *especially* : an inferior or mongrel dog

2 a *chiefly British* : a clumsy, churlish, or eccentric person **b** : a small child
tym·bal \'tim-bəl\ *noun* [alteration of *timbal*] (1929)
: the vibrating membrane in the shrilling organ of a cicada
tym·pan \'tim-pən\ *noun* [in sense 1, from Middle English, from Old English *timpana*, from Latin *tympanum*; in other senses, from Medieval Latin & Latin *tympanum*] (before 12th century)
1 : DRUM
2 : a sheet (as of paper or cloth) placed between the impression surface of a press and the paper to be printed
3 : TYMPANUM 2
tym·pa·ni, tym·pa·nist *variant of* TIMPANI, TIMPANIST
tym·pan·ic \tim-'pa-nik\ *adjective* [Latin & New Latin *tympanum*] (1808)
: of, relating to, or being a tympanum
tympanic membrane *noun* (1860)
: a thin membrane that closes externally the cavity of the middle ear and functions in the mechanical reception of sound waves and in their transmission to the site of sensory reception — called also *eardrum*; see EAR illustration
tym·pa·ni·tes \,tim-pə-'nī-tēz\ *noun* [Middle English, from Late Latin, from Greek *tympanitēs*, from *tympanon*] (14th century)
: a distension of the abdomen caused by accumulation of gas in the intestinal tract or peritoneal cavity
— tym·pa·nit·ic \-'ni-tik\ *adjective*
tym·pa·num \'tim-pə-nəm\ *noun, plural* **-na** \-nə\ *also* **-nums** [Medieval Latin & Latin; Medieval Latin, eardrum, from Latin, drum, architectural panel, from Greek *tympanon* drum, kettledrum; perhaps akin to Greek *typtein* to beat] (1619)
1 a : TYMPANIC MEMBRANE (2) : MIDDLE EAR **b** : a thin tense membrane covering an organ of hearing of an insect — see INSECT illustration **c** : a membranous resonator in a sound-producing organ
2 a : the recessed usually triangular face of a pediment

1 tympanum 2a

within the frame made by the upper and lower cornices **b** : the space within an arch and above a lintel or a subordinate arch
tym·pa·ny \-nē\ *noun, plural* **-nies** [Medieval Latin *tympanias*, from Greek, from *tympanon*] (1528)
1 : TYMPANITES
2 : BOMBAST, TURGIDITY
Tyn·dar·e·us \tin-'dar-ē-əs\ *noun* [Latin, from Greek]
: a king of Sparta and husband of Leda in Greek mythology
tyne *variant of* TINE
typ·al \'tī-pəl\ *adjective* (1853)
1 : serving as a type : TYPICAL
2 : of or relating to a type
¹type \'tīp\ *noun, often attributive* [Middle English, from Late Latin *typus*, from Latin & Greek; Latin *typus* image, from Greek *typos* blow, impression, model, from *typtein* to strike, beat; akin to Sanskrit *tupati* he injures and probably to Latin *stupēre* to be benumbed] (15th century)
1 a : a person or thing (as in the Old Testament) believed to foreshadow another (as in the New Testament) **b** : one having qualities of a higher category : MODEL **c** : a lower taxonomic category selected as a standard of reference for a higher category; *also* : a specimen or series of specimens on which a taxonomic species or subspecies is actually based

2 : a distinctive mark or sign
3 a (1) : a rectangular block usually of metal bearing a relief character from which an inked print can be made (2) : a collection of such blocks ⟨a font of *type*⟩ (3) : alphanumeric characters for printing ⟨the *type* for this book has been photoset⟩ **b** : TYPEFACE ⟨italic *type*⟩ **c** : printed letters **d** : matter set in type
4 a : qualities common to a number of individuals that distinguish them as an identifiable class: as (1) : the morphological, physiological, or ecological characters by which relationship between organisms may be recognized (2) : the form common to all instances of a linguistic element **b** : a typical and often superior specimen **c** : a member of an indicated class or variety of people ⟨the guests were mostly urban *types* —Lucy Cook⟩ **d** : a particular kind, class, or group ⟨oranges of the seedless *type*⟩ ⟨leaders of the new *type* . . . did England yeoman's service —G. M. Trevelyan⟩ **e** : something distinguishable as a variety : SORT ⟨what *type* of food do you like?⟩ ☆

\ə\ abut \ᵊ\ kitten \ər\ **further** \a\ ash \ā\ ace
\ä\ mop, mar \au̇\ out \ch\ chin \e\ bet \ē\ **easy**
\g\ go \i\ hit \ī\ ice \j\ job \ŋ\ sing \ō\ go
\ȯ\ law \ȯi\ boy \th\ **thin** \t͟h\ the \ü\ loot \u̇\ foot
\y\ yet \zh\ vision *see also* Guide to Pronunciation

²type *verb* **typed; typ·ing** (1596)
transitive verb
1 : to represent beforehand as a type **:** PREFIGURE
2 a : to produce a copy of **b :** to represent in terms of typical characteristics **:** TYPIFY
3 : to produce (as a character or document) on a typewriter; *also* **:** KEYBOARD
4 : to identify as belonging to a type: as **a :** to determine the natural type of (as a blood sample) **b :** TYPECAST
intransitive verb
: to write something on a typewriter or enter data into a computer by way of a keyboard
— **type·able** \'tī-pə-bəl\ *adjective*
type A *adjective* (1970)
: relating to, characteristic of, having, or being a personality that is marked by impatience, aggressiveness, and competitiveness and that is held to be associated with increased risk of cardiovascular disease ⟨*type A* behavior⟩
type·cast \'tīp-ˌkast\ *transitive verb* **-cast; -cast·ing** (1927)
1 : to cast (an actor or actress) in a part calling for the same characteristics as those possessed by the performer
2 : to cast (an actor or actress) repeatedly in the same type of role
3 : STEREOTYPE ⟨*typecast* as the grubby, unbeautiful place which is full of life —Miles Kington⟩
type·face \-ˌfās\ *noun* (1887)
1 : the face of printing type
2 : all type of a single design
type·found·er \-ˌfaún-dər\ *noun* (1797)
: one engaged in the design and production of metal printing type for hand composition
— **type·found·ing** \-diŋ\ *noun*
type genus *noun* (1840)
: the genus of a taxonomic family or subfamily from which the name of the family or subfamily is formed
type I error \'tīp-ˈwən-\ *noun* (1947)
: rejection of the null hypothesis in statistical testing when it is true
type·script \'tīp-ˌskript\ *noun* [*type* + manuscript] (1893)
: a typewritten manuscript; *especially* **:** one intended for use as printer's copy
type·set \-ˌset\ *transitive verb* **-set; -set·ting** (1945)
: to set in type **:** COMPOSE
type·set·ter \-ˌse-tər\ *noun* (1883)
: one that sets type
type·set·ting \-ˌse-tiŋ\ *noun* (1846)
: the process of setting material in type or into a form to be used in printing; *also* **:** the process of producing graphic matter (as through a computer system)
type species *noun* (1840)
: the species of a genus with which the generic name is permanently associated
type specimen *noun* (circa 1891)
: a specimen or individual designated as type of a species or lesser group and serving as the final criterion of the characteristics of that group
type·style \'tīp-ˌstī(ə)l\ *noun* (1954)
: TYPEFACE
type II error \-ˈtü-\ *noun* (1947)
: acceptance of the null hypothesis in statistical testing when it is false
type·write \'tīp-ˌrīt\ *verb* **-wrote** \-ˌrōt\; **-writ·ten** \-ˌri-t°n\ [back-formation from *typewriter*] (1887)
transitive verb
: TYPE 3
intransitive verb
: TYPE
type·writ·er \-ˌrī-tər\ *noun* (1868)
1 : a machine for writing in characters similar to those produced by printer's type by means of keyboard-operated types striking a ribbon to transfer ink or carbon impressions onto the paper
2 : TYPIST

type·writ·ing \-ˌrī-tiŋ\ *noun* (1867)
1 : the act or study of or skill in using a typewriter
2 : writing produced with a typewriter
typ·ey *also* **typy** \'tī-pē\ *adjective* **typ·i·er; -est** [¹*type*] (1923)
: characterized by strict conformance to type; *also* **:** exhibiting superior bodily conformation ⟨a sound *typey* heifer⟩
typh·lo·sole \'ti-flə-ˌsōl\ *noun* [Greek *typhlos* blind + *sōlēn* pipe, channel — more at DEAF] (1859)
: a longitudinal fold of the intestinal wall that projects into the cavity especially in bivalve mollusks, annelids, and starfishes
Ty·pho·eus \tī-ˈfō-ˌyüs, -ˌyəs\ *noun* [Latin, from Greek *Typhōeus*]
: TYPHON
— **Ty·phoe·an** \-ˈfē-ən\ *adjective*
¹ty·phoid \'tī-ˌfoid, (ˌ)tī-ˈ\ *adjective* [New Latin *typhus*] (1800)
1 : of, relating to, or suggestive of typhus
2 : [²*typhoid*] **:** of, relating to, or constituting typhoid
²typhoid *noun* (1861)
1 : TYPHOID FEVER
2 : a disease of domestic animals resembling human typhus or typhoid
typhoid fever *noun* (1845)
: a communicable disease marked especially by fever, diarrhea, prostration, headache, and intestinal inflammation and caused by a bacterium (*Salmonella typhi*)
Typhoid Mary *noun, plural* **Typhoid Marys** [*Typhoid Mary*, nickname of Mary Mallon (died 1938) Irish cook in U.S. who was found to be a typhoid carrier] (1931)
: one that is by force of circumstances a center from which something undesirable spreads
Ty·phon \'tī-ˌfän\ *noun* [Latin, from Greek *Typhōn*]
: a monster with a tremendous voice who according to classical mythology was father of Cerberus, the Chimera, and the Sphinx
ty·phoon \tī-ˈfün\ *noun* [alteration (influenced by Chinese — Guangdong — *daaih-fùng*, from *daaih* big + *fùng* wind) of earlier *touffon*, from Arabic *ṭūfān* hurricane, from Greek *typhōn* violent storm] (1771)
1 : a tropical cyclone occurring in the region of the Philippines or the China sea
2 : WHIRLWIND 2a ⟨a veritable *typhoon* of interest and corporate investment —Norman Sklarewitz⟩
ty·phus \'tī-fəs\ *noun* [New Latin, from Greek *typhos* fever; akin to Greek *typhein* to smoke — more at DEAF] (1785)
: any of various bacterial diseases caused by rickettsias: as **a :** a severe human febrile disease that is caused by one (*Rickettsia prowazekii*) transmitted especially by body lice and is marked by high fever, stupor alternating with delirium, intense headache, and a dark red rash **b :** MURINE TYPHUS **c :** TSUTSUGAMUSHI DISEASE
typ·ic \'ti-pik\ *adjective* (1610)
: TYPICAL 1
typ·i·cal \'ti-pi-kəl\ *adjective* [Late Latin *typicalis*, from *typicus*, from Greek *typikos*, from *typos* model — more at TYPE] (1612)
1 : constituting or having the nature of a type **:** SYMBOLIC
2 a : combining or exhibiting the essential characteristics of a group ⟨*typical* suburban houses⟩ **b :** conforming to a type ⟨a specimen *typical* of the species⟩
synonym see REGULAR
— **typ·i·cal·i·ty** \ˌti-pə-ˈka-lə-tē\ *noun*
— **typ·i·cal·ness** \'ti-pi-kəl-nəs\ *noun*
typ·i·cal·ly \'ti-pi-k(ə-)lē\ *adverb* (1605)
1 : in a typical manner ⟨*typically* American⟩
2 : on a typical occasion **:** in typical circumstances ⟨*typically*, members of our staff receive little . . . recognition —Brendan Gill⟩
typ·i·fy \'ti-pə-ˌfī\ *transitive verb* **-fied; -fy·ing** (1634)

1 : to represent in typical fashion **:** to constitute a typical mark or instance of ⟨realism . . . that *typified* his earlier work —*Current Biography*⟩
2 : to embody the essential or salient characteristics of **:** be the type of
— **typ·i·fi·ca·tion** \ˌti-pə-fə-ˈkā-shən\ *noun*
typ·ist \'tī-pist\ *noun* (1885)
: one who types or enters data into a computer especially as a job
ty·po \'tī-(ˌ)pō\ *noun, plural* **typos** [short for *typographical (error)*] (1892)
: an error (as of spelling) in typed or typeset material
ty·po·graph \'tī-pə-ˌgraf\ *transitive verb* (circa 1933)
: to produce (stamps) by letterpress
ty·pog·ra·pher \tī-ˈpä-grə-fər\ *noun* (1643)
: a person (as a compositor, printer, or designer) who specializes in the design, choice, and arrangement of type matter
ty·po·graph·ic \ˌtī-pə-ˈgra-fik\ *or* **ty·po·graph·i·cal** \-fi-kəl\ *adjective*
: of, relating to, or occurring or used in typography or typeset matter ⟨a *typographic* character⟩ ⟨a *typographical* error⟩
— **ty·po·graph·i·cal·ly** \-fi-k(ə-)lē\ *adverb*
ty·pog·ra·phy \tī-ˈpä-grə-fē\ *noun* [Medieval Latin *typographia*, from Greek *typos* impression, cast + *-graphia* -graphy — more at TYPE] (1610)
1 : letterpress printing
2 : the style, arrangement, or appearance of typeset matter
ty·po·log·i·cal \ˌtī-pə-ˈlä-ji-kəl\ *adjective* (1845)
: of or relating to typology or types
— **ty·po·log·i·cal·ly** \-ji-k(ə-)lē\ *adverb*
ty·pol·o·gy \tī-ˈpä-lə-jē\ *noun, plural* **-gies** (1845)
1 : a doctrine of theological types; *especially* **:** one holding that things in Christian belief are prefigured or symbolized by things in the Old Testament
2 : study of or analysis or classification based on types or categories
— **ty·pol·o·gist** \-jist\ *noun*
Tyr \'tir\ *noun* [Old Norse *Týr*; akin to Old English *Tīw* Tiu — more at DEITY]
: a god of war in Norse mythology
ty·ra·mine \'tī-rə-ˌmēn\ *noun* [International Scientific Vocabulary *tyrosine* + *amine*] (1910)
: a phenolic amine $C_8H_{11}NO$ found in various foods and beverages (as cheese and red wine) that has a sympathomimetic action and is derived from tyrosine
ty·ran·ni·cal \tə-ˈra-ni-kəl, tī-\ *also* **ty·ran·nic** \-nik\ *adjective* [Latin *tyrannicus*, from Greek *tyrannikos*, from *tyrannos* tyrant] (15th century)
: being or characteristic of a tyrant or tyranny **:** DESPOTIC ⟨*tyrannical* rule⟩ ⟨a *tyrannical* ruler⟩
— **ty·ran·ni·cal·ly** \-ni-k(ə-)lē\ *adverb*
— **ty·ran·ni·cal·ness** \-kəl-nəs\ *noun*
ty·ran·ni·cide \tə-ˈra-nə-ˌsīd, tī-\ *noun* [in sense 1, from French, from Latin *tyrannicidium*, from *tyrannus* + *-i-* + *-cidium* -cide (killing); in sense 2, from French, from Latin *tyrannicida*, from *tyrannus* + *-i-* + *-cida* -cide (killer)] (1650)
1 : the act of killing a tyrant
2 : the killer of a tyrant
tyr·an·nise *British variant of* TYRANNIZE
tyr·an·nize \'tir-ə-ˌnīz\ *verb* **-nized; -niz·ing** (15th century)
intransitive verb
: to exercise arbitrary oppressive power or severity ⟨some ways the living *tyrannize* over the dying —Thomas Powers⟩

transitive verb
: to treat tyrannically : OPPRESS
— **tyr·an·niz·er** *noun*

ty·ran·no·saur \tə-'ra-nə-ˌsȯr, tī-\ *noun* [New Latin *Tyrannosaurus*, genus name, from Greek *tyrannos* tyrant + *sauros* lizard] (1924)
: a very large bipedal carnivorous dinosaur (*Tyrannosaurus rex*) with small forelegs that occurs in the Upper Cretaceous of North America

ty·ran·no·sau·rus \tə-ˌra-nə-'sȯr-əs, (ˌ)tī-\ *noun* [New Latin] (1905)
: TYRANNOSAUR

tyr·an·nous \'tir-ə-nəs\ *adjective* (15th century)
: marked by tyranny; *especially* : unjustly severe
— **tyr·an·nous·ly** *adverb*

tyr·an·ny \'tir-ə-nē\ *noun, plural* **-nies** [Middle English *tyrannie*, from Middle French, from Medieval Latin *tyrannia*, from Latin *tyrannus* tyrant] (14th century)
1 : oppressive power ⟨every form of *tyranny* over the mind of man —Thomas Jefferson⟩; *especially* : oppressive power exerted by government ⟨the *tyranny* of a police state⟩
2 a : a government in which absolute power is vested in a single ruler; *especially* : one characteristic of an ancient Greek city-state **b** : the office, authority, and administration of a tyrant
3 : a rigorous condition imposed by some outside agency or force ⟨living under the *tyranny* of the clock —Dixon Wecter⟩
4 : a tyrannical act

ty·rant \'tī-rənt\ *noun* [Middle English *tirant*, from Old French *tyran, tyrant*, from Latin *tyr-*

annus, from Greek *tyrannos*] (14th century)
1 a : an absolute ruler unrestrained by law or constitution **b** : a usurper of sovereignty
2 a : a ruler who exercises absolute power oppressively or brutally **b** : one resembling an oppressive ruler in the harsh use of authority or power

tyrant flycatcher *noun* (circa 1783)
: any of various large American flycatchers (family Tyrannidae) that are usually strictly insectivorous and have a flattened bill often hooked at the tip and usually bristly at the gape

tyre *chiefly British variant of* TIRE

Tyr·i·an purple \'tir-ē-ən-\ *noun* [*Tyre*, maritime city of ancient Phoenicia] (circa 1586)
: a crimson or purple dye that is related to indigo, obtained by the ancient Greeks and Romans from gastropod mollusks, and now made synthetically

ty·ro \'tī-(ˌ)rō\ *noun, plural* **tyros** *often attributive* [Medieval Latin, from Latin *tiro* young soldier, tyro] (1611)
: a beginner in learning : NOVICE
synonym see AMATEUR

ty·ro·ci·dine *also* **ty·ro·ci·din** \ˌtī-rə-'sī-d°n\ *noun* [*tyrothricin* + *gramicidin*] (1940)
: a basic polypeptide antibiotic produced by a soil bacillus (*Bacillus brevis*)

Ty·ro·le·an *also* **Ty·ro·li·an** \tə-'rō-lē-ən, tī-\ *adjective* (1805)
1 : of or relating to the Tirol
2 *of a hat* : of a style originating in the Tirol and marked by soft often green felt, a narrow brim and pointed crown, and an ornamental feather

ty·ros·i·nase \tə-'rä-sə-ˌnās, tī-, -ˌnāz\ *noun* (1896)
: a copper-containing enzyme that promotes the oxidation of phenols (as tyrosine) and is widespread in plants and animals

ty·ro·sine \'tī-rə-ˌsēn\ *noun* [International Scientific Vocabulary, irregular from Greek *tyros* cheese — more at BUTTER] (1857)
: a phenolic amino acid $C_9H_{11}NO_3$ that is a precursor of several important substances (as epinephrine and melanin)

ty·ro·thri·cin \ˌtī-rə-'thrī-s°n\ *noun* [New Latin *Tyrothoric-, Tyrothrix*, genus name formerly applied to various bacteria including *Bacillus brevis*] (1940)
: an antibiotic mixture that consists chiefly of tyrocidine and gramicidin, is usually extracted from a soil bacillus (*Bacillus brevis*) as a gray to brown powder, and is used for local applications especially for infection caused by gram-positive bacteria

tzaddik *noun, plural* **tzaddikim** *variant of* ZADDIK

tzar \'zär, '(t)sär\ *variant of* CZAR

tzi·gane \(t)sē-'gän\ *noun* [French, from Hungarian *cigány*] (1763)
1 : GYPSY 1
2 : ROMANY 2

tzim·mes \'tsi-məs\ *noun* [Yiddish *tsimes*, from Middle High German *z, zuo* at, too + *imbīz* light meal] (1892)
: a sweetened combination of vegetables (as carrots and potatoes) or of meat and carrots often with dried fruits (as prunes) that is stewed or baked in a casserole

tzi·tzis, tzi·tzit *variant of* ZIZITH

U

U *is the twenty-first letter of the English alphabet. It is a cursive form of the letter* V, *with which it was once used interchangeably, both letters having the value of either the modern vowel* U *or the modern consonant* V. *By the 10th century,* V *came to be preferred as the capital form used at the beginning of a word, and* U *as the cursive form used in the middle of a word. Since the consonant sound usually occurred at the beginning and the vowel sound in the middle of words,* V *gradually became specialized to represent the former and* U *the latter, but small* u *and small* v *were used interchangeably as late as the 13th century. In dictionaries of English,* U *and* V *were not given separate alphabetical positions until about 1800. The vowel sounds of* u *in Old English were the ones which it still retains in most of the languages of Europe, that of the vowel in* tool, *and the vowel in* wood, *but Modern English* u *represents various other sounds as well.*

u \'yü\ *noun, plural* **u's** *or* **us** \'yüz\ *often capitalized, often attributive* (before 12th century) **1 a** : the 21st letter of the English alphabet **b** : a graphic representation of this letter **c** : a speech counterpart of orthographic *u* **2** : a graphic device for reproducing the letter *u* **3** : one designated *u* especially as the 21st in order or class **4** [abbreviation for *unsatisfactory*] **a** : a grade rating a student's work as unsatisfactory **b** : one graded or rated with a U **5** : something shaped like the letter U

U \'yü\ *adjective* [*upper class*] (1954) : characteristic of the upper classes

Uban·gi \yü-'baŋ-gē, ü-, -'baŋ-ē\ *noun* [*Ubangi-Shari*, Africa] (1942) : a woman of the district of Kyabé village in Chad with lips pierced and distended to unusual dimensions with wooden disks — not used technically

ubi·qui·none \yü-'bi-kwə-ˌnōn, ˌyü-bə-kwi-'nōn\ *noun* [blend of Latin *ubique* everywhere and English *quinone*; from its widespread occurrence in nature] (1958) : any of a group of lipid-soluble quinones that contain a long isoprenoid side chain and that function in the part of cellular respiration comprising oxidative phosphorylation as electron-carrying coenzymes in the transport of electrons from organic substrates to oxygen especially along the chain of reactions leading from the Krebs cycle

ubiq·ui·tous \yü-'bi-kwə-təs\ *adjective* (1837) : existing or being everywhere at the same time : constantly encountered : WIDESPREAD
— **ubiq·ui·tous·ly** *adverb*
— **ubiq·ui·tous·ness** *noun*

ubiq·ui·ty \-kwə-tē\ *noun* [Latin *ubique* everywhere, from *ubi* where + *-que*, enclitic generalizing particle; akin to Latin *quis* who and to Latin *-que* and — more at WHO, SESQUI-] (1597) : presence everywhere or in many places especially simultaneously : OMNIPRESENCE

U–boat \'yü-ˌbōt\ *noun* [translation of German *U-boot*, short for *Unterseeboot*, literally, undersea boat] (1916) : a German submarine

ud·der \'ə-dər\ *noun* [Middle English, from Old English *üder;* akin to Old High German *ütar* udder, Latin *uber*, Greek *outhar*, Sanskrit *üdhar*] (before 12th century) **1** : a large pendulous organ consisting of two or more mammary glands enclosed in a common envelope and each provided with a single nipple — see COW illustration

2 : MAMMARY GLAND

UFO \ˌyü-(ˌ)ef-'ō\ *noun, plural* **UFO's** *or* **UFOs** \-'ōz\ [*unidentified flying object*] (1953) : an unidentified flying object; *especially* : FLYING SAUCER

ufol·o·gy \yü-'fä-lə-jē\ *noun, often UFO capitalized* [*UFO* + *-logy*] (1959) : the study of unidentified flying objects
— **ufo·log·i·cal** \ˌyü-fə-'lä-ji-kəl\ *adjective, often UFO capitalized*
— **ufol·o·gist** \yü-'fä-lə-jist\ *noun, often UFO capitalized*

¹Uga·rit·ic \ˌyü-gə-'ri-tik, ˌü-gə-\ *noun* (1936) : the Semitic language of ancient Ugarit closely related to Phoenician and Hebrew

²Ugaritic *adjective* (1938) : of, relating to, or characteristic of the ancient city of Ugarit, its inhabitants, or Ugaritic

ugh \often read as 'əg *or* 'ək *or* 'ə\ *interjection* (1837) — used to indicate the sound of a cough or grunt or to express disgust or horror

Ug·li \'ə-glē\ *trademark* — used for a tangelo

ug·li·fy \'ə-gli-ˌfī\ *transitive verb* **-fied; -fy·ing** (1576) : to make ugly
— **ug·li·fi·ca·tion** \ˌə-gli-fə-'kā-shən\ *noun*

ug·li·ness \'ə-glē-nəs\ *noun* (14th century) **1** : the quality or state of being ugly **2** : something that is ugly

¹ug·ly \'ə-glē\ *adjective* **ug·li·er; -est** [Middle English, from Old Norse *uggligr*, from *uggr* fear; akin to Old Norse *ugga* to fear] (13th century) **1** : FRIGHTFUL, DIRE **2 a** : offensive to the sight : HIDEOUS **b** : offensive or unpleasant to any sense **3** : morally offensive or objectionable ⟨corruption—the *ugliest* stain of all⟩ **4 a** : likely to cause inconvenience or discomfort ⟨the *ugly* truth⟩ **b** : SURLY, QUARRELSOME ⟨an *ugly* disposition⟩ ⟨the crowd got *ugly*⟩
— **ug·li·ly** \-glə-lē\ *adverb*

²ugly *adverb* (14th century) : in an ugly manner ⟨was acting *ugly*⟩

Ugly American *noun* [*The Ugly American* (1958), collection of stories by Eugene Burdick (died 1965) and William J. Lederer (born 1912) American authors] (1965) : an American in a foreign country whose behavior is offensive to the people of that country

ugly duckling *noun* [*The Ugly Duckling*, story by Hans Christian Andersen] (1883) : one that appears very unpromising but often has great potential

Ugri·an \'yü-grē-ən, 'ü-\ *noun* [Old Russian *Ugre* Hungarians] (1841) : a member of a division of the Finno-Ugric peoples that includes the Hungarians and two peoples of western Siberia
— **Ugrian** *adjective*

Ugric \-grik\ *adjective* (1854) : of, relating to, or characteristic of the languages of the Ugrians

ug·some \'əg-səm\ *adjective* [Middle English, from *uggen* to fear, inspire fear, from Old Norse *ugga* to fear] (15th century) *archaic* : FRIGHTFUL, LOATHSOME

uh–huh *two m's or two n's separated by the voiceless sound* h; 'əⁿ-(ˌ)həⁿ, (ˌ)əⁿ-'\ *interjection* (1899) — used to indicate affirmation, agreement, or gratification

uh–lan \'ü-ˌlän, ü-'; 'yü-lən, 'ü-\ *noun* [German, from Polish *ulan*, from Turkish *oğlan* boy, servant] (1753) : any of a body of Prussian light cavalry originally modeled on Tatar lancers

uh–oh \'ə-ˌō, *usually with strong glottal stops before the vowels*\ *interjection* (1971) — used to indicate dismay or concern

uh–uh *two m's or two n's preceded by glottal stops;* 'əⁿ-ˌəⁿ\ *interjection* (circa 1924) — used to indicate negation

Ui·ghur *also* **Ui·gur** \'wē-ˌgùr\ *noun* [Uighur *Uighur*] (1747) **1** : a member of a Turkic people powerful in Mongolia and eastern Turkestan between the 8th and 12th centuries A.D. who constitute a majority of the population of Chinese Turkestan **2** : the Turkic language of the Uighurs
— **Uighur** *also* **Uigur** *adjective*

uil·leann pipes \'i-lən-\ *noun plural, often capitalized* [*uilleann* from Irish, genitive singular of *uillinn* elbow, from Old Irish *uilen;* akin to Old English *eln* ell — more at ELL] (1906) : an Irish bagpipe with air supplied by a bellows held under and worked by the elbow

uin·ta·ite *also* **uin·tah·ite** \yü-'in-tə-ˌīt\ *noun* [*Uinta, Uintah*, mountains in Utah] (1888) : a black lustrous asphalt occurring especially in Utah

Uit·land·er \'āt-ˌlan-dər, 'aùt-, -ˌlän-\ *noun* [Afrikaans, from Middle Dutch *utelander* foreigner, from *utelant* foreign territory, from *ute* out + *lant* land] (1892) : FOREIGNER; *especially* : a British resident in the former republics of the Transvaal and Orange Free State

ukase \yü-'kās, -'kāz, 'yü-ˌ; ü-'käz\ *noun* [French & Russian; French, from Russian *ukaz*, from *ukazat'* to show, order; akin to Old Church Slavonic *u-* away, Latin *au-*, Sanskrit *ava-* and to Old Church Slavonic *kazati* to show] (1729) **1** : a proclamation by a Russian emperor or government having the force of law **2** : EDICT

uke \'yük\ *noun* (1921) : UKULELE

uki·yo·e *also* **uki·yo·ye** \ü-ˌkē-ō-'yä, -'ā\ *noun* [Japanese *ukiyo-e* genre picture, from *ukiyo* world, life + *e* picture] (1879) : a Japanese art movement that flourished from the 17th to the 19th century and produced paintings and prints depicting the everyday life and interests of the common people; *also* : the paintings and prints themselves

Ukrai·ni·an \yü-'krā-nē-ən *also* -'krī-\ *noun* (1823) **1** : a native or inhabitant of Ukraine **2** : the Slavic language of the Ukrainian people
— **Ukrainian** *adjective*

uku·le·le *also* **uke·le·le** \ˌyü-kə-'lā-lē, ˌü-\ *noun* [Hawaiian *'ukulele*, from *'uku* flea + *lele* jumping] (1896)

: a small guitar of Portuguese origin popularized in Hawaii in the 1880s and strung typically with four strings ◆

ukulele

-ular *adjective suffix* [Latin *-ularis,* from *-ulus, -ula, -ulum* -ule + *-aris* -ar]
: of, relating to, or resembling ⟨valv*ular*⟩

ul·cer \'əl-sər\ *noun* [Middle English, from Latin *ulcer-, ulcus;* akin to Greek *helkos* wound] (14th century)
1 : a break in skin or mucous membrane with loss of surface tissue, disintegration and necrosis of epithelial tissue, and often pus
2 : something that festers and corrupts like an open sore
— **ulcer** *verb*

ul·cer·ate \'əl-sə-ˌrāt\ *verb* **-at·ed; -at·ing** (15th century)
intransitive verb
: to become affected with or as if with an ulcer
transitive verb
: to affect with or as if with an ulcer
ul·cer·a·tion \ˌəl-sə-'rā-shən\ *noun* (14th century)
1 : the process of becoming ulcerated : the state of being ulcerated
2 : ULCER
— **ul·cer·a·tive** \'əl-sə-ˌrā-tiv, 'əls-rə-, 'əl-sə-rə-\ *adjective*

ulcerative colitis *noun* (circa 1928)
: a nonspecific inflammatory disease of the colon of unknown cause characterized by diarrhea with discharge of mucus and blood, cramping abdominal pain, and inflammation and edema of the mucous membrane with patches of ulceration

ul·cero·gen·ic \ˌəl-sə-rō-'je-nik\ *adjective* (1950)
: tending to produce or develop into ulcers or ulceration

ul·cer·ous \'əls-rəs, 'əl-sə-\ *adjective* (1577)
1 : being or marked by an ulceration ⟨*ulcerous* lesions⟩
2 : affected with or as if with an ulcer : ULCERATED

-ule *noun suffix* [French & Latin; French, from Latin *-ulus,* masculine diminutive suffix, *-ula,* feminine diminutive suffix, *-ulum,* neuter diminutive suffix]
: little one ⟨duct*ule*⟩

ule·ma *or* **ula·ma** \ˌü-lə-'mä\ *noun* [Arabic, Turkish, & Persian; Turkish & Persian *'ulemā,* from Arabic *'ulamā*] (1688)
1 *plural in construction* : the body of mullahs
2 : MULLAH

-ulent *adjective suffix* [Latin *-ulentus*]
: that abounds in (a specified thing) ⟨floccu*lent*⟩

ulex·ite \'yü-lək-ˌsīt\ *noun* [George L. *Ulex* (died 1883) German chemist] (1867)
: a mineral consisting of a hydrous borate of sodium and calcium and usually occurring in loosely packed white fibers that transmit light lengthwise with nearly undiminished intensity

ul·lage \'ə-lij\ *noun* [Middle English *ulage,* from Middle French *eullage* act of filling a cask, from *eullier* to fill a cask, from Old French *ouil* eye, bunghole, from Latin *oculus* eye — more at EYE] (15th century)
: the amount that a container (as a tank or cask) lacks of being full

ul·na \'əl-nə\ *noun* [New Latin, from Latin, elbow — more at ELL] (1541)
: the bone on the little-finger side of the human forearm; *also* : a corresponding part of the forelimb of vertebrates above fishes
— **ul·nar** \-nər, -ˌnär\ *adjective*

ul·ster \'əl-stər\ *noun* [*Ulster,* Ireland] (1876)
: a long loose overcoat of Irish origin made of heavy material (as frieze)

ul·te·ri·or \ˌəl-'tir-ē-ər\ *adjective* [Latin, farther, further, comparative of (assumed) Latin *ulter* situated beyond, from *uls* beyond; akin to Latin *ollus, ille,* that one, Old Irish in*doll* beyond] (1646)
1 a : FURTHER, FUTURE **b :** more distant : REMOTER **c :** situated on the farther side : THITHER
2 : going beyond what is openly said or shown and especially what is proper ⟨*ulterior* motives⟩
— **ul·te·ri·or·ly** *adverb*

ul·ti·ma \'əl-tə-mə\ *noun* [Latin, feminine of *ultimus* last] (circa 1864)
: the last syllable of a word

ul·ti·ma·cy \'əl-tə-mə-sē\ *noun, plural* **-cies** (1842)
1 : the quality or state of being ultimate
2 : ULTIMATE 1

ul·ti·ma ra·tio \ˌúl-tə-mə-'rä-tē-ˌō\ *noun* [New Latin] (1780)
: the final argument; *also* : the last resort (as force)

¹ul·ti·mate \'əl-tə-mət\ *adjective* [Medieval Latin *ultimatus* last, final, from Late Latin, past participle of *ultimare* to come to an end, be last, from Latin *ultimus* farthest, last, final, superlative of (assumed) Latin *ulter* situated beyond] (1654)
1 a : most remote in space or time : FARTHEST **b :** last in a progression or series ⟨their *ultimate* destination was Paris⟩ **c :** EVENTUAL ⟨they hoped for *ultimate* success⟩ **d :** the best or most extreme of its kind : UTMOST ⟨the *ultimate* sacrifice⟩
2 : arrived at as the last result ⟨the *ultimate* question⟩
3 a : BASIC, FUNDAMENTAL ⟨the *ultimate* nature of things —A. N. Whitehead⟩ **b :** ORIGINAL ⟨the *ultimate* source⟩ **c :** incapable of further analysis, division, or separation
4 : MAXIMUM
synonym see LAST
— **ul·ti·mate·ness** *noun*

²ultimate *noun* (1681)
1 : something ultimate; *especially* : FUNDAMENTAL
2 : ACME

³ul·ti·mate \-mət, -ˌmāt\ *verb* **-mat·ed; -mat·ing** (circa 1834)
: END

ul·ti·mate·ly \-mət-lē\ *adverb* (1652)
1 : in the end : FINALLY, FUNDAMENTALLY
2 : EVENTUALLY

ul·ti·ma Thu·le \ˌəl-tə-mə-'thü-lē, -'thyü-\ *noun* [Latin, farthest Thule] (1665)
: THULE

ul·ti·ma·tum \ˌəl-tə-'mā-təm, -'mä-\ *noun, plural* **-tums** *or* **-ta** \-tə\ [New Latin, from Medieval Latin, neuter of *ultimatus* final] (1731)
: a final proposition, condition, or demand; *especially* : one whose rejection will end negotiations and cause a resort to force or other direct action

ul·ti·mo \'əl-tə-ˌmō\ *adjective* [Latin *ultimo mense* in the last month] (1616)
: of or occurring in the month preceding the present

ul·ti·mo·gen·i·ture \ˌəl-tə-mō-'je-nə-ˌchùr, -ni-chər, -nə-ˌtyùr, -nə-ˌtùr\ *noun* [Latin *ultimus* last + English prim*ogeniture*] (1882)
: a system of inheritance by which the youngest child succeeds to the estate

¹ul·tra \'əl-trə\ *adjective* [*ultra-*] (1818)
1 : going beyond others or beyond due limit
2 : EXTREME

²ultra *noun* [*ultra-*] (1819)
: one that is ultra : EXTREMIST

ultra- *prefix* [Latin, from *ultra* beyond, adverb & preposition, from (assumed) Latin *ulter* situated beyond — more at ULTERIOR]
1 : beyond in space : on the other side : TRANS- ⟨*ultra*violet⟩
2 : beyond the range or limits of : transcending : SUPER- ⟨*ultra*microscopic⟩

3 : beyond what is ordinary, proper, or moderate : excessively : extremely ⟨*ultra*modern⟩

ul·tra·care·ful
ul·tra·ca·su·al
ul·tra·cau·tious
ul·tra·chic
ul·tra·civ·i·lized
ul·tra·clean
ul·tra·cold
ul·tra·com·mer·cial
ul·tra·com·pact
ul·tra·com·pe·tent
ul·tra·con·ser·va·tive
ul·tra·con·tem·po·rary
ul·tra·con·ve·nient
ul·tra·cool
ul·tra·crit·i·cal
ul·tra·dem·o·crat·ic
ul·tra·dense
ul·tra·dis·tance
ul·tra·dis·tant
ul·tra·dry
ul·tra·ef·fi·cient
ul·tra·en·er·get·ic
ul·tra·ex·clu·sive
ul·tra·fa·mil·iar
ul·tra·fast
ul·tra·fas·tid·i·ous
ul·tra·fem·i·nine
ul·tra·fine
ul·tra·glam·or·ous
ul·tra·haz·ard·ous
ul·tra·heat
ul·tra·heavy
ul·tra·high
ul·tra·hip
ul·tra·hot
ul·tra·hu·man
ul·tra·left
ul·tra·left·ism
ul·tra·left·ist
ul·tra·lib·er·al
ul·tra·lib·er·al·ism
ul·tra·light·weight
ul·tra·low
ul·tra·mas·cu·line
ul·tra·mil·i·tant
ul·tra·min·i·a·tur·ized
ul·tra·mod·ern
ul·tra·mod·ern·ist
ul·tra·na·tion·al·ism
ul·tra·na·tion·al·ist

ul·tra·na·tion·al·is·tic
ul·tra·or·tho·dox
ul·tra·par·a·dox·i·cal
ul·tra·pa·tri·ot·ic
ul·tra·phys·i·cal
ul·tra·pow·er·ful
ul·tra·prac·ti·cal
ul·tra·pre·cise
ul·tra·pre·ci·sion
ul·tra·pro·fes·sion·al
ul·tra·pro·gres·sive
ul·tra·pure
ul·tra·qui·et
ul·tra·rad·i·cal
ul·tra·rap·id
ul·tra·rare
ul·tra·rar·e·fied
ul·tra·ra·tio·nal
ul·tra·re·al·ism
ul·tra·re·al·ist
ul·tra·re·al·is·tic
ul·tra·re·fined
ul·tra·re·li·able
ul·tra·re·spect·able
ul·tra·rev·o·lu·tion·ary
ul·tra·rich
ul·tra·right
ul·tra·right·ist
ul·tra·ro·man·tic
ul·tra·roy·al·ist
ul·tra·safe
ul·tra·se·cret
ul·tra·seg·re·ga·tion·ist
ul·tra·sen·si·tive
ul·tra·se·ri·ous
ul·tra·sharp
ul·tra·sim·ple
ul·tra·slick
ul·tra·slow
ul·tra·small
ul·tra·smart
ul·tra·smooth
ul·tra·soft
ul·tra·so·phis·ti·cat·ed
ul·tra·thin
ul·tra·vac·u·um
ul·tra·vi·o·lence
ul·tra·vi·o·lent
ul·tra·vir·ile
ul·tra·vi·ril·i·ty
ul·tra·wide

◆ **WORD HISTORY**
ukulele In Hawaiian *'ukulele* means literally "jumping flea," a creature with little resemblance to a small guitar. It is likely that this improbable name became attached to the instrument in a rather roundabout way. Edward Purvis, a former British army officer living in Hawaii as an official at the court of King Kalakaua, is said to have been given the nickname *'ukulele* because he was a small and lively man. In 1879 Portuguese immigrants to the Hawaiian Islands from Madeira brought with them several musical instruments. Among these was the *machete,* a small four-stringed guitar. Purvis, being fond of music, was taken with the new instrument and soon learned to play it. When the *machete* became a Hawaiian favorite, it took the name of its popularizer, and its Portuguese name and origin were soon forgotten.

ul·tra·ba·sic \ˌəl-trə-ˈbā-sik\ *adjective* [International Scientific Vocabulary] (1881)
: extremely basic; *specifically* **:** very low in silica and rich in iron and magnesium minerals — **ultrabasic** *noun*

ul·tra·cen·trif·u·gal \-ˌsen-ˈtri-fyə-gəl, -fi-gəl\ *adjective* (1930)
: of, relating to, or obtained by means of an ultracentrifuge
— **ul·tra·cen·trif·u·gal·ly** \-gə-lē\ *adverb*

¹**ul·tra·cen·tri·fuge** \-ˈsen-trə-ˌfyüj\ *noun* (1924)
: a high-speed centrifuge able to sediment colloidal and other small particles and used especially in determining sizes of such particles and molecular weights of large molecules

²**ultracentrifuge** *transitive verb* (1930)
: to subject to an ultracentrifuge
— **ul·tra·cen·tri·fu·ga·tion** \-ˌsen-trə-fyü-ˈgā-shən\ *noun*

ul·tra·fiche \ˈəl-trə-ˌfēsh\ *noun* (1969)
: a microfiche whose microimages are of printed matter reduced 90 or more times

ul·tra·fil·tra·tion \ˌəl-trə-fil-ˈtrā-shən\ *noun* (1908)
: filtration through a medium (as a semipermeable capillary wall) which allows small molecules (as of water) to pass but holds back larger ones (as of protein)
— **ul·tra·fil·trate** \-ˈfil-ˌtrāt\ *noun*

ultrahigh frequency *noun* (1932)
: a radio frequency between superhigh frequency and very high frequency — see RADIO FREQUENCY table

ul·tra·ism \ˈəl-trə-ˌi-zəm\ *noun* (1821)
1 : the principles of those who advocate extreme measures (as radicalism)
2 : an instance or example of radicalism
— **ul·tra·ist** \-trə-ist\ *adjective or noun*
— **ul·tra·is·tic** \ˌəl-trə-ˈis-tik\ *adjective*

¹**ul·tra·light** \ˈəl-trə-ˌlīt\ *adjective* (1974)
: extremely light in mass or weight ⟨an *ultralight* alloy⟩ ⟨an *ultralight* pullover⟩

²**ultralight** *noun* (1980)
: a very light recreational aircraft typically for one person that is powered by a small gasoline engine

ul·tra·maf·ic \ˌəl-trə-ˈma-fik\ *adjective* (1933)
: ULTRABASIC

ul·tra·mar·a·thon \-ˈmar-ə-ˌthän\ *noun* (1977)
: a footrace longer than a marathon
— **ul·tra·mar·a·thon·er** \-ˌthä-nər\ *noun*

¹**ul·tra·ma·rine** \-mə-ˈrēn\ *noun* [Medieval Latin *ultramarinus* coming from beyond the sea, from Latin *ultra-* + *mare* sea — more at MARINE] (1598)
1 a (1) **:** a blue pigment prepared by powdering lapis lazuli (2) **:** a similar pigment prepared from kaolin, soda ash, sulfur, and charcoal **b :** any of several related pigments
2 : a vivid blue

²**ultramarine** *adjective* (1652)
: situated beyond the sea

ul·tra·mi·cro \ˌəl-trə-ˈmī-(ˌ)krō\ *adjective* (1937)
: being or dealing with something smaller than micro

ul·tra·mi·cro·scope \ˌəl-trə-ˈmī-krə-ˌskōp\ *noun* [back-formation from *ultramicroscopic*] (1906)
: an apparatus for making visible by scattered light particles too small to be perceived by an ordinary microscope

ul·tra·mi·cro·scop·ic \-ˌmī-krə-ˈskä-pik\ *also* **ul·tra·mi·cro·scop·i·cal** \-pi-kəl\ *adjective* [International Scientific Vocabulary] (1870)
1 : too small to be seen with an ordinary microscope
2 : of or relating to an ultramicroscope
— **ul·tra·mi·cro·scop·i·cal·ly** \-pi-k(ə-)lē\ *adverb*

ul·tra·mi·cro·tome \-ˈmī-krə-ˌtōm\ *noun* (1946)
: a microtome for cutting extremely thin sections for electron microscopy
— **ul·tra·mi·crot·o·my** \-mī-ˈkrä-tə-mē\ *noun*

ul·tra·min·i·a·ture \-ˈmi-nē-ə-ˌchùr, -ˈmi-ni-ˌchùr, -ˈmin-yə-, -chər, -ˌtyùr, -ˌtùr\ *adjective* (1942)
: SUBMINIATURE

ul·tra·mon·tane \-ˈmän-ˌtān, -ˌmän-ˈ\ *adjective* [Medieval Latin *ultramontanus*, from Latin *ultra-* + *mont-, mons* mountain — more at MOUNT] (circa 1618)
1 : of or relating to countries or peoples beyond the mountains (as the Alps)
2 : favoring greater or absolute supremacy of papal over national or diocesan authority in the Roman Catholic Church
— **ultramontane** *noun, often capitalized*
— **ul·tra·mon·tan·ism** \-ˈmän-t°n-ˌi-zəm\ *noun*

ul·tra·short \-ˈshòrt\ *adjective* (1926)
1 : having a wavelength below 10 meters ⟨*ultrashort* radiation⟩
2 : very short in duration ⟨an *ultrashort* pulse of light⟩

ul·tra·son·ic \-ˈsä-nik\ *adjective* (1923)
1 : having a frequency above the human ear's audibility limit of about 20,000 hertz — used of waves and vibrations
2 : utilizing, produced by, or relating to ultrasonic waves or vibrations ⟨*ultrasonic* testing of metal⟩
— **ul·tra·son·i·cal·ly** \-ni-k(ə-)lē\ *adverb*

ul·tra·son·ics \ˌəl-trə-ˈsä-niks\ *noun plural* (1924)
1 : ultrasonic vibrations or compressional waves
2 *singular in construction* **:** the study of ultrasonic vibrations and their associated phenomena
3 : ultrasonic devices

ul·tra·so·nog·ra·phy \-sə-ˈnä-grə-fē, -sō-\ *noun* [*ultrason*ic + *-o-* + *-graphy*] (1951)
: ULTRASOUND 2
— **ul·tra·so·nog·ra·pher** \-fər\ *noun*
— **ul·tra·so·no·graph·ic** \-ˌsō-nə-ˈgra-fik, -ˌsä-\ *adjective*

ul·tra·sound \ˈəl-trə-ˌsaùnd\ *noun* (1923)
1 : vibrations of the same physical nature as sound but with frequencies above the range of human hearing
2 : the diagnostic or therapeutic use of ultrasound and especially a technique involving the formation of a two-dimensional image used for the examination and measurement of internal body structures and the detection of bodily abnormalities — called also *sonography*
3 : a diagnostic examination using ultrasound

ul·tra·struc·ture \ˈəl-trə-ˌstrək-chər\ *noun* (1939)
: biological structure and especially fine structure (as of a cell) not visible through an ordinary microscope
— **ul·tra·struc·tur·al** \ˌəl-trə-ˈstrək-chə-rəl, -ˈstrək-shrəl\ *adjective*
— **ul·tra·struc·tur·al·ly** *adverb*

ul·tra·vi·o·let \ˌəl-trə-ˈvī-(ə-)lət\ *adjective* (1840)
1 : situated beyond the visible spectrum at its violet end — used of radiation having a wavelength shorter than wavelengths of visible light and longer than those of X rays
2 : relating to, producing, or employing ultraviolet radiation
— **ultraviolet** *noun*

ul·tra vi·res \ˌəl-trə-ˈvī-(ˌ)rēz\ *adverb or adjective* [New Latin, literally, beyond power] (1793)
: beyond the scope or in excess of legal power or authority

ul·u·lant \ˈəl-yə-lənt\ *adjective* (1868)
: having a howling sound **:** WAILING ⟨dark wasteland . . . *ululant* with bitter wind —Rudi Blesh⟩

ul·u·late \-ˌlāt\ *intransitive verb* **-lat·ed; -lat·ing** [Latin *ululatus*, past participle of *ululare*, of imitative origin] (1623)
: HOWL, WAIL
— **ul·u·la·tion** \ˌəl-yə-ˈlā-shən\ *noun*

ul·va \ˈəl-və\ *noun* [New Latin, genus name, from Latin, sedge] (1706)
: SEA LETTUCE

Ulys·ses \yù-ˈli-(ˌ)sēz\ *noun* [Latin *Ulysses, Ulixes*, from Greek *Oulixes, Olysseus, Odysseus*]
: ODYSSEUS

um·bel \ˈəm-bəl\ *noun* [New Latin *umbella*, from Latin, umbrella — more at UMBRELLA] (1597)
: a racemose inflorescence typical of the carrot family in which the axis is very much contracted so that the pedicels appear to spring from the same point to form a flat or rounded flower cluster — see INFLORESCENCE illustration

um·bel·late \ˈəm-bə-ˌlāt, ˌəm-ˈbe-lət\ *adjective* (1760)
1 : bearing, consisting of, or arranged in umbels
2 : resembling an umbel in form

um·bel·lif·er \ˌəm-ˈbe-lə-fər\ *noun* [New Latin *Umbelliferae*, group name, feminine plural of *umbellifer* bearing umbels] (1718)
: a plant of the carrot family

um·bel·lif·er·ous \ˌəm-bə-ˈli-f(ə-)rəs\ *adjective* (1662)
: of or relating to the carrot family ⟨*umbelliferous* flower heads⟩

¹**um·ber** \ˈəm-bər\ *noun* [probably from obsolete English, shade, color, from Middle English *umbre* shade, shadow, from Middle French, from Latin *umbra* — more at UMBRAGE] (1568)
1 : a brown earth that is darker in color than ocher and sienna because of its content of manganese and iron oxides and is highly valued as a permanent pigment either in the raw or burnt state
2 a : a moderate to dark yellowish brown **b :** a moderate brown

²**umber** *transitive verb* **um·bered; um·ber·ing** \-b(ə-)riŋ\ (1610)
: to darken with or as if with umber

³**umber** *adjective* (1802)
: of, relating to, or having the characteristics of umber; *specifically* **:** of the color of umber

¹**um·bil·i·cal** \ˌəm-ˈbi-li-kəl, *British also* ˌəm-bə-ˈlī-kəl\ *adjective* (1541)
1 : of, relating to, or used at the navel
2 : of or relating to the central region of the abdomen

²**umbilical** *noun* (1774)
: UMBILICAL CORD 2

umbilical cord *noun* (1753)
1 : a cord arising from the navel that connects the fetus with the placenta; *also* **:** YOLK STALK
2 : a tethering or supply line (as for an astronaut outside a spacecraft or a diver underwater)

um·bil·i·cate \ˌəm-ˈbi-li-kət\ *or* **um·bil·i·cat·ed** \-lə-ˌkā-təd\ *adjective* (1698)
1 : depressed like a navel
2 : having an umbilicus
— **um·bil·i·ca·tion** \ˌəm-ˌbi-lə-ˈkā-shən\ *noun*

um·bi·li·cus \ˌəm-ˈbi-li-kəs, ˌəm-bə-ˈlī-\ *noun, plural* **um·bi·li·ci** \ˌəm-ˈbi-li-ˌkī, -ˌkē; ˌəm-bə-ˈlī-ˌkī, -ˌsī\ *or* **um·bi·li·cus·es** [Latin — more at NAVEL] (circa 1615)
1 a : NAVEL 1 **b :** any of several morphological depressions; *especially* **:** HILUM 1
2 : a central point **:** CORE, HEART

um·bles \ˈəm-bəlz\ *noun plural* [Middle English, alteration of *nombles*, from Middle French, plural of *nomble* fillet of beef, pork loin, modification of Latin *lumbulus*, diminutive of *lumbus* loin — more at LOIN] (15th century)
: the edible viscera of an animal and especially of a deer or hog

um·bo \'əm-(,)bō\ *noun, plural* **um·bo·nes** \,əm-'bō-(,)nēz\ *or* **umbos** [Latin; akin to Latin *umbilicus* — more at NAVEL] (1721)
1 : the boss of a shield
2 a : a rounded elevation: as **a** : an inward projection of the tympanic membrane of the ear **b** : one of the lateral prominences just above the hinge of a bivalve shell
— **um·bo·nal** \'əm-bə-nᵊl, ,əm-'bō-\ *adjective*
— **um·bo·nate** \'əm-bə-,nāt, ,əm-'bō-nət\ *adjective*

um·bra \'əm-brə\ *noun, plural* **umbras** *or* **um·brae** \-(,)brē, -,brī [Latin] (1638)
1 : a shaded area
2 a : a conical shadow excluding all light from a given source; *specifically* : the conical part of the shadow of a celestial body excluding all light from the primary source **b** : the central dark part of a sunspot
— **um·bral** \-brəl\ *adjective*

um·brage \'əm-brij\ *noun* [Middle English, from Middle French, from Latin *umbraticum*, neuter of *umbraticus* of shade, from *umbratus*, past participle of *umbrare* to shade, from *umbra* shade, shadow; akin to Lithuanian *unksmė* shadow] (15th century)
1 : SHADE, SHADOW
2 : shady branches : FOLIAGE
3 a : an indistinct indication : vague suggestion : HINT **b** : a reason for doubt : SUSPICION
4 : a feeling of pique or resentment at some often fancied slight or insult ⟨took *umbrage* at the speaker's remarks⟩
synonym see OFFENSE

um·bra·geous \,əm-'brā-jəs\ *adjective* (1587)
1 a : affording shade **b** : spotted with shadows
2 : inclined to take offense easily
— **um·bra·geous·ly** *adverb*
— **um·bra·geous·ness** *noun*

¹um·brel·la \,əm-'bre-lə, *especially Southern* 'əm-\ *noun* [Italian *ombrella*, modification of Latin *umbella*, diminutive of *umbra*] (1611)
1 : a collapsible shade for protection against weather consisting of fabric stretched over hinged ribs radiating from a central pole; *especially* : a small one for carrying in the hand
2 : the bell-shaped or saucer-shaped largely gelatinous structure that forms the chief part of the body of most jellyfishes
3 : something which provides protection: as **a** : defensive air cover (as over a battlefront) **b** : a heavy barrage
4 : something which covers or embraces a broad range of elements or factors ⟨decided to expand . . . by building new colleges under a federation *umbrella* —Diane Ravitch⟩

²umbrella *transitive verb* **-laed; -la·ing** (circa 1800)
: to protect, cover, or provide with an umbrella

umbrella plant *noun* (1874)
: an African sedge (*Cyperus alternifolius*) that has large terminal whorls of slender leaves and is often grown as an ornamental

umbrella tree *noun* (1738)
1 : a magnolia (*Magnolia tripetala*) of the eastern U.S. having large leaves clustered at the ends of the branches
2 : any of various trees or shrubs resembling an umbrella especially in the arrangement of leaves or the shape of the crown

Um·bri·an \'əm-brē-ən\ *noun* (1601)
1 : a native or inhabitant of Umbria
2 : the Italic language of ancient Umbria — see INDO-EUROPEAN LANGUAGES table
— **Umbrian** *adjective*

Um·bun·du \,əm-'bùn-(,)dü\ *noun* (circa 1895)
: a Bantu language of central Angola

umi·ak \'ü-mē-,ak\ *noun* [Inuit *umiaq*] (1769)
: an open Eskimo boat made of a wooden frame covered with hide

¹um·laut \'üm-,laùt, 'ùm-\ *noun* [German, from *um-* around, transformation + *Laut* sound] (1852)
1 a : the change of a vowel that is caused by partial assimilation to a succeeding sound or that occurs as a reflex of the former presence of a succeeding sound which has been lost or altered (as to mark pluralization in *goose, geese* or *mouse, mice*) **b** : a vowel resulting from such partial assimilation
2 : a diacritical mark ¨ placed over a vowel to indicate a more central or front articulation — compare DIAERESIS

²umlaut *transitive verb* (1879)
1 : to produce by umlaut
2 : to write or print an umlaut over

¹ump \'əmp\ *noun* (1912)
: UMPIRE 2

²ump *intransitive verb* (1928)
: to act as umpire

um·pire \'əm-,pīr\ *noun* [Middle English *oumpere*, alteration (from misdivision of *a noumpere*) of *noumpere*, from Middle French *nomper* not equal, not paired, from *non-* + *per* equal, from Latin *par*] (15th century)
1 : one having authority to decide finally a controversy or question between parties: as **a** : one appointed to decide between arbitrators who have disagreed **b** : an impartial third party chosen to arbitrate disputes arising under the terms of a labor agreement
2 : an official in a sport who rules on plays
3 : a military officer who evaluates maneuvers
◇

²umpire *verb* **um·pired; um·pir·ing** (1609)
transitive verb
: to supervise or decide as umpire
intransitive verb
: to act as umpire

ump·teen \'əm(p)-,tēn, ,əm(p)-'\ *adjective* [blend of *umpty* (such and such) and *-teen* (as in *thirteen*)] (1918)
: very many : indefinitely numerous
— **ump·teenth** \-,tēn(t)th, -'tēn(t)th\ *adjective*

¹un- \,ən, *often* 'ən *before* '-stressed syllable\ *prefix* [Middle English, from Old English; akin to Old High German *un-* un-, Latin *in-*, Greek *a-, an-*, Old English *ne* not — more at NO]
1 : not : IN-, NON- — in adjectives formed from adjectives ⟨*un*ambitious⟩ ⟨*un*skilled⟩ or participles ⟨*un*dressed⟩, in nouns formed from nouns ⟨*un*availability⟩, and rarely in verbs formed from verbs ⟨*un*be⟩; sometimes in words that have a meaning that merely negates that of the base word and are thereby distinguished from words that prefix *in-* or a variant of it (as *im-*) to the same base word and have a meaning positively opposite to that of the base word ⟨*un*artistic⟩ ⟨*un*moral⟩
2 : opposite of : contrary to — in adjectives formed from adjectives ⟨*un*constitutional⟩ ⟨*un*graceful⟩ ⟨*un*mannered⟩ or participles ⟨*un*believing⟩ and in nouns formed from nouns ⟨*un*rest⟩

²un- *prefix* [Middle English *un-, on-*, alteration of *and-* against — more at ANTE-]
1 : do the opposite of : reverse (a specified action) — DE- 1a, DIS- 1a — in verbs formed from verbs ⟨*un*bend⟩ ⟨*un*dress⟩ ⟨*un*fold⟩
2 a : deprive of : remove (a specified thing) from : remove — in verbs formed from nouns ⟨*un*frock⟩ ⟨*un*sex⟩ **b** : release from : free from — in verbs formed from nouns ⟨*un*hand⟩ **c** : remove from : extract from : bring out of — in verbs formed from nouns ⟨*un*bosom⟩ **d** : cause to cease to be — in verbs formed from nouns ⟨*un*man⟩
3 : completely ⟨*un*loose⟩

un·abrad·ed
un·ab·sorbed
un·ab·sor·bent
un·ac·a·dem·ic
un·ac·a·dem·i·cal·ly
un·ac·cent·ed
un·ac·cept·ed
un·ac·cli·mat·ed
un·ac·cli·ma·tized
un·ac·com·mo·dat·ed
un·ac·com·mo·dat·ing
un·ac·cred·it·ed
un·ac·cul·tur·at·ed
un·achieved
un·ac·knowl·edged
un·ac·quaint·ed

un·act·able
un·act·ed
un·ac·tor·ish
un·adapt·able
un·adapt·ed
un·ad·dressed
un·ad·ju·di·cat·ed
un·ad·just·ed
un·ad·mired
un·ad·mit·ted
un·adopt·able
un·adult
un·ad·ven·tur·ous
un·ad·ver·tised
un·aes·thet·ic
un·af·fect·ing
un·af·fec·tion·ate
un·af·fec·tion·ate·ly
un·af·fil·i·at·ed
un·af·flu·ent
un·af·ford·able
un·afraid
un·ag·gres·sive
un·aid·ed
un·air-con·di·tioned
un·akin
un·alien·at·ed
un·alike
un·al·le·vi·at·ed
un·al·lo·cat·ed
un·al·lur·ing
un·al·tered
un·am·bi·tious
un·ame·na·ble
un·amend·ed
un·ami·a·ble
un·am·or·tized
un·am·pli·fied
un·amus·ing
un·an·a·lyz·able
un·an·a·lyzed
un·an·no·tat·ed
un·an·nounced
un·apol·o·giz·ing
un·ap·par·ent
un·ap·peased
un·ap·pre·ci·at·ed
un·ap·pre·cia·tive
un·ap·pro·pri·at·ed

un·ap·proved
un·ar·gu·able
un·ar·gu·ably
un·ar·mored
un·ar·ro·gant
un·ar·tis·tic
un·as·pi·rat·ed
un·as·sailed
un·as·sem·bled
un·as·signed
un·as·sim·i·la·ble
un·as·sim·i·lat·ed
un·as·so·ci·at·ed
un·as·suaged
un·ath·let·ic
un·at·tain·able
un·at·tend·ed
un·at·ten·u·at·ed
un·at·test·ed
un·at·trib·ut·able
un·at·trib·ut·ed
un·at·tuned
un·au·dit·ed
un·au·then·tic
un·au·tho·rized
un·au·to·mat·ed
un·avail·abil·i·ty
un·avail·able
un·avowed
un·awak·ened
un·award·ed
un·awe·some
un·ban
un·bap·tized
un·barbed
un·bar·ri·cad·ed
un·be·hold·en
un·bel·lig·er·ent
un·be·loved
un·be·mused
un·billed
un·bit·ten
un·bit·ter
un·bleached
un·blem·ished
un·blend·ed
un·blood·ed
un·book·ish
un·bought

\ə\ abut \ᵊ\ kitten \ər\ further \a\ ash \ā\ ace
\ä\ mop, mar \aù\ out \ch\ chin \e\ bet \ē\ easy
\g\ go \i\ hit \ī\ ice \j\ job \ŋ\ sing \ō\ go
\ò\ law \òi\ boy \th\ thin \th\ the \ü\ loot \ù\ foot
\y\ yet \zh\ vision *see also* Guide to Pronunciation

un·bowd·ler·ized
un·brack·et·ed
un·brake
un·breach·able
un·break·able
un·bridge·able
un·bridged
un·briefed
un·bright
un·bril·liant
un·bruised
un·brushed
un·bud·get·ed
un·buf·fered
un·build·able
un·bulky
un·bu·reau·crat·ic
un·bur·ied
un·burn·able
un·burned
un·burnt
un·busi·ness·like
un·busy
un·but·tered
un·cal·ci·fied
un·cal·cined
un·cal·i·brat·ed
un·called
un·cal·loused
un·can·celed
un·can·did
un·can·did·ly
un·ca·non·i·cal
un·cap
un·cap·i·tal·ized
un·cap·tioned
un·cap·tur·able
un·cared—for
un·car·ing
un·car·pet·ed
un·case
un·cas·trat·ed
un·cat·a·loged
un·catch·able
un·catchy
un·cat·e·go·riz·able
un·caught
un·cen·sored
un·cen·so·ri·ous
un·cen·sured
un·cer·ti·fied
un·chal·lenge·able
un·chal·lenged
un·chal·leng·ing
un·changed
un·chan·neled
un·chap·er·oned
un·char·is·mat·ic
un·charm·ing
un·char·tered
un·chau·vin·is·tic
un·check·able
un·checked
un·chew·able
un·chewed
un·chic
un·child·like
un·chlo·ri·nat·ed
un·cho·reo·graphed
un·chris·tened
un·chron·i·cled
un·chro·no·log·i·cal
un·church·ly
un·cil·i·at·ed
un·cin·e·mat·ic
un·clad
un·claimed
un·clar·i·fied
un·clas·si·fi·able
un·cleaned
un·clear
un·cli·chéd
un·clip
un·cloy·ing
un·co·alesce
un·coat·ed

un·coat·ing
un·cod·ed
un·cod·i·fied
un·co·erced
un·co·er·cive
un·co·er·cive·ly
un·col·lect·ed
un·col·lect·ible
un·co·lored
un·com·bat·ive
un·combed
un·com·bined
un·come·ly
un·com·ic
un·com·mer·cial·
 ized
un·com·pas·sion·ate
un·com·pel·ling
un·com·pen·sat·ed
un·com·pla·cent
un·com·plet·ed
un·com·pound·ed
un·com·pre·hend·ed
un·com·pu·ter·ized
un·con·cealed
un·con·fessed
un·con·fined
un·con·firmed
un·con·found·ed
un·con·fuse
un·con·ju·gat·ed
un·con·nect·ed
un·con·quered
un·con·se·crat·ed
un·con·strained
un·con·strict·ed
un·con·struc·tive
un·con·sumed
un·con·sum·mat·ed
un·con·tain·able
un·con·tam·i·nat·ed
un·con·tem·plat·ed
un·con·tem·po·rary
un·con·ten·tious
un·con·test·ed
un·con·tract·ed
un·con·tra·dict·ed
un·con·trived
un·con·trolled
un·con·tro·ver·sial
un·con·tro·ver·sial·ly
un·con·vert·ed
un·con·vinced
un·con·voyed
un·cooked
un·cooled
un·co·op·er·a·tive
un·co·or·di·nat·ed
un·copy·right·able
un·cor·rect·able
un·cor·rect·ed
un·cor·re·lat·ed
un·cor·rob·o·rat·ed
un·cor·rupt
un·count·able
un·cou·ra·geous
un·cov·e·nant·ed
un·coy
un·cracked
un·crate
un·cra·zy
un·cre·a·tive
un·cre·den·tialed
un·cred·it·ed
un·crip·pled
un·cropped
un·cross·able
un·crowd·ed
un·crush·able
un·cuff
un·cul·ti·va·ble
un·cul·ti·vat·ed
un·cul·tured
un·cured
un·cu·ri·ous
un·cur·rent

un·cur·tained
un·cus·tom·ar·i·ly
un·cus·tom·ary
un·cute
un·cyn·i·cal
un·cyn·i·cal·ly
un·dam·aged
un·damped
un·dance·able
un·dat·ed
un·dec·a·dent
un·de·cid·abil·i·ty
un·de·cid·able
un·de·cid·ed
un·de·ci·pher·able
un·de·ci·phered
un·de·clared
un·de·com·posed
un·dec·o·rat·ed
un·ded·i·cat·ed
un·de·feat·ed
un·de·fend·ed
un·de·filed
un·de·fin·able
un·de·fined
un·de·fo·li·at·ed
un·de·formed
un·del·e·gat·ed
un·de·liv·er·able
un·de·liv·ered
un·de·lud·ed
un·de·mand·ing
un·de·nom·i·na·
 tion·al
un·de·pend·able
un·de·scrib·able
un·de·served
un·de·serv·ing
un·des·ig·nat·ed
un·de·sired
un·de·tect·able
un·de·tect·ed
un·de·ter·min·able
un·de·ter·mined
un·de·terred
un·de·vel·oped
un·di·ag·nos·able
un·di·ag·nosed
un·di·a·lec·ti·cal
un·di·dac·tic
un·dif·fer·en·ti·at·ed
un·di·gest·ed
un·di·gest·ible
un·dig·ni·fied
un·di·lut·ed
un·di·min·ished
un·dimmed
un·dis·charged
un·dis·ci·plined
un·dis·closed
un·dis·cour·aged
un·dis·cov·er·able
un·dis·cov·ered
un·dis·crim·i·nat·ing
un·dis·cussed
un·dis·mayed
un·dis·pu·ta·ble
un·dis·put·ed
un·dis·solved
un·dis·tin·guished
un·dis·tort·ed
un·dis·tract·ed
un·dis·trib·ut·ed
un·dis·turbed
un·di·vid·ed
un·do·able
un·doc·ile
un·doc·tored
un·doc·tri·naire
un·doc·u·ment·ed
un·do·mes·tic
un·do·mes·ti·cat·ed
un·dot·ted
un·doubt·able
un·doubt·ing
un·drained

un·dra·ma·tized
un·drilled
un·dubbed
un·dulled
un·du·pli·cat·ed
un·dyed
un·dy·nam·ic
un·ea·ger
un·ear·marked
un·eat·able
un·eat·en
un·ec·cen·tric
un·eco·log·i·cal
un·ed·i·fy·ing
un·ed·u·ca·ble
un·ed·u·cat·ed
un·elab·o·rate
un·elect·able
un·elect·ed
un·elec·tri·fied
un·em·bar·rassed
un·em·bel·lished
un·em·bit·tered
un·em·phat·ic
un·em·phat·i·cal·ly
un·em·pir·i·cal
un·en·chant·ed
un·en·closed
un·en·cour·ag·ing
un·en·dear·ing
un·en·dur·able
un·en·dur·able·ness
un·en·dur·ably
un·en·force·able
un·en·forced
un·en·larged
un·en·light·ened
un·en·light·en·ing
un·en·riched
un·en·ter·pris·ing
un·en·thu·si·as·tic
un·en·thu·si·as·ti·
 cal·ly
un·en·vi·able
un·en·vi·ous
un·erot·ic
un·es·cap·able
un·es·tab·lished
un·eth·i·cal
un·eval·u·at·ed
un·ex·am·ined
un·ex·celled
un·ex·cit·able
un·ex·cit·ed
un·ex·cit·ing
un·ex·cused
un·ex·ot·ic
un·ex·pend·ed
un·ex·pired
un·ex·plain·able
un·ex·plained
un·ex·plod·ed
un·ex·plored
un·ex·posed
un·ex·pressed
un·ex·pur·gat·ed
un·ex·traor·di·nary
un·faked
un·fa·mous
un·fan·cy
un·fas·tid·i·ous
un·fea·si·ble
un·felt
un·fem·i·nine
un·fenced
un·fer·ment·ed
un·fer·tile
un·fer·til·ized
un·filled
un·fired
un·flam·boy·ant
un·flashy
un·fly·able
un·fond
un·forced
un·fore·see·able

un·fore·seen
un·for·est·ed
un·for·giv·able
un·forked
un·for·mu·lat·ed
un·forth·com·ing
un·for·ti·fied
un·fos·sil·if·er·ous
un·framed
un·free
un·free·dom
un·friv·o·lous
un·ful·fill·able
un·ful·filled
un·fun·ny
un·fur·nished
un·fused
un·gal·lant
un·gal·lant·ly
un·gar·nished
un·ge·nial
un·gen·teel
un·gen·tle
un·gen·tle·man·ly
un·gen·tri·fied
un·ger·mi·nat·ed
un·gift·ed
un·gim·micky
un·glam·or·ized
un·glam·or·ous
un·glazed
un·grace·ful
un·grace·ful·ly
un·grad·ed
un·grasp·able
un·ground
un·grouped
un·guess·able
un·guid·ed
un·hack·neyed
un·ham·pered
un·harmed
un·har·ness
un·har·vest·ed
un·hatched
un·healed
un·health·ful
un·heat·ed
un·hedged
un·heed·ed
un·heed·ing
un·help·ful
un·help·ful·ly
un·her·ald·ed
un·he·ro·ic
un·hin·dered
un·hip
un·his·tor·i·cal
un·ho·mog·e·nized
un·hon·ored
un·hope·ful
un·housed
un·hu·mor·ous
un·hurt
un·hy·dro·lyzed
un·hy·gien·ic
un·hy·phen·at·ed
un·hys·ter·i·cal
un·hys·ter·i·cal·ly
un·iden·ti·fi·able
un·iden·ti·fied
un·ideo·log·i·cal
un·id·i·om·at·ic
un·ig·nor·able
un·il·lu·mi·nat·ing
un·imag·i·na·tive
un·imag·i·na·tive·ly
un·im·mu·nized
un·im·paired
un·im·pas·sioned
un·im·ped·ed
un·im·por·tant
un·im·pos·ing
un·im·pressed
un·im·pres·sive
un·in·cor·po·rat·ed

un·in·dexed
un·in·dict·ed
un·in·dus·tri·al·ized
un·in·fect·ed
un·in·flat·ed
un·in·flect·ed
un·in·flu·enced
un·in·for·ma·tive
un·in·for·ma·tive·ly
un·in·formed
un·in·gra·ti·at·ing
un·in·hab·it·able
un·in·hab·it·ed
un·ini·ti·at·ed
un·in·jured
un·in·oc·u·lat·ed
un·in·spect·ed
un·in·spired
un·in·spir·ing
un·in·struct·ed
un·in·struc·tive
un·in·su·lat·ed
un·in·sur·able
un·in·sured
un·in·te·grat·ed
un·in·tel·lec·tu·al
un·in·tel·li·gent
un·in·tel·li·gent·ly
un·in·tel·li·gi·bil·i·ty
un·in·tel·li·gi·ble
un·in·tel·li·gi·ble-
 ness
un·in·tel·li·gi·bly
un·in·tend·ed
un·in·ten·tion·al
un·in·ten·tion·al·ly
un·in·ter·est·ing
un·in·ter·rupt·ed
un·in·ter·rupt·ed·ly
un·in·tim·i·dat·ed
un·in·ven·tive
un·in·vit·ed
un·in·vit·ing
un·in·volved
un·iron·i·cal·ly
un·ir·ra·di·at·ed
un·ir·ri·gat·ed
un·is·sued
un·jad·ed
un·joint·ed
un·jus·ti·fi·able
un·jus·ti·fi·ably
un·jus·ti·fied
un·kept
un·knot
un·knowl·edge·able
un·ko·sher
un·la·beled
un·la·dy·like
un·la·ment·ed
un·laun·dered
un·learn·able
un·leav·ened
un·lib·er·at·ed
un·li·censed
un·lik·able
un·lined
un·lis·ten·able
un·lit
un·lit·er·ary
un·liv·able
un·lo·cal·ized
un·lov·able
un·loved
un·lov·ing
un·lyr·i·cal
un·ma·cho
un·mag·ni·fied
un·ma·li·cious
un·ma·li·cious·ly
un·man·age·able
un·man·age·ably
un·man·aged
un·ma·nip·u·lat·ed
un·mapped
un·marked

un·mar·ket·able
un·marred
un·mas·cu·line
un·match·able
un·matched
un·meant
un·mea·sur·able
un·mea·sured
un·mech·a·nized
un·med·i·cat·ed
un·me·lo·di·ous
un·me·lo·di·ous·ness
un·mem·o·ra·ble
un·mem·o·ra·bly
un·mer·it·ed
un·mer·ry
un·met
un·me·tab·o·lized
un·mil·i·tary
un·milled
un·mined
un·mix
un·mix·able
un·mixed
un·mod·ern·ized
un·mod·i·fied
un·mod·ish
un·mo·lest·ed
un·mon·i·tored
un·mo·ti·vat·ed
un·mount·ed
un·mov·able
un·moved
un·mu·si·cal
un·name·able
un·named
un·need·ed
un·ne·go·tia·ble
un·neu·rot·ic
un·news·wor·thy
un·no·tice·able
un·no·ticed
un·nour·ish·ing
un·ob·jec·tion·able
un·ob·serv·able
un·ob·served
un·ob·struct·ed
un·ob·tain·able
un·of·fi·cial
un·of·fi·cial·ly
un·open·able
un·opened
un·op·posed
un·or·dered
un·orig·i·nal
un·or·na·ment·ed
un·os·ten·ta·tious
un·os·ten·ta·tious·ly
un·owned
un·ox·y·gen·at·ed
un·paint·ed
un·par·a·sit·ized
un·par·don·able
un·pass·able
un·pas·teur·ized
un·pas·to·ral
un·pat·ent·able
un·pa·tri·ot·ic
un·paved
un·pe·dan·tic
un·peeled
un·per·ceived
un·per·cep·tive
un·per·form·able
un·per·formed
un·per·suad·ed
un·per·sua·sive
un·per·turbed
un·pic·tur·esque
un·planned
un·plau·si·ble
un·play·able
un·pleased
un·pleas·ing
un·plowed

un·po·et·ic
un·po·liced
un·pol·ished
un·pol·lut·ed
un·posed
un·prac·ti·cal
un·pre·dict·abil·i·ty
un·pre·dict·able
un·pre·dict·ably
un·prej·u·diced
un·pre·med·i·tat·ed
un·pre·pared
un·pre·pared·ness
un·pre·pos·sess·ing
un·pressed
un·pres·sured
un·pres·sur·ized
un·pret·ty
un·priv·i·leged
un·prob·lem·at·ic
un·pro·cessed
un·pro·duced
un·pro·duc·tive
un·pro·fes·sion·al
un·pro·gram·ma·ble
un·pro·grammed
un·pro·gres·sive
un·prompt·ed
un·pro·nounce·able
un·pro·pi·tious
un·pros·per·ous
un·pro·tect·ed
un·prov·able
un·proved
un·prov·en
un·pro·voked
un·pruned
un·pub·li·cized
un·pub·lished
un·punc·tu·al
un·punc·tu·al·i·ty
un·punc·tu·at·ed
un·pun·ished
un·quan·ti·fi·able
un·quench·able
un·ques·tioned
un·raised
un·ranked
un·rat·ed
un·rav·ished
un·reach·able
un·reached
un·read·able
un·read·i·ness
un·ready
un·re·al·iz·able
un·re·al·ized
un·re·cep·tive
un·re·claim·able
un·re·claimed
un·rec·og·niz·able
un·rec·og·niz·ably
un·rec·og·nized
un·rec·on·cil·able
un·rec·on·ciled
un·re·cord·ed
un·re·cov·er·able
un·re·cov·ered
un·re·cy·cla·ble
un·re·deem·able
un·re·deemed
un·re·dressed
un·re·fined
un·re·flec·tive
un·re·formed
un·re·frig·er·at·ed
un·reg·is·tered
un·reg·u·lat·ed
un·re·hearsed
un·re·in·forced
un·re·lat·ed
un·re·laxed
un·re·li·abil·i·ty
un·re·li·able
un·re·lieved
un·re·liev·ed·ly

un·re·luc·tant
un·re·mark·able
un·re·mark·ably
un·re·mem·bered
un·rem·i·nis·cent
un·re·mov·able
un·re·peat·able
un·re·pen·tant
un·re·pen·tant·ly
un·re·port·ed
un·rep·re·sen·ta·tive
un·rep·re·sen·ta·tive·ness
un·rep·re·sent·ed
un·re·pressed
un·re·sis·tant
un·re·solv·able
un·re·solved
un·re·spect·able
un·re·spon·sive
un·re·spon·sive·ly
un·re·spon·sive·ness
un·rest·ful
un·re·stored
un·re·strict·ed
un·re·touched
un·re·turn·able
un·re·vealed
un·re·view·able
un·re·viewed
un·re·vised
un·rev·o·lu·tion·ary
un·re·ward·ed
un·re·ward·ing
un·rhe·tor·i·cal
un·rhymed
un·rhyth·mic
un·rid·able
un·ri·fled
un·rip·ened
un·ro·man·tic
un·ro·man·ti·cal·ly
un·ro·man·ti·cized
un·roofed
un·rushed
un·safe
un·sal·able
un·sal·a·ried
un·salt·ed
un·sal·vage·able
un·sanc·tioned
un·san·i·tary
un·sat·is·fied
un·scal·able
un·scarred
un·scent·ed
un·sched·uled
un·schol·ar·ly
un·screened
un·scrip·tur·al
un·sea·soned
un·sea·wor·thy
un·se·cured
un·seed·ed
un·seg·ment·ed
un·self-con·scious
un·self-con·scious·ly
un·self-con·scious·ness
un·sell·able
un·sen·sa·tion·al
un·sen·si·tized
un·sent
un·sen·ti·men·tal
un·sep·a·rat·ed
un·se·ri·ous
un·se·ri·ous·ness
un·served
un·ser·vice·able
un·sex·u·al
un·sexy
un·shad·ed
un·shak·able
un·shak·ably

un·shak·en
un·shape·ly
un·shared
un·sharp
un·shav·en
un·shelled
un·shock·able
un·shorn
un·showy
un·signed
un·sink·able
un·size
un·slaked
un·smart
un·smil·ing
un·smoothed
un·soiled
un·sol·dier·ly
un·so·lic·it·ed
un·solv·able
un·solved
un·sort·ed
un·sound·ed
un·sown
un·spe·cial·ized
un·spec·i·fi·able
un·spe·cif·ic
un·spec·i·fied
un·spec·tac·u·lar
un·spent
un·spir·i·tu·al
un·split
un·spoiled
un·spoilt
un·spo·ken
un·sprayed
un·stained
un·stan·dard·ized
un·star·tling
un·stat·ed
un·stayed
un·ster·ile
un·ster·il·ized
un·stint·ed
un·stitch
un·stop·per
un·strained
un·strat·i·fied
un·stuffy
un·styl·ish
un·sub·dued
un·sub·si·dized
un·sub·stan·ti·at·ed
un·sub·tle
un·sub·tly
un·suit·abil·i·ty
un·suit·able
un·suit·ably
un·suit·ed
un·sul·lied
un·su·per·vised
un·sup·port·able
un·sup·port·ed
un·sure
un·sur·pass·able
un·sur·passed
un·sur·prised
un·sus·cep·ti·ble
un·sus·pect·ed
un·sus·pect·ing
un·sus·pi·cious
un·sus·tain·able
un·sweet·ened
un·sym·pa·thet·ic
un·sym·pa·thet·i·cal·ly
un·syn·chro·nized
un·sys·tem·at·ic
un·sys·tem·at·i·cal·ly
un·sys·tem·a·tized
un·tact·ful
un·tagged
un·taint·ed
un·tal·ent·ed
un·tam·able

un·tamed
un·tanned
un·tar·nished
un·taxed
un·teach·able
un·tech·ni·cal
un·tem·pered
un·ten·ant·ed
un·tend·ed
un·ten·ured
un·test·able
un·test·ed
un·the·o·ret·i·cal
un·threat·en·ing
un·thrifty
un·till·able
un·tilled
un·to·geth·er
un·trace·able
un·tra·di·tion·al
un·tra·di·tion·al·ly
un·trained
un·tram·meled
un·trans·formed
un·trans·lat·abil·i·ty
un·trans·lat·able
un·trans·lat·ed
un·trav·eled
un·tra·versed
un·treat·ed
un·trendy
un·trimmed
un·trust·ing
un·trust·wor·thy
un·tuck
un·tuft·ed
un·typ·i·cal

un·typ·i·cal·ly
un·un·der·stand·able
un·us·able
un·uti·lized
un·vac·ci·nat·ed
un·var·ied
un·vary·ing
un·ven·ti·lat·ed
un·ver·bal·ized
un·ver·i·fi·able
un·versed
un·vi·a·ble
un·vis·it·ed
un·want·ed
un·war·like
un·war·rant·ed
un·wa·ver·ing
un·wa·ver·ing·ly
un·waxed
un·weaned
un·wear·able
un·weath·ered
un·wed
un·weight·ed
un·wel·come
un·white
un·willed
un·win·na·ble
un·wom·an·ly
un·won
un·work·abil·i·ty
un·work·able
un·worked
un·wor·ried
un·wound·ed
un·wo·ven
un·young

un·abashed \ˌən-ə-'basht\ *adjective* (1571)
: not abashed : UNDISGUISED, UNAPOLOGETIC
— **un·abash·ed·ly** \-'bash-əd-lē\ *adverb*

un·abat·ed \ˌən-ə-'bā-təd\ *adjective* (circa 1611)
: not abated : being at full strength or force
— **un·abat·ed·ly** *adverb*

un·able \ˌən-'ā-bəl\ *adjective* (14th century)
: not able : INCAPABLE: as **a** : UNQUALIFIED, INCOMPETENT **b** : IMPOTENT, HELPLESS

un·abridged \ˌən-ə-'brijd\ *adjective* (1599)
1 : not abridged : COMPLETE ⟨an *unabridged* reprint of a novel⟩
2 : being the most complete of its class : not based on one larger ⟨an *unabridged* dictionary⟩

un·ac·cept·able \ˌən-ik-'sep-tə-bəl, -ak-\ *adjective* (15th century)
: not acceptable : not pleasing or welcome
— **un·ac·cept·abil·i·ty** \-ˌsep-tə-'bi-lə-tē\ *noun*
— **un·ac·cept·ably** \-'sep-tə-blē\ *adverb*

un·ac·com·pa·nied \ˌən-ə-'kəmp-nēd, -'kämp-; -'kəm-pə-, -'käm-\ *adjective* (1545)
: not accompanied; *especially* : being without instrumental accompaniment

un·ac·count·able \ˌən-ə-'kaún-tə-bəl\ *adjective* (1643)
1 : not to be accounted for : INEXPLICABLE, STRANGE
2 : not to be called to account : not responsible
— **un·ac·count·abil·i·ty** \-ˌkaún-tə-'bi-lə-tē\ *noun*

un·ac·count·ably \-'kaún-tə-blē\ *adverb* (1694)
1 : in an unaccountable manner ⟨looking *unaccountably* upset⟩ ⟨heat was *unaccountably* disappearing⟩
2 : for reasons that are hard to understand ⟨*unaccountably*, he stayed right there⟩

un·ac·count·ed \-'kaún-təd\ *adjective* (1689)

\ə\ abut \ᵊ\ kitten \ər\ further \a\ ash \ā\ ace \ä\ mop, mar \aú\ out \ch\ chin \e\ bet \ē\ easy \g\ go \i\ hit \ī\ ice \j\ job \ŋ\ sing \ō\ go \ó\ law \ói\ boy \th\ thin \t͟h\ the \ü\ loot \ú\ foot \y\ yet \zh\ vision *see also* Guide to Pronunciation

: not accounted : UNEXPLAINED — often used with *for*

un·ac·cus·tomed \,ən-ə-'kəs-təmd\ *adjective* (1526)
1 : not customary : not usual or common
2 : not habituated — usually used with *to*

una cor·da \,ü-nə-'kòr-də, -(,)dä\ *adverb or adjective* [Italian, literally, one string] (circa 1849)
: with soft pedal depressed — used as a direction in piano music

un·adorned \,ən-ə-'dòrnd\ *adjective* (1634)
: not adorned : lacking embellishment or decoration : PLAIN, SIMPLE

un·adul·ter·at·ed \,ən-ə-'dəl-tə-,rā-təd\ *adjective* (circa 1719)
1 : not adulterated : PURE ⟨*unadulterated* food⟩
2 : COMPLETE, UNQUALIFIED ⟨an *unadulterated* fool⟩
— un·adul·ter·at·ed·ly *adverb*

un·ad·vised \,ən-əd-'vīzd\ *adjective* (14th century)
1 : done without due consideration : RASH ⟨*unadvised* and dangerous dealings with the terrorists⟩
2 : not prudent : ILL-ADVISED ⟨done with *unadvised* haste⟩
— un·ad·vis·ed·ly \-'vī-zəd-lē\ *adverb*

un·af·fect·ed \,ən-ə-'fek-təd\ *adjective* (circa 1586)
1 : not influenced or changed mentally, physically, or chemically
2 : free from affectation : GENUINE
— un·af·fect·ed·ly *adverb*
— un·af·fect·ed·ness *noun*

un·ag·ing *or* **un·age·ing** \,ən-'ā-jiŋ\ *adjective* (1860)
: AGELESS

una·kite \'yü-nə-,kīt\ *noun* [*Unaka* Mountains, Tenn. & N.C. + ¹-*ite*] (1874)
: an altered igneous rock that is usually opaque with green, black, pink, and white flecks and is usually used as a gemstone

un·alien·able \,ən-'āl-yə-nə-bəl, -'ā-lē-ə-\ *adjective* (1611)
: INALIENABLE

un·aligned \,ən-ə-'līnd\ *adjective* (circa 1934)
: NONALIGNED

un·al·loyed \,ən-ə-'lòid\ *adjective* (1667)
: not alloyed : UNMIXED, UNQUALIFIED, PURE ⟨*unalloyed* metals⟩ ⟨*unalloyed* happiness⟩

un·al·ter·able \,ən-'òl-t(ə-)rə-bəl\ *adjective* (1611)
: not capable of being altered or changed ⟨an *unalterable* resolve⟩ ⟨*unalterable* hatred⟩
— un·al·ter·abil·i·ty \,ən-,òl-t(ə-)rə-'bi-lə-tē\ *noun*
— un·al·ter·able·ness \,ən-'òl-t(ə-)rə-bəl-nəs\ *noun*
— un·al·ter·ably \-blē\ *adverb*

un·am·big·u·ous \,ən-am-'bi-gyə-wəs\ *adjective* (1751)
: not ambiguous : CLEAR, PRECISE
— un·am·big·u·ous·ly *adverb*

un·am·biv·a·lent \-'bi-və-lənt\ *adjective* (1945)
: not ambivalent : CLEAR-CUT, DEFINITE
— un·am·biv·a·lent·ly *adverb*

un–Amer·i·can \,ən-ə-'mer-ə-kən\ *adjective* (1818)
: not American : not characteristic of or consistent with American customs, principles, or traditions

un·an·chored \,ən-'aŋ-kərd\ *adjective* (1651)
1 : not anchored : not at anchor
2 : not having a firm basis or foundation

un·aneled \,ən-ə-'nē(ə)ld\ *adjective* [*un-* + *aneled*, past participle of *anele* to anoint, from Middle English, from *an* on + *elen* to anoint, from *ele* oil, from Old English, from Latin *oleum* — more at OIL] (1602)
archaic : not having received extreme unction

un·anes·the·tized \,ən-ə-'nes-thə-,tīzd\ *adjective* (1950)
: not having been subjected to an anesthetic

una·nim·i·ty \,yü-nə-'ni-mə-tē\ *noun* (15th century)
: the quality or state of being unanimous

unan·i·mous \yù-'na-nə-məs\ *adjective* [Latin *unanimus*, from *unus* one + *animus* mind — more at ONE, ANIMATE] (1624)
1 : being of one mind : AGREEING
2 : formed with or indicating unanimity : having the agreement and consent of all
— unan·i·mous·ly *adverb*

un·an·swer·able \,ən-'an(t)s-rə-bəl, -'an(t)-sə-\ *adjective* (1613)
: not capable of being answered; *also* : IRREFUTABLE
— un·an·swer·abil·i·ty \,ən-,an(t)s-rə-'bi-lə-tē, -,an(t)-sə-\ *noun*
— un·an·swer·ably \,ən-'an(t)s-rə-blē, -'an(t)-sə-\ *adverb*

un·an·swered \,ən-'an(t)-sərd\ *adjective* (14th century)
1 : not answered ⟨*unanswered* letters⟩
2 : scored in succession during a period in which an opponent fails to score ⟨scored 20 *unanswered* points in the last quarter⟩

un·an·tic·i·pat·ed \,ən-an-'ti-sə-,pā-təd\ *adjective* (circa 1779)
: not anticipated : UNEXPECTED, UNFORESEEN
— un·an·tic·i·pat·ed·ly *adverb*

un·apol·o·get·ic \,ən-ə-,pä-lə-'je-tik\ *adjective* (1834)
: not apologetic : offered, put forward, or being such without apology or qualification ⟨an *unapologetic* liberal⟩
— un·apol·o·get·i·cal·ly \-ti-k(ə-)lē\ *adverb*

un·ap·peal·able \,ən-ə-'pē-lə-bəl\ *adjective* (1635)
: not appealable : not subject to appeal

un·ap·peal·ing \-'pē-liŋ\ *adjective* (circa 1846)
: not appealing : UNATTRACTIVE
— un·ap·peal·ing·ly \-liŋ-lē\ *adverb*

un·ap·peas·able \-'pē-zə-bəl\ *adjective* (1561)
: not to be appeased : IMPLACABLE
— un·ap·peas·ably \-blē\ *adverb*

un·ap·pe·tiz·ing \,ən-'a-pə-,tī-ziŋ\ *adjective* (1884)
: not appetizing : INSIPID, UNATTRACTIVE
— un·ap·pe·tiz·ing·ly \-ziŋ-lē\ *adverb*

un·ap·pre·ci·a·tion \,ən-ə-,prē-shē-'ā-shən\ *noun* (1886)
: failure to appreciate something

un·ap·proach·able \,ən-ə-'prō-chə-bəl\ *adjective* (1581)
1 : not approachable : physically inaccessible
2 : discouraging intimacies : RESERVED
— un·ap·proach·abil·i·ty \-,prō-chə-'bi-lə-tē\ *noun*
— un·ap·proach·ably \-'prō-chə-blē\ *adverb*

un·apt \,ən-'apt\ *adjective* (circa 1513)
1 : INAPPROPRIATE, UNSUITABLE ⟨an *unapt* quote⟩
2 : not accustomed and not likely ⟨a teacher *unapt* to tolerate carelessness⟩
3 : DULL, BACKWARD ⟨*unapt* scholars⟩
— un·apt·ly \-'ap(t)-lē\ *adverb*
— un·apt·ness \-nəs\ *noun*

un·arm \,ən-'ärm\ *transitive verb* (1560)
: DISARM

un·armed \-'ärmd\ *adjective* (14th century)
1 : not armed or armored
2 : having no hard and sharp projections (as spines, spurs, or claws)

un·ar·tic·u·lat·ed \,ən-är-'ti-kyə-,lā-təd\ *adjective* (circa 1700)
: not articulated; *especially* : not carefully reasoned or analyzed

una·ry \'yü-nə-rē\ *adjective* [Latin *unus* one + English -*ary*] (1576)
: having, consisting of, or acting on a single element, item, or component : MONADIC

un·ashamed \,ən-ə-'shāmd\ *adjective* (1600)
: not ashamed : being without guilt, self-consciousness, or doubt

— un·asham·ed·ly \-'shā-məd-lē\ *adverb*

un·asked \,ən-'as(k)t\ *adjective* (13th century)
1 : not being asked : UNINVITED
2 : not asked ⟨*unasked* questions⟩
3 : not asked for ⟨*unasked* advice⟩

un·as·sail·able \,ən-ə-'sā-lə-bəl\ *adjective* (1596)
: not assailable : not liable to doubt, attack, or question
— un·as·sail·abil·i·ty \-,sā-lə-ə-'bi-lə-tē\ *noun*
— un·as·sail·able·ness \-'sā-lə-bəl-nəs\ *noun*
— un·as·sail·ably \-blē\ *adverb*

un·as·ser·tive \,ən-ə-'sər-tiv\ *adjective* (1861)
: not assertive : MODEST, SHY
— un·as·ser·tive·ly *adverb*

un·as·sist·ed \,ən-ə-'sis-təd\ *adjective* (1614)
1 : not assisted : lacking help
2 : made or performed without an assist ⟨an *unassisted* double play⟩

un·as·suage·able \,ən-ə-'swā-jə-bəl\ *adjective* (circa 1611)
: not capable of being assuaged

un·as·sum·ing \,ən-ə-'sü-miŋ\ *adjective* (1726)
: not assuming : not arrogant or presuming : MODEST, RETIRING
— un·as·sum·ing·ness *noun*

un·at·tached \,ən-ə-'tacht\ *adjective* (1796)
1 a : not assigned or committed (as to a particular task, organization, or person); *especially* : not married or engaged **b :** not seized as security for a legal judgment
2 : not joined or united ⟨*unattached* buildings⟩

un·at·trac·tive \-'trak-tiv\ *adjective* (circa 1775)
: not attractive : PLAIN, DULL
— un·at·trac·tive·ly *adverb*
— un·at·trac·tive·ness *noun*

un·avail·ing \-'vā-liŋ\ *adjective* (1670)
: not availing : FUTILE, USELESS
— un·avail·ing·ly \-liŋ-lē\ *adverb*
— un·avail·ing·ness *noun*

un·av·er·age \,ən-'a-v(ə-)rij\ *adjective* (1962)
: not average : UNUSUAL, OUTSTANDING

un·avoid·able \,ən-ə-'vòi-də-bəl\ *adjective* (1577)
: not avoidable : INEVITABLE
— un·avoid·ably \-blē\ *adverb*

¹un·aware \-ə-'war, -'wer\ *adverb* (1592)
: UNAWARES

²unaware *adjective* (1704)
: not aware : IGNORANT
— un·aware·ly *adverb*
— un·aware·ness *noun*

un·awares \-'warz, -'werz\ *adverb* [*un-* + *aware* + -*s*, adverb suffix, from Middle English, from -*s*, genitive singular ending of nouns — more at -s] (1535)
1 : without design, attention, preparation, or premeditation
2 : without warning : SUDDENLY, UNEXPECTEDLY

un·backed \,ən-'bakt\ *adjective* (1609)
: lacking support or aid

¹un·bal·ance \,ən-'ba-lən(t)s\ *transitive verb* (1856)
: to put out of balance; *especially* : to derange mentally

²unbalance *noun* (1887)
: lack of balance : IMBALANCE

un·bal·anced \-lən(t)st\ *adjective* (1650)
: not balanced: as **a :** not in equilibrium **b :** mentally disordered or deranged **c :** not adjusted so as to make credits equal to debits ⟨an *unbalanced* account⟩

un·bal·last·ed \-'ba-lə-stəd\ *adjective* (1657)
: not furnished with or steadied by ballast : UNSTEADY

un·ban·dage \-'ban-dij\ *transitive verb* (1840)
: to remove a bandage from

un·bar \,ən-'bär\ *transitive verb* (14th century)
: to remove a bar from : UNBOLT, OPEN

un·bar·bered \-'bär-bərd\ *adjective* (1845)
: having long and especially unkempt hair

un·barred \-'bärd\ *adjective* (1603)
1 : not secured by a bar : UNLOCKED
2 : not marked with bars

un·bat·ed \-'bā-təd\ *adjective* (1596)
1 : UNABATED
2 *archaic* : not blunted

un·be \-'bē\ *intransitive verb* (15th century)
archaic : to lack or cease to have being

un·bear·able \ˌən-'bar-ə-bəl, -'ber-\ *adjective* (15th century)
: not bearable : UNENDURABLE
— **un·bear·ably** \-blē\ *adverb*

un·beat·able \-'bē-tə-bəl\ *adjective* (1897)
1 : not capable of being defeated
2 : possessing unsurpassable qualities
— **un·beat·ably** \-blē\ *adverb*

un·beat·en \-'bē-t²n\ *adjective* (13th century)
1 : not pounded or beaten : not whipped
2 : not traversed : UNTROD
3 : not defeated

un·beau·ti·ful \-'byü-ti-fəl\ *adjective* (15th century)
: not beautiful : UNATTRACTIVE
— **un·beau·ti·ful·ly** \-f(ə-)lē\ *adverb*

un·be·com·ing \ˌən-bi-'kə-miŋ\ *adjective* (1598)
: not becoming ⟨an *unbecoming* dress⟩; *especially* : not according with the standards appropriate to one's position or condition of life ⟨*unbecoming* conduct⟩
synonym see INDECOROUS
— **un·be·com·ing·ly** \-miŋ-lē\ *adverb*
— **un·be·com·ing·ness** *noun*

un·be·knownst \ˌən-bi-'nōn(t)st\ *also* **un·be·known** \-'nōn\ *adjective* [¹*un*- + obsolete English *beknown* known; *unbeknownst,* irregular from *unbeknown*] (1636)
: happening without one's knowledge : UNKNOWN — usually used with *to*

un·be·lief \ˌən-bə-'lēf\ *noun* (12th century)
: incredulity or skepticism especially in matters of religious truth

un·be·liev·able \-'lē-və-bəl\ *adjective* (1548)
: too improbable for belief ⟨the plot is unreal and *unbelievable*⟩; *also* : of such a superlative degree as to be hard to believe ⟨the destruction was *unbelievable*⟩ ⟨made an *unbelievable* catch in center field⟩
— **un·be·liev·ably** \-blē\ *adverb*

un·be·liev·er \-'lē-vər\ *noun* (1526)
1 : one that does not believe : an incredulous person : DOUBTER, SKEPTIC
2 : one that does not believe in a particular religious faith

un·be·liev·ing \-'lē-viŋ\ *adjective* (14th century)
: marked by unbelief : INCREDULOUS, SKEPTICAL
— **un·be·liev·ing·ly** \-viŋ-lē\ *adverb*

un·belt·ed \ˌən-'bel-təd\ *adjective* (1814)
: not furnished with a belt

un·bend \-'bend\ *verb* **-bent** \-'bent\; **-bend·ing** (13th century)
transitive verb
1 : to free from flexure : make or allow to become straight ⟨*unbend* a bow⟩
2 : to cause (as the mind) to relax
3 a : to unfasten (as a sail) from a spar or stay **b** : to cast loose (as a rope) : UNTIE
intransitive verb
1 : to relax one's severity, stiffness, or austerity
2 : to cease to be bent : become straight

un·bend·able \-'ben-də-bəl\ *adjective* (circa 1775)
: SINGLE-MINDED, FIRM

un·bend·ing \-'ben-diŋ\ *adjective* [¹*un*-] (circa 1688)
1 : not bending : UNYIELDING, INFLEXIBLE ⟨an *unbending* will⟩
2 : aloof or unsocial in manner : RESERVED

un·be·seem·ing \ˌən-bi-'sē-miŋ\ *adjective* (1583)
: not befitting : UNBECOMING

un·bi·ased \ˌən-'bī-əst\ *adjective* (1647)
1 : free from bias; *especially* : free from all prejudice and favoritism : eminently fair
2 : having an expected value equal to a population parameter being estimated ⟨an *unbiased* estimate of the population mean⟩
synonym see FAIR
— **un·bi·ased·ness** \-əs(t)-nəs\ *noun*

un·bib·li·cal \ˌən-'bi-bli-kəl\ *adjective* (1828)
: contrary to or unsanctioned by the Bible

un·bid·den \-'bi-d²n\ *also* **un·bid** \-'bid\ *adjective* [Middle English *unbiden, unbeden,* from Old English *unbeden,* from *un*- + *beden,* past participle of *biddan* to entreat — more at BID] (before 12th century)
: not bidden : UNASKED, UNINVITED

un·bind \-'bīnd\ *transitive verb* **-bound** \-'baund\; **-bind·ing** (before 12th century)
1 : to remove a band from : free from fastenings : UNTIE, UNFASTEN
2 : to set free : RELEASE

un·bit·ted \-'bi-təd\ *adjective* [²*bit*] (circa 1586)
: UNBRIDLED, UNCONTROLLED

un·blenched \-'blencht\ *adjective* (1634)
: not disconcerted : UNDAUNTED

un·blessed *also* **un·blest** \ˌən-'blest\ *adjective* (14th century)
1 : not blessed
2 : EVIL, ACCURSED

un·blind·ed \-'blīn-dəd\ *adjective* (circa 1611)
: not blinded; *especially* : free from illusion

un·blink·ing \-'bliŋ-kiŋ\ *adjective* (circa 1909)
1 : not blinking
2 : not showing signs of emotion, doubt, or confusion
— **un·blink·ing·ly** \-kiŋ-lē\ *adverb*

un·block \-'bläk\ *transitive verb* (1611)
: to free from being blocked

un·blush·ing \-'blə-shiŋ\ *adjective* (1595)
1 : not blushing
2 : SHAMELESS, UNABASHED
— **un·blush·ing·ly** \-shiŋ-lē\ *adverb*

un·bod·ied \-'bä-dēd\ *adjective* (1532)
1 : having no body : INCORPOREAL; *also* : freed from the body ⟨*unbodied* souls⟩
2 : FORMLESS

un·bolt \ˌən-'bōlt\ *transitive verb* (circa 1598)
: to open or unfasten by withdrawing a bolt

¹un·bolt·ed \-'bōl-təd\ *adjective* [²*bolt*] (circa 1580)
: not fastened by bolts

²unbolted *adjective* [⁴*bolt*] (1598)
: not sifted ⟨*unbolted* flour⟩

un·bon·net·ed \ˌən-'bä-nə-təd\ *adjective* (1604)
: BAREHEADED

un·born \-'bȯrn\ *adjective* (before 12th century)
1 : not born : not brought into life
2 : still to appear : FUTURE
3 : existing without birth

un·bos·om \ˌən-'bu̇-zəm *also* -'bü-\ (1588)
transitive verb
1 : to give expression to : DISCLOSE, REVEAL
2 : to disclose the thoughts or feelings of (oneself)
intransitive verb
: to unbosom oneself

un·bound \-'baund\ *adjective* (before 12th century)
: not bound: as **a** (1) : not fastened (2) : not confined **b** : not having the leaves fastened together ⟨an *unbound* book⟩ **c** : not bound together with other issues ⟨*unbound* periodicals⟩ **d** : not held in chemical or physical combination

un·bound·ed \-'baun-dəd\ *adjective* (1593)
1 : having no limit
2 : UNRESTRAINED, UNCONTROLLED
— **un·bound·ed·ness** *noun*

un·bowed \ˌən-'baud\ *adjective* (14th century)
1 : not bowed down
2 : not subdued ⟨bloodied but *unbowed*⟩

un·box \-'bäks\ *transitive verb* (1611)
: to remove from a box

un·brace \-'brās\ *transitive verb* (1593)
1 : to free or detach by or as if by untying or removing a brace or bond
2 : ENFEEBLE, WEAKEN

un·braid \-'brād\ *transitive verb* (circa 1828)
: to separate the strands of : UNRAVEL

un·branched \-'brancht\ *adjective* (1665)
1 : having no branches ⟨a straight *unbranched* trunk⟩
2 : not divided into branches ⟨a leaf with *unbranched* veins⟩

un·brand·ed \-'bran-dəd\ *adjective* (1886)
1 : not marked with the owner's name or mark ⟨*unbranded* cattle⟩
2 : not sold under a brand name

un·breath·able \-'brē-thə-bəl\ *adjective* (1846)
: not fit for being breathed

un·bred \-'bred\ *adjective* (1662)
1 *obsolete* : ILL-BRED
2 : not taught : UNTRAINED
3 : not bred : never having been bred ⟨an *unbred* heifer⟩

un·bri·dle \ˌən-'brī-d²l\ *transitive verb* (15th century)
: to free or loose from a bridle; *broadly* : to set loose : free from restraint

un·bri·dled \-'brī-d²ld\ *adjective* (14th century)
1 : UNRESTRAINED ⟨*unbridled* enthusiasm⟩
2 : not confined by a bridle

un·broke \-'brōk\ *adjective* (14th century)
: UNBROKEN

un·bro·ken \ˌən-'brō-kən\ *adjective* (14th century)
: not broken: as **a** : not violated **b** : WHOLE, INTACT **c** : not subdued : UNTAMED; *especially* : not trained for service or use ⟨*unbroken* colts⟩ **d** : CONTINUOUS ⟨miles of *unbroken* forest⟩ **e** : not plowed **f** : not disorganized (advanced in *unbroken* ranks⟩

un·buck·le \-'bə-kəl\ (14th century)
transitive verb
: to loose the buckle of : UNFASTEN
intransitive verb
1 : to loosen buckles
2 : RELAX

un·budge·able \-'bə-jə-bəl\ *adjective* (1929)
: not able to be budged or changed : INFLEXIBLE
— **un·budge·ably** \-blē\ *adverb*

un·budg·ing \-'bə-jiŋ\ *adjective* (circa 1934)
: not budging : resisting movement or change
— **un·budg·ing·ly** \-jiŋ-lē\ *adverb*

un·build \ˌən-'bild\ *verb* **-built** \-'bilt\; **-build·ing** (1607)
transitive verb
: to pull down : DEMOLISH, RAZE
intransitive verb
: to destroy something

un·built \-'bilt\ *adjective* (15th century)
1 : not built : not yet constructed
2 : not built on ⟨an *unbuilt* plot⟩

un·bun·dle \-'bən-d²l\ (1969)
intransitive verb
: to give separate prices for equipment and supporting services
transitive verb
: to price separately

un·bur·den \-'bər-d²n\ *transitive verb* (1538)
1 : to free or relieve from a burden
2 : to relieve oneself of (as cares, fears, or worries) : cast off

un·bur·dened \-'bər-d²nd\ *adjective* (1548)
: not burdened : having no weight or load

un·but·ton \-'bə-t²n\ (14th century)
transitive verb
1 : to loose the buttons of
2 : to open by or as if by loosing buttons

\ə\ abut \ᵊ\ kitten \ər\ further \a\ ash \ā\ ace
\ä\ mop, mar \au̇\ out \ch\ chin \e\ bet \ē\ easy
\g\ go \i\ hit \ī\ ice \j\ job \ŋ\ sing \ō\ go
\ȯ\ law \ȯi\ boy \th\ thin \t̶h\ the \ü\ loot \u̇\ foot
\y\ yet \zh\ vision *see also* Guide to Pronunciation

intransitive verb
: to undo buttons
un·but·toned \-t°nd\ *adjective* (1583)
1 a : not buttoned **b** : not provided with buttons
2 : not under constraint : free and unrestricted in action and expression
un·cage \,ən-'kāj\ *transitive verb* (1620)
: to release from or as if from a cage : free from restraint
un·cal·cu·lat·ed \-'kal-kyə-,lā-təd\ *adjective* (circa 1828)
: not planned or thought out beforehand : SPONTANEOUS
un·cal·cu·lat·ing \-,lā-tiŋ\ *adjective* (circa 1828)
: not based on or marked by calculation
un·called–for \,ən-'kȯl(d)-,fȯr\ *adjective* (circa 1656)
1 : not called for or needed : UNNECESSARY
2 : being or offered without provocation or justification ⟨an *uncalled-for* display of temper⟩ ⟨*uncalled-for* insults⟩
un·can·ny \-'ka-nē\ *adjective* (1843)
1 a : seeming to have a supernatural character or origin : EERIE, MYSTERIOUS **b** : being beyond what is normal or expected : suggesting superhuman or supernatural powers ⟨an *uncanny* sense of direction⟩
2 *chiefly Scottish* : SEVERE, PUNISHING
synonym see WEIRD
— **un·can·ni·ly** \-'ka-n°l-ē\ *adverb*
— **un·can·ni·ness** \-'ka-nē-nəs\ *noun*
un·caused \-'kȯzd\ *adjective* (circa 1628)
: having no antecedent cause
un·ceas·ing \-'sē-siŋ\ *adjective* (14th century)
: never ceasing : CONTINUOUS, INCESSANT
— **un·ceas·ing·ly** \-siŋ-lē\ *adverb*
un·cel·e·brat·ed \-'se-lə-,brā-təd\ *adjective* (1660)
1 : not formally honored or commemorated
2 : not famous : OBSCURE
un·cer·e·mo·ni·ous \,ən-,ser-ə-'mō-nē-əs\ *adjective* (1598)
1 : not ceremonious : INFORMAL
2 : ABRUPT, RUDE ⟨an *unceremonious* dismissal⟩
— **un·cer·e·mo·ni·ous·ly** *adverb*
— **un·cer·e·mo·ni·ous·ness** *noun*
un·cer·tain \,ən-'sər-t°n\ *adjective* (14th century)
1 : INDEFINITE, INDETERMINATE ⟨the time of departure is *uncertain*⟩
2 : not certain to occur : PROBLEMATICAL
3 : not reliable : UNTRUSTWORTHY
4 a : not known beyond doubt : DUBIOUS **b** : not having certain knowledge : DOUBTFUL **c** : not clearly identified or defined
5 : not constant : VARIABLE, FITFUL
— **un·cer·tain·ly** *adverb*
— **un·cer·tain·ness** \-t°n-(n)əs\ *noun*
un·cer·tain·ty \-t°n-tē\ *noun* (14th century)
1 : the quality or state of being uncertain : DOUBT
2 : something that is uncertain ☆
uncertainty principle *noun* (1929)
: a principle in quantum mechanics: it is impossible to discern simultaneously and with high accuracy both the position and the momentum of a particle (as an electron) — called also *Heisenberg uncertainty principle*
un·chain \,ən-'chān\ *transitive verb* (1582)
: to free by or as if by removing a chain : set loose
un·chancy \-'chan(t)-sē\ *adjective* (1533)
1 *chiefly Scottish* : ILL-FATED
2 *chiefly Scottish* : DANGEROUS
un·change·able \-'chān-jə-bəl\ *adjective* (14th century)
: not changing or to be changed : IMMUTABLE
— **un·change·abil·i·ty** \,ən-,chān-jə-'bi-lə-tē\ *noun*
— **un·change·able·ness** \,ən-'chān-jə-bəl-nəs\ *noun*
— **un·chan·ge·ably** \-blē\ *adverb*
un·chang·ing \-'chān-jiŋ\ *adjective* (1593)
: CONSTANT, INVARIABLE

— **un·chang·ing·ly** \-jiŋ-lē\ *adverb*
— **un·chang·ing·ness** *noun*
un·char·ac·ter·is·tic \,ən-,kar-ik-tə-'ris-tik\ *adjective* (1753)
: not characteristic : not typical or distinctive
— **un·char·ac·ter·is·ti·cal·ly** \-ti-k(ə-)lē\ *adverb*
un·charge \,ən-'chärj\ *transitive verb* (1602)
obsolete : ACQUIT
un·charged \-'chärjd\ *adjective* (1815)
: not charged; *specifically* : having no electric charge
un·char·i·ta·ble \-'char-ə-tə-bəl\ *adjective* (15th century)
: lacking in charity : severe in judging : HARSH
— **un·char·i·ta·ble·ness** *noun*
— **un·char·i·ta·bly** \-blē\ *adverb*
un·chart·ed \-'chär-təd\ *adjective* (circa 1847)
: not recorded or plotted on a map, chart, or plan; *broadly* : UNKNOWN ⟨*uncharted* territory⟩
un·chaste \-'chāst\ *adjective* (14th century)
: not chaste : lacking in chastity
— **un·chaste·ly** *adverb*
— **un·chaste·ness** \-'chās(t)-nəs\ *noun*
un·chas·ti·ty \-'chas-tə-tē\ *noun* (14th century)
: the quality or state of being unchaste
un·chiv·al·rous \-'shi-vəl-rəs\ *adjective* (circa 1846)
: not chivalrous : lacking in chivalry
— **un·chiv·al·rous·ly** *adverb*
un·choke \-'chōk\ *transitive verb* (1588)
: to clear of obstruction
un·chris·tian \-'kris-chən, -'krish-\ *adjective* (1555)
1 : not of the Christian faith
2 a : contrary to the Christian spirit or character **b** : UNCIVILIZED, BARBAROUS
un·church \-'chərch\ *transitive verb* (circa 1620)
1 : to expel from a church : EXCOMMUNICATE
2 : to deprive of a church or of status as a church
un·churched \-'chərcht\ *adjective* (1681)
: not belonging to or connected with a church
unci *plural of* UNCUS
¹un·cial \'ən(t)-shəl, -sē-əl\ *adjective* [Late Latin *unciales* (*litterae*) uncial (letters), from Latin, plural of *uncialis* weighing an ounce, from *uncia* twelfth part, ounce — more at OUNCE] (1712)
: written in the style or size of uncials
— **un·cial·ly** *adverb*
²uncial *noun* (circa 1775)
1 : a hand-writing used especially in Greek and Latin manuscripts of the 4th to the 8th centuries A.D. and made with somewhat rounded separated majuscules but having cursive forms for some letters

ROMAN UNCIAL

uncials

2 : an uncial letter
3 : a manuscript written in uncial
un·ci·form \'ən(t)-sə-,fȯrm\ *adjective* [New Latin *unciformis*, from Latin *uncus* hook + -*formis* -form — more at ANGLE] (circa 1734)
: hook-shaped : UNCINATE
un·ci·na·ri·a·sis \,ən-,si-nə-'rī-ə-səs\ *noun* [New Latin, from *Uncinaria*, genus that includes hookworms, from Latin *uncinus* hook] (1903)
: ANCYLOSTOMIASIS
un·ci·nate \'ən(t)-sə-,nāt\ *adjective* [Latin *uncinatus*, from *uncinus* hook, from *uncus*] (circa 1760)
: bent at the tip like a hook : HOOKED ⟨an *uncinate* achene⟩
un·cir·cu·lat·ed \,ən-'sər-kyə-,lā-təd\ *adjective* (1917)
: issued for use as money but kept out of circulation (as for preservation in a collection)
un·cir·cum·cised \,ən-'sər-kəm-,sīzd\ *adjective* (14th century)

1 : not circumcised
2 : spiritually impure : HEATHEN
— **un·cir·cum·ci·sion** \,ən-,sər-kəm-'si-zhən\ *noun*
un·civ·il \,ən-'si-vəl\ *adjective* (1553)
1 : not civilized : BARBAROUS
2 : lacking in courtesy : ILL-MANNERED, IMPOLITE
3 : not conducive to civic harmony and welfare
— **un·civ·il·ly** \-və-lē\ *adverb*
un·civ·i·lized \-'si-və-,līzd\ *adjective* (1607)
1 : not civilized : BARBAROUS
2 : remote from settled areas : WILD
un·clamp \-'klamp\ *transitive verb* (1809)
: to loosen the clamp of : to free from a clamp
un·clar·i·ty \-'klar-ə-tē\ *noun, plural* -ties (1923)
: lack of clarity : AMBIGUITY, OBSCURITY
un·clasp \-'klasp\ (1530)
transitive verb
1 : to open the clasp of
2 : to open or cause to be opened (as a clenched hand)
intransitive verb
: to loosen a hold
un·clas·si·cal \-'kla-si-kəl\ *adjective* (1725)
: not classical; *especially* : unconcerned with the classics
un·clas·si·fied \-'kla-sə-,fīd\ *adjective* (1865)
1 : not placed or belonging in a class
2 : not subject to a security classification
un·cle \'əŋ-kəl\ *noun* [Middle English, from Old French, from Latin *avunculus* mother's brother; akin to Old English *ēam* uncle, Welsh *ewythr* uncle, Latin *avus* grandfather] (14th century)
1 a : the brother of one's father or mother **b** : the husband of one's aunt
2 : one who helps, advises, or encourages
3 — used as a cry of surrender ⟨was forced to cry *uncle*⟩
4 *capitalized* : UNCLE SAM
un·clean \,ən-'klēn\ *adjective* (before 12th century)
1 : morally or spiritually impure
2 : infected with a harmful supernatural contagion; *also* : prohibited by ritual law for use or contact
3 : DIRTY, FILTHY
4 : lacking in clarity and precision of conception or execution
— **un·clean·ness** \-'klēn-nəs\ *noun*
¹un·clean·ly \-'klen-lē\ *adjective* (before 12th century)
: morally or physically unclean
— **un·clean·li·ness** *noun*
²un·clean·ly \-'klēn-lē\ *adverb* (before 12th century)
: in an unclean manner
un·clench \-'klench\ (1699)

☆ SYNONYMS
Uncertainty, doubt, dubiety, skepticism, suspicion, mistrust mean lack of sureness about someone or something. UNCERTAINTY may range from a falling short of certainty to an almost complete lack of conviction or knowledge especially about an outcome or result (assumed the role of manager without hesitation or *uncertainty*). DOUBT suggests both uncertainty and inability to make a decision (plagued by *doubts* as to what to do). DUBIETY stresses a wavering between conclusions (felt some *dubiety* about its practicality). SKEPTICISM implies unwillingness to believe without conclusive evidence (an economic forecast greeted with *skepticism*). SUSPICION stresses lack of faith in the truth, reality, fairness, or reliability of something or someone (regarded the stranger with *suspicion*). MISTRUST implies a genuine doubt based upon suspicion (had a great *mistrust* of doctors).

transitive verb
1 : to open from a clenched position
2 : to release from a grip
intransitive verb
: to become unclasped or relaxed
Un·cle Sam \ˌən-kəl-ˈsam\ *noun* [expansion of *U.S.*, abbreviation of *United States*] (1813)
1 : the U.S. government
2 : the American nation or people
¹Uncle Tom \-ˈtäm\ *noun* [*Uncle Tom,* pious and faithful black slave in *Uncle Tom's Cabin* (1851–52) by Harriet Beecher Stowe] (1922)
1 : a black who is overeager to win the approval of whites (as by obsequious behavior or uncritical acceptance of white values and goals)
2 : a member of a low-status group who is overly subservient to or cooperative with authority ⟨the worst floor managers and supervisors by far are women . . . Some of them are regular *Uncle Toms* —Jane Fonda⟩
— **Uncle Tom·ism** \-ˈtä-ˌmi-zəm\ *noun*
²Uncle Tom *intransitive verb* **Uncle Tommed; Uncle Tom·ming** (1947)
: to behave like an Uncle Tom
un·climb·able \ˌən-ˈklī-mə-bəl\ *adjective* (1553)
: not able to be climbed
— **un·climb·able·ness** *noun*
un·clinch \ˌən-ˈklinch\ *transitive verb* (1598)
: UNCLENCH
un·cloak \-ˈklōk\ (1598)
transitive verb
1 : to remove a cloak or cover from
2 : REVEAL, UNMASK
intransitive verb
: to take off a cloak
un·clog \-ˈkläg\ *transitive verb* (1607)
: to free from a difficulty or obstruction
un·close \-ˈklōz\ (14th century)
transitive verb
1 : OPEN
2 : DISCLOSE, REVEAL
intransitive verb
: to become opened
un·closed \-ˈklōzd\ *adjective* (15th century)
: not closed or settled **:** not concluded
un·clothe \-ˈklōth\ *transitive verb* (14th century)
1 : to strip of clothes
2 : DIVEST, UNCOVER
un·clothed \-ˈklōthd\ *adjective* (15th century)
: not clothed
un·cloud·ed \-ˈklau̇-dəd\ *adjective* (1594)
: not covered by clouds **:** not darkened or obscured **:** CLEAR
— **un·cloud·ed·ly** *adverb*
un·club·ba·ble \ˌən-ˈklə-bə-bəl\ *adjective* (circa 1764)
: UNSOCIABLE 1
un·clut·ter \-ˈklə-tər\ *transitive verb* (1930)
: to remove clutter from **:** make neat and orderly
un·clut·tered \-ˈtərd\ *adjective* (1925)
: not cluttered
¹un·co \ˈən-(ˌ)kō, -kə\ *adjective* [Middle English (Scots) *unkow,* alteration of Middle English *uncouth*] (15th century)
1 *chiefly Scottish* **a :** STRANGE, UNKNOWN **b :** UNCANNY, WEIRD
2 *chiefly Scottish* **:** EXTRAORDINARY
²unco *adverb* (1724)
: EXTREMELY, REMARKABLY, UNCOMMONLY
³unco *noun, plural* **uncos** (1785)
1 *plural, chiefly Scottish* **:** NEWS, TIDINGS
2 *chiefly Scottish* **:** STRANGER
un·cock \ˌən-ˈkäk\ *transitive verb* (circa 1775)
: to remove the hammer of (a firearm) from a cocked position
un·cof·fin \-ˈkȯ-fən\ *transitive verb* (1836)
: to remove from or as if from a coffin
un·cof·fined \-fənd\ *adjective* (1648)
: not placed in a coffin
un·coil \ˌən-ˈkȯi(ə)l\ (1713)
transitive verb
: to release from a coiled state **:** UNWIND

intransitive verb
: to become uncoiled
un·coiled \-ˈkȯi(ə)ld\ *adjective* (1713)
: not coiled
un·coined \-ˈkȯind\ *adjective* (15th century)
1 : not minted ⟨*uncoined* metal⟩
2 : not fabricated **:** NATURAL
un·com·fort·able \ˌən-ˈkəm(p)(f)-tə(r)-bəl, -ˈkəm(p)-fə(r)-tə-bəl, -ˈkəm-fə(r)-bəl\ *adjective* (1592)
1 : causing discomfort or annoyance ⟨an *uncomfortable* chair⟩ ⟨an *uncomfortable* performance⟩
2 : feeling discomfort **:** UNEASY ⟨was *uncomfortable* with them⟩
— **un·com·fort·ably** \-blē\ *adverb*
un·com·mer·cial \ˌən-kə-ˈmər-shəl\ *adjective* (1768)
1 : not engaged in or related to commerce
2 : not based on commercial principles
3 : not likely to result in financial success ⟨an *uncommercial* book⟩
un·com·mit·ted \ˌən-kə-ˈmi-təd\ *adjective* (1598)
: not committed; *specifically* **:** not pledged to a particular belief, allegiance, or program
un·com·mon \ˌən-ˈkä-mən\ *adjective* (1611)
1 : not ordinarily encountered **:** UNUSUAL
2 : REMARKABLE, EXCEPTIONAL
synonym see INFREQUENT
— **un·com·mon·ly** *adverb*
— **un·com·mon·ness** \-mən-nəs\ *noun*
un·com·mu·ni·ca·ble \ˌən-kə-ˈmyü-ni-kə-bəl\ *adjective* (14th century)
: INCOMMUNICABLE
un·com·mu·ni·ca·tive \-ˈmyü-nə-ˌkā-tiv, -ni-kə-tiv\ *adjective* (1691)
: not disposed to talk or impart information **:** RESERVED
un·com·pet·i·tive \-ˈpe-tə-tiv\ *adjective* (1885)
: not competitive **:** unable to compete
— **un·com·pet·i·tive·ness** *noun*
un·com·plain·ing \-ˈplā-niŋ\ *adjective* (1744)
: not complaining **:** PATIENT
— **un·com·plain·ing·ly** \-niŋ-lē\ *adverb*
un·com·pli·cat·ed \ˌən-ˈkäm-plə-ˌkā-təd\ *adjective* (circa 1775)
1 a : not complicated by something outside itself **b :** not involving medical complications ⟨an *uncomplicated* peptic ulcer⟩
2 : not complex **:** SIMPLE ⟨*uncomplicated* machinery⟩
un·com·pli·men·ta·ry \ˌən-ˌkäm-plə-ˈmen-tə-rē, -ˈmen-trē\ *adjective* (1842)
: not complimentary **:** DEROGATORY
un·com·pre·hend·ing \-pri-ˈhen-diŋ\ *adjective* (1838)
: not comprehending **:** lacking understanding
— **un·com·pre·hend·ing·ly** \-diŋ-lē\ *adverb*
un·com·pro·mis·able \ˌən-ˈkäm-prə-ˌmī-zə-bəl\ *adjective* (1958)
: not able to be compromised
un·com·pro·mis·ing \-ˌmī-ziŋ\ *adjective* (circa 1828)
: not making or accepting a compromise **:** making no concessions **:** INFLEXIBLE, UNYIELDING
— **un·com·pro·mis·ing·ly** \-ziŋ-lē\ *adverb*
— **un·com·pro·mis·ing·ness** \-nəs\ *noun*
un·con·ceiv·able \ˌən-kən-ˈsē-və-bəl\ *adjective* (circa 1607)
: INCONCEIVABLE
un·con·cern \ˌən-kən-ˈsərn\ *noun* (1711)
1 : lack of care or interest **:** INDIFFERENCE
2 : freedom from excessive concern or anxiety
un·con·cerned \-ˈsərnd\ *adjective* (circa 1635)
1 : not involved **:** not having any part or interest
2 : not anxious or upset **:** free of worry
synonym see INDIFFERENT
— **un·con·cerned·ly** \-ˈsər-nəd-lē, -ˈsərnd-lē\ *adverb*

— **un·con·cerned·ness** \-ˈsər-nəd-nəs, -ˈsərn(d)-nəs\ *noun*
un·con·di·tion·al \ˌən-kən-ˈdish-nəl, -ˈdi-shə-nᵊl\ *adjective* (1666)
1 : not conditional or limited **:** ABSOLUTE, UNQUALIFIED ⟨*unconditional* surrender⟩
2 : UNCONDITIONED 2
— **un·con·di·tion·al·ly** *adverb*
un·con·di·tioned \-ˈdi-shənd\ *adjective* (circa 1631)
1 : not subject to conditions or limitations
2 a : not dependent on or subjected to conditioning or learning **:** NATURAL ⟨*unconditioned* responses⟩ **b :** producing an unconditioned response ⟨*unconditioned* stimuli⟩
un·con·form·able \-ˈfȯr-mə-bəl\ *adjective* (1594)
1 : not conforming
2 : exhibiting geological unconformity
— **un·con·form·ably** \-blē\ *adverb*
un·con·for·mi·ty \-ˈfȯr-mə-tē\ *noun* (circa 1600)
1 *archaic* **:** lack of conformity
2 a : lack of continuity in deposition between rock strata in contact corresponding to a period of nondeposition, weathering, or erosion **b :** the surface of contact between unconformable strata
un·con·ge·nial \-ˈjē-nyəl, -nē-əl\ *adjective* (circa 1775)
1 : not sympathetic or compatible ⟨*uncongenial* roommates⟩
2 a : not fitted **:** UNSUITABLE ⟨a soil *uncongenial* to most crops⟩ **b :** not to one's taste **:** DISAGREEABLE ⟨an *uncongenial* task⟩
— **un·con·ge·nial·i·ty** \-ˌjē-nē-ˈa-lə-tē, -ˌjēn-ˈya-\ *noun*
un·con·quer·able \ˌən-ˈkäŋ-k(ə-)rə-bəl\ *adjective* (1598)
1 : incapable of being conquered **:** INDOMITABLE ⟨an *unconquerable* will⟩
2 : incapable of being surmounted ⟨*unconquerable* difficulties⟩
— **un·con·quer·ably** \-blē\ *adverb*
un·con·scio·na·ble \-ˈkän(t)-sh(ə-)nə-bəl\ *adjective* (1570)
1 : not guided or controlled by conscience **:** UNSCRUPULOUS ⟨an *unconscionable* villain⟩
2 a : EXCESSIVE, UNREASONABLE ⟨found an *unconscionable* number of defects in the car⟩ **b :** shockingly unfair or unjust ⟨*unconscionable* sales practices⟩
— **un·con·scio·na·bil·i·ty** \ˌən-ˌkän(t)-sh(ə-)nə-ˈbi-lə-tē\ *noun*
— **un·con·scio·na·ble·ness** \ˌən-ˈkän(t)-sh(ə-)nə-bəl-nəs\ *noun*
— **un·con·scio·na·bly** \-blē\ *adverb*
¹un·con·scious \ˌən-ˈkän(t)-shəs\ *adjective* (1712)
1 a : not knowing or perceiving **:** not aware **b :** free from self-awareness
2 a : not possessing mind or consciousness ⟨*unconscious* matter⟩ **b** (1) **:** not marked by conscious thought, sensation, or feeling ⟨*unconscious* motivation⟩ (2) **:** of or relating to the unconscious **c :** having lost consciousness ⟨was *unconscious* for three days⟩
3 : not consciously held or deliberately planned or carried out ⟨*unconscious* bias⟩
— **un·con·scious·ly** *adverb*
— **un·con·scious·ness** *noun*
²unconscious *noun* (1912)
: the part of the psychic apparatus that does not ordinarily enter the individual's awareness and that is manifested especially by slips of the tongue or dissociated acts or in dreams
un·con·sid·ered \ˌən-kən-ˈsi-dərd\ *adjective* (1587)
1 : not considered or worth consideration
2 : not resulting from consideration

\ə\ **abut** \ᵊ\ **kitten** \ər\ **further** \a\ **ash** \ā\ **ace** \ä\ **mop, mar** \au̇\ **out** \ch\ **chin** \e\ **bet** \ē\ **easy** \g\ **go** \i\ **hit** \ī\ **ice** \j\ **job** \ŋ\ **sing** \ō\ **go** \ȯ\ **law** \ȯi\ **boy** \th\ **thin** \t͟h\ **the** \ü\ **loot** \u̇\ **foot** \y\ **yet** \zh\ **vision** *see also* Guide to Pronunciation

un·con·sol·i·dat·ed \-'sä-lə-ˌdā-təd\ *adjective* (circa 1775)
: loosely arranged ⟨*unconsolidated* subsidiaries⟩; *especially* : not stratified ⟨*unconsolidated* soil⟩

un·con·sti·tu·tion·al \-ən-ˌkän(t)-stə-'tü-shnəl, -'tyü-, -shə-nᵊl\ *adjective* (1734)
: not according or consistent with the constitution of a body politic (as a nation)
— **un·con·sti·tu·tion·al·i·ty** \-ˌtü-shə-'na-lə-tē, -ˌtyü-\ *noun*
— **un·con·sti·tu·tion·al·ly** *adverb*

un·con·straint \ˌən-kən-'strānt\ *noun* (1711)
: freedom from constraint : EASE

un·con·struct·ed \-'strək-təd\ *adjective* (1970)
of clothing : manufactured without added material for padding, stiffening, or shape retention

un·con·trol·la·ble \-'trō-lə-bəl\ *adjective* (1593)
1 *archaic* : free from control by a superior power : ABSOLUTE
2 : incapable of being controlled : UNGOVERNABLE
— **un·con·trol·la·bil·i·ty** \-ˌtrō-lə-ə-'bi-lə-tē\ *noun*
— **un·con·trol·la·bly** \-'trō-lə-blē\ *adverb*

un·con·ven·tion·al \-'vench-nəl, -'ven(t)-shə-nᵊl\ *adjective* (1839)
: not conventional : not bound by or in accordance with convention : being out of the ordinary
— **un·con·ven·tion·al·i·ty** \-ˌven(t)-shə-'na-lə-tē\ *noun*
— **un·con·ven·tion·al·ly** *adverb*

un·con·vinc·ing \-'vin(t)-siŋ\ *adjective* (1653)
: not convincing : IMPLAUSIBLE
— **un·con·vinc·ing·ly** \-siŋ-lē\ *adverb*
— **un·con·vinc·ing·ness** *noun*

un·cool \ˌən-'kül\ *adjective* (1953)
1 : lacking in assurance
2 : failing to accord with the current styles (as of dress or behavior) of a particular group

un·cork \ˌən-'kȯrk\ *transitive verb* (1727)
1 : to draw a cork from
2 a : to release from a sealed or pent-up state ⟨*uncork* a surprise⟩ b : to let go : RELEASE ⟨*uncork* a wild pitch⟩

un·corked \-'kȯrkt\ *adjective* (1791)
: not provided with a cork

un·cor·set·ed \-'kȯr-sə-təd\ *adjective* (1856)
1 : not wearing a corset
2 : not controlled or inhibited ⟨*uncorseted* freedom⟩

un·count·ed \-'kaȯn-təd\ *adjective* (15th century)
1 : not counted
2 : INNUMERABLE

un·cou·ple \-'kə-pəl\ *transitive verb* (14th century)
1 : to release (dogs) from a couple
2 : DETACH, DISCONNECT ⟨*uncouple* railroad cars⟩
— **un·cou·pler** \-p(ə-)lər\ *noun*

un·couth \-'küth\ *adjective* [Middle English, from Old English *uncūth*, from *un-* + *cūth* familiar, known; akin to Old High German *kund* known, Old English *can* know — more at CAN] (before 12th century)
1 a *archaic* : not known or not familiar to one : seldom experienced : UNCOMMON, RARE b *obsolete* : MYSTERIOUS, UNCANNY
2 a : strange or clumsy in shape or appearance : OUTLANDISH b : lacking in polish and grace : RUGGED ⟨*uncouth* verse⟩ c : awkward and uncultivated in appearance, manner, or behavior
— **un·couth·ly** *adverb*
— **un·couth·ness** *noun*

un·cov·er \-'kə-vər\ (14th century)
transitive verb
1 : to make known : bring to light : DISCLOSE, REVEAL
2 : to expose to view by removing some covering

3 a : to take the cover from b : to remove the hat from
4 : to deprive of protection
intransitive verb
1 : to remove a cover or covering
2 : to take off the hat as a token of respect

un·cov·ered \-'vərd\ *adjective* (15th century)
: not covered: as a : not supplied with a covering b : not covered by insurance or included in a social insurance or welfare program c : not covered by collateral ⟨an *uncovered* note⟩

un·cre·at·ed \ˌən-krē-'ā-təd\ *adjective* (circa 1549)
1 : not existing by creation : ETERNAL, SELF-EXISTENT
2 : not yet created

un·crit·i·cal \ˌən-'kri-ti-kəl\ *adjective* (1659)
1 : not critical : lacking in discrimination
2 : showing lack or improper use of critical standards or procedures
— **un·crit·i·cal·ly** \-k(ə-)lē\ *adverb*

un·cross \-'krȯs\ *transitive verb* (1599)
: to change from a crossed position

un·crown \-'kraȯn\ *transitive verb* (14th century)
: to take the crown from : DEPOSE, DETHRONE

un·crum·ple \-'krəm-pəl\ *transitive verb* (1611)
: to restore to an original smooth condition

un·crys·tal·ized \-'kris-tə-ˌlīzd\ *adjective* (1759)
: not crystallized; *also* : not finally or definitely formed

unc·tion \'əŋ(k)-shən\ *noun* [Middle English *unctioun*, from Latin *unction-*, *unctio*, from *unguere* to anoint — more at OINTMENT] (14th century)
1 : the act of anointing as a rite of consecration or healing
2 : something used for anointing : OINTMENT, UNGUENT
3 a : religious or spiritual fervor or the expression of such fervor b : exaggerated, assumed, or superficial earnestness of language or manner : UNCTUOUSNESS

unc·tu·ous \'əŋ(k)-chə-wəs, -chəs, -shwəs\ *adjective* [Middle English, from Middle French or Medieval Latin; Middle French *unctueux*, from Medieval Latin *unctuosus*, from Latin *unctus* act of anointing, from *unguere* to anoint] (14th century)
1 a : FATTY, OILY b : smooth and greasy in texture or appearance
2 : PLASTIC ⟨fine *unctuous* clay⟩
3 : full of unction; *especially* : revealing or marked by a smug, ingratiating, and false earnestness or spirituality
— **unc·tu·ous·ly** *adverb*
— **unc·tu·ous·ness** *noun*

un·curl \ˌən-'kər(-ə)l\ (1588)
intransitive verb
: to become straightened out from a curled or coiled position
transitive verb
: to straighten the curls of : UNROLL

un·cus \'əŋ-kəs\ *noun, plural* **un·ci** \'əŋ-ˌkī, -ˌkē; 'ən-ˌsī\ [New Latin, from Latin, hook — more at ANGLE] (1826)
: a hooked anatomical part or process

un·cut \ˌən-'kət\ *adjective* (1548)
1 : not cut down or cut into
2 : not shaped by cutting ⟨an *uncut* diamond⟩
3 *of a book* : not having the folds of the leaves slit
4 : not abridged, curtailed, or expurgated ⟨the *uncut* version of the film⟩
5 : not diluted or adulterated ⟨*uncut* vinegar⟩ ⟨*uncut* heroin⟩

un·daunt·able \ˌən-'dȯn-tə-bəl, -'dän-\ *adjective* (1587)
: incapable of being daunted : FEARLESS

un·daunt·ed \-təd\ *adjective* (1587)
: courageously resolute especially in the face of danger or difficulty : not discouraged
— **un·daunt·ed·ly** *adverb*

un·dead \ˌən-'ded\ *noun, plural* **undead** (1897)
1 : VAMPIRE 1
2 : ZOMBIE 1b

un·de·bat·able \ˌən-di-'bā-tə-bəl\ *adjective* (1869)
: not subject to debate : INDISPUTABLE
— **un·de·bat·ably** \-blē\ *adverb*

un·de·ceive \ˌən-di-'sēv\ *transitive verb* (1598)
: to free from deception, illusion, or error

un·de·cil·lion \ˌən-di-'sil-yən\ *noun, often attributive* [Latin *undecim* eleven (from *unus* one + *decem* ten) + English *-illion* (as in *million*) — more at ONE, TEN] (1931)
— see NUMBER table

un·dec·y·le·nic acid \ˌən-ˌde-sə-'le-nik-, -'lē-\ *noun* [*undecylene* ($C_{11}H_{22}$)] (1879)
: an acid $C_{11}H_{20}O_2$ found in perspiration, obtained commercially from castor oil, and used in the treatment of fungal infections (as ringworm) of the skin

un·dem·o·crat·ic \ˌən-ˌde-mə-'kra-tik\ *adjective* (1839)
: not democratic : not agreeing with democratic practice or ideals
— **un·dem·o·crat·i·cal·ly** \-ti-k(ə-)lē\ *adverb*

un·de·mon·stra·tive \ˌən-di-'män(t)-strə-tiv\ *adjective* (1846)
: restrained in expression of feeling : RESERVED
— **un·de·mon·stra·tive·ly** *adverb*
— **un·de·mon·stra·tive·ness** *noun*

un·de·ni·able \ˌən-di-'nī-ə-bəl\ *adjective* (1547)
1 : plainly true : INCONTESTABLE
2 : unquestionably excellent or genuine ⟨an applicant with *undeniable* references⟩
— **un·de·ni·able·ness** *noun*
— **un·de·ni·ably** \-blē\ *adverb*

¹**un·der** \'ən-dər\ *adverb* & *preposition*, from Old English; akin to Old High German *untar* under, Latin *inferus* situated beneath, lower, *infra* below, Sanskrit *adha*] (before 12th century)
1 : in or into a position below or beneath something
2 : below or short of some quantity, level, or limit ⟨$10 or *under*⟩ — often used in combination ⟨*under*staffed⟩
3 : in or into a condition of subjection, subordination, or unconsciousness
4 : down to defeat, ruin, or death
5 : so as to be covered

²**under** *preposition* (before 12th century)
1 : below or beneath so as to be overhung, surrounded, covered, protected, or concealed by ⟨*under* sunny skies⟩ ⟨a soft heart *under* a stern exterior⟩ ⟨*under* cover of darkness⟩
2 a : subject to the authority, control, guidance, or instruction of ⟨served *under* the general⟩ ⟨*under* the terms of the contract⟩ b : receiving or undergoing the action or effect of ⟨*under* pressure⟩ ⟨courage *under* fire⟩ ⟨*under* the influence of alcohol⟩ ⟨the image of a point *under* a mapping⟩
3 : within the group or designation of ⟨*under* this heading⟩
4 : less or lower than (as in size, amount, or rank); *especially* : falling short of a standard or required degree ⟨*under* the legal age⟩ ⟨*under* par⟩

³**under** *adjective* (14th century)
1 a : lying or placed below, beneath, or on the ventral side — often used in combination ⟨*under*lip⟩ b : facing or protruding downward
2 : lower in rank or authority : SUBORDINATE
3 : lower than usual, proper, or desired in amount, quality, or degree ⟨an *under* dose of medicine⟩

un·der·achiev·er \ˌən-dər-ə-'chē-vər\ *noun* (1952)
: a person and especially a student who fails to attain a predicted level of achievement or does not do as well as expected

— **un·der·achieve** \-ə-'chēv\ *intransitive verb*

— **un·der·achieve·ment** \-mənt\ *noun*

un·der·act \,ən-dər-'akt\ (circa 1623)
transitive verb
: to perform (a dramatic part) with restraint for effect : UNDERPLAY
intransitive verb
: to perform feebly or with restraint

un·der·ac·tive \-'ak-tiv\ *adjective* (1959)
: characterized by an abnormally low level of activity ⟨an *underactive* thyroid gland⟩
— **un·der·ac·tiv·i·ty** \-'ti-və-tē\ *noun*

un·der·age \,ən-dər-'āj\ *adjective* (1594)
1 : of less than mature or legal age
2 : done by or involving underage persons ⟨*underage* drinking⟩

un·der·ap·pre·ci·at·ed \,ən-dər-ə-'prē-shē-,ā-təd\ *adjective* (1968)
: not duly appreciated

¹**un·der·arm** \'ən-dər-'ärm\ *adjective* (1816)
1 : UNDERHAND 4
2 : placed under or on the underside of the arm ⟨*underarm* seams⟩

²**un·der·arm** \,ən-dər-'ärm\ *adverb* (circa 1909)
: UNDERHAND

³**un·der·arm** \'ən-dər-,ärm\ *noun* (1923)
1 : ARMPIT 1
2 : the part of a garment that covers the underside of the arm

un·der·bel·ly \'ən-dər-,be-lē\ *noun* (1607)
1 : the underside of a body or mass
2 : a vulnerable area

un·der·bid \,ən-dər-'bid\ *verb* -**bid**; -**bid·ding** (circa 1677)
transitive verb
1 : to bid less than (a competing bidder)
2 : to bid (a hand of cards) at less than the strength of the hand warrants
intransitive verb
: to bid too low
— **un·der·bid·der** *noun*

un·der·body \'ən-dər-,bä-dē\ *noun* (1879)
: the lower part of something: as **a** : the lower part of an animal's body : UNDERPARTS **b** : the lower parts of the body of a vehicle

un·der·boss \'ən-dər-,bòs\ *noun* (1942)
: a boss ranking next below the head of a branch of a crime syndicate

un·der·bred \,ən-dər-'bred\ *adjective* (1650)
: marked by lack of good breeding : ILL-BRED

un·der·brim \'ən-dər-,brim\ *noun* (1886)
: a facing on the underside of a hat brim

un·der·brush \'ən-dər-,brəsh\ *noun* (1775)
1 : shrubs, bushes, or small trees growing beneath large trees in a wood or forest : BRUSH
2 : a tangled, obstructing, or impeding mass

un·der·bud·get·ed \,ən-dər-'bə-jə-təd\ *adjective* (1965)
: provided with an inadequate budget

un·der·cap·i·tal·ized \-'ka-pə-tᵊl-,īzd, -'kap-tᵊl-\ *adjective* (1967)
: having too little capital for efficient operation

un·der·card \'ən-dər-,kärd\ *noun* (1948)
: a program (as of boxing matches) supporting the featured match

un·der·car·riage \'ən-dər-,kar-ij\ *noun* (circa 1796)
1 : a supporting framework (as of an automobile)
2 *chiefly British* : the landing gear of an airplane

un·der·charge \,ən-dər-'chärj\ *transitive verb* (1633)
: to charge (as a person) too little
— **undercharge** \'ən-dər-,\ *noun*

un·der·class \'ən-dər-,klas\ *noun* (1918)
: the lowest social stratum usually made up of disadvantaged minority groups

un·der·class·man \,ən-dər-'klas-mən\ *noun* (1871)
: a member of the freshman or sophomore class in a school or college

un·der·clothes \'ən-dər-,klō(th)z\ *noun plural* (circa 1859)
: UNDERWEAR

un·der·cloth·ing \-,klō-thiŋ\ *noun* (1835)
: UNDERWEAR

un·der·coat \-,kōt\ *noun* (1648)
1 : a coat or jacket worn under another
2 : a growth of short hair or fur partly concealed by the longer and usually coarser guard hairs of a mammal
3 a : a coat (as of paint) applied as a base for another coat **b** : UNDERCOATING
4 *dialect* : PETTICOAT

un·der·coat·ing \-,kō-tiŋ\ *noun* (1922)
: a usually asphalt-based waterproof coating applied to the underside of a vehicle

un·der·cool \,ən-dər-'kül\ *transitive verb* (1902)
: SUPERCOOL

un·der·count \-'kaunt\ *transitive verb* (1951)
: to count fewer than the actual number of
— **undercount** *noun*

un·der·cov·er \-'kə-vər\ *adjective* (1920)
: acting or executed in secret; *specifically* : employed or engaged in spying or secret investigation ⟨an *undercover* agent⟩

un·der·croft \'ən-dər-,kròft\ *noun* [Middle English, from *under* + *crofte* crypt, from Middle Dutch, from Medieval Latin *crupta*, from Latin *crypta* — more at CRYPT] (14th century)
: a subterranean room; *especially* : a vaulted chamber under a church

un·der·cur·rent \-,kər-ənt, -,kə-rənt\ *noun* (1683)
1 : a current below the upper currents or surface
2 : a hidden opinion, feeling, or tendency often contrary to the one publicly shown
— **undercurrent** *adjective*

¹**un·der·cut** \,ən-dər-'kət\ *verb* -**cut**; -**cut·ting** (1598)
transitive verb
1 : to cut away the underpart of ⟨*undercut* a vein of ore⟩
2 : to cut away material from the underside of (an object) so as to leave an overhanging portion in relief
3 : to offer to sell at lower prices than or to work for lower wages than (a competitor)
4 : to cut obliquely into (a tree) below the main cut and on the side toward which the tree will fall
5 : to strike (a ball) with a downward glancing blow so as to give a backspin or elevation to the shot
6 : to undermine or destroy the force, value, or effectiveness of ⟨inflation *undercuts* consumer buying power⟩
intransitive verb
: to perform the action of cutting away beneath

²**un·der·cut** \'ən-dər-,kət\ *noun* (1859)
1 *British* : TENDERLOIN 1
2 : the action or result of cutting away from the underside or lower part of something
3 : a notch cut in the base of a tree before felling to determine the direction of falling and to prevent splitting

un·der·de·vel·oped \,ən-dər-di-'ve-ləpt\ *adjective* (1892)
1 : not normally or adequately developed ⟨*underdeveloped* muscles⟩ ⟨an *underdeveloped* film⟩
2 : having a relatively low economic level of industrial production and standard of living (as from lack of capital) ⟨*underdeveloped* nations⟩
— **un·der·de·vel·op·ment** \-ləp-mənt\ *noun*

un·der·dog \'ən-dər-,dòg\ *noun* (1887)
1 : a loser or predicted loser in a struggle or contest
2 : a victim of injustice or persecution

un·der·done \,ən-dər-'dən\ *adjective* (1683)
: not thoroughly cooked : RARE

un·der·draw·ers \'ən-dər-,dró(-ə)rz\ *noun plural* (1894)
: an article of underwear for the lower body

un·der·ed·u·cat·ed \,ən-dər-'e-jə-,kā-təd\ *adjective* (1856)
: poorly educated

un·der·em·pha·sis \,ən-dər-'em(p)-fə-səs\ *noun* (1964)
: less emphasis than is possible or desirable

un·der·em·pha·size \-,sīz\ *transitive verb* (1967)
: to fail to emphasize adequately

un·der·em·ployed \,ən-dər-im-'plòid\ *adjective* (1908)
: having less than full-time, regular, or adequate employment

un·der·em·ploy·ment \-'plòi-mənt\ *noun* (1910)
1 : the condition in which people in a labor force are employed at less than full-time or regular jobs or at jobs inadequate with respect to their training or economic needs
2 : the condition of being underemployed

un·der·es·ti·mate \,ən-dər-'es-tə-,māt\ *transitive verb* (1812)
1 : to estimate as being less than the actual size, quantity, or number
2 : to place too low a value on : UNDERRATE
— **un·der·es·ti·mate** \-mət\ *noun*
— **un·der·es·ti·ma·tion** \-,es-tə-'mā-shən\ *noun*

un·der·ex·pose \,ən-dər-ik-'spōz\ *transitive verb* (1861)
: to expose insufficiently; *especially* : to expose (as film) to insufficient radiation (as light)
— **un·der·ex·po·sure** \-'spō-zhər\ *noun*

un·der·feed \,ən-dər-'fēd\ *transitive verb* -**fed** \-'fed\; -**feed·ing** (1659)
: to feed with too little food

un·der·fi·nanced \-fə-'nan(t)st, -'fī-,, -fī-'\ *adjective* (1922)
: inadequately financed

un·der·foot \-'füt\ *adverb* (13th century)
1 : under the foot especially against the ground ⟨trampled the flowers *underfoot*⟩
2 : below, at, or before one's feet ⟨warm sand *underfoot*⟩
3 : in the way ⟨children always getting *underfoot*⟩

un·der·fund \-'fənd\ *transitive verb* (1968)
: to provide insufficient funds for

un·der·fur \'ən-dər-,fər\ *noun* (1877)
: an undercoat of fur especially when thick and soft

un·der·gar·ment \-,gär-mənt\ *noun* (1530)
: a garment to be worn under another

un·der·gird \,ən-dər-'gərd\ *transitive verb* (1526)
1 *archaic* : to make secure underneath ⟨took measures to *undergird* the ship —Acts 27:17 (Revised Standard Version)⟩
2 : to form the basis or foundation of : STRENGTHEN, SUPPORT ⟨facts and statistics subtly *undergird* his commentary —Susan Q. Stranahan⟩

un·der·glaze \'ən-dər-,glāz\ *adjective* (1879)
: applied or suitable for applying before the glaze is put on ⟨*underglaze* decorations⟩ ⟨*underglaze* colors⟩
— **underglaze** *noun*

un·der·go \,ən-dər-'gō\ *transitive verb* -**went** \-'went\; -**gone** \-'gòn *also* \-'gän\; -**go·ing** \-'gō-iŋ, -'gò(-)iŋ\ (14th century)
1 : to submit to : ENDURE
2 : to go through : EXPERIENCE
3 *obsolete* : UNDERTAKE
4 *obsolete* : to partake of

un·der·grad \'ən-dər-,grad\ *noun* (1827)
: UNDERGRADUATE

un·der·grad·u·ate \,ən-dər-'gra-jə-wət, -,wāt; -'graj-wət\ *noun* (1630)
: a student at a college or university who has not taken a first and especially a bachelor's degree
— **undergraduate** *adjective*

¹un·der·ground \,ən-dər-'graund\ *adverb* (1571)
1 : beneath the surface of the earth
2 : in or into hiding or secret operation

²underground \'ən-dər-,\ *noun* (1594)
1 : a subterranean space or channel
2 : an underground city railway system
3 a : a movement or group organized in strict secrecy among citizens especially in an occupied country for maintaining communications, popular solidarity, and concerted resistive action pending liberation **b :** a clandestine conspiratorial organization set up for revolutionary or other disruptive purposes especially against a civil order **c :** an unofficial, unsanctioned, or illegal but informal movement or group; *especially* **:** a usually avant-garde group or movement that functions outside the establishment

³un·der·ground \'ən-dər-,graund\ *adjective* (1610)
1 : being, growing, operating, or situated below the surface of the ground
2 : conducted by secret means
3 a : existing outside the establishment ⟨an *underground* literary reputation⟩ **b :** existing outside the purview of tax collectors or statisticians ⟨the *underground* economy⟩
4 a : produced or published outside the establishment especially by the avant-garde ⟨*underground* movies⟩ ⟨*underground* newspapers⟩ **b :** of or relating to the avant-garde underground ⟨an *underground* moviemaker⟩ ⟨an *underground* theater⟩

un·der·ground·er \'ən-dər-,graun-dər\ *noun* (1882)
: a member of the underground

Underground Railroad *noun* (1842)
: a system of cooperation among active antislavery people in the U.S. before 1863 by which fugitive slaves were secretly helped to reach the North or Canada — called also *Underground Railway*

un·der·growth \'ən-dər-,grōth\ *noun* (1600)
: low growth on the floor of a forest including seedlings and saplings, shrubs, and herbs

¹un·der·hand \'ən-dər-,hand\ *adverb* (1538)
1 a : in a clandestine manner **b** *archaic* **:** in a quiet or unobtrusive manner
2 : with the target seen below the hand holding the bow
3 : with an underhand motion ⟨bowl *underhand*⟩ ⟨pitch *underhand*⟩

²underhand *adjective* (1545)
1 : aimed so that the target is seen below the hand holding the bow ⟨*underhand* shooting at long range⟩
2 : UNDERHANDED
3 : done so as to evade notice
4 : made with the hand brought forward and up from below the shoulder level

¹un·der·hand·ed \,ən-dər-'han-dəd\ *adverb* (circa 1822)
: UNDERHAND

²underhanded *adjective* (1853)
: marked by secrecy, chicanery, and deception
: not honest and aboveboard **:** SLY
synonym see SECRET
— **un·der·hand·ed·ly** *adverb*
— **un·der·hand·ed·ness** *noun*

un·der·in·flat·ed \,ən-dər-in-'flā-təd\ *adjective* (1928)
: not sufficiently inflated ⟨*underinflated* tires⟩
— **un·der·in·fla·tion** \-'flā-shən\ *noun*

un·der·in·sured \-'shurd\ *adjective* (1893)
: not sufficiently insured

un·der·in·vest·ment \,ən-dər-in-'ves(t)-mənt\ *noun* (1940)
: an insufficient amount of investment

un·der·laid \,ən-dər-'lād\ *adjective* (before 12th century)
1 : laid or placed underneath
2 : having something laid or lying underneath

¹un·der·lay \-'lā\ *transitive verb* **-laid** \-'lād\; **-lay·ing** (before 12th century)
1 : to cover, line, or traverse the bottom of **:** give support to on the underside or below
2 : to raise or support by something laid under

²un·der·lay \'ən-dər-,\ *noun* (1612)
: something that is or is designed to be laid under

un·der·lay·ment \,ən-dər-'lā-mənt\ *noun* (1949)
: UNDERLAY

un·der·let \,ən-dər-'let\ *transitive verb* **-let; -let·ting** (1677)
1 : to let below the real value
2 : SUBLET

un·der·lie \-'lī\ *transitive verb* **-lay** \-'lā\; **-lain** \-'lān\; **-ly·ing** \-'lī-iŋ\ (before 12th century)
1 *archaic* **:** to be subject or amenable to
2 : to lie or be situated under
3 : to be at the basis of **:** form the foundation of **:** SUPPORT ⟨ideas *underlying* the revolution⟩
4 : to exist as a claim or security superior and prior to (another)

¹un·der·line \'ən-dər-,līn, ,ən-dər-'\ *transitive verb* (1721)
1 : to mark (as a word) with a line underneath
2 : to put emphasis on **:** STRESS
3 : to show clearly or emphatically

²un·der·line \'ən-dər-,līn\ *noun* (1886)
1 : the outline of a quadruped's underbody; *also* **:** the ventral surface of a quadruped's body
2 : a horizontal line placed underneath something

un·der·ling \'ən-dər-liŋ\ *noun* (12th century)
: one who is under the orders of another **:** SUBORDINATE, INFERIOR

un·der·lip \'ən-dər-'lip\ *noun* (1669)
: the lower lip

un·der·ly·ing \,ən-dər-'lī-iŋ\ *adjective* (1611)
1 a : lying beneath or below ⟨the *underlying* rock is shale⟩ **b :** BASIC, FUNDAMENTAL ⟨an investigation of the *underlying* issues⟩
2 : evident only on close inspection **:** IMPLICIT
3 : anterior and prior in claim ⟨*underlying* mortgage⟩
4 : of or being present in deep structure ⟨*underlying* word order⟩

un·der·ly·ing·ly \-'lī-iŋ-lē\ *adverb* (1973)
: in deep structure

un·der·manned \,ən-dər-'mand\ *adjective* (circa 1867)
: inadequately staffed

un·der·mine \-'mīn\ *transitive verb* (14th century)
1 : to excavate the earth beneath **:** form a mine under **:** SAP
2 : to wash away supporting material from under
3 : to subvert or weaken insidiously or secretly
4 : to weaken or ruin by degrees
synonym see WEAKEN

un·der·most \'ən-dər-,mōst\ *adjective* (1555)
: lowest in relative position
— **undermost** *adverb*

¹un·der·neath \,ən-dər-'nēth\ *preposition* [Middle English *undernethe*, preposition & adverb, from Old English *underneothan*, from *under* + *neothan* below — more at BENEATH] (before 12th century)
1 a : directly beneath ⟨write the date *underneath* the address⟩ **b :** close under especially so as to be hidden ⟨treachery lying *underneath* a mask of friendliness⟩ ⟨wore a swimsuit *underneath* his slacks⟩
2 : under subjection to

²underneath *adverb* (before 12th century)
1 : under or below an object or a surface **:** BENEATH
2 : on the lower side

— **underneath** *adjective*

un·der·nour·ished \,ən-dər-'nər-isht, -'nə-risht\ *adjective* (1910)
1 : supplied with less than the minimum amount of the foods essential for sound health and growth
2 : poorly supplied with vital elements or qualities ⟨*undernourished* independent libraries⟩
— **un·der·nour·ish·ment** \-'nər-ish-mənt, -'nə-rish-\ *noun*

un·der·nu·tri·tion \-nü-'tri-shən, -nyü-\ *noun* (circa 1889)
: deficient bodily nutrition due to inadequate food intake or faulty assimilation

un·der·paint·ing \'ən-dər-,pān-tiŋ\ *noun* (1866)
: preliminary painting; *especially* **:** such painting done on a canvas or panel and covered completely or partially by the final layers of paint

un·der·pants \'ən-dər-,pan(t)s\ *noun plural* (1925)
: a usually short undergarment for the lower trunk **:** DRAWERS

word history see PANTALOON

un·der·part \-,pärt\ *noun* (1662)
1 : a part lying on the lower side especially of a bird or mammal
2 : a subordinate or auxiliary part or role

un·der·pass \-,pas\ *noun* (1903)
: a crossing of a highway and another way (as a road or railroad) at different levels; *also* **:** the lower level of such a crossing

un·der·pay \,ən-dər-'pā\ *transitive verb* **-paid** \-'pād\; **-pay·ing** (1817)
: to pay less than what is normal or required ⟨*underpay* taxes⟩
— **un·der·pay·ment** *noun*

un·der·pin \-'pin\ *transitive verb* (1522)
1 : SUPPORT, SUBSTANTIATE ⟨*underpin* a thesis with evidence⟩
2 : to form part of, strengthen, or replace the foundation of ⟨*underpin* a structure⟩ ⟨*underpin* a sagging building⟩

un·der·pin·ning \'ən-dər-,pi-niŋ\ *noun* (1538)
1 : the material and construction (as a foundation) used for support of a structure
2 : something that serves as a foundation **:** BASIS, SUPPORT — often used in plural ⟨the philosophical *underpinnings* of educational methods⟩
3 : UNDERWEAR — usually used in plural
4 : a person's legs — usually used in plural

un·der·play \,ən-dər-'plā\ (1896)
intransitive verb
: to play a role with subdued force
transitive verb
1 : to act or present (as a role or a scene) with restraint **:** PLAY DOWN
2 : to play a card lower than (a held high card)

un·der·plot \'ən-dər-,plät\ *noun* (1668)
: SUBPLOT 1

un·der·pop·u·lat·ed \,ən-dər-'pä-pyə-,lā-təd\ *adjective* (1884)
: having a lower density of population than is normal or desirable

un·der·pow·ered \-'pau(-ə)rd\ *adjective* (1905)
1 : driven by an engine of insufficient power
2 : having or supplied with insufficient power

un·der·pre·pared \-prə-'pard, -'perd\ *adjective* (1964)
: inadequately prepared

un·der·price \-'prīs\ *transitive verb* (1756)
1 : to price below what is normal or below the real value
2 : to undercut (a competitor) in prices

un·der·priv·i·leged \-'priv-lijd, -'pri-və-\ *adjective* (1896)
1 : deprived through social or economic condition of some of the fundamental rights of all members of a civilized society
2 : of or relating to underprivileged people ⟨*underprivileged* areas of the city⟩

un·der·pro·duc·tion \-prə-'dək-shən\ *noun* (1887)
: the production of less than enough to satisfy the demand or of less than the usual amount

un·der·proof \,ən-dər-'prüf\ *adjective* (1857)
: containing less alcohol than proof spirit

un·der·pub·li·cized \-'pə-blə-,sīzd\ *adjective* (1966)
: insufficiently publicized

un·der·rate \,ən-də(r)-'rāt\ *transitive verb* (1650)
: to rate too low : UNDERVALUE

un·der·re·act \-rē-'akt\ *intransitive verb* (1965)
: to react with less than appropriate force or intensity

un·der·re·port \-ri-'pōrt, -'pòrt\ *transitive verb* (1949)
: to report to be less than is actually the case : UNDERSTATE ⟨*underreports* his income⟩ ⟨the number of cases has been *underreported*⟩

un·der·rep·re·sent·ed \-,re-pri-'zen-təd\ *adjective* (1884)
: inadequately represented
— **un·der·rep·re·sen·ta·tion** \-,zen-'tā-shən, -zən-\ *noun*

¹un·der·run \-'rən\ *transitive verb* **-ran** \-'ran\; **-run; -run·ning** (1547)
1 : to pass along under in order to examine (a cable)
2 : to pass or extend under

²un·der·run \'ən-də(r)-,rən\ *noun* (1926)
: the amount by which something produced (as a cut of lumber) falls below an estimate

un·der·sat·u·rat·ed \,ən-dər-'sa-chə-,rā-təd\ *adjective* (circa 1828)
: less than normally or adequately saturated

¹un·der·score \'ən-dər-,skōr, -,skòr\ *transitive verb* (1771)
1 : to draw a line under : UNDERLINE
2 : to make evident : EMPHASIZE, STRESS
3 : to provide (action on film) with accompanying music

²underscore *noun* (1901)
1 : a line drawn under a word or line especially for emphasis or to indicate intent to italicize
2 : music accompanying the action and dialogue of a film

¹un·der·sea \,ən-dər-'sē\ *adjective* (1613)
1 : being or carried on under the sea or under the surface of the sea ⟨*undersea* oil deposits⟩ ⟨*undersea* fighting⟩
2 : designed for use under the surface of the sea ⟨an *undersea* fleet⟩

²undersea *or* **un·der·seas** \-'sēz\ *adverb* (1684)
: under the sea : beneath the surface of the sea ⟨photographs taken *undersea*⟩

un·der·sec·re·tary \,ən-dər-'se-krə-,ter-ē, -'se-kə-\ *noun* (1687)
: a secretary immediately subordinate to a principal secretary ⟨*undersecretary* of health⟩

un·der·sell \,ən-dər-'sel\ *transitive verb* **-sold** \-'sōld\; **-sell·ing** (1622)
1 : to sell articles cheaper than ⟨*undersell* a competitor⟩ ⟨we will not be *undersold*⟩
2 : to sell cheaper than ⟨imported cars that *undersell* domestic ones⟩

un·der·served \-'sərvd\ *adjective* (1710)
: provided with inadequate service

un·der·sexed \-'sekst\ *adjective* (1931)
: deficient in sexual desire

un·der·shirt \'ən-dər-,shərt\ *noun* (1648)
: a collarless undergarment with or without sleeves
— **un·der·shirt·ed** *adjective*

un·der·shoot \,ən-dər-'shüt\ *transitive verb* **-shot** \-'shät\; **-shoot·ing** (circa 1661)
1 : to shoot short of or below (a target)
2 : to fall short of (a runway) in landing an airplane

un·der·shorts \'ən-dər-,shòrts\ *noun plural* (1949)
: SHORT 4b

un·der·shot \'ən-dər-,shät\ *adjective* (1610)

1 : moved by water passing beneath ⟨an *undershot* wheel⟩
2 : having the lower incisor teeth or lower jaw projecting beyond the upper when the mouth is closed

un·der·shrub \'ən-dər-,shrəb, *especially Southern* -,srəb\ *noun* (1598)
: SUBSHRUB

un·der·side \'ən-dər-,sīd, ,ən-dər-'\ *noun* (1680)
1 : the side or surface lying underneath
2 : a side usually hidden from sight; *specifically* : the more unpleasant or reprehensible side ⟨the *underside* of politics⟩

un·der·signed \'ən-dər-,sīnd\ *noun, plural* **undersigned** (1643)
: one whose name is signed at the end of a document ⟨the *undersigned* all agree⟩

un·der·sized \,ən-dər-'sīzd\ *also* **un·der·size** \-'sīz\ *adjective* (1706)
: of a size less than is common, proper, normal, or average ⟨*undersized* trout⟩

un·der·skirt \'ən-dər-,skərt\ *noun* (1861)
: a skirt worn under an outer skirt; *especially* : PETTICOAT

un·der·slung \,ən-dər-'sləŋ\ *adjective* (1903)
1 *of a vehicle frame* : suspended below the axles
2 : having a low center of gravity

un·der·spin \'ən-dər-,spin\ *noun* (1901)
: BACKSPIN

un·der·staffed \,ən-dər-'staft\ *adjective* (1891)
: inadequately staffed
— **un·der·staff·ing** \-'sta-fiŋ\ *noun*

un·der·stand \,ən-dər-'stand\ *verb* **-stood** \-'stüd\; **-stand·ing** [Middle English, from Old English *understandan*, from *under* + *standan* to stand] (before 12th century)
transitive verb
1 a : to grasp the meaning of ⟨*understand* Russian⟩ **b** : to grasp the reasonableness of ⟨his behavior is hard to *understand*⟩ **c** : to have thorough or technical acquaintance with or expertness in the practice of ⟨*understand* finance⟩ **d** : to be thoroughly familiar with the character and propensities of ⟨*understands* children⟩
2 : to accept as a fact or truth or regard as plausible without utter certainty ⟨we *understand* that he is returning from abroad⟩
3 : to interpret in one of a number of possible ways
4 : to supply in thought as though expressed ⟨"to be married" is commonly *understood* after the word *engaged*⟩
intransitive verb
1 : to have understanding : have the power of comprehension
2 : to achieve a grasp of the nature, significance, or explanation of something
3 : to believe or infer something to be the case
4 : to show a sympathetic or tolerant attitude toward something ☆
— **un·der·stand·abil·i·ty** \-,stan-də-'bi-lə-tē\ *noun*
— **un·der·stand·able** \-'stan-də-bəl\ *adjective*

un·der·stand·ably \,ən-dər-'stan-də-blē\ *adverb* (circa 1921)
: as can be easily understood : for understandable reasons ⟨is *understandably* nervous⟩

¹un·der·stand·ing \,ən-dər-'stan-diŋ\ *noun* (before 12th century)
1 : a mental grasp : COMPREHENSION
2 a : the power of comprehending; *especially* : the capacity to apprehend general relations of particulars **b** : the power to make experience intelligible by applying concepts and categories
3 a : friendly or harmonious relationship **b** : an agreement of opinion or feeling : adjustment of differences **c** : a mutual agreement not formally entered into but in some degree binding on each side
4 : EXPLANATION, INTERPRETATION

5 : SYMPATHY 3a

²understanding *adjective* (13th century)
1 *archaic* : KNOWING, INTELLIGENT
2 : endowed with understanding : TOLERANT, SYMPATHETIC
— **un·der·stand·ing·ly** \-'stan-diŋ-lē\ *adverb*

un·der·state \,ən-dər-'stāt\ *transitive verb* (1824)
1 : to represent as less than is the case
2 : to state or present with restraint especially for effect
— **un·der·state·ment** \-mənt\ *noun*

un·der·stat·ed \-'stā-təd\ *adjective* (circa 1909)
: avoiding obvious emphasis or embellishment
— **un·der·stat·ed·ly** *adverb*

un·der·steer \'ən-dər-,stir\ *noun* (1936)
: the tendency of an automobile to turn less sharply than the driver intends
— **un·der·steer** \,ən-dər-'\ *intransitive verb*

un·der·stood \,ən-dər-'stüd\ *adjective* (1605)
1 : fully apprehended
2 : agreed upon
3 : IMPLICIT

un·der·sto·ry \'ən-dər-,stōr-ē, -,stòr-\ *noun* (1902)
1 : an underlying layer of vegetation; *specifically* : the vegetative layer and especially the trees and shrubs between the forest canopy and the ground cover
2 : the plants that form the understory

un·der·strap·per \-,stra-pər\ *noun* [³*under* + *strapper* one who harnesses horses] (circa 1704)
: a petty agent or subordinate : UNDERLING

un·der·strength \,ən-dər-'streŋ(k)th\ *adjective* (1925)
: deficient in strength; *especially* : lacking sufficient or prescribed personnel

¹un·der·study \'ən-dər-,stə-dē, ,ən-dər-'\ (1874)
intransitive verb
: to study another actor's part in order to substitute in an emergency
transitive verb
: to prepare (as a part) as understudy; *also* : to prepare as understudy to (as an actor)

²un·der·study \'ən-dər-,stə-dē\ *noun* (1882)
: one who is prepared to act another's part or take over another's duties

un·der·sup·ply \,ən-dər-sə-'plī\ *noun* (1848)
: an inadequate supply or amount

¹un·der·sur·face \'ən-dər-,sər-fəs\ *noun* (1733)
: UNDERSIDE

²un·der·sur·face \,ən-dər-'sər-fəs\ *adjective* (circa 1934)
: existing or moving below the surface

un·der·take \,ən-dər-'tāk\ *verb* **-took** \-'tük\; **-tak·en** \-'tā-kən\; **-tak·ing** (14th century)

☆ SYNONYMS
Understand, comprehend, appreciate mean to have a clear or complete idea of. UNDERSTAND and COMPREHEND are very often interchangeable. UNDERSTAND may, however, stress the fact of having attained a firm mental grasp of something ⟨orders that were fully *understood* and promptly obeyed⟩. COMPREHEND may stress the process of coming to grips with something intellectually ⟨I have trouble *comprehending* your reasons for doing this⟩. APPRECIATE implies a just evaluation or judgment of a thing's value or nature ⟨failed to *appreciate* the risks involved⟩.

\ə\ abut \ᵊ\ kitten \ər\ further \a\ ash \ā\ ace
\ä\ mop, mar \aù\ out \ch\ chin \e\ bet \ē\ easy
\g\ go \i\ hit \ī\ ice \j\ job \ŋ\ sing \ō\ go
\ò\ law \òi\ boy \th\ thin \th\ the \ü\ loot \ù\ foot
\y\ yet \zh\ vision *see also* Guide to Pronunciation

transitive verb
1 : to take upon oneself **:** set about **:** ATTEMPT ⟨*undertake* a task⟩ ⟨*undertake* to learn to swim⟩
2 : to put oneself under obligation to perform; *also* **:** to accept as a charge or responsibility ⟨the lawyer who *undertook* the case⟩
3 : GUARANTEE, PROMISE
intransitive verb
archaic **:** to give surety or assume responsibility

un·der·tak·er \ˌən-dər-ˈtā-kər, *2 is* ˈən-dər-ˌ\ *noun* (1615)
1 : one that undertakes **:** one that takes the risk and management of business **:** ENTREPRENEUR
2 : one whose business is to prepare the dead for burial and to arrange and manage funerals
3 : an Englishman taking over forfeited lands in Ireland in the 16th and 17th centuries

un·der·tak·ing \ˈən-dər-ˌtā-kiŋ, ˌən-dər-ˈ; *1b is* ˈən-dər-, *only*\ *noun* (15th century)
1 a : the act of one who undertakes or engages in a project or business **b :** the business of an undertaker
2 : something undertaken **:** ENTERPRISE
3 : PLEDGE, GUARANTEE

un·der·ten·ant \ˈən-dər-ˌte-nənt\ *noun* (1546)
: one who holds lands or tenements by a sublease

under–the–counter *adjective* [from the hiding of illicit wares under the counter of stores where they are sold] (1926)
: surreptitious and usually irregular or illicit ⟨*under-the-counter* liquor sales⟩

under–the–table *adjective* (1948)
: covert and usually unlawful ⟨*under-the-table* payoffs⟩

un·der·thrust \ˌən-dər-ˈthrəst\ *transitive verb* **-thrust; -thrust·ing** (1893)
: to insert (a faulted rock mass) into position under a passive rock mass

un·der·tone \ˈən-dər-ˌtōn\ *noun* (1806)
1 : a low or subdued utterance or accompanying sound
2 : a quality (as of emotion) underlying the surface of an utterance or action
3 : a subdued color; *specifically* **:** a color seen through and modifying another color

un·der·tow \-ˌtō\ *noun* (1817)
1 : the current beneath the surface that sets seaward or along the beach when waves are breaking upon the shore
2 : an underlying current, force, or tendency that is in opposition to what is apparent

un·der·trick \-ˌtrik\ *noun* (1903)
: any of the tricks by which a declarer in bridge falls short of making the contract

un·der·used \ˌən-dər-ˈyüzd\ *adjective* (1960)
: not fully used

un·der·uti·lize \ˌən-dər-ˈyü-tᵊl-ˌīz\ *transitive verb* (1951)
: to utilize less than fully or below the potential use
— **un·der·uti·li·za·tion** \ˈən-dər-ˌyü-tᵊl-ə-ˈzā-shən\ *noun*

un·der·val·u·a·tion \ˌən-dər-ˌval-yə-ˈwā-shən\ *noun* (1653)
1 : the act of undervaluing
2 : a value below the real worth

un·der·val·ue \-ˈval-(ˌ)yü\ *transitive verb* (1599)
1 : to value, rate, or estimate below the real worth ⟨*undervalue* stock⟩
2 : to treat as having little value ⟨was *undervalued* as a poet⟩

un·der·wa·ter \ˌən-dər-ˈwȯ-tər, -ˈwä-\ *adjective* (1627)
1 : lying, growing, worn, or operating below the surface of the water
2 : being below the waterline of a ship
— **underwater** *adverb*

un·der·way \ˌən-dər-ˈwā\ *adjective* (1743)
: occurring, performed, or used while traveling or in motion ⟨*underway* replenishment of fuel⟩

under way *adverb* [probably from Dutch *onderweg*, from Middle Dutch *onderwegen*, literally, under or among the ways] (1751)
1 : in motion **:** not at anchor or aground
2 : into motion from a standstill
3 : in progress **:** AFOOT ⟨preparations were *under way*⟩ ⟨the season got *under way* with a bang⟩

un·der·wear \ˈən-dər-ˌwar, -ˌwer\ *noun* (circa 1879)
: clothing or an article of clothing worn next to the skin and under other clothing

under weigh *adverb* [by folk etymology] (1777)
: UNDER WAY

¹un·der·weight \ˌən-dər-ˈwāt\ *noun* (1596)
: weight below normal, average, or requisite weight

²underweight *adjective* (1890)
: weighing less than the normal or requisite amount

un·der·whelm \-ˈhwelm, -ˈwelm\ *transitive verb* [under + over*whelm*] (1949)
: to fail to impress or stimulate

¹un·der·wing \ˈən-dər-ˌwiŋ\ *noun* (1535)
1 : one of the posterior wings of an insect
2 : any of various noctuid moths (especially genus *Catocala*) that have the hind wings banded with contrasting colors (as red and black) — called also *underwing moth*
3 : the underside of a bird's wing

²underwing *adjective* (1896)
: placed or growing underneath the wing ⟨*underwing* rockets⟩

un·der·wood \ˈən-dər-ˌwu̇d\ *noun* (14th century)
: UNDERGROWTH, UNDERBRUSH

un·der·wool \-ˌwu̇l\ *noun* (1939)
: short woolly underfur

un·der·world \-ˌwərld\ *noun* (1608)
1 : the place of departed souls **:** HADES
2 *archaic* **:** EARTH
3 : the side of the earth opposite to one **:** ANTIPODES
4 : a social sphere below the level of ordinary life; *especially* **:** the world of organized crime

un·der·write \ˈən-də(r)-ˌrīt, ˌən-də(r)-ˈ\ *verb* **-wrote** \-ˌrōt, -ˈrōt\; **-writ·ten** \-ˌri-tᵊn, -ˈri-tᵊn\; **-writ·ing** \-ˌrī-tiŋ, -ˈrī-\ (15th century)
transitive verb
1 : to write under or at the end of something else
2 : to set one's name to (an insurance policy) for the purpose of thereby becoming answerable for a designated loss or damage on consideration of receiving a premium percent **:** insure on life or property; *also* **:** to assume liability for (a sum or risk) as an insurer
3 : to subscribe to **:** agree to
4 a : to purchase (as security issue) usually on a fixed date at a fixed price with a view to public distribution **b :** to guarantee financial support of
intransitive verb
: to work as an underwriter

un·der·writ·er \ˈən-də(r)-ˌrī-tər\ *noun* (1622)
1 : one that underwrites **:** GUARANTOR
2 a : one that underwrites a policy of insurance **:** INSURER **b :** one who selects risks to be solicited or rates the acceptability of risks solicited
3 : one that underwrites a security issue

un·de·scend·ed \ˌən-di-ˈsen-dəd\ *adjective* (1701)
: retained within the inguinal region rather than descending into the scrotum ⟨an *undescended* testis⟩

un·de·sign·ing \ˌən-di-ˈzī-niŋ\ *adjective* (1697)
: having no ulterior or fraudulent purpose **:** SINCERE

¹un·de·sir·able \-ˈzī-rə-bəl\ *adjective* (1667)
: not desirable **:** UNWANTED
— **un·de·sir·abil·i·ty** \-ˌzī-rə-ˈbi-lə-tē\ *noun*

— **un·de·sir·able·ness** \-ˈzī-rə-bəl-nəs\ *noun*
— **un·de·sir·ably** \-blē\ *adverb*

²undesirable *noun* (1883)
: one that is undesirable

un·de·vi·at·ing \ˌən-ˈdē-vē-ˌā-tiŋ\ *adjective* (1732)
: keeping a true course **:** UNSWERVING ⟨served their country with *undeviating* loyalty and devotion⟩
— **un·de·vi·at·ing·ly** \-tiŋ-lē\ *adverb*

un·dies \ˈən-dēz\ *noun plural* [by shortening & alteration] (1900)
: UNDERWEAR; *especially* **:** women's underwear

un·dine \ˌən-ˈdēn, ˈən-ˌ\ *noun* [New Latin *undina*, from Latin *unda* wave — more at WATER] (1657)
: an elemental being in the theory of Paracelsus inhabiting water **:** WATER NYMPH

un·dip·lo·mat·ic \ˌən-ˌdi-plə-ˈma-tik\ *adjective* (1828)
: not diplomatic; *especially* **:** TACTLESS
— **un·dip·lo·mat·i·cal·ly** \-ti-k(ə-)lē\ *adverb*

un·di·rect·ed \ˌən-də-ˈrek-təd, -dī-\ *adjective* (1596)
: not directed **:** not planned or guided ⟨*undirected* efforts⟩

un·dis·guised \ˌən-dis-ˈgīzd\ *adjective* (circa 1500)
: not disguised or concealed **:** FRANK, OPEN
— **un·dis·guis·ed·ly** \-ˈgī-zəd-lē\ *adverb*

un·dis·so·ci·at·ed \ˌən-di-ˈsō-shē-ˌā-təd, -sē-\ *adjective* (1899)
: not electrolytically dissociated

un·do \ˌən-ˈdü, ˈən-\ *verb* **-did** \-ˈdid\; **-done** \-ˈdən\; **-do·ing** \-ˈdü-iŋ\ (before 12th century)
transitive verb
1 : to open or loose by releasing a fastening
2 : to make of no effect or as if not done **:** make null **:** REVERSE
3 a : to ruin the worldly means, reputation, or hopes of **b :** to disturb the composure of **:** UPSET ⟨she's come *undone*⟩ **c :** SEDUCE 3
intransitive verb
: to come open or apart
— **un·do·er** \-ˈdü-ər\ *noun*

un·dock \-ˈdäk\ (1750)
intransitive verb
: to move away from a dock (as at sailing time)
transitive verb
: UNCOUPLE ⟨*undock* the shuttle from the space station⟩

un·dog·mat·ic \ˌən-dȯg-ˈma-tik, -däg-\ *adjective* (1857)
: not dogmatic **:** not committed to dogma
— **un·dog·mat·i·cal·ly** \-ti-k(ə-)lē\ *adverb*

un·do·ing \-ˈdü-iŋ\ *noun* (14th century)
1 : an act of loosening **:** UNFASTENING
2 : RUIN; *also* **:** a cause of ruin ⟨greed was to prove his *undoing*⟩
3 : ANNULMENT, REVERSAL

un·done \-ˈdən\ *adjective* (14th century)
: not done **:** not performed or finished

un·dou·ble \ˌən-ˈdə-bəl\ *verb* (circa 1611)
: UNFOLD, UNCLENCH

un·dou·bled \-ˈdə-bəld\ *adjective* (1598)
: not doubled

un·doubt·ed \-ˈdau̇-təd\ *adjective* (15th century)
: not doubted **:** GENUINE, UNDISPUTED
— **un·doubt·ed·ly** *adverb*

un·dra·mat·ic \ˌən-drə-ˈma-tik\ *adjective* (1754)
: lacking dramatic force or quality **:** UNSPECTACULAR
— **un·dra·mat·i·cal·ly** \-ti-k(ə-)lē\ *adverb*

un·drape \ˌən-ˈdrāp\ *transitive verb* (1869)
: to strip of drapery **:** UNVEIL

un·draw \-ˈdrȯ\ *transitive verb* **-drew** \-ˈdrü\; **-drawn** \-ˈdrȯn\; **-draw·ing** (1677)
: to draw aside (as a curtain) **:** OPEN

un·dreamed \-'drem(p)t, -'drēmd\ *also* **un·dreamt** \-'drem(p)t\ *adjective* (1611)
: not dreamed : not thought of : UNIMAGINED ⟨technical advances *undreamed* of a few years ago⟩

¹**un·dress** \-'dres\ (1596)
transitive verb
1 : to remove the clothes or covering of : DIVEST, STRIP
2 : EXPOSE, REVEAL
intransitive verb
: to take off one's clothes : DISROBE

²**undress** *noun* (1683)
1 : informal dress: as **a** : a loose robe or dressing gown **b** : ordinary dress — compare FULL DRESS
2 : the state of being undressed

un·dressed \,ən-'drest\ *adjective* (1535)
: not dressed: as **a** : partially, improperly, or informally clothed **b** : not fully processed or finished ⟨*undressed* hides⟩ **c** : not cared for or tended ⟨an *undressed* wound⟩ ⟨*undressed* fields⟩

un·drink·able \,ən-'driŋ-kə-bəl\ *adjective* (1611)
: unsuitable or unpleasant to drink

un·drunk \-'drəŋk\ *adjective* (1637)
: not swallowed

un·due \-'dü, -'dyü\ *adjective* (14th century)
1 : not due : not yet payable
2 : exceeding or violating propriety or fitness : EXCESSIVE

un·du·lant \'ən-jə-lənt, 'ən-dyə-, 'ən-də-\ *adjective* (circa 1830)
1 : rising and falling in waves
2 : having a wavy form, outline, or surface ⟨played her approach shot onto the *undulant* green⟩

undulant fever *noun* (1896)
: a persistent human brucellosis marked by remittent fever, pain and swelling in the joints, and great weakness and contracted by contact with infected domestic animals or consumption of their products

¹**un·du·late** \'ən-jə-lət, 'ən-dyə-, 'ən-də-, -,lāt\ *or* **un·du·lat·ed** \-,lā-təd\ *adjective* [Latin *undulatus*, from (assumed) Latin *undula*, diminutive of Latin *unda* wave — more at WATER] (1658)
: having a wavy surface, edge, or markings ⟨the *undulate* margin of a leaf⟩

²**un·du·late** \-,lāt\ *verb* **-lat·ed; -lat·ing** [Late Latin *undula* small wave, from (assumed) Latin] (1664)
intransitive verb
1 : to form or move in waves : FLUCTUATE
2 : to rise and fall in volume, pitch, or cadence
3 : to present a wavy appearance
transitive verb
: to cause to move in a wavy, sinuous, or flowing manner
synonym see SWING

un·du·la·tion \,ən-jə-'lā-shən, ,ən-dyə-, ,ən-də-\ *noun* (1646)
1 a : a rising and falling in waves **b** : a wavelike motion to and fro in a fluid or elastic medium propagated continuously among its particles but with little or no permanent translation of the particles in the direction of the propagation : VIBRATION
2 : the pulsation caused by the vibrating together of two tones not quite in unison
3 : a wavy appearance, outline, or form : WAVINESS

un·du·la·to·ry \'ən-jə-lə-,tōr-ē, 'ən-dyə-, 'ən-də-, -,tòr-\ *adjective* (1728)
: of or relating to undulation : moving in or resembling waves : UNDULATING

undulatory theory *noun* (circa 1828)
: WAVE THEORY

un·du·ly \,ən-'dü-lē, -'dyü-\ *adverb* (14th century)
: in an undue manner : EXCESSIVELY

un·du·ti·ful \-'dü-ti-fəl, -'dyü-\ *adjective* (1582)
: not dutiful

— **un·du·ti·ful·ly** \-fə-lē\ *adverb*
— **un·du·ti·ful·ness** *noun*

un·dy·ing \-'dī-iŋ\ *adjective* (14th century)
: not dying : IMMORTAL, PERPETUAL

un·earned \-'ərnd\ *adjective* (13th century)
1 : not gained by labor, service, or skill ⟨*unearned* income⟩
2 : scored as a result of an error by the opposing team ⟨an *unearned* run⟩

unearned increment *noun* (1871)
: an increase in the value of property (as land) that is due to no labor or expenditure of the owner but to natural causes (as the increase of population) that create an increased demand for it

un·earth \,ən-'ərth\ *transitive verb* (15th century)
1 : to dig up out of or as if out of the earth : EXHUME ⟨*unearth* a hidden treasure⟩ ⟨*unearth* a forgotten photo album⟩
2 : to make known or public : bring to light ⟨*unearth* a plot⟩
synonym see DISCOVER

un·earth·ly \-lē\ *adjective* (1611)
: not earthly: as **a** : not terrestrial ⟨*unearthly* radio sources⟩ **b** : PRETERNATURAL, SUPERNATURAL ⟨an *unearthly* light⟩ **c** : WEIRD, EERIE ⟨*unearthly* howls⟩ **d** : not mundane : IDEAL ⟨*unearthly* love⟩ **e** : ABSURD 1, UNGODLY ⟨getting up at an *unearthly* hour⟩
— **un·earth·li·ness** *noun*

un·ease \,ən-'ēz\ *noun* (14th century)
: mental or spiritual discomfort: as **a** : vague dissatisfaction : MISGIVING **b** : ANXIETY, DISQUIET **c** : lack of ease (as in social relations) : EMBARRASSMENT

un·eas·i·ly \-'ē-zə-lē\ *adverb* (14th century)
: in an uneasy manner

¹**un·easy** \-'ē-zē\ *adjective* (13th century)
1 : causing physical or mental discomfort ⟨*uneasy* news of captures and killings —Marjory S. Douglas⟩
2 : not easy : DIFFICULT
3 : marked by lack of ease : AWKWARD, EMBARRASSED ⟨gave an *uneasy* laugh⟩
4 : APPREHENSIVE, WORRIED
5 : RESTLESS, UNQUIET
6 : PRECARIOUS, UNSTABLE ⟨an *uneasy* truce⟩
— **un·eas·i·ness** *noun*

²**uneasy** *adverb* (1596)
: UNEASILY

un·eco·nom·ic \,ən-,e-kə-'nä-mik, -,ē-kə-\ *or* **un·eco·nom·i·cal** \-mi-kəl\ *adjective* (1840)
: not economically practicable ⟨*uneconomic* transportation routes⟩; *also* : COSTLY, WASTEFUL ⟨an *uneconomic* nuclear technology⟩

un·ed·it·ed \,ən-'e-də-təd\ *adjective* (1829)
: not edited: as **a** : left unrevised **b** : not yet edited ⟨*unedited* books⟩ ⟨*unedited* films⟩

un·emo·tion·al \,ən-i-'mō-shnəl, -shə-n°l\ *adjective* (1876)
: not emotional: as **a** : not easily aroused or excited : COLD **b** : involving a minimum of emotion : INTELLECTUAL
— **un·emo·tion·al·ly** *adverb*

un·em·ploy·able \,ən-im-'plói-ə-bəl\ *adjective* (1887)
: not acceptable for employment
— **un·em·ploy·abil·i·ty** \-,plói-ə-'bi-lə-tē\ *noun*
— **unemployable** *noun*

un·em·ployed \-'plóid\ *adjective* (1600)
: not employed: **a** : not being used **b** : not engaged in a gainful occupation **c** : not invested
— **unemployed** *noun*

un·em·ploy·ment \-'plói-mənt\ *noun* (1888)
1 : the state of being unemployed : involuntary idleness of workers; *also* : the rate of such unemployment
2 : UNEMPLOYMENT COMPENSATION

unemployment compensation *noun* (1944)
: compensation paid at regular intervals (as by a government agency) to an unemployed worker and especially one who has been laid off — called also *unemployment benefit*

unemployment insurance *noun* (1923)
: social insurance against involuntary unemployment that provides unemployment compensation for a limited period to unemployed workers; *also* : UNEMPLOYMENT COMPENSATION

un·en·cum·bered \,ən-in-'kəm-bərd\ *adjective* (1722)
: free of encumbrance

un·end·ing \,ən-'en-diŋ\ *adjective* (1661)
: never ending : ENDLESS
— **un·end·ing·ly** \-diŋ-lē\ *adverb*

un–En·glish \,ən-'iŋ-glish *also* -'iŋ-lish\ *adjective* (1633)
1 : not characteristically English
2 : not agreeing with standard or generally accepted usage of the English language

¹**un·equal** \,ən-'ē-kwəl\ *adjective* (1565)
1 a : not of the same measurement, quantity, or number as another **b** : not like or not the same as another in degree, worth, or status
2 : not uniform : VARIABLE, UNEVEN
3 a : badly balanced or matched ⟨an *unequal* contest⟩ **b** : contracted between unequals ⟨*unequal* marriages⟩ **c** *archaic* : not equable
4 *archaic* : not equitable : UNJUST
5 : INADEQUATE, INSUFFICIENT ⟨*unequal* to the task⟩
— **un·equal·ly** \-kwə-lē\ *adverb*

²**unequal** *noun* (1600)
: one that is not equal to another

³**unequal** *adverb* (1602)
archaic : in an unequal manner ⟨*unequal* match'd —Shakespeare⟩

un·equaled *or* **un·equalled** \-kwəld\ *adjective* (1600)
: not equaled : UNPARALLELED

un·equiv·o·ca·bly \,ən-i-'kwi-və-kə-blē\ *adverb* [by alteration] (1917)
nonstandard : UNEQUIVOCALLY

un·equiv·o·cal \,ən-i-'kwi-və-kəl\ *adjective* (1784)
1 : leaving no doubt : CLEAR, UNAMBIGUOUS
2 : UNQUESTIONABLE ⟨production of *unequivocal* masterpieces —Carole Cook⟩

un·equiv·o·cal·ly \-kə-lē, -klē\ *adverb* (1794)
: in an unequivocal manner

un·err·ing \,ən-'er-iŋ, ,ən-'ər-\ *adjective* (1621)
: committing no error : FAULTLESS, UNFAILING
— **un·err·ing·ly** \-iŋ-lē\ *adverb*

un·es·sen·tial \,ən-ə-'sen(t)-shəl\ *adjective* (circa 1656)
1 : not essential : DISPENSABLE, UNIMPORTANT
2 *archaic* : void of essence : INSUBSTANTIAL

un·Eu·ro·pe·an \,ən-,yür-ə-'pē-ən\ *adjective* (1846)
: not characteristically European

un·even \,ən-'ē-vən\ *adjective* (before 12th century)
1 a *archaic* : UNEQUAL 1a **b** : ODD 3a
2 a : not even : not level or smooth : RUGGED, RAGGED ⟨large *uneven* teeth⟩ ⟨*uneven* handwriting⟩ **b** : varying from the straight or parallel **c** : not uniform : IRREGULAR ⟨*uneven* combustion⟩ **d** : varying in quality ⟨an *uneven* performance⟩
3 : UNEQUAL 3a ⟨an *uneven* confrontation⟩
synonym see ROUGH
— **un·even·ly** *adverb*
— **un·even·ness** \-və(n)-nəs\ *noun*

un·event·ful \,ən-i-'vent-fəl\ *adjective* (1800)
: marked by no noteworthy or untoward incidents : PLACID
— **un·event·ful·ly** \-fə-lē\ *adverb*
— **un·event·ful·ness** \-nəs\ *noun*

un·ex·am·pled \,ən-ig-'zam-pəld\ *adjective* (1610)

: having no example or parallel : UNPRECE-DENTED

un·ex·cep·tion·able \,ən-ik-'sep-sh(ə-)nə-bəl\ *adjective* [*un-* + obsolete *exception* to take exception, object] (1664)
: not open to objection or criticism : beyond reproach : UNIMPEACHABLE
— **un·ex·cep·tion·able·ness** *noun*
— **un·ex·cep·tion·ably** \-blē\ *adverb*

un·ex·cep·tion·al \-shnəl, -shə-nᵊl\ *adjective* (1806)
: not out of the ordinary : COMMONPLACE

un·ex·er·cised \,ən-'ek-sər-,sīzd\ *adjective* (14th century)
1 : having terms that are not implemented ⟨*un-exercised* options⟩
2 : not subjected to exercise ⟨*unexercised* muscles⟩

un·ex·pect·ed \,ən-ik-'spek-təd\ *adjective* (circa 1586)
: not expected : UNFORESEEN
— **un·ex·pect·ed·ly** *adverb*
— **un·ex·pect·ed·ness** *noun*

un·ex·ploit·ed \,ən-ik-'splói-təd\ *adjective* (1888)
: not exploited or developed : not taken advantage of

un·ex·pres·sive \,ən-ik-'spre-siv\ *adjective* (1600)
1 *obsolete* : INEFFABLE
2 : not expressive : failing to convey the feeling or meaning intended

un·fad·ing \,ən-'fā-diŋ\ *adjective* (1652)
1 : not losing color or freshness
2 : not losing value or effectiveness
— **un·fad·ing·ly** \-diŋ-lē\ *adverb*

un·fail·ing \,ən-'fā-liŋ\ *adjective* (14th century)
: not failing or liable to fail: **a** : CONSTANT, UNFLAGGING ⟨*unfailing* courtesy⟩ **b** : EVERLASTING, INEXHAUSTIBLE ⟨a subject of *unfailing* interest⟩ **c** : INFALLIBLE, SURE ⟨an *unfailing* test⟩
— **un·fail·ing·ly** \-liŋ-lē\ *adverb*

un·fair \,ən-'far, -'fer\ *adjective* (1700)
1 : marked by injustice, partiality, or deception : UNJUST
2 : not equitable in business dealings
— **un·fair·ness** *noun*

un·fair·ly *adverb* (1713)
: in an unfair manner

un·faith \,ən-'fāth, 'ən-,\ *noun* (15th century)
: absence of faith : DISBELIEF

un·faith·ful \,ən-'fāth-fəl\ *adjective* (15th century)
: not faithful: **a** : not adhering to vows, allegiance, or duty : DISLOYAL **b** : not faithful to marriage vows **c** : INACCURATE, UNTRUSTWORTHY
— **un·faith·ful·ly** \-fə-lē\ *adverb*
— **un·faith·ful·ness** *noun*

un·fall·en \,ən-'fó-lən\ *adjective* (1653)
: not morally fallen : INNOCENT 1a

un·fal·si·fi·able \,ən-,fól-sə-'fī-ə-bəl\ *adjective* (circa 1934)
: not capable of being proved false ⟨*unfalsifiable* hypotheses⟩

un·fal·ter·ing \,ən-'fól-t(ə-)riŋ\ *adjective* (1727)
: not wavering or weakening : FIRM
— **un·fal·ter·ing·ly** \-t(ə-)riŋ-lē\ *adverb*

un·fa·mil·iar \,ən-fə-'mil-yər\ *adjective* (1594)
: not familiar: **a** : not well-known : STRANGE ⟨an *unfamiliar* place⟩ **b** : not well acquainted ⟨*unfamiliar* with the subject⟩
— **un·fa·mil·iar·i·ty** \-,mil-'yar-ə-tē, -,mil-ē-'yar-\ *noun*
— **un·fa·mil·iar·ly** \-'mil-yər-lē\ *adverb*

un·fash·ion·able \-'fa-sh(ə-)nə-bəl\ *adjective* (1648)
1 : not in keeping with the current fashion ⟨*unfashionable* clothes⟩
2 : not favored socially ⟨*unfashionable* neighborhoods⟩
— **un·fash·ion·able·ness** \-bəl-nəs\ *noun*
— **un·fash·ion·ably** \-blē\ *adverb*

un·fas·ten \-'fa-sᵊn\ *transitive verb* (15th century)
: to make loose: as **a** : UNPIN, UNBUCKLE **b** : UNDO ⟨*unfasten* a button⟩ **c** : DETACH ⟨*unfasten* a boat from its moorings⟩

un·fa·thered \-'fä-thərd\ *adjective* (1597)
1 : having no father : ILLEGITIMATE, BASTARD
2 : having no known origin ⟨*unfathered* slanders⟩

un·fath·om·able \-'fa-thə-mə-bəl\ *adjective* (1640)
: not capable of being fathomed: **a** : impossible to comprehend **b** : IMMEASURABLE

un·fa·vor·able \-'fā-v(ə-)rə-bəl, -'fā-vər-bəl\ *adjective* (1548)
1 a : OPPOSED, CONTRARY **b** : expressing disapproval : NEGATIVE ⟨*unfavorable* reviews⟩
2 : not propitious : DISADVANTAGEOUS
3 : not pleasing
— **un·fa·vor·able·ness** *noun*
— **un·fa·vor·ably** \-blē\ *adverb*

un·fa·vor·ite \-'fā-v(ə-)rət, -'fā-vərt\ *adjective* (circa 1934)
: not being a favorite; *especially* : being regarded with special disfavor or dislike

un·fazed \,ən-'fāzd\ *adjective* (1945)
: not fazed : UNDAUNTED

un·feel·ing \-'fē-liŋ\ *adjective* (before 12th century)
1 : devoid of feeling : INSENSATE ⟨an *unfeeling* corpse⟩
2 : devoid of kindness or sympathy : HARD-HEARTED, CRUEL ⟨an *unfeeling* wretch⟩
— **un·feel·ing·ly** \-liŋ-lē\ *adverb*
— **un·feel·ing·ness** *noun*

un·feigned \-'fānd\ *adjective* (14th century)
: not feigned or hypocritical : GENUINE
synonym see SINCERE
— **un·feign·ed·ly** \-'fā-nəd-lē, -'fānd-lē\ *adverb*

un·fet·ter \-'fe-tər\ *transitive verb* (14th century)
1 : to free from fetters ⟨*unfetter* a prisoner⟩
2 : EMANCIPATE, LIBERATE ⟨*unfetter* the mind from prejudice⟩

un·fet·tered \-tərd\ *adjective* (1601)
: FREE, UNRESTRAINED

un·fil·ial \,ən-'fi-lē-əl, -'fil-yəl\ *adjective* (1611)
: not observing the obligations of a child to a parent : UNDUTIFUL
— **un·fil·ial·ly** *adverb*

un·fil·tered \,ən-'fil-tərd\ *adjective* (circa 1775)
1 : not filtered ⟨*unfiltered* wine⟩; *also* : not modified, processed, or refined ⟨*unfiltered* commercial publicity material —Paul Grimes⟩
2 : lacking a filter ⟨an *unfiltered* cigarette⟩

un·find·able \,ən-'fīn-də-bəl\ *adjective* (1791)
: not capable of being found

un·fin·ished \-'fi-nisht\ *adjective* (1539)
: not finished: **a** : not brought to an end or to the desired final state **b** : being in a rough state : UNPOLISHED **c** : subjected to no other processes (as bleaching or dyeing) after coming from the loom

¹un·fit \-'fit\ *adjective* (1545)
: not fit: **a** : not adapted to a purpose : UNSUITABLE **b** : not qualified : INCAPABLE, INCOMPETENT **c** : physically or mentally unsound
— **un·fit·ly** *adverb*
— **un·fit·ness** *noun*

²unfit *transitive verb* (1611)
: to make unfit : DISABLE, DISQUALIFY

un·fit·ted \,ən-'fi-təd\ *adjective* (1592)
: not adapted : UNQUALIFIED

un·fit·ting \-'fi-tiŋ\ *adjective* (1534)
: not fitting : UNSUITABLE

un·fix \-'fiks\ *transitive verb* (1597)
1 : to loosen from a fastening : DETACH, DISENGAGE
2 : to make unstable : UNSETTLE

un·flag·ging \-'fla-giŋ\ *adjective* (1715)
1 : not flagging : TIRELESS
2 : UNRELENTING 2

— **un·flag·ging·ly** \-giŋ-lē\ *adverb*

un·flap·pa·ble \-'fla-pə-bəl\ *adjective* [¹*un-* + ¹*flap* (state of excitement) + *-able*] (1954)
: marked by assurance and self-control
— **un·flap·pa·bil·i·ty** \-,fla-pə-'bi-lə-tē\ *noun*
— **un·flap·pa·bly** \-'fla-pə-blē\ *adverb*

un·flat·ter·ing \-'fla-tə-riŋ\ *adjective* (1581)
: not flattering; *especially* : UNFAVORABLE
— **un·flat·ter·ing·ly** \-riŋ-lē\ *adverb*

un·fledged \,ən-'flejd\ *adjective* (1611)
1 : not feathered : not ready for flight
2 : not fully developed : IMMATURE ⟨an *un-fledged* writer⟩

un·flinch·ing \-'flin-chiŋ\ *adjective* (1728)
: not flinching or shrinking : STEADFAST, UNCOMPROMISING
— **un·flinch·ing·ly** \-chiŋ-lē\ *adverb*

un·fo·cused *also* **un·fo·cussed** \-'fō-kəst\ *adjective* (1886)
1 : not adjusted to a focus
2 : not concentrated on one point or objective ⟨*unfocused* rage⟩

un·fold \-'fōld\ *verb* (before 12th century)
transitive verb
1 a : to open the folds of : spread or straighten out : EXPAND ⟨*unfolded* the map⟩ **b** : to remove (as a package) from the folds : UNWRAP
2 : to open to the view : REVEAL; *especially* : to make clear by gradual disclosure and often by recital
intransitive verb
1 a : to open from a folded state : open out : EXPAND **b** : BLOSSOM
2 : DEVELOP, EVOLVE ⟨as the story *unfolds*⟩
3 : to open out gradually to the view or understanding : become known ⟨a panorama *unfolds* before their eyes⟩
— **un·fold·ment** \-'fōl(d)-mənt\ *noun*

un·fold·ed *adjective* (1683)
: not folded

un·for·get·ta·ble \,ən-fər-'ge-tə-bəl\ *adjective* (1806)
: incapable of being forgotten : MEMORABLE
— **un·for·get·ta·bly** \-'ge-tə-blē\ *adverb*

un·for·giv·ing \,ən-fər-'gi-viŋ\ *adjective* (1713)
1 : unwilling or unable to forgive
2 : having or making no allowance for error or weakness ⟨an *unforgiving* environment where false moves can prove fatal —Jaclyn Fierman⟩
— **un·for·giv·ing·ness** *noun*

un·formed \-'fórmd\ *adjective* (14th century)
: not arranged in regular shape, order, or relations; *especially* : IMMATURE, UNDEVELOPED

¹un·for·tu·nate \-'fórch-nət, -'fór-chə-\ *adjective* (15th century)
1 a : not favored by fortune : UNSUCCESSFUL, UNLUCKY ⟨an *unfortunate* young man⟩ **b** : marked or accompanied by or resulting in misfortune ⟨an *unfortunate* decision⟩
2 a : INFELICITOUS, UNSUITABLE ⟨an *unfortunate* choice of words⟩ **b** : DEPLORABLE, REGRETTABLE ⟨an *unfortunate* lack of taste⟩

²unfortunate *noun* (1683)
: an unfortunate person

un·for·tu·nate·ly \-lē\ *adverb* (circa 1548)
1 : in an unfortunate manner ⟨the marriage turned out *unfortunately*⟩
2 : it is unfortunate ⟨*unfortunately* for him your letter has let the cat out of the bag —G. B. Shaw⟩

un·found·ed \,ən-'faùn-dəd\ *adjective* (1648)
: lacking a sound basis : GROUNDLESS, UNWARRANTED

un·freeze \-'frēz\ *transitive verb* **-froze** \-'frōz\; **-fro·zen** \-'frō-zᵊn\; **-freez·ing** (1584)
1 : to cause to thaw
2 : to remove from a freeze

un·fre·quent·ed \,ən-frē-'kwen-təd; ,ən-'frē-kwən-\ *adjective* (1588)
: not often visited or traveled over

un·friend·ed \,ən-'fren-dəd\ *adjective* (1513)
: having no friends : not befriended

un·friend·li·ness \-'fren(d)-lē-nəs\ *noun* (circa 1684)
: the quality or state of being unfriendly : HOSTILITY

un·friend·ly \-'fren(d)-lē\ *adjective* (15th century)
: not friendly: as **a** : HOSTILE, UNSYMPATHETIC **b** : INHOSPITABLE, UNFAVORABLE

un·frock \-'fräk\ *transitive verb* (1644)
: DEFROCK

un·froz·en \-'frō-zªn\ *adjective* (1596)
: not frozen ⟨*unfrozen* ground⟩

un·fruit·ful \-'früt-fəl\ *adjective* (14th century)
: not fruitful: as **a** : not producing offspring : BARREN **b** : yielding no valuable result : UNPROFITABLE ⟨an *unfruitful* conference⟩
— **un·fruit·ful·ly** \-fə-lē\ *adverb*
— **un·fruit·ful·ness** *noun*

un·fund·ed \-'fən-dəd\ *adjective* (circa 1775)
1 : not funded : FLOATING ⟨an *unfunded* debt⟩
2 : not provided with funds ⟨*unfunded* schools⟩

un·furl \-'fər(-ə)l\ (1641)
transitive verb
: to release from a furled state
intransitive verb
: to open out from or as if from a furled state : UNFOLD

un·fussy \-'fə-sē\ *adjective* (1825)
: not fussy: as **a** : not particular : UNCONCERNED **b** : not cluttered with pretentious or nonessential matters : UNCOMPLICATED
— **un·fuss·i·ly** \-'fə-sə-lē\ *adverb*

un·gain·ly \-'gān-lē\ *adjective* (1611)
1 a : lacking in smoothness or dexterity : CLUMSY **b** : hard to handle : UNWIELDY
2 : having an awkward appearance : UGLY
— **un·gain·li·ness** *noun*

un·gen·er·os·i·ty \,ən-,je-nə-'rä-sə-tē, -'räs-tē\ *noun* (1757)
: lack of generosity

un·gen·er·ous \,ən-'jen-rəs, -'je-nə-\ *adjective* (1641)
: not generous: **a** : PETTY, MEAN **b** : deficient in liberality : STINGY
— **un·gen·er·ous·ly** *adverb*

un·gird \-'gərd\ *transitive verb* (before 12th century)
: to divest of a restraining band or girdle : UNBIND

un·girt \-'gərt\ *adjective* (14th century)
1 : having the belt or girdle off or loose
2 : lacking in discipline or compactness : LOOSE, SLACK

un·glue \-'glü\ *transitive verb* (circa 1548)
: to separate by or as if by dissolving an adhesive

un·glued \-'glüd\ *adjective* (1922)
: UPSET, DISORDERED

un·god·li·ness \,ən-'gäd-lē-nəs *also* -'gòd-\ *noun* (1526)
: the quality or state of being ungodly

un·god·ly \-lē\ *adjective* (1526)
1 a : denying or disobeying God : IMPIOUS, IRRELIGIOUS **b** : contrary to moral law : SINFUL, WICKED
2 : OUTRAGEOUS ⟨gets up at an *ungodly* hour⟩

un·got·ten \-'gä-tªn\ *or* **un·got** \-'gät\ *adjective* (15th century)
1 *obsolete* : not begotten
2 : not obtained

un·gov·ern·able \-'gə-vər-nə-bəl\ *adjective* (1673)
: not capable of being governed, guided, or restrained
synonym see UNRULY

un·gra·cious \-'grā-shəs\ *adjective* (13th century)
1 *archaic* : WICKED
2 : not courteous : RUDE
3 : not pleasing : DISAGREEABLE
— **un·gra·cious·ly** *adverb*
— **un·gra·cious·ness** *noun*

un·gram·mat·i·cal \,ən-grə-'ma-ti-kəl\ *adjective* (1654)

: not following rules of grammar
— **un·gram·mat·i·cal·i·ty** \-,ma-tə-'ka-lə-tē\ *noun*

un·grate·ful \,ən-'grāt-fəl\ *adjective* (1533)
1 : showing no gratitude : making a poor return
2 : DISAGREEABLE; *also* : THANKLESS
— **un·grate·ful·ly** \-fə-lē\ *adverb*
— **un·grate·ful·ness** *noun*

un·grudg·ing \-'grə-jiŋ\ *adjective* (circa 1774)
: being without envy or reluctance

un·gual \'əŋ-gwəl, 'ən-\ *adjective* [Latin *unguis* nail, claw, hoof — more at NAIL] (1834)
: of, relating to, or resembling a nail, claw, or hoof

un·guard \,ən-'gärd\ *transitive verb* [back-formation from *unguarded*] (1745)
: to leave unprotected

un·guard·ed \-'gär-dəd\ *adjective* (circa 1593)
1 : vulnerable to attack : UNPROTECTED
2 : free from guile or wariness : DIRECT, INCAUTIOUS
— **un·guard·ed·ly** *adverb*
— **un·guard·ed·ness** *noun*

un·guent \'əŋ-gwənt, 'ən-; 'ən-jənt\ *noun* [Middle English, from Latin *unguentum* — more at OINTMENT] (15th century)
: a soothing or healing salve : OINTMENT

un·guis \'əŋ-gwəs, 'ən-\ *noun, plural* **un·gues** \-,gwēz\ [Latin — more at NAIL] (circa 1790)
: a nail, claw, or hoof especially on a digit of a vertebrate

¹un·gu·late \'əŋ-gyə-lət, 'ən-, -,lät\ *adjective* [Late Latin *ungulatus,* from Latin *ungula* hoof, from *unguis* nail, hoof] (1839)
1 : having hoofs
2 : of or relating to the ungulates

²ungulate *noun* [New Latin *Ungulata,* from Late Latin, neuter plural of *ungulatus*] (circa 1842)
: a hoofed typically herbivorous quadruped mammal (as a ruminant, swine, camel, hippopotamus, horse, tapir, rhinoceros, elephant, or hyrax) of a polyphyletic group formerly considered a major mammalian taxon (Ungulata)

un·hair \,ən-'har, -'her\ *transitive verb* (14th century)
archaic : to deprive of hair

un·hal·low \-'ha-(,)lō\ *transitive verb* (1535)
archaic : to make profane

un·hal·lowed \-(,)lōd\ *adjective* (before 12th century)
1 : not blessed : UNCONSECRATED, UNHOLY
2 a : unsanctioned by or showing lack of reverence for religion : IMPIOUS, PROFANE **b** : contrary to accepted standards : IMMORAL

un·hand \,ən-'hand\ *transitive verb* (1602)
: to remove the hand from : let go

un·hand·some \-'han(t)-səm\ *adjective* (1530)
: not handsome: as **a** : not beautiful : HOMELY **b** : UNBECOMING, UNSEEMLY **c** : lacking in courtesy or taste : RUDE
— **un·hand·some·ly** *adverb*

un·handy \-'han-dē\ *adjective* (1664)
1 : hard to handle : INCONVENIENT
2 : lacking in skill or dexterity : AWKWARD
— **un·hand·i·ly** \-də-lē\ *adverb*
— **un·hand·i·ness** \-dē-nəs\ *noun*

un·hap·pi·ly \,ən-'ha-pə-lē\ *adverb* (14th century)
1 : UNFORTUNATELY **2** ⟨*unhappily,* medicine has not yet found a cure —Diana Trilling⟩
2 : in an unhappy manner : without pleasure ⟨practiced law *unhappily* for a few years⟩

un·hap·py \-'ha-pē\ *adjective* (14th century)
1 : not fortunate : UNLUCKY
2 : not cheerful or glad : SAD, WRETCHED
3 a : causing or subject to misfortune : INAUSPICIOUS **b** : INFELICITOUS, INAPPROPRIATE
— **un·hap·pi·ness** *noun*

un·healthy \-'hel-thē\ *adjective* (1595)

1 : not conducive to health ⟨an *unhealthy* climate⟩
2 : not in good health : SICKLY, DISEASED
3 a : DANGEROUS, RISKY **b** : BAD, INJURIOUS **c** : morally contaminated : CORRUPT, UNWHOLESOME ⟨an *unhealthy* imagination⟩
— **un·health·i·ly** \-thə-lē\ *adverb*
— **un·health·i·ness** \-thē-nəs\ *noun*

un·heard \-'hərd\ *adjective* (14th century)
1 a : not perceived by the ear **b** : not given a hearing
2 *archaic* : UNHEARD-OF

un·heard-of \-,əv, -,äv\ *adjective* (1592)
: previously unknown; *especially* : UNPRECEDENTED

un·hes·i·tat·ing \-'he-zə-,tā-tiŋ\ *adjective* (1753)
: not hesitating : not checked or qualified
— **un·hes·i·tat·ing·ly** \-tiŋ-lē\ *adverb*

un·hinge \-'hinj\ *transitive verb* (1616)
1 : to remove (as a door) from the hinges
2 : to make unstable : UNSETTLE, DISRUPT ⟨*unhinge* the balance of world peace⟩ ⟨pressure that would *unhinge* a less experienced person⟩

un·hitch \-'hich\ *transitive verb* (1706)
: to free from or as if from being hitched

un·ho·ly \,ən-'hō-lē\ *adjective* (before 12th century)
1 : showing disregard for what is holy : WICKED
2 : SHOCKING, OUTRAGEOUS
— **un·ho·li·ness** *noun*

un·hood \-'hùd\ *transitive verb* (1575)
: to remove a hood or covering from

un·hook \-'hùk\ *transitive verb* (1611)
1 : to remove from a hook
2 : to unfasten by disengaging a hook
3 : to free from a habit or dependency

un·hoped \-'hōpt\ *adjective* (14th century)
archaic : not hoped for or expected

un·horse \-'hòrs\ *transitive verb* (14th century)
: to dislodge from or as if from a horse

un·hou·seled \-'haù-zəld\ *adjective* (1532)
archaic : not having received the Eucharist especially shortly before death

un·hur·ried \-'hər-ēd, -'hə-rēd\ *adjective* (circa 1774)
: not hurried : LEISURELY
— **un·hur·ried·ly** *adverb*

uni- *prefix* [Middle English, from Middle French, from Latin, from *unus* — more at ONE]
: one : single ⟨*unicellular*⟩

uni·al·gal \,yü-nē-'al-gəl\ *adjective* (1914)
: of, relating to, or derived from a single algal individual or cell ⟨a *unialgal* culture⟩

Uni·ate *or* **Uni·at** \'yü-nē-,at, 'ü-\ *noun* [Ukrainian *uniat, uniyat* one in favor of the union of the Greek and Roman Catholic churches, from *uniya* union, from Polish *unija,* from Late Latin *unio* — more at UNION] (1833)
: a Christian of a church adhering to an Eastern rite and discipline but submitting to papal authority
— **Uniate** *adjective*

uni·ax·i·al \,yü-nē-'ak-sē-əl\ *adjective* (circa 1828)
1 : having only one axis
2 : of or relating to only one axis

uni·cam·er·al \,yü-ni-'kam-rəl, -'ka-mə-\ *adjective* [*uni-* + Late Latin *camera* room, chamber — more at CHAMBER] (1853)
: having or consisting of a single legislative chamber
— **uni·cam·er·al·ly** *adverb*

uni·cel·lu·lar \,yü-ni-'sel-yə-lər\ *adjective* (1858)
: having or consisting of a single cell

\ə\ abut \ª\ kitten \ər\ **further** \a\ ash \ā\ ace
\ä\ mop, mar \aù\ out \ch\ chin \e\ bet \ē\ easy
\g\ go \i\ hit \ī\ ice \j\ job \ŋ\ sing \ō\ go
\ò\ law \òi\ boy \th\ thin \th\ the \ü\ loot \ù\ foot
\y\ yet \zh\ vision *see also* Guide to Pronunciation

uni·corn \'yü-nə-ˌkȯrn\
noun [Middle English *uni-
corne,* from Old French,
from Late Latin *unicornis,*
from Latin, having one
horn, from *uni-* + *cornu*
horn — more at HORN]
(13th century)
: a mythical animal general-
ly depicted with the body
and head of a horse, the
hind legs of a stag, the tail
of a lion, and a single horn
in the middle of the fore-
head ◇

unicorn

unicorn plant *noun* (1796)
: DEVIL'S CLAW
uni·cy·cle \'yü-ni-ˌsī-kəl\ *noun* [*uni* + *-cycle*
(as in *tricycle*)] (1869)
: a vehicle that has a single
wheel and is usually propelled
by pedals
— **uni·cy·clist** \-ˌsī-
k(ə-)list\ *noun*
uni·di·men·sion·al \ˌyü-ni-
də-'mench-nəl, -'men(t)-
shə(-ə)n°l *also* -ˌdī-\ *adjective*
(1883)
: ONE-DIMENSIONAL
— **uni·di·men·sion·al·i-
ty** \-ˌmen(t)-shə-'na-lə-tē\
noun
uni·di·rec·tion·al \ˌyü-ni-də-
'rek-shnəl, -dī-, -shə-n°l\ *adjective* (1883)
1 : involving, functioning, moving, or respon-
sive in a single direction
2 : not subject to change or reversal of direc-
tion
— **uni·di·rec·tion·al·ly** *adverb*
unidirectional current *noun* (1883)
: DIRECT CURRENT
uni·fi·ca·tion \ˌyü-nə-fə-'kā-shən\ *noun*
(1851)
: the act, process, or result of unifying : the
state of being unified
uni·fo·li·ate \-'fō-lē-ət\ *adjective* [*uni-* + Latin
folium leaf — more at BLADE] (1849)
1 : having only one leaf
2 : UNIFOLIOLATE
uni·fo·li·o·late \-'fō-lē-ə-ˌlāt\ *adjective* [*uni-*
+ Late Latin *foliolum* leaflet, diminutive of
Latin *folium* leaf] (circa 1859)
of a leaf : compound but having only a single
leaflet and distinguishable from a simple leaf
by the basal joint
¹uni·form \'yü-nə-ˌfȯrm\ *adjective* [Middle
French *uniforme,* from Latin *uniformis,* from
uni- + *-formis* -form] (1538)
1 : consistent in conduct or opinion ⟨*uniform*
interpretation of laws⟩
2 : having always the same form, manner, or
degree : not varying or variable
3 : of the same form with others : conforming
to one rule or mode : CONSONANT
4 : presenting an unvaried appearance of sur-
face, pattern, or color ⟨*uniform* red brick hous-
es⟩
5 : relating to or being convergence of a series
whose terms are functions in such manner that
the absolute value of the difference between
the sum of the first *n* terms of the series and
the sum of all terms can be made arbitrarily
small for all values of the domain of the func-
tions by choosing the *n*th term sufficiently far
along in the series
— **uni·form·ly** \'yü-nə-ˌfȯrm-lē, ˌyü-nə-'\
adverb
— **uni·form·ness** \'yü-nə-ˌfȯrm-nəs\ *noun*
²uniform *transitive verb* (circa 1681)
1 : to bring into uniformity
2 : to clothe with a uniform
³uniform *noun* (1748)
: dress of a distinctive design or fashion worn
by members of a particular group and serving
as a means of identification; *broadly* : distinc-
tive or characteristic clothing

Uniform (circa 1956)
— a communication code word for the letter
u
uni·for·mi·tar·i·an \ˌyü-nə-ˌfȯr-mə-'ter-ē-ən\
noun (1840)
1 : an adherent of the doctrine of uniformitar-
ianism
2 : an advocate of uniformity
— **uniformitarian** *adjective*
uni·for·mi·tar·i·an·ism \-ē-ə-ˌni-zəm\ *noun*
(1865)
: a geological doctrine that existing processes
acting in the same manner as at present are
sufficient to account for all geological changes
— compare CATASTROPHISM
uni·for·mi·ty \ˌyü-nə-'fȯr-mə-tē\ *noun, plural*
-ties (15th century)
1 : the quality or state of being uniform
2 : an instance of uniformity
uni·fy \'yü-nə-ˌfī\ *transitive verb* **-fied; -fy-
ing** [Late Latin *unificare,* from Latin *uni-* +
-ficare -fy] (1502)
: to make into a unit or a coherent whole
: UNITE
— **uni·fi·able** \-ˌfī-ə-bəl\ *adjective*
— **uni·fi·er** \-ˌfī-(-ə)r\ *noun*
uni·lat·er·al \ˌyü-ni-'la-tə-rəl, -'la-trəl\ *adjec-
tive* (1802)
1 a : done or undertaken by one person or par-
ty **b** : of, relating to, or affecting one side of a
subject : ONE-SIDED **c** : constituting or relating
to a contract or engagement by which an ex-
press obligation to do or forbear is imposed on
only one party
2 a : having parts arranged on one side ⟨a *uni-
lateral* raceme⟩ **b** : occurring on, performed
on, or affecting one side of the body or one of
its parts ⟨*unilateral* exophthalmos⟩
3 : UNILINEAL
4 : having only one side
— **uni·lat·er·al·ly** *adverb*
uni·lin·e·al \-'li-nē-əl\ *adjective* (1952)
: tracing descent through either the maternal
or paternal line only
uni·lin·e·ar \ˌyü-ni-'li-nē-ər\ *adjective* (1851)
: developing in or involving a series of stages
usually from the primitive to the more ad-
vanced ⟨a *unilinear* cultural sequence⟩
uni·lin·gual \ˌyü-ni-'liŋ-gwəl, -gyə-wəl\ *ad-
jective* [*uni-* + Latin *lingua* tongue, language
— more at TONGUE] (1866)
: composed in or using one language only
un·il·lu·sioned \ˌən-i-'lü-zhənd\ *adjective*
(1926)
: free from illusion
uni·loc·u·lar \ˌyü-ni-'lä-kyə-lər\ *adjective*
(1753)
: containing a single cavity
un·imag·in·able \ˌən-ə-'maj-nə-bəl, -'ma-jə-\
adjective (1611)
: not imaginable or comprehensible
— **un·imag·in·ably** \-blē\ *adverb*
un·im·peach·able \ˌən-im-'pē-chə-bəl\ *ad-
jective* (1784)
: not impeachable : not to be called in ques-
tion : not liable to accusation : IRREPROACH-
ABLE, BLAMELESS
— **un·im·peach·ably** \-blē\ *adverb*
¹un·im·proved \-'prüvd\ *adjective* (1602)
obsolete : not reproved or admonished
²unimproved *adjective* (1665)
: not improved: as **a** : not tilled, built on, or
otherwise improved for use ⟨*unimproved* land⟩
b : not used or employed advantageously
⟨wasted time and *unimproved* opportunities⟩ **c**
: not selectively bred for better quality or pro-
ductiveness
un·in·hib·it·ed \ˌən-in-'hi-bə-təd\ *adjective*
(1880)
: free from inhibition; *also* : boisterously in-
formal
— **un·in·hib·it·ed·ly** *adverb*
— **un·in·hib·it·ed·ness** *noun*
un·ini·tiate \ˌən-ə-'ni-sh(ē-)ət\ *adjective*
(1801)
: not initiated : INEXPERIENCED

— **uninitiate** *noun*
un·in·ter·est \ˌən-'in-trəst, -'in-tə-rəst, -tə-
ˌrest, -tərst; -'in-ˌtrest\ *noun* (1890)
: lack of interest
uninterested *adjective* (1661)
: not interested : not having the mind or feel-
ings engaged
usage see DISINTERESTED
uni·nu·cle·ate \ˌyü-ni-'nü-klē-ət, -'nyü-\ *ad-
jective* (1885)
: having a single nucleus ⟨a *uninucleate* yeast
cell⟩
¹union \'yün-yən\ *noun* [Middle English, from
Middle French, from Late Latin *union-, unio*
oneness, union, from Latin *unus* one — more
at ONE] (15th century)
1 a : an act or instance of uniting or joining
two or more things into one: as (1) : the for-
mation of a single political unit from two or
more separate and independent units (2) : a
uniting in marriage; *also* : SEXUAL INTER-
COURSE (3) : the growing together of severed
parts **b** : a unified condition : COMBINATION,
JUNCTION ⟨a gracious *union* of excellence and
strength⟩
2 : something that is made one : something
formed by a combining or coalition of parts or
members: as **a** : a confederation of indepen-
dent individuals (as nations or persons) for
some common purpose **b** (1) : a political unit
constituting an organic whole formed usually
from previously independent units (as England
and Scotland in 1707) which have surrendered
their principal powers to the government of
the whole or to a newly created government
(as the U.S. in 1789) (2) *capitalized* : the fed-
eral union of states during the period of the
U.S. Civil War **c** *capitalized* : an organization
on a college or university campus providing
recreational, social, cultural, and sometimes
dining facilities; *also* : the building housing
such an organization **d** : the set of all elements
belonging to one or more of a given collection
of two or more sets — called also *join, sum* **e**
: LABOR UNION
3 a : a device emblematic of the union of two
or more sovereignties borne on a national flag
typically in the upper inner corner or constitut-
ing the whole design of the flag **b** : the upper
inner corner of a flag
4 : any of various devices for connecting parts
(as of a machine); *especially* : a coupling for
pipes or pipes and fittings

◇ WORD HISTORY
unicorn The two-horned African rhinocer-
os was quite familiar in the ancient Mediter-
ranean world, even to the urban populaces
of Alexandria and Rome, where specimens
are reported to have been exhibited. The
Greeks dubbed the animal *rhinokerōs,* literal-
ly, "nose-horned one"—an appropriate name,
since the rhinoceros's primary horn protrudes
from above its snout, unlike the horns of oth-
er ungulates, which grow above the brow.
The single-horned Indian rhinoceros, on the
other hand, was never observed firsthand by
ancient authors, and descriptions of it are
rather garbled. By late antiquity legend had
shaped out of the Indian rhinoceros a mythi-
cal animal, the *monokerōs* ("single-horned
one"). This animal is described in the *Physi-
ologus,* an anonymous 4th century Greek
prototype of the medieval bestiary, as having
most of the physical features we now associ-
ate with the unicorn. The *Physiologus* intro-
duces as well the belief that the fierce uni-
corn can only be subdued by a virgin, and
attaches to this trait a Christian interpreta-
tion, that the taming of the unicorn symboliz-
es Christ's incarnation in a virgin. Authors
writing in Latin translated Greek *monokerōs*
as *unicornis* or *unicornuus,* the ultimate
source of English *unicorn.*

²union *adjective* (1707)
: of, relating to, dealing with, or constituting a union; *especially, capitalized* : of, relating to, or being the side favoring the Union in the U.S. Civil War ⟨*Union* troops⟩

union card *noun* (1874)
1 : a card certifying personal membership in good standing in a labor union
2 : something that resembles a union card especially in being necessary for employment or in providing evidence of in-group status

union church *noun* (1847)
: a local church uniting members of diverse denominational backgrounds in an interdenominational congregation

un·ion·i·sa·tion, union·ise *British variant of* UNIONIZATION, UNIONIZE

union·ism \'yün-yə-,ni-zəm\ *noun* (1845)
: the principle or policy of forming or adhering to a union: as **a** *capitalized* : adherence to the policy of a firm federal union between the states of the United States especially during the Civil War period **b** : the principles, theory, advocacy, or system of trade unions

union·ist \-nist\ *noun* (1799)
: an advocate or supporter of union or unionism

union·i·za·tion \,yün-yə-nə-'zā-shən\ *noun* (1896)
1 : the quality or state of being unionized
2 : the action of unionizing

union·ize \'yün-yə-,nīz\ *verb* **-ized; -iz·ing** (1890)
transitive verb
: to organize into a labor union
intransitive verb
: to form or join a labor union

unionized *adjective* (1900)
: characterized by the presence of labor unions ⟨*unionized* states⟩

union jack *noun* (1674)
1 : a jack consisting of the union of a national ensign
2 *U&J capitalized* : the state flag of the United Kingdom consisting of the union of the British national ensign

union shop *noun* (1904)
: an establishment in which the employer by agreement is free to hire nonmembers as well as members of the union but retains nonmembers on the payroll only on condition of their becoming members of the union within a specified time

union suit *noun* (1892)
: an undergarment with shirt and drawers in one piece

uni·pa·ren·tal \,yü-ni-pə-'ren-t°l\ *adjective* (1900)
: having or involving a single parent; *especially* : PARTHENOGENETIC
— **uni·pa·ren·tal·ly** \-t°l-ē\ *adverb*

unique \yu̇-'nēk\ *adjective* [French, from Latin *unicus,* from *unus* one — more at ONE] (1602)
1 : being the only one : SOLE ⟨his *unique* concern was his own comfort⟩ ⟨I can't walk away with a *unique* copy. Suppose I lost it? —Kingsley Amis⟩ ⟨the *unique* factorization of a number into prime factors⟩
2 a : being without a like or equal : UNEQUALED ⟨could stare at the flames, each one new, violent, *unique* —Robert Coover⟩ **b** : distinctively characteristic : PECULIAR 1 ⟨this is not a condition *unique* to California —Ronald Reagan⟩
3 : UNUSUAL ⟨a very *unique* ball-point pen⟩ ⟨we were fairly *unique,* the sixty of us, in that there wasn't one good mixer in the bunch —J. D. Salinger⟩ □
synonym see STRANGE
— **unique·ly** *adverb*

union suit

— **unique·ness** *noun*

¹uni·sex \'yü-nə-,seks\ *noun* (1966)
: the state or condition of not being distinguishable (as by hair or clothing) as to sex

²unisex *adjective* (1968)
1 : not distinguishable as male or female ⟨a *unisex* face⟩
2 : suitable or designed for both males and females ⟨*unisex* clothes⟩

uni·sex·u·al \,yü-nə-'sek-sh(ə-)wəl, -shəl\ *adjective* (circa 1802)
1 : of, relating to, or restricted to one sex: **a** : male or female but not hermaphroditic **b** : DICLINOUS ⟨a *unisexual* flower⟩
2 : UNISEX
— **uni·sex·u·al·i·ty** \-,sek-shə-'wa-lə-tē\ *noun*

uni·son \'yü-nə-sən, -nə-zən\ *noun* [Middle French, from Medieval Latin *unisonus* having the same sound, from Latin *uni-* + *sonus* sound — more at SOUND] (1575)
1 a : identity in musical pitch; *specifically* : the interval of a perfect prime **b** : the state of being so tuned or sounded **c** : the writing, playing, or singing of parts in a musical passage at the same pitch or in octaves
2 : a harmonious agreement or union : CONCORD
— **unison** *adjective*
— **in unison 1** : in perfect agreement : so as to harmonize exactly **2** : at the same time : SIMULTANEOUSLY

¹unit \'yü-nət\ *noun* [back-formation from *unity*] (1570)
1 a : the first and least natural number : ONE **b** : a single quantity regarded as a whole in calculation
2 : a determinate quantity (as of length, time, heat, or value) adopted as a standard of measurement: as **a** : an amount of work used in education in calculating student credits **b** : an amount of a biologically active agent (as a drug or antigen) required to produce a specific result under strictly controlled conditions
3 a : a single thing, person, or group that is a constituent of a whole **b** : a part of a military establishment that has a prescribed organization (as of personnel and materiel) **c** : a piece or complex of apparatus serving to perform one particular function **d** : a part of a school course focusing on a central theme **e** : a local congregation of Jehovah's Witnesses

²unit *adjective* (1844)
: being, relating to, or measuring one unit

unit·age \'yü-nə-tij\ *noun* (1935)
1 : specifications of the amount constituting a unit
2 : amount in units

uni·tard \'yü-nə-,tärd\ *noun* [*uni-* + leo*tard*] (1961)
: a close-fitting one-piece garment for the torso, legs, feet, and often the arms

uni·tar·i·an \,yü-nə-'ter-ē-ən\ *noun* [New Latin *unitarius,* from Latin *unitas* unity] (1687)
1 a *often capitalized* : one who believes that the deity exists only in one person **b** *capitalized* : a member of a denomination that stresses individual freedom of belief, the free use of reason in religion, a united world community, and liberal social action
2 : an advocate of unity or a unitary system
— **unitarian** *adjective, often capitalized*
— **uni·tar·i·an·ism** \-ē-ə-,ni-zəm\ *noun, often capitalized*

uni·tary \'yü-nə-,ter-ē\ *adjective* (1861)
1 a : of or relating to a unit **b** : based on or characterized by unity or units
2 : having the character of a unit : UNDIVIDED, WHOLE
— **uni·tar·i·ly** \,yü-nə-'ter-ə-lē\ *adverb*

unit cell *noun* (1915)
: the simplest polyhedron that embodies all the structural characteristics of and by indefinite repetition makes up the lattice of a crystal

unit character *noun* (1902)

: a natural character inherited on an all-or-none basis; *especially* : one dependent on the presence or absence of a single gene

unit circle *noun* (1955)
: a circle having a radius of 1

¹unite \yu̇-'nīt\ *verb* **unit·ed; unit·ing** [Middle English, from Latin *unire,* from *unus* one — more at ONE] (15th century)
transitive verb
1 a : to put together to form a single unit **b** : to cause to adhere **c** : to link by a legal or moral bond
2 : to possess (as qualities) in combination
intransitive verb
1 a : to become one or as if one **b** : to become combined by or as if by adhesion or mixture
2 : to act in concert
synonym see JOIN
— **unit·er** *noun*

²unite \'yü-,nīt\ *noun* [obsolete *unite* united, from Middle English *unit,* from Late Latin *unitus,* past participle] (1604)
: an old British gold 20-shilling piece issued first by James I in 1604 for the newly united England and Scotland — called also *Jacobus*

unit·ed \yu̇-'nī-təd\ *adjective* (1552)
1 : made one : COMBINED
2 : relating to or produced by joint action
3 : being in agreement : HARMONIOUS
— **unit·ed·ly** *adverb*

United Nations Day *noun* (1947)
: October 24 observed in commemoration of the founding of the United Nations

Unit·ed States \yu̇-'nī-təd-, *especially* Southern 'yü-,\ *noun plural but singular or plural in construction* (1617)
: a federation of states especially when forming a nation in a usually specified territory ⟨advocating a *United States* of Europe⟩

uni·tive \'yü-nə-tiv, yu̇-'nī-\ *adjective* (1526)
: characterized by or tending to produce union

unit·ize \'yü-nə-,tīz\ *transitive verb* **-ized; -iz·ing** (1860)
1 : to form or convert into a unit
2 : to divide into units ⟨the added cost of *unitizing* bulk products⟩
— **unit·i·za·tion** \,yü-nə-tə-'zā-shən\ *noun*

unit membrane *noun* [from its being the basic structural unit of the cell] (1959)

□ **USAGE** **unique** Many commentators have objected to the comparison or modification (as by *somewhat* or *very*) of *unique;* the statement that a thing is either unique or it is not has often been repeated by them. Objections are based chiefly on the assumption that *unique* has but a single absolute sense, an assumption contradicted by information readily available in a dictionary. *Unique* dates back to the 17th century but was little used until the end of the 18th when, according to the Oxford English Dictionary, it was reacquired from French. H. J. Todd entered it as a foreign word in his edition (1818) of Johnson's Dictionary, characterizing it as "affected and useless." Around the middle of the 19th century it ceased to be considered foreign and came into considerable popular use. With popular use came a broadening of application beyond the original two meanings (here numbered 1 and 2a). In modern use both comparison and modification are widespread and standard but are confined to the extended senses 2b and 3. When sense 1 or sense 2a is intended, *unique* is used without qualifying modifiers.

\ə\ abut \°\ kitten \ər\ further \a\ ash \ā\ ace
\ä\ mop, mar \au̇\ out \ch\ chin \e\ bet \ē\ easy
\g\ go \i\ hit \ī\ ice \j\ job \ŋ\ sing \ō\ go
\ȯ\ law \ȯi\ boy \th\ thin \th̲\ the \ü\ loot \u̇\ foot
\y\ yet \zh\ vision *see also* Guide to Pronunciation

: a 3-layered membrane that consists of an inner lipid layer surrounded by a protein layer on each side

unit rule *noun* (1884)
: a rule under which a delegation to a national political convention casts its entire vote as a unit as determined by a majority vote

uni·trust \'yü-ni-ˌtrəst\ *noun* (1970)
: a trust from which the beneficiary receives annually a fixed percentage of the fair market value of its assets

units place *noun* (1937)
: the place just to the left of the decimal point in a number expressed in the Arabic system of writing numbers

unit train *noun* (1964)
: a railway train that transports a single commodity directly from producer to consumer

unit trust *noun* (1936)
1 *British* : MUTUAL FUND
2 : an investment company whose portfolio consists of long-term bonds that are held to maturity

uni·ty \'yü-nə-tē\ *noun, plural* **-ties** [Middle English *unite*, from Middle French *unité*, from Latin *unitat-*, *unitas*, from *unus* one — more at ONE] (14th century)
1 a : the quality or state of not being multiple : ONENESS **b** (1) : a definite amount taken as one or for which 1 is made to stand in calculation ⟨in a table of natural sines the radius of the circle is regarded as *unity*⟩ (2) : IDENTITY ELEMENT
2 a : a condition of harmony : ACCORD **b** : continuity without deviation or change (as in purpose or action)
3 a : the quality or state of being made one : UNIFICATION **b** : a combination or ordering of parts in a literary or artistic production that constitutes a whole or promotes an undivided total effect; *also* : the resulting singleness of effect or symmetry and consistency of style and character
4 : a totality of related parts : an entity that is a complex or systematic whole
5 : any of three principles of dramatic structure derived by French classicists from Aristotle's *Poetics* and requiring a play to have a single action represented as occurring in one place and within one day
6 *capitalized* : a 20th century American religious movement that emphasizes spiritual sources of health and prosperity

¹uni·va·lent \ˌyü-ni-'vā-lənt\ *adjective* (1898)
1 : MONOVALENT
2 : being a chromosomal univalent

²univalent *noun* (1912)
: a chromosome that lacks a synaptic mate

uni·valve \'yü-ni-ˌvalv\ *noun* (1668)
1 : a mollusk with a shell consisting of one valve; *especially* : GASTROPOD
2 : the shell of a univalve
— **univalve** *adjective*

uni·var·i·ate \ˌyü-ni-'ver-ē-ət, -'var-\ *adjective* (1928)
: characterized by or depending on only one random variable ⟨a *univariate* linear model⟩

¹uni·ver·sal \ˌyü-nə-'vər-səl\ *adjective* [Middle English, from Middle French, from Latin *universalis*, from *universum* universe] (14th century)
1 : including or covering all or a whole collectively or distributively without limit or exception
2 a : present or occurring everywhere **b** : existent or operative everywhere or under all conditions ⟨*universal* cultural patterns⟩
3 a : embracing a major part or the greatest portion (as of mankind) ⟨a *universal* state⟩ ⟨*universal* practices⟩ **b** : comprehensively broad and versatile ⟨a *universal* genius⟩
4 a : affirming or denying something of all members of a class or of all values of a variable **b** : denoting every member of a class ⟨a *universal* term⟩

5 : adapted or adjustable to meet varied requirements (as of use, shape, or size) ⟨a *universal* gear cutter⟩
— **uni·ver·sal·ly** \-s(ə-)lē\ *adverb*
— **uni·ver·sal·ness** \-səl-nəs\ *noun*

²universal *noun* (1553)
1 : one that is universal: as **a** : a universal proposition in logic **b** : a predicable of traditional logic **c** : a general concept or term or something in reality to which it corresponds : ESSENCE
2 a : a behavior pattern or institution (as the family) existing in all cultures **b** : a culture trait characteristic of all normal adult members of a particular society

universal donor *noun* (1922)
: a person who belongs to ABO blood group O and can donate blood to any recipient

universal grammar *noun* (1751)
: the study of general principles believed to underlie the grammatical phenomena of all languages; *also* : such principles viewed as part of an innate human capacity for learning a language

uni·ver·sal·ism \ˌyü-nə-'vər-sə-ˌli-zəm\ *noun* (1805)
1 *often capitalized* **a** : a theological doctrine that all human beings will eventually be saved **b** : the principles and practices of a liberal Christian denomination founded in the 18th century originally to uphold belief in universal salvation and now united with Unitarianism
2 : something that is universal in scope
3 : the state of being universal : UNIVERSALITY
— **uni·ver·sal·ist** \-s(ə-)list\ *noun or adjective, often capitalized*

uni·ver·sal·is·tic \-ˌvər-sə-'lis-tik\ *adjective* (1872)
: of or relating to the whole : universal in scope or nature

uni·ver·sal·i·ty \-(ˌ)vər-'sa-lə-tē\ *noun* (14th century)
1 : the quality or state of being universal
2 : universal comprehensiveness in range

uni·ver·sal·ize \-'vər-sə-ˌlīz\ *transitive verb* **-ized; -iz·ing** (1642)
: to make universal : GENERALIZE
— **uni·ver·sal·i·za·tion** \-ˌvər-sə-lə-'zā-shən\ *noun*

universal joint *noun* (1676)
: a shaft coupling capable of transmitting rotation from one shaft to another not collinear with it — called also *universal coupling*

universal joint

universal motor *noun* (1925)
: an electric motor that can be used on either an alternating or a direct current supply

Universal Product Code *noun* (1974)
: a combination of a bar code and numbers by which a scanner can identify a product and usually assign a price

universal recipient *noun* (1922)
: a person who belongs to ABO blood group AB and can receive blood from any donor

Universal time *noun* (1882)
: GREENWICH MEAN TIME

uni·verse \'yü-nə-ˌvərs\ *noun* [Latin *universum*, from neuter of *universus* entire, whole, from *uni-* + *versus* turned toward, from past participle of *vertere* to turn — more at WORTH] (1589)
1 : the whole body of things and phenomena observed or postulated : COSMOS: as **a** : a systematic whole held to arise by and persist through the direct intervention of divine power **b** : the world of human experience **c** (1) : the entire celestial cosmos (2) : MILKY WAY GALAXY (3) : an aggregate of stars comparable to the Milky Way galaxy

2 : a distinct field or province of thought or reality that forms a closed system or self-inclusive and independent organization
3 : POPULATION 4
4 : a set that contains all elements relevant to a particular discussion or problem
5 : a great number or quantity ⟨a large enough *universe* of stocks . . . to choose from —G. B. Clairmont⟩

universe of discourse (1881)
: an inclusive class of entities that is tacitly implied or explicitly delineated as the subject of a statement, discourse, or theory

uni·ver·si·ty \ˌyü-nə-'vər-sə-tē, -'vər-stē\ *noun, plural* **-ties** [Middle English *universite*, from Middle French *université*, from Medieval Latin *universitat-*, *universitas*, from Latin *universus*] (14th century)
1 : an institution of higher learning providing facilities for teaching and research and authorized to grant academic degrees; *specifically* : one made up of an undergraduate division which confers bachelor's degrees and a graduate division which comprises a graduate school and professional schools each of which may confer master's degrees and doctorates
2 : the physical plant of a university

univ·o·cal \yü-'ni-və-kəl\ *adjective* [Late Latin *univocus*, from Latin *uni-* + *voc-*, *vox* voice — more at VOICE] (1599)
: having one meaning only
— **univ·o·cal·ly** \-k(ə-)lē\ *adverb*

un·joined \ˌən-'jȯind\ *adjective* (1538)
: not joined

un·just \ˌən-'jəst\ *adjective* (14th century)
1 : characterized by injustice : UNFAIR
2 *archaic* : DISHONEST, FAITHLESS
— **un·just·ly** *adverb*
— **un·just·ness** \-'jəs(t)-nəs\ *noun*

un·kempt \ˌən-'kem(p)t\ *adjective* [*un-* + *kempt* combed, neat] (1579)
1 : deficient in order or neatness ⟨*unkempt* individuals⟩ ⟨*unkempt* hotel rooms⟩; *also* : ROUGH, UNPOLISHED ⟨*unkempt* prose⟩
2 : not combed ⟨*unkempt* hair⟩

un·kenned \-'kend\ *adjective* (14th century)
chiefly dialect : UNKNOWN, STRANGE

un·ken·nel \-'ke-nᵊl\ *transitive verb* (1575)
1 a : to drive (as a fox) from a hiding place or den **b** : to free (dogs) from a kennel
2 : to bring out into the open : UNCOVER

un·kind \-'kīnd\ *adjective* (13th century)
1 : not pleasing or mild : INCLEMENT ⟨an *unkind* climate⟩
2 : lacking in kindness or sympathy : HARSH, CRUEL
— **un·kind·ness** \-'kīn(d)-nəs\ *noun*

¹un·kind·ly \-'kīn(d)-lē\ *adjective* (13th century)
: not kindly
— **un·kind·li·ness** *noun*

²unkindly *adverb* (14th century)
: in an unkind manner ⟨dwells *unkindly* long on his final decline —A. H. Johnston⟩

un·kink \ˌən-'kiŋk\ (1891)
transitive verb
: to free from kinks : STRAIGHTEN
intransitive verb
: to become lax or loose : RELAX

un·knit \-'nit\ *verb* **-knit** *or* **-knit·ted; -knit·ting** (before 12th century)
: UNDO, UNRAVEL

un·know·able \ˌən-'nō-ə-bəl\ *adjective* (14th century)
: not knowable; *especially* : lying beyond the limits of human experience or understanding
— **un·know·abil·i·ty** \-ˌnō-ə-'bi-lə-tē\ *noun*

¹un·know·ing \-'nō-iŋ\ *adjective* (14th century)
: not knowing
— **un·know·ing·ly** \-iŋ-lē\ *adverb*

²unknowing *noun* (14th century)
: IGNORANCE

¹un·known \-'nōn\ *adjective* (14th century)

: not known or not well-known; *also* : having an unknown value ⟨an *unknown* quantity⟩

²**unknown** *noun* (1597)
1 : one that is not known or not well-known; *especially* : a person who is little known (as to the public)
2 : something that requires discovery, indentification, or clarification: as **a** : a symbol (as *x, y,* or *z*) in a mathematical equation representing an unknown quantity **b** : a specimen (as of bacteria or mixed chemicals) required to be identified as an exercise in appropriate laboratory techniques

Unknown Soldier *noun* (1923)
: an unidentified soldier whose body is selected to receive national honors as a representative of all of the same nation who died in a war and especially in one of the world wars

un·lace \ˌən-ˈlās\ *transitive verb* (14th century)
1 : to loose by undoing a lacing
2 *obsolete* : UNDO, DISGRACE

un·lade \-ˈlād\ *verb* **-lad·ed; -laded** *or* **-laden** \-ˈlā-dᵊn\; **-lad·ing** (14th century)
transitive verb
1 : to take the load or cargo from
2 : DISCHARGE, UNLOAD
intransitive verb
: to discharge cargo

un·lash \-ˈlash\ *transitive verb* (1748)
: to untie the lashing of

un·latch \-ˈlach\ (1642)
transitive verb
: to open or loose by lifting the latch
intransitive verb
: to become loosed or opened

un·law·ful \ˌən-ˈlȯ-fəl\ *adjective* (14th century)
1 : not lawful : ILLEGAL
2 : not morally right or conventional
— **un·law·ful·ly** \-f(ə-)lē\ *adverb*
— **un·law·ful·ness** \-fəl-nəs\ *noun*

un·lay \-ˈlā\ *verb* **-laid** \-ˈlād\; **-lay·ing** (1726)
transitive verb
: to untwist the strands of (as a rope)
intransitive verb
: UNTWIST

un·lead·ed \-ˈle-dəd\ *adjective* (circa 1891)
1 : not having leads between the lines in printing
2 : not treated or mixed with lead or lead compounds ⟨*unleaded* fuels⟩

un·learn \-ˈlərn\ *transitive verb* (15th century)
1 : to put out of one's knowledge or memory
2 : to undo the effect of : discard the habit of

un·learned \-ˈlər-nəd *for 1, 2,* -ˈlərnd *for 3*\ *adjective* (15th century)
1 : possessing inadequate learning or education; *especially* : deficient in scholarly attainments
2 : characterized by or revealing ignorance
3 : not gained by study or training
synonym see IGNORANT

un·leash \-ˈlēsh\ *transitive verb* (circa 1671)
: to free from or as if from a leash : let loose

¹**un·less** \ən-ˈles, ˈən-ˌ\ *conjunction* [Middle English *unlesse*, alteration of *onlesse*, from *on + lesse* less] (1509)
1 : except on the condition that : under any other circumstance than
2 : without the accompanying circumstance or condition that : but that : BUT

²**unless** *preposition* (circa 1532)
: except possibly : EXCEPT

un·let·tered \ˌən-ˈle-tərd\ *adjective* (14th century)
1 a : lacking facility in reading and writing and ignorant of the knowledge to be gained from books **b** : ILLITERATE
2 : not marked with letters
synonym see IGNORANT

un·licked \-ˈlikt\ *adjective* (1593)
1 : lacking proper form or shape
2 *archaic* : not licked dry

¹**un·like** \-ˈlīk\ *adjective* (13th century)

: not like: as **a** : marked by lack of resemblance : DIFFERENT ⟨the two books are quite *unlike*⟩ **b** : marked by inequality : UNEQUAL ⟨contributed *unlike* amounts⟩
— **un·like·ness** *noun*

²**unlike** *preposition* (1593)
: not like: as **a** : different from **b** : not characteristic of **c** : in a different manner from

un·like·li·hood \ˌən-ˈlī-klē-ˌhu̇d\ *noun* (1548)
1 : IMPROBABILITY
2 : something unlikely

un·like·li·ness \-nəs\ *noun* (1614)
: IMPROBABILITY

un·like·ly \-ˈlī-klē\ *adjective* (14th century)
1 : not likely : IMPROBABLE
2 : likely to fail : UNPROMISING

un·lim·ber \ˌən-ˈlim-bər\ (1802)
transitive verb
1 : to detach the limber from and so make ready ⟨*unlimber* a gun for action⟩
2 : to prepare for operation or performance ⟨*unlimbered* his banjo and began to play⟩
intransitive verb
: to perform the task of preparing something for action

un·lim·it·ed \-ˈli-mə-təd\ *adjective* (15th century)
1 : lacking any controls : UNRESTRICTED
2 : BOUNDLESS, INFINITE
3 : not bounded by exceptions : UNDEFINED
— **un·lim·it·ed·ly** *adverb*

un·link \-ˈliŋk\ (1600)
transitive verb
: to unfasten the links of : SEPARATE, DISCONNECT
intransitive verb
: to become detached

un·linked \-ˈliŋ(k)t\ *adjective* (1966)
: not belonging to the same genetic linkage group ⟨*unlinked* genes⟩

un·list·ed \-ˈlis-təd\ *adjective* (1644)
1 : not appearing on a list; *especially* : not appearing in a telephone book ⟨*unlisted* numbers⟩
2 : being or involving a security not listed formally on an organized exchange : OVER-THE-COUNTER

un·live \-ˈliv\ *transitive verb* (1614)
: ANNUL, REVERSE

un·load \ˌən-ˈlōd\ (1523)
transitive verb
1 a (1) : to take off : DELIVER (2) : to take the cargo from **b** : to give outlet to : pour forth ⟨*unloaded* her bitter feelings⟩
2 : to relieve of something burdensome, unwanted, or oppressive ⟨*unloaded* the pack animals⟩ ⟨*unloaded* himself to his friend⟩
3 : to draw the charge from ⟨*unloaded* the gun⟩
4 : to sell or dispose of especially in large quantities : DUMP
5 : to hit or propel with a great release of power ⟨*unloaded* his ninth homer⟩
intransitive verb
1 : to perform the act of unloading
2 : to release or deliver something especially with power ⟨*unloaded* on the ball⟩
— **un·load·er** *noun*

un·lock \-ˈläk\ (15th century)
transitive verb
1 : to unfasten the lock of
2 : OPEN, UNDO
3 : to free from restraints or restrictions ⟨the shock *unlocked* a flood of tears⟩
4 : to furnish a key to : DISCLOSE
intransitive verb
: to become unfastened or freed from restraints

un·looked–for \-ˈlu̇kt-ˌfȯr\ *adjective* (1535)
: not foreseen : UNEXPECTED

un·loose \ˌən-ˈlüs\ *transitive verb* (14th century)
1 : to relax the strain of ⟨*unloose* a grip⟩
2 : to release from or as if from restraints : set free

3 : to loosen the ties of ⟨*unloose* traditional social bonds⟩

un·loos·en \-ˈlü-sᵊn\ *transitive verb* (15th century)
: UNLOOSE

un·love·ly \-ˈləv-lē\ *adjective* (14th century)
: not likable : DISAGREEABLE, UNPLEASANT
— **un·love·li·ness** \-lē-nəs\ *noun*

un·luck·i·ly \ˌən-ˈlə-kə-lē\ *adverb* (1530)
: UNFORTUNATELY ⟨*unluckily*, it has a nasty way of turning to rain —Ambrose Bierce⟩ ⟨his ascent being *unluckily* a little out of the perpendicular —T. L. Peacock⟩

un·lucky \-ˈlə-kē\ *adjective* (1530)
1 : marked by adversity or failure ⟨an *unlucky* year⟩
2 : likely to bring misfortune : INAUSPICIOUS
3 : having or meeting with bad luck ⟨*unlucky* people⟩
4 : producing dissatisfaction : REGRETTABLE
— **un·luck·i·ness** \-lə-kē-nəs\ *noun*

un·made \ˌən-ˈmād\ *adjective* (13th century)
: not made ⟨an *unmade* bed⟩

un·make \-ˈmāk\ *transitive verb* **-made** \-ˈmād\; **-mak·ing** (15th century)
1 : to cause to disappear : DESTROY
2 : to deprive of rank or office : DEPOSE
3 : to deprive of essential characteristics : change the nature of

un·man \ˌən-ˈman\ *transitive verb* (circa 1600)
1 : to deprive of manly vigor, fortitude, or spirit
2 : CASTRATE, EMASCULATE
synonym see UNNERVE

un·man·ly \-ˈman-lē\ *adjective* (circa 1547)
: not manly: as **a** : being of weak character : COWARDLY **b** : EFFEMINATE
— **un·man·li·ness** \-lē-nəs\ *noun*

un·manned \-ˈmand\ *adjective* (1544)
1 : not manned ⟨an *unmanned* spaceflight⟩
2 *of a hawk* : not trained

un·man·nered \-ˈma-nərd\ *adjective* (1594)
1 : marked by a lack of good manners : RUDE
2 : characterized by an absence of artificiality : UNAFFECTED
— **un·man·nered·ly** *adverb*

¹**un·man·ner·ly** \-ˈma-nər-lē\ *adverb* (14th century)
: in an unmannerly fashion

²**unmannerly** *adjective* (14th century)
: not mannerly : DISCOURTEOUS
— **un·man·ner·li·ness** \-lē-nəs\ *noun*

un·mar·ried \-ˈmar-ēd\ *adjective* (14th century)
: not married: **a** : not now or previously married **b** : being divorced or widowed
— **unmarried** *noun*

un·mask \ˌən-ˈmask\ (1602)
transitive verb
1 : to remove a mask from
2 : to reveal the true nature of : EXPOSE
intransitive verb
: to remove one's mask

un·mean·ing \-ˈmē-niŋ\ *adjective* (1704)
1 : lacking intelligence : VAPID
2 : having no meaning : SENSELESS

un·me·di·at·ed \ˌən-ˈmē-dē-ˌā-təd\ *adjective* (1648)
: not mediated : not communicated or transformed by an intervening agency ⟨experience *unmediated* by artifice⟩

un·meet \-ˈmēt\ *adjective* (circa 1529)
: not meet : UNSUITABLE, IMPROPER

¹**un·men·tion·able** \-ˈmen(t)-sh(ə-)nə-bəl\ *adjective* (1837)
: not fit or allowed to be mentioned or discussed : UNSPEAKABLE

²**unmentionable** *noun* (1928)
: one that is not to be mentioned or discussed: as **a** *plural* : ³PANT 1 **b** *plural* : UNDERWEAR

un·mer·ci·ful \ən-'mər-si-fəl\ *adjective* (15th century)
1 : not merciful : MERCILESS
2 : EXCESSIVE, EXTREME ⟨chatted for an *unmerciful* length of time⟩
— **un·mer·ci·ful·ly** \-f(ə-)lē\ *adverb*

un·mind·ful \-'mīn(d)-fəl\ *adjective* (14th century)
: not conscientiously aware, attentive, or heedful : INATTENTIVE, CARELESS

un·mis·tak·able \ən-mə-'stā-kə-bəl\ *adjective* (1666)
: not capable of being mistaken or misunderstood : CLEAR
— **un·mis·tak·ably** \-blē\ *adverb*

un·mit·i·gat·ed \ən-'mi-tə-ˌgā-təd\ *adjective* (1599)
1 : not lessened : UNRELIEVED ⟨sufferings *unmitigated* by any hope of early relief⟩
2 : being so definitely what is stated as to offer little chance of change or relief ⟨an *unmitigated* evil⟩
— **un·mit·i·gat·ed·ly** *adverb*
— **un·mit·i·gat·ed·ness** *noun*

un·mold \ən-'mōld\ *transitive verb* (circa 1900)
: to remove from a mold

un·moor \-'mur\ (15th century)
transitive verb
: to loosen from or as if from moorings
intransitive verb
: to cast off moorings

un·mor·al \-'mór-əl, -'mär-\ *adjective* (1841)
1 : having no moral perception or quality; *also* **:** not influenced or guided by moral considerations
2 : lying outside the bounds of morals or ethics : AMORAL
— **un·mo·ral·i·ty** \ˌən-mə-'ra-lə-tē, -mó-\ *noun*

un·muf·fle \ən-'mə-fəl\ *transitive verb* (1611)
: to free from something that muffles

un·muz·zle \-'mə-zəl\ *transitive verb* (1601)
: to free from or as if from a muzzle

un·my·elin·at·ed \-'mī-ə-lə-ˌnā-təd\ *adjective* (1919)
: lacking a myelin sheath

un·nail \ən-'nā(ə)l\ *transitive verb* (15th century)
: to unfasten by removing nails

un·nat·u·ral \ən-'na-chə-rəl, -'nach-rəl\ *adjective* (15th century)
1 : not being in accordance with nature or consistent with a normal course of events
2 a : not being in accordance with normal human feelings or behavior : PERVERSE **b :** lacking ease and naturalness : CONTRIVED ⟨her manner was forced and *unnatural*⟩ **c :** inconsistent with what is reasonable or expected ⟨an *unnatural* alliance⟩
synonym see IRREGULAR
— **un·nat·u·ral·ly** \-'na-chə-rə-lē, -'nach-rə-, -'na-chər-\ *adverb*
— **un·nat·u·ral·ness** \-'na-chə-rəl-nəs, -'nach-rəl-\ *noun*

un·nec·es·sar·i·ly \ˌən-ˌne-sə-'ser-ə-lē\ *adverb* (1594)
: not by necessity : to an unnecessary degree

un·nec·es·sary \ən-'ne-sə-ˌser-ē\ *adjective* (1548)
: not necessary

un·nerve \ən-'nərv\ *transitive verb* (1601)
1 : to deprive of courage, strength, or steadiness
2 : to cause to become nervous : UPSET ☆
— **un·nerv·ing·ly** \-'nər-viṅ-lē\ *adverb*

un·nil·hex·i·um \ˌyü-nʲl-'hek-sē-əm\ *noun* [New Latin, from *unnil*- (from Latin *unus* one + *nil* nothing, zero) + Greek *hex* six + New Latin *-ium* — more at ONE, NIL, SIX] (1981)
: the chemical element of atomic number 106 — see ELEMENT table

un·nil·pen·ti·um \-'pen-tē-əm\ *noun* [New Latin, from *unnil*- + Greek *pente* five + New Latin *-ium* — more at FIVE] (1981)

: the chemical element of atomic number 105 — see ELEMENT table

un·nil·qua·di·um \-'kwä-dē-əm\ *noun* [New Latin, from *unnil*- + *quadr*i- + *-ium*] (1979)
: the chemical element of atomic number 104 — see ELEMENT table

un·num·bered \ən-'nəm-bərd\ *adjective* (14th century)
1 : INNUMERABLE
2 : not having an identifying number ⟨*unnumbered* pages⟩

un·ob·tru·sive \ˌən-əb-'trü-siv, -ziv\ *adjective* (1743)
: not obtrusive : not blatant, arresting, or aggressive : INCONSPICUOUS
— **un·ob·tru·sive·ly** *adverb*
— **un·ob·tru·sive·ness** *noun*

un·oc·cu·pied \ən-'ä-kyə-ˌpīd\ *adjective* (14th century)
: not occupied: as **a :** not busy : UNEMPLOYED **b :** not lived in : EMPTY

un·or·ga·nized \-'ór-gə-ˌnīzd\ *adjective* (circa 1828)
1 : not organized: as **a :** not brought into a coherent or well-ordered whole **b :** not belonging to a labor union
2 : not having the characteristics of a living organism

un·or·tho·dox \-'ór-thə-ˌdäks\ *adjective* (1657)
: not orthodox
— **un·or·tho·dox·ly** *adverb*

un·or·tho·doxy \-ˌdäk-sē\ *noun* (circa 1704)
1 : the quality or state of being unorthodox
2 : something (as an opinion or doctrine) that is unorthodox

un·pack \ˌən-'pak\ (15th century)
transitive verb
1 a : to remove the contents of ⟨*unpack* a trunk⟩ **b :** UNBURDEN, REVEAL ⟨must . . . *unpack* my heart with words —Shakespeare⟩
2 : to remove or undo from packing or a container ⟨*unpacked* his gear⟩
3 : to analyze the nature of by examining in detail : EXPLICATE ⟨*unpack* a concept⟩
intransitive verb
: to engage in unpacking a container
— **un·pack·er** *noun*

un·paged \-'pājd\ *adjective* (1874)
: having no page numbers

un·paid \-'pād\ *adjective* (14th century)
1 : not paid ⟨*unpaid* volunteer⟩
2 : not paying a salary ⟨an *unpaid* position⟩

un·paired \-'pard, -'perd\ *adjective* (1648)
1 : not paired; *especially* **:** not matched or mated
2 : characterized by the absence of pairing ⟨electrons in the *unpaired* state⟩

un·pal·at·able \-'pa-lə-tə-bəl\ *adjective* (1682)
1 : not palatable : DISTASTEFUL
2 : UNPLEASANT, DISAGREEABLE
— **un·pal·at·abil·i·ty** \ən-ˌpa-lə-tə-'bi-lə-tē\ *noun*

un·par·al·leled \ən-'par-ə-ˌleld, -ləld\ *adjective* (1594)
: having no parallel; *especially* **:** having no equal or match : unique in kind or quality

un·par·lia·men·ta·ry \ˌən-ˌpär-lə-'men-tə-rē, -ˌpärl-yə-, -'men-trē\ *adjective* (1626)
: contrary to the practice of parliamentary bodies

un·peg \ˌən-'peg\ *transitive verb* (1602)
1 : to remove a peg from
2 : to unfasten by or as if by removing a peg

un·peo·ple \-'pē-pəl\ *transitive verb* (circa 1533)
: DEPOPULATE

un·peo·pled \ən-'pē-pəld\ *adjective* (circa 1586)
: not filled with or occupied by people

un·per·fect \-'pər-fikt\ *adjective* (14th century)
: IMPERFECT

un·per·son \'ən-ˌpər-sʲn, -ˌpər-\ *noun* (1949)

: an individual who usually for political or ideological reasons is removed completely from recognition or consideration

un·pick \ən-'pik\ *transitive verb* (circa 1775)
: to undo (as sewing) by taking out stitches

un·pile \-'pī(ə)l\ *transitive verb* (1611)
: to take or disentangle from a pile

un·pin \-'pin\ *transitive verb* (14th century)
1 : to remove a pin from
2 : to loosen, free, or unfasten by or as if by removing a pin

un·placed \ən-'plāst\ *adjective* (1512)
1 : not placed : not having a definite or assigned place ⟨taxonomically *unplaced* organisms⟩
2 : not finishing in one of the first three places in a horse race

un·pleas·ant \-'ple-zʲnt\ *adjective* (1538)
: not pleasant : not amiable or agreeable : DISPLEASING ⟨*unpleasant* odors⟩
— **un·pleas·ant·ly** *adverb*

un·pleas·ant·ness *noun* (1548)
1 : the quality or state of being unpleasant
2 : an unpleasant situation, experience, or event

un·plug \ˌən-'pləg\ *transitive verb* (circa 1775)
1 a : to take a plug out of **b :** to remove an obstruction from
2 a : to remove (as an electric plug) from a socket or receptacle **b :** to disconnect from an electric circuit by removing a plug ⟨*unplug* the refrigerator⟩

un·plumbed \-'pləmd\ *adjective* (1623)
1 : not tested with a plumb line
2 a : not measured with a plumb **b :** not thoroughly explored

un·po·lar·ized \-'pō-lə-ˌrīzd\ *adjective* (circa 1828)
: not polarized; *specifically* **:** having a random pattern of vibrations

un·po·lit·i·cal \ˌən-pə-'li-ti-kəl\ *adjective* (1643)
: APOLITICAL 1

un·pop·u·lar \ˌən-'pä-pyə-lər\ *adjective* (1647)
: not popular : viewed or received unfavorably by the public
— **un·pop·u·lar·i·ty** \ˌən-ˌpä-pyə-'lar-ə-tē\ *noun*

un·prec·e·dent·ed \ˌən-'pre-sə-ˌden-təd\ *adjective* (1623)
: having no precedent : NOVEL, UNEXAMPLED
— **un·prec·e·dent·ed·ly** *adverb*

un·preg·nant \ˌən-'preg-nənt\ *adjective* (1602)
obsolete **:** INEPT 1

un·pre·tend·ing \ˌən-pri-'ten-diṅ\ *adjective* (1697)
: UNPRETENTIOUS

un·pre·ten·tious \-'ten(t)-shəs\ *adjective* (1859)
: free from ostentation, elegance, or affectation : MODEST ⟨*unpretentious* homes⟩
— **un·pre·ten·tious·ly** *adverb*
— **un·pre·ten·tious·ness** *noun*

☆ **SYNONYMS**
Unnerve, enervate, unman, emasculate mean to deprive of strength or vigor and the capacity for effective action. UNNERVE implies marked often temporary loss of courage, self-control, or power to act ⟨*unnerved* by the near collision⟩. ENERVATE suggests a gradual physical or moral weakening (as through luxury or indolence) until one is too feeble to make an effort ⟨a nation's youth *enervated* by affluence and leisure⟩. UNMAN implies a loss of manly vigor, fortitude, or spirit ⟨a soldier *unmanned* by the terrors of battle⟩. EMASCULATE stresses a depriving of characteristic force by removing something essential ⟨an amendment that *emasculates* existing safeguards⟩.

un·prin·ci·pled \ˌən-ˈprin(t)-s(ə-)pəld, -sə-bəld\ *adjective* (1644)
: lacking moral principles : UNSCRUPULOUS
— **un·prin·ci·pled·ness** *noun*

un·print·able \-ˈprin-tə-bəl\ *adjective* (1871)
: unfit to be printed

un·pro·fessed \ˌən-prə-ˈfest\ *adjective* (15th century)
: not professed 〈an *unprofessed* aim〉

un·prof·it·able \ˌən-ˈprä-fə-tə-bəl, -ˈpräf-tə-bəl\ *adjective* (14th century)
: not profitable : producing no gain, good, or result
— **un·prof·it·able·ness** *noun*
— **un·prof·it·ably** \-blē\ *adverb*

un·prom·is·ing \-ˈprä-mə-siŋ\ *adjective* (1663)
: appearing unlikely to prove worthwhile or result favorably
— **un·prom·is·ing·ly** \-siŋ-lē\ *adverb*

un·pro·nounced \ˌən-prə-ˈnaün(t)st\ *adjective* (1611)
: not pronounced; *especially* : MUTE

un·pub·lish·able \-ˈpə-bli-shə-bəl\ *adjective* (1815)
: UNPRINTABLE

un·qual·i·fied \ˌən-ˈkwä-lə-ˌfīd\ *adjective* (1556)
1 : not fit : not having requisite qualifications
2 : not modified or restricted by reservations : COMPLETE 〈an *unqualified* denial〉
— **un·qual·i·fied·ly** \-ˌfī(-ə)d-lē\ *adverb*

un·ques·tion·able \-ˈkwes-chə-nə-bəl, -ˈkwesh-\ *adjective* (1631)
: not questionable : INDISPUTABLE 〈*unquestionable* evidence〉
— **un·ques·tion·ably** \-blē\ *adverb*

un·ques·tion·ing \-ˈkwes-chə-niŋ, -ˈkwesh-\ *adjective* (circa 1828)
: not questioning : not expressing or marked by doubt or hesitation 〈*unquestioning* obedience〉
— **un·ques·tion·ing·ly** \-niŋ-lē\ *adverb*

un·qui·et \-ˈkwī-ət\ *adjective* (1523)
1 : not quiet : AGITATED, TURBULENT
2 : physically, emotionally, or mentally restless : UNEASY
— **un·qui·et·ly** *adverb*
— **un·qui·et·ness** *noun*

un·quote \ˈən-ˌkwōt *also* -ˌkōt\ *noun* (1915)
— used orally to indicate the end of a direct quotation

un·rav·el \ˌən-ˈra-vəl\ (1603)
transitive verb
1 a : to disengage or separate the threads of : DISENTANGLE **b** : to cause to come apart by or as if by separating the threads of
2 : to resolve the intricacy, complexity, or obscurity of : clear up 〈*unravel* a mystery〉
intransitive verb
: to become unraveled

un·read \-ˈred\ *adjective* (15th century)
1 : not read : left unexamined
2 : lacking the experience or the benefits of reading 〈*unread* in political science〉

un·re·al \-ˈrē(-ə)l, -ˈri(-ə)l\ *adjective* (1605)
: lacking in reality, substance, or genuineness : ARTIFICIAL, ILLUSORY; *also* : INCREDIBLE, FANTASTIC

un·re·al·is·tic \ˌən-ˌrē-ə-ˈlis-tik, -ˌri-ə-\ *adjective* (1865)
: not realistic : inappropriate to reality or fact
— **un·re·al·is·ti·cal·ly** \-ti-k(ə-)lē\ *adverb*

un·re·al·i·ty \ˌən-rē-ˈa-lə-tē\ *noun* (1751)
1 a : the quality or state of being unreal : lack of substance or validity **b** : something unreal, insubstantial, or visionary : FIGMENT
2 : ineptitude in dealing with reality

un·rea·son \ˌən-ˈrē-zⁿn, ˈən-ˌ\ *noun* (1827)
: the absence of reason or sanity : IRRATIONALITY, MADNESS

un·rea·son·able \-ˈrēz-nə-bəl, -ˈrē-zⁿn-ə-bəl\ *adjective* (14th century)
1 a : not governed by or acting according to reason 〈*unreasonable* people〉 **b** : not conformable to reason : ABSURD 〈*unreasonable* beliefs〉

2 : exceeding the bounds of reason or moderation 〈working under *unreasonable* pressure〉
— **un·rea·son·able·ness** \-nəs\ *noun*
— **un·rea·son·ably** \-blē\ *adverb*

un·rea·soned \-ˈrē-zⁿnd\ *adjective* (1790)
: not founded on reason or reasoning

un·rea·son·ing \-ˈrēz-niŋ, -ˈrē-zⁿn-iŋ\ *adjective* (1751)
: not reasoning; *especially* : not moderated or controlled by reason 〈*unreasoning* fear〉
— **un·rea·son·ing·ly** \-ˈrēz-niŋ-lē, -ˈrē-zⁿn-iŋ-\ *adverb*

un·re·con·struct·ed \ˌən-ˌrē-kən-ˈstrək-təd\ *adjective* (1867)
: not reconciled to some political, economic, or social change 〈an *unreconstructed* rebel〉; *also* : holding stubbornly to a particular belief, view, place, or style 〈an *unreconstructed* New Yorker〉

un·reel \ˌən-ˈrē(ə)l\ (1567)
transitive verb
1 : to unwind from a reel
2 : to perform successfully 〈*unreeled* a 66-yard pass play〉
3 : REEL OFF 2
intransitive verb
1 : to become unwound
2 : to be presented 〈the dress rehearsal *unreeled* flawlessly〉

un·reeve \-ˈrēv\ *transitive verb* **-rove** \-ˈrōv\ *or* **-reeved; -reev·ing** (1600)
: to withdraw (a rope) from an opening (as a ship's block or thimble)

un·re·gen·er·ate \ˌən-ri-ˈje-nə-rət, -ˈjen-rət\ *adjective* (1589)
1 : not regenerate 〈the *unregenerate* condition of humanity〉 〈*unregenerate* pagans〉
2 a : not reformed : UNRECONSTRUCTED 〈*unregenerate* liberals〉 〈*unregenerate* Confederates〉 **b** : OBSTINATE, STUBBORN 〈struggling against *unregenerate* impulses〉 〈his *unregenerate* competitiveness〉
— **un·re·gen·er·ate·ly** *adverb*

un·re·lent·ing \-ˈlen-tiŋ\ *adjective* (1588)
1 : not softening or yielding in determination : HARD, STERN 〈an *unrelenting* leader〉
2 : not letting up or weakening in vigor or pace : CONSTANT 〈the *unrelenting* struggle〉
— **un·re·lent·ing·ly** \-tiŋ-lē\ *adverb*

un·re·marked \-ˈmärkt\ *adjective* (circa 1775)
: not remarked : UNNOTICED

un·re·mit·ting \-ˈmi-tiŋ\ *adjective* (1728)
: not remitting : CONSTANT, INCESSANT
— **un·re·mit·ting·ly** \-tiŋ-lē\ *adverb*

un·re·quit·ed \ˌən-ri-ˈkwī-təd\ *adjective* (1542)
: not requited : not reciprocated or returned in kind 〈*unrequited* love〉

un·re·serve \-ˈzərv\ *noun* (1751)
: absence of reserve : FRANKNESS

un·re·served \-ˈzərvd\ *adjective* (1539)
1 : not limited or partial : ENTIRE, UNQUALIFIED 〈*unreserved* enthusiasm〉
2 : not cautious or reticent : FRANK, OPEN
3 : not set aside for special use
— **un·re·serv·ed·ly** \-ˈzər-vəd-lē\ *adverb*
— **un·re·served·ness** \-ˈzər-vəd-nəs, -ˈzərv(d)-nəs\ *noun*

un·rest \ˌən-ˈrest\ *noun* (14th century)
: a disturbed or uneasy state : TURMOIL

un·re·strained \ˌən-ri-ˈstränd\ *adjective* (circa 1600)
1 : not restrained : IMMODERATE, UNCONTROLLED 〈*unrestrained* proliferation of technology〉
2 : free of constraint : SPONTANEOUS 〈felt happy and *unrestrained*〉
— **un·re·strain·ed·ly** \-ˈstrā-nəd-lē\ *adverb*
— **un·re·strained·ness** \-ˈstrā-nəd-nəs, -ˈsträn(d)-nəs\ *noun*

un·re·straint \-ˈstränt\ *noun* (1804)
: freedom from or lack of restraint

un·rid·dle \ˌən-ri-ˈdⁿl\ *transitive verb* (circa 1586)

: to find the explanation of : FIGURE OUT, SOLVE 〈*unriddle* a puzzle〉 〈no trouble *unriddling* three-part syllogisms —*New Yorker*〉; *also* : to make understandable : EXPLAIN 〈just trying to *unriddle* the man —Helen Dudar〉

un·rig \-ˈrig\ *transitive verb* (circa 1580)
: to strip of rigging 〈*unrig* a ship〉

un·righ·teous \-ˈrī-chəs\ *adjective* (before 12th century)
1 : not righteous : SINFUL, WICKED
2 : UNJUST, UNMERITED 〈intolerable and *unrighteous* interference in their lives —W. W. Wagar〉
— **un·righ·teous·ly** *adverb*
— **un·righ·teous·ness** *noun*

un·ripe \-ˈrīp\ *adjective* (13th century)
1 : not ripe : IMMATURE
2 : not ready : UNPREPARED
— **un·ripe·ness** *noun*

un·ri·valed *or* **un·ri·valled** \ˌən-ˈrī-vəld\ *adjective* (1591)
: having no rival : INCOMPARABLE, SUPREME

un·roll \-ˈrōl\ (15th century)
transitive verb
1 : to unwind a roll of : open out : UNCOIL
2 : to spread out like a scroll for reading or inspection : UNFOLD, REVEAL
intransitive verb
: to be unrolled : UNWIND

un·roof \-ˈrüf, -ˈrúf\ *transitive verb* (1598)
: to strip off the roof or covering of

¹un·round \-ˌən-ˈraünd\ *transitive verb* (1874)
1 : to pronounce (a sound) without lip rounding or with decreased lip rounding
2 : to spread (the lips) laterally 〈necessary to *unround* the lips in pronouncing \ē\〉

²unround *adjective* (1958)
: pronounced with the lips not rounded

un·ruf·fled \ˌən-ˈrə-fəld\ *adjective* (1659)
1 : poised and serene especially in the face of setbacks or confusion
2 : not ruffled : SMOOTH 〈*unruffled* water〉
synonym see COOL

un·ruly \ˌən-ˈrü-lē\ *adjective* [Middle English *unreuly*, from *un-* + *reuly* disciplined, from *reule* rule] (15th century)
: not readily ruled, disciplined, or managed 〈an *unruly* crowd〉 〈a mane of *unruly* hair〉 ☆
— **un·rul·i·ness** *noun*

un·sad·dle \ˌən-ˈsa-dⁿl\ (14th century)
transitive verb
1 : to take the saddle from

☆ **SYNONYMS**
Unruly, ungovernable, intractable, refractory, recalcitrant, willful, headstrong mean not submissive to government or control. UNRULY implies lack of discipline or incapacity for discipline and often connotes waywardness or turbulence of behavior 〈*unruly* children〉. UNGOVERNABLE implies either an escape from control or guidance or a state of being unsubdued and incapable of controlling oneself or being controlled by others 〈*ungovernable* rage〉. INTRACTABLE suggests stubborn resistance to guidance or control 〈*intractable* opponents of the hazardous-waste dump〉. REFRACTORY stresses resistance to attempts to manage or to mold 〈special schools for *refractory* children〉. RECALCITRANT suggests determined resistance to or defiance of authority 〈acts of sabotage by a *recalcitrant* populace〉. WILLFUL implies an obstinate determination to have one's own way 〈a *willful* disregard for the rights of others〉. HEADSTRONG suggests self-will impatient of restraint, advice, or suggestion 〈a *headstrong* young calvary officer〉.

2 : to throw from the saddle
intransitive verb
: to remove the saddle from a horse
un·said \-'sed\ *adjective* (before 12th century)
: not said; *especially* **:** not spoken aloud
un·sat·is·fac·to·ry \-,sa-təs-'fak-t(ə-)rē\ *adjective* (circa 1650)
: not satisfactory
— **un·sat·is·fac·to·ri·ly** \-t(ə-)rə-lē\ *adverb*
— **un·sat·is·fac·to·ri·ness** \-t(ə-)rē-nəs\ *noun*
un·sat·u·rate \-'sa-chə-rət, -'sach-rət\ *noun* (1934)
: an unsaturated chemical compound
un·sat·u·rat·ed \-'sa-chə-,rā-təd\ *adjective* (1758)
: not saturated: as **a :** capable of absorbing or dissolving more of something ⟨an *unsaturated* solution⟩ **b :** able to form products by chemical addition; *especially* **:** containing double or triple bonds between carbon atoms
un·saved \,ən-'sāvd\ *adjective* (1648)
: not saved; *especially* **:** not absolved from eternal punishment **:** not regenerate
un·sa·vory \-'sā-və-rē, -'sāv-rē\ *adjective* (13th century)
1 : INSIPID, TASTELESS
2 a : unpleasant to taste or smell **b :** DISAGREEABLE, DISTASTEFUL ⟨an *unsavory* assignment⟩; *especially* **:** morally offensive
un·say \-'sā, *Southern also* -'se\ *transitive verb* **-said** \-'sed\; **-say·ing** \-'sā-iŋ\ (15th century)
: to make as if not said **:** RECANT, RETRACT
un·say·able \-'sā-ə-bəl\ *adjective* (1870)
: not sayable **:** not easily expressed or related
un·scathed \-'skā<u>th</u>d\ *adjective* (14th century)
: wholly unharmed **:** not injured
un·schooled \-'sküld\ *adjective* (1589)
1 : not schooled **:** UNTAUGHT, UNTRAINED ⟨an *unschooled* woodsman⟩
2 : not artificial **:** NATURAL ⟨*unschooled* talent⟩
un·sci·en·tif·ic \,ən-,sī-ən-'ti-fik\ *adjective* (circa 1775)
: not scientific: as **a :** not used in scientific work **b :** not being in accord with the principles and methods of science ⟨*unscientific* management of woodlands⟩ ⟨an *unscientific* survey⟩ **c :** not showing scientific knowledge or familiarity with scientific methods
— **un·sci·en·tif·i·cal·ly** \-fi-k(ə-)lē\ *adverb*
un·scram·ble \,ən-'skram-bəl\ *transitive verb* (circa 1920)
1 : to separate (as a conglomeration or tangle) into original components **:** RESOLVE, CLARIFY
2 : to restore (scrambled communication) to intelligible form
— **un·scram·bler** \-b(ə-)lər\ *noun*
un·screw \-'skrü\ (1605)
transitive verb
1 : to draw the screws from
2 : to loosen or withdraw by turning
intransitive verb
: to become or admit of being unscrewed
un·script·ed \-'skrip-təd\ *adjective* (circa 1950)
: not following a prepared script
un·scru·pu·lous \-'skrü-pyə-ləs\ *adjective* (1803)
: not scrupulous **:** UNPRINCIPLED
— **un·scru·pu·lous·ly** *adverb*
— **un·scru·pu·lous·ness** *noun*
un·seal \-'sē(ə)l\ *transitive verb* (15th century)
: to break or remove the seal of
un·sealed \-'sē(ə)ld\ *adjective* (14th century)
: not sealed
un·seam \,ən-'sēm\ *transitive verb* (1592)
: to open the seams of
un·search·able \-'sər-chə-bəl\ *adjective* (14th century)
: not capable of being searched or explored **:** INSCRUTABLE
— **un·search·ably** \-blē\ *adverb*

un·sea·son·able \-'sēz-nə-bəl, -'sē-z°n-ə-\ *adjective* (15th century)
1 : occurring at other than the proper time **:** UNTIMELY
2 : not being in season
3 a : not normal for the season of the year ⟨*unseasonable* weather⟩ **b :** marked by unseasonable weather ⟨an *unseasonable* summer⟩
— **un·sea·son·able·ness** *noun*
— **un·sea·son·ably** \-blē\ *adverb*
un·seat \-'sēt\ *transitive verb* (1596)
1 : to dislodge from one's seat especially on horseback
2 : to remove from a place or position; *especially* **:** to remove from political office
¹un·seem·ly \-'sēm-lē\ *adjective* (14th century)
: not seemly: as **a :** not according with established standards of good form or taste ⟨*unseemly* bickering⟩ **b :** not suitable for time or place **:** INAPPROPRIATE, UNSEASONABLE
synonym see INDECOROUS
— **un·seem·li·ness** \-lē-nəs\ *noun*
²unseemly *adverb* (14th century)
: in an unseemly manner
un·seen \,ən-'sēn\ *adjective* (13th century)
1 : not seen or perceived
2 : SIGHT 1 ⟨an *unseen* translation⟩
un·seg·re·gat·ed \-'se-gri-,gā-təd\ *adjective* (1905)
: not segregated; *especially* **:** free from racial segregation
un·se·lect·ed \,ən-sə-'lek-təd\ *adjective* (circa 1891)
: not selected **:** chosen at random
un·se·lec·tive \-'lek-tiv\ *adjective* (circa 1925)
: not marked by selection **:** RANDOM, INDISCRIMINATE
— **un·se·lec·tive·ly** \-lē\ *adverb*
un·self·ish \,ən-'sel-fish\ *adjective* (1698)
: not selfish **:** GENEROUS
— **un·self·ish·ly** *adverb*
— **un·self·ish·ness** *noun*
un·sell \-'sel\ *transitive verb* **-sold** \-'sōld\; **-sell·ing** (circa 1929)
1 : to dissuade from a belief in the truth, value, or desirability of something ⟨ads that *unsell* the public on energy consumption⟩
2 : to discourage a belief in the truth, value, or desirability of ⟨I *unsold* the coat he wanted and sold him another⟩
un·set \-'set\ *adjective* (14th century)
: not set: as **a :** not fixed in a setting **:** UNMOUNTED ⟨*unset* diamonds⟩ **b :** not firmed or solidified ⟨*unset* concrete⟩
un·set·tle \,ən-'se-t°l\ (1598)
transitive verb
1 : to loosen or move from a settled state or condition **:** make unstable **:** DISORDER
2 : to perturb or agitate mentally or emotionally **:** DISCOMPOSE
intransitive verb
: to become unsettled
un·set·tled \-'se-t°ld\ *adjective* (1591)
: not settled: as **a (1) :** not calm or tranquil **:** DISTURBED ⟨*unsettled* political conditions⟩ **(2) :** likely to vary widely especially in the near future **:** VARIABLE ⟨*unsettled* weather⟩ **(3) :** not settled down ⟨*unsettled* dust⟩ **b (1) :** not decided or determined **:** DOUBTFUL ⟨an *unsettled* state of mind⟩ **(2) :** not resolved or worked out **:** UNDECIDED ⟨an *unsettled* question⟩ **c :** characterized by irregularity ⟨an *unsettled* life⟩ **d :** not inhabited or populated ⟨*unsettled* land⟩ **e :** mentally unbalanced **f (1) :** not disposed of according to law ⟨an *unsettled* estate⟩ **(2) :** not paid or discharged ⟨*unsettled* debts⟩
— **un·set·tled·ness** \-t°l(d)-nəs\ *noun*
un·set·tling \,ən-'set-liŋ, -'se-t°l-iŋ\ *adjective* (1665)
: having the effect of upsetting, disturbing, or discomposing ⟨*unsettling* images of the war⟩
un·set·tle·ment \-t°l-mənt\ *noun* (1648)
1 : an act, process, or instance of unsettling

2 : the quality or state of being unsettled
un·sew \,ən-'sō\ *transitive verb* **-sewed**; **-sewn** \-'sōn\ *or* **-sewed**; **-sew·ing** (14th century)
: to undo the sewing of
un·sex \-'seks\ *transitive verb* (1605)
1 : to deprive of sex or sexual power
2 : to deprive of the qualities typical of one's sex
un·shack·le \-'sha-kəl\ *transitive verb* (1611)
: to free from shackles
un·shaped \-'shāpt\ *adjective* (1572)
: not shaped: as **a :** not dressed or finished to final form ⟨an *unshaped* timber⟩ **b :** imperfect in form or formulation ⟨*unshaped* ideas⟩
un·shap·en \-'shā-pən\ *adjective* [Middle English, from ¹*un-* + *shapen,* past participle of *shapen* to shape] (14th century)
: UNSHAPED
un·sheathe \,ən-'shē<u>th</u>\ *transitive verb* (circa 1542)
: to draw from or as if from a sheath or scabbard
un·ship \-'ship\ (15th century)
transitive verb
1 : to take out of a ship **:** DISCHARGE, UNLOAD
2 : to remove (as an oar or tiller) from position **:** DETACH
intransitive verb
: to become or admit of being detached or removed
un·shod \,ən-'shäd\ *adjective* (before 12th century)
: not wearing or provided with shoes
¹un·sight \-'sīt\ *transitive verb* (1615)
: to prevent from seeing
²unsight *adjective* (circa 1622)
: not sighted or examined
un·sight·ly \,ən-'sīt-lē\ *adjective* (15th century)
: not pleasing to the sight **:** not comely
— **un·sight·li·ness** \-lē-nəs\ *noun*
un·skilled \-'skild\ *adjective* (1581)
1 : not skilled in a branch of work **:** lacking technical training ⟨an *unskilled* worker⟩
2 : not requiring skill ⟨*unskilled* jobs⟩
3 : marked by lack of skill ⟨produced *unskilled* poems⟩
un·skill·ful \-'skil-fəl\ *adjective* (1565)
: not skillful **:** lacking in skill or proficiency
— **un·skill·ful·ly** \-fə-lē\ *adverb*
— **un·skill·ful·ness** *noun*
un·slak·able \,ən-'slā-kə-bəl\ *adjective* (1820)
: unable to be slaked **:** UNQUENCHABLE ⟨an *unslakable* thirst⟩ ⟨an *unslakable* desire for excellence⟩
un·sling \-'sliŋ\ *transitive verb* **-slung** \-'sləŋ\; **-sling·ing** \-'sliŋ-iŋ\ (1630)
1 : to take off the slings of especially aboard ship **:** release from slings
2 : to remove from being slung ⟨*unslung* the carbine⟩
un·snap \-'snap\ *transitive verb* (1862)
: to loosen or free by or as if by undoing a snap
un·snarl \-'snär(-ə)l\ *transitive verb* (1555)
: to disentangle a snarl in
un·so·cia·ble \,ən-'sō-shə-bəl\ *adjective* (1600)
1 : having or showing a disinclination for social activity **:** SOLITARY, RESERVED
2 : not conducive to sociability
— **un·so·cia·bil·i·ty** \,ən-,sō-shə-'bi-lə-tē\ *noun*
— **un·so·cia·ble·ness** \,ən-'sō-shə-bəl-nəs\ *noun*
— **un·so·cia·bly** \-blē\ *adverb*
un·so·cial \-'sō-shəl\ *adjective* (1731)
: lacking a taste or desire for society or close association; *also* **:** marked by or arising from such a lack ⟨an *unsocial* disposition⟩
— **un·so·cial·ly** \-'sō-sh(ə-)lē\ *adverb*
un·sold \-'sōld\ *adjective* (14th century)
: not sold

un·so·phis·ti·cat·ed \ˌən-sə-ˈfis-tə-ˌkā-təd\ *adjective* (1630)
: not sophisticated: as **a** : not changed or corrupted **: GENUINE b** (1) : not worldly-wise : lacking social or economic sophistication (2) : lacking complexity of structure **: SIMPLE, STRAIGHTFORWARD** ⟨an *unsophisticated* analysis⟩ ⟨*unsophisticated* rhythms⟩
synonym see NATURAL

un·so·phis·ti·ca·tion \-ˌfis-tə-ˈkā-shən\ *noun* (1825)
: lack of or freedom from sophistication

un·sought \ˌən-ˈsȯt\ *adjective* (13th century)
: not searched for or sought out ⟨*unsought* compliments⟩

un·sound \-ˈsau̇nd\ *adjective* (14th century)
: not sound: as **a** : not healthy or whole **b** : not mentally normal : not wholly sane **c** : not firmly made, placed, or fixed **d** : not valid or true **: INVALID, SPECIOUS**
— **un·sound·ly** \-ˈsau̇n(d)-lē\ *adverb*
— **un·sound·ness** \-ˈsau̇n(d)-nəs\ *noun* (1586)
1 : the quality or state of being unsound
2 : something (as a disease, injury, or defect) that causes one to be unsound

un·spar·ing \-ˈspar-iŋ, -ˈsper-\ *adjective* (circa 1586)
1 : not merciful or forbearing **: HARD, RUTHLESS**
2 : not frugal **: LIBERAL, PROFUSE**
— **un·spar·ing·ly** \-iŋ-lē\ *adverb*

un·speak \-ˈspēk\ *transitive verb* (1605)
obsolete **: UNSAY**

un·speak·able \-ˈspē-kə-bəl\ *adjective* (14th century)
1 a : incapable of being expressed in words **: UNUTTERABLE b** : inexpressibly bad **: HORRENDOUS**
2 : that may not or cannot be spoken ⟨the bawdy thoughts that come into one's head — the *unspeakable* words —L. P. Smith⟩ ⟨*unspeakable* collections of consonants —Rosemary Jellis⟩
— **un·speak·ably** \-blē\ *adverb*

un·sports·man·like \-ˈspȯrts-mən-ˌlīk, -ˈspȯrts-\ *adjective* (1754)
: not characteristic of or exhibiting good sportsmanship : not sportsmanlike

un·spot·ted \-ˈspä-təd\ *adjective* (14th century)
: not spotted : free from spot or stain; *especially* : free from moral stain

un·sprung \-ˈsprəŋ\ *adjective* (1600)
: not sprung; *especially* : not equipped with springs

un·sta·ble \-ˈstā-bəl\ *adjective* (13th century)
: not stable : not firm or fixed : not constant: as **a** : not steady in action or movement **: IRREGULAR** ⟨an *unstable* pulse⟩ **b** : wavering in purpose or intent **: VACILLATING c** : lacking steadiness : apt to move, sway, or fall ⟨an *unstable* tower⟩ **d** (1) : liable to change or alteration ⟨an *unstable* economy⟩ ⟨*unstable* weather⟩ (2) : readily changing (as by decomposing) in chemical composition or biological activity **e** : characterized by lack of emotional control
synonym see INCONSTANT
— **un·sta·ble·ness** *noun*
— **un·sta·bly** \-b(ə-)lē\ *adverb*

¹**un·steady** \ˌən-ˈste-dē\ *transitive verb* (1532)
: to make unsteady

²**unsteady** *adjective* (1598)
: not steady: as **a** : not firm or solid : not fixed in position **: UNSTABLE b** : marked by change or fluctuation **: CHANGEABLE c** : not uniform or even **: IRREGULAR**
— **un·stead·i·ly** \-ˈste-dᵊl-ē\ *adverb*
— **un·stead·i·ness** \-ˈste-dē-nəs\ *noun*

un·step \-ˈstep\ *transitive verb* (1853)
: to remove (a mast) from a step

un·stick \-ˈstik\ *transitive verb* **-stuck** \-ˈstək\; **-stick·ing** (1706)
: to release from a state of adhesion

un·stint·ing \-ˈstin-tiŋ\ *adjective* (1845)
: not restricting or holding back : giving or being given freely or generously ⟨an *unstinting* volunteer⟩ ⟨*unstinting* praise⟩
— **un·stint·ing·ly** *adverb*

un·stop \-ˈstäp\ *transitive verb* (14th century)
1 : to free from an obstruction **: OPEN**
2 : to remove a stopper from

un·stop·pa·ble \-ˈstä-pə-bəl\ *adjective* (1836)
: incapable of being stopped
— **un·stop·pa·bly** \-blē\ *adverb*

un·strap \-ˈstrap\ *transitive verb* (1828)
: to remove or loose a strap from

un·stressed \-ˈstrest\ *adjective* (1883)
1 : not bearing a stress or accent ⟨*unstressed* syllables⟩
2 : not subjected to stress ⟨*unstressed* wires⟩

un·string \-ˈstriŋ\ *transitive verb* **-strung** \-ˈstrəŋ\; **-string·ing** \-ˈstriŋ-iŋ\ (1611)
1 : to loosen or remove the strings of
2 : to remove from a string
3 : to make weak, disordered, or unstable ⟨was *unstrung* by the news⟩

un·struc·tured \-ˈstrək-chərd\ *adjective* (1936)
: lacking structure or organization: as **a** : not formally organized in a set or conventional pattern ⟨an *unstructured* question⟩ ⟨feel insecure in an *unstructured* situation⟩ **b** : not having a system or hierarchy typical of an organized society

un·stuck \ˌən-ˈstək\ *adjective* (1934)
: brought into a state of disarray, discomposure, or incoherence ⟨the deal came *unstuck*⟩

un·stud·ied \-ˈstə-dēd\ *adjective* (14th century)
: not studied: as **a** : not acquired by study **b** : not forced : not done or planned for effect

un·sub·stan·tial \ˌən-səb-ˈstan(t)-shəl\ *adjective* (15th century)
: not substantial : lacking substance, firmness, or strength
— **un·sub·stan·ti·al·i·ty** \-ˌstan(t)-shē-ˈa-lə-tē\ *noun*
— **un·sub·stan·tial·ly** \ˌən-səb-ˈstan(t)-sh(ə-)lē\ *adverb*

un·suc·cess \ˌən-sək-ˈses\ *noun* (circa 1586)
: lack of success **: FAILURE**

un·suc·cess·ful \-fəl\ *adjective* (1617)
: not successful : not meeting with or producing success
— **un·suc·cess·ful·ly** \-fə-lē\ *adverb*

un·sung \ˌən-ˈsəŋ\ *adjective* (15th century)
1 : not sung
2 : not celebrated or praised (as in song or verse) ⟨an *unsung* hero⟩

un·sur·pris·ing \ˌən-sə(r)-ˈprī-ziŋ\ *adjective* (1671)
: not surprising or unexpected
— **un·sur·pris·ing·ly** \-ziŋ-lē\ *adverb* (1950)
1 : as is not surprising ⟨matters complicate, *unsurprisingly* —Stanley Kauffmann⟩
2 : in an unsurprising manner ⟨the story ended *unsurprisingly*⟩

un·swathe \-ˈswäth, -ˈswȯth, -ˈswāth\ *transitive verb* (14th century)
: to free from something that swathes

un·swear \-ˈswar, -ˈswer\ *verb* **-swore** \-ˈswȯr, -ˈswȯr\; **-sworn** \-ˈswȯrn, -ˈswȯrn\; **swear·ing** (1596)
intransitive verb
archaic : to unsay or retract something sworn
transitive verb
archaic : to recant or recall (as an oath) especially by a second oath

un·swerv·ing \-ˈswər-viŋ\ *adjective* (1694)
1 : not swerving or turning aside
2 : STEADY, UNFALTERING ⟨*unswerving* loyalty⟩

un·sym·met·ri·cal \ˌən-sə-ˈme-tri-kəl\ *adjective* (circa 1755)
: ASYMMETRIC
— **un·sym·met·ri·cal·ly** \-k(ə-)lē\ *adverb*

un·tan·gle \ˌən-ˈtaŋ-gəl\ *transitive verb* (1550)
1 : to loose from tangles or entanglement
2 : straighten out
synonym see EXTRICATE

un·tapped \-ˈtapt\ *adjective* (circa 1775)

1 : not subjected to tapping ⟨an *untapped* keg⟩
2 : not drawn upon or utilized ⟨as yet *untapped* markets⟩

un·taught \-ˈtȯt\ *adjective* (14th century)
1 : not instructed or trained **: IGNORANT**
2 : NATURAL, SPONTANEOUS ⟨*untaught* kindness⟩

un·teach \-ˈtēch\ *transitive verb* **-taught** \-ˈtȯt\; **-teach·ing** (1532)
1 : to cause to unlearn something
2 : to teach the contrary of

un·ten·a·ble \-ˈte-nə-bəl\ *adjective* (1647)
1 : not able to be defended
2 : not able to be occupied
— **un·ten·a·bil·i·ty** \ˌən-ˌte-nə-ˈbi-lə-tē\ *noun*

un·tent·ed \-ˈten-təd\ *adjective* [¹un- + obsolete English *tented,* past participle of *tent* to probe] (1605)
archaic : not probed or dressed ⟨the *untented* woundings of a father's curse —Shakespeare⟩

un·teth·er \-ˈte-thər\ *transitive verb* (circa 1775)
: to free from a tether

un·think \-ˈthiŋk\ *transitive verb* **-thought** \-ˈthȯt\; **-think·ing** (circa 1600)
: to put out of mind

un·think·able \-ˈthiŋ-kə-bəl\ *adjective* (15th century)
1 : not capable of being grasped by the mind
2 : being contrary to what is reasonable, desirable, or probable : being out of the question
— **un·think·abil·i·ty** \ˌən-ˌthiŋ-kə-ˈbi-lə-tē\ *noun*
— **un·think·ably** \ˌən-ˈthiŋ-kə-blē\ *adverb*

un·think·ing \ˌən-ˈthiŋ-kiŋ\ *adjective* (1676)
1 : not taking thought **: HEEDLESS, UNMINDFUL**
2 : not indicating thought or reflection
3 : not having the power of thought
— **un·think·ing·ly** \-kiŋ-lē\ *adverb*

un·thought \-ˈthȯt\ *adjective* (circa 1548)
: not anticipated **: UNEXPECTED** — often used with *of* ⟨an *unthought*-of development⟩

un·thread \ˌən-ˈthred\ *transitive verb* (1595)
1 : to draw or take out a thread from
2 : to loosen the threads or connections of
3 : to make one's way through ⟨*unthread* a maze⟩

un·throne \-ˈthrōn\ *transitive verb* (1611)
: to remove from or as if from a throne

un·ti·dy \-ˈtī-dē\ *adjective* (14th century)
1 a : not neat **: SLOVENLY b** : not neat or orderly in habits or procedure ⟨an *untidy* mind⟩
2 a : not neatly organized or carried out ⟨an *untidy* manuscript⟩ **b** : conducive to a lack of neatness ⟨*untidy* tasks like bathing the baby —New Yorker⟩
— **un·ti·di·ly** \-ˈtī-dᵊl-ē\ *adverb*
— **un·ti·di·ness** \-ˈtī-dē-nəs\ *noun*

un·tie \-ˈtī\ *verb* **-tied; -ty·ing** *or* **-tie·ing** (before 12th century)
transitive verb
1 : to free from something that ties, fastens, or restrains **: UNBIND**
2 a : to disengage the knotted parts of **b : DISENTANGLE, RESOLVE** ⟨*untie* a traffic jam⟩
intransitive verb
: to become loosened or unbound

¹**un·til** \ən-ˈtil, -ˈtel; ˈən-ˌ, -tᵊl\ *preposition* [Middle English, from *un-* up to, until (akin to Old English *oth* to, until, Old High German *unt* up to, until, Old English *ende* end) + *til, till* till] (13th century)
1 *chiefly Scottish* **: TO**
2 — used as a function word to indicate continuance (as of an action or condition) to a specified time ⟨stayed *until* morning⟩
3 : BEFORE 2 ⟨not available *until* tomorrow⟩ ⟨we don't open *until* ten⟩

²**until** *conjunction* (14th century)

: up to the time that : up to such time as ⟨play continued *until* it got dark⟩ ⟨never able to relax *until* he took up fishing⟩ ⟨ran *until* he was breathless⟩

¹un·time·ly \ˌən-ˈtīm-lē\ *adverb* (13th century)
1 : at an inopportune time : UNSEASONABLY
2 : before the due, natural, or proper time : PREMATURELY ⟨went *untimely* to the grave⟩

²untimely *adjective* (1535)
1 : occurring or done before the due, natural, or proper time : too early : PREMATURE ⟨*untimely* death⟩
2 : INOPPORTUNE, UNSEASONABLE ⟨an *untimely* joke⟩ ⟨*untimely* frost⟩
— **un·time·li·ness** *noun*

un·time·ous \-ˈtī-məs\ *adjective* (15th century)
chiefly Scottish : UNTIMELY

un·tir·ing \-ˈtī-riŋ\ *adjective* (1822)
: not becoming tired : INDEFATIGABLE ⟨an *untiring* worker⟩
— **un·tir·ing·ly** *adverb*

un·ti·tled \-ˈtī-tᵊld\ *adjective* (1590)
1 *obsolete* : having no title or right to rule
2 : not named ⟨an *untitled* novel⟩
3 : not called by a title ⟨*untitled* nobility⟩

un·to \ˈən-(ˌ)tü\ *preposition* [Middle English, from *un-* up to, until + *to*] (14th century)
1 : TO
2 — used as a function word to indicate reference or concern ⟨they became a world *unto* themselves —Anne T. Fleming⟩

un·told \ˌən-ˈtōld\ *adjective* (15th century)
1 : too great or numerous to count : INCALCULABLE, VAST
2 a : not told or related **b** : kept secret

un·touch·abil·i·ty \ˌən-ˌtə-chə-ˈbi-lə-tē\ *noun* (1919)
: the quality or state of being untouchable; *especially* : the state of being an untouchable

¹un·touch·able \ˌən-ˈtə-chə-bəl\ *adjective* (1567)
1 a : forbidden to the touch : not to be handled **b** : exempt from criticism or control
2 : lying beyond reach
3 : disagreeable or defiling to the touch

²untouchable *noun* (1909)
: one that is untouchable; *specifically* : a member of a large formerly segregated hereditary group in India having in traditional Hindu belief the quality of defiling by contact a member of a higher caste

un·touched \ˌən-ˈtəcht\ *adjective* (14th century)
1 : not subjected to touching : not handled
2 : not described or dealt with
3 a : not tasted **b** : being in the first or a primeval state or condition
4 : not influenced : UNAFFECTED

un·to·ward \ˌən-ˈtō(-ə)rd, -ˈtȯ(-ə)rd; ˌən-tə-ˈwȯrd\ *adjective* (1526)
1 : difficult to guide, manage, or work with : UNRULY, INTRACTABLE
2 a : marked by trouble or unhappiness : UNLUCKY **b** : not favorable : ADVERSE, UNPROPITIOUS ⟨*untoward* side effects⟩
3 : IMPROPER, INDECOROUS
— **un·to·ward·ly** *adverb*
— **un·to·ward·ness** *noun*

un·tread \ˌən-ˈtred\ *transitive verb* (1592)
archaic : to tread back : RETRACE

un·tried \-ˈtrīd\ *adjective* (1526)
1 : not tested or proved by experience or trial
2 : not tried in court

un·trod \-ˈträd\ *or* **un·trod·den** \-ˈträ-dᵊn\ *adjective* (1593)
: not trod : UNTRAVERSED

un·trou·bled \-ˈtrə-bəld\ *adjective* (15th century)
1 : not given trouble : not made uneasy
2 : CALM, TRANQUIL

un·true \-ˈtrü\ *adjective* (before 12th century)
1 : not faithful : DISLOYAL
2 : not according with a standard of correctness : not level or exact

3 : not according with the facts : FALSE
— **un·tru·ly** \-ˈtrü-lē\ *adverb*

un·truss \-ˈtrəs\ (1577)
transitive verb
1 *archaic* : UNTIE, UNFASTEN — used in the phrase *untruss one's points*
2 *archaic* : UNDRESS
intransitive verb
archaic : to unfasten or take off one's clothes and especially one's breeches

un·truth \ˌən-ˈtrüth, ˈən-ˌ\ *noun* (before 12th century)
1 *archaic* : DISLOYALTY
2 : lack of truthfulness : FALSITY
3 : something that is untrue : FALSEHOOD

un·truth·ful \-ˈtrüth-fəl\ *adjective* (circa 1843)
: not containing or telling the truth : FALSE, INACCURATE ⟨*untruthful* report⟩
synonym see DISHONEST
— **un·truth·ful·ly** \-fə-lē\ *adverb*
— **un·truth·ful·ness** *noun*

un·tune \-ˈtün, -ˈtyün\ *transitive verb* (1598)
1 : to put out of tune
2 : DISARRANGE, DISCOMPOSE

un·tu·tored \-ˈtü-tərd, -ˈtyü-\ *adjective* (1593)
1 a : having no formal learning or training **b** : NAIVE, UNSOPHISTICATED
2 : not produced or developed by instruction : NATIVE ⟨*untutored* shrewdness⟩
synonym see IGNORANT

un·twine \-ˈtwīn\ (15th century)
transitive verb
1 : to unwind the twisted or tangled parts of : DISENTANGLE
2 : to remove by unwinding
intransitive verb
: to become disentangled or unwound

un·twist \ˌən-ˈtwist\ (1538)
transitive verb
: to separate the twisted parts of : UNTWINE
intransitive verb
: to become untwined

un·twist·ed \-ˈtwis-təd\ *adjective* (1575)
: not twisted

un·used \-ˈyüzd, *in the phrase "unused to"* usually -ˈyüs(t)\ *adjective* (14th century)
1 : not habituated : UNACCUSTOMED ⟨*unused* to crowds⟩
2 : not used: as **a** : FRESH, NEW ⟨set an *unused* canvas on the easel⟩ **b** : not put to use : IDLE ⟨*unused* land⟩ **c** : not consumed : ACCRUED ⟨*unused* sick leave⟩

un·usu·al \-ˈyü-zhə-wəl, -zhəl; -ˈyüzh-wəl\ *adjective* (1582)
: not usual : UNCOMMON, RARE
— **un·usu·al·ly** *adverb*
— **un·usu·al·ness** *noun*

un·ut·ter·able \ˌən-ˈə-tə-rə-bəl\ *adjective* (circa 1586)
: being beyond the powers of description : INEXPRESSIBLE
— **un·ut·ter·ably** \-blē\ *adverb*

un·val·ued \-ˈval-(ˌ)yüd, -yəd\ *adjective* (1586)
1 *obsolete* : INVALUABLE
2 a : not important or prized : DISREGARDED **b** : not appraised

un·var·nished \-ˈvär-nisht\ *adjective* (1604)
1 a : not adorned or glossed : PLAIN, STRAIGHTFORWARD ⟨told the *unvarnished* truth⟩ **b** : ARTLESS, FRANK ⟨the *unvarnished* candor of old people and children —Janet Flanner⟩
2 : not coated with or as if with varnish : CRUDE, UNFINISHED

un·veil \ˌən-ˈvā(ə)l\ (1599)
transitive verb
1 : to remove a veil or covering from
2 : to make public : DIVULGE, REVEAL
intransitive verb
: to throw off a veil or protective cloak

un·veiled \-ˈvā(ə)ld\ *adjective* (1606)
: not veiled : OPEN, REVEALED

un·vo·cal \ˌən-ˈvō-kəl\ *adjective* (1773)
1 : not eloquent or outspoken : INARTICULATE
2 : not musical : DISCORDANT

un·voice \-ˈvȯis\ *transitive verb* (1637)

: DEVOICE

un·voiced \-ˈvȯist\ *adjective* (1859)
1 : not verbally expressed
2 : VOICELESS 2

un·war·rant·able \-ˈwȯr-ən-tə-bəl, -ˈwär-\ *adjective* (1612)
: not justifiable : INEXCUSABLE
— **un·war·rant·ably** \-blē\ *adverb*

un·wary \ˌən-ˈwar-ē, -ˈwer-\ *adjective* (1579)
: not alert : easily fooled or surprised : HEEDLESS, GULLIBLE
— **un·wari·ly** \-ˈwar-ə-lē, -ˈwer-\ *adverb*
— **un·wari·ness** \-ˈwar-ē-nəs, -ˈwer-\ *noun*

¹un·washed \-ˈwȯsht, -ˈwäsht\ *adjective* (14th century)
1 : not cleaned with or as if with soap and water
2 : IGNORANT, PLEBEIAN
— **un·washed·ness** *noun*

²unwashed *noun* (1830)
: an ignorant or underprivileged group : RABBLE — usually used with *great* ⟨the great *unwashed*⟩

un·watch·able \ˌən-ˈwä-chə-bəl, -ˈwȯ-\ *adjective* (1886)
: not suitable or fit for watching : tending to discourage watching

un·wea·ried \-ˈwir-ēd\ *adjective* (13th century)
: not tired or jaded : FRESH
— **un·wea·ried·ly** *adverb*

un·weave \-ˈwēv\ *transitive verb* **-wove** \-ˈwōv\; **-wo·ven** \-ˈwō-vən\; **-weav·ing** (1542)
: DISENTANGLE, UNRAVEL

un·weet·ing \-ˈwē-tiŋ\ *adjective* (14th century)
archaic : UNWITTING
— **un·weet·ing·ly** \-tiŋ-lē\ *adverb, archaic*

un·weight \-ˈwāt\ (circa 1939)
transitive verb
: to reduce momentarily the force exerted by (as a ski) upon a surface by shifting the weight or position of one's body
intransitive verb
: to unweight something by shifting the weight or position of one's body

un·well \ˌən-ˈwel\ *adjective* (15th century)
1 : being in poor health : AILING, SICK
2 : undergoing menstruation

un·whole·some \-ˈhōl-səm\ *adjective* (13th century)
1 : detrimental to physical, mental, or moral well-being : UNHEALTHY ⟨*unwholesome* food⟩ ⟨*unwholesome* pastimes⟩
2 a : CORRUPT, UNSOUND **b** : offensive to the senses : LOATHSOME
— **un·whole·some·ly** *adverb*

un·wieldy \-ˈwē(ə)l-dē\ *adjective* (1530)
: not easily managed, handled, or used (as because of bulk, weight, complexity, or awkwardness) : CUMBERSOME
— **un·wield·i·ly** \-ˈwēl-də-lē\ *adverb*
— **un·wield·i·ness** \-dē-nəs\ *noun*

un·will·ing \-ˈwi-liŋ\ *adjective* (before 12th century)
: not willing: **a** : LOATH, RELUCTANT ⟨was *unwilling* to learn⟩ **b** : done or given reluctantly ⟨*unwilling* approval⟩ **c** : offering opposition : OBSTINATE ⟨an *unwilling* student⟩
— **un·will·ing·ly** \-liŋ-lē\ *adverb*
— **un·will·ing·ness** *noun*

un·wind \-ˈwīnd\ *verb* **-wound** \-ˈwaȯnd\; **-wind·ing** (14th century)
transitive verb
1 a : to cause to uncoil : wind off : UNROLL **b** : to free from or as if from a binding or wrapping **c** : to release from tension : RELAX
2 *archaic* : to trace to the end ⟨*unwinding* the labyrinth and bringing the hero out —Laurence Sterne⟩
intransitive verb
1 : to become uncoiled or disentangled : UNFOLD
2 : to become released from tension

un·wis·dom \ˌən-'wiz-dəm\ *noun* (before 12th century)
: lack of wisdom : FOOLISHNESS, FOLLY

un·wise \-'wīz\ *adjective* (before 12th century)
: lacking wisdom or good sense : FOOLISH, IMPRUDENT
— **un·wise·ly** *adverb*

un·wish \-'wish\ *transitive verb* (1594)
obsolete : to wish away

un·wit·ting \-'wi-tiŋ\ *adjective* (before 12th century)
1 : not knowing : UNAWARE ⟨kept the truth from their *unwitting* friends⟩
2 : not intended : INADVERTENT ⟨an *unwitting* mistake⟩
— **un·wit·ting·ly** \-tiŋ-lē\ *adverb*

un·wont·ed \-'wȯn-təd, -'wōn- *also* -'wən- *or* -'wän-\ *adjective* (1553)
1 : being out of the ordinary : RARE, UNUSUAL
2 : not accustomed by experience
— **un·wont·ed·ly** *adverb*
— **un·wont·ed·ness** *noun*

un·world·ly \-'wər(-ə)l-dlē, -'wərl-lē\ *adjective* (1707)
1 : not of this world : UNEARTHLY; *specifically* : SPIRITUAL
2 a : not wise in the ways of the world : NAIVE **b** : not swayed by mundane considerations
— **un·world·li·ness** \-'wərl(d)-lē-nəs\ *noun*

un·worn \-'wȯrn, -'wȯrn\ *adjective* (circa 1586)
1 a : not impaired by use : not worn away **b** : not worn : NEW
2 : not jaded : FRESH, ORIGINAL

un·wor·thy \ˌən-'wər-<u>th</u>ē\ *adjective* (13th century)
1 a : lacking in excellence or value : POOR, WORTHLESS **b** : BASE, DISHONORABLE
2 : not meritorious : UNDESERVING ⟨*unworthy* of attention⟩
3 : not deserved : UNMERITED ⟨*unworthy* treatment⟩
4 : inappropriate to one's condition or station ⟨actions *unworthy* of a gentleman⟩
— **un·wor·thi·ly** \-thə-lē\ *adverb*
— **un·wor·thi·ness** \-thē-nəs\ *noun*

un·wrap \-'rap\ *transitive verb* (14th century)
: to remove the wrapping from : DISCLOSE ⟨*unwrap* a package⟩ ⟨*unwrap* evidence in a criminal case⟩

un·wreathe \-'rē<u>th</u>\ *transitive verb* (1591)
: UNCOIL, UNTWIST

un·writ·ten \-'ri-tᵊn\ *adjective* (14th century)
1 : not expressed in writing : ORAL, TRADITIONAL
2 : containing no writing : BLANK

unwritten constitution *noun* (1890)
: a constitution not embodied in a single document but based chiefly on custom and precedent as expressed in statutes and judicial decisions

unwritten law *noun* (1641)
: law based chiefly on custom rather than legislative enactments

un·yield·ing \ˌən-'yē(ə)l-diŋ\ *adjective* (1658)
1 : characterized by lack of softness or flexibility
2 : characterized by firmness or obduracy
— **un·yield·ing·ly** \-diŋ-lē\ *adverb*

un·yoke \-'yōk\ (before 12th century)
transitive verb
1 : to free from a yoke or harness
2 : to take apart : DISJOIN
intransitive verb
1 *archaic* : to unharness a draft animal
2 *archaic* : to cease from work

un·zip \-'zip\ (1939)
transitive verb
: to zip open
intransitive verb
: to open by or as if by means of a zipper

¹up \'əp\ *adverb* [partly from Middle English *up* upward, from Old English *ūp;* partly from Middle English *uppe* on high, from Old English; both akin to Old High German *ūf* up and

probably to Latin *sub* under, Greek *hypo* under, *hyper* over — more at OVER] (before 12th century)
1 a (1) : in or into a higher position or level; *especially* : away from the center of the earth (2) : from beneath the ground or water to the surface (3) : from below the horizon (4) : UPSTREAM (5) : in or into an upright position ⟨sit *up*⟩; *especially* : out of bed **b** : upward from the ground or surface ⟨pull *up* a daisy⟩ **c** : so as to expose a particular surface
2 : with greater intensity ⟨speak *up*⟩
3 a : in or into a better or more advanced state **b** : at an end ⟨your time is *up*⟩ **c** : in or into a state of greater intensity or excitement **d** : in a continual sequence : in continuance from a point or to a point ⟨from third grade *up*⟩ ⟨at prices of $10 and *up*⟩ ⟨*up* until now⟩
4 a (1) : into existence, evidence, prominence, or prevalence ⟨put *up* several new buildings⟩ (2) : into operation or practical form **b** : into consideration or attention ⟨bring *up* for discussion⟩
5 : into possession or custody
6 a : ENTIRELY, COMPLETELY ⟨button *up* your coat⟩ **b** — used as an intensifier ⟨clean *up* the house⟩
7 : in or into storage : BY ⟨lay *up* supplies⟩
8 a : so as to arrive or approach **b** : in a direction conventionally the opposite of down: (1) : to windward (2) : NORTHWARD (3) : to or at the top (4) : to or at the rear of a theatrical stage
9 : in or into parts
10 : to a stop — usually used with *draw, bring, fetch,* or *pull*
11 : for each side ⟨the score is 15 *up*⟩

²up *adjective* (before 12th century)
1 a : risen above the horizon ⟨the sun is *up*⟩ **b** : STANDING **c** : being out of bed **d** : relatively high ⟨the river is *up*⟩ ⟨was well *up* in her class⟩ **e** : being in a raised position : LIFTED ⟨windows are *up*⟩ **f** : being in a state of completion : CONSTRUCTED, BUILT **g** : having the face upward **h** : mounted on a horse ⟨a new jockey *up*⟩ **i** : grown above a surface ⟨the corn is *up*⟩ **j** (1) : moving, inclining, or directed upward ⟨the *up* escalator⟩ (2) : bound in a direction regarded as up
2 a (1) : marked by agitation, excitement, or activity (2) : positive or upbeat in mood or demeanor **b** : being above a former or normal level (as of quantity or intensity) ⟨attendance is *up*⟩ ⟨the wind is *up*⟩ **c** : exerting enough power (as for operation) ⟨sail when steam is *up*⟩ **d** : READY; *specifically* : highly prepared **e** : going on : taking place ⟨find out what is *up*⟩
3 a : risen from a lower position ⟨men *up* from the ranks⟩ **b** : being at the same level or point ⟨did not feel *up* to par⟩ **c** (1) : well informed : ABREAST ⟨*up* on the news⟩ (2) : being on schedule ⟨*up* on his homework⟩ **d** : being ahead of one's opponent
4 a : presented for or undergoing consideration ⟨contract *up* for negotiation⟩; *also* : charged before a court ⟨*up* for robbery⟩ **b** : being the one whose turn it is ⟨you're *up* next⟩
5 *of a quark* : having an electric charge of +⅔, zero charm, and zero strangeness — compare ⁴DOWN 6
— **up against** : confronted with : face-to-face with ⟨the problem we are *up against*⟩
— **up to 1** : capable of performing or dealing with ⟨feels *up to* her role⟩ **2** : engaged in ⟨what is he *up to*⟩ **3** : being the responsibility of ⟨it's *up to* me⟩

³up *preposition* (1509)
1 a — used as a function word to indicate motion to or toward or situation at a higher point of ⟨went *up* the stairs⟩ **b** : up into or in the ⟨went *up* attic⟩
2 a : in a direction regarded as being toward or near the upper end or part of ⟨lives a few

miles *up* the coast⟩ ⟨walked *up* the street⟩ **b** : toward or near a point closer to the source or beginning of ⟨sail *up* the river⟩
3 : in the direction opposite to ⟨sailed *up* the wind⟩

⁴up *noun* (1536)
1 : one in a high or advantageous position
2 : an upward slope
3 : a period or state of prosperity or success
4 : ³UPPER

⁵up *verb* **upped** \'əpt\ *or in intransitive verb 2* **up; upped; up·ping; ups** *or in intransitive verb 2* **up** (1643)
intransitive verb
1 a : to rise from a lying or sitting position **b** : to move upward : ASCEND
2 — used with *and* and another verb to indicate that the action of the following verb was either surprisingly or abruptly initiated ⟨he *up* and married a showgirl⟩
transitive verb
1 : RAISE, LIFT
2 a : to advance to a higher level: (1) : INCREASE (2) : PROMOTE 1a **b** : RAISE 8d, e

up–and–com·ing \ˌəp-ən(d)-'kə-miŋ, ˌəp-ᵊm-\ *adjective* (1926)
: gaining prominence and likely to advance or succeed
— **up–and–com·er** \-'kə-mər\ *noun*

up–and–down \-'daun\ *adjective* (circa 1755)
1 : marked by alternate upward and downward movement, action, or surface
2 : PERPENDICULAR

up and down *adverb* (12th century)
1 : TO AND FRO ⟨paced *up and down*⟩
2 : alternately upward and downward ⟨jump *up and down*⟩
3 *archaic* : here and there especially throughout an area
4 : with regard to every particular : THOROUGHLY ⟨knew the territory *up and down*⟩
— **up and down** *preposition*

up–and–up \'əp-ən-'əp\ *noun* (1863)
: an honest or respectable course — used in the phrase *on the up-and-up*

Upa·ni·shad \ü-'pä-ni-ˌshäd, yü-'pa-nə-ˌshad\ *noun* [Sanskrit *upaniṣad*] (1805)
: one of a class of Vedic treatises dealing with broad philosophic problems
— **Upa·ni·shad·ic** \(ˌ)ü-ˌpä-ni-'shä-dik, (ˌ)yü-ˌpa-nə-'sha-dik\ *adjective*

upas \'yü-pəs\ *noun* [Indonesian Malay *pohon upas* poison tree] (1783)
1 : a tall tropical Asian tree (*Antiaris toxicaria*) of the mulberry family with a latex that contains poisonous glucosides used as an arrow poison; *also* : a poisonous concentrate of the juice or latex of a upas
2 : a poisonous or harmful influence or institution

¹up·beat \'əp-ˌbēt\ *noun* (1869)
1 : an unaccented beat in a musical measure; *specifically* : the last beat of the measure
2 : an increase in activity or prosperity ⟨business that is on the *upbeat*⟩

²upbeat *adjective* (1947)
: CHEERFUL, OPTIMISTIC

up–bow \'əp-ˌbō\ *noun* (circa 1890)
: a stroke in playing a bowed instrument in which the bow is moved across the strings from the tip to the heel

up·braid \ˌəp-'brād\ *transitive verb* [Middle English *upbreyden,* from Old English *upbregdan,* probably from *ūp* up + *bregdan* to snatch, move suddenly — more at BRAID] (14th century)
1 : to criticize severely : find fault with
2 : to reproach severely : scold vehemently
synonym see SCOLD
— **up·braid·er** *noun*

up·bring·ing \'əp-ˌbriŋ-iŋ\ *noun* (1520)
: early training; *especially* **:** a particular way of bringing up a child ⟨had a strict *upbringing*⟩

up·build \ˌəp-'bild\ *transitive verb* **-built** \-'bilt\; **-build·ing** (1513)
: BUILD UP

up·cast \'əp-ˌkast\ *noun* (1890)
: something cast up

up·chuck \'əp-ˌchək\ *verb* (1936)
: VOMIT

up close *adverb or adjective* (1851)
: at close range

up·coast \'əp-ˌkōst\ *adverb* (1909)
: up the coast

up·com·ing \'əp-ˌkə-miŋ\ *adjective* (1944)
: FORTHCOMING, APPROACHING

up·coun·try \'əp-ˌkən-trē\ *adjective* (1835)
: of, relating to, or characteristic of an inland, upland, or outlying region
— **up–country** *noun*
— **up–country** \'əp-'\ *adverb*

¹up·date \ˌəp-'dāt\ *transitive verb* (1910)
: to bring up to date

²up·date \'əp-ˌdāt\ *noun* (1965)
1 : an act or instance of updating
2 : current information for updating something
3 : an up-to-date version, account, or report

up·do \'əp-ˌ(ˌ)dü\ *noun, plural* **updos** [*up*-swept hair*do*] (1938)
: an upswept hairdo

up·draft \'əp-ˌdraft, -ˌdráft\ *noun* (circa 1887)
: an upward movement of gas (as air)

up·end \ˌəp-'end\ (1823)
transitive verb
1 : to set or stand on end; *also* **:** OVERTURN 1
2 a : to affect to the point of being upset or flurried ⟨a . . . literary shocker, designed to *upend* the credulous matrons —Wolcott Gibbs⟩ **b :** DEFEAT, BEAT
intransitive verb
: to rise on an end

up·field \'əp-'fē(ə)ld\ *adverb or adjective* (circa 1934)
: in or into the part of the field toward which the offensive team is headed

up–front \ˌəp-'frənt, 'əp-ˌ\ *adjective* (1945)
: being or coming in or at the front: as **a** (1) **:** being in a conspicuous or leading position (2) **:** FRANK, FORTHRIGHT **b :** playing in a front line (as in football) **c :** paid or payable in advance

up front *adverb* (1937)
1 : in or at the front
2 : in advance
3 : in an up-front manner **:** FRANKLY

¹up·grade \'əp-ˌgrād\ *noun* (1873)
1 : an upward grade or slope
2 : INCREASE, RISE
3 : IMPROVEMENT 2b

²up·grade \'əp-ˌgrād, ˌəp-'\ *transitive verb* (1901)
: to raise or improve the grade of: as **a :** to improve (livestock) by use of purebred sires **b :** to advance to a job requiring a higher level of skill especially as part of a training program **c :** to raise the quality of **d :** to raise the classification and usually the price of without improving the quality **e :** to extend the usefulness of (as a device)
— **up·grad·abil·i·ty** *or* **up·grade·abil·i·ty** \ˌəp-ˌgrā-də-'bi-lə-tē\ *noun*
— **up·grad·able** *or* **up·grade·able** \ˌəp-'grā-də-bəl\ *adjective*

up·growth \'əp-ˌgrōth\ *noun* (1844)
: the process of growing upward **:** DEVELOPMENT; *also* **:** a product or result of this

up·heav·al \ˌəp-'hē-vəl, (ˌ)ə-'pē-\ *noun* (1838)
1 : the action or an instance of upheaving especially of part of the earth's crust
2 : extreme agitation or disorder **:** radical change; *also* **:** an instance of this

up·heave \ˌəp-'hēv, (ˌ)ə-'pēv\ (14th century)
transitive verb
: to heave up **:** LIFT
intransitive verb
: to move upward especially with power

— **up·heav·er** *noun*

¹up·hill \'əp-ˌhil\ *noun* (1548)
: rising ground **:** ASCENT

²up·hill \-'hil\ *adverb* (1607)
1 : upward on a hill or incline
2 : against difficulties ⟨seemed to be talking *uphill* —Willa Cather⟩

³up·hill \-ˌhil\ *adjective* (1613)
1 : situated on elevated ground
2 a : going up **:** ASCENDING **b :** being the higher one or part especially of a set; *specifically* **:** being nearer the top of an incline
3 : DIFFICULT, LABORIOUS

up·hold \(ˌ)əp-'hōld\ *transitive verb* **-held** \-'held\; **-hold·ing** (13th century)
1 a : to give support to **b :** to support against an opponent
2 a : to keep elevated **b :** to lift up
synonym see SUPPORT
— **up·hold·er** *noun*

up·hol·ster \(ˌ)əp-'hōl-stər, (ˌ)ə-'pōl-\ *transitive verb* **-stered; -ster·ing** \-st(ə-)riŋ\ [back-formation from *upholstery*] (1864)
: to furnish with or as if with upholstery
— **up·hol·ster·er** \-stər-ər\ *noun*

up·hol·stery \-st(ə-)rē\ *noun, plural* **-ster·ies** [Middle English *upholdester* upholsterer, from *upholden* to uphold, from *up* + *holden* to hold] (1649)
: materials (as fabric, padding, and springs) used to make a soft covering especially for a seat

up·keep \'əp-ˌkēp\ *noun* (1884)
1 : the act of maintaining in good condition **:** the state of being maintained in good condition
2 : the cost of maintaining in good condition

up·land \'əp-lənd, -ˌland\ *noun* (1566)
1 : high land especially at some distance from the sea **:** PLATEAU
2 : ground elevated above the lowlands along rivers or between hills
— **upland** *adjective*
— **up·land·er** \-lən-dər, -ˌlan-\ *noun*

upland cotton *noun* (1819)
: a widely cultivated American cotton plant (*Gossypium hirsutum*) having short- to medium-staple fibers

upland sandpiper *noun* (circa 1890)
: a large North American sandpiper (*Bartramia longicauda*) that frequents fields and prairies — called also *upland plover*

upland sandpiper

¹up·lift \(ˌ)əp-'lift\ (14th century)
transitive verb
1 : to lift up **:** ELEVATE; *especially* **:** to cause (a portion of the earth's surface) to rise above adjacent areas
2 : to improve the spiritual, social, or intellectual condition of
intransitive verb
: RISE
— **up·lift·er** *noun*

²up·lift \'əp-ˌlift\ *noun* (circa 1845)
1 : an act, process, result, or cause of uplifting: as **a** (1) **:** the uplifting of a part of the earth's surface (2) **:** an uplifted mass of land **b :** a bettering of a condition especially spiritually, socially, or intellectually **c** (1) **:** influences intended to uplift (2) **:** a social movement to improve especially morally or culturally
2 : a brassiere designed to hold the breasts up

up·link \'əp-ˌliŋk\ *noun* (1968)
1 : a communications channel for transmissions to a spacecraft; *also* **:** the transmissions themselves
2 : a facility on earth for transmitting to a spacecraft

up·load \(ˌ)əp-'lōd, 'əp-ˌ\ *transitive verb* (1983)
: to transfer (information) from a microcomputer to a remote computer usually with a modem

up·man·ship \'əp-mən-ˌship\ *noun* (1959)
: ONE-UPMANSHIP

up·mar·ket \'əp-'mär-kət\ *adjective* (1972)
: UPSCALE
— **upmarket** *adverb*

up·most \'əp-ˌmōst\ *adjective* (1560)
: UPPERMOST

¹up·on \ə-'pȯn, -'pän\ *preposition* (13th century)
: ON

²up·on \ə-'pȯn, -'pän\ *adverb* (14th century)
1 *obsolete* **:** on the surface **:** on it
2 *obsolete* **:** THEREAFTER, THEREON

¹up·per \'ə-pər\ *adjective* [Middle English, comparative of ²*up*] (14th century)
1 a : higher in physical position, rank, or order **b :** farther inland ⟨the *upper* Mississippi⟩
2 : constituting the branch of a bicameral legislature that is usually smaller and more restricted in membership and possesses greater traditional prestige than the lower house
3 a : constituting a stratum relatively near the earth's surface **b** *capitalized* **:** being a later epoch or series of the period or system named ⟨*Upper* Cretaceous⟩ ⟨*Upper* Paleolithic⟩
4 : NORTHERN ⟨*upper* Manhattan⟩

²upper *noun* (1789)
: one that is upper: as **a :** the parts of a shoe or boot above the sole **b :** an upper tooth or denture **c :** an upper berth
— **on one's uppers :** in straitened circumstances **:** DESTITUTE

³upper *noun* [*up* + ²*-er*] (circa 1968)
1 : a stimulant drug; *especially* **:** AMPHETAMINE
2 : something that induces a state of good feeling or exhilaration

¹up·per·case \ˌə-pər-'kās\ *adjective* [from the compositor's practice of keeping capital letters in the upper of a pair of type cases] (1738)
: CAPITAL 1

²uppercase *noun* (circa 1916)
: capital letters

³uppercase *transitive verb* **-cased; -cas·ing** (1949)
: to print or set in capital letters

upper case *noun* (1683)
: a type case containing capitals and usually small capitals, fractions, symbols, and accents

upper–class *adjective* (1837)
: of, relating to, or characteristic of the upper class

upper class *noun* (1839)
: a social class occupying a position above the middle class and having the highest status in a society

up·per·class·man \ˌə-pər-'klas-mən\ *noun* (1871)
: a member of the junior or senior class in a school or college

upper crust *noun* (1836)
: the highest social class or group; *especially* **:** the highest circle of the upper class
— **upper–crust** *adjective*

up·per·cut \'ə-pər-ˌkət\ *noun* (1842)
: a swinging blow (as in boxing) directed upward with a bent arm
— **uppercut** *verb*

upper hand *noun* (15th century)
: MASTERY, ADVANTAGE, CONTROL ⟨was determined not to let the opposition get the *upper hand*⟩

up·per·most \'ə-pər-ˌmōst\ *adverb* (15th century)
: in or into the highest or most prominent position
— **uppermost** *adjective*

up·per·part \-ˌpärt\ *noun* (1526)
: a part lying on the upper side (as of a bird)

upper respiratory *adjective* (1950)
: of, affecting, or being the part of the respiratory system that includes the nose, nasal passages, and nasopharynx ⟨*upper respiratory* tract⟩ ⟨*upper respiratory* infection⟩

up·pish \ˈə-pish\ *adjective* (circa 1734)
: UPPITY
— **up·pish·ly** *adverb*
— **up·pish·ness** *noun*

up·pi·ty \ˈə-pə-tē\ *adjective* [probably from *up* + *-ity* (as in *persnickity*, variant of *persnickety*)] (1880)
: putting on or marked by airs of superiority : ARROGANT, PRESUMPTUOUS ⟨*uppity* technicians⟩ ⟨a small *uppity* country⟩
— **up·pi·ti·ness** *also* **up·pi·ty·ness** *noun*

up·raise \(ˌ)əp-ˈrāz\ *transitive verb* (14th century)
: to raise or lift up : ELEVATE

up·rate \ˈəp-ˌrāt\ *transitive verb* (1965)
: UPGRADE; *specifically* : to improve the power output of (as an engine)

up·rear \-ˈrir\ (14th century)
transitive verb
1 : to lift up
2 : ERECT
intransitive verb
: RISE

¹up·right \ˈəp-ˌrīt\ *adjective* (before 12th century)
1 a : PERPENDICULAR, VERTICAL **b** : erect in carriage or posture **c** : having the main axis or a main part perpendicular ⟨*upright* freezer⟩
2 : marked by strong moral rectitude ☆
— **up·right·ly** *adverb*
— **up·right·ness** *noun*

²upright *adverb* (1590)
: vertically upward : in an upright position

³upright *noun* (1683)
1 : the state of being upright : PERPENDICULAR ⟨a pillar out of *upright*⟩
2 : something that stands upright; *especially* : a football goalpost — usually used in plural
3 : UPRIGHT PIANO

upright piano *noun* (circa 1890)
: a piano with vertical frame and strings — compare GRAND PIANO

¹up·rise \ˌəp-ˈrīz\ *intransitive verb* **up·rose** \-ˈrōz\; **up·ris·en** \-ˈri-zᵊn\; **up·ris·ing** \-ˈrī-ziŋ\ (14th century)
1 a : to rise to a higher position **b** (1) : STAND UP (2) : to get out of bed **c** : to come into view especially from below the horizon
2 : to rise up in sound
— **up·ris·er** \ˌəp-ˈrī-zər, ˈəp-ˌ\ *noun*

²up·rise \ˈəp-ˌrīz\ *noun* (15th century)
1 : an act or instance of uprising
2 : an upward slope

up·ris·ing \ˈəp-ˌrī-ziŋ\ *noun* (13th century)
: an act or instance of rising up; *especially* : a usually localized act of popular violence in defiance usually of an established government
synonym see REBELLION

up·riv·er \ˈəp-ˈri-vər\ *adverb or adjective* (1774)
: toward or at a point nearer the source of a river

up·roar \ˈəp-ˌrȯr, -ˌrȯr\ *noun* [by folk etymology from Middle Dutch *oproer*, from *op* up (akin to Old English *ūp*) + *roer* motion; akin to Old English *hrēran* to stir] (1526)
: a state of commotion, excitement, or violent disturbance ◇

up·roar·i·ous \ˌəp-ˈrȯr-ē-əs, -ˈrȯr-\ *adjective* (1819)
1 : marked by uproar
2 : very noisy and full
3 : extremely funny ⟨an *uproarious* comedy⟩
— **up·roar·i·ous·ly** *adverb*
— **up·roar·i·ous·ness** *noun*

up·root \(ˌ)əp-ˈrüt, -ˈrüt\ *transitive verb* (circa 1620)
1 : to remove as if by pulling up
2 : to pull up by the roots
3 : to displace from a country or traditional habitat
synonym see EXTERMINATE
— **up·root·ed·ness** *noun*
— **up·root·er** *noun*

up·rush \ˈəp-ˌrəsh\ *noun* (1871)

1 : an upward rush (as of gas or liquid)
2 : a sudden increase

ups and downs *noun plural* (1659)
: alternating rise and fall especially in fortune

up·scale \ˈəp-ˈskāl\ *adjective* (1966)
: relating to, being, or appealing to affluent consumers; *also* : of a superior quality
— **upscale** *adverb or transitive verb*

¹up·set \(ˌ)əp-ˈset\ *verb* **-set; -set·ting** (1677)
transitive verb
1 : to thicken and shorten (as a heated bar of iron) by hammering on the end : SWAGE
2 : to force out of the usual upright, level, or proper position : OVERTURN
3 a : to trouble mentally or emotionally : disturb the poise of **b** : to throw into disorder **c** : INVALIDATE **d** : to defeat unexpectedly
4 : to cause a physical disorder in; *specifically* : to make somewhat ill
intransitive verb
: to become overturned
synonym see DISCOMPOSE
— **up·set·ter** *noun*

²up·set \ˈəp-ˌset\ *noun* (1804)
1 : an act of overturning : OVERTURN
2 a (1) : an act of throwing into disorder : DERANGEMENT (2) : a state of disorder : CONFUSION **b** : an unexpected defeat
3 a : a minor physical disorder ⟨a stomach *upset*⟩ **b** : an emotional disturbance ⟨went through a big *upset* after his father's death⟩
4 a : a part of a rod (as the head on a bolt) that is upset **b** : the expansion of a bullet on striking

³up·set \(ˌ)əp-ˈset\ *adjective* (1805)
: emotionally disturbed or agitated ⟨was too *upset* to speak to him⟩

up·set price \ˈəp-ˌset-\ *noun* (1814)
: the minimum price set for property offered at auction or public sale

up·shift \ˈəp-ˌshift\ *intransitive verb* (1952)
: to shift an automotive vehicle into a higher gear
— **upshift** *noun*

up·shot \ˈəp-ˌshät\ *noun* (1604)
: the final result : OUTCOME

¹up·side \ˈəp-ˌsīd\ *noun* [²up + ¹side] (1927)
1 : an upward trend (as of prices)
2 : a positive aspect

²up·side \ˈəp-ˈsīd\ *preposition* [perhaps from ¹up + -side (as in *alongside*)] (1929)
: up on or against the side of ⟨layin' in this death cell, writin' my time *upside* the wall —Lonnie Johnson⟩ ⟨if they wish to knock a thug *upside* the head, they do so —Robert MacKenzie⟩

up·side down \ˈəp-ˌsīd-ˈdaún\ *adverb* [alteration of Middle English *up so doun*, from *up* + *so* + *doun* down] (15th century)
1 : in such a way that the upper and the lower parts are reversed in position
2 : in or into great disorder
— **upside–down** *adjective*

upside–down cake *noun* (1930)
: a cake baked with its batter covering an arrangement of fruit (as pineapple) and served fruit side up

up·si·lon \ˈüp-sə-ˌlän, ˈyüp-, ˈəp-, -lən, *British usually* yüp-ˈsī-lən\ *noun* [Middle Greek *y psilon*, literally, simple *y*; from the desire to distinguish it from *oi*, which was pronounced the same in later Greek] (1621)
1 : the 20th letter of the Greek alphabet — see ALPHABET table
2 : any of a group of unstable electrically neutral elementary particles of the meson family that have a mass about 10 times that of a proton

up·spring \ˌəp-ˈspriŋ\ *intransitive verb* **-sprang** \-ˈspraŋ\ *or* **-sprung** \-ˈsprəŋ\; **-sprung; -spring·ing** \-ˈspriŋ-iŋ\ (before 12th century)
1 : to spring up
2 : to come into being

¹up·stage \ˈəp-ˈstāj\ *adverb* (1870)

1 : toward or at the rear of a theatrical stage
2 : away from a motion-picture or television camera

²upstage *adjective* (1918)
1 [³*upstage*] : HAUGHTY
2 : of or relating to the rear of a stage

³up·stage \ˌəp-ˈstāj\ *transitive verb* (1921)
1 : to draw attention away from
2 : to force out (an actor) to face away from the audience by staying upstage
3 : to treat snobbishly

⁴up·stage \ˈəp-ˌstāj\ *noun* (circa 1931)
: the part of a stage that is farthest from the audience or camera

¹up·stairs \ˌəp-ˈstarz, -ˈsterz\ *adverb* (1596)
1 : up the stairs : on or to a higher floor
2 : to or at a high altitude or higher position ⟨kicked *upstairs* to company management⟩
3 : in the head : INTELLECTUALLY ⟨a little slow *upstairs* —Tom Clancy⟩

²up·stairs \ˈəp-ˈ\ *adjective* (1782)
: situated above the stairs especially on an upper floor ⟨an *upstairs* bedroom⟩

³up·stairs \ˈəp-ˈ, ˈəp-ˌ\ *noun plural but singular or plural in construction* (1842)
: the part of a building above the ground floor

up·stand·ing \ˌəp-ˈstan-diŋ, ˈəp-ˌ\ *adjective* (before 12th century)
1 : ERECT, UPRIGHT
2 : marked by integrity
— **up·stand·ing·ness** *noun*

¹up·start \ˌəp-ˈstärt\ *intransitive verb* (14th century)
: to jump up (as to one's feet) suddenly

²up·start \ˈəp-ˌstärt\ *noun* (1555)

☆ SYNONYMS
Upright, honest, just, conscientious, scrupulous, honorable mean having or showing a strict regard for what is morally right. UPRIGHT implies a strict adherence to moral principles ⟨a stern and *upright* minister⟩. HONEST stresses adherence to such virtues as truthfulness, candor, fairness ⟨known for being *honest* in business dealings⟩. JUST stresses conscious choice and regular practice of what is right or equitable ⟨workers given *just* compensation⟩. CONSCIENTIOUS and SCRUPULOUS imply an active moral sense governing all one's actions and painstaking efforts to follow one's conscience ⟨*conscientious* in the completion of her assignments⟩ ⟨*scrupulous* in carrying out the terms of the will⟩. HONORABLE suggests a firm holding to codes of right behavior and the guidance of a high sense of honor and duty ⟨a difficult but *honorable* decision⟩.

◇ WORD HISTORY
uproar Despite appearances to the contrary, the *-roar* part of the word *uproar* has no etymological connection with the sound made by some animals. In Dutch *oproer* means "revolt, uprising," having been compounded from *op* "up," and *roer* "motion." When the word was borrowed into English, its Dutch meaning was initially retained, but through the process known as folk etymology its spelling and meaning were altered to fit already familiar English words. English speakers assumed that the *-roar* in *uproar* did indeed refer to loud cries or sounds, and so the word went from meaning "uprising" to meaning "a state of commotion."

\ə\ **abut** \ᵊ\ **kitten** \ər\ **further** \a\ **ash** \ā\ **ace** \ä\ **mop, mar** \aú\ **out** \ch\ **chin** \e\ **bet** \ē\ **easy** \g\ **go** \i\ **hit** \ī\ **ice** \j\ **job** \ŋ\ **sing** \ō\ **go** \ȯ\ **law** \ȯi\ **boy** \th\ **thin** \ṯẖ\ **the** \ü\ **loot** \ú\ **foot** \y\ **yet** \zh\ **vision** *see also* Guide to Pronunciation

1 : one that has risen suddenly (as from a low position to wealth or power) **:** PARVENU; *especially* **:** one that claims more personal importance than is warranted
2 : a start-up enterprise
— **up·start** \'əp-\ *adjective*

up·state \'əp-ˌstāt\ *noun* (1901)
: the chiefly northerly sections of a state; *also* : the chiefly rural part of a state when the major metropolitan area is in the south
— **up·state** \-'stāt\ *adverb or adjective*
— **up·stat·er** \-'stā-tər\ *noun*

up·stream \'əp-'strēm\ *adverb or adjective* (1681)
1 : in the direction opposite to the flow of a stream
2 : toward a portion of the production stream closer to basic extractive or manufacturing processes ⟨make most of its money *upstream*, selling cheap crude . . . to refineries —John Quirt⟩

up·stroke \'əp-ˌstrōk\ *noun* (1828)
: a stroke (as of a pen) made in an upward direction

up·surge \'əp-ˌsərj\ *noun* (1917)
: a rapid or sudden rise

¹up·sweep \'əp-ˌswēp\ *intransitive verb* **-swept** \-ˌswept\; **-sweep·ing** (1791)
: to sweep upward

²upsweep *noun* (circa 1891)
1 : an upward sweep
2 : an upswept hairdo

up·swept \'əp-ˌswept\ *adjective* (1938)
: swept upward; *especially* : brushed up to the top of the head ⟨*upswept* hair⟩

up·swing \'əp-ˌswiŋ\ *noun* (1924)
1 : an upward swing
2 : a marked increase or improvement — often used in the phrase *on the upswing*

up·take \'əp-ˌtāk\ *noun* [Scots *uptake* to understand] (1816)
1 : UNDERSTANDING, COMPREHENSION ⟨quick on the *uptake*⟩
2 : a flue leading upward
3 : an act or instance of absorbing and incorporating especially into a living organism

up–tem·po \'əp-ˌtem-(ˌ)pō\ *adjective* (1948)
: having a fast-moving tempo (as in jazz)

¹up·throw \'əp-ˌthrō\ *transitive verb* **-threw** \-ˌthrü\; **-thrown** \-ˌthrōn\; **-throw·ing** (1600)
: to throw or thrust upward

²upthrow *noun* (1807)
: an upward displacement (as of a rock stratum) **:** UPHEAVAL, UPTHRUST

¹up·thrust \'əp-ˌthrəst\ *transitive verb* (1845)
: to thrust up; *especially* : to elevate (a part of the earth's surface) in an upthrust
intransitive verb
: to rise with an upward thrust

²upthrust *noun* (1846)
: an upward thrust; *specifically* : an uplift of part of the earth's crust

up·tick \'əp-ˌtik\ *noun* [²*up* + ³*tick*] (1955)
: INCREASE, RISE

up·tight \'əp-'tīt\ *adjective* (1934)
1 a : being tense, nervous, or uneasy **b** : ANGRY, INDIGNANT **c** : rigidly conventional
2 : being in financial difficulties
— **up·tight·ness** \(ˌ)əp-'tīt-nəs\ *noun*

up·tilt \ˌəp-'tilt\ *transitive verb* (1849)
: to tilt upward

up·time \'əp-ˌtīm\ *noun* (1958)
: time during which a piece of equipment (as a computer) is functioning or able to function

up to *preposition* (13th century)
1 — used as a function word to indicate extension as far as a specified place ⟨sank *up to* his knees in the mud⟩
2 — used as a function word to indicate a limit or boundary ⟨*up to* 50,000 copies a month⟩ ⟨worked *up to* the last minute⟩

up–to–date *adjective* (1888)
1 : extending up to the present time **:** including the latest information ⟨*up-to-date* maps⟩

2 : abreast of the times **:** MODERN ⟨*up-to-date* methods⟩
— **up–to–date·ly** *adverb*
— **up–to–date·ness** *noun*

up–to–the–minute *adjective* (1912)
1 : extending up to the immediate present **:** including the very latest information
2 : marked by complete up-to-dateness

¹up·town \'əp-ˌtaùn\ *adjective* (1838)
1 : of or relating to uptown
2 : UPSCALE, FASHIONABLE
— **uptown** *adverb*

²up·town \'əp-ˌtaùn\ *noun* (1844)
: the upper part of a town or city; *especially* : the residential district

up·trend \'əp-ˌtrend\ *noun* (1926)
: an upturn especially in business or economic activity

¹up·turn \'əp-ˌtərn, ˌəp-'\ (1567)
transitive verb
1 : to turn up or over
2 : to direct upward
intransitive verb
: to turn upward

²up·turn \'əp-ˌtərn\ *noun* (1864)
: an upward turn especially toward better conditions or higher prices

¹up·ward \'əp-wərd\ *or* **up·wards** \-wərdz\ *adverb* (before 12th century)
1 a : in a direction from lower to higher ⟨the kite rose *upward*⟩ **b** (1) : toward the source (as of a river) (2) : toward the interior (as of a region) **c** : in a higher position ⟨held out his hand, palm *upward*⟩ **d** : in the upper parts **:** toward the head **:** ABOVE ⟨from the waist *upward*⟩
2 : toward a higher or better condition or level ⟨young lawyers moving *upward*⟩
3 a : to an indefinitely greater amount, figure, or rank ⟨from $5 *upward*⟩ **b** : toward a greater amount or higher number, degree, or rate ⟨attendance figures have risen *upward*⟩
4 : toward or into later years ⟨from youth *upward*⟩

²upward *adjective* (1607)
1 : directed toward or situated in a higher place or level **:** ASCENDING
2 : rising to a higher pitch
— **up·ward·ly** *adverb*
— **up·ward·ness** *noun*

upward mobility *noun* (1949)
: the capacity or facility for rising to a higher social or economic position
— **upwardly mobile** *adjective*

upwards of *also* **upward of** *adverb* (1721)
: more than **:** in excess of ⟨they cost *upwards of* $25⟩

up·well \ˌəp-'wel\ *intransitive verb* (1885)
: to well up; *specifically* : to move or flow upward

up·well·ing \-'we-liŋ\ *noun* (1868)
: the process or an instance of rising or appearing to rise to the surface and flowing outward; *especially* : the process of upward movement to the surface of marine often nutrient-rich lower waters especially along some shores due to the offshore drift of surface water (as from the action of winds and the Coriolis force)

up·wind \'əp-'wind\ *adverb or adjective* (1838)
: in the direction from which the wind is blowing

¹ur- *or* **uro-** *combining form* [New Latin, from Greek *our-*, *ouro-*, from *ouron* urine, from *ourein* to urinate — more at URINE]
1 : urine ⟨*ur*ic⟩
2 : urinary tract ⟨*uro*logy⟩
3 : urinary and ⟨*uro*genital⟩
4 : urea ⟨*ur*acil⟩

²ur- *or* **uro-** *combining form* [New Latin, from Greek *our-*, *ouro-*, from *oura* tail — more at ASS]
: tail ⟨*uro*pod⟩

³ur- \'ùr\ *prefix, often capitalized* [German, from Old High German *ir-*, *ur-* thoroughly (perfective prefix) — more at ABIDE]
1 : original **:** primitive ⟨*ur*-form⟩
2 : original version of ⟨*ur*text⟩
3 : prototypical **:** ARCH- ⟨*ur*-anticommunist⟩

ura·cil \'yùr-ə-ˌsil, -səl\ *noun* [International Scientific Vocabulary ¹*ur-* + *acet* + *-il* (substance relating to)] (1890)
: a pyrimidine base $C_4H_4N_2O_2$ that is one of the four bases coding genetic information in the polynucleotide chain of RNA — compare ADENINE, CYTOSINE, GUANINE, THYMINE

urae·us \yù-'rē-əs\ *noun, plural* **uraei** \-'rē-ˌī\ [New Latin, from Late Greek *ouraios*, a kind of snake] (1832)
: a representation of the sacred asp (*Naja haje*) appearing in ancient Egyptian art and especially on the headdress of rulers and serving as a symbol of sovereignty

uraeus

Ural–Al·ta·ic \ˌyùr-əl-al-'tā-ik\ *noun* (1853)
: a postulated language family comprising the Uralic and Altaic languages
— **Ural–Altaic** *adjective*

Ura·li·an \yù-'rā-lē-ən, -'ra-\ *adjective* (1801)
1 : of or relating to the Ural mountains
2 : URALIC

¹Ural·ic \yù-'ra-lik\ *noun* (1861)
: a language family comprising the Finno-Ugric and Samoyed languages

²Uralic *adjective* (1880)
: of, relating to, or constituting the Finno-Ugric and Samoyed languages

Ura·nia \yù-'rā-nē-ə, -nyə\ *noun* [Latin, from Greek *Ourania*]
: the Greek Muse of astronomy

Ura·ni·an \yù-'rā-nē-ən, -nyən\ *adjective* (1844)
: of or relating to the planet Uranus

ura·ni·nite \yù-'rā-nə-ˌnīt\ *noun* [German *Uranin* uraninite (from New Latin *uranium*) + English *-ite*] (1879)
: a mineral that is basically a black octahedral or cubic oxide of uranium which contains thorium, lead, and rare earth elements and is the chief ore of uranium

ura·ni·um \yù-'rā-nē-əm\ *noun, often attributive* [New Latin, from *Uranus*] (circa 1797)
: a silvery heavy radioactive polyvalent metallic element that is found especially in pitchblende and uraninite and exists naturally as a mixture of three isotopes of mass number 234, 235, and 238 in the proportions of 0.006 percent, 0.71 percent, and 99.28 percent respectively — see ELEMENT table ◆

uranium hexa·flu·o·ride \-ˌhek-sə-'flòr-ˌīd, -'flùr-\ *noun* (1899)

◇ WORD HISTORY
uranium In Greek mythology the god of the heavens was known as *Ouranos,* literally "sky, heaven," and the muse of astronomy as *Ourania.* The Romans latinized these figures as *Uranus* and *Urania.* Uranus was the father of the god Saturn and the grandfather of Jupiter. In 1781 the English astronomer Sir William Herschel discovered by telescope the seventh planet of our solar system. Because the planets long familiar to astronomy were named after Roman gods, the German astronomer Johann Bode suggested the name *Uranus,* an especially apt choice since the fifth and sixth planets were Jupiter and Saturn respectively. In 1789 the German chemist Martin Klaproth discovered a new element and later gave it the name *uranium,* after the planet that had been recently discovered.

: a volatile compound UF$_6$ of uranium and fluorine that is used in one major process of enriching uranium in uranium 235

uranium 238 *noun* (1942)
: an isotope of uranium of mass number 238 that is the most abundant and stable uranium isotope, that is not fissionable but can be used to produce a fissionable isotope of plutonium, and that has a half-life of 4.51×10^9 years

uranium 235 *noun* (1940)
: a light isotope of uranium of mass number 235 that when bombarded with slow neutrons undergoes rapid fission into smaller atoms with the release of neutrons and energy and that is used in nuclear power plants and atomic bombs

ura·nog·ra·phy \ˌyu̇r-ə-ˈnä-grə-fē\ *noun* [Greek *ouranographia* description of the heavens, from *ouranos* sky + *-graphia* -graphy] (1675)
: the construction of celestial representations (as maps)

Ura·nus \ˈyu̇r-ə-nəs, yu̇-ˈrā-\ *noun* [Late Latin, from Greek *Ouranos*]
1 : the sky personified as a god and father of the Titans in Greek mythology
2 : the planet seventh in order from the sun — see PLANET table □

ura·nyl \ˈyu̇r-ə-ˌnil, yu̇-ˈrā-nᵊl\ *noun* [International Scientific Vocabulary, from New Latin *uranium* + International Scientific Vocabulary *-yl*] (1850)
: a bivalent radical UO$_2$

urate \ˈyu̇r-ˌāt\ *noun* [French, from *urique* uric, from English *uric*] (1800)
: a salt of uric acid
— **urat·ic** \yu̇-ˈra-tik\ *adjective*

ur·ban \ˈər-bən\ *adjective* [Latin *urbanus,* from *urbs* city] (1619)
: of, relating to, characteristic of, or constituting a city

ur·bane \ˌər-ˈbān\ *adjective* [Latin *urbanus* urban, urbane] (circa 1623)
: notably polite or finished in manner
: POLISHED
synonym see SUAVE
— **ur·bane·ly** *adverb*

ur·ban·i·sa·tion, ur·ban·ise *British variant of* URBANIZATION, URBANIZE

ur·ban·ism \ˈər-bə-ˌni-zəm\ *noun* (1889)
1 : the characteristic way of life of city dwellers
2 a : the study of the physical needs of urban societies **b** : CITY PLANNING
3 : URBANIZATION

ur·ban·ist \ˈər-bə-nist\ *noun* (1930)
: a specialist in city planning
— **ur·ban·is·tic** \ˌər-bə-ˈnis-tik\ *adjective*
— **ur·ban·is·ti·cal·ly** \-ti-k(ə)lē\ *adverb*

ur·ban·ite \ˈər-bə-ˌnīt\ *noun* (1897)
: a person who lives in a city

ur·ban·i·ty \ˌər-ˈba-nə-tē\ *noun, plural* **-ties** (1535)
1 : the quality or state of being urbane
2 *plural* : urbane acts or conduct

ur·ban·i·za·tion \ˌər-bə-nə-ˈzā-shən\ *noun* (1888)
: the quality or state of being urbanized or the process of becoming urbanized

ur·ban·ize \ˈər-bə-ˌnīz\ *transitive verb* **-ized; -iz·ing** (1884)
1 : to cause to take on urban characteristics ⟨*urbanized* areas⟩
2 : to impart an urban way of life to ⟨*urbanize* migrants from rural areas⟩

ur·ban·ol·o·gy \ˌər-bə-ˈnä-lə-jē\ *noun* (1961)
: a study dealing with specialized problems of cities (as planning, education, sociology, and politics)
— **ur·ban·ol·o·gist** \-jist\ *noun*

urban renewal *noun* (1954)
: a construction program to replace or restore substandard buildings in an urban area

urban sprawl *noun* (1958)
: the spreading of urban developments (as houses and shopping centers) on undeveloped land near a city

ur·ce·o·late \ˌər-ˈsē-ə-lət, ˌər-sē-ə-ˌlāt\ *adjective* [New Latin *urceolatus,* from Latin *urceolus,* diminutive of *urceus* pitcher] (1760)
: shaped like an urn ⟨the *urceolate* corolla of a blueberry⟩

ur·chin \ˈər-chən\ *noun* [Middle English, from Middle French *herichon, heriçon,* from (assumed) Old French *eriz,* from Latin *ericius,* from *eris;* akin to Greek *chēr* hedgehog] (14th century)
1 *archaic* : HEDGEHOG 1a
2 : a mischievous youngster : SCAMP
3 : SEA URCHIN

urd \ˈu̇rd, ˈərd\ *noun* [Hindi] (circa 1934)
: an annual Asian legume (*Vigna mungo* synonym *Phaseolus mungo*) widely grown in warm regions for its edible blackish seed, for green manure, or for forage; *also* : the seed

Ur·du \ˈu̇r-(ˌ)dü, ˈər-\ *noun* [Hindi *urdū,* from Persian *zabān-e-urdū-e-muallā* language of the Exalted Camp (the imperial bazaar in Delhi)] (1796)
: an Indo-Aryan language that has the same colloquial basis as standard Hindi, is an official language of Pakistan, and is widely used by Muslims in urban areas of India

-ure *noun suffix* [Middle English, from Old French, from Latin *-ura*]
1 : act : process ⟨expo*sure*⟩
2 : office : function; *also* : body performing (such) a function ⟨legisla*ture*⟩

urea \yu̇-ˈrē-ə\ *noun* [New Latin, from French *urée,* from *urine*] (1806)
: a soluble weakly basic nitrogenous compound CO(NH$_2$)$_2$ that is the chief solid component of mammalian urine and an end product of protein decomposition, is synthesized from carbon dioxide and ammonia, and is used especially in synthesis (as of resins and plastics) and in fertilizers and animal rations

urea–formaldehyde *noun* (1928)
: a thermosetting synthetic resin made by condensing urea with formaldehyde

ure·ase \ˈyu̇r-ē-ˌās, -ˌāz\ *noun* (1892)
: an enzyme that catalyzes the hydrolysis of urea

ure·din·i·um \ˌyu̇r-ə-ˈdi-nē-əm\ *noun, plural* **-ia** \-nē-ə\ [New Latin, from Latin *uredin-, uredo* burning, blight, from *urere* to burn — more at EMBER] (1905)
: a usually reddish or black mass of hyphae and spores of a rust fungus forming pustules that rupture the host's cuticle
— **ure·din·i·al** \-nē-ə\ *adjective*

ure·do·spore \yu̇-ˈrē-də-ˌspōr, -ˌspȯr\ *also* **ure·dio·spore** \-ˈrē-dē-ə-\ *or* **ure·din·io·spore** \yu̇-ˈdi-nē-ə-\ *noun* [New Latin *ure*d*ium uredinium (from Latin *uredo*) + English *-o-* + *spore*] (1875)
: one of the thin-walled spores that are produced by the uredinial hyphae of rust fungi and spread the fungus vegetatively

ure·ide \ˈyu̇r-ē-ˌīd\ *noun* (1857)
: a cyclic or acyclic acyl derivative of urea

ure·mia \yu̇-ˈrē-mē-ə\ *noun* [New Latin] (circa 1857)
1 : accumulation in the blood of constituents normally eliminated in the urine that produces a severe toxic condition and usually occurs in severe kidney disease
2 : the toxic bodily condition associated with uremia ⟨the patient was in *uremia*⟩
— **ure·mic** \-mik\ *adjective*

ureo·tel·ic \yu̇-ˌrē-ə-ˈte-lik, ˌyu̇r-ē-ō-\ *adjective* [*urea* + *-o-* + *tel-* + *-ic;* from the fact that urea is the end product] (1924)
: excreting nitrogen mostly in the form of urea ⟨*ureotelic* mammals⟩
— **ureo·te·lism** \-ˈte-ˌli-zəm, ˌyu̇r-ē-ˈä-tᵊl-ˌi-zəm\ *noun*

ure·ter \ˈyu̇r-ə-tər\ *noun* [New Latin, from Greek *ourētēr,* from *ourein* to urinate — more at URINE] (1543)
: a duct that carries away the urine from a kidney to the bladder or cloaca
— **ure·ter·al** \yu̇-ˈrē-tə-rəl\ *or* **ure·ter·ic** \ˌyu̇r-ə-ˈter-ik\ *adjective*

ure·thane \ˈyu̇r-ə-ˌthān\ *or* **ure·than** \-ˌthan\ *noun* [French *uréthane,* from *ur-* ¹ur- + *éth*eth- + *-ane*] (1838)
1 a : a crystalline compound C$_3$H$_7$NO$_2$ that is the ethyl ester of carbamic acid and is used especially as a solvent and medicinally as an antineoplastic agent **b** : an ester of carbamic acid other than the ethyl ester
2 : POLYURETHANE

ure·thra \yu̇-ˈrē-thrə\ *noun, plural* **-thras** *or* **-thrae** \-(ˌ)thrē\ [Late Latin, from Greek *ourēthra,* from *ourein* to urinate] (1634)
: the canal that in most mammals carries off the urine from the bladder and in the male serves also as a genital duct
— **ure·thral** \-thrəl\ *adjective*

ure·thri·tis \ˌyu̇r-i-ˈthrī-təs\ *noun* [New Latin] (circa 1823)
: inflammation of the urethra

ure·thro·scope \yu̇-ˈrē-thrə-ˌskōp\ *noun* [International Scientific Vocabulary] (1868)
: an instrument for viewing the interior of the urethra

¹urge \ˈərj\ *verb* **urged; urg·ing** [Latin *urgēre* to press, push, entreat — more at WREAK] (1560)
transitive verb
1 : to present, advocate, or demand earnestly or pressingly ⟨his conviction was upheld on a theory never *urged* at his . . . trial —Leon Friedman⟩
2 : to undertake the accomplishment of with energy, swiftness, or enthusiasm ⟨*urge* the attack⟩
3 a : SOLICIT, ENTREAT **b** : to serve as a motive or reason for
4 : to force or impel in an indicated direction or into motion or greater speed ⟨the dog *urged* the sheep toward the gate⟩
5 : STIMULATE, PROVOKE
intransitive verb
: to declare, advance, or press earnestly a statement, argument, charge, or claim
— **urg·er** *noun*

²urge *noun* (circa 1618)
1 : the act or process of urging
2 : a force or impulse that urges; *especially* : a continuing impulse toward an activity or goal

ur·gen·cy \ˈər-jən(t)-sē\ *noun, plural* **-cies** (1540)
1 : the quality or state of being urgent : INSISTENCE
2 : a force or impulse that impels or constrains : URGE

\ə\ **abut** \ᵊ\ **kitten** \ər\ **further** \a\ **ash** \ā\ **ace**
\ä\ **mop, mar** \au̇\ **out** \ch\ **chin** \e\ **bet** \ē\ **easy**
\g\ **go** \i\ **hit** \ī\ **ice** \j\ **job** \ŋ\ **sing** \ō\ **go**
\ȯ\ **law** \ȯi\ **boy** \th\ **thin** \th\ **the** \ü\ **loot** \u̇\ **foot**
\y\ **yet** \zh\ **vision** *see also* Guide to Pronunciation

ur·gent \'ər-jənt\ *adjective* [Middle English, from Middle French, from Latin *urgent-, urgens,* present participle of *urgēre*] (15th century)
1 a : calling for immediate attention : PRESSING ⟨*urgent* appeals⟩ **b :** conveying a sense of urgency
2 : urging insistently : IMPORTUNATE
— **ur·gent·ly** *adverb*
-urgy *noun combining form* [New Latin *-urgia,* from Greek *-ourgia,* from *-ourgos* working, from *-o-* + *ergon* work — more at WORK]
: technique or art of dealing or working with (such) a product, matter, or tool ⟨metall*urgy*⟩
-uria *noun combining form* [New Latin, from Greek *-ouria,* from *ouron* urine, from *ourein* to urinate — more at URINE]
1 : presence of (a specified substance) in urine ⟨albumin*uria*⟩
2 : condition of having (such) urine ⟨poly*uria*⟩; *especially* **:** abnormal or diseased condition marked by the presence of (a specified substance) ⟨py*uria*⟩
uri·al \'ur-ē-əl, -ˌäl\ *noun* [Panjabi *huṛeāl*] (1860)
: an upland wild sheep (*Ovis vignei*) of southern and central Asia which is reddish brown and the males of which have a beard from the neck to the chest

urial

uric \'yur-ik\ *adjective* (1797)
: of, relating to, or found in urine
uric acid *noun* (1800)
: a white odorless and tasteless nearly insoluble acid $C_5H_4N_4O_3$ that is the chief nitrogenous waste present in the urine especially of lower vertebrates (as birds and reptiles), is present in small quantity in human urine, and occurs pathologically in renal calculi and the tophi of gout
uri·co·su·ric \ˌyur-i-kə-'shur-ik, -'sur-\ *adjective* [irregular from *uric*] (circa 1947)
: relating to or promoting the excretion of uric acid in the urine
uri·co·tel·ic \ˌyur-i-kō-'te-lik\ *adjective* [*uric* + *-o-* + *tel-* + *-ic;* from the fact that uric acid is the end product] (1924)
: excreting nitrogen mostly in the form of uric acid ⟨birds are typical *uricotelic* animals⟩
— **uri·co·tel·ism** \-'te-ˌli-zəm, -'kä-tᵊl-ˌi-zəm\ *noun*
uri·dine \'yur-ə-ˌdēn\ *noun* [International Scientific Vocabulary ¹*ur-* + *-idine*] (1911)
: a pyrimidine nucleoside $C_9H_{12}N_2O_6$ that is composed of uracil attached to ribose, is derived by hydrolysis from nucleic acids, and in the form of phosphate derivatives plays an important role in carbohydrate metabolism
Uri·el \'yur-ē-əl\ *noun* [Hebrew *Ūrī'ēl*]
: one of the four archangels named in Hebrew tradition
Urim and Thum·mim \ˌyur-ə-mən(d)-'thə-məm, ˌur-; ˌur-ēm-ən(d)-'tu-mēm\ *noun plural* [part translation of Hebrew *ūrīm wĕthummīm*] (1537)
: sacred lots used in early times by the Hebrews
urin- *or* **urino-** *combining form* [Middle English, from Old French, from Latin *urina* urine]
: ¹UR- ⟨*urino*genital⟩ ⟨*urinary*⟩
uri·nal \'yur-ə-nᵊl, *British also* yu-'rī-nᵊl\ *noun* [Middle English, from Middle French, from Late Latin, from Latin *urina*] (13th century)
1 : a vessel for receiving urine
2 a : a building or enclosure with facilities for urinating **b :** a fixture used for urinating

uri·nal·y·sis \ˌyur-ə-'na-lə-səs\ *noun, plural* **-y·ses** [New Latin, irregular from *urin-* + *analysis*] (1889)
: chemical analysis of urine
uri·nary \'yur-ə-ˌner-ē\ *adjective* (1578)
1 : relating to, occurring in, affecting, or constituting the organs concerned with the formation and discharge of urine ⟨*urinary* system⟩ ⟨*urinary* calculi⟩
2 : of, relating to, or for urine
3 : excreted as or in urine
urinary bladder *noun* (1728)
: a membranous sac in many vertebrates that serves for the temporary retention of urine and discharges by the urethra
uri·nate \'yur-ə-ˌnāt\ *intransitive verb* **-nat·ed; -nat·ing** (1599)
: to discharge urine : MICTURATE
— **uri·na·tion** \ˌyur-ə-'nā-shən\ *noun*
urine \'yur-ən\ *noun* [Middle English, from Middle French, from Latin *urina,* from *urinari* to dive; akin to Sanskrit *vār* water and perhaps to Sanskrit *varṣati* it rains, Greek *ourein* to urinate] (14th century)
: waste material that is secreted by the kidney in vertebrates, is rich in end products of protein metabolism together with salts and pigments, and forms a clear amber and usually slightly acid fluid in mammals but is semisolid in birds and reptiles
— **urin·ous** \'yur-ə-nəs\ *adjective*
uri·no·gen·i·tal \ˌyur-ə-nō-'je-nə-tᵊl\ *adjective* (1836)
: UROGENITAL
uri·nom·e·ter \ˌyur-ə-'nä-mə-tər\ *noun* [International Scientific Vocabulary] (1843)
: a small hydrometer for determining the specific gravity of urine
urn \'ərn\ *noun* [Middle English *urne,* from Latin *urna*] (14th century)
1 : a vessel that is typically an ornamental vase on a pedestal and that is used for various purposes (as preserving the ashes of the dead after cremation)
2 : a closed vessel usually with a spigot for serving a hot beverage ⟨a coffee *urn*⟩
uro- — see UR-
uro·ca·nic acid \ˌyur-ə-'kā-nik-, -'ka-\ *noun* [¹*ur-* + *canine* + *-ic;* from its being first obtained from the urine of a dog] (circa 1903)
: a crystalline acid $C_6H_6N_2O_2$ that is normally present in human skin
uro·chor·date \ˌyur-ə-'kor-dət, -ˌdāt\ *noun* [New Latin *Urochordata,* former group name, from ²*ur-* + *chordatus* having a notochord, from *chorda* notochord, from Latin, string, cord — more at CORD] (1948)
: TUNICATE
— **urochordate** *adjective*
uro·chrome \'yur-ə-ˌkrōm\ *noun* (1864)
: a yellow pigment to which the color of normal urine is principally due
uro·dele \'yur-ə-ˌdēl\ *noun* [French *urodèle,* ultimately from Greek *oura* tail + *dēlos* evident, showing — more at ASS] (1842)
: any of an order (Caudata synonym Urodela) of amphibians (as newts) that have a tail throughout life
— **urodele** *adjective*
uro·gen·i·tal \ˌyur-ō-'je-nə-tᵊl\ *adjective* [International Scientific Vocabulary] (1848)
: of, relating to, or being the organs or functions of excretion and reproduction
uro·ki·nase \ˌyur-ō-'kī-ˌnās, -ˌnāz\ *noun* (1952)
: an enzyme that is produced by the kidney and found in urine, that activates plasminogen, and that is used therapeutically to dissolve blood clots (as in the heart)
uro·lith \'yur-ə-ˌlith\ *noun* [International Scientific Vocabulary] (circa 1900)
: a calculus in the urinary tract
uro·lith·i·a·sis \ˌyur-ə-li-'thī-ə-səs\ *noun* [New Latin] (circa 1860)

: a condition that is characterized by the formation or presence of calculi in the urinary tract
uro·log·ic \ˌyur-ə-'lä-jik\ *also* **uro·log·i·cal** \-ji-kəl\ *adjective* (1855)
: of or relating to the urinary tract or to urology
urol·o·gist \yu-'rä-lə-jist\ *noun* (1889)
: a physician who specializes in the urinary or urogenital tract
— **urol·o·gy** \-jē\ *noun*
-uronic *adjective suffix* [Greek *ouron* urine]
: connected with urine — in names of certain aldehyde-acids derived from sugars or compounds of such acids ⟨hyal*uronic*⟩
uron·ic acid \yu-'rä-nik-\ *noun* (1925)
: any of a class of acidic compounds of the general formula $HOOC(CHOH)_nCHO$ that contain both carboxylic and aldehydic groups, are oxidation products of sugars, and occur combined in many polysaccharides and in urine
uro·pod \'yur-ə-ˌpäd\ *noun* [International Scientific Vocabulary ²*ur-* + Greek *pod-, pous* foot — more at FOOT] (circa 1890)
: either of the flattened lateral appendages of the last abdominal segment of a crustacean; *broadly* **:** an abdominal appendage of a crustacean
uro·py·gi·al gland \ˌyur-ə-'pī-jē-əl-\ *noun* (1870)
: a large gland that occurs in most birds, opens dorsally at the base of the tail feathers, and usually secretes an oily fluid which the bird uses in preening its feathers — called also *oil gland*
uro·py·gi·um \ˌyur-ə-'pī-jē-əm\ *noun* [New Latin, from Greek *ouropygion,* from *ouro-* ²*ur-* + *pygē* rump] (1771)
: the fleshy and bony prominence at the posterior extremity of a bird's body that supports the tail feathers
uro·style \'yur-ə-ˌstīl\ *noun* [International Scientific Vocabulary ²*ur-* + Greek *stylos* pillar — more at STEER] (1875)
: a long unsegmented bone that represents a number of fused vertebrae and forms the posterior part of the vertebral column of frogs and toads
Ur·sa Ma·jor \ˌər-sə-'mā-jər\ *noun* [Latin (genitive *Ursae Majoris*), literally, greater bear]
: a constellation that is the most conspicuous of the northern constellations, is situated near the north pole of the heavens, and contains the stars forming the Big Dipper two of which are in a line indicating the direction of the North Star — called also *Great Bear*
Ursa Mi·nor \-'mī-nər\ *noun* [Latin (genitive *Ursae Minoris*), literally, lesser bear]
: a constellation that includes the north pole of the heavens and the stars which form the Little Dipper with the North Star at the tip of the handle — called also *Little Bear*
ur·sine \'ər-ˌsīn\ *adjective* [Latin *ursinus,* from *ursus* bear — more at ARCTIC] (circa 1550)
1 : of or relating to a bear or the bear family (Ursidae)
2 : suggesting or characteristic of a bear ⟨a lumbering *ursine* gait⟩
Ur·su·line \'ər-sə-lən, -ˌlīn, -ˌlēn\ *noun* [New Latin *Ursulina,* from *Ursula* Saint Ursula, legendary Christian martyr] (1693)
: a member of any of several Roman Catholic teaching orders of nuns; *especially* **:** a member of a teaching order founded by Saint Angela Merici in Brescia, Italy, in 1535
ur·text \'ur-ˌtekst\ *noun* [German, from ³*ur-* + *Text* text] (circa 1932)
: the original text (as of a musical score)
ur·ti·car·ia \ˌər-tə-'kar-ē-ə, -'ker-\ *noun* [New Latin, from Latin *urtica* nettle] (circa 1771)
: an allergic disorder marked by raised edematous patches of skin or mucous membrane and usually intense itching and caused by contact

with a specific precipitating factor (as a food, drug, or inhalant) either externally or internally
— **ur·ti·car·i·al** \-ē-əl\ *adjective*

ur·ti·cate \'ər-tə-ˌkāt\ *intransitive verb* **-cated; -cat·ing** [Medieval Latin *urticatus,* past participle of *urticare* to sting, from Latin *urtica*] (1843)
: to produce wheals or itching; *especially* : to induce urticaria
— **ur·ti·ca·tion** \ˌər-tə-'kā-shən\ *noun*

urus \'yu̇r-əs\ *noun* [Latin, of Germanic origin; akin to Old High German *ūro* aurochs — more at AUROCHS] (1601)
: AUROCHS 1

uru·shi·ol \yu̇-'rü-shē-ˌȯl, u̇-', -ˌōl\ *noun* [International Scientific Vocabulary, from Japanese *urushi* lacquer + International Scientific Vocabulary ¹-*ol*] (1908)
: a mixture of pyrocatechol derivatives with saturated or unsaturated side chains of 15 or 17 carbon atoms that is an oily toxic irritant principle present in poison ivy and some related plants (genus *Rhus*) and in oriental lacquers derived from such plants

us \'əs\ *pronoun* [Middle English, from Old English *ūs;* akin to Old High German *uns* us, Latin *nos*] *objective case of* WE

us·able *also* **use·able** \'yü-zə-bəl\ *adjective* (14th century)
1 : capable of being used
2 : convenient and practicable for use
— **us·abil·i·ty** \ˌyü-zə-'bi-lə-tē\ *noun*
— **us·able·ness** \'yü-zə-bəl-nəs\ *noun*
— **us·ably** \-blē\ *adverb*

us·age \'yü-sij, -zij\ *noun* [Middle English, from Middle French, from *us* use] (14th century)
1 a : firmly established and generally accepted practice or procedure **b** : a uniform certain reasonable lawful practice existing in a particular locality or occupation and binding persons entering into transactions chiefly on the basis of presumed familiarity **c** : the way in which words and phrases are actually used (as in a particular form or sense) in a language community
2 a : the action, amount, or mode of using (a decrease in the *usage* of electricity) **b** : manner of treating (suffered ill *usage* at the hands of his captors)
synonym see HABIT

us·ance \'yü-zᵊn(t)s\ *noun* (14th century)
1 : USAGE 1a
2 : USE, EMPLOYMENT
3 a *obsolete* : USURY **b** : INTEREST
4 : the time allowed by custom for payment of a bill of exchange in foreign commerce

¹use \'yüs\ *noun* [Middle English *us,* from Old French, from Latin *usus,* from *uti* to use] (13th century)
1 a : the act or practice of employing something : EMPLOYMENT, APPLICATION (he made good *use* of his spare time) **b** : the fact or state of being used (a dish in daily *use*) **c** : a method or manner of employing or applying something (gained practice in the *use* of the camera)
2 a (1) : habitual or customary usage (2) : an individual habit or group custom **b** : a liturgical form or observance; *especially* : a liturgy having modifications peculiar to a local church or religious order
3 a : the privilege or benefit of using something (gave him the *use* of her car) **b** : the ability or power to use something (as a limb or faculty) **c** : the legal enjoyment of property that consists in its employment, occupation, exercise, or practice (she had the *use* of the estate for life)
4 a : a particular service or end (put learning to practical *use*) **b** : the quality of being suitable for employment (saving things that might be of *use*) **c** : the occasion or need to employ (took only what they had *use* for)

5 a : the benefit in law of one or more persons; *specifically* : the benefit or profit of property established in one other than the legal possessor **b** : a legal arrangement by which such benefits and profits are so established
6 : a favorable attitude : LIKING (had no *use* for modern art)

²use \'yüz\ *verb* **used** \'yüzd, *in the phrase* "used to" *usually* 'yüs(t)\; **us·ing** \'yü-ziŋ\ (14th century)
transitive verb
1 *archaic* : ACCUSTOM, HABITUATE
2 : to put into action or service : avail oneself of : EMPLOY
3 : to consume or take (as liquor or drugs) regularly
4 : to carry out a purpose or action by means of : UTILIZE; *also* : MANIPULATE 2b (*used* him only as a means up the corporate ladder)
5 : to expend or consume by putting to use — often used with *up*
6 : to behave toward : act with regard to : TREAT (*used* the prisoners cruelly)
7 : STAND 1d (the house could *use* a coat of paint)
intransitive verb
— used in the past with *to* to indicate a former fact or state (claims winters *used* to be harder) (didn't *use* to smoke so much) ☆

used \'yüzd, *in the phrase* "used to" *usually* 'yüs(t)\ *adjective* (14th century)
1 : employed in accomplishing something
2 : that has endured use; *specifically* : SECONDHAND (a *used* car)
3 : ACCUSTOMED, HABITUATED

use·ful \'yüs-fəl\ *adjective* (1595)
1 : capable of being put to use; *especially* : serviceable for an end or purpose
2 : of a valuable or productive kind (do something *useful* with your life)
— **use·ful·ly** \-fə-lē\ *adverb*

use·ful·ness *noun* (1617)
: the quality of having utility and especially practical worth or applicability

use·less \'yü-sləs\ *adjective* (1593)
: having or being of no use: **a** : INEFFECTUAL **b** : not able to give service or aid : INEPT
— **use·less·ly** *adverb*
— **use·less·ness** *noun*

us·er \'yü-zər\ *noun* (15th century)
: one that uses

user fee *noun* (1967)
: an excise tax often in the form of a license or supplemental charge levied to fund a public service — called also *user's fee*

us·er–friend·ly \ˌyü-zər-'fren(d)-lē\ *adjective* (1977)
: easy to learn, use, understand, or deal with
— **user–friendliness** *noun*

use up *transitive verb* (1833)
: to exhaust of strength or useful properties (land that has been *used up*)

Ushak \ü-'shäk\ *variant of* OUSHAK

¹ush·er \'ə-shər\ *noun* [Middle English *ussher,* from Middle French *ussier,* from (assumed) Vulgar Latin *ustiarius* doorkeeper, from Latin *ostium, ustium* door, mouth of a river — more at OSTIUM] (14th century)
1 a : an officer or servant who has the care of the door of a court, hall, or chamber **b** : an officer who walks before a person of rank **c** : one who escorts persons to their seats (as in a theater)
2 *archaic* : an assistant teacher

²usher *verb* **ush·ered; ush·er·ing** \'ə-sh(ə-)riŋ\ (1596)
transitive verb
1 : to conduct to a place
2 : to precede as an usher, forerunner, or harbinger
3 : to cause to enter : INTRODUCE (a new theory *ushered* into the world)
intransitive verb
: to serve as an usher (*usher* at a wedding)

ush·er·ette \ˌə-shə-'ret\ *noun* (1925)
: a girl or woman who is an usher (as in a theater)

usher in *transitive verb* (circa 1600)
1 : to serve to bring into being (a discovery that *ushered in* a period of prosperity)
2 : to mark or observe the beginning of (*ushered in* the new year with much merrymaking)
synonym see BEGIN

us·nea \'əs-nē-ə, 'əz-\ *noun* [New Latin, from Arabic *ushnah* moss] (circa 1597)
: any of a genus (*Usnea*) of widely distributed lichens (as old-man's beard) that have a grayish or yellow pendulous freely branched thallus

us·que·baugh \'əs-kwi-ˌbȯ, -ˌbä\ *noun* [Irish *uisce beathadh*] (1581)
Irish & Scottish : WHISKEY

¹usu·al \'yü-zhə-wəl, -zhəl; 'yüzh-wəl\ *adjective* [Middle English, from Late Latin *usualis,* from Latin *usus* use] (14th century)
1 : accordant with usage, custom, or habit : NORMAL
2 : commonly or ordinarily used (followed his *usual* route)
3 : found in ordinary practice or in the ordinary course of events : ORDINARY ☆
— **usu·al·ly** \'yü-zhə-wə-lē, -zhə-lē; 'yüzh-wə-lē, 'yüzh-lē\ *adverb*
— **usu·al·ness** \'yü-zhə-wəl-nəs, -zhəl-; 'yüzh-wəl-nəs\ *noun*
— **as usual** : in the accustomed or habitual way (*as usual* they were late)

²usual *noun* (1589)
: something usual

usu·fruct \'yü-zə-ˌfrəkt, -sə-\ *noun* [Latin *ususfructus,* from *usus et fructus* use and enjoyment] (circa 1630)
1 : the legal right of using and enjoying the fruits or profits of something belonging to another
2 : the right to use or enjoy something

¹usu·fruc·tu·ary \ˌyü-zə-'frək-chə-ˌwer-ē, -sə-\ *noun* (circa 1618)

1 : one having the usufruct of property
2 : one having the use or enjoyment of something

²usufructuary *adjective* (1710)
: of, relating to, or having the character of a usufruct

usu·rer \'yü-zhər-ər, 'yüzh-rər\ *noun* (14th century)
: one that lends money especially at an exorbitant rate

usu·ri·ous \yu̇-'zhu̇r-ē-əs, -'zu̇r-\ *adjective* (1610)
1 : practicing usury
2 : involving usury **:** of the character of usury
— **usu·ri·ous·ly** *adverb*
— **usu·ri·ous·ness** *noun*

usurp \yu̇-'sərp *also* -'zərp\ *verb* [Middle English, from Middle French *usurper*, from Latin *usurpare* to take possession of without legal claim, from *usu* (ablative of *usus* use) + *rapere* to seize — more at RAPID] (14th century)
transitive verb
1 a : to seize and hold (as office, place, or powers) in possession by force or without right ⟨*usurp* a throne⟩ **b :** to take or make use of without right ⟨*usurped* the rights to her life story⟩
2 : to take the place of by or as if by force **:** SUPPLANT ⟨must not let stock responses based on inherited prejudice *usurp* careful judgment⟩
intransitive verb
: to seize or exercise authority or possession wrongfully
— **usur·pa·tion** \,yü-sər-'pā-shən *also* ,yü-zər-\ *noun*
— **usurp·er** \yu̇-'sər-pər *also* -'zər-\ *noun*

usu·ry \'yü-zhə-rē, 'yüzh-rē\ *noun, plural* **-ries** [Middle English, from Medieval Latin *usuria,* alteration of Latin *usura,* from *usus,* past participle of *uti* to use] (14th century)
1 *archaic* **:** INTEREST
2 : the lending of money with an interest charge for its use; *especially* **:** the lending of money at exorbitant interest rates
3 : an unconscionable or exorbitant rate or amount of interest; *specifically* **:** interest in excess of a legal rate charged to a borrower for the use of money

ut \'ət, 'üt, 'u̇t\ *noun* [Middle English, first note in the diatonic scale, from Medieval Latin, from the syllable sung to this note in a medieval hymn to Saint John the Baptist] (14th century)
: a syllable used for the first note in the diatonic scale in an early solmization system and later replaced by *do*

Ute \'yüt\ *noun, plural* **Ute** *or* **Utes** [short for earlier *Utah, Utaw,* from American Spanish *Yuta*] (1776)
1 : a member of an American Indian people originally ranging through Utah, Colorado, Arizona, and New Mexico
2 : the Uto-Aztecan language of the Ute people

uten·sil \yu̇-'ten(t)-səl, 'yü-,\ *noun* [Middle English, vessels for domestic use, from Middle French *utensile*, from Latin *utensilia,* from neuter plural of *utensilis* useful, from *uti* to use] (14th century)
1 : an implement, instrument, or vessel used in a household and especially a kitchen
2 : a useful tool or implement
synonym see IMPLEMENT

uter·ine \'yü-tə-,rīn, -rən\ *adjective* [Middle English, from Late Latin *uterinus,* from Latin *uterus*] (15th century)
1 : born of the same mother but by a different father
2 : of, relating to, or affecting the uterus ⟨*uterine* cancer⟩

uter·us \'yü-tə-rəs, 'yü-trəs\ *noun, plural* **uteri** \'yü-tə-,rī\ *also* **uter·us·es** [Latin, belly, womb; probably akin to Greek *hoderos* belly, Sanskrit *udara*] (1615)

1 : an organ of the female mammal for containing and usually for nourishing the young during development previous to birth — called also *womb*
2 : a structure in some lower animals analogous to the uterus in which eggs or young develop

Uther \'ü-thər, 'yü-\ *noun*
: a legendary British king and father of Arthur

utile \'yü-t°l, 'yü-,tīl\ *adjective* [Middle French, from Latin *utilis*] (15th century)
: USEFUL

uti·lise *British variant of* UTILIZE

¹util·i·tar·i·an \(,)yü-,ti-lə-'ter-ē-ən\ *noun* (circa 1780)
: an advocate or adherent of utilitarianism

²utilitarian *adjective* (1802)
1 : of or relating to or advocating utilitarianism
2 : marked by utilitarian views or practices
3 a : of, relating to, or aiming at utility **b :** exhibiting or preferring mere utility ⟨spare *utilitarian* furnishings⟩

util·i·tar·i·an·ism \-ē-ə-,ni-zəm\ *noun* (1827)
1 : a doctrine that the useful is the good and that the determining consideration of right conduct should be the usefulness of its consequences; *specifically* **:** a theory that the aim of action should be the largest possible balance of pleasure over pain or the greatest happiness of the greatest number
2 : utilitarian character, spirit, or quality

¹util·i·ty \yü-'ti-lə-tē\ *noun, plural* **-ties** [Middle English *utilite,* from Middle French *utilité,* from Latin *utilitat, utilitas,* from *utilis* useful, from *uti* to use] (14th century)
1 : fitness for some purpose or worth to some end
2 : something useful or designed for use
3 a : PUBLIC UTILITY **b** (1) **:** a service (as light, power, or water) provided by a public utility (2) **:** equipment or a piece of equipment to provide such service or a comparable service
4 : a program or routine designed to perform or facilitate especially routine operations (as copying files or editing text) on a computer

²utility *adjective* (1851)
1 : capable of serving as a substitute in various roles or positions ⟨a *utility* infielder⟩
2 a : kept to provide a useful product or service rather than for show or as a pet ⟨*utility* livestock⟩ ⟨a *utility* dog⟩ **b :** being of a usable but inferior grade ⟨*utility* beef⟩
3 : serving primarily for utility rather than beauty **:** UTILITARIAN
4 : designed or adapted for general use ⟨a *utility* knife⟩
5 : of or relating to a utility ⟨a *utility* company⟩

uti·lize \'yü-t°l-,īz\ *transitive verb* **-lized; -lizing** [French *utiliser,* from *utile*] (1807)
: to make use of **:** turn to practical use or account ⟨I'm a great person for *utilizing* waste power —Robert Frost⟩
synonym see USE
— **uti·liz·able** \-,ī-zə-bəl\ *adjective*
— **uti·li·za·tion** \,yü-t°l-ə-'zā-shən\ *noun*
— **uti·liz·er** \'yü-t°l-,ī-zər\ *noun*

¹ut·most \'ət-,mōst, *especially Southern* -məst\ *adjective* [Middle English, alteration of *utmest,* from Old English *ūtmest,* superlative adjective, from *ūt* out, adverb — more at OUT] (before 12th century)
1 : situated at the farthest or most distant point **:** EXTREME ⟨the *utmost* point of the earth —John Hunt⟩
2 : of the greatest or highest degree, quantity, number, or amount ⟨a matter of *utmost* concern⟩

²utmost *noun* (before 12th century)
1 : the most possible **:** the extreme limit **:** the highest attainable point or degree ⟨the *utmost* in reliability⟩
2 : the highest, greatest, or best of one's abilities, powers, and resources ⟨will do our *utmost* to help⟩

Uto–Az·tec·an \,yü-tō-'az-,te-kən\ *noun* [*Ute* + *-o-* + *Aztec*] (1891)
: a family of American Indian languages spoken by peoples from the U.S. Great Basin south to Central America
— **Uto–Aztecan** *adjective*

uto·pia \yu̇-'tō-pē-ə\ *noun* [*Utopia,* imaginary and ideal country in *Utopia* (1516) by Sir Thomas More, from Greek *ou* not, no + *topos* place] (1610)
1 : an imaginary and indefinitely remote place
2 *often capitalized* **:** a place of ideal perfection especially in laws, government, and social conditions
3 : an impractical scheme for social improvement ◆

¹uto·pi·an \-pē-ən\ *adjective, often capitalized* (1551)
1 : of, relating to, or having the characteristics of a utopia; *especially* **:** having impossibly ideal conditions especially of social organization
2 : proposing or advocating impractically ideal social and political schemes ⟨*utopian* idealists⟩
3 : impossibly ideal **:** VISIONARY ⟨recognised the *utopian* nature of his hopes —C. S. Kilby⟩
4 : believing in, advocating, or having the characteristics of utopian socialism ⟨*utopian* doctrines⟩ ⟨*utopian* novels⟩

²utopian *noun* (circa 1873)
1 : one that believes in the perfectibility of human society
2 : one that proposes or advocates utopian schemes

uto·pi·an·ism \-pē-ə-,ni-zəm\ *noun* (circa 1661)
1 : a utopian idea or theory
2 *often capitalized* **:** the body of ideas, views, or aims of a utopian

utopian socialism *noun* (circa 1923)
: socialism based on a belief that social ownership of the means of production can be achieved by voluntary and peaceful surrender of their holdings by propertied groups
— **utopian socialist** *noun*

uto·pism \'yü-tə-,pi-zəm, yu̇-'tō-\ *noun* (1888)
: UTOPIANISM 2
— **utopist** \yu̇-'tō-pist\ *noun*
— **uto·pis·tic** \,yü-tə-'pis-tik, yu̇-,tō-\ *adjective*

utri·cle \'yü-tri-kəl\ *noun* [Latin *utriculus,* diminutive of *uter* leather bag] (1731)
: any of various small pouches or saccate parts of an animal or plant body: **a :** the part of the membranous labyrinth of the inner ear into which the semicircular canals open **b :** a small usually indehiscent one-seeded fruit with thin membranous pericarp
— **utric·u·lar** \yu̇-'tri-kyə-lər\ *adjective*

utric·u·lus \yu̇-'tri-kyə-ləs\ *noun* [Latin, small bag] (1847)
: UTRICLE a

¹ut·ter \'ə-tər\ *adjective* [Middle English, remote, from Old English *ūtera* outer, comparative adjective from *ūt* out, adverb — more at OUT] (15th century)
: carried to the utmost point or highest degree : ABSOLUTE, TOTAL ⟨*utter* darkness⟩ ⟨*utter* strangers⟩
— **ut·ter·ly** *adverb*

²utter *verb* [Middle English *uttren*, from *utter* outside, adverb, from Old English *ūtor*, comparative of *ūt* out] (15th century)
transitive verb
1 *obsolete* : to offer for sale
2 a : to send forth as a sound **b** : to give utterance to : PRONOUNCE, SPEAK **c** : to give public expression to : express in words
3 : to put (as currency) into circulation; *specifically* : to circulate (as a counterfeit note) as if legal or genuine ⟨*utter* false tokens⟩
4 : to put forth or out : DISCHARGE
intransitive verb
: to make a statement or sound
synonym see EXPRESS
— **ut·ter·able** \'ə-tə-rə-bəl\ *adjective*
— **ut·ter·er** \'ə-tər-ər\ *noun*

¹ut·ter·ance \'ə-tə-rən(t)s, 'ə-trən(t)s\ *noun* [Middle English *uttraunce*, modification of Middle French *outrance* — more at OUTRANCE] (15th century)
archaic : the last extremity : BITTER END

²ut·ter·ance \'ə-tə-rən(t)s *also* 'ə-trən(t)s\ *noun* (15th century)

1 : something uttered; *especially* : an oral or written statement : a stated or published expression
2 : vocal expression : SPEECH
3 : power, style, or manner of speaking

¹ut·ter·most \'ə-tər-ˌmōst\ *adjective* [Middle English, alteration of *uttermest*, from ¹*utter* + *-mest* (as in *utmest* utmost)] (14th century)
1 : OUTERMOST
2 : EXTREME, UTMOST

²uttermost *noun* (14th century)
: UTMOST ⟨to the *uttermost* of our capacity —H. S. Truman⟩

U-turn \'yü-ˌtərn\ *noun* (1930)
1 : a turn resembling the letter U; *especially* : a 180-degree turn made by a vehicle in a road
2 : something (as a reversal of policy) resembling a U-turn

U-val·ue \'yü-ˌval-(ˌ)yü\ *noun* [*unit*] (1949)
: a measure of the heat transmission through a building part (as a wall or window) or a given thickness of a material (as insulation) with lower numbers indicating better insulating properties — compare R-VALUE

uva·rov·ite \yü-'vär-ə-ˌvīt, ü-\ *noun* [German *Uwarowit*, from Count Sergei S. *Uvarov* (died 1855) Russian statesman] (1837)
: an emerald green calcium-chromium garnet

uvea \'yü-vē-ə\ *noun* [Medieval Latin, from Latin *uva* grape] (1525)
: the posterior pigmented layer of the iris; *also* : the iris and ciliary body together with the choroid coat
— **uve·al** \-vē-əl\ *adjective*

uve·itis \ˌyü-vē-'ī-təs\ *noun* [New Latin] (circa 1848)
: inflammation of the uvea of the eye

uvu·la \'yü-vyə-lə\ *noun, plural* **-las** *or* **-lae** \-ˌlē, -ˌlī\ [Middle English, from Medieval Latin, diminutive of Latin *uva* cluster of grapes, uvula; probably akin to Greek *oa* service tree, Old English *īw* yew — more at YEW] (14th century)
: the pendent fleshy lobe in the middle of the posterior border of the soft palate

uvu·lar \-lər\ *adjective* (1843)
1 : of or relating to the uvula ⟨*uvular* glands⟩
2 : produced with the aid of the uvula ⟨a *uvular* sound⟩

ux·o·ri·al \ˌək-'sōr-ē-əl, -'sȯr-; ˌəg-'zōr-, -'zȯr-\ *adjective* [Latin *uxorius*] (1800)
: of, relating to, or characteristic of a wife

ux·or·i·cide \ˌək-'sȯr-ə-ˌsīd, -'sär-; ˌəg-'zȯr-, -'zär-\ *noun* (1860)
1 [Medieval Latin *uxoricidium*, from Latin *uxor* wife + *-i-* + *-cidium* -cide] : murder of a wife by her husband
2 [Latin *uxor* + English *-i-* + *-cide*] : a wife murderer

ux·o·ri·ous \ˌək-'sȯr-ē-əs, -'sȯr-; ˌəg-'zȯr-, -'zȯr-\ *adjective* [Latin *uxorius* uxorious, uxorial, from *uxor* wife] (1598)
: excessively fond of or submissive to a wife
— **ux·o·ri·ous·ly** *adverb*
— **ux·o·ri·ous·ness** *noun*

Uz·bek \'u̇z-ˌbek, 'əz-, u̇z-\ *or* **Uz·beg** \-ˌbeg, -'beg\ *noun* (1616)
1 : a member of a Turkic people of Uzbekistan and adjacent regions of central Asia
2 : the Turkic language of the Uzbek people

V

V *is the twenty-second letter of the English alphabet.* V *and* U *are varieties of the same character,* U *being the cursive form, and the two letters were once used indiscriminately (see* U*). The letter* W*, a doubled* V *called "double* u*," is a survival of this interchangeable use.* V *does not occur in the oldest English texts; its sound was represented in the middle of words by* F*. The letter was probably introduced into English during the later Middle Ages by French scribes.* V *is from the Latin alphabet, where it was used both as a vowel and as a consonant (first with the value of English* w*, and later with that of* v*). Latin derived the letter from a western alphabetic form of the Greek upsilon (see* Y*). In Greek it was used as a vowel, but it originated in a Phoenician character,* wāw*, which had the value of a consonant (see* F*). In English* V *represents the sound of the second consonant in* love*. Small* v *originated as a miniaturized form of the capital letter.*

v \'vē\ *noun, plural* **v's** *or* **vs** \'vēz\ *often capitalized, often attributive* (15th century)
1 a : the 22d letter of the English alphabet **b :** a graphic representation of this letter **c :** a speech counterpart of orthographic *v*
2 : FIVE — see NUMBER table
3 : a graphic device for reproducing the letter *v*
4 : one designated *v* especially as the 22d in order or class
5 : something shaped like the letter V

va·can·cy \'vā-kən(t)-sē\ *noun, plural* **-cies** (1599)
1 *archaic* **:** an interval of leisure
2 : physical or mental inactivity or relaxation **:** IDLENESS
3 a : a vacating of an office, post, or piece of property **b :** the time such office or property is vacant
4 : a vacant office, post, or tenancy
5 : empty space **:** VOID; *specifically* **:** an unoccupied site for an atom or ion in a crystal
6 : the state of being vacant **:** VACUITY

va·cant \'vā-kənt\ *adjective* [Middle English, from Old French, from Latin *vacant-, vacans,* present participle of *vacare* to be empty, be free] (14th century)
1 : not occupied by an incumbent, possessor, or officer ⟨a *vacant* office⟩ ⟨*vacant* thrones⟩
2 : being without content or occupant ⟨a *vacant* seat in a bus⟩ ⟨a *vacant* room⟩
3 : free from activity or work **:** DISENGAGED ⟨*vacant* hours⟩
4 : devoid of thought, reflection, or expression ⟨a *vacant* smile⟩
5 : not lived in ⟨*vacant* houses⟩
6 a : not put to use ⟨*vacant* land⟩ **b :** having no heir or claimant **:** ABANDONED ⟨a *vacant* estate⟩
synonym see EMPTY
— **va·cant·ly** *adverb*
— **va·cant·ness** *noun*

va·cate \'vā-ˌkāt, vā-'\ *verb* **va·cat·ed; va·cat·ing** [Latin *vacatus,* past participle of *vacare*] (1643)
transitive verb
1 : to make legally void **:** ANNUL
2 a : to deprive of an incumbent or occupant **b :** to give up the incumbency or occupancy of
intransitive verb
: to vacate an office, post, or tenancy

¹va·ca·tion \vā-'kā-shən, və-\ *noun, often attributive* [Middle English *vacacioun,* from Middle French *vacation,* from Latin *vacation-, vacatio* freedom, exemption, from *vacare*] (14th century)
1 : a respite or a time of respite from something **:** INTERMISSION

2 a : a scheduled period during which activity (as of a court or school) is suspended **b :** a period of exemption from work granted to an employee for rest and relaxation
3 : a period spent away from home or business in travel or recreation ⟨had a restful *vacation* at the beach⟩
4 : an act or an instance of vacating

²vacation *intransitive verb* **-tioned; -tioning** \-sh(ə-)niŋ\ (1896)
: to take or spend a vacation
— **va·ca·tion·er** \-sh(ə-)nər\ *noun*

va·ca·tion·ist \-sh(ə-)nist\ *noun* (1885)
: a person taking a vacation

va·ca·tion·land \-shən-ˌland\ *noun* (1927)
: an area with recreational attractions and facilities for vacationists

vac·ci·nal \'vak-sə-nᵊl, vak-'sē-\ *adjective* (circa 1860)
: of or relating to vaccine or vaccination

vac·ci·nate \'vak-sə-ˌnāt\ *verb* **-nat·ed; -nat·ing** (1803)
transitive verb
1 : to inoculate (a person) with cowpox virus in order to produce immunity to smallpox
2 : to administer a vaccine to usually by injection
intransitive verb
: to perform or practice vaccination
— **vac·ci·na·tor** \-ˌnā-tər\ *noun*

vac·ci·na·tion \ˌvak-sə-'nā-shən\ *noun* (1800)
1 : the act of vaccinating
2 : the scar left by vaccinating

vac·cine \vak-'sēn, 'vak-ˌ\ *noun* [Latin *vaccinus,* adjective, of or from cows, from *vacca* cow; akin to Sanskrit *vaśa* cow] (1803)
1 : matter or a preparation containing the virus of cowpox in a form used for vaccination
2 : a preparation of killed microorganisms, living attenuated organisms, or living fully virulent organisms that is administered to produce or artificially increase immunity to a particular disease ◇
— **vaccine** *adjective*

vac·ci·nee \ˌvak-sə-'nē\ *noun* (1889)
: a vaccinated individual

vac·cin·ia \vak-'si-nē-ə\ *noun* [New Latin, from *vaccinus*] (1803)
1 : COWPOX
2 : the virus that is the causative agent of cowpox
— **vac·cin·i·al** \-nē-əl\ *adjective*

vac·il·late \'va-sə-ˌlāt\ *intransitive verb* **-lat·ed; -lat·ing** [Latin *vacillatus,* past participle of *vacillare* to sway, waver — more at WINK] (1597)
1 a : to sway through lack of equilibrium **b :** FLUCTUATE, OSCILLATE

2 : to waver in mind, will, or feeling **:** hesitate in choice of opinions or courses
synonym see HESITATE
— **vac·il·lat·ing·ly** \-ˌlā-tiŋ-lē\ *adverb*
— **vac·il·la·tor** \-ˌlā-tər\ *noun*

vac·il·la·tion \ˌva-sə-'lā-shən\ *noun* (15th century)
1 : an act or instance of vacillating
2 : inability to take a stand **:** IRRESOLUTION, INDECISION

va·cu·i·ty \va-'kyü-ə-tē, və-\ *noun, plural* **-ties** [Latin *vacuitas,* from *vacuus* empty] (1541)
1 : an empty space
2 : the state, fact, or quality of being vacuous
3 : something (as an idea) that is vacuous or inane

vac·u·o·late \'va-kyə-(ˌ)wō-ˌlāt\ *or* **vac·u·o·lat·ed** \-ˌlā-təd\ *adjective* (1859)
: containing one or more vacuoles ⟨highly *vacuolated* cells⟩

vac·u·o·la·tion \ˌva-kyə-(ˌ)wō-'lā-shən\ *noun* (1858)
: the development or formation of vacuoles

vac·u·ole \'va-kyə-ˌwōl\ *noun* [French, literally, small vacuum, from Latin *vacuum*] (1853)
1 : a small cavity or space in the tissues of an organism containing air or fluid
2 : a cavity or vesicle in the cytoplasm of a cell usually containing fluid — see CELL illustration
— **vac·u·o·lar** \ˌva-kyə-'wō-lər, -ˌlär\ *adjective*

vac·u·ous \'va-kyə-wəs\ *adjective* [Latin *vacuus*] (1655)
1 : emptied of or lacking content
2 : marked by lack of ideas or intelligence **:** STUPID, INANE ⟨a *vacuous* mind⟩ ⟨a *vacuous* expression⟩
3 : devoid of serious occupation **:** IDLE
synonym see EMPTY
— **vac·u·ous·ly** *adverb*
— **vac·u·ous·ness** *noun*

¹vac·u·um \'va-(ˌ)kyüm, -kyəm\ *noun, plural* **vac·u·ums** *or* **vac·ua** \-kyə-wə\ [Latin, from neuter of *vacuus* empty, from *vacare* to be empty] (1550)
1 : emptiness of space
2 a : a space absolutely devoid of matter **b :** a space partially exhausted (as to the highest degree possible) by artificial means (as an air pump) **c :** a degree of rarefaction below atmospheric pressure

3 a : a state or condition resembling a vacuum **:** VOID ⟨the power *vacuum* in Indochina after the departure of the French —Norman Cousins⟩ **b :** a state of isolation from outside influences ⟨people who live in a *vacuum* . . . so that the world outside them is of no moment —W. S. Maugham⟩
4 : a device creating or utilizing a partial vacuum; *especially* **:** VACUUM CLEANER
²**vacuum** *adjective* (1825)
1 : of, containing, producing, or utilizing a partial vacuum ⟨separated by means of *vacuum* distillation⟩
2 : of or relating to a vacuum device or system
³**vacuum** (1922)
transitive verb
: to use a vacuum device (as a vacuum cleaner) on
intransitive verb
: to operate a vacuum device
vacuum bottle *noun* (1910)
: THERMOS
vacuum cleaner *noun* (1903)
: a household appliance for cleaning (as floors, carpets, or upholstery) by suction — called also *vacuum sweeper*
vacuum flask *noun* (1917)
: THERMOS
vacuum gauge *noun* (circa 1864)
: a gauge indicating degree of rarefaction below atmospheric pressure
vacuum–packed *adjective* (circa 1926)
: having much of the air removed before being hermetically sealed
vacuum pan *noun* (1833)
: a tank with a vacuum pump for rapid evaporation and condensation (as of sugar syrup) by boiling at a low temperature
vacuum pump *noun* (circa 1858)
: a pump for exhausting gas from an enclosed space
vacuum tube *noun* (1859)
: an electron tube evacuated to a high degree of vacuum
va·de me·cum \ˌvä-dē-ˈmē-kəm, ˌvä-dē-ˈmā-\ *noun, plural* **vade mecums** [Latin, go with me] (1629)
1 : a book for ready reference **:** MANUAL
2 : something regularly carried about by a person
va·dose \ˈvā-ˌdōs\ *adjective* [Latin *vadosus* shallow, from *vadum*, noun, shallow, ford; akin to Latin *vadere* to go — more at WADE] (1894)
: of, relating to, or being water or solutions in the earth's crust above the permanent groundwater level
vag- *or* **vago-** *combining form* [International Scientific Vocabulary, from New Latin *vagus*]
: vagus nerve ⟨*vag*al⟩ ⟨*vago*tomy⟩
¹**vag·a·bond** \ˈva-gə-ˌbänd\ *adjective* [Middle English, from Middle French, from Late Latin *vagabundus*, from Latin *vagari* to wander] (15th century)
1 : moving from place to place without a fixed home **:** WANDERING
2 a : of, relating to, or characteristic of a wanderer **b :** leading an unsettled, irresponsible, or disreputable life
— **vag·a·bond·ish** \-ˌbän-dish\ *adjective*
²**vagabond** *noun* (15th century)
: one leading a vagabond life; *especially* **:** TRAMP
— **vag·a·bond·age** \-ˌbän-dij\ *noun*
— **vag·a·bond·ism** \-ˌbän-di-zəm\ *noun*
³**vagabond** *intransitive verb* (1586)
: to wander in the manner of a vagabond **:** roam about
va·gal \ˈvā-gəl\ *adjective* [International Scientific Vocabulary] (1854)
: of, relating to, mediated by, or being the vagus nerve
— **va·gal·ly** \-gə-lē\ *adverb*
va·gar·i·ous \vā-ˈger-ē-əs, və-, -ˈgar-\ *adjective* (1798)
: marked by vagaries **:** CAPRICIOUS, WHIMSICAL

— **va·gar·i·ous·ly** *adverb*
va·ga·ry \ˈvā-gə-rē; və-ˈger-ē, -ˈgar-, vā-; *also* ˈva-gə-rē\ *noun, plural* **-ries** [probably from Latin *vagari* to wander, from *vagus* wandering] (1573)
: an erratic, unpredictable, or extravagant manifestation, action, or notion
synonym see CAPRICE
vag·ile \ˈva-jəl, -ˌjīl\ *adjective* [International Scientific Vocabulary, from Latin *vagus* wandering] (circa 1890)
: free to move about ⟨*vagile* organisms⟩
— **va·gil·i·ty** \və-ˈji-lə-tē, va-\ *noun*
va·gi·na \və-ˈjī-nə\ *noun, plural* **-nae** \-ˌ)nē\ *or* **-nas** [Latin, literally, sheath] (1682)
1 : a canal in a female mammal that leads from the uterus to the external orifice of the genital canal
2 : a canal that is similar in function or location to the vagina and occurs in various animals other than mammals
vag·i·nal \ˈva-jə-n°l\ *adjective* (1726)
1 : of or relating to a theca
2 : of, relating to, or affecting the genital vagina
— **vag·i·nal·ly** \-n°l-ē\ *adverb*
vag·i·nis·mus \ˌva-jə-ˈniz-məs\ *noun* [New Latin, from Latin *vagina*] (1866)
: a painful spasmodic contraction of the vagina
vag·i·ni·tis \ˌva-jə-ˈnī-təs\ *noun* [New Latin] (1846)
: inflammation of the vagina or of a sheath (as a tendon sheath)
va·got·o·my \vā-ˈgä-tə-mē\ *noun, plural* **-mies** [International Scientific Vocabulary] (circa 1903)
: surgical division of the vagus nerve
va·go·to·nia \ˌvā-gə-ˈtō-nē-ə\ *noun* [New Latin] (circa 1915)
: excessive excitability of the vagus nerve resulting typically in vasomotor instability, constipation, and sweating
— **va·go·ton·ic** \-ˈtä-nik\ *adjective*
va·gran·cy \ˈvā-grən(t)-sē\ *noun, plural* **-cies** (1641)
1 : VAGARY
2 : the state or action of being vagrant
3 : the offense of being a vagrant
¹**va·grant** \ˈvā-grənt\ *noun* [Middle English *vagraunt*, probably modification of Middle French *waucrant, wacrant* wandering, from Old French, from present participle of *waucrer, wacrer* to roll, wander, of Germanic origin; akin to Old English *wealcan* to roll — more at WALK] (15th century)
1 a : one who has no established residence and wanders idly from place to place without lawful or visible means of support **b :** one (as a prostitute or drunkard) whose conduct constitutes statutory vagrancy
2 : WANDERER, ROVER
²**vagrant** *adjective* (15th century)
1 : wandering about from place to place usually with no means of support
2 a : having a fleeting, wayward, or inconstant quality **b :** having no fixed course **:** RANDOM
— **va·grant·ly** *adverb*
va·grom \ˈvā-grəm\ *adjective* [by alteration] (1599)
: VAGRANT
vague \ˈvāg\ *adjective* **vagu·er; vagu·est** [Middle French, from Latin *vagus*, literally, wandering] (1548)
1 a : not clearly expressed **:** stated in indefinite terms ⟨*vague* accusation⟩ **b :** not having a precise meaning ⟨*vague* term of abuse⟩
2 a : not clearly defined, grasped, or understood **:** INDISTINCT ⟨only a *vague* notion of what's needed⟩; *also* **:** SLIGHT ⟨a *vague* hint of a thickening waistline⟩ ⟨hasn't the *vaguest* idea⟩ **b :** not clearly felt or sensed **:** somewhat subconscious ⟨a *vague* longing⟩
3 : not thinking or expressing one's thoughts clearly or precisely ⟨*vague* about dates and places⟩

4 : lacking expression **:** VACANT
5 : not sharply outlined **:** HAZY
synonym see OBSCURE
— **vague·ly** *adverb*
— **vague·ness** *noun*
va·gus nerve \ˈvā-gəs-\ *noun* [New Latin *vagus nervus*, literally, wandering nerve] (1840)
: either of the 10th pair of cranial nerves that arise from the medulla and supply chiefly the viscera especially with autonomic sensory and motor fibers — called also *vagus*
vail \ˈvā(ə)l\ *transitive verb* [Middle English *valen*, partly from Middle French *valer* (short for *avaler* to let fall) & partly short for Middle English *avalen* to let fall, from Middle French *avaler*, from Old French, from *aval* downward, from *a* to (from Latin *ad*) + *val* valley — more at AT, VALE] (14th century)
: to lower often as a sign of respect or submission
vain \ˈvān\ *adjective* [Middle English, from Middle French, from Latin *vanus* empty, vain — more at WANE] (14th century)
1 : having no real value **:** IDLE, WORTHLESS
2 : marked by futility or ineffectualness **:** UNSUCCESSFUL, USELESS ⟨*vain* efforts to escape⟩
3 *archaic* **:** FOOLISH, SILLY
4 : having or showing undue or excessive pride in one's appearance or achievements **:** CONCEITED ☆
synonym see FUTILE
— **vain·ly** *adverb*
— **vain·ness** \ˈvān-nəs\ *noun*
— **in vain 1 :** to no end **:** without success or result **2 :** in an irreverent or blasphemous manner ⟨you shall not take the name of the Lord your God *in vain* —Deuteronomy 5:11 (Revised Standard Version)⟩
vain·glo·ri·ous \ˌvān-ˈglōr-ē-əs, -ˈglȯr-\ *adjective* (15th century)
: marked by vainglory **:** BOASTFUL
— **vain·glo·ri·ous·ly** *adverb*
— **vain·glo·ri·ous·ness** *noun*
vain·glo·ry \ˈvān-ˌglōr-ē, -ˌglȯr-, ˌvān-ˈ\ *noun* (14th century)
1 : excessive or ostentatious pride especially in one's achievements
2 : vain display or show **:** VANITY
vair \ˈvar, ˈver\ *noun* [Middle English *veir*, from Old French *vair*, from *vair*, adjective, variegated, from Latin *varius* variegated, various] (14th century)
: the bluish gray and white fur of a squirrel prized for ornamental use in medieval times
Vaish·na·va \ˈvīsh-nə-və\ *noun* [Sanskrit *vaiṣṇava* of Vishnu, from *Viṣṇu* Vishnu] (1815)
: a member of a major Hindu sect devoted to the cult of Vishnu
— **Vaishnava** *adjective*
— **Vaish·na·vism** \-ˌvi-zəm\ *noun*

☆ SYNONYMS
Vain, nugatory, otiose, idle, empty, hollow mean being without worth or significance. VAIN implies either absolute or relative absence of value ⟨*vain* promises⟩. NUGATORY suggests triviality or insignificance ⟨a monarch with *nugatory* powers⟩. OTIOSE suggests that something serves no purpose and is either an encumbrance or a superfluity ⟨a film without a single *otiose* scene⟩. IDLE suggests being incapable of worthwhile use or effect ⟨*idle* speculations⟩. EMPTY and HOLLOW suggest a deceiving lack of real substance or soundness or genuineness ⟨an *empty* attempt at reconciliation⟩ ⟨a *hollow* victory⟩.

\ə\ abut \°\ kitten \ər\ **further** \a\ **ash** \ā\ **ace**
\ä\ **mop, mar** \au̇\ **out** \ch\ **chin** \e\ **bet** \ē\ **easy**
\g\ **go** \i\ **hit** \ī\ **ice** \j\ **job** \ŋ\ **sing** \ō\ **go**
\ȯ\ **law** \ȯi\ **boy** \th\ **thin** \t͟h\ **the** \ü\ **loot** \u̇\ **foot**
\y\ **yet** \zh\ **vision** *see also* Guide to Pronunciation

Vais·ya \'vīsh-yə, 'vī-shə\ *noun* [Sanskrit *vaiśya,* from *viś* settlement; akin to Greek *oikos* house — more at VICINITY] (1665)
: a Hindu of an upper caste traditionally assigned to commercial and agricultural occupations

va·lance \'va-lən(t)s, 'vā-\ *noun* [Middle English *vallance,* perhaps from *Valence,* France] (15th century)
1 : a drapery hung along the edge of a bed, table, altar, canopy, or shelf
2 : a short drapery or wood or metal frame used as a decorative heading to conceal the top of curtains and fixtures
— **va·lanced** \-lən(t)st\ *adjective*

vale \'vā(ə)l\ *noun* [Middle English, from Middle French, from Old French *val,* from Latin *valles, vallis;* perhaps akin to Latin *volvere* to roll — more at VOLUBLE] (14th century)
1 : VALLEY, DALE
2 : WORLD ⟨this *vale* of tears⟩

val·e·dic·tion \,va-lə-'dik-shən\ *noun* [Latin *valedicere* to say farewell, from *vale* farewell + *dicere* to say — more at DICTION] (1614)
1 : an act of bidding farewell
2 : VALEDICTORY

val·e·dic·to·ri·an \-,dik-'tōr-ē-ən, -'tȯr-\ *noun* (1759)
: the student usually having the highest rank in a graduating class who delivers the valedictory address at the commencement exercises

¹val·e·dic·to·ry \-'dik-t(ə-)rē\ *adjective* [Latin *valedicere*] (1651)
: of or relating to a valediction : expressing or containing a farewell

²valedictory *noun, plural* **-ries** (1779)
: an address or statement of farewell or leave-taking

va·lence \'vā-lən(t)s\ *noun* [Late Latin *valentia* power, capacity, from Latin *valent-, valens,* present participle of *valēre* to be strong — more at WIELD] (1884)
1 : the degree of combining power of an element as shown by the number of atomic weights of a univalent element (as hydrogen) with which the atomic weight of the element will combine or for which it can be substituted or with which it can be compared
2 a : relative capacity to unite, react, or interact (as with antigens or a biological substrate)
b : the degree of attractiveness an individual, activity, or object possesses as a behavioral goal

valence band *noun* (1953)
: the range of permissible energy values that are the highest energies an electron of an atom can have and still be associated with the atom and be used to form bonds — compare CONDUCTION BAND

valence electron *noun* (1923)
: a single electron or one of two or more electrons in the outer shell of an atom that is responsible for the chemical properties of the atom

Va·len·cia orange \və-'len-ch(ē-)ə, -len(t)-sē-ə\ *noun* [*Valencia,* Spain] (1858)
: a sweet orange of a juicy thin-skinned cultivar grown in the U.S. — called also *Valencia*

Va·len·ci·ennes \və-,len(t)-sē-'en(z), ,va-lən-sē-\ *noun* [*Valenciennes,* France] (1717)
: a fine bobbin lace

-valent *adjective combining form* [International Scientific Vocabulary, from Latin *valent-, valens*]
1 : having a (specified) valence or valences ⟨bi*valent*⟩ ⟨multi*valent*⟩
2 : having (so many) chromosomal strands or homologous chromosomes ⟨uni*valent*⟩

val·en·tine \'va-lən-,tīn\ *noun* (15th century)
1 : a sweetheart chosen or complimented on Saint Valentine's Day
2 a : a gift or greeting sent or given especially to a sweetheart on Saint Valentine's Day; es-

pecially **:** a greeting card sent on this day **b** **:** something (as a movie or piece of writing) expressing uncritical praise or affection **:** TRIBUTE

Valentine's Day *also* **Valentine Day** *noun* (1668)
: SAINT VALENTINE'S DAY

val·er·ate \'va-lə-,rāt\ *noun* (1852)
: a salt or ester of valeric acid

va·le·ri·an \və-'lir-ē-ən\ *noun* [Middle English, from Middle French or Medieval Latin; Middle French *valeriane,* from Medieval Latin *valeriana,* probably from feminine of *valerianus* of Valeria, from *Valeria,* Roman province formerly part of Pannonia] (14th century)
1 : any of a genus (*Valeriana* of the family Valerianaceae, the valerian family) of perennial herbs many of which possess medicinal properties
2 : a drug consisting of the dried rootstock and roots of the garden heliotrope (*Valeriana officinalis*) formerly used as a carminative and sedative

va·le·ric acid \və-'lir-ik-, -'ler-\ *noun* [*valerian;* from its occurrence in the root of valerian] (1857)
: any of four isomeric fatty acids $C_5H_{10}O_2$ or a mixture of these; *especially* **:** a liquid acid of disagreeable odor obtained from valerian or made synthetically and used especially in organic synthesis

¹val·et \'va-lət, 'va-(,)lā, va-'lā\ *noun* [Middle French *vaslet, varlet, valet* young nobleman, page, domestic servant, from (assumed) Medieval Latin *vassellittus,* diminutive of Medieval Latin *vassus* servant — more at VASSAL] (1567)
1 a : a man's male servant who performs personal services (as taking care of clothing) **b :** an employee (as of a hotel or a public facility) who performs personal services for customers
2 : a device (as a rack or tray) for holding clothing or personal effects

²valet *transitive verb* (1840)
: to serve as a valet

va·let de cham·bre \(,)va-lā-də-'shäⁿbr'\ *noun, plural* **va·lets de chambre** *same*\ [French, literally, chamber valet] (1646)
: VALET 1a

valet parking *noun* (1960)
: a service that provides parking of motor vehicles by an attendant

¹val·e·tu·di·nar·i·an \,va-lə-,tü-d°n-'er-ē-ən, -,tyü-\ *noun* [Latin *valetudinarius* sickly, infirm, from *valetudin-, valetudo* state of health, sickness, from *valēre* to be strong, be well — more at WIELD] (1703)
: a person of a weak or sickly constitution; *especially* **:** one whose chief concern is being or becoming a chronic invalid

²valetudinarian *adjective* (1713)
: of, relating to, or characteristic of a valetudinarian **:** SICKLY, WEAK

val·e·tu·di·nar·i·an·ism \-ē-ə-,ni-zəm\ *noun* (1839)
: the condition or state of mind of a valetudinarian

¹val·e·tu·di·nary \-'tü-d°n-,er-ē, -'tyü-\ *adjective* [Latin *valetudinarius*] (1581)
: VALETUDINARIAN

²valetudinary *noun, plural* **-nar·ies** (1665)
: VALETUDINARIAN

val·gus \'val-gəs\ *adjective* [New Latin, from Latin, bowlegged] (1884)
: of, relating to, or being a deformity in which an anatomical part is turned outward away from the midline of the body to an abnormal degree ⟨*valgus* deformity of the ankle⟩
— **valgus** *noun*

Val·hal·la \val-'ha-lə *also* väl-'hä-\ *noun* [German & Old Norse; German *Walhalla,* from Old Norse *Valhǫll,* literally, hall of the slain, from *valr* (akin to Old English *wæl* slaughter, the slain) + *hǫll* hall; akin to Old English *heall* hall]

: the great hall in Norse mythology where the souls of heroes slain in battle are received

val·iance \'val-yən(t)s\ *noun* (15th century)
: VALOR

val·ian·cy \-yən(t)-sē\ *noun* (15th century)
: VALOR

¹val·iant \'val-yənt\ *adjective* [Middle English *valiaunt,* from Middle French *vaillant,* from Old French, from present participle of *valoir* to be of worth, from Latin *valēre* to be strong — more at WIELD] (14th century)
1 : possessing or acting with bravery or boldness **:** COURAGEOUS ⟨*valiant* soldiers⟩
2 : marked by, exhibiting, or carried out with courage or determination **:** HEROIC ⟨*valiant* feats⟩
— **val·iant·ly** *adverb*
— **val·iant·ness** *noun*

²valiant *noun* (1609)
: a valiant person

val·id \'va-ləd\ *adjective* [Middle French or Medieval Latin; Middle French *valide,* from Medieval Latin *validus,* from Latin, strong, from *valēre*] (1571)
1 : having legal efficacy or force; *especially* **:** executed with the proper legal authority and formalities ⟨a *valid* contract⟩
2 a : well-grounded or justifiable **:** being at once relevant and meaningful ⟨a *valid* theory⟩
b : logically correct ⟨a *valid* argument⟩ ⟨*valid* inference⟩
3 : appropriate to the end in view **:** EFFECTIVE ⟨every craft has its own *valid* methods⟩
4 *of a taxon* **:** conforming to accepted principles of sound biological classification ☆
— **va·lid·i·ty** \və-'li-də-tē, va-\ *noun*
— **val·id·ly** \'va-ləd-lē\ *adverb*

val·i·date \'va-lə-,dāt\ *transitive verb* **-dat·ed; -dat·ing** (1648)
1 a : to make legally valid **b :** to grant official sanction to by marking **c :** to confirm the validity of (an election); *also* **:** to declare (a person) elected
2 : to support or corroborate on a sound or authoritative basis ⟨experiments designed to *validate* the hypothesis⟩
synonym see CONFIRM

val·i·da·tion \,va-lə-'dā-shən\ *noun* (circa 1656)
: an act, process, or instance of validating; *especially* **:** the determination of the degree of validity of a measuring device

va·line \'va-,lēn, 'vā-\ *noun* [International Scientific Vocabulary, from *valeric (acid)*] (1907)
: a crystalline essential amino acid $C_5H_{11}NO_2$ that is one of the building blocks of plant and animal proteins

va·lise \və-'lēs\ *noun* [French, from Italian *valigia*] (1615)
: SUITCASE

Val·i·um \'va-lē-əm, 'val-yəm\ *trademark*
— used for a preparation of diazepam

Val·ky·rie \val-'kir-ē *also* val-'kī-rē, 'val-kə-rē\ *noun* [German & Old Norse; German

☆ **SYNONYMS**
Valid, sound, cogent, convincing, telling mean having such force as to compel serious attention and usually acceptance. VALID implies being supported by objective truth or generally accepted authority ⟨a *valid* reason for being absent⟩ ⟨a *valid* marriage⟩. SOUND implies a basis of flawless reasoning or of solid grounds ⟨a *sound* proposal for reviving the economy⟩. COGENT may stress either weight of sound argument and evidence or lucidity of presentation ⟨the prosecutor's *cogent* summation won over the jury⟩. CONVINCING suggests a power to overcome doubt, opposition, or reluctance to accept ⟨a *convincing* argument for welfare reform⟩. TELLING stresses an immediate and crucial effect striking at the heart of a matter ⟨a *telling* example of bureaucratic waste⟩.

Walküre, from Old Norse *valkyrja,* literally, chooser of the slain; akin to Old English *wœl-cyrige* witch, Old Norse *valr* the slain, Old High German *kiosan* to choose — more at CHOOSE]
: any of the maidens of Odin who choose the heroes to be slain in battle and conduct them to Valhalla

val·late \'va-ˌlāt\ *adjective* [Latin *vallatus,* past participle of *vallare* to surround with a wall, from *vallum* wall, rampart — more at WALL] (1878)
: having a raised edge surrounding a depression ⟨*vallate* papillae of the tongue⟩

val·lec·u·la \va-'le-kyə-lə, və-\ *noun, plural* **-u·lae** \-kyə-ˌlē, -ˌlī\ [New Latin, from Late Latin, little valley, diminutive of Latin *valles* valley — more at VALE] (1859)
: an anatomical groove, channel, or depression; *especially* **:** one between the base of the tongue and the epiglottis
— **val·lec·u·lar** \-lər\ *adjective*

val·ley \'va-lē\ *noun, plural* **valleys** [Middle English *valey,* from Old French *valee,* from *val* valley — more at VALE] (14th century)
1 a : an elongate depression of the earth's surface usually between ranges of hills or mountains **b :** an area drained by a river and its tributaries
2 : a low point or condition
3 a : HOLLOW, DEPRESSION **b :** the place of meeting of two slopes of a roof that form on the plan a reentrant angle

valley fever *noun* [from its prevalence in the San Joaquin valley of California] (1938)
: COCCIDIOIDOMYCOSIS

Va·lois \'val-ˌwä, val-'\ *adjective* [Philippe de *Valois* (Philip VI of France)] (circa 1888)
: of or relating to the French royal house that ruled from 1328 to 1589

va·lo·nia \və-'lō-nē-ə, -nyə\ *noun* [Italian *vallonia,* from Middle Greek *balanidia,* plural of *balanidion,* diminutive of Greek *balanos* acorn — more at GLAND] (1722)
: dried acorn cups especially from a Eurasian evergreen oak (*Quercus macrolepis* synonym *Q. aegilops*) used in tanning or dressing leather

val·or \'va-lər\ *noun* [Middle English, from Middle French *valour,* from Medieval Latin *valor* value, valor, from Latin *valēre* to be strong — more at WIELD] (15th century)
: strength of mind or spirit that enables a person to encounter danger with firmness **:** personal bravery

val·o·rize \'va-lə-ˌrīz\ *transitive verb* **-rized; -riz·ing** [Portuguese *valorizar,* from *valor* value, price, from Medieval Latin] (circa 1906)
: to enhance or try to enhance the price, value, or status of by organized and usually governmental action ⟨using subsidies to *valorize* coffee⟩
— **val·o·ri·za·tion** \ˌva-lə-rə-'zā-shən\ *noun*

val·or·ous \'va-lə-rəs\ *adjective* (15th century)
: VALIANT
— **val·or·ous·ly** *adverb*

val·our \'va-lər\ *chiefly British variant of* VALOR

val·po·li·cel·la \ˌväl-ˌpō-lə-'che-lə, ˌval-\ *noun, often capitalized* [*Valpolicella,* district in northern Italy] (1903)
: a dry red Italian table wine

Val·sal·va maneuver \val-'sal-və-\ *noun* [Antonio Maria *Valsalva* (died 1723) Italian anatomist] (1886)
: the process of making a forceful attempt at expiration while holding the nostrils closed and keeping the mouth shut for the purpose of testing the patency of the eustachian tubes or of adjusting middle ear pressure — called also *Valsalva*

valse \'väls\ *noun* [French, from German *Walzer* — more at WALTZ] (1796)
: WALTZ; *specifically* **:** a concert waltz

¹valu·able \'val-yə-bəl, -yə-wə-bəl\ *adjective* (1589)
1 a : having monetary value **b :** worth a good price
2 a : having desirable or esteemed characteristics or qualities ⟨*valuable* friendships⟩ **b :** of great use or service ⟨*valuable* advice⟩
— **valu·able·ness** *noun*
— **valu·ably** \-blē\ *adverb*

²valuable *noun* (circa 1775)
: a usually personal possession (as jewelry) of relatively great monetary value — usually used in plural

valuable consideration *noun* (1638)
: an equivalent or compensation having value that is given for something acquired or promised (as money or marriage) and that may consist either in a benefit accruing to one party or a loss falling upon the other

val·u·ate \'val-yə-ˌwāt\ *transitive verb* **-at·ed; -at·ing** (1873)
: to place a value on **:** APPRAISE

val·u·a·tion \ˌval-yə-'wā-shən\ *noun* [Middle French, from *valuer* to value, from *value*] (1529)
1 : the act or process of valuing; *specifically* **:** appraisal of property
2 : the estimated or determined market value of a thing
3 : judgment or appreciation of worth or character
— **val·u·a·tion·al** \-shnəl, -shə-nᵊl\ *adjective*
— **val·u·a·tion·al·ly** *adverb*

val·u·a·tor \'val-yə-ˌwā-tər\ *noun* (1731)
: one that valuates; *specifically* **:** one that appraises

¹val·ue \'val-(ˌ)yü\ *noun* [Middle English, from Middle French, from (assumed) Vulgar Latin *valuta,* from feminine of *valutus,* past participle of Latin *valēre* to be worth, be strong — more at WIELD] (14th century)
1 : a fair return or equivalent in goods, services, or money for something exchanged
2 : the monetary worth of something **:** marketable price
3 : relative worth, utility, or importance ⟨a good *value* at the price⟩ ⟨the *value* of base stealing in baseball⟩ ⟨had nothing of *value* to say⟩
4 a : a numerical quantity that is assigned or is determined by calculation or measurement ⟨let x take on positive *values*⟩ ⟨a *value* for the age of the earth⟩ **b :** precise signification ⟨*value* of a word⟩
5 : the relative duration of a musical note
6 a : relative lightness or darkness of a color **:** LUMINOSITY **b :** the relation of one part in a picture to another with respect to lightness and darkness
7 : something (as a principle or quality) intrinsically valuable or desirable ⟨sought material *values* instead of human *values* —W. H. Jones⟩
8 : DENOMINATION 2
— **val·ue·less** \-(ˌ)yü-ləs, -yə-\ *adjective*
— **val·ue·less·ness** *noun*

²value *transitive verb* **val·ued; val·u·ing** (15th century)
1 a : to estimate or assign the monetary worth of **:** APPRAISE ⟨*value* a necklace⟩ **b :** to rate or scale in usefulness, importance, or general worth **:** EVALUATE
2 : to consider or rate highly **:** PRIZE, ESTEEM ⟨*values* your opinion⟩
synonym see ESTIMATE, APPRECIATE
— **val·u·er** \-yə-wər\ *noun*

value-added tax *noun* (1935)
: an incremental excise that is levied on the value added at each stage of the processing of a raw material or the production and distribution of a commodity and that typically has the impact of a sales tax on the ultimate consumer

val·ued \'val-(ˌ)yüd, -yəd\ *adjective* (1595)

: having a value or values especially of a specified kind or number — often used in combination ⟨real-*valued*⟩

val·ue–free \'val-(ˌ)yü-'frē\ *adjective* (1948)
: making or having no value judgments ⟨*value-free* distinctions⟩ ⟨*value-free* economics⟩

value judgment *noun* (1899)
: a judgment assigning a value (as good or bad) to something

va·lu·ta \və-'lü-tə, -'(ˌ)tä\ *noun* [Italian, value, from (assumed) Vulgar Latin *valuta*] (1920)
1 : the agreed upon or exchange value of a currency
2 : FOREIGN EXCHANGE 2

val·vate \'val-ˌvāt\ *adjective* (1829)
: having valves or parts resembling a valve; *especially* **:** meeting at the edges without overlapping in the bud (as in the calyx of a mallow)

valve \'valv\ *noun* [Latin *valva;* akin to Latin *volvere* to roll — more at VOLUBLE] (14th century)
1 *archaic* **:** a leaf of a folding or double door
2 [New Latin *valva,* from Latin] **:** a structure especially in a vein or lymphatic that closes temporarily a passage or orifice or permits movement of fluid in one direction only
3 a : any of numerous mechanical devices by which the flow of liquid, gas, or loose material in bulk may be started, stopped, or regulated by a movable part that opens, shuts, or partially obstructs one or more ports or passageways; *also* **:** the movable part of such a device **b :** a device in a brass instrument for quickly channeling air flow through an added length of tube in order to change the fundamental tone by some definite interval **c** *chiefly British* **:** ELECTRON TUBE
4 [New Latin *valva,* from Latin] **:** one of the distinct and usually movably articulated pieces of which the shell of some shell-bearing animals (as lamellibranch mollusks, brachiopods, and barnacles) consists
5 [New Latin *valva,* from Latin] **a :** one of the segments or pieces into which a dehiscing capsule or legume separates **b :** the portion of various anthers (as of the barberry) resembling a lid **c :** one of the two encasing membranes of a diatom
— **valved** \'valvd\ *adjective*
— **valve·less** \'valv-ləs\ *adjective*

val·vu·la \'val-vyə-lə\ *noun, plural* **-lae** \-ˌlē, -ˌlī\ [New Latin, diminutive of Latin *valva*] (1615)
: a small valve or fold

val·vu·lar \'val-vyə-lər\ *adjective* (1797)
1 : resembling or functioning as a valve; *also* **:** opening by valves
2 : of, relating to, or affecting a valve especially of the heart ⟨*valvular* heart disease⟩

val·vu·li·tis \ˌval-vyə-'lī-təs\ *noun* [New Latin] (circa 1891)
: inflammation of a valve especially of the heart

va·moose \va-'müs, va-\ *intransitive verb* **va·moosed; va·moos·ing** [Spanish *vamos* let us go, suppletive 1st plural imperative (from Latin *vadere* to go) of *ir* to go, from Latin *ire* — more at WADE, ISSUE] (1840)
: to depart quickly

¹vamp \'vamp\ *verb* [²*vamp*] (1599)
transitive verb
1 a : to provide (a shoe) with a new vamp **b :** to piece (something old) with a new part **:** PATCH ⟨*vamp* up old sermons⟩
2 : INVENT, FABRICATE ⟨*vamp* up an excuse⟩
intransitive verb
: to play a musical vamp
— **vamp·er** *noun*

\ə\ **abut** \ᵊ\ **kitten** \ər\ **further** \a\ **ash** \ā\ **ace**
\ä\ **mop, mar** \au̇\ **out** \ch\ **chin** \e\ **bet** \ē\ **easy**
\g\ **go** \i\ **hit** \ī\ **ice** \j\ **job** \ŋ\ **sing** \ō\ **go**
\ȯ\ **law** \ȯi\ **boy** \th\ **thin** \th̲\ **the** \ü\ **loot** \u̇\ **foot**
\y\ **yet** \zh\ **vision** *see also* Guide to Pronunciation

²vamp *noun* [Middle English *vampe* sock, from Old French *avantpié*, from *avant*- fore- + *pié* foot, from Latin *ped-*, *pes* — more at VANGUARD, FOOT] (1654)
1 : the part of a shoe upper or boot upper covering especially the forepart of the foot and sometimes also extending forward over the toe or backward to the back seam of the upper
2 [¹*vamp*] **:** a short introductory musical passage often repeated several times (as in vaudeville) before a solo or between verses

³vamp *noun* [short for *vampire*] (circa 1911)
: a woman who uses her charm or wiles to seduce and exploit men
— **vamp·ish** \'vam-pish\ *adjective*

⁴vamp *transitive verb* (circa 1915)
: to practice seductive wiles on

vam·pire \'vam-ˌpīr\ *noun* [French, from German *Vampir*, from Serbo-Croatian *vampir*] (1734)
1 : the reanimated body of a dead person believed to come from the grave at night and suck the blood of persons asleep
2 a : one who lives by preying on others **b :** a woman who exploits and ruins her lover
3 : VAMPIRE BAT
— **vam·pir·ish** \-ish\ *adjective*

vampire bat *noun* (1790)
: any of several Central and South American bats (*Desmodus rotundus*, *Diaemus youngi*, and *Diphylla ecaudata*) of the subfamily Desmodontinae of the family Phyllostomidae) that feed on the blood of birds and mammals and especially domestic animals and that are sometimes vectors of equine trypanosomiasis and of rabies; *also* **:** any of several other bats (as of the families Megadermatidae and Phyllostomidae) that do not feed on blood but are sometimes reputed to do so

vampire bat

vam·pir·ism \-ˌpīr-ˌi-zəm\ *noun* (1794)
1 : belief in vampires
2 : the actions of a vampire

¹van \'van\ *noun* [Middle English, from Middle French, from Latin *vannus* — more at WINNOW] (14th century)
1 *dialect English* **:** a winnowing device (as a fan)
2 : WING 1a

²van *noun* [by shortening] (1610)
: VANGUARD

³van *noun* [short for *caravan*] (1829)
1 a : a usually enclosed wagon or motortruck used for transportation of goods or animals; *also* **:** CARAVAN 2a **b :** a multipurpose enclosed motor vehicle having a boxlike shape, rear or side doors, and side panels often with windows **c :** a detachable passenger cabin transportable by aircraft or truck
2 *chiefly British* **:** an enclosed railroad freight or baggage car

⁴van *transitive verb* **vanned; van·ning** (1840)
: to transport by van

van·a·date \'va-nə-ˌdāt\ *noun* [New Latin *vanadium* + English ¹*-ate*] (1835)
: a salt derived from vanadium pentoxide and containing pentavalent vanadium

va·na·di·um \və-'nā-dē-əm\ *noun* [New Latin, from Old Norse *Vanadís* Freya] (1833)
: a grayish malleable ductile metallic element found combined in minerals and used especially to form alloys (as vanadium steel) — see ELEMENT table

vanadium pentoxide *noun* (1885)
: a yellowish red compound V_2O_5 used especially in glass manufacture and as a catalyst

Van Al·len belt \van-'a-lən-\ *noun* [James A. *Van Allen*] (1958)
: a belt of intense radiation in the magnetosphere composed of energetic charged particles trapped by the earth's magnetic field; *also* **:** a similar belt surrounding another planet

va·nas·pa·ti \və-'nəs-pə-tē, -'näs-\ *noun* [Sanskrit, forest tree, soma plant, literally, lord of the forest, from *vana* forest + *pati* lord, master — more at POTENT] (1941)
: a hydrogenated vegetable fat used as a butter substitute in India

van·dal \'van-dᵊl\ *noun* [Latin *Vandalii* (plural), of Germanic origin] (1555)
1 *capitalized* **:** a member of a Germanic people who lived in the area south of the Baltic between the Vistula and the Oder, overran Gaul, Spain, and northern Africa in the 4th and 5th centuries A.D. and in 455 sacked Rome
2 : one who willfully or ignorantly destroys, damages, or defaces property belonging to another or to the public ◇
— **vandal** *adjective, often capitalized*
— **Van·dal·ic** \van-'da-lik\ *adjective*

van·dal·ise *British variant of* VANDALIZE

van·dal·ism \'van-dᵊl-ˌi-zəm\ *noun* (1798)
: willful or malicious destruction or defacement of public or private property

van·dal·is·tic \ˌvan-dᵊl-'is-tik\ *adjective* (1897)
: of or relating to vandalism

van·dal·ize \'van-dᵊl-ˌīz\ *transitive verb* **-ized; -iz·ing** (1845)
: to subject to vandalism **:** DAMAGE
— **van·dal·i·za·tion** \ˌvan-dᵊl-ə-'zā-shən\ *noun*

van·da orchid \'van-də-\ *noun* [New Latin, from Hindi *vandā* mistletoe, from Sanskrit, a parasitic plant] (1943)
: any of a large genus (*Vanda*) of Indo-Malayan epiphytic orchids often grown for their loose racemes of showy flowers — called also *vanda*

Van de Graaff generator \'van-də-ˌgraf-\ *noun* [Robert J. *Van de Graaff* (died 1967) American physicist] (1937)
: an apparatus for the production of electrical discharges at high voltage commonly consisting of an insulated hollow conducting sphere that accumulates in its interior the charge continuously conveyed from a source of direct current by an endless belt of flexible nonconducting material

van der Waals forces \'van-dər-ˌwölz-, 'vän-dər-ˌvälz-\ *noun plural* [Johannes D. *van der Waals* (died 1923) Dutch physicist] (1926)
: the relatively weak attractive forces that act on neutral atoms and molecules and that arise because of the electric polarization induced in each of the particles by the presence of other particles

Van·dyke \van-'dīk, vən-\ *noun* [Sir Anthony *Vandyke*] (1755)
1 a : a wide collar with a deeply indented edge **b :** one of several V-shaped points forming a decorative edging **c :** a border of such points
2 : a trim pointed beard
— **van·dyked** \-'dīkt\ *adjective*

Vandyke brown *noun* [from its use by the painter Vandyke] (circa 1850)
: a natural brown-black pigment of organic matter obtained from bog earth or peat or lignite deposits; *also* **:** any of various synthetic brown pigments

Vandyke 2

vane \'vān\ *noun* [Middle English (southern dialect), from Old English *fana* banner; akin to Old High German *fano* cloth, Latin *pannus* cloth, rag] (15th century)
1 a : a movable device attached to an elevated object (as a spire) for showing the direction of

the wind **b :** one that is changeable or inconstant
2 : a thin flat or curved object that is rotated about an axis by a flow of fluid or that rotates to cause a fluid to flow or that redirects a flow of fluid ⟨the *vanes* of a windmill⟩
3 : the web or flat expanded part of a feather — see FEATHER illustration
4 : a feather fastened to the shaft near the nock of an arrow
word history see VIXEN
— **vaned** \'vānd\ *adjective*

van·guard \'van-ˌgärd *also* 'van-\ *noun* [Middle English *vantgard*, from Middle French *avant-garde*, from Old French, from *avant*-fore- (from *avant* before, from Late Latin *abante*) + *garde* guard — more at ADVANCE] (15th century)
1 : the troops moving at the head of an army
2 : the forefront of an action or movement
— **van·guard·ism** \-ˌgär-ˌdi-zəm\ *noun*
— **van·guard·ist** \-dist\ *noun*

¹va·nil·la \və-'ni-lə, -'ne-\ *noun* [New Latin, from Spanish *vainilla* vanilla (plant and fruit), diminutive of *vaina* sheath, from Latin *vagina* sheath, vagina] (1662)
1 a : VANILLA BEAN **b :** a commercially important extract of the vanilla bean that is used especially as a flavoring
2 : any of a genus (*Vanilla*) of tropical American climbing epiphytic orchids

²vanilla *adjective* (1846)
1 : flavored with vanilla
2 : lacking distinction **:** PLAIN, ORDINARY

vanilla bean *noun* (1874)
: the long capsular fruit of a vanilla (especially *Vanilla planifolia*) that is an important article of commerce

van·il·lin \'va-nᵊl-ən\ *noun* (circa 1868)
: a crystalline phenolic aldehyde $C_8H_8O_3$ that is extracted from vanilla beans or prepared synthetically and is used especially in flavoring and in perfumery

Va·nir \'vän-ˌir\ *noun plural* [Old Norse]
: a race of Norse gods who become united with the Aesir

van·ish \'va-nish\ *verb* [Middle English *vanisshen*, from Middle French *evaniss-*, stem of *evanir*, from (assumed) Vulgar Latin *exvanire*, alteration of Latin *evanescere* to dissipate like vapor, vanish, from *e-* + *vanescere* to vanish, from *vanus* empty] (14th century) *intransitive verb*
1 a : to pass quickly from sight **:** DISAPPEAR **b :** to pass completely from existence

2 : to assume the value zero
transitive verb
: to cause to disappear
— **van·ish·er** *noun*

van·ish·ing cream *noun* (1916)
: a cosmetic preparation that is less oily than cold cream and is used chiefly as a foundation for face powder

van·ish·ing·ly \'va-ni-shiŋ-lē\ *adverb* (1870)
: so as to be almost nonexistent or invisible ⟨the difference is *vanishingly* small⟩

vanishing point *noun* (1797)
1 : a point at which receding parallel lines seem to meet when represented in linear perspective
2 : a point at which something disappears or ceases to exist

van·i·ty \'va-nə-tē\ *noun, plural* **-ties** [Middle English *vanite*, from Old French *vanité*, from Latin *vanitat-, vanitas* quality of being empty or vain, from *vanus* empty, vain — more at WANE] (13th century)
1 : something that is vain, empty, or valueless
2 : the quality or fact of being vain
3 : inflated pride in oneself or one's appearance **:** CONCEIT
4 : a fashionable trifle or knicknack
5 a : ³COMPACT a **b :** a small case or handbag for toilet articles used by women
6 : DRESSING TABLE

vanity fair *noun, often V&F capitalized* [*Vanity-Fair*, a fair held in the frivolous town of Vanity in *Pilgrim's Progress* (1678) by John Bunyan] (1816)
: a scene or place characterized by frivolity and ostentation

vanity plate *noun* (1966)
: a license plate bearing letters or numbers designated by the owner of the vehicle

vanity press *noun* (1950)
: a publishing house that publishes books at the author's expense — called also *vanity publisher*

van·ner \'va-nər\ *noun* (1927)
: a person who owns a usually customized van

van·pool \'van-ˌpül\ *noun* (1973)
: an arrangement by which a group of people commute to work in a van
— **van·pool·ing** *noun*

van·quish \'vaŋ-kwish, 'van-\ *transitive verb* [Middle English *venquissen*, from Middle French *venquis*, preterit of *veintre* to conquer, from Latin *vincere* — more at VICTOR] (14th century)
1 : to overcome in battle **:** subdue completely
2 : to defeat in a conflict or contest
3 : to gain mastery over (an emotion, passion, or temptation)
synonym see CONQUER
— **van·quish·able** \-kwi-shə-bəl\ *adjective*
— **van·quish·er** *noun*

van·tage \'van-tij\ *noun* [Middle English, from Anglo-French, from Middle French *avantage* — more at ADVANTAGE] (14th century)
1 *archaic* **:** BENEFIT, GAIN
2 : superiority in a contest
3 : a position giving a strategic advantage, commanding perspective, or comprehensive view
4 : ADVANTAGE 4
— **to the vantage** *obsolete* **:** in addition

vantage point *noun* (1865)
: a position or standpoint from which something is viewed or considered; *especially* **:** POINT OF VIEW

van·ward \'van-wərd\ *adjective* (1820)
: located in the vanguard **:** ADVANCED
— **vanward** *adverb*

va·pid \'va-pəd, 'vā-\ *adjective* [Latin *vapidus* flat-tasting; akin to Latin *vappa* vapid wine and perhaps to Latin *vapor* steam] (circa 1656)
: lacking liveliness, tang, briskness, or force **:** FLAT, DULL ⟨a gossipy, *vapid* woman, obsessed by her own elegance —R. F. Delder-

field⟩ ⟨London was not all *vapid* dissipation —V. S. Pritchett⟩
synonym see INSIPID
— **va·pid·ly** *adverb*
— **va·pid·ness** *noun*

va·pid·i·ty \va-'pi-də-tē, vā-, və-\ *noun, plural* **-ties** (circa 1721)
1 : the quality or state of being vapid
2 : something vapid

¹va·por \'vā-pər\ *noun* [Middle English *vapour*, from Middle French *vapeur*, from Latin *vapor* steam, vapor] (14th century)
1 : diffused matter (as smoke or fog) suspended floating in the air and impairing its transparency
2 a : a substance in the gaseous state as distinguished from the liquid or solid state **b :** a substance (as gasoline, alcohol, mercury, or benzoin) vaporized for industrial, therapeutic, or military uses; *also* **:** a mixture (as the explosive mixture in an internal combustion engine) of such a vapor with air
3 a : something unsubstantial or transitory **:** PHANTASM **b :** a foolish or fanciful idea
4 *plural* **a** *archaic* **:** exhalations of bodily organs (as the stomach) held to affect the physical or mental condition **b :** a depressed or hysterical nervous condition

²vapor *intransitive verb* **va·pored; va·por·ing** \-p(ə-)riŋ\ (15th century)
1 a : to rise or pass off in vapor **b :** to emit vapor
2 : to indulge in bragging, blustering, or idle talk
— **va·por·er** \-pər-ər\ *noun*

vapor barrier *noun* (circa 1941)
: a layer of material (as roofing paper or polyethylene film) used to retard or prevent the absorption of moisture into a construction (as a wall or floor)

va·po·ret·to \ˌvä-pə-'re-(ˌ)tō\ *noun, plural* **-ret·ti** \-'re-tē\ *also* **-ret·tos** [Italian, diminutive of *vapore* steamboat, from French *vapeur*, from *bateau à vapeur* steamboat] (1926)
: a motorboat serving as a canal bus in Venice, Italy

va·por·ing \'vā-p(ə-)riŋ\ *noun* (circa 1630)
: the act or speech of one that vapors; *specifically* **:** an idle, extravagant, or high-flown expression or speech — usually used in plural

va·por·ise *British variant of* VAPORIZE

va·por·ish \'vā-p(ə-)rish\ *adjective* (circa 1644)
1 : resembling or suggestive of vapor
2 : given to fits of the vapors
— **va·por·ish·ness** *noun*

va·por·ize \'vā-pə-ˌrīz\ *verb* **-ized; -iz·ing** (1803)
transitive verb
1 : to convert (as by the application of heat or by spraying) into vapor
2 : to cause to become dissipated
intransitive verb
1 : to become vaporized
2 : VAPOR 2
— **va·por·iz·able** \-ˌrī-zə-bəl\ *adjective*
— **va·por·i·za·tion** \ˌvā-pər-ə-'zā-shən\ *noun*

va·por·iz·er \'vā-pə-ˌrī-zər\ *noun* (circa 1846)
: one that vaporizes: as **a :** ATOMIZER **b :** a device for converting water or a medicated liquid into a vapor for inhalation

vapor lock *noun* (1926)
: partial or complete interruption of flow of a fluid (as fuel in an internal combustion engine) caused by the formation of bubbles of vapor in the feeding system

va·por·ous \'vā-p(ə-)rəs\ *adjective* (1527)
1 : consisting or characteristic of vapor
2 : producing vapors **:** VOLATILE
3 : containing or obscured by vapors **:** MISTY
4 a : ETHEREAL, UNSUBSTANTIAL **b :** consisting of or indulging in vaporings
— **va·por·ous·ly** *adverb*
— **va·por·ous·ness** *noun*

vapor pressure *noun* (1875)

: the pressure exerted by a vapor that is in equilibrium with its solid or liquid form — called also *vapor tension*

vapor trail *noun* (1941)
: CONTRAIL

va·por·ware \'vā-pər-ˌwar, -ˌwer\ *noun* (1984)
: a new computer-related product that has been widely advertised but is not yet available

va·pory \'vā-p(ə-)rē\ *adjective* (1598)
: VAPOROUS, MISTY

va·pour *chiefly British variant of* VAPOR

va·que·ro \vä-'ker-(ˌ)ō\ *noun, plural* **-ros** [Spanish — more at BUCKAROO] (1826)
: HERDSMAN, COWBOY

va·ra \'vär-ə\ *noun* [American Spanish, from Spanish, pole, from Latin, forked pole, from feminine of *varus* bent, bow-legged] (1831)
: a Texas unit of length equal to 33.33 inches (84.66 centimeters)

vari- *or* **vario-** *combining form* [Latin *varius*]
1 : varied **:** diverse ⟨*varicolored*⟩
2 : variation **:** variability ⟨*variometer*⟩

var·ia \'ver-ē-ə, 'var-\ *noun plural* [New Latin, from Latin, neuter plural of *varius* various] (1926)
: MISCELLANY; *especially* **:** a literary miscellany

¹var·i·able \'ver-ē-ə-bəl, 'var-\ *adjective* [Middle English, from Middle French, from Latin *variabilis*, from *variare* to vary] (14th century)
1 a : able or apt to vary **:** subject to variation or changes ⟨*variable* winds⟩ ⟨*variable* costs⟩ **b :** FICKLE, INCONSTANT
2 : characterized by variations
3 : having the characteristics of a variable
4 : not true to type **:** ABERRANT — used of a biological group or character
— **var·i·abil·i·ty** \ˌver-ē-ə-'bi-lə-tē, ˌvar-\ *noun*
— **var·i·able·ness** \'ver-ē-ə-bəl-nəs, 'var-\ *noun*
— **var·i·ably** \-blē\ *adverb*

²variable *noun* (1816)
1 a : a quantity that may assume any one of a set of values **b :** a symbol representing a variable
2 : something that is variable
3 : VARIABLE STAR

variable rate mortgage *noun* (1975)
: ADJUSTABLE RATE MORTGAGE

variable star *noun* (1788)
: a star whose brightness changes usually in more or less regular periods

var·i·ance \'ver-ē-ən(t)s, 'var-\ *noun* (14th century)
1 : the fact, quality, or state of being variable or variant **:** DIFFERENCE, VARIATION ⟨yearly *variance* in crops⟩
2 : the fact or state of being in disagreement **:** DISSENSION, DISPUTE
3 : a disagreement between two parts of the same legal proceeding that must be consonant
4 : a license to do some act contrary to the usual rule ⟨a zoning *variance*⟩
5 : the square of the standard deviation
synonym see DISCORD
— **at variance :** not in harmony or agreement

¹var·i·ant \'ver-ē-ənt, 'var-\ *adjective* (14th century)
1 *obsolete* **:** VARIABLE
2 : manifesting variety, deviation, or disagreement
3 : varying usually slightly from the standard form ⟨*variant* readings⟩

²variant *noun* (1848)
: one of two or more persons or things exhibiting usually slight differences: as **a :** one that exhibits variation from a type or norm **b :** one of two or more different spellings (as *labor*

and *labour*) or pronunciations (as of *economics* \ek-, ēk-\) of the same word **c** : one of two or more words (as *geographic* and *geographical*) or word elements (as *mon-* and *mono-*) of essentially the same meaning differing only in the presence or absence of an affix

var·i·ate \'ver-ē-ət, 'var-, -āt\ *noun* (1899)
: RANDOM VARIABLE

var·i·a·tion \ˌver-ē-'ā-shən, ˌvar-\ *noun* (14th century)
1 a : the act or process of varying : the state or fact of being varied **b** : an instance of varying **c** : the extent to which or the range in which a thing varies
2 : DECLINATION 6
3 a : a change of algebraic sign between successive terms of a sequence **b** : a measure of the change in data, a variable, or a function
4 : the repetition of a musical theme with modifications in rhythm, tune, harmony, or key
5 a : divergence in the characteristics of an organism from the species or population norm or average **b** : something (as an individual or group) that exhibits variation
6 a : a solo dance in classic ballet **b** : a repetition in modern ballet of a movement sequence with changes
— **var·i·a·tion·al** \-shnəl, -shə-nᵊl\ *adjective*
— **var·i·a·tion·al·ly** *adverb*

var·i·cel·la \ˌvar-ə-'se-lə\ *noun* [New Latin, irregular diminutive of *variola*] (circa 1771)
: CHICKEN POX

var·i·co·cele \'var-ə-kō-ˌsēl\ *noun* [New Latin, from Latin *varic-, varix* + New Latin *-o-* + *-cele*] (1736)
: a varicose enlargement of the veins of the spermatic cord

vari·col·ored \'ver-i-ˌkə-lərd, 'var-\ *adjective* (1665)
: having various colors : VARIEGATED ⟨the *varicolored* breeding plumage of a bird⟩; *also* : of various colors

var·i·cose \'var-ə-ˌkōs\ *also* **var·i·cosed** \-ˌkōst\ *adjective* [Latin *varicosus* full of dilated veins, from *varic-, varix* dilated vein] (circa 1730)
1 : abnormally swollen or dilated ⟨*varicose* veins⟩
2 : affected with varicose veins ⟨*varicose* legs⟩

var·i·cos·i·ty \ˌvar-ə-'kä-sə-tē\ *noun, plural* **-ties** (circa 1842)
1 : the quality or state of being abnormally or markedly swollen or dilated
2 : VARIX

var·ied \'ver-ēd, 'var-\ *adjective* (1588)
1 : VARIOUS, DIVERSE
2 : VARIEGATED 1
— **var·ied·ly** *adverb*

var·ie·gate \'ver-ē-ə-ˌgāt, 'ver-i-ˌgāt, 'var-\ *transitive verb* **-gat·ed; -gat·ing** [Latin *variegatus*, past participle of *variegare*, from *varius* various + *-egare* (akin to Latin *agere* to drive) — more at AGENT] (1653)
1 : to diversify in external appearance especially with different colors : DAPPLE
2 : to enliven or give interest to by means of variety
— **var·ie·ga·tor** \-ˌgā-tər\ *noun*

var·ie·gat·ed \-ˌgā-təd\ *adjective* (1661)
1 : having discrete markings of different colors ⟨*variegated* leaves⟩
2 : VARIED 1

variegated cutworm *noun* (1922)
: a widespread noctuid moth (*Peridroma saucia*) whose larva is destructive to crops

var·ie·ga·tion \ˌver-ē-ə-'gā-shən, ˌver-i-'gā-, ˌvar-\ *noun* (1646)
: the act of variegating : the state of being variegated; *especially* : diversity of colors

var·i·er \'ver-ē-ər, 'var-\ *noun* (1860)
: one that varies

¹va·ri·etal \və-'rī-ə-tᵊl\ *adjective* (1866)

1 : of, relating to, or characterizing a variety ⟨*varietal* name⟩; *also* : being a variety in distinction from an individual or species
2 : of, relating to, or producing a varietal

²varietal *noun* (1950)
: a wine bearing the name of the principal grape from which it is made

va·ri·ety \və-'rī-ə-tē\ *noun, plural* **-ties** [Middle French or Latin; Middle French *variété*, from Latin *varietat-, varietas*, from *varius* various] (15th century)
1 : the quality or state of having different forms or types : MULTIFARIOUSNESS
2 : a number or collection of different things especially of a particular class : ASSORTMENT
3 a : something differing from others of the same general kind : SORT **b** : any of various groups of plants or animals ranking below a species : SUBSPECIES
4 : VARIETY SHOW

variety meat *noun* (circa 1946)
: an edible part (as the liver or tongue) of a slaughter animal other than skeletal muscle

variety show *noun* (1882)
: a theatrical entertainment of successive separate performances (as of songs, dances, skits, acrobatic feats, and trained animal acts)

variety store *noun* (circa 1768)
: a retail store that carries a wide variety of merchandise especially of low unit value

vario- — SEE VARI-

va·ri·o·la \və-'rī-ə-lə, ˌver-ē-'ō-lə, ˌvar-\ *noun* [New Latin, from Medieval Latin, pustule, pox, from Late Latin, pustule, probably from *varius* various] (1543)
: SMALLPOX

var·i·om·e·ter \ˌver-ē-'ä-mə-tər, ˌvar-\ *noun* (circa 1900)
1 : an instrument for measuring magnetic declination
2 : an aeronautical instrument for indicating rate of climb

¹var·i·o·rum \ˌver-ē-'ōr-əm, ˌvar-, -'òr-\ *noun* [Latin *variorum* of various persons (genitive plural masculine of *varius*), in the phrase *cum notis variorum* with the notes of various persons] (1728)
1 : an edition or text with notes by different persons
2 : an edition containing variant readings of the text

²variorum *adjective* (1763)
: relating to or being a variorum; *also* : VARIANT ⟨*variorum* readings⟩

¹var·i·ous \'ver-ē-əs, 'var-\ *adjective* [Latin *varius*] (1552)
1 *archaic* : VARIABLE, INCONSTANT
2 : VARICOLORED ⟨birds of *various* plumage⟩
3 a : of differing kinds : MULTIFARIOUS **b** : dissimilar in nature or form : UNLIKE ⟨animals as *various* as the jaguar and the sloth⟩
4 : having a number of different aspects or characteristics ⟨a *various* place⟩ ⟨a *various* talent⟩
5 : of an indefinite number greater than one ⟨stop at *various* towns⟩
6 : INDIVIDUAL, SEPARATE ⟨rate increases granted in the *various* states⟩
synonym see DIFFERENT
— **var·i·ous·ness** *noun*

²various *pronoun, plural in construction* (1877)
: an indefinite number of separate individuals greater than one ⟨conversations with people from *various* of the schools —Patricia Linden⟩

var·i·ous·ly *adverb* (1627)
1 : in various ways : at various times ⟨was *variously* occupied teaching, farming, and clerking⟩
2 : by various designations ⟨known *variously* as principal, headmaster, and rector⟩

vari·sized \'ver-i-ˌsīzd, 'var-\ *adjective* (1936)
: of various sizes

va·ris·tor \və-'ris-tər, ve-\ *noun* [*vari-* + *resistor*] (1937)

: an electrical resistor whose resistance depends on the applied voltage

var·ix \'var-iks\ *noun, plural* **var·i·ces** \'var-ə-ˌsēz\ [Middle English, from Latin *varic-, varix*] (14th century)
: an abnormally dilated and lengthened vein, artery, or lymph vessel; *especially* : a varicose vein

var·let \'vär-lət\ *noun* [Middle English, from Middle French *vaslet, varlet* young nobleman, page — more at VALET] (15th century)
1 a : ATTENDANT, MENIAL **b** : a knight's page
2 : a base unprincipled person : KNAVE

var·let·ry \-lə-trē\ *noun* (1606)
archaic : RABBLE

var·mint \'vär-mənt\ *noun* [alteration of *vermin*] (1539)
1 : an animal considered a pest; *specifically* : one classed as vermin and unprotected by game law
2 : a contemptible person : RASCAL; *broadly* : PERSON, FELLOW

¹var·nish \'vär-nish\ *noun* [Middle English *vernish*, from Middle French *vernis*, from Old Italian or Medieval Latin; Old Italian *vernice*, from Medieval Latin *veronic-, veronix sandarac*] (14th century)
1 a : a liquid preparation that when spread and allowed to dry on a surface forms a hard lustrous typically transparent coating **b** : the covering or glaze given by the application of varnish **c** (1) : something that suggests varnish by its gloss (2) : a coating (as of deposits in an internal combustion engine) comparable to varnish
2 : outside show : ¹GLOSS
3 *chiefly British* : a liquid nail polish
— **var·nishy** \-ni-shē\ *adjective*

²varnish *transitive verb* (14th century)
1 : to apply varnish to
2 : to cover or conceal (as something unpleasant) with something that gives a fair appearance : ²GLOSS
3 : ADORN, EMBELLISH
— **var·nish·er** \'vär-ni-shər\ *noun*

varnish tree *noun* (1758)
: any of various trees yielding a milky juice from which in some cases varnish or lacquer is prepared; *especially* : a Japanese sumac (*Rhus vernicflua*)

var·si·ty \'vär-sə-tē, -stē\ *noun, plural* **-ties** [by shortening & alteration from *university*] (1646)
1 *British* : UNIVERSITY
2 a : the principal squad representing a university, college, school, or club especially in a sport **b** : REGULAR 1d

Var·so·vi·an \ˌvär-'sō-vē-ən\ *noun* [French *varsovien*, from *Varsovie* Warsaw] (1764)
: a native or resident of Warsaw, Poland

Va·ru·na \'vär-ə-nə\ *noun* [Sanskrit *Varuṇa*]
: a chief Vedic god responsible for natural and moral order in the cosmos

var·us \'var-əs, 'ver-\ *noun* [New Latin, from Latin, bent, knock-kneed] (1800)
: a deformed position of a bodily part characterized by bending or turning inward toward the midline of the body to an abnormal degree ⟨a moderate right metatarsus *varus* —*Journal American Medical Association*⟩
— **varus** *adjective*

varve \'värv\ *noun* [Swedish *varv* turn, layer; akin to Old Norse *hvarf* ring, Old English *hweorfan* to turn — more at WHARF] (1912)
: a pair of layers of alternately finer and coarser silt or clay believed to comprise an annual cycle of deposition in a body of still water
— **varved** \'värvd\ *adjective*

vary \'ver-ē, 'var-\ *verb* **var·ied; vary·ing** [Middle English *varien*, from Middle French or Latin; Middle French *varier*, from Latin *variare*, from *varius* various] (14th century)
transitive verb

1 a : to make a partial change in **:** make different in some attribute or characteristic **b :** to make differences between items in **:** DIVERSIFY **2 :** to present under new aspects ⟨*vary* the rhythm and harmonic treatment⟩ *intransitive verb* **1 :** to exhibit or undergo change ⟨the sky was constantly *varying*⟩ **2 :** DEVIATE, DEPART **3 :** to take on successive values ⟨*y varies* inversely with *x*⟩ **4 :** to exhibit divergence in structural or physiological characters from the typical form **synonym** see CHANGE — **vary·ing·ly** \-iŋ-lē\ *adverb*

varying hare *noun* (1781)
: SNOWSHOE HARE

vas \'vas\ *noun, plural* **va·sa** \'vā-zə\ [New Latin, from Latin, vessel] (1651)
: an anatomical vessel **:** DUCT
— **va·sal** \-zəl\ *adjective*

vas- *or* **vaso-** *combining form* [New Latin, from Latin *vas*]
1 : vessel: as **a :** blood vessel ⟨*vaso*motor⟩ **b :** vas deferens ⟨*vas*ectomy⟩ **2 :** vascular and ⟨*vaso*vagal⟩ **3 :** vasomotor ⟨*vaso*active⟩

va·sa ef·fer·en·tia \'vā-zə-,e-fə-'ren(t)-sh(ē-)ə\ *noun plural* [New Latin, literally, efferent vessels] (circa 1860)
: the 12 to 20 ductules that lead from the rete of the testis to the vas deferens and except near their commencement are greatly convoluted and form the compact head of the epididymis

vas·cu·lar \'vas-kyə-lər\ *adjective* [New Latin *vascularis*, from Latin *vasculum* small vessel, diminutive of *vas*] (1672)
1 : of or relating to a channel for the conveyance of a body fluid (as blood of an animal or sap of a plant) or to a system of such channels; *also* **:** supplied with or made up of such channels and especially blood vessels ⟨a *vascular* tumor⟩ ⟨a *vascular* system⟩ **2 :** marked by vigor and ardor **:** SPIRITED, PASSIONATE
— **vas·cu·lar·i·ty** \,vas-kyə-'lar-ə-tē\ *noun*

vascular bundle *noun* (circa 1884)
: a strand of specialized vascular tissue of higher plants consisting mostly of xylem and phloem

vascular cylinder *noun* (circa 1889)
: STELE

vas·cu·lar·i·za·tion \,vas-kyə-lə-rə-'zā-shən\ *noun* (1818)
: the process of becoming vascular; *also* **:** abnormal or excessive formation of blood vessels (as in the retina or on the cornea)

vascular plant *noun* (1861)
: a plant having a specialized conducting system that includes xylem and phloem **:** TRACHEOPHYTE

vascular ray *noun* (1672)
: a band of usually parenchymatous cells partly in the xylem and partly in the phloem of a plant root or stem that conducts fluids radially and appears in a cross section like a spoke of a wheel

vascular tissue *noun* (1815)
: plant tissue concerned mainly with conduction; *especially* **:** the specialized tissue of higher plants consisting essentially of phloem and xylem

vas·cu·la·ture \'vas-kyə-lə-,chùr, -,tyùr, -,tùr\ *noun* [Latin *vasculum* vessel + English *-ature* (as in *musculature*)] (circa 1927)
: the arrangement of blood vessels in an organ or part

vas·cu·li·tis \,vas-kyə-'lī-təs\ *noun, plural* **-lit·i·des** \-'li-tə-,dēz\ [New Latin, from Latin *vasculum* vessel] (circa 1900)
: inflammation of a blood or lymph vessel

vas·cu·lum \'vas-kyə-ləm\ *noun, plural* **-la** \-lə\ [New Latin, from Latin, small vessel] (1782)

: a usually metal and commonly cylindrical or flattened covered box used in collecting plants

vas def·er·ens \'vas-'de-fə-rənz, -,renz\ *noun, plural* **va·sa def·er·en·tia** \'vā-zə-,de-fə-'ren(t)-sh(ē-)ə\ [New Latin, literally, deferent vessel] (1578)
: a spermatic duct especially of a higher vertebrate that in the human male is a thick-walled tube about two feet (0.61 meters) long that begins at and is continuous with the tail of the epididymis and eventually joins the duct of the seminal vesicle to form the ejaculatory duct

vase *US oftenest* 'vās; *Canadian usually & US also* 'vāz; *British usually, Canadian also, & US sometimes* 'väz\ *noun* [French, from Latin *vas* vessel] (1563)
: a usually round vessel of greater depth than width used chiefly as an ornament or for holding flowers ▢
— **vase·like** \-,līk\ *adjective*

va·sec·to·mize \və-'sek-tə-,mīz, vā-'zek-\ *transitive verb* **-mized; -miz·ing** (1900)
: to perform a vasectomy on

va·sec·to·my \-tə-mē\ *noun, plural* **-mies** [International Scientific Vocabulary] (1899)
: surgical division or resection of all or part of the vas deferens usually to induce sterility

Vas·e·line \'va-sə-,lēn, ,va-sə-'\ *trademark*
— used for petroleum jelly

va·so·ac·tive \,vā-zō-'ak-tiv\ *adjective* (circa 1921)
: affecting the blood vessels especially in respect to the degree of their relaxation or contraction
— **va·so·ac·tiv·i·ty** \-ak-'ti-və-tē\ *noun*

va·so·con·stric·tion \-kən-'strik-shən\ *noun* [International Scientific Vocabulary] (1899)
: narrowing of the lumen of blood vessels especially as a result of vasomotor action

va·so·con·stric·tive \-'strik-tiv\ *adjective* (1890)
: inducing vasoconstriction

va·so·con·stric·tor \-tər\ *noun* (1877)
: an agent (as a sympathetic nerve fiber or a drug) that induces or initiates vasoconstriction

va·so·di·la·tion \-dī-'lā-shən, -də-\ *or* **va·so·di·la·ta·tion** \-,di-lə-'tā-shən, -,dī-lə-\ *noun* [International Scientific Vocabulary] (1896)
: widening of the lumen of blood vessels

va·so·di·la·tor \-dī-'lā-tər, -'dī-,lā-\ *noun* (1881)
: an agent (as a parasympathetic nerve fiber or a drug) that induces or initiates vasodilation

va·so·mo·tor \,vā-zə-'mō-tər\ *adjective* [International Scientific Vocabulary] (1865)
: of, relating to, or being nerves or centers controlling the size of blood vessels

va·so·pres·sin \,vā-zō-'pres-ᵊn\ *noun* [from *Vasopressin*, a trademark] (1927)
: a polypeptide hormone secreted by the posterior lobe of the pituitary gland that increases blood pressure and decreases urine flow — called also *antidiuretic hormone*

va·so·pres·sor \-'pre-sər\ *adjective* (1928)
: causing a rise in blood pressure by exerting a vasoconstrictor effect
— **vasopressor** *noun*

va·so·spasm \'vā-zō-,spa-zəm\ *noun* [International Scientific Vocabulary] (circa 1909)
: sharp and often persistent contraction of a blood vessel reducing its caliber and blood flow
— **va·so·spas·tic** \,vā-zō-'spas-tik\ *adjective*

va·so·to·cin \,vā-zə-'tō-sᵊn\ *noun* [*vaso-* + *oxytocin*] (circa 1963)
: a polypeptide pituitary hormone of most vertebrates below mammals that is probably the phylogenetic precursor of oxytocin and vasopressin

va·so·va·gal \,vā-zō-'vā-gəl\ *adjective* (circa 1923)
: of, relating to, or involving both vascular and vagal factors

vas·sal \'va-səl\ *noun* [Middle English, from Middle French, from Medieval Latin *vassal-*

lus, from *vassus* servant, vassal, of Celtic origin; akin to Welsh *gwas* young man, servant] (14th century)
1 : a person under the protection of a feudal lord to whom he has vowed homage and fealty **:** a feudal tenant **2 :** one in a subservient or subordinate position
— **vassal** *adjective*

vas·sal·age \-sə-lij\ *noun* (1594)
1 : the state of being a vassal **2 :** the homage, fealty, or services due from a vassal **3 :** a position of subordination or submission (as to a political power)

¹vast \'vast\ *adjective* [Latin *vastus;* akin to Old High German *wuosti* empty, desolate, Old Irish *fás*] (1575)
: very great in size, amount, degree, intensity, or especially in extent or range
synonym see ENORMOUS
— **vast·ly** *adverb*
— **vast·ness** \'vas(t)-nəs\ *noun*

²vast *noun* (1604)
: a boundless space ⟨the *vast* of heaven —John Milton⟩

vas·ti·tude \'vas-tə-,tüd, -,tyüd\ *noun* [Latin *vastitudo*, from *vastus*] (1623)
: IMMENSITY, VASTNESS

vasty \'vas-tē\ *adjective* (1596)
: VAST ⟨call spirits from the *vasty* deep —Shakespeare⟩

¹vat \'vat\ *noun* [Middle English *fat, vat,* from Old English *fæt;* akin to Old High German *vaz* vessel, Lithuanian *puodas* pot] (13th century)
1 : a large vessel (as a cistern, tub, or barrel) especially for holding liquors in an immature state or preparations for dyeing or tanning **2 :** a liquor containing a dye converted into a soluble reduced colorless or weakly colored form that on textile material steeped in the liquor and exposed to the air is converted by oxidation to the original insoluble dye and precipitated in the fiber
word history see VIXEN

²vat *transitive verb* **vat·ted; vat·ting** (1784)
: to put into or treat in a vat

vat dye *noun* (circa 1903)
: a water-insoluble generally fast dye used in the form of a vat liquor — called also *vat color*

vat–dyed \'vat-'dīd\ *adjective* (circa 1947)
: dyed with one or more vat dyes

vat·ic \'va-tik\ *adjective* [Latin *vates* seer, prophet; akin to Old English *wōth* poetry, Old High German *wuot* madness, Old Irish *fáith* seer, poet] (1603)
: PROPHETIC, ORACULAR

Vat·i·can \'va-ti-kən\ *noun* [Latin *Vaticanus* Vatican Hill (in Rome)] (1555)

▢ USAGE
vase This little word of four letters, one of which is silent, provokes two long-standing pronunciation questions. Should the *a* have the sound of *a* in *are* or *ate,* and should the *s* have the sound of *s* in *case* or *rase*? Swift and Byron rhymed *vase* with *face* and *place,* but all four possibilities have been advocated in the past, along with a fifth variant which rhymed with *gauze*. One also finds a variety of spellings over the centuries to match each pronunciation. To some ears the \'väz\ variant sounds more elegant, but the others are also established by long usage and are equally acceptable. Which is the dominant form depends on where you are in the English-speaking world, as noted above.

\ə\ abut \ᵊ\ kitten \ər\ further \a\ ash \ā\ ace
\ä\ mop, mar \au̇\ out \ch\ chin \e\ bet \ē\ easy
\g\ go \i\ hit \ī\ ice \j\ job \ŋ\ sing \ō\ go
\ȯ\ law \ȯi\ boy \th\ thin \th̲\ the \ü\ loot \u̇\ foot
\y\ yet \zh\ vision *see also* Guide to Pronunciation

1 : the papal headquarters in Rome
2 : the papal government
— **Vatican** *adjective*

va·tic·i·nal \və-'ti-s°n-əl, va-\ *adjective* [Latin *vaticinus,* from *vaticinari* to foretell, prophesy] (1586)
: PROPHETIC

va·tic·i·nate \-s°n-,āt\ *verb* **-nat·ed; -nat·ing** [Latin *vaticinatus,* past participle of *vaticinari,* from *vates* + *-cinari* (akin to Latin *canere* to sing) — more at CHANT] (circa 1623)
: PROPHESY, PREDICT
— **va·tic·i·na·tor** \-,ā-tər\ *noun*

va·tic·i·na·tion \-,ti-s°n-'ā-shən\ *noun* (1603)
1 : PREDICTION
2 : the act of prophesying

va·tu \'vä-,tü\ *noun, plural* **vatu** [probably alteration of *Vanuatu*] (1981)
— see MONEY table

vaude·ville \'vȯd-vəl, 'väd-, 'vȯd-, -,vil; 'vȯ-də-, 'vä-, 'vō-\ *noun* [French, from Middle French, popular satirical song, alteration of *vaudevire,* from *vau-de-Vire* valley of Vire, town in northwest France where such songs were composed] (1739)
1 : a light often comic theatrical piece frequently combining pantomime, dialogue, dancing, and song
2 : stage entertainment consisting of various acts (as performing animals, acrobats, comedians, dancers, or singers)
— **vaude·vil·lian** \,vȯd-'vil-yən, ,väd-, ,vȯd-; 'vȯ-də-, 'vä-, 'vō-\ *noun or adjective*

Vau·dois \vō-'dwä, 'vō-,\ *noun plural* [Middle French, from Medieval Latin *Valdenses*] (1560)
: WALDENSES

¹vault \'vȯlt\ *noun* [Middle English *voute,* from Middle French, from (assumed) Vulgar Latin *volvita* turn, vault, from feminine of *volvitus,* alteration of Latin *volutus,* past participle of *volvere* to roll — more at VOLUBLE] (14th century)
1 a : an arched structure of masonry usually forming a ceiling or roof **b :** something (as the sky) resembling a vault **c :** an arched or dome-shaped anatomical structure
2 a : a space covered by an arched structure; *especially* **:** an underground passage or room **b :** an underground storage compartment **c :** a room or compartment for the safekeeping of valuables
3 a : a burial chamber **b :** a prefabricated container usually of metal or concrete into which a casket is placed at burial
— **vaulty** \'vȯl-tē\ *adjective*

²vault *transitive verb* (14th century)
: to form or cover with or as if with a vault
: ARCH

³vault *verb* [Middle French *volter,* from Old Italian *voltare,* from (assumed) Vulgar Latin *volvitare* to turn, leap, frequentative of Latin *volvere*] (1538)
intransitive verb
1 : to bound vigorously; *especially* **:** to execute a leap using the hands or a pole
2 : to do or achieve something as if by a leap
transitive verb
: to leap over; *especially* **:** to leap over by or as if by aid of the hands or a pole

⁴vault *noun* (1576)
: an act of vaulting **:** LEAP

vault·ed \'vȯl-təd\ *adjective* (1533)
1 : built in the form of a vault **:** ARCHED
2 : covered with a vault

vault·er \-tər\ *noun* (circa 1552)
: one that vaults; *especially* **:** an athlete who competes in the pole vault

¹vault·ing \-tiŋ\ *noun* (1512)
: vaulted construction

²vaulting *adjective* (1593)
1 : reaching or stretching for the heights ⟨*vaulting* ambition⟩ ⟨a *vaulting* imagination⟩
2 : designed for use in vaulting or in gymnastic exercises ⟨a *vaulting* block⟩

— **vault·ing·ly** \-tiŋ-lē\ *adverb*

vaulting horse *noun* (circa 1875)
1 : a gymnastics apparatus used in vaulting that consists of a padded rectangular or cylindrical form supported in a horizontal position above the floor
2 : an event in which vaults are made over a vaulting horse

¹vaunt \'vȯnt, 'vänt\ *verb* [Middle English, from Middle French *vanter,* from Late Latin *vanitare,* frequentative of (assumed) Latin *vanare,* from Latin *vanus* vain] (15th century)
intransitive verb
: to make a vain display of one's own worth or attainments **:** BRAG
transitive verb
: to call attention to pridefully and often boastfully ⟨people who *vaunt* their ingenuity⟩
synonym see BOAST
— **vaunt·er** *noun*
— **vaunt·ing·ly** \'vȯn-tiŋ-lē, 'vän-\ *adverb*

²vaunt *noun* (15th century)
1 : a vainglorious display of what one is or has or has done
2 : a bragging assertive statement

vaunt–cou·ri·er \'vȯnt-'kür-ē-ər, vänt-, -'kȯr-ē-, -'kȯ-rē-, -'kə-rē-\ *noun* [Middle French *avant-courrier,* literally, advance courier] (1560)
archaic **:** FORERUNNER

vaunt·ed \'vȯn-təd, 'vän-\ *adjective* (1579)
: highly or widely praised or boasted about ⟨his own much *vaunted* ferocity —Calvin Tomkins⟩

vaunt·ful \'vȯnt-fəl, 'vänt-\ *adjective* (1590)
: VAINGLORIOUS, BOASTFUL

vaunty \'vȯn-tē, 'vän-\ *adjective* (1724)
Scottish **:** PROUD, BOASTFUL, VAIN

vav *variant of* WAW

vav·a·sor *or* **vav·a·sour** \'va-və-,sȯr, -,sȯr, -,sür\ *noun* [Middle English *vavasour,* from Middle French *vavassor,* probably from Medieval Latin *vassus vassorum* vassal of vassals] (14th century)
: a feudal tenant ranking directly below a baron

va·ward \'vaù-,ȯrd, -,wȯrd\ *noun* [Middle English *vauntwarde, vaward,* from Old North French *avantwarde,* from *avant* before (from Late Latin *abante*) + *warde* guard, from *warder* to guard — more at ADVANCE, REWARD] (1597)
archaic **:** the foremost part **:** FOREFRONT ⟨the *vaward* of our youth —Shakespeare⟩

VCR \,vē-(,)sē-'är\ *noun* [videocassette recorder] (1971)
: a videotape recorder that uses videocassettes

V–day \'vē-,dā\ *noun* [victory day] (1941)
: a day of victory

've \v, əv\ *verb* [by contraction]
: HAVE ⟨we've been there⟩

Ve·adar \'vā-,ä-,där, 'vä-ə-\ *noun* [Hebrew *wĕ-Adhār,* literally, and Adar (i.e., the second Adar)] (circa 1864)
: the intercalary month of the Jewish calendar following Adar in leap years — see MONTH table

¹veal \'vē(ə)l\ *noun* [Middle English *veel,* from Middle French, from Latin *vitellus* small calf, diminutive of *vitulus* calf — more at WETHER] (14th century)
1 : the flesh of a young calf
2 : CALF; *especially* **:** VEALER

²veal *transitive verb* (1847)
: to kill and dress (a calf) for veal

veal·er \'vē-lər\ *noun* (circa 1895)
: a calf grown for or suitable for veal

vealy \'vē-lē\ *adjective* (1769)
1 : resembling or suggesting veal or a calf
2 : IMMATURE

¹vec·tor \'vek-tər\ *noun* [New Latin, from Latin, carrier, from *vehere* to carry — more at WAY] (1846)
1 a : a quantity that has magnitude and direction and that is commonly represented by a directed line segment whose length represents the magnitude and whose orientation in space

represents the direction; *broadly* **:** an element of a vector space **b :** a course or compass direction especially of an airplane
2 a : an organism (as an insect) that transmits a pathogen **b :** POLLINATOR a
3 : a sequence of genetic material (as a transposon or the genome of a bacteriophage) used to introduce specific genes into the genome of an organism
— **vector** *adjective*
— **vec·to·ri·al** \vek-'tȯr-ē-əl, -'tȯr-\ *adjective*
— **vec·to·ri·al·ly** \-ə-lē\ *adverb*

veal 1: *A* wholesale cuts: *1* leg, *2* loin, *3* flank, *4* rib, *5* breast, *6* shoulder, *7* shank; *B* retail cuts: *1* hind shank, *2* heel of round, *3* round, *4* rump roast, *5* sirloin steak, *6* loin chops, *7* kidney chops, *8* flank, *9* breast, *10* rib roast, *11* blade steak, *12* arm steak, *13* shoulder roast, *14* foreshank

²vector *transitive verb* **vec·tored; vec·tor·ing** \-t(ə-)riŋ\ (1941)
1 : to guide (as an airplane, its pilot, or a missile) in flight by means of a radioed vector
2 : to change the direction of (the thrust of a jet engine) for steering

vector product *noun* (1878)
: a vector *c* whose length is the product of the lengths of two vectors *a* and *b* and the sine of their included angle, whose direction is perpendicular to their plane, and whose direction is that in which a right-handed screw with axis *c* will move along *c* when *a* is rotated into *b* — called also *cross product*

vector space *noun* (1937)
: a set representing a generalization of a system of vectors and consisting of elements which comprise a commutative group under addition, each of which is left unchanged under multiplication by the multiplicative identity of a field, and for which multiplication by the multiplicative operation of the field is commutative, closed, distributive such that both $c(A + B) = cA + cB$ and $(c + d)A = cA + dA$, and associative such that $(cd)A = c(dA)$ where *A, B* are vectors and *c, d* are elements of the field

vector sum *noun* (circa 1890)
: the sum of a number of vectors that for the sum of two vectors is geometrically represented by the diagonal of a parallelogram whose sides represent the two vectors being added

Ve·da \'vā-də\ *noun* [Sanskrit, literally, knowledge; akin to Greek *eidenai* to know — more at WIT] (1734)
: any of four canonical collections of hymns, prayers, and liturgical formulas that comprise the earliest Hindu sacred writings

ve·da·lia \vi-'dāl-yə\ *noun* [New Latin, genus name] (1889)
: an Australian ladybug (*Rodolia cardinalis*) introduced to many countries to control scale insects

Ve·dan·ta \vā-'dän-tə, və-, -'dan-\ *noun* [Sanskrit *Vedānta,* literally, end of the Veda, from *Veda* + *anta* end; akin to Old English *ende* end] (1788)
: an orthodox system of Hindu philosophy developing especially in a qualified monism on the speculations of the Upanishads on ultimate reality and the liberation of the soul
— **Ve·dan·tism** \-'dän-,ti-zəm, -'dan-\ *noun*
— **Ve·dan·tist** \-'dän-tist, -'dan-\ *noun*

Ve·dan·tic \-'dän-tik, -'dan-\ *adjective* (1882)
1 : of or relating to the Vedanta philosophy
2 : VEDIC

Ved·da *or* **Ved·dah** \'ve-də\ *noun* [Sinhalese *vedda* hunter] (1681)
: a member of an aboriginal people of Sri Lanka

Ved·doid \'ve-ˌdȯid\ *noun* (1928)
: a member of an ancient race of southern Asia characterized by wavy to curly hair, chocolate-brown skin color, and slender body build
— **Veddoid** *adjective*

ve·dette \vi-'det\ *noun* [French, from Italian *vedetta*, alteration of *veletta*, probably from Spanish *vela* watch, from *velar* to keep watch, from Latin *vigilare* to wake, watch, from *vigil* awake — more at VIGIL] (circa 1702)
: a mounted sentinel stationed in advance of pickets

Ve·dic \'vā-dik\ *adjective* (1848)
: of or relating to the Vedas, the language in which they are written, or Hindu history and culture between 1500 B.C. and 500 B.C.

vee \'vē\ *noun* (circa 1883)
1 : something shaped like the letter V
2 : the letter *v*

vee·jay \'vē-ˌjā\ *noun* [video jockey] (1981)
: an announcer of a program (as on television) that features music videos

vee·na *variant of* VINA

veep \'vēp\ *noun* [from *v. p.* (abbreviation for *vice president*)] (1949)
: VICE PRESIDENT

¹veer \'vir\ *transitive verb* [Middle English *veren*, of Low German or Dutch origin; akin to Middle Dutch *vieren* to slacken, Middle Low German *vīren*] (15th century)
: to let out (as a rope)

²veer *verb* [Middle French *virer*, from Old French, to throw with a twisting motion, perhaps modification of Latin *vibrare* to wave, propel suddenly — more at VIBRATE] (1582)
intransitive verb
1 *of the wind* : to shift in a clockwise direction — compare BACK
2 : to change direction or course
3 : to wear ship
transitive verb
: to direct to a different course; *specifically* : WEAR 7
synonym see SWERVE
— **veer·ing·ly** \-iŋ-lē\ *adverb*

³veer *noun* (1611)
: a change in course or direction ⟨a *veer* to the right⟩

vee·ry \'vir-ē\ *noun, plural* **veeries** [probably imitative] (1838)
: a thrush (*Catharus fuscescens*) common in the eastern U.S.

veg \'vej\ *noun, plural* **veg** (1918)
chiefly British : VEGETABLE

Ve·ga \'vē-gə, 'vā-\ *noun* [New Latin, from Arabic *(al-Nasr) al-Wāqi'*, literally, the falling (vulture)]
: a star of the first magnitude that is the brightest in the constellation Lyra

veg·an \'vē-gən *also* 'vā- *also* 've-jən *or* -ˌjan\ *noun* [by contraction from *vegetarian*] (1944)
: a strict vegetarian who consumes no animal food or dairy products; *also* : one who abstains from using animal products (as leather)
— **veg·an·ism** \'vē-gə-ˌni-zəm, 'vā-gə-, 've-jə-\ *noun*

¹veg·e·ta·ble \'vej-tə-bəl, 've-jə-\ *adjective* [Middle English, from Medieval Latin *vegetabilis* vegetative, from *vegetare* to grow, from Latin, to animate, from *vegetus* lively, from *vegēre* to enliven — more at WAKE] (15th century)
1 a : of, relating to, constituting, or growing like plants **b** : consisting of plants : VEGETATIONAL
2 : made or obtained from plants or plant products
3 : resembling or suggesting a plant (as in inertness or passivity)

²vegetable *noun* (1582)
1 : PLANT 1b
2 : a usually herbaceous plant (as the cabbage, bean, or potato) grown for an edible part that is usually eaten as part of a meal; *also* : such edible part
3 : a human being whose mental and physical functioning is severely impaired (as from accident or disease)

vegetable ivory *noun* (1842)
1 : the hard white opaque endosperm of the ivory nut that takes a high polish and is used as a substitute for ivory
2 : IVORY NUT

vegetable marrow *noun* (1816)
: any of various smooth-skinned elongated summer squashes with creamy white to deep green skins

vegetable oil *noun* (1797)
: an oil of plant origin; *especially* : a fatty oil from seeds or fruits

vegetable oyster *noun* (circa 1818)
: SALSIFY

vegetable pear *noun* (1887)
: CHAYOTE

vegetable wax *noun* (1815)
: a wax of plant origin secreted commonly in thin flakes by the walls of epidermal cells

veg·e·ta·bly \'vej-tə-blē, 've-jə-\ *adverb* (1651)
: in the manner of or like a vegetable

veg·e·tal \'vej-ə-tᵊl\ *adjective* [Medieval Latin *vegetare* to grow] (15th century)
1 : VEGETABLE
2 : VEGETATIVE
3 : of or relating to the vegetal pole of an egg or to that part of an egg from which the endoderm normally develops ⟨*vegetal* blastomeres⟩

vegetal pole *noun* (1896)
: the point on the surface of an egg that is diametrically opposite to the animal pole and usually marks the center of the protoplasm containing more yolk, dividing more slowly and into larger blastomeres than that about the animal pole, and giving rise to the hypoblast of the embryo

¹veg·e·tar·i·an \ˌve-jə-'ter-ē-ən\ *noun* [²*vegetable* + *-arian*] (1839)
1 : one who believes in or practices vegetarianism
2 : HERBIVORE

²vegetarian *adjective* (1849)
1 : of or relating to vegetarians
2 : consisting wholly of vegetables, fruits, and sometimes eggs or dairy products ⟨a *vegetarian* diet⟩

veg·e·tar·i·an·ism \-ē-ə-ˌni-zəm\ *noun* (circa 1851)
: the theory or practice of living on a diet made up of vegetables, fruits, grains, nuts, and sometimes eggs or dairy products

veg·e·tate \'ve-jə-ˌtāt\ *verb* **-tat·ed; -tat·ing** [Medieval Latin *vegetatus*, past participle of *vegetare* to grow] (1605)
intransitive verb
1 a : to grow in the manner of a plant; *also* : to grow exuberantly or with proliferation of fleshy or warty outgrowths **b** : to produce vegetation
2 : to lead a passive existence without exertion of body or mind
transitive verb
: to establish vegetation in or on

veg·e·ta·tion \ˌve-jə-'tā-shən\ *noun* (1564)
1 : the act or process of vegetating
2 : inert existence
3 : plant life or total plant cover (as of an area)
4 : an abnormal growth upon a body part
— **veg·e·ta·tion·al** \-shnəl, -shə-nᵊl\ *adjective*

veg·e·ta·tive \'ve-jə-ˌtā-tiv\ *adjective* (14th century)
1 a (1) : growing or having the power of growing (2) : of, relating to, or engaged in nutritive and growth functions as contrasted with reproductive functions ⟨a *vegetative* nucleus⟩
b : promoting plant growth ⟨the *vegetative* properties of soil⟩ **c** : of, relating to, or involving propagation by nonsexual processes or methods
2 : relating to, composed of, or suggesting vegetation ⟨*vegetative* cover⟩
3 : of or relating to the division of nature comprising the plant kingdom
4 : affecting, arising from, or relating to involuntary bodily functions
5 : VEGETABLE 3
— **veg·e·ta·tive·ly** *adverb*
— **veg·e·ta·tive·ness** *noun*

ve·gete \və-'jēt\ *adjective* [Latin *vegetus* — more at VEGETABLE] (1639)
archaic : LIVELY, HEALTHY

veg·gie *also* **veg·ie** \'ve-jē\ *noun* [by shortening & alteration] (1955)
1 : VEGETABLE
2 *slang* : VEGETARIAN

veg out \'vej-\ *intransitive verb* **vegged out; veg·ging out** [short for *vegetate*] (1980)
: to spend time idly or passively

ve·he·mence \'vē-ə-mən(t)s\ *noun* (15th century)
: the quality or state of being vehement : INTENSITY

ve·he·ment \-mənt\ *adjective* [Middle English, from Middle French, from Latin *vehement-, vehemens, vement-, vemens*] (15th century)
: marked by forceful energy : POWERFUL ⟨a *vehement* wind⟩: as **a** : intensely emotional : IMPASSIONED, FERVID ⟨*vehement* patriotism⟩ **b** (1) : deeply felt ⟨a *vehement* suspicion⟩ (2) : forcibly expressed ⟨*vehement* denunciations⟩ **c** : bitterly antagonistic ⟨a *vehement* debate⟩
— **ve·he·ment·ly** *adverb*

ve·hi·cle \'vē-ə-kəl *also* 'vē-ˌhi-kəl\ *noun* [French *véhicule*, from Latin *vehiculum* carriage, conveyance, from *vehere* to carry — more at WAY] (1612)
1 a : an inert medium (as a syrup) in which a medicinally active agent is administered **b** : any of various media acting usually as solvents, carriers, or binders for active ingredients or pigments
2 : an agent of transmission : CARRIER
3 : a medium through which something is expressed, achieved, or displayed
4 : a means of carrying or transporting something : CONVEYANCE: as **a** : MOTOR VEHICLE **b** : a piece of mechanized equipment

ve·hic·u·lar \vē-'hi-kyə-lər\ *adjective* (1616)
1 a : of, relating to, or designed for vehicles and especially motor vehicles **b** : transported by vehicle **c** : caused by or resulting from the operation of a vehicle ⟨*vehicular* homicide⟩
2 : serving as a vehicle

V–8 \'vē-'āt\ *noun* (1942)
: an internal combustion engine having two banks of four cylinders each with the banks at an angle to each other; *also* : an automobile having such an engine

¹veil \'vā(ə)l\ *noun* [Middle English *veile*, from Old North French, from Latin *vela*, plural of *velum* sail, awning, curtain] (13th century)
1 a : a length of cloth worn by women as a covering for the head and shoulders and often especially in Eastern countries for the face; *specifically* : the outer covering of a nun's headdress **b** : a length of veiling or netting worn over the head or face or attached for protection or ornament to a hat or headdress **c** : any of various liturgical cloths; *especially* : a cloth used to cover the chalice
2 : the cloistered life of a nun

\ə\ abut \ᵊ\ kitten \ər\ further \a\ ash \ā\ ace
\ä\ mop, mar \au̇\ out \ch\ chin \e\ bet \ē\ easy
\g\ go \i\ hit \ī\ ice \j\ job \ŋ\ sing \ō\ go
\ȯ\ law \ȯi\ boy \th\ thin \th\ the \ü\ loot \u̇\ foot
\y\ yet \zh\ vision *see also* Guide to Pronunciation

3 : a concealing curtain or cover of cloth
4 : something that hides or obscures like a veil
5 : a covering body part or membrane: as **a** : VELUM **b** : CAUL
²**veil** (14th century)
transitive verb
: to cover, provide, obscure, or conceal with or as if with a veil
intransitive verb
: to put on or wear a veil
veiled \'vā(ə)ld\ *adjective* (1593)
1 a : having or wearing a veil or a concealing cover ⟨a *veiled* hat⟩ **b :** characterized by a softening tonal distortion
2 : obscured as if by a veil : DISGUISED ⟨*veiled* threats⟩
veil·ing \'vā-liŋ\ *noun* (14th century)
1 : VEIL
2 : any of various light sheer fabrics
¹**vein** \'vān\ *noun* [Middle English *veine*, from Old French, from Latin *vena*] (14th century)
1 a : a narrow water channel in rock or earth or in ice **b** (1) : LODE 2, 3 (2) : a bed of useful mineral matter
2 : BLOOD VESSEL; *especially* : any of the tubular branching vessels that carry blood from the capillaries toward the heart
3 a : any of the vascular bundles forming the framework of a leaf **b :** any of the thickened cuticular ribs that serve to stiffen the wings of an insect
4 : something suggesting veins (as in reticulation); *specifically* : a wavy variegation (as in marble)
5 a : a distinctive mode of expression : STYLE **b :** a pervasive element or quality : STRAIN **c** : a line of thought or action
6 a : a special aptitude : TALENT **b :** a usually transitory and casually attained mood **c :** top form : FETTLE
— **vein·al** \'vā-nºl\ *adjective*
²**vein** *transitive verb* (1502)
: to pattern with or as if with veins
veined \'vānd\ *adjective* (circa 1529)
: patterned with or as if with veins : having venation : STREAKED ⟨a *veined* leaf⟩ ⟨*veined* marble⟩ ⟨*veined* cheese⟩
vein·er \'vā-nər\ *noun* (1895)
: a small V gouge used in wood carving
vein·ing \'vā-niŋ\ *noun* (1826)
: a pattern of veins : VENATION
vein·let \'vān-lət\ *noun* (1831)
: a small vein
veiny \'vā-nē\ *adjective* (1611)
: full of veins : noticeably veined
ve·la·men \və-'lā-mən\ *noun, plural* **ve·lam·i·na** \-'la-mə-nə\ [New Latin, from Latin, covering, from *velare* to cover, from *velum* curtain] (1882)
: the thick corky epidermis of aerial roots of an epiphytic orchid that absorbs water from the atmosphere
ve·lar \'vē-lər\ *adjective* [New Latin *velaris*, from *velum*] (1876)
1 : formed with the back of the tongue touching or near the soft palate ⟨the *velar* \k\ of \'kül\ *cool*⟩
2 : of, forming, or relating to a velum and especially the soft palate
— **velar** *noun*
ve·lar·i·um \vi-'lar-ē-əm, -'ler-\ *noun, plural* **-ia** \-ē-ə\ [Latin, from *velum* curtain] (1834)
: an awning over an ancient Roman theater or amphitheater
ve·lar·i·za·tion \,vē-lə-rə-'zā-shən\ *noun* (1915)
1 : the quality or state of being velarized
2 : an act or instance of velarizing
ve·lar·ize \'vē-lə-,rīz\ *transitive verb* **-ized; -iz·ing** (1915)
: to modify (as the \l\ of \'pül\ *pool*) by a simultaneous velar articulation
Vel·cro \'vel-(,)krō\ *trademark*
— used for a closure consisting of a piece of fabric of small hooks that sticks to a corresponding fabric of small loops

veld *or* **veldt** \'velt, 'felt\ *noun* [Afrikaans *veld*, from Dutch, field; akin to Old English *feld* field] (1835)
: a grassland especially of southern Africa usually with scattered shrubs or trees
ve·li·ger \'vē-lə-jər, 've-\ *noun* [New Latin, from *velum* + *-ger* bearing, from *gerere* to bear] (1877)
: a larval mollusk in the stage when it has developed the velum
vel·le·i·ty \ve-'lē-ə-tē, və-\ *noun, plural* **-ties** [New Latin *velleitas*, from Latin *velle* to wish, will — more at WILL] (1618)
1 : the lowest degree of volition
2 : a slight wish or tendency : INCLINATION
¹**vel·lum** \'ve-ləm\ *noun* [Middle English *velim*, from Middle French *veelin*, from *veelin*, adjective, of a calf, from *veel* calf — more at VEAL] (15th century)
1 : a fine-grained unsplit lambskin, kidskin, or calfskin prepared especially for writing on or for binding books
2 : a strong cream-colored paper
²**vellum** *adjective* (1565)
1 : of, resembling, or bound in vellum
2 : slightly rough ⟨paper with a *vellum* finish⟩
ve·lo·ce \vā-'lō-(,)chā\ *adverb or adjective* [Italian, from Latin *veloc-, velox*] (circa 1823)
: in a rapid manner — used as a direction in music
ve·lo·cim·e·ter \,vē-lō-'si-mə-tər, ,ve-\ *noun* [*velocity* + *-meter*] (1842)
: a device for measuring speed (as of fluid flow or sound)
ve·loc·i·pede \və-'lä-sə-,pēd\ *noun* [French *vélocipède*, from Latin *veloc-, velox* + *ped-, pes* foot — more at FOOT] (1818)
: a lightweight wheeled vehicle propelled by the rider: as **a** *archaic* : BICYCLE **b** : TRICYCLE **c** : a 3-wheeled railroad handcar
ve·loc·i·ty \və-'lä-sə-tē, -'läs-tē\ *noun, plural* **-ties** [Middle French *velocité*, from Latin *velocitat-, velocitas*, from *veloc-, velox* quick; probably akin to Latin *vegēre* to enliven — more at WAKE] (circa 1550)
1 a : quickness of motion : SPEED ⟨the *velocity* of sound⟩ **b :** rapidity of movement ⟨[my horse's] strong suit is grace & personal comeliness, rather than *velocity* —Mark Twain⟩ **c** : speed imparted to something ⟨the power pitcher relies on *velocity* —Tony Scherman⟩
2 : the rate of change of position along a straight line with respect to time : the derivative of position with respect to time
3 a : rate of occurrence or action : RAPIDITY ⟨the *velocity* of historical change —R. J. Lifton⟩ ⟨the narrative leaps from one frantic episode to another with impressive *velocity* —James Atlas⟩ **b :** rate of turnover ⟨the *velocity* of money⟩
ve·lo·drome \'vē-lə-,drōm, 've-, 'vā-\ *noun* [French *vélodrome*, from *vélo* cycle (short for *vélocipède*) + *-drome*] (1895)
: a track designed for cycling
ve·lour *or* **ve·lours** \və-'lùr\ *noun, plural* **ve·lours** \-'lùrz\ [French *velours* velvet, velour, from Middle French *velours, velour*, from Old French *velos*, from Old Provençal *velos*, from Latin *villosus* shaggy, from *villus* shaggy hair — more at VELVET] (circa 1706)
1 : any of various fabrics with a pile or napped surface resembling velvet used in heavy weights for upholstery and curtains and in lighter weights for clothing; *also* : the article of clothing itself
2 : a fur felt (as of rabbit or nutria) finished with a long velvety nap and used especially for hats
ve·lou·té \və-,lü-'tā\ *noun* [French, literally, velvetiness, from Middle French *velluté*, from Old Provençal *velut* velvety, from (assumed) Vulgar Latin *villutus*] (1830)

: a white sauce made of chicken, veal, or fish stock and cream and thickened with butter and flour
ve·lum \'vē-ləm\ *noun, plural* **ve·la** \-lə\ [New Latin, from Latin, curtain] (1753)
1 : a membrane or membranous part resembling a veil or curtain: as **a** : SOFT PALATE **b** : an annular membrane projecting inward from the margin of the umbrella in some jellyfishes (as the hydromedusans)
2 : a swimming organ that is especially well developed in the later larval stages of many marine gastropods
ve·lure \ve-'lùr, vel-'yùr, 'vel-yər\ *noun* [modification of Middle French *velour*] (1587)
obsolete : VELVET; *also* : a fabric resembling velvet
¹**vel·vet** \'vel-vət\ *noun* [Middle English *veluet, velvet*, from Middle French *velu* shaggy, from (assumed) Vulgar Latin *villutus*, from Latin *villus* shaggy hair; akin to Latin *vellus* fleece — more at WOOL] (14th century)
1 : a clothing and upholstery fabric (as of silk, rayon, or wool) characterized by a short soft dense warp pile
2 a : something suggesting velvet **b :** a characteristic (as softness or smoothness) of velvet
3 : the soft vascular skin that envelops and nourishes the developing antlers of deer
4 a : the winnings of a player in a gambling game **b :** a profit or gain beyond ordinary expectation
— **vel·vet·like** \-,līk\ *adjective*
²**velvet** *adjective* (14th century)
1 : made of or covered with velvet; *also* : clad in velvet
2 : resembling or suggesting velvet : VELVETY ⟨a *velvet* voice⟩
velvet ant *noun* (1748)
: any of various solitary usually brightly colored and hairy fossorial wasps (family Mutillidae) with the female wingless
velvet bean *noun* (1898)
: an annual legume (*Mucuna deeringiana* synonym *Stizolobium deeringianum*) grown especially in the southern U.S. for green manure and grazing; *also* : its seed often used as stock feed
vel·ve·teen \,vel-və-'tēn\ *noun* (1776)
1 : a clothing fabric usually of cotton in twill or plain weaves made with a short close weft pile in imitation of velvet
2 : *plural* : clothes made of velveteen
vel·vety \'vel-və-tē\ *adjective* (1752)
1 : soft and smooth like velvet ⟨*velvety* hair⟩
2 : smooth to the taste : MILD ⟨a *velvety* wine⟩
ven- *or* **veni-** *or* **veno-** *combining form* [Latin *vena*]
: vein ⟨*veni*puncture⟩ ⟨*veno*graphy⟩
ve·na \'vē-nə\ *noun, plural* **ve·nae** \-(,)nē\ [Middle English, from Latin] (14th century)
: VEIN
ve·na ca·va \,vē-nə-'kā-və\ *noun, plural* **ve·nae ca·vae** \-(,)nē-'kā-(,)vē\ [New Latin, literally, hollow vein] (1598)
: any of the large veins by which in air-breathing vertebrates the blood is returned to the right atrium of the heart
— **vena ca·val** \-vəl\ *adjective*
ve·nal \'vē-nºl\ *adjective* [Latin *venalis*, from *venum* (accusative) sale; akin to Greek *ōneisthai* to buy, Sanskrit *vasna* price] (1652)
1 : capable of being bought or obtained for money or other valuable consideration : PURCHASABLE; *especially* : open to corrupt influence and especially bribery : MERCENARY ⟨a *venal* legislator⟩
2 : originating in, characterized by, or associated with corrupt bribery ⟨a *venal* arrangement with the police⟩
— **ve·nal·i·ty** \vi-'na-lə-tē\ *noun*
— **ve·nal·ly** \'vē-nºl-ē\ *adverb*

ve·na·tion \ve-'nā-shən, vē-\ *noun* [Latin *vena* vein] (1646)
: an arrangement or system of veins (as in the tissue of a leaf or the wing of an insect)

venation a:
*1 parallel-veined,
2 net-veined,
3 dichotomously
veined*

vend \'vend\ *verb* [Latin *vendere* to sell, transitive verb, contraction for *venum dare* to give for sale] (1622)
intransitive verb
: to dispose of something by sale **:** SELL; *also* **:** to engage in selling
transitive verb
1 a : to sell especially as a hawker or peddler **b :** to sell by means of vending machines
2 : to utter publicly

Ven·da \'ven-də\ *noun* (1908)
: a Bantu language spoken by a people of Northern Transvaal; *also* **:** a member of this people

vend·ee \ven-'dē\ *noun* (1547)
: one to whom a thing is sold **:** BUYER

ven·det·ta \ven-'de-tə\ *noun* [Italian, literally, revenge, from Latin *vindicta* — more at VINDICTIVE] (1855)
1 : BLOOD FEUD
2 : an often prolonged series of retaliatory, vengeful, or hostile acts or exchange of such acts ⟨waged a personal *vendetta* against those who opposed his nomination⟩

ven·deuse \vän-'də(r)z, vän-'düz\ *noun* [French, feminine of *vendeur* salesman, from Middle French] (1913)
: a saleswoman especially in the fashion industry

vend·ible *or* **vend·able** \'ven-də-bəl\ *adjective* (14th century)
: capable of being vended **:** SALABLE
— **vend·ibil·i·ty** \ven-də-'bi-lə-tē\ *noun*

vending machine *noun* (circa 1895)
: a coin-operated machine for selling merchandise

ven·dor \'ven-dər, *for 1 also* ven-'dòr\ *also* **vend·er** \-dər\ *noun* [Middle French *vendeur*, from *vendre* to sell, from Latin *vendere*] (1594)
1 : one that vends **:** SELLER
2 : VENDING MACHINE

ven·due \'ven-,dü, 'vän-, 'fen-, -,dyü; ven-', vän-'\ *noun* [obsolete French, from Middle French, from *vendre*] (1668)
: a public sale at auction

¹ve·neer \və-'nir\ *noun* [German *Furnier*, from *furnieren* to veneer, from French *fournir* to furnish, equip — more at FURNISH] (1702)
1 : a thin sheet of a material: as **a :** a layer of wood of superior value or excellent grain to be glued to an inferior wood **b :** any of the thin layers bonded together to form plywood
2 : a protective or ornamental facing (as of brick or stone)
3 : a superficial or deceptively attractive appearance, display, or effect **:** FACADE, GLOSS

²veneer *transitive verb* (1728)
1 : to overlay or plate (as a common wood) with a thin layer of finer wood for outer finish or decoration; *broadly* **:** to face with a material giving a superior surface
2 : to cover over with a veneer; *especially* **:** to conceal (as a defect of character) under a superficial and deceptive attractiveness
— **ve·neer·er** *noun*

ve·neer·ing *noun* (circa 1706)
1 : a veneered surface
2 : material used as veneer

ven·er·a·ble \'ve-nər-(ə-)bəl, 'ven-rə-bəl\ *adjective* (15th century)
1 : deserving to be venerated — used as a ti-

tle for an Anglican archdeacon or for a Roman Catholic who has been accorded the lowest of three degrees of recognition for sanctity
2 : made sacred especially by religious or historical association
3 a : calling forth respect through age, character, and attainments; *broadly* **:** conveying an impression of aged goodness and benevolence
b : impressive by reason of age ⟨under *venerable* pines⟩
synonym see OLD
— **ven·er·a·bil·i·ty** \,ve-nə-rə-'bi-lə-tē, ,ven-rə-\ *noun*
— **ven·er·a·ble·ness** \'ve-nər(-ə)-bəl-nəs, 'ven-rə-\ *noun*
— **ven·er·a·bly** \-blē\ *adverb*

ven·er·ate \'ve-nə-,rāt\ *transitive verb* **-at·ed; -at·ing** [Latin *veneratus*, past participle of *venerari*, from *vener-, venus* love, charm — more at WIN] (circa 1623)
1 : to regard with reverential respect or with admiring deference
2 : to honor (as an icon or a relic) with a ritual act of devotion
synonym see REVERE
— **ven·er·a·tor** \-,rā-tər\ *noun*

ven·er·a·tion \,ve-nə-'rā-shən\ *noun* (15th century)
1 : respect or awe inspired by the dignity, wisdom, dedication, or talent of a person
2 : the act of venerating
3 : the condition of one that is venerated

ve·ne·re·al \və-'nir-ē-əl\ *adjective* [Middle English *venerealle*, from Latin *venereus*, from *vener-, venus* love, sexual desire] (15th century)
1 : of or relating to sexual pleasure or indulgence
2 a : resulting from or contracted during sexual intercourse ⟨*venereal* infections⟩ **b :** of, relating to, or affected with venereal disease ⟨a high *venereal* rate⟩ **c :** involving the genital organs ⟨*venereal* sarcoma⟩

venereal disease *noun* (1658)
: a contagious disease (as gonorrhea or syphilis) that is typically acquired in sexual intercourse — compare STD

¹ven·ery \'ve-nə-rē\ *noun* [Middle English *venerie*, from Middle French, from *vener* to hunt, from Latin *venari* — more at VENISON] (14th century)
1 : the art, act, or practice of hunting
2 : animals that are hunted **:** GAME

²venery *noun* [Middle English *venerie*, from Medieval Latin *veneria*, from Latin *vener-, venus* sexual desire] (15th century)
1 : the pursuit of or indulgence in sexual pleasure
2 : SEXUAL INTERCOURSE

ve·ne·sec·tion \'ve-nə-,sek-shən, 'vē-\ *noun* [New Latin *venae section-, venae sectio*, literally, cutting of a vein] (1661)
: the operation of opening a vein for letting blood **:** PHLEBOTOMY

Ven·e·ti \'ve-nə-,tī\ *noun plural* [Latin *Veneti*] (1881)
1 : an ancient people in Gaul conquered by Caesar in 56 B.C.
2 : an ancient people in northeastern Italy allied politically to the Romans

ve·ne·tian blind \və-'nē-shən-\ *noun* [*Venetian* of Venice, Italy] (1770)
: a blind (as for a window) having numerous horizontal slats that may be set simultaneously at any of several angles so as to vary the amount of light admitted

venetian glass *noun, often V capitalized* (circa 1845)
: often colored glassware made at Murano near Venice of a soda-lime metal and typically elaborately decorated (as with gilt, enamel, or engraving)

Venetian red *noun* (circa 1753)
: an earthy hematite used as a pigment; *also* **:** a synthetic iron oxide pigment

Ve·net·ic \və-'ne-tik\ *adjective* [Latin *veneticus* of the Veneti, from *Veneti*] (1902)
: the language of the ancient Veneti of Italy — see INDO-EUROPEAN LANGUAGES table
— **Venetic** *adjective*

venge \'venj\ *transitive verb* **venged; veng·ing** [Middle English, from Middle French *vengier*, from Old French] (14th century)
archaic **:** AVENGE

ven·geance \'ven-jən(t)s\ *noun* [Middle English, from Old French, from *vengier* to avenge, from Latin *vindicare* to lay claim to, avenge — more at VINDICATE] (14th century)
: punishment inflicted in retaliation for an injury or offense **:** RETRIBUTION
— **with a vengeance 1 :** with great force or vehemence **2 :** to an extreme or excessive degree

venge·ful \'venj-fəl\ *adjective* [obsolete English *venge* revenge] (1586)
: REVENGEFUL: as **a :** seeking to avenge **b :** serving to gain vengeance
— **venge·ful·ly** \-fə-lē\ *adverb*
— **venge·ful·ness** *noun*

V–en·gine \'vē-\ *noun* (circa 1922)
: an internal combustion engine whose cylinders are arranged in two banks forming an acute or right angle

veni- *or* **veno-** — see VEN-

ve·ni·al \'vē-nē-əl, -nyəl\ *adjective* [Middle English, from Middle French, from Late Latin *venialis*, from Latin *venia* favor, indulgence, pardon; akin to Latin *venus* love, charm — more at WIN] (14th century)
: of a kind that can be remitted **:** FORGIVABLE, PARDONABLE; *also* **:** meriting no particular censure or notice **:** EXCUSABLE ⟨*venial* faults⟩
— **ve·nial·ly** *adverb*
— **ve·nial·ness** *noun*

venial sin *noun* (14th century)
: a sin that is relatively slight or that is committed without full reflection or consent and so according to Thomist theology does not deprive the soul of sanctifying grace — compare MORTAL SIN

ve·ni·punc·ture \'vē-nə-,pəŋ(k)-chər, 've-\ *noun* (circa 1924)
: surgical puncture of a vein especially for the withdrawal of blood or for intravenous medication

ve·ni·re \və-'nī-rē\ *noun* [*venire facias*] (1665)
: an entire panel from which a jury is drawn

ve·ni·re fa·ci·as \-,fā-shē-əs\ *noun* [Middle English, from Medieval Latin, you should cause to come] (15th century)
: a judicial writ directing the sheriff to summon a specified number of qualified persons to serve as jurors

ve·ni·re·man \və-'nī-rē-mən, -'nir-ē-\ *noun* (1776)
: a member of a venire

ven·i·son \'ve-nə-sən *also* -zən, *British usually* 'ven-zən\ *noun, plural* **venisons** *also* **venison** [Middle English, from Old French *veneison* hunting, game, from Latin *venation-, venatio*, from *venari* to hunt, pursue; akin to Sanskrit *vanoti* he strives for — more at WIN] (14th century)
: the edible flesh of a game animal and especially a deer

Ve·ni·te \və-'nī-tē, -'nē-,tā\ *noun* [Middle English, from Latin, O come, from *venire* to come; from the opening word of Psalms 95:1 — more at COME] (13th century)
: a liturgical chant composed of parts of Psalms 95 and 96

\ə\ abut \ᵊ\ kitten \ər\ further \a\ ash \ā\ ace \ä\ mop, mar \aù\ out \ch\ chin \e\ bet \ē\ easy \g\ go \i\ hit \ī\ ice \j\ job \ŋ\ sing \ō\ go \ò\ law \òi\ boy \th\ thin \th̶\ the \ü\ loot \ù\ foot \y\ yet \zh\ vision *see also* Guide to Pronunciation

Venn diagram \'ven-\ *noun* [John *Venn* (died 1923) English logician] (1918)
: a graph that employs closed curves and especially circles to represent logical relations between and operations on sets and the terms of propositions by the inclusion, exclusion, or intersection of the circles

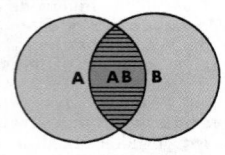

Venn diagram: *AB* represents the intersection of sets *A* and *B*

ve·nog·ra·phy \vi-'nä-grə-fē, vā-\ *noun* [International Scientific Vocabulary] (1935)
: roentgenography of a vein after injection of an opaque substance

¹ven·om \'ve-nəm\ *noun* [Middle English *venim, venom,* from Old French *venim,* from (assumed) Vulgar Latin *venimen,* alteration of Latin *venenum* magic charm, drug, poison; akin to Latin *venus* love, charm — more at WIN] (13th century)
1 : poisonous matter normally secreted by some animals (as snakes, scorpions, or bees) and transmitted to prey or an enemy chiefly by biting or stinging; *broadly* **:** material that is poisonous
2 : ILL WILL, MALEVOLENCE ◇

²venom *transitive verb* (14th century)
: ENVENOM

ven·om·ous \'ve-nə-məs\ *adjective* (14th century)
1 : full of venom: as **a :** POISONOUS, ENVENOMED **b :** NOXIOUS, PERNICIOUS ⟨expose a *venomous* dope ring —Don Porter⟩ **c :** SPITEFUL, MALEVOLENT ⟨*venomous* criticism⟩
2 : having a venom-producing gland and able to inflict a poisoned wound ⟨*venomous* snakes⟩
— **ven·om·ous·ly** *adverb*
— **ven·om·ous·ness** *noun*

ve·nous \'vē-nəs\ *adjective* [Latin *venosus,* from *vena* vein] (1626)
1 : of, relating to, or full of veins ⟨a *venous* rock⟩ ⟨a *venous* system⟩
2 *of blood* **:** having passed through the capillaries and given up oxygen for the tissues and become charged with carbon dioxide
— **ve·nous·ly** *adverb*

¹vent \'vent\ *transitive verb* [Middle English, probably from Middle French *esventer* to expose to the air, from *es-* ex- (from Latin *ex-*) + *vent* wind, from Latin *ventus* — more at WIND] (14th century)
1 : to provide with a vent
2 a : to serve as a vent for ⟨chimneys *vent* smoke⟩ **b :** DISCHARGE, EXPEL **c :** to give often vigorous or emotional expression to
3 : to relieve by means of a vent
synonym see EXPRESS

²vent *noun* (1508)
1 : an opportunity or means of escape, passage, or release **:** OUTLET ⟨finally gave *vent* to his pent-up hostility⟩
2 : an opening for the escape of a gas or liquid or for the relief of pressure: as **a :** the external opening of the rectum or cloaca **:** ANUS **b :** PIPE 3c, FUMAROLE **c :** an opening at the breech of a muzzle-loading gun through which fire is touched to the powder **d** *chiefly Scottish* **:** CHIMNEY, FLUE
— **vent·less** \-ləs\ *adjective*

³vent *noun* [Middle English *vente,* alteration of *fente,* from Middle French, slit, fissure, from *fendre* to split, from Latin *findere* — more at BITE] (15th century)
: a slit in a garment; *specifically* **:** an opening in the lower part of a seam (as of a jacket or skirt)
— **vent·less** *adjective*

vent·age \'ven-tij\ *noun* (1602)
: a small hole (as a flute stop)

ven·tail \'ven-,tāl\ *noun* [Middle English, from Middle French *ventaille,* from *vent* wind] (15th century)
: the lower movable front of a medieval helmet

ven·ter \'ven-tər\ *noun* [Anglo-French, from Latin, belly, womb; perhaps akin to Old High German *wanast* paunch, Latin *vesica* bladder, Sanskrit *vasti*] (1544)
1 : a wife or mother that is a source of offspring
2 : a protuberant and often hollow anatomical structure: as **a :** the undersurface of the abdomen of an arthropod **b :** the swollen basal portion of an archegonium in which an egg develops

ven·ti·fact \'ven-tə-,fakt\ *noun* [Latin *ventus* + English art*ifact*] (1911)
: a stone worn, polished, or faceted by wind-blown sand

ven·ti·late \'ven-t²l-,āt\ *transitive verb* **-lat·ed; -lat·ing** [Late Latin *ventilatus,* past participle of *ventilare,* from Latin, to fan, winnow, from *ventus* wind — more at WIND] (1527)
1 a : to examine, discuss, or investigate freely and openly **:** EXPOSE ⟨*ventilating* family quarrels in public⟩ **b :** to make public **:** UTTER ⟨*ventilated* their objections at length⟩
2 *archaic* **:** to free from chaff by winnowing
3 a : to expose to air and especially to a current of fresh air for purifying, curing, or refreshing ⟨*ventilate* stored grain⟩; *also* **:** OXYGENATE, AERATE ⟨*ventilate* blood in the lungs⟩ **b :** to subject the lungs to ventilation ⟨artificially *ventilate* a patient in respiratory distress⟩
4 a *of a current of air* **:** to pass or circulate through so as to freshen **b :** to cause fresh air to circulate through (as a room or mine)
5 : to provide an opening in (a burning structure) to permit escape of smoke and heat

ven·ti·la·tion \,ven-t²l-'ā-shən\ *noun* (1519)
1 : the act or process of ventilating
2 a : circulation of air ⟨a room with good *ventilation*⟩ **b :** the circulation and exchange of gases in the lungs or gills that is basic to respiration
3 : a system or means of providing fresh air

ven·ti·la·tor \'ven-t²l-,ā-tər\ *noun* (1743)
: one that ventilates: as **a :** a contrivance for introducing fresh air or expelling foul or stagnant air **b :** RESPIRATOR 2

ven·ti·la·to·ry \'ven-t²l-ə-,tōr-ē, -,tȯr-\ *adjective* (1850)
: of, relating to, or provided with ventilation ⟨*ventilatory* capacity of the lung⟩

ventr- *or* **ventro-** *combining form* [Latin *ventr-, venter* belly]
: ventral and ⟨*ventro*lateral⟩

¹ven·tral \'ven-trəl\ *adjective* [French, from Latin *ventralis,* from *ventr-, venter*] (1739)
1 a : of or relating to the belly **:** ABDOMINAL **b :** being or located near or on the anterior or lower surface of an animal opposite the back
2 : being or located on the lower surface of a dorsiventral plant structure
— **ven·tral·ly** \-trə-lē\ *adverb*

²ventral *noun* (1834)
: a ventral part (as a scale or fin)

ventral root *noun* (circa 1923)
: the one of the two roots of a spinal nerve that passes ventrally from the spinal cord and consists of motor fibers — compare DORSAL ROOT

ven·tri·cle \'ven-tri-kəl\ *noun* [Middle English, from Latin *ventriculus,* from diminutive of *ventr-, venter* belly] (14th century)
: a cavity of a bodily part or organ: as **a :** a chamber of the heart which receives blood from a corresponding atrium and from which blood is forced into the arteries — see HEART illustration **b :** any of the system of communicating cavities in the brain that are continuous with the central canal of the spinal cord — see BRAIN illustration

ven·tri·cose \-,kōs\ *adjective* [New Latin *ventricosus,* from Latin *ventr-, venter* + *-icosus* (as in *varicosus* varicose)] (1756)
: markedly swollen, distended, or inflated especially on one side ⟨*ventricose* corollas⟩

ven·tric·u·lar \ven-'tri-kyə-lər, vən-\ *adjective* (1822)
: of, relating to, or being a ventricle ⟨*ventricular* fibrillation⟩ ⟨*ventricular* pressure⟩ ⟨*ventricular* myocardium⟩

ven·tric·u·lus \ven-'tri-kyə-ləs, vən-\ *noun,* *plural* **-li** \-,lī, -,lē\ [New Latin, from Latin, diminutive of *venter*] (1693)
: a digestive cavity: as **a :** STOMACH **b :** GIZZARD 1a **c :** the digestive part of an insect's stomach

ven·tril·o·quism \ven-'tri-lə-,kwi-zəm\ *noun* [Late Latin *ventriloquus* ventriloquist, from Latin *ventr-, venter* + *loqui* to speak; from the belief that the voice is produced from the ventriloquist's stomach] (circa 1797)
: the production of the voice in such a way that the sound seems to come from a source other than the vocal organs of the speaker
— **ven·tril·o·qui·al** \,ven-trə-'lō-kwē-əl\ *adjective*
— **ven·tril·o·qui·al·ly** \-ə-lē\ *adverb*

ven·tril·o·quist \ven-'tri-lə-kwist\ *noun* (circa 1656)
: one who uses or is skilled in ventriloquism; *especially* **:** one who provides entertainment by using ventriloquism to carry on an apparent conversation with a hand-manipulated dummy
— **ven·tril·o·quis·tic** \(,)ven-,tri-lə-'kwis-tik\ *adjective*

ven·tril·o·quize \ven-'tri-lə-,kwīz\ *verb* **-quized; -quiz·ing** (1844)
intransitive verb
: to use ventriloquism
transitive verb
: to utter in the manner of a ventriloquist

ven·tril·o·quy \-kwē\ *noun* (1584)
: VENTRILOQUISM

ven·tro·lat·er·al \,ven-,trō-'la-tə-rəl, -'la-trəl\ *adjective* (1835)
: ventral and lateral

ven·tro·me·di·al \-'mē-dē-əl\ *adjective* (1908)
: ventral and medial

¹ven·ture \'ven(t)-shər\ *verb* **ven·tured; ven·tur·ing** \'ven(t)-sh(ə-)riŋ\ [Middle English *venteren,* by shortening & alteration

◇ **WORD HISTORY**
venom The Romans called their goddess of love *Venus,* a word that must first have meant simply "charm" or "epitome of qualities that arouse sexual desire" and was later applied to the goddess who personified sexual attractiveness. The unattested noun stem *venes-* that underlies the later attested Latin word *Venus* must also have meant "magical charm" or "magical power to propitiate the gods," to judge by its verbal derivative *venerari* "to solicit the favor of (a deity), worship." (From *veneratus,* the past participle of this verb, English has borrowed *venerate.*) Another derivative of *venes-* was, in its reconstructed shape, *venesnom,* which became Latin *venenum* "magical charm, potent drug." *Venenum* also developed the sense "deadly substance, poison," and in this meaning after some restructuring in spoken Latin became Old French *venim,* which Middle English borrowed as *venim* or *venom.* The word *poison* itself, the French outcome of Latin *potio,* first meant merely "drink" and then "drink with magical power" (hence English *potion*). The change in sense from the latter meaning to "deadly substance," which took place during the word's passage from Latin to French, is similar to the shift that produced *venom.*

from *aventuren,* from *aventure* adventure]
(15th century)
transitive verb
1 : to expose to hazard **:** RISK, GAMBLE ⟨*ventured* a buck or two on the race⟩
2 : to undertake the risks and dangers of **:** BRAVE ⟨*ventured* the stormy sea⟩
3 : to offer at the risk of rebuff, rejection, or censure ⟨*venture* an opinion⟩
intransitive verb
: to proceed especially in the face of danger
— **ven·tur·er** \'ven(t)-sh(ə-)rər\ *noun*
²**venture** *noun* (15th century)
1 *obsolete* **:** DESTINY, FORTUNE, CHANCE
2 a : an undertaking involving chance, risk, or danger; *especially* **:** a speculative business enterprise **b :** a venturesome act
3 : something (as money or property) at hazard in a speculative venture
— **at a venture :** at random ⟨a certain man drew a bow *at a venture,* and smote the king —1 Kings 22:34 (Authorized Version)⟩
venture capital *noun* (1943)
: capital (as retained corporate earnings or individual savings) invested or available for investment in the ownership element of new or fresh enterprise — called also *risk capital*
— **venture capitalist** *noun*
ven·ture·some \'ven(t)-shər-səm\ *adjective* (1661)
1 : involving risk **:** HAZARDOUS ⟨a *venturesome* journey⟩
2 : inclined to court or incur risk or danger **:** DARING ⟨a *venturesome* hunter⟩
synonym see ADVENTUROUS
— **ven·ture·some·ly** *adverb*
— **ven·ture·some·ness** *noun*
ven·tu·ri \ven-'tür-ē\ *noun* [G. B. *Venturi* (died 1822) Italian physicist] (1887)
: a short tube with a tapering constriction in the middle that causes an increase in the velocity of flow of a fluid and a corresponding decrease in fluid pressure and that is used especially in measuring fluid flow or for creating a suction (as for driving aircraft instruments or drawing fuel into the flow stream of a carburetor)
ven·tur·ous \'ven(t)-sh(ə-)rəs\ *adjective* (1565)
: VENTURESOME
— **ven·tur·ous·ly** *adverb*
— **ven·tur·ous·ness** *noun*
ven·ue \'ven-,yü\ *noun* [Middle English *venyw* action of coming, from Middle French *venue,* from *venir* to come, from Latin *venire* — more at COME] (1531)
1 a : the place or county in which take place the alleged events from which a legal action arises **b :** the place from which a jury is drawn and in which trial is held ⟨requested a change of *venue*⟩ **c :** a statement showing that a case is brought to the proper court or authority
2 : LOCALE 1
ve·nule \'vēn-(,)yü(ə)l, 'ven-\ *noun* [Latin *venula,* diminutive of *vena* vein] (circa 1850)
: a small vein; *especially* **:** any of the minute veins connecting the capillaries with the larger systemic veins
Ve·nus \'vē-nəs\ *noun* [Middle English, from Latin *Vener-, Venus*]
1 : the Roman goddess of love and beauty — compare APHRODITE
2 : the planet second in order from the sun — see PLANET table
Ve·nus·berg \-,bərg\ *noun*
: a mountain in central Germany containing a cavern where in medieval legend Venus held court
Ve·nus·hair \-,har, -,her\ *noun* (1548)
: a delicate maidenhair fern (*Adiantum capillus-veneris*) that grows chiefly on wet calcareous rocks
Ve·nu·sian \vi-'nü-zhən, -'nyü-\ *adjective* (1874)
: of or relating to the planet Venus

Ve·nus's–flow·er–bas·ket \'vē-nə-səz-, 'vē-nəs-\ *noun* (1872)
: any of several glass sponges (genus *Euplectella*) of the western Pacific and Indian oceans — called also *Venus flower basket*
Ve·nus's–fly·trap \-'flī-,trap\ *noun* (1770)
: an insectivorous plant (*Dionaea muscipula*) of the sundew family of the Carolina coast with the leaf apex modified into an insect trap — called also *Venus flytrap*
ve·ra·cious \və-'rā-shəs\ *adjective* [Latin *verac-, verax* — more at VERY] (1677)
1 : TRUTHFUL, HONEST
2 : marked by truth **:** ACCURATE
— **ve·ra·cious·ly** *adverb*
— **ve·ra·cious·ness** *noun*

Venus's-flytrap

ve·rac·i·ty \və-'ra-sə-tē\ *noun,* *plural* **-ties** (circa 1623)
1 : devotion to the truth **:** TRUTHFULNESS
2 : power of conveying or perceiving truth
3 : conformity with truth or fact **:** ACCURACY
4 : something true ⟨makes lies sound like *veracities*⟩
ve·ran·da *or* **ve·ran·dah** \və-'ran-də\ *noun* [Hindi *varandā*] (1711)
: a usually roofed open gallery or portico attached to the exterior of a building
ve·ran·daed *also* **ve·ran·dahed** \-dəd\ *adjective* (1818)
: having a veranda
ve·rap·a·mil \və-'ra-pə-,mil\ *noun* [International Scientific Vocabulary *valeric* (acid) + *-apam-* (probably alteration of *amino* + *propyl*) + *nitrile*] (1967)
: a calcium channel blocker $C_{27}H_{38}N_2O_4$ used especially in the form of its hydrochloride
ve·rat·ri·dine \və-'ra-trə-,dēn\ *noun* [*veratrine* + *-idine*] (1907)
: a poisonous alkaloid $C_{36}H_{51}NO_{11}$ occurring especially in sabadilla seed
ve·ra·trine \'ver-ə-,trēn, və-'ra-trən\ *noun* [New Latin *veratrina,* from *Veratrum,* genus of herbs] (1822)
: a poisonous irritant mixture of alkaloids from sabadilla seed that has been used as a counterirritant and insecticide
ve·ra·trum \və-'rā-trəm\ *noun* [New Latin, genus name, from Latin, hellebore] (1577)
: HELLEBORE 2
verb \'vərb\ *noun* [Middle English *verbe,* from Middle French, from Latin *verbum* word, verb — more at WORD] (14th century)
: a word that characteristically is the grammatical center of a predicate and expresses an act, occurrence, or mode of being, that in various languages is inflected for agreement with the subject, for tense, for voice, for mood, or for aspect, and that typically has rather full descriptive meaning and characterizing quality but is sometimes nearly devoid of these especially when used as an auxiliary or linking verb
— **verb·less** \'vər-bləs\ *adjective*
¹**ver·bal** \'vər-bəl\ *adjective* [Middle French or Late Latin; Middle French, from Late Latin *verbalis,* from Latin *verbum* word] (15th century)
1 a : of, relating to, or consisting of words ⟨*verbal* instructions⟩ **b :** of, relating to, or involving words rather than meaning or substance ⟨a consistency that is merely *verbal* and scholastic —B. N. Cardozo⟩ **c :** consisting of or using words only and not involving action ⟨a *verbal* protest⟩
2 : of, relating to, or formed from a verb ⟨a *verbal* adjective⟩
3 : spoken rather than written ⟨a *verbal* contract⟩
4 : VERBATIM, WORD-FOR-WORD ⟨a *verbal* translation⟩
5 : of or relating to facility in the use and comprehension of words ⟨*verbal* aptitude⟩ ☐

— **ver·bal·ly** \-bə-lē\ *adverb*
²**verbal** *noun* (1530)
: a word that combines characteristics of a verb with those of a noun or adjective — compare GERUND, INFINITIVE, PARTICIPLE
verbal auxiliary *noun* (circa 1958)
: an auxiliary verb
ver·bal·ism \'vər-bə-,li-zəm\ *noun* (1787)
1 a : a verbal expression **:** TERM **b :** PHRASING, WORDING
2 : words used as if they were more important than the realities they represent ⟨the emancipation of science from *verbalism* —G. A. L. Sarton⟩
3 a : a wordy expression of little meaning **b :** VERBOSITY
ver·bal·ist \-list\ *noun* (circa 1609)
1 : one who stresses words above substance or reality
2 : a person who uses words skillfully
— **ver·bal·is·tic** \,vər-bə-'lis-tik\ *adjective*
ver·bal·ize \'vər-bə-,līz\ *verb* **-ized; -iz·ing** (1609)
intransitive verb
1 : to speak or write verbosely
2 : to express something in words
transitive verb
1 : to convert into a verb
2 : to name or describe in words
— **ver·bal·i·za·tion** \,vər-bə-lə-'zā-shən\ *noun*
— **ver·bal·iz·er** \'vər-bə-,lī-zər\ *noun*
verbal noun *noun* (circa 1706)
: a noun derived directly from a verb or verb stem and in some uses having the sense and constructions of a verb
¹**ver·ba·tim** \(,)vər-'bā-təm\ *adverb* [Middle English, from Medieval Latin, from Latin *verbum* word] (15th century)
: in the exact words **:** word for word
²**verbatim** *adjective* (1737)
: being in or following the exact words **:** WORD-FOR-WORD
ver·be·na \(,)vər-'bē-nə\ *noun* [New Latin, genus of herbs or subshrubs, from Latin, leafy

\ə\ abut \ᵊ\ kitten \ər\ further \a\ ash \ā\ ace
\ä\ mop, mar \aủ\ out \ch\ chin \e\ bet \ē\ easy
\g\ go \i\ hit \ī\ ice \j\ job \ŋ\ sing \ō\ go
\ȯ\ law \ȯi\ boy \th\ thin \ṯh\ the \ü\ loot \ủ\ foot
\y\ yet \zh\ vision *see also* Guide to Pronunciation

branch used ceremonially or medicinally — more at VERVAIN⟩ (1562)
: VERVAIN; *especially* : any of numerous garden plants of hybrid origin widely grown for their showy spikes of white, pink, red, or blue flowers which are borne in profusion over a long season

ver·biage \'vər-bē-ij *also* -bij\ *noun* [French, from Middle French *verbier* to chatter, from *verbe* speech, from Latin *verbum* word] (circa 1721)
1 : a profusion of words usually of little or obscure content ⟨such a tangled maze of evasive *verbiage* as a typical party platform —Marcia Davenport⟩
2 : manner of expressing oneself in words : DICTION ⟨sportswriters guarded their *verbiage* so jealously —Raymond Sokolov⟩

ver·bi·cide \'vər-bə-ˌsīd\ *noun* [Latin *verbum* word + English *-cide*] (1858)
1 : deliberate distortion of the sense of a word (as in punning)
2 : one who distorts the sense of a word

ver·bid \'vər-bəd\ *noun* (1914)
: VERBAL

ver·big·er·a·tion \(ˌ)vər-ˌbi-jə-'rā-shən\ *noun* [International Scientific Vocabulary, from Latin *verbigerare* to talk, chat, from *verbum* word + *gerere* to carry, wield — more at WORD] (1886)
: continual repetition of stereotyped phrases (as in some forms of mental illness)

ver·bose \(ˌ)vər-'bōs\ *adjective* [Latin *verbosus*, from *verbum*] (1672)
1 : containing more words than necessary : WORDY ⟨a *verbose* reply⟩; *also* : impaired by wordiness ⟨a *verbose* style⟩
2 : given to wordiness ⟨a *verbose* orator⟩
synonym see WORDY
— **ver·bose·ly** *adverb*
— **ver·bose·ness** *noun*
— **ver·bos·i·ty** \-'bä-sə-tē\ *noun*

ver·bo·ten \vər-'bō-t°n, fər-, ver-\ *adjective* [German, from Old High German *farboten*, past participle of *farbioten* to forbid (akin to Old English *forbēodan* to forbid), from *far-, fur-* for- + *biotan* to offer — more at BID] (1912)
: not allowed : FORBIDDEN; *especially* : prohibited by dictate

verb sap \'vərb-'sap\ (1841)
: VERBUM SAP

ver·bum sap \ˌvər-bəm-'sap\ [short for New Latin *verbum sapienti* (*sat est*) a word to the wise (is sufficient)] (1818)
: enough said — used to indicate that something left unsaid may or should be inferred

ver·dant \'vər-d°nt\ *adjective* [modification of Middle French *verdoyant*, from present participle of *verdoyer* to be green, from Old French *verdoier*, from *verd, vert* green, from Latin *viridis*, from *virēre* to be green] (1581)
1 a : green in tint or color ⟨*verdant* grass⟩ **b** : green with growing plants ⟨*verdant* fields⟩
2 : unripe in experience or judgment : GREEN 9a, b
— **ver·dan·cy** \-d°n(t)-sē\ *noun*
— **ver·dant·ly** \-d°nt-lē\ *adverb*

verd an·tique *or* **verde an·tique** \ˌvərd-ˌan-'tēk\ *noun* [Italian *verde antico*, literally, ancient green] (1745)
: a green mottled or veined serpentine marble or calcareous serpentine much used for indoor decoration especially by the ancient Romans

ver·der·er *also* **ver·der·or** \'vər-dər-ər\ *noun* [Anglo-French, from Old French *verdier*, from *verd* green] (circa 1538)
: a onetime English judicial officer in charge of the king's forest

ver·dict \'vər-(ˌ)dikt\ *noun* [alteration of Middle English *verdit*, from Anglo-French, from Old French *ver* true (from Latin *verus*) + *dit* saying, dictum, from Latin *dictum* — more at VERY] (1533)
1 : the finding or decision of a jury on the matter submitted to it in trial

2 : OPINION, JUDGMENT

ver·di·gris \'vər-də-ˌgrēs, -, -ˌgris, -grəs *also* -ˌgrē\ *noun* [Middle English *vertegrez*, from Old French *vert de Grice*, literally, green of Greece] (14th century)
1 a : a green or greenish blue poisonous pigment resulting from the action of acetic acid on copper and consisting of one or more basic copper acetates **b** : normal copper acetate $Cu(C_2H_3O_2)_2 \cdot H_2O$
2 : a green or bluish deposit especially of copper carbonates formed on copper, brass, or bronze surfaces

ver·din \'vər-d°n\ *noun* [French, a green songbird of Indochina, alteration of *verdon, verdun* bunting, yellowhammer, from *vert* green, from Old French *verd, vert*] (1881)
: a very small yellow-headed titmouse (*Auriparus flaviceps*) found from Texas to California and southward

ver·dure \'vər-jər *also* -dyər\ *noun* [Middle English, from Middle French, from *verd* green] (14th century)
1 : the greenness of growing vegetation; *also* : such vegetation itself
2 : a condition of health and vigor
— **ver·dur·ous** \'vərj-rəs; 'ver-jə-rəs, -dyə-\ *adjective*

ver·dured \'vər-jərd *also* -dyərd\ *adjective* (circa 1718)
: covered with verdure

¹verge \'vərj\ *noun* [Middle English, from Middle French, from Latin *virga* rod, stripe] (15th century)
1 a (1) : a rod or staff carried as an emblem of authority or symbol of office (2) *obsolete* : a stick or wand held by a person being admitted to tenancy while he swears fealty **b** : the spindle of a watch balance; *especially* : a spindle with pallets in an old vertical escapement **c** : the male intromittent organ of any of various invertebrates
2 a : something that borders, limits, or bounds: as (1) : an outer margin of an object or structural part (2) : the edge of roof covering (as tiling) projecting over the gable of a roof (3) *British* : a paved or planted strip of land at the edge of a road : SHOULDER **b** : BRINK, THRESHOLD ⟨a country on the *verge* of destruction —Archibald MacLeish⟩

²verge *intransitive verb* **verged; verg·ing** (1787)
1 : to be contiguous
2 : to be on the verge or border

³verge *intransitive verb* **verged; verg·ing** [Latin *vergere* to bend, incline — more at WRENCH] (1610)
1 a *of the sun* : to incline toward the horizon : SINK **b** : to move or extend in some direction or toward some condition
2 : to be in transition or change

verg·er \'vər-jər\ *noun* (15th century)
1 *chiefly British* : an attendant that carries a verge (as before a bishop or justice)
2 : a church official who keeps order during services or serves as an usher or a sacristan

ve·rid·i·cal \və-'ri-di-kəl\ *adjective* [Latin *veridicus*, from *verus* true + *dicere* to say — more at VERY, DICTION] (1653)
1 : TRUTHFUL, VERACIOUS ⟨tried . . . to supply . . . a *veridical* background to the events and people portrayed —Laura Krey⟩
2 : not illusory : GENUINE ⟨it is assumed that . . . perception is *veridical* —George Lakoff⟩
— **ve·rid·i·cal·i·ty** \-ˌri-də-'ka-lə-tē\ *noun*
— **ve·rid·i·cal·ly** \-'ri-di-k(ə-)lē\ *adverb*

ver·i·fi·able \ˌver-ə-'fī-ə-bəl\ *adjective* (1593)
: capable of being verified
— **ver·i·fi·abil·i·ty** \ˌver-ə-ˌfī-ə-'bi-lə-tē\ *noun*
— **ver·i·fi·able·ness** *noun*

ver·i·fi·ca·tion \ˌver-ə-fə-'kā-shən\ *noun* (1523)
: the act or process of verifying : the state of being verified

ver·i·fy \'ver-ə-ˌfī\ *transitive verb* **-fied; -fy·ing** [Middle English *verifien*, from Middle French *verifier*, from Medieval Latin *verificare*, from Latin *verus* true] (14th century)
1 : to confirm or substantiate in law by oath
2 : to establish the truth, accuracy, or reality of
synonym see CONFIRM
— **ver·i·fi·er** \-ˌfī-(ə)r\ *noun*

ver·i·ly \'ver-ə-lē\ *adverb* [Middle English *verraily*, from *verray* very] (14th century)
1 : in truth : CERTAINLY
2 : TRULY, CONFIDENTLY

veri·sim·i·lar \ˌver-ə-'si-mə-lər, -'sim-lər\ *adjective* [Latin *verisimilis*] (1681)
1 : having the appearance of truth : PROBABLE
2 : depicting realism (as in art or literature)
— **veri·sim·i·lar·ly** *adverb*

veri·si·mil·i·tude \-sə-'mi-lə-ˌtüd, -ˌtyüd\ *noun* [Latin *verisimilitudo*, from *verisimilis* verisimilar, from *veri similis* like the truth] (1603)
1 : the quality or state of being verisimilar
2 : something verisimilar
— **veri·si·mil·i·tu·di·nous** \-ˌmi-lə-'tüd-nəs, -'tyüd-; -'tü-d°n-əs, -'tyü-\ *adjective*

ve·rism \'vir-ˌi-zəm, 'ver-\ *noun* [Italian *verismo*, from *vero* true, from Latin *verus*] (1892)
: artistic use of contemporary everyday material in preference to the heroic or legendary especially in grand opera
— **ve·rist** \-ist\ *noun or adjective*
— **ve·ris·tic** \vir-'is-tik, ver-\ *adjective*

ve·ris·mo \vā-'rēz-(ˌ)mō\ *noun* [Italian] (circa 1908)
: VERISM; *also* : REALISM 3

ver·i·ta·ble \'ver-ə-tə-bəl\ *adjective* [Middle English, from Middle French, from *verité*] (15th century)
: being in fact the thing named and not false, unreal, or imaginary — often used to stress the aptness of a metaphor ⟨a *veritable* mountain of references⟩
— **ver·i·ta·ble·ness** *noun*
— **ver·i·ta·bly** \-blē\ *adverb*

vé·ri·té \ˌver-ə-'tā\ *noun* [*cinema verité*] (1966)
: the art or technique of filming (as a motion picture) so as to convey candid realism

ver·i·ty \'ver-ə-tē\ *noun, plural* **-ties** [Middle English, from Middle French *verité*, from Latin *veritat-, veritas*, from *verus* true] (14th century)
1 : the quality or state of being true or real
2 : something (as a statement) that is true; *especially* : a fundamental and inevitably true value ⟨such eternal *verities* as honor, love, and patriotism⟩
3 : the quality or state of being truthful or honest ⟨the king-becoming graces, as justice, *verity* —Shakespeare⟩

ver·juice \'vər-ˌjüs\ *noun* [Middle English *verjus*, from Middle French *vert jus*, literally, green juice] (14th century)
1 : the sour juice of crab apples or of unripe fruit (as grapes or apples); *also* : an acid liquor made from verjuice
2 : acidity of disposition or manner

ver·meil *noun* [Middle French, from *vermeil*, adjective — more at VERMILION] (1590)
1 \vər-məl, -ˌmāl\ : VERMILION
2 \ver-'mā\ : gilded silver
— **vermeil** *adjective*

vermi- *combining form* [New Latin, from Late Latin, from Latin *vermis* — more at WORM]
: worm ⟨*vermi*form⟩

ver·mi·cel·li \ˌvər-mə-'che-lē, -'se-\ *noun* [Italian, from plural of *vermicello*, diminutive of *verme* worm, from Latin *vermis*] (1669)
: pasta made in long solid strings smaller in diameter than spaghetti

ver·mi·cide \'vər-mə-ˌsīd\ *noun* (1849)
: an agent that destroys worms

ver·mic·u·lar \(ˌ)vər-'mi-kyə-lər\ *adjective* [New Latin *vermicularis*, from Latin *vermiculus*, diminutive of *vermis*] (1672)

1 a : resembling a worm in form or motion **b
:** VERMICULATE
2 : of, relating to, or caused by worms

ver·mic·u·late \-lət\ *or* **ver·mic·u·lat·ed**
\-ˌlā-təd\ *adjective* [Latin *vermiculatus,* from
vermiculus] (1605)
1 : TORTUOUS, INVOLUTE
2 : full of worms : WORM-EATEN
3 a : VERMIFORM **b :** marked with irregular fine
lines or with wavy impressed lines ⟨a *vermicu-
late* nut⟩
— **ver·mic·u·la·tion** \-ˌmi-kyə-'lā-shən\
noun

ver·mic·u·lite \(ˌ)vər-'mi-kyə-ˌlīt\ *noun* [Lat-
in *vermiculus* little worm] (1824)
: any of various micaceous minerals that are
hydrous silicates resulting usually from expan-
sion of the granules of mica at high tempera-
tures to give a lightweight highly water-
absorbent material

ver·mi·form \'vər-mə-ˌförm\ *adjective* [New
Latin *vermiformis,* from *vermi-* + *-formis*
-form] (circa 1730)
: resembling a worm in shape

vermiform appendix *noun* (1778)
: a narrow blind tube usually about three to
four inches (7.6 to 10.2 centimeters) long that
extends from the cecum in the lower right-
hand part of the abdomen

ver·mi·fuge \'vər-mə-ˌfyüj\ *adjective* (1697)
: serving to destroy or expel parasitic worms
: ANTHELMINTIC
— **vermifuge** *noun*

ver·mil·ion *also* **ver·mil·lion** \vər-'mil-yən\
noun [Middle English *vermilioun,* from Old
French *vermeillon,* from *vermeil,* adjective,
bright red, vermilion, from Late Latin *ver-
miculus* kermes, from Latin, little worm] (13th
century)
1 : a bright red pigment consisting of mercuric
sulfide; *broadly* **:** any of various red pigments
2 : a vivid reddish orange

ver·min \'vər-mən\ *noun, plural* **vermin**
[Middle English, from Middle French, from
(assumed) Vulgar Latin *verminum,* from Latin
verminare to be infested with maggots, have
racking pains, from *vermina* racking pains]
(14th century)
1 a : small common harmful or objectionable
animals (as lice or fleas) that are difficult to
control **b :** birds and mammals that prey on
game **c :** animals that at a particular time and
place compete (as for food) with humans or
domestic animals
2 : an offensive person

ver·min·ous \'vər-mə-nəs\ *adjective* (circa
1616)
1 : consisting of or being vermin : NOXIOUS
2 : forming a breeding place for or infested by
vermin : FILTHY ⟨*verminous* garbage⟩
3 : caused by vermin ⟨*verminous* disease⟩

ver·mouth \vər-'müth\ *noun* [French *vermout,*
from German *Wermut* wormwood, from Old
High German *wermuota* — more at WORM-
WOOD] (1806)
: a dry or sweet aperitif wine flavored with ar-
omatic herbs and often used in mixed drinks

¹ver·nac·u·lar \və(r)-'na-kyə-lər\ *adjective*
[Latin *vernaculus* native, from *verna* slave
born in the master's house, native] (1601)
1 a : using a language or dialect native to a re-
gion or country rather than a literary, cultured,
or foreign language **b :** of, relating to, or being
a nonstandard language or dialect of a place,
region, or country **c :** of, relating to, or being
the normal spoken form of a language
2 : applied to a plant or animal in the common
native speech as distinguished from the Latin
nomenclature of scientific classification
3 : of, relating to, or characteristic of a period,
place, or group; *especially* **:** of, relating to, or
being the common building style of a period
or place ◇
— **ver·nac·u·lar·ly** *adverb*

²vernacular *noun* (circa 1706)

1 : a vernacular language, expression, or mode
of expression
2 : the mode of expression of a group or class
3 : a vernacular name of a plant or animal

ver·nac·u·lar·ism \və(r)-'na-kyə-lə-ˌri-zəm\
noun (circa 1841)
: a vernacular word or idiom

ver·nal \'vər-n°l\ *adjective* [Latin *vernalis,* al-
teration of *vernus,* from *ver* spring; akin to
Greek *ear* spring, Sanskrit *vasanta*] (1534)
1 : of, relating to, or occurring in the spring
⟨*vernal* equinox⟩ ⟨*vernal* sunshine⟩
2 : fresh or new like the spring; *also* **:** YOUTH-
FUL
— **ver·nal·ly** \-n°l-ē\ *adverb*

ver·nal·i·za·tion \ˌvər-n°l-ə-'zā-shən\ *noun*
(1933)
: the act or process of hastening the flowering
and fruiting of plants by treating seeds, bulbs,
or seedlings so as to induce a shortening of the
vegetative period
— **ver·nal·ize** \'vər-n°l-ˌīz\ *transitive verb*

ver·na·tion \(ˌ)vər-'nā-shən\ *noun* [New Latin
vernation-, vernatio, from Latin *vernare* to be-
have as in spring, from *vernus* vernal] (1793)
: the arrangement of foliage leaves within the
bud

Ver·ner's law \'ver-nərz-\ *noun* [Karl A. *Ver-
ner*] (1878)
: a statement in historical linguistics: in medial
or final position in voiced environments and
when the immediately preceding vowel did
not bear the principal accent in Proto-Indo-
European, the Proto-Germanic voiceless frica-
tives *f, þ,* and *χ* derived from the Proto-Indo-
European voiceless stops *p, t,* and *k* and the
Proto-Germanic voiceless fricative *s* derived
from Proto-Indo-European *s* became the
voiced fricatives *b̄, ð̄, ḡ,* and *z* represented in
various recorded Germanic languages by *b, d,
g,* and *r*

ver·ni·cle *or* **ver·na·cle** \'vər-ni-kəl\ *noun*
[Middle English *vernicle,* from Middle French
veronique, vernicle, from Medieval Latin
veronica] (14th century)
: ²VERONICA

¹ver·ni·er \'vər-nē-ər\ *noun* [Pierre *Vernier*]
(1766)
1 : a short scale made to slide along the divi-
sions of a graduated instrument for indicating
parts of divisions
2 a : a small auxiliary device used with a
main device to obtain fine adjustment **b :** any
of two or more small supplementary rocket
engines or gas nozzles on a missile or a rocket
vehicle for making fine adjustments in the
speed or course or controlling the attitude —
called also *vernier engine*

²vernier *adjective* (1788)
: having or comprising a vernier

vernier caliper *noun* (circa 1876)
: a measuring device that consists of a main
scale with a fixed jaw and a sliding jaw with
an attached vernier

ver·nis·sage \ˌver-ni-'säzh\ *noun* [French,
day reserved for an exhibition opens reserved for
artists to varnish and put finishing touches to
their paintings, literally, varnishing, from *ver-
nis* varnish — more at VARNISH] (1912)
: a private showing or preview of an art exhi-
bition

¹ve·ron·i·ca \və-'rä-ni-kə\ *noun* [New Latin,
genus of herbs] (1527)
: SPEEDWELL

²veronica *noun* [Medieval Latin, from *Veron-
ica,* legendary saint of the 1st century A.D.]
(circa 1700)
: an image of Christ's face said to have been
impressed on the cloth that Saint Veronica
gave him to wipe his face with on the way to
his crucifixion; *also* **:** a cloth resembling the
legendary one of Saint Veronica

³veronica *noun* [Spanish *verónica,* from Saint
Veronica] (1926)

: a pase in bullfighting in which the cape is
swung slowly away from the charging bull
while the matador keeps his feet in the same
position

Vé·ro·nique *also* **Ve·ro·nique** \ˌvā-rȯ-'nēk\
adjective [French *Véronique* Veronica] (1907)
: prepared or garnished with usually white
seedless grapes ⟨sole *Véronique*⟩

ver·ru·ca \və-'rü-kə\ *noun, plural* **-cae**
\-(ˌ)kē, -ˌkī, -ˌsī\ [Latin, wart, hillock; akin to
Lithuanian *viršus* summit and probably to Old
English *wearte* wart — more at WART] (1565)
1 : a wart or warty skin lesion
2 : a warty elevation on a plant or animal sur-
face

verruca vul·ga·ris \-ˌvəl-'gar-əs, -'ger-\ *noun*
[New Latin, literally, common verruca] (1903)
: WART 1a

ver·ru·cose \və-'rü-ˌkōs\ *adjective* (1686)
: covered with warty elevations

ver·sal \'vər-səl, 'vär-\ *adjective* [short for *uni-
versal*] (1592)
archaic **:** ENTIRE, WHOLE ⟨as pale as any clout
in the *versal* world —Shakespeare⟩

ver·sant \'vər-s°nt\ *adjective* [Latin *versant-,
versans,* present participle of *versare, versari*
to turn, occupy oneself, meditate] (1645)
1 *archaic* **:** EXPERIENCED, PRACTICED
2 : CONVERSANT

ver·sa·tile \'vər-sə-t°l, *especially British* -ˌtīl\
adjective [French or Latin; French, from Latin
versatilis turning easily, from *versare* to turn,
frequentative of *vertere*] (1605)
1 : changing or fluctuating readily : VARIABLE
⟨a *versatile* disposition⟩
2 : embracing a variety of subjects, fields, or
skills; *also* **:** turning with ease from one thing
to another
3 a (1) **:** capable of turning forward or back-
ward : REVERSIBLE ⟨a *versatile* toe of a bird⟩ (2)
: capable of moving laterally and up and down
⟨*versatile* antennae⟩ **b** *of an anther* **:** having
the filaments attached at or near the middle so
as to swing freely
4 : having many uses or applications ⟨*versatile*
building material⟩
— **ver·sa·tile·ly** \-t°l-(l)ē, -ˌtīl-lē\ *adverb*
— **ver·sa·tile·ness** \-t°l-nəs, -ˌtīl-nəs\
noun

ver·sa·til·i·ty \ˌvər-sə-'ti-lə-tē\ *noun* (circa
1755)

◇ WORD HISTORY
vernacular In ancient Rome, where
slaves constituted most of the labor force, a
distinction was made between a slave born
within a master's household, called in Latin a
verna, and one who was acquired by other
means. From *verna* the Romans derived the
adjective *vernaculus,* meaning "domestic,
homegrown" or "native, indigenous," presum-
ably created by analogy with *masculus*
"male" (noun and adjective), originally a di-
minutive of *mas* "male animal." *Vernaculus*
was applied to language peculiar to the in-
habitants of a particular area as well as to a
wide variety of other things that were local or
domestic. When Latin *vernaculus* was angli-
cized as *vernacular* in the early 17th century
its scope was restricted to language, and it
meant "using local rather than literary or for-
eign speech." A relatively modern application
of *vernacular* is its use in distinguishing the
common native names of plants and animals
from the Latin nomenclature of scientific clas-
sification, the vernacular name for *Ursus arc-
tos horribilis* being, for example, *grizzly bear.*

: the quality or state of being versatile ⟨a writer of great *versatility*⟩

vers de so·ci·é·té \ˌver-də-ˌsō-sē-ə-'tā\ *noun* [French, society verse] (1796)
: witty and typically ironic light verse

¹**verse** \'vərs\ *noun* [Middle English *vers*, from Old French & Old English; both from Latin *versus*, literally, turning, from *vertere* to turn — more at WORTH] (before 12th century)
1 : a line of metrical writing
2 a (1) : metrical language (2) : metrical writing distinguished from poetry especially by its lower level of intensity (3) : POETRY 2 b : POEM c : a body of metrical writing (as of a period or country)
3 : STANZA
4 : one of the short divisions into which a chapter of the Bible is traditionally divided

²**verse** *verb* **versed; vers·ing** (before 12th century)
intransitive verb
: to make verse : VERSIFY
transitive verb
1 : to tell or celebrate in verse
2 : to turn into verse

³**verse** *transitive verb* **versed; vers·ing** [back-formation from *versed*, from Latin *versatus*, past participle of *versari* to be active, be occupied (in), passive of *versare* to turn] (1673)
: to familiarize by close association, study, or experience ⟨well *versed* in the theater⟩

vers·et \'vər-sət, -ˌset; ˌvər-'set\ *noun* [Middle English, from Old French, diminutive of *vers* verse] (13th century)
: a short verse especially from a sacred book (as the Koran)

ver·si·cle \'vər-si-kəl\ *noun* [Middle English, from Latin *versiculus*, diminutive of *versus* verse] (14th century)
1 : a short verse or sentence (as from a psalm) said or sung by a leader in public worship and followed by a response from the people
2 : a little verse

ver·sic·u·lar \ˌvər-'si-kyə-lər\ *adjective* [Latin *versiculus* little verse] (1812)
: of or relating to verses or versicles

ver·si·fi·ca·tion \ˌvər-sə-fə-'kā-shən\ *noun* (1603)
1 : the making of verses
2 a : metrical structure : PROSODY b : a particular metrical structure or style
3 : a version in verse of something originally in prose

ver·si·fi·er \'vər-sə-ˌfī(-ə)r\ *noun* (14th century)
: one that versifies; *especially* : a writer of light or inferior verse

ver·si·fy \-ˌfī\ *verb* **-fied; -fy·ing** [Middle English *versifien*, from Middle French *versifier*, from Latin *versificare*, from *versus* verse, line] (14th century)
intransitive verb
: to compose verses
transitive verb
1 : to relate or describe in verse
2 : to turn into verse

ver·sion \'vər-zhən, -shən\ *noun* [Middle French, from Medieval Latin *version-, versio* act of turning, from Latin *vertere* to turn — more at WORTH] (1582)
1 : a translation from another language; *especially* : a translation of the Bible or a part of it
2 a : an account or description from a particular point of view especially as contrasted with another account b : an adaptation of a literary work ⟨the movie *version* of the novel⟩ c : an arrangement of a musical composition
3 : a form or variant of a type or original ⟨an experimental *version* of the plane⟩
4 a : a condition in which an organ and especially the uterus is turned from its normal position b : manual turning of a fetus in the uterus to aid delivery
— **ver·sion·al** \'vərzh-nəl, 'vərsh-; 'vər-zhən°l, -shə-\ *adjective*

vers li·bre \ver-'lēbr\ *noun, plural* **vers li·bres** *same*\ [French] (1902)
: FREE VERSE

vers–li·brist \-'lē-brist\ *noun* [French *vers-libriste*] (1916)
: a writer of free verse

ver·so \'vər-(ˌ)sō\ *noun, plural* **versos** [New Latin *verso* (*folio*) the page being turned] (1839)
1 : the side of a leaf (as of a manuscript) that is to be read second
2 : a left-hand page — compare RECTO

verst \'vərst\ *noun* [French *verste* & German *Werst*; both from Russian *versta*; akin to Latin *vertere* to turn] (1555)
: a Russian unit of distance equal to 0.6629 mile (1.067 kilometers)

ver·sus \'vər-səs, -səz\ *preposition* [Medieval Latin, towards, against, from Latin, adverb, so as to face, from past participle of *vertere* to turn] (15th century)
1 : AGAINST
2 : in contrast to or as the alternative of ⟨free trade *versus* protection⟩

vert \'vərt\ *noun* [Middle English *verte*, from Middle French *vert*, from *vert* green — more at VERDANT] (15th century)
1 a : green forest vegetation especially when forming cover or providing food for deer b : the right or privilege (as in England) of cutting living wood or sometimes of pasturing animals in a forest
2 : the heraldic color green

ver·te·bra \'vər-tə-brə, -ˌbrä\ *noun, plural* **-brae** \-ˌbrā, -(ˌ)brē, -brə\ *or* **-bras** [Latin, joint, vertebra, from *vertere* to turn] (1578)
: one of the bony or cartilaginous segments composing the spinal column, consisting in some lower vertebrates of several distinct elements which never become united, and in higher vertebrates having a short more or less cylindrical body whose ends articulate by pads of elastic or cartilaginous tissue with those of adjacent vertebrae and a bony arch that encloses the spinal cord

ver·te·bral \(ˌ)vər-'tē-brəl, 'vər-tə-\ *adjective* (circa 1681)
1 : of, relating to, or being vertebrae or the vertebral column : SPINAL
2 : composed of or having vertebrae

vertebral canal *noun* (1831)
: a canal that contains the spinal cord and is delimited by the arches on the dorsal side of the vertebrae — called also *spinal canal*

vertebral column *noun* (1822)
: SPINAL COLUMN

¹**ver·te·brate** \'vər-tə-brət, -ˌbrāt\ *adjective* [New Latin *vertebratus*, from Latin, jointed, from *vertebra*] (1826)
1 a : having a spinal column b : of or relating to the vertebrates
2 : organized or constructed in orderly or developed form

²**vertebrate** *noun* [New Latin *Vertebrata*, from neuter plural of *vertebratus*] (1826)
: any of a subphylum (Vertebrata) of chordates that possess a spinal column including the mammals, birds, reptiles, amphibians, and fishes

ver·tex \'vər-ˌteks\ *noun, plural* **ver·ti·ces** \'vər-tə-ˌsēz\ *also* **ver·tex·es** [Latin *vertic-, vertex, vortic-, vortex* whirl, whirlpool, top of the head, summit, from *vertere* to turn] (1570)
1 a : the point opposite to and farthest from the base in a figure b : a point (as of an angle, polygon, polyhedron, graph, or network) that terminates a line or curve or comprises the intersection of two or more lines or curves c : a point where an axis of an ellipse, parabola, or hyperbola intersects the curve itself
2 : the top of the head
3 : a principal or highest point : SUMMIT ⟨the *vertex* of the hill⟩

ver·ti·cal \'vər-ti-kəl\ *adjective* [Middle French or Late Latin; Middle French, from Late Latin *verticalis*, from Latin *vertic-, vertex*] (1559)
1 a : situated at the highest point : directly overhead or in the zenith b *of an aerial photograph* : taken with the camera pointing straight down or nearly so
2 a : perpendicular to the plane of the horizon or to a primary axis : UPRIGHT b (1) : located at right angles to the plane of a supporting surface (2) : lying in the direction of an axis : LENGTHWISE
3 a : relating to, involving, or integrating economic activity from basic production to point of sale ⟨*vertical* monopoly⟩ b : of, relating to, or comprising persons of different status ⟨the *vertical* arrangement of society⟩ ☆
— **vertical** *noun*
— **ver·ti·cal·i·ty** \ˌvər-tə-'ka-lə-tē\ *noun*
— **ver·ti·cal·ly** \'vər-ti-k(ə-)lē\ *adverb*
— **ver·ti·cal·ness** \-kəl-nəs\ *noun*

vertical angle *noun* (1571)
: either of two angles lying on opposite sides of two intersecting lines

vertical circle *noun* (1559)
: a great circle of the celestial sphere whose plane is perpendicular to that of the horizon

vertical file *noun* (1906)
: a collection of articles (as pamphlets and clippings) that is maintained (as in a library) to answer brief questions or to provide points of information not easily located

vertical union *noun* (1933)
: INDUSTRIAL UNION

ver·ti·cil \'vər-tə-ˌsil\ *noun* [New Latin *verticillus*, diminutive of Latin *vertex* whirl] (1793)
: a circle of similar parts (as flowers around a stem or sensory hairs around an antennal joint) about the same point on the axis : WHORL

ver·ti·cil·late \ˌvər-tə-'si-lət\ *adjective* (circa 1793)
: arranged in verticils

ver·ti·cil·li·um wilt \ˌvər-tə-'si-lē-əm-\ *noun* [New Latin *Verticillium*, from *verticillus*] (1916)
: a wilt disease of various plants that is caused by a soil-borne imperfect fungus (genus *Verticillium*)

ver·tig·i·nous \(ˌ)vər-'ti-jə-nəs\ *adjective* [Latin *vertiginosus*, from *vertigin-, vertigo*] (1608)
1 a : characterized by or suffering from vertigo or dizziness b : inclined to frequent and often pointless change : INCONSTANT
2 : causing or tending to cause dizziness ⟨the *vertiginous* heights⟩
3 : marked by turning : ROTARY ⟨the *vertiginous* motion of the earth⟩
— **ver·tig·i·nous·ly** *adverb*

ver·ti·go \'vər-ti-ˌgō\ *noun, plural* **-goes** *or* **-gos** [Latin *vertigin-, vertigo*, from *vertere* to turn] (1528)
1 a : a disordered state in which the individual or the individual's surroundings seem to whirl dizzily b : a dizzy confused state of mind
2 : disordered vertiginous movement as a symptom of disease in lower animals; *also* : a disease (as gid) causing this

ver·tu \ˌvər-'tü, ver-\ *variant of* VIRTU

☆ SYNONYMS
Vertical, perpendicular, plumb mean being at right angles to a base line. VERTICAL suggests a line or direction rising straight upward toward a zenith ⟨the side of the cliff is almost *vertical*⟩. PERPENDICULAR may stress the straightness of a line making a right angle with any other line, not necessarily a horizontal one ⟨the parallel bars are *perpendicular* to the support posts⟩. PLUMB stresses an exact verticality determined (as with a plumb line) by earth's gravity ⟨make sure that the wall is *plumb*⟩.

ver·vain \'vər-ˌvān\ *noun* [Middle English *verveine*, from Middle French, from Latin *verbena* leafy branch; akin to Latin *verber* rod, Lithuanian *virbas*, and perhaps to Greek *rhabdos* rod] (14th century)
: any of a genus (*Verbena* of the family Verbenaceae, the vervain family) of chiefly American plants that have bracted spicate flowers, a regular corolla with a 5-lobed limb, and a fruit that separates into four nutlets

verve \'vərv\ *noun* [French, fantasy, caprice, animation, from Latin *verba*, plural of *verbum* word — more at WORD] (1697)
1 *archaic* : special ability or talent
2 a : the spirit and enthusiasm animating artistic composition or performance : VIVACITY **b** : ENERGY, VITALITY

ver·vet monkey \'vər-vət-\ *noun* [French *vervet*] (1893)
: a monkey of any of several African races of a guenon (*Cercopithecus aethiops*) having the face, chin, hands, and feet black — called also *vervet*

vervet monkey

¹very \'ver-ē\ *adjective* **veri·er; -est** [Middle English *verray, verry*, from Old French *verai*, from (assumed) Vulgar Latin *veracus*, alteration of Latin *verac-, verax* truthful, from *verus* true; akin to Old English *wǣr* true, Old High German *wāra* trust, care, Greek *ēra* (accusative) favor] (13th century)
1 a : properly entitled to the name or designation : TRUE ⟨the fierce hatred of a *very* woman —J. M. Barrie⟩ **b** : ACTUAL, REAL ⟨the *very* blood and bone of our grammar —H. L. Smith (died 1972)⟩ **c** : SIMPLE, PLAIN ⟨in *very* truth⟩
2 a : being exactly as stated ⟨the *very* heart of the city⟩ **b** : exactly suitable or necessary ⟨the *very* thing for the purpose⟩
3 a : ABSOLUTE, UTTER ⟨the *veriest* fool alive⟩ **b** : UNQUALIFIED, SHEER ⟨the *very* shame of it⟩
4 — used as an intensive especially to emphasize identity ⟨before my *very* eyes⟩
5 : MERE, BARE ⟨the *very* thought terrified him⟩
6 : being the same one : SELFSAME ⟨the *very* man I saw⟩
7 : SPECIAL, PARTICULAR ⟨the *very* essence of truth is plainness and brightness —John Milton⟩
synonym see SAME

²very *adverb* (14th century)
1 : in actual fact : TRULY ⟨the *very* best store in town⟩ ⟨told the *very* same story⟩
2 : to a high degree : EXCEEDINGLY ⟨*very* hot⟩ ⟨didn't hurt *very* much⟩ □

very hard *adjective* (circa 1943)
of cheese : suitable chiefly for grating

very high frequency *noun* (1920)
: a radio frequency between ultrahigh frequency and high frequency — see RADIO FREQUENCY table

Ve·ry light \'ver-ē-, 'vir-ē-\ *noun* [Edward W. *Very* (died 1910) American naval officer] (1917)
: a pyrotechnic signal in a system of signaling using white or colored balls of fire projected from a special pistol

very low–density lipoprotein *noun* (1977)
: VLDL

very low frequency *noun* (1938)
: a radio frequency between low frequency and voice frequency — see RADIO FREQUENCY table

Ve·ry pistol \'ver-ē-, 'vir-ē-\ *noun* (1915)
: a pistol for firing Very lights

Very Reverend \'ver-ē-\ (circa 1828)
— used as a title for various ecclesiastical officials (as cathedral deans and canons, rectors

of Roman Catholic colleges and seminaries, and superiors of some religious houses)

ves·i·cal \'ve-si-kəl\ *adjective* [Latin *vesica* bladder — more at VENTER] (1797)
: of or relating to the urinary bladder ⟨*vesical* burning⟩

ves·i·cant \-kənt\ *noun* [Latin *vesica* bladder, blister] (1661)
: an agent (as a drug or a chemical weapon) that induces blistering
— **vesicant** *adjective*

ves·i·cle \'ve-si-kəl\ *noun* [Middle French *vesicule*, from Latin *vesicula* small bladder, blister, from diminutive of *vesica*] (1578)
1 a : a membranous and usually fluid-filled pouch (as a cyst, vacuole, or cell) in a plant or animal **b** : a small abnormal elevation of the outer layer of skin enclosing a watery liquid : BLISTER **c** : a pocket of embryonic tissue that is the beginning of an organ
2 : a small cavity in a mineral or rock

ve·sic·u·lar \və-'si-kyə-lər, ve-\ *adjective* [New Latin *vesicula* vesicle, from Latin, small bladder] (1715)
1 : containing, composed of, or characterized by vesicles ⟨*vesicular* lava⟩
2 : having the form or structure of a vesicle
3 : of or relating to vesicles
— **ve·sic·u·lar·i·ty** \-ˌsi-kyə-'lar-ə-tē\ *noun*

vesicular stomatitis *noun* (circa 1903)
: an acute virus disease especially of various domesticated animals (as horses and cows) that is marked by erosive blisters in and about the mouth and that much resembles foot-and-mouth disease

ve·sic·u·late \və-'si-kyə-ˌlāt, ve-\ *verb* **-lat·ed; -lat·ing** (1865)
transitive verb
: to make vesicular
intransitive verb
: to become vesicular
— **ve·sic·u·la·tion** \-ˌsi-kyə-'lā-shən\ *noun*

¹ves·per \'ves-pər\ *noun* [Middle English, from Latin, evening, evening star — more at WEST] (14th century)
1 *capitalized, archaic* : EVENING STAR
2 : a vesper bell
3 *archaic* : EVENING, EVENTIDE

²vesper *adjective* (1791)
: of or relating to vespers or the evening

ves·per·al \'ves-p(ə-)rəl\ *adjective* (circa 1623)
: VESPER ⟨a *vesperal* breeze⟩

ves·pers \'ves-pərz\ *noun plural but singular or plural in construction, often capitalized* [French *vespres*, from Medieval Latin *vesperae*, from Latin, plural of *vespera* evening; akin to Latin *vesper* evening star] (1611)
1 : the sixth of the canonical hours that is said or sung in the late afternoon
2 : a service of evening worship

ves·per·til·ian \ˌves-pər-'ti-lē-ən, -'til-yən\ *adjective* [Latin *vespertilio* bat, from *vesper*] (1874)
: of, relating to, or resembling a bat ⟨flaunts *vespertilian* wing and cloven hoof —Robert Graves⟩

ves·per·tine \'ves-pər-ˌtīn\ *adjective* [Latin *vespertinus*, from *vesper*] (1502)
1 : of, relating to, or occurring in the evening ⟨*vespertine* shadows⟩
2 : active, flowering, or flourishing in the evening : CREPUSCULAR

ves·pid \'ves-pəd\ *noun* [ultimately from Latin *vespa* wasp — more at WASP] (circa 1900)
: any of a cosmopolitan family (Vespidae) of chiefly social wasps that usually live in colonies like bees
— **vespid** *adjective*

ves·pine \'ves-ˌpīn\ *adjective* [Latin *vespa* wasp] (1843)
: of, relating to, or resembling wasps and especially vespid wasps

ves·sel \'ve-səl\ *noun* [Middle English, from Middle French *vaissel*, from Late Latin *vas-*

cellum, diminutive of Latin *vas* vase, vessel] (14th century)
1 a : a container (as a hogshead, bottle, kettle, cup, or bowl) for holding something **b** : a person into whom some quality (as grace) is infused ⟨a child of light, a true *vessel* of the Lord —H. J. Laski⟩
2 : a watercraft bigger than a rowboat; *especially* : SHIP 1
3 a : a tube or canal (as an artery) in which a body fluid is contained and conveyed or circulated **b** : a conducting tube in the xylem of a vascular plant formed by the fusion and loss of end walls of a series of cells

¹vest \'vest\ *verb* [Middle English, from Middle French *vestir* to clothe, invest, from Latin *vestire* to clothe, from *vestis* clothing, garment — more at WEAR] (15th century)
transitive verb
1 a : to place or give into the possession or discretion of some person or authority; *especially* : to give to a person a legally fixed immediate right of present or future enjoyment of (as an estate) **b** : to grant or endow with a particular authority, right, or property ⟨the retirement plan *vests* the workers absolutely with the company's contribution after 10 years of continuous employment⟩
2 : to clothe with or as if with a garment; *especially* : to robe in ecclesiastical vestments
intransitive verb
1 : to become legally vested
2 : to put on garments; *especially* : to put on ecclesiastical vestments

²vest *noun* [French *veste*, from Italian, from Latin *vestis* garment] (1613)
1 *archaic* **a** : a loose outer garment : ROBE **b** : CLOTHING, GARB
2 a : a man's sleeveless garment for the upper body usually worn under a suit coat; *also* : a similar garment for women **b** : a protective usually sleeveless garment (as a life preserver) that extends to the waist **c** : an insulated sleeveless waist-length garment often worn under or in place of a coat
3 a *chiefly British* : a man's sleeveless undershirt **b** : a knitted undershirt for women

□ USAGE
very The propriety of using *very* to modify a participial adjective, as in "very pleased" or "very flattering," has been the subject of considerable speculation since the 1870s. *Very,* an intensifier, does not modify verbs—you can "try hard" but you can't "try very"—and it was thus a matter of dispute whether *very* could modify participles. Many commentators believe that *very much* rather than *very* alone should be used. However, the question is not one of propriety, but of grammar. Participles have been moving into the class of adjectives since at least the 17th century. And one of the surest signs that a participle is established as an adjective is its being modified by *very.* The transition from verb form to adjective is a gradual one, and at any given time there will be participles that will sound right with *very* to some people and wrong to others. So writers have to trust their ear and use *very* where it sounds right and *very much* (or something else) where *very* alone sounds wrong. Dictionaries will not always be helpful. Participial adjectives are often omitted when their meaning is simply the meaning of the verb so that the space they would take up can be devoted to more words.

\ə\ abut \ʹ\ kitten \ər\ further \a\ ash \ā\ ace
\ä\ mop, mar \aú\ out \ch\ chin \e\ bet \ē\ easy
\g\ go \h\ hit \ī\ ice \j\ job \ŋ\ sing
\ō\ law \ói\ boy \th\ thin \t̲h̲\ the \ü\ loot \ú\ foot
\y\ yet \zh\ vision *see also* Guide to Pronunciation

4 : a plain or decorative piece used to fill in the front neckline of a woman's outer garment (as a waist, coat, or gown)
— **vest·like** \-ˌlīk\ *adjective*

ves·ta \'ves-tə\ *noun* [Latin *Vesta*]
1 *capitalized* : the Roman goddess of the hearth — compare HESTIA
2 : a short match with a shank of wax-coated threads; *also* : a short wooden match

¹ves·tal \'ves-tᵊl\ *adjective* (15th century)
1 : of or relating to the Roman goddess Vesta
2 a : of or relating to a vestal virgin **b** : CHASTE

²vestal *noun* (1549)
: VESTAL VIRGIN

vestal virgin *noun* (1600)
1 : a virgin consecrated to the Roman goddess Vesta and to the service of watching the sacred fire perpetually kept burning on her altar
2 : a chaste woman

vest·ed \'ves-təd\ *adjective* (1766)
1 : fully and unconditionally guaranteed as a legal right, benefit, or privilege ⟨the *vested* benefits of the pension plan⟩
2 : having a vest ⟨a *vested* suit⟩

vested interest *noun* (1818)
1 a : an interest (as a title to an estate) carrying a legal right of present or future enjoyment **b** : a right vested in an employee under a pension plan
2 : a special concern or stake in maintaining or influencing a condition, arrangement, or action especially for selfish ends
3 : one having a vested interest in something; *specifically* : a group enjoying benefits from an existing economic or political privilege

vest·ee \ve-'stē\ *noun* (1915)
1 : DICKEY; *especially* : one made to resemble a vest and worn under a coat
2 : VEST 4

ves·ti·ary \'ves-tē-ˌer-ē, 'vesh-chē-\ *noun* [Middle English *vestiarie*, from Middle French, *vestry* — more at VESTRY] (15th century)
1 : a room where clothing is kept
2 : CLOTHING, RAIMENT

ves·tib·u·lar \ve-'sti-byə-lər\ *adjective* (circa 1839)
: of, relating to, or functioning as a vestibule

ves·ti·bule \'ves-tə-ˌbyü(ə)l\ *noun* [Latin *vestibulum*] (1728)
1 : any of various bodily cavities especially when serving as or resembling an entrance to some other cavity or space: as **a** : the central cavity of the bony labyrinth of the ear or the parts of the membranous labyrinth that it contains **b** : the part of the left ventricle below the aortic orifice **c** : the space between the labia minora containing the orifice of the urethra **d** : the part of the mouth cavity outside the teeth and gums
2 a : a passage, hall, or room between the outer door and the interior of a building : LOBBY **b** : an enclosed entrance at the end of a railway passenger car
3 : a course that offers access (as to something new)
— **ves·ti·buled** \-ˌbyü(ə)ld\ *adjective*

vestibule school *noun* (1918)
: a school organized in an industrial plant to train new workers in specific skills

ves·tib·u·lo·co·chle·ar nerve \ve-ˌsti-byə-lō-'kō-klē-ər-, -'kä-\ *noun* (1962)
: AUDITORY NERVE

ves·tige \'ves-tij\ *noun* [French, from Latin *vestigium* footstep, footprint, track, vestige] (1602)
1 a (1) : a trace, mark, or visible sign left by something (as an ancient city or a condition or practice) vanished or lost (2) : the smallest quantity or trace **b** : FOOTPRINT 1
2 : a bodily part or organ that is small and degenerate or imperfectly developed in comparison to one more fully developed in an earlier stage of the individual, in a past generation, or

in closely related forms
synonym see TRACE
— **ves·ti·gial** \ve-'sti-jē-əl, -jəl\ *adjective*
— **ves·ti·gial·ly** *adverb*

vest·ing \'ves-tiŋ\ *noun* (1944)
: the conveying to an employee of the inalienable right to share in a pension fund especially in the event of termination of employment prior to the normal retirement age; *also* : the right so conveyed

vest·ment \'ves(t)-mənt\ *noun* [Middle English *vestement*, from Middle French, from Latin *vestimentum*, from *vestire* to clothe] (14th century)
1 a : an outer garment; *especially* : a robe of ceremony or office **b** *plural* : CLOTHING, GARB
2 : a covering resembling a garment
3 : one of the articles of the ceremonial attire and insignia worn by ecclesiastical officiants and assistants as indicative of their rank and appropriate to the rite being celebrated
— **vest·men·tal** \ves(t)-'men-tᵊl\ *adjective*

vest–pocket *adjective* (1848)
1 : adapted to fit into the vest pocket ⟨a *vest-pocket* edition of a book⟩
2 : of very small size or scope

vest–pocket park *noun* (1966)
: a very small urban park

ves·try \'ves-trē\ *noun, plural* **vestries** [Middle English *vestrie*, probably modification of Middle French *vestiarie*, from Medieval Latin *vestiarium*, from Latin *vestire*; from its use as a robing room for the clergy] (14th century)
1 a : SACRISTY **b** : a room used for church meetings and classes
2 a : the business meeting of an English parish **b** : an elective body in an Episcopal parish composed of the rector and a group of elected parishioners administering the temporal affairs of the parish

ves·try·man \-trē-mən\ *noun* (1614)
: a member of a vestry

¹ves·ture \'ves-chər, 'vesh-\ *noun* [Middle English, from Middle French, from *vestir* to clothe — more at VEST] (14th century)
1 a : a covering garment (as a robe or vestment) **b** : CLOTHING, APPAREL
2 : something that covers like a garment

²vesture *transitive verb* **ves·tured; ves·tur·ing** (1555)
: to cover with vesture : CLOTHE

ve·su·vi·an \və-'sü-vē-ən\ *noun* [*Vesuvian*] (1853)
: a match used especially formerly for lighting cigars

Ve·su·vi·an \və-'sü-vē-ən\ *adjective* (1673)
1 : of, relating to, or resembling the volcano Vesuvius
2 : marked by sudden outbursts ⟨has a *Vesuvian* temper, but quickly controls himself —Sidney Shalett⟩

ve·su·vi·an·ite \-vē-ə-ˌnīt\ *noun* (circa 1888)
: IDOCRASE

¹vet \'vet\ *noun* (1862)
: VETERINARIAN, VETERINARY

²vet *transitive verb* **vet·ted; vet·ting** (1891)
1 a : to provide veterinary care for (an animal) or medical care for (a person) **b** : to subject (a person or animal) to a physical examination or checkup
2 : to subject to expert appraisal or correction : EVALUATE

³vet *adjective or noun* (1848)
: VETERAN

vetch \'vech\ *noun* [Middle English *vecche*, from Old North French *veche*, from Latin *vicia*; perhaps akin to Latin *vincire* to bind] (14th century)
: any of a genus (*Vicia*) of herbaceous twining leguminous plants including some grown for fodder and green manure

vetch·ling \-liŋ\ *noun* (1578)
: any of various leguminous herbs (genus *Lathyrus* and especially *L. pratensis*)

vet·er·an \'ve-tə-rən, 've-trən\ *noun* [Latin *veteranus*, from *veteranus*, *adjective*, old, of

long experience, from *veter-*, *vetus* old — more at WETHER] (1509)
1 a : an old soldier of long service **b** : a former member of the armed forces
2 : a person of long experience in some occupation or skill (as politics or the arts)
— **veteran** *adjective*

Veterans Day *noun* (1952)
: November 11 set aside in commemoration of the end of hostilities in 1918 and 1945 and observed as a legal holiday in the U.S. to honor the veterans of the armed forces

veterans' preference *noun* (circa 1941)
: preferential treatment given qualified veterans of the U.S. armed forces under federal or state law; *specifically* : special consideration (as by allowance of points) on a civil service examination

vet·er·i·nar·i·an \ˌve-tə-rə-'ner-ē-ən, ˌve-trə-, ˌve-t²n-\ *noun* (1646)
: a person qualified and authorized to practice veterinary medicine

¹vet·er·i·nary \'ve-tə-rə-ˌner-ē, 've-trə-, 've-t²n-\ *adjective* [Latin *veterinarius* of beasts of burden, from *veterinae* beasts of burden, from feminine plural of *veterinus* of beasts of burden; akin to Latin *veter-*, *vetus* old] (1790)
: of, relating to, or being the science and art of prevention, cure, or alleviation of disease and injury in animals and especially domestic animals

²veterinary *noun, plural* **-nar·ies** (1861)
: VETERINARIAN

veterinary surgeon *noun* (circa 1802)
British : VETERINARIAN

vet·i·ver \'ve-tə-vər\ *noun* [French *vétiver*, from Tamil *veṭṭivēr*] (circa 1858)
: an East Indian grass (*Vetiveria zizanioides*) cultivated in warm regions especially for its fragrant roots which are used especially in woven goods (as mats) and in perfumes; *also* : its root

¹ve·to \'vē-(ˌ)tō\ *noun, plural* **vetoes** [Latin, I forbid, from *vetare* to forbid] (1629)
1 : an authoritative prohibition : INTERDICTION
2 a : a power of one department or branch of a government to forbid or prohibit finally or provisionally the carrying out of projects attempted by another department; *especially* : a power vested in a chief executive to prevent permanently or temporarily the enactment of measures passed by a legislature **b** (1) : the exercise of such authority (2) : a message communicating the reasons of an executive and especially the president of the U.S. for vetoing a proposed law

²veto *transitive verb* (1706)
: to refuse to admit or approve : PROHIBIT; *also* : to refuse assent to (a legislative bill) so as to prevent enactment or cause reconsideration
— **ve·to·er** \-ˌtō-(-ə)r\ *noun*

ve·to–proof \-ˌprüf\ *adjective* (1972)
: having enough potential votes to be enacted over a veto or to override vetoes consistently ⟨a *veto-proof* bill⟩

vex \'veks\ *transitive verb* **vexed** *also* **vext; vex·ing** [Middle English, from Middle French *vexer*, from Latin *vexare* to agitate, harry; probably akin to Latin *vehere* to convey — more at WAY] (15th century)
1 a : to bring trouble, distress, or agitation to ⟨the restaurant is *vexed* by slow service⟩ **b** : to bring physical distress to ⟨a headache *vexed* him all morning⟩ **c** : to irritate or annoy by petty provocations : HARASS ⟨*vexed* by the children⟩ **d** : PUZZLE, BAFFLE ⟨a problem to *vex* the keenest wit⟩
2 : to shake or toss about
synonym see ANNOY

vex·a·tion \vek-'sā-shən\ *noun* (15th century)
1 : the act of harassing or vexing : TROUBLING
2 : the quality or state of being vexed : IRRITATION
3 : a cause of trouble : AFFLICTION

vex·a·tious \-shəs\ *adjective* (1534)

1 a : causing vexation **:** DISTRESSING **b :** intended to harass
2 : full of disorder or stress **:** TROUBLED
— **vex·a·tious·ly** *adverb*
— **vex·a·tious·ness** *noun*
vexed \'vekst\ *adjective* (1657)
: debated or discussed at length ⟨a *vexed* question⟩
vexed·ly \'vek-səd-lē, 'vekst-lē\ *adverb* (1748)
: with vexation
vex·il·lol·o·gy \,vek-sə-'lä-lə-jē\ *noun* [Latin *vexillum*] (1959)
: the study of flags
— **vex·il·lo·log·ic** \(,)vek-si-lə-'lä-jik\ *or*
vex·il·lo·log·i·cal \-'lä-ji-kəl\ *adjective*
— **vex·il·lol·o·gist** \,vek-sə-'lä-lə-jist\ *noun*
vex·il·lum \vek-'si-ləm\ *noun, plural* **-la** \-lə\ [Latin; akin to Latin *velum* curtain, awning] (1726)
1 : a square flag of the ancient Roman cavalry
2 : the web or vane of a feather
via \'vī-ə, 'vē-ə\ *preposition* [Latin, ablative of *via* way — more at WAY] (1779)
1 : by way of
2 : through the medium or agency of; *also*
: by means of
vi·a·ble \'vī-ə-bəl\ *adjective* [French, from Middle French, from *vie* life, from Latin *vita* — more at VITAL] (circa 1832)
1 : capable of living; *especially* **:** capable of surviving outside the mother's womb without artificial support ⟨the normal human fetus is usually *viable* by the end of the seventh month⟩
2 : capable of growing or developing ⟨*viable* seeds⟩ ⟨*viable* eggs⟩
3 a : capable of working, functioning, or developing adequately ⟨*viable* alternatives⟩ **b** **:** capable of existence and development as an independent unit ⟨the colony is now a *viable* state⟩ **c** (1) **:** having a reasonable chance of succeeding ⟨a *viable* candidate⟩ (2) **:** financially sustainable ⟨a *viable* enterprise⟩
— **vi·a·bil·i·ty** \,vī-ə-'bi-lə-tē\ *noun*
— **vi·a·bly** \'vī-ə-blē\ *adverb*
via·duct \'vī-ə-,dəkt\ *noun* [Latin *via* way, road + English aqu*educt*] (1816)
: a long elevated roadway usually consisting of a series of short spans supported on arches, piers, or columns

viaduct

vi·al \'vī(-ə)l\ *noun* [Middle English *fiole, viole*, from Middle French *fiole*, from Old Provençal *fiola*, from Latin *phiala* — more at PHIAL] (14th century)
: a small closed or closable vessel especially for liquids
via me·dia \,vī-ə-'mē-dē-ə, ,vē-ə-'mä-dē-ə, -'me-\ *noun* [Latin] (1834)
: a middle way
vi·and \'vī-ənd\ *noun* [Middle English, from Middle French *viande*, from Medieval Latin *vivanda* food, alteration of Latin *vivenda*, neuter plural of *vivendus*, gerundive of *vivere* to live — more at QUICK] (15th century)
1 : an item of food; *especially* **:** a choice or tasty dish
2 *plural* **:** PROVISIONS, FOOD
vi·at·i·cum \vī-'a-ti-kəm, vē-\ *noun, plural* **-cums** *or* **-ca** \-kə\ [Latin — more at VOYAGE] (1562)
1 : the Christian Eucharist given to a person in danger of death
2 a : an allowance (as of transportation or supplies and money) for traveling expenses **b** **:** provisions for a journey
vibe \'vīb\ *noun* (1967)

: VIBRATION **4** ⟨seems to be in on every conversation, every deal, every *vibe* that is winging through the room —Albert Goldman⟩ — usually used in plural ⟨got bad *vibes* from him⟩
vibes \'vībz\ *noun plural* (1940)
: VIBRAPHONE
— **vib·ist** \'vī-bist\ *noun*
vi·bra·harp \'vī-brə-,härp\ *noun* [from *Vibra-Harp*, a trademark] (1930)
: VIBRAPHONE
— **vi·bra·harp·ist** \-,här-pist\ *noun*
vi·brance \'vī-brən(t)s\ *noun* (1921)
: VIBRANCY
vi·bran·cy \'vī-brən(t)-sē\ *noun* (circa 1890)
: the quality or state of being vibrant
vi·brant \-brənt\ *adjective* (1616)
1 a (1) **:** oscillating or pulsating rapidly (2) **:** pulsating with life, vigor, or activity ⟨a *vibrant* personality⟩ **b** (1) **:** readily set in vibration (2) **:** RESPONSIVE, SENSITIVE
2 : sounding as a result of vibration **:** RESONANT ⟨a *vibrant* voice⟩
3 : BRIGHT **4** ⟨a *vibrant* orange⟩
— **vi·brant·ly** *adverb*
vi·bra·phone \'vī-brə-,fōn\ *noun* [Latin *vibra-* + International Scientific Vocabulary *-phone*] (1926)
: a percussion instrument resembling the xylophone but having metal bars and motor-driven resonators for sustaining the tone and producing a vibrato
— **vi·bra·phon·ist** \-,fō-nist\ *noun*

vibraphone

vi·brate \'vī-,brāt, *especially* British vī-'\ *verb* **vi·brat·ed; vi·brat·ing** [Latin *vibratus*, past participle of *vibrare* to brandish, wave, rock — more at WIPE] (1616)
transitive verb
1 : to swing or move to and fro
2 : to emit with or as if with a vibratory motion
3 : to mark or measure by oscillation ⟨a pendulum *vibrating* seconds⟩
4 : to set in vibration
intransitive verb
1 a : to move to and fro or from side to side **:** OSCILLATE **b** **:** FLUCTUATE, VACILLATE ⟨*vibrate* between two choices⟩
2 : to have an effect as or as if of vibration ⟨music, when soft voices die, *vibrates* in the memory —P. B. Shelley⟩
3 : to be in a state of vibration **:** QUIVER
4 : to respond sympathetically **:** THRILL ⟨*vibrate* to the opportunity⟩
synonym see SWING
vi·bra·tile \'vī-brə-t⁸l, -,tīl\ *adjective* (circa 1826)
1 : characterized by vibration
2 : adapted to or used in vibratory motion ⟨the *vibratile* organs of insects⟩
vi·bra·tion \vī-'brā-shən\ *noun* (1655)
1 a : a periodic motion of the particles of an elastic body or medium in alternately opposite directions from the position of equilibrium when that equilibrium has been disturbed (as when a stretched cord produces musical tones or particles of air transmit sounds to the ear) **b** **:** the action of vibrating **:** the state of being vibrated or in vibratory motion: as (1) **:** OSCILLATION (2) **:** a quivering or trembling motion **:** QUIVER
2 : an instance of vibration
3 : vacillation in opinion or action **:** WAVERING
4 a : a characteristic emanation, aura, or spirit that infuses or vitalizes someone or something and that can be instinctively sensed or experienced — often used in plural **b** **:** a distinctive usually emotional atmosphere capable of being sensed — usually used in plural
— **vi·bra·tion·al** \-shnəl, -shə-n⁸l\ *adjective*
— **vi·bra·tion·less** \-shən-ləs\ *adjective*

vi·bra·to \vi-'brä-(,)tō, vī-\ *noun, plural* **-tos** [Italian, from past participle of *vibrare* to vibrate, from Latin] (circa 1876)
: a slightly tremulous effect imparted to vocal or instrumental tone for added warmth and expressiveness by slight and rapid variations in pitch
— **vi·bra·to·less** \-ləs\ *adjective*
vi·bra·tor \'vī-,brā-tər\ *noun* (1862)
: one that vibrates or causes vibration: as **a** **:** a vibrating electrical apparatus used in massage or for sexual stimulation **b** **:** a vibrating device (as in an electric bell or buzzer)
vi·bra·to·ry \'vī-brə-,tōr-ē, -,tȯr-\ *adjective* (1728)
1 : consisting in, capable of, or causing vibration or oscillation
2 : characterized by vibration
vib·rio \'vi-brē-,ō\ *noun, plural* **-rios** [New Latin, *Vibrion-, Vibrio*, from Latin *vibrare* to wave] (circa 1864)
: any of a genus (*Vibrio*) of short rigid motile bacteria typically shaped like a comma or an S
— **vib·ri·on·ic** \,vi-brē-'ä-nik\ *adjective*
vib·ri·on \'vi-brē-,än\ *noun* [New Latin *Vibrion-, Vibrio*] (1882)
: VIBRIO; *also* **:** a motile bacterium
vib·ri·o·sis \,vi-brē-'ō-səs\ *noun, plural* **-o·ses** \-,sēz\ [New Latin, from *Vibrio*] (1950)
: abortion in sheep and cattle caused by a bacterium (*Campylobacter fetus* synonym *Vibrio fetus*) that invades the uterine and placental capillaries, interferes with fetal nutrition, and causes the death of the developing fetus
vi·bris·sa \vī-'bri-sə, və-\ *noun, plural* **vi·bris·sae** \vī-'bri-(,)sē; və-'bri-(,)sē, -,sī\ [Medieval Latin, from Latin *vibrare*] (circa 1693)
1 : one of the stiff hairs that are located especially about the nostrils or on other parts of the face in many mammals and that often serve as tactile organs
2 : one of the bristly feathers near the mouth of many and especially insectivorous birds that may help to prevent the escape of insects
vi·bur·num \vī-'bər-nəm\ *noun* [New Latin, from Latin, a viburnum] (circa 1731)
: any of a genus (*Viburnum*) of widely distributed shrubs or trees of the honeysuckle family with simple leaves and white or rarely pink cymose flowers
vic·ar \'vi-kər\ *noun* [Middle English, from Latin *vicarius*, from *vicarius* vicarious] (14th century)
1 : one serving as a substitute or agent; *specifically* **:** an administrative deputy
2 : an ecclesiastical agent: as **a** **:** a Church of England incumbent receiving a stipend but not the tithes of a parish **b** **:** a member of the Episcopal clergy or laity who has charge of a mission or chapel **c** **:** a member of the clergy who exercises a broad pastoral responsibility as the representative of a prelate
— **vic·ar·ship** \-,ship\ *noun*
vic·ar·age \'vi-k(ə-)rij\ *noun* (15th century)
1 : the benefice of a vicar
2 : the house of a vicar
3 : VICARIATE 1
vicar apostolic *noun, plural* **vicars apostolic** (1766)
: a Roman Catholic titular bishop who administers a territory not organized as a diocese
vic·ar·ate \'vi-kə-rət, -,rāt\ *noun* (1883)
: VICARIATE
vicar–general *noun, plural* **vicars–general** (15th century)
: an administrative deputy of a Roman Catholic or Anglican bishop or of the head of a religious order
vi·car·i·al \vī-'ker-ē-əl, və-, -'kar-\ *adjective* [Latin *vicarius*] (1617)

\ə\ abut \'ə\ kitten \ər\ further \a\ ash \ā\ ace
\ä\ mop, mar \au̇\ out \ch\ chin \e\ bet \ē\ easy
\g\ go \i\ hit \ī\ ice \j\ job \ŋ\ sing \ō\ go
\ȯ\ law \ȯi\ boy \th\ thin \t͟h\ the \ü\ loot \u̇\ foot
\y\ yet \zh\ vision *see also* Guide to Pronunciation

1 : VICARIOUS 1
2 : of or relating to a vicar

vi·car·i·ance \-ē-ən(t)s\ *noun* (1957)
: fragmentation of the environment (as by splitting of a tectonic plate) in contrast to dispersal as a factor in promoting biological evolution by division of large populations into isolated subpopulations — called also *vicariance biogeography*

vi·car·i·ant \-ē-ənt\ *adjective* [translation of German *vikarirend*, present participle of *vikarieren* to act as a substitute, from *Vikar* representative, proxy, from Middle High German *vicar*, from Latin *vicarius* substitute] (1952)
: of, relating to, or being the process of vicariance or organisms that evolved through this process ⟨the possible *vicariant* origin of the Antillean arthropod fauna⟩
— vicariant *noun*

vi·car·i·ate \-ē-ət\ *noun* [Medieval Latin *vicariatus*, from Latin *vicarius* vicar] (1610)
1 : the office, jurisdiction, or tenure of a vicar
2 : the office or district of a governmental administrative deputy

vi·car·i·ous \vī-'ker-ē-əs, və-, -'kar-\ *adjective* [Latin *vicarius*, from *vicis* change, alternation, stead — more at WEEK] (1637)
1 a : serving instead of someone or something else **b :** that has been delegated ⟨*vicarious* authority⟩
2 : performed or suffered by one person as a substitute for another or to the benefit or advantage of another **:** SUBSTITUTIONARY ⟨a *vicarious* sacrifice⟩
3 : experienced or realized through imaginative or sympathetic participation in the experience of another
4 : occurring in an unexpected or abnormal part of the body instead of the usual one ⟨bleeding from the gums sometimes occurs in the absence of the normal discharge from the uterus in *vicarious* menstruation⟩
— vi·car·i·ous·ly *adverb*
— vi·car·i·ous·ness *noun*

Vicar of Christ (1570)
: POPE 1

¹vice \'vīs\ *noun* [Middle English, from Old French, from Latin *vitium* fault, vice] (14th century)
1 a : moral depravity or corruption **:** WICKEDNESS **b :** a moral fault or failing **c :** a habitual and usually trivial defect or shortcoming **:** FOIBLE ⟨suffered from the *vice* of curiosity⟩
2 : BLEMISH, DEFECT
3 : a physical imperfection, deformity, or taint
4 a *often capitalized* **:** a character representing one of the vices in an English morality play **b :** BUFFOON, JESTER
5 : an abnormal behavior pattern in a domestic animal detrimental to its health or usefulness
6 : sexual immorality; *especially* **:** PROSTITUTION

synonym see FAULT, OFFENSE

²vice *chiefly British variant of* VISE

³vice \'vīs *also* 'vī-sē\ *preposition* [Latin, ablative of *vicis* change, alternation, stead — more at WEEK] (1770)
: in the place of ⟨I will preside, *vice* the absent chairman⟩; *also* **:** rather than

vice- \'vīs, ,vīs\ *prefix* [Middle English *vis-*, *vice-*, from Middle French, from Late Latin *vice-*, from Latin *vice*, ablative of *vicis*]
: one that takes the place of ⟨*vice*-chancellor⟩

vice admiral *noun* [Middle French *visamiral*, from *vis-* vice- + *amiral* admiral] (1520)
: a commissioned officer in the navy or coast guard who ranks above a rear admiral and whose insignia is three stars

vice–chan·cel·lor \'vīs-'chan(t)-s(ə-)lər, ,vīs-\ *noun* [Middle English *vichauncellor*, from Middle French *vischancelier*, from *vis-* + *chancelier* chancellor] (15th century)
1 : an officer ranking next below a chancellor and serving as deputy to the chancellor

2 : chief administrative officer in a British university
3 : a judge appointed to act for or to assist a chancellor

vice–con·sul \-'kän(t)-səl\ *noun* (1559)
: a consular officer subordinate to a consul general or to a consul

vice-ge·ren·cy \-'jir-ən(t)-sē\ *noun, plural* **-cies** (1596)
: the office or jurisdiction of a vicegerent

vice-ge·rent \-'jir-ənt\ *noun* [Medieval Latin *vicegerent-, vicegerens*, from Late Latin *vice-* + Latin *gerent-, gerens*, present participle of *gerere* to carry, carry on] (1536)
: an administrative deputy of a king or magistrate

vi·cen·ni·al \vī-'se-nē-əl\ *adjective* [Late Latin *vicennium* period of 20 years, from Latin *vicies* 20 times + *annus* year; akin to Latin *viginti* twenty — more at VIGESIMAL, ANNUAL] (circa 1859)
: occurring once every 20 years

vice presidency *noun* (1804)
: the office of vice president

vice president *noun* (1574)
1 : an officer next in rank to a president and usually empowered to serve as president in that officer's absence or disability
2 : any of several officers serving as a president's deputies in charge of particular locations or functions
— vice presidential *adjective*

vice-re·gal \'vīs-'rē-gəl, ,vīs-\ *adjective* (1836)
: of or relating to a viceroy or viceroyalty
— vice·re·gal·ly \-gə-lē\ *adverb*

vice–re·gent \-'rē-jənt\ *noun* (1556)
: a regent's deputy

vice–reine \'vīs-,rān\ *noun* [French, from *vice-* + *reine* queen, from Latin *regina*, feminine of *reg-, rex* king — more at ROYAL] (1823)
1 : the wife of a viceroy
2 : a woman who is a viceroy

vice·roy \'vīs-,rȯi\ *noun* [Middle French *viceroi*, from *vice-* + *roi* king, from Latin *reg-, rex*] (1524)
1 : the governor of a country or province who rules as the representative of a king or sovereign
2 : a showy American nymphalid butterfly (*Limenitis archippus*) closely mimicking the monarch in coloration but smaller

vice·roy·al·ty \'vīs-,rȯi(-ə)l-tē, ,vīs-\ *noun* (1703)
: the office, jurisdiction, or term of service of a viceroy

vice·roy·ship \'vīs-,rȯi-,ship\ *noun* (1609)
: VICEROYALTY

vice squad *noun* (1905)
: a police squad charged with enforcement of laws concerning gambling, pornography, prostitution, and the illegal use of liquor and narcotics

vice ver·sa \,vī-si-'vər-sə, 'vīs-'vər-\ *adverb* [Latin] (1601)
: with the order changed **:** with the relations reversed **:** CONVERSELY

vi·chys·soise \,vi-shē-'swäz, ,vē-\ *noun* [French, from feminine of *vichyssois* of Vichy, from *Vichy*, France] (1939)
: a soup made of pureed leeks or onions and potatoes, cream, and chicken stock and usually served cold

Vi·chy water \'vi-shē-\ *noun* (circa 1858)
: a natural sparkling mineral water from Vichy, France; *also* **:** an imitation of or substitute for this

vic·i·nage \'vi-sᵊn-ij, 'vis-nij\ *noun* [Middle English *vesinage*, from Middle French, from *vesin* neighboring, from Latin *vicinus*] (14th century)
: a neighboring or surrounding district **:** VICINITY

vic·i·nal \'vi-sᵊn-əl, 'vis-nəl\ *adjective* [Latin *vicinalis*, from *vicinus* neighbor, from *vicinus*, adjective, neighboring] (circa 1623)

1 : of or relating to a limited district **:** LOCAL
2 : of, relating to, or substituted in adjacent sites in a molecule ⟨a *vicinal* disulfide group⟩

vi·cin·i·ty \və-'si-nə-tē\ *noun, plural* **-ties** [Middle French *vicinité*, from Latin *vicinitat-, vicinitas*, from *vicinus* neighboring, from *vicus* row of houses, village; akin to Gothic *weihs* village, Old Church Slavonic *vĭsĭ*, Greek *oikos, oikia* house] (1560)
1 : the quality or state of being near **:** PROXIMITY
2 : a surrounding area or district **:** NEIGHBORHOOD
3 : NEIGHBORHOOD 3b

vi·cious \'vi-shəs\ *adjective* [Middle English, from Middle French *vicieus*, from Latin *vitiosus* full of faults, corrupt, from *vitium* vice] (14th century)
1 : having the nature or quality of vice or immorality **:** DEPRAVED
2 : DEFECTIVE, FAULTY; *also* **:** INVALID
3 : IMPURE, NOXIOUS
4 a : dangerously aggressive **:** SAVAGE ⟨a *vicious* dog⟩ **b :** marked by violence or ferocity **:** FIERCE ⟨a *vicious* fight⟩
5 : MALICIOUS, SPITEFUL ⟨*vicious* gossip⟩
6 : worsened by internal causes that reciprocally augment each other ⟨a *vicious* wage-price spiral⟩ ☆
— vi·cious·ly *adverb*
— vi·cious·ness *noun*

vicious circle *noun* (circa 1792)
1 : a chain of events in which the response to one difficulty creates a new problem that aggravates the original difficulty
2 : an argument or definition that begs the question

vi·cis·si·tude \və-'si-sə-,tüd, vī-, -,tyüd\ *noun* [Middle French, from Latin *vicissitudo*, from *vicissim* in turn, from *vicis* change, alternation — more at WEEK] (circa 1576)
1 a : the quality or state of being changeable **:** MUTABILITY **b :** natural change or mutation visible in nature or in human affairs
2 a : a favorable or unfavorable event or situation that occurs by chance **:** a fluctuation of state or condition ⟨the *vicissitudes* of daily life⟩ **b :** a difficulty or hardship attendant on a way of life, a career, or a course of action and usually beyond one's control **c :** alternating change **:** SUCCESSION

vi·cis·si·tu·di·nous \və-,si-sə-'tüd-nəs, (,)vī-, -'tyüd-; -'tü-dᵊn-əs, -'tyü-\ *adjective* [Latin *vicissitudin-, vicissitudo*] (circa 1846)
: marked by or filled with vicissitudes

vic·tim \'vik-təm\ *noun* [Middle English *vyctym*, from Latin *victima;* perhaps akin to Old High German *wîh* holy] (15th century)
1 : a living being sacrificed to a deity or in the performance of a religious rite

2 : one that is acted on and usually adversely affected by a force or agent ⟨the schools are *victims* of the social system⟩: as **a** (1) : one that is injured, destroyed, or sacrificed under any of various conditions ⟨a *victim* of cancer⟩ ⟨a *victim* of the auto crash⟩ ⟨a murder *victim*⟩ (2) : one that is subjected to oppression, hardship, or mistreatment ⟨a frequent *victim* of political attacks⟩ **b** : one that is tricked or duped ⟨a con man's *victim*⟩
— **vic·tim·hood** \-,hu̇d\ *noun*
vic·tim·ise *British variant of* VICTIMIZE
vic·tim·ize \'vik-tə-,mīz\ *transitive verb* **-ized; -iz·ing** (1830)
1 : to make a victim of
2 : to subject to deception or fraud : CHEAT
— **vic·tim·i·za·tion** \,vik-tə-mə-'zā-shən\ *noun*
— **vic·tim·iz·er** \'vik-tə-,mī-zər\ *noun*
vic·tim·less \'vik-təm-ləs\ *adjective* (1965)
: having no victim : not of a nature that may produce a complainant ⟨a *victimless* crime⟩
vic·tim·ol·o·gy \,vik-tə-'mä-lə-jē\ *noun* (1958)
1 : the study of victims and victimization
2 : the claim that the problems of a person or group are the result of victimization
— **vic·tim·ol·o·gist** \-jist\ *noun*
vic·tor \'vik-tər\ *noun* [Middle English, from Latin, from *vincere* to conquer, win; akin to Old English *wīgan* to fight, Lithuanian *veikti* to be active] (14th century)
: one that defeats an enemy or opponent : WINNER
— **victor** *adjective*
Victor (1942)
— a communications code word for the letter *v*
vic·to·ria \vik-'tōr-ē-ə, -'tȯr-\ *noun* [Queen *Victoria*] (circa 1864)
: a low four-wheeled pleasure carriage for two with a folding top and a raised seat in front for the driver
Victoria Cross *noun* (1856)
: a bronze Maltese cross awarded to members of the British armed services for acts of remarkable valor
Victoria Day *noun* [Queen *Victoria*] (1901)
1 : formerly May 24 and now the Monday preceding May 25 observed in Canada as a legal holiday
2 : COMMONWEALTH DAY
¹Vic·to·ri·an \vik-'tōr-ē-ən, -'tȯr-\ *adjective* (1839)
1 : of, relating to, or characteristic of the reign of Queen Victoria of England or the art, letters, or tastes of her time
2 : typical of the moral standards, attitudes, or conduct of the age of Victoria especially when considered stuffy or hypocritical
²Victorian *noun* (1876)
1 : a person living during Queen Victoria's reign; *especially* : a representative figure of that time
2 : a typically large and ornate house built during Queen Victoria's reign
Vic·to·ri·ana \(,)vik-,tōr-ē-'a-nə, -,tȯr-, -'ä-, -'ā-\ *noun* [Queen *Victoria* + English -*ana*] (1940)
: materials concerning or characteristic of the Victorian age; *also* : a collection of such materials
Vic·to·ri·an·ism \vik-'tōr-ē-ə-,ni-zəm, -'tȯr-\ *noun* (1905)
1 : a typical instance or product of Victorian expression, taste, or conduct
2 : the quality or state of being Victorian especially in taste or conduct
vic·to·ri·ous \vik-'tōr-ē-əs, -'tȯr-\ *adjective* (14th century)
1 a : having won a victory **b** : of, relating to, or characteristic of victory
2 : evincing moral harmony or a sense of fulfillment : FULFILLED
— **vic·to·ri·ous·ly** *adverb*
— **vic·to·ri·ous·ness** *noun*

vic·to·ry \'vik-t(ə-)rē\ *noun, plural* **-ries** [Middle English, from Middle French *victorie*, from Latin *victoria*, from *victor*] (14th century)
1 : the overcoming of an enemy or antagonist
2 : achievement of mastery or success in a struggle or endeavor against odds or difficulties
Vic·tro·la \vik-'trō-lə\ *trademark*
— used for a phonograph
¹vict·ual \'vi-t°l\ *noun* [alteration of Middle English *vitaille*, from Middle French, from Late Latin *victualia*, plural, provisions, victuals, from neuter plural of *victualis* of nourishment, from Latin *victus* nourishment, way of living, from *vivere* to live — more at QUICK] (1523)
1 : food usable by people
2 *plural* : supplies of food : PROVISIONS
²victual *verb* **-ualed** *or* **-ualled; -ual·ing** *or* **-ual·ling** (1558)
transitive verb
: to supply with food
intransitive verb
1 : EAT
2 : to lay in provisions
vict·ual·ler *or* **vict·ual·er** \'vi-t°l-ər\ *noun* (1568)
1 : the keeper of a restaurant or tavern
2 : one that provisions an army, a navy, or a ship with food
3 : an army or navy provision ship
vi·cu·ña *or* **vi·cu·na** \vi-'kün-yə, vī-; vī-'kü-nə, və-, -'kyü-\ *noun* [Spanish *vicuña*, from Quechua *wik'uña*] (1604)
1 : a wild ruminant (*Vicugna vicugna* synonym *Lama vicugna*) of the Andes from Peru to Argentina that is related to the llama and alpaca
2 a : the wool from the vicuña's fine lustrous undercoat **b** : a fabric made of vicuña wool; *also* : a sheep's wool imitation of this

vicuña 1

vi·de \'vī-dē, 'vē-,dā\ *imperative verb* [Latin, from *vidēre* to see — more at WIT] (1565)
: SEE — used to direct a reader to another item
vi·de·li·cet \və-'de-lə-,set, vī-; vi-'dā-li-,ket\ *adverb* [Middle English, from Latin, from *vidēre* to see + *licet* it is permitted, from *licēre* to be permitted] (15th century)
: that is to say : NAMELY
¹vid·eo \'vi-dē-,ō\ *noun* [Latin *vidēre* to see + -*o* (as in *audio*)] (1937)
1 : TELEVISION; *also* : the visual portion of television
2 : VIDEOTAPE: as **a** : a recording of a motion picture or television program for playing through a television set **b** : a videotaped performance of a song often featuring an interpretation of the lyrics through visual images
²video *adjective* (1938)
1 : being, relating to, or used in the transmission or reception of the television image ⟨*video* channel⟩ — compare AUDIO
2 : being, relating to, or involving images on a television screen or computer display ⟨*video* terminal⟩
vid·eo·cas·sette \,vi-dē-ō-kə-'set, -ka-\ *noun* (1970)
1 : a case containing videotape for use with a VCR
2 : a recording (as of a movie) on a videocassette
videocassette recorder *noun* (1976)
: VCR
vid·eo·con·fer·enc·ing \-'kän-f(ə-)rən(t)-siŋ, -fərn(t)-\ *noun* (1977)

: the holding of a conference among people at remote locations by means of transmitted audio and video signals
— **vid·eo·con·fer·ence** \-'känf(ə-)rən(t)s, -fərn(t)s\ *noun*
vid·eo·disc *or* **vid·eo·disk** \'vi-dē-ō-,disk\ *noun* (1967)
1 : a disc similar in appearance and use to a phonograph record on which programs have been recorded for playback on a television set; *also* : OPTICAL DISK
2 : a recording (as of a movie) on a videodisc
video game *noun* (1973)
: an electronic game played by means of images on a video screen and often emphasizing fast action
vid·e·og·ra·phy \,vi-dē-'ä-grə-fē\ *noun* (1972)
: the practice or art of recording images with a video camera
— **vid·e·og·ra·pher** \-fər\ *noun*
vid·eo·land \-,land\ *noun* (1967)
: television as a medium or industry
vid·eo·phile \'vi-dē-ə-,fīl\ *noun* (1966)
: a person fond of video; *especially* : one interested in video equipment or in producing videos
vid·eo·phone \'vi-dē-ə-,fōn\ *noun* (circa 1950)
: a telephone equipped for transmission of video as well as audio signals so that users can see each other
¹vid·eo·tape \'vi-dē-ō-,tāp\ *noun* (1953)
: a recording of visual images and sound (as of a television production) made on magnetic tape; *also* : the magnetic tape used for such a recording
²videotape *transitive verb* (1958)
: to make a videotape of ⟨*videotape* a show⟩ ⟨*videotape* the president's speech⟩
videotape recorder *noun* (1953)
: a device for recording and playing back videotapes — called also *video recorder*
vid·eo·tex \-,teks\ *also* **vid·eo·text** \-,tekst\ *noun* [²*video* + -*tex* (alteration of *text*)] (1978)
: an electronic data retrieval system in which usually textual information is transmitted via telephone or cable-television lines and displayed on a television set or video display terminal; *especially* : such a system that is interactive — compare TELETEXT
video vé·ri·té \-,ver-ə-'tā\ *noun* [cinema *verité*] (1969)
: the filming or videotaping of a television program (as a documentary) so as to convey candid realism
vi·dette *variant of* VEDETTE
vid·i·con \'vi-di-,kän\ *noun, often capitalized* [²*video* + *icon*oscope] (1950)
: a camera tube using the principle of photoconductivity
vi·du·ity \vi-'dü-ə-tē, -'dyü-\ *noun* [Middle English (Scots) *viduite*, from Middle French *viduite*, from Latin *viduitat-*, *viduitas*, from *vidua* widow — more at WIDOW] (15th century)
: WIDOWHOOD
vie \'vī\ *verb* **vied; vy·ing** \'vī-iŋ\ [modification of Middle French *envier* to invite, challenge, wager, from Latin *invitare* to invite] (1577)
intransitive verb
: to strive for superiority : CONTEND, COMPETE
transitive verb
archaic : WAGER, HAZARD; *also* : to exchange in rivalry : MATCH
— **vi·er** \'vī(-ə)r\ *noun*
Vi·en·na sausage \vē-'e-nə-\ *noun* [*Vienna*, Austria] (circa 1902)
: a short slender frankfurter

Viet·cong \vē-'et-'käŋ, vyet-, ,vē-ət-, vēt-, -'kȯŋ\ *noun, plural* **Vietcong** [Vietnamese *Việt-cộng*] (1957)
: a guerrilla member of the Vietnamese communist movement

Viet·minh \-'min\ *noun, plural* **Vietminh** [Vietnamese *Việt-Minh,* short for *Việt-Nam Độc-Lập Đồng-Minh* League for the Independence of Vietnam] (1945)
: an adherent of the Vietnamese communist movement from 1941 to 1951

Viet·nam·ese \vē-,et-nə-'mēz, ,vyet-, ,vē-ət-, ,vēt-, -na-, -nä-, -'mēs\ *noun, plural* **Vietnamese** (1947)
1 : a native or inhabitant of Vietnam
2 : the language of the largest group in Vietnam and the official language of the country
— **Vietnamese** *adjective*

¹view \'vyü\ *noun* [Middle English *vewe,* from Middle French *veue, vue,* from Old French, from feminine of *veu, vu,* past participle of *veeir, voir* to see, from Latin *vidēre* — more at WIT] (15th century)
1 : the act of seeing or examining : INSPECTION; *also* : SURVEY ⟨a *view* of English literature⟩
2 a : a mode or manner of looking at or regarding something **b** : an opinion or judgment colored by the feeling or bias of its holder ⟨in my *view* the conference has no chance of success⟩
3 : SCENE, PROSPECT ⟨the lovely *view* from the balcony⟩
4 : extent or range of vision : SIGHT ⟨tried to keep the ship in *view*⟩ ⟨sat high in the bleachers to get a good *view*⟩
5 : something that is looked toward or kept in sight : OBJECT ⟨studied hard with a *view* to getting an A⟩
6 : the foreseeable future ⟨no hope in *view*⟩
7 : a pictorial representation
synonym see OPINION
— **in view of** : in regard to : in consideration of
— **on view** : open to public inspection : on exhibition

²view *transitive verb* (1523)
1 : to look at attentively : SCRUTINIZE, OBSERVE ⟨*view* an exhibit⟩ ⟨*view* the landscape⟩
2 a : SEE, WATCH ⟨*view* a film⟩ **b** : to look on in a particular light : REGARD ⟨doesn't *view* himself as a rebel⟩
3 : to survey or examine mentally : CONSIDER ⟨*view* all sides of a question⟩
— **view·able** \-ə-bəl\ *adjective*

view·data \'vyü-,dā-tə also -,da-\ *noun* (1975)
: a videotex system usually employing telephone lines

view·er \'vyü-ər\ *noun* (15th century)
: one that views: as **a** : a person legally appointed to inspect and report on property **b** : an optical device used in viewing **c** : a person who watches television

view·er·ship \-,ship\ *noun* (1954)
: a television audience especially with respect to size or makeup

view·find·er \'vyü-,fīn-dər\ *noun* (1889)
: a device on a camera for showing the area of the subject to be included in the picture

view hal·loo \,vyü-hə-'lü\ *interjection* (1761)
— used in fox hunting on seeing a fox break cover

view·ing *noun* (1535)
: an act of seeing, watching, or taking a look; *especially* : an instance or the practice of watching television

view·less \'vyü-ləs\ *adjective* (1603)
1 : not perceivable : INVISIBLE
2 : affording no view
3 : expressing no views or opinions
— **view·less·ly** *adverb*

view·point \-,pȯint\ *noun* (1855)
: POINT OF VIEW, STANDPOINT

viewy \'vyü-ē\ *adjective* (1848)
1 : possessing visionary, impractical, or fantastic views

2 : spectacular or arresting in appearance : SHOWY

vig \'vig\ *noun* (1968)
: VIGORISH

vi·ga \'vē-gə\ *noun* [Spanish, beam, rafter] (1844)
: one of the heavy rafters and especially a log supporting the roof in American Indian and Spanish architecture of the Southwest

vi·ges·i·mal \vī-'je-sə-məl\ *adjective* [Latin *vicesimus, vigesimus* twentieth; akin to Latin *viginti* twenty, Greek *eikosi*] (circa 1656)
: based on the number 20

vig·il \'vi-jəl\ *noun* [Middle English *vigile,* from Old French, from Late Latin & Latin; Late Latin *vigilia* watch on the eve of a feast, from Latin, wakefulness, watch, from *vigil* awake, watchful; akin to Latin *vigēre* to be vigorous, *vegēre* to enliven — more at WAKE] (13th century)
1 a : a watch formerly kept on the night before a religious feast with prayer or other devotions **b** : the day before a religious feast observed as a day of spiritual preparation **c** : evening or nocturnal devotions or prayers — usually used in plural
2 : the act of keeping awake at times when sleep is customary; *also* : a period of wakefulness
3 : an act or period of watching or surveillance : WATCH

vig·i·lance \'vi-jə-lən(t)s\ *noun* (1533)
: the quality or state of being vigilant

vigilance committee *noun* (1835)
: a committee of vigilantes

vig·i·lant \'vi-jə-lənt\ *adjective* [Middle English, from Middle French, from Latin *vigilant-, vigilans,* from present participle of *vigilare* to keep watch, stay awake, from *vigil* awake] (15th century)
: alertly watchful especially to avoid danger
synonym see WATCHFUL
— **vig·i·lant·ly** *adverb*

vig·i·lan·te \,vi-jə-'lan-tē\ *noun* [Spanish, watchman, guard, from *vigilante* vigilant, from Latin *vigilant-, vigilans*] (1865)
: a member of a volunteer committee organized to suppress and punish crime summarily (as when the processes of law appear inadequate); *broadly* : a self-appointed doer of justice
— **vig·i·lan·tism** \-'lan-,ti-zəm\ *noun*

vigil light *noun* (circa 1931)
: a candle lighted devotionally (as in a Roman Catholic church) before a shrine or image — called also *vigil candle*

vi·gin·til·lion \,vī-,jin-'til-yən\ *noun, often attributive* [Latin *viginti* twenty + English *-illion* (as in *million*) — more at VIGESIMAL] (circa 1903)
— see NUMBER table

vi·gne·ron \,vēn-yə-'rōn\ *noun* [Middle English, from Middle French, from Old French *vineron,* from *vine, vigne* vine, vineyard] (15th century)
: WINEGROWER

¹vi·gnette \vin-'yet, vēn-\ *noun* [French, from Middle French *vignete,* from diminutive of *vigne* vine — more at VINE] (1751)
1 : a running ornament (as of vine leaves, tendrils, and grapes) put on or just before a title page or at the beginning or end of a chapter; *also* : a small decorative design or picture so placed
2 a : a picture (as an engraving or photograph) that shades off gradually into the surrounding paper **b** : the pictorial part of a postage stamp design as distinguished from the frame and lettering
3 a : a short descriptive literary sketch **b** : a brief incident or scene (as in a play or movie)
— **vi·gnett·ist** \-'ye-tist\ *noun*

²vignette *transitive verb* **vi·gnett·ed; vi·gnett·ing** (1853)
1 : to finish (as a photograph) in the manner of a vignette

2 : to describe briefly
— **vi·gnett·er** *noun*

vig·or \'vi-gər\ *noun* [Middle English, from Middle French *vigor,* from Latin, from *vigēre* to be vigorous] (14th century)
1 : active bodily or mental strength or force
2 : active healthy well-balanced growth especially of plants
3 : intensity of action or effect : FORCE
4 : effective legal status

vig·or·ish \'vi-gə-rish\ *noun* [perhaps from Ukrainian *vygrash* or Russian *vyigrysh* winnings, profit] (1912)
1 : a charge taken (as by a bookie or a gambling house) on bets; *also* : the degree of such a charge ⟨a *vigorish* of five percent⟩
2 : interest paid to a moneylender

vi·go·ro·so \,vi-gə-'rō-(,)sō, ,vē-, -(,)zō\ *adjective or adverb* [Italian, literally, vigorous, from Middle French *vigorous*] (circa 1724)
: energetic in style — used as a direction in music

vig·or·ous \'vi-g(ə-)rəs\ *adjective* [Middle English, from Middle French, from Old French, from *vigor*] (14th century)
1 : possessing vigor : full of physical or mental strength or active force : STRONG ⟨a *vigorous* youth⟩ ⟨a *vigorous* plant⟩
2 : done with vigor : carried out forcefully and energetically ⟨*vigorous* exercises⟩ ☆
— **vig·or·ous·ly** *adverb*
— **vig·or·ous·ness** *noun*

vig·our \'vi-gər\ *chiefly British variant of* VIGOR

Vi·king \'vī-kiŋ\ *noun* [Old Norse *vīkingr*] (1807)
1 a : one of the pirate Norsemen plundering the coasts of Europe in the 8th to 10th centuries **b** *not capitalized* : SEA ROVER
2 : SCANDINAVIAN

vile \'vī(ə)l\ *adjective* **vil·er** \'vī-lər\; **vil·est** \-ləst\ [Middle English, from Old French *vil,* from Latin *vilis*] (14th century)
1 a : morally despicable or abhorrent ⟨nothing is so *vile* as intellectual dishonesty⟩ **b** : physically repulsive : FOUL ⟨a *vile* slum⟩
2 : of little worth or account : COMMON; *also* : MEAN
3 : tending to degrade ⟨*vile* employments⟩
4 : disgustingly or utterly bad : OBNOXIOUS, CONTEMPTIBLE ⟨*vile* weather⟩ ⟨had a *vile* temper⟩
synonym see BASE
— **vile·ly** \'vī(ə)l-lē\ *adverb*
— **vile·ness** *noun*

vil·i·fi·ca·tion \,vi-lə-fə-'kā-shən\ *noun* (1630)
1 : the act of vilifying : ABUSE
2 : an instance of vilifying : a defamatory utterance

vil·i·fy \'vi-lə-,fī\ *transitive verb* **-fied; -fy·ing** [Middle English *vilifien,* from Late Latin *vilificare,* from Latin *vilis* cheap, vile] (15th century)
1 : to lower in estimation or importance

☆ **SYNONYMS**
Vigorous, energetic, strenuous, lusty, nervous mean having or showing great vitality and force. VIGOROUS further implies showing no signs of depletion or diminishing of freshness or robustness ⟨as *vigorous* as a youth half his age⟩. ENERGETIC suggests a capacity for intense activity ⟨an *energetic* campaigner⟩. STRENUOUS suggests a preference for coping with the arduous or the challenging ⟨the *strenuous* life on an oil rig⟩. LUSTY implies exuberant energy and capacity for enjoyment ⟨a *lusty* appetite for life⟩. NERVOUS suggests especially the forcibleness and sustained effectiveness resulting from mental vigor ⟨full of *nervous* energy⟩.

2 : to utter slanderous and abusive statements against **:** DEFAME

synonym see MALIGN

— **vil·i·fi·er** \-ˌfī(-ə)r\ *noun*

vil·i·pend \'vi-lə-ˌpend\ *transitive verb* [Middle English, from Middle French *vilipender*, from Medieval Latin *vilipendere*, from Latin *vilis* + *pendere* to weigh, estimate] (15th century)

1 : to hold or treat as of little worth or account **:** CONTEMN

2 : to express a low opinion of **:** DISPARAGE

vill \'vil\ *noun* [Anglo-French, from Old French *ville* village] (1596)

1 : a division of a hundred **:** TOWNSHIP

2 : VILLAGE

vil·la \'vi-lə\ *noun* [Italian, from Latin; akin to Latin *vicus* village — more at VICINITY] (1611)

1 : a country estate

2 : the rural or suburban residence of a wealthy person

3 *British* **:** a detached or semidetached urban residence with yard and garden space

vil·la·dom \'vi-lə-dəm\ *noun* (1880) *British* **:** the world constituted by villas and their occupants

vil·lage \'vi-lij\ *noun, often attributive* [Middle English, from Middle French, from Old French, from *ville* farm, village, from Latin *villa*] (14th century)

1 a : a settlement usually larger than a hamlet and smaller than a town **b :** an incorporated minor municipality

2 : the residents of a village

3 : something (as an aggregation of burrows or nests) suggesting a village

4 : a territorial area having the status of a village especially as a unit of local government

vil·lag·er \'vi-li-jər\ *noun* (1570) **:** an inhabitant of a village

vil·lag·ery \'vi-lij-rē, -li-jə-\ *noun* (1590) **:** VILLAGES

vil·lain \'vi-lən\ *noun* [Middle English *vilain, vilein*, from Middle French, from Medieval Latin *villanus*, from Latin *villa*] (14th century)

1 : an uncouth person **:** BOOR

2 : VILLEIN

3 : a deliberate scoundrel or criminal

4 : a scoundrel in a story or play

5 : a person or thing blamed for a particular evil or difficulty ⟨automation as the *villain* in job . . . displacement —M. H. Goldberg⟩ ◆

vil·lain·ess \-lə-nəs\ *noun* (1586) **:** a woman who is a villain

vil·lain·ous \-lə-nəs\ *adjective* (15th century)

1 a : befitting a villain (as in evil, depraved, or vile character) ⟨a *villainous* attack⟩ **b :** being or having the character of a villain **:** DEPRAVED ⟨the *villainous* foe⟩

2 : highly objectionable **:** WRETCHED

synonym see VICIOUS

— **vil·lain·ous·ly** *adverb*

— **vil·lain·ous·ness** *noun*

vil·lainy \-lə-nē\ *noun, plural* **-lain·ies** (13th century)

1 : villainous conduct; *also* **:** a villainous act

2 : the quality or state of being villainous **:** DEPRAVITY

vil·la·nel·la \ˌvi-lə-'ne-lə\ *noun, plural* **-nel·le** \-'ne-lē\ [Italian, from *villano* villein, peasant, from Medieval Latin *villanus*] (1596)

1 : a 16th century Italian rustic part-song unaccompanied and in free form

2 : an instrumental piece in the style of a rustic dance

vil·la·nelle \ˌvi-lə-'nel\ *noun* [French, from Italian *villanella*] (1877) **:** a chiefly French verse form running on two rhymes and consisting typically of five tercets and a quatrain in which the first and third lines of the opening tercet recur alternately at the end of the other tercets and together as the last two lines of the quatrain

vil·lat·ic \vi-'la-tik\ *adjective* [Latin *villaticus*, from *villa*] (1671)

: RURAL

-ville \ˌvil, *especially Southern* vəl\ *noun suffix* [*-ville*, suffix occurring in names of towns, from French, from Old French, from *ville* village]

: place, category, or quality of a specified nature ⟨dull*ville*⟩

vil·lein \'vi-lən, 'vi-ˌlān, vi-'lān\ *noun* [Middle English *vilain, vilein* — more at VILLAIN] (14th century)

1 : a free common villager or village peasant of any of the feudal classes lower in rank than the thane

2 : a free peasant of a feudal class lower than a sokeman and higher than a cotter

3 : an unfree peasant standing as the slave of a feudal lord but free in legal relations with respect to all others

vil·len·age \'vi-lə-nij\ *noun* [Middle English *vilenage*, from Middle French, from Old French, from *vilein, vilain*] (14th century)

1 : tenure at the will of a feudal lord by villein services

2 : the status of a villein

vil·li·form \'vi-lə-ˌfȯrm\ *adjective* [International Scientific Vocabulary] (1849) **:** having the form or appearance of villi

vil·los·i·ty \vi-'lä-sə-tē\ *noun, plural* **-ties** (1777)

1 : the state of being villous

2 : a villous patch or area

vil·lous \'vi-ləs\ *adjective* [Middle English, from Latin *villosus* hairy, shaggy, from *villus*] (14th century)

1 : covered or furnished with villi

2 : having soft long hairs ⟨leaves *villous* underneath⟩ — compare PUBESCENT

vil·lus \'vi-ləs\ *noun, plural* **vil·li** \'vi-ˌlī, -(ˌ)lē\ [New Latin, from Latin, tuft of shaggy hair — more at VELVET] (circa 1704) **:** a small slender often vascular process: as **a :** one of the minute finger-shaped processes of the mucous membrane of the small intestine that serve in the absorption of nutriment **b :** one of the branching processes of the surface of the chorion of the developing embryo of most mammals that help to form the placenta

vim \'vim\ *noun* [Latin, accusative of *vis* strength; akin to Greek *is* strength, Sanskrit *vaya* meal, strength] (1843) **:** robust energy and enthusiasm

vi·na \'vē-nə\ *noun* [Sanskrit *vīṇā*] (1788) **:** a stringed instrument of India having usually four strings on a long bamboo fingerboard with movable frets and a gourd resonator at each end

vina

vi·na·ceous \vī-'nā-shəs, vi-\ *adjective* [Latin *vinaceus* of wine, from *vinum* wine — more at WINE] (1688) **:** of the color wine

vin·ai·grette \ˌvi-ni-'gret\ *noun* [French, from *vinaigre* vinegar] (1699)

1 : a sauce made typically of oil and vinegar, onions, parsley, and herbs and used especially on cold meats or fish — called also *vinaigrette dressing, vinaigrette sauce*

2 : a small ornamental box or bottle with perforated top used for holding an aromatic preparation (as smelling salts)

vi·nal \'vī-ˌnal\ *noun* [poly*vinyl* *al*cohol] (circa 1939) **:** a synthetic textile fiber that is a long-chain polymer consisting largely of vinyl alcohol units

vin·blas·tine \(ˌ)vin-'blas-ˌtēn\ *noun* [contrac-tion of *vincaleukoblastine*, from *vinca* + *leukoblast* developing leukocyte, from *leuk-* + *-blast*] (1962) **:** an alkaloid $C_{46}H_{58}N_4O_9$ from Madagascar periwinkle used especially in the form of its sulfate to treat human neoplastic diseases

vin·ca \'viŋ-kə\ *noun* [New Latin, short for Latin *vincapervinca* periwinkle] (1868) **:** ¹PERIWINKLE

Vin·cen·tian \vin-'sen(t)-shən\ *noun* (1854)

1 : a member of the Roman Catholic Congregation of the Mission founded by Saint Vincent de Paul in Paris, France, in 1625 and devoted to missions and seminaries

2 : a native or inhabitant of the island of Saint Vincent

— **Vincentian** *adjective*

Vin·cent's angina \'vin(t)-sən(t)s-, (ˌ)vanⁿ-'säⁿz-\ *noun* [Jean Hyacinthe *Vincent* (died 1950) French bacteriologist] (circa 1903) **:** Vincent's infection in which the ulceration has spread to surrounding tissues (as of the pharynx and tonsils) — called also *trench mouth*

Vincent's infection *noun* (circa 1922) **:** a progressive painful disease of the mouth that is marked especially by dirty gray ulceration of the mucous membranes, spontaneous hemorrhaging of the gums, and a foul odor to the breath and that is associated with the presence of large numbers of a bacillus (*Fusobacterium nucleatum* synonym *F. fusiforme*) and a spirochete (*Treponema vincentii* synonym *Borrelia vincentii*) in the lesions — called also *trench mouth*

vin·ci·ble \'vin(t)-sə-bəl\ *adjective* [Latin *vincibilis*, from *vincere* to conquer — more at VICTOR] (1548) **:** capable of being overcome or subdued

vin·cris·tine \(ˌ)vin-'kris-ˌtēn\ *noun* [*vin*circa + Latin *crista* crest + English ²*-ine* — more at CREST] (circa 1962) **:** an alkaloid $C_{46}H_{56}N_4O_{10}$ from Madagascar periwinkle used especially in the form of its sulfate to treat some human neoplastic diseases (as leukemias)

vin·cu·lum \'viŋ-kyə-ləm\ *noun, plural* **-lums** *or* **-la** \-lə\ [Latin, from *vincire* to bind] (1661)

1 : a unifying bond **:** LINK, TIE

\ə\ abut \ᵊ\ kitten \ər\ further \a\ ash \ā\ ace
\ä\ mop, mar \au̇\ out \ch\ chin \e\ bet \ē\ easy
\g\ go \i\ hit \ī\ ice \j\ job \ŋ\ sing \ō\ go
\ȯ\ law \ȯi\ boy \th\ thin \th̲\ the \ü\ loot \u̇\ foot
\y\ yet \zh\ vision *see also* Guide to Pronunciation

2 : a straight horizontal mark that is placed over two or more members of a compound mathematical expression and is equivalent to parentheses or brackets placed around them (as in $a - b - c = a - [b - c]$)

vin·da·loo \'vin-də-ˌlü\ *noun* [probably from Konkani *vindalu*, from Indo-Portuguese (Portuguese creole of India) *vinh d'alho*, literally, wine of garlic, from Portuguese *vinho de alho*] (1888)
: a curried dish of Indian origin made with meat or shellfish, garlic, and wine or vinegar

vin·di·ca·ble \'vin-di-kə-bəl\ *adjective* (1647)
: capable of being vindicated

vin·di·cate \'vin-də-ˌkāt\ *transitive verb* **-cat·ed; -cat·ing** [Latin *vindicatus*, past participle of *vindicare* to lay claim to, avenge, from *vindic-, vindex* claimant, avenger] (1570)
1 *obsolete* **:** to set free **:** DELIVER
2 : AVENGE
3 a : to free from allegation or blame **b** (1) **:** CONFIRM, SUBSTANTIATE (2) **:** to provide justification or defense for **:** JUSTIFY **c :** to protect from attack or encroachment **:** DEFEND
4 : to maintain a right to
synonym see EXCULPATE, MAINTAIN
— **vin·di·ca·tor** \-ˌkā-tər\ *noun*

vin·di·ca·tion \ˌvin-də-'kā-shən\ *noun* (1613)
: an act of vindicating **:** the state of being vindicated; *specifically* **:** justification against denial or censure **:** DEFENSE

vin·dic·a·tive \vin-'di-kə-tiv\ *adjective* (1521)
1 *obsolete* **:** VINDICTIVE, VENGEFUL
2 *archaic* **:** PUNITIVE

vin·dic·a·to·ry *adjective* (1647)
1 \'vin-di-kə-ˌtōr-ē, -ˌtôr-\ **:** providing vindication **:** JUSTIFICATORY
2 \vin-'di-kə-\ **:** PUNITIVE, RETRIBUTIVE

vin·dic·tive \vin-'dik-tiv\ *adjective* [Latin *vindicta* revenge, vindication, from *vindicare*] (1616)
1 a : disposed to seek revenge **:** VENGEFUL **b :** intended for or involving revenge
2 : intended to cause anguish or hurt **:** SPITEFUL
— **vin·dic·tive·ly** *adverb*
— **vin·dic·tive·ness** *noun*

¹vine \'vīn\ *noun* [Middle English, from Middle French, from Old French *vigne*, from Latin *vinea* vine, vineyard, from feminine of *vineus* of wine, from *vinum* wine — more at WINE] (14th century)
1 : GRAPE 2
2 a : a plant whose stem requires support and which climbs by tendrils or twining or creeps along the ground; *also* **:** the stem of such a plant **b :** any of various sprawling herbaceous plants (as a tomato or potato) that lack specialized adaptations for climbing

²vine *intransitive verb* **vined; vin·ing** (1796)
: to form or grow in the manner of a vine

vine·dress·er \'vīn-ˌdre-sər\ *noun* (1560)
: a person who cultivates and prunes grapevines

vin·e·gar \'vi-ni-gər\ *noun* [Middle English *vinegre*, from Middle French *vinaigre*, from *vin* wine (from Latin *vinum*) + *aigre* keen, sour — more at EAGER] (14th century)
1 : a sour liquid obtained by fermentation of dilute alcoholic liquids and used as a condiment or preservative
2 : ill humor **:** SOURNESS
3 : VIM

vin·e·gared \-gərd\ *adjective* (1861)
: flavored or marinated with vinegar

vinegar eel *noun* (circa 1839)
: a minute nematode worm (*Turbatrix aceti*) often found in great numbers in vinegar or acid fermenting vegetable matter

vinegar fly *noun* [from its breeding in pickles] (1901)
: DROSOPHILA

vin·e·gar·ish \'vi-ni-g(ə-)rish\ *adjective* (1648)
: VINEGARY 2

vin·e·gary \'vi-ni-g(ə-)rē\ *adjective* (circa 1730)
1 a : resembling vinegar **:** SOUR **b :** flavored with vinegar
2 : disagreeable, bitter, or irascible in character or manner

vin·ery \'vīn-rē, 'vī-nə-\ *noun, plural* **-er·ies** (15th century)
: an area or building in which vines are grown

vine·yard \'vin-yərd\ *noun* (14th century)
1 : a planting of grapevines
2 : a sphere of activity **:** field of endeavor ⟨toilers in the *vineyard* of diplomacy —Daniel Schorr⟩

vine·yard·ist \-yər-dist\ *noun* (1848)
: a person who owns or cultivates a vineyard

vingt–et–un \ˌvan-tā-'ən\ *noun* [French, literally, twenty-one] (1772)
: BLACKJACK 5

vi·ni·cul·ture \'vi-nə-ˌkəl-chər, 'vī-\ *noun* [Latin *vinum* + International Scientific Vocabulary *-i- + culture*] (1871)
: VITICULTURE

vi·nif·era \vī-'ni-f(ə-)rə\ *adjective* [New Latin, from Latin *vinifer* wine-producing, from *vinum* wine] (1900)
: of, relating to, being, or derived from a common European grape (*Vitis vinifera*) that is the chief source of Old World wine grapes and table grapes
— **vinifera** *noun*

vi·ni·fi·ca·tion \ˌvi-nə-fə-'kā-shən, ˌvī-\ *noun* [French, from *vin* wine + *-i- + -fication*] (1880)
: the conversion of fruit juices (as grape juice) into wine by fermentation

vin·i·fy \'vi-nə-ˌfī, 'vī-\ *transitive verb* **-fied; -fy·ing** [probably back-formation from *vinification*] (1969)
1 : to make wine from (grapes often of a specified kind)
2 : to make (wine) from grapes

vi·no \'vē-(ˌ)nō\ *noun* [Italian & Spanish, from Latin *vinum*] (circa 1919)
: WINE

vi·nos·i·ty \vī-'nä-sə-tē\ *noun, plural* **-ties** (1658)
: the characteristic body, flavor, and color of a wine

vi·nous \'vī-nəs\ *adjective* [Latin *vinosus*, from *vinum* wine] (1664)
1 : of, relating to, or made with wine ⟨*vinous* medications⟩
2 : showing the effects of the use of wine
3 : VINACEOUS
— **vi·nous·ly** *adverb*

¹vin·tage \'vin-tij\ *noun* [Middle English, alteration of *vendage*, from Middle French *vendenge*, from Latin *vindemia* grape-gathering, vintage, from *vinum* wine, grapes + *demere* to take off, from *de-* + *emere* to take — more at WINE, REDEEM] (15th century)
1 a (1) **:** a season's yield of grapes or wine from a vineyard (2) **:** WINE; *especially* **:** a usually superior wine all or most of which comes from a single year **b :** a collection of contemporaneous and similar persons or things **:** CROP
2 : the act or time of harvesting grapes or making wine
3 a : a period of origin or manufacture ⟨a piano of 1845 *vintage*⟩ **b :** length of existence **:** AGE

²vintage *adjective* (1601)
1 *of wine* **:** of, relating to, or produced in a particular vintage
2 : of old, recognized, and enduring interest, importance, or quality **:** CLASSIC
3 a : dating from the past **:** OLD **b :** OUTMODED, OLD-FASHIONED
4 : of the best and most characteristic — used with a proper noun ⟨*vintage* Shaw: a wise and winning comedy —*Time*⟩

vin·tag·er \'vin-ti-jər\ *noun* (1589)
: a person concerned with the production of grapes and wine

vintage year *noun* (1933)

1 : a year of outstanding distinction or success
2 : a year in which a vintage wine is produced

vint·ner \'vint-nər\ *noun* [Middle English *vineter*, from Middle French *vinetier*, from Medieval Latin *vinetarius*, from Latin *vinetum* vineyard, from *vinum* wine] (15th century)
1 : a wine merchant
2 : a person who makes wine

viny \'vī-nē\ *adjective* **vin·i·er; -est** (1570)
1 : of, relating to, or resembling vines ⟨*viny* plants⟩
2 : covered with or abounding in vines

vi·nyl \'vī-nᵊl\ *noun* [International Scientific Vocabulary, from Latin *vinum* wine] (1863)
1 : a univalent group $CH_2 = CH$ derived from ethylene by removal of one hydrogen atom
2 : a polymer of a vinyl compound or a product (as a resin or a textile fiber) made from such a polymer
— **vi·nyl·ic** \vī-'ni-lik\ *adjective*

vinyl alcohol *noun* (1873)
: an unstable compound $CH_2 = CHOH$ isolated only in the form of its polymers or derivatives

vinyl chloride *noun* (1872)
: a flammable gaseous carcinogenic compound C_2H_3Cl that is used especially to make vinyl resins

vi·nyl·i·dene \vī-'ni-lə-ˌdēn\ *noun* [International Scientific Vocabulary *vinyl + -ide + -ene*] (1898)
: a bivalent group $CH_2 = C$ derived from ethylene by removal of two hydrogen atoms from one carbon atom

vinyl resin *noun* (1934)
: any of various thermoplastic resinous materials that are essentially polymers of vinyl compounds

vi·ol \'vī-(ə)l, 'vī-(ˌ)ōl\ *noun* [Middle English, from Middle French *viole* viol, viola, from Old Provençal *viola* viol] (15th century)
: a bowed stringed instrument chiefly of the 16th and 17th centuries made in treble, alto, tenor, and bass sizes and distinguished from members of the violin family especially in having a deep body, a flat back, sloping shoulders, usually six strings, a fretted fingerboard, and a low-arched bridge

¹vi·o·la \vī-'ō-lə, vē-; 'vī-ə-\ *noun* [Middle English, from Latin] (15th century)
: VIOLET 1a; *especially* **:** any of various garden hybrids with solitary white, yellow, or purple often variegated flowers resembling but smaller than typical pansies

²vi·o·la \vē-'ō-lə\ *noun* [Italian & Spanish, viol, viola, from Old Provençal, viol] (circa 1724)
: a musical instrument of the violin family that is intermediate in size and compass between the violin and cello and is tuned a fifth below the violin
— **vi·o·list** \-list\ *noun*

vi·o·la·ble \'vī-ə-lə-bəl\ *adjective* (1552)
: capable of being or likely to be violated
— **vi·o·la·bil·i·ty** \ˌvī-ə-lə-'bi-lə-tē\ *noun*
— **vi·o·la·ble·ness** \'vī-ə-lə-bəl-nəs\ *noun*
— **vi·o·la·bly** \-blē\ *adverb*

vi·o·la·ceous \ˌvī-ə-'lā-shəs\ *adjective* [Latin *violaceus*, from *viola* violet] (1657)
: of the color violet

vi·o·la da gam·ba \vē-ˌō-lə-də-'gäm-bə, -'gam-\ *noun, plural* **vi·o·las da gamba** \-ləz-də-\ *or* **vi·o·le da gamba** \-(ˌ)lā-\ [Italian, leg viol] (1597)
: a bass member of the viol family having a range approximating the cello
— **vi·o·list da gamba** \-lis(t)-də-\ *noun*

viola d'amo·re \-də-'mȯr-ē, -'mȯr-, -(ˌ)ā\ *noun, plural* **violas d'amore** *or* **viole d'amore** [Italian, viol of love] (circa 1700)
: a tenor viol having usually seven gut and seven wire strings

¹vi·o·late \'vī-ə-ˌlāt\ *transitive verb* **-lat·ed; -lat·ing** [Middle English, from Latin *violatus*, past participle of *violare*, probably from *violentus* violent] (15th century)
1 : BREAK, DISREGARD ⟨*violate* the law⟩

2 : to do harm to the person or especially the chastity of; *specifically* **:** RAPE
3 : to fail to show proper respect for **:** PROFANE ⟨*violate* a shrine⟩
4 : INTERRUPT, DISTURB ⟨*violate* the peace of a spring evening —Nancy Larter⟩
— **vi·o·la·tive** \-ˌlā-tiv\ *adjective*
— **vi·o·la·tor** \-ˌlā-tər\ *noun*
²**vi·o·late** \ˈvī-ə-lət\ *adjective* (1503)
archaic **:** subjected to violation
vi·o·la·tion \ˌvī-ə-ˈlā-shən\ *noun* (15th century)
: the act of violating **:** the state of being violated: as **a :** INFRINGEMENT, TRANSGRESSION; *specifically* **:** an infringement of the rules in sports that is less serious than a foul and usually involves technicalities of play **b :** an act of irreverence or desecration **:** PROFANATION **c :** DISTURBANCE, INTERRUPTION **d :** RAPE, RAVISHMENT
vi·o·lence \ˈvī-ə-lən(t)s\ *noun* (14th century)
1 a : exertion of physical force so as to injure or abuse (as in effecting illegal entry into a house) **b :** an instance of violent treatment or procedure
2 : injury by or as if by distortion, infringement, or profanation **:** OUTRAGE
3 a : intense, turbulent, or furious and often destructive action or force ⟨the *violence* of the storm⟩ **b :** vehement feeling or expression **:** FERVOR; *also* **:** an instance of such action or feeling **c :** a clashing or jarring quality **:** DISCORDANCE
4 : undue alteration (as of wording or sense in editing a text)
vi·o·lent \-lənt\ *adjective* [Middle English, from Middle French, from Latin *violentus*; akin to Latin *vis* strength — more at VIM] (14th century)
1 : marked by extreme force or sudden intense activity ⟨a *violent* attack⟩
2 a : notably furious or vehement ⟨a *violent* denunciation⟩ **b :** EXTREME, INTENSE ⟨*violent* pain⟩ ⟨*violent* colors⟩
3 : caused by force **:** not natural ⟨a *violent* death⟩
4 a : emotionally agitated to the point of loss of self-control ⟨a mental patient becoming *violent*⟩ **b :** prone to commit acts of violence ⟨*violent* prison inmates⟩
— **vi·o·lent·ly** *adverb*
violent storm *noun* (circa 1881)
: STORM 1c(1) — see BEAUFORT SCALE table
vi·o·let \ˈvī-(ə-)lət\ *noun* [Middle English, from Middle French *violete*, diminutive of *viole* violet, from Latin *viola*] (14th century)
1 a : any of a genus (*Viola* of the family Violaceae, the violet family) of chiefly herbs with alternate stipulate leaves and showy flowers in spring and cleistogamous flowers in summer; *especially* **:** one with smaller usually solid-colored flowers as distinguished from the usually larger-flowered violas and pansies **b :** any of several plants of genera other than that of the violet — compare DOGTOOTH VIOLET
2 : any of a group of colors of reddish blue hue, low lightness, and medium saturation
vi·o·lin \ˌvī-ə-ˈlin\ *noun* [Italian *violino*, diminutive of *viola*] (1579)
: a bowed stringed instrument having four strings tuned at intervals of a fifth and a usual range from G below middle C upward for more than 4½ octaves and having a shallow body, shoulders at right angles to the neck, a fingerboard without frets, and a curved bridge
— **vi·o·lin·ist** \-ist\ *noun*
— **vi·o·lin·is·tic** \-ə-lə-ˈnis-tik\ *adjective*

violet 1a

vi·o·lon·cel·lo \ˌvī-ə-lən-ˈche-(ˌ)lō, ˌvē-ə-\ *noun* [Italian, diminutive of *violone*, augmentative of *viola*] (circa 1724)
: CELLO
— **vi·o·lon·cel·list** \-ˈche-list\ *noun*
vio·my·cin \ˌvī-ə-ˈmī-sᵊn\ *noun* [*violet* + *-mycin*; from the color of the soil organism] (1950)
: a polypeptide antibiotic $C_{25}H_{43}N_{13}O_{10}$ that is produced by several soil actinomycetes (genus *Streptomyces*) and is administered in the form of its sulfate in the treatment of tuberculosis
VIP \ˌvē-ˌī-ˈpē\ *noun, plural* **VIPs** \-ˈpēz\ [*very important person*] (1933)
: a person of great influence or prestige; *especially* **:** a high official with special privileges
vi·per \ˈvī-pər\ *noun* [Middle French *vipere*, from Latin *vipera*] (1526)
1 a : a common Eurasian venomous snake (*Vipera berus*) that attains a length of two feet (0.6 meter), varies in color from red, brown, or gray with dark markings to black, and is usually not fatal to humans; *broadly* **:** any of a family (Viperidae) of venomous snakes that includes Old World snakes (subfamily Viperinae) and the pit vipers **b :** a venomous or reputedly venomous snake
2 : a vicious or treacherous person
vi·per·ine \-pə-ˌrīn\ *adjective* (circa 1550)
: of, relating to, or resembling a viper **:** VENOMOUS
vi·per·ish \-p(ə-)rish\ *adjective* (1755)
: spitefully vituperative **:** VENOMOUS
vi·per·ous \-p(ə-)rəs\ *adjective* (1535)
1 : VIPERINE
2 : having the qualities attributed to a viper **:** MALIGNANT, VENOMOUS
— **vi·per·ous·ly** *adverb*
viper's bugloss *noun* (1597)
: a coarse Old World herb (*Echium vulgare*) of the borage family that is naturalized in North America and has showy blue tubular flowers with exserted stamens — called also *blueweed*
vi·ra·go \və-ˈrä-(ˌ)gō, -ˈrā-; ˈvir-ə-ˌgō\ *noun, plural* **-goes** *or* **-gos** [Middle English, from Latin *viragin-*, *virago*, from *vir* man — more at VIRILE] (14th century)
1 : a loud overbearing woman **:** TERMAGANT
2 : a woman of great stature, strength, and courage
— **vi·rag·i·nous** \və-ˈra-jə-nəs\ *adjective*
vi·ral \ˈvī-rəl\ *adjective* (1937)
: of, relating to, or caused by a virus
— **vi·ral·ly** \-rə-lē\ *adverb*
vir·e·lay \ˈvir-ə-ˌlā\ *noun* [Middle English, from Middle French *virelai*] (14th century)
: a chiefly French verse form consisting of stanzas of indeterminate length and number with alternating long and short lines and interlaced rhyme (as *abab bcbc cdcd dada*)
vi·re·mia \vī-ˈrē-mē-ə\ *noun* [New Latin, from *virus* + *-emia*] (1946)
: the presence of virus in the blood of a host
— **vi·re·mic** \-mik\ *adjective*
vir·eo \ˈvir-ē-ˌō\ *noun, plural* **-e·os** [Latin, a small bird, from *virēre* to be green] (1834)
: any of various small insectivorous American oscine birds (family Vireonidae and especially genus *Vireo*) that are chiefly olivaceous and grayish in color
vires *plural of* VIS
vi·res·cence \və-ˈre-sᵊn(t)s, vī-\ *noun* (circa 1888)
: the state or condition of becoming green; *especially* **:** such a condition due to the development of chloroplasts in plant organs (as petals) normally white or colored
vi·res·cent \-sᵊnt\ *adjective* [Latin *virescent-*, *virescens*, present participle of *virescere* to become green, inchoative of *virēre* to be green] (1826)
1 : beginning to be green **:** GREENISH
2 : developing or displaying virescence
vir·ga \ˈvər-gə\ *noun* [New Latin, from Latin, branch, rod, streak in the sky suggesting rain] (1938)
: wisps of precipitation evaporating before reaching the ground
¹**vir·gate** \ˈvər-ˌgāt\ *noun* [Medieval Latin *virgata*, from *virga*, a land measure, from Latin, rod] (1655)
: an old English unit of land area equal to one quarter of a hide or one quarter of an acre
²**virgate** *adjective* [New Latin *virgatus*, from Latin, made of twigs, from *virga*] (1821)
: shaped like a rod or wand ⟨a *virgate* one-flowered branch⟩
¹**vir·gin** \ˈvər-jən\ *noun* [Middle English, from Old French *virgine*, from Latin *virgin-*, *virgo* young woman, virgin] (13th century)
1 a : an unmarried woman devoted to religion **b** *capitalized* **:** VIRGO
2 a : an absolutely chaste young woman **b :** an unmarried girl or woman
3 *capitalized* **:** VIRGIN MARY
4 a : a person who has not had sexual intercourse **b :** a person who is inexperienced in a usually specified sphere of activity ⟨a *virgin* in politics⟩
5 : a female animal that has never copulated
²**virgin** *adjective* (14th century)
1 : free of impurity or stain **:** UNSULLIED
2 : CHASTE
3 : characteristic of or befitting a virgin **:** MODEST
4 : FRESH, UNSPOILED; *specifically* **:** not altered by human activity ⟨a *virgin* forest⟩
5 a (1) **:** being used or worked for the first time (2) *of a metal* **:** produced directly from ore by primary smelting **b :** INITIAL, FIRST
6 *of a vegetable oil* **:** obtained from the first light pressing and without heating
¹**vir·gin·al** \ˈvər-jə-nᵊl, ˈvərj-nəl\ *adjective* (15th century)
1 : of, relating to, or characteristic of a virgin or virginity; *especially* **:** PURE, CHASTE
2 : PRISTINE, UNSULLIED
— **vir·gin·al·ly** *adverb*
²**virginal** *noun* [probably from Latin *virginalis* of a virgin, from *virgin-*, *virgo*] (1530)
: a small rectangular spinet having no legs and only one wire to a note and popular in the 16th and 17th centuries — often used in plural; called also *pair of virginals*
— **vir·gin·al·ist** \ˈvər-jə-nᵊl-ist, ˈvərj-nə-list\ *noun*
virgin birth *noun* (1652)
1 : birth from a virgin
2 *often V&B capitalized* **:** the theological doctrine that Jesus was miraculously begotten of God and born of a virgin mother
Vir·gin·ia bluebells \vər-ˈjin-yə-, -ˈji-nē-ə-\ *noun plural* [*Virginia*, state of the U.S.] (circa 1922)
: BLUEBELL 2b
Virginia creeper *noun* (1704)
: a common North American tendril-climbing vine (*Parthenocissus quinquefolia*) of the grape family with palmately compound leaves and bluish black berries — called also *woodbine*
Virginia fence *noun* (1671)
: WORM FENCE — called also *Virginia rail fence*
Virginia ham *noun* (1824)

\ə\ abut	\ᵊ\ kitten	\ər\ further	\a\ ash	\ā\ ace	
\ä\ mop, mar	\au̇\ out	\ch\ chin	\e\ bet	\ē\ easy	
\g\ go	\i\ hit	\ī\ ice	\j\ job	\ŋ\ go	
\ȯ\ law	\ȯi\ boy	\th\ thin	\t͟h\ the	\ü\ loot	\u̇\ foot
\y\ yet	\zh\ vision		*see also* Guide to Pronunciation		

: a dry-cured, smoked, and aged ham especially from a peanut-fed hog

Virginia pine *noun* (1897)
: a pine (*Pinus virginiana*) of the eastern U.S. that has short needles occurring in pairs — called also *Jersey pine*

Virginia rail *noun* (1813)
: an American long-billed rail (*Rallus limicola*) that has gray cheeks

Virginia reel *noun* (1817)
: an American dance in which two lines of couples face each other and all couples in turn participate in a series of figures

Virginia snakeroot *noun* (1694)
: a birthwort (*Aristolochia serpentaria*) of the eastern U.S. with oblong leaves cordate at the base and a solitary basal very irregular flower

vir·gin·i·ty \(ˌ)vər-ˈji-nə-tē\ *noun, plural* **-ties** (14th century)
1 : the quality or state of being virgin; *especially* : MAIDENHOOD
2 : the unmarried life : CELIBACY, SPINSTERHOOD

Virgin Mary *noun*
: the mother of Jesus

virgin's bower *noun* (1597)
: any of several usually small-flowered and climbing clematises (especially *Clematis virginiana*)

virgin wool *noun* (1915)
: wool not used before in manufacture

Vir·go \ˈvər-(ˌ)gō, ˈvir-\ *noun* [Latin (genitive *Virginis*), literally, virgin]
1 : a zodiacal constellation on the celestial equator that lies due south of the handle of the Big Dipper and is pictured as a woman holding a spike of grain
2 a : the 6th sign of the zodiac in astrology — see ZODIAC table **b** : one born under the sign of Virgo
— **Vir·go·an** *noun*

vir·gule \ˈvər-(ˌ)gyü(ə)l\ *noun* [French, from Latin *virgula* small stripe, obelus, from diminutive of *virga* rod] (1837)
: DIAGONAL 3

vi·ri·ci·dal \ˌvī-rə-ˈsī-dᵊl\ *adjective* [New Latin *virus* + English *-i-* + *-cide*] (1924)
: VIRUCIDAL
— **vi·ri·cide** \ˈvī-rə-ˌsīd\ *noun*

vir·id \ˈvir-əd\ *adjective* [Latin *viridis* green] (1600)
: vividly green : VERDANT

vir·i·des·cent \ˌvir-ə-ˈde-sᵊnt\ *adjective* [Latin *viridis* green] (circa 1847)
: slightly green : GREENISH

vi·rid·i·an \və-ˈri-dē-ən\ *noun* [Latin *viridis*] (1882)
: a chrome green that is a hydrated oxide of chromium

vi·rid·i·ty \və-ˈri-də-tē\ *noun* [Middle English *viridite*, from Middle French *viridité*, from Latin *viriditat-, viriditas*, from *viridis*] (15th century)
1 a : the quality or state of being green **b** : the color of grass or foliage
2 : naive innocence

vir·ile \ˈvir-əl, ˈvir-ˌīl, *British also* ˈvir-ˌīl\ *adjective* [Middle French or Latin; Middle French *viril*, from Latin *virilis*, from *vir* man, male; akin to Old English & Old High German *wer* man, Sanskrit *vīra*] (15th century)
1 : having the nature, properties, or qualities of an adult male; *specifically* : capable of functioning as a male in copulation
2 : ENERGETIC, VIGOROUS
3 a : characteristic of or associated with men : MASCULINE **b** : having traditionally masculine traits especially to a marked degree
4 : MASTERFUL, FORCEFUL
— **vir·ile·ly** *adverb*

vir·il·ism \ˈvir-ə-ˌli-zəm\ *noun* (1922)
: the appearance of secondary male characteristics in the female

vi·ril·i·ty \və-ˈri-lə-tē, *British also* vī-\ *noun* (1586)

: the quality or state of being virile: **a** : MANHOOD **b** : manly vigor : MASCULINITY

vi·ri·on \ˈvī-rē-ˌän, ˈvir-ē-\ *noun* [French, from *virien* viral (from *virus* virus) + *-on* ²-on] (1959)
: a complete virus particle that consists of an RNA or DNA core with a protein coat sometimes with external envelopes and that is the extracellular infective form of a virus

virl \ˈvər(-ə)l\ *noun* [Middle English *virole* — more at FERRULE] (15th century)
Scottish : FERRULE 1

vi·roid \ˈvī-ˌroid\ *noun* [New Latin *virus* + English *-oid*] (1971)
: any of several causative agents of plant disease that consist solely of a single-stranded RNA of low molecular weight arranged in a closed loop or a linear chain

vi·rol·o·gy \vī-ˈrä-lə-jē\ *noun* [New Latin *virus* + International Scientific Vocabulary *-logy*] (circa 1935)
: a branch of science that deals with viruses
— **vi·ro·log·i·cal** \ˌvī-rə-ˈlä-ji-kəl\ *or* **vi·ro·log·ic** \-jik\ *adjective*
— **vi·ro·log·i·cal·ly** \-ji-k(ə-)lē\ *adverb*
— **vi·rol·o·gist** \vī-ˈrä-lə-jist\ *noun*

vir·tu \ˌvər-ˈtü, vir-\ *noun* [Italian *virtù*, literally, virtue, from Latin *virtut-, virtus*] (1722)
1 : a love of or taste for curios or objets d'art
2 : productions of art especially of a curious or antique nature : OBJETS D'ART

vir·tu·al \ˈvər-chə-wəl, -chəl; ˈvərch-wəl\ *adjective* [Middle English, possessed of certain physical virtues, from Medieval Latin *virtualis*, from Latin *virtus* strength, virtue] (1654)
1 : being such in essence or effect though not formally recognized or admitted 〈a *virtual* dictator〉
2 : of, relating to, or using virtual memory
3 : of, relating to, or being a hypothetical particle whose existence is inferred from indirect evidence 〈*virtual* photons〉 — compare REAL 3

virtual image *noun* (1859)
: an image (as seen in a plane mirror) formed of points from which divergent rays (as of light) seem to emanate without actually doing so

vir·tu·al·i·ty \ˌvər-chə-ˈwa-lə-tē\ *noun, plural* **-ties** (1646)
1 : ESSENCE
2 : potential existence : POTENTIALITY

vir·tu·al·ly \ˈvər-chə-wə-lē, -chə-lē; ˈvərch-wə-lē\ *adverb* (15th century)
1 : almost entirely : NEARLY
2 : for all practical purposes 〈*virtually* unknown〉

virtual memory *noun* (1959)
: external memory (as magnetic disks) for a computer that can be used as if it were an extension of the computer's internal memory — called also *virtual storage*

virtual reality *noun* (1989)
: an artificial environment which is experienced through sensory stimuli (as sights and sounds) provided by a computer and in which one's actions partially determine what happens in the environment

vir·tue \ˈvər-(ˌ)chü\ *noun* [Middle English *virtu*, from Old French, from Latin *virtut-, virtus* strength, manliness, virtue, from *vir* man — more at VIRILE] (13th century)
1 a : conformity to a standard of right : MORALITY **b** : a particular moral excellence
2 *plural* : an order of angels — see CELESTIAL HIERARCHY
3 : a beneficial quality or power of a thing
4 : manly strength or courage : VALOR
5 : a commendable quality or trait : MERIT
6 : a capacity to act : POTENCY
7 : chastity especially in a woman
— **vir·tue·less** \-(ˌ)chü-ləs\ *adjective*
— **by virtue of** *or* **in virtue of** : through the force of : by authority of

vir·tu·o·sa \ˌvər-chü-ˈō-sə, -zə\ *noun* [Italian, feminine of *virtuoso*] (1668)

: a girl or woman who is a virtuoso

vir·tu·os·i·ty \-ˈä-sə-tē\ *noun, plural* **-ties** (1673)
1 : a taste for or interest in virtu
2 : great technical skill (as in the practice of a fine art)

vir·tu·o·so \-ˈō-(ˌ)sō, -(ˌ)zō\ *noun, plural* **-sos** *or* **-si** \-(ˌ)sē, -(ˌ)zē\ [Italian, from *virtuoso*, adjective, virtuous, skilled, from Late Latin *virtuosus* virtuous, from Latin *virtus*] (1651)
1 : an experimenter or investigator especially in the arts and sciences : SAVANT
2 : one skilled in or having a taste for the fine arts
3 : one who excels in the technique of an art; *especially* : a highly skilled musical performer (as on the violin)
4 : a person who has great skill at some endeavor 〈a computer *virtuoso*〉 〈a *virtuoso* at public relations〉
— **vir·tu·o·sic** \-ˈō-sik, -zik\ *adjective*
— **virtuoso** *adjective*

vir·tu·ous \ˈvər-chə-wəs, ˈvərch-wəs\ *adjective* (14th century)
1 : POTENT, EFFICACIOUS
2 a : having or exhibiting virtue **b** : morally excellent : RIGHTEOUS
3 : CHASTE
synonym see MORAL
— **vir·tu·ous·ly** *adverb*
— **vir·tu·ous·ness** *noun*

vi·ru·cid·al \ˌvī-rə-ˈsī-dᵊl\ *adjective* [New Latin, *virus* + English *-cide*] (1925)
: having the capacity to or tending to destroy or inactivate viruses 〈*virucidal* agents〉 〈*virucidal* activity〉
— **vi·ru·cide** \ˈvī-rə-ˌsīd\ *noun*

vir·u·lence \ˈvir-ə-lən(t)s, ˈvir-yə-\ *noun* (1663)
: the quality or state of being virulent: as **a** : extreme bitterness or malignity of temper : RANCOR **b** : MALIGNANCE, VENOMOUSNESS 〈ameliorate the *virulence* of a disease〉 **c** : the relative capacity of a pathogen to overcome body defenses

vir·u·len·cy \-lən(t)-sē\ *noun* (circa 1617)
: VIRULENCE

vir·u·lent \-lənt\ *adjective* [Middle English, from Latin *virulentus*, from *virus* poison] (14th century)
1 a : marked by a rapid, severe, and malignant course 〈a *virulent* infection〉 **b** : able to overcome bodily defensive mechanisms 〈a *virulent* pathogen〉
2 : extremely poisonous or venomous
3 : full of malice : MALIGNANT 〈*virulent* racists〉
4 : objectionably harsh or strong
— **vir·u·lent·ly** *adverb*

vir·u·lif·er·ous \ˌvir-ə-ˈli-f(ə-)rəs, ˌvir-yə-\ *adjective* [*virulence* + *-iferous*] (circa 1899)
: containing, producing, or conveying an agent of infection and especially a virus 〈*viruliferous* insects〉

vi·rus \ˈvī-rəs\ *noun* [Latin, venom, poisonous emanation; akin to Greek *ios* poison, Sanskrit *viṣa*; in senses 2 & 4, from New Latin, from Latin] (1599)
1 *archaic* : VENOM 1
2 a : the causative agent of an infectious disease **b** : any of a large group of submicroscopic infective agents that are regarded either as extremely simple microorganisms or as extremely complex molecules, that typically contain a protein coat surrounding an RNA or DNA core of genetic material but no semipermeable membrane, that are capable of growth and multiplication only in living cells, and that cause various important diseases in humans, lower animals, or plants; *also* : FILTERABLE VIRUS **c** : a disease caused by a virus
3 : something that poisons the mind or soul 〈the force of this *virus* of prejudice —V. S. Waters〉
4 : a computer program usually hidden within another seemingly innocuous program that

produces copies of itself and inserts them into other programs and that usually performs a malicious action (as destroying data)

vis \'vis\ *noun, plural* **vi·res** \'vī-ˌrēz\ [Latin — more at VIM] (1601)
: FORCE, POWER

¹**vi·sa** \'vē-zə *also* -sə\ *noun* [French, from Latin, neuter plural of *visus,* past participle] (1831)
1 : an endorsement made on a passport by the proper authorities denoting that it has been examined and that the bearer may proceed
2 : a signature of formal approval by a superior or upon a document

²**visa** *transitive verb* **vi·saed** \-zəd, -səd\; **vi·sa·ing** \-zə-iŋ, -sə-\ (circa 1847)
: to give a visa to (a passport)

vis·age \'vi-zij\ *noun* [Middle English, from Old French, from *vis* face, from Latin *visus* sight, from *vidēre* to see — more at WIT] (14th century)
1 : the face, countenance, or appearance of a person or sometimes an animal
2 : ASPECT, APPEARANCE ⟨grimy *visage* of a mining town⟩
— **vis·aged** \-zijd\ *adjective*

¹**vis-à-vis** \ˌvēz-ə-'vē, ˌvēs-, *also* -ä-'vē\ *preposition* [French, literally, face-to-face] (1755)
1 : face-to-face with
2 : in relation to
3 : as compared with

²**vis-à-vis** *noun, plural* **vis-à-vis** \-ə-'vē(z), -ä-\ (circa 1757)
1 : one that is face-to-face with another
2 a : ESCORT, DATE **b** : COUNTERPART
3 : TÊTE-À-TÊTE 1

³**vis-à-vis** *adverb* (1870)
: in company : TOGETHER

Vi·sa·yan \və-'sī-ən\ *variant of* BISAYAN

vis·ca·cha \vis-'kä-chə\ *noun* [Spanish *vizcacha,* from Quechua *wisk'acha*] (1604)
: any of several South American burrowing rodents (genera *Lagostomus* and *Lagidium*) closely related to the chinchilla

viscera *plural of* VISCUS

viscacha

vis·cer·al \'vi-sə-rəl, 'vis-rəl\ *adjective* (1575)
1 : felt in or as if in the viscera : DEEP ⟨*visceral* conviction⟩
2 : not intellectual : INSTINCTIVE, UNREASONING ⟨*visceral* drives⟩
3 : dealing with crude or elemental emotions : EARTHY ⟨a *visceral* novel⟩
4 : of, relating to, or located on or among the viscera : SPLANCHNIC
— **vis·cer·al·ly** \-rə-lē\ *adverb*

vis·cid \'vi-səd\ *adjective* [Late Latin *viscidus,* from Latin *viscum* birdlime — more at VISCOUS] (1635)
1 a : having an adhesive quality : STICKY **b** : having a glutinous consistency : VISCOUS
2 : covered with a sticky layer
— **vis·cid·i·ty** \vi-'si-də-tē\ *noun*
— **vis·cid·ly** \'vi-səd-lē\ *adverb*

vis·co·elas·tic \ˌvis-kō-ə-'las-tik\ *adjective* [*viscous* + *-o-* + *elastic*] (1935)
: having appreciable and conjoint viscous and elastic properties ⟨such *viscoelastic* materials as asphalt⟩; *also* : constituting or relating to the state of viscoelastic materials ⟨*viscoelastic* data⟩ ⟨*viscoelastic* properties⟩
— **vis·co·elas·tic·i·ty** \-ˌlas-'ti-sə-tē, -'tis-tē\ *noun*

vis·com·e·ter \vis-'kä-mə-tər\ *noun* [*viscos*ity + *-meter*] (circa 1883)
: an instrument with which to measure viscosity
— **vis·co·met·ric** \ˌvis-kə-'me-trik\ *adjective*
— **vis·com·e·try** \-mə-trē\ *noun*

¹**vis·cose** \'vis-ˌkōs, -ˌkōz\ *noun* [obsolete *viscose,* adjective, viscous] (1896)
1 : a viscous golden-brown solution made by treating cellulose with caustic alkali solution and carbon disulfide and used in making rayon and films of regenerated cellulose
2 : viscose rayon

²**viscose** *adjective* (1900)
: of, relating to, or made from viscose

vis·co·sim·e·ter \ˌvis-kə-'si-mə-tər\ *noun* [International Scientific Vocabulary *viscos*ity + *-meter*] (circa 1868)
: VISCOMETER
— **vis·cosi·met·ric** \(ˌ)vis-ˌkä-sə-'me-trik\ *adjective*

vis·cos·i·ty \vis-'kä-sə-tē\ *noun, plural* **-ties** [Middle English *viscosite,* from Middle French *viscosité,* from Medieval Latin *viscositat-, viscositas,* from Late Latin *viscosus* viscous] (15th century)
1 : the quality or state of being viscous
2 : the property of resistance to flow in a fluid or semifluid
3 : the ratio of the tangential frictional force per unit area to the velocity gradient perpendicular to the direction of flow of a liquid — called also *coefficient of viscosity*

viscosity index *noun* (1929)
: an arbitrary number assigned as a measure of the constancy of the viscosity of a lubricating oil with change of temperature with higher numbers indicating viscosities that change little with temperature

vis·count \'vī-ˌkaunt\ *noun* [Middle English *viscounte,* from Middle French *viscomte,* from Medieval Latin *vicecomit-, vicecomes,* from Late Latin *vice-* vice- + *comit-, comes* count — more at COUNT] (15th century)
: a member of the peerage in Great Britain ranking below an earl and above a baron
— **vis·count·cy** \-ˌkaun(t)-sē\ *noun*
— **vis·count·y** \-ˌkaun-tē\ *noun*

vis·count·ess \-ˌkaun-təs\ *noun* (15th century)
1 : the wife or widow of a viscount
2 : a woman who holds the rank of viscount in her own right

vis·cous \'vis-kəs\ *adjective* [Middle English *viscouse,* from Late Latin *viscosus* full of birdlime, viscous, from Latin *viscum* mistletoe, birdlime; akin to Old High German *wīhsila* cherry, Greek *ixos* mistletoe] (14th century)
1 : VISCID
2 : having or characterized by viscosity ⟨*viscous* flow⟩
— **vis·cous·ly** *adverb*
— **vis·cous·ness** *noun*

vis·cus \'vis-kəs\ *noun, plural* **vis·cera** \'vi-sə-rə\ [Latin (plural *viscera*)] (1651)
1 : an internal organ of the body; *especially* : one (as the heart, liver, or intestine) located in the great cavity of the trunk proper
2 *plural* : HEART 4

¹**vise** \'vīs\ *noun* [Middle French *vis* screw, something winding, from Latin *vitis* vine — more at WITHY] (1500)
1 : any of various tools with two jaws for holding work that close usually by a screw, lever, or cam
2 : something likened to a vise ⟨economic *vise* of slow growth and rampant price increases —David Milne⟩
— **vise·like** \-ˌlīk\ *adjective*

vise 1

²**vise** *transitive verb* **vised; vis·ing** (1602)
: to hold, force, or squeeze with or as if with a vise

¹**vi·sé** \'vē-ˌzā, vē-'\ *transitive verb* **vi·séd** or **vi·séed; vi·sé·ing** [French, past participle of *viser* to visa, from *visa*] (1810)
: VISA

²**visé** *noun* (1842)
: VISA

Vish·nu \'vish-(ˌ)nü\ *noun* [Sanskrit *Viṣṇu*] (1638)
: the preserver god of the Hindu sacred triad — compare BRAHMA, SIVA

vis·i·bil·i·ty \ˌvi-zə-'bi-lə-tē\ *noun, plural* **-ties** (1581)
1 : the quality or state of being visible
2 a : the degree of clearness of the atmosphere; *specifically* : the greatest distance toward the horizon at which prominent objects can be identified with the naked eye **b** : capability of being readily noticed **c** : capability of affording an unobstructed view **d** : PUBLICITY 2d
3 : a measure of the ability of radiant energy to evoke visual sensation

vis·i·ble \'vi-zə-bəl\ *adjective* [Middle English, from Middle French or Latin; Middle French, from Latin *visibilis,* from *visus,* past participle of *vidēre* to see] (14th century)
1 a : capable of being seen ⟨stars *visible* to the naked eye⟩ **b** : situated in the region of the electromagnetic spectrum perceptible to human vision ⟨*visible* light⟩ — used of radiation having a wavelength between about 400 nanometers and 700 nanometers
2 a : exposed to view ⟨the *visible* horizon⟩ **b** : CONSPICUOUS
3 : capable of being discovered or perceived : RECOGNIZABLE ⟨no *visible* means of support⟩
4 : ACCESSIBLE 4
5 : devised to keep a particular part or item always in full view or readily seen or referred to ⟨a *visible* index⟩
— **vis·i·ble·ness** *noun*
— **vis·i·bly** \-blē\ *adverb*

visible speech *noun* (1865)
1 : a set of phonetic symbols based on symbols for articulatory position
2 : speech reproduced spectrographically

Vis·i·goth \'vi-zə-ˌgäth\ *noun* [Late Latin *Visigothi,* plural] (1611)
: a member of the western division of the Goths
— **Vis·i·goth·ic** \ˌvi-zə-'gä-thik\ *adjective*

¹**vi·sion** \'vi-zhən\ *noun* [Middle English, from Old French, from Latin *vision-, visio,* from *vidēre* to see — more at WIT] (14th century)
1 a : something seen in a dream, trance, or ecstasy; *especially* : a supernatural appearance that conveys a revelation **b** : an object of imagination **c** : a manifestation to the senses of something immaterial ⟨look, not at *visions,* but at realities —Edith Wharton⟩
2 a : the act or power of imagination **b** (1) : mode of seeing or conceiving (2) : unusual discernment or foresight ⟨a man of *vision*⟩ **c** : direct mystical awareness of the supernatural usually in visible form
3 a : the act or power of seeing : SIGHT **b** : the special sense by which the qualities of an object (as color, luminosity, shape and size) constituting its appearance are perceived and which is mediated by the eye
4 a : something seen **b** : a lovely or charming sight
— **vi·sion·al** \'vizh-nəl, 'vi-zhə-nᵊl\ *adjective*
— **vi·sion·al·ly** *adverb*

²**vision** *transitive verb* **vi·sioned; vi·sion·ing** \'vi-zhə-niŋ, 'vizh-niŋ\ (1795)
: ENVISION

¹**vi·sion·ary** \'vi-zhə-ˌner-ē\ *adjective* (1648)
1 a : of the nature of a vision : ILLUSORY **b** : incapable of being realized or achieved : UTOPIAN ⟨a *visionary* scheme⟩ **c** : existing only in imagination : UNREAL
2 a : able or likely to see visions **b** : disposed to reverie or imagining : DREAMY

3 : of, relating to, or characterized by visions or the power of vision
4 : having or marked by foresight and imagination ⟨a *visionary* leader⟩ ⟨a *visionary* invention⟩
synonym see IMAGINARY
— **vi·sion·ar·i·ness** \-ē-nəs\ *noun*
²**visionary** *noun, plural* **-ar·ies** (1702)
1 : one whose ideas or projects are impractical : DREAMER
2 : one who sees visions : SEER
vi·sioned \'vi-zhənd\ *adjective* (1510)
1 : seen in a vision ⟨a *visioned* face⟩
2 : produced by or experienced in a vision ⟨*visioned* agony⟩
3 : endowed with vision : INSPIRED
vi·sion·less \'vi-zhən-ləs\ *adjective* (1820)
1 : SIGHTLESS, BLIND ⟨*visionless* eyes⟩
2 : lacking vision or inspiration ⟨a *visionless* leader⟩
¹**vis·it** \'vi-zət\ *verb* **vis·it·ed** \'vi-zə-təd, 'viz-təd\; **vis·it·ing** \'vi-zə-tiŋ, 'viz-tiŋ\ [Middle English, from Old French *visiter*, from Latin *visitare*, frequentative of *visere* to go to see, frequentative of *vidēre* to see] (13th century) *transitive verb*
1 a *archaic* : COMFORT — used of the Deity ⟨*visit* us with Thy salvation —Charles Wesley⟩ **b** (1) : AFFLICT ⟨*visited* his people with distempers —Tobias Smollett⟩ (2) : INFLICT, IMPOSE ⟨*visited* his wrath upon them⟩ **c** : AVENGE ⟨*visited* the sins of the fathers upon the children⟩ : to present itself to come over momentarily ⟨was *visited* by a strange notion⟩
2 : to go to see in order to comfort or help
3 a : to pay a call on as an act of friendship or courtesy **b** : to reside with temporarily as a guest **c** : to go to see or stay at (a place) for a particular purpose (as business or sightseeing) **d** : to go or come officially to inspect or oversee ⟨a bishop *visiting* his parishes⟩ *intransitive verb*
1 : to make a visit; *also* : to make frequent or regular visits
2 : CHAT, CONVERSE
²**visit** *noun* (1621)
1 a : a short stay : CALL **b** : a brief residence as a guest : an extended stay : SOJOURN
2 : a journey to and stay or short sojourn at a place
3 : an official or professional call or tour : VISITATION
4 : the act of a naval officer in boarding a merchant ship on the high seas in exercise of the right of search
vis·it·a·ble \'vi-zə-tə-bəl, 'viz-tə-\ *adjective* (1605)
1 : subject to or allowing visitation or inspection
2 : socially eligible to receive visits
vis·i·tant \'vi-zə-tənt, 'viz-tənt\ *noun* (1599)
1 : VISITOR; *especially* : one thought to come from a spirit world
2 : a migratory bird that appears at intervals for a limited period
— **visitant** *adjective*
vis·i·ta·tion \,vi-zə-'tā-shən\ *noun* (14th century)
1 : an instance of visiting: as **a** : an official visit (as for inspection) **b** : ²WAKE 3 **c** : temporary custody of a child granted to a noncustodial parent ⟨*visitation* rights⟩
2 a : a special dispensation of divine favor or wrath **b** : a severe trial : AFFLICTION
3 *capitalized* : the visit of the Virgin Mary to Elizabeth recounted in Luke and celebrated July 2 by a Christian feast
vis·i·ta·to·ri·al \,vi-zə-tə-'tōr-ē-əl, ,viz-tə-, -'tȯr-\ *adjective* (1688)
: of or relating to visitation or to a judicial visitor or superintendent
visiting *adjective* (1949)
: invited to join or attend an institution (as a university) for a limited time ⟨a *visiting* professor⟩ ⟨a *visiting* fellow⟩
visiting card *noun* (1782)

: a small card presented when visiting that bears the name and sometimes the address of the visitor
visiting fireman *noun* (1926)
: a usually important or influential visitor whom it is desirable or expedient to entertain impressively
visiting nurse *noun* (circa 1924)
: a nurse employed by a hospital or social-service agency to perform public health services and especially to visit sick persons in a community
vis·i·tor \'vi-zə-tər, 'viz-tər\ *noun* (15th century)
: one that visits; *especially* : one that makes formal visits of inspection
vi·sive \'vi-ziv, 'vī-siv\ *adjective* [Medieval Latin *visivus*, from Latin *visus*, past participle of *vidēre* to see — more at WIT] (1543) *archaic* : of, relating to, or serving for vision
vi·sor \'vī-zər\ *noun* [Middle English *viser*, from Anglo-French, from Old French *visiere*, from *vis* face — more at VISAGE] (14th century)
1 : the front piece of a helmet; *especially* : a movable upper piece
2 a : a face mask **b** : DISGUISE
3 a : a projecting front on a cap for shading the eyes **b** : a usually movable flat sunshade attached at the top of an automobile windshield
— **vi·sored** \-zərd\ *adjective*
— **vi·sor·less** \-zər-ləs\ *adjective*
vis·ta \'vis-tə\ *noun* [Italian, sight, from *visto*, past participle of *vedere* to see, from Latin *vidēre* — more at WIT] (1644)
1 : a distant view through or along an avenue or opening : PROSPECT
2 : an extensive mental view (as over a stretch of time or a series of events)
vis·taed \'vis-təd\ *adjective* (1835)
1 : affording or made to form a vista
2 : seen in or as if in a vista
¹**vi·su·al** \'vi-zhə-wəl, -zhəl; 'vizh-wəl\ *adjective* [Middle English, from Late Latin *visualis*, from Latin *visus* sight, from *vidēre* to see] (1603)
1 : of, relating to, or used in vision ⟨*visual* organs⟩
2 : attained or maintained by sight ⟨*visual* impressions⟩
3 : VISIBLE
4 : producing mental images : VIVID
5 : done or executed by sight only ⟨*visual* navigation⟩
6 : of, relating to, or employing visual aids
— **vi·su·al·ly** \'vi-zhə-wə-lē, -zhə-lē; 'vizh-wə-lē\ *adverb*
²**visual** *noun* (1938)
: something (as a picture, chart, or film) that appeals to the sight and is variously used (as for illustration, demonstration, or promotion) — usually used in plural
visual acuity *noun* (1889)
: the relative ability of the visual organ to resolve detail that is usually expressed as the reciprocal of the minimum angular separation in minutes of two lines just resolvable as separate and that forms in the average human eye an angle of one minute
visual aid *noun* (1911)
: an instructional device (as a chart, map, or model) that appeals chiefly to vision; *especially* : an educational motion picture or filmstrip
visual field *noun* (1880)
: the entire expanse of space visible at a given instant without moving the eyes — called also *field of vision*
vi·su·al·ise British variant of VISUALIZE
vi·su·al·i·za·tion \,vi-zhə-wə-lə-'zā-shən, ,vi-zhə-lə-, ,vizh-wə-lə-\ *noun* (1883)
1 : formation of mental visual images
2 : the act or process of interpreting in visual terms or of putting into visible form
3 : the process of making an internal organ visible by the introduction (as by swallowing,

by an injection, or by an enema) of a radiopaque substance followed by roentgenography
vi·su·al·ize \'vi-zhə-wə-,līz, 'vi-zhə-,līz, 'vizh-wə-,līz\ *verb* **-ized; -iz·ing** (1863) *transitive verb*
: to make visible: as **a** : to see or form a mental image of : ENVISAGE **b** : to make (an organ) visible by roentgenographic visualization *intransitive verb*
: to form a mental visual image
vi·su·al·iz·er \-,lī-zər\ *noun* (1886)
: one that visualizes; *especially* : a person whose mental imagery is prevailingly visual
visual literacy *noun* (1971)
: the ability to recognize and understand ideas conveyed through visible actions or images (as pictures)
visual purple *noun* (1878)
: a photosensitive red or purple pigment in the retinal rods of various vertebrates; *especially* : RHODOPSIN
vi·ta \'vē-tə, 'vī-tə\ *noun, plural* **vi·tae** \'vē-,tī, -,tē\ [Latin, literally, life] (1939)
1 : a brief biographical sketch
2 : CURRICULUM VITAE
vi·tal \'vī-t³l\ *adjective* [Middle English, from Middle French, from Latin *vitalis* of life, from *vita* life; akin to Latin *vivere* to live — more at QUICK] (14th century)
1 a : existing as a manifestation of life **b** : concerned with or necessary to the maintenance of life ⟨*vital* organs⟩ ⟨blood and other *vital* fluids⟩
2 : full of life and vigor : ANIMATED
3 : characteristic of life or living beings
4 a : fundamentally concerned with or affecting life or living beings: as (1) : tending to renew or refresh the living : INVIGORATING (2) : destructive to life : MORTAL **b** : of the utmost importance
5 : recording data relating to lives
6 : of, relating to, or constituting the staining of living tissues
synonym see ESSENTIAL
— **vi·tal·ly** \-t³l-ē\ *adverb*
vital capacity *noun* (1852)
: the breathing capacity of the lungs expressed as the number of cubic inches or cubic centimeters of air that can be forcibly exhaled after a full inspiration
vi·tal·ism \'vī-t³l-,i-zəm\ *noun* (1822)
1 : a doctrine that the functions of a living organism are due to a vital principle distinct from physicochemical forces
2 : a doctrine that the processes of life are not explicable by the laws of physics and chemistry alone and that life is in some part self-determining
— **vi·tal·ist** \-t³l-ist\ *noun or adjective*
— **vi·tal·is·tic** \,vī-t³l-'is-tik\ *adjective*
vi·tal·i·ty \vī-'ta-lə-tē\ *noun, plural* **-ties** (1592)
1 a : the peculiarity distinguishing the living from the nonliving **b** : capacity to live and develop; *also* : physical or mental vigor especially when highly developed
2 a : power of enduring **b** : lively and animated character
vi·tal·ize \'vī-t³l-,īz\ *transitive verb* **-ized; -iz·ing** (1678)
: to endow with vitality : ANIMATE
— **vi·tal·i·za·tion** \,vī-t³l-ə-'zā-shən\ *noun*
vi·tals \'vī-t³lz\ *noun plural* (circa 1610)
1 : vital organs (as the heart, liver, lungs, and brain)
2 : essential parts
vital signs *noun plural* (circa 1919)
: signs of life; *specifically* : the pulse rate, respiratory rate, body temperature, and often blood pressure of a person
vital statistics *noun plural* (1837)
1 : statistics relating to births, deaths, marriages, health, and disease

2 : facts (as physical dimensions or quantities) considered to be interesting or important; *especially* **:** a woman's bust, waist, and hip measurements

vi·ta·min \'vī-tə-mən, *British usually* 'vi-\ *noun* [Latin *vita* life + International Scientific Vocabulary *amine*] (1912) **:** any of various organic substances that are essential in minute quantities to the nutrition of most animals and some plants, act especially as coenzymes and precursors of coenzymes in the regulation of metabolic processes but do not provide energy or serve as building units, and are present in natural foodstuffs or sometimes produced within the body

vitamin A *noun* (1920) **:** any of several fat-soluble vitamins (as retinol) found especially in animal products (as egg yolk, milk, or fish-liver oils) or a mixture of them whose lack in the animal body causes epithelial tissues to become keratinous (as in the eye with resulting visual defects)

vitamin B *noun* (1920) **1 :** VITAMIN B COMPLEX **2** *or* **vitamin B₁** \-'bē-'wən\ **:** THIAMINE

vitamin B complex *noun* (1928) **:** a group of water-soluble vitamins found especially in yeast, seed germs, eggs, liver and flesh, and vegetables that have varied metabolic functions and include coenzymes and growth factors — called also *B complex*; compare BIOTIN, CHOLINE, NICOTINIC ACID, PANTOTHENIC ACID

vitamin B₆ \-'bē-'siks\ *noun* (1934) **:** pyridoxine or a closely related compound found widely in combined form and considered essential to vertebrate nutrition

vitamin B₁₂ \-'bē-'twelv\ *noun* (1948) **1 :** a complex cobalt-containing compound $C_{63}H_{88}CoN_{14}O_{14}P$ that occurs especially in liver, is essential to normal blood formation, neural function, and growth, and is used especially in treating pernicious and related anemias and in animal feed as a growth factor — called also *cyanocobalamin* **2 :** any of several compounds similar to vitamin B₁₂ in action but having different chemistry

vitamin B₂ \-'bē-'tü\ *noun* (1928) **:** RIBOFLAVIN

vitamin C *noun* (1920) **:** a water-soluble vitamin $C_6H_8O_6$ found in plants and especially in fruits and leafy vegetables or made synthetically and used in the prevention and treatment of scurvy and as an antioxidant for foods — called also *ascorbic acid*

vitamin D *noun* (1921) **:** any or all of several fat-soluble vitamins chemically related to steroids, essential for normal bone and tooth structure, and found especially in fish-liver oils, egg yolk, and milk or produced by activation (as by ultraviolet irradiation) of sterols: as **a** *or* **vitamin D₂** \-'dē-'tü\ **:** CALCIFEROL **b** *or* **vitamin D₃** \-'dē-'thrē\ **:** CHOLECALCIFEROL

vitamin E *noun* (1925) **:** any of several fat-soluble vitamins that are chemically tocopherols, are essential in the nutrition of various vertebrates in which their absence is associated with infertility, degenerative changes in muscle, or vascular abnormalities, are found especially in leaves and in seed germ oils, and are used chiefly in animal feeds and as antioxidants

vitamin G *noun* (1929) **:** RIBOFLAVIN

vitamin H *noun* (circa 1935) **:** BIOTIN

vitamin K *noun* [Danish *koagulation* coagulation] (1935) **1 :** either of two naturally occurring fat-soluble vitamins $C_{31}H_{46}O_2$ and $C_{41}H_{56}O_2$ essential for the clotting of blood because of their role in the production of prothrombin — called also respectively *vitamin K₁*, *vitamin K₂*

2 : any of several synthetic compounds closely related chemically to natural vitamins K₁ and K₂ and of similar biological activity

vi·tel·line \vī-'te-lən, -,lēn, -,līn\ *adjective* [Middle English, from Middle French *vitellin*, from Medieval Latin *vitellinus*, from Latin *vitellus*] (15th century) **1 :** resembling the yolk of an egg especially in yellow color **2 :** of, relating to, or producing yolk

vitelline membrane *noun* (1845) **:** a membrane that encloses the egg proper, corresponds to the plasmalemma of an ordinary cell, and in many animals forms the fertilization membrane by separating from the plasma membrane immediately after fertilization

vi·tel·lo·gen·e·sis \vī-,te-lō-'je-nə-səs, və-\ *noun* [New Latin, from Latin *vitellus* + New Latin *-o- + genesis*] (1947) **:** yolk formation

vi·tel·lus \-'te-ləs\ *noun* [Latin] (1728) **:** the egg cell proper including the yolk but excluding any albuminous or membranous envelopes; *also* **:** YOLK 1c

vi·ti·ate \'vi-shē-,āt\ *transitive verb* **-at·ed; -at·ing** [Latin *vitiatus*, past participle of *vitiare*, from *vitium* fault, vice] (1534) **1 :** to make faulty or defective **:** IMPAIR ⟨the comic impact is *vitiated* by obvious haste —William Styron⟩ **2 :** to debase in moral or aesthetic status ⟨a mind *vitiated* by prejudice⟩ **3 :** to make ineffective ⟨fraud *vitiates* a contract⟩ *synonym* see DEBASE — **vi·ti·a·tion** \,vi-shē-'ā-shən\ *noun* — **vi·ti·a·tor** \'vi-shē-,ā-tər\ *noun*

vi·ti·cul·ture \'vi-tə-,kəl-chər, 'vī-\ *noun* [Latin *vitis* vine + English *culture* — more at WITHY] (1872) **:** the cultivation or culture of grapes especially for wine making — **vi·ti·cul·tur·al** \,vi-tə-'kəl-chə-rəl, ,vī-, -'kəlch-rəl\ *adjective* — **vi·ti·cul·tur·al·ly** *adverb* — **vi·ti·cul·tur·ist** \-rist\ *noun*

vit·i·li·go \,vi-t°l-'ī-(,)gō, -'ē-\ *noun* [New Latin, from Latin, tetter] (1842) **:** a skin disorder manifested by smooth white spots on various parts of the body

vit·rec·to·my \və-'trek-tə-mē\ *noun, plural* **-mies** [*vitreous* humor + *-ectomy*] (1968) **:** surgical removal of all or part of the vitreous humor

¹vit·re·ous \'vi-trē-əs\ *adjective* [Latin *vitreus*, from *vitrum* glass] (1646) **1 :** of, relating to, derived from, or consisting of glass **2 a :** resembling glass (as in color, composition, brittleness, or luster) **:** GLASSY ⟨*vitreous* rocks⟩ **b :** characterized by low porosity and usually translucence due to the presence of a glassy phase ⟨*vitreous* china⟩ **3 :** of, relating to, or constituting the vitreous humor

²vitreous *noun* (1869) **:** VITREOUS HUMOR

vitreous humor *noun* (1663) **:** the clear colorless transparent jelly that fills the eyeball posterior to the lens — see EYE illustration

vitreous silica *noun* (1925) **:** a chemically stable and refractory glass made from silica alone — compare QUARTZ GLASS

vit·ri·fy \'vi-trə-,fī\ *verb* **-fied; -fy·ing** [Middle French *vitrifier*, from Latin *vitrum* glass] (1594) *transitive verb* **:** to convert into glass or a glassy substance by heat and fusion *intransitive verb* **:** to become vitrified — **vit·ri·fi·able** \,vi-trə-'fī-ə-bəl\ *adjective*

— **vit·ri·fi·ca·tion** \,vi-trə-fə-'kā-shən\ *noun*

vi·trine \və-'trēn\ *noun* [French, from *vitre* pane of glass, from Old French, from Latin *vitrum*] (1880) **:** a glass showcase or cabinet especially for displaying fine wares or specimens

vit·ri·ol \'vi-trē-əl\ *noun* [Middle English, from Middle French, from Medieval Latin *vitriolum*, alteration of Late Latin *vitreolum*, neuter of *vitreolus* glassy, from Latin *vitreus* vitreous] (14th century) **1 a :** a sulfate of any of various metals (as copper, iron, or zinc); *especially* **:** a glassy hydrate of such a sulfate **b :** OIL OF VITRIOL **2 :** something felt to resemble vitriol especially in caustic quality; *especially* **:** virulence of feeling or of speech — **vit·ri·ol·ic** \,vi-trē-'ä-lik\ *adjective*

vit·ta \'vi-tə\ *noun, plural* **vit·tae** \'vi-tē, 'vi-,tē, 'vi-,tī\ [New Latin, from Latin, fillet; akin to Latin *viēre* to plait — more at WIRE] (1819) **1 :** STRIPE, STREAK **2 :** one of the oil tubes in the fruits of plants of the carrot family

vit·tles \'vi-t°lz\ *noun plural* (14th century) **:** VICTUALS

vi·tu·per·ate \vī-'tü-pə-,rāt, və-, -'tyü-\ *verb* **-at·ed; -at·ing** [Latin *vituperatus*, past participle of *vituperare*, from *vitium* fault + *parare* to make, prepare — more at PARE] (1542) *transitive verb* **:** to abuse or censure severely or abusively **:** BERATE *intransitive verb* **:** to use harsh condemnatory language *synonym* see SCOLD — **vi·tu·per·a·tor** \-,rā-tər\ *noun*

vi·tu·per·a·tion \(,)vī-,tü-pə-'rā-shən, və-, -'tyü-\ *noun* (15th century) **1 :** sustained and bitter railing and condemnation **:** vituperative utterance **2 :** an act or instance of vituperating *synonym* see ABUSE

vi·tu·per·a·tive \vī-'tü-p(ə-)rə-tiv, -pə-,rā-\ *adjective* (1727) **:** uttering or given to censure **:** containing or characterized by verbal abuse — **vi·tu·per·a·tive·ly** *adverb*

vi·tu·per·a·to·ry \-p(ə-)rə-,tōr-ē, -,tòr-\ *adjective* (1586) **:** VITUPERATIVE

vi·va \'vē-və, -,vä\ *interjection* [Italian & Spanish, long live, from 3d person singular present subjunctive of *vivere* to live, from Latin — more at QUICK] (circa 1700) — used to express goodwill or approval

¹vi·va·ce \vē-'vä-(,)chā, -chē\ *adverb or adjective* [Italian, vivacious, from Latin *vivac-, vivax*] (1683) **:** in a brisk spirited manner — used as a direction in music

²vivace *noun* (circa 1683) **:** a musical composition or movement in vivace tempo

vi·va·cious \və-'vā-shəs *also* vī-\ *adjective* [Latin *vivac-, vivax*, literally, long-lived, from *vivere* to live] (circa 1645) **:** lively in temper, conduct, or spirit **:** SPRIGHTLY *synonym* see LIVELY — **vi·va·cious·ly** *adverb* — **vi·va·cious·ness** *noun*

vi·vac·i·ty \-'va-sə-tē\ *noun* (15th century) **:** the quality or state of being vivacious

vi·van·dière \,vē-,vän²-'dir\ *noun* [French, feminine of Middle French *vivandier*, from Medieval Latin *vivanda* food — more at VIAND] (1848)

: a female sutler

vi·var·i·um \vī-'var-ē-əm, -'ver-\ *noun, plural* **-ia** \-ē-ə\ *or* **-i·ums** [Latin, park, preserve, from *vivus* alive — more at QUICK] (1853)
: a terrarium used especially for small animals

¹vi·va vo·ce \ˌvī-və-'vō-(ˌ)sē *or (as if from* Italian) \ˌvē-və-'vō-(ˌ)chā\ *adverb* [Medieval Latin, with the living voice] (1563)
: by word of mouth : ORALLY

²viva voce *adjective* (1654)
: expressed or conducted by word of mouth : ORAL

³viva voce *noun* (1842)
: an examination conducted viva voce — called also *viva*

vi·vax malaria \'vī-ˌvaks-\ *noun* [New Latin *vivax*, specific epithet of *Plasmodium vivax*, parasite causing tertian] (circa 1941)
: malaria caused by a plasmodium (*Plasmodium vivax*) that induces paroxysms at 48-hour intervals

vi·ver·rid \vī-'ver-əd\ *noun* [New Latin *Viverridae*, from *Viverra*, type genus, from Latin *viverra* ferret; akin to Old English *ācweorna* squirrel, Lithuanian *voverė*] (1902)
: any of a family (*Viverridae*) of carnivorous mammals (as a civet, a genet, or a mongoose) that are rarely larger than a domestic cat but are long, slender, and like a weasel in build with short more or less retractile claws and rounded feet
— **viverrid** *adjective*

vi·vers \'vē-vərz, 'vī-\ *noun plural* [Middle French *vivres*, plural of *vivre* food, from *vivre* to live, from Latin *vivere*] (1536)
chiefly Scottish : VICTUALS, FOOD

Viv·i·an *or* **Viv·i·en** \'vi-vē-ən\ *noun*
: the mistress of Merlin in Arthurian legend — called also *Lady of the Lake*

viv·id \'vi-vəd\ *adjective* [Latin *vividus*, from *vivere* to live — more at QUICK] (1638)
1 : having the appearance of vigorous life or freshness : LIVELY ⟨a *vivid* sketch⟩
2 *of a color* : very strong : very high in chroma
3 : producing a strong or clear impression on the senses : SHARP, INTENSE; *specifically* : producing distinct mental images ⟨a *vivid* description⟩
4 : acting clearly and vigorously ⟨a *vivid* imagination⟩
synonym see GRAPHIC
— **viv·id·ly** *adverb*
— **viv·id·ness** *noun*

viv·if·ic \vī-'vi-fik\ *adjective* [Latin *vivificus*] (1551)
: imparting spirit or vivacity

viv·i·fy \'vi-və-ˌfī\ *transitive verb* **-fied; -fy·ing** [Middle French *vivifier*, from Late Latin *vivificare*, from Latin *vivificus* enlivening, from *vivus* alive — more at QUICK] (1545)
1 : to endue with life or renewed life : ANIMATE ⟨rains that *vivify* the barren hills⟩
2 : to impart vitality or vividness to ⟨concentrating this union of quality and meaning in a way which *vivifies* both —John Dewey⟩
synonym see QUICKEN
— **viv·i·fi·ca·tion** \ˌvi-və-fə-'kā-shən\ *noun*
— **viv·i·fi·er** \'vi-və-ˌfī(-ə)r\ *noun*

vi·vip·a·ri·ty \ˌvī-və-'par-ət-ē, ˌvi-\ *noun* (1864)
: the quality or state of being viviparous

vi·vip·a·rous \vī-'vi-p(ə-)rəs, və-\ *adjective* [Latin *viviparus*, from *vivus* alive + *-parus* -parous] (1646)
1 : producing living young instead of eggs from within the body in the manner of nearly all mammals, many reptiles, and a few fishes
2 : germinating while still attached to the parent plant ⟨the *viviparous* seed of the mangrove⟩
— **vi·vip·a·rous·ly** *adverb*

viv·i·sect \'vi-və-ˌsekt\ *verb* [back-formation from *vivisection*] (1864)
transitive verb

: to perform vivisection on : subject to vivisection
intransitive verb
: to practice vivisection
— **viv·i·sec·tor** \-ˌsek-tər\ *noun*

viv·i·sec·tion \ˌvi-və-'sek-shən, 'vi-və-\ *noun* [Latin *vivus* + English *section*] (1707)
1 : the cutting of or operation on a living animal usually for physiological or pathological investigation; *broadly* : animal experimentation especially if considered to cause distress to the subject
2 : minute or pitiless examination or criticism
— **viv·i·sec·tion·al** \ˌvi-və-'sek-shnəl, -shə-nᵊl\ *adjective*
— **viv·i·sec·tion·ist** \-'sek-sh(ə-)nist\ *noun*

vix·en \'vik-sən\ *noun* [(assumed) Middle English (southern dialect) *vixen*, alteration of Middle English *fixen*, from Old English *fyxe*, feminine of *fox*] (1590)
1 : a shrewish ill-tempered woman
2 : a female fox ◆
— **vix·en·ish** \-s(ə-)nish\ *adjective*

viz·ard \'vi-zərd, -ˌzärd\ *noun* [alteration of Middle English *viser* mask, visor] (circa 1555)
1 : a mask for disguise or protection
2 : DISGUISE, GUISE

viz·ca·cha *variant of* VISCACHA

vi·zier \və-'zir\ *noun* [Turkish *vezir*, from Arabic *wazīr*] (1599)
: a high executive officer of various Muslim countries and especially of the Ottoman Empire
— **vi·zier·ate** \-'zir-ət, -'zir-ˌāt\ *noun*
— **vi·zier·ial** \-'zir-ē-əl\ *adjective*
— **vi·zier·ship** \-'zir-ˌship\ *noun*

vi·zor *variant of* VISOR

vizs·la \'vēz-lə, 'vēs-, 'vizh-\ *noun* [Hungarian] (1945)
: any of a breed of hunting dogs of Hungarian origin that resemble the weimaraner but have a rich deep red coat and brown eyes

vizsla

VLDL \ˌvē-(ˌ)el-(ˌ)dē-'el\ *noun* [*very low-density lipoprotein*] (1977)
: a plasma lipoprotein that is produced primarily by the liver with lesser amounts contributed by the intestine, that contains relatively large amounts of triglycerides compared to protein, and that leaves a residue of cholesterol in the tissues during the process of conversion to LDL — compare HDL

V neck *noun* (1905)
: a V-shaped neck of a garment; *also* : a garment (as a sweater) with a V-shaped neck
— **V-necked** *adjective*

vo·ca·ble \'vō-kə-bəl\ *noun* [Middle French, from Latin *vocabulum*, from *vocare* to call, from *vox* voice — more at VOICE] (1530)
: TERM; *specifically* : a word composed of various sounds or letters without regard to its meaning

vo·cab·u·lar \vō-'ka-byə-lər, və-\ *adjective* [back-formation from *vocabulary*] (1608)
: of or relating to words or phraseology : VERBAL

vo·cab·u·lary \vō-'ka-byə-ˌler-ē, və-\ *noun, plural* **-lar·ies** [Middle French *vocabulaire*, probably from Medieval Latin *vocabularium*, from neuter of *vocabularius* verbal, from Latin *vocabulum*] (1532)
1 : a list or collection of words or of words and phrases usually alphabetically arranged and explained or defined : LEXICON
2 a : a sum or stock of words employed by a language, group, individual, or work or in a field of knowledge **b** : a list or collection of terms or codes available for use (as in an indexing system)

3 : a supply of expressive techniques or devices (as of an art form)

vocabulary entry *noun* (circa 1934)
: a word (as the noun *book*), hyphenated or open compound (as the verb *book-match* or the noun *book review*), word element (as the affix *pro-*), abbreviation (as *agt*), verbalized symbol (as *Na*), or term (as *man in the street*) entered alphabetically in a dictionary for the purpose of definition or identification or expressly included as an inflected form (as the noun *mice* or the verb *saw*) or as a derived form (as the noun *godlessness* or the adverb *globally*) or related phrase (as *one for the book*) run on at its base word and usually set in a type (as boldface) readily distinguishable from that of the lightface running text which defines, explains, or identifies the entry

¹vo·cal \'vō-kəl\ *adjective* [Middle English, from Latin *vocalis*, from *voc-, vox* voice — more at VOICE] (14th century)
1 a : uttered by the voice : ORAL **b** : produced in the larynx : uttered with voice
2 : relating to, composed or arranged for, or sung by the human voice ⟨*vocal* music⟩
3 : VOCALIC
4 a : having or exercising the power of producing voice, speech, or sound **b** : EXPRESSIVE **c** : full of voices : RESOUNDING **d** : given to expressing oneself freely or insistently : OUTSPOKEN **e** : expressed in words
5 : of, relating to, or resembling the voice ⟨*vocal* impairment⟩
— **vo·cal·i·ty** \vō-'ka-lə-tē\ *noun*
— **vo·cal·ly** \'vō-kə-lē\ *adverb*

²vocal *noun* (1582)
1 : a vocal sound
2 : a usually accompanied musical composition for the human voice : SONG; *also* : a performance of such a composition

vocal cords *noun plural* (1852)
: either of two pairs of folds of mucous membranes that project into the cavity of the larynx and have free edges extending dorsoventrally toward the middle line

vocal folds *noun plural* (1924)
: the lower pair of vocal cords each of which when drawn taut, approximated to the contralateral member of the pair, and subjected to a flow of breath produces the voice

¹vo·cal·ic \vō-'ka-lik, və-\ *adjective* [Latin *vocalis* vowel, from *vocalis* vocal] (1814)
1 : marked by or consisting of vowels

2 a : being or functioning as a vowel **b :** of, relating to, or associated with a vowel
— **vo·cal·i·cal·ly** \-li-k(ə-)lē\ *adverb*

²vocalic *noun* (1924)
: a vowel sound or sequence in its function as the most sonorous part of a syllable

vo·cal·ise *British variant of* VOCALIZE

vo·cal·ism \'vō-kə-ˌli-zəm\ *noun* (circa 1859)
1 : VOCALIZATION
2 : vocal art or technique : SINGING
3 a : the vowel system of a language or dialect **b :** the pattern of vowels in a word or paradigm

vo·cal·ist \-kə-list\ *noun* (1834)
: ¹SINGER

vo·cal·ize \'vō-kə-ˌlīz\ *verb* **-ized; -iz·ing** (1669)
transitive verb
1 : to give voice to : UTTER; *specifically* **:** SING
2 a : to make voiced rather than voiceless **:** VOICE **b :** to convert to a vowel
3 : to furnish (as a consonantal Hebrew or Arabic text) with vowels or vowel points
intransitive verb
1 : to utter vocal sounds
2 : SING; *specifically* **:** to sing without words
— **vo·cal·i·za·tion** \ˌvō-kə-lə-'zā-shən\ *noun*
— **vo·cal·iz·er** \'vō-kə-ˌlī-zər\ *noun*

vo·ca·tion \vō-'kā-shən\ *noun* [Middle English *vocacioun*, from Latin *vocation-, vocatio* summons, from *vocare* to call, from *vox* voice — more at VOICE] (15th century)
1 a : a summons or strong inclination to a particular state or course of action; *especially* **:** a divine call to the religious life **b :** an entry into the priesthood or a religious order
2 a : the work in which a person is regularly employed : OCCUPATION **b :** the persons engaged in a particular occupation
3 : the special function of an individual or group

vo·ca·tion·al \-shnəl, -shə-nᵊl\ *adjective* (1652)
1 : of, relating to, or concerned with a vocation
2 : of, relating to, or being in training in a skill or trade to be pursued as a career
— **vo·ca·tion·al·ly** *adverb*

vo·ca·tion·al·ism \-shnə-ˌli-zəm, -shə-nᵊl-ˌi-zəm\ *noun* (1924)
: emphasis on vocational training in education
— **vo·ca·tion·al·ist** \-list, -ist\ *noun*

¹voc·a·tive \'vä-kə-tiv\ *adjective* [Middle English *vocatif*, from Middle French, from Latin *vocativus*, from *vocatus*, past participle of *vocare*] (15th century)
1 : of, relating to, or being a grammatical case marking the one addressed (as Latin *Domine* in *miserere, Domine* "have mercy, O Lord")
2 *of a word or word group* **:** marking the one addressed (as *mother* in "mother, come here")
— **voc·a·tive·ly** *adverb*

²vocative *noun* (circa 1522)
1 : the vocative case of a language
2 : a form in the vocative case

vo·cif·er·ant \vō-'si-fə-rənt\ *adjective* (1609)
: CLAMOROUS, VOCIFEROUS

vo·cif·er·ate \-ˌrāt\ *verb* **-at·ed; -at·ing** [Latin *vociferatus*, past participle of *vociferari*, from *voc-, vox* voice + *ferre* to bear — more at VOICE, BEAR] (1599)
transitive verb
: to utter loudly : SHOUT
intransitive verb
: to cry out loudly : CLAMOR
— **vo·cif·er·a·tion** \-ˌsi-fə-'rā-shən\ *noun*
— **vo·cif·er·a·tor** \-'si-fə-ˌrā-tər\ *noun*

vo·cif·er·ous \vō-'si-f(ə-)rəs\ *adjective* (circa 1611)
: marked by or given to vehement insistent outcry ☆
— **vo·cif·er·ous·ly** *adverb*
— **vo·cif·er·ous·ness** *noun*

vo·cod·er \'vō-ˌkō-dər\ *noun* [*voice coder*] (1939)

: an electronic mechanism that reduces speech signals to slowly varying signals transmittable over communication systems of limited frequency bandwidth

vod·ka \'väd-kə\ *noun* [Russian, from *voda* water; akin to Old English *wæter* water] (circa 1803)
: a colorless liquor of neutral spirits distilled from a mash (as of rye or wheat)

vodka martini *noun* (1948)
: a martini made with vodka instead of gin

vo·dun *also* **vo·doun** \vō-'düⁿ\ *noun* [Haitian Creole] (1920)
: VOODOO 1

vo·gie \'vō-gē\ *adjective* [origin unknown] (1712)
Scottish **:** PROUD, VAIN

¹vogue \'vōg\ *noun* [Middle French, action of rowing, course, fashion, from Old Italian *voga*, from *vogare* to row] (1571)
1 *archaic* **:** the leading place in popularity or acceptance
2 a : popular acceptation or favor : POPULARITY **b :** a period of popularity
3 : one that is in fashion at a particular time
synonym see FASHION
— **vogue** *adjective*

²vogue *intransitive verb* [from *Vogue*, a fashion magazine] **vogued; vogu·ing** *or* **vogue·ing** (1989)
: to strike poses in campy imitation of fashion models especially as a kind of dance
— **vogu·er** \'vō-gər\ *noun*

vogu·ish \'vō-gish\ *adjective* (1926)
1 : FASHIONABLE, SMART
2 : suddenly or temporarily popular
— **vogu·ish·ness** *noun*

¹voice \'vȯis\ *noun* [Middle English, from Old French *vois*, from Latin *voc-, vox*; akin to Old High German *giwahanen* to mention, Greek *epos* word, speech, Sanskrit *vāk* voice] (14th century)
1 a : sound produced by vertebrates by means of lungs, larynx, or syrinx; *especially* **:** sound so produced by human beings **b** (1) **:** musical sound produced by the vocal folds and resonated by the cavities of head and throat (2) **:** the power or ability to produce musical tones (3) **:** SINGER (4) **:** one of the melodic parts in a vocal or instrumental composition (5) **:** condition of the vocal organs with respect to production of musical tones (6) **:** the use of the voice (as in singing or acting) ⟨studying *voice*⟩ **c :** expiration of air with the vocal cords drawn close so as to vibrate audibly (as in uttering vowels and consonant sounds as \v\ or \z\) **d :** the faculty of utterance ⟨lost my *voice*⟩
2 : a sound resembling or suggesting vocal utterance
3 : an instrument or medium of expression ⟨the party became the *voice* of the workers⟩
4 a : wish, choice, or opinion openly or formally expressed ⟨the *voice* of the people⟩ **b :** right of expression; *also* **:** influential power
5 : distinction of form or a system of inflections of a verb to indicate the relation of the subject of the verb to the action which the verb expresses ⟨active and passive *voices*⟩
— **with one voice :** without dissent
: UNANIMOUSLY

²voice *transitive verb* **voiced; voic·ing** (15th century)
1 : to express in words : UTTER ⟨*voice* a complaint⟩
2 : to adjust for producing the proper musical sounds
3 : to pronounce (as a consonant) with voice
synonym see EXPRESS

voice box *noun* (1912)
: LARYNX

voiced \'vȯist\ *adjective* (1593)
1 : having or furnished with a voice especially of a specified kind — often used in combination ⟨soft-*voiced*⟩
2 : uttered with vocal cord vibration ⟨a *voiced* consonant⟩

voice·ful \'vȯis-fəl\ *adjective* (circa 1611)
: having a voice or vocal quality; *also* **:** having a loud voice or many voices
— **voice·ful·ness** *noun*

voice·less \-ləs\ *adjective* (1535)
1 : having no voice : MUTE
2 : not voiced : SURD ⟨a *voiceless* consonant⟩
— **voice·less·ly** *adverb*
— **voice·less·ness** *noun*

voice mail *noun* (1981)
: an electronic communication system in which spoken messages are recorded or digitized for later playback to the intended recipient

voice–over \'vȯis-ˌō-vər\ *noun* (circa 1947)
1 a : the voice of an unseen narrator speaking (as in a motion picture or television commercial) **b :** the voice of a visible character (as in a motion picture) expressing unspoken thoughts
2 : a recording of a voice-over

voice part *noun* (1776)
: VOICE 1b(4)

voice·print \'vȯis-print\ *noun* [*voice* + *fingerprint*] (1962)
: an individually distinctive pattern of certain voice characteristics that is spectrographically produced

voic·er \'vȯi-sər\ *noun* (1879)
: one that voices; *specifically* **:** one that voices organ pipes

voice vote *noun* (1924)
: a parliamentary vote taken by calling for ayes and noes and estimating which response is stronger

¹void \'vȯid\ *adjective* [Middle English *voide*, from Old French, from (assumed) Vulgar Latin *vocitus*, alteration of Latin *vocivus, vacivus* empty, from *vacare* to be empty] (14th century)
1 a : not occupied : VACANT ⟨a *void* bishopric⟩ **b :** not inhabited : DESERTED
2 : containing nothing ⟨*void* space⟩
3 : IDLE, LEISURE
4 a : being without : DEVOID ⟨a nature *void* of all malice⟩ **b :** having no members or examples; *specifically, of a suit* **:** having no cards represented in a particular hand
5 : VAIN, USELESS
6 a : of no legal force or effect : NULL ⟨a *void* contract⟩ **b :** VOIDABLE
synonym see EMPTY
— **void·ness** *noun*

²void *noun* (1616)
1 a : OPENING, GAP **b :** empty space : EMPTINESS, VACUUM

☆ **SYNONYMS**
Vociferous, clamorous, blatant, strident, boisterous, obstreperous mean so loud or insistent as to compel attention. VOCIFEROUS implies a vehement shouting or calling out ⟨*vociferous* cries of protest and outrage⟩. CLAMOROUS may imply insistency as well as vociferousness in demanding or protesting ⟨*clamorous* demands for prison reforms⟩. BLATANT implies an offensive bellowing or insensitive loudness ⟨*blatant* rock music⟩ ⟨a *blatant* clamor for impeachment⟩. STRIDENT suggests harsh and discordant noise ⟨heard the *strident* cry of the crow⟩. BOISTEROUS suggests a noisiness and turbulence due to high spirits ⟨a *boisterous* crowd of party goers⟩. OBSTREPEROUS suggests unruly and aggressive noisiness and resistance to restraint ⟨the *obstreperous* demonstrators were removed from the hall⟩.

\ə\ **abut** \ᵊ\ **kitten** \ər\ **further** \a\ **ash** \ā\ **ace**
\ä\ **mop, mar** \aů\ **out** \ch\ **chin** \e\ **bet** \ē\ **easy**
\g\ **go** \i\ **hit** \ī\ **ice** \j\ **job** \ŋ\ **sing** \ō\ **go**
\ȯ\ **law** \ȯi\ **boy** \th\ **thin** \t͟h\ **the** \ü\ **loot** \ů\ **foot**
\y\ **yet** \zh\ **vision** *see also* Guide to Pronunciation

2 : the quality or state of being without something : LACK, ABSENCE
3 : a feeling of want or hollowness
4 : absence of cards of a particular suit in a hand originally dealt to a player

³**void** verb [Middle English, from Middle French *vuidier*, from (assumed) Vulgar Latin *vocitare*, from *vocitus*] (14th century)
transitive verb
1 a : to make empty or vacant : CLEAR **b** *archaic* : VACATE, LEAVE
2 : DISCHARGE, EMIT ⟨*void* excrement⟩
3 : NULLIFY, ANNUL ⟨*void* a contract⟩
intransitive verb
: to eliminate solid or liquid waste from the body
— **void·er** noun

void·able \'vȯi-də-bəl\ adjective (15th century)
: capable of being voided; *specifically* : capable of being adjudged void
— **void·able·ness** noun

void·ance \'vȯi-dᵊn(t)s\ noun (14th century)
1 : the act of voiding
2 *of a benefice* : the state of being without an incumbent

void·ed \'vȯi-dəd\ adjective (circa 1539)
: having the inner part cut away or left vacant with a narrow border left at the sides — used of a heraldic charge

voi·là or **voi·la** \vwä-'lä\ interjection [French, literally, see there] (1739)
— used to call attention, to express satisfaction or approval, or to suggest an appearance as if by magic

voile \'vȯi(ə)l\ noun [French, veil, from Latin *vela*, neuter plural of *velum*] (1889)
: a fine soft sheer fabric used especially for women's summer clothing or curtains

voir dire \'vwär-'dir, 'wär-\ noun [Anglo-French, from Old French, to speak the truth] (1676)
: a preliminary examination to determine the competency of a witness or juror

vo·lant \'vō-lənt\ adjective [Middle French, from Latin *volant-, volans*, present participle of *volare* to fly] (1572)
1 : having the wings extended as if in flight — used of a heraldic bird
2 : flying or capable of flying
3 : QUICK, NIMBLE

vo·lan·te \vō-'län-(,)tā\ adjective [Italian, literally, flying, from Latin *volant-, volans*, present participle] (circa 1854)
: moving with light rapidity — used as a direction in music

Vo·la·pük \'vō-lə-,pùk, 'vä-\ noun [Volapük, literally, world's speech, from *vol* of the world (genitive of *vol* world, modification of English *world*) + *pük* speech, modification of English *speak*] (1885)
: an artificial international language based largely on English but with some root words from German, French, and Latin

vo·lar \'vō-lər, -,lär\ adjective [Latin *vola* hollow in the palm of the hand or sole of the foot] (1814)
: relating to the palm of the hand or the sole of the foot; *specifically* : located on the same side as the palm of the hand ⟨the *volar* part of the forearm⟩

¹**vol·a·tile** \'vä-lə-tᵊl, especially British -,tīl\ adjective [French, from Latin *volatilis*, from *volare* to fly] (1605)
1 : readily vaporizable at a relatively low temperature
2 : flying or having the power to fly
3 a : LIGHTHEARTED, LIVELY **b :** easily aroused ⟨*volatile* suspicions⟩ **c :** tending to erupt into violence : EXPLOSIVE
4 a : unable to hold the attention fixed because of an inherent lightness or fickleness of disposition **b :** characterized by or subject to rapid or unexpected change
5 : difficult to capture or hold permanently : EVANESCENT, TRANSITORY

— **vol·a·tile·ness** noun
— **vol·a·til·i·ty** \,vä-lə-'ti-lə-tē\ noun

²**volatile** noun (1686)
: a volatile substance

volatile oil noun (1800)
: an oil that vaporizes readily; *especially* : ESSENTIAL OIL

vol·a·til·ise British variant of VOLATILIZE

vol·a·til·ize \'vä-lə-tᵊl-,īz, British also və-'la-\ verb **-ized; -iz·ing** (1657)
transitive verb
: to make volatile; *especially* : to cause to pass off in vapor
intransitive verb
: to pass off in vapor
— **vol·a·til·iz·able** \-,ī-zə-bəl\ adjective
— **vol·a·til·i·za·tion** \,vä-lə-tᵊl-ə-'zā-shən, British also və-,la-\ noun

vol–au–vent \,vȯ-lō-'väⁿ\ noun [French, literally, flight in the wind] (1828)
: a baked patty shell filled with meat, fowl, game, or seafood in sauce

¹**vol·ca·nic** \väl-'ka-nik, vȯl- also -'kä-\ adjective (1774)
1 a : of, relating to, or produced by a volcano **b :** characterized by volcanoes ⟨a *volcanic* range⟩ **c :** made of materials from volcanoes
2 : explosively violent : VOLATILE ⟨*volcanic* emotions⟩
— **vol·ca·ni·cal·ly** \-ni-k(ə-)lē\ adverb

²**volcanic** noun (1894)
: a volcanic rock

volcanic glass noun (circa 1840)
: natural glass produced by the cooling of molten lava too rapidly to permit crystallization

vol·ca·nic·i·ty \,väl-kə-'ni-sə-tē, ,vȯl-\ noun (1836)
: VOLCANISM

vol·ca·nism \'väl-kə-,ni-zəm, 'vȯl-\ noun (circa 1864)
: volcanic action or activity

vol·ca·no \väl-'kā-(,)nō, vȯl-\ noun, plural **-noes** or **-nos** [Italian or Spanish; Italian *vulcano*, from Spanish *volcán*, ultimately from Latin *Volcanus* Vulcan] (1613)
1 : a vent in the crust of the earth or another planet from which usually molten or hot rock and steam issue; *also* : a hill or mountain composed wholly or in part of the ejected material
2 : something of explosively violent potential

vol·ca·no·log·i·cal \,väl-kə-nᵊl-'ä-ji-kəl, ,vȯl-\ also **vol·ca·no·log·ic** \-jik\ adjective (circa 1891)
: of, relating to, or involving volcanology or volcanic phenomena ⟨*volcanological* processes that shape the planets⟩

vol·ca·nol·o·gy \,väl-kə-'nä-lə-jē, ,vȯl-\ noun (1886)
: a branch of science that deals with volcanic phenomena
— **vol·ca·nol·o·gist** \-jist\ noun

¹**vole** \'vōl\ noun [French, probably from *voler* to fly — more at VOLLEY] (1679)
: GRAND SLAM 1

²**vole** noun [earlier *vole-mouse*, from *vole-* (of Scandinavian origin; akin to Old Norse *vǫllr* field) + *mouse*; akin to Old English *weald* forest — more at WOLD] (1805)
: any of various small rodents (*Microtus* and related genera) that typically have a stout body, rather blunt nose, and short ears, inhabit both moist meadows and dry uplands and do much damage to crops, and are closely related to muskrats and lemmings

vo·li·tion \vō-'li-shən, və-\ noun [French, from Medieval Latin *volition-, volitio*, from Latin *vol-* (stem of *velle* to will, wish) + *-ition-, -itio* (as in Latin *position-, positio* position) — more at WILL] (1615)
1 : an act of making a choice or decision; *also* : a choice or decision made
2 : the power of choosing or determining : WILL

— **vo·li·tion·al** \-'lish-nəl, -'li-shə-nᵊl\ adjective

vol·i·tive \'vä-lə-tiv\ adjective (1660)
1 : of or relating to the will
2 : expressing a wish or permission

volks·lied \'fōks-,lēt, 'fȯlks-\ noun, plural **volks·lie·der** \-,lē-dər\ [German, from *Volk* people + *Lied* song] (circa 1854)
: a folk song

¹**vol·ley** \'vä-lē\ noun, plural **volleys** [Middle French *volee* flight, from *voler* to fly, from Latin *volare*] (1573)
1 a : a flight of missiles (as arrows) **b :** simultaneous discharge of a number of missile weapons **c :** one round per gun in a battery fired as soon as a gun is ready without regard to order **d** (1) **:** the flight of the ball (as in volleyball or tennis) or its course before striking the ground; *also* : a return of the ball before it touches the ground (2) **:** a kick of the ball in soccer before it rebounds (3) **:** the exchange of the shuttlecock in badminton following the serve
2 a : a burst or emission of many things or a large amount at once ⟨received a *volley* of angry letters⟩ ⟨a *volley* of praise⟩ **b :** a burst of simultaneous or immediately sequential nerve impulses passing to an end organ, synapse, or center

²**volley** verb **vol·leyed; vol·ley·ing** (1591)
transitive verb
1 : to discharge in or as if in a volley
2 : to propel (an object) while in the air and before touching the ground; *especially* : to hit (a tennis ball) on the volley
intransitive verb
1 : to become discharged in or as if in a volley
2 : to make a volley; *specifically* : to volley an object of play (as in tennis)
— **vol·ley·er** noun

vol·ley·ball \'vä-lē-,bȯl\ noun (1896)
: a game played by volleying an inflated ball over a net; *also* : the ball used in this game

vol·plane \'väl-,plān, 'vȯl-\ intransitive verb **vol·planed; vol·plan·ing** [French *vol plané* gliding flight] (1909)
1 : to glide in or as if in an airplane
2 : GLIDE 3

Vol·sci \'vȯl-,skē, 'väl-,sī\ noun plural [Latin] (circa 1909)
: a people of ancient Italy dwelling between the Latins and Samnites

Vol·scian \'väl-shən, 'vȯl-skē-ən\ *noun, plural*
Volscians (1513)
1 : a member of the Volsci
2 : the Italic language of the Volsci
— **Volscian** *adjective*

¹**volt** \'vōlt, 'vȯlt\ *noun* [French *volte*, from
Italian *volta* turn, from *voltare* to turn, from
(assumed) Vulgar Latin *volvitare*, frequenta-
tive of Latin *volvere* to roll — more at VOLU-
BLE] (1688)
1 : a leaping movement in fencing to avoid a
thrust
2 a : a tread or gait in which a horse going
sideways makes a turn around a center **b** : a
circle traced by a horse in this movement

²**volt** \'vōlt\ *noun* [Alessandro *Volta*] (1873)
: the practical meter-kilogram-second unit of
electrical potential difference and electromo-
tive force equal to the difference of potential
between two points in a conducting wire car-
rying a constant current of one ampere when
the power dissipated between these two points
is equal to one watt and equivalent to the po-
tential difference across a resistance of one
ohm when one ampere is flowing through it

volt·age \'vōl-tij\ *noun* (1890)
1 : electric potential or potential difference ex-
pressed in volts
2 : intensity of feeling

voltage divider *noun* (1922)
: a resistor or series of resistors provided with
taps at certain points and used to provide vari-
ous potential differences from a single power
source

vol·ta·ic \väl-'tā-ik, vōl-, vȯl-\ *adjective*
[Alessandro *Volta*] (1812)
: of, relating to, or producing direct electric
current by chemical action (as in a battery)
: GALVANIC ⟨*voltaic* cell⟩

volt–am·pere \'vōlt-'am-,pir *also* -,per\ *noun*
(1896)
: a unit of electric measurement equal to the
product of a volt and an ampere that for direct
current constitutes a measure of power equiva-
lent to a watt

volte–face \,vȯlt-'fäs, ,vȯl-tə-\ *noun* [French,
from Italian *voltafaccia*, from *voltare* to turn +
faccia face, from (assumed) Vulgar Latin *facia*
— more at VOLT, FACE] (1819)
: a reversal in policy : ABOUT-FACE

volt·me·ter \'vōlt-,mē-tər\ *noun* [International
Scientific Vocabulary] (1882)
: an instrument (as a galvanometer) for mea-
suring in volts the differences in potential be-
tween different points of an electrical circuit

vol·u·ble \'väl-yə-bəl\ *adjective* [Middle
French or Latin; Middle French, from Latin
volubilis, from *volvere* to roll; akin to Old En-
glish *wealwian* to roll, Greek *eilyein* to roll,
wrap] (15th century)
1 : easily rolling or turning : ROTATING
2 : characterized by ready or rapid speech
: GLIB, FLUENT
synonym see TALKATIVE
— **vol·u·bil·i·ty** \,väl-yə-'bi-lə-tē\ *noun*
— **vol·u·ble·ness** \'väl-yə-bəl-nəs\ *noun*
— **vol·u·bly** \-blē\ *adverb*

¹**vol·ume** \'väl-yəm, -(,)yüm\ *noun* [Middle
English, from Middle French, from Latin *volu-
men* roll, scroll, from *volvere* to roll] (14th
century)
1 a : a series of printed sheets bound typically
in book form : BOOK **b** : a series of issues of a
periodical **c** : ALBUM 1c
2 : SCROLL 1a
3 : the amount of space occupied by a three-
dimensional object as measured in cubic units
(as quarts or liters) : cubic capacity — see
METRIC SYSTEM table, WEIGHT table
4 a (1) : AMOUNT; *also* : BULK, MASS (2) : a con-
siderable quantity **b** : the amount of a sub-
stance occupying a particular volume **c** : mass
or the representation of mass in art or architec-
ture

5 : the degree of loudness or the intensity of a
sound; *also* : LOUDNESS
synonym see BULK
— **vol·umed** \-yəmd, -(,)yümd\ *adjective*

VOLUME FORMULAS

FIGURE	FORMULA	MEANING OF LETTERS
cube	$V= a^3$	a=length of one edge
rectangular solid	$V= lwh$	l=length of base; w=width of base; h=height
pyramid	$V = \dfrac{Ah}{3}$	A=area of base; h=height
cylinder	$V= \pi r^2 h$	$\pi = 3.1416$; r=radius of the base; h=height
cone	$V = \dfrac{\pi r^2 h}{3}$	$\pi = 3.1416$; r=radius of the base; h=height
sphere	$V = \dfrac{4\pi r^3}{3}$	$\pi = 3.1416$; r=radius

²**volume** *verb* **vol·umed; vol·um·ing**
(1815)
transitive verb
: to send or give out in volume
intransitive verb
: to roll or rise in volume

³**volume** *adjective* (circa 1945)
: involving large quantities ⟨offered *volume*
discounts⟩

vol·u·me·ter \'väl-yù-,mē-tər\ *noun* [Interna-
tional Scientific Vocabulary, blend of *volume*
and *-meter*] (1829)
: an instrument for measuring volumes (as of
gases or liquids) directly or (as of solids) by
displacement of a liquid

vol·u·met·ric \,väl-yù-'me-trik\ *adjective*
(1857)
: of, relating to, or involving the measurement
of volume
— **vol·u·met·ri·cal·ly** \-tri-k(ə-)lē\ *adverb*

vo·lu·mi·nos·i·ty \və-,lü-mə-'nä-sə-tē\ *noun*
(1782)
: the quality or state of being voluminous

vo·lu·mi·nous \və-'lü-mə-nəs\ *adjective* [Late
Latin *voluminosus*, from Latin *volumin-, volu-
men*] (1611)
1 : consisting of many folds, coils, or convo-
lutions : WINDING
2 a : having or marked by great volume or
bulk : LARGE ⟨long *voluminous* tresses⟩; *also*
: FULL ⟨a *voluminous* skirt⟩ **b** : NUMEROUS ⟨try-
ing to keep track of *voluminous* slips of paper⟩
3 a : filling or capable of filling a large vol-
ume or several volumes ⟨a *voluminous* litera-
ture on the subject⟩ **b** : writing or speaking
much or at great length
— **vo·lu·mi·nous·ly** *adverb*
— **vo·lu·mi·nous·ness** *noun*

vol·un·ta·rism \'vä-lən-tə-,ri-zəm\ *noun*
(1838)
1 : the principle or system of doing something
by or relying on voluntary action or volunteers
2 : a theory that conceives will to be the dom-
inant factor in experience or in the world
— **vol·un·ta·rist** \-rist\ *noun*
— **vol·un·ta·ris·tic** \,vä-lən-tə-'ris-tik\ *ad-
jective*

¹**vol·un·tary** \'vä-lən-,ter-ē\ *adjective* [Middle
English, from Latin *voluntarius*, from *voluntas*
will, from *velle* to will, wish — more at
WILL] (14th century)
1 : proceeding from the will or from one's
own choice or consent
2 : unconstrained by interference : SELF-DETER-
MINING

3 : done by design or intention : INTENTIONAL
⟨*voluntary* manslaughter⟩
4 : of, relating to, subject to, or regulated by
the will ⟨*voluntary* behavior⟩
5 : having power of free choice
6 : provided or supported by voluntary action
⟨a *voluntary* organization⟩
7 : acting or done of one's own free will with-
out valuable consideration or legal obligation
☆
— **vol·un·tar·i·ly** *adverb*
— **vol·un·tar·i·ness** *noun*

²**voluntary** *noun, plural* **-tar·ies** (1598)
1 a : a prefatory often extemporized musical
piece **b** : an improvisatory organ piece played
before, during, or after a religious service
2 : one who participates voluntarily : VOLUN-
TEER

vol·un·tary·ism \'vä-lən-,ter-ē,-i-zəm\ *noun*
(1835)
: VOLUNTARISM
— **vol·un·tary·ist** \-ē-ist\ *noun*

voluntary muscle *noun* (1788)
: muscle (as most striated muscle) under vol-
untary control

¹**vol·un·teer** \,vä-lən-'tir\ *noun* [obsolete
French *voluntaire* (now *volontaire*), from *vol-
untaire*, adjective, voluntary, from Latin *vol-
untarius*] (circa 1618)
1 : a person who voluntarily undertakes or ex-
presses a willingness to undertake a service: as
a : one who enters into military service volun-
tarily **b** (1) : one who renders a service or
takes part in a transaction while having no le-
gal concern or interest (2) : one who receives a
conveyance or transfer of property without
giving valuable consideration
2 : a volunteer plant
3 *capitalized* [*Volunteers of America*] : a
member of a quasi-military religious and phil-
anthropic organization founded in 1896 by
Commander and Mrs. Ballington Booth

²**volunteer** *adjective* (1649)
1 : being, consisting of, or engaged in by vol-
unteers ⟨a *volunteer* army⟩ ⟨*volunteer* activi-
ties to help the mentally handicapped⟩
2 : growing spontaneously without direct hu-
man control or supervision especially from
seeds lost from a previous crop ⟨*volunteer*
corn plants⟩

³**volunteer** (circa 1755)
intransitive verb
: to offer oneself as a volunteer
transitive verb
: to offer or bestow voluntarily ⟨*volunteer*
one's services⟩

vol·un·teer·ism \,vä-lən-'tir,-i-zəm\ *noun*
(1844)
1 : VOLUNTARISM 1
2 : the act or practice of doing volunteer work
in community service

\ə\ abut \ᵊ\ kitten \ər\ **further** \a\ ash \ā\ **ace**
\ä\ mop, mar \au̇\ out \ch\ **chin** \e\ bet \ē\ **easy**
\g\ go \i\ hit \ī\ **ice** \j\ **job** \ŋ\ sing \ō\ **go**
\ȯ\ **law** \ȯi\ **boy** \th\ **thin** \t͟h\ **the** \ü\ loot \u̇\ **foot**
\y\ **yet** \zh\ vision *see also* Guide to Pronunciation

vo·lup·tu·ary \və-'ləp(t)-shə-,wer-ē\ *noun, plural* **-ar·ies** (circa 1610)
: a person whose chief interests are luxury and the gratification of sensual appetites
— **voluptuary** *adjective*

vo·lup·tu·ous \-shə-wəs, -shəs\ *adjective* [Middle English, from Latin *voluptuosus*, irregular from *voluptas* pleasure, from *volup* pleasurable; akin to Greek *elpesthai* to hope, Latin *velle* to wish — more at WILL] (14th century)
1 a : full of delight or pleasure to the senses : conducive to or arising from sensuous or sensual gratification : LUXURIOUS ⟨a *voluptuous* dance⟩ ⟨*voluptuous* ornamentation⟩ **b** : suggesting sensual pleasure by fullness and beauty of form ⟨*voluptuous* nudes⟩
2 : given to or spent in enjoyments of luxury, pleasure, or sensual gratifications ⟨a long and *voluptuous* holiday —Edmund Wilson⟩
synonym see SENSUOUS
— **vo·lup·tuous·ly** *adverb*
— **vo·lup·tuous·ness** *noun*

vo·lute \və-'lüt\ *noun* [Latin *voluta*, from feminine of *volutus*, past participle of *volvere* to roll — more at VOLUBLE] (circa 1696)
1 : a spiral or scroll-shaped form
2 : a spiral scroll-shaped ornament forming the chief feature of the Ionic capital
3 a : any of various marine gastropod mollusks (family Volutidae) with a thick short-spired shell **b** : the shell of a volute
— **volute** *or* **vo·lut·ed** \-'lü-təd\ *adjective*

vo·lu·tin \'väl-yə-,tin, və-'lü-tᵊn\ *noun* [German, from New Latin *volutans*, specific epithet of the bacterium *Spirillum volutans* in which it was first found] (1908)
: a granular basophilic substance that is thought to be a nucleic acid compound and that is common in microorganisms

vol·va \'väl-və, 'vȯl-\ *noun* [New Latin, from Latin *volva, vulva* integument — more at VULVA] (circa 1753)
: a membranous sac or cup about the base of the stipe in many gill fungi

vol·vox \-,väks\ *noun* [New Latin, from Latin *volvere* to roll] (1798)
: any of a genus (*Volvox*) of flagellated unicellular green algae that form spherical colonies

volva

vol·vu·lus \'väl-vyə-ləs, 'vȯl-\ *noun* [New Latin, from Latin *volvere*] (1679)
: a twisting of the intestine upon itself that causes obstruction

vo·mer \'vō-mər\ *noun* [New Latin, from Latin, plowshare] (circa 1704)
: a bone of the skull of most vertebrates that is situated below the ethmoid region and in the human skull forms part of the nasal septum
— **vo·mer·ine** \'vō-mə-,rīn\ *adjective*

¹vom·it \'vä-mət\ *noun* [Middle English, from Middle French, from Latin *vomitus*, from *vomere* to vomit; akin to Old Norse *vāma* seasickness, Greek *emein* to vomit] (14th century)
1 : an act or instance of disgorging the contents of the stomach through the mouth; *also* : the disgorged matter
2 : EMETIC

²vomit (15th century)
intransitive verb
1 : to disgorge the stomach contents
2 : to spew forth : BELCH, GUSH
transitive verb
1 : to disgorge (the contents of the stomach) through the mouth
2 : to eject violently or abundantly : SPEW
3 : to cause to vomit
— **vom·it·er** *noun*

vom·i·to·ry \'vä-mə-,tōr-ē, -,tȯr-\ *noun, plural* **-ries** [Late Latin *vomitorium*, from Latin *vomere*; from its disgorging the spectators] (1730)
: an entrance piercing the banks of seats of a theater, amphitheater, or stadium

vom·i·tus \'vä-mə-təs\ *noun* [Latin] (circa 1899)
: material discharged by vomiting

V–1 \'vē-'wən\ *noun* [German, abbreviation for *Vergeltungswaffe 1*, literally, reprisal weapon 1] (1944)
: BUZZ BOMB

¹voo·doo \'vü-(,)dü\ *noun, plural* **voodoos** [Louisiana Creole *voudou*, probably from Ewe *vódũ* tutelary deity, demon] (1850)
1 : a religion that is derived from African polytheism and ancestor worship and is practiced chiefly in Haiti
2 a : a person who deals in spells and necromancy **b** (1) : a sorcerer's spell : HEX (2) : a hexed object : CHARM
— **voodoo** *adjective*

²voodoo *transitive verb* (1880)
: to bewitch by or as if by means of voodoo : HEX

voo·doo·ism \'vü-(,)dü-,i-zəm\ *noun* (1865)
1 : VOODOO 1
2 : the practice of witchcraft
— **voo·doo·ist** \-ist\ *noun*
— **voo·doo·is·tic** \,vü-(,)dü-'is-tik\ *adjective*

vo·ra·cious \vȯ-'rā-shəs, və-\ *adjective* [Latin *vorac-, vorax*, from *vorare* to devour; akin to Old English *ācweorran* to guzzle, Latin *gurges* whirlpool, Greek *bibrōskein* to devour] (1635)
1 : having a huge appetite : RAVENOUS
2 : excessively eager : INSATIABLE ⟨a *voracious* reader⟩ ☆
— **vo·ra·cious·ly** *adverb*
— **vo·ra·cious·ness** *noun*

vo·rac·i·ty \vȯ-'ra-sə-tē, və-\ *noun* (1526)
: the quality or state of being voracious

vor·la·ge \'fōr-,lä-gə, 'fȯr-\ *noun* [German, literally, forward position, from *vor* fore + *Lage* position] (1936)
: the position of a skier leaning forward from the ankles usually without lifting the heels from the skis

-vorous *adjective combining form* [Latin *-vorus*, from *vorare* to devour]
: eating : feeding on ⟨frugi*vorous*⟩

vor·tex \'vȯr-,teks\ *noun, plural* **vor·ti·ces** \'vȯr-tə-,sēz\ *also* **vor·tex·es** \'vȯr-,tek-səz\ [New Latin *vortic-, vortex*, from Latin *vertex, vortex* whirlpool — more at VERTEX] (1652)
1 a : a mass of fluid (as a liquid) with a whirling or circular motion that tends to form a cavity or vacuum in the center of the circle and to draw toward this cavity or vacuum bodies subject to its action; *especially* : WHIRLPOOL, EDDY **b** : a region within a body of fluid in which the fluid elements have an angular velocity
2 : something that resembles a whirlpool ⟨the hellish *vortex* of battle —*Time*⟩

vor·ti·cal \'vȯr-ti-kəl\ *adjective* (1653)
: of, relating to, or resembling a vortex : SWIRLING
— **vor·ti·cal·ly** \-k(ə-)lē\ *adverb*

vor·ti·cel·la \,vȯr-tə-'se-lə\ *noun, plural* **-cel·lae** \-'se-(,)lē\ *or* **-cellas** [New Latin, from Latin *vortic-, vortex*] (1787)
: any of a genus (*Vorticella*) of stalked bell-shaped ciliates

vor·ti·cism \'vȯr-tə-,si-zəm\ *noun* [Latin *vortic-, vortex*] (1914)
: an English abstract art movement from about 1912–15 embracing cubist and futurist concepts
— **vor·ti·cist** \-sist\ *noun*

vor·tic·i·ty \vȯr-'ti-sə-tē\ *noun* (1888)
1 : the state of a fluid in vortical motion; *broadly* : vortical motion
2 : a measure of vortical motion; *especially* : a vector measure of local rotation in a fluid flow

vor·ti·cose \'vȯr-ti-,kōs\ *adjective* (1783)
archaic : VORTICAL

vo·ta·ress \'vō-tə-rəs\ *noun* (1589)
: a female votary

vo·ta·rist \-rist\ *noun* (1603)
: VOTARY

vo·ta·ry \'vō-tə-rē\ *noun, plural* **-ries** [Latin *votum* vow] (1546)
1 *archaic* : a sworn adherent
2 a : ENTHUSIAST, DEVOTEE **b** : a devoted admirer
3 a : a devout or zealous worshiper **b** : a staunch believer or advocate

¹vote \'vōt\ *noun* [Middle English (Scots), from Latin *votum* vow, wish — more at VOW] (15th century)
1 a : a usually formal expression of opinion or will in response to a proposed decision; *especially* : one given as an indication of approval or disapproval of a proposal, motion, or candidate for office **b** : the total number of such expressions of opinion made known at a single time (as at an election) **c** : an expression of opinion or preference that resembles a vote **d** : BALLOT 1
2 : the collective opinion or verdict of a body of persons expressed by voting
3 : the right to cast a vote; *specifically* : the right of suffrage : FRANCHISE
4 a : the act or process of voting ⟨brought the question to a *vote*⟩ **b** : a method of voting
5 : a formal expression of a wish, will, or choice voted by a meeting
6 a : VOTER **b** : a group of voters with some common and identifying characteristics ⟨the labor *vote*⟩
7 *chiefly British* **a** : a proposition to be voted on; *especially* : a legislative money item **b** : APPROPRIATION

²vote *verb* **vot·ed; vot·ing** (1552)
intransitive verb
1 : to express one's views in response to a poll; *especially* : to exercise a political franchise
2 : to express an opinion ⟨consumers . . . *vote* with their dollars —Lucia Mouat⟩
transitive verb
1 : to choose, endorse, decide the disposition of, defeat, or authorize by vote
2 a : to adjudge by general agreement : DECLARE **b** : to offer as a suggestion : PROPOSE ⟨*vote* we all go home⟩
3 a : to cause to vote in a given way **b** : to cause to be cast for or against a proposal
4 : to vote in accordance with or in the interest of ⟨*vote* your conscience⟩ ⟨*voted* their pocketbooks⟩

vote·less \'vōt-ləs\ *adjective* (1672)
: having no vote; *especially* : denied the political franchise

vot·er \'vō-tər\ *noun* (circa 1578)
: one that votes or has the legal right to vote

voting machine *noun* (1900)
: a mechanical device for recording and counting votes cast in an election

☆ SYNONYMS
Voracious, gluttonous, ravenous, rapacious mean excessively greedy. VORACIOUS applies especially to habitual gorging with food or drink ⟨teenagers are often *voracious* eaters⟩. GLUTTONOUS applies to one who delights in eating or acquiring things especially beyond the point of necessity or satiety ⟨an admiral who was *gluttonous* for glory⟩. RAVENOUS implies excessive hunger and suggests violent or grasping methods of dealing with food or with whatever satisfies an appetite ⟨a nation with a *ravenous* lust for territorial expansion⟩. RAPACIOUS often suggests excessive and utterly selfish acquisitiveness or avarice ⟨*rapacious* developers indifferent to environmental concerns⟩.

vo·tive \'vō-tiv\ *adjective* [Latin *votivus*, from *votum* vow] (1597)
1 : consisting of or expressing a vow, wish, or desire ⟨a *votive* prayer⟩
2 : offered or performed in fulfillment of a vow or in gratitude or devotion
— **vo·tive·ly** *adverb*
— **vo·tive·ness** *noun*

votive candle *noun* (1824)
1 : a candle lit in devotion or gratitude
2 : a small squat candle

votive mass *noun* (1738)
: a mass celebrated for a special intention (as for a wedding or funeral) in place of the mass of the day

vo·tress \'vō-trəs\ *noun* [by alteration] (1590)
archaic : VOTARESS

¹vouch \'vau̇ch\ *verb* [Middle English *vochen*, *vouchen*, from Middle French *vocher*, from Latin *vocare* to call, summon, from *vox* voice — more at VOICE] (14th century)
transitive verb
1 : to summon into court to warrant or defend a title
2 *archaic* **a** : ASSERT, AFFIRM **b** : ATTEST
3 *archaic* : to cite or refer to as authority or supporting evidence
4 a : PROVE, SUBSTANTIATE **b** : to verify (a business transaction) by examining documentary evidence
intransitive verb
1 : to give a guarantee : become surety
2 a : to supply supporting evidence or testimony **b** : to give personal assurance
synonym see CERTIFY

²vouch *noun* (1603)
obsolete : ALLEGATION, DECLARATION

vouch·ee \vau̇-'chē\ *noun* (15th century)
: a person for whom another vouches

¹vouch·er \'vau̇-chər\ *noun* [Middle French *vocher*, *voucher* to vouch] (circa 1523)
1 : an act of vouching
2 a : a piece of supporting evidence : PROOF **b** : a documentary record of a business transaction **c** : a written affidavit or authorization : CERTIFICATE **d** : a form or check indicating a credit against future purchases or expenditures

²voucher *transitive verb* (1609)
1 : to establish the authenticity of
2 : to prepare a voucher for

³voucher *noun* [¹*vouch* + ²-*er*] (1612)
archaic : one that guarantees : SURETY

vouch·safe \vau̇ch-'sāf, 'vau̇ch-,\ *transitive verb* **vouch·safed; vouch·saf·ing** (1587)
1 a : to grant or furnish often in a gracious or condescending manner **b** : to give by way of reply ⟨refused to *vouchsafe* an explanation⟩
2 : to grant as a privilege or special favor
synonym see GRANT
— **vouch·safe·ment** \vau̇ch-'sāf-mənt\ *noun*

vous·soir \vü-'swär, 'vü-,\ *noun* [French, from (assumed) Vulgar Latin *volsorium*, from Latin *volvere* to roll — more at VOLUBLE] (1728)
: one of the wedge-shaped pieces forming an arch or vault — see ARCH illustration

Vou·vray \vü-'vrā\ *noun* [French, from *Vouvray*, village in France] (1885)
: a semidry to semisweet white wine from the Loire Valley of France that is often produced as a sparkling wine

¹vow \'vau̇\ *noun* [Middle English *vowe*, from Old French *vou*, from Latin *votum*, from neuter of *votus*, past participle of *vovēre* to vow; akin to Greek *euchesthai* to pray, vow, Sanskrit *vāghat* sacrificer] (14th century)
: a solemn promise or assertion; *specifically* : one by which a person is bound to an act, service, or condition

²vow (14th century)
transitive verb
1 : to promise solemnly : SWEAR
2 : to bind or consecrate by a vow
intransitive verb
: to make a vow
— **vow·er** \'vau̇(-ə)r\ *noun*

³vow *transitive verb* [Middle English, short for *avowen*] (14th century)
: AVOW, DECLARE

vow·el \'vau̇(-ə)l\ *noun* [Middle English, from Middle French *vouel*, from Latin *vocalis* — more at VOCALIC] (14th century)
1 : one of a class of speech sounds in the articulation of which the oral part of the breath channel is not blocked and is not constricted enough to cause audible friction; *broadly* : the one most prominent sound in a syllable
2 : a letter or other symbol representing a vowel — usually used in English of *a, e, i, o, u,* and sometimes *y*

vow·el·ize \'vau̇-(ə-)līz\ *transitive verb* **-ized; -iz·ing** (1883)
: to furnish with vowel points

vowel point *noun* (1764)
: a mark placed below or otherwise near a consonant in some languages (as Hebrew) and representing the vowel sound that precedes or follows the consonant sound

vowel rhyme *noun* (1838)
: ASSONANCE 2b

vox po·pu·li \'väks-'pä-pyü-,lī, -pyə-(,)lē, -pə-(,)lē\ *noun* [Latin, voice of the people] (circa 1550)
: popular sentiment

¹voy·age \'vȯi-ij, 'vȯ(-)ij\ *noun* [Middle English, from Old French *voiage*, from Late Latin *viaticum*, from Latin, traveling money, from neuter of *viaticus* of a journey, from *via* way — more at WAY] (14th century)
1 : an act or instance of traveling : JOURNEY
2 : a course or period of traveling by other than land routes
3 : an account of a journey especially by sea

²voyage *verb* **voy·aged; voy·ag·ing** (15th century)
intransitive verb
: to take a trip : TRAVEL
transitive verb
: SAIL, TRAVERSE
— **voy·ag·er** *noun*

voya·geur \,vȯi-ə-'zhər, ,vwä-yä-\ *noun* [Canadian French, from French, traveler, from *voyager* to travel, from *voyage* voyage, from Old French *voiage*] (1793)
: a man employed by a fur company to transport goods to and from remote stations especially in the Canadian Northwest

voy·eur \vwä-'yər, vȯi-'ər\ *noun* [French, literally, one who sees, from Middle French, from *voir* to see, from Latin *vidēre* — more at WIT] (1900)
1 : one obtaining sexual gratification from seeing sex organs and sexual acts; *broadly* : one who habitually seeks sexual stimulation by visual means
2 : a prying observer who is usually seeking the sordid or the scandalous
— **voy·eur·ism** \-,i-zəm\ *noun*
— **voy·eur·is·tic** \,vwä-(,)yər-'is-tik, ,vȯi-ər-\ *adjective*
— **voy·eur·is·ti·cal·ly** \-ti-k(ə-)lē\ *adverb*

vroom \'vrüm, və-'rüm\ *intransitive verb* [imitative of the noise of an engine] (1965)
: to operate a motor vehicle at high speed or so as to create a great deal of engine noise

V sign *noun* (1942)
: a sign made by raising the index and middle fingers in a V and used as a victory salute or a gesture of approval

V–2 \'vē-'tü\ *noun* [German, abbreviation for *Vergeltungswaffe 2*, literally, reprisal weapon 2] (1944)
: a rocket-propelled bomb of German invention

vug \'vəg\ *noun* [Cornish dialect *vooga* underground chamber, from Latin *fovea* small pit] (1818)
: a small unfilled cavity in a lode or in rock
— **vug·gy** \'və-gē\ *adjective*

Vul·can \'vəl-kən\ *noun* [Latin *Volcanus, Vulcanus*]
: the Roman god of fire and metalworking — compare HEPHAESTUS

vul·ca·ni·an \,vəl-'kā-nē-ən\ *adjective* (1602)
1 *capitalized* : of or relating to Vulcan or to working in metals (as iron)
2 : of or relating to a volcanic eruption in which highly viscous or solid lava is blown into fragments and dust

vul·ca·nic·i·ty \,vəl-kə-'ni-sə-tē\ *noun* (1873)
: VOLCANISM

vul·ca·ni·sate, vul·ca·ni·sa·tion, vul·ca·nise *British variant of* VULCANIZATE, VULCANIZATION, VULCANIZE

vul·ca·nism \'vəl-kə-,ni-zəm\ *noun* (1877)
: VOLCANISM

vul·ca·ni·zate \'vəl-kə-nə-,zāt, ,vəl-kə-'nī-\ *noun* [back-formation from *vulcanization*] (1926)
: a vulcanized product

vul·ca·ni·za·tion \,vəl-kə-nə-'zā-shən\ *noun* (1846)
: the process of treating crude or synthetic rubber or similar plastic material chemically to give it useful properties (as elasticity, strength, and stability)

vul·ca·nize \'vəl-kə-,nīz\ *verb* **-nized; -niz·ing** [International Scientific Vocabulary, from Latin *Vulcanus* Vulcan, fire] (1846)
transitive verb
: to subject to vulcanization
intransitive verb
: to undergo vulcanization
— **vul·ca·niz·er** *noun*

vulcanized fiber *noun* [from *Vulcanized Fibre*, a trademark] (circa 1884)
: a tough substance made by treatment of cellulose and used for luggage and electrical insulation and in packaging

vul·ca·nol·o·gy \,vəl-kə-'nä-lə-jē\ *noun* [International Scientific Vocabulary] (1858)
: VOLCANOLOGY
— **vul·ca·nol·o·gist** \-jist\ *noun*

vul·gar \'vəl-gər\ *adjective* [Middle English, from Latin *vulgaris* of the mob, vulgar, from *volgus, vulgus* mob, common people] (14th century)
1 a : generally used, applied, or accepted **b** : understood in or having the ordinary sense ⟨they reject the *vulgar* conception of miracle —W. R. Inge⟩
2 : VERNACULAR ⟨the *vulgar* name of a plant⟩
3 a : of or relating to the common people : PLEBEIAN **b** : generally current : PUBLIC ⟨the *vulgar* opinion of that time⟩ **c** : of the usual, typical, or ordinary kind
4 a : lacking in cultivation, perception, or taste : COARSE **b** : morally crude, undeveloped, or unregenerate : GROSS **c** : ostentatious or excessive in expenditure or display : PRETENTIOUS
5 a : offensive in language : EARTHY **b** : lewdly or profanely indecent
synonym see COMMON, COARSE
— **vul·gar·ly** *adverb*

vulgar era *noun* (1716)
: CHRISTIAN ERA

vul·gar·i·an \,vəl-'gar-ē-ən, -'ger-\ *noun* (1804)
: a vulgar person

vul·gar·ise *British variant of* VULGARIZE

vul·gar·ism \'vəl-gə-,ri-zəm\ *noun* (circa 1676)
1 : VULGARITY
2 a : a word or expression originated or used chiefly by illiterate persons **b** : a coarse word or phrase : OBSCENITY

vul·gar·i·ty \,vəl-'gar-ə-tē\ *noun, plural* **-ties** (1579)
1 : something vulgar

2 : the quality or state of being vulgar

vul·gar·ize \'vəl-gə-,rīz\ *transitive verb* **-ized; -iz·ing** (1709)
1 : to diffuse generally : POPULARIZE
2 : to make vulgar : COARSEN
— **vul·gar·i·za·tion** \,vəl-gə-rə-'zā-shən\ *noun*
— **vul·gar·iz·er** \'vəl-gə-,rī-zər\ *noun*

Vulgar Latin *noun* (1818)
: the nonclassical Latin of ancient Rome including the speech of plebeians and the informal speech of the educated established by comparative evidence as the chief source of the Romance languages

vul·gate \'vəl-,gāt, -gət\ *noun* [Medieval Latin *vulgata,* from Late Latin *vulgata editio* edition in general circulation] (1728)
1 *capitalized* : a Latin version of the Bible authorized and used by the Roman Catholic Church
2 : a commonly accepted text or reading
3 : the speech of the common people and especially of uneducated people

vul·gus \'vəl-gəs\ *noun* [probably alteration of obsolete *vulgars* English sentences to be translated into Latin] (1856)
: a short composition in Latin verse formerly common as an exercise in some English public schools

vul·ner·a·ble \'vəl-n(ə-)rə-bəl, 'vəl-nər-bəl\ *adjective* [Late Latin *vulnerabilis,* from Latin *vulnerare* to wound, from *vulner-, vulnus* wound; probably akin to Latin *vellere* to pluck, Greek *oulē* wound] (1605)
1 : capable of being physically wounded
2 : open to attack or damage : ASSAILABLE
3 : liable to increased penalties but entitled to increased bonuses after winning a game in contract bridge
— **vul·ner·a·bil·i·ty** \,vəl-n(ə-)rə-'bi-lə-tē\ *noun*
— **vul·ner·a·ble·ness** \'vəl-n(ə-)rə-bəl-nəs, 'vəl-nər-bəl-\ *noun*
— **vul·ner·a·bly** \-blē\ *adverb*

¹vul·ner·ary \'vəl-nə-,rer-ē\ *adjective* [Latin *vulnerarius,* from *vulner-, vulnus*] (1599)
: used for or useful in healing wounds ⟨*vulnerary* plants⟩

²vulnerary *noun, plural* **-ar·ies** (1601)
: a vulnerary remedy

vul·pine \'vəl-,pīn\ *adjective* [Latin *vulpinus,* from *vulpes* fox; perhaps akin to Greek *alōpēx* fox — more at ALOPECIA] (1628)
1 : of, relating to, or resembling a fox
2 : FOXY, CRAFTY

vul·ture \'vəl-chər\ *noun* [Middle English, from Latin *vultur*] (14th century)

1 : any of various large raptorial birds (families Accipitridae and Cathartidae) that are related to the hawks, eagles, and falcons but have weaker claws and the head usually naked and that subsist chiefly or entirely on carrion
2 : a rapacious or predatory person
— **vul·tur·ish** \-chə-rish\ *adjective*

vul·tur·ine \-chə-,rīn\ *adjective* (1647)
1 : of, relating to, or characteristic of vultures
2 : RAPACIOUS, PREDATORY ⟨*vulturine* legislators⟩

vul·tur·ous \'vəl-chə-rəs, 'vəlch-rəs\ *adjective* (1623)
: resembling a vulture especially in rapacity or scavenging habits

vul·va \'vəl-və\ *noun, plural* **vul·vae** \-,vē, -,vī\ [New Latin, from Latin *volva, vulva* womb, female genitals; akin to Sanskrit *ulva* womb and perhaps to Latin *volvere* to roll — more at VOLUBLE] (circa 1577)
: the external parts of the female genital organs
— **vul·val** \'vəl-vəl\ *or* **vul·var** \-vər, -,vär\ *adjective*

vul·vo·vag·i·ni·tis \,vəl-(,)vō-,va-jə-'nī-təs\ *noun* [New Latin] (1897)
: coincident inflammation of the vulva and vagina

vying *present participle of* VIE

W *is the twenty-third letter of the English alphabet. In form and origin,* W *is a ligature,* VV *or* UU, *called "double* u," *which was introduced into English by French scribes in the 11th century to replace an Old English runic character called* wynn. *The sound of* w *is usually a consonant, as in* we. *In English, with minor exceptions,* w *represents a vowel only in diphthongs, as in* few *and* how. W *appears also in the frequent consonantal group* wh, *as in* what *and* white. *Written* W *is silent in some words, as* wrist *and* answer. *Words with* W *are almost wholly of Germanic origin, either by inheritance through Old English or by borrowing from Old Norse or from Old North French. In the latter, Germanic loanwords appear with* w *instead of with the* gu *or* g *that prevails in central Old French and in Modern French (as seen in Old North French* wage *"pledge" contrasting with Old French* guage *"pledge"). Small* w *was formed by a simple reduction in the size of the capital.*

w \'də-bəl-(ˌ)yü, 'də-bə-; 'dəb-(ˌ)yü, -yə; 'dəb-yē\ *noun, plural* **w's** *or* **ws** \-(ˌ)yüz, -yəz, -yēz\ *often capitalized, often attributive* (15th century)
1 a : the 23d letter of the English alphabet **b :** a graphic representation of this letter **c :** a speech counterpart of orthographic *w*
2 : a graphic device for reproducing the letter *w*
3 : one designated *w* especially as the 23d in order or class
4 : something shaped like the letter W
W *noun* (1960)
: W PARTICLE
wab·ble \'wä-bəl\ *variant of* WOBBLE
Wac \'wak\ *noun* [Women's Army Corps] (1943)
: a member of the Women's Army Corps
wacked–out *variant of* WHACKED-OUT
wacko \'wa-(ˌ)kō\ *adjective* [by alteration] (1975)
: WACKY
— **wacko** *noun*
wacky \'wa-kē\ *adjective* **wack·i·er; -est** [perhaps from English dialect *whacky* fool] (circa 1935)
: absurdly or amusingly eccentric or irrational : CRAZY
— **wack·i·ly** \'wa-kə-lē\ *adverb*
— **wack·i·ness** \'wa-kē-nəs\ *noun*
¹**wad** \'wäd\ *noun* [Medieval Latin *wadda*] (1573)
1 : a small mass, bundle, or tuft: as **a :** a soft mass especially of a loose fibrous material variously used (as to stop an aperture, pad a garment, or hold grease around an axle) **b** (1) : a soft plug used to retain a powder charge or to avoid windage especially in a muzzle-loading gun (2) **:** a felt or paper disk used to separate the components of a shotgun cartridge **c :** a small mass of a chewing substance ⟨a *wad* of gum⟩
2 : a considerable amount (as of money)
3 a : a roll of paper money **b :** MONEY
²**wad** *transitive verb* **wad·ded; wad·ding** (1579)
1 a : to insert a wad into ⟨*wad* a gun⟩ **b :** to hold in by a wad ⟨*wad* a bullet in a gun⟩
2 : to form into a wad or wadding; *especially* : to roll or crush into a tight wad
3 : to stuff or line with some soft substance
— **wad·der** *noun*
wad·ding \'wä-diŋ\ *noun* (1627)
1 : wads or material for making wads
2 : a soft mass or sheet of short loose fibers used for stuffing or padding

¹**wad·dle** \'wä-dᵊl\ *intransitive verb* **wad·dled; wad·dling** \'wäd-liŋ, 'wä-dᵊl-iŋ\ [frequentative of *wade*] (1592)
1 : to walk with short steps swinging the forepart of the body from side to side
2 : to move clumsily in a manner suggesting a waddle
— **wad·dler** \'wäd-lər, 'wä-dᵊl-ər\ *noun*
²**waddle** *noun* (1691)
: an awkward clumsy swaying gait
¹**wad·dy** \'wä-dē\ *noun, plural* **waddies** [Dharuk (Australian aboriginal language of the Port Jackson area) *wadi* stick, wooden weapon] (circa 1790)
Australian **:** CLUB 1a
²**waddy** *transitive verb* **wad·died; wad·dy·ing** (1833)
Australian **:** to attack or beat with a waddy
³**wad·dy** *or* **wad·die** \'wä-dē\ *noun, plural* **waddies** [origin unknown] (1897)
West **:** COWBOY
¹**wade** \'wād\ *verb* **wad·ed; wad·ing** [Middle English, from Old English *wadan;* akin to Old High German *watan* to go, wade, Latin *vadere* to go] (13th century)
intransitive verb
1 : to step in or through a medium (as water) offering more resistance than air
2 : to move or proceed with difficulty or labor
3 : to set to work or attack with determination or vigor — used with *in* or *into* ⟨*wade* into a task⟩
transitive verb
: to pass or cross by wading
— **wad·able** *or* **wade·able** \'wā-də-bəl\ *adjective*
²**wade** *noun* (1665)
: an act of wading ⟨a *wade* in the brook⟩
Wade–Giles \'wād-'gīlz\ *noun* [Thomas F. Wade (died 1895) British diplomat & Herbert A. Giles (died 1935) British sinologist] (1943)
: a system for romanizing Chinese ideograms in which tones are indicated by superscript numbers and consonantal aspiration is indicated by an apostrophe — compare PINYIN
wad·er \'wā-dər\ *noun* (1673)
1 : one that wades
2 : SHOREBIRD; *also* **:** WADING BIRD
3 *plural* **:** high waterproof boots or a one-piece waterproof garment usually consisting of pants with attached boots that are used for wading (as when fishing)
wa·di \'wä-dē\ *noun* [Arabic *wādiy*] (1839)
1 : the bed or valley of a stream in regions of southwestern Asia and northern Africa that is usually dry except during the rainy season and that often forms an oasis **:** GULLY, WASH

2 : a shallow usually sharply defined depression in a desert region
wading bird *noun* (circa 1843)
: any of an order (Ciconiiformes) of long-legged birds (as herons, bitterns, storks, and flamingos) that wade in water in search of food
wading pool *noun* (1921)
: a shallow pool of portable or permanent construction used by children for wading

waders

wad·mal *or* **wad·mol** *or* **wad·mel** \'wäd-məl\ *noun* [Middle English *wadmale*, from Old Norse *vathmāl*, literally, standard cloth, from *vāth* cloth, clothing + *māl* measure; akin to Latin *metiri* to measure — more at WEED, MEASURE] (14th century)
: a coarse rough woolen fabric formerly used in the British Isles and Scandinavia for protective coverings and warm clothing
wae·sucks \'wā-ˌsəks\ *interjection* [Scots *wae* woe (from Middle English *wa*) + *sucks*, alteration of English *sakes* — more at WOE] (circa 1774)
Scottish **:** used to express pity
Waf \'waf\ *noun* [Women in the Air Force] (1948)
: a member of the women's component of the air force formed after World War II
¹**wa·fer** \'wā-fər\ *noun* [Middle English, from Old North French *waufre*, of Germanic origin; akin to Middle Dutch *wafel, wafer* waffle] (14th century)
1 a : a thin crisp cake, candy, or cracker **b :** a round thin piece of unleavened bread used in the celebration of the Eucharist
2 : an adhesive disk of dried paste with added coloring matter used as a seal
3 a : a thin disk or ring resembling a wafer and variously used (as for a valve or diaphragm) **b :** a thin slice of semiconductor (as silicon) used as a base for an electronic component or circuit
²**wafer** *transitive verb* **wa·fered; wa·fer·ing** \-f(ə-)riŋ\ (1748)
1 : to seal, close, or fasten with a wafer
2 : to divide (as a silicon rod) into wafers
waff \'waf\ *noun* [English dialect *waff* to wave] (1600)
1 *chiefly Scottish* **:** a waving motion
2 *chiefly Scottish* **:** PUFF, GUST
¹**waf·fle** \'wä-fəl, 'wò-\ *noun* [Dutch *wafel*, from Middle Dutch *wafel, wafer;* akin to Old English *wefan* to weave] (1744)
: a crisp cake of batter baked in a waffle iron
²**waffle** *intransitive verb* **waf·fled; waf·fling** \-f(ə-)liŋ\ [frequentative of obsolete *woff* to yelp, of imitative origin] (1868)
1 : EQUIVOCATE, VACILLATE; *also* **:** YO-YO, FLIP-FLOP
2 : to talk or write foolishly **:** BLATHER ⟨can *waffle . . .* tiresomely off the point —*Times Literary Supplement*⟩
— **waf·fler** \-f(ə-)lər\ *noun*
³**waffle** *noun* (circa 1888)
: empty or pretentious words **:** TRIPE
waffle iron *noun* (1794)
: a cooking utensil having two hinged metal parts that shut upon each other and impress surface projections on waffles that are being cooked
waf·fle-stomp·er \'wä-fəl-ˌstäm-pər, 'wò-, -ˌstòm-\ *noun* [from the pattern left by the soles] (1972)

\ə\ **abut** \ᵊ\ **kitten** \ər\ **further** \a\ **ash** \ā\ **ace**
\ä\ **mop, mar** \au̇\ **out** \ch\ **chin** \e\ **bet** \ē\ **easy**
\g\ **go** \i\ **hit** \ī\ **ice** \j\ **job** \ŋ\ **sing** \ō\ **go**
\ò\ **law** \òi\ **boy** \th\ **thin** \t̶h̶\ **the** \ü\ **loot** \u̇\ **foot**
\y\ **yet** \zh\ **vision** *see also* Guide to Pronunciation

: a hiking boot with a lug sole

¹waft \'wäft, 'waft\ *verb* [(assumed) Middle English *waughten* to guard, convoy, from Middle Dutch or Middle Low German *wachten* to watch, guard; akin to Old English *wæccan* to watch — more at WAKE] (circa 1562)
intransitive verb
: to move or go lightly on or as if on a buoyant medium
transitive verb
: to cause to move or go lightly by or as if by the impulse of wind or waves
— **waft·er** *noun*

²waft *noun* (1607)
1 : something (as an odor) that is wafted : WHIFF
2 : a slight breeze : PUFF
3 : the act of waving
4 : a pennant or flag used to signal or to show wind direction

waft·age \'wäf-tij, 'waf-\ *noun* (1558)
: the act of wafting or state of being wafted; *broadly* : CONVEYANCE

waf·ture \'wäf(t)-shər, 'waf(t)-\ *noun* (1601)
: the act of waving or a wavelike motion

¹wag \'wag\ *verb* **wagged; wag·ging** [Middle English *waggen*; akin to Middle High German *wacken* to totter, Old English *wegan* to move — more at WAY] (13th century)
intransitive verb
1 : to be in motion : STIR
2 : to move to and fro or up and down especially with quick jerky motions
3 : to move in chatter or gossip ⟨scandal caused tongues to *wag*⟩
4 *archaic* : DEPART
5 : WADDLE
transitive verb
1 : to swing to and fro or up and down especially with quick jerky motions : SWITCH; *specifically* : to nod (the head) or shake (a finger) at (as in assent or mild reproof)
2 : to move (as the tongue) animatedly in conversation
— **wag·ger** *noun*

²wag *noun* (1589)
: an act of wagging : SHAKE

³wag *noun* [probably short for obsolete English *waghalter* gallows bird, from English ¹*wag* + *halter*] (circa 1553)
1 : WIT, JOKER
2 *obsolete* : a young man : CHAP

¹wage \'wāj\ *noun* [Middle English, pledge, wage, from Old North French, of Germanic origin; akin to Gothic *wadi* pledge — more at WED] (14th century)
1 a : a payment usually of money for labor or services usually according to contract and on an hourly, daily, or piecework basis — often used in plural **b** *plural* : the share of the national product attributable to labor as a factor in production
2 : RECOMPENSE, REWARD — usually used in plural but singular or plural in construction (the *wages* of sin is death —Romans 6:23 (Revised Standard Version))
— **wage·less** \'wāj-ləs\ *adjective*

²wage *verb* **waged; wag·ing** [Middle English, to pledge, give as security, from Old North French *wagier*, from *wage*] (15th century)
transitive verb
: to engage in or carry on ⟨*wage* war⟩ ⟨*wage* a campaign⟩
intransitive verb
: to be in process of occurring ⟨the riot *waged* for several hours —*American Guide Series: Maryland*⟩

wage earner *noun* (1885)
: a person who works for wages or salary

¹wa·ger \'wā-jər\ *noun* [Middle English, pledge, bet, from Anglo-French *wageure*, from Old North French *wagier* to pledge] (14th century)

1 a : something (as a sum of money) risked on an uncertain event : STAKE **b** : something on which bets are laid : GAMBLE ⟨do a stunt as a *wager*⟩
2 *archaic* : an act of giving a pledge to take and abide by the result of some action

²wager *verb* **wa·gered; wa·ger·ing** \'wāj-riŋ, 'wā-jə-\ (1602)
intransitive verb
: to make a bet
transitive verb
: to risk or venture on a final outcome; *specifically* : to lay as a gamble : BET ⟨*wager* $5 on a horse⟩
— **wa·ger·er** \'wā-jər-ər\ *noun*

wage scale *noun* (1902)
: a schedule of wage rates for related tasks; *broadly* : the general level of wages in an industry or region

wage slave *noun* (1886)
: a person dependent on wages or a salary for a livelihood

wage-work·er \'wāj-,wər-kər\ *noun* (1876)
: WAGE EARNER

wag·gery \'wa-gə-rē\ *noun, plural* **-ger·ies** (1594)
1 : mischievous merriment : PLEASANTRY
2 : JEST; *especially* : PRACTICAL JOKE

wag·gish \'wa-gish\ *adjective* (1589)
1 : resembling or characteristic of a wag ⟨a *waggish* friend⟩ ⟨a *waggish* prose style⟩
2 : done or made in waggery or for sport : HUMOROUS ⟨*waggish* spoofs of popular songs⟩
— **wag·gish·ly** *adverb*
— **wag·gish·ness** *noun*

¹wag·gle \'wa-gəl\ *verb* **wag·gled; wag·gling** \-g(ə-)liŋ\ [frequentative of ¹*wag*] (1594)
transitive verb
: to move frequently one way and the other : WAG
intransitive verb
: to reel, sway, or move from side to side : WAG
— **wag·gly** \-g(ə-)lē\ *adjective*

²waggle *noun* (circa 1866)
1 : an instance of waggling : a jerky motion back and forth or up and down
2 : a preliminary swinging of a golf club head back and forth over the ball before the swing

wag·gon *chiefly British variant of* WAGON

¹Wag·ne·ri·an \väg-'nir-ē-ən, -'ner-\ *adjective* [Richard *Wagner*] (1873)
: of, relating to, characteristic, or suggestive of Wagner or his music or theories

²Wagnerian *noun* (1882)
: an admirer of the musical theories and style of Wagner

Wag·ner·ite \'väg-nə-,rīt\ *noun* (1855)
: WAGNERIAN

¹wag·on \'wa-gən\ *noun* [Dutch *wagen*, from Middle Dutch — more at WAIN] (15th century)
1 a : a usually four-wheel vehicle for transporting bulky commodities and drawn originally by animals **b** : a lighter typically horse-drawn vehicle for transporting goods or passengers **c** : PADDY WAGON
2 *British* : a railway freight car
3 : a low four-wheel vehicle with an open rectangular body and a retroflex tongue made for the play or use (as for carrying newspapers) of a child
4 : a small wheeled table used for the service of a dining room
5 : a delivery truck ⟨milk *wagon*⟩
6 : STATION WAGON
— **off the wagon** : no longer abstaining from alcoholic beverages
— **on the wagon** : abstaining from alcoholic beverages

²wagon (1606)
intransitive verb
: to travel or transport goods by wagon

transitive verb : to transport (goods) by wagon

wag·on·er \'wa-gə-nər\ *noun* (1544)
1 : a person who drives a wagon or transports goods by wagon
2 *capitalized, obsolete* : BOÖTES

wag·on·ette \,wa-gə-'net\ *noun* (circa 1858)
: a light wagon with two facing seats along the sides behind a transverse front seat

wa·gon–lit \vȧ-gōⁿ-lē\ *noun, plural* **wagons–lits** *or* **wagon–lits** \-gōⁿ-lē(z)\ [French, from *wagon* railroad car + *lit* bed] (1884)
: a railroad sleeping car

wagon master *noun* (1645)
: a person in charge of one or more wagons

wagon train *noun* (1810)
: a column of wagons (as of supplies for a group of settlers) traveling overland

wag·tail \'wag-,tāl\ *noun* (1510)
: any of various chiefly Old World oscine birds (family Motacillidae) related to the pipits and having a trim slender body and a very long tail that they habitually jerk up and down

Wah·ha·bi *also* **Wa·ha·bi** \wə-'hä-bē, wä-\ *noun* [Arabic *wahhābīy*, from *wahhābī*, from Muḥammad born 'Abd al-*Wahhāb* (Abdul-Wahhab) (died 1787) Arabian religious reformer] (1807)
: a member of a puritanical Muslim sect founded in Arabia in the 18th century by Muhammad ibn-Abdul Wahhab and revived by ibn-Saud in the 20th century
— **Wah·ha·bism** \-'hä-,bi-zəm\ *noun*
— **Wah·ha·bite** \-,bīt\ *adjective or noun*

wa·hi·ne \wä-'hē-nē, -(,)nä\ *noun* [Maori & Hawaiian, woman] (1773)
1 : a Polynesian woman
2 : a female surfer

¹wa·hoo \'wä-,hü, 'wȯ-\ *noun, plural* **wa·hoos** [origin unknown] (1770)
: WINGED ELM

²wahoo *noun, plural* **wahoos** [Dakota *wáhu*, from *wá-* arrow + *hu* wood] (1857)
: a shrubby North American spindle tree (*Euonymus atropurpureus*) having purple capsules which in dehiscence expose the scarlet-ariled seeds — called also *burning bush*

³wahoo *noun, plural* **wahoos** [origin unknown] (circa 1900)
: a large vigorous mackerel (*Acanthocybium solandri*) that is common in warm seas and esteemed as a food and sport fish

⁴wa·hoo \wä-'hü\ *interjection* (circa 1924)
chiefly West — used to express exuberance or enthusiasm or to attract attention

wah·wah pedal *variant of* WA-WA PEDAL

¹waif \'wāf\ *noun* [Middle English, from Old North French, adjective, lost, unclaimed, probably of Scandinavian origin; akin to Old Norse *veif* something flapping, *veifa* to be in movement — more at WIPE] (14th century)
1 a : a piece of property found (as washed up by the sea) but unclaimed **b** *plural* : stolen goods thrown away by a thief in flight
2 a : something found without an owner and especially by chance **b** : a stray person or animal; *especially* : a homeless child
— **waif·like** \-,līk\ *adjective*

²waif *noun* (1530)
: WAFT 4

¹wail \'wā(ə)l\ *verb* [Middle English, of Scandinavian origin; akin to Old Norse *væla, væla* to wail; akin to Old Norse *vei* woe — more at WOE] (14th century)
intransitive verb
1 : to express sorrow audibly : LAMENT
2 : to make a sound suggestive of a mournful cry
3 : to express dissatisfaction plaintively : COMPLAIN
transitive verb
archaic : BEWAIL
— **wail·er** \'wā-lər\ *noun*

²wail *noun* (15th century)
1 : the act or practice of wailing : loud lamentation
2 a : a usually prolonged cry or sound expressing grief or pain **b** : a sound suggestive of wailing ⟨the *wail* of an air-raid siren⟩ **c** : a querulous expression of grievance : COMPLAINT

wail·ful \'wā(ə)l-fəl\ *adjective* (1544)
1 : uttering a sound suggestive of wailing
2 : expressing grief or pain : SORROWFUL, MOURNFUL
— **wail·ful·ly** \-fə-lē\ *adverb*

wailing wall *noun* (1919)
1 *capitalized* : a surviving section of the wall which in ancient times formed a part of the enclosure of Herod's temple near the Holy of Holies and at which Jews traditionally gather for prayer and religious lament
2 : a source of comfort and consolation in misfortune

wain \'wān\ *noun* [Middle English, wagon, chariot, from Old English *wægn*; akin to Middle Dutch *wagen* wagon, Old English *wegan* to move — more at WAY] (before 12th century)
1 : a usually large and heavy vehicle for farm use
2 *capitalized* [short for *Charles's Wain*] : BIG DIPPER

¹wain·scot \'wān-skət, -ˌskōt, -ˌskät\ *noun* [Middle English, from Middle Dutch *wagenschot*, probably from *wagen* wagon + *schot* shot, crossbar] (14th century)
1 *British* : a fine grade of oak imported for woodwork
2 a (1) : a usually paneled wooden lining of an interior wall (2) : a lining of an interior wall irrespective of material **b** : the lower three or four feet (about one meter) of an interior wall when finished differently from the remainder of the wall

²wainscot *transitive verb* **-scot·ed** *or* **-scot·ted; -scot·ing** *or* **-scot·ting** (circa 1570)
: to line with or as if with boards or paneling

wain·scot·ing *or* **wain·scot·ting** \-ˌskō-tiŋ, -ˌskä-, -skə-\ *noun* (1580)
1 : WAINSCOT 2
2 : material used to wainscot a surface

wain·wright \'wān-ˌrīt\ *noun* (before 12th century)
: a maker and repairer of wagons

waist \'wāst\ *noun* [Middle English *wast;* akin to Old English *wæstm* growth, *weaxan* to grow — more at WAX] (14th century)
1 a : the narrowed part of the body between the thorax and hips **b** : the greatly constricted basal part of the abdomen of some insects (as wasps and flies)
2 : the part of something corresponding to or resembling the human waist: as **a** (1) : the part of a ship's deck between the poop and forecastle (2) : the middle part of a sailing ship between foremast and mainmast **b** : the middle section of the fuselage of an airplane
3 : a garment or the part of a garment covering the body from the neck to the waistline or just below: **a** : BODICE 1 **b** : BLOUSE
4 : WAISTLINE 1b
— **waist·ed** \'wā-stəd\ *adjective*

waist·band \'wās(t)-ˌband\ *noun* (1584)
: a band (as of trousers or a skirt) fitting around the waist

waist·coat \'wes-kət, 'wās(t)-ˌkōt\ *noun* (1519)
1 : an ornamental garment worn under a doublet
2 *chiefly British* : VEST 2a
— **waist·coat·ed** \-ˌkō-təd\ *adjective*

waist·line \'wāst-ˌlīn\ *noun* (1896)
1 a : an arbitrary line encircling the narrowest part of the waist **b** : the part of a garment that

covers the waistline or may be above or below it as fashion dictates
2 : body circumference at the waist

¹wait \'wāt\ *verb* [Middle English, from Old North French *waitier* to watch, of Germanic origin; akin to Old High German *wahta* watch, Old English *wæccan* to watch — more at WAKE] (14th century)
transitive verb
1 : to stay in place in expectation of : AWAIT
2 : to delay serving (a meal)
3 : to serve as waiter for ⟨*wait* tables⟩
intransitive verb
1 a : to remain stationary in readiness or expectation ⟨*wait* for a train⟩ **b** : to pause for another to catch up — usually used with *up*
2 a : to look forward expectantly ⟨just *waiting* to see his rival lose⟩ **b** : to hold back expectantly ⟨*waiting* for a chance to strike⟩
3 : to serve at meals — usually used in such phrases as *wait on tables* or *wait on table*
4 a : to be ready and available ⟨slippers *waiting* by the bed⟩ **b** : to remain temporarily neglected or unrealized ◻
— **wait on** *also* **wait upon 1 a** : to attend as a servant **b** : to supply the wants of : SERVE
2 : to make a formal call on **3** : to wait for
— **wait up** : to delay going to bed : stay up

²wait *noun* [Middle English *waite* watchman, public musician, wait, from Old North French *waitman*, watch, watchman, of Germanic origin; akin to Old High German *wahta* watch] (14th century)
1 a : a hidden or concealed position — used chiefly in the expression *lie in wait* **b** : a state or attitude of watchfulness and expectancy ⟨anchored in *wait* for early morning fishing —Fred Zimmer⟩
2 a : one of a band of public musicians in England employed to play for processions or public entertainments **b** (1) : one of a group who serenade for gratuities especially at the Christmas season (2) : a piece of music by such a group
3 : an act or period of waiting ⟨a long *wait* in line⟩

wait·er \'wā-tər\ *noun* (15th century)
1 : one that waits on another; *especially* : a person who waits tables (as in a restaurant)
2 : a tray on which something (as a tea service) is carried : SALVER

waiting game *noun* (1890)
: a strategy in which one or more participants withhold action temporarily in the hope of having a favorable opportunity for more effective action later

waiting list *noun* (1897)
: a list or roster of those waiting (as for election to a club or admission to an educational institution)

waiting room *noun* (1683)
: a room (as in a doctor's office) for the use of persons (as patients) who are waiting

wait out *transitive verb* (1941)
: to await an end to ⟨*wait* the storm *out*⟩

wait·per·son \'wāt-ˌpər-s°n\ *noun* (1976)
: a waiter or waitress

wait·ress \'wā-trəs\ *noun* (1834)
: a woman who waits tables (as in a restaurant)
usage see -ESS
— **waitress** *intransitive verb*

waive \'wāv\ *transitive verb* **waived; waiving** [Middle English *weiven,* from Old North French *weyver,* from *waif* lost, unclaimed — more at WAIF] (14th century)
1 *archaic* : GIVE UP, FORSAKE
2 : to throw away (stolen goods)
3 *archaic* : to shunt aside (as a danger or duty) : EVADE
4 a : to relinquish voluntarily (as a legal right) ⟨*waive* a jury trial⟩ **b** : to refrain from pressing or enforcing (as a claim or rule) : FORGO

5 : to put off from immediate consideration : POSTPONE
6 : to dismiss with or as if with a wave of the hand ⟨*waived* the problem aside⟩
7 : to place (a ball player) on waivers; *also* : to release after placing on waivers
synonym see RELINQUISH

waiv·er \'wā-vər\ *noun* [Anglo-French *weyver,* from Old North French *weyver* to abandon, waive] (1628)
1 : the act of intentionally relinquishing or abandoning a known right, claim, or privilege; *also* : the legal instrument evidencing such an act
2 : the act of a club's waiving the right to claim a professional ball player who is being removed from another club's roster — often used in the phrase *on waivers* denoting the process by which a player to be removed from a roster is made available to other clubs ⟨was placed on *waivers* before being released⟩

Wa·kash·an \wȯ-'ka-shən, 'wȯ-ˌ\ *noun* (circa 1895)
: a family of American Indian languages spoken in coastal areas of British Columbia and northwest Washington

¹wake \'wāk\ *verb* **woke** \'wōk\ *also* **waked** \'wākt\; **wo·ken** \'wō-kən\ *or* **waked** *also* **woke; wak·ing** [partly from Middle English *waken* (past *wook,* past participle *waken*), from Old English *wacan* to awake (past *wōc,* past participle *wacen*); partly from Middle English *wakien, waken* (past & past participle *waked*), from Old English *wacian* to be awake (past *wacode,* past participle *wacod*); akin to Old English *wæccan* to watch, Latin *vegēre* to enliven] (before 12th century)
intransitive verb
1 a : to be or remain awake **b** *archaic* : to remain awake on watch especially over a corpse **c** *obsolete* : to stay up late in revelry
2 : AWAKE — often used with *up*
transitive verb
1 : to stand watch over (as a dead body); *especially* : to hold a wake over
2 a : to rouse from or as if from sleep : AWAKE — often used with *up* **b** : STIR, EXCITE ⟨*woke* up latent possibilities —Norman Douglas⟩ **c** : to arouse conscious interest in : ALERT — usually used with *to* ⟨*woke* the publishers to

◻ **USAGE**

wait American dialectologists have evidence showing *wait on* (sense 3) to be more a Southern than a Northern form in speech. Handbook writers universally denigrate *wait on* and prescribe *wait for* in writing. Our evidence from printed sources does not show a regional preference; it does show that the handbooks' advice is not based on current usage (settlement of the big problems still *waited on* Russia —*Time*⟩ ⟨I couldn't make out . . . whether Harper was *waiting on* me for approval —E. B. White⟩ ⟨the staggering bill that *waited on* them at the white commissary downtown —Maya Angelou⟩. One reason for the continuing use of *wait on* may lie in its being able to suggest protracted or irritating waits better than *wait for* ⟨for two days I've been *waiting on* weather —Charles A. Lindbergh⟩ ⟨the boredom of black Africans sitting there, *waiting on* the whims of a colonial bureaucracy —Vincent Canby⟩ ⟨doesn't care to sit around *waiting on* a House that's virtually paralyzed —Glenn A. Briere⟩. *Wait on* is less common than *wait for,* but if it seems natural, there is no reason to avoid it.

\ə\ **abut** \ᵊ\ **kitten** \ər\ **further** \a\ **ash** \ā\ **ace**
\ä\ **mop, mar** \au̇\ **out** \ch\ **chin** \e\ **bet** \ē\ **easy**
\g\ **go** \i\ **hit** \ī\ **ice** \j\ **job** \ŋ\ **sing** \ō\ **go**
\ȯ\ **law** \ȯi\ **boy** \th\ **thin** \th̲\ **the** \ü\ **loot** \u̇\ **foot**
\y\ **yet** \zh\ **vision** *see also* Guide to Pronunciation

the fact that there was an enormous . . . audience —Harrison Smith⟩ □
— **wak·er** *noun*
²**wake** *noun* (13th century)
1 : the state of being awake
2 a (1) **:** an annual English parish festival formerly held in commemoration of the church's patron saint (2) **:** VIGIL 1a **b :** the festivities originally connected with the wake of an English parish church — usually used in plural but singular or plural in construction **c** *British* **:** an annual holiday or vacation — usually used in plural but singular or plural in construction
3 : a watch held over the body of a dead person prior to burial and sometimes accompanied by festivity
³**wake** *noun* [of Scandinavian origin; akin to Old Norse *vǫk* hole in ice] (circa 1547)
1 : the track left by a moving body (as a ship) in a fluid (as water); *broadly* **:** a track or path left
2 : AFTERMATH 3
— **in the wake of 1 :** close behind and in the same path of travel ⟨*in the wake of* trappers and . . . riflemen came . . . settlers —American Guide Series: Indiana*⟩ **2 :** as a result of **:** as a consequence of ⟨power vacuums left *in the wake of* the second world war —A. M. Schlesinger (born 1917)⟩
wake·ful \'wāk-fəl\ *adjective* (1549)
: not sleeping or able to sleep **:** SLEEPLESS
— **wake·ful·ly** \-fə-lē\ *adverb*
— **wake·ful·ness** *noun*
wake·less \'wā-kləs\ *adjective* (1824)
: SOUND, UNBROKEN ⟨*wakeless* sleep⟩
wak·en \'wā-kən\ *verb* **wak·ened; wak·en·ing** \'wāk-niŋ, 'wā-kə-\ [Middle English *waknen*, from Old English *wæcnian*; akin to Old Norse *vakna* to awaken, Old English *wæccan* to watch] (before 12th century)
intransitive verb
: AWAKE — often used with *up*
transitive verb
: to rouse especially out of sleep **:** WAKE
wak·en·er \'wāk-nər, 'wā-kə-\ *noun* (1573)
archaic **:** one that causes to waken
wake·rife \'wāk-ˌrīf\ *adjective* [Middle English (Scots) *walkryfe*, from *walk* awake (from *waken, walken* to wake) + *ryfe* rife] (15th century)
Scottish **:** WAKEFUL, ALERT
wake-rob·in \'wāk-ˌrä-bən\ *noun* (circa 1530)
1 : TRILLIUM
2 : JACK-IN-THE-PULPIT
wake-up \'wāk-ˌəp\ *adjective* (1946)
: serving to wake up ⟨a *wake-up* call⟩ ⟨a *wake-up* cup of coffee⟩
wak·ing \'wā-kiŋ\ *adjective* (1567)
: passed in a conscious or alert state ⟨every *waking* hour⟩
Wal·den·ses \wȯl-'den(t)-ˌsēz, wäl-\ *noun plural* [Middle English *Waldensis*, from Medieval Latin *Waldenses, Valdenses*, from Peter Waldo (or *Valdo*)] (1537)
: a Christian sect arising in southern France in the 12th century, adopting Calvinist doctrines in the 16th century, and later living chiefly in Piedmont
— **Wal·den·sian** \-'den(t)-shən, -'den(t)-sē-ən\ *adjective or noun*
Wal·dorf salad \'wȯl-ˌdȯrf-\ *noun* [Waldorf-Astoria Hotel, New York City] (1902)
: a salad made typically of diced apples, celery, nuts, and mayonnaise
¹**wale** \'wā(ə)l\ *noun* [Middle English, from Old English *walu*; akin to Old Norse *vǫlr* staff and perhaps to Old Norse *valr* round, Latin *volvere* to roll — more at VOLUBLE] (before 12th century)
1 a : a streak or ridge made on the skin especially by the stroke of a whip **:** WEAL **b :** a narrow raised surface **:** RIDGE
2 : any of a number of strakes usually of extra thick and strong planks in the sides of a wooden ship — usually used in plural

3 a : one of a series of even ribs in a fabric **b :** the texture especially of a fabric
4 : a horizontal constructional member (as of timber or steel) used for bracing vertical members
²**wale** *transitive verb* **waled; wal·ing** (15th century)
: to mark (as the skin) with welts
³**wale** *noun* [Middle English (Scots & northern dialect) *wal*, from *wale*; akin to Old High German *wala* choice, Old English *wyllan* to wish — more at WILL] (14th century)
1 *dialect British* **:** CHOICE
2 *dialect British* **:** the best part **:** PICK
⁴**wale** *verb* (14th century)
dialect British **:** CHOOSE
wal·er \'wā-lər\ *noun, often capitalized* [New South *Wales*, Australia] (1849)
: a horse from New South Wales; *especially* **:** a rather large rugged saddle horse of mixed ancestry formerly exported in quantity from Australia to British India for military use
Wal·hal·la \väl-'hä-lə\ *noun* [German]
: VALHALLA
¹**walk** \'wȯk\ *verb* [partly from Middle English *walken* (past *welk*, past participle *walken*), from Old English *wealcan* to roll, toss, journey about (past *weolc*, past participle *wealcen*) and partly from Middle English *walkien* (past *walked*, past participle *walked*), from Old English *wealcian* to roll up, muffle up; akin to Middle Dutch *walken* to knead, press, full] (before 12th century)
intransitive verb
1 a *obsolete* **:** ROAM, WANDER **b** *of a spirit* **:** to move about in visible form **:** APPEAR **c** *of a ship* **:** to make headway
2 a : to move along on foot **:** advance by steps **b :** to come or go easily or readily **c :** to go on foot for exercise or pleasure **d :** to go at a walk
3 a : to pursue a course of action or way of life **:** conduct oneself **:** BEHAVE ⟨*walk* warily⟩ **b :** to be or act in association **:** continue in union ⟨the British and American peoples will . . . *walk* together side by side . . . in peace —Sir Winston Churchill⟩ **c :** WALK OUT ⟨the workers didn't like the new contract so they *walked*⟩
4 : to go to first base as a result of a base on balls
5 *of an inanimate object* **a :** to move in a manner that is suggestive of walking **b :** to stand with an appearance suggestive of strides ⟨pylons *walking* across the valley⟩
6 *of an astronaut* **:** to move about in space outside a spacecraft
transitive verb
1 a : to pass on foot or as if on foot through, along, over, or upon **:** TRAVERSE, PERAMBULATE ⟨*walk* the streets⟩ ⟨*walk* a tightrope⟩ **b :** to perform or accomplish by going on foot ⟨*walk* guard⟩
2 a : to cause (an animal) to go at a walk **:** take for a walk ⟨*walking* a dog⟩ **b** (1) **:** to cause to move by walking ⟨*walked* her bicycle up the hill⟩ (2) **:** to haul (as an anchor) by walking round the capstan
3 : to follow on foot for the purpose of measuring, surveying, or inspecting ⟨*walk* a boundary⟩
4 a : to accompany on foot **:** walk with ⟨*walked* her home⟩ **b :** to compel to walk (as by a command) **c :** to bring to a specified condition by walking ⟨*walked* us off our feet⟩
5 : to move (an object) in a manner suggestive of walking
6 : to perform (a dance) at a walking pace ⟨*walk* a quadrille⟩
7 : to give a base on balls to
— **walk away from 1 :** to outrun or get the better of without difficulty **2 :** to survive (an accident) with little or no injury
— **walk off with 1 a :** to steal and take away **b :** to take over unexpectedly from someone else **:** STEAL 1d ⟨*walked off with* the

show⟩ **2 :** to win or gain especially by outdoing one's competitors without difficulty
— **walk on :** to take advantage of **:** ABUSE
— **walk over :** to treat contemptuously
— **walk the plank 1 :** to walk under compulsion over the side of a ship into the sea **2 :** to resign an office or position under compulsion
— **walk through 1 :** to go through (as a theatrical role or familiar activity) perfunctorily (as in an early stage of rehearsal) **2 :** to guide (as a novice) through an unfamiliar or complex procedure step-by-step **3 :** to deal with or carry out perfunctorily
²**walk** *noun* (14th century)
1 a : an act or instance of going on foot especially for exercise or pleasure ⟨go for a *walk*⟩ **b :** SPACE WALK
2 : an accustomed place of walking **:** HAUNT
3 : a place designed for walking: **a :** a railed platform above the roof of a dwelling house **b** (1) **:** a path specially arranged or paved for walking (2) **:** SIDEWALK **c :** a public avenue for promenading **:** PROMENADE **d :** ROPEWALK
4 : a place or area of land in which animals feed and exercise with minimal restraint
5 : distance to be walked ⟨a quarter mile *walk* from here⟩
6 *British* **:** a ceremonial procession
7 : manner of living **:** CONDUCT, BEHAVIOR
8 a : the gait of a biped in which the feet are lifted alternately with one foot not clear of the ground before the other touches **b :** the gait of a quadruped in which there are always at least two feet on the ground; *specifically* **:** a four-beat gait of a horse in which the feet strike the ground in the sequence near hind, near fore, off hind, off fore **c :** a low rate of speed ⟨the shortage of raw materials slowed production to a *walk*⟩
9 : a route regularly traversed by a person in the performance of a particular activity (as patrolling, begging, or vending)
10 : characteristic manner of walking ⟨his *walk* is just like his father's⟩
11 a : social or economic status ⟨all *walks* of life⟩ **b** (1) **:** range or sphere of action **:** FIELD, PROVINCE (2) **:** VOCATION
12 : BASE ON BALLS
walk·about \'wȯ-kə-ˌbau̇t\ *noun* (1908)
1 : a short period of wandering bush life engaged in by an Australian aborigine as an occasional interruption of regular work

□ USAGE
wake *Wake* has such a large selection of forms for the past and past participle because it is the modern result of the coalescence of two old verbs, one with regular parts, one with irregular. What makes *wake* interesting is that preference for these forms has changed over time and is still changing. The regular *waked* was the prevalent form in the 16th, 17th, and 18th centuries. During the 19th century *woke* came into wide use for the past tense while *waked* continued as the past participle. In the 20th century *woken* has emerged as a strong contender to be the dominant past participle. These changes have not taken place uniformly, and they seem to have become prevalent in British English earlier than they did in American English. For instance *woken* seems to be the usual past participle for British writers ⟨in the mornings he was *woken* by his butler —Julian Huxley⟩ ⟨one night he was *woken* by someone coming into the bedroom —Graham Greene⟩ while in American English *waked* and *woken* are both used ⟨during the night he has *waked* up sweating —Mary McCarthy⟩ ⟨he had *woken* them, clearing his throat —John Updike⟩. *Woke* is much less frequent as a past participle than *waked* and *woken*.

2 : a walking tour **:** walking trip

walk·a·thon \ˈwȯ-kə-ˌthän\ *noun* [*walk* + *-athon*] (1932)
: a walk covering a considerable distance organized especially to raise money for a cause

walk·away \ˈwȯ-kə-ˌwā\ *noun* (1888)
: an easily won contest

walk·er \ˈwȯ-kər\ *noun* (14th century)
1 : one that walks: as **a :** a competitor in a walking race **b :** a peddler going on foot **c :** a temporary male escort of socially prominent women attending usually public events
2 : something used in walking: as **a :** a framework designed to support a baby learning to walk or an infirm or handicapped person **b :** a walking shoe

walk·ie–talk·ie \ˌwȯ-kē-ˈtȯ-kē, ˈwȯ-kē-ˌ\ *noun* (1939)
: a compact easily transportable battery‑operated radio transmitting and receiving set

¹walk–in \ˈwȯk-ˌin\ *adjective* (1926)
1 : large enough to be walked into ⟨a *walk-in* closet⟩
2 : arranged so as to be entered directly rather than through a lobby ⟨a *walk-in* apartment⟩
3 a : being a person who walks in without an appointment ⟨a *walk-in* blood donor⟩ **b :** of or relating to such persons ⟨*walk-in* clinic⟩

²walk–in \ˈwȯk-ˌin\ *noun* (1944)
1 : a walk-in refrigerator or cold storage room
2 : an easy election victory
3 : one who walks in without an appointment

¹walk·ing \ˈwȯ-kiŋ\ *noun* (15th century)
1 : the action of one that walks ⟨*walking* is good exercise⟩
2 : the condition of a surface for one going on foot ⟨the *walking* is slippery⟩

²walking *adjective* (15th century)
1 a : able to walk **:** AMBULATORY ⟨the *walking* wounded⟩ **b :** being the personification of a nonhuman quality or thing ⟨a *walking* encyclopedia⟩
2 a : used for or in walking ⟨*walking* shoes⟩ **b :** characterized by or consisting of the action of walking ⟨a *walking* tour⟩
3 : that moves or appears to move in a manner suggestive of walking; *especially* **:** that swings or rocks back and forth ⟨*walking* beam⟩
4 : guided or operated by a person on foot ⟨a *walking* plow⟩

walking catfish *noun* (1968)
: an Asian freshwater catfish (*Clarias batrachus* of the family Clariidae) that is able to move about on land and has become established in Florida waters

walking delegate *noun* (1889)
: a labor union representative appointed to visit members and their places of employment, to secure enforcement of union rules and agreements, and at times to represent the union in dealing with employers

walking leaf *noun* (1826)
: any of a family (Phylliidae) of phasmid insects with wings and legs resembling leaves

walking papers *noun plural* (1825)
: DISMISSAL, DISCHARGE — called also *walking ticket*

walking pneumonia *noun* (1964)
: a usually mild pneumonia caused by a mycoplasma (*Mycoplasma pneumoniae*) and characterized by malaise, cough, and often fever

walking stick *noun* (1580)
1 : a stick used in walking
2 *usually* **walk·ing·stick :** STICK INSECT; *especially* **:** a phasmid insect (*Diapheromera femorata*) common in parts of the U.S.

walkingstick

Walk·man \ˈwȯk-mən, -ˌman\ *trademark*
— used for a small portable radio or cassette player listened to by means of headphones or earphones

walk–on \ˈwȯk-ˌȯn, -ˌän\ *noun* (1902)
1 : a minor part (as in a dramatic production); *also* **:** an actor having such a part
2 : a college athlete who tries out for an athletic team without having been recruited or offered a scholarship

walk·out \ˈwȯk-ˌaut\ *noun* (1888)
1 : STRIKE 3a
2 : the action of leaving a meeting or organization as an expression of disapproval

walk out *intransitive verb* (1840)
1 : to leave suddenly often as an expression of disapproval
2 : to go on strike
— **walk out on :** to leave in the lurch **:** ABANDON, DESERT

walk·over \ˈwȯk-ˌō-vər\ *noun* (1838)
1 : a one-sided contest **:** an easy or uncontested victory
2 : a horse race with only one starter

walk–through \ˈwȯk-ˌthrü\ *noun* (1940)
1 : a perfunctory performance of a play or acting part (as in an early stage of rehearsal)
2 : a television rehearsal without cameras

¹walk–up \ˈwȯk-ˌəp\ *adjective* (1919)
1 : located above the ground floor in a building with no elevator ⟨a *walk-up* apartment⟩
2 : consisting of several stories and having no elevator ⟨a *walk-up* tenement⟩
3 : designed to allow pedestrians to be served without entering a building ⟨the *walk-up* window of a bank⟩

²walk–up *noun* (1924)
: a building or apartment house of several stories that has no elevator; *also* **:** an apartment or office in such a building

walk·way \ˈwȯk-ˌwā\ *noun* (1792)
: a passage for walking **:** WALK

Wal·ky·rie \väl-ˈkir-ē *also* väl-ˈkī-rē *or* ˈväl-kə-rē\ *noun* [German *Walküre* & Old Norse *valkyrja*]
: VALKYRIE

¹wall \ˈwȯl\ *noun* [Middle English, from Old English *weall*; akin to Middle High German *wall*; both from Latin *vallum* rampart, from *vallus* stake, palisade; perhaps akin to Old Norse *vǫlr* staff — more at WALE] (before 12th century)
1 a : a high thick masonry structure forming a long rampart or an enclosure chiefly for defense — often used in plural **b :** a masonry fence around a garden, park, or estate **c :** a structure that serves to hold back pressure (as of water or sliding earth)
2 : one of the sides of a room or building connecting floor and ceiling or foundation and roof
3 : the side of a footpath next to buildings
4 : an extreme or desperate position or a state of defeat, failure, or ruin — usually used in the phrase *to the wall*
5 : a material layer enclosing space ⟨the *wall* of a container⟩ ⟨heart *walls*⟩
6 : something resembling a wall (as in appearance, function, or effect); *especially* **:** something that acts as a barrier or defense ⟨a *wall* of reserve⟩ ⟨tariff *wall*⟩
— **walled** \ˈwȯld\ *adjective*
— **wall–like** \ˈwȯl-ˌlīk\ *adjective*
— **up the wall** *slang* **:** into a state of intense agitation, annoyance, or frustration ⟨the noise drove me *up the wall*⟩

²wall *transitive verb* (13th century)
1 a : to provide, cover with, or surround with or as if with a wall ⟨*wall* in the garden⟩ **b :** to separate by or as if by a wall ⟨*walled* off half the house⟩
2 a : IMMURE **b :** to close (an opening) with or as if with a wall

³wall *verb* [Middle English (Scots) *wawlen*, probably from Middle English *wawil-* (in *wawil-eghed* walleyed)] (15th century)
intransitive verb
of the eyes **:** to roll in a dramatic manner
transitive verb
: to roll (one's eyes) in a dramatic manner

wal·la·by \ˈwä-lə-bē\ *noun, plural* **wallabies** *also* **wallaby** [Dharuk (Australian aboriginal language of the Port Jackson area) *walaba*] (circa 1798)
: any of various small or medium-sized kangaroos (especially genus *Macropus*) — compare ROCK WALLABY

Wal·lace's line \ˈwä-lə-səz-\ *noun* [Alfred Russel *Wallace*] (1868)
: a hypothetical boundary that separates the highly distinctive floras and faunas of the Oriental and Australian biogeographic regions and passes between the islands of Bali and Lombok in Indonesia, between Borneo and Sulawesi, and between the Philippines and the Moluccas

wal·lah \ˈwä-lə, *in combination usually* ˌwä-lə\ *noun* [Hindi *-vālā* one in charge, from Sanskrit *pāla* protector, from *pālayati, pārayati* he guards; akin to Sanskrit *piparti* he brings over, saves, Old English *faran* to go — more at FARE] (1782)
: a person who is associated with a particular work or who performs a specific duty or service — usually used in combination ⟨the book *wallah* was an itinerant peddler —George Orwell⟩

wal·la·roo \ˌwä-lə-ˈrü\ *noun, plural* **-roos** [Dharuk (Australian aboriginal language of the Port Jackson area) *walaru*] (1827)
1 : a large reddish gray kangaroo (*Macropus robustus*) — called also *euro*
2 : either of two kangaroos (*Macropus antelopinus* and *M. bernardus*) related to the wallaroo

wall·board \ˈwȯl-ˌbōrd, -ˌbȯrd\ *noun* (1906)
: a structural boarding of any of various materials (as wood pulp, gypsum, or plastic) made in large rigid sheets and used especially for sheathing interior walls and ceilings

wal·let \ˈwä-lət\ *noun* [Middle English *walet*] (14th century)
1 : a bag for carrying miscellaneous articles while traveling
2 a : a folding pocketbook with compartments for personal papers and usually unfolded paper money; *also* **:** BILLFOLD **b :** a container that resembles a money wallet: as (1) **:** a usually flexible folding case fitted for carrying specific items (as tools or fishing flies) (2) **:** FOLDER 3

wall·eye \ˈwȯ-ˌlī\ *noun* [back-formation from *walleyed*] (1523)
1 a : an eye with a whitish or bluish white iris **b :** an eye with an opaque white cornea
2 a : strabismus in which the eye turns outward away from the nose **b :** an eye affected with divergent strabismus
3 : a large vigorous North American freshwater food and sport fish (*Stizostedion vitreum*) that has prominent eyes and is related to the perches but resembles the true pike — called also *walleyed pike*

wall·eyed \-ˈlīd\ *adjective* [by folk etymology from Middle English *wawil-eghed*, part translation of Old Norse *vagl-eygr* walleyed, from *vagl* beam (akin to Greek *ochleus* bar, Old English *wegan* to move, carry) + *eygr* eyed — more at WAY] (15th century)
1 : having walleyes or affected with walleye
2 : marked by a wild irrational staring of the eyes

walleye pollack *noun* (1907)

\ə\ abut	\ᵊ\ kitten	\ər\ further	\a\ ash	\ā\ ace	
\ä\ mop, mar	\au̇\ out	\ch\ chin	\e\ bet	\ē\ easy	
\g\ go	\i\ hit	\ī\ ice	\j\ job	\ŋ\ sing	\ō\ go
\ȯ\ law	\ȯi\ boy	\th\ thin	\t͟h\ the	\ü\ loot	\u̇\ foot
\y\ yet	\zh\ vision	*see also* Guide to Pronunciation			

: POLLACK 2

wall·flow·er \'wȯl-ˌflau̇(-ə)r\ *noun* (1578)
1 a : any of several Old World herbaceous or somewhat woody perennial plants (genus *Cheiranthus*) of the mustard family; *especially* **:** a hardy erect herb (*C. cheiri*) widely cultivated for its showy fragrant flowers **b :** any of a related genus (*Erysimum*) of plants with showy flowers
2 : a person who from shyness or unpopularity remains on the sidelines of a social activity (as a dance)
Wal·loon \wä-'lün\ *noun* [Middle French *Wallon*, adjective & noun, of Germanic origin; probably akin to Old High German *Walah* Celtic, Roman, Old English *Wealh* Celt, Welshman — more at WELSH] (1567)
1 : a member of a people of southern and southeastern Belgium and adjacent parts of France
2 : a French dialect of the Walloons
— **Walloon** *adjective*
¹**wal·lop** \'wä-ləp\ *verb* [Middle English *walopen* to gallop, from Old North French *waloper*] (1579)
intransitive verb
1 : to boil noisily
2 a : to move with reckless or disorganized haste **:** advance in a headlong rush **b :** WALLOW, FLOUNDER
transitive verb
1 a : to thrash soundly **:** LAMBASTE **b :** to beat by a wide margin **:** TROUNCE
2 : to hit with force **:** SOCK
— **wal·lop·er** *noun*
²**wallop** *noun* [Middle English, gallop, from Old North French *walop*, from *waloper* to gallop] (circa 1823)
1 a : a powerful blow **:** PUNCH **b :** something resembling a wallop especially in suddenness of force **c :** the ability (as of a boxer) to hit hard
2 a : emotional, sensory, or psychological force or influence **:** IMPACT ⟨a novel that packs a *wallop*⟩ **b :** an exciting emotional response **:** THRILL
3 *British* **:** BEER
wal·lop·ing *adjective* (circa 1847)
1 : LARGE, WHOPPING
2 : exceptionally fine or impressive **:** SMASHING
¹**wal·low** \'wä-(ˌ)lō\ *intransitive verb* [Middle English *walwen*, from Old English *wealwian* to roll — more at VOLUBLE] (before 12th century)
1 : to roll oneself about in an indolent or ungainly manner
2 : to billow forth **:** SURGE
3 : to devote oneself entirely; *especially* **:** to take unrestrained pleasure **:** DELIGHT
4 a : to become abundantly supplied **:** LUXURIATE ⟨a family that *wallows* in money⟩ **b :** to indulge oneself immoderately ⟨*wallowing* in self-pity⟩
5 : to become or remain helpless ⟨allowed them to *wallow* in their ignorance⟩
— **wal·low·er** \'wä-lə-wər\ *noun*
²**wallow** *noun* (15th century)
1 : an act or instance of wallowing
2 a : a muddy area or one filled with dust used by animals for wallowing **b :** a depression formed by or as if by the wallowing of animals
3 : a state of degradation or degeneracy
wall painting *noun* (1688)
: FRESCO
¹**wall·pa·per** \'wȯl-ˌpā-pər\ *noun* (1827)
: decorative paper for the walls of a room
²**wallpaper** (1924)
transitive verb
: to provide the walls of (a room) with wallpaper
intransitive verb
: to put wallpaper on a wall
wall plate *noun* (14th century)
: PLATE 5

wall plug *noun* (1888)
: an electric receptacle in a wall
wall rock *noun* (1876)
: a rock through which a fault or vein runs
wall rocket *noun* (1611)
: any of several Old World herbs (genus *Diplotaxis*) of the mustard family; *especially* **:** a yellow-flowered European herb (*D. tenuifolia*) adventive in North America
Wall Street \'wȯl-\ *noun* [*Wall Street*, New York City, site of the New York Stock Exchange] (1836)
: the influential financial interests of the U.S. economy
Wall Street·er \-ˌstrē-tər\ *noun* (1885)
: a person who is involved in Wall Street
wall system *noun* (1968)
: a set of shelves often with cabinets or bureaus that can be variously arranged along a wall
wall–to–wall *adjective* (1946)
1 : covering the entire floor ⟨*wall-to-wall* carpeting⟩
2 a : covering or filling one entire space or time ⟨a party crammed with *wall-to-wall* bodies⟩ **b :** occurring or found everywhere **:** UBIQUITOUS
wal·ly \'wä-lē\ *adjective* [probably from ³*wale*] (circa 1520)
Scottish **:** FINE, STURDY
wal·ly-drai·gle \'wä-lē-ˌdrā-gəl, 'wä-lē-\ *noun* [origin unknown] (1508)
chiefly Scottish **:** a feeble, imperfectly developed, or slovenly creature
wal·nut \'wȯl-(ˌ)nət\ *noun* [Middle English *walnut*, from Old English *wealhhnutu*, literally, foreign nut, from *Wealh* Welshman, foreigner + *hnutu* nut — more at WELSH, NUT] (before 12th century)
1 a : a nut of any of a genus (*Juglans* of the family Juglandaceae, the walnut family) of trees; *especially* **:** the large edible nut of a Eurasian tree (*J. regia*) with a hard richly figured wood **b :** a tree that bears walnuts **c :** the wood of a walnut that is often used for cabinetmaking and veneers
2 : a moderate reddish brown ◇
Wal·pur·gis·nacht \väl-'pu̇r-gəs-ˌnäkt\ *noun* [German] (1822)
: WALPURGIS NIGHT
Wal·pur·gis Night \väl-'pu̇r-gəs-\ *noun* [part translation of German *Walpurgisnacht*, from *Walpurgis* Saint Walburga (died A.D. 779) English saint whose feast day falls on May Day + German *Nacht* night] (1823)
1 : the eve of May Day on which witches are held to ride to an appointed rendezvous
2 : something (as an event or situation) having a nightmarish quality
wal·rus \'wȯl-rəs, 'wäl-\ *noun, plural* **walrus** *or* **wal·rus·es** [Dutch, of Scandinavian origin; akin to Danish & Norwegian *hvalros* walrus, Old Norse *rosmhvalr*] (1728)
: a large gregarious marine mammal (*Odobenus rosmarus* of the family Odobenidae) related to the seal that is found in Arctic seas, has long ivory tusks, a tough wrinkled hide, and stiff whiskers, and feeds mostly on bivalve mollusks
Wal·ter Mit·ty \ˌwȯl-tər-'mi-tē\ *noun* [*Walter Mitty*, daydreaming hero of a story by James Thurber] (1949)
: a commonplace unadventurous person who seeks escape from reality through daydreaming
— **Walter Mit·ty·ish** \-ish\ *adjective*
¹**waltz** \'wȯl(t)s\ *noun* [German *Walzer*, from *walzen* to roll, dance, from Old High German *walzan* to turn, roll — more at WELTER] (1781)
1 : a ballroom dance in ¾ time with strong accent on the first beat and a basic pattern of step-step-close
2 : music for a waltz or a concert composition in ¾ time
²**waltz** (circa 1794)

intransitive verb
1 : to dance a waltz
2 : to move or advance in a lively or conspicuous manner **:** FLOUNCE
3 a : to advance easily and successfully **:** BREEZE — often used with *through* **b :** to approach boldly — used with *up* ⟨can't just *waltz* up and introduce ourselves⟩
transitive verb
1 : to dance a waltz with
2 : to grab and lead (as a person) unceremoniously **:** MARCH
— **waltz·er** *noun*
¹**wam·ble** \'wäm-bəl\ *intransitive verb* **wambled; wam·bling** \-b(ə-)liŋ\ [Middle English *wamlen;* akin to Danish *vamle* to become nauseated, Latin *vomere* to vomit — more at VOMIT] (14th century)
1 a : to feel nausea **b** *of a stomach* **:** RUMBLE 1
2 : to move unsteadily or with a weaving or rolling motion
²**wamble** *noun* (1552)
1 : a wambling especially of the stomach
2 : a reeling or staggering gait or movement
wame \'wäm\ *noun* [Middle English, alteration of *wamb* — more at WOMB] (15th century)
chiefly Scottish **:** BELLY
Wam·pa·no·ag \ˌwäm-pə-'nō-(ˌ)ag, ˌwȯm-\ *noun, plural* **Wampanoag** *or* **Wampanoags** [Narraganset, literally, easterners] (1676)
: a member of an American Indian people of Rhode Island east of Narragansett Bay and neighboring parts of Massachusetts
wam·pum \'wäm-pəm\ *noun* [short for *wampumpeag*] (1636)
1 : beads of polished shells strung in strands, belts, or sashes and used by North American Indians as money, ceremonial pledges, and ornaments
2 : MONEY
wam·pum·peag \-ˌpēg\ *noun* [Massachuset *wampompeag*, from *wampan* white + *api* string + *-ag*, plural suffix] (1627)
: WAMPUM
¹**wan** \'wän\ *adjective* **wan·ner; wan·nest** [Middle English, from Old English *wann* dark, livid] (14th century)
1 a : suggestive of poor health **:** SICKLY, PALLID **b :** lacking vitality **:** FEEBLE
2 : DIM, FAINT
3 : LANGUID ⟨a *wan* smile⟩
— **wan·ly** *adverb*
— **wan·ness** \'wän-nəs\ *noun*

◇ WORD HISTORY
walnut The English walnut (*Juglans regia*) is not native to England in spite of its name. This tree, important for both its wood and fruit, was known in southern Europe long before it was introduced to northern Europeans, to whom the only readily available nut was the hazelnut. *Wealhhnutu*, the Old English ancestor of *walnut*, reflects the foreign origin of the walnut: it is a compound of *wealh* "stranger, foreigner" and *hnutu* "nut." Other Germanic words of later date, such as Middle Low German *walnut* (from which ultimately Modern German *Walnuss* comes), Middle High German *walhisch nuz*, and Old Norse *valhnot*, contain the same elements. They have a parallel in a Medieval Latin name for the walnut, *nux gallica*, literally, "Gallic or French nut." Old English *wealh* "foreigner" is buried in other Modern English words in addition to *walnut*. *Wealh* was applied to the Celtic speakers who opposed the Anglo-Saxons' invasion of Britain—despite being the indigenous inhabitants they were "foreigners" to the Germanic tribes—and *Wealas*, the plural of *wealh*, developed into Modern English *Wales*, now designating the land where Celtic Britons took refuge and maintained their ancient speech.

²wan *intransitive verb* **wanned; wan·ning** (1582)
: to grow or become pale or sickly

wand \'wänd\ *noun* [Middle English, slender stick, from Old Norse *vǫndr*; probably akin to Old English *windan* to wind, twist — more at WIND] (15th century)
1 : a slender staff carried in a procession : VERGE
2 : a slender rod used by conjurers and magicians
3 : a slat 6 feet by 2 inches used as a target in archery; *also* : a narrow strip of paper pasted vertically on a target face
4 : any of various pipelike devices; *especially* : the rigid tube between the hose and the nozzle of a vacuum cleaner
5 : a handheld device used to enter information (as from a bar code) into a computer

wan·der \'wän-dər\ *verb* **wan·dered; wan·der·ing** \-d(ə-)riŋ\ [Middle English *wandren*, from Old English *wandrian*; akin to Middle High German *wandern* to wander, Old English *windan* to wind, twist] (before 12th century)
intransitive verb
1 a : to move about without a fixed course, aim, or goal **b** : to go idly about : RAMBLE
2 : to follow a winding course : MEANDER
3 a : to deviate (as from a course) : STRAY **b** : to go astray morally : ERR **c** : to lose normal mental contact : stray in thought
transitive verb
: to roam over ☆
— **wander** *noun*
— **wan·der·er** \-dər-ər\ *noun*

¹wandering *adjective* (before 12th century)
: characterized by aimless, slow, or pointless movement: as **a** : that winds or meanders ⟨a *wandering* course⟩ **b** : not keeping a rational or sensible course : VAGRANT **c** : NOMADIC ⟨*wandering* tribes⟩ **d** *of a plant* : having long runners or tendrils

²wandering *noun* (14th century)
1 : a going about from place to place — often used in plural
2 : movement away from the proper, normal, or usual course or place — often used in plural

Wandering Jew *noun*
1 : a Jew of medieval legend condemned by Christ to wander the earth till Christ's second coming
2 *W not capitalized* : any of several plants (genera *Zebrina* and *Tradescantia*) of the spiderwort family; *especially* : either of two trailing or creeping plants (*Z. pendula* and *T. fluminensis*) cultivated for their showy and often white-striped foliage

wan·der·lust \'wän-dər-ˌləst\ *noun* [German, from *wandern* to wander + *Lust* desire, pleasure] (1902)
: strong longing for or impulse toward wandering

¹wane \'wān\ *intransitive verb* **waned; wan·ing** [Middle English, from Old English *wanian*; akin to Old High German *wanōn* to wane, Old English *wan* wanting, deficient, Latin *vanus* empty, vain] (before 12th century)
1 : to decrease in size, extent, or degree : DWINDLE: as **a** : to diminish in phase or intensity — used chiefly of the moon **b** : to become less brilliant or powerful : DIM **c** : to flow out : EBB
2 : to fall gradually from power, prosperity, or influence
synonym see ABATE

²wane *noun* (14th century)
1 a : the act or process of waning ⟨strength on the *wane*⟩ **b** : a period or time of waning; *specifically* : the period from full phase of the moon to the new moon
2 [Middle English, defect, from Old English *wana*; akin to Middle English *wan* deficient] : a defect in lumber characterized by bark or a lack of wood at a corner or edge

wan·gle \'waŋ-gəl\ *verb* **wan·gled; wan·gling** \-g(ə-)liŋ\ [perhaps alteration of *waggle*] (circa 1820)
intransitive verb
1 : to extricate oneself (as from difficulty) : WIGGLE
2 : to resort to trickery or devious methods
transitive verb
1 : SHAKE, WIGGLE
2 : to adjust or manipulate for personal or fraudulent ends
3 : to make or get by devious means : FINAGLE ⟨*wangle* an invitation⟩
— **wan·gler** \-g(ə-)lər\ *noun*

wan·i·gan *or* **wan·ni·gan** \'wä-ni-gən\ *noun* [Ojibwa *waʼnikkaʼn* pit] (circa 1848)
: a shelter (as for sleeping, eating, or storage) often mounted on wheels or tracks and towed by tractor or mounted on a raft or boat

wan·ion \'wän-yən\ *noun* [from the obsolete phrase *in the waniand* unluckily, literally, in the waning (moon), from Middle English, from *waniand, wanen* northern present participle of *wanien, wanen* to wane] (1549)
archaic : PLAGUE, VENGEANCE — used in the phrase *with a wanion*

Wan·kel engine \'väŋ-kəl-, 'waŋ-\ *noun* [Felix *Wankel* (died 1988) German engineer] (1961)
: an internal combustion rotary engine that has a rounded triangular rotor functioning as a piston and rotating in a space in the engine and that has only two major moving parts

wan·na·be \'wä-nə-ˌbē\ *noun* [from the phrase *want to be*] (1981)
: a person who wants or aspires to be someone or something else or who tries to look or act like someone else

¹want \'wȯnt *also* 'wänt & 'wənt\ *verb* [Middle English, from Old Norse *vanta*; akin to Old English *wan* deficient] (13th century)
intransitive verb
1 : to be needy or destitute
2 : to have or feel need ⟨never *wants* for friends⟩
3 : to be necessary or needed
4 : to desire to come, go, or be ⟨the cat *wants* in⟩ ⟨*wants* out of the deal⟩
transitive verb
1 : to fail to possess especially in customary or required amount : LACK ⟨the answer *wanted* courtesy⟩
2 a : to have a strong desire for ⟨*wanted* a chance to rest⟩ **b** : to have an inclination to : LIKE ⟨say what you *want*, he is efficient⟩
3 a : to have need of : REQUIRE ⟨the motor *wants* a tune-up⟩ **b** : to suffer from the lack of ⟨thousands still *want* food and shelter⟩
4 : OUGHT — used with the infinitive ⟨you *want* to be very careful what you say —Claudia Cassidy⟩
5 : to wish or demand the presence of
6 : to hunt or seek in order to apprehend ⟨*wanted* for murder⟩
synonym see DESIRE

²want *noun* (14th century)
1 a : DEFICIENCY, LACK ⟨suffers from a *want* of good sense⟩ **b** : grave and extreme poverty that deprives one of the necessities of life
2 : something wanted : NEED, DESIRE
3 : personal defect : FAULT
synonym see POVERTY

want ad *noun* (1897)
: a newspaper advertisement stating that something (as an employee, employment, or a specified item) is wanted

¹want·ing *adjective* (15th century)
1 : not present or in evidence : ABSENT
2 a : not being up to standards or expectations **b** : lacking in ability or capacity : DEFICIENT

²wanting *preposition* (1693)
1 : LESS, MINUS ⟨a month *wanting* two days⟩
2 : WITHOUT ⟨a book *wanting* a cover⟩

¹wan·ton \'wȯn-tᵊn, 'wän-\ *adjective* [Middle English, from *wan-* deficient, wrong, mis- (from Old English *wan-* deficient) + *to-*

wen, past participle of *teen* to draw, train, discipline, from Old English *tēon* — more at TOW] (14th century)
1 a *archaic* : hard to control : UNDISCIPLINED, UNRULY **b** : playfully mean or cruel : MISCHIEVOUS
2 a : LEWD, BAWDY **b** : causing sexual excitement : LUSTFUL, SENSUAL
3 a : MERCILESS, INHUMANE ⟨*wanton* cruelty⟩ **b** : having no just foundation or provocation : MALICIOUS ⟨a *wanton* attack⟩
4 : being without check or limitation: as **a** : luxuriantly rank ⟨*wanton* vegetation⟩ **b** : unduly lavish : EXTRAVAGANT
— **wan·ton·ly** *adverb*
— **wan·ton·ness** \-tᵊn-nəs\ *noun*

²wanton *noun* (1526)
1 : a pampered person or animal : PET; *especially* : a spoiled child
2 : a frolicsome child or animal
3 a : one given to self-indulgent flirtation or trifling — used especially in the phrase *play the wanton* **b** : a lewd or lascivious person

³wanton (1582)
intransitive verb
: to be wanton or act wantonly
transitive verb
: to pass or waste wantonly or in wantonness
— **wan·ton·er** *noun*

wa·pen·take \'wa-pən-ˌtāk, 'wä-\ *noun* [Middle English, from Old English *wǣpentæc*, from Old Norse *vápnatak* act of grasping weapons, from *vápn* weapon + *tak* act of grasping, from *taka* to take; probably from the brandishing of weapons as an expression of approval when the chief of the wapentake entered upon his office — more at WEAPON, TAKE] (before 12th century)
: a subdivision of some English shires corresponding to a hundred

wa·pi·ti \'wä-pə-tē\ *noun, plural* **wapiti** *or* **wapitis** [Shawnee *waʼpiti*, literally, white rump] (1806)
: ELK 1b

wap·pen·schaw·ing \'wa-pən-ˌshȯ(-)iŋ, 'wä-\ *noun* [Middle English (northern dialect) *wapynschawing*, from *wapen* weapon (from Old Norse *vápn*) + *schawing*, gerund of *schawen* to show, from Old English *scēawian* to look, look at — more at WEAPON, SHOW] (15th century)
: an inspection or muster of soldiers formerly held at various times in each district of Scotland

☆ **SYNONYMS**
Wander, roam, ramble, rove, traipse, meander mean to go about from place to place usually without a plan or definite purpose. WANDER implies an absence of or an indifference to a fixed course ⟨fond of *wandering* about the square just watching the people⟩. ROAM suggests wandering about freely and often far afield ⟨liked to *roam* through the woods⟩. RAMBLE stresses carelessness and indifference to one's course or objective ⟨the speaker *rambled* on without ever coming to the point⟩. ROVE suggests vigorous and sometimes purposeful roaming ⟨armed brigands *roved* over the countryside⟩. TRAIPSE implies a course that is erratic but may sometimes be purposeful ⟨*traipsed* all over town looking for the right dress⟩. MEANDER implies a winding or intricate course suggestive of aimless or listless wandering ⟨the river *meanders* for miles through rich farmland⟩.

\ə\ abut \ᵊ\ kitten \ər\ further \a\ ash \ā\ ace
\ä\ mop, mar \au̇\ out \ch\ chin \e\ bet \ē\ easy
\g\ go \i\ hit \ī\ ice \j\ job \ŋ\ sing
\ō\ law \ȯi\ boy \th\ thin \t̲h̲\ the \ü\ loot \u̇\ foot
\y\ yet \zh\ vision *see also* Guide to Pronunciation

¹war \ˈwȯr\ *noun, often attributive* [Middle English *werre*, from Old North French, of Germanic origin; akin to Old High German *werra* strife; akin to Old High German *werran* to confuse] (12th century) **1 a** (1) **:** a state of usually open and declared armed hostile conflict between states or nations (2) **:** a period of such armed conflict (3) : STATE OF WAR **b :** the art or science of warfare **c** (1) *obsolete* **:** weapons and equipment for war (2) *archaic* **:** soldiers armed and equipped for war **2 a :** a state of hostility, conflict, or antagonism **b :** a struggle or competition between opposing forces or for a particular end ⟨a class *war*⟩ ⟨a *war* against disease⟩ **c :** VARIANCE, ODDS 3

— **war·less** \-ləs\ *adjective*

²war *intransitive verb* **warred; war·ring** (13th century) **1 :** to be in active or vigorous conflict **2 :** to engage in warfare

³war \ˈwär\ *adverb or adjective* [Middle English *werre*, from Old Norse *verri*, adjective, *verr*, adverb; akin to Old English *wiersa* worse — more at WORSE] (13th century) *chiefly Scottish* **:** WORSE

⁴war \ˈwär\ *transitive verb* **warred; war·ring** (15th century) *Scottish* **:** WORST, OVERCOME

war baby *noun* (1901) **:** a person born or conceived during a war

¹war·ble \ˈwȯr-bəl\ *noun* [Middle English *werble* tune, from Old North French, of Germanic origin; akin to Middle High German *wirbel* whirl, tuning peg, Old High German *wirbil* whirlwind — more at WHIRL] (14th century) **1 :** a melodious succession of low pleasing sounds **2 :** a musical trill **3 :** the action of warbling

²warble *verb* **war·bled; war·bling** \-b(ə-)liŋ\ (15th century) *intransitive verb* **1 :** to sing in a trilling manner or with many turns and variations **2 :** to become sounded with trills, quavers, and rapid modulations in pitch **3 :** SING *transitive verb* **:** to render with turns, runs, or rapid modulations : TRILL

³warble *noun* [perhaps of Scandinavian origin; akin to obsolete Swedish *varbulde* boil, from *var* pus + *bulde* swelling] (circa 1585) **1 :** a swelling under the hide especially of the back of cattle, horses, and wild mammals caused by the maggot of a botfly or warble fly **2 :** the maggot of a warble fly

— **war·bled** \-bəld\ *adjective*

warble fly *noun* (1877) **:** any of various dipteran flies (family Oestridae) whose larvae live under the skin of various mammals and cause warbles

war·bler \ˈwȯr-blər\ *noun* (1611) **1 :** one that warbles : SINGER, SONGSTER **2 a :** any of numerous small Old World oscine birds (family Sylviidae) many of which are noted songsters and are closely related to the thrushes **b :** any of numerous small brightly colored American oscine birds (family Parulidae) with a usually weak and unmusical song — called also *wood warbler*

war·bon·net \ˈwȯr-ˌbä-nət\ *noun* (1845) **:** an American Indian ceremonial headdress with a feathered extension down the back

war bride *noun* (1916) **1 :** a woman who marries a serviceman ordered into active service in time of war **2 :** a woman who marries a serviceman especially of a foreign nation met during a time of war

war chest *noun* (1901) **:** a fund accumulated to finance a war; *broadly* **:** a fund earmarked for a specific purpose, action, or campaign

war club *noun* (1776) **:** a club-shaped implement used as a weapon especially by American Indians

war crime *noun* (1906) **:** a crime (as genocide or maltreatment of prisoners) committed during or in connection with war — usually used in plural

— **war criminal** *noun*

war cry *noun* (1748) **1 :** a cry used by a body of fighters in war **2 :** a slogan used especially to rally people to a cause

¹ward \ˈwȯrd\ *noun* [Middle English, from Old English *weard;* akin to Old High German *warta* act of watching, Old English *warian* to beware of, guard, *wær* careful — more at WARY] (before 12th century) **1 a :** the action or process of guarding **b :** a body of guards **2 :** the state of being under guard; *especially* **:** CUSTODY **3 a :** the inner court of a castle or fortress **b :** a division (as a cell or block) of a prison **c :** a division in a hospital; *especially* **:** a large room in a hospital where a number of patients often requiring similar treatment are accommodated **4 a :** a division of a city for representative, electoral, or administrative purposes **b :** a division of some English and Scottish counties corresponding to a hundred **c :** the Mormon local congregation having auxiliary organizations (as Sunday schools and relief societies) and one or more quorums of each office of the Aaronic priesthood **5 :** a projecting ridge of metal in a lock casing or keyhole permitting only the insertion of a key with a corresponding notch; *also* **:** a corresponding notch in a bit of a key **6 :** a person or thing under guard, protection, or surveillance: as **a :** a minor subject to wardship **b :** a person who by reason of incapacity (as minority or lunacy) is under the protection of a court either directly or through a guardian appointed by the court — called also *ward of court* **c :** a person or body of persons under the protection or tutelage of a government **7 :** a means of defense : PROTECTION

— **ward·ed** \ˈwȯr-dəd\ *adjective*

²ward *transitive verb* [Middle English, from Old English *weardian;* akin to Old High German *wartēn* to watch, Old Norse *vartha* to guard, Old English *weard* ward] (before 12th century) **1 :** to keep watch over **:** GUARD **2 :** to turn aside (something threatening) **:** DEFLECT — usually used with *off*

¹-ward *also* **-wards** *adjective suffix* [-ward from Middle English, from Old English *-weard;* akin to Old High German *-wart, -wert* -ward, Latin *vertere* to turn; *-wards* from *-wards,* adverb suffix — more at WORTH] **1 :** that moves, tends, faces, or is directed toward ⟨river*ward*⟩ **2 :** that occurs or is situated in the direction of ⟨left*ward*⟩

²-ward *or* **-wards** *adverb suffix* [-ward from Middle English, from Old English *-weard,* from *-weard,* adjective suffix; *-wards* from Middle English, from Old English *-weardes,* genitive singular neuter of *-weard,* adjective suffix] **1 :** in a (specified) spatial or temporal direction ⟨up*ward*⟩ ⟨after*ward*⟩

2 : toward a (specified) point, position, or area ⟨earth*ward*⟩

war dance *noun* (1711) **:** a dance performed (as by American Indians) in preparation for battle or in celebration of victory

ward·ed \ˈwȯr-dəd\ *adjective* (1572) **:** provided with a ward ⟨a *warded* lock⟩

war·den \ˈwȯr-d°n\ *noun* [Middle English *wardein,* from Old North French, from *warder* to guard, of Germanic origin; akin to Old High German *wartēn* to watch] (13th century) **1 :** one having care or charge of something : GUARDIAN, KEEPER **2 a :** REGENT 2 **b :** the governor of a town, district, or fortress **c :** a member of the governing body of a guild **3 a :** an official charged with special supervisory duties or with the enforcement of specified laws or regulations ⟨game *warden*⟩ ⟨air raid *warden*⟩ **b :** an official in charge of the operation of a prison **c :** any of various British officials having designated administrative functions ⟨*warden* of the mint⟩ **4 a :** one of two ranking lay officers of an Episcopal parish **b :** any of various British college officials whose duties range from the administration of academic matters to the supervision of student discipline

war·den·ship \-ˌship\ *noun* (15th century) **:** the office, jurisdiction, or powers of a warden

¹ward·er \ˈwȯr-dər\ *noun* [Middle English, from Anglo-French *wardere,* from *warde* act of guarding, of Germanic origin; akin to Old High German *warta* act of watching] (15th century) **1 :** WATCHMAN, PORTER **2** *British* **a :** WARDEN **b :** a prison guard

²war·der *noun* [Middle English, staff, perhaps from *warden* to ward] (circa 1548) **:** a truncheon used by a king or commander in chief to signal orders

ward heeler *noun* (1888) **:** a worker for a political boss in a ward or other local area

ward·ress \ˈwȯr-drəs\ *noun* (1878) **:** a woman supervising female prisoners (as in a prison)

ward·robe \ˈwȯr-ˌdrōb\ *noun* [Middle English *warderobe,* from Old North French, from *warder* to guard + *robe* robe] (14th century) **1 a :** a room or closet where clothes are kept **b :** CLOTHESPRESS **c :** a large trunk in which clothes may be hung upright **2 a :** a collection of wearing apparel (as of one person or for one activity) ⟨a summer *wardrobe*⟩ **b :** a collection of stage costumes and accessories **3 :** the department of a royal or noble household entrusted with the care of wearing apparel, jewels, and personal articles

ward·room \ˈwȯr-ˌdrüm, -ˌdrum\ *noun* (1758) **:** the space in a warship allotted for living quarters to the commissioned officers excepting the captain; *specifically* **:** the mess assigned to these officers

ward·ship \ˈwȯrd-ˌship\ *noun* (15th century) **1 a :** care and protection of a ward **b :** the right to the custody of an infant heir of a feudal tenant and of the heir's property **2 :** the state of being under a guardian

¹ware \ˈwar, ˈwer\ *adjective* [Middle English *war, ware* careful, aware, from Old English *wær* — more at WARY] (before 12th century) **1 :** AWARE, CONSCIOUS ⟨was *ware* of black looks cast at me —Mary Webb⟩ **2** *archaic* **:** WARY, VIGILANT

²ware *transitive verb* **wared; war·ing** [Middle English, from Old English *warian;* akin to Old High German *biwarōn* to protect, Old English *wær* aware] (before 12th century) **:** to beware of **:** AVOID — used chiefly as a command to hunting animals

warbonnet

³**ware** *noun* [Middle English, from Old English *waru;* akin to Middle High German *ware* ware and probably to Sanskrit *vasna* price — more at VENAL] (before 12th century)
1 a : manufactured articles, products of art or craft, or farm produce **:** GOODS — often used in combination ⟨tin*ware*⟩ **b :** an article of merchandise
2 : articles (as pottery or dishes) of fired clay ⟨earthen*ware*⟩
3 : an intangible item (as a service or ability) that is a marketable commodity

⁴**ware** *transitive verb* **wared; war·ing** [Middle English, from Old Norse *verja* to clothe, invest, spend — more at WEAR] (14th century)
Scottish **:** SPEND, EXPEND

¹**ware·house** \'war-ˌhau̇s, 'wer-\ *noun* (14th century)
: a structure or room for the storage of merchandise or commodities

²**ware·house** \-ˌhau̇z, -ˌhau̇s\ *transitive verb* (1799)
1 : to deposit, store, or stock in or as if in a warehouse
2 : to confine or house (a person) in conditions suggestive of a warehouse

ware·house·man \-ˌhau̇s-mən\ *noun* (1635)
: a person who manages or works in a warehouse

ware·hous·er \-ˌhau̇-zər, -sər\ *noun* (circa 1927)
: WAREHOUSEMAN

ware·room \'war-ˌrüm, 'wer-, -ˌru̇m\ *noun* (1811)
: a room in which goods are exhibited for sale

war·fare \'wȯr-ˌfar, -ˌfer\ *noun* [Middle English, from *werre, warre* war + *fare* journey, passage — more at FARE] (15th century)
1 : military operations between enemies **:** HOSTILITIES, WAR; *also* **:** an activity undertaken by a political unit (as a nation) to weaken or destroy another ⟨economic *warfare*⟩
2 : struggle between competing entities **:** CONFLICT

war·fa·rin \'wȯr-fə-rən\ *noun* [*W*isconsin *A*lumni *R*esearch *F*oundation (its patentee) + coum*arin*] (1950)
: a crystalline anticoagulant compound $C_{19}H_{16}O_4$ used as a rodent poison and in medicine

war footing *noun* (1847)
: the condition of being prepared to undertake or maintain war

war–game (1942)
transitive verb
: to plan or conduct in the manner of a war game ⟨*war-gamed* an invasion —*Newsweek*⟩
intransitive verb
: to conduct a war game

war game *noun* (1828)
1 : a simulated battle or campaign to test military concepts and usually conducted in conferences by officers acting as the opposing staffs
2 : a two-sided umpired training maneuver with actual elements of the armed forces participating

war hawk *noun* (1798)
: one who clamors for war; *especially* **:** an American jingo favoring war with Britain around 1812

war·head \'wȯr-ˌhed\ *noun* (1898)
: the section of a missile containing the explosive, chemical, or incendiary charge

war·horse \-ˌhȯrs\ *noun* (1653)
1 : a horse used in war **:** CHARGER
2 : a person with long experience in a field; *especially* **:** a veteran soldier or public person (as a politician)
3 : something (as a work of art or musical composition) that has become overly familiar or hackneyed due to much repetition in the standard repertoire

war·i·son \'war-ə-sən\ *noun* [probably a misunderstanding by Sir Walter Scott in the *Lay*

of the Last Minstrel (1805) of Middle English *waryson* reward, from Old North French *warison* defense, possessions, from *warir* to protect, provide, of Germanic origin; akin to Old High German *werien* to defend — more at WEIR] (1805)
: a bugle call to attack

war·like \'wȯr-ˌlīk\ *adjective* (15th century)
1 *obsolete* **:** ready for war **:** equipped to fight
2 : fit for, disposed to, or fond of war **:** BELLICOSE
3 : of, relating to, or useful in war
4 : befitting or characteristic of war or a soldier

war·lock \-ˌläk\ *noun* [Middle English *warloghe,* from Old English *wǣrloga* one that breaks faith, the Devil, from *wǣr* faith, troth + *-loga* (from *lēogan* to lie); akin to Old English *wǣr* true — more at VERY, LIE] (14th century)
1 : a man practicing the black arts **:** SORCERER — compare WITCH
2 : CONJURER

war·lord \-ˌlȯrd\ *noun* (1856)
1 : a supreme military leader
2 : a military commander exercising civil power by force usually in a limited area
— **war·lord·ism** \-ˌlȯr-di-zəm\ *noun*

¹**warm** \'wȯrm\ *adjective* [Middle English, from Old English *wearm;* akin to Old High German *warm* warm and probably to Lithuanian *virti* to cook, boil] (before 12th century)
1 a : having or giving out heat to a moderate or adequate degree **b :** serving to maintain or preserve heat especially to a satisfactory degree ⟨a *warm* sweater⟩ **c :** feeling or causing sensations of heat brought about by strenuous exertion
2 : comfortably established **:** SECURE
3 a : marked by strong feeling **:** ARDENT **b :** marked by excitement, disagreement, or anger ⟨the argument grew *warm*⟩
4 : marked by or readily showing affection, gratitude, cordiality, or sympathy ⟨a *warm* welcome⟩ ⟨*warm* regards⟩
5 : emphasizing or exploiting sexual imagery or incidents
6 : accompanied or marked by extreme danger or duress
7 : newly made **:** FRESH ⟨a *warm* scent⟩
8 : having the color or tone of something that imparts heat; *specifically* **:** of a hue in the range yellow through orange to red
9 : near to a goal, object, or solution sought
— **warm·ish** \'wȯr-mish\ *adjective*
— **warm·ness** \'wȯrm-nəs\ *noun*

²**warm** (before 12th century)
transitive verb
1 : to make warm
2 a : to infuse with a feeling of love, friendship, well-being, or pleasure **b :** to fill with anger, zeal, or passion
3 : to reheat (cooked food) for eating — often used with *over*
4 : to make ready for operation or performance by preliminary exercise or operation — often used with *up*
intransitive verb
1 : to become warm
2 a : to become ardent, interested, or receptive — usually used with *to* or *toward* ⟨*warmed* to the idea⟩ **b :** to become filled with affection or love — used with *to* or *toward*
3 : to experience feelings of pleasure **:** BASK
4 : to become ready for operation or performance by preliminary activity — often used with *up*

³**warm** *adverb* (before 12th century)
: WARMLY — usually used in combination ⟨*warm*-clad⟩

warm–blood·ed \'wȯrm-'blə-dəd\ *adjective* (1793)
1 : having warm blood; *specifically* **:** having a relatively high and constant body temperature relatively independent of the surroundings
2 : fervent or ardent in spirit
— **warm–blood·ed·ness** *noun*

warmed–over \'wȯrmd-'ō-vər\ *adjective* (1887)
1 : not fresh or new **:** STALE ⟨*warmed-over* ideas⟩
2 : heated again ⟨*warmed-over* beans⟩

warm·er \'wȯr-mər\ *noun* (circa 1595)
: one that warms; *especially* **:** a device for keeping something warm ⟨a hand *warmer*⟩

warm front *noun* (circa 1921)
: an advancing edge of a warm air mass

warm–heart·ed \'wȯrm-'här-təd\ *adjective* (circa 1520)
: marked by ready affection, cordiality, generosity, or sympathy
— **warm–heart·ed·ness** *noun*

warming pan *noun* (15th century)
: a long-handled covered pan filled with live coals that is used to warm a bed

warm·ly \'wȯrm-lē\ *adverb* (1529)
1 : in a manner characterized or accompanied by warmth of emotion
2 : in a manner that causes or maintains warmth

war·mon·ger \'wȯr-ˌmən-gər, -ˌmäŋ-\ *noun* (1590)
: one who urges or attempts to stir up war **:** JINGO
— **war·mon·ger·ing** \-g(ə-)riŋ\ *noun*

war·mouth \'wȯr-ˌmau̇th\ *noun* [origin unknown] (circa 1883)
: a freshwater sunfish (*Lepomis gulosus*) chiefly of the eastern U.S. — called also *warmouth bass*

warm spot *noun* (1951)
: a lasting affection for a particular person or object

warmth \'wȯrm(p)th\ *noun* (13th century)
1 : the quality or state of being warm in temperature
2 : the quality or state of being warm in feeling ⟨a child needing human *warmth* and family life⟩
3 : a glowing effect produced by the use of warm colors

warm–up \'wȯrm-ˌəp\ *noun* (1915)
1 : the act or an instance of warming up; *also* **:** a preparatory activity or procedure
2 : a suit for exercise or casual wear consisting of a jacket or sweatshirt and pants — often used in plural; called also *warm-up suit*

warm up *intransitive verb* (1846)
: to engage in exercise or practice especially before entering a game or contest; *broadly* **:** to get ready

warn \'wȯrn\ *verb* [Middle English, from Old English *warnian;* akin to Old High German *warnōn* to take heed, Old English *wær* careful, aware — more at WARY] (before 12th century)
transitive verb
1 a : to give notice to beforehand especially of danger or evil **b :** to give admonishing advice to **:** COUNSEL **c :** to call to one's attention **:** INFORM
2 : to order to go or stay away — often used with *off*
intransitive verb
: to give a warning
— **warn·er** *noun*

¹**warn·ing** \'wȯr-niŋ\ *noun* (before 12th century)
1 : the act of warning **:** the state of being warned ⟨he had *warning* of his illness⟩
2 : something that warns or serves to warn; *especially* **:** a notice or bulletin that alerts the public that a tornado has been reported in the immediate vicinity or that the approach of a severe storm is imminent

\ə\ **abut** \ᵊ\ **kitten** \ər\ **further** \a\ **ash** \ā\ **ace**
\ä\ **mop, mar** \au̇\ **out** \ch\ **chin** \e\ **bet** \ē\ **easy**
\g\ **go** \i\ **hit** \ī\ **ice** \j\ **job** \ŋ\ **sing** \ō\ **go**
\ȯ\ **law** \ȯi\ **boy** \th\ **thin** \t̲h̲\ **the** \ü\ **loot** \u̇\ **foot**
\y\ **yet** \zh\ **vision** *see also* Guide to Pronunciation

²warning *adjective* (circa 1552)
: serving as an alarm, signal, summons, or admonition ⟨*warning* bell⟩ ⟨*warning* shot⟩
— **warn·ing·ly** \ˈwȯr-niŋ-lē\ *adverb*

warning coloration *noun* (circa 1928)
: conspicuous coloration possessed by an animal (as an insect) otherwise effectively but not obviously defended that serves to warn off potential enemies

warning track *noun* (1966)
: a usually dirt or cinder strip around the outside edge of a baseball outfield to warn a fielder when running to make a catch that the fence is near — called also *warning path*

war of nerves (1939)
: a conflict characterized by psychological tactics (as bluff, threats, and intimidation) designed primarily to create confusion, indecision, or breakdown of morale

¹warp \ˈwȯrp\ *noun* [Middle English, from Old English *wearp;* akin to Old High German *warf* warp, Old English *weorpan* to throw, Old Norse *verpa*] (before 12th century)
1 a : a series of yarns extended lengthwise in a loom and crossed by the weft **b :** FOUNDATION, BASE ⟨the *warp* of the economic structure is agriculture —*American Guide Series: North Carolina*⟩
2 : a rope for warping or mooring a ship or boat
3 [²*warp*] **a :** a twist or curve that has developed in something originally flat or straight ⟨a *warp* in a door panel⟩ **b :** a mental twist or aberration
— **warp·age** \ˈwȯr-pij\ *noun*

²warp (14th century)
transitive verb
1 : to arrange (yarns) so as to form a warp
2 a : to turn or twist out of or as if out of shape; *especially* **:** to twist or bend out of a plane **b :** to cause to judge, choose, or act wrongly or abnormally **:** PERVERT **c :** DISTORT 1 ⟨intellect and learning . . . *warped* by prejudices —Irving Wallace⟩ **d :** to deflect from a course
3 : to move (as a ship) by hauling on a line attached to a fixed object
intransitive verb
1 : to become warped
2 : to move a ship by warping
synonym see DEFORM
— **warp·er** *noun*

war paint *noun* (1826)
1 : paint put on parts of the body (as the face) by American Indians as a sign of going to war
2 : MAKEUP 3a

warp and woof *noun* (1842)
: FOUNDATION, BASE ⟨the vigorous Anglo-Saxon base had become the *warp and woof* of English speech —H. R. Warfel⟩

war party *noun* (1755)
1 : a group of American Indians on the warpath
2 : a usually jingoistic political party advocating or upholding a war

war·path \ˈwȯr-ˌpath, -ˌpȧth\ *noun* (1755)
1 : the route taken by a party of American Indians going on a warlike expedition or to a war
2 : a hostile course of action or frame of mind

warp beam *noun* (circa 1833)
: a roll on which warp is wound for a loom

warp knit *noun* (1946)
: a knit fabric produced by machine with the yarns running in a lengthwise direction — compare WEFT KNIT
— **warp–knit·ted** \-ˈni-təd\ *adjective*
— **warp knitting** *noun*

war·plane \ˈwȯr-ˌplān\ *noun* (circa 1911)
: a military airplane; *specifically* **:** one armed for combat

war power *noun* (1766)
: the power to make war; *specifically* **:** an extraordinary power exercised usually by the ex-

ecutive branch of a government in the prosecution of a war

¹war·rant \ˈwȯr-ənt, ˈwär-\ *noun* [Middle English, protector, warrant, from Old North French *warant,* modification of a Germanic noun represented by Old High German *werēnto* guarantor, from present participle of *werēn* to warrant; akin to Old High German *wāra* trust, care — more at VERY] (14th century)
1 a (1) : SANCTION, AUTHORIZATION; *also* **:** evidence for or token of authorization (2) **:** GUARANTEE, SECURITY **b (1) :** GROUND, JUSTIFICATION (2) **:** CONFIRMATION, PROOF
2 a : a commission or document giving authority to do something; *especially* **:** a writing that authorizes a person to pay or deliver to another and the other to receive money or other consideration **b :** a precept or writ issued by a competent magistrate authorizing an officer to make an arrest, a seizure, or a search or to do other acts incident to the administration of justice **c :** an official certificate of appointment issued to an officer of lower rank than a commissioned officer **d (1) :** a short-term obligation of a governmental body (as a municipality) issued in anticipation of revenue (2) **:** an instrument issued by a corporation giving to the holder the right to purchase the capital stock of the corporation at a stated price either prior to a stipulated date or at any future time
— **war·rant·less** \-ləs\ *adjective*

²warrant *transitive verb* [Middle English, from Old North French *warantir,* from *warant*] (14th century)
1 a : to declare or maintain with certainty **:** be sure that ⟨I'll *warrant* he'll be here by noon⟩ **b :** to assure (a person) of the truth of what is said
2 a : to guarantee to a person good title to and undisturbed possession of (as an estate) **b :** to provide a guarantee of the security of (as title to property sold) usually by an express covenant in the deed of conveyance **c :** to guarantee to be as represented **d :** to guarantee (as goods sold) especially in respect of the quality or quantity specified
3 : to guarantee security or immunity to **:** SECURE ⟨I'll *warrant* him from drowning —Shakespeare⟩
4 : to give warrant or sanction to **:** AUTHORIZE ⟨the law *warrants* this procedure⟩
5 a : to give proof of the authenticity or truth of **b :** to give assurance of the nature of or for the undertaking of **:** GUARANTEE
6 : to serve as or give adequate ground or reason for ⟨promising enough to *warrant* further consideration⟩

war·rant·able \ˈwȯr-ən-tə-bəl, ˈwär-\ *adjective* (1581)
: capable of being warranted **:** JUSTIFIABLE
— **war·rant·able·ness** *noun*
— **war·rant·ably** \-blē\ *adverb*

war·ran·tee \ˌwȯr-ən-ˈtē, ˌwär-\ *noun* (1706)
: the person to whom a warranty is made

warrant officer *noun* (1693)
1 : an officer in the armed forces holding rank by virtue of a warrant and ranking above a noncommissioned officer and below a commissioned officer
2 : a commissioned officer ranking below an ensign in the navy or coast guard and below a second lieutenant in the marine corps

war·ran·tor \ˌwȯr-ən-ˈtȯr, ˌwär-; ˈwȯr-ən-tər, ˈwär-\ *also* **war·rant·er** \ˈwȯr-ən-tər, ˈwär-\ *noun* (1583)
: one that warrants or gives a warranty

war·ran·ty \ˈwȯr-ən-tē, ˈwär-\ *noun, plural* **-ties** [Middle English *warantie,* from Old North French, from *warantir* to warrant] (14th century)
1 a : a real covenant binding the grantor of an estate and his heirs to warrant and defend the

title **b :** a collateral undertaking that a fact regarding the subject of a contract is or will be as it is expressly or by implication declared or promised to be
2 : something that authorizes, sanctions, supports, or justifies **:** WARRANT
3 : a usually written guarantee of the integrity of a product and of the maker's responsibility for the repair or replacement of defective parts

warranty deed *noun* (1779)
: a deed warranting that the grantor has a good title free and clear of all liens and encumbrances and will defend the grantee against all claims

war·ren \ˈwȯr-ən, ˈwär-\ *noun* [Middle English *warenne,* from Old North French, probably of Germanic origin; akin to Old High German *werien* to defend, protect — more at WEIR] (15th century)
1 *chiefly British* **a :** a place legally authorized for keeping small game (as hare or pheasant) **b :** the privilege of hunting game in such a warren
2 a (1) : an area (as of uncultivated ground) where rabbits breed (2) **:** a structure where rabbits are kept or bred **b :** the rabbits of a warren
3 a : a crowded tenement or district **b :** a maze of passageways or cubbies

war·ren·er \-ə-nər\ *noun* (13th century)
1 : GAMEKEEPER
2 : a person who maintains a rabbit warren

war·rior \ˈwȯr-yər, ˈwȯr-ē-ər, ˈwär-ē-\ *also* ˈwär-yər\ *noun, often attributive* [Middle English *werriour,* from Old North French *werreiour,* from *werreier* to make war, from *werre* war — more at WAR] (14th century)
: a man engaged or experienced in warfare; *broadly* **:** a person engaged in some struggle or conflict ⟨poverty *warriors*⟩

war room *noun* (1914)
1 : a room at a military headquarters where maps showing the current status of troops in battle are maintained
2 : a room (as at a business headquarters) used for conferences and planning that is often specially equipped (as with computers, maps, or charts)

war·saw grouper \ˈwȯr-(ˌ)sȯ-\ *noun* [*warsaw* modification of American Spanish *guasa*] (1949)
: any of several large groupers (especially *Epinephelus nigritus*) — called also *warsaw*

war·ship \ˈwȯr-ˌship\ *noun* (1533)
: a naval vessel

war·sle *or* **wars·tle** \ˈwä(r)-səl\ *verb* [Middle English *werstelen, warstelen,* alteration of *wrestlen, wrastlen*] (14th century)
Scottish **:** WRESTLE, STRUGGLE
— **warsle** *noun, Scottish*

war story *noun* (1981)
: a story of a memorable personal experience typically involving an element of danger, hardship, or adventure ⟨politicians swapping *war stories* from past campaigns⟩

wart \ˈwȯrt\ *noun* [Middle English, from Old English *wearte;* akin to Old High German *warza* wart, Old Church Slavonic *vrědŭ* injury] (before 12th century)
1 a : a horny projection on the skin usually of the extremities that is caused by a virus — called also *verruca vulgaris* **b :** any of numerous similar skin lesions
2 : an excrescence or protuberance resembling a true wart; *especially* **:** a glandular excrescence or hardened protuberance on a plant
3 a : one that suggests a wart especially in smallness, unpleasantness, or unattractiveness **b :** DEFECT, IMPERFECTION — often used in the phrase *warts and all*
— **wart·ed** \ˈwȯr-təd\ *adjective*
— **wart·less** \ˈwȯrt-ləs\ *adjective*
— **warty** \ˈwȯr-tē\ *adjective*

wart·hog \'wȯrt-ˌhȯg, -ˌhäg\ noun (1840)
: a wild African hog (Phacochoerus aethiopicus) which has large protruding tusks and the males of which have two pairs of rough warty excrescences on the face

warthog

war·time \'wȯr-ˌtīm\ noun, often attributive (14th century)
: a period during which a war is in progress

warts–and–all adjective (1930)
: showing defects or imperfections frankly : not idealized ⟨a warts-and-all biography⟩

war whoop noun (1739)
: a war cry especially of American Indians

wary \'war-ē, 'wer-\ adjective **war·i·er; -est**
[¹ware, from Middle English war, ware, from Old English wær careful, aware, wary; akin to Old High German giwar aware, attentive, Latin vereri to fear, Greek horan to see] (15th century)
: marked by keen caution, cunning, and watchful prudence especially in detecting and escaping danger
synonym see CAUTIOUS
— **war·i·ly** \'war-ə-lē, 'wer-\ adverb
— **war·i·ness** \'war-ē-nəs, 'wer-\ noun

war zone noun (1914)
1 : a zone in which belligerents are waging war
2 : a designated area especially on the high seas within which rights of neutrals are not respected by a belligerent nation in time of war

was [Middle English, from Old English, 1st & 3d singular past indicative of wesan to be; akin to Old Norse vera to be, var was, Sanskrit vasati he lives, dwells] past 1st & 3d singular of BE

wa·sa·bi \'wä-sə-bē\ noun [Japanese] (1903)
1 : a condiment that is prepared from the thick pungent greenish root of an Asian herb (Eutrema wasabi) of the mustard family and is similar in flavor and use to horseradish; also : the root
2 : the herb that yields wasabi

¹wash \'wȯsh, 'wäsh, chiefly Midland also 'wȯrsh or 'wärsh\ verb [Middle English, from Old English wascan; akin to Old High German waskan to wash and perhaps to Old English wæter water] (before 12th century)
transitive verb
1 a : to cleanse by or as if by the action of liquid (as water) **b** : to remove (as dirt) by rubbing or drenching with liquid
2 : to cleanse (fur) by licking or by rubbing with a paw moistened with saliva
3 a : to flush or moisten (a bodily part or injury) with a liquid **b** (1) : to wet thoroughly : DRENCH (2) : to overspread with light : SUFFUSE **c** : to pass a liquid (as water) over or through especially so as to carry off material from the surface or interior
4 : to flow along or dash or overflow against ⟨waves washing the shore⟩
5 : to move, carry, or deposit by or as if by the force of water in motion ⟨houses washed away by the flood⟩
6 a : to subject (as crushed ore) to the action of water to separate valuable material **b** : to separate (particles) from a substance (as ore) by agitation with or in water **c** (1) : to pass through a bath to carry off impurities or soluble components (2) : to pass (a gas or gaseous mixture) through or over a liquid to purify it especially by removing soluble components
7 a : to cover or daub lightly with or as if with an application of a thin liquid (as whitewash or varnish) **b** : to depict or paint by a broad sweep of thin color with a brush
8 : to cause to swirl ⟨washing coffee around in his cup⟩

9 : LAUNDER 3 ⟨how the mob washes its money through corrupt bankers —Vincent Teresa⟩
intransitive verb
1 : to wash oneself or a part of one's body
2 : to become worn away by the action of water
3 : to clean something by rubbing or dipping in water
4 a : to become carried along on water : DRIFT ⟨cakes of ice washing along⟩ **b** : to pour, sweep, or flow in a stream or current ⟨waves of pioneers washing westward —Green Peyton⟩
5 : to serve as a cleansing agent ⟨this soap washes thoroughly⟩
6 a : to undergo laundering ⟨this dress doesn't wash well⟩ **b** (1) : to undergo testing successfully : WORK 4 ⟨an interesting theory, but it just won't wash⟩ (2) : to gain acceptance : inspire belief ⟨the story didn't wash with me⟩
— **wash one's hands of** : to disclaim interest in, responsibility for, or further connection with

²wash noun (15th century)
1 a : a piece of ground washed by the sea or river **b** : BOG, MARSH **c** (1) : a shallow body of water (2) : a shallow creek **d** West : the dry bed of a stream — called also dry wash
2 a : the act or process or an instance of washing or being washed **b** : articles to be washed, being washed, or having been washed
3 : the surging action of waves
4 a : worthless especially liquid waste : REFUSE **b** : an insipid beverage **c** : vapid writing or speech
5 a : a sweep or splash especially of color made by or as if by a long stroke of a brush **b** : a thin coat of paint (as watercolor) **c** : a thin liquid used for coating a surface (as a wall)
6 : LOTION
7 : loose or eroded surface material of the earth (as rock debris) transported and deposited by running water
8 a : BACKWASH 1 **b** : a disturbance in the air produced by the passage of an airfoil or propeller
9 : a situation in which losses and gains or advantages and disadvantages balance each other

³wash adjective (1634)
1 : WASHABLE ⟨wash fabric⟩
2 : involving essentially simultaneous purchase and sale of the same security ⟨spurious market activity resulting from wash trading⟩

wash·able \'wȯ-shə-bəl, 'wä-\ adjective (1821)
: capable of being washed without damage
— **wash·abil·i·ty** \ˌwȯ-shə-'bi-lət-ē, ˌwä-\ noun

wash–and–wear adjective (1956)
: of, relating to, or constituting a fabric or garment that needs little or no ironing after washing

wash·a·te·ria also **wash·e·te·ria** \ˌwä-shə-'tir-ē-ə, ˌwȯ-\ noun [²wash + -ateria or -eteria (as in cafeteria)] (1937)
chiefly Southern : a self-service laundry

wash·ba·sin \'wȯsh-ˌbā-s°n, 'wäsh-\ noun (1812)
: WASHBOWL

wash·board \'wȯsh-ˌbȯrd, 'wäsh-, -ˌbȯrd\ noun (1742)
1 : a broad thin plank along a gunwale or on the sill of a lower deck port to keep out the sea
2 : BASEBOARD
3 a : a corrugated rectangular surface that is used for scrubbing clothes or as a percussion instrument **b** : a road or pavement so worn by traffic as to be corrugated transversely

wash·bowl \-ˌbōl\ noun (1816)
: a large bowl for water that is used to wash one's hands and face

wash·cloth \-ˌklȯth\ noun (circa 1900)
: a cloth that is used for washing one's face and body — called also facecloth, washrag

wash down transitive verb (1600)

1 : to move or carry downward by action of a liquid; especially : to facilitate the passage of (food) down the gullet with accompanying swallows of liquid ⟨pizza washed down with beer⟩
2 : to wash the whole length or extent of ⟨washed down and scrubbed the front porch⟩

wash drawing noun (1889)
: watercolor painting in or chiefly in washes especially in black, white, and gray tones only

washed–out \'wȯsht-'aůt, 'wäsht-\ adjective (1796)
1 : faded in color
2 : depleted in vigor or animation : EXHAUSTED

washed–up \'wȯsht-'əp, 'wäsht-\ adjective (1928)
: no longer successful, skillful, popular, or needed

wash·er \'wȯ-shər, 'wä-\ noun (13th century)
1 : a flat thin ring or a perforated plate used in joints or assemblies to ensure tightness, prevent leakage, or relieve friction
2 : one that washes; especially : WASHING MACHINE

wash·er·man \-mən\ noun (1715)
: LAUNDRYMAN; also : a man operating any of various industrial washing machines

wash·er·wom·an \-ˌwů-mən\ noun (1632)
: a woman whose occupation is washing clothes : LAUNDRESS

wash·house \'wȯsh-ˌhaůs, 'wäsh-\ noun (1577)
: a building used or equipped for washing; especially : one for washing clothes

wash·ing \'wȯ-shiŋ, 'wä-\ noun (13th century)
1 : the act or action of one that cleanses with water
2 : material obtained by washing
3 : articles washed or to be washed : WASH

washing machine noun (circa 1754)
: a machine for washing; especially : one for washing clothes and household linen

washing soda noun (1865)
: a transparent crystalline hydrated sodium carbonate — called also sal soda

Wash·ing·ton pie \'wȯ-shiŋ-tən-, 'wä-, chiefly Midland also 'wȯr-shiŋ- or 'wär-shiŋ-\ noun [George Washington] (1905)
: cake layers put together with a jam or jelly filling

Washington's Birthday noun [George Washington] (1829)
1 : February 22 formerly observed as a legal holiday in most of the states of the U.S.
2 : the third Monday in February observed as a legal holiday in most of the states of the U.S. — called also Presidents' Day

wash·out \'wȯsh-ˌaůt, 'wäsh-\ noun (1873)
1 a : the washing out or away of something and especially of earth in a roadbed by a freshet **b** : a place where earth is washed away
2 : one that fails to measure up : FAILURE: as **a** : one who fails in a course of training or study **b** : an unsuccessful enterprise or undertaking

wash out (1555)
transitive verb
1 : to wash free of an extraneous substance (as dirt)
2 a : to cause to fade by or as if by laundering **b** : to deplete the strength or vitality of **c** : to eliminate as useless or unsatisfactory : REJECT
3 a : to destroy or make useless by the force or action of water ⟨the storm washed out the bridge⟩ **b** : RAIN OUT ⟨the game was washed out⟩
intransitive verb
1 : to become depleted of color or vitality : FADE
2 : to fail to meet requirements or measure up to a standard

wash·rag \'wȯsh-,rag, 'wäsh-\ *noun* (1890)
: WASHCLOTH

wash·room \-,rüm, -,rum\ *noun* (1806)
: a room that is equipped with washing and toilet facilities : LAVATORY

wash·stand \-,stand\ *noun* (1789)
1 : a stand holding articles needed for washing one's face and hands
2 : a washbowl permanently set in place and attached to water and drainpipes

wash·tub \-,təb\ *noun* (1602)
: a tub in which clothes are washed or soaked

wash·up \-,əp\ *noun* (1884)
: the act or process of washing clean

wash up (1751)
transitive verb
1 : to get rid of by washing ⟨*wash up* the spilled milk⟩
2 : EXHAUST, FINISH
intransitive verb
1 : to wash one's face and hands
2 *British* : to wash the dishes after a meal
3 : to be deposited by or as if by a swell of waves ⟨seaweed *washed up* on the shore⟩

wash·wom·an \'wȯsh-,wu̇-mən, 'wäsh-\ *noun* (1590)
: WASHERWOMAN

washy \'wȯ-shē, 'wä-\ *adjective* **wash·i·er; -est** (1615)
1 a : WEAK, WATERY ⟨*washy* tea⟩ **b** : deficient in color : PALLID **c** : lacking in vigor, individuality, or definiteness
2 : lacking in condition and in firmness of flesh

wasn't \'wə-z°nt, 'wä-, *dialect also* 'wə-t°n(t)\ (circa 1849)
: was not

wasp \'wäsp, 'wȯsp\ *noun* [Middle English *waspe,* from Old English *wæps, wæsp;* akin to Old High German *wafsa* wasp, Latin *vespa* wasp] (before 12th century)
1 : any of numerous social or solitary winged hymenopterous insects (especially families Sphecidae and Vespidae) that usually have a slender smooth body with the abdomen attached by a narrow stalk, well-developed wings, biting mouthparts, and in the females and workers an often formidable sting, and that are largely carnivorous and often provision their nests with caterpillars, insects, or spiders killed or paralyzed by stinging for their larvae to feed on — compare BEE

wasp 1

2 : any of various hymenopterous insects (as a chalcid or ichneumon fly) other than wasps with larvae that are parasitic on other arthropods
— **wasp·like** \-,līk\ *adjective*

WASP *or* **Wasp** \'wäsp, 'wȯsp\ *noun, often attributive* [*w*hite *A*nglo-*S*axon *P*rotestant] (1957)
: an American of Northern European and especially British ancestry and of Protestant background; *especially* : a member of the dominant and the most privileged class of people in the U.S. — sometimes used disparagingly
— **Wasp·dom** \-dəm\ *noun*
— **Wasp·ish** \'wäs-pish, 'wȯs-\ *adjective*
— **Wasp·ish·ness** *noun*
— **Waspy** \-pē\ *adjective*

wasp·ish \'wäs-pish, 'wȯs-\ *adjective* (1566)
1 : resembling a wasp in behavior; *especially* : SNAPPISH, PETULANT
2 : resembling a wasp in form; *especially* : slightly built
— **wasp·ish·ly** *adverb*
— **wasp·ish·ness** *noun*

wasp waist *noun* (1870)
: a very slender waist
— **wasp–waist·ed** \'wäsp-'wā-stəd, 'wȯsp-\ *adjective*

¹was·sail \'wä-səl *also* wä-'sā(ə)l\ *noun* [Middle English *wæs hæil,* from Old Norse *ves heill* be well, from *ves* (imperative singular of *vera* to be) + *heill* healthy — more at WAS, WHOLE] (13th century)
1 : an early English toast to someone's health
2 : a hot drink that is made with wine, beer, or cider, spices, sugar, and usually baked apples and is traditionally served in a large bowl especially at Christmastime
3 : riotous drinking : REVELRY

²wassail (14th century)
intransitive verb
1 : to indulge in wassail : CAROUSE
2 *dialect English* : to sing carols from house to house at Christmas
transitive verb
: to drink to the health or thriving of

was·sail bowl \'wä-səl-\ *noun* (1606)
1 : a bowl that is used for the serving of wassail
2 : WASSAIL 2

was·sail·er \'wä-sə-lər *also* wä-'sā-lər\ *noun* (1634)
1 : one that carouses : REVELER
2 *archaic* : one who goes about singing carols

Was·ser·mann reaction \'wä-sər-mən-, 'vä-\ *noun* [August von *Wassermann*] (1911)
: the complement-fixing reaction that occurs in a positive complement-fixation test for syphilis using the serum of an infected individual

Wassermann test *noun* (1909)
: a test for the detection of syphilitic infection using the Wassermann reaction — called also *Wasserman*

wast \'wəst, 'wäst\ *archaic past 2d singular of* BE

wast·age \'wā-stij\ *noun* (1756)
: loss, decrease, or destruction of something (as by use, decay, erosion, or leakage); *especially* : wasteful or avoidable loss of something valuable

¹waste \'wāst\ *noun* [Middle English *waste, wast;* in sense 1, from Old North French *wast,* from *wast,* adjective, desolate, waste, from Latin *vastus;* in other senses, from Middle English *wasten* to waste — more at VAST] (13th century)
1 a : a sparsely settled or barren region : DESERT **b** : uncultivated land **c** : a broad and empty expanse (as of water)
2 : the act or an instance of wasting : the state of being wasted
3 a : loss through breaking down of bodily tissue **b** : gradual loss or decrease by use, wear, or decay
4 a : damaged, defective, or superfluous material produced by a manufacturing process: as (1) : material rejected during a textile manufacturing process and used usually for wiping away dirt and oil ⟨cotton *waste*⟩ (2) : SCRAP (3) : an unwanted by-product of a manufacturing process, chemical laboratory, or nuclear reactor ⟨toxic *waste*⟩ ⟨hazardous *waste*⟩ ⟨nuclear *waste*⟩ **b** : refuse from places of human or animal habitation: as (1) : GARBAGE, RUBBISH (2) : EXCREMENT — often used in plural (3) : SEWAGE **c** : material derived by mechanical and chemical weathering of the land and moved down sloping surfaces or carried by streams to the sea

²waste *verb* **wast·ed; wast·ing** [Middle English, from Old North French *waster,* from Latin *vastare,* from *vastus* desolate, waste] (13th century)
transitive verb
1 : to lay waste; *especially* : to damage or destroy gradually and progressively ⟨reclaiming land *wasted* by strip-mining⟩
2 : to cause to shrink in physical bulk or strength : EMACIATE, ENFEEBLE
3 : to wear away or diminish gradually : CONSUME

4 a : to spend or use carelessly : SQUANDER **b** : to allow to be used inefficiently or become dissipated
5 : KILL; *also* : to injure severely
intransitive verb
1 : to lose weight, strength, or vitality — often used with *away*
2 a : to become diminished in bulk or substance **b** : to become consumed
3 : to spend money or consume property extravagantly or improvidently
synonym see RAVAGE
— **waste one's breath** : to accomplish nothing by speaking

³waste *adjective* [Middle English *waste, wast,* from Old North French *wast*] (14th century)
1 a (1) : being wild and uninhabited : DESOLATE (2) : ARID, EMPTY **b** : not cultivated : not productive
2 : being in a ruined or devastated condition
3 [¹waste] **a** : discarded as worthless, defective, or of no use : REFUSE ⟨*waste* material⟩ **b** : excreted from or stored in inert form in a living body as a byproduct of vital activity ⟨*waste* disposal in birds⟩
4 [¹waste] : serving to conduct or hold refuse material; *specifically* : carrying off superfluous water
5 : WASTED 4

waste·bas·ket \'wās(t)-,bas-kət\ *noun* (1850)
: a receptacle for refuse and especially for wastepaper — called also *wastepaper basket*

wasted *adjective* (15th century)
1 : laid waste : RAVAGED
2 : impaired in strength or health : EMACIATED
3 *archaic* : gone by : ELAPSED ⟨the chronicle of *wasted* time —Shakespeare⟩
4 : unprofitably used, made, or expended ⟨*wasted* effort⟩
5 *slang* : intoxicated from drugs or alcohol

waste·ful \'wāst-fəl\ *adjective* (14th century)
: given to or marked by waste : LAVISH, PRODIGAL
— **waste·ful·ly** \-fə-lē\ *adverb*
— **waste·ful·ness** *noun*

waste·land \'wāst-,land *also* -lənd\ *noun* (14th century)
1 : barren or uncultivated land ⟨a desert *wasteland*⟩
2 : an ugly often devastated or barely inhabitable place or area
3 : something (as a way of life) that is spiritually and emotionally arid and unsatisfying

waste·pa·per \'wās(t)-'pā-pər\ *noun* (1585)
: paper discarded as used, superfluous, or not fit for use

waste pipe *noun* (circa 1512)
: a pipe for carrying off waste fluid

wast·er \'wā-stər\ *noun* (14th century)
1 a (1) : one that spends or consumes extravagantly and without thought for the future (2) : a dissolute person **b** : one that uses wastefully or causes or permits waste ⟨a procedure that is a *waster* of time⟩ **c** : one that lays waste : DESTROYER
2 : an imperfect or inferior manufactured article or object

waste·wa·ter \'wāst-,wȯ-tər, -,wä-\ *noun* (15th century)
: water that has been used (as in a manufacturing process) : SEWAGE

wast·ing \'wā-stiŋ\ *adjective* (13th century)
1 : laying waste : DEVASTATING
2 : undergoing or causing decay or loss of strength ⟨*wasting* diseases such as tuberculosis⟩

wast·rel \'wās-trəl *also* 'wäs-\ *noun* [irregular from ²*waste*] (circa 1841)
1 : VAGABOND, WAIF
2 : one who dissipates resources foolishly and self-indulgently : PROFLIGATE

¹watch \'wäch, 'wȯch\ *verb* [Middle English *wacchen,* from Old English *wæccan* — more at WAKE] (before 12th century)
intransitive verb

1 a : to keep vigil as a devotional exercise **b :** to be awake during the night
2 a : to be attentive or vigilant **b :** to keep guard
3 a : to keep someone or something under close observation **b :** to observe as a spectator ⟨the country *watched* as stocks fell sharply⟩
4 : to be expectant : WAIT ⟨*watch* for the signal⟩
transitive verb
1 : to keep under guard
2 a : to observe closely in order to check on action or change ⟨being *watched* by the police⟩ **b :** to look at : OBSERVE ⟨sat and *watched* the crowd⟩ **c :** to look on at ⟨*watch* television⟩ ⟨*watch* a ball game⟩
3 a : to take care of : TEND **b :** to be careful of ⟨*watches* his diet⟩
4 : to be on the alert for : BIDE ⟨*watched* her opportunity⟩
— **watch it :** look out : be careful ⟨*watch it* when you handle the glassware⟩
— **watch one's step :** to proceed with extreme care : act or talk warily
— **watch over :** to have charge of : SUPERINTEND

²watch *noun* (before 12th century)
1 a : the act of keeping awake to guard, protect, or attend **b** *obsolete* **:** the state of being wakeful **c :** a wake over a dead body **d :** a state of alert and continuous attention **e :** close observation : SURVEILLANCE **f :** a notice or bulletin that alerts the public to the possibility of severe weather conditions occurring in the near future ⟨winter storm *watch*⟩
2 a : any of the definite divisions of the night made by ancient peoples **b :** one of the indeterminate intervals marking the passage of night — usually used in plural ⟨the silent *watches* of the night⟩
3 a : LOOKOUT, WATCHMAN **b** *archaic* **:** the office or function of a sentinel or guard
4 a : a body of soldiers or sentinels making up a guard **b :** a watchman or body of watchmen formerly assigned to patrol the streets of a town at night, announce the hours, and act as police
5 a (1) **:** a portion of time during which a part of a ship's company is on duty (2) **:** the part of a ship's company required to be on duty during a particular watch (3) **:** a sailor's assigned duty period **b :** a period of duty : SHIFT **c :** a term as holder especially of an overseeing or managerial office ⟨the business grew on her *watch*⟩
6 : a portable timepiece designed to be worn (as on the wrist) or carried in the pocket — compare CLOCK

watch·able \'wä-chə-bəl, 'wȯ-\ *adjective* (1954)
: worth watching
— **watchable** *noun*
watch and ward *noun* (14th century)
1 : continuous unbroken vigilance and guard
2 : service as a watchman or sentinel required from a feudal tenant
watch·band \'wäch-,band, 'wȯch-\ *noun* (1924)
: the bracelet or strap of a wristwatch
watch cap *noun* (1886)
: a knitted close-fitting usually navy-blue cap worn especially by enlisted men in the U.S. navy in cold or stormy weather
watch·case \'wäch-,kās, 'wȯch-\ *noun* (1671)
: the outside metal covering of a watch
¹watch·dog \-,dȯg\ *noun* (1610)
1 : a dog kept to guard property
2 : one that guards against loss, waste, theft, or undesirable practices
²watchdog *transitive verb* (1902)
: to act as watchdog for
watch·er \'wä-chər, 'wȯ-\ *noun* (1509)
: one that watches: **a :** one that sits up or continues awake at night **b :** WATCHMAN **c** (1) **:** one that keeps watch beside a dead person

(2) **:** one that attends a sick person at night **d :** a person who closely follows or observes someone or something ⟨a Supreme Court *watcher*⟩ — often used in combination ⟨celebrity-*watchers*⟩ **e :** a representative of a party or candidate who is stationed at the polls on an election day to watch the conduct of officials and voters
watch fire *noun* (1801)
: a fire lighted as a signal or for the use of a guard
watch·ful \'wäch-fəl, 'wȯch-\ *adjective* (1548)
1 *archaic* **a :** not able or accustomed to sleep or rest : WAKEFUL **b :** causing sleeplessness **c :** spent in wakefulness : SLEEPLESS
2 : carefully observant or attentive : being on the watch ☆
— **watch·ful·ly** \-fə-lē\ *adverb*
— **watch·ful·ness** *noun*
watch·mak·er \-,mā-kər\ *noun* (1630)
: one that makes or repairs watches or clocks
— **watch·mak·ing** \-,mā-kiŋ\ *noun*
watch·man \-mən\ *noun* (15th century)
: a person who keeps watch : GUARD
watch night *noun* (1742)
: a devotional service lasting until after midnight especially on New Year's Eve
watch out *intransitive verb* (1845)
: to be vigilant or alert : be on the lookout ⟨you'd better *watch out*⟩ ⟨*watch out* for the tree!⟩
watch pocket *noun* (1831)
: a small pocket just below the front waistband of men's trousers
watch·tow·er \'wäch-,taur, 'wȯch-\ *noun* (1544)
: a tower for a lookout
watch·word \-,wərd\ *noun* (15th century)
1 : a word or phrase used as a sign of recognition among members of the same society, class, or group
2 a : a word or motto that embodies a principle or guide to action of an individual or group : SLOGAN ⟨"safety" is our *watchword*⟩ **b :** a guiding principle ⟨change is the *watchword* for both parties⟩
¹wa·ter \'wȯ-tər, 'wä-\ *noun, often attributive* [Middle English, from Old English *wæter;* akin to Old High German *wazzar* water, Greek *hydōr,* Latin *unda* wave] (before 12th century)
1 a : the liquid that descends from the clouds as rain, forms streams, lakes, and seas, and is a major constituent of all living matter and that when pure is an odorless, tasteless, very slightly compressible liquid oxide of hydrogen H_2O which appears bluish in thick layers, freezes at 0° C and boils at 100° C, has a maximum density at 4° C and a high specific heat, is feebly ionized to hydrogen and hydroxyl ions, and is a poor conductor of electricity and a good solvent **b :** a natural mineral water — usually used in plural
2 : a particular quantity or body of water: as **a** (1) *plural* **:** the water occupying or flowing in a particular bed (2) *chiefly British* **:** LAKE, POND **b :** a quantity or depth of water adequate for some purpose (as navigation) **c** *plural* (1) **:** a band of seawater abutting on the land of a particular sovereignty and under the control of that sovereignty (2) **:** the sea of a particular part of the earth **d :** WATER SUPPLY ⟨threatened to turn off the *water*⟩
3 : travel or transportation on water ⟨we went by *water*⟩
4 : the level of water at a particular state of the tide : TIDE
5 : liquid containing or resembling water: as **a** (1) **:** a pharmaceutical or cosmetic preparation made with water (2) **:** a watery solution of a gaseous or readily volatile substance — compare AMMONIA WATER **b** *archaic* **:** a distilled fluid (as an essence); *especially* **:** a distilled alcoholic liquor **c :** a watery fluid (as tears, urine, or sap) formed or circulating in a living body **d :** AMNIOTIC FLUID; *also* **:** BAG OF WATERS

6 a : the degree of clarity and luster of a precious stone **b :** degree of excellence ⟨a scholar of the first *water*⟩
7 : WATERCOLOR
8 a : capital stock not representing assets of the issuing company and not backed by earning power **b :** fictitious or exaggerated asset entries that give a stock an unrealistic book value
— **above water :** out of difficulty
²water (before 12th century)
transitive verb
1 : to moisten, sprinkle, or soak with water
2 : to supply with water for drink
3 : to supply water to
4 : to treat with or as if with water; *specifically* **:** to impart a lustrous appearance and wavy pattern to (cloth) by calendering
5 a : to dilute by the addition of water — often used with *down* ⟨*water* down the punch⟩ **b :** to add to the aggregate par value of (securities) without a corresponding addition to the assets represented by the securities
intransitive verb
1 : to form or secrete water or watery matter (as tears or saliva)
2 : to get or take water: as **a :** to take on a supply of water **b :** to drink water
water bag *noun* (1638)
1 : a bag for holding water; *especially* **:** one designed to keep water cool for drinking by evaporation through a slightly porous surface
2 : the fetal membranes enclosing the amniotic fluid — used especially of domestic animals
water balance *noun* (1911)
: the ratio between the water assimilated into the body and that lost from the body; *also* **:** the condition of the body when this ratio approximates unity
water ballet *noun* (1926)
: a synchronized sequence of movements performed by a group of swimmers
water bear *noun* (1852)
: TARDIGRADE
Water Bearer *noun*
: AQUARIUS 1, 2a
water bed *noun* (1844)
: a bed whose mattress is a watertight bag filled with water
water beetle *noun* (circa 1668)
: any of numerous oval flattened aquatic beetles (especially family Dytiscidae) that swim by means of their fringed hind legs which act together as oars
wa·ter·bird \'wȯ-tər-,bərd, 'wä-\ *noun* (15th century)
: a swimming or wading bird — compare WATERFOWL
water biscuit *noun* (circa 1790)
: a cracker of flour and water and sometimes fat

☆ **SYNONYMS**
Watchful, vigilant, wide-awake, alert mean being on the lookout especially for danger or opportunity. WATCHFUL is the least explicit term ⟨the *watchful* eye of the department supervisor⟩. VIGILANT suggests intense, unremitting, wary watchfulness ⟨eternally *vigilant* in the safeguarding of democracy⟩. WIDE-AWAKE applies to watchfulness for opportunities and developments more often than dangers ⟨*wide-awake* companies latched onto the new technology⟩. ALERT stresses readiness or promptness in meeting danger or in seizing opportunity ⟨*alert* traders anticipated the stock market's slide⟩.

\ə\ **abut** \ᵊ\ **kitten** \ər\ **further** \a\ **ash** \ā\ **ace**
\ä\ **mop, mar** \aú\ **out** \ch\ **chin** \e\ **bet** \ē\ **easy**
\g\ **go** \i\ **hit** \ī\ **ice** \j\ **job** \ŋ\ **sing** \ō\ **go**
\ȯ\ **law** \ȯi\ **boy** \th\ **thin** \t̲h̲\ **the** \ü\ **loot** \ú\ **foot**
\y\ **yet** \zh\ **vision** *see also* Guide to Pronunciation

water blister *noun* (1895)
: a blister with a clear watery content that is not purulent or sanguineous

water bloom *noun* (1903)
: an accumulation of algae and especially of blue-green algae at or near the surface of a body of water

water boatman *noun* (1815)
1 : BACK SWIMMER
2 : any of various aquatic bugs (family Corixidae) with one pair of legs modified into paddles

wa·ter·borne \'wȯ-tər-ˌbōrn, 'wä-, -ˌbȯrn\ *adjective* (circa 1559)
: supported or carried by water ⟨*waterborne* commerce⟩ ⟨*waterborne* infection⟩

water boy *noun* (1859)
: one who keeps a group (as of football players) supplied with drinking water

wa·ter·buck \'wȯ-tər-ˌbək, 'wä-\ *noun, plural* **waterbuck** *or* **waterbucks** (1850)
: an antelope (*Kobus ellipsiprymnus*) of sub-Saharan Africa that commonly frequent streams or wet areas

water buffalo *noun* (circa 1890)
: an often domesticated Asian buffalo (*Bubalus bubalis* synonym *B. arnee*)

water bug *noun* (1750)
: any of various small arthropods and especially insects that frequent damp or wet places: as **a**

water buffalo

: GERMAN COCKROACH **b** : WATER BOATMAN **c** : any of various large aquatic bugs (family Belostomatidae) with the hind legs flattened and used for swimming

water cannon *noun* (1964)
: a large truck-mounted nozzle for directing a high-pressure stream of water (as at a crowd of rioters or demonstrators)

water chestnut *noun* (1854)
1 : any of a genus (*Trapa* and especially *T. natans* of the family Trapaceae, the water-chestnut family) of Old World aquatic herbs sometimes grown as ornamentals; *also* : its edible nutlike spiny fruit
2 : a whitish crunchy vegetable used especially in Chinese cooking that is the peeled and often sliced tuber of a sedge (*Eleocharis dulcis* synonym *E. tuberosa*) native to Asia but widely cultivated elsewhere; *also* : the tuber or the sedge itself

water clock *noun* (1601)
: an instrument designed to measure time by the fall or flow of a quantity of water — called also *clepsydra*

water closet *noun* (1755)
1 : a compartment or room for defecation and excretion into a toilet bowl
2 : a toilet bowl and its accessories

wa·ter·col·or \'wȯ-tər-ˌkə-lər, 'wä-\ *noun* (1596)
1 : a paint of which the liquid is a water dispersion of the binding material (as glue, casein, or gum)
2 : the art or method of painting with watercolors
3 : a picture or design executed in watercolors
— **watercolor** *adjective*
— **wa·ter·col·or·ist** \-ˌkə-lə-rist\ *noun*

wa·ter·cool·er \'wȯ-tər-ˌkü-lər, 'wä-\ *noun* (1846)
: a device for dispensing refrigerated drinking water

wa·ter·course \'wȯ-tər-ˌkōrs, -ˌkȯrs\ *noun* (1510)
1 : a natural or artificial channel through which water flows
2 : a stream of water (as a river, brook, or underground stream)

wa·ter·craft \-ˌkraft\ *noun* (1566)
1 : skill in aquatic activities (as managing boats)
2 a : SHIP, BOAT **b** : craft for water transport

wa·ter·cress \-ˌkres\ *noun* (14th century)
: any of several water-loving cresses; *especially* : a perennial European cress (*Nasturtium officinale*) naturalized in the U.S. and used especially in salads or as a potherb

water cycle *noun* (1928)
: HYDROLOGIC CYCLE

water dog *noun* (14th century)
1 : any of several large American salamanders; *especially* : any of a genus (*Necturus* of the family Proteidae) with external gills
2 : a person (as a skilled sailor) who is quite at ease in or on water

water down *transitive verb* (1850)
: to reduce or temper the force or effectiveness of
— **wa·tered-down** *adjective*

wa·ter·er \'wȯ-tər-ər, 'wä-\ *noun* (1549)
: one that waters: as **a** : a person who obtains or supplies drinking water **b** : a device used for supplying water to livestock and poultry — called also *drinker*

wa·ter·fall \-ˌfȯl\ *noun* (before 12th century)
1 a : a perpendicular or very steep descent of the water of a stream **b** : an artificial waterfall (as in a hotel lobby or a nightclub)
2 : something resembling a waterfall

water flea *noun* (circa 1585)
: any of various small active dark or brightly colored aquatic crustaceans (as a daphnia or cyclops)

¹wa·ter·flood \-ˌfləd\ *noun* (1928)
: the process of waterflooding an oil well

²waterflood *intransitive verb* (1928)
: to pump water into the ground around an oil well nearing depletion in order to loosen and force out additional oil

wa·ter·fowl \'wȯ-tər-ˌfau̇l, 'wä-\ *noun* (14th century)
1 : a bird that frequents water; *especially* : a swimming bird
2 waterfowl *plural* : swimming game birds as distinguished from upland game birds and shorebirds

wa·ter·fowl·er \-ˌfau̇-lər\ *noun* (1968)
: a hunter of waterfowl
— **wa·ter·fowl·ing** \-liŋ\ *noun*

wa·ter·front \-ˌfrənt\ *noun* (1766)
: land, land with buildings, or a section of a town fronting or abutting on a body of water

water gap *noun* (1756)
: a pass in a mountain ridge through which a stream runs — compare WIND GAP

water garden *noun* (1891)
1 : a garden in which aquatic plants predominate
2 : a garden built about a stream or pool as a central feature

water gas *noun* (1851)
: a poisonous flammable gaseous mixture that consists chiefly of carbon monoxide and hydrogen with small amounts of methane, carbon dioxide, and nitrogen, is usually made by blowing air and then steam over red-hot coke or coal, and is used as a fuel or after carbureting as an illuminant

Wa·ter·gate \-ˌgāt\ *noun* [*Watergate*, apartment and office complex in Washington, D.C.; from the scandal following the break-in at the Democratic National Committee headquarters there in 1972] (1973)
: a scandal usually involving abuses of office, skulduggery, and a cover-up

water gate *noun* (14th century)
1 : a gate (as of a building) giving access to a body of water
2 : FLOODGATE

water gauge *noun* (circa 1706)
: an instrument to measure or find the depth or quantity of water or to indicate the height of its surface especially in a steam boiler

water glass *noun* (1612)

1 : a glass vessel (as a drinking glass) for holding water
2 : an instrument consisting of an open box or tube with a glass bottom used for examining objects in or under water
3 : a substance that consists usually of the silicate of sodium, is found in commerce as a glassy mass, a stony powder, or dissolved in water as a viscous syrupy liquid, and is used especially as a cement, a protective coating, and as a fireproofing agent

water gun *noun* (1951)
: WATER PISTOL

water hammer *noun* (circa 1890)
: a concussion or sound of concussion of moving water against the sides of a containing pipe or vessel (as a steam pipe)

water haul *noun* [from the figure of a fishing net that catches nothing but water] (1823)
: a fruitless effort

water heater *noun* (circa 1876)
: an apparatus for heating and usually storing hot water (as for domestic use)

water hemlock *noun* (1764)
: a tall poisonous Eurasian perennial herb (*Cicuta virosa*) of the carrot family; *also* : any of several poisonous North American plants (especially *Cicuta maculata* and *C. douglasii*) of the same genus

water hen *noun* (circa 1529)
: any of various birds (as a coot or gallinule) of the rail family

water hole *noun* (circa 1653)
1 : a natural hole or hollow containing water
2 : a hole in a surface of ice

water hyacinth *noun* (circa 1890)
: a showy floating aquatic plant (*Eichhornia crassipes*) of the family Pontederiaceae) of tropical America that often clogs waterways (as in the southern U.S.)

water ice *noun* (1818)
: a frozen dessert of water, sugar, and flavoring

watering can *noun* (1692)
: a vessel usually with a spout used to sprinkle or pour water especially on plants — called also *watering pot*

watering hole *noun* (1955)
: a place where people gather socially; *especially* : WATERING PLACE 3

watering place *noun* (15th century)
1 : a place where water may be obtained; *especially* : one where animals and especially livestock come to drink
2 : a health or recreational resort featuring mineral springs or bathing
3 : a place (as a nightclub, bar, or lounge) where drink is available

wa·ter·ish \'wȯ-tər-ish, 'wä-\ *adjective* (1542)
: somewhat watery
— **wa·ter·ish·ness** *noun*

water jacket *noun* (1869)
: an outer casing which holds water or through which water circulates to cool the interior; *specifically* : the enclosed space surrounding the cylinder block of an internal combustion engine and containing the cooling liquid

water jump *noun* (1875)
: an obstacle (as in a steeplechase) consisting of a pool, stream, or ditch of water

wa·ter·leaf \'wȯ-tər-ˌlēf, 'wä-\ *noun, plural* **-leafs** \-ˌlēfs\ (1760)
: any of a genus (*Hydrophyllum* of the family Hydrophyllaceae, the waterleaf family) of perennial North American woodland herbs with lobed or pinnate toothed leaves and cymes of bell-shaped flowers

wa·ter·less \-ləs\ *adjective* (before 12th century)
1 : lacking or destitute of water : DRY
2 : not requiring water (as for cooling or cooking)
— **wa·ter·less·ness** *noun*

water level *noun* (1563)

1 : an instrument to show the level by means of the surface of water in a trough or in a U-shaped tube
2 : the surface of still water: as **a :** the level assumed by the surface of a particular body or column of water **b :** the waterline of a vessel

water lily *noun* (15th century)
: any of various aquatic plants (especially genera *Nymphaea* and *Nuphar* of the family Nymphaeaceae, the water-lily family) with floating leaves and usually showy flowers; *broadly* **:** an aquatic plant (as a water hyacinth) with showy flowers

wa·ter·line \'wȯ-tər-ˌlīn, 'wä-\ *noun* (circa 1625)
: a line that marks the level of the surface of water on something: as **a** (1) **:** the point on the hull of a ship or boat to which the water rises (2) **:** a line marked on the outside of a ship that corresponds with the water's surface when the ship is afloat on an even keel under specified conditions of loading **b :** SHORELINE 1

wa·ter·log \-ˌlȯg, -ˌläg\ *transitive verb* [back-formation from *waterlogged*] (1779)
: to make waterlogged

wa·ter·logged \-ˌlȯgd, -ˌlägd\ *adjective* [¹water + log to accumulate in the hold] (circa 1776)
1 : so filled or soaked with water as to be heavy or hard to manage ⟨*waterlogged* boats⟩
2 : saturated with water ⟨*waterlogged* soil⟩

wa·ter·loo \ˌwȯ-tər-'lü, ˌwä-\ *noun, plural* **-loos** [*Waterloo*, Belgium, scene of Napoleon's defeat in 1815] (1816)
: a decisive or final defeat or setback

water main *noun* (1803)
: a pipe or conduit for conveying water

wa·ter·man \'wȯ-tər-mən, 'wä-\ *noun* (15th century)
: one who works or lives on the water: as **a :** a man who makes his living from the water (as by fishing) **b :** a boatman who plies for hire usually on inland waters or harbors

wa·ter·man·ship \-ˌship\ *noun* (1882)
: the business, skill, or art of a waterman: as **a :** technique or expertness in rowing **b :** technique or expertness in swimming

¹wa·ter·mark \'wȯ-tər-ˌmärk, 'wä-\ *noun* (1678)
1 : a mark indicating the height to which water has risen
2 : a marking in paper resulting from differences in thickness usually produced by pressure of a projecting design in the mold or on a processing roll and visible when the paper is held up to the light; *also* **:** the design of or the metal pattern producing the marking

²watermark *transitive verb* (1866)
1 : to mark (paper) with a watermark
2 : to impress (a given design) as a watermark

wa·ter·mel·on \-ˌme-lən\ *noun* (1615)
1 : a large oblong or roundish fruit with a hard green or white rind often striped or variegated, a sweet watery pink, yellowish, or red pulp, and usually many seeds
2 : a widely grown African vine (*Citrullus lanatus* synonym *C. vulgaris*) of the gourd family that bears watermelons

water meter *noun* (circa 1858)
: an instrument for recording the quantity of water passing through a particular outlet

water milfoil *noun* (1578)
: any of a genus (*Myriophyllum* of the family Haloragaceae) of aquatic plants with finely pinnate submersed leaves

water mill *noun* (15th century)
: a mill whose machinery is moved by water

water moccasin *noun* (1821)
1 : a venomous semiaquatic pit viper (*Agkistrodon piscivorus*) chiefly of the southeastern U.S. that is closely related to the copperhead — called also *cottonmouth, cottonmouth moccasin*
2 : an American water snake (genus *Nerodia*)

water mold *noun* (1899)
: an aquatic fungus (as of the genus *Saprolegnia*)

water nymph *noun* (14th century)
: a nymph (as a naiad, Nereid, or Oceanid) associated with a body of water

water moccasin 1

water oak *noun* (1687)
: any of several American oaks (especially *Quercus nigra*) that thrive in wet soils

water of crystallization (1791)
: water of hydration present in many crystallized substances that is usually essential for maintenance of a particular crystal structure

water of hydration (1889)
: water that is chemically combined with a substance to form a hydrate and can be expelled (as by heating) without essentially altering the composition of the substance

water on the knee (circa 1934)
: an accumulation of inflammatory exudate in the knee joint often following an injury

water ouzel *noun* (1622)
: DIPPER 2

water parting *noun* (1859)
: DIVIDE 2a

water pepper *noun* (circa 1538)
: an annual smartweed (*Polygonum hydropiper*) of moist soils with extremely acrid peppery juice

water pimpernel *noun* (circa 1760)
: either of two small white-flowered herbs (*Samolus valerandi* of Eurasia and *S. floribundus* synonym *S. parviflorus* of America) of the primrose family that grow in wet places

water pipe *noun* (15th century)
1 : a pipe for conveying water
2 : a smoking device that consists of a bowl mounted on a vessel of water which is provided with a long tube and arranged so that smoke is drawn through the water where it is cooled and up the tube to the mouth

water pistol *noun* (1905)
: a toy pistol designed to squirt a jet of liquid — called also *water gun, squirt gun*

water plantain *noun* (circa 1538)
: any of a genus (*Alisma* of the family Alismataceae, the water-plantain family) of marsh or aquatic herbs with acrid sap and scapose 3-petaled flowers

water polo *noun* (1884)
: a goal game similar to soccer that is played in water by teams of swimmers using a ball resembling a soccer ball

wa·ter·pow·er \'wȯ-tər-ˌpau̇(-ə)r, 'wä-\ *noun* (1817)
1 : the power of water employed to move machinery
2 : a fall of water suitable for being used to move machinery

water privilege *noun* (1804)
: the right to use water especially as a source of mechanical power

¹wa·ter·proof \'wȯ-tər-ˌprüf, 'wä-\ *adjective* (1736)
: impervious to water; *especially* **:** covered or treated with a material (as a solution of rubber) to prevent permeation by water
— **wa·ter·proof·ness** *noun*

²waterproof *noun* (1799)
1 : a waterproof fabric
2 *chiefly British* **:** RAINCOAT

³waterproof *transitive verb* (1841)
: to make waterproof
— **wa·ter·proof·er** *noun*

wa·ter·proof·ing \-ˌprü-fiŋ\ *noun* (1845)
1 a : the act or process of making something waterproof **b :** the condition of being made waterproof
2 : something (as a coating) capable of imparting waterproofness

water rat *noun* (1552)
1 : a rodent that frequents water

2 : a waterfront loafer or petty thief

wa·ter-re·pel·lent \ˌwȯ-tə(r)-ri-'pe-lənt, ˌwä-\ *adjective* (1896)
: treated with a finish that is resistant but not impervious to penetration by water

wa·ter-re·sis·tant \-ri-'zis-tənt\ *adjective* (1921)
: WATER-REPELLENT

water right *noun* (1793)
: a right to the use of water (as for irrigation); *especially* **:** RIPARIAN RIGHT

water sapphire *noun* (circa 1741)
: a deep blue cordierite sometimes used as a gem

wa·ter·scape \'wȯ-tər-ˌskāp, 'wä-\ *noun* (circa 1854)
: a water or sea view **:** SEASCAPE 1

water scorpion *noun* (1681)
: any of numerous aquatic bugs (family Nepidae) with the end of the abdomen prolonged by a long breathing tube

wa·ter·shed \'wȯ-tər-ˌshed, 'wä-\ *noun* (1803)
1 a : DIVIDE 2a **b :** a region or area bounded peripherally by a divide and draining ultimately to a particular watercourse or body of water
2 : a crucial dividing point, line, or factor **:** TURNING POINT
— **watershed** *adjective*

water shield *noun* (circa 1818)
: an aquatic plant (*Brasenia schreberi*) of the water-lily family having floating oval leaves with a gelatinous coating and small dull purple flowers; *also* **:** any of a related genus (*Cabomba*)

¹wa·ter·side \'wȯ-tər-ˌsīd, 'wä-\ *noun* (14th century)
: the margin of a body of water **:** WATERFRONT

²waterside *adjective* (1663)
1 : employed along the waterside ⟨*waterside* workers⟩; *also* **:** of or relating to the workers along the waterside ⟨a *waterside* strike⟩
2 : of, relating to, or located on the waterside ⟨a *waterside* café⟩

water ski *noun* (1931)
: a ski used in planing over water while being towed by a speedboat
— **wa·ter-ski** *intransitive verb*

wa·ter-ski·er \'wȯ-tər-ˌskē-ər, 'wä-\ *noun* (1931)
: one that water-skis

wa·ter-ski·ing \-ˌskē-iŋ\ *noun* (1931)
: the sport of planing and jumping on water skis

water snake *noun* (1601)
: any of various snakes (especially genus *Nerodia* formerly included in the genus *Natrix*) that frequent or inhabit fresh waters and feed largely on aquatic animals

wa·ter-soak \'wȯ-tər-ˌsōk, 'wä-\ *transitive verb* (1791)
: to soak in water

water spaniel *noun* (1566)
: a spaniel of either of two breeds: **a :** AMERICAN WATER SPANIEL **b :** IRISH WATER SPANIEL

water spot *noun* (1939)
: a physiological disorder of citrus fruits in the rainy season in which the epidermal air spaces of the rind become filled with liquid

wa·ter·spout \'wȯ-tər-ˌspau̇t, 'wä-\ *noun* (14th century)
1 : a pipe, duct, or orifice from which water is spouted or through which it is carried
2 : a funnel-shaped or tubular column of rotating cloud-filled wind usually extending from the underside of a cumulus or cumulonimbus cloud down to a cloud of spray torn up by the whirling winds from the surface of an ocean or lake

water sprite *noun* (1798)

: a sprite believed to inhabit or haunt water — WATER NYMPH

water sprout *noun* (circa 1892)
: an extremely vigorous shoot from an adventitious or latent bud on a tree — compare SUCKER 2

water strider *noun* (1849)
: any of various long-legged bugs (family Gerridae) that move about on the surface of the water

water supply *noun* (circa 1882)
: a source, means, or process of supplying water (as for a community) usually including reservoirs, tunnels, and pipelines

water table *noun* (15th century)
1 : a stringcourse or similar member when projecting so as to throw off water
2 : the upper limit of the portion of the ground wholly saturated with water

water taxi *noun* (1928)
: a boat functioning (as within a harbor) as a taxi

wa·ter·thrush \'wȯ-tər-,thrəsh, 'wä-\ *noun* (circa 1813)
: either of two North American warblers (*Seiurus noveboracensis* and *S. motacilla*) found near freshwater (as a stream)

wa·ter·tight \,wȯ-tər-'tīt, ,wä-\ *adjective* (14th century)
1 : of such tight construction or fit as to be impermeable to water except when under sufficient pressure to produce structural discontinuity
2 : leaving no possibility of misconstruction or evasion ⟨a *watertight* lease⟩
— **wa·ter·tight·ness** *noun*

water tower *noun* (circa 1883)
: a tower or standpipe serving as a reservoir to deliver water at a required head

water turkey *noun* (1836)
: a New World anhinga (*Anhinga anhinga*)

water vapor *noun* (1880)
: water in a vaporous form especially when below boiling temperature and diffused (as in the atmosphere)

water–vascular system *noun* (1870)
: a system of canals in echinoderms containing a circulating watery fluid that is used for the movement of the tentacles and tube feet

water wagon *noun* (1904)
: a wagon or motortruck equipped with a tank or barrels for hauling water or for sprinkling
— **on the water wagon :** abstaining from alcoholic beverages **:** on the wagon

water wave *noun* (1882)
: a method or style of setting hair by dampening with water and forming into waves
— **wa·ter–waved** \'wȯ-tər-,wāvd, 'wä-\ *adjective*

wa·ter·way \'wȯ-tər-,wā, 'wä-\ *noun* (15th century)
1 : a way or channel for water
2 : a navigable body of water

wa·ter·weed \-,wēd\ *noun* (1842)
: any of various aquatic plants (as a pondweed) with inconspicuous flowers — compare WATER LILY

wa·ter·wheel \-,hwēl, -,wēl\ *noun* (15th century)
1 : a wheel made to rotate by direct action of water
2 : a wheel for raising water

water wings *noun plural* (1907)
: a pneumatic device that buoys the body of a swimmer and is used especially in learning to swim

water witch *noun* (1817)
: one that dowses for water
— **water witch·ing** \-,wi-chiŋ\ *noun*

waterwheel 1

water witch·er \-,wi-chər\ *noun* (1917)
: WATER WITCH

wa·ter·works \'wȯ-tər-,wərks, 'wä-\ *noun plural* (circa 1586)
1 : an ornamental fountain or cascade
2 : the system of reservoirs, channels, mains, and pumping and purifying equipment by which a water supply is obtained and distributed (as to a city)
3 : the shedding of tears **:** TEARS

wa·ter·worn \-,wōrn, -,wȯrn\ *adjective* (1815)
: worn, smoothed, or polished by the action of water

wa·tery \'wȯ-tə-rē, 'wä-\ *adjective* (before 12th century)
1 a : consisting of, filled with, or surrounded by water **b :** containing, sodden with, or yielding water or a thin liquid ⟨a *watery* solution⟩ ⟨*watery* vesicles⟩
2 a : resembling water or watery matter especially in thin fluidity, soggy texture, paleness, or lack of savor ⟨*watery* blood⟩ ⟨*watery* sunlight⟩ ⟨a *watery* soup⟩ **b :** exhibiting weakness and vapidity **:** WISHY-WASHY ⟨a *watery* writing style⟩
— **wa·ter·i·ly** \-tə-rə-lē\ *adverb*
— **wa·ter·i·ness** \-tə-rē-nəs\ *noun*

wa·ter·zooi \'vä-tər-,zȯi\ *noun* [Flemish, from *water* water + *zooi* quantity of cooked food] (1949)
: a stew of fish or chicken and vegetables in a seasoned stock thickened with cream and egg yolks

Wat·son–Crick \,wät-sən-'krik\ *adjective* (1964)
: of or relating to the Watson-Crick model ⟨*Watson-Crick* helix⟩ ⟨*Watson-Crick* structure⟩ ⟨*Watson-Crick* base pairs⟩

Watson–Crick model *noun* [J. D. *Watson* & F. H. C. *Crick*] (1958)
: a model of DNA structure in which the molecule is a cross-linked double-stranded helix, each strand is composed of alternating links of phosphate and deoxyribose, and the strands are cross-linked by pairs of purine and pyrimidine bases projecting inward from the deoxyribose sugars and joined by hydrogen bonds with adenine paired with thymine and with cytosine paired with guanine — compare DOUBLE HELIX

watt \'wät\ *noun* [James *Watt* (died 1819)] (1882)
: the absolute meter-kilogram-second unit of power equal to the work done at the rate of one joule per second or to the power produced by a current of one ampere across a potential difference of one volt **:** ¹⁄₇₄₆ horsepower

watt·age \'wä-tij\ *noun* (1903)
: amount of power expressed in watts

Wat·teau \(,)wä-'tō\ *adjective* [Antoine *Watteau*] (1873)
1 *of women's dress* **:** having back pleats falling loosely from neckline to hem
2 *of a hat* **:** shallow-crowned and having a wide brim turned up at the back to hold flower trimmings

watt–hour \'wät-'au̇(-ə)r\ *noun* (1888)
: a unit of work or energy equivalent to the power of one watt operating for one hour

¹wat·tle \'wä-tᵊl\ *noun* [Middle English *wattel,* from Old English *watel;* akin to Old High German *wadal* bandage] (before 12th century)
1 a : a fabrication of poles interwoven with slender branches, withes, or reeds and used especially formerly in building **b :** material for such construction **c** *plural* **:** poles laid on a roof to support thatch
2 : a fleshy dependent process usually about the head or neck (as of a bird)
3 *Australian* **:** ACACIA 2
— **wat·tled** \-tᵊld\ *adjective*

²wattle *transitive verb* **wat·tled; wat·tling** \'wät-liŋ, 'wä-tᵊl-iŋ\ (14th century)
1 : to form or build of or with wattle

2 a : to form into wattle **:** interlace to form wattle **b :** to unite or make solid by interweaving light flexible material

wattle and daub *noun* (1808)
: a framework of woven rods and twigs covered and plastered with clay and used in building construction

wat·tle·bird \'wä-tᵊl-,bərd\ *noun* (1819)
: any of several Australasian honeyeaters (genus *Anthochaera*) having fleshy pendulous ear wattles

watt·me·ter \'wät-,mē-tər\ *noun* [International Scientific Vocabulary] (1887)
: an instrument for measuring electric power in watts

Wa·tu·si \wä-'tü-sē\ *noun, plural* **Watusi** *also* **Watusis** (1899)
: TUTSI

¹wave \'wāv\ *verb* **waved; wav·ing** [Middle English, from Old English *wafian* to wave with the hands; akin to *wæfan* to clothe and perhaps to Old English *wefan* to weave] (before 12th century)
intransitive verb
1 : to motion with the hands or with something held in them in signal or salute
2 : to float, play, or shake in an air current **:** move loosely to and fro **:** FLUTTER
3 *of water* **:** to move in waves **:** HEAVE
4 : to become moved or brandished to and fro
5 : to move before the wind with a wavelike motion ⟨field of *waving* grain⟩
6 : to follow a curving line or take a wavy form **:** UNDULATE
transitive verb
1 : to swing (something) back and forth or up and down
2 : to impart a curving or undulating shape to ⟨*waved* her hair⟩
3 a : to motion to (someone) to go in an indicated direction or to stop **:** FLAG, SIGNAL ⟨checked his name and *waved* him on⟩ ⟨*waved* down a passing car⟩ **b :** to gesture with (the hand or an object) in greeting or farewell or in homage **c :** to dismiss or put out of mind **:** DISREGARD — usually used with *aside* or *off* **d :** to convey by waving ⟨*waved* farewell⟩
4 : BRANDISH, FLOURISH ⟨*waved* a pistol menacingly⟩
synonym see SWING

²wave *noun* (1526)
1 a : a moving ridge or swell on the surface of a liquid (as of the sea) **b :** open water
2 a : a shape or outline having successive curves **b :** a waviness of the hair **c :** an undulating line or streak or a pattern formed by such lines
3 : something that swells and dies away: as **a :** a surge of sensation or emotion ⟨a *wave* of anger swept over her⟩ **b :** a movement sweeping large numbers in a common direction ⟨*waves* of protest⟩ **c :** a peak or climax of activity ⟨a *wave* of buying⟩
4 : a sweep of hand or arm or of some object held in the hand used as a signal or greeting
5 : a rolling or undulatory movement or one of a series of such movements passing along a surface or through the air
6 : a movement like that of an ocean wave: as **a :** a surging movement of a group ⟨a big new *wave* of women politicians⟩ **b :** one of a succession of influxes of people migrating into a region **c** (1) **:** a moving group of animals of one kind (2) **:** a sudden rapid increase in a population **d :** a line of attacking or advancing troops or airplanes **e :** a display of people in a large crowd (as at a sports event) successively rising, lifting their arms overhead, and quickly sitting so as to form a swell moving through the crowd
7 a : a disturbance or variation that transfers energy progressively from point to point in a medium and that may take the form of an elastic deformation or of a variation of pressure,

electric or magnetic intensity, electric potential, or temperature **b :** one complete cycle of such a disturbance
8 : a marked change in temperature **:** a period of hot or cold weather
9 : an undulating or jagged line constituting a graphic representation of an action
— **wave·less** \'wāv-ləs\ *adjective*
— **wave·less·ly** *adverb*
— **wave·like** \-ˌlīk\ *adjective*

Wave \'wāv\ *noun* [*W*omen *A*ccepted for *Vol*unteer *E*mergency *S*ervice] (1942)
: a woman serving in the navy

wave band *noun* (1923)
: a band of radio-wave frequencies

waved \'wāvd\ *adjective* (1599)
: having a wavelike form or outline: as **a** **:** having wavy lines of color **:** WATERED ⟨*waved* cloth⟩ **b :** marked by undulations **:** CURVING ⟨the *waved* cutting edge of a bread knife⟩

wave equation *noun* (1926)
: a partial differential equation of the second order whose solutions describe wave phenomena

wave·form \'wāv-ˌform\ *noun* (1845)
: a usually graphic representation of the shape of a wave that indicates its characteristics (as frequency and amplitude) — called also *waveshape*

wave front *noun* (circa 1864)
: a surface composed at any instant of all the points just reached by a vibrational disturbance in its propagation through a medium

wave·guide \'wāv-ˌgīd\ *noun* (1932)
: a device (as a duct, coaxial cable, or glass fiber) designed to confine and direct the propagation of electromagnetic waves (as light); *especially* **:** a metal tube for channeling ultrahigh-frequency waves

wave·length \-ˌleŋ(k)th\ *noun* (1850)
1 : the distance in the line of advance of a wave from any one point to the next point of corresponding phase
2 : a particular course or line of thought especially as related to mutual understanding ⟨two people on different *wavelengths*⟩

wave·let \-lət\ *noun* (circa 1810)
: a little wave **:** RIPPLE

wave mechanics *noun plural but singular or plural in construction* (1926)
1 : the mathematical description of atomic and subatomic particles in terms of their wave characteristics
2 : QUANTUM MECHANICS

wave number *noun* (1873)
: the number of waves per unit distance of radiant energy of a given wavelength **:** the reciprocal of the wavelength

wave of the future (1940)
: an idea, product, or movement that is viewed as representing forces or a trend that will inevitably prevail

wave packet *noun* (1928)
: a pulse of radiant energy that is the resultant of a number of wave trains of differing wavelengths

¹wa·ver \'wā-vər\ *intransitive verb* **wa·vered; wa·ver·ing** \'wāv-riŋ, 'wā-və-riŋ\ [Middle English; akin to Old English *wǣfre* restless, *wafian* to wave with the hands — more at WAVE] (14th century)
1 : to vacillate irresolutely between choices **:** fluctuate in opinion, allegiance, or direction
2 a : to weave or sway unsteadily to and fro **:** REEL, TOTTER **b :** QUIVER, FLICKER ⟨*wavering* flames⟩ **c :** to hesitate as if about to give way **:** FALTER
3 : to give an unsteady sound **:** QUAVER
synonym SEE SWING, HESITATE
— **wa·ver·er** \'wā-vər-ər\ *noun*
— **wa·ver·ing·ly** \'wāv-riŋ-lē, 'wā-və-\ *adverb*

²waver *noun* (1519)
: an act of wavering, quivering, or fluttering

³wav·er \'wā-vər\ *noun* (1835)
: one that waves

wa·very \'wāv-rē, 'wā-və-rē\ *adjective* (1820)
: that waves **:** WAVERING

wave·shape \'wāv-ˌshāp\ *noun* (1907)
: WAVEFORM

wave theory *noun* (1833)
: a theory in physics: light is transmitted from luminous bodies to the eye and other objects by an undulatory movement — called also *undulatory theory*

wave train *noun* (1897)
: a succession of similar waves at equal intervals

wavy \'wā-vē\ *adjective* **wav·i·er; -est** (circa 1586)
1 : rising or swelling in waves; *also* **:** abounding in waves ⟨*wavy* hair⟩
2 : moving with an undulating motion **:** FLUCTUATING; *also* **:** marked by wavering
3 : marked by undulation **:** ROLLING
— **wav·i·ly** \'wā-və-lē\ *adverb*
— **wav·i·ness** \-vē-nəs\ *noun*

waw \'väv, 'vov\ *noun* [Hebrew *wāw*] (14th century)
: the 6th letter of the Hebrew alphabet — see ALPHABET table

wa–wa pedal \'wä-ˌwä-\ *noun* [imitative] (1968)
: an electronic device that is connected to an amplifier and operated by a foot pedal and that is used (as with an electric guitar) to produce a fluctuating muted effect

¹wax \'waks\ *noun* [Middle English, from Old English *weax*; akin to Old High German *wahs* wax, Lithuanian *vaškas*] (before 12th century)
1 : a substance that is secreted by bees and is used by them for constructing the honeycomb, that is a dull yellow solid plastic when warm, and that is composed of a mixture of esters, cerotic acid, and hydrocarbons — called also *beeswax*
2 : any of various substances resembling beeswax: as **a** **:** any of numerous substances of plant or animal origin that differ from fats in being less greasy, harder, and more brittle and in containing principally compounds of high molecular weight (as fatty acids, alcohols, and saturated hydrocarbons) **b :** a solid substance (as ozokerite or paraffin wax) of mineral origin consisting usually of hydrocarbons of high molecular weight **c :** a pliable or liquid composition used especially in uniting surfaces, excluding air, making patterns or impressions, or producing a polished surface
3 : something likened to wax as soft, impressionable, or readily molded
4 : a waxy secretion; *especially* **:** CERUMEN
5 : a phonograph recording
— **wax·like** \'waks-ˌlīk\ *adjective*

²wax *transitive verb* (14th century)
1 : to treat or rub with wax usually for polishing or stiffening
2 : to record on phonograph records

³wax *intransitive verb* [Middle English, from Old English *weaxan*; akin to Old High German *wahsan* to increase, Greek *auxanein*, Latin *augēre* — more at EKE] (before 12th century)
1 a : to increase in size, numbers, strength, prosperity, or intensity **b :** to grow in volume or duration **c :** to grow toward full development
2 : to increase in phase or intensity — used chiefly of the moon, other satellites, and inferior planets
3 : to assume a (specified) characteristic, quality, or state **:** BECOME ⟨*wax* indignant⟩

⁴wax *noun* (14th century)
: INCREASE, GROWTH — usually used in the phrase *on the wax*

⁵wax *noun* [perhaps from ³*wax*] (1854)
: a fit of temper **:** RAGE

wax bean *noun* (1897)
: a kidney bean with pods that turn creamy yellow to bright yellow when mature enough for use as snap beans

wax·bill \'waks-ˌbil\ *noun* (1757)

: any of numerous Old World oscine birds (family Estrildidae and especially genus *Estrilda*) having white, pink, or reddish bills of a waxy appearance

waxed paper *noun* (1853)
: paper coated or treated with wax to make it resistant to water and grease and used especially as a wrapping

wax·en \'wak-sən\ *adjective* (before 12th century)
1 : made of or covered with wax
2 : resembling wax: as **a** **:** easily molded **:** PLIABLE **b :** seeming to lack vitality or animation **:** PALLID **c :** lustrously smooth

wax·er \'wak-sər\ *noun* (circa 1875)
1 : a device for applying wax
2 : one whose work is applying or polishing with wax

wax·ing *noun* (15th century)
1 : the act of applying wax (as in polishing)
2 : the process of removing body hair with a depilatory wax

wax light *noun* (1599)
: a wax candle **:** TAPER

wax moth *noun* (1766)
: a dull brownish or ashen pyralid moth (*Galleria mellonella*) with a larva that feeds on the comb wax of the honeybee

wax museum *noun* (1953)
: a place where wax effigies (as of famous historical persons) are exhibited

wax myrtle *noun* (1806)
: any of a genus (*Myrica* of the family Myricaceae, the wax-myrtle family) of trees or shrubs with aromatic foliage; *especially* **:** a shrub (*M. cerifera*) of the eastern U.S. having small hard berries with a thick coating of white wax used for candles

wax palm *noun* (circa 1828)
: any of several palms that yield wax: as **a** **:** an Andean pinnate-leaved palm (*Ceroxylon alpinum* synonym *C. andicola*) whose stem yields a resinous wax used in candles **b :** CARNAUBA

wax paper *noun* (circa 1844)
: WAXED PAPER

wax·wing \'waks-ˌwiŋ\ *noun* (1817)
: any of a genus (*Bombycilla*) of American and Eurasian chiefly brown to gray oscine birds (as a cedar waxwing) having a showy crest, red waxy material on the tips of the secondaries, and a yellow band on the tip of the tail

wax·work \-ˌwərk\ *noun* (1697)
1 : an effigy in wax usually of a person
2 *plural but singular or plural in construction* **:** WAX MUSEUM

waxy \'wak-sē\ *adjective* **wax·i·er; -est** (1552)
1 : made of, abounding in, or covered with wax **:** WAXEN ⟨a *waxy* surface⟩ ⟨*waxy* berries⟩
2 : resembling wax: as **a** **:** readily shaped or molded **b :** marked by smooth or lustrous whiteness ⟨a *waxy* complexion⟩
— **wax·i·ness** *noun*

¹way \'wā\ *noun* [Middle English, from Old English *weg*; akin to Old High German *weg* way, Old English *wegan* to move, Latin *vehere* to carry, *via* way] (before 12th century)
1 a : a thoroughfare for travel or transportation from place to place **b :** an opening for passage ⟨this door is the only *way* out of the room⟩
2 : the course traveled from one place to another **:** ROUTE
3 a : a course (as a series of actions or se-

waxwing

quence of events) leading in a direction or toward an objective ⟨led the *way* to eventual open heart operations —*Current Biography*⟩ **b** (1) **:** a course of action ⟨took the easy *way* out⟩ (2) **:** opportunity, capability, or fact of doing as one pleases ⟨always manages to get her own *way*⟩ **c :** a possible decision, action, or outcome **:** POSSIBILITY ⟨they were rude—no two *ways* about it⟩

4 a : manner or method of doing or happening; *also* **:** method of accomplishing **:** MEANS **b :** FEATURE, RESPECT ⟨in no *way* resembles her mother⟩ **c :** a usually specified degree of participation in an activity or enterprise ⟨active in real estate in a small *way*⟩

5 a : characteristic, regular, or habitual manner or mode of being, behaving, or happening ⟨knows nothing of the *ways* of women⟩ **b :** ability to get along well or perform well ⟨she has a *way* with kids⟩ ⟨a *way* with words⟩

6 : the length of a course **:** DISTANCE ⟨has come a long *way* in her studies⟩ ⟨still have a *way* to go⟩

7 : movement or progress along a course ⟨worked her *way* up the corporate ladder⟩

8 a : DIRECTION ⟨is coming this *way*⟩ **b :** PARTICIPANT — usually used in combination ⟨three-*way* discussion⟩

9 : state of affairs **:** CONDITION, STATE ⟨that's the *way* things are⟩

10 a *plural but sometimes singular in construction* **:** an inclined structure upon which a ship is built or supported in launching **b** *plural* **:** the guiding surfaces on the bed of a machine along which a table or carriage moves

11 : CATEGORY, KIND — usually used in the phrase *in the way of* ⟨doesn't require much in the *way* of expensive equipment —*Forbes*⟩

12 : motion or speed of a ship or boat through the water

synonym see METHOD

— **all the way :** to the full or entire extent **:** as far as possible ⟨ran *all the way* home⟩ ⟨seated *all the way* in the back⟩

— **by the way :** by way of interjection or digression **:** INCIDENTALLY

— **by way of 1 :** for the purpose of **2 :** by the route through **:** VIA

— **in a way 1 :** within limits **:** with reservations **2 :** from one point of view

— **in one's way** *also* **in the way 1 :** in a position to be encountered by one **:** in or along one's course ⟨an opportunity had been put *in my way* —Ellen Glasgow⟩ **2 :** in a position to hinder or obstruct

— **on the way** *or* **on one's way :** moving along in one's course **:** in progress

— **out of the way 1 :** WRONG, IMPROPER ⟨didn't know I'd said anything *out of the way*⟩ **2 a :** in or to a secluded place **b :** UNUSUAL, REMARKABLE ⟨there's nothing *out of the way* about the plan⟩ **3 :** DONE, COMPLETED ⟨got his homework *out of the way*⟩

— **the way 1 :** in view of the manner in which ⟨you'd think she was rich, *the way* she spends money⟩ **2 :** LIKE, AS ⟨we have cats the *way* other people have mice —James Thurber⟩

²way *adjective* (1799)

: of, connected with, or constituting an intermediate point on a route ⟨visited five major countries plus *way* points⟩

³way *adverb* (1849)

1 a : AWAY 7 ⟨is *way* ahead of the class⟩ **b :** by far **:** MUCH ⟨ate *way* too much⟩

2 : all the way ⟨pull the switch *way* back⟩

— **from way back :** of long standing ⟨friends *from way back*⟩

way·bill \ˈwā-ˌbil\ *noun* (1821)

: a document prepared by the carrier of a shipment of goods that contains details of the shipment, route, and charges

way·far·er \ˈwā-ˌfar-ər, -ˌfer-\ *noun* [Middle English *weyfarere*, from *wey*, *way* way + *-farere* traveler, from *faren* to go — more at FARE] (15th century)

: a traveler especially on foot

— **way·far·ing** \-ˌfar-iŋ, -ˌfer-\ *adjective*

wayfaring tree *noun* (1597)

: a Eurasian shrub (*Viburnum lantana*) that has large ovate leaves and dense cymes of small white flowers and is common along waysides

way·go·ing \ˈwā-ˌgō-ən, -iŋ\ *noun* (1633) *chiefly Scottish* **:** the act of leaving **:** DEPARTURE

Way·land \ˈwā-lən(d)\ *noun* [Old English *Wēland*]

: an heroic smith of Germanic legend

way·lay \ˈwā-ˌlā\ *transitive verb* **-laid** \-ˌlād\; **-lay·ing** (1513)

: to lie in wait for or attack from ambush

way·less \-ləs\ *adjective* (12th century)

: having no road or path

Way of the Cross (1868)

: STATIONS OF THE CROSS

way–out \ˈwā-ˈaút\ *adjective* (1954)

: FAR-OUT

ways \ˈwāz\ *noun plural but singular in construction* [Middle English *wayes*, from genitive of ¹*way*] (1588)

1 : WAY 6 ⟨a long *ways* from home⟩

-ways *adverb suffix* [Middle English, from *ways*, genitive of *way*]

: in (such) a way, course, direction, or manner ⟨side*ways*⟩

ways and means *noun plural* (15th century)

1 : methods and resources for accomplishing something and especially for defraying expenses

2 *W&M often capitalized* **a :** methods and resources for raising the necessary revenues for the expenses of a nation or state **b :** a legislative committee concerned with this function

way·side \ˈwā-ˌsīd\ *noun* (15th century)

: the side of or land adjacent to a road or path

— **wayside** *adjective*

— **by the wayside :** out of consideration **:** into a condition of neglect or disuse — usually used with *fall*

way station *noun* (1850)

1 : an intermediate station between principal stations on a line of travel (as a railroad)

2 : an intermediate stopping place

way·ward \ˈwā-wərd\ *adjective* [Middle English, short for *awayward* turned away, from *away*, adverb + *-ward*] (14th century)

1 : following one's own capricious, wanton, or depraved inclinations **:** UNGOVERNABLE

2 : following no clear principle or law **:** UNPREDICTABLE

3 : opposite to what is desired or expected **:** UNTOWARD ⟨*wayward* fate⟩

synonym see CONTRARY

— **way·ward·ly** *adverb*

— **way·ward·ness** *noun*

way·worn \-ˌwōrn, -ˌwórn\ *adjective* (1788)

: wearied by traveling

we \ˈwē\ *pronoun, plural in construction* [Middle English, from Old English *wē*; akin to Old High German *wir* we, Sanskrit *vayam*] (before 12th century)

1 : I and the rest of a group that includes me **:** you and I **:** you and I and another or others **:** I and another or others not including you — used as pronoun of the first person plural; compare I, OUR, OURS, US

2 : ¹I — used by sovereigns; used by writers to keep an impersonal character

weak \ˈwēk\ *adjective* [Middle English *weike*, from Old Norse *veikr*; akin to Old English *wīcan* to yield, Greek *eikein* to give way, Sanskrit *vijate* he speeds, flees] (14th century)

1 : lacking strength: as **a :** deficient in physical vigor **:** FEEBLE, DEBILITATED **b :** not able to sustain or exert much weight, pressure, or strain **c :** not able to resist external force or withstand attack

2 a : mentally or intellectually deficient **b :** not firmly decided **:** VACILLATING **c :** resulting from or indicating lack of judgment or discernment **d :** not able to withstand temptation or persuasion ⟨the spirit is willing but the flesh is *weak*⟩

3 : not factually grounded or logically presented ⟨a *weak* argument⟩

4 a : not able to function properly **b** (1) **:** lacking skill or proficiency ⟨tutoring for *weaker* students⟩ (2) **:** indicative of a lack of skill or aptitude ⟨history was my *weakest* subject⟩ **c :** wanting in vigor of expression or effect

5 a : deficient in the usual or required ingredients **:** DILUTE ⟨*weak* coffee⟩ **b :** lacking normal intensity or potency ⟨*weak* strain of virus⟩

6 a : not having or exerting authority or political power ⟨*weak* government⟩ **b :** INEFFECTIVE, IMPOTENT

7 : of, relating to, or constituting a verb or verb conjugation that in English forms the past tense and past participle by adding the suffix *-ed* or *-d* or *-t*

8 a : bearing the minimal degree of stress occurring in the language ⟨*weak* syllable⟩ **b :** having little or no stress and obscured vowel sound ⟨'*d* is the *weak* form of *would*⟩

9 : tending toward a lower price ⟨a *weak* market⟩

10 : ionizing only slightly in solution ⟨*weak* acids and bases⟩ ☆

— **weak·ly** *adverb*

weak anthropic principle *noun* (1985)

: ANTHROPIC PRINCIPLE a

weak·en \ˈwē-kən\ *verb* **weak·ened; weak·en·ing** \ˈwēk-niŋ, ˈwē-kə-\ (1530)

transitive verb

1 : to make weak **:** lessen the strength of

2 : to reduce in intensity or effectiveness

intransitive verb

: to become weak ☆

— **weak·en·er** \ˈwēk-nər, ˈwē-kə-\ *noun*

weak·fish \'wēk-ˌfish\ *noun* [obsolete Dutch *weekvis*, from Dutch *week* soft + *vis* fish; from its tender flesh] (1791)
1 : a common marine bony fish (*Cynoscion regalis* of the family Sciaenidae) that is a sport and food fish of the eastern coast of the U.S. — called also *sea trout*
2 : any of several fishes congeneric with the weakfish

weak force *noun* (1971)
: a fundamental physical force that governs interactions between hadrons and leptons (as in the emission and absorption of neutrinos) and is responsible for particle decay processes (as beta decay) in radioactivity, that is 10^5 times weaker than the strong force, and that acts over distances smaller than those between nucleons in an atomic nucleus — called also *weak interaction, weak nuclear force*; compare ELECTROMAGNETISM 2a, GRAVITY 3a(2), STRONG FORCE

weak·heart·ed \-'här-təd\ *adjective* (1549)
: lacking courage : FAINTHEARTED

weak·ish \'wē-kish\ *adjective* (1594)
: somewhat weak ⟨*weakish* tea⟩

weak–kneed \'wēk-'nēd\ *adjective* (1863)
: lacking willpower or resolution

weak·ling \'wē-kliŋ\ *noun* (1548)
: one that is weak in body, character, or mind
— **weakling** *adjective*

weak·ly \'wē-klē\ *adjective* (1577)
: FEEBLE, WEAK
— **weak·li·ness** *noun*

weak–mind·ed \'wēk-'mīn-dəd\ *adjective* (1716)
: having or indicating a weak mind: **a** : lacking in judgment or good sense : FOOLISH **b** : FEEBLEMINDED
— **weak–mind·ed·ness** *noun*

weak·ness \-nəs\ *noun* (14th century)
1 : the quality or state of being weak; *also* : an instance or period of being weak ⟨agreed in a moment of *weakness* to go along⟩
2 : FAULT, DEFECT
3 a : a special desire or fondness ⟨has a *weakness* for chocolates⟩ **b** : an object of special desire or fondness ⟨pizza is my *weakness*⟩

weak side *noun* (1940)
1 : the side of a football formation having the smaller number of players; *specifically* : the side of a formation away from the tight end
2 : the side of a court or field (as in basketball or soccer) away from the ball
— **weak·side** \'wēk-ˌsīd\ *adjective*

weak sister *noun* (1857)
: a member of a group who needs aid; *also* : something that is weak and ineffective as compared with others in the group

¹weal \'wē(ə)l\ *noun* [Middle English *wele*, from Old English *wela;* akin to Old English *wel* well] (before 12th century)
1 : a sound, healthy, or prosperous state : WELL-BEING
2 *obsolete* : BODY POLITIC, COMMONWEAL

²weal *noun* [alteration of *wale*] (circa 1798)
: WELT

weald \'wē(ə)ld\ *noun* [the *Weald*, England, from Middle English *weeld*, from Old English *weald* forest — more at WOLD] (before 12th century)
1 : a heavily wooded area : FOREST ⟨the *Weald* of Kent⟩
2 : a wild or uncultivated usually upland region

wealth \'welth *also* 'weltth\ *noun* [Middle English *welthe*, from *wele* weal] (13th century)
1 *obsolete* : WEAL, WELFARE
2 : abundance of valuable material possessions or resources
3 : abundant supply : PROFUSION
4 a : all property that has a money value or an exchangeable value **b** : all material objects that have economic utility; *especially* : the stock of useful goods having economic value in existence at any one time ⟨national *wealth*⟩

wealthy \'wel-thē *also* 'welt-thē\ *adjective*
wealth·i·er; -est (15th century)
1 : having wealth : extremely affluent
2 : characterized by abundance : AMPLE
synonym see RICH
— **wealth·i·ly** \-thə-lē\ *adverb*
— **wealth·i·ness** \-thē-nəs\ *noun*

wean \'wēn\ *transitive verb* [Middle English *wenen*, from Old English *wenian* to accustom, wean; akin to Old English *wunian* to be used to — more at WONT] (before 12th century)
1 : to accustom (as a child) to take food otherwise than by nursing
2 : to detach from a source of dependence ⟨being *weaned* off the medication⟩ ⟨*wean* the bears from human food —*Sports Illustrated*⟩; *also* : to free from a usually unwholesome habit or interest ⟨*wean* him off his excessive drinking⟩ ⟨settling his soldiers on the land . . ., *weaning* them from habits of violence —Geoffrey Carnall⟩
3 : to accustom to something from an early age — used in the passive especially with *on* ⟨students *weaned* on the microcomputer⟩ ⟨I was *weaned* on greasepaint —Helen Hayes⟩ ⟨the principles upon which he had been *weaned* —J. A. Michener⟩

wean·er \'wē-nər\ *noun* (1579)
1 : one that weans
2 : a young animal recently weaned from its mother

wean·ling \'wēn-liŋ\ *noun* (1532)
: a child or animal newly weaned
— **wean·ling** *adjective*

¹weap·on \'we-pən\ *noun* [Middle English *wepen*, from Old English *wǣpen;* akin to Old High German *wāffan* weapon, Old Norse *vāpn*] (before 12th century)
1 : something (as a club, knife, or gun) used to injure, defeat, or destroy
2 : a means of contending against another

²weapon *transitive verb* (before 12th century)
: ARM

weap·on·less \-ləs\ *adjective* (before 12th century)
: lacking weapons : UNARMED

weap·on·ry \-rē\ *noun* (1844)
1 : WEAPONS
2 : the science of designing and making weapons

¹wear \'war, 'wer\ *verb* **wore** \'wōr, 'wȯr\; **worn** \'wōrn, 'wȯrn\; **wear·ing** [Middle English *weren*, from Old English *werian;* akin to Old Norse *verja* to clothe, invest, spend, Latin *vestis* clothing, garment, Greek *hennynai* to clothe] (before 12th century)
transitive verb
1 : to bear or have on the person ⟨*wore* a coat⟩
2 a : to use habitually for clothing, adornment, or assistance ⟨*wears* a toupee⟩ ⟨*wear* glasses⟩ **b** : to carry on the person ⟨*wear* a sword⟩
3 a : to hold the rank or dignity or position signified by (an ornament) ⟨*wear* the royal crown⟩ **b** : EXHIBIT, PRESENT ⟨*wore* a happy smile⟩ ⟨commend the book for *wearing* its research so lightly —Brad Leithauser⟩ **c** : to show or fly (a flag or colors) on a ship
4 a : to cause to deteriorate by use **b** : to impair or diminish by use or attrition : consume or waste gradually ⟨letters on the stone *worn* away by weathering⟩
5 : to produce gradually by friction or attrition ⟨*wear* a hole in the rug⟩
6 : to exhaust or lessen the strength of : WEARY, FATIGUE
7 : to cause (a ship) to go about with the stern presented to the wind
8 *British* : to accept or tolerate without complaint : put up with — usually used in negative constructions ⟨your mates wouldn't *wear* it —Colin MacInnes⟩
intransitive verb
1 a : to endure use : last under use or the passage of time ⟨material that will *wear* for years⟩
b : to retain quality or vitality

2 a : to diminish or decay through use ⟨the heels of his shoes began to *wear*⟩ **b** : to diminish or fail with the passage of time ⟨the effect of the drug *wore* off⟩ ⟨the day *wore* on⟩ **c** : to grow or become by attrition or use
3 *of a ship* : to change to an opposite tack by turning the stern to the wind — compare TACK
— **wear·er** *noun*
— **wear on** : IRRITATE, FRAY
— **wear the trousers** *or* **wear the pants** : to have the controlling authority in a household
— **wear thin 1** : to become weak or ready to give way ⟨my patience was *wearing thin*⟩ **2** : to become trite, unconvincing, or out-of-date ⟨an argument that quickly *wore thin*⟩

²wear *noun* (15th century)
1 : the act of wearing : the state of being worn : USE ⟨clothes for everyday *wear*⟩
2 a : clothing or an article of clothing usually of a particular kind; *especially* : clothing worn for a special occasion or popular during a specific period **b** : FASHION, VOGUE
3 : wearing quality : durability under use
4 : the result of wearing or use : diminution or impairment due to use ⟨*wear*-resistant surface⟩

¹wear·able \'war-ə-bəl, 'wer-\ *adjective* (1590)
: capable of being worn : suitable to be worn
— **wear·abil·i·ty** \ˌwar-ə-'bi-lə-tē, ˌwer-\ *noun*

²wearable *noun* (1711)
: GARMENT — usually used in plural

wear and tear *noun* (1666)
: the loss, injury, or stress to which something is subjected by or in the course of use; *especially* : normal depreciation

wear down *transitive verb* (1803)
: to weary and overcome by persistent resistance or pressure

wea·ri·ful \'wir-ē-fəl\ *adjective* (15th century)
1 : causing weariness; *especially* : TEDIOUS
2 : full of weariness : WEARIED
— **wea·ri·ful·ly** \-fə-lē\ *adverb*
— **wea·ri·ful·ness** *noun*

wea·ri·less \'wir-ē-ləs\ *adjective* (15th century)
: TIRELESS
— **wea·ri·less·ly** *adverb*

¹wear·ing \'war-iŋ, 'wer-\ *adjective* (15th century)
: intended for wear ⟨*wearing* apparel⟩

²wearing *adjective* (1811)
: subjecting to or inflicting wear; *especially* : causing fatigue ⟨a *wearing* journey⟩
— **wear·ing·ly** \-iŋ-lē\ *adverb*

wea·ri·some \'wir-ē-səm\ *adjective* (15th century)
: causing weariness : TIRESOME
— **wea·ri·some·ly** *adverb*
— **wea·ri·some·ness** *noun*

wear out (14th century)
transitive verb
1 : TIRE, EXHAUST
2 : to make useless especially by long or hard usage
3 : ERASE, EFFACE
4 : to endure through : OUTLAST ⟨*wear out* a storm⟩
5 : to consume (as time) tediously ⟨*wear out* idle days⟩
intransitive verb
: to become useless from long or excessive wear or use

¹wea·ry \'wir-ē\ *adjective* **wea·ri·er; -est** [Middle English *wery*, from Old English *wērig;* akin to Old High German *wuorag* intoxicated and perhaps to Greek *aōros* sleep] (before 12th century)

1 : exhausted in strength, endurance, vigor, or freshness
2 : expressing or characteristic of weariness
3 : having one's patience, tolerance, or pleasure exhausted — used with *of*
4 : WEARISOME
— **wea·ri·ly** \'wir-ə-lē\ *adverb*
— **wea·ri·ness** \'wir-ē-nəs\ *noun*
²**weary** *verb* **wea·ried; wea·ry·ing** (before 12th century)
intransitive verb
: to become weary
transitive verb
: to make weary
synonym see TIRE

wea·sand \'wē-z°nd, 'wi-z°n(d)\ *noun* [Middle English *wesand,* from (assumed) Old English *wāsend* gullet; akin to Old English *wāsend* gullet, Old High German *weisunt* windpipe] (before 12th century)
: THROAT, GULLET; *also* : TRACHEA
¹**wea·sel** \'wē-zəl\ *noun, plural* **weasels** [Middle English *wesele,* from Old English *weosule;* akin to Old High German *wisula* weasel] (before 12th century)
1 *or plural* **weasel :** any of various small slender active carnivorous mammals (genus *Mustela* of the family Mustelidae, the weasel family) that are able to prey

weasel 1

on animals (as rabbits) larger than themselves, are mostly reddish brown with white or yellowish underparts, and in northern forms turn white in winter
2 : a light self-propelled tracked vehicle built either for traveling over snow, ice, or sand or as an amphibious vehicle
²**weasel** *intransitive verb* **wea·seled; wea·sel·ing** \'wēz-liŋ, 'wē-zə-\ [*weasel word*] (1900)
1 : to use weasel words : EQUIVOCATE
2 : to escape from or evade a situation or obligation — often used with *out*
wea·sel·ly *also* **wea·sely** \'wēz-lē, 'wē-zə-\ *adjective* (1838)
: resembling or suggestive of a weasel
weasel word *noun* [from the weasel's reputed habit of sucking the contents out of an egg while leaving the shell superficially intact] (1900)
: a word used in order to evade or retreat from a direct or forthright statement or position
¹**weath·er** \'we-thər\ *noun* [Middle English *weder,* from Old English; akin to Old High German *wetar* weather, Old Church Slavonic *vetrŭ* wind] (before 12th century)
1 : the state of the atmosphere with respect to heat or cold, wetness or dryness, calm or storm, clearness or cloudiness
2 : state or vicissitude of life or fortune
3 : disagreeable atmospheric conditions: as **a** : RAIN, STORM **b :** cold air with dampness
4 : WEATHERING
— **under the weather 1 :** ILL **2 :** DRUNK 1a
²**weather** *verb* **weath·ered; weath·er·ing** \'weth-riŋ, 'we-thə-\ (15th century)
transitive verb
1 : to expose to the open air : subject to the action of the elements
2 : to bear up against and come safely through ⟨*weather* a storm⟩ ⟨*weather* a crisis⟩
intransitive verb
: to undergo or endure the action of the elements
³**weather** *adjective* (circa 1625)
: of or relating to the side facing the wind — compare LEE
weath·er·abil·i·ty \,weth-rə-'bi-lə-tē, ,we-thə-\ *noun* (1947)

: capability of withstanding the weathering process ⟨*weatherability* of a plastic⟩
weath·er-beat·en \'we-thər,bē-t°n\ *adjective* (1530)
1 : toughened, tanned, or bronzed by the weather ⟨a *weather-beaten* face⟩
2 : worn or damaged by exposure to weather
weath·er·board \-,bōrd, -,bórd\ *noun* (circa 1540)
1 : CLAPBOARD, SIDING
2 : the weather side of a ship
— **weath·er·board·ed** *adjective*
weath·er·board·ing \-,bōr-diŋ, -,bór-\ *noun* (1632)
: CLAPBOARDS, SIDING
weath·er-bound \-,baúnd\ *adjective* (1590)
: kept in port or at anchor or from travel or sport by bad weather
weather bureau *noun* (1871)
: a bureau engaged in the collection of weather reports as a basis for weather predictions, storm warnings, and the compiling of statistical records
weath·er-burned \'we-thər,bərnd\ *adjective* (1906)
: browned by sun and wind
weath·er·cast \-,kast\ *noun* [¹*weather* + ²*forecast*] (1866)
: a weather forecast especially on radio or television
weath·er·cast·er \-,kas-tər\ *noun* (1607)
: a weather forecaster especially on radio or television
weath·er·cock \-,käk\ *noun* (13th century)
1 : a vane often in the figure of a cock mounted so as to turn freely with the wind and show its direction
2 : a person or thing that changes readily or often
weather deck *noun* (1850)
: a deck having no overhead protection from the weather
weath·ered \'we-thərd\ *adjective* (1789)
1 : seasoned by exposure to the weather
2 : altered in color, texture, composition, or form by such exposure or by artificial means producing a similar effect ⟨*weathered* oak⟩
weather eye *noun* (1839)
1 : an eye quick to observe coming changes in the weather
2 : constant and shrewd watchfulness and alertness
weath·er·glass \'we-thər,glas\ *noun* (1626)
: a simple instrument for showing changes in atmospheric pressure by the changing level of liquid in a spout connected with a closed reservoir; *broadly* : BAROMETER
weathering *noun* (1548)
: the action of the elements in altering the color, texture, composition, or form of exposed objects; *specifically* **:** the physical disintegration and chemical decomposition of earth materials at or near the earth's surface
weath·er·ize \'we-thə-,rīz\ *transitive verb* **-ized; -iz·ing** (1943)
: to make (as a house) better protected against winter weather (as by adding insulation)
— **weath·er·i·za·tion** \,weth-rə-'za-shən, ,we-thə-\ *noun*
weath·er·ly \'we-thər-lē\ *adjective* (1729)
: able to sail close to the wind with little leeway
weath·er·man \-,man\ *noun* (1859)
: one who reports and forecasts the weather **:** METEOROLOGIST
weather map *noun* (1871)
: a map or chart showing the principal meteorological elements at a given hour and over an extended region
weath·er·per·son \'we-thər,pər-s°n\ *noun* (1974)
: a person who reports and forecasts the weather **:** METEOROLOGIST
weath·er·proof \'we-thər,prüf\ *adjective* (1620)

: able to withstand exposure to weather without damage or loss of function
— **weatherproof** *transitive verb*
— **weath·er·proof·ness** *noun*
weather ship *noun* (1946)
: a ship that makes observations for use by meteorologists
weather station *noun* (circa 1895)
: a station for taking, recording, and reporting meteorological observations
weather strip *noun* (1846)
: a strip of material to cover the joint of a door or window and the sill, casing, or threshold so as to exclude rain, snow, and cold air — called also *weather stripping*
— **weath·er-strip** *transitive verb*
weather vane *noun* (circa 1721)
: VANE 1a
weath·er-wise \'we-thər,wīz\ *adjective* (14th century)
1 : skillful in forecasting changes in the weather
2 : skillful in forecasting changes in opinion or feeling ⟨a *weather-wise* politician⟩
weath·er·worn \-,wōrn, -,wórn\ *adjective* (1609)
: worn by exposure to the weather
¹**weave** \'wēv\ *verb* **wove** \'wōv\ *or* **weaved; wo·ven** \'wō-vən\ *or* **weaved; weav·ing** [Middle English *weven,* from Old English *wefan;* akin to Old High German *weban* to weave, Greek *hyphainein* to weave, *hyphos* web] (before 12th century)
transitive verb
1 a : to form (cloth) by interlacing strands (as of yarn); *specifically* **:** to make (cloth) on a loom by interlacing warp and filling threads **b :** to interlace (as threads) into cloth **c :** to make (as a basket) by intertwining
2 : SPIN 2 — used of spiders and insects
3 : to interlace especially so as to form a texture, fabric, or design
4 a : to produce by elaborately combining elements **:** CONTRIVE **b :** to unite in a coherent whole **c :** to introduce as an appropriate element **:** work in — usually used with *in* or *into*
5 : to direct (as the body) in a winding or zigzag course especially to avoid obstacles
intransitive verb
1 : to work at weaving : make cloth
2 : to move in a devious, winding, or zigzag course especially to avoid obstacles
²**weave** *noun* (1581)
1 : something woven; *especially* **:** woven cloth
2 : any of the patterns or methods for interlacing the threads of woven fabrics
³**weave** *intransitive verb* **weaved; weav·ing** [Middle English *weven* to move to and fro, wave; akin to Old Norse *veifa* to be in movement — more at WIPE] (1596)
: to move waveringly from side to side : SWAY
weav·er \'wē-vər\ *noun* (14th century)
1 : one that weaves especially as an occupation
2 : WEAVERBIRD
weav·er·bird \-,bərd\ *noun* (1826)
: any of numerous Old World passerine birds (family Ploceidae) that resemble finches and mostly construct elaborate nests of interlaced vegetation
weaver's knot *noun* (1532)
: SHEET BEND — called also *weaver's hitch*
¹**web** \'web\ *noun* [Middle English, from Old English; akin to Old Norse *vefr* web, Old English *wefan* to weave] (before 12th century)
1 : a fabric on a loom or in process of being removed from a loom
2 a : COBWEB, SPIDERWEB **b :** a network of silken thread spun especially by the larvae of various insects (as a tent caterpillar) and usually serving as a nest or shelter
3 : a tissue or membrane of an animal or plant; *especially* **:** that uniting fingers or toes

either at their bases (as in humans) or for a greater part of their length (as in many water-birds)
4 a : a thin metal sheet, plate, or strip **b :** the plate connecting the upper and lower flanges of a girder or rail **c :** the arm of a crank
5 : something resembling a web: **a :** SNARE, ENTANGLEMENT ⟨a *web* of intrigue⟩ ⟨ensnared in a *web* of folly —David A. Stockman⟩ **b :** an intricate pattern or structure suggestive of something woven **:** NETWORK ⟨a *web* of little roads⟩ ⟨a complex *web* of relationships⟩
6 : the series of barbs implanted on each side of the shaft of a feather **:** VANE
7 a : a continuous sheet of paper manufactured or undergoing manufacture on a paper machine **b :** a roll of paper for use in a rotary printing press
8 : the part of a ribbed vault between the ribs
— **webbed** \'webd\ *adjective*
— **web-like** \'web-ˌlīk\ *adjective*
²**web** *verb* **webbed; web-bing** (1604)
intransitive verb
: to construct or form a web
transitive verb
1 : to cover with a web or network
2 : ENSNARE, ENTANGLE
3 : to provide with a web
web-bing \'we-biŋ\ *noun* (1796)
1 : a strong narrow closely woven tape designed for bearing weight and used especially for straps, harness, or upholstery
2 : TRAP 3c
web-by \'we-bē\ *adjective* (1661)
: of, relating to, or consisting of a web
we-ber \'we-bər, 'vā-bər\ *noun* [Wilhelm E. Weber (died 1891) German physicist] (1891)
: the practical meter-kilogram-second unit of magnetic flux equal to that flux which in linking a circuit of one turn produces in it an electromotive force of one volt as the flux is reduced to zero at a uniform rate in one second **:** 10^8 maxwells
web-fed \'web-ˌfed\ *adjective* (1947)
: of, relating to, or printed by a web press
web-foot *noun* (1765)
1 \'web-ˌfut\ **:** a foot having webbed toes
2 \-ˌfut\ **:** an animal having web feet
— **web–foot-ed** \-'fu-təd\ *adjective*
web member *noun* (circa 1890)
: one of the several members joining the top and bottom chords of a truss or lattice girder
web-off-set \'web-'òf-ˌset\ *noun, often attributive* (1959)
: offset printing by web press
web press *noun* (1875)
: a press that prints a continuous roll of paper
web spinner *noun* (circa 1907)
: an insect that spins a web; *especially* **:** any of an order (Embioptera synonym Embiidina) of small slender insects with biting mouthparts that live in silken tunnels which they spin
web-ster \'web-stər\ *noun* [Middle English, from Old English *webbestre* female weaver, from *webbian* to weave; akin to Old English *wefan* to weave] (12th century)
archaic **:** WEAVER 1
web-work \'web-ˌwərk\ *noun* (1790)
: WEB 5b ⟨a vast *webwork* of real estate holdings⟩
web-worm \-ˌwərm\ *noun* (1797)
: any of various caterpillars that are more or less gregarious and spin large webs
wed \'wed\ *verb* **wed-ded** *also* **wed; wed-ding** [Middle English *wedden*, from Old English *weddian*; akin to Middle High German *wetten* to pledge, Old English *wedd* pledge, Old High German *wetti*, Gothic *wadi*, Latin *vad-, vas* bail, security] (before 12th century)
transitive verb
1 : to take for wife or husband by a formal ceremony **:** MARRY
2 : to join in marriage
3 : to unite as if by the bond of marriage
intransitive verb
: to enter into matrimony

— **wed-der** *noun*
we'd \'wēd\ (1603)
: we had **:** we would **:** we should
Wed-dell seal \wi-'del-, 'we-dᵊl-\ *noun* [James *Weddell* (died 1834) English navigator] (1914)
: a vocal Antarctic hair seal (*Leptonychotes weddelli*) noted for its deep dives in search of food
wed-ding \'we-diŋ\ *noun, often attributive* (before 12th century)
1 : a marriage ceremony usually with its accompanying festivities **:** NUPTIALS
2 : an act, process, or instance of joining in close association
3 : a wedding anniversary or its celebration — usually used in combination ⟨a golden *wedding*⟩
wedding cake *noun* (1648)
1 : a usually elaborately decorated and tiered cake made for the celebration of a wedding
2 : something (as a large building) likened to a wedding cake especially in elaborate ornamentation
wedding march *noun* (1850)
: a march of slow tempo and stately character composed or played to accompany the bridal procession
wedding ring *noun* (14th century)
: a ring often of plain gold or platinum given by the groom to the bride during the wedding service; *also* **:** a similar ring given by the bride to the groom in a double-ring service
we-del \'vā-dᵊl\ *intransitive verb* [German *Wedeln*] (circa 1963)
: to ski downhill by means of wedeln
we-deln \'vā-dᵊln\ *noun* [German, from *wedeln*, literally, to fan, wag the tail, from *Wedel* fan, tail, from Old High German *wadal*; akin to Old Norse *vēli* bird's tail] (circa 1957)
: a style of skiing in which a skier rhythmically swings the rear of the skis from side to side while following the fall line
¹**wedge** \'wej\ *noun* [Middle English *wegge*, from Old English *wecg*; akin to Old High German *wecki* wedge, Lithuanian *vagis*] (before 12th century)
1 : a piece of a substance (as wood or iron) that tapers to a thin edge and is used for splitting wood and rocks, raising heavy bodies, or for tightening by being driven into something
2 a : something (as a policy) causing a breach or separation **b :** something used to initiate an action or development
3 : something wedge-shaped: as **a :** an array of troops or tanks in the form of a wedge **b :** the wedge-shaped stroke in cuneiform characters **c :** a shoe having a heel extending from the back of the shoe to the front of the shank and a tread formed by an extension of the sole **d :** an iron golf club with a broad low-angled face for maximum loft
²**wedge** *verb* **wedged; wedg-ing** (15th century)
transitive verb
1 : to fasten or tighten by driving in a wedge
2 a : to force or press (something) into a narrow space **:** CRAM **b :** to force (one's way) into or through ⟨*wedged* his way into the crowd⟩
3 : to separate or force apart with or as if with a wedge
intransitive verb
: to become wedged
wedged \'wejd, 'we-jəd\ *adjective* (1552)
: shaped like a wedge
wedg-ie \'we-jē\ *noun* (1939)
1 : a shoe having a wedge-shaped piece serving as the heel and joining the half sole to form a continuous flat undersurface
2 : the condition of having one's clothing wedged between the buttocks especially from having one's pants or underpants yanked up from behind as a prank — often used with *get* or *give*
Wedg-wood \'wej-ˌwùd\ *trademark*

— used for ceramic wares (as bone china or jasper)
wedgy \'we-jē\ *adjective* (1799)
: resembling a wedge in shape
wed-lock \'wed-ˌläk\ *noun* [Middle English *wedlok*, from Old English *wedlāc* marriage bond, from *wedd* pledge + *-lāc*, suffix denoting activity] (13th century)
: the state of being married **:** MARRIAGE, MATRIMONY
— **out of wedlock :** with the natural parents not legally married to each other
Wednes-day \'wenz-dē, -(ˌ)dā; *British also* 'we-dᵊnz-\ *noun* [Middle English, from Old English *wōdnesdæg* (akin to Old Norse *ōthinsdagr* Wednesday); akin to Old English *Wōden* Odin and *dæg* day] (before 12th century)
: the fourth day of the week
— **Wednes-days** \-dēz, -(ˌ)dāz\ *adverb*
wee \'wē\ *adjective* [Middle English *we*, from *we*, noun, little bit, from Old English *wǣge* weight; akin to Old English *wegan* to move, weigh — more at WAY] (15th century)
1 : very small **:** DIMINUTIVE
2 : very early ⟨*wee* hours of the morning⟩
¹**weed** \'wēd\ *noun* [Middle English, from Old English *wēod* weed, herb; akin to Old Saxon *wiod* weed] (before 12th century)
1 a (1) : a plant that is not valued where it is growing and is usually of vigorous growth; *especially* **:** one that tends to overgrow or choke out more desirable plants **(2) :** a weedy growth of plants **b :** an aquatic plant; *especially* **:** SEAWEED **c (1) :** TOBACCO **(2) :** MARIJUANA
2 a : an obnoxious growth, thing, or person **b :** something like a weed in detrimental quality; *especially* **:** an animal unfit to breed from
²**weed** (before 12th century)
intransitive verb
: to remove weeds or something harmful
transitive verb
1 a : to clear of weeds ⟨*weed* a garden⟩ **b (1) :** to free from something hurtful or offensive **(2) :** to remove the less desirable portions of
2 : to get rid of (something harmful or superfluous) — often used with *out*
³**weed** *noun* [Middle English *wede*, from Old English *wǣd, gewǣde*; akin to Old Norse *vāth* cloth, clothing and perhaps to Lithuanian *austi* to weave] (before 12th century)
1 : GARMENT — often used in plural
2 a : dress worn as a sign of mourning (as by a widow) — usually used in plural **b :** a band of crape worn on a man's hat as a sign of mourning — usually used in plural
weed-er \'wē-dər\ *noun* (15th century)
: one that weeds; *specifically* **:** any of various devices for removing weeds from an area
weedy \'wē-dē\ *adjective* **weed-i-er; -est** (15th century)
1 : abounding with or consisting of weeds
2 : resembling a weed especially in rank growth or ready propagation
3 : noticeably lean and scrawny **:** LANKY
— **weed-i-ness** *noun*
week \'wēk\ *noun* [Middle English *weke*, from Old English *wicu, wucu*; akin to Old High German *wehha* week and perhaps to Latin *vicis* change, alternation, Old High German *wehsal* exchange] (before 12th century)
1 a : any of a series of 7-day cycles used in various calendars; *especially* **:** a 7-day cycle beginning on Sunday and ending on Saturday **b (1) :** a week beginning with a specified day or containing a specified holiday ⟨the *week* of the 18th⟩ ⟨Easter *week*⟩ **(2) :** a week appointed for public recognition of some cause ⟨Fire Prevention *Week*⟩

\ə\ **abut** \ᵊ\ **kitten** \ər\ **further** \a\ **ash** \ā\ **ace**
\ä\ **mop, mar** \aù\ **out** \ch\ **chin** \e\ **bet** \ē\ **easy**
\g\ **go** \i\ **hit** \ī\ **ice** \j\ **job** \ŋ\ **sing** \ō\ **go**
\ò\ **law** \òi\ **boy** \th\ **thin** \t̲h̲\ **the** \ü\ **loot** \ù\ **foot**
\y\ **yet** \zh\ **vision** *see also* Guide to Pronunciation

2 a : any seven consecutive days **b :** a series of regular working, business, or school days during each 7-day period
3 : a time seven days before or after a specified day ⟨last Sunday *week*⟩
week·day \'wēk-,dā\ *noun* (15th century)
: a day of the week except Sunday or sometimes except Saturday and Sunday
week·days \-,dāz\ *adverb* (1777)
: on weekdays repeatedly **:** on any weekday ⟨takes a bus *weekdays*⟩
¹week·end \'wēk-,end\ *noun* (1638)
: the end of the week; *specifically* **:** the period between the close of one working or business or school week and the beginning of the next
²weekend *intransitive verb* (1901)
: to spend the weekend
³weekend *adjective* (1935)
: active in a specified role only on weekends or part-time ⟨a *weekend* father⟩ ⟨*weekend* athletes⟩
weekend bag *noun* (1921)
: a suitcase of a size to carry clothing and personal articles for a weekend trip — called also *weekend case*
week·end·er \'wēk-'en-dər\ *noun* (1880)
1 : one that vacations or visits for a weekend
2 : WEEKEND BAG
week·ends \'wēk-,en(d)z\ *adverb* (1892)
: on weekends repeatedly **:** on any weekend ⟨travels *weekends*⟩
week·long \'wēk-'lȯŋ\ *adjective* (1898)
: lasting a week
¹week·ly \'wē-klē\ *adverb* (15th century)
: every week **:** once a week **:** by the week
²weekly *adjective* (15th century)
1 : occurring, appearing, or done weekly
2 : reckoned by the week
³weekly *noun, plural* **weeklies** (1833)
: a weekly newspaper or periodical
week·night \'wēk-,nīt\ *noun* (1859)
: a weekday night
week·nights \-,nīts\ *adverb* (1965)
: on weeknights repeatedly **:** on any weeknight
ween \'wēn\ *transitive verb* [Middle English *wenen*, from Old English *wēnan*; akin to Old Norse *væna* to hope and probably to Latin *venus* love, charm — more at WIN] (before 12th century)
archaic **:** IMAGINE
wee·nie \'wē-nē\ *noun* [alteration of *wienie*] (circa 1906)
1 : FRANKFURTER
2 *slang* **:** PENIS
3 : NERD ⟨computer *weenies*⟩
wee·ny \'wē-nē\ *also* **ween·sy** \'wēn(t)-sē\ *adjective* [alteration of *wee*] (circa 1781)
: exceptionally small **:** TINY
weep \'wēp\ *verb* **wept** \'wept\; **weep·ing** [Middle English *wepen*, from Old English *wēpan*; akin to Old High German *wuoffan* to weep, Old Church Slavonic *vabiti* to call to] (before 12th century)
transitive verb
1 : to express deep sorrow for usually by shedding tears **:** BEWAIL
2 : to pour forth (tears) from the eyes
3 : to exude (a fluid) slowly **:** OOZE
intransitive verb
1 : to express passion (as grief) by shedding tears
2 a : to give off or leak fluid slowly **:** OOZE **b** *of a fluid* **:** to flow sluggishly or in drops
3 : to droop over **:** BEND
weep·er \'wē-pər\ *noun* (14th century)
1 a : one that weeps **b :** a professional mourner
2 : a small statue of a figure in mourning on a funeral monument
3 : a badge of mourning worn especially in the 18th and 19th centuries
4 *plural* **:** long and flowing side-whiskers
5 : TEARJERKER
weep hole *noun* (1851)
: a hole (as in a wall or foundation) that is designed to drain off accumulated water

weep·ie \'wē-pē\ *noun* (1928)
: TEARJERKER
weep·ing \'wē-piŋ\ *adjective* (before 12th century)
1 : TEARFUL
2 *archaic* **:** RAINY
3 : having slender pendent branches
weeping willow *noun* (circa 1731)
: an Asian willow (*Salix babylonica*) introduced into North America that has slender pendent branches
weepy \'wē-pē\ *adjective* (1863)
: inclined to weep **:** TEARFUL
weet \'wēt\ *verb* [Middle English *weten*, alteration of *witen* — more at WIT] (14th century)
archaic **:** KNOW
wee·vil \'wē-vəl\ *noun* [Middle English *wevel*, from Old English *wifel*; akin to Old High German *wibil* beetle, Old English *wefan* to weave] (before 12th century)
: any of a superfamily (Curculionoidea) of beetles which have the head prolonged into a more or less distinct snout and which include many that are injurious especially as larvae to nuts, fruit, and grain or to living plants; *especially* **:** any of a family (Curculionidae) having a well-developed snout curved downward with the jaws at the tip and clubbed usually elbowed antennae

weevil

— **wee·vily** *or* **wee·vil·ly** \'wēv-lē, 'wē-və-lē\ *adjective*
weft \'weft\ *noun* [Middle English, from Old English; akin to Old Norse *veptr* weft, Old English *wefan* to weave — more at WEAVE] (before 12th century)
1 a : a filling thread or yarn in weaving **b :** yarn used for the weft
2 : WEB, FABRIC; *also* **:** an article of woven fabric
weft knit *noun* (1943)
: a knit fabric produced in machine or hand knitting with the yarns running crosswise or in a circle — compare WARP KNIT
— **weft–knit·ted** \-,ni-təd\ *adjective*
— **weft knit·ting** *noun*
wei·ge·la \wī-'jē-lə\ *noun* [New Latin, from Christian E. *Weigel* (died 1831) German physician] (1846)
: any of a genus (*Weigela*) of showy shrubs of the honeysuckle family; *especially* **:** one (*W. florida*) of China widely grown for its usually pink or red flowers
¹weigh \'wā\ *verb* [Middle English *weyen*, from Old English *wegan* to move, carry, weigh — more at WAY] (before 12th century)
transitive verb
1 : to ascertain the heaviness of by or as if by a balance
2 a : OUTWEIGH **b :** COUNTERBALANCE **c :** to make heavy **:** WEIGHT — often used with *down*
3 : to consider carefully especially by balancing opposing factors or aspects in order to reach a choice or conclusion **:** EVALUATE
4 : to heave up (an anchor) preparatory to sailing
5 : to measure or apportion (a definite quantity) on or as if on a scales
intransitive verb
1 a : to have a certain heaviness **:** experience a specific force due to gravity **b :** to register a weight (as on a scales) — used with *in* or *out*; compare WEIGH IN
2 : to merit consideration as important **:** COUNT ⟨evidence will *weigh* heavily against him⟩
3 a : to press down with or as if with a heavy weight **b :** to have a saddening or disheartening effect
4 : to weigh anchor
synonym see CONSIDER
— **weigh·able** \'wā-ə-bəl\ *adjective*
— **weigh·er** *noun*
²weigh *noun* [alteration of *way*] (1777)

: WAY — used in the phrase *under weigh*
weigh down *transitive verb* (14th century)
1 : to cause to bend down **:** OVERBURDEN
2 : OPPRESS, DEPRESS
weigh–in \'wā-,in\ *noun* (1939)
: an act or instance of weighing in as a contestant especially in sport
weigh in *intransitive verb* (1868)
1 : to have oneself or one's possessions (as baggage) weighed; *especially* **:** to have oneself weighed in connection with an athletic contest
2 : to enter as a participant
¹weight \'wāt\ *noun* [Middle English *wight*, *weght*, from Old English *wiht*; akin to Old Norse *vætt* weight, Old English *wegan* to weigh] (before 12th century)
1 a : the amount that a thing weighs **b** (1) **:** the standard or established amount that a thing should weigh (2) **:** one of the classes into which contestants in a sports event are divided according to body weight (3) **:** poundage required to be carried by a horse in a handicap race
2 a : a quantity or thing weighing a fixed and usually specified amount **b :** a heavy object (as a metal ball) thrown, put, or lifted as an athletic exercise or contest
3 a : a unit of weight or mass — see METRIC SYSTEM table **b :** a piece of material (as metal) of known specified weight for use in weighing articles **c :** a system of related units of weight
4 a : something heavy **:** LOAD **b :** a heavy object to hold or press something down or to counterbalance
5 a : BURDEN, PRESSURE **b :** the quality or state of being ponderous **c :** CORPULENCE
6 a : relative heaviness **:** MASS **b :** the force with which a body is attracted toward the earth or a celestial body by gravitation and which is equal to the product of the mass and the local gravitational acceleration
7 a : the relative importance or authority accorded something **b :** measurable influence especially on others
8 : overpowering force
9 : the quality (as lightness) that makes a fabric or garment suitable for a particular use or season — often used in combination ⟨summer-*weight*⟩
10 : a numerical coefficient assigned to an item to express its relative importance in a frequency distribution
11 : the degree of thickness of the strokes of a type character
synonym see IMPORTANCE, INFLUENCE
²weight *transitive verb* (1647)
1 : to oppress with a burden ⟨*weighted* down with cares⟩
2 a : to load or make heavy with or as if with a weight **b :** to increase in heaviness by adding an ingredient
3 a : WEIGH 1 **b :** to feel the weight of **:** HEFT
4 : to assign a statistical weight to
5 : to cause to incline in a particular direction by manipulation ⟨the tax structure . . . which was *weighted* so heavily in favor of the upper classes —A. S. Link⟩
6 : to shift the burden of weight upon ⟨*weight* the inside ski⟩
weight·ed *adjective* (circa 1732)
1 : made heavy **:** LOADED ⟨*weighted* silk⟩
2 a : having a statistical weight attached ⟨a *weighted* test score⟩ **b :** compiled or calculated from weighted data ⟨a *weighted* mean⟩
3 : INCLINED 1
weight·less \'wāt-ləs\ *adjective* (circa 1547)
: having little weight **:** lacking apparent gravitational pull
— **weight·less·ly** *adverb*
— **weight·less·ness** *noun*
weight lifter *noun* (1897)
: one that lifts barbells in competition or as an exercise
— **weight lifting** *noun*
weight man *noun* (circa 1949)

WEIGHTS AND MEASURES[1]

UNIT	ABBREVIATION OR SYMBOL	EQUIVALENTS IN OTHER UNITS OF SAME SYSTEM	METRIC EQUIVALENT
WEIGHT			
Avoirdupois[2]			
ton			
short ton		20 short hundredweight, 2000 pounds	0.907 metric ton
long ton		20 long hundredweight, 2240 pounds	1.016 metric tons
hundredweight	cwt		
short hundredweight		100 pounds, 0.05 short ton	45.359 kilograms
long hundredweight		112 pounds, 0.05 long ton	50.802 kilograms
pound	lb *or* lb avdp *also* #	16 ounces, 7000 grains	0.454 kilogram
ounce	oz *or* oz avdp	16 drams, 437.5 grains, 0.0625 pound	28.350 grams
dram	dr *or* dr avdp	27.344 grains, 0.0625 ounce	1.772 grams
grain	gr	0.037 dram, 0.002286 ounce	0.0648 gram
Troy			
pound	lb t	12 ounces, 240 pennyweight, 5760 grains	0.373 kilogram
ounce	oz t	20 pennyweight, 480 grains, 0.083 pound	31.103 grams
pennyweight	dwt *also* pwt	24 grains, 0.05 ounce	1.555 grams
grain	gr	0.042 pennyweight, 0.002083 ounce	0.0648 gram
Apothecaries'			
pound	lb ap	12 ounces, 5760 grains	0.373 kilogram
ounce	oz ap *or* ℥	8 drams, 480 grains, 0.083 pound	31.103 grams
dram	dr ap *or* ʒ	3 scruples, 60 grains	3.888 grams
scruple	s ap *or* ℈	20 grains, 0.333 dram	1.296 grams
grain	gr	0.05 scruple, 0.002083 ounce, 0.0166 dram	0.0648 gram
CAPACITY			
U.S. liquid measure			
gallon	gal	4 quarts (231 cubic inches)	3.785 liters
quart	qt	2 pints (57.75 cubic inches)	0.946 liter
pint	pt	4 gills (28.875 cubic inches)	473.176 milliliters
gill	gi	4 fluid ounces (7.219 cubic inches)	118.294 milliliters
fluid ounce	fl oz *or* f℥	8 fluid drams (1.805 cubic inches)	29.573 milliliters
fluid dram	fl dr *or* f ʒ	60 minims (0.226 cubic inch)	3.697 milliliters
minim	min *or* ♍	¹⁄₆₀ fluid dram (0.003760 cubic inch)	0.061610 milliliter
U.S. dry measure			
bushel	bu	4 pecks (2150.42 cubic inches)	35.239 liters
peck	pk	8 quarts (537.605 cubic inches)	8.810 liters
quart	qt	2 pints (67.201 cubic inches)	1.101 liters
pint	pt	½ quart (33.600 cubic inches)	0.551 liter
British imperial liquid and dry measure			
bushel	bu	4 pecks (2219.36 cubic inches)	36.369 liters
peck	pk	2 gallons (554.84 cubic inches)	9.092 liters
gallon	gal	4 quarts (277.420 cubic inches)	4.546 liters
quart	qt	2 pints (69.355 cubic inches)	1.136 liters
pint	pt	4 gills (34.678 cubic inches)	568.26 milliliters
gill	gi	5 fluid ounces (8.669 cubic inches)	142.066 milliliters
fluid ounce	fl oz *or* f℥	8 fluid drams (1.7339 cubic inches)	28.412 milliliters
fluid dram	fl dr *or* f ʒ	60 minims (0.216734 cubic inch)	3.5516 milliliters
minim	min *or* ♍	¹⁄₆₀ fluid dram (0.003612 cubic inch)	0.059194 milliliter
LENGTH			
mile	mi	5280 feet, 1760 yards, 320 rods	1.609 kilometers
rod	rd	5.50 yards, 16.5 feet	5.029 meters
yard	yd	3 feet, 36 inches	0.9144 meter
foot	ft *or* '	12 inches, 0.333 yard	30.48 centimeters
inch	in *or* "	0.083 foot, 0.028 yard	2.54 centimeters
AREA			
square mile	sq mi *or* mi^2	640 acres, 102,400 square rods	2.590 square kilometers
acre		4840 square yards, 43,560 square feet	0.405 hectare, 4047 square meters
square rod	sq rd *or* rd^2	30.25 square yards, 0.00625 acre	25.293 square meters
square yard	sq yd *or* yd^2	1296 square inches, 9 square feet	0.836 square meter
square foot	sq ft *or* ft^2	144 square inches, 0.111 square yard	0.093 square meter
square inch	sq in *or* in^2	0.0069 square foot, 0.00077 square yard	6.452 square centimeters
VOLUME			
cubic yard	cu yd *or* yd^3	27 cubic feet, 46,656 cubic inches	0.765 cubic meter
cubic foot	cu ft *or* ft^3	1728 cubic inches, 0.0370 cubic yard	0.028 cubic meter
cubic inch	cu in *or* in^3	0.00058 cubic foot, 0.000021 cubic yard	16.387 cubic centimeters

[1] For U.S. equivalents of the metric units see Metric System table.
[2] The U.S. uses the avoirdupois units as the common system of measuring weight.

: an athlete who competes in any of the field events in which a weight is thrown or put

weight room *noun* (1973)
: a room containing equipment for weight training

weight training *noun* (1955)
: a system of conditioning involving lifting weights especially for strength and endurance

weighty \'wā-tē\ *adjective* **weight·i·er; -est** (15th century)
1 a : of much importance or consequence **:** MOMENTOUS **b :** SOLEMN
2 a : weighing a considerable amount **b :** heavy in proportion to its bulk ⟨*weighty* metal⟩
3 : POWERFUL, TELLING ⟨*weighty* arguments⟩
synonym see HEAVY
— **weight·i·ly** \'wā-tᵊl-ē\ *adverb*
— **weight·i·ness** \'wā-tē-nəs\ *noun*

wei·ma·ra·ner \,vī-mə-'rä-nər, ,wī-; 'vī-mə-,, 'wī-\ *noun* [German, from *Weimar*, Germany] (1943)
: any of a breed of large light gray usually short-haired pointers of German origin

wei·ner *variant of* WIENER

weir \'war, 'wer, 'wir\ *noun* [Middle English *were*, from Old English *wer*; akin to Old Norse *ver* fishing place, Old High German *werien, werren* to defend] (before 12th century)
1 : a fence or enclosure set in a waterway for taking fish
2 : a dam in a stream or river to raise the water level or divert its flow

¹weird \'wird\ *noun* [Middle English *wird, werd*, from Old English *wyrd*; akin to Old Norse *urthr* fate, Old English *weorthan* to become — more at WORTH] (before 12th century)
1 : FATE, DESTINY; *especially* **:** ill fortune
2 : SOOTHSAYER ◆

²weird *adjective* (15th century)
1 : of, relating to, or caused by witchcraft or the supernatural **:** MAGICAL
2 : of strange or extraordinary character **:** ODD, FANTASTIC ☆
— **weird·ly** *adverb*
— **weird·ness** *noun*

weird·ie \'wir-dē\ *or* **weirdy** *noun, plural* **weird·ies** (1894)
: WEIRDO

weirdo \'wir-(,)dō\ *noun, plural* **weird·os** (circa 1955)
: a person who is extraordinarily strange or eccentric

Weird Sisters *noun plural*
: FATES

wei·sen·hei·mer *variant of* WISENHEIMER

weka \'we-kə\ *noun* [Maori] (1845)
: a flightless New Zealand rail (*Gallirallus australis*)

welch \'welch\ *variant of* WELSH

Welch \'welch\ *variant of* WELSH

¹wel·come \'wel-kəm\ *transitive verb* **wel·comed; wel·com·ing** [Middle English, from Old English *welcuman, wylcumian*, from *wilcuma*, noun] (before 12th century)
1 : to greet hospitably and with courtesy or cordiality
2 : to accept with pleasure the occurrence or presence of ⟨*welcomes* danger⟩
— **wel·com·er** *noun*

²welcome *interjection* [Middle English, alteration of *wilcume*, from Old English, from *wilcuma* desirable guest (akin to Old High German *willicomo* desirable guest); akin to Old English *willa*, *will* desire, *cuman* to come — more at WILL, COME] (12th century)
— used to express a greeting to a guest or newcomer upon arrival

³welcome *adjective* (12th century)
1 : received gladly into one's presence or companionship ⟨was always *welcome* in their home⟩
2 : giving pleasure **:** received with gladness or delight especially in response to a need ⟨a *welcome* relief⟩

3 : willingly permitted or admitted ⟨he was *welcome* to come and go —W. M. Thackeray⟩
4 — used in the phrase "You're welcome" as a reply to an expression of thanks
— **wel·come·ly** *adverb*
— **wel·come·ness** *noun*

⁴welcome *noun* (1525)
1 : a greeting or reception usually upon arrival
2 : the state of being welcome ⟨overstayed their *welcome*⟩

welcome mat *noun* (1946)
: something likened to a mat placed before an entrance as a sign of welcome

¹weld \'weld\ *verb* [alteration of obsolete English *well* to weld, from Middle English *wellen* to boil, well, weld — more at WELL] (1599)
intransitive verb
: to become or be capable of being welded
transitive verb
1 a : to unite (metallic parts) by heating and allowing the metals to flow together or by hammering or compressing with or without previous heating **b :** to unite (plastics) in a similar manner by heating **c :** to repair (as an article) by this method **d :** to produce or create as if by such a process
2 : to unite or reunite closely or intimately
— **weld·able** \'wel-də-bəl\ *adjective*

²weld *noun* (1831)
1 : a welded joint
2 : union by welding **:** the state or condition of being welded

weld·er \'wel-dər\ *noun* (circa 1828)
: one that welds: as **a** *or* **wel·dor :** one whose work is welding **b :** a machine used in welding

weld·ment \'wel(d)-mənt\ *noun* (1941)
: a unit formed by welding together an assembly of pieces

¹wel·fare \'wel-,far, -,fer\ *noun* [Middle English, from the phrase *wel faren* to fare well] (14th century)
1 : the state of doing well especially in respect to good fortune, happiness, well-being, or prosperity
2 a : aid in the form of money or necessities for those in need **b :** an agency or program through which such aid is distributed

²welfare *adjective* (1904)
1 : of, relating to, or concerned with welfare and especially with improvement of the welfare of disadvantaged social groups ⟨*welfare* legislation⟩
2 : receiving public welfare benefits ⟨*welfare* families⟩

welfare state *noun* (1941)
1 : a social system based on the assumption by a political state of primary responsibility for the individual and social welfare of its citizens
2 : a nation or state characterized by the operation of the welfare state system

wel·far·ism \'wel-,far-,i-zəm, -,fer-\ *noun* (1949)
: the complex of policies, attitudes, and beliefs associated with the welfare state
— **wel·far·ist** \-ist\ *noun or adjective*

wel·kin \'wel-kən\ *noun* [Middle English, literally, cloud, from Old English *wolcen*; akin to Old High German *wolkan* cloud] (12th century)
1 a : the vault of the sky **:** FIRMAMENT **b :** the celestial abode of God or the gods **:** HEAVEN
2 : the upper atmosphere

¹well \'wel\ *noun* [Middle English *welle*, from Old English *welle*; akin to Old English *weallan* to bubble, boil, Old High German *wella* wave, Lithuanian *vilnis*] (before 12th century)
1 a : an issue of water from the earth **:** a pool fed by a spring **b :** SOURCE, ORIGIN
2 a : a pit or hole sunk into the earth to reach a supply of water **b :** a shaft or hole sunk to obtain oil, brine, or gas
3 a : an enclosure in the middle of a ship's hold to protect from damage and facilitate the

inspection of the pumps **b :** a compartment in the hold of a fishing boat in which fish are kept alive
4 : an open space extending vertically through floors of a structure
5 : a space having a construction or shape suggesting a well for water
6 a : something resembling a well in being damp, cool, deep, or dark **b :** a deep vertical hole **c :** a source from which something may be drawn as needed
7 : a pronounced minimum of a variable in physics ⟨a potential *well*⟩

²well [Middle English, from Old English *wellan* to cause to well; akin to Old English *weallan* to bubble, boil] (before 12th century)
intransitive verb
1 : to rise to the surface and usually flow forth ⟨tears *welled* from her eyes⟩
2 : to rise like a flood of liquid ⟨longing *welled* up in his breast⟩
transitive verb
: to emit in a copious free flow

³well *adverb* **bet·ter** \'be-tər\; **best** \'best\ [Middle English *wel*, from Old English; akin to Old High German *wela* well, Old English *wyllan* to wish — more at WILL] (before 12th century)
1 a : in a good or proper manner **:** JUSTLY, RIGHTLY **b :** satisfactorily with respect to conduct or action ⟨did *well* in math⟩
2 : in a kindly or friendly manner ⟨spoke *well* of your idea⟩
3 a : with skill or aptitude **:** EXPERTLY ⟨paints *well*⟩ **b :** SATISFACTORILY **c :** with good appearance or effect **:** ELEGANTLY ⟨carried himself *well*⟩
4 : with careful or close attention **:** ATTENTIVELY
5 : to a high degree ⟨*well* deserved the honor⟩ ⟨a *well*-equipped kitchen⟩ — often used as an intensifier or qualifier ⟨there are . . . vacancies pretty *well* all the time —*Listener*⟩
6 : FULLY, QUITE ⟨*well* worth the price⟩

☆ **SYNONYMS**
Weird, eerie, uncanny mean mysteriously strange or fantastic. WEIRD may imply an unearthly or supernatural strangeness or it may stress queerness or oddness ⟨*weird* creatures from another world⟩. EERIE suggests an uneasy or fearful consciousness that mysterious and malign powers are at work ⟨an *eerie* calm preceded the bombing raid⟩. UNCANNY implies disquieting strangeness or mysteriousness ⟨an *uncanny* resemblance between total strangers⟩.

◇ **WORD HISTORY**
weird *Weird* is a northern English and Scots outcome of Old English *wyrd*, the Anglo-Saxons' name for the unpredictable and uncontrollable force determining the outcome of human events that in Modern English we call *fate*. As early as the late 8th century, *wyrde*, the plural of *wyrd*, served as an Old English gloss for *Parcae*, the Latin name for the Fates, three goddesses who spun, measured, and cut the thread of life. In the 15th and 16th centuries Scots authors employed *werd* or *weird* attributively in the phrase *weird sisters* to refer to the Fates of classical myth. Shakespeare adopted this usage in his tragedy *Macbeth*, in which the *weird sisters* are depicted not in their ancient guise but rather as three witches. Subsequent adjectival use of *weird* to mean "unearthly," "mysterious," or "odd" has grown out of a reinterpretation of *weird* in the Shakespearean phrase, most notably by the Romantic poets Shelley and Keats in the early 19th century.

7 a : in a way appropriate to the facts or circumstances **:** FITTINGLY, RIGHTLY **b :** in a prudent manner **:** SENSIBLY — used with *do*
8 : in accordance with the occasion or circumstances **:** with propriety or good reason ⟨cannot *well* refuse⟩
9 a : as one could wish **:** FAVORABLY **b :** with material success **:** ADVANTAGEOUSLY ⟨married *well*⟩
10 a : EASILY, READILY ⟨could *well* afford a new car⟩ **b :** in all likelihood **:** INDEED ⟨it may *well* be true⟩
11 : in a prosperous or affluent manner ⟨he lives *well*⟩
12 : to an extent approaching completeness **:** THOROUGHLY ⟨after being *well* dried with a sponge⟩
13 : without doubt or question **:** CLEARLY ⟨*well* knew the penalty⟩
14 : in a familiar manner ⟨knew her *well*⟩
15 : to a large extent or degree **:** CONSIDERABLY, FAR ⟨*well* over a million⟩
usage see GOOD
— **as well 1 :** in addition **:** ALSO ⟨there were other features *as well*⟩ **2 :** to the same extent or degree **:** as much ⟨open *as well* to the poor as to the rich⟩ **3 :** with equivalent, comparable, or more favorable effect ⟨might just *as well* have stayed home⟩
⁴**well** *interjection* (before 12th century)
1 — used to indicate resumption of discourse or to introduce a remark
2 — used to express surprise or expostulation
⁵**well** *adjective* (before 12th century)
1 a : PROSPEROUS, WELL-OFF **b :** being in satisfactory condition or circumstances
2 : being in good standing or favor
3 : SATISFACTORY, PLEASING ⟨all's *well* that ends well⟩
4 : ADVISABLE, DESIRABLE ⟨it might be *well* for you to leave⟩
5 a : free or recovered from infirmity or disease **:** HEALTHY ⟨a *well* man⟩ **b :** completely cured or healed ⟨the wound is nearly *well*⟩
6 : pleasing or satisfactory in appearance
7 : being a cause for thankfulness **:** FORTUNATE ⟨it is *well* that this has happened⟩
synonym see HEALTHY
usage see GOOD
we'll \'wē(ə)l, wil\ (1578)
: we will **:** we shall
well·ad·just·ed \ˌwel-ə-'jəs-təd\ *adjective* (1692)
: WELL-BALANCED 2
well·ad·vised \'wel-əd-'vīzd\ *adjective* (14th century)
1 : acting with wisdom, wise counsel, or proper deliberation **:** PRUDENT
2 : resulting from, based on, or showing careful deliberation or wise counsel ⟨*well-advised* plans⟩
well·ap·point·ed \'wel-ə-'pȯin-təd\ *adjective* (1530)
: having good and complete equipment **:** properly fitted out ⟨a *well-appointed* house⟩
wel·la·way \ˌwe-lə-'wā, 'we-lə-ˌ\ *interjection* [Middle English *welaway*, from Old English *wēilāwei*, literally, woe! lo! woe!, alteration of *wālāwā*, from *wā* woe + *lā* lo + *wā* woe — more at WOE] (before 12th century)
archaic — used to express sorrow or lamentation
well·ba·lanced \'wel-'ba-lən(t)st\ *adjective* (1629)
1 : nicely or evenly balanced, arranged, or regulated ⟨a *well-balanced* diet⟩ ⟨a *well-balanced* attack in football⟩
2 : emotionally or psychologically untroubled
well·be·ing \'wel-'bē-iŋ\ *noun* (circa 1613)
: the state of being happy, healthy, or prosperous **:** WELFARE
well·be·loved \ˌwel-bi-'ləvd\ *adjective* (14th century)
1 : sincerely and deeply loved ⟨my *well-beloved* wife⟩

2 : sincerely respected — used in various ceremonial forms of address
well·born \'wel-'bȯrn\ *adjective* (before 12th century)
: born of noble or wealthy lineage
well·bred \-'bred\ *adjective* (1597)
1 : having or displaying good breeding **:** REFINED
2 : having a good pedigree ⟨*well-bred* swine⟩
well·con·di·tioned \ˌwel-kən-'di-shənd\ *adjective* (15th century)
1 : characterized by proper disposition, morals, or behavior
2 : having a good physical condition **:** SOUND
well deck *noun* (1888)
: a space on the weather deck of a ship lying at a lower level between a raised forecastle and the bridge superstructure
well·de·fined \ˌwel-di-'fīnd\ *adjective* (1704)
1 : having clearly distinguishable limits, boundaries, or features ⟨a *well-defined* scar⟩
2 : clearly stated or described ⟨*well-defined* policies⟩
well·dis·posed \-dis-'pōzd\ *adjective* (14th century)
: having a good disposition; *especially* **:** disposed to be friendly, favorable, or sympathetic
well·done \'wel-'dən\ *adjective* (15th century)
1 : rightly or properly performed
2 : cooked thoroughly
Wel·ler·ism \'we-lə-ˌri-zəm\ *noun* [Sam *Weller*, witty servant of Mr. Pickwick in the story *Pickwick Papers* (1836–37) by Charles Dickens] (1839)
: an expression of comparison comprising a usually well-known quotation followed by a facetious sequel (as "'every one to his own taste,' said the old woman as she kissed the cow")
well·fa·vored \'wel-'fā-vərd\ *adjective* (15th century)
: GOOD-LOOKING, HANDSOME
— **well·fa·vored·ness** *noun*
well·fixed \-'fikst\ *adjective* (1822)
: having plenty of money or property
well·found \-'faùnd\ *adjective* (1793)
: fully furnished **:** properly equipped ⟨a *well-found* ship⟩
well·found·ed \-'faùn-dəd\ *adjective* (14th century)
: based on excellent reasoning, information, judgment, or grounds
well·groomed \-'grümd, -'grùmd\ *adjective* (1886)
1 : well-dressed and scrupulously neat ⟨*well-groomed* men⟩
2 : made neat, tidy, and attractive down to the smallest details ⟨a *well-groomed* lawn⟩
well·ground·ed \-'graùn-dəd\ *adjective* (14th century)
1 : having a firm foundation ⟨*well-grounded* in Latin and Greek⟩
2 : WELL-FOUNDED
well·han·dled \-'han-dᵊld\ *adjective* (15th century)
1 : managed or administered efficiently
2 : having been handled a great deal ⟨*well-handled* goods held for sale⟩
well·head \'wel-ˌhed\ *noun* (14th century)
1 : the source of a spring or a stream
2 : principal source **:** FOUNTAINHEAD
3 : the top of or a structure built over a well
wellhead price *noun* (1953)
: the price less transportation costs charged by the producer for petroleum or natural gas
well·heeled \-'hē(ə)ld\ *adjective* (1897)
: having plenty of money **:** WELL-FIXED
wel·lie *or* **wel·ly** \'we-lē\ *noun, plural* **wellies** [by shortening & alteration] (1961)
chiefly British **:** WELLINGTON — usually used in plural
well·in·formed \-in-'fȯrmd\ *adjective* (15th century)
1 : having extensive knowledge especially of current topics and events

2 : thoroughly knowledgeable in a particular subject
Wel·ling·ton \'we-liŋ-tən\ *noun* [Arthur Wellesley, 1st Duke of *Wellington*] (1817)
: a boot having a loose top with the front usually coming to or above the knee — usually used in plural
well·in·ten·tioned \ˌwel-in-'ten(t)-shənd\ *adjective* (1598)
: WELL-MEANING
well·knit \'wel-'nit\ *adjective* (15th century)
: firmly knit ⟨a *well-knit* group⟩; *especially* **:** firmly and strongly constructed, compacted, or framed ⟨a *well-knit* drama⟩
well·known \-'nōn\ *adjective* (15th century)
: fully or widely known
well·mean·ing \-'mē-niŋ\ *adjective* (1532)
1 : having good intentions ⟨*well-meaning* but misguided idealists⟩
2 : based on good intentions ⟨*well-meaning* advice⟩
well·meant \-'ment\ *adjective* (15th century)
: WELL-MEANING 2
well·ness \'wel-nəs\ *noun* (1654)
: the quality or state of being in good health especially as an actively sought goal ⟨*wellness* clinics⟩ ⟨lifestyles that promote *wellness*⟩
well·nigh \-'nī\ *adverb* (12th century)
: ALMOST, NEARLY ⟨*well-nigh* impossible⟩
well·off \-'ȯf\ *adjective* (1733)
1 : being in good condition or favorable circumstances ⟨doesn't know when he's *well-off*⟩
2 : having no lack — usually used with *for*
3 a : being in easy or affluent circumstances **:** WELL-TO-DO **b :** suggesting prosperity ⟨the house had a sleek *well-off* look⟩
well·oiled \-'ȯild\ *adjective* (1847)
: smoothly functioning ⟨a *well-oiled* political machine⟩
well·or·dered \-'ȯr-dərd\ *adjective* (1589)
1 : having an orderly procedure or arrangement ⟨a *well-ordered* household⟩
2 : partially ordered with every subset containing a first element and exactly one of the relationships "greater than", "less than", or "equal to" holding for any given pair of elements
— **well·or·der·ing** \-'ȯrd-riŋ, -'ȯr-də-\ *noun*
well·read \-'red\ *adjective* (1596)
: well informed or deeply versed through reading ⟨*well-read* in history⟩
well·round·ed \-'raùn-dəd\ *adjective* (1875)
: fully or broadly developed: as **a :** having a broad educational background ⟨schools that turn out *well-rounded* graduates⟩ **b :** COMPREHENSIVE ⟨a *well-rounded* program of activities⟩
well·set \-'set\ *adjective* (14th century)
1 : well or firmly established ⟨*well-set* in his own values —William Johnson⟩
2 : strongly built ⟨a *well-set* athlete⟩
well·spo·ken \'wel-'spō-kən\ *adjective* (15th century)
1 : speaking well, fitly, or courteously
2 : spoken with propriety ⟨*well-spoken* words⟩
well·spring \-ˌspriŋ\ *noun* (before 12th century)
: a source of continual supply ⟨a *wellspring* of information⟩
well·tak·en \-'tā-kən\ *adjective* (1761)
: WELL-GROUNDED, JUSTIFIABLE ⟨your point is *well-taken*⟩
well·thought·of \ˌwel-'thȯt-ˌəv, -ˌäv\ *adjective* (1579)
: being of good repute
well·timed \'wel-'tīmd\ *adjective* (circa 1656)
: happening at an opportune moment **:** TIMELY ⟨a *well-timed* announcement⟩
well·to·do \ˌwel-tə-'dü\ *adjective* (1825)

\ə\ abut \ᵊ\ kitten \ər\ further \a\ ash \ā\ ace
\ä\ mop, mar \aù\ out \ch\ chin \e\ bet \ē\ easy
\g\ go \i\ hit \ī\ ice \j\ job \ŋ\ sing \ō\ go
\ȯ\ law \ȯi\ boy \th\ thin \th\ the \ü\ loot \ù\ foot
\y\ yet \zh\ vision *see also* Guide to Pronunciation

: having more than adequate financial resources : PROSPEROUS ⟨a *well-to-do* family⟩

well–turned \'wel-'tərnd\ *adjective* (1616)
1 : symmetrically shaped or rounded : SHAPELY
2 : concisely and appropriately expressed ⟨a *well-turned* phrase⟩
3 : expertly rounded or turned ⟨a *well-turned* column⟩

well–wish·er \'wel-,wi-shər, -'wi-\ *noun* (1590)
: one that wishes well to another
— **well–wish·ing** \-shiŋ\ *adjective or noun*

well–worn \-'wōrn, -'wȯrn\ *adjective* (1621)
1 a : made trite by overuse : HACKNEYED ⟨a *well-worn* quotation⟩ **b** : having been much used or worn ⟨*well-worn* shoes⟩
2 *archaic* : worn well or properly

welsh \'welsh, 'welch\ *intransitive verb* [probably from *Welsh*, adjective] (1905)
1 : to avoid payment — used with *on* ⟨*welshed* on his debts⟩
2 : to break one's word : RENEGE ⟨*welshed* on their promises⟩
— **welsh·er** *noun*

Welsh \'welsh *also* 'welch\ *noun* [Middle English *Walsche, Welsse,* from *walisch, welisch,* adjective, Welsh, from Old English *wælisc, welisc* Celtic, Welsh, foreign, from Old English *Wealh* Celtic, Welshman, foreigner, of Celtic origin; akin to the source of Latin *Volcae,* a Celtic people of southeastern Gaul] (before 12th century)
1 : the Celtic language of the Welsh people
2 *plural in construction* : the natives or inhabitants of Wales
3 : WELSH PONY
— **Welsh** *adjective*

Welsh black *noun* (1919)
: any of a breed of hardy medium-sized thick-haired horned black cattle of Welsh origin that are raised for meat and milk

Welsh cob *noun* (1947)
: any of a breed of medium-sized cobby horses that were developed by interbreeding Welsh mountain ponies with larger horses

Welsh corgi *noun* (1926)
: a short-legged long-backed dog with foxy head of either of two breeds of Welsh origin: **a** : CARDIGAN WELSH CORGI **b** : PEMBROKE WELSH CORGI

Welsh·man \-mən\ *noun* (13th century)
: a native or inhabitant of Wales

Welsh corgi: *1* Pembroke, *2* Cardigan

Welsh mountain pony *noun* (1947)
: any of a breed of small sturdy ponies native to the mountains of Wales that do not exceed 12.2 hands (124 centimeters) in height

Welsh pony *noun* (1771)
: a pony of any of several breeds of Welsh origin; *especially* : any of a breed of riding and light draft ponies measuring 12.2 to 13.2 hands (124 to 134 centimeters) in height

Welsh rabbit *noun* (1725)
: melted often seasoned cheese poured over toast or crackers

Welsh rare·bit \-'rar-bət, -'rer-\ *noun* [by alteration] (1785)
: WELSH RABBIT

Welsh springer spaniel *noun* (circa 1929)
: any of a breed of red and white or orange and white small-eared springer spaniels of Welsh origin

Welsh terrier *noun* (1885)
: any of a breed of wiry-coated terriers resembling Airedales but smaller and developed in Wales for hunting

Welsh·wom·an \'welsh-,wu̇-mən *also* 'welch-\ *noun* (15th century)
: a woman who is a native or inhabitant of Wales

¹welt \'welt\ *noun* [Middle English *welte*] (15th century)
1 : a strip between a shoe sole and upper through which they are stitched or stapled together
2 : a doubled edge, strip, insert, or seam (as on a garment) for ornament or reinforcement
3 a : a ridge or lump raised on the body usually by a blow **b** : a heavy blow

²welt *transitive verb* (15th century)
1 : to furnish with a welt
2 a : to raise a welt on the body of **b** : to hit hard

welt·an·schau·ung \'velt-,än-,shau̇-əŋ\ *noun, plural* **weltanschauungs** \-əŋz\ *or* **welt·an·schau·ung·en** \-əŋ-ən\ *often capitalized* [German, from *Welt* world + *Anschauung* view] (1868)
: a comprehensive conception or apprehension of the world especially from a specific standpoint

¹wel·ter \'wel-tər\ *intransitive verb* **weltered; wel·ter·ing** \-t(ə-)riŋ\ [Middle English; akin to Middle Dutch *welteren* to roll, Old High German *walzan,* Lithuanian *volioti,* Latin *volvere* — more at VOLUBLE] (14th century)
1 a : WRITHE, TOSS; *also* : WALLOW **b** : to rise and fall or toss about in or with waves
2 : to become deeply sunk, soaked, or involved
3 : to be in turmoil

²welter *noun* (1596)
1 : a state of wild disorder : TURMOIL
2 : a chaotic mass or jumble ⟨a bewildering *welter* of data⟩

³welter *noun* (1900)
: WELTERWEIGHT

wel·ter·weight \'wel-tər-,wāt\ *noun* [welter (probably from ¹welt) + weight] (circa 1892)
: a boxer in a weight division having a maximum limit of 147 pounds — compare LIGHTWEIGHT, MIDDLEWEIGHT

welt·schmerz \'velt-,shmerts\ *noun, often capitalized* [German, from *Welt* world + *Schmerz* pain] (1875)
1 : mental depression or apathy caused by comparison of the actual state of the world with an ideal state
2 : a mood of sentimental sadness

¹wen \'wen\ *noun* [Middle English *wenn,* from Old English; akin to Middle Low German *wene* wen] (before 12th century)
: an abnormal growth or a cyst protruding from a surface especially of the skin

²wen *variant of* WYNN

¹wench \'wench\ *noun* [Middle English *wenche,* short for *wenchel* child, from Old English *wencel;* akin to Old High German *wankōn* to totter, waver and probably to Old High German *winchan* to stagger — more at WINK] (14th century)
1 a : a young woman : GIRL **b** : a female servant
2 : a lewd woman : PROSTITUTE

²wench *intransitive verb* (1599)
: to consort with lewd women; *especially* : to practice fornication
— **wench·er** *noun*

wend \'wend\ *verb* [Middle English, from Old English *wendan;* akin to Old High German *wenten* to turn, Old English *windan* to twist — more at WIND] (before 12th century)
intransitive verb
: to direct one's course : TRAVEL
transitive verb
: to proceed on (one's way) : DIRECT

Wend \'wend\ *noun* [German *Wende,* from Old High German *Winida;* akin to Old English *Winedas,* plural, Wends] (1786)
: a member of a Slavic people of eastern Germany

¹Wend·ish \'wen-dish\ *adjective* (1614)
: of or relating to the Wends or their language

²Wendish *noun* (1617)
: the West Slavic language of the Wends

went [Middle English, past & past participle of *wenden* to wend] *past of* GO

wen·tle·trap \'wen-t²l-,trap\ *noun* [Dutch *wenteltrap* winding stair, from Middle Dutch *wendeltrappe,* from *wendel* turning + *trappe* stairs] (1758)
: any of a family (Epitoniidae) of marine snails with usually white shells; *also* : one of the shells

wept *past and past participle of* WEEP

were [Middle English *were* (suppletive singular past subjunctive & 2d singular past indicative of *been* to be), *weren* (suppletive past plural of *been*), from Old English *wǣre* (singular past subjunctive & 2d singular past indicative of *wesan* to be), *wǣron* (past plural indicative of *wesan*), *wǣren* (past plural subjunctive of *wesan*) — more at WAS] *past 2d singular, past plural, or past subjunctive of* BE

we're \'wir, 'wər, 'wē-ər\ (1608)
: we are

weren't \(')wərnt, 'wər-ənt\ (1865)
: were not

were·wolf \'wir-,wu̇lf, 'wer-, 'wər-\ *noun, plural* **were·wolves** \-,wu̇lvz\ [Middle English, from Old English *werwulf* (akin to Old High German *werwolf* werewolf), from *wer* man + *wulf* wolf — more at VIRILE, WOLF] (before 12th century)
: a person transformed into a wolf or capable of assuming a wolf's form

wer·gild \'wər-,gild\ *or* **wer·geld** \-,geld\ *noun* [Middle English *wergeld,* from Old English, from *wer* man + *-geld, geld* payment, tribute — more at GELD] (13th century)
: the value set in Anglo-Saxon and Germanic law upon human life in accordance with rank and paid as compensation to the kindred or lord of a slain person

wert \'wərt\ *archaic past 2d singular of* BE

wes·kit \'wes-kət\ *noun* [alteration of *waistcoat*] (1856)
: VEST 2a

Wes·ley·an·ism \'wes-lē-ə-,ni-zəm *also* 'wez-\ *noun* (1774)
: METHODISM 1; *specifically* : the system of Arminian Methodism taught by John Wesley
— **Wes·ley·an** \-lē-ən\ *adjective or noun*

¹west \'west\ *adverb* [Middle English, from Old English; akin to Old High German *westar* to the west and probably to Latin *vesper* evening, Greek *hesperos*] (before 12th century)
: to, toward, or in the west

²west *adjective* (before 12th century)
1 : situated toward or at the west ⟨the *west* exit⟩
2 : coming from the west ⟨a *west* wind⟩

³west *noun* (12th century)
1 a : the general direction of sunset : the direction to the left of one facing north **b** : the compass point directly opposite to east
2 *capitalized* **a** : regions or countries lying to the west of a specified or implied point of orientation **b** : the noncommunist countries of Europe and America
3 : the end of a church opposite the chancel
4 *often capitalized* **a** : the one of four positions at 90-degree intervals that lies to the west or at the left of a diagram **b** : a person (as a bridge player) occupying this position during a specified activity

west·bound \'wes(t)-,bau̇nd\ *adjective* (1881)
: traveling or heading west

west by north (1760)
: a compass point that is one point north of due west : N78°45′W

west by south (1577)
: a compass point that is one point south of due west : S78°45′W

west·er \'wes-tər\ *intransitive verb* **west-ered; west·er·ing** \-t(ə-)riŋ\ [Middle English *westren*, from ¹*west*] (14th century) : to turn or move westward ⟨the half moon *westers* low —A. E. Housman⟩

¹**west·er·ly** \'wes-tər-lē\ *adjective or adverb* [obsolete *wester* western] (15th century) **1** : situated toward or belonging to the west ⟨the *westerly* end of the farm⟩ **2** : coming from the west ⟨a *westerly* breeze⟩

²**westerly** *noun, plural* **-lies** (1876) : a wind from the west

¹**west·ern** \'wes-tərn\ *adjective* [Middle English *westerne*, from Old English; akin to Old High German *westrōni* western, Old English *west*] (before 12th century) **1 a** : coming from the west ⟨a *western* storm⟩ **b** : lying toward the west **2** *capitalized* : of, relating to, or characteristic of a region conventionally designated West: as **a** : steeped in or stemming from the Greco-Roman traditions **b** : of or relating to the noncommunist countries of Europe and America **c** : of or relating to the American West **3** *capitalized* : of or relating to the Roman Catholic or Protestant segment of Christianity ⟨*Western* liturgies⟩ — **west·ern·most** \-ˌmōst\ *adjective*

²**western** *noun* (1612) **1** : one that is produced in or characteristic of a western region and especially the western U.S. **2** *often capitalized* : a novel, story, motion picture, or broadcast dealing with life in the western U.S. especially during the latter half of the 19th century

Western blot *noun* [after *Southern blot*] (1983) : a blot that consists of a nitrocellulose sheet containing spots of protein for identification by a suitable molecular probe and is used especially for the detection of antibodies — **Western blotting** *noun*

West·ern·er \'wes-tə(r)-nər\ *noun* (1599) **1** : a native or inhabitant of the West; *especially* : a native or resident of the western part of the U.S. **2** : one advocating the adoption of western European culture especially in 19th century Russia

western hemisphere *noun, often W&H capitalized* (1624) : the half of the earth comprising North and South America and surrounding waters

west·ern·i·sa·tion, west·ern·ise *British variant of* WESTERNIZATION, WESTERNIZE

west·ern·i·za·tion \ˌwes-tər-nə-'zā-shən\ *noun, often capitalized* (1904) : conversion to or adoption of western traditions or techniques

west·ern·ize \'wes-tər-ˌnīz\ *verb* **-ized; -iz·ing** *often capitalized* (1837) *transitive verb* : to imbue with qualities native to or associated with a western region and especially the noncommunist countries of Europe and America *intransitive verb* : to become westernized

western omelet *noun* (1951) : an omelet made usually with diced ham, green pepper, and onion — called also *Denver omelet*

western red cedar *noun* (1886) : RED CEDAR 2; *also* : its wood

western saddle *noun, often W capitalized* (1897) : a deep-seated saddle with a high pommel and broad skirts and fenders used originally by cattlemen — called also *stock saddle;* see SADDLE illustration

western sandwich *noun* (1926) : a sandwich filled with a western omelet — called also *Denver sandwich*

western swing *noun* (1973)

: swing music played typically on country-music instruments (as guitar, fiddle, or steel guitar)

West Germanic *noun* (1894) : a subdivision of the Germanic languages including English, Frisian, Dutch, and German — see INDO-EUROPEAN LANGUAGES table

West Highland white terrier *noun* (circa 1904) : any of a breed of small white long-coated terriers developed in Scotland — called also *West·ie* \'wes-tē\

West Highland white terrier

west·ing \'wes-tiŋ\ *noun* (1628) : westerly progress : a going westward

west–northwest *noun* (15th century) : a compass point that is two points north of due west : N67°30′W

West·pha·lian ham \wes(t)-'fāl-yən-, -'fā-lē-ən-\ *noun* [*Westphalia,* Germany] (1664) : a ham of distinctive flavor produced by smoking with juniper brush

West Saxon *noun* (14th century) **1** : a member or a descendant of the Saxons who occupied England largely south of the Thames, west of the Downs, and east of Dartmoor **2** : a dialect of Old English used as the chief literary dialect in England before the Norman Conquest

west–southwest *noun* (1555) : a compass point that is two points south of due west : S67°30′W

¹**west·ward** \'wes-twərd\ *adverb or adjective* (before 12th century) : toward the west — **west·wards** \-twərdz\ *adverb*

²**westward** *noun* (1652) : westward direction or part ⟨sail to the *westward*⟩

¹**wet** \'wet\ *adjective* **wet·ter; wet·test** [Middle English, partly from past participle of *weten* to wet & partly from Old English *wæt* wet; akin to Old Norse *vātr* wet, Old English *wæter* water] (before 12th century) **1 a** : consisting of, containing, covered with, or soaked with liquid (as water) **b** *of natural gas* : containing appreciable quantities of readily condensable hydrocarbons **2** : RAINY **3** : still moist enough to smudge or smear ⟨*wet* paint⟩ **4 a** : DRUNK 1a ⟨a *wet* driver⟩ **b** : having or advocating a policy permitting the manufacture and sale of alcoholic beverages ⟨a *wet* county⟩ ⟨a *wet* candidate⟩ **5** : preserved in liquid **6** : employing or done by means of or in the presence of water or other liquid ⟨*wet* extraction of copper⟩ **7** : overly sentimental **8** *British* : lacking strength of character : WEAK, SPINELESS ⟨thought him *wet* and violence petrified him —William Golding⟩ **b** : belonging to the moderate or liberal wing of the Conservative party ☆ — **wet·ly** *adverb* — **wet·ness** *noun* — **all wet** : completely wrong : in error — **wet behind the ears** : IMMATURE, INEXPERIENCED

²**wet** *noun* (before 12th century) **1** : WATER; *also* : MOISTURE, WETNESS **2** : rainy weather : RAIN **3** : an advocate of a policy permitting the sale of intoxicating liquors **4** *British* : one who is wet

³**wet** *verb* **wet** *or* **wet·ted; wet·ting** [Middle English, from Old English *wǣtan,* from *wǣt,* adjective] (before 12th century) *transitive verb* **1** : to make wet **2** : to urinate in or on *intransitive verb* **1** : to become wet **2** : URINATE — **wet one's whistle** : to take a drink especially of liquor

wet·back \'wet-ˌbak\ *noun* [from the practice of wading or swimming the Rio Grande where it forms the U.S.-Mexico border] (1929) : a Mexican who enters the U.S. illegally — sometimes taken to be offensive

wet bar *noun* (1967) : a bar for mixing drinks (as in a home) that contains a sink with running water

wet blanket *noun* (1857) : one that quenches or dampens enthusiasm or pleasure

wet down *transitive verb* (1840) : to dampen by sprinkling with water

wet dream *noun* (1851) : an erotic dream culminating in orgasm and in the male accompanied by seminal emission

weth·er \'we-thər\ *noun* [Middle English, ram, from Old English; akin to Old High German *widar* ram, Latin *vitulus* calf, *vetus* old, Greek *etos* year] (before 12th century) : a male sheep castrated before sexual maturity; *also* : a castrated male goat

wet·land \'wet-ˌland, -lənd\ *noun* (1778) : land or areas (as tidal flats or swamps) containing much soil moisture — usually used in plural

wet–nurse *transitive verb* (1784) **1** : to act as wet nurse to **2** : to give constant and often excessive care to

wet nurse *noun* (1620) : a woman who cares for and suckles children not her own

wet suit *noun* (1955) : a close-fitting suit made of material (as sponge rubber) that traps a thin layer of water against the body to retain body heat and that is worn (as by a skin diver) especially in cold water

wet·ta·bil·i·ty \ˌwe-tə-'bi-lə-tē\ *noun* (1913) : the quality or state of being wettable : the degree to which something can be wet

wet·ta·ble \'we-tə-bəl\ *adjective* (1885) : capable of being wetted

wet·ter \'we-tər\ *noun* (1737) : one that wets; *also* : WETTING AGENT

wetting agent *noun* (1927)

☆ **SYNONYMS**
Wet, damp, dank, moist, humid mean covered or more or less soaked with liquid. WET usually implies saturation but may suggest a covering of a surface with water or something (as paint) not yet dry ⟨slipped on the *wet* pavement⟩. DAMP implies a slight or moderate absorption and often connotes an unpleasant degree of moisture ⟨clothes will mildew if stored in a *damp* place⟩. DANK implies a more distinctly disagreeable or unwholesome dampness ⟨a prisoner in a cold, *dank* cell⟩. MOIST applies to what is slightly damp or not felt as dry ⟨treat the injury with *moist* heat⟩. HUMID applies to the presence of much water vapor in the air ⟨a hot, *humid* climate⟩.

\ə\ abut \ᵊ\ kitten \ər\ further \a\ ash \ā\ ace
\ä\ mop, mar \au̇\ out \ch\ chin \e\ bet \ē\ easy
\g\ go \i\ hit \ī\ ice \j\ job \ŋ\ sing \ō\ go
\ȯ\ law \ȯi\ boy \th\ thin \th\ the \ü\ loot \u̇\ foot
\y\ yet \zh\ vision *see also* Guide to Pronunciation

: a substance that by becoming adsorbed prevents a surface from being repellent to a wetting liquid and is used especially in mixing solids with liquids or spreading liquids on surfaces

wet·tish \'we-tish\ *adjective* (1648)
: somewhat wet : MOIST

wet wash *noun* (1916)
: laundry returned damp and not ironed

we've \'wēv\ (1742)
: we have

¹**whack** \'hwak, 'wak\ *verb* [probably imitative of the sound of a blow] (1719)
transitive verb
1 a : to strike with a smart or resounding blow **b** : to cut into or as if with a whack : CHOP **2** *chiefly British* : to get the better of : DEFEAT
intransitive verb
: to strike a smart or resounding blow
— **whack·er** *noun*

²**whack** *noun* (1736)
1 a : a smart or resounding blow; *also* : the sound of or as if of such a blow **b** : a critical attack
2 : PORTION, SHARE
3 : CONDITION, STATE
4 a : an opportunity or attempt to do something ⟨take a *whack* at it⟩ **b** : a single action or occasion ⟨borrowed $50 all at one *whack*⟩
— **out of whack 1** : out of proper order or shape ⟨threw his knee *out of whack*⟩ **2** : not in accord ⟨feeling *out of whack* with her contemporaries —S. E. Rubin⟩

whacked–out \'(h)wakt-,aut, ,(h)wakt-'\ *adjective* (1967)
1 : WORN-OUT, EXHAUSTED
2 : WACKY ⟨a *whacked-out* parody⟩
3 : STONED ⟨*whacked-out* on drugs⟩

¹**whack·ing** \'hwa-kiŋ, 'wa-\ *adjective* (1806)
: very large : WHOPPING

²**whacking** *adverb* (1853)
: VERY ⟨a *whacking* good story⟩

whacko \'hwa-(,)kō, 'wa-\ *variant of* WACKO

whack off *verb* (1969)
: MASTURBATE — usually considered vulgar

whack up *transitive verb* (circa 1893)
: to divide into shares

whacky \'hwa-kē, 'wa-\ *variant of* WACKY

¹**whale** \'hwā(ə)l, 'wā(ə)l\ *noun, plural* **whales** *often attributive* [Middle English, from Old English *hwæl*; akin to Old High German *hwal* whale and perhaps to Latin *squalus* sea fish] (before 12th century)
1 *or plural* **whale** : CETACEAN; *especially* : one (as a sperm whale or killer whale) of larger size
2 : one that is impressive especially in size ⟨a *whale* of a difference⟩ ⟨a *whale* of a good time⟩
— **whale·like** \-,līk\ *adjective*

²**whale** *intransitive verb* **whaled; whal·ing** (1700)
: to engage in whale fishing

³**whale** *transitive verb* **whaled; whal·ing** [origin unknown] (circa 1790)
1 : LASH, THRASH
2 : to strike or hit vigorously
3 : to defeat soundly

whale·back \'hwā(ə)l-,bak, 'wā(ə)l-\ *noun* (1886)
: something shaped like the back of a whale

whale·boat \-,bōt\ *noun* (1682)
1 : a long narrow rowboat made with both ends sharp and raking, often steered with an oar, and formerly used by whalers for hunting whales
2 : a long narrow rowboat or motorboat resembling the original whaleboats and often carried by warships and merchant ships

whale·bone \-,bōn\ *noun* (1601)
1 : BALEEN
2 : an article made of whalebone

whalebone whale *noun* (1725)
: BALEEN WHALE

whal·er \'hwā-lər, 'wā-\ *noun* (1684)
1 : a person or ship engaged in whale fishing

2 : WHALEBOAT 2

whale shark *noun* (circa 1885)
: a shark (*Rhincodon typus*) of warm waters that has small teeth, feeds chiefly on plankton strained by its gill rakers, may attain a length of up to 60 feet (18.3 meters), and is the largest known fish

whal·ing \'hwā-liŋ, 'wā-\ *noun* (1688)
: the occupation of catching and extracting commercial products from whales

¹**wham** \'hwam, 'wam\ *noun* [imitative] (1739)
1 : a solid blow
2 : the loud sound of a hard impact

²**wham** *or* **wham·mo** \'hwa-(,)mō, 'wa-\ *adverb* (1924)
: with violent abruptness ⟨everything seemed to be going well, when *wham* the deal fell through⟩

³**wham** *verb* **whammed; wham·ming** (1925)
transitive verb
: to propel, strike, or beat so as to produce a loud impact
intransitive verb
: to hit or explode with a loud impact

wham·my \'hwa-mē, 'wa-\ *noun, plural* **whammies** [probably from ¹*wham*] (1940)
1 a : a supernatural power bringing bad luck **b** : a magic curse or spell
2 : a potent force or attack; *specifically* : a paralyzing or lethal blow

¹**whang** \'hwaŋ, 'waŋ\ *noun* [alteration of Middle English *thong, thwang*] (1536)
1 *dialect* **a** : THONG **b** : RAWHIDE
2 *British* : a large piece : CHUNK
3 : PENIS — often considered vulgar

²**whang** (1684)
transitive verb
1 *dialect* : BEAT, THRASH
2 : to propel or strike with force
intransitive verb
: to beat or work with force or violence

³**whang** *noun* [imitative] (circa 1824)
: a loud sharp vibrant or resonant sound

⁴**whang** (1875)
intransitive verb
: to make a whang
transitive verb
: to strike with a whang

whan·gee \hwaŋ-'ē, waŋ-, -'gē\ *noun* [probably modification of Chinese (Beijing) *huáng* bamboo] (1790)
1 : any of several Chinese bamboos (genus *Phyllostachys*)
2 : a walking stick or riding crop of whangee

whap \'hwäp, 'wäp\ *variant of* WHOP

wharf \'hworf, 'worf\ *noun, plural* **wharves** \'hworvz, 'worvz\ *also* **wharfs** [Middle English, from Old English *hwearf* embankment, wharf; akin to Old English *hweorfan* to turn, Old High German *hwerban*, Greek *karpos* wrist] (before 12th century)
1 : a structure built along or at an angle from the shore of navigable waters so that ships may lie alongside to receive and discharge cargo and passengers
2 *obsolete* : the bank of a river or the shore of the sea

wharf·age \'hwor-fij, 'wor-\ *noun* (15th century)
1 a : the provision or the use of a wharf **b** : the handling or stowing of goods on a wharf
2 : the charge for the use of a wharf
3 : the wharf accommodations of a place : WHARVES

wharf·in·ger \-fən-jər\ *noun* [irregular from *wharfage*] (1552)
: the operator or manager of a commercial wharf

wharf·mas·ter \'hworf-,mas-tər, 'worf-\ *noun* (1618)
: the manager of a wharf : WHARFINGER

¹**what** \'hwät, 'hwət, 'wät, 'wət\ *pronoun* [Middle English, from Old English *hwæt*, neuter of *hwā* who — more at WHO] (before 12th century)

1 a (1) — used as an interrogative expressing inquiry about the identity, nature, or value of an object or matter ⟨*what* is this⟩ ⟨*what* is wealth without friends⟩ ⟨*what* hath God wrought⟩ (2) — often used to ask for repetition of an utterance or part of an utterance not properly heard or understood ⟨you said *what*⟩ **b** (1) *archaic* : WHO 1 — used as an interrogative expressing inquiry about the identity of a person (2) — used as an interrogative expressing inquiry about the character, nature, occupation, position, or role of a person ⟨*what* do you think I am, a fool⟩ ⟨*what* is she, that all our swains commend her —Shakespeare⟩ **c** — used as an exclamation expressing surprise or excitement and frequently introducing a question ⟨*what*, no breakfast⟩ **d** — used in expressions directing attention to a statement that the speaker is about to make ⟨you know *what*⟩ **e** — used at the end of a question to express inquiry about additional possibilities ⟨is it raining, or snowing, or *what*⟩ **f** *chiefly British* — used at the end of an utterance as a form of tag question ⟨a clever play, *what*⟩
2 *chiefly dialect* : ⁴THAT 1, WHICH 3, WHO 3
3 : that which : the one or ones that ⟨no income but *what* he gets from his writings⟩ — sometimes used in reference to a clause or phrase that is yet to come or is not yet complete ⟨gave also, *what* is more valuable, understanding⟩
4 a : WHATEVER 1a ⟨say *what* you will⟩ **b** *obsolete* : WHOEVER
— **what for 1** : for what purpose or reason : WHY — usually used with the other words of a question between *what* and *for* ⟨*what* did you do that *for*⟩ except when used alone **2** : harsh treatment especially by blows or by a sharp reprimand ⟨gave him *what for* in violent Spanish —*New Yorker*⟩
— **what have you** : WHATNOT ⟨novels, plays, short stories, travelogues, and *what have you* —Haldeen Braddy⟩
— **what if 1** : what will or would be the result if **2** : what does it matter if
— **what of 1** : what is the situation with respect to **2** : what importance can be assigned to
— **what's what** : the true state of things ⟨knows *what's what* when it comes to fashion⟩
— **what though** : what does it matter if ⟨*what though* the rose have prickles, yet 'tis plucked —Shakespeare⟩

²**what** *adverb* (before 12th century)
1 *obsolete* : WHY
2 : in what respect : HOW ⟨*what* does he care⟩
3 — used to introduce prepositional phrases in parallel construction or a prepositional phrase that expresses cause and usually has more than one object; used principally before phrases beginning with *with* ⟨*what* with unemployment increasing⟩ ⟨*what* with the war, *what* with the sweat, *what* with the gallows, and *what* with poverty, I am custom-shrunk —Shakespeare⟩

³**what** *adjective* (13th century)
1 a — used as an interrogative expressing inquiry about the identity, nature, or value of a person, object, or matter ⟨*what* minerals do we export⟩ **b** : how remarkable or striking for good or bad qualities — used especially in exclamatory utterances and dependent clauses ⟨*what* mountains⟩ ⟨remember *what* fun we had⟩ ⟨*what* a suggestion⟩ ⟨*what* a charming girl⟩
2 a (1) : WHATEVER 1a (2) : ANY ⟨ornament of *what* description soever⟩ **b** : the . . . that : as much or as many . . . as ⟨rescued *what* survivors they found⟩

what all \'hwä-,dol, 'wä-, '(h)wə-\ *pronoun* (1702)
: WHATNOT

what·cha·ma·call·it \'hwä-chə-mə-,ko-lət, 'wä-, '(h)wə-\ *noun* [alteration of *what you may call it*] (1928)

: THINGAMAJIG

¹what·ev·er \hwät-'e-vər, wät-, (ˌ)(h)wət-\ *pronoun* (14th century)
1 a : anything or everything that ⟨take *whatever* you want⟩ **b :** no matter what ⟨*whatever* he says, they won't believe him⟩ **c :** WHATNOT ⟨buffalo or rhinoceros or *whatever* —Alan Moorehead⟩
2 : WHAT 1a(1) — used to express astonishment or perplexity ⟨*whatever* do you mean by that⟩

²whatever *adjective* (14th century)
1 a : any . . . that **:** all . . . that ⟨buy peace . . . on *whatever* terms could be obtained —C. S. Forester⟩ **b :** no matter what ⟨money, in *whatever* hands, will confer power — Samuel Johnson⟩
2 : of any kind at all — used after the substantive it modifies with *any* or with an expressed or implied negative ⟨in any order *whatever* —W. G. Moulton⟩ ⟨no food *whatever*⟩

³whatever *adverb* (1870)
: in any case **:** whatever the case may be — sometimes used interjectionally to suggest the unimportance of a decision between alternatives

what-if \ˌhwät-'if, ˌwät-, ˌ(h)wət-\ *noun* (1970)
: a suppositional question

what·ness \'hwät-nəs, 'wät-, '(h)wət-\ *noun* (1611)
: QUIDDITY 1

¹what·not \'hwät-ˌnät, 'wät-, '(h)wət-\ *pronoun* [*what not?*] (1540)
: any of various other things that might also be mentioned ⟨paper clips, pins, and *whatnot*⟩

²whatnot *noun* (1602)
1 : a nondescript person or thing
2 : a light open set of shelves for bric-a-brac

what·sit \'hwät-sət, 'wät-, 'wət-\ *or* **what·sis** \-səs\ *also* **what-is-it** \-iz-ət\ *noun* [*whatsit* & *whatsis* contraction of *what-is-it*] (circa 1882)
: THINGAMAJIG

what·so·ev·er \ˌhwät-sə-'we-vər, ˌwät-, ˌ(h)wət-\ *pronoun or adjective* (13th century)
: WHATEVER

whaup \'hwȯp, 'wȯp\ *noun, plural* **whaup** *also* **whaups** [imitative] (circa 1512)
chiefly Scottish **:** a European curlew (*Numenius arquata*)

wheal \'hwēl, 'wēl\ *noun* [alteration of ¹*wale*] (1808)
: a suddenly formed elevation of the skin surface: as **a :** WELT **b :** a flat burning or itching eminence on the skin

wheat \'hwēt, 'wēt\ *noun, often attributive* [Middle English *whete*, from Old English *hwǣte*; akin to Old High German *weizzi* wheat, *hwīz*, *wīz* white — more at WHITE] (before 12th century)
1 : a cereal grain that yields a fine white flour, is the chief breadstuff of temperate climates, is used also in pastas (as macaroni or spaghetti), and is important in animal feeds
2 : any of various annual grasses (genus *Triticum* and especially *T. aestivum* and *T. turgidum*) of wide climatic adaptability that are cultivated in most temperate areas for the wheat they yield
3 : a light yellow

wheat bread *noun* (14th century)
: a bread made of a combination of white and whole wheat flours as distinguished from bread made entirely of white or whole wheat flour

wheat cake *noun* (1772)
: a pancake made of wheat flour

wheat-ear \'hwēt-ˌir, 'wēt-\ *noun* [back-formation from earlier *wheatears* wheatear, probably by folk etymology or euphemism from *white* + *arse*] (1591)
: any of various small thrushes (genus *Oenanthe*); *especially* **:** a white-rumped one (*O. oenanthe*) of Eurasia and northern North America

¹wheat·en \'hwē-t°n, 'wē-\ *adjective* (before 12th century)
: of, relating to, or made of wheat

²wheaten *noun* (circa 1931)
: a pale yellowish to ruddy fawn color characteristic of the coat of some dogs

wheat germ *noun* (1897)
: the embryo of the wheat kernel separated in milling and used especially as a source of vitamins and protein

wheat rust *noun* (1884)
: a destructive disease of wheat caused by rust fungi; *also* **:** a fungus (as *Puccinia graminis*) causing a wheat rust

Wheat·stone bridge \'hwēt-ˌstōn-, 'wēt-, *chiefly British* -stən-\ *noun* [Sir Charles *Wheatstone*] (1872)
: a bridge for measuring electrical resistances that consists of a conductor joining two branches of a circuit

whee \'hwē, 'wē\ *interjection* (1898)
— used to express delight or exuberance

whee·dle \'hwē-d°l, 'wē-\ *verb* **whee·dled**; **whee·dling** \'(h)wēd-liŋ, '(h)wē-d°l-iŋ\ [origin unknown] (circa 1661)
transitive verb
1 : to influence or entice by soft words or flattery
2 : to gain or get by wheedling ⟨*wheedle* one's way into favor⟩
intransitive verb
: to use soft words or flattery

¹wheel \'hwē(ə)l, 'wē(ə)l\ *noun, often attributive* [Middle English, from Old English *hweogol*, *hwēol*; akin to Old Norse *hvēl* wheel, Greek *kyklos* circle, wheel, Sanskrit *cakra*, Latin *colere* to cultivate, inhabit, Sanskrit *carati* he moves, wanders] (before 12th century)
1 : a circular frame of hard material that may be solid, partly solid, or spoked and that is capable of turning on an axle
2 : a contrivance or apparatus having as its principal part a wheel: as **a :** a chiefly medieval instrument of torture designed for mutilating a victim (as by stretching or disjointing) **b :** BICYCLE **c :** any of many revolving disks or drums used as gambling paraphernalia **d :** POTTER'S WHEEL **e :** STEERING WHEEL
3 a : an imaginary turning wheel symbolizing the inconstancy of fortune **b :** a recurring course, development, or action **:** CYCLE
4 : something resembling a wheel in shape or motion: as **a :** a round flat cheese **b :** a firework that rotates while burning **c :** a propeller on a boat
5 a : a curving or circular movement **b :** a rotation or turn usually about an axis or center; *specifically* **:** a turning movement of troops or ships in line in which the units preserve alignment and relative positions as they change direction
6 a : a moving or essential part of something compared to a machine ⟨the *wheels* of government⟩ **b :** a directing or controlling force **c :** a person of importance especially in an organization ⟨a big *wheel*⟩
7 : the refrain or burden of a song
8 a : a circuit of theaters or places of entertainment **b :** a sports league
9 *plural, slang* **:** a wheeled vehicle; *especially* **:** AUTOMOBILE
— **wheel·less** \'hwē(ə)l-ləs, 'wē(ə)l-\ *adjective*

²wheel (13th century)
intransitive verb
1 : to turn on or as if on an axis **:** REVOLVE
2 : to change direction as if revolving on a pivot ⟨the battalion would have *wheeled* to the

wheel 1: *1* hub, *2* spoke, *3* felly, *4* tire

flank —Walter Bernstein⟩ ⟨her mind will *wheel* around to the other extreme —Liam O'Flaherty⟩
3 : to move or extend in a circle or curve ⟨birds in *wheeling* flight⟩ ⟨valleys where young cotton *wheeled* slowly in fanlike rows —William Faulkner⟩
4 : to drive or go on or as if on wheels or in a wheeled vehicle
transitive verb
1 : to cause to turn on or as if on an axis **:** ROTATE
2 : to convey or move on or as if on wheels or in a wheeled vehicle; *especially* **:** to drive (a vehicle) at high speed
3 : to cause to change direction as if revolving on a pivot
4 : to make or perform in a circle or curve
— **wheel and deal :** to make deals or do business especially shrewdly or briskly

wheel and axle *noun* (circa 1773)
: a mechanical device consisting of a grooved wheel turned by a cord or chain with a rigidly attached axle (as for winding up a weight) together with the supporting standards

wheel animal *noun* (1788)
: ROTIFER

wheel animalcule *noun* (1834)
: ROTIFER

¹wheel·bar·row \'hwē(ə)l-ˌbar-(ˌ)ō, 'wē(ə)l-\ *noun* (14th century)
: a small usually single-wheeled vehicle that is used for carrying small loads and is fitted with handles at the rear by which it can be pushed and guided

²wheelbarrow *transitive verb* (1721)
: to convey in a wheelbarrow

wheel·base \'hwē(ə)l-ˌbās, 'wē(ə)l-\ *noun* (1886)
: the distance in inches between the front and rear axles of an automotive vehicle

wheel bug *noun* (1815)
: a large North American bug (*Arilus cristatus*) that has a high serrated crest on its prothorax and preys on other insects

wheel·chair \'hwē(ə)l-ˌcher, 'wē(ə)l-, -ˌchar\ *noun* (circa 1700)
: a chair mounted on wheels especially for the use of disabled persons

wheeled \'hwē(ə)ld, 'wē(ə)ld\ *adjective* (1606)
1 : equipped with wheels ⟨*wheeled* vehicles⟩
2 : moving or functioning by means of wheels ⟨*wheeled* traffic⟩

wheel·er \'hwē-lər, 'wē-\ *noun* (1683)
1 : one that wheels
2 : a draft animal (as a horse) pulling in the position nearest the front wheels of a wagon
3 : something (as a vehicle or ship) that has wheels — used especially in combination ⟨side-*wheeler*⟩

wheeler and dealer *noun, plural* **wheelers and dealers** (1966)
: WHEELER-DEALER

wheel·er–deal·er \ˌhwē-lər-'dē-lər, ˌwē-\ *noun* (1954)
: a shrewd operator especially in business or politics

wheel·horse \'hwē(ə)l-ˌhȯrs, 'wē(ə)l-\ *noun* (1708)
1 : a horse (as in a tandem) in a position nearest the wheels
2 : a steady and effective worker especially in a political body

wheel·house \-ˌhaùs\ *noun* (1835)
: PILOTHOUSE

wheel·ie \'hwē-lē, 'wē-\ *noun* (circa 1965)
: a maneuver in which a wheeled vehicle (as a bicycle) is momentarily balanced on its rear wheel or wheels

\ə\ abut \ˀ\ kitten \ər\ further \a\ ash \ā\ ace
\ä\ mop, mar \aù\ out \ch\ chin \e\ bet \ē\ easy
\g\ go \i\ hit \ī\ ice \j\ job \ŋ\ sing \ō\ go
\ȯ\ law \ȯi\ boy \th\ thin \th\ the \ü\ loot \ù\ foot
\y\ yet \zh\ vision *see also* Guide to Pronunciation

wheel·ing \'hwē-liŋ, 'wē-\ *noun* (15th century)
1 : the act or process of one that wheels
2 : the condition of a road relative to passage on wheels

wheel lock *noun* (1670)
: a gun's lock for a muzzle-loading firearm in which sparks are struck from a flint or a piece of iron pyrites by a revolving wheel

wheel·man \'hwē(ə)l-mən, 'wē)l-\ *noun* (1865)
1 a : HELMSMAN **b :** the driver of an automobile
2 : CYCLIST

wheels·man \'hwē(ə)lz-mən, 'wē)lz-\ *noun* (1866)
: one who steers with a wheel; *especially*
: HELMSMAN

wheel–thrown \'hwēl-,thrōn, 'wēl-\ *adjective* (1975)
: made on a potter's wheel ⟨*wheel-thrown* pottery⟩

wheel·work \'hwē(ə)l-,wərk, 'wē(ə)l-\ *noun* (1670)
: wheels in gear and their connections in a machine or mechanism

wheel·wright \-,rīt\ *noun* (13th century)
: a maker and repairer of wheels and wheeled vehicles

¹wheen \'hwēn, 'wēn\ *adjective* [Middle English (Scots) *quheyne*, from Old English *hwǣne, hwēne*, somewhat, from instrumental of *hwōn* little, few] (14th century)
dialect British **:** FEW 2

²wheen *noun* (1680)
dialect British **:** a considerable number or amount

¹wheeze \'hwēz, 'wēz\ *intransitive verb*
wheezed; wheez·ing [Middle English *whesen*, probably of Scandinavian origin; akin to Old Norse *hvæsa* to hiss; akin to Old English *hwǣst* action of blowing, Sanskrit *śvasiti* he blows, snorts] (15th century)
1 : to breathe with difficulty usually with a whistling sound
2 : to make a sound resembling that of wheezing

²wheeze *noun* (1834)
1 : a sound of wheezing
2 a : an often repeated and widely known joke used especially by entertainers **b :** a trite saying or proverb

wheezy \'hwē-zē, 'wē-\ *adjective* **wheez·i·er; -est** (1818)
1 : inclined to wheeze
2 : having a wheezing sound
— **wheez·i·ly** \-zə-lē\ *adverb*
— **wheez·i·ness** \-zē-nəs\ *noun*

¹whelk \'hwelk, 'welk, 'wilk\ *noun* [Middle English *welke*, from Old English *weoloc*; akin to Middle Dutch *willoc* whelk and perhaps to Latin *volvere* to turn — more at VOLUBLE] (before 12th century)
: any of numerous large marine snails (as of the genus *Buccinum*); *especially* **:** one (*B. undatum*) much used as food in Europe

²whelk \'hwelk, 'welk\ *noun* [Middle English *whelke*, from Old English *hwylca*, from *hwelian* to suppurate] (before 12th century)
: PAPULE, PUSTULE

whelm \'hwelm, 'welm\ *verb* [Middle English] (14th century)
transitive verb
1 : to turn (as a dish or vessel) upside down usually to cover something **:** cover or engulf completely with usually disastrous effect
2 : to overcome in thought or feeling **:** OVERWHELM
intransitive verb
: to pass or go over something so as to bury or submerge it

whelk

¹whelp \'hwelp, 'welp\ *noun* [Middle English, from Old English *hwelp*; akin to Old High German *hwelf* whelp] (before 12th century)
1 : any of the young of various carnivorous mammals and especially of the dog
2 : a young boy or girl

²whelp (13th century)
transitive verb
: to give birth to — used of various carnivores and especially the dog
intransitive verb
: to bring forth young

¹when \'hwen, 'wen, (h)wən\ *adverb* [Middle English, from Old English *hwanne, hwenne*; akin to Old High German *hwanne* when, Old English *hwā* who — more at WHO] (before 12th century)
1 : at what time ⟨*when* will you return⟩
2 a : at or during which time **b :** and then
3 : at a former and usually less prosperous time ⟨brag fondly of having known him *when* —Vance Packard⟩

²when *conjunction* [Middle English, from Old English *hwanne, hwenne*, from *hwanne, hwenne*, adverb] (before 12th century)
1 a : at or during the time that **:** WHILE ⟨went fishing *when* he was a boy⟩ **b :** just at the moment that ⟨stop writing *when* the bell rings⟩ **c :** at any or every time that ⟨*when* he listens to music, he falls asleep⟩
2 : in the event that **:** IF ⟨a contestant is disqualified *when* he disobeys the rules⟩
3 a : considering that ⟨why use water at all *when* you can drown in it —Stuart Chase⟩ **b :** in spite of the fact that **:** ALTHOUGH ⟨quit politics *when* I might have had a great career in it⟩
4 : the time or occasion at or in which ⟨tomorrow is *when* we must decide⟩ ⟨humor is *when* you laugh —Earl Rovit⟩

³when \'hwen, 'wen\ *pronoun* (14th century)
: what or which time ⟨life-long homes for those . . . who have lived here since *when* —Kim Waller⟩

⁴when *noun* (1616)
: the time in which something is done or comes about ⟨troubled his head very little about the hows and *whens* of life —Laurence Sterne⟩

when·as \hwe-'naz, we-, (h)wə-\ *conjunction* [Middle English (Scots) *when as*, from Middle English *when* + *as*] (15th century)
archaic **:** WHEN

¹whence \'hwen(t)s, 'wen(t)s\ *adverb* [Middle English *whennes*, from *whenne* whence (from Old English *hwanon*) + *-s*, adverb suffix, from *-s*, genitive singular ending; akin to Old High German *hwanān* whence, Old English *hwā* who] (13th century)
: from what place, source, or cause ⟨then *whence* comes this paradox —*Changing Times*⟩
— **from whence :** from what place, source, or cause ⟨no one could tell me *from whence* the gold had come —Graham Greene⟩

²whence *conjunction* (14th century)
1 : from what place, source, or cause ⟨inquired *whence* the water came —Maria Edgeworth⟩
2 a : from or out of which place, source, or cause ⟨the lawless society *whence* the ballads sprang —DeLancey Ferguson⟩ **b :** by reason of which fact **:** WHEREFORE ⟨nothing broke — *whence* I infer that my bones are not yet chalky —O. W. Holmes (died 1935)⟩

whence·so·ev·er \'hwen(t)(s)-sə-,we-vər, 'wen(t)(s)-\ *conjunction* (1511)
: from whatever place or source

¹when·ev·er \hwe-'ne-vər, we-, (h)wə-\ *conjunction* (14th century)
: at any or every time that

²whenever *adverb* (1667)
: at whatever time

¹when·so·ev·er \'hwen(t)-sə-,we-vər, 'wen(t)-\ *conjunction* (14th century)
: WHENEVER

²whensoever *adverb* (1526)

obsolete **:** at any time whatever

¹where \'hwer, 'hwar, 'wer, 'war, (,)(h)wər\ *adverb* [Middle English, from Old English *hwǣr*; akin to Old High German *hwār* where, Old English *hwā* who — more at WHO] (before 12th century)
1 a : at, in, or to what place ⟨*where* is the house⟩ ⟨*where* are we going⟩ **b :** at, in, or to what situation, position, direction, circumstances, or respect ⟨*where* does this plan lead⟩ ⟨*where* am I wrong⟩
2 *archaic* **:** HERE, THERE ⟨lo, *where* it comes again —Shakespeare⟩

²where *conjunction* (13th century)
1 a : at, in, or to what place ⟨knows *where* the house is⟩ **b :** at, in, or to what situation, position, direction, circumstances, or respect ⟨shows *where* the plan leads⟩ **c :** the place or point at, in, or to which ⟨couldn't see from *where* he was sitting⟩ ⟨kept that horse and gentled him to *where* I finally rode him —William Faulkner⟩
2 : WHEREVER ⟨goes *where* she likes⟩
3 a : at, in, or to which place ⟨the town *where* she lives⟩ **b :** at or in which ⟨has reached the size *where* traffic is a problem⟩ ⟨two fireplaces *where* you can bake bread in the ovens —Randall Jarrell⟩
4 a : at, in, or to the place at, in, or to which ⟨stay *where* you are⟩ ⟨send him away *where* he'll forget⟩ **b :** in a case, situation, or respect in which ⟨outstanding *where* endurance is called for⟩
5 : THAT ⟨I've read *where* they do it that way in some Middle Eastern countries —Andy Rooney⟩

³where \'hwer, 'hwar, 'wer, 'war\ *noun* (15th century)
1 : PLACE, LOCATION ⟨the *where* and the how of the accident⟩
2 : what place, source, or cause ⟨I know *where* that comes from⟩
— **where it's at 1 a :** a place of central interest or activity **b :** something (as a topic or field of interest) of primary concern or importance ⟨education is *where it's at*⟩ **2 :** the true nature of things
— **where one is at :** one's true position, state, or nature

¹where·abouts \-ə-,bauts\ *also* **whereabout** \-,baut\ *adverb* [Middle English *wheraboutes* (from *wher aboute* + *-s*, adverb suffix) & *wher aboute*, from *where, wher* where + *about, aboute* about — more at WHENCE] (14th century)
: about where **:** near what place ⟨*whereabouts* is the house⟩

²whereabouts *also* **whereabout** *conjunction* (14th century)
1 *obsolete* **:** on what business or errand
2 : near what place **:** WHERE ⟨know *whereabouts* he lives⟩

³whereabouts *noun plural but singular or plural in construction, also* **whereabout** (1605)
: the place or general locality where a person or thing is ⟨their present *whereabouts* are a secret⟩

¹where·as \hwer-'az, hwar-, wer-, war-, (,)(h)wər-\ *conjunction* [Middle English *where as*, from *where* + *as*] (14th century)
1 a : while on the contrary **b :** ALTHOUGH
2 : in view of the fact that **:** SINCE — used especially to introduce a preamble

²whereas *noun* (1795)
1 : an introductory statement of a formal document **:** PREAMBLE
2 : a conditional or qualifying statement

where·at \-'at\ *conjunction* (15th century)
1 : at or toward which
2 : in consequence of which **:** WHEREUPON

¹where·by \-'bī\ *conjunction* (13th century)
: by, through, or in accordance with which

²whereby *adverb* (14th century)
obsolete **:** by what **:** HOW

¹where·fore \'hwer-ˌfōr, 'hwar-, 'wer-, 'war-, -ˌför\ *adverb* [Middle English *wherfor, wherfore,* from *where, wher* + *for, fore* for] (13th century)
1 : for what reason or purpose : WHY
2 : THEREFORE

²wherefore *noun* (1590)
: an answer or statement giving an explanation : REASON ⟨wants to know the whys and *wherefores*⟩

where·from \-ˌfrəm, -ˌfräm\ *conjunction* (15th century)
: from which

¹where·in \hwer-'in, hwar-, wer-, war-, (ˌ)(h)wər-\ *adverb* (13th century)
: in what : in what particular or respect ⟨*wherein* was I wrong⟩

²wherein *conjunction* (15th century)
1 a : in which : WHERE ⟨the city *wherein* he lives⟩ **b** : during which
2 : in what way : HOW ⟨showed me *wherein* I was wrong⟩

where·in·to \-'in-(ˌ)tü\ *conjunction* (1539)
: into which

¹where·of \-'əv, -'äv\ *conjunction* (13th century)
1 *archaic* : with or by which
2 : of what ⟨knows *whereof* she speaks⟩
3 a : of which ⟨books *whereof* the best are lost⟩ **b** : of whom

²whereof *adverb* (15th century)
archaic : of what ⟨*whereof* are you made —Shakespeare⟩

¹where·on \-'ȯn, -'än\ *conjunction* (13th century)
1 *archaic* : on what ⟨tell me *whereon* the likelihood depends —Shakespeare⟩
2 : on which ⟨the base *whereon* it rests⟩

²whereon *adverb* (15th century)
archaic : on what ⟨*whereon* do you look —Shakespeare⟩

where·so·ev·er \'hwer-sə-ˌwe-vər, 'hwar-, 'wer-, 'war-\ *conjunction* (13th century)
: WHEREVER

where·through \'hwer-ˌthrü, 'hwar-, 'wer-, 'war-\ *conjunction* (13th century)
: through which

¹where·to \-ˌtü\ *adverb* (13th century)
: to what place, purpose, or end ⟨*whereto* tends all this —Shakespeare⟩

²whereto *conjunction* (14th century)
: to which

where·un·to \hwer-'ən-(ˌ)tü, hwar-, wer-, war-, (ˌ)(h)wər-\ *adverb or conjunction* (15th century)
: WHERETO

where·up·on \'hwer-ə-ˌpȯn, 'hwar-, 'wer-, 'war-, -ˌpän\ *conjunction* (14th century)
1 : on which
2 : closely following and in consequence of which

¹where·ev·er \hwer-'e-vər, hwar-, wer-, war-, (ˌ)(h)wər-\ *adverb* (13th century)
1 : where in the world ⟨*wherever* did you get that tie⟩
2 : anywhere at all ⟨explore northward or *wherever* —Bernard De Voto⟩

²wherever *conjunction* (14th century)
1 : at, in, or to any or all places that ⟨thrives *wherever* he goes⟩
2 : in any circumstance in which ⟨*wherever* it is possible, we try to help⟩

¹where·with \'hwer-ˌwith, 'hwar-, 'wer-, 'war-, -ˌwith\ *pronoun* (13th century)
archaic : that with or by which — used with an infinitive ⟨so shall I have *wherewith* to answer him —Psalms 119:42 (Authorized Version)⟩

²wherewith *adverb* (13th century)
obsolete : with what ⟨*wherewith* shall it be salted —Matthew 5:13 (Authorized Version)⟩

³wherewith *conjunction* (14th century)
: with or by means of which ⟨metal tools *wherewith* to break ground —Russell Lord⟩

¹where·with·al \'hwer-wi-ˌthȯl, 'hwar-, 'wer-, 'war-, -ˌthȯl\ *conjunction* [*where* + ²*withal*] (1534)
: WHEREWITH

²wherewithal *pronoun* (1583)
: WHEREWITH

³wherewithal *noun* (1659)
: MEANS, RESOURCES; *specifically* : MONEY ⟨didn't have the *wherewithal* for an expensive dinner⟩

wher·ry \'hwer-ē, 'wer-\ *noun, plural* **wher·ries** [Middle English *whery*] (15th century)
1 : any of various light boats: as **a** : a long light rowboat made sharp at both ends and used to transport passengers on rivers and about harbors **b** : a racing scull for one person
2 : a large light barge, lighter, or fishing boat varying in type in different parts of Great Britain

¹whet \'hwet, 'wet\ *transitive verb* **whet·ted; whet·ting** [Middle English *whetten,* from Old English *hwettan;* akin to Old High German *wezzen* to whet, *waz* sharp] (before 12th century)
1 : to sharpen by rubbing on or with something (as a stone) ⟨*whet* a knife⟩
2 : to make keen or more acute : EXCITE, STIMULATE ⟨*whet* the appetite⟩
— **whet·ter** *noun*

²whet *noun* (circa 1628)
1 *dialect* **a** : a spell of work done with a scythe between the time it is sharpened and the time it needs to be sharpened again **b** : TIME, WHILE
2 : something that sharpens or makes keen: **a** : GOAD, INCITEMENT **b** : APPETIZER; *also* : a drink of liquor

¹wheth·er \'hwe-thər, 'we-, (ˌ)(h)wə-\ *pronoun* [Middle English, from Old English *hwæther, hwether;* akin to Old High German *hwedar* which of two, Latin *uter,* Greek *poteros,* Old English *hwā* who — more at WHO] (before 12th century)
1 *archaic* : which one of the two
2 *archaic* : whichever one of the two

²whether *conjunction* (before 12th century)
— used as a function word usually with correlative *or* or with *or whether* to indicate (1) until the early 19th century a direct question involving alternatives; (2) an indirect question involving stated or implied alternatives ⟨decide *whether* he should agree or raise objections⟩ ⟨wondered *whether* to stay⟩; (3) alternative conditions or possibilities ⟨see me no more, *whether* he be dead or no —Shakespeare⟩ ⟨seated him next to her *whether* by accident or design⟩
— **whether or no** *or* **whether or not**
: in any case

whet·stone \'hwet-ˌstōn, 'wet-\ *noun* (before 12th century)
: a stone for whetting edge tools

whew *often read as* 'hwü, 'wü, 'hyü; *the interjection is a whistle concluded with a voiceless* ü\ *noun* [imitative] (1513)
: a whistling sound or a sound like a half-formed whistle uttered as an exclamation ⟨gave a long *whew* when he realized the size of the job⟩ — used interjectionally chiefly to express amazement, discomfort, or relief

whey \'hwā, 'wā\ *noun* [Middle English, from Old English *hwæg;* akin to Middle Dutch *wey* whey] (before 12th century)
: the watery part of milk that is separated from the coagulable part or curd especially in the process of making cheese and that is rich in lactose, minerals, and vitamins and contains lactalbumin and traces of fat
— **whey·like** \-ˌlīk\ *adjective*

whey–face \'hwā-ˌfās, 'wā-\ *noun* (1605)
: a person having a pale face (as from fear)
— **whey–faced** \-ˌfāst\ *adjective*

¹which \'hwich, 'wich\ *adjective* [Middle English, of what kind, which, from Old English *hwilc;* akin to Old High German *wilīh* of what

kind, which, Old English *hwā* who, *gelīk* like — more at WHO, LIKE] (before 12th century)
1 : being what one or ones out of a group — used as an interrogative ⟨*which* tie should I wear⟩ ⟨kept a record of *which* employees took their vacations in July⟩
2 : WHICHEVER ⟨it will not fit, turn it *which* way you like⟩
3 — used as a function word to introduce a nonrestrictive relative clause and to modify a noun in that clause and to refer together with that noun to a word or word group in a preceding clause or to an entire preceding clause or sentence or longer unit of discourse ⟨in German, *which* language might . . . have been the medium of transmission —Thomas Pyles⟩ ⟨that this city is a rebellious city . . . : for *which* cause was this city destroyed —Ezra 4:15 (Authorized Version)⟩

²which *pronoun* (before 12th century)
1 : what one or ones out of a group — used as an interrogative ⟨*which* of those houses do you live in⟩ ⟨*which* of you want tea and *which* want lemonade⟩ ⟨he is swimming or canoeing, I don't know *which*⟩
2 : WHICHEVER ⟨take *which* you like⟩
3 — used as a function word to introduce a relative clause; used in any grammatical relation except that of a possessive; used especially in reference to animals, inanimate objects, groups, or ideas ⟨the bonds *which* represent the debt —G. B. Robinson⟩ ⟨the Samnite tribes, *which* settled south and southeast of Rome —Ernst Pulgram⟩; used freely in reference to persons as recently as the 17th century ⟨our Father *which* art in heaven —Matthew 6:9 (Authorized Version)⟩, and still occasionally so used but usually with some implication of emphasis on the function or role of the person rather than on the person as such ⟨chiefly they wanted husbands, *which* they got easily —Lynn White⟩; used by speakers on all educational levels and by many reputable writers, though disapproved by some grammarians, in reference to an idea expressed by a word or group of words that is not necessarily a noun or noun phrase ⟨he resigned that post, after *which* he engaged in ranching —Current Biography⟩
usage see ⁴THAT, WHOSE

¹which·ev·er \hwich-'e-vər, wich-\ *adjective* (14th century)
: being whatever one or ones out of a group : no matter which ⟨its soothing . . . effect will be the same *whichever* way you take it —Punch⟩

²whichever *pronoun* (15th century)
: whatever one or ones out of a group ⟨take two of the four elective subjects, *whichever* you prefer⟩

which·so·ev·er \ˌhwich-sə-'we-vər, ˌwich-\ *pronoun or adjective* (15th century)
archaic : WHICHEVER

whick·er \'hwi-kər, 'wi-\ *intransitive verb* **whick·ered; whick·er·ing** \-k(ə-)riŋ\ [imitative] (1753)
: NEIGH, WHINNY
— **whicker** *noun*

whid \'hwid, 'wid\ *intransitive verb* **whid·ded; whid·ding** [Scots *whid* silent rapid motion] (1728)
Scottish : to move nimbly and silently

¹whiff \'hwif, 'wif\ *noun* [origin unknown] (1591)
1 a : a quick puff or slight gust especially of air, odor, gas, smoke, or spray **b** : an inhalation of odor, gas, or smoke **c** : a slight puffing or whistling sound
2 : a slight trace or indication
3 : STRIKEOUT

²**whiff** (1591)
intransitive verb
1 : to move with or as if with a puff of air
2 : to emit whiffs **:** PUFF
3 : to inhale an odor
4 : STRIKE OUT 3
transitive verb
1 a : to carry or convey by or as if by a whiff **:** BLOW **b :** to expel or puff out in a whiff **:** EXHALE **c :** SMOKE 3
2 : FAN 8

whif·fet \'hwi-fət, 'wi-\ *noun* [probably alteration of *whippet*] (1839)
: a small, young, or unimportant person

whif·fle \'hwi-fəl, 'wi-\ *verb* **whif·fled; whif·fling** \-f(ə-)liŋ\ [probably frequentative of *whiff*] (1568)
intransitive verb
1 a *of the wind* **:** to blow unsteadily or in gusts **b :** VACILLATE
2 : to emit or produce a light whistling or puffing sound
transitive verb
: to blow, disperse, emit, or expel with or as if with a whiff

¹**whif·fler** \'hwi-flər, 'wi-\ *noun* [alteration of earlier *wifler*, from obsolete *wifle* battle-ax] (1539)
British **:** one that clears the way for a procession

²**whif·fler** \'hwi-f(ə-)lər, 'wi-\ *noun* [*whiffle*] (1607)
1 : a person who frequently changes opinions or course
2 : a person who uses shifts and evasions in argument

whif·fle·tree \'hwi-fəl-(ˌ)trē, 'wi-\ *noun* [alteration of *whippletree*] (circa 1806)
: the pivoted swinging bar to which the traces of a harness are fastened and by which a vehicle or implement is drawn

1 whiffletree

Whig \'hwig, 'wig\ *noun* [short for *Whiggamore*, member of a Scottish group that marched to Edinburgh in 1648 to oppose the court party] (circa 1680)
1 : a member or supporter of a major British political group of the late 17th through early 19th centuries seeking to limit the royal authority and increase parliamentary power — compare TORY
2 : an American favoring independence from Great Britain during the American Revolution
3 : a member or supporter of an American political party formed about 1834 in opposition to the Jacksonian Democrats, associated chiefly with manufacturing, commercial, and financial interests, and succeeded about 1854 by the Republican party
— Whig *adjective*
— Whig·gism \'hwi-ˌgi-zəm\ *noun*

Whig·gery \'hwi-gə-rē, 'wi-\ *noun* (1714)
: the principles or practices of Whigs

Whig·gish \'hwi-gish, 'wi-\ *adjective* (1684)
1 : characteristic of Whigs or Whiggery
2 : of, relating to, or characterized by a view which holds that history follows a path of inevitable progression and improvement and which judges the past in light of the present

whig·ma·lee·rie \ˌhwig-mə-'lir-ē, ˌwig-\ *noun* [origin unknown] (1730)
1 *chiefly Scottish* **:** WHIM
2 *chiefly Scottish* **:** an odd or fanciful contrivance **:** GIMCRACK

¹**while** \'hwī(ə)l, 'wī(ə)l\ *noun* [Middle English, from Old English *hwīl*; akin to Old High German *hwīla* time, Latin *quies* rest, quiet] (before 12th century)
1 : a period of time especially when short and marked by the occurrence of an action or a condition **:** TIME ⟨stay here for a *while*⟩
2 : the time and effort used (as in the performance of an action) **:** TROUBLE ⟨worth your *while*⟩

²**while** *conjunction* (12th century)
1 a : during the time that ⟨take a nap *while* I'm out⟩ **b :** as long as ⟨*while* there's life there's hope⟩
2 a : when on the other hand **:** WHEREAS ⟨easy for an expert, *while* it is dangerous for a novice⟩ **b :** in spite of the fact that **:** ALTHOUGH ⟨*while* respected, he is not liked⟩
3 : similarly and at the same time that ⟨*while* the book will be welcomed by scholars, it will make an immediate appeal to the general reader —*British Book News*⟩

³**while** *preposition* (15th century)
dialect British **:** UNTIL

⁴**while** *transitive verb* **whiled; whil·ing** (1635)
: to cause to pass especially without boredom or in a pleasant manner — usually used with *away* ⟨*while* away the time⟩

¹**whiles** \'hwī(ə)lz, 'wī(ə)lz\ *conjunction* [Middle English, from *while* + *-s*, adverb suffix — more at WHENCE] (13th century)
archaic **:** WHILE

²**whiles** *adverb* (15th century)
chiefly Scottish **:** SOMETIMES

¹**whi·lom** \'hwī-ləm, 'wī-\ *adverb* [Middle English, literally, at times, from Old English *hwīlum*, dative plural of *hwīl* time, while] (13th century)
archaic **:** FORMERLY

²**whilom** *adjective* (1837)
: FORMER

whilst \'hwī(ə)lst, 'wī(ə)lst\ *conjunction* [Middle English *whilest*, alteration of *whiles*] (14th century)
chiefly British **:** WHILE

whim \'hwim, 'wim\ *noun* [short for *whim-wham*] (1697)
1 : a capricious or eccentric and often sudden idea or turn of the mind **:** FANCY
2 : a large capstan that is made with one or more radiating arms to which a horse may be yoked and that is used in mines for raising ore or water
synonym see CAPRICE

whim·brel \'hwim-brəl, 'wim-\ *noun* [origin unknown] (circa 1531)
: a small curlew (*Numenius phaeopus*) chiefly of the northern regions of North America and Eurasia; *broadly* **:** any small curlew

¹**whim·per** \'hwim-pər, 'wim-\ *intransitive verb* **whim·pered; whim·per·ing** \-p(ə-)riŋ\ [imitative] (1513)
1 : to make a low whining plaintive or broken sound
2 : to complain or protest with or as if with a whimper

²**whimper** *noun* (circa 1700)
1 : a whimpering cry or sound
2 : a petulant complaint or protest

whim·si·cal \'hwim-zi-kəl, 'wim-\ *adjective* [*whimsy*] (1653)
1 : full of, actuated by, or exhibiting whims
2 a : resulting from or characterized by whim or caprice; *especially* **:** lightly fanciful **b :** subject to erratic behavior or unpredictable change
— whim·si·cal·i·ty \ˌhwim-zə-'ka-lə-tē, ˌwim-\ *noun*
— whim·si·cal·ly \'hwim-zi-k(ə-)lē, 'wim-\ *adverb*
— whim·si·cal·ness \-kəl-nəs\ *noun*

whim·sy *also* **whim·sey** \'hwim-zē, 'wim-\ *noun, plural* **whimsies** *also* **whimseys** [irregular from *whim-wham*] (1605)
1 : WHIM, CAPRICE
2 : the quality or state of being whimsical or fanciful ⟨the designer's new line showed a touch of *whimsy*⟩

3 : a fanciful or fantastic device, object, or creation especially in writing or art

whim–wham \'hwim-ˌhwam, 'wim-ˌwam\ *noun* [origin unknown] (1500)
1 : a whimsical object or device especially of ornament or dress
2 : FANCY, WHIM
3 *plural* **:** JITTERS

whin \'hwin, 'win\ *noun* [Middle English *whynne*, of Scandinavian origin; akin to Norwegian *kvein* bent grass] (15th century)
: GORSE

whin·chat \'hwin-ˌchat, 'win-\ *noun* [*whin*] (1678)
: a small brown and buff European singing bird (*Saxicola rubetra*) of grassy meadows

¹**whine** \'hwīn, 'wīn\ *verb* **whined; whin·ing** [Middle English, from Old English *hwīnan* to whiz; akin to Old Norse *hvīna* to whiz] (13th century)
intransitive verb
1 a : to utter a high-pitched plaintive or distressed cry **b :** to make a sound similar to such a cry ⟨the wind *whined* in the chimney⟩
2 : to complain with or as if with a whine
3 : to move or proceed with the sound of a whine ⟨the bullet *whined* . . . across the ice —Berton Roueché⟩
transitive verb
: to utter or express with or as if with a whine
— whin·er *noun*
— whin·ing·ly \'hwī-niŋ-lē, 'wī-\ *adverb*

²**whine** *noun* (1633)
1 a : a prolonged high-pitched cry usually expressive of distress or pain **b :** a sound resembling such a cry
2 : a complaint uttered with or as if with a whine
— whiny *or* **whin·ey** \'hwī-nē, 'wī-\ *adjective*

whing–ding \'wiŋ-ˌdiŋ, 'hwiŋ-\ *noun* [by alteration] (circa 1945)
: WINGDING

whinge \'hwinj, 'winj\ *intransitive verb* **whinged; whing·ing** *or* **whinge·ing** [from (assumed) Middle English, from Old English *hwinsian*; akin to Old High German *winsōn* to moan] (12th century)
British **:** to complain fretfully **:** WHINE

¹**whin·ny** \'hwi-nē, 'wi-\ *verb* **whin·nied; whin·ny·ing** [probably imitative] (1530)
intransitive verb
: to neigh especially in a low or gentle way
transitive verb
: to utter with or as if with a whinny

²**whinny** *noun, plural* **whinnies** (circa 1823)
1 : the neigh of a horse especially when low or gentle
2 : a sound resembling a neigh

whin·stone \'hwin-ˌstōn, 'win-\ *noun* [*whin*, a hard rock] (1513)
: basaltic rock **:** TRAP; *also* **:** any of various other dark resistant rocks (as chert)

¹**whip** \'hwip, 'wip\ *verb* **whipped; whip·ping** [Middle English *wippen, whippen*; akin to Middle Dutch *wippen* to move up and down, sway, Old English *wīpian* to wipe] (14th century)
transitive verb
1 : to take, pull, snatch, jerk, or otherwise move very quickly and forcefully ⟨*whipped* out his gun —Green Peyton⟩
2 a (1) **:** to strike with a slender lithe implement (as a lash or rod) especially as a punishment (2) **:** SPANK **b :** to drive or urge on by or as if by using a whip **c :** to strike as a lash does ⟨rain *whipped* the pavement⟩
3 a : to bind or wrap (as a rope or fishing rod) with cord for protection and strength **b :** to wind or wrap around something
4 : to belabor with stinging words **:** ABUSE
5 : to seam or hem with shallow overcasting stitches
6 : to overcome decisively **:** DEFEAT

7 : to stir up : INCITE — usually used with *up* ⟨trying to *whip* up a new emotion —Ellen Glasgow⟩
8 : to produce in a hurry — usually used with *up* ⟨a sketch . . . an artist might *whip* up —*N.Y. Times*⟩
9 : to fish (water) with rod, line, and artificial lure
10 : to beat (as eggs or cream) into a froth with a utensil (as a whisk or fork)
11 : to gather together or hold together for united action in the manner of a party whip
intransitive verb
1 : to proceed nimbly or quickly ⟨*whipping* through the supper dishes —C. B. Davis⟩
2 : to thrash about flexibly in the manner of a whiplash ⟨a flag . . . *whipping* out from its staff —H. A. Calahan⟩
— **whip·per** *noun*
— **whip into shape :** to bring forcefully to a desired state or condition
²whip *noun* (14th century)
1 : an instrument consisting usually of a handle and lash forming a flexible rod that is used for whipping
2 : a stroke or cut with or as if with a whip
3 a : a dessert made by whipping a portion of the ingredients ⟨prune *whip*⟩ **b :** a kitchen utensil made of braided or coiled wire or perforated metal with a handle and used in whipping
4 : one that handles a whip : as **a :** a driver of horses : COACHMAN **b :** WHIPPER-IN 1
5 a : a member of a legislative body appointed by a political party to enforce party discipline and to secure the attendance of party members at important sessions **b** *often capitalized* **:** a notice of forthcoming business sent weekly to each member of a political party in the British House of Commons
6 : a whipping or thrashing motion
7 : the quality of resembling a whip especially in being flexible
8 : a flexible vertical rod radio antenna — called also *whip antenna*
— **whip·like** \'hwip-ˌlīk, 'wip-\ *adjective*
whip·cord \'hwip-ˌkȯrd, 'wip-\ *noun* [from its use in making whips] (14th century)
1 : a thin tough cord made of braided or twisted hemp or catgut
2 : a cloth that is made of hard-twisted yarns and has fine diagonal cords or ribs
whip hand *noun* (1680)
1 : positive control : ADVANTAGE
2 : the hand holding the whip in driving
whip in *transitive verb* (1742)
1 : to collect or keep together (members of a political party) for legislative action
2 : to keep (hounds in a pack) from scattering by use of a whip
whip·lash \'hwip-ˌlash, 'wip-\ *noun* (circa 1580)
1 : the lash of a whip
2 : something resembling a blow from a whip ⟨the *whiplash* of fear —R. S. Banay⟩
3 : WHIPLASH INJURY
whiplash injury *noun* (circa 1953)
: injury resulting from a sudden sharp whipping movement of the neck and head (as of a person in a vehicle that is struck head-on or from the rear by another vehicle)
whip·per-in \ˌhwip-ər-'in, ˌwi-\ *noun, plural* **whip·pers-in** \-pərz-\ (1739)
1 : a huntsman's assistant who whips in the hounds
2 : WHIP 5a
whip·per·snap·per \'hwip-ər-ˌsna-pər, 'wi-\ *noun* [alteration of *snippersnapper*] (1700)
: a diminutive, insignificant, or presumptuous person
whip·pet \'hwip-ət, 'wi-\ *noun* [probably from ¹*whip*] (1610)
: any of a breed of small swift slender dogs that are widely used for racing
whipping *noun* (1540)

1 : the act of one that whips: as **a :** a severe beating or chastisement **b :** a stitching with small overcasting stitches
2 : material used to whip or bind
whipping boy *noun* (1647)
1 : a boy formerly educated with a prince and punished in his stead
2 : SCAPEGOAT 2
whipping cream *noun* (1921)
: a cream suitable for whipping that by law contains not less than 30 percent butterfat
whipping post *noun* (1600)
: a post to which offenders are tied to be legally whipped
whip·ple·tree \'hwi-pəl-(ˌ)trē, 'wi-\ *noun* [perhaps irregular from *whip* + *tree*] (1733)
: WHIFFLETREE
whip·poor·will \'hwi-pər-ˌwil, ˌhwi-pər-', 'wi-, ˌwi-\ *noun* [imitative] (1709)
: a nocturnal nightjar (*Caprimulgus vociferus*) of eastern North America with a loud repeated call suggestive of its name

whippoorwill

whip·py \'hwi-pē, 'wi-\ *adjective* **whip·pi·er; -est** (1867)
1 : unusually resilient : SPRINGY ⟨a *whippy* fishing rod⟩
2 : of, relating to, or resembling a whip
whip-round \'hwip-ˌraůnd, 'wip-\ *noun* (1887)
chiefly British **:** a collection of money made usually for a benevolent purpose ⟨had a *whip-round* to help the couple pay for a Paris honeymoon —*The People*⟩
¹whip·saw \'hwip-ˌsȯ, 'wip-\ *noun* [²*whip*] (1538)
: a narrow pit saw averaging from 5 to 7½ feet (1.5 to 2.3 meters) in length
²whipsaw *transitive verb* (1842)
1 : to saw with a whipsaw
2 : to beset or victimize in two opposite ways at once, by a two-phase operation, or by the collusive action of two opponents ⟨wage earners were *whipsawed* by inflation and high taxes⟩
whip·sawed \-ˌsȯd\ *adjective* (1892)
: subjected to a double market loss through trying inopportunely to recoup a loss by a subsequent short sale of the same security
whip scorpion *noun* (circa 1890)
: any of an order (Uropygi) of arachnids somewhat resembling true scorpions but having a long slender caudal process and no sting
whip stall *noun* (1924)
: a stall during a vertical climb in which the nose of the airplane whips violently forward and then downward
¹whip·stitch \'hwip-ˌstich, 'wip-\ *transitive verb* (1592)
: WHIP 5
²whipstitch *noun* (1640)
: a shallow overcasting stitch
whip·stock \-ˌstäk\ *noun* (circa 1530)
: the handle of a whip
whip·worm \-ˌwərm\ *noun* (1875)
: a parasitic nematode worm (genus *Trichuris*) with a body that is thickened posteriorly and that is very long and slender anteriorly; *especially* **:** one (*T. trichiura*) of the human intestine
¹whir *also* **whirr** \'hwər, 'wər\ *verb* **whirred; whir·ring** [Middle English (Scots) *quirren*, probably of Scandinavian origin; akin to Danish *hvirre* to whirl, whirl] (15th century)
intransitive verb
: to fly, revolve, or move rapidly with a whir
transitive verb
: to move or carry rapidly with a whir
²whir *also* **whirr** *noun* (1677)
: a continuous fluttering or vibratory sound made by something in rapid motion

¹whirl \'hwər(-ə)l, 'wər(-ə)l\ *verb* [Middle English, probably of Scandinavian origin; akin to Old Norse *hvirfla* to whirl; akin to Old High German *wirbil* whirlwind, Old English *hweorfan* to turn — more at WHARF] (14th century)
intransitive verb
1 : to move in a circle or similar curve especially with force or speed
2 a : to turn on or around an axis like a wheel **:** ROTATE **b :** to turn abruptly around or aside **:** WHEEL
3 : to pass, move, or go quickly ⟨*whirled* down the hallway⟩
4 : to become giddy or dizzy : REEL ⟨my head is *whirling*⟩
transitive verb
1 : to drive, impel, or convey with or as if with a rotary motion
2 a : to cause to turn usually rapidly on or around an axis **:** ROTATE **b :** to cause to turn abruptly around or aside
3 *obsolete* **:** to throw or hurl violently with a revolving motion
— **whirl·er** \'hwər-lər, 'wər-\ *noun*
²whirl *noun* (15th century)
1 a : a rapid rotating or circling movement **b :** something undergoing such a movement
2 a : a busy or fast-paced succession of events **:** BUSTLE ⟨a *whirl* of activity⟩ ⟨the social *whirl*⟩ **b :** a confused or disturbed mental state **:** TURMOIL ⟨a *whirl* of febrile excitement —Emily Skeel⟩
3 : an experimental or brief attempt **:** TRY ⟨gave it a *whirl*⟩
whirl·i·gig \'hwər-li-ˌgig, 'wər-\ *noun* [Middle English *whirlegigg*, from *whirlen* to whirl + *gigg* top — more at GIG] (15th century)
1 : a child's toy having a whirling motion
2 : MERRY-GO-ROUND
3 a : one that continuously whirls, moves, or changes **b :** a whirling or circling course (as of events)
whirligig beetle *noun* (1855)
: any of a family (Gyrinidae) of beetles with two pairs of eyes and clubbed antennae that live mostly on the surface of water where they swim swiftly about in circles
whirl·pool \'hwər(-ə)l-ˌpül, 'wər(-ə)l-\ *noun* (1529)
1 a : a confused tumult and bustle **:** WHIRL **b :** a magnetic or impelling force by which something may be engulfed ⟨refusing to be drawn into this *whirlpool* of intrigue —A. D. White⟩
2 a : water moving rapidly in a circle so as to produce a depression in the center into which floating objects may be drawn **:** EDDY, VORTEX **b :** WHIRLPOOL BATH
whirlpool bath *noun* (circa 1916)
: a therapeutic bath in which all or part of the body is exposed to forceful whirling currents of hot water
¹whirl·wind \-ˌwind\ *noun* (14th century)
1 : a small rotating windstorm of limited extent
2 a : a confused rush **:** WHIRL **b :** a violent or destructive force or agency
²whirlwind *adjective* (1614)
: resembling a whirlwind especially in speed or force ⟨a *whirlwind* campaign⟩ ⟨a *whirlwind* romance⟩
¹whirl·y \'hwər-lē, 'wər-\ *adjective* (15th century)
: marked by or exhibiting a whirling motion
²whirly *noun, plural* **whirl·ies** (1914)
: a small whirlwind
whirly·bird \-ˌbərd\ *noun* (1951)
: HELICOPTER

whir·ry \'hwər-ē, 'wər-, '(h)wə-rē\ *verb* **whir·ried; whir·ry·ing** [perhaps blend of *whir* and *hurry*] (1582)
transitive verb
Scottish **:** to convey quickly
intransitive verb
Scottish **:** HURRY

¹**whish** \'hwish, 'wish\ *verb* [imitative] (1518)
transitive verb
: to urge on or cause to move with a whish
intransitive verb
1 : to make a sibilant sound
2 : to move with a whish especially at high speed ⟨an elevator . . . *whishes* down to the lower level —Natalie Cooper⟩
²**whish** *noun* (circa 1802)
: a rushing sound **:** SWISH

whisht \'hwisht, 'wisht\ *intransitive verb* [Middle English; imitative] (15th century)
chiefly Irish **:** HUSH — often used interjectionally to enjoin silence

¹**whisk** \'hwisk, 'wisk\ *noun* [Middle English *wisk*, probably of Scandinavian origin; akin to Old Norse *visk* wisp; akin to Old English *wiscian* to plait] (14th century)
1 : a quick light brushing or whipping motion
2 a : a usually wire kitchen utensil used for beating food by hand **b :** a flexible bunch (as of twigs, feathers, or straw) attached to a handle for use as a brush
²**whisk** (15th century)
intransitive verb
: to move nimbly and quickly
transitive verb
1 : to move or convey briskly ⟨*whisked* the children off to bed⟩
2 : to mix or fluff up by or as if by beating with a whisk ⟨*whisk* egg whites⟩
3 : to brush or wipe off lightly
whisk broom *noun* (1857)
: a small broom with a short handle used especially as a clothes brush

whis·ker \'hwis-kər, 'wis-\ *noun* [singular of *whiskers* mustache, from ²*whisk*] (circa 1600)
1 a : a hair of the beard **b** *plural* (1) *archaic* **:** MUSTACHE (2) **:** the part of the beard growing on the sides of the face or on the chin **c :** HAIRBREADTH ⟨lost the race by a *whisker*⟩
2 : one of the long projecting hairs or bristles growing near the mouth of an animal (as a cat or bird)
3 : an outrigger extending on each side of the bowsprit to spread the jib and flying jib guys — usually used in plural
4 a : a shred or filament resembling a whisker **b :** a thin hairlike crystal (as of sapphire or copper) of exceptional mechanical strength used especially to reinforce composite structural material
— **whis·kered** \-kərd\ *adjective*
— **whis·kery** \-k(ə-)rē\ *adjective*

whis·key *or* **whis·ky** \'hwis-kē, 'wis-\ *noun, plural* **whiskeys** *or* **whiskies** [Irish *uisce beathadh* & Scottish Gaelic *uisge beatha*, literally, water of life] (1715)
1 : a liquor distilled from the fermented mash of grain (as rye, corn, or barley)
2 : a drink of whiskey ◇
Whiskey (circa 1952)
— a communication code word for the letter *w*

whiskey sour *noun* (circa 1889)
: a cocktail usually consisting of whiskey, sugar, and lemon juice shaken with ice

¹**whis·per** \'hwis-pər, 'wis-\ *verb* **whispered; whis·per·ing** \-p(ə-)riŋ\ [Middle English, from Old English *hwisperian;* akin to Old High German *hwispalōn* to whisper, Old Norse *hvīsla* — more at WHISTLE] (before 12th century)
intransitive verb
1 : to speak softly with little or no vibration of the vocal cords especially to avoid being overheard
2 : to make a sibilant sound that resembles whispering

transitive verb
1 : to address in a whisper
2 : to utter or communicate in or as if in a whisper
²**whisper** *noun* (1595)
1 : something communicated by or as if by whispering; *especially* **:** RUMOR ⟨*whispers* of scandal⟩
2 a : an act or instance of whispering; *especially* **:** speech without vibration of the vocal cords **b :** a sibilant sound that resembles whispered speech
3 : HINT, TRACE

whis·per·er \-pər-ər\ *noun* (1547)
: one that whispers; *specifically* **:** RUMORMONGER

¹**whispering** *noun* (before 12th century)
1 a : whispered speech **b :** GOSSIP, RUMOR
2 : a sibilant sound **:** WHISPER
²**whispering** *adjective* (1547)
1 : making a sibilant sound
2 : spreading confidential and especially derogatory reports ⟨*whispering* tongues can poison truth —S. T. Coleridge⟩
— **whis·per·ing·ly** \-p(ə-)riŋ-lē\ *adverb*
whispering campaign *noun* (1920)
: the systematic dissemination by word of mouth of derogatory rumors or charges especially against a candidate for public office
whis·pery \'hwis-p(ə-)rē, 'wis-\ *adjective* (1834)
1 : resembling a whisper
2 : full of whispers

¹**whist** \'hwist, 'wist\ *intransitive verb* [Middle English; imitative] (14th century)
dialect British **:** to be silent **:** HUSH — often used interjectionally to enjoin silence
²**whist** *adjective* (15th century)
: QUIET, SILENT
³**whist** *noun* [alteration of earlier *whisk,* probably from ²*whisk;* from whisking up the tricks] (1663)
: a card game for four players in two partnerships that is played with a pack of 52 cards and that scores one point for each trick in excess of six

¹**whis·tle** \'hwi-səl, 'wi-\ *noun, often attributive* [Middle English, from Old English *hwistle;* akin to Old Norse *hvīsla* to whisper] (before 12th century)
1 a : a small wind instrument in which sound is produced by the forcible passage of breath through a slit in a short tube ⟨police *whistle*⟩ **b :** a device through which air or steam is forced into a cavity or against a thin edge to produce a loud sound ⟨a factory *whistle*⟩
2 a : a shrill clear sound produced by forcing breath out or air in through the puckered lips **b :** the sound produced by a whistle **c :** a signal given by or as if by whistling
3 : a sound that resembles a whistle; *especially* **:** a shrill clear note of or as if of a bird
²**whistle** *verb* **whis·tled; whis·tling** \-s(ə-)liŋ\ (before 12th century)
intransitive verb
1 a : to utter a shrill clear sound by blowing or drawing air through the puckered lips **b :** to utter a shrill note or call resembling a whistle **c :** to make a shrill clear sound especially by rapid movement ⟨the wind *whistled*⟩ **d :** to blow or sound a whistle
2 a : to give a signal or issue an order or summons by or as if by whistling **b :** to make a demand without result ⟨did a sloppy job so he can *whistle* for his money⟩
transitive verb
1 a : to send, bring, signal, or call by or as if by whistling **b :** to charge (as a basketball or hockey player) with an infraction
2 : to produce, utter, or express by whistling ⟨*whistle* a tune⟩
— **whis·tle·able** \-sə-lə-bəl\ *adjective*
— **whistle in the dark :** to keep up one's courage by or as if by whistling
whis·tle–blow·er \-ˌblō(-ə)r\ *noun* (1970)

: one who reveals something covert or who informs against another ⟨pledges to protect *whistle-blowers* who fear reprisals —*Wall Street Journal*⟩
— **whis·tle–blow·ing** \-ˌblō-iŋ\ *noun*
whis·tler \'hwi-s(ə-)lər, 'wi-\ *noun* (before 12th century)
: one that whistles: as **a :** any of various birds; *especially* **:** any of numerous Australian and Polynesian oscine birds (especially genus *Pachycephala*) that are related to the shrikes and have a whistling call **b :** a large mountain marmot (*Marmota caligata*) of northwestern North America **c :** a broken-winded horse **d :** a very-low-frequency radio signal that is generated by lightning discharge, travels along the earth's magnetic-field lines, and produces a sound resembling a whistle of descending pitch in radio receivers
¹**whis·tle–stop** \'hwi-səl-ˌstäp, 'wi-\ *noun, often attributive* (circa 1925)
1 a : a small station at which trains stop only on signal **:** FLAG STOP **b :** a small community
2 : a brief personal appearance especially by a political candidate usually on the rear platform of a train during the course of a tour
²**whistle–stop** *intransitive verb* (1952)
: to make a tour especially in a political campaign with many brief personal appearances in small communities
whistling *noun* (14th century)
: the act or sound of one that whistles **:** WHISTLE
whistling swan *noun* (1785)
: a native North American swan (*Cygnus columbianus* synonym *Olor columbianus*) that calls with a soft musical note, breeds in the Arctic tundra, and winters in shallow fresh or salt water especially along the eastern and western coasts of the U.S.
whit \'hwit, 'wit\ *noun* [Middle English, probably alteration of *wiht, wight* creature, thing — more at WIGHT] (15th century)
: the smallest part or particle imaginable **:** BIT ⟨what some people will do for a *whit* of publicity —Patrick Quinn⟩
¹**white** \'hwīt, 'wīt\ *adjective* **whit·er; whit·est** [Middle English, from Old English *hwīt;* akin to Old High German *hwīz* white and probably to Old Church Slavonic *světŭ* light, Sanskrit *śveta* white, bright] (before 12th century)
1 a : free from color **b :** of the color of new snow or milk; *specifically* **:** of the color white **c :** light or pallid in color ⟨*white* lips⟩ ⟨lips *white* with fear⟩ **d :** lustrous pale gray **:** SILVERY; *also* **:** made of silver
2 a : being a member of a group or race characterized by reduced pigmentation and usually

◇ **WORD HISTORY**
whiskey Of the relatively few English words that have come from the Celtic languages, certainly one of the most common is *whiskey. Whiskey* (or *whisky*) is a shortening from earlier *whiskeybae, usquebaugh,* and many other variants, all of which are borrowed from either Irish *uisce beathadh* or Scottish Gaelic *uisge beatha,* a drink traditionally distilled from malted barley. Both of these phrases mean literally "water of life" and are ultimately translations of Medieval Latin *aqua vitae,* a phrase that writers on alchemy used to describe distilled spirits. *Aqua vitae* turns up in other guises elsewhere in Europe. In Scandinavia it was directly borrowed into Danish, Norwegian, and Swedish as *akvavit,* usually rendered in English as *aquavit,* a clear liquor flavored with caraway seeds. French *eau-de-vie,* on the other hand, is, like the Gaelic expression, a translation from Latin; today it is applied to a clear brandy usually distilled from fermented fruit juice.

specifically distinguished from persons belonging to groups marked by black, brown, yellow, or red skin coloration **b :** of, relating to, characteristic of, or consisting of white people **c :** marked by upright fairness
3 : free from spot or blemish: as **a** (1) **:** free from moral impurity **:** INNOCENT (2) **:** marked by the wearing of white by the woman as a symbol of purity ⟨a *white* wedding⟩ **b :** unmarked by writing or printing **c :** not intended to cause harm ⟨a *white* lie⟩ ⟨*white* magic⟩ **d :** FAVORABLE, FORTUNATE ⟨one of the *white* days of his life —Sir Walter Scott⟩
4 a : wearing or habited in white **b :** marked by the presence of snow **:** SNOWY ⟨a *white* Christmas⟩
5 a : heated to the point of whiteness **b :** notably ardent **:** PASSIONATE ⟨*white* fury⟩
6 a : conservative or reactionary in political outlook and action **b :** instigated or carried out by reactionary forces as a counterrevolutionary measure ⟨a *white* terror⟩
7 : of, relating to, or constituting a musical tone quality characterized by a controlled pure sound, a lack of warmth and color, and a lack of resonance
8 : consisting of a wide range of frequencies — used of light, sound, and electromagnetic radiation
— **whit·ish** \'hwī-tish, 'wī-\ *adjective*

²white *noun* (before 12th century)
1 : the achromatic object color of greatest lightness characteristically perceived to belong to objects that reflect diffusely nearly all incident energy throughout the visible spectrum
2 a : a white or light-colored part of something: as (1) **:** a mass of albuminous material surrounding the yolk of an egg (2) **:** the white part of the ball of the eye (3) **:** the light-colored pieces in a two-handed board game; *also* **:** the player by whom these are played (4) **:** the area of a page unmarked by writing, printing, or illustration **b** (1) *archaic* **:** a white target (2) **:** the fifth or outermost circle of an archery target; *also* **:** a shot that hits it
3 : one that is or approaches white in color: as **a :** white clothing — often used in plural **b :** WHITE WINE **c :** a white mammal (as a horse or a hog) **d** (1) **:** a white-colored product (as flour, pins, or sugar) — usually used in plural (2) **:** any of numerous butterflies (subfamily Pierinae of the family Pieridae) that usually have the ground color of the wings white and are related to the sulphur butterflies
4 *plural* **:** LEUKORRHEA
5 : a person belonging to a light-skinned race
6 *often capitalized* **:** a member of a conservative or reactionary political group

³white *transitive verb* **whit·ed; whit·ing** [Middle English, from *white*, adjective] (before 12th century)
archaic **:** WHITEN

white amur \-ä-'mür\ *noun* [*amur* from *Amur* River] (1968)
: GRASS CARP

white ant *noun* (1684)
: TERMITE

white ash *noun* (1683)
: an American ash (*Fraxinus americana*) having compound leaves with a pale green or silvery white underside; *also* **:** its hard brownish wood

white·bait \'hwīt-,bāt, 'wīt-\ *noun* (1758)
1 : the young of any of several European herrings and especially of the common herring (*Clupea harengus*) or of the sprat (*C. sprattus*)
2 : any of various small fishes likened to the European whitebait and used as food

white bass *noun* (1813)
: a North American freshwater bony fish (*Morone chrysops* of the family Percichthyidae) that is used for food

white bean *noun* (1969)
: a dried white kidney bean seed; *also* **:** a plant that is a source of white beans

white·beard \'hwīt-,bird, 'wīt-\ *noun* (15th century)
: an old man **:** GRAYBEARD

white birch *noun* (1789)
1 : PAPER BIRCH; *also* **:** GRAY BIRCH
2 : either of two European birches (*Betula pubescens* and *B. pendula*) with white or ash-colored bark that are often planted as ornamentals in the U.S.

white blood cell *noun* (1885)
: any of the blood cells that are colorless, lack hemoglobin, contain a nucleus, and include the lymphocytes, monocytes, neutrophils, eosinophils, and basophils — called also *white blood corpuscle*

white book *noun* (15th century)
: an official report of government affairs bound in white

white–bread \'hwīt-'bred, 'wīt-\ *adjective* (1979)
: being, typical of, or having qualities (as blandness) associated with the white middle class

white·cap \'hwīt-,kap, 'wīt-\ *noun* (1773)
: a wave crest breaking into white foam — usually used in plural

white cedar *noun* (1674)
1 : a strong-scented evergreen swamp tree (*Chamaecyparis thyoides*) of the cypress family that occurs along the eastern coast of the U.S. and that has smaller leaves than an arborvitae and globose cones with peltate scales; *also* **:** its wood
2 : NORTHERN WHITE CEDAR

white cell *noun* (1861)
: WHITE BLOOD CELL

white chip *noun* (1897)
1 : a white-colored poker chip usually of minimum value
2 : a thing or quantity of little worth — compare BLUE CHIP

white chocolate *noun* (1923)
: a confection of cocoa butter, sugar, milk solids, lecithin, and flavorings

white clover *noun* (before 12th century)
: a Eurasian clover (*Trifolium repens*) with round heads of white flowers that is widely used in lawn and pasture grass-seed mixtures and is an important source of nectar for bees — called also *white Dutch clover*

white–col·lar \'hwīt-'kä-lər, 'wīt-\ *adjective* (1920)
: of, relating to, or constituting the class of salaried employees whose duties do not call for the wearing of work clothes or protective clothing — compare BLUE-COLLAR

white crappie *noun* (circa 1926)
: a silvery North American sunfish (*Pomoxis annularis*) with 5 or 6 protruding spines on the dorsal fins that is used as a panfish and often for stocking small ponds

white–crowned sparrow \'hwīt-'kraünd-, 'wīt-\ *noun* (1839)
: a migratory sparrow (*Zonotrichia leucophrys*) that breeds in northern and western North America and has a grayish breast, pink bill, and head striped with black and white

whit·ed \'hwīt-təd, 'wī-\ *adjective* (14th century)
1 : covered with white or whiting and especially with whitewash
2 : made white **:** WHITENED

whited sepulcher *noun* [from the simile in Matthew 23:27 (Authorized Version)] (1582)
: a person inwardly corrupt or wicked but outwardly or professedly virtuous or holy **:** HYPOCRITE

white dwarf *noun, plural* **white dwarfs** (1924)
: a small whitish star of low intrinsic brightness usually with a mass approximately equal to that of the sun but with a density many times larger

white elephant *noun* (15th century)
1 : an Indian elephant of a pale color that is sometimes venerated in India, Sri Lanka, Thailand, and Myanmar
2 a : a property requiring much care and expense and yielding little profit **b :** an object no longer of value to its owner but of value to others **c :** something of little or no value

white·face \'hwīt-,fās, 'wīt-\ *noun* (1709)
1 : a white-faced animal; *specifically* **:** HEREFORD
2 : dead-white facial makeup ⟨a clown in *whiteface*⟩

white–faced \-'fāst\ *adjective* (1595)
1 : having a wan pale face
2 : having the face white in whole or in part — used especially of an animal otherwise dark in color

white feather *noun* [from the superstition that a white feather in the plumage of a gamecock is a mark of a poor fighter] (circa 1785)
: a mark or symbol of cowardice — used chiefly in the phrase *show the white feather*

white·fish \'hwīt-,fish, 'wīt-\ *noun* (15th century)
1 a : any of various freshwater salmonid food fishes (especially of genera *Coregonus* and *Prosopium*) **b :** any of various fishes resembling the true whitefishes **c** *British* **:** any of various market fishes with white flesh that is not oily
2 : the flesh of a whitefish especially as an article of food

white flag *noun* (1600)
1 : a flag of plain white used as a flag of truce or as a token of surrender
2 : a token of weakness or yielding

white flight *noun* (1967)
: the departure of white families usually from urban neighborhoods undergoing racial integration or from cities implementing school desegregation

white–fly \'hwīt-,flī, 'wīt-\ *noun* (circa 1889)
: any of numerous small homopterous insects (family Aleyrodidae) that are injurious plant pests

white–foot·ed mouse \'hwīt-,fù-təd, 'wīt-\ *noun* (1869)
: any of various largely nocturnal mice (genus *Peromyscus*) of North and Central America typically having whitish feet and underparts; *especially* **:** a common woodland mouse (*P. leucopus*) of North America

white-footed mouse

white friar *noun, often W&F capitalized* [from his white habit] (15th century)
: CARMELITE

white–fringed beetle \'hwīt-,frinj(d)-, 'wīt-\ *noun* (1939)
: any of a genus (*Graphognathus*) of South American flightless beetles of which one (*G. leucoloma*) has been accidentally introduced into the southeastern U.S. where it is a pest on cultivated plants

white gas *noun* (1926)
: unleaded gasoline — called also *white gasoline*

white gold *noun* (1666)
: a pale alloy of gold especially with nickel or palladium that resembles platinum in appearance

white goods *noun plural* (circa 1871)
1 a : white fabrics especially of cotton or linen **b :** articles (as sheets, towels, or curtains) originally or typically made of white cloth

\ə\ abut \ᵊ\ kitten \ər\ further \a\ ash \ā\ ace
\ä\ mop, mar \aü\ out \ch\ chin \e\ bet \ē\ easy
\g\ go \i\ hit \ī\ ice \j\ job \ŋ\ sing \ō\ go
\o\ law \oi\ boy \th\ thin \t͟h\ the \ü\ loot \ù\ foot
\y\ yet \zh\ vision *see also* Guide to Pronunciation

2 : major household appliances (as stoves and refrigerators) that are typically finished in white enamel

white grub *noun* (circa 1817)
: a grub that is a destructive pest of grass roots and is the larva of various beetles and especially june bugs

White·hall \'hwīt-,hȯl, 'wīt-\ *noun* [*Whitehall*, thoroughfare of London in which are located the chief offices of British government] (1827)
: the British government

white·head \-,hed\ *noun* (circa 1931)
: MILIUM

white–head·ed \-'he-dəd\ *adjective* (1525)
1 : having the hair, fur, or plumage of the head white or very light
2 : specially favored : FORTUNATE — used especially in the phrase *white-headed boy*

white heat *noun* (circa 1710)
1 : a temperature (as for copper and iron from 1500° to 1600° C) which is higher than red heat and at which a body becomes brightly incandescent
2 : a state of intense mental or physical strain, emotion, or activity

white hole *noun* (1971)
: a hypothetical extremely dense celestial object that radiates enormous amounts of energy and matter — compare BLACK HOLE 1

white hope *noun* (1911)
1 : a white contender for a boxing championship held by a black; *also* : one who is felt to represent whites
2 : one from whom much is expected; *especially* : a person undertaking a difficult task

white–hot \'hwīt-'hät, 'wīt-\ *adjective* (1820)
1 : being at or radiating white heat
2 : ardently zealous : FERVID

White House \-,haús\ *noun* [the *White House*, mansion in Washington, D.C., assigned to the use of the president of the U.S.] (1811)
1 : the executive department of the U.S. government
2 : a residence of the president of the U.S.

white hunter *noun* (1945)
: a white man serving as guide and professional hunter to an African safari

white knight *noun* (1951)
1 : one that comes to the rescue of another; *especially* : a corporation invited to buy out a second corporation in order to prevent an undesired takeover by a third
2 : one that champions a cause

white–knuck·le \'hwīt-'nə-kəl, 'wīt-\ *also* **white–knuck·led** \-kəld\ *adjective* (1974)
: showing or causing tense nervousness ⟨a *white-knuckle* ride on a roller coaster⟩

white lead *noun* (15th century)
: any of several white lead-containing pigments; *especially* : a heavy poisonous basic carbonate of lead of variable composition that is marketed as a powder or as a paste in linseed oil, has good hiding power, and is used chiefly in exterior paints

white lightning *noun* (1915)
: MOONSHINE 3

white line *noun* (15th century)
: a band or edge of something white; *especially* : a stripe painted on a road and used to guide traffic

white list \-,list\ *noun* (1900)
: a list of approved or favored items — compare BLACKLIST
— white–list·ed \-,lis-təd\ *adjective*

white–liv·ered \-'li-vərd\ *adjective* [from the former belief that the choleric temperament depends on the body's producing large quantities of yellow bile] (1549)
: PUSILLANIMOUS, LILY-LIVERED

white·ly \'hwīt-lē, 'wīt-\ *adverb* (14th century)
: with an effect of whiteness : so as to show or appear white

white man's burden *noun* ["The White Man's Burden" (1899), poem by Rudyard Kipling] (1911)

: the alleged duty of the white peoples to manage the affairs of the less developed nonwhite peoples

white matter *noun* (circa 1847)
: neural tissue that consists largely of myelinated nerve fibers, has a whitish color, and underlies the gray matter of the brain and spinal cord or is gathered into nerves

white metal *noun* (1613)
1 : any of several light-colored alloys used especially as a base for plated silverware and ornaments and novelties
2 : any of several lead-base or tin-base alloys (as babbitt) used especially for bearings, fusible plugs, and type metal

white mustard *noun* (1731)
: a Eurasian mustard (*Brassica hirta*) grown for its seeds which yield mustard and mustard oil

whit·en \'hwī-t²n, 'wī-\ *verb* **whit·ened; whit·en·ing** \'hwīt-niŋ, 'wīt-, -²n-iŋ\ (14th century)
transitive verb
: to make white or whiter ⟨snow *whitened* the hills⟩
intransitive verb
: to become white or whiter

whit·en·er \'hwīt-nər, 'wīt-; 'hwī-t²n-ər, 'wī-\ *noun* (1611)
: one that whitens; *specifically* : an agent (as a bleach) used to impart whiteness to something

white·ness \'hwīt-nəs, 'wīt-\ *noun* (before 12th century)
1 : the quality or state of being white: as **a** : white color **b** : PALLOR, PALENESS **c** : freedom from stain : CLEANNESS
2 : white substance

whitening *noun* (1601)
1 : the act or process of making or becoming white
2 : something that is used to make white : WHITING

white noise *noun* (1943)
: a heterogeneous mixture of sound waves extending over a wide frequency range

white oak *noun* (1634)
: any of various oaks (especially *Quercus alba* of eastern North America) with acorns that mature in one year and leaf veins that never extend beyond the margin of the leaf; *also* : its hard strong durable wood

white oak: leaves and acorns

white oil *noun* (circa 1900)
: any of various colorless odorless tasteless mineral oils used especially in medicine and in pharmaceutical and cosmetic preparations

white·out \'hwīt-,aùt, 'wīt-\ *noun* [*white* + black*out*] (1942)
: a surface weather condition in a snow-covered area (as a polar region) in which no object casts a shadow, the horizon cannot be seen, and only dark objects are discernible; *also* : a blizzard that severely reduces visibility

white pages *noun plural* (1952)
: the section of a telephone directory that lists individuals and businesses alphabetically

white paper *noun* (1899)
1 : a government report on any subject; *especially* : a British publication that is usually less extensive than a blue book
2 : a detailed or authoritative report

white pepper *noun* (14th century)
: a pungent condiment that consists of the fruit of an East Indian plant (*Piper nigrum*) ground after the black husk has been removed

white perch *noun* (1775)

1 : a silvery anadromous bass (*Morone americana*) chiefly of the coast and coastal streams of the eastern U.S.
2 : FRESHWATER DRUM
3 : WHITE CRAPPIE

white pine *noun* (1682)
1 a : a tall-growing pine (*Pinus strobus*) of eastern North America with long needles in clusters of five — called also *eastern white pine* **b** : any of several trees that resemble the white pine especially in having leaves in bundles of five
2 : the wood of a white pine and especially of the eastern white pine

white–pine blister rust *noun* (1911)
: a destructive disease of white pine caused by a rust fungus (*Cronartium ribicola*) that passes part of its complex life cycle on currant or gooseberry bushes; *also* : this fungus

white potato *noun* (circa 1890)
: POTATO 2b

white rice *noun* (1923)
: rice from which the hull and bran have been removed by milling

white room *noun* (1961)
: CLEAN ROOM

White Russian *noun* (1850)
1 : BELORUSSIAN
2 : a cocktail made of vodka, coffee liqueur, and cream or milk

white rust *noun* (circa 1848)
: any of various plant diseases caused by a fungus (genus *Albugo* of the order Peronosporales) and characterized by the presence of masses of white spores that escape through ruptures of the host tissue; *also* : a fungus causing a white rust

white sale *noun* (1914)
: a sale of white goods

white sauce *noun* (1723)
: a sauce consisting essentially of a roux with milk, cream, or stock and seasoning

white sea bass *noun* (1884)
: a large croaker (*Atractoscion nobilis*) of the Pacific coast that is an important sport and food fish

white shark *noun* (1674)
: GREAT WHITE SHARK

white slave *noun* (1882)
: a woman or girl held unwillingly for purposes of commercial prostitution

white slav·er \-'slā-ər\ *noun* (1912)
: one engaged in white-slave traffic

white slavery *noun* (1857)
: enforced prostitution

white·smith \'hwīt-,smith, 'wīt-\ *noun* (14th century)
1 : TINSMITH
2 : a worker in iron who finishes or polishes the work

white space *noun* (1849)
: the areas of a page without print or pictures

white spruce *noun* (1770)
1 : any of several spruces; *especially* : a widely distributed spruce (*Picea glauca*) of coniferous forests of Canada and the northern U.S. that has short stiff blue-green needles and slender cones
2 : the wood of a white spruce; *especially* : the light pale tough straight-grained wood of the common white spruce (*Picea glauca*) used especially for construction and as a source of paper pulp

white sucker *noun* (circa 1902)
: a common and widespread edible sucker (*Catostomus commersoni*) of the U.S. and Canada

white supremacist *noun* (1945)
: an advocate of or believer in white supremacy

white supremacy *noun* (1867)
: a doctrine based on a belief in the inherent superiority of the white race over the black race and the correlative necessity for the subordination of blacks to whites in all relationships

white·tail \'hwīt-,tāl, 'wīt-\ *noun* (1872)
: WHITE-TAILED DEER

white–tailed deer \-'tāld-\ *noun* (1849)
: a North American deer (*Odocoileus virginianus*) with a rather long tail white on the undersurface and the males of which have forward-arching antlers

white-tailed deer

white·throat \'hwīt-,thrōt, 'wīt-\ *noun* (1676)
: any of several birds with white on the throat: as **a** : an Old World warbler (*Sylvia communis*) with rusty upper parts and largely pale buff underparts **b** : WHITE-THROATED SPARROW

white–throat·ed sparrow \-,thrō-təd-\ *noun* (1811)
: a common brown sparrow (*Zonotrichia albicollis*) chiefly of eastern North America with a black-and-white striped crown and a white patch on the throat

white–tie *adjective* (1936)
: characterized by or requiring the wearing of formal evening clothes consisting of white tie and tailcoat for men and a formal gown for women ⟨a *white-tie* dinner⟩ — compare BLACK-TIE

white trash *noun singular but plural in construction* (1831)
: POOR WHITE — usually used disparagingly

white·wall \'hwīt-,wȯl, 'wīt-\ *noun* (1953)
: an automobile tire having a white band on the sidewall

white walnut *noun* (1743)
1 : BUTTERNUT 1
2 : the light-colored wood of a butternut

¹white·wash \'hwīt-,wȯsh, 'wīt-, -,wäsh\ *transitive verb* (1591)
1 : to whiten with whitewash
2 a : to gloss over or cover up (as vices or crimes) **b** : to exonerate by means of a perfunctory investigation or through biased presentation of data
3 : to hold (an opponent) scoreless in a game or contest
— **white·wash·er** *noun*

²whitewash *noun* (1689)
1 : a liquid composition for whitening a surface: as **a** : a preparation for whitening the skin **b** : a composition (as of lime and water or whiting, size, and water) for whitening structural surfaces
2 : an act or instance of glossing over or of exonerating
3 : a defeat in a contest in which the loser fails to score

white·wash·ing *noun* (1663)
: an act or instance of applying whitewash; *also* : WHITEWASH 3

white water *noun* (1586)
: frothy water (as in breakers, rapids, or falls)
— **white–water** *adjective*

white way *noun* [the *Great White Way*, nickname for the theatrical section of Broadway, New York City] (1909)
: a brilliantly lighted street or avenue especially in a city's business or theater district

white whale *noun* (circa 1834)
: a cetacean (*Delphinapterus leucas*) that is about 10 feet (3.0 meters) long and white when adult — called also *beluga*

white whale

white wine *noun* (14th century)
: a wine ranging in color from faintly yellow to amber that is produced from the juice alone of dark- or light-colored grapes

white·wing \'hwīt-,wiŋ, 'wīt-\ *noun* (1898)
: a person and especially a street sweeper wearing a white uniform

white·wood \-,wu̇d\ *noun* (1663)
1 : any of various trees with pale or white wood: as **a** : TULIP TREE 1 **b** : an Australian tree (*Atalaya hemiglauca*) of the soapberry family
2 : the wood of a whitewood; *especially* : TULIPWOOD 1

whit·ey \'hwī-tē, 'wī-\ *noun, often capitalized* (1828)
: the white man : white society — usually used disparagingly

white zinfandel *noun* (1976)
: a blush wine made from zinfandel grapes

¹whith·er \'hwi-thər, 'wi-\ *adverb* [Middle English, from Old English *hwider*; akin to Latin *quis* who and to Old English *hider* hither — more at WHO, HITHER] (before 12th century)
1 : to what place ⟨*whither* will they go⟩
2 : to what situation, position, degree, or end ⟨*whither* will this abuse drive him⟩

²whither *conjunction* (before 12th century)
1 a : to what place ⟨knew *whither* to go —Daniel Defoe⟩ **b** : to what situation, position, degree, or end
2 a : to the place at, in, or to which **b** : to which place
3 : to whatever place

whith·er·so·ev·er \,hwi-thər-sə-'we-vər, ,wi-\ *conjunction* (14th century)
: to whatever place ⟨will go *whithersoever* you lead⟩

whith·er·ward \'hwi-thər-wərd, 'wi-\ *adverb* (13th century)
archaic : toward what or which place

¹whit·ing \'hwī-tiŋ, 'wī-\ *noun* [Middle English, from Middle Dutch *witinc*, from *wit* white; akin to Old English *hwīt* white] (15th century)
: any of various marine food fishes: as **a** : a common European fish (*Merlangus merlangus*) of the cod family **b** : SILVER HAKE

²whiting *noun* [Middle English, from gerund of *whiten* to white] (15th century)
: calcium carbonate ground into fine powder, washed, and used especially as a pigment and extender, in putty, and in rubber compounding and paper coating

whit·low \'hwit-(,)lō, 'wit-\ *noun* [Middle English *whitflawe, whitflowe, whitlowe*] (14th century)
: a deep usually suppurative inflammation of the finger or toe especially near the end or around the nail — called also *felon*

Whit·mon·day \'hwit-,mən-dē, 'wit-, -'mən-\ *noun* [*Whit*sunday + *Monday*] (1557)
: the day after Whitsunday observed as a legal holiday in England, Wales, and Ireland

Whit·sun \'hwit-sən, 'wit-\ *adjective* [Middle English *Whitson*, from *Whitsonday*] (14th century)
: of, relating to, or observed on Whitsunday or at Whitsuntide

Whit·sun·day \-'sən-dē, -sən-,dā\ *noun* [Middle English *Whitsonday*, from Old English *hwīta sunnandæg*, literally, white Sunday; probably from the custom of wearing white robes by those newly baptized at this season] (12th century)
: PENTECOST 2

Whit·sun·tide \-sən-,tīd\ *noun* (13th century)
: the week beginning with Whitsunday and especially the first three days of this week

¹whit·tle \'hwi-t²l, 'wi-\ *noun* [Middle English *whittel*, alteration of *thwitel*, from *thwiten* to whittle, from Old English *thwītan*; akin to Old Norse *thveita* to hew] (15th century)
archaic : a large knife

²whittle *verb* **whit·tled; whit·tling** \'hwit-liŋ, 'wit-; 'hwi-t²l-iŋ, 'wi-\ (1552)
transitive verb
1 a : to pare or cut off chips from the surface of (wood) with a knife **b** : to shape or form by so paring or cutting

2 : to reduce, remove, or destroy gradually as if by cutting off bits with a knife : PARE ⟨*whittle* down expenses⟩
intransitive verb
1 : to cut or shape something (as wood) by or as if by paring it with a knife
2 : to wear oneself or another out with fretting
— **whit·tler** \'hwit-lər, 'wit-; 'hwi-t²l-ər, 'wi-\ *noun*

whit·tling *noun* (1854)
1 : the act or art of whittling
2 : a piece cut away in whittling

whit·tret \'hwi-trət, 'wi-\ *noun* [Middle English *whitrat*, from *white, whit* white + *rat* rat] (15th century)
chiefly Scottish : WEASEL

whity *or* **whit·ey** \'hwī-tē, 'wī-\ *adjective* (1593)
: somewhat white : WHITISH — usually used in combination

¹whiz *or* **whizz** \'hwiz, 'wiz\ *verb* **whizzed; whiz·zing** [imitative] (1547)
intransitive verb
1 : to hum, whir, or hiss like a speeding object (as an arrow or ball) passing through air
2 : to fly or move swiftly especially with a whiz
transitive verb
: to cause to whiz; *especially* : to rotate very rapidly

²whiz *or* **whizz** *noun, plural* **whiz·zes** (1620)
1 : a hissing, buzzing, or whirring sound
2 : a movement or passage of something accompanied by a whizzing sound

³whiz *noun, plural* **whiz·zes** [probably by shortening & alteration] (1914)
: WIZARD 3 ⟨a *whiz* at math⟩

whiz–bang *also* **whizz–bang** \'hwiz-,baŋ, 'wiz-, -'baŋ\ *noun* (1915)
: one that is conspicuous for noise, speed, excellence, or startling effect
— **whiz–bang** *adjective*

whiz kid *also* **whizz kid** *noun* [³*whiz*] (circa 1942)
: a person who is unusually intelligent, clever, or successful especially at an early age

whiz·zer \'hwi-zər, 'wi-\ *noun* (1881)
: one that whizzes; *especially* : a centrifugal machine for drying something (as grain, sugar, or nitrated cotton)

who \'hü, ü\ *pronoun* [Middle English, from Old English *hwā;* akin to Old High German *hwer*, interrogative pronoun, who, Latin *quis*, Greek *tis*, Latin *qui*, relative pronoun, who] (before 12th century)
1 : what or which person or persons — used as an interrogative ⟨*who* was elected?⟩ ⟨find out *who* they are⟩; used by speakers on all educational levels and by many reputable writers, though disapproved by some grammarians, as the object of a verb or a following preposition ⟨*who* did I see but a Spanish lady —Padraic Colum⟩ ⟨do not know *who* the message is from —G. K. Chesterton⟩
2 : the person or persons that : WHOEVER
3 — used as a function word to introduce a relative clause; used especially in reference to persons ⟨my father, *who* was a lawyer⟩ but also in reference to groups ⟨a generation *who* had known nothing but war —R. B. West⟩ or to animals ⟨dogs *who* . . . fawn all over tramps —Nigel Balchin⟩ or to inanimate objects especially with the implication that the reference is really to a person ⟨earlier sources *who* maintain a Davidic ancestry —F. M. Cross⟩; used by speakers on all educational levels and by many reputable writers, though disapproved by some grammarians, as the object of a verb or a following preposition ⟨a

character *who* we are meant to pity —*Times Literary Supplement*⟩
usage see WHOM, THAT
— **as who** *archaic* **:** as one that **:** as if someone
— **as who should say** *archaic* **:** so to speak
— **who is who** *or* **who's who** *or* **who was who :** the identity of or the noteworthy facts about each of a number of persons
whoa \'wō, 'hō, 'hwō\ *imperative verb* [Middle English *whoo, who*] (15th century)
— a command (as to a draft animal) to stand still
who'd \'hüd\ (1640)
: who had **:** who would
who·dun·it *also* **who·dun·nit** \hü-'də-nət\ *noun* [alteration of *who done it?*] (1930)
: a detective story or mystery story
who·ev·er \hü-'e-vər\ *pronoun* (13th century)
: whatever person **:** no matter who — used in any grammatical relation except that of a possessive ⟨sells to *whoever* has the money to buy⟩
¹**whole** \'hōl\ *adjective* [Middle English *hool* healthy, unhurt, entire, from Old English *hāl;* akin to Old High German *heil* healthy, unhurt, Old Norse *heill,* Old Church Slavonic *cělŭ*] (before 12th century)
1 a (1) **:** free of wound or injury **:** UNHURT (2) **:** recovered from a wound or injury **:** RESTORED (3) **:** being healed ⟨*whole* of an ancient evil, I sleep sound —A. E. Housman⟩ **b :** free of defect or impairment **:** INTACT **c :** physically sound and healthy **:** free of disease or deformity **d :** mentally or emotionally sound
2 : having all its proper parts or components **:** COMPLETE, UNMODIFIED ⟨*whole* milk⟩ ⟨a *whole* egg⟩
3 a : constituting the total sum or undiminished entirety **:** ENTIRE ⟨owns the *whole* island⟩ **b :** each or all of the ⟨took part in the *whole* series of athletic events⟩
4 a : constituting an undivided unit **:** UNBROKEN, UNCUT ⟨a *whole* roast suckling pig⟩ **b :** directed to one end **:** CONCENTRATED ⟨promised to give it his *whole* attention⟩
5 a : seemingly complete or total ⟨the *whole* idea is to help, not hinder⟩ **b :** very great in quantity, extent, or scope ⟨feels a *whole* lot better now⟩
6 : constituting the entirety of a person's nature or development ⟨educate the *whole* student⟩
7 : having the same father and mother ⟨*whole* brother⟩ ☆
synonym see PERFECT
— **whole·ness** *noun*
²**whole** *noun* (14th century)
1 : a complete amount or sum **:** a number, aggregate, or totality lacking no part, member, or element
2 : something constituting a complex unity **:** a coherent system or organization of parts fitting or working together as one
— **in whole :** to the full or entire extent **:** WHOLLY — usually used in the phrase *in whole or in part*
— **on the whole 1 :** in view of all the circumstances or conditions **:** all things considered **2 :** in general **:** in most instances **:** TYPICALLY
³**whole** *adverb* (14th century)
1 : WHOLLY, ENTIRELY ⟨a *whole* new age group —Henry Chauncey⟩
2 : as a complete entity
whole cloth *noun* (1840)
: pure fabrication — usually used in the phrase *out of whole cloth*
whole gale *noun* (circa 1805)
: wind having a speed of 55 to 63 miles (88 to 101 kilometers) per hour — see BEAUFORT SCALE table
whole·heart·ed \'hōl-'här-təd\ *adjective* (1840)

1 : completely and sincerely devoted, determined, or enthusiastic ⟨a *wholehearted* student of social problems⟩
2 : marked by complete earnest commitment **:** free from all reserve or hesitation ⟨gave the proposal *wholehearted* approval⟩
synonym see SINCERE
— **whole·heart·ed·ly** *adverb*
whole–hog *adjective* (1829)
: committed without reservation **:** THOROUGHGOING ⟨a *whole-hog* patriot⟩
¹**whole hog** *noun* (1829)
: the whole way or farthest limit — usually used adverbially in the phrase *go the whole hog*
²**whole hog** *adverb* (1844)
: to the fullest extent **:** without reservation **:** COMPLETELY ⟨accepting *whole hog* the standards . . . of the majority —R. B. Kaplan⟩
whole–life \'hōl-'līf\ *adjective* (1845)
: of, relating to, or being life insurance with a fixed premium for the life of the policyholder and a cash value that can be redeemed on sale of the policy or can be the basis of low-interest loans
whole note *noun* (1597)
: a musical note equal in time value to four quarter notes or two half notes — see NOTE illustration
whole number *noun* (1557)
: any of the set of nonnegative integers; *also* **:** INTEGER
whole rest *noun* (circa 1890)
: a musical rest corresponding in time value to a whole note — see REST illustration
¹**whole·sale** \'hōl-,sāl\ *noun* (15th century)
: the sale of commodities in quantity usually for resale (as by a retail merchant)
²**wholesale** *adjective* (1642)
1 : performed or existing on a large scale especially without discrimination ⟨*wholesale* slaughter⟩
2 : of, relating to, or engaged in the sale of commodities in quantity ⟨a *wholesale* grocer⟩
³**wholesale** *adverb* (1759)
: in a wholesale manner
⁴**wholesale** *verb* **whole·saled; whole·sal·ing** (1800)
transitive verb
: to sell (something) in quantity usually for resale
intransitive verb
: to sell in quantity usually for resale
whole·sal·er \'hōl-,sā-lər\ *noun* (1857)
: a merchant middleman who sells chiefly to retailers, other merchants, or industrial, institutional, and commercial users mainly for resale or business use
whole·some \'hōl-səm\ *adjective* (13th century)
1 : promoting health or well-being of mind or spirit
2 : promoting health of body
3 a : sound in body, mind, or morals **b :** having the simple health or vigor of normal domesticity
4 a : based on well-grounded fear **:** PRUDENT ⟨a *wholesome* respect for the law⟩ **b :** SAFE ⟨it wouldn't be *wholesome* for you to go down there —Mark Twain⟩
synonym see HEALTHFUL, HEALTHY
— **whole·some·ly** *adverb*
— **whole·some·ness** *noun*
whole–souled \'hōl-'sōld\ *adjective* (1834)
: moved by ardent enthusiasm or single-minded devotion **:** WHOLEHEARTED
whole step *noun* (circa 1899)
: a musical interval (as C–D or G–A) comprising two half steps — called also *whole tone*
whole wheat *adjective* (1880)
: made of ground entire wheat kernels
who·lis·tic \hō-'lis-tik\ *variant of* HOLISTIC
whol·ly \'hō(l)-lē\ *adverb* [Middle English *hoolly,* from *hool* whole] (14th century)

1 : to the full or entire extent **:** COMPLETELY ⟨a *wholly* owned subsidiary⟩
2 : to the exclusion of other things **:** SOLELY ⟨a book dealing *wholly* with herbs⟩
whom \'hüm, üm\ *pronoun, objective case of* WHO [Middle English, from Old English *hwām,* dative of *hwā* who] (before 12th century)
— used as an interrogative or relative; used as object of a verb or a preceding preposition ⟨to know for *whom* the bell tolls —John Donne⟩ or less frequently as the object of a following preposition ⟨the man *whom* you wrote to⟩ though now often considered stilted especially as an interrogative and especially in oral use; occasionally used as predicate nominative with a copulative verb or as subject of a verb especially in the vicinity of a preposition or a verb of which it might mistakenly be considered the object ⟨*whom* say ye that I am —Matthew 16:15 (Authorized Version)⟩ ⟨people . . . *whom* you never thought would sympathize —Shea Murphy⟩ □
whom·ev·er \hü-'me-vər\ *pronoun, objective case of* WHOEVER
¹**whomp** \'hwämp, 'hwȯmp, 'wämp, 'wȯmp\ *noun* [imitative] (1926)
: a loud slap, crash, or crunch
²**whomp** (1942)
intransitive verb
: to strike with a sharp noise or thump
transitive verb
1 : to hit or slap sharply
2 : to defeat decisively **:** TROUNCE
3 : to create or put together especially hastily — usually used with *up*
whomp up *transitive verb* (1949)

☆ **SYNONYMS**
Whole, entire, total, all mean including everything or everyone without exception. WHOLE implies that nothing has been omitted, ignored, abated, or taken away ⟨read the *whole* book⟩. ENTIRE may suggest a state of completeness or perfection to which nothing can be added ⟨the *entire* population was wiped out⟩. TOTAL implies that everything has been counted, weighed, measured, or considered ⟨the *total* number of people present⟩. ALL may equal WHOLE, ENTIRE, or TOTAL ⟨*all* proceeds go to charity⟩.

□ **USAGE**
whom Observers of the language have been predicting the demise of *whom* from about 1870 down to the present day ⟨one of the pronoun cases is visibly disappearing—the objective case *whom* —R. G. White (1870)⟩ ⟨*whom* is dying out in England, where "Whom did you see?" sounds affected —Anthony Burgess (1980)⟩. Our evidence shows that no one—English or not—should expect *whom* to disappear momentarily; it shows every indication of persisting quite a while yet. Actual usage of *who* and *whom*—accurately described at the entries in this dictionary—does not appear to be markedly different from the usage of Shakespeare's time. But the 18th century grammarians, propounding rules and analogies, rejecting other rules and analogies, and usually justifying both with appeals to Latin or Greek, have intervened between us and Shakespeare. It seems clear that the grammarians' rules have had little effect on the traditional uses. One thing they have accomplished is to encourage hypercorrect uses of *whom* ⟨*whom* shall I say is calling?⟩. Another is that they have made some people unsure of themselves ⟨said he was asked to step down, although it is not known exactly *who* or *whom* asked him —*Redding (Connecticut) Pilot*⟩.

: to stir up : AROUSE

whom·so \'hüm-(,)sō\ *pronoun, objective case of* WHOSO

whom·so·ev·er \,hüm-sə-'we-vər\ *pronoun, objective case of* WHOSOEVER

¹whoop \'hüp, 'hu̇p, 'hwüp, 'hwu̇p, 'wüp, 'wu̇p\ *verb* [Middle English *whopen*, from Middle French *houpper*, of imitative origin] (14th century)
intransitive verb
1 : to utter a whoop in expression of eagerness, enthusiasm, or enjoyment : SHOUT
2 : to utter the cry of an owl : HOOT
3 : to make the characteristic whoop of whooping cough
4 a : to go or pass with a loud noise **b** : to be rushed through by acclamation or with noisy support ⟨the bill *whooped* through both houses⟩
transitive verb
1 a : to utter or express with a whoop **b** : to urge, drive, or cheer on with a whoop
2 : to agitate in behalf of
3 : RAISE, BOOST ⟨*whoop* up the price⟩
— whoop it up 1 : to celebrate riotously : CAROUSE **2** : to stir up enthusiasm

²whoop *noun* (1593)
1 a : a loud yell expressive of eagerness, exuberance, or jubilation — often used interjectionally **b** : a shout of hunters or of men in battle or pursuit
2 : the cry of an owl : HOOT
3 : the crowing intake of breath following a paroxysm in whooping cough
4 : a minimum amount or degree : the least bit ⟨not worth a *whoop*⟩

whoop–de–do *or* **whoop–de–doo** \,h(w)üp-dē-'dü, ,h(w)u̇p-, -tē-\ *noun* [probably irregular from ²*whoop*] (1929)
1 : noisy and exuberant or attention-getting activity (as at a social affair or in a political campaign)
2 : a lively social affair
3 : agitated public discussion or debate

¹whoop·ee \'(h)wu̇-(,)pē, '(h)wü-; (h)wu̇-'pē, (h)wü-\ *interjection* [irregular from ²*whoop*] (1845)
— used to express exuberance

²whoop·ee \'(h)wu̇-(,)pē, '(h)wü-\ *noun* (1924)
1 : boisterous convivial fun : MERRYMAKING — usually used with *make*
2 : sexual play — usually used with *make*

whoopee cushion *noun* (1953)
: a cushion that makes a sound like the breaking of wind when sat upon

whoop·er \'h(w)ü-pər\ *noun* (1660)
: one that whoops; *specifically* : WHOOPING CRANE

whooper swan *noun* (1880)
: a chiefly Eurasian swan (*Cygnus cygnus*) with a yellow and black bill — compare TRUMPETER SWAN

whooping cough *noun* (circa 1670)
: an infectious disease especially of children caused by a bacterium (*Bordetella pertussis*) and marked by a convulsive spasmodic cough sometimes followed by a crowing intake of breath — called also *pertussis*

whooping crane *noun* (circa 1730)
: a large white nearly extinct North American crane (*Grus americana*) noted for its loud trumpeting call

whoop·la \'h(w)üp-,lä, 'h(w)u̇p-,lä\ *noun* [alteration of *hoopla*] (1931)
1 : HOOPLA
2 : boisterous merrymaking

whoops \'(w)u̇(ə)ps\ *variant of* OOPS

whooping crane

¹whoosh \'hwu̇sh, 'wu̇sh, '(h)wu̇sh\ *noun* [imitative] (1880)
: a swift or explosive rush; *also* : the sound created by such a rush — often used interjectionally

²whoosh (1909)
intransitive verb
: to rush past or move explosively ⟨cars *whooshing* along the expressway⟩
transitive verb
: to move (a person or thing) with or as if with a whoosh

¹whop \'hwäp, 'wäp\ *transitive verb* **whopped; whop·ping** [Middle English *whappen*, alteration of *wappen* to throw violently] (15th century)
1 : to pull or whip out
2 a : BEAT, STRIKE **b** : to defeat totally

²whop *noun* (15th century)
: a heavy blow : THUMP

whop·per \'hwä-pər, 'wä-\ *noun* [¹*whop*] (circa 1785)
1 : something unusually large or otherwise extreme of its kind
2 : an extravagant or monstrous lie

whop·ping \'hwä-piŋ, 'wä-\ *adjective* (circa 1625)
: extremely large; *also* : EXTRAORDINARY, INCREDIBLE

¹whore \'hȯr, 'hȯr, 'hu̇r\ *noun* [Middle English *hore*, from Old English *hōre*; akin to Old Norse *hōra* whore, *hōrr* adulterer, Latin *carus* dear — more at CHARITY] (before 12th century)
1 : a woman who engages in sexual acts for money : PROSTITUTE; *also* : a promiscuous or immoral woman
2 : a male who engages in sexual acts for money
3 : a venal or unscrupulous person

²whore *verb* **whored; whor·ing** (1583)
intransitive verb
1 : to have unlawful sexual intercourse as or with a whore
2 : to pursue a faithless, unworthy, or idolatrous desire
transitive verb
obsolete : to corrupt by lewd intercourse : DEBAUCH

whore·dom \'hȯr-dəm, 'hȯr-, 'hu̇r-\ *noun* [Middle English *hordom* sexual immorality, idolatrous practices, from Old Norse *hōrdōmr* adultery, from *hōrr*] (12th century)
1 : the practice of whoring : PROSTITUTION
2 : faithless, unworthy, or idolatrous practices or pursuits

whore·house \'hȯr-,hau̇s, 'hȯr-, 'hu̇r-\ *noun* (14th century)
: a building in which prostitutes are available : BORDELLO

whore·mas·ter \-,mas-tər\ *noun* (14th century)
: a man consorting with whores or given to lechery

whore·mon·ger \-,məŋ-gər, -,mäŋ-\ *noun* (1526)
: WHOREMASTER

whore·son \'hȯr-sᵊn, 'hȯr-, 'hu̇r-\ *noun, often attributive* (14th century)
1 : BASTARD
2 : a coarse fellow — used as a generalized term of abuse

Whorf·ian hypothesis \'wȯr-fē-ən-, 'hwȯr-\ *noun* [Benjamin Lee *Whorf* (died 1941) American anthropologist] (1954)
: a theory in linguistics: one's language determines one's conception of the world

whor·ish \'hȯr-ish, 'hȯr-, 'hu̇r-\ *adjective* (1535)
: of or befitting a whore

whorl \'hwȯr(-ə)l, 'wȯr(-ə)l, '(h)wȯr(-ə)l\ *noun* [Middle English *wharle, worle*, probably alteration of *whirle*, from *whirlen* to whirl] (15th century)
1 : a drum-shaped section on the lower part of a spindle in spinning or weaving machinery

serving as a pulley for the tape drive that rotates the spindle
2 : an arrangement of similar anatomical parts (as leaves) in a circle around a point on an axis
3 : something that whirls, coils, or spirals or whose form suggests such movement : SWIRL ⟨*whorls* of snow⟩
4 : one of the turns of a univalve shell
5 : a fingerprint in which the central papillary ridges turn through at least one complete circle

whorled \'hwȯr(-ə)ld, 'wȯr(-ə)ld, '(h)wȯr(-ə)ld\ *adjective* (circa 1776)
: having or arranged in whorls ⟨leaves *whorled* at the nodes of the stem⟩

whor·tle·ber·ry \'hwər-tᵊl-,ber-ē, 'wər-\ *noun* [alteration of earlier *hurtleberry*, from Middle English *hurtilberye*, irregular from Old English *horte* whortleberry + Middle English *berye* berry] (1578)
1 : a European blueberry (*Vaccinium myrtillus*); *also* : its glaucous blackish edible berry
2 : BLUEBERRY

¹whose \'hüz, üz\ *adjective* [Middle English *whos*, genitive of *who, what*] (before 12th century)
: of or relating to whom or which especially as possessor or possessors ⟨*whose* gorgeous vesture heaps the ground —Robert Browning⟩, agent or agents ⟨the law courts, *whose* decisions were important —F. L. Mott⟩, or object or objects of an action ⟨the first poem *whose* publication he ever sanctioned —J. W. Krutch⟩

²whose *pronoun, singular or plural in construction* (13th century)
: that which belongs to whom — used without a following noun as a pronoun equivalent in meaning to the adjective *whose* ⟨tell me *whose* it was —Shakespeare⟩ □

whose·so·ev·er \,hüz-sə-'we-vər\ *adjective* (1611)
: of or relating to whomsoever ⟨*whosesoever* sins ye remit —John 20:23 (Authorized Version)⟩

who·so \'hü-(,)sō\ *pronoun* (12th century)
: WHOEVER

who·so·ev·er \,hü-sə-'we-vər\ *pronoun* (13th century)

: WHOEVER

who's who \ˌhüz-'hü\ *noun, often both Ws capitalized* (1917)
1 : a compilation of brief biographical sketches of prominent persons in a particular field ⟨a *who's who* of sports figures⟩
2 : the leaders of a group : ELITE; *also* : a listing of such figures

whump \'hwəmp, 'wəmp\ *intransitive verb* [imitative] (1897)
: BANG, THUMP
— **whump** *noun*

¹**why** \'hwī, 'wī\ *adverb* [Middle English, from Old English *hwȳ*, instrumental case of *hwæt* what — more at WHAT] (before 12th century)
: for what cause, reason, or purpose ⟨*why* did you do it?⟩

²**why** *conjunction* (before 12th century)
1 : the cause, reason, or purpose for which ⟨know *why* you did it⟩ ⟨that is *why* you did it⟩
2 : for which : on account of which ⟨know the reason *why* you did it⟩

³**why** *noun, plural* **whys** (14th century)
1 : REASON, CAUSE ⟨wants to know the *whys* and wherefores⟩
2 : a baffling problem : ENIGMA

⁴**why** *interjection* (1519)
— used to express mild surprise, hesitation, approval, disapproval, or impatience ⟨*why*, here's what I was looking for⟩

whyd·ah \'hwi-də, 'wi-\ *noun* [alteration of *widow (bird)*] (1783)
: any of various mostly black and white African weaverbirds (genera *Euplectes* and *Vidua*) often kept as cage birds and distinguished in the male by long drooping tail feathers during the breeding season

¹**wick** \'wik\ *noun* [Middle English *weke, wicke*, from Old English *wēoce*; akin to Old High German *wiohha* wick, Middle Irish *figid* he weaves] (before 12th century)
: a bundle of fibers or a loosely twisted, braided, or woven cord, tape, or tube usually of soft spun cotton threads that by capillary attraction draws up to be burned a steady supply of the oil in lamps or the melted tallow or wax in candles

²**wick** *transitive verb* (1949)
: to carry (as moisture) by capillary action — often used with *away* ⟨a fabric that *wicks* away perspiration⟩

¹**wick·ed** \'wi-kəd\ *adjective* [Middle English, alteration of *wicke* wicked] (13th century)
1 : morally very bad : EVIL
2 a : FIERCE, VICIOUS ⟨a *wicked* dog⟩ **b** : disposed to or marked by mischief : ROGUISH ⟨does *wicked* impersonations⟩
3 a : disgustingly unpleasant : VILE ⟨a *wicked* odor⟩ **b** : causing or likely to cause harm, distress, or trouble ⟨a *wicked* storm⟩
4 : going beyond reasonable or predictable limits : of exceptional quality or degree ⟨throws a *wicked* fastball⟩
— **wick·ed·ly** *adverb*

²**wicked** *adverb* (1980)
: VERY, EXTREMELY ⟨*wicked* fast⟩

wick·ed·ness *noun* (14th century)
1 : the quality or state of being wicked
2 : something wicked

wick·er \'wi-kər\ *noun* [Middle English *wiker*, of Scandinavian origin; akin to Swedish dialect *vikker* willow, Old Norse *veikr* weak — more at WEAK] (14th century)
1 : a small pliant twig or branch : OSIER, WITHE
2 a : WICKERWORK **b** : something made of wicker
— **wicker** *adjective*

wick·er·work \-ˌwərk\ *noun* (1719)
: work consisting of interlaced osiers, twigs, or rods ⟨a cage of *wickerwork*⟩

wick·et \'wi-kət\ *noun* [Middle English *wiket*, from Old North French, of Germanic origin; akin to Old Norse *vik* corner, *vīkja* to move, turn] (13th century)
1 : a small gate or door; *especially* : one forming part of or placed near a larger gate or door

2 : an opening like a window; *especially* : a grilled or grated window through which business is transacted
3 a : either of the two sets of three stumps topped by two crosspieces and set 66 feet apart at which the ball is bowled in cricket **b** : an area 10 feet wide bounded by these wickets **c** : one innings of a batsman; *specifically* : one that is not completed or never begun ⟨win by three wickets⟩
4 : an arch or hoop in croquet

wick·ing \'wi-kin\ *noun* (1847)
: material for wicks

wick·i·up \'wi-kē-ˌəp\ *noun* [Fox (Algonquian language of the Fox, Sauk, and Kickapoo Indians) *wiʼkiyaʼpi* house] (1852)
: a hut used by the nomadic Indians of the arid regions of the western and southwestern U.S. with a usually oval base and a rough frame covered with reed mats, grass, or brushwood; *also* : a rude temporary shelter or hut

wickiup

wid·er·shins \'wi-dər-shənz\ *adverb* [Middle Low German *wedder-sinnes*, from Middle High German *widersinnes*, from *widersinnen* to go against, from *wider* back against (from Old High German *widar*) + *sinnen* to travel, go; akin to Old High German *sendan* to send — more at WITH, SEND] (1513)
: in a left-handed, wrong, or contrary direction
: COUNTERCLOCKWISE — compare DEASIL

wid·dy \'wi-dē\ *noun, plural* **widdies** [Middle English (Scots), from Middle English *withy*] (15th century)
1 *Scottish & dialect English* : a rope of osiers
2 *Scottish & dialect English* : a hangman's noose

¹**wide** \'wīd\ *adjective* **wider; wid·est** [Middle English, from Old English *wīd*; akin to Old High German *wīt* wide] (before 12th century)
1 a : having great extent : VAST ⟨a *wide* area⟩ **b** : extending over a vast area : EXTENSIVE ⟨a *wide* reputation⟩ **c** : extending throughout a specified area or scope — usually used in combination ⟨nation*wide*⟩ ⟨industry-*wide*⟩ **d** : COMPREHENSIVE, INCLUSIVE ⟨a *wide* assortment⟩
2 a : having a specified extension from side to side ⟨3 feet *wide*⟩ **b** : having much extent between the sides : BROAD ⟨a *wide* doorway⟩ **c** : fully opened ⟨*wide*-eyed⟩ **d** : LAX 4
3 a : extending or fluctuating considerably between limits ⟨a *wide* variation⟩ **b** : straying or deviating from something specified — used with *of* ⟨the accusation was *wide* of the truth⟩
4 *of an animal ration* : relatively rich in carbohydrate as compared with protein
synonym see BROAD
— **wide·ness** *noun*

²**wide** *adverb* **wid·er; wid·est** (before 12th century)
1 a : over a great distance or extent : WIDELY ⟨searched far and *wide*⟩ **b** : over a specified distance, area, or extent — usually in combination ⟨expanded the business country-*wide*⟩
2 a : so as to leave much space or distance between **b** : so as to pass at or clear by a considerable distance ⟨ran *wide* around left end⟩
3 : to the fullest extent : COMPLETELY, FULLY ⟨*wide* open⟩

wide–an·gle \'wīd-'aŋ-gəl\ *adjective* (1878)
1 : having or covering an angle of view wider than the ordinary — used especially of lenses of shorter than normal focal length
2 : having, involving the use of, or relating to a wide-angle lens ⟨a *wide-angle* shot⟩

wide–awake \ˌwīd-ə-'wāk\ *noun* (1837)
1 : a soft felt hat with a low crown and a wide brim

2 : SOOTY TERN

wide–awake *adjective* (1818)
1 : fully awake
2 : alertly watchful especially for advantages or opportunities
synonym see WATCHFUL

wide·band \'wīd-ˌband\ *adjective* (1935)
: BROADBAND

wide–body \'wīd-ˌbä-dē\ *noun* (1968)
: a large jet aircraft

wide–eyed \'wīd-'īd\ *adjective* (1853)
1 : having the eyes wide open especially with wonder or astonishment
2 : having or marked by unsophisticated or uncritical acceptance or admiration : NAIVE ⟨*wide-eyed* innocence⟩

wide·ly *adverb* (1579)
1 : over or through a wide area ⟨has traveled *widely*⟩
2 : to a great extent ⟨departed *widely* from the previous edition⟩
3 : by or among a large well-dispersed group of people ⟨a *widely* known political figure⟩
4 : over a broad range ⟨persons with *widely* fluctuating incomes —*Current Biography*⟩

wide·mouthed \'wīd-'maůthd, -'maůth\ *adjective* (1593)
1 : having one's mouth opened wide (as in awe)
2 : having a wide mouth ⟨*widemouthed* jars⟩

wid·en \'wī-dⁿn\ *verb* **wid·ened; wid·en·ing** \'wīd-niŋ, 'wī-dⁿn-iŋ\ (1650)
transitive verb
: to increase the width, scope, or extent of
intransitive verb
: to become wide or wider
— **wid·en·er** \'wīd-nər, 'wī-dⁿn-ər\ *noun*

wide–open \'wīd-'ō-pən, -ˌō-\ *adjective* (1852)
: having virtually no limits or restrictions ⟨a *wide-open* town⟩

wide–out \'wīd-ˌaůt\ *noun* (1979)
: WIDE RECEIVER

wide–rang·ing \'wīd-ˌrān-jin\ *adjective* (1816)
: extensive in scope : COMPREHENSIVE ⟨*wide-ranging* interests⟩

wide receiver *noun* (1968)
: a football receiver who normally lines up several yards to the side of the offensive formation

wide–screen *adjective* (1931)
: of or relating to a projected picture whose aspect ratio is substantially greater than 1.33:1

wide·spread \'wīd-'spred\ *adjective* (1705)
1 : widely diffused or prevalent ⟨*widespread* public interest⟩
2 : widely extended or spread out ⟨low, *widespread* hood and fenders —*Time*⟩ ⟨a *widespread* erosion surface —C. B. Hitchcock⟩

wide–spread·ing \-ˌspre-din\ *adjective* (1591)
: stretching or extending over a wide space or area ⟨*wide-spreading* thatch roofs —*Nat'l Geographic*⟩

wid·get \'wi-jət\ *noun* [alteration of *gadget*] (1926)
1 : GADGET
2 : an unnamed article considered for purposes of hypothetical example

wid·ish \'wī-dish\ *adjective* (1845)
: somewhat wide

¹**wid·ow** \'wi-(ˌ)dō\ *noun* [Middle English *widewe*, from Old English *wuduwe*; akin to Old High German *wituwa* widow, Latin *vidua*, Sanskrit *vidhavā*, Latin -*videre* to separate] (before 12th century)
1 a : a woman who has lost her husband by death and usually has not remarried **b** : GRASS WIDOW 2 **c** : a woman whose husband leaves her alone frequently or for long periods to engage in a usually specified activity ⟨a golf *widow*⟩
2 : an extra hand or part of a hand of cards dealt face down and usually placed at the disposal of the highest bidder

3 : a single usually short last line (as of a paragraph) separated from its related text and appearing at the top of a printed page or column

²**widow** transitive verb (14th century)
1 : to cause to become a widow or widower
2 obsolete **:** to survive as the widow of
3 : to deprive of something greatly valued or needed

wid·ow·er \'wi-də-wər\ noun [Middle English widewer, alteration of wedow widow, widower, from Old English wuduwa widower; akin to Old English wuduwe widow] (14th century)
: a man who has lost his wife by death and usually has not remarried

wid·ow·er·hood \-ˌhu̇d\ noun (1796)
1 : the fact or state of being a widower
2 : the period during which a man remains a widower

wid·ow·hood \'wi-dō-ˌhu̇d, -də-\ noun (before 12th century)
1 : the fact or state of being a widow
2 : the period during which a woman remains a widow
3 : WIDOWERHOOD

widow's cruse noun [from the widow's cruse of oil that miraculously supplies Elijah during a famine (I Kings 17:8–16)] (1816)
: an inexhaustible supply

widow's peak noun (1849)
: a point formed by the hairline in front

widow's walk noun (1937)
: a railed observation platform atop a usually coastal house

width \'width, 'witth\ noun [¹wide] (1627)
1 : the horizontal measurement taken at right angles to the length **:** BREADTH
2 : largeness of extent or scope
3 : a measured and cut piece of material 〈a width of calico〉

wield \'wē(ə)ld\ transitive verb [Middle English welden to control, from Old English wieldan; akin to Old High German waltan to rule, Latin valēre to be strong, be worth] (before 12th century)
1 chiefly dialect **:** to deal successfully with **:** MANAGE
2 : to handle (as a tool) especially effectively 〈wield a broom〉
3 a : to exert one's authority by means of 〈wield influence〉 **b :** have at one's command or disposal 〈did not wield appropriate credentials —G. W. Bonham〉
— wield·er noun

wieldy \'wē(ə)l-dē\ adjective (14th century)
: capable of being wielded easily

wie·ner \'wē-nər, 'wē-nē also 'wi-nē\ noun [short for wienerwurst] (1900)
: FRANKFURTER

Wie·ner schnit·zel \'vē-nər-,shnit-səl, 'wē-nər-,snit-\ noun [German, literally, Vienna cutlet] (1862)
: a thin breaded veal cutlet

wie·ner·wurst \'wē-nə(r)-,wərst also -,wu̇rst sometimes -,wu̇sht or -,wu̇st; also with v for w\ noun [German, from Wiener of Vienna + Wurst sausage] (1889)
1 : VIENNA SAUSAGE
2 : FRANKFURTER

wie·nie \'wē-nē also 'wi-nē\ noun [by shortening & alteration from wienerwurst] (1897)
: FRANKFURTER

wife \'wīf\ noun, plural **wives** \'wīvz\ [Middle English wif, from Old English wīf; akin to Old High German wīb wife] (before 12th century)
1 a dialect **:** WOMAN **b :** a woman acting in a specified capacity — used in combination 〈fishwife〉
2 : a female partner in a marriage
— wife·hood \'wīf-,hu̇d, 'wī-,fu̇d\ noun
— wife·less \'wī-fləs\ adjective

¹**wife·like** \'wī-,flīk\ adverb (1598)
: in a wifely manner

²**wifelike** adjective (1613)
: WIFELY

wife·ly \'wī-flē\ adjective (before 12th century)
: of, relating to, or befitting a wife
— wife·li·ness \-flē-nəs\ noun

Wif·fle \'wi-f°l\ trademark
— used for a hollow plastic ball with cutouts in one hemisphere

wif·ty \'wif-tē\ adjective [origin unknown] (1979)
: DITSY

¹**wig** \'wig\ noun [short for periwig] (1675)
1 a : a manufactured covering of natural or synthetic hair for the head **b :** TOUPEE 2
2 : an act of wigging **:** REBUKE

²**wig** verb **wigged; wig·ging** (1829)
transitive verb
: to scold severely **:** REBUKE
intransitive verb
slang **:** to lose one's composure or reason **:** FLIP — usually used with out

wig·an \'wi-gən\ noun [Wigan, England] (circa 1875)
: a stiff plain-weave cotton fabric used for interlining

wi·geon or **wid·geon** \'wi-jən\ noun, plural **wigeon** or **wigeons** or **widgeon** or **widgeons** [origin unknown] (1513)
: any of several freshwater ducks (genus Anas): as **a :** an Old World duck (Anas penelope) with a large white patch on each wing and in the male with a red brown head and a buff crown **b :** BALDPATE 2

wigged \'wigd\ adjective (1777)
: wearing a wig especially of a specified kind 〈the mute, blond-wigged . . . member of the team —Current Biography〉

wigged-out \'wigd-'au̇t\ adjective (1970)
slang **:** having lost touch with reality **:** CRAZY

¹**wig·gle** \'wi-gəl\ verb **wig·gled; wig·gling** \-g(ə-)liŋ\ [Middle English wiglen, from or akin to Middle Dutch or Middle Low German wiggelen to totter; akin to Old English wegan to move — more at WAY] (13th century)
intransitive verb
1 : to move to and fro with quick jerky or shaking motions **:** JIGGLE
2 : to proceed with or as if with twisting and turning movements **:** WRIGGLE
transitive verb
: to cause to wiggle

²**wiggle** noun (1816)
1 : the act of wiggling
2 : shellfish or fish in cream sauce with peas
— wig·gly \'wi-g(ə-)lē\ adjective

wig·gler \'wi-g(ə-)lər\ noun (1859)
1 : a larva or pupa of the mosquito — called also wriggler
2 : one that wiggles

¹**wight** \'wīt\ noun [Middle English, creature, thing, from Old English wiht; akin to Old High German wiht creature, thing, Old Church Slavonic veštĭ thing] (before 12th century)
: a living being **:** CREATURE; especially **:** a human being

²**wight** adjective [Middle English, of Scandinavian origin; akin to Old Norse vīgr skilled in fighting (neuter vīgt); akin to Old English wīgan to fight — more at VICTOR] (13th century)
archaic **:** VALIANT, STALWART

wig·let \'wig-lət\ noun (1831)
: a small wig used especially to enhance a hairstyle

¹**wig·wag** \'wig-,wag\ verb [English dialect wig to move + English wag] (1892)
transitive verb
1 : to signal by wigwagging
2 : to cause to wigwag
intransitive verb
1 : to send a signal by or as if by a flag or light waved according to a code
2 : to make a signal (as by waving the hand or arm)

²**wigwag** noun (1886)
: the art or practice of wigwagging

wig·wam \'wig-,wäm\ noun [Eastern Abenaki wìkəwàm house] (1628)
: a hut of the American Indians of the Great Lakes region and eastward having typically an arched framework of poles overlaid with bark, rush mats, or hides; also **:** a rough hut

wigwam

wil·co \'wil-(ˌ)kō\ interjection [will comply] (circa 1938)
— used especially in radio and signaling to indicate that a message received will be complied with

¹**wild** \'wī(ə)ld\ adjective [Middle English wilde, from Old English; akin to Old High German wildi wild, Welsh gwyllt] (before 12th century)
1 a : living in a state of nature and not ordinarily tame or domesticated 〈wild duck〉 **b** (1) **:** growing or produced without human aid or care 〈wild honey〉 (2) **:** related to or resembling a corresponding cultivated or domesticated organism **c :** of or relating to wild organisms 〈the wild state〉
2 a : not inhabited or cultivated 〈wild land〉 **b :** not amenable to human habitation or cultivation; also **:** DESOLATE
3 a (1) **:** not subject to restraint or regulation **:** UNCONTROLLED; also **:** UNRULY (2) **:** emotionally overcome 〈wild with grief〉; also **:** passionately eager or enthusiastic 〈was wild to own a toy train —J. C. Furnas〉 **b :** marked by turbulent agitation **:** STORMY 〈a wild night〉 **c :** going beyond normal or conventional bounds **:** FANTASTIC 〈wild ideas〉; also **:** SENSATIONAL **d :** indicative of strong passion, desire, or emotion 〈a wild gleam of delight in his eyes —Irish Digest〉
4 : UNCIVILIZED, BARBARIC
5 : characteristic of, appropriate to, or expressive of wilderness, wildlife, or a simple or uncivilized society
6 a : deviating from the intended or expected course 〈wild spelling —C. W. Cunnington〉 〈the throw was wild〉; also **:** tending to throw inaccurately **b :** having no basis in known or surmised fact 〈a wild guess〉
7 of a playing card **:** able to represent any card designated by the holder
— wild·ish \'wīl-dish\ adjective
— wild·ness \-nəs\ noun

²**wild** adverb (1549)
: in a wild manner: as **a :** without regulation or control **b :** off an intended or expected course

³**wild** noun (1596)
1 : a sparsely inhabited or uncultivated region or tract **:** WILDERNESS
2 : a wild, free, or natural state or existence

wild bergamot noun (1843)
: a fragrant North American herbaceous mint (Monarda fistulosa) having a terminal capitate cluster of rather large pink or purple flowers

wild boar noun (13th century)
: an Old World wild hog (Sus scrofa) from which most domestic swine have been derived

wild card noun [wild card, playing card with arbitrarily determined value] (1972)
1 : one picked to fill a leftover playoff or tournament berth after regularly qualifying competitors have all been determined
2 : an unknown or unpredictable factor

wild carrot noun (circa 1538)
: QUEEN ANNE'S LACE

\ə\ abut \ə\ kitten \ər\ further \a\ ash \ā\ ace
\ä\ mop, mar \au̇\ out \ch\ chin \e\ bet \ē\ easy
\g\ go \i\ hit \ī\ ice \j\ job \ŋ\ sing \ō\ go
\ȯ\ law \ȯi\ boy \th\ thin \th\ the \ü\ loot \u̇\ foot
\y\ yet \zh\ vision see also Guide to Pronunciation

¹wild·cat \'wī(ə)l(d)-ˌkat\ *noun, plural* **wild-cats** (14th century)
1 a : a cat (*Felis silvestris*) of Eurasia and Africa that resembles but is heavier in build than the domestic tabby cat and is usually held to be among the ancestors of the domestic cat **b** *or plural* **wildcat :** any of various small or medium-sized cats (as the lynx or ocelot) **c :** a feral domestic cat
2 : a savage quick-tempered person
3 a : wildcat money **b :** a wildcat oil or gas well **c :** a wildcat strike
²wildcat *adjective* (1838)
1 a (1) **:** financially irresponsible or unreliable ⟨*wildcat* banks⟩ (2) **:** issued by a financially irresponsible banking establishment ⟨*wildcat* currency⟩ **b :** operating, produced, or carried on outside the bounds of standard or legitimate business practices ⟨*wildcat* insurance schemes —H. H. Reichard⟩ **c :** of, relating to, or being an oil or gas well drilled in territory not known to be productive **d :** initiated by a group of workers without formal union approval or in violation of a contract ⟨a *wildcat* strike⟩ ⟨*wildcat* work stoppages⟩
2 a *of a cartridge* **:** having a bullet of standard caliber but using an expanded case or a case designed for a bullet of greater caliber necked down for the smaller bullet **b** *of a firearm* **:** using wildcat cartridges
³wildcat *intransitive verb* **wild·cat·ted; wild·cat·ting** (1883)
: to prospect and drill an experimental oil or gas well or sink a mine shaft in territory not known to be productive
wild·cat·ter \-ˌka-tər\ *noun* (1883)
1 : one that drills wells in the hope of finding oil in territory not known to be an oil field
2 : one that promotes unsafe and unreliable enterprises; *especially* **:** one that sells stocks in such enterprises
3 : one that designs, builds, or fires wildcat cartridges and firearms
4 : a worker who goes out on a wildcat strike
wild celery *noun* (1874)
: TAPE GRASS
wil·de·beest \'wil-də-ˌbēst\ *noun, plural* **wildebeests** *also* **wildebeest** [Afrikaans *wildebees*, from *wilde* wild + *bees* ox] (1824)
: GNU
wil·der \'wil-dər\ *verb* [probably irregular from *wilderness*] (1613)
transitive verb
1 *archaic* **:** to lead astray
2 *archaic* **:** BEWILDER, PERPLEX
intransitive verb
archaic **:** to move at random **:** WANDER
— wil·der·ment \-mənt\ *noun, archaic*
wil·der·ness \'wil-dər-nəs\ *noun* [Middle English, from *wildern* wild, from Old English *wilddēoren* of wild beasts] (13th century)
1 a (1) **:** a tract or region uncultivated and uninhabited by human beings (2) **:** an area essentially undisturbed by human activity together with its naturally developed life community **b :** an empty or pathless area or region ⟨in remote *wildernesses* of space groups of nebulae are found —G. W. Gray (died 1960)⟩ **c :** a part of a garden devoted to wild growth
2 *obsolete* **:** wild or uncultivated state
3 a : a confusing multitude or mass **:** an indefinitely great number or quantity ⟨I would not have given it for a *wilderness* of monkeys —Shakespeare⟩ **b :** a bewildering situation ⟨those moral *wildernesses* of civilized life —Norman Mailer⟩
wilderness area *noun, often W&A capitalized* (1928)
: an often large tract of public land maintained essentially in its natural state and protected against introduction of intrusive artifacts (as roads and buildings)
wild–eyed \'wī(ə)ld-ˈīd\ *adjective* (1817)
1 : having a wild expression in the eyes
2 : consisting of or favoring extreme or visionary ideas ⟨*wild-eyed* schemes⟩

wild·fire \-ˌfīr\ *noun* (12th century)
1 : a sweeping and destructive conflagration especially in a wilderness or a rural area
2 : GREEK FIRE
3 : a phosphorescent glow (as ignis fatuus or fox fire)
4 : a destructive leaf-spot disease of tobacco caused by several strains of a bacterium (*Pseudomonas syringae*)
— like wildfire : very rapidly
wild·flow·er \-ˌflau̇(-ə)r\ *noun* (1797)
: the flower of a wild or uncultivated plant or the plant bearing it
wild·fowl \-ˌfau̇l\ *noun* (before 12th century)
: a game bird; *especially* **:** a game waterfowl (as a wild duck or goose)
— wild·fowl·er \-ˌfau̇-lər\ *noun*
— wild·fowl·ing \-liŋ\ *noun*
wild geranium *noun* (1840)
: a common geranium (*Geranium maculatum*) of eastern North America with deeply parted leaves and flowers of rosy purple; *also* **:** any of several related geraniums
wild ginger *noun* (1804)
: a North American perennial herb (*Asarum canadense*) of the birthwort family with a pungent creeping rhizome
wild–goose chase *noun* (1592)
: a complicated or lengthy and usually fruitless pursuit or search
wild hyacinth *noun* (1847)
: any of several plants with flowers suggestive of hyacinths: as **a :** a camas (*Camassia scilloides*) of the central U.S. and southern Ontario with white racemose flowers **b :** BLUEBELL 2a **c :** any of several western North American plants (genus *Brodiaea*) of the lily family with grasslike basal leaves and variously colored flowers
wild indigo *noun* (1744)
: BAPTISIA; *especially* **:** a tumbleweed (*Baptisia tinctoria*) with bright yellow flowers and trifoliolate leaves
¹wild·ing \'wīl-diŋ\ *noun* [¹*wild* + ²-*ing*] (circa 1525)
1 a : a plant growing uncultivated in the wild either as a native or an escape; *especially* **:** a wild apple or crab apple **b :** the fruit of a wilding
2 : a wild animal
²wilding *adjective* (1697)
: not domesticated or cultivated **:** WILD
wild·land \'wī(ə)l(d)-ˌland\ *noun* (1813)
: land that is uncultivated or unfit for cultivation
wild·life \-ˌlīf\ *noun, often attributive* (1879)
: living things and especially mammals, birds, and fishes that are neither human nor domesticated
wild·ling \-liŋ\ *noun* (1840)
: WILDING
wild·ly \'wī(ə)l(d)-lē\ *adverb* (14th century)
1 : in a wild manner ⟨was talking *wildly*⟩
2 : EXTREMELY 2 ⟨*wildly* popular⟩
wild marjoram *noun* (1550)
: OREGANO 1
wild mustard *noun* (1597)
: CHARLOCK
wild oat *noun* (15th century)
1 : any of several wild grasses (genus *Avena*); *especially* **:** a European annual weed (*A. fatua*) common in meadows and pastures
2 *plural* **:** offenses and indiscretions ascribed to youthful exuberance — usually used in the phrase *sow one's wild oats*
wild pansy *noun* (circa 1900)
: JOHNNY-JUMP-UP
wild pink *noun* (1814)
: an American catchfly (*Silene caroliniana*) of the eastern U.S. with pink or whitish flowers
wild pitch *noun* (1867)
: a baseball pitch not hit by the batter that cannot be caught or controlled by the catcher with ordinary effort and that enables a base runner to advance — compare PASSED BALL
wild rice *noun* (1748)

: a tall aquatic North American perennial grass (*Zizania aquatica*) that yields an edible grain; *also* **:** the grain
wild rye *noun* (circa 1500)
: any of several grasses (genus *Elymus*)
wild sarsaparilla *noun* (1814)
: a common North American perennial herb (*Aralia nudicaulis*) of the ginseng family with long-stalked basal compound leaves, umbels of greenish flowers, and an aromatic root used as a substitute of true sarsaparilla
wild type *noun* (1914)
: a phenotype, genotype, or gene that predominates in a natural population of organisms or strain of organisms in contrast to that of natural or laboratory mutant forms; *also* **:** an organism or strain displaying the wild type
— wild–type *adjective*
Wild West *noun* (1849)
: the western U.S. in its frontier period characterized by roughness and lawlessness
— Wild West *adjective*
wild·wood \'wī(ə)l(d)-ˌwu̇d\ *noun* (12th century)
: a wood unaltered or unfrequented by humans
¹wile \'wī(ə)l\ *noun* [Middle English *wil*, probably of Scandinavian origin; akin to Old Norse *vēl* deceit, artifice] (12th century)
1 : a trick or stratagem intended to ensnare or deceive; *also* **:** a beguiling or playful trick
2 : skill in outwitting **:** TRICKERY, GUILE
synonym see TRICK
²wile *transitive verb* **wiled; wil·ing** (14th century)
1 : to lure by or as if by a magic spell **:** ENTICE
2 [by alteration] **:** WHILE
¹will \wəl, (ə)l, ²l, 'wil\ *verb, past* **would** \wəd, (ə)d, 'wu̇d\; *present singular & plural* **will** [Middle English (1st & 3d singular present indicative), from Old English *wille* (infinitive *wyllan*); akin to Old High German *wili* (3d singular present indicative) wills, Latin *velle* to wish, will] (before 12th century)
transitive verb
: DESIRE, WISH ⟨call it what you *will*⟩
verbal auxiliary
1 — used to express desire, choice, willingness, consent, or in negative constructions refusal ⟨no one *would* take the job⟩ ⟨if we *will* all do our best⟩ ⟨*will* you please stop that racket⟩
2 — used to express frequent, customary, or habitual action or natural tendency or disposition ⟨*will* get angry over nothing⟩ ⟨*will* work one day and loaf the next⟩
3 — used to express futurity ⟨tomorrow morning I *will* wake up in this first-class hotel suite —Tennessee Williams⟩
4 — used to express capability or sufficiency ⟨the back seat *will* hold three passengers⟩
5 — used to express probability and often equivalent to the simple verb ⟨that *will* be the milkman⟩
6 a — used to express determination, insistence, persistence, or willfulness ⟨I have made up my mind to go and go I *will*⟩ **b** — used to express inevitability ⟨accidents *will* happen⟩
7 — used to express a command, exhortation, or injunction ⟨you *will* do as I say, at once⟩
intransitive verb
: to have a wish or desire ⟨whether we *will* or no⟩
usage see SHALL
— if you will : if you wish to call it that ⟨a kind of preoccupation, or obsession *if you will* —Louis Auchincloss⟩
²will \'wil\ *noun* [Middle English, from Old English *willa* will, desire; akin to Old English *wille*] (before 12th century)
1 : DESIRE, WISH: as **a :** DISPOSITION, INCLINATION ⟨where there's a *will* there's a way⟩ **b :** APPETITE, PASSION **c :** CHOICE, DETERMINATION
2 a : something desired; *especially* **:** a choice or determination of one having authority or

power **b** (1) *archaic* **:** REQUEST, COMMAND (2) [from the phrase *our will is* which introduces it] **:** the part of a summons expressing a royal command
3 : the act, process, or experience of willing **:** VOLITION
4 a : mental powers manifested as wishing, choosing, desiring, or intending **b :** a disposition to act according to principles or ends **c :** the collective desire of a group ⟨the *will* of the people⟩
5 : the power of control over one's own actions or emotions ⟨a man of iron *will*⟩
6 : a legal declaration of a person's wishes regarding the disposal of his or her property or estate after death; *especially* **:** a written instrument legally executed by which a person makes disposition of his or her estate to take effect after death
— **at will :** as one wishes **:** as or when it pleases or suits oneself
³**will** \'wil\ *verb* (before 12th century)
transitive verb
1 a : to order or direct by a will **b :** to dispose of by or as if by a will **:** BEQUEATH
2 a : to determine by an act of choice **b :** DECREE, ORDAIN ⟨Providence *wills* it⟩ **c :** INTEND, PURPOSE **d :** to cause or change by an act of will; *also* **:** to try to do so
intransitive verb
1 : to exercise the will
2 : CHOOSE
willed \'wild\ *adjective* (14th century)
1 : having a will especially of a specified kind — usually used in combination ⟨strong-*willed*⟩
2 : DELIBERATE
wil·lem·ite \'wi-lə-ˌmīt\ *noun* [German *Willemit*, from *Willem* (William) I (died 1843) king of the Netherlands] (circa 1841)
: a mineral consisting of a silicate of zinc, occurring in hexagonal prisms and in massive or granular forms, and varying in color
wil·let \'wi-lət\ *noun, plural* **willet** [imitative] (1791)
: a large American shorebird (*Catoptrophorus semipalmatus*) that resembles the greater yellowlegs but has a thicker bill and gray legs and that displays a black and white wing pattern when in flight
will·ful *or* **wil·ful** \'wil-fəl\ *adjective* (13th century)
1 : obstinately and often perversely self-willed
2 : done deliberately **:** INTENTIONAL
synonym see UNRULY
— **will·ful·ly** \-fə-lē\ *adverb*
— **will·ful·ness** *noun*
Wil·liam Tell \ˌwil-yəm-'tel\ *noun*
: an heroic archer in Swiss legend who complies with an order to shoot an apple off his son's head
wil·lies \'wi-lēz\ *noun plural* [origin unknown] (circa 1896)
: a fit of nervousness **:** JITTERS — used with *the*
will·ing \'wi-liŋ\ *adjective* (14th century)
1 : inclined or favorably disposed in mind **:** READY
2 : prompt to act or respond
3 : done, borne, or accepted by choice or without reluctance
4 : of or relating to the will or power of choosing **:** VOLITIONAL
synonym see VOLUNTARY
— **will·ing·ly** \-liŋ-lē\ *adverb*
— **will·ing·ness** *noun*
wil·li·waw \'wi-li-ˌwȯ\ *noun* [origin unknown] (1842)
1 a : a sudden violent gust of cold land air common along mountainous coasts of high latitudes **b :** a sudden violent wind
2 : a violent commotion
will–less \'wil-ləs\ *adjective* (1747)
1 : involving no exercise of the will **:** INVOLUNTARY ⟨*will-less* obedience⟩
2 : not exercising the will ⟨*will-less* slaves⟩

will–o'–the–wisp \ˌwil-ə-thə-'wisp\ *noun* [*Will* (nickname for *William*) + *of* + *the* + *wisp*] (1661)
1 : IGNIS FATUUS 1
2 : a delusive or elusive goal
— **will–o'–the–wisp** *adjective*
wil·low \'wi-(ˌ)lō\ *noun* [Middle English *wilghe, wilowe*, from Old English *welig*; akin to Middle High German *wilge* willow] (before 12th century)
1 : any of a genus (*Salix* of the family Salicaceae, the willow family) of trees and shrubs bearing catkins of apetalous flowers and including forms of value for wood, osiers, or tanbark and a few ornamentals
2 : an object made of willow wood; *especially* **:** a cricket bat
— **wil·low·like** \-lō-ˌlīk\ *adjective*
willow herb *noun* (1578)
: any of a genus (*Epilobium*) of herbs of the evening-primrose family; *especially* **:** FIREWEED 2
wil·low·ware \'wi-lə-ˌwar, 'wi-lō-, -ˌwer\ *noun* (circa 1885)
: dinnerware that is usually blue-and-white and that is decorated with a story-telling design featuring a large willow tree by a little bridge
wil·lowy \'wi-lə-wē\ *adjective* (1766)
1 : abounding with willows
2 : resembling a willow: **a :** PLIANT **b :** gracefully tall and slender
will·pow·er \'wil-ˌpau̇(-ə)r\ *noun* (1874)
: energetic determination
will to power (1907)
1 : the drive of the superman in the philosophy of Nietzsche to perfect and transcend the self through the possession and exercise of creative power
2 : a conscious or unconscious desire to exercise authority over others
wil·ly–nil·ly \ˌwi-lē-'ni-lē\ *adverb or adjective* [alteration of *will I nill I* or *will ye nill ye* or *will he nill he*] (1608)
1 : by compulsion **:** without choice
2 : in a haphazard or spontaneous manner
Wilms' tumor \'vilm-zəz-, 'vilmz-\ *noun* [Max *Wilms* (died 1918) German surgeon] (circa 1910)
: a malignant tumor of the kidney that primarily affects children and is made up of embryonic elements
Wil·son's disease \'wil-sənz-\ *noun* [Samuel A. K. *Wilson* (died 1937) English neurologist] (circa 1915)
: a hereditary disease that is determined by an autosomal recessive gene and is marked especially by cirrhotic changes in the liver and severe mental disorder due to a ceruloplasmin deficiency and resulting inability to metabolize copper
¹**wilt** \'wȯlt, 'wilt\ *archaic present 2d singular of* WILL
²**wilt** \'wilt\ *verb* [alteration of earlier *welk*, from Middle English *welken*, probably from Middle Dutch; akin to Old High German *erwelkēn* to wilt] (circa 1691)
intransitive verb
1 a : to lose turgor from lack of water ⟨the plants *wilted* in the heat⟩ **b :** to become limp
2 : to grow weak or faint **:** LANGUISH
transitive verb
: to cause to wilt
³**wilt** \'wilt\ *noun* (1855)
1 : an act or instance of wilting **:** the state of being wilted
2 a : a disorder (as a fungus disease) of plants marked by loss of turgidity in soft tissues with subsequent drooping and often shriveling — called also *wilt disease* **b :** a destructive virus disease of various caterpillars marked by visceral liquefaction and shriveling of the body
Wil·ton \'wil-tᵊn\ *noun* [*Wilton*, borough in England] (1774)

: a carpet woven with loops like the Brussels carpet but having a velvet cut pile and being generally of better materials
wily \'wī-lē\ *adjective* **wil·i·er; -est** (14th century)
: full of wiles **:** CRAFTY
synonym see SLY
— **wil·i·ly** \-lə-lē\ *adverb*
— **wil·i·ness** \-lē-nəs\ *noun*
¹**wim·ble** \'wim-bəl\ *noun* [Middle English, from Anglo-French, from Middle Dutch *wimmel* auger; akin to Middle Low German *wimmel* auger] (13th century)
: any of various instruments for boring holes
²**wimble** *transitive verb* **wim·bled; wim·bling** \-b(ə-)liŋ\ (15th century)
archaic **:** to bore with or as if with a wimble
wimp \'wimp\ *noun* [origin unknown] (1920)
: a weak, cowardly, or ineffectual person
— **wimp·i·ness** \'wim-pē-nəs\ *noun*
— **wimp·ish** \'wim-pish\ *adjective*
— **wimp·ish·ness** \-nəs\ *noun*
— **wimpy** \'wim-pē\ *adjective*
¹**wim·ple** \'wim-pəl\ *noun* [Middle English *wimpel*, from Old English; perhaps akin to Old English *wīpian* to wipe] (before 12th century)
1 : a cloth covering worn over the head and around the neck and chin especially by women in the late medieval period and by some nuns
2 *Scottish* **a :** a crafty turn **:** TWIST **b :** CURVE, BEND

wimple 1

²**wimple** *verb* **wim·pled; wim·pling** \-p(ə-)liŋ\ (13th century)
transitive verb
1 : to cover with or as if with a wimple **:** VEIL
2 : to cause to ripple
intransitive verb
1 *archaic* **:** to fall or lie in folds
2 *chiefly Scottish* **:** to follow a winding course **:** MEANDER
3 : RIPPLE
wimp out *intransitive verb* (1982)
: to behave like a wimp **:** chicken out; *especially* **:** to choose the easiest course of action
¹**win** \'win\ *verb* **won** \'wən\; **win·ning** [Middle English *winnen*, from Old English *winnan* to struggle; akin to Old High German *winnan* to struggle and probably to Latin *venus* sexual desire, charm, Sanskrit *vanas* desire, *vanoti* he strives for] (before 12th century)
transitive verb
1 a : to get possession of by effort or fortune **b :** to obtain by work **:** EARN ⟨striving to *win* a living from the sterile soil⟩
2 a : to gain in or as if in battle or contest **b :** to be the victor in ⟨*won* the war⟩
3 a : to make friendly or favorable to oneself or to one's cause — often used with *over* ⟨*won* him over with persuasive arguments⟩ **b :** to induce to accept oneself in marriage
4 a : to obtain (as ore, coal, or clay) by mining **b :** to prepare (as a vein or bed) for regular mining **c :** to recover (as metal) from ore
5 : to reach by expenditure of effort
intransitive verb
1 : to gain the victory in a contest **:** SUCCEED
2 : to succeed in arriving at a place or a state
— **win·less** \'win-ləs\ *adjective*
— **win·na·ble** \'wi-nə-bəl\ *adjective*
²**win** *noun* (1862)

\ə\ abut \ᵊ\ kitten \ər\ further \a\ ash \ā\ ace \ä\ mop, mar \au̇\ out \ch\ chin \e\ bet \ē\ easy \g\ go \i\ hit \ī\ ice \j\ job \ŋ\ sing \ō\ go \ȯ\ law \ȯi\ boy \th\ thin \t͟h\ the \ü\ loot \u̇\ foot \y\ yet \zh\ vision *see also* Guide to Pronunciation

: VICTORY; *especially* **:** first place at the finish (as of a horse race)

wince \'win(t)s\ *intransitive verb* **winced;** **winc·ing** [Middle English *wynsen* to kick impatiently, from (assumed) Old North French *wincier* to turn aside, of Germanic origin; akin to Old High German *wankōn* to totter — more at WENCH] (circa 1748)
: to shrink back involuntarily (as from pain)
: FLINCH
synonym see RECOIL
— **wince** *noun*

¹winch \'winch\ *noun* [Middle English *winche* roller, reel, from Old English *wince;* akin to Old English *wincian* to wink] (before 12th century)
1 : any of various machines or instruments for hauling or pulling; *especially* **:** a powerful machine with one or more drums on which to coil a rope, cable, or chain for hauling or hoisting
: WINDLASS
2 : a crank with a handle for giving motion to a machine (as a grindstone)

winch 1

²winch *transitive verb* (1529)
: to hoist or haul with or as if with a winch
— **winch·er** *noun*

Win·ches·ter \'win-ˌches-tər\ *adjective* [from the code name used by the original developer] (1973)
: relating to or being computer disk technology that permits high-density storage by sealing the rigid metal disks within the disk drive mechanism as protection against dust

¹wind \'wind, *archaic or poetic* 'wīnd\ *noun, often attributive* [Middle English, from Old English; akin to Old High German *wint* wind, Latin *ventus*, Greek *aēnai* to blow, Sanskrit *vāti* it blows] (before 12th century)
1 a : a natural movement of air of any velocity; *especially* **:** the earth's air or the gas surrounding a planet in natural motion horizontally **b :** an artificially produced movement of air **c :** SOLAR WIND, STELLAR WIND
2 a : a destructive force or influence **b :** a force or agency that carries along or influences **:** TENDENCY, TREND ⟨withstood the *winds* of popular opinion —Felix Frankfurter⟩
3 a : BREATH 4a **b :** BREATH 2a **c :** the pit of the stomach **:** SOLAR PLEXUS
4 : gas generated in the stomach or the intestines
5 a : compressed air or gas **b** *archaic* **:** AIR
6 : something that is insubstantial: as **a :** mere talk **:** idle words **b :** NOTHING, NOTHINGNESS **c :** vain self-satisfaction
7 a : air carrying a scent (as of a hunter or game) **b :** slight information especially about something secret **:** INTIMATION ⟨got *wind* of the plan⟩
8 a : musical wind instruments especially as distinguished from strings and percussion **b** *plural* **:** players of wind instruments
9 a : a direction from which the wind may blow **:** a point of the compass; *especially* **:** one of the cardinal points **b :** the direction from which the wind is blowing
— **wind·less** \-ləs\ *adjective*
— **wind·less·ly** *adverb*
— **before the wind :** in the same direction as the main force of the wind
— **close to the wind :** as nearly as possible against the main force of the wind
— **have the wind of 1 :** to be to windward of **2 :** to be on the scent of **3 :** to have a superior position to
— **in the wind :** about to happen **:** ASTIR, AFOOT ⟨change is *in the wind*⟩
— **near the wind 1 :** close to the wind **2 :** close to a point of danger **:** near the permissible limit
— **off the wind :** away from the direction from which the wind is blowing

— **on the wind :** toward the direction from which the wind is blowing
— **to the wind** *or* **to the winds :** ASIDE, AWAY ⟨threw caution *to the wind*⟩
— **under the wind 1 :** to leeward **2 :** in a place protected from the wind **:** under the lee

²wind \'wind\ (15th century)
transitive verb
1 : to detect or follow by scent
2 : to expose to the air or wind **:** dry by exposing to air
3 : to make short of breath
4 : to regulate the wind supply of (an organ pipe)
5 : to rest (as a horse) in order to allow the breath to be recovered
intransitive verb
1 : to scent game
2 *dialect* **:** to pause for breath

³wind \'wīnd, 'wind\ *verb* **wind·ed** \'wīn-dəd, 'win-\ *or* **wound** \'waůnd\; **wind·ing** [¹*wind*] (1586)
transitive verb
1 : to cause (as a horn) to sound by blowing **:** BLOW
2 : to sound (as a call or note) on a horn ⟨*wound* a rousing call —R. L. Stevenson⟩
intransitive verb
: to produce a sound on a horn

⁴wind \'wīnd\ *verb* **wound** \'waůnd\ *also* **wind·ed; wind·ing** [Middle English, from Old English *windan* to twist, move with speed or force, brandish; akin to Old High German *wintan* to wind, Umbrian oha*vendu* let him turn aside] (before 12th century)
transitive verb
1 a *obsolete* **:** WEAVE **b :** ENTANGLE, INVOLVE **c :** to introduce sinuously or stealthily **:** INSINUATE
2 a : to encircle or cover with something pliable **:** bind with loops or layers **b :** to turn completely or repeatedly about an object **:** COIL, TWINE **c** (1) **:** to hoist or haul by means of a rope or chain and a windlass (2) **:** to move (a ship) by hauling on a capstan **d** (1) **:** to tighten the spring of ⟨*wind* a clock⟩ (2) *obsolete* **:** to make tighter **:** TIGHTEN, TUNE (3) **:** CRANK **e :** to raise to a high level (as of excitement or tension) — usually used with *up*
3 a : to cause to move in a curving line or path **b** *archaic* **:** to turn the course of; *especially* **:** to lead (a person) as one wishes **c** (1) **:** to cause (as a ship) to change direction **:** TURN (2) **:** to turn (a ship) end for end **d :** to traverse on a curving course ⟨the river *winds* the valley⟩ **e :** to effect by or as if by curving
intransitive verb
1 : BEND, WARP
2 a : to have a curving course or shape **:** extend in curves **b :** to proceed as if by winding
3 : to move so as to encircle something
4 : to turn when lying at anchor

⁵wind \'wīnd\ *noun* (14th century)
1 : a mechanism (as a winch) for winding
2 : an act of winding **:** the state of being wound
3 : COIL, TURN
4 : a particular method of winding

wind·age \'win-dij\ *noun* [¹*wind*] (circa 1710)
1 a : the space between the projectile of a smoothbore gun and the surface of the bore **b :** the difference between the diameter of the bore of a muzzle-loading rifled cannon and that of the projectile cylinder
2 a : the amount of sight deflection necessary to compensate for wind displacement in aiming a gun **b** (1) **:** the influence of the wind in deflecting the course of a projectile (2) **:** the amount of deflection due to the wind
3 : the surface exposed (as by a ship) to the wind

wind·bag \'win(d)-ˌbag\ *noun* (1827)
: an exhaustively talkative person

wind–bell \-ˌbel\ *noun* (1901)
1 : WIND CHIME — usually used in plural

2 : a bell that is light enough to be moved and sounded by the wind

wind–blast \-ˌblast\ *noun* (1942)
: the destructive effect of air friction on a pilot ejected from a high-speed airplane

wind–blown \-ˌblōn\ *adjective* (1600)
: blown by the wind; *especially* **:** having a permanent set or character of growth determined by the prevailing winds ⟨*windblown* trees⟩

wind–borne \-ˌbȯrn, -ˌbȯrn\ *adjective* (1842)
: carried by the wind ⟨*wind-borne* pollen⟩ ⟨*wind-borne* soil deposits⟩

wind–break \-ˌbrāk\ *noun* (1861)
: a growth of trees or shrubs serving to break the force of wind; *broadly* **:** a shelter (as a fence) from the wind

wind–break·er \-ˌbrā-kər\ *noun* [from a trademark] (1918)
: an outer jacket made of wind-resistant material

wind–bro·ken \-ˌbrō-kən\ *adjective* (1603)
of a horse **:** affected with pulmonary emphysema or heaves

wind–burn \-ˌbərn\ *noun* (1925)
: irritation of the skin caused by wind
— **wind–burned** \-ˌbərnd\ *adjective*

Wind·cheat·er \'win(d)-ˌchē-tər\ *trademark*
— used for a windbreaker

wind–chill \'win(d)-ˌchil\ *noun* (1939)
: a still-air temperature that would have the same cooling effect on exposed human skin as a given combination of temperature and wind speed — called also *chill factor, windchill factor, windchill index*

wind chime *noun* (1927)
: a cluster of small often sculptured pieces (as of metal or glass) suspended so as to chime when blown by the wind — usually used in plural

wind down (1952)
intransitive verb
1 : to draw gradually toward an end
2 : RELAX, UNWIND
transitive verb
: to cause a gradual lessening of usually with the intention of bringing to an end

wind·er \'wīn-dər\ *noun* [⁴*wind*] (1552)
: one that winds: as **a :** a worker or machine that winds thread and yarn **b :** a key for winding a mechanism (as a clock) **c :** a step that is wider at one end than at the other (as in a spiral staircase)

wind·fall \'win(d)-ˌfȯl\ *noun* (15th century)
1 : something (as a tree or fruit) blown down by the wind
2 : an unexpected, unearned, or sudden gain or advantage

wind farm *noun* (1980)
: an area of land with a cluster of wind turbines for driving electrical generators

wind–flow·er \-ˌflaů(-ə)r\ *noun* (1551)
: ANEMONE 1

wind–gall \-ˌgȯl\ *noun* (circa 1534)
: a soft tumor or synovial swelling on a horse's leg in the region of the fetlock joint

wind gap *noun* (1769)
: a notch in the crest of a mountain ridge **:** a pass not occupied by a stream — compare WATER GAP

wind harp *noun* (1813)
: AEOLIAN HARP

wind–hov·er \'wind-ˌhə-vər, -ˌhä-\ *noun* (1674)
British **:** KESTREL

¹wind·ing \'wīn-diŋ\ *noun* (before 12th century)
1 : material (as wire) wound or coiled about an object (as an armature); *also* **:** a single turn of the wound material
2 a : the act of one that winds **b :** the manner of winding something
3 : a curved or sinuous course, line, or progress

²winding *adjective* (1530)

: marked by winding: as **a** : having a curved or spiral course or form ⟨a *winding* stairway⟩ **b** : having a course that winds ⟨a *winding* road⟩

wind·ing–sheet \'wīn-diŋ-ˌshēt\ *noun* (15th century)
: a sheet in which a corpse is wrapped

wind·ing–up \ˌwīn-diŋ-'əp\ *noun* (circa 1858)
British : the process of liquidating the assets of a partnership or corporation in order to pay creditors and make distributions to partners or shareholders upon dissolution

wind instrument *noun* (1582)
: a musical instrument (as a trumpet, clarinet, or organ) sounded by wind; *especially* : one sounded by the player's breath

wind·jam·mer \'win(d)-ˌja-mər\ *noun* (1880)
: a sailing ship; *also* : one of its crew
— **wind·jam·ming** \-miŋ\ *noun*

¹**wind·lass** \'win(d)-ləs\ *noun* [Middle English *wyndlas*, alteration of *wyndas*, from Old Norse *vindāss*, from *vinda* to wind (akin to Old High German *wintan* to wind) + *āss* pole; akin to Gothic *ans* beam] (15th century)
: any of various machines for hoisting or hauling: as **a** : a horizontal barrel supported on vertical posts and turned by a crank so that the hoisting rope is wound around the barrel **b** : a steam or electric winch with horizontal or vertical shaft and two drums used to raise a ship's anchor

²**windlass** *transitive verb* (1834)
: to hoist or haul with a windlass

win·dle·straw \'win-dᵊl-ˌströ, 'wi-nᵊl-\ *noun* [(assumed) Middle English, from Old English *windelstrēaw*, from *windel* basket (from *windan* to wind) + *strēaw* straw] (before 12th century)
British : a dry thin stalk of grass

¹**wind·mill** \'win(d)-ˌmil\ *noun* (14th century)
1 a : a mill or machine operated by the wind usually acting on oblique vanes or sails that radiate from a horizontal shaft; *especially* : a wind-driven water pump or electric generator **b** : the wind-driven wheel of a windmill
2 : something that resembles or suggests a windmill; *especially* : a calisthenic exercise that involves alternately lowering each outstretched hand to touch the toes of the opposite foot
3 [from the episode in *Don Quixote* by Cervantes in which the hero attacks windmills under the illusion that they are giants] : an imaginary wrong, evil, or opponent — usually used in the phrase *to tilt at windmills*

²**windmill** (1914)
transitive verb
: to cause to move like a windmill
intransitive verb
: to move like a windmill; *especially* : to spin from the force of wind

win·dow \'win-(ˌ)dō\ *noun, often attributive* [Middle English *windowe*, from Old Norse *vindauga*, from *vindr* wind (akin to Old English *wind*) + *auga* eye; akin to Old English *ēage* eye — more at EYE] (13th century)
1 a : an opening especially in the wall of a building for admission of light and air that is usually closed by casements or sashes containing transparent material (as glass) and capable of being opened and shut **b** : WINDOWPANE **c** : a space behind a window of a retail store containing displayed merchandise **d** : an opening in a partition or wall through which business is conducted ⟨a bank teller's *window*⟩
2 : a means of entrance or access; *especially* : a means of obtaining information ⟨a *window* on history⟩
3 : an opening (as a shutter, slot, or valve) that resembles or suggests a window
4 : the transparent panel or opening of a window envelope
5 : the framework (as a shutter or sash with its fittings) that closes a window opening
6 : CHAFF 4

7 : a range of wavelengths in the electromagnetic spectrum to which a planet's atmosphere is transparent
8 a : an interval of time within which a rocket or spacecraft must be launched to accomplish a particular mission **b** : an interval of time during which certain conditions or an opportunity exists ⟨a *window* of vulnerability⟩
9 : an area at the limits of the earth's sensible atmosphere through which a spacecraft must pass for successful reentry
10 : any of the areas into which a computer display may be divided and on which distinctly different types of information are displayed
◇
— **win·dow·less** \-dō-ləs, -də-\ *adjective*
— **out the window** : out of existence, use, or consideration

window box *noun* (circa 1885)
: a box designed to hold soil for growing plants at a windowsill

window dressing *noun* (1895)
1 : the display of merchandise in a retail store window
2 a : the act or an instance of making something appear deceptively attractive or favorable **b** : something used to create a deceptively favorable or attractive impression
— **win·dow–dress** \'win-dō-ˌdres\ *transitive verb*
— **window dresser** *noun*

win·dowed \'win-(ˌ)dōd, -dəd\ *adjective* (15th century)
: having windows especially of a specified kind — often used in combination

window envelope *noun* (1914)
: an envelope having an opening through which the address on the enclosure is visible

win·dow·pane \'win-dō-ˌpān, -də-\ *noun* (1819)
1 : a pane in a window
2 : TATTERSALL

window seat *noun* (circa 1745)
1 : a seat built into a window recess
2 : a seat next to a window (as in a bus or airplane)

window shade *noun* (1810)
: a shade or curtain for a window

win·dow–shop \'win-dō-ˌshäp, -də-\ *intransitive verb* (1922)
: to look at the displays in retail store windows without going inside the stores to make purchases
— **win·dow–shop·per** *noun*

win·dow·sill \-ˌsil\ *noun* (1703)
: the horizontal member at the bottom of a window opening

wind·pipe \'win(d)-ˌpīp\ *noun* (1530)
: TRACHEA 1

wind–pol·li·nat·ed \-'pä-lə-ˌnā-təd\ *adjective* (1884)
: pollinated by wind-borne pollen

wind·proof \-'prüf\ *adjective* (1616)
: impervious to wind ⟨a *windproof* jacket⟩

wind rose \'wind-ˌrōz\ *noun* [German *Windrose* compass card] (1846)
: a diagram showing for a given place the relative frequency or frequency and strength of winds from different directions

¹**wind·row** \'win(d)-ˌrō\ *noun* (circa 1534)
1 a : a row of hay raked up to dry before being baled or stored **b** : a similar row of cut vegetation (as grain) for drying
2 : a row heaped up by or as if by the wind
3 a : a long low ridge of road-making material scraped to the side of a road **b** : BANK, RIDGE, HEAP

²**windrow** *transitive verb* (1729)
: to form (as hay) into a windrow

wind–screen \'win(d)-ˌskrēn\ *noun* (1858)
1 : a screen that protects against the wind
2 *chiefly British* : WINDSHIELD

wind shake *noun* (1545)
: shake in timber attributed to high winds

wind shear *noun* (1941)

: a radical shift in wind speed and direction that occurs over a very short distance

wind·shield \'win(d)-ˌshēld\ *noun* (1902)
: a transparent screen (as of glass) in front of the occupants of a vehicle

wind sock *noun* (1928)
: a truncated cloth cone open at both ends and mounted in an elevated position to indicate the direction of the wind

Wind·sor chair \'win-zər-\ *noun* [*Windsor*, England] (1740)
: a wooden chair with spindle back, raking legs, and usually a saddle seat — called also *Windsor*

Windsor knot *noun* [probably after Edward, Duke of *Windsor*] (1947)
: a symmetrical necktie knot that is wider than the usual four-in-hand knot

Windsor tie *noun* (1895)
: a broad necktie usually tied in a loose bow

Windsor chair

wind sprint *noun* (1948)
: a sprint performed as a training exercise to develop breathing capacity especially during exertion

wind·storm \'win(d)-ˌstȯrm\ *noun* (14th century)
: a storm marked by high wind with little or no precipitation

Wind·surf·er \-ˌsər-fər\ *trademark*
— used for a sailboard

wind·surf·ing \-ˌsər-fiŋ\ *noun* (1969)
: the sport or activity of riding a sailboard
— **wind·surf** \-ˌsərf\ *intransitive verb*

wind·swept \'win(d)-ˌswept\ *adjective* (1812)
: swept by or as if by wind

wind tee *noun* (1932)
: a large weather vane shaped like a horizontal letter T on or near a landing field

wind·throw \'win(d)-ˌthrō\ *noun* (1916)
: the uprooting and overthrowing of trees by the wind

wind tunnel *noun* (1911)
: a tunnellike passage through which air is blown at a known velocity to investigate air flow around an object (as an airplane part or model) placed in the passage

◇ WORD HISTORY
window To the ancient inhabitants of cold regions around the world, a window in a dwelling was a practical feature only when glass had become available to provide light and a view while sealing the opening from the weather. Consequently, in English and other tongues of northern Europe words for "window" developed relatively late, being either borrowings from languages of the Mediterranean region, where glass was known much earlier, or entirely new coinages. A metaphor common to several northern European languages equated the window in a dwelling with the human or animal eye, both being means of seeing out. In Old English "window" was *ēagduru*, literally, "eye-door," or *ēagthyrel* "eye-hole." The latter survived into early Middle English as *eie thurl*, but was soon supplanted by *windowe*, a loan from Old Norse *vindauga*, literally, "wind eye." *Windowe* in its turn competed for a while with *fenestre*, a borrowing from the Old French descendant of Latin *fenestra*, but the French loan died out in early Modern English, leaving us with *window* as our usual word.

\ə\ abut \ᵊ\ kitten \ər\ further \a\ ash \ā\ ace
\ä\ mop, mar \aů\ out \ch\ chin \e\ bet \ē\ easy
\g\ go \i\ hit \ī\ ice \j\ job \ŋ\ sing \ō\ go
\ȯ\ law \ȯi\ boy \th\ thin \t̲h̲\ the \ü\ loot \ů\ foot
\y\ yet \zh\ vision *see also* Guide to Pronunciation

wind turbine *noun* (1909)
: a wind-driven turbine for generating electricity

¹wind·up \'wīn-ˌdəp\ *noun* (1665)
1 a : the act of bringing to an end **b :** a concluding act or part : FINISH
2 a : a series of regular and distinctive motions (as swinging the arms) made by a pitcher preparatory to releasing a pitch **b :** an exaggerated backswing (as in tennis)

²windup *adjective* (1784)
: operated by a spring mechanism wound by hand

wind up (1583)
transitive verb
1 : to bring to a conclusion : END
2 a : to put in order for the purpose of bringing to an end ⟨*winds up* the meeting⟩ **b** *British* : to effectuate a winding up
intransitive verb
1 a : to come to a conclusion **b :** to arrive in a place, situation, or condition at the end or as a result of a course of action ⟨*wound up* as millionaires⟩
2 : to make a pitching windup

¹wind·ward \'win-(d)wərd\ *noun* (1549)
: the side or direction from which the wind is blowing
— to windward : into or in an advantageous position

²windward *adjective* (1627)
: being in or facing the direction from which the wind is blowing — compare LEEWARD

wind·way \'win(d)-ˌwā\ *noun* (circa 1875)
: a passage for air (as in an organ pipe)

windy \'win-dē\ *adjective* **wind·i·er; -est** (before 12th century)
1 a (1) : WINDSWEPT (2) : marked by strong wind or by more wind than usual **b :** VIOLENT, STORMY
2 : FLATULENT 1 ⟨a *windy* bellyache⟩
3 a : VERBOSE, BOMBASTIC **b :** lacking substance : EMPTY
— wind·i·ly \-də-lē\ *adverb*
— wind·i·ness \-dē-nəs\ *noun*

¹wine \'wīn\ *noun, often attributive* [Middle English *win*, from Old English *wīn*; akin to Old High German *wīn* wine; both from Latin *vinum* wine, probably of non-Indo-European origin; akin to the source of Greek *oinos* wine] (before 12th century)
1 a : the fermented juice of fresh grapes used as a beverage **b :** wine or a substitute used in Christian communion services
2 : the usually fermented juice of a plant product (as a fruit) used as a beverage
3 : something that invigorates or intoxicates
4 : a dark red

²wine *verb* **wined; win·ing** (1829)
intransitive verb
: to drink wine
transitive verb
: to give wine to ⟨*wined* and dined his friends⟩

wine cellar *noun* (14th century)
: a room for storing wines; *also* : a stock of wines

wine cooler *noun* (1815)
1 : a vessel or container in which wine is cooled
2 : a usually carbonated beverage that contains a mixture of wine and fruit juice

wine·glass \'wīn-ˌglas\ *noun* (1709)
: a stemware drinking glass for wine

wine·grow·er \-ˌgrō(-ə)r\ *noun* (1844)
: a person who cultivates a vineyard and makes wine

wine·press \'wīn-ˌpres\ *noun* (1526)
: a vat in which juice is expressed from grapes by treading or by means of a plunger

win·ery \'wī-nə-rē, 'wīn-rē\ *noun, plural* **-er·ies** (1882)
: a wine-making establishment

wine·shop \'wīn-ˌshäp\ *noun* (1848)
: a tavern that specializes in serving wine

wine·skin \-ˌskin\ *noun* (1821)
: a bag that is made from the skin of an animal (as a goat) and that is used for holding wine

wine taster *noun* (1632)
1 : one who tastes and evaluates wine especially professionally
2 : a small shallow vessel used to sample wine

win·ey *variant of* WINY

¹wing \'win\ *noun, often attributive* [Middle English *winge*, of Scandinavian origin; akin to Danish & Swedish *vinge* wing; akin to Sanskrit *vāti* it blows — more at WIND] (13th century)

wing 1a: *1* coverts, *2* primaries, *3* secondaries

1 a : one of the movable feathered or membranous paired appendages by means of which a bird, bat, or insect is able to fly; *also* : such an appendage even though rudimentary if possessed by an animal belonging to a group characterized by the power of flight **b :** any of various anatomical structures especially of a flying fish or flying lemur providing means of limited flight
2 : an appendage or part resembling a wing in appearance, position, or function: as **a :** a device worn under the arms to aid a person in swimming or staying afloat **b :** ALA **c :** a turned-back or extended edge on an article of clothing **d :** a sidepiece at the top of an armchair **e** (1) : a foliaceous, membranous, or woody expansion of a plant especially along a stem or on a samara or capsule (2) : either of the two lateral petals of a papilionaceous flower **f :** a vane of a windmill or arrow **g :** SAIL **h :** an airfoil that develops a major part of the lift which supports a heavier-than-air aircraft **i** *chiefly British* : FENDER d
3 : a means of flight or rapid progress
4 : the act or manner of flying : FLIGHT
5 : a side or outlying region or district
6 : a part or feature usually projecting from and subordinate to the main or central part ⟨the servants' *wing* of the mansion⟩
7 a : one of the pieces of scenery at the side of a stage **b** *plural* : the area at the side of the stage out of sight
8 a : a left or right section of an army or fleet : FLANK **b :** one of the offensive positions or players on either side of a center position in certain team sports; *also* : FLANKER
9 a : either of two opposing groups within an organization or society : FACTION **b :** a section of an organized body (as a legislative chamber) representing a group or faction holding distinct opinions or policies — compare LEFT WING, RIGHT WING
10 a : a unit of the U.S. Air Force higher than a group and lower than a division **b :** two or more squadrons of naval airplanes
11 : a dance step marked by a quick outward and inward rolling glide of one foot
12 *plural* : insignia consisting of an outspread pair of stylized bird's wings which are awarded on completion of prescribed training to a qualified pilot, aircrew member, or military balloon pilot
— wingy \'win-ē\ *adjective*
— in the wings 1 : out of sight in the stage wings **2 :** close at hand in the background : readily available ⟨had a plan waiting *in the wings*⟩
— on the wing 1 : in flight : FLYING **2 :** in motion
— under one's wing : under one's protection : in one's care

²wing (1591)
transitive verb
1 a : to fit with wings **b :** to enable to fly or move swiftly
2 a : to traverse with or as if with wings **b :** to effect or achieve by flying

3 : to let fly : DISPATCH ⟨would start to *wing* punches —A. J. Liebling⟩
4 a : to wound in the wing : disable the wing of ⟨*winged* the duck⟩ **b :** to wound (as with a bullet) without killing ⟨*winged* by a sniper⟩
5 : to do or perform without preparation or guidelines : IMPROVISE ⟨*winging* it⟩
intransitive verb
: to go with or as if with wings : FLY

wing and wing *adverb* (1781)
: with sails extended on both sides

wing·back \'win-ˌbak\ *noun* (1933)
: an offensive back in football who lines up outside the tight end; *also* : the position of such a player

wing bar *noun* (1855)
: a line of contrasting color across the middle of a bird's wing made by markings on the wing coverts

wing case *noun* (1661)
: ELYTRON

wing chair *noun* (1904)
: an upholstered armchair with high solid back and sides that provide a rest for the head and protection from drafts

wing commander *noun* (1914)
: a commissioned officer in the British air force who ranks with a lieutenant colonel in the army

wing covert *noun* (1815)
: one of the feathers covering the bases of the wing quills

wing-ding \'win-ˌdin\ *noun* [origin unknown] (1944)
: a wild, lively, or lavish party

winged \'wind *also except for* 1a(2) 'win-əd\ *adjective* (14th century)
1 a (1) : having wings ⟨*winged* seeds⟩ (2) : having wings of a specified kind — used in combination ⟨strong-*winged*⟩ **b :** using wings in flight
2 a : soaring with or as if with wings : ELEVATED **b :** SWIFT, RAPID

winged bean \'wind-\ *noun* (1910)
: an Asian twining legume (*Psophocarpus tetragonolobus*) cultivated in warm regions for its edible high-protein 4-winged pods; *also* : its pod

winged elm *noun* (1820)
: an elm (*Ulmus alata*) of the U.S. having twigs and young branches with prominent corky projections

wing·er \'win-ər\ *noun* (1896)
: a player (as in soccer or ice hockey) in a wing position

wing-foot·ed \'win-'fu̇-təd\ *adjective* (1591)
1 : having winged feet
2 : SWIFT

wing·less \'win-ləs\ *adjective* (1591)
: having no wings or very rudimentary wings
— wing·less·ness *noun*

wing·let \'win-lət\ *noun* (1816)
: a small wing; *also* : a small nearly vertical airfoil at an airplane's wingtip that reduces drag by inhibiting turbulence

wing·like \-ˌlīk\ *adjective* (circa 1804)
: resembling a wing in form or lateral position

wing·man \-mən\ *noun* (1942)
: a pilot who flies behind and outside the leader of a flying formation

wing nut *noun* (circa 1900)
: a nut with wings that provide a grip for the thumb and finger

wing·over \'win-ˌō-vər\ *noun* (1927)
: a flight maneuver in which a plane is put into a climbing turn until nearly stalled after which the nose is allowed to fall while the turn is continued until normal flight is attained in a direction opposite to that in which the maneuver was entered

wing shooting *noun* (1881)
: the act or practice of shooting at game birds in flight or at flying targets

wing·span \'win-ˌspan\ *noun* (circa 1917)
: the distance from the tip of one of a pair of wings to that of the other; *also* : SPAN 2c

wing·spread \-ˌspred\ *noun* (1897)
: the spread of the wings : WINGSPAN; *specifically* : the extreme measurement between the tips or outer margins of the wings (as of a bird or insect)

wing tip *noun* (circa 1908)
1 : a toe cap having a point that extends back toward the throat of the shoe and curving sides that extend toward the shank
2 : a shoe having a wing tip
3 a : the edge or outer margin of a bird's wing **b** *usually* **wingtip** : the outer end of an airplane wing

¹wink \'wiŋk\ *verb* [Middle English, from Old English *wincian;* akin to Old High German *winchan* to stagger, wink and perhaps to Latin *vacillare* to sway, Sanskrit *vañcati* he goes crookedly] (before 12th century)
intransitive verb
1 : to shut one eye briefly as a signal or in teasing
2 : to close and open the eyelids quickly
3 : to avoid seeing or noting something — usually used with *at*
4 : to gleam or flash intermittently : TWINKLE
5 a : to come to an end — usually used with *out* **b** : to stop shining — usually used with *out*
6 : to signal a message with a light
transitive verb
1 : to cause to open and shut
2 : to affect or influence by or as if by blinking the eyes

²wink *noun* (14th century)
1 : a brief period of sleep : NAP
2 a : a hint or sign given by winking **b** : an act of winking
3 : the time of a wink : INSTANT ⟨quick as a *wink*⟩
4 : a flicker of the eyelids : BLINK

wink·er \'wiŋ-kər\ *noun* (1549)
1 : one that winks
2 : a horse's blinder

¹win·kle \'wiŋ-kəl\ *noun* [by shortening] (1585)
: ²PERIWINKLE

²winkle *intransitive verb* **win·kled; win·kling** \-k(ə-)liŋ\ [frequentative of *wink*] (1791)
: TWINKLE

³winkle *transitive verb* **win·kled; win·kling** \-k(ə-)liŋ\ [¹*winkle;* from the process of extracting a winkle from its shell] (1918)
chiefly British : to displace, extract, or evict from a position — usually used with *out*

win·ner \'wi-nər\ *noun* (14th century)
: one that wins: as **a** : one that is successful especially through praiseworthy ability and hard work **b** : a victor especially in games and sports **c** : one that wins admiration **d** : a shot in a court game that is not returned and that scores for the player making it

winner's circle *noun* (1951)
: an enclosure near a racetrack where the winning horse and jockey are brought for photographs and awards

Win·nie \'wi-nē\ *noun* [*winner* + *-ie*] (circa 1944)
: an award presented annually by a professional organization for notable achievement in fashion design

¹win·ning \'wi-niŋ\ *noun* (14th century)
1 : the act of one that wins : VICTORY
2 : something won: as **a** : a captured territory : CONQUEST **b** : money won by success in a game or competition — usually used in plural

²winning *adjective* (15th century)
1 a : of or relating to winning : that wins ⟨the *winning* ticket⟩ **b** : successful especially in competition ⟨a *winning* team⟩
2 : tending to please or delight ⟨a *winning* smile⟩
— **win·ning·ly** \-niŋ-lē\ *adverb*

win·nock \'wi-nək\ *noun* [Middle English (Scots) *windok, windowe*] (15th century)

Scottish : WINDOW

¹win·now \'wi-(ˌ)nō\ *verb* [Middle English *winewen,* from Old English *windwian* to fan, winnow; akin to Old High German *winton* to fan, Latin *vannus* winnowing fan, *ventus* wind — more at WIND] (before 12th century)
transitive verb
1 a (1) : to remove (as chaff) by a current of air (2) : to get rid of (something undesirable or unwanted) : REMOVE — often used with *out* ⟨*winnow* out certain inaccuracies —Stanley Walker⟩ **b** (1) : SEPARATE, SIFT ⟨an old hand at *winnowing* what is true and significant —Oscar Lewis⟩ (2) : SELECT
2 a : to treat (as grain) by exposure to a current of air so that waste matter is eliminated **b** : to free of unwanted or inferior elements : PARE
3 : to blow on : FAN ⟨the wind *winnowing* his thin white hair —*Time*⟩
intransitive verb
1 : to separate chaff from grain by fanning
2 : to separate desirable and undesirable elements
— **win·now·er** \'wi-nə-wər\ *noun*

²winnow *noun* (1580)
1 : a device for winnowing
2 a : the action of winnowing **b** : a motion resembling that of winnowing

wino \'wī-(ˌ)nō\ *noun, plural* **win·os** (circa 1915)
: one who is chronically addicted to drinking wine

win·some \'win(t)-səm\ *adjective* [Middle English *winsum,* from Old English *wynsum,* from *wynn* joy; akin to Old High German *wunna* joy, Latin *venus* desire — more at WIN] (before 12th century)
1 : generally pleasing and engaging often because of a childlike charm and innocence
2 : CHEERFUL, GAY
— **win·some·ly** *adverb*
— **win·some·ness** *noun*

¹win·ter \'win-tər\ *noun* [Middle English, from Old English; akin to Old High German *wintar* winter, and perhaps to Lithuanian *vanduo* water, Old English *wæter* — more at WATER] (before 12th century)
1 : the season between autumn and spring comprising in the northern hemisphere usually the months of December, January, and February or as reckoned astronomically extending from the December solstice to the March equinox
2 : the colder half of the year
3 : YEAR ⟨happened many *winters* ago⟩
4 : a period of inactivity or decay

²winter *verb* **win·tered; win·ter·ing** \'win-t(ə-)riŋ\ (14th century)
intransitive verb
1 : to pass the winter
2 : to feed or find food during the winter — used with *on*
transitive verb
: to keep, feed, or manage during the winter

³winter *adjective* (15th century)
1 : of, relating to, or suitable for winter ⟨a *winter* vacation⟩ ⟨*winter* clothes⟩
2 : sown in the autumn and harvested in the following spring or summer ⟨*winter* wheat⟩ ⟨*winter* rye⟩ — compare SUMMER

winter aconite *noun* (1794)
: a small European perennial herb (*Eranthis hyemalis*) of the buttercup family grown for its bright yellow flowers which often bloom through the snow

win·ter·ber·ry \'win-tər-ˌber-ē\ *noun* (1759)
1 : an eastern North American shrub (*Ilex verticillata*) of the holly family with clusters of axillary flowers, usually bright red berries, and deciduous leaves that turn black in the fall — called also *black alder*
2 : a shrub (*Ilex laevigata*) of the holly family similar to the winterberry but of more restricted range

winter crookneck *noun* (circa 1909)

: any of several crooknecks that are winter squashes of the pumpkin group noted for their keeping qualities

win·ter·er \'win-tər-ər\ *noun* (1783)
: one that winters; *specifically* : a winter resident or visitor

winter flounder *noun* (1814)
: a rusty brown flounder (*Pseudopleuronectes americanus* of the family Pleuronectidae) of the northwestern Atlantic important as a market fish especially in winter

win·ter·green \'win-tər-ˌgrēn\ *noun* (1548)
1 : any of a genus (*Pyrola* of the family Pyrolaceae, the wintergreen family) of evergreen perennial herbs (as the shinleafs) that have basal leaves and racemose flowers
2 a : any of a genus (*Gaultheria*) of evergreen plants of the heath family; *especially* : a low creeping evergreen shrub (*G. procumbens*) of North America with white flowers and spicy red berries — compare CHECKERBERRY **b** (1) : an essential oil from this plant (2) : the flavor of this oil ⟨*wintergreen* lozenges⟩

win·ter·ize \'win-tə-ˌrīz\ *transitive verb* **-ized; -iz·ing** (1934)
: to make ready for winter or winter use and especially resistant or proof against winter weather ⟨*winterize* a car⟩
— **win·ter·i·za·tion** \ˌwin-tə-rə-'zā-shən\ *noun*

win·ter·kill \'win-tər-ˌkil\ (circa 1806)
transitive verb
: to kill (as a plant) by exposure to winter conditions
intransitive verb
: to die as a result of exposure to winter conditions
— **winterkill** *noun*

win·ter·ly \'win-tər-lē\ *adjective* (1559)
: of, relating to, or occurring in winter : WINTRY

winter melon *noun* (circa 1900)
1 : any of several muskmelons (as a casaba or honeydew melon) that are fruits of a cultivated vine (*Cucumis melo indorus*)
2 : a large white-fleshed melon that is the fruit of an Asian vine (*Benincasa hispida*) and is used especially in Chinese cooking

winter quarters *noun plural but singular or plural in construction* (1641)
: a winter residence or station (as of a military unit or a circus)

winter savory *noun* (1597)
: a perennial European mint (*Satureja montana*) with leaves used for seasoning — compare SUMMER SAVORY

winter squash *noun* (1775)
: any of various hard-shelled squashes that belong to cultivars derived from several species (especially *Cucurbita maxima, C. moschata,* and *C. pepo*) and that can be stored for several months

win·ter·tide \'win-tər-ˌtīd\ *noun* (before 12th century)
: WINTERTIME

win·ter·time \-ˌtīm\ *noun* (14th century)
: the season of winter

win through *intransitive verb* (1644)
: to survive difficulties and reach a desired or satisfactory end

win·tle \'wi-nᵊl, 'win-tᵊl\ *intransitive verb* **win·tled; win·tling** \'win(t)-liŋ; 'wi-nᵊl-iŋ, 'win-tᵊl-\ [perhaps from Flemish *windtelen* to reel] (1786)
1 *Scottish* : STAGGER, REEL
2 *Scottish* : WRIGGLE

win·try \'win-trē\ *also* **win·tery** \'win-t(ə-)rē\ *adjective* **win·tri·er; -est** [Old English *wintrig,* from *winter*] (before 12th century)
1 : of, relating to, or characteristic of winter

\ə\ abut \ᵊ\ kitten \ər\ further \a\ ash \ā\ ace
\ä\ mop, mar \au̇\ out \ch\ chin \e\ bet \ē\ easy
\g\ go \i\ hit \ī\ ice \j\ job \ŋ\ sing \ō\ go
\ȯ\ law \ȯi\ boy \th\ thin \t͟h\ the \ü\ loot \u̇\ foot
\y\ yet \zh\ vision *see also* Guide to Pronunciation

2 a : weathered by or as if by winter **:** AGED, HOARY **b :** CHEERLESS, CHILLING ⟨a *wintry* greeting⟩
— **win·tri·ness** \'win-trē-nəs\ *noun*
winy \'wī-nē\ *adjective* **win·i·er; -est** (14th century)
1 : having the taste or qualities of wine **:** VINOUS
2 *of the air* **:** crisply fresh **:** EXHILARATING
¹**winze** \'winz\ *noun* [alteration of earlier *winds,* probably from plural of ⁵*wind*] (1757)
: a steeply inclined passageway in a mine
²**winze** *noun* [Flemish or Dutch *wensch* wish] (1785)
Scottish **:** CURSE
¹**wipe** \'wīp\ *verb* **wiped; wip·ing** [Middle English *wipen,* from Old English *wīpian;* akin to Old High German *wīfan* to wind around, Latin *vibrare* to brandish, and probably to Old Norse *veipa* to be in movement, Sanskrit *vepate* it trembles] (before 12th century)
transitive verb
1 a : to rub with or as if with something soft for cleaning **b :** to clean or dry by rubbing **c :** to draw, pass, or move for or as if for rubbing or cleaning
2 a : to remove by or as if by rubbing **b :** to expunge completely ⟨*wipe* from memory the gruesome scenes —*American Guide Series: Delaware*⟩
3 : to spread by or as if by wiping
intransitive verb
: to make a motion of or as if of wiping something
— **wipe one's boots on :** to treat with indignity
— **wipe the floor with** *or* **wipe the ground with :** to defeat decisively
²**wipe** *noun* (1550)
1 a : BLOW, STRIKE **b :** JEER, GIBE
2 a : an act or instance of wiping **b :** a transition from one scene or picture to another (as in movies or television) made by a line moving across the screen
3 : something (as a towel) used for wiping
wiped out *adjective* (1965)
slang **:** INTOXICATED, HIGH
wipe·out \'wīp-ˌaut\ *noun* (1921)
1 : the act or an instance of wiping out **:** complete or utter destruction
2 : a fall or crash caused usually by losing control
wipe out (1535)
transitive verb
: to destroy completely **:** ANNIHILATE
intransitive verb
: to fall or crash usually as a result of losing control
wip·er \'wī-pər\ *noun* (1552)
1 : one that wipes
2 a : something (as a towel or sponge) used for wiping **b :** a moving contact for making connections with the terminals of an electrical device (as a rheostat) **c :** a usually motor-driven arm with a flexible blade for wiping a window (as the windshield of an automobile or airplane)
¹**wire** \'wīr\ *noun, often attributive* [Middle English, from Old English *wīr;* akin to Old High German *wiara* fine gold work, Latin *viēre* to plait, and probably to Greek *iris* rainbow] (before 12th century)
1 a : metal in the form of a usually very flexible thread or slender rod **b :** a thread or rod of such material
2 a : WIREWORK **b :** the meshwork of parallel or woven wire on which the wet web of paper forms
3 : something (as a thin plant stem) that is wirelike
4 *plural* **a :** a system of wires used to operate the puppets in a puppet show **b :** hidden influences controlling the action of a person or organization

5 a : a line of wire for conducting electrical current — compare CORD 3b **b :** a telephone or telegraph wire or system; *especially* **:** WIRE SERVICE **c :** TELEGRAM, CABLEGRAM
6 : fencing or a fence of usually barbed wire
7 : the finish line of a race
8 : WIREHAIR
— **wire·like** \-ˌlīk\ *adjective*
— **under the wire 1 :** at the finish line **2 :** at the last moment
²**wire** *verb* **wired; wir·ing** (15th century)
transitive verb
1 : to provide with wire **:** use wire on for a specific purpose
2 : to send or send word to by telegraph
3 : to connect by or as if by a wire
intransitive verb
: to send a telegraphic message
— **wir·er** \'wīr-ər\ *noun*
wire cloth *noun* (1798)
: a fabric of woven metallic wire (as for strainers)
wired \'wīrd\ *adjective* (15th century)
1 : reinforced by wire (as for strength)
2 : furnished with wires (as for electric connections)
3 : bound with wire ⟨a *wired* container⟩
4 : having a wirework netting or fence
5 : feverishly excited
wire·draw \'wīr-ˌdrȯ\ *transitive verb* (1598)
1 : to draw or stretch forcibly **:** ELONGATE
2 : to draw or spin out to great length, tenuity, or overrefinement **:** ATTENUATE
— **wire·draw·er** \-ˌdrȯ-(ə)r\ *noun*
wire·drawn \-ˌdrȯn\ *adjective* (1603)
: excessively minute and subtle ⟨curious speculations, *wiredrawn* comparisons, obsolete erudition —Virginia Woolf⟩
wire fox terrier *noun* (1929)
: a wirehaired fox terrier
wire fraud *noun* (1976)
: fraud committed using a means of electronic communication (as a telephone)
wire gauge *noun* (1833)
1 : a gauge especially for measuring the diameter of wire or the thickness of sheet metal
2 : any of various systems consisting of a series of standard sizes used in describing the diameter of wire or the thickness of sheet metal
wire gauze *noun* (1816)
: a gauzelike wire cloth
wire grass *noun* (1751)
: any of various grasses or rushes having wiry culms or leaves: as **a :** a European slender-stemmed meadow grass (*Poa compressa*) widely naturalized in the U.S. and Canada **b :** any of several coarse grasses (genus *Aristida*) with a 3-awned lemma that grow extensively in open dry, sandy, or sterile areas especially of the southeastern and south-central U.S.
wire·hair \'wīr-ˌhar, -ˌher\ *noun* (1884)
: a wirehaired dog or cat
wire·haired \-'hard, -'herd\ *adjective* (1801)
: having a stiff wiry outer coat of hair — used especially of a dog or cat; compare ROUGH, SMOOTH
wirehaired pointing griffon *noun* (1929)
: any of a breed of dogs of Dutch origin that both hunt and retrieve and have a long head and a harsh wiry often chestnut or white and chestnut colored coat
wirehaired terrier *noun* (circa 1885)
: WIRE FOX TERRIER
¹**wire·less** \'wīr-ləs\ *adjective* (1894)
1 : having no wire or wires
2 *chiefly British* **:** of or relating to radiotelegraphy, radiotelephony, or radio
²**wireless** *noun* (1903)
1 : WIRELESS TELEGRAPHY
2 : two-way wireless transmission of sound using radio waves
3 *chiefly British* **:** RADIO

wireless telegraphy *noun* (1898)
: telegraphy carried on by radio waves and without connecting wires — called also *wireless telegraph*
wireless telephone *noun* (1894)
: RADIOTELEPHONE
wire·man \'wīr-mən\ *noun* (circa 1548)
1 : a maker of or worker with wire; *especially* **:** LINEMAN 1
2 : WIRETAPPER
wire netting *noun* (1801)
: a wire cloth coarser than wire gauze
wire·pho·to \'wīr-'fō-(ˌ)tō\ *noun* [from *Wirephoto,* a trademark] (1935)
: a photograph transmitted by electrical signals over telephone wires
wire–pull·er \-ˌpu̇-lər\ *noun* (1832)
: one who uses secret or underhanded means to influence the acts of a person or organization
— **wire–pull·ing** \-ˌpu̇-liŋ\ *noun*
wire recorder *noun* (1943)
: a magnetic recorder using a thin wire as the recording medium
— **wire–re·cord·ing** *noun*
wire rope *noun* (1841)
: a rope formed wholly or chiefly of wires
wire service *noun* (1944)
: a news agency that sends out syndicated news copy to subscribers by wire or by satellite transmission
¹**wire·tap** \'wīr-ˌtap\ *verb* (1904)
intransitive verb
: to tap a telephone or telegraph wire in order to get information
transitive verb
: to tap the telephone of
²**wiretap** *noun* (1948)
1 : the act or an instance of wiretapping
2 : an electrical connection for wiretapping
wire·tap·per \-ˌtap-ər\ *noun* (1893)
: one that taps telephone or telegraph wires
wire·work \-ˌwərk\ *noun* (1587)
1 : a work of wires; *especially* **:** meshwork, netting, or grillwork of wire ⟨plan the *wirework* for new circuitry⟩
2 : walking on wires especially by acrobats
wire·worm \-ˌwərm\ *noun* (1790)
: any of the slender hard-coated larvae of various click beetles that include some destructive especially to plant roots
wir·ing \'wīr-iŋ\ *noun* (1809)
1 : the act of providing or using wire
2 : a system of wires; *especially* **:** an arrangement of wires used for electric distribution
wir·ra \'wir-ə\ *interjection* [from Irish *a Mhuire,* literally, Mary!] (1829)
Irish — usually used to express lament, grief, or concern
wiry \'wīr-ē\ *adjective* **wir·i·er** \'wī-rē-ər\; **-est** (1588)
1 a *archaic* **:** made of wire **b :** resembling wire especially in form and flexibility **c** *of sound* **:** produced by or suggestive of the vibration of wire ⟨the violinist . . . often let his tone go nasal and *wiry* —D. J. Henahan⟩
2 : being lean, supple, and vigorous **:** SINEWY
— **wir·i·ly** \'wī-rə-lē\ *adverb*
— **wir·i·ness** \-rē-nəs\ *noun*
wis \'wis\ *verb* [by misdivision from *iwis* (understood as *I wis,* with *wis* taken to be an archaic present indicative of ¹*wit*) (1508)
archaic **:** KNOW
wis·dom \'wiz-dəm\ *noun* [Middle English, from Old English *wīsdōm,* from *wīs* wise] (before 12th century)
1 a : accumulated philosophic or scientific learning **:** KNOWLEDGE **b :** ability to discern inner qualities and relationships **:** INSIGHT **c :** good sense **:** JUDGMENT **d :** generally accepted belief ⟨challenges what has become accepted *wisdom* among many historians —Robert Darnton⟩
2 : a wise attitude or course of action

3 : the teachings of the ancient wise men
synonym see SENSE

Wisdom *noun*
: a didactic book included in the Roman Catholic canon of the Old Testament and corresponding to the Wisdom of Solomon in the Protestant Apocrypha — see BIBLE table

Wisdom of Sol·o·mon \-'sä-lə-mən\
: a didactic book included in the Protestant Apocrypha — see BIBLE table

wisdom tooth *noun* [from being cut usually in the late teens] (1848)
: the third molar that is the last tooth to erupt on each side of the upper and lower jaws in humans

¹wise \'wīz\ *noun* [Middle English, from Old English *wīse;* akin to Old High German *wīsa* manner, Greek *eidos* form, *idein* to see — more at WIT] (before 12th century)
: MANNER, WAY ⟨in any *wise*⟩

²wise *adjective* **wis·er; wis·est** [Middle English *wis,* from Old English *wīs;* akin to Old High German *wīs* wise, Old English *witan* to know — more at WIT] (before 12th century)
1 a : characterized by wisdom **:** marked by deep understanding, keen discernment, and a capacity for sound judgment **b :** exercising sound judgment **:** PRUDENT
2 a : evidencing or hinting at the possession of inside information **:** KNOWING **b :** possessing inside information **c :** CRAFTY, SHREWD
3 *archaic* **:** skilled in magic or divination
4 : INSOLENT, SMART-ALECKY, FRESH ☆
— **wise·ly** *adverb*
— **wise·ness** *noun*

³wise *verb* **wised; wis·ing** (1905)
transitive verb
: to give instruction or information to **:** TEACH — usually used with *up*
intransitive verb
: to become informed or knowledgeable **:** LEARN — used with *up*

⁴wise *transitive verb* **wised; wis·ing** [Middle English, from Old English *wīsian;* akin to Old Norse *vīsa* to show the way, Old English *wīs* wise] (before 12th century)
1 *chiefly Scottish* **a :** DIRECT, GUIDE **b :** ADVISE, PERSUADE
2 *chiefly Scottish* **:** to divert or impel in a given direction **:** SEND

-wise *adverb combining form* [Middle English, from Old English *-wīsan,* from *wīse* manner]
1 a : in the manner of ⟨crab*wise*⟩ ⟨fan*wise*⟩ **b :** in the position or direction of ⟨slant*wise*⟩ ⟨clock*wise*⟩
2 : with regard to **:** in respect of ⟨dollar*wise*⟩

wise·acre \'wī-₁zā-kər\ *noun* [Middle Dutch *wijssegger* soothsayer, modification of Old High German *wīzzago;* akin to Old English *wītega* soothsayer, *witan* to know] (1595)
: one who pretends to knowledge or cleverness; *especially* **:** SMART ALECK

wise·ass \'wīz-₁as\ *noun* (1971)
: SMART ALECK

¹wise·crack \'wīz-₁krak\ *noun* (1924)
: a clever or sarcastic remark

²wisecrack *intransitive verb* (1924)
: to make a wisecrack
— **wise·crack·er** *noun*

wised–up \'wīzd-'əp\ *adjective* (1926)
: KNOWING 1

wise guy \'wīz-₁gī\ *noun* (1896)
: SMART ALECK

wise man *noun* (before 12th century)
1 : a man of unusual learning, judgment, or insight **:** SAGE
2 : a man versed in esoteric lore (as of magic or astrology); *especially* **:** MAGUS 1b

wi·sen·hei·mer \'wī-z°n-₁hī-mər\ *noun* [²*wise* + *-enheimer* (as in family names such as *Guggenheimer, Oppenheimer*)] (1904)
: SMART ALECK

wi·sent \'vē-₁zent\ *noun* [German, from Old High German *wisant* — more at BISON] (1866)
: a European bison (*Bison bonasus*) sometimes considered conspecific with the North American buffalo (*B. bison*) — called also *aurochs*

wisent

wise·wom·an \'wīz-₁wû-mən\ *noun* (14th century)
: a woman versed in charms, conjuring, or fortune-telling

¹wish \'wish\ *verb* [Middle English *wisshen,* from Old English *wȳscan;* akin to Old High German *wunsken* to wish, Sanskrit *vāñchati* he wishes, *vanoti* he strives for — more at WIN] (before 12th century)
transitive verb
1 : to have a desire for (as something unattainable) ⟨*wished* he could live his life over⟩
2 : to give expression to as a wish **:** BID ⟨*wish* them good night⟩
3 a : to give form to (a wish) **b :** to express a wish for **c :** to request in the form of a wish **:** ORDER **d :** to desire (a person or thing) to be as specified ⟨cannot *wish* our problems away⟩
4 : to confer (something unwanted) on someone **:** FOIST
intransitive verb
1 : to have a desire **:** WANT
2 : to make a wish
synonym see DESIRE
— **wish·er** *noun*

²wish *noun* (14th century)
1 a : an act or instance of wishing or desire **:** WANT **b :** an object of desire **:** GOAL
2 a : an expressed will or desire **:** MANDATE **b :** a request or command couched as a wish
3 : an invocation of good or evil fortune on someone

wisha \'wi-shə\ *interjection* [Irish *mhuise*] (1826)
chiefly Irish — used as an intensive or to express surprise

wish·bone \'wish-₁bōn\ *noun* [from the superstition that when two persons pull it apart the one getting the longer fragment will have a wish granted] (1853)
1 : a forked bone in front of the breastbone in a bird consisting chiefly of the two clavicles fused at their median or lower end
2 : a variation of the T formation in which the halfbacks line up farther from the line of scrimmage than the fullback does

wish·ful \'wish-fəl\ *adjective* (1593)
1 a : expressive of a wish **:** HOPEFUL **b :** having a wish **:** DESIROUS
2 : according with wishes rather than reality
— **wish·ful·ly** \-fə-lē\ *adverb*
— **wish·ful·ness** *noun*

wish fulfillment *noun* (1908)
: the gratification of a desire especially symbolically (as in dreams, daydreams, or neurotic symptoms)

wishful thinking *noun* (1932)
: the attribution of reality to what one wishes to be true or the tenuous justification of what one wants to believe

wish·ing *adjective* (circa 1530)
1 *archaic* **:** WISHFUL
2 : regarded as having the power to grant wishes ⟨threw a coin in the *wishing* well⟩

wish list *noun* (1972)
: a list of desired but often realistically unobtainable items

wish–wash \'wish-₁wôsh, -₁wäsh\ *noun* [reduplication of ²*wash*] (1786)
1 : a weak drink
2 : insipid talk or writing

wishy–washy \'wi-shē-₁wô-shē, -₁wä-\ *adjective* [reduplication of *washy*] (circa 1693)
1 : lacking in character or determination **:** INEFFECTUAL
2 : lacking in strength or flavor **:** WEAK
— **wishy–wash·i·ness** *noun*

¹wisp \'wisp\ *noun* [Middle English] (14th century)
1 : a small handful (as of hay or straw)
2 a : a thin strip or fragment **b :** a thready streak ⟨a *wisp* of smoke⟩ **c :** something frail, slight, or fleeting ⟨a *wisp* of a girl⟩ ⟨a *wisp* of a smile⟩
3 *archaic* **:** WILL-O'-THE-WISP
— **wisp·i·ly** \'wis-pə-lē\ *adverb*
— **wisp·i·ness** \'wis-pē-nəs\ *noun*
— **wispy** \'wis-pē\ *adjective*

²wisp (1753)
transitive verb
1 : to roll into a wisp
2 : to make wisps of ⟨a cigarette *wisping* smoke at the corner of his mouth —Raymond Chandler⟩
intransitive verb
: to emerge or drift in wisps ⟨her hair began to *wisp* into her eyes —Mary Manning⟩

wisp·ish \'wis-pish\ *adjective* (1896)
: resembling a wisp **:** INSUBSTANTIAL

wist \'wist\ *transitive verb* [alteration of *wis*] (1508)
archaic **:** KNOW

wis·te·ria \wis-'tir-ē-ə\ *or* **wis·tar·ia** \-'tir-ē-ə *also* -'ter-\ *noun* [New Latin *Wisteria,* from Caspar *Wistar* (died 1818) American physician] (1842)
: any of a genus (*Wisteria*) of chiefly Asian mostly woody leguminous vines that have pinnately compound leaves and long racemes of showy blue, white, purple, or rose papilionaceous flowers and that include several grown as ornamentals

wist·ful \'wist-fəl\ *adjective* [blend of *wishful* and obsolete English *wistly* intently] (1714)
1 : full of yearning or desire tinged with melancholy; *also* **:** inspiring such yearning ⟨a *wistful* memoir⟩

wisteria

☆ **SYNONYMS**
Wise, sage, sapient, judicious, prudent, sensible, sane mean having or showing sound judgment. WISE suggests great understanding of people and of situations and unusual discernment and judgment in dealing with them ⟨*wise* beyond his tender years⟩. SAGE suggests wide experience, great learning, and wisdom ⟨the *sage* advice of my father⟩. SAPIENT suggests great sagacity and discernment ⟨the *sapient* musings of an old philosopher⟩. JUDICIOUS stresses a capacity for reaching wise decisions or just conclusions ⟨*judicious* parents using kindness and discipline in equal measure⟩. PRUDENT suggests exercise of the restraint of sound practical wisdom and discretion ⟨a *prudent* decision to wait out the storm⟩. SENSIBLE applies to action guided and restrained by good sense and rationality ⟨a *sensible* woman who was not fooled by flattery⟩. SANE stresses mental soundness, rationality, and levelheadedness ⟨remained *sane* even in times of crises⟩.

\ə\ **abut** \°\ **kitten** \ər\ **further** \a\ **ash** \ā\ **ace**
\ä\ **mop, mar** \aù\ **out** \ch\ **chin** \e\ **bet** \ē\ **easy**
\g\ **go** \i\ **hit** \ī\ **ice** \j\ **job** \ŋ\ **sing** \ō\ **go**
\ò\ **law** \òi\ **boy** \th\ **thin** \th\ **the** \ü\ **loot** \ù\ **foot**
\y\ **yet** \zh\ **vision** *see also* Guide to Pronunciation

2 : musingly sad **: PENSIVE**
— **wist·ful·ly** \-fə-lē\ *adverb*
— **wist·ful·ness** *noun*

¹wit \'wit\ *verb* **wist** \'wist\; **wit·ting** *present 1st & 3d singular* **wot** \'wät\ [Middle English *witen* (1st & 3d singular present *wot,* past *wiste*), from Old English *witan* (1st & 3d singular present *wāt,* past *wisse, wiste*); akin to Old High German *wizzan* to know, Latin *vidēre* to see, Greek *eidenai* to know, *idein* to see] (before 12th century)
1 *archaic* **: KNOW**
2 *archaic* **:** to come to know **: LEARN**

²wit *noun* [Middle English, from Old English; akin to Old High German *wizzi* knowledge, Old English *witan* to know] (before 12th century)
1 a : MIND, MEMORY **b :** reasoning power **: INTELLIGENCE**
2 a : SENSE 2a — usually used in plural (alone and warming his five *wits,* the white owl in the belfry sits —Alfred Tennyson) **b** (1) **:** mental soundness **: SANITY** — usually used in plural (2) **:** mental capability and resourcefulness **: INGENUITY**
3 a : astuteness of perception or judgment **: ACUMEN b :** the ability to relate seemingly disparate things so as to illuminate or amuse **c** (1) **:** a talent for banter or persiflage (2) **:** a witty utterance or exchange **d :** clever or apt humor
4 a : a person of superior intellect **: THINKER b :** an imaginatively perceptive and articulate individual especially skilled in banter or persiflage ☆
— **at one's wit's end** *or* **at one's wits' end :** at a loss for a means of solving a problem

wi·tan \'wi-ˌtän\ *noun plural* [Old English, plural of *wita* sage, adviser; akin to Old High German *wizzo* sage; akin to Old High German *witan* to know] (1807)
: members of the witenagemot

¹witch \'wich\ *noun* [Middle English *wicche,* from Old English *wicca,* masculine, wizard & *wicce,* feminine, witch; akin to Middle High German *wicken* to bewitch, Old English *wigle* divination, and perhaps to Old High German *wīh* holy — more at VICTIM] (before 12th century)
1 : one that is credited with usually malignant supernatural powers; *especially* **:** a woman practicing usually black witchcraft often with the aid of a devil or familiar **: SORCERESS** — compare WARLOCK
2 : an ugly old woman **: HAG**
3 : a charming or alluring girl or woman
— **witch·like** \'wich-ˌlīk\ *adjective*
— **witchy** \'wi-chē\ *adjective*

²witch (14th century)
transitive verb
1 : to affect injuriously with witchcraft
2 *archaic* **:** to influence or beguile with allure or charm
intransitive verb
: DOWSE

witch·craft \'wich-ˌkraft\ *noun* (before 12th century)
1 a : the use of sorcery or magic **b :** communication with the devil or with a familiar
2 : an irresistible influence or fascination

witch doctor *noun* (1718)
: a professional worker of magic usually in a primitive society who often works to cure sickness

witch·ery \'wi-chə-rē, 'wich-rē\ *noun, plural* **-er·ies** (1546)
1 a : the practice of witchcraft **: SORCERY b :** an act of witchcraft
2 : an irresistible fascination

witches' brew *noun* (1929)
: a potent or fearsome mixture (a *witches' brew* of untamed sex and brutality —Harrison Smith)

witch·es'–broom \'wi-chəz-ˌbrüm, -ˌbrum\ *noun* (1881)

: an abnormal tufted growth of small branches on a tree or shrub caused especially by fungi or viruses

witches' Sabbath *noun* (circa 1676)
: a midnight assembly of witches, devils, and sorcerers for the celebration of rites and orgies

witch·grass \'wich-ˌgras\ *noun* [probably alteration of *quitch (grass)*] (1790)
1 : QUACK GRASS
2 [¹*witch*] **:** a North American grass (*Panicum capillare*) with slender brushy panicles that is often a weed on cultivated land

witch ha·zel \'wich-ˌhā-zəl\ *noun* [*witch,* a tree with pliant branches, from Middle English *wyche,* from Old English *wice;* probably akin to Old English *wīcan* to yield — more at WEAK] (circa 1542)
1 : any of a genus (*Hamamelis* of the family Hamamelidaceae, the witch-hazel family) of shrubs or small trees with slender-petaled yellow flowers borne in late fall or early spring; *especially* **:** one (*H. virginiana*) of eastern North America that blooms in the fall
2 : an alcoholic solution of a distillate of the bark of a witch hazel (*H. virginiana*) used as a soothing and mildly astringent lotion

witch–hunt \'wich-ˌhənt\ *noun* (1885)
1 : a searching out for persecution of persons accused of witchcraft
2 : the searching out and deliberate harassment of those (as political opponents) with unpopular views
— **witch–hunt·er** *noun*
— **witch–hunt·ing** *noun or adjective*

¹witch·ing \'wi-chiŋ\ *noun* (before 12th century)
: the practice of witchcraft **: SORCERY**

²witching *adjective* (14th century)
: of, relating to, or suitable for sorcery or supernatural occurrences (the very *witching* time of night —Shakespeare)

witch of Agne·si \-ˌän-'yä-zē\ *noun* [Maria Gaetana *Agnesi* (died 1799) Italian mathematician; *witch,* translation of Italian *versiera* cubic curve (influenced by Italian *versiera* female demon)] (1875)
: a plane cubic curve that is symmetric about the y-axis and approaches the x-axis as an asymptote that is constructed by drawing lines from the origin intersecting an upright circle tangent to the x-axis at the origin and taking the locus of points of intersection of pairs of lines parallel to the x-axis and y-axis each pair of which consists of a line parallel to the x-axis through the point where a line through the origin intersects the circle and a line parallel to the y-axis through the point where the same line through the origin intersects the line parallel to the x-axis through the point of intersection of the circle and the y-axis and that has the equation $x^2y = 4a^2(2a - y)$ — called also WITCH

witch·weed \'wich-ˌwēd\ *noun* (1904)
: any of a genus (*Striga*) of yellow-flowered Old World plants of the snapdragon family that are damaging root parasites of grasses (as sorghum and maize) and that include one (*S. lutea*) which is an introduced pest in parts of the southeastern U.S.

¹wite \'wīt\ *transitive verb* **wit·ed; wit·ing** [Middle English, from Old English *wītan;* akin to Old High German *wīzan* to blame, Old English *witan* to know] (before 12th century)
chiefly Scottish **: BLAME**

²wite *noun* (13th century)
chiefly Scottish **: BLAME, RESPONSIBILITY**

wi·te·na·ge·mot *or* **wi·te·na·ge·mote** \'wi-tᵊn-ə-gə-ˌmōt, -yə-ˌmōt\ *noun* [Old English *witena gemōt,* from *witena* (genitive plural of *wita* sage, adviser) + *gemōt* gemot] (before 12th century)
: an Anglo-Saxon council made up of a varying number of nobles, prelates, and influential officials and convened from time to time to advise the king on administrative and judicial matters

with \'with, 'with, wəth, wəth\ *preposition* [Middle English, against, from, with, from Old English; akin to Old English *wither* against, Old High German *widar* against, back, Sanskrit *vi* apart] (before 12th century)
1 a : in opposition to **: AGAINST** (had a fight *with* his brother) **b :** so as to be separated or detached from (broke *with* her family)
2 a — used as a function word to indicate a participant in an action, transaction, or arrangement (works *with* his father) (a talk *with* a friend) (got into an accident *with* the car) **b** — used as a function word to indicate the object of attention, behavior, or feeling (get tough *with* him) (angry *with* me) **c :** in respect to **:** so far as concerns (on friendly terms *with* all nations) **d** — used to indicate the object of an adverbial expression of imperative force (off *with* his head) **e :** OVER, ON (no longer has any influence *with* them) **f :** in the performance, operation, or use of (the trouble *with* this machine)
3 a — used as a function word to indicate the object of a statement of comparison or equality (a dress identical *with* her hostess's) **b** — used as a function word to express agreement or sympathy (must conclude, *with* you, that the painting is a forgery) **c :** on the side of **:** FOR (if he's for lower taxes, I'm *with* him) **:** as well as (can pitch *with* the best of them)
4 a — used as a function word to indicate combination, accompaniment, presence, or addition (heat milk *with* honey) (went there *with* her) (his money, *with* his wife's, comes to a million) **b :** inclusive of (costs $5 *with* the tax)
5 a : in the judgment or estimation of (stood well *with* her classmates) **b :** in or according to the experience or practice of (*with* many of us, our ideas seem to fall by the wayside —W. J. Reilly)
6 a — used as a function word to indicate the means, cause, agent, or instrumentality (hit him *with* a rock) (pale *with* anger) (threatened *with* tuberculosis) (he amused the crowd *with* his antics) **b** *archaic* **:** by the direct act of
7 a — used as a function word to indicate manner of action (ran *with* effort) (acknowledge your contribution *with* thanks) **b** — used as a function word to indicate an attendant fact or circumstance (stood there *with* his hat on) **c** — used as a function word to indicate a result attendant on a specified action (got off *with* a light sentence)
8 a (1) **:** in possession of **: HAVING** (came *with* good news) (2) **:** in the possession or care of (left the money *with* her mother) **b :** characterized or distinguished by (a person *with* a sharp nose)

9 a — used as a function word to indicate a close association in time ⟨*with* the outbreak of war they went home⟩ ⟨mellows *with* time⟩ **b** : in proportion to ⟨the pressure varies *with* the depth⟩

10 a : in spite of : NOTWITHSTANDING ⟨a really tip-top man, *with* all his wrongheadedness —H. J. Laski⟩ **b** : except for ⟨finds that, *with* one group of omissions and one important addition, they reflect that curriculum —Gilbert Highet⟩

11 : in the direction of ⟨*with* the wind⟩ ⟨*with* the grain⟩

¹with·al \wi-ˈthȯl, -ˈthȯl\ *adverb* [Middle English, from *with* + *all, al* all] (13th century)
1 : together with this : BESIDES ⟨a supporter of all constructive work and *withal* an excellent businessman —A. W. Long⟩
2 *archaic* : THEREWITH 1
3 : on the other hand : NEVERTHELESS

²withal *preposition* (14th century)
archaic : WITH — used postpositively with a relative or interrogative pronoun as object

with·draw \with-ˈdrȯ, with-\ *verb* **-drew** \-ˈdrü\; **-drawn** \-ˈdrȯn\; **-draw·ing** \-ˈdrȯ(-)iŋ\ [Middle English, from *with* from + *drawen* to draw] (13th century)
transitive verb
1 a : to take back or away : REMOVE ⟨pressure upon educational administrators to *withdraw* academic credit —J. W. Scott⟩ **b** : to remove from use or cultivation **c** : to remove (money) from a place of deposit **d** : to turn away (as the eyes) from an object of attention ⟨*withdrew* her gaze⟩ **e** : to draw (as a curtain) back or aside
2 a : to remove from consideration or set outside a group ⟨*withdrew* his name from the list of nominees⟩ ⟨*withdrew* their child from the school⟩ **b** (1) : TAKE BACK, RETRACT (2) : to recall or remove (a motion) under parliamentary procedure
intransitive verb
1 a : to move back or away : RETIRE **b** : to draw back from a battlefield : RETREAT
2 a : to remove oneself from participation **b** : to become socially or emotionally detached ⟨had *withdrawn* farther and farther into herself —Ethel Wilson⟩
3 : to recall a motion under parliamentary procedure
— **with·draw·able** \-ˈdrȯ-ə-bəl\ *adjective*

with·draw·al \-ˈdrȯ(-ə)l\ *noun* (1749)
1 a : the act of taking back or away something that has been granted or possessed **b** : removal from a place of deposit or investment **c** (1) : the discontinuance of administration or use of a drug (2) : a period following the discontinuance of an addicting drug that is marked by often painful physical and psychological symptoms ⟨a heroin addict going through *withdrawal*⟩
2 a : retreat or retirement especially into a more secluded or less exposed place or position **b** : an operation by which a military force disengages from the enemy **c** (1) : social or emotional detachment (2) : a pathological retreat from objective reality (as in some schizophrenic states)
3 : RETRACTION, REVOCATION ⟨threatened us with *withdrawal* of consent⟩
4 a : the act of drawing someone or something back from or out of a place or position **b** : COITUS INTERRUPTUS

withdrawing room *noun* (1591)
: a room to retire to (as from a dining room); *especially* : DRAWING ROOM

with·drawn \with-ˈdrȯn, with-\ *adjective* (1615)
1 : removed from immediate contact or easy approach : ISOLATED
2 : socially detached and unresponsive : exhibiting withdrawal : INTROVERTED
— **with·drawn·ness** \-ˈdrȯn-nəs\ *noun*

withe \ˈwith, ˈwith, ˈwīth\ *noun* [Middle English, from Old English *withthe;* akin to Old English *wīthig* withy] (before 12th century)
: a slender flexible branch or twig; *especially* : one used as a band or line

¹with·er \ˈwi-thər\ *verb* **with·ered; with·er·ing** \ˈwith-riŋ, ˈwi-thə-\ [Middle English *widren;* probably akin to Middle English *weder* weather] (14th century)
intransitive verb
1 : to become dry and sapless; *especially* : to shrivel from or as if from loss of bodily moisture
2 : to lose vitality, force, or freshness
transitive verb
1 : to cause to wither
2 : to make speechless or incapable of action : STUN ⟨*withered* him with a look —Dorothy Sayers⟩

²wither *noun* (1607)
chiefly British : WITHERS

withering *adjective* (1579)
: acting or serving to cut down or destroy : DEVASTATING ⟨a *withering* fire from the enemy⟩
— **with·er·ing·ly** \ˈwith-riŋ-lē, ˈwi-thə-\ *adverb*

with·er·ite \ˈwi-thə-ˌrīt\ *noun* [German *Witherit,* irregular from William *Withering* (died 1799) English physician] (1794)
: a mineral consisting of a carbonate of barium in the form of white or gray twin crystals or columnar or granular masses

withe rod *noun* (1846)
: a North American viburnum (*Viburnum cassinoides*) with tough slender shoots

with·ers \ˈwi-thərz\ *noun plural* [probably from obsolete English *wither-* against, from Middle English, from Old English, from *wither* against; from the withers being the parts which resist the pull in drawing a load — more at WITH] (1580)
1 : the ridge between the shoulder bones of a horse — see HORSE illustration
2 : a part corresponding to the withers in a quadruped other than a horse

with·er·shins \ˈwi-thər-shənz\ *variant of* WIDDERSHINS

with·hold \with-ˈhōld, with-\ *verb* **-held** \-ˈheld\; **-hold·ing** [Middle English, from *with* from + *holden* to hold — more at WITH] (13th century)
transitive verb
1 : to hold back from action : CHECK
2 *archaic* : to keep in custody
3 : to refrain from granting, giving, or allowing ⟨*withhold* permission⟩
4 : to deduct (withholding tax) from income
intransitive verb
: FORBEAR, REFRAIN
synonym see KEEP
— **with·hold·er** *noun*

withholding tax *noun* (1940)
: a deduction (as from wages, fees, or dividends) levied at a source of income as advance payment on income tax

¹with·in \wi-ˈthin, -ˈthin\ *adverb* [Middle English *withinne,* from Old English *withinnan,* from *with* + *innan* inwardly, within, from *in*] (before 12th century)
1 : in or into the interior : INSIDE
2 : in one's inner thought, disposition, or character : INWARDLY ⟨search *within* for a creative impulse —Kingman Brewster, Jr.⟩

²within *preposition* (12th century)
1 — used as a function word to indicate enclosure or containment
2 — used as a function word to indicate situation or circumstance in the limits or compass of: as **a** : before the end of ⟨gone *within* a week⟩ **b** (1) : not beyond the quantity, degree, or limitations of ⟨live *within* your income⟩ (2) : in or into the scope or sphere of ⟨*within* the jurisdiction of the state⟩ (3) : in or into the range of ⟨*within* reach⟩ ⟨*within* sight⟩ (4) — used as a function word to indicate a specified

difference or margin ⟨came *within* two points of a perfect mark⟩ ⟨*within* a mile of the town⟩
3 : to the inside of : INTO

³within *noun* (15th century)
: an inner place or area ⟨revolt from *within*⟩

⁴within *adjective* (1748)
: being inside : ENCLOSED ⟨the *within* indictment⟩

with·in·doors \wi-ˌthin-ˈdȯrz, -ˌthin-, -ˈdȯrz\ *adverb* (1581)
: INDOORS

with·it \ˈwi-thət, -thət\ *adjective* (1959)
: socially or culturally up-to-date ⟨the intelligent, disaffected, *with-it* young —Eliot Fremont-Smith⟩

¹with·out \wi-ˈthaut, -ˈthaut\ *preposition* [Middle English *withoute,* from Old English *withūtan,* from *with* + *ūtan* outside, from *ūt* out — more at OUT] (before 12th century)
1 : OUTSIDE
2 — used as a function word to indicate the absence or lack of something or someone ⟨fight *without* fear⟩ ⟨left *without* him⟩ ⟨looks *without* seeing⟩

²without *adverb* (before 12th century)
1 : on the outside : EXTERNALLY
2 : with something lacking or absent ⟨has learned to do *without*⟩

³without *conjunction* (14th century)
chiefly dialect : UNLESS ⟨you don't know about me *without* you have read a book —Mark Twain⟩

⁴without *noun* (15th century)
: an outer place or area ⟨came from *without*⟩

with·out·doors \wi-ˌthaut-ˈdȯrz, -ˌthaut-\ *adverb* (1617)
: OUTDOORS

with·stand \with-ˈstand, with-\ *transitive verb* **-stood** \-ˈstud\; **-stand·ing** [Middle English, from Old English *withstandan,* from *with* against + *standan* to stand] (before 12th century)
1 a : to stand up against : oppose with firm determination; *especially* : to resist successfully **b** : to be proof against : resist the effect of ⟨*withstand* the impact of a landing —Current Biography⟩
2 *archaic* : to stop or obstruct the course of
synonym see OPPOSE

¹withy \ˈwi-thē\ *noun, plural* **with·ies** [Middle English, from Old English *wīthig;* akin to Old High German *wīda* willow, Latin *vitis* vine, *viēre* to plait — more at WIRE] (before 12th century)
1 : WILLOW; *especially* : OSIER 1
2 : a flexible slender twig or branch (as of osier) : WITHE

²withy \ˈwi-thē, ˈwi-thē, ˈwī-thē\ *adjective* [*withe*] (1598)
: flexibly tough

wit·less \ˈwit-ləs\ *adjective* (before 12th century)
1 : destitute of wit or understanding : FOOLISH
2 : mentally deranged : CRAZY ⟨drive one *witless* with anxiety —William Styron⟩
— **wit·less·ly** *adverb*
— **wit·less·ness** *noun*

wit·ling \-liŋ\ *noun* (1693)
1 : a would-be wit
2 : a person of little wit

wit·loof \ˈwit-ˌlōf, -ˌlüf\ *noun* [Dutch dialect *witloof* chicory, from Dutch *wit* white + *loof* foliage] (1885)
: CHICORY 1; *also* : ENDIVE 2

¹wit·ness \ˈwit-nəs\ *noun* [Middle English *witnesse,* from Old English *witnes* knowledge, testimony, witness, from ²*wit*] (before 12th century)
1 : attestation of a fact or event : TESTIMONY

2 : one that gives evidence; *specifically* **:** one who testifies in a cause or before a judicial tribunal
3 : one asked to be present at a transaction so as to be able to testify to its having taken place
4 : one who has personal knowledge of something
5 a : something serving as evidence or proof **:** SIGN **b :** public affirmation by word or example of usually religious faith or conviction ⟨the heroic *witness* to divine life —*Pilot*⟩
6 *capitalized* **:** a member of the Jehovah's Witnesses

²witness (14th century)
transitive verb
1 : to testify to **:** ATTEST
2 : to act as legal witness of
3 : to furnish proof of **:** BETOKEN
4 a : to have personal or direct cognizance of **:** see for oneself ⟨*witnessed* the historic event⟩ **b :** to take note of ⟨our grammar — *witness* our verb system—is a marvel of flexibility, variety, and exactitude —Charlton Laird⟩
5 : to constitute the scene or time of ⟨structures . . . which this striking Dorset hilltop once *witnessed* —*Times Literary Supplement*⟩
intransitive verb
1 : to bear witness **:** TESTIFY
2 : to bear witness to one's religious convictions ⟨opportunity to *witness* for Christ —Billy Graham⟩
synonym see CERTIFY

wit·ness–box \-ˌbäks\ *noun* (1806)
chiefly British **:** an enclosure in which a witness sits or stands while testifying in court

witness stand *noun* (1853)
: a stand or an enclosure from which a witness gives evidence in a court

wit·ted \'wi-təd\ *adjective* (14th century)
: having wit or understanding — usually used in combination ⟨dull-*witted*⟩ ⟨quick-*witted*⟩

wit·ti·cism \'wi-tə-ˌsi-zəm\ *noun* [*witty* + *-cism* (as in *criticism*)] (1651)
: a cleverly witty and often biting or ironic remark

¹wit·ting \'wi-tⁿn, -tiŋ\ *noun* (14th century)
1 *chiefly dialect* **:** knowledge or awareness of something **:** COGNIZANCE
2 *chiefly dialect* **:** information obtained or communicated **:** NEWS

²wit·ting \-tiŋ\ *adjective* (circa 1520)
1 : cognizant or aware of something **:** CONSCIOUS
2 : done deliberately **:** INTENTIONAL
— **wit·ting·ly** \-tiŋ-lē\ *adverb*

wit·tol \'wi-tⁿl\ *noun* [Middle English *wetewold*, from *weten, witen* to know + *cokewold* cuckold — more at WIT] (15th century)
1 *archaic* **:** a man who knows of his wife's infidelity and puts up with it
2 *archaic* **:** a witless person

wit·ty \'wi-tē\ *adjective* **wit·ti·er; -est** (before 12th century)
1 *archaic* **:** having good intellectual capacity **:** INTELLIGENT
2 : amusingly or ingeniously clever in conception or execution ⟨the costumes are sumptuous and *witty* —Virgil Thomson⟩ ⟨the musical background is . . . often *witty* —Wolcott Gibbs⟩
3 : marked by or full of wit **:** smartly facetious or jocular
4 : quick or ready to see or express illuminating or amusing relationships or insights ☆
— **wit·ti·ly** \'wi-tⁿl-ē\ *adverb*
— **wit·ti·ness** \'wi-tē-nəs\ *noun*

wive \'wīv\ *verb* **wived; wiv·ing** [Middle English, from Old English *wīfian*, from *wīf* woman, wife] (before 12th century)
intransitive verb
: to marry a woman
transitive verb
1 : to marry to a woman
2 : to take for a wife

wives *plural of* WIFE

wiz \'wiz\ *noun* (1902)
: WIZARD 3

¹wiz·ard \'wi-zərd\ *noun* [Middle English *wysard*, from *wis, wys* wise] (15th century)
1 *archaic* **:** a wise man **:** SAGE
2 : one skilled in magic **:** SORCERER
3 : a very clever or skillful person

²wizard *adjective* (1579)
1 *archaic* **:** having magical influence or power
2 *archaic* **:** of or relating to wizardry **:** ENCHANTED
3 *chiefly British* **:** worthy of the highest praise **:** EXCELLENT

wiz·ard·ly \'wi-zərd-lē\ *adjective* (1588)
1 : having characteristics of a wizard
2 : marvelous in construction or operation ⟨uses *wizardly* circuitry to distort images —*Time*⟩

wiz·ard·ry \'wi-zə(r)-drē\ *noun, plural* **-ries** (1583)
1 : the art or practices of a wizard **:** SORCERY
2 a : a seemingly magical transforming power or influence ⟨electronic *wizardry*⟩ **b :** great skill or cleverness in an activity

¹wiz·en \'wi-zⁿn *also* 'wē-\ *verb* **wiz·ened; wiz·en·ing** \'wiz-niŋ *also* 'wēz-; 'wi-zⁿn-iŋ *also* 'wē-\ [Middle English *wisenen*, from Old English *wisnian*; akin to Old High German *wesanēn* to wither, Lithuanian *vysti*] (before 12th century)
intransitive verb
: to become dry, shrunken, and wrinkled often as a result of aging or of failing vitality
transitive verb
: to cause to wizen

²wizen *adjective* [alteration of *wizened*] (1786)
: that is wizened

woad \'wōd\ *noun* [Middle English *wod*, from Old English *wād*; akin to Old High German *weit* woad, Latin *vitrum*] (before 12th century)
: a European herb (*Isatis tinctoria*) of the mustard family formerly grown for the blue dyestuff yielded by its leaves; *also* **:** this dyestuff

¹wob·ble \'wä-bəl\ *verb* **wob·bled; wob·bling** \-b(ə-)liŋ\ [probably from Low German *wabbeln*; akin to Old English *wæfre* restless — more at WAVER] (1657)
intransitive verb
1 a : to move or proceed with an irregular rocking or staggering motion or unsteadily and clumsily from side to side **b :** TREMBLE, QUAVER
2 : WAVER, VACILLATE
transitive verb
: to cause to wobble
— **wob·bler** \-b(ə-)lər\ *noun*
— **wob·bli·ness** \'wä-blē-nəs\ *noun*
— **wob·bly** \'wä-b(ə-)lē\ *adjective*

²wobble *noun* (1699)
1 a : a hobbling or rocking unequal motion (as of a wheel unevenly mounted) **b :** an uncertainly directed movement
2 : an intermittent variation (as in volume of sound)

Wob·bly \'wä-blē\ *noun, plural* **Wobblies** [origin unknown] (1914)
: a member of the Industrial Workers of the World

Wo·den \'wō-dⁿn\ *noun* [Old English *Wōden*]
: ODIN

wodge \'wäj\ *noun* [probably alteration of *wedge*] (1860)
chiefly British **:** a bulky mass or chunk **:** LUMP, WAD

¹woe \'wō\ *interjection* [Middle English *wa, wo*, from Old English *wā*; akin to Old Norse *vei*, interjection, woe, Latin *vae*] (before 12th century)
— used to express grief, regret, or distress

²woe *noun* (13th century)
1 : a condition of deep suffering from misfortune, affliction, or grief
2 : ruinous trouble **:** CALAMITY, AFFLICTION ⟨economic *woes*⟩
synonym see SORROW

woe·be·gone \'wō-bi-ˌgȯn *also* -ˌgän\ *adjective* [Middle English *wo begon*, from *wo*, noun + *begon*, past participle of *begon* to go about, beset, from Old English *begān*, from *be-* + *gān* to go — more at GO] (14th century)
1 : strongly affected with woe **:** WOEFUL
2 a : exhibiting great woe, sorrow, or misery ⟨a *woebegone* expression⟩ **b :** being in a sorry state ⟨*woebegone* tattered clothes⟩
— **woe·be·gone·ness** *noun*

woe·ful *also* **wo·ful** \'wō-fəl\ *adjective* (14th century)
1 : full of woe **:** GRIEVOUS ⟨*woeful* prophecies⟩
2 : involving or bringing woe
3 : lamentably bad or serious **:** DEPLORABLE ⟨*woeful* ignorance⟩
— **woe·ful·ly** \-f(ə-)lē\ *adverb*
— **woe·ful·ness** \-fəl-nəs\ *noun*

wog \'wäg, 'wȯg\ *noun* [perhaps short for *golliwog*] (circa 1929)
chiefly British **:** a dark-skinned foreigner; *especially* **:** one from the Middle East or Far East — usually used disparagingly

wok \'wäk\ *noun* [Chinese (Guangdong) *wohk*] (1952)
: a bowl-shaped cooking utensil used especially in stir-frying

woke *past and past participle of* WAKE
woken *past participle of* WAKE

wold \'wōld\ *noun* [Middle English *wald, wold*, from Old English *weald, wald* forest; akin to Old High German *wald* forest, Old Norse *vȯllr* field] (before 12th century)
1 : a usually upland area of open country
2 *capitalized* **:** a hilly or rolling region — used in names of various English geographical areas ⟨Yorkshire *Wolds*⟩

¹wolf \'wu̇lf\ *noun, plural* **wolves** \'wu̇lvz\ *often attributive* [Middle English, from Old English *wulf*; akin to Old High German *wolf* wolf, Latin *lupus*, Greek *lykos*] (before 12th century)
1 *plural also* **wolf a :** any of various large predatory canids (genus *Canis*) that live and hunt in packs and resemble the related dogs; *especially* **:** GRAY WOLF — compare COYOTE, JACKAL **b :** the fur of a wolf
2 a (1) **:** a fierce, rapacious, or destructive person (2) **:** a man forward, direct, and zealous in amatory attentions to women **b :** dire poverty **:** STARVATION ⟨keep the *wolf* from the door⟩ **c :** the maggot of a warble fly
3 [German; from the howling sound] **a** (1) **:** dissonance in some chords on organs, pianos, or other instruments with fixed tones tuned by unequal temperament (2) **:** an instance of such dissonance **b :** a harshness due to faulty vibration in various tones in a bowed instrument
— **wolf·like** \'wu̇lf-ˌlīk\ *adjective*
— **wolf in sheep's clothing :** one who cloaks a hostile intention with a friendly manner

²wolf *transitive verb* (1862)
: to eat greedily **:** DEVOUR

wolf·ber·ry \'wu̇lf-ˌber-ē\ *noun* (circa 1834)

: a white-berried North American shrub (*Symphoricarpos occidentalis*) of the honeysuckle family

wolf dog *noun* (1652)
1 : any of various large dogs formerly kept for hunting wolves
2 : the offspring of a wolf and a domestic dog

wolf·er \'wu̇l-fər\ *noun* (1872)
: a hunter of wolves

wolff·ian body \'wu̇l-fē-ən-\ *noun, often W capitalized* [Kaspar Friedrich *Wolff*] (circa 1844)
: MESONEPHROS

Wolffian duct *noun* (1879)
: the duct of the mesonephros that persists in the female chiefly as part of a vestigial organ and in the male as the duct system leaving the testis and including the epididymis, vas deferens, and ejaculatory duct

wolf·fish \'wu̇l-ˌfish\ *noun* (1569)
: any of several large marine blennies (genus *Anarhichas* of the family Anarhicadidae) having strong canine teeth in the front of the jaws and molar teeth on the sides and that feed chiefly on shellfish, starfish, and sea urchins

wolf·hound \'wu̇lf-ˌhau̇nd\ *noun* (1786)
: any of several large dogs used especially formerly in hunting large animals (as wolves)

wolf·ish \'wu̇l-fish\ *adjective* (1570)
1 : of or relating to wolves
2 a : suggestive of a wolf ⟨*wolfish* mongrel dogs —Hoffman Birney⟩ ⟨a *wolfish* and withdrawn youth —Marshall Frady⟩ **b** : befitting or characteristic of a wolf ⟨a *wolfish* appetite⟩
— **wolf·ish·ly** *adverb*
— **wolf·ish·ness** *noun*

wolf pack *noun* (1941)
: a group of submarines that make a coordinated attack on shipping

wol·fram \'wu̇l-frəm\ *noun* [German] (1757)
1 : WOLFRAMITE
2 : TUNGSTEN

wol·fram·ite \'wu̇l-frə-ˌmīt\ *noun* [German *Wolframit*, from *Wolfram*] (circa 1868)
: a mineral that consists of a tungstate of iron and manganese usually of a brownish or grayish black color and slightly metallic luster, occurs in monoclinic crystals and in granular or columnar masses, and is used as a source of tungsten

wolfs·bane \'wu̇lfs-ˌbān\ *noun* (1548)
: MONKSHOOD; *especially* : a highly variable yellow-flowered poisonous European herb (*Aconitum vulparia*)

wolf spider *noun* (1608)
: any of various active wandering ground spiders (family Lycosidae)

wolf whistle *noun* (1946)
: a distinctive whistle sounded by a boy or man to express sexual admiration for a girl or woman in his vicinity

wol·las·ton·ite \'wu̇-lə-stə-ˌnīt, 'wä-\ *noun* [William H. *Wollaston*] (1823)
: a triclinic mineral consisting of a native calcium silicate occurring usually in cleavable masses

Wo·lof \'wō-ˌlȯf\ *noun* (1823)
: a Niger-Congo language of Senegambia

wol·ver·ine \ˌwu̇l-və-'rēn\ *noun, plural* **wolverines** [probably irregular from *wolv-* (as in *wolves*)] (1574)
1 *plural also* **wolverine a** : a carnivorous usually solitary mammal (*Gulo gulo*) of the weasel family of northern forests and associated tundra that is blackish with a light brown band on each side of the body and is noted especially for its strength **b** : the fur of the wolverine

wolverine 1a

2 *capitalized* : a native or resident of Michigan — used as a nickname

wom·an \'wu̇-mən, *especially Southern* 'wȯ-ər 'wȧ-\ *noun, plural* **wom·en** \'wi-mən\ [Middle English, from Old English *wīfman*, from *wīf* woman, wife + *man* human being, man] (before 12th century)
1 a : an adult female person **b** : a woman belonging to a particular category (as by birth, residence, membership, or occupation) — usually used in combination ⟨council*woman*⟩
2 : WOMENKIND
3 : distinctively feminine nature : WOMANLINESS
4 : a female servant or personal attendant
5 a *chiefly dialect* : WIFE **b** : MISTRESS **c** : GIRLFRIEND 2 ◇
— **woman** *adjective*
— **wom·an·less** \-ləs\ *adjective*

wom·an·hood \-ˌhu̇d\ *noun* (14th century)
1 a : the state of being a woman **b** : the distinguishing character or qualities of a woman or of womankind
2 : WOMAN, WOMENKIND

wom·an·ise *British variant of* WOMANIZE

wom·an·ish \'wu̇-mə-nish\ *adjective* (14th century)
1 : characteristic of or suitable for a woman
2 : unsuitable to a man or to a strong character of either sex : EFFEMINATE ⟨*womanish* fears⟩
— **wom·an·ish·ly** *adverb*
— **wom·an·ish·ness** *noun*

wom·an·ize \'wu̇-mə-ˌnīz\ *verb* **-ized; -izing** (1593)
transitive verb
: to make effeminate
intransitive verb
: to pursue multiple casual relationships with women
— **wom·an·iz·er** *noun*

wom·an·kind \'wu̇-mən-ˌkīnd\ *noun singular but singular or plural in construction* (14th century)
: WOMENKIND

¹wom·an·like \-ˌlīk\ *adjective* (15th century)
: WOMANLY

²womanlike *adverb* (15th century)
: in the manner of a woman

wom·an·ly \-lē\ *adjective* (13th century)
1 : having qualities generally associated with a woman
2 : appropriate in character to a woman
— **wom·an·li·ness** *noun*

woman of letters (1818)
1 : a woman who is a scholar
2 : a woman who is an author

woman of the street (1928)
: PROSTITUTE

wom·an·pow·er \'wu̇-mən-ˌpau̇(-ə)r\ *noun* (1938)
: women available and prepared for work (as in industry or a particular line of endeavor)

woman's rights *noun plural* (1840)
1 : legal, political, and social rights for women equal to those of men
2 : FEMINISM 2

woman suffrage *noun* (1867)
: possession and exercise of suffrage by women

womb \'wüm\ *noun* [Middle English *wamb, womb*, from Old English; akin to Old High German *wamba* belly] (before 12th century)
1 : UTERUS
2 a : a cavity or space that resembles a womb in containing and enveloping **b** : a place where something is generated
— **wombed** \'wümd\ *adjective*

wom·bat \'wäm-ˌbat\ *noun* [Dharuk (Australian aboriginal language of the Port Jackson area) *wambat*] (1798)
: any of several stocky Australian marsupials (genera

wombat

Vombatus and *Lasiorhinus* of the family Vombatidae) resembling small bears

wom·en·folk \'wi-mən-ˌfōk\ *also* **wom·en·folks** \-ˌfōks\ *noun plural* (1833)
: WOMEN

wom·en·kind \-ˌkīnd\ *noun* (14th century)
: female human beings : women especially as distinguished from men

women's rights *noun plural* (1632)
: WOMAN'S RIGHTS

women's room *noun* (circa 1937)
: LADIES' ROOM

wom·mera \'wä-mə-rə\ *variant of* WOOMERA

¹won \'wən, 'wȯn\ *intransitive verb* **wonned; won·ning** [Middle English, from Old English *wunian* — more at WONT] (before 12th century)
archaic : DWELL 2a, ABIDE 2

²won \'wən\ *past and past participle of* WIN

³won \'wən\ *noun, plural* **won** [Korean *wŏn*] (circa 1917)
— see MONEY table

¹won·der \'wən-dər\ *noun* [Middle English, from Old English *wundor;* akin to Old High German *wuntar* wonder] (before 12th century)
1 a : a cause of astonishment or admiration : MARVEL ⟨it's a *wonder* you weren't killed⟩ **b** : MIRACLE
2 : the quality of exciting amazed admiration
3 a : rapt attention or astonishment at something awesomely mysterious or new to one's experience **b** : a feeling of doubt or uncertainty

²wonder *verb* **won·dered; won·der·ing** \-d(ə-)riŋ\ (before 12th century)
intransitive verb
1 a : to be in a state of wonder **b** : to feel surprise
2 : to feel curiosity or doubt
transitive verb
: to be curious or in doubt about
— **won·der·er** \-dər-ər\ *noun*

³wonder *adjective* (12th century)
: WONDROUS, WONDERFUL: as **a** : exciting

◇ **WORD HISTORY**
woman *Woman* is descended from Old English *wīfman,* made up of *wīf* "woman" and *man* "human being." This seemingly redundant compound, with no counterpart in other Germanic languages, forms a pair with Old English *wæpnedman* or *wæpenman* "male human," literally, "weaponed man" or "weapon man," in which *wæpen* serves as a euphemism for the organ specific to males. Phrases such as *bitweone wepmon & wimmane* "between man and woman" are found in Middle English, but only up to about 1300, after which *wepman* is entirely supplanted by simple *man* in the sense "male human." *Wīfman* lasted, however, becoming in Middle English *wimman* (written *f*) of the Old English word blended into the following \m\ and the vowel of the first syllable shortened. The Modern English plural *\'wi-mən* perpetuates this vowel, while a further change, in which the initial *i* was altered to *u* under influence of the preceding \w\ sound, resulted in Middle English *wumman,* continued by the Modern English singular \'wu̇-mən\. Both the *i* and the *u* variants were also lengthened, ultimately producing early Modern English variants with *wee-* and *wo-* in the first syllable. The latter has provided our spelling—though not our pronunciation—for both singular *woman* and plural *women.*

amazement or admiration **b :** effective or efficient far beyond anything previously known or anticipated

wonder drug *noun* (1939)
: MIRACLE DRUG

won·der·ful \'wən-dər-fəl\ *adjective* (before 12th century)
1 : exciting wonder **:** MARVELOUS, ASTONISHING ⟨a sight *wonderful* to behold⟩
2 : unusually good **:** ADMIRABLE
— **won·der·ful·ly** \-f(ə-)lē\ *adverb*
— **won·der·ful·ness** \-fəl-nəs\ *noun*

won·der·land \'wən-dər-,land, -lənd\ *noun* (1790)
1 : an imaginary place of delicate beauty or magical charm
2 : a place that excites admiration or wonder

won·der·ment \-mənt\ *noun* (1535)
1 : ASTONISHMENT, SURPRISE
2 : a cause or occasion for wonder
3 : curiosity about something

won·der·work \-də(r)-,wərk\ *noun* (before 12th century)
: a marvelous act, work, or accomplishment

won·der–work·er \-,wər-kər\ *noun* (1599)
: one that performs wonders

won·der–work·ing \-,kiŋ\ *adjective* (1594)
: producing wonders

won·drous \'wən-drəs\ *adjective* [Middle English, alteration of *wonders,* from genitive of ¹*wonder*] (15th century)
: that is to be marveled at **:** EXTRAORDINARY
— **wondrous** *adverb, archaic*
— **won·drous·ly** *adverb*
— **won·drous·ness** *noun*

wonk \'wäŋk, 'wȯŋk\ *noun* [origin unknown] (1954)
: NERD

won·ky \'wän-kē\ *adjective* [probably alteration of English dialect *wankle,* from Middle English *wankel,* from Old English *wancol;* akin to Old High German *wankōn* to totter — more at WENCH] (1919)
1 *British* **:** UNSTEADY, SHAKY
2 *British* **:** AWRY, WRONG

¹**wont** \'wȯnt, 'wōnt *also* 'wənt, 'wänt\ *adjective* [Middle English *woned, wont,* from past participle of *wonen* to dwell, be used to, from Old English *wunian;* akin to Old High German *wonēn* to dwell, be used to, Sanskrit *vanoti* he strives for — more at WIN] (before 12th century)
1 : ACCUSTOMED, USED ⟨got up early as he is *wont* to do⟩
2 : INCLINED, APT ⟨revealing as letters are *wont* to be —Gladys M. Wrigley⟩

²**wont** *verb* **wont; wont** *or* **wont·ed; wont·ing** (15th century)
transitive verb
: ACCUSTOM, HABITUATE
intransitive verb
: to have the habit of doing something

³**wont** *noun* (1530)
: habitual way of doing **:** USE
synonym see HABIT

won't \'wōnt; *New England, upstate New York, northern Pennsylvania* ,wənt, 'wənt; *greater New York City* 'wünt; *eastern South Carolina* 'wünt, 'wŭnt\ (1652)
: will not

wont·ed \'wȯn-təd, 'wōn- *also* 'wən- *or* 'wän-\ *adjective* (15th century)
: usual or ordinary especially by reason of established habit ⟨flashed his *wonted* grin⟩
synonym see USUAL
— **wont·ed·ly** *adverb*
— **wont·ed·ness** *noun*

won·ton \'wän-,tän\ *noun* [Chinese (Guangdong) *wàhn-tān*] (1934)
: filled pockets of noodle dough served boiled in soup or fried

woo \'wü\ *verb* [Middle English *wowen,* from Old English *wōgian*] (before 12th century)
transitive verb
1 : to sue for the affection of and usually marriage with **:** COURT

2 : to solicit or entreat especially with importunity
3 : to seek to gain or bring about
intransitive verb
: to court a woman
— **woo·er** *noun*

¹**wood** \'wüd, 'wōd, 'wŭd\ *adjective* [Middle English, from Old English *wōd* insane; akin to Old High German *wuot* madness — more at VATIC] (before 12th century)
archaic **:** violently mad

²**wood** \'wŭd\ *noun* [Middle English *wode,* from Old English *widu, wudu;* akin to Old High German *witu* wood, Old Irish *fid* tree] (before 12th century)
1 a : a dense growth of trees usually greater in extent than a grove and smaller than a forest — often used in plural but singular or plural in construction **b :** WOODLAND
2 a : the hard fibrous substance consisting basically of xylem that makes up the greater part of the stems, branches, and roots of trees or shrubs beneath the bark and is found to a limited extent in herbaceous plants **b :** wood suitable or prepared for some use (as burning or building)
3 a : something made of wood **b :** a golf club having a thick wooden head; *also* **:** a golf club having a similar head made of metal
— **out of the woods :** clear of danger or difficulty

³**wood** \'wŭd\ *adjective* (1538)
1 : WOODEN
2 : suitable for cutting or working with wood ⟨a *wood* saw⟩
3 *or* **woods** \'wŭdz\ **:** living, growing, or existing in woods ⟨*woods* trails⟩

⁴**wood** \'wŭd\ (1630)
intransitive verb
: to gather or take on wood
transitive verb
: to cover with a growth of trees or plant with trees

wood alcohol *noun* (1861)
: METHANOL

wood anemone *noun* (1657)
: any of several anemones; *especially* **:** one (*Anemone quinquefolia*) of North America with solitary often pink-tinged flowers

wood bet·o·ny \-'be-tⁿn-ē\ *noun* [Middle English *betone,* from Old French *betoine,* from Latin *vettonica, betonica,* from *Vettones,* an ancient people inhabiting the Iberian peninsula] (1657)
: a lousewort (*Pedicularis canadensis*) of eastern North America with yellow or reddish flowers in bracted spikes

wood·bine \'wŭd-,bīn\ *noun* [Middle English *wodebinde,* from Old English *wudubinde,* from *wudu* wood + *bindan* to tie, bind; from its winding around trees] (before 12th century)
1 : any of several honeysuckles; *especially* **:** a Eurasian twining shrub (*Lonicera periclymenum*)
2 : VIRGINIA CREEPER

wood·block \-,bläk\ *noun* (1837)
: WOODCUT
— **wood–block** *adjective*

wood–bor·ing \-,bōr-iŋ, -,bȯr-\ *adjective* (1815)
: excavating galleries in wood in feeding or in constructing a nest — used chiefly of an insect

wood carving *noun* (1847)
: the art of fashioning or ornamenting objects of wood by cutting with a sharp handheld implement; *also* **:** an object of wood so fashioned or ornamented
— **wood–carv·er** \-,kär-vər\ *noun*

wood·chat shrike \'wŭd-,chat-\ *noun* (1781)
: a European shrike (*Lanius senator*) — called also *woodchat*

wood·chop·per \-,chä-pər\ *noun* (1779)
: one engaged especially in chopping down trees

wood·chuck \-,chək\ *noun* [by folk etymology from a word of Algonquian origin; akin to Narraganset *ockqutchaun* woodchuck] (1674)
: a grizzled thickset marmot (*Marmota monax*) chiefly of Alaska, Canada, and the northeastern U.S. — called also *groundhog*

wood·cock \'wŭd-,käk\ *noun, plural* **woodcocks** (before 12th century)
1 *or plural* **woodcock :** a widespread Old World woodland bird (*Scolopax rusticola*) that is related to the sandpipers and snipes; *also* **:** a smaller related game bird (*Scolopax minor* synonym *Philohela minor*) of eastern North America
2 [from the ease with which the woodcock is snared] *archaic* **:** SIMPLETON

wood·craft \-,kraft\ *noun* (14th century)
1 : skill and practice in anything relating to the woods and especially in maintaining oneself and making one's way in the woods
2 : skill in shaping or constructing articles from wood

wood·cut \-,kət\ *noun* (1662)
1 : a relief printing surface consisting of a wooden block with a usually pictorial design cut with the grain
2 : a print from a woodcut

wood·cut·ter \-,kə-tər\ *noun* (1761)
: one that cuts wood

wood·cut·ting \-,kə-tiŋ\ *noun* (1683)
1 : the action or occupation of cutting wood or timber
2 : the producing of woodcuts

wood duck *noun* (1777)
: a showy American duck (*Aix sponsa*) which nests in tree cavities and the males of which have a large crest and iridescent plumage varied with green, purple, black, white, and chestnut

wood duck

wood ear *noun* (1917)
: TREE EAR

wood·ed \'wŭ-dəd\ *adjective* (1605)
: covered with growing trees

wood·en \'wŭ-dⁿn\ *adjective* (1538)
1 : made or consisting of wood
2 : lacking ease or flexibility **:** awkwardly stiff
— **wood·en·ly** *adverb*
— **wood·en·ness** \-dⁿn-(n)əs\ *noun*

wood engraving *noun* (1816)
1 : a relief printing surface consisting of a wooden block with a usually pictorial design cut in the end grain
2 : a print from a wood engraving

wood·en·head \'wŭ-dⁿn-,hed\ *noun* (1831)
: BLOCKHEAD

wood·en·head·ed \,wŭ-dⁿn-'he-dəd\ *adjective* (circa 1854)
: DENSE, STUPID

wooden Indian *noun* (1879)
: a wooden image of a standing American Indian brave used especially formerly as a sign for a cigar store

wood·en·ware \'wŭ-dⁿn-,war, -,wer\ *noun* (1647)
: articles made of wood for domestic use

wood fiber *noun* (1875)
: any of various fibers in or associated with xylem

¹**wood·land** \'wŭd-lənd, -,land\ *noun* (before 12th century)
: land covered with woody vegetation **:** TIMBERLAND, FOREST
— **wood·land·er** \-lən-dər, -,lan-\ *noun*

²**woodland** *adjective* (14th century)
1 : growing, living, or existing in woodland
2 : of, relating to, or being woodland

wood·lore \'wŭd-,lōr, -,lȯr\ *noun* (1918)
: knowledge of the woods

wood·lot \-,lät\ *noun* (1643)

: a restricted area of woodland usually privately maintained as a source of fuel, posts, and lumber

wood louse *noun* (1611)
: a terrestrial isopod crustacean (suborder Oniscoidea) with a flattened elliptical body often capable of being rolled into a ball — called also *pill bug, sow bug*

wood·man \'wùd-mən\ *noun* (15th century)
1 : WOODSMAN
2 *capitalized* [Modern *Woodmen* of America & *Woodmen* of the World] : a member of either of two independent benevolent and fraternal societies

wood·note \-,nōt\ *noun* [from its likeness to the call of a bird in the woods] (1632)
: verbal expression that is natural and artless

wood nymph *noun* (1577)
: a nymph living in woods — called also *dryad*

wood·peck·er \'wùd-,pe-kər\ *noun* (circa 1530)
: any of numerous birds (family Picidae) with zygodactyl feet, stiff spiny tail feathers used in climbing or resting on tree trunks, a usually extensile tongue, a very hard bill used to drill the bark or wood of trees for insect food or to excavate nesting cavities, and generally showy parti-colored plumage

wood·pile \-,pīl\ *noun* (circa 1552)
: a pile of wood (as firewood)
— in the woodpile : doing or responsible for covert mischief

wood pulp *noun* (1866)
: pulp from wood used in making cellulose derivatives (as paper or rayon)

wood pussy *noun* (circa 1899)
: SKUNK

wood rat *noun* (1763)
: any of numerous cricetid rodents (especially genus *Neotoma*) of North and Central America with soft fur, well-furred tails, and large ears

wood ray *noun* (1925)
: XYLEM RAY

wood·ruff \'wùd-(,)rəf\ *noun* [Middle English *woderove*, from Old English *wudurofe*, from *wudu* wood + *-rofe* (of unknown origin)] (before 12th century)
1 : any of a genus (*Asperula*) of Old World herbs of the madder family
2 : a small Eurasian and North African sweet-scented herb (*Galium odoratum* synonym *Asperula odorata*) used in perfumery and for flavoring wine

¹wood·shed \-,shed\ *noun* (1844)
1 : a shed for storing wood and especially firewood
2 : a place, means, or session for administering discipline

²woodshed *intransitive verb* **-shed·ded; -shed·ding** [probably from the former use of woodsheds for private practicing] (1936)
: PRACTICE; *especially* : to practice on a musical instrument

wood shot *noun* (1927)
1 : a golf shot played with a wood
2 : a stroke in a racket game in which the ball or shuttlecock is hit with the frame of the racket rather than the strings

woods·man \'wùdz-mən\ *noun* (1688)
: a person who frequents or works in the woods; *especially* : one skilled in woodcraft

wood sorrel *noun* (1525)
: any of a genus (*Oxalis* of the family Oxalidaceae, the wood-sorrel family) of herbs with acid sap, compound leaves, and regular flowers; *especially* : either of two stemless herbs (*O. montana* of North America and *O. acetosella* of Eurasia) with trifoliolate leaves

wood spirit *noun* (1842)
: METHANOL

wood stork *noun* (1884)
: a white stork (*Mycteria americana*) with black wing flight feathers and tail that frequents wooded swamps from the southeastern U.S. to Argentina — called also *wood ibis*

wood·stove \'wùd-,stōv\ *noun* (1847)
: a stove that uses wood for fuel

wood sugar *noun* (circa 1900)
: XYLOSE

woodsy \'wùd-zē\ *adjective* (1860)
: characteristic or suggestive of woods

wood tar *noun* (1857)
: tar obtained by the destructive distillation of wood either as a deposit from pyroligneous acid or as a residue from the distillation of the acid or of wood turpentine

wood tick *noun* (1668)
: any of several ixodid ticks: as **a** : a widely distributed tick (*Dermacentor andersoni*) of western North America that is a vector of Rocky Mountain spotted fever **b** : AMERICAN DOG TICK

wood turning *noun* (circa 1876)
: the art or process of fashioning wooden pieces or blocks into various forms and shapes by means of a lathe

wood turpentine *noun* (circa 1909)
: TURPENTINE 2b

wood warbler *noun* (1817)
: WARBLER 2b

wood·wind \'wùd-,wind\ *noun* (1876)
1 : any of a group of wind instruments (as a clarinet, flute, oboe, or saxophone) that are characterized by a cylindrical or conical tube of wood or metal usually ending in a slightly flared bell, that produce tones by the vibration of one or two reeds in the mouthpiece or by the passing of air over a mouth hole, and that usually have finger holes or keys by which the player may produce all the tones within an instrument's range
2 *plural* : the woodwind section of a band or orchestra

wood·work \-,wərk\ *noun* (1650)
1 : work made of wood; *especially* : interior fittings (as moldings or stairways) of wood
2 : a place or state of concealment, seclusion, or anonymity ⟨witnesses came out of the *woodwork* when a reward was offered⟩

¹wood·work·ing \-,wər-kiŋ\ *adjective* (1872)
: used for woodworking

²woodworking *noun* (1875)
: the act, process, or occupation of working wood into a useful or desired form
— wood·work·er \-kər\ *noun*

wood·worm \'wùd-,wərm\ *noun* (1725)
: an insect larva (as of a furniture beetle) that bores especially in dead wood; *also* : an infestation of woodworms

¹woody \'wù-dē\ *adjective* **wood·i·er; -est** (14th century)
1 : abounding or overgrown with woods
2 a : of or containing wood or wood fibers : LIGNEOUS ⟨*woody* tissues⟩ **b** : having woody parts : rich in xylem and associated structures ⟨*woody* plants⟩
3 : characteristic of or suggestive of wood ⟨wine with a *woody* flavor⟩
— wood·i·ness *noun*

²woody *or* **wood·ie** \'wù-dē\ *noun, plural* **woodies** [alteration of ³*wood*] (1961)
: a wood-paneled station wagon

¹woof \'wùf, 'wüf\ *noun* [alteration of Middle English *oof*, from Old English *ōwef*, from *ō-* (from *on*) + *wefan* to weave — more at WEAVE] (before 12th century)
1 a : WEFT 1a **b** : woven fabric; *also* : the texture of such a fabric
2 : a basic or essential element or material

²woof \'wùf\ *intransitive verb* [imitative] (1804)
1 : to make the low gruff sound typically produced by a dog
2 : to express oneself in a usually stylized boastful, aggressive, or exaggeratedly deceitful manner

³woof *noun* (1839)
1 : a low gruff sound typically produced by a dog
2 : a low note emitted by sound reproducing equipment

woof·er \'wù-fər\ *noun* (1935)
: a loudspeaker usually larger than a tweeter, responsive only to the lower acoustic frequencies, and used for reproducing sounds of low pitch — compare TWEETER

wool \'wùl\ *noun, often attributive* [Middle English *wolle*, from Old English *wull*; akin to Old High German *wolla* wool, Latin *vellus* fleece, *lana* wool] (before 12th century)
1 : the soft wavy or curly hypertrophied undercoat of various hairy mammals and especially the sheep made up of a matrix of keratin fibers and covered with minute scales
2 : a product of wool; *especially* : a woven fabric or garment of such fabric
3 a : a dense felted pubescence especially on a plant : TOMENTUM **b** : a filamentous mass — usually USED in combination; compare MINERAL WOOL, STEEL WOOL

wooled *also* **woolled** \'wùld\ *adjective* (circa 1859)
: having wool especially of a specified kind — used in combination ⟨long-*wooled*⟩

¹wool·en *or* **wool·len** \'wù-lən\ *adjective* (before 12th century)
1 : made of wool
2 : of or relating to the manufacture or sale of woolen products ⟨*woolen* mills⟩ ⟨the *woolen* industry⟩

²woolen *or* **woollen** *noun* (14th century)
1 : a fabric made of wool and especially of woolen yarns having a fuzzy or napped face (as for use in clothing or blankets) — compare WORSTED
2 : garments of woolen fabric — usually used in plural

wool fat *noun* (1875)
: wool grease especially after refining : LANOLIN

wool–gath·er \'wùl-,ga-thər, -,ge-thər\ *intransitive verb* (1850)
: to indulge in woolgathering
— wool·gath·er·er \-thər-ər\ *noun*

wool·gath·er·ing \-,ga-th(ə-)riŋ, -,ge-th(ə-)riŋ\ *noun* (1553)
: indulgence in idle daydreaming

wool grease *noun* (1875)
: a fatty slightly sticky wax coating the surface of the fibers of sheep's wool — compare WOOL FAT

¹wool·ly *also* **wooly** \'wù-lē\ *adjective* **wool·li·er; -est** (1578)
1 a : of, relating to, or bearing wool **b** : resembling wool
2 a : lacking in clearness or sharpness of outline ⟨a *woolly* TV picture⟩ **b** : marked by mental confusion ⟨*woolly* thinking⟩
3 : marked by boisterous roughness or lack of order or restraint ⟨where the West is still *woolly* —Paul Schubert⟩ — used especially in the phrase *wild and woolly*
— wool·li·ly \-lə-lē\ *adverb*
— wool·li·ness *noun*

²wool·ly *also* **wool·ie** *or* **wooly** \'wù-lē\ *noun, plural* **wool·lies** *also* **wool·ies** (circa 1865)
1 : a garment made from wool; *especially* : underclothing of knitted wool — usually used in plural
2 *West & Australian* : SHEEP

woolly aphid *noun* (1842)
: any of several plant lice (especially genus *Eriosoma*) covered with a dense coat of white filaments — called also *woolly aphis*

woolly bear *noun* (circa 1841)
: any of various rather large very hairy moth caterpillars; *especially* : one of a tiger moth

wool·ly–head·ed \,wù-lē-'he-dəd\ *adjective* (1650)
1 : having hair suggesting wool

2 : marked by vague or confused perception or thinking

wool·ly mammoth *noun* (1933)
: a heavy-coated mammoth (*Mammuthus primigenius*) of the colder parts of the northern hemisphere

wool·pack \'wùl-,pak\ *noun* (14th century)
1 : a wrapper of strong fabric into which fleeces are packed for shipment
2 : the complete package of wool and wrapper

wool·sack \-,sak\ *noun* (14th century)
1 *archaic* **:** WOOLPACK 2
2 : a cushion that is the official seat of the Lord Chancellor or his deputy in presiding over the House of Lords

wool·shed \-,shed\ *noun* (1850)
: a building or range of buildings (as on an Australian sheep station) in which sheep are sheared and wool is prepared for market

wool·skin \-,skin\ *noun* (15th century)
: a sheepskin having the wool still on it

wool·sort·er's disease \'wùl-,sòr-tərz-\ *noun* (1880)
: pulmonary anthrax resulting especially from inhalation of bacterial spores (*Bacillus anthracis*) from contaminated wool or hair

wool stapler *noun* (1709)
: a dealer in wool

woom·era \'wù-mə-rə\ *noun* [Dharvk (Australian aboriginal language of the Port Jackson area) *wumera*] (1817)
: a wooden rod with a hooked end used by Australian aborigines for throwing a spear

woops \'(w)ù(ə)ps\ *variant of* OOPS

woo·zy \'wü-zē, 'wù-\ *adjective* **woo·zi·er; -est** [origin unknown] (1897)
1 : mentally unclear or hazy ⟨seems a little *woozy*, not quite knowing what to say —J. A. Lukacs⟩
2 : affected with dizziness, mild nausea, or weakness
— woo·zi·ly *adverb*
— woo·zi·ness *noun*

wop \'wäp\ *noun, often capitalized* [Italian dialect *guappo* swaggerer, tough, from Spanish *guapo*, probably from Middle French dialect *vape, wape* weak, insipid, from Latin *vappa* wine gone flat] (1908)
: ITALIAN — usually used disparagingly

Worces·ter \'wùs-tər\ *noun* (1802)
: low-fired porcelain containing a frit and steatite produced at Worcester, England, from about 1751 — called also *Worcester china, Worcester porcelain*

Worces·ter·shire sauce \'wùs-tə(r)-,shir-, -shər- *also* -,shīr-\ *noun* [*Worcestershire*, England, where it was originally made] (1843)
: a pungent sauce whose ingredients include soy, vinegar, and garlic

¹word \'wərd\ *noun* [Middle English, from Old English; akin to Old High German *wort* word, Latin *verbum*, Greek *eirein* to say, speak, Hittite *weriya-* to call, name] (before 12th century)
1 a : something that is said **b** *plural* (1) **:** TALK, DISCOURSE ⟨putting one's feelings into *words*⟩ (2) **:** the text of a vocal musical composition **c :** a brief remark or conversation ⟨would like to have a *word* with you⟩
2 a (1) **:** a speech sound or series of speech sounds that symbolizes and communicates a meaning without being divisible into smaller units capable of independent use (2) **:** the entire set of linguistic forms produced by combining a single base with various inflectional elements without change in the part of speech elements **b** (1) **:** a written or printed character or combination of characters representing a spoken word ⟨the number of *words* to a line⟩ — sometimes used with the first letter of a real or pretended taboo word prefixed often as a humorous euphemism ⟨we were not afraid to use the d *word* and talk about death —Erma Bombeck⟩ ⟨the first man to utter the f *word* on British TV —*Time*⟩ (2) **:** any segment of written or printed discourse ordinarily appearing

between spaces or between a space and a punctuation mark **c :** a number of bytes processed as a unit and conveying a quantum of information in communication and computer work
3 : ORDER, COMMAND ⟨don't move till I give the *word*⟩
4 *often capitalized* **a :** LOGOS **b :** GOSPEL 1a **c :** the expressed or manifested mind and will of God
5 a : NEWS, INFORMATION ⟨sent *word* that he would be late⟩ **b :** RUMOR
6 : the act of speaking or of making verbal communication
7 : SAYING, PROVERB
8 : PROMISE, DECLARATION ⟨kept her *word*⟩
9 : a quarrelsome utterance or conversation — usually used in plural ⟨they had *words* and parted⟩
10 : a verbal signal **:** PASSWORD
— good word 1 : a favorable statement ⟨put in a *good word* for me⟩ **2 :** good news ⟨what's the *good word*⟩
— in a word : in short
— in so many words 1 : in exactly those terms ⟨implied that such actions were criminal but did not say so *in so many words*⟩ **2 :** in plain forthright language ⟨*in so many words*, she wasn't fit to be seen —Jean Stafford⟩
— of few words : not inclined to say more than is necessary **:** LACONIC
— of one's word : that can be relied on to keep a promise — used only after *man* or *woman*
— upon my word : with my assurance **:** INDEED, ASSUREDLY ⟨*upon my word*, I've never heard of such a thing⟩

²word (13th century)
intransitive verb
archaic **:** SPEAK
transitive verb
: to express in words **:** PHRASE

word·age \'wər-dij\ *noun* (1829)
1 a : WORDS **b :** VERBIAGE 1
2 : the number or quantity of words
3 : WORDING

word–association test *noun* (1946)
: a test of personality and mental function in which the subject is required to respond to each of a series of words with the first one that comes to mind or with one of a specified class of words

word·book \'wərd-,bùk\ *noun* (1598)
: VOCABULARY, DICTIONARY

word class *noun* (1914)
: a linguistic form class whose members are words; *especially* **:** PART OF SPEECH

word–for–word *adjective* (1611)
: being in the exact words **:** VERBATIM

word for word *adverb* (14th century)
: in the exact words **:** VERBATIM

word–hoard \'wərd-,hōrd, -,hȯrd\ *noun* [translation of Old English *wordhord*] (circa 1869)
: a supply of words **:** VOCABULARY

word·ing \'wər-diŋ\ *noun* (1649)
: the act or manner of expressing in words **:** PHRASEOLOGY

word·less \'wərd-ləs\ *adjective* (15th century)
1 : not expressed in or accompanied by words
2 : SILENT, SPEECHLESS
— word·less·ly *adverb*
— word·less·ness *noun*

word·mon·ger \-,məŋ-gər, -,mäŋ-\ *noun* (1590)
: a writer who uses words for show or without particular regard for meaning

word–mon·ger·ing \-g(ə-)riŋ\ *noun* (1879)
: the use of empty or bombastic words

word–of–mouth \,wərd-ə(v)-'maùth\ *adjective* (1802)
: orally communicated; *also* **:** generated from or reliant on oral publicity ⟨*word-of-mouth* customers⟩ ⟨a *word-of-mouth* business⟩

word of mouth (1553)
: oral communication; *especially* **:** oral often inadvertent publicity

word order *noun* (1892)
: the order or arrangement of words in a phrase, clause, or sentence

word·play \'wərd-,plā\ *noun* (1855)
: verbal wit

word processing *noun* (1970)
: the production of typewritten documents (as business letters) with automated and usually computerized typing and text-editing equipment
— word process *verb*

word processor *noun* (1970)
: a keyboard-operated terminal usually with a video display and a magnetic storage device for use in word processing; *also* **:** software (as for a computer system) to perform word processing

word·smith \'wərd-,smith\ *noun* (1896)
: a person who works with words; *especially* **:** a skillful writer
— word·smith·ery \-,smi-thə-rē\ *noun*

word square *noun* (circa 1879)
: a series of words of equal length arranged in a square pattern to read the same horizontally and vertically

word stress *noun* (circa 1914)
: the manner in which stresses are distributed on the syllables of a word — called also *word accent*

wordy \'wər-dē\ *adjective* **word·i·er; -est** (12th century)
1 : using or containing many and usually too many words
2 : of or relating to words **:** VERBAL ☆
— word·i·ly \'wər-dᵊl-ē\ *adverb*
— word·i·ness \'wər-dē-nəs\ *noun*

wore *past of* WEAR

¹work \'wərk\ *noun* [Middle English *werk, work*, from Old English *werc, weorc*; akin to Old High German *werc*, Greek *ergon*, Avestan *varazem* activity] (before 12th century)
1 : activity in which one exerts strength or faculties to do or perform something: **a :** sustained physical or mental effort to overcome obstacles and achieve an objective or result **b :** the labor, task, or duty that is one's accustomed means of livelihood **c :** a specific task, duty, function, or assignment often being a part or phase of some larger activity
2 a : energy expended by natural phenomena **b :** the result of such energy ⟨sand dunes are the *work* of sea and wind⟩ **c :** the transference of energy that is produced by the motion of the point of application of a force and is measured by multiplying the force and the displacement of its point of application in the line of action
3 a : something that results from a particular manner or method of working, operating, or devising ⟨careful police *work*⟩ ⟨clever camera *work*⟩ **b :** something that results from the use or fashioning of a particular material ⟨porcelain *work*⟩
4 a : a fortified structure (as a fort, earthen barricade, or trench) **b** *plural* **:** structures in engineering (as docks, bridges, or embankments) or mining (as shafts or tunnels)
5 *plural but singular or plural in construction* **:** a place where industrial labor is carried on **:** PLANT, FACTORY

☆ SYNONYMS
Wordy, verbose, prolix, diffuse mean using more words than necessary to express thought. WORDY may also imply loquaciousness or garrulity (a *wordy* speech). VERBOSE suggests a resulting dullness, obscurity, or lack of incisiveness or precision (the *verbose* position papers). PROLIX suggests unreasonable and tedious dwelling on details (habitually transformed brief anecdotes into *prolix* sagas). DIFFUSE stresses lack of compactness and pointedness of style (*diffuse* memoirs that are so many shaggy-dog stories).

6 *plural* **:** the working or moving parts of a mechanism ⟨*works* of a clock⟩
7 a : something produced or accomplished by effort, exertion, or exercise of skill ⟨this book is the *work* of many hands⟩ **b :** something produced by the exercise of creative talent or expenditure of creative effort **:** artistic production
8 *plural* **:** performance of moral or religious acts ⟨salvation by *works*⟩
9 a : effective operation **:** EFFECT, RESULT ⟨wait for time to do its healing *work*⟩ **b :** manner of working **:** WORKMANSHIP, EXECUTION
10 : the material or piece of material that is operated upon at any stage in the process of manufacture
11 *plural* **a :** everything possessed, available, or belonging ⟨the whole *works*, rod, reel, tackle box, went overboard⟩ ⟨ordered pizza with the *works*⟩ **b :** subjection to drastic treatment **:** all possible abuse — usually used with *get* ⟨get the *works*⟩ or *give* ⟨gave them the *works*⟩
☆ ☆
— **at work 1 :** engaged in working **:** BUSY; *especially* **:** engaged in one's regular occupation **2 :** having effect **:** OPERATING, FUNCTIONING
— **in the works :** in process of preparation, development, or completion
— **in work 1 :** in process of being done **2** *of a horse* **:** in training
— **out of work :** without regular employment **:** JOBLESS

²**work** *adjective* (14th century)
1 : used for work ⟨*work* elephant⟩
2 : suitable or styled for wear while working ⟨*work* clothes⟩
3 : involving or engaged in work ⟨*work* gang⟩ ⟨*work* hours⟩

³**work** *verb* **worked** \'wərkt\ *or* **wrought** \'rȯt\; **work·ing** [Middle English *werken*, *worken*, from Old English *wyrcan;* akin to Old English *weorc*] (before 12th century)
transitive verb
1 : to bring to pass **:** EFFECT ⟨*work* miracles⟩
2 a : to fashion or create a useful or desired product by expending labor or exertion on **:** FORGE, SHAPE ⟨*work* flint into tools⟩ **b :** to make or decorate with needlework; *especially* **:** EMBROIDER
3 a : to prepare for use by stirring or kneading **b :** to bring into a desired form by a gradual process of cutting, hammering, scraping, pressing, or stretching ⟨*work* cold steel⟩
4 : to set or keep in motion, operation, or activity **:** cause to operate or produce ⟨a pump *worked* by hand⟩ ⟨*work* farmland⟩
5 : to solve (a problem) by reasoning or calculation — often used with *out*
6 a : to cause to toil or labor ⟨*worked* their horses nearly to death⟩ **b :** to make use of **:** EXPLOIT **c :** to control or guide the operation of ⟨switches are *worked* from a central tower⟩
7 a : to carry on an operation or perform a job through, at, in, or along ⟨the salespeople *worked* both sides of the street⟩ ⟨a sportscaster hired to *work* the game⟩ **b :** to greet and talk with in a friendly way in order to ingratiate oneself or achieve a purpose ⟨politicians *working* the crowd⟩ ⟨*worked* the room⟩
8 : to pay for or achieve with labor or service ⟨*worked* my way through college⟩ ⟨*worked* my way up in the company⟩
9 a : to get (oneself or an object) into or out of a condition or position by gradual stages **b :** CONTRIVE, ARRANGE ⟨we can *work* it so that you can take your vacation⟩
10 a : to practice trickery or cajolery on for some end ⟨*worked* the management for a free ticket⟩ **b :** EXCITE, PROVOKE ⟨*worked* myself into a rage⟩
intransitive verb
1 a : to exert oneself physically or mentally especially in sustained effort for a purpose or under compulsion or necessity **b :** to perform or carry through a task requiring sustained ef-

fort or continuous repeated operations ⟨*worked* all day over a hot stove⟩ **c :** to perform work or fulfill duties regularly for wages or salary
2 : to function or operate according to plan or design ⟨hinges *work* better with oil⟩
3 : to exert an influence or tendency
4 : to produce a desired effect or result **:** SUCCEED
5 a : to make way slowly and with difficulty **:** move or progress laboriously ⟨*worked* up to the presidency⟩ **b :** to sail to windward
6 : to permit of being worked **:** react in a specified way to being worked ⟨this wood *works* easily⟩
7 a : to be in agitation or restless motion **b :** FERMENT 1 **c :** to move slightly in relation to another part **d :** to get into a specified condition by slow or imperceptible movements ⟨the knot *worked* loose⟩
usage see WRECK
— **work on 1 :** AFFECT ⟨*worked on* my sympathies⟩ **2 :** to strive to influence or persuade
— **work upon :** to have effect upon **:** operate on **:** INFLUENCE

work·a·ble \'wər-kə-bəl\ *adjective* (1545)
1 : capable of being worked
2 : PRACTICABLE, FEASIBLE ⟨a *workable* system⟩
— **work·a·bil·i·ty** \ˌwər-kə-'bi-lə-tē\ *noun*
— **work·a·ble·ness** \'wər-kə-bəl-nəs\ *noun*
work·a·day \'wər-kə-ˌdā\ *adjective* [alteration of earlier *workyday*, from obsolete *workyday*, noun *workday*] (1554)
1 : of, relating to, or suited for working days
2 : ORDINARY, PROSAIC
work·a·hol·ic \ˌwər-kə-'hȯ-lik, -'hä-\ *noun* [*work* + *-aholic*, alteration of *-oholic* (as in *alcoholic*)] (1968)
: a compulsive worker
— **workaholic** *adjective*
— **work·a·hol·ism** \'wər-kə-ˌhȯ-ˌli-zəm, -ˌhä-\ *noun*
work·bag \'wərk-ˌbag\ *noun* (1775)
: a bag for implements or materials for work; *especially* **:** a bag for needlework
work·bas·ket \-ˌbas-kət\ *noun* (1743)
: a basket for needlework
work·bench \-ˌbench\ *noun* (1781)
: a bench on which work especially of mechanics, machinists, and carpenters is performed
work·boat \-ˌbōt\ *noun* (1937)
: a boat used for work purposes (as commercial fishing and ferrying supplies) rather than for sport or for passenger or naval service
work·book \-ˌbu̇k\ *noun* (1910)
1 : a worker's manual
2 : a booklet outlining a course of study
3 : a record of work done
4 : a student's book of problems to be solved directly on the pages
work·box \-ˌbäks\ *noun* (1605)
: a box for work instruments and materials
work camp *noun* (1933)
: a camp for workers: as **a :** PRISON CAMP 1 **b :** a short-term group project in which individuals from one or more religious organizations volunteer their labor
work·day \'wərk-ˌdā\ *noun* (15th century)
1 : a day on which work is performed as distinguished from a day off
2 : the period of time in a day during which work is performed
— **workday** *adjective*
worked \'wərkt\ *adjective* (1740)
: that has been subjected to some process of development, treatment, or manufacture ⟨a newly *worked* field⟩
worked up *adjective* (1903)
: emotionally aroused **:** EXCITED
work·er \'wər-kər\ *noun* (14th century)
1 a : one that works especially at manual or industrial labor or with a particular material — often used in combination **b :** a member of the working class
2 : any of the sexually underdeveloped and usually sterile members of a colony of social

ants, bees, wasps, or termites that perform most of the labor and protective duties of the colony
worker–priest *noun* (1949)
: a French Roman Catholic priest who for missionary purposes spends part of each weekday as a worker in a secular job
workers' compensation *noun* (1948)
: a system of insurance that reimburses an employer for damages that must be paid to an employee for injury occurring in the course of employment
work ethic *noun* (1951)
: a belief in work as a moral good
work·fare \'wərk-ˌfar, -ˌfer\ *noun* [*work* + wel*fare*] (1968)
: a welfare program in which recipients are required to perform usually public-service work
work farm *noun* (1953)
: a farm on which persons guilty of minor law violations are confined
work·folk \'wərk-ˌfȯk\ *or* **work·folks** \-ˌfȯks\ *noun plural* (15th century)
: working people; *especially* **:** farm workers
work·force \'wərk-ˌfȯrs, -ˌfȯrs\ *noun* (1943)
1 : the workers engaged in a specific activity or enterprise ⟨the factory's *workforce*⟩
2 : the number of workers potentially assignable for any purpose ⟨the nation's *workforce*⟩
work·horse \'wərk-ˌhȯrs\ *noun* (1543)
1 : a horse used chiefly for labor as distinguished from driving, riding, or racing

☆ **SYNONYMS**
Work, labor, travail, toil, drudgery, grind mean activity involving effort or exertion. WORK may imply activity of body, of mind, of a machine, or of a natural force ⟨too tired to do any *work*⟩. LABOR applies to physical or intellectual work involving great and often strenuous exertion ⟨farmers demanding fair compensation for their *labor*⟩. TRAVAIL is bookish for labor involving pain or suffering ⟨years of *travail* were lost when the house burned⟩. TOIL implies prolonged and fatiguing labor ⟨his lot would be years of backbreaking *toil*⟩. DRUDGERY suggests dull and irksome labor ⟨an editorial job with a good deal of *drudgery*⟩. GRIND implies labor exhausting to mind or body ⟨the *grind* of the assembly line⟩.

Work, employment, occupation, calling, pursuit, métier, business mean a specific sustained activity engaged in especially in earning one's living. WORK may apply to any purposeful activity whether remunerative or not ⟨her *work* as a hospital volunteer⟩. EMPLOYMENT implies work for which one has been engaged and is being paid by an employer ⟨your *employment* with this firm is hereby terminated⟩. OCCUPATION implies work in which one engages regularly especially as a result of training ⟨his *occupation* as a trained auto mechanic⟩. CALLING applies to an occupation viewed as a vocation or profession ⟨the ministry seemed my true *calling*⟩. PURSUIT suggests a trade, profession, or avocation followed with zeal or steady interest ⟨her family considered medicine the only proper *pursuit*⟩. MÉTIER implies a calling or pursuit for which one believes oneself to be especially fitted ⟨acting was my one and only *métier*⟩. BUSINESS suggests activity in commerce or the management of money and affairs ⟨the *business* of managing a hotel⟩.

\ə\ abut \ᵊ\ kitten \ər\ **further** \a\ ash \ā\ ace
\ä\ mop, mar \au̇\ out \ch\ chin \e\ bet \ē\ easy
\g\ go \i\ hit \ī\ ice \j\ job \ŋ\ sing \ō\ go
\ȯ\ law \ȯi\ boy \th\ thin \t̲h̲\ the \ü\ loot \u̇\ foot
\y\ yet \zh\ vision *see also* Guide to Pronunciation

2 a (1) **:** a person who performs most of the work of a group task (2) **:** a hardworking person **b :** a markedly useful or durable vehicle, craft, or machine **c :** HORSE 7

work·house \-ˌhaus\ *noun* (1652)
1 *British* **:** POORHOUSE
2 : a house of correction for persons guilty of minor law violations

work in *transitive verb* (1675)
1 : to insert or cause to penetrate by repeated or continued effort
2 : to interpose or insinuate gradually or unobtrusively ⟨*worked in* a few topical jokes⟩

¹work·ing *noun* (14th century)
1 : the manner of functioning or operating **:** OPERATION — usually used in plural
2 : an excavation or group of excavations made in mining, quarrying, or tunneling — usually used in plural

²working *adjective* (1613)
1 : engaged in work ⟨a *working* journalist⟩
2 : adequate to permit work to be done ⟨a *working* majority⟩
3 : assumed or adopted to permit or facilitate further work or activity ⟨*working* draft⟩
4 : spent at work ⟨*working* life⟩
5 : being in use or operation ⟨a *working* farm⟩

working asset *noun* (circa 1914)
: an asset other than a capital asset

working capital *noun* (circa 1901)
: capital actively turned over in or available for use in the course of business activity: **a** **:** the excess of current assets over current liabilities **b :** all capital of a business except that invested in capital assets

working–class *adjective* (1839)
: of, relating to, deriving from, or suitable to the class of wage earners ⟨*working-class* virtues⟩ ⟨*working-class* family⟩

working class *noun* (1789)
: the class of people who work for wages usually at manual labor

working day *noun* (15th century)
: WORKDAY

working dog *noun* (1891)
: a dog fitted by size, breeding, or training for useful work (as draft or herding) especially as distinguished from one fitted primarily for pet, show, or sporting use

working fluid *noun* (1903)
: a fluid working substance

work·ing·man \ˈwər-kiŋ-ˌman\ *noun* (1638)
: one who works for wages usually at manual labor

working papers *noun plural* (1928)
: official documents legalizing the employment of a minor

working substance *noun* (1897)
: a usually fluid substance that through changes of temperature, volume, and pressure is the means of carrying out thermodynamic processes or cycles (as in a heat engine)

work·ing·wom·an \ˈwər-kiŋ-ˌwu̇-mən\ *noun* (1853)
: WORKWOMAN

work·less \ˈwər-kləs\ *adjective* (15th century)
: being without work **:** UNEMPLOYED
— **work·less·ness** *noun*

work·load \ˈwərk-ˌlōd\ *noun* (1943)
1 : the amount of work or of working time expected or assigned
2 : the amount of work performed or capable of being performed (as by a mechanical device) usually within a specific period

work·man \ˈwərk-mən\ *noun* (before 12th century)
1 : WORKINGMAN
2 : ARTISAN

work·man·like \-ˌlīk\ *adjective* (1739)
: characterized by the skill and efficiency typical of a good workman

work·man·ly \-lē\ *adjective* (1545)
: WORKMANLIKE

work·man·ship \-ˌship\ *noun* (1523)
1 : something effected, made, or produced **:** WORK

2 : the art or skill of a workman **:** CRAFTSMANSHIP; *also* **:** the quality imparted to a thing in the process of making ⟨a vase of exquisite *workmanship*⟩

work·mate \ˈwərk-ˌmāt\ *noun* (1851)
chiefly British **:** a fellow worker

workmen's compensation insurance *noun* (circa 1917)
: WORKERS' COMPENSATION

work of art (1834)
1 : a product of one of the fine arts; *especially* **:** a painting or sculpture of high artistic quality
2 : something giving high aesthetic satisfaction to the viewer or listener

work off *transitive verb* (1678)
: to dispose of or get rid of by work or activity

work·out \ˈwərk-ˌau̇t\ *noun* (circa 1894)
1 : a practice or exercise to test or improve one's fitness for athletic competition, ability, or performance
2 : a test of one's ability, capacity, stamina, or suitability

work out (1534)
transitive verb
1 a : to bring about by labor and exertion ⟨*work out* your own salvation —Philippians 2:12 (Authorized Version)⟩ **b :** to solve (as a problem) by a process of reasoning or calculation **c :** to devise, arrange, or achieve by resolving difficulties ⟨after many years of wrangling, *worked out* a definite agreement —A. A. Butkus⟩ **d :** DEVELOP ⟨the final situation is not *worked out* with psychological profundity —Leslie Rees⟩
2 : to discharge (as a debt) by labor
3 : to exhaust (as a mine) by working
intransitive verb
1 a : to prove effective, practicable, or suitable ⟨how this will actually *work out* I don't know —Milton Kotler⟩ **b :** to amount to a total or calculated figure — used with *at* or *to*
2 : to engage in a workout ⟨*works out* in gymnasiums . . . to keep in shape —*Current Biography*⟩

work over *transitive verb* (1874)
1 : to do over **:** REWORK ⟨saved the play by *working* the first act *over*⟩
2 : to subject to thorough examination, study, or treatment ⟨shelf stock *worked over* by shoppers⟩
3 : to beat up or manhandle with thoroughness ⟨the gang *worked* me *over*⟩

work·peo·ple \ˈwərk-ˌpē-pəl\ *noun plural* (1708)
chiefly British **:** WORKERS, EMPLOYEES

work·piece \-ˌpēs\ *noun* (1926)
: a piece of work in process of manufacture

work·place \-ˌplās\ *noun* (circa 1828)
: a place (as a shop or factory) where work is done

work print *noun* (1937)
: a completely edited motion-picture print used as a guide in cutting the original negative from which the final production prints will be made

work·room \ˈwərk-ˌrüm, -ˌru̇m\ *noun* (1828)
: a room used for work

work·shop \-ˌshäp\ *noun* (1562)
1 : a small establishment where manufacturing or handicrafts are carried on
2 : WORKROOM
3 : a usually brief intensive educational program for a relatively small group of people that focuses especially on techniques and skills in a particular field

work song *noun* (1911)
: a song sung in rhythm with work

work·sta·tion \-ˌstā-shən\ *noun* (1931)
1 : an area with equipment for the performance of a specialized task usually by a single individual
2 a : an intelligent terminal or personal computer usually connected to a computer network **b :** a powerful microcomputer used especially for scientific or engineering work

work stoppage *noun* (1945)

: concerted cessation of work by a group of employees usually more spontaneous and less serious than a strike

work–study program *noun* (1946)
: a program planned to give high school or college students work experience

work·ta·ble \ˈwərk-ˌtā-bəl\ *noun* (1790)
: a table for holding working materials and implements; *especially* **:** a small table with drawers and other conveniences for needlework

work–to–rule *noun* (1950)
: the practice of working to the strictest interpretation of the rules as a job action

work·up \ˈwərk-ˌəp\ *noun* (1939)
: an intensive diagnostic study

work·up \ˈwərk-ˌəp\ *noun* (1903)
: an unintended mark on a printed sheet caused by the rising of spacing material

work up (15th century)
transitive verb
1 : to stir up **:** ROUSE
2 : to produce by mental or physical work ⟨*worked up* a comedy act⟩ ⟨*worked up* a sweat in the gymnasium⟩
intransitive verb
: to rise gradually in intensity or emotional tone

work·week \ˈwərk-ˌwēk\ *noun* (1921)
: the hours or days of work in a calendar week ⟨40-hour *workweek*⟩ ⟨a 5-day *workweek*⟩ ⟨a shortened *workweek*⟩

work·wom·an \-ˌwu̇-mən\ *noun* (circa 1530)
: a woman who works

¹world \ˈwər(-ə)ld\ *noun* [Middle English, from Old English *woruld* human existence, this world, age (akin to Old High German *weralt* age, world); akin to Old English *wer* man, *eald* old — more at VIRILE, OLD] (before 12th century)
1 a : the earthly state of human existence **b :** life after death — used with a qualifier ⟨the next *world*⟩
2 : the earth with its inhabitants and all things upon it
3 : individual course of life **:** CAREER
4 : the inhabitants of the earth **:** the human race
5 a : the concerns of the earth and its affairs as distinguished from heaven and the life to come **b :** secular affairs
6 : the system of created things **:** UNIVERSE
7 a : a division or generation of the inhabitants of the earth distinguished by living together at the same place or at the same time ⟨the medieval *world*⟩ **b :** a distinctive class of persons or their sphere of interest ⟨the academic *world*⟩ ⟨the sports *world*⟩
8 : human society ⟨withdraw from the *world*⟩
9 : a part or section of the earth that is a separate independent unit
10 : the sphere or scene of one's life and action ⟨living in your own little *world*⟩
11 : an indefinite multitude or a great quantity or distance ⟨makes a *world* of difference⟩ ⟨a *world* away⟩
12 : the whole body of living persons **:** PUBLIC ⟨announced their discovery to the *world*⟩
13 : KINGDOM 5 ⟨the animal *world*⟩
14 : a celestial body (as a planet)
— **for all the world :** in every way **:** EXACTLY ⟨copies which look *for all the world* like the original⟩
— **in the world :** among innumerable possibilities **:** EVER — used as an intensive ⟨what *in the world* is it⟩
— **out of this world :** of extraordinary excellence **:** SUPERB

²world *adjective* (13th century)
1 : of or relating to the world ⟨a *world* championship⟩
2 a : extending or found throughout the world **:** WORLDWIDE ⟨brought about *world* peace⟩ **b :** involving or applying to part of or the whole world ⟨a *world* tour⟩ ⟨a *world* state⟩

world–beat·er \'wərl(d)-ˌbē-tər\ noun (circa 1888)
: one that excels all others of its kind : CHAMPION

world–class adjective (1950)
: being of the highest caliber in the world ⟨a world-class polo player⟩

world federalism noun (1950)
1 : federalism on a worldwide basis
2 W&F capitalized **a** : the principles and policies of the World Federalists **b** : the body or movement composed of World Federalists

world federalist noun (1951)
1 : an adherent or advocate of world federalism
2 W&F capitalized : a member of a movement arising after World War II advocating the formation of a federal union of the nations of the world with limited but positive governmental powers

world·ling \'wərl(-ə)ld-liŋ, 'wərl-liŋ\ noun (1549)
: a person engrossed in the concerns of this present world

world·ly \'wər(-ə)ld-lē, 'wərl-lē\ adjective (before 12th century)
1 : of, relating to, or devoted to this world and its pursuits rather than to religion or spiritual affairs
2 : WORLDLY-WISE
synonym see EARTHLY
— **world·li·ness** noun

world·ly–mind·ed \ˌwərl(d)-lē-'mīn-dəd\ adjective (1601)
: devoted to or engrossed in worldly interests
— **world·ly–mind·ed·ness** noun

world·ly–wise \'wərl(d)-lē-ˌwīz\ adjective (15th century)
: possessing a practical and often shrewd understanding of human affairs
synonym see SOPHISTICATED

world power noun (1860)
: a political unit (as a nation or state) powerful enough to affect the entire world by its influence or actions

world premiere noun (1925)
: the first regular performance (as of a theatrical production) anywhere in the world

World Series noun [from World Series, annual championship of U.S. major-league baseball] (1951)
: a contest or event that is the most important or prestigious of its kind ⟨the World Series of the equestrian world⟩

world's fair noun (1850)
: an international exposition featuring exhibits and participants from all over the world

world–shak·ing \'wərl(d)-ˌshā-kiŋ\ adjective (1598)
: EARTHSHAKING

world soul noun (1848)
: an animating spirit or creative principle related to the world as the soul is to the individual being

world·view \-ˌvyü\ noun (1858)
: WELTANSCHAUUNG

world war noun (1909)
: a war engaged in by all or most of the principal nations of the world; especially, both Ws capitalized : either of two such wars of the first half of the 20th century

world–wea·ry \'wərl-ˌwir-ē\ adjective (1768)
: feeling or showing fatigue from or boredom with the life of the world and especially material pleasures
— **world–wea·ri·ness** noun

¹**world·wide** \-'wīd\ adjective (1632)
: extended throughout or involving the entire world

²**worldwide** adverb (1892)
: throughout the world

¹**worm** \'wərm\ noun, often attributive [Middle English, from Old English wyrm serpent,

worm; akin to Old High German wurm serpent, worm, Latin vermis worm] (before 12th century)
1 a : EARTHWORM; broadly : an annelid worm **b** : any of numerous relatively small elongated usually naked and soft-bodied animals: as (1) : an insect larva; especially : one that is a destructive grub, caterpillar, or maggot (2) : SHIPWORM (3) : BLINDWORM
2 a : a human being who is an object of contempt, loathing, or pity : WRETCH **b** : something that torments or devours from within
3 archaic : SNAKE, SERPENT
4 : HELMINTHIASIS — usually used in plural
5 : something (as a mechanical device) spiral or vermiculate in form or appearance: as **a** : the thread of a screw **b** : a short revolving screw whose threads gear with the teeth of a worm wheel or a rack **c** : a spiral condensing tube used in distilling **d** : ARCHIMEDES' SCREW; also : a conveyor working on the principle of such a screw
6 : a usually small self-contained computer program that invades computers on a network and usually performs a malicious action
— **worm-like** \-ˌlīk\ adjective

²**worm** (1610)
intransitive verb
: to move or proceed sinuously or insidiously
transitive verb
1 a : to proceed or make (one's way) insidiously or deviously ⟨worm their way into positions of power —Bill Franzen⟩ **b** : to insinuate or introduce (oneself) by devious or subtle means **c** : to cause to move or proceed in or as if in the manner of a worm
2 : to wind rope or yarn spirally round and between the strands of (a cable or rope) before serving
3 : to obtain or extract by artful or insidious questioning or by pleading, asking, or persuading — usually used with out of
4 : to treat (an animal) with a drug to destroy or expel parasitic worms

worm–eat·en \'wərm-ˌē-t°n\ adjective (14th century)
1 a : eaten or burrowed by worms ⟨worm-eaten timber⟩ **b** : PITTED
2 : WORN-OUT, ANTIQUATED

worm·er \'wər-mər\ noun (circa 1934)
: a drug used in veterinary medicine to worm an animal

worm fence noun (1652)
: a zigzag fence consisting of interlocking rails supported by crossed poles — called also snake fence, Virginia fence

worm gear noun (circa 1876)
1 : WORM WHEEL
2 : a gear of a worm and a worm wheel working together

worm fence

worm·hole \'wərm-ˌhōl\ noun (1593)
1 : a hole or passage burrowed by a worm
2 : a hypothetical structure of space-time envisioned as a long thin tunnel connecting points that are separated in space and time

worm·seed \-ˌsēd\ noun (15th century)
: any of various plants whose seeds possess anthelmintic properties: as **a** : any of several artemisias **b** : a goosefoot (Chenopodium ambrosioides)

worm's–eye \'wərm-ˌzī\ adjective (1908)
: seen from ground level or from the lowest levels of a hierarchy ⟨the bird's-eye view of the executive and the worm's-eye view of the employee —Current Biography⟩

worm snake noun (1885)
: a reddish terrestrial colubrid snake (Carphophis amoenus) of the eastern U.S.

worm wheel noun (1677)
: a toothed wheel gearing with the thread of a worm

worm·wood \'wərm-ˌwu̇d\ noun [Middle English wormwode, alteration of wermode, from Old English wermōd; akin to Old High German wermuota wormwood] (15th century)
1 : ARTEMISIA; especially : a European plant (Artemisia absinthium) that has silvery silky-haired leaves and drooping yellow nearly globular flower heads and yields a bitter dark green oil used in absinthe
2 : something bitter or grievous : BITTERNESS

wormy \'wər-mē\ adjective **worm·i·er; -est** (15th century)
1 : containing, abounding in, or infested with or as if with worms ⟨wormy flour⟩ ⟨a wormy dog⟩; also : damaged by worms : WORM-EATEN ⟨wormy timbers⟩
2 : resembling or suggestive of a worm

worn past participle of WEAR

worn–out \'wōrn-'au̇t, 'wȯrn-\ adjective (1589)
: exhausted or used up by or as if by wear

wor·ri·ment \'wər-ē-mənt, 'wə-rē-\ noun (1833)
: an act or instance of worrying; also : TROUBLE, WORRY

wor·ri·some \-səm\ adjective (1845)
1 : causing distress or worry
2 : inclined to worry or fret
— **wor·ri·some·ly** adverb
— **wor·ri·some·ness** noun

¹**wor·ry** \'wər-ē, 'wə-rē\ verb **wor·ried; wor·ry·ing** [Middle English worien, from Old English wyrgan; akin to Old High German wurgen to strangle, Lithuanian veržti to constrict] (before 12th century)
transitive verb
1 dialect British : CHOKE, STRANGLE
2 a : to harass by tearing, biting, or snapping especially at the throat **b** : to shake or pull at with the teeth ⟨a terrier worrying a rat⟩ **c** : to touch or disturb something repeatedly **d** : to change the position of or adjust by repeated pushing or hauling
3 a : to assail with rough or aggressive attack or treatment : TORMENT **b** : to subject to persistent or nagging attention or effort
4 : to afflict with mental distress or agitation : make anxious
intransitive verb
1 dialect British : STRANGLE, CHOKE
2 : to move, proceed, or progress by unceasing or difficult effort : STRUGGLE
3 : to feel or experience concern or anxiety : FRET ☆
— **wor·ried·ly** \-(r)ēd-lē, -(r)əd-\ adverb

☆ SYNONYMS
Worry, annoy, harass, harry, plague, pester, tease mean to disturb or irritate by persistent acts. WORRY implies an incessant goading or attacking that drives one to desperation ⟨pursued a policy of worrying the enemy⟩. ANNOY implies disturbing one's composure or peace of mind by intrusion, interference, or petty attacks ⟨you're doing that just to annoy me⟩. HARASS implies petty persecutions or burdensome demands that exhaust one's nervous or mental power ⟨harassed on all sides by creditors⟩. HARRY may imply heavy oppression or maltreatment ⟨the strikers had been harried by thugs⟩. PLAGUE implies a painful and persistent affliction ⟨plagued all her life by poverty⟩. PESTER stresses the repetition of petty attacks ⟨constantly pestered with trivial complaints⟩. TEASE suggests an attempt to break down one's resistance or rouse to wrath ⟨children teased the dog⟩.

\ə\ abut \ᵊ\ kitten \ər\ further \a\ ash \ā\ ace
\ä\ mop, mar \au̇\ out \ch\ chin \e\ bet \ē\ easy
\g\ go \i\ hit \ī\ ice \j\ job \ŋ\ sing \ō\ go
\ȯ\ law \ȯi\ boy \th\ thin \th\ the \ü\ loot \u̇\ foot
\y\ yet \zh\ vision see also Guide to Pronunciation

— **wor·ri·er** \-(r)ē-ər\ *noun*
²**worry** *noun, plural* **worries** (1804)
1 a : mental distress or agitation resulting from concern usually for something impending or anticipated **:** ANXIETY **b :** an instance or occurrence of such distress or agitation
2 : a cause of worry **:** TROUBLE, DIFFICULTY
synonym see CARE
worry beads *noun plural* (1956)
: a string of beads that can be fingered to keep one's hands occupied
wor·ry·wart \'wər-ē-,wȯrt, 'wə-rē-\ *noun* (1936)
: one who is inclined to worry unduly
¹**worse** \'wərs\ *adjective, comparative of* BAD *or of* ILL [Middle English *werse, worse,* from Old English *wiersa, wyrsa;* akin to Old High German *wirsiro* worse] (before 12th century)
1 : of more inferior quality, value, or condition
2 a : more unfavorable, difficult, unpleasant, or painful **b :** more faulty, unsuitable, or incorrect **c :** less skillful or efficient
3 : bad, evil, or corrupt in a greater degree **:** more reprehensible
4 : being in poorer health **:** SICKER
²**worse** *noun* (before 12th century)
: one that is worse ⟨thought he was an atheist and *worse* —Van Wyck Brooks⟩
³**worse** *adverb, comparative of* BAD *or of* ILL (before 12th century)
1 : in a worse manner **:** to a worse extent or degree
2 : what is worse
wors·en \'wərs-°n\ *verb* **wors·ened; wors·en·ing** \'wərs-niŋ, 'wər-s°n-iŋ\ (13th century)
transitive verb
: to make worse
intransitive verb
: to become worse
wors·er \'wər-sər\ *adjective or adverb* (15th century)
archaic **:** WORSE ⟨I cannot hate thee *worser* than I do —Shakespeare⟩
¹**wor·ship** \'wər-shəp\ *noun* [Middle English *worshipe* worthiness, respect, reverence paid to a divine being, from Old English *weorth-scipe* worthiness, respect, from *weorth* worthy, worth + *-scipe* -ship] (before 12th century)
1 *chiefly British* **:** a person of importance — used as a title for various officials (as magistrates and some mayors)
2 : reverence offered a divine being or supernatural power; *also* **:** an act of expressing such reverence
3 : a form of religious practice with its creed and ritual
4 : extravagant respect or admiration for or devotion to an object of esteem ⟨*worship* of the dollar⟩
²**worship** *verb* **-shiped** *or* **-shipped; -ship·ing** *or* **-ship·ping** (13th century)
transitive verb
1 : to honor or reverence as a divine being or supernatural power
2 : to regard with great or extravagant respect, honor, or devotion
intransitive verb
: to perform or take part in worship or an act of worship
synonym see REVERE
— **wor·ship·er** *or* **wor·ship·per** *noun*
wor·ship·ful \'wər-shəp-fəl\ *adjective* (14th century)
1 a *archaic* **:** NOTABLE, DISTINGUISHED **b** *chiefly British* — used as a title for various persons or groups of rank or distinction
2 : giving or expressing worship or veneration
— **wor·ship·ful·ly** \-fə-lē\ *adverb*
— **wor·ship·ful·ness** *noun*
wor·ship·less \-shə-pləs\ *adjective* (1765)
: lacking worship or worshipers
¹**worst** \'wərst\ *adjective, superlative of* BAD *or of* ILL [Middle English *werste, worste,* from Old English *wierresta, wyrsta,* superlative of the root of Old English *wiersa* worse] (before 12th century)

1 : most corrupt, bad, evil, or ill
2 a : most unfavorable, difficult, unpleasant, or painful **b :** most unsuitable, faulty, unattractive, or ill-conceived **c :** least skillful or efficient
3 : most wanting in quality, value, or condition
— **the worst way :** very much ⟨such men . . . need indoctrination *the worst way* —J. G. Cozzens⟩ — often used with *in* ⟨wanted a new bicycle in *the worst way*⟩
²**worst** *adverb, superlative of* ILL *or* ILLY *or of* BAD *or* BADLY (before 12th century)
1 : to the extreme degree of badness or inferiority
2 : to the greatest or highest degree ⟨groups who need the subsidies *worst* lose out —T. W. Arnold⟩
³**worst** *noun, plural* **worst** (14th century)
: one that is worst
— **at worst :** under the worst circumstances
⁴**worst** *transitive verb* (1636)
: to get the better of **:** DEFEAT
worst–case *adjective* (1964)
: involving, projecting, or providing for the worst possible circumstances or outcome of a given situation
wor·sted \'wu̇s-təd, 'wər-stəd\ *noun* [Middle English, from *Worsted* (now *Worstead*), England] (13th century)
: a smooth compact yarn from long wool fibers used especially for firm napless fabrics, carpeting, or knitting; *also* **:** a fabric made from worsted yarns
— **worsted** *adjective*
¹**wort** \'wərt, 'wȯrt\ *noun* [Middle English, from Old English *wyrt* root, herb, plant — more at ROOT] (before 12th century)
: PLANT; *especially* **:** an herbaceous plant — usually used in combination ⟨louse*wort*⟩
²**wort** *noun* [Middle English, from Old English *wyrt;* akin to Middle High German *würze* brewer's wort, Old English *wyrt* root, herb] (before 12th century)
: a liquid formed by soaking mash in hot water and then fermented to make beer
¹**worth** \'wərth\ *intransitive verb* [Middle English, from Old English *weorthan;* akin to Old High German *werdan* to become, Latin *vertere* to turn, Lithuanian *versti* to overturn, Sanskrit *vartate* he turns] (before 12th century)
archaic **:** BECOME — usually used in the phrase *woe worth*
²**worth** *adjective* [Middle English, from Old English *weorth* worthy, of (a specified) value; akin to Old High German *werd* worthy, worth] (before 12th century)
1 *archaic* **:** having monetary or material value
2 *archaic* **:** ESTIMABLE
— **for all one is worth :** to the fullest extent of one's value or ability
³**worth** *noun* (before 12th century)
1 a : monetary value ⟨farmhouse and lands of little *worth*⟩ **b :** the equivalent of a specified amount or figure ⟨a dollar's *worth* of gas⟩
2 : the value of something measured by its qualities or by the esteem in which it is held ⟨a literary heritage of great *worth*⟩
3 a : moral or personal value ⟨trying to teach human *worth*⟩ **b :** MERIT, EXCELLENCE ⟨a field in which we have proved our *worth*⟩
4 : WEALTH, RICHES
⁴**worth** *preposition* (13th century)
1 a : equal in value to **b :** having assets or income equal to
2 : deserving of ⟨well *worth* the effort⟩
— **worth one's salt :** of substantial or significant value or merit
worth·ful \'wərth-fəl\ *adjective* (before 12th century)
1 : full of merit ⟨a good and *worthful* person⟩
2 : having value ⟨the *worthful* aspects of their culture⟩
worth·less \'wərth-ləs\ *adjective* (1588)

1 a : lacking worth **:** VALUELESS ⟨*worthless* currency⟩ **b :** USELESS ⟨*worthless* to continue searching⟩
2 : CONTEMPTIBLE, DESPICABLE
— **worth·less·ly** *adverb*
— **worth·less·ness** *noun*
worth·while \-'hwī(ə)l, -'wī(ə)l\ *adjective* (1900)
1 : being worth the time or effort spent
2 : WORTHY 1
— **worth·while·ness** *noun*
¹**wor·thy** \'wər-thē\ *adjective* **wor·thi·er; -est** (13th century)
1 a : having worth or value **:** ESTIMABLE ⟨a *worthy* cause⟩ **b :** HONORABLE, MERITORIOUS ⟨*worthy* candidates⟩
2 : having sufficient worth or importance ⟨*worthy* to be remembered⟩
— **wor·thi·ly** \'wər-thə-lē\ *adverb*
— **wor·thi·ness** \-thē-nəs\ *noun*
²**worthy** *noun, plural* **worthies** (14th century)
: a worthy or prominent person
-wor·thy \,wər-thē\ *adjective combining form*
1 : fit or safe for ⟨a sea*worthy* vessel⟩
2 : of sufficient worth for ⟨a news*worthy* event⟩
¹**wot** *present 1st & 3d singular of* WIT
²**wot** \'wät\ *verb* **wot·ted; wot·ting** [Middle English, alteration of *witen* — more at WIT] (14th century)
chiefly British **:** KNOW — often used with *of*
would \wəd, əd, d, 'wu̇d\ *past of* WILL [Middle English *wolde,* from Old English; akin to Old High German *wolta* wished, desired] (before 12th century)
1 a *archaic* **:** WISHED, DESIRED **b** *archaic* **:** wish for **:** WANT **c** (1) **:** strongly desire **:** WISH ⟨I *would* I were young again⟩ — often used without a subject and with *that* in a past or conditional construction ⟨*would* that I had heeded your advice⟩ (2) — used in auxiliary function with *rather* or *sooner* to express preference ⟨he *would* sooner die than face them⟩
2 a — used in auxiliary function to express wish, desire, or intent ⟨those who *would* forbid gambling⟩ **b** — used in auxiliary function to express willingness or preference ⟨as ye *would* that men should do to you —Luke 6:31 (Authorized Version)⟩ **c** — used in auxiliary function to express plan or intention ⟨said we *would* come⟩
3 — used in auxiliary function to express custom or habitual action ⟨we *would* meet often for lunch⟩
4 — used in auxiliary function to express consent or choice ⟨*would* put it off if he could⟩
5 a — used in auxiliary function in the conclusion of a conditional sentence to express a contingency or possibility ⟨if he were coming, he *would* be here now⟩ **b** — used in auxiliary function in a noun clause (as one completing a statement of desire, request, or advice) ⟨we wish that he *would* go⟩
6 — used in auxiliary function to express probability or presumption in past or present time ⟨*would* have won if I had not tripped⟩
7 : COULD ⟨the barrel *would* hold 20 gallons⟩
8 — used in auxiliary function to express a request with which voluntary compliance is expected ⟨*would* you please help us⟩
9 — used in auxiliary function to express doubt or uncertainty ⟨the explanation . . . *would* seem satisfactory⟩
10 : SHOULD ⟨knew I *would* enjoy the trip⟩ ⟨*would* be glad to know the answer⟩ □
would–be \'wu̇d-'bē\ *adjective* (1647)
: desiring, professing, or having the potential to be
would·est \'wu̇-dəst\ *archaic past 2d singular of* WILL
wouldn't \'wu̇-d°nt, -d°n, *dialect also* 'wu̇-t°n(t) *or* ,wu̇nt\ (circa 1828)
: would not
wouldst \wədst, 'wu̇dst, wətst\ *archaic past 2d singular of* WILL

¹wound \'wünd, *archaic or dialect* 'waůnd\ *noun* [Middle English, from Old English *wund;* akin to Old High German *wunta* wound] (before 12th century)
1 a : an injury to the body (as from violence, accident, or surgery) that involves laceration or breaking of a membrane (as the skin) and usually damage to underlying tissues **b** : a cut or breach in a plant due to external violence
2 : a mental or emotional hurt or blow
3 : something resembling a wound in appearance or effect; *especially* : a rift in or blow to a political body or social group

²wound (before 12th century)
transitive verb
: to cause a wound to or in
intransitive verb
: to inflict a wound

³wound \'waůnd\ *past and past participle of* WIND

¹wound·ed \'wün-dəd\ *noun plural* (before 12th century)
: wounded persons

²wounded *adjective* (14th century)
: injured, hurt by, or suffering from a wound

wound·less \'wün(d)-ləs\ *adjective* (1579)
1 : free from wounds : UNWOUNDED
2 *obsolete* : INVULNERABLE ⟨the *woundless* air —Shakespeare⟩

wove *past of* WEAVE
¹woven *past participle of* WEAVE
²wo·ven \'wō-vən\ *noun* (1930)
: a woven fabric

wove paper \'wōv-\ *noun* [*wove* (archaic past participle of *weave*)] (1815)
: paper made with a revolving roller covered with wires so woven as to produce no fine lines running across the grain — compare LAID PAPER

¹wow \'waů\ *interjection* (1513)
— used to express strong feeling (as pleasure or surprise)

²wow *noun* (1920)
: a striking success : HIT

³wow *transitive verb* (1924)
: to excite to enthusiastic admiration or approval

⁴wow *noun* [imitative] (1932)
: a distortion in reproduced sound consisting of a slow rise and fall of pitch caused by speed variation in the reproducing system

wow·ser \'waů-zər\ *noun* [origin unknown] (1899)
chiefly Australian : an obtrusively puritanical person

W particle *noun* [*weak*] (1963)
: either of two particles about 80 times heavier than a proton that along with the Z particle are transmitters of the weak force and that can have a positive or negative charge

¹wrack \'rak\ *noun* [Middle English *wrak,* from Middle Dutch or Middle Low German; akin to Old English *wræc* something driven by the sea] (14th century)
1 a : a wrecked ship **b** : WRECKAGE **c** : WRECK **d** *dialect* : the violent destruction of a structure, machine, or vehicle
2 a : marine vegetation; *especially* : KELP **b** : dried seaweeds

²wrack *noun* [Middle English, from Old English *wræc* misery, punishment, something driven by the sea; akin to Old English *wrecan* to drive, punish — more at WREAK] (15th century)
1 : RUIN, DESTRUCTION
2 : a remnant of something destroyed

³wrack *transitive verb* (1562)
: to utterly ruin : WRECK

⁴wrack *verb* [by alteration] (circa 1555)
: ⁴RACK

⁵wrack *noun* (1591)
: ³RACK 2

⁶wrack *noun* (1796)
: ¹RACK

wrack·ful \'rak-fəl\ *adjective* (1558)
: DESTRUCTIVE

wraith \'rāth\ *noun, plural* **wraiths** \'rāths *also* 'rāthz\ [origin unknown] (1513)
1 a : the exact likeness of a living person seen usually just before death as an apparition **b** : GHOST, SPECTER
2 : an insubstantial form or semblance : SHADOW
3 : a barely visible gaseous or vaporous column
— **wraith·like** \-,līk\ *adjective*

¹wran·gle \'raŋ-gəl\ *verb* **wran·gled; wran·gling** \-g(ə-)liŋ\ [Middle English; akin to Old High German *ringan* to struggle — more at WRING] (14th century)
intransitive verb
1 : to dispute angrily or peevishly : BICKER
2 : to engage in argument or controversy
transitive verb
1 : to obtain by persistent arguing or maneuvering : WANGLE
2 [back-formation from *wrangler*] : to herd and care for (livestock and especially horses) on the range

²wrangle *noun* (1547)
1 : an angry, noisy, or prolonged dispute or quarrel
2 : the action or process of wrangling

wran·gler \-g(ə-)lər\ *noun* (circa 1515)
1 : a bickering disputant
2 [short for *horse-wrangler,* probably part translation of Mexican Spanish *caballerango* groom] : a ranch hand who takes care of the saddle horses; *broadly* : COWBOY

¹wrap \'rap\ *verb* **wrapped; wrap·ping** [Middle English *wrappen*] (14th century)
transitive verb
1 a : to cover especially by winding or folding **b** : to envelop and secure for transportation or storage : BUNDLE **c** : ENFOLD, EMBRACE **d** : to coil, fold, draw, or twine (as string or cloth) around something
2 a : SURROUND, ENVELOP **b** : to suffuse or surround with an aura or state ⟨the affair was *wrapped* in scandal⟩ **c** : to involve completely : ENGROSS — usually used with *up*
3 : to conceal or obscure as if by enveloping
4 : to enclose as if with a protective covering
5 : to finish filming or videotaping ⟨*wrap* a movie⟩
intransitive verb
1 : to wind, coil, or twine so as to encircle or cover something
2 : to put on clothing : DRESS — usually used with *up*
3 : to be subject to covering, enclosing, or packaging — usually used with *up*
4 : to come to completion in filming or videotaping

²wrap *noun* (15th century)
1 a (1) : WRAPPER, WRAPPING (2) : material used for wrapping ⟨plastic *wrap*⟩ **b** : an article of clothing that may be wrapped round a person; *especially* : an outer garment (as a coat or shawl) **c** : BLANKET
2 : a single turn or convolution of something wound round an object
3 *plural* **a** : RESTRAINT **b** : a shroud of secrecy ⟨a plan kept under *wraps*⟩
4 : the completion of a schedule or session for filming or videotaping

³wrap *adjective* (1948)
: WRAPAROUND 1

¹wrap·around \'rap-ə-,raůnd\ *noun* (1924)
1 : a garment (as a dress) made with a full-length opening and adjusted to the figure by wrapping around
2 : an object that encircles or especially curves and laps over another

²wraparound *adjective* (1926)
1 : made to be wrapped around something and especially the body ⟨a *wraparound* skirt⟩
2 a : shaped to follow a contour; *especially* : made to curve from the front around to the side ⟨*wraparound* sunglasses⟩ ⟨*wraparound*

terraces⟩ **b** : extending laterally to the outermost limits of the field of vision ⟨a *wraparound* movie screen⟩

wrap·per \'ra-pər\ *noun* (15th century)
1 : that in which something is wrapped: as **a** : a tobacco leaf used for the outside covering especially of cigars **b** (1) : JACKET 3c(1) (2) : the paper cover of a book not bound in boards **c** : a paper wrapped around a newspaper or magazine in the mail
2 : one that wraps
3 : an article of clothing worn wrapped around the body

wrap·ping \'ra-piŋ\ *noun* (14th century)
: something used to wrap an object : WRAPPER

wrap–up \'rap-,əp\ *noun* (1951)
1 : a summarizing report
2 : a concluding part : FINALE

wrap up *transitive verb* (circa 1568)
1 : SUMMARIZE, SUM UP
2 a : to bring to a usually successful conclusion **b** : CINCH, SEW UP ⟨has the nomination *wrapped up*⟩

wrasse \'ras\ *noun, plural* **wrasses** *also* **wrasse** [Cornish *gwragh, wragh* hag, wrasse] (circa 1672)
: any of a large family (Labridae) of elongate compressed usually brilliantly colored marine bony fishes that usually bury themselves in sand at night and include important food fishes as well as a number of popular aquarium fishes

¹wrath \'rath, *chiefly British* 'rȯth\ *noun* [Middle English, from Old English *wræththo,* from *wrāth* wroth — more at WROTH] (before 12th century)
1 : strong vengeful anger or indignation
2 : retributory punishment for an offense or a crime : divine chastisement
synonym see ANGER

²wrath *adjective* [alteration of *wroth*] (1535)
archaic : WRATHFUL

wrath·ful \-fəl\ *adjective* (14th century)
1 : filled with wrath : IRATE

☐ **USAGE**

would *Would have* is sometimes substituted for the past subjunctive *had* in the subordinate clause of a conditional sentence ⟨if we *would have* known Max was going to die [we] should have made sound movies of him —Ernest Hemingway (letter)⟩. Most of the evidence for this construction comes from speech, and it must be common in student writing for it is mentioned as something to avoid in student handbooks dating from 1920 to the present. It is occasionally found in edited writing ⟨if the spurious signal *would have* turned up during the brief period it took to punch the keys, it would have triggered an actual abort —*N. Y. Times*⟩ ⟨if this *would have* been a real . . . test of his critical powers, in another sense it could have proved a greater surety for his critical survival —Louis Kronenberger⟩. The origin and development of this construction are imperfectly known, but it has been found as far back as the second half of the 19th century ⟨these characteristics, fixed and unchangeable as bone in Mr. Casaubon, might have remained longer unfelt by Dorothea . . . if he *would have* held her hands between his and listened —George Eliot⟩. It is apparently well established in speech, where it tends not to be noticed. It is better avoided in writing, however, where it tends to attract unfavorable notice.

\ə\ abut \ᵊ\ kitten \ər\ further \a\ ash \ā\ ace
\g\ go \i\ hit \ī\ ice \j\ job \ŋ\ sing \ō\ go
\ȯ\ law \ȯi\ boy \th\ thin \th\ the \ü\ loot \ů\ foot
\y\ yet \zh\ vision *see also* Guide to Pronunciation

2 : arising from, marked by, or indicative of wrath
— **wrath·ful·ly** \-fə-lē\ *adverb*
— **wrath·ful·ness** *noun*
wrathy \'ra-thē, *chiefly British* 'rȯ-\ *adjective* (1828)
: WRATHFUL

wreak \'rēk *also* 'rek\ *transitive verb* [Middle English *wreken*, from Old English *wrecan* to drive, punish, avenge; akin to Old High German *rehhan* to avenge and perhaps to Latin *urgēre* to drive on, urge] (before 12th century)
1 a *archaic* : AVENGE **b** : to cause the infliction of (vengeance or punishment)
2 : to give free play or course to (malevolent feeling)
3 : BRING ABOUT, CAUSE ⟨*wreak* havoc⟩
usage see WRECK

wreath \'rēth\ *noun, plural* **wreaths** \'rēthz, 'rēths\ [Middle English *wrethe,* from Old English *writha;* akin to Old English *wrīthan* to twist — more at WRITHE] (before 12th century)
: something intertwined into a circular shape; *especially* : GARLAND, CHAPLET

wreathe \'rēth\ *verb* **wreathed; wreath·ing** [*wreath*] (1530)
transitive verb
1 a : to shape into a wreath **b** : INTERWEAVE **c** : to cause to coil about something
2 : to twist or contort so as to show folds or creases
3 : to encircle or adorn with or as if with a wreath
intransitive verb
1 : to twist in coils : WRITHE
2 a : to take on the shape of a wreath **b** : to move or extend in circles or spirals

wreathy \'rē-thē, -thē\ *adjective* (1644)
1 : having the form of a wreath
2 : constituting a wreath

¹wreck \'rek\ *noun* [Middle English *wrek,* from Anglo-French, of Scandinavian origin; akin to Old Norse *rek* wreck; akin to Old English *wrecan* to drive] (13th century)
1 : something cast up on the land by the sea especially after a shipwreck
2 a : SHIPWRECK **b** : the action of wrecking or fact or state of being wrecked : DESTRUCTION
3 a : a hulk or the ruins of a wrecked ship **b** : the broken remains of something wrecked or otherwise ruined **c** : something disabled or in a state of ruin or dilapidation; *also* : a person or animal of broken constitution, health, or spirits

²wreck (15th century)
transitive verb
1 : to cast ashore
2 a : to reduce to a ruinous state by or as if by violence **b** : SHIPWRECK **c** : to ruin, damage, or imperil by a wreck **d** : to involve in disaster or ruin
3 : BRING ABOUT, WREAK ⟨*wreck* havoc⟩
intransitive verb
1 : to become wrecked
2 : to rob, salvage, or repair wreckage or a wreck □

wreck·age \'re-kij\ *noun* (1837)
1 : the act of wrecking : the state of being wrecked
2 a : something that has been wrecked **b** : broken and disordered parts or material from something wrecked

wreck·er \'re-kər\ *noun* (1802)
1 a : one that searches for or works on the wrecks of ships (as for rescue or for plunder) **b** : TOW TRUCK
2 : one that wrecks; *especially* : one whose work is the demolition of buildings

wrecker's ball *noun* (1967)
: a heavy iron or steel ball swung or dropped by a derrick to demolish old buildings — called also *wrecking ball*

wrecking bar *noun* (1924)

: a small crowbar with a claw for pulling nails at one end and a slight bend for prying at the other end

wren \'ren\ *noun* [Middle English *wrenne,* from Old English *wrenna;* akin to Old High German *rentilo* wren] (before 12th century)
1 : any of a family (Troglodytidae) of numerous small more or less brown oscine singing birds; *especially* : a very small widely distributed bird (*Troglodytes troglodytes*) that has a short erect tail and is noted for its song
2 : any of various small singing birds resembling the true wrens in size and habits

wren 1

¹wrench \'rench\ *verb* [Middle English, from Old English *wrencan;* akin to Old High German *renken* to twist and perhaps to Latin *vergere* to bend, incline] (before 12th century)
intransitive verb
1 : to move with a violent twist; *also* : to undergo twisting
2 : to pull or strain at something with violent twisting
transitive verb
1 : to twist violently
2 : to injure or disable by a violent twisting or straining
3 : CHANGE; *especially* : DISTORT, PERVERT
4 a : to pull or tighten by violent twisting or with violence **b** : to snatch forcibly : WREST
5 : to cause to suffer mental anguish : RACK
— **wrench·ing·ly** \'ren-chin-lē\ *adverb*

²wrench *noun* (1530)
1 a : a violent twisting or a pull with or as if with twisting **b** : a sharp twist or sudden jerk straining muscles or ligaments; *also* : the resultant injury (as of a joint) **c** : a distorting or perverting alteration **d** : acute emotional distress : sudden violent mental change
2 : a hand or power tool for holding, twisting, or turning an object (as a bolt or nut)
3 : MONKEY WRENCH 2

¹wrest \'rest\ *transitive verb* [Middle English *wrasten, wresten,* from Old English *wrǣstan;* akin to Old Norse *reista* to bend and probably to Old English *wrigian* to turn — more at WRY] (before 12th century)
1 : to pull, force, or move by violent wringing or twisting movements
2 : to gain with difficulty by or as if by force, violence, or determined labor

²wrest *noun* (14th century)
1 : the action of wresting : WRENCH
2 *archaic* : a key or wrench used for turning pins in a stringed instrument (as a harp or piano)

¹wres·tle \'re-səl, 'ra-\ *verb* **wres·tled; wres·tling** \'res-lin, 'ras-; 're-sᵊl-in, 'ra-\ [Middle English *wrastlen, wrestlen,* from Old English *wrǣstlian,* frequentative of *wrǣstan*] (before 12th century)
intransitive verb
1 : to contend by grappling with and striving to trip or throw an opponent down or off balance
2 : to combat an opposing tendency or force ⟨*wrestling* with his conscience⟩
3 : to engage in deep thought, consideration, or debate
4 : to engage in or as if in a violent or determined struggle ⟨*wrestling* with cumbersome luggage⟩
transitive verb
1 a : to engage in (a match, bout, or fall) in wrestling **b** : to wrestle with ⟨*wrestle* an alligator⟩
2 : to move, maneuver, or force with difficulty
— **wres·tler** \'res-lər, 'ras-; 're-sᵊl-ər, 'ra-\ *noun*

²wrestle *noun* (1593)
: the action or an instance of wrestling : STRUGGLE; *especially* : a wrestling bout

wres·tling \'res-lin, 'ras-; 're-sᵊl-in, 'ra-\ *noun* (before 12th century)
: a sport or contest in which two unarmed individuals struggle hand to hand with each attempting to subdue or unbalance the other

wretch \'rech\ *noun* [Middle English *wrecche,* from Old English *wrecca* outcast, exile; akin to Old High German *hrechjo* fugitive, Old English *wrecan* to drive, drive out — more at WREAK] (before 12th century)
1 : a miserable person : one who is profoundly unhappy or in great misfortune
2 : a base, despicable, or vile person

wretch·ed \'re-chəd\ *adjective* [Middle English, irregular from *wretch*] (12th century)
1 : deeply afflicted, dejected, or distressed in body or mind
2 : extremely or deplorably bad or distressing ⟨was in *wretched* health⟩ ⟨a *wretched* accident⟩
3 a : being or appearing mean, miserable, or contemptible ⟨dressed in *wretched* old clothes⟩ **b** : very poor in quality or ability : INFERIOR ⟨*wretched* workmanship⟩
— **wretch·ed·ly** *adverb*
— **wretch·ed·ness** *noun*

¹wrig·gle \'ri-gəl\ *verb* **wrig·gled; wrig·gling** \-g(ə-)lin\ [Middle English, from or akin to Middle Low German *wriggeln* to wriggle; akin to Old English *wrigian* to turn — more at WRY] (15th century)
intransitive verb
1 : to move the body or a bodily part to and fro with short writhing motions like a worm : SQUIRM
2 : to move or advance by twisting and turning
3 : to extricate or insinuate oneself or reach a goal as if by wriggling
transitive verb
1 : to cause to move in short quick contortions
2 : to introduce, insinuate, or bring into a state or place by or as if by wriggling
— **wrig·gly** \-g(ə-)lē\ *adjective*

²wriggle *noun* (1709)
1 : a short or quick writhing motion or contortion
2 : a formation or marking of sinuous design

wrig·gler \'ri-g(ə-)lər\ *noun* (1631)
: one that wriggles; *especially* : WIGGLER 1

wright \'rīt\ *noun* [Middle English, from Old English *wyrhta, wryhta* worker, maker; akin to Old English *weorc* work — more at WORK] (before 12th century)

: a worker skilled in the manufacture especially of wooden objects — usually used in combination ⟨ship*wright*⟩ ⟨wheel*wright*⟩

wring \'riŋ\ *verb* **wrung** \'rəŋ\; **wring·ing** \'riŋ-iŋ\ [Middle English, from Old English *wringan;* akin to Old High German *ringan* to struggle, Lithuanian *rengtis* to bend down, Old English *wyrgan* to strangle — more at WORRY] (before 12th century)
transitive verb
1 : to squeeze or twist especially so as to make dry or to extract moisture or liquid ⟨*wring* a towel dry⟩
2 : to extract or obtain by or as if by twisting and compressing ⟨*wring* water from a towel⟩ ⟨*wring* a confession from the suspect⟩
3 a : to twist so as to strain or sprain into a distorted shape ⟨I could *wring* your neck⟩ **b :** to twist together (clasped hands) as a sign of anguish
4 : to affect painfully as if by wringing **:** TORMENT ⟨a tragedy that *wrings* the heart⟩
intransitive verb
: SQUIRM, WRITHE
— **wring** *noun*

wring·er \'riŋ-ər\ *noun* (14th century)
: one that wrings: as **a :** a machine or device for pressing out liquid or moisture ⟨a clothes *wringer*⟩ **b :** something that causes pain, hardship, or exertion

¹wrin·kle \'riŋ-kəl\ *noun* [Middle English, back-formation from *wrinkled* twisted, winding, probably from Old English *gewrinclod*, past participle of *gewrinclian* to wind, from *ge-*, perfective prefix + *-wrinclian* (akin to *wrencan* to wrench) — more at CO-] (15th century)
1 : a small ridge or furrow especially when formed on a surface by the shrinking or contraction of a smooth substance **:** CREASE; *specifically* **:** one in the skin especially when due to age, worry, or fatigue
2 a : METHOD, TECHNIQUE **b :** a change in a customary procedure or method **c :** something new or different **:** INNOVATION
3 : IMPERFECTION, IRREGULARITY
— **wrin·kly** \-k(ə-)lē\ *adjective*

²wrinkle *verb* **wrin·kled; wrin·kling** \-k(ə-)liŋ\ (1523)
intransitive verb
: to become marked with or contracted into wrinkles
transitive verb
: to contract into wrinkles **:** PUCKER

wrist \'rist\ *noun* [Middle English, from Old English; akin to Middle High German *rist* wrist, ankle, Old English *wrǣstan* to twist — more at WREST] (before 12th century)
1 : the joint or the region of the joint between the human hand and the arm or a corresponding part on a lower animal
2 : the part of a garment or glove covering the wrist

wrist·band \'ris(t)-,band\ *noun* (1571)
1 : the part of a sleeve covering the wrist
2 : a band encircling the wrist

wrist·let \'ris(t)-lət\ *noun* (circa 1847)
: a band encircling the wrist; *especially* **:** a close-fitting knitted band attached to the top of a glove or the end of a sleeve

wrist·lock \'rist-,läk\ *noun* (1921)
: a wrestling hold in which one contestant is thrown or made helpless by a twisting grip on the wrist

wrist pin *noun* (circa 1875)
: a stud or pin that forms a journal (as in a crosshead) for a connecting rod

wrist shot *noun* (circa 1899)
: a quick usually short-range shot in ice hockey made while the puck is against the blade of the stick by snapping the blade quickly forward

wrist·watch \'rist-,wäch\ *noun* (1896)
: a small watch that is attached to a bracelet or strap and is worn around the wrist

wrist wrestling *noun* (1968)

: a form of arm wrestling in which opponents interlock thumbs instead of gripping hands

wristy \'ris-tē\ *adjective* **wrist·i·er; -est** (1867)
: involving or using a lot of wrist movement (as in stroking a ball)

writ \'rit\ *noun* [Middle English, from Old English; akin to Old English *wrītan* to write] (before 12th century)
1 : something written **:** WRITING ⟨Sacred *Writ*⟩
2 a : a formal written document; *specifically* **:** a legal instrument in epistolary form issued under seal in the name of the English monarch **b :** an order or mandatory process in writing issued in the name of the sovereign or of a court or judicial officer commanding the person to whom it is directed to perform or refrain from performing an act specified therein ⟨*writ* of detinue⟩ ⟨*writ* of entry⟩ ⟨*writ* of execution⟩ **c :** the power and authority of the issuer of such a written order — usually used with *run* ⟨outside the United States where . . . our *writ* does not run —Dean Acheson⟩

writ·able \'rī-tə-bəl\ *adjective* (1782)
: capable of being put in writing

write \'rīt\ *verb* **wrote** \'rōt\; **writ·ten** \'ri-t°n\ *also* **writ** \'rit\ *or dialect* **wrote; writ·ing** \'rī-tiŋ\ [Middle English, from Old English *wrītan* to scratch, draw, inscribe; akin to Old High German *rīzan* to tear and perhaps to Greek *rhīnē* file, rasp] (before 12th century)
transitive verb
1 a : to form (as characters or symbols) on a surface with an instrument (as a pen) **b :** to form (as words) by inscribing the characters or symbols of on a surface **c :** to spell in writing ⟨words *written* alike but pronounced differently⟩ **d :** to cover, fill, or fill in by writing ⟨*wrote* ten pages⟩ ⟨*write* a check⟩
2 : to set down in writing: as **a :** DRAW UP, DRAFT ⟨*write* a will⟩ **b** (1) **:** to be the author of **:** COMPOSE ⟨*writes* poems and essays⟩ (2) **:** to compose in musical form ⟨*write* a string quartet⟩ **c :** to express in literary form ⟨if I could *write* the beauty of your eyes —Shakespeare⟩ **d :** to communicate by letter ⟨*writes* that they are coming⟩ **e :** to use or exhibit (a specific script, language, or literary form or style) in writing ⟨*write* Braille⟩ ⟨*writes* French with ease⟩ **f :** to write contracts or orders for; *especially* **:** UNDERWRITE ⟨*write* life insurance⟩
3 : to make a permanent impression of
4 : to communicate with in writing ⟨we'll *write* you when we get there⟩
5 : ORDAIN, FATE ⟨so be it, it is *written* —D. C. Peattie⟩
6 : to make evident or obvious ⟨guilt *written* on his face⟩
7 : to force, effect, introduce, or remove by writing ⟨*write* oneself into fame and fortune —Charles Lee⟩
8 : to take part in or bring about (something worth recording)
9 a : to introduce (information) into the storage device or medium of a computer **b :** to transfer (information) from the main memory of a computer to a storage or output device
10 : SELL ⟨*write* a stock option⟩
intransitive verb
1 a : to make significant characters or inscriptions; *also* **:** to permit or be adapted to writing **b :** to form or produce written letters, words, or sentences
2 : to compose, communicate by, or send a letter
3 a : to produce a written work **b :** to compose music □
— **write one's own ticket :** to select a course of action or position entirely according to one's wishes
— **writ large :** on a larger scale or in a more prominent manner ⟨the problems of modern totalitarianism are only our own problems *writ large* —*Times Literary Supplement*⟩
— **writ small :** on a smaller scale

write–down \'rīt-,daůn\ *noun* (1932)

: a deliberate reduction in the book value of an asset (as to reflect the effect of obsolescence)

write down (1588)
transitive verb
1 : to record in written form
2 a : to depreciate, disparage, or injure by writing **b :** to reduce in status, rank, or value; *especially* **:** to reduce the book value of
intransitive verb
: to write so as to appeal to a lower level of taste, comprehension, or intelligence

write–in \'rīt-,in\ *noun* (1932)
1 : a vote cast by writing in the name of a candidate
2 : a candidate whose name is written in

write in *transitive verb* (14th century)
1 : to insert in a document or text
2 a : to insert (a name not listed on a ballot or voting machine) in an appropriate space **b :** to cast (a vote) in this manner

write–off \'rīt-,óf\ *noun* (1905)
1 : an elimination of an item from the books of account
2 : a reduction in book value of an item (as by way of depreciation)

write off *transitive verb* (1682)
1 a : to reduce the estimated or book value of **:** DEPRECIATE **b :** to take off the books **:** CANCEL ⟨*write off* a bad debt⟩
2 : to regard or concede to be lost ⟨most were content to *write off* 1979 and look optimistically ahead —*Money*⟩; *also* **:** DISMISS ⟨was *written off* as an expatriate highbrow —Brendan Gill⟩

write out *transitive verb* (1548)
: to write especially in a full and complete form

writ·er \'rī-tər\ *noun* (before 12th century)
: one that writes: as **a :** AUTHOR **b :** one who writes stock options

writ·er·ly \'rī-tər-lē\ *adjective* (1957)
: of, relating to, or typical of a writer

writer's block *noun* (1950)
: a psychological inhibition preventing a writer from proceeding with a piece

writer's cramp *noun* (1853)
: a painful spasmodic cramp of muscles of the hand or fingers brought on by excessive writing

write–up \'rīt-,əp\ *noun* (1885)
1 : a written account; *especially* **:** a flattering article
2 : a deliberate increase in the book value of an asset (as to reflect the effect of inflation)

write up *transitive verb* (15th century)
1 : to make a write-up of
2 : to report (a person) especially for some violation of law or rules

□ **USAGE**

write Back in the 18th century, the past participles *wrote* and *writ* were both in common use ⟨I have *wrote* him word —George Washington⟩ ⟨I ought to have *wrote* to you long since —Benjamin Franklin⟩ ⟨you will have thought me very inexcusable for not having *writ* to you —Richard Brinsley Sheridan⟩. We can still find *writ* in the Civil War era ⟨I have *writ* to George again —Walt Whitman⟩ and it has continued in the 20th century in much diminished use—chiefly in facetious text ⟨yes, Little Eva, the foregoing sentence was *writ* deliberate —James J. Kilpatrick⟩ and in the fixed phrase *writ large* ⟨museums are collections *writ large* —*Smithsonian*⟩. *Written* is the usual past participle now; *wrote* has dropped out of standard use.

\ə\ abut	\ᵊ\ kitten	\ər\ further	\a\ ash	\ā\ ace	
\ä\ mop, mar	\au̇\ out	\ch\ chin	\e\ bet	\ē\ easy	
\g\ go	\i\ hit	\ī\ ice	\j\ job	\ŋ\ sing	\ō\ go
\ȯ\ law	\ȯi\ boy	\th\ thin	\t͟h\ the	\ü\ loot	\u̇\ foot
\y\ yet	\zh\ vision		*see also* Guide to Pronunciation		

writhe \'rīth\ *verb* **writhed; writh·ing** [Middle English, from Old English *wrīthan;* akin to Old Norse *rītha* to twist] (before 12th century)
transitive verb
1 a : to twist into coils or folds **b :** to twist so as to distort **:** WRENCH **c :** to twist (the body or a bodily part) in pain
2 : INTERTWINE
intransitive verb
1 : to move or proceed with twists and turns
2 : to twist from or as if from pain or struggling
3 : to suffer keenly
— **writhe** *noun*
writh·en \'ri-thən\ *adjective* [Middle English, from Old English, from past participle of *wrīthan*] (before 12th century)
: being twisted or contorted ⟨*writhen* trees⟩ ⟨a *writhen* smile⟩
writ·ing \'rī-tiŋ\ *noun* (13th century)
1 : the act or process of one who writes: as **a :** the act or art of forming visible letters or characters; *specifically* **:** HANDWRITING 1 **b :** the act or practice of literary or musical composition
2 : something written: as **a :** letters or characters that serve as visible signs of ideas, words, or symbols **b :** a letter, note, or notice used to communicate or record **c :** a written composition **d :** INSCRIPTION
3 : a style or form of composition
4 : the occupation of a writer; *especially* **:** the profession of authorship
— **writing on the wall :** HANDWRITING ON THE WALL
writing desk *noun* (1611)
: a desk that often has a sloping top for writing on; *also* **:** a portable case that contains writing materials and has a surface for writing
writing paper *noun* (1548)
: paper that is usually finished with a smooth surface and sized and that can be written on with ink
Writ·ings \'rī-tiŋz\ *noun plural* [translation of Late Hebrew *kĕthūbhīm*] (14th century)
: HAGIOGRAPHA
writ of assistance (1706)
1 : a writ issued to a law officer (as a sheriff or marshal) for the enforcement of a court order or decree; *especially* **:** one used to enforce an order for the possession of lands
2 : a writ used especially in colonial America authorizing a law officer to search in unspecified locations for unspecified illegal goods
writ of certiorari (circa 1532)
: CERTIORARI
writ of error (15th century)
: a common law writ directing an inferior court to remit the record of a legal action to the reviewing court in order that an error of law may be corrected if it exists
writ of extent (circa 1861)
: a writ formerly used to recover debts of record to the British crown and under which the lands, goods, and person of the debtor might all be seized to secure payment
writ of habeas corpus (1771)
: HABEAS CORPUS
writ of mandamus (circa 1861)
: MANDAMUS
writ of prohibition (circa 1876)
: a writ issued by a superior court to prevent an inferior court from acting beyond its jurisdiction
writ of right *noun* (15th century)
1 : a common law writ for restoring to its owner property held by another
2 : a writ granted as a matter of right
writ of summons (1660)
: a writ issued on behalf of the British monarch summoning a lord spiritual or a lord temporal to attend parliament
¹wrong \'rȯŋ\ *noun* [Middle English, from Old English *wrang*, from (assumed) *wrang*, adjective, wrong] (before 12th century)

1 a : an injurious, unfair, or unjust act **:** action or conduct inflicting harm without due provocation or just cause **b :** a violation or invasion of the legal rights of another; *especially* **:** TORT
2 : something wrong, immoral, or unethical; *especially* **:** principles, practices, or conduct contrary to justice, goodness, equity, or law
3 : the state, position, or fact of being or doing wrong: as **a :** the state of being mistaken or incorrect **b :** the state of being guilty
synonym see INJUSTICE
²wrong *adjective* **wrong·er** \'rȯŋ-ər\; **wrong·est** \'rȯŋ-əst\ [Middle English, from (assumed) Old English *wrang*, of Scandinavian origin; akin to Old Norse *rangr* awry, wrong; akin to Old English *wringan* to wring] (13th century)
1 : not according to the moral standard **:** SINFUL, IMMORAL ⟨thought that war was *wrong*⟩
2 : not right or proper according to a code, standard, or convention **:** IMPROPER ⟨it was *wrong* not to thank your host⟩
3 : not according to truth or facts **:** INCORRECT ⟨gave a *wrong* date⟩
4 : not satisfactory (as in condition, results, health, or temper)
5 : not in accordance with one's needs, intent, or expectations ⟨took the *wrong* bus⟩
6 : of, relating to, or constituting the side of something that is usually held to be opposite to the principal one, that is the one naturally or by design turned down, inward, or away, or that is the least finished or polished
— **wrong·ly** \'rȯŋ-lē\ *adverb*
— **wrong·ness** *noun*
— **wrong side of the tracks :** a rundown or unfashionable neighborhood
³wrong *adverb* (13th century)
1 : without accuracy **:** INCORRECTLY ⟨guessed *wrong*⟩
2 : without regard for what is proper or just
3 : in a wrong direction
4 a : in an unsuccessful or unfortunate way **b :** out of working order or condition
5 : in a false light ⟨don't get me *wrong*⟩
⁴wrong *transitive verb* **wronged; wrong·ing** \'rȯŋ-iŋ\ (14th century)
1 a : to do wrong to **:** INJURE, HARM **b :** to treat disrespectfully or dishonorably **:** VIOLATE
2 : DEFRAUD — usually used with *of*
3 : DISCREDIT, MALIGN ☆
— **wrong·er** \'rȯŋ-ər\ *noun*
wrong·do·er \'rȯŋ-ˌdü-ər\ *noun* (15th century)
: one that does wrong; *especially* **:** one who transgresses moral laws
wrong·do·ing \-ˌdü-iŋ\ *noun* (14th century)
1 : evil or improper behavior or action
2 : an instance of doing wrong
wronged *adjective* (circa 1547)
: being injured unjustly **:** suffering a wrong
wrong·ful \'rȯŋ-fəl\ *adjective* (14th century)
1 : WRONG, UNJUST
2 a : having no legal sanction **:** UNLAWFUL **b :** ILLEGITIMATE
— **wrong·ful·ly** \-fə-lē\ *adverb*
— **wrong·ful·ness** *noun*
wrong·head·ed \'rȯŋ-ˈhe-dəd\ *adjective* (1732)
: stubborn in adherence to wrong opinion or principles ⟨a *wrongheaded* policy⟩
— **wrong·head·ed·ly** *adverb*
— **wrong·head·ed·ness** *noun*
wrote *past and dialect past participle of* WRITE
wroth \'rȯth *also* 'rōth\ *adjective* [Middle English, from Old English *wrāth;* akin to Old High German *reid* twisted, Old English *wrīthan* to writhe] (before 12th century)
: intensely angry **:** highly incensed **:** WRATHFUL
¹wrought \'rȯt\ *past and past participle of* WORK
usage see WRECK
²wrought *adjective* [Middle English, from past participle of *worken* to work] (14th century)

1 : worked into shape by artistry or effort ⟨carefully *wrought* essays⟩
2 : elaborately embellished **:** ORNAMENTED
3 : processed for use **:** MANUFACTURED ⟨*wrought* silk⟩
4 : beaten into shape by tools **:** HAMMERED — used of metals
5 : deeply stirred **:** EXCITED — often used with *up* ⟨gets easily *wrought* up over nothing⟩
wrought iron *noun* (1678)
: a commercial form of iron that is tough, malleable, and relatively soft, contains less than 0.3 percent and usually less than 0.1 percent carbon, and carries 1 or 2 percent of slag mechanically mixed with it
wrung *past and past participle of* WRING
¹wry \'rī\ *verb* **wried; wry·ing** [Middle English *wrien*, from Old English *wrigian* to turn; akin to Middle High German *rigel* kerchief wound around the head, Greek *rhiknos* shriveled, Avestan *urvisyeiti* he turns] (14th century)
intransitive verb
: TWIST, WRITHE
transitive verb
: to pull out of or as if out of proper shape **:** make awry
²wry *adjective* **wry·er** \'rī-(ə)r\; **wry·est** \'rī-əst\ (1523)
1 : having a bent or twisted shape or condition ⟨a *wry* smile⟩; *especially* **:** turned abnormally to one side ⟨a *wry* neck⟩
2 : WRONGHEADED
3 : cleverly and often ironically or grimly humorous
— **wry·ly** \'rī-lē\ *adverb*
— **wry·ness** *noun*
wry·neck \'rī-ˌnek\ *noun* (1585)
1 : either of two Old World woodpeckers (*Jynx torquilla* or *J. ruficollis*) that differ from the typical woodpeckers in having soft tail feathers and a peculiar manner of writhing the neck
2 : TORTICOLLIS
Wu \'wü\ *noun* [Chinese (Beijing) *Wú*, historical kingdom coextensive with the dialect area] (1908)
: a group of Chinese dialects spoken principally in Jiangsu and Zhejiang provinces
wud \'wüd\ *adjective* [alteration of ¹*wood*] (1772)
chiefly Scottish **:** INSANE, MAD
wul·fen·ite \'wül-fə-ˌnīt\ *noun* [German *Wulfenit*, from F. X. von *Wulfen* (died 1805) Austrian mineralogist] (1849)
: a tetragonal mineral that is a complex oxide of lead and molybdenum and occurs especially in bright orange-yellow tabular crystals
wun·der·kind \'vun-dər-ˌkint\ *noun, plural* **wun·der·kin·der** \-ˌkin-dər\ [German, from *Wunder* wonder + *Kind* child] (1891)
: a child prodigy; *also* **:** one who succeeds in a competitive or highly difficult field or profession at an early age
wurst \'wərst *also* 'wurst *sometimes* 'wusht *or*

☆ SYNONYMS
Wrong, oppress, persecute, aggrieve mean to injure unjustly or outrageously. WRONG implies inflicting injury either unmerited or out of proportion to what one deserves ⟨a penal system that had *wronged* him⟩. OPPRESS suggests inhumane imposing of burdens one cannot endure or exacting more than one can perform ⟨a people *oppressed* by a warmongering tyrant⟩. PERSECUTE implies a relentless and unremitting subjection to annoyance or suffering ⟨a child *persecuted* by constant criticism⟩. AGGRIEVE implies suffering caused by an infringement or denial of rights ⟨a legal aid society representing *aggrieved* minority groups⟩.

'wu̇st; *also with* v *for* w\ *noun* [German, from Old High German] (1855)

: SAUSAGE

wurzel *noun* [short for *mangel-wurzel*] (circa 1888)

: MANGEL

wuss \'wu̇s\ *also* **wus·sy** \'wu̇-sē\ *noun, plural* **wuss·es** *also* **wus·sies** [origin unknown] (1983)

: WIMP

— **wussy** *adjective*

wuth·er \'wə-t͟hər\ *intransitive verb* [alteration of *whither* to rush, bluster, hurl] (circa 1825)

dialect English **:** to blow with a dull roaring sound

Wy·an·dot \'wī-ən-ˌdät *also* 'wīn-\ *noun* (1749)

: a member of an American Indian group formed in the 17th century by Hurons and other Indians fleeing the Iroquois

wy·an·dotte \-ˌdät\ *noun* [probably from *Wyandotte* Wyandot] (1884)

: any of a U.S. breed of medium-sized domestic fowls raised for meat and eggs

Wyc·liff·ite \'wi-klə-ˌfīt\ *noun* [John *Wycliffe*] (1580)

: LOLLARD

— **Wycliffite** *adjective*

wye \'wī\ *noun* (1857)

1 : a Y-shaped part or object

2 : the letter *y*

wy·lie·coat \'wī-lē-ˌkōt, 'wi-\ *noun* [Middle English (Scots) *wyle cot*] (15th century)

1 *chiefly Scottish* **:** a warm undergarment

2 *chiefly Scottish* **:** PETTICOAT

wynd \'wīnd\ *noun* [Middle English (Scots) *wynde*, probably from *wynden* to wind, proceed, go, from Old English *windan* to twist — more at WIND] (15th century)

chiefly Scottish **:** a very narrow street

wynn *or* **wyn** \'win\ *noun* [Old English *wynn*, literally, joy — more at WINSOME] (before 12th century)

: a runic letter used in Old English and Middle English to represent the consonant \w\

WYS·I·WYG \'wi-zē-ˌwig, -zə-\ *adjective* [*w*hat *y*ou *s*ee *i*s *w*hat *y*ou *g*et] (1982)

: of, relating to, or being a display generated by word-processing or desktop-publishing software that exactly reflects the appearance of the printed document

wy·vern \'wī-vərn\ *noun* [alteration of Middle English *wyvere* viper, from Old North French *wivre*, modification of Latin *vipera*] (1610)

: a mythical animal usually represented as a 2-legged winged creature resembling a dragon

X *is the twenty-fourth letter of the English alphabet. Its form and pronunciation are from Latin, as is its name. The letter came into Latin from a western Greek alphabet in which it had the value of* ks. *In an eastern Greek alphabet and in classical Greek, the same sign stood for the letter* chi, *which represented the breathy, guttural sound heard in English at the end of Scottish* loch, *while that of* ks *was indicated by the letter* xi. *In English,* x *represents an unusually wide variety of sounds for a consonant letter. Most prominent are these five: the sound of* ks *as in* tax, *of* z *as in* xylophone, *of* gz *as in* exact, *of* ksh *as in one pronunciation of* anxious, *and of* gzh *as in one pronunciation of* luxurious. *Initial* X *occurs most often in words of Greek origin, where it is pronounced like* z *and stands for classical Greek* xi. *In the middle and at the end of words, however,* X *appears frequently in words of Latin origin, directly or through French, such as* axis *and* mix. *Small* x *developed through the miniaturizing of the capital form.*

¹**x** \'eks\ *noun, plural* **x's** *or* **xs** \'ek-səz\ *often capitalized, often attributive* (before 12th century)
1 a : the 24th letter of the English alphabet **b** : a graphic representation of this letter **c** : a speech counterpart of orthographic *x*
2 : TEN — see NUMBER table
3 : a graphic device for reproducing the letter *x*
4 : one designated *x* especially as the 24th in order or class, or the first in an order or class that includes x, y, and sometimes z
5 : an unknown quantity
6 : something shaped like or marked with the letter X

²**x** *transitive verb* **x-ed** *also* **x'd** *or* **xed** \'ekst\; **x-ing** *or* **x'ing** \'ek-siŋ\ (circa 1849)
1 : to mark with an *x*
2 : to cancel or obliterate with a series of *x*'s — usually used with *out*

X \'eks\ *adjective* (1950)
of a motion picture : of such a nature that admission is denied to persons under a specified age (as 17) — used before the adoption of *NC-17*

Xan·a·du \'za-nə-,dü, -,dyü\ *noun* [*Xanadu*, locality in *Kubla Khan* (1798), poem by Samuel T. Coleridge] (1919)
: an idyllic, exotic, or luxurious place

xanth- *or* **xantho-** *combining form* [New Latin, from Greek, from *xanthos*]
: yellow ⟨*xanthene*⟩

xan·than gum \'zan-thən-\ *noun* [*xanth-* (from New Latin *Xanthomonas,* genus name) + ³*-an*] (1964)
: a polysaccharide that is produced by fermentation of carbohydrates by a gram-negative bacterium (*Xanthomonas campestris* of the family Pseudomonadaceae) and is a thickening and suspending agent used especially in pharmaceuticals and prepared foods — called also *xanthan*

xan·thate \'zan-,thāt\ *noun* (1831)
: a salt or ester of any of various thio acids and especially $C_3H_6OS_2$

xan·thene \-,thēn\ *noun* (1898)
1 : a white crystalline heterocyclic compound $C_{13}H_{10}O$; *also* : an isomer of this that is the parent of the colored forms of the xanthene dyes
2 : any of various derivatives of xanthene

xanthene dye *noun* (1930)
: any of various brilliant fluorescent yellow to pink to bluish red dyes that are characterized by the presence of the xanthene nucleus

xan·thine \'zan-,thēn\ *noun* [International Scientific Vocabulary] (1857)
: a feebly basic compound $C_5H_4N_4O_2$ that occurs especially in animal or plant tissue, is derived from guanine and hypoxanthine, and

yields uric acid on oxidation; *also* : any of various derivatives of this

Xan·thip·pe \zan-'thi-pē, -'ti-\ *or* **Xan·tip·pe** \-'ti-pē\ *noun* [Greek *Xanthippē,* shrewish wife of Socrates] (1691)
: an ill-tempered woman

xan·thone \'zan-,thōn\ *noun* [International Scientific Vocabulary] (circa 1894)
: a ketone $C_{13}H_8O_2$ that is the parent of several natural yellow pigments

xan·tho·phyll \'zan(t)-thə-,fil\ *noun* [French *xanthophylle,* from *xanth-* + *-phylle* -phyll] (1838)
: any of several neutral yellow to orange carotenoid pigments that are oxygen derivatives of carotenes; *especially* : LUTEIN

Xa·ve·ri·an Brother \zā-'vir-ē-ən-, za-\ *noun* [*Xaverian* of Saint Francis Xavier] (1882)
: a member of a Roman Catholic congregation of lay brothers founded by Theodore J. Ryken in Bruges, Belgium, in 1839 and dedicated to education

x-ax·is \'eks-,ak-səs\ *noun* (1886)
1 : the axis in a plane Cartesian coordinate system parallel to which abscissas are measured
2 : one of the three axes in a three-dimensional rectangular coordinate system

X band *noun* (circa 1946)
: a segment of the superhigh-frequency radio spectrum that lies between 5.2 GHz and 10.9 GHz and is used especially for radars and for spacecraft communication

X chromosome *noun* (1911)
: a sex chromosome that usually occurs paired in each female cell and single in each male cell in species in which the male typically has two unlike sex chromosomes — compare Y CHROMOSOME

x-co·or·di·nate \,eks-kō-'órd-nət; -'ór-d°n-ət, -də-,nät\ *noun* (1927)
: a coordinate whose value is determined by measuring parallel to an x-axis; *specifically* : ABSCISSA

xe·bec \'zē-,bek, zi-'\ *noun* [modification of French *chebec,* from Arabic *shabbāk*] (1756)
: a usually 3-masted Mediterranean sailing ship with long overhanging bow and stern

xen- *or* **xeno-** *combining form* [Late Latin, from Greek, from *xenos* stranger, guest, host]
1 : guest : foreigner ⟨*xenophobia*⟩
2 : strange : foreign ⟨*xenolith*⟩

xe·nia \'zē-nē-ə, -nyə\ *noun* [New Latin, from Greek, hospitality, from *xenos* host] (1899)
: the effect of genes introduced by pollen especially on endosperm and embryo development

xe·no·bi·ot·ic \,ze-nō-bī-'ä-tik, ,zē-, -bē-\ *noun* (1965)

: a chemical compound (as a drug, pesticide, or carcinogen) that is foreign to a living organism
— **xenobiotic** *adjective*

xe·no·di·ag·no·sis \-,dī-ig-'nō-səs\ *noun* [New Latin] (circa 1929)
: the detection of a parasite (as of humans) by feeding a suitable intermediate host (as an insect) on supposedly infected material (as blood) and later examining the host for the parasite
— **xe·no·di·ag·nos·tic** \-'näs-tik\ *adjective*

xe·no·ge·ne·ic \-jə-'nē-ik\ *adjective* [*xen-* + *-geneic* (as in *isogeneic*)] (1961)
: derived from, originating in, or being a member of another species

xe·no·graft \'ze-nə-,graft, 'zē-\ *noun* (1961)
: HETEROGRAFT

xe·no·lith \'ze-n°l-,ith, 'zē-\ *noun* (1894)
: a fragment of a rock included in another rock
— **xe·no·lith·ic** \,ze-n°l-'i-thik, ,zē-\ *adjective*

xe·non \'zē-,nän, 'ze-\ *noun* [Greek, neuter of *xenos* strange] (1898)
: a heavy, colorless, and relatively inert gaseous element that occurs in air as about one part in 20 million by volume and is used especially in thyratrons and specialized flashtubes — see ELEMENT table

xe·no·phile \'ze-nə-,fīl, 'zē-\ *noun* [International Scientific Vocabulary] (1948)
: one attracted to foreign things (as styles or people)

xe·no·phobe \'ze-nə-,fōb, 'zē-\ *noun* [International Scientific Vocabulary] (1922)
: one unduly fearful of what is foreign and especially of people of foreign origin
— **xe·no·pho·bic** \,ze-nə-'fō-bik, ,zē-\ *adjective*
— **xe·no·pho·bi·cal·ly** \-bi-k(ə-)lē\ *adverb*

xe·no·pho·bia \,ze-nə-'fō-bē-ə, ,zē-\ *noun* [New Latin] (1903)
: fear and hatred of strangers or foreigners or of anything that is strange or foreign

xe·no·tro·pic \-'trä-pik, -trō-\ *adjective* (1973)
: replicating or reproducing only in cells other than those of the host species ⟨*xenotropic* viruses⟩

xer- *or* **xero-** *combining form* [Late Latin, from Greek *xēr-, xēro-,* from *xēros*]
: dry ⟨*xeric*⟩ ⟨*xerophyte*⟩

xe·ric \'zir-ik, 'zer-\ *adjective* (1926)
: characterized by, relating to, or requiring only a small amount of moisture ⟨a *xeric* habitat⟩ ⟨a *xeric* plant⟩ — compare HYDRIC, MESIC

Xeri·scape \'zir-ə-,skāp, 'zer-\ *trademark*
— used for a water-conserving method of landscaping in arid or semiarid climates

xe·ro·der·ma pig·men·to·sum \,zir-ə-'dər-mə-,pig-mən-'tō-səm, -,men-\ *noun* [New Latin, literally, pigmented dryness of the skin] (1884)
: a genetic condition inherited as a recessive autosomal trait that is caused by a defect in mechanisms that repair DNA mutations (as those caused by ultraviolet light) and is characterized by the development of pigment abnormalities and multiple skin cancers in body areas exposed to the sun

xe·rog·ra·phy \zə-'rä-grə-fē\ *noun* [International Scientific Vocabulary] (1948)
1 : a process for copying graphic matter by the action of light on an electrically charged photoconductive insulating surface in which the latent image is developed with a resinous powder
2 : XERORADIOGRAPHY
— **xe·ro·graph·ic** \,zir-ə-'gra-fik\ *adjective*
— **xe·ro·graph·i·cal·ly** \-fi-k(ə-)lē\ *adverb*

xe·roph·i·lous \zə-'rä-fə-ləs\ *or* **xe·ro·phile** \'zir-ə-,fīl\ *adjective* (1863)

: thriving in or tolerant or characteristic of a xeric environment

— **xe·roph·i·ly** \zə-'rä-fə-lē\ *noun*

xe·roph·thal·mia \ˌzir-ˌäf-'thal-mē-ə, -ˌäp-'thal-\ *noun* [Late Latin, from Greek *xērophthalmia*, from *xēr-* xer- + *ophthalmia* ophthalmia] (circa 1656)
: a dry thickened lusterless condition of the eyeball resulting especially from a severe systemic deficiency of vitamin A

— **xe·roph·thal·mic** \-mik\ *adjective*

xe·ro·phyte \'zir-ə-ˌfīt\ *noun* (1897)
: a plant structurally adapted for life and growth with a limited water supply especially by means of mechanisms that limit transpiration or that provide for the storage of water

— **xe·ro·phyt·ic** \ˌzir-ə-'fi-tik\ *adjective*
— **xe·ro·phyt·ism** \'zir-ə-ˌfī-ˌti-zəm\ *noun*

xe·ro·ra·di·og·ra·phy \ˌzir-ō-ˌrā-dē-'ä-grə-fē\ *noun* (1949)
: radiography used especially in mammographic screening for breast cancer that produces an image using X rays in a manner similar to the way an image is produced by light in xerography

xe·ro·ther·mic \ˌzir-ə-'thər-mik\ *adjective* (1904)
1 : characterized by heat and dryness
2 : adapted to or thriving in a hot dry environment

xe·rox \'zir-ˌäks, 'zē-ˌräks\ *transitive verb* [from *Xerox*] (1965)
1 : to copy on a Xerox copier
2 : to make (a copy) on a Xerox copier

Xe·rox \'zir-ˌäks, 'zē-ˌräks\ *trademark*
— used for a xerographic copier

x-height \'eks-ˌhīt, -ˌhītth\ *noun* (circa 1945)
: the height of a lowercase x used to represent the height of the main body of a lowercase letter

Xho·sa \'kō-sə, 'hō-, 'kō- *or with* ȯ *for* ō\ *noun* (1801)
1 : a member of a Bantu-speaking people of Eastern Cape province
2 : a Bantu language of the Xhosas

xi \'zī, 'ksī\ *noun, plural* **xis** [Greek *xei*] (1823)
: the 14th letter of the Greek alphabet — see ALPHABET table

x-in·ter·cept \'eks-'in-tər-ˌsept\ *noun* (circa 1939)
: the x-coordinate of a point where a line, curve, or surface intersects the x-axis

xi·phi·ster·num \ˌzi-fə-'stər-nəm, ˌzi-\ *noun, plural* **-na** \-nə\ [New Latin, from Greek *xiphos* sword + New Latin *sternum*] (circa 1860)
: XIPHOID PROCESS

xi·phoid \'zī-ˌfȯid, 'zi-\ *noun* [New Latin *xiphoides*, from Greek *xiphoeidēs*, from *xiphos*] (circa 1860)
: XIPHOID PROCESS

— **xiphoid** *adjective*

xiphoid process *noun* (1873)
: the segment of the human sternum that is the third and closest to the feet

x-ir·ra·di·a·tion \ˌeks-i-ˌrā-dē-'ā-shən\ *noun, often capitalized* (1927)
: X-RADIATION 1

Xmas \'kris-məs *also* 'eks-məs\ *noun* [*X* (symbol for *Christ*, from the Greek letter chi (X), initial of *Christos* Christ) + *-mas* (in *Christmas*)] (1551)
: CHRISTMAS

x-ra·di·a·tion \ˌeks-ˌrā-dē-'ā-shən\ *noun, often capitalized* (1896)
1 : exposure to X rays
2 : radiation composed of X rays

X-rated \'eks-'rā-təd\ *adjective* (1970)
1 : having a rating of X; *broadly* : relating to or characterized by explicit sexual material or activity ⟨an *X-rated* book⟩
2 : OBSCENE, VULGAR ⟨an *X-rated* gesture⟩

Xray \'eks-ˌrā\ (1943)
— a communications code word for the letter x ◇

x-ray \'eks-ˌrā\ *transitive verb, often capitalized* (1899)
: to examine, treat, or photograph with X rays

X ray \'eks-ˌrā\ *noun* (1896)
1 : any of the electromagnetic radiations of the same nature as visible radiation but having an extremely short wavelength of less than 100 angstroms that is produced by bombarding a metallic target with fast electrons in vacuum or by transition of atoms to lower energy states and that has the properties of ionizing a gas upon passage through it, of penetrating various thicknesses of all solids, of producing secondary radiations by impinging on material bodies, of acting on photographic films and plates as light does, and of causing fluorescent screens to emit light
2 : a photograph obtained by use of X rays
— **X-ray** *adjective*

X–ray astronomy *noun* (1963)
: astronomy dealing with investigations of celestial bodies by means of the X rays they emit

X–ray diffraction *noun* (1924)
: a scattering of X rays by the atoms of a crystal that produces an interference effect so that the diffraction pattern gives information on the structure of the crystal or the identity of a crystalline substance

X–ray star *noun* (1964)
: a luminous celestial object emitting a major portion of its radiation in the form of X rays
— called also *X-ray source*

X–ray therapy *noun* (1926)
: medical treatment (as of cancer) by controlled application of X rays

X–ray tube *noun* (1896)
: a vacuum tube in which a concentrated stream of electrons strikes a metal target and produces X rays

x–sec·tion \'krȯs-'sek-shən, -ˌsek-\ *noun* [*x*, rebus for *cross*] (1962)
: CROSS SECTION
— **x–sec·tion·al** \-shnəl, -shə-nʳl\ *adjective*

xu \'sü\ *noun, plural* **xu** [Vietnamese, from French *sou* sou] (1948)
1 : a coin formerly minted by South Vietnam equivalent to the cent
2 — see *dong* at MONEY table

xyl- *or* **xylo-** *combining form* [Latin, from Greek, from *xylon*]
1 : wood ⟨*xylophone*⟩
2 : xylene ⟨*xyl*idine⟩

xy·lan \'zī-ˌlan\ *noun* [International Scientific Vocabulary] (circa 1894)
: a yellow gummy pentosan that yields xylose on hydrolysis and is abundantly present in plant cell walls and woody tissue

xy·lem \'zī-ləm, -ˌlem\ *noun* [German, from Greek *xylon*] (1873)
: a complex tissue in the vascular system of higher plants that consists of vessels, tracheids, or both usually together with wood fibers and parenchyma cells, functions chiefly in conduction of water and dissolved minerals but also in support and food storage, and typically constitutes the woody element (as of a plant stem) — compare PHLOEM

xylem ray *noun* (1875)
: a vascular ray or portion of a vascular ray located in xylem — called also *wood ray;* compare PHLOEM RAY

xy·lene \'zī-ˌlēn\ *noun* [International Scientific Vocabulary] (1851)
: any of three toxic flammable oily isomeric aromatic hydrocarbons C_8H_{10} that are dimethyl homologues of benzene and are usually obtained from petroleum or natural gas distillates; *also* : a mixture of xylenes and ethyl benzene used chiefly as a solvent

xy·li·dine \'zī-lə-ˌdēn\ *noun* [International Scientific Vocabulary] (1850)
: any or a mixture of six toxic liquid or low-melting crystalline isomeric amino derivatives $C_8H_{11}N$ of the xylenes used chiefly as intermediates for azo dyes and in organic synthesis

xy·li·tol \'zī-lə-ˌtȯl, -ˌtōl\ *noun* (1891)
: a crystalline alcohol $C_5H_{12}O_5$ that is a derivative of xylose, is obtained especially from birch bark, and is used as a sweetener

xy·log·ra·phy \zī-'lä-grə-fē\ *noun* [French *xylographie*, from *xyl-* + *-graphie* -graphy] (1816)
: the art of making engravings on wood especially for printing

— **xy·lo·graph** \'zī-lə-ˌgraf\ *noun*
— **xy·log·ra·pher** \zī-'lä-grə-fər\ *noun*
— **xy·lo·graph·ic** \ˌzī-lə-'gra-fik\ *also* **xy·lo·graph·i·cal** \-fi-kəl\ *adjective*

xy·lol \'zī-ˌlȯl, -ˌlōl\ *noun* [International Scientific Vocabulary] (1851)
: XYLENE

xy·loph·a·gous \zī-'lä-fə-gəs\ *adjective* [Greek *xylophagos*, from *xyl-* + *-phagos* -phagous] (1739)
: feeding on or in wood

xy·lo·phone \'zī-lə-ˌfōn *also* 'zi-\ *noun* (1866)
: a percussion instrument consisting of a series of wooden bars graduated in length to produce the musical scale, supported on belts of straw or felt, and sounded by striking with two small wooden hammers

xylophone

— **xy·lo·phon·ist** \-ˌfō-nist\ *noun*

xy·lose \'zī-ˌlōs, -ˌlōz\ *noun* [International Scientific Vocabulary] (circa 1894)
: a crystalline aldose sugar $C_5H_{10}O_5$ that is not fermentable with ordinary yeasts and occurs especially as a constituent of xylans from which it is obtained by hydrolysis

◇ WORD HISTORY

Xray On November 8, 1895, Wilhelm Conrad Röntgen was conducting an experimental investigation in Würzburg, Germany, of the properties of cathode rays. He noticed that a fluorescent surface in the neighborhood of a cathode-ray tube would become luminous even if shielded from the direct light of the tube. A thick metal object placed between the tube and the affected surface impaired the fluorescence and cast a dark shadow. An object made of a less dense substance such as wood cast only a weak shadow. Röntgen's explanation for this phenomenon was that the tube produced some type of invisible radiation which could pass through substances that blocked ordinary visible light. Because he did not know the nature of this radiation he had discovered, he named it *X-Strahl*, based on the mathematical use of *x* to designate an unknown quantity. His German name was translated into English as *X ray*.

Y *is the twenty-fifth letter of the English alphabet. It comes from the Latin, which borrowed it from the Greek* upsilon *and used it as a vowel in the writing of Greek words. In Greek,* Y *was an eastern and classical form of the* V *which had been borrowed earlier from the western Greek alphabet by Latin. In English,* Y *is used as both a consonant and a vowel. At the beginning of a word or syllable, it is usually pronounced as a consonant with slight or no audible friction (as in* yes*); in the middle or at the end of a syllable, it is usually a vowel, with various values (as in* myth, happy, my, myrrh, *and* martyr*). In certain archaic forms such as the* ye *of "ye olde tavern,"* Y *represents an Old and Middle English character called* thorn *and is pronounced like* th*. This use caused confusion in later English speakers, who interpreted words like* ye *as though pronounced with the sound of consonant* y*. Actually, such words were originally pronounced with the* th *sound.*

y \'wī\ *noun, plural* **y's** *or* **ys** \'wīz\ *often capitalized, often attributive* (before 12th century) **1 a :** the 25th letter of the English alphabet **b :** a graphic representation of this letter **c :** a speech counterpart of orthographic *y* **2 :** a graphic device for reproducing the letter *y* **3 :** one designated *y* especially as the 25th in order or class or the second in order or class when x is made the first **4 :** something shaped like the letter Y

Y \'wī\ *noun* (circa 1915) **:** YMCA, YWCA

¹-y *also* **-ey** \ē; *in some dialects, especially British, Southern, & New England, often* i *but not shown at individual entries\ adjective suffix* [Middle English, from Old English *-ig;* akin to Old High German *-īg -y*, Latin *-icus*, Greek *-ikos*, Sanskrit *-ika*] **1 a :** characterized by **:** full of ⟨blossom*y*⟩ ⟨dirt*y*⟩ ⟨mudd*y*⟩ ⟨clay*ey*⟩ **b :** having the character of **:** composed of ⟨ic*y*⟩ ⟨wax*y*⟩ **c :** like **:** like that of ⟨home*y*⟩ ⟨wintr*y*⟩ — often with a disparaging connotation ⟨stag*y*⟩ **2 a :** tending or inclined to ⟨sleep*y*⟩ ⟨chatt*y*⟩ **b :** giving occasion for (specified) action ⟨tear*y*⟩ **c :** performing (specified) action ⟨curl*y*⟩

²-y \same\ *noun suffix, plural* **-ies** [Middle English *-ie*, from Old French, from Latin *-ia*, from Greek *-ia*, *-eia*] **1 :** state **:** condition **:** quality ⟨beggar*y*⟩ **2 :** activity, place of business, or goods dealt with ⟨chandler*y*⟩ ⟨laundr*y*⟩ **3 :** whole body or group ⟨soldier*y*⟩

³-y *noun suffix, plural* **-ies** [Middle English *-ie*, from Anglo-French, from Latin *-ium*] **:** instance of a (specified) action ⟨entreat*y*⟩ ⟨inquir*y*⟩

⁴-y — see -IE

yab·ber \'ya-bər\ *noun* [probably modification of Wuywurung (Australian aboriginal language of the Melbourne area) *yaba* speak] (1855) *Australian* **:** TALK, JABBER ⟨all *yabber* and chatter ceased around the campfires —Francis Birtles⟩
— yabber *intransitive verb*

¹yacht \'yät\ *noun* [obsolete Dutch *jaght*, from Middle Low German *jacht*, short for *jachtschip*, literally, hunting ship] (1557) **1 :** any of various recreational watercraft: as a **:** a sailboat used for racing **b :** a large usually motor-driven craft used for pleasure cruising

²yacht *intransitive verb* (1836) **:** to race or cruise in a yacht
yacht club *noun* (1834) **:** a club organized to promote and regulate yachting and boating
yacht·ing *noun* (1836) **:** the action, fact, or pastime of racing or cruising in a yacht
yachts·man \'yäts-mən\ *noun* (1862) **:** a person who owns or sails a yacht

YAG \'yag\ *noun* [*y*ttrium *a*luminum *g*arnet] (1964) **:** a synthetic yttrium aluminum garnet of marked hardness and high refractive index that is used especially as a gemstone and in laser technology

ya·gi \'yä-gē, 'ya-\ *noun* [Hidetsugu *Yagi* (born 1886) Japanese engineer] (1943) **:** a highly directional and selective shortwave antenna consisting of a horizontal conductor of one or two dipoles connected with the receiver or transmitter and of a set of nearly equal insulated dipoles parallel to and on a level with the horizontal conductor

ya·hoo \'yā-(,)hü, 'yä-\ *noun, plural* **yahoos** (1726) **1** *capitalized* **:** a member of a race of brutes in Swift's *Gulliver's Travels* who have the form and all the vices of humans **2 :** a boorish, crass, or stupid person
— ya·hoo·ism \-,i-zəm\ *noun*

Yah·weh \'yä-(,)wā, -(,)vā\ *also* **Yah·veh** \-(,)vā\ *noun* [Hebrew *Yahweh*] (1869) **:** GOD 1a — used especially by the Hebrews; compare TETRAGRAMMATON

Yah·wism \-,wi-zəm, -,vi-\ *noun* (1867) **:** the worship of Yahweh among the ancient Hebrews

Yah·wis·tic \yä-'wis-tik, -'vis-\ *adjective* (1874) **1 :** characterized by the use of *Yahweh* as the name of God **2 :** of or relating to Yahwism

¹yak \'yak\ *noun, plural* **yaks** *also* **yak** [Tibetan *gyagk*] (1795) **:** a large long-haired wild or domesticated ox (*Bos grunniens* synonym *B. mutus*) of Tibet and adjacent elevated parts of central Asia

yak

²yak \'yäk, 'yak\ *noun* [imitative] (1948) **1** *slang* **:** LAUGH **2** *slang* **:** JOKE, GAG

³yak *also* **yack** *intransitive verb* **yakked** *also* **yacked; yak·king** *also* **yack·ing** [probably imitative] (1949) **:** to talk persistently **:** CHATTER

⁴yak *also* **yack** \'yak\ *noun* (1950) **:** persistent or voluble talk

Yak·i·ma \'ya-kə-,mò\ *noun, plural* **Yakima** *or* **Yakimas** (1838) **1 :** a member of a group of Shahaptian peoples of the lower Yakima River valley, south central Washington **2 :** the language of the Yakima people

ya·ki·to·ri \,yä-ki-'tòr-ē\ *noun* [Japanese, grilled chicken, from *yaki* broil, roast + *tori* bird] (1962) **:** bite-sized marinated pieces of beef, seafood, or chicken on skewers

y'all \'yòl\ *variant of* YOU-ALL

yam \'yam\ *noun* [earlier *iname*, from Portuguese *inhame* & Spanish *ñame*, of African origin; akin to Fulani *nyami* to eat] (1657) **1 :** the edible starchy tuberous root of various plants (genus *Dioscorea* of the family Dioscoreaceae) used as a staple food in tropical areas; *also* **:** a plant producing yams **2 :** a moist-fleshed and usually orange-fleshed sweet potato

ya·men \'yä-mən\ *noun* [Chinese (Beijing) *yámen*] (1747) **:** the headquarters or residence of a Chinese government official or department

yam·mer \'ya-mər\ *intransitive verb* **yammered; yam·mer·ing** \'ya-mə-riŋ, 'yam-riŋ\ [Middle English *yameren*, alteration of *yomeren* to murmur, be sad, from Old English *gēomrian*; akin to Old High German *jāmaron* to be sad] (15th century) **1 a :** to utter repeated cries of distress or sorrow **b :** WHIMPER **2 :** to utter persistent complaints **:** WHINE **3 :** to talk persistently or volubly and often loudly ⟨caused the purists to *yammer* for censorship —D. W. Maurer⟩
— yammer *noun*

yang \'yäŋ, 'yaŋ\ *noun* [Chinese (Beijing) *yáng*] (1671) **:** the masculine active principle in nature that in Chinese cosmology is exhibited in light, heat, or dryness and that combines with yin to produce all that comes to be

¹yank \'yaŋk\ *noun* [origin unknown] (circa 1864) **:** a strong sudden pull **:** JERK

²yank (1822) *intransitive verb* **:** to pull on something with a quick vigorous movement *transitive verb* **1 :** to pull or extract with a quick vigorous movement **2 :** to remove in or as if in an abrupt manner ⟨*yanked* the story from the evening edition⟩

Yank \'yaŋk\ *noun* (1778) **:** YANKEE

◇ WORD HISTORY
yacht In the 16th century the Dutch developed a kind of shallow-draft, fast-moving ship for use in coastal waters and river estuaries. These vessels were called by the name *jaght*, short for Middle Low German *jachtschip* or Middle Dutch *jageschip*, literally "hunting ship" or "pursuit ship," though *jacht* may simply imply that the boat was a speedy one. The name appears in 16th and 17th century English documents in a variety of forms, such as *yoath* and *yaught*. The form *jacht* or *yacht* became widespread after 1660, when King Charles II, on his return from exile on the Continent, was given such a craft, dubbed the *Mary*, by the Dutch East India Company. The king chose to use the boat for excursions and racing, and the word *yacht* became attached to other vessels used for the same purposes, the earliest being copied after the design of the *Mary*. Today the word *yacht* is applied to a wide variety of luxuriously outfitted craft—powerboats as well as sailboats—that are designed for pleasure cruising.

¹**Yan·kee** \'yaŋ-kē\ *noun* [origin unknown] (1758)
1 a : a native or inhabitant of New England **b** : a native or inhabitant of the northern U.S.
2 : a native or inhabitant of the U.S.
— **Yan·kee·dom** \-kē-dəm\ *noun*
— **Yan·kee·ism** \-kē-ˌi-zəm\ *noun*
²**Yankee** (1952)
— a communications code word for the letter *y*

Yan·kee–Doo·dle \ˌyaŋ-kē-'dü-d°l\ *noun* [*Yankee Doodle,* popular song during the American Revolution] (1770)
: YANKEE

yan·qui \'yäŋ-kē\ *noun, often capitalized* [Spanish, from English ¹*Yankee*] (1928)
: a citizen of the U.S. as distinguished from a Latin American

yan·tra \'yən-trə, 'yan-, 'yän-\ *noun* [Sanskrit] (1877)
: a geometrical diagram used like an icon usually in meditation

¹**yap** \'yap\ *intransitive verb* **yapped; yap·ping** [imitative] (1668)
1 : to bark snappishly **:** YELP
2 : to talk in a shrill insistent way **:** CHATTER
— **yap·per** *noun*
²**yap** *noun* (1826)
1 a : a quick sharp bark **:** YELP **b** : shrill insistent talk **:** CHATTER
2 : an unsophisticated, ignorant, or uncouth person **:** BUMPKIN
3 *slang* **:** MOUTH

Ya·qui \'yä-kē\ *noun* (1861)
1 : a member of an American Indian people of Sonora, Mexico
2 : the Uto-Aztecan language of the Yaqui people

Yar·bor·ough \'yär-ˌbər-ə, -ˌbə-rə, -b(ə-)rə\ *noun* [Charles Anderson Worsley, 2d Earl of *Yarborough* (died 1897) English nobleman said to have bet a thousand to one against the dealing of such a hand] (1900)
: a hand in bridge or whist containing no ace and no card higher than a nine

¹**yard** \'yärd\ *noun* [Middle English, from Old English *geard* enclosure, yard; akin to Old High German *gart* enclosure, Latin *hortus* garden] (before 12th century)
1 a : a small usually walled and often paved area open to the sky and adjacent to a building **:** COURT **b** : the grounds of a building or group of buildings
2 : the grounds immediately surrounding a house that are usually covered with grass
3 a : an enclosure for livestock (as poultry) **b** (1) **:** an area with its buildings and facilities set aside for a particular business or activity (2) **:** an assembly or storage area **c :** a system of tracks for storage and maintenance of cars and making up trains
4 : a locality in a forest where deer herd in winter
²**yard** *adjective* (15th century)
1 : of, relating to, or employed in the yard surrounding a building ⟨*yard* light⟩
2 : of, relating to, or employed in a railroad yard ⟨a *yard* engine⟩
³**yard** (1758)
transitive verb
1 : to drive into or confine in a restricted area **:** HERD, PEN
2 : to deliver to or store in a yard
intransitive verb
: to congregate in or as if in a yard
⁴**yard** *noun* [Middle English *yarde,* from Old English *gierd* twig, measure, yard; akin to Old High German *gart* stick, Latin *hasta* spear] (before 12th century)
1 : any of various units of measure: as **a** : a unit of length equal in the U.S. to 0.9144 meter — see WEIGHT table **b** : a unit of volume equal to a cubic yard
2 a : a great length or quantity ⟨remembered *yards* of facts and figures⟩ **b** *slang* : one hundred dollars

3 : a long spar tapered toward the ends to support and spread the head of a square sail, lateen, or lugsail
4 : a slender horn-shaped glass about three feet tall; *also* : the amount it contains ⟨a *yard* of ale⟩
— **the whole nine yards :** all of a related set of circumstances, conditions, or details ⟨who could learn the most about making records, about electronics and engineering, *the whole nine yards* —Stephen Stills⟩ — sometimes used adverbially with *go* to indicate an all-out effort

¹**yard·age** \'yär-dij\ *noun* [¹*yard*] (1867)
1 : the use of a livestock enclosure for animals in transit provided by a railroad at a station
2 : a charge made by a railroad for the use of a livestock enclosure
²**yardage** *noun* [⁴*yard*] (1900)
1 a : an aggregate number of yards **b** : the length, extent, or volume of something as measured in yards
2 : YARD GOODS

yard·arm \'yärd-ˌärm\ *noun* (1553)
: either end of the yard of a square-rigged ship

yard·bird \-ˌbərd\ *noun* [¹*yard*] (circa 1941)
1 : a soldier assigned to a menial task or restricted to a limited area as a disciplinary measure
2 : an untrained or inept enlisted man

yard goods *noun plural* (1905)
: fabrics sold by the yard **:** PIECE GOODS

yard grass *noun* [¹*yard*] (1822)
: a coarse annual grass (*Eleusine indica*) with digitate spikes that is widely distributed as a weed — called also *goosegrass*

yard line *noun* (1949)
: any of a series of marked or imaginary lines one yard apart on a football field that are parallel to the goal lines and that indicate the distance to the nearest goal line

yard–long bean \ˌyärd-'loŋ-\ *noun* (1926)
: the edible 1- to 3-foot (0.3- to 0.9- meter) long thin stringless fruit of a plant of a subspecies (*Vigna unguiculata sesquipedalis*) of the cowpea; *also* : the plant

yard·man \'yärd-mən, -ˌman\ *noun* (circa 1825)
1 : a person employed to do outdoor work (as mowing lawns)
2 : a person who works in the yard of a commercial establishment; *especially* : one who supervises the handling of building materials in a lumberyard
3 : a railroad hand employed in yard service

yard·mas·ter \-ˌmas-tər\ *noun* (1864)
: the person in charge of operations in a railroad yard

yard sale *noun* (1972)
: GARAGE SALE

yard·stick \'yärd-ˌstik\ *noun* (1816)
1 a : a graduated measuring stick three feet (0.9144 meter) long **b** : a standard basis of calculation
2 : a standard for making a critical judgment **:** CRITERION
synonym see STANDARD

yare \'yar, 'yer, 'yär\ *adjective* [Middle English, from Old English *gearu;* akin to Old High German *garo* ready] (before 12th century)
1 *archaic* **:** set for action **:** READY
2 *or* **yar** \'yär\ **a :** characterized by speed and agility **:** NIMBLE, LIVELY **b** : HANDY 1c, MANEUVERABLE
— **yare** *adverb, archaic*
— **yare·ly** *adverb, archaic*

yar·mul·ke *also* **yar·mel·ke** \'yä-mə-kə, 'yär-mə(l)-kə\ *noun* [Yiddish *yarmlke,* from Polish *jarmułka* & Ukrainian *yarmulka* skullcap, of Turkic origin; akin to Turkish *yağmurluk* rainwear] (1903)
: a skullcap worn especially by Orthodox and Conservative Jewish males in the synagogue and the home

¹**yarn** \'yärn\ *noun* [Middle English, from Old English *gearn;* akin to Old High German *garn* yarn, Greek *chordē* string, Latin *hernia* rupture, Sanskrit *hira* band] (before 12th century)
1 a : a continuous often plied strand composed of either natural or man-made fibers or filaments and used in weaving and knitting to form cloth **b** : a similar strand of another material (as metal, glass, or plastic)
2 : a narrative of adventures; *especially* : a tall tale
²**yarn** *intransitive verb* (1812)
: to tell a yarn
— **yarn·er** *noun*

yarn–dye \'yärn-ˌdī\ *transitive verb* (1885)
: to dye before weaving or knitting

yar·row \'yar-(ˌ)ō\ *noun* [Middle English *yarowe,* from Old English *gearwe;* akin to Old High German *garwa* yarrow] (before 12th century)
: a widely naturalized strong-scented Eurasian composite herb (*Achillea millefolium*) with finely dissected leaves and small usually white corymbose flowers; *also* : any of several congeneric plants

yash·mak *also* **yas·mak** \'yash-ˌmak, 'yas-\ *noun* [Turkish *yaşmak*] (1844)
: a veil worn by Muslim women that is wrapped around the upper and lower parts of the face so that only the eyes remain exposed to public view

yat·a·ghan \'ya-tə-ˌgan, 'ya-ti-gən\ *noun* [Turkish *yatağan*] (1819)
: a long knife or short saber that lacks a guard for the hand at the juncture of blade and hilt and that usually has a double curve to the edge and a nearly straight back

yauld \'yȯl(d)\ *adjective* [origin unknown] (1786)
chiefly Scottish **:** VIGOROUS, ENERGETIC

yau·pon \'yü-ˌpän *also* 'yȯ-, 'yȯ-\ *noun* [Catawba *yápą,* from *yą-* tree + *pą* leaf] (1709)
: a holly (*Ilex vomitoria*) of the southeastern U.S. that has smooth elliptical leaves and emetic and purgative properties

yau·tia \'yaü-tē-ə\ *noun* [American Spanish *yautía,* from Taino] (1899)
: any of several aroid plants (genus *Xanthosoma* and especially *X. sagittifolium*) chiefly of tropical America with starchy edible shaggy brown tubers that are cooked and eaten like yams or potatoes; *especially* : one of these tubers

¹**yaw** \'yȯ\ *noun* [origin unknown] (1546)
1 : the action of yawing; *especially* : a side to side movement
2 : the extent of the movement in yawing
²**yaw** *intransitive verb* (1586)
1 a *of a ship* **:** to deviate erratically from a course (as when struck by a heavy sea); *especially* : to move from side to side **b** *of an airplane, spacecraft, or projectile* : to turn by angular motion about the vertical axis
2 : ALTERNATE ⟨restlessly *yawing* between apparent extremes —Martin Kasindorf⟩

yawl \'yȯl\ *noun* [Low German *jolle*] (1670)
1 : a ship's small boat **:** JOLLY BOAT
2 : a fore-and-aft rigged sailboat carrying a mainsail and one or more jibs with a mizzenmast far aft

yawl 2

¹**yawn** \'yȯn, 'yän\ *verb* [Middle English *yenen, yanen,* from Old English *ginian;* akin to Old High German *ginēn* to yawn, Latin *hiare,* Greek *chainein*] (before 12th century)
intransitive verb
1 : to open wide **:** GAPE
2 : to open the mouth wide usually as an involuntary reaction to fatigue or boredom
transitive verb
1 : to utter with a yawn
2 : to accomplish with or impel by yawns ⟨his grandchildren *yawned* him to bed —L. L. King⟩
²**yawn** *noun* (1602)
1 : GAP, CAVITY
2 : a deep usually involuntary intake of breath through the wide open mouth often as an involuntary reaction to fatigue or boredom; *also* **:** a reaction resembling a yawn ⟨a . . . success at the box office but drew only *yawns* from critics —*Current Biography*⟩
3 : ⁵BORE
yawn·er *noun* (1687)
1 : one that yawns
2 : something that causes boredom ⟨the show was a real *yawner*⟩
yawn·ing *adjective* (before 12th century)
1 : wide open **:** CAVERNOUS ⟨a *yawning* hole⟩ ⟨a dreadful, *yawning* gap of . . . weeks —*Times Educational Supplement*⟩
2 : showing fatigue or boredom by yawns ⟨a *yawning* audience⟩
— **yawn·ing·ly** \'yȯ-niŋ-lē\ *adverb*
¹**yawp** *or* **yaup** \'yȯp\ *intransitive verb* [Middle English *yolpen*] (14th century)
1 : to make a raucous noise **:** SQUAWK
2 : CLAMOR, COMPLAIN
— **yawp·er** *noun*
²**yawp** *also* **yaup** *noun* (1824)
1 : a raucous noise **:** SQUAWK
2 : something suggestive of a raucous noise; *specifically* **:** rough vigorous language
yawp·ing *noun* (1876)
: a strident utterance
yaws \'yȯz\ *noun plural but singular or plural in construction* [probably from an English-based creole of the Caribbean] (1679)
: an infectious contagious tropical disease caused by a spirochete (*Treponema pertenue*) closely resembling the causative agent of syphilis and marked by ulcerating lesions with later bone involvement — called also *frambesia*
y–ax·is \'wī-,ak-səs\ *noun* (1875)
1 : the axis of a plane Cartesian coordinate system parallel to which ordinates are measured
2 : one of the three axes in a three-dimensional rectangular coordinate system
Y chromosome *noun* (1911)
: a sex chromosome that is characteristic of male cells in species in which the male typically has two unlike sex chromosomes — compare X CHROMOSOME
yclept *or* **ycleped** [Middle English, from Old English *geclipod,* past participle of *clipian* to cry out, name] *past participle of* CLEPE
y–co·or·di·nate \,wī-kō-'ȯrd-nət, -'ȯr-dᵊn-ət, -də-,nāt\ *noun* (1927)
: a coordinate whose value is determined by measuring parallel to a y-axis; *specifically* **:** ORDINATE
¹**ye** \'yē\ *pronoun* [Middle English, from Old English *gē;* akin to Old High German *ir* you — more at YOU] (before 12th century)
: YOU 1 — used originally only as a plural pronoun of the second person in the subjective case and now used especially in ecclesiastical or literary language and in various English dialects
word history see YOU
²**ye** \yē, yə; *originally same as* ¹THE\ *definite article* [alteration of Middle English *þe* the, from Old English *þē;* from the use of the letter *y* by printers and scribes of late Middle English to represent þ (*th*) of earlier manuscripts] (1551)
archaic **:** THE ⟨*Ye* Olde Gifte Shoppe⟩
¹**yea** \'yā\ *adverb* [Middle English *ye, ya,* from Old English *gēa;* akin to Old High German *jā* yes] (before 12th century)
1 : YES — used in oral voting
2 : more than this **:** not only so but — used as a function word to introduce a more explicit or emphatic phrase ⟨yet the impression, *yea* the evidence, is inescapable —J. G. Harrison⟩
²**yea** *noun* (13th century)
1 : AFFIRMATION, ASSENT
2 a : an affirmative vote **b :** a person casting a yea vote
yeah \'ye-ə, 'yeủ, 'ya-ə\ *adverb* [by alteration] (1902)
: YES
yean \'yēn, ēn\ *intransitive verb* [Middle English *yenen,* from (assumed) Old English *gēeanian,* from Old English *ge-,* perfective prefix + *ēanian* to yean; akin to Latin *agnus* lamb, Greek *amnos*] (1548)
: to bring forth young — used of a sheep or goat
yean·ling \-liŋ, -lən\ *noun* (1637)
: LAMB, KID 1a
year \'yir\ *noun* [Middle English *yere,* from Old English *gēar;* akin to Old High German *jār* year, Greek *hōros* year, *hōra* season, hour] (before 12th century)
1 a : the period of about 365¼ solar days required for one revolution of the earth around the sun **b :** the time required for the apparent sun to return to an arbitrary fixed or moving reference point in the sky **c :** the time in which a planet completes a revolution about the sun ⟨a *year* of Jupiter⟩
2 a : a cycle in the Gregorian calendar of 365 or 366 days divided into 12 months beginning with January and ending with December **b :** a period of time equal to one year of the Gregorian calendar but beginning at a different time
3 : a calendar year specified usually by a number ⟨died in the *year* 1900⟩
4 *plural* **:** a time or era having a special significance ⟨their glory *years*⟩
5 a : 12 months that constitute a measure of age or duration ⟨her 21st *year*⟩ — often used in combination ⟨a *year*-old child⟩ **b** *plural* **:** AGE ⟨an adult in *years* but a child in understanding⟩; *also* **:** the final stage of the normal life span
6 : a period of time (as the usually nine-month period in which a school is in session) other than a calendar year
year·book \-,bùk\ *noun* (1710)
1 : a book published yearly as a report or summary of statistics or facts **:** ANNUAL
2 : a school publication that is compiled usually by a graduating class and that serves as a record of the year's activities
¹**year–end** \'yir-'end\ *noun* (1872)
: the end of usually the fiscal year
²**year–end** *adjective* (1899)
: made, occurring, or existing at the year-end ⟨a *year-end* report⟩
year·ling \'yir-liŋ, 'yər-lən\ *noun* (15th century)
: one that is a year old: as **a :** an animal one year old or in the second year of its age **b :** a racehorse between January 1st of the year after the year in which it was foaled and the next January 1st
— **yearling** *adjective*
year·long \'yir-'lȯŋ\ *adjective* (1813)
: lasting through a year
¹**year·ly** \'yir-lē\ *adjective* (before 12th century)
1 : reckoned by the year
2 : occurring, appearing, made, done, or acted upon every year or once a year **:** ANNUAL
²**yearly** *adverb* (before 12th century)
: every year **:** ANNUALLY
Yearly Meeting *noun* (1688)
: an organization uniting several Quarterly Meetings of the Society of Friends
yearn \'yərn\ *intransitive verb* [Middle English *yernen,* from Old English *giernan;* akin to Old High German *gerōn* to desire, Latin *hortari* to urge, encourage, Greek *chairein* to rejoice] (before 12th century)
1 : to long persistently, wistfully, or sadly
2 : to feel tenderness or compassion
synonym see LONG
— **yearn·er** *noun*
— **yearn·ing·ly** \'yər-niŋ-lē\ *adverb*
yearn·ing *noun* (before 12th century)
: a tender or urgent longing
year of grace (14th century)
: a calendar year of the Christian era ⟨the *year of grace* 1993⟩
year–round \'yir-'raùnd\ *adjective* (1924)
: occurring, effective, employed, staying, or operating for the full year **:** not seasonal ⟨a *year-round* resort⟩
— **year–round** *adverb*
— **year–round·er** \-'raùn-dər\ *noun*
yea–say·er \'yā-,sā-ər, -,se(-ə)r\ *noun* (1920)
1 : one whose attitude is that of confident affirmation
2 : YES-MAN
¹**yeast** \'yēst, *especially Southern & Midland* 'ēst\ *noun* [Middle English *yest,* from Old English *gist;* akin to Old High German *jesen, gesen* to ferment, Greek *zein* to boil] (before 12th century)
1 a : a yellowish surface froth or sediment that occurs especially in saccharine liquids (as fruit juices) in which it promotes alcoholic fermentation, consists largely of cells of a fungus (family Saccharomycetaceae), and is used especially in the making of alcoholic liquors and as a leaven in baking **b :** a commercial product containing yeast plants in a moist or dry medium **c** (1) **:** a minute fungus (especially *Saccharomyces cerevisiae*) that is present and functionally active in yeast, usually has little or no mycelium, and reproduces by budding (2) **:** any of various similar fungi (especially orders Endomycetales and Moniliales)
2 *archaic* **:** the foam or spume of waves
3 : something that causes ferment or activity ⟨were all seething with the *yeast* of revolt —J. F. Dobie⟩
²**yeast** *intransitive verb* (1819)
: FERMENT, FROTH
yeasty \'yē-stē, 'ē-stē\ *adjective* **yeast·i·er; -est** (1598)
1 : of, relating to, or resembling yeast
2 a : IMMATURE, UNSETTLED **b :** marked by change **c :** full of vitality **d :** FRIVOLOUS 1a, 2
— **yeast·i·ness** \-stē-nəs\ *noun*
yech *or* **yecch** \'yək, 'yək̲, 'yek, 'yek̲\ *interjection* (1969)
— used to express rejection or disgust
yegg \'yeg, 'yäg\ *noun* [origin unknown] (1903)
: SAFECRACKER; *also* **:** ROBBER
¹**yell** \'yel\ *verb* [Middle English, from Old English *giellan;* akin to Old High German *gellan* to yell, Old English *galan* to sing] (before 12th century)
intransitive verb
1 : to utter a loud cry, scream, or shout
2 : to give a cheer usually in unison
transitive verb
: to utter or declare with or as if with a yell **:** SHOUT
— **yell·er** *noun*
²**yell** *noun* (14th century)
1 : SCREAM, SHOUT
2 : a usually rhythmic cheer used especially in schools or colleges to encourage athletic teams
¹**yel·low** \'ye-(,)lō, *dialect* 'ye-lər *or* 'ya-\ *adjective* [Middle English *yelwe, yelow,* from Old English *geolu;* akin to Old High German *gelo* yellow, Latin *helvus* light bay, Greek *chlōros* greenish yellow, Sanskrit *hari* yellowish] (before 12th century)

1 a : of the color yellow **b :** become yellowish through age, disease, or discoloration **:** SALLOW **c :** having a yellow or light brown complexion or skin
2 a : featuring sensational or scandalous items or ordinary news sensationally distorted ⟨*yellow* journalism⟩ **b :** MEAN, COWARDLY
— **yel·low·ish** \'ye-lə-wish\ *adjective*

²yellow *noun* (before 12th century)
1 : something yellow or marked by a yellow color: as **a :** a person having yellow or light brown skin **b :** the yolk of an egg
2 a : a color whose hue resembles that of ripe lemons or sunflowers or is that of the portion of the spectrum lying between green and orange **b :** a pigment or dye that colors yellow
3 *plural* **:** JAUNDICE
4 *plural but singular in construction* **:** any of several plant diseases caused especially by mycoplasma-like organisms and marked by yellowing of the foliage and stunting

³yellow (1598)
transitive verb
: to make yellow **:** give a yellow tinge or color to ⟨*yellowed* by time⟩
intransitive verb
: to become or turn yellow

yellow bile *noun* (1881)
: a humor believed in medieval physiology to be secreted by the liver and to cause irascibility

yellow birch *noun* (1787)
: a North American birch (*Betula alleghaniensis* synonym *B. lutea*) with thin lustrous gray or yellow bark forming plates with ragged edges in older trees; *also* **:** its strong hard dark brown to reddish brown wood

yel·low–dog \,ye-lō-'dȯg, -lə-'dȯg\ *adjective* (1880)
1 : MEAN, CONTEMPTIBLE
2 : of or relating to opposition to trade unionism or a labor union

yellow–dog contract *noun* (1920)
: an employment contract in which a worker disavows membership in and agrees not to join a labor union in order to get a job

yellow dwarf *noun* (1928)
: any of several virus diseases especially of cereal grasses (as oats and barley) characterized by yellowing and stunting

yellow fever *noun* (1739)
: an acute destructive infectious disease of warm regions marked by sudden onset, prostration, fever, albuminuria, jaundice, and often hemorrhage and caused by a virus transmitted by the yellow-fever mosquito

yellow–fever mosquito *noun* (1905)
: a small dark-colored mosquito (*Aedes aegypti*) that is the usual vector of yellow fever

yel·low·fin tuna \'ye-lō-,fin-, 'ye-lə-\ *noun* (1922)
: a rather small and nearly cosmopolitan tuna (*Thunnus albacares*) with yellowish fins — called also *yellowfin*

yellow–green alga *noun* (1930)
: any of a class (Xanthophyceae of the division Chrysophyta) of algae with the chlorophyll masked by brown or yellow pigment

yel·low·ham·mer \'ye-lō-,ha-mər, 'ye-lə-\ *noun* [alteration of earlier *yelambre*, from (assumed) Middle English *yelwambre*, from Middle English *yelwe* yellow + (assumed) Middle English *ambre* yellowhammer, from Old English *amore*; akin to Old High German *amaro* yellowhammer, *amari* emmer] (1556)
1 : a common Palearctic finch (*Emberiza citrinella*) having the male largely bright yellow — called also *yellow bunting*
2 : YELLOW-SHAFTED FLICKER

yellow jack *noun* (1836)
1 : YELLOW FEVER
2 : a yellowish carangid marine food fish (*Caranx bartholomaei*) found from Massachusetts to Brazil

yellow jacket *noun* (1796)

1 : any of various small yellow-marked vespid wasps (especially genus *Vespula*) that commonly nest in the ground and can sting repeatedly and painfully
2 *slang* **:** pentobarbital especially in a yellow capsule

yellow jessamine *noun* (1709)
: a twining evergreen shrub (*Gelsemium sempervirens* of the family Loganiaceae) with fragrant yellow flowers — called also *yellow jasmine*

yel·low·legs \'ye-lō-,legz, 'ye-lə-, -,lāgz\ *noun plural but singular or plural in construction* (1772)
: either of two American shorebirds with yellow legs: **a :** GREATER YELLOWLEGS **b :** LESSER YELLOWLEGS

yellow ocher *noun* (15th century)
1 : a mixture of limonite usually with clay and silica used as a pigment
2 : a moderate orange yellow

yellow pages *noun plural, often Y&P capitalized* (1952)
: the section of a telephone book that lists business and professional firms alphabetically by category and that includes classified advertising; *also* **:** a listing of products or services that is independently published

yellow perch *noun* (1805)
: a common North American freshwater bony fish (*Perca flavescens*) of the perch family that is yellowish with dark green bands and is an excellent food and sport fish

yellow peril *noun, often Y&P capitalized* (1898)
1 : a danger to Western civilization held to arise from expansion of the power and influence of eastern Asian peoples
2 : a threat to Western living standards from the influx of eastern Asian laborers willing to work for very low wages

yellow pine *noun* (1709)
1 : any of several North American pines (as a Ponderosa pine or longleaf pine) with yellowish wood
2 : the wood of a yellow pine

yellow poplar *noun* (1774)
1 : TULIP TREE 1
2 : TULIPWOOD 1

yellow rain *noun* (1979)
: a yellow substance reported to occur as a mist or as spots on rocks and vegetation in Southeast Asia and variously held to be a chemical warfare agent used in the Vietnam War or a natural substance similar if not identical to pollen or the feces of bees

yel·low–shaft·ed flicker \'ye-lō-,shaf-təd-, 'ye-lə-\ *noun* (1888)
: a flicker of eastern North America that is golden yellow on the underside of the tail and wings, has a red mark on the nape, and in the male has a black streak on each cheek

yellow spot *noun* (1869)
: MACULA LUTEA

yel·low·tail \'ye-lō-,tāl, 'ye-lə-\ *noun, plural* **yellowtail** *or* **yellowtails** (1709)
: any of various fishes having a yellow or yellowish tail: as **a :** any of several carangid fishes (genus *Seriola*); *especially* **:** a sport fish (*S. lalandei*) of the California coast and southward that reaches a length of about three feet (one meter) **b :** SILVER PERCH a **c :** a common snapper (*Ocyurus chrysurus*) that is a sport and food fish of the tropical western Atlantic and West Indies and is olive above and broadly striped with yellow along the sides and on the tail — called also *yellowtail snapper*

yel·low·throat \-,thrōt\ *noun* (1702)
: any of several largely olive American warblers (genus *Geothlypis*); *especially* **:** one (*G. trichas*) with yellow breast and throat and a whitish belly

yel·low·ware \-,war, -,wer\ *noun* (1785)
: pottery made from buff clay and covered with a yellowish transparent clay

yel·low·wood \-,wu̇d\ *noun* (1666)

1 : any of various trees having yellowish wood or yielding a yellow extract; *especially* **:** a leguminous tree (*Cladrastis lutea*) of the southern U.S. having showy white fragrant flowers and yielding a yellow dye
2 : the wood of a yellowwood tree

¹yelp \'yelp\ *noun* [²*yelp*] (1501)
: a sharp shrill bark or cry (as of a dog); *also* **:** SQUEAL

²yelp *verb* [Middle English, to boast, cry out, from Old English *gielpan* to boast, exult; akin to Old High German *gelph* outcry] (1553)
intransitive verb
: to utter a sharp quick shrill cry ⟨dogs *yelp*⟩
transitive verb
: to utter with a yelp

yelp·er \'yel-pər\ *noun* (1673)
1 : one that yelps; *especially* **:** a yelping dog
2 : an instrument used by hunters to produce a call or whistle imitating the yelp of the wild turkey hen

¹yen \'yen\ *noun, plural* **yen** [Japanese *en*] (1875)
— see MONEY table

²yen *noun* [obsolete English argot *yen-yen* craving for opium, from Chinese (Guangdong) *yīn-yáhn*, from *yīn* opium + *yáhn* craving] (1906)
: a strong desire or propensity **:** LONGING; *also* **:** URGE

³yen *intransitive verb* **yenned; yen·ning** (1919)
: to have an intense desire **:** LONG, YEARN

yen–shee \'yen-'shē\ *noun* [Chinese (Guangdong) *yīn-sí*, from *yīn* opium + *sí* excrement, filth] (1882)
: the residue formed in the bowl of an opium pipe by smoking

yen·ta \'yen-tə\ *noun* [Yiddish *yente*, from the name *Yente*] (1923)
: one that meddles; *also* **:** BLABBERMOUTH, GOSSIP

yeo·man \'yō-mən\ *noun* [Middle English *yoman*] (14th century)
1 a : an attendant or officer in a royal or noble household **b :** a person attending or assisting another **:** RETAINER **c :** YEOMAN OF THE GUARD **d :** a naval petty officer who performs clerical duties
2 a : a person who owns and cultivates a small farm; *specifically* **:** one belonging to a class of English freeholders below the gentry **b :** a person of the social rank of yeoman
3 : one that performs great and loyal service ⟨did a *yeoman's* job in seeing the program through⟩

¹yeo·man·ly \-lē\ *adverb* (14th century)
archaic **:** in a manner befitting a yeoman **:** BRAVELY

²yeomanly *adjective* (1576)
1 : of, relating to, or having the rank of a yeoman
2 : becoming or suitable to a yeoman **:** STURDY, LOYAL

yeoman of the guard (circa 1520)
: a member of a military corps attached to the British royal household that serves as ceremonial attendants of the sovereign and as warders of the Tower of London

yeo·man·ry \'yō-mən-rē\ *noun* (14th century)
1 : the body of yeomen; *specifically* **:** the body of small landed proprietors of the middle class
2 : a British volunteer cavalry force created from yeomen in 1761 as a home defense force and reorganized in 1907 as part of the territorial force

yep \'yep, *or with glottal stop instead of* p\ *adverb* [by alteration] (1891)
: YES

-yer — see -ER

yer·ba ma·té \ˌyer-bə-ˈmä-ˌtā, ˌyәr-\ *noun* [American Spanish *yerba mate,* from *yerba* herb + *mate* maté] (1839) : MATÉ

¹yerk \ˈyәrk\ *transitive verb* [Middle English, to bind tightly] (circa 1520)
1 *dialect* : to beat vigorously : THRASH
2 *dialect* : to attack or excite vigorously : GOAD

²yerk *noun* (1581)
1 *Scottish* : a lashing out : KICK
2 *dialect* : JERK 1

¹yes \ˈyes\ *adverb* [Middle English, from Old English *gēse*] (before 12th century)
1 — used as a function word to express assent or agreement ⟨are you ready? *Yes,* I am⟩
2 — used as a function word usually to introduce a correction or contradiction of a negative assertion or direction ⟨don't say that! *Yes,* I will⟩
3 — used as a function word to introduce a more emphatic or explicit phrase
4 — used as a function word to indicate uncertainty or polite interest or attentiveness

²yes *noun* (1712)
: an affirmative reply : YEA

ye·shi·va *also* **ye·shi·vah** \yә-ˈshē-vә\ *noun,* *plural* **yeshivas** *or* **ye·shi·vot** \-ˌshē-ˈvōt, -ˈvōth\ [Late Hebrew *yĕshībhāh*] (1851)
1 : a school for talmudic study
2 : an Orthodox Jewish rabbinical seminary
3 : a Jewish day school providing secular and religious instruction

yes–man \ˈyes-ˌman\ *noun* (1913)
: a person who agrees with everything that is said; *especially* : one who endorses or supports without criticism every opinion or proposal of an associate or superior

yes·ter \ˈyes-tәr\ *adjective* (1577)
archaic : of or relating to yesterday

¹yes·ter·day \ˈyes-tәr-dē, -(ˌ)dā\ *adverb* [Middle English *yisterday,* from Old English *giestran dæg,* from *giestran* yesterday + *dæg* day; akin to Old High German *gestaron* yesterday, Latin *heri,* Greek *chthes*] (before 12th century)
1 : on the day last past : on the day preceding today
2 : at a time not long past : only a short time ago ⟨I wasn't born *yesterday*⟩
— **yesterday** *adjective*

²yesterday *noun* (before 12th century)
1 : the day last past : the day next before the present
2 : recent time : time not long past
3 : past time — usually used in plural

¹yes·ter·night \ˈyes-tәr-ˌnīt\ *adverb* [Middle English, from Old English *gystran niht,* from *giestran* yesterday + *niht* night] (before 12th century)
archaic : on the night last past

²yesternight *noun* (1513)
: the night last past

yes·ter·year \ˈyes-tәr-ˌyir\ *noun* [*yester*day + *year*] (1870)
1 : last year
2 : time gone by; *especially* : the recent past
— **yesteryear** *adverb*

yes·treen \ye-ˈstrēn\ *noun* [Middle English (Scots) *yistrevin,* from *yister*day + *evin* evening, alteration of Middle English *even*] (1785)
chiefly Scottish : last evening or night
— **yestreen** *adverb*

¹yet \ˈyet\ *adverb* [Middle English, from Old English *gīet;* akin to Old Frisian *ieta* yet] (before 12th century)
1 a : in addition : BESIDES ⟨gives *yet* another reason⟩ **b** : EVEN 2c ⟨a *yet* higher speed⟩ **c** : on top of everything else : no less ⟨had wells going dry. Between two large lakes, *yet* —J. H. Buzard⟩
2 a (1) : up to now : so far ⟨hasn't done much *yet*⟩ — often used to imply the negative of a following infinitive ⟨have *yet* to win a game⟩

(2) : at this or that time : so soon as now ⟨not time to go *yet*⟩ **b** : continuously up to the present or a specified time : STILL ⟨is *yet* a new country⟩ **c** : at a future time : EVENTUALLY ⟨may *yet* see the light⟩
3 : NEVERTHELESS, HOWEVER
— **as yet** : up to the present or a specified time
— **yet again** : one more time ⟨arrived late *yet again*⟩

²yet *conjunction* (13th century)
: but nevertheless : BUT

ye·ti \ˈye-tē, ˈyā-\ *noun* [Tibetan] (1937)
: ABOMINABLE SNOWMAN

yeuk \ˈyük\ *intransitive verb* [Middle English (northern) *yukyn,* from Old English *giccan* — more at ITCH] (15th century)
chiefly Scottish : ITCH

yew \ˈyü\ *noun* [Middle English *ew,* from Old English *īw;* akin to Old High German *īwa* yew, Middle Irish *eó*] (before 12th century)
1 a : any of a genus (*Taxus* of the family Taxaceae, the yew family) of evergreen trees and shrubs with stiff linear leaves and fruits with a fleshy aril: as (1) : a long-lived Eurasian tree or shrub (*T. baccata*) — called also *English yew* (2) : a low straggling bush (*T. canadensis*) of the eastern U.S. and Canada **b** : the wood of a yew; *especially* : the heavy fine-grained wood of English yew
2 *archaic* : an archery bow made of yew

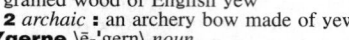
yew 1a

Ygerne \ē-ˈgern\ *noun*
: IGRAINE

Ygg·dra·sil \ˈig-drә-ˌsil\ *noun* [Old Norse]
: a huge ash tree in Norse mythology that overspreads the world and binds earth, hell, and heaven together

YHWH \ˈyä-(ˌ)wä, -(ˌ)vä\ *noun*
: YAHWEH — compare TETRAGRAMMATON

Yid \ˈyid\ *noun* [Yiddish, from Middle High German *Jüde,* from Old High German *Judeo,* from Latin *Judaeus* — more at JEW] (circa 1874)
: JEW — usually taken to be offensive

Yid·dish \ˈyi-dish\ *noun* [Yiddish *yidish,* short for *yidish daytsh,* literally, Jewish German, from Middle High German *jüdisch diutsch,* from *jüdisch* Jewish (from *Jude* Jew) + *diutsch* German] (1886)
: a High German language written in Hebrew characters that is spoken by Jews and descendants of Jews of central and eastern European origin
— **Yiddish** *adjective*

Yid·dish·ism \ˈyi-di-ˌshi-zәm\ *noun* (1904)
1 : a usage, word, phrase, or idiom peculiar to Yiddish
2 : a movement characterized by advocacy of the Yiddish language and culture
— **Yid·dish·ist** \-shist\ *noun or adjective*

¹yield \ˈyē(ә)ld\ *verb* [Middle English, from Old English *gieldan;* akin to Old High German *geltan* to pay] (before 12th century)
transitive verb
1 *archaic* : RECOMPENSE, REWARD
2 : to give or render as fitting, rightfully owed, or required
3 : to give up possession of on claim or demand: as **a** : to give up (as one's breath) and so die **b** : to surrender or relinquish to the physical control of another : hand over possession of **c** : to surrender or submit (oneself) to another **d** : to give (oneself) up to an inclination, temptation, or habit **e** : to relinquish one's possession of (as a position of advantage or point of superiority) ⟨*yield* precedence⟩
4 a : to bear or bring forth as a natural product especially as a result of cultivation ⟨the tree always *yields* good fruit⟩ **b** : to produce or furnish as return ⟨this soil should *yield* good

crops⟩ **c** (1) : to produce as return from an expenditure or investment : furnish as profit or interest ⟨a bond that *yields* 12 percent⟩ (2) : to produce as revenue : BRING IN ⟨the tax is expected to *yield* millions⟩
5 : to give up (as a hit or run) in baseball ⟨*yielded* two runs in the third inning⟩
intransitive verb
1 : to be fruitful or productive : BEAR, PRODUCE
2 : to give up and cease resistance or contention : SUBMIT, SUCCUMB
3 : to give way to pressure or influence : submit to urging, persuasion, or entreaty
4 : to give way under physical force (as bending, stretching, or breaking)
5 a : to give place or precedence : acknowledge the superiority of someone else **b** : to be inferior ⟨our dictionary *yields* to none⟩ **c** : to give way to or become succeeded by someone or something else
6 : to relinquish the floor of a legislative assembly ☆

²yield *noun* (15th century)
1 : something yielded : PRODUCT; *especially* : the amount or quantity produced or returned ⟨*yield* of wheat per acre⟩
2 : the capacity of yielding produce

yield·er \ˈyēl-dәr\ *noun* (1590)
: one that yields: as **a** : a person who surrenders, concedes, or gives in **b** : something that yields produce or products

yield·ing \-diŋ\ *adjective* (1533)
1 : PRODUCTIVE ⟨a high-*yielding* wheat⟩
2 : lacking rigidity or stiffness : FLEXIBLE
3 : disposed to submit or comply

yikes \ˈyīks\ *interjection* [probably alteration of *yoicks*] (1957)
— used to express fear or astonishment

yin \ˈyin\ *noun* [Chinese (Beijing) *yīn*] (1671)
: the feminine passive principle in nature that in Chinese cosmology is exhibited in darkness, cold, or wetness and that combines with yang to produce all that comes to be

Yin·glish \ˈyiŋ-glish, -lish\ *noun* [blend of *Yiddish* and *English*] (1951)
: English marked by numerous borrowings from Yiddish

y–in·ter·cept \ˈwī-ˈin-tәr-ˌsept\ *noun* (circa 1939)
: the y-coordinate of a point where a line, curve, or surface intersects the y-axis

yip \ˈyip\ *intransitive verb* **yipped; yip·ping** [imitative] (1907)
1 : to bark sharply, quickly, and often continuously

☆ **SYNONYMS**
Yield, submit, capitulate, succumb, relent, defer mean to give way to someone or something that one can no longer resist. YIELD may apply to any sort or degree of giving way before force, argument, persuasion, or entreaty ⟨*yields* too easily in any argument⟩. SUBMIT suggests full surrendering after resistance or conflict to the will or control of another ⟨a repentant sinner vowing to *submit* to the will of God⟩. CAPITULATE stresses the fact of ending all resistance and may imply either a coming to terms (as with an adversary) or hopelessness in the face of an irresistible opposing force ⟨officials *capitulated* to the protesters' demands⟩. SUCCUMB implies weakness and helplessness to the one that gives way or an overwhelming power to the opposing force ⟨a stage actor *succumbing* to the lure of Hollywood⟩. RELENT implies a yielding through pity or mercy by one who holds the upper hand ⟨finally *relented* and let the children stay up late⟩. DEFER implies a voluntary yielding or submitting out of respect or reverence for or deference and affection toward another ⟨I *defer* to your superior expertise in these matters⟩. See in addition RELINQUISH.

2 : to utter a short sharp cry
— **yip** *noun*

yip·pee \'yi-pē\ *interjection* (1914)
— used to express exuberant delight or triumph

yip·pie \'yi-pē\ *noun* [*Youth International Party* + *-ie* (as in *hippie*)] (1968)
: a person belonging to or identified with a politically active group of hippies

yips \'yips\ *noun plural* [origin unknown] (1962)
: a state of nervous tension affecting an athlete (as a golfer) in the performance of a crucial action ⟨had a bad case of the *yips* on short putts⟩

-yl \əl, əl, (,)il, ,ēl, *chiefly British* ,īl\ *noun combining form* [Greek *hylē* matter, material, literally, wood]
: chemical and usually univalent group ⟨ethyl⟩

ylang-ylang \,ē-,läŋ-'ē-,läŋ\ *noun* [Tagalog] (1876)
1 : a tree (*Cananga odorata* synonym *Canangium odoratum*) of the custard-apple family of the Malay Archipelago, the Philippines, and adjacent areas that has very fragrant greenish yellow flowers
2 : a perfume distilled from the flowers of the ylang-ylang tree

YMCA \,wī-,em-(,)sē-'ā\ *noun* [*Young Men's Christian Association*] (1881)
: an international organization that promotes the spiritual, intellectual, social, and physical welfare originally of young men

YMHA \,wī-,em-,ā-'chā\ *noun* [*Young Men's Hebrew Association*] (1918)
: an organization that promotes the religious, intellectual, social, and physical welfare of Jewish young men

Ymir \'ē-,mir\ *noun* [Old Norse]
: a giant from whose body the gods create the world in Norse mythology

yo \'yō\ *interjection* [Middle English *yo, io*, interjection] (15th century)
— used especially to call attention, to indicate attentiveness, or to express affirmation

yob \'yäb\ *noun* [backward spelling for *boy*] (1908)
British : YOBBO

yob·bo \'yä-bō\ *noun, plural* **yobbos** *or* **yob·boes** [*yob* + *-o*] (1922)
1 *British* : LOUT, YOKEL
2 *British* : HOODLUM

yock \'yäk\ *variant of* ²YAK

yod \'yōd, 'yüd\ *noun* [Hebrew *yōdh*] (1735)
: the 10th letter of the Hebrew alphabet — see ALPHABET table

¹yo·del \'yō-dᵊl\ *verb* **-deled** *or* **-delled**; **-del·ing** *or* **-del·ling** \'yōd-liŋ, 'yō-dᵊl-iŋ\ [German *jodeln*] (1838)
intransitive verb
: to sing by suddenly changing from a natural voice to a falsetto and back; *also* : to shout or call in a similar manner
transitive verb
: to sing (a tune) by yodeling
— **yo·del·er** \'yōd-lər, 'yō-dᵊl-ər\ *noun*

²yodel *noun* (1849)
: a song or refrain sung by yodeling; *also* : a yodeled shout or cry

yo·ga \'yō-gə\ *noun* [Sanskrit, literally, yoking, from *yunakti* he yokes; akin to Latin *jungere* to join — more at YOKE] (1820)
1 *capitalized* : a Hindu theistic philosophy teaching the suppression of all activity of body, mind, and will in order that the self may realize its distinction from them and attain liberation
2 : a system of exercises for attaining bodily or mental control and well-being
— **yo·gic** \-gik\ *adjective, often capitalized*

yogh \'yōk, 'yōg, 'yōk͟\ *noun* [Middle English] (14th century)
: the letter ȝ used especially in Middle English chiefly to represent voiced and voiceless velar and palatal fricatives

yo·gi \'yō-gē\ *also* **yo·gin** \-gən, -,gin\ *noun* [Sanskrit *yogin*, from *yoga*] (1619)
1 : a person who practices yoga
2 *capitalized* : an adherent of Yoga philosophy
3 : a markedly reflective or mystical person

yo·gurt *also* **yo·ghurt** \'yō-gərt\ *noun* [Turkish *yoğurt*] (1625)
: a fermented slightly acid often flavored semisolid food made of whole or skimmed cow's milk and milk solids to which cultures of two bacteria (*Lactobacillus bulgaricus* and *Streptococcus thermophilus*) have been added

yo·him·bine \yō-'him-,bēn, -bən\ *noun* [International Scientific Vocabulary, from *yohimbé*, a tropical African tree (*Corynanthe yohimbe*) from which it is obtained] (1898)
: an alkaloid $C_{21}H_{26}N_2O_3$ that is a weak blocker of alpha-adrenergic receptors and has been used as an aphrodisiac

yoicks \'yȯiks\ *interjection* (1774)
— used as a cry of encouragement to foxhounds

¹yoke \'yōk\ *noun, plural* **yokes** [Middle English *yok*, from Old English *geoc*; akin to Old High German *joh* yoke, Latin *jugum*, Greek *zygon*, Sanskrit *yuga*, Latin *jungere* to join] (before 12th century)
1 a : a wooden bar or frame by which two draft animals (as oxen) are joined at the heads or necks for working together **b** : an arched device formerly laid on the neck of a defeated person **c** : a frame fitted to a person's shoulders to carry a load in two equal portions **d** : a bar by which the end of the tongue of a wagon or carriage is suspended from the collars of the harness **e** (1) : a crosspiece on the head of a boat's rudder (2) : the control device for an airplane's ailerons that is mounted on a column which also serves to operate the elevator **f** : a frame from which a bell is hung **g** : a clamp or similar piece that embraces two parts to hold or unite them in position
2 *plural usually* **yoke** : two animals yoked or worked together
3 a (1) : an oppressive agency (2) : SERVITUDE, BONDAGE **b** : TIE, LINK; *especially* : MARRIAGE
4 : a fitted or shaped piece at the top of a skirt or at the shoulder of various garments

²yoke *verb* **yoked**; **yok·ing** (before 12th century)
transitive verb
1 a (1) : to put a yoke on (2) : to join in or with a yoke **b** : to attach a draft animal to; *also* : to attach (a draft animal) to something
2 : to join as if by a yoke
3 : to put to work
intransitive verb
: to become joined or linked

yoke·fel·low \'yōk-,fe-(,)lō\ *noun* (1526)
: a close companion : MATE

yo·kel \'yō-kəl\ *noun* [perhaps from English dialect *yokel* green woodpecker, of imitative origin] (circa 1812)
: a naive or gullible inhabitant of a rural area or small town

yolk \'yōk, 'yelk (*in cultivated speech, especially Southern*), *also* 'yōlk, 'yȯlk, 'yälk, 'yȯlk\ *also* **yoke** \'yōk\ *noun* [Middle English *yolke*, from Old English *geoloca*, from *geolu* yellow — more at YELLOW] (before 12th century)
1 a : the yellow spheroidal mass of stored food that forms the inner portion of the egg of a bird or reptile and is surrounded by the white — see EGG illustration **b** *archaic* : the whole contents of an ovum consisting of a protoplasmic formative portion and an inert nutritive portion **c** : material stored in an ovum that supplies food to the developing embryo and consists chiefly of proteins, lecithin, and cholesterol
2 [akin to Middle Dutch *ieke* yolk (of wool), Old English *ēowu* ewe] : oily material in unprocessed sheep wool consisting of wool fat, suint, and debris
— **yolked** *adjective*
— **yolky** *adjective*

yolk sac *noun* (1861)
: a membranous sac that is attached to an embryo and encloses food yolk, that is continuous in most forms through the yolk stalk with the intestinal cavity of the embryo, that being abundantly supplied with blood vessels is throughout embryonic life and in some forms later the chief organ of nutrition, and that in placental mammals is nearly vestigial and functions chiefly prior to the elaboration of the placenta

yolk stalk *noun* (1900)
: the narrow tubular stalk connecting the yolk sac with the embryo

Yom Kip·pur \,yōm-ki-'pu̇r, ,yȯm-, ,yäm-; -'ki-pər, -(,)pu̇r\ *noun* [Hebrew *yōm kippūr*, literally, day of atonement] (1854)
: a Jewish holiday observed with fasting and prayer on the 10th day of Tishri in accordance with the rites described in Leviticus 16 — called also *Day of Atonement*

¹yon \'yän\ *adjective* [Middle English, from Old English *geon*; akin to Old High German *iener*, adjective, that, Greek *enē* day after tomorrow] (before 12th century)
: YONDER

²yon *pronoun* (14th century)
dialect : that or those yonder

³yon *adverb* (15th century)
1 : YONDER
2 : THITHER ⟨ran hither and *yon*⟩

¹yond \'yänd\ *adverb* [Middle English, from Old English *geond*; akin to Old English *geon*] (before 12th century)
archaic : YONDER

²yond *adjective* (13th century)
dialect : YONDER

¹yon·der \'yän-dər\ *adverb* [Middle English, from *yond* + *-er* (as in *hither*)] (14th century)
: at or in that indicated more or less distant place usually within sight

²yonder *adjective* (14th century)
1 : farther removed : more distant
2 : being at a distance within view or at a place or in a direction known or indicated

³yonder *pronoun* (14th century)
: something that is or is in an indicated more or less distant place

yo·ni \'yō-nē\ *noun* [Sanskrit, vulva] (1799)
: a stylized representation of the female genitalia symbolizing the feminine principle in Hindu cosmology — compare LINGAM
— **yo·nic** \'yō-nik\ *adjective*

yoo–hoo \'yü-(,)hü\ *interjection* (circa 1924)
— used to attract attention or as a call to persons

yore \'yōr, 'yȯr\ *noun* [Middle English, from *yore*, adverb, long ago, from Old English *gēara*, from *gēar* year — more at YEAR] (14th century)
: time past and especially long past — usually used in the phrase *of yore*

York·ie \'yȯr-kē\ *noun* [by shortening & alteration] (1946)
: YORKSHIRE TERRIER

York·ist \'yȯr-kist\ *adjective* [Edward, Duke of *York* (Edward IV of England)] (1823)
: of or relating to the English royal house that ruled from 1461 to 1485
— **Yorkist** *noun*

York rite \'yȯrk-\ *noun* [*York*, England] (circa 1878)
1 : a ceremonial observed by one of the Masonic systems
2 : a system or organization that observes the York rite and confers in the U.S. 13 degrees of which the last three are in commanderies of Knights Templar — compare SCOTTISH RITE

York·shire \'yȯrk-,shir, -shər\ *noun* (1902)

\ə\ abut \ᵊ\ kitten \ər\ further \a\ ash \ā\ ace
\ä\ mop, mar \au̇\ out \ch\ chin \e\ bet \ē\ easy
\g\ go \i\ hit \ī\ ice \j\ job \ŋ\ sing \ō\ go
\ȯ\ law \ȯi\ boy \th\ thin \t͟h\ the \ü\ loot \u̇\ foot
\y\ yet \zh\ vision *see also* Guide to Pronunciation

: a white swine of any of several breeds or strains originated in Yorkshire, England

Yorkshire pudding *noun* (1747)
: batter consisting of eggs, flour, and milk that is baked in meat drippings

Yorkshire terrier *noun* (1872)
: any of a breed of compact toy terriers with long straight silky hair mostly bluish gray but tan on the head and chest

Yor·u·ba \'yȯr-ə-bə\ *noun, plural* **Yoruba** *or* **Yorubas** (1841)
: a Niger-Congo language of southwestern Nigeria and parts of Benin and Togo; *also* : a member of any of the Yoruba-speaking peoples of this region
— **Yo·ru·ban** \'yȯr-ə-bən\ *noun or adjective*

you \'yü, yə *also* yē\ *pronoun* [Middle English, from Old English *ēow,* dative & accusative of *gē* you; akin to Old High German *iu,* dative of *ir* you, Sanskrit *yūyam* you] (before 12th century)
1 : the one or ones being addressed — used as the pronoun of the second person singular or plural in any grammatical relation except that of a possessive ⟨*you* may sit in that chair⟩ ⟨*you* are my friends⟩ ⟨can I pour *you* a cup of tea⟩; used formerly only as a plural pronoun of the second person in the dative or accusative case as direct or indirect object of a verb or as object of a preposition; compare THEE, THOU, YE, YOUR, YOURS
2 : ONE 2a □ ◇

you-all \yü-'ȯl, 'yü-,; 'yȯl\ *pronoun* (1824)
chiefly Southern : YOU — usually used in addressing two or more persons or sometimes one person as representing also another or others

you'd \'yüd, 'yu̇d, yəd\ (1602)
: you had : you would

you'll \'yü(ə)l, 'yu̇l, yəl\ (1592)
: you will : you shall

¹**young** \'yəŋ\ *adjective* **youn·ger** \'yəŋ-gər\; **youn·gest** \'yəŋ-gəst\ [Middle English *yong,* from Old English *geong;* akin to Old High German *jung* young, Latin *juvenis*] (before 12th century)
1 a : being in the first or an early stage of life, growth, or development **b** : JUNIOR 1a **c** : of an early, tender, or desirable age for use as food or drink ⟨fresh *young* lamb⟩ ⟨a *young* wine⟩
2 : having little experience
3 a : recently come into being : NEW **b** : YOUTHFUL 5
4 : of, relating to, or having the characteristics of youth or a young person
5 *capitalized* : representing a new or rejuvenated especially political group or movement
— **young·ish** \'yəŋ-ish\ *adjective*
— **young·ness** \'yəŋ-nəs\ *noun*

²**young** *noun, plural* **young** (before 12th century)
1 *plural* **a** : young persons : YOUTH **b** : immature offspring especially of lower animals
2 : a single recently born or hatched animal
— **with young** : PREGNANT — used of a female animal

young·ber·ry \'yəŋ-,ber-ē\ *noun* [B. M. *Young* (flourished 1900) American fruit grower] (1927)
: the large sweet reddish black fruit of a cultivar of a hybrid bramble closely related to the boysenberry and loganberry and grown in the western and southern U.S.; *also* : a bramble bearing youngberries

youn·ger \'yəŋ-gər\ *noun* (before 12th century)
: an inferior in age : JUNIOR — usually used with a possessive pronoun ⟨is several years his *younger*⟩

youn·gest \'yəŋ-gəst\ *noun, plural* **youngest** (13th century)
: one that is the least old; *especially* : the youngest child or member of a family

young·ling \'yəŋ-liŋ\ *noun* (before 12th century)

: one that is young; *especially* : a young person or animal
— **youngling** *adjective*

young·ster \'yəŋ(k)-stər\ *noun* (1589)
1 a : a young person : YOUTH **b** : CHILD
2 : a young mammal, bird, or plant especially of a domesticated or cultivated breed or type

Young Turk *noun* [*Young Turks,* a 20th century revolutionary party in Turkey] (1908)
: an insurgent or a member of an insurgent group especially in a political party : RADICAL; *broadly* : one advocating changes within a usually established group

youn·ker \'yəŋ-kər\ *noun* [Dutch *jonker* young nobleman] (1513)
1 : a young man
2 : CHILD, YOUNGSTER

your \yər, 'yu̇r, 'yōr, 'yȯr\ *adjective* [Middle English, from Old English *ēower;* akin to Old English *ēow* you — more at YOU] (before 12th century)
1 : of or relating to you or yourself or yourselves especially as possessor or possessors ⟨*your* bodies⟩, agent or agents ⟨*your* contributions⟩, or object or objects of an action ⟨*your* discharge⟩
2 : of or relating to one or oneself ⟨when you face the north, east is at *your* right⟩
3 — used with little or no meaning almost as an equivalent to the definite article *the* ⟨a trait . . . that sets him apart from *your* average professor —James Breckenridge⟩

you're \yər, 'yu̇r, 'yōr, 'yȯr, ,yü-ər\ (1593)
: you are

yours \'yu̇rz, 'yōrz, 'yȯrz\ *pronoun, singular or plural in construction* [Middle English from *your* + *-s* -'s] (1526)
: that which belongs to you — used without a following noun as a pronoun equivalent in meaning to the adjective *your;* often used especially with an adverbial modifier in the complimentary close of a letter ⟨*yours* truly⟩
— **yours truly** : I, ME, MYSELF ⟨I can take care of *yours* truly⟩

your·self \yər-'self, *Southern also* -'sef\ *pronoun* (14th century)
1 a : that identical one that is you — used reflexively ⟨you might hurt *yourself*⟩, for emphasis ⟨carry them *yourself*⟩, or in absolute constructions **b** : your normal, healthy, or sane condition
2 : ONESELF □

your·selves \-'selvz, *Southern also* -'sevz\ *pronoun plural* (1523)
1 : those identical ones that are you — used reflexively ⟨get *yourselves* a treat⟩, for emphasis, or in absolute constructions
2 : your normal, healthy, or sane condition

youth \'yüth\ *noun, plural* **youths** \'yüthz, 'yüths\ *often attributive* [Middle English *youthe,* from Old English *geoguth;* akin to Old English *geong* young — more at YOUNG] (before 12th century)
1 a : the time of life when one is young; *especially* : the period between childhood and maturity **b** : the early period of existence, growth, or development
2 a : a young person; *especially* : a young male between adolescence and maturity **b** : young persons or creatures — usually plural in construction
3 : the quality or state of being youthful : YOUTHFULNESS

youth·ful \'yüth-fəl\ *adjective* (1590)
1 : of, relating to, or characteristic of youth
2 : being young and not yet mature
3 : marked by or possessing youth
4 : having the vitality or freshness of youth : VIGOROUS
5 : having accomplished or undergone little erosion
— **youth·ful·ly** \-fə-lē\ *adverb*
— **youth·ful·ness** *noun*

youth hostel *noun* (1929)
: HOSTEL 2b

□ USAGE

you Just about everybody agrees that the use of *you* to address the reader contributes to informality and directness, and helps avoid labored circumlocutions to boot. But when *you* is used indefinitely ⟨in seventh grade they were always assigning *you* to write about things like farm produce — Russell Baker⟩ some commentators are reluctant to consider it acceptable, preferring *one* instead. *One* sometimes presents problems of pronoun agreement in American English; in British English "one does what one can" is normal, but the second *one* sounds a bit odd to American ears. Should it be replaced with *he, she, he or she, they?* The question is neatly sidestepped by using *you. You* is appropriately used for *one* in all contexts except the most formal.

yourself *Yourself* and, less often, *yourselves* turn up in contexts in which *you* might be used ⟨get me some good left-handers like *yourself* and Robinson —Robert Frost (letter)⟩. Such use has been censured in handbooks by many of the same authors who have censured the similar use of *myself.* But the commentators have failed to note that such use is not random, but rather is confined to contexts in which the person addressed is the subject of the discourse rather than a participant in it. A letter written to Alfred Lord Tennyson makes this point: "How are you standing this tropical heat, and Mrs. Tennyson? Let us have a good account of yourselves." The *you* is in direct address— Tennyson is a participant here. But the *yourselves*—the plural showing more certainly than *you* alone would that Mrs. Tennyson is to be included—makes the Tennysons the subjects about whom the writer wants to hear. Substituting *you,* or even *you both,* for *yourselves* sounds awkward. This use of the reflexive is standard in English and is found especially in conversation, dialogue, and letters.

◇ WORD HISTORY

you Any English speaker who has studied another European language has discovered that most foreign tongues have more than one word corresponding to *you.* Typically there are separate forms to express distinctions of number and grammatical function. Many languages also use different forms depending on degree of familiarity with the person addressed; a common pattern, exemplified by French and Russian, is to address an elder, social superior, or stranger with the plural pronoun. The leveling of all these possibilities into one word, *you,* is in fact relatively recent in our language. Early Modern English inherited four second person pronouns: *thou* and *thee* as subject and object forms for singular usage, and *ye* and *you* for plural. However, in weakly stressed positions both *ye* and *you* were pronounced \yə\, which led to the blurring of the grammatical distinction between them. *You* emerged predominant around 1600. In the 14th century English had copied French and begun to use *ye* and *you* as a polite mode of addressing a single person. *You* gradually became the common neutral form, while *thou* and *thee* conveyed either intimacy or disrespect. By the late 17th century, use of *thou* and *thee* was confined to the church, Quaker speech, and rural dialects.

youth·quake \-ˌkwāk\ *noun* [*youth* + *earth-quake*] (1966)
: the impact of the values, tastes, and mores of youth on the established norms of society

you've \'yüv, yəv\ (1691)
: you have

¹yowl \'yau̇(ə)l\ *verb* [Middle English] (13th century)
intransitive verb
1 : to utter a loud long cry of grief, pain, or distress **:** WAIL
2 : to complain or protest with or as if with yowls
transitive verb
: to express with yowling

²yowl *noun* (15th century)
: a loud long mournful wail or howl (as of a cat)

¹yo-yo \'yō-(ˌ)yō\ *noun, plural* **yo-yos** [perhaps from a language of the Philippines] (1915)
1 : a thick grooved double disk with a string attached to its center which is made to fall and rise to the hand by unwinding and rewinding on the string
2 : one that resembles a yo-yo especially in moving up and down unexpectedly or repeatedly
3 : a stupid or foolish person

²yo-yo *adjective* (1932)
: shifting back and forth or up and down uncertainly or unexpectedly

³yo-yo *intransitive verb* **yo-yoed; yo-yo-ing** (1967)
: to move from one position to another repeatedly **:** FLUCTUATE

yt·ter·bi·um \i-'tər-bē-əm\ *noun* [New Latin, from *Ytterby*, town in southern Sweden] (1879)
: a metallic element of the rare-earth group that resembles yttrium and occurs with it and related elements in several minerals — see ELEMENT table

yt·tri·um \'i-trē-əm\ *noun* [New Latin, from *yttria* yttrium oxide (Y_2O_3), irregular from *Ytterby*, town in southern Sweden] (1822)
: a metallic element usually included among the rare-earth metals which it resembles chemically and with which it usually occurs in minerals — see ELEMENT table

yu·an \'yü-ən, yu̇-'än\ *noun, plural* **yuan** [Chinese (Beijing) *yuán*] (1914)

1 — see MONEY table
2 : the dollar of the Republic of China (Taiwan)

yu·ca \'yü-kə\ *noun* [New Latin *jucca*, from Taino *yuca*] (1555)
: CASSAVA

Yu·ca·tec \'yü-kə-ˌtek\ *noun* [Spanish *yucateco*] (1843)
1 : a member of an American Indian people of the Yucatán peninsula, Mexico
2 : the Mayan language of the Yucatecs
— **Yu·ca·tec·an** \ˌyü-kə-'te-kən\ *adjective or noun*

yuc·ca \'yə-kə\ *noun* [New Latin, from Spanish *yuca*, of unknown origin] (1664)
1 : any of a genus (*Yucca*) of sometimes arborescent plants of the agave family that occur in warm regions chiefly of western North America and have often rigid fibrous-margined leaves on a woody base and bear a large panicle of white blossoms
2 : CASSAVA

yucca

¹yuck \'yək\ *variant of* ²YAK

²yuck *also* **yuk** *interjection* (1966)
— used to express rejection or disgust (spending hours over some dish and getting, "*yuck*, I hate that" —Anne Dowie)

yucky \'yə-kē\ *adjective* [²*yuck*] (1970)
: OFFENSIVE, DISTASTEFUL

yu·ga \'yu̇-gə, 'yü-\ *noun* [Sanskrit, yoke, age — more at YOKE] (1784)
: one of the four ages of a Hindu world cycle

yuk \'yək\ *variant of* ²YAK

yule \'yü(ə)l\ *noun, often capitalized* [Middle English *yol*, from Old English *gēol*; akin to Old Norse *jōl*, a pagan midwinter festival] (before 12th century)
: the feast of the nativity of Jesus Christ **:** CHRISTMAS

Yule log *noun* (1725)
: a large log formerly put on the hearth on Christmas Eve as the foundation of the fire

yule·tide \'yü(ə)l-ˌtīd\ *noun, often capitalized* (15th century)

: CHRISTMASTIDE

Yu·man \'yü-mən\ *noun* (1891)
: an American Indian language family of southwestern U.S. and northern Mexico
— **Yuman** *adjective*

yum·my \'yə-mē\ *adjective* **yum·mi·er; -est** [*yum-yum*] (1899)
: highly attractive or pleasing; *especially* **:** DELICIOUS, DELECTABLE

yum-yum \'yəm-'yəm\ *interjection* (1878)
— used to express pleasurable satisfaction especially in the taste of food

¹yup \'yəp\ *variant of* YEP

²yup *noun* (1983)
: YUPPIE

Yu·pik \'yü-pək\ *noun, plural* **Yupiks** *or* **Yupik** [Central Alaskan Yupik *yúppik*, literally, authentic person] (1951)
1 : the language of the Eskimo people of southwestern Alaska
2 : a member of the Yupik-speaking people

yup·pie \'yə-pē\ *noun, often capitalized* [probably from *y*oung *u*rban *p*rofessional + *-ie*] (1983)
: a young college-educated adult who is employed in a well-paying profession and who lives and works in or near a large city

yurt \'yu̇rt\ *noun* [Russian dialect *yurta*, of Turkic origin; akin to Turkish *yurt* home] (1784)
: a circular domed tent of skins or felt stretched over a collapsible lattice framework and used by pastoral peoples of inner Asia; *also* : a structure that resembles a yurt usually in size and design

yurt

YWCA \ˌwī-ˌdə-bəl-yu̇-(ˌ)sē-'ā, -ˌdə-bə-yu̇-\ *noun* [*Y*oung *W*omen's *C*hristian *A*ssociation] (1887)
: an international organization that promotes the spiritual, intellectual, social, and physical welfare originally of young women

YWHA \-ˌāch-'ā\ *noun* [*Y*oung *W*omen's *H*ebrew *A*ssociation] (1918)
: an organization that promotes the religious, intellectual, social, and physical welfare of Jewish young women

Z *is the twenty-sixth and last letter of the English alphabet. It comes from Latin, which borrowed it, after the Roman conquest of the eastern Mediterranean, from the Greek zeta and used it to render that letter in words from Greek. The Greek letter is from Phoenician zayin. In English, the letter is usually pronounced as in* maze, *but that sound is more often represented by* s *than by* z. *It sometimes has the palatalized sound of* z *in* azure. *The letter Z occurs for a Middle English character called* yogh, *which looked like cursive* z *but had the sound of* y, *in a few Scottish words such as* capercailzie *"a European grouse" and names such as* Mackenzie. *English Z occurs in some native words, such as* graze *and* ooze, *to represent the voiced sound of an earlier written* s *(that is, an* s *pronounced with vibration of the vocal cords), but for the most part it is restricted to loanwords, especially from Greek. Small* z *developed through a simple reduction in size of the capital form. The name of this letter is usually* zee *in American English but usually* zed *in other varieties.* Zed *comes by way of French and Latin from Greek* zeta.

z \'zē, *Canadian, British, & Australian* 'zed, *chiefly dialect* 'i-zərd\ *noun, plural* **z's** *or* **zs** *often capitalized, often attributive* (before 12th century)
1 a : the 26th and last letter of the English alphabet **b :** a graphic representation of this letter **c :** a speech counterpart of orthographic *z*
2 : a graphic device for reproducing the letter *z*
3 : one designated *z* especially as the 26th in order or class or the third in order or class when *x* is made the first
4 : something shaped like the letter Z
5 : WINK 1 — usually used in plural ⟨catch some *z's* before dinner⟩
Z *noun* (1967)
: Z PARTICLE
za·ba·glio·ne \,zä-bəl-'yō-nē\ *noun* [Italian] (1899)
: a whipped dessert consisting of a mixture of egg yolks, sugar, and usually Marsala wine that is often served on fruit
Zach·a·ri·as \,za-kə-'rī-əs\ *noun* [Late Latin, from Greek, from Hebrew *Zĕkharyāh*]
: ZECHARIAH
zad·dik \'tsä-dik\ *noun, plural* **zad·dik·im** \tsä-'di-kəm\ [Yiddish *tsadek*, from Hebrew *ṣaddīq* just, righteous] (1873)
1 : a righteous and saintly person by Jewish religious standards
2 : the spiritual leader of a modern Hasidic community
zaf·tig \'zäf-tig, 'zȯf-\ *adjective* [Yiddish *zaftik* juicy, succulent, from *zaft* juice, sap, from Middle High German *saf, saft*, from Old High German *saf* — more at SAP] (circa 1936)
of a woman **:** having a full rounded figure **:** pleasingly plump
¹zag \'zag\ *noun* [zig*zag*] (1793)
1 a : one of the sharp turns, angles, or alterations in a zigzag course **b :** one of the short straight lines or sections of a zigzag course at an angle to a zig
2 : ZIG 2
²zag *intransitive verb* **zagged; zag·ging** (1900)
: to execute a zag — usually contrasted with *zig*
zaire \'zīr, zä-'ir\ *noun, plural* **zaires** *or* **zaire** [French *zaïre*, from *Zaïre*, former country in central Africa] (1967)
— see MONEY table
za·mia \'zā-mē-ə\ *noun* [New Latin, from Latin *zamiae nuces*, false manuscript reading for *azaniae nuces* pine nuts] (1819)
: any of a genus (*Zamia* of the family Zamiaceae) of American cycads with a short thick woody base, a crown of palmlike leaves, and oblong cones
za·min·dar *or* **ze·min·dar** \'za-mən-,där, 'ze-; zə-,mēn-'där\ *noun* [Hindi *zamīndār*, from Persian, from *zamīn* land + *-dār* holder] (1683)
1 : a collector of the land revenue of a district for the government during the period of Mogul rule in India
2 : a feudal landlord in British India paying the government a fixed revenue
za·min·dari *or* **ze·min·dary** \,za-mən-'där-ē, ,ze-; zə-,mēn-\ *noun, plural* **-dar·is** *or* **-dar·ies** [Hindi *zamīndārī*, from Persian, from *zamīndār*] (1757)
1 : the system of landholding and revenue collection by zamindars
2 : the land held or administered by a zamindar
zan·der \'zan-dər, 'tsän-\ *noun, plural* **zander** *or* **zanders** [German] (1854)
: a pike perch (*Stizostedion lucioperca*) of central Europe related to the walleye
¹za·ny \'zā-nē\ *noun, plural* **zanies** [Italian *zanni*, a traditional masked clown, from Italian dialect *Zanni*, nickname for Italian *Giovanni* John] (1588)
1 : a subordinate clown or acrobat in old comedies who mimics ludicrously the tricks of the principal **:** MERRY-ANDREW
2 : a slavish follower **:** TOADY
3 a : one who acts the buffoon to amuse others **b :** NUT, KOOK
²zany *adjective* **za·ni·er; -est** (1616)
1 : being or having the characteristics of a zany
2 : fantastically or absurdly ludicrous
— **za·ni·ly** \'zā-nə-lē, 'zā-nᵊl-ē\ *adverb*
— **za·ni·ness** \'zā-nē-nəs\ *noun*
¹zap \'zap\ *interjection* [imitative] (1929)
1 — used to express a sound made by or as if by a gun
2 — used to indicate a sudden or instantaneous occurrence
²zap *verb* **zapped; zap·ping** (1942)
transitive verb
1 a : to get rid of, destroy, or kill especially with or as if with sudden force **b :** to hit with or as if with a sudden concentrated application of force or energy **c :** to irradiate especially with microwaves
2 a : to propel suddenly or speedily **b :** to transport instantaneously

3 : to avoid watching (as a television commercial) by changing channels especially with a remote control or by fast-forwarding a videotape
intransitive verb
1 : to move with speed or force
2 : to change television channels using a remote control
³zap *noun* (1963)
: a pungent or zestful quality **:** ZIP; *also* **:** a sudden forceful blow
za·pa·te·ado \,zä-pə-tā-'ä-(,)dō, ,sä-pə-tā-'aù\ *noun* [Spanish, from *zapatear* to strike or tap with the shoe, from *zapato* shoe] (1845)
: a Latin-American dance marked by rhythmic stamping or tapping of the feet
za·pa·teo \,zä-pə-'tā-(,)ō, ,sä-\ *noun* [Spanish, from *zapatear*] (1922)
: ZAPATEADO
Za·po·tec \,zä-pə-'tek, ,sä-\ *noun* (1797)
: a member of an American Indian people of Oaxaca state, Mexico
zap·per \'za-pər\ *noun* (1969)
: one that zaps: as **a :** an electronic device designed to attract and kill insects **b :** a person who habitually changes channels (as to avoid commercials) **c :** a remote control device used for zapping
zap·py \'za-pē\ *adjective* (1969)
: ZIPPY
za·re·ba *or* **za·ri·ba** \zə-'rē-bə\ *noun* [Arabic *zarībah* enclosure] (1849)
: an improvised stockade constructed in parts of Africa especially of thorny bushes
zar·zue·la \,zär-zə-'wä-lə, ,zär-'zwä-\ *noun* [Spanish, probably from *La Zarzuela*, royal residence near Madrid where it was first performed] (1888)
: a usually comic Spanish operetta
z-ax·is \'zē-,ak-səs; *Canadian, British, & Australian* 'zed-\ *noun* (circa 1949)
: one of the axes in a three-dimensional rectangular coordinate system
za·yin \'zä-yən, 'zī-(ə)n\ *noun* [Hebrew] (1823)
: the 7th letter of the Hebrew alphabet — see ALPHABET table
z–co·or·di·nate \,zē-kō-'ȯrd-nət; -'ȯr-d°n-ət, -də-,nät; *Canadian, British, & Australian* ,zed-\ *noun* (circa 1956)
: a coordinate whose value is determined by measuring parallel to a z-axis
zeal \'zē(ə)l\ *noun* [Middle English *zele*, from Late Latin *zelus*, from Greek *zēlos*] (15th century)
: eagerness and ardent interest in pursuit of something **:** FERVOR
synonym see PASSION
zeal·ot \'ze-lət\ *noun* [Late Latin *zelotes*, from Greek *zēlōtēs*, from *zēlos*] (1537)
1 *capitalized* **:** a member of a fanatical sect arising in Judea during the first century A.D. and militantly opposing the Roman domination of Palestine
2 : a zealous person; *especially* **:** a fanatical partisan
zeal·ot·ry \'ze-lə-trē\ *noun, plural* **-ries** (1656)
: excess of zeal **:** fanatical devotion
zeal·ous \'ze-ləs\ *adjective* (1535)
: filled with or characterized by zeal ⟨*zealous* missionaries⟩
— **zeal·ous·ly** *adverb*
— **zeal·ous·ness** *noun*
ze·a·tin \'zē-ə-tən\ *noun* [New Latin *Zea*, genus of grasses including Indian corn + kine*tin*] (1963)
: a cytokinin first isolated from the endosperm of Indian corn
ze·bra \'zē-brə, *Canadian & British also* 'ze-\ *noun, plural* **zebras** [Portuguese *zebra, zebro* wild ass, perhaps from Latin *equiferus*, kind of wild horse, from *equus* horse + *ferus* wild — more at EQUINE, FIERCE] (1600)
1 *plural also* **zebra :** any of several fleet African mammals (*Equus burchelli, E. grevyi,*

and *E. zebra*) related to the horse but distinctively and conspicuously patterned in stripes of black or dark brown and white or buff **2** [from the shirts patterned in black and white stripes worn by football referees] **:** REFEREE 2 **3 :** ZEBRA CROSSING
— **ze·brine** \-ˌbrīn\ *adjective or noun*
ze·bra crossing \'zē-brə-, 'zē-\ *noun* (1950) *British* **:** a crosswalk marked by a series of broad white stripes to indicate a crossing point at which pedestrians have the right of way
zebra finch *noun* (1889) **:** a small largely gray-and-white Australian waxbill (*Poephila guttata*) that has black bars on the tail coverts and is often kept as a cage bird
zebra fish *noun* (1771) **:** any of various barred fishes; *especially* **:** a very small blue-and-silver-striped Indian danio (*Brachydanio rerio* synonym *Danio rerio*) often kept in the tropical aquarium
zebra mussel *noun* (1883) **:** a freshwater Eurasian lamellibranch mollusk (*Dreissena polymorpha*) that was accidentally introduced into the Great Lakes and is spreading to surrounding waterways where it colonizes and clogs water intake pipes and competes with native fish for food
ze·bra·wood \'zē-brə-ˌwủd, 'zē-\ *noun* (1783) **1 :** any of several trees or shrubs having mottled or striped wood: as **a :** any of various leguminous African timber trees (genus *Brachystegia*) **b :** a tall South American timber tree (*Astronium fraxinifolium*) of the cashew family **2 :** the wood of a zebrawood
ze·bu \'zē-(ˌ)bü, -(ˌ)byü\ *noun* [French *zébu*] (1774) **:** any of various breeds of domestic oxen developed in India that are often considered conspecific with the common ox (*Bos taurus*) or sometimes as a separate species (*B. indicus*) and are characterized by a large fleshy hump over the shoulders, a dewlap, pendulous ears, and marked resistance to the injurious effects of heat and insect attack

zebu

Zeb·u·lun \'ze-byə-lən\ *noun* [Hebrew *Zĕbhūlūn*] **:** a son of Jacob and the traditional eponymous ancestor of one of the tribes of Israel
zec·chi·no \ze-'kē-(ˌ)nō, tse-\ *noun, plural* **-ni** \-(ˌ)nē\ *or* **-nos** [Italian — more at SEQUIN] (1617) **:** SEQUIN
Zech·a·ri·ah \ˌze-kə-'rī-ə\ *noun* [Hebrew *Zĕkharyāh*] **1 :** a Hebrew prophet of the 6th century B.C. **2 :** a prophetic book of canonical Jewish and Christian Scripture — see BIBLE table
ze·chin \'ze-kən, ze-'kēn\ *noun* [Italian *zecchino*] (1575) **:** SEQUIN
zed \'zed\ *noun* [Middle English, from Middle French *zede*, from Late Latin *zeta* zeta, from Greek *zēta*] (15th century) *chiefly British* **:** the letter *z*
zee \'zē\ *noun* (1677) **:** the letter *z*
ze·in \'zē-ən\ *noun* [New Latin *Zea*, genus of grasses including Indian corn, from Greek *zeai*, plural, wheat; akin to Sanskrit *yava* barley] (1822) **:** a protein from Indian corn that lacks lysine and tryptophan and is used especially in making textile fibers, plastics, printing inks, coatings, and adhesives and sizes

zeit·ge·ber \'tsīt-ˌgā-bər, 'zīt-\ *noun* [German, from *Zeit* time + *Geber* giver] (1964) **:** an environmental agent or event (as the occurrence of light or dark) that provides the stimulus setting or resetting a biological clock of an organism
zeit·geist \'tsīt-ˌgīst, 'zīt-\ *noun, often capitalized* [German, from *Zeit* + *Geist* spirit] (1884) **:** the general intellectual, moral, and cultural climate of an era
zel·ko·va \'zel-kə-və, zel-'kō-və\ *noun* [New Latin, from Russian *zel'kova, zel'kva*, from Georgian *dzelkva*] (circa 1890) **:** a tall widely spreading Japanese tree (*Zelkova serrata*) of the elm family that is often used as an ornamental and shade tree in place of the American elm because of its resistance to Dutch elm disease
zemst·vo \'zem(p)st-(ˌ)vō, -və\ *noun, plural* **zemstvos** [Russian; akin to Russian *zemlya* earth, land, Latin *humus* — more at HUMBLE] (1865) **:** one of the district and provincial assemblies established in Russia in 1864
Zen \'zen\ *noun* [Japanese, religious meditation] (1727) **:** a Japanese sect of Mahayana Buddhism that aims at enlightenment by direct intuition through meditation
ze·na·na \zə-'nä-nə\ *noun* [Hindi *zanāna*, from Persian, from *zan* woman] (1760) **:** HAREM 1a
Zend-Aves·ta \ˌzend-ə-'ves-tə\ *noun* [French, from Middle Persian *Avastāk va Zand* Avesta and commentary] (1630) **:** AVESTA
ze·ner diode \'zē-nər, 'zē-\ *noun, often* Z *capitalized* [Clarence M. Zener (born 1905) American physicist] (1957) **:** a silicon semiconductor device used especially as a voltage regulator
ze·nith \'zē-nəth, *Canadian also* & *British usually* 'ze-nəth, -nith\ *noun* [Middle English *senith*, from Middle French *cenith*, from Medieval Latin, from Old Spanish *zenit*, modification of Arabic *samt* (*ar-ra's*) way (over one's head)] (14th century) **1 :** the point of the celestial sphere that is directly opposite the nadir and vertically above the observer **2 :** the highest point reached in the heavens by a celestial body **3 :** culminating point **:** ACME ⟨at the *zenith* of his powers —John Buchan⟩ ◆
ze·nith·al \-nə-thəl\ *adjective* (1860) **1 :** of, relating to, or located at or near the zenith **2 :** showing correct directions from the center ⟨a *zenithal* map⟩
ze·o·lite \'zē-ə-ˌlīt\ *noun* [Swedish *zeolit*, from Greek *zein* to boil + *-o-* + Swedish *-lit* -lite, from French *-lite* — more at YEAST] (circa 1777) **:** any of various hydrous silicates that are analogous in composition to the feldspars, occur as secondary minerals in cavities of lavas, and can act as ion-exchangers; *also* **:** any of various natural or synthesized silicates of similar structure used especially in water softening and as adsorbents and catalysts
— **ze·o·lit·ic** \ˌzē-ə-'li-tik\ *adjective*
Zeph·a·ni·ah \ˌze-fə-'nī-ə\ *noun* [Hebrew *Ṣĕphanyāh*] **1 :** a Hebrew prophet of the 7th century B.C. **2 :** an apocalyptic book of canonical Jewish and Christian Scripture — see BIBLE table
zeph·yr \'ze-fər\ *noun* [Middle English *Zephirus*, west wind (personified), from Latin *Zephyrus*, god of the west wind & *zephyrus* west wind, zephyr, from Greek *Zephyros* & *zephyros*] (1611) **1 a :** a breeze from the west **b :** a gentle breeze **2 :** any of various lightweight fabrics and articles of clothing
Zeph·y·rus \'ze-fə-rəs\ *noun* [Latin]

: the Greek god of the west wind
zep·pe·lin \'ze-p(ə-)lən\ *noun* [Count Ferdinand von *Zeppelin*] (1900) **:** a rigid airship consisting of a cylindrical trussed and covered frame supported by internal gas cells; *broadly* **:** AIRSHIP

zeppelin

zerk \'zərk\ *noun* [Oscar U. *Zerk* (died 1968) American (Austrian-born) inventor] (1926) **:** a grease fitting
¹ze·ro \'zē-(ˌ)rō, 'zir-(ˌ)ō\ *noun, plural* **zeros** *also* **zeroes** [French or Italian; French *zéro*, from Italian *zero*, from Medieval Latin *zephirum*, from Arabic *ṣifr*] (1604) **1 a :** the arithmetical symbol 0 or ∅ denoting the absence of all magnitude or quantity **b :** ADDITIVE IDENTITY; *specifically* **:** the number between the set of all negative numbers and the set of all positive numbers **c :** a value of an independent variable that makes a function equal to zero ⟨+2 and −2 are *zeros* of $f(x)=x^2-4$⟩ **2** — see NUMBER table **3 a** (1) **:** the point of departure in reckoning; *specifically* **:** the point from which the graduation of a scale (as of a thermometer) begins (2) **:** the temperature represented by the zero mark on a thermometer **b :** the setting or adjustment of the sights of a firearm that causes it to shoot to point of aim at a desired range **4 :** an insignificant person or thing **:** NONENTITY **5 a :** a state of total absence or neutrality **b :** the lowest point **:** NADIR **6 :** something arbitrarily or conveniently designated zero
²zero *adjective* (1810) **1 a :** of, relating to, or being a zero **b :** having no magnitude or quantity **:** not any ⟨*zero* growth⟩ **c** (1) **:** having no phonetic manifestation ⟨the *zero* modification in the past tense of *cut*⟩ (2) **:** having no modified inflectional form ⟨a *zero* plural⟩ **2 a** *of a cloud ceiling* **:** limiting vision to 50 feet (15 meters) or less **b** *of horizontal visibility* **:** limited to 165 feet (50.3 meters) or less
³zero (1913) *transitive verb* **1 :** to determine or adjust the zero of (as a rifle)

\ə\ **abut** \ᵊ\ **kitten** \ər\ **further** \a\ **ash** \ā\ **ace** \ä\ **mop, mar** \aủ\ **out** \ch\ **chin** \e\ **bet** \ē\ **easy** \g\ **go** \i\ **hit** \ī\ **ice** \j\ **job** \ŋ\ **sing** \ō\ **go** \ȯ\ **law** \ȯi\ **boy** \th\ **thin** \t̲h̲\ **the** \ü\ **loot** \ủ\ **foot** \y\ **yet** \zh\ **vision** *see also* Guide to Pronunciation

2 a : to concentrate firepower on the exact range of — usually used with *in* **b :** to bring to bear on the exact range of a target — usually used with *in*
intransitive verb
1 : to adjust fire on a specific target — usually used with *in*
2 : to close in on or focus attention on an objective — usually used with *in*

zero–based *or* **zero–base** *adjective* (1970)
: having each item justified on the basis of cost or need ⟨*zero-based* budgeting⟩

zero coupon *adjective* (1979)
: of, relating to, or being an investment security that is sold at a deep discount, is redeemable at face value on maturity, and that pays no periodic interest ⟨*zero coupon* municipal bonds⟩

zero gravity *noun* (1951)
: the state or condition of lacking apparent gravitational pull : WEIGHTLESSNESS

zero hour *noun* [from its being marked by the count of zero in a countdown] (1917)
1 a : the hour at which a planned military operation is scheduled to start **b :** the time at which a usually significant or notable event is scheduled to take place
2 : a time when a vital decision or decisive change must be made

zero–sum *adjective* (1944)
: of, relating to, or being a situation (as a game or relationship) in which a gain for one side entails a corresponding loss for the other side

ze·roth \'zē-(,)rōth, 'zir-(,)ōth\ *adjective* (1896)
: being numbered zero in a series; *also* : ZERO 1 ⟨the *zeroth* power of a number⟩

zero tillage *noun* (1963)
: NO-TILLAGE

zero vector *noun* (circa 1901)
: a vector which is of zero length and all of whose components are zero

zero–zero *adjective* (circa 1939)
1 : characterized by or being atmospheric conditions that reduce ceiling and visibility to zero
2 : limited to zero by atmospheric conditions

zest \'zest\ *noun* [obsolete French (now *zeste*), orange or lemon peel (used as flavoring)] (circa 1674)
1 : a piece of the peel or of the thin outer skin of an orange or lemon used as flavoring
2 : an enjoyably exciting quality : PIQUANCY
3 : keen enjoyment : RELISH, GUSTO ◇
— **zest·ful** \-fəl\ *adjective*
— **zest·ful·ly** \-fə-lē\ *adverb*
— **zest·ful·ness** *noun*
— **zest·less** \-ləs\ *adjective*

zest·er \'zes-tər\ *noun* (1973)
: a small utensil for peeling zest

zesty \'zes-tē\ *adjective* **zest·i·er; -est** (1930)
: having or characterized by zest

ze·ta \'zā-tə, 'zē-\ *noun* [Greek *zēta*] (1823)
: the 6th letter of the Greek alphabet — see ALPHABET table

zeug·ma \'züg-mə\ *noun* [Latin, from Greek, literally, joining, from *zeugnynai* to join; akin to Latin *jungere* to join — more at YOKE] (1523)
: the use of a word to modify or govern two or more words usually in such a manner that it applies to each in a different sense or makes sense with only one (as in "opened the door and her heart to the homeless boy")

Zeus \'züs\ *noun* [Greek]
: the king of the gods and husband of Hera in Greek mythology — compare JUPITER

zib·e·line *or* **zib·el·line** \'zi-bə-,lēn, -,līn\ *noun* [Middle French, sable, from Old Italian *zibellino*, of Slavic origin; akin to Russian *sobol'* sable] (1892)
: a soft lustrous wool fabric with mohair, alpaca, or camel's hair

zi·do·vu·dine \zi-'dō-vyü-,dēn\ *noun* [by shortening & alteration from *azidothymidine*] (1987)

: AZIDOTHYMIDINE

¹zig \'zig\ *noun* [zigzag] (1840)
1 a : one of the sharp turns, angles, or alterations in a zigzag course **b :** one of the short straight lines or sections of a zigzag course at an angle to a zag
2 : a sharp alteration or change of direction (as in a process or policy) ⟨the quick *zigs* and zags of his international maneuverings —*N.Y. Times*⟩

²zig *intransitive verb* **zigged; zig·ging** (1940)
: to execute a zig — usually contrasted with zag

zig·gu·rat \'zi-gə-,rat\ *noun* [Akkadian *ziqqurratu*] (1877)
: an ancient Mesopotamian temple tower consisting of a lofty pyramidal structure built in successive stages with outside staircases and a shrine at the top

ziggurat

¹zig·zag \'zig-,zag\ *noun* [French] (1712)
: one of a series of short sharp turns, angles, or alterations in a course; *also* : something having the form or character of such a series ⟨a blouse with green *zigzags*⟩ ⟨endured the *zigzags* of policy —Richard Bernstein⟩

²zigzag *adverb* (circa 1730)
: in or by a zigzag path or course

³zigzag *adjective* (1750)
: having short sharp turns or angles ⟨a *zigzag* trail⟩

⁴zigzag *verb* **zig·zagged; zig·zag·ging** (1777)
transitive verb
: to form into a zigzag or move along a zigzag course
intransitive verb
: to lie in, proceed along, or consist of a zigzag course

zilch \'zilch\ *adjective or noun* [origin unknown] (circa 1966)
: ZERO, NOTHING

zil·lion \'zil-yən\ *noun* [*z* + *-illion* (as in *million*)] (1934)
: an indeterminately large number ⟨*zillions* of mosquitoes⟩
— **zil·lionth** \-yən(t)th\ *adjective*

zil·lion·aire \,zil-yə-'nar, -'ner\ *noun* [*zillion* + *-aire* (as in *millionaire*)] (1946)
: an immeasurably wealthy person

zin \'zin\ *noun, often capitalized* (1980)
: ZINFANDEL

¹zinc \'ziŋk\ *noun, often attributive* [German *Zink*] (1651)
: a bluish white solid metallic element of low to intermediate hardness that is ductile when pure but in the commercial form is brittle at ordinary temperatures and becomes ductile on slight heating, occurs abundantly in minerals, is an essential micronutrient for both plants and animals, and is used especially as a protective coating for iron and steel — see ELEMENT table

²zinc *transitive verb* **zinced** *or* **zincked** \'ziŋ(k)t\; **zinc·ing** *or* **zinck·ing** \'ziŋ-kiŋ\ (1841)
: to treat or coat with zinc : GALVANIZE

zinc blende *noun* (1842)
: SPHALERITE

zinc chloride *noun* (1851)
: a poisonous caustic deliquescent salt $ZnCl_2$ used especially as a wood preservative, drying agent, and catalyst

zinc·ite \'ziŋ-,kīt\ *noun* [German *Zinkit*, from *Zink*] (1854)

: a brittle deep-red to orange-yellow hexagonal mineral that consists essentially of zinc oxide and occurs in massive or granular form

zinc oxide *noun* (1849)
: an infusible white solid ZnO used especially as a pigment, in compounding rubber, and in pharmaceutical and cosmetic preparations

zinc oxide ointment *noun* (1936)
: an ointment that contains about 20 percent of zinc oxide and is used in treating skin disorders

zinc sulfate *noun* (1851)
: a crystalline salt $ZnSO_4$ used especially in making a white paint pigment, in printing and dyeing, in sprays and fertilizers, and in medicine as an astringent, emetic, and weak antiseptic

zinc sulfide *noun* (1851)
: a fluorescent white to yellowish compound ZnS used especially as a white pigment and a phosphor

zinc white *noun* (1847)
: a white pigment that consists of zinc oxide

zin·eb \'zi-,neb\ *noun* [zinc + ethylene + *bis*-] (1950)
: a zinc-containing agricultural fungicide $C_4H_6N_2S_4Zn$ used on fruits and vegetables

zin·fan·del \'zin-fən-,del\ *noun* [origin unknown] (1896)
: a dry red table wine made from a small black grape that is grown chiefly in California; *also* : the grape

¹zing \'ziŋ\ *noun* [imitative] (1911)
1 : a shrill humming noise
2 a : an enjoyably exciting or stimulating quality : ZEST ⟨really put some *zing* into this industry —Erwin Fine⟩ **b :** a sharply piquant flavor ⟨barbecue sauce with *zing*⟩

²zing (1920)
intransitive verb
1 : to make or move with a humming sound
2 : ZIP, SPEED
transitive verb
1 : to hit suddenly : ZAP
2 : to criticize in a pointed or witty manner

zing·er \'ziŋ-ər\ *noun* (1955)
1 : something causing or meant to cause interest, surprise, or shock
2 : a pointed witty remark or retort

zingy \'ziŋ-ē\ *adjective* **zing·i·er; -est** [¹zing] (1945)
1 : enjoyably exciting ⟨a *zingy* musical⟩
2 : strikingly attractive or appealing ⟨wore a *zingy* new outfit⟩
3 : sharply piquant ⟨a *zingy* salad⟩

zin·nia \'zi-nē-ə, 'zē-; 'zin-yə, 'zēn-\ *noun* [New Latin, from Johann G. *Zinn* (died 1759) German botanist] (1767)
: any of a small genus (*Zinnia*) of tropical

◇ WORD HISTORY
zest *Zest* was borrowed into English in the 17th century from French *zest* (now spelled *zeste*), meaning "orange or lemon peel." In French the word appears to be related to the onomatopoeic interjection *zeste*, which expressed suddenness of occurrence or contemptuous dismissal (somewhat like English *poof*). As a noun, *zeste* could refer to something of no importance or value. Apparently because a rind, shell, or the like is usually worthless, *zeste* was applied more specifically to the membrane enclosing the sections of a nut and then the peel of a citrus fruit. Belying the logic of its name, however, citrus peel turned out to be quite useful as a flavoring in drinks or food. Upon borrowing the word, English extended the "flavoring" meaning of *zest* beyond the culinary domain, and in the 18th century the word began to denote any quality that adds enjoyment or piquancy to something. By the end of that century it could simply mean "keen enjoyment."

American composite herbs and low shrubs with showy flower heads and long-lasting ray flowers

Zi·on \'zī-ən\ *noun* [Middle English *Sion*, from Old English, citadel in Palestine which was the nucleus of Jerusalem, from Late Latin, from Greek *Seiōn*, from Hebrew *Ṣīyōn*] (14th century)
1 a : the Jewish people **:** ISRAEL **b :** the Jewish homeland that is symbolic of Judaism or of Jewish national aspiration **c :** the ideal nation or society envisaged by Judaism
2 : HEAVEN
3 : UTOPIA

Zi·on·ism \'zī-ə-,ni-zəm\ *noun* (1896)
: an international movement originally for the establishment of a Jewish national or religious community in Palestine and later for the support of modern Israel
— **Zi·on·ist** \-nist\ *adjective or noun*
— **Zi·on·is·tic** \,zī-ə-'nis-tik\ *adjective*

¹zip \'zip\ *verb* **zipped; zip·ping** [imitative of the sound of a speeding object] (1852)
intransitive verb
1 : to move, act, or function with speed and vigor
2 : to travel with a sharp hissing or humming sound
transitive verb
1 : to impart speed or force to
2 : to add zest, interest, or life to — often used with *up*
3 : to transport or propel with speed

²zip *noun* (1875)
1 : a sudden sharp hissing or sibilant sound
2 : ENERGY, VIM
— **zip·less** \-ləs\ *adjective*

³zip *noun* [origin unknown] (circa 1900)
: NOTHING, ZERO ⟨the final score was 27 to *zip*⟩

⁴zip *noun* (1920)
chiefly British **:** ZIPPER

⁵zip *verb* **zipped; zip·ping** [back-formation from *zipper*] (1932)
transitive verb
1 a : to close or open with or as if with a zipper **b :** to enclose or wrap by fastening a zipper
2 : to cause (a zipper) to open or shut
intransitive verb
: to become open, closed, or attached by means of a zipper

⁶zip *noun, often* Z&I&P *capitalized* (1965)
: ZIP CODE

zip–code *transitive verb* (1964)
: to furnish with a zip code

zip code *noun, often* Z&I&P *capitalized* [*z*one *i*mprovement *p*lan] (1963)
: a number that identifies each postal delivery area in the U.S.

zip fastener *noun* (1927)
chiefly British **:** ZIPPER

zip gun *noun* (1950)
: a crudely homemade single-shot pistol

¹zip·per \'zi-pər\ *noun* [from *Zipper*, a trademark] (1926)
: a fastener consisting of two rows of metal or plastic teeth on strips of tape and a sliding piece that closes an opening by drawing the teeth together

²zipper *transitive verb* (1930)
: ⁵ZIP

zip·pered \-pərd\ *adjective* (1939)
: equipped with a zipper

zip·py \'zi-pē\ *adjective* **zip·pi·er; -est** (1904)
: full of zip **:** BRISK, SNAPPY

zi·ram \'zī-,ram\ *noun* [*zi*nc + dithiocar*bam*ate] (1949)
: an organic zinc salt $C_6H_{12}N_2S_4Zn$ used especially as an agricultural fungicide

zir·con \'zər-,kän, -kən\ *noun* [German, modification of French *jargon* jargoon, zircon, from Italian *giargone*] (1794)
: a tetragonal mineral consisting of a silicate of zirconium and occurring usually in brown or grayish square prisms of adamantine luster

or sometimes in transparent forms which are used as gems

zir·co·nia \,zər-'ko-nē-ə\ *noun* [New Latin, from International Scientific Vocabulary *zircon*] (1797)
: a white crystalline compound ZrO_2 used especially in refractories, in thermal and electric insulation, in abrasives, and in enamels and glazes — called also *zirconium oxide*

zir·co·ni·um \,zər-'kō-nē-əm\ *noun* [New Latin, from International Scientific Vocabulary *zircon*] (1808)
: a steel-gray strong ductile metallic element with a high melting point that occurs widely in combined form (as in zircon), is highly resistant to corrosion, and is used especially in alloys and in refractories and ceramics — see ELEMENT table

zit \'zit\ *noun* [origin unknown] (circa 1966)
slang **:** PIMPLE 1

zith·er \'zi-thər, -thər\ *noun* [German, from Latin *cithara* cithara — more at CITHER] (1850)
: a stringed instrument having usually 30 to 40 strings over a shallow horizontal soundboard and played with pick and fingers
— **zith·er·ist** \-thə-rist, -thə-\ *noun*

zither

zi·ti \'zē-tē\ *noun, plural* **ziti** [Italian, plural of *zito*, alteration of *zita* piece of tubular pasta, probably short for *maccheroni di zita*, literally, bride's macaroni] (circa 1845)
: medium-sized tubular pasta

zi·zith \'tsit-səs, tsēt-'sēt\ *noun plural* [Hebrew *ṣīṣīth*] (1675)
: the fringes or tassels worn on traditional or ceremonial garments by Jewish males as reminders of the commandments of Deuteronomy 22:12 and Numbers 15:37–41

Z line *noun* (1916)
: any of the dark thin lines across a striated muscle fiber that mark the boundaries between adjacent sarcomeres

zlo·ty \'zlo-tē\ *noun, plural* **zlo·tys** \-tēz\ *or* **zloty** [Polish *złoty*] (1915)
— see MONEY table

zo- *or* **zoo-** *combining form* [Greek *zōi-, zōio-*, from *zōion*; akin to Greek *zōē* life — more at QUICK]
1 : animal **:** animal kingdom or kind ⟨*zoo*id⟩ ⟨*zoo*logy⟩
2 [Greek *zō-* alive, from *zōos*; akin to Greek *zōē*] **:** motile ⟨*zoo*spore⟩

-zoa \'zō-ə\ *noun plural combining form* [New Latin, from Greek *zōia*, plural of *zōion*]
: animals — in taxa ⟨Meta*zoa*⟩ ⟨Proto*zoa*⟩

zo·an·thar·i·an \,zō-ən-'ther-ē-ən, -'thar-\ *noun* [ultimately from *zo-* + Greek *anthos* flower — more at ANTHOLOGY] (1887)
: any of a subclass (Zoantharia) of anthozoans having a hexamerous arrangement of tentacles or septa or both and including most of the recent corals and sea anemones
— **zoantharian** *adjective*

zo·di·ac \'zō-dē-,ak\ *noun* [Middle English, from Middle French *zodiaque*, from Latin *zodiacus*, from Greek *zōidiakos*, from *zōidiakos*, adjective, of carved figures, of the zodiac, from *zōidion* carved figure, sign of the zodiac, from diminutive of *zōion* living being, figure; akin to Greek *zōē* life] (14th century)
1 a : an imaginary band in the heavens centered on the ecliptic that encompasses the apparent paths of all the planets except Pluto and is divided into 12 constellations or signs each taken for astrological purposes to extend 30 degrees of longitude **b :** a figure representing the signs of the zodiac and their symbols
2 : a cyclic course ⟨a *zodiac* of feasts and fasts —R. W. Emerson⟩
— **zo·di·a·cal** \zō-'dī-ə-kəl, zə-\ *adjective*

SIGNS OF THE ZODIAC

NUMBER and NAME	SYMBOL	SUN ENTERS
1 Aries the Ram	♈	March 21
2 Taurus the Bull	♉	April 20
3 Gemini the Twins	♊	May 21
4 Cancer the Crab	♋	June 22
5 Leo the Lion	♌	July 23
6 Virgo the Virgin	♍	August 23
7 Libra the Balance	♎	September 23
8 Scorpio the Scorpion	♏	October 24
9 Sagittarius the Archer	♐	November 22
10 Capricorn the Goat	♑	December 22
11 Aquarius the Water Bearer	♒	January 20
12 Pisces the Fishes	♓	February 19

zodiacal light *noun* (1734)
: a diffuse glow seen in the west after twilight and in the east before dawn

zo·ea \zō-'ē-ə\ *noun, plural* **zo·eae** \-'ē-,ē\ *or* **zo·eas** \-'ē-əz\ [New Latin, from Greek *zōē* life] (circa 1890)
: a free-swimming planktonic larval form of many decapod crustaceans and especially crabs that has a relatively large cephalothorax, conspicuous eyes, and fringed antennae and mouthparts

zof·tig \'zof-tig\ *variant of* ZAFTIG

¹-zoic *adjective combining form* [Greek *zōikos* of animals, from *zōion* animal — more at ZO-]
: having a (specified) animal mode of existence ⟨holo*zoic*⟩

²-zoic *adjective combining form* [Greek *zōē* life]
: of, relating to, or being a (specified) geological era ⟨Archeo*zoic*⟩ ⟨Meso*zoic*⟩

zois·ite \'zoi-,sīt\ *noun* [German *Zoisit*, from Baron Sigismund *Zois* von Edelstein (died 1819) Slovenian nobleman] (1805)
: an orthorhombic mineral that consists of a basic silicate of calcium and aluminum and is related to epidote

zom·bie *also* **zom·bi** \'zäm-bē\ *noun* [Louisiana Creole or Haitian Creole *zôbi*, of Bantu origin; akin to Kimbundu *nzúmbe* ghost] (circa 1871)
1 *usually* zombi **a :** the supernatural power that according to voodoo belief may enter into and reanimate a dead body **b :** a will-less and speechless human in the West Indies capable only of automatic movement who is held to have died and been supernaturally reanimated
2 a : a person held to resemble the so-called walking dead; *especially* **:** AUTOMATON **b :** a

\ə\ abut \ᵊ\ kitten \ər\ further \a\ ash \ā\ ace \ä\ mop, mar \aů\ out \ch\ chin \e\ bet \ē\ easy \g\ go \i\ hit \ī\ ice \j\ job \ŋ\ sing \ō\ go \ȯ\ law \ȯi\ boy \th\ thin \t̲h̲\ the \ü\ loot \ů\ foot \y\ yet \zh\ vision *see also* Guide to Pronunciation

person markedly strange in appearance or behavior

3 : a mixed drink made of several kinds of rum, liqueur, and fruit juice ◆

— **zom·bie·like** \-bē-ˌlīk\ *adjective*

zom·bi·fy \'zäm-bə-ˌfī\ *transitive verb* **-fied; -fy·ing** (1946)

: to turn (a human being) into a zombie

— **zom·bi·fi·ca·tion** \ˌzäm-bə-fə-'kā-shən\ *noun*

zom·bi·ism \-bē-ˌi-zəm\ *noun* (1932)

: the beliefs and practices of the cult of the zombi

zon·al \'zō-nᵊl\ *adjective* (1873)

1 : of, relating to, affecting, or having the form of a zone ⟨a *zonal* boundary⟩

2 : of, relating to, or being a soil or a major soil group marked by well-developed characteristics that are determined primarily by the action of climate and organisms especially vegetation — compare AZONAL, INTRAZONAL

— **zon·al·ly** \-nᵊl-ē\ *adverb*

zo·na pel·lu·ci·da \ˌzō-nə-pə-'lü-sə-də, -pel-'yü-\ *noun, plural* **zo·nae pel·lu·ci·dae** \-(ˌ)nē . . . -(ˌ)dē, -ˌnī . . . -ˌdī\ [New Latin, transparent zone] (1841)

: the transparent more or less elastic outer layer or envelope of a mammalian ovum often traversed by numerous radiating striae

zo·na·tion \zō-'nā-shən\ *noun* (1902)

1 : structure or arrangement in zones

2 : distribution of kinds of organisms in biogeographic zones

¹zone \'zōn\ *noun* [Middle English, from Latin *zona* belt, zone, from Greek *zōnē;* akin to Lithuanian *juosti* to gird] (15th century)

1 a : any of five great divisions of the earth's surface with respect to latitude and temperature — compare FRIGID ZONE, TEMPERATE ZONE, TORRID ZONE **b** : a portion of the surface of a sphere included between two parallel planes

2 *archaic* : GIRDLE, BELT

3 a : an encircling anatomical structure **b** (1) : a subdivision of a biogeographic region that supports a similar fauna and flora throughout its extent (2) : such a zone dominated by a particular life form **c** : a distinctive belt, layer, or series of layers of earth materials (as rock)

4 : a region or area set off as distinct from surrounding or adjoining parts

5 : one of the sections of an area or territory created for a particular purpose: as **a** : a zoned section of a city **b** : any of the eight concentric bands of territory centered on a given postal shipment point designated as a distance bracket for U.S. parcel post to which mail is charged at a single rate **c** : a distance within which the same fare is charged by a common carrier **d** : an area on a field of play **e** : a stretch of roadway or a space in which certain traffic regulations are in force

²zone *transitive verb* **zoned; zon·ing** (1795)

1 : to surround with a zone : ENCIRCLE

2 : to arrange in or mark off into zones; *specifically* : to partition (a city, borough, or township) by ordinance into sections reserved for different purposes (as residence or business)

— **zon·er** *noun*

³zone *adjective* (1795)

1 : ZONAL 1

2 : of, relating to, or being a system of defense (as in basketball or football) in which each player guards an assigned area rather than a specified opponent

zone out *intransitive verb* (1984)

: to become oblivious to one's surroundings especially in order to relax

zone refining *noun* (1952)

: a technique for the purification of a crystalline material and especially a metal in which a molten region travels through the material to be refined, picks up impurities at its advancing

edge, and then allows the purified part to recrystallize at its opposite edge — called also *zone melting*

— **zone–refined** *adjective*

Zon·ian \'zō-nē-ən, -nyən\ *noun* (1910)

: a U.S. citizen who lives in the Panama Canal Zone

zonk \'zäŋk, 'zȯŋk\ *verb* [probably imitative] (1950)

transitive verb

: STUN, STUPEFY; *also* : STRIKE, ZAP — often used with *out*

intransitive verb

: to pass out from or as if from alcohol or a drug — often used with *out*

zonked \'zäŋkt, 'zȯŋ(k)t\ *adjective* (circa 1959)

: stupefied by or as if by alcohol or a drug

zonked–out \-'aút\ *adjective* (1967)

: ZONKED

Zon·ti·an \'zän-tē-ən\ *noun* [*Zonta International,* a service club] (1934)

: a member of a service club made up of executive women each of whom is a sole representative of one business or profession in a community

zoo \'zü\ *noun, plural* **zoos** [short for *zoological garden*] (circa 1847)

1 a : ZOOLOGICAL GARDEN **b** : a collection of living animals usually for public display

2 : a place, situation, or group marked by crowding, confusion, or unrestrained behavior ⟨the convention was a *zoo*⟩

zoo- — see ZO-

zo·oe·ci·um *or* **zo·e·ci·um** \zō-'ē-shē-əm\ *noun, plural* **-cia** [New Latin, from *zo-* + Greek *oikia* house — more at VICINITY] (1880)

: a sac or chamber secreted and lived in by a bryozoan zooid

zoo·gen·ic \ˌzō-ə-'je-nik\ *adjective* [International Scientific Vocabulary] (circa 1864)

: caused by or associated with animals or their activities ⟨*zoogenic* humus⟩

zoo·ge·og·ra·phy \ˌzō-ə-jē-'ä-grə-fē\ *noun* [International Scientific Vocabulary] (1868)

: a branch of biogeography concerned with the geographical distribution of animals and especially with the determination of the areas characterized by special groups of animals and the study of the causes and significance of such groups

— **zoo·ge·og·ra·pher** \-fər\ *noun*

— **zoo·geo·graph·ic** \-ˌjē-ə-'gra-fik\ *or* **zoo·geo·graph·i·cal** \-fi-kəl\ *adjective*

— **zoo·geo·graph·i·cal·ly** \-fi-k(ə-)lē\ *adverb*

zo·oid \'zō-ˌȯid\ *noun* (1851)

: one of the asexually produced individuals of a compound organism (as a bryozoan, hydroid, or coral colony)

zoo·keep·er \'zü-ˌkē-pər\ *noun* (1924)

: one who maintains or cares for animals in a zoo

zooks \'zúks\ *interjection* [short for *gadzooks*] (1634)

archaic — used as a mild oath

zo·ol·a·try \zō-'ä-lə-trē, zə-'wä-\ *noun* [New Latin *zoolatria,* from *zo-* + Late Latin *-latria* -latry] (1817)

: animal worship

zoo·log·i·cal \ˌzō-ə-'lä-ji-kəl\ *also* **zoo·log·ic** \-jik\ *adjective* (1807)

1 : of, relating to, or occupied with zoology

2 : of, relating to, or affecting lower animals often as distinguished from humans

— **zoo·log·i·cal·ly** \-ji-k(ə-)lē\ *adverb*

zoological garden *noun* (1829)

: a garden or park where wild animals are kept for exhibition

zo·ol·o·gy \zō-'ä-lə-jē, zə-'wä-\ *noun* [New Latin *zoologia,* from *zo-* + *-logia* -logy] (1669)

1 : a branch of biology concerned with the classification and the properties and vital phenomena of animals

2 a : animal life (as of a region) : FAUNA **b** : the properties and vital phenomena exhibited by an animal, animal type, or group

— **zo·ol·o·gist** \-jist\ *noun*

¹zoom \'züm\ *verb* [imitative] (1886)

intransitive verb

1 a : to move with a loud low hum or buzz **b** : to go speedily : ZIP

2 *of an airplane* : to climb for a short time at an angle greater than that which can be maintained in steady flight so that the machine is carried upward at the expense of stored kinetic energy

3 : to focus a camera or microscope on an object using a zoom lens so that the object's apparent distance from the observer changes — often used with *in* or *out*

4 : to increase sharply ⟨retail sales *zoomed*⟩

transitive verb

: to cause to zoom □

²zoom *noun* (1918)

1 a : an act or process of zooming; *especially* : a sharp upward movement **b** : an image created by zooming

2 : a zooming sound

3 : ZOOM LENS

zoom lens *noun* (1936)

: a lens (as of a camera or projector) in which the image size can be varied continuously while the image remains in focus

zoo·mor·phic \ˌzō-ə-'mȯr-fik\ *adjective* [International Scientific Vocabulary] (1872)

1 : having the form of an animal

2 : of, relating to, or being a deity conceived of in animal form or with animal attributes

— **zoo·morph** \'zō-ə-ˌmȯrf\ *noun*

-zoon *noun combining form, plural* **-zoa** [New Latin, from Greek *zōion*]
: animal : zooid ⟨spermato*zoon*⟩

zoo·no·sis \zō-'ä-nə-səs, ‚zō-ə-'nō-səs\ *noun, plural* **-no·ses** \-‚sēz\ [New Latin, from *zo-* + Greek *nosos* disease] (1876)
: a disease communicable from animals to humans under natural conditions
— **zoo·not·ic** \‚zō-ə-'nä-tik\ *adjective*

zoo·phil·ic \‚zō-ə-'fi-lik\ *or* **zo·oph·i·lous** \zō-'ä-fə-ləs, zə-'wä-\ *adjective* (1886)
: having an attraction to or preference for animals; *especially, of an insect* : preferring animals to humans as a source of food

zoo·phyte \'zō-ə-‚fīt\ *noun* [Greek *zōophyton*, from *zōi-, zō-* zo- + *phyton* plant — more at PHYT-] (1621)
: an invertebrate animal (as a coral or sponge) more or less resembling a plant in appearance or mode of growth

zoo·plank·ter \'zō-ə-‚plaŋ(k)-tər\ *noun* [*zo-* + *plankter*] (1943)
: a planktonic animal

zoo·plank·ton \‚zō-ə-'plaŋ(k)-tən, -‚tän\ *noun* (1901)
: plankton composed of animals
— **zoo·plank·ton·ic** \-‚plaŋ(k)-'tä-nik\ *adjective*

zoo·spo·ran·gi·um \‚zō-ə-spə-'ran-jē-əm\ *noun* [New Latin] (1874)
: a spore case or sporangium bearing zoospores

zoo·spore \'zō-ə-‚spōr, -‚spȯr\ *noun* [International Scientific Vocabulary] (1846)
: an independently motile spore; *especially* : a motile usually naked and flagellated asexual spore especially of an alga or lower fungus
— **zoo·spor·ic** \‚zō-ə-'spȯr-ik, -'spȯr-\ *adjective*

zo·os·ter·ol \zō-'äs-tə-‚rȯl, -‚rōl\ *noun* (1926)
: a sterol (as cholesterol) of animal origin — compare PHYTOSTEROL

zoo·tech·ni·cal \‚zō-ə-'tek-ni-kəl\ *adjective* (1926)
: of or relating to the technology of animal husbandry
— **zoo·tech·nics** \-'tek-niks\ *noun plural but singular or plural in construction*

zoot suit \'züt-\ *noun* [coined by Harold C. Fox (born 1910) American clothier and bandleader] (1942)
: a suit of extreme cut typically consisting of a thigh-length jacket with wide padded shoulders and peg pants with narrow cuffs
— **zoot–suit·er** \-‚sü-tər\ *noun*

zooty \'zü-tē\ *adjective* (1946)
: typical of a zoot-suiter : flashy in manner or style ⟨a *zooty* haircut⟩

zo·o·xan·thel·la \‚zō-ə-zan-'the-lə\ *noun, plural* **-lae** \-‚(‚)lē\ [New Latin, from *zo-* + *xanth-* + *-ella* (diminutive suffix)] (circa 1891)
: any of various symbiotic dinoflagellates that live within the cells of other organisms (as reef-building coral polyps)

zo·ri \'zōr-ē, 'zȯr-\ *noun, plural* **zori** *also* **zoris** [Japanese *zōri*] (1823)
: a flat thonged sandal usually made of straw, cloth, leather, or rubber

Zorn's lemma \'zȯrnz-, 'tsȯrnz-\ *noun* [Max August *Zorn* (died 1993) German mathematician] (circa 1950)
: a lemma in set theory: if a set S is partially ordered and if each subset for which every pair of elements is related by exactly one of the relationships "less than," "equal to," or "greater than" has an upper bound in S, then S contains at least one element for which there is no greater element in S — compare AXIOM OF CHOICE

Zo·ro·as·tri·an·ism \‚zōr-ə-'was-trē-ə-‚ni-zəm\ *noun* (1854)
: a Persian religion founded in the 6th century B.C. by the prophet Zoroaster, promulgated in the Avesta, and characterized by worship of a supreme god Ahura Mazda who requires good

deeds for help in his cosmic struggle against the evil spirit Ahriman
— **Zo·ro·as·tri·an** \-trē-ən\ *adjective or noun*

zoster *noun* [Latin, from Greek *zōstēr* girdle; akin to Greek *zōnē* zone] (circa 1706)
: HERPES ZOSTER

Zou·ave \zù-'äv\ *noun* [French, from Berber *Zwāwa*, Berber tribe] (1830)
1 : a member of a French infantry unit originally composed of Algerians wearing a brilliant uniform and conducting a quick spirited drill
2 : a member of a military unit adopting the dress and drill of the Zouaves

zounds \'zaùn(d)z, 'zün(d)z, 'zwaùn(d)z, 'zwün(d)z\ *interjection* [euphemism for *God's wounds*] (circa 1600)
— used as a mild oath

zow·ie \'zaù-ē\ *interjection* [imitative of the sound of a speeding vehicle] (1902)
— used to express astonishment or admiration especially in response to something sudden or speedy

zoy·sia \'zȯi-shə, -zhə, -sē-ə, -zē-ə\ *noun* [New Latin, alteration of *Zoisia*, from Karl von *Zois* (died 1800) German botanist] (1924)
: any of a genus (*Zoysia*) of creeping perennial grasses of southeastern Asia and New Zealand having fine wiry leaves and including some suitable for lawn grasses especially in warm regions

Z particle *noun* (1979)
: a neutral elementary particle about 90 times heavier than a proton that along with the W particle is a transmitter of the weak force — called also Z^0 or Z^0 particle

zuc·chet·to \zù-'ke-(‚)tō, tsü-\ *noun, plural* **-tos** [Italian, diminutive of *zucca* gourd, head] (1853)
: a small round skullcap worn by Roman Catholic ecclesiastics in colors that vary according to the rank of the wearer

zuc·chi·ni \zù-'kē-nē\ *noun, plural* **-ni** *or* **-nis** [Italian, plural of *zucchino*, diminutive of *zucca* gourd] (1929)
: a summer squash of bushy growth with smooth cylindrical usually dark green fruits; *also* : its fruit

¹Zu·lu \'zü-(‚)lü\ *noun, plural* **Zulu** *or* **Zulus** (1824)
1 : a member of a Bantu-speaking people of Natal
2 : the Bantu language of the Zulus
— **Zulu** *adjective*

²Zulu (1952)
— a communications code word for the letter *z*

Zu·ni \'zü-nē\ *also* **Zu·ñi** \'zün-yē\ *noun, plural* **Zuni** *or* **Zunis** *also* **Zuñi** *or* **Zuñis** [American Spanish *Zuñi*] (1834)
1 : a member of an American Indian people of western New Mexico
2 : the language of the Zuni people

zup·pa in·gle·se \‚tsü-pə-iŋ-'glā-(‚)zā, ‚zü-, -in-, -(‚)sä\ *noun, often I capitalized* [Italian, literally, English soup] (1941)
: a dessert consisting of sponge cake and custard or pudding that is flavored with rum, covered with cream, and garnished with fruit

zwie·back \'swē-‚bak, 'swī-, 'zwē-, 'zwī-, -‚bäk\ *noun* [German, literally, twice baked, from *zwie-* twice (from Old High German *zwi-*) + *backen* to bake, from Old High German *bahhan* — more at TWI-, BAKE] (1894)
: a usually sweetened bread enriched with eggs that is baked and then sliced and toasted until dry and crisp

Zwing·li·an \'zwiŋ-glē-ən, 'swiŋ-, -lē-; 'tsfiŋ-lē-\ *adjective* (1532)
: of or relating to Ulrich Zwingli or his teachings and especially his doctrine that Christ's presence in the Eucharist is not corporeal but symbolic

— **Zwinglian** *noun*
— **Zwing·li·an·ism** \-ə-‚ni-zəm\ *noun*

zwit·ter·ion \'tsvi-tər-‚ī-‚än *also* 'zwi-\ *noun* [German, from *Zwitter* hybrid (from Old High German *zwitaran*, from *zwi-*) + *Ion* ion — more at TWI-] (1906)
: a dipolar ion
— **zwit·ter·ion·ic** \‚zwi-tər-ī-'ä-nik, ‚swi-\ *adjective*

zy·de·co \'zī-də-‚kō\ *noun, often attributive* [perhaps modification of French *les haricots* beans, from the Cajun dance tune *Les Haricots Sont Pas Salés*] (1960)
: popular music of southern Louisiana that combines tunes of French origin with elements of Caribbean music and the blues and that features guitar, washboard, and accordion

zyg- *or* **zygo-** *combining form* [New Latin, from Greek, from *zygon* — more at YOKE]
1 : yoke ⟨*zygo*morphic⟩
2 : pair ⟨*zygo*dactyl⟩
3 : union ⟨*zygo*spore⟩

zyg·apoph·y·sis \‚zī-gə-'pä-fə-səs\ *noun, plural* **-y·ses** \-‚sēz\ [New Latin] (1854)
: any of the articular processes of the neural arch of a vertebra of which there are usually two anterior and two posterior

zy·go·dac·tyl \‚zī-gə-'dak-t³l\ *adjective* [International Scientific Vocabulary *zyg-* + Greek *daktylos* toe] (1831)
: having the toes arranged two in front and two behind — used of a bird

zy·go·dac·ty·lous \-tə-ləs\ *adjective* (circa 1828)
: ZYGODACTYL

zy·go·ma \zī-'gō-mə\ *noun, plural* **-ma·ta** \-mə-tə\ *also* **-mas** [New Latin *zygomat-, zygoma*, from Greek *zygōma*, from *zygoun* to join, from *zygon* yoke] (circa 1684)
1 a : ZYGOMATIC ARCH **b** : a slender bony process of the zygomatic arch
2 : ZYGOMATIC BONE

zy·go·mat·ic \‚zī-gə-'ma-tik\ *adjective* (1709)
: of, relating to, constituting, or situated in the region of the zygoma and especially the zygomatic arch

zygomatic arch *noun* (1825)
: the arch of bone that extends along the front or side of the skull beneath the orbit

zygomatic bone *noun* (1709)
: a bone of the side of the face below the eye that in mammals forms part of the zygomatic arch and part of the orbit — called also *cheekbone*

zygomatic process *noun* (1741)
: any of several bony processes that enter into or strengthen the zygomatic arch

zy·go·mor·phic \‚zī-gə-'mȯr-fik\ *adjective* (1875)
: having one or more similar parts unequal in size or form so that the whole structure is capable of division into essentially symmetrical halves by only one longitudinal plane passing through the axis ⟨the flower of the pea is *zygomorphic*⟩
— **zy·go·mor·phy** \'zī-gə-‚mȯr-fē\ *noun*

zy·gos·i·ty \zī-'gä-sə-tē\ *noun* [probably from *-zygous*] (1946)
: the makeup or characteristics of a particular zygote

zy·go·spore \'zī-gə-‚spōr, -‚spȯr\ *noun* [International Scientific Vocabulary] (1851)
: a thick-walled spore of some algae and fungi that is formed by union of two similar sexual cells, usually serves as a resting spore, and produces the sporophytic phase of the plant — compare OOSPORE

zy·gote \'zī-‚gōt\ *noun* [Greek *zygōtos* yoked,

\ə\ abut \³\ kitten \ər\ **further** \a\ **ash** \ā\ **ace**
\ä\ mop, mar \aù\ **out** \ch\ **chin** \e\ **bet** \ē\ **easy**
\g\ **go** \i\ **hit** \ī\ **ice** \j\ **job** \ŋ\ **sing** \ō\ **go**
\ȯ\ **law** \ȯi\ **boy** \th\ **thin** \th\ **the** \ü\ **loot** \ù\ **foot**
\y\ **yet** \zh\ **vision** *see also* Guide to Pronunciation

from *zygoun* to join — more at ZYGOMA] (circa 1887)
: a cell formed by the union of two gametes; *broadly* **:** the developing individual produced from such a cell
— **zy·got·ic** \zī-'gä-tik\ *adjective*
zy·go·tene \'zī-gə-,tēn\ *noun* [International Scientific Vocabulary] (1911)
: the stage of meiotic prophase which immediately follows the leptotene and during which synapsis of homologous chromosomes occurs
— **zygotene** *adjective*
-zygous *adjective combining form* [Greek *-zygos* yoked, from *zygon* yoke — more at YOKE]

: having (such) a zygotic constitution ⟨hetero*zygous*⟩
zym- *or* **zymo-** *combining form* [International Scientific Vocabulary, from Greek, leaven, from *zymē* — more at JUICE]
1 : yeast ⟨*zymosan*⟩
2 : enzyme ⟨*zymogen*⟩
zy·mase \'zī-,mās, -,māz\ *noun* [International Scientific Vocabulary] (1875)
: an enzyme or enzyme complex of yeast that promotes fermentation of sugar
-zyme *noun combining form* [Greek *zymē* leaven]
: enzyme ⟨lyso*zyme*⟩

zy·mo·gen \'zī-mə-jən\ *noun* [International Scientific Vocabulary] (1877)
: an inactive protein precursor of an enzyme secreted by living cells and activated by catalysis (as by a kinase or an acid) — called also *proenzyme*
zy·mo·gram \'zī-mə-,gram\ *noun* (1957)
: an electrophoretic strip (as of starch gel) or a representation of it exhibiting the pattern of separated enzymes and especially isoenzymes after electrophoresis
zy·mo·san \'zī-mə-,san\ *noun* [*zym-* + *-osan* (as in *hexosan*)] (1943)
: an insoluble largely polysaccharide fraction of yeast cell walls

Abbreviations

AND SYMBOLS FOR CHEMICAL ELEMENTS

The following list of abbreviations is not intended to be all-inclusive; it does, however, contain many of those most commonly used as well as all the abbreviations that are used in the text of this work. Symbols for chemical elements are also included. Most of these abbreviations have been normalized to one form. In practice, however, there is considerable variation in the use of periods and in capitalization (as *mph, m.p.h., Mph,* and *MPH*), and stylings other than those given in this dictionary are often acceptable. For a small number of abbreviations about which the question of punctuation is raised very frequently, a note is added at the entry.

For a list of special signs and symbols not readily alphabetizable, see the section Signs and Symbols in the back matter.

a absent, acceleration, acre, adult, alto, anode, answer, ante, anterior, are, area, atto-, author

A ace, adenine, ampere, argon

Å angstrom unit

aa ana

AA administrative assistant, Alcoholics Anonymous, antiaircraft, associate in arts, author's alterations

AAA Agricultural Adjustment Administration, American Automobile Association

AAAL American Academy of Arts and Letters

AAAS American Association for the Advancement of Science

AAFP American Academy of Family Physicians

AAMC American Association of Medical Colleges

A and M agricultural and mechanical, ancient and modern

A and R artists and repertory

AAR against all risks

AARP American Association of Retired Persons

AAS associate in applied science

AASCU American Association of State Colleges and Universities

AAU Amateur Athletic Union

AAUP American Association of University Professors

AAUW American Association of University Women

ab about

AB able-bodied seaman, airborne, airman basic, Alberta, [New Latin *artium baccalaureus*] bachelor of arts

ABA Amateur Boxing Association, American Bankers Association, American Bar Association, American Booksellers Association

abbr abbreviation

ABC American Bowling Congress, American Broadcasting Companies, Australian Broadcasting Corporation

ABCD accelerated business collection and delivery

abd *or* **abdom** abdomen, abdominal

abl ablative

abn airborne

abp archbishop

abr abridged, abridgment

abs absolute, abstract

ABS American Bible Society, antilock braking system

abstr abstract

ac account, acre

Ac actinium, altocumulus

AC air-conditioning, alternating current, [Medieval Latin *ante Christum*] before Christ; [Latin *ante cibum*] before meals; area code, athletic club

acad academic, academy

acc accusative

accel accelerando

acct account, accountant

accus accusative

ACE American Council on Education

ack acknowledge, acknowledgment

ACLU American Civil Liberties Union

ACP African, Caribbean and Pacific (states), American College of Physicians

acpt acceptance

ACS American Chemical Society, American College of Surgeons

act active, actor, actual

ACT Action for Children's Television, American College Test, Association of Classroom Teachers, Australian Capital Territory

actg acting

ACV actual cash value, air-cushion vehicle

AD active duty, after date, anno Domini — often printed in small capitals and often punctuated; assembly district, assistant director, athletic director

A/D analog/digital

ADA American Dental Association, Americans for Democratic Action, average daily attendance

ADC aide-de-camp, Aid to Dependent Children, Air Defense Command, assistant division commander

ADD American Dialect Dictionary, attention deficit disorder

addn addition

addnl additional

ADF automatic direction finder

ad int ad interim

ADIZ air defense identification zone

adj adjective, adjunct, adjustment, adjutant

ad loc [Latin *ad locum*] to or at the place

adm administration, administrative

ADM admiral

admin administration, administrative

adv adverb, [Latin *adversus*] against; advertisement, advertising, advisory

ad val ad valorem

advt advertisement

AEC Atomic Energy Commission

AEF American Expeditionary Force

aeq [Latin *aequalis*] equal

aero aeronautical, aeronautics

aet *or* **aetat** [Latin *aetatis*] of age, aged

af affix

AF air force, audio frequency

AFB air force base

AFC American Football Conference, automatic frequency control

A/1C airman first class

AFDC Aid to Families with Dependent Children

aff affirmative

afft affidavit

AFL American Football League

AFL–CIO American Federation of Labor and Congress of Industrial Organizations

AFP alpha-fetoprotein

Afr Africa, African

aft afternoon

AFT American Federation of Teachers, automatic fine tuning

AFTRA American Federation of Television and Radio Artists

Ag [Latin *argentum*] silver

AG adjutant general, attorney general

AGC advanced graduate certificate

agcy agency

agl above ground level

agr *or* **agric** agricultural, agriculture

agt agent

AH ampere-hour, anno hegirae, arts and humanities

AHL American Hockey League

AI ad interim, airborne intercept, air interception, artificial insemination, artificial intelligence

AIA American Institute of Architects

AID Agency for International Development, artificial insemination by donor

AIM American Indian Movement

AK Alaska

aka also known as

AKC American Kennel Club

Al aluminum

AL Alabama, American League, American Legion

Ala Alabama

ALA American Library Association

Alb Albania, Albanian

alc alcohol

ALCS American League Championship Series

ald alderman

alg algebra

alk alkaline

alky alkalinity

ALS amyotrophic lateral sclerosis, autographed letter signed

alt alternate, altitude, alto

Alta Alberta

alum aluminum

alw allowance

Am America, American, americium

AM airmail, Air Medal, [Latin *anno mundi*] in the year of the world — often printed in small capitals; ante meridiem — often not capitalized and often punctuated; [New Latin *artium magister*] master of arts

AMA American Medical Association

amb ambassador

amdt amendment

AmE American English

Amer America, American

AmerInd American Indian

AMG allied military government

Amn airman

amp hr ampere-hour

AMSLAN American Sign Language

amt amount

AMU atomic mass unit

AMVETS American Veterans (of World War II)

an annum

AN airman (Navy)

ANA American Nurses Association

anal analogy, analysis, analytic

anat anatomical, anatomy

anc ancient

ANC African National Congress

Angl Anglican

anhyd anhydrous

ann annals, annual

anon anonymous, anonymously

ANOVA analysis of variance

ans answer

ANSI American National Standards Institute

ant antenna, antonym

Ant Antarctica, Antrim

anthrop anthropological, anthropology

antiq antiquarian, antiquary

AO account of, and others

aor aorist

ap apostle, apothecaries'

AP additional premium, adjective phrase, airplane, American plan, antipersonnel, arithmetic progression, armor-piercing, Associated Press, author's proof

APB all points bulletin

APC armored personnel carrier

API air position indicator

APO army post office

Apoc Apocalypse, Apocrypha, apocryphal

app apparatus, appendix, appliance

appl applied

appro approval

approx approximate, approximately

appt appoint, appointed, appointment

apptd appointed

Apr April

APR annual percentage rate

apt apartment, aptitude

aq aqua, aqueous

ar arrival, arrive

Ar Arabic, argon

AR accounts receivable, acknowledgment of receipt, all rail, all risks, annual return, Arkansas, army regulation, autonomous republic

Arab Arabian, Arabic

ARC AIDS-related complex, American Red Cross
arch archaic, archery, architect, architectural, architecture
Arch Archbishop
archeol archeology
arg argent, argument
Arg Argentina
arith arithmetic, arithmetical
Ariz Arizona
Ark Arkansas
Arm Armagh, Armenian
ARM adjustable rate mortgage
ARP air-raid precautions
arr arranged, arrival, arrive
ARRT American Registry of Radiologic Technologists
art article, artificial, artillery
arty artillery
ARV American Revised Version
ARVN Army of the Republic of Vietnam (South Vietnam)
As altostratus, arsenic
AS after sight, airspeed, American Samoa, Anglo-Saxon, antisubmarine, associate in science
ASAP as soon as possible
asb asbestos
ASCAP American Society of Composers, Authors and Publishers
ASE American Stock Exchange
ASEAN Association of Southeast Asian Nations
asgd assigned
asgmt assignment
ASI airspeed indicator
ASL American Sign Language
ASPCA American Society for the Prevention of Cruelty to Animals
ASR airport surveillance radar, air-sea rescue
assn association
assoc associate, associated, association
ASSR Autonomous Soviet Socialist Republic
asst assistant, assorted
asstd assented, assorted
assy assembly
Assyr Assyrian
AST Alaska standard time
ASTM American Society for Testing and Materials
ASTP army specialized training program
astrol astrologer, astrology
astron astronomer, astronomy
ASV American Standard Version
ASW antisubmarine warfare
at airtight, atmosphere, atomic
At astatine
AT air temperature, ampere-turn, automatic transmission
ATC air traffic control
Atl Atlantic
atm atmosphere, atmospheric
ATM automated teller machine, automatic teller machine
at no atomic number
att attached, attention, attorney
attn attention
attrib attributive, attributively
atty attorney
atty gen attorney general
ATV all-terrain vehicle
at wt atomic weight
Au [Latin *aurum*] gold; author
AU angstrom unit, astronomical unit
AUC [Latin *ab urbe condita*] from the year of the founding of the city (of Rome)
aud audit, auditor
aug augmentative
Aug August
Aus Austria, Austrian
AUS Army of the United States
Austral Australia, Australian
auth authentic, author, authorized
auto automatic
aux auxiliary verb
av avenue, average, avoirdupois

AV ad valorem, audiovisual, Authorized Version
AVC automatic volume control
avdp avoirdupois
ave avenue
avg average
avn aviation
AW actual weight, aircraft warning, articles of war, automatic weapon
AWACS airborne warning and control system
ax axiom, axis
AYC American Youth Congress
AYD American Youth for Democracy
AYH American Youth Hostels
az azimuth, azure
AZ Arizona
b bachelor, bacillus, back, bag, bale, bass, basso, bat, Baumé, before, Bible, billion, bishop, black, blue, bolivar, book, born, bottom, brick, brightness, British, bulb, butut
B boron
Ba barium
BA bachelor of arts, batting average, Buenos Aires
BAA bachelor of applied arts
BAAE bachelor of aeronautical and astronautical engineering
bac [Medieval Latin *baccalaureus*] bachelor
bact bacterial, bacteriology, bacterium
BAE bachelor of aeronautical engineering, bachelor of agricultural engineering, bachelor of architectural engineering, bachelor of art education, bachelor of arts in education
BAEd bachelor of arts in education
BAeE bachelor of aeronautical engineering
BAEE bachelor of arts in elementary education
BAg bachelor of agriculture
bal balance
BAM bachelor of applied mathematics, bachelor of arts in music
B and B bed-and-breakfast
B and E breaking and entering
b and w black and white
Bap *or* **Bapt** Baptist
bar barometer, barometric, barrel
Bar Baruch
BAr bachelor of architecture
BAR Browning automatic rifle
Bart baronet
BAS bachelor of applied science, bachelor of arts and sciences
BAT bachelor of arts in teaching
Bav Bavaria, Bavarian
BB bachelor of business, ball bearing, base on balls, blue book, B'nai B'rith
BBA bachelor of business administration
BBB Better Business Bureau
BBC British Broadcasting Corporation
BBE bachelor of business education
bbl barrel, barrels
BBQ barbecue
BBS bulletin board system
BC before Christ — often printed in small capitals and often punctuated; British Columbia
BCD bad conduct discharge
BCE bachelor of chemical engineering, bachelor of civil engineering, before the Christian Era — often punctuated; before the Common Era — often punctuated
bcf billion cubic feet
BCh bachelor of chemistry
BChE bachelor of chemical engineering
BCL bachelor of canon law, bachelor of civil law
bcn beacon
BCS bachelor of chemical science, bachelor of commercial science
bd barrels per day, board, bound, boundary, bundle

BD bachelor of divinity, bank draft, bills discounted, bomb disposal, brought down
BDA bachelor of dramatic art
bd ft board foot
bdl *or* **bdle** bundle
bdrm bedroom
Be beryllium
BE bachelor of education, bachelor of engineering, bill of exchange, Black English
Bé Baumé
BEC Bureau of Employees' Compensation
BEd bachelor of education
Beds Bedfordshire
BEE bachelor of electrical engineering
bef before
BEF British Expeditionary Force
beg begin, beginning
Belg Belgian, Belgium
BEM bachelor of engineering of mines, British Empire Medal
BEngr bachelor of engineering
BEngS bachelor of engineering science
Berks Berkshire
bet between
BeV billion electron volts
BEV Black English vernacular
bf boldface
BF bachelor of forestry, board foot, brought forward
BFA bachelor of fine arts
bg background, bag, beige, being
BG *or* **B Gen** brigadier general
BH bill of health, Brinell hardness
bhd bulkhead
BHL bachelor of Hebrew letters, bachelor of Hebrew literature
BHN Brinell hardness number
bhp bishop
Bi bismuth
BIA bachelor of industrial administration, Bureau of Indian Affairs
bib Bible, biblical
bibliog bibliography
bid [Latin *bis in die*] twice a day
BID bachelor of industrial design
BIE bachelor of industrial engineering
bil billion
biog biographer, biographical, biography
biol biologic, biological, biologist, biology
BJ bachelor of journalism
bk bank, book, break, brook
Bk berkelium
bkg banking, bookkeeping, breakage
bkgd background
bks barracks
bkt basket, bracket
bl bale, barrel, black, block, blue
BL bachelor of law, bachelor of letters, baseline, bats left, bill of lading, breadth-length
bld blond, blood
bldg building
bldr builder
BLEVE boiling liquid expanding vapor explosion
BLitt *or* **BLit** [Medieval Latin *baccalaureus litterarum*] bachelor of letters, bachelor of literature
blk black, block, bulk
BLM Bureau of Land Management
BLS bachelor of liberal studies, bachelor of library science, Bureau of Labor Statistics
blvd boulevard
bm beam
BM bachelor of medicine, bachelor of music, basal metabolism, bill of material, board measure, bowel movement, bronze medal
BME bachelor of mechanical engineering, bachelor of mining engineering, bachelor of music education
BMOC big man on campus
BMR basal metabolic rate
BMS bachelor of marine science
BMT bachelor of medical technology

BMX bicycle motocross
bn baron, battalion, beacon, been
BN bachelor of nursing, bank note, Bureau of Narcotics
BNDD Bureau of Narcotics and Dangerous Drugs
BNS bachelor of naval sciences
BO back order, best offer, body odor, box office, branch office, buyer's option
BOD biochemical oxygen demand, biological oxygen demand
BOQ bachelor officers' quarters
bor borough
bot botanical, botanist, botany, bottle, bottom, bought
botan botanical
bp baptized, base pair, birthplace, bishop
BP batting practice, beautiful people, before the present, bills payable, blood pressure, blueprint, boiling point
bpd barrels per day
BPE bachelor of petroleum engineering, bachelor of physical education
BPh bachelor of philosophy
BPH benign prostatic hyperplasia; benign prostatic hypertrophy
BPharm bachelor of pharmacy
bpi bits per inch, bytes per inch
bpl birthplace
BPOE Benevolent and Protective Order of Elks
bps bits per second
BPW Board of Public Works, Business and Professional Women's Clubs
br branch, brass, brown
Br Britain, British, bromine
BR bats right, bedroom, bills receivable
Braz Brazil, Brazilian
BRE bachelor of religious education, business reply envelope
Breck Brecknockshire
brig brigade, brigadier
Brig Gen brigadier general
Brit Britain, British
brl barrel
bros brothers
BS bachelor of science, balance sheet, bill of sale, British standard, bullshit — sometimes considered vulgar
BSA bachelor of science in agriculture, Boy Scouts of America
BSAA bachelor of science in applied arts
BSAE bachelor of science in aeronautical engineering, bachelor of science in agricultural engineering, bachelor of science in architectural engineering
BSAg bachelor of science in agriculture
BSArch bachelor of science in architecture
BSB bachelor of science in business
BSc bachelor of science
BSCE bachelor of science in chemical engineering
BSCh bachelor of science in chemistry
BSEc *or* **BSEcon** bachelor of science in economics
BSEd *or* **BSE** bachelor of science in education
BSEE bachelor of science in electrical engineering, bachelor of science in elementary education
BSFor bachelor of science in forestry
BSFS bachelor of science in foreign service
BSI British Standards Institution
bskt basket
BSL bachelor of sacred literature, bachelor of science in languages, bachelor of science in law, bachelor of science in linguistics
BSME bachelor of science in mechanical engineering
bsmt basement
BSN bachelor of science in nursing
BSW bachelor of social work

Bt baronet

btry battery

Btu British thermal unit

bu bureau, bushel

Bucks Buckinghamshire

buff buffalo

Bulg Bulgaria, Bulgarian

bull bulletin

bur bureau

bus business

BV Blessed Virgin

bvt brevet

BW bacteriological warfare, biological warfare, black and white

BWI British West Indies

bx box

BX base exchange

by billion years

BYO bring your own

BYOB bring your own beer, bring your own booze, bring your own bottle

byp bypass

c calm, calorie, Canadian, canceled, candle, carat, case, castle, catcher, Catholic, cedi, cent, centavo, center, centi-, centime, centimeter, centum, century, chairman, chapter, circa, circuit, circumference, clockwise, cloudy, cocaine, codex, coefficient, college, colon, color, colt, [Latin *congius*] gallon; congress, conservative, contralto, copyright, cost, cubic, cup, curie

C capacitance, carbon, Celsius, centigrade, Coulomb, cytosine

ca circa

Ca calcium

CA California, Central America, certified acupuncturist, chartered accountant, chief accountant, chronological age, commercial agent, controller of accounts, current account

CAB Civil Aeronautics Board

CAD computer-aided design

CAF cost and freight

CAFE corporate average fuel economy

CAGS Certificate of Advanced Graduate Study

CAI computer-aided instruction, computer-assisted instruction

cal calendar, caliber, calorie, small calorie

Cal California, large calorie

calc calculate, calculated

Calif California

cam camera

CAM computer-aided manufacturing

Cambs Cambridgeshire

can canceled, cancellation, cannon, canto

Can *or* **Canad** Canada, Canadian

canc canceled

C and F cost and freight

C and W country and western

Cant Canticle of Canticles, Cantonese

cap capacity, capital, capitalize, capitalized

CAP Civil Air Patrol

caps capitals, capsule

Capt captain

Car Carlow

CAR civil air regulations

card cardinal

CARE Cooperative for American Relief to Everywhere

CAS certificate of advanced study

cat catalog, catalyst

CAT clear-air turbulence, college ability test, computerized axial tomography

cath cathedral, cathode

CATV community antenna television

caus causative

cav cavalry, cavity

CAVU ceiling and visibility unlimited

Cb columbium, cumulonimbus

CBC Canadian Broadcasting Corporation

CBD cash before delivery, central business district

CBE commander of the Order of the British Empire, companion of the Order of the British Empire

CBI computer-based instruction, Cumulative Book Index

CBO Congressional Budget Office

CBS Columbia Broadcasting System

CBW chemical and biological warfare

cc cubic centimeter

Cc cirrocumulus

CC carbon copy, chief clerk, common carrier, community college, country club

CCC Civilian Conservation Corps

CCD Confraternity of Christian Doctrine

CCF Chinese communist forces

cckw counterclockwise

CCTV closed-circuit television

CCU cardiac care unit, coronary care unit, critical care unit

ccw counterclockwise

cd candela, candle, cord

Cd cadmium

CD carried down, certificate of deposit, civil defense, [French *corps diplomatique*] diplomatic corps

CDC Centers for Disease Control

CDD certificate of disability for discharge

cdg commanding

Cdn Canadian

CDP certificate in data processing

CDR commander

CDT central daylight time

Ce cerium

CE chemical engineer, civil engineer, Christian Era — often punctuated; Common Era — often punctuated; Corps of Engineers

CEA College English Association, Council of Economic Advisors

CED Committee for Economic Development

cem cement

CEMF counter electromotive force

cent centigrade, central, centum, century

Cent Central

CENTO Central Treaty Organization

CERN [*Conseil Européen pour la Recherche Nucléaire*] European Organization for Nuclear Research

cert certificate, certification, certified, certify

CETA Comprehensive Employment and Training Act

CEU continuing education credit

cf calf, [Latin *confer*, imperative of *conferre* to compare] compare

Cf californium

CF carried forward, centrifugal force, cost and freight, cystic fibrosis

CFC chlorofluorocarbon

CFI certified flight instructor, chief flying instructor; cost, freight, and insurance

CFL Canadian Football League

cfm cubic feet per minute

CFO chief financial officer

CFP Certified Financial Planner

cfs cubic feet per second

cg centigram

CG center of gravity, coast guard, commanding general

cgs centimeter-gram-second

CGT [French *Confédération Germanénérale du Travail*] General Confederation of Labor

ch chain, champion, chaplain, chapter, chief, child, children, church

CH clearinghouse, courthouse, customhouse

chan channel

chap chapter

CHD coronary heart disease

chem chemical, chemist, chemistry

Ches Cheshire

chg change, charge

Chin Chinese

chm chairman, checkmate

Chmn chairman

chron chronicle, chronological, chronology

Chron Chronicles

Ci cirrus, curie

CI cast iron, certificate of insurance, Channel Islands

CIA Central Intelligence Agency, certified internal auditor

cía [Spanish *compañía*] company

CIAA Central Intercollegiate Athletic Association

CIC counterintelligence corps

CID Criminal Investigation Department, cubic inch displacement

cie [French *compagnie*] company

CIF central information file; cost, insurance, and freight

C in C commander in chief

CIP Cataloging in Publication

cir circle, circuit, circular, circumference

circ circular

cit citation, cited, citizen

civ civil, civilian, civilization

CIWS close-in weapons system

CJ chief justice

ck cask, check

cl centiliter, claiming, class, clause, close, closet, cloth

Cl chlorine

CL carload, center line, civil law, common law

cld called, cleared

CLEP College Level Examination Program

clin clinical

clk clerk

clo clothing

clr clear, clearance

CLU chartered life underwriter

cm centimeter, cumulative

Cm curium

CM center matched, circular mil, common meter, [Commonwealth of the Northern Mariana Islands] Northern Mariana Islands, Congregation of the Mission

CMA certified medical assistant

cmd command

cmdg commanding

cmdr commander

CMG Companion of the Order of St. Michael and St. George

cml commercial

CMSgt chief master sergeant

CMV cytomegalovirus

CN credit note

CNC computer numerical control

CNO chief of naval operations

CNS central nervous system

co company, county

Co cobalt

CO cash order, Colorado, commanding officer, conscientious objector

c/o care of

cod codex

COD carrier onboard delivery, cash on delivery, collect on delivery

coeff *or* **coef** coefficient

C of C Chamber of Commerce

C of S chief of staff

cog cognate

col colonial, colony, color, colored, column, counsel

col *or* **coll** collateral, collect, collected, collection, college, collegiate

Col colonel, Colorado, Colossians

COL colonel, cost of living

COLA cost-of-living allowance

collat collateral

colloq colloquial

Colo Colorado

colog cologarithm

com comedy, comic, comma

COM computer output microfilm, computer output microfilmer

comb combination, combined, combining, combustion

comd command

comdg commanding

comdr commander

comdt commandant

COMECON Council for Mutual Economic Assistance

coml commercial

comm command, commandant, commander, commanding, commentary, commerce, commercial, commission, commissioned, commissioner, committee, common, commoner, commonwealth, commune, communication, communist, community

commo commodore

comp comparative, compare, compensation, compiled, compiler, composition, compositor, compound, comprehensive, comptroller

compd compound

comr commissioner

con [Latin *conjunx*] consort; consolidated, const, continued

conc concentrate, concentrated, concentration, concrete

concn concentration

cond condition, conductivity

conf conference, confidential

Confed Confederate

cong congress, congressional

conj conjunction, conjunctive

Conn Connecticut

cons consecrated, conservative, consigned, consignment, consol, consolidated, consonant, constable, constitution, construction, consul, consulting

consol consolidated

const constant, constitution, constitutional, construction

constr construction

cont containing, contents, continent, continental, continued, control

contd continued

contg containing

contr contract, contraction, contralto, contrary, control, controller

contrib contribution, contributor

conv convention, conventional, convertible, convocation

COO chief operating officer

cop copper, copulative, copy, copyright

cor corner, coroner, corpus, corresponding

Cor Corinthians

CORE Congress of Racial Equality

Corn Cornish, Cornwall

corp corporal, corporation

corr correct, corrected, correction, correspondence, correspondent, corresponding, corrupt, corruption

cos companies, consul, consulship, cosine, counties

COS cash on shipment, chief of staff

cosec cosecant

cot cotangent

cp compare, coupon

CP candlepower, Cape Province, center of pressure, cerebral palsy, charter party, chemically pure, command post, Communist party, Congregation of the Passion, custom of port

CPA certified public accountant

CPB Corporation for Public Broadcasting

CPCU chartered property casualty underwriter

cpd compound

CPFF cost plus fixed fee

cpi characters per inch

CPI consumer price index

cpl complete, compline

Cpl corporal

CPM cost per thousand

CPO chief petty officer

CPOM master chief petty officer

CPOS senior chief petty officer

CPR cardiopulmonary resuscitation

CPS cards per second, certified professional secretary, characters per second, Civilian Public Service, cycles per second

CPSC Consumer Product Safety Commission

CPT captain

cpu central processing unit

CQ call to quarters, charge of quarters, commercial quality

cr center, circular, commander, cream, creased, credit, creditor, creek, crescendo

Cr chromium

CR carrier's risk, cathode ray, class rate, conditioned reflex, conditioned response, consciousness-raising, Costa Rica, current rate

CRC Civil Rights Commission

cresc crescendo

crim criminal

crim con criminal conversation

criminol criminologist, criminology

crit critical, criticism, criticized

CRNA certified registered nurse anesthetist

CRT carrier route

cryst crystalline, crystallized

cs case, cases, census, consciousness, consul

Cs cesium, cirrostratus

CS capital stock, cesarean section, chief of staff, Christian Science practitioner, civil service, conditioned stimulus, county seat

CSA Confederate States of America

csc cosecant

CSC Civil Service Commission

CSF cerebrospinal fluid

CSM command sergeant major

CST central standard time

ct carat, cent, count, county, court

CT central time, certificated teacher, certified teacher, code telegram, computed tomography, computerized tomography, Connecticut

CTC centralized traffic control

ctf certificate

ctn carton, cotangent

c to c center to center

ctr center, counter

cu cubic, cumulative

Cu cumulus, [Latin *cuprum*] copper

CU close-up

cum cumulative

Cumb Cumbria

cur currency, current

cv *or* **cvt** convertible

CV cardiovascular, chief value, curriculum vitae

CVA Columbia Valley Authority

cw clockwise

CW chemical warfare, chief warrant officer, continuous wave

CWO cash with order, chief warrant officer

cwt hundredweight

CY calendar year

cyl cylinder

CYO Catholic Youth Organization

cytol cytological, cytology

CZ Canal Zone

d date, daughter, day, dead, deceased, deci-, degree, [Latin *denarius, denarii*] penny, pence; depart, departure, diameter, differential, dimensional, distance, dorsal, drive, driving

D Democrat, derivative, deuterium, Dutch

da deka-

DA days after acceptance, delayed action, deposit account, Dictionary of Americanisms, district attorney, doctor of arts, documents against acceptance, documents for acceptance, don't answer

DAB Dictionary of American Biography

DAE Dictionary of American English

dag dekagram

DAH Dictionary of American History

dal dekaliter

dam dekameter

Dan Daniel, Danish

D & C dilation and curettage

DAR Daughters of the American Revolution

DARE Dictionary of American Regional English

DARPA Defense Advanced Research Projects Agency

dat dative

DAT differential aptitude test, digital audiotape

dau daughter

DAV Disabled American Veterans

db debenture

dB decibel

DB daybook

d/b/a doing business as

DBA doctor of business administration

DBE Dame Commander of the Order of the British Empire

DBH diameter at breast height

dbl *or* **dble** double

DBMS data base management system

DBS direct broadcast satellite

DC [Italian *da capo*] from the beginning; decimal classification, direct current, District of Columbia, doctor of chiropractic, double crochet

DChE doctor of chemical engineering

DCL doctor of canon law, doctor of civil law

dd dated, delivered

DD days after date, demand draft, dishonorable discharge, doctor of divinity, due date

DDC Dewey Decimal Classification

DDD direct distance dialing

DDS doctor of dental science, doctor of dental surgery

DE defensive end, Delaware, doctor of engineering

DEA Drug Enforcement Administration

deb debenture

dec deceased, declaration, declared, declination, decorated, decorative, decrease, decrescendo

Dec December

decd deceased

def defendant, defense, deferred, defined, definite, definition

deg degree

del delegate, delegation, delete

Del Delaware

dely delivery

dem demonstrative, demurrage

Dem Democrat, Democratic

Den Denmark

dent dental, dentist, dentistry

dep depart, department, departure, deponent, deposed, deposit, depot, deputy

depr depreciation, depression

dept department

der *or* **deriv** derivation, derivative

Derbys Derbyshire

derm dermatologist, dermatology

det detached, detachment, detail, determine

detd determined

detn detention, determination

Deut Deuteronomy

dev deviation

Devon Devonshire

DEW distant early warning

DF damage free, direction finder, direction finding

DFA doctor of fine arts

DFC Distinguished Flying Cross

dft defendant, draft

dg decigram

DG [Late Latin *Dei gratia*] by the grace of God; director general

DH doctor of humanities

DHL doctor of Hebrew letters, doctor of Hebrew literature

DI drill instructor

dia diameter

diag diagonal, diagram

dial dialect, dialectical

diam diameter

dict dictionary

dif *or* **diff** difference

dig digest

dil dilute

dim dimension, diminished, diminuendo, diminutive

dimin diminuendo

din dinar

DIN [German *Deutsche Industrie-Normen*] German Industrial Standards

dip diploma

dir direction, director

dis discharge, discount, distance

disc discount

disp dispensary

diss dissertation

dist distance, district

distn distillation

distr distribute, distribution

div divided, dividend, division, divorced

DIY do it yourself

DJ district judge, doctor of jurisprudence, dust jacket

DJIA Dow-Jones Industrial Average

dk dark, deck, dock

dl deciliter

DL disabled list

DLitt *or* **DLit** [New Latin *doctor litterarum*] doctor of letters, doctor of literature

DLO dead letter office, dispatch loading only

DLS doctor of library science

dm decimeter

DM deutsche mark

DMA doctor of musical arts

DMD [New Latin *dentariae medicinae doctor*] doctor of dental medicine

DMin doctor of ministry

DML doctor of modern languages

DMZ demilitarized zone

dn down

DNB Dictionary of National Biography

DNF did not finish

DNR do not resuscitate

do ditto

DO defense order, doctor of osteopathy

DOA dead on arrival

DOB date of birth

doc document

DOD Department of Defense

DOE Department of Energy

dol dollar

dom domestic, dominant, dominion

Don Donegal

Dors Dorset

DOS disk operating system

DOT Department of Transportation

doz dozen

DP data processing, degree of polymerization, dew point, doctor of podiatry, double play

DPE doctor of physical education

DPh doctor of philosophy

DPH department of public health, doctor of public health

DPM doctor of podiatric medicine

dpt department, deponent

DPT diphtheria, pertussis, tetanus

DQ disqualification, disqualify

dr debtor, drachma, dram, drive, drum

Dr doctor

DR dead reckoning, dining room

dram dramatic, dramatist

DS [Italian *dal segno*] from the sign; days after sight, detached service, document signed

DSc doctor of science

DSC Distinguished Service Cross, doctor of surgical chiropody

DSM Distinguished Service Medal

DSO Distinguished Service Order

DSP [Latin *decessit sine prole*] died without issue

DST daylight saving time, doctor of sacred theology

DSW doctor of social welfare, doctor of social work

DT daylight time, doctor of theology, double time

DTh doctor of theology

DTP desktop publishing; diphtheria, tetanus, pertussis

Du Dutch

Dub Dublin

DUI driving under the influence

Dumf Gal Dumfries and Galloway

dup duplex, duplicate

Dur Durham

DV [Latin *Deo volente*] God willing; Douay Version

DVM doctor of veterinary medicine

DW deadweight, delayed weather, distilled water, dust wrapper

DWI driving while intoxicated, Dutch West Indies

dwt deadweight ton, pennyweight

DX distance

dy delivery, deputy, duty

Dy dysprosium

dynam dynamics

dz dozen

e earth, east, easterly, eastern, edge, eldest, ell, empty, end, energy, erg, error, excellent

E electromotive force, energy, English, exponent

ea each

E and OE errors and omissions excepted

EB eastbound

EBC Educational Broadcasting Corporation

EBV Epstein-Barr virus

EC European Community

eccl ecclesiastic, ecclesiastical

Eccles Ecclesiastes

Ecclus Ecclesiasticus

ECG electrocardiogram

ECM electronic countermeasure, European Common Market

ecol ecological, ecology

econ economics, economist, economy

ECT electroconvulsive therapy

Ecua Ecuador

ed edited, edition, editor, education

EDB ethylene dibromide

EdD doctor of education

EDD English Dialect Dictionary

EDP electronic data processing

EdS specialist in education

EDT eastern daylight time

educ education, educational

EE electrical engineer

EEC European Economic Community

EEG electroencephalogram, electroencephalograph

EENT eye, ear, nose, and throat

EEO equal employment opportunity

eff efficiency

EFT *or* **EFTS** electronic funds transfer (system)

e.g. [Latin *exempli gratia*] for example

Eg Egypt, Egyptian

EGF epidermal growth factor

Egypt Egyptian

EHF extremely high frequency

EHP effective horsepower, electric horsepower

EHV extra high voltage

EKG [German *Elektrokardiogramm*] electrocardiogram, electrocardiograph

el elevation

elec electric, electrical, electricity

elem elementary

elev elevation

ELF extremely low frequency

Eliz Elizabethan

EM electromagnetic, electron microscope, electron microscopy, end matched, engineer of mines, enlisted man

emer emeritus

EMG electromyogram, electromyograph, electromyography

emp emperor, empress

EMP electromagnetic pulse

emu electromagnetic unit

enc *or* **encl** enclosure

ency *or* **encyc** encyclopedia

ENE east-northeast

eng engine, engineer, engineering

Eng England, English

engr engineer, engraved, engraver, engraving
enl enlarged, enlisted
ENS ensign
ENT ear, nose, and throat
entom *or* **entomol** entomological, entomology
env envelope
EO executive order
EOE equal opportunity employer
EOM end of month
EP estimated position, European plan, extended play
EPA Environmental Protection Agency
Eph *or* **Ephes** Ephesians
Episc Episcopal
eq equal, equation
equip equipment
equiv equivalency, equivalent
Er erbium
ER earned run, emergency room
ERA earned run average, Equal Rights Amendment
ERISA Employee Retirement Income Security Act
Es einsteinium
ESB electrical stimulation of the brain
Esd Esdras
ESE east-southeast
Esk Eskimo
ESL English as a second language
ESOP employee stock ownership plan
esp especially
Esq *or* **Esqr** esquire
est established, estimate, estimated
EST eastern standard time
Esth Esther
Et ethyl
ET eastern time
ETA estimated time of arrival
et al [Latin *et alii* (masculine), *et aliae* (feminine), or *et alia* (neuter)] and others
etc et cetera
ETD estimated time of departure
ETO European theater of operations
et seq [Latin *et sequens*] and the following one; [Latin *et sequentes* (masculine & feminine plural), or *et sequentia* (neuter plural)] and the following ones
et ux [Latin *et uxor*] and wife
ETV educational television
Eu europium
Eur Europe, European
eV electron volt
EVA extravehicular activity
eval evaluation
evap evaporate
evg evening
EW enlisted woman
ex example, exchange, executive, express, extra
Ex Exodus
exc excellent, except
exch exchange, exchanged
excl exclude, excluded, excluding
exhbn exhibition
Exod Exodus
exor executor
exp expense, experience, experiment, experimental, exponent, export, express
expt experiment
exptl experimental
expwy expressway
exrx executrix
ext extension, exterior, external, externally, extra, extract
Ez *or* **Ezr** Ezra
Ezech Ezechiel
Ezek Ezekiel
f failure, false, family, faraday, feast, female, feminine, femto-, fermi, fine, finish, fluid, fluidness, focal length, [*following*] and the following one; force, forte, fragile, frequency, from, full
F Fahrenheit, farad, fluorine, French, Friday

FA field artillery, fielding average, football association
FAA Federal Aviation Administration, free of all average
fac facsimile, faculty
FADM fleet admiral
Fah *or* **Fahr** Fahrenheit
fam familiar, family
F and A fore and aft
FAO Food and Agriculture Organization of the United Nations
FAQ fair average quality, frequently asked question
far farthing
FAS firsts and seconds, free alongside (ship)
fasc fascicle
fath fathom
FB foreign body, freight bill
FBI Federal Bureau of Investigation
FC fire control, fire controlman, follow copy, food control, footcandle
FCA Farm Credit Administration
FCC Federal Communications Commission
fcp foolscap
fcy fancy
FD fire department, free dock
FDA Food and Drug Administration
FDIC Federal Deposit Insurance Corporation
Fe [Latin *ferrum*] iron
Feb February
fec [Latin *fecit*] he made it
fed federal, federation
fedn federation
fem female, feminine
FEMA Federal Emergency Management Agency
FEPA Fair Employment Practices Act
FEPC Fair Employment Practices Commission
Ferm Fermanagh
FET Federal excise tax, field-effect transistor
ff folios, [*following*] and the following ones; fortissimo
FHA Federal Housing Administration
FICA Federal Insurance Contributions Act
fict fiction, fictitious
fi fa fieri facias
FIFO first in, first out
fig figurative, figuratively, figure
fin finance, financial, finish
Finn Finnish
FIO free in and out
fl flanker, floor, florin, [Latin *floruit*] flourished; fluid
FL Florida, focal length, foreign language
Fla Florida
fl dr fluid dram
Flem Flemish
Flint *or* **Flints** Flintshire
FLIR forward-looking infrared
fl oz fluid ounce
FLSA Fair Labor Standards Act
fm fathom
Fm fermium
FM field manual
FMCS Federal Mediation and Conciliation Service
fn footnote
fo *or* **fol** folio
FO field officer, field order, finance officer, flight officer, foreign office, forward observer
FOB free on board
FOC free of charge
FOE Fraternal Order of Eagles
FOIA Freedom of Information Act
for foreign, forestry
FOR free on rail
forz forzando
FOS free on steamer
FOT free on truck
4WD four-wheel drive
fow first open water
fp freezing point
FPA Foreign Press Association, free of particular average

FPC fish protein concentrate
fpm feet per minute
FPO fleet post office
fps feet per second, foot-pound-second, frames per second
fr father, franc, friar, from
Fr France, francium, French, Friday
FRB Federal Reserve Board
freq frequency, frequent, frequentative, frequently
FRG Federal Republic of Germany
Fri Friday
FRM fixed rate mortgage
FRS Federal Reserve System
frt freight
frwy freeway
fs femtosecond
FS filmstrip, Foreign Service
FSH follicle-stimulating hormone
FSLIC Federal Savings and Loan Insurance Corporation
FSO Foreign Service Officer
ft feet, foot, fort
FT Fourier transform, free throw, full time
FTC Federal Trade Commission
FTE full-time equivalent
fth fathom
ft lb foot-pound
FTP file transfer protocol
fund fundamental
fur furlong
fut future
FV [Latin *folio verso* the page being turned] on the back of the page
fwd foreword, forward
FWD front-wheel drive
FX foreign exchange
FY fiscal year
FYI for your information
g acceleration of gravity, game, gauge, gelding, gender, good, gram, grand, gravity
G German, giga-, guanine, Gulf
ga gauge
Ga gallium, Georgia
GA Gamblers Anonymous, general agent, general assembly, general average, general of the army, Georgia
GAAP generally accepted accounting principles
gal gallery, gallon
Gal Galatians
galv galvanized
GAO General Accounting Office
gar garage
GAR Grand Army of the Republic
GATT General Agreement on Tariffs and Trade
gaz gazette
GB Great Britain
GBF Great Books Foundation
GC gas chromatograph, gas chromatography
GCA ground-controlled approach
GCB Knight Grand Cross of the Bath
GCD greatest common divisor
GCF greatest common factor
gd good
Gd gadolinium
GDR German Democratic Republic
Ge germanium
GE gilt edges
GED General Educational Development (tests), general equivalency diploma
GEM ground-effect machine
gen general, genitive, genus
Gen Genesis
Gen AF general of the air force
genl general
geog geographic, geographical, geography
geol geologic, geological, geology
geom geometric, geometrical, geometry
ger gerund
Ger German, Germany
GeV giga-electron-volt
GHQ general headquarters
GHz gigahertz

gi gill
GI galvanized iron, gastrointestinal, general issue, government issue
Gib *or* **Gibr** Gibraltar
GIGO garbage in, garbage out
GIT Group Inclusive Tour
Gk Greek
Glos Gloucestershire
gm gram
GM general manager, grand master, guided missile
GMT Greenwich mean time
GMW gram-molecular weight
gn guinea
GNI gross national income
GNP gross national product
GO general order
GOP Grand Old Party (Republican)
Goth Gothic
gov government, governor
govt government
gp group
GP general practice, general practitioner, geometric progression
GPA grade point average
GPD gallons per day
GPH gallons per hour
GPM gallons per minute
GPO general post office, Government Printing Office
GPS gallons per second
GQ general quarters
gr grade, grain, gram, gravity, gross
Gr Greece, Greek
grad graduate, graduated
gram grammar, grammatical
Gramp Grampian
GRAS generally recognized as safe
GRE Graduate Record Examination
gro gross
GRP glass-reinforced plastic
GRU [Russian *Glavnoe razvedyvatel'noe upravlenie*] Chief Intelligence Directorate
gr wt gross weight
GS general staff, giant slalom, government service, ground speed
GSA General Services Administration, Girl Scouts of America
GSC general staff corps
GSL Guaranteed Student Loan
GSO general staff officer
GSR galvanic skin response
GST Greenwich sidereal time
GSUSA Girl Scouts of the United States of America
gt gilt top, great
GT gross ton
Gt Brit Great Britain
gtd guaranteed
Gtr Man Greater Manchester
gtt [Latin *gutta*, plural *guttae*] drop
GU genitourinary, Guam
GUI graphical user interface
GUT grand unified theory, grand unification theory
GWRBI game winning run batted in
Gwyn Gwynedd
gyn *or* **gynecol** gynecology
Gy Sgt gunnery sergeant
h half, harbor, hard, hardness, hecto-, height, hit, horse, hour, humidity, hundred, Hungary, husband
H Hamiltonian, henry, heroin, hydrogen
ha hectare
HA hour angle
Hab Habacuc, Habakkuk
hab corp habeas corpus
Hag Haggai
Hants Hampshire
Hb hemoglobin
HBM Her Britannic Majesty, His Britannic Majesty
HC Holy Communion, House of Commons, hydrocarbon
HCF highest common factor
HCG human chorionic gonadotropin
HCL high cost of living
hd head
HD heavy-duty
hdbk handbook

hdkf handkerchief
HDTV high-definition television
hdwe hardware
He helium
HE Her Excellency, high explosive, His Eminence, His Excellency
Heb Hebrew, Hebrews
her heraldry
Heref/Worcs Hereford and Worcester
Herts Hertfordshire
HEW Department of Health, Education, and Welfare
hex hexagon
hf half
Hf hafnium
HF height finding, high frequency, home forces
hg hectogram, heliogram, hemoglobin
Hg [New Latin *hydrargyrum,* literally, water silver] mercury
HGH human growth hormone
hgt height
hgwy highway
HH Her Highness, His Highness, His Holiness
HHD [New Latin *humanitatum doctor*] doctor of humanities
HHS Department of Health and Human Services
HI Hawaii, high intensity, humidity index
hist historian, historical, history
Hitt Hittite
HJ [Latin *hic jacet*] here lies
HJR House joint resolution
hl hectoliter
HL House of Lords
hld hold
hlqn harlequin
HLS [Latin *hoc loco situs*] laid in this place; holograph letter signed
hlt halt
hm hectometer
HM Her Majesty, Her Majesty's, His Majesty, His Majesty's
HMAS Her Majesty's Australian ship, His Majesty's Australian ship
HMBS Her Majesty's British ship, His Majesty's British ship
HMC Her Majesty's Customs, His Majesty's Customs
HMCS Her Majesty's Canadian ship, His Majesty's Canadian ship
HMS Her Majesty's ship, His Majesty's ship
HN head nurse
Ho holmium
hom homiletics, homily
hon honor, honorable, honorary
Hon *or* **Hond** Honduras
HOPE Health Opportunity for People Everywhere
hor horizontal
hort horticultural, horticulture
Hos Hosea
hosp hospital
HOV high-occupancy vehicle
hp horsepower
HP half pay, high pressure
HPA high-power amplifier
HPF highest possible frequency, high power field
HPV human-powered vehicle
HQ headquarters
hr here, hour
HR home run, House of Representatives
H Res House resolution
HRH Her Royal Highness, His Royal Highness
hrzn horizon
HS high school
HSL high-speed launch
HST Hawaiian standard time, hypersonic transport
ht height
HT half time, halftone, hardtop, Hawaii time, high-tension, high tide, [Latin *hoc tempore*] at this time; [Latin *hoc titulo*] under this title
http hypertext transfer protocol

HUAC House Un-American Activities Committee
HUD Department of Housing and Urban Development
Humber Humberside
Hung Hungarian, Hungary
hv have
HV high velocity, high voltage
HVAC heating, ventilating, and air-conditioning
hvy heavy
hw how
HW high water, highway, hot water
HWM high-water mark
hwy highway
hyd hydraulics, hydrostatics
hyp hypothesis, hypothetical
Hz hertz
i industrial, initial, intelligence, intensity, intransitive, island, isle
I electric current, Indian, interstate, iodine, Israeli
Ia *or* **IA** Iowa
IAA indoleacetic acid
IAAF International Amateur Athletic Federation
IABA International Amateur Boxing Association
IAEA International Atomic Energy Agency
IALC instrument approach and landing chart
IAM International Association of Machinists and Aerospace Workers
IAP international airport
IAS indicated airspeed
IATA International Air Transport Association
IAU International Association of Universities, International Astronomical Union
ib *or* **ibid** ibidem
IB in bond, incendiary bomb
IBRD International Bank for Reconstruction and Development
ICA International Cooperative Alliance
ICAO International Civil Aviation Organization
ICC International Chamber of Commerce, Interstate Commerce Commission
Ice Iceland
ICE internal combustion engine, International Cultural Exchange
Icel Icelandic
ICF intermediate care facility
ICFTU International Confederation of Free Trade Unions
ICJ International Court of Justice
ICRC International Committee of the Red Cross
ICU intensive care unit
id idem
ID Idaho, identification, independent distributor, industrial design, inner diameter, inside dimensions, intelligence department, internal diameter
IDA International Development Association
IDP international driving permit
i.e. [Latin *id est*] that is
IE industrial engineer
IEEE The Institute of Electrical and Electronics Engineers
IF intermediate frequency
IFC International Finance Corporation
IFF identification, friend or foe
IFO identified flying object
IFR instrument flight rules
Ig immunoglobulin
IG inspector general
IGY International Geophysical Year
ihp indicated horsepower
IIE Institute of Industrial Engineers
IL Illinois
ILA International Longshoremen's Association
ILGWU International Ladies' Garment Workers' Union
ill illustrated, illustration, illustrator
Ill Illinois

illust *or* **illus** illustrated, illustration
ILO International Labor Organization
ILS instrument landing system
IL–2 interleukin-2
IM individual medley, intramural
IMCO Inter-Governmental Maritime Consultative Organization
IMF International Monetary Fund
imit imitative
immed immediate, immediately
immun immunity, immunization
immunol immunology
imp imperative, imperfect, imperial, import, imported
IMP international match point
imperf imperfect, imperforate
in inch, inlet
In indium
IN Indiana
inc incomplete, incorporated, increase
incl include, included, including, inclusive
incog incognito
incr increase, increased
ind independent, index, industrial, industry
Ind Indian, Indiana
IND investigational new drug
IndE industrial engineer
indef indefinite
indic indicative
indiv individual
indn indication
Indon Indonesia, Indonesian
indus industrial, industry
inf infantry, infinitive
INF intermediate range nuclear forces
infl influenced
INH [*iso-nicotinic acid hydrazide*] isoniazid
inorg inorganic
INP International News Photo
inq inquire
INRI [Latin *Iesus Nazarenus Rex Iudaeorum*] Jesus of Nazareth, King of the Jews
ins inches, insurance
INS Immigration and Naturalization Service, inertial navigation system
insol insoluble
insp inspector
inst instant, institute, institution, institutional
instr instructor, instrument, instrumental
insur insurance
int intelligence, intercept, interest, interim, interior, interjection, interleaved, intermediate, internal, international, interpreter, intersection, interval, interview, intransitive
intel intelligence
interj interjection
Interpol International Criminal Police Organization
interrog interrogative
intl *or* **intnl** international
intrans intransitive
in trans [Latin *in transitu*] in transit
introd introduction
inv inventor, invoice
I/O input/output
IOC International Olympic Committee
IOM Isle of Man
Ion Ionic
IOOF Independent Order of Odd Fellows
IORM Improved Order of Red Men
IOW Isle of Wight
IP initial point, innings pitched, intermediate pressure
IPA individual practice association
ipm inches per minute
IPO initial public offering
ips inches per second
IPTS International Practical Temperature Scale
iq [Latin *idem quod*] the same as
Ir iridium, Irish

IR information retrieval, infrared, inland revenue, intelligence ratio, internal revenue
IRA Irish Republican Army
IRBM intermediate range ballistic missile
Ire Ireland
irid iridescent
irred irredeemable
irreg irregular
IRS Internal Revenue Service
is island, isle
Isa *or* **Is** Isaiah
ISBN International Standard Book Number
ISC interstate commerce
isl island
ISO International Organization for Standardization
isoln isolation
Isr Israel, Israeli
ISSN International Standard Serial Number
isth isthmus
ISV International Scientific Vocabulary
It Italian, Italy
ital italic, italicized
Ital Italian
ITO International Trade Organization
ITU International Telecommunication Union, International Typographical Union
ITV instructional television
IU international unit
IV intravenous, intravenously
IVF in vitro fertilization
IW inside width, isotopic weight
IWW Industrial Workers of the World
j jack, journal, judge, justice
J joule, jump shot
JA joint account, judge advocate
JAG judge advocate general
Jam Jamaica
Jan January
Jas James
Jav Javanese
JBS John Birch Society
JC junior college
JCAHO Joint Commission on Accreditation of Healthcare Organizations
JCB [New Latin *juris canonici baccalaureus*] bachelor of canon law
JCD [New Latin *juris canonici doctor*] doctor of canon law
JCL [New Latin *juris canonici licentiatus*] licentiate in canon law
JCS joint chiefs of staff
jct junction
JD [New Latin *juris doctor*] doctor of jurisprudence, doctor of law; [New Latin *jurum doctor*] doctor of laws; justice department, juvenile delinquent
Jer Jeremiah, Jeremias
jg junior grade
JIT job instruction training, just in time
Jn *or* **Jno** John
JND just noticeable difference
jnr *British* junior
Jo Joel
Jon Jonah, Jonas
Josh Joshua
jour journal, journeyman
Jp Japanese
JP jet propulsion, justice of the peace
Jpn Japan, Japanese
Jr junior
JSD [New Latin *juris scientiae doctor*] doctor of science of law
jt *or* **jnt** joint
Jud Judith
Judg Judges
Jul July
jun junior
Jun June
junc junction
juv juvenile
JV junior varsity

k karat, kindergarten, king, kitchen, knit, knot, koruna, kosher — often enclosed in a circle; kyat
K [New Latin *kalium*] potassium; Kelvin, kilometer
ka [German *Kathode*] cathode
Kan *or* **Kans** Kansas
kb kilobar, kilobase
KB kilobyte
kbar kilobar
kc kilocycle
KC Kansas City, King's Counsel, Knights of Columbus
kcal kilocalorie, kilogram calorie
KCB knight commander of the Order of the Bath
kc/s kilocycles per second
KD kiln-dried, knockdown, knocked down
Ker Kerry
keV kilo-electron volt
kg keg, kilogram, king
kG kilogauss
KG knight of the Order of the Garter
KGB [Russian *Komitet gosudarstvennoĭ bezopasnosti*] (Soviet) State Security Committee
kgps kilograms per second
kHz kilohertz
KIA killed in action
Kild Kildare
Kilk Kilkenny
kit kitchen
kJ kilojoule
KJV King James Version
KKK Ku Klux Klan
kl kiloliter
km kilometer
kmh *or* **kmph** kilometers per hour
kmps kilometers per second
kn knot
K of C Knights of Columbus
Kor Korea, Korean
kPa kilopascal
kpc kiloparsec
kph kilometers per hour
Kr krypton
KS Kansas, Kaposi's sarcoma
kt karat, knight, knot
KT kiloton
kV kilovolt
kW kilowatt
kWh kilowatt-hour
Ky *or* **KY** Kentucky
l lady, lake, lambert, land, large, late, left, [Latin *libra*] pound; line, liquid, lira, lire, liter, little, low
L Lagrangian, Latin, long
La lanthanum, Louisiana
LA law agent, legislative assistant, Los Angeles, Louisiana
Lab Labrador
lam laminated
Lam Lamentations
Lancs Lancashire
lang language
lat latitude
Lat Latin, Latvia
LAT local apparent time
lav lavatory
lb [Latin *libra*] pound
LB Labrador
LBO leveraged buyout
lc lowercase
LC landing craft, left center, letter of credit, Library of Congress
LCD least common denominator, lowest common denominator
LCDR lieutenant commander
LCL less-than-carload lot
LCM least common multiple, lowest common multiple, [New Latin *legis comparativae magister*] master of comparative law
LCpl lance corporal
LCS League Championship Series
LCT local civil time
ld load, lord
LD learning disabled, learning disability; lethal dose — often used with a numerical subscript to indicate the percent of a test group of organisms

the dose is expected to kill ⟨LD$_{50}$⟩; line of departure
LDC less developed country
ldg landing, loading
LDH lactate dehydrogenase, lactic dehydrogenase
ldr leader
LDS Latter-day Saints
LE leading edge
lea leather
Leb Lebanese, Lebanon
lect lecture, lecturer
leg legal, legato, legislative, legislature
legis legislation, legislative, legislature
Leics Leicestershire
Leit Leitrim
LEM lunar excursion module
LEP limited English proficiency, limited English proficient
Lev *or* **Levit** Leviticus
lf lightface
LF ledger folio, low frequency
lg large, long
LH left hand, lower half, luteinizing hormone
LHD [New Latin *litterarum humaniorum doctor*] doctor of humane letters, doctor of humanities
li link
Li lithium
LI Long Island
lib liberal, librarian, library
lic license
lieut lieutenant
LIFO last in, first out
Lim Limerick
lin lineal, linear
Lincs Lincolnshire
ling linguistics
liq liquid, liquor
lit liter, literal, literally, literary, literature
lith lithographic, lithography
Lith Lithuanian
Litt B *or* **Lit B** [Medieval Latin *litterarum baccalaureus*] bachelor of letters, bachelor of literature
Litt D *or* **Lit D** [Medieval Latin *litterarum doctor*] doctor of letters, doctor of literature
Lk Luke
ll lines
LL lending library, limited liability, lower left
LLB [New Latin *legum baccalaureus*] bachelor of laws
LLD [New Latin *legum doctor*] doctor of laws
LLM [New Latin *legum magister*] master of laws
lm lumen
LM Legion of Merit, long meter, lunar module
LMG light machine gun
LMT local mean time
ln lane, natural logarithm
lndg landing
LNG liquefied natural gas
LOA length overall
loc cit [Latin *loco citato*] in the place cited
log logic
Lond London, Londonderry
long longitude
Long Longford
loq [Latin *loquitur*] he speaks, she speaks
LOS line of scrimmage, line of sight
Loth Lothian
Lou Louth
LP low pressure
LPG liquefied petroleum gas
LPGA Ladies Professional Golf Association
Lr lawrencium
LR living room, log run, lower right
LRT light-rail transit
LRV light-rail vehicle

LS left side, letter signed, library science, [Latin *locus sigilli*] place of the seal; long shot
LSAT Law School Admission Test
LSI large-scale integrated circuit, large-scale integration
LSM letter-sorting machine
LSS lifesaving service, lifesaving station, life-support system
LST landing ship, tank; local sidereal time
lt light
Lt lieutenant
LT long ton, low-tension
LTC lieutenant colonel, long term care
Lt Col lieutenant colonel
Lt Comdr lieutenant commander
ltd limited
LTG *or* **Lt Gen** lieutenant general
lt gov lieutenant governor
LTh licentiate in theology
LTJG lieutenant, junior grade
LTL less than truckload
ltr letter, lighter
LTS launch telemetry station, launch tracking system
Lu lutetium
lub lubricant, lubricating
Luth Lutheran
lv leave
LVT landing vehicle, tracked
LW low water
LWM low-water mark
LWV League of Women Voters
lx lux
LZ landing zone
m male, manual, married, martyr, masculine, mass, measure, meridian, [Latin *meridies*] noon; meter, middle, mile, [Latin *mille*] thousand; milli-, minute, molal, molality, molar, molarity, mole, month, moon, morning, muscle
m- meta-
M Mach, March, May, medium, mega-, million, monsieur
mA milliampere
MA [Medieval Latin *magister artium*] master of arts; Massachusetts, mental age, Middle Ages
MAA master of applied arts
Mac Machabees
Mac *or* **Macc** Maccabees
MAC military airlift command
mach machine, machinery, machinist
MAD mutual assured destruction
MAE *or* **MA Ed** master of arts in education
mag magnesium, magnetism, magneto, magnitude
Maj major
Maj Gen major general
Mal Malachi
MALS master of arts in liberal studies, master of arts in library science
man manual
Man Manitoba
M&A mergers and acquisitions
manuf manufacture, manufacturing
MAO monoamine oxidase
MAP modified American plan
mar maritime
Mar March
MARC machine readable cataloging
MARV maneuverable reentry vehicle
masc masculine
MASH mobile army surgical hospital
Mass Massachusetts
MAT master of arts in teaching, Miller analogy test
math mathematical, mathematician
matric matriculated, matriculation
Matt Matthew
MATV master antenna television
max maximum
mb millibar
MB bachelor of medicine, Manitoba, megabyte, municipal borough
MBA master of business administration
mbd million barrels per day
MBD minimal brain dysfunction

MBE member of the Order of the British Empire
MBO management by objective
MBS Mutual Broadcasting System
mc megacycle, millicurie
MC member of Congress
MCAT Medical College Admission Test
MCC mission control center
mcf thousand cubic feet
mcg microgram
MCL Marine Corps League, master of civil law, master of comparative law
MCP male chauvinist pig
MCPO master chief petty officer
Md Maryland, mendelevium
MD [New Latin *medicinae doctor*] doctor of medicine; [Italian *mano destra*] right hand; Maryland, medical department, months after date, muscular dystrophy
MDC more developed country
MDiv master of divinity
mdnt midnight
mdse merchandise
MDT mountain daylight time
Me Maine, methyl
ME Maine, managing editor, mechanical engineer, medical examiner
Mea Meath
meas measure
mech mechanical, mechanics
med medicine, medieval, medium
Med Mediterranean
MEd master of education
meg megohm
MEGO my eyes glaze over
MEK methyl ethyl ketone
mem member, memoir, memorial
MEng master of English
MEP member of the European Parliament
mer meridian
Mersey Merseyside
met meteorological, meteorology, metropolitan
metal *or* **metall** metallurgical, metallurgy
metaph metaphysics
METO Middle East Treaty Organization
MeV million electron volts
Mex Mexican, Mexico
mf mezzo forte
mF millifarad
MF medium frequency, microfiche
MFA master of fine arts
mfd manufactured
mfg manufacturing
MFH master of foxhounds
MFN most favored nation
mfr manufacture, manufacturer
mg milligram
Mg magnesium
MG machine gun, major general, military government
mgal milligal
MGB [Russian *Ministerstvo gosudarstvennoĭ bezopasnosti*] Ministry of State Security
mgd million gallons per day
mgr manager, monseigneur, monsignor
mgt *or* **mgmt** management
MGy Sgt master gunnery sergeant
MH medal of honor, mental health, mobile home
MHA master of hospital administration
MHC major histocompatibility complex
MHD magnetohydrodynamic, magnetohydrodynamics
mhg mahogany
MHW mean high water
MHz megahertz
mi mile, mileage, mill
MI Michigan, military intelligence
Mic Micah
MIC methyl isocyanate
Mich Michigan

MICR magnetic ink character recognition
mid middle
Middx Middlesex
Mid Glam Mid Glamorgan
midn midshipman
mil military, million
min minim, minimum, mining, minister, minor, minute
Minn Minnesota
MIO minimum identifiable odor
MIPS *or* **mips** million instructions per second
misc miscellaneous
Miss Mississippi
mixt mixture
mk mark, markka
Mk Mark
mks meter-kilogram-second
mkt market
mktg marketing
ml milliliter
mL millilambert
MLA Member of the Legislative Assembly
MLD median lethal dose, minimum lethal dose
MLF multilateral force
Mlle [French] mademoiselle
Mlles [French] mesdemoiselles
MLS master of library science
MLW mean low water
mm millimeter
MM [French] messieurs; mutatis mutandis
Mme [French] madame
Mmes [French] mesdames
mmf magnetomotive force
MMPI Minnesota Multiphasic Personality Inventory
Mn manganese
MN magnetic north, Minnesota
MNC multinational company, multinational corporation
mo month
Mo Missouri, molybdenum, Monday
MO mail order, medical officer, Missouri, modus operandi, money order
mod moderate, modification, modified, modulo, modulus
modif modification
mol mole, molecular, molecule
MOL manned orbiting laboratory
mol wt molecular weight
MOM middle of month
mon monastery, monetary
Mon Monaghan, Monday
Mont Montana
mor morocco
MOR middle of the road
morph morphology
mos months
MOS metal-oxide semiconductor, military occupational specialty
MOSFET metal-oxide-semiconductor field-effect transistor
MP melting point, member of parliament, metropolitan police, milepost, military police, military policeman
MPA master of public administration
MPAA Motion Picture Association of America
mpg miles per gallon
mph miles per hour
MPH master of public health
MPhil master of philosophy
MPM meters per minute
MPS meters per second
MPV multi-purpose vehicle
MPX multiplex
mR milliroentgen
MR map reference, mentally retarded
MRE meals ready to eat
MRI magnetic resonance imaging
mRNA messenger RNA
ms millisecond
MS [Italian *mano sinistra*] left hand; manuscript, master of science, military science, Mississippi, motor ship, multiple sclerosis
MSc master of science
msec millisecond

msg message
MSG master sergeant, monosodium glutamate
msgr monseigneur, monsignor
MSgt master sergeant
MSH melanocyte-stimulating hormone
MSL mean sea level
MSN master of science in nursing
MSS manuscripts
MST mountain standard time
MSW master of social welfare, master of social work
mt mount, mountain
Mt Matthew
MT machine translation, metric ton, Montana, mountain time
mtg meeting, mortgage
mtge mortgage
mth month
mtn mountain
MTO Mediterranean theater of operations
mun *or* **munic** municipal
mus museum, music, musical, musician
mV millivolt
MV main verb, mean variation, motor vessel
MVD [Russian *Ministerstvo vnutrennikh del*] Ministry of Internal Affairs
MVP most valuable player
mW milliwatt
MW megawatt
MWe megawatts electric
mxd mixed
my million years
myc *or* **mycol** mycology
Myr million years
n name, nano-, navy, net, neuter, *usually italic* neutron, noon, normal, north, northern, note, noun, number
N newton, nitrogen
Na [New Latin *natrium*] sodium
NA national association, no account, North America, not applicable, not available
NAACP National Association for the Advancement of Colored People
NAB New American Bible
NAD no appreciable disease
Nah Nahum
NAIA National Association of Intercollegiate Athletes
NAS National Academy of Sciences, naval air station
NASA National Aeronautics and Space Administration
NASCAR National Association for Stock Car Auto Racing
NASD National Association of Securities Dealers
NASL North American Soccer League
NASW National Association of Social Workers
nat national, native, natural
natl national
NATO North Atlantic Treaty Organization
naut nautical
nav naval, navigable, navigation
Nb niobium
NB New Brunswick, northbound, nota bene
NBA National Basketball Association, National Boxing Association
NBC National Broadcasting Company
NBS National Bureau of Standards
NC no charge, no credit, North Carolina, nurse corps
NCAA National Collegiate Athletic Association
NCE New Catholic Edition
NCV no commercial value
nd no date
Nd neodymium
ND doctor of naturopathy, North Dakota
N Dak North Dakota
NDE near-death experience
NDP New Democratic Party (Canadian)

Ne neon
NE Nebraska, New England, no effects, northeast
NEA National Education Association, National Endowment for the Arts
Neb *or* **Nebr** Nebraska
NEB New English Bible
NED New English Dictionary
neg negative, negotiable
Neh Nehemiah
NEH National Endowment for the Humanities
NEI not elsewhere included
nem con [New Latin *nemine contradicente*] no one contradicting
nem diss [New Latin *nemine dissentiente*] no one dissenting
NEP New Economic Policy
NES not elsewhere specified
Neth Netherlands
neurol neurological, neurology
neut neuter
Nev Nevada
New Eng New England
NF Newfoundland, no funds
NFC National Football Conference
NFL National Football League
Nfld Newfoundland
NFP natural family planning
NFS not for sale
ng nanogram
NG national guard, no good
NGF nerve growth factor
NGO nongovernmental organization
NGU nongonococcal urethritis
NH never hinged, New Hampshire
NHL National Hockey League
Ni nickel
NIC newly industrialized country, newly industrializing country
NIH National Institutes of Health, not invented here
NIMBY not in my backyard
NIT National Invitational Tournament
NIU network interface unit
NJ New Jersey
NKVD [Russian *Narodnyĭ komissariat vnutrennikh del*] People's Commissariat of Internal Affairs
NL National League, new line, night letter, [Latin *non licet*] it is not permitted; north latitude
NLCS National League Championship Series
NLF National Liberation Front
NLRB National Labor Relations Board
NLT night letter
nm nanometer
NM nautical mile, New Mexico, no mark, not marked
N Mex New Mexico
NMHA National Mental Health Association
NMI no middle initial
NMR nuclear magnetic resonance
NNE north-northeast
NNW north-northwest
no north, northern, [Latin *numero,* ablative of *numerus*] number
No nobelium
NOAA National Oceanic and Atmospheric Administration
NOIBN not otherwise indexed by name
nom nominative
non obst *or* **non obs** non obstante
non seq non sequitur
NOP not otherwise provided for
Nor Norway, Norwegian
NORAD North American Air Defense Command
Norf Norfolk
norm normal
Northants Northamptonshire
Norw Norway, Norwegian
nos numbers
NOS not otherwise specified
Notts Nottinghamshire
nov novelist
Nov November

NOW National Organization for Women
NO$_x$ nitrogen oxide
np no pagination, no place (of publication)
Np neptunium
NP neuropsychiatric, neuropsychiatry, no protest, notary public, noun phrase
NPF not provided for
NPN nonprotein nitrogen
NPR National Public Radio
NPS National Park Service
nr near
NR not rated
NRA National Recovery Administration, National Rifle Association
NRC National Research Council, Nuclear Regulatory Commission
ns *also* **nsec** nanosecond
Ns nimbostratus
NS new series, new style, not specified, not sufficient, Nova Scotia
NSA National Security Agency
NSC National Security Council
NSF National Science Foundation, not sufficient funds
NSW New South Wales
NT New Territories, New Testament, Northern Territory, Northwest Territories
Nthmb Northumberland
NTP normal temperature and pressure
NTSB National Transportation Safety Board
nt wt *or* **n wt** net weight
NU name unknown
num numeral
Num *or* **Numb** Numbers
numis numismatic, numismatical, numismatics
NV Nevada, nonvoting
NW northwest
NWT Northwest Territories
NY New York
NYC New York City
NYSE New York Stock Exchange
NZ New Zealand
o ocean, ohm, old, order, oriental, over
O Ohio, oxygen, [New Latin *octarius*] pint
o- ortho-
o/a on or about
OAS Organization of American States
OASDHI Old Age, Survivors, Disability, and Health Insurance
OAU Organization of African Unity
ob [Latin *obiit*] he died, she died; observation
Ob *or* **Obad** Obadiah
OB obstetric, obstetrician, obstetrics
OBE officer of the Order of the British Empire, out-of-body experience
OB–GYN obstetrician gynecologist, obstetrics gynecology
obj object, objective
obl oblique, oblong
obstet obstetrical, obstetrics
obv obverse
oc ocean
OC off center, officer candidate, on center, on course, over-the-counter
occas occasionally
oceanog oceanography
OCR optical character reader, optical character recognition
OCS officer candidate school
oct octavo
Oct October
OD doctor of optometry, [Latin *oculus dexter*] right eye; officer of the day, olive drab, on demand, outside diameter, outside dimension, overdraft, overdrawn
Oe oersted
OECD Organization for Economic Cooperation and Development
OED Oxford English Dictionary
OEO Office of Economic Opportunity
OER officer efficiency report
OES Order of the Eastern Star
OF outfield
off office, officer, official

offic official
OG officer of the guard, original gum
OH Ohio
OHMS on Her Majesty's service, on His Majesty's service
OIT Office of International Trade
OJ orange juice
OJT on-the-job training
OK Oklahoma, outer keel
Okla Oklahoma
OM order of merit
OMB Office of Management and Budget
ON or **Ont** Ontario
OOD officer of the deck
op operation, operative, operator, opportunity, opus
OP observation post, out of print
op cit [Latin *opere citato*] in the work cited
OPEC Organization of Petroleum Exporting Countries
opp opposite
opt optical, optician, optics, option, optional
OR operating room, operational research, operations research, Oregon, owner's risk, own recognizance
orch orchestra
ord order, ordnance
Ore or **Oreg** Oregon
org organic, organization, organized
orig original, originally, originator
Ork Orkney
ornith ornithology
ORV off-road vehicle
Os osmium
OS [Latin *oculus sinister*] left eye; old series, old style, ordinary seaman, out of stock
OSHA Occupational Safety and Health Administration
OSS Office of Strategic Services
OT occupational therapy, Old Testament, overtime
OTA Office of Technology Assessment
OTB offtrack betting
OTC over-the-counter
OTR occupational therapist, registered
OTS officers' training school
OW one-way
Oxfam Oxford Committee for Famine Relief
Oxon [Medieval Latin *Oxonia*] Oxford; Oxfordshire, [Medieval Latin *Oxoniensis*] of Oxford
oz [obsolete Italian *onza* (now *oncia*)] ounce, ounces

p page, pages, parental generation, part, participle, past, pater, pawn, pence, penny, per, peseta, peso, petite, piano, pico-, pint, pipe, pitch, pole, port, power, pro, proton, purl
P phosphorus, pressure, [French *poids*] weight
p- para-
Pa pascal, Pennsylvania, protactinium
PA particular average, passenger agent, Pennsylvania, per annum, personal appearance, personal assistant, power amplifier, power of attorney, press agent, private account, professional association, public address, purchasing agent
Pac Pacific
PAC political action committee
paleon paleontology
pam pamphlet
Pan Panama
p and h postage and handling
P&I principal and interest
P&L profit and loss
par paragraph, parallel, parish
para paragraph
part participial, participle, particular
PAS para-aminosalicylic acid
pass passenger, passive
pat patent
PAT point after touchdown
path or **pathol** pathological, pathology

PAYE *British* pay as you earn
payt payment
pb paperback
Pb [Latin *plumbum*] lead
PB personal best, power brakes
PB&J peanut butter and jelly
PBS Public Broadcasting Service
pc parsec
PC Peace Corps, percent, percentage, politically correct, postcard, [Latin *post cibum*] after meals; printed circuit, professional corporation
PCP pneumocystis carinii pneumonia, primary care physician
PCR polymerase chain reaction
pct percent, percentage
pd paid
Pd palladium
PD per diem, police department, postal district, potential difference, program director, public domain
PDA predicted drift angle, public display of affection
PDD past due date
PDT Pacific daylight time
PE physical education, printer's error, probable error, professional engineer
P/E price/earnings
PEI Prince Edward Island
pen peninsula
PEN International Association of Poets, Playwrights, Editors, Essayists and Novelists
Penn or **Penna** Pennsylvania
per period, person
perf perfect, perforated, performance
perh perhaps
perm permanent
perp perpendicular
pers person, personal, personnel
Pers Persia, Persian
pert pertaining
pet petroleum
Pet Peter
PET positron-emission tomography
pf personal foul, pfennig, picofarad, preferred
PF power factor, pianoforte, [Italian *più forte*] louder
PFC or **Pfc** private first class
pfd preferred
PFD personal flotation device
pg page, picogram
Pg Portugal, Portuguese
PG paying guest, postgraduate, prostaglandin
PGA Professional Golfers' Association
ph phase
PH pinch hit, public health, Purple Heart
phar pharmacopoeia, pharmacy
pharm pharmaceutical, pharmacist, pharmacy
PhB [New Latin *philosophiae baccalaureus*] bachelor of philosophy
PhD [New Latin *philosophiae doctor*] doctor of philosophy
phil or **philol** philological, philology
Phil Philippians
philos philosopher, philosophy
phon phonetics
photog photographic, photography
phr phrase
phys physical, physics
physiol physiologist, physiology
PI Philippine Islands, private investigator, programmed instruction
PID pelvic inflammatory disease
PIK payment in kind
PIN personal identification number
PINS persons in need of supervision
pinx [Latin *pinxit*] he painted it, she painted it
PIRG Public Interest Research Group
pizz pizzicato
pk park, peak, peck, pike
PK preacher's kid
pkg package
pkt packet, pocket
PKU phenylketonuria
pkwy parkway

pl place, plate, plural
PL partial loss, private line, Public Law
plat plateau, platoon
PLC *British* public limited company
plf plaintiff
PLO Palestine Liberation Organization
pls please
PLSS portable life-support system
pm phase modulation, premium
Pm promethium
PM paymaster, permanent magnet, police magistrate, postmaster, post meridiem — often not capitalized and often punctuated; postmortem, prime minister, provost marshal
pmk postmark
PMS premenstrual syndrome
pmt payment
PN promissory note
pnxt [Latin *pinxit*] he painted it, she painted it
Po polonium
PO [Latin *per os*] by mouth, orally; petty officer, postal order, post office, purchase order
POB post office box
POC port of call
POD pay on delivery, post office department
POE port of embarkation, port of entry
Pol Poland, Polish
polit political, politician
poly polytechnic
pon pontoon
pop population
POP point of purchase
por portable, portrait
POR pay on return, price on request
port portable, portrait
Port Portugal, Portuguese
pos position, positive
POS point of sale
poss possessive
pot potential, potentiometer
POV point of view
pp pages, [Latin *per procurationem*] by proxy; pianissimo
PP parcel post, past participle, postpaid, prepaid
ppa per power of attorney
ppb parts per billion
ppd postpaid, prepaid
PPI plan position indicator
ppm parts per million
PPS [New Latin *post postscriptum*] an additional postscript
ppt parts per thousand, parts per trillion, precipitate
pptn precipitation
PQ Province of Quebec
pr pair, price, printed
Pr praseodymium, propyl
PR payroll, proportional representation, public relations, Puerto Rico
PRC People's Republic of China
prec preceding
pred predicate
pref preface, preference, preferred, prefix
prem premium
prep preparatory, preposition
prepd prepared
prepg preparing
prepn preparation
pres present, president
Presb Presbyterian
prev previous, previously
prf proof
prim primary, primitive
prin principal, principle
priv private, privately, privative
PRN [Latin *pro re nata*] for the emergency, as needed
PRO public relations officer
prob probable, probably, probate, problem
proc proceedings
prod product, production
prof professional
prog program

proj project, projector
prom promontory
pron pronoun, pronounced, pronunciation
prop property, proposition, proprietor
pros prosody
Prot Protestant
prov province, provincial, provisional
Prov Proverbs
prox proximo
Pruss Prussian
ps picosecond
Ps or **Psa** Psalms
PS [New Latin *postscriptum*] postscript; power steering, power supply, public school
PSA public service announcement
psec picosecond
pseud pseudonym, pseudonymous
psf pounds per square foot
PSG platoon sergeant
psi pounds per square inch
psig pounds per square inch gauge
PST Pacific standard time
psych psychology
psychol psychologist, psychology
pt part, payment, pint, point, port
Pt platinum
PT Pacific time, part-time, physical therapy, physical training
pta peseta
PTA Parent-Teacher Association
pte *British* private
ptg printing
PTO Parent-Teacher Organization, please turn over, power takeoff
PTSD post-traumatic stress disorder
PTV public television
Pty *British* proprietary
Pu plutonium
PU pickup
pub public, publication, publicity, published, publisher, publishing
publ publication, published, publisher
PUD pickup and delivery
pulv [Latin *pulvis*] powder
PUSH People United to Serve Humanity
PV photovoltaic, polyvinyl
PVA polyvinyl acetate
PVC polyvinyl chloride
PVO private voluntary organization
pvt private
PVT pressure, volume, temperature
PW prisoner of war
PWA person with AIDS
pwr power
PWR pressurized water reactor
pwt pennyweight
PX please exchange, post exchange
PYO pick your own
q quart, quartile, quarto, queen, query, question, quetzal, quire
QA quality assurance
QB quarterback, queen's bench
QC quality control, queen's counsel
qd [Latin *quaque die*] daily
QED quantum electrodynamics, [Latin *quod erat demonstrandum*] which was to be demonstrated
QEF [Latin *quod erat faciendum*] which was to be done
QEI [Latin *quod erat inveniendum*] which was to be found out
QF quick-firing
qid [Latin *quater in die*] four times a day
Qld Queensland
qm [Latin *quoque matutino*] every morning
QM quartermaster
QMC quartermaster corps
QMG quartermaster general
qp or **q pl** [Latin *quantum placet*] as much as you please
qq questions
qq v [Latin *quae vide*] which (*plural*) see
qr quarter, quire
qs [Latin *quantum sufficit*] as much as suffices
qt quantity, quart

qtd quartered
qto quarto
qty quantity
qu *or* **ques** question
quad quadrant
qual qualitative, quality
quant quantitative
quar quarterly
Que Quebec
quot quotation
qv [Latin *quod vide*] which see
qy query
r rabbi, radius, rain, range, Rankine, rare, real, Reaumur, recto, red, repeat, rerun, resistance, right, river, roentgen, rook, rough, run
R radial, radical — used especially of a univalent hydrocarbon radical; recipe; registered trademark — often enclosed in a circle; regular, Republican
ra range
Ra radium
RA regular army, right ascension, Royal Academician, Royal Academy
RAAF Royal Australian Air Force
rad radical, radian, radiator, radio, radius, radix
RADM rear admiral
RAF Royal Air Force
R & B rhythm and blues
R and R rest and recreation, rest and recuperation
rap rapid
Rb rubidium
RBC red blood cells, red blood count
RBE relative biological effectiveness
RC Red Cross, resistance-capacitance, Roman Catholic
RCAF Royal Canadian Air Force
RCMP Royal Canadian Mounted Police
RCN Royal Canadian Navy
rct recruit
rd road, rod, round
RD registered dietitian, rural delivery
RDA recommended daily allowance, recommended dietary allowance
RDF radio direction finder, radio direction finding, Rapid Deployment Force, refuse-derived fuel
Re rhenium
REA Rural Electrification Administration
reas reasonable
rec receipt, record, recording, recreation
recd received
recip reciprocal, reciprocity
rec sec recording secretary
rect receipt, rectangle, rectangular, rectified
red reduce, reduction
ref reference, referred, refining, reformed, refunding
refl reflex, reflexive
refr refraction
refrig refrigerating, refrigeration
reg region, register, registered, registration, regular
regd registered
regt regiment
REIT real estate investment trust
rel relating, relative, released, religion, religious
relig religion
rep repair, repeat, report, reporter, representative, republic
Rep Republican
repl replace, replacement
rept report
req request, require, required, requisition
reqd required
res research, reservation, reserve, reservoir, residence, resident, resolution
RES reticuloendothelial system
resp respective, respectively
ret retain, retired, return
retd retained, retired, returned
rev revenue, reverse, review, reviewed, revised, revision, revolution
Rev Revelation, reverend

Revd *British* reverend
rf refunding
RF radio frequency
RFD rural free delivery
RFP request for proposal
Rh rhodium
RH relative humidity, right hand
rhet rhetoric
RHIP rank has its privileges
RI refractive index, Rhode Island
RIA radioimmunoassay
RICO Racketeer Influenced and Corrupt Organizations (Act)
RIF reduction in force
RIO radar intercept officer
RIP [Latin *requiescat in pace*] may he rest in peace, may she rest in peace; [Latin *requiescant in pace*] may they rest in peace
RISC reduced instruction-set computer; reduced instruction-set computing
rit ritardando
riv river
RJ road junction
rm ream, room
rms root-mean-square
Rn radon
RN Royal Navy
rnd round
RNZAF Royal New Zealand Air Force
ROC Republic of China (Taiwan)
ROG receipt of goods
ROI return on investment
ROK Republic of Korea (South Korea)
Rom Roman, Romance, Romania, Romanian, Romans
ROP record of production, run-of-paper
ROR release on own recognizance
Ros *or* **Rosc** Roscommon
rot rotating, rotation
ROTC Reserve Officers' Training Corps
RP Received Pronunciation, relief pitcher, reply paid, reprint, reprinting, Republic of the Philippines
RPh registered pharmacist
rpm revolutions per minute
rps revolutions per second
rpt repeat, report
RQ respiratory quotient
RR railroad, rural route
RRT registered record technician
RS Received Standard, recording secretary, revised statutes, right side, Royal Society
RSA Republic of South Africa
RSFSR [Russian *Rossiĭskaya Sovetskaya Federativnaya Sotsialisticheskaya Respublika*] Russian Soviet Federated Socialist Republic
RSV Revised Standard Version
RSVP [French *répondez s'il vous plaît*] please reply
RSWC right side up with care
rt right, route
RT radiologic technologist, radiotelephone, respiratory therapy, room temperature, round-trip
rte route
rtw ready-to-wear
Ru ruthenium
Rum Rumania, Rumanian
Russ Russia, Russian
RV Revised Version
RW radiological warfare, right worshipful, right worthy
rwy *or* **ry** railway
s sabbath, saint, schilling, scruple, second, secondary, section, senate, series, shilling, [Latin *signa*] label; siemens, signor, sine, singular, small, smooth, snow, society, son, sou, south, southern, subject, symmetrical
S satisfactory, short, standard deviation of a sample, sulfur, svedberg
Sa Saturday
SA Salvation Army, seaman apprentice, sex appeal, [Latin *sine anno* without year] without date; South Af-

rica, South America, South Australia, subject to approval
sac sacrifice
SAC special agent in charge, Strategic Air Command
SAD seasonal affective disorder
SAE self-addressed envelope, Society of Automotive Engineers, stamped addressed envelope
SAG Screen Actors Guild
sal salary
SALT Strategic Arms Limitation Talks
Sam *or* **Saml** Samuel
san sanatorium
S&H shipping and handling
S and M sadism and masochism, sadist and masochist
sanit sanitary, sanitation
SAR search and rescue
SASE self-addressed stamped envelope
Sask Saskatchewan
sat saturate, saturated, saturation
Sat Saturday
satd saturated
S Aust South Australia
sb substantive
Sb [Latin *stibium*] antimony
SB [New Latin *scientiae baccalaureus*] bachelor of science; simultaneous broadcast, southbound
SBA Small Business Administration
SBN Standard Book Number
sc scale, scene, science, scilicet, screw, [Latin *sculpsit*] he carved it, she carved it, he engraved it, she engraved it
Sc scandium, Scots, stratocumulus
SC small capitals, South Carolina, supercalendered, supreme court
Scand Scandinavia, Scandinavian
SCAT School and College Ability Test, supersonic commercial air transport
ScD doctor of science
sch school
sci science, scientific
SCID severe combined immune deficiency, severe combined immunodeficiency
scil scilicet
SCLC Southern Christian Leadership Conference
Scot Scotland, Scottish
SCPO senior chief petty officer
script scripture
sct scout
sctd scattered
sd said, sewed
SD sea-damaged, sine die, South Dakota, special delivery, stage direction, standard deviation
S Dak South Dakota
SDI Strategic Defense Initiative
SDRs special drawing rights
SDS Students for a Democratic Society
Se selenium
SE self-explanatory, southeast, Standard English, stock exchange, straight edge
SEAL sea, air, land (team)
SEATO Southeast Asia Treaty Organization
sec secant, second, secondary, secretary, section, [Latin *secundum*] according to; security
SEC Securities and Exchange Commission
sect section, sectional
secy secretary
sed sediment, sedimentation
sel select, selected, selection
sem semicolon, seminar, seminary
Sem Semitic
sen senate, senator, senior
sep separate, separated
Sep September
SEP simplified employee pension
sepd separated
sepg separating
sepn separation

Sept September
seq [Latin *sequens, sequentes, sequentia*] the following
seqq [Latin *sequentia*] the following ones
ser serial, series, service
Serb Serbian
serg *or* **sergt** sergeant
serv service
SES socioeconomic status
sess session
sf *or* **sfz** sforzando
SF sacrifice fly, science fiction, sinking fund, square feet, square foot
SFC sergeant first class
SG senior grade, sergeant, solicitor general, *often not capitalized* specific gravity; surgeon general
sgd signed
Sgt sergeant
Sgt Maj sergeant major
sh share
Shak Shakespeare
shd should
Shet Shetland
SHF superhigh frequency
shipt shipment
shp shaft horsepower
shpt shipment
sht sheet
shtg shortage
Si silicon
SI [French *Système International d'Unités*] International System of Units
SIDS sudden infant death syndrome
sig signal, signature, signor
Sig [Latin *signa*] label
SIG special interest group
sigill [Latin *sigillum*] seal
sin sine
sing singular
SIS Secret Intelligence Service (British)
SJ Society of Jesus
SK Saskatchewan
sl slightly, slip, slow
SL salvage loss, sea level, south latitude
SLAN [Latin *sine loco, anno, (vel) nomine*] without place, year, or name
SLBM submarine-launched ballistic missile
sld sailed, sealed, sold
SLE systemic lupus erythematosus
Slo Sligo
SLR single-lens reflex
sm small
Sm samarium
SM [New Latin *scientiae magister*] master of science; sergeant major, service mark, soldier's medal, stage manager, station master
S–M *or* **S/M** sadomasochism, sadomasochist
SMA sergeant major of the army
SMaj sergeant major
SMSA Standard Metropolitan Statistical Area
SMSgt senior master sergeant
SMV slow-moving vehicle
Sn [Late Latin *stannum*] tin
SN seaman
SNCC Student Nonviolent Coordinating Committee
SNF skilled nursing facility
SNG substitute natural gas, synthetic natural gas
Snr *British* senior
so south, southern
SO seller's option, strikeout
soc social, society, sociology
sociol sociology, sociology
sol solicitor, soluble, solution
soln solution
Som Somersetshire
SOP standard operating procedure, standing operating procedure
soph sophomore
SO$_x$ sulfur oxide
sp special, species, specific, specimen, spelling, spirit

Sp Spain, Spanish

SP self-propelled, shore patrol, shore patrolman, shore police, [Latin *sine prole*] without issue; single pole, specialist

Span Spanish

SPCA Society for the Prevention of Cruelty to Animals

SPCC Society for the Prevention of Cruelty to Children

spd speed

spec special, specialist, specifically, specification

specif specific, specifically

SPF sun protection factor

sp gr specific gravity

sp ht specific heat

SPOT satellite positioning and tracking

spp species (*plural*)

SPQR [Latin *senatus populusque Romanus*] the senate and the people of Rome; small profits, quick returns

sps [Latin *sine prole superstite*] without surviving issue

sq squadron, square

Sr senior, senor, señor, sister, strontium

SR seaman recruit, sedimentation rate, shipping receipt

Sra senora, señora

SRO standing room only

Srta senorita, señorita

ss scilicet — used in legal documents, [Latin *semis*] one half

SS saints, same size, Social Security, steamship, sworn statement

SSA Social Security Administration

SSE south-southeast

SSG or **SSgt** staff sergeant

SSI supplemental security income

SSM staff sergeant major

SSN Social Security number

ssp subspecies

SSPE subacute sclerosing panencephalitis

SSR Soviet Socialist Republic

SSS Selective Service System

SSW south-southwest

st stanza, state, stitch, stone, street

St saint, stratus

ST short ton, single throw, standard time

sta station, stationary

Staffs Staffordshire

START strategic arms limitation talks

stat [Latin *statim*] immediately; statute

STB [New Latin *sacrae theologiae baccalaureus*] bachelor of sacred theology; [New Latin *scientiae theologicae baccalaureus*] bachelor of theology

stbd starboard

std standard

STD [New Latin *sacrae theologiae doctor*] doctor of sacred theology

Ste [French *sainte*] saint (female)

ster or **stg** sterling

stge storage

stk stock

STL [New Latin *sacrae theologiae licentiatus*] licentiate of sacred theology

STM [New Latin *sacrae theologiae magister*] master of sacred theology, scanning tunneling microscope; scanning tunneling microscopy

STOL short takeoff and landing

stor storage

STP standard temperature and pressure

str steamer, strophe

stud student

STV subscription television

Su Sunday

sub subaltern, subscription, subtract, suburb

subj subject, subjunctive

suff sufficient, suffix

Suff Suffolk

Sun Sunday

sup superior, supplement, supplementary, supply, supra

supp or **suppl** supplement, supplementary

supr supreme

supt superintendent

supvr supervisor

sur surface

surg surgeon, surgery, surgical

surv survey, surveying, surveyor

Suss Sussex

sv sailing vessel, saves, [Latin *sub verbo* or *sub voce*] under the word

svc or **svce** service

svgs savings

sw switch

Sw Sweden

SW seawater, shipper's weight, shortwave, southwest

SWAK sealed with a kiss

SWAT Special Weapons and Tactics

Swed Sweden, Swedish

SWG standard wire gauge

Switz Switzerland

syl or **syll** syllable

sym symbol, symmetrical

syn synonym, synonymous, synonymy

syst system

t metric ton, tablespoon, target, teaspoon, technical, temperature, [Latin *tempore*] in the time of; tense, tension, tertiary, time, ton, township, transitive, troy, true

T tera-, tesla, thymine, toddler, tritium, T-shirt

Ta tantalum

TA teaching assistant, transactional analysis

TAC Tactical Air Command

TAG the adjutant general

tan tangent

TAT thematic apperception test

taxon taxonomic, taxonomy

Tay Tayside

tb tablespoon, tablespoonful

Tb terbium

TB thoroughbred, trial balance, tubercle bacillus

TBA *often not capitalized* to be announced

TBD to be determined

tbs or **tbsp** tablespoon, tablespoonful

TBS talk between ships

tc tierce

Tc technetium

TC terra-cotta, till countermanded

TCE trichloroethylene

tchr teacher

TD tank destroyer, touchdown, Treasury Department

TDD telecommunications device for the deaf

TDN total digestible nutrients

TDY temporary duty

Te tellurium

tec technical, technician

tech technical, technically, technician, technological, technology

technol technological, technology

TEFL teaching English as a foreign language

tel telegram, telegraph, telephone

teleg telegraphy

temp temperance, template, temporal, temporary, [Latin *tempore*] in the time of

Tenn Tennessee

ter terrace, territory

terr territory

TESL teaching English as a second language

TESOL Teachers of English to Speakers of Other Languages

Test Testament

Tex Texas

TF task force, territorial force

tfr transfer

TFR total fertility rate

TG transformational grammar, type genus

TGIF thank God it's Friday

tgt target

TGV [French *train à grande vitesse*] high-speed train

Th thorium, Thursday

TH true heading

Thai Thailand

ThD [New Latin *theologiae doctor*] doctor of theology

theat theater, theatrical

theol theological, theology

therm thermometer

Thess Thessalonians

ThM [New Latin *theologiae magister*] master of theology

Thurs or **Thur** or **Thu** Thursday

Ti titanium

TIA transient ischemic attack

tid [Latin *ter in die*] three times a day

Tim Timothy

TIN taxpayer identification number

tinc tincture

Tip Tipperary

tit title

Tit Titus

tk tank, truck

tkt ticket

Tl thallium

TL total loss, truckload

TLC tender loving care, thin-layer chromatography

TLO total loss only

tlr tailor, trailer

Tm thulium

TM trademark, transcendental meditation

TMJ temporomandibular joint

TMO telegraph money order

tn ton, town, train

TN Tennessee, true north

TNF tumor necrosis factor

tng training

tnpk turnpike

TO table of organization, telegraph office, traditional orthography, turn over

Tob Tobit

TOEFL Test of English as a Foreign Language

tol tolerance

tonn tonnage

topo topographic, topographical

topog topography

tot total

TOT time on target

tp title page, township

TP triple play

TPA tissue plasminogen activator

tpk or **tpke** turnpike

tps townships, troops

tr translated, translation, translator, transpose, troop, trustee

trag tragedy, tragic

trans transaction, transitive, translated, translation, translator, transmission, transportation, transverse

transf transfer, transferred

transl translated, translation

transp transportation

trav travel, traveler, travels

treas treasurer, treasury

trib tributary

trit triturate

trop tropic, tropical

ts tensile strength

TSgt technical sergeant

TSH thyroid-stimulating hormone

tsp teaspoon, teaspoonful

TSS toxic shock syndrome

TT telegraphic transfer, teletypewriter, Trust Territories

TTY teletypewriter

Tu Tuesday

TU trade union, transmission unit

TUC Trades Union Congress

Tues or **Tue** Tuesday

Turk Turkey, Turkish

TV terminal velocity, transvestite

TVA Tennessee Valley Authority

2WD two-wheel drive

twp township

TWX teletypewriter exchange

TX Texas

Tyr Tyrone

u uncle, unit, unsymmetrical, upper

U [*Union of Orthodox Hebrew Congregations*] kosher certification — often enclosed in a circle; university, unsatisfactory, uracil, uranium

UAE United Arab Emirates

UAR United Arab Republic

UAW United Automobile Workers

UC undercharge, uppercase

ugt urgent

UHF ultrahigh frequency

UI unemployment insurance

UK United Kingdom

ult ultimate, ultimo

UMWA United Mine Workers of America

UN United Nations

unan unanimous

Unc uncirculated

UNCF United Negro College Fund

UNESCO United Nations Educational, Scientific, and Cultural Organization

Unh unnilhexium

uni uniform

UNICEF [*United Nations International Children's Emergency Fund,* its former name] United Nations Children's Fund

univ universal, university

unp unpaged

Unp unnilpentium

Unq unnilquadium

UNRWA United Nations Relief and Works Agency

uns unsymmetrical

UP underproof, Upper Peninsula (of Michigan)

UPC Universal Product Code

UPI United Press International

urol urological, urology

US [Latin *ubi supra*] where above mentioned; United States, [Latin *ut supra*] as above

USA United States Army, United States of America

USAF United States Air Force

USCG United States Coast Guard

USDA United States Department of Agriculture

USES United States Employment Service

USG United States government

USGA United States Golf Association

USGS United States Geological Survey

USIA United States Information Agency

USMC United States Marine Corps

USN United States Navy

USNR United States Naval Reserve

USNS United States Naval Ship

USO United Service Organizations

USP United States Pharmacopeia

USPS United States Postal Service

USS United States ship

USSR Union of Soviet Socialist Republics

USTA United States Tennis Association

usu usual, usually

UT Universal time, Utah

UTC Coordinated Universal Time

ut dict [Latin *ut dictum*] as directed

util utility

UV ultraviolet

UW underwriter

ux [Latin *uxor*] wife

UXB unexploded bomb

v vector, velocity, verb, verse, verso, versus, very, vice, victory, vide, voice, voltage, volume, vowel

V vanadium, volt

Va Virginia

VA Veterans Administration, vicar apostolic, vice admiral, Virginia, visual aid, volt-ampere

vac vacuum

VADM vice admiral

vag vagrancy

val value, valued

var variable, variant, variation, variety, various

VAR visual-aural range, volt-ampere reactive

VAT value-added tax

vb verb, verbal

VC veterinary corps, vice-chancellor, vice-consul, Victoria Cross, Vietcong

VD vapor density, various dates, venereal disease

VDRL venereal disease research laboratory

VDT video display terminal

VDU visual display unit

veg vegetable

vel vellum, velocity

Ven venerable

ver verse

vert vertebrate, vertical

VF very fair, very fine, video frequency, visual field, voice frequency

VFD volunteer fire department

VFR visual flight rules

VFW Veterans of Foreign Wars

VG very good, vicar-general

VHF very high frequency

vi verb intransitive, [Latin *vide infra*] see below

VI Virgin Islands, viscosity index, volume indicator

vic vicinity

Vic Victoria

vil village

VIN vehicle identification number

vis visibility, visible, visual

VISTA Volunteers in Service to America

viz videlicet

VJ veejay

VLF very low frequency

VMD [New Latin *veterinariae medicinae doctor*] doctor of veterinary medicine

VNA Visiting Nurse Association

VOA Voice of America

voc vocational, vocative

vocab vocabulary

vol volcano, volume, volunteer

VOM volt-ohmmeter

VOR very-high-frequency omnidirectional radio range

vou voucher

VP variable pitch, various places, verb phrase, vice president

VRM variable rate mortgage

vs verse, versus

VS veterinary surgeon, [Latin *vide supra*] see above

vss verses, versions

V/STOL vertical or short takeoff and landing

vt verb transitive

Vt Vermont

VT vacuum tube, variable time, Vermont, voice tube

VTOL vertical takeoff and landing

VTR videotape recorder

VU volume unit

Vulg Vulgate

vv verses, vice versa

w warden, water, week, weight, Welsh, west, western, white, wicket, wide, width, wife, with, withdrawal, work

W energy, [German *Wolfram*] tungsten; watt

WA Washington, Western Australia

war warrant

Warks Warwickshire

Wash Washington

Wat Waterford

WATS Wide-Area Telecommunications Service

W Aust Western Australia

Wb weber

WB water ballast, waybill, weather bureau, westbound, wheelbase

WBC white blood cells

WBF wood-burning fireplace

WC water closet, without charge

WCTU Women's Christian Temperance Union

wd wood, word, would

WD War Department

We *or* **Wed** Wednesday

Westm Westmeath, Westmorland

Wex Wexford

wf wrong font

WFTU World Federation of Trade Unions

wh which, white

WH watt-hour, withholding

whf wharf

WHO World Health Organization

whr watt-hour

whs *or* **whse** warehouse

whsle wholesale

wi when issued

WI West Indies, Wisconsin, wrought iron

WIA wounded in action

Wick Wicklow

wid widow, widower

Wilts Wiltshire

Wis *or* **Wisc** Wisconsin

Wisd Wisdom

wk week, work

wkly weekly

WL waterline, wavelength

wm wattmeter

wmk watermark

WNW west-northwest

WO warrant officer

w/o without

WOC without compensation

WP weather permitting, wettable powder, white phosphorus, without prejudice, word processing, word processor

WPA Works Progress Administration

wpc watts per candle, watts per channel

WPI Wholesale Price Index

WPM words per minute

wpn weapon

WR warehouse receipt, world record

WRAC Women's Royal Army Corps

WRAF Women's Royal Air Force

WRNS Women's Royal Naval Service

wrnt warrant

WRVS Women's Royal Voluntary Service

WSW west-southwest

wt weight

WT watertight, wireless telegraphy

wtd wanted

WV *or* **W Va** West Virginia

WVS Women's Voluntary Services

WW warehouse warrant, with warrants, world war

w/w wall-to-wall

WWW World Wide Web

WY *or* **Wyo** Wyoming

x cross, ex, experimental, extra

X–C cross-country

XD *or* **x div** ex dividend

Xe xenon

XL extra large, extra long

Xn Christian

Xnty Christianity

XO executive officer

XS extra small

XW ex warrants

y yard, year, yeoman

Y yttrium

YA young adult

Yb ytterbium

YB yearbook

YBP years before present

yd yard

yeo *or* **yeom** yeomanry

YO year old

YOB year of birth

Yorks Yorkshire

yr year, younger, your

yrbk yearbook

YT Yukon Territory

Yug Yugoslavia

z zero, zone

Z *or* **ZD** zenith distance

Zach Zacharias

Zech Zechariah

Zeph Zephaniah

ZI zone of interior

Zn [azimuth + *north*] azimuth; zinc

zool zoological, zoology

ZPG zero population growth

Zr zirconium

Foreign Words and Phrases

ab·eunt stu·dia in mo·res \'ä-be-,ûnt-'stü-dē-,ä-,in-'mō-,räs\ [Latin] **:** practices zealously pursued pass into habits

à bien·tôt \à-byaⁿ-tō\ [French] **:** so long

ab in·cu·na·bu·lis \,äb-,iŋ-kû-'nä-bû-,lēs\ [Latin] **:** from the cradle **:** from infancy

à bon chat, bon rat \à-bōⁿ-'shà bōⁿ-'rà\ [French] **:** to a good cat, a good rat **:** retaliation in kind

à bouche ou·verte \à-bü-shü-vert\ [French] **:** with open mouth **:** eagerly **:** uncritically

ab ovo us·que ad ma·la \'äb-'ō-vō-,ûs-kwe-,äd-'mä-lä\ [Latin] **:** from egg to apples **:** from soup to nuts **:** from beginning to end

à bras ou·verts \à-brà-zü-ver\ [French] **:** with open arms **:** cordially

ab·sit in·vi·dia \'äb-,sit-in-'wi-dē-,ä\ [Latin] **:** let there be no envy or ill will

ab uno dis·ce om·nes \äb-'ü-nō-,dis-ke-'óm-,näs\ [Latin] **:** from one learn to know all

ab ur·be con·di·ta \äb-'ûr-be-'kón-di-,tä\ [Latin] **:** from the founding of the city (Rome, founded 753 B.C.) — used by the Romans in reckoning dates

ab·usus non tol·lit usum \'ä,-bü-sûs-,nōn-,tó-lit-'ü-sûm\ [Latin] **:** abuse does not take away use, i.e., is not an argument against proper use

à compte \à-'kōⁿt\ [French] **:** on account

à coup sûr \à-kü-sûr\ [French] **:** with sure stroke **:** surely

acte gra·tuit \àk-tə -grà-tw^yē\ [French] **:** gratuitous impulsive act

ad ar·bi·tri·um \,ad-är-'bi-trē-ûm\ [Latin] **:** at will **:** arbitrarily

ad as·tra per as·pe·ra \ad-'as-trə-,pər-'as-pə-rä\ [Latin] **:** to the stars by hard ways — motto of Kansas

ad ex·tre·mum \,ad-ik-'strē-məm\ [Latin] **:** to the extreme **:** at last

ad ka·len·das Grae·cas \,äd-kä-'len-däs-'grī-,käs\ [Latin] **:** at the Greek calends **:** never (since the Greeks had no calends)

ad ma·jo·rem Dei glo·ri·am \äd-mä-'yōr-,em-'de-,ē-'glōr-ē-,äm, -'yòr-, -'glór-\ [Latin] **:** to the greater glory of God — motto of the Society of Jesus

ad pa·tres \äd-'pä-,träs\ [Latin] **:** (gathered) to his fathers **:** deceased

ad re·fe·ren·dum \äd-,re-fe-'ren-dùm\ [Latin] **:** for reference **:** for further consideration by one having the authority to make a final decision

à droite \à-drwàt\ [French] **:** to or on the right hand

ad un·guem \äd-'ûŋ-,gwem\ [Latin] **:** to the fingernail **:** to a nicety **:** exactly (from the use of the fingernail to test the smoothness of marble)

ad utrum·que pa·ra·tus \äd-ü-'trùm-kwe-pä-'rä-tùs\ [Latin] **:** prepared for either (event)

ad vi·vum \äd-'wē-,wùm\ [Latin] **:** to the life

ae·gri som·nia \'ī-grē-'sóm-nē-,ä\ [Latin] **:** a sick man's dreams

ae·quam ser·va·re men·tem \'ī-,kwäm-ser-,wä-rä-'men-,tem\ [Latin] **:** to preserve a calm mind

ae·quo ani·mo \,ī-,kwō-'ä-ni-,mō\ [Latin] **:** with even mind **:** calmly

ae·re per·en·ni·us \'ī-rä-pe-'re-nē-,ús\ [Latin] **:** more lasting than bronze

à gauche \à-gōsh\ [French] **:** to or on the left hand

age quod agis \'ä-ge-,kwód-'ä-,gis\ [Latin] **:** do what you are doing **:** to the business at hand

à grands frais \à-gräⁿ-fre\ [French] **:** at great expense

à huis clos \à-w^yē-klō\ [French] **:** with closed doors

aide–toi, le ciel t'ai·dera \ed-twà lə-'syel-te-drà\ [French] **:** help yourself (and) heaven will help you

aî·né \e-nä\ [French] **:** elder **:** senior (masculine)

aî·née \e-nä\ [French] **:** elder **:** senior (feminine)

à l'aban·don \à-là-bän-dōⁿ\ [French] **:** carelessly **:** in disorder

à la belle étoile \à-là-bel-ä-twàl\ [French] **:** under the beautiful star **:** in the open air at night

à la bonne heure \à-là-bò-nœr\ [French] **:** at a good time **:** well and good **:** all right

à la fran·çaise \à-là-fräⁿ-sez\ [French] **:** in the French manner

à l'amé·ri·caine \à-là-mä-rē-ken\ [French] **:** in the American manner **:** of the American kind

à l'an·glaise \à-läⁿ-glez\ [French] **:** in the English manner

à la page \à-là-pàzh\ [French] **:** at the page **:** up-to-the-minute

à la russe \à-là-rēs\ [French] **:** in the Russian manner

alea jac·ta est \'ä-lē-,ä-,yäk-tä-'est\ [Latin] **:** the die is cast

à l'im·pro·viste \à-laⁿ-prò-vēst\ [French] **:** unexpectedly

ali·quan·do bo·nus dor·mi·tat Ho·me·rus \,ä-li-,kwän-dō-'bó-nùs-dòr-'mē-,tät-hō-'mer-ùs\ [Latin] **:** sometimes (even) good Homer nods

alis vo·lat pro·pri·is \'ä-,lēs-'wò-,lät-'prō-prē-,ēs\ [Latin] **:** she flies with her own wings — motto of Oregon

al–ki \'al-,kī, -kē\ [Chinook Jargon] **:** by and by — motto of Washington

alo·ha oe \ä-,lō-hä-'ói, -'ō-ē\ [Hawaiian] **:** love to you **:** greetings **:** farewell

al·ter Chris·tus \,äl-ter-'kris-tùs\ [Latin] **:** another Christ

al·ter idem \,òl-tər-'ī-,dem, ,äl-ter-'ē-\ [Latin] **:** second self

a max·i·mis ad mi·ni·ma \ä-'mäk-si-,mēs-,äd-'mi-ni-,mä\ [Latin] **:** from the greatest to the least

à mer·veille \à-mer-vey\ [French] **:** marvelously

ami·cus hu·ma·ni ge·ne·ris \à-'mē-kùs-hü-,mä-nē-'ge-ne-ris\ [Latin] **:** friend of the human race

ami·cus us·que ad aras \-,ùs-kwe-,äd-'är-,äs\ [Latin] **:** a friend as far as to the altars, i.e., except in what is contrary to one's religion; *also* **:** a friend to the last extremity

ami de cour \à-,mē-də-'kùr\ [French] **:** court friend **:** insincere friend

amor pa·tri·ae \'ä-,mòr-'pä -trē-,ī\ [Latin] **:** love of one's country

amor vin·cit om·nia \'ä-,mòr,-wiŋ-kit-'óm-nē-ä\ [Latin] **:** love conquers all things

an·cienne no·blesse \äⁿ-syen-nò-bles\ [French] **:** old-time nobility **:** the French nobility before the Revolution of 1789

an·guis in her·ba \,äŋ-gwis-in-'her-,bä\ [Latin] **:** snake in the grass

ani·mal bi·pes im·plu·me \'ä-ni-,mäl,-bi-,päs-im-'plü-me\ [Latin] **:** two-legged animal without feathers (i.e., the human race)

ani·mis opi·bus·que pa·ra·ti \'ä-ni-,mēs,-ó-pi-'bùs-kwe-pä-'rä-tē\ [Latin] **:** prepared in mind and resources — one of the mottoes of South Carolina

an·no ae·ta·tis su·ae \'ä-nō-ī-,tä-tis-'sü-,ī\ [Latin] **:** in the (specified) year of his (or her) age

an·no mun·di \,ä-nō-'mûn-dē\ [Latin] **:** in the year of the world — used in reckoning dates from the supposed period of the creation of the world, especially as fixed by James Ussher at 4004 B.C. or by the Jews at 3761 B.C.

an·no ur·bis con·di·tae \,ä-nō-,ûr-bis-'kón-di-,tī\ [Latin] **:** in the year of the founded city (Rome, founded 753 B.C.)

an·nu·it coep·tis \,ä-nü-,it-'kóip-,tēs\ [Latin] **:** He (God) has approved our beginnings — motto on the reverse of the Great Seal of the United States

à peu près \à-pœ-pre\ [French] **:** nearly **:** approximately

à pied \à-pyä\ [French] **:** on foot

après moi le dé·luge \à-pre-mwà-lə-dā-lūzh\ *or* **après nous le déluge** \à-pre-nü-\ [French] **:** after me the deluge — attributed to Louis XV

à pro·pos de bottes \à-prə-pō-də-bót\ [French] **:** apropos of boots — used to change the subject

à pro·pos de rien \-ryaⁿ\ [French] **:** apropos of nothing

aqua et ig·ni in·ter·dic·tus \,ä-kwä-et-'ig-nē-,in-ter-'dik-tùs\ [Latin] **:** forbidden to be furnished with water and fire **:** outlawed

Ar·ca·des am·bo \'är-kä-,des-'äm-bō\ [Latin] **:** both Arcadians **:** two persons of like occupations or tastes; *also* **:** two rascals

ar·gu·men·tum ad ba·cu·lum \,är-gù-'men-tùm-,äd-'bä-kù-lùm\ [Latin] **:** argument of the staff **:** appeal to force

ar·rec·tis au·ri·bus \ä-'rek-,tēs-'aù-ri-,bùs\ [Latin] **:** with ears pricked up **:** attentively

ar·ri·ve·der·ci \,är-ē-vä-'der-chē\ [Italian] **:** till we meet again **:** farewell

ars est ce·la·re ar·tem \,ärs-,est-kä-,lär-ā-'är-,tem\ [Latin] **:** it is (true) art to conceal art

ars lon·ga, vi·ta bre·vis \,ärs-'lóŋ-,gä ,wē-,tä-'bre-wis\ [Latin] **:** art is long, life is short

a ter·go \ä-'ter-(,)gō\ [Latin] **:** from behind

à tort et à tra·vers \à-,tòr-ā-à-trà-ver\ [French] **:** wrong and crosswise **:** at random **:** without rhyme or reason

au bout de son la·tin \ō-büd-sōⁿ-là-taⁿ, -bü-də-\ [French] **:** at the end of one's Latin **:** at the end of one's mental resources

au con·traire \ō-kōⁿ-trer\ [French] **:** on the contrary

au·de·mus ju·ra nos·tra de·fen·de·re \aù-'dā-mùs,-yùr-ä-'nò-strä-dā-'fen-de-rä\ [Latin] **:** we dare defend our rights — motto of Alabama

au·den·tes for·tu·na ju·vat \aù-'den-,täs-fòr-,tü-nä-'yù-,wät\ [Latin] **:** fortune favors the bold

au·di al·te·ram par·tem \'aù-,dē-,äl-te-,räm-'pär-,tem\ [Latin] **:** hear the other side

au fait \ō-fet, -fe\ [French] **:** to the point **:** fully competent **:** fully informed **:** socially correct

au fond \ō-fōⁿ\ [French] **:** at bottom **:** fundamentally

au grand sé·rieux \ō-gräⁿ-sä-ryœ\ [French] **:** in all seriousness

au mieux \ō-myœ\ [French] **:** on the best terms **:** on intimate terms

\ə\ abut \^ə\ kitten \ər\ further \a\ ash \ā\ ace \ä\ mop, mar \aù\ out \ch\ chin \e\ bet \ē\ easy \g\ go \i\ hit \ī\ ice \j\ job \ŋ\ sing \ō\ go \ò\ law \òi\ boy \th\ thin \t̲h̲\ the \ü\ loot \ù\ foot \y\ yet \zh\ vision *see also* Guide to Pronunciation

au pays des aveugles les borgnes sont rois \ō-pā-ē-dā-zá-vœgl³-lā-bȯrn^y-ə-sȯⁿ-rwá, -rwä\ [French] **:** in the country of the blind the one-eyed men are kings

au·rea me·di·o·cri·tas \àu-rē-ä-me-dē-'ó-kri-,täs\ [Latin] **:** the golden mean

au reste \ō-rest\ [French] **:** for the rest **:** besides

au sé·rieux \ō-sā-ryœ̄\ [French] **:** seriously

au·spi·ci·um me·li·o·ris ae·vi \àu-'spi-kē-,ùm-,me-lē-,ōr-is-'ī-,wē\ [Latin] **:** an omen of a better age — motto of the Order of St. Michael and St. George

aus·si·tôt dit, aus·si·tôt fait \ō-sē-tō-dē ō-sē-tō-fe\ [French] **:** no sooner said than done

aut Cae·sar aut ni·hil \àut-'kī-sär-,àut-'ni-,hil\ [Latin] **:** either a Caesar or nothing

aut Caesar aut nul·lus \-'nù-lùs\ [Latin] **:** either a Caesar or a nobody

au·tres temps, au·tres mœurs \ō-trə-täⁿ ō-trə-mœrs\ [French] **:** other times, other customs

aut vin·ce·re aut mo·ri \àut-'wiŋ-ke-rä-,àut-'mó-,rē\ [Latin] **:** either to conquer or to die

aux armes \ō-zárm\ [French] **:** to arms

avant la lettre \á-väⁿ-lä-letr³\ [French] **:** before the letter **:** before a (specified) name existed

avant–pro·pos \á-väⁿ-prò-pō\ [French] **:** preface

ave at·que va·le \'ä-,wā-,ät-kwe-'wä-,lā\ [Latin] **:** hail and farewell

à vo·tre san·té \á-vȯt-säⁿ-tā, -vȯ-trə-\ [French] **:** to your health — used as a toast

beaux yeux \bō-zyœ̄\ [French] **:** beautiful eyes **:** beauty of face

bel·la fi·gu·ra \'bel-lə-fē-'gü-rä\ [Italian] **:** fine appearance or impression

belle laide \bel-led\ [French] **:** beautiful ugly woman **:** woman who is attractive though not conventionally beautiful

bel·lum om·ni·um con·tra om·nes \'be-lúm-'òm-nē-ùm-,kón-trä-'óm-,nās\ [Latin] **:** war of all against all

bien en·ten·du \byä-näⁿ-täⁿ-dœ\ [French] **:** well understood **:** of course

bien–pen·sant \byä-paⁿ-säⁿ\ [French] **:** right-minded **:** one who holds orthodox views

bien·sé·ance \byä-sā-äⁿs\ [French] **:** propriety

bien vu \byä-vœ\ [French] **:** well regarded

bis dat qui ci·to dat \'bis-,dät-kwē-'ki-tō-,dät\ [Latin] **:** he gives twice who gives promptly

bon ap·pé·tit \bó-ná-pā-tē\ [French] **:** good appetite **:** enjoy your meal

bon gré, mal gré \'bōⁿ,grä-'mál,grä\ [French] **:** whether with good grace or bad **:** willy-nilly

bo·nis avi·bus \,bó-,nēs-'ä-wi,bùs\ [Latin] **:** under good auspices

bon·jour \bōⁿ-zhür\ [French] **:** good day **:** good morning

bonne foi \bón-fwä\ [French] **:** good faith

bon·soir \bōⁿ-swár\ [French] **:** good evening

bru·tum ful·men \,brü-tùm-'fùl-men\ [Latin] **:** insensible thunderbolt **:** a futile threat or display of force

ca·dit quae·stio \,kä-dit-'kwī-stē-,ō\ [Latin] **:** the question drops **:** the argument collapses

ca·pable de tout \ká-,pábl³-də-tü\ [French] **:** capable of anything **:** unpredictable

carte d'iden·ti·té \kárt-dē-däⁿ-tē-tā\ [French] **:** identity card

cau·sa si·ne qua non \'kaù-,sä-,si-nā-kwä-'nōn\ [Latin] **:** an indispensable cause or condition

ça va sans dire \sá-vá-säⁿ-dēr\ [French] **:** it goes without saying

ca·ve·at lec·tor \'ká-vē-,ät-'lek,tór, 'ka-\ [Latin] **:** let the reader beware

ca·ve ca·nem \,kä-wā-'kä-,nem\ [Latin] **:** beware the dog

ce·dant ar·ma to·gae \'kā-,dänt-,är-mə-'tō-,gī\ [Latin] **:** let arms yield to the toga **:** let military power give way to civil power — motto of Wyoming

ce n'est que le pre·mier pas qui coûte \snek-lə-prə-myä-pä-kē-küt\ [French] **:** it is only the first step that costs

c'est–à–dire \se-tá-dēr\ [French] **:** that is to say **:** namely

c'est au·tre chose \se-tōt-shōz, -tō-trə-\ [French] **:** that's a different thing

c'est la guerre \se-là-ger\ [French] **:** that's war **:** it cannot be helped

c'est la vie \se-là-vē\ [French] **:** that's life **:** that's how things happen

c'est plus qu'un crime, c'est une faute \se-plœ-kœⁿ-krēm se-tœn-fōt\ [French] **:** it is worse than a crime, it is a blunder

ce·te·ra de·sunt \,kā-te,rä-'dā-,sùnt\ [Latin] **:** the rest is missing

cha·cun à son goût \shá-kœⁿ-ná-sōⁿ-gü\ [French] **:** everyone to his taste

châ·teau en Es·pagne \shä-tō-äⁿ-nes-pán^y\ [French] **:** castle in Spain **:** a visionary project

cher·chez la femme \sher-shä-là-fám\ [French] **:** look for the woman

che sa·rà, sa·rà \,kā-sä-,rä-sä-'rä\ [Italian] **:** what will be, will be

che·val de ba·taille \shə-vál-də-bá-tä^y\ [French] **:** warhorse **:** argument constantly relied on **:** favorite subject

ci–gît \sē-zhē\ [French] **:** here lies — used preceding a name on a tombstone

co·gi·to, er·go sum \'kō-gi-,tō,-er-gō-'sùm\ [Latin] **:** I think, therefore I exist

co·mé·die hu·maine \kȯ-mā-dē-œ-men\ [French] **:** human comedy **:** the whole variety of human life

comédie lar·moy·ante \-lár-mwá-yäⁿt\ [French] **:** tearful comedy **:** sentimental comedy

comme ci, comme ça \kȯm-sē-kȯm-sá\ [French] **:** so-so

com·pa·gnon de voy·age \kōⁿ-pá-n^yōⁿ-də-vwá-yäzh\ [French] **:** traveling companion

compte ren·du \kōⁿt-räⁿ-dœ\ [French] **:** report (as of proceedings in an investigation)

con·cor·dia dis·cors \kón-'kȯr-dē-ä-'dis-,kȯrs\ [Latin] **:** discordant harmony

con·fes·sio fi·dei \kȯn-'fe-sē-ō-'fi-dē-,ē\ [Latin] **:** confession of faith

con·temp·tus mun·di \kȯn-'tem(p)-tùs-'mùn-dē\ [Latin] **:** contempt for the world

cor·rup·tio op·ti·mi pes·si·ma \kȯ-'rùp-tē-,ō-'äp-ti-,mē-'pe-si-,mä\ [Latin] **:** the corruption of the best is the worst of all

coup de maî·tre \küd-metr³, kü-də-\ [French] **:** masterstroke

coup d'es·sai \kü-dā-se\ [French] **:** experiment **:** trial

coûte que coûte \küt-kə-küt\ [French] **:** cost what it may

cre·do quia ab·sur·dum est \,krä-dō-'kwē-ä-äp-,sùr-dùm-'est\ [Latin] **:** I believe it because it is absurd

cre·do ut in·tel·li·gam \,krä-dō-,ùt-in-'te-lē-,gäm\ [Latin] **:** I believe so that I may understand

cres·cit eun·do \,kres-kit-'eùn-dō\ [Latin] **:** it grows as it goes — motto of New Mexico

crise de conscience \krēz-də-kōⁿ-syäⁿs\ [French] **:** crisis of conscience **:** agonizing period of moral uncertainty

crise de nerfs or **crise des nerfs** \krēz-də-ner\ [French] **:** crisis of nerves **:** nervous collapse **:** hysterical fit

crux cri·ti·co·rum \'krúks-,kri-ti-'kȯr-ùm\ [Latin] **:** crux of critics

cuj·us re·gio, ej·us re·li·gio \'kü-yùs-'re-gē-,ō,e-yùs-re-'li-gē-,ō\ [Latin] **:** whose region, his or her religion **:** subjects are to accept the religion of their ruler

cum gra·no sa·lis \,kùm-,grä-nō-'sä-lis\ [Latin] **:** with a grain of salt

cur·sus ho·no·rum \'kúr-sùs-hȯ-'nō-rùm\ [Latin] **:** course of honors **:** succession of offices of increasing importance

cus·tos mo·rum \,kùs-tōs-'mōr-ùm\ [Latin] **:** guardian of manners or morals **:** censor

d'ac·cord \dá-kȯr\ [French] **:** in accord **:** agreed

dame d'hon·neur \dám-dȯ-nœr\ [French] **:** lady-in-waiting

dam·nant quod non in·tel·li·gunt \'däm-,nänt-,kwȯd-,nōn-in-'te-li-,gùnt\ [Latin] **:** they condemn what they do not understand

de bonne grâce \də-bȯn-gräs\ [French] **:** with good grace **:** willingly

de gus·ti·bus non est dis·pu·tan·dum \dā-'gùs-tə-,bùs-,nōn-,est-,dis-pü-'tän-,dúm\ [Latin] **:** there is no disputing about tastes

Dei gra·tia \,de-,ē-'grä-tē-,ä\ [Latin] **:** by the grace of God

de in·te·gro \dā-'in-te-,grō\ [Latin] **:** anew **:** afresh

de l'au·dace, en·core de l'au·dace, et tou·jours de l'au·dace \də-lō-'dás äⁿ-'kȯr-də-lō-dás ā-tü-'zhür-də-lō-dás\ [French] **:** audacity, more audacity, and ever more audacity

de·len·da est Car·tha·go \dā-'len-dä-,est-kär-'tä-gō\ [Latin] **:** Carthage must be destroyed

de·li·ne·a·vit \dā-,lē-nä-'ä-wit\ [Latin] **:** he (or she) drew it

de mal en pis \də-má-läⁿ-pē\ [French] **:** from bad to worse

de mi·ni·mis non cu·rat lex \dā-'mi-ni-,mēs-,nōn-,kü-,rät-'leks\ [Latin] **:** the law takes no account of trifles

de mor·tu·is nil ni·si bo·num \dā-'mȯr-tù-,ēs-,nēl-,ni-sē-'bȯ-,nùm\ [Latin] **:** of the dead (say) nothing but good

de nos jours \də-nō-zhür\ [French] **:** of our time **:** contemporary — used postpositively especially after a proper name

Deo fa·ven·te \,dā-ō-fä-'ven-tā\ [Latin] **:** with God's favor

Deo gra·ti·as \,dā-ō-'grä-tē-,äs\ [Latin] **:** thanks (be) to God

de pro·fun·dis \,dā-prō-'fùn-dēs, -'fən-\ [Latin] **:** out of the depths

der Geist der stets ver·neint \dər-'gīst-dər-,shtäts-fer-'nīnt\ [German] **:** the spirit that ever denies — applied originally to Mephistopheles

de·si·pe·re in lo·co \dā-'si-pe-rä-in-'lō-kō\ [Latin] **:** to indulge in trifling at the proper time

De·us ab·scon·di·tus \,dā-ús-,äp-'skȯn-di-,tús\ [Latin] **:** hidden God **:** God unknowable by the human mind

De·us vult \,dā-ùs-'wúlt\ [Latin] **:** God wills it — rallying cry of the First Crusade

di·es fau·stus \,dē-,ās-'faù-stùs\ [Latin] **:** lucky day

dies in·fau·stus \-'in-,faù-stùs\ [Latin] **:** unlucky day

dies irae \-'ē-,rī, -,rä\ [Latin] **:** day of wrath — used of the Judgment Day

Dieu et mon droit \dyœ̄-ā-mōⁿ-drwä\ [French] **:** God and my right — motto on the British royal arms

Dieu vous garde \dyœ̄-vü-gárd\ [French] **:** God keep you

di·ri·go \'dē-ri-,gō\ [Latin] **:** I direct — motto of Maine

dis ali·ter vi·sum \,dēs-,ä-li-,ter-'wē-,sùm\ [Latin] **:** the Gods decreed otherwise

dis·cor·dia con·cors \dis-'kȯr-dē-ä-'kȯn-,kȯrs\ [Latin] **:** harmonious discord **:** harmony or unity gained by combining disparate or conflicting elements

di·tat De·us \,dē-,tät-'dā-,ùs\ [Latin] **:** God enriches — motto of Arizona

di·vi·de et im·pe·ra \'dē-wi-,de-,et-'im-pe-,rä\ [Latin] **:** divide and rule

do·cen·do dis·ci·mus \dȯ-,ken-dō-'dis-ki-,mùs\ [Latin] **:** we learn by teaching

dol·ce stil nuo·vo \'dȯl-chä-stēl-'nwȯ-vō\ [Italian] **:** sweet new style

Do·mi·ne, di·ri·ge nos \'dȯ-mi-,ne-'dē-ri-,ge-'nōs\ [Latin] **:** Lord, direct us — motto of the City of London

Do·mi·nus vo·bis·cum \'dȯ-mi-,nùs-wō-'bēs-,kùm\ [Latin] **:** the Lord be with you

dul·ce et de·co·rum est pro pa·tria mo·ri \,dúl-,ke-et-de-'kȯr-ùm-,est-prō-,pä-trē-,ä-'mó-,rē\ [Latin] **:** it is sweet and seemly to die for one's country

dum spi·ro, spe·ro \,dùm-'spē-rō-'spä-rō\ [Latin] **:** while I breathe, I hope — one of the mottoes of South Carolina

dum vi·vi·mus vi·va·mus \,dùm-'wē-wē-,mùs-wē-'wä-mùs\ [Latin] **:** while we live, let us live

d'un cer·tain âge \dœⁿ-ser-te-näzh\ [French] **:** of a certain age **:** no longer young

dux fe·mi·na fac·ti \,dúks-,fā-mi-nä-'fäk-,tē\ [Latin] **:** a woman was leader of the exploit

ec·ce sig·num \,e-ke-'sig-,nùm\ [Latin] **:** behold the sign **:** look at the proof

e con·tra·rio \,ā-kȯn-'trär-ē-,ō\ [Latin] **:** on the contrary

écra·sez l'in·fâme \ā-krä-zā-laⁿ-fäm\ [French] **:** crush the infamous thing

eheu fu·ga·ces la·bun·tur an·ni \ā-,heú-fù-'gä-,käs-lä-'bùn-,túr-'ä-,nē\ [Latin] **:** alas! the fleeting years glide on

ein' fes·te Burg ist un·ser Gott \īn-ˌfes-tə-'bu̇rk-ist-ˌu̇n-zər-'gȯt\ [German] **:** a mighty fortress is our God

em·bar·ras de ri·chesses *or* **embarras de ri·chesse** \äⁿ-bȧ-räd-rē-shes, -rä-də-\ [French] **:** embarrassing surplus of riches **:** confusing abundance

em·bar·ras de choix \äⁿ-bȧ-rä-də-shwȧ\ *or* **embarras du choix** \-du̇-shwȧ\ [French] **:** embarrassing variety of choice

en ami \äⁿ-nȧ-mē\ [French] **:** as a friend

en ef·fet \äⁿ-nā-fe\ [French] **:** in fact **:** indeed

en fa·mille \äⁿ-fȧ-mēy\ [French] **:** in or with one's family **:** at home **:** informally

en·fant ché·ri \äⁿ-fäⁿ-shä-rē\ [French] **:** loved or pampered child **:** one that is highly favored

en·fant gâ·té \äⁿ-fäⁿ-gä-tā\ [French] **:** spoiled child

en·fants per·dus \äⁿ-fäⁿ-per-dœ\ [French] **:** lost children **:** soldiers sent to a dangerous post

en·fin \äⁿ-faⁿ\ [French] **:** in conclusion **:** in a word

en gar·çon \äⁿ-gȧr-sōⁿ\ [French] **:** as or like a bachelor

en garde \äⁿ-gȧrd\ [French] **:** on guard

en pan·tou·fles \äⁿ-päⁿ-tüflᵊ\ [French] **:** in slippers **:** at ease **:** informally

en plein air \äⁿ-ple-ner\ [French] **:** in the open air

en plein jour \äⁿ-plaⁿ-zhu̇r\ [French] **:** in broad day

en poste \äⁿ-pȯst\ [French] **:** in a diplomatic post

en re·tard \äⁿr-(ə-)tȧr\ [French] **:** behind time **:** late

en re·traite \äⁿr-(ə-)tret\ [French] **:** in retreat **:** in retirement

en re·vanche \äⁿr-(ə-)väⁿsh\ [French] **:** in return **:** in compensation

en se·condes noces \äⁿs-gōⁿd-nȯs, äⁿ-sə-\ [French] **:** in a second marriage

en·se pe·tit pla·ci·dam sub li·ber·ta·te qui·e·tem \ˌen-se-pe-tit-'plä-ki-ˌdäm-sub-ˌlē-ber-ˌtä-te-kwē-'ä-ˌtem\ [Latin] **:** with the sword she seeks calm repose under liberty **:** by the sword we seek peace, but peace only under liberty — motto of Massachusetts

eo ip·so \ā-ō-'ip-(ˌ)sō\ [Latin] **:** by that itself **:** by that fact alone

épa·ter le bour·geois \ā-pȧ-tä-lə-bür-zhwȧ\ *or* **épater les bourgeois** \-lā-bür-\ [French] **:** to shock the middle classes

e plu·ri·bus unum \ˌē-ˌplu̇r-ə-bəs-'(y)ü-nəm, ˌā-ˌplu̇r-i-bu̇s-'ü-nu̇m\ [Latin] **:** one out of many — used on the Great Seal of the U.S. and on several U.S. coins

ep·pur si muo·ve \āp-ˌpür-sē-'mwȯ-vā\ [Italian] **:** and yet it does move — attributed to Galileo after recanting his assertion of the earth's motion

Erin go bragh \ˌer-ən-gə-'brȯ, -gō-'brä\ [Irish *go brách* or *go bráth*, lit., till doomsday] **:** Ireland forever

er·ra·re hu·ma·num est \e-'rär-ā-hü-ˌmä-nùm-'est\ [Latin] **:** to err is human

es·prit de l'es·ca·lier \es-prēd-les-kȧ-lyā\ *or* **esprit d'es·ca·lier** \-prē-des-\ [French] **:** wit of the staircase **:** repartee thought of only too late, on the way home

es·se quam vi·de·ri \'e-sā-ˌkwäm-wi-'dā-rē\ [Latin] **:** to be rather than to seem — motto of North Carolina

est mo·dus in re·bus \est-'mȯ-ˌdùs-in-'rä-ˌbùs\ [Latin] **:** there is a proper measure in things, i.e., the golden mean should always be observed

es·to per·pe·tua \'es-ˌtō-per-'pe-tù-ˌä\ [Latin] **:** may she endure forever — motto of Idaho

et hoc ge·nus om·ne \et-ˌhōk-ˌge-nùs-'ȯm-ne\ *or* **et id genus omne** \et-ˌid-\ [Latin] **:** and everything of this kind

et in Ar·ca·dia ego \et-in-ˌär-ˌkä-dē-ä-'e-gō\ [Latin] **:** I too (lived) in Arcadia

et sic de si·mi·li·bus \et-ˌsēk-dä-si-'mi-li-ˌbùs\ [Latin] **:** and so of like things

et tu Bru·te \et-'tü-ˌbrü-te\ [Latin] **:** thou too, Brutus — exclamation attributed to Julius Caesar on seeing his friend Brutus among his assassins

eu·re·ka \yu̇-'rē-kä\ [Greek] **:** I have found it — motto of California

Ewig—Weib·li·che \ˌā-vik-'vīp-li-kə\ [German] **:** eternal feminine

ex·al·té \eg-zȧl-tā\ [French] **:** emotionally excited or elated **:** fanatic

ex ani·mo \eks-'ä-ni-ˌmō\ [Latin] **:** from the heart **:** sincerely

ex·cel·si·or \ik-'sel-sē-ər, eks-'kel-sē-ˌȯr\ [Latin] **:** still higher — motto of New York

ex·cep·tio pro·bat re·gu·lam de re·bus non ex·cep·tis \eks-'kep-tē-ō-ˌprō-bät-'rä-gù-ˌläm-dā-'rä-ˌbùs-ˌnōn-eks-'kep-ˌtēs\ [Latin] **:** an exception establishes the rule as to things not excepted

ex·cep·tis ex·ci·pi·en·dis \eks-'kep-ˌtēs-eks-ˌki-pē-'en-ˌdēs\ [Latin] **:** with the proper or necessary exceptions

ex·i·tus ac·ta pro·bat \'ek-si-ˌtùs-ˌäk-tä-'prō-ˌbät\ [Latin] **:** the outcome justifies the deed

ex li·bris \eks-'lē-bris\ [Latin] **:** from the books of — used on bookplates

ex me·ro mo·tu \eks-ˌmer-ō-'mō-tü\ [Latin] **:** out of mere impulse **:** of one's own accord

ex ne·ces·si·ta·te rei \eks-ne-ˌke-si-'tä-te-'rä(-ˌē)\ [Latin] **:** from the necessity of the case

ex ni·hi·lo ni·hil fit \eks-'ni-hi-ˌlō-ˌni-ˌhil-'fit\ [Latin] **:** from nothing nothing is produced

ex pe·de Her·cu·lem \eks-ˌpe-de-'her-kù-ˌlem\ [Latin] **:** from the foot (we may judge of the size of) Hercules **:** from a part we may judge of the whole

ex·per·to cre·de \eks-ˌper-tō-'krä-de\ *or* **ex·perto cre·di·te** \-'krä-di-ˌte\ [Latin] **:** believe one who has had experience **:** trust me

ex un·gue le·o·nem \eks-'ùŋ-gwe-le-'ō-ˌnem\ [Latin] **:** from the claw (we may judge of) the lion **:** from a part we may judge of the whole

ex vi ter·mi·ni \eks-ˌwē-'ter-mə-ˌnē\ [Latin] **:** from the force of the term

fa·ci·le prin·ceps \fä-ki-le-'priŋ-ˌkeps\ [Latin] **:** easily first

fa·ci·lis de·scen·sus Aver·no \'fä-ki-ˌlis-dā-ˌskän-ˌsùs-ä-'wer-nō\ *or* **facilis descensus Aver·ni** \-(ˌ)nē\ [Latin] **:** the descent to Avernus is easy **:** the road to evil is easy

fa·çon de par·ler \fȧ-sōⁿ-də-pȧr-lā\ [French] **:** manner of speaking **:** figurative or conventional expression

faire suivre \fer-swᵊēvrᵊ\ [French] **:** have forwarded **:** please forward

fas est et ab ho·ste do·ce·ri \fäs-'est-et-äb-'hȯ-ste-dȯ-'kā-(ˌ)rē\ [Latin] **:** it is right to learn even from an enemy

Fa·ta vi·am in·ve·ni·ent \ˌfä-tä-'wē-ˌäm-in-'we-nē-ˌent\ [Latin] **:** the Fates will find a way

fat·ti mas·chii, pa·ro·le fe·mi·ne \ˌfät-tē-'mäs-ˌkē pä-ˌrō-lā-'fä-mē-ˌnä\ [Italian] **:** deeds are males, words are females **:** deeds are more effective than words — motto of Maryland, where it is generally interpreted as meaning "manly deeds, womanly words"

faux bon·homme \fō-bȯ-nȯm\ [French] **:** pretended good fellow

faux—naïf \fō-nä-ēf\ [French] **:** spuriously or affectedly childlike **:** artfully simple

fe·lix cul·pa \'fā-liks-'kùl-pä\ [Latin] **:** fortunate fault — used especially of original sin in relation to the consequent coming of Christ

femme de cham·bre \fȧm-də-shäⁿbrᵊ\ [French] **:** chambermaid **:** lady's maid

fe·sti·na len·te \fe-ˌstē-nä-'len-ˌtä\ [Latin] **:** make haste slowly

feux d'ar·ti·fice \fœ-dȧr-tē-fēs\ [French] **:** fireworks **:** display of wit

fi·at ex·pe·ri·men·tum in cor·po·re vi·li \'fē-ˌät-ek-ˌsper-ē-'men-ˌtùm-in-ˌkȯr-pȯ-re-'wē-lē\ [Latin] **:** let experiment be made on a worthless body

fi·at ju·sti·tia, ru·at cae·lum \ˌfē-ˌät-yùs-'ti-tē-ä ˌrù-ˌät-'kī-ˌlùm\ [Latin] **:** let justice be done though the heavens fall

fi·at lux \fē-ˌät-'lùks\ [Latin] **:** let there be light

Fi·dei De·fen·sor \ˌfi-de-ē-dā-'fän-ˌsȯr\ [Latin] **:** Defender of the Faith — a title of the sovereigns of England

fi·dus Acha·tes \fē-dùs-ä-'kä-ˌtās\ [Latin] **:** faithful Achates **:** trusty friend

fille de cham·bre \fēy-də-shäⁿbrᵊ\ [French] **:** lady's maid

fille d'hon·neur \fēy-dȯ-nœr\ [French] **:** maid of honor

fils \fēs\ [French] **:** son — used originally after French and now also after other family names to distinguish a son from his father

fi·nem re·spi·ce \ˌfē-ˌnem-'rä-spi-ˌke\ [Latin] **:** consider the end

fi·nis co·ro·nat opus \ˌfē-nis-kȯ-ˌrō-ˌnät-'ō-ˌpùs\ [Latin] **:** the end crowns the work

flo·re·at \'flō-re-ˌät\ [Latin] **:** may (he, she, or it) flourish — usually followed by a name

fluc·tu·at nec mer·gi·tur \'flùk-tù-ˌät-ˌnek-'mer-gi-ˌtùr\ [Latin] **:** it is tossed by the waves but does not sink — motto of Paris

fo·lie de gran·deur *or* **fo·lie des gran·deurs** \fȯ-lē-də-gräⁿ-dœr\ [French] **:** delusion of greatness **:** megalomania

force de frappe \fȯrs-də-frȧp\ [French] **:** military striking force especially with nuclear weapons

fors·an et haec olim me·mi·nis·se ju·va·bit \ˌfȯr-ˌsän-et-'hīk-ˌō-lim-me-mi-'ni-se-yù-'wä-bit\ [Latin] **:** perhaps this too will be a pleasure to look back on one day

for·tes for·tu·na ju·vat \ˌfȯr-ˌtäs-fȯr-ˌtü-nä-'yù-ˌwät\ [Latin] **:** fortune favors the brave

fron·ti nul·la fi·des \ˌfrȯn-ˌtē-ˌnù-lä-'fi-ˌdäs\ [Latin] **:** no reliance can be placed on appearance

fu·it Ili·um \'fù-it-'i-le-ùm\ [Latin] **:** Troy has been (i.e., is no more)

fu·ror lo·quen·di \ˌfùr-ˌȯr-lȯ-'kwen-(ˌ)dē\ [Latin] **:** rage for speaking

furor po·e·ti·cus \-pȯ-'ā-ti-kùs\ [Latin] **:** poetic frenzy

furor scri·ben·di \-skrē-'ben-(ˌ)dē\ [Latin] **:** rage for writing

Gal·gen·hu·mor \'gäl-gən-hü-ˌmȯr\ [German] **:** gallows humor

Gal·li·ce \'gä-li-ˌke\ [Latin] **:** in French **:** after the French manner

gar·çon d'hon·neur \gȧr-sōⁿ-dȯ-nœr\ [French] **:** bridegroom's attendant

garde du corps \gȧrd-du-kȯr\ [French] **:** bodyguard

gar·dez la foi \gȧr-dā-lȧ-fwä\ [French] **:** keep faith

gau·de·a·mus igi·tur \ˌgau̇-dē-'ä-mùs-'i-gi-ˌtùr\ [Latin] **:** let us be merry

gens d'é·glise \zhäⁿ-dā-glēz\ [French] **:** church people **:** clergy

gens de guerre \zhäⁿ-də-ger\ [French] **:** military people **:** soldiery

gens du monde \zhäⁿ-du-mōⁿd\ [French] **:** people of the world **:** fashionable people

gno·thi se·au·ton \'gnō-thē-ˌse-au̇-'tȯn\ [Greek] **:** know thyself

goût de ter·roir \gü-də-te-rwȧr\ [French] **:** taste of the earth

grande école \grä̃-dā-kȯl\ [French] **:** great school **:** French institution of higher education for postbaccalaureate professional or technological training

grand monde \grä̃-mōⁿd\ [French] **:** great world **:** high society

gros·so mo·do \ˌgrȯs-(ˌ)sō-'mȯ-(ˌ)dō\ [Italian] **:** roughly

guerre à ou·trance \ger-ä-ü-träⁿs\ [French] **:** war to the uttermost

gu·ten Tag \ˌgü-tən-'täk\ [German] **:** good day

has·ta la vis·ta \ˌäs-tə-lä-'vēs-tə\ [Spanish] **:** good-bye

haute vul·ga·ri·sa·tion \ōt-vùl-gȧ-rē-zä-syōⁿ\ [French] **:** high popularization **:** effective presentation of a difficult subject to a general audience

haut goût \ō-gü\ [French] **:** high flavor **:** slight taint of decay

hic et nunc \ˌhēk-et-'nùŋk\ [Latin] **:** here and now

hic et ubi·que \ˌhēk-et-ù-'bē-kwe\ [Latin] **:** here and everywhere

hic ja·cet \hik-'jä-sət, hēk-'yä-ket\ [Latin] **:** here lies — used preceding a name on a tombstone

hinc il·lae la·cri·mae \ˌhiŋk-ˌi-ˌlī-'lä-kri-ˌmī\ [Latin] **:** hence those tears

hoc age \hōk-'ä-ge\ [Latin] **:** do this **:** apply yourself to what you are about

hoc opus, hic la·bor est \hōk-'ȯ-ˌpùs-ˌhēk-'lä-ˌbȯr-'est\ [Latin] **:** this is the hard work, this is the toil

homme d'af·faires \ȯm-dȧ-fer\ [French] **:** man of business **:** business agent

homme d'es·prit \-des-prē\ [French] **:** man of wit

\ə\ **abut** \ᵊ\ **kitten** \ər\ **further** \a\ **ash** \ā\ **ace**
\ä\ **mop, mar** \au̇\ **out** \ch\ **chin** \e\ **bet** \ē\ **easy**
\g\ **go** \i\ **hit** \ī\ **ice** \j\ **job** \ŋ\ **sing** \ō\ **go**
\ȯ\ **law** \ȯi\ **boy** \th\ **thin** \th̲\ **the** \ü\ **loot** \u̇\ **foot**
\y\ **yet** \zh\ **vision** *see also* Guide to Pronunciation

homme moyen sen·suel \óm-mwȧ-yaⁿ-sän-sw°el\ [French] **:** the average nonintellectual man

ho·mo sum: hu·ma·ni nil a me ali·e·num pu·to \'hò-mō-,sùm hü-,mä-nē-'nēl-ä-,mā-,ä-lē-'ā-,nùm-'pù-tō\ [Latin] **:** I am a human being: I regard nothing of human concern as foreign to my interests

ho·ni soit qui mal y pense \ò-nē-swȧ-kē-mál-ē-päⁿs\ [French] **:** shamed be he who thinks evil of it — motto of the Order of the Garter

hon·nête homme \ò-net-òm\ [French] **:** honest man **:** respectable and honorable citizen of the middle class

hors com·merce \ór-kò-mers\ [French] **:** outside the trade **:** not offered through regular commercial channels

hu·ma·num est er·ra·re \hü-,mä-nùm-,est-e-'rär-ā\ [Latin] **:** to err is human

ich dien \ik-'dēn\ [German] **:** I serve — motto of the Prince of Wales

ici on parle fran·çais \ē-sē-ōⁿ-párl-fräⁿ-se, -pȧr-lə-\ [French] **:** French is spoken here

idées re·çues \ē-dār-(ə-)sū\ [French] **:** received ideas **:** conventional opinions

id est \id-'est\ [Latin] **:** that is

ig·no·ran·tia ju·ris ne·mi·nem ex·cu·sat \,ig-nó-,rän-tē-ä-'yùr-is-'nä-mi-,nem-eks-'kü-,sät\ [Latin] **:** ignorance of the law excuses no one

ig·no·tum per ig·no·ti·us \ig-'nō-tùm,-per-ig-'nō-tē-,ùs\ [Latin] **:** (explaining) the unknown by means of the more unknown

il faut cul·ti·ver no·tre jar·din \ēl-fō-kūēl-tē-vā-,nót-zhár-daⁿ, -nó-trə-zhár-\ [French] **:** we must cultivate our garden **:** we must tend to our own affairs

ils ne pas·se·ront pas \ēl-nə-pás-rōⁿ-pä, -pá-sə-rōⁿ-\ [French] **:** they shall not get past

in ae·ter·num \,in-ī-'ter-,nùm\ [Latin] **:** forever

in du·bio \in-'dù-bē-,ō\ [Latin] **:** in doubt **:** undetermined

in fu·tu·ro \,in-fù-'tùr-ō\ [Latin] **:** in the future

in hoc sig·no vin·ces \in-hōk-'sig-nō-'wiŋ-,kās\ [Latin] **:** by this sign (the Cross) you will conquer

in li·mi·ne \in-'lē-mi-,ne\ [Latin] **:** on the threshold **:** at the beginning

In·nig·keit \'i-ni(k)-,kīt\ [German] **:** poignant intimacy of feeling — used especially of music

in om·nia pa·ra·tus \in-'óm-nē-ä-pä-'rä-,tùs\ [Latin] **:** ready for all things

in par·ti·bus in·fi·de·li·um \in-'pär-ti-,bùs,-in-fi-'dā-lē-,ùm\ [Latin] **:** in the regions of the infidels — used of a titular bishop having no diocesan jurisdiction, usually in non-Christian countries

in prae·sen·ti \,in-prī-'sen-,tē\ [Latin] **:** at the present time

in sae·cu·la sae·cu·lo·rum \in-'sī-kù-,lä,-sī-kù-'lòr-ùm, -'sä-kù-,lä,-sä-\ [Latin] **:** for ages of ages **:** forever and ever

in·shal·lah \, in-shä-'lä\ [Arabic] **:** if Allah wills **:** God willing

in sta·tu quo an·te bel·lum \in-'stä-,tü-kwō-,än-te-'be-lùm\ [Latin] **:** in the same state as before the war

in·te·ger vi·tae sce·le·ris·que pu·rus \,in-te-,ger-'wē-,tī-,ske-le-'ris-kwe-'pù-rùs\ [Latin] **:** upright of life and free from wickedness

in·ter nos \,in-ter-'nōs\ [Latin] **:** between ourselves

in·tra mu·ros \in-trä-'mü-,rōs\ [Latin] **:** within the walls

in usum Del·phi·ni \in-'ü-sùm-del-'fē-nē\ [Latin] **:** for the use of the Dauphin **:** expurgated

in utrum·que pa·ra·tus \,in-ü-'trùm-kwe-pä-'rä-,tùs\ [Latin] **:** prepared for either (event)

in·ve·nit \in-'wā-nit\ [Latin] **:** he or she devised it

in vi·no ve·ri·tas \in-wē-nō-'wā-ri-,täs\ [Latin] **:** there is truth in wine

in·vi·ta Mi·ner·va \in-,wē-,tä-mi-'ner-,wä\ [Latin] **:** Minerva being unwilling **:** without natural talent or inspiration

ip·sis·si·ma ver·ba \ip-,si-si-,mä-'wer-,bä\ [Latin] **:** the very words

ira fu·ror bre·vis est \,ē-rä-'fùr-,ór-'bre-wis-,est\ [Latin] **:** anger is a brief madness

j'ac·cuse \zhá-küz\ [French] **:** I accuse **:** bitter denunciation

jac·ta alea est \'yäk-,tä-,ä-lē-,ä-'est\ [Latin] **:** the die is cast

j'adoube \zhá-düb\ [French] **:** I adjust — used in chess when touching a piece without intending to move it

ja·nu·is clau·sis \,yä-nù-,ēs-'klaù-,sēs\ [Latin] **:** behind closed doors

je main·tien·drai \zhə-maⁿ-tyaⁿ-drā\ [French] **:** I will maintain — motto of the Netherlands

jeu de mots \zhœd-mō, zhœ-də-\ [French] **:** play on words **:** pun

Jo·an·nes est no·men eius \yō-'ä-nās-est-,nō-men-'ā-yùs\ [Latin] **:** John is his name — motto of Puerto Rico

jo·lie laide \zhò-lē-led\ [French] **:** good-looking ugly woman **:** woman who is attractive though not conventionally pretty

jour·nal in·time \zhür-nál-aⁿ-tēm\ [French] **:** intimate journal **:** private diary

jus di·vi·num \,yüs-di-'wē-,nùm\ [Latin] **:** divine law

jus·ti·tia om·ni·bus \yùs-,ti-tē-,ä-'óm-ni-,bùs\ [Latin] **:** justice for all — motto of the District of Columbia

j'y suis, j'y reste \zhē-sw°ē-zhē-rest\ [French] **:** here I am, here I remain

Kin·der, Kir·che, Kü·che \'kin-dər 'kir-kə 'kœ-kə\ [German] **:** children, church, kitchen

kte·ma es aei \kə-)'tä-,mä-,es-ä-'ā\ [Greek] **:** a possession for ever — applied to a work of art or literature of enduring significance

la belle dame sans mer·ci \lȧ-bel-dám-säⁿ-mer-sē\ [French] **:** the beautiful lady without mercy

la·bo·ra·re est ora·re \'lä-bō-,rär-ā-,est-'ō-,rär-ā\ [Latin] **:** to work is to pray

la·bor om·nia vin·cit \'lä-,bòr-,óm-nē-,ä-'wiŋ-kit\ [Latin] **:** labor conquers all things — motto of Oklahoma

la·cri·mae re·rum \lä-kri-,mī-'rä-,rùm\ [Latin] **:** tears for things **:** pity for misfortune; also **:** tears in things **:** tragedy of life

lais·sez–al·ler or **lais·ser–al·ler** \le-sā-à-lā\ [French] **:** letting go **:** lack of restraint

lap·sus ca·la·mi \,läp-sùs-'kä-lä-,mē, ,lap-səs-'ka-lə-,mī\ [Latin] **:** slip of the pen

lap·sus lin·guae \,lap-səs-'liŋ-,gwī, ,läp-,sùs-\ [Latin] **:** slip of the tongue

la reine le veut \lȧ-ren-lə-vœ̄\ [French] **:** the queen wills it

la·scia·te ogni spe·ran·za, voi ch'en·tra·te \läsh-'shä-tā-,ō-nº̄ē-spä-'rän-tsä-,vō-ē-kän-'trä-tā\ [Italian] **:** abandon all hope, ye who enter

lau·da·tor tem·po·ris ac·ti \laù-'dä-,tòr-,tem-pó-ris-'äk-,tē\ [Latin] **:** one who praises past times

laus Deo \laùs-'dā-ō\ [Latin] **:** praise (be) to God

Le·bens·welt \'lā-bəns-,velt\ [German] **:** life world **:** world of lived experience

le cœur a ses rai·sons que la rai·son ne con·naît point \lə-kœr-à-sā-re-zōⁿk-la-re-zōⁿ-kò-ne-pwaⁿ, -zōⁿ-nə-\ [French] **:** the heart has its reasons that reason knows nothing of

le roi est mort, vive le roi \lə-rwä-e-mór vēv-lə-rwä\ [French] **:** the king is dead, long live the king

le roi le veut \lə-rwä-lə-vœ̄\ [French] **:** the king wills it

le roi s'avi·se·ra \lə-rwä-sá-vēz-rà\ [French] **:** the king will consider

le style, c'est l'homme \lə-stēl-se-lóm\ [French] **:** the style is the man

l'état, c'est moi \lā-tá-se-mwà\ [French] **:** the state, it is I

l'étoile du nord \lā-twál-dṻ-nór\ [French] **:** the star of the north — motto of Minnesota

Lie·der·kranz \'lē-dər-,kränts\ [German] **:** wreath of songs **:** German singing society

lit·tera scrip·ta ma·net \,li-te-,rä-,skrip-tä-'mä-net\ [Latin] **:** the written letter abides

lo·cus in quo \,lò-kùs-in-'kwō\ [Latin] **:** place in which

l'union fait la force \lē-nyōⁿ-fe-lä-fórs\ [French] **:** union makes strength — motto of Belgium

lu·sus na·tu·rae \lü-sùs-nä-'tùr-ē, -'tùr-,ī\ [Latin] **:** freak of nature

ma foi \mȧ-fwä\ [French] **:** my faith! **:** indeed

mag·na est ve·ri·tas et prae·va·le·bit \,mäg-nä-,est-'wā-ri-,täs-et-,prī-wä-'lā-bit\ [Latin] **:** truth is mighty and will prevail

mag·ni no·mi·nis um·bra \,mäg-nē-,nō-mi-nis-'ùm-brä\ [Latin] **:** the shadow of a great name

ma·ha·lo \'mä-hä-lō\ [Hawaiian] **:** thank you

mai·son de san·té \mā-zōⁿd-sä̈ⁿ-tā, -zōⁿ-də-\ [French] **:** private hospital **:** asylum

ma·lade ima·gi·naire \mȧ-lȧd-ē-mȧ-zhē-ner\ [French] **:** imaginary invalid **:** hypochondriac

ma·lis avi·bus \mä-,lēs-'ä-wi-,bùs\ [Latin] **:** under evil auspices

mal vu \mȧl-vṻ\ [French] **:** badly regarded **:** disapproved of

ma·no a ma·no \,mä-nō-ä-'mä-nō\ [Spanish] **:** hand to hand **:** in direct competition or confrontation

man spricht Deutsch \män-shprikt-'dóich\ [German] **:** German spoken

ma·riage de con·ve·nance \má-ryàzh-də-kōⁿv-näⁿs\ [French] **:** marriage of convenience

ma·ri com·plai·sant \mȧ-rē-kōⁿ-ple-zäⁿ\ [French] **:** complaisant husband **:** cuckold who accepts his wife's infidelity

mau·vaise honte \mò-vez-ōⁿt\ [French] **:** bad shame **:** bashfulness

mau·vais quart d'heure \mò-ve-kár-dœr\ [French] **:** bad quarter hour **:** an uncomfortable though brief experience

me·den agan \(,)mä-,den-'ä-,gän\ [Greek] **:** nothing in excess

me·dio tu·tis·si·mus ibis \'me-dē-,ō-tü-,ti-si-müs-'ē-bis\ [Latin] **:** you will go most safely by the middle course

me ju·di·ce \mä-'yü-di-ke\ [Latin] **:** I being judge **:** in my judgment

mens sa·na in cor·po·re sa·no \mäns-'sä-nä-in-,kòr-pó-re-'sä-nō\ [Latin] **:** a sound mind in a sound body

met·teur en scène \me-tœr-äⁿ-sen\ [French] **:** one who puts on the stage **:** director of a play or film

me·um et tu·um \,mē-əm,-et-'tü-əm, ,me-ùm,-et-'tü-ùm\ [Latin] **:** mine and thine **:** distinction of private property

mi·ra·bi·le vi·su \mi-,rä-bi-lā-'wē-sü\ [Latin] **:** wonderful to behold

mi·ra·bi·lia \, mir-ə-'bi-lē-,ä\ [Latin] **:** wonders **:** miracles

mœurs \mœr(s)\ [French] **:** mores **:** attitudes, customs, and manners of a society

mo·le ru·it sua \'mō-le-'rù-it-,sù-ä\ [Latin] **:** it collapses from its own bigness

monde \mōⁿd\ [French] **:** world **:** fashionable world **:** society

mon·ta·ni sem·per li·be·ri \mòn-,tä-nē-,sem-per-'lē-be-,rē\ [Latin] **:** mountaineers are always free — motto of West Virginia

mo·nu·men·tum ae·re per·en·ni·us \,mō-nù-'men-tùm-,ī-re-pe-'re-nē-ùs\ [Latin] **:** a monument more lasting than bronze — used of an immortal work of art or literature

mo·re suo \,mòr-ā-'sü-ō\ [Latin] **:** in his (or her) own manner

mo·ri·tu·ri te sa·lu·ta·mus \,mòr-i-'tùr-ē-,tē-,sä-lù-'tä-mùs\ or **mo·ri·tu·ri te sa·lu·tant** \-'sä-lù-,tänt\ [Latin] **:** we (or those) who are about to die salute thee

mul·tum in par·vo \,mùl-tùm-in-'pär-vō, -'pär-wō\ [Latin] **:** much in little

mu·sée ima·gi·naire \mṻ-zä-ē-má-zhē-ner\ [French] **:** imaginary museum

mu·ta·to no·mi·ne de te fa·bu·la nar·ra·tur \mü-,tä-tō-'nō-mi-ne-,dä-,tä-'fä-bù-lä-nä-'rä-,tur\ [Latin] **:** with the name changed the story applies to you

my·ster·i·um tre·men·dum \mi-'ster-ē-,ùm-tre-'men-dúm\ [Latin] **:** overwhelming mystery

na·tu·ram ex·pel·las fur·ca, ta·men us·que re·cur·ret \nä-'tü-,räm-ek-,spe-läs-'fùr-,kä ,tä-men-'ùs-kwe-re-'kúr-et\ [Latin] **:** you may drive nature out with a pitchfork, but she will keep coming back

na·tu·ra non fa·cit sal·tum \nä-'tü-rä-,nōn-,fä-kit-'sal-,tùm\ [Latin] **:** nature makes no leap

ne ce·de ma·lis \nä-,kä-de-'mä-,lēs\ [Latin] **:** yield not to misfortunes

ne·mo me im·pu·ne la·ces·sit \'nä-mō-'mä-im-,pü-nä-lä-'ke-sit\ [Latin] **:** no one attacks me with impunity — motto of Scotland and of the Order of the Thistle

ne quid ni·mis \,nä-,kwid-'ni-mis\ [Latin] **:** not anything in excess

n'est–ce pas? \nes-pä\ [French] **:** isn't it so?

nicht wahr? \nikt-'vär\ [German] **:** not true? **:** isn't it so?

nil ad·mi·ra·ri \'nēl-,äd-mi-'rär-ē\ [Latin] **:** to be excited by nothing **:** equanimity

nil de·spe·ran·dum \'nēl-,dā-spä-'rän-dùm\ [Latin] **:** never despair

nil si·ne nu·mi·ne \'nēl-,si-nä-'nü-mi-ne\ [Latin] **:** nothing without the divine will — motto of Colorado

n'im·porte \naⁿ-pȯrt\ [French] **:** it's no matter

no·lens vo·lens \,nō-,lenz-'vō-,lenz\ [Latin] **:** unwilling (or) willing — willy-nilly

non om·nia pos·su·mus om·nes \nōn-'ȯm-nē-ä-,pȯ-sü-müs-'ȯm-,nās\ [Latin] **:** we can't all (do) all things

non om·nis mo·ri·ar \nōn-'ȯm-nis-'mȯr-ē-,är\ [Latin] **:** I shall not wholly die

non sans droict \nōⁿ-säⁿ-drwä\ [Old French] **:** not without right — motto on Shakespeare's coat of arms

non sum qua·lis eram \nōn-,süm-,kwä-lis-'er-,äm\ [Latin] **:** I am not what I used to be

nos·ce te ip·sum \,nȯs-ke-,tā-'ip-,süm\ [Latin] **:** know thyself

nos·tal·gie de la boue \nȯs-tȧl-zhēd-là-bü, -zhē-də-\ [French] **:** yearning for the mud **:** attraction to what is unworthy, crude, or degrading

nous avons chan·gé tout ce·la \nü-zȧ-vōⁿ-shäⁿ-zhä-tü-sə-là\ [French] **:** we have changed all that

nous ver·rons ce que nous ver·rons \nü-ve-rōⁿs-kə-nü-ve-rōⁿ, -rōⁿ-sə-kə-\ [French] **:** we shall see what we shall see

no·vus ho·mo \,nȯ-wùs-'hȯ-mō\ [Latin] **:** new man **:** man newly ennobled **:** upstart

novus or·do se·clo·rum \-'ȯr-,dō-sā-'klōr-üm\ [Latin] **:** a new cycle of the ages — motto on the reverse of the Great Seal of the United States

nu·gae \'nü-,gī\ [Latin] **:** trifles

nuit blanche \nwē-blä'sh\ [French] **:** white night **:** a sleepless night

nyet \'nyet\ [Russian] **:** no

O al·ti·tu·do \'ō-,äl-ti-'tü-,dō\ [Latin] **:** O (the) height **:** feeling of spiritual exaltation

ob·iit \'ȯ-bē-,it\ [Latin] **:** he or she died

ob·scu·rum per ob·scu·ri·us \ȯb-'skyùr-üm-,per-ȯb-'skyùr-ē-ùs\ [Latin] **:** (explaining) the obscure by means of the more obscure

ode·rint dum me·tu·ant \'ō-de-,rint-,düm-me-tü-,änt\ [Latin] **:** let them hate, so long as they fear

odi et amo \'ō-,dē-et-'ä-(,)mō\ [Latin] **:** I hate and I love

omer·tà \ȯ-'mer-tä\ [Italian] **:** submission **:** code chiefly among members of the criminal underworld that enjoins private vengeance and the refusal to give information to outsiders (as the police)

om·ne ig·no·tum pro mag·ni·fi·co \,ȯm-ne-ig-'nō-,tüm-prō-mäg-'ni-fi-,kō\ [Latin] **:** everything unknown (is taken) as grand **:** the unknown tends to be exaggerated in importance or difficulty

om·nia mu·tan·tur, nos et mu·ta·mur in il·lis \,ȯm-nē-ä-mü-'tän-,tùr ,nōs-,et-mü-,tä-mùr-in-'i-,lēs\ [Latin] **:** all things are changing, and we are changing with them

om·nia vin·cit amor \'ȯm-nē-ä-'wiṇ-kit-'ä-,mȯr\ [Latin] **:** love conquers all

onus pro·ban·di \,ō-nùs-prō-'ban,dī, -dē\ [Latin] **:** burden of proof

ora pro no·bis \,ō-rä-prō-'nō-,bēs\ [Latin] **:** pray for us

ore ro·tun·do \,ōr-ē-rō-'tən-dō\ [Latin] **:** with round mouth **:** eloquently

oro y pla·ta \,ōr-ō-ē-'plä-tə\ [Spanish] **:** gold and silver — motto of Montana

o tem·po·ra! o mo·res! \ō-'tem-pȯ-rä-ō-'mō-,räs\ [Latin] **:** oh the times! oh the manners!

oti·um cum dig·ni·ta·te \'ō-tē-,üm-kùm-,dig-ni-'tä-te\ [Latin] **:** leisure with dignity

où sont les neiges d'an·tan? \ü-sōⁿ-lā-nezh-däⁿ-täⁿ\ [French] **:** where are the snows of yesteryear?

outre–mer \ütr°-mer\ [French] **:** overseas **:** distant lands

pal·li·da Mors \,pa-li-dä-'mȯrz\ [Latin] **:** pale Death

pa·nem et cir·cen·ses \,pä-,nem-et-kir-'kän-,säs\ [Latin] **:** bread and circuses **:** provision of the means of life and recreation by government to appease discontent

pan·ta rhei \,pän-,tä-'rä, ,pan-tə-'rä\ [Greek] **:** all things are in flux

par avance \pár-á-väⁿs\ [French] **:** in advance **:** by anticipation

par avion \pár-á-vyōⁿ\ [French] **:** by airplane — used on airmail

par ex·em·ple \pár-ág-zäⁿplᵃ\ [French] **:** for example

pars pro to·to \'pärs-(,)prō-'tō-(,)tō\ [Latin] **:** part (taken) for the whole

par·tu·ri·unt mon·tes, nas·ce·tur ri·di·cu·lus mus \pär-'tùr-ē-,ùnt-'mȯn-,täs nás-'kā-,tùr-ri-,di-kù-lús-'müs\ [Latin] **:** the mountains are in labor, and a ridiculous mouse will be brought forth

pa·ter pa·tri·ae \'pä-,ter-'pä-trē-,ī\ [Latin] **:** father of his country

pau·cis ver·bis \,paù-,kēs-'wer-,bēs\ [Latin] **:** in a few words

pax vo·bis·cum \,päks-vō-'bēs-,küm\ [Latin] **:** peace (be) with you

peine forte et dure \,pen-fȯr-tā-dūr\ [French] **:** strong and hard punishment **:** torture

per an·gus·ta ad au·gus·ta \per-'än-,gùs-tä-äd-'aù-,gù-,stä, per-,äⁿ-\ [Latin] **:** through difficulties to honors

père \per\ [French] **:** father — used originally after French and now also after other family names to distinguish a father from his son

per·eant qui an·te nos nos·tra dix·e·runt \'per-e-,änt-kwē-,än-te-'nōs-trä-dēk-'sä-,rùnt\ [Latin] **:** may they perish who have expressed our bright ideas before us

per·eunt et im·pu·tan·tur \'per-e-,ùnt-et-,im-pú-'tän-,tùr\ [Latin] **:** they (the hours) pass away and are reckoned on (our) account

per·fide Al·bion \per-fēd-ál-byōⁿ\ [French] **:** perfidious Albion (England)

peu à peu \pœ̄-á-pœ̄\ [French] **:** little by little

peu de chose \pœ̄d-shȯz, pœ̄-də-\ [French] **:** a trifle

pièce d'oc·ca·sion \pyes-dȯ-kä-zyōⁿ\ [French] **:** piece for a special occasion

pièce jus·ti·fi·ca·tive \pyes-zhūes-tē-fē-ká-tēv\ [French] **:** justificatory paper **:** document serving as evidence

pièce mon·tée \pyes-mōⁿ-tä\ [French] **:** set piece **:** food that has been decoratively shaped or arranged

pinx·it \'piṇk-sit\ [Latin] **:** he or she painted it

place aux dames \plás-ō-dám\ [French] **:** (make) room for the ladies

ple·no ju·re \,plä-nō-'yür-e\ [Latin] **:** with full right

plus ça change, plus c'est la même chose \plūe-sá-shäⁿzh plūe-se-là-mem-shōz\ [French] **:** the more that changes, the more it's the same thing — often shortened to *plus ça change*

plus roy·a·liste que le roi \plūe-rwá-yá-lēst-kəl-rwä\ [French] **:** more royalist than the king

po·cas pa·la·bras \,pō-käs-pä-'lä-vräs\ [Spanish] **:** few words

po·eta nas·ci·tur, non fit \pȯ-,ä-tä-'näs-ki-,tùr nōn-'fit\ [Latin] **:** a poet is born, not made

point de re·père \pwaⁿ-də-rā-per\ [French] **:** point of reference

pol·li·ce verso \,pȯ-li-ke-'wer-sō\ [Latin] **:** with thumb turned **:** with a gesture or expression of condemnation

post hoc, er·go prop·ter hoc \'pȯst-,hōk ,er-gō-'prȯp-ter-,hōk\ [Latin] **:** after this, therefore on account of it (a fallacy of argument)

post ob·itum \pȯst-'ȯ-bi-,tüm\ [Latin] **:** after death

pour ac·quit \pür-à-kē\ [French] **:** received payment

pour le mé·rite \pür-lə-mä-rēt\ [French] **:** for merit

pour rire \pür-rēr\ [French] **:** for laughing **:** not to be taken seriously

pri·mum non no·ce·re \,prē-mùm-,nōn-nȯ-'kā-rä\ [Latin] **:** the first thing (is) to do no harm

pro aris et fo·cis \prō-,ä-,rēs-et-'fȯ-,kēs\ [Latin] **:** for altars and firesides

pro bo·no pu·bli·co \prō-,bȯ-nō-'pü-bli-,kō\ [Latin] **:** for the public good

pro hac vi·ce \prō-,häk-'wi-ke\ [Latin] **:** for this occasion

pro pa·tria \prō-'pä-trē-,ä\ [Latin] **:** for one's country

pro re·ge, le·ge, et gre·ge \prō-'rā-,ge-'lā-,ge-et-'gre-,ge\ [Latin] **:** for the king, the law, and the people

pro re na·ta \prō-,rā-'nä-tä\ [Latin] **:** for an occasion that has arisen **:** as needed — used in medical prescriptions

quand même \käⁿ-mem\ [French] **:** even so **:** all the same

quan·tum mu·ta·tus ab il·lo \,kwän-tüm-mü-'tä-tús-äb-'i-lō\ [Latin] **:** how changed from what he once was

quan·tum suf·fi·cit \,kwän-təm-'sə-fə-,kit\ [Latin] **:** as much as suffices **:** a sufficient quantity — used chiefly in medical prescriptions

¿quién sa·be? \kyän-'sä-vä\ [Spanish] **:** who knows?

qui fa·cit per ali·um fa·cit per se \kwē-,fä-kit-,per-'ä-lē-,üm-fä-kit-,per-'sä\ [Latin] **:** he who does (something) through another does it through himself

quis cus·to·di·et ip·sos cus·to·des? \,kwis-,kùs-'tō-dē-,et-,ip-,sōs-kùs-'tō-,däs\ [Latin] **:** who will keep the keepers themselves?

qui s'ex·cuse s'ac·cuse \kē-'sek-,skūez-'sá-,kūez\ [French] **:** he who excuses himself accuses himself

quis se·pa·ra·bit? \,kwis-,sä-pə-'rä-bit\ [Latin] **:** who shall separate (us)? — motto of the Order of St. Patrick

qui trans·tu·lit sus·ti·net \kwē-'träns-tù-,lit-'sùs-tù-,net\ [Latin] **:** He who transplanted sustains (us) — motto of Connecticut

qui va là? \kē-vá-là\ [French] **:** who goes there?

quo·ad hoc \,kwȯ-,äd-'hōk\ [Latin] **:** as far as this **:** to this extent

quod erat de·mon·stran·dum \,kwȯd-'er-,ät-,de-mən-'stran-dəm, -,dä-,mȯn-'strän-,dùm\ [Latin] **:** which was to be proved

quod erat fa·ci·en·dum \-,fä-kē-'en-,dùm\ [Latin] **:** which was to be done

quod sem·per, quod ubi·que, quod ab om·ni·bus \,kwȯd-'sem-,per kwȯd-'ù-bi-,kwä ,kwȯd-äb-'ȯm-ni-,bùs, ,kwȯd-ù-'bē-(,)kwä-\ [Latin] **:** what (has been held) always, everywhere, by everybody

quod vi·de \kwȯd-'wi-,de\ [Latin] **:** which see

quo·rum pars mag·na fui \'kwȯr-ùm-,pärs-,mäg-nä-'fù-ē\ [Latin] **:** in which I played a great part

quos de·us vult per·de·re pri·us de·men·tat \,kwōs-'dä-ùs-,wült-'per-dä-rä,pri-ùs-dä-'men-,tät\ [Latin] **:** those whom a god wishes to destroy he first drives mad

quot ho·mi·nes, tot sen·ten·ti·ae \,kwȯt-'hȯ-mi-,nās-,tȯt-sen-'ten-tē-,ī\ [Latin] **:** there are as many opinions as there are men

quo va·dis? \kwō-'wä-dis, -'vä-dəs\ [Latin] **:** whither are you going?

rai·son d'état \re-zōⁿ-dä-tá\ [French] **:** reason of state

re·cu·ler pour mieux sau·ter \rə-kūe-lā-pür-myœ̄-sō-tä\ [French] **:** to draw back in order to make a better jump

reg·nat po·pu·lus \,reg-,nät-'pȯ-pù-,lùs\ [Latin] **:** the people rule — motto of Arkansas

re in·fec·ta \,rā-in-'fek-,tä\ [Latin] **:** the business being unfinished **:** without accomplishing one's purpose

re·li·gio lo·ci \re-'li-gē-,ō-'lȯ-,kē\ [Latin] **:** religious sanctity of a place

rem acu te·ti·gis·ti \rem-'ä-,kü-,te-ti-'gis-tē\ [Latin] **:** you have touched the point with a needle **:** you have hit the nail on the head

ré·pon·dez s'il vous plaît \rā-pōⁿ-dä-sēl-vü-ple\ [French] **:** reply, if you please

re·qui·es·cat in pa·ce \,rā-kwē-'es-,kät-in-'pä-,ke, ,rā-kwē-'es-,kät-in-'pä-,chä\ [Latin] **:** may he or she rest in peace — used on tombstones

re·spi·ce fi·nem \'rā-spi-,ke-'fē-,nem\ [Latin] **:** look to the end **:** consider the outcome

re·sur·gam \re-'sùr-,gäm\ [Latin] **:** I shall rise again

re·te·nue \rət-nē\ [French] **:** self-restraint **:** reserve

re·ve·nons à nos mou·tons \rəv-nōⁿ-à-nō-mü-tōⁿ\ [French] **:** let us return to our sheep **:** let us get back to the subject

ruse de guerre \rūez-də-ger\ [French] **:** war stratagem

rus in ur·be \,rüs-in-'ùr-,be\ [Latin] **:** country in the city

sae·va in·dig·na·tio \,sī-wä-,in-dig-'nä-tē-ō\ [Latin] **:** fierce indignation

\ə\ abut \ᵊ\ kitten \ər\ further \a\ ash \ā\ ace \ä\ mop, mar \aù\ out \ch\ chin \e\ bet \ē\ easy \g\ go \i\ hit \ī\ ice \j\ job \ŋ\ sing \ō\ go \ȯ\ law \ȯi\ boy \th\ thin \t͟h\ the \ü\ loot \ù\ foot \y\ yet \zh\ vision *see also* Guide to Pronunciation

sal At·ti·cum \sal-'a-ti-kəm\ [Latin] **:** Attic salt **:** wit

salle à man·ger \sȧl-ȧ-mäⁿ-zhā\ [French] **:** dining room

sa·lon des re·fu·sés \sȧ-lòⁿ-dār-(ə-)fūē-zā\ [French] **:** salon of the refused **:** exhibition of art that has been rejected by an official body

sal·to mor·ta·le \säl-tō-mór-'tä-lā\ [Italian] **:** deadly jump **:** full somersault **:** dangerous or crucial undertaking

sa·lus po·pu·li su·pre·ma lex es·to \sä-,lüs-'pò-pù,lē-sù,-prä-mä-,leks-'es-tō\ [Latin] **:** let the welfare of the people be the supreme law — motto of Missouri

sanc·ta sim·pli·ci·tas \,säŋk-tä-sim-'pli-ki-,täs\ [Latin] **:** holy simplicity — often used ironically in reference to another's naïveté

sans doute \säⁿ-'düt\ [French] **:** without doubt

sans gêne \säⁿ-zhen\ [French] **:** without embarrassment or constraint

sans peur et sans re·proche \säⁿ-pœr-ā-säⁿ-rə-'pròsh\ [French] **:** without fear and without reproach

sans sou·ci \säⁿ-sü-sē\ [French] **:** without worry

sa·yo·na·ra \,sī-ə-'när-ə, ,sä-yə-\ [Japanese] **:** good-bye

scène à faire \sen-ȧ-fer\ [French] **:** obligatory scene

sculp·sit \'skəlp-sət, 'skülp-sit\ [Latin] **:** he or she carved it

scu·to bo·nae vo·lun·ta·tis tu·ae co·ro·nas·ti nos \'skü-,tō-'bò-,nī-,vò-lùn-,tä-tis-'tù-,ī-'kòr-ò-,näs-tē-'nòs\ [Latin] **:** Thou hast crowned us with the shield of Thy good will — a motto on the Great Seal of Maryland

se·cun·dum ar·tem \se-,kùn-dùm-'är-,tem\ [Latin] **:** according to the art **:** according to the accepted practice of a profession or trade

secundum na·tu·ram \-nä-'tü-,räm\ [Latin] **:** according to nature **:** naturally

se de·fen·den·do \sā-,dā-,fen-'den-dō\ [Latin] **:** in self-defense

se ha·bla es·pa·ñol \sā-,äv-lä-,äs-pä-'nʸól\ [Spanish] **:** Spanish spoken

sem·per ea·dem \,sem-,per-'e-ä-,dem\ [Latin] **:** always the same (feminine) — motto of Queen Elizabeth I

sem·per fi·de·lis \,sem-pər-fə-'dā-ləs\ [Latin] **:** always faithful — motto of the U.S. Marine Corps

sem·per idem \,sem-,per-'ē-,dem\ [Latin] **:** always the same (masculine)

sem·per pa·ra·tus \,sem-pər-pə-'rä-təs\ [Latin] **:** always prepared — motto of the U.S. Coast Guard

se non è ve·ro, è ben tro·va·to \sā-,nōn-e-'vä-rō-ē-,ben-trō-'vä-tō\ [Italian] **:** even if it is not true, it is well conceived

sic itur ad as·tra \sēk-'i-,tùr-,äd-'äs-trə\ [Latin] **:** thus one goes to the stars **:** such is the way to immortality

sic sem·per ty·ran·nis \,sik-,sem-pər-tə-'ra-nəs\ [Latin] **:** thus ever to tyrants — motto of Virginia

sic trans·it glo·ria mun·di \sēk-'trän-sit-,glōr-ē-ä-'mùn-dē\ [Latin] **:** so passes away the glory of the world

sic·ut pa·tri·bus sit De·us no·bis \,sē-,kùt-'pä-tri-,bùs-sit-,dā-ùs-'nō-,bēs\ [Latin] **:** as to our fathers may God be to us — motto of Boston

si jeu·nesse sa·vait, si vieil·lesse pou·vait! \sē-'zhœ-nes-'sȧ-ve sē-'vye-yes-'pü-ve\ [French] **:** if youth only knew, if age only could!

si·lent le·ges in·ter ar·ma \,si-,lent-'lā-,gās-,in-ter-'är-mä\ [Latin] **:** the laws are silent in the midst of arms

s'il vous plaît \sēl-vü-ple\ [French] **:** if you please

si·mi·lia si·mi·li·bus cu·ran·tur \si-'mi-lē-ä-si-'mi-li-,bùs-kü-'rän-,tùr\ [Latin] **:** like is cured by like

si·mi·lis si·mi·li gau·det \'si-mi-lis-'si-mi-lē-'gaú-,det\ [Latin] **:** like takes pleasure in like

si mo·nu·men·tum re·qui·ris, cir·cum·spi·ce \,sē-,mò-nù-,men-tùm-re-'kwē-ris kir-'kùm-spi-ke\ [Latin] **:** if you seek his monument, look around — epitaph of Sir Christopher Wren in St. Paul's, London, of which he was architect

sim·pliste \saⁿ-'plēst\ [French] **:** simplistic **:** overly simple or naive

si quae·ris pen·in·su·lam amoe·nam, cir·cum·spi·ce \sē-'kwī-ris-pä-'nin-sə-,läm-,äm-,näm kir-'kùm-spi-ke\ [Latin] **:** if you seek a beautiful peninsula, look around — motto of Michigan

sis·te vi·a·tor \sis-te-wē-'ä-,tòr\ [Latin] **:** stop, traveler — used on Roman roadside tombs

si vis pa·cem, pa·ra bel·lum \sē-'wēs-'pä-,kem 'pä-rä-'be-,lùm\ [Latin] **:** if you wish peace, prepare for war

sol·vi·tur am·bu·lan·do \'sòl-wi-,tùr-,äm-bù-'län-dō\ [Latin] **:** it is solved by walking **:** the problem is solved by a practical experiment

splen·di·de men·dax \,splen-di-,dā-'men-,däks\ [Latin] **:** nobly untruthful

spo·lia opi·ma \,spò-lē-ä-ō-'pē-mä\ [Latin] **:** rich spoils **:** the arms taken by the victorious from the vanquished general

Sta·bat Ma·ter \,stä-bät-'mä-ter\ [Latin] **:** the mother was standing — title of a Latin hymn

sta·tus in quo \,stä-,tùs-,in-'kwō\ [Latin] **:** state in which **:** the existing state

sta·tus quo an·te bel·lum \'stä-,tùs-kwō-,än-te-'be-lùm\ [Latin] **:** the state existing before the war

Stim·mung \shti-mùŋ\ [German] **:** tone **:** mood **:** atmosphere

sua·vi·ter in mo·do, for·ti·ter in re \'swä-wi-,ter-in-'mó-dō 'fór-,ti-,ter-in-'rā\ [Latin] **:** gently in manner, strongly in deed

sub ver·bo \,sùb-'wer-bō, ,səb-'vər-bō\ or **sub vo·ce** \,sùb-'wō-ke, ,səb-'vō-sē\ [Latin] **:** under the word — introducing a cross-reference in a dictionary or index

sunt la·cri·mae re·rum \,sùnt-,lä-kri-,mī-'rä-rùm\ [Latin] **:** there are tears for things **:** tears attend trials

suo ju·re \,sù-ō-'yùr-e\ [Latin] **:** in his (or her) own right

suo lo·co \-'ló-kō\ [Latin] **:** in its proper place

suo Mar·te \-'mär-te\ [Latin] **:** by one's own exertions

sur place \sūr-plȧs\ [French] **:** in place **:** on the spot

su·um cui·que \,sù-ùm-'kwi-kwe\ [Latin] **:** to each his own

tant mieux \täⁿ-myœ\ [French] **:** so much the better

tant pis \-pē\ [French] **:** so much the worse **:** too bad

tem·po·ra mu·tan·tur, nos et mu·ta·mur in il·lis \,tem-pò-rä-mü-'tän-,tùr ,nòs-et-mü-,tä-mùr-in-'i-,lēs\ [Latin] **:** the times are changing, and we are changing with them

tem·pus edax re·rum \'tem-pùs-,a-däks-'rä-rùm\ [Latin] **:** time, that devours all things

tem·pus fu·git \,tem-pəs-'fyü-jət, ,tem-pùs-'fü-git\ [Latin] **:** time flies

ti·meo Da·na·os et do·na fe·ren·tes \,ti-mē-,ō-'dä-nä-,ōs-et-,dō-nä-fe-'ren-,täs\ [Latin] **:** I fear the Greeks even when they bring gifts

to·ti·dem ver·bis \,tó-ti-,dem-'wer-,bēs\ [Latin] **:** in so many words

to·tis vi·ri·bus \,tō-,tēs-'wē-ri-,bùs\ [Latin] **:** with all one's might

to·to cae·lo \,tō-tō-'kī-lō\ or **toto coe·lo** \-'kòi-lō\ [Latin] **:** by the whole extent of the heavens **:** diametrically

tou·jours per·drix \tü-zhür-per-drē\ [French] **:** always partridge **:** too much of a good thing

tour d'ho·ri·zon \tür-dò-rē-zōⁿ\ [French] **:** circuit of the horizon **:** general survey

tous frais faits \tü-fre-fe\ [French] **:** all expenses defrayed

tout à fait \tü-tȧ-fe\ [French] **:** altogether **:** quite

tout au con·traire \tü-tō-kōⁿ-trer\ [French] **:** quite the contrary

tout à vous \tü-tȧ-vü\ [French] **:** wholly yours **:** at your service

tout bien ou rien \tü-'byaⁿ-nü-'ryaⁿ\ [French] **:** everything well (done) or nothing (attempted)

tout com·pren·dre c'est tout par·don·ner \tü-kōⁿ-präⁿ-drə se-tü-pȧr-dò-nā\ [French] **:** to understand all is to forgive all

tout court \tü-kür\ [French] **:** quite short **:** and nothing more **:** simply **:** just; *also* **:** brusquely

tout de même \tüt-mem\ [French] **:** all the same **:** nevertheless

tout de suite \tüt-swʸēt\ [French] **:** immediately; *also* **:** all at once **:** consecutively

tout en·sem·ble \tü-täⁿ-säⁿblᵊ\ [French] **:** all together **:** general effect

tout est per·du fors l'hon·neur \tü-te-per-dⁱē-fòr-lò-nœr\ or **tout est perdu hors l'honneur** \-dⁱē-òr-\ [French] **:** all is lost save honor

tout le monde \tü-lə-mōⁿd\ [French] **:** all the world **:** everybody

tra·hi·son des clercs \trȧ-ē-zòⁿ-dā-klerk\ [French] **:** treason of the intellectuals

tranche de vie \träⁿsh-də-'vē\ [French] **:** slice of life

tria junc·ta in uno \,tri-ä-'yùŋk-tä-in-'ü-nō\ [Latin] **:** three joined in one — motto of the Order of the Bath

trist·esse \trē-stes\ [French] **:** melancholy

tru·di·tur di·es die \'trü-di-,tùr-'di-,äs-'di-,ä\ [Latin] **:** day is pushed forth by day **:** one day hurries on another

tu·e·bor \,tü-'ā-,bòr\ [Latin] **:** I will defend — a motto on the Great Seal of Michigan

ua mau ke ea o ka ai·na i ka po·no \,ù-ä-'mä-ù-kā-'ā-ä-ō-kä-'ā-ē-nä-,ē-kä-'pō-nō\ [Hawaiian] **:** the life of the land is perpetuated in righteousness — motto of Hawaii

über al·les \,ūē-ber-'ä-les\ [German] **:** above everything else

ue·ber·mensch \'ūē-bər-,mench\ [German] **:** superman

ul·ti·ma ra·tio re·gum \'ùl-ti-mä-,rä-tē-ō-'rā-gùm\ [Latin] **:** the final argument of kings, i.e., war

und so wei·ter \ùnt-zō-'vī-tər\ [German] **:** and so on

uno ani·mo \,ü-nō-'ä-ni-,mō\ [Latin] **:** with one mind **:** unanimously

ur·bi et or·bi \,ùr-bē-,et-'òr-bē\ [Latin] **:** to the city (Rome) and the world **:** to everyone

uti·le dul·ci \,ü-ti-le-'dùl-,kē\ [Latin] **:** the useful with the agreeable

ut in·fra \ùt-'in-frä\ [Latin] **:** as below

ut su·pra \ùt-'sü-prä\ [Latin] **:** as above

va·de re·tro me, Sa·ta·na \,wä-de-'rä-trō-,mä-'sä-tä-,nä\ [Latin] **:** get thee behind me, Satan

va et vient \vȧ-ā-vyaⁿ\ [French] **:** coming and going **:** active movement **:** traffic

vae vic·tis \,wī-'wik-,tēs\ [Latin] **:** woe to the vanquished

va·ria lec·tio \,wär-ē-ä-'lek-tē-,ō\ plural **va·ri·ae lec·ti·o·nes** \'wär-ē-,ī-,lek-tē-'ō-,nās\ [Latin] **:** variant reading

va·ri·um et mu·ta·bi·le sem·per fe·mi·na \,wär-ē-ùm-,et-,mü-'tä-bi-le-,sem-,per-'fä-mi-nä\ [Latin] **:** woman is ever a fickle and changeable thing

ve·di Na·po·li e poi mo·ri \vä-dē-'nä-pō-lē-ä-,pò-ē-'mò-rē\ [Italian] **:** see Naples and then die

ve·ni, vi·di, vi·ci \,wä-nē-,wē-dē-'wē-kē , ,vā-nē-,vē-dē-'vē-chē\ [Latin] **:** I came, I saw, I conquered

ven·tre à terre \väⁿ-trȧ-ter\ [French] **:** belly to the ground **:** at very great speed

ver·ba·tim ac lit·te·ra·tim \wer-'bä-tim-,äk-,li-te-'rä-tim\ [Latin] **:** word for word and letter for letter

ver·bum sat sa·pi·en·ti est \,wer-bùm-'sät-,sä-pē-'en-tē-,est\ [Latin] **:** a word to the wise is sufficient

vieux jeu \vyœ-zhœ\ [French] **:** old game **:** old hat

vin·cit om·nia ve·ri·tas \,wiŋ-kit-'òm-nē-ä-'wä-ri-,täs\ [Latin] **:** truth conquers all things

vin·cu·lum ma·tri·mo·nii \,wiŋ-kù-lùm-,mä-tri-'mō-nē-,ē\ [Latin] **:** bond of marriage

vin du pays \vaⁿ-dⁱē-pä-ē\ or **vin de pays** \vaⁿ-də-\ [French] **:** wine of the locality

vir·gi·ni·bus pu·e·ris·que \wir-'gi-ni-bùs-,pù-e-'rēs-kwe\ [Latin] **:** for girls and boys

vir·go in·tac·ta \,vir-,gō-in-'täk-tä\ [Latin] **:** untouched virgin

vir·tu·te et ar·mis \wir-'tü-te-,et-'är-mēs\ [Latin] **:** by valor and arms — motto of Mississippi

vis me·di·ca·trix na·tu·rae \,wēs-,me-di-kä-triks-nä-'tü-,rī\ [Latin] **:** the healing power of nature

vi·ta nuo·va \,vē-tä-'nwó-vä\ [Italian] **:** new life

vive la dif·fé·rence \vēv-lä-dē-fā-räⁿs, vē-və-\ [French] **:** long live the difference (between the sexes)

vive la reine \vēv-lä-ren\ [French] **:** long live the queen

vive le roi \vēv-lə-rwä\ [French] **:** long live the king

vix·e·re for·tes an·te Aga·mem·no·na \wik-,sä-re-'fòr-,tēs-,än-te-,ä-gä-'mem-nò-,nä\ [Latin] **:** brave men lived before Agamemnon

vogue la ga·lère \vòg-lȧ-gȧ-ler\ [French] **:** let the galley be kept rowing **:** keep on, whatever may happen

voi·là tout \vwȧ-lä-tü\ [French] **:** that's all

vo·lup·té \vò-lue̅p-tā\ [French] **:** pleasure **:** sensuality

vou·lu \vü-lue̅\ [French] **:** willed **:** contrived or forced

vox et prae·te·rea ni·hil \'wōks-et-prī-'ter-e-ä-'ni-,hil\ [Latin] **:** voice and nothing more

vox po·pu·li vox Dei \wōks-'pò-pu̇-,lē-,wōks-'dā-ē\ [Latin] **:** the voice of the people is the voice of God

Wan·der·jahr \'vän-dər-,yär\ [German] **:** year of wandering

Welt·bild \'velt-,bilt\ [German] **:** conception of the world

Wert·frei·heit \'vert-,frī-,hīt\ [German] **:** freedom from value judgments **:** ethical neutrality

wie geht's? \vē-'gāts\ [German] **:** how goes it?

Wis·sen·schaft \'vi-sən-,shäft\ [German] **:** learning **:** science

wun·der·bar \'vu̇n-dər-,bär\ [German] **:** wonderful

Biographical Names

This section contains the names of many notable persons both living and dead. Persons are generally entered under the name or title by which they are most commonly known. Entries typically consist of last name, personal names, birth and death dates, nationality, and occupation or status. Also included, when appropriate, are pseudonyms, original names, epithets, alternate names, reign names, and titles. The pronunciation and end-of-line division of elements in boldface are usually shown. the pronunciation and end-of-line division of names or titles in italics or roman are given only occasionally. Transliterations of names from alphabets other than the roman have been made as exact and consistent as possible. For most Chinese names, the traditional Wade-Giles system has been used. The Pinyin system has been used only for Chinese still living or recently deceased.

A number of names contain connectives like *d'*, *de*, *di*, *van*, and *von*. With some exceptions, chiefly American or British, names are not alphabetized under these connectives but rather under the principal element of the surname. If the surname of a person is usually construed as containing this connective, the entry appears at the principal element and the connective appears immediately after, separated by a comma:

Gogh, van . . . Vincent

If the full name contains a connective which is not usually construed as an inseparable part of the surname, then the connective follows the personal name.

Bee·tho·ven . . . Ludwig van

Birth and death dates about which there is little or no doubt are entered without qualification. Doubtful dates are followed by a question mark, and approximate dates are preceded by the word *circa*. In some instances only the years of principal activity are given, preceded by the word *flourished*. The dates of a reign or other term of office are enclosed in parentheses.

At the end of many entries are derivative adjectives with such endings as *-ian*, *-ic*, or *-esque*. While it is possible to form these derivative from any name, only the more common are shown:

Dan·te . . .— **Dan·te·an** . . . *or* **Dan·tes·can** . . . *or* **Dan·tesque** . . . *adjective*

Abbreviations used in the entries in this section are listed in the Abbreviations and Symbols for Chemical Elements section of the back matter.

Ab·bey \'a-bē\ Edwin Austin 1852–1911 Am. painter & illustrator

Ab·bott \'a-bət\ Berenice 1898–1991 Am. photographer

Abbott Sir John Joseph Caldwell 1821–1893 Canad. politician; prime minister (1891–92)

Abbott Lyman 1835–1922 Am. clergyman & author

Ab·del·ka·der \,ab-,del-'kä-dər\ *or* Abd al-Qā-dir \,ab-dəl-\ 1808–1883 Arab leader in Algeria

'Ab·dor·rah·mān Khān \,ab-,dòr-rə-'män-'kän\ *circa* 1844–1901 emir of Afghanistan (1880–1901)

Ab·dül·a·ziz \,ab-,dü-lə-'zēz\ 1830–1876 Ottoman sultan (1861–76)

Ab·dül·ha·mīd II \,ab-,dül-hä-'mēd\ 1842–1918 Ottoman sultan (1876–1909)

Abd·ul·lah \,ab-zə-'lä\ 1882–1951 *'Abd Allāh ibn al-Husayn* emir of Transjordan (1921–46); king of Jordan (1946–51)

Ab·dül·me·cid I \,ab-,dül-mə-'jēd\ 1823–1861 Ottoman sultan (1839–61)

Abel \'ā-bəl\ Sir Frederick Augustus 1827–1902 Eng. chemist

Ab·e·lard \'a-bə-,lärd\ Peter *French* Pierre **Alé·lard** *or* **Abai·lard** \,a-bā-'lär\ 1079–?1144 *husband of Héloïse* Fr. philosopher & theologian

Ab·er·crom·bie *or* **Ab·er·crom·by** \'a-bər-,kräm-bē, -,krəm-\ James 1706–1781 Brit. general in America

Abercromby Sir Ralph 1734–1801 Brit. general

Ab·er·nathy \'a-bər-,na-thē\ Ralph David 1926–1990 Am. clergyman & civil rights leader

Ab·ing·ton \'a-biŋ-tən\ Fanny 1737–1815 née *Frances Barton* Eng. actress

Abruz·zi Duke of the — see LUIGI AMEDEO

Abū al-Qā·sim *or* **Abul Ka·sim** \ə-,bül-'kä-səm\ *Latin* **Al·bu·ca·sis** \al-byù-'kā-səs\ *circa* 936–*circa* 1013 Span. Arab physician & medical writer

Abū Bakr \ə-,bü-'ba-kər\ *circa* 573–634 1st caliph of Mecca

Ach·e·son \'a-chə-sən\ Dean Gooderham 1893–1971 Am. statesman

Ac·ton \'ak-tən\ 1st Baron 1834–1902 *John Emer-ich Edward Dal·berg-Acton* \'dal-,bərg-\ Eng. historian

Ad·am \'a-dəm\ Robert 1728–1792 & his brother James 1730–1794 Scot. architects & furniture designers

Ad·ams \'a-dəmz\ Ansel Easton 1902–1984 Am. photographer

Adams Charles Francis 1807–1886 *son of J.Q.* Am. author & diplomat

Adams Franklin Pierce 1881–1960 *known as F.P.A.* Am. journalist

Adams Henry Brooks 1838–1918 *son of C.F.* Am. historian

Adams James Truslow 1878–1949 Am. historian

Adams John 1735–1826 Am. diplomat; 2d president of the U.S. (1797–1801)

Adams John Quin·cy \'kwin-zē, 'kwin(t)-sē\ 1767–1848 *son of John* 6th president of the U.S. (1825–29)

Adams Maude 1872–1953 originally *Maude Kiskadden* Am. actress

Adams Samuel 1722–1803 Am. Revolutionary patriot

Adams Samuel Hopkins 1871–1958 Am. author

Ad·dams \'a-dəmz\ Jane 1860–1935 Am. social worker

Ad·di·son \'a-də-sən\ Joseph 1672–1719 Eng. essayist & poet — **Ad·di·so·nian** \,a-də-'sō-nē-ən, -nyən\ *adjective*

Ade \'ād\ George 1866–1944 Am. humorist & playwright

Ade·nau·er \'a-dᵊn-,aủ(-ə)r, 'ä-\ Konrad 1876–1967 chancellor of West Germany (1949–63)

Ad·ler \'äd-lər, 'ad-\ Alfred 1870–1937 Austrian psychiatrist

Ad·ler \'ad-lər\ Cyrus 1863–1940 Am. educator & scholar

Ad·ler \'ad-lər\ Felix 1851–1933 Am. educator & reformer

Ad·ler \'ad-lər\ Mortimer Jerome 1902– Am. philosopher

Adri·an \'ā-drē-ən\ name of 6 popes: especially **IV** (*Nicholas Break·spear* \'brāk-,spi(ə)r\) 1100?–1159 the only Eng. pope (1154–59)

Adrian Rom. emperor — see HADRIAN

Adrian Edgar Douglas 1889–1977 1st Baron of *Cambridge* Eng. physiologist

Æ — see George William RUSSELL

Æl·fric \'al-frik\ circa 955–circa 1010 Eng. abbot & writer

Aeneas Silvius or **Sylvius** — see PIUS II

Aes·chi·nes \'es-kə-,nēz, 'ēs-\ 389–314 B.C. Athenian orator

Aes·chy·lus \'es-kə-ləs, 'ēs-\ 525–456 B.C. Greek dramatist — **Aes·chy·le·an** \,es-kə-'lē-ən, ,ēs-\ adjective

Ae·sop \'ē-,säp, -səp\ Greek fabulist; probably legendary

Aeth·el·berht \'a-thəl-,berkt\ or **Eth·el·bert** \'e-thəl-,bert, -thəl-, -,bərt\ or **Aed·il·berct** \'a-d⁰l-,berkt\ died 616 king of Kent (560–616)

Aeth·el·red \'a-thəl-,red\ or **Eth·el·red II** \'e-thəl-\ 968?–1016 the Unready king of England (978–1016)

Afon·so \ə-'fōⁿ(n)-sü\ name of 6 kings of Portugal: especially **I Hen·ri·ques** \āⁿ-'rē-kish\ 1109?–1185 (1st king of Portugal; 1139–85); **V** 1432–1481 (reigned 1438–81)

Aga Khan III \,ä-gə-'kän, ,a-\ 1877–1957 Aga Sultan Sir Mohammed Shah imam of a branch of Shiism (1885–1957)

Aga Khan IV 1936– grandson of preceding, Shah Karim imam of a branch of Shiism (1957–)

Ag·as·siz \'a-gə-(,)sē\ Alexander 1835–1910 son of J.L.R. Am. zoologist

Agassiz (Jean) Louis (Rodolphe) 1807–1873 Am. (Swiss-born) naturalist

Agath·o·cles \ə-'ga-thə-,klēz\ 361–289 B.C. tyrant of Syracuse

Agee \'ā-(,)jē\ James 1909–1955 Am. author

Ages·i·la·us II \ə-,je-sə-'lā-əs\ circa 444–360 B.C. king of Sparta (399–360)

Ag·nes \'ag-nəs\ Saint died A.D. 304 virgin martyr

Ag·new \'ag-,nü, -,nyü\ Spi·ro \'spir-(,)ō\ Theodore 1918–1996 Am. politician; vice president of the U.S. (1969–73)

Ag·non \'ag-,nän\ Shmuel Yosef 1888–1970 Israeli (Austrian-born) author

Agric·o·la \ə-'gri-kə-lə\ Gnaeus Julius A.D. 40–93 Rom. general

Agrip·pa \ə-'gri-pə\ Marcus Vipsanius 63?–12 B.C. Rom. statesman

Ag·rip·pi·na \a-grə-'pī-nə, -'pē-\ the elder circa 14 B.C.–A.D. 33 daughter of Agrippa, wife of Germanicus Caesar, mother of Caligula

Agrippina the younger A.D. 15?–59 daughter of preceding & mother of Emperor Nero

Agui·nal·do \,ä-gē-'näl-(,)dō\ Emilio 1869–1964 Filipino leader

Ah·med III \ä-'met, -'med\ 1673–1736 Ottoman sultan (1703–30)

Ai·ken \'ā-kən\ Conrad Potter 1889–1973 Am. writer

Ai·ley \'ā-lē\ Alvin 1931–1989 Am. dancer & choreographer

Ains·worth \'ānz-(,)wərth\ (William) Harrison 1805–1882 Eng. novelist

Āi·shah \'ä-ē-shə\ 611–678 favorite wife of Muhammad

Ak·bar \'ak-bər, -,bär\ 1542–1605 Mughal emperor of India (1556–1605)

à Kempis — see THOMAS À KEMPIS

Aken·side \'ā-kən-,sīd\ Mark 1721–1770 Eng. poet & physician

Akhe·na·ton \,äk-'nä-tⁿn, ,ä-kə-\ also **Ikh·na·ton** \ik-'nä-tⁿn\ Amenhotep IV king of Egypt (1379–1362 B.C.)

Aki·ba ben Jo·seph \ä-'ki-vä-ben-'jō-zəf\ A.D. 40–135 Jewish sage & martyr in Palestine

Aki·hi·to \,ä-kē-'hē-(,)tō\ 1933– emperor of Japan (1989–)

'Ālam·gīr \'ä-ləm-,gir\ Muhī-ud-Dīn Muhammad 1618–1707 Au·rang·zeb \,aù-rəŋ-'zeb, ò-, -'zēb\ Mughal emperor of India

Alanbrooke Viscount — see Sir Alan Francis BROOKE

Alar·cón, de \,ä-,lär-'kōn, -'kón\ Pedro Antonio 1833–1891 Span. writer & statesman

Al·a·ric \'a-lə-rik\ circa 370–410 Visigoth king; conqueror of Rome

Alaric II died 507 Visigoth king; issued legal code

Al·bee \'ól-(,)bē, 'al-\ Edward Franklin 1928–Am. dramatist

Albemarle Duke of — see George MONCK

Al·bé·niz \äl-'bā-(,)nēs, -(,)nēth\ Isaac 1860–1909 Span. pianist & composer

Al·bers \'al-bərz, 'äl-bərs\ Josef 1888–1976 Am. (Ger.-born) painter

Al·bert I \'al-bərt\ 1875–1934 king of Belgium (1909–34)

Albert Carl Bert 1908– Am. politician

Albert of Saxe–Coburg–Gotha 1819–1861 prince consort of Queen Victoria of Great Britain (1840–61)

Al·ber·tus Mag·nus \al-'bər-təs-'mag-nəs\ Saint circa 1200–1280 Albert Count von Boll·städt \'ból-,shtet\ Ger. philosopher & theologian

Al·boin \'al-,bóin, -bə-wən\ died 572 Lombard king (circa 565–572)

Al·bright \'ól-,brīt\ Madeleine Korbel 1937–U.S. secretary of state (1997–)

Albucasis — see ABŪ AL-QĀSIM

Al·bu·quer·que, de \'al-bə-,kər-kē, ,al-bə-'\ Afonso 1453–1515 Port. viceroy & conqueror in India

Al·cae·us \al-'sē-əs\ circa 620–circa 580 B.C. Greek poet

Al·ci·bi·a·des \,al-sə-'bī-ə-,dēz\ circa 450–404 B.C. Athenian general & politician

Al·cott \'ól-kət, 'al-, -,kät\ Amos Bronson 1799–1888 Am. teacher & philosopher

Alcott Louisa May 1832–1888 daughter of A.B. Am. author

Al·cuin \'al-kwən\ circa 732–804 Anglo-Saxon theologian & scholar

Al·da \'äl-də, 'ól-, 'al-\ Frances 1883–1952 originally *Frances Davis* N.Z.-born soprano

Al·den \'ól-dən\ John 1599?–1687 Mayflower Pilgrim

Al·der \'äl-dər\ Kurt 1902–1958 Ger. chemist

Al·drich \'ól-drich\ Thomas Bailey 1836–1907 Am. author

Al·drin \'ól-drən\ Edwin Eugene Jr. 1930–Am. astronaut

Alei·chem Sha·lom \,shò-ləm-ə-'lā-kəm, ,shō-\ 1859–1916 pseudonym of Sholem Ra·bin·o·witz \rə-'bi-nə-,wits\ Am. (Russ.-born) humorist

Alei·x·an·dre \,ä-lek-'sän-dre\ Vicente 1898–1984 Span. poet

Ale·mán \,ä-lā-'män\ Mateo 1547–circa 1614 Span. novelist

Alemán Val·dés \väl-'des\ Miguel 1902–1983 Mex. lawyer; president of Mexico (1946–52)

Alem·bert, d' \,da-ləm-'bar, -'ber\ Jean Le Rond 1717–1783 Fr. mathematician & philosopher

Al·ex·an·der \,a-lig-'zan-dər, ,e-\ name of 8 popes: especially **VI** (*Rodrigo Borgia*) 1431–1503 (pope 1492–1503)

Alexander III of Macedon 356–323 B.C. the Great king (336–323)

Alexander Russian **Alek·sandr** \ä-lik-'sän-dər\ name of 3 emperors of Russia: **I** 1777–1825 (reigned 1801–25); **II** 1818–1881 (reigned 1855–81); **III** 1845–1894 (reigned 1881–94)

Alexander Serbian **Alek·san·dar Obre·no·vić** \,ä-lik-'sän-dər-ō-'bre-nə-,vich\ 1876–1903 king of Serbia (1889–1903)

Alexander Harold Rupert Leofric George 1891–1969 1st Earl Alexander of Tunis Brit. field marshal; governor-general of Canada (1946–52)

Alexander I 1888–1934 king of Yugoslavia (1929–34)

Alexander Nev·sky \'nev-skē, 'nef-\ circa 1220–1263 Russ. saint & military hero

Alexander Se·ve·rus \sə-'vir-əs\ A.D. 208–235 Rom. emperor (222–235)

Alex·is I Mi·khay·lo·vich \ə-,lek-səs-mi-ˈkī-lə-,vich\ 1629–1676 father of Peter the Great czar of Russia (1645–76)

Alexis Pe·tro·vich \pe-'trō-vich\ 1690–1718 son of Peter the Great czarevitch of Russia

Alex·i·us I Com·ne·nus \ə-'lek-sē-əs-,käm-'nē-nəs\ 1048–1118 Byzantine emperor (1081–1118)

Al·fie·ri \,al-fē-'er-ē\ Conte Vittorio 1749–1803 Ital. tragic poet

Al·fon·so XIII \al-'fän(t)-(,)sō, -'fän-(,)zō\ 1886–1941 king of Spain (1886–1931)

Al·fred or **Æl·fred** \'al-frəd, -fərd\ 849–899 the Great king of Wessex (871–899)

Alf·vén \(,)al(f)-'vän, -'ven\ Hannes Olof Gösta 1908–1995 Swed. astrophysicist

Al·ger \'al-jər\ Horatio 1832–1899 Am. author

Al·gren \'ól-grən\ Nelson 1909–1981 Am. author

'Alī \ä-'lē, 'ä-lē\ Arabic **'Alī ibn Abī Tā·lib** \-,i-bən-,ä-bē-'tä-lib\ circa 600–661 cousin & son-in-law of Muhammad 4th orthodox caliph (656–661)

Ali Pa·şa \'pä-shə, 'pa-; pə-'shä\ 1741–1822 the Lion of Janina Turk. pasha

Ali \ä-'lē\ Muhammad 1942– originally Cassius Marcellus Clay Am. boxer

Al·lais \ä-lā\ Maurice 1911– Fr. economist

Al·len \'a-lən\ Ethan 1738–1789 Am. Revolutionary soldier

Allen William 1532–1594 Eng. cardinal

Al·len·by \'a-lən-bē\ Edmund Henry Hynman 1861–1936 1st Viscount Allenby of Megiddo and Felixstowe Brit. field marshal

Allen·de Gos·sens \ä-,yen-dā-'gò-,sen(t)s\ Salvador 1908–1973 Chilean Marxist; president of Chile (1970–73)

Al·leyne \'a-lən, -,lēn, -,lān\ Edward 1566–1626 Eng. actor

All·ston \'ól-stən\ Washington 1779–1843 Am. painter

Al·ma–Tad·e·ma \,al-mə-'ta-də-mə\ Sir Lawrence 1836–1912 Eng. (Du.-born) painter

Alt·man \'ólt-mən\ Sidney 1939– Am. (Canad.-born) biophysicist

Alva Duke of — see ÁLVAREZ DE TOLEDO

Al·va·ra·do, de \,äl-vä-'rä-thō\ Pedro circa 1485–1541 Span. conquistador

Ál·va·rez \'al-və-,rez\ Luis Walter 1911–1988 Am. physicist

Ál·va·rez de To·le·do \'äl-vä-,räth-thā-tō-'lā-thō\ Fernando 1507–1582 3d Duke of Al·ba \'al-bə\ or Al·va \'al-və\ Span. general

Alvarez Quin·te·ro \kēn-'tä-rō\ Serafín 1871–1938 & his brother Joaquín 1873–1944 Span. dramatist

Ama·ti \ä-'mä-tē, ə-\ family of Ital. violin makers of Cremona: especially Nicolò 1596–1684

Am·brose \'am-,brōz\ Saint 339–397 bishop of Milan — **Am·bro·sian** \am-'brō-zhən, -zē-ən\ adjective

Amen·ho·tep \,ä-mən-'hō-,tep, ,a-\ or **Am·e·no·phis** \,a-mə-'nō-fəs\ name of 4 kings of Egypt: especially **III** (1417–1379 B.C.); **IV**— see AKHENATON

Amerigo Vespucci — see VESPUCCI

Am·herst \'a-(,)mərst\ Jeffrey 1717–1797 Baron Amherst Brit. general; governor-general of Brit. No. America (1760–63)

Amis \'ā-məs\ Kingsley 1922–1995 Eng. author

Am·père \äⁿ-'per\ André-Marie 1775–1836 Fr. physicist

Amund·sen \'ä-mən-sən\ Roald 1872–1928 Norw. polar explorer

Anac·re·on \ə-'na-krē-ən\ circa 582–circa 485 B.C. Greek poet

An·ax·ag·o·ras \,a-,nak-'sa-gə-rəs\ circa 500–circa 428 B.C. Greek philosopher — **An·ax·ag·o·re·an** \-,sa-gə-'rē-ən\ adjective

Anax·i·man·der \ə-'nak-sə-,man-dər\ 610–circa 547 B.C. Greek philosopher & astronomer — **Anax·i·man·dri·an** \ə-,nak-sə-'man-drē-ən\ adjective

An·ders \'än-dərs, -dərz\ Władysław 1892–1970 Pol. general

An·der·sen \'an-dər-sən\ Hans Christian 1805–1875 Dan. writer

An·der·son \'an-dər-sən\ Carl David 1905–1991 Am. physicist

Anderson John 1882–1958 1st Viscount Wa·ver·ley \'wā-vər-lē\ Brit. politician

Anderson Dame Judith 1898–1992 originally Frances Margaret Anderson Austral. actress

Anderson Marian 1897–1993 Am. contralto

Anderson Maxwell 1888–1959 Am. dramatist

Anderson Philip Warren 1923– Am. physicist

Anderson Sherwood 1876–1941 Am. writer

An·drás·sy \'òn-,drä-shē\ Gyula, count; father 1823–1890 & son 1860–1929 Hung. statesmen

An·dré \'an-drē, 'än-(,)drā\ John 1750–1780 Brit. spy

An·drea del Sar·to \än-'drā-ə-,del-'sär-(,)tō\ 1486–1530 *Andrea d'Agnolo* Florentine painter

An·dre·ot·ti \,än-drā-'ä-(,)tē\ Giulio 1919– prime minister of Italy (1972–73; 1976–79; 1989–92)

An·drews \'an-,drüz\ Roy Chapman 1884–1960 Am. naturalist

An·dre·yev \än-'drā-yəf\ Leonid Nikolayevich 1871–1919 Russ. author

An·drić \'än-drich\ Ivo 1892–1975 Serbo-Croatian author

An·dro·pov \an-'drò-,póv\ Yuri Vladimirovich 1914–1984 Russ. politician; president U.S.S.R. (1982–84); 1st secretary of Communist party (1982–84)

An·dros \'an-,dräs, -drəs\ Sir Edmund 1637–1714 Brit. colonial governor in America

An·fin·sen \'an-fən-sən\ Christian Boehmer 1916–1995 Am. chemist

An·ge·la Me·ri·ci \'an-jə-lə-mə-'rē-chē\ Saint 1474?–1540 Ital. religious & founder of Ursuline order

An·ge·li·co \an-'je-li-,kō\ Fra *circa* 1400–1455 originally *Guido di Pietro* Florentine painter

An·gell \'än-jəl\ Sir Norman 1872–1967 originally *Ralph Norman Angell Lane* Eng. author & lecturer

Ång·ström \'aŋ-strəm, 'òŋ-\ Anders Jonas 1814–1874 Swed. physicist

An·na Iva·nov·na \'a-nə-ē-'vä-nəv-nə\ 1693–1740 empress of Russia (1730–40)

An·nan \'a-,nan, 'ä-,nän\ Kofi 1938– Ghanaian U.N. official; secretary-general (1997–)

Anne \'an\ 1665–1714 *daughter of James II* queen of Great Britain (1702–14)

Anne of Austria 1601–1666 *consort of Louis XIII of France* regent (1643–51) for her son Louis XIV

Anne of Cleves \'klēvz\ 1515–1557 *4th wife of Henry VIII of England*

Annunzio, D' Gabriele — see D'ANNUNZIO

Anouilh \a-'nü-ē\ Jean 1910–1987 Fr. dramatist

An·selm \'an-,selm\ Saint 1033/34–1109 archbishop of Canterbury (1093–1109)

An·tall \'òn-,tòl\ József 1932–1993 prime minister of Hungary (1990–93)

An·tho·ny \'an(t)-thə-nē, *chiefly British* 'an-tə-\ Saint *circa* 250–355 Egypt. monk

Anthony Mark — see Marcus ANTONIUS

Anthony Susan Brownell 1820–1906 Am. suffragist

Anthony *or* **An·to·ny** \'an-tə-nē\ **of Padua** Saint 1195–1231 Franciscan friar

An·tig·o·nus I \an-'ti-gə-nəs\ 382–301 B.C. *Antigonus Cyclops* general of Alexander the Great & king of Macedonia (306–301)

An·ti·o·chus \an-'tī-ə-kəs\ name of 13 Seleucid kings of Syria: especially **III** *the Great* 242–187 B.C. (reigned 223–187),**IV** *Epiph·a·nes* \i-'pi-fə-,nēz\ *circa* 215–164 B.C. (reigned 175–164)

An·tip·a·ter \an-'ti-pə-tər\ *circa* 397–*circa* 319 B.C. Macedonian general

An·tis·the·nes \an-'tis-thə-,nēz\ *circa* 445–*circa* 365 B.C. Athenian philosopher

An·to·ne·scu \,an-tə-'nes-(,)kü\ Ion \'yòn\ 1882–1946 Romanian general; dictator (1940–44)

An·to·ni·nus \an-tə-'nī-nəs\ Marcus Au·re·lius \ò-'rēl-yəs, -'rē-lē-əs\ A.D. 121–180 *nephew, son-in-law, and adopted son of Antoninus Pius* Rom. emperor (161–180) & Stoic philosopher

Antoninus Pi·us \-'pī-əs\ A.D. 86–161 Rom. emperor (138–161)

An·to·ni·us \an-'tō-nē-əs\ Marcus *English* Mark *or* Marc An·to·ny \'an-tə-nē\ *or* An·tho·ny \'an(t)-thə-nē, *chiefly Brit* 'an-tə-\ *circa* 82–30 B.C. Rom. orator, triumvir, & general

Apel·les \ə-'pe-lēz\ 4th century B.C. Greek painter

Apol·li·naire \ə-,pä-lə-'nar, -'ner\ Guillaume 1880–1918 originally *Wilhelm Apollinaris de Kos·tro·wit·zki* \,kòs-trə-'vēt-skē\ Fr. poet

Apol·lo·ni·us \,a-pə-'lō-nē-əs\ **of Rhodes** 3d century B.C. Greek poet — **Apol·lo·nian** \-nē-ən, -nyən\ *adjective*

Appius Claudius — see CLAUDIUS

Appleseed Johnny — see John CHAPMAN

Ap·ple·ton \'a-pəl-tən\ Sir Edward 1892–1965 Eng. physicist

Apraks·in *or* **Aprax·in** \ə-'prak-sən\ Fyodor Matveyevich 1661–1728 Russ. admiral

Ap·u·le·ius \,a-pə-'lā-əs\ Lucius *circa* A.D. 124– after 170? Rom. philosopher & rhetorician

Aquinas Saint Thomas — see THOMAS AQUINAS

Aqui·no \ə-'kē-nō\ Corazon 1933– president of Philippines (1986–92)

'Ar·a·fāt \är-ə-'fät, 'ar-ə-,fat\ Yāsir 1929– *Raḥmān 'Abd Arra'ūf Al-Qudwah* Palestinian politician leader

Ar·am \'ar-əm, 'er-\ Eugene 1704–1759 Eng. philologist & murderer

Ara·nha \ə-'ran-yə\ Oswaldo 1894–1960 Braz. lawyer & politician

Ar·ber \'är-bər\ Werner 1929– Swiss microbiologist

Arblay, d' Madame — see Fanny BURNEY

Ar·buth·not \är-'bəth-nət, 'är-bəth-,nät\ John 1667–1735 Scot. physician & author

Ar·cher \'är-chər\ William 1856–1924 Scot. critic & dramatist

Ar·chi·me·des \,är-kə-'mē-dēz\ *circa* 287–212 B.C. Greek mathematician & inventor — **Ar·chi·me·de·an** \-'mē-dē-ən, -mi-\ *adjective*

Ar·chi·pen·ko \,är-kə-'peŋ-(,)kō\ Aleksandr Porfiryevich 1887–1964 Am. (Ukrainian-born) sculptor

Are·ti·no \,ar-ə-'tē-(,)nō\ Pietro 1492–1556 Ital. satirist

Ar·gall \'är-,gòl, -gəl\ Sir Samuel *circa* 1572–*circa* 1626 Eng. mariner

Argyll 9th Duke of — see John D.S. CAMPBELL

Ar·i·as Sán·chez \'är-ē-,äs-'sän-chez\ Oscar 1941– president of Costa Rica (1986–90)

Ari·os·to \,är-ē-'ò-(,)stō\ Ludovico 1474–1533 Ital. poet

Ar·is·tar·chus \,ar-ə-'stär-kəs\ *circa* 217–145 B.C. Greek grammarian

Aristarchus of Samos *flourished circa* 270 B.C. Greek astronomer

Ar·is·tide \,ar-i-'stēd, à-rē-stēd\ Jean-Bertrand 1953– president of Haiti (1991; 1994–96)

Ar·is·ti·des *or* **Ar·is·tei·des** \,ar-ə-'stī-dēz\ *circa* 530–*circa* 468 B.C. *the Just* Athenian statesman

Ar·is·tip·pus \,ar-ə-'sti-pəs\ *circa* 435–366 B.C. Greek philosopher

Ar·is·toph·a·nes \,ar-ə-'stä-fə-,nēz\ *circa* 450–*circa* 388 B.C. Athenian dramatist — **Ar·is·to·phan·ic** \,ar-ə-stə-'fa-nik\ *adjective*

Aristophanes of Byzantium *circa* 257–180 B.C. Greek scholar

Ar·is·tot·le \'ar-ə-,stä-t°l\ 384–322 B.C. Greek philosopher

Ar·i·us \'ar-ē-əs, 'er-\ *circa* A.D. 250–336 Greek theologian

Ark·wright \'ärk-,rīt\ Sir Richard 1732–1792 Eng. inventor

Ar·len \'är-lən\ Michael 1895–1956 originally *Dik·ran* \'di-krän\ *Kou·youm·djian* \kü-'yüm-jē-ən\ Brit. (Bulg.-born) novelist

Ar·min·i·us \är-'mi-nē-əs\ *or* **Ar·min** \är-'mēn\ 18 B.C.?–A.D. 19 sometimes *Her·mann* \'her-,män\ Ger. hero

Arminius Jacobus 1560–1609 *Jacob Har·men·sen* \'här-mən-sən\ or *Her·mansz* \'her-,män(t)s\ Du. theologian

Ar·mour \'är-mər\ Philip Danforth 1832–1901 Am. industrialist

Arm·strong \'ärm-,stròŋ\ Hamilton Fish 1893–1973 Am. editor

Armstrong Louis 1901–1971 *Satch·mo* \'sach-,mō\ Am. jazz musician

Armstrong Neil Alden 1930– Am. astronaut

Armstrong William George 1810–1900 Baron *Armstrong of Cragside* Eng. inventor & industrialist

Arm·strong–Jones \'ärm-,stròŋ-'jōnz\ Antony Charles Robert 1930– Earl of *Snowdon* Eng. photographer

Arne \'ärn\ Thomas Augustine 1710–1778 Eng. composer

Ar·nold \'är-n°ld\ Benedict 1741–1801 Am. Revolutionary general & traitor

Arnold Henry Harley 1886–1950 *Hap Arnold* Am. general

Arnold Matthew 1822–1888 *son of Thomas* Eng. poet & critic — **Ar·nold·ian** \är-'nòl-dē-ən\ *adjective*

Arnold Thomas 1795–1842 Eng. educator

Ar·nold·son \'är-nəld-sən\ Klas Pontus 1844–1916 Swed. pacifist

Arou·et \är-we\ François-Marie — see VOLTAIRE

Arp \'ärp\ Jean (or Hans) 1887–1966 Fr. artist & poet

Ár·pád \'är-,päd\ *died* 907 Hung. national hero

Ar·rau \ä-'raú\ Claudio 1903–1991 Am. (Chilean-born) pianist

Ar·rhe·ni·us \ə-'rē-nē-əs, -'rā-\ Svante August 1859–1927 Swed. physicist & chemist

Ar·row \'ar-(,)ō\ Kenneth Joseph 1921– Am. economist

Ar·son·val, d' \'där-s°n-,väl\ Jacques Arsène 1851–1940 Fr. biophysicist

Ar·ta·xer·xes \,är-tə(g)-'zərk-,sēz\ name of 3 Pers. kings: **I** *died* 425 B.C. (reigned 465–25); **II** *died* 359/58 B.C. (reigned 404–359/58); **III** *died* 338 B.C. (reigned 359/58–338)

Ar·te·vel·de, van \vän-'är-tə-,vel-də\ Jacob *circa* 1295–1345 & his son Philip 1340–1382 Flem. leaders

Ar·thur \'är-thər\ Chester Alan 1829–1886 21st president of the U.S. (1881–85)

As·bury \'az-,ber-ē, -b(ə-)rē\ Francis 1745–1816 Methodist bishop

Asch \'ash\ Sho·lem \'shò-ləm, 'shō-\ *or* Sha·lom \shə-'lōm\ *or* Sho·lom \'shó-ləm, 'shó-, 'shō-\ 1880–1957 Am. (Pol.-born) Yiddish writer

As·cham \'as-kəm\ Roger 1515–1568 Eng. scholar & author

Ashburton Baron — see Alexander BARING

Ash·croft \'ash-,kròft\ Dame Peggy 1907–1991 Brit. actress

Ashton Winifred — see Clemence DANE

Ashur·ba·ni·pal *also* **As·sur·ba·ni·pal** *or* **Asur·ba·ni·pal** \,ä-sər-'bä-nə-,päl, ,ä-shər-\ king of Assyria (668–627 B.C.)

Aśo·ka *or* **Ashō·ka** \ə-'shō-kə, -'sō-\ *died* 238 or 232 B.C. king of India (*circa* 265–238 or *circa* 273–232 B.C.)

As·pa·sia \as-'pā-zh(ē-)ə\ 470?–410 B.C. *consort of Pericles*

As·quith \'as-,kwith, -kwəth\ Herbert Henry 1852–1928 1st Earl of *Oxford and Asquith* Brit. statesman

Assad, al- \al-'ä-,säd\ Hafiz 1928– president of Syria (1971–)

As·ser \'ä-sər\ Tobias Michael Carel 1838–1913 Du. jurist

Astaire \ə-'star, -'ster\ Fred 1899–1987 Am. dancer & actor

As·ton \'as-tən\ Francis William 1877–1945 Eng. physicist

As·tor \'as-tər\ John Jacob 1763–1848 Am. (Ger.-born) fur trader & capitalist

Astor Nancy Witcher 1879–1964 Viscountess *Astor* 1st woman member of Brit. Parliament (1919–45)

As·tu·ri·as \ə-'stúr-ē-əs, -'styúr-\ Miguel Angel 1899–1974 Guatemalan author

Ata·huall·pa *or* **Ata·hual·pa** \,ä-tə-'wäl-pə\ *circa* 1502–1533 last Incan king of Peru

Ath·a·na·si·us \,a-thə-'nā-zh(ē-)əs, -sh(ē-)əs\ Saint *circa* 293–373 Greek (Egyptian-born) church father

Ath·el·stan \'a-thəl-,stan\ *died* 939 Anglo-Saxon ruler

Ath·er·ton \'a-thər-t°n\ Gertrude Franklin 1857–1948 née *Horn* Am. novelist

'At·tār \'a-tər, -,tär\ Farīdied od-Dīn Mohammad ebn Ebrāhīm *circa* 1142–*circa* 1220 Pers. mystical poet

At·ti·la \'a-t°l-ə, ə-'ti-lə\ 406?–453 *the Scourge of God* king of the Huns

Att·lee \'at-lē\ Clement Richard 1883–1967 1st Earl *Attlee* Eng. politician

At·tucks \'a-təks\ Crispus 1723?–1770 Am. patriot

At·wood \'at-,wúd\ Margaret Eleanor 1939– Canad. author

Au·ber \ō-'ber\ Daniel-François-Esprit 1782–1871 Fr. composer

Au·chin·closs \'ò-kən-,kläs\ Louis Stanton 1917– Am. writer

Au·den \'ȯ-d⁽ᵊ⁾n\ Wystan Hugh 1907–1973 Am. (Eng.-born) poet — **Au·den·esque** \ˌȯ-d⁽ᵊ⁾n-'esk\ *adjective*

Au·du·bon \'ȯ-də-bən, -ˌbän\ John James 1785–1851 Am. (Haitian-born) artist & ornithologist

Au·er·bach \'au̇(-ə)r-ˌbäk, -ˌbäk\ Berthold 1812–1882 Ger. novelist

Au·gier \ō-'zhā, -'zhyā; ˌō-zhē-'ā\ Émile 1820–1889 Fr. poet & dramatist

Au·gus·tine \'ȯ-gə-ˌstēn; ȯ-'gəs-tən, ə-\ Saint 354–430 church father; bishop of Hippo (396–430)

Augustine *also* **Aus·tin** \'ȯs-tən, 'äs-\ Saint *died* 604 *Apostle of the English* 1st archbishop of Canterbury (601–04)

Au·gus·tus \ȯ-'gəs-təs, ə-\ 63 B.C.–A.D. 14 originally *Gaius Oc·ta·vi·us* \äk-'tā-vē-əs\ then *Gaius Julius Caesar* 1st Rom. emperor (27 B.C.–A.D. 14)

Aung San Suu Kyi \'ȯŋ-ˌsän-'sü-ˌchē\ 1945– Burmese human rights activist

Aurangzeb — see ʿĀLAMGĪR

Au·re·lian \ȯ-'rēl-yən\ *circa* A.D. 215–275 *Lucius Domitius Aurelianus* Rom. emperor (270–275)

Au·riol \ȯr-ē-'ȯl, -'ȯl\ Vincent 1884–1966 Fr. politician; 1st president of 4th Republic (1947–54)

Au·ro·bin·do \ˌȯr-ə-'bin-dō\ Sri 1872–1950 originally *Sri Aurobindo Ghose* \'gōs\ Indian seer, poet, & nationalist

Aus·ten \'ȯs-tən, 'äs-\ Jane 1775–1817 Eng. novelist

Aus·tin \'ȯs-tən, 'äs-\ Alfred 1835–1913 Eng. poet; poet laureate (1896–1913)

Austin John 1790–1859 Eng. jurist

Austin John Langshaw 1911–1960 Eng. philosopher

Austin Mary 1868–1934 née *Hunter* Am. novelist

Austin Stephen Fuller 1793–1836 Am. colonizer in Texas

Avebury 1st Baron — see LUBBOCK

Avenzoar — see IBN ZUHR

Aver·ro·ës *or* **Aver·rho·ës** \ə-'ver-ə-ˌwēz, ˌa-və-'rō-(ˌ)ēz\ 1126–1198 *also Ibn-Rushd* Span. Arab philosopher & physician

Avery \'ā-və-rē, 'äv-rē\ Milton Clark 1885–1965 Am. artist

Av·i·cen·na \ˌa-və-'se-nə\ 980–1037 *also Ibn Sīnā* Islamic (Pers.-born) philosopher & scientist

Ávi·la Ca·ma·cho \'ä-vē-lə-kə-'mä-(ˌ)chō\ Manuel 1897–1955 Mex. soldier & politician; president of Mexico (1940–46)

Avo·ga·dro \ˌa-və-'gä-(ˌ)drō, ˌä-\ Amedeo 1776–1856 *Conte di Quaregna e Ceretto* Ital. chemist & physicist

Avon Earl of — see Anthony EDEN

Ax·el·rod \'ak-səl-ˌräd\ Julius 1912– Am. biochemist

Ay·de·lotte \'ā-d⁽ᵊ⁾l-ˌät\ Frank 1880–1956 Am. educator

Ayer \'ar, 'er\ Sir Alfred Jules 1910–1989 Eng. philosopher

Ayl·win Azó·car \'āl-win-ä-'sō-kär\ Patricio 1918– president of Chile (1990–94)

Aza·ña y Di·az \ə-'thän-yə-ē-'thē-äth\ Manuel 1880–1940 Span. politician; president of Spain (1936–39)

Ba'al Shem Tov — see ISRAEL BEN ELIEZER

Bab·bitt \'ba-bət\ Bruce Edward 1938– U.S. secretary of interior (1993–)

Babbitt Irving 1865–1933 Am. scholar

Ba·beuf \bä-'bəf, bȧ-bœf\ François-Noël 1760–1797 Fr. agitator

Bab·ing·ton \'ba-biŋ-tən\ Anthony 1561–1586 Eng. conspirator against Queen Elizabeth I

Bab·son \'bab-sən\ Roger Ward 1875–1967 Am. statistician

Bā·bur \'bä-bər\ 1483–1530 *Zahīr-ud-Dīn Muhammad* founder of Mogul dynasty of India; emperor (1526–30)

Ba·bu·ren \bä-'bœ̄-rən, -'bir-ən\ Dirck van *circa* 1590–1624 Du. painter

Bach \'bäk, 'bäk\ Carl Philipp Emanuel 1714–1788 *son of J.S.* Ger. composer

Bach Johann Christian 1735–1782 *son of J.S.* Ger. organist & composer

Bach Johann Sebastian 1685–1750 Ger. organist & composer

Bach Wilhelm Friedemann 1710–1784 *son of J.S.* Ger. organist & composer

Ba·con \'bā-kən\ Francis 1561–1626 1st Baron *Ver·u·lam* \'ver-(y)ə-ləm\ Viscount *St. Al·bans* \sänt-'ȯl-bənz, sənt-\ Eng. philosopher

Bacon Francis 1909–1992 Brit. (Irish-born) painter

Bacon Nathaniel 1647–1676 Am. colonial leader

Bacon Roger *circa* 1220–1292 Eng. philosopher and scientist

Ba·den-Pow·ell \'bā-d⁽ᵊ⁾n-'pō-əl\ Robert Stephenson Smyth 1857–1941 1st Baron of *Gilwell* founder of Boy Scout movement

Ba·do·glio \bə-'dōl-(ˌ)yō\ Pietro 1871–1956 Ital. general; prime minister (1943–44)

Bae·yer, von \'bā-ər\ Adolf 1835–1917 Ger. chemist

Baf·fin \'ba-fən\ William *circa* 1584–1622 Eng. navigator

Bage·hot \'ba-jət\ Walter 1826–1877 Eng. economist & journalist

Ba·gra·tion \bä-ˌgrä-tē-'ȯn, -ˌgrät-sē-; ˌbä-grə-'tyȯn\ Prince Pyotr Ivanovich 1765–1812 Russ. general

Ba·hā' Al·lāh *or* **Ba·ha·ul·lah** \bä-'hä-ù-'lä\ Mīrzā Ḥoseyn Alī Nūrī 1817–1892 Pers. founder of the Bahā'ī faith

Bai·ley \'bā-lē\ Liberty Hyde 1858–1954 Am. botanist

Bailey Nathan *or* Nathaniel *died* 1742 Eng. lexicographer

Bailey Pearl Mae 1918–1990 Am. singer

Bail·lie \'bā-lē\ Joanna 1762–1851 Scot. dramatist & poet

Bain \'bān\ Alexander 1818–1903 Scot. psychologist

Baird \'bard, 'berd\ John Logie 1888–1946 *father of television* Scot. inventor

Bairns·fa·ther \'barnz-ˌfä-thər, 'bernz-\ Bruce 1888–1959 Eng. cartoonist

Ba·jer \'bī-(ə)r\ Fredrik 1837–1922 Dan. statesman & writer

Ba·ker \'bā-kər\ James Addison 1930– U.S. secretary of treasury (1985–88); secretary of state (1989–92)

Baker Newton Diehl 1871–1937 Am. statesman

Baker Ray Stannard 1870–1946 pseudonym *David Gray·son* \'grās-⁰n\ Am. author

Baker Sir Samuel White 1821–1893 Eng. explorer in Africa

Bakst \'bäkst\ Léon 1866–1924 originally *Lev Samoylovich Rosenberg* Russ. painter

Ba·ku·nin \bə-'kün-yən, bä-, -'kü-nən\ Mikhail Aleksandrovich 1814–1876 Russ. anarchist

Bal·an·chine \ˌba-lən-'shēn, 'ba-lən-,\ George 1904–1983 *Georgy Melitonovich Balanchivadze* Am. (Russ.-born) choreographer

Bal·bo \'bäl-(ˌ)bō\ Italo 1896–1940 Ital. aviator & politician

Bal·boa \bal-'bō-ə\ Vasco Núñez de 1475–1519 Span. explorer & conquistador

Balch \'bȯlch\ Emily Greene 1867–1961 Am. economist & sociologist

Bald·win I \'bȯl-dwən\ 1058?–1118 *brother of Godfrey of Bouillon* king of Jerusalem (1100–18)

Baldwin James 1924–1987 Am. writer

Baldwin James Mark 1861–1934 Am. psychologist

Baldwin Stanley 1867–1947 1st Earl *Baldwin of Bewd·ley* \'byüd-lē\ Eng. statesman

Balfe \'balf\ Michael William 1808–1870 Irish composer & singer

Bal·four \'bal-fər, -ˌfȯr, -ˌfȯr\ Arthur James 1848–1930 1st Earl of Balfour; Brit. philosopher & statesman

Ba·liol *or* **Bal·liol** \'bāl-yəl\ John de 1249–1315 king of Scotland (1292–96)

Ball \'bȯl\ John *died* 1381 Eng. priest & social agitator

Bal·lan·tyne \'ba-lən-ˌtīn\ James 1772–1833 Scot. printer

Bal·ti·more \'bȯl-tə-ˌmȯr, -ˌmȯr, -mər\ David 1938– Am. microbiologist

Baltimore Baron — see George CALVERT

Bal·zac \'bȯl-ˌzak, 'bal-,\ *French* bȧl-zȧk\ Honoré de 1799–1850 Fr. novelist — **Bal·za·cian** \bȯl-'zä-shən, bal-, -'za-kē-ən\ *adjective*

Ban·croft \'ban-ˌkrȯft, 'baŋ-\ George 1800–1891 Am. historian

Bancroft Richard 1544–1610 Eng. prelate; archbishop of Canterbury (1604–10)

Ban·del·lo \ban-'de-(ˌ)lō, bän-\ Matteo 1485–1561 Ital. writer

Bangs \'baŋz\ John Kendrick 1862–1922 Am. humorist

Banks \'baŋ(k)s\ Sir Joseph 1743–1820 Eng. naturalist

Ban·ting \'ban-tiŋ\ Sir Frederick Grant 1891–1941 Canad. physician

Ba·ra·nov \bə-'rä-nəf\ Aleksandr Andreyevich 1747–1819 Russ. fur trader; 1st governor of Russ. America

Bá·rány \'bär-ˌän-yə\ Robert 1876–1936 Austrian physician

Barbarossa — see FREDERICK I

Bar·ba·ros·sa \ˌbär-bə-'rä-sə, -'rȯ-\ *died* 1546 *Khayr ad-Dīn* Barbary pirate

Bar·ber \'bär-bər\ Samuel 1910–1981 Am. composer

Bar·bie \'bär-bē\ Klaus 1913–1991 Ger. Nazi leader

Bar·busse \bär-büs; bär-'büs, -'byüs\ Henri 1873–1935 Fr. author

Bar·clay \'bär-klē\ Robert 1648–1690 Scot. Quaker author

Bar·clay de Tol·ly \ˌbär-'klī-də-'tō-lē, -'klä-\ Prince Mikhail 1761–1818 Russ. field marshal

Bar·deen \bär-'dēn\ John 1908–1991 Am. physicist

Ba·rents \'bar-ən(t)s, 'bär-\ Willem *circa* 1550–1597 Du. navigator

Bar·ing \'bar-iŋ, 'ber-\ Alexander 1774–1848 1st Baron *Ash·bur·ton* \'ash-ˌbər-t⁽ᵊ⁾n\ Brit. financier & diplomat

Baring Evelyn 1841–1917 1st Earl of *Cro·mer* \'krō-mər\ Brit. diplomat

Bark·la \'bär-klə\ Charles Glover 1877–1944 Eng. physicist

Bark·ley \'bär-klē\ Al·ben \'al-bən\ William 1877–1956 Am. lawyer & politician; vice president of U.S. (1949–53)

Bar·low \'bär-ˌlō\ Joel 1754–1812 Am. poet & diplomat

Bar·nard \'bär-nərd, -ˌnärd\ Christiaan Neethling 1922– So. African surgeon

Bar·nard \'bär-nərd\ George Grey 1863–1938 Am. sculptor

Barnevelt Jan van Olden — see OLDENBARNEVELT

Bar·num \'bär-nəm\ Phineas Taylor 1810–1891 Am. showman — **Bar·num·esque** \ˌbär-nə-'mesk\ *adjective*

Ba·ro·ja \bä-'rō-(ˌ)hä\ Pío 1872–1956 Span. writer

Barozzi Giacomo — see VIGNOLA

Bar·rès \ba-'res\ Auguste-Maurice 1862–1923 Fr. novelist & politician

Bar·rie \'bar-ē\ Sir James Matthew 1860–1937 Scot. novelist & dramatist

Bar·ros \'bär-üsh\ João de *circa* 1496–1570 Port. historian

Bar·row \'bar-(ˌ)ō\ Isaac 1630–1677 Eng. mathematician & theologian

Bar·ry \bä-rē\ Jeanne Bécu 1743–1793 *Comtesse du Barry* mistress of Louis XV of France

Bar·ry \'bar-ē\ Philip 1896–1949 Am. dramatist

Bar·ry·more \'bar-i-ˌmȯr, -ˌmȯr\ family of Am. actors: Maurice 1847–1905 originally *Herbert Blythe;* his wife Georgiana Emma 1854–1893 *daughter of John Drew;* their children Lionel 1878–1954, Ethel 1879–1959, & John Blythe 1882–1942

Bart \'bär\ *or* **Barth** \'bärt\ Jean 1650–1702 Fr. naval hero

Barth \'bärth\ John Simmons 1930– Am. author

Barth \'bärt, 'bärth\ Karl 1886–1968 Swiss theologian — **Barth·ian** \'bär-tē-ən, -thē-\ *adjective*

Bar·thol·di \bär-'täl-dē, -'tȯl-, -'thäl-, -'thȯl-\ Frédéric-Auguste 1834–1904 Fr. sculptor

Bar·thol·o·mew \bär-'thä-lə-ˌmyü\ 1940– archbishop of Constantinople and ecumenical patriarch (1991–)

Bart·lett \'bärt-lət\ John 1820–1905 Am. publisher & editor

Bar·tók \'bär-ˌtäk, -ˌtȯk\ Bé·la \'bā-lə\ 1881–1945 Hung. composer

Bar·to·lom·meo \ˌbär-ˌtō-lə-'mā-(ˌ)ō\ Fra 1472–1517 *Baccio della Porta* Florentine painter

Bar·ton \'bär-tᵊn\ Clara 1821–1912 in full *Clarissa Harlowe Barton* founder of Am. Red Cross Society

Barton Sir Derek Harold Richard 1918– Brit. chemist

Bar·tram \'bär-trəm\ John 1699–1777 Am. botanist

Bartram William 1739–1823 *son of John* Am. naturalist

Ba·ruch \bə-'rük\ Bernard Man·nes \'ma-nəs\ 1870–1965 Am. businessman & statesman

Ba·rysh·ni·kov \bə-'rish-nə-ˌkóf\ Mikhail 1948– Am. (Latvian-born) ballet dancer

Bashō — see MATSUO

Ba·sie \'bā-sē\ William 1904–1984 *Count* Am. bandleader & composer

Bas·il \'bā-zəl, 'ba-, -səl\ *or* **Ba·sil·i·us** \bə-'si-lē-əs, -'zi-\ Saint *circa* 329–379 *the Great* church father; bishop of Caesarea

Bas·ker·ville \'bas-kər-ˌvil\ John 1706–1775 Eng. typographer

Ba·sov \'bä-ˌsóf, -ˌsòv\ Nikolay Gennadiyevich 1922– Russ. physicist

Bates \'bāts\ Katharine Lee 1859–1929 Am. poet & educator

Ba·tis·ta y Zal·dí·var \bə-'tēs-tə-ˌē-zäl-'dē-ˌvär\ Fulgencio 1901–1973 Cuban soldier; president of Cuba (1940–44; 1952–59)

Bat·tā·nī, al- \ˌal-bə-'tä-nē\ *circa* 858–929 *Al·ba·te·gni* \ˌal-bə-'tän-yē\ *or Al·ba·te·ni·us* \-'tē-nē-əs\ Arab astronomer

Bau·de·laire \bōd-'lar, -'ler\ Charles-Pierre 1821–1867 Fr. poet — **Bau·de·lair·ean** *also* **Bau·de·lair·ian** \-ē-ən\ *adjective*

Bau·douin \bō-'dwaⁿ\ 1930–1993 king of Belgium (1951–93)

Baum \'bäm\ Lyman Frank 1856–1919 Am. journalist & writer

Baum \'baúm\ Vicki 1888–1960 Am. (Austrian-born) novelist

Bau·mé \bō-'mā\ Antoine 1728–1804 Fr. chemist

Bax·ter \'bak-stər\ Richard 1615–1691 Eng. Puritan scholar & writer

Ba·yard \'bī-ərd, 'bā-ərd, *French* bá-yàr\ Pierre Terrail *circa* 1473–1524 *Seigneur de Bayard* Fr. military hero

Bayle \'bā(ə)l, 'bel\ Pierre 1647–1706 Fr. philosopher & critic

Beaconsfield Earl of — see Benjamin DISRAELI

Bea·dle \'bē-dᵊl\ George Wells 1903–1989 Am. biologist

Beard \'bird\ Charles Austin 1874–1948 & his wife Mary née *Ritter* 1876–1958 Am. historians

Beard Daniel Carter 1850–1941 Am. painter, illustrator, & organizer of Boy Scouts in U.S.

Beards·ley \'birdz-lē\ Aubrey Vincent 1872–1898 Eng. illustrator — **Beards·ley·esque** \ˌbirdz-lē-'yesk\ *adjective*

Be·a·trix \'bā-ə-ˌtriks\ 1938– queen of the Netherlands (1980–)

Beat·tie \'bē-tē\ James 1735–1803 Scot. poet

Beau·fort \'bō-fərt\ Sir Francis 1774–1857 Brit. admiral

Beaufort Henry *circa* 1374–1447 Eng. cardinal & statesman

Beau·har·nais, de \ˌbō-ˌär-'nā\ Fr. family including: Vicomte Alexandre 1760–1794 general; his wife Joséphine 1763–1814 later the *1st wife of Napoleon I;* their son Eugène 1781–1824 prince of Eich·stätt \'īk-ˌshtet\; their daughter Hortense \òr-'täⁿs\ 1783–1837 *wife of Louis Bonaparte & mother of Napoleon III*

Beau·mar·chais \ˌbō-ˌmär-'shā\ Pierre-Augustin Caron de 1732–1799 Fr. dramatist & businessman

Beau·mont \'bō-ˌmänt, -mənt\ Francis 1584–1616 Eng. dramatist

Beau·mont \-ˌmänt\ William 1785–1853 Am. surgeon

Beau·re·gard \'bōr-ə-ˌgärd, 'bòr-\ Pierre Gustave Toutant 1818–1893 Am. Confederate general

Beau·voir, de \də-bō-'vwär\ Simone 1908–1986 Fr. author

Bea·ver·brook \'bē-vər-ˌbrúk\ 1st Baron 1879–1964 *William Maxwell Aitken* Brit. (Canad.-born) newspaper publisher

Be·bel \'bā-bəl\ August 1840–1913 Ger. Social Democrat leader & writer

Beck·er \'be-kər\ Gary Stanley 1930– Am. economist

Beck·et \'be-kət\ Saint Thomas *circa* 1118–1170 *Thomas à Becket* archbishop of Canterbury (1162–70)

Beck·ett \'be-kət\ Samuel 1906–1989 Irish author in France — **Beck·ett·ian** \be-'ke-tē-ən\ *adjective*

Beck·ford \'bek-fərd\ William 1760–1844 Eng. author

Bec·que·rel \be-'krel, ˌbe-kə-'rel\ family of Fr. physicists including: Antoine-César 1788–1878; his son Alexandre-Edmond 1820–1891; the latter's son Antoine-Henri 1852–1908

Bed·does \'be-(ˌ)dōz\ Thomas Lovell 1803–1849 Eng. writer

Bede \'bēd\ *or* **Bae·da** *or* **Be·da** \'bē-də\ Saint *circa* 672–735 *the Venerable Bede* Anglo-Saxon scholar, historian, & theologian

Bedford Duke of — see JOHN OF LANCASTER

Bed·norz \'bed-ˌnòrts\ Johannes Georg 1950– Ger. physicist

Bee·be \'bē-bē\ Charles William 1877–1962 Am. naturalist & explorer

Bee·cham \'bē-chəm\ Sir Thomas 1879–1961 Eng. conductor

Bee·cher \'bē-chər\ Henry Ward 1813–1887 Am. clergyman

Beecher Lyman 1775–1863 *father of H.W. & of Harriet Beecher Stowe* Am. Presbyterian clergyman

Beer·bohm \'bir-ˌbōm, -bəm\ Sir Max 1872–1956 Eng. critic & caricaturist

Beer·naert \'ber-ˌnärt\ Auguste Marie François 1829–1912 Belg. statesman

Bee·tho·ven \'bā-ˌtō-vən\ Ludwig van 1770–1827 Ger. composer — **Bee·tho·ve·nian** \ˌbā-ˌtō-'vē-nyən\ *adjective*

Be·gin \'bā-gin\ Me·na·chem \mə-'nä-kəm\ 1913–1992 prime minister of Israel (1977–83)

Be·han \'bē-ən\ Brendan Francis 1923–1964 Irish dramatist

Beh·ring \'ber-iŋ\ Emil von 1854–1917 Ger. bacteriologist

Behr·man \'ber-mən\ Samuel Nathaniel 1893–1973 Am. dramatist

Bé·ké·sy \'bā-kə-shē\ Georg von 1899–1972 Am. (Hung.-born) physicist

Be·las·co \bə-'las-(ˌ)kō\ David 1853–1931 Am. dramatist & producer

Bel·i·sar·i·us \ˌbe-lə-'sar-ē-əs, -'ser-\ *circa* 505–565 Byzantine general

Bell \'bel\ Alexander Graham 1847–1922 Am. (Scot.-born) inventor

Bel·la·my \'be-lə-mē\ Edward 1850–1898 Am. author

Bel·lay, du \ˌdü-bə-'lā, ˌdyü-\ Joachim *circa* 1522–1560 Fr. poet

Bel·li·ni \bə-'lē-nē\ family of Venetian painters including: Jacopo *circa* 1400–*circa* 1470 and his sons Gentile *circa* 1429–1507 and Giovanni *circa* 1430–1516

Bellini Vincenzo 1801–1835 Ital. composer

Bel·loc \'be-ˌläk, -lək\ (Joseph-Pierre) Hilaire 1870–1953 Eng. author

Bel·low \'be-(ˌ)lō\ Saul 1915– Am. (Canad.-born) writer

Bel·lows \'be-(ˌ)lōz\ George Wesley 1882–1925 Am. painter & lithographer

Be·lo \'be-(ˌ)lü\ Carlos Filipe Xi·men·es \shē-'me-nēsh\ 1948– Indonesian bishop & peace activist

Be·na·cer·raf \be-'na-sə-ˌräf\ Baruj 1920– Am. (Venezuelan-born) pathologist

Be·na·ven·te y Mar·tí·nez \be-nə-'ven-tē-ˌē-ˌmär-'tē-nəs\ Jacinto 1866–1954 Span. dramatist

Bench·ley \'bench-lē\ Robert Charles 1889–1945 Am. humorist

Ben·e·dict \'be-nə-ˌdikt\ name of 15 popes: especially **XIV** (*Prospero Lambertini*) 1675–1758 (pope 1740–58); **XV** (*Giacomo della Chiesa*) 1854–1922 (pope 1914–22)

Benedict of Nur·sia \'nər-sh(ē-)ə\ Saint *circa* 480–*circa* 547 Ital. founder of Benedictine order

Benedict Ruth 1887–1948 née *Fulton* Am. anthropologist

Be·neš \'be-ˌnesh\ Edvard 1884–1948 Czech statesman; president (1935–38; 1940–48)

Be·nét \bə-'nā\ Stephen Vincent 1898–1943 *brother of W.R.* Am. poet

Benét William Rose 1886–1950 Am. poet, novelist, & editor

Ben–Gu·rion \ˌben-gür-'yón, ben-'gúr-ē-ən\ David 1886–1973 Israeli (Pol.-born) statesman; prime minister of Israel (1949–53; 1955–63)

Ben·ja·min \'ben-jə-mən\ Judah Philip 1811–1884 Am. Confederate statesman & lawyer

Ben·nett \'be-nət\ (Enoch) Arnold 1867–1931 Eng. novelist

Bennett James Gordon 1795–1872 Am. (Scot.-born) journalist

Bennett Richard Bedford 1870–1947 *Viscount Bennett* Canad. prime minister (1930–35)

Be·noît de Sainte–Maure \ben-'wä-də-(ˌ)sa⁽n⁾t-'mòr\ 12th century Fr. trouvère

Ben·son \ben(t)-sən\ Edward White 1829–1896 Brit. prelate; archbishop of Canterbury (1882–96)

Ben·tham \'ben(t)-thəm\ Jeremy 1748–1832 Eng. jurist & philosopher

Ben·tinck \'ben-ti(ŋ)k\ Lord William Cavendish 1774–1839 *son of W.H.C.* 1st governor-general of India (1833)

Bentinck William Henry Cavendish 1738–1809 3d Duke of *Portland* Brit. prime minister (1783; 1807–09)

Bent·ley \'bent-lē\ Richard 1662–1742 Eng. clergyman, scholar, & critic

Ben·ton \'ben-tᵊn\ Thomas Hart 1782–1858 *Old Bullion* Am. politician

Benton Thomas Hart 1889–1975 Am. painter

Bé·ran·ger \bā-rä⁽ⁿ⁾-zhā\ Pierre-Jean de 1780–1857 Fr. poet

Ber·dya·yev \bərd-'yä-yəf, bər-'jä-\ Nikolay Aleksandrovich 1874–1948 Russ. philosopher

Ber·en·son \'ber-ən-sən\ Bernard 1865–1959 Am. (Lith.-born) art critic

Berg \'berg\ Alban 1885–1935 Austrian composer

Berg \'bərg\ Paul 1926– Am. chemist

Bergerac, de Cyrano — see CYRANO DE BERGERAC

Ber·gi·us \'ber-gē-əs\ Friedrich 1884–1949 Ger. chemist

Berg·man \'bərg-mən, *Swedish* 'ber-ē-màn\ Ingmar 1918– Swed. film & theater director

Berg·son \'berg-sən, berk-sō⁽ⁿ⁾\ Henri-Louis 1859–1941 Fr. philosopher — **Berg·son·ian** \berg-'sō-nē-ən, berk-\ *adjective*

Berg·ström \'berg-strəm, 'bar-ē-strùm\ K. Sune D. 1916– Swed. biochemist

Be·ria *or* **Be·ri·ya** \'ber-ē-ə\ Lavrenty Pavlovich 1899–1953 Russ. politician

Be·ring \'ber-iŋ, 'bir-\ Vitus Jonassen 1681–1741 Dan. navigator

Berke·ley \'bär-klē, 'bər-\ George 1685–1753 Irish bishop & philosopher

Berke·ley \'bər-klē\ Sir William 1606–1677 colonial governor of Virginia

Ber·lich·ing·en \'ber-li-ˌkiŋ-ən\ Götz *or* Gottfried von 1480–1562 Ger. knight

Ber·lin \(ˌ)bər-'lin\ Irving 1888–1989 Am. (Russ.-born) composer

Ber·li·ner \'bər-lə-nər\ Emile 1851–1929 Am. (Ger.-born) inventor

Ber·li·oz \'ber-lē-ˌōz\ Hector 1803–1869 in full *Louis-Hector Berlioz* Fr. composer — **Ber·li·oz·ian** \ˌber-lē-'ō-zē-ən\ *adjective*

Ber·na·dette de Lourdes \ˌbər-nə-'det\ Saint 1844–1879 *Marie-Bernarde Sou·bi·rous* \ˌsü-bē-'rü\ Fr. religious

Bernadotte Jean Baptiste Jules — see CHARLES XIV JOHN

Ber·nard \ber-'när\ Claude 1813–1878 Fr. physiologist

Ber·nard of Clair·vaux \bər-'närd-əv-ˌklar-'vō, ber-'när-, -ˌkler-\ Saint 1090–1153 Fr. ecclesiastic — **Ber·nar·dine** \'bər-nə(r)-ˌdēn\ *adjective*

Ber·nar·din de Saint–Pierre \ˌber-nər-'da⁽ⁿ⁾-də-ˌsänt-pē-'er\ Jacques-Henri 1737–1814 Fr. author

Berners Baron — see TYRWHITT-WILSON

Bern·hardt \'bərn-ˌhärt, ber-'när\ Sarah 1844–1923 originally *Henriette-Rosine Bernard* \ber-när\ Fr. actress

Ber·ni·ni \ber-'nē-nē\ Gian *or* Giovanni Lorenzo 1598–1680 Ital. sculptor, architect, & painter

Bern·stein \'bərn-ˌstīn *also* -ˌstēn\ Leonard 1918–1990 Am. conductor & composer

Bern·storff \'bern-ˌshtòrf\ Johann-Heinrich 1862–1939 Graf *von Bernstorff* Ger. diplomat

Ber·ry·man \'ber-ē-mən\ John 1914–1972 Am. poet

Ber·thier \ber-'tyā\ Louis-Alexandre 1753–1815 Prince *de Neuchâtel;* Prince *de Wagram* Fr. soldier; marshal of France

Ber·til·lon \ˌber-tē-'yōⁿ\ Alphonse 1853–1914 Fr. criminologist

Ber·ton \'bər-tᵊn\ Pierre 1920– Canad. writer

Ber·ze·li·us \(ˌ)bər-'zē-lē-əs, ber-'zā-\ Baron Jöns Jakob 1779–1848 Swed. chemist

Bes·ant \'be-sᵊnt, -zᵊnt\ Annie 1847–1933 née *Wood* Eng. theosophist

Bes·se·mer \'be-sə-mər\ Sir Henry 1813–1898 Eng. engineer

Best \'best\ Charles Herbert 1899–1978 Canad. (Am.-born) physiologist

Be·tan·court \ˌbe-ˌtän-'kùr(t), -tän-\ Rómulo 1908–1981 Venezuelan president (1959–64)

Be·the \'bā-tə\ Hans Albrecht 1906– Am. (Ger.-born) physicist

Beth·mann–Holl·weg \'bet-mən-'hȯl-ˌväg, -ˌmän-\ Theobald Theodor Friedrich Alfred von 1856–1921 Ger. statesman; chancellor (1909–17)

Be·thune \bə-'thün, -'thyün\ Mary 1875–1955 née *McLeod* Am. educator

Bet·je·man \'be-chə-mən\ Sir John 1906–1984 Brit. author; poet laureate (1972–84)

Bet·tel·heim \'be-təl-ˌhīm\ Bruno 1903–1990 Am. (Austrian-born) psychologist

Bet·ter·ton \'be-tər-tᵊn\ Thomas *circa* 1635–1710 Eng. actor

Bev·er·idge \'be-və-rij, 'bev-rij\ Albert Jeremiah 1862–1927 Am. politician & historian

Beveridge William Henry 1879–1963 1st Baron *Beveridge of Tug·gal* \'tə-gəl\ Eng. economist

Bev·in \'be-vən\ Ernest 1881–1951 Brit. labor leader & politician

Beyle Marie-Henri — see STENDHAL

Bhu·mi·bol Adul·ya·dej \'pü-mē-ˌpȯn-ä-'dùn-lə-ˌdāt—*sic*\ 1927– king of Thailand (1946–)

Bhut·to \'bü-tō\ Benazir 1953– prime minister of Pakistan (1988–90; 1993–96)

Bi·dault \bē-'dō\ Georges 1899–1983 Fr. statesman

Bid·dle \'bi-dᵊl\ John 1615–1662 founder of Eng. Unitarianism

Biddle Nicholas 1786–1844 Am. financier

Bien·ville \bē-'en-ˌvil, -vəl; byaⁿ-'vēl\ Jean-Baptiste Le Moyne, sieur de 1680–1768 Fr. colonial governor of Louisiana

Bierce \'birs\ Ambrose Gwinnett 1842–?1914 Am. author

Bier·stadt \'bir-ˌstat\ Albert 1830–1902 Am. (Ger.-born) painter

Bing·ham \'biŋ-əm\ George Caleb 1811–1879 Am. painter

Bin·nig \'bi-nik\ Gerd 1947– Ger. physicist

Bi·on \'bī-ˌän, -ən\ *flourished* 100 B.C. Greek bucolic poet

Birk·beck \'bər(k)-ˌbek\ George 1776–1841 Eng. physician

Bir·ken·head \'bər-kən-ˌhed\ 1st Earl of 1872–1930 *Frederick Edwin Smith* Eng. jurist & statesman

Bi·ron \'bē-ˌrȯn\ Ernst Johann 1690–1772 originally *Büh·ren* \'bū̇-rən\ Duke of *Kurland* Ger. politician in Russia

Bish·op \'bi-shəp\ Elizabeth 1911–1979 Am. poet

Bishop John Michael 1936– Am. microbiologist

Bis·marck \'biz-ˌmärk\ Prince Otto Eduard Leopold von 1815–1898 in full *Bismarck-Schön·hau·sen* \-shȯn-'hau̇-zᵊn\ 1st chancellor of Ger. Empire (1871–90) — **Bis·marck·ian** \biz-'mär-kē-ən\ *adjective*

Bi·zet \bē-'zā\ Alexandre-César-Léopold 1838–1875 called *Georges* Fr. composer

Bjørn·son \'byǝrn-sǝn\ Bjørnstjerne Martinius 1832–1910 Norw. poet, dramatist, & novelist

Black \'blak\ Hugo LaFayette 1886–1971 Am. jurist & politician

Black Sir James Whyte 1924– Brit. pharmacologist

Black·ett \'bla-kət\ Patrick Maynard Stuart 1897–1974 Brit. physicist

Black Hawk \'blak-ˌhȯk\ 1767–1838 *Ma-ka-ta-i-me-she-kia-kiak* Sauk Indian chief

Black·more \'blak-ˌmȯr, -ˌmȯr\ Richard Doddridge 1825–1900 Eng. novelist

Black·mun \'blak-mən\ Harry Andrew 1908– Am. jurist

Black·stone \'blak-ˌstōn, *chiefly British* -stən\ Sir William 1723–1780 Eng. jurist

Black·well \'blak-ˌwel, -wəl\ Elizabeth 1821–1910 Am. physician

Black·wood \'blak-ˌwu̇d\ William 1776–1834 Scot. publisher

Blaine \'blān\ James Gillespie 1830–1893 Am. statesman

Blair \'blar, 'bler\ Tony 1953– *Anthony Charles Lynton Blair* Brit. prime minister (1997–)

Blake \'blāk\ Eugene Carson 1906–1985 Am. clergyman

Blake Robert 1599–1657 Eng. admiral

Blake William 1757–1827 Eng. artist, poet, & mystic — **Blak·ean** \'blā-kē-ən\ *adjective*

Blanc \'blaŋk\ Melvin Jerome 1908–1989 *Mel* Am. actor

Blas·co Ibá·ñez \'bläs-(ˌ)kō-ē-'bän-(ˌ)yäs\ Vicente 1867–1928 Span. novelist

Bla·vat·sky \blä-'vat-skē, -'vät-\ Helena Petrovna 1831–1891 née *Hahn* Russ. traveler & theosophist

Blé·riot \'bler-ē-ˌō\ Louis 1872–1936 Fr. engineer & pioneer aviator

Bligh \'blī\ William 1754–1817 Eng. naval officer

Bloch \'bläk, 'blȯk, 'blȯk\ Ernest 1880–1959 Am. (Swiss-born) composer

Bloch \'bläk\ Felix 1905–1983 Am. physicist

Bloch \'bläk, 'blȯk, 'blȯk\ Konrad Emil 1912– Am. (Ger.-born) biochemist

Block \'bläk\ Herbert Lawrence 1909– *Herblock* \'hər-ˌbläk\ Am. editorial cartoonist

Bloem·ber·gen \'blüm-ˌbər-gən\ Nicolaas 1920– Am. (Du.-born) physicist

Bloom·er \'blü-mər\ Amelia 1818–1894 née *Jenks* Am. reformer

Bloom·field \'blüm-ˌfēld\ Leonard 1887–1949 Am. linguist — **Bloom·field·ian** \ˌblüm-'fēl-dē-ən\ *adjective*

Blü·cher \'blü-kər, 'blu̇-kər\ Gebhard Leberecht von 1742–1819 prince of *Wahlstatt* Pruss. field marshal

Blum \'blüm\ Léon 1872–1950 Fr. politician; provisional president (1946–47)

Blum·berg \'bləm-ˌbərg, 'blüm-\ Baruch Samuel 1925– Am. virologist

Bluntsch·li \'blünch-lē\ Johann Kaspar 1808–1881 Swiss legal scholar

Boabdil — see MUḤAMMAD XI

Boadicea — see BOUDICCA

Bo·as \'bō-ˌaz\ Franz 1858–1942 Am. (Ger.-born) anthropologist & ethnologist — **Bo·as·ian** \bō-'a-zē-ən, -zh(ē-)ən\ *adjective*

Bo·ba·dil·la \ˌbō-bə-'dē-yə\ Francisco de *died* 1502 Span. viceroy of Indies

Boc·cac·cio \bō-'kä-ch(ē-)ō\ Giovanni 1313–1375 Ital. author

Boc·che·ri·ni \ˌbä-kə-'rē-nē\ Luigi 1743–1805 Ital. composer

Bod·ley \'bäd-lē\ Sir Thomas 1545–1613 Eng. diplomat & founder of Bodleian library

Bo·do·ni \bə-'dō-nē\ Giambattista 1740–1813 Ital. printer & type designer

Bo·e·thi·us \bō-'ē-thē-əs\ Anicius Manlius Severinus *circa* 480–524 Rom. philosopher

Boh·len \'bō-lən\ Charles Eustis 1904–1974 Am. diplomat

Böh·me \'bə(r)m-ə, 'bœ̄-mə\ Ja·kob \'yä-ˌkȯp\ 1575–1624 Ger. mystic

Bohr \'bȯr, 'bȯr\ Aage Niels 1922– *son of Niels* Dan. physicist

Bohr Niels Henrik David 1885–1962 Dan. physicist

Bo·iar·do \bȯi-'är-(ˌ)dō, bō-'yär-\ Matteo Maria 1441?–1494 Ital. poet

Boi·leau–Des·pré·aux \'bwä-lō-ˌdā-prē-'ō\ Nicolas 1636–1711 Fr. critic & poet

Boj·er \'bȯi-ər\ Johan \yō-'hän\ 1872–1959 Norw. writer

Bok \'bäk\ Edward William 1863–1930 Am. (Du.-born) editor

Bo·leyn \bu̇-'lin, -'lēn; 'bu̇-lən\ Anne 1507?–1536 *2d wife of Henry VIII of England & mother of Queen Elizabeth I*

Bol·ger \'bäl-jər, 'bȯl-\ James Brendan 1935– prime minister of New Zealand (1990–)

Bo·ling·broke \'bä-liŋ-ˌbru̇k, 'bü-, *United States also* 'bō-liŋ-, -ˌbrȯk\ 1st Viscount 1678–1751 *Henry St. John* \'sin-jən, *US also* (ˌ)sānt-ˌjän, sənt-\ Eng. statesman

Bo·lí·var \bō-'lē-ˌvär, 'bä-lə-vär, -vər\ Si·món \sē-ˌmōn-bə-'lē-ˌvär, 'sī-mən-ˌbä-lə-ˌvär, -vər\ 1783–1830 So. Am. liberator

Böll \'bȯl, 'bœl\ Heinrich Theodor 1917–1985 Ger. writer

Bo·na·parte \'bō-nə-ˌpärt\ *Italian* **Buo·na·par·te** \ˌbwȯ-nə-'pär-tē\ Corsican family including Na·po·léon \nə-'pōl-yən, -'pō-lē-ən\ (*q.v.*) & his brothers: Joseph 1768–1844 king of Naples & Spain; Lucien 1775–1840 prince of Ca·ni·no \kə-'nē-(ˌ)nō\; Louis 1778–1846 *father of Napoléon III* king of Holland; Jérôme 1784–1860 king of Westphalia

Bonar Law — see LAW

Bon·a·ven·tu·ra \ˌbä-nə-ˌven-'tùr-ə, -'tyúr-\ *or* **Bon·a·ven·ture** \ˌbä-nə-'ven-chər, 'bä-nə-ˌ\ Saint *circa* 1217–1274 *the Seraphic Doctor* Ital. philosopher

Bone \'bōn\ Sir Muirhead 1876–1953 Scot. etcher & painter

Bon·heur \bä-'nər\ Rosa 1822–1899 *Marie-Rosalie* Fr. painter

Bon·i·face \'bä-nə-fəs, -ˌfäs\ Saint *circa* 675–754 *Wynfrid* or *Wynfrith* Eng. missionary in Germany

Boniface name of 9 popes: especially **VIII** (*Benedict Caetani*) *circa* 1235(or 1240)–1303 (pope 1294–1303)

Bon·nard \bȯ-'när\ Pierre 1867–1947 Fr. painter

Bon·er *or* **Bon·ner** \'bä-nər\ Edmund *circa* 1500–1569 Eng. prelate

Bon·net \bȯ-'nā\ Georges-Étienne 1889–1973 Fr. politician & diplomat

Bon·ney \'bä-nē\ William originally *Henry* 1859–1881 *Billy the Kid* Am. outlaw

Bon·temps \bän-'täm\ Arna Wendell 1902–1973 Am. writer

Boone \'bün\ Daniel 1734–1820 Am. pioneer

Booth \'büth, *chiefly British* 'büth\ family of Am. actors: Junius Brutus 1796–1852 *b* in England & his sons Edwin Thomas 1833–1893 & John Wilkes 1838–1865 assassin of Lincoln

Booth William 1829–1912 Eng. founder of Salvation Army *father of:* William Bramwell 1856–1929 Salvation Army general; Ballington 1857–1940 founder of Volunteers of America; Evangeline Cory 1865–1950 Salvation Army general

Boothe Clare — see Clare Boothe LUCE

Bo·rah \'bȯr-ə, 'bȯr-\ William Edgar 1865–1940 Am. politician

Bor·den \'bȯr-dᵊn\ Sir Robert (Laird) 1854–1937 Canad. lawyer & statesman; prime minister (1911–20)

Bor·det \bȯr-'dā\ Jules 1870–1961 Belg. bacteriologist

Bor·ges \'bȯr-ˌhäs\ Jorge Luis 1899–1986 Argentine author

Bor·gia \'bȯr-(ˌ)jä, -jə, -zhə\ Cesare 1475(or 1476)–1507 *son of Rodrigo* Ital. cardinal & military leader

Borgia Lucrezia 1480–1519 *daughter of Rodrigo* duchess of Ferrara

Borgia Rodrigo — see Pope ALEXANDER VI

Bor·glum \'bȯr-gləm\ (John) Gut·zon \'gət-sən\ (de la Mothe) 1867–1941 Am. sculptor

Bo·ris III \'bȯr-əs, 'bȯr-, 'bär-\ 1894–1943 czar of Bulgaria (1918–43)

Bor·laug \'bȯr-ˌlȯg\ Norman Ernest 1914– Am. agronomist

Born \'bȯrn\ Max 1882–1970 Ger. physicist

Bo·ro·din \ˌbȯr-ə-'dēn, ˌbär-\ Aleksandr Porfiryevich 1833–1887 Russ. composer & chemist

Bor·row \'bär-(ˌ)ō\ George Henry 1803–1881 Eng. author

Bosch \'bäsh, 'bȯsh\ Carl 1874–1940 Ger. industrial chemist

Bosch \'bäsh, 'bȯsh, *Dutch* 'bȯs\ Hieronymus *circa* 1450–*circa* 1516 Du. painter

Bo·sco \'bäs-kō\ Saint Giovanni Melchior 1815–1888 *Don Bosco* Ital. religious & founder of Society of St. Francis de Sales

Bose \'bōs, 'bȯs, 'bȯsh\ Sir Ja·ga·dis \ˌjə-gə-'dēs\ Chan·dra \'chən-drə\ 1858–1937 Indian physicist & plant physiologist

Bos·suet \bȯ-'swā\ Jacques-Bénigne 1627–1704 Fr. bishop

Bos·well \'bäz-ˌwel, -wəl\ James 1740–1795 Scot. biographer & diarist

\ə\ abut \ᵊ\ kitten \ər\ further \a\ ash \ā\ ace \ä\ mop, mar \au̇\ out \ch\ chin \e\ bet \ē\ easy \g\ go \i\ hit \ī\ ice \j\ job \ŋ\ sing \ō\ go \ȯ\ law \ȯi\ boy \th\ thin \t̷h\ the \ü\ loot \u̇\ foot \y\ yet \zh\ vision *see also* Guide to Pronunciation

Bo·tha \'bō-tə, 'bú(ə)-\ Louis 1862–1919 Boer general; 1st prime minister of Transvaal (1907) & of Union of So. Africa (1910–19)

Botha Pieter Willem 1916– prime minister of Republic of So. Africa (1978–89)

Bo·the \'bō-tə\ Walther Wilhelm Georg Franz 1891–1957 Ger. physicist

Bot·ti·cel·li \,bä-tə-'che-lē\ Sandro 1445–1510 *Alessandro di Mariano Filipepi* Ital. painter

Bou·cher \bü-'shā\ François 1703–1770 Fr. painter

Bou·ci·cault \'bü-si-,kō\ *or* **Bour·ci·cault** \'búr-\ Dion 1820(or 1822)–1890 *Dionysius Lardner Boursiquot* Am. (Irish-born) actor & dramatist

Bou·dic·ca \bü-'di-kə\ *also* **Bo·a·di·cea** \,bō-ə-də-'sē-ə\ *died* A.D. 60 ancient Brit. queen

Bou·gain·ville \'bü-gən-,vil, bü-ga^n-'vēl\ Louis-Antoine de 1729–1811 Fr. navigator

Bou·lan·ger \bü-lä^n-zhā\ Georges-Ernest-Jean-Marie 1837–1891 Fr. general

Boulanger Nadia-Juliette 1887–1979 Fr. music teacher & conductor

Bou·lez \bü-'lez\ Pierre 1925– Fr. composer & conductor

Bour·bon \'búr-bən, bür-'bō^n\ Charles de 1490–1527 Duc *de Bourbon* Fr. general; constable of France

Bour·geois \búrzh-'wä, 'búrzh-,\ Léon-Victor-Auguste 1851–1925 Fr. statesman

Bour·get \búr-'zhā\ Paul-Charles-Joseph 1852–1935 Fr. author

Bour·gui·ba \búr-'gē-bə\ Habib ibn Ali 1903– Tunisian president (1957–87)

Bou·tros–Gha·li \'bü-trōs-'gä-lē\ Boutros 1922– Egypt. U.N. official; secretary-general (1992–96)

Bo·vet \bō-'vā\ Daniele 1907–1992 Ital. (Swiss-born) pharmacologist

Bow·ditch \'baú-dich\ Nathaniel 1773–1838 Am. mathematician & astronomer

Bow·ell \'bō-əl\ Sir Mackenzie 1823–1917 Canad. politician; prime minister of Canada (1894–96)

Bow·en \'bō-ən\ Elizabeth 1899–1973 Irish author

Bow·ie \'bü-ē, 'bō-\ James 1796–1836 hero of Texas revolution

Bowles \'bōlz\ Chester 1901–1986 Am. economist & diplomat

Boy·den \'bói-d^n\ Seth 1788–1870 Am. inventor

Boyd Orr \'bóid-'ór, -'ór\ John 1880–1971 Baron *Boyd-Orr of Brechin Mearns* Scot. agriculturist

Boyle \'bói(ə)l\ Kay 1902–1992 Am. author

Boyle Robert 1627–1691 Brit. physicist & chemist

Brad·bury \'brad-,ber-ē, -b(ə-)rē\ Ray Douglas 1920– Am. writer

Brad·dock \'bra-dək\ Edward 1695–1755 Brit. general in America

Brad·ford \'brad-fərd\ Gamaliel 1863–1932 Am. biographer

Bradford William 1590–1657 Pilgrim father; 2d governor of Plymouth colony

Bradford William 1663–1752 Am. printer

Brad·ley \'brad-lē\ Francis Herbert 1846–1924 Eng. philosopher — **Brad·le·ian** *also* **Brad·ley·an** \'brad-lē-ən, brad-\ *adjective*

Bradley Henry 1845–1923 Eng. philologist & lexicographer

Bradley Omar Nelson 1893–1981 Am. general

Brad·street \'brad-,strēt\ Anne *circa* 1612–1672 née *Dudley; wife of Simon* Am. poet

Bradstreet Simon 1603–1697 colonial governor of Massachusetts

Bra·dy \'brā-dē\ Mathew B. 1823?–1896 Am. photographer

Bragg \'brag\ Braxton 1817–1876 Am. Confederate general

Bragg Sir (William) Lawrence 1890–1971 *son of W.H.* Eng. physicist

Bragg Sir William Henry 1862–1942 Eng. physicist

Brahe \'brä; 'brä-hē, -hə\ Ty·cho \'tē-(,)kō, 'tī-\ 1546–1601 Dan. astronomer

Brahms \'brämz\ Johannes 1833–1897 Ger. composer & pianist — **Brahms·ian** \'bräm-zē-ən\ *adjective*

Braille \'brā(ə)l, 'brī\ Louis 1809–1852 Fr. blind teacher of the blind

Bra·man·te \brə-'män-tē, -(,)tā\ Donato 1444–1514 originally *Donato d'Agnolo* or *d'Angelo* Ital. architect

Bran·cu·si \bran-'kü-sē\ Constantin 1876–1957 Fr. (Romanian-born) sculptor

Bran·deis \'bran-,dīs, -,dīz\ Louis Dembitz 1856–1941 Am. jurist

Bran·des \'brän-dəs\ Georg Morris 1842–1927 Dan. literary critic

Brandt \'bränt, 'brant\ Wil·ly \'vi-lē, 'wi-\ 1913–1992 originally *Herbert Ernst Karl Frahm* W. Ger. politician; chancellor of West Germany (1969–74)

Brant \'brant\ Joseph 1742–1807 *Thayendanegea* Mohawk Indian chief

Bran·ting \'bran-tiŋ\ Karl Hjal·mar \'yäl-,mär\ 1860–1925 Swed. statesman & socialist leader

Braque \'brak, 'bräk\ Georges 1882–1963 Fr. painter

Brat·tain \'bra-t^n\ Walter Houser 1902–1987 Am. physicist

Brau·chitsch \'braú-kich, -kich\ Heinrich Alfred Hermann Walther von 1881–1948 Ger. general

Braun \'braún\ Karl Ferdinand 1850–1918 Ger. physicist

Braun Wernher von 1912–1977 Am. (Ger.-born) engineer

Breas·ted \'bres-təd\ James Henry 1865–1935 Am. orientalist

Brecht \'brekt, 'brekt\ Bertolt 1898–1956 Ger. dramatist — **Brecht·ian** \'brek-tē-ən, 'brek-\ *adjective*

Breck·in·ridge \'bre-kən-(,)rij\ John Cabell 1821–1875 Am. politician; vice president of the U.S. (1857–61)

Bren·nan \'bre-nən\ William Joseph, Jr. 1906–

Bre·ton \brə-tō^n\ André 1896–1966 Fr. surrealist poet

Brew·ster \'brü-stər\ William 1567–1644 Pilgrim father

Brey·er \'brī-ər\ Stephen Gerald 1938– Am. jurist

Brezh·nev \'brezh-,nef\ Leonid Ilyich 1906–1982 Russ. politician; president of U.S.S.R. (1960–64; 1977–82); 1st secretary of Communist party (1964–82)

Bri·an \'brī-ən, 'brēn\ *also* **Brian Bo·ru** \bə-'rü\ 941–1014 king of Ireland (1002–14)

Bri·and \brē-ä^n\ Aristide 1862–1932 Fr. statesman

Brid·ger \'bri-jər\ James 1804–1881 Am. pioneer & scout

Brid·ges \'bri-jəz\ Robert Seymour 1844–1930 Eng. poet; poet laureate (1913–30)

Bridg·man \'brij-mən\ Percy Williams 1882–1961 Am. physicist

Bright \'brīt\ John 1811–1889 Eng. orator & statesman

Brig·it \'bri-jət, 'brē-yit\ *also* **Brid·get** \'bri-jət\ *or* **Brig·id** \'bri-jəd, 'brē-jid\ *or* **Brighid** \'brēd\ Saint *died circa* 524–528 *Bride of Kildare* or *Bride of Ireland* a patron saint of Ireland

Bril·lat–Sa·va·rin \brē-'yä-,sa-və-'ra^n, -'sa-və-ra^n\ Anthelme 1755–1826 Fr. gastronome

Brit·ten \'bri-t^n\ (Edward) Benjamin 1913–1976 Baron *Britten of Aldeburgh* Eng. composer

Brock·house \'bräk-,haús\ Bertram Neville 1918– Canad. physicist

Brod·sky \'bräd-skē\ Joseph 1940–1996 originally *Iosip Aleksandrovich Brodsky* Am. (Russ.-born) poet & essayist

Bro·gan \'brō-gən\ Sir Denis William 1900–1974 Brit. historian

Broglie \'brói\ Louis-Victor-Pierre-Raymond de 1892–1987 Fr. physicist

Bron·të \brän-tē, -(,)tā\ a family of Eng. writers: Charlotte 1816–1855 & her sisters Emily 1818–1848 & Anne 1820–1849

Brooke \'brúk\ Sir Alan Francis 1883–1963 1st Viscount *Al·an·brooke* \'a-lən-,brúk\ Brit. field marshal

Brooke Edward William 1919– Am. politician

Brooke Rupert 1887–1915 Eng. poet

Brooks \'brúks\ Gwendolyn Elizabeth 1917– Am. poet

Brooks Phillips 1835–1893 Am. bishop

Brooks Van Wyck \van-'wīk, vən-\ 1886–1963 Am. essayist & critic

Brow·der \'braú-dər\ Earl 1891–1973 Am. Communist politician

Brown \'braún\ Charles Brockden 1771–1810 Am. novelist

Brown Ford Mad·ox \'ma-dəks\ 1821–1893 Eng. painter

Brown Herbert Charles 1912– Am. (Eng.-born) chemist

Brown Jesse 1944– U.S. secretary of veteran affairs (1993–)

Brown John 1800–1859 *Old Brown of Osa·wat·o·mie* \,ō-sə-'wä-tə-mē\ Am. abolitionist

Brown Michael Stuart 1941– Am. biochemist

Brown Ronald Harmon 1941–1996 U.S. secretary of commerce (1993–96)

Browne \'braún\ Charles Farrar 1834–1867 pseudonym *Ar·te·mus* \'är-tə-məs\ *Ward* Am. humorist

Browne Sir Thomas 1605–1682 Eng. physician & author

Brow·ning \'braú-niŋ\ Elizabeth Barrett 1806–1861 *wife of Robert* Eng. poet

Browning Robert 1812–1889 Eng. poet

Broz Josip — see TITO

Bruce \'brüs\ Sir David 1855–1931 Brit. physician & bacteriologist

Bruce Robert — see ROBERT I the Bruce

Bruce Stanley Melbourne 1883–1967 1st Viscount *Bruce of Melbourne* Austral. statesman; prime minister (1923–29)

Bruck·ner \'brúk-nər\ Anton 1824–1896 Austrian composer — **Bruck·ner·ian** \,brúk-'ner-ē-ən\ *adjective*

Brue·ghel *or* **Breu·ghel** \'brü-gəl, 'brói-, *Dutch* 'brœ-kəl\ family of Flem. painters including: Pieter *circa* 1525(or 1530)–1569 & his sons Pieter 1564–1638 & Jan 1568–1625

Brum·mell \'brə-məl\ George Bryan 1778–1840 *Beau Brummell* Eng. dandy

Bru·nel·le·schi \,brü-n°l-'es-kē\ *or* **Bru·nel·le·sco** \-(,)kō\ Filippo 1377–1446 Ital. architect

Bru·ne·tière \,brü-nə-'tyer, ,brē-\ Vincent de Paul-Marie-Ferdinand 1849–1906 Fr. critic

Brü·ning \'brü-niŋ, 'brē-\ Heinrich 1885–1970 chancellor of Germany (1930–32)

Bru·no \'brü-(,)nō\ Giordano 1548–1600 Ital. philosopher

Bru·tus \'brü-təs\ Marcus Junius 85–42 B.C. Rom. politician & conspirator

Bry·an \'brī-ən\ William Jennings 1860–1925 Am. lawyer & politician

Bry·ant \'brī-ənt\ William Cullen 1794–1878 Am. poet & editor

Bu·ber \'bü-bər\ Martin 1878–1965 Israeli (Austrian-born) philosopher

Buch·an \'bə-kən, -,kən\ Sir John 1875–1940 1st Baron *Tweeds·muir* \'twēdz-,myúr\ Scot. author; governor-general of Canada (1935–40)

Bu·chan·an \byü-'ka-nən, bə-\ James 1791–1868 Am. politician & diplomat; 15th president of the U.S. (1857–61)

Buchanan James McGill 1919– Am. economist

Buch·man \'búk-mən, 'bək-\ Frank Nathan Daniel 1878–1961 Am. evangelist

Buch·ner \'búk-nər, 'bük-\ Eduard 1860–1917 Ger. chemist

Buck \'bək\ Pearl 1892–1973 née *Sy·den·strick·er* \'sī-d°n-,stri-kər\ Am. novelist

Buckingham 1st & 2d Dukes of — see VILLIERS

Buck·ley \'bə-klē\ William Frank 1925– Am. editor & writer

Buck·ner \'bək-nər\ Simon Bolivar 1823–1914 Am. Confederate general & politician

Buckner Simon Bolivar 1886–1945 *son of preceding* Am. general

Buddha — see SIDDHĀRTHA GAUTAMA

Bu·den·ny \bü-'dyò-nē, bú-'de-\ Semyon Mikhaylovich 1883–1973 Russ. general

Buffalo Bill — see William Frederick CODY

Buf·fon \,bə-'fō^n, byü-, bǖ-\ Comte Georges-Louis Leclerc de 1707–1788 Fr. naturalist

Buis·son \bwē-'sō^n\ Ferdinand-Édouard 1841–1932 Fr. educator

Bu·kha·rin \bü-'kär-ən\ Nikolay Ivanovich 1888–1938 Russ. Communist leader & editor

Bul·finch \'búl-,finch\ Charles 1763–1844 Am. architect

Bul·ga·nin \búl-'ga-nən\ Nikolay Aleksandrovich 1895–1975 Russ. politician & marshal

Bull \'búl\ Ole \'ō-lə\ Bornemann 1810–1880 Norw. violinist

Bul·litt \'bu̇-lət\ William Christian 1891–1967 Am. diplomat

Bü·low \'byü-(ˌ)lō, 'bē-\ Bernhard Heinrich Martin Karl 1849–1929 Prince *von Bülow* Ger. diplomat & statesman; chancellor of Germany (1900–09)

Bult·mann \'bu̇lt-ˌmän\ Rudolf Karl 1884–1976 Ger. theologian — **Bult·mann·ian** \bu̇lt-'mä-nē-ən\ *adjective*

Bul·wer \'bu̇l-wər\ William Henry Lytton Earle 1801–1872 *brother of 1st Baron Lytton* Brit. diplomat

Bulwer–Lytton — see LYTTON

Bunche \'bənch\ Ralph Johnson 1904–1971 Am. diplomat

Bu·nin \'bün-yən, -ˌyēn; 'bü-nən, -ˌnēn\ Ivan Alekseyevich 1870–1953 Russ. poet & novelist

Bun·ker \'bəŋ-kər\ Ellsworth 1894–1984 Am. diplomat

Bun·sen \'bün-zən, 'bən(t)-sən\ Robert Wilhelm 1811–1899 Ger. chemist

Bun·yan \'bən-yən\ John 1628–1688 Eng. preacher & author

Buonaparte Ital. spelling of BONAPARTE

Bur·bage \'bər-bij\ Richard *circa* 1567–1619 Eng. actor

Bur·bank \'bər-ˌbaŋk\ Luther 1849–1926 Am. horticulturist

Burch·field \'bərch-ˌfēld\ Charles Ephraim 1893–1967 Am. painter

Bur·ger \'bər-gər\ Warren Earl 1907–1995 Am. jurist; chief justice U.S. Supreme Court (1969–86)

Bür·ger \'bu̇r-gər, 'bir-, 'bu̇ēr-\ Gottfried August 1747–1794 Ger. poet

Bur·gess \'bər-jəs\ Anthony 1917–1993 Brit. writer

Burgess (Frank) Gelett 1866–1951 Am. humorist & illustrator

Burgess Thornton Waldo 1874–1965 Am. writer

Burghley *or* **Burleigh** 1st Baron — see William CECIL

Bur·goyne \(ˌ)bər-'gȯin, 'bər-ˌ\ John 1722–1792 Brit. general in America

Burk \'bərk\ Martha Jane 1852?–1903 née *Cannary* \'ka-nə-rē\ pseudonym *Calamity Jane* Am. frontier figure

Burke \'bərk\ Edmund 1729–1797 Brit. statesman & orator — **Burk·ean** *or* **Burk·ian** \'bər-kē-ən\ *adjective*

Bur·lin·game \'bər-lən-ˌgām\ Anson 1820–1870 Am. diplomat

Burne–Jones \'bərn-'jōnz\ Sir Edward Coley \'kō-lē\ 1833–1898 original surname *Jones* Eng. painter & designer

Bur·net \(ˌ)bər-'net, 'bər-nət\ Sir (Frank) Macfarlane 1899–1985 Austral. physician

Bur·nett \(ˌ)bər-'net, 'bər-nət\ Frances Eliza 1849–1924 née *Hodg·son* \'häj-sən\ Am. (Eng.-born) writer

Bur·ney \'bər-nē\ Fanny 1752–1840 originally *Frances; Madame d'Ar·blay* \'där-ˌblā\ Eng. novelist & diarist

Burns \'bərnz\ Robert 1759–1796 Scot. poet — **Burns·ian** \'bərn-zē-ən\ *adjective*

Burn·side \'bərn-ˌsīd\ Ambrose Everett 1824–1881 Am. general

Burr \'bər\ Aaron 1756–1836 3d vice president of the U.S. (1801–05)

Bur·roughs \'bər-(ˌ)ōz, 'bə-(ˌ)rōz\ Edgar Rice 1875–1950 Am. writer

Burroughs John 1837–1921 Am. naturalist

Burroughs William Seward 1914–1997 Am. writer

Bur·ton \'bər-tᵊn\ Harold Hitz 1888–1964 Am. jurist

Burton Richard 1925–1984 Brit. actor

Burton Sir Richard Francis 1821–1890 Brit. explorer & orientalist

Burton Robert 1577–1640 Eng. clergyman & author

Bush \'bu̇sh\ George Herbert Walker 1924– Am. politician; 41st president of the U.S. (1989–93)

Bush Van·ne·var \və-'nē-vər\ 1890–1974 Am. electrical engineer

Bu·so·ni \byü-'zō-nē, bü-\ Ferruccio Benvenuto 1866–1924 Ital. composer & pianist

Bu·sta·man·te y Sir·vén \bü-stä-'män-(ˌ)tā-ē-sir-'ven\ Antonio Sán·chez \'sän-(ˌ)chez\ 1865–1951 Cuban jurist

Bu·te·nandt \'bü-tᵊn-ˌänt\ Adolph Friedrich Johann 1903–1995 Ger. chemist

But·ler \'bət-lər\ Benjamin Franklin 1818–1893 Am. general & politician

Butler Joseph 1692–1752 Eng. theologian

Butler Nicholas Murray 1862–1947 Am. educator

Butler Samuel 1612–1680 Eng. satirical poet

Butler Samuel 1835–1902 Eng. novelist & satirist

Bux·te·hu·de \ˌbu̇k-stə-'hü-də\ Dietrich 1637–1707 Dan. organist & composer

Byng \'biŋ\ George 1663–1733 1st Viscount *Torrington* Brit. admiral

Byng Julian Hedworth George 1862–1935 1st Viscount *Byng of Vimy* Brit. general; governor-general of Canada (1921–26)

Byrd \'bərd\ Richard Evelyn 1888–1957 Am. admiral & polar explorer

Byrnes \'bərnz\ James Francis 1879–1972 Am. politician & jurist

By·ron \'bī-rən\ Lord 1788–1824 in full *George Gordon Byron*, 6th Baron *Byron* Eng. poet — **By·ron·ic** \bī-'rä-nik\ *adjective*

Ca·be·za de Va·ca \kə-'bā-zə-də-'vä-kə\ Álvar Núñez *circa* 1490–*circa* 1560 Span. explorer

Ca·ble \'kā-bəl\ George Washington 1844–1925 Am. novelist

Cab·ot \'ka-bət\ John *circa* 1450–*circa* 1499 It. *Giovanni Ca·bo·to* \kä-'bō-(ˌ)tō\ Venetian navigator & explorer for England

Cabot Sebastian 1476?–1557 *son of John* Eng. navigator & explorer

Ca·bral \kə-'bräl\ Pedro Álvares 1467(or 1468)–1520 Port. navigator

Ca·bril·ho \kə-'brē-(ˌ)yō, -'bri-(ˌ)lō\ João Rodrigues *died* 1543 Spanish *Juan Rodríguez Cabrillo* Span. (Port.-born) explorer in Mexico & California

Ca·bri·ni \kə-'brē-nē\ Saint Frances Xavier 1850–1917 *Mother Cabrini* 1st Am. citizen canonized (1946)

Cade \'kād\ John *died* 1450 *Jack Cade* Eng. rebel

Cad·il·lac \'ka-dᵊl-ˌak, *French* kả-dē-yảk\ Antoine de la Mothe, sieur de 1658–1730 Fr. founder of Detroit

Caed·mon \'kad-mən\ *flourished* 658–680 Anglo-Saxon poet

Cae·sar \'sē-zər\ Gaius Julius 100–44 B.C. Rom. general, statesman, & writer

Cage \'kāj\ John Milton 1912–1992 Am. composer

Ca·glio·stro \kal-'yȯ-(ˌ)strō, käl-\ Count Alessandro di 1743–1795 originally *Giuseppe Bal·sa·mo* \'bäl-sə-ˌmō\ Ital. adventurer

Caine \'kān\ Sir (Thomas Henry) Hall 1853–1931 Eng. novelist

Calamity Jane — see Martha Jane BURK

Cal·der \'kȯl-dər\ Alexander 1898–1976 Am. sculptor

Cal·de·ra Rod·rí·guez \käl-'thä-rä-rȯth-'rē-gäs\ Rafael 1916– president of Venezuela (1969–74; 1994–)

Cal·de·rón de la Bar·ca \ˌkäl-də-'rōn-dā-lə-'bär-kə\ Pedro 1600–1681 Span. dramatist & poet

Cal·de·rón Sol \ˌkäl-dā-'rōn-'sȯl\ Armando 1949– president of El Salvador (1994–)

Cald·well \'kȯl-ˌdwel, -dwəl, 'käl-\ Erskine 1903–1987 Am. novelist

Caldwell (Janet) Taylor 1900–1985 Am. (Eng.-born) author

Cal·houn \kal-'hün\ John Caldwell 1782–1850 Am. politician; vice president of the U.S. (1825–32)

Ca·lig·u·la \kə-'li-gyə-lə\ A.D. 12–41 *Gaius Caesar* Rom. emperor (37–41)

Cal·la·ghan \'ka-lə-hən, -ˌhan\ (Leonard) James 1912– Brit. prime minister (1976–79)

Callaghan Morley Edward 1903–1990 Canad. author

Cal·las \'ka-ləs, 'kä-\ Maria 1923–1977 originally *Maria Anna Sofia Cecilia Kalogeropoulos* Am. soprano

Cal·les \'kä-ˌyās\ Plutarco Elías 1877–1945 Mex. general; president of Mexico (1924–28)

Cal·lim·a·chus \kə-'li-mə-kəs\ 5th century B.C. Greek sculptor

Callimachus *circa* 305–*circa* 240 B.C. Greek scholar & Alexandrian librarian

Cal·lis·the·nes \kə-'lis-thə-ˌnēz\ *circa* 360–328 B.C. Greek philosopher & historian

Cal·lis·tra·tus \kə-'lis-trə-təs\ *died* 355 B.C. Athenian orator & general

Cal·vert \'kal-vərt\ George 1580?–1632 1st Baron *Baltimore* Eng. proprietor in America

Calvert Leonard 1606–1647 *son of George* governor of Maryland province (1634–47)

Cal·vin \'kal-vən\ John 1509–1564 originally *Jean Chau·vin* \shō-vaⁿ\ *or* *Caul·vin* \kȯl-vaⁿ\ Fr. theologian & reformer

Calvin Melvin 1911–1997 Am. chemist

Camacho Manuel Ávila — see ÁVILA CAMACHO

Cam·ba·cé·rès \ˌkäⁿ-ˌba-sā-'res, -ˌbä-\ Jean-Jacques-Régis de 1753–1824 Duc de *Parme* Fr. jurist; counselor of Napoléon I

Cambridge 1st Baron of — see Edgar Douglas ADRIAN

Cam·by·ses II \kam-'bī-(ˌ)sēz\ *died* 522 B.C. *son of Cyrus II the Great* king of Persia (529–22)

Cam·den \'kam-dən\ William 1551–1623 Eng. antiquarian & historian

Cam·er·on of Loch·iel \'ka-mə-rən-əv-lä-'kē(ə)l, ˌkam-rən-, -'kē(ə)l\ 1629–1719 Sir *Ewen Cameron* Scot. chieftain

Cameron of Lochiel 1695?–1748 *Donald Cameron; the gentle Lochiel* Scot. chieftain

Ca·mões \kə-'mōiⁿsh\ *English* **Ca·mo·ens** \kə-'mō-ənz, 'ka-mə-wənz\ Luiz Vaz de 1524(or 1525)–1580 Port. poet

Camp \'kamp\ Walter Chauncey 1859–1925 Am. football coach

Camp·bell \'kam-bəl, 'ka-məl\ Alexander 1788–1866 Am. (Irish-born) founder of Disciples of Christ

Campbell Colin 1792–1863 original surname *Mac·li·ver* \mə-'klē-vər\; Baron *Clyde* Brit. field marshal

Campbell John 1705–1782 4th Earl of *Lou·doun* \'lau̇-dᵊn\ Brit. general in America

Campbell John Douglas Sutherland 1845–1914 9th Duke of *Argyll* governor-general of Canada (1878–83)

Campbell Joseph 1904–1987 Am. mythologist & folklorist

Campbell Kim 1947– originally *Avril Phaedra Campbell* prime minister of Canada (1993)

Campbell Thomas 1777–1844 Brit. poet

Camp·bell–Ban·ner·man \-'ba-nər-mən\ Sir Henry 1836–1908 Brit. statesman; prime minister (1905–08)

Cam·pi \'käm-(ˌ)pē\ Ital. family of painters in Cremona including: Galeazzo 1477–1536 & his three sons Giulio 1502–1572, Antonio 1536–*circa* 1591, & Vincenzo 1536–1591

Cam·pi·on \'kam-pē-ən\ Thomas 1567–1620 Eng. poet & composer

Ca·mus \kả-mœ̄\ Albert 1913–1960 Fr. novelist, essayist, & dramatist

Ca·na·let·to \ˌka-nᵊl-'e-(ˌ)tō\ 1697–1768 originally *Giovanni Antonio Canal* Ital. painter

Can·by \'kan-bē\ Henry Seidel \'sī-dᵊl\ 1878–1961 Am. editor & author

Can·dolle \käⁿ-dȯl\ Augustin Pyrame de 1778–1841 Swiss botanist

Can·dra·gup·ta \ˌkən-drə-'gu̇p-tə\ *or* **Chan·dra·gup·ta** \ˌchən-\ *died circa* 297 B.C. Indian emperor (*circa* 321–*circa* 297 B.C.)

Can·dra Gup·ta II \ˌkən-drə-'gu̇p-tə\ *also* **Chan·dra Gup·ta II** \ˌchən-\ Indian ruler of Gupta dynasty (*circa* 380–*circa* 415)

Ca·net·ti \kə-'ne-tē\ Elias 1905–1994 Brit. (Bulg.-born) author writing in German

Canfield Dorothy — see Dorothy Canfield FISHER

Can·ning \'ka-niŋ\ Charles John 1812–1862 Earl *Canning* Brit. governor-general of India (1856–58); 1st viceroy of India (1858–62)

Canning George 1770–1827 *father of C.J.* Brit. statesman; prime minister (1827)

Canning Stratford 1786–1880 1st Viscount *Stratford de Red·cliffe* \'red-ˌklif\ Brit. diplomat

Can·non \'ka-nən\ Joseph Gurney 1836–1926 *Uncle Joe* Am. politician

Ca·no·va \kə-'nō-və, -'nȯ-\ Antonio 1757–1822 Ital. sculptor

Ca·nute \kə-'nüt, -'nyüt\ *died* 1035 *the Great* king of England (1016–35); of Denmark (1018–35); of Norway (1028–35)

\ə\ abut \ᵊ\ kitten \ər\ further \a\ ash \ā\ ace
\ä\ mop, mar \au̇\ out \ch\ chin \e\ bet \ē\ easy
\g\ go \i\ hit \ī\ ice \j\ job \ŋ\ sing \ō\ go
\ȯ\ law \ȯi\ boy \th\ thin \tẖ\ the \ü\ loot \u̇\ foot
\y\ yet \zh\ vision *see also* Guide to Pronunciation

Ča·pek \'chä-ˌpek\ Ka·rel \'kär-əl\ 1890–1938 Czech novelist & dramatist

Capet Hugh — see HUGH CAPET

Ca·pone \kə-'pōn\ Alphonse 1899–1947 *Scarface* Am. gangster

Ca·pote \kə-'pō-tē\ Truman 1924–1984 Am. writer

Cap·ra \'ka-prə\ Frank 1897–1991 Am. film director & producer — **Cap·ra·esque** \ˌka-prə-'esk\ adjective

Car·a·cal·la \ˌkar-ə-'ka-lə\ A.D. 188–217 *Marcus Aurelius Antoninus* originally *Bas·si·a·nus* \ˌba-sē-'ä-nəs\ Rom. emperor (211–217)

Ca·rat·a·cus \kə-'ra-ti-kəs\ also **Ca·rac·ta·cus** \-'rak-ti-\ *Welsh* **Ca·ra·doc** or **Ca·ra·dog** \kə-'rä-(ˌ)dȯg\ 1st century A.D. Brit. chieftain

Ca·ra·vag·gio \ˌkar-ə-'vä-j(ē-ˌ)ō, -'vä-zhō\ Michelangelo da 1573–1610 *Michelangelo Merisi* Ital. painter — **Ca·ra·vag·gesque** \ˌkär-ə-ˌvä-'jesk\ adjective

Car·ber·ry \'kär-ˌber-ē, -bə-rē\ John Joseph 1904– Am. cardinal

Cár·de·nas \'kär-dᵊn-ˌäs, 'kär-thä-ˌnäs\ Lázaro 1895–1970 Mex. general & politician; president of Mexico (1934–40)

Car·do·so \kär-'dō-(ˌ)zü\ Fernando Henrique 1931– president of Brazil (1995–)

Car·do·zo \kär-'dō-(ˌ)zō\ Benjamin Nathan 1870–1938 Am. jurist

Car·duc·ci \kär-'dü-(ˌ)chē\ Giosuè 1835–1907 Ital. poet

Ca·rew \kə-'rü; 'kar-ē, 'ker-\ Thomas 1595?–?1640 Eng. poet

Car·ey \'kar-ē, 'ker-\ George Leonard 1935– archbishop of Canterbury (1991–)

Carl XVI Gus·taf \'kärl-'gəs-ˌtäv, -'gȯs-, -ˌtäf\ 1946– king of Sweden (1973–)

Carle·ton \'kär(-ə)l-tən\ Sir Guy 1724–1808 1st Baron *Dorchester* Brit. general & administrator in America

Car·los \'kär-ləs, -ˌlōs\ Don 1788–1855 infante & pretender to Span. throne

Carlos de Aus·tria \-thä-'aů-strē-ə\ Don 1545–1568 *son of Philip II of Spain* prince of Asturias & heir to Span. throne

Car·lo·ta \kär-'lō-tə, -'lä-\ 1840–1927 *Marie-Charlotte-Amélie-Augustine-Victoire-Clémentine-Léopoldine* empress of Mexico (1864–67)

Car·lyle \kär-'lī(ə)l, 'kär-\ Thomas 1795–1881 Scot. essayist & historian — **Car·lyl·ean** or **Car·lyl·ian** \kär-'lī-lē-ən\ adjective

Car·mo·na \kär-'mō-nə\ António Óscar de Fragoso 1869–1951 Port. general; president of Portugal (1928–51)

Car·nap \'kär-ˌnap\ Rudolf 1891–1970 Am. (Ger.-born) philosopher

Car·ne·gie \'kär-'ne-gē, 'kär-nə-gē\ Andrew 1835–1919 Am. (Scot.-born) industrialist & philanthropist

Car·not \kär-'nō\ Lazare-Nicolas-Marguerite 1753–1823 Fr. statesman & general

Carnot Marie-François-Sadi 1837–1894 president of France (1887–94)

Car·ol II \'kar-əl\ 1893–1953 king of Romania (1930–40)

Car·pac·cio \kär-'pä-ch(ē-ˌ)ō\ Vittore *circa* 1460–1525(or 1526) Ital. painter

Car·ran·za \kə-'ran-zə, -'rän-\ Venustiano 1859–1920 president of Mexico (1915–20)

Car·rel \kə-'rel, 'kar-əl\ Alexis 1873–1944 Fr. surgeon & biologist

Car·rère \kə-'rer\ John Merven 1858–1911 Am. architect

Car·roll \'kar-əl\ Charles 1737–1832 *Carroll of Carrollton* Am. patriot

Carroll Lewis — see Charles Lutwidge DODGSON — **Car·roll·ian** \kə-'rō-lē-ən\ adjective

Car·son \'kär-sᵊn\ Christopher 1809–1868 *Kit* \'kit\ *Carson* Am. scout

Carson Rachel Louise 1907–1964 Am. scientist & writer

Carte, D'Oy·ly \ˌdȯi-lē-'kärt\ Richard 1844–1901 Eng. opera impresario

Car·ter \'kär-tər\ Elliott Cook 1908– Am. composer

Carter Howard 1874–1939 Eng. archaeologist

Carter Jimmy 1924– *James Earl Carter, Jr.* Am. politician; 39th president of the U.S. (1977–81)

Car·ter·et \ˌkär-tə-'ret, 'kär-tə-\ John 1690–1763 Earl *Gran·ville* \'gran-ˌvil\ Eng. statesman

Car·tier \kär-'tyā, 'kär-tē-ˌā\ George Étienne 1814–1873 Canad. politician

Cartier Jacques 1491–1557 Fr. navigator & explorer

Cart·wright \'kärt-ˌrīt\ Edmund 1743–1823 Eng. inventor

Ca·ru·so \kə-'rü-(ˌ)sō, -(ˌ)zō\ En·ri·co \en-'rē-(ˌ)kō\ 1873–1921 originally *Errico* Ital. tenor

Car·ver \'kär-vər\ George Washington *circa* 1864–1943 Am. botanist

Carver John 1576–1621 Eng. *Mayflower* Pilgrim; 1st governor of Plymouth colony

Cary \'kar-ē, 'ker-ē\ (Arthur) Joyce (Lunel) 1888–1957 Brit. novelist

Cary Henry Francis 1772–1844 Eng. clergyman & translator

Ca·sals \kə-'sälz, -'zälz\ Pablo 1876–1973 Catalan *Pau* Span.-born cellist, conductor, & composer

Ca·sa·no·va \ˌka-zə-'nō-və, ˌka-sə-\ Giovanni Giacomo 1725–1798 Chevalier *de Seingalt* Ital. adventurer

Ca·sau·bon \kə-'sȯ-bən, ˌka-zō-'bōⁿ\ Isaac 1559–1614 Fr. theologian & scholar

Case·ment \'kās-mənt\ Sir Roger David 1864–1916 Irish rebel

Ca·si·mir-Pé·rier \ˌka-zə-ˌmir-'per-ē-ˌā\ Jean-Paul-Pierre 1847–1907 Fr. statesman; president of France (1894–95)

Cas·lon \'kaz-lən\ William 1692–1766 Eng. typefounder

Cass \'kas\ Lewis 1782–1866 Am. statesman

Cas·satt \kə-'sat\ Mary Stevenson 1845–1926 Am. painter in France

Cas·sin \ka-'saⁿ, kä-\ René-Samuel 1887–1976 Fr. statesman

Cas·si·o·do·rus \ˌka-sē-ə-'dōr-əs, -'dȯr-\ Flavius Magnus Aurelius *circa* 490–*circa* 585 Rom. statesman & author

Cas·sius Lon·gi·nus \'ka-sh(ē-)əs-ˌlän-'jī-nəs, -s(ē-)əs-\ Gaius *died* 42 B.C. Rom. general & conspirator

Cas·te·lar y Ri·poll \ˌkas-tə-'lär-ē-rē-'pōl'\ Emilio 1832–1899 Span. statesman & writer

Ca·stel·ve·tro \kä-ˌstel-'ve-(ˌ)trō\ Lodovico *circa* 1505–1571 Ital. critic & philologist

Ca·sti·glio·ne \ˌkäs-tēl-'yō-(ˌ)nā\ Baldassare 1478–1529 Ital. writer

Cas·ti·lho \kash-'tēl-(ˌ)yü, -kas-\ Antônio Feliciano de 1800–1875 Port. poet

Castlereagh Viscount — see Robert STEWART

Cas·tro \'kas-(ˌ)trō, 'käs-\ Cipriano 1858–1924 Venezuelan general; president of Venezuela (1902–08)

Cas·tro \'käs-(ˌ)trō\ Inés \ē-'näs\ de 1320?–1355 Span. noblewoman

Castro (Ruz) \'rüs\ Fi·del \fē-'del\ 1926– Cuban leader (1959–)

Cates·by \'kāts-bē\ Mark 1679?–1749 Eng. naturalist

Catesby Robert 1573–1605 Eng. rebel

Cath·er \'ka-thər\ Willa Sibert 1873–1947 Am. novelist

Cath·er·ine \'ka-th(ə-)rən\ name of 1st, 5th, & 6th wives of Henry VIII of England: Catherine of Aragon 1485–1536; Catherine Howard 1520?–1542; Catherine Parr \'pär\ 1512–1548

Catherine I 1684–1727 *wife of Peter the Great* empress of Russia (1725–27)

Catherine II 1729–1796 *the Great* empress of Russia (1762–96)

Catherine of Bra·gan·za \brə-'gan-zə\ 1638–1705 *queen of Charles II of England*

Cath·er·ine de Mé·di·cis \-də-ˌmä-dē-'sēs, -'me-də-(ˌ)chē also kä-'trēn-\ *Italian* **Ca·te·ri·na de' Me·di·ci** \ˌkä-tā-'rē-nä-dā-'me-də-(ˌ)chē\ 1519–1589 *queen of Henry II of France*

Cat·i·line \'ka-tᵊl-ˌīn\ *circa* 108–62 B.C. *Lucius Sergius Cat·i·li·na* \ˌka-tᵊl-'ī-nə, -'ē-nə\ Rom. politician & conspirator

Cat·lin \'kat-lən\ George 1796–1872 Am. artist

Ca·to \'kā-(ˌ)tō\ Marcus Porcius 234–149 B.C. *the Elder; the Censor* Rom. statesman

Cato Marcus Porcius 95–46 B.C. *the Younger; great-grandson of preceding* Rom. statesman

Catt \'kat\ Carrie Chapman 1859–1947 née *Lane* Am. suffragist

Cat·tell \kə-'tel\ James McKeen 1860–1944 Am. psychologist & educator

Cat·ton \'ka-tᵊn\ (Charles) Bruce 1899–1978 Am. journalist & historian

Ca·tul·lus \kə-'tə-ləs\ Gaius Valerius *circa* 84–*circa* 54 B.C. Rom. poet

Cau·lain·court \ˌkō-ˌlaⁿ-'kůr\ Marquis Armand-Augustin-Louis de 1773–1827 Fr. general & diplomat

Ca·vell \'ka-vəl, kə-'vel\ Edith Louisa 1865–1915 Eng. nurse

Cav·en·dish \'ka-vən-(ˌ)dish\ Henry 1731–1810 Eng. scientist

Cavendish Spencer Compton 1833–1908 8th Duke of *Devonshire* Eng. statesman

Cavendish Sir William 1505?–1557 Eng. statesman

Cavendish William 1640–1707 1st Duke of *Devonshire* Eng. statesman

Ca·vour \kə-'vůr, kä-\ Con·te \'kōn-(ˌ)tā\ Camillo Benso di 1810–1861 Ital. statesman

Ca·xi·as \kə-'shē-əs\ Du·que \'dü-kə\ de 1803–1880 *Luiz Alves de Lima e Silva* Braz. general & statesman

Cax·ton \'kak-stən\ William *circa* 1422–1491 1st Eng. printer

Ceau·șes·cu \chaů-'shes-(ˌ)kü\ Nicolae 1918–1989 president of Romania (1974–1989)

Cech \'chek\ Thomas Robert 1947– Am. biochemist

Cec·il \'se-səl, 'si-\ (Edgar Algernon) Robert 1864–1958 1st Viscount *Cecil of Chel·wood* \'chel-ˌwůd\ Eng. statesman

Cecil Lord (Edward Christian) David 1902–1986 Eng. biographer

Cecil Robert 1563–1612 1st Earl of *Salisbury* & 1st Viscount *Cran·borne* \'kran-ˌbȯrn\ Eng. statesman

Cecil Robert Arthur Talbot Gas·coyne- \'gas-ˌkȯin\ 1830–1903 3d Marquis of *Salis·bury* \'sȯlz-b(ə-)rē, 'sälz-\ Eng. statesman

Cecil William 1520–1598 1st Baron *Burgh·ley* or *Bur·leigh* \'bər-lē\ Eng. statesman

Ce·la \'sā-lə\ Camilo José 1916– Span. writer

Cel·li·ni \chə-'lē-nē\ Ben·ve·nu·to \ˌben-və-'nü-(ˌ)tō\ 1500–1571 Ital. goldsmith & sculptor

Cel·sius \'sel-sē-əs, -shəs\ Anders 1701–1744 Swed. astronomer

Cen·ci \'chen-(ˌ)chē\ Be·a·tri·ce \ˌbā-ä-'trē-(ˌ)chā\ 1577–1599 Ital. woman executed for parricide

Cer·van·tes \sər-'van-ˌtēz, -'vän-ˌtās\ Miguel de 1547–1616 full surname *Cervantes Saa·ve·dra* \ˌsä-(ə-)'vä-drə\ Span. writer

Cé·zanne \sā-'zan\ Paul 1839–1906 Fr. painter — **Cé·zann·esque** \(ˌ)sā-ˌza-'nesk\ adjective

Cha·bri·er \ˌshä-brē-'ā, ˌsha-\ (Alexis-) Emmanuel 1841–1894 Fr. composer

Chad·wick \'chad-(ˌ)wik\ Sir James 1891–1974 Eng. physicist

Cha·gall \shə-'gäl, -'gal\ Marc 1887–1985 Russ. painter in France

Chag·a·tai \ˌcha-gə-'tī\ or **Jag·a·tai** \ˌja-\ *died* 1241 *2d son of Genghis Khan* Mongol ruler

Chain \'chān\ Ernst Boris 1906–1979 Brit. (Ger.-born) biochemist

Cha·lia·pin \shəl-'yä-(ˌ)pēn, -pən\ Fyodor Ivanovich 1873–1938 Russ. basso

Chal·mers \'chal-mərz, 'chä-mərz\ Alexander 1759–1834 Scot. biographer & editor

Cham·ber·lain \'chām-bər-lən\ Joseph 1836–1914 & his sons Sir (Joseph) Austen 1863–1937 & (Arthur) Neville 1869–1940 Brit. statesmen

Chamberlain Owen 1920– Am. physicist

Cham·ber·lin \'chām-bər-lən\ Thomas Chrowder \'kraů-dər\ 1843–1928 Am. geologist

Cham·bers \'chām-bərz\ Robert 1802–1871 Scot. publisher & editor

Cham·bord \shäⁿ-'bȯr\ Comte de 1820–1883 *Henri-Charles-Ferdinand-Marie Dieudonné d'Artois Duc de Bordeaux* Bourbon claimant to Fr. throne

Cha·mor·ro \chä-'mȯr-(ˌ)rō\ Violeta Barrios de 1929– president of Nicaragua (1990–97)

Cham·plain \sham-'plān, shäⁿ-'plaⁿ\ Samuel de *circa* 1567–1635 Fr. navigator, explorer, & founder of Quebec

Cham·pol·lion \shäⁿ-pȯl-yōⁿ\ Jean-François 1790–1832 Fr. Egyptologist

Cham·pol·lion–Fi·geac \-fē-zhák\ Jacques-Joseph 1778–1867 *brother of preceding* Fr. archaeologist

Chan·dra·gup·ta — see CANDRAGUPTA

Chandra Gupta II — see CANDRA GUPTA II

Chan·dra·se·khar \ˌchən-drə-'shā-kär\ Subrahmanyan 1910–1995 Am. (Indian-born) physicist

Cha·nel \shə-'nel, sha-\ Gabrielle 1883–1971 *Co·co* \'kō-(,)kō\ *Chanel* Fr. fashion designer & perfumer

Chang Hsüeh–liang \'jäŋ-shù-'ā-lē-'äŋ\ *son of Chang Tso-lin* 1898– Chin. general

Chang Tso–lin \-'(t)sō-'lin\ 1873–1928 Chin. general

Chan·ning \'cha-niŋ\ William Ellery 1780–1842 Am. clergyman

Chao K'uang–yin \'jaù-'kwäŋ-'yin\ 927–976 *T'ai Tsu* \'tīd-'zü\ Chin. emperor (960–976) & founder of Sung dynasty

Chap·lin \'cha-plən\ Sir Charles Spencer 1889–1977 Brit. actor & producer — **Chap·lin·esque** \,cha-plə-'nesk\ *adjective*

Chap·man \'chap-mən\ Frank Mich·ler \'mi-klər\ 1864–1945 Am. ornithologist

Chapman George 1559?–1634 Eng. dramatist & translator

Chapman John 1774–1845 *Johnny Ap·ple·seed* \'ap-əl-,sēd\ Am. pioneer

Char·cot \shär-'kō, 'shär-\ Jean-Mar·tin \'zhän-mär-'taⁿ\ 1825–1893 Fr. neurologist

Char·din \shär-'daⁿ\ Jean-Baptiste-Siméon 1699–1779 Fr. painter

Char·le·magne \'shär-lə-,mān\ 742–814 *Charles the Great* or *Charles I* Frankish king (768–814) & emperor of the West (800–814)

Charles I \'chär(-ə)lz\ 1600–1649 *Charles Stuart* king of Great Britain (1625–49)

Charles II 1630–1685 *son of Charles I* king of Great Britain (1660–85)

Charles 1948– *son of Elizabeth II* prince of Wales

Charles 1771–1847 archduke of Austria

Charles I 1887–1922 *Charles Francis Joseph; nephew of Francis Ferdinand* emperor of Austria & (as *Charles IV*) king of Hungary (1916–18)

Charles I or **II** 823–877 *the Bald* king of France as *Charles I* (840–877); Holy Roman emperor as *Charles II* (875–877)

Charles IV 1294–1328 *the Fair* king of France (1322–28)

Charles V 1337–1380 *the Wise* king of France (1364–80)

Charles VI 1368–1422 *the Mad* or *the Beloved* king of France (1380–1422)

Charles VII 1403–1461 king of France (1422–61)

Charles IX 1550–1574 king of France (1560–74)

Charles X 1757–1836 king of France (1824–30)

Charles V 1500–1558 Holy Rom. emperor (1519–56); king of Spain as *Charles I* (1516–56)

Charles XII 1682–1718 king of Sweden (1697–1718)

Charles Prince 1903–1983 *brother of King Leopold* regent of Belgium (1944–50)

Charles XIV John 1763–1844 originally *Jean-Baptiste-Jules Ber·na·dotte* \ber-nà-dòt\ king of Sweden & Norway (1818–44)

Charles Edward 1720–1788 *the Young Pretender; (Bonnie) Prince Charlie* Brit. prince

Charles Mar·tel \-mär-'tel\ *circa* 688–741 *grandfather of Charlemagne* Frankish ruler (719–741)

Charlotte Empress of Mexico — see CARLOTA

Char·pak \shär-pák\ Georges 1924– Fr. (Pol.-born) physicist

Chase \'chās\ Mary Ellen 1887–1973 Am. educator & author

Chase Sal·mon \'sa-mən, 'sal-\ Portland 1808–1873 Am. statesman; chief justice U.S. Supreme Court (1864–73)

Cha·teau·bri·and \(,)sha-,tō-brē-'äⁿ\ Vi·comte \vē-kōⁿt\ François-Auguste-René de 1768–1848 Fr. author

Chatham 1st Earl of — see William PITT

Chatrian Alexandre — see ERCKMANN-CHATRIAN

Chat·ter·jee \'cha-tər-jē\ Ban·kim \'bòṇ-kim\ Chan·dra \'chən-(,)drə\ 1838–1894 Indian novelist

Chat·ter·ton \'cha-tər-t^ən\ Thomas 1752–1770 Eng. poet

Chau·cer \'chò-sər\ Geoffrey *circa* 1342–1400 Eng. poet — **Chau·ce·ri·an** \chò-'sir-ē-ən\ *adjective*

Chau·temps \shō-täⁿ\ Camille 1885–1963 Fr. lawyer & politician; premier (1930; 1933–34; 1937–38)

Chavannes, de — see PUVIS DE CHAVANNES

Chá·vez \'chä-vəs, -,vez\ Carlos 1899–1978 Mex. conductor & composer

Chee·ver \'chē-vər\ John 1912–1982 Am. writer

Che·khov *also* **Che·kov** \'che-,kòf, -,kòv\ Anton Pavlovich 1860–1904 Russ. dramatist & writer — **Che·kho·vi·an** \che-'kō-vē-ən\ *adjective*

Ché·nier \shän-'yā\ André-Marie de 1762–1794 Fr. poet

Chen·nault \shə-'nólt\ Claire Lee 1890–1958 Am. general

Cheops — see KHUFU

Che·ren·kov \chə-'reŋ-kəf\ Pavel Alekseyevich 1904–1990 Russ. physicist

Cher·nen·ko \cher-'n^yeŋ-kō\ Konstantin Ustinovich 1911–1985 Soviet politician; president U.S.S.R. (1984–85); 1st secretary of Communist party (1984–85)

Cher·ny·shev·sky \,cher-ni-'shef-skē, -'shev-\ Nikolay Gavrilovich 1829–1889 Russ. revolutionary & author

Che·ru·bi·ni \,ker-ə-'bē-nē, ,kä-rü-\ (Maria) Lu·i·gi \lü-'ē-(,)jē\ Carlo Zenobio Salvatore 1760–1842 Ital. composer

Ches·ter·field \'ches-tər-,fēld\ 4th Earl of 1694–1773 *Philip Dormer Stan·hope* \'sta-nəp\ Eng. statesman & author

Ches·ter·ton \'ches-tər-t^ən\ Gilbert Keith 1874–1936 Eng. journalist & author — **Ches·ter·to·nian** \,ches-tər-'tō-nē-ən, -nyən\ *adjective*

Che·va·lier \shə-'val-(,)yā\ Mau·rice \mò-'rēs\ 1888–1972 Fr. entertainer

Chiang Kai–shek \jē-'äŋ-kī-'shek, ,chaŋ-\ 1887–1975 pinyin *Jiang Jie-shī* \jē-'äŋ-jē-'ā-'shē\ Chin. general & politician; president of China (1948–49; Taiwan, 1950–75)

Chi·ca·go \shə-'kä-(,)gō, -'kò-, -gə\ Judy 1939– originally surname *Cohen* Am. artist

Ch'ien–lung \che-'en-'lùŋ\ 1711–1799 Chin. emperor (1736–96)

Chi·ka·ma·tsu \,chē-kə-'mät-(,)sü\ Monzaemon 1653–1724 *the Shakespeare of Japan* Jp. dramatist

Child \'chī(ə)ld\ Francis James 1825–1896 Am. philologist & ballad editor

Childe \'chī(ə)ld\ Vere Gordon 1892–1957 Brit. anthropologist & archaeologist

Chil·ders \'chil-dərz\ Erskine Hamilton 1905–1974 Irish (Eng.-born) politician; president of Ireland (1973–74)

Ch'in Shih Huang Ti \'chin-'shir-'hwäŋ-'dē\ *circa* 259–210 B.C. prename *Cheng* \'jeŋ\ Chin. emperor (221–210 B.C.)

Chip·pen·dale \'chi-pən-,dāl\ Thomas 1718–1779 Eng. cabinetmaker

Chi·rac \shē-rák\ Jacques-René 1932– prime minister of France (1974–76; 1986–88); president (1995–)

Chi·ri·co, De \'kir-i-,kō, 'kē-ri-\ Gior·gio \'jòr-(,)jō\ 1888–1978 Ital. painter

Choate \'chōt\ Joseph Hodges 1832–1917 Am. lawyer & diplomat

Choate Rufus 1799–1859 Am. jurist

Choi·seul \shwä-'zəl, -'zər(-ə), -'zœl\ Étienne-François de 1719–1785 Duc *de Choiseul* Fr. statesman

Chom·sky \'chäm(p)-skē\ (Avram) Noam 1928– Am. linguist — **Chom·sky·an** *also* **Chom·ski·an** \-skē-ən\ *adjective*

Cho·pin \'shō-,pan, -,paⁿ\ Frédéric François 1810–1849 Pol. pianist & composer

Chou En–lai \'jō-'en-'lī\ 1898–1976 pinyin *Zhou Enlai* Chin. Communist politician

Chré·tien \krā-tyaⁿ\ (Joseph Jacques) Jean 1934– prime minister of Canada (1993–)

Chré·tien de Troyes \krā-tyaⁿ-də-trwä\ *flourished* 1170 Fr. trouvère

Christ Jesus — see JESUS

Chris·tian X \'kris-chən, 'krish-\ 1870–1947 king of Denmark (1912–47)

Chris·tie \'kris-tē\ Dame Agatha 1890–1976 née *Miller* Eng. writer

Chris·ti·na \kris-'tē-nə\ 1626–1689 *daughter of Gustav II Adolphus* queen of Sweden (1632–54)

Chris·tine de Pi·san \krēs-tēn-də-pē-zäⁿ\ 1364–*circa* 1430 Fr. poet

Chris·tophe \krē-stóf\ Henri 1767–1820 king of Haiti (1811–20)

Chris·to·pher \'kris-tə-fər\ Warren Minor 1925– U.S. secretary of state (1993–97)

Chris·ty \'kris-tē\ Howard Chandler 1873–1952 Am. artist

Chry·sos·tom \'kri-səs-təm, kri-'säs-təm\ Saint John *circa* 347–407 church father & patriarch of Constantinople

Chu Hsi \'jü-'shē\ 1130–1200 Chin. philosopher

Chun Doo–Hwan \'jún-'dō-'hwän\ 1931– president of So. Korea (1980–88)

Church \'chərch\ Frederic Edwin 1826–1900 Am. painter

Chur·chill \'chər-,chil, 'chərch-,hil\ John 1650–1722 1st Duke of *Marl·bor·ough* \'märl-,bər-ə, 'mòl-, -,bə-rə, -b(ə-)rə\ Eng. general

Churchill Randolph Henry Spencer 1849–1895 Lord *Randolph Churchill* Brit. statesman

Churchill Sir Winston Leonard Spencer 1874–1965 *son of Lord Randolph* Brit. statesman; prime minister (1940–45; 1951–55) — **Chur·chill·ian** \,chər-'chi-lē-ən, 'chərch-'hi-\ *adjective*

Chu Teh \'jü-'de\ 1886–1976 Chin. general

Cia·no \'chä-(,)nō\ Galeazzo 1903–1944 Conte *di Cortellazzo* Ital. statesman

Ciar·di \'chär-dē\ John 1916–1986 Am. poet

Cib·ber \'si-bər\ Col·ley \'kä-lē\ 1671–1757 Eng. dramatist & actor; poet laureate (1730–57)

Cic·ero \'si-sə-,rō\ Marcus Tullius 106–43 B.C. Rom. statesman, orator, & author — **Cic·ero·nian** \,si-sə-'rō-nyən, -nē-ən\ *adjective*

Cid, El \'sid\ *circa* 1043–1099 *Rodrigo Dí·az de Vi·variant* \'dē-,äs-də-vē-'vär, -,äz-\ Span. soldier & hero

Çil·ler \chi-'lesh\ Tan·su \tän-'sü\ 1946– prime minister of Turkey (1993–96)

Ci·ma·bue \,chē-mə-'bü-(,)ā\ Giovanni *circa* 1251–1302 originally *Bencivieni di Pepo* Florentine painter

Ci·mon \'sī-mən, -,män\ *circa* 570–*circa* 451 B.C. Athenian general & statesman

Cin·cin·na·tus \,sin(t)-sə-'na-təs, -'nä-\ Lucius Quinctius *born circa* 519 B.C. Rom. general & statesman

Clare \klar, 'kler\ John 1793–1864 Eng. poet

Clare of Assisi Saint 1194–1253 Ital. religious

Clarendon Earl of — see Edward HYDE

Clark \'klärk\ Champ \'champ\ 1850–1921 *James Beau·champ* \'bē-chəm\ *Clark* Am. politician

Clark George Rogers 1752–1818 Am. soldier & frontiersman

Clark Joe 1939– *Charles Joseph* Canad. politician; prime minister (1979–80)

Clark Kenneth Bancroft 1914– Am. psychologist

Clark Kenneth Mackenzie 1903–1983 Baron *Clark of Saltwood* Brit. art historian

Clark Mark Wayne 1896–1984 Am. general

Clark Tom Campbell 1899–1977 Am. jurist

Clark William 1770–1838 *brother of G.R.* Am. explorer

Clarke \'klärk\ Charles Cow·den \'kaù-d^ən\ 1787–1877 & his wife Mary Victoria Cowden-Clarke 1809–1898 Eng. Shakespearean scholars

Claude \'klōd\ Albert 1898–1983 Belg. physiologist in U.S.

Claude Lor·rain \klōd-lò-raⁿ\ 1600–1682 pseudonym of *Claude Gel·lée* \zhə-lā\ Fr. painter

Clau·di·us \'klò-dē-əs\ Rom. generals including: **Ap·pi·us** \'a-pē-əs\ **Claudius Cras·sus** \'kra-səs\ consul (471 & 451 B.C.) & decemvir (451–450 B.C.); **Appius Claudius Cae·cus** \'sē-kəs\ censor (312–307 B.C.), consul (307 & 296 B.C.), & dictator

Claudius I 10 B.C.–A.D. 54 *Tiberius Claudius Drusus Ne·ro* \'nē-(,)rō, 'nir-(,)ō\ *Germanicus* Rom. emperor (41–54)

Claudius II A.D. 214–270 *Marcus Aurelius Claudius Gothicus* Rom. emperor (268–270)

Clau·se·witz \'klaù-zə-,vits\ Carl von 1780–1831 Pruss. general & military strategist — **Clau·se·witz·ian** \,klaù-zə-'vit-sē-ən\ *adjective*

Clay \'klā\ Henry 1777–1852 Am. statesman & orator

Clay Lucius Du Bi·gnon \dù-'bin-yən\ 1897–1978 Am. general

Cle·an·thes \klē-'an-,thēz\ 331(or 330)–232(or 231) B.C. Greek Stoic philosopher

Cle·ar·chus \klē-'är-kəs\ 5th century B.C. Greek soldier; governor of Byzantium

Cleis·the·nes \'klīs-thə-ˌnēz\ *or* **Clis·the·nes** \'klis-\ *circa* 570–after 508 B.C. Athenian statesman

Cle·men·ceau \ˌkle-mən-'sō, klä-mäⁿ-sō\ Georges 1841–1929 Fr. statesman

Clem·ens \'kle-mənz\ Samuel Langhorne 1835–1910 pseudonym *Mark Twain* \'twān\ Am. writer

Clem·ent \'kle-mənt\ name of 14 popes: especially **VII** (*Giulio de'Me·di·ci* \'me-də-(ˌ)chē\) 1478–1534 (pope 1523–34)

Cle·men·ti \'klə-'men-tē\ Muzio 1752–1832 Ital. pianist & composer in England

Clement of Alexandria Saint *circa* 150–between 211 and 215 *Titus Flavius Cle·mens* \'kle-ˌmenz\ Greek Christian theologian & church father

Cle·om·e·nes \klē-'ä-mə-ˌnēz\ name of 3 kings of Sparta: especially **III** (reigned 235–222 B.C.)

Cle·o·pa·tra \ˌklē-ə-'pa-trə, -'pä-\ 69–30 B.C. queen of Egypt (51–30)

Cleve·land \'klēv-lənd\ (Stephen) Grover 1837–1908 22d & 24th president of the U.S. (1885–89; 1893–97)

Cli·burn \'klī-bərn\ Van 1934– *Harvey Lavan Cliburn* Am. pianist

Clin·ton \'klin-tⁿn\ De Witt 1769–1828 Am. statesman

Clinton George 1739–1812 vice president of the U.S. (1805–12)

Clinton Sir Henry 1738–1795 Eng. general in America

Clinton William Jefferson 1946– Am. politician; 42d president of the U.S. (1993–)

Clive \'klīv\ Robert 1725–1774 Baron *Clive of Plassey* Brit. general & founder of the empire of Brit. India

Cloots \'klōts\ Baron de 1755–1794 *Jean-Baptiste du Val-de-Grâce;* known as *An·a·char·sis* \ˌa-nə-'kär-səs\ *Cloots* Pruss.-Fr. revolutionary

Clough \'kləf\ Arthur Hugh 1819–1861 Eng. poet

Clo·vis I \'klō-vəs\ *German* **Chlod·wig** \'klōt-(ˌ)vik\ *circa* 466–511 king of the Salian Franks (481–511)

Clyde Baron — see Colin CAMPBELL

Cnut \kə-'nüt, -'nyüt\ *variant of* CANUTE

Coase \'kōz\ Ronald Harry 1910– Am. (Brit.-born) economist

Coates \'kōts\ Joseph Gordon 1878–1943 N.Z. statesman

Cobb \'käb\ Tyrus Raymond 1886–1961 *Ty* Am. baseball player

Cob·bett \'kä-bət\ William 1763–1835 pseudonym *Peter Porcupine* Eng. political writer

Cob·den \'käb-dən\ Richard 1804–1865 Eng. statesman & economist

Cobham Lord — see Sir John OLDCASTLE

Co·chise \kō-'chēs\ 1812?–1874 Chiricahua Apache Indian chief

Cock·croft \'kä(k)-ˌkròft\ Sir John Douglas 1897–1967 Brit. physicist

Coc·teau \käk-'tō, kòk-\ Jean 1889–1963 Fr. author & artist

Co·dy \'kō-dē\ William Frederick 1846–1917 *Buffalo Bill* Am. scout & showman

Coen \'kün\ Jan Pieterszoon 1587–1629 Du. colonial governor & founder of Du. East Indian empire

Coeur de Lion — see RICHARD I of England

Cof·fin \'kò-fən, 'kä-\ Robert Peter Tristram 1892–1955 Am. author

Cog·gan \'kä-gən\ Frederick Donald 1909– archbishop of Canterbury (1974–80)

Co·han \kō-ˌhan\ George Michael 1878–1942 Am. actor, dramatist, & producer

Co·hen \'kō-ən\ Stanley 1922– Am. biochemist

Cohen William Sebastian 1940– U.S. secretary of defense (1997–)

Cohn \'kōn\ Ferdinand Julius 1828–1898 Ger. botanist

Coke \'kük, 'kōk\ Sir Edward 1552–1634 *Lord Coke* Eng. jurist

Col·bert \kòl-'ber, 'kōl-\ Jean-Baptiste 1619–1683 Fr. statesman & financier

Cole \'kōl\ Thomas 1801–1848 Am. (Eng.-born) painter

Cole·pep·er *or* **Cul·pep·er** \'kəl-ˌpe-pər\ Thomas 1635–1689 2d Baron *Colepeper* Eng. colonial administrator; governor of Virginia

Cole·ridge \'kōl-rij, 'kō-lə-rij\ Samuel Taylor 1772–1834 Eng. poet — **Cole·ridg·ean** *also* **Cole·ridg·ian** \ˌkōl-'ri-jē-ən, ˌkō-lə-\ *adjective*

Col·et \'kä-lət\ John 1466(or 1467)–1519 Eng. theologian & scholar

Co·lette \kò-'let\ Sidonie-Gabrielle 1873–1954 Fr. author

Col·fax \'kōl-ˌfaks\ Schuy·ler \'skī-lər\ 1823–1885 vice president of the U.S. (1869–73)

Co·li·gny \ˌkò-lēn-'yē, kə-'lēn-yē\ Gaspard II de 1519–1572 *Seigneur de Châtillon* Fr. admiral & Huguenot leader

Col·lier \'käl-yər, 'kä-lē-ər\ Jeremy 1650–1726 Eng. clergyman

Collier John Payne 1789–1883 Eng. editor

Collier Peter Fen·e·lon \'fe-nⁿl-ən\ 1849–1909 Am. publisher

Col·lins \'kä-lənz\ Michael 1890–1922 Irish revolutionary

Collins Michael 1930– Am. astronaut

Collins William 1721–1759 Eng. poet

Collins (William) Wilkie 1824–1889 Eng. novelist

Col·lor de Mel·lo \kō-'lòr-də-'me-lü\ Fernando Affonso 1949– president of Brazil (1990–92)

Col·man \'kōl-mən\ George 1732–1794 Eng. dramatist

Col·um \'kä-ləm\ Pad·raic \'pòth-rig\ 1881–1972 Am. (Irish-born) writer

Co·lum·ba \kə-'ləm-bə\ *Irish* **Col·um** \'kə-ləm\ *or* **Col·um·cille** \kə-'ləm-ˌkil\ Saint *circa* 521–597 Irish missionary in Scotland

Co·lum·bus \kə-'ləm-bəs\ Christopher *It* Christoforo **Co·lom·bo** \kə-'ləm-(ˌ)bō\ *Sp* Cristóbal **Co·lón** \kə-'lōn\ 1451–1506 Genoese navigator & explorer for Spain

Co·me·ni·us \kə-'mē-nē-əs\ John Amos *Czech* Jan Ámos **Ko·men·ský** \'kò-mən-skē\ 1592–1670 Czech theologian & educator

Com·ma·ger \'kä-mi-jər\ Henry Steele 1902– Am. historian

Com·mo·dus \'kä-mə-dəs\ Lucius Aelius Aurelius A.D. 161–192 Rom. emperor (180–192)

Com·mo·ner \'kä-mə-nər\ Barry 1917– Am. biologist & educator

Com·mynes *or* **Co·mines** *or* **Com·mines** \kò-'mēn\ Philippe de *circa* 1447–1511 Fr. politician & chronicler

Comp·ton \'käm(p)-tən\ Arthur Holly 1892–1962 Am. physicist

Compton Karl Taylor 1887–1954 *brother of A.H.* Am. physicist

Com·stock \'käm-ˌstäk *also* 'kəm-\ Anthony 1844–1915 Am. reformer

Comte \'kōⁿ(n)t\ Auguste 1798–1857 in full *Isidore-Auguste-Marie-François-Xavier* Fr. mathematician & philosopher

Conan Doyle — see DOYLE

Co·nant \'kō-nənt\ James Bryant 1893–1978 Am. chemist & educator

Con·dé \kōⁿ-'dā\ Prince de 1621–1686 *Louis II de Bour·bon* \'bùr-bən, bùr-'bōⁿ\; Duc *d'En·ghien* \däⁿ-gaⁿ\ Fr. general

Con·don \'kän-dən\ Edward Uhler 1902–1974 Am. physicist

Con·dor·cet \kōⁿ-dòr-sā\ Marquis de 1743–1794 *Marie-Jean-Antoine-Nicholas de Ca·ri·tat* \ˌkar-ə-'tä\ Fr. philosopher & politician

Con·fu·cius \kən-'fyü-shəs\ *Chinese* **K'ung–Fu–tzu** \'kùŋ-'fü-'dzü\ *or* **K'ung–tzu** \kùŋ-'dzü\ 551–479 B.C. Chin. philosopher

Con·greve \'kän-ˌgrēv, 'käŋ-\ William 1670–1729 Eng. dramatist

Con·ing·ham \'kə-niŋ-ˌham, *chiefly British* -niŋ-əm\ Sir Arthur 1895–1948 Brit. air marshal

Con·rad \'kän-ˌrad\ Joseph 1857–1924 originally *Józef Teodor Konrad Kor·ze·niow·ski* \ˌkò-zhən-'yòf-skē, -'yòv-\ Brit. (Ukrainian-born of Pol. parents) novelist — **Con·rad·ian** \ˌkän-'ra-dē-ən\ *adjective*

Con·sta·ble \'kən(t)-stə-bəl, 'kän(t)-\ John 1776–1837 Eng. painter

Cons·tant de Re·becque \kōⁿ-'stäⁿ-də-rə-'bek\ Benjamin 1767–1830 Fr. writer & politician

Con·stan·tine \'kän(t)-stən-ˌtēn, -ˌtīn\ name of 2 kings of Greece: **I** 1868–1923 (reigned 1913–17; 1920–22); **II** (reigned 1964–73; deposed)

Constantine I *died* 337 *the Great* Rom. emperor (306–337) — **Con·stan·tin·ian** \ˌkän(t)s-tən-'ti-nē-ən\ *adjective*

Con·ta·ri·ni \ˌkän-tə-'rē-nē\ Venetian family including especially Gasparo 1483–1542 cardinal & diplomat

Con·ti \'kōn-tē, 'kän-\ Niccolò de' *circa* 1395–1469 Venetian traveler

Cook \'kük\ James 1728–1779 Eng. navigator & explorer

Cooke \'kük\ (Alfred) Al·is·tair \'a-lə-stər\ 1908– Am. (Brit.-born) essayist & journalist

Cooke Terence James 1921–1983 Am. cardinal

Coo·lidge \'kü-lij\ (John) Calvin 1872–1933 30th president of the U.S. (1923–29)

Cooper Anthony Ashley — see SHAFTESBURY

Coo·per \'kü-pər, 'kù-\ James Fen·i·more \'fen-ə-ˌmòr, -ˌmòr\ 1789–1851 Am. novelist

Cooper Leon N. 1930– Am. physicist

Cooper Peter 1791–1883 Am. manufacturer & philanthropist

Co·per·ni·cus \kō-'pər-ni-kəs\ Nicolaus *Pol* Mikołaj **Ko·per·nik** \kò-'per-nēk\ *or* Niklas **Kop·per·nigk** \'kä-pər-ˌnik\ 1473–1543 Pol. astronomer

Cop·land \'kō-plənd\ Aaron 1900–1990 Am. composer

Cop·ley \'kä-plē\ John Sin·gle·ton \'siŋ-gəl-tən\ 1738–1815 Am. portrait painter

Co·que·lin \ˌkòk-'laⁿ, ˌkò-kə-\ Benoît-Constant 1841–1909 Fr. actor

Cor·bu·sier, Le \lə-kòr-büs-'yä\ 1887–1965 originally *Charles-Édouard Jean·ne·ret* \zhän-'re\ Fr. (Swiss-born) architect, painter, & sculptor

Cor·day \kòr-'dā, 'kòr-\ Charlotte 1768–1793 *Marie-Anne-Charlotte Corday d'Ar·mont* \där-'mōⁿ\ Fr. patriot

Co·rel·li \kə-'re-lē\ Arcangelo 1653–1713 Ital. violinist & composer

Co·rey \'kòr-ē, 'kòr-\ Elias James 1928– Am. chemist

Co·ri \'kòr-ē, 'kòr-\ Carl Ferdinand 1896–1984 & his wife Ger·ty \'ger-tē\ Theresa 1896–1957 née *Rad·nitz* \'räd-ˌnits\ Am. (Czech-born) biochemists

Cor·mack \'kòr-mək\ Allan MacLeod 1924– Am. (So. African-born) physicist

Cor·neille \kòr-'nā\ Pierre 1606–1684 Fr. dramatist

Cor·ne·lia \kòr-'nēl-yə, -'nē-lē-ə\ 2d century B.C. *Mother of the Gracchi* Rom. matron

Cornelia *died* 67? B.C. *wife of Julius Caesar*

Cor·ne·lius \kòr-'nāl-yəs, -'nē-lē-əs\ Pe·ter \'pä-tər\ von 1783–1867 Ger. painter

Cor·nell \kòr-'nel\ Ezra 1807–1874 Am. financier & philanthropist

Cornell Katharine 1893–1974 Am. actress

Corn·forth \'kòrn-fərth, -ˌfòrth, -ˌfòrth\ John Warcup 1917– Brit. (Austral.-born) chemist

Corn·wal·lis \kòrn-'wä-ləs\ 1st Marquis 1738–1805 *Charles Cornwallis* Brit. general & statesman

Co·ro·na·do \ˌkòr-ə-'nä-(ˌ)dō, ˌkär-\ Francisco Vásquez de *circa* 1510–1554 Span. explorer & conquistador

Co·rot \kə-'rō, kò-\ Jean-Baptiste-Camille 1796–1875 Fr. painter

Cor·reg·gio \kə-'re-j(ē-ˌ)ō\ 1494–1534 *Antonio Allegri da Correggio* Ital. painter

Cor·ri·gan \'kòr-i-gən\ Mairead 1944– Irish peace worker

Cor·tés \kòr-'tez, 'kòr-\ Hernán *or* Hernando 1485–1547 Span. conquistador

Cos·grave \ˌkäz-ˌgräv\ Liam 1920– prime minister of Ireland (1973–77)

Cosgrave William Thomas 1880–1965 *father of Liam* Irish statesman

Cos·ta Ca·bral \ˌkòsh-tə-kə-'bräl, ˌkòs-\ António Bernardo da 1803–1889 Conde *de Thomar* Port. statesman

Cos·tel·lo \'käs-tə-ˌlō\ John Aloysius 1891–1976 prime minister of Ireland (1948–51; 1954–57)

Cot·ton \'kä-tⁿn\ Charles 1630–1687 Eng. author & translator

Cotton John 1585–1652 Am. (Eng.-born) Puritan clergyman

Co·ty \kò-'tē, kō-\ René-Jules-Gustave 1882–1962 Fr. lawyer; 2d president of Fourth Republic (1954–59)

Cou·lomb \kü-'lōⁿ', 'kü-ˌläm, -ˌlòm, kü-'\ Charles-Augustin de 1736–1806 Fr. physicist

Cou·pe·rin \ˌkü-'praⁿ', ˌkü-pə-\ François 1668–1733 Fr. composer

Cou·pe·rus \kü-'pā-rəs, -'per-əs\ Louis Marie Anne 1863–1923 Du. novelist

Cour·bet \kur-'bā\ Gustave 1819–1877 Fr. painter

Cour·nand \kur-'nän\ André Frédéric 1895–1988 Am. (Fr.-born) physiologist

Cou·sin \kü-zaⁿ\ Victor 1792–1867 Fr. philosopher

Cous·ins \'kə-zⁿnz\ Norman 1912–1990 Am. editor & essayist

Cous·teau \kü-'stō\ Jacques-Yves 1910–1997 Fr. marine explorer

Co·var·ru·bias \ˌkō-və-'rü-bē-əs\ Miguel 1904–1957 Mex. artist

Cov·er·dale \'kə-vər-ˌdāl\ Miles 1488?–1569 Eng. Bible translator

Cow·ard \'kau̇(-ə)rd\ Sir Noël Peirce 1899–1973 Eng. actor & dramatist

Cow·ell \'kau̇(-ə)l\ Henry Dixon 1887–1965 Am. composer

Cowl \'kau̇(ə)l\ Jane 1883–1950 originally *Cowles* Am. actress

Cow·ley \'kau̇-lē\ Abraham 1618–1667 Eng. poet

Cowley Malcolm 1898–1989 Am. literary critic

Cow·per \'kü-pər, 'ku̇-, 'kau̇-\ William 1731–1800 Eng. poet

Cox·ey \'käk-sē\ Jacob Sechler 1854–1951 Am. political reformer

Coz·zens \'kə-zⁿnz\ James Gould 1903–1978 Am. author

Crabbe \'krab\ George 1754–1832 Eng. poet

Craig·av·on \krā-'ga-vən\ 1st Viscount 1871–1940 *James Craig* Brit. statesman; 1st prime minister of Northern Ireland (1921–40)

Crai·gie \'krā-gē\ Sir William Alexander 1867–1957 Brit. philologist & lexicographer

Cram \'kram\ Donald James 1919– Am. chemist

Cram Ralph Adams 1863–1942 Am. architect & author

Cra·nach \'krä-ˌnäk\ Lucas 1472–1553 Ger. painter & engraver

Cranborne Viscount — see Robert CECIL

Crane \'krān\ (Harold) Hart 1899–1932 Am. poet

Crane Stephen 1871–1900 Am. writer

Crane Walter 1845–1915 Eng. artist

Cran·mer \'kran-mər\ Thomas 1489–1556 Eng. reformer; archbishop of Canterbury (1533–56)

Cras·sus \'kra-səs\ Marcus Licinius 115?–53 B.C. *Di·ves* \'dī-(ˌ)vēz\ Rom. politician

Cray \'krā\ Seymour R. 1925–1996 Am. computer scientist

Crazy Horse \'krā-zē-ˌhȯrs\ 1842–1877 *Ta·sunko-witko* or *Tashunca-Uitco* Sioux Indian chief

Cré·bil·lon \ˌkrā-bē-'yōⁿ\ 1674–1762 pseudonym of *Prosper Jolyot* Fr. dramatist

Cre·mer \'krē-mər\ Sir William Randal 1838–1908 Eng. pacifist

Cres·ton \'kres-tən\ Paul 1906–1985 originally *Giuseppe Guttoveggio* Am. composer

Crève·coeur \krev-'kər, ˌkrev-, -'ku̇r\ Michel-Guillaume-Jean de 1735–1813 pseudonym *J. Hector St. John* Am. (Fr.-born) essayist

Crich·ton \'krī-tⁿn\ James 1560–1582 *the Admirable Crichton* Scot. man of letters

Crick \'krik\ Francis Harry Compton 1916– Brit. biophysicist

Crile \'krī(ə)l\ George Washington 1864–1943 Am. surgeon

Cripps \'krips\ Sir (Richard) Stafford 1889–1952 Brit. statesman

Cri·spi \'kris-pē, 'krēs-\ Francesco 1819–1901 Ital. statesman; premier (1887–91; 1893–96)

Cris·ti·ani \ˌkris-tē-'ä-nē\ Alfredo 1947– president of El Salvador (1989–94)

Cro·ce \'krō-(ˌ)chā\ Benedetto 1866–1952 Ital. philosopher & statesman

Crock·ett \'krä-kət\ David 1786–1836 *Davy* Am. frontiersman & politician

Croe·sus \'krē-səs\ died *circa* 546 B.C. king of Lydia (*circa* 560–546)

Cro·ker \'krō-kər\ John Wilson 1780–1857 Brit. essayist & editor

Cromer 1st Earl of — see Evelyn BARING

Cromp·ton \'kräm(p)-tən\ Samuel 1753–1827 Eng. inventor

Crom·well \'kräm-ˌwel, 'krȯm-, 'krəm-, -wəl\ Oliver 1599–1658 Eng. general & statesman; lord protector of England (1653–58) — **Crom·well·ian** \kräm-'we-lē-ən, ˌkrȯm-\ *adjective*

Cromwell Richard 1626–1712 *son of Oliver* lord protector (1658–59)

Cromwell Thomas 1485?–1540 Earl of *Essex* Eng. statesman

Cro·nin \'krō-nən\ Archibald Joseph 1896–1981 Eng. physician & novelist

Cronin James Watson 1931– Am. physicist

Cron·jé \krȯn-'yä\ Piet Arnoldus *circa* 1835–1911 Boer leader & general

Crookes \'kru̇ks\ Sir William 1832–1919 Eng. physicist & chemist

Cross \'krȯs\ Wilbur Lucius 1862–1948 Am. educator & politician

Crouse \'krau̇s\ Russel 1893–1966 Am. journalist & dramatist

Cru·den \'krü-dⁿn\ Alexander 1701–1770 Scot. compiler of a biblical concordance

Cruik·shank \'kru̇k-ˌshaŋk\ George 1792–1878 Eng. caricaturist & illustrator

Crut·zen \'krət-sən, 'kru̇t-\ Paul J. 1933– Du. chemist

Cruz \'krüs\ Juana Inés de la 1651–1695 originally *Juana Inés de Asbaje* Mex. religious & poet

Cud·worth \'kəd-(ˌ)wərth\ Ralph 1617–1688 Eng. philosopher

Cul·pep·er \'kəl-ˌpe-pər\ *variant of* COLEPEPER

Cum·mings \'kə-miŋz\ Edward Estlin 1894–1962 known as *e. e. cummings* Am. poet

Cu·nha \'kün-yə\ Tris·tão da \ˌtris-tən-də-'kü-nə, trēsh-,tau̇ⁿ-də-'kün-yə, trēs-\ 1460–1540 Port. navigator & explorer

Cun·ning·ham \'kə-niŋ-ˌham, *chiefly British* -niŋ-əm\ Allan 1784–1842 Scot. author

Cunningham Merce 1919?– Am. choreographer

Cuo·mo \'kwō-(ˌ)mō\ Andrew Mark 1957– U.S. secretary of housing and urban development (1997–)

Cu·rie \kyu̇-'rē, 'kyu̇r-(ˌ)ē\ Eve 1904– *daughter of Marie & Pierre* Am. (Fr.-born) author

Curie Marie 1867–1934 née *Maria Skło·dow·ska* \skłō-'dȯf-skə, -'dȯv-\ Fr. (Pol.-born) chemist

Curie Pierre 1859–1906 *husband of Marie* Fr. chemist

Curie Joliot — see JOLIOT-CURIE

Curl \'kər(-ə)l\ Robert Floyd 1933– Am. chemist

Cur·ley \'kər-lē\ James Michael 1874–1958 Am. politician

Cur·ri·er \'kər-ē-ər, 'kə-rē-\ Nathaniel 1813–1888 Am. lithographer

Cur·ry \'kər-ē, 'kə-rē\ John Steuart 1897–1946 Am. painter

Cur·tin \'kər-tⁿn\ John 1885–1945 Austral. prime minister (1941–45)

Cur·tis \'kər-təs\ Charles 1860–1936 vice president of the U.S. (1929–33)

Curtis Cyrus Hermann Kotzschmar 1850–1933 Am. publisher

Curtis George Ticknor 1812–1894 Am. lawyer & writer

Curtis George William 1824–1892 Am. author & editor

Cur·tiss \'kər-təs\ Glenn Hammond 1878–1930 Am. aviator & inventor

Cur·ti·us \'kər-tē-əs\ Ernst 1814–1896 Ger. historian & archaeologist

Cur·wen \'kər-wən\ John 1816–1880 Eng. music teacher

Cur·zon \'kər-zⁿn\ George Nathaniel 1859–1925 1st Baron & 1st Marquis *Curzon of Ked·le·ston* \'ke-dⁿl-stən\ Eng. statesman; viceroy of India (1899–1905)

Cush·ing \'ku̇-shiŋ\ Caleb 1800–1879 Am. lawyer & diplomat

Cushing Harvey 1869–1939 Am. surgeon

Cushing Richard James 1895–1970 Am. cardinal

Cush·man \'ku̇sh-mən\ Charlotte Saunders 1816–1876 Am. actress

Cus·ter \'kəs-tər\ George Armstrong 1839–1876 Am. general

Cuth·bert \'kəth-bərt\ Saint 635?–687 Eng. monk

Cu·vier \'kü-vē-ˌā, 'kyü-, ˌkū-vyä\ Baron Georges 1769–1832 originally *Jean-Léopold-Nicolas-Frédéric Cuvier* Fr. naturalist

Cuyp *or* **Cuijp** \'kīp\ Aelbert Jacobsz 1620–1691 Du. painter

Cyn·e·wulf \'ki-nə-ˌwu̇lf\ *or* **Cyn·wulf** \'kin-ˌwu̇lf\ 9th century Anglo-Saxon poet

Cyp·ri·an \'si-prē-ən\ Saint *died* 258 *Thascius Caecilius Cyprianus* Christian martyr; bishop of Carthage (*circa* 248–258)

Cy·ran·kie·wicz \ˌ(t)sir-ən-'kyä-vich\ Józef 1911–1989 Pol. politician; prime minister (1947–52; 1954–70)

Cy·ra·no de Ber·ge·rac \'sir-ə-ˌnō-də-'ber-zhə-ˌrak\ Savinien de 1619–1655 Fr. poet & soldier

Cyr·il \'sir-əl\ Saint *circa* 827–869 *Constantine* apostle to the Slavs

Cy·rus II \'sī-rəs\ *circa* 585–*circa* 529 B.C. *the Great* or *the Elder* king of Persia (*circa* 550–529)

Cyrus 424?–401 B.C. *the Younger* Persian prince & satrap

Czer·ny \'cher-nē, 'chər-\ Carl 1791–1857 Austrian pianist & composer

D' \d-\ **De** \də-, di-; *in Dutch names* dē-\, **Du** \dü, dyü-, də-\, etc. for many names beginning with these elements see the specific family names

Da·guerre \də-'ger\ Louis-Jacques-Mandé 1789–1851 Fr. painter & inventor

Daim·ler \'dīm-lər\ Gottlieb Wilhelm 1834–1900 Ger. automotive manufacturer

Da·kin \'dā-kən\ Henry Drysdale 1880–1952 Eng. chemist

Da·la·dier \də-'lä-dē-ˌā, ˌda-lə-'dyä\ Édouard 1884–1970 Fr. statesman

Da·lai La·ma \ˌdä-ˌlī-'lä-mə\ 1935– *Tenzin Gyatso* Tibetan religious & political leader

D' Al·bert \'dal-bərt\ Eugen Francis Charles 1864–1932 Scot. pianist & composer

Dalcroze Émile Jaques — see Émile JAQUES-DALCROZE

Dale \'dā(ə)l\ Sir Henry Hallett 1875–1968 Eng. physiologist

Dale Sir Thomas *died* 1619 Eng. colonial administrator in Virginia

Da·lén \də-'län\ Nils Gustaf 1869–1937 Swed. inventor

Da·ley \'dā-lē\ Richard Joseph 1902–1976 Am. politician

Daley William Michael 1948– *son of Richard* U.S. secretary of commerce (1997–)

Dalhousie Earl & Marquis of — see RAMSAY

Da·lí \'dä-lē, *by himself* dä-'lē\ Salvador 1904–1989 Span. surrealistic painter — **Da·li·esque** \ˌdä-lē-'esk\ *adjective*

Dal·las \'da-ləs, -lis\ George Mifflin 1792–1864 vice president of the U.S. (1845–49)

Dal·rym·ple \dal-'rim-pəl, 'dal-,\ Sir James 1619–1695 1st Viscount *Stair* \'ster\ Scot. jurist

Dalrymple Sir John 1673–1747 2d Earl of *Stair* Brit. general & statesman

Dal·ton \'dȯl-tⁿn\ Baron 1887–1962 *Hugh Dalton* Brit. politician

Dalton John 1766–1844 Eng. chemist & physicist

Da·ly \'dā-lē\ (John) Augustin 1838–1899 Am. dramatist & theater manager

Dam \'dam, 'däm\ (Carl Peter) Henrik 1895–1976 Dan. biochemist

Da·mien \'dā-mē-ən, ˌda-mē-'aⁿ\ Father 1840–1889 originally *Joseph de Veuster* Belg. Roman Catholic missionary in Hawaiian Islands

Dam·pi·er \'dam-pē-ər\ William 1652–1715 Eng. buccaneer & navigator

Dam·rosch \'dam-ˌräsh\ Walter Johannes 1862–1950 Am. (Ger.-born) musician & conductor

Da·na \'dā-nə\ Charles Anderson 1819–1897 Am. newspaper editor

Dana James Dwight 1813–1895 Am. geologist

Dana Richard Henry 1815–1882 Am. lawyer & author

Dane \'dān\ Clemence 1888–1965 pseudonym of *Winifred Ashton* \'ash-tən\ Eng. novelist

Dan·iel \'dan-yəl\ Samuel 1562?–1619 Eng. poet

Dan·iels \'dan-yəlz\ Josephus 1862–1948 Am. journalist & statesman

Da·ni·lo·va \də-'nē-lə-və\ Aleksandra 1903?–1997 Am. (Russ.-born) choreographer & dancer

D'An·nun·zio \dä-'nün(t)-sē-ˌō\ Gabriele 1863–1938 Ital. author & soldier

\ə\ abut	\ⁿ\ kitten	\ər\ further \a\ ash \ā\ ace
\ä\ mop, mar	\au̇\ out	\ch\ chin \e\ bet \ē\ easy
\g\ go	\i\ hit	\ī\ ice \j\ job \ŋ\ sing \ō\ go
\ȯ\ law	\ȯi\ boy	\th\ thin \t̟h\ the \ü\ loot \u̇\ foot
\y\ yet	\zh\ vision	*see also* Guide to Pronunciation

Dan·te \'dän-(,)tā, 'dan-, -(,)tē\ 1265–1321 *Dante* or *Durante Ali·ghie·ri* \,ä-lə-'gyer-ē\ Ital. poet — **Dan·te·an** \dän-'tē-ən, 'dän-\ *or* **Dan·tes·can** \dan-'tes-kən, dän-\ *or* **Dan·tesque** \-'tesk\ *adjective*

Dan·ton \dän-'tōⁿ\ Georges-Jacques 1759–1794 Fr. revolutionary

Dare \'dar, 'der\ Virginia 1587–? 1st child born in America of Eng. parents

Da·ri·us \də-'rī-əs\ name of 3 kings of Persia: especially **I** 550–486 B.C. (reigned 522–486) *Darius Hys·tas·pes* \his-'tas-pəs\; *the Great*

Dar·lan \där-'läⁿ\ Jean-Louis-Xavier-François 1881–1942 Fr. admiral

Darn·ley \'därn-lē\ Lord 1545–1567 *Henry Stewart* or *Stuart; husband of Mary, Queen of Scots*

Dar·row \'dar-(,)ō\ Clarence Seward 1857–1938 Am. lawyer & author

Dar·win \'där-wən\ Charles Robert 1809–1882 Eng. naturalist

Darwin Erasmus 1731–1802 *grandfather of C. R.* Eng. physiologist & poet

Dau·bi·gny \dō-bēn-'yē, dō-'bē-nyē\ Charles-François 1817–1878 Fr. painter

Dau·det \dō-'dā\ Alphonse 1840–1897 Fr. novelist

Daudet Léon 1867–1942 *son of Alphonse* Fr. journalist & writer

Dau·mier \dō-myā, 'dō-mē-,ā\ Honoré 1808–1879 Fr. caricaturist & painter

Daus·set \dō-se, -sā\ Jean-Baptiste-Gabriel 1916– Fr. physician

Dav·e·nant *or* **D'Av·e·nant** \'dav-nənt, 'da-və-\ Sir William 1606–1668 Eng. poet & dramatist; poet laureate (1638–68)

Dav·en·port \'da-vən-,pört, 'da-vᵊm-, -,pórt\ John 1597–1670 Am. (Eng.-born) clergyman & founder of New Haven colony

Da·vid I \'dā-vəd\ *circa* 1082–1153 king of Scotland (1124–53)

Da·vid \dä-vət\ Gerard *circa* 1460–1523 Du. painter

Da·vid \dä-vēd\ Jacques-Louis 1748–1825 Fr. painter

Da·vid d'An·gers \däⁿ-'zhā\ Pierre-Jean 1788–1856 Fr. sculptor

Da·vid·son \'dä-vəd-sən\ Jo 1883–1952 Am. sculptor

Davidson Randall Thomas 1848–1930 archbishop of Canterbury (1903–28)

Da·vies \'dä-vēz\ Arthur Bowen 1862–1928 Am. painter

Davies (William) Robertson 1913–1995 Canad. author

Dá·vi·la Pa·di·lla \'dä-vi-lə-pä-'dē-yə\ Agustín 1562–1604 Mex. monk & historian

Da·vis \'dā-vəs\ Bet·te \'be-tē\ 1908–1989 originally *Ruth Elizabeth Davis* Am. actress

Davis Dwight Filley 1879–1945 Am. statesman

Davis Elmer Holmes 1890–1958 Am. radio broadcaster & news commentator

Davis Harold Le·noir \lə-'nōr, -'nör\ 1896–1960 Am. writer

Davis Jefferson 1808–1889 Am. statesman; president of Confederate states (1861–65)

Davis Miles 1926–1991 Am. jazz composer & musician

Da·vis·son \'dā-və-sən\ Clinton Joseph 1881–1958 Am. physicist

Da·vout \da-'vü\ Louis-Nicolas 1770–1823 Duc *d'Au·er·städt* \daú-(,)ər-,stet\ & *Prince d'Eck·mühl* \'dek-,myül\ marshal of France

Da·vy \'dā-vē\ Sir Humphry 1778–1829 Eng. chemist

Dawes \'dóz\ Charles Gates 1865–1951 Am. lawyer & financier; vice president of U.S. (1925–29)

Daw·son \'dó-sᵊn\ Sir John William 1820–1899 Canad. geologist

Day \'dā\ Clarence Shepard, Jr. 1874–1935 Am. author

Day Thomas 1748–1789 Eng. author

Day William Rufus 1849–1923 Am. statesman & jurist

Da·yan \dī-'än\ Moshe 1915–1981 Israeli soldier & politician

Day–Le·wis \'dā-'lü-əs\ Cecil 1904–1972 pseudonym *Nicholas Blake* Brit. writer; poet laureate (1968–72)

De·ák \'dā-,äk\ Fe·renc \'fer-,en(t)s\ 1803–1876 Hung. statesman

Dean \'dēn\ Sir Patrick 1909–1994 Brit. diplomat

Deane \'dēn\ Silas 1737–1789 Am. lawyer & diplomat

De·bierne \də-'byern\ André-Louis 1874–1949 Fr. chemist

De·breu \də-'brœ\ Gerard 1921– Am. (Fr.-born) economist

Debs \'debz\ Eugene Victor 1855–1926 Am. socialist

De·bus·sy \,de-byü-'sē, ,dā-; də-'byü-sē\ (Achille-) Claude 1862–1918 Fr. composer — **De·bus·sy·an** \,de-byü-'sē-ən, ,dā-; də-'byü-sē-ən\ *adjective*

De·bye \də-'bī\ Peter Joseph William 1884–1966 Am. (Du.-born) physicist

De·ca·tur \di-'kā-tər\ Stephen 1779–1820 Am. naval officer

De·cazes \də-käz\ Duc Élie 1780–1860 Fr. statesman

De·cius \'dē-sh(ē-)əs\ Gaius Messius Quintus Trajanus *circa* 201–251 Rom. emperor (249–51)

Dee·ping \'dē-piŋ\ (George) Warwick 1877–1950 Eng. novelist

Deere \'dir\ John 1804–1886 Am. inventor

Def·fand, du \dü-fäⁿ\ Marquise 1697–1780 née *Marie de Vichy-Cham·rond* \də-vē-shē-shäⁿ-rōⁿ\ Fr. woman of letters

De·foe \di-'fō\ Daniel 1660–1731 Eng. journalist & novelist

De For·est \di-'fór-əst, -'fär-\ Lee 1873–1961 Am. inventor

De·gas \də-gä\ (Hilaire-Germain-) Edgar 1834–1917 Fr. artist

de Gaulle Charles — see GAULLE

De Gennes \də-zhen\ Pierre-Gilles 1932– Fr. physicist

Deh·melt \'dā-məlt\ Hans Georg 1922– Am. (Ger.-born) physicist

Dei·sen·hof·er \'dī-zən-,hō-fər\ Johann 1943– Ger. biochemist

Dek·ker \'de-kər\ Thomas 1572?–?1632 Eng. dramatist

de Klerk \də-'klərk, -'klerk\ Frederik Willem 1936– president of Republic of So. Africa (1989–94); vice president (1994–)

de Koo·ning \də-'kō-niŋ\ Willem 1904–1997 Am. (Du.-born) painter

de Kruif \də-'krīf\ Paul Henry 1890–1971 Am. bacteriologist & author

De·la·croix \,de-lə-'k(r)wä\ (Ferdinand-Victor-) Eugène 1798–1863 Fr. painter

de la Mare \de-lə-'mar, -'mer\ Walter John 1873–1956 Eng. poet & novelist

De·land \də-'land\ Margaret 1857–1945 née *Margaretta Wade Campbell* Am. novelist

De La Rey \de-lə-'rī, -'rā\ Jacobus Hercules 1847–1914 Boer general & statesman

De·la·roche \,de-lə-'rōsh, -'rósh\ (Hippolyte-) Paul 1797–1859 Fr. painter

De·la·vigne \,de-lə-'vēnʸ, -'vēn-yə\ Jean-François-Casimir 1793–1843 Fr. poet & dramatist

De La Warr \də-lə-,war, -,wer\ Baron 1577–1618 *Thomas West; Lord Delaware* Eng. colonial administrator in America

Del·brück \'del-,brʊk, -,brük\ Max 1906–1981 Am. (Ger.-born) biologist

De·led·da \dā-'le-də, də-\ Grazia 1875–1936 Ital. author

De·libes \də-'lēb\ (Clément-Philibert-) Léo 1836–1891 Fr. composer

De·lius \'dē-lē-əs, 'dēl-yəs\ Frederick 1862–1934 Eng. composer

Del·la Rob·bia \,de-lə-'rä-bē-ə, -'rō-\ Luca 1399(or 1400)–1482 originally *Luca di Simone di Marco* Florentine sculptor

De Long \də-'lóŋ\ George Washington 1844–1881 Am. naval officer & explorer

De·lorme *or* **de l'Orme** \de-'lórm\ Philibert 1515?–1570 Fr. architect

de Mille \də-'mil\ Agnes George 1905–1993 Am. dancer & choreographer

De·Mille \də-'mil\ Cec·il \'se-səl\ Blount \'blənt\ 1881–1959 Am. film director & producer

De·moc·ri·tus \di-'mä-krə-təs\ *circa* 460–*circa* 370 B.C. *the Laughing Philosopher* Greek philosopher

De Mor·gan \di-'mór-gən\ William Frend 1839–1917 Eng. artist & novelist

De·mos·the·nes \di-'mäs-thə-,nēz\ 384–322 B.C. Athenian orator & statesman — **De·mos·then·ic** \di-,mäs-'the-nik, ,dē-, -'thē-\ *adjective*

Demp·sey \'dem(p)-sē\ William Harrison 1895–1983 *Jack* Am. boxer

Deng Xiaoping — see TENG HSIAO-P'ING

De·ni·ker \dā-nē-'ker\ Joseph 1852–1918 Fr. anthropologist

De·nis *or* **De·nys** \'de-nəs, də-nē\ Saint *died* 258? 1st bishop of Paris & patron saint of France

Dent \'dent\ Joseph Mal·a·by \'ma-lə-bē\ 1849–1926 Eng. publisher

De·pew \di-'pyü\ Chauncey Mitchell 1834–1928 Am. lawyer & politician

De Quin·cey \di-'kwin(t)-sē, -'kwin-zē\ Thomas 1785–1859 Eng. author

De·rain \də-raⁿ\ André 1880–1954 Fr. painter

Der·ri·da \de-rē-dä\ Jacques 1930– Fr. philosopher & critic — **Der·ri·de·an** *also* **Der·ri·di·an** \,de-ri-'dē-ən\ *adjective*

Der·zha·vin \der-'zhä-vən\ Gavrila Romanovich 1743–1816 Russ. poet

De·sai \də-'sī\ Morarji Ranchhodji 1896–1995 prime minister of India (1977–79)

De·saix de Vey·goux \də-'sā-də-(,)vā-'gü\ Louis-Charles-Antoine 1768–1800 Fr. general

De·sargues \dā-'zärg\ Gérard *or* Girard 1591–1661 Fr. mathematician

Des·cartes \dā-'kärt\ René 1596–1650 Latin *Renatus Cartesius* Fr. mathematician & philosopher

Des·cha·nel \,dā-shə-'nel\ Paul-Eugène-Louis 1855–1922 Fr. statesman; president of France (1920)

De Se·ver·sky \də-sə-'ver-skē\ Alexander Procofieff 1894–1974 Am. (Russ.-born) aeronautical engineer

Des·mou·lins \dā-mü-laⁿ\ Camille 1760–1794 *Lucie-Simplice-Camille-Benoît Desmoulins* Fr. revolutionary

de Soto Hernando — see SOTO, DE

Des Prez Josquin — see JOSQUIN DES PREZ

Des·saix \də-'sā\ Comte Joseph-Marie 1764–1834 Fr. general

Des·sa·lines \,dā-sə-'lēn, ,de-\ Jean-Jacques 1758?–1806 emperor as *Jacques I* \zhäk\ of Haiti (1804–06)

De·taille \də-'tī\ (Jean-Baptiste-) Édouard 1848–1912 Fr. painter

De·us Ra·mos \'dā-əsh-'ra-(,)müsh\ João \'zhwaúⁿ\ de 1830–1896 Port. poet

De Va·le·ra \də-və-'ler-ə, -'lir-ə\ Ea·mon \'ā-mən\ 1882–1975 Irish politician; prime minister of Ireland (1937–48; 1951–54; 1957–59); president of Ireland (1959–73)

De Vere \də-'vir\ Aubrey Thomas 1814–1902 Irish poet

Dev·er·eux \'de-və-,rüks, -,rü\ Robert 1566–1601 2d Earl of *Essex* Eng. soldier & courtier

Devonshire dukes of — see CAVENDISH

De Vo·to \di-'vō-(,)tō\ Bernard Augustine 1897–1955 Am. author

De Vries Hugo — see VRIES, DE

Dew·ar \'dü-ər, 'dyü-\ Sir James 1842–1923 Scot. chemist & physicist

De Wet Christiaan Rudolph — see WET, DE

Dew·ey \'dü-ē, 'dyü-\ George 1837–1917 Am. admiral

Dewey John 1859–1952 Am. philosopher & educator — **Dew·ey·an** \-ən\ *adjective*

Dewey Melvil 1851–1931 Am. librarian

Dewey Thomas Edmund 1902–1971 Am. lawyer & politician

De Witt Johan — see WITT, DE

De Witte Emanuel — see WITT, DE

Dia·ghi·lev \dē-'ä-gə,lef\ Sergey Pavlovich 1872–1929 Russ. ballet producer & art critic

Di·as \'dē-,äsh\ Bartholomew *circa* 1450–1500 Port. navigator

Dí·az \'dē-,äts\ Armando 1861–1928 Duca *della Vittoria* Ital. general; marshal of Italy

Dí·az \'dē-,äs, -,äz\ Porfirio 1830–1915 *José de la Cruz Porfirio* Mex. general; president of Mexico (1877–80; 1884–1911)

Díaz de Vivar — see CID

Dí·az Or·daz \'dē-əs-ór-'däz\ Gustavo 1911–1979 president of Mexico (1964–70)

Dick \'dik\ George Frederick 1881–1967 & Gladys Henry 1881–1963 Am. physicians

Dick·ens \'di-kənz\ Charles John Huffam 1812–1870 pseudonym *Boz* \'böz\ Eng. novelist — **Dick·en·si·an** \di-'ken-zē-ən, -sē-\ *adjective*

Dick·ey \'di-kē\ James Lafayette 1923–1997 Am. poet, novelist, & critic

Dick·in·son \'di-kən-sən\ Emily Elizabeth 1830–1886 Am. poet

Dickinson John 1732–1808 Am. statesman

Di·de·rot \dē-'drō, 'dē-də-,rō\ Denis 1713–1784 Fr. encyclopedist

Die·fen·ba·ker \'dē-fən-,bā-kər\ John George 1895–1979 prime minister of Canada (1957–63)

Diels \'dē(ə)lz, 'dē(ə)ls\ Otto Paul Hermann 1876–1954 Ger. chemist

Die·sel \'dē-zəl, -səl\ Rudolf 1858–1913 Ger. mechanical engineer

Die·trich \'dē-trik, -trik\ Marlene 1901?–1992 Am. (Ger.-born) actress & singer

Diez \'dēts\ Friedrich Christian 1794–1876 Ger. philologist

Dig·by \'dig-bē\ Sir Ken·elm \'ke-,nelm\ 1603–1665 Eng. naval commander, diplomat, & author

Dill \'dil\ Sir John Greer 1881–1944 Brit. general

Dil·lon \'di-lən\ John 1851–1927 Irish nationalist politician

Di·Mag·gio \də-'mä-zhē-(,)ō, -'ma-jē-(,)ō, -'ma-jō\ Joseph Paul 1914– Am. baseball player

Di·mi·tri·os I \thē-'mē-trē-ôs; də-'mē-trē-əs\ 1914–1991 archbishop of Constantinople and ecumenical patriarch (1972–91)

Di·ne·sen \'dē-nə-sən, 'dī-\ Isak \'ē-,säk\ 1885–1962 pseudonym of *Karen Christence Dinesen*, Baroness *Blixen-Finecke* Dan. author

Din·wid·die \din-'wi-dē\ Robert 1693–1770 Eng. colonial administrator in America

Di·o·cle·tian \,dī-ə-'klē-shən\ 245(or 248)–313(or 316) *Gaius Aurelius Valerius Diocletianus* Rom. emperor (284–305)

Di·og·e·nes \dī-'ä-jə-,nēz\ *died circa* 320 B.C. Greek Cynic philosopher

Di·o·ny·sius \,dī-ə-'ni-shē-əs, -sē-əs, -shəs; -'nī-sē-əs\ *circa* 430–367 B.C. *the Elder* Greek tyrant of Syracuse (405–367)

Dionysius *the Younger* tyrant of Syracuse (367–356; 354–343 B.C.)

Dionysius Ex·ig·u·us \eg-'zi-gyə-wəs\ *circa* 500–*circa* 560 Christian monk

Dionysius of Alexandria Saint *circa* 200–*circa* 265 theologian & bishop of Alexandria (247)

Dionysius of Hal·i·car·nas·sus \,ha-lə-(,)kär-'na-səs\ *flourished circa* 20 B.C. Greek scholar

Di·rac \di-'rak\ Paul Adrien Maurice 1902–1984 Eng. physicist

Dirk·sen \'dərk-sən\ Everett McKinley 1896–1969 Am. politician

Dis·ney \'diz-nē\ Walter Elias 1901–1966 Am. film producer

Dis·rae·li \diz-'rā-lē\ Benjamin 1804–1881 1st Earl of *Bea·cons·field* \'bē-kənz-,fēld\ Brit. politician & author; prime minister (1868; 1874–80)

Dit·mars \'dit-,märz\ Raymond Lee 1876–1942 Am. naturalist

Dix \'diks\ Dorothea Lynde 1802–1887 Am. social reformer

Dix Dorothy — see Elizabeth Meriwether GILMER

Dix·on \'dik-sən\ Jeremiah *died* 1777 Eng. surveyor in America

Dmow·ski \də-'móf-skē, -'móv-\ Roman 1864–1939 Pol. statesman

Dö·be·rei·ner \'də(r)-bə-,rī-nər, 'dœ-\ Johann Wolfgang 1780–1849 Ger. chemist

Do·bie \'dō-bē\ James Frank 1888–1964 Am. folklorist

Do·brée \'dō-,brā\ Bon·a·my \'bä-nə-mē\ 1891–1974 Eng. scholar

Dob·son \'däb-sən\ (Henry) Austin 1840–1921 Eng. poet & essayist

Dodge \'däj\ Mary Elizabeth 1831–1905 née *Mapes* \'māps\ Am. author

Dodg·son \'däd-sən, 'däj-\ Charles Lut·widge \'lət-wij\ 1832–1898 pseudonym *Lewis Car·roll* \'kar-əl\ Eng. mathematician & writer

Dods·ley \'dädz-lē\ Robert 1703–1764 Eng. author & bookseller

Do·her·ty \'dō-ər-tē, 'dō-, 'dä-\ Peter Charles 1940– Am. (Austral.-born) immunologist

Doi·sy \'dói-zē\ Edward Adelbert 1893–1986 Am. biochemist

Dole \'dōl\ Robert Joseph 1923– Am. politician

Dole Sanford Ballard 1844–1926 Am. jurist; president (1894–1900) & governor (1900–03) of Hawaii

Doll·fuss \'dól-,füs\ Engelbert 1892–1934 Austrian statesman

Do·magk \'dō-,mäk\ Gerhard 1895–1964 Ger. bacteriologist

Do·me·ni·chi·no \(,)dō-,mā-nə-'kē-(,)nō\ 1581–1641 *Domenico Zam·pie·ri* \,tsäm-pē-'er-ē, ,zäm-\ Ital. painter

Do·min·go \dō-'miŋ-gō\ Placido 1941– Span. tenor

Dom·i·nic \'dä-mə-(,)nik\ Saint *circa* 1170–1221 *Domingo de Guz·mán* \güz-'män, güs-\ Span.-born founder of the Dominican order of friars

Do·mi·tian \də-'mi-shən\ A.D. 51–96 *Titus Flavius Domitianus* Rom. emperor (81–96)

Don·a·tel·lo \,dä-nə-'te-(,)lō\ 1386?–1466 *Donato de Betto di Bardi* Florentine sculptor

Don·gen \'dóŋ-ən\ Kees van 1877–1968 originally *Cornelis Theodorus Maria Dongen* Fr. (Du.-born) painter

Dö·nitz \'dœ(r)-nəts, 'dœ-\ Karl 1891–1980 Ger. admiral

Don·i·zet·ti \,dä-nə(d)-'ze-tē, ,dō-\ Gaetano 1797–1848 Ital. composer — **Don·i·zet·ti·an** \-'ze-tē-ən\ *adjective*

Donne \'dän *also* 'dən\ John 1572–1631 Eng. poet & clergyman — **Donn·ean** *or* **Donn·ian** \'də-nē-ən, 'dä-\ *adjective*

Don·o·van \'dä-nə-vən, 'də-\ William Joseph 1883–1959 *Wild Bill* Am. lawyer & general

Doo·lit·tle \'dü-,li-t'l\ James Harold 1896–1993 Am. aviator & general

Dopp·ler \'dä-plər\ Christian Johann 1803–1853 Austrian physicist

Do·ra·ti \də-'rä-tē\ An·tal \'än-,täl\ 1906–1988 Am. (Hung.-born) conductor

Do·ré \dó-'rā, də-\ (Paul-) Gustave 1832–1883 Fr. illustrator & painter

Dor·ge·les \,dór-zhə-'les\ Roland 1886–1973 Fr. novelist

Dor·nier \'dórn-,yā\ Claudius 1884–1969 Ger. airplane builder

Dorr \'dór\ Thomas Wilson 1805–1854 Am. lawyer & politician

Dorset 1st Earl of — see Thomas SACKVILLE

Dos Pas·sos \däs-'pa-səs\ John Roderigo 1896–1970 Am. writer

Dos·to·yev·sky \däs-tə-'yef-skē, -'yev-\ Fyodor Mikhaylovich 1821–1881 Russ. novelist — **Dos·to·yev·ski·an** *or* **Dos·to·ev·ski·an** \-skē-ən\ *adjective*

Dou *or* **Douw** \'daú\ Gerrit *or* Gerard 1613–1675 Du. painter

Dou·ble·day \'də-bəl-,dā\ Abner 1819–1893 Am. soldier & reputed inventor of baseball

Dough·ty \'daú-tē\ Charles Montagu 1843–1926 Eng. poet & traveler

Doug·las \'də-gləs\ John Shol·to \'shól-(,)tō\ 1844–1900 8th Marquis & Earl of *Queens·ber·ry* \'kwēnz-,ber-ē, -b(ə-)rē\ Scot. boxing patron

Douglas Stephen Arnold 1813–1861 Am. politician

Douglas William Orville 1898–1980 Am. jurist

Douglas–Home — see HOME

Douglas of Kir·tle·side \'kər-t'l-,sīd\ 1st Baron 1893–1969 *William Sholto Douglas* Brit. air marshal

Doug·lass \'də-gləs\ Frederick 1817–1895 originally *Frederick Augustus Washington Bailey* Am. abolitionist

Dou·mer \dü-'mer\ Paul 1857–1932 president of France (1931–32)

Dou·mergue \dü-'merg\ Gaston 1863–1937 Fr. statesman; president of France (1924–31)

Dow·den \'daú-d'n\ Edward 1843–1913 Irish literary critic

Dow·ie \'daú-ē\ John Alexander 1847–1907 Am. (Scot.-born) religious leader

Dow·son \'daú-s'n\ Ernest Christopher 1867–1900 Eng. lyric poet

Dox·ia·dis \,dók-sē-'ä-thēs\ Konstantinos Apostolos 1913–1975 Greek architect

Doyle \'dói(ə)l\ Sir Arthur Co·nan \'kō-nən\ 1859–1930 Brit. physician, novelist, & detective-story writer

D'Oyly Carte — see CARTE, D'OYLY

Drach·mann \'dräk-mən\ Holger Henrik Herholdt 1846–1908 Dan. writer

Dra·co \'drā-(,)kō\ late 7th century B.C. Athenian lawgiver

Drake \'drāk\ Sir Francis 1540(or 1543)–1596 Eng. navigator & buccaneer

Dra·per \'drā-pər\ Henry 1837–1882 Am. astronomer

Dray·ton \'drā-t'n\ Michael 1563–1631 Eng. poet

Drei·ser \'drī-sər, -zər\ Theodore 1871–1945 Am. editor & novelist — **Drei·ser·ian** \,drī-'ser-ē-ən, -'zər-\ *adjective*

Drew \'drü\ John 1827–1862 Am. (Irish-born) actor

Drew John 1853–1927 *son of preceding* Am. actor

Drey·fus \'drī-fəs, 'drā-; dre-füs\ Alfred 1859–1935 Fr. army officer

Driesch \'drēsh\ Hans Adolf Eduard 1867–1941 Ger. biologist & philosopher

Drink·wa·ter \'driŋk-,wó-tər, -,wä-\ John 1882–1937 Eng. writer

Drou·et \drü-'e, -'ā\ Jean-Baptiste 1765–1844 Comte *d'Er·lon* \der-'lōⁿ\ Fr. general; marshal of France

Drum·mond \'drə-mənd\ Henry 1851–1897 Scot. clergyman & writer

Drummond William Henry 1854–1907 Canad. (Irish-born) poet

Drummond of Haw·thorn·den \'hó-,thórn-dən\ William 1585–1649 Scot. poet

Dru·sus \'drü-səs\ 38–9 B.C. *Ne·ro* \'nē-(,)rō, 'nir-(,)ō\ *Claudius Drusus Ger·man·i·cus* \(,)jer-'ma-ni-kəs\ Rom. general

Dry·den \'drī-d'n\ John 1631–1700 Eng. poet & dramatist; poet laureate (1668–88) — **Dry·de·ni·an** \drī-'dē-nē-ən, -'de-\ *adjective*

Du Barry Comtesse — see Jeanne BARRY

Du·bois \dü-'bwä, dyü-; dē-'bwä\ Paul 1829–1905 Fr. sculptor

Dubois (François-Clément-) Théodore 1837–1924 Fr. composer

DuBois \dü-'bóis, dyü-\ William Edward Burghardt 1868–1963 Am. educator & writer

Du·buf·fet \,dü-bə-'fā, ,dyü-; dē-bü-fe\ Jean 1901–1985 Fr. artist

Du Cange \dü-'käⁿzh, dyü-\ Sieur Charles Du Fresne 1610–1688 Fr. scholar & glossarist

Du Chail·lu \də-'shal-(,)yü, -'shī-(,)ü\ Paul Belloni 1831–1903 Am. (Fr.-born) explorer in Africa

Du·champ \dü-'shäⁿ, dyü-\ Marcel 1887–1968 Fr. painter — **Du·champ·ian** \-'shäm-pē-ən\ *adjective*

Du·com·mun \,dü-kə-'mœⁿ, ,dyü-\ Élie 1833–1906 Swiss journalist

Dudevant Aurore — see George SAND

Dud·ley \'dəd-lē\ Robert 1532(or 1533)–1588 1st Earl of *Leicester* Eng. courtier

Dudley Thomas 1576–1653 Eng. colonial administrator in America

Duf·fer·in and Ava \,də-fə-rin-ən(d)-'ä-və\ 1st Marquis of 1826–1902 *Frederick Temple Hamilton-Temple-Blackwood* Brit. diplomat

Duff–Gor·don \'dəf-'gór-d'n\ Lady Lucie 1821–1869 Eng. author

Duf·fy \'də-fē\ Sir Charles Gavan 1816–1903 Irish nationalist & Austral. politician

Du·fy \dü-'fē, dyü-\ Raoul 1877–1953 Fr. painter

Du Gard Roger Martin — see MARTIN DU GARD

Du Guesclin Bertrand — see GUESCLIN

Du·ha·mel \,dü-ä-'mel, ,dyü-; dē-à-mel\ Georges 1884–1966 Fr. writer

Du·ka·kis \dü-'kä-kis\ Michael Stanley 1933– Am. politician

Duke \dük, 'dyük\ Benjamin Newton 1855–1929 & his brother James Buchanan 1856–1925 Am. tobacco industrialists

Dul·bec·co \(,)dəl-'be-(,)kō\ Renato 1914– Am. (Ital.-born) virologist

Dul·les \'də-ləs\ John Foster 1888–1959 Am. diplomat; secretary of state (1953–59)

Du·mas \dü-'mä, dyü-; 'd(y)ü-,\ Alexandre 1802–1870 *Dumas père* \'per\ Fr. novelist & dramatist

Dumas Alexandre 1824–1895 *Dumas fils* \'fēs\ Fr. novelist & dramatist

du Mau·rier \dü-'mór-ē-,ā, dyü-\ Dame Daphne 1907–1989 Brit. writer

du Maurier George Louis Palmella Busson 1834–1896 *grandfather of preceding* Brit. artist & novelist

Du·mou·riez \dü-'mür-ē-,ā, dyü-\ Charles-François du Périer 1739–1823 Fr. general

Du·nant \dü-'näⁿ, dyü-\ Jean-Henri 1828–1910 Swiss philanthropist & founder of the Red Cross

Dun·bar \'dən-,bär\ Paul Laurence 1872–1906 Am. poet

Dunbar \'dən-,bär, ,dən-'\ William 1460?–?1530 Scot. poet

Dun·can \'dəŋ-kən\ Isadora 1877–1927 Am. dancer

Dun·das \,dən-'das\ Henry 1742–1811 1st Viscount *Melville* & Baron *Dun·ira* \,də-'nir-ə\ Brit. statesman

Dun·lop \,dən-'läp, 'dən-,\ John Boyd 1840–1921 Scot. inventor

Dunne \'dən\ Finley Peter 1867–1936 Am. humorist

Du·nois \dün-'wä, dyün-\ Comte de 1403–1468 *Jean d'Orléans; the Bastard of Orléans* Fr. general

Dun·sa·ny \,dən-'sā-nē\ 18th Baron 1878–1957 *Edward John Moreton Drax Plunkett* Irish poet & dramatist

Duns Sco·tus \'dənz-'skō-təs\ John 1266?–1308 Scot. scholastic theologian

Dun·stan \'dən(t)-stən\ Saint 924–988 archbishop of Canterbury (959–988)

Du·pleix \dü-'pleks, dyü-\ Marquis Joseph·François 1697–1763 Fr. colonial administrator in India

Duplessis–Mornay — see Philippe de MORNAY

Du Pont \dü-'pänt, dyü-; 'd(y)ü-,\ Éleuthère Irénée 1771–1834 *son of P.S. Du Pont de Nemours* Am. (Fr.-born) industrialist

Du Pont de Ne·mours \-də-nə-'mùr\ Pierre-Samuel 1739–1817 Fr. economist & statesman

Du·quesne \dü-'kān, dyü-\ Marquis Abraham 1610–1688 Fr. naval officer

Du·rant \dù-'rant, dyü-\ William James 1885–1981 Am. educator & writer

Dü·rer \'dùr-ər, 'dyùr-, 'dūr-\ Albrecht 1471–1528 Ger. painter & engraver — **Dü·rer·esque** \,dùr-ər-'esk, ,dyùr-, ,dūr-\ *adjective*

D'Ur·fey \'dər-fē\ Thomas 1653–1723 Eng. songwriter & dramatist

Durk·heim \'dùr-'kem\ Émile 1858–1917 Fr. sociologist — **Durk·heim·ian** \-'ke-mē-ən\ *adjective*

Du·roc \dù-'räk, dyù-\ Géraud-Christophe-Michel 1772–1813 Duc *de Fri·oul* \frē-ül\ Fr. general under Napoleon

Dur·rell \'dər-əl, 'də-rəl\ Lawrence 1912–1990 Eng. novelist & poet

Dür·ren·matt \'dùr-ən-,mät, 'dùr-\ Friedrich 1921–1990 Swiss author

Du·ruy \dùr-'wē, dūr-rw°ē\ Victor 1811–1894 Fr. historian

Du·se \'dü-(,)zā\ Eleonora 1858–1924 Ital. actress

Du·tra \'dü-trə\ Eurico Gaspar 1885–1974 Braz. general; president of Brazil (1946–51)

Du·va·lier \dù-'val-(,)yā, dyù-\ François 1907–1971 *Papa Doc* president of Haiti (1957–71)

Du·ve \'dü-və\ Christian René Marie Joseph 1917– Belg. (Eng.-born) physiologist

Du Vi·gneaud \dü-'vēn-(,)yō, dyù-\ Vincent 1901–1978 Am. biochemist

Dvo·řák \(də-)'vȯr-,zhäk\ Antonín 1841–1904 Bohemian composer

Dwig·gins \'dwi-gənz\ William Addison 1880–1956 Am. type designer

Dwight \'dwīt\ Timothy 1752–1817 Am. clergyman; president Yale U. (1795–1817)

Dwight Timothy 1828–1916 *grandson of preceding* Am. clergyman; president Yale U. (1886–99)

Dwyfor Earl of — see LLOYD GEORGE

Dyce \'dīs\ Alexander 1798–1869 Scot. editor

Dy·er \'dī(-ə)r\ John 1699–1757 Brit. poet

Dyer Mary *died* 1660 Am. Quaker martyr

Eads \'ēdz\ James Buchanan 1820–1887 Am. engineer & inventor

Ea·kins \'ā-kənz\ Thomas 1844–1916 Am. artist

Ear·hart \'er-,härt, 'ir-\ Amelia 1897–1937 Am. aviator

Ear·ly \'ər-lē\ Ju·bal \'jü-bəl\ Anderson 1816–1894 Am. Confederate general

Earp \'ərp\ Wyatt 1848–1929 Am. lawman

East·man \'ēst-mən\ George 1854–1932 Am. inventor & industrialist

Eastman Max Forrester 1883–1969 Am. editor & writer

Ea·ton \'ē-t°n\ Theophilus 1590–1658 Eng. colonial administrator in America; governor of New Haven colony (1638–58)

Ebert \'ā-bərt\ Friedrich 1871–1925 president of Germany (1919–25)

Ec·cles \'e-kəlz\ Sir John Carew 1903–1997 Austral. physiologist

Eccles Marriner Stoddard 1890–1977 Am. banker & economist

Eche·ga·ray y Ei·za·guir·re \,ā-chə-gə-'rī-,ē-,ā-thə-'gwir-(,)ā, -sə-'gwir-\ José 1832–1916 Span. dramatist

Eche·ver·ría Ál·va·rez \,ā-chə-və-'rē-ə-'al-və-,rez, ,e-chə-\ Luis 1922– president of Mexico (1970–76)

Eck \'ek\ Johann 1486–1543 originally *Maier* Ger. Roman Catholic theologian

Ecke·hart \'e-kə-,härt\ *or* **Eck·art** *or* **Eck·hart** \'ek-,härt, 'e-,kärt\ Johannes 1260?–?1327 *Meister Eckehart* Ger. mystic

Eck·er·mann \'e-kər-,män, -mən\ Johann Peter 1792–1854 Ger. writer

Ed·ding·ton \'e-diŋ-tən\ Sir Arthur Stanley 1882–1944 Eng. astronomer

Ed·dy \'e-dē\ Mary Morse 1821–1910 née *Baker* Am. founder of the Christian Science Church

Ed·el·man \'e-d°l-mən\ Gerald Maurice 1929– Am. biochemist

Eden \'ē-d°n\ (Robert) Anthony 1897–1977 Earl of *Avon* \'ā-vən\ Eng. statesman; prime minister (1955–57)

Edge·worth \'ej-(,)wərth\ Maria 1767–1849 Brit. novelist

Edinburgh Duke of — see PHILIP

Ed·i·son \'e-də-sən\ Thomas Alva 1847–1931 Am. inventor

Ed·mund *or* **Ead·mund II** \'ed-mənd\ *circa* 993–1016 *Ironside* king of the English (1016)

Ed·ward \'ed-wərd\ name of 8 post-Norman Eng. (Brit.) kings: **I** 1239–1307 (reigned 1272–1307); **II** 1284–1327 (reigned 1307–27); **III** 1312–1377 (reigned 1327–77); **IV** 1442–1483 (reigned 1461–70; 1471–83); **V** 1470–1483 (reigned 1483); **VI** 1537–1553 (reigned 1547–53) *son of Henry VIII & Jane Seymour*; **VII** 1841–1910 (reigned 1901–10) *Albert Edward, son of Victoria*; **VIII** 1894–1972 (reigned 1936; abdicated) Duke of *Windsor, son of George V*

Edward 1330–1376 *the Black Prince; son of Edward III* prince of Wales

Edward *or* **Ead·ward** \'ed-\ 1003?–1066 *the Confessor* king of the English (1042–66)

Ed·wards \'ed-wərdz\ Jonathan 1703–1758 Am. theologian — **Ed·ward·ean** \ed-'wär-dē-ən, -'wȯr-\ *adjective*

Ed·win *or* **Ead·wine** \'ed-wən\ 585?–633 king of Northumbria (616–633)

Egas Mo·niz \'ā-gäs-mō-'nēz\ António Caetano de Abreu Freire 1874–1955 Port. neurologist & politician

Eg·bert \'eg-bərt\ *died* 839 king of the West Saxons (802–839) & 1st king of the English (828–839)

Eg·gle·ston \'e-gəl-stən\ Edward 1837–1902 Am. writer

Eggleston George Cary 1839–1911 *brother of Edward* Am. writer

Eg·mond \'eg-,mänt\ *or* **Eg·mont** Lamoraal 1522–1568 Graaf *van Egmond* Flem. general & statesman

Eh·ren·burg \'er-ən-,bùrg, -,bùrk\ Ilya Grigoryevich 1891–1967 Russ. writer

Ehr·lich \'er-lik\ Paul 1854–1915 Ger. bacteriologist

Ehr·lich \'ər-lik\ Paul Ralph 1932– Am. biologist

Eif·fel \'ī-fəl, e-fel\ Alexandre-Gustave 1832–1923 Fr. engineer

Ei·gen \'ī-gən\ Manfred 1927– Ger. chemist

Eijk·man \'īk-,män, 'āk-\ Christiaan 1858–1930 Du. pathologist

Ein·stein \'īn-,stīn\ Albert 1879–1955 Am. (Ger.-born) physicist — **Ein·stein·ian** \īn-'stī-nē-ən\ *adjective*

Eint·ho·ven \'īnt-,hō-vən, 'änt-\ Willem 1860–1927 Du. physiologist

Ei·sen·how·er \'ī-z°n-,haù(-ə)r\ Dwight David 1890–1969 Am. general; 34th president of the U.S. (1953–61)

Ei·sen·stein \'ī-z°n-,stīn\ Sergey Mikhaylovich 1898–1948 Soviet (Russ.-born) film director

El·a·gab·a·lus \,el-ə-'ga-bə-ləs\ *Greek* **He·li·o·gab·a·lus** \,hē-lē-ō-'ga-bə-ləs\ 204–222 Rom. emperor (218–222)

El·ders \'el-dərz\ (Minnie) Joycelyn 1933– U.S. surgeon general (1993–94)

El·don \'el-dən\ 1st Earl of 1751–1838 *John Scott* Eng. jurist

El·ea·nor \'e-lə-nər, -,nȯr\ **of Aquitaine** 1122?–1204 *queen of Louis VII of France (divorced 1152) & of Henry II of England*

Eleanor of Castile 1246–1290 *queen of Edward I of England*

Eleanor of Provence 1223–1291 *queen of Henry III of England*

El·gar \'el-,gär, -gər\ Sir Edward 1857–1934 Eng. composer

El·i·on \'e-lē-ən\ Gertrude Belle 1918– Am. biochemist

El·iot \'e-lē-ət, 'el-yət\ Charles William 1834–1926 Am. educator; president Harvard U. (1869–1909)

Eliot George 1819–1880 pseudonym of *Mary Ann (or Marian) Evans* Eng. novelist

Eliot Sir John 1592–1632 Eng. statesman

Eliot John 1604–1690 *apostle to the Indians* Am. clergyman

Eliot Thomas Stearns 1888–1965 Brit. (Am.-born) poet & critic — **El·i·ot·ian** \,e-lē-'ō-tē-ən, -'ȯsh(ē-)ən\ *adjective* — **El·i·ot·ic** \,e-lē-'ä-tik\ *adjective*

Eliz·a·beth \i-'li-zə-bəth\ name of 2 Eng. (Brit.) queens: **I** 1533–1603 *daughter of Henry VIII & Anne Boleyn* (reigned 1558–1603); **II** 1926– *Elizabeth Alexandra Mary; daughter of George VI* (reigned 1952–)

Elizabeth *also* **Elizabeth Stu·art** \-'stü-ərt, -'styü-; 'stü-(ə)rt, 'styü-(ə)rt\ 1596–1662 *queen of Frederick V of Bohemia*

Elizabeth 1900– *Elizabeth Angela Marguerite Bowes-Ly·on* \'bōz-'lī-ən\; *queen of George VI of Great Britain*

Elizabeth 1843–1916 pseudonym *Car·men Syl·va* \'kär-mən-'sil-və\ queen of Romania & writer

Elizabeth Pe·trov·na \pə-'trȯv-nə\ 1709–1762 empress of Russia (1741–62)

Ellenborough 1st Baron — see LAW

El·ling·ton \'e-liŋ-tən\ Edward Kennedy 1899–1974 *Duke Ellington* Am. bandleader & composer

El·liott \'e-lē-ət, 'el-yət\ Maxine 1868–1940 pseudonym of *Jessie Dermot* Am. actress

El·lis \'e-ləs\ Alexander John 1814–1890 original surname *Sharpe* Eng. philologist

Ellis (Henry) Have·lock \'hav-,läk, -lək\ 1859–1939 Eng. psychologist & writer

El·li·son \'e-lə-sən\ Ralph Waldo 1914–1994 Am. writer

Ells·worth \'elz-(,)wərth\ Lincoln 1880–1951 Am. explorer

Ellsworth Oliver 1745–1807 Am. jurist; chief justice U.S. Supreme Court (1796–1800)

El·man \'el-mən\ Mi·scha \'mē-shə\ 1891–1967 Am. (Russ.-born) violinist

El·phin·stone \'el-fən-,stōn, *chiefly British* -stən\ Mount·stu·art \maùnt-'st(y)ü-ərt\ 1779–1859 Brit. statesman in India

Elphinstone William 1431–1514 Scot. bishop & statesman

El·yot \'e-lē-ət, 'el-yət\ Sir Thomas 1490?–1546 Eng. scholar & diplomat

El·y·tis \'e-'lē-(,)tēs\ Odysseus 1911–1996 Greek poet

El·ze·vir *or* **El·ze·vier** \'el-zə-,vir\ family of Du. printers including especially Lodewijk or Louis 1546?–1617, his son Bonaventura 1583–1652, & his grandson Abraham 1592–1652

Em·er·son \'e-mər-sən\ Ralph Waldo 1803–1882 Am. essayist & poet — **Em·er·so·nian** \,e-mər-'sō-nē-ən, -nyən\ *adjective*

Em·met \'e-mət\ Robert 1778–1803 Irish nationalist & rebel

Em·ped·o·cles \em-'pe-də-,klēz\ *circa* 490–430 B.C. Greek philosopher & statesman

Endara (Galimany) \en-'där-ə,-,gä-lē-'mä-nē\ Guillermo 1936– president of Panama (1989–94)

En·de·cott *or* **En·di·cott** \'en-di-kət, -də-,kät\ John 1588–1665 colonial governor of Massachusetts

En·ders \'en-dərz\ John Franklin 1897–1985 Am. bacteriologist

Enes·cu \ə-'nes-(,)kü\ Gheorghe *or* George *Fr* **Enes·co** \-(,)kō\ Georges 1881–1955 Romanian composer

Eng·els \'eŋ-gəlz, -əlz, *German* 'eŋ-əls\ Friedrich 1820–1895 Ger. socialist

En·ver Pa·şa \'en-ˌver-'pä-shə, -'pa-shə, -pə-'shä\ 1881–1922 Turk. soldier & politician

Epam·i·non·das \i-ˌpa-mə-'nän-dəs\ circa 410–362 B.C. Theban general & statesman

Ep·ic·te·tus \ˌe-pik-'tē-təs\ circa A.D. 55–circa 135 Greek Stoic philosopher in Rome — **Ep·ic·te·tian** \-'tē-shən\ adjective

Ep·i·cu·rus \ˌe-pi-'kyŭr-əs\ 341–270 B.C. Greek philosopher

Ep·stein \'ep-ˌstīn\ Sir Jacob 1880–1959 Brit. (Am.-born) sculptor

Eras·mus \i-'raz-məs\ Desiderius 1466?–1536 Du. scholar — **Eras·mi·an** \-mē-ən\ adjective

Er·a·tos·the·nes \ˌer-ə-'täs-thə-ˌnēz\ circa 276–circa 194 B.C. Greek astronomer

Erck·mann–Cha·tri·an \'erk-ˌmän-shä-trē-'äⁿ, -ˌsha-\ joint pseudonym of *Émile Erckmann* 1822–1899 & *Alexandre Chatrian* 1826–1890 Fr. authors

Er·dos \'er-ˌdərsh\ Paul 1913–1996 Hung. mathematician

Er·hard \'er-härt\ Ludwig 1897–1977 chancellor of West Germany (1963–66)

Er·ics·son \'er-ik-sən\ John 1803–1889 Am. (Swed.-born) engineer & inventor

Erig·e·na \i-'ri-jə-nə\ John Sco·tus \'skō-təs\ circa 810–circa 877 Scot. (Irish-born) philosopher & theologian

Er·ik \'er-ik\ the Red 10th century Norw. navigator & explorer

Eriksson Leif — see LEIF ERIKSSON

Er·lan·der \er-'län-dər\ Tage Frithiof 1901–1985 Swed. politician

Er·lang·er \'ər-ˌlaŋ-ər\ Joseph 1874–1965 Am. physiologist

Er·len·mey·er \'ər-lən-ˌmī(-ə)r\ er, \-ˌer-\ Richard August Carl Emil 1825–1909 Ger. chemist

Ernst \'ern(t)st, 'ərn(t)st\ Max 1891–1976 Ger. painter

Ernst Richard Robert 1933– Swiss chemist

Er·skine \'ər-skən\ John 1879–1951 Am. educator & writer

Erskine of Car·nock \'kär-nək\ John 1695–1768 Scot. jurist

Er·vine \'ər-vən\ St. John \sänt-'jän, sənt-; 'sin-jən\ Greer 1883–1971 Irish dramatist & novelist

Erz·ber·ger \'erts-ˌber-gər\ Matthias 1875–1921 Ger. statesman

Es·a·ki \ə-'sä-kē\ Leo 1925– Jp. physicist

Esch·er \'e-shər, 'es-kər\ Maurits Cornelis 1898–1972 Du. graphic artist

Esh·kol \esh-'kôl\ Levi 1895–1969 prime minister of Israel (1963–69)

Es·par·te·ro \ˌes-pər-'ter-(ˌ)ō\ Baldomero 1793–1879 Conde de Luchana Span. general & statesman

Es·qui·vel \ˌä-skē-'vel\ Adolfo Pérez 1931– Argentine sculptor and dissident

Es·sen \'e-sᵊn\ Count Hans Henrik von 1755–1824 Swed. field marshal & statesman

Essex 2d Earl of — see DEVEREUX

Es·taing, d' \des-taⁿ\ Comte Jean-Baptiste-Charles-Henri-Hector 1729–1794 Fr. admiral

Este \'es-(ˌ)tä\ Ital. princely family beginning with *Alberto Az·zo II* \'äd-(ˌ)zō\ 996–1097 & ending with *Er·co·le III* \'er-kə-ˌlā\ *Rinaldo* 1727–1803

Es·ter·ha·zy \'es-tər-ˌhä-zē\ Marie-Charles-Ferdinand-Walsin 1847–1923 Fr. army officer

Es·tienne \ā-'tyen\ or **Étienne** Fr. family of printers & booksellers including especially: Henri I circa 1470–1520; his son Robert 1503–1559; & Robert's son Henri II 1528–1598

Es·tra·da Pal·ma \ā-'strä-thə-'päl-mə\ Tomás 1835–1908 1st president of Cuba (1902–06)

Ethelbert — see AETHELBERHT

Ethelred — see AETHELRED

Eth·er·ege \'e-th(ə-)rij\ Sir George 1635?–1692 Eng. dramatist

Euck·en \'ôi-kən\ Rudolf Christoph 1846–1926 Ger. philosopher

Eu·clid \'yü-kləd\ flourished circa 300 B.C. Greek geometer

Eu·gene \yü-'jēn, 'yü-ˌ\ French ē-zhen\ 1663–1736 *François-Eugène de Savoie-Carignan* prince of Savoy & Austrian general

Eu·gé·nie \yü-jā-nē; yü-'jä-nē, -'jē-; French ē-zhā-nē\ 1826–1920 *Eugénia Maria de Montijo de Guzmán; wife of Napoleon III* empress of the French (1853–71)

Eu·ler \'ôi-lər\ Leonhard 1707–1783 Swiss mathematician & physicist

Eu·ler–Chel·pin \'ôi-lər-'kel-pən\ Hans Karl August Simon von 1873–1964 Swed. (Ger.-born) chemist

Eu·rip·i·des \yū-'ri-pə-ˌdēz\ circa 484–406 B.C. Greek dramatist — **Eu·rip·i·de·an** \-ˌri-pə-'dē-ən\ adjective

Eus·den \'yüz-dən\ Laurence 1688–1730 Eng. poet; poet laureate (1718–30)

Eu·se·bi·us of Caesarea \yü-'sē-bē-əs\ circa 260–circa 339 theologian & church historian

Eu·sta·chio \eù-'stä-kē-ˌō\ Bartolomeo 1520–1574 Latin *Eu·sta·chius* \yü-'stä-kē-əs, -'stä-sh(ē-)əs\ Ital. anatomist

Ev·ans \'e-vənz\ Sir Arthur John 1851–1941 Eng. archaeologist

Evans Herbert McLean 1882–1971 Am. anatomist & embryologist

Evans Maurice 1901–1989 Am. (Eng.-born) actor

Evans Rudolph 1878–1960 Am. sculptor

Evans Walker 1903–1975 Am. photographer

Ev·arts \'e-vərts\ William Maxwell 1818–1901 Am. lawyer & statesman

Ev·att \'e-vət\ Herbert Vere 1894–1965 Austral. jurist & statesman

Eve·lyn \'ēv-lən, 'ev-\ John 1620–1706 Eng. diarist

Ev·er·ett \'ev-rət, 'e-və-\ Edward 1794–1865 Am. clergyman, orator, & statesman

Ewald \'i-ˌväl\ Johannes 1743–1781 Dan. poet & dramatist

Ew·ell \'yü-əl\ Richard Stoddert 1817–1872 Am. Confederate general

Eyck, van \van-'īk\ Hubert or Huybrecht circa 1370–1426 & his brother Jan before 1395–1441 Flem. painters

Eze·kiel \i-'zēk-yəl\ Moses Jacob 1844–1917 Am. sculptor

Fa·bio·la \ˌfa-bē-'ō-lə, fə-'byō-\ 1928– queen of King Baudouin I of Belgium

Fa·bi·us \'fā-bē-əs\ died 203 B.C. *Quintus Fabius Maximus Verrucosus Cunc·ta·tor* \ˌkəŋk-'tā-tər\ Rom. general against Hannibal

Fa·bre \'fäbrᵊ\ Jean-Henri 1823–1915 Fr. entomologist

Fad·den \'fa-dᵊn\ Sir Arthur William 1895–1973 Austral. statesman

Fad·i·man \'fa-də-mən\ Clifton 1904– Am. writer & editor

Fahd \'fäd\ 1923– Fahd ibn 'Abd al-'Azīz as-Sa'ūd king of Saudi Arabia (1982–)

Fah·ren·heit \'far-ən-ˌhīt, 'fär-\ Daniel Gabriel 1686–1736 Ger. physicist

Fair·banks \'far-ˌbaŋ(k)s, 'fer-\ Charles Warren 1852–1918 Am. lawyer & politician; vice president of U.S. (1905–09)

Fairbanks Douglas Elton 1883–1939 Am. actor

Fair·child \'far-ˌchīld, 'fer-\ David Grandison 1869–1954 Am. botanist

Fair·fax \'far-ˌfaks, 'fer-\ Baron Thomas 1612–1671 Eng. general

Fairfax Baron Thomas 1692–1782 proprietor in Virginia

Fai·sal \'fī-səl, 'fā-\ circa 1906–1975 king of Saudi Arabia (1964–75)

Fai·sal I Arabic **Fay·ṣal** \'fī-səl, 'fā-\ 1885–1933 king of Syria (1920), of Iraq (1921–1933)

Faisal II Arabic **Fay·ṣal** 1935–1958 king of Iraq (1939–58)

Fa·lier \'fal-'yer\ or **Fa·lie·ro** \-(ˌ)ō\ Marino 1274–1355 doge of Venice (1354–55)

Fal·ken·hau·sen \'fäl-kən-ˌhaù-zᵊn, 'fal-\ Ludwig 1844–1936 Freiherr *von Falkenhausen* Ger. general

Fal·ken·hayn \'fäl-kən-ˌhīn, 'fal-\ Erich von 1861–1922 Ger. general

Falkner William — see FAULKNER

Fal·la \'fä-yə, 'fäl-\ Manuel de 1876–1946 Span. composer

Fal·lières \fal-'yer\ Clément-Armand 1841–1931 Fr. statesman; president of France (1906–13)

Fan·euil \'fan-yəl, 'fa-nᵊl, 'fan-yə-wəl\ Peter 1700–1743 Am. merchant

Far·a·day \'far-ə-ˌdā, -dē\ Michael 1791–1867 Eng. chemist & physicist

Fa·ri·na \fə-'rē-nə\ Salvatore 1846–1918 Ital. novelist

Far·ley \'fär-lē\ James Aloysius 1888–1976 Am. politician

Far·man \fär-'mäⁿ, 'fär-mən\ Henri 1874–1958 & his brother Maurice 1877–1964 Fr. pioneer aviators and airplane manufacturers

Far·mer \'fär-mər\ Fannie Merritt 1857–1915 Am. cookery expert

Farmer James Leonard 1920– Am. civil rights leader

Far·ne·se \fär-'nā-zē, -sē\ Alessandro 1545–1592 Duke of *Parma* Ital. general in Span. service

Fa·rouk I \fə-'rük\ Arabic **Fā·rūq al–Aw·wal** \fär-'ük-al-'a-wal\ 1920–1965 king of Egypt (1936–52; abdicated)

Far·quhar \'fär-kər, -kwər\ George 1678–1707 Brit. dramatist

Far·ra·gut \'far-ə-gət\ David Glasgow 1801–1870 Am. admiral

Far·rar \'far-ər\ Frederic William 1831–1903 Eng. clergyman & writer

Far·rar \fə-'rär\ Geraldine 1882–1967 Am. soprano

Far·rell \'far-əl\ James Thomas 1904–1979 Am. novelist

Farrell Suzanne 1945– Am. dancer

Fa·ruk variant of FAROUK

Fāt·i·mah \'fa-tə-mə\ circa 606–633 *az-Zahrā' ('Shining One')* daughter of Muḥammad

Faulk·ner \'fôk-nər\ William Cuthbert 1897–1962 originally *Falkner* Am. novelist — **Faulk·ner·ian** \fôk-'nir-ē-ən, -'ner-\ adjective

Faure \'fôr, 'fŏr\ François-Félix 1841–1899 Fr. statesman; president of France (1895–99)

Fau·ré \fō-'rā\ Gabriel-Urbain 1845–1924 Fr. composer

Faus·ta \'fô-stə, 'faù-\ 289–326 *Flavia Maximiana Fausta; wife of Constantine the Great* Rom. empress

Fawkes \'fôks\ Guy 1570–1606 Eng. conspirator

Fech·ner \'fek-nər, 'fek\ Gustav Theodor 1801–1887 Ger. physicist & psychologist

Feif·fer \'fī-fər\ Jules 1929– Am. cartoonist and writer

Fei·ning·er \'fī-niŋ-ər\ Lyonel Charles Adrian 1871–1956 Am. painter

Feke \'fēk\ Robert circa 1705–circa 1750 Am. painter

Fel·li·ni \fə-'lē-nē\ Federico 1920–1993 Ital. film director — **Fel·li·ni·esque** \fə-ˌlē-nē-'esk\ adjective

Fell·tham \'fel-thəm\ Owen 1602?–1668 Eng. writer

Fé·ne·lon \ˌfā-nᵊl-'ōⁿ, fen-'lōⁿ\ François de Salignac de La Mothe- 1651–1715 Fr. prelate & writer

Feng Yü–hsiang \'fəŋ-'yü-shē-'äŋ\ 1882–1948 Chin. general

Fer·ber \'fər-bər\ Edna 1887–1968 Am. writer

Fer·di·nand I \'fər-dᵊn-ˌand\ 1503–1564 Holy Roman emperor (1558–64)

Ferdinand II 1578–1637 king of Bohemia (1617–19; 1620–27) & of Hungary (1618–25); Holy Roman emperor (1619–37)

Ferdinand III 1608–1657 king of Hungary (1625–47); Holy Roman emperor (1637–57)

Ferdinand I 1861–1948 king of Bulgaria (1908–18)

Ferdinand I 1016(or 1018)–1065 the Great king of Castile (1035–65); of León (1037–65)

Ferdinand II of Aragon or **V** of Castile 1452–1516 the Catholic; husband of Isabella I king of Castile (1474–1504); of Aragon (1479–1516); of Naples (1504–16); founder of the Span. monarchy

Ferdinand VII 1784–1833 king of Spain (1808; 1814–33)

Fer·mat \fer-'mä\ Pierre de 1601–1665 Fr. mathematician

Fer·mi \'fer-(ˌ)mē\ Enrico 1901–1954 Am. (Ital.-born) physicist

Fer·nán·dez \fər-'nan-ˌdez\ Juan circa 1536–circa 1604 Span. navigator

Fernández de Cór·do·ba \-thä-'kòr-də-bə, -və\ Gon·za·lo \gòn-'zä-lò\ 1453–1515 *El Gran Capitán* Span. soldier & statesman

Fer·re·ro \fə-'rer-(ˌ)ō\ Guglielmo 1871–1943 Ital. historian & author

Fes·sen·den \'fe-sᵊn-dən\ William Pitt 1806–1869 Am. politician; secretary of the treasury (1864–65)

\ə\ abut	\ᵊ\ kitten	\ər\ **further** \a\ ash \ā\ ace
\ä\ mop, mar	\aù\ out	\ch\ chin \e\ bet \ē\ easy
\g\ go	\i\ hit	\ī\ ice \j\ job
\ŋ\ sing	\ō\ go	\ô\ law \òi\ boy \th\ thin \th\ the \ü\ loot \ù\ foot
\y\ yet	\zh\ vision	see also Guide to Pronunciation

Fes·tus \'fes-təs\ Porcius *died circa* A.D. 62 Rom. procurator of Judea (58 or 60–62)

Feucht·wang·er \'fóikt-ˌväŋ-ər, 'fóikt-\ Li·on \'lē-ˌón\ 1884–1958 Ger. novelist & dramatist

Feuil·let \fə-'yä\ Octave 1821–1890 Fr. novelist & dramatist

Feyn·man \'fīn-mən\ Richard Phillips 1918–1988 Am. physicist

Fi·bi·ger \'fē-bē-gər\ Johannes Andreas Grib 1867–1928 Dan. pathologist

Fich·te \'fik-tə, 'fik-\ Johann Gottlieb 1762–1814 Ger. philosopher — **Fich·te·an** \-tē-ən\ *adjective*

Fied·ler \'fēd-lər\ Arthur 1894–1979 Am. conductor

Field \'fē(ə)ld\ Cyrus West 1819–1892 Am. financier

Field Eugene 1850–1895 Am. poet & journalist

Field Marshall 1834–1906 Am. merchant

Field·ing \'fē(ə)l-diŋ\ Henry 1707–1754 Eng. novelist

Fields \'fē(ə)ldz\ W.C. 1880–1946 originally *William Claude Dukenfield* Am. actor

Figl \'fē-gəl\ Leopold 1902–1965 Austrian politician

Fi·guei·re·do \ˌfē-ge-'rā-(ˌ)dü\ João Baptista de Oliveira 1918– president of Brazil (1979–85)

Fi·gue·roa \ˌfē-gə-'rō-ə\ Francisco de *circa* 1536– *circa* 1620 Span. poet

Fill·more \'fil-ˌmōr, -ˌmór\ Millard 1800–1874 13th president of the U.S. (1850–53)

Fin·lay \fin-'lī\ Carlos Juan 1833–1915 Cuban physician & biologist

Finn·bo·ga·dót·tir \'fin-ˌbō-gə-ˌdō-tər\ Vigdís 1930– president of Iceland (1980–96)

Fin·sen \'fin(t)-sən\ Niels Ryberg 1860–1904 Dan. physician

Fir·bank \'fər-ˌbaŋk\ (Arthur Annesley) Ronald 1886–1926 Eng. author — **Fir·bank·ian** \ˌfər-'baŋ-kē-ən\ *adjective*

Fir·daw·sī *or* **Fer·dow·sī** \fər-'daù-sē, -'dó-\ *or* **Fir·du·si** \-'dü-\ *or* **Fir·dou·si** \-'daù-, -'dó-\ *circa* 935–*circa* 1020(or 1026) originally *Abū ol-Qāsem Manṣūr* Pers. poet

Fire·stone \'fīr-ˌstōn\ Harvey Samuel 1868–1938 Am. industrialist

Fi·scher \'fi-shər\ Edmond Henri 1920– Am. (Chin.-born of Fr. parents) biochemist

Fischer Emil 1852–1919 Ger. chemist

Fischer Ernst Otto 1918– Ger. chemist

Fischer Hans 1881–1945 Ger. chemist

Fi·scher–Dies·kau \'fi-shər-'dēs-ˌkaù\ Dietrich 1925– Ger. baritone

Fish \'fish\ Hamilton 1808–1893 Am. statesman

Fish·bein \'fish-ˌbīn\ Morris 1889–1976 Am. physician & editor

Fish·er \'fi-shər\ Dorothy 1879–1958 *Dorothea Frances* née *Can·field* \'kan-ˌfēld\ Am. novelist

Fisher Irving 1867–1947 Am. economist

Fisher John Arbuthnot 1841–1920 1st Baron *Fisher of Kil·ver·stone* \'kil-vər-stən\ Brit. admiral

Fisher Mary Frances Kennedy 1908–1992 Am. writer

Fiske \'fisk\ John 1842–1901 originally *Edmund Fisk Green* Am. philosopher & historian

Fitch \'fich\ (William) Clyde 1865–1909 Am. dramatist

Fitch John 1743–1798 Am. inventor

Fitch Val Logsdon 1923– Am. physicist

Fitz·ger·ald \fits-'jer-əld\ Ella 1917–1996 Am. singer

Fitzgerald Francis Scott Key 1896–1940 Am. writer

FitzGerald Edward 1809–1883 Eng. poet & translator

FitzGerald Garret 1926– prime minister of Ireland (1981–87)

Fitz·her·bert \fits-'hər-bərt\ Maria Anne 1756–1837 née *Smythe; wife of George IV of England*

Flagg \'flag\ James Montgomery 1877–1960 Am. illustrator

Flag·stad \'flag-ˌstad, *Norwegian* 'fläg-ˌstä\ Kirsten \'kish-tən, 'kir-ˌstən\ 1895–1962 Norw. soprano

Fla·min·i·us \flə-'mi-nē-əs\ Gaius *died* 217 B.C. Rom. general & statesman

Flam·ma·rion \flä-ˌmar-ē-'ōⁿ\ (Nicolas-) Camille 1842–1925 Fr. astronomer & writer

Flan·a·gan \'fla-ni-gən\ Edward Joseph 1886–1948 Am. (Irish-born) Roman Catholic priest & founder of Boys Town

Flan·din \flä"-da"\ Pierre-Étienne 1889–1958 Fr. politician; premier (1934–35)

Flau·bert \flō-'ber\ Gustave 1821–1880 Fr. novelist — **Flau·ber·tian** \-'bər-shən, -'ber-tē-ən\ *adjective*

Flax·man \'flaks-mən\ John 1755–1826 Eng. sculptor

Fleet·wood \'flēt-ˌwùd\ Charles *died* 1692 Eng. general

Flem·ing \'fle-miŋ\ Sir Alexander 1881–1955 Brit. bacteriologist

Fleming Ian Lancaster 1908–1964 Brit. writer

Fleming Sir John Ambrose 1849–1945 Eng. electrical engineer

Fletch·er \'fle-chər\ John 1579–1625 Eng. dramatist

Fleu·ry \ˌflər-'ē\ André-Hercule de 1653–1743 Fr. cardinal & statesman

Fleury Claude 1640–1723 Fr. ecclesiastical historian

Flint \'flint\ Austin: father 1812–1886 & son 1836–1915 Am. physicians

Flo·res \'flór-ˌās, 'flór-\ Juan José 1800–1864 Ecuadorian soldier; president of Ecuador (1830–35; 1839–45)

Flo·rey \'flór-ē, 'flór-\ Sir Howard Walter 1898–1968 Brit. pathologist

Flo·rio \'flór-ē-ˌō, 'flór-\ John *circa* 1553–*circa* 1625 Eng. lexicographer & translator

Flo·ry \'flór-ē, 'flór-\ Paul John 1910–85 Am. chemist

Flo·tow \'flō-(ˌ)tō\ Friedrich 1812–1883 Freiherr *von Flotow* Ger. composer

Foch \'fosh, 'fäsh\ Ferdinand 1851–1929 Fr. general; marshal of France

Fo·gel \'fō-gəl\ Robert William 1926– Am. economist

Fo·kine \'fó-ˌkēn, fó-'\ Michel 1880–1942 Am. (Russ.-born) choreographer

Fok·ker \'fä-kər, 'fó-\ Anthony Herman Gerard 1890–1939 Am. (Du.-born) aircraft designer & builder

Fol·ger \'fōl-jər\ Henry Clay 1857–1930 Am. bibliophile

Fon·tanne \fän-'tan, 'fän-\ Lynn 1887?–1983 *wife of Alfred Lunt* Am. (Eng.-born) actress

Fon·teyn \fän-'tān, 'fän-\ Dame Margot 1919–1991 originally *Margot Hook·ham* \'hù-kəm\ Eng. ballerina

Foote \'fùt\ Andrew Hull 1806–1863 Am. admiral

Foote Samuel 1720–1777 Eng. actor & playwright

Foote Shelby 1916– Am. historian & novelist

Forbes–Rob·ert·son \'fórbz-'rä-bərt-sən\ Sir Johnston 1853–1937 Eng. actor

Ford \'fórd, 'fórd\ Ford Mad·ox \'ma-dəks\ 1873–1939 originally *Huef·fer* \'hü-fər; 'hwe-fər, 'we-\ Eng. author

Ford Gerald Rudolph 1913– Am. politician; 38th president of the U.S. (1974–77)

Ford Henry 1863–1947 Am. automobile manufacturer

Ford John 1586–?1639 Eng. dramatist

For·es·ter \'fór-əs-tər, 'fär-\ Cecil Scott 1899–1966 Brit. writer

For·rest \'fór-əst, 'fär-\ Edwin 1806–1872 Am. actor

Forrest Nathan Bedford 1821–1877 Am. Confederate general

For·res·tal \'fór-əs-tᵊl, 'fär-, -ˌtòl\ James Vincent 1892–1949 Am. banker; 1st secretary of defense (1947–49)

Forss·mann \'fórs-ˌmän\ Werner Theodor Otto 1904–1979 Ger. surgeon

For·ster \'fór-stər\ Edward Morgan 1879–1970 Brit. novelist — **For·ste·ri·an** \fór-'stir-ē-ən\ *adjective*

For·syth \fór-'sīth, fər-\ John 1780–1841 Am. statesman

For·tas \'fór-təs\ Abe 1910–1982 Am. jurist

Fos·dick \'fäz-(ˌ)dik\ Harry Emerson 1878–1969 Am. clergyman

Fos·sey \'fó-sē, 'fä-\ Dian 1932–1985 Am. ethologist

Fos·ter \'fós-tər, 'fäs-\ Stephen Collins 1826–1864 Am. songwriter

Foster William Zebulon 1881–1961 Am. Communist

Fou·cault \fü-'kō\ Jean-Bernard-Léon 1819–1868 Fr. physicist

Fou·qué \fü-'kā\ Friedrich Heinrich Karl de la Motte \mót\ 1777–1843 Freiherr *Fouqué* Ger. author

Fou·quet *or* **Fouc·quet** \fü-'kā\ Nicolas 1615–1680 Fr. government official

Fou·quier–Tin·ville \fü-kyä-ta"-'vēl\ Antoine-Quentin 1746–1795 Fr. politician

Four·dri·nier \ˌfór-drə-'nir, ˌfór-; fùr'dri-nē-ər, fór-, fór-\ Henry 1766–1854 & his brother Sealy *died* 1847 Eng. papermakers & inventors

Fou·ri·er \'fùr-ē-ˌā\ (François-Marie-) Charles 1772–1837 Fr. sociologist & reformer

Fow·ler \'faù-lər\ Henry Watson 1858–1933 Eng. lexicographer

Fowler William Alfred 1911–1995 Am. physicist

Fox \'fäks\ Charles James 1749–1806 Eng. statesman & orator

Fox George 1624–1691 Eng. preacher & founder of Society of Friends

Fox Henry 1705–1774 1st Baron *Hol·land* \'hä-lənd\ Brit. statesman

Foxe \'fäks\ John 1516–1587 Eng. martyrologist

Foxe *or* **Fox** Richard *circa* 1448–1528 Eng. prelate & statesman

Fra·go·nard \ˌfra-gə-'när\ Jean-Honoré 1732–1806 Fr. artist

France \'fran(t)s, frä"s\ Anatole 1844–1924 pseudonym of *Jacques-Anatole-François Thibault* Fr. novelist & satirist

Francesca Piero della — see PIERO DELLA FRANCESCA

Francesca da Rimini — see POLENTA

Fran·cis I \'fran(t)-səs\ 1494–1547 king of France (1515–47)

Francis II 1768–1835 last Holy Roman emperor (1792–1806); emperor of Austria (as *Francis I*) 1804–35

Francis Fer·di·nand \'fər-də-ˌnand, 'fer-dē-ˌnänt\ 1863–1914 archduke of Austria

Francis Jo·seph I \'jō-səf, 'yō-sef\ 1830–1916 emperor of Austria (1848–1916)

Francis of Assisi Saint 1181(or 1182)–1226 in full *Francesco di Pietro di Bernardone* Ital. friar; founder of Franciscan order

Francis of Sales \'sä(ə)lz\ Saint 1567–1622 Fr. Roman Catholic bishop of Geneva

Franck \'fräŋk\ César Auguste 1822–1890 Fr. (Belg.-born) organist & composer

Franck James 1882–1964 Am. (Ger.-born) physicist

Francke \'fräŋ-kə\ Kuno 1855–1930 Am. (Ger.-born) historian & educator

Fran·co \'fräŋ-(ˌ)kō, 'fraŋ-\ Francisco 1892–1975 *Francisco Paulino Hermenegildo Teódulo Franco Bahamonde* Span. general & head of Span. state (1936–75)

Frank \'fraŋk, 'fräŋk\ Anne 1929–1945 Ger.-born diarist during the Holocaust

Frank Ilya Mikhaylovich 1908–1990 Russ. physicist

Frank·en·thal·er \'fraŋ-kən-ˌtä-lər, -ˌthä-\ Helen 1928– Am. artist

Frank·furt·er \'fraŋk-fə(r)-tər, -ˌfər-\ Felix 1882–1965 Am. (Austrian-born) jurist

Frank·lin \'fraŋ-klən\ Benjamin 1706–1790 Am. statesman & philosopher

Franklin Sir John 1786–1847 Eng. arctic explorer

Franklin Rosalind Elsie 1920–1958 Eng. biophysicist

Franks \'fraŋks\ Oliver Shewell 1905–1992 Baron *Franks of Headington* Eng. philosopher & diplomat

Fra·ser \'frā-zər, -zhər\ James Earle 1876–1953 Am. sculptor

Fraser (John) Malcolm 1930– prime minister of Australia (1975–83)

Fraser Peter 1884–1950 N.Z. statesman; prime minister (1940–49)

Fraun·ho·fer \'fraùn-ˌhō-fər\ Joseph von 1787–1826 Bavarian optician & physicist

Fra·zer \'frā-zər, -zhər\ Sir James George 1854–1941 Scot. anthropologist

Fré·chette \frā-'shet\ Louis-Honoré 1839–1908 Canad. poet

Fred·er·ick I \'fre-d(ə-)rik\ *circa* 1123–1190 *Frederick Bar·ba·ros·sa* \ˌbär-bə-'rä-sə, -'rò-\ Holy Roman emperor (1152–90)

Frederick II 1194–1250 Holy Roman emperor (1215–50); king of Sicily (1198–1250)

Frederick I 1657–1713 king of Prussia (1701–13)

Frederick II 1712–1786 *the Great* king of Prussia (1740–86)

Frederick IX 1899–1972 king of Denmark (1947–72)

Frederick William 1620–1688 *the Great Elector* elector of Brandenburg (1640–88)

Frederick William name of 4 kings of Prussia: **I** 1688–1740 (reigned 1713–40); **II** 1744–1797 (reigned 1786–97); **III** 1770–1840 (reigned 1797–1840); **IV** 1795–1861 (reigned 1840–61)

Free·man \'frē-mən\ Douglas Sou·thall \'saủ-,thôl, -,thôl\ 1886–1953 Am. editor & historian

Freeman Mary Eleanor 1852–1930 née *Wilkins* Am. writer

Fre·ge \'frā-gə\ (Friedrich Ludwig) Gottlob 1848–1925 Ger. mathematician & philosopher

Frei Ru·íz-Ta·gle \'frā-rủ-'ēs-'tä-glä\ Eduardo 1941–　president of Chile (1994–　)

Fre·ling·huy·sen \'frē-liŋ,hī-z°n\ Frederick Theodore 1817–1885 Am. statesman

Fré·mont \'frē-,mänt\ John Charles 1813–1890 Am. general & explorer

French \'french\ Daniel Chester 1850–1931 Am. sculptor

Fre·neau \fri-'nō\ Philip Morin 1752–1832 Am. poet

Fres·co·bal·di \,fres-kə-'bäl-dē, -'bôl-\ Girolamo 1583–1643 Ital. composer

Fres·nel \frā-'nel\ Augustin-Jean 1788–1827 Fr. physicist

Freud \'frȯid\ Sigmund 1856–1939 Austrian neurologist

Frey·berg \'frī-,bərg\ 1st Baron 1889–1963 *Bernard Cyril Freyberg* N.Z. general

Frey·tag \'frī-,täk, -,täg\ Gustav 1816–1895 Ger. author

Frick \'frik\ Henry Clay 1849–1919 Am. industrialist

Fried \'frēt, 'frēd\ Alfred Hermann 1864–1921 Austrian pacifist

Fried·man \'frēd-mən\ Jerome Isaac 1930–　Am. physicist

Friedman Milton 1912–　　Am. economist

Frie·drich \'frē-drik\ Caspar David 1774–1840 Ger. painter

Frisch \'frish\ Karl von 1886–1982 Austrian zoologist

Frisch Ragnar 1895–1973 Norw. economist

Fro·bi·sher \'frō-bi-shər\ Sir Martin 1535?–1594 Eng. navigator

Froe·bel *or* **Frö·bel** \'frā-bəl, 'frē-, 'frœ-\ Friedrich Wilhelm August 1782–1852 Ger. educator

Froh·man \'frō-mən\ Charles 1860–1915 Am. theater manager

Frois·sart \'frȯi-,särt, frwä-'sär\ Jean 1333?–*circa* 1405 Fr. chronicler

Fromm \'frȯm, 'främ\ Erich 1900–1980 Am. (Ger.-born) psychoanalyst

Fron·di·zi \frän-'dē-zē, -sē\ Arturo 1908–1995 Argentine president (1958–62)

Fron·te·nac et Pal·lu·au \frōⁿ-tə-nák-ā-pä-lw°ō\ Comte de 1622–1698 *Louis de Buade* \'bwᵁäd\ Fr. general & colonial administrator in America

Frost \'frȯst\ Robert Lee 1874–1963 Am. poet — **Frost·ian** \'frȯs-tē-ən, -stē-\ *adjective*

Froude \'früd\ James Anthony 1818–1894 Eng. historian

Fry \'frī\ Christopher 1907–　Eng. dramatist

Frye \'frī\ (Herman) Northrop 1912–1991 Canad. literary critic

Fu-'ād I \fủ-'äd\ 1868–1936 sultan (1917–22) & king (1922–36) of Egypt

Fu·en·tes \fủ-'en-,tās\ Carlos 1928–　Mex. author

Fuer·tes \'fyùr-(,)tēz\ Louis Agassiz 1874–1927 Am. illustrator

Fu·gard \fü-'gärd\ Athol 1932–　So. African playwright

Fu·ji·mo·ri \,fü-jē-'mó-rē\ Alberto 1938–　president of Peru (1990–　)

Fu·kui \'fủ-kủ-ē, fủ-'kủ-ē\ Kenichi 1918–　Jp. chemist

Ful·bright \'fủl-,brīt\ (James) William 1905–1995 Am. politician

Ful·ler \'fủ-lər\ Melville Weston 1833–1910 Am. jurist; chief justice U.S. Supreme Court (1888–1910)

Fuller (Richard) Buckminster 1895–1983 Am. engineer

Fuller (Sarah) Margaret 1810–1850 Marchioness *Os·so·li* \'ȯ-sə-(,)lē\ Am. critic & reformer

Fuller Thomas 1608–1661 Eng. divine & author

Ful·ton \'fủl-t°n\ Robert 1765–1815 Am. engineer & inventor

Funk \'fuŋk, 'fəŋk\ Casimir 1884–1967 Am. (Pol.-born) biochemist

Funk \'fəŋk\ Isaac Kauffman 1839–1912 Am. editor & publisher

Fun·ston \'fən(t)-stən\ Frederick 1865–1917 Am. general

Fur·ness \'fər-nəs, -,nes\ Horace Howard: father 1833–1912 & son 1865–1930 Am. Shakespeare scholars

Fur·ni·vall \'fər-nə-vəl\ Frederick James 1825–1910 Eng. philologist

Furt·wäng·ler \'fủrt-,veŋ-lər\ (Gustav Heinrich Ernst Martin) Wilhelm 1886–1954 Ger. conductor

Ga·ble \'gā-bəl\ (William) Clark 1901–1960 Am. actor

Ga·bo \'gä-(,)bō\ Naum 1890–1977 originally *Naum Pevs·ner* \'pevz-nər\ Am. (Russ.-born) sculptor

Ga·bor \'gä-(,)bȯr, gə-'bȯr\ Dennis 1900–1979 Brit. (Hung.-born) physicist

Ga·bo·riau \,gə-'bȯr-ē-,ō\ Émile 1832(or 1833 or 1835)–*circa* 1873 Fr. writer

Ga·bri·eli \,gä-brē-'e-lē\ Giovanni *circa* 1556–1612 Ital. composer

Gad·ha·fi \gə-'dä-fē, kə-, -'da-\ Mu'ammar Muhammad al–1942–　Libyan leader (1969–　)

Gads·den \'gadz-dən\ James 1788–1858 Am. army officer & diplomat

Ga·ga·rin \gə-'gär-ən\ Yu·ry \'yủr-ē\ Alekseyevich 1934–1968 Russ. astronaut

Gage \'gāj\ Thomas 1721–1787 Brit. general & colonial governor in America

Gail·lard \gil-'yärd\ David DuBose \dü-'bōz, dyü-\ 1859–1913 Am. army officer & engineer

Gaines \'gānz\ Edmund Pendleton 1777–1849 Am. general

Gains·bor·ough \'gānz-,bər-ə, -,bə-rə, -b(ə-)rə\ Thomas 1727–1788 Eng. painter

Gait·skell \'gāt-skəl\ Hugh Todd Naylor 1906–1963 Eng. politician

Ga·ius \'gā-əs, 'gī-əs\ *flourished* A.D. 130–180 Rom. jurist

Gaj·du·sek \'gī-də-,shek\ D(aniel) Carleton 1923–　Am. virologist

Gal·ba \'gal-bə, 'gȯl-\ Servius Sulpicius 3 B.C.–A.D. 69 Rom. emperor (68–69)

Gal·braith \'gal-,brāth\ John Kenneth 1908–　Am. (Canad.-born) economist — **Galbraith·ian** \,gal-'brā-thē-ən, -'brāth-yən\ *adjective*

Gale \'gā(ə)l\ Zona 1874–1938 Am. novelist

Ga·len \'gā-lən\ A.D. 129–*circa* 199 Greek physician & writer — **Ga·len·ic** \gə-'le-nik\ *or* **Ga·len·i·cal** \-ni-kəl\ *adjective*

Ga·le·ri·us \gə-'lir-ē-əs\ *died* 311 *Gaius Galerius Valerius Maximianus* Rom. emperor (305–311)

Ga·li·leo \,ga-lə-'lē-(,)ō, -'lā-\ 1564–1642 in full *Galileo Galilei* Ital. astronomer & physicist

Gal·land \ga-'läⁿ\ Antoine 1646–1715 Fr. orientalist & translator

Gal·la·tin \'ga-lə-t°n\ (Abraham Alfonse) Albert 1761–1849 Am. (Swiss-born) financier & statesman

Gal·lau·det \,ga-lə-'det\ Thomas Hopkins 1787–1851 Am. teacher of the hearing- and speech-impaired

Gal·le·gos Frei·re \gä-'yā-(,)gōs-'frā-(,)rā\ Rómulo 1884–1969 Venezuelan novelist; president of Venezuela (1948)

Gal·li-Cur·ci \,ga-li-'kùr-chē, ,gä-, -'kər-\ Amelita 1889–1963 née *Galli* Am. (Ital.-born) soprano

Gal·lie·ni \,gal-yā-'nē, gal-'yā-nē\ Joseph-Simon 1849–1916 Fr. general & colonial administrator

Gal·li·e·nus \,ga-lē-'ē-nəs, -'ā-nəs\ Publius Licinius Valerianus Egnatius *died* 268 Rom. emperor (253–268)

Gal·lup \'ga-ləp\ George Horace 1901–1984 Am. statistician

Ga·lois \gal-'wä\ Évariste 1811–1832 Fr. mathematician

Gals·wor·thy \'gȯlz-,wər-thē\ John 1867–1933 Eng. novelist & dramatist

Galt \'gȯlt\ John 1779–1839 Scot. novelist

Gal·ton \'gȯl-t°n\ Sir Francis 1822–1911 Eng. scientist — **Gal·to·nian** \gȯl-'tō-nē-ən, -nyən\ *adjective*

Gal·va·ni \gal-'vä-nē, gäl-\ Luigi 1737–1798 Ital. physician & physicist

Gál·vez \'gäl-,ves\ José 1729–1787 Marqués *de la Sonora* Span. jurist & colonial administrator

Ga·ma, da \dä-'ga-mə, -'gä-\ Vas·co \'vas-kō, 'väs-\ *circa* 1460–1524 Port. navigator & explorer

Ga·mar·ra \gə-'mär-ə\ Augustín 1785–1841 Peruvian general; president of Peru (1829–33; 1839–41)

Gam·bet·ta \gam-'be-tə, ,gäⁿ-bə-'tä\ Léon Michel 1838–1882 Fr. lawyer & statesman

Ga·me·lin \,gam-'laⁿ, ,gam-'lan\ Maurice-Gustave 1872–1958 Fr. general

Gan·dhi \'gän-dē, 'gan-\ In·dira \in-'dir-ə, 'in-də-rə\ Nehru 1917–1984 *daughter of Jawaharlal Nehru* prime minister of India (1966–77; 1980–84)

Gandhi Mohandas Karamchand 1869–1948 *Mahat·ma* \mə-'hät-mə, -'hat-\ Indian nationalist leader — **Gan·dhi·an** \-ən\ *adjective*

Gandhi Ra·jiv \rä-'jēv\ Ratna 1944–1991 *son of Indira* prime minister of India (1984–89)

Gar·a·mond \'gar-ə-,mänd, ,gar-ə-'mōⁿ\ *or* **Gar·a·mont** \-,mänt, -'mōⁿ\ Claude *circa* 1480–1561 Fr. typefounder

Gar·rand \gə-'rand, 'gar-ənd\ John Cantius 1888–1974 Am. (Canad.-born) inventor

Gar·bo \'gär-(,)bō\ Greta 1905–1990 originally *Greta Lovisa Gustafsson* Am. (Swed.-born) actress — **Gar·bo·esque** \,gär-bō-'wesk\ *adjective*

Gar·cía Gu·tiér·rez \gär-'sē-ə-gü-'tyer-əs\ Antonio 1813–1884 Span. dramatist

García Íñi·guez \-'ēn-yi-,gäs\ Calixto 1839–1898 Cuban revolutionary

García Lor·ca \-'lȯr-kə\ Federico 1898–1936 Span. poet & dramatist

García Már·quez \-'mär-,käs\ Gabriel 1928–　Colombian author

García Mo·re·no \-mə-'rā-(,)nō\ Gabriel 1821–1875 Ecuadorian journalist; president of Ecuador (1861–65; 1869–75)

Gar·ci·la·so de la Ve·ga \,gär-si-'lä-sō-,dā-lə-'vā-gə\ 1539–1616 *El Inca* Peruvian historian

Gar·den \'gär-d°n\ Mary 1874–1967 Am. (Scot.-born) soprano

Gar·di·ner \'gärd-nər, 'gär-d°n-ər\ Samuel Rawson 1829–1902 Eng. historian

Gardiner Stephen *circa* 1482–1555 Eng. prelate & statesman

Gard·ner \'gärd-nər\ Erle Stanley 1889–1970 Am. writer

Gar·field \'gär-,fēld\ James Abram 1831–1881 20th president of the U.S. (1881)

Gar·i·bal·di \,gar-ə-'bȯl-dē\ Giuseppe 1807–1882 Ital. patriot — **Gar·i·bal·di·an** \-dē-ən\ *adjective*

Gar·land \'gär-lənd\ (Hannibal) Hamlin 1860–1940 Am. novelist

Gar·ner \'gär-nər\ John Nance 1868–1967 Am. politician; vice president of the U.S. (1933–41)

Gar·nett \'gär-nət\ Constance 1862–1946 née *Black* Eng. translator

Gar·rick \'gar-ik\ David 1717–1779 Eng. actor

Gar·ri·son \'gar-ə-sən\ William Lloyd 1805–1879 Am. abolitionist

Gar·shin \'gär-shən\ Vsevolod Mikhaylovich 1855–1888 Russ. writer

Gar·vey \'gär-vē\ Marcus Moziah 1887–1940 Jamaican black leader

Gary \gar-ē, 'ger-ē\ Elbert Henry 1846–1927 Am. industrialist

Gas·coigne \'gas-,kȯin\ George *circa* 1525–1577 Eng. poet

Gas·kell \'gas-kəl\ Elizabeth Cleghorn 1810–1865 née *Stevenson* Eng. novelist

Gas·ser \'ga-sər\ Herbert Spencer 1888–1963 Am. physiologist

Gates \'gāts\ Horatio *circa* 1728–1806 Am. general in Revolution

Gau·guin \gō-gaⁿ\ (Eugène-Henri-) Paul 1848–1903 Fr. painter — **Gau·guin·esque** \(,)gō-,ga-'nesk\ *adjective*

Gaulle, de \di-'gōl, -'gȯl\ Charles-André-Marie-Joseph 1890–1970 Fr. general & politician; president of Fifth Republic (1958–69)

Gauss \'gaús\ Carl Friedrich 1777–1855 Ger. mathematician & astronomer

Gautama Buddha — see SIDDHĀRTHA GAUTAMA

Gau·tier \gō-tyā\ Théophile 1811–1872 Fr. author

Gay \'gā\ John 1685–1732 Eng. poet & dramatist

Gay–Lus·sac \'gā-lə-'sak\ Joseph-Louis 1778–1850 Fr. chemist & physicist

Geber — see JĀBIR IBN ḤAYYĀN

Ged·des \'ge-dēz\ Norman Bel 1893–1958 Am. designer

Gei·kie \'gē-kē\ Sir Archibald 1835–1924 Scot. geologist

Gei·sel \'gī-zəl\ Theodor Seuss 1904–1991 pseudonym *Dr. Seuss* \'süs\ Am. writer & illustrator

Gellée Claude — see CLAUDE LORRAIN

Gell–Mann \'gel-,män\ Murray 1929– Am. physicist

Ge·net \zhə-'nā\ Edmond-Charles-Édouard 1763–1834 Fr. diplomat in U.S.

Genet Jean 1910–1986 Fr. dramatist & novelist

Gen·ghis Khan \'jeŋ-gəs-'kän, ,geŋ-\ *circa* 1162–1227 Mongol conqueror

Gen·ser·ic \'gen(t)-sə-rik, 'jen(t)-\ or **Gai·se·ric** \'gī-zə-(,)rik, -sə-\ *died* 477 king of the Vandals (428–477)

Gen·ti·le da Fa·bri·a·no \jen-'tē-lē-də-,fä-brē-'ä-(,)nō\ *circa* 1370–1427 originally *Niccolo di Giovanni di Massio* Ital. painter

Gen·ti·les·chi \jen-t°l-'es-kē\ Orazio Lomi *circa* 1562–*circa* 1647 & his daughter Artemisia *circa* 1597–after 1651 Ital. painters

Geof·frey of Monmouth \'jef-rē-əv-'män-məth\ *circa* 1100–1154 Brit. ecclesiastic & chronicler

George \'jȯrj\ Saint 3d century Christian martyr & patron saint of England

George name of 6 kings of Great Britain: **I** 1660–1727 (reigned 1714–27); **II** 1683–1760 (reigned 1727–60); **III** 1738–1820 (reigned 1760–1820); **IV** 1762–1830 (reigned 1820–30); **V** 1865–1936 (reigned 1910–36); **VI** 1895–1952 (reigned 1936–52)

George name of 2 kings of Greece: **I** 1845–1913 (reigned 1863–1913); **II** 1890–1947 (reigned 1922–23; 1935–47)

George David Lloyd — see David LLOYD GEORGE

George Henry 1839–1897 Am. economist

Ge·rard \jə-'rärd, 'jer-,ärd\ Charles 1618?–1694 1st Baron *Gerard of Bran·don* \'bran-dən\; Viscount *Brandon* Eng. Royalist commander

Gé·rard \zhā-'rär\ Comte Étienne-Maurice 1773–1852 Fr. Napoleonic general; marshal of France

Ger·hard·sen \'ger-,här-s°n\ Einar Henry 1897–1987 Norw. politician

Gé·ri·cault \zhā-ri-'kō\ (Jean-Louis-André-) Théodore 1791–1824 Fr. painter

Ger·man·i·cus Cae·sar \jər-,ma-ni-kə(s)-'sē-zər\ 15 B.C.–A.D. 19 Rom. general

Gé·rôme \zhā-'rōm\ Jean-Léon 1824–1904 Fr. painter

Ge·ron·i·mo \jə-'rä-nə-,mō\ 1829–1909 *Goyathlay* Chiricahua Apache leader

Ger·ry \'ger-ē\ Elbridge 1744–1814 Am. politician; vice president of the U.S. (1813–14)

Gersh·win \'gər-shwən\ George 1898–1937 originally *Jacob Gershvin* Am. composer

Ge·sell \gə-'zel\ Arnold Lucius 1880–1961 Am. psychologist & pediatrician

Ges·ner \'ges-nər\ Conrad 1516–1565 Swiss naturalist

Get·ty \'ge-tē\ Jean Paul 1892–1976 Am. business executive

Gha·zā·lī, al- \,al-gə-'za-lē\ 1058–1111 *Abu Ḥāmid Muḥammad ibn Muḥammad aṭ-Ṭūsī al-Ghazālī* Islamic jurist, theologian, & mystic

Ghi·ber·ti \gē-'ber-tē\ Lorenzo *circa* 1378–1455 Florentine goldsmith, painter, & sculptor

Ghir·lan·da·jo or **Ghir·lan·da·io** \gir-lən-'dä-(,)yō\ Domenico 1449–1494 originally *Domenico di Tommaso Bigordi* Florentine painter

Ghose Sri Aurobindo — see AUROBINDO

Gia·co·met·ti \jä-kə-'me-tē\ Alberto 1901–1966 Swiss artist

Giae·ver \'yā-vər\ Ivar 1929– Am. (Norw.-born) physicist

Gi·auque \jē-'ōk\ William Francis 1895–1982 Am. chemist

Gib·bon \'gi-bən\ Edward 1737–1794 Eng. historian — **Gib·bon·ian** \gi-'bō-nē-ən\ *adjective*

Gib·bons \'gi-bənz\ James 1834–1921 Am. cardinal

Gibbons Orlando 1538–1625 Eng. organist & composer

Gibbs \'gibz\ James 1682–1754 Brit. architect

Gibbs Josiah Willard 1839–1903 Am. mathematician & physicist

Gib·ran or **Jib·ran** \jə-'brän\ Kahlil 1883–1931 *Jubrān Khalīl Jubrān* Lebanese novelist, poet, & artist in U.S.

Gib·son \'gib-sən\ Charles Dana 1867–1944 Am. illustrator

Gibson William 1914– Am. dramatist

Gide \'zhēd\ André 1869–1951 Fr. novelist, critic, & essayist

Giel·gud \'gil-,gùd, 'gēl-\ Sir (Arthur) John 1904– Eng. actor

Gie·rek \'gyer-ək\ Edward 1913– 1st secretary of Polish Communist party (1970–80)

Gie·se·king \'gē-zə-kiŋ\ Walter Wilhelm 1895–1956 Ger. (Fr.-born) pianist

Gil·bert \'gil-bərt\ Cass 1859–1934 Am. architect

Gilbert Sir Humphrey *circa* 1539–1583 Eng. navigator

Gilbert Walter 1932– Am. biochemist

Gilbert William 1540–1603 Eng. physician & physicist

Gilbert Sir William Schwenck 1836–1911 Eng. librettist & poet — **Gil·bert·ian** \gil-'bər-tē-ən\ *adjective*

Gil·les·pie \gə-'les-pē\ John Birks 1917–1993 *Dizzy* Am. jazz musician

Gil·lette \jə-'let\ King Camp 1855–1932 Am. inventor & manufacturer

Gillette William Hooker 1855–1937 Am. actor

Gil·man \'gil-mən\ Alfred Goodman 1941– Am. pharmacologist

Gilman Daniel Coit \'kȯit\ 1831–1908 Am. educator; president Johns Hopkins U. (1875–1901)

Gil·mer \'gil-mər\ Elizabeth 1870–1951 née *Mer·i·weth·er* \'mer-ə-,we-thər\ pseudonym *Dorothy Dix* \'diks\ Am. journalist

Gil·pin \'gil-pən\ Charles Sidney 1878–1930 Am. actor

Gi·na·ste·ra \,hē-nə-ə-'ster-ə\ Alberto Evaristo 1916–1983 Argentine composer

Gin·grich \'giŋ-(,)grich, -(,)rich\ Newton Leroy 1943– Am. politician

Gins·berg \'ginz-,bərg\ Allen 1926–1997 Am. poet

Gins·burg \'ginz-,bərg\ Ruth Bader 1933– Am. jurist

Gior·gio·ne \(,)jȯr-'jō-nē\ *circa* 1477–1511 *Giorgione da Castelfranco* Venetian painter

Giot·to \'jȯ(t)-(,)tō, jē-'ä-(,)tō\ 1266/67(or 1276?)–1337 *Giotto di Bondone* Florentine painter, architect, & sculptor

Gi·rard \zhē-'rär\ Jean-Baptiste 1765–1850 Swiss Franciscan & educator

Gi·rard \jə-'rärd\ Stephen 1750–1831 Am. (Fr.-born) financier

Gi·raud \zhē-'rō\ Henri-Honoré 1879–1949 Fr. general

Gi·rau·doux \,zhē-rō-'dü\ (Hyppolyte-) Jean 1882–1944 Fr. writer

Gir·tin \'gər-t°n\ Thomas 1775–1802 Eng. painter

Gis·card d'Es·taing \zhis-kär-des-ta*n*, ,kär-des-'taŋ\ Valéry 1926– president of France (1974–81)

Gis·sing \'gi-siŋ\ George Robert 1857–1903 Eng. novelist

Giu·lio Ro·ma·no \,jül-yō-rə-'mä-(,)nō\ *circa* 1499–1546 *Giulio di Pietro di Filippo de' Gianuzzi* Ital. painter & architect

Gjel·le·rup \'ge-lə-,rüp\ Karl 1857–1919 Dan. writer

Glad·stone \'glad-,stōn, *chiefly British* -stən\ William Ewart 1809–1898 Brit. statesman; prime minister (1868–74; 1880–85; 1886; 1892–94) — **Glad·ston·ian** \glad-'stō-nē-ən\ *adjective*

Gla·ser \'glā-zər\ Donald Arthur 1926– Am. physicist

Glas·gow \'glas-(,)kō, -(,)gō; 'glaz-(,)gō\ Ellen Anderson Gholson 1873–1945 Am. novelist

Glash·ow \'gla-(,)shō\ Sheldon Lee 1932– Am. physicist

Glas·pell \'glas-,pel\ Susan 1882–1948 Am. novelist & dramatist

Glass \'glas\ Carter 1858–1946 Am. statesman

Glass Philip 1937– Am. composer

Gla·zu·nov \'gla-zə-,nȯf, -,nȯv, ,glä-zù-'\ Aleksandr Konstantinovich 1865–1936 Russ. composer

Glen·dow·er \glen-'daú-(ə)r\ Owen *circa* 1359–*circa* 1416 Welsh rebel

Glenn \'glen\ John Herschel 1921– Am. astronaut & politician

Glick·man \'glik-mən\ Daniel Robert 1941– U.S. secretary of agriculture (1995–)

Glin·ka \'gliŋ-kə\ Mikhail Ivanovich 1804–1857 Russ. composer

Gloucester Duke of — see HUMPHREY

Glov·er \'glə-vər\ John 1732–1797 Am. general in Revolution

Glover Sarah Ann 1785–1867 Eng. music teacher

Gluck \'glúk\ Alma 1884–1938 née (*Reba*) *Fiersohn* Am. (Romanian-born) soprano

Gluck Christoph Willibald 1714–1787 Ger. composer

Go·bat \gō-'bä\ Charles Albert 1834–1914 Swiss statesman

God·dard \'gä-dərd\ Robert Hutchings 1882–1945 Am. physicist

God·frey of Bouillon \,gäd-frē\ *French* **Gode·froy de Bouillon** \gȯt-frwä\ *circa* 1060–1100 Fr. crusader

Go·dol·phin \gə-'däl-fən\ Sidney 1645–1712 1st Earl of *Godolphin* Eng. statesman

Go·doy \gō-'dȯi\ Manuel de 1767–1851 Span. statesman

Go·du·nov \gō-d°n-,ȯf, 'gȯ-, 'gä-\ Boris Fyodorovich *circa* 1551–1605 czar of Russia (1598–1605)

God·win \'gäd-wən\ or **God·wine** \'gäd-(,)wi-nə\ *died* 1053 earl of Wessex

Godwin William 1756–1836 Eng. philosopher & novelist — **God·win·ian** \gäd-'wi-nē-ən\ *adjective*

Godwin–Aus·ten \-'ȯs-tən, -'äs-\ Henry Haversham 1834–1923 Eng. explorer & geologist

Goeb·bels \'gœ(r)-bəlz, 'gœ-bəls\ (Paul) Joseph 1897–1945 Ger. Nazi propagandist

Goe·ring *variant of* GÖRING

Goes \'güs\ Hugo van der *circa* 1440–1482 Du. painter

Goe·thals \'gō-thəlz\ George Washington 1858–1928 Am. general & engineer

Goe·the \'gœ(r)-tə, 'gœ-tə\ Johann Wolfgang von 1749–1832 Ger. poet & dramatist — **Goe·the·an** \-tē-ən\ *adjective*

Gogh, van \van-'gō, -'gäk, -'kȯk, *British also* -'gȯf\ Vincent Willem 1853–1890 Du. painter

Go·gol \'gȯ-gəl, 'gō-,gȯl\ Nikolay Vasilyevich 1809–1852 Russ. writer — **Go·gol·ian** \gȯ-'gōl-yən, gō-'gȯl\ *adjective*

Gold·berg \'gōl(d)-,bərg\ Arthur Joseph 1908–1990 Am. lawyer and jurist; U.S. ambassador to U.N. (1965–68)

Gol·den·wei·ser \'gōl-dən-,wī-zər\ Alexander Alexandrovich 1880–1940 Am. (Russ.-born) anthropologist & sociologist

Gol·ding \'gōl-diŋ\ William Gerald 1911–1993 Eng. author

Gol·do·ni \gäl-'dō-nē, gȯl-\ Carlo 1707–1793 Ital. dramatist

Gold·smith \'gōl(d)-,smith\ Oliver 1730–1774 Brit. author

Gold·stein \'gōl(d)-,stīn\ Joseph Leonard 1940– Am. medical geneticist

Gold·wa·ter \'gōld-,wȯ-tər, -,wä-\ Barry Morris 1909– Am. politician

Gold·wyn \'gōl-dwən\ Samuel 1879?–1974 originally *Schmuel Gelbfisz* Am. (Pol.-born) motion-picture producer

Gol·gi \'gȯl-(,)jē\ Camillo \kä-'mēl-(,)lō\ 1843(or 1844)–1926 Ital. physician

Gol·lancz \gə-'lan(t)s\ Sir Hermann 1852–1930 Eng. Semitic scholar

Gó·mez \'gō-,mez\ Juan Vicente 1864–1935 Venezuelan general & politician; dictator (1908–35)

Gom·pers \'gäm-pərz\ Samuel 1850–1924 Am. (Brit.-born) labor leader

Go·muł·ka \gō-'mùl-kə, -'məl-\ Władysław 1905–1982 Pol. politician

Gon·çal·ves Di·as \gən-'säl-vəs-'dē-əs\ Antônio 1823–1864 Braz. poet

Gon·cha·ro·va \gən-'chär-ə-və\ Nathalie 1883–1962 Russ. artist

Gon·court \gōⁿ-'kür\ Edmond-Louis-Antoine Huot de 1822–1896 & his brother Jules-Alfred Huot de 1830–1870 Fr. novelists & collaborators

Gon·do·mar \ˌgän-də-'mär\ Conde de 1567–1626 *Diego Sarmiento de Acuña* Span. diplomat

Gon·za·ga \gən-'zä-gə, gän-, -'za-\ Saint Aloysius 1568–1591 Ital. Jesuit

Gon·zá·lez \gən-'zä-ləs\ Manuel 1833–1893 Mex. general; president of Mexico (1880–84)

Gon·za·lo de Cór·do·ba — see FERNÁNDEZ DE CÓRDOBA

Goo·dall \'gü-(ˌ)dȯl, -(ˌ)däl\ Jane 1934– Brit. ethologist

Good·hue \'gùd-(ˌ)hyü, -(ˌ)yü\ Bertram Grosvenor 1869–1924 Am. architect

Good·man \'gùd-mən\ Benjamin David 1909–1986 *Benny Goodman* Am. musician and bandleader

Good·rich \'gùd-(ˌ)rich\ Samuel Griswold 1793–1860 pseudonym *Peter Parley* \'pär-lē\ Am. writer

Good·year \'gùd-ˌyir\ Charles 1800–1860 Am. inventor

Gor·ba·chev \ˌgȯr-bə-'chȯf, -'chef; 'gȯr-bə-ˌ\ Mikhail Sergeyevich 1931– Soviet politician; 1st secretary of Communist party (1985–91); president of U.S.S.R. (1990–91)

Gor·cha·kov \ˌgȯr-chə-'kȯf, -'kȯv\ Prince Aleksandr Mikhaylovich 1798–1883 Russ. statesman & diplomat

Gor·di·mer \'gȯr-də-mər\ Nadine 1923– So. African writer

Gor·din \'gȯr-dᵊn\ Jacob 1853–1909 Am. (Russ.-born) Yiddish dramatist

Gor·don \'gȯr-dᵊn\ Charles George 1833–1885 *Chinese Gordon, Gordon Pasha* Brit. soldier

Gordon Charles William 1860–1937 pseudonym *Ralph Connor* Canad. clergyman & novelist

Gordon Lord George 1751–1793 Eng. political agitator

Gore \'gōr, 'gȯr\ Albert, Jr. 1948– Am. politician; vice president of the U.S. (1993–)

Go·re·my·kin \ˌgȯr-ə-'mē-kən\ Ivan Logginovich 1839–1917 Russ. statesman; prime minister (1906; 1914–16)

Gor·gas \'gȯr-gəs\ William Crawford 1854–1920 Am. army surgeon & sanitation expert

Gö·ring \'gər-iŋ, 'ger-, 'gȯr-\ Hermann 1893–1946 Ger. Nazi politician

Gor·ky \'gȯr-kē\ Maksim 1868–1936 pseudonym of *Aleksey Maksimovich Pesh·kov* \'pesh-ˌkȯf, -ˌkȯv\ Russ. writer

Gor·ky \'gȯr-kē\ Arshile 1905–1948 Am. (Armenian-born) artist

Gort Viscount — see VEREKER

Gosse \'gäs\ Sir Edmund William 1849–1928 Eng. poet & critic

Gott·schalk \'gä-ˌchȯk, 'gät-ˌshȯk\ Louis Moreau 1829–1869 Am. composer

Gou·dy \'gau-dē\ Frederic William 1865–1947 Am. type designer

Gough \'gäf\ Hugh 1779–1869 1st Viscount *Gough* Eng. field marshal

Gould \'güld\ Jay 1836–1892 originally *Jason Gould* Am. financier

Gou·nod \gü-'nō, 'gü-ˌnō\ Charles-François 1818–1893 Fr. composer

Gour·mont \gür-'mōⁿ\ Remy de 1858–1915 Fr. writer

Gove \'gōv\ Philip Babcock 1902–1972 Am. lexicographer

Gow·da \'gō-(ˌ)dä\ Haradanahalli Doddegowda Deve \'de-(ˌ)vä, -ve\ 1933– prime minister of India (1996–)

Gow·er \'gaü-(ə)r, 'gō-(ə)r, 'gȯ(-ə)r\ John 1330?–1408 Eng. poet

Go·ya y Lu·cien·tes \'gȯi-ə-ˌē-,lü-sē-'en-ˌtäs\ Francisco José de 1746–1828 Span. painter — **Go·ya·esque** \ˌgȯi-ə-'esk\ *or* **Go·yesque** \gȯi-'yesk\ *adjective*

Goy·en *or* **Goij·en, van** \van-'gȯi-ən, 'k̲ȯi-\ Jan Josephszoon 1596–1656 Du. painter

Grac·chus \'gra-kəs\ Gaius Sempronius 153–121 B.C. & his brother Tiberius Sempronius 163–133 B.C. *the Grac·chi* \'gra-ˌkī\ Rom. statesmen

Gra·ham \'grā-əm, 'gra(-ə)m\ John 1648–1689 *Graham of Claverhouse; Bonnie Dundee;* 1st Viscount of *Dundee* Scot. Jacobite

Graham Martha 1893–1991 Am. choreographer & dancer

Graham Thomas 1805–1869 Scot. chemist

Graham William Franklin 1918– *Billy Graham* Am. evangelist

Gra·hame \'grā-əm, 'gra(-ə)m\ Kenneth 1859–1932 Brit. writer

Gramme \'gram\ Zénobe Théophile 1826–1901 Belg. engineer

Gra·na·dos \grə-'nä-(ˌ)dōs, -(ˌ)thōs\ Enrique 1867–1916 Span. composer

Gran·di \'grän-(ˌ)dē\ Dino 1895–1988 Conte *di Mordano* Ital. Fascist politician

Gra·nit \grä-'nēt\ Ragnar Arthur 1900–1991 Swed. (Finn.-born) physiologist

Grant \'grant\ Ulysses 1822–1885 originally *Hiram Ulysses Grant* Am. general; 18th president of the U.S. (1869–77)

Gran·ville–Bar·ker \'gran-ˌvil-'bär-kər\ Harley Granville 1877–1946 Eng. actor, manager, & dramatist

Grass \'gräs\ Günter Wilhelm 1927– Ger. writer

Grasse \'gras, 'gräs\ François-Joseph-Paul 1722–1788 Comte *de Grasse* & Marquis *de Grasse-Tilly* \-tē-'yē\ Fr. naval officer

Gra·tian \'grā-sh(ē-)ən\ *Latin* **Flavius Gratianus** 359–383 Rom. emperor (367–383)

Grat·tan \'gra-tᵊn\ Henry 1746–1820 Irish orator & statesman

Grau San Mar·tín \'grau̇-ˌsan-(ˌ)mär-'tēn, -ˌsän-\ Ramón 1887–1969 Cuban physician & politician; president of Cuba (1944–48)

Graves \'grāvz\ Robert Ranke 1895–1985 Brit. author

Gray \'grā\ Asa 1810–1888 Am. botanist

Gray Thomas 1716–1771 Eng. poet

Grayson David — see Ray Stannard BAKER

Gra·zia·ni \ˌgrät-sē-'ä-nē\ Rodolfo 1882–1955 Marchese *di Neghelli* Ital. marshal & colonial administrator

Gre·co, El \el-'gre-(ˌ)kō *also* -'grā-\ 1541–1614 *Doménikos Theotokópoulos* Span. (Cretan-born) painter

Gree·ley \'grē-lē\ Horace 1811–1872 Am. journalist & politician

Gree·ly \'grē-lē\ Adolphus Washington 1844–1935 Am. general & arctic explorer

Green \'grēn\ John Richard 1837–1883 Eng. historian

Green Julien 1900– Fr. novelist

Green William 1873–1952 Am. labor leader

Gree·na·way \'grē-nə-ˌwā\ Catherine 1846–1901 *Kate* Eng. illustrator

Greene \'grēn\ Graham 1904–1991 Brit. novelist

Greene Nathanael 1742–1786 Am. general in Revolution

Greene Robert 1558?–1592 Eng. poet & dramatist

Gree·nough \'grē-ˌnō\ Horatio 1805–1852 Am. sculptor

Greg·o·ry \'gre-g(ə-)rē\ Saint 240–332 *the Illuminator* apostle & founder of the Armenian Church

Gregory name of 16 popes: especially **I** Saint *circa* 540–604 *the Great* (pope 590–604); **VII** Saint originally *Hil·de·brand* \'hil-də-ˌbrand\ *circa* 1020–1085 (pope 1073–85); **XIII** originally *Ugo Buon·com·pa·gni* \ˈü-gō-bwȯn-kōm-'pän-yē\ 1502–1585 (pope 1572–85)

Gregory Isabella Augusta 1852–1932 *Lady Gregory* née *Persse* Irish dramatist

Gregory of Nys·sa \'ni-sə\ Saint *circa* 335–*circa* 394 Eastern church father

Gregory of Tours Saint 538–594 Frankish ecclesiastic & historian

Gren·fell \'gren-ˌfel, -fəl\ Sir Wilfred Thomason 1865–1940 Eng. medical missionary

Gren·ville \'gren-ˌvil, -vəl\ George 1712–1770 Eng. statesman

Grenville *or* **Greyn·ville** \'grän-\ Sir Richard 1542–1591 Brit. naval commander

Gresh·am \'gre-shəm\ Sir Thomas 1519–1579 Eng. financier

Greuze \'grə(r)z, 'grōēz\ Jean-Baptiste 1725–1805 Fr. painter

Gré·vy \grā-'vē\ (François-Paul-) Jules 1807–1891 Fr. lawyer; 3d president of the Republic (1879–87)

Grey \'grā\ 2d Earl 1764–1845 *Charles Grey* Eng. statesman; prime minister (1830–34)

Grey Edward 1862–1933 Viscount *Grey of Fal·lo·don* \'fa-lə-dᵊn\ Eng. politician

Grey Lady Jane 1537–1554 titular queen of England for 9 days

Grey Zane 1875–1939 Am. novelist

Grieg \'grēg\ Edvard Hagerup 1843–1907 Norw. composer

Grieve Christopher Murray — see Hugh MACDIARMID

Grif·fin \'gri-fən\ Walter Burley 1876–1937 Am. architect

Grif·fith \'gri-fəth\ Arthur 1872–1922 Irish journalist & nationalist

Griffith David Lewelyn Wark 1875–1948 Am. motion-picture producer & director

Gri·gnard \grēn-'yär\ (François-Auguste-) Victor 1871–1935 Fr. chemist

Grill·par·zer \'gril-ˌpärt-sər\ Franz 1791–1872 Austrian dramatist & poet

Grimm \'grim\ Jacob 1785–1863 & his brother Wilhelm 1786–1859 Ger. philologists & folklorists

Gris \'grēs\ Juan 1887–1927 *José Victoriano González* Span. painter in France

Gro·fé \'grō-,fā\ Fer·de \'fər-dē\ 1892–1972 Am. conductor & composer

Gro·lier de Ser·vières \ˌgrōl-'yä-də-,ser-vē-'er, 'grōl-yər-\ Jean 1479–1565 Vicomte *d'Aguisy* Fr. bibliophile

Gro·my·ko \grə-'mē-(ˌ)kō, grō-\ Andrey Andreyevich 1909–1989 Russ. economist & diplomat; president of U.S.S.R. (1985–88)

Groo·te \'grō-tə\ Gerhard 1340–1384 *Ge·rar·dus Mag·nus* \jə-ˌrär-dəs-'mag-nəs\ Du. religious reformer

Gro·pi·us \'grō-pē-əs\ Walter 1883–1969 Am. (Ger.-born) architect

Grop·per \'grä-pər\ William 1897–1977 Am. artist

Gros·ve·nor \'grōv-nər, 'grō-və-\ Gilbert Hovey 1875–1966 Am. geographer and editor

Grosz \'grōs\ George 1893–1959 Am. (Ger.-born) painter

Grote \'grōt\ George 1794–1871 Eng. historian

Gro·tius \'grō-sh(ē-)əs\ Hugo 1583–1645 *Huigh de Groot* \də-'grōt\ Du. jurist & statesman

Grou·chy \grü-'shē\ Emmanuel 1766–1847 Marquis *de Grouchy* Fr. general

Grove \'grōv\ Sir George 1820–1900 Eng. musicologist

Groves \'grōvz\ Leslie Richard 1896–1970 Am. general

Grü·ne·wald \'grü-nə-ˌwȯld, 'grüē-nə-ˌvält\ Matthias *circa* 1455–1528 Ger. painter

Gryph·i·us \'gri-fē-əs\ Andreas 1616–1664 *German Greif* \'grīf\ Ger. poet & dramatist

Guar·ne·ri·us \gwär-'ner-ē-əs\ *Latin* **Guar·ne·ri·us** \gwär-'nir-ē-əs, -'ner-\ family of Ital. violin makers: especially Giuseppe Antonio 1687–1745

Gu·de·ri·an \gü-'der-ē-ən\ Heinz Wilhelm 1888–1954 Ger. general

Gue·dal·la \gwi-'da-lə\ Philip 1889–1944 Eng. writer

Gue·rin \'ger-ən\ Jules 1866–1946 Am. painter

Gues·clin \ges-'klaⁿ\ Bertrand du *circa* 1320–1380 Fr. soldier

Guesde \ged\ Jules 1845–1922 *Mathieu Basile* Fr. socialist

Guest \'gest\ Edgar Albert 1881–1959 Am. journalist & poet

Gue·va·ra \ge-'vär-ə, gä-\ Ernesto 1928–1967 *Che* Latin-Am. (Argentine-born) revolutionary leader

Gui·do of Arezzo \'gwē-(ˌ)dō\ *or* **Guido Areti·nus** \ˌar-ə-'tē-nəs\ *circa* 991–1050 Benedictine monk & music reformer

Guil·laume \gē-'yōm\ Charles Édouard 1861–1938 Fr. physicist

Guille·min \gē(-ə)-'maⁿ\ Roger Charles Louis 1924– Am. (Fr.-born) physiologist

Guiscard Robert — see ROBERT GUISCARD

Guise \gēz\ 1st Duc de 1519–1563 *François de Lorraine* Fr. soldier & politician

Guise 3d Duc de 1550–1588 *Henri I de Lorraine* Fr. soldier & politician

Gui·te·ras \gē-'ter-əs\ Juan 1852–1925 Cuban physician

Gui·zot \gē-'zō\ François-Pierre-Guillaume 1787–1874 Fr. historian & statesman

\ə\ abut \ᵊ\ kitten \ər\ further \a\ ash \ā\ ace
\ä\ mop, mar \au̇\ out \ch\ chin \e\ bet \ē\ easy
\g\ go \i\ hit \ī\ ice \j\ job \ŋ\ sing \ō\ go
\ȯ\ law \ȯi\ boy \th\ thin \t̲h̲\ the \ü\ loot \u̇\ foot
\y\ yet \zh\ vision *see also* Guide to Pronunciation

Gull·strand \'gəl-ˌstrand\ Allvar 1862–1930 Swed. ophthalmologist

Gun·nars·son \'gə-nər-sən\ Gunnar 1889–1975 Icelandic writer

Gun·ter \'gən-tər\ Edmund 1581–1626 Eng. mathematician

Gus·tav \'güs-ˌtäv\ *or* **Gus·ta·vus** \(ˌ)gə-'stä-vəs, -'stä-\ name of 6 kings of Sweden, the first 4 of the Vasa dynasty: **I** (*Gustav Eriksson*) 1496?–1560 (reigned 1523–60); **II** (*Gustav Adolph*)1594–1632 (reigned 1611–32); **III** 1746–1792 (reigned 1771–92); **IV** (*Gustav Adolph*) 1778–1837 (reigned 1792–1809); **V** 1858–1950 (reigned 1907–50); **VI** (*Gustav Adolph*)1882–1973 (reigned 1950–73)

Gu·ten·berg \'gü-t⁵n-ˌbərg\ Johannes *circa* 1390–1468 Ger. inventor of printing from movable type

Guth·rie \'gə-thrē\ Woodrow Wilson 1912–1967 *Woody* Am. folksinger

Gutz·kow \'güts-(ˌ)kō\ Karl Ferdinand 1811–1878 Ger. journalist, novelist, & dramatist

Guz·mán Blan·co \güs-ˌmän-'bläŋ-(ˌ)kō\ Antonio 1829–1899 Venezuelan soldier & statesman; dictator of Venezuela (1870–89)

Gwin·nett \gwi-'net\ Button *circa* 1735–1777 Am. Revolutionary leader

Gwyn *or* **Gwynn** *or* **Gwynne** \'gwin\ Eleanor 1650–1687 *Nell* Eng. actress *mistress of Charles II*

Haa·kon VII \'hȯ-kən, -ˌkän\ 1872–1957 king of Norway (1905–57)

Haa·vel·mo \'hȯ-vəl-ˌmō\ Trygve 1911– Norw. economist

Ha·ber \'hä-bər\ Fritz 1868–1934 Ger. chemist

Há·cha \'hä-(ˌ)kä\ Emil 1872–1945 Czech jurist & statesman

Had·field \'had-ˌfēld\ Sir Robert Abbott 1858–1940 Eng. metallurgist

Had·ley \'had-lē\ Henry Kimball 1871–1937 Am. composer

Had·ow \'ha-(ˌ)dō\ Sir (William) Henry 1859–1937 Eng. educator & musicologist

Ha·dri·an \'hā-drē-ən\ *variant of* ADRIAN

Hadrian A.D. 76–138 Rom. emperor (117–138)

Haeck·el \'he-kəl\ Ernst Heinrich 1834–1919 Ger. biologist & philosopher

Hā·fez \hä-'fez\ 1325(or 1326)–1389(or 1390) *Moḥammad Shams od-Dīn Hāfez* Pers. poet

Hag·gard \'ha-gərd\ Sir (Henry) Rider 1856–1925 Eng. novelist

Hahn \'hän\ Otto 1879–1968 Ger. physical chemist

Hah·ne·mann \'hä-nə-mən\ (Christian Friedrich) Samuel 1755–1843 Ger. physician

Haider Ali — see HYDER ALI

Haig \'hāg\ 1st Earl 1861–1928 *Douglas Haig* Brit. field marshal

Hai·le Se·las·sie \'hī-lē-sə-'la-sē, -'lä-\ 1892–1975 Ras *Tafari* emperor of Ethiopia (1930–36; 1941–74)

Hak·luyt \'hak-ˌlüt\ Richard *circa* 1552–1616 Eng. geographer & historian

Hal·dane \'hȯl-ˌdān, -dən\ John Burdon Sanderson 1892–1964 *son of J.S.* Brit. biologist

Haldane John Scott 1860–1936 Brit. physiologist

Haldane Richard Burdon 1856–1928 Viscount *Haldane of Cloan* \'klōn\; *brother of J.S.* Brit. lawyer, philosopher, & statesman

Hal·der \'häl-dər\ Franz 1884–1972 Ger. general

Hale \'hā(ə)l\ Edward Everett 1822–1909 Am. Unitarian clergyman & writer

Hale George Ellery 1868–1938 Am. astronomer

Hale Sir Matthew 1609–1676 Eng. jurist

Hale Nathan 1755–1776 Am. Revolutionary hero

Ha·lé·vy \ˌ(h)a-lā-'vē, ˌ(h)ä-\ (Jacques-François-) Fromental (-Elíe) 1799–1862 pseudonym of *Élie Lé·vy* \lä-'vē\ Fr. composer

Halévy Ludovic 1834–1908 *nephew of preceding* Fr. dramatist & novelist

Hal·i·fax \'ha-lə-ˌfaks\ Earl of 1881–1959 *Edward Frederick Lindley Wood* Eng. statesman & diplomat

Hall \'hȯl\ Charles Francis 1821–1871 Am. arctic explorer

Hall Charles Martin 1863–1914 Am. chemist & manufacturer

Hall Granville Stanley 1844–1924 Am. psychologist & educator

Hall James Norman 1887–1951 Am. novelist

Hal·lam \'ha-ləm\ Henry 1777–1859 Eng. historian

Hal·leck \'ha-lək, -lik\ Fitz-Greene 1790–1867 Am. poet

Halleck Henry Wager 1815–1872 Am. general

Hal·ley \'ha-lē *also* 'hā-lē\ Edmond *or* Edmund 1656–1742 Eng. astronomer

Hals \'hälz, 'häls\ Frans *circa* 1581–1666 Du. painter

Hal·sey \'hȯl-sē, -zē\ William Frederick 1882–1959 Am. admiral

Hal·sted \'hȯl-stəd, -ˌsted\ William Stewart 1852–1922 Am. surgeon

Ham·bro \'häm-ˌbrō\ Carl Joachim 1885–1964 Norw. statesman

Ha·mil·car Bar·ca \hə-'mil-ˌkär-'bär-kə, 'ha-məl-\ *or* **Bar·cas** \'bär-kəs\ 270?–229(or 228) B.C. *father of Hannibal* Carthaginian general

Ham·il·ton \'ha-məl-tən, -t⁵n\ Alexander 1755–1804 Am. statesman

Hamilton Edith 1867–1963 Am. classicist

Hamilton Lady Emma 1765–1815 née *Amy Lyon* mistress of Lord Nelson

Ham·lin \'ham-lən\ Hannibal 1809–1891 Am. politician; vice president of the U.S. (1861–65)

Ham·mar·skjöld \'ha-mər-ˌsheld, 'häm-, -ˌshuld, -ˌsheld\ Dag \'däg\ Hjalmar Agne Carl 1905–1961 Swed. U.N. official; secretary-general (1953–61)

Ham·mer·stein \'ha-mər-ˌstīn, -ˌsten\ Oscar 1846–1919 Am. (Ger.-born) theater impresario

Hammerstein Oscar 1895–1960 *grandson of preceding* Am. lyricist & librettist

Ham·mett \'ha-met\ (Samuel) Dashiell 1894–1961 Am. writer

Ham·mond \'ha-mənd\ John Hays 1855–1936 Am. mining engineer

Hammond John Hays 1888–1965 *son of preceding* Am. electrical engineer & inventor

Hammond Laurens 1895–1973 Am. inventor

Ham·mu·ra·bi \ˌha-mə-'rä-bē\ *or* **Ham·mu·ra·pi** \-'rä-pē\ died 1750 B.C. king of Babylon (1792–50)

Hamp·den \'ham(p)-dən\ John 1594–1643 Eng. statesman

Hampden Walter 1879–1955 stage name of *W. H. Dougherty* Am. actor

Hamp·ton \'ham(p)-tən\ Wade 1751?–1835 Am. general

Hampton Wade 1818–1902 *grandson of preceding* Am. politician & Confederate general

Ham·sun \'häm-sən\ Knut 1859–1952 pseudonym of *Knut Pedersen* Norw. writer

Han·cock \'han-ˌkäk\ John 1737–1793 Am. statesman in Revolution

Hancock Winfield Scott 1824–1886 Am. general & politician

Hand \'hand\ (Billings) Learned 1872–1961 Am. jurist

Han·del \'han-d⁵l\ George Frideric 1685–1759 Brit. (Ger.-born) composer — **Han·de·li·an** \han-'dē-lē-ən\ adjective

Han·dy \'han-dē\ William Christopher 1873–1958 Am. blues musician

Han·na \'ha-nə\ Marcus Alonzo 1837–1904 *Mark* Am. businessman & politician

Han·nay \'ha-ˌnā, 'ha-nē\ James Owen 1865–1950 Irish clergyman & novelist

Han·ni·bal \'ha-nə-bəl\ 247–183 B.C. *son of Hamilcar Barca* Carthaginian general

Han·no \'ha-(ˌ)nō\ 3d century B.C. *the Great* Carthaginian statesman

Ha·no·taux \ˌa-nə-'tō, ˌä-\ (Albert-Auguste-) Gabriel 1853–1944 Fr. historian & statesman

Han·sard \'han-ˌsärd, 'han(t)-sərd\ Luke 1752–1828 Eng. printer

Han·son \'han(t)-sən\ Howard 1896–1981 Am. composer

Hans·son \'han(t)-sən\ Per Albin 1885–1946 Swed. statesman

Han Wu Ti \'hän-'wü-'dē\ 156–87 B.C. originally *Liu Ch'e* often called *Wu Ti* Chin. emperor (140–87)

Han Yü \'hän-'yü\ 768–824 *Han Wen-kung* Chin. poet, essayist, & philosopher

Har·bach \'här-ˌbäk\ Otto Abels 1873–1963 Am. dramatist & librettist

Har·de·ca·nute *or* **Har·di·ca·nute** \ˌhär-di-kə-'nüt, -'nyüt\ *circa* 1019–1042 king of Denmark (1028–42) and of England (1040–42)

Har·den \'här-d⁵n\ Sir Arthur 1865–1940 Eng. chemist

Harden Maximilian 1861–1927 originally *Felix Ernst Witkowski* Ger. writer

Har·den·berg \'här-d⁵n-ˌbərg, -ˌberk\ Prince Karl August von 1750–1822 Pruss. statesman

Har·ding \'här-diŋ\ Warren Gamaliel 1865–1923 29th president of the U.S. (1921–23)

Har·dy \'här-dē\ Thomas 1840–1928 Eng. novelist & poet — **Har·dy·esque** \ˌhär-dē-'esk\ adjective

Har·greaves \'här-ˌgrēvz\ James died 1778 Eng. inventor

Har·ing·ton *or* **Har·ring·ton** \'har-iŋ-tən\ Sir John 1561–1612 Eng. writer & translator

Ha·rī·rī, al– \ˌal-hə-'rir-ē\ 1054–1122 Arab scholar & poet

Har·lan \'här-lən\ John Marshall 1833–1911 & his grandson 1899–1971 Am. jurists

Har·ley \'här-lē\ Robert 1661–1724 1st Earl of *Oxford* Eng. statesman

Harms·worth \'härmz-(ˌ)wərth\ Alfred Charles William 1865–1922 Viscount *North·cliffe* \'nȯrth-ˌklif\ Eng. publisher & politician

Harmsworth Harold Sidney 1868–1940 1st Viscount *Roth·er·mere* \'rä-thər-mir\ *brother of A.C.W.* Eng. publisher & politician

Har·old \'har-əld\ name of 2 kings of the English: **I** died 1040 *Harold Hare·foot* \'har-ˌfut, 'her-\ (reigned 1035–40); **II** *circa* 1022–1066 (reigned 1066)

Harold name of 3 kings of Norway: especially **III** *Hard·raa·de* \'hȯr-ˌrȯ-də\ 1015–1066 (reigned 1045–66)

Har·ri·man \'har-ə-mən\ William Aver·ell \'āv-rəl, 'ā-və-\ 1891–1986 Am. businessman, diplomat, & politician

Har·ris \'har-əs\ Barbara Clementine 1930– Am. bishop

Harris Frank 1856–1931 Am. (Irish-born) writer

Harris Joel Chandler 1848–1908 Am. writer

Harris Roy 1898–1979 Am. composer

Harris William Torrey 1835–1909 Am. philosopher & educator

Har·ri·son \'har-ə-sən\ Benjamin 1833–1901 *grandson of W. H. Harrison* 23d president of the U.S. (1889–93)

Harrison Frederic 1831–1923 Eng. writer & philosopher

Harrison Sir Rex 1908–1990 originally *Reginald Carey Harrison* Brit. actor

Harrison William Henry 1773–1841 9th president of the U.S. (1841)

Har·san·yi \'här-'shä-nē\ John Charles 1920– Am. (Hung.-born) economist

Hart \'härt\ Albert Bushnell 1854–1943 Am. historian & editor

Hart Basil Henry Liddell — see LIDDELL HART

Hart Lorenz 1895–1943 Am. lyricist

Hart Moss 1904–1961 Am. librettist & dramatist

Hart Sir Robert 1835–1911 Brit. diplomat

Hart William Surrey 1872–1946 Am. actor

Harte \'härt\ Francis Brett 1836–1902 *Bret Harte* Am. writer

Hart·line \'härt-ˌlīn\ Haldan Keffer 1903–1983 Am. biophysicist

Har·tung \'här-ˌtuŋ\ Hans 1904–1989 Fr. (Ger.-born) painter

Hā·rūn ar–Ra·shīd \hə-'rün-är-rə-'shēd\ 763(or 766)–809 *Hārūn ar-Rashīd ibn Muhammad al-Mahdī ibn al-Manṣūr al-'Abbāsī* caliph of Baghdad (786–809)

Har·vard \'här-vərd\ John 1607–1638 Am. clergyman & benefactor

Har·vey \'här-vē\ George Brinton McClellan 1864–1928 Am. journalist & diplomat

Harvey Sir John Martin 1863–1944 Eng. actor & producer

Harvey William 1578–1657 Eng. physician & anatomist

Has·dru·bal \'haz-ˌdrü-bəl, haz-'\ died 207 B.C. *brother of Hannibal* Carthaginian general

Ha·shi·mo·to \ˌhä-shē-'mō-(ˌ)tō\ Ryutaro 1937– prime minister of Japan (1996–)

Has·sam \'ha-səm\ (Frederick) Childe 1859–1935 Am. artist

Has·sel \'hä-səl\ Odd 1897–1981 Norw. chemist

Hass·ler \'häs-lər\ Hans Leo 1564–1612 Ger. composer

Has·tings \'hās-tiŋz\ 1st Marquess of 1754–1826 *Francis Raw·don-Hastings* \'rȯ-d⁵n-\ Brit. general & colonial administrator

Hastings Warren 1732–1818 Eng. statesman & administrator in India

Haugh·ey \'hȯ-hē\ Charles James 1925– prime minister of Ireland (1979–81; 1982; 1987–92)

Haupt·man \'haupt-mən\ Herbert Aaron 1917– Am. biophysicist

Haupt·mann \'haupt-,män\ Gerhart 1862–1946 Ger. writer

Haus·ho·fer \'haus-,hō-fər\ Karl Ernst 1869–1946 Ger. general & geographer

Hauss·mann \ōs-'män, 'haus-mən\ Baron Georges-Eugène 1809–1891 Fr. administrator

Ha·vel \'hä-vel, -vəl\ Vá·clav \'vät-,släf\ 1936– Czech writer & politician; president of Czechoslovakia (1989–92); president of Czech Republic (1993–)

Have·lock \'hav-,läk, -lək\ Sir Henry 1795–1857 Brit. general

Hawke \'hȯk\ 1st Baron 1705–1781 *Edward Hawke* Eng. admiral

Hawke Robert James Lee 1929– prime minister of Australia (1983–91)

Haw·king \'hȯ-kiŋ\ Stephen William 1942– Brit. physicist

Haw·kins \'hȯ-kənz\ Sir Anthony Hope 1863–1933 pseudonym *Anthony Hope* Eng. novelist & dramatist

Hawkins *or* **Haw·kyns** Sir John 1532–1595 Eng. admiral

Haw·orth \'hau-ərth\ Sir (Walter) Norman 1883–1950 Eng. chemist

Haw·thorne \'hȯ-,thȯrn\ Nathaniel 1804–1864 Am. author

Hay \'hā\ John Milton 1838–1905 Am. statesman

Haydn \'hī-dᵊn\ (Franz) Joseph 1732–1809 Austrian composer

Hay·ek \'hī-,ak\ Friedrich August von 1899–1992 Brit. (Austrian-born) economist

Hayes \'hāz\ Helen 1900–1993 *Helen Hayes Brown* Am. actress

Hayes Isaac Israel 1832–1881 Am. arctic explorer

Hayes Roland 1887–1977 Am. tenor

Hayes Rutherford Birchard 1822–1893 19th president of the U.S. (1877–81)

Haynes \'hānz\ Elwood 1857–1925 Am. inventor

Hays \'hāz\ Will Harrison 1879–1954 Am. lawyer & politician

Ha·zard \ä-'zär\ Paul-Gustave-Marie-Camille 1878–1944 Fr. literary historian

Haz·litt \'haz-lət, 'häz-\ William 1778–1830 Eng. essayist

Hea·ly \'hē-lē\ Timothy Michael 1855–1931 Irish statesman

Hea·ney \'hē-nē\ Sea·mus \'shā-məs\ 1939– Irish poet

Hearn \'hərn\ Laf·ca·dio \laf-'kä-dē-,ō\ 1850–1904 Jp. *Yakumo Koizumi* Am. (Greek-born) writer in Japan

Hearst \'hərst\ William Randolph 1863–1951 Am. newspaper publisher

Heath \'hēth\ Edward 1916– Brit. prime minister (1970–74)

Heav·i·side \'he-vē-,sīd\ Oliver 1850–1925 Eng. physicist

Heb·bel \'he-bəl\ (Christian) Friedrich 1813–1863 Ger. dramatist

He·ber \'hē-bər\ Reginald 1783–1826 Eng. prelate & hymn writer

Hé·bert \ā-'ber\ Jacques-René 1757–1794 Fr. radical journalist

He·din \hā-'dēn\ Sven Anders 1865–1952 Swed. explorer

Heem \'hām\ Jan Davidsz de 1606–1683(or 1684) Du. painter

He·gel \'hā-gəl\ Georg Wilhelm Friedrich 1770–1831 Ger. philosopher

Hei·deg·ger \'hī-,de-gər, 'hī-di-gər\ Martin 1889–1976 Ger. philosopher — **Hei·deg·ger·ian** \,hī-di-'gar-ē-ən, -'ger-\ *adjective*

Hei·den·stam \'hā-dᵊn-,stam, -,stäm\ (Carl Gustaf) Verner von 1859–1940 Swed. writer

Hei·fetz \'hī-fəts\ Ja·scha \'yä-shə\ 1901–1987 Am. (Russ.-born) violinist

Hei·ne \'hī-nə *also* -nē\ Heinrich 1797–1856 Ger. poet & critic

Hei·sen·berg \'hī-zᵊn-bərg, -,berk\ Werner Karl 1901–1976 Ger. physicist

Heliogabalus — *see* ELAGABALUS

Hel·ler \'he-lər\ Joseph 1923– Am. novelist

Hell·man \'hel-mən\ Lillian 1905–1984 Am. dramatist

Helm·holtz \'helm-,hōlts\ Hermann Ludwig Ferdinand von 1821–1894 Ger. physicist, anatomist, & physiologist

Hé·lo·ïse \'ā-lə-,wēz, 'e-lə-\ *circa* 1098–1164 *wife of Abelard* Fr. abbess

Hel·vé·tius \hel-'vā-sh(ē-)əs, -'vē-; ,(h)el-,vās-'yüs, -'yœs\ Claude-Adrien 1715–1771 Fr. philosopher

He·mans \'he-mənz, 'hē-\ Felicia Dorothea 1793–1835 *née Browne* Eng. poet

Hem·inge *or* **Hem·minge** \'he-miŋ\ John *circa* 1556–1630 Eng. actor

Hem·ing·way \'he-miŋ-,wā\ Ernest Miller 1899–1961 Am. writer & journalist — **Hem·ing·way·esque** \,he-miŋ-,wā-'esk\ *adjective*

Hench \'hench\ Philip Showalter 1896–1965 Am. physician

Hen·der·son \'hen-dər-sən\ Arthur 1863–1935 Brit. labor leader & statesman

Henderson Sir Nev·ile \'ne-vəl\ Meyrick 1882–1942 Brit. diplomat

Hen·dricks \'hen-driks\ Thomas Andrews 1819–1885 Am. politician; vice president of the U.S. (1885)

Hen·gist *or* **Hen·gest** \'heŋ-gəst, -,gist\ & *his brother* **Hor·sa** \'hȯr-sə\ 5th century Jute invaders of Britain

Hen·ley \'hen-lē\ William Ernest 1849–1903 Eng. editor & author

Hen·ne·pin \'he-nə-pən, ,e-nə-'paⁿ\ Louis 1626– after 1701 Belg. friar & explorer in America

Hen·ri \'hen-rī\ Robert 1865–1929 Am. painter

Hen·ry \'hen-rē\ name of 8 kings of England: **I** 1068–1135 (reigned 1100–35); **II** 1133–1189 (reigned 1154–89); **III** 1207–1272 (reigned 1216–72); **IV** 1366–1413 (reigned 1399–1413); **V** 1387–1422 (reigned 1413–22); **VI** 1421–1471 (reigned 1422–61 & 1470–71); **VII** 1457–1509 (reigned 1485–1509); **VIII** 1491–1547 (reigned 1509–47)

Henry name of 4 kings of France: **I** *circa* 1008–1060 (reigned 1031–60); **II** 1519–1559 (reigned 1547–59); **III** 1551–1589 (reigned 1574–89); **IV** (Henry III of Navarre) 1553–1610 (reigned 1589–1610)

Henry 1394–1460 *the Navigator* Port. prince

Henry Joseph 1797–1878 Am. physicist

Henry O. — *see* William Sydney PORTER

Henry Patrick 1736–1799 Am. statesman & orator

Hens·lowe \'henz-(,)lō\ Philip *circa* 1550–1616 Eng. theater manager

Hep·burn \'hep-(,)bərn\ Katharine 1907– Am. actress

Hep·ple·white \'he-pəl-,hwīt, -,wīt\ George *died* 1786 Eng. cabinetmaker and designer

Hep·worth \'hep-(,)wərth\ Dame Barbara 1903–1975 Brit. sculptor

Her·a·clei·tus *or* **Her·a·cli·tus** \,her-ə-'klī-təs\ *circa* 540–*circa* 480 B.C. Greek philosopher — **Her·a·cli·te·an** \-'klī-tē-ən, -,klī-'tē-\ *adjective*

He·ra·cli·us \,her-ə-'klī-əs, hi-'ra-klē-\ *circa* 575–641 Byzantine emperor (610–641)

Her·bart \'her-,bärt\ Johann Friedrich 1776–1841 Ger. philosopher & educator

Her·bert \'hər-bərt\ George 1593–1633 Eng. divine & poet

Herbert Victor 1859–1924 Am. (Irish-born) composer & conductor

Herbert William 1580–1630 3d Earl of *Pembroke* Eng. statesman & patron

Herblock — *see* Herbert Lawrence BLOCK

Her·der \'her-dər\ Johann Gottfried von 1744–1803 Ger. philosopher

He·re·dia \ā-rā-'dyä, (h)ā-'rä-dē-ə\ José María de 1842–1905 Fr. (Cuban-born) poet

Her·ford \'hər-fərd\ Oliver 1863–1935 Eng. writer & illustrator

He·ring \'her-iŋ, 'hā-riŋ\ Ewald 1834–1918 Ger. physiologist & psychologist

Her·ki·mer \'hər-kə-mər\ Nicholas 1728–1777 Am. general

Her·man \'hər-mən\ Alexis 1947– U.S. secretary of labor (1997–)

Herman Woodrow Charles 1913–1987 *Woody Herman* Am. musician & bandleader

Hern·don \'hərn-dən\ William Henry 1818–1891 Am. lawyer

He·ro \'hē-(,)rō, 'hir-(,)ō\ *or* **He·ron** \'hē-,rän\ 1st century A.D. Greek scientist

Her·od \'her-əd\ 73–4 B.C. *the Great* Rom. king of Judea (37–4)

Herod An·ti·pas \'an-tə-pəs, -,pas\ 21 B.C.–A.D. 39 *son of preceding* Rom. tetrarch of Galilee (4 B.C.–A.D. 39)

He·rod·o·tus \hi-'rä-də-təs\ *circa* 484–between 430 and 420 B.C. Greek historian — **He·rod·o·te·an** \-,rä-də-'tē-ən\ *adjective*

Her·re·ra \(h)ə-'rer-ə\ Francisco de 1576–*circa* 1656 *el Viejo* Span. painter

Her·rick \'her-ik\ Robert 1591–1674 Eng. poet

Her·riot \,er-ē-'ō\ Édouard 1872–1957 Fr. statesman

Hersch·bach \'hərsh-,bäk\ Dudley Robert 1932– Am. chemist

Her·schel \'hər-shəl\ Sir John Frederick William 1792–1871 & *his father* Sir William 1738–1822 Eng. astronomers

Her·sey \'hər-sē\ John Richard 1914–1993 Am. novelist

Her·shey \'hər-shē\ Alfred Day 1908–1997 Am. geneticist

Her·ter \'hər-tər\ Christian Archibald 1895–1966 Am. diplomat; secretary of state (1959–61)

Hertz \'herts, 'härts\ Gustav Ludwig 1887–1975 Ger. physicist

Hertz Heinrich Rudolf 1857–1894 Ger. physicist

Hert·zog \'hert-,sȯk\ James Barry Munnik 1866–1942 So. African general

Herz·berg \'hərts-,bərg\ Gerhard 1904– Canad. (Ger.-born) physicist

Herzl \'hert-sᵊl\ Theodor 1860–1904 Austrian (Hung.-born) Zionist

He·si·od \'hē-sē-əd, 'he-\ *flourished circa* 800 B.C. Greek poet

Hess \'hes\ Dame Myra 1890–1965 Eng. pianist

Hess (Walther Richard) Rudolf 1894–1987 Ger. Nazi politician

Hess Victor Franz 1883–1964 Austrian physicist

Hess Walter Rudolf 1881–1973 Swiss physiologist

Hes·se \'he-sə\ Hermann 1877–1962 Ger. author

He·ve·sy \'he-və-shē, -,ve-shē\ Georg Karl 1885–1966 Hung. chemist

Hew·ish \'hyü-ish\ Antony 1924– Brit. astronomer

Hey·drich \'hī-drik, -drik\ Reinhard 1904–1942 *the Hangman* Ger. Nazi administrator

Hey·er·dahl \'hā-ər-,däl\ Thor 1914– Norw. explorer & writer

Hey·mans \ā-'män(t)s, -'man(t)s\ Corneille-Jean-François 1892–1968 Belg. physiologist

Hey·rov·ský \'hā-,rȯf-skē, -,rȯv-\ Jaroslav 1890–1967 Czech chemist

Hey·se \'hī-zə\ Paul Johann Ludwig von 1830–1914 Ger. writer

Hey·ward \'hā-wərd\ (Edwin) Du·Bose \dü-'bōz, dyü-\ 1885–1940 Am. author

Hey·wood \'hā-,wud\ John 1497?–?1580 Eng. author

Heywood Thomas 1574?–1641 Eng. dramatist

Hick·ok \'hi-,käk\ James Butler 1837–1876 *Wild Bill* Am. scout & U.S. marshal

Hicks \'hiks\ Edward 1780–1849 Am. painter

Hicks Sir John Richard 1904–1989 Brit. economist

Hi·ero I \'hī-ə-,rō\ *or* **Hi·er·on** \-,rän\ *died* 467(or 466) B.C. tyrant of Syracuse (478–467 or 466)

Hieronymus Saint Eusebius — *see* JEROME

Hig·gin·son \'hi-gən-sən\ Thomas Wentworth Storrow 1823–1911 Am. clergyman & writer

Hil·bert \'hil-bərt\ David 1862–1943 Ger. mathematician

Hildebrand — *see* Pope GREGORY VII

Hill \'hil\ Ambrose Powell 1825–1865 Am. Confederate general

Hill Archibald Vivian 1886–1977 Eng. physiologist

Hill James Jerome 1838–1916 Am. financier

Hill Sir Rowland 1795–1879 Eng. postal reformer

Hil·la·ry \'hi-lə-rē\ Sir Edmund Percival 1919– N.Z. mountaineer & explorer

Hil·lel \'hi-ləl, -,lel\ 1st century B.C.–1st century A.D. Jewish teacher

Hil·liard \'hil-yərd\ Nicholas 1547–1619 Eng. painter

Hill·man \'hil-mən\ Sidney 1887–1946 Am. labor leader

Hil·ton \'hil-tᵊn\ Conrad Nicholson 1887–1979 Am. hotelier

Hilton James 1900–1954 Eng. novelist

Himm·ler \'him-lər\ Heinrich 1900–1945 Ger. Nazi politician

Hin·de·mith \'hin-də-ˌmit, -ˌmith, -mət, -ˌməth\ Paul 1895–1963 Am. (Ger.-born) violist & composer

Hin·den·burg \'hin-dən-ˌbərg, -ˌbu̇rg\ Paul von 1847–1934 *Paul Ludwig Hans Anton von Beneckendorff und von Hindenburg* Ger. field marshal; president of Germany (1925–34)

Hin·shel·wood \'hint-shəl-ˌwu̇d\ Sir Cyril Norman 1897–1967 Brit. chemist

Hip·par·chus \hi-'pär-kəs\ *died* 514 B.C. tyrant of Athens (527–514)

Hipparchus *or* **Hip·par·chos** \hi-'pär-kəs\ *flourished* 146–127 B.C. Greek astronomer

Hip·pi·as \'hi-pē-əs\ *died* 490 B.C. *brother of Hipparchus* ruled Athens with his brother

Hip·poc·ra·tes \hi-'pä-krə-ˌtēz\ *circa* 460–*circa* 377 B.C. *father of medicine* Greek physician

Hi·ro·hi·to \ˌhir-ō-'hē-(ˌ)tō\ 1901–1989 emperor of Japan (1926–89)

Hi·ro·shi·ge \ˌhir-ə-'shē-ˌgā\ Ando 1797–1858 Jp. artist

Hitch·cock \'hich-ˌkäk\ Sir Alfred Joseph 1899–1980 Brit. film director — **Hitch·cock·ian** \hich-'kä-kē-ən\ *adjective*

Hitchcock Edward 1793–1864 Am. geologist

Hitch·ings \'hi-chiŋz\ George Herbert 1905– Am. biochemist

Hit·ler \'hit-lər\ Adolf 1889–1945 Ger. chancellor & führer — **Hit·ler·ian** \hit-'lir-ē-ən, -'ler-\ *adjective*

Hit·ti \'hi-tē\ Philip Khuri 1886–1978 Am. (Lebanese-born) orientalist

Hit·torf \'hi-ˌtȯrf\ Johann Wilhelm 1824–1914 Ger. physicist

Hoare \'hōr, 'hȯr\ Sir Samuel John Gurney 1880–1959 Viscount *Templewood* Eng. statesman

Ho·bart \'hō-ˌbärt, -bərt\ Garret Augustus 1844–1899 Am. politician; vice president of the U.S. (1897–99)

Hob·be·ma \'hä-bə-mə\ Mein·dert *or* Meyn·dert \'mīn-ˌdert\ 1638–1709 Du. painter

Hobbes \'häbz\ Thomas 1588–1679 Eng. philosopher

Hoc·cleve \'häk-ˌlēv\ *or* **Oc·cleve** \'äk-\ Thomas 1368(or 1369)–*circa* 1450 Eng. poet

Ho Chi Minh \'hō-'chē-'min, -'shē-\ 1890–1969 originally *Nguyen That Thanh* president of No. Vietnam (1945–69)

Hock·ing \'hä-kiŋ\ William Ernest 1873–1966 Am. philosopher

Hodg·kin \'häj-kin\ Sir Alan Lloyd 1914– Brit. physiologist

Hodgkin Dorothy Mary Crowfoot 1910–1994 Brit. physicist

Hoe \'hō\ Richard March 1812–1886 *son of Robert* Am. inventor

Hoe Robert 1784–1833 Am. (Eng.-born) printing-press manufacturer

Ho·fer \'hō-fər\ Andreas 1767–1810 Tyrolese patriot

Hof·fa \'hä-fə\ James Riddle 1913–?1975 Am. labor leader

Hoff·man \'häf-mən, 'hȯf-\ Mal·vi·na \mal-'vē-nə\ 1887–1966 Am. sculptor

Hoff·mann \'häf-mən, 'hȯf-, -ˌmän\ August Heinrich 1798–1874 Ger. poet, philologist, & historian

Hoffmann Ernst Theodor Wilhelm 1776–1822 known as *Ernst Theodor Amadeus Hoffmann* Ger. composer, writer, & illustrator

Hoffmann Roald 1937– Am. (Pol.-born) chemist

Hof·mann \'häf-mən, 'hȯf-, -ˌmän\ August Wilhelm von 1818–1892 Ger. chemist

Hofmann Hans 1880–1966 Am. (Ger.-born) painter

Hofmann Josef Casimir 1876–1957 Pol. pianist

Hof·manns·thal \'hȯf-ˌmənz-ˌtäl, 'hȯf-\ Hugo von 1874–1929 Austrian poet & dramatist

Hof·stadt·er \'hȯf-ˌsta-tər\ Robert 1915–1990 Am. physicist

Ho·garth \'hō-ˌgärth\ William 1697–1764 Eng. painter & engraver — **Ho·garth·ian** \hō-'gär-thē-ən\ *adjective*

Hog·ben \'hȯg-bən, 'häg-\ Lancelot Thomas 1895–1975 Eng. scientist

Hogg \'hȯg, 'häg\ James 1770–1835 *the Ettrick Shepherd* Scot. poet

Ho·hen·zol·lern \ˌhō-ənt-'sȯ-lərn\ Michael — *see* MICHAEL

Ho·ku·sai \'hō-ku̇-ˌsī, ˌhō-ku̇-'\ Katsushika 1760–1849 Jp. artist

Hol·bein \'hōl-ˌbīn, 'hȯl-\ Hans 1465?–1524 *the Elder* & Hans 1497?–1543 *the Younger* Ger. painters

Hol·berg \'hōl-ˌberg\ Baron 1684–1754 *Ludwig Holberg* Dan. (Norw.-born) author

Hol·i·day \'hä-lə-ˌdā\ Eleanora 1915–1959 *Billie* Am. jazz singer

Hol·in·shed \'hä-lən-ˌshed\ *or* **Hol·lings·head** \-liŋz-ˌhed\ Raphael *died circa* 1580 Eng. chronicler

Hol·land \'hä-lənd\ John Philip 1840–1914 Am. (Irish-born) inventor

Holland Sir Sidney George 1893–1961 prime minister of New Zealand (1945–57)

Hol·ley \'hä-lē\ Robert William 1922–1993 Am. biochemist

Holman–Hunt William — *see* Holman HUNT

Holmes \'hōmz, 'hōlmz\ Oliver Wendell 1809–1894 Am. physician & author

Holmes Oliver Wendell 1841–1935 *son of preceding* Am. jurist

Holst \'hōlst\ Gustav Theodore 1874–1934 Eng. composer

Holt \'hōlt\ Harold Edward 1908–1967 Austral. politician; prime minister (1966–67)

Holt Luther Emmett 1855–1924 Am. pediatrician

Hol·yoake \'hōl-ˌyōk, 'hō-lē-ˌōk\ Sir Keith Jacka 1904–1983 prime minister of New Zealand (1960–72)

Home \'hyüm, 'hōm\ Sir Alec Douglas- 1903–1995 Brit. prime minister (1963–64)

Home William Douglas- 1912–1992 Brit. dramatist

Ho·mer \'hō-mər\ 9th–8th? century B.C. Greek epic poet

Homer Winslow 1836–1910 Am. artist

Ho·neck·er \'hō-nə-kər\ Erich 1912–1994 general secretary of East German Communist party (1971–89)

Ho·neg·ger \ˌȯ-nā-'ger, '(h)ä-ni-gər\ Arthur 1892–1955 Fr. composer

Ho·no·ri·us \hə-'nȯr-ē-əs, -'nȯr-\ Flavius 384–423 Rom. emperor of the West (395–423)

Hont·horst \'hȯnt-ˌhȯrst\ Gerrit van 1590–1656 Du. painter

Hooch *or* **Hoogh** \'hōk\ Pieter de 1629–after 1684 Du. painter

Hood \'hu̇d\ John Bell 1831–1879 Am. Confederate general

Hood Samuel 1724–1816 1st Viscount *Hood* Brit. admiral

Hood Thomas 1799–1845 Eng. poet

Hooke \'hu̇k\ Robert 1635–1703 Eng. scientist

Hook·er \'hu̇-kər\ Joseph 1814–1879 Am. general

Hooker Sir Joseph Dalton 1817–1911 Eng. botanist

Hooker Richard 1554–1600 Eng. theologian

Hooker Thomas 1586?–1647 Eng. Puritan clergyman & founder of Connecticut

Hoo·ton \'hü-tᵊn\ Earnest Albert 1887–1954 Am. anthropologist

Hoo·ver \'hü-vər\ Herbert Clark 1874–1964 31st president of the U.S. (1929–33)

Hoover John Edgar 1895–1972 Am. criminologist; F.B.I. director (1924–72)

Hope \'hōp\ Anthony — *see* Sir Anthony Hope HAWKINS

Hope Victor Alexander John 1887–1951 8th Earl of *Hope·toun* \'hōp-tən\ & 2d Marquis of *Lin·lith·gow* \lin-'lith-(ˌ)gō\ Brit. soldier; viceroy of India (1936–43)

Hop·kins \'häp-kənz\ Sir Frederick Gow·land \'gau̇-lənd\ 1861–1947 Eng. biochemist

Hopkins Gerard Manley 1844–1889 Eng. poet

Hopkins Harry Lloyd 1890–1946 Am. politician & administrator

Hopkins Johns \'jänz\ 1795–1873 Am. financier

Hopkins Mark 1802–1887 Am. educator

Hop·kin·son \'häp-kən-sən\ Francis 1737–1791 Am. lawyer & satirist

Hop·pe \'hä-pē\ William Frederick 1887–1959 Am. billiard player

Hop·per \'hä-pər\ Edward 1882–1967 Am. artist

Hopper Grace 1906–1992 Am. admiral, mathematician, & computer scientist

Hopper (William) DeWolf 1858–1935 Am. actor

Hop·wood \'häp-ˌwu̇d\ (James) Avery 1882–1928 Am. dramatist

Hor·ace \'hȯr-əs, 'här-\ 65–8 B.C. *Quintus Horatius Flaccus* Rom. poet & satirist — **Ho·ra·tian** \hə-'rā-shən\ *adjective*

Hore–Be·li·sha \ˌhȯr-bə-'lē-shə, 'hȯr-\ Leslie 1893–1957 Eng. politician

Hor·na·day \'hȯr-nə-ˌdā\ William Temple 1854–1937 Am. zoologist

Hor·ney \'hȯr-ˌnī\ Karen 1885–1952 née *Danielsen* Am. (Ger.-born) psychoanalyst & author

Ho·ro·witz \'hȯr-ə-ˌwits, 'här-\ Vladimir 1903–1989 Am. (Russ.-born) pianist

Horsa *see* HENGIST

Hor·ta \'hȯr-tə\ José Ramos 1950– Indonesian peace activist

Hortense de Beauharnais — *see* BEAUHARNAIS

Hor·thy de Nagy·bán·ya \'hȯr-tē-dä-'näj-ˌbän-ya\ Miklós 1868–1957 Hung. admiral; regent of Hungary (1920–44)

Hou·di·ni \hü-'dē-nē\ Harry 1874–1926 originally *Erik Weisz* Am. (Hung.-born) magician

Hou·don \'hü-ˌdän, ü-dōⁿ\ Jean-Antoine 1741–1828 Fr. sculptor

Houns·field \'hau̇nz-ˌfē(ə)ld\ Godfrey Newbold 1919– Brit. engineer & inventor

House \'hau̇s\ Edward Mandell 1858–1938 *Colonel House* Am. diplomat

Hous·man \'hau̇s-mən\ Alfred Edward 1859–1936 Eng. classical scholar & poet

Housman Laurence 1865–1959 *brother of preceding* Eng. writer & illustrator

Hous·say \ü-'sī\ Bernardo Alberto 1887–1971 Argentine physiologist

Hous·ton \'hyü-stən, 'yü-\ Samuel 1793–1863 Am. general; president of the Republic of Texas (1836–38; 1841–44)

How·ard \'hau̇-(ə)rd\ Catherine — *see* CATHERINE

Howard Henry 1517?–1547 Earl of *Surrey* Eng. soldier & poet

Howard John Winston 1939– prime minister of Australia (1996–)

Howard Oliver Otis 1830–1909 Am. general & educator

Howard Sidney Coe 1891–1939 Am. dramatist

Howe \'hau̇\ Ed 1853–1937 *Edgar Watson* Am. journalist

Howe Elias 1819–1867 Am. inventor

Howe Julia 1819–1910 née *Ward* Am. suffragist & reformer

Howe Richard 1726–1799 *Earl Howe* Eng. admiral

Howe William 1729–1814 5th Viscount *Howe; brother of preceding* Eng. general in America

How·ells \'hau̇-əlz\ William Dean 1837–1920 Am. author

Hr·dlič·ka \'hərd-lich-ˌkä\ Aleš \'ä-ˌlesh\ 1869–1943 Am. (Bohemian-born) anthropologist

Hsüan–t'ung \shü-'än-'tu̇ŋ\ — *see* P'U-I

Hua Kuo·feng \'hwä-'gwō-'feŋ\ 1920– pinyin *Hua Guo·feng* Chin. premier (1976–80)

Huás·car \'wäs-ˌkär\ *died* 1532 Inca prince

Hub·bard \'hə-bərd\ Elbert Green 1856–1915 Am. writer

Hub·ble \'hə-bəl\ Edwin Powell 1889–1953 Am. astronomer

Hu·bel \'hyü-bəl, 'yü-\ David Hunter 1926– Am. (Canad.-born) neurobiologist

Hu·ber \'hü-bər, 'hyü-\ Robert 1937– Ger. biochemist

Hud·son \'həd-sən\ Henry *died* 1611 Eng. navigator & explorer

Hudson Manley Ottmer 1886–1960 Am. jurist

Hudson William Henry 1841–1922 Eng. naturalist & writer

Huer·ta \'wer-tə, ü-'er-\ Victoriano 1854–1916 Mex. general; provisional president of Mexico (1913–14)

Hug·gins \'hə-gənz\ Charles Brenton 1901–1997 Am. (Canad.-born) physician

Huggins Sir William 1824–1910 Eng. astron.

Hugh Ca·pet \'hyü-'kā-pət, -'ka-, -ka-'pā\ *circa* 938–996 king of France (987–996)

Hughes \'hyüz *also* 'yüz\ Charles Evans 1862–1948 Am. jurist; chief justice U.S. Supreme Court (1930–41)

Hughes Howard Robard 1905–1976 Am. businessman

Hughes (James) Langston 1902–1967 Am. writer

Hughes Ted 1930– Brit. poet; poet laureate (1984–)

Hughes Thomas 1822–1896 Eng. jurist, reformer, & writer

Hughes William Morris 1864–1952 Austral. statesman

Hu·go \'hyü-(,)gō, 'yü-\ Victor-Marie 1802–1885 Fr. poet, novelist, & dramatist — **Hu·go·esque** \,hyü-(,)gō-'esk, ,yü-\ *adjective*

Hui·zin·ga \'hī-ziŋ-gə\ Johan 1872–1945 Du. historian

Hü·le·gü \hü-'lā-(,)gü\ *circa* 1217–*circa* 1265 *grandson of Genghis Khan* Mongol ruler

Hull \'həl\ Cordell 1871–1955 Am. statesman; secretary of state (1933–44)

Hull Isaac 1773–1843 Am. naval officer

Hull William 1753–1825 Am. general

Hulse \'həls\ Russell Alan 1950– Am. physicist

Hu·mā·yun \hü-'mä-,yün\ 1508–1556 Mughal emperor of India (1530–56)

Hum·boldt \'həm-,bōlt, 'həm-\ (Friedrich Wilhelm Karl Heinrich) Alexander von 1769–1859 Ger. naturalist, traveler, & statesman

Humboldt (Karl) Wilhelm von 1767–1835 *brother of preceding* Ger. philologist & diplomat

Hume \'hyüm *also* 'yüm\ David 1711–1776 Scot. philosopher & historian — **Hum·ean** *or* **Hum·ian** \'(h)yü-mē-ən\ *adjective*

Hum·per·dinck \'hüm-pər-,diŋk, 'həm-\ Engelbert 1854–1921 Ger. composer

Hum·phrey \'həm(p)-frē\ 1391–1447 *son of Henry IV* Duke of *Gloucester* (*the Good Duke*) & Earl of *Pembroke* Eng. statesman & book collector

Humphrey Hubert Horatio 1911–1978 Am. politician; vice president of the U.S. (1965–69)

Hun·e·ker \'hə-ni-kər\ James Gibbons 1860–1921 Am. critic

Hung–wu \'hùŋ-'wü\ 1328–1398 *Chu Yüan-chang* \'jü-yü-'än-'jäŋ\ Chin. emperor (1368–98); founder of Ming dynasty

Hunt \'hənt\ (James Henry) Leigh 1784–1859 Eng. writer

Hunt (William) Hol·man \'hōl-mən\ 1827–1910 Eng. painter

Hun·ter \'hən-tər\ John 1728–1793 Brit. anatomist & surgeon

Hun·ting·ton \'hən-tiŋ-tən\ Collis Potter 1821–1900 Am. railroad builder

Huntington Ellsworth 1876–1947 Am. geographer & explorer

Huntington Henry Edwards 1850–1927 Am. bibliophile

Huntington Samuel 1731–1796 Am. Revolutionary politician

Hun·tzi·ger \(h)ənt-sē-'zher\ Charles-Léon-Clément 1880–1941 Fr. general

Hu·nya·di \'hün-,yä-dē, -,yō-\ Já·nos \'yä-(,)nōsh\ 1407?–1456 Hung. soldier & hero

Hur·ley \'hər-lē\ Patrick Jay 1883–1963 Am. lawyer & diplomat

Hurst \'hərst\ Sir Cecil James Barrington 1870–1963 Eng. jurist

Hurst Fannie 1889–1968 Am. writer

Hus \'həs, 'hüs\ Jan 1372(or 1373)–1415 Bohemian religious reformer

Hu·sák \'hü-(,)säk, 'hyü-\ Gustav 1913–1991 president of Czechoslovakia (1975–87)

Hu·sayn ibn ʿAlī \hü-'sän-,i-bən-ä-'lē\ *circa* 1854–1931 1st king of the Hejaz (1916–24)

Hu Shih \'hü-'shir\ 1891–1962 Chin. philosopher

Hus·sein I \hü-'sän\ 1935– king of Jordan (1952–)

Hussein Saddam al-Tikriti 1937– president of Iraq (1979–)

Hus·serl \'hú-sə-rəl\ Edmund 1859–1938 Ger. philosopher — **Hus·serl·ian** \hü-'sər-lē-ən\ *adjective*

Hus·ton \'hyü-stən, 'yü-\ John 1906–1987 Am. motion-picture director, writer, & actor

Hu·szár \'hù-,sär\ Károly 1882–1941 Hung. journalist & politician

Hutch·ins \'hə-chənz\ Robert Maynard 1899–1977 Am. educator

Hutch·in·son \'hə-chə(n)-sən\ Anne 1591–1643 née *Marbury* Am. (Eng.-born) religious dissident

Hutchinson Thomas 1711–1780 Am. colonial administrator

Hut·ten \'hú-t°n\ Ulrich von 1488–1523 Ger. humanist & supporter of Luther

Hux·ley \'həks-lē\ Al·dous \'ōl-dəs\ Leonard 1894–1963 *brother of J.S.* Eng. novelist & critic — **Hux·lei·an** \,həks-'lē-ən, 'həks-lē-\ *or* **Hux·ley·an** \'həks-lē-ən\ *adjective*

Huxley Andrew Fielding 1917– Brit. physiologist & educator

Huxley Sir Julian Sorell 1887–1975 *grandson of T.H.* Eng. biologist

Huxley Thomas Henry 1825–1895 Eng. biologist

Huy·gens \'hī-gənz, 'hói-\ Christian 1629–1695 Du. mathematician, physicist, & astronomer

Huys·mans \wē-'smä°s\ Camille 1871–1968 Belg. politician

Huysmans Joris-Karl 1848–1907 originally *Georges-Charles* Fr. novelist

Hy·att \'hī-ət\ Alpheus 1838–1902 Am. naturalist

Hyde \'hīd\ Douglas 1860–1949 pseudonym *An Craoibhín Aoibhinn* Irish author; president of Republic of Ireland (1938–45)

Hyde Edward 1609–1674 1st Earl of *Clar·en·don* \'klar-ən-dən, 'kler-\ Eng. statesman & historian

Hy·der Ali *or* **Hai·dar Ali** \'hī-dər-ä-'lē\ 1722–1782 Indian ruler & soldier

Hy·mans \'hī-,män(t)s, ē-mä°s\ Paul 1865–1941 Belg. statesman

Hy·pse·lan·tes \,ēp-sə-'län-dēs\ *variant of* YPSILANTIS

Ibáñez Vicente Blasco — see BLASCO IBÁÑEZ

Iber·ville \ē-bər-,vil, -,vēl; 'ī-bər-,vil\ Sieur d' 1661–1706 *Pierre Le Moyne* \'mwàn\ Fr.-Canad. explorer & founder of Louisiana

Ibn–Khal·dūn \,i-bən-,kal-'dün, -,kal-\ 1332–1406 Arab historian

Ibn–Rushd \,i-bən-'rùsht\ — see AVERROËS

Ibn Sa·ʿūd \,i-bən-sä-'üd, -'saùd\ *circa* 1880–1953 king of Saudi Arabia (1932–53)

Ibn Zuhr \,i-bən-'zúr\ *Latin* **Av·en·zo·ar** \,a-vən-'zō-ər, -zō-'är\ *or* **Abu·me·ron** \,a-byü-'mer-,än\ *circa* 1090–1162 Muslim physician

Ibrā·hīm Pa·sha \i-,brä-'him-'pä-shə, -'pa-shə, -pə-'shä\ 1789–1848 Egypt. general & viceroy

Ib·sen \'ib-sən, 'ip-\ Henrik 1828–1906 Norw. poet & dramatist — **Ib·se·ni·an** \ib-'sē-nē-ən, ip-, -'se-nē-\ *or* **Ib·sen·esque** \,ib-sə-'nesk, ,ip-\ *adjective*

Ick·es \'i-kəs\ Harold LeClair 1874–1952 Am. politician

Ic·ti·nus \ik-'tī-nəs\ 5th century B.C. Greek architect

Ig·na·tius \ig-'nā-sh(ē-)əs\ Saint *died circa* A.D. 110 *Theophorus* bishop of Antioch & church father

Ignatius of Loyola Saint 1491–1556 originally *Iñigo de Oñaz y Loyola* Span. religious & founder of Society of Jesus — **Ig·na·tian** \-sh(ē-)ən\ *adjective*

Ike·da \ē-'kä-də, -'ke-\ Hayato 1899–1965 Jp. politician; prime minister (1960–64)

Ikhnaton — see AKHENATON

Il·ies·cu \i-lē-'es-(,)kü, il-'yes-\ Ion 1930– president of Romania (1989–96)

Im·mel·mann \'i-məl-,män, -mən\ Max 1890–1916 Ger. aviator

In·dy, d' \'dan-dē; dan-'dē, da°-\ (Paul-Marie-Théodore-) Vincent 1851–1931 Fr. composer

Inés de Castro — see CASTRO

Inge \'iŋj\ William 1913–1973 Am. playwright

Inge \'iŋ\ William Ralph 1860–1954 Eng. prelate & author

In·ger·soll \'iŋ-gər-,sól, -səl\ Robert Green 1833–1899 Am. orator

In·gres \'a°(ŋ)grə\ Jean-Auguste-Dominique 1780–1867 Fr. painter

In·ness \'i-nəs\ George: father 1825–1894 & son 1854–1926 Am. painters

In·no·cent \'i-nə-sənt\ name of 13 popes: especially **II** *died* 1143 (pope 1130–43); **III** 1160(or 1161)–1216 (pope 1198–1216); **IV** *died* 1254 (pope 1243–54); **XI** 1611–1689 (pope 1676–89)

İnö·nü \,i-nə-'nü, -'nyü\ İs·met \is-'met\ 1884–1973 Turk. statesman; president of Turkey (1938–50); premier (1961–65)

In·sull \'in(t)-səl\ Samuel 1859–1938 Am. (Eng.-born) financier

Io·nes·co \,ē-ə-'nes-(,)kō\ Eugène 1909–1994 Fr. (Rom.-born) dramatist

Ipa·tieff \i-'pä-tē-,ef, -'pä-chəf\ Vladimir Nikolayevich 1867–1952 Am. (Russ.-born) chemist

Ire·dell \'īr-,del\ James 1751–1799 Am. jurist

Ire·ton \'īr-t°n\ Henry 1611–1651 Eng. soldier & politician

Iri·go·yen \,ir-i-'gó-,yen\ Hi·pó·li·to \ē-'pó-lē-,tō\ 1852–1933 president of Argentina (1916–22; 1928–30)

Iron·side \'ī(-ə)rn-,sīd\ William Edmund 1880–1959 1st Baron *Ironside* Brit. field marshal

Ir·ving \'ər-viŋ\ Sir Henry 1838–1905 originally *John Henry Brodribb* Eng. actor

Irving Washington 1783–1859 Am. essayist, novelist, & historian

Ir·win \'ər-wən\ William Henry 1873–1948 *Will Irwin* Am. journalist

Isaacs \'ī-ziks, -zəks\ Sir Isaac Alfred 1855–1948 Austral. jurist & statesman; governor-general of Australia (1931–36)

Isaacs Rufus Daniel — see Marquis of READING

Is·a·bel·la I \,i-zə-'be-lə\ 1451–1504 *wife of Ferdinand V of Castile* queen of Castile (1474–1504) & of Aragon (1479–1504)

Ish·er·wood \'i-shər-,wúd\ Christopher William Bradshaw 1904–1986 Am. (Brit.-born) writer

Ishii \ē-shē-,ē, 'i-\ Viscount Kikujiro 1866–1945 Jp. diplomat

Is·i·dore of Seville \'i-zə-,dōr, -,dòr\ Saint *circa* 560–636 Latin *Isidorus Hispalensis* Span. prelate & scholar

Iskander Bey — see SKANDERBEG

Is·mā·ʿīl Pa·sha \is-,mä-,ēl-'pä-shə, -'pa-shə, -pə-'shä\ 1830–1895 viceroy of Egypt (1863–79)

Isoc·ra·tes \ī-'sä-krə-,tēz\ 436–338 B.C. Athenian orator

Is·ra·el ben Eli·ezer \'iz-rē-əl-,ben-,e-lē-'ā-zər\ *circa* 1700–1760 *Baʿal Shem Tov* \'bā-(ə)l-'shem-'tóv\ Pol.-Jewish religious leader

Ito \'ē-(,)tō\ Prince Hirobumi 1841–1909 Jp. statesman

Itur·bi \i-'túr-bē\ José 1895–1980 Span.-born pianist & conductor

Itur·bi·de \,ē-,túr-'bē-(,)thā\ Agustín de 1783–1824 Mex. soldier; emperor of Mexico (1822–23)

Ivan III \ē-'vän, 'ī-vən\ **Va·si·lye·vich** \və-'sil-yə-,vich\ 1440–1505 *the Great* grand prince of Russia (1462–1505)

Ivan IV Vasilyevich 1530–1584 *the Terrible* ruler of Russia (1533–84)

Ives \'īvz\ Charles Edward 1874–1954 Am. composer — **Ives·ian** \'īv-zē-ən\ *adjective*

Ives James Merritt 1824–1895 Am. lithographer

Iyeyasu *or* **Ieyasu** — see TOKUGAWA

Jā·bir ibn Hay·yān \'ja-,bir-,i-bən-hī-'yan\ Abū Mūsā *circa* 721–*circa* 851 Latin *Ge·ber* \'ja-,bir, 'ga-, 'ge-\ Arab alchemist & mystic

Jack·son \'jak-sən\ Andrew 1767–1845 Am. general; 7th president of the U.S. (1829–37) — **Jack·son·ian** \jak-'sō-nē-ən\ *adjective*

Jackson Helen Maria Hunt 1830–1885 née *Fiske* Am. novelist

Jackson Jesse Louis 1941– Am. clergyman & political activist

Jackson Mahalia 1911–1972 Am. gospel singer

Jackson Robert Hough·wout \'haú-ət\ 1892–1954 Am. jurist

Jackson Thomas Jonathan 1824–1863 *Stonewall* \'stōn-,wòl\ *Jackson* Am. Confederate general

Ja·cob \zhà-kòb\ François 1920– Fr. geneticist

Ja·co·po del·la Quer·cia \yä-'kō-(,)pō-,dā-lə-'kwer-chä\ *circa* 1374–1438 Ital. sculptor

Jac·quard \zhà-'kär, 'ja-,kärd\ Joseph-Marie 1752–1834 Fr. inventor

Jacques I — see Jean-Jacques DESSALINES

Jag·a·tai — see CHAGATAI

Ja·hān·gīr \jə-'hän-,gir\ 1569–1627 emperor of India (1605–27)

Ja·lāl ad–Dīn ar–Rū·mī \jə-'lä-lə-'dē-när-'rü-mē\ *circa* 1207–1273 Pers. poet

\ə\ abut \°\ kitten \ər\ further \a\ ash \ā\ ace
\ä\ mop, mar \aú\ out \ch\ chin \e\ bet \ē\ easy
\g\ go \i\ hit \ī\ ice \j\ job \ŋ\ sing \ō\ go
\ò\ law \òi\ boy \th\ thin \th\ the \ü\ loot \ú\ foot
\y\ yet \zh\ vision *see also* Guide to Pronunciation

James \'jāmz\ name of 6 kings of Scotland & 2 kings of Great Britain: especially **VI** 1566–1625 of Scotland (reigned 1567–1603) *or* **I** of Great Britain (reigned 1603–25); **II** 1633–1701 (reigned 1685–88)

James Henry 1811–1882 Am. philosopher

James Henry 1843–1916 *son of preceding* Brit. (Am.-born) writer — **James·ian** \'jām-zē-ən\ *adjective*

James Jesse Woodson 1847–1882 Am. outlaw

James Phyllis Dorothy 1920– Brit. writer

James William 1842–1910 *brother of Henry* Am. psychologist & philosopher — **James·ian** \'jām-zē-ən\ *adjective*

James Edward 1688–1766 *James Francis Edward Stuart; the Old Pretender* Brit. prince

Jame·son \'jām-sən, 'je-mə-sən\ Sir Leander Starr 1853–1917 *Doctor Jameson* Scot. physician & administrator in So. Africa

Jā·mī \'jä-mē\ 1414–1492 Pers. poet & mystic

Ja·ná·ček \'yä-nə-ˌchek\ Leoš 1854–1928 Czech composer

Jan·sen \'jan(t)-sən, 'yän(t)-\ Cor·ne·lis \kȯr-'nā-ləs\ 1585–1638 L. *Cornelius Jansenius* Du. Roman Catholic theologian

Jaques–Dal·croze \'zhäk-ˌdal-'krōz, 'zhak-\ Émile 1865–1950 Swiss composer & creator of eurythmics

Ja·rīr \jə-'rir\ *circa* 650–*circa* 729 Arab poet

Jar·rell \jə-'rel, ja-\ Randall 1914–1965 Am. writer

Ja·ru·zel·ski \ˌyär-ü-'zel-skē\ Woj·ciech \'vȯi-ˌchek\ Witold 1923– general; 1st secretary of the Communist party in Poland (1981–89)

Jas·pers \'yäs-pərs\ Karl Theodor 1883–1969 Ger. philosopher

Jauregg Julius Wagner von — see WAGNER VON JAUREGG

Jau·rès \zhō-res\ Jean-Joseph-Marie-Auguste 1859–1914 Fr. socialist

Jay \'jā\ John 1745–1829 Am. jurist & statesman; 1st chief justice U.S. Supreme Court (1789–95)

Jeanne d'Arc — see JOAN OF ARC

Jeans \'jēnz\ Sir James Hopwood 1877–1946 Eng. physicist, astronomer, & author

Jebb \'jeb\ Sir Richard Claverhouse 1841–1905 Scot. scholar

Jef·fers \'je-fərz\ (John) Robinson 1887–1962 Am. poet

Jef·fer·son \'je-fər-sən\ Thomas 1743–1826 3d president of the U.S. (1801–09) — **Jef·fer·so·nian** \je-fər-'sō-nē-ən, -nyən\ *adjective*

Jef·frey \'je-frē\ Lord Francis 1773–1850 Scot. critic & jurist

Jef·freys \'je-frēz\ George 1645–1689 1st Baron *Jeffreys of Wem* Eng. jurist

Jel·li·coe \'je-li-ˌkō\ 1st Earl 1859–1935 *John Rushworth Jellicoe* Brit. admiral

Jen·ner \'je-nər\ Edward 1749–1823 Eng. physician — **Jen·ne·ri·an** \je-'nir-ē-ən\ *adjective*

Jenner Sir William 1815–1898 Eng. physician

Jen·sen \'yen-zən\ (Johannes) Hans Daniel 1907–1973 Ger. physicist

Jen·sen \'yen(t)-sən, 'jen(t)-\ Johannes Vilhelm 1873–1950 Dan. poet & novelist

Jen·son \'jen-sən, zhäⁿ-sōⁿ\ Nicolas *circa* 1420–1480 Fr. printer & engraver in Venice

Jerne \'yer-ne\ Niels Kai 1911–1994 Dan. (Eng.-born) immunologist

Je·rome \jə-'rōm *also* 'jer-əm\ Saint *circa* 347–419(or 420) Latin *Eusebius Hi·eron·y·mus* \ˌhī-ə-'rä-nə-məs, hi-\ church father

Jer·vis \'jär-vəs, 'jär-\ John 1735–1823 Earl of *St. Vincent* Brit. admiral

Jes·per·sen \'yes-pər-sən\ (Jens) Otto Harry 1860–1943 Dan. philologist

Je·sus \'jē-zəs, -zəz\ *or* **Jesus Christ** \'krīst\ *or* **Christ Jesus** *circa* 6 B.C.–*circa* A.D. 30 *Jesus of Nazareth; the Son of Mary* source of the Christian religion & Savior in the Christian faith

Jev·ons \'je-vənz\ William Stanley 1835–1882 Eng. economist

Jew·ett \'jü-ət\ Sarah Orne 1849–1909 Am. writer

Ji·ang Ze·min \jē-'äŋ-zə-'min\ 1926– general secretary of Chin. Communist party (1989–); president of China (1993–)

Ji·mé·nez \hē-'mä-nəs\ Juan Ramón 1881–1958 Span. poet

Jiménez de Cis·ne·ros \-ˌdä-sis-'ner-əs\ Francisco 1436–1517 Span. prelate & statesman

Jin·nah \'ji-(ˌ)nä, 'ji-nə\ Mohammed Ali 1876–1948 Indian politician; 1st governor-general of dominion of Pakistan (1947–48)

Jo·achim \yō-'ä-kim, -ˌkim; 'yō-ə-ˌkim, -ˌkim\ Joseph 1831–1907 Hung. violinist

Joan of Arc \ˌjōn-əv-'ärk\ *French* **Jeanne d'Arc** \zhän-därk\ Saint *circa* 1412–1431 *the Maid of Orleans* Fr. national heroine

Jodl \'yō-dᵊl\ Alfred 1890–1946 Ger. general

Jof·fre \zhȯfrᵉ\ Joseph-Jacques-Césaire 1852–1931 Fr. field marshal; marshal of France

John \'jän\ name of 21 popes: especially **XXIII** (*Angelo Giuseppe Roncalli*) 1881–1963 (pope 1958–63)

John 1167–1216 *John Lack·land* \'lak-ˌland\ king of England (1199–1216)

John I 1357–1433 *the Great* king of Portugal (1385–1433)

John Augustus Edwin 1878–1961 Brit. painter & etcher

John of Austria 1547–1578 Don *John* Span. general

John of Gaunt \'gȯnt, 'gänt\ 1340–1399 Duke of *Lancaster; son of Edward III of England*

John of Lancaster 1389–1435 Duke of *Bedford; son of Henry IV of England*

John of Leiden *circa* 1509–1536 Du. Anabaptist

John of Salisbury 1115(or 1120)–1180 Eng. ecclesiastic

John of the Cross 1542–1591 *Juan de Yepes y Álvarez* Span. mystic & poet

John Paul \'pȯl\ name of 2 popes: especially **II** (*Karol Wojtyla*) 1920– (pope 1978–)

John III So·bies·ki \sō-'byes-kē, ˌsō-bē-'es-\ 1629–1696 king of Poland (1674–96)

John·son \'jän(t)-sən\ Andrew 1808–1875 17th president of the U.S. (1865–69) — **John·so·nian** \jän-'sō-nē-ən, -nyən\ *adjective*

Johnson (Jonathan) Eastman 1824–1906 Am. painter

John·son \'yün-sȯn\ Eyvind 1900–1976 Swed. author

John·son \'jän(t)-sən\ James Weldon 1871–1938 Am. author

Johnson Lyndon Baines 1908–1973 Am. politician; 36th president of the U.S. (1963–69) — **John·so·nian** \jän-'sō-nē-ən, -nyən\ *adjective*

Johnson Philip Cortelyou 1906– Am. architect

Johnson Richard Mentor 1780–1850 vice president of the U.S. (1837–41)

Johnson Samuel 1709–1784 *Dr. Johnson* Eng. lexicographer & author — **John·so·nian** \jän-'sō-nē-ən, -nyən\ *adjective*

Johnson Sir William 1715–1774 Brit. administrator in America

John·ston \'jän(t)-stən, -sən\ Albert Sidney 1803–1862 Am. Confederate general

Johnston Joseph Eggleston 1807–1891 Am. Confederate general

Join·ville \zhwaⁿ-'vē(ə)l\ Jean de *circa* 1224–1317 Fr. chronicler

Jó·kai \'yō-ˌkȯi\ Mór 1825–1904 Hung. novelist & dramatist

Jo·liot–Cu·rie \'zhȯl-ˌyō-kyü-'rē, -'kyür-(ˌ)ē\ (Jean) Frédéric 1900–1958 originally *Joliot* Fr. physicist

Joliot–Curie Irène 1897–1956 formerly *Irène Curie-Joliot, daughter of Marie & Pierre Curie & wife of preceding* Fr. physicist

Jol·liet *or* **Jo·liet** \zhȯl-'yā\ Louis 1645–1700 Fr. explorer

Jo·mi·ni \ˌzhō-mə-'nē\ Henri de 1779–1869 Swiss-born soldier & military strategist

Jones \'jōnz\ Anson 1798–1858 president of the Republic of Texas (1844–46)

Jones Daniel 1881–1967 Eng. phonetician

Jones Howard Mumford 1892–1980 Am. educator & critic

Jones In·i·go \'i-ni-ˌgō\ 1573–1652 Eng. architect

Jones John Paul 1747–1792 originally *John Paul* Am. (Scot.-born) naval officer

Jones Thomas Hudson 1892–1969 Am. sculptor

Jon·son \'jän(t)-sən\ Benjamin 1572–1637 *Ben Jonson* Eng. dramatist — **Jon·so·nian** \jän-'sō-nē-ən, -nyən\ *adjective*

Jop·lin \'jä-plən\ Scott 1868–1917 Am. pianist & composer

Jor·daens \'yȯr-ˌdän(t)s\ Jacob 1593–1678 Flem. painter

Jor·dan \'jȯr-dᵊn\ David Starr 1851–1931 Am. biologist & educator

Jo·seph \'jō-zəf *also* -səf\ *circa* 1840–1904 *In·mut-too-yah-lat-lat* Nez Percé Indian chief

Joseph II 1741–1790 Holy Roman emperor (1765–90)

Jo·se·phine \'jō-zə-ˌfēn\ Empress — see BEAUHARNAIS

Jo·seph·son \'jō-zəf-sən *also* -səf-\ Brian David 1940– Brit. physicist

Jo·se·phus \jō-'sē-fəs\ Flavius *circa* A.D. 37–*circa* 100 Jewish historian

Jos·quin des Prez \zhȯ-'skaⁿ-de-'prā\ *or* **Des·prez** \de-'prā\ *circa* 1440–1521 Fr. composer

Jou·bert \zhü-'ber\ Joseph 1754–1824 Fr. essayist & moralist

Joubert \yü-'ber, yō-\ Petrus Jacobus 1834–1900 known as *Piet Joubert* Boer general & statesman

Jou·haux \zhü-ō\ Léon 1879–1954 Fr. trade-union leader

Joule \'jül\ James Prescott 1818–1889 Eng. physicist

Jour·dan \zhùr-'däⁿ\ Comte Jean-Baptiste 1762–1833 Fr. soldier; marshal of France

Jo·vi·an \'jō-vē-ən\ *circa* 331–364 *Flavius Jovianus* Rom. emperor (363–364)

Jow·ett \'jaù-ət, 'jō-\ Benjamin 1817–1893 Eng. Greek scholar

Joyce \'jȯis\ James Augustine 1882–1941 Irish writer — **Joyc·ean** \'jȯi-sē-ən\ *adjective*

Juan Car·los \'(h)wän-'kär-ˌlōs\ 1938– king of Spain (1975–)

Juan Manuel Don — see MANUEL

Juá·rez \'hwär-əs, 'wär-\ Benito Pablo 1806–1872 Mex. lawyer; president of Mexico (1861–65; 1867–72)

Judas Maccabaeus — see MACCABEES

Ju·gur·tha \jü-'gər-thə\ *or* **Iu·gur·tha** \yù-\ *circa* 160–104 B.C. king of Numidia (118–105 B.C.)

Ju·lian \'jül-yən\ *circa* 331–363 *Flavius Claudius Julianus, the Apostate* Rom. emperor (361–363)

Ju·li·ana \ˌjü-lē-'a-nə\ 1909– *daughter of Wilhelmina* queen of the Netherlands (1948–80)

Jung \'yùŋ\ Carl Gustav 1875–1961 Swiss psychologist

Ju·nius \'jü-nyəs, -nē-əs\ Franciscus 1589–1677 Eng. (Ger.-born) philologist

Jun·kers \'yùṅ-kərz, -kərs\ Hugo 1859–1935 Ger. airplane designer & builder

Ju·not \zhü-'nō\ Andoche 1771–1813 Duc d'Abran·tès \ˌda-ˌbräⁿ-'tes\ Fr. general

Jus·se·rand \zhēs-räⁿ, zhü-sə-\ Jean-(Adrien-Antoine-) Jules 1855–1932 Fr. scholar & diplomat

Jus·tin \'jəs-tən\ Saint *circa* 100–*circa* 165 *Justin (the) Martyr* church father

Jus·tin·i·an I \jə-'sti-nē-ən\ 483–565 *the Great* Byzantine emperor (527–565)

Ju·ve·nal \'jü-və-nᵊl\ A.D. 55 to 60–*circa* 127 *Decimus Junius Juvenalis* Rom. poet & satirist — **Ju·ve·na·lian** \ˌjü-və-'näl-yən\ *adjective*

Ká·dár \'kä-ˌdär\ János 1912–1989 1st secretary of Hung. Communist party (1956–88)

Kaf·ka \'käf-kə, 'kaf-\ Franz 1883–1924 Czech-born author writing in German

Ka·ga·wa \kä-'gä-wə\ Toyohiko 1888–1960 Jp. social reformer

Kai·ser \'kī-zər\ Henry John 1882–1967 Am. industrialist

Kalb \'kälp, 'kalb\ Johann 1721–1780 Baron *de Kalb* \di-'kalb\ Ger. general in Am. Revolution

Kā·li·dā·sa \ˌkä-li-'dä-sə\ 5th century A.D. Indian dramatist & poet

Ka·li·nin \kə-'lē-nyən, -nyən\ Mikhail Ivanovich 1875–1946 Russ. politician; formal head of Soviet state (1919–46)

Ka·me·ha·me·ha I \kə-ˌmä-ə-'mä-(ˌ)hä\ 1758?–1819 *the Great* king of Hawaii (1795–1819)

Ka·me·nev \'käm-yə-ˌnef, 'kam-; 'kä-mə-, 'ka-\ Lev Borisovich 1883–1936 Russ. Communist leader

Ka·mer·lingh On·nes \ˌkä-mər-liṅ-'ȯn-əs\ Heike 1853–1926 Du. physicist

Kan·din·sky \kan-'din(t)-skē\ Wassily 1866–1944 Russ. painter

Kane \'kān\ Elisha Kent 1820–1857 Am. arctic explorer

K'ang-hsi \'käŋ-'shē\ 1654–1722 Chin. emperor (1661–1722)

Kant \'kant, 'känt\ Immanuel 1724–1804 Ger. philosopher

Kan·to·ro·vich \\,kän-tə-'rȯ-vich\\ Leonid Vitaly-evich 1912–1986 Russ. economist

Ka·pit·sa \\'kä-pyit-sə\\ Pyotr Leonidovich 1894–1984 Russ. physicist

Kar·a·george \\,kar-ə-'jȯrj\\ 1762–1817 originally *George Petrović Karageorge* Serbian nationalist & founder of Kar·a·geor·ge·vić \\-'jȯr-jə-,vich\\ dynasty

Ka·ra·jan \\,kär-ə-,yän\\ Herbert von 1908–1989 Austrian conductor

Ka·ra·man·lis \\,kär-ə-,män-'lēs, -'män-,\\ Konstantinos 1907– prime minister (1974–80) & president (1980–85; 1990–95) of Greece

Karle \\'kärl\\ Jerome 1918– Am. physical chemist

Karl·feldt \\'kär(ə)l-,felt\\ Erik Axel 1864–1931 Swed. poet

Ká·ro·lyi \\'kar-əl-yē, 'kär-\\ Count Mihály 1875–1955 Hung. politician

Kar·rer \\'kär-ər\\ Paul 1889–1971 Swiss chemist

Kar·sa·vi·na \\kär-'sä-və-nə, -'sa-\\ Tamara 1885–1978 Russ. dancer

Kast·ler \\käst-ler\\ Alfred 1902–1984 Fr. physicist

Kastrioti George — see SKANDERBEG

Katz \\'kats\\ Sir Bernhard 1911– Brit. (Ger.-born) biophysicist

Kauf·man \\'kȯf-mən\\ George Simon 1889–1961 Am. dramatist

Kau·nitz \\'kau̇-nəts\\ Wenzel Anton von 1711–1794 Prince *von Kaunitz-Rietberg* Austrian statesman

Kaut·sky \\'kau̇t-skē\\ Karl Johann 1854–1938 Ger. socialist writer

Ka·wa·ba·ta \\,kä-wə-'bä-tə, kə-'wä-bə-,tä\\ Yasunari 1899–1972 Jp. writer

Kaye–Smith \\'kā-'smith\\ Sheila 1887–1956 Eng. novelist

Ka·zan·tza·kis \\,kä-z°n-'tsä-kēs, -'chä-\\ Nikos 1885–1957 Greek poet, novelist, & translator

Kean \\'kēn\\ Edmund 1789–1833 Eng. actor

Kear·ny \\'kär-nē\\ Philip 1814–1862 Am. general

Keat·ing \\'kē-tiŋ\\ Paul John 1944– prime minister of Australia (1991–96)

Keats \\'kēts\\ John 1795–1821 Eng. poet — **Keats·ian** \\'kēt-sē-ən\\ *adjective*

Ke·ble \\'kē-bəl\\ John 1792–1866 Eng. clergyman & poet

Ke·fau·ver \\'kē-,fȯ-vər\\ (Carey) Estes 1903–1963 Am. politician

Kei·tel \\'kī-t°l\\ Wilhelm 1882–1946 Ger. field marshal

Kek·ko·nen \\'ke-kə-nən, -,nen\\ Urho Kaleva 1900–1986 president of Finland (1956–81)

Kel·ler \\'ke-lər\\ Helen Adams 1880–1968 Am. deaf & blind lecturer

Kel·logg \\'ke-,lȯg, -,läg\\ Frank Billings 1856–1937 Am. statesman

Kel·vin \\'kel-vən\\ 1st Baron 1824–1907 *William Thomson* Brit. mathematician & physicist

Ke·mal Ata·türk \\kə-'mal-'a-tə-,tȯrk, -'ä-\\ 1881–1938 originally *Mus·ta·fa Ke·mal* \\mü-stä-'fä-kä-'mäl\\ Turk. general; president of Turkey (1923–38)

Kem·ble \\'kem-bəl\\ Frances Anne 1809–1893 *Fanny* Eng. actress

Kemble John Philip 1757–1823 Eng. actor

Kempis Thomas à — see THOMAS À KEMPIS

Ken *or* **Kenn** \\'ken\\ Thomas 1637–1711 Eng. prelate & hymn writer

Ken·dall \\'ken-d°l\\ Edward Calvin 1886–1972 Am. biochemist

Kendall Henry Way 1926– Am. physicist

Ken·drew \\'ken-(,)drü\\ Sir John Cowdery 1917– Brit. chemist

Ken·nan \\'ke-nən\\ George Frost 1904– Am. historian & diplomat

Kennedy \\'ke-nə-dē\\ Anthony M. 1936– Am. jurist

Kennedy John Fitzgerald 1917–1963 Am. politician; 35th president of the U.S. (1961–63) — **Ken·ne·dy·esque** \\,ke-nə-dē-'esk\\ *adjective*

Kennedy Joseph Patrick 1888–1969 *father of J. F. & R. F.* Am. businessman & diplomat

Kennedy Robert Francis 1925–1968 Am. politician; attorney-general (1961–64)

Ken·nel·ly \\'ke-n°l-ē\\ Arthur Edwin 1861–1939 Am. engineer

Ken·ny \\'ke-nē\\ Elizabeth 1880–1952 *Sister Kenny* Austral. nurse & physiotherapist

Kent \\'kent\\ James 1763–1847 Am. jurist

Kent Rockwell 1882–1971 Am. painter & illustrator

Ken·yon \\'ken-yən\\ John Samuel 1874–1959 Am. phonetician

Ke·o·kuk \\'kē-ə-,kək\\ 1780?–1848 *Kiyo'kaga* Sauk & Fox tribal leader

Kep·ler \\'ke-plər\\ Johannes 1571–1630 Ger. astronomer — **Kep·ler·ian** \\ke-'plir-ē-ən, -'pler-\\ *adjective*

Kep·pel \\'ke-pəl\\ 1st Viscount 1725–1786 *Augustus Keppel* Brit. admiral

Ker \\'ker, 'kər, 'kär\\ William Paton 1855–1923 Brit. scholar

Ke·ren·sky \\'ker-ən-skē, ke-'ren-\\ Aleksandr Fyodorovich 1881–1970 Russ. revolutionary

Kern \\'kərn\\ Jerome David 1885–1945 Am. composer

Ker·ou·ac \\'ker-ə-,wak\\ Jack 1922–1969 *Jean-Louis* Am. writer

Kes·sel·ring \\'ke-səl-riŋ\\ Albert 1885–1960 Ger. field marshal

Ket·ter·ing \\'ke-tə-riŋ\\ Charles Franklin 1876–1958 Am. electrical engineer & inventor

Key \\'kē\\ Francis Scott 1779–1843 Am. lawyer & author of "The Star-Spangled Banner"

Keynes \\'kānz\\ John Maynard 1883–1946 1st Baron *Keynes of Tilton* Eng. economist

Key·ser·ling \\'kī-zər-liŋ\\ Hermann Alexander 1880–1946 Graf *Keyserling* Ger. philosopher & writer

Kha·cha·tu·ri·an \\,kä-chə-'tu̇r-ē-ən, ,ka-\\ Aram Ilich 1903–1978 Soviet (Armenian-born) composer

Kha·da·fy *variant of* GADHAFI

Khā·lid \\'ka-lid, 'kä-\\ *in full* Khālid ibn ʿAbd al-ʿAzīz ibn ʿAbd ar-Raḥmān al-Saʿūd 1913–1982 king of Saudi Arabia (1975–82)

Kha·me·nei \\kä-'mä-nä\\ Hojatolislam Sayyed Ali 1939– religious leader of Iran (1989–)

Khayyám Omar — see OMAR KHAYYÁM

Khe·ra·skov \\kə-'räs-kəf\\ Mikhail Matveyevich 1733–1807 Russ. poet

Kho·mei·ni \\kō-'mā-nē, kō-, hō-\\ Ayatollah Ruholla Mussaui 1900–1989 religious leader of Iran (1979–89)

Kho·ra·na \\kō-'rä-nə\\ Har Gobind 1922– Am. (Indian-born) biochemist

Khru·shchev \\krüsh-'chȯf, -'chȯv; 'krüsh-,; krü-'shȯf, -'shȯv; 'krü-,; *also with* e *for* ȯ\\ Ni·ki·ta \\nə-'kē-tə\\ Sergeyevich 1894–1971 Soviet politician; premier of Soviet Union (1958–64) — **Khru·shchev·ian** \\krüsh-'chȯ-vē-ən, -'chȯ- *also* -'che-; krü-'shȯ-, -'shō- *also* -'she-\\ *adjective* — **Khru·shchev·ite** \\krüsh-'chȯ-,vīt, -'che-,vīt, 'krüsh-,; krü-'shȯ-, -'she-, 'krü-,\\ *adjective*

Khu·fu \\'kü-(,)fü\\ *Greek* **Che·ops** \\'kē-,äps\\ 26th century B.C. king of Egypt & pyramid builder

Khwā·riz·mī, al– \\al-'kwär-əz-mē, -'kwȯr-\\ *circa* 780–*circa* 850 Muḥammad ibn Mūsā al-Khwārizmī Islamic (Persian-born) mathematician & astronomer

Kidd \\'kid\\ William *circa* 1645–1701 *Captain Kidd* Scot. pirate

Kie·ran \\'kir-ən\\ John Francis 1892–1981 Am. journalist

Kier·ke·gaard \\'kir-kə-,gär(d), -,gȯr\\ Søren Aabye 1813–1855 Dan. philosopher & theologian — **Kier·ke·gaard·ian** \\,kir-kə-'gär-dē-ən, -'gȯr-\\ *adjective*

Kie·sing·er \\'kē-ziŋ-ər\\ Kurt Georg 1904–1988 chancellor of West Germany (1966–69)

Kil·lian \\'ki-lē-ən, 'kil-yən\\ James Rhyne 1904–1988 Am. educator

Kil·mer \\'kil-mər\\ (Alfred) Joyce 1886–1918 Am. poet

Kim Il Sung \\'kim-'il-'səŋ, -'su̇ŋ\\ 1912–1994 No. Korean Communist leader (1948–94) and president (1972–94)

Kim·mel \\'ki-məl\\ Husband Edward 1882–1968 Am. admiral

Kim Young Sam \\'kim-'yəŋ-'säm, -'sam\\ 1927– president of So. Korea (1993–)

Kin·di, al– \\al-'kin-dē\\ *died circa* 870 Arab philosopher

King \\'kiŋ\\ Ernest Joseph 1878–1956 Am. admiral

King Martin Luther, Jr. 1929–1968 Am. clergyman & civil rights leader

King Rufus 1755–1827 Am. politician & diplomat

King William Lyon Mackenzie 1874–1950 Canad. statesman; prime minister (1921–26; 1926–30; 1935–48)

King William Rufus de Vane 1786–1853 Am. politician; vice president of the U.S. (1853)

Kings·ley \\'kiŋz-lē\\ Charles 1819–1875 Eng. clergyman & novelist

Kin·kaid \\kin-'kād\\ Thomas Cassin 1888–1972 Am. admiral

Kin·sey \\'kin-zē\\ Alfred Charles 1894–1956 Am. sexologist

Kip·ling \\'kip-liŋ\\ (Joseph) Rud·yard \\'rəd-yərd, 'rə-jərd\\ 1865–1936 Eng. author — **Kip·ling·esque** \\,kip-liŋ-'esk\\ *adjective*

Kir·by–Smith \\,kər-bē-'smith\\ Edmund 1824–1893 originally surname *Smith* Am. Confederate general

Kirch·hoff \\'kir-,kȯf\\ Gustav Robert 1824–1887 Ger. physicist

Kirch·ner \\'kirk-nər, 'kirk-\\ Ernst Ludwig 1880–1938 Ger. painter

Ki·rov \\'kē-,rȯf, -,rȯv\\ Sergey Mironovich 1886–1934 Soviet politician

Kir·wan \\'kər-wən\\ Richard 1733–1812 Irish chemist

Kis·sin·ger \\'ki-s°n-jər\\ Henry Alfred 1923– Am. (Ger.-born) scholar & government official; secretary of state (1973–77)

Kitch·e·ner \\'kich-nər, 'ki-chə-\\ Horatio Herbert 1850–1916 1st Earl *Kitchener of Khartoum and of Broome* Brit. field marshal

Kit·tredge \\'ki-trij\\ George Lyman 1860–1941 Am. educator

Klee \\'klā\\ Paul 1879–1940 Swiss painter

Klein \\'klīn\\ Lawrence Robert 1920– Am. economist

Kleist \\'klīst\\ (Bernd) Heinrich Wilhelm von 1777–1811 Ger. dramatist

Kleist (Paul Ludwig) Ewald von 1881–1954 Ger. field marshal

Klem·per·er \\'klem-pər-ər\\ Otto 1885–1973 Ger. conductor

Klitz·ing \\'klit-siŋ\\ Klaus von 1943– Ger. physicist

Klop·stock \\'kläp-,stäk, 'klȯp-,shtȯk\\ Friedrich Gottlieb 1724–1803 Ger. poet

Klug \\'klüg\\ Aaron 1926– So. African (Lith.-born) molecular biologist

Knel·ler \\'ne-lər, 'kne-\\ Sir Godfrey 1646(or 1649)–1723 originally *Gottfried Kniller* Eng. (Ger.-born) painter

Knox \\'näks\\ Henry 1750–1806 Am. general in Revolution

Knox John *circa* 1514–1572 Scot. religious reformer

Knox Philander Chase 1853–1921 Am. statesman

Knud·sen \\'nüd-sən, 'knüd-\\ William Signius 1879–1948 Am. (Dan.-born) industrialist & administrator

Knut \\'knüt, 'knyüt\\ *variant of* CANUTE

Koch \\'kȯk, 'kȯk, *or* ō *or* ä *for* ȯ\\ Robert 1843–1910 Ger. bacteriologist

Ko·cher \\'kȯ-kər, -,kər\\ Emil Theodor 1841–1917 Swiss surgeon

Kock \\'kȯk\\ Charles-Paul de 1793–1871 Fr. novelist & dramatist

Ko·dály \\'kō-,dī\\ Zol·tán \\'zȯl-,tän\\ 1882–1967 Hung. composer

Koest·ler \\'kes(t)-lər\\ Arthur 1905–1983 Brit. (Hung.-born) writer

Kohl \\'kōl\\ Helmut 1930– chancellor of West Germany (1982–90) chancellor of Germany (1990–)

Koh·ler \\'kō-lər\\ Foy David 1908–1990 Am. diplomat

Köhler \\'krē-ler\\ Georges J. F. 1946–1995 Ger. immunologist

Koi·so \\'kȯi-(,)sō, 'kō-ē-(,)sō\\ Kuniaki 1880–1950 Jp. general

Kokh·ba \\'kȯk-bä\\ Bar *died* A.D. 135 originally *Sim·e·on bar Ko·zi·ba* \\'si-mē-ən-bär-'kȯ-zē-,bä\\ Jewish leader in Palestine

Ko·kosch·ka \\kō-'kȯsh-kə\\ Oskar 1886–1980 Brit. (Austrian-born) painter

Kol·chak \\kȯl-'chäk\\ Aleksandr Vasilyevich 1873–1920 Russ. admiral & counterrevolutionary

Kol·lon·tay \\,kä-lən-'tī\\ Aleksandra Mikhaylovna 1872–1952 Russ. diplomat

Koll·witz \'kōl-ˌwits, 'kȯl-ˌvits\ Käthe 1867–1945 Ger. artist

Kol·mo·go·rov \kəl-mə-'gȯ-rəf\ Andrey Nikolayevich 1903–1987 Soviet mathematician

Kol·tsov \kȯlt-'sȯf, -'sȯv\ Aleksey Vasilyevich 1808–1842 Russ. poet

Ko·mu·ra \kō-'mu̇r-ä, 'kȯ-mə-ˌrä\ Marquis Jutarō 1855–1911 Jp. diplomat

Kon·dí·lis \kȯn-'dē-ləs, -lēs\ Géorgios 1879–1936 Greek general & politician

Ko·nev \'kȯn-ˌyef, -ˌyev, -yəf\ Ivan Stepanovich 1897–1973 Soviet general

Ko·noe \kə-'nō-(ˌ)ā\ Prince Fumimaro 1891–1945 Jp. statesman

Koo \'kü\ Vi Kyuin Wel·ling·ton \'we-liŋ-tən\ 1888–1985 originally *Ku Wei-chün* Chin. statesman & diplomat

Koop·mans \'küp-mənz, 'kōp-ˌmänz\ Tjalling Charles 1910–1985 Am. (Du.-born) economist

Kopernik *or* **Koppernigk** — see COPERNICUS

Korn·berg \'kȯrn-ˌbərg\ Arthur 1918– Am. biochemist

Korn·gold \'kȯrn-ˌgōld, -ˌgȯlt\ Erich Wolfgang 1897–1957 Am. (Austrian-born) composer, conductor, & pianist

Kor·ni·lov \kȯr-'nē-ləf\ Lavr Georgiyevich 1870–1918 Russ. general & counterrevolutionary

Ko·ro·len·ko \ˌkȯr-ə-'len-(ˌ)kō, ˌkär-\ Vladimir Galaktionovich 1853–1921 Russ. novelist

Kor·zyb·ski \kə-'zhip-skē, kȯr-'zib-\ Alfred Habdank Skarbek 1879–1950 Am. (Pol.-born) scientist & writer

Koś·ciusz·ko \kȯsh-'chüsh-(ˌ)kō, ˌkä-sē-'əs-ˌkō\ Tadeusz Andrzej Bonawentura 1746–1817 Pol. patriot & soldier in Am. Revolution

Kos·sel \'kȯ-səl\ Albrecht 1853–1927 Ger. biochemist

Kos·suth \'kä-ˌsüth, kä-'; ˌkȯ-ˌshüt\ La·jos \'lȯi-ˌȯsh\ 1802–1894 Hung. patriot & statesman

Ko·sy·gin \kə-'sē-gən\ Aleksey Nikolayevich 1904–1980 Soviet politician; premier of Soviet Union (1964–80)

Kot·ze·bue \'kät-sə-ˌbü, 'kȯt-\ August Friedrich Ferdinand von 1761–1819 Ger. dramatist

Kous·se·vitz·ky \ˌkü-sə-'vit-skē\ Serge \'sərj, 'serzh\ 1874–1951 *Sergey Aleksandrovich Kusevitsky* Am. (Russ.-born) conductor

Krafft–Ebing \'kräft-'ā-biŋ, 'kraft-\ Richard 1840–1902 Freiherr *von Krafft-Ebing* Ger. neurologist

Krebs \'krebz\ Edwin Gerhard 1918– Am. biochemist

Krebs Sir Hans Adolf 1900–1981 Brit. (Ger.-born) biochemist

Kreis·ky \'krī-skē\ Bruno 1911–1990 chancellor of Austria (1970–83)

Kreis·ler \'krīs-lər\ Fritz 1875–1962 Am. (Austrian-born) violinist

Krogh \'krȯg\ (Schack) August Steenberg 1874–1949 Dan. physiologist

Kro·pot·kin \krə-'pät-kən\ Pyotr Alekseyevich 1842–1921 Russ. geographer & revolutionary

Kro·to \'krō-(ˌ)tō\ Sir Harold Walter 1939– Brit. chemist

Kru·ger \'krü-gər *Afrikaans* 'krē-ər\ Paul 1825–1904 *Stephanus Johannes Paulus* So. African statesman

Krupp \'krùp, 'krəp\ family of Ger. munition makers: including Friedrich 1787–1826; his son Alfred 1812–1887; Alfred's son Friedrich Alfred 1854–1902; Friedrich Alfred's daughter Bertha 1886–1957; & Bertha's son Alfried 1907–1967

Krup·ska·ya \'krùp-skə-yə\ Nadezhda Konstantinovna 1869–1939 *wife of Lenin* Russ. revolutionary

Krutch \'krüch\ Joseph Wood 1893–1970 Am. author & critic

Ku·bi·tschek de Oli·vei·ra \'kü-bə-ˌchek-dā-ȯ-lē-'vā-rə\ Juscelino 1902–1976 president of Brazil (1956–61)

Ku·blai Khan \'kü-ˌblə-'kän, -ˌblī-\ 1215–1294 founder of Mongol dynasty in China

Ku·brick \'kü-brik, 'kyü-\ Stanley 1928– Am. film director, writer, & producer

Kuhn \'kün\ Richard 1900–1967 Austrian chemist

Kuhn Thomas Samuel 1922–1996 Am. philosopher & scientist — **Kuhn·ian** \'kü-nē-ən\ *adjective*

Kun \'kün\ Bé·la \'bā-lə\ 1885–1937 Hung. Communist

Kung \'gùŋ\ Prince 1833–1898 Manchu statesman

K'ung \'kùŋ\ H. H. 1881–1967 originally *K'ung Hsiang-hsi* Chin. statesman

Ku·ro·pat·kin \ˌkùr-ə-'pat-kən, -'pät-\ Aleksey Nikolayevich 1848–1921 Russ. general

Ku·ro·sa·wa \ˌkùr-ə-'saù-ə\ Akira 1910– Jp. filmmaker

Kusch \'kùsh\ Polykarp 1911–1993 Am. (Ger.-born) physicist

Ku·tu·zov \kə-'tü-ˌzȯf, -ˌzȯv\ Mikhail Illarionovich 1745–1813 Prince of *Smolensk* Russ. field marshal

Kuz·nets \'kəz-(ˌ)nets\ Simon 1901–1985 Am. (Ukrainian-born) economist

Kyd *or* **Kid** \'kid\ Thomas 1558–1594 Eng. dramatist

Kynewulf *variant of* CYNEWULF

La Bru·yère \ˌlä-brü-'yer, -brē-'er\ Jean de 1645–1696 Fr. moralist

La·chaise \lə-'shāz\ Gaston 1882–1935 Am. (Fr.-born) sculptor

La Farge \lə-'färzh, -'färj\ John 1835–1910 Am. artist

La Farge Oliver Hazard Perry 1901–1963 Am. writer & anthropologist

La·fa·yette \ˌlä-fē-'et, ˌla-; la-\ Marquis de 1757–1834 *Marie-Joseph-Paul-Yves-Roch-Gilbert du Motier* Fr. general & statesman

Laf·fite *or* **La·fitte** \lə-'fēt, la-\ Jean *circa* 1780–*circa* 1826 Fr. pirate in America

La Fol·lette \lə-'fä-lət\ Robert Marion 1855–1925 Am. politician

La·fon·taine \ˌlä-fōⁿ-'ten\ Henri 1854–1943 Belg. lawyer & statesman

La Fon·taine \ˌlä-fōⁿ-'ten\ Jean 1621–1695 Fr. poet

La·ger·kvist \'lä-gər-ˌkvist, -ˌkwist\ Pär Fabian 1891–1974 Swed. dramatist, poet, & novelist

La·ger·löf \'lä-gər-ˌlə(r)v\ Selma Ottiliana Lovisa 1858–1940 Swed. novelist & poet

La·grange \lə-'gräⁿj, la-\ Joseph-Louis 1736–1813 Comte *de Lagrange* Fr. mathematician

La Guar·dia \lə-'gwär-dē-ə\ Fi·o·rel·lo \ˌfē-ə-'re-(ˌ)lō\ Henry 1882–1947 Am. politician

Laing \'laŋ\ Ronald David 1927–1989 Brit. psychiatrist — **Laing·ian** \-ē-ən\ *adjective*

Lake \'lāk\ Simon 1866–1945 Am. naval architect

La·marck \lə-'märk\ Jean-Baptiste de Monet de 1744–1829 Chevalier *de Lamarck* Fr. naturalist

La·mar·tine \ˌlä-ˌmär-'tēn, ˌla-mər-\ Alphonse-Marie-Louis de Prat de 1790–1869 Fr. poet

Lamas Carlos Saavedra — see Carlos SAAVEDRA LAMAS

Lamb \'lam\ Charles 1775–1834 Eng. essayist & critic

Lamb William 1779–1848 2d Viscount *Melbourne* Eng. statesman

Lamb Willis Eugene 1913– Am. physicist

Lam·bert \'lam-bərt\ John 1619–1683 Eng. general

Lam·masch \'lä-ˌmäsh\ Heinrich 1853–1920 Austrian jurist

La Motte–Fouqué — see FOUQUÉ

L'Amour \lä-'mȯr, -'mùr\ Louis Dearborn 1908–1988 Am. writer

Land \'land\ Edwin Herbert 1909–1991 Am. inventor & industrialist

Lan·dau \län-'daù\ Lev Davidovich 1908–1968 Russ. physicist

Lan·dis \'lan-dəs\ Ken·e·saw \'ke-nə-ˌsȯ\ Mountain 1866–1944 Am. jurist & baseball commissioner

Lan·don \'lan-dən\ Alfred Mossman 1887–1987 Am. politician

Lan·dor \'lan-ˌdȯr\ Walter Savage 1775–1864 Eng. author

Lan·dow·ska \lan-'dȯf-skə, -'dȯv-\ Wanda Louise 1879–1959 Pol. pianist

Land·seer \'lan(d)-ˌsir\ Sir Edwin Henry 1802–1873 Eng. painter

Land·stei·ner \'lan(d)-ˌstī-nər, 'länt-ˌshtī-\ Karl 1868–1943 Am. (Austrian-born) pathologist

Lane \'lān\ Edward William 1801–1876 Eng. orientalist

Lan·franc \'lan-ˌfraŋk\ 1005?–1089 Ital.-born prelate in England

Lang \'laŋ\ Andrew 1844–1912 Scot. scholar & author

Lang Cosmo Gordon 1864–1945 Brit. prelate; archbishop of Canterbury (1928–42)

Lange \'läŋ-ə\ Christian Louis 1869–1938 Norw. pacifist & historian

Lange \'lȯŋ-ē\ David Russell 1942– prime minister of New Zealand (1984–89)

Lang·er \'laŋ-ər\ Susanne Knauth 1895–1985 Am. philosopher & educator

Lang·land \'laŋ-lənd\ William *circa* 1330–*circa* 1400 Eng. poet

Lang·ley \'laŋ-lē\ Samuel Pierpont 1834–1906 Am. astronomer & airplane pioneer

Lang·muir \'laŋ-ˌmyùr\ Irving 1881–1957 Am. chemist

Lang·ton \'laŋ(k)-tən\ Stephen *died* 1228 Eng. prelate

Lang·try \'laŋ(k)-trē\ Lillie 1853–1929 née (*Emilie Charlotte*) *Le Breton*; the *Jersey Lily* Brit. actress

La·nier \lə-'nir\ Sidney 1842–1881 Am. poet

Lan·kes·ter \'laŋ-kəs-tər; 'lan-ˌkes-, 'laŋ-\ Sir Edwin Ray 1847–1929 Eng. zoologist

Lannes \'län, 'lan\ Jean 1769–1809 Duc *de Montebello* Fr. soldier

Lan·sing \'lan(t)-siŋ\ Robert 1864–1928 Am. lawyer & statesman

Lao·tzu \'laùd-'zə\ originally *Li Erh* \'lē-'er\ 6th century B.C. Chin. philosopher

La Pé·rouse \ˌlä-pā-'rüz, -pə-\ Comte de 1741–1788 *Jean-François de Galoup* Fr. navigator & explorer

La·place \lə-'pläs\ Pierre-Simon 1749–1827 Marquis *de Laplace* Fr. astronomer & mathematician

Lard·ner \'lärd-nər\ Ring 1885–1933 in full *Ringgold Wilmer Lardner* Am. writer

La·re·do Brú \lə-'rā-dō-'brü\ Federico 1875–1946 Cuban soldier; president of Cuba (1936–40)

La Roche·fou·cauld \ˌlä-ˌrȯsh-fü-'kō, -ˌrȯsh-\ François 1613–1680 Duc *de La Rochefoucauld* Fr. writer & moralist

La·rousse \lä-'rüs\ Pierre-Athanase 1817–1875 Fr. grammarian & lexicographer

Lar·tet \lär-'tā\ Édouard-Armand-Isidore-Hippolyte 1801–1871 Fr. archaeologist

La Salle \lə-'sal\ Sieur de 1643–1687 *René-Robert Cavelier* Fr. explorer in America

Las Ca·sas \läs-'kä-səs\ Bartolomé de 1474–1566 Span. Dominican missionary & historian

Las·ki \'las-kē\ Harold Joseph 1893–1950 Eng. politician scientist

Las·salle \lə-'sal, -'säl\ Ferdinand 1825–1864 Ger. socialist

Lat·i·mer \'la-tə-mər\ Hugh *circa* 1485–1555 Eng. religious reformer

La Tour \lə-'tùr\ Georges de 1593–1652 Fr. painter

La Tour Maurice-Quentin de 1704–1788 Fr. painter

La·trobe \lə-'trōb\ Benjamin Henry 1764–1820 Am. (Eng.-born) architect & engineer

Lat·ti·more \'la-tə-ˌmōr, -ˌmȯr\ Owen 1900–1989 Am. orientalist

Lattimore Richmond 1906–1984 Am. poet & translator

Lau·bach \'laù-ˌbäk\ Frank Charles 1884–1970 Am. educator & missionary

Laud \'lȯd\ William 1573–1645 Eng. prelate; archbishop of Canterbury (1633–45) — **Laud·ian** \'lȯ-dē-ən\ *adjective*

Lau·der \'lȯ-dər\ Sir Harry Maclennan 1870–1950 Scot. singer

Laue \'laù-ə\ Max von 1879–1960 Ger. physicist

Laugh·ton \'lȯ-tⁿn\ Charles 1899–1962 Am. (Eng.-born) actor

Lau·rence \'lȯr-ən(t)s, 'lär-\ (Jean) Margaret 1926–1987 née *Wemyss* Can. author

Lau·ren·cin \lȯ-räⁿ-saⁿ\ Marie 1885–1956 Fr. painter

Lau·ri·er \'lȯr-ē-ˌā, 'lär-\ Sir Wilfrid 1841–1919 Canad. statesman

Lautrec — see TOULOUSE-LAUTREC

La·val \lə-'val, -'väl\ Pierre 1883–1945 Fr. politician

La Val·lière \ˌlä-val-'yer\ Duchesse de 1644–1710 *Françoise-Louise de La Baume Le Blanc* mistress of Louis XIV of France

La·ve·ran \ˌla-və-'räⁿ\ Charles-Louis-Alphonse 1845–1922 Fr. physiologist & bacteriologist

La Vé·ren·drye \ˌlä-ˌver-ən-'drē, -'ver-ən-ˌdrī\ Sieur de 1685–1749 *Pierre Gaultier de Varennes* Canad. explorer in America

La·very \'lā-və-rē, 'la-; 'lāv-rē, 'lav-\ Sir John 1856–1941 Brit. painter

La·voi·sier \ləv-'wä-zē-ˌā\ Antoine-Laurent 1743–1794 Fr. chemist

Law \'lȯ\ (Andrew) Bon·ar \'bä-nər\ 1858–1923 Brit. (Canad.-born) statesman

Law Edward 1750–1818 1st Baron *El·len·bor·ough* \e-lən-ˌbȯr-ə, -ˌbä-rə, -brə\ Eng. jurist

Law John 1671–1729 Scot. financier & speculator

Law William 1686–1761 Eng. writer

Lawes \'lȯz\ Henry 1596–1662 Eng. composer

Lawes Lewis Edward 1883–1947 Am. penologist

Law·rence \'lȯr-ən(t)s, 'lär-\ David 1888–1973 Am. journalist

Lawrence David Herbert 1885–1930 Eng. novelist — **Law·renc·ian** \lȯ-'ren(t)-sē-ən\ *or* **Law·ren·tian** *or* **Lau·ren·tian** \-sh(ē-)ən\ *adjective*

Lawrence Ernest Orlando 1901–1958 Am. physicist

Lawrence Gertrude 1898–1952 originally *Gertrud Alexandra Dagmar Lawrence Klasen* Eng. actress

Lawrence James 1781–1813 Am. naval officer

Lawrence Sir Thomas 1769–1830 Eng. painter

Lawrence Thomas Edward 1888–1935 *Lawrence of Arabia* later surname *Shaw* Brit. archaeologist, soldier, & writer

Lax·ness \'läks-ˌnes\ Halldór Kiljan 1902– Icelandic writer

Lay·a·mon \'lī-ə-mən, 'lā-\ *flourished* 1200 Eng. poet

Lay·ard \'lā-ˌärd, -ərd\ Sir Austen Henry 1817–1894 Eng. archaeologist & diplomat

Lea·cock \'lē-ˌkäk\ Stephen Butler 1869–1944 Canad. economist & humorist

Leadbelly — see Huddie LEDBETTER

Lea·hy \'lā-(ˌ)hē\ William Daniel 1875–1959 Am. admiral

Lea·key \'lē-kē\ Louis Seymour Bazett 1903–1972 Brit. paleontologist

Leakey Mary Douglas 1913–1996 *wife of preceding* Brit. paleontologist

Lean \'lēn\ Sir David 1908–1991 Brit. film director

Lear \'lir\ Edward 1812–1888 Eng. painter & nonsense poet

Lea·vis \'lē-vəs\ Frank Raymond 1895–1978 Eng. critic — **Lea·vis·ian** \lē-'vi-zh(ē-)ən\ *adjective* — **Lea·vis·ite** \'lē-və-ˌsīt\ *adjective*

Le·brun \lə-'brœⁿ(n), -'brœⁿ\ Albert 1871–1950 Fr. statesman; president of France (1932–40)

Lebrun Mme. Vigée- — see VIGÉE-LEBRUN

Le Brun *or* **Le·brun** \lə-'brœⁿ(n), -'brœⁿ\ Charles 1619–1690 Fr. painter

Le Car·ré \lə-kä-'rā\ John 1931– pseudonym of *David Corn·well* \'kȯrn-ˌwel\ Eng. novelist

Lecky \'le-kē\ William Edward Hartpole 1838–1903 Irish historian

Le·conte de Lisle \lə-'kōⁿ(n)t-də-'lē(ə)l\ Charles-Marie 1818–1894 originally *Leconte* Fr. poet

Le Corbusier — see CORBUSIER

Led·bet·ter \'led-ˌbe-tər\ Huddie 1888–1949 *Lead·bel·ly* \'led-ˌbe-lē\ Am. blues singer

Le·der·berg \'lā-dər-ˌbərg\ Joshua 1925– Am. geneticist

Led·er·man \'lā-dər-mən\ Leon Max 1922– Am. physicist

Le Duc Tho \'lā-'dək-'tō\ 1911–1990 Vietnamese diplomat

Lee \'lē\ Ann 1736–1784 Am. (Eng.-born) Shaker

Lee Charles 1731–1782 Am. (Eng.-born) general

Lee David Morris 1931– Am. physicist

Lee Fitzhugh 1835–1905 *nephew of R. E. Lee* Am. gen.

Lee Francis Lightfoot 1734–1797 Am. statesman in Revolution

Lee Henry 1756–1818 *Light-Horse Harry* Am. general

Lee Richard Henry 1732–1794 Am. statesman in Revolution

Lee Robert Edward 1807–1870 Am. Confederate general

Lee Sir Sidney 1859–1926 Eng. editor & scholar

Lee Yuan Tseh 1936– Am. (Taiwanese-born) chemist

Lee Tsung–Dao \'lē-'dzuṇ-'dau\ 1926– Chin. physicist

Leeu·wen·hoek \'lā-vən-ˌhu̇k\ Antonie van 1632–1723 Du. naturalist

Le·feb·vre \lə-'fevrᵊ\ François-Joseph 1755–1820 Duc *de Dantzig* Fr. general; marshal of France

Le Gal·lienne \lə-'gal-yən\ Eva 1899–1991 Am. (Eng.-born) actress

Le Gallienne Richard 1866–1947 Eng. writer

Le·gen·dre \lə-'zhäⁿdrᵊ\ Adrien-Marie 1752–1833 Fr. mathematician

Lé·ger \lā-'zhā\ Alexis Saint-Léger 1887–1975 pseudonym *St. John Perse* \saⁿ-ˌjȯn-'pers\ Fr. diplomat & poet

Léger Fernand 1881–1955 Fr. painter

Le·guía y Sal·ce·do \lə-'gē-ə-ˌē-säl-'sā-(ˌ)dō, -(ˌ)thō\ Augusto Bernardino 1863–1932 Peruvian banker; president of Peru (1908–12; 1919–30)

Le·hár \'lā-ˌhär\ Franz 1870–1948 Hung. composer

Leh·man \'lē-mən\ Herbert Henry 1878–1963 Am. banker & politician

Leh·mann \'lā-ˌmän\ Lot·te \'lȯ-tə\ 1888–1976 Ger. soprano

Lehn \'lān\ Jean-Marie 1939– Fr. chemist

Leib·niz \'līb-nəts, *German* 'līp-nits\ Gottfried Wilhelm 1646–1716 Ger. philosopher & mathematician — **Leib·niz·ian** \līb-'nit-sē-ən, līp-\ *adjective*

Lei·bo·vitz \'lē-bō-ˌvits\ Annie 1949– Am. photographer

Leicester 1st Earl of — see Robert DUDLEY; see also de MONTFORT

Leif Er·iks·son \ˌlāv-'er-ik-sən, ˌlēf-\ *or* **Er·ics·son** *same*\ *flourished* 1000 *son of Erik the Red* Norw. explorer

Leigh·ton \'lā-tᵊn\ Frederick 1830–1896 Baron *Leighton of Stretton* Eng. painter

Leins·dorf \'līnz-ˌdȯrf, 'līn(t)s-\ Erich 1912–1993 Am. (Austrian-born) conductor

Le·jeune \lə-'jün\ John Archer 1867–1942 Am. marine-corps general

Le·land \'lē-lənd\ John 1506?–1552 Eng. antiquarian

Leloir \lā-'lwär\ Luis Federico 1906–1987 Argentine biochemist

Le·ly \'lē-lē\ Sir Peter 1618–1680 originally *Pieter Van der Faes* Brit. (Westphalian-born) painter

Le·maî·tre \lə-'metrᵊ\ (François-Élie) Jules 1853–1914 Fr. writer

Lemaître (Abbé) Georges Henri 1894–1966 Belg. astrophysicist

Le Moyne Pierre — see IBERVILLE

Le·nard \'lā-ˌnärt\ Philipp 1862–1947 Ger. physicist

Len·clos \läⁿ-klō\ Anne de 1620–1705 *Ninon de Lenclos* Fr. courtesan

L'En·fant \läⁿ-ˌfänt, läⁿ-fäⁿ\ Pierre-Charles 1754–1825 Am. (Fr.-born) architect & engineer

Le·nin \'le-nən\ 1870–1924 originally *Vladimir Ilyich Ul·ya·nov* \ül-'yä-nəf, -ˌnȯf, -ˌnȯv\ Russ. Communist leader

Leo \'lē-(ˌ)ō\ name of 13 popes: especially **I** Saint *died* 461 (pope 440–61); **III** Saint *died* 816 (pope 795–816); **XIII** 1810–1903 (pope 1878–1903)

Leon·ard \'le-nərd\ William Ellery 1876–1944 Am. educator & poet

Le·o·nar·do da Vin·ci \ˌlē-ə-'när-(ˌ)dō-də-'vin-chē, ˌlā-, -'vēn-\ 1452–1519 It. painter, sculptor, architect, & engineer — **Le·o·nar·desque** \ˌlē-ə-ˌnär-'desk, ˌlā-\ *adjective*

Le·on·ca·val·lo \ˌlā-ˌän-kə-'vä-(ˌ)lō\ Ruggiero 1858–1919 Ital. composer & librettist

Le·on·i·das \lē-'ä-nə-dəs\ *died* 480 B.C. Greek hero; king of Sparta (490?–480)

Le·ont·ief \lē-'ȯnt-yəf, lyē-\ Wassily 1906– Am. (Russ.-born) economist

Le·o·par·di \ˌlā-ə-'pär-dē\ Giacomo 1798–1837 Ital. poet

Le·o·pold I \'lē-ə-ˌpōld\ 1640–1705 king of Hungary (1655–1705) & Holy Roman emperor (1658–1705)

Leopold II 1747–1792 Holy Roman emperor (1790–92)

Leopold I 1790–1865 king of Belgium (1831–65)

Leopold II 1835–1909 king of Belgium (1865–1909)

Leopold III 1901–1983 king of Belgium (1934–51)

Lep·i·dus \'le-pə-dəs\ Marcus Aemilius *died* 13(or 12) B.C. Rom. triumvir

Ler·mon·tov \'ler-mən-ˌtȯf, -ˌtȯv\ Mikhail Yuryevich 1814–1841 Russ. poet & novelist

Ler·ner \'lər-nər\ Alan Jay 1918–1986 Am. dramatist & librettist

Le·sage \lə-'säzh\ Alain-René 1668–1747 Fr. novelist & dramatist

Le·sche·tiz·ky \ˌle-shə-'tit-skē\ Theodor 1830–1915 Pol. pianist & composer

Les·seps \'le-seps, 'le-səps\ Ferdinand-Marie de 1805–1894 Vicomte *de Lesseps* Fr. diplomat & promoter of Suez Canal

Les·sing \'le-sin\ Gotthold Ephraim 1729–1781 Ger. critic & dramatist

L'Es·trange \lə-'strānj\ Sir Roger 1616–1704 Eng. journalist & translator

Leu·tze \'lȯit-sə\ Emanuel 1816–1868 Am. (Ger.-born) painter

Le·ver \'lē-vər\ Charles James 1806–1872 Brit. novelist

Le·vi-Mon·tal·ci·ni \ˌlā-vē-ˌmȯn-täl-'chē-nē\ Rita 1909– Am. (Ital.-born) neurologist

Lé·vi-Strauss \ˌlā-vē-'straus, ˌle-vē-\ Claude 1908– Fr. (Belg.-born) social anthropologist — **Lé·vi-Strauss·i·an** \-'strau-sē-ən\ *adjective*

Lew·es \'lü-əs\ George Henry 1817–1878 Eng. philosopher & critic

Lew·is \'lü-əs\ Sir (William) Arthur 1915–1991 Brit. economist

Lewis Cecil Day — see DAY-LEWIS

Lewis Clive Staples 1898–1963 Eng. novelist & essayist

Lewis Edward B. 1918– Am. biologist

Lewis Isaac Newton 1858–1931 Am. army officer & inventor

Lewis John Llewellyn 1880–1969 Am. labor leader

Lewis Matthew Gregory 1775–1818 *Monk Lewis* Eng. author

Lewis Meriwether 1774–1809 Am. explorer

Lewis (Harry) Sinclair 1885–1951 Am. novelist

Lewis (Percy) Wyndham 1882–1957 Brit. painter & author

Ley \'lī\ Robert 1890–1945 Ger. Nazi leader

Lib·by \'li-bē\ Willard Frank 1908–1980 Am. chemist

Lich·ten·stein \'lik-tən-ˌstīn, -ˌstēn\ Roy 1923– Am. artist

Li·cin·i·us \lə-'si-nē-əs\ *died* 325 *Valerius Licinianus Licinius* Rom. emperor (308–324)

Lid·dell Hart \'li-dᵊl-'härt\ Sir Basil Henry 1895–1970 Eng. military scientist

Lie \'lē\ Jonas 1833–1908 Norw. novelist & dramatist

Lie Trygve Halvdan 1896–1968 Norw. lawyer; secretary-general of U.N. (1946–52)

Lie·big \'lē-big\ Justus von 1803–1873 Freiherr *von Liebig* Ger. chemist

Lieb·knecht \'lēp-ˌknekt, -ˌnekt\ Karl 1871–1919 Ger. socialist leader

Li·far \'lē-ˌfär, lē-'\ Serge 1905–1986 Fr. (Russ.-born) choreographer & dancer

Li Hung–chang \'lē-'huṇ-'jäṇ\ 1823–1901 Chin. statesman

Lil·ien·thal \'lil-yən-ˌtäl, -ˌthȯl\ Otto 1848–1896 Ger. aeronautical engineer

Li·li·u·o·ka·la·ni \li-ˌlē-ə-ō-(ˌ)wō-kə-'lä-nē\ 1838–1917 *Lydia Paki Liliuokalani; Liliu Kamakaeha* queen of the Hawaiian Islands (1891–93)

Lil·lo \'li-(ˌ)lō\ George 1693–1739 Eng. dramatist

Li·món \li-'mōn\ José Arcadio 1908–1972 Am. (Mex.-born) dancer & choreographer

Lin·a·cre \'li-ni-kər\ Thomas *circa* 1460–1524 Eng. humanist & physician

Lin·coln \'liṇ-kən\ Abraham 1809–1865 16th president of the U.S. (1861–65) — **Lin·coln·esque** \ˌliṇ-kə-'nesk\ *or* **Lin·coln·ian** \liṇ-'kō-nē-ən\ *adjective*

Lincoln Benjamin 1733–1810 Am. general in Revolution

Lind \'lind\ Jenny 1820–1887 originally *Johanna Maria; the Swedish Nightingale* Swed. soprano

Lind·bergh \'lin(d)-ˌbərg\ Anne Spencer 1906– née *Morrow; wife of C. A.* Am. author

Lindbergh Charles Augustus 1902–1974 Am. aviator

Lind·ley \'lin(d)-lē\ John 1799–1865 Eng. botanist — **Lind·ley·an** \-lē-ən\ *adjective*

Lind·say \'lin-zē\ Howard 1889–1968 Am. dramatist & actor

Lindsay (Nicholas) Va·chel \'vā-chəl, 'va-\ 1879–1931 Am. poet

Link·la·ter \'liŋk-ˌlā-tər, -lə-tər\ Eric 1899–1974 Brit. writer

Linlithgow Marquis of — see HOPE

Lin·nae·us \lə-'nē-əs, -'nā-\ Carolus 1707–1778 Sw. *Carl von Lin·né* \lə-'nā\ Swed. botanist

Lin Yü–t'ang \'lin-'yü-'täŋ\ 1895–1976 Chin. author & philologist

Li·o·tard \ˌlē-ō-'tär\ Jean-Étienne 1702–1789 Swiss painter

Lip·chitz \'lip-shits\ Jacques 1891–1973 Am. (Latvian-born) sculptor

Li Peng \'lē-'pəŋ, -'peŋ\ 1928– Chin. Communist leader (1987–)

Lip·mann \'lip-mən\ Fritz Albert 1899–1986 Am. (Ger.-born) biochemist

Li Po \'lē-'bō, -'pō\ 701–762 Chin. poet

Lip·pi \'li-pē\ Fra Filippo *circa* 1406–1469 Florentine painter

Lippi Filippo *or* Filippino *circa* 1457–1504 *son of preceding* Florentine painter

Lipp·mann \lēp-'män, -'man\ Gabriel 1845–1921 Fr. physicist

Lipp·mann \'lip-mən\ Walter 1889–1974 Am. journalist & author

Lips·comb \'lips-kəm\ William Nunn, Jr. 1919– Am. chemist

Lip·ton \'lip-tən\ Sir Thomas Johnstone 1850–1931 Eng. merchant & yachtsman

Li Shih–min — see T'ANG T'AI TSUNG

Lisle, de — see LECONTE DE LISLE, ROUGET DE LISLE

Lis·ter \'lis-tər\ Joseph 1827–1912 1st Baron *Lister of Lyme Regis* Eng. surgeon

Liszt \'list\ Franz 1811–1886 Hung. pianist & composer — **Liszt·ian** \'lis-tē-ən\ *adjective*

Lit·tle·ton *or* **Lyt·tel·ton** \'li-t°l-tən\ *or* **Lut·tel·ton** \'lə-\ Sir Thomas 1422–1481 Eng. jurist

Lit·tré \li-'trā\ Maximilien-Paul-Émile 1801–1881 Fr. lexicographer

Lit·vi·nov \lit-'vē-ˌnóf, -ˌnóv, -ˌnəf\ Maksim Maksimovich 1876–1951 Soviet diplomat

Liu Shao–ch'i \lē-'ü-'shaú-'chē\ 1898–1974 Chin. Communist politician

Liv·ing·ston \'li-viŋ-stən\ Robert R. 1746–1813 Am. statesman

Liv·ing·stone \'li-viŋ-stən\ David 1813–1873 Scot. missionary & explorer in Africa

Livy \'li-vē\ 59 B.C.–A.D. 17 *Titus Livius* Rom. historian

Lloyd George \'lóid-'jórj\ David 1863–1945 1st Earl of *Dwy·for* \'dü-ē-ˌvór\ Brit. statesman; prime minister (1916–22)

Llull \'lyül°\ Ramon *circa* 1235–1316 *Raymond Lul·ly* \'lú-lē\ Catalan mystic & poet

Lo·ba·chev·sky \ˌlō-bə-'chef-skē, ˌlä-, -'chev-\ Nikolay Ivanovich 1792–1856 Russ. mathematician

Lo·ben·gu·la \ˌlō-bən-'gü-lə, -'gyü-\ *circa* 1836–1894 Zulu king of the Matabele

Locke \'läk\ John 1632–1704 Eng. philosopher — **Lock·ean** *also* **Locke·ian** \'lä-kē-ən\ *adjective*

Lock·hart \'lä-kərt, -ˌkärt; 'läk-ˌhärt\ John Gibson 1794–1854 Scot. novelist & biographer

Lock·yer \'lä-kyər\ Sir Joseph Norman 1836–1920 Eng. astronomer

Lodge \'läj\ Henry Cabot 1850–1924 Am. statesman & author

Lodge Henry Cabot 1902–1985 *grandson of preceding* Am. politician & diplomat

Lodge Sir Oliver Joseph 1851–1940 Eng. physicist

Lodge Thomas 1558–1625 Eng. poet & dramatist

Loeb \'lōb\ Jacques 1859–1924 Am. (Ger.-born) physiologist

Loewe \'lō\ Frederick 1901–1988 Am. (Austrian-born) composer

Loewi \'lō-ē\ Otto 1873–1961 Am. (Ger.-born) pharmacologist

Löff·ler \'le-flər\ Friedrich August Johannes 1852–1915 Ger. bacteriologist

Lo·max \'lō-ˌmaks\ John Avery 1867–1948 and his son Alan 1915– Am. folklorists

Lombard Peter — see PETER LOMBARD

Lom·bro·so \lóm-'brō-(ˌ)sō\ Ce·sa·re \'chā-zä-ˌrā\ 1836–1909 Ital. physician & psychiatrist

Lon·don \'lən-dən\ John Griffith 1876–1916 *Jack* Am. writer

Long \'lóŋ\ Crawford Williamson 1815–1878 Am. surgeon

Long Hu·ey \'hyü-ē\ Pierce 1893–1935 Am. politician

Long Stephen Harriman 1784–1864 Am. army officer & explorer

Long·fel·low \'lóŋ-ˌfe-(ˌ)lō\ Henry Wads·worth \'wädz-(ˌ)wərth\ 1807–1882 Am. poet

Lon·gi·nus \län-'jī-nəs\ 1st century A.D. Greek critic

Long·street \'lóŋ-ˌstrēt\ James 1821–1904 Am. Confederate general

Lönn·rot \'lœn-ˌrüt\ Elias 1802–1884 Finn. folklorist

Lons·dale \'länz-ˌdāl\ Frederick 1881–1954 Brit. dramatist

Ló·pez \'lō-ˌpez\ Carlos Antonio 1790–1862 president of Paraguay (1844–62)

López Francisco Solano 1827–1870 *son of preceding* president of Paraguay (1862–70)

López Ma·te·os \-mə-'tā-əs, -ˌ)ōs\ Adolfo 1910–1969 president of Mexico (1958–64)

López Por·til·lo \-pór-'tē-yō\ José 1920– president of Mexico (1976–82)

Lorca Federico García — see Federico GARCÍA LORCA

Lo·rentz \'lór-ˌen(t)s, 'lór-\ Hendrik Antoon 1853–1928 Du. physicist

Lo·renz \'lór-ˌen(t)s, 'lór-\ Konrad 1903–1989 Ger. (Austrian-born) ethologist

Lorrain Claude — see CLAUDE LORRAIN

Lo·thair I \lō-'tar, -'ter, -'thar, -'ther, 'lō-ˌ\ 795–855 Holy Roman emperor (840–855)

Lothair (*or* **III**) 1075–1137 king of Germany & Holy Roman emperor (1125–37)

Lo·ti \lō-'tē, lò-\ Pierre 1850–1923 pseudonym of *Louis-Marie-Julien Viaud* Fr. naval officer & novelist

Lou·bet \lü-'bā\ Émile-François 1838–1929 Fr. statesman; president of France (1899–1906)

Loudoun 4th Earl of — see John CAMPBELL

Lou·is \'lü-ē, lù-'ē\ name of 18 kings of France: especially **I** 778–840 (reigned 814–840); **V** (*le Fainéant*) 967–987 (reigned—last Carolingian—986–987); **IX** (*Saint*) 1214–1270 (reigned 1226–70); **XI** 1423–1483 (reigned 1461–83); **XII** 1462–1515 (reigned 1498–1515); **XIII** 1601–1643 (reigned 1610–43); **XIV** 1638–1715 (reigned 1643–1715); **XV** 1710–1774 (reigned 1715–74); **XVI** 1754–1793 (reigned 1774–92; guillotined); **XVII** 1785–1795 (nominally reigned 1793–95); **XVIII** 1755–1824 (reigned 1814–15; 1815–24)

Louis IV 1283?–1347 Duke of *Bavaria* king of Germany & Holy Roman emperor (1314–47)

Louis II de Bourbon — see CONDÉ

Louis–Napoléon — see NAPOLÉON III

Louis Phi·lippe \-fi-'lēp\ 1773–1850 *the Citizen King* king of the French (1830–48)

Louverture — see TOUSSAINT-LOUVERTURE

Louÿs \lü-'ē\ Pierre 1870–1925 Fr. writer

Love·lace \'ləv-ˌlās\ Richard 1618–1657 Eng. poet

Lov·ell \'lə-vəl\ Sir (Alfred Charles) Bernard 1913– Brit. astronomer

Lov·er \'lə-vər\ Samuel 1797–1868 Irish novelist

Low \'lō\ Sir David Alexander Cecil 1891–1963 Brit. cartoonist

Low·ell \'lō-əl\ Amy 1874–1925 Am. poet & critic

Lowell James Russell 1819–1891 Am. poet, essayist, & dramatist

Lowell Percival 1855–1916 *brother of Amy* Am. astronomer

Lowell Robert Traill Spence 1917–1977 Am. poet

Lowes \'lōz\ John Livingston 1867–1945 Am. educator

Lowndes \'laún(d)z\ William Thomas 1798–1843 Eng. bibliographer

Low·ry \'laú-(ə)r-ē\ (Clarence) Malcolm 1909–1957 Brit. writer

Loyola Saint Ignatius — see IGNATIUS OF LOYOLA

Lub·bock \'lə-bək\ Sir John 1834–1913 1st Baron *Ave·bury* \'āv-b(ə-)rē, 'ā-\ *son of Sir J. W.* Eng. financier & author

Lubbock Sir John William 1803–1865 Eng. astronomer & mathematician

Luc·an \'lü-kən\ A.D. 39–65 *Marcus Annaeus Lucanus* Rom. poet

Lu·cas \'lü-kəs\ Robert Emerson, Jr. 1937– Am. economist

Luce \'lüs\ Clare 1903–1987 née *Boothe* \'büth\ *wife of H. R.* Am. dramatist, politician, & diplomat

Luce Henry Robinson 1898–1967 Am. editor & publisher

Lu·cre·tius \lü-'krē-sh(ē-)əs\ *circa* 96–*circa* 55 B.C. *Titus Lucretius Carus* Rom. poet & philosopher — **Lu·cre·tian** \-shən\ *adjective*

Lu·cul·lus \lü-'kə-ləs\ Lucius Licinius *circa* 117–58(or 56) B.C. Rom. general & epicure

Lu·den·dorff \'lü-d°n-ˌdórf\ Erich Friedrich Wilhelm 1865–1937 Ger. general

Lu Hsün \'lü-'shün\ 1881–1936 pseudonym of *Chou Shu-Jen* Chin. writer

Lu·i·gi Ame·deo \lə-'wē-jē-ˌä-mə-'dā-(ˌ)ō\ 1873–1933 Duca *D'Abruz·zi* \dä-'brüt-tsē\ & Prince of *Savoy-Aosta* Ital. explorer & naval officer

Lul·ly \lü-'lē\ Jean-Baptiste 1632–1687 Fr. (Ital.-born) composer

Lully Raymond — see Ramon LLULL

Lunt \'lənt\ Alfred 1893–1977 *husband of Lynn Fontanne* Am. actor

Lu·ria \'lür-ē-ə\ Salvador Edward 1912–1991 Am. (Ital.-born) microbiologist

Lu·ther \'lü-thər\ Martin 1483–1546 Ger. Reformation leader

Lu·thu·li \lü-'tü-lē, -'thü-\ Albert John 1898–1967 So. African reformer

Lux·em·burg \'lək-səm-ˌbərg, 'lúk-səm-ˌbúrk\ Rosa 1870–1919 Ger. socialist leader

Lwoff \'lwóf\ André-Michael 1902–1995 Fr. microbiologist

Lyau·tey \lē-ˌō-'tā\ Louis-Hubert-Gonzalve 1854–1934 Fr. soldier & colonial administrator

Ly·cur·gus \lī-'kər-gəs\ 9th century B.C. Spartan lawgiver

Lyd·gate \'lid-ˌgāt, -gət\ John *circa* 1370–*circa* 1450 Eng. poet

Ly·ell \'lī-əl\ Sir Charles 1797–1875 Brit. geologist

Lyly \'li-lē\ John 1554?–1606 Eng. author

Lynd \'lind\ Robert Staugh·ton \'stó-t°n\ 1892–1970 & his wife Helen née *Merrell* 1896–1982 Am. sociologists

Ly·nen \'lü-nən\ Feodor Felix Konrad 1911–1979 Ger. biochemist

Ly·on \'lī-ən\ Mary 1797–1849 Am. educator

Ly·ons \'lī-ənz\ Joseph Aloysius 1879–1939 Austral. statesman; prime minister (1931–39)

Ly·san·der \lī-'san-dər\ *died* 395 B.C. Spartan commander

Ly·sen·ko \lə-'sen-(ˌ)kō\ Trofim Denisovich 1898–1976 Soviet biologist

Lys·i·as \'li-sē-əs\ *circa* 445–after 380 B.C. Athenian orator

Ly·sim·a·chus \lī-'si-mə-kəs\ *circa* 355–*circa* 281 B.C. Macedonian general under Alexander the Great; king of Thrace (306)

Ly·sip·pus \lī-'si-pəs\ 4th century B.C. Greek sculptor

Lyt·ton \'li-t°n\ 1st Baron 1803–1873 *Edward George Earle Bul·wer-Lytton* \'búl-wər-\; *brother of Sir Henry Bulwer* Eng. author

Lytton 1st Earl of 1831–1891 (*Edward*) *Robert Bulwer-Lytton*; pseudonym *Owen Meredith; son of preceding* Brit. statesman & poet

Mac·Ar·thur \mə-'kär-thər\ Arthur 1845–1912 Am. general

MacArthur Charles 1895–1956 Am. dramatist

MacArthur Douglas 1880–1964 *son of Arthur* Am. general

Ma·cau·lay \mə-'kó-lē\ Dame Rose 1881–1958 Eng. novelist

Macaulay Thomas Babington 1800–1859 1st Baron *Macaulay* Eng. historian, author, & statesman

Mac·beth \mək-'beth\ *died* 1057 king of Scotland (1040–57)

Mac·Bride \mək-'brīd\ Seán 1904–1988 Irish statesman

Mac·ca·bees \'ma-kə-ˌbēz\ Judas *or* Judah *died* 161 B.C. surname *Mac·ca·ba·eus* \ˌma-kə-'bē-əs\ Jewish patriot

Mac·Di·ar·mid \mək-'dər-məd, -mət\ Hugh 1892–1978 pseudonym of *Christopher Murray Grieve* \'grēv\ Scot. poet

Mac·don·ald \mək-'dä-n°ld\ George 1824–1905 Scot. novelist & poet

Macdonald Sir John Alexander 1815–1891 Canad. statesman; 1st prime minister of Dominion of Canada (1867–73; 1878–91)

Mac·Don·ald \mək-'dä-n°ld\ (James) Ramsay 1866–1937 Brit. statesman

Mac·don·ough \mək-'dä-nə, -'də-\ Thomas 1783–1825 Am. naval officer

Mac·Dow·ell \mək-'daù-(ə)l\ Edward Alexander 1860–1908 Am. composer

Mach \'mäk, 'mäk\ Ernst 1838–1916 Austrian physicist & philosopher

Ma·cha·do y Mo·ra·les \mä-'chä-dō-,ē-mə-'rä-ləs\ Gerardo 1871–1939 president of Cuba (1925–33)

Ma·chi·a·vel·li \,ma-kē-ə-'ve-lē\ Niccolò 1469–1527 Ital. political philosopher

Mac·Kaye \mə-'kī\ Percy 1875–1956 Am. poet & dramatist

Mack·en·sen \'mä-kən-zən\ August von 1849–1945 Ger. field marshal

Mac·ken·zie \mə-'ken-zē\ Alexander 1822–1892 Canad. (Scot.-born) statesman; prime minister (1873–78)

Mackenzie Sir Alexander Campbell 1847–1935 Brit. composer & conductor

Mackenzie Sir Compton 1883–1972 Eng. novelist

Mackenzie William Lyon 1795–1861 Canad. (Scot.-born) insurgent leader

Mac·kin·der \mə-'kin-dər\ Sir Halford John 1861–1947 Eng. geographer

Maclaren Ian — see John WATSON

Mac·Leish \mə-'klēsh\ Archibald 1892–1982 Am. poet & administrator

Mac·Len·nan \mə-'kle-nən\ (John) Hugh 1907–1990 Canad. novelist

Mac·leod \mə-'klaùd\ John James Rickard 1876–1935 Scot. physiologist

Mac–Ma·hon \,mäk-,mä-'ōⁿ; mək-'ma(-ə)n, -'män\ Marie-Edme-Patrice-Maurice 1808–1893 Comte de Mac-Mahon; duc de Magenta marshal (1859) & president (1873–79) of France

Mac·mil·lan \mək-'mi-lən\ (Maurice) Harold 1894–1986 Brit. prime minister (1957–63)

Mac·Mil·lan \mək-'mi-lən\ Donald Baxter 1874–1970 Am. explorer

Mac·Neice \mək-'nēs\ Louis 1907–1963 Irish poet

Mac·pher·son \mək-'fər-sᵊn\ James 1736–1796 Scot. writer

Mac·rea·dy \mə-'krē-dē\ William Charles 1793–1873 Eng. actor

Ma·da·ria·ga y Ro·jo \,mä-də-rē-'ä-gə-(,)ē-'rō-(,)hō\ Salvador de 1886–1978 Span. writer & diplomat

Ma·de·ro \mə-'der-(,)ō\ Francisco Indalecio 1873–1913 president of Mexico (1911–13)

Mad·i·gan \'ma-də-gən\ Edward R. 1936–1994 U.S. secretary of agriculture (1991–93)

Mad·i·son \'ma-də-sən\ Dolley 1768–1849 née (Dorothea) Payne; wife of James Am. socialite

Madison James 1751–1836 4th president of the U.S. (1809–17) — **Mad·i·so·nian** \,ma-də-'sō-nē-ən, -nyən\ adjective

Mae·ce·nas \mi-'sē-nəs\ Gaius circa 70–8 B.C. Rom. statesman & patron of literature

Maes \'mäs\ Nicolaes 1634–1693 also called Nicolas Maas Du. painter

Mae·ter·linck \'mä-tər-,liŋk also 'me-, 'ma-\ Maurice-Polydore-Marie-Bernard 1862–1949 Belg. poet, dramatist, & essayist — **Mae·ter·linck·ian** \,mä-tər-'liŋ-kē-ən, ,me-, ,ma-\ adjective

Ma·gel·lan \mə-'je-lən, chiefly British -'ge-\ Ferdinand circa 1480–1521 Pg. Fernão de Magalhães Pg. navigator & explorer

Ma·gi·not \,ma-zhə-'nō, ,ma-jə-\ André 1877–1932 Fr. politician

Ma·gritte \mə-'grēt\ René-François-Ghislain 1898–1967 Belg. painter

Mag·say·say \mäg-'sī-,sī, -,sī-'sī\ Ramon 1907–1957 president of Philippines (1953–57)

Mah·fouz \'mäk-füz\ Naguib 1911– Egypt. writer

Mah·ler \'mä-lər\ Gustav 1860–1911 Austrian composer — **Mah·ler·ian** \mä-'lir-ē-ən, -'ler-\ adjective

Mah·mud II \mä-'müd\ 1785–1839 Ottoman sultan (1808–39)

Mail·er \'mā-lər\ Norman 1923– Am. author

Mail·lol \mä-'yól, -'yōl\ Aristide 1861–1944 Fr. sculptor

Mai·mon·i·des \mī-'mä-nə-,dēz\ Moses 1135–1204 Hebrew Moses ben Maimon Jewish philosopher, jurist, & physician

Maine \'mān\ Sir Henry James Sumner 1822–1888 Eng. jurist

Main·te·non \,maⁿ(n)-tᵊn-'ōⁿ, maⁿ(n)t-'nōⁿ\ Marquise de 1635–1719 Françoise d'Aubigné; consort of Louis XIV

Mait·land \'māt-lənd\ Frederic William 1850–1906 Eng. historian

Ma·jor \'mā-jər\ John 1943– Brit. prime minister (1990–97)

Mal·a·mud \'ma-lə-(,)məd\ Bernard 1914–1986 Am. writer

Ma·lan \mə-'lan, -'län\ Daniel François 1874–1959 So. African editor; prime minister (1948–54)

Mal·colm X \'mal-kəm-'eks\ 1925–1965 originally Malcolm Little Am. civil rights leader

Male·branche \,mal-'bräⁿsh, mäl-; ,ma-lə-, ,mä-\ Nicolas de 1638–1715 Fr. philosopher

Ma·len·kov \mə-'len-,kóf, -,kóv, -'len-kəf; ,ma-lən-'kóf, -'kóv\ Georgy Maksimilianovich 1902–1988 Soviet politician

Mal·herbe \ma-'lerb, mä-\ François de 1555–1628 Fr. poet

Ma·li·nov·sky \,ma-lə-'nóf-skē, ,mä-, -'nóv-\ Rodion Yakovlevich 1898–1967 Soviet general

Ma·li·now·ski \,ma-lə-'nóf-skē, ,mä-, -'nóv-\ Bronislaw Kasper 1884–1942 Am. (Pol.-born) anthropologist

Mal·lar·mé \,ma-,lär-'mä\ Stéphane 1842–1898 Fr. poet

Ma·lone \mə-'lōn\ Edmond 1741–1812 Irish scholar

Mal·o·ry \'ma-lə-rē, 'mal-rē\ Sir Thomas flourished 1470 Eng. author

Mal·pi·ghi \mal-'pē-gē, -'pi-\ Marcello 1628–1694 Ital. anatomist — **Mal·pi·ghi·an** \-ən\ adjective

Mal·raux \mal-'rō\ André 1901–1976 Fr. writer & art historian

Mal·thus \'mal-thəs\ Thomas Robert 1766–1834 Eng. economist

Mam·et \'ma-mət\ David Alan 1947– Am. dramatist

Man·del \mäⁿ(n)-'del\ Georges 1885–1944 originally Louis-Georges Rothschild Fr. politician

Man·de·la \man-'de-lə\ Nelson Rolihlahla 1918– So. African black political leader; president of So. Africa (1994–)

Man·del·brot \'man-dəl-,brōt\ Benoit 1924– Am. (Pol.-born) mathematician & scientist

Man·de·ville \'man-də-,vil\ Bernard de 1670–1733 Brit. (Du.-born) satirist & philosopher

Mandeville Sir John flourished 1356 pseudonym of an unidentified travel writer

Ma·net \ma-'nā, mä-\ Édouard 1832–1883 Fr. painter

Ma·nil·i·us \mə-'ni-lē-əs\ Gaius 1st century B.C. Rom. politician

Mann \'man\ Horace 1796–1859 Am. educator

Mann \'män, 'man\ Thomas 1875–1955 Am. (Ger.-born) author

Man·ner·heim \'mä-nər-,hām, 'ma-, -,hīm\ Baron Carl Gustaf Emil von 1867–1951 Finn. general & statesman

Man·ning \'ma-niŋ\ Henry Edward 1808–1892 Eng. cardinal

Mans·field \'mans-,fēld, 'manz-\ Katherine 1888–1923 pseudonym of Kathleen Mansfield Beauchamp \'bē-chəm\ Brit. (N.Z.-born) writer

Man·son \'man(t)-sən\ Sir Patrick 1844–1922 Brit. parasitologist

Man·stein \'män-shtīn\ Fritz Erich von 1887–1973 original surname von Lewinski Ger. field marshal

Man·sur, al- \,al-,man-'sùr\ 709(to 714)–775 in full Abū Ja'far al-Manṣūr or al-Manṣūr al-'Abbāsī Arab caliph (754–775) & founder of Baghdad

Man·te·gna \män-'tän-yə\ Andrea 1431–1506 Ital. painter & engraver

Man·uel \män-'wel\ Don Juan 1282–1349 Span. nobleman & writer

Man·zo·ni \man(d)-'zō-nē\ Alessandro Francesco Tommaso Antonio 1785–1873 Ital. novelist & poet

Mao Tse-tung \'maù-(')(d)zə-'dùŋ, -(')tsə-\ 1893–1976 pinyin Mao Ze-dong Chin. Communist; leader of People's Republic of China (1949–76)

Map \'map\ Walter circa 1140–circa 1209 Eng. writer

Ma·rat \mə-'rä\ Jean-Paul 1743–1793 Fr. (Swiss-born) revolutionary

Mar·cel·lus \mär-'se-ləs\ Marcus Claudius 268?–208 B.C. Rom. general

March 1st Earl of — see Roger de MORTIMER

Mar·co·ni \mär-'kō-nē\ Guglielmo 1874–1937 Ital. physicist & inventor

Marco Polo — see POLO

Mar·cos \'mär-(,)kōs\ Ferdinand Edralin 1917–1989 president of the Philippines (1965–86)

Mar·cus \'mär-kəs\ Rudolph Arthur 1923– Am. (Canad.-born) chemist

Marcus Aurelius — see Marcus Aurelius AN-TONINUS

Mar·cu·se \mär-'kü-zə\ Herbert 1898–1979 Am. (Ger.-born) social & political philosopher

Mar·ga·ret \'mär-g(ə-)rət\ of Angoulême 1492–1549 queen of Henry II of Navarre & writer

Margaret of Anjou 1430–1482 queen of Henry VI of England

Margaret of Valois or **Margaret of France** 1553–1615 queen consort of Henry of Navarre

Margaret Rose \'rōz\ 1930– princess of Great Britain

Mar·gre·the II \mär-'grā-tə\ 1940– queen of Denmark (1972–)

Ma·ria The·re·sa \mə-'rē-ə-tə-'rā-sə, -'rä-zə\ 1717–1780 wife of Holy Roman Emperor Francis I archduchess of Austria & queen of Hungary & Bohemia

Ma·rie \mə-'rē\ 1875–1938 queen of Romania (1914–27); queen dowager (1927–38)

Marie An·toi·nette \,an-two-'net, -tə-\ 1755–1793 daughter of Maria Theresa & wife of Louis XVI of France

Ma·rie–Lou·ise \mə-'rē-lə-'wēz, -'lwēz\ 1791–1847 daughter of Francis II of Austria & 2d wife of Napoléon I

Ma·rie de Mé·di·cis \mə-'rē-də-'me-də-(,)chē, -,mä-də-'sē(s)\ 1573–1642 2d wife of Henry IV of France regent for Louis XIII

Mar·in \'mar-ən\ John Cheri 1870–1953 Am. painter

Ma·ri·net·ti \,mar-ə-'ne-tē, ,mär-\ (Emilio) Filippo Tommaso 1876–1944 Ital. poet

Ma·ri·ni \mə-'rē-nē\ or **Ma·ri·no** \-(,)nō\ Giambattista 1569–1625 Ital. poet

Mar·i·on \'mer-ē-ən, 'mar-ē-\ Francis 1732?–1795 the Swamp Fox Am. general in Revolution

Ma·ri·otte \mär-yòt\ Edme circa 1620–1684 Fr. physicist

Mar·i·tain \,mar-ə-'taⁿ\ Jacques 1882–1973 Fr. philosopher & diplomat

Mar·i·us \'mer-ē-əs, 'mar-\ Gaius circa 157–86 B.C. Rom. general

Ma·ri·vaux \,mar-ə-'vō\ Pierre Carlet de Chamblain de 1688–1763 Fr. dramatist & novelist

Mark Antony or **Anthony** — see Marcus ANTO-NIUS

Mark·ham \'mär-kəm\ Beryl 1902–1986 Brit. aviator

Markham Edwin 1852–1940 originally Charles Edward Anson Markham Am. poet

Mar·ko·va \mär-'kō-və\ Dame Ali·cia \ə-'lē-sē-ə\ 1910– originally Lilian Alicia Marks Eng. dancer

Mar·ko·witz \'mär-kə-,wits\ Harry M. 1927– Am. economist

Marlborough 1st Duke of — see John CHURCHILL

Mar·lowe \'mär-,lō\ Christopher 1564–1593 Eng. dramatist — **Mar·lo·vi·an** \mär-'lō-vē-ən, -vyən\ adjective

Marlowe Julia 1866–1950 originally Sarah Frances Frost Am. (Eng.-born) actress

Mar·mont \mär-'mōⁿ\ Auguste-Frédéric-Louis Viesse de 1774–1852 Duc de Raguse Fr. general; marshal of France

Mar·mon·tel \,mär-(,)mōⁿ-'tel\ Jean-François 1723–1799 Fr. author

Ma·rot \ma-'rō\ Clément 1496?–1544 Fr. poet

Mar·quand \mär-'kwänd\ John Phillips 1893–1960 Am. novelist

\ə\ abut \ᵊ\ kitten \ər\ further \a\ ash \ā\ ace
\ä\ mop, mar \aù\ out \ch\ chin \e\ bet \ē\ easy
\g\ go \i\ hit \ī\ ice \j\ job \ŋ\ sing \ō\ go
\ò\ law \òi\ boy \th\ thin \t͟h\ the \ü\ loot \ù\ foot
\y\ yet \zh\ vision see also Guide to Pronunciation

Mar·quette \mär-'ket\ Jacques 1637–1675 *Père* \,pir, ,per\ *Marquette* Fr.-born Jesuit missionary & explorer in America

Mar·quis \'mär-kwəs\ Donald Robert Perry 1878–1937 Am. humorist

Mar·ry·at \'mar-ē-ət\ Frederick 1792–1848 Eng. naval commander & novelist

Marsh \'märsh\ Dame (Edith) Ngaio \'nī-(,)ō\ 1899–1982 N.Z. writer

Mar·shall \'mär-shəl\ Alfred 1842–1924 Eng. economist

Marshall George Catlett 1880–1959 Am. general & statesman

Marshall John 1755–1835 Am. jurist; chief justice U.S. Supreme Court (1801–35)

Marshall Thomas Riley 1854–1925 vice president of the U.S. (1913–21)

Marshall Thurgood 1908–1993 Am. jurist

Mar·sil·i·us \mär-'si-lē-əs\ **of Padua** *circa* 1280–*circa* 1343 Ital. scholar

Mar·ston \'mär-stən\ John 1576–1634 Eng. dramatist

Martel Charles — see CHARLES MARTEL

Mar·tens \'mär-tⁿz\ Fyodor Fyodorovich 1845–1909 Russ. jurist

Martens Wilfried 1936– prime minister of Belgium (1979–92)

Mar·tial \'mär-shəl\ *circa* A.D. 40–*circa* 103 *Marcus Valerius Martialis* Rom. epigrammatist

Mar·tin \'mär-tⁿn, mär-taⁿ\ Saint *circa* 316–397 *Martin of Tours* patron saint of France

Mar·tin \'mär-tⁿn\ Archer John Porter 1910– Brit. chemist

Martin Glenn Luther 1886–1955 Am. airplane manufacturer

Martin Homer Dodge 1836–1897 Am. painter

Martin Joseph William 1884–1968 Am. publisher & politician

Martin Lynn Morley 1939– U.S. secretary of labor (1991–93)

Mar·tin du Gard \mär-taⁿ-dü-gär\ Roger 1881–1958 Fr. author

Mar·ti·neau \'mär-tⁿn-,ō\ Harriet 1802–1876 Eng. novelist & economist

Martineau James 1805–1900 *brother of Harriet* Eng. theologian & philosopher

Mar·ti·ni \mär-'tē-nē\ Simone *circa* 1284–1344 Ital. painter

Mar·tin·son \'mär-tēn-(,)sòn\ Harry Edmund 1904–1978 Swed. author

Mar·vell \'mär-vəl\ Andrew 1621–1678 Eng. poet & satirist

Marx \'märks\ Karl Heinrich 1818–1883 Ger. political philosopher & socialist

Mary I \'mer-ē, 'mar-ē, 'mä-rē\ 1516–1558 *Mary Tudor; Bloody Mary* queen of England (1553–58)

Mary II 1662–1694 joint Brit. sovereign with William III

Mary Stuart 1542–1587 *Mary, Queen of Scots* queen of Scotland (1542–67)

Ma·sac·cio \mə-'zä-ch(ē-,)ō\ 1401–1428 originally *Tommaso di Giovanni di Simone Guidi* Ital. painter

Ma·sa·ryk \'mä-sə-(,)rik, 'ma-\ Jan \'yän, 'yan\ Gar·rigue \gə-'rēg\ 1886–1948 *son of T. G.* Czech diplomat & politician

Masaryk To·máš \'tò-,mäsh, 'tä-məs\ Garrigue 1850–1937 Czech philosopher & statesman; 1st president of Czechoslovakia (1918–35)

Ma·sca·gni \mä-'skän-yē, ma-\ Pietro 1863–1945 Ital. composer

Mase·field \'mās-,fēld\ John 1878–1967 Eng. author; poet laureate (1930–67)

Mas·i·nis·sa *or* **Mas·si·nis·sa** \,ma-sə-'ni-sə\ *circa* 240–148 B.C. king of Numidia

Ma·son \'mā-sⁿn\ Charles 1728–1786 Eng. astronomer & surveyor

Mason George 1725–1792 Am. statesman in Revolution

Mas·sa·soit \,ma-sə-'sòit\ *died* 1661 Wampanoag Indian chief

Mas·sé·na \,ma-sā-'nä, mə-'sä-nə\ André 1758–1817 Duc *de Rivoli*; Prince *d'Ess·ling* \des-lēn\ Fr. general

Mas·se·net \,ma-sⁿn-'ā, ma-'snä\ Jules-Émile Frédéric 1842–1912 Fr. composer

Mas·sey \'ma-sē\ William Ferguson 1856–1925 N.Z. statesman

Mas·sine \ma-'sēn\ Léonide 1896–1979 originally *Leonid Fedorovich Miassin* Am. (Russ.-born) dancer & choreographer

Mas·sin·ger \'ma-sⁿn-jər\ Philip 1583–1640 Eng. dramatist

Mas·son \'ma-sⁿn\ David 1822–1907 Scot. editor & author

Mas·sys \'mä-,sīs\ *or* **Mat·sys** \'mät-sīs\ *or* **Mes·sys** \'me-sīs\ *or* **Met·sys** \'met-sīs\ Quentin *circa* 1466–1530 Flem. painter

Mas·ters \'mas-tərz\ Edgar Lee 1869–1950 Am. author

Math·er \'ma-thər, -thər\ Cotton 1663–1728 Am. clergyman & author

Mather Increase 1639–1723 *father of Cotton* Am. clergyman & author; president Harvard College (1685–1701)

Ma·tisse \ma-'tēs, mə-\ Henri-Émile-Benoît 1869–1954 Fr. painter

Ma·tsuo \mät-'sü-ō, mät-sü-ō\ Ba·shō \'bä-,shō\ 1644–1694 pseudonym of *Matsuo Munefusa* Jp. haiku poet

Ma·tsu·o·ka \,mat-sə-'wō-kə, ,mät-, -(,)kä\ Yō·suke 1880–1946 Jp. statesman

Mat·te·ot·ti \,ma-tē-'ō-tē, ,mä-, -'ò-\ Giacomo 1885–1924 Ital. socialist

Mat·thews \'ma-(,)thyüz\ (James) Brander 1852–1929 Am. educator & author

Maugham \'mòm\ (William) Somerset 1874–1965 Eng. novelist & dramatist

Mau·nou·ry \mō-nə-'rē\ Michel-Joseph 1847–1923 Fr. general

Mau·pas·sant \,mō-pə-'säⁿ\ (Henri-René-Albert-) Guy de 1850–1893 Fr. writer

Mau·riac \mòr-'yäk, ,mór-ē-'äk\ François 1885–1970 Fr. author

Mau·rice \'mòr-əs, 'mär-; mò-'rēs\ *German* **Mo·ritz** \'mōr-əts, 'mòr-\ 1521–1553 elector of Saxony (1547–53) & general

Maurice of Nassau 1567–1625 Prince of *Orange* Du. general & statesman

Mau·rois \mòr-'wä\ André 1885–1967 pseudonym of *Émile-Salomon-Wilhelm Her·zog* \'er-,zòg\ Fr. writer

Mau·ry \'mòr-ē, 'mär-\ Matthew Fontaine 1806–1873 Am. naval officer & oceanographer

Mau·ser \'maù-zər\ Peter Paul 1838–1914 & his brother Wilhelm 1834–1882 Ger. inventors

Maw·son \'mò-sⁿn\ Sir Douglas 1882–1958 Austral. explorer & geologist

Max·im \'mak-səm\ Sir Hiram Stevens 1840–1916 Brit. (Am.-born) inventor

Maxim Hudson 1853–1927 *brother of Sir Hiram* Am. inventor

Max·i·mil·ian \,mak-sə-'mil-yən\ 1832–1867 *brother of Francis Joseph I of Austria* emperor of Mexico (1864–67)

Maximilian I 1459–1519 Holy Roman emperor (1493–1519)

Maximilian II 1527–1576 Holy Roman emperor (1564–76)

Max·well \'maks-,wel, -wəl\ James Clerk \'klärk\ 1831–1879 Scot. physicist — **Max·wel·li·an** \maks-'we-lē-ən\ *adjective*

May \'mā\ Sir Thomas Erskine 1815–1886 1st Baron *Farn·bor·ough* \'färn-,bər-ə, -,bə-rə, -b(ə-)rə\ Eng. jurist

Ma·ya·kov·ski \,mä-yə-'kòf-skē, -'kòv-\ Vladimir Vladimirovich 1893–1930 Russ. poet

May·er \'mī(-ə)r\ Maria Goeppert 1906–1972 Am. (Ger.-born) physicist

Mayo \'mā-(,)ō\ Charles Horace 1865–1939 & his brother William James 1861–1939 Am. surgeons

Ma·za·rin \,ma-zə-'raⁿ\ Jules 1602–1661 Fr. cardinal & statesman

Ma·zo·wie·cki \,mä-zō-'vyet-skē\ Tadeusz 1927– prime minister of Poland (1989–91)

Maz·zi·ni \mät-'sē-nē, mäd-'zē-\ Giuseppe 1805–1872 Ital. patriot

Mc·Adoo \'ma-kə-,dü\ William Gibbs 1863–1941 Am. administrator

M'·Car·thy \mə-'kär-thē *also* -tē\ Justin 1830–1912 Irish writer & politician

Mc·Car·thy \mə-'kär-thē *also* -tē\ Eugene Joseph 1916– Am. politician

McCarthy Joseph Raymond 1908–1957 Am. politician

McCarthy Mary Therese 1912–1989 Am. writer

Mc·Clel·lan \mə-'kle-lən\ George Brinton 1826–1885 Am. general & politician

Mc·Clin·tock \mə-'klin-tək\ Barbara 1902–1992 Am. botanist

Mc·Clos·key \mə-'kläs-kē\ John 1810–1885 1st Am. cardinal

Mc·Cloy \mə-'klòi\ John Jay 1895–1989 Am. banker & government official

Mc·Clure \mə-'klùr\ Samuel Sidney 1857–1949 Am. (Irish-born) editor & publisher

Mc·Cor·mack \mə-'kòr-mək, -mik\ John 1884–1945 Am. (Irish-born) tenor

McCormack John William 1891–1980 Am. politician

Mc·Cor·mick \mə-'kòr-mik\ Cyrus Hall 1809–1884 Am. inventor

McCormick Robert Rutherford 1880–1955 Am. newspaper publisher

Mc·Cul·lers \mə-'kə-lərz\ Carson 1917–1967 née *Smith* Am. writer

Mc·Dow·ell \mək-'daù(-ə)l\ Ephraim 1771–1830 Am. surgeon

McDowell Irvin 1818–1885 Am. general

Mc·Gill \mə-'gil\ James 1744–1813 Canad. (Scot.-born) businessman & philanthropist

Mc·Gov·ern \mə-'gə-vərn\ George Stanley 1922– Am. politician

Mc·Guf·fey \mə-'gə-fē\ William Holmes 1800–1873 Am. educator

Mc·Ken·na \mə-'ke-nə\ Sio·bhan \shə-'vòn\ 1923?–1986 Irish actress

Mc·Kim \mə-'kim\ Charles Follen 1847–1909 Am. architect

Mc·Kin·ley \mə-'kin-lē\ William 1843–1901 25th president of the U.S. (1897–1901)

Mc·Lu·han \mə-'klü-ən\ (Herbert) Marshall 1911–1980 Canad. educator

Mc·Ma·hon \mək-'mä(-ə)n\ Sir William 1908–1988 prime minister of Australia (1971–72)

Mc·Mil·lan \mək-'mi-lən\ Edwin Mattison 1907–1991 Am. chemist

Mc·Na·mara \,mak-nə-'mar-ə, 'mak-nə-,mar-ə\ Robert Strange 1916– U.S. secretary of defense (1961–68)

Mc·Naugh·ton \mək-'nò-tⁿn\ Andrew George Latta 1887–1966 Canad. general & diplomat

Mead \'mēd\ Margaret 1901–1978 Am. anthropologist

Meade \'mēd\ George Gordon 1815–1872 Am. general

Meade James Edward 1907–1995 Brit. economist

Mea·ny \'mē-nē\ George 1894–1980 Am. labor leader

Med·a·war \'me-də-wər\ Peter Brian 1915–1987 Eng. anatomist

Me·dei·ros \mə-'der-əs, -(,)ōs\ Humberto 1915–1983 Am. (Port.-born) cardinal

Me·di·ci, de' \'me-də-(,)chē\ Catherine — see CATHERINE DE MÉDICIS

Medici, de' Cosimo 1389–1464 *the Elder* Florentine financier & ruler

Medici, de' Cosimo I 1519–1574 *the Great;* Duke of *Florence;* Grand Duke of *Tuscany*

Medici, de' Giulio — see CLEMENT VII

Medici, de' Lorenzo 1449–1492 *the Magnificent* Florentine statesman, ruler, & patron

Me·di·na-Si·do·nia \mə-'dē-nə-sə-'dòn-yə\ Duque de *died* 1619 *Alonso Pérez de Guzmán* Span. admiral

Meer van Delft, van der — see Jan VERMEER

Meigh·en \'mē-ən\ Arthur 1874–1960 Canad. statesman; prime minister (1920–21; 1926)

Me·ir \me-'ir\ Golda 1898–1978 originally *Goldie Mabovitch*, later *Goldie Myerson* prime minister of Israel (1969–74)

Meis·so·nier \,mā-sⁿn-'yä\ Jean-Louis-Ernest 1815–1891 Fr. painter

Meit·ner \'mīt-nər\ Li·se \'lē-zə\ 1878–1968 Ger. physicist

Me·lanch·thon \mə-'laŋ(k)-thən, -tən\ Philipp 1497–1560 original surname *Schwartzerd* Ger. scholar & religious reformer

Mel·ba \'mel-bə\ Dame Nellie 1861–1931 originally *Helen Porter Mitchell* Austral. soprano

Mel·chers \'mel-chərz\ (Julius) Gari 1860–1932 Am. painter

Mel·chi·or \'mel-kē-,òr\ Lau·ritz \'laù-rəts\ Lebrecht Hommel 1890–1973 Am. (Dan.-born) tenor

Mel·lon \'me-lən\ Andrew William 1855–1937 Am. financier

Mel·ville \'mel-,vil\ Herman 1819–1891 Am. author

Mem·ling \'mem-liŋ\ *or* **Mem·linc** \-liŋk\ Hans *circa* 1430–1494 Flem. painter

Me·nan·der \mə-'nan-dər\ 342–292 B.C. Greek dramatist

Men·chú \'men-ˌchü\ Rigoberta 1959– Guatemalan human rights activist

Mencius — see MENG-TZU

Menck·en \'meŋ-kən, 'men-\ Henry Louis 1880–1956 Am. editor — **Menck·e·nian** \meŋ-'kē-nē-ən, men-\ *adjective*

Men·del \'men-dᵊl\ Gregor Johann 1822–1884 Austrian botanist — **Men·del·ian** \men-'de-lē-ən, -'dē-\ *adjective*

Men·de·le·yev \ˌmen-də-'lā-əf\ Dmitry Ivanovich 1834–1907 Russ. chemist

Men·dels·sohn \'men-dᵊl-sən\ Moses 1729–1786 Ger. philosopher

Mendelssohn–Bar·thol·dy \-bär-'tōl-dē, -'thōl-\ (Jakob Ludwig) Felix 1809–1847 *grandson of preceding* Ger. composer, pianist, & conductor — **Men·dels·sohn·ian** \ˌmen-dᵊl-'sō-nē-ən, -nyən\ *adjective*

Mendès–France \maⁿ-des-fräⁿs\ Pierre 1907–1982 Fr. statesman

Men·do·za \men-'dō-zə\ Antonio de *circa* 1490–1552 Span. colonial governor

Men·e·lik II \'me-nᵊl-(ˌ)ik\ 1844–1913 emperor of Ethiopia (1889–1913)

Men·em \'me-ˌnem, -nəm\ Carlos Saúl 1930– president of Argentina (1989–)

Me·nén·dez de Av·i·lés \mə-'nen-dəs-dā-ˌä-və-'lās\ Pedro 1519–1574 Span. navigator & explorer

Me·nes \'mē-(ˌ)nēz\ *flourished circa* 3100 B.C. king of Egypt

Mengs \'meŋ(k)s\ Anton Raphael 1728–1779 Ger. painter

Meng-tzu \'məŋ-'dzü\ *circa* 371–*circa* 289 B.C. originally *Meng K'o* Latin *Men·cius* \'men-ch(ē-)əs\ Chin. philosopher

Men·ning·er \'me-niŋ-ər\ Karl Augustus 1893–1990 Am. psychiatrist

Men·no Si·mons \'me-nō-'sē-mōns, -'sī-\ 1469–1561 Dutch religious reformer

Me·not·ti \mə-'nä-tē, -'nȯ-\ Gian Carlo 1911– Am. (Ital.-born) composer

Me·nu·hin \'men-yə-wən\ Ye·hu·di \yə-'hü-dē\ 1916– Am. violinist

Men·zies \'men-(ˌ)zēz\ Sir Robert Gordon 1894–1978 Austral. statesman; prime minister (1939–41; 1949–66)

Mer·ca·tor \(ˌ)mər-'kā-tər\ Gerardus 1512–1594 *Gerhard Kremer* Flem. cartographer

Mer·cier \mer-'syā, 'mer-sē-ˌā\ Désiré-Joseph 1851–1926 Belg. cardinal & philosopher

Mer·e·dith \'mer-ə-dəth\ George 1828–1909 Eng. novelist & poet

Meredith Owen — see E. R. Bulwer-LYTTON

Mer·gen·tha·ler \'mər-gən-ˌthä-lər, 'mer-gən-ˌtä-\ Ottmar 1854–1899 Am. (Ger.-born) inventor

Mé·ri·mée \'mer-ə-ˌmā, ˌmä-rə-\ Prosper 1803–1870 Fr. writer

Mer·ri·field \'mer-i-ˌfēld\ Robert Bruce 1921– Am. biochemist

Mer·ton \'mər-tᵊn\ Thomas 1915–1968 Am. religious & author

Mes·mer \'mez-mər, 'mes-\ Franz *or* Friedrich Anton 1734–1815 Ger. physician

Mes·sa·la (*or* **Mes·sal·la**) **Cor·vi·nus** \mə-'säl-ə-ˌkȯr-'vī-nəs\ Marcus Valerius *circa* 64 B.C.–A.D. 8 Rom. general & statesman

Mes·sa·li·na \ˌme-sə-'lī-nə, -'lē-\ Valeria *circa* A.D. 22–48 *3d wife of Emperor Claudius*

Mes·ser·schmitt \'me-sər-ˌshmit\ Willy 1898–1978 Ger. aircraft designer & manufacturer

Mes·sier \mäs-yā, 'me-sē-ˌā\ Charles 1730–1817 Fr. astronomer

Meš·tro·vić \'mesh-trə-ˌvich, 'mes-\ Ivan 1883–1962 Am. (Yugoslavian-born) sculptor

Me·tax·as \me-ˌtäk-'säs\ Ioannis 1871–1941 Greek general & dictator

Metch·ni·koff \'mech-nə-ˌkȯf\ Élie 1845–1916 originally *Ilya Ilich Mech·ni·kov* \'myäch-nyi-ˌkȯf\ Fr. (Russ.-born) zoologist & bacteriologist

Met·ter·nich \'me-tər-(ˌ)nik, -(ˌ)niH\ Klemens Wenzel Nepomuk Lothar 1773–1859 Fürst *von Metternich* Austrian statesman — **Met·ter·nich·ian** \ˌme-tər-'ni-kē-ən, -kē-ən\ *adjective*

Mey·er \'mī(-ə)r\ Annie 1867–1951 née *Nathan* Am. educator & writer

Mey·er·beer \'mī-ər-ˌbir, -ˌber\ Giacomo 1791–1864 originally *Jakob Liebmann Beer* Ger. composer

Mey·er·hof \'mī-ər-ˌhȯf\ Otto 1884–1951 Ger. biochemist

Mfume \əm-'fü-mā, ùm-\ Kwei·si \kwä-'ē-sē\ 1948– Am. civil rights leader

Mi·chael \'mī-kəl\ *Romanian* **Mi·hai** \mē-'hī\ 1921– *Michael Hohenzollern* king of Romania (1927–30; 1940–47)

Mich·el \'mi-kəl\ Hartmut 1948– Ger. biochemist

Mi·chel·an·ge·lo \ˌmī-kə-'lan-jə-ˌlō, ˌmi-, ˌmē-kə-'län-\ 1475–1564 *Michelangelo di Lodovico Buonarroti Simoni* Ital. sculptor, painter, architect, & poet — **Mi·chel·an·ge·lesque** \-ˌlan-jə-'lesk\ *adjective*

Mi·che·let \mēsh-'lā, ˌmē-shə-\ Jules 1798–1874 Fr. historian

Mi·chel·son \'mī-kəl-sən\ Albert Abraham 1852–1931 Am. (Ger.-born) physicist

Mich·e·ner \'mich-nər, 'mi-chə-\ James Albert 1907– Am. author

Mi·chu·rin \myi-'chür-yin\ Ivan Vladimirovich 1855–1935 Soviet horticulturist

Mic·kie·wicz \mits-'kyā-vich\ Adam 1798–1855 Pol. poet

Mid·dle·ton \'mi-dᵊl-tən\ Thomas 1570?–1627 Eng. dramatist

Mies van der Ro·he \ˌmēs-van-də-'rō(-ə), ˌmēz-\ Ludwig 1886–1969 Am. (Ger.-born) architect — **Mies·ian** \'mē-sē-ən, 'mē-shən\ *adjective*

Mi·haj·lo·vić \mi-'hī-lə-ˌvich\ Dragoljub 1893–1946 *Draža* \'drä-zhə\ Yugoslav general

Mi·ki \'mē-kē\ Tak·eo \'tä-kā-ō\ 1907–1988 prime minister of Japan (1974–76)

Mi·ko·yan \ˌmē-kō-'yän\ Ana·stas \ˌä-nə-'stäs\ Ivanovich 1895–1978 Soviet politician; head of Presidium (1964–65)

Miles \'mī(ə)lz\ Nelson Appleton 1839–1925 Am. general

Mi·lhaud \mē-'yō\ Darius 1892–1974 Fr. composer

Mill \'mil\ James 1773–1836 Scot. philosopher, historian, & economist

Mill John Stuart 1806–1873 *son of James* Eng. philosopher & economist

Mil·lais \'mi-ˌlā, mi-'lā\ Sir John Everett 1829–1896 Eng. painter

Mil·lay \mi-'lā\ Edna St. Vincent 1892–1950 Am. poet

Mil·ler \'mi-lər\ Arthur 1915– Am. dramatist & novelist

Miller Henry 1891–1980 Am. writer

Miller Joa·quin \wä-'kēn, wȯ-\ 1837–1913 pseudonym of *Cincinnatus Hiner Miller* Am. poet

Miller Merton Howard 1923– Am. economist

Miller Perry Gilbert Eddy 1905–1963 Am. literary critic & scholar

Miller William 1782–1849 Am. religious leader

Mil·le·rand \mēl-räⁿ, mel-lə-\ Alexandre 1859–1943 Fr. statesman; president of France (1920–24)

Mil·les \'mi-ləs\ Carl 1875–1955 Am. (Swed.-born) sculptor

Mil·let \mē-'yā, mi-'lā\ Jean-François 1814–1875 Fr. painter

Mil·li·kan \'mi-li-kən\ Robert Andrews 1868–1953 Am. physicist

Mil·man \'mil-mən\ Henry Hart 1791–1868 Eng. poet & historian

Milne \'mil(n)\ Alan Alexander 1882–1956 Eng. poet & dramatist

Mi·losz \'mē-lȯsh\ Czeslaw 1911– Pol. writer

Mil·stein \'mil-ˌstīn, -ˌstēn\ César 1927– Brit. (Argentine-born) immunologist

Mil·ti·a·des \mil-'tī-ə-ˌdēz\ *circa* 554–?489 B.C. *the Younger* Athenian general

Mil·ton \'mil-tᵊn\ John 1608–1674 Eng. poet — **Mil·to·nian** \mil-'tō-nē-ən, -nyən\ *or* **Mil·ton·ic** \-'tä-nik\ *adjective*

Mil·yu·kov \ˌmil-yə-'kȯf, -'kȯv\ Pavel Nikolayevich 1859–1943 Russ. politician & historian

Mi·not \'mī-nət\ George Richards 1885–1950 Am. physician

Min·ton \'min-tᵊn\ Sherman 1890–1965 Am. jurist

Min·u·it \'min-yə-wət\ *or* **Min·ne·wit** \'mi-nə-ˌwit\ Peter 1580–1638 Du. colonial administrator in America

Mi·ra·beau \'mir-ə-ˌbō\ Comte de 1749–1791 *Honoré-Gabriel Riqueti* Fr. orator & revolutionary

Mi·ró \mē-'rō\ Joan \zhù-'än\ 1893–1983 Span. painter

Mirr·lees \'mər-ˌlēz\ James Alexander 1936– Brit. economist

Mi·shi·ma \'mē-shi-ˌmä, mə-'shē-mə\ Yukio 1925–1970 Jp. writer

Mis·tral \mi-'sträl, -'stral\ Frédéric 1830–1914 Provençal poet

Mis·tral \mi-'sträl, -'stral\ Gabriela 1889–1957 originally *Lucila Godoy Alcayaga* Chilean poet & educator

Mitch·ell \'mi-chəl\ John 1870–1919 Am. labor leader

Mitchell Margaret Munnerlyn 1900–1949 Am. novelist

Mitchell Maria 1818–1889 Am. astronomer

Mitchell Peter Dennis 1920– Brit. chemist

Mitchell William 1879–1936 *Billy* Am. general

Mit·ford \'mit-fərd\ Mary Russell 1787–1855 Eng. novelist & dramatist

Mitford William 1744–1827 Eng. historian

Mith·ra·da·tes VI Eu·pa·tor \ˌmi-thrə-'dā-tēz-'yü-ˌpā-tər\ *died* 63 B.C. *the Great* king of Pontus (120–63)

Mi·tro·pou·los \mə-'trä-pə-ləs\ Di·mi·tri \də-'mē-trē\ 1896–1960 Am. (Greek-born) conductor

Mit·ter·rand \ˌmē-ter-'äⁿ\ François-Maurice 1916–1996 president of France (1981–95)

Mo·bu·tu Se·se Se·ko \mə-'bü-(ˌ)tü-'sā-sā-'sā-(ˌ)kō\ 1930–1997 originally *Joseph-Désiré Mobutu* president of Zaire (1965–97)

Mo·di·glia·ni \ˌmȯ-dēl-'yä-nē, -dᵊl-\ Amedeo 1884–1920 Ital. painter

Modigliani Franco 1918– Am. (Ital.-born) economist

Mo·djes·ka \mə-'jes-kə\ Helena 1840–1909 Am. (Pol.-born) actress

Mo·ham·mad Re·za Pah·la·vi \mō-'ha-məd-ri-'zä-'pa-lə-(ˌ)vē, -'hä-\ 1919–1980 shah of Iran (1941–79)

Mo·ham·med *variant of* MUHAMMAD

Mois·san \mwä-'säⁿ\ Henri 1852–1907 Fr. chemist

Mo·ley \'mō-lē\ Raymond Charles 1886–1975 Am. journalist

Mo·lière \mōl-'yer, 'mōl-\ 1622–1673 originally *Jean-Baptiste Poquelin* Fr. actor & dramatist

Mo·li·na \mō-'lē-nə\ Mario José 1943– Am. (Mex.-born) chemist

Molina Tirso de — see TIRSO DE MOLINA

Mol·nár \'mōl-ˌnär, 'mȯl-\ Fe·renc \'fer-ən(t)s\ 1878–1952 Hung. author

Mo·lo·tov \'mäl-ə-ˌtȯf, 'mȯ-, 'mō-, -ˌtȯv\ Vyacheslav Mikhaylovich 1890–1986 original surname *Skryabin* Soviet statesman

Molt·ke \'mōlt-kə\ Helmuth Karl Bernhard 1800–1891 Graf *von Moltke* Pruss. field marshal

Momm·sen \'mȯm-zən\ Theodor 1817–1903 Ger. scholar & historian

Monck *or* **Monk** \'məŋk\ George 1608–1670 1st Duke of *Al·be·marle* \'al-bə-ˌmärl\ Eng. general

Mon·dale \'män-ˌdāl\ Walter Frederick 1928– Am. politician; vice president of the U.S. (1977–81)

Mon·dri·an \'mȯn-drē-ˌän\ Piet 1872–1944 *Pieter Cornelis Mondriaan* Du. painter

Mo·net \mō-'nā\ Claude 1840–1926 Fr. painter

Mo·ne·ta \mō-'nä-tə\ Ernesto Teodoro 1833–1918 Ital. journalist & pacifist

Mo·niz Antonio Egas — see EGAS MONIZ

Monk \'məŋk\ Thelonious Sphere 1920–1982 Am. jazz musician

Mon·mouth \'mən-məth, 'män-\ Duke of 1649–1685 *James Scott, son of Charles II of England* Eng. rebel & claimant to the throne

Mon·net \mȯ-'ne\ Jean-Omer-Marie-Gabriel 1888–1979 Fr. economist & diplomat

Mo·nod \mȯ-'nō\ Jacques-Lucien 1910–1976 Fr. biochemist

Mon·roe \mən-'rō\ James 1758–1831 5th president of U.S. (1817–25)

Mon·ta·gna \mȯn-'tän-yə\ Bartolommeo *circa* 1450–1523 Ital. painter

Mon·ta·gu \'män-tə-ˌgyü, 'mən-\ Lady Mary Wortley 1689–1762 Eng. letter writer & poet

\ə\ abut \ᵊ\ kitten \ər\ further \a\ ash \ā\ ace \ä\ mop, mar \au\ out \ch\ chin \e\ bet \ē\ easy \g\ go \i\ hit \ī\ ice \j\ job \ŋ\ sing \ō\ go \ȯ\ law \ȯi\ boy \th\ thin \th\ the \ü\ loot \ù\ foot \y\ yet \zh\ vision *see also* Guide to Pronunciation

Mon·taigne \män-'tān, mōⁿ-ten'\ Michel Eyquem de 1533–1592 Fr. essayist

Mon·ta·le \mōn-'tä-(ˌ)lā\ Eugenio 1896–1981 Ital. poet

Mont·calm de Saint–Véran \mänt-'kälm-də-ˌsäⁿ-vā-'räⁿ, -'käm-\ Marquis de 1712–1759 *Louis-Joseph de Montcalm-Grozon* Fr. field marshal

Mon·tes·pan \mōⁿ-tes-päⁿ, 'män-tə-ˌspan\ Marquise de 1641–1707 née (*Françoise-Athénaïs*) *Rochechouart de Mortemart* mistress of Louis XIV

Mon·tes·quieu \ˌmän-təs-'kyü, -'kyə(r), -'kyœ̄\ Baron *de La Brède et de* 1689–1755 *Charles-Louis de Secondat* Fr. lawyer & political philosopher

Mon·tes·so·ri \ˌmän-tə-'sōr-ē, -'sòr-\ Maria 1870–1952 Ital. physician & educator

Mon·teux \mōⁿ-'tə(r), -'tœ̄\ Pierre 1875–1964 Am. (Fr.-born) conductor

Mon·te·ver·di or **Mon·te·ver·de** \ˌmän-tə-'ver-dē, -'vər-\ Claudio 1567–1643 Ital. composer

Mon·te·zu·ma II \ˌmän-tə-'zü-mə\ or **Moc·te·zu·ma** \ˌmäk-tə-\ 1466–1520 last Aztec emperor of Mexico (1502–20)

Mont·fort \'mänt-fərt, mōⁿ-'fòr\ Simon de 1165?–1218 *Simon IV de Montfort l'Amaury* Fr. soldier

Mont·fort \'mänt-fərt\ Simon de *circa* 1208–1265 Earl of *Leicester* Eng. soldier & statesman

Mont·gol·fier \mänt-'gäl-fē-ər, -fē-ˌā\ Joseph-Michel 1740–1810 & his brother Jacques-Étienne 1745–1799 Fr. inventors & balloonists

Mont·gom·ery \(ˌ)mən(t)-'gəm-rē, -ˌmän(t)-, -'gäm-; -'gə-mə-, -'gä-\ Bernard Law 1887–1976 1st Viscount *Montgomery of Alamein* Brit. field marshal

Montgomery Lucy Maud 1874–1942 Canad. novelist

Mont·mo·ren·cy \ˌmänt-mə-'ren(t)-sē\ Anne 1493–1567 1st duc *de Montmorency* Fr. soldier; constable (1537)

Mon·trose \män-'trōz\ 1st Marquess of 1612–1650 *James Graham* Scot. Royalist

Moo·dy \'mü-dē\ Dwight Lyman 1837–1899 Am. evangelist

Moore \'mōr, 'mòr, 'mùr\ George 1852–1933 Irish author

Moore George Edward 1873–1958 Eng. philosopher

Moore Henry 1898–1986 Brit. sculptor

Moore John Bassett 1860–1947 Am. jurist

Moore Marianne Craig 1887–1972 Am. poet

Moore Stanford 1913–1982 Am. biochemist

Moore Thomas 1779–1852 Irish poet

Mo·ra·via \mò-'rä-vē-ə\ Alberto 1907–1990 pseudonym of *Alberto Pincherle* Ital. writer

More \'mōr, 'mòr\ Hannah 1745–1833 Eng. religious writer

More Henry 1614–1687 Eng. philosopher

More Paul Elmer 1864–1937 Am. essayist & critic

More Sir Thomas 1478–1535 *Saint* Eng. statesman & author

Mo·reau \mò-rō\ (Jean-) Victor-Marie 1763–1813 Fr. general

Mor·gan \'mòr-gən\ Daniel 1736–1802 Am. general in Revolution

Morgan Sir Henry 1635–1688 Eng. buccaneer

Morgan John Hunt 1825–1864 Am. Confederate cavalry officer

Morgan John Pier·pont \'pir-ˌpänt\ 1837–1913 Am. financier

Morgan John Pierpont 1867–1943 *son of J. P.* Am. financier

Morgan Thomas Hunt 1866–1945 Am. geneticist

Morgan William Wilson 1906–1994 Am. astronomer

Mor·gen·thau \'mòr-gən-ˌthò\ Henry 1891–1967 U.S. secretary of the treasury (1934–45)

Mor·i·son \'mòr-ə-sən, 'mär-\ Samuel Eliot 1887–1976 Am. historian

Morison Stanley 1889–1968 Eng. type designer

Mo·ri·sot \mò-rē-zō\ Berthe 1841–1895 Fr. painter

Mor·ley \'mòr-lē\ Christopher Darlington 1890–1957 Am. writer

Morley John 1838–1923 Viscount *Morley* Eng. statesman & writer

Mor·nay \mòr-nā\ Philippe de 1549–1623 Seigneur *du Plessis-Marly;* usually called *Du·ples·sis-Mor·nay* \dū̄-plä-sē-mòr-ne\ Fr. Huguenot

Mor·ris \'mòr-əs, 'mär-\ Gou·ver·neur \ˌgə-və(r)-'nir\ 1752–1816 Am. statesman & diplomat

Morris Robert 1734–1806 Am. financier & statesman

Morris William 1834–1896 Eng. poet, artist, & socialist

Mor·ri·son \'mòr-ə-sən, 'mär-\ Herbert Stanley 1888–1965 Baron *Morrison of Lambeth* Eng. politician

Morrison Robert 1782–1834 Scot. missionary

Morrison Toni 1931– originally *Chloe Anthony Wofford* Am. novelist

Morse \'mòrs\ Samuel Finley Breese 1791–1872 Am. artist & inventor

Mor·ti·mer \'mòr-tə-mər\ Roger de 1287–1330 1st Earl of *March* & 8th Baron of *Wigmore* Welsh rebel

Mor·ton \'mòr-tⁿn\ Levi Parsons 1824–1920 Am. banker & politician; vice president of the U.S. (1889–93)

Morton William Thomas Green 1819–1868 Am. dentist

Mos·by \'mōz-bē\ John Singleton 1833–1916 Am. Confederate cavalry officer

Moś·cic·ki \mòsh-'chēt-skē, -'chit-\ Ignacy 1867–1946 Pol. chemist; president of Poland (1926–39)

Mo·ses \'mō-zəz *also* -zəs\ Anna Mary née *Robertson* 1860–1961 *Grandma Moses* Am. painter

Mos·ley \'mōz-lē\ Sir Oswald Er·nald \'ər-nⁿld\ 1896–1980 Eng. politician

Möss·bau·er \'mœs-ˌbaù-(ə)r, 'mes-\ Rudolf Ludwig 1929– Ger. physicist

Moth·er·well \'mə-thər-ˌwel, -wəl\ Robert 1915–1991 Am. artist

Mo Ti — see MO-TZU

Mot·ley \'mät-lē\ John Lothrop 1814–1877 Am. historian

Mo·ton \'mō-tⁿn\ Robert Russa 1867–1940 Am. educator

Mott \'mät\ John Raleigh 1865–1955 Am. religious leader

Mott Lucretia 1793–1880 née *Coffin* Am. social reformer

Mott Sir Nevill Francis 1905–1996 Brit. physicist

Mot·tel·son \'mō-tⁿl-sən, -(ˌ)sòn\ Ben Roy 1926– Dan. (Am.-born) physicist

Mot·teux \mä-'tə(r), 'mä-\ Peter Anthony 1660–1718 Brit. (Fr.-born) dramatist & translator

Mo–tzu \'mōd-'zə\ 470?–?391 B.C. originally *Mo Ti* \'mō-'dē\ Latin *Mi·cius* \'mē-sh(ē-)əs\ Chin. philosopher

Moul·ton \'mōl-tⁿn\ Forest Ray 1872–1952 Am. astronomer

Moul·trie \'mül-trē, 'mōl-\ William 1730–1805 Am. general in Revolution

Mount·bat·ten \maùnt-'ba-tⁿn\ Louis 1900–1979 1st Earl *Mountbatten of Burma* Brit. admiral; 1st governor-general of India (1947–48); chief of defense staff (1959–65)

Mountbatten Philip, Duke of Edinburgh — see Prince PHILIP

Mow·at \'mō-ət\ Farley McGill 1921– Canad. writer

Mo·zart \'mōt-ˌsärt\ Wolfgang Amadeus 1756–1791 Austrian composer — **Mo·zart·ean** or **Mo·zart·ian** \mōt-'sär-tē-ən\ *adjective*

Mu·bar·ak \mù-'bär-ək\ Muhammad Hosni 1929– president of Egypt (1981–)

Muench \'minch\ Aloisius Joseph 1889–1962 Am. cardinal

Mu·ga·be \mù-'gä-bē\ Robert Gabriel 1924– prime minister of Zimbabwe (1980–87); executive president (1987–)

Mug·ge·ridge \'mə-gə-ˌrij\ Malcolm Thomas 1903–1990 Brit. writer & social critic

Mu·ham·mad \mō-'ha-məd, -'hä- *also* mü-\ *circa* 570–632 *Abū al-Qāsim Muḥammad ibn 'Abd Allāh ibn 'Abd al-Muṭṭalib ibn Hāshim* Arab prophet & founder of Islam

Mu·ham·mad \mō-'ha-məd, mü-\ Elijah 1897–1975 originally *E. Poole* Am. religious leader

Muhammad XI \mō-'ha-məd, mü-\ *died* 1527 *Abū 'Abd Allāh Muḥammad* Spanish *Bo·ab·dil* \bō-äv-'dēl\ last sultan of Granada

Müh·len·berg \'myü-lən-ˌbərg\ Henry Melchior 1711–1787 Am. (Ger.-born) Lutheran clergyman

Muir \'myùr\ John 1838–1914 Am. (Scot.-born) naturalist

Mul·ler \'mə-lər\ Hermann Joseph 1890–1967 Am. geneticist

Mül·ler \'myü-lər, 'mi-, 'mə-\ (Friedrich) Max 1823–1900 Brit. (Ger.-born) philologist

Müller Johann 1436–1476 *Regiomontanus* Ger. astronomer

Müller Karl Alexander 1927– Swiss physicist

Müller Paul Hermann 1899–1965 Swiss chemist

Mul·li·ken \'mə-lə-kən\ Robert Sanderson 1896–1986 Am. chemist & physicist

Mul·lis \'mə-lis\ Kary Banks 1944– Am. biochemist

Mul·ro·ney \məl-'rü-nē\ (Martin) Brian 1939– Canad. politician; prime minister (1984–93)

Mum·ford \'məm(p)-fərd\ Lewis 1895–1990 Am. writer

Munch \'munch, 'mēnch\ Charles 1891–1968 Fr.-born conductor

Munch \'muŋk\ Edvard 1863–1944 Norw. painter

Münch·hau·sen \'muŋk-ˌhaù-zⁿn\ Karl Friedrich Hieronymus von 1720–1797 Baron *Mun·chau·sen* \'mən-ˌchaù-zⁿn, 'mün-\ Ger. hunter, soldier, & raconteur

Mu·ñoz Ma·rín \(ˌ)mün-'yōs-mə-'rēn, -'yōz-\ Luis 1898–1980 Puerto Rican politician

Mun·ro \(ˌ)mən-'rō\ Alice 1931– née *Laidlaw* Canad. writer

Munro Hector Hugh 1870–1916 pseudonym *Saki* Scot. writer

Mün·ster·berg \'mun(t)-stər-ˌbərg, 'myun(t)-, 'mən(t)-\ Hugo 1863–1916 Am. (Ger.-born) psychologist

Mu·ra·sa·ki \ˌmur-ə-'sä-kē, ˌmyur-\ Shikibu 978?–?1026 Jp. court lady & novelist

Mu·rat \myu-'rä, mu̇-\ Joachim 1767–1815 Fr. general; marshal of France; king of Naples (1808–15)

Mur·doch \'mər-dək, -ˌdäk\ Dame (Jean) Iris 1919– Brit. (Irish-born) writer

Mu·ril·lo \myu-'ri-(ˌ)lō; mù-'rē-(ˌ)ō, myù-\ Bartolomé Esteban 1617–1682 Span. painter

Mur·phy \'mər-fē\ Frank 1890–1949 Am. jurist

Murphy William Parry 1892–1987 Am. physician

Mur·ray \'mər-ē, -mə-'rē\ (George) Gilbert Aimé 1866–1957 Brit. classical scholar

Murray Sir James Augustus Henry 1837–1915 Brit. lexicographer

Murray Joseph Edward 1919– Am. surgeon

Murray Lindley 1745–1826 Am. grammarian

Murray Philip 1886–1952 Am. labor leader

Mur·row \'mər-(ˌ)ō, 'mə-(ˌ)rō\ Edward Roscoe 1908–1965 Am. journalist

Mus·set \myü-'sā\ (Louis-Charles-) Alfred de 1810–1857 Fr. poet

Mus·so·li·ni \ˌmü-sə-'lē-nē, ˌmu̇-\ Be·ni·to \bə-'nē-(ˌ)tō\ 1883–1945 *Il Du·ce* \ēl-'dü-(ˌ)chā\ Ital. Fascist premier (1922–43)

Mus·sorg·sky \mu̇-'sòrg-skē, -'zòrg-\ Mo·dest \mō-'dest\ Petrovich 1839–1881 Russ. composer

Mustafa Kemal — see KEMAL ATATÜRK

Mu·tsu·hi·to \ˌmüt-sə-'hē-(ˌ)tō, -'hä- *also* mü-\ 1852–1912 *Mei·ji* \'mā-(ˌ)jē\ emperor of Japan (1867–1912)

Mu·zo·re·wa \ˌmü-zə-'rä-wə\ Abel Tendekayi 1925– prime minister of Zimbabwe Rhodesia (1979–80)

Myr·dal \'mur-ˌdäl, 'mər-, 'mir\ Alva 1902–1986 Swed. sociologist & diplomat

Myrdal (Karl) Gunnar 1898–1987 Swed. economist

My·ron \'mī-rən\ *flourished circa* 480–440 B.C. Greek sculptor

Na·bo·kov \nə-'bò-kəf\ Vladimir Vladimirovich 1899–1977 Am. (Russ.-born) novelist & poet — **Na·bo·ko·vi·an** \ˌna-bə-'kō-vē-ən\ *adjective*

Na·der \'nā-dər\ Ralph 1934– Am. consumer advocate

Nai·du \'nī-(ˌ)dü\ Sarojini 1879–1949 Indian poet & reformer

Na·ka·so·ne \ˌnä-kə-'sō-nē\ Yasuhiro 1918– prime minister of Japan (1982–87)

Na·mier \'nā-ˌmir\ Sir Lewis Bernstein 1888–1960 Brit. historian

Nā·nak \'nä-nək\ 1469–1539 founder of the Sikh faith in India

Nan·sen \'nän(t)-sən, 'nan(t)-\ Frid·tjof \'fri-ˌchòf\ 1861–1930 Norw. arctic explorer, zoologist, & statesman

Na·pier \'nā-pē-ər, -ˌpir; nə-'pir\ Sir Charles James 1782–1853 Brit. general

Napier or **Ne·per** \'nā-pər\ John 1550–1617 Laird of *Mer·chis·ton* \'mər-kə-stən\ Scot. mathematician

Napier Robert Cornelis 1810–1890 1st Baron *Napier of Mag·da·la* \\'mag-də-lə\\ Brit. field marshal

Na·po·léon I \\nə-'pōl-yən, -'pō-lē-ən\\ *or* **Napoléon Bo·na·parte** \\'bō-nə-ˌpärt\\ 1769–1821 emperor of the French (1804–15) — **Na·po·le·on·ic** \\nə-ˌpō-lē-'ä-nik\\ *adjective*

Napoléon II 1811–1832 Duc *de Reichstadt; son of Napoléon I & Marie Louise*

Napoléon III 1808–1873 *Louis-Napoléon; son of Louis Bonaparte & nephew of Napoléon I* emperor of the French (1852–71)

Nar·vá·ez \\när-'vä-ˌās\\ Pánfilo de *circa* 1480–1528 Span. soldier

Nash \\'nash\\ John F. 1928– Am. economist

Nash Ogden 1902–1971 Am. poet

Nash *or* **Nashe** \\'nash\\ Thomas 1567–1601 Eng. satirist & dramatist

Nash Walter 1882–1968 prime minister of New Zealand (1957–60)

Na·smyth \\'nā-ˌsmith, 'nāz-məth\\ Alexander 1758–1840 Scot. painter

Nas·ser \\'nä-sər, 'na-\\ Ga·mal \\gə-'mäl\\ Ab·del \\'äb-dᵊl\\ 1918–1970 Egypt. politician; president of Egypt (1956–70)

Nast \\'nast\\ Thomas 1840–1902 Am. (Ger.-born) cartoonist

Na·than \\'nā-thən\\ George Jean 1882–1958 Am. editor & drama critic

Na·thans \\'nā-thənz\\ Daniel 1928– Am. microbiologist

Na·tion \\'nā-shən\\ Car·ry \\'kar-ē\\ Amelia 1846–1911 née *Moore* Am. temperance agitator

Nat·ta \\'nät-(ˌ)tä\\ Giulio 1903–1979 Ital. chemist

Neb·u·cha·drez·zar II \\ˌne-byə-kə-'dre-zər, -bə-\\ *or* **Neb·u·chad·nez·zar** \\-kəd-'ne-\\ *circa* 630–562 B.C. Chaldean king of Babylon (605–562)

Nec·ker \\nā-'ker, 'ne-kər\\ Jacques 1732–1804 *father of Mme. de Staël* Fr. (Swiss-born) financier & statesman

Né·el \\nā-el\\ Louis-Eugène-Félix 1904– Fr. physicist

Neh·er \\'nā-(ə)r\\ Erwin 1944– Ger. biochemist

Neh·ru \\'ner-(ˌ)ü, 'nā-(ˌ)rü\\ Ja·wa·har·lal \\jə-'wä-hər-ˌläl\\ 1889–1964 *son of Motilal* Indian nationalist; prime minister (1947–64)

Nehru Pan·dit \\'pən-dət\\ Mo·ti·lal \\'mō-tᵊl-ˌäl\\ 1861–1931 Indian nationalist

Neil·son \\'nē(ə)l-sən\\ William Allan 1869–1946 Am. (Scot.-born) educator; president Smith College (1917–39)

Nel·son \\'nel-sən\\ Horatio 1758–1805 Viscount *Nelson* Brit. admiral

Nem·e·rov \\'ne-mə-ˌröf, -ˌröv\\ Howard 1920–1991 Am. writer; poet laureate (1988–90)

Ne·pos \\'nē-ˌpäs, 'ne-\\ Cornelius *circa* 100–*circa* 25 B.C. Rom. historian

Ne·ri \\'ner-ē, 'nā-rē\\ Saint Philip 1515–1595 Italian *Filippo Neri* Ital. founder (1564) of "Fathers of the Oratory"

Nernst \\'nern(t)st\\ Walther Hermann 1864–1941 Ger. physicist & chemist

Ne·ro \\'nē-(ˌ)rō, 'nir-(ˌ)ō\\ A.D. 37–68 *Nero Claudius Caesar Drusus Germanicus* originally *Lucius Domitius Ahenobarbus* Rom. emperor 54–68 — **Ne·ro·ni·an** \\ni-'rō-nē-ən\\ *or* **Ne·ron·ic** \\-'rä-nik\\ *adjective*

Ne·ru·da \\nā-'rü-də, -(ˌ)thä\\ Pablo 1904–1973 *Neftalí Ricardo Reyes Basoalto* Chilean poet & diplomat

Ner·va \\'nər-və\\ Marcus Cocceius *circa* A.D. 30–98 Rom. emperor (96–98)

Ner·vi \\'ner-vē\\ Pier Luigi 1891–1979 Ital. engineer & architect

Nes·to·ri·us \\ne-'stōr-ē-əs, -'stör-\\ *died circa* 451 patriarch of Constantinople (428–431)

Net·an·ya·hu \\ˌne-ˌtän-'yä-(ˌ)hü, ˌnet-ᵊn-\\ Benjamin 1949– Israeli diplomat & politician; prime min. of Israel (1996–)

Neu·rath \\'nȯi-ˌrät\\ Konstantin 1873–1956 Freiherr *von Neurath* Ger. diplomat

Nev·el·son \\'ne-vəl-sən\\ Louise 1900–1988 Am. (Russ.-born) sculptor

Neville Richard — see Earl of WARWICK

Nev·in \\'ne-vən\\ Ethelbert Woodbridge 1862–1901 Am. composer

Nev·ins \\'ne-vənz\\ Allan 1890–1971 Am. historian

New·bolt \\'nü-ˌbōlt, 'nyü-\\ Sir Henry John 1862–1938 Eng. author

New·comb \\'nü-kəm, 'nyü-\\ Simon 1835–1909 Am. (Canad.-born) astronomer

New·man \\'nü-mən, 'nyü-\\ John Henry 1801–1890 Eng. cardinal & writer

New·ton \\'nü-tᵊn, 'nyü-\\ Sir Isaac 1642–1727 Eng. mathematician & physicist — **New·to·ni·an** \\nü-'tō-nē-ən, nyü-, -'nyən\\ *adjective*

Ney \\'nā\\ Michel 1769–1815 Duc *d'Elchingen; Prince de la Moskova* Fr. soldier; marshal of France

Nich·o·las \\'ni-k(ə-)ləs\\ Saint 4th century Christian prelate

Nicholas name of 2 czars of Russia: **I** 1796–1855 (reigned 1825–55); **II** 1868–1918 (reigned 1894–1917)

Nicholas *Russian* **Ni·ko·lay Ni·ko·lay·e·vich** \\'nyē-kə-ˌlī-,nyē-kə-'lī(-ə)-ˌvyich\\ 1856–1929 Russ. grand duke & army officer

Nicholas of Cu·sa \\-'kyü-sə, -zə\\ 1401–1464 Ger. cardinal, mathematician, & philosopher

Nich·ol·son \\'ni-kəl-sən\\ Ben 1894–1982 Brit. painter

Ni·ci·as \\'ni-shē-əs, -sē-\\ *died* 413 B.C. Athenian general & statesman

Nic·o·lay \\'ni-kə-ˌlā\\ John George 1832–1901 Am. biographer

Ni·co·let \\'ni-kə-'lā, -'let\\ Jean 1598–1642 Fr. explorer in No. America

Ni·colle \\nē-kȯl\\ Charles-Jean-Henri 1866–1936 Fr. physician & bacteriologist

Nic·ol·son \\'ni-kəl-sən\\ Sir Harold George 1886–1968 Eng. biographer & diplomat

Nie·buhr \\'nē-ˌbu̇r, -ˌbȯr\\ Barthold Georg 1776–1831 Ger. historian, statesman, & philologist

Niebuhr Rein·hold \\'rīn-ˌhōld\\ 1892–1971 Am. theologian — **Nie·buhr·ian** \\nē-'bu̇r-ē-ən\\ *adjective*

Niel·sen \\'nē(ə)l-sən\\ Carl August 1865–1931 Dan. composer

Niem·ce·wicz \\nyemt-'sā-vich\\ Julian Ursyn 1758–1841 Pol. patriot & writer

Nie·mey·er \\'nē-ˌmī(-ə)r\\ Oscar 1907– in full *Oscar Niemeyer Soares Filho* Braz. architect

Nie·möl·ler \\'nē-ˌmə(r)l-ər, -ˌmœl-\\ (Friedrich Gustav Emil) Martin 1892–1984 Ger. Protestant theologian

Nietz·sche \\'nē-chə, -chē\\ Friedrich Wilhelm 1844–1900 Ger. philosopher — **Nietz·sche·an** \\-chē-ən\\ *adjective*

Night·in·gale \\'nī-tᵊn-ˌgāl, -tiŋ-\\ Florence 1820–1910 Eng. nurse & philanthropist

Ni·jin·ska \\nə-'zhin-skə, -'jin-\\ Bro·ni·sła·wa \\ˌbrä-nə-'slä-və\\ 1891–1972 *sister of following* Russ. (Pol.-born) dancer & choreographer

Ni·jin·sky \\nə-'zhin-skē, -'jin-\\ Vas·lav \\'vät-släf\\ Fomich 1890–1950 Russ. dancer

Nils·son \\'nil-sən\\ Birgit 1918– Swed. soprano

Nim·itz \\'ni-məts\\ Chester William 1885–1966 Am. admiral

Nin \\'nēn\\ Anaïs 1903–1977 Am. (Fr.-born) author

Ni·ren·berg \\'nir-ən-ˌbərg\\ Marshall Warren 1927– Am. geneticist

Nit·ti \\'nē-tē, 'nē-\\ Francesco Saverio 1868–1953 Ital. economist & politician

Nix·on \\'nik-sən\\ Richard Milhous 1913–1994 Am. politician; 37th president of the U.S. (1969–74) — **Nix·on·esque** \\nik-sə-'nesk\\ *or* **Nix·o·ni·an** \\nik-'sō-nē-ən, -nyən\\ *adjective*

Nkru·mah \\en-'krü-mə, eŋ-\\ Kwa·me \\'kwä-mē\\ 1909–1972 prime minister (1952–60) & 1st president (1960–66) of Ghana

No·bel \\nō-'bel\\ Alfred Bernhard 1833–1896 Swed. manufacturer, inventor, & philanthropist

No·bi·le \\'nō-bə-ˌlā\\ Umberto 1885–1978 Ital. arctic explorer & aeronautical engineer

No·el–Ba·ker \\ˌnō-əl-'bā-kər\\ Philip John 1889–1982 Brit. politician

No·gu·chi \\nō-'gü-chē\\ Hideyo 1876–1928 Am. (Jp.-born) bacteriologist

Noguchi Isamu 1904–1988 Am. sculptor

Nor·dau \\'nȯr-ˌdau̇\\ Max Simon 1849–1923 originally *Süd·feld* \\'züt-ˌfelt\\ Ger. (Hung.-born) physician, author, & Zionist

Nor·den·ski·öld \\'nu̇r-dᵊn-ˌshȯld, -ˌshu̇ld, -ˌshēld\\ Baron (Nils) Adolf Erik 1832–1901 Swed. arctic explorer

Nor·ris \\'nȯr-əs, 'när-\\ Benjamin Franklin 1870–1902 *Frank; brother of C. G.* Am. novelist

Norris Charles Gilman 1881–1945 Am. novelist

Norris George William 1861–1944 Am. statesman

Nor·rish \\'nȯr-ish\\ Ronald George Wreyford 1897–1978 Brit. chemist

North \\'nȯrth\\ Christopher — see John WILSON

North Douglass Cecil 1920– Am. economist

North Frederick 1732–1792 *Lord North* Eng. statesman; prime minister (1770–82)

North Sir Thomas 1535–?1603 Eng. translator

Northcliffe Viscount — see Alfred C. W. HARMSWORTH

Nor·throp \\'nȯr-thrəp\\ John Howard 1891–1987 Am. biochemist

Nor·ton \\'nȯr-tᵊn\\ Charles Eliot 1827–1908 Am. author & educator

Norton Thomas 1532–1584 Eng. lawyer & poet

Nos·tra·da·mus \\ˌnäs-trə-'dä-məs, ˌnōs-, -'dā-\\ 1503–1566 *Michel de Notredame* or *Nostredame* Fr. physician & astrologer

No·vel·lo \\nō-'ve-(ˌ)lō\\ Antonia Coello 1944– U.S. surgeon general (1990–93)

Noyes \\'nȯiz\\ Alfred 1880–1958 Eng. poet

Nu·re·yev \\nü-'rā-yəf\\ Rudolf Hametovich 1938–1993 Russ.-born ballet dancer

Nüss·lein–Vol·hard \\'nu̇s-,līn-'fōl-ˌhärt\\ Christiane 1942– Ger. biologist

Nut·ting \\'nə-tiŋ\\ Wallace 1861–1941 Am. antiquarian

Nye \\'nī\\ Edgar Wilson 1850–1896 *Bill Nye* Am. humorist

Oates \\'ōts\\ Joyce Carol 1938– Am. writer

Oates Titus 1649–1705 Brit. fabricator of the Popish Plot

O'·Boyle \\ō-'bȯi(ə)l\\ Patrick Aloysius 1896–1987 Am. cardinal

Obrenović Alexander I — see ALEXANDER

O'·Ca·sey \\ō-'kā-sē\\ Sean \\'shȯn\\ 1880–1964 originally *John Casey* Irish dramatist

Occleve — see Thomas HOCCLEVE

Ochoa \\ō-'chō-ə\\ Severo 1905–1993 Am. (Span.-born) biochemist

Ochs \\'äks\\ Adolph Simon 1858–1935 Am. newspaper publisher

Ock·ham *or* **Oc·cam** \\'ä-kəm\\ William of *circa* 1285–?1349 Eng. philosopher — **Ock·ham·is·tic** *or* **Oc·cam·is·tic** \\ˌä-kə-'mis-tik\\ *adjective*

O'·Con·nell \\ō-'kä-nᵊl\\ Daniel 1775–1847 Irish nationalist

O'Connell William Henry 1859–1944 Am. cardinal

O'·Con·nor \\ō-'kä-nər\\ (Mary) Flannery 1925–1964 Am. writer

O'Connor Frank 1903–1966 pseudonym of *Michael John O'Donovan* Irish author

O'Connor Sandra Day 1930– Am. jurist

O'Connor Thomas Power 1848–1929 *Tay Pay* \\'tā-'pā\\ Irish journalist

Octavius — see AUGUSTUS

Odets \\ō-'dets\\ Clifford 1906–1963 Am. dramatist

Odo·a·cer \\ˌō-dō-ˌwä-sər, 'ä-\\ *also* **Odo·va·car** *or* **Odo·va·kar** \\-ˌvä-kər\\ 433–493 1st barbarian ruler of Italy (476–493)

Oe \\'ō-e\\ Kenzaburo 1935– Jp. writer

Oeh·len·schläg·er \\'ə(r)-lən-ˌshlā-gər, 'ēl-\\ Adam Gottlob 1779–1850 Dan. poet & dramatist

O'·Fao·láin \\ō-fə-'lȯn\\ Seán \\'shȯn\\ 1900–1991 Irish author

Of·fen·bach \\'ȯ-fən-ˌbäk, -ˌbäk\\ Jacques 1819–1880 Fr. composer

O'·Fla·her·ty \\ō-'fla-(h)ər-tē\\ Li·am \\'lē-əm\\ 1896–1984 Irish novelist

Og·den \\'ȯg-dən, 'äg-\\ Charles Kay 1889–1957 Brit. psychologist

Ogle·thorpe \\'ō-gəl-ˌthȯrp\\ James Edward 1696–1785 Eng. philanthropist, general, & founder of Georgia

Ögö·dei \\'ȯ-gə-ˌdā\\ *also* **Oga·dai** \\-ˌdī\\ *or* **Og·dai** \\'ȯ-ˌdī\\ *or* **Uge·dei** \\'ü-gə-ˌdā\\ 1185–1241 Mongol Khan (1229–41)

O'·Hara \\ō-'har-ə\\ John Henry 1905–1970 Am. author

O'·Hig·gins \\ō-'hi-gənz, ō-'ē-gən(t)s\\ Bernardo 1778–1842 *Liberator of Chile* Chilean soldier & statesman

\\ə\\ abut \\ᵊ\\ kitten \\ər\\ further \\a\\ ash \\ā\\ ace \\ä\\ mop, mar \\au̇\\ out \\ch\\ chin \\e\\ bet \\ē\\ easy \\g\\ go \\i\\ hit \\ī\\ ice \\j\\ job \\ŋ\\ sing \\ō\\ go \\ȯ\\ law \\ȯi\\ boy \\th\\ thin \\th\\ the \\ü\\ loot \\u̇\\ foot \\y\\ yet \\zh\\ vision *see also* Guide to Pronunciation

Ohi·ra \ō-'hir-ə\ Masayoshi 1910–1980 prime minister of Japan (1978–80)

Oh·lin \'ō-lin\ Bertil Gotthard 1899–1979 Swed. economist

Ohm \'ōm\ Georg Simon 1787–1854 Ger. physicist

Ois·trakh \'ois-träk\ David Fyodorovich 1908–1974 Russ. violinist

O'·Keeffe \ō-'kēf\ Georgia 1887–1986 Am. painter

O'·Kel·ly \ō-'ke-lē\ Seán \'shòn\ Thomas 1883–1966 Irish journalist; president of Republic of Ireland (1945–59)

O'Kelly Seu·mas \'shā-məs\ 1881–1918 Irish writer

Olaf \'ō-ləf, -läf, -laf; 'ü-läf\ name of 5 kings of Norway: especially **Olaf I Trygg·va·son** \'trig-və-sən\ circa 964–1000 (reigned 995–1000); **Olaf II Har·alds·son** \'har-əl(d)-sən\ Saint Olaf 995?–1030 (reigned 1016–28); **Olaf V** 1903–1991 (reigned 1957–91)

Olah \'ō-lä\ George Andrew 1927– Am. (Hung.-born) chemist

Old·cas·tle \'ōl(d)-,ka-səl\ Sir John 1377?–1417 Baron Cob·ham \-'kä-bəm\ Eng. Lollard leader

Ol·den·bar·ne·velt \,ōl-dən-'bär-nə-vəlt\ Johan van 1547–1619 Du. statesman

Oliv·i·er \ō-'li-vē-,ā\ Laurence Kerr 1907–1989 Baron Olivier of Brighton Eng. actor

Olm·sted \'ōm-,sted, 'äm-, -stəd\ Frederick Law 1822–1903 Am. landscape architect

Omar Khay·yám \,ō-,mär-,kī-'yäm, ,ō-mər-, -'yam\ 1048?–1122 Pers. poet & astronomer

O'·Neill \ō-'nē(ə)l\ Eugene Gladstone 1888–1953 Am. dramatist

On·ions \'ən-yənz\ Charles Talbut 1873–1965 Eng. lexicographer

On·sa·ger \'òn-,sä-gər\ Lars 1903–1976 Am. (Norw.-born) chemist

Op·pen·heim \'ä-pən-,hīm\ Edward Phillips 1866–1946 Eng. novelist

Op·pen·hei·mer \'ä-pən-,hī-mər\ (Julius) Robert 1904–1967 Am. physicist

Or·ca·gna \ôr-'kän-yə\ Andrea circa 1308–circa 1368 Andrea di Cione Florentine painter, sculptor, & architect

Or·czy \'òrt-sē\ Baroness Em·mus·ka \'e-məsh-kə\ 1865–1947 Eng. (Hung.-born) novelist & dramatist

Orff \'òrf\ Carl 1895–1982 Ger. composer

Or·i·gen \'òr-ə-jən, 'är-\ 185?–?254 Greek (Egypt.-born) Christian writer, teacher, & mystic

Or·lan·do \ôr-'lan-(,)dō, -'län-\ Vittorio Emanuele 1860–1952 Ital. statesman

Or·man·dy \'òr-mən-dē\ Eugene 1899–1985 Am. (Hung.-born) conductor

Oroz·co \ō-'rò-(,)skō\ José Clemente 1883–1949 Mex. painter

Ør·sted \'ə(r)-stəd, 'œr-\ Hans Christian 1777–1851 Dan. physicist & chemist

Or·te·ga y Gas·set \ôr-'tā-gə-,ē-gä-'set\ José 1883–1955 Span. philosopher, writer, & statesman

Or·well \'òr-,wel, -wəl\ George 1903–1950 pseudonym of Eric Blair Eng. author — **Or·well·ian** \òr-'we-lē-ən\ adjective

Os·born \'äz-bòrn, -bərn\ Henry Fairfield 1857–1935 Am. paleontologist

Os·borne \'äz-bòrn, -,bórn, -,bōrn\ John James 1929–1994 Brit. dramatist

Osborne Thomas Mott 1859–1926 Am. penologist

Os·car II \'äs-kər\ 1829–1907 king of Sweden (1872–1907) & of Norway (1872–1905)

Osce·o·la \,ä-sē-'ō-lə, ,ō-\ circa 1800–1838 Seminole Indian chief

Osh·er·off \'ä-shər-,òf\ Douglas Dean 1945– Am. physicist

Os·ler \'ōs-lər, 'ōz-\ Sir William 1849–1919 Canad. physician

Os·man I \òs-'män\ 1258–circa 1326 founder of the Ottoman Empire

Os·me·ña \ōz-'mān-yə, ōs-\ Sergio 1878–1961 president of Philippine Commonwealth (1944–46)

Os·si·etz·ky \,ä-sē-'et-skē\ Carl von 1889–1938 Ger. writer & pacifist

Ossoli Marchioness — see Margaret FULLER

Ost·wald \'òst-,wòld, -,vòld\ Friedrich Wilhelm 1853–1932 Ger. physical chemist & philosopher

Otis \'ō-təs\ Elwell Stephen 1838–1909 Am. general

Otis Harrison Gray 1837–1917 Am. general & journalist

Otis James 1725–1783 Am. statesman in Revolution

Ot·ter·bein \'ä-tər-,bīn\ Philip William 1726–1813 Am. (Ger.-born) clergyman

Ot·to I \'ä-(,)tō\ 912–973 the Great Holy Roman emperor (936–973)

Ot·way \'ät-,wā\ Thomas 1652–1685 Eng. dramatist

Ou·ida — see Marie Louise de la RAMÉE

Ov·id \'ä-vəd\ 43 B.C.–?A.D. 17 Publius Ovidius Naso Rom. poet — **Ovid·ian** \ä-'vi-dē-ən\ adjective

Ow·en \'ō-ən\ Robert 1771–1858 Welsh social reformer

Owen Wilfred 1893–1918 Brit. poet

Ox·en·stier·na \'úk-sen-,sher-nä\ Count Axel Gustafsson 1583–1654 Swed. statesman

Oxford Earl of — see Robert HARLEY

Paa·si·ki·vi \'pä-sə-,kē-vē\ Ju·ho \'yü-(,)hó\ Kusti 1870–1956 Finn. businessman; president of Finland (1946–56)

Pa·de·rew·ski \,pa-də-'ref-skē, -'rev-\ Ignacy \ēn-'yäs\ Jan \'yän\ 1860–1941 Pol. pianist, composer, & statesman

Pa·ga·ni·ni \,pa-gə-'nē-nē, ,pä-\ Niccolò 1782–1840 Ital. violinist

Page \'pāj\ Thomas Nelson 1853–1922 Am. novelist & diplomat

Page Walter Hines 1855–1918 Am. journalist & diplomat

Pag·et \'pa-jət\ Sir James 1814–1899 Eng. surgeon & pathologist

Pahlavi — see REZA SHAH PAHLAVI & MOHAMMAD REZA PAHLAVI

Paine \'pān\ Albert Bigelow 1861–1937 Am. author

Paine Thomas 1737–1809 Am. (Eng.-born) political philosopher & author

Pain·le·vé \paⁿ-lə-vä\ Paul 1863–1933 Fr. mathematician & statesman

Pa·la·de \pə-'lä-dē\ George Emil 1912– Am. (Romanian-born) biologist

Pa·le·stri·na \,pa-lə-'strē-nə\ Giovanni Pierluigi da circa 1525–1594 Ital. composer

Pa·ley \'pā-lē\ Grace 1922– née Goodside Am. writer

Paley William 1743–1805 Eng. theologian & philosopher

Pal·grave \'pal-,grāv, 'pòl-\ Francis Turner 1824–1897 Eng. writer

Pal·la·dio \pə-'lä-dē-,ō\ Andrea 1508–1580 Ital. architect

Palma Tomás Estrada — see ESTRADA PALMA

Palm·er \'pä-mər, 'päl-mər\ Alice Elvira 1855–1902 née Freeman; wife of G. H. Am. educator

Palmer Daniel David 1845–1913 Am. chiropractor

Palmer George Herbert 1842–1933 Am. scholar & educator

Palm·er·ston \'pä-mər-stən, 'päl-\ 3d Viscount 1784–1865 Henry John Temple Eng. statesman; prime minister (1855–58; 1859–65) — **Palm·er·sto·nian** \,pä-mər-'stō-nē-ən, ,päl-, -nyən\ adjective

Palm·gren \'päm-grən, 'pälm-\ Selim 1878–1951 Finn. pianist & composer

Pā·ni·ni \'pä-nə-(,)nē, 'pän-yə-; pä-'nē-nē\ flourished circa 400 B.C. Indian grammarian of Sanskrit

Pank·hurst \'paŋk-,hərst\ Emmeline 1858–1928 née Goulden Eng. suffragist

Pan·ni·ni or **Pa·ni·ni** \pä-'nē-(,)nē\ Giovanni Paolo 1691–1765 Ital. painter

Pa·nof·sky \pä-'nòf-skē\ Erwin 1892–1968 Am. (Ger.-born) art historian

Pa·o·li \'paú-lē, ,pä-ō-(,)lē\ Pasquale 1725–1807 Corsican patriot

Pa·pan·dre·ou \,pä-pän-'drā-ü\ Andreas Georgios 1919–1996 prime minister of Greece (1981–89; 1993–96)

Pa·pen \'pä-pən\ Franz von 1879–1969 Ger. diplomat

Pap·pen·heim \'pä-pən-,hīm, 'pa-\ Gottfried Heinrich 1594–1632 Graf zu Pappenheim Ger. general

Par·a·cel·sus \,par-ə-'sel-səs\ 1493–1541 pseudonym of Philippus Aureolus Theophrastus Bombast von Hohenheim Swiss-born alchemist & physician

Pa·re·to \pə-'rā-(,)tō\ Vilfredo 1848–1923 Ital. economist & sociologist

Pa·ris \pä-'rēs, pə-\ (Bruno-Paulin-) Gaston 1839–1903 Fr. philologist

Par·is \'par-əs\ Matthew died 1259 Eng. monk & historian

Park Chung Hee \'pärk-'chən-'hē\ 1917–1979 So. Korean leader (1961–79) & president (1963–79)

Park \'pärk\ Mungo 1771–1806 Scot. explorer

Par·ker \'pär-kər\ Dorothy 1893–1967 née Rothschild Am. writer

Parker Sir Gilbert 1862–1932 Canad. author

Parker Matthew 1504–1575 Eng. theologian

Parker Theodore 1810–1860 Am. Unitarian clergyman

Parkes \'pärks\ Sir Henry 1815–1896 Austral. statesman

Park·man \'pärk-mən\ Francis 1823–1893 Am. historian

Parks \'pärks\ Rosa Lee 1913– Am. civil rights activist

Parley Catherine — see CATHERINE

Par·men·i·des \pär-'me-nə-,dēz\ born circa 515 B.C. Greek philosopher

Par·mi·gia·no \,pär-mi-jä-'nē-(,)nō\ or **Par·mi·gia·no** \-mə-'jä-(,)nō\ 1503–1540 Girolamo Francesco Maria Mazzuoli or Mazzola Ital. painter

Par·nell \pär-'nel\ Charles Stewart 1846–1891 Irish nationalist

Parr Catherine — see CATHERINE

Par·ring·ton \'par-iŋ-tən\ Vernon Louis 1871–1929 Am. literary historian

Par·rish \'par-ish\ Maxfield Frederick 1870–1966 Am. painter

Par·ry \'par-ē\ Sir William Edward 1790–1855 Eng. explorer

Par·sons \'pär-sᵊnz\ Talcott 1902–1979 Am. sociologist

Parsons William 1800–1867 3d Earl of Rosse Irish astronomer

Pas·cal \pa-'skal, päs-kål\ Blaise 1623–1662 Fr. mathematician & philosopher — **Pas·cal·ian** \pa-'ska-lē-ən\ adjective

Pa·šić \pä-(,)shich\ Nicola \'nē-kō-lä\ 1845–1926 Serbian & Yugoslav statesman

Pass·field \'pas-,feld\ 1st Baron — see WEBB

Pas·sy \pa-'sē, pä-\ Frédéric 1822–1912 Fr. economist & statesman

Passy Paul-Édouard 1859–1940 son of preceding Fr. phonetician

Pas·ter·nak \'pas-tər-,nak\ Boris Leonidovich 1890–1960 Soviet (Russ.-born) poet, novelist, & translator

Pas·teur \pas-'tər\ Louis 1822–1895 Fr. chemist & microbiologist — **Pas·teur·ian** \-ē-ən\ adjective

Pa·ter \'pā-tər\ Walter Horatio 1839–1894 Eng. essayist & critic

Pat·more \'pat-,mōr, -,mòr\ Coventry Kersey Dighton 1823–1896 Eng. poet

Pa·ton \'pā-tᵊn\ Alan Stewart 1903–1988 So. African writer

Pat·rick \'pa-trik\ Saint 5th century A.D. apostle & patron saint of Ireland

Pat·ti \'pa-tē, pä-\ Adelina 1843–1919 Am. (Span.-born) soprano

Pat·ti·son \'pa-tə-sən\ Mark 1813–1884 Eng. scholar & author

Pat·ton \'pa-tᵊn\ George Smith 1885–1945 Am. general

Paul \'pòl\ name of 6 popes: especially **III** 1468–1549 (pope 1534–49); **V** 1552–1621 (pope 1605–21); **VI** (Giovanni Battista Montini) 1897–1978 (pope 1963–78)

Paul I 1754–1801 emperor of Russia (1796–1801)

Paul I 1901–1964 king of Greece (1947–64)

Paul Jean — see RICHTER

Paul \'paúl\ Wolfgang 1913–1993 Ger. physicist

Paul–Bon·cour \,pòlᵇⁿ-'kúr\ Joseph 1873–1972 Fr. lawyer & statesman

Paul·ding \'pòl-diŋ\ James Kirke 1778–1860 Am. author

Pau·li \'paú-lē\ Wolfgang 1900–1958 Am. (Austrian-born) physicist

Pau·ling \'pȯ-liŋ\ Li·nus \'lī-nəs\ Carl 1901–1994 Am. chemist

Pau·lus \'paù-ləs\ Friedrich 1890–1957 Ger. field marshal

Pau·lus \'pȯ-ləs\ Julius 2d–3d century A.D. Rom. jurist

Pau·sa·ni·as \pȯ-'sä-nē-əs\ *flourished* A.D. 143–176 Greek historian & geographer

Pav·lov \'päv-ˌlȯf, 'pav-, -ˌlȯv\ Ivan Petrovich 1849–1936 Russ. physiologist — **Pav·lov·ian** \pav-'lȯ-vē-ən, -'lȯ-; -'lȯ-fē-\ *adjective*

Pav·lo·va \'pav-lə-və, pav-'lō-\ Anna 1882–1931 Russ. ballerina

Paz \'päs, 'päz\ Octavio 1914– Mex. author

Pea·body \'pē-ˌbä-dē, -bə-dē\ Endicott 1857–1944 Am. educator

Peabody George 1795–1869 Am. merchant & philanthropist

Pea·cock \'pē-ˌkäk\ Thomas Love 1785–1866 Eng. novelist & poet

Peale \'pē(ə)l\ Charles Willson 1741–1827 & his brother James 1749–1831 & Charles's son Rembrandt 1778–1860 Am. painters

Pear·son \'pir-sᵊn\ Karl 1857–1936 Eng. mathematician

Pearson Lester Bowles 1897–1972 prime minister of Canada (1963–68)

Pea·ry \'pir-ē\ Robert Edwin 1856–1920 Am. polar explorer

Pe·der·sen \'pē-dər-sən\ Charles John 1904–1989 Am. (Korean-born) chemist

Pe·dro \'pā-drō, -drü\ Dom; name of 2 emperors of Brazil: **I** 1798–1834 (reigned as emperor 1822–31; as king of Portugal 1826); **II** 1825–1891 (reigned 1831–89)

Peel \'pē(ə)l\ Sir Robert 1788–1850 Eng. statesman

Peele \'pē(ə)l\ George 1556–1596 Eng. dramatist & poet

Pei \'pā\ Ieoh Ming 1917– Am. (Chin.-born) architect

Peirce \'pərs, 'pirs\ Charles Sanders 1839–1914 Am. physicist, mathematician, & logician — **Peirc·ean** \'pər-sē-ən, 'pir-\ *adjective*

Pei·sis·tra·tus or **Pi·sis·tra·tus** \pi-'sis-trə-təs, pə-\ *died* 527 B.C. Athenian tyrant

Pe·la·gius \pə-'lā-j(ē-)əs\ *circa* 354–after 418 Brit. monk & theologian

Pe·lop·i·das \pə-'lä-pə-dəs\ *died* 364 B.C. Theban general

Pe·ña \'pe-nyə, 'pā-\ Federico Fabian 1947– U.S. secretary of transportation (1993–97); secretary of energy (1997–)

Pen·de·rec·ki \ˌpen-də-'ret-skē\ Krzysztof 1933– Pol. composer

Penn \'pen\ Sir William 1621–1670 Eng. admiral

Penn William 1644–1718 *son of preceding* Eng. Quaker & founder of Pennsylvania

Pen·nell \'pen-ᵊl, pə-'nel\ Joseph 1857–1926 Am. etcher

Pen·rose \'pen-ˌrōz, pen-'rōz\ Roger 1931– Brit. mathematician & physicist

Pen·zi·as \'pent-sē-əs\ Arno Allan 1933– Am. (Ger.-born) physicist

Pép·in III \pe-pən\ 714?–768 *the Short* king of the Franks (751–768)

Pepys \'pēps\ Samuel 1633–1703 Eng. diarist — **Pepys·ian** \'pēp-sē-ən\ *adjective*

Per·cy \'pər-sē\ Sir Henry 1364–1403 *Hotspur* Eng. soldier

Percy Thomas 1729–1811 Eng. antiquarian & poet

Percy Walker 1916–1990 Am. writer

Per·el·man \'per-əl-mən (*his own pron.*), 'pər(-ə)l-\ Sidney Joseph 1904–1979 Am. writer

Per·es \'per-(ˌ)ez\ Shimon 1923– Israeli foreign minister (1986–88; 1992–95); prime minister (1995–96)

Pé·rez Gal·dós \'per-əs-(ˌ)gäl-'dōs\ Benito 1843–1920 Span. writer

Pérez Ro·drí·guez \-ˌrȯth-'rē-gäs\ Carlos Andrés 1922– president of Venezuela (1974–79; 1989–93)

Per·go·le·si \ˌpər-gə-'lā-zē, ˌper-gə-'lā-sē\ Giovanni Battista 1710–1736 Ital. composer

Per·i·cles \'per-ə-ˌklēz\ *circa* 495–429 B.C. Athenian statesman — **Per·i·cle·an** \ˌper-ə-'klē-ən\ *adjective*

Per·kins \'pər-kənz\ Frances 1880–1965 Am. public official

Perl \'pərl\ Martin 1927– Am. physicist

Perl·man \'per(-ə)l-mən, 'pər(-ə)l-\ Itzhak 1945– Israeli violinist

Pe·rón \pā-'rōn, pə-\ Juan Domingo 1895–1974 Argentine politician; president of Argentina (1946–55; 1973–74)

Per·rault \pə-'rō, pe-\ Charles 1628–1703 Fr. writer

Per·rin \pə-'raⁿ(n), pe-\ Jean-Baptiste 1870–1942 Fr. physicist

Per·ry \'per-ē\ Bliss 1860–1954 Am. educator & critic

Perry Matthew Calbraith 1794–1858 Am. commodore

Perry Oliver Hazard 1785–1819 *brother of preceding* Am. naval officer

Perry Ralph Barton 1876–1957 Am. philosopher & educator

Perse St. John — see Aléxis Saint-Léger LÉGER

Per·shing \'pər-shiŋ, -zhiŋ\ John Joseph 1860–1948 Am. general

Per·sius \'pər-shəs, 'pər-sē-əs\ A.D. 34–62 *Aulus Persius Flaccus* Rom. satirist

Pe·ru·gi·no \ˌper-ə-'jē-(ˌ)nō\ *circa* 1450–1523 *Pietro di Cristoforo Vannucci* Ital. painter

Per·utz \pə-'rüts\ Max Ferdinand 1914– Brit. (Austrian-born) chemist

Pe·ruz·zi \pə-'rüt-sē, pā-\ Baldassare 1481–1536 Ital. architect & painter

Pes·ta·loz·zi \ˌpes-tə-'lät-sē\ Johann Heinrich 1746–1827 Swiss educator

Pé·tain \pā-taⁿ\ Philippe 1856–1951 Fr. general; marshal of France; premier of Vichy France (1940–44)

Pe·ter I \'pē-tər\ 1672–1725 *the Great* czar of Russia (1682–1725)

Peter I 1844–1921 king of Serbia (1903–21)

Peter II 1923–1970 king of Yugoslavia (1934–45)

Peter Cla·ver \'klä-vər\ Saint 1581–1654 Span. Jesuit missionary

Peter Lom·bard \'läm-ˌbärd\ *circa* 1095–1160 Latin *Petrus Lombardus* Ital. theologian

Peter the Hermit *circa* 1050–1115 Fr. preacher of the 1st Crusade

Pe·ters \'pā-tərz, -tərs\ Carl 1856–1918 Ger. explorer

Pe·ter·son \'pē-tər-sən\ Roger Tory 1908–1996 Am. ornithologist

Pe·tő·fi \'pe-tə-fē\ Sán·dor \'shän-ˌdȯr\ 1823–1849 Hung. poet

Pe·trarch \'pē-ˌträrk, 'pe-\ 1304–1374 Italian *Francesco Petrarca* Ital. poet — **Pe·trarch·an** \pē-'trär-kən, pe-\ *adjective*

Pe·trie \'pē-trē\ Sir (William Matthew) Flin·ders \'flin-dərz\ 1853–1942 Eng. Egyptologist

Pe·tro·ni·us \pi-'trō-nē-əs\ *died* A.D. 66 in full probably *Titus Petronius Niger* Rom. satirist — **Pe·tro·ni·an** \-nē-ən\ *adjective*

Pet·ty \'pe-tē\ Sir William 1623–1687 Eng. political economist

Pevs·ner \'pevz-nər\ Antoine 1886–1962 *brother of Naum Gabo* Fr. (Russ.-born) sculptor & painter

Pevsner Sir Nikolaus 1902–1983 Brit. (Ger.-born) art historian

Phae·drus \'fē-drəs\ 5th century B.C. Greek philosopher

Phaedrus *circa* 15 B.C.–*circa* A.D. 50 Rom. fabulist

Phid·i·as \'fi-dē-əs\ *flourished circa* 490–430 B.C. Greek sculptor

Phil·ip \'fi-ləp\ 1639?–1676 *Met·a·com·et* \ˌme-tə-'kä-mət\ Wampanoag Indian chief

Philip name of 6 kings of France: especially **II** or **Philip Augustus** 1165–1223 (reigned 1179–1223); **IV** (*the Fair*) 1268–1314 (reigned 1285–1314); **VI** 1293–1350 (reigned 1328–50)

Philip name of 5 kings of Spain: especially **II** 1527–1598 (reigned 1556–98); **V** 1683–1746 (reigned 1700–24, 1724–46)

Philip II 382–336 B.C. king of Macedon (359–336)

Philip III 1396–1467 *the Good* Duke of Burgundy (1419–67)

Philip Prince 1921– *consort of Queen Elizabeth II of Great Britain* 3d Duke of *Edinburgh*

Phil·ips \'fi-ləps\ Ambrose 1674–1749 *Nam·by-Pam·by* \ˌnam-bē-'pam-bē\ Eng. poet & dramatist

Phil·lips \'fi-ləps\ Wendell 1811–1884 Am. orator & reformer

Phill·potts \'fil-ˌpäts\ Eden 1862–1960 Eng. novelist & dramatist

Phi·lo Ju·dae·us \'fī-(ˌ)lō-jü-'dē-əs, -'dā-\ *circa* 13 B.C.–A.D. 45 to 50 Jewish philosopher of Alexandria

Pho·ci·on \'fō-sē-ˌän\ *circa* 402–318 B.C. Athenian general & statesman

Phyfe \'fīf\ Duncan 1768–1854 Am. (Scot.-born) cabinetmaker

Pia·get \pyä-'zhā\ Jean 1896–1980 Swiss psychologist — **Pia·get·ian** \ˌpyä-ə-'je-tē-ən, pyä-'zhä-ən\ *adjective*

Pi·card \pē-'kär, pi-'kärd\ Jean 1620–1682 Fr. astronomer

Pi·cas·so \pi-'kä-(ˌ)sō, -'ka-\ Pablo 1881–1973 Span. painter & sculptor in France

Pic·card \pi-'kär, -'kärd\ Auguste 1884–1962 Swiss physicist

Piccard Jacques-Ernest-Jean 1922– *son of Auguste* Swiss (Belg.-born) oceanographer

Pick·er·ing \'pi-k(ə-)riŋ\ Edward Charles 1846–1919 & his brother William Henry 1858–1938 Am. astronomers

Pick·ett \'pi-kət\ George Edward 1825–1875 Am. Confederate general

Pi·co del·la Mi·ran·do·la \'pē-(ˌ)kō-ˌde-lə-mə-'ran-də-lə, -'rän-\ Conte Giovanni 1463–1494 Ital. humanist

Pierce \'pirs\ Franklin 1804–1869 14th president of the U.S. (1853–57)

Pie·ro del·la Fran·ces·ca \'pyer-ō-ˌde-lə-fran-'ches-kə, -frän-\ or **de·Fran·ces·chi** \-dā-frän-'ches-kē, -frän-\ *circa* 1420–1492 Ital. painter

Pike \'pīk\ Zebulon Montgomery 1779–1813 Am. general & explorer

Pi·late \'pī-lət\ Pon·tius \'pän-chəs, 'pən-chəs\ *died* after A.D. 36 Rom. procurator of Judea (26–*circa* 36)

Pit·sud·ski \pil-'süt-skē, -'züt-\ Józef Klemens 1867–1935 Pol. general & statesman

Pin·chot \'pin-shō\ Gifford 1865–1946 Am. conservationist & politician

Pinck·ney \'piŋk-nē\ Charles Cotesworth 1746–1825 Am. statesman

Pin·dar \'pin-dər, -ˌdär\ *circa* 522–*circa* 438 B.C. Greek poet

Pi·ne·ro \pə-'nir-(ˌ)ō, -'ner-\ Sir Arthur Wing 1855–1934 Eng. dramatist

Pin·ker·ton \'piŋ-kər-tᵊn\ Allan 1819–1884 Am. (Scot.-born) detective

Pi·no·chet Ugar·te \ˌpē-nō-'chet-ü-'gär-tā\ Augusto 1915– Chilean general; president of Chile (1974–90)

Pin·ter \'pin-tər\ Harold 1930– Eng. dramatist — **Pin·ter·esque** \ˌpin-tə-'resk\ *adjective*

Pin·tu·ric·chio \ˌpin-tə-'rē-kē-ˌō\ *circa* 1454–1513 *Bernardino di Betto di Biago* Ital. painter

Pin·zón \pin-'zōn\ Martín Alonso *circa* 1441–1493 & his brother Vicente Yáñez *circa* 1460–*circa* 1523 Span. navigators & explorers

Pioz·zi \pē-'ȯt-sē\ Hester Lynch 1741–1821 *Mrs. Thrale* \'thrā(ə)l\ Eng. writer

Pi·ran·del·lo \ˌpir-ən-'de-(ˌ)lō\ Luigi 1867–1936 Ital. author — **Pi·ran·del·li·an** \-'de-lē-ən\ *adjective*

Pi·ra·ne·si \ˌpir-ə-'nä-zē\ Giambattista 1720–1778 Ital. architect, painter, & engraver

Pire \'pir\ Dominique Georges 1910–1969 Belg. humanitarian

Pi·sa·no \pi-'sä-(ˌ)nō, -'zä-\ Giovanni *circa* 1250–after 1314 & his father Nicola *circa* 1220–1278(or 1284) Ital. sculptors

Pisistratus — see PEISISTRATUS

Pis·sar·ro \pə-'sär-(ˌ)ō\ Camille 1830–1903 Fr. painter

Pis·ton \'pis-tən\ Walter Hamor 1894–1976 Am. composer

Pit·man \'pit-mən\ Sir Isaac 1813–1897 Eng. phonographer

Pitt \'pit\ William 1708–1778 Earl of *Chatham; the Elder Pitt* Eng. statesman

Pitt William 1759–1806 *the Younger Pitt; son of preceding* Eng. statesman

Pitt–Riv·ers \'pit-'ri-vərz\ Augustus Henry 1827–1900 Eng. archaeologist

\ə\ abut \ᵊ\ kitten \ər\ further \a\ ash \ā\ ace
\ä\ mop, mar \aú\ out \ch\ chin \e\ bet \ē\ easy
\g\ go \i\ hit \ī\ ice \j\ job \ŋ\ sing \ō\ go
\ȯ\ law \ȯi\ boy \th\ thin \th̶\ the \ü\ loot \ú\ foot
\y\ yet \zh\ vision *see also* Guide to Pronunciation

Pi·us \\'pī-əs\\ name of 12 popes: especially **II** (*Enea Silvio Piccolomini* or *Ae·ne·as Sil·vi·us* \\i-'nē-əs-'sil-vē-əs\\ or *Syl·vi·us* \\'sil-vē-əs\\) 1405–1464 (pope 1458–64); **VII** 1742–1823 (pope 1800–23); **IX** 1792–1878 (pope 1846–78); **X** 1835–1914 (pope 1903–14); **XI** (*Ambrogio Damiano Achille Ratti*) 1857–1939 (pope 1922–39); **XII** (*Eugenio Pacelli*) 1876–1958 (pope 1939–58)

Pi·zar·ro \\pə-'zär-(ˌ)ō\\ Francisco *circa* 1475–1541 Span. conquistador

Planck \\'pläŋk\\ Max Karl Ernst Ludwig 1858–1947 Ger. physicist

Plan·tin \\plä"-ta"\\ Christophe *circa* 1520–1589 Fr. printer

Plath \\'plath\\ Sylvia 1932–1963 Am. poet

Pla·to \\'plā-(ˌ)tō\\ *circa* 428–348(or 347) B.C. Greek philosopher

Plau·tus \\'plȯ-təs\\ Titus Maccius *circa* 254–184 B.C. Rom. dramatist — **Plau·tine** \\'plȯ-ˌtīn\\ *adjective*

Ple·kha·nov \\plə-'kä-ˌnȯf, pli-'kä-\\ Georgy Valentinovich 1857–1918 Russ. Marxist philosopher

Ple·ven \\plä-'ven\\ René 1901–1993 Fr. politician

Pliny \\'pli-nē\\ A.D. 23–79 *Gaius Plinius Secundus; the Elder* Rom. scholar

Pliny A.D. 61(or 62)–*circa* 113 *Gaius Plinius Caecilius Secundus; the Younger; nephew of preceding* Rom. author

Plo·ti·nus \\plō-'tī-nəs\\ A.D. 205–270 Rom. (Egypt.-born) philosopher — **Plo·tin·i·an** \\-'ti-nē-ən\\ *adjective*

Plu·tarch \\'plü-ˌtärk\\ *circa* A.D. 46–after 119 Greek biographer & moralist — **Plu·tarch·an** \\'plü-'tär-kən\\ *or* **Plu·tarch·ian** \\-kē-ən\\ *adjective*

Po·ca·hon·tas \\ˌpō-kə-'hän-təs\\ *circa* 1595–1617 *daughter of Powhatan* Am. Indian

Pod·gor·ny \\pəd-'gȯr-nē\\ Nikolay Viktorovich 1903–1983 Soviet politician; head of Presidium (1965–77)

Poe \\'pō\\ Edgar Allan 1809–1849 Am. poet & short-story writer

Poin·ca·ré \\ˌpwa"-ˌkä-'rā\\ Jules-Henri 1854–1912 Fr. mathematician

Poincaré Raymond 1860–1934 *cousin of J. H.* Fr. statesman; president of France (1913–20)

Po·lan·yi \\pō-'län-yē\\ John Charles 1929– Canad. (Ger.-born) chemist

Pole \\'pōl, 'pül\\ Reginald 1500–1558 Eng. cardinal; archbishop of Canterbury (1556–58)

Po·len·ta \\pō-'len-tə\\ Francesca da *died* 1283(or 1284) *Fran·ces·ca da Ri·mi·ni* \\ˌfran-'ches-kə-dä-'ri-mə-(ˌ)nē, ˌfrän-, -'rē-\\ Ital. noblewoman famous for tragic adulterous love affair

Po·li·tian \\pə-'li-shən\\ 1454–1494 *Angelo Poliziano* or *Angelo Ambrogini* Ital. classical scholar & poet

Polk \\'pōk\\ James Knox 1795–1849 11th president of the U.S. (1845–49)

Pol·lio \\'pä-lē-ˌō\\ Gaius Asinius 76 B.C.–A.D. 4 Rom. soldier, orator, & politician

Pol·lock \\'pä-lək\\ Sir Frederick 1845–1937 Eng. jurist

Pollock (Paul) Jackson 1912–1956 Am. painter

Po·lo \\'pō-(ˌ)lō\\ Mar·co \\'mär-(ˌ)kō\\ 1254–1324 Venetian traveler

Po·lyb·i·us \\pə-'li-bē-əs\\ *circa* 200–*circa* 118 B.C. Greek historian

Pol·y·carp \\'pä-li-ˌkärp\\ Saint 2d century Christian martyr & Apostolic Father; bishop of Smyrna

Pol·y·cli·tus *or* **Pol·y·clei·tus** \\ˌpä-li-'klī-təs\\ 5th century B.C. Greek sculptor & architect

Po·lyc·ra·tes \\pə-'li-krə-ˌtēz\\ *died circa* 522 B.C. tyrant of Samos

Pol·y·do·rus \\ˌpä-li-'dȯr-əs, -'dȯr-\\ 1st century B.C. Rhodian sculptor

Pol·yg·no·tus \\ˌpä-lig-'nō-təs\\ *circa* 500–*circa* 440 B.C. Greek painter

Pom·pa·dour \\'päm-pə-ˌdȯr, -ˌdȯr, -ˌdu̇r\\ Madame de 1721–1764 *Jeanne-Antoinette Poisson; mistress of Louis XV*

Pom·pey \\'päm-pē\\ 106–48 B.C. *Gnaeus Pompeius Magnus; the Great* Rom. general & statesman

Pom·pi·dou \\'päm-pi-ˌdü\\ Georges-Jean-Raymond 1911–1974 Fr. politician; premier (1962–68) & president (1969–74) of France

Ponce de Le·ón \\ˌpän(t)-sə-,dä-lē-'ōn, ˌpänts-də-, -'lē-ən\\ Juan 1460–1521 Span. explorer

Pon·chi·el·li \\ˌpȯŋ-kē-'e-lē\\ Amilcare 1834–1886 Ital. composer

Pons \\'pänz, 'pō"s\\ Lily 1904–1976 Am. (Fr.-born) soprano

Pon·selle \\pän-'sel\\ Rosa Melba 1897–1981 Am. soprano

Pon·ti·ac \\'pän-tē-ˌak\\ *circa* 1720–1769 Ottawa Indian chief

Pon·top·pi·dan \\pän-'tä-pə-ˌdan\\ Henrik 1857–1943 Dan. novelist

Pon·tor·mo \\pōn-'tȯr-(ˌ)mō\\ Jacopo da 1494–1557 originally *J. Carrucci* Ital. painter

Pope \\'pōp\\ Alexander 1688–1744 Eng. poet — **Pop·ean** *also* **Pop·ean** \\'pō-pē-ən\\ *adjective*

Pope John 1822–1892 Am. general

Por·son \\'pȯr-sᵊn\\ Richard 1759–1808 Eng. scholar

Por·tal \\'pȯr-tᵊl, 'pȯr-\\ Charles Frederick Algernon 1893–1971 1st Viscount *Portal of Hungerford* Brit. air marshal

Por·ter \\'pȯr-tər, 'pȯr-\\ Cole Albert 1891–1964 Am. composer & lyricist

Porter David 1780–1843 & his son David Dixon 1813–1891 Am. naval officers

Porter Eliot Furness 1901–1990 Am. photographer

Porter Gene 1868–1924 née *Stratton* Am. novelist

Porter Sir George 1920– Brit. chemist

Porter Katherine Anne 1890–1980 Am. writer

Porter Noah 1811–1892 Am. philosopher & lexicographer

Porter Rodney Robert 1917–1985 Brit. biochemist

Porter William Sydney 1862–1910 pseudonym *O. Hen·ry* \\(ˌ)ō-'hen-rē\\ Am. short-story writer

Portland Duke of — see BENTINCK

Post \\'pōst\\ Emily 1872–1960 née *Price* Am. columnist & writer

Po·tem·kin \\pə-'tyȯm(p)-kən, pō-'tem(p)-\\ Grigory Aleksandrovich 1739–1791 Russ. field marshal & statesman

Pot·ter \\'pä-tər\\ Beatrix 1866–1943 Brit. writer & illustrator

Potter Paul *or* Paulus 1625–1654 Du. painter

Pou·lenc \\'pü-ˌlaŋk\\ Fran·cis \\frä"-sēs\\ 1899–1963 Fr. composer

Pound \\'pau̇nd\\ Ezra Loomis 1885–1972 Am. poet — **Pound·ian** \\'pau̇n-dē-ən\\ *adjective*

Pound Roscoe 1870–1964 Am. jurist

Pound·mak·er \\'pau̇nd-ˌmä-kər\\ 1826–1886 Canad. Cree chief

Pous·sin \\pü-sa"\\ Nicolas 1594–1665 Fr. painter

Pow·ell \\'pau̇-(ə)l\\ Adam Clayton 1908–1972 Am. clergyman & politician

Pow·ell \\'pō-əl, 'pau̇-(ə)l\\ Anthony 1905– Eng. writer

Powell Cecil Frank 1903–1969 Brit. physicist

Pow·ell \\'pau̇-(ə)l\\ Colin Luther 1937– Am. general

Powell John Wesley 1834–1902 Am. geologist & explorer

Powell Lewis Franklin 1907– Am. jurist

Pow·ell \\'pō-əl, 'pau̇(-ə)l\\ Michael Latham 1905–1990 Brit. film director, writer, & producer

Pow·ers \\'pau̇-(ə)rz\\ Hiram 1805–1873 Am. sculptor

Pow·ha·tan \\ˌpau̇-ə-'tan, pau̇-'ha-tᵊn\\ 1550?–1618 *Wa-hun-sen-a-cawh* or *Wahunsonacock; father of Pocahontas* Am. Indian chief

Pow·ys \\'pō-əs\\ John Cow·per \\'kü-pər\\ 1872–1963 & his brothers Theodore Francis 1875–1953 & Llewelyn 1884–1939 Eng. authors

Pra·do Ugar·te·che \\'prä-(ˌ)dō-,ü-gär-'tä-chē\\ Manuel 1889–1967 Peruvian banker; president of Peru (1939–45; 1956–62)

Pra·ja·dhi·pok \\prə-'chä-ti-ˌpäk\\ 1893–1941 king of Siam (1925–35)

Pratt \\'prat\\ Edwin John 1883–1964 Canad. poet

Prax·it·e·les \\prak-'si-tᵊl-ˌēz\\ *flourished* 370–330 B.C. Athenian sculptor — **Prax·it·e·le·an** \\(ˌ)prak-ˌsi-tᵊl-'ē-ən\\ *adjective*

Pre·ble \\'pre-bəl\\ Edward 1761–1807 Am. naval officer

Pregl \\'prä-gəl\\ Fritz 1869–1930 Austrian chemist

Pre·log \\'pre-ˌlȯg\\ Vladimir 1906– Swiss (Bosnian-born) chemist

Pres·cott \\'pres-kət *also* -ˌkät\\ William Hickling 1796–1859 Am. historian

Pre·to·ri·us \\pri-'tȯr-ē-əs, -'tȯr-\\ Andries Wilhelmus Jacobus 1798–1853 & his son Marthinus Wessels 1819–1901 So. African Du. colonizers & soldiers

Pré·vost d'Ex·iles \\prä-'vō-,deg-'zē(ə)l\\ Antoine-François 1697–1763 Fr. abbé & writer

Price \\'prīs\\ (Mary) Le·on·tyne \\lē-'än-ˌtēn; 'lē-ən-ˌ, 'lä-\\ 1927– Am. soprano

Pride \\'prīd\\ Thomas *died* 1658 Eng. Parliamentarian commander

Priest·ley \\'prēst-lē\\ John Boynton 1894–1984 Eng. author

Priestley Joseph 1733–1804 Eng. clergyman & chemist

Pri·go·gine \\prə-'gō-zhən, -(ˌ)gō-'zhēn\\ Ilya 1917– Belg. (Russ.-born) chemist

Pri·mo de Ri·ve·ra y Or·ba·ne·ja \\'prē-(ˌ)mō-thä-ri-'ver-ə-ˌē-,ȯr-bə-'nä-(ˌ)hä\\ Miguel 1870–1930 Marqués *de Estella* Span. general & politician

Primrose Archibald Philip — see ROSEBERY

Prior \\'prī-(ə)r\\ Matthew 1664–1721 Eng. poet

Pri·scian \\'pri-shən, 'pri-shē-ən\\ *flourished* A.D. 500 *Priscianus Caesariensis* Latin grammarian at Constantinople

Pro·clus \\'prō-kləs, 'prä-\\ 410?–485 Greek philosopher

Pro·co·pi·us \\prə-'kō-pē-əs\\ 6th century Byzantine historian

Pro·kho·rov \\ˌprȯ-kə-'rȯf\\ Aleksandr Mikhaylovich 1916– Russ. physicist

Pro·kof·iev \\prə-'kȯf-yəf, -ˌyef, -ˌyev\\ Sergey Sergeyevich 1891–1953 Russ. composer — **Pro·kof·iev·ian** \\-ˌkȯf-'ye-vē-ən\\ *adjective*

Pro·per·tius \\prō-'pər-sh(ē-)əs\\ Sextus *circa* 50–*circa* 15 B.C. Rom. poet

Pro·tag·o·ras \\prō-'ta-gə-rəs\\ *circa* 485–410 B.C. Greek philosopher — **Pro·tag·o·re·an** \\-ˌta-gə-'rē-ən\\ *adjective*

Prou·dhon \\prü-dō"\\ Pierre-Joseph 1809–1865 Fr. journalist

Proust \\'prüst\\ Marcel 1871–1922 Fr. novelist — **Proust·ian** \\'prü-stē-ən\\ *adjective*

Prynne \\'prin\\ William 1600–1669 Eng. Puritan pamphleteer

Prze·val·sky \\ˌpər-zhə-'väl-skē, ˌpshə-'väl-\\ Nikolay Mikhaylovich 1839–1888 Russ. explorer

Ptol·e·my \\'tä-lə-mē\\ name of 15 kings of Egypt 323–30 B.C.

Ptolemy 2d century A.D. *Claudius Ptolemaeus* Alexandrian astronomer

Puc·ci·ni \\pü-'chē-nē\\ Giacomo 1858–1924 Ital. composer — **Puc·ci·ni·an** \\-nē-ən\\ *adjective*

P'u·i \\'pü-ˌē, -ˌyē\\ Henry 1906–1967 *Hsüan-T'ung* Chin. emperor (1908–12); last of Manchu dynasty; puppet emperor of Manchukuo (1934–45)

Pu·las·ki \\pə-'las-kē, pyü-\\ Kazimierz 1747–1779 Pol. soldier in Am. Revolution

Pu·lit·zer \\'pu̇-lət-sər (*family's pron.*), 'pyü-\\ Joseph 1847–1911 Am. (Hung.-born) journalist

Pull·man \\'pu̇l-mən\\ George Mortimer 1831–1897 Am. inventor

Pu·pin \\pyü-'pēn, pü-\\ Michael Idvorsky 1858–1935 Am. (Hung.-born) physicist & inventor

Pur·cell \\(ˌ)pər-'sel\\ Edward Mills 1912–1997 Am. physicist

Pur·cell \\'pər-səl, (ˌ)pər-'sel\\ Henry *circa* 1659–1695 Eng. composer

Pur·chas \\'pər-chəs\\ Samuel *circa* 1577–1626 Eng. compiler of travel books

Pur·ky·ně *or* **Pur·kin·je** \\'pu̇r-kən-ˌyä\\ Jan Evangelista 1787–1869 Bohemian physiologist

Pu·sey \\'pyü-zē\\ Edward Bouverie 1800–1882 Eng. theologian

Push·kin \\'pu̇sh-kən\\ Aleksandr Sergeyevich 1799–1837 Russ. poet — **Push·kin·ian** \\'pu̇sh-'ki-nē-ən\\ *adjective*

Put·nam \\'pət-nəm\\ Israel 1718–1790 Am. general in Revolution

Putnam Rufus 1738–1824 *cousin of preceding* Am. general in Revolution

Pu·vis de Cha·vannes \\pē-vē-də-shá-vän, -vēs-; pyü-ˌvē(s)-də-shä-'vän\\ Pierre-Cécile 1824–1898 Fr. painter & muralist

Pye \\'pī\\ Henry James 1745–1813 Eng. poet laureate (1790–1813)

Pyle \\'pī(ə)l\\ Ernest Taylor 1900–1945 *Ernie* Am. journalist

Pym \\'pim\\ John 1584–1643 Eng. statesman

Pyn·chon \'pin-chən\ Thomas 1937– Am. writer — **Pyn·chon·esque** \,pin-chə-'nesk\ *adjective*
Pyr·rhus \'pir-əs\ 319–272 B.C. king of Epirus (306–302; 297–272 B.C.)
Py·thag·o·ras \pə-'tha-gə-rəs, pī-\ *circa* 580–*circa* 500 B.C. Greek philosopher & mathematician
Qad·da·fi *variant of* GADHAFI
Qua·dros \'kwä-,drōs\ Jânio da Silva 1917–1992 president of Brazil (1960–61)
Quarles \'kwór(-ə)lz, 'kwär(-ə)lz\ Francis 1592–1644 Eng. poet
Qua·si·mo·do \kwä-'zē-mə-,dō\ Salvatore \,säl-vä-'tō-(,)rä\ 1901–1968 Ital. poet & critic
Quayle \'kwā(ə)l\ James Danforth 1947– *Dan* Am. politician; vice president of the U.S. (1989–93)
Queensberry Marquis of — see DOUGLAS
Quercia, della Jacopo — see JACOPO DELLA QUERCIA
Ques·nay \kā-'nā\ François 1694–1774 Fr. physician & economist
Que·zon y Mo·li·na \kā-,sòn-,ē-mə-'lē-nə\ Manuel Luis 1878–1944 president of the Philippine Commonwealth (1935–44)
Quid·de \'kvi-də, 'kwi-\ Ludwig 1858–1941 Ger. historian & pacifist
Quil·ler–Couch \'kwi-lər-'küch\ Sir Arthur Thomas 1863–1944 pseudonym *Q* Eng. author
Quin·cy \'kwin-zē, 'kwin(t)-sē\ Josiah 1744–1775 Am. lawyer
Quine \'kwīn\ Willard Van Orman 1908– Am. philosopher
Quin·te·ro Serafín & Joaquín — see ALVAREZ QUINTERO
Quin·til·ian \kwin-'til-yən\ *circa* A.D. 35–*circa* 100 *Marcus Fabius Quintilianus* Rom. rhetorician
Qui·ri·no \ki-'rē-(,)nō\ Elpidio 1890–1956 president of the Philippine Republic (1948–53)
Quoirez Françoise — see Françoise SAGAN
Ra·be·lais \'ra-bə-,lā, ,ra-bə-'lā\ François *circa* 1483–1553 Fr. humorist & satirist
Ra·bi \'rä-bē\ Isidor Isaac 1898–1988 Am. (Austrian-born) physicist
Ra·bin \rä-'bēn\ Yitzhak 1922–1995 prime minister of Israel (1974–77; 1992–95)
Rabinowitz Solomon — see Shalom ALEICHEM
Rach·ma·ni·noff \räk-'mä-nə-,nóf\ Sergey Vasilyevich 1873–1943 Russ. composer, pianist, & conductor
Ra·cine \ra-'sēn, rə-\ Jean 1639–1699 Fr. dramatist — **Ra·cin·ian** \ra-'si-nē-ən, rə-\ *adjective*
Rack·ham \'ra-kəm\ Arthur 1867–1939 Brit. illustrator
Rad·cliffe \'rad-,klif\ Ann 1764–1823 née *Ward* Eng. novelist
Ra·detz·ky \rə-'det-skē\ Joseph 1766–1858 Graf *Radetzky von Radetz* Austrian field marshal
Rae \'rā\ John 1813–1893 Scot. explorer
Rae·burn \'rā-(,)bərn\ Sir Henry 1756–1823 Scot. painter
Rae·der \'rā-dər\ Erich 1876–1960 Ger. admiral
Rae·me·kers \'rä-,mä-kərz, -kərs\ Louis 1869–1956 Du. cartoonist
Raf·san·ja·ni \,räf-sän-'jä-nē\ Ali Akbar Hashemi 1934– president of Iran (1989–97)
Rag·lan \'ra-glən\ 1st Baron 1788–1855 *FitzRoy James Henry Somerset* Brit. field marshal
Rai·mon·di \rī-'män-dē, -'mōn-\ Marcantonio *circa* 1480–*circa* 1534 Ital. engraver
Rai·nier III \rə-'nir, ra-, rā-\ 1923– prince of Monaco (1949–)
Rain·wa·ter \'rān-,wò-tər, -,wä-\ L(eo) James 1917–1986 Am. physicist
Ra·ja·go·pa·la·cha·ri \'rä-jə-(,)gō-,pä-lə-'chär-ē\ Chakravarti 1879–1972 Indian politician; governor-general of India (1948–50)
Ra·leigh *or* **Ra·legh** \'rò-lē, 'rä- *also* 'ra-\ Sir Walter 1554–1618 Eng. courtier, navigator, & historian
Ra·ma·krish·na \,rä-mə-'krish-nə\ 1836–1886 Hindu religious
Ra·man \'rä-mən\ Sir Chan·dra·se·kha·ra \,chən-drə-'shā-kə-rə\ Venkata 1888–1970 Indian physicist
Ra·meau \ra-'mō\ Jean-Philippe 1683–1764 Fr. composer
Ra·mée \rə-'mā\ Marie Louise de la 1839–1908 pseudonym *Oui·da* \'wē-də\ Eng. novelist

Ra·món y Ca·jal \rə-'mōn-ē-kə-'häl\ Santiago 1852–1934 Span. histologist
Ra·mos \'rä-(,)mōs\ Fidel V. 1928– president of the Philippines (1992–)
Ram·say \'ram-zē\ Allan 1686–1758 Scot. poet
Ramsay James Andrew Broun 1812–1860 10th Earl & 1st Marquis of *Dal·hou·sie* \dal-'haú-zē\ Brit. colonial administrator
Ramsay Sir William 1852–1916 Brit. chemist
Ram·ses \'ram-,sēz\ *or* **Ram·e·ses** \'ra-mə-,sēz\ name of 11 kings of Egypt: especially **II** (reigned 1304–1237 B.C.); **III** (reigned 1198–1166 B.C.)
Ram·sey \'ram-zē\ (Arthur) Michael 1904–1988 archbishop of Canterbury (1961–74)
Ramsey Norman Foster 1915– Am. physicist
Rand \'rand\ Ayn \'īn\ 1905–1982 Am. (Russ.-born) writer
Ran·dolph \'ran-,dälf\ Asa Philip 1889–1979 Am. labor leader
Randolph Edmund Jennings 1753–1813 Am. statesman
Randolph John 1773–1833 *John Randolph of Roanoke* Am. statesman
Ran·jit Singh \'rən-jət-'siṇ\ 1780–1839 *Lion of the Punjab* founder of Sikh kingdom
Ran·ke \'räṇ-kə\ Leopold von 1795–1886 Ger. historian
Ran·som \'ran(t)-səm\ John Crowe 1888–1974 Am. educator & poet
Rao \'raú, 'rä-ō\ Pamulaparti Venkata Narasimha 1921– prime minister of India (1991–96)
Ra·pha·el \'ra-fē-əl, 'rä-, 'rä-\ 1483–1520 Italian *Raffaello Sanzio* Ital. painter — **Ra·pha·el·esque** \,ra-fē-ə-'lesk, ,rä-, \ *adjective*
Rask \'rask, 'räsk\ Rasmus Kristian 1787–1832 Dan. philologist & orientalist
Ras·mus·sen \'ras-mə-sən, 'räs-,mú-s°n\ Knud Johan Victor 1879–1933 Dan. explorer & ethnologist
Ras·pu·tin \ra-'spyü-t°n, -'spü-, -'spù-\ Grigory Yefimovich 1872–1916 Russ. mystic
Rausch·en·berg \'raú-shən-,berg\ Robert 1925– Am. artist
Ra·vel \ra-'vel, ra-\ Mau·rice \mó-'rēs\ Joseph 1875–1937 Fr. composer — **Ra·vel·ian** \rə-'vel-yən, ra-, -lē-ən\ *adjective*
Raw·lin·son \'rò-lən-sən\ Sir Henry Cres·wicke \'kre-zik\ 1810–1895 Eng. orientalist
Ray \'rā\ John 1627–1705 Eng. naturalist
Ray Satyajit 1921–1992 Indian film director, writer, & producer
Ray·burn \'rā-(,)bərn\ Samuel Taliaferro 1882–1961 Am. politician
Ray·leigh \'rā-lē\ Lord 1842–1919 *John William Strutt* Eng. mathematician & physicist
Read \'rēd\ George 1733–1798 Am. statesman in Revolution
Read Sir Herbert 1893–1968 Eng. writer
Reade \'rēd\ Charles 1814–1884 Eng. novelist & dramatist
Read·ing \'re-diṇ\ 1st Marquis of 1860–1935 *Rufus Daniel Isaacs* Brit. statesman; viceroy of India (1921–26)
Rea·gan \'rā-gən\ Ronald Wilson 1911– Am. actor & politician; 40th president of the U.S. (1981–89) — **Rea·gan·esque** \,rā-gə-'nesk\ *adjective*
Ré·au·mur \,rā-ō-'myùr, -'mūr\ René-Antoine Ferchault de 1683–1757 Fr. naturalist & physicist
Ré·ca·mier \rā-'ka-mē-,ā, rā-kà-myä\ Jeanne-Françoise-Julie-Adélaïde 1777–1849 Fr. society wit
Red Cloud \'red-,klaúd\ 1822–1909 Sioux Indian chief
Red·mond \'red-mənd\ John Edward 1856–1918 Irish politician
Re·don \rə-'dōⁿ\ Odilon 1840–1916 Fr. artist
Reed \'rēd\ John 1887–1920 Am. journalist, poet, & Communist
Reed Stanley Forman 1884–1980 Am. jurist
Reed Thomas Brackett 1839–1902 Am. politician
Reed Walter 1851–1902 Am. army surgeon
Reg·u·lus \'re-gyə-ləs\ Marcus Atilius *died circa* 250 B.C. Rom. general
Rehn·quist \'ren-,kwist, 'reṇ-kwəst\ William Hubbs 1924– Am. jurist; chief justice U.S. Supreme Court (1986–)
Reich \'rīk\ Wilhelm 1897–1957 Austrian psychologist — **Reich·ian** \'rī-kē-ən\ *adjective*

Reich·stein \'rīk-,shtīn, -,stīn\ Tadeus 1897–1996 Swiss (Pol.-born) chemist
Reid \'rēd\ Thomas 1710–1796 Scot. philosopher
Reid Whitelaw 1837–1912 Am. journalist & diplomat
Rei·ner \'rī-nər\ Fritz 1888–1963 Am. (Hung.-born) conductor
Reines \'rīnz\ Frederick 1918– Am. physicist
Rein·hardt \'rīn-,härt\ Max 1873–1943 originally surname *Goldmann* Austrian theater director
Re·marque \rə-'märk\ Erich Maria 1898–1970 Am. (Ger.-born) novelist
Rem·brandt \'rem-,brant *also* -,bränt\ 1606–1669 in full *Rembrandt Harmensz* (or *Harmenszoon*) *van Rijn* (or *Ryn*) Du. painter — **Rem·brandt·esque** \,rem-,bran-'tesk, -,brän-\ *adjective*
Rem·ing·ton \'re-miṇ-tən\ Frederic 1861–1909 Am. artist
Rem·sen \'rem(p)-sən, 'rem-zən\ Ira 1846–1927 Am. chemist
Re·nan \rə-'nä⁰(n)\ Joseph Ernest 1823–1892 Fr. philologist & historian
Re·nault \rə-'nō\ Louis 1843–1918 Fr. jurist & pacifist
Re·ni \'rā-nē\ Guido 1575–1642 Ital. painter
Ren·ner \'re-nər\ Karl 1870–1950 president of Austria (1945–50)
Re·no \'rē-(,)nō\ Janet 1938– U.S. attorney-general (1993–)
Re·noir \'ren-,wär, rən-'\ Jean 1894–1979 *son of P.-A.* Fr. film director & writer
Renoir Pierre-Auguste 1841–1919 Fr. painter
Ren·wick \'ren-(,)wik\ James 1818–1895 Am. architect
Rep·plier \'re-,plir, -plē-ər\ Agnes 1855–1950 Am. essayist
Re·spi·ghi \rə-'spē-gē, re-\ Ottorino 1879–1936 Ital. composer
Res·ton \'res-tən\ James Barrett 1909–1995 Am. journalist
Retz \'rets, *Fr* re(s)\ Cardinal de 1613–1679 *Jean-François-Paul de Gondi* Fr. ecclesiastic & politician
Reuch·lin \'rói-klən; -,klēn, rói-\ Johannes 1455–1522 *Cap·nio* \'kap-nē-,ō\ Ger. humanist
Reu·ter \'rói-tər\ Baron Paul Julius von 1816–1899 originally *Israel Beer Josaphat* Brit. (Ger.-born) journalist
Reu·ther \'rü-thər\ Walter Philip 1907–1970 Am. labor leader
Re·vere \ri-'vir\ Paul 1735–1818 Am. patriot & silversmith
Rex·roth \'reks-,róth\ Kenneth 1905–1982 Am. writer
Rey·mont \'rā-,mänt\ *or* **Rej·ment** \'rā-,ment\ Wła·dy·sław \vlä-'di-,släf\ Sta·ni·sław \stä-'nē-,släf\ 1867–1925 Pol. novelist
Rey·naud \rā-'nō\ Paul 1878–1966 premier of France (1940)
Reyn·olds \'re-n°l(d)z\ Sir Joshua 1723–1792 Eng. painter
Re·za Shah Pah·lavi \ri-'zä-'shä-'pa-lə-(,)vē, -'shō-\ 1878–1944 *father of Mohammad Reza Pahlavi* shah of Iran (1925–41)
Rhee \'rē\ Syng·man \'siṇ-mən, 'sig-\ 1875–1965 So. Korean politician; president of So. Korea (1948–60)
Rhodes \'rōdz\ Cecil John 1853–1902 Brit. administrator & financier in So. Africa
Rhond·da \'rän-də, -thə\ 1st Viscount 1856–1918 *David Alfred Thomas* Brit. industrialist & administrator
Rib·ben·trop \'ri-bən-,träp, -,trōp\ Joachim von 1893–1946 Ger. diplomat
Ri·be·ra \rē-'ber-ə\ José (or Jusepe) de 1591–1652 *Lo Spa·gno·let·to* \,lō-,spän-yə-'le-(,)tō\ Span. painter & etcher in Naples
Ri·car·do \ri-'kär-(,)dō\ David 1772–1823 Eng. economist
Rice \'rīs\ Elmer Leopold 1892–1967 originally *Elmer Reizenstein* Am. dramatist
Rich \'rich\ Adrienne Cecile 1929– Am. poet
Rich·ard \'ri-chərd\ name of 3 kings of England: **I** (*Coeur de Li·on* \,kər-də-'lī-ən, -'lē-; -lē-'ō⁰\)

1157–1199 (reigned 1189–99); **II** 1367–1400 (reigned 1377–99); **III** 1452–1485 (reigned 1483–85)

Richards Dickinson Woodruff 1895–1973 Am. physician

Richards Theodore William 1868–1928 Am. chemist

Rich·ard·son \'ri-chərd-sən\ Henry Handel 1870–1946 pseudonym of *Ethel Florence Lindesay Richardson* Austral. novelist

Richardson Henry Hobson 1838–1886 Am. architect

Richardson Sir Owen Willans 1879–1959 Eng. physicist

Richardson Sir Ralph David 1902–1983 Brit. actor

Richardson Robert Coleman 1937– Am. physicist

Richardson Samuel 1689–1761 Eng. novelist

Ri·che·lieu \'ri-shə-,lü, -shəl-,yü; rē-shə-lyœ̄\ Duc de 1585–1642 *Armand-Jean du Plessis* Fr. cardinal & statesman

Ri·chet \rē-'shā\ Charles Robert 1850–1935 Fr. physiologist

Rich·ter \'rik-tər\ Burton 1931– Am. physicist

Richter Charles Francis 1900–1985 Am. seismologist

Rich·ter \'rik-tər, 'rik-\ Jean Paul Friedrich 1763–1825 pseudonym *Jean Paul* \'zhän-'paůl\ Ger. writer

Ric·i·mer \'ri-sə-mər\ Flavius *died* 472 Rom. general

Rick·en·back·er \'ri-kən-,ba-kər\ Edward Vernon 1890–1973 Am. aviator

Rick·o·ver \'ri-,kō-vər\ Hyman George 1900–1986 Am. admiral

Ride \'rīd\ Sally Kristen 1951– Am. astronaut

Rid·ley \'rid-lē\ Nicholas *circa* 1503–1555 Eng. reformer & martyr

Ri·el \rē-'el\ Louis 1844–1885 Canad. insurgent

Rie·mann \'rē-,män\ Georg Friedrich Bernhard 1826–1866 Ger. mathematician — **Rie·mann·ian** \rē-'mä-nē-ən\ *adjective*

Rien·zo \'ryent-sō\ Cola di 1313–1354 prename *Niccolò* Ital. leader

Ries·man \'rēs-mən\ David 1909– Am. social scientist

Riis \'rēs\ Jacob August 1849–1914 Am. (Dan.-born) social reformer

Ri·ley \'rī-lē\ James Whit·comb \'hwit-kəm, 'wit-\ 1849–1916 Am. poet

Riley Richard Wilson 1933– U.S. secretary of education (1993–)

Ril·ke \'ril-kə, -kē\ Rai·ner \'rī-nər\ Maria 1875–1926 Ger. poet

Rim·baud \ra(m)-'bō, 'ram-,\ (Jean-Nicholas-)Arthur 1854–1891 Fr. poet

Rimini Francesca da — see POLENTA

Rim·sky-Kor·sa·kov \,rim(p)-skē-'kör-sə-,kôf, -,kóv, -,kór-sə-\ Nikolay Andreyevich 1844–1908 Russ. composer

Rine·hart \'rīn-,härt\ Mary 1876–1958 née *Roberts* Am. writer

Rí·os \'rē-,ōs\ Juan Antonio 1888–1946 president of Chile (1942–46)

Rip·ley \'ri-plē\ George 1802–1880 Am. literary critic & socialist

Ri·ve·ra \ri-'ver-ə\ Diego 1886–1957 Mex. painter

Riv·ers \'ri-vərz\ Larry 1923– Am. artist

Ri·zal \ri-'zäl, -'säl\ José Protasio 1861–1896 Filipino patriot

Riza Shah Pahlavi *variant of* REZA SHAH PAHLAVI

Riz·zio \'rit-sē-,ō\ *or* **Ric·cio** \'ri-chē-,ō\ David *circa* 1533–1566 Ital. musician & favorite of Mary, Queen of Scots

Robbe–Gril·let \,ró-bə-grē-'yā\ Alain 1922– Fr. writer

Robbia, della Luca — see DELLA ROBBIA

Rob·bins \'rä-bənz\ Frederick Chapman 1916– Am. physician

Robbins Jerome 1918– Am. dancer & choreographer

Rob·ert I \'rä-bərt\ *died* 1035 *the Devil* Duke of Normandy (1027–35) *father of William the Conqueror*

Robert I 1274–1329 *the Bruce* \'brüs\ king of Scotland (1306–1329)

Robert Guis·card \-gē-'skär\ *circa* 1015–1085 *Robert de Hauteville* Norman military leader

Rob·erts \'rä-bərts\ Sir Charles George Douglas 1860–1943 Canad. poet

Roberts Frederick Sleigh 1832–1914 1st Earl *Roberts* Brit. field marshal

Roberts Kenneth 1885–1957 Am. novelist

Roberts Owen Josephus 1875–1955 Am. jurist

Roberts Richard John 1943– Am. (Brit.-born) biologist

Rob·ert·son \'rä-bərt-sən\ William 1721–1793 Scot. historian

Robe·son \'rōb-sən\ Paul Bustill 1898–1976 Am. actor & singer

Robes·pierre \'rōbz-,pir, -,pyer; ,rō-,bes-'pyer\ Maximilien-François-Marie-Isidore de 1758–1794 Fr. revolutionary

Rob·in·son \'rä-bən-sən\ Edwin Arlington 1869–1935 Am. poet

Robinson George Frederick Samuel 1827–1909 1st Marquis & 2d Earl of *Ripon* Brit. statesman

Robinson James Harvey 1863–1936 Am. historian

Robinson Sir Robert 1886–1975 Eng. chemist

Ro·cham·beau \,rō-,sham-'bō\ Comte de 1725–1807 *Jean-Baptiste-Donatien de Vimeur* Fr. field marshal

Rocke·fel·ler \'rä-ki-,fe-lər\ John Davison father 1839–1937 & son 1874–1960 Am. oil magnates & philanthropists

Rockefeller Nelson Aldrich 1908–1979 *grandson & son of preceding* Am. politician; vice president of the U.S. (1974–77)

Rock·ing·ham \'rä-kiŋ-əm, *United States also* -kiŋ-,ham\ 2d Marquis of 1730–1782 *Charles Watson-Wentworth* Eng. statesman

Rock·ne \'räk-nē\ Knute \'nüt\ Kenneth 1888–1931 Am. (Norw.-born) football coach

Rock·well \'räk-,wel, -wəl\ Norman 1894–1978 Am. illustrator

Rod·bell \'räd-(,)bel\ Martin 1925– Am. biochemist

Ro·de \'rō-thə\ Hel·ge \'hel-gə\ 1870–1937 Dan. poet

Rod·gers \'rä-jərz\ Richard 1902–1979 Am. composer

Ro·din \rō-,da(n)\ (François-)Auguste(-René) 1840–1917 Fr. sculptor — **Ro·din·esque** \,rō-,da-'nesk\ *adjective*

Rod·ney \'räd-nē\ George Bryd·ges \'bri-jəz\ 1718–1792 1st Baron *Rodney* Eng. admiral

Roeb·ling \'rō-bliŋ\ John Augustus 1806–1869 Am. (Ger.-born) civil engineer

Roentgen — see RÖNTGEN

Roe·rich \'rər-ik, 'rer-\ Nikolay Konstantinovich 1874–1947 Russ. painter

Roeth·ke \'ret-kē, 'reth-\ Theodore 1908–1963 Am. poet

Rog·ers \'rä-jərz\ Bruce 1870–1957 Am. printer & book designer

Rogers Carl Ranson 1902–1987 Am. psychologist

Rogers Henry Hut·tle·ston \'hə-t°l-stən\ 1840–1909 Am. financier

Rogers Robert 1731–1795 Am. frontiersman

Rogers William Penn Adair 1879–1935 *Will* Am. actor & humorist

Ro·get \rō-'zhā, 'rō-,\ Peter Mark 1779–1869 Eng. physician & scholar

Rohr·er \'rör-ər\ Heinrich 1933– Swiss physicist

Roh Tae Woo \'rō-'tā-'ü, 'nō-, -'wü\ 1932– president of So. Korea (1988–93)

Ro·kos·sov·sky \,rä-kə-'sóf-skē, -'sóv-\ Konstantin Konstantinovich 1896–1968 marshal of Soviet Union

Rolfe \'rälf\ John 1585–1622 Eng. colonist

Rol·land \rō-'län, ró-\ Romain 1866–1944 Fr. author

Röl·vaag \'rōl-,väg\ Ole \'ō-lə\ Ed·vart \'ed-,värt\ 1876–1931 Am. (Norw.-born) educator & novelist

Ro·mains \rō-'maⁿ\ Jules 1885–1972 pseudonym of *Louis-Henri-Jean Farigoule* Fr. author

Romano Giulio — see GIULIO ROMANO

Ro·ma·nov *or* **Ro·ma·noff** \'rō-mä-nəf, 'rō-mə-,näf\ Michael 1596–1645 1st czar (1613–45) of Russ. Romanov dynasty (1613–1917)

Rom·berg \'räm-,bərg\ Sigmund 1887–1951 Am. (Hung.-born) composer

Rom·mel \'rä-məl\ Erwin Johannes Eugen 1891–1944 Ger. field marshal

Rom·ney \'räm-nē, 'rəm-\ George 1734–1802 Eng. painter

Ron·sard \rōⁿ-'sär\ Pierre de 1524–1585 Fr. poet

Rönt·gen *or* **Roent·gen** \'rent-gən, 'rənt-, -jən; 'ren-chən, 'rən-\ Wilhelm Conrad 1845–1923 Ger. physicist

Roo·se·velt \'rō-zə-vəlt (*Roosevelts'* usual pron.), -,velt *also* 'rü-\ (Anna) Eleanor 1884–1962 née *Roosevelt*, wife of F.D. Am. humanitarian & writer

Roosevelt Franklin Del·a·no \'de-lə-,nō\ 1882–1945 32d president of the U.S. (1933–45) — **Roo·se·velt·ian** \,rō-zə-'vel-tē-ən, -sh(ē-)ən\ *adjective*

Roosevelt Theodore 1858–1919 26th president of the U.S. (1901–09)

Root \'rüt, 'rút\ Elihu 1845–1937 Am. lawyer & statesman

Ro·sa \'rō-zə\ Salvator 1615–1673 Ital. painter & poet

Rose·bery \'rōz-,ber-ē, -b(ə-)rē\ 5th Earl of 1847–1929 *Archibald Philip Prim·rose* \'prim-,rōz\ Eng. statesman

Rose·crans \'rō-zə-,kranz, 'rōz-,kran(t)s\ William Starke 1819–1898 Am. general

Ro·sen·berg \'rō-z°n-,bərg, -,berg\ Alfred 1893–1946 Ger. Nazi & writer

Ro·sen·wald \'rō-z°n-,wóld\ Julius 1862–1932 Am. merchant & philanthropist

Ross \'rós\ Betsy 1752–1836 née *Griscom* reputed maker of 1st Am. flag

Ross Sir James Clark 1800–1862 Scot. explorer

Ross Sir John 1777–1856 *uncle of preceding* Scot. explorer

Ross Sir Ronald 1857–1932 Brit. physician

Rosse Earl of — see William PARSONS

Ros·set·ti \rō-'ze·tē, -'se-\ Christina Georgina 1830–1894 *sister of D.G.* Eng. poet

Rossetti Dante Gabriel 1828–1882 Eng. painter & poet

Ros·si \'rō-sē\ Bruno 1905–1993 Am. (Ital.-born) physicist

Ros·si·ni \rō-'sē-nē, rə-\ Gio·ac·chi·no \,jō-ə-'kē-(,)nō\ Antonio 1792–1868 Ital. composer — **Ros·si·ni·an** \-'sē-nē-ən\ *adjective*

Ros·tand \rō-stäⁿ, 'räs-,tand\ Edmond 1868–1918 Fr. poet & dramatist

Ro·ta \'rō-(,)tä\ Nino 1911–1979 Ital. composer

Rot·blat \'rät-,blat, 'rót-\ Joseph 1908– Brit. (Pol.-born) physicist

Roth \'róth\ Philip 1933– Am. writer

Roth·ko \'räth-(,)kō\ Mark 1903–1970 Am. (Russ.-born) painter

Roth·schild \'róth(s)-,chīld, 'rós-, *German* 'rōt-,shilt\ Mayer Amschel 1744–1812 Ger. financier

Rothschild Nathan Mayer 1777–1836 *son of preceding* financier in London

Rou·ault \rü-'ō\ Georges 1871–1958 Fr. painter

Rou·get de Lisle \(,)rü-'zhā-də-'lē(ə)l\ Claude-Joseph 1760–1836 Fr. army officer & composer

Rous \'raús\ Francis Peyton 1879–1970 Am. pathologist

Rous·seau \rü-'sō, 'rü-,\ Henri-Julien-Félix 1844–1910 *le Douanier* Fr. painter

Rousseau Jean-Jacques 1712–1778 Fr. (Swiss-born) philosopher & writer — **Rous·seau·esque** \rü-sō-'esk, ,rü-\ *or* **Rous·seau·ian** \-'sō-ē-ən\ *adjective*

Rousseau (Pierre-Étienne-) Théodore 1812–1867 Fr. painter

Rowe \'rō\ Nicholas 1674–1718 Eng. poet & dramatist; poet laureate (1715–18)

Row·land \'rō-lənd\ Frank Sherwood 1927– Am. chemist

Row·land·son \'rō-lən(d)-sən\ Thomas 1756–1827 Eng. caricaturist

Row·ley \'rō-lē, 'raú-\ William 1585?–?1642 Eng. actor & dramatist

Ro·xas y Acu·ña \'rō-,häs-,ē-ə-'kün-yə\ Manuel 1892–1948 Philippine statesman; president of the Philippine Republic (1946–48)

Royce \'róis\ Josiah 1855–1916 Am. philosopher

Rub·bia \'rü-bē-ə\ Carlo 1934– Ital. physicist

Ru·bens \'rü-bənz\ Peter Paul 1577–1640 Flem. painter — **Ru·ben·si·an** \rü-'ben-zē-ən\ *adjective*

Ru·bin \'rü-bən\ Robert Edward 1938– U.S. secretary of treasury (1995–)

Ru·bin·stein \'rü-bən-ˌstīn\ An·ton \än-'tȯn\ 1829–1894 Russ. pianist & composer

Rubinstein Arthur 1887–1982 Am. (Pol.-born) pianist

Rud·olf \'rü-ˌdälf\ 1858–1889 archduke & crown prince of Austria

Rudolf I 1218–1291 Holy Roman emperor (1273–91); 1st of the Hapsburgs

Ruis·dael or **Ruys·dael** \'rīz-ˌdäl, 'rīs-\ Jacob van 1628(or 1629)–1682 & his uncle Salomon van circa 1602–1670 Du. painters

Rumford Count — see Benjamin THOMPSON

Run·cie \'rən(t)-sē\ Robert Alexander Kennedy 1921– archbishop of Canterbury (1980–91)

Rund·stedt \'run(t)-ˌshtet\ Karl Rudolf Gerd von 1875–1953 Ger. field marshal

Ru·ne·berg \'rü-nə-ˌbȯrg, -ˌber-ē\ Johan Ludvig 1804–1877 Finn. poet

Run·yon \'rən-yən\ (Alfred) Da·mon \'dā-mən\ 1884–1946 Am. author — **Run·yon·esque** \ˌrən-yə-'nesk\ adjective

Ru·pert \'rü-pərt\ Prince 1619–1682 Count Palatine of Rhine & Duke of Bavaria Eng. (Ger.-born) Royalist general & admiral

Rush \'rəsh\ Benjamin 1745–1813 Am. physician & patriot

Rush Richard 1780–1859 son of preceding Am. diplomat & statesman

Rush·die \'rush-(ˌ)dē, 'rush-\ (Ahmed) Salman 1947– Brit. (Indian-born) writer

Rusk \'rəsk\ (David) Dean 1909–1994 U.S. secretary of state (1961–69)

Rus·ka \'rus-kə\ Ernst August Friedrich 1906–1988 Ger. physicist

Rus·kin \'rəs-kən\ John 1819–1900 Eng. essayist, critic, & reformer — **Rus·kin·ian** \ˌrəs-'ki-nē-ən\ adjective

Rus·sell \'rə-səl\ Bertrand Arthur William 1872–1970 3d Earl Russell Eng. mathematician & philosopher

Russell Charles Taze 1852–1916 Am. religious leader

Russell George William 1867–1935 pseudonym Æ \'ā-ē, 'ā\ Irish author

Russell John 1792–1878 1st Earl Russell of Kingston Russell Brit. statesman

Russell Lillian 1861–1922 Helen Louise Leonard Am. singer & actress

Rus·tin \'rəs-tən\ Bayard 1910–1987 Am. civil rights leader

Ruth \'rüth\ George Herman 1895–1948 Babe Ruth or the Babe Am. baseball player — **Ruth·ian** \'rü-thē-ən\ adjective

Ruth·er·ford \'rə-thə(r)-fərd, -thə(r)-\ Ernest 1871–1937 1st Baron Rutherford of Nelson Brit. physicist

Rutherford Joseph Franklin 1869–1942 Am. leader of Jehovah's Witnesses

Rut·ledge \'rət-lij\ John 1739–1800 Am. statesman & jurist; chief justice U.S. Supreme Court (1795)

Rutledge Wiley Blount \'blənt\ 1894–1949 Am. jurist

Ru·žič·ka \'rü-ˌzhich-kə, -ˌzich-, -ˌzhits-\ Leopold 1887–1976 Swiss (Croatian-born) chemist

Ry·der \'rī-dər\ Albert Pinkham 1847–1917 Am. painter

Rydz–Śmig·ły \'rits-'shmē-glē\ Edward 1886–1941 Pol. general

Ryle \'rī(ə)l\ Sir Martin 1918–1984 Brit. astronomer

Saa·ri·nen \'sär-ə-nən\ Ee·ro \'er-(ˌ)ō\ 1910–1961 Am. architect

Saarinen (Gottlieb) Eliel 1873–1950 father of preceding Finn. architect

Saa·ve·dra La·mas \sä-'vä-drə-'lä-məs, -'vä-thrə-\ Carlos 1878–1959 Argentine lawyer & diplomat

Sa·ba·tier \ˌsa-bə-'tyā\ Paul 1854–1941 Fr. chemist

Sa·ba·ti·ni \ˌsa-bə-'tē-nē, ˌsä-\ Rafael 1875–1950 Eng. (Ital.-born) author

Sa·bin \'sā-bin\ Albert Bruce 1906–1993 Am. physician

Sac·a·ga·wea also **Sac·a·ja·wea** \ˌsa-kə-jə-'wē-ə\ 1786?–1812 Am. Indian guide

Sac·co \'sa-(ˌ)kō\ Nicola 1891–1927 & **Van·zet·ti** \van-'ze-tē\ Bartolomeo 1888–1927 Am. (Ital.-born) anarchists

Sachs \'zäks\ Hans 1494–1576 Ger. poet & Meistersinger

Sachs \'saks, 'zäks\ Nelly 1891–1970 Swed. (Ger.-born) dramatist & poet

Sack·ville \'sak-ˌvil\ Thomas 1536–1608 1st Earl of Dorset Eng. poet & diplomat

Sackville–West \-'west\ Victoria Mary 1892–1962 Vita Eng. writer

Sā·dāt \sə-'dat, -'dät\ Anwar el- 1918–1981 president of Egypt (1970–81)

Sade, de \də-'säd\ Comte Donatien-Alphonse-François 1740–1814 Marquis de Sade Fr. writer of erotica

Sa·gan \sä-'gäⁿ\ Françoise 1935– pseudonym of Françoise Quoi·rez \kwȧ-rä\ Fr. writer

Sage \'säj\ Russell 1816–1906 Am. financier

St. Den·is \sānt-'de-nəs, sənt-\ Ruth 1878–1968 Am. dancer & choreographer

Sainte–Beuve \saⁿt-'bœv; sānt-'bə(r)v, sənt-\ Charles-Augustin 1804–1869 Fr. critic & author

Saint–Gau·dens \sānt-'gȯ-dᵊnz, sənt-\ Augustus 1848–1907 Am. (Irish-born) sculptor

St. John Henry — see BOLINGBROKE

Saint–Just \saⁿ-zhœst; sānt-'jəst, sənt-\ Louis-Antoine-Léon de 1767–1794 Fr. revolutionary

St. Lau·rent \saⁿ-lȯ-räⁿ\ Louis Stephen 1882–1973 Canad. politician; prime minister (1948–57)

Saint–Pierre — see BERNARDIN DE SAINT-PIERRE

Saint–Saëns \saⁿ-säⁿs\ (Charles-) Camille 1835–1921 Fr. composer

Saints·bury \'sānts-ˌber-ē, -b(ə-)rē\ George Edward Bateman 1845–1933 Eng. critic

Saint–Si·mon \saⁿ-sē-mōⁿ\ Claude-Henri de Rouvroy 1760–1825 Comte de Saint-Simon Fr. philosopher & social scientist

Saint–Simon Louis de Rouvroy 1675–1755 Duc de Saint-Simon Fr. soldier, statesman, & writer

Sai·on·ji \sī-'än-jē, -'ȯn-\ Prince Kimmochi 1849–1940 Jp. statesman

Sa·kha·rov \'sä-kə-ˌrȯf, -kə-, -ˌrȯv\ Andrey Dmitriyevich 1921–1989 Russ. physicist

Sa·ki \'sä-kē\ — see H. H. MUNRO

Sak·mann \'zäk-ˌmän, 'säk-\ Bert 1942– Ger. biochemist

Sal·a·din \'sa-lə-ˌdēn, -dən; ˌsa-lə-'dēn\ 1137(or 1138)–1193 Salāḥ Ad-dīn Yūsuf Ibn Ayyūb Syrian commander & vizier in Egypt

Sa·lam \sä-'läm\ Abdus 1926– Pakistani physicist

Sa·la·zar \ˌsa-lə-'zär, ˌsä-\ Antonio de Oliveira 1889–1970 Port. dictator (1932–68)

Sa·li·nas de Gor·ta·ri \sä-'lē-näs-thä-gȯr-'tä-rē\ Carlos 1948– president of Mexico (1988–94)

Sal·in·ger \'sa-lən-jər\ Jerome David 1919– Am. novelist

Salisbury 1st Earl of & 3d Marquis of — see CECIL

Salk \'sȯ(l)k\ Jonas Edward 1914–1995 Am. physician

Sal·lust \'sa-ləst\ circa 86–35(or 34) B.C. Gaius Sallustius Crispus Rom. historian & politician — **Sal·lus·ti·an** \sə-'ləs-tē-ən, sä-\ adjective

Sal·o·mon \'sa-lə-mən\ Haym 1740–1785 Am. (Pol.-born) merchant

Sam·per Pi·za·no \'säm-per-pē-'sä-nō\ Ernesto 1950– president of Colombia (1994–)

Sam·u·el·son \'sam-yə(-wə)l-sən\ Paul Anthony 1915– Am. economist

Sam·u·els·son \'sam-yə(-wə)l-sən\ Bengt I. 1934– Swed. biochemist

Sánchez de Bustamante y Sirvén Antonio — see BUSTAMANTE Y SIRVÉN

Sand \'sand, 'säⁿ(n)d, säⁿ\ George 1804–1876 pseudonym of Amandine-Aurore-Lucie (or -Lucile) Du·de·vant \dᵊd-väⁿ, dᵊ-də-\ née Dupin Fr. writer

Sand·burg \'san(d)-ˌbərg\ Carl 1878–1967 Am. author

San·gal·lo \sän-'gä-(ˌ)lō, säŋ-\ Giuliano da 1445?–1516 Florentine architect & sculptor

Sang·er \'saŋ-ər\ Frederick 1918– Brit. chemist

Sanger Margaret 1883–1966 née Higgins Am. birth-control leader

San Mar·tín \ˌsan-(ˌ)mär-'tēn, ˌsän-\ José de 1778–1850 So. Am. soldier & statesman

San·ta An·na \ˌsan-tə-'a-nə, ˌsän-tə-'ä-nə\ Antonio López de 1794–1876 Mex. general, revolutionary, & president

San·tan·der \ˌsän-tän-'der, ˌsan-ˌtan-\ Francisco de Paula 1792–1840 Colombian general & politician

San·ta·ya·na \ˌsan-tə-'yä-nə, ˌsan-tē-'ä-, ˌsän-\ George 1863–1952 Am. (Span.-born) poet & philosopher

San·tos–Du·mont \ˌsan-təs-dü-'mänt, -dyü-; säⁿ-tōs-dᵊ-'mōⁿ\ Alberto 1873–1932 Fr. (Braz.-born) aviation pioneer

Sa·pir \sə-'pir\ Edward 1884–1939 Am. (Pomeranian-born) anthropologist & linguist

Sap·pho also **Psap·pho** \'sa-(ˌ)fō\ flourished circa 610–circa 580 B.C. Greek poet

Sar·da·na·pa·lus or **Sar·da·na·pal·lus** \ˌsär-dᵊn-'a-p(ə-)ləs, -dᵊn-ə-'pä-ləs\ king of Assyria; sometimes identified with Ashurbanipal (reigned 668–627 B.C.)

Sar·dou \sär-'dü\ Victorien 1831–1908 Fr. dramatist

Sar·gent \'sär-jənt\ John Sing·er \'siŋ-ər\ 1856–1925 Am. painter

Sar·gon II \'sär-ˌgän, -gən\ king of Assyria (722–705 B.C.)

Sa·roy·an \sə-'rȯi-ən\ William 1908–1981 Am. writer

Sar·tre \'särtrᵊ\ Jean-Paul 1905–1980 Fr. philosopher, dramatist, & novelist — **Sar·tre·an** or **Sar·tri·an** \'sär-trē-ən\ adjective

Sas·soon \sa-'sün, sə-\ Siegfried Lorraine 1886–1967 Eng. writer

Sa·tie \sa-'tē, sä-\ Erik-Alfred-Leslie 1866–1925 Fr. composer

Sa·ud \sä-'üd\ 1902–1969 king of Saudi Arabia (1953–64)

Saus·sure \sō-'sūr\ Ferdinand de 1857–1913 Swiss linguist — **Saus·sur·ean** also **Saus·sur·ian** \sō-'sūr-ē-ən, sȯ-\ adjective

Sav·age \'sa-vij\ Michael Joseph 1872–1940 prime minister of New Zealand (1935–40)

Savage Richard 1697?–1743 Eng. poet

Sa·vo·na·ro·la \ˌsa-və-nə-'rō-lə, sə-,vä-nə-'rō-\ Gi·ro·la·mo \ji-'rō-lə-ˌmō\ 1452–1498 Ital. reformer

Saxe \'saks\ Hermann-Maurice 1696–1750 Comte de Saxe Fr. general

Saxo Gram·mat·i·cus \ˌsak-(ˌ)sō-grə-'ma-ti-kəs\ circa 1150–after 1216 Dan. historian

Say·ers \'sā-ərz, 'serz\ Dorothy Leigh 1893–1957 Eng. writer

Sca·lia \skə-'lē-ə\ Antonin 1936– Am. jurist

Scal·i·ger \'ska-lə-jər\ Joseph Justus 1540–1609 Fr. scholar

Scaliger Julius Caesar 1484–1558 father of preceding Ital. physician

Scanderbeg — see SKANDERBEG

Scar·lat·ti \skär-'lä-tē\ (Pietro) Alessandro Gaspare 1660–1725 & his son (Giuseppe) Domenico 1685–1757 Ital. composers

Scar·ron \ska-'rōⁿ\ Paul 1610–1660 Fr. author

Schacht \'shäkt, 'shäkt\ (Horace Greeley) Hjalmar \'yäl-ˌmär\ 1877–1970 Ger. financier

Schal·ly \'sha-lē\ Andrew Victor 1926– Am. (Pol.-born) physiologist

Scharn·horst \'shärn-ˌhȯrst\ Gerhard Johann David von 1755–1813 Pruss. general

Schar·wen·ka \shär-'veŋ-kə\ (Ludwig) Philipp 1847–1917 & his brother (Franz) Xaver 1850–1924 Ger. pianists & composers

Schaw·low \'shȯ-(ˌ)lō\ Arthur Leonard 1921– Am. physicist

Schei·de·mann \'shī-də-ˌmän\ Philipp 1865–1939 Ger. politician

Schel·ling \'she-liŋ\ Friedrich Wilhelm Joseph von 1775–1854 Ger. philosopher — **Schel·ling·ian** \she-'liŋ-ē-ən\ adjective

Schia·pa·rel·li \skē-ˌä-pə-'re-lē, ska-\ Giovanni Virginio 1835–1910 Ital. astronomer

Schick \'shik\ Bé·la \'bā-lə\ 1877–1967 Am. (Hung.-born) pediatrician

Schil·ler \'shi-lər\ (Johann Christoph) Friedrich von 1759–1805 Ger. poet & dramatist

Schin·dler \'shind-lər\ Oskar 1908–1974 Ger. humanitarian

Schi·rach \'shē-ˌräk, -ˌräk\ Baldur von 1907–1974 Ger. Nazi politician

Schle·gel \'shlā-gəl\ August Wilhelm von 1767–1845 Ger. author

Schlegel Friedrich von 1772–1829 *brother of preceding* Ger. philosopher & writer

Schlei·cher \'shlī-kər, -kər\ Kurt von 1882–1934 Ger. soldier & politician

Schlei·er·ma·cher \'shlī-ər-,mä-kər, -kər\ Friedrich Ernst Daniel 1768–1834 Ger. theologian & philosopher

Schle·sing·er \'shlā-ziŋ-ər, 'shle-sin-jər\ Arthur Meier father 1888–1965 & son 1917– Am. historians

Schley \'shlī, 'slī\ Winfield Scott 1839–1909 Am. admiral

Schlie·mann \'shlē-,män\ Heinrich 1822–1890 Ger. archaeologist

Schmidt \'shmit\ Helmut 1918– chancellor of West Germany (1974–82)

Schna·bel \'shnä-bəl\ Ar·tur \'är-,tùr\ 1882–1951 Austrian pianist & composer

Schnitz·ler \'shnits-lər\ Arthur 1862–1931 Austrian dramatist & novelist

Schoen·berg \'shö(r)n-,bərg, 'shēn-,berk\ Arnold Franz Walter 1874–1951 Am. (Austrianborn) composer — **Schoen·berg·ian** \-,bər-gē-ən\ *adjective*

Scho·field \'skō-,fēld\ John McAllister 1831–1906 Am. general

Scho·pen·hau·er \'shō-pən-,haú(-ə)r\ Arthur 1788–1860 Ger. philosopher — **Scho·penhau·er·ian** \,shō-pən-'haú-(ə-)rē-ən\ *adjective*

Schrief·fer \'shrē-fər\ John Robert 1931– Am. physicist

Schrö·ding·er \'shrē-diŋ-ər, shrä-\ Erwin 1887–1961 Austrian physicist

Schu·bert \'shü-bərt, -,bert\ Franz Peter 1797–1828 Austrian composer — **Schu·bert·ian** \shü-'bər-tē-ən, -'ber-\ *adjective*

Schultz \'shúlts\ Theodore 1902– Am. economist

Schulz \'shúlts\ Charles Monroe 1922– Am. cartoonist

Schu·man \'shü-,män, -mən\ Robert 1886–1963 Fr. statesman

Schu·man \'shü-mən\ William Howard 1910–1992 Am. composer

Schu·mann \'shü-,män, mən\ Robert 1810–1856 Ger. composer

Schu·mann–Heink \'shü-mən-'hīŋk\ Ernestine 1861–1936 née *Roessler* Am. (Austrian-born) contralto

Schur·man \'shúr-mən, 'shər-\ Jacob Gould 1854–1942 Am. philosopher & diplomat

Schurz \'shúrts, 'shərts\ Carl 1829–1906 Am. (Ger.-born) lawyer, general, & politician

Schusch·nigg \'shúsh-(,)nik, -(,)nig\ Kurt von 1897–1977 Austrian statesman

Schuy·ler \'skī-lər\ Philip John 1733–1804 Am. general & statesman

Schwartz \'shwórts\ Melvin 1932– Am. physicist

Schwarz·kopf \'shwórts-,kóf, 'swórts-\ H. Norman 1934– Am. general

Schwarz·kopf \'shvärts-,kópf\ (Olga Maria) Elisabeth Friederike 1915– Ger. (Pol.-born) soprano

Schweit·zer \'shwīt-sər, 'shvīt-, 'swīt-\ Albert 1875–1965 Fr. theologian, philosopher, missionary physician, & music scholar

Schwing·er \'shwiŋ-ər\ Julian Seymour 1918– Am. physicist

Scip·io \'si-pē-,ō, 'skī-\ **Aemilianus Af·ri·ca·nus** \-,a-frə-'ka-nəs, -'kä-, -'kä-\ **Numantinus** Publius Cornelius 185(or 184)–129 B.C. *Scipio the Younger* Rom. general

Scipio Africanus Publius Cornelius 236–184(or 183) B.C. *Scipio the Elder* Rom. general

Scopes \'skōps\ John Thomas 1900–1970 Am. teacher

Scott \'skät\ Dred \'dred\ 1795?–1858 Am. slave

Scott Sir George Gilbert 1811–1878 Eng. architect

Scott Robert Falcon 1868–1912 Eng. polar explorer

Scott Sir Walter 1771–1832 Scot. poet & novelist

Scott Winfield 1786–1866 Am. general

Scotus Duns — see DUNS SCOTUS

Scotus John — see ERIGENA

Scria·bin *or* **Skrya·bin** \skrē-'ä-bən\ Aleksandr Nikolayevich 1872–1915 Russ. composer

Scribe \'skrēb\ Augustin-Eugène 1791–1861 Fr. dramatist

Scu·dé·ry \,skü-də-'rē, skü-dā-rē\ Madeleine de 1607–1701 *Sa·pho* \sä-fō\ Fr. poet, novelist, & hostess of literary salon

Sea·borg \'sē-,bórg\ Glenn Theodore 1912– Am. chemist

Sears \'sirz\ Richard Warren 1863–1914 Am. merchant

See \'sē\ Thomas Jefferson Jackson 1866–1962 Am. astronomer & mathematician

Seeckt \'zäkt\ Hans von 1866–1936 Ger. army officer

See·ger \'sē-gər\ Peter 1919– *Pete* Am. folksinger

Se·fe·ri·a·des \,se-,fer-'yä-,thēs\ Giorgos Stylianou 1900–1971 pseudonym *George Se·fer·is* \se-'fer-ēs\ Greek diplomat & poet

Se·go·via \sä-'gō-vyə, -vē-ə\ Andrés 1893?–1987 Span. guitarist & composer

Se·grè \sə-'grā, sā-\ Emilio Gino 1905–1989 Am. (Ital.-born) physicist

Sei·fert \'zī-fərt\ Jaroslav 1901–1986 Czech poet

Se·ja·nus \si-'jä-nəs\ Lucius Aelius *died* A.D. 31 Rom. conspirator

Sel·den \'sel-dən\ George Baldwin 1846–1922 Am. lawyer & inventor

Selden John 1584–1654 Eng. jurist & antiquarian

Se·leu·cus I Ni·ca·tor \sə-,lü-kəs-'nī-,kā-tər\ 358(to 354)–281 B.C. Macedonian general & founder of Seleucid dynasty

Sel·kirk \'sel-,kərk\ Alexander 1676–1721 Scot. marooned sailor

Sel·ten \'zel-t°n\ Reinhard 1930– Ger. economist

Se·me·nov \sə-'myó-nəf\ Nikolay Nikolayevich 1896–1986 Soviet chemist

Semmes \'semz\ Raphael 1809–1877 Am. Confederate admiral

Sen·e·ca \'se-ni-kə\ Lucius Annaeus 4 B.C.?–A.D. 65 Rom. statesman, dramatist, & philosopher — **Sen·e·can** \-kən\ *adjective*

Sen·ghor \seŋ-'gór, säⁿ-'gór\ Léopold Sédar 1906– president of Senegal (1960–80)

Sen·nach·er·ib \sə-'na-kə-rəb\ *died* 681 B.C. king of Assyria (704–681)

Se·quoya *or* **Se·quoy·ah** *or* **Se·quoia** \si-'kwói-ə\ *circa* 1760–1843 *George Guess* Cherokee Indian scholar

Ser·kin \'sər-kən\ Rudolf 1903–1991 Am. (Bohemian-born) pianist

Ser·ra \'ser-ə\ Ju·ní·pe·ro \hü-'nē-pə-,rō\ 1713–1784 originally *Miguel José* Span. missionary in Mexico & California

Ser·to·ri·us \(,)sər-'tōr-ē-əs, -'tór-\ Quintus *circa* 123–72 B.C. Rom. general & statesman

Ser·ve·tus \(,)sər-'vē-təs\ Michael 1511?–1553 Span. *Miguel Serveto* Span. theologian & physician

Ser·vice \'sər-vəs\ Robert William 1874–1958 Canad. writer

Ses·sions \'se-shənz\ Roger Huntington 1896–1985 Am. composer

Se·ton \'sē-t°n\ Saint Elizabeth Ann née *Bayley* 1774–1821 *Mother Seton* Am. religious leader

Seton Ernest Thompson 1860–1946 original surname *Thompson* Am. (Eng.-born) writer & illustrator

Seu·rat \sə-'rä\ Georges 1859–1891 Fr. painter

Seuss — see Theodor Seuss GEISEL

Se·ve·rus \sə-'vir-əs\ Lucius Septimius A.D. 146–211 Rom. emperor (193–211)

Sé·vi·gné \,sā-(,)vēn-'yā, sā-'vēn-(,)yä\ Marquise de 1626–1696 née *(Marie) de Rabutin-Chantal* Fr. letter writer

Sew·ard \'sü-ərd, 'sú-(ə)rd\ William Henry 1801–1872 Am. statesman; secretary of state (1861–69)

Sew·ell \'sü-əl\ Anna 1820–1878 Brit. writer

Sey·mour \'sē-,mōr, -,mòr\ Jane 1509?–1537 *3d wife of Henry VIII of England & mother of Edward VI*

Seyss–In·quart \'zīs-'iŋk-,värt\ Ar·tur \'är-,túr\ 1892–1946 Austrian Nazi politician

Shack·le·ton \'sha-kəl-tən\ Sir Ernest Henry 1874–1922 Brit. polar explorer

Shad·well \'shad-,wel, -wəl\ Thomas 1642?–1692 Eng. dramatist; poet laureate (1688–92)

Shaf·ter \'shaf-tər\ William Rufus 1835–1906 Am. general

Shaftes·bury \'shaf(t)s-,ber-ē, -b(ə-)rē\ 1st Earl of 1621–1683 *Anthony Ashley Coo·per* \'kü-pər, 'kú-\ Eng. statesman

Shāh Jā·han \'shä-jə-'hän\ 1592–1666 Mughal emperor of India (1628–57 or 58)

Shahn \'shän\ Ben 1898–1969 Am. (Lithuanianborn) painter

Shake·speare \'shāk-,spir\ William 1564–1616 Eng. dramatist & poet

Sha·la·la \shə-'lā-lə, -'lä-\ Donna Edna 1941– U.S. secretary of health & human services (1993–)

Sha·mir \shə-'mēr\ Yitzhak 1914– original surname *Yizernitzky* prime minister of Israel (1983–92)

Sha·piro \shə-'pir-(,)ō\ Karl Jay 1913– Am. poet & critic

Sha·rif \shä-'rēf\ Nawaz 1949– prime minister of Pakistan (1990–93)

Sharp \'shärp\ Phillip Allen 1944– Am. biologist

Sharpe \'shärp\ William Forsyth 1934– Am. economist

Shas·tri \'shäs-trē\ Lal \'läl\ Bahadur 1904–1966 prime minister of India (1964–66)

Shaw \'shó\ George Bernard 1856–1950 Brit. (Irish-born) author

Shaw Thomas Edward — see T. E. LAWRENCE

Shawn \'shón\ Ted 1891–1972 Am. dancer & choreographer

Shays \'shāz\ Daniel 1747?–1825 Am. soldier & insurrectionist

Shee·ler \'shē-lər\ Charles 1883–1965 Am. painter & photographer

Shel·don \'shel-dən\ William Herbert 1898–1977 Am. psychologist & physical anthropologist

Shel·ley \'she-lē\ Mary Woll·stone·craft \'wúl-stən-,kraft\ 1797–1851 née *Godwin; wife of P. B.* Eng. novelist

Shelley Percy Bysshe \'bish\ 1792–1822 Eng. poet — **Shel·ley·an** \'she-lē-ən\ *or* **Shel·ley·esque** \,she-lē-'esk\ *adjective*

Shen·stone \'shen-,stōn, 'shen(t)-stən\ William 1714–1763 Eng. poet

Shep·ard \'she-pərd\ Alan Bartlett 1923– Am. astronaut

Sher·a·ton \'sher-ə-t°n\ Thomas 1751–1806 Eng. furniture designer

Sher·i·dan \'sher-ə-d°n\ Philip Henry 1831–1888 Am. general

Sheridan Richard Brins·ley \'brinz-lē\ 1751–1816 Irish dramatist & orator

Sher·man \'shər-mən\ James Schoolcraft 1855–1912 vice president of the U.S. (1909–12)

Sherman John 1823–1900 *brother of W. T.* Am. statesman

Sherman Roger 1721–1793 Am. jurist & statesman

Sherman William Tecumseh 1820–1891 Am. general — **Sher·man·esque** \,shər-mə-'nesk\ *adjective*

Sher·riff \'sher-əf\ Robert Cedric 1896–1975 Eng. writer

Sher·ring·ton \'sher-iŋ-tən\ Sir Charles Scott 1857–1952 Eng. physiologist

Sher·wood \'shər-,wúd *also* 'sher-\ Robert Emmet 1896–1955 Am. dramatist

Shev·ard·nad·ze \,she-vər(d)-'näd-zə\ Eduard Amvrosiyevich 1928– Soviet foreign minister (1985–90; 1991); president of Republic of Georgia (1992–)

Shev·chen·ko *or* **Šev·čen·ko** \shef-'chen-(,)kō\ Taras Hryhorovych 1814–1861 Ukrainian poet

Shi·de·ha·ra \,shē-də-'här-ə\ Kijūrō Baron 1872–1951 Jp. statesman

Shi·ge·mit·su \,shē-gə-'mit-(,)sü, ,shi-\ Mamoru 1887–1957 Jp. diplomat

Shih Huang-ti — see CH'IN SHIH HUANG TI

Shi·rer \'shīr-ər\ William Lawrence 1904–1993 Am. author

Shir·ley \'shər-lē\ James 1596–1666 Eng. dramatist

Shock·ley \'shä-klē\ William Bradford 1910–1989 Am. physicist

Sho·lo·khov \'shó-lə-,kóf, -,kóv\ Mikhail Aleksandrovich 1905–1984 Soviet (Russ.-born) novelist

Sho·sta·ko·vich \,shäs-tə-'kō-vich, ,shós-, -'kó-\ Dmi·try \də-'mē-trē\ Dmitriyevich 1906–1975 Soviet (Russ.-born) composer

Shull \'shəl\ Clifford Glenwood 1915– Am. physicist

Shultz \'shŭlts\ George Pratt 1920– U.S. secretary of labor (1969–70); secretary of the treasury (1972–73); secretary of state (1982–89)

Shute \'shüt\ Nev·il \'ne-vəl\ 1899–1960 pseudonym of *Nevil Shute Norway* Eng. aeronautical engineer & writer

Shver·nik \'shver-nik\ Nikolay Mikhaylovich 1888–1970 Soviet politician; chairman of the Presidium (1946–54)

Si·be·lius \sə-'bāl-yəs, -'bā-lē-əs\ Jean \'zhän, 'yän\ 1865–1957 Finn. composer

Sick·les \'si-kəlz\ Daniel Edgar 1825–1914 Am. general & politician

Sid·dhār·tha Gau·ta·ma \si-'där-tə-'gaú-tə-mə, -'gó-\ *circa* 563–*circa* 483 B.C. *The Bud·dha* \'bü-də, 'bú-\ Indian philosopher & founder of Buddhism

Sid·dons \'si-dᵊnz\ Sarah 1755–1831 née *Kemble* Eng. actress

Sid·ney \'sid-nē\ Sir Philip 1554–1586 Eng. poet, statesman, & soldier

Sieg·bahn \'sēg-,bän\ Kai Manne 1918– Swed. physicist

Siegbahn Karl Manne Georg 1886–1978 Swed. physicist *father of preceding*

Sie·mens \'sē-mənz\ Sir William 1823–1883 Brit. (Ger.-born) inventor

Sien·kie·wicz \shen-'kyā-vich\ Henryk 1846–1916 pseudonym *Litwos* Pol. novelist

Sie·yès \sē-,ā-'yes\ Emmanuel-Joseph 1748–1836 Fr. revolutionary

Sig·is·mund \'si-gəs-mənd\ 1368–1437 Holy Roman emperor (1433–37)

Sigs·bee \'sigz-bē\ Charles Dwight 1845–1923 Am. admiral

Si·gurds·son \'si-gərd-sən, -,gərth-\ Jón \'yōn\ 1811–1879 Icelandic statesman & author

Si·kor·ski \sə-'kòr-skē\ Władysław 1881–1943 Pol. general & statesman

Si·kor·sky \sə-'kòr-skē\ Igor Ivan 1889–1972 Am. (Russ.-born) aeronautical engineer

Sil·lan·pää \'si-lən-,pa\ Frans Eemil 1888–1964 Finn. novelist

Si·lo·ne \si-'lō-nē\ Ignazio 1900–1978 pseudonym of *Secondo Tranquilli* Ital. author

Si·me·non \sē-mə-'nōⁿ\ Georges-Joseph-Christian 1903–1989 Fr. (Belg.-born) writer

Sim·e·on Sty·li·tes \'si-mē-ən-stə-'lī-tēz, -,stī-\ Saint *circa* 390–459 Syrian ascetic & pillar dweller

Si·mon \sē-'mōⁿ\ Claude 1913– Fr. writer

Si·mon \'sī-mən\ 1st Viscount 1873–1954 *John Allsebrook Simon* Brit. jurist & statesman

Simon Herbert Alexander 1916– Am. economist

Simon Neil 1927– Am. dramatist

Si·mon·i·des \sī-'mä-nə-,dēz\ **of Ceos** *circa* 556–*circa* 468? B.C. Greek poet

Sims \'simz\ William Sow·den \'saú-dᵊn\ 1858–1936 Am. admiral

Sin·clair \sin-'kler, siṇ-\ Upton Beall \'bel\ 1878–1968 Am. writer & politician

Sing·er \'siṇ-ər\ Isaac Ba·shev·is \bə-'she-vəs\ 1904–1991 Am. (Pol.-born) author

Singer Isaac Merritt 1811–1875 Am. inventor

Singh \'siṇ, 'siⁿ-hə\ Vishwanath Pratap 1931– prime minister of India (1989–90)

Si·quei·ros \si-'kā-(,)rōs\ David Alfaro 1896–1974 Mex. painter

Si·rāj-ud-Daw·lah \sə-,räj-ə-'daú-lə\ *circa* 1732–1757 nawab of Bengal (1756–57)

Sis·ley \'siz-lē, sēs-le\ Alfred 1839–1899 Fr. (Eng.-born) painter

Sis·mon·di \sis-'män-dē, sēs-mōⁿ-dē\ Jean-Charles-Léonard Simonde de 1773–1842 Swiss historian & economist

Sit·ter \'si-tər\ Willem de 1872–1934 Du. astronomer

Sit·ting Bull \,si-tiṇ-'búl\ *circa* 1831–1890 Sioux leader

Sit·well \'sit-,wel, -wəl\ Sir George Reres·by \'rirz-bē\ 1860–1943 & his 3 children: Dame Edith 1887–1964; Sir Osbert 1892–1969; & Sachev·er·ell \sə-'she-və-rəl\ 1897–1988 Eng. authors

Skan·der·beg *or* **Scan·der·beg** \'skan-dər-,beg\ 1405–1468 originally *George Kas·tri·o·ti* \,käs-trē-'ō-(,)tē\ Turk. *Is·kan·der Bey* \i-skän-'der-'bā\ Albanian hero

Skeat \'skēt\ Walter William 1835–1912 Eng. philologist

Skel·ton \'skel-tᵊn\ John *circa* 1460–1529 Eng. poet — **Skel·ton·ic** \skel-'tä-nik\ *adjective*

Skin·ner \'ski-nər\ Burrhus Frederic 1904–1990 Am. psychologist — **Skin·ner·ian** \ski-'nir-ē-ən, -'ner-\ *adjective*

Skinner Cornelia Otis 1901–1979 *daughter of Otis* Am. actress

Skinner Otis 1858–1942 Am. actor

Ško·da \'skō-də, 'shkó-(,)dä\ Emil von 1839–1900 Czech engineer & industrialist

Sla·ter \'slā-tər\ Rodney Earl 1955– U.S. secretary of transportation (1997–)

Slater Samuel 1768–1835 Am. (Eng.-born) industrialist

Sli·dell \slī-'del, *by collateral descendants* 'slī-dᵊl\ John 1793–1871 Am. Confederate diplomat

Sloan \'slōn\ John French 1871–1951 Am. painter

Slo·cum \'slō-kəm\ Henry Warner 1827–1894 Am. general

Slo·nim·sky \slō-'nim(p)-skē\ Nicolas 1894–1995 Am. (Russ.-born) composer & musicologist

Small·ey \'smò-lē\ Richard Errett 1943– Am. chemist

Sme·ta·na \'sme-tᵊn-ə\ Be·dřich \'be-dər-,zhik\ 1824–1884 Czech composer

Šmig·ly–Rydz Edward — see RYDZ-ŚMIGŁY

Smith \'smith\ Adam 1723–1790 Scot. economist

Smith Alfred Emanuel 1873–1944 Am. politician

Smith Bessie 1894(or 1898)–1937 Am. blues singer

Smith David 1906–1965 Am. sculptor

Smith Edmund Kirby — see KIRBY-SMITH

Smith Hamilton Othanel 1931– Am. microbiologist

Smith John *circa* 1580–1631 Eng. explorer & colonist

Smith Joseph 1805–1844 Am. founder of Mormon Church

Smith Michael 1932– Canad. (Brit-born) biochemist

Smith Sydney 1771–1845 Eng. essayist

Smith Walter Be·dell \bə-'del\ 1895–1961 Am. general & diplomat

Smith William 1769–1839 Eng. geologist

Smith–Dor·ri·en \'smith-'dòr-ē-ən, -'där-\ Sir Horace Lockwood 1858–1930 Brit. general

Smith·son \'smith-sən\ James 1765–1829 Brit. chemist & mineralogist & benefactor of Smithsonian Institution

Smol·lett \'smä-lət\ Tobias George 1721–1771 Brit. author

Smuts \'sməts, 'smœts\ Jan \'yän\ Christiaan 1870–1950 So. African field marshal; prime minister (1919–24; 1939–48)

Smyth \'smīth\ Henry DeWolf 1898–1986 Am. physicist

Snell \'snel\ George Davis 1903–1996 Am. research geneticist

Snor·ri Stur·lu·son \'snòr-ē-'stər-lə-sən, ,snär-\ 1179–1241 Icelandic statesman & historian

Snow \'snō\ Charles Percy 1905–1980 Baron *Snow* Eng. novelist & physicist

Snow·den \'snō-dᵊn\ Philip 1864–1937 1st Viscount *Snowden of Ick·orn·shaw* \'i-,kòrn-,shò\ Eng. politician

Snow·don \'snō-dᵊn\ Earl of — see ARMSTRONG-JONES

Sny·ders \'snī-dərs\ Frans 1579–1657 Flem. painter

Soar·es \'swär-ish\ Mário 1924– prime minister of Portugal (1976–78; 1983–85) & president (1986–96)

Sobieski John — see JOHN III SOBIESKI

So·ci·nus \sō-'sī-nəs\ Faustus 1539–1604 *Fausto Soz·zi·ni* or *So·ci·ni* or *So·zi·ni* \sòt-'sē-nē\ Ital. theologian

Soc·ra·tes \'sä-krə-,tēz\ *circa* 470–399 B.C. Greek philosopher

Sod·dy \'sä-dē\ Frederick 1877–1956 Eng. chemist

Sö·der·blom \'sə(r)-dər-,blüm, 'sē-\ Nathan 1866–1931 Swed. theologian

So·do·ma \sō-'dō-mə\ Il 1477–1549 *Giovanni Antonio Bazzi* Ital. painter

So·lon \'sō-lən, -,län\ *circa* 630–*circa* 560 B.C. Athenian lawgiver

So·low \'sō-lō\ Robert Merton 1924– Am. economist

Sol·zhe·ni·tsyn \,sōl-zhə-'nēt-sən, ,sól-\ Aleksandr Isayevich 1918– Russ. novelist

Som·er·ville \'sə-mər-,vil\ Sir James Fownes 1882–1949 Brit. admiral

Son·tag \'sän-,tag\ Susan 1933– Am. writer

Soong Ai-ling \'súŋ-'ī-'liŋ\ 1888–1973 *wife of H. H. K'ung*

Soong Ch'ing-ling \-'chiŋ-'liŋ\ 1892–1981 *wife of Sun Yat-sen*

Soong Mei-ling \-'mā-'liŋ\ 1897– *wife of Chiang Kai-shek*

Soong Tzu-wen *or* **Tse-ven** *or* **Tsŭ-wên** \-'tsŭ-'wən\ 1894–1971 *T. V. Soong; brother of preceding* Chin. financier & statesman

Soph·o·cles \'sä-fə-,klēz\ *circa* 496–406 B.C. Greek dramatist — **Soph·o·cle·an** \,sä-fə-'klē-ən\ *adjective*

Sor·del·lo \sòr-'de-(,)lō\ *circa* 1200–before 1269 Ital. troubadour

So·rol·la y Bas·ti·da \sə-'ròl-yə-,ē-bä-'stē-də, -'ròi-ə-, -'stē-tha\ Joaquín 1863–1923 Span. painter

So·to, de \thä-'sōt-(,)ō, di-\ Hernando 1496(or 1499 or 1500)–1542 Span. explorer

Soult \sült\ Nicolas-Jean de Dieu 1769–1851 Duc de Dal·ma·tie \dàl-má-sē\ Fr. soldier; marshal of France

Sou·sa \'sü-zə, 'sü-sə\ John Philip 1854–1932 *the March King* Am. bandmaster & composer

Sou·ter \'sü-tər\ David 1939– Am. jurist

South \'saúth\ Robert 1634–1716 Eng. clergyman

Sou·they \'saú-thē, 'sə-thē\ Robert 1774–1843 Eng. author; poet laureate (1813–43)

Sou·tine \sü-'tēn\ Chaim 1893–1943 Fr. (Lith.-born) painter

So·yin·ka \shò-'yiŋ-ka\ Wo·le \'wò-lā\ 1934– Nigerian dramatist & poet

Spaak \'späk\ Paul-Henri Charles 1899–1972 Belg. lawyer & politician; premier (1938–39; 1947–50); secretary-general of NATO (1957–61)

Spaatz \'späts\ Carl 1891–1974 Am. general

Spal·ding \'spòl-diŋ\ Albert 1888–1953 Am. violinist & composer

Spark \'spärk\ Muriel Sarah 1918– née *Camberg* Brit. writer

Sparks \'spärks\ Jar·ed \'jar-əd, 'jer-\ 1789–1866 Am. historian

Spar·ta·cus \'spär-tə-kəs\ *died* 71 B.C. Rom. slave & insurrectionist

Spell·man \'spel-mən\ Francis Joseph 1889–1967 Am. cardinal

Spe·mann \'shpā-,män\ Hans 1869–1941 Ger. embryologist

Spen·cer \'spen(t)-sər\ Herbert 1820–1903 Eng. philosopher

Spen·der \'spen-dər\ Stephen Harold 1909–1995 Eng. poet & critic

Speng·ler \'shpeŋ-lər, 'speŋ-\ Oswald 1880–1936 Ger. philosopher

Spen·ser \'spen(t)-sər\ Edmund 1552–1599 Eng. poet — **Spen·se·ri·an** \spen-'sir-ē-ən\ *adjective*

Sper·ry \'sper-ē\ Elmer Ambrose 1860–1930 Am. inventor

Sperry Roger Wolcott 1913–1994 Am. psychobiologist

Spiel·berg \'spē(ə)l-,bərg\ Steven 1947– Am. motion-picture director, writer, & producer — **Spiel·berg·ian** \,spēl-'bər-gē-ən\ *adjective*

Spi·no·za \spi-'nō-zə\ Benedict de 1632–1677 Hebrew prename *Baruch* Du. philosopher

Spit·te·ler \'shpi-tᵊl-ər, 'spi-; 'shpit-lər, 'spit-,dem\ Carl 1845–1924 pseudonym *Felix Tan·dem* \'tän-,dem\ Swiss writer

Spock \'späk\ Benjamin McLane 1903– Am. physician

Spode \'spōd\ Josiah 1754–1827 Eng. potter

Spru·ance \'sprü-ən(t)s\ Raymond Ames 1886–1969 Am. admiral

Spy·ri \'shpir-ē, 'spir-\ Johanna 1827–1901 née *Heusser* Swiss author

Staël, de \də-'stäl, -stäl\ Mme. Anne-Louise-Germaine 1766–1817 née *Necker* Baronne de Staël-Holstein Fr. writer & hostess of literary salon

Ståhl·berg \'stòl-,bərg, -,ber-ē\ Kaarlo Ju·ho \'yü-(,)hò\ 1865–1952 Finn. statesman

Stair Viscount & Earl of — see DALRYMPLE

\ə\ abut \ᵊ\ kitten \ər\ further \a\ ash \ā\ ace
\ä\ mop, mar \aú\ out \ch\ chin \e\ bet \ē\ easy
\g\ go \i\ hit \ī\ ice \j\ job \ŋ\ go \ō\ go
\ò\ law \òi\ boy \th\ thin \th\ the \ü\ loot \ú\ foot
\y\ yet \zh\ vision *see also* Guide to Pronunciation

Sta·lin \'stä-lən, 'sta-, -,lēn\ Joseph 1879–1953 *Iosif Vissarionovich Dzhu·gash·vi·li* \,jü-gəsh-'vē-lē\ Soviet leader

Stan·dish \'stan-dish\ Myles *or* Miles 1584?–1656 Am. colonist

Stan·is·lav·sky \,sta-ni-'släf-skē\ Konstantin 1863–1938 pseudonym of *Konstantin Sergeyevich Alekseyev* Russ. actor, director, & producer

Stan·is·law I \'sta-nə-,slòv, -,släv\ **Lesz·czyń·ski** \lesh-'chin-skē\ 1677–1766 king of Poland (1704–09; 1733–35)

Stan·ley \'stan-lē\ Edward George Geoffrey Smith 1799–1869 Earl of *Derby* Brit. statesman

Stanley Sir Henry Morton 1841–1904 originally *John Rowlands* Brit. explorer

Stanley Wendell Meredith 1904–1971 Am. biochemist

Stan·ton \'stan-tⁿn\ Edwin McMasters 1814–1869 Am. lawyer & secretary of war (1862–68)

Stanton Elizabeth 1815–1902 née *Cady* Am. suffragist

Star·hem·berg \'stär-əm-,bərg, 'shtär-əm-,berk\ Ernst Rüdiger 1899–1956 Fürst *von Starhemberg* Austrian politician

Stark \'stärk\ Harold Raynsford 1880–1972 Am. admiral

Stark \'shtärk, 'stärk\ Johannes 1874–1957 Ger. physicist

Stark \'stärk\ John 1728–1822 Am. general in Revolution

Sta·tius \'stā-sh(ē-)əs\ Publius Papinius *circa* A.D. 45–96 Rom. poet

Stau·ding·er \'shtaú-diŋ-ər, 'staú-\ Hermann 1881–1965 Ger. chemist

Steele \'stē(ə)l\ Sir Richard 1672–1729 Brit. essayist & dramatist

Steen \'stān\ Jan 1626–1679 Du. painter

Ste·fans·son \'ste-fən-sən\ Vil·hjal·mur \'vil-,yaúl-mər\ 1879–1962 Am. (Canad.-born) explorer

Stef·fens \'ste-fənz\ (Joseph) Lincoln 1866–1936 Am. journalist

Stei·chen \'stī-kən\ Edward Jean 1879–1973 Am. photographer

Stein \'stīn\ Gertrude 1874–1946 Am. writer

Stein William Howard 1911–1980 Am. biochemist

Stein \'shtīn, 'stīn\ (Heinrich Friedrich) Karl 1757–1831 Freiherr *vom und zum Stein* Pruss. statesman

Stein·beck \'stīn-,bek\ John Ernst 1902–1968 Am. novelist

Stein·berg·er \'stīn-,bər-gər\ Jack 1921– Am. (Ger.-born) physicist

Stei·nem \'stī-nəm\ Gloria 1934– Am. feminist writer & editor

Stein·metz \'stīn-,mets, 'stīn-\ Charles Proteus 1865–1923 Am. (Ger.-born) electrical engineer

Sten·dhal \sten-'däl, stan-, *French* staⁿ-dàl\ 1783–1842 pseudonym of *Marie-Henri Beyle* \'bel\ Fr. writer — **Sten·dhal·ian** \-'dä-lē-ən\ *adjective*

Ste·phen \'stē-vən\ *circa* 1097–1154 king of England (1135–54)

Stephen Sir Leslie 1832–1904 Eng. philosopher, critic, & biographer

Ste·phens \'stē-vənz\ Alexander Hamilton 1812–1883 Am. politician; vice president of the Confederate states

Stephens James 1882–1950 Irish poet & novelist

Ste·phen·son \'stē-vən-sən\ George 1781–1848 Eng. inventor & founder of railroads

Stephenson Robert 1803–1859 *son of George* Eng. engineer

Stern \'stərn\ Isaac 1920– Am. (Russ.-born) violinist

Stern Otto 1888–1969 Am. (Ger.-born) physicist

Stern·berg \'stərn-,bərg\ George Miller 1838–1915 Am. physician & bacteriologist

Sterne \'stərn\ Laurence 1713–1768 Brit. novelist

Stet·tin·i·us \stə-'ti-nē-əs, ste-\ Edward Reilly 1900–1949 Am. financier & statesman

Steu·ben \'stü-bən, 'styü-, 'shtói-\ Baron Friedrich Wilhelm Ludolf Gerhard Augustin von 1730–1794 Pruss.-born general in Am. Revolution

Ste·vens \'stē-vənz\ John 1749–1838 Am. inventor

Stevens John Paul 1920– Am. jurist

Stevens Thaddeus 1792–1868 Am. politician

Stevens Wallace 1879–1955 Am. poet

Ste·ven·son \'stē-vən-sən\ Ad·lai \'ad-lē, -(,)lā\ Ewing 1835–1914 Am. politician; vice president of U.S. (1893–97)

Stevenson Adlai Ewing 1900–1965 *grandson of preceding* Am. politician

Stevenson Robert Louis Balfour 1850–1894 Scot. author

Stew·art \'stü-ərt, 'styü-; 'st(y)ù(-ə)rt\ Du·gald \'dü-gəld\ 1753–1828 Scot. philosopher

Stewart Potter 1915–1985 Am. jurist

Stewart Robert 1769–1822 Viscount *Cas·tle·reagh* \'ka-səl-,rā\ Eng. statesman

Steyn \'stīn\ Marthinus Theunis 1857–1916 So. African statesman

Stieg·litz \'stē-gləts, -,glits\ Alfred 1864–1946 Am. photographer

Stig·ler \'sti-glər\ George J. 1911–1991 Am. economist

Stil·i·cho \'sti-li-,kō\ Flavius *circa* 365–408 Rom. general & statesman

Still \'stil\ Andrew Taylor 1828–1917 Am. founder of osteopathy

Stil·well \'stil-,wel, -wəl\ Joseph Warren 1883–1946 Am. general

Stim·son \'stim(p)-sən\ Henry Lewis 1867–1950 Am. statesman

Stin·nes \'shti-nəs, 'sti-\ Hugo 1870–1924 Ger. industrialist

Stir·ling \'stər-liŋ\ James Frazer 1926–1992 Brit. architect

Stock·hau·sen \'shtòk-,haú-zən, 'stäk-\ Karlheinz 1928– Ger. composer & theorist

Stock·mar \'stäk-,mär\ Christian Friedrich 1787–1863 Baron *von Stockmar* Anglo-Belg. statesman

Stock·ton \'stäk-tən\ Francis Richard 1834–1902 *Frank R. Stockton* Am. writer

Stod·dard \'stä-dərd\ Richard Henry 1825–1903 Am. poet & critic

Sto·ker \'stō-kər\ Bram 1847–1912 Brit. writer

Stokes \'stōks\ Sir Frederick Wilfrid Scott 1860–1927 Eng. engineer & inventor

Sto·kow·ski \stə-'kòf-skē, -'kòv- *also* -'kaú-\ Leopold Antoni Stanislaw Boleslawowicz 1882–1977 Am. (Eng.-born) conductor

Stone \'stōn\ Harlan Fiske 1872–1946 Am. jurist; chief justice U.S. Supreme Court (1941–46)

Stone Irving 1903–1989 original surname *Tennenbaum* Am. writer

Stone Lucy 1818–1893 Am. suffragist

Stone Sir (John) Richard Nicholas 1913–1991 Eng. economist

Stoph \'shtòf, 'stòf\ Willi 1914– prime minister of East Germany (1976–89)

Sto·ry \'stòr-ē, 'stòr-ē\ Joseph 1779–1845 Am. jurist

Story William Wetmore 1819–1895 *son of preceding* Am. sculptor

Stow \'stō\ John 1525–1605 Eng. historian & antiquarian

Stowe \'stō\ Harriet Elizabeth 1811–1896 née *Beecher* Am. author

Stra·bo \'strā-(,)bō\ 64(or 63) B.C.–after A.D. 23 Greek geographer

Stra·chey \'strā-chē\ (Evelyn) John St. Loe 1901–1963 Eng. socialist

Strachey (Giles) Lytton 1880–1932 Eng. biographer

Stra·di·va·ri \,stra-də-'vär-ē, -'var-, -'ver-\ Antonio 1644–1737 Latin *Antonius Strad·i·var·i·us* \,stra-də-'vär-ē-əs, -'ver-\ Ital. violin maker

Straf·ford \'stra-fərd\ 1st Earl of 1593–1641 *Thomas Wentworth* Eng. statesman

Stratford de Redcliffe Viscount — see Stratford CANNING

Strath·co·na \strath-'kō-nə\ **and Mount Roy·al** 1st Baron 1820–1914 *Donald Alexander Smith* Canad. (Scot.-born) railroad builder & politician

Straus \'shtraús, 'straús\ Oscar 1870–1954 Fr. (Austrian-born) composer

Strauss \'shtraús, 'straús\ David Friedrich 1808–1874 Ger. theologian & philosopher

Strauss Johann father 1804–1849 & his sons Johann Baptist 1825–1899 & Josef 1827–1870 Austrian composers

Strauss Ri·chard \'ri-,kärt, -,kärt\ 1864–1949 Ger. composer — **Strauss·ian** \'strau-sē-ən, 'shtraú-\ *adjective*

Stra·vin·sky \strə-'vin(t)-skē\ Igor \'ē-,gòr\ Fyodorovich 1882–1971 Am. (Russ.-born) composer — **Stra·vin·sky·an** *or* **Stra·vin·ski·an** \-skē-ən\ *adjective*

Strei·cher \'shtrī-kər, 'strī-, -kər\ Julius 1885–1946 Ger. Nazi administrator

Stre·se·mann \'shtrā-zə-,män, 'strä-\ Gustav 1878–1929 Ger. politician

Strij·dom \'strī-dəm, 'strä-\ Johannes Gerhardus 1893–1958 prime minister of So. Africa (1954–58)

Strind·berg \'strin(d)-,bərg, *Swedish* 'strind-,ber-ē\ August 1849–1912 Swed. dramatist & novelist — **Strind·berg·ian** \strin(d)-'bər-gē-ən\ *adjective*

Stroess·ner \'stres-nər\ Alfredo 1912– president of Paraguay (1954–89)

Stru·en·see \'shtrü-ən-,zā, 'strü-\ Johann Friedrich 1737–1772 Graf *Struensee* Dan. (Ger.-born) physician & politician

Stu·art \'stü-ərt, 'styü-; 'st(y)ù(-ə)rt\ — see CHARLES I & MARY STUART

Stuart Charles *the Young Pretender* — see CHARLES EDWARD

Stuart Gilbert Charles 1755–1828 Am. painter

Stuart James Ewell Brown 1833–1864 *Jeb Stuart* Am. Confederate general

Stuart James Francis Edward *the Old Pretender* — see JAMES EDWARD

Stubbs \'stəbz\ George 1724–1806 Eng. painter

Stubbs William 1825–1901 Eng. historian & prelate

Stülp·na·gel \'shtúlp-,nä-gəl, 'stúlp-, 'shtɛlp-\ Karl Heinrich von 1886–1944 Ger. general

Sturluson — see SNORRI STURLUSON

Štur·sa \'shtúr-sə\ Jan \'yän\ 1880–1925 Czech sculptor

Stuy·ve·sant \'stī-və-sənt\ Peter *circa* 1610–1672 Du. colonial administrator in America

Sty·ron \'stī-rən\ William 1925– Am. writer

Sua·rez Gon·zá·lez \'swär-əz-gən-'zä-ləs\ Adolfo 1932– prime minister of Spain (1976–81)

Su·choc·ka \sü-'kòt-,skä\ Hanna 1946– prime minister of Poland (1992–93)

Suck·ling \'sə-kliŋ\ Sir John 1609–1642 Eng. Cavalier poet

Su·cre \'sü-(,)krā\ Antonio José de 1795–1830 So. Am. liberator

Sue \'sü, 'sē\ Eugène 1804–1857 originally *Marie-Joseph Sue* Fr. novelist

Sue·to·ni·us \swē-'tō-nē-əs, ,sü-ə-'tō-\ *circa* A.D. 69–after 122 *Gaius Suetonius Tranquillus* Rom. biographer & historian

Su·gi·ya·ma \,sü-gē-'yä-mə\ Hajime 1880–1945 Jp. field marshal

Su·har·to \sə-'här-(,)tō, sù-\ 1921– president of Indonesia (1967–)

Su·kar·no \sü-'kär-(,)nō\ 1901–1970 president of Indonesian Republic (1945–67)

Sü·ley·man *or* **So·li·man** *or* **Su·lei·man I** \'sü-lā-,män, -li-\ 1494(or 1495)–1566 *the Magnificent* Ottoman sultan (1520–66)

Sul·la \'sə-lə\ 138–78 B.C. *Lucius Cornelius Sulla Felix* Rom. general & politician

Sul·li·van \'sə-lə-vən\ Sir Arthur Seymour 1842–1900 Eng. composer

Sullivan John 1740–1795 Am. general in Revolution

Sullivan John Lawrence 1858–1918 Am. boxer

Sullivan John Lawrence 1899–1982 Am. lawyer & administrator

Sullivan Louis Henri 1856–1924 Am. architect

Sul·ly \'sə-lē, (,)sə-'lē, sɛl-lē\ Duc de 1560–1641 *Maximilien de Béthune* Baron *de Ros·ny* \də-rō-'nē\ Fr. statesman

Sul·ly \'sə-lē\ Thomas 1783–1872 Am. (Eng.-born) painter

Sul·ly Prud·homme \sɛl-lē-prɛ̄-dəm\ 1839–1907 pseudonym of *René-François-Armand Prudhomme* Fr. poet & critic

Sum·ner \'səm-nər\ Charles 1811–1874 Am. statesman & orator

Sumner James Batcheller 1887–1955 Am. biochemist

Sumner William Graham 1840–1910 Am. sociologist & educator

Sun·day \'sən-dē\ William Ashley 1862–1935 *Billy* Am. evangelist

Sun Yat-sen \'sùn-'yät-'sen\ 1866–1925 originally *Sun Wen* or *Sun Chung-shan* Chin. statesman

Surrey Earl of — see Henry HOWARD

Sur·tees \'sər-(,)tēz\ Robert Smith 1803–1864 Eng. novelist & editor

Suth·er·land \'sə-<u>th</u>ər-lənd\ Earl Wilbur, Jr. 1915–1974 Am. physiologist

Sutherland Dame Joan 1926– Austral. soprano

Sut·ter \'sə-tər, 'sü-\ John Augustus 1803–1880 originally *Johann August Suter* Am. (Ger.-born) pioneer

Sutt·ner \'zùt-nər, 'sùt-\ Bertha 1843–1914 née *Kinsky* Baroness *von Suttner* Austrian writer & pacifist

Su·vo·rov \sù-'vòr-əf, -'vär-\ Aleksandr Vasilyevich 1729–1800 Russ. field marshal

Sved·berg \'sved-,bərg, *Swedish* -,ber-ē\ The *or* Theodor 1884–1971 Swed. chemist

Sver·drup \'sver-drəp\ Otto Neumann 1855–1930 Norw. explorer

Sver·rir \'sver-ər\ *circa* 1149–1202 *Sverrir Sigurds·son* \'si-gərd-sən\ king of Norway (1184–1202)

Swe·den·borg \'swē-d°n-,bòrg\ Emanuel 1688–1772 originally *Svedberg* Swed. philosopher & religious writer

Swee·linck \'swā-liŋk\ Jan Pieterszoon 1562–1621 Du. organist & composer

Sweet \'swēt\ Henry 1845–1912 Eng. phonetician

Swift \'swift\ Gustavus Franklin 1839–1903 Am. meatpacker

Swift Jonathan 1667–1745 Eng. satirist — **Swift·ian** \'swif-tē-ən\ *adjective*

Swin·burne \'swin-(,)bərn\ Algernon Charles 1837–1909 Eng. poet — **Swin·burn·ian** \swin-'bər-nē-ən\ *adjective*

Swin·ner·ton \'swi-nər-t°n\ Frank Arthur 1884–1982 Eng. novelist & critic

Sylva Carmen — see ELIZABETH Queen of Romania

Sy·ming·ton \'sī-miŋ-tən\ (William) Stuart 1901–1988 Am. industrialist & politician

Sy·monds \'si-mən(d)z, 'sī-\ John Addington 1840–1893 Eng. scholar

Sy·mons \'si-mənz, 'sī-\ Arthur William 1865–1945 Brit. poet & critic

Synge \'siŋ\ John Millington 1871–1909 Irish poet & dramatist

Synge Richard Laurence Millington 1914– Brit. biochemist

Szell \'sel, 'zel\ George 1897–1970 Am. (Hung.-born) conductor

Szent–Györ·gyi \sänt-'jórj, -'jór-jē\ Albert von Nagyrapolt 1893–1986 Am. (Hung.-born) chemist

Szi·lard \'zi-,lärd, zə-'lärd\ Leo 1898–1964 Am. (Hung.-born) physicist

Szold \'zōld\ Henrietta 1860–1945 Am. Zionist & founder of Hadassah

Szym·bor·ska \shim-'bór-skə\ Wis·la·wa \vēs-'wä-və\ 1923– Pol. poet

Tac·i·tus \'ta-sə-təs\ Cornelius *circa* A.D. 56–*circa* 120 Rom. historian — **Tac·i·te·an** \,ta-sə-'tē-ən\ *adjective*

Taft \'taft\ Lo·ra·do \lə-'rä-(,)dō\ 1860–1936 Am. sculptor

Taft Robert Alphonso 1889–1953 *son of W. H.* Am. politician

Taft William Howard 1857–1930 27th president of the U.S. (1909–13); chief justice U.S. Supreme Court (1921–30)

Ta·gore \tə-'gòr, -'gór\ Ra·bin·dra·nath \rə-'bin-drə-,nät\ 1861–1941 Indian poet

Taine \'tān, 'ten\ Hippolyte-Adolphe 1828–1893 Fr. philosopher & critic

Tait \'tāt\ Archibald Campbell 1811–1882 archbishop of Canterbury (1869–82)

T'ai–tsu — see CHAO K'UANG-YIN

Ta·ke·shi·ta \tä-'kā-shə-,tä\ Noboru 1924– prime minister of Japan (1987–89)

Tall·chief \'tòl-,chēf\ Maria 1925– Am. dancer

Tal·ley·rand–Pé·ri·gord \'ta-lē-,ran(d)-,per-ə-'gór, *French* tál-rä°-\ Charles-Maurice de 1754–1838 Prince de *Bénévent* Fr. statesman

Ta·ma·yo \tə-'mī-(,)ō\ Rufino 1899–1991 Mex. painter

Tamerlane *or* **Tamburlaine** — see TIMUR

Tamm \'täm, 'tam\ Igor Yevgenyevich 1895–1971 Soviet physicist

Tan·cred \'taŋ-krəd\ 1078?–1112 Norman leader in 1st Crusade

Tan·dy \'tan-dē\ Jessica 1909–1994 Am. (Brit.-born) actress

Ta·ney \'tò-nē\ Roger Brooke 1777–1864 Am. jurist; chief justice U.S. Supreme Court (1836–64)

Tan·ge \'tän-gā\ Kenzo 1913– Jp. architect

T'ang T'ai Tsung \'täŋ-'tī-'dzùŋ\ 600–649 originally *Li Shih-min* \'le-'shir-'min\ Chin. emperor

Tan·guy \tä°-'gē\ Yves 1900–1955 Am. (Fr.-born) artist

Tar·bell \'tär-bəl\ Ida Minerva 1857–1944 Am. author

Tar·dieu \tär-'dyə(r), -'dyœ\ André-Pierre-Gabriel-Amédée 1876–1945 Fr. statesman

Tar·king·ton \'tär-kiŋ-tən\ (Newton) Booth 1869–1946 Am. novelist

Tas·man \'taz-mən\ Abel Janszoon 1603?–?1659 Du. navigator & explorer

Tas·so \'tä-(,)sō, 'tä-\ Tor·qua·to \tòr-'kwä-(,)tō\ 1544–1595 Ital. poet

Tate \'tāt\ (John Orley) Allen 1899–1979 Am. poet & critic

Tate Nahum 1652–1715 Brit. dramatist; poet laureate (1692–1715)

Ta·tum \'tā-təm\ Edward Lawrie 1909–1975 Am. biochemist

Taube \'taúb\ Henry 1915– Am. (Canad.-born) chemist

Taw·ney \'tò-nē\ Richard Henry 1880–1962 Eng. economic historian

Tay·lor \'tā-lər\ (James) Bay·ard \'bī-ərd, 'bā-\ 1825–1878 Am. writer

Taylor (Joseph) Deems 1885–1966 Am. composer & music critic

Taylor Edward 1645?–1729 Am. clergyman & poet

Taylor Jeremy 1613–1667 Eng. prelate & author

Taylor Joseph Hooton 1941– Am. physicist

Taylor Maxwell Davenport 1901–1987 Am. general

Taylor Richard Edward 1929– Canad. physicist

Taylor Tom 1817–1880 Eng. dramatist

Taylor Zachary 1784–1850 12th president of the U.S. (1849–50)

Tchai·kov·sky \chī-'kóf-skē, chə-, -'kóv-\ Pyotr Ilich 1840–1893 Russ. composer — **Tchai·kov·sky·an** *or* **Tchai·kov·ski·an** \-skē-ən\ *adjective*

Teas·dale \'tēz-,dāl\ Sara 1884–1933 Am. poet

Te·cum·seh \tə-'kəm(p)-sə, -sē\ *or* **Te·cum·tha** \-'kəm(p)-thə\ *or* **Ti·kam·the** \-'kəm(p)-thə, -'käm(p)-\ 1768–1813 Shawnee Indian chief

Ted·der \'te-dər\ 1st Baron 1890–1967 *Arthur William Tedder* Brit. air marshal

Teil·hard de Char·din \tā-yár-də-shàr-da°\ Pierre 1881–1955 Fr. philosopher & paleontologist

Tek·a·kwitha \,te-kə-'kwi-thə\ *or* **Teg·a·kwitha** \,te-gə-\ *or* **Teg·a·kouita** \,te-gə-'kwi-tə\ Ka·teri \'kä-tə-rē\ 1656–1680 *Lily of the Mohawks* Am. Indian religious

Te·le·mann \'tā-lə-,män, 'tē-\ Georg Philipp 1681–1767 Ger. composer

Tel·ler \'te-lər\ Edward 1908– Am. (Hung.-born) physicist

Téllez Gabriel — see TIRSO DE MOLINA

Tem·in \'te-mən\ Howard Martin 1934–1994 Am. oncologist

Tem·ple \'tem-pəl\ Frederick 1821–1902 archbishop of Canterbury (1896–1902)

Temple Shirley 1928– Am. actress & politician

Temple Sir William 1628–1699 Brit. statesman

Temple William 1881–1944 *son of Frederick* archbishop of Canterbury (1942–44)

Templewood Viscount — see HOARE

Teng Hsiao–p'ing *or* **Deng Xiao·ping** \'dəŋ-'shaú-'piŋ\ 1904–1997 Chin. Communist leader (1977–97)

Te·niers \tə-'nirs, tä-'nyä\ David *the Elder* 1582–1649 & *the Younger* 1610–1690 Flem. painters

Ten·niel \'ten-yəl\ Sir John 1820–1914 Eng. cartoonist & illustrator

Ten·ny·son \'te-nə-sən\ Alfred 1809–1892 1st Baron *Tennyson* known as *Alfred, Lord Tennyson* Eng. poet; poet laureate (1850–92) — **Ten·ny·so·nian** \,te-nə-'sō-nē-ən, -nyən\ *adjective*

Ter·borch *or* **Ter Borch** \tər-'bórk, -'bòrk\ Gerard 1617–1681 Du. painter

Ter·brug·ghen \tər-'brü-gən\ Hendrik 1588–1629 Du. painter

Ter·ence \'ter-ən(t)s 186(or 185)–?159 B.C. *Publius Terentius Afer* Rom. dramatist

Te·re·sa \tə-'rā-zə, -'rē-sə\ Mother 1910–1997 *Agnes Gonxha Bojaxhiu* Albanian religious in India

Teresa of Avila Saint 1515–1582 Span. Carmelite & mystic

Te·resh·ko·va \,ter-əsh-'kó-və, -'kō-\ Valentina Vladimirovna 1937– Soviet (Russ.-born) cosmonaut

Ter·hune \(,)tər-'hyün\ Albert Payson 1872–1942 Am. author

Ter·ry \'ter-ē\ (Alice) Ellen 1847–1928 Eng. actress

Ter·tul·lian \(,)tər-'təl-yən\ *circa* A.D. 155(or 160)–after 220 *Quintus Septimius Florens Tertullianus* church father

Tes·la \'tes-lə\ Nikola 1856–1943 Am. (Croatian-born) electrical engineer & inventor

Tet·zel *or* **Te·zel** \'tet-səl\ Johann *circa* 1465–1519 Ger. Dominican friar

Thack·er·ay \'tha-k(ə-)rē\ William Makepeace 1811–1863 Eng. author — **Thack·er·ay·an** \-k(ə-)rē-ən\ *adjective*

Tha·les \'thā-(,)lēz\ *of Miletus* 625?–?547 B.C. Greek philosopher — **Tha·le·sian** \thā-'lē-zhən\ *adjective*

Thant \'thant, 'thänt\ U \'ü\ 1909–1974 Burmese U.N. official; secretary-general (1961–71)

Thatch·er \'tha-chər\ Margaret Hilda 1925– née *Roberts* Brit. prime minister (1979–90)

Thayer \'thar, 'ther, 'thā-ər\ Sylvanus 1785–1872 *father of West Point* Am. army officer & educator

Thei·ler \'tī-lər\ Max 1899–1972 Am. (So. African-born) microbiologist

The·mis·to·cles \thə-'mis-tə-,klēz\ *circa* 524–*circa* 460 B.C. Athenian general & statesman

The·oc·ri·tus \thē-'ä-krə-təs\ *circa* 310–250 B.C. Greek poet

The·od·o·ric \thē-'ä-də-rik\ 454?–526 *the Great* king of the Ostrogoths (493–526)

The·o·do·sius I \,thē-ə-'dō-sh(ē-)əs\ 347–395 *the Great* Rom. general & emperor (379–395)

The·o·phras·tus \,thē-ə-'fras-təs\ *circa* 372–*circa* 287 B.C. Greek philosopher & naturalist

The·o·rell \,tā-ə-'rel\ Axel Hugo Theodor 1903–1982 Swed. biochemist

Theresa Saint — see TERESA OF AVILA

Thes·pis \'thes-pəs\ 6th century B.C. Greek poet

Thiers \tē-'er\ Louis-Adolphe 1797–1877 Fr. statesman & historian

Tho·mas \tò-'mä\ (Charles-Louis-)Ambroise 1811–1896 Fr. composer

Thom·as \'tä-məs\ Augustus 1857–1934 Am. dramatist

Thomas Clarence 1948– Am. jurist

Thomas Dyl·an \'di-lən\ Marlais 1914–1953 Welsh poet

Thomas Edward Donnall 1920– Am. physician

Thomas Lowell Jackson 1892–1981 Am. traveler, journalist, & author

Thomas Norman Mat·toon \ma-'tün, mə-\ 1884–1968 Am. socialist politician

Thomas Seth 1785–1859 Am. clock manufacturer

Thomas (Christian Friedrich) Theodore 1835–1905 Am. (Ger.-born) conductor

Thomas à Becket — SEE BECKET

Thomas à Kem·pis \ə-'kem-pəs, (,)ä-'kem-\ 1379(or 1380)–1471 originally *Thomas Hemerken* Du. ecclesiastic & writer

Thomas Aqui·nas \ə-'kwī-nəs\ Saint 1224(or 1225)–1274 Italian *Tommaso d'Aquino* Ital. religious & philosopher

Thomas of Er·cel·doune \'ər-səl-,dün\ *flourished* 1220–1297 *Thomas the Rhymer* and *Thomas Learmont* Scot. seer & poet

Thomp·son \'täm(p)-sən\ Benjamin 1753–1814 Count *Rum·ford* \'rəm(p)-fərd\ Brit. (Am.-born) physicist & statesman

Thompson Dorothy 1894–1961 Am. journalist

Thompson Francis 1859–1907 Eng. poet

Thompson Sir John Sparrow David 1844–1894 Canad. statesman; prime minister (1892–94)

\ə\ abut \°\ kitten \ər\ further \a\ ash \ā\ ace
\ä\ mop, mar \aú\ out \ch\ chin \e\ bet \ē\ easy
\g\ go \i\ hit \ī\ ice \j\ job \ŋ\ sing \ō\ go
\ò\ law \òi\ boy \th\ thin \<u>th</u>\ the \ü\ loot \ú\ foot
\y\ yet \zh\ vision *see also* Guide to Pronunciation

Thom·son \'täm(p)-sən\ Sir George Pag·et \'pa-jət\ 1892–1975 *son of Sir Joseph John* Eng. physicist

Thomson James 1700–1748 Scot. poet

Thomson James 1834–1882 *B. V.* or *Bysshe Vanolis* Scot. poet

Thomson John Arthur 1861–1933 Scot. biologist

Thomson Sir Joseph John 1856–1940 Eng. physicist

Thomson Virgil Garnett 1896–1989 Am. composer & critic

Thomson William — see Baron KELVIN

Tho·reau \thə-'rō, thō-; 'thȯr-(ˌ)ō, 'thȯr-(ˌ)ō\ Henry David 1817–1862 originally *David Henry Thoreau* Am. writer — **Tho·reau·vi·an** \thə-'rō-vē-ən, thō-\ *adjective*

Tho·rez \tȯ-'rez\ Maurice 1900–1964 Fr. politician

Thorn·dike \'thȯrn-ˌdīk\ Edward Lee 1874–1949 Am. psychologist

Thorndike Lynn 1882–1965 Am. historian

Thorndike Dame (Agnes) Sybil 1882–1976 Brit. actress

Thorn·ton \'thȯrn-tᵊn\ William 1759–1828 Am. architect

Thorpe \'thȯrp\ James Francis 1888–1953 *Jim* Am. athlete

Thor·vald·sen or **Thor·wald·sen** \'tȯr-ˌwȯl-sən, 'thȯr-; 'tur-ˌväl-sən\ Ber·tel \'ber-tᵊl\ 1768(or 1770)–1844 Dan. sculptor

Thras·y·bu·lus \ˌthra-sə-'byü-ləs\ *died* 388 B.C. Athenian general

Thu·cyd·i·des \thü-'si-də-ˌdēz, thyü-\ *died circa* 401 B.C. Greek historian — **Thu·cyd·i·de·an** \(ˌ)thü-ˌsi-də-'dē-ən, (ˌ)thyü-\ *adjective*

Thur·ber \'thər-bər\ James Grover 1894–1961 Am. writer — **Thur·ber·esque** \ˌthər-bə-'resk\ *adjective*

Thut·mo·se \thüt-'mō-sə\ name of 4 kings of Egypt: especially **III** *died* 1450 B.C. (reigned 1504–1450 B.C.)

Thys·sen \'ti-sᵊn\ Fritz 1873–1951 Ger. industrialist

Tib·bett \'ti-bət\ Lawrence Mervil 1896–1960 Am. baritone

Ti·be·ri·us \tī-'bir-ē-əs\ 42 B.C.–A.D. 37 *Tiberius Claudius Nero Caesar Augustus* Rom. emperor (14–37)

Ti·bul·lus \tə-'bə-ləs\ Albius *circa* 55–*circa* 19 B.C. Rom. poet

Tieck \'tēk\ (Johann) Ludwig 1773–1853 Ger. author

Tie·po·lo \tē-'ä-pə-ˌlō, -'e-\ Giovanni Battista 1696–1770 Ital. painter

Tif·fa·ny \'ti-fə-nē\ Charles Lewis 1812–1902 Am. jeweler

Tiffany Louis Comfort 1848–1933 *son of C.L.* Am. painter & stained-glass artist

Tig·lath-pi·le·ser III \ˌti-ˌglath-(ˌ)pī-'lē-zər-, -pə-\ *died* 727 B.C. king of Assyria (745–727)

Til·den \'til-dən\ Samuel Jones 1814–1886 Am. politician

Til·dy \'til-dē\ Zol·tán \'zōl-ˌtän\ 1889–1961 Hung. politician

Til·lich \'ti-lik, -lik\ Paul Johannes 1886–1965 Am. (Ger.-born) theologian

Til·lot·son \'ti-lət-sən\ John 1630–1694 Eng. prelate

Til·ly \'ti-lē\ Graf von 1559–1632 *Johann Tserclaes* \tsər-'kläs\ Bavarian general

Ti·mo·shen·ko \ˌti-mə-'sheŋ-(ˌ)kō\ Sem·yon \səm-'yȯn\ Konstantinovich 1895–1970 Soviet marshal

Tim·ur \'ti-(ˌ)mur\ or **Timur Lenk** \-'leŋk\ 1336–1405 English *Tam·er·lane* \'ta-mər-ˌlān\ or *Tam·bur·laine* \'tam-bər-ˌlān\ Turkic conqueror

Tin·ber·gen \'tin-ber-kə(n)\ Jan 1903–1994 Du. economist

Tinbergen Nikolaas 1907–1988 *brother of Jan* Du. ethologist

Ting \'tiŋ\ Samuel Chao Chung 1936– Am. physicist

Ting·ley \'tiŋ-lē\ Katherine Augusta 1847–1929 née *Westcott* Am. theosophist

Tin·to·ret·to \ˌtin-tə-'re-(ˌ)tō\ *circa* 1518–1594 *Jacopo Robusti* Ital. painter

Ti·pu or **Tip·pu Sul·tan** \ˌti-(ˌ)pü-'sul-ˌtän\ 1749(or 1753)–1799 sultan of Mysore (1782–99)

Tir·pitz \'tir-pəts, 'tər-\ Alfred von 1849–1930 Ger. admiral

Tir·so de Mo·li·na \'tir-(ˌ)sō-ˌdä-mə-'lē-nə\ *circa* 1584–1648 pseudonym of *Gabriel Te·llez* \'tā(l)-yäth\ Span. dramatist

Ti·se·li·us \tə-'sā-lē-əs, -'zā-\ Arne Wilhelm Kaurin 1902–1971 Swed. biochemist

Ti·so \'tē-(ˌ)sō\ Josef or Joseph 1887–1947 Slovak priest & politician

Titch·e·ner \'ti-chə-nər\ Edward Bradford 1867–1927 Am. psychologist

Ti·tian \'ti-shən\ *circa* 1488–1576 *Tiziano Vecellio* Ital. painter — **Ti·tian·esque** \ˌti-shə-'nesk\ *adjective*

Ti·to \'tē-(ˌ)tō\ 1892–1980 originally *Josip Broz* \'brȯz, 'brōz\ usually called *Marshal Tito* leader of Yugoslavia (1943–80)

Ti·tus \'tī-təs\ A.D. 39–81 *Titus Flavius Vespasianus* Rom. emperor (79–81)

To·bin \'tō-bən\ James 1918– Am. economist

Tocque·ville \'tōk-ˌvil, 'tȯk-, 'täk-, -ˌvēl, -vəl\ Alexis-Charles-Henri Clérel de 1805–1859 Fr. statesman & author

Todd \'täd\ Sir Alexander Robertus 1907–1997 Brit. chemist

Todt \'tōt\ Fritz 1891–1942 Ger. military engineer

To·gliat·ti \tōl-'yä-tē\ Pal·mi·ro \päl-'mē-(ˌ)rō\ 1893–1964 Ital. politician

Tō·gō \'tō-(ˌ)gō\ Marquis Heihachirō 1848–1934 Jp. admiral

Tō·jō \'tō-(ˌ)jō\ Hideki 1884–1948 Jp. general & politician

To·ku·ga·wa \ˌtō-kù-'gä-wə\ Ieyasu 1543–1616 originally *Matsudaira Takechiyo* Jp. shogun (1603–05); founder of last Jp. shogunate (1603–1867)

Tol·kien \'tȯl-ˌkēn\ John Ronald Reuel 1892–1973 Eng. author — **Tol·kien·esque** \ˌtȯl-(ˌ)kē-'nesk\ *adjective*

Tol·ler \'tȯ-lər, 'tä-\ Ernst 1893–1939 Ger. dramatist & politician

Tol·stoy \tȯl-'stȯi, tōl-', täl-', 'tȯl-ˌ, 'tōl-ˌ, 'täl-\ Count Lev Nikolayevich 1828–1910 Russ. novelist, philosopher, & mystic — **Tol·stoy·an** also **Tol·stoi·an** \-ən\ *adjective*

Tom·baugh \'täm-ˌbȯ\ Clyde William 1906–1997 Am. astronomer

Tom·ma·si·ni \ˌtä-mə-'zē-nē\ Vincenzo 1878–1950 Ital. composer

To·mo·na·ga \ˌtō-mə-'nä-gə, -mō-\ Shin'ichirō 1906–1979 Jp. physicist

Tomp·kins \'täm(p)-kənz\ Daniel D. 1774–1825 Am. politician; vice president of the U.S. (1817–25)

Tone \'tōn\ (Theobald) Wolfe 1763–1798 Irish revolutionary

To·ne·ga·wa \ˌtō-nə-'gä-wə\ Susumu 1939– Am. (Jp.-born) biologist

Tooke \'tuk\ (John) Horne 1736–1812 Eng. political radical & philologist

Toombs \'tümz\ Robert Augustus 1810–1885 Am. politician

Tor·que·ma·da \ˌtȯr-kə-'mä-də, -thə\ Tomás de 1420–1498 Span. grand inquisitor

Tor·ri·cel·li \ˌtȯr-ə-'che-lē, ˌtär-\ Evangelista 1608–1647 Ital. mathematician & physicist

Tos·ca·ni·ni \ˌtäs-kə-'nē-nē, ˌtȯs-\ Ar·tu·ro \är-'tur-(ˌ)ō\ 1867–1957 Ital. conductor

Tou·louse-Lau·trec (–Mon·fa) \tü-ˌlüz-lō-'trek(-mōⁿ-'fä)\ Henri-Marie-Raymond de 1864–1901 Fr. painter

Tour·neur \'tər-nər\ Cyril *circa* 1575–1626 Eng. dramatist

Tous·saint–Lou·ver·ture \'tü-ˌsaⁿ-'lü-vər-ˌtür, -ˌtyür\ *circa* 1743–1803 originally *François-Dominique Toussaint* Haitian general & liberator

Townes \'taunz\ Charles Hard 1915– Am. physicist

Toyn·bee \'tȯin-bē\ Arnold Joseph 1889–1975 Eng. historian

Tra·jan \'trā-jən\ A.D. 53–117 originally *Marcus Ulpius Traiánus* usually called *Germanicus* Rom. emperor (98–117)

Trau·bel \'trau-bəl\ Helen 1903–1972 Am. soprano

Tree \'trē\ Sir Herbert Draper Beerbohm 1853–1917 Eng. actor-manager

Treitsch·ke \'trīch-kə\ Heinrich von 1834–1896 Ger. historian

Tre·vel·yan \tri-'vel-yən, -'vil-\ George Macaulay 1876–1962 Eng. historian

Trevelyan Sir George Otto 1838–1928 *father of preceding* Eng. politician, biographer, & historian

Trol·lope \'trä-ləp\ Anthony 1815–1882 Eng. novelist — **Trol·lo·pi·an** \trä-'lō-pē-ən\ *adjective*

Tromp \'trȯmp, 'trämp\ Maarten Harpertszoon 1598–1653 Du. admiral

Trots·ky \'trät-skē also 'trȯt-\ Leon 1879–1940 originally *Lev Davidovich Bronstein* Russ. Communist leader

Tru·deau \trü-(ˌ)dō, trü-'\ Pierre Elliott 1919– Canad. politician; prime minister (1968–79; 1980–84)

Tru·ji·llo Mo·li·na \trü-'hē-(ˌ)yō-mə-'lē-nə\ Rafael Leónidas 1891–1961 Dominican general & politician; president of Dominican Republic (1930–38; 1942–52)

Tru·man \'trü-mən\ Harry S. 1884–1972 33d president of the U.S. (1945–53)

Trum·bull \'trəm-bəl\ John 1756–1843 Am. painter

Trumbull Jonathan 1710–1785 *father of preceding* Am. statesman

Truth \'trüth\ Sojourner *circa* 1797–1883 Am. evangelist & reformer

Ts'ao Chan \'tsau-'jän\ 1715?–1763 *Ts'ao Hsüeh-ch'in* Chin. novelist

Tschaikovsky *variant of* TCHAIKOVSKY

Tu Fu \'tü-'fü\ 712–770 Chin. poet

Tub·man \'təb-mən\ Harriet *circa* 1820–1913 Am. abolitionist

Tubman William Vacanarat Shadrach 1895–1971 Liberian lawyer; president of Liberia (1944–71)

Tuch·man \'tək-mən\ Barbara 1912–1989 Am. historian

Tu·dor \'tü-dər, 'tyü-\ Antony 1908 (or 1909)–1987 Am. (Brit.-born) ballet dancer & choreographer

Tul·sī·dās \ˌtul-sē-'däs\ 1543?–1623 Hindu poet

Tup·per \'tə-pər\ Sir Charles 1821–1915 Canad. politician; prime minister (1896)

Tu·renne \tü-'ren\ Vicomte de 1611–1675 *Henri de La Tour d'Auvergne* marshal of France

Tur·ge·nev \tür-'gän-yəf, -'gen-\ Ivan Sergeyevich 1818–1883 Russ. novelist

Tur·got \tür-'gō\ Anne-Robert-Jacques 1727–1781 Baron *de l'Aulne* \'lōn\ Fr. statesman & economist

Tur·ner \'tər-nər\ Frederick Jackson 1861–1932 Am. historian

Turner Joseph Mallord William 1775–1851 Eng. painter

Turner Nat 1800–1831 Am. slave insurrectionist

Tut·ankh·a·men \ˌtü-ˌtaŋ-'kä-mən, -ˌtäŋ-\ or **Tut·ankh·a·ten** \-'kä-tᵊn\ *circa* 1370–1352 B.C. king of Egypt (1361–1352 B.C.)

Tutu \'tü-ˌtü\ Desmond Mpilo 1931– So. African clergyman & political activist

Twacht·man \'twäkt-mən\ John Henry 1853–1902 Am. painter

Twain Mark — see CLEMENS

Tweed \'twēd\ William Marcy 1823–1878 *Boss Tweed* Am. politician

Tweedsmuir — see BUCHAN

Ty·ler \'tī-lər\ Anne 1941– Am. writer

Tyler John 1790–1862 10th president of the U.S. (1841–45)

Tyler Wat \'wät\ or Walter *died* 1381 Eng. leader of Peasants' Revolt (1381)

Tyn·dale or **Tin·dal** or **Tin·dale** \'tin-dᵊl\ William *circa* 1494–1536 Eng. reformer & translator

Tyn·dall \'tin-dᵊl\ John 1820–1893 Brit. physicist

Tyr·whitt-Wil·son \'tir-ət-'wil-sən\ Gerald Hugh 1883–1950 14th Baron *Ber·ners* \'bər-nərz\ Eng. composer & painter

Tz'u-hsi \'tsü-'shē\ 1835–1908 Chin. empress dowager

Uc·cel·lo \ü-'che-(ˌ)lō\ Paolo 1397–1475 originally *Paolo di Dono* Florentine painter

Udall \'yü-ˌdȯl, 'yü-dᵊl\ Nicholas 1505–1556 Eng. schoolmaster & dramatist

Ugar·te \ü-'gär-tē\ Manuel 1874–1951 Argentine writer

Uh·land \'ü-ˌlänt\ Johann Ludwig 1787–1862 Ger. poet & historian

Ul·bricht \'ul-(ˌ)brikt, -(ˌ)brikt\ Walter 1893–1973 East German politician

Ul·fi·las \'ul-fə-ˌläs, 'əl-, -ləs, -ˌlas\ or Goth. **Wul·fi·la** \'wul-fə-lə\ *circa* 311–*circa* 382 Gothic missionary

Ul·pi·an \'əl-pē-ən\ *died* A.D. 228 *Domitius Ulpianus* Rom. jurist

Um·ber·to \(ˌ)əm-'ber-(ˌ)tō\ name of 2 kings of Italy: **I** 1844–1900 Duke of *Savoy* (reigned 1878–

1900); **II** 1904–1983 Prince of *Piedmont;* Count of *Sarre* (reigned 1946)

Una·mu·no y Ju·go \ˌü-nə-ˈmü-(ˌ)nō-ē-ˈhü-(ˌ)gō\ Miguel de 1864–1936 Span. philosopher & writer

Un·cas \ˈəŋ-kəs\ 1588?–?1683 Pequot Indian chief

Und·set \ˈuṅ-ˌset\ Si·grid \ˈsi-grē, -grəd\ 1882–1949 Norw. novelist

Uno \ˈu̇-(ˌ)nō\ Sousuke 1922– prime minister of Japan (1989)

Un·ter·mey·er \ˈən-tər-ˌmī(-ə)r\ Louis 1885–1977 Am. poet

Up·dike \ˈəp-ˌdīk\ John Hoyer 1932– Am. writer

Up·john \ˈəp-ˌjän\ Richard 1802–1878 Am. (Eng.-born) architect

Up·ton \ˈəp-tən\ Emory 1839–1881 Am. general & author

Ur·ban \ˈər-bən\ name of 8 popes: especially **II** (*Odo* \ˈō-(ˌ)dō\ *of Lagery)* circa 1035–1099 (pope 1088–99)

Urey \ˈyu̇r-ē\ Harold Clayton 1893–1981 Am. chemist

Ur·quhart \ˈər-kərt, -ˌkärt\ or **Ur·chard** \ˈər-chərd\ Sir Thomas 1611–1660 Scot. author & translator

Ussh·er \ˈə-shər\ James 1581–1656 Irish prelate

Utril·lo \yü-ˈtri-(ˌ)lō, ˌyü-trē-ˈō, ˌē-\ Maurice 1883–1955 Fr. painter

Val·de·mar \ˈväl-də-ˌmär, ˈval-\ or **Wal·de·mar** \ˈwȯl-\ name of 4 kings of Denmark: especially **I** 1131–1182 (reigned 1157–82)

Valdes Peter — see WALDO

Val·di·via \val-ˈdē-vē-ä\ Pedro de *circa* 1498–1553 Span. conquistador

Va·lens \ˈvā-lənz, -ˌlenz\ 328?–378 Rom. emperor of the East (364–378)

Val·en·tin·ian \ˌva-lən-ˈti-nē-ən, -ˈtin-yən\ *Latin* **Val·en·tin·i·a·nus** \ˈva-lən-ˌti-nē-ˈä-nəs\ name of 3 Rom. emperors: **I** 321–375 (reigned 364–375), **II** 371–392 (reigned 375–392), **III** 419–455 (reigned 425–455)

Valera Eamon de — see DE VALERA

Va·le·ra y Al·ca·lá Ga·lia·no \və-ˈler-ə-ē-ˌal-kə-ˈlä-ˌga-lē-ˈä-(ˌ)nō, -ˌäl-kə-, -ˌgä-\ Juan 1824–1905 Span. writer & statesman

Va·le·ri·an \və-ˈlir-ē-ən\ *died* A.D. 260 *Publius Licinius Valerianus* Rom. emperor (253–260)

Va·lé·ry \va-lā-ˈrē, ˈva-lə-rē\ (Ambroise-) Paul-Toussaint-Jules 1871–1945 Fr. poet & philosopher

Val·le·jo \və-ˈlā-(ˌ)ō, -ˈyä-(ˌ)(h)ō\ Mariano Guadalupe 1808–1890 Am. soldier & pioneer

Van Al·len \van-ˈa-lən\ James Alfred 1914– Am. physicist

Van·brugh \ˈvan-brə, van-ˈbrü\ Sir John 1664–1726 Eng. dramatist & architect

Van Bu·ren \van-ˈbyu̇r-ən, vən-\ Martin 1782–1862 8th president of the U.S. (1837–41)

Van·cou·ver \van-ˈkü-vər\ George 1757–1798 Eng. navigator & explorer

Van·de·grift \ˈvan-də-ˌgrift\ Alexander Archer 1887–1973 Am. marine-corps general

Van·den·berg \ˈvan-dən-ˌbərg\ Arthur Hendrick 1884–1951 Am. journalist & politician

Van·der·bilt \ˈvan-dər-ˌbilt\ Cornelius 1794–1877 Am. industrialist

van der Meer \ˌvän-dər-ˈmer\ Simon 1925– Du. physicist

Van Dine — see Willard Huntington WRIGHT

van Dongen Kees — see DONGEN

Van Do·ren \van-ˈdȯr-ən, -ˈdȯr-\ Carl Clinton 1885–1950 & his brother Mark 1894–1972 Am. writers & editors

Van Dyck or **Van·dyke** \van-ˈdīk, vən-\ Sir Anthony 1599–1641 Flem. painter

Vane \ˈvān\ Sir Henry 1613–1662 *the Younger* Eng. statesman

Vane John R. 1927– Eng. pharmacologist

Van Eyck — see EYCK, VAN

van Gogh Vincent Willem — see GOGH, VAN

Van·ier \ˈvän-yā\ Georges-Philéas 1888–1967 Canad. politician; governor-general (1959–67)

Van Rens·se·laer \ˌvan-ˌren(t)-sə-ˈlir, -ˌren-ˈslir, vən-; -ˈren(t)-s(ə-)lər\ Stephen 1764–1839 Am. general & politician

van't Hoff \vänt-ˈhȯf, vant-\ Jacobus Hen·dri·cus \hen-ˈdrē-kəs\ 1852–1911 Du. physical chemist

Van Vleck \van-ˈvlek\ John Hasbrouck 1899–1980 Am. physicist

Vanzetti Bartolomeo — see Nicola SACCO

Va·rèse \və-ˈräz, -ˈrez\ Edgard 1883–1965 originally *Edgar Victor Achille Charles Varèse* Am. (Fr.-born) composer

Var·gas \ˈvär-gəs\ Getúlio Dornelles 1883–1954 Braz. lawyer; president of Brazil (1930–45; 1951–54)

Var·mus \ˈvär-məs\ Harold Elliot 1939– Am. microbiologist

Var·ro \ˈvar-(ˌ)ō\ Marcus Terentius 116–27 B.C. Rom. scholar

Va·sa·ri \və-ˈzär-ē\ Giorgio 1511–1574 Ital. artist & art historian

Vasco da Gama — see GAMA

Va·tu·tin \və-ˈtü-tin\ Nikolay Fyodorovich 1900–1944 Soviet general

Vau·ban \vō-ˈbäⁿ\ Sébastien Le Prestre de 1633–1707 Fr. military engineer; marshal of France

Vaughan \ˈvȯn, ˈvän\ Henry 1621?–1695 Brit. poet

Vaughan Sarah Lois 1924–1990 Am. singer

Vaughan Wil·liams \-ˈwil-yəmz\ Ralph 1872–1958 Eng. composer

Veb·len \ˈve-blən\ Thor·stein \ˈthȯr-ˌstīn\ Bunde 1857–1929 Am. sociologist & economist — **Veb·le·ni·an** \ve-ˈblē-nē-ən\ *adjective*

Ve·ga \ˈvā-gə\ Lo·pe \ˈlō-(ˌ)pā\ de 1562–1635 *Lope Félix de Vega Carpio* Span. dramatist

Ve·láz·quez \və-ˈlas-kəs, -ˈläs-, -kwiz, -(ˌ)käs\ Diego Rodríguez de Silva 1599–1660 Span. painter

Ven·dôme \väⁿ(ˌ)-ˈdōm\ Duc de 1654–1712 *Louis-Joseph* Fr. soldier

Ve·ni·zé·los \ˌve-nə-ˈzā-ləs, -ˈze-ləs\ Eleuthérios 1864–1936 Greek statesman

Ver·di \ˈver-dē\ Giuseppe Fortunio Francesco 1813–1901 Ital. composer — **Ver·di·an** \-ən\ *adjective*

Ve·re·ker \ˈver-ə-kər\ John Standish Surtees Prendergast 1886–1946 6th Viscount *Gort* \ˈgȯrt\ Brit. soldier

Ve·re·shcha·gin \ˌver-əsh-ˈchä-gən, ˌver-ə-ˈshä-\ Vasily Vasilyevich 1842–1904 Russ. painter

Vergil — see VIRGIL

Ver·laine \ver-ˈlän, -ˈlen\ Paul 1844–1896 Fr. poet

Ver·meer \vər-ˈmer, -ˈmir\ Jan 1632–1675 also called *Jan van der Meer van Delft* \van-dər-ˈmer-van-ˈdelft, -ˈmir-\ Du. painter

Verne \ˈvərn, ˈvern\ Jules \ˈjülz, ˈzhüēl\ 1828–1905 Fr. writer

Ver·ner \ˈver-nər\ Karl Adolph 1846–1896 Dan. philologist

Ver·ni·er \vern-ˈyā, ˈvər-nē-ər\ Pierre *circa* 1580–1637 Fr. mathematician

Ver·non \ˈvər-nən\ Edward 1684–1757 Eng. admiral

Ve·ro·ne·se \ˌver-ə-ˈnā-sē, -zē\ Paolo 1528–1588 originally *Paolo Caliari* Ital. painter

Ver·ra·za·no or **Ver·raz·za·no** \ˌver-ə-ˈzä-(ˌ)nō, -ət-ˈsä-\ Giovanni da 1485?–?1528 Florentine navigator & explorer

Ver·roc·chio \və-ˈrō-kē-ˌō\ Andrea del 1435–1488 originally *Andrea di Michele Cione* Florentine sculptor & painter

Verulam — see Francis BACON

Ve·rus \ˈvir-əs\ Lucius Aurelius A.D. 130–169 originally *Lucius Ceionius Commodus* Rom. emperor (161–169)

Ver·woerd \fər-ˈvu̇rt, fer-\ Hendrik Frensch 1901–1966 So. African politician; prime minister (1958–66)

Ve·sa·li·us \və-ˈsā-lē-əs, -ˈzā-\ Andreas 1514–1564 Belg. anatomist

Ve·sey \ˈvē-sē\ Denmark *circa* 1767–1822 Am. slave insurrectionist

Ves·pa·sian \ve-ˈspā-zh(ē-)ən\ A.D. 9–79 *Titus Flavius Sabinus Vespasianus* Rom. emperor (69–79)

Ves·puc·ci \ve-ˈspü-chē, -ˈspyü\ Ame·ri·go \ə-ˈmer-i-ˌgō, ˌä-me-ˈrē-(ˌ)gō\ 1454–1512 Latin *Amer·i·cus Ves·pu·cius* \ə-ˈmer-ə-kəs, ˌves-ˈpyü-sh(ē-)əs\ Ital. navigator & explorer

Vick·rey \ˈvi-krē\ William Spencer 1914–1996 Am. (Canad.-born) economist

Vi·co \ˈvē-kō\ Giambattista 1668–1744 Ital. philosopher

Vic·tor Em·man·u·el I \ˈvik-tər-i-ˈman-yə-wəl\ 1759–1824 king of Sardinia (1802–21)

Victor Emmanuel II 1820–1878 king of Sardinia-Piedmont (1849–61) & 1st king of Italy (1861–78)

Victor Emmanuel III 1869–1947 king of Italy (1900–46)

Vic·to·ria \vik-ˈtōr-ē-ə, -ˈtȯr-\ 1819–1901 *Alexandrina Victoria* queen of Great Britain (1837–1901)

Victoria Tomás Luis de *circa* 1548–1611 Span. composer

Vi·da \ˈvē-də\ Marco Girolamo *circa* 1490–1566 Ital. poet

Vi·gée–Le·brun \vē-ˈzhā-lə-ˈbrəⁿ(n), -ˈbrœⁿ\ Marie-Louise-Élisabeth 1755–1842 Fr. painter

Vi·gno·la \vēn-ˈyō-lə\ Giacomo da 1507–1573 *Giacomo Ba·roz·zi* \bä-ˈrót-sē\ Ital. architect

Vi·gny \vēn-ˈyē\ Alfred-Victor de 1797–1863 Fr. author

Vil·la \ˈvē-yə\ Francisco usually called Pan·cho \ˈpän-(ˌ)chō, ˈpan-\ 1878–1923 originally *Doroteo Arango* Mex. bandit & revolutionary

Vil·la-Lo·bos \ˌvē-lə-ˈlō-(ˌ)bōsh, -(ˌ)bōs, -bəs\ Heitor \ˈā-ˌtȯr\ 1887–1959 Braz. composer

Vil·lard \və-ˈlär(d)\ Oswald Garrison 1872–1949 Am. journalist

Vil·lars \vi-ˈlär\ Claude-Louis-Hector 1653–1734 Duc de *Villars* Fr. soldier; marshal of France

Ville·neuve \ˌvēl-ˈnə(r)v, -ˈnœv\ Pierre-Charles-Jean-Baptiste-Silvestre de 1763–1806 Fr. admiral

Vil·liers \ˈvil-yərz, ˈvi-lərz\ George 1592–1628 1st Duke of *Buck·ing·ham* \ˈbə-kiŋ-əm, *United States also* -kiŋ-ˌham\ Eng. courtier & politician

Villiers George 1628–1687 2d Duke of *Buckingham, son of preceding* Eng. courtier & dramatist

Vil·lon \vē-ˈyōⁿ *also* -ˈlōⁿ\ François 1431–after 1463 originally *François de Montcorbier* or *Des Loges* Fr. poet

Vil·lon \vē-ˈlōⁿ, -ˈyōⁿ\ Jacques 1875–1963 originally *Gaston Duchamp; brother of Marcel Duchamp* Fr. painter

Vin·cent de Paul \ˈvin(t)-sənt-də-ˈpȯl\ Saint 1581–1660 Fr. religious

Vinci, da Leonardo — see LEONARDO DA VINCI

Vi·no·gra·doff \ˌvi-nə-ˈgra-ˌdȯf\ Sir Paul Gavrilovitch 1854–1925 Brit. (Russ.-born) jurist & historian

Vin·son \ˈvin(t)-sən\ Frederick Moore 1890–1953 Am. jurist; chief justice U.S. Supreme Court (1946–53)

Viol·let–le–Duc \ˌvē-ə-ˈlä-lə-ˈdük, -ˈdyük; vyȯ-le-lə-ˈdük\ Eugène-Emmanuel 1814–1879 Fr. architect

Vir·chow \ˈfir-(ˌ)kō, ˈvir-\ Rudolf 1821–1902 Ger. pathologist

Vir·gil \ˈvər-jəl\ 70–19 B.C. *Publius Vergilius Maro* Rom. poet — **Vir·gil·ian** *also* **Ver·gil·ian** \(ˌ)vər-ˈji-lē-ən\ *adjective*

Vir·ta·nen \ˈvir-tə-ˌnen\ Art·tu·ri \ˈär-tə-rē\ Ilmari 1895–1973 Finn. biochemist

Vi·tru·vi·us \və-ˈtrü-vē-əs\ *flourished* 1st century B.C. *Marcus Vitruvius Pollio* Rom. architect & engineer

Vi·val·di \vi-ˈväl-dē, -ˈvȯl-\ Antonio Lucio 1678–1741 Ital. composer

Vla·di·mir I \ˈvla-də-ˌmir, vlə-ˈdē-ˌmir\ Saint *circa* 956–1015 grand prince of Kiev (980–1015)

Vla·minck \vlə-ˈmaŋk\ Maurice de 1876–1958 Fr. painter

Vo·gler \ˈfō-glər\ Georg Joseph 1749–1814 Abt \äpt, apt\ or Abbé *Vogler* Ger. composer & writer

Vol·stead \ˈväl-ˌsted, ˈvȯl-, ˈvōl-, -stəd\ Andrew John 1860–1947 Am. legislator

Vol·ta \ˈvōl-tə, ˈväl-, ˈvȯl-\ Conte Alessandro Giuseppe Antonio Anastasio 1745–1827 Ital. physicist

Vol·taire \vōl-ˈtar, väl-, vȯl-, -ˈter\ 1694–1778 originally *François-Marie Arouet* Fr. writer — **Vol·tair·ean** or **Vol·tair·ian** \-ˈtar-ē-ən, -ˈter-\ *adjective*

Von Braun Wernher — see BRAUN

Von Eu·ler \fȯn-ˈȯi-lər\ Ulf Svante 1905–1983 Swed. physiologist

Von·ne·gut \ˈvä-ni-gət\ Kurt 1922– Am. writer

\ə\ abut \ᵊ\ kitten \ər\ further \a\ ash \ā\ ace
\ä\ mop, mar \au̇\ out \ch\ chin \e\ bet \ē\ easy
\g\ go \i\ hit \ī\ ice \j\ job \ŋ\ sing \ō\ go
\ȯ\ law \ȯi\ boy \th\ thin \t͟h\ the \ü\ loot \u̇\ foot
\y\ yet \zh\ vision *see also* Guide to Pronunciation

Vo·ro·shi·lov \,vór-ə-'shē-,lóf, ,vär-, -,lóv\ Kliment Yefremovich 1881–1969 Soviet marshal; chairman of the Presidium (1953–60)

Vor·ster \'fór-stər\ Balthazar Johannes 1915–1983 prime minister of Republic of So. Africa (1966–78)

Voz·ne·sen·sky \,väz-nə-'sen(t)-skē\ Andrey 1933– Soviet (Russ.-born) poet

Vries, de \də-'vrēs\ Hugo Marie 1848–1935 Du. botanist & geneticist

Vuil·lard \vwē-'yär\ (Jean-)Édouard 1868–1940 Fr. painter

Vy·shin·sky \və-'shin(t)-skē\ Andrey Yanuaryevich 1883–1954 Soviet lawyer, politician, & diplomat

Waals, van der \'van-dər-,wólz\ Johannes Diderik 1837–1923 Du. physicist

Wace \'wās, 'wäs\ circa 1100–after 1174 Anglo-Norman poet

Wag·ner \'väg-nər\ (Wilhelm) Ri·chard \'ri-,kärt, -,kärt\ 1813–1883 Ger. composer

Wagner von Jau·regg or **Wagner–Jau·regg** \-'yaú-,rek\ Julius 1857–1940 Austrian neurologist & psychiatrist

Wain·wright \'wān-,rīt\ Jonathan Mayhew 1883–1953 Am. general

Wainwright Richard father 1817–1862 & his son 1849–1926 Am. naval officers

Waite \'wāt\ Morrison Remick 1816–1888 Am. jurist; chief justice U.S. Supreme Court (1874–88)

Waks·man \'wäks-mən, 'waks-\ Sel·man \'sel-mən\ Abraham 1888–1973 Am. (Ukrainian-born) microbiologist

Wal·cott \'wäl-(,)kät\ Derek Alton 1930– West Indian poet & playwright

Wald \'wóld\ George 1906–1997 Am. biologist

Wald Lillian D. 1867–1940 Am. social worker

Waldemar — see VALDEMAR

Wal·der·see \'väl-dər-,zā, 'wól-\ Alfred von 1832–1904 Ger. soldier

Wald·heim \'vält-,hīm\ Kurt 1918– Austrian U.N. official; secretary-general (1972–82); president of Austria (1986–92)

Wal·do \'wól-(,)dō, 'wäl-\ or **Val·des** \'val-(,)dās, 'väl-\ Peter died before 1218 Fr. religious leader

Wa·łe·sa \vä-'len(t)-sə, wä-; vä-'weⁿ-sə\ Lech \'lek, 'lek\ 1943– Pol. politician; president of Poland (1990–95)

Walk·er \'wó-kər\ Alice Malsenior 1944– Am. writer

Walker Francis Am·a·sa \'a-mə-sə\ 1840–1897 Am. economist

Walker William 1824–1860 Am. filibuster

Wal·lace \'wä-ləs\ Alfred Russel 1823–1913 Eng. naturalist

Wallace George Corley 1919– Am. politician

Wallace Henry Agard \'ā-,gärd\ 1888–1965 Am. agriculturist, editor, & politician; vice president of the U.S. (1941–45)

Wallace Lewis 1827–1905 Lew Am. lawyer, general, & novelist

Wallace Sir William circa 1270–1305 Scot. patriot

Wal·lach \'wä-läk, 'väl-\ Otto 1847–1931 Ger. chemist

Wal·len·berg \'wä-lən-,bərg, Swedish -,ber-ē\ Raoul 1912–1947? Swed. diplomat & hero of the Holocaust

Wal·len·stein \'vä-lən-,shtīn, 'wä-lən-,stīn\ Albrecht Eusebius Wenzel von 1583–1634 Duke of Friedland and Mecklenburg; Prince of Sagan Austrian general

Wal·ler \'wä-lər\ Edmund 1606–1687 Eng. poet

Waller Thomas Wright 1904–1943 Fats Am. pianist & composer

Wal·pole \'wól-,pōl, 'wäl-\ Horace 1717–1797 originally Horatio 4th Earl of Or·ford \'ór-fərd\ Eng. author

Walpole Sir Hugh Seymour 1884–1941 Eng. novelist

Walpole Sir Robert 1676–1745 1st Earl of Orford; father of Horace Eng. statesman — **Wal·pol·ian** \wól-'pō-lē-ən, wäl-\ adjective

Wal·ter \'väl-tər, 'wól-\ Bruno 1876–1962 originally Bruno Schle·sing·er \'shlä-ziŋ-ər\ Am. (Ger.-born) conductor

Wal·ther von der Vo·gel·wei·de \'väl-tər-,fón-dər-'fō-gəl-,vī-də\ circa 1170–circa 1230 Ger. minnesinger & poet

Wal·ton \'wól-tᵊn\ Ernest Thomas Sinton 1903–1995 Irish physicist

Walton Izaak \'ī-zik, -zək\ 1593–1683 Eng. writer

Walton Sir William Turner 1902–1983 Eng. composer

Wan·a·ma·ker \'wä-nə-,mā-kər\ John 1838–1922 Am. merchant

Wang Ching–wei \'wäŋ-'jiŋ-'wā\ 1883–1944 Chin. politician

War·beck \'wór-,bek\ Perkin 1474–1499 Flem. imposter & pretender to the English throne

War·burg \'wór-,bərg, 'vär-,búrk\ Otto Heinrich 1883–1970 Ger. biochemist

Ward \'wórd\ Aaron Montgomery 1843–1913 Am. merchant

Ward Ar·te·mas \'är-tə-məs\ 1727–1800 Am. general in Revolution

Ward Artemus — see Charles Farrar BROWNE

Ward Barbara 1914–1981 Baroness Jackson of Lodsworth Eng. economist

Ward Sir Joseph George 1856–1930 N.Z. statesman

Ward Mary Augusta 1851–1920 Mrs. Humphry Ward née Arnold Eng. novelist

War·hol \'wór-,hól, -,hōl\ Andy 1928?–1987 originally Andrew Warhola Am. artist & filmmaker — **War·hol·ian** \(,)wór-'hó-lē-ən, -'hō-\ adjective

War·ner \'wór-nər\ Charles Dudley 1829–1900 Am. editor & essayist

War·ren \'wór-ən, 'wär-\ Earl 1891–1974 Am. jurist; chief justice U.S. Supreme Court (1953–69)

Warren Gou·ver·neur \,gə-və(r)-'nir\ Kemble 1830–1882 Am. general

Warren Joseph 1741–1775 Am. physician & general in Revolution

Warren Robert Penn 1905–1989 Am. author & educator; poet laureate (1986–87)

War·ton \'wór-tᵊn\ Thomas 1728–1790 Eng. literary historian & critic; poet laureate (1785–90)

War·wick \'wär-ik, United States also 'wór-ik, 'wór-(,)wik\ Earl of 1428–1471 Richard Nev·ille \'ne-vəl\; the Kingmaker Eng. soldier & statesman

Wash·ing·ton \'wó-shiŋ-tən, 'wä-, chiefly Midland also 'wór- or 'wär-\ Book·er \'bú-kər\ Tal·ia·ferro \'tä-lə-vər\ 1856–1915 Am. educator

Washington George 1732–1799 Am. general; 1st president of the U.S. (1789–97) — **Wash·ing·to·nian** \,wó-shiŋ-'tō-nē-ən, ,wä-, ,wór-, ,wär-, -nyən\ adjective

Was·mo·sy \wäs-'mō-sē\ Juan Carlos 1939– president of Paraguay (1993–)

Was·ser·mann \'wä-sər-mən, 'vä-\ August von 1866–1925 Ger. bacteriologist

Was·ser·stein \'wä-sər-,stīn\ Wendy 1950– Am. dramatist

Wa·ters \'wó-tərz, 'wä-\ Ethel 1896–1977 Am. actress & singer

Wat·son \'wät-sən\ James Dewey 1928– Am. geneticist

Watson John 1850–1907 pseudonym Ian Maclar·en \mə-'klar-ən\ Scot. clergyman & author

Watson John Broadus 1878–1958 Am. psychologist

Watson Sir (John) William 1858–1935 Eng. poet

Watson–Watt \-'wät\ Sir Robert Alexander 1892–1973 Scot. physicist

Watt \'wät\ James 1736–1819 Scot. inventor

Wat·teau \wä-'tō, vä-\ (Jean-) Antoine 1684–1721 Fr. painter

Wat·ter·son \'wä-tər-sən, 'wó-\ Henry 1840–1921 Am. journalist & politician

Watts \'wäts\ George Frederic 1817–1904 Eng. painter & sculptor

Watts Isaac 1674–1748 Eng. theologian & hymn writer

Watts–Dun·ton \-'dən-tᵊn\ Walter Theodore 1832–1914 Eng. critic & poet

Waugh \'wó\ Evelyn Arthur St. John 1903–1966 Eng. writer

Wa·vell \'wä-vəl\ 1st Earl 1883–1950 Archibald Percival Wavell Brit. field marshal; viceroy of India (1943–47)

Wayne \'wān\ Anthony 1745–1796 Mad Anthony Am. general in Revolution

Webb \'web\ Beatrice 1858–1943 née Potter; wife of S.J. Eng. socialist

Webb Sidney James 1859–1947 1st Baron Passfield Eng. socialist

We·ber \'vā-bər\ Ernst Heinrich 1795–1878 Ger. physiologist

Weber Carl Maria von 1786–1826 Ger. composer & conductor

Weber Max 1864–1920 Ger. sociologist & economist — **We·be·ri·an** \vā-'bir-ē-ən\ adjective

Web·er \'we-bər\ Max 1881–1961 Am. (Russ.-born) painter

We·bern \'vā-bərn\ Anton von 1883–1945 Austrian composer

Web·ster \'web-stər\ Daniel 1782–1852 Am. statesman & orator

Webster John circa 1580–circa 1625 Eng. dramatist

Webster Noah 1758–1843 Am. lexicographer & author

Wedg·wood \'wej-,wúd\ Josiah 1730–1795 Eng. potter

Weems \'wēmz\ Mason Locke 1759–1825 Parson Weems Am. clergyman & biographer

We·ge·ner \'vā-gə-nər\ Alfred Lothar 1880–1930 Ger. geophysicist & meteorologist

Weill \'wī(ə)l, 'vī(ə)l\ Kurt \'kúrt\ 1900–1950 Am. (Ger.-born) composer

Wein·berg \'wīn-,bərg\ Steven 1933– Am. physicist

Wein·ber·ger \'wīn-,bər-gər\ Caspar Willard 1917– U.S. secretary of defense (1981–87)

Weir \'wir\ Robert Walter 1803–1889 Am. painter

Weis·mann \'vīs-,män, 'wīs-mən\ August Friedrich Leopold 1834–1914 Ger. biologist

Weiz·mann \'vīts-mən, 'wīts-\ Chaim \'kīm, 'hīm\ Azriel 1874–1952 Israeli (Russ.-born) chemist; 1st president of Israel (1949–52)

Welch \'welch, 'welsh\ William Henry 1850–1934 Am. pathologist

Wel·ler \'we-lər\ Thomas Huckle 1915– Am. virologist

Welles \'welz\ (George) Or·son \'ór-sᵊn\ 1915–1985 Am. film & theater director, writer, producer, & actor

Welles Gideon 1802–1878 Am. politician & writer

Welles Sumner 1892–1961 Am. diplomat

Welles·ley \'welz-lē\ 1st Marquis of 1760–1842 Richard Colley Wellesley Brit. statesman; governor-general of India (1797–1805)

Wel·ling·ton \'we-liŋ-tən\ 1st Duke of 1769–1852 Arthur Wellesley; the Iron Duke Brit. general & statesman

Wells \'welz\ Herbert George 1866–1946 Eng. novelist & historian — **Wells·ian** \'wel-zē-ən\ adjective

Wel·ty \'wel-tē\ Eudora 1909– Am. writer

Wen·ces·las \'wen(t)-sə-,slós, -sləs\ German **Wen·zel** \'ven(t)-səl\ 1361–1419 king of Germany & Holy Roman emperor (1378–1400) & (as Wenceslas IV) king of Bohemia (1378–1419)

Wen·dell \'wen-dᵊl\ Barrett 1855–1921 Am. scholar

Went·worth \'went-(,)wərth\ William Charles 1793–1872 Austral. statesman

Wer·fel \'ver-fəl\ Franz 1890–1945 Ger. author

Wer·ner \'ver-nər\ Alfred 1866–1919 Swiss chemist

Wes·ley \'wes-lē, 'wez-\ Charles 1707–1788 brother of John Eng. Methodist preacher & hymn writer

Wesley John 1703–1791 Eng. evangelist & founder of Methodism

West \'west\ Benjamin 1738–1820 Am. painter

West Nathanael 1903–1940 originally Nathan Wallenstein Weinstein Am. novelist

West Dame Rebecca 1892–1983 pseudonym of Cicily Isabel Andrews née Fairfield Eng. critic & novelist

West Thomas — see DE LA WARR

Wes·ter·marck \'wes-tər-,märk\ Edward Alexander 1862–1939 Finn. philosopher & anthropologist

Wes·ting·house \'wes-tiŋ-,haús\ George 1846–1914 Am. inventor

Wet, de \də-'vet\ Christiaan Rudolf 1854–1922 Boer soldier & politician

Wey·den \'vī-dᵊn, 'vā-\ Rogier van der 1399?–1464 Flem. painter

Wey·gand \vā-gäⁿ\ Maxime 1867–1965 Fr. general

Whar·ton \'hwór-tᵊn, 'wór-\ Edith Newbold 1862–1937 née Jones Am. novelist

Whate·ly \'hwāt-lē, 'wāt-\ Richard 1787–1863 Eng. theologian & logician

Wheat·ley \'hwēt-lē, 'wēt-\ Phillis 1753?–1784 Am. (African-born) poet

Wheat·stone \'hwēt-,stōn, 'wēt-, *chiefly British* -stən\ Sir Charles 1802–1875 Eng. physicist & inventor

Whee·ler \'hwē-lər, 'wē-\ Joseph 1836–1906 Am. general

Wheeler William Almon 1819–1887 Am. politician; vice president of the U.S. (1877–81)

Whee·lock \'hwē-,läk, 'wē-\ Eleazar 1711–1779 Am. clergyman & educator

Whip·ple \'hwi-pəl, 'wi-\ George Hoyt 1878–1976 Am. pathologist

Whis·tler \'hwis-lər, 'wis-\ James Abbott McNeill 1834–1903 Am. painter & etcher — **Whis·tler·ian** \hwis-'lir-ē-ən, wis-\ *adjective*

White \'hwīt\ Andrew Dickson 1832–1918 Am. educator & diplomat

White Byron Raymond 1917– Am. jurist & politician

White Edward Douglass 1845–1921 Am. jurist; chief justice U.S. Supreme Court (1910–21)

White Elwyn Brooks 1899–1985 Am. journalist & writer

White Gilbert 1720–1793 Eng. clergyman & naturalist

White Patrick Victor Martindale 1912–1990 Austral. writer

White Stanford 1853–1906 Am. architect

White Stewart Edward 1873–1946 Am. writer

White Theodore Harold 1915–1986 Am. writer

White William Allen 1868–1944 Am. journalist & writer

White·field \'hwit-,fēld, 'hwīt-, 'wit-, 'wīt-\ George 1714–1770 Eng. Methodist revivalist

White·head \'hwīt-,hed, 'wīt-\ Alfred North 1861–1947 Eng. mathematician & philosopher

Whitehead William 1715–1785 Eng. dramatist; poet laureate (1757–85)

Whit·man \'hwit-mən, 'wit-\ Marcus 1802–1847 & his wife Narcissa 1808–1847 née *Prentiss* Am. missionaries & pioneers

Whitman Walt \'wôlt\ 1819–1892 originally *Walter* Am. poet — **Whit·man·esque** \,hwit-mə-'nesk, ,wit-\ *or* **Whit·man·ian** \hwit-'mā-nē-ən, wit-\ *adjective*

Whit·ney \'hwit-nē, 'wit-\ Eli 1765–1825 Am. inventor

Whitney Josiah Dwight 1819–1896 Am. geologist

Whitney William Dwight 1827–1894 *brother of J.D.* Am. philologist

Whit·ta·ker \'hwi-ti-kər, 'wit-\ Charles Evans 1901–1973 Am. jurist

Whit·ti·er \'hwi-tē-ər, 'wit-\ John Greenleaf 1807–1892 Am. poet

Wic·lif *or* **Wick·liffe** *variant of* WYCLIFFE

Wi·dor \vē-'dôr\ Charles-Marie 1844–1937 Fr. organist & composer

Wie·land \'vē-,länt\ Christoph Martin 1733–1813 Ger. author

Wieland Heinrich 1877–1957 Ger. chemist

Wien \'vēn\ Wilhelm 1864–1928 Ger. physicist

Wie·ner \'wē-nər\ Norbert 1894–1964 Am. mathematician

Wie·schaus \'wē-,shaus\ Eric F. 1947– Am. biologist

Wie·sel \vē-'zel, wē-\ El·ie \'e-lē\ 1928– Am. (Rom.-born) writer

Wie·sel \vē-'səl\ Torsten N. 1924– Swed. neurobiologist

Wig·gin \'wi-gən\ Kate Douglas 1856–1923 Am. writer & educator

Wig·ner \'wig-nər\ Eugene Paul 1902–1995 Am. (Hung.-born) physicist

Wil·ber·force \'wil-bər-,fôrs, -,fôrs\ William 1759–1833 Eng. philanthropist & abolitionist

Wil·bur \'wil-bər\ Richard Purdy 1921– Am. poet & translator; poet laureate (1987–88)

Wilde \'wī(ə)ld\ Oscar Fingal O'Flahertie Wills 1854–1900 Irish writer — **Wil·de·an** \'wīl-dē-ən\ *adjective*

Wil·der \'wīl-dər\ Thornton Niven 1897–1975 Am. author

Wi·ley \'wī-lē\ Harvey Washington 1844–1930 Am. chemist & reformer

Wil·hel·mi·na \,wil-(,)hel-'mē-nə, ,wi-lə-'mē-\ 1880–1962 queen of the Netherlands (1890–1948)

Wilkes \'wilks\ Charles 1798–1877 Am. naval officer & explorer

Wilkes John 1725–1797 Eng. politician

Wil·kins \'wil-kənz\ Sir George Hubert 1888–1958 Austral. explorer

Wilkins Mary Eleanor — see Mary E. FREEMAN

Wilkins Maurice Hugh Frederick 1916– Brit. biophysicist

Wilkins Roy 1901–1981 Am. civil rights leader

Wil·kin·son \'wil-kən-sən\ Ellen Cicely 1891–1947 Eng. politician

Wilkinson Sir Geoffrey 1921–1996 Brit. chemist

Wilkinson James 1757–1825 Am. general & adventurer

Wil·lard \'wi-lərd\ Emma 1787–1870 née *Hart* Am. educator

Willard Frances Elizabeth Caroline 1839–1898 Am. educator & reformer

Will·cocks \'wil-,käks\ Sir William 1852–1932 Brit. engineer

Wil·liam \'wil-yəm\ name of 4 kings of England: **I** (*the Conqueror*) circa 1028–1087 (reigned 1066–87); **II** (*Ru·fus* \'rü-fəs\) circa 1056–1100 (reigned 1087–1100); **III** 1650–1702 (reigned 1689–1702—see MARY); **IV** 1765–1837 (reigned 1830–37)

William I 1533–1584 *the Silent* prince of Orange & founder of the Du. Republic

William I 1797–1888 *Wilhelm Friedrich Ludwig* king of Prussia (1861–88) Ger. emperor (1871–88)

William II 1859–1941 *Friedrich Wilhelm Viktor Albert* Ger. emperor & king of Prussia (1888–1918)

William 1882–1951 *Friedrich Wilhelm Victor August Ernst* crown prince of Germany (1888–1918)

William of Malmes·bury \'mämz-,ber-ē, 'mälmz-, -b(ə-)rē\ circa 1090–circa 1143 Eng. historian

Wil·liams \'wil-yəmz\ Elizabeth 1943– *Betty* Irish peace worker

Williams Ralph Vaughan — see VAUGHAN WILLIAMS

Williams Roger 1603?–1683 Am. (Eng.-born) clergyman & founder of Rhode Island colony

Williams Tennessee 1911–1983 originally *Thomas Lanier Williams* Am. dramatist

Williams William Carlos 1883–1963 Am. writer

Will·kie \'wil-kē\ Wendell Lewis 1892–1944 Am. politician

Wil·loch \'vi-lək\ Kå·re \'kôr-ə\ Isaachsen 1928– prime minister of Norway (1981–86)

Will·stät·ter \'vil-,shte-tər, 'wil-,ste-\ Richard 1872–1942 Ger. chemist

Wil·son \'wil-sən\ Charles Thomson Rees 1869–1959 Scot. physicist

Wilson Edmund 1895–1972 Am. writer

Wilson Sir (James) Harold 1916–1995 Brit. prime minister (1964–70; 1974–76)

Wilson Henry 1812–1875 originally *Jeremiah Jones Colbath* Am. politician; vice president of the U.S. (1873–75)

Wilson John 1785–1854 pseudonym *Christopher North* Scot. author

Wilson Kenneth G. 1936– Am. physicist

Wilson Robert Woodrow 1936– Am. physicist

Wilson (Thomas) Wood·row \'wu-,drō\ 1856–1924 28th president of the U.S. (1913–21) — **Wil·so·ni·an** \wil-'sō-nē-ən\ *adjective*

Winck·el·mann \'viŋ-kəl-,män, 'wiŋ-kəl-mən\ Johann Joachim 1717–1768 Ger. archaeologist & art historian

Win·daus \'vin-,daus\ Adolf Otto Reinhold 1876–1959 Ger. chemist

Win·disch-grätz \,vin-dish-'grets\ Alfred Candidus Ferdinand 1787–1862 Fürst *zu Windischgrätz* Austrian field marshal

Windsor Duke of — see EDWARD VIII

Win·gate \'win-,gāt, -gət\ Orde \'ôrd\ Charles 1903–1944 Brit. general

Wingate Sir (Francis) Reginald 1861–1953 Brit. general

Wins·low \'winz-,lō\ Edward 1595–1655 governor of Plymouth colony

Win·sor \'win-zər\ Justin 1831–1897 Am. librarian & historian

Win·throp \'win(t)-thrəp\ John 1588–1649 1st governor of Massachusetts Bay colony

Winthrop John 1606–1676 *son of preceding* governor of Connecticut colony

Winthrop John 1638–1707 *son of preceding* governor of Connecticut colony

Wise \'wīz\ Stephen Samuel 1874–1949 Am. (Hung.-born) rabbi

Wise Thomas James 1859–1937 Eng. bibliophile & forger

Wise·man \'wīz-mən\ Nicholas Patrick Stephen 1802–1865 Eng. cardinal & author

Wiss·ler \'wis-lər\ Clark 1870–1947 Am. anthropologist

Wis·ter \'wis-tər\ Owen 1860–1938 Am. novelist

With·er \'wi-thər\ George 1588–1667 Eng. poet & pamphleteer

Witt, de \də-'vit\ Johan 1625–1672 Du. statesman

Wit·te \'vi-tə\ Sergey Yulyevich 1849–1915 Russ. statesman

Wit·te, de \də-'vi-tə\ Emanuel 1617–1692 Du. painter

Wit·te·kind \'vi-tə-,kint\ *or* **Wi·du·kind** \'vē-də-\ died circa 807 Saxon warrior

Witt·gen·stein \'vit-gən-,shtīn, -,stīn\ Ludwig Josef Johan 1889–1951 Brit. (Austrian-born) philosopher — **Witt·gen·stein·ian** \,vit-gən-'shtī-nē-ən, -'stī-\ *adjective*

Wit·tig \'vi-tik\ Georg 1897–1987 Ger. chemist

Wode·house \'wud-,haus\ Sir Pel·ham \'pe-ləm\ Grenville 1881–1975 Am. (Eng.-born) writer

Wof·fing·ton \'wä-fiŋ-tən\ Margaret circa 1714–1760 *Peg* Irish actress

Wol·cott \'wul-kət\ Oliver 1726–1797 *son of Roger* Am. politician

Wolcott Oliver 1760–1833 *son of preceding* Am. politician

Wolcott Roger 1679–1767 Am. colonial administrator

Wolf \'vôlf\ Friedrich August 1759–1824 Ger. philologist

Wolf Hugo Philipp Jakob 1860–1903 Austrian composer

Wolfe \'wulf\ Charles 1791–1823 Irish poet

Wolfe James 1727–1759 Brit. general

Wolfe Thomas Clayton 1900–1938 Am. novelist

Wolff \'vôlf\ Caspar Friedrich 1734–1794 Ger. anatomist

Wolff *or* **Wolf** \vôlf\ Christian 1679–1754 Freiherr *von Wolff* Ger. philosopher & mathematician

Wol·fram von Esch·en·bach \'wul-främ-vän-'e-shən-,bäk, 'vôl-främ-, -,bäk\ circa 1170–circa 1220 Ger. poet & minnesinger

Wol·las·ton \'wu-lə-stən\ William Hyde 1766–1828 Eng. chemist & physicist

Woll·stone·craft \'wul-stən-,kraft\ Mary 1759–1797 *wife of William Godwin & mother of M.W. Shelley* Eng. feminist & writer

Wolse·ley \'wulz-lē\ 1st Viscount 1833–1913 *Garnet Joseph Wolseley* Brit. field marshal

Wol·sey \'wul-zē\ Thomas circa 1475–1530 Eng. cardinal & statesman

Wood \'wud\ Grant 1892–1942 Am. painter

Wood Leonard 1860–1927 Am. physician & general

Wood·ward \'wud-wərd\ Robert Burns 1917–1979 Am. chemist

Woolf \'wulf\ (Adeline) Virginia 1882–1941 née *Stephen* Eng. author

Wooll·cott \'wul-kət\ Alexander 1887–1943 Am. writer

Wool·ley \'wu-lē\ Sir Charles Leonard 1880–1960 Eng. archaeologist

Wool·worth \'wul-(,)wərth\ Frank Winfield 1852–1919 Am. merchant

Worces·ter \'wus-tər\ Joseph Emerson 1784–1865 Am. lexicographer

Worde \'wôrd\ Wynkyn de *died* 1534? Eng. (Alsatian-born) printer

Words·worth \'wərdz-(,)wərth\ William 1770–1850 Eng. poet; poet laureate (1843–50) — **Words·worth·ian** \,wərdz-'wər-thē-ən, -thē-\ *adjective*

Wot·ton \'wu-t°n, 'wä-\ Sir Henry 1568–1639 Eng. diplomat & poet

\ə\ abut	\°\ kitten	\ər\ **further**	\a\ **ash**	\ā\ **ace**	
\ä\ **mop, mar**		\au̇\ **out**	\ch\ **chin**	\e\ **bet**	\ē\ **easy**
\g\ **go**	\i\ **hit**	\ī\ **ice**	\j\ **job**	\ŋ\ **sing**	\ō\ **go**
\ȯ\ **law**	\ȯi\ **boy**	\th\ **thin**	\t̲h̲\ **the**	\ü\ **loot**	\u̇\ **foot**
\y\ **yet**	\zh\ **vision**		*see also* Guide to Pronunciation		

Wran·gel \'raŋ-gəl\ Baron Pyotr Nikolayevich 1878–1928 Russ. general

Wren \'ren\ Sir Christopher 1632–1723 Eng. architect

Wright \'rīt\ Frank Lloyd 1867–1959 Am. architect

Wright Joseph 1734–1797 *Wright of Derby* Eng. painter

Wright Louis Booker 1899–1984 Am. educator & librarian

Wright Or·ville \'ȯr-vəl\ 1871–1948 & his brother Wilbur 1867–1912 Am. pioneers in aviation

Wright Richard 1908–1960 Am. author

Wright Willard Huntington 1888–1939 pseudonym *S. S. Van Dine* \van-'dīn, vən-\ Am. writer

Wundt \'vunt\ Wilhelm 1832–1920 Ger. physiologist & psychologist

Wu–ti — see HAN WU TI

Wy·att *or* **Wy·at** \'wī-ət\ Sir Thomas 1503–1543 Eng. poet & diplomat

Wych·er·ley \'wi-chər-lē\ William 1640–1716 Eng. dramatist

Wyc·liffe \'wi-,klif, -kləf\ John *circa* 1330–1384 Eng. religious reformer & theologian — **Wyc·liff·ian** \wi-'kli-fē-ən\ *adjective*

Wy·eth \'wī-əth\ Andrew Newell 1917– Am. painter

Wyeth Newell Convers 1882–1945 *father of A. N.* Am. painter

Wyld \'wī(ə)ld\ Henry Cecil Kennedy 1870–1945 Eng. lexicographer

Wy·lie \'wī-lē\ Elinor Morton 1885–1928 *Mrs. William Rose Benét, née Hoyt* Am. poet & novelist

Wylie Philip Gordon 1902–1971 Am. writer

Wynd·ham \'win-dəm\ George 1863–1913 Eng. politician & writer

Xan·thip·pe \zan-'thi-pē, -'ti-\ 5th century B.C. *wife of Socrates*

Xa·vi·er \'zāv-yər, 'zā-vē-ər, ig-'zā-\ Saint Francis 1506–1552 Spanish *Francisco Ja·vier* \hä-'vyer\ Span. Jesuit missionary

Xe·noc·ra·tes \zi-'nä-krə-,tēz\ 396–314 B.C. Greek philosopher

Xe·noph·a·nes \zi-'nä-fə-,nēz\ *circa* 560–*circa* 478 B.C. Greek philosopher

Xen·o·phon \'ze-nə-fən\ *circa* 431–*circa* 352 B.C. Greek historian

Xer·xes I \'zərk-,sēz\ *circa* 519–465 B.C. *the Great* king of Persia (486–465)

Yale \'yā(ə)l\ Elihu 1649–1721 Eng. (Am.-born) colonial administrator

Yal·ow \'ya-(,)lō\ Rosalyn Sussman 1921– Am. med. physicist

Ya·ma·ga·ta \,yä-mə-'gä-tə\ Prince Aritomo 1838–1922 Jp. general & statesman

Ya·ma·mo·to \,yä-mə-'mō-(,)tō\ Isoroku 1884–1943 Jp. admiral

Ya·ma·shi·ta \yä-'mä-shi-,tä\ Tomoyuki 1885–1946 Jp. general

Yang Chen Ning \'yäŋ-'jən-'niŋ\ 1922– Chin. physicist

Yeats \'yāts\ William Butler 1865–1939 Irish poet & dramatist — **Yeats·ian** \'yāt-sē-ən\ *adjective*

Yelt·sin \'yelt-sən, 'yel-sin\ Boris Nikolayevich 1931– president of Russian Federation (1990–)

Yen Hsi–shan \'yen-'shē-'shän\ 1883–1960 Chin. general

Yer·kes \'yər-kēz\ Charles Ty·son \'tī-sᵊn\ 1837–1905 Am. financier

Yev·tu·shen·ko \,yef-tə-'sheŋ-(,)kō\ Yevgeny Aleksandrovich 1933– Soviet (Russ.-born) writer

Yo·nai \'yō-,nī\ Mitsumasa 1880–1948 Jp. admiral & statesman

York \'yȯrk\ Alvin Cullum 1887–1964 Am. soldier

Yo·shi·hi·to \,yō-shi-'hē-(,)tō\ 1879–1926 emperor of Japan (1912–26)

You·mans \'yü-mənz\ Vincent 1898–1946 Am. composer

Young \'yəŋ\ Andrew Jackson, Jr. 1932– U.S. ambassador to U.N. (1977–79)

Young Brig·ham \'bri-gəm\ 1801–1877 Am. Mormon leader

Young Edward 1683–1765 Eng. poet

Young Francis Brett 1884–1954 Eng. novelist

Young Owen D. 1874–1962 Am. lawyer

Young Whitney Moore 1921–1971 Am. civil rights leader

Young·hus·band \'yəŋ-,həz-bənd\ Sir Francis Edward 1863–1942 Brit. explorer & author

Your·ce·nar \,yür-sə-'när\ Marguerite 1903–1987 original surname *de Crayencour* Fr. author

Yp·si·lan·tis \,ip-sə-'lan-tē\ Alexandros 1792–1828 & his brother Demetrios 1793–1832 Greek revolutionaries

Yüan Shih–k'ai \yü-'än-'shir-'kī, -'shē\ 1859–1916 Chin. soldier & statesman; president of China (1913–16)

Yu·ka·wa \yü-'kä-wə\ Hideki 1907–1981 Jp. physicist

Yung–lo \'yuŋ-'lō\ 1360–1424 originally *Chu Ti;* often called *Ch'eng Tsu* Chin. emperor (1402–24)

Zagh·lūl \zag-'lül\ Sa'd \'säd\ 1857–1927 *Sa'd Zaghlūl Pasha ibn Ibrāhīm* Egypt. statesman

Za·ha·roff \zə-'här-əf, -,ȯf\ Sir Basil 1849–1936 originally *Basileios Zacharias* Fr. (Russ.-born) banker & armament contractor

Za·i·mis \zä-'ē-məs, -mēs\ Alexandros 1855–1936 Greek statesman

Zan·gwill \'zaŋ-,gwil, -,wil\ Israel 1864–1926 Eng. dramatist & novelist

Ze·dil·lo Pon·ce de Le·ón \sā-'thē-(,)yō-'pȯn-sā-(,)thä-lā-'ōn\ Ernesto 1951– president of Mexico (1994–)

Zee·man \'zā-,män, -mən\ Pieter 1865–1943 Du. physicist

Zeng·er \'zeŋ-gər, -ər\ John Peter 1697–1746 Am. (Ger.-born) journalist & printer

Ze·no of Citium \'zē-(,)nō-əv-'si-sh(ē-)-əm\ *circa* 335–*circa* 263 B.C. Greek philosopher & founder of Stoic school

Zeno of Elea \'ē-lē-ə\ *circa* 495–*circa* 430 B.C. Greek philosopher

Ze·no·bia \zə-'nō-bē-ə\ *died* after A.D. 274 queen of Palmyra (267 or 268–272)

Zep·pe·lin \,tse-pə-'lēn, 'ze-p(ə-)lən\ Ferdinand Adolf August Heinrich 1838–1917 Graf *von Zeppelin* Ger. general & aeronaut

Zer·ni·ke \'zer-ni-kə, 'zər-\ Frits 1888–1966 Du. physicist

Zeux·is \'zük-səs\ 5th century B.C. Greek painter

Zhao Zi·yang *or* **Chao Tzu–yang** \'jaù-(d)zə-'yäŋ\ 1919– Chin. Communist leader (1987–89)

Zhda·nov \zhə-'dä-nəf, 'shtä-\ Andrey Aleksandrovich 1896–1948 Soviet politician

Zhu·kov \'zhü-,kȯf, -,kȯv\ Georgy Konstantinovich 1896–1974 Soviet marshal

Zieg·feld \'zig-,feld, 'zēg- *also* -,fēld, -fəld\ Florenz 1869–1932 Am. theatrical producer

Zieg·ler \'tsē-glər\ Karl 1898–1973 Ger. chemist

Zim·mer·mann \'zi-mər-mən, 'tsi-mər-,män\ Arthur 1864–1940 Ger. statesman

Zin·ker·na·gel \'tsiŋ-kər-,näg-ᵊl\ Rolf Martin 1944– Swiss immunologist

Zi·nov·yev *or* **Zi·nov·iev** \zyi-'nȯf-yəf\ Grigory Yevseyevich 1883–1936 originally *Ovsel Gershon Aronov Radomyslsky* Soviet revolutionary

Zins·ser \'zin(t)-sər\ Hans 1878–1940 Am. bacteriologist

Zin·zen·dorf \'zin-zən-,dȯrf, 'tsin-sən-\ Nikolaus Ludwig 1700–1760 Graf *von Zinzendorf* religious reformer

Žiž·ka \'zhish-kə\ Count Jan *circa* 1376–1424 Bohemian general & Hussite leader

Zog I \'zȯg\ 1895–1961 prename *Ahmed Bey Zogu* king of the Albanians (1928–39)

Zo·la \'zō-lə, 'zō-,lä, zō-'lä\ Émile 1840–1902 Fr. novelist — **Zo·la·esque** \zō-lə-'esk, -lä-\ *adjective*

Zorn \'sȯrn, 'zȯrn\ Anders Leonhard 1860–1920 Swed. painter, etcher, & sculptor

Zo·ro·as·ter \'zȯr-ə-,was-tər, 'zȯr-\ *Old Iranian* **Zar·a·thu·shtra** \,zar-ə-'thüsh-trə, -'thəsh-, -'thüs-, -'thəs-\ *circa* 628–*circa* 551 B.C. founder of Zoroastrianism

Zor·ri·lla y Mo·ral \zə-'rē-yə-,ē-mə-'räl\ José 1817–1893 Span. poet & dramatist

Zsig·mon·dy \'zhig-,mȯn-dē\ Richard 1865–1929 Ger. chemist

Zu·lo·a·ga \,zü-lə-'wä-gə\ Ignacio 1870–1945 Span. painter

Zur·ba·rán \,zúr-bə-'rän\ Francisco de 1598–1664 Span. painter

Zweig \'zwīg, 'swīg, 'tsvīk\ Arnold 1887–1968 Ger. author

Zweig Stefan 1881–1942 Austrian writer

Zwing·li \'zwiŋ-glē, 'swiŋ-, -lē; 'tsfiŋ-lē\ Huldrych 1484–1531 Swiss Reformation leader

Geographical Names

This section gives basic information about the countries of the world and their most important regions, cities, and physical features. The information includes spelling, end-of-line division, and pronunciation of the name, nature of the feature, its location, and for the more important entries statistical data. Cities in the United States having 19,000 or more inhabitants at the 1990 census and incorporated places in Canada having 21,500 or more inhabitants at the 1991 census have been included.

This section complements the A–Z vocabulary by entering many derivative forms:

Ab·ys·sin·ia . . . — **Ab·ys·sin·ian** . . . *adjective or noun*

Cos·ta Ri·ca . . . — **Cos·ta Ri·can** . . . *adjective or noun*

Mo·na·co . . . — **Mo·na·can** . . . *adjective or noun* — **Mon·e·gasque** . . . *adjective or noun*

The abbreviations used are listed in the back-matter section Abbreviations and Symbols for Chemical Elements. The letters N, E, S, and W when not followed by a period indicate direction and are not part of a place-name; thus N Vietnam indicates northern Vietnam and not North Vietnam. The symbol ✳ denotes a capital. Areas, altitudes, and lengths are given first in conventional units with metric equivalents in parentheses.

The Pinyin transliteration of place-names for the People's Republic of China is the first spelling shown; the Wade-Giles transliteration is second. Where no variant is given, the two spellings are identical.

Aa·chen \'ä-kən, -kən\ *or French* **Aix-la-Cha-pelle** \,äks-,lä-shä-'pel, ,eks-\ city W Germany near Belgian & Dutch borders *pop* 241,861

Aai·ún, El \,el-ī-'ün\ *or* **Laa·youne** *or* **La'youn** \lä-'yün\ town NW Africa ✳ of Western Sahara

Aalborg — see ÅLBORG

Aalst \'älst\ *or* **Alost** \à-'lòst\ commune *central* Belgium WNW of Brussels *pop* 76,382

Aa·rau \'är-,aù\ commune N Switzerland ✳ of Aargau canton *pop* 15,836

Aa·re \'är-ə\ *or* **Aar** \'är\ river 183 *mi* (294 *km*), *central* & N Switzerland flowing E & NE into the Rhine

Aar·gau \'är-,gaù\ *or French* **Ar·go·vie** \,àr-gō-'vē\ canton N Switzerland ✳ Aarau *area* 542 *sq mi* (1409 *sq km*), *pop* 489,567

Aarhus — see ÅRHUS

Ab·a·co \'a-bə-,kō\ two islands of Bahamas (**Great Abaco** & **Little Abaco**) N of New Providence Is. *area* 776 *sq mi* (2018 *sq km*)

Aba·dan \,ä-bə-'dän, ,a-bə-'dan\ **1** island W Iran in delta of Shatt-al-Arab **2** town & port on Abadan Is.

Aba·kan \,ə-bə-'kän\ town S Russia in Asia ✳ of Khakassia *pop* 158,000

Abay *or* **Ab·bai** \ä-'bī\ the upper course of the Blue Nile

Ab·be·ville \àb-'vēl, 'a-bi-,vil\ commune N France on the Somme NW of Amiens *pop* 24,588

Ab·er·dare \,a-bər-'dar, -'der\ town S Wales in Mid Glamorgan *pop* 36,621

Ab·er·deen 1 \'a-bər-,dēn\ city NE S.Dak. *pop* 24,927 **2** \,a-bər-'dēn\ *or* **Ab·er·deen·shire** \-,shir, -shər\ former county NE Scotland ✳ Aberdeen **3** city & port NE Scotland ✳ of Grampian *pop* 211,080 — **Ab·er·do·ni·an** \,a-bər-'dō-nē-ən\ *adjective or noun*

Ab·er·yst·wyth \,a-bə-'ris-,twith, -'rəs-\ borough W Wales in Dyfed on Cardigan Bay *pop* 8666

Ab·i·djan \,ä-bē-'jän, ,a-bi-\ city & port ✳ of Ivory Coast *pop* 1,934,342

Abila — see MUSA (Jebel)

Ab·i·lene \'a-bə-,lēn\ city NW *central* Tex. *pop* 106,654

Ab·i·tibi \,a-bə-'ti-bē\ **1** lake Canada on E boundary of Ontario *area* 356 *sq mi* (926 *sq km*) **2** river 230 *mi* (368 *km*) Canada flowing N into Moose River

Ab·khaz Republic \ab-'kaz, əb-'käs\ autonomous republic NW Republic of Georgia on Black Sea ✳ Sukhumi *area* 3320 *sq mi* (8599 *sq km*), *pop* 533,800 — **Ab·khas** \-'käs\ *noun* — **Ab·kha·sian** *or* **Ab·kha·zian** \-'kā-zh(ē-)ən, -'kä-zē-ən\ *adjective or noun*

Abo·mey \,a-bō-'mā, ə-'bō-mē\ city S Benin *pop* 54,418

Abruz·zi \ä-'brüt-sē, ə-\ region *central* Italy bordering on the Adriatic & including highest of the Apennines ✳ L'Aquila *pop* 1,249,388; with Molise (to S), formerly comprised **Abruzzi e Molise** \ä-'mò-li-,zā\ region

Ab·sa·ro·ka Range \ab-'sär-ə-kə, -'sór-kē, -'zòr-\ mountain range S Mont. & NW Wyo. E of Yellowstone National Park — see FRANCS PEAK

Ab·se·con Inlet \ab-'sē-kən\ inlet SE N.J. between barrier islands N of Atlantic City

Abu Dha·bi \,ä-bü-'dä-bē, -'thä-\ **1** sheikhdom, member of United Arab Emirates **2** town, its ✳ & ✳ of United Arab Emirates *pop* 347,000

Abu·ja \ä-'bü-jä\ city *central* Nigeria, its ✳ since 1991

Abu Qir \,a-bü-'kir, ,ä-\ **1** bay N Egypt between Alexandria & Rosetta mouth of the Nile **2** village on this bay

Abu Sim·bel \,ä-,bü-'sim-bəl\ locality S Egypt on left bank of the Nile SW of Aswân; site of two rock temples which were moved 1964–66 to higher ground when area was flooded after completion of Aswan High Dam

Aby·dos \ə-'bī-dəs\ **1** ancient town Asia Minor on the Heliespont **2** ancient town S Egypt on left bank of the Nile S of Thebes

Abyla — see MUSA (Jebel)

Ab·ys·sin·ia \,a-bə-'si-nē-ə, -nyə\ — see ETHIOPIA — **Ab·ys·sin·ian** \-nē-ən, -nyən\ *adjective or noun*

Aca·dia \ə-'kā-dē-ə\ *or French* **Aca·die** \à-kà-'dē\ NOVA SCOTIA — an early name

Acadia National Park section of coast of Maine including chiefly mountainous areas on Mount Desert Is. & Isle au Haut

Aca·pul·co \,ä-kä-'pül-(,)kō, ,a-\ *or* **Acapulco de Juá·rez** \dā-'hwär-,es, thä-\ city & port S Mexico in Guerrero on the Pacific *pop* 592,187

Ac·ar·na·nia \,a-kər-'nä-nē-ə, -'nä-nyə\ region W Greece on Ionian Sea — **Ac·ar·na·nian** \,a-kər-'nä-nē-ən, -'nä-nyən\ *adjective or noun*

Ac·cad \'a-,kad, 'ä-,käd\ — see AKKAD — **Ac·ca·di·an** \ə-'kā-dē-ən, -'kä-\ *adjective or noun*

Ac·cra \'ä-krə, 'a-; ə-'krä\ city & port ✳ of Ghana on Gulf of Guinea *pop* 867,459

Ac·cring·ton \'a-kriŋ-tən\ town NW England in SE Lancashire N of Manchester

Achaea \ə-'kē-ə\ *or* **Acha·ia** \ə-'kī-ə, -'kā-\ region S Greece in N Peloponnese bordering on Gulfs of Corinth & Patras — **Achae·an** \ə-'kē-ən\ *or* **Acha·ian** \ə-'kī-ən, -'kā-\ *adjective or noun*

Ach·e·lo·us \,a-kə-'lō-əs\ *or New Greek* **Akhe·ló·os** \,ä-ke-'lò-ōs\ river 137 *mi* (220 *km*) W Greece flowing S to Ionian Sea

Ach·ill \'a-kəl\ island 15 *mi* (24 *km*) long NW Ireland in County Mayo

Achray, Loch \ə-'krā\ lake *central* Scotland in SW Tayside

Acon·ca·gua \,ä-kōn-'kä-gwä\ mountain 22,834 *ft* (6960 *m*) W Argentina WNW of Mendoza near Chilean border; highest in Andes & western hemisphere

Açores — see AZORES

Acragas — see AGRIGENTO

Acre \'ä-krē, -(,)krä\ state W Brazil bordering on Peru & Bolivia ✳ Rio Branco *area* 59,343 *sq mi* (153,698 *sq km*), *pop* 417,437

Acre \'ä-kər, 'ā-kər, 'ä-krə\ *or Hebrew* **'Ak·ko** *or Old Testament* **Ac·cho** \'ä-kō, 'ä-\ *or New Testament* **Ptol·e·ma·ïs** \,tä-lə-'mā-əs\ city & port NW Israel N of Mt. Carmel *pop* 37,400

Ac·te \'ak-tē\ *or Greek* **Aktí** \'äk-'tē\ peninsula NE Greece, the most easterly of the three peninsulas of Chalcidice — see ATHOS

Ac·ti·um \'ak-shē-əm, 'ak-tē-\ promontory & ancient town W Greece in NW Acarnania

Adak \'ä-,dak\ island SW Alaska in Andreanof group

Adalia — see ANTALYA

Ad·ams, Mount \'a-dəmz\ **1** mountain 5798 *ft* (1767 *m*) N N.H. in White Mountains N of Mt. Washington **2** mountain 12,307 *ft* (3751 *m*) SW Wash. in Cascade Range SSE of Mt. Rainier

Ad·am's Bridge \'a-dəmz\ chain of shoals 30 *mi* (48 *km*) long between Sri Lanka & SE India

Adam's Peak *or Sinhalese* **Sa·ma·na·la** \'sə-mə-nə-lə\ mountain 7360 *ft* (2243 *m*) S *central* Sri Lanka

Ada·na \'ä-dä-nä, ə-'dä-nə\ *or formerly* **Sey·han** \sā-'hän\ city S Turkey on Seyhan River *pop* 916,150

Ada·pa·za·rı \,ä-də-,pä-zə-'rı\ city NW Turkey E of Istanbul *pop* 171,225

Ad Dam·mām \,äd-däm-'mäm\ *or* **Dam·mam** \də-'mäm\ town & port Saudi Arabia on Persian Gulf

Ad·dis Aba·ba \'ä-dis-'ä-bä-bä, ,ä-dəs-'a-bə-bə\ city *central* Ethiopia, its ✳ *pop* 1,408,068

Ad·di·son \'a-də-sən\ village NE Ill. W of Chicago *pop* 32,058

Ad·e·laide \'a-d'l-,ād\ city Australia ✳ of S. Australia *metropolitan area pop* 917,000

Aden \'ä-d'n, 'ā-\ **1** former Brit. protectorate S Arabia comprising coast area between Yemen on W & Oman on E; became part of People's Democratic Republic of Yemen 1967 *area* 112,000 *sq mi* (291,200 *sq km*) **2** former Brit. colony on coast of & surrounded by Aden protectorate comprising Aden & Little Aden peninsulas, a small area of hinterland, & Perim Is.; became part of People's Democratic Republic of Yemen 1967 *area* 75 *sq mi* (195 *sq km*) **3** city & port S Yemen; formerly ✳ of People's Democratic Republic of Yemen & before that ✳ of Aden colony & protectorate *pop* 240,370

Aden, Gulf of arm of Indian Ocean between Aden & Somalia

Adi·ge \'ä-dē-,jä\ river 255 *mi* (410 *km*) N Italy flowing SE into the Adriatic

Ad·i·ron·dack Mountains \,a-də-'rän-,dak\ mountains NE N.Y.

Adjar·i·an Autonomous Republic \ə-'jär-ē-ən\ *or* **Adzhar** \'ä-jär, ə-'jär\ *or* **Adzhar·ia** *or* **Ajar·ia** \ə-'jär-ē-ə\ autonomous republic SW Republic of Georgia on Black Sea ✳ Batumi *area* 1158 *sq mi* (2999 *sq km*), *pop* 381,500

Ad·mi·ral·ty Inlet \'ad-m(ə-)rəl-tē\ branch of Puget Sound NW Washington

Admiralty Island island 90 *mi* (145 *km*) long SE Alaska in N Alexander Archipelago

Admiralty Islands islands W Pacific N of New Guinea in Bismarck Archipelago *area* 800 *sq mi* (2080 *sq km*), *pop* 30,160

Adour \ä-'dür\ river 208 *mi* (335 *km*) SW France flowing from the Pyrenees NW & W into Bay of Biscay

Adri·an \'ā-drē-ən\ city SE Mich. SW of Detroit *pop* 22,097

Adrianople — see EDIRNE

Adri·at·ic Sea \,ā-drē-'a-tik, ,a-\ arm of the Mediterranean between Italy & Balkan Peninsula

Ad·vent Bay \'ad-,vent, -vənt\ inlet of Arctic Ocean West Spitsbergen on W coast

Ad·wa \'äd-(,)wä\ town N Ethiopia S of Asmara *pop* 17,476

Ady·gea *or* **Ady·ge·ya** \,ä-də-'gā-ə\ republic S Russia in Europe ✳ Maykop *area* 2934 *sq mi* (7599 *sq km*), *pop* 437,400

Adzhar *or* **Adzharia** — see ADJARIAN AUTONOMOUS REPUBLIC — **Adzhar** *noun* — **Adzhar·i·an** \ə-'jär-ē-ən\ *adjective or noun*

Aegates — see EGADI

Ae·ge·an Islands \i-'jē-ən\ islands Aegean Sea including the Cyclades & the Northern & Southern Sporades

Aegean Sea arm of the Mediterranean between Asia Minor & Greece

Ae·gi·na \i-'jī-nə\ *or Greek* **Aí·yi·na** \'e-yē-,nä\ island & ancient state SE Greece in Saronic Gulf — **Ae·gi·ne·tan** \,ē-jə-'nē-t°n\ *adjective or noun*

Ae·gos·pot·a·mi \,ē-gə-'spä-tə-,mī\ *or* **Ae·gos·pot·a·mos** \-məs\ river & town of ancient Thrace in the Chersonese

Aemilia — see EMILIA-ROMAGNA

Ae·o·lis \'ē-ə-ləs\ *or* **Ae·o·lia** \ē-'ō-lē-ə, -'ōl-yə\ ancient country of NW Asia Minor

Ae·to·lia \ē-'tō-lē-ə, -'tōl-yə\ region W *central* Greece N of Gulf of Patras & E of Acarnania — **Ae·to·lian** \-lē-ən, -yən\ *adjective or noun*

Afars and the Issas, French Territory of the — see DJIBOUTI

Af·ghan·i·stan \af-'ga-nə-,stan, -'gä-nə-,stän\ country W Asia E of Iran; a republic ✳ Kabul *area* 250,775 *sq mi* (649,507 *sq km*), *pop* 18,052,000

Afog·nak \ə-'fòg-,nak, -'fäg-\ island S Alaska N of Kodiak Is.

Af·ri·ca \'a-fri-kə *also* \-ä-\ continent of the eastern hemisphere S of the Mediterranean & adjoining Asia on NE *area* 11,677,239 *sq mi* (30,244,049 *sq km*)

Af·yon \ä-'fyòn\ *or* **Afyon·ka·ra·hi·sar** \ä-'fyòn-,kär-ə-hi-'sär\ city W *central* Turkey *pop* 98,618

Aga·dir \,ä-gə-'dir, ,a-\ city & port SW Morocco *pop* 110,479

Aga·na \ä-'gä-nyä\ town ✳ of Guam on W coast *pop* 1139

Agar·ta·la \,ə-gər-tə-'lä\ city E India ✳ of Tripura *pop* 157,636

Ag·ate Fossil Beds National Monument \'a-gət\ reservation W Nebr.

Ag·a·wam \'a-gə-,wäm\ town SW Mass. *pop* 27,323

Age·nais \,ä-zhə-'nā\ *or* **Age·nois** \,ä-zhe-'nwä\ ancient region SW France S of Périgord ✳ Agen

Aghrim — see AUGHRIM

Ag·in·court \'a-jin-,kòrt, 'ä-zhən-,kùr\ *or French* **Azin·court** \,á-za°-'kür\ village N France WNW of Arras

Ag·no \'äg-(,)nō\ river 128 *mi* (206 *km*) Philippines in NW Luzon

Agou·ra Hills \ə-'gür-ə\ city SW Calif. W of Los Angeles *pop* 20,390

Agra \'ä-grə, 'ə-\ **1** region N India roughly equivalent to present Uttar Pradesh excluding Oudh region **2** city N India in W Uttar Pradesh SSE of Delhi *pop* 891,790

Agri Dagi — see ARARAT

Agri·gen·to \,ä-grē-'jen-(,)tō, ,a-\ *or formerly* **Gir·gen·ti** \jər-'jen-tē\ *or ancient* **Ag·ri·gen·tum** \,a-grə-'jen-təm\ *or* **Ac·ra·gas** \'ä-krä-,gäs\ commune Italy in SW Sicily near coast *pop* 54,603

Agua·di·lla \,ä-gwä-'thē-yä\ city NW Puerto Rico *pop* 59,335

Aguas·ca·lien·tes \,ä-gwä-,skäl-'yen-,täs\ **1** state *central* Mexico *area* 2158 *sq mi* (5589 *sq km*), *pop* 719,659 **2** city, its ✳ *pop* 506,384

Agul·has, Cape \ə-'gə-ləs\ headland Republic of S. Africa in S Western Cape province; southernmost point of Africa, at 34°50'S, 20°E

Ahag·gar Mountains \ə-'hä-gər, ,ä-\ *or* **Hog·gar Mountains** \'hä-gər, hə-'gär\ mountains S Algeria in W *central* Sahara; highest Tahat 9842 *ft* (3000 *m*)

Ah·mad·abad \'ä-mə-də-,bäd, -,bad\ city W India N of Bombay in Gujarat *pop* 2,954,526

Ah·vaz \ä-'väz\ *or* **Ah·waz** \ä-'wäz\ city SW Iran on the Karun *pop* 579,826

Ai·ken \'ā-kən\ city W S.C. SW of Columbia *pop* 19,872

Ail·sa Craig \'āl-zə-,krāg\ small rocky island Scotland S of Arran at mouth of Firth of Clyde

Ain \'a°\ river 120 *mi* (195 *km*) E France rising in Jura Mountains & flowing SSW into the Rhône

Aintab — see GAZIANTEP

Air·drie \'ar-drē, 'er-\ burgh S *central* Scotland in Strathclyde E of Glasgow *pop* 45,643

Aire \'ar, 'er\ river 70 *mi* (113 *km*) N England in W Yorkshire flowing to the Ouse; its valley is **Aire·dale** \-,dāl\

Aisne \'ān\ river *about* 165 *mi* (265 *km*) N France flowing NW & W from Argonne Forest into the Oise near Compiègne

Aix–en–Pro·vence \,āks-ä°-prō-'vä°s, ,eks-\ *or* **Aix** \'āks, 'eks\ city SE France N of Marseille *pop* 126,854

Aix–la–Chapelle — see AACHEN

Aix–les–Bains \,āks-lā-'ba°, ,eks-\ commune E France N of Chambéry *pop* 24,826

Ajac·cio \ä-'yä-(,)chō, ä-zhäk-'syō\ city & port France in Corsica *pop* 59,318

Ajan·ta \ə-'jən-tə\ village W *central* India in N *central* Maharashtra in Ajanta Range NNE of Aurangabad; caves

Ajaria — see ADJARIAN AUTONOMOUS REPUBLIC

Ajax \'ā-,jaks\ town Canada in SE Ontario *pop* 57,350

'Aj·man \,äj-'män\ sheikhdom, member of United Arab Emirates

Aj·mer \əj-'mir, -'mer\ city NW India in Rajasthan SW of Delhi *pop* 402,700

Akhelóos — see ACHELOUS

Ak·hi·sar \,äk-hi-'sär, ,ä-ki-\ *or ancient* **Thy·a·ti·ra** \,thī-ə-'tī-rə\ city W Turkey in Asia NE of Izmir *pop* 151,957

Aki·ta \ä-'kē-tä, ä-kē-,tä\ city & port Japan in N Honshu on Sea of Japan *pop* 302,359

Ak·kad *or* **Ac·cad** \'a-,kad, 'ä-,käd\ **1** the N division of ancient Babylonia **2** *or* **Aga·de** \ə-'gä-də\ ancient city, its ✳

Akkerman — see BELGOROD-DNESTROVSKI

'Akko — see ACRE

Ak·ron \'a-krən\ city NE Ohio SE of Cleveland *pop* 223,019

Ak·sum *also* **Ax·um** \'äk-,süm\ town N Ethiopia ✳ of an ancient kingdom (the Axumite Empire)

Aktí — see ACTE

Akyab — see SITTWE

Al·a·bama \,a-lə-'ba-mə\ **1** river 315 *mi* (507 *km*) S Ala. flowing SW into Tensaw & Mobile rivers — see TALLAPOOSA **2** state SE U.S. ✳ Montgomery *area* 51,705 *sq mi* (133,916 *sq km*), *pop* 4,040,587 — **Al·a·bam·i·an** \-'ba-mē-ən\ *or* **Al·a·bam·an** \-'ba-mən\ *adjective or noun*

Ala·go·as \,ä-lə-'gō-əs\ state NE Brazil ✳ Maceió *area* 11,238 *sq mi* (29,184 *sq km*), *pop* 2,512,515

Alai \ä-,lī\ mountain range SW Kyrgyzstan; highest peak 19,554 *ft* (5960 *m*)

Al 'A·mā·rah \al-ha-'mä-rə\ city SE Iraq on the Tigris

Al·a·me·da \,a-lə-'mē-də\ city & port W Calif. on island in San Francisco Bay near Oakland *pop* 76,459

Alamein, El — see EL ALAMEIN

Al·a·mo·gor·do \,a-lə-mə-'gòr-(,)dō\ city S N.Mex. *pop* 27,596

Åland \'ō-,län(d)\ *or* **Ahv·e·nan·maa** \'ä-ve-nän-,mä\ **1** archipelago SW Finland in Baltic Sea ✳ Mariehamn **2** island, chief of this group

Ala·nia \ə-'lä-nyə, -nē-ə\ *or* **North Os·se·tia** \,ä-'sē-sh(ē-)ə\ autonomous republic SE Russia in Europe on the N slopes of Caucasus Mountains ✳ Vladikavkaz *area* 3089 *sq mi* (8001 *sq km*), *pop* 695,000

Al–'Aqabah — see AQABA

Ala·şe·hir \,a-lə-shə-'hir, ,ä-\ *or ancient* **Phila·delphia** city W Turkey 75 *mi* (121 *km*) E of Izmir *pop* 36,535

Alas·ka \ə-'las-kə\ state (territory 1912–59) of the U.S. NW N. America ✳ Juneau *area* 591,004 *sq mi* (1,530,700 *sq km*), *pop* 550,043 — **Alas·kan** \-kən\ *adjective or noun*

Alaska, Gulf of inlet of the Pacific off S Alaska between Alaska Peninsula on W & Alexander Archipelago on E

Alaska Peninsula peninsula SW Alaska SW of Cook Inlet

Alaska Range mountain range S Alaska extending from Alaska Peninsula to Yukon boundary — see MCKINLEY (Mount)

Ala Tau \'ä-lə-'tau\ several ranges of the Tian Shan mountain system E Kazakhstan & Kyrgyzstan around & NE of Issyk Kul

Ala·va \'ä-lə-və\ province N Spain S of Vizcaya; in Basque Country ✳ Vitoria *area* 1176 *sq mi* (3046 *sq km*), *pop* 272,447

Al·a·va, Cape \'a-lə-və\ cape NW Wash. S of Cape Flattery; westernmost point of conterminous U.S., at 124°44'W

Al–'Ayzarīyah — see BETHANY 2

Al·ba·ce·te \,äl-bä-'sā-tä\ **1** province SE Spain N of Murcia province *area* 5737 *sq mi* (14,859 *sq km*), *pop* 342,677 **2** commune, its ✳ *pop* 130,023

Al·ba Lon·ga \,al-bə-'lòn-gə\ ancient city *central* Italy SE of Rome

Al·ban Hills \'òl-bən, 'al-\ *or ancient* **Al·ba·nus Mons** \àl-'bä-nəs-'mȯn(t)s\ mountain group Italy SE of Rome

Al·ba·nia \al-'bā-nē-ə, -nyə *also* òl-\ **1** ancient country Europe in E Caucasus region on W side of Caspian Sea **2** country S Europe in Balkan Peninsula on the Adriatic; a republic ✻ Tiranë *area* 11,100 *sq mi* (28,749 *sq km*), *pop* 3,357,000

Al·ba·no, Lake \al-'bä-(,)nō, äl-\ *or ancient* **Al·ba·nus La·cus** \àl-'bä-nəs-'lä-kəs\ lake Italy SE of Rome

Al·ba·ny \'òl-bə-nē\ **1** city SW Ga. *pop* 78,122 **2** city ✻ of N.Y., on Hudson River *pop* 101,082 **3** city NW Oreg. S of Salem *pop* 29,462 **4** \'al-\ river 610 *mi* (982 *km*) Canada in N Ontario flowing E into James Bay — **Al·ba·ni·an** \òl-'bä-nē-ən\ *adjective or noun*

Al Basrah — see BASRA

Al·be·marle Sound \'al-bə-,märl\ inlet of Atlantic Ocean NE N.C.

Al·bert, Lake \'al-bərt\ lake 100 *mi* (161 *km*) long E Africa between Uganda & Democratic Republic of the Congo in course of the Victoria Nile

Al·ber·ta \al-'bər-tə\ province W Canada ✻ Edmonton *area* 246,422 *sq mi* (638,232 *sq km*), *pop* 2,545,553 — **Al·ber·tan** \-'bər-tᵊn\ *adjective or noun*

Albert Nile — see NILE

Albertville — see KALEMIE

Al·bi \al-'bē\ commune S France NE of Toulouse *pop* 48,707

Al Biqa — see BEKAA

Ål·borg *or* **Aal·borg** \'òl-,bȯrg\ city & port Denmark in NE Jutland *pop* 155,664

Al·bu·quer·que \'al-bə-,kər-kē\ city *central* N.Mex. *pop* 384,736 — **Al·bu·quer·que·an** \-kē-ən\ *noun*

Al·ca·mo \'äl-kä-,mō\ commune Italy in NW Sicily *pop* 43,231

Al·ca·traz \'al-kə-,traz\ island Calif. in San Francisco Bay

Al·coy \äl-'kȯi\ commune E Spain N of Alicante *pop* 65,514

Al·da·bra \àl-'dä-brə\ island (atoll) NW Indian Ocean N of Madagascar, chief of Aldabra group belonging to Seychelles

Al·dan \àl-'dän\ river 1393 *mi* (2241 *km*) E Russia in Asia, in Sakha Republic flowing into the Lena

Al·der·ney \'òl-dər-nē\ island in English Channel, northernmost of the Channel Islands ✻ St. Anne *area* 3 *sq mi* (7.8 *sq km*), *pop* 2086

Al·der·shot \'òl-dər-,shät\ borough S England in NE Hampshire *pop* 32,654

Aleksandrovsk — see ZAPOROZH 'YE

Aleksandrovsk–Grushevski — see SHAKHTY

Alen·çon \,a-,län-'sōⁿ\ city NW France N of Le Mans *pop* 32,917

Alep·po \ə-'le-(,)pō\ *or ancient* **Be·roea** \bə-'rē-ə\ city N Syria *pop* 1,445,000 — **Alep·pine** \ə-'le-pən, -,pīn, -,pēn\ *adjective or noun*

Ales·san·dria \,ä-le-'sän-drē-ä\ commune NW Italy *pop* 90,475

Aleu·tian Islands \ə-'lü-shən\ islands SW Alaska extending in an arc 1700 *mi* (2735 *km*) SW & W from Alaska Peninsula — see ANDREANOF ISLANDS, FOX ISLANDS, NEAR ISLANDS, RAT ISLANDS

Aleutian Range mountain range SW Alaska, the SW extension of Alaska Range, running along NW shore of Cook Inlet to SW tip of Alaska Peninsula with mountains of the Aleutian chain forming its SW extension — see SHISHALDIN

Al·ex·an·der Archipelago \,a-lig-'zan-dər, ,e-\ archipelago of *about* 1100 islands SE Alaska — see ADMIRALTY ISLAND, BARANOF, CHICHAGOF, KUPREANOF, PRINCE OF WALES ISLAND, REVILLAGIGEDO ISLAND

Alexander I Island island Antarctica W of base of Antarctic Peninsula

Alexandretta — see ISKENDERUN

Al·ex·an·dria \,a-lig-'zan-drē-ə, ,e-\ **1** city *central* La. *pop* 49,188 **2** city N Va. on the Potomac S of Washington, D.C. *pop* 111,183 **3** city & port N Egypt between Lake Mareotis & the Mediterranean *pop* 3,170,000 — **Al·ex·an·dri·an** \-drē-ən\ *adjective or noun*

Al Fayyûm — see EL FAIYÛM

Al·föld \'òl-,fə(r)ld, -,fœld\ the central plain of Hungary

Al Fu·jay·rah \,àl-fü-'jī-rə\ *or* **Fu·jai·rah** \-'jī-rə\ sheikhdom, member of United Arab Emirates *area* 450 *sq mi* (1166 *sq km*)

Al·gar·ve \àl-'gär-və, al-\ medieval Moorish kingdom now a province of Portugal on S coast

Al·ge·ci·ras \,al-jə-'sir-əs, ,äl-hā-'thē-räs\ city & port SW Spain W of Gibraltar on Bay of Algeciras *pop* 101,256

Al·ge·ria \al-'jir-ē-ə\ country NW Africa bordering on the Mediterranean ✻ Algiers *area* 918,497 *sq mi* (2,390,315 *sq km*), *pop* 22,971,000 — **Al·ge·ri·an** \-ē-ən\ *adjective or noun*

Al·giers \al-'jirz\ **1** former Barbary state N Africa now Algeria **2** city & port ✻ of Algeria on Bay of Algiers (inlet of Mediterranean) *pop* 1,365,400 — **Al·ge·rine** \,al-jə-'rēn\ *adjective or noun*

Al·goa Bay \al-'gō-ə\ inlet of Indian Ocean S Republic of S. Africa on SE coast of Eastern Cape province

Al Hamad — see HAMAD, AL

Al·ham·bra \al-'ham-brə, *for 2 also* ə-'lam-brə\ **1** city SW Calif. E of Los Angeles *pop* 82,106 **2** hill in Granada, Spain; site of remains of the palace of the Moorish kings

Al–Ha·sa \àl-'hä-sä\ *or* **Hasa** region NE Saudi Arabia in E Nejd bordering on Persian Gulf

Al Ḥijāz — see HEJAZ

Al Hu·day·dah \,àl-hȯ-'dā-də, -dī-\ *or* **Ho·dei·da** \hō-'dā-də\ city & port W Yemen *pop* 155,110

Al Hu·fuf \,àl-hȯ-'füf\ *or* **Ho·fuf** \hō-'füf\ city NE Saudi Arabia in E Nejd

Al·i·ba·tes Flint Quarries National Monument \,a-lə-'bä-tēz\ archaeological site N Tex. NE of Amarillo

Ali·can·te \,a-lə-'kan-tē, ,ä-lē-'kän-tä\ **1** province E Spain on the Mediterranean S of Valencia province *area* 2264 *sq mi* (5864 *sq km*), *pop* 1,292,563 **2** city & port, its ✻ *pop* 265,473

Al·ice \a-ləs\ city S Tex. W of Corpus Christi *pop* 19,788

Ali·garh \,ə-lē-'gər, 'a-lē-,gär\ city N India in NW Uttar Pradesh N of Agra *pop* (including old town of **Ko·il** \'kō-əl\) 480,520

Al Ittihad — see MADINAT ASH SHA'B

Al Jazirah — see GEZIRA

Al Jizah — see GIZA

Al Khums \àl-'kȯms, al-'kümz\ town & port Libya ESE of Tripoli; nearby are ruins of ancient Leptis Magna

Alk·maar \'alk-,mär\ commune NW Netherlands *pop* 91,817

Al Ku·frah \àl-'kü-frə\ *or* **Ku·fra** \'kü-frə\ group of five oases SE Libya

Al Kut city SE *central* Iraq on the Tigris SE of Baghdad

Al·lah·abad \'a-lä-hä-,bäd, 'a-lə-hə-,bad\ city N India in S Uttar Pradesh on the Ganges W of Varanasi *pop* 806,486

Al·le·ghe·ny \,a-lə-'gā-nē *also* -'ge-\ river 325 *mi* (523 *km*) W Pa. & SW N.Y. uniting with the Monongahela at Pittsburgh to form the Ohio — **Al·le·ghe·ni·an** \-'gä-nē-ən, -'ge-\ *adjective*

Allegheny Mountains mountains of Appalachian system E U.S. in Pa., Md., Va., & W.Va.

Al·len Park \'a-lən\ city SE Mich. WSW of Detroit *pop* 31,092

Allenstein — see OLSZTYN

Al·len·town \'a-lən-,taȯn\ city E Pa. on the Lehigh *pop* 105,090

Al·lep·pey \ə-'le-pē\ city & port S India in Kerala *pop* 174,606

Al·li·ance \ə-'lī-ən(t)s\ city NE Ohio NE of Canton *pop* 23,376

Al·lier \al-'yā\ river *about* 250 *mi* (402 *km*) S *central* France flowing to the Loire

Al·ma \'al-mə\ **1** river 50 *mi* (80 *km*) in SW Crimea **2** city Canada in E Quebec on the Saguenay *pop* 25,910

Al·ma-Ata \,äl-'mä-ə-'tä\ *or* **Al·maty** \əl-'mä-tē\ *or formerly* **Ver·nyi** \'vern-yē\ city SE Kazakhstan, its ✻ *pop* 1,156,200

Al·ma·dén \,äl-mä-'dän, -'thän\ town S *central* Spain in Sierra Morena *pop* 8012

Al Mansurah — see EL MANSÛRA

Al·me·lo \'äl-mə-,lō\ commune E Netherlands *pop* 63,383

Al·me·ría \,al-mā-'rē-ä\ **1** province S Spain SE of Granada province *area* 3388 *sq mi* (8775 *sq km*), *pop* 455,496 **2** city & port, its ✻ *pop* 155,120

Al Minya — see EL MINYA

Al Mu·kal·la \,àl-mü-'kà-lä\ *or* **Mu·kal·la** \mü-'ka-lə\ town & port Yemen on Gulf of Aden; chief town of the Hadhramaut

Al Mukhā — see MOCHA

Alor \'ä-,lȯr, 'ä-\ island Indonesia in Lesser Sunda Is. N of Timor; with **Pan·tar** \'pan-,tär\, forms **Alor Islands** group

Alor Se·tar \sə-'tär\ city Malaysia in NW Peninsular Malaysia ✻ of Kedah *pop* 66,179

Alost — see AALST

Al·phe·us \al-'fē-əs\ *or New Greek* **Al·fiós** \àl-'fyȯs\ river *about* 75 *mi* (121 *km*) S Greece in W Peloponnese flowing NW into Ionian Sea

Alps \'alps\ mountain system S *central* Europe extending from Mediterranean coast at border between France & Italy into Slovenia, Croatia, Bosnia and Herzegovina, Montenegro, & W Serbia — see MONT BLANC

Al·sace \al-'sas, -'säs; àl-'zàs\ *or German* **El·sass** \'el-,zäs\ *or ancient* **Al·sa·tia** \al-'sä-sh(ē-)ə\ region & former province NE France between Rhine River & Vosges Mountains — **Al·sa·tian** \al-'sä-shən\ *adjective or noun*

Alsace–Lor·raine \-lə-'rān, -lȯ-\ region NE France including Alsace & part of Lorraine

Al·sek \'al-,sek\ river 260 *mi* (418 *km*) NW Canada & SE Alaska flowing S into the Pacific

Al·ta California \'al-tə\ former Spanish & Mexican province (1772–1848) comprising the present state of Calif. - a name used to differentiate it from Baja California

Al·tai \,al-'tī\ mountain system *central* Asia between Mongolia (republic) & Xinjiang Uygur region of W China & between Kazakhstan & Russia in Asia — see TABUN BOGDO

Al·ta·ma·ha \,òl-tə-mə-,hò\ river 137 *mi* (220 *km*) SE Ga. formed by junction of the Ocmulgee & the Oconee & flowing SE into **Altamaha Sound** (estuary)

Al·ta·mi·ra \,àl-tä-'mē-rä\ caverns N Spain WSW of Santander

Al·ta·monte Springs \'al-tə-,mänt\ city *central* Fla. *pop* 34,879

Al·tay *or* **Al·tai** \al-'tī\ territory SW Russia in Asia ✻ Barnaul *area* 101,042 *sq mi* (261,699 *sq km*), *pop* 2,666,000

Alt·dorf \'alt-,dȯrf, 'ält-\ *or* **Al·torf** \'al-,tȯrf, 'äl-\ town *central* Switzerland ✻ of Uri canton *pop* 8249

Al·ten·burg \'äl-tᵊn-,bȯrg\ city E *central* Germany E of Weimar *pop* 48,926

Al·to Adi·ge \'àl-tō-'ä-dē-,jä\ *or* **Upper Adige** *or* **South Tirol** district N Italy in S Tirol in N Trentino-Alto Adige region

Al·ton \'òl-tᵊn\ city SW Ill. on the Mississippi *pop* 32,905

Al·too·na \al-'tü-nə\ city S *central* Pa. *pop* 51,881

Alto Paraná — see PARANÁ

Al·trinc·ham \'òl-triŋ-əm\ borough NW England in Greater Manchester SSW of Manchester *pop* 39,641

Al·tun *or* **Al·tyn** \àl-'tün\ mountain range W China in S Xinjiang Uygur; highest peak *about* 25,000 *ft* (7620 *m*)

Al·tus \'al-təs\ city SW Okla. *pop* 21,910

Al·vin \'al-vən\ city SE Tex. S of Houston *pop* 19,220

Ama·do·ra \,à-mə-'dȯr-ə, -'dȯr-\ city W Portugal *pop* 95,518

Ama·ga·sa·ki \,ä-mä-gä-'sä-kē\ city Japan in W *central* Honshu on Osaka Bay *pop* 497,333

Amal·fi \ä-'mäl-fē\ commune & port S Italy in Campania on Gulf of Salerno — **Amal·fi·an** \-fē-ən\ *adjective or noun*

Ama·mi \ä-'mä-mē\ island group W Pacific in *central* Ryukyus *area* 498 *sq mi* (1295 *sq km*)

Ama·pá \,à-mə-'pä\ state N Brazil NW of Amazon delta ✻ Macapá *area* 54,965 *sq mi* (142,359 *sq km*), *pop* 289,050

Am·a·ril·lo \,a-mə-'ri-(,)lō, -lə\ city NW Tex. *pop* 157,615 — **Am·a·ril·lo·an** \-'ri-lō-ən\ *noun*

Am·a·zon \'a-mə-,zän, -zən\ river *about* 3900 *mi* (6276 *km*) N S. America flowing from Peruvian

Andes into the Atlantic in N Brazil — see UCAYALI, SOLIMÕES

Ama·zo·nas \ˌä-mə-'zō-nəs\ state NW Brazil ✻ Manaus *area* 604,032 *sq mi* (1,564,443 *sq km*), *pop* 2,088,682

Ama·zo·nia \ˌa-mə-'zō-nē-ə\ region N S. America, the basin of the Amazon

Am·ba·to \äm-'bä-(ˌ)tō\ city *central* Ecuador S of Quito *pop* 124,166

Am·bon \äm-'bòn, 'am-ˌbän\ *or* **Am·boi·na** \am-'bòi-nə\ **1** island E Indonesia in the Moluccas S of Ceram *area* 314 *sq mi* (816 *sq km*) **2** city & port on Ambon Is. *pop* 276,955

Am·bra·cian Gulf \am-'brā-shən\ *or* **Gulf of Ar·ta** \'är-tə\ *or Greek* **Am·vra·ki·kós Kól·pos** \ˌäm-'vrä-kē-ˌkòs-'kòl-ˌpòs\ inlet of Ionian Sea 25 *mi* (40 *km*) long W Greece in S Epirus

Am·brose \ˌäm-ˌbròz\ dredged channel SE N.Y. at entrance to N.Y. harbor N of Sandy Hook; 40 *ft* (12 *m*) deep, 2000 *ft* (606 *m*) at widest point

Am·chit·ka \am-'chit-kə\ island SW Alaska at E end of Rat group

Amer·i·ca \ə-'mer-ə-kə\ **1** either continent (N. America or S. America) of the western hemisphere **2** *or* **the Amer·i·cas** \-kəz\ the lands of the western hemisphere including N., Central, & S. America & the W. Indies **3** UNITED STATES OF AMERICA

American Samoa *or* **Eastern Samoa** island group of S Samoa SW America ✻ Pago Pago (on Tutuila Is.) *area* 76 *sq mi* (198 *sq km*), *pop* 49,600

Amers·foort \'ä-mərz-ˌfòrt, -mərs-, -ˌfòrt\ commune *central* Netherlands NE of Utrecht *pop* 104,390

Ames \'āmz\ city *central* Iowa N of Des Moines *pop* 47,198

Am·ga \əm-'gä\ river 800 *mi* (1280 *km*) E *central* Russia in Asia, flowing NE to the Aldan

Am·hara \am-'har-ə, äm-'här-ə\ former kingdom (now a province) NW Ethiopia ✻ Gondar

Am·herst \'a-(ˌ)mərst, *chiefly by outsiders* 'am-ˌhərst\ town W *central* Mass. N of Springfield *pop* 35,228

Amiens \äm-'yaⁿ\ city N France on the Somme *pop* 136,234

Amin·di·vi \ˌə-mən-'dē-vē\ island group India in the N Laccadives

Am·i·rante \'a-mə-ˌrant\ islands W Indian Ocean SW of Seychelles; a dependency of Seychelles

Am·man \ä-'män, a-, -'man\ *or ancient* **Phila·delphia** *or biblical* **Rab·bah Am·mon** \'ra-bə-'a-mən\ *or* **Rab·bath Am·mon** \'ra-bəth\ city ✻ of Jordan, NE of Dead Sea *pop* 1,213,300

Am·mon \'a-mən\ ancient country NW Arabia E of Gilead ✻ Rabbah

Ammonium — see SIWA

Amne Machin — see A'NYÊMAQÊN

Amo — see BLACK

Amor·gós \ˌä-(ˌ)mòr-'gòs\ island Greece in the Aegean in SE Cyclades SE of Naxos *area* 47 *sq mi* (122 *sq km*)

Amoy — see XIAMEN

Am·ra·va·ti \əm-'rä-və-tē, äm-\ *or formerly* **Am·rao·ti** \-'raù-tē\ city *central* India in NE Maharashtra, chief city of Berar region *pop* 421,576

Am·rit·sar \əm-'rit-sər\ city N India in NW Punjab *pop* 709,456

Am·ster·dam \'am(p)-stər-ˌdam, *for 2 also* 'äm(p)-stər-ˌdäm\ **1** city E N.Y. on the Mohawk *pop* 20,714 **2** city & port, official ✻ of Netherlands *pop* 713,407 — **Am·ster·dam·mer** \-ˌda-mər, -ˌdä-mər\ *noun*

Amu Dar'ya \ˌä-mü-'där-yə\ *or ancient* **Ox·us** \'äk-səs\ river over 1500 *mi* (2400 *km*), *central* & W Asia flowing from Pamir plateau into Aral Sea

Amund·sen Gulf \'ä-mən-sən, 'a-\ arm of Beaufort Sea N Canada

Amundsen Sea arm of the S Pacific W Antarctica off Marie Byrd Land

Amur \ä-'mür\ *or* **Chin Hei·long** *or* **Hei–lung** \'hä-'lùn\ river *about* 1780 *mi* (2865 *km*) E Asia formed by junction of the Shilka & the Argun, flowing into the Pacific at N end of Tatar Strait, & forming part of boundary between China & Russia

Ana·dyr \ˌä-nə-'dir, ˌa-\ river 694 *mi* (1117 *km*) E Russia in Asia flowing S & E to Gulf of Anadyr

Anadyr, Gulf of *or* **Gulf of Ana·dir** \ˌä-nə-'dir, ˌa-\ inlet of N Bering Sea E Russia in Asia S of Chukchi Peninsula

An·a·heim \'a-nə-ˌhīm\ city SW Calif. E of Long Beach *pop* 266,406

Aná·huac \ä-'nä-ˌwäk\ the central plateau of Mexico

An·a·to·lia \ˌa-nə-'tō-lē-ə, -'tòl-yə\ the part of Turkey comprising the peninsula of Asia Minor

An·cas·ter \'aŋ-ˌkas-tər, 'an-\ town Canada in SE Ontario W of Hamilton *pop* 21,988

An–ch'ing — see ANQING

An·chor·age \'aŋ-k(ə-)rij\ city S *central* Alaska at head of Cook Inlet *pop* 226,338

An·co·hu·ma \ˌäŋ-kō-'ü-mä, -'hü-\ mountain peak 20,958 *ft* (6388 *m*) W Bolivia; highest in the Illampu massif

An·co·na \aŋ-'kō-nə, an-\ city & port *central* Italy ✻ of Marche on the Adriatic *pop* 101,179

An·da·lu·sia \ˌan-də-'lü-zh(ē-)ə\ *or Spanish* **An·da·lu·cía** \ˌän-dä-(ˌ)lü-'sē-ä\ region S Spain including Sierra Nevada & valley of the Guadalquivir — **An·da·lu·sian** \ˌan-də-'lü-zhən\ *adjective or noun*

An·da·man and Nic·o·bar \'an-də-mən...ni-kə-ˌbar, -ˌman-\ union territory India comprising Andaman & Nicobar groups ✻ Port Blair *area* 3202 *sq mi* (8293 *sq km*), *pop* 280,661

Andaman Islands islands India in Bay of Bengal S of Myanmar & N of Nicobar Islands *area* 2461 *sq mi* (6374 *sq km*) — **An·da·man·ese** \ˌan-də-mə-'nēz, -'nēs\ *adjective or noun*

Andaman Sea sea SE Asia, the E section of Bay of Bengal

An·der·lecht \'an-dər-ˌlekt\ commune *central* Belgium, *pop* 87,884

An·der·matt \'än-dər-ˌmät\ commune *central* Switzerland S of Altdorf

An·der·son \'an-dər-sən\ **1** city *central* Ind. *pop* 59,459 **2** city NW S.C. *pop* 26,184 **3** river 430 *mi* (692 *km*) Canada in Northwest Territories flowing W & N into Beaufort Sea

An·des \'an-(ˌ)dēz\ mountain system of S. America extending along W coast from Panama to Tierra del Fuego — see ACONCAGUA — **An·de·an** \'an-(ˌ)dē-ən, an-'\ *adjective* — **An·dine** \'an-ˌdēn, -ˌdīn\ *adjective*

An·dhra Pra·desh \ˌän-drə-prə-'dāsh, -'desh\ state SE India N of Tamil Nadu state bordering on Bay of Bengal ✻ Hyderabad *area* 106,272 *sq mi* (275,244 *sq km*), *pop* 66,508,008

An·di·zhan *or* **An·di·jon** \ˌan-di-'zhan, ˌän-di-'zhän\ city Uzbekistan ESE of Tashkent *pop* 298,300

An·dor·ra \an-'dòr-ə, -'där-ə\ country SW Europe in E Pyrenees between France & Spain; a republic ✻ Andorra la Vella *area* 180 *sq mi* (482 *sq km*), *pop* 57,100 — **An·dor·ran** \-ən\ *adjective or noun*

An·do·ver \'an-ˌdō-vər, -də-\ town NE Mass. *pop* 29,151

An·dre·a·nof Islands \ˌan-drē-'a-ˌnòf, ˌän-drä-'ä-nəf\ islands SW Alaska in *central* Aleutian chain — see ADAK, ATKA

An·dria \'än-drē-ə\ commune SE Italy in Puglia *pop* 89,762

Andropov — see RYBINSK

An·dros **1** \'an-drəs\ island, largest of Bahamas *area* 1600 *sq mi* (4160 *sq km*) **2** \'an-drəs, -ˌdräs; 'än-ˌdròs\ island 25 *mi* (40 *km*) long Greece in N Cyclades

An·dros·cog·gin \ˌan-drə-'skä-gən\ river 157 *mi* (253 *km*) NE N.H. & SW Maine flowing into the Kennebec

Ane·to, Pi·co de \'pē-(ˌ)kō-ˌdā-ä-'nä-(ˌ)tō\ *or French* **Pic de Né·thou** \ˌpēk-də-(ˌ)nä-'tü\ mountain 11,168 *ft* (3404 *m*) NE Spain; highest in the Pyrenees

An·ga·ra \ˌäŋ-gə-'rä, ˌaŋ-gə-'rä\ river 1100 *mi* (1770 *km*) Russia, flowing from Lake Baikal into the Yenisey — see TUNGUSKA

An·garsk \ən-'gärsk\ city S Russia in Asia on the Angara NW of Irkutsk *pop* 269,000

An·gel Falls \'än-jəl\ waterfall 3212 *ft* (979 *m*) SE Venezuela on Auyán-tepuí mountain in a headstream of the Caroní

An·gers \äⁿ-'zhā\ city W France ENE of Nantes *pop* 146,163

Ang·kor \'aŋ-ˌkòr\ ruins of ancient city NW Cambodia N of Tonle Sap; ✻ of the Khmers

An·gle·sey *or* **An·gle·sea** \'aŋ-gəl-sē\ **1** *or ancient* **Mo·na** \'mō-nə\ island NW Wales **2** former county comprising Anglesey Is. & Holyhead Is. ✻ Llangefni

Anglia 1 — see ENGLAND **2** — see EAST ANGLIA — **An·gli·an** \'aŋ-glē-ən\ *adjective or noun*

Anglo–Egyptian Sudan — see SUDAN

An·go·la \aŋ-'gō-lə, an-\ country SW Africa S of mouth of the Congo; until 1975 a dependency of Portugal ✻ Luanda *area* 481,351 *sq mi* (1,251,513 *sq km*), *pop* 10,609,000 — **An·go·lan** \-lən\ *adjective or noun*

An·gou·lême \ˌäⁿ-gü-'lām, -'lem\ city W France *pop* 46,194

An·gou·mois \ˌäⁿ-gü-'mwä\ region & former duchy & province W France S of Poitou ✻ Angoulême

An·guil·la \aŋ-'gwi-lə, an-\ island Brit. West Indies NW of St. Kitts *area* 35 *sq mi* (91 *sq km*) — **An·guil·lan** \-'gwi-lən\ *adjective or noun*

An·gus \'aŋ-gəs\ *or earlier* **For·far** \'fòr-fər\ *or* **For·far·shire** \-ˌshir, -shər\ former county E Scotland ✻ Forfar

An·halt \'än-ˌhält\ former state *central* Germany ✻ Dessau

An·hui *or* **An·hwei** \'än-'hwā, -'wā\ province E China W of Jiangsu ✻ Hefei *area* 54,015 *sq mi* (140,439 *sq km*), *pop* 56,180,813

An·i·ak·chak Crater \ˌa-nē-'ak-ˌchak\ active volcano SW Alaska on Alaska Peninsula in **Aniakchak National Monument;** crater 6 *mi* (10 *km*) in diameter

A·ni–ma–ch'ing — see A'NYÊMAQÊN

An·jou \'an-jü, äⁿ-'zhü\ **1** region & former province NW France in Loire valley ✻ Angers **2** town Canada in S Quebec *pop* 37,210

An·ka·ra \'aŋ-kə-rə, 'äŋ-\ *or formerly* **An·go·ra** \aŋ-'gōr-ə, an-, -'gòr-\ *or ancient* **An·cy·ra** \an-'sī-rə\ city ✻ of Turkey in N *central* Anatolia *pop* 2,559,471

Ann, Cape \'an\ peninsula NE Mass.

An·na·ba \ä-'nä-bə\ *or formerly* **Bône** \'bōn\ commune & port NE Algeria NE of Constantine *pop* 305,526

An Na·fūd \ˌän-nä-'füd\ *or* **Na·fud** \na-'füd\ desert N Saudi Arabia in N Nejd

An Na·jaf \ˌän-'nä-ˌjäf\ city S *central* Iraq W of the Euphrates *pop* 242,603

An·nam \a-'nam, ə-; 'a-ˌnam\ region & former kingdom E Indochina in *central* Vietnam ✻ Hue *area about* 57,000 *sq mi* (148,200 *sq km*)

An·nap·o·lis \ə-'na-pə-ləs\ city & port ✻ of Md. *pop* 33,187

Annapolis Basin inlet of Bay of Fundy Canada in W Nova Scotia

An·na·pur·na \ˌa-nə-'pùr-nə, -'pər-\ massif N Nepal in the Himalayas; highest peak 26,504 *ft* (8078 *m*)

Ann Ar·bor \(ˌ)an-'är-bər\ city SE Mich. W of Detroit *pop* 109,592

An·ne·cy \ân-'sē\ city E France ENE of Lyons *pop* 51,143

An Nhon \'än-'nòn\ *or formerly* **Binh Dinh** \'bin-'din\ city *central* Vietnam in S Annam

An·nis·ton \'a-nə-stən\ city NE Ala. *pop* 26,623

An·qing *or* **An–ch'ing** \'än-'chiŋ\ *or* **An·king** \'än-'kiŋ\ *or formerly* **Hwai·ning** \'hwī-'niŋ\ city E China in Anhui on the Chang *pop* 250,718

An·shan \'än-'shän\ city NE China in E *central* Liaoning SSW of Shenyang *pop* 1,203,986

An·ta·kya \ˌän-tä-'kyä\ *or* **An·ta·ki·yah** \-'kē-yə\ *or ancient* **An·ti·och** \'an-tē-ˌäk\ city S Turkey on the Orontes *pop* 123,871

An·tal·ya \ˌän-täl-'yä\ *or formerly* **Ada·lia** \ə-'dä-lē-ə\ city & port SW Turkey on Gulf of Antalya *pop* 378,208

An·ta·nan·a·ri·vo \ˌän-tä-ˌnä-nä-'rē-(ˌ)vō\ *or Malagasy* **Ta·nan·a·ri·vo** \tə-ˌna-nä-'rē-(ˌ)vō\ *or formerly* **Ta·nan·a·rive** \tə-'na-nə-ˌrēv\ city ✻ of Madagascar *pop* 802,390

Ant·arc·tic \ant-'ärk-tik, -'är-tik\ region including Antarctica, Antarctic Peninsula, and the Antarctic Ocean

Ant·arc·ti·ca \-'ärk-ti-kə, -'är-ti-\ body of land around the S. Pole; a plateau covered by a great ice cap & mountain peaks *area about* 5,500,000 *sq mi* (14,300,000 *sq km*), divided into **West Antarctica** (including Antarctic Peninsula) & **East Antarctica** by Transantarctic Mountains

Antarctic Archipelago — see PALMER ARCHIPELAGO

Antarctic Ocean ocean surrounding Antarctica including the southern regions of the S. Atlantic, S. Pacific, & Indian oceans especially S of *about* 60°S

Antarctic Peninsula or *formerly* **Palmer Peninsula** peninsula *about* 700 *mi* (1126 *km*) long W Antarctica and S end of S. America

An·tibes \än̄-ˈtēb\ city & port SE France SW of Nice *pop* 70,688

Antibes, Cap d' — see CAP D'ANTIBES

An·ti·cos·ti Island \ˌan-tə-ˈkȯ-stē\ island E Canada in E Quebec at mouth of the St. Lawrence *area* 3043 *sq mi* (7912 *sq km*)

An·tie·tam Creek \an-ˈtē-təm\ creek S Pa. & N Md. flowing S into the Potomac N of Harpers Ferry, W.Va.

An·ti·gua \an-ˈtē-gə, -gwə\ **1** island Brit. West Indies in the Leewards *area* 108 *sq mi* (281 *sq km*); with Barbuda an independent nation (**Antigua and Barbuda**) since 1981 (*pop* 83,000) — see WEST INDIES ASSOCIATED STATES **2** or **Antigua Guatemala** city S central Guatemala; former ✱ of Guatemala *pop* 20,715 — **An·ti·guan** \an-ˈtē-gən, -gwən\ *adjective or noun*

An·ti–Leb·a·non \ˌan-ti-ˈle-bə-nən, -ˌnän\ mountain range SW Asia E of Bekaa Valley on Syria-Lebanon border — see HERMON (Mount)

An·til·les \an-ˈti-lēz\ the W. Indies excluding Bahamas — see GREATER ANTILLES, LESSER ANTILLES — **An·til·le·an** \an-ˈti-lē-ən\

An·ti·och \ˈan-tē-ˌäk\ **1** city W Calif. NE of Oakland *pop* 62,195 **2** — see ANTAKYA **3** ancient city Asia Minor in Pisidia, at certain periods within boundaries of Phrygia; ruins in W *central* Turkey — **An·ti·o·chene** \an-ˈtī-ə-ˌkēn, ˌan-tē-(ˌ)ä-ˈkēn\ *adjective or noun* — **An·ti·och·i·an** \ˌan-tē-ˈō-kē-ən, -ˈä-\ *adjective or noun*

An·ti·sa·na \ˌan-tē-ˈsä-nə\ volcano 18,714 *ft* (5704 *m*) N central Ecuador

An·to·fa·gas·ta \ˌän-tō-fä-ˈgäs-tä\ city & port N Chile W of Santiago *pop* 218,754

An·trim \ˈan-trəm\ **1** traditional county NE Northern Ireland **2** district E Northern Ireland, established 1974 *area* 217 *sq mi* (564 *sq km*), *pop* 44,322

An·tsi·ra·na·na \ˌän-tsē-ˈrä-nə-nə\ or *formerly* **Di·é·go–Suá·rez** \dē-ˈä-gō-ˈswä-res\ city & port Madagascar near N tip of island *pop* 54,418

Antung — see DANDONG

Ant·werp \ˈant-ˌwərp, ˈan-ˌtwərp\ or *French* **An·vers** \äⁿ-ˈver(s)\ or *Flemish* **Ant·wer·pen** \ˈänt-ˌver-pə(n)\ **1** province N Belgium *area* 1104 *sq mi* (2870 *sq km*), *pop* 1,605,167 **2** city & port, its ✱, on the Schelde *pop* 467,518

Anu·ra·dha·pu·ra \ə-ˈnür-ə-də-ˌpùr-ə\ town N central Sri Lanka; an ancient ✱ of Ceylon *pop* 37,000

An·yang \ˈän-ˈyäŋ\ **1** city E China in N Henan *pop* 480,668 **2** city NW S. Korea *pop* 361,577

A'·nyê·ma·qên \ˈä-ˌnyä-mä-ˈchen\ or **Am·ne Ma·chin** \ˈäm-nē-mä-ˈchin\ or **A·ni–ma·ch'ing** \ˈä-nē-ˈmä-ˈchiŋ\ range of the Kunlun Mountains W China in E *central* Qinghai; highest peak *about* 20,500 *ft* (6250 *m*)

An·zio \ˈänt-sē-ˌō, ˈan-zē-ˌō\ city & port Italy SSE of Rome *pop* 33,523

Ao·mo·ri \ˈä-ˈō-mō-rē\ city & port N Japan in NE Honshu on Mutsu Bay *pop* 287,354

Aorangi — see COOK (Mount)

Aos·ta \ä-ˈō-stä\ **1** commune NW Italy in Piedmont at junction of Great & Little Saint Bernard passes *pop* 36,339 **2** — see VALLE D'AOSTA

Ap·a·lach·i·co·la \ˌa-pə-ˌla-chi-ˈkō-lə\ river 90 *mi* (145 *km*) NW Fla. flowing from Lake Seminole S into **Apalachicola Bay** (inlet of Gulf of Mexico)

Apa·po·ris \ˌä-pä-ˈpȯr-(ˌ)ēs, -ˈpȯr-\ river *about* 550 *mi* (885 *km*) S Colombia flowing SE into the Japurá on Colombia-Brazil boundary

Apel·doorn \ˈä-pəl-ˌdȯrn, -ˌdȯrn\ commune E central Netherlands N of Arnhem *pop* 148,745

Ap·en·nines \ˈa-pə-ˌnīnz\ mountain chain Italy extending the length of the peninsula — see CORNO (Monte) — **Ap·en·nine** \-ˌnīn\ *adjective*

Apia \ä-ˈpē-ä\ town & port Samoa ✱ of Western Samoa on Upolu Is.

Apo, Mount \ˈä-(ˌ)pō\ volcano 9692 *ft* (2954 *m*) S Philippines in SE Mindanao; highest peak in the Philippines

Ap·pa·la·chia \ˌa-pə-ˈlā-chə, -ˈlä-chə, -ˈlā-shə\ region E U.S. comprising Appalachian Mountains from S central N.Y. to *central* Ala.

Ap·pa·la·chian Mountains \ˌa-pə-ˈlā-ch(ē-)ən, -sh(ē-)ən; -ˈla-ch(ē-)ən\ mountain system E N. America extending from SE Quebec, Newfoundland, & New Brunswick SW to N Ala.; highest peak Mt. Mitchell 6684 *ft* (2037 *m*)

Ap·pen·zell \ˈa-pən-ˌzel, ˈä-pən(t)-ˌsel\ former canton NE Switzerland, now divided into two cantons (formerly half cantons): **Appenzell Inner Rhodes** \ˈrōdz\ or *German* **Appenzell Inner Rho·den** \ˈi-nə(r)-ˈrō-dᵊn\ (✱ Appenzell *area* 67 *sq mi* or 174 *sq km*, *pop* 13,656) & **Appenzell Outer Rhodes** or *German* **Appenzell Aus·ser Rhoden** \ˈaù-sə(r)\ (✱ Herisau *area* 94 *sq mi* or 243 *sq km*, *pop* 51,167)

Ap·pi·an Way \ˈa-pē-ən\ ancient paved highway extending from Rome to the Adriatic

Ap·ple·ton \ˈa-pəl-tən\ city E Wis. *pop* 65,695

Apple Valley **1** town SE Calif. N of San Bernardino *pop* 46,079 **2** city SE Minn. *pop* 34,598

Apra Harbor \ˈä-prä\ seaport Guam on W coast

Ap·she·ron \ˌap-shi-ˈrȯn\ peninsula E Azerbaijan projecting into the Caspian Sea

Apu·lia — see PUGLIA — **Apu·lian** \ə-ˈpyül-yən, -ˈpyü-lē-ən\ *adjective or noun*

Apu·re \ä-ˈpü-rā\ river 509 *mi* (819 *km*) W Venezuela flowing E into the Orinoco

Apu·rí·mac \ˌä-pü-ˈrē-ˌmäk\ river 428 *mi* (689 *km*) S & *central* Peru flowing N to unite with the Urubamba forming the Ucayali

Aqa·ba \ˈä-kä-bə\ or **Al-ˈA·qa·bah** \ˌäl-\ or *ancient* **Elath** \ˈē-ˌlath\ town & port SW Jordan on border of Israel at head of NE arm (**Gulf of Aqaba**) of Red Sea

Aquid·neck Island \ə-ˈkwid-ˌnek\ or **Rhode Island** island SE R.I. in Narragansett Bay; site of city of Newport

Aq·ui·taine \ˈa-kwə-ˌtān\ old region of SW France comprising area later known as Guienne ✱ Toulouse

Aq·ui·ta·nia \ˌa-kwə-ˈtā-nyə, -nē-ə\ a Roman division of SW Gaul under Caesar consisting of country between Pyrenees & Garonne River & under Augustus expanded to Loire & Allier rivers — **Aq·ui·ta·nian** \-nyən, -nē-ən\ *adjective or noun*

'Ara·bah, Wadi \ˈwä-dē-ˈär-ä-bə\ or **Wadi al–ˈArabah** or **Wadi el–ˈArabah** \-ˌäl-, -ˌel-\ valley extending S from Dead Sea to Gulf of Aqaba

Arabian Desert desert E Egypt between the Nile & the Red Sea

Arabian Peninsula or **Ara·bia** \ə-ˈrā-bē-ə\ peninsula SW Asia *about* 1200 *mi* (1930 *km*) long & 1300 *mi* (2090 *km*) wide including Saudi Arabia, Yemen, & Persian Gulf States; in early times divided into **Arabia Pe·traea** \pə-ˈtrē-ə\, "Rocky Arabia", the NW part; **Arabia De·ser·ta** \di-ˈzər-tə\, "Desert Arabia", the N part; & **Arabia Fe·lix** \ˈfē-liks\, "Fertile Arabia", the main part but by some geographers restricted to Yemen

Arabian Sea sea, NW section of the Indian Ocean between India & Arabian Peninsula

Ar·a·by \ˈar-ə-bē\ ARABIA

Ara·ca·ju \ˌär-ə-kə-ˈzhü\ city & port NE Brazil ✱ of Sergipe *pop* 293,285

Arad \ä-ˈräd\ city W Romania on the Mures *pop* 191,428

Ara·fu·ra Sea \ˌä-rä-ˈfü-rä\ sea between N Australia & W New Guinea

Ar·a·gon \ˈar-ə-ˌgän, -gən; ˌä-rä-ˈgōn\ region NE Spain bordering on France; once an independent kingdom ✱ Saragossa — **Ar·a·go·nese** \ˌar-ə-gə-ˈnēz, -ˈnēs\ *adjective or noun*

Ara·gua·ia or **Ara·gua·ya** \ˌär-ä-ˈgwī-ə\ river *about* 1365 *mi* (2195 *km*), *central* Brazil flowing N into the Tocantins

Arāk \ä-ˈräk, ä-ˈrak\ city W Iran SW of Tehran *pop* 265,349

Ara·kan \ˌar-ə-ˈkän, -ˈkan\ coast region SW Myanmar on Bay of Bengal; chief town Sittwe

Araks \ə-ˈräks\ or **Aras** \ä-ˈräs\ or *ancient* **Arax·es** \ə-ˈrak-(ˌ)sēz\ river 635 *mi* (1022 *km*) W Asia rising in mountains of Turkish Armenia & flowing E to join the Kura in E Azerbaijan

Ar·al Sea \ˈar-əl\ or *formerly* **Lake Aral** brackish lake between Kazakhstan & Kyrgyzstan *area formerly* more than 25,500 *sq mi* (66,000 *sq km*)

Ar·am \ˈar-əm, ˈer-\ ancient Syria — its Hebrew name

Ar·an Islands \ˈar-ən\ islands W Ireland off coast of Galway; largest island Inishmore

Aran·sas Bay \ə-ˈran(t)-səs\ inlet of Gulf of Mexico S Tex. NE of Corpus Christi Bay between mainland & St. Joseph Is.

Aransas Pass channel S Tex. between Mustang & St. Joseph islands leading to Corpus Christi & Aransas bays

Ar·a·rat \ˈar-ə-ˌrat\ or **Ag·ri Da·gi** \ä-grē-dä-ˈgē\ mountain 16,946 *ft* (5165 *m*) E Turkey near border of Iran

Ara·val·li Range \ə-ˈrä-və-(ˌ)lē\ mountain range NW India E of Thar Desert; highest peak Mt. Abu 5650 *ft* (1722 *m*)

Ar·bil or **Ir·bil** or **Er·bil** \ər-ˈbēl\ city N Iraq E of Mosul *pop* 460,758

Ar·bon \är-ˈbōⁿ\ commune NE Switzerland *pop* 11,333

Ar·buck·le Mountains \ˈär-ˌbək-ᵊl\ hilly region S *central* Okla.

Ar·ca·dia \är-ˈkā-dē-ə\ **1** city SW Calif. ENE of Los Angeles *pop* 48,290 **2** mountainous region S Greece in *central* Peloponnese

Archangel, Gulf of — see DVINA GULF

Arch·es National Park \ˈär-chəz\ reservation E Utah including wind-eroded natural arch formations

Ar·cos de la Fron·te·ra \ˈär-kōs-ˌthä-lä-frōn-ˈtä-rä\ commune SW Spain NE of Cádiz *pop* 26,946

Ar·cot \är-ˈkät\ city SE India in N Tamil Nadu WSW of Madras; once ✱ of the nawabs of Carnatic *pop* 45,193

Arc·tic \ˈärk-tik, ˈär-tik\ the Arctic Ocean and lands in it and adjacent to it

Arctic Archipelago archipelago N & E Northwest Territories, Canada in Arctic Ocean

Arctic Ocean ocean N of the Arctic Circle

Arctic Red river 310 *mi* (499 *km*) Canada in W Northwest Territories, flowing N into the Mackenzie

Ar·cueil \är-ˈkəi, -ˈkü-ē\ commune N France S of Paris *pop* 20,303

Ar·da·bil or **Ar·de·bil** \ˌär-də-ˈbēl\ city NW Iran in E Azerbaijan region *pop* 281,973

Ar·den \ˈär-dᵊn\ district *central* England in SW Warwickshire W of Stratford-upon-Avon; site of former **Forest of Arden**

Ar·dennes \är-ˈden\ wooded plateau region in NE France, W Luxembourg, & SE Belgium E of the Meuse

Ard·more \ˈärd-ˌmȯr, -ˌmȯr\ city S Okla. *pop* 23,079

Ards \ˈärdz\ district E Northern Ireland, established 1974 *area* 143 *sq mi* (372 *sq km*), *pop* 64,026

Are·ci·bo \ˌä-rä-ˈsē-(ˌ)bō\ city & port N Puerto Rico *pop* 93,385

Are·na, Point \ə-ˈrē-nə\ promontory N Calif. in the Pacific *about* midway between Cape Mendocino & San Francisco Bay

Are·qui·pa \ˌä-rä-ˈkē-pä\ city S Peru at foot of El Misti *pop* 621,700

Arez·zo \ä-ˈret-(ˌ)sō, ä-\ commune *central* Italy in Tuscany *pop* 91,527

Ar·gen·tan \ˌär-zhən-ˈtäⁿ\ commune NW France in Normandy NNW of Alençon *pop* 16,063

Ar·gen·teuil \ˌär-zhən-ˈtəi, -ˈtü-ē\ commune N France on the Seine NNW of Paris *pop* 94,162

Ar·gen·ti·na \ˌär-jən-ˈtē-nə\ or **the Ar·gen·tine** \ˈär-jən-ˌtīn, -ˌtēn\ country S S. America between the Andes & the Atlantic S of the Pilcomayo; a federal republic ✱ Buenos Aires *area* 1,072,156 *sq mi* (2,776,884 *sq km*), *pop* 33,070,000 — **Ar·gentine** *adjective or noun* — **Ar·gen·tin·ean** or **Ar·gen·tin·i·an** \ˌär-jən-ˈti-nē-ən\ *adjective or noun*

Ar·gi·nu·sae \ˌär-jə-ˈnü-(ˌ)sē, -ˈnyü-\ group of small islands in the Aegean SE of Lesbos

Ar·go·lis \'är-gə-ləs\ district & ancient country S Greece in E Peloponnese comprising a plain around Argos & area between Gulf of Argolis & Saronic Gulf — **Ar·gol·ic** \är-'gä-lik\ *adjective*

Argolis, Gulf of inlet of the Aegean S Greece on E coast of Peloponnese

Ar·gonne \är-'gòn, -'gän\ wooded plateau NE France S of the Ardennes near Belgian border between the Meuse & the Aisne

Ar·gos \'är-ga, -gäs\ town Greece in E Peloponnese on Argive plain at head of Gulf of Argolis; once a Greek city-state

Argovie — see AARGAU

Ar·guel·lo, Point \är-'gwe-(,)lō\ cape SW Calif. WNW of Santa Barbara

Ar·gun \'är-gün\ river 450 *mi* (724 *km*) NE Asia forming boundary between Inner Mongolia (China) & Russia & uniting with the Shilka to form the Amur

Ar·gyll \är-'gīl, är-,gīl\ *or* **Ar·gyll·shire** \-,shir, -shər\ former county W Scotland ✱ Lochgilphead

Ar·hus *or* **Aar·hus** \'òr-,hüs\ city & port Denmark in E Jutland on the Kattegat *pop* 259,493

Aria \'är-ē-ə, ə-'rī-ə\ **1** an E province of ancient Persian Empire; district now in NW Afghanistan & E Iran **2** — see HERAT

Ari·ca \ə-'rē-kə\ city & port N Chile *pop* 177,330 — see TACNA

Ar·i·ma·thea \,ar-ə-mə-'thē-ə\ town in ancient Palestine; location not certainly identified

Ariminum — see RIMINI

Ari·pua·nã \,är-ē-pwə-'nä"\ river 400 *mi* (644 *km*) W central Brazil rising in Mato Grosso state & flowing N into the Madeira

Arius — see HARI

Ar·i·zo·na \,ar-ə-'zō-nə\ state SW U.S. ✱ Phoenix *area* 113,909 *sq mi* (296,163 *sq km*), *pop* 3,665,228 — **Ar·i·zo·nan** \-nən\ *or* **Ar·i·zo·nian** \-nē-ən, -nyən\ *adjective or noun*

Ar·kan·sas \'är-kən-,sò; *1 is also* är-'kan-zəs\ **1** river 1450 *mi* (2334 *km*) SW *central* U.S. rising in *central* Colo. & flowing E & SE through S Kans., NE Okla., & Ark. into the Mississippi **2** state S *central* U.S. ✱ Little Rock *area* 53,187 *sq mi* (137,754 *sq km*), *pop* 2,350,725 — **Ar·kan·san** \-'kan-zən\ *adjective or noun*

Ar·khan·gel'sk \är-'kan-gelsk, ər-'kän-gilsk\ *or* **Arch·an·gel** \'är,kän-jəl\ city & port Russia in Europe on the Northern Dvina *pop* 414,000

Arl·berg \'är(-ə)l-,bərg, -,berk\ Alpine valley, pass, & tunnel W Austria in the Tirol

Arles \'är(-ə)l\ **1** medieval kingdom E & SE France; also called Kingdom of Burgundy **2** *or ancient* **Ar·e·las** \'ar-ə-,las\ *or* **Ar·e·la·te** \,ar-ə-'lä-tē\ city SE France on the Rhône *pop* 52,593 — **Ar·le·sian** \är-'lē-zhən\ *noun*

Ar·ling·ton \'är-liŋ-tən\ **1** town E Mass. NW of Boston *pop* 44,630 **2** city N Tex. E of Fort Worth *pop* 261,721 **3** unincorporated population center N Va. *pop* 170,936

Arlington Heights village NE Ill. NW of Chicago *pop* 75,460

Ar·lon \är-'lōⁿ\ commune SE Belgium ✱ of Luxembourg province *pop* 23,422

Ar·magh \är-'mä, 'är-,\ **1** traditional county SE Northern Ireland **2** district S Northern Ireland, established 1974 *area* 260 *sq mi* (676 *sq km*), *pop* 51,331 **3** town *central* Armagh district, Northern Ireland *pop* 49,100

Ar·ma·gnac \,är-mán-'yák\ district SW France in old province of Gascony; chief town Auch

Ar·me·nia \är-'mē-nē-ə, -nyə\ **1** *or biblical* **Min·ni** \'mi-,nī\ former kingdom W Asia in mountainous region SE of Black Sea & SW of Caspian Sea; area now divided between Armenia, Turkey, & Iran **2** independent country SE Europe; a constituent republic (**Armenian Republic**) of the U.S.S.R. 1936–91 ✱ Yerevan *area* 11,506 *sq mi* (29,800 *sq km*), *pop* 3,426,000 — see LESSER ARMENIA

Ar·men·tières \,är-mä"-'tyer, -,är-mən-'tirz\ commune N France W of Lille *pop* 26,240

Ar·mor·i·ca \är-'mór-ə-kə, -'mär-\ **1** *or* **Ar·e·mor·i·ca** \,ar-ə-\ ancient region NW France between the Seine & the Loire **2** BRITTANY

Arn·hem \'ärn-,hem, 'är-nəm\ commune E Netherlands ✱ of Gelderland province *pop* 132,928

Arn·hem Land \'är-nəm\ region N Australia on N coast of Northern Territory

Ar·no \'är-(,)nō\ *or ancient* **Ar·nus** \-nəs\ river 150 *mi* (241 *km*) *central* Italy flowing W from the Apennines through Florence into Ligurian Sea

Aroos·took \ə-'rüs-tək, -'rüs-\ river 140 *mi* (225 *km*) N Maine flowing NE across New Brunswick border & into St. John River

Ar·ran \'ar-ən\ island SW Scotland in Firth of Clyde *area* 165 *sq mi* (429 *sq km*)

Ar·ras \ä-'räs, 'ar-əs\ city N France SSW of Lille *pop* 42,715

Arsanias — see MURAT

Arta, Gulf of — see AMBRACIAN GULF

Ar·tois \är-'twä\ former province N France between Flanders & Picardy ✱ Arras

Aru·ba \ə-'rü-bə\ internally self-governing Dutch island off NW Venezuela; chief town Oranjestad *area* 69 *sq mi* (179 *sq km*), *pop* 69,000

Aru Islands *or formerly* **Aroe Islands** \'är-(,)ü\ islands E Indonesia S of W New Guinea *area* 3305 *sq mi* (8593 *sq km*), *pop* 29,604

Arun·a·chal Pra·desh \ə-rə-,nä-chəl-prə-'däsh, -'desh\ *or formerly* **North East Frontier Agency** state NE India N of Assam ✱ Itanagar *area* 32,269 *sq mi* (83,577 *sq km*), *pop* 864,558

Aru·wi·mi \,ä-rü-'wē-mē\ river 620 *mi* (998 *km*) N Democratic Republic of the Congo flowing SW & W into Congo River

Ar·vada \är-'va-də\ city N *central* Colo. NW of Denver *pop* 89,235

Ar·wad \är-'wad, -'wäd\ *or biblical* **Ar·vad** \'är-,vad\ island Syria off coast of S Latakia

Asa·hi·ka·wa \ä-sə-hē-'kä-wə, ä-,sä-'hē-kä-\ *or* **Asa·hi·ga·wa** \-'gä-wə, -gä-wə\ city Japan in *central* Hokkaido *pop* 361,736

Asa·ma \ä-'sä-mä\ *or* **Asa·ma·ya·ma** \ä-,sä-mä-'yä-mä\ volcano 8300 *ft* (2530 *m*) Japan in *central* Honshu

Asan·sol \ə-'sənsòl\ city NE India in W. Bengal *pop* 261,836

As·cen·sion \ə-'sen(t)-shən\ island in S Atlantic belonging to Brit. colony of St. Helena *area* 34 *sq mi* (88 *sq km*), *pop* 1400

As·co·li Pi·ce·no \'äs-kō-(,)lē-pē-'chā-(,)nō\ *or ancient* **As·cu·lum Pi·ce·num** \-as-kyə-ləm-(,)pī-'sē-nəm\ commune *central* Italy in Marche NE of Rome *pop* 52,371

Ascoli Sa·tri·a·no \ä-,sä-trē-'ä-(,)nō\ *or ancient* **As·cu·lum Ap·u·lum** \,as-kyə-ləm-'a-pyə-ləm\ *or* **Aus·cu·lum Apulum** \,òs-\ commune SE Italy in Puglia S of Foggia

As·cot \'as-kət\ village S England in Berkshire SW of London

As·cut·ney, Mount \ə-'skət-nē\ mountain 3320 *ft* (1012 *m*) SE Vt.

Ashan·ti \ə-'shan-tē, -'shän-\ region *central* Ghana; formerly a native kingdom & later a Brit. colony ✱ Kumasi *area* 9417 *sq mi* (24,390 *sq km*), *pop* 2,090,100

Ash·bur·ton \'ash-,bər-t°n\ river *about* 400 *mi* (644 *km*) Australia in NW Western Australia flowing NW into Indian Ocean

Ash·dod \'ash-,däd\ city & port Israel W of Jerusalem *pop* 76,600

Ashe·ville \'ash-,vil, -vəl\ city W N.C. *pop* 61,607

Ashkh·a·bad \'ash-kə-,bad, -,bäd\ *or* **Ash·ga·bat** \'äsh-gə-,bät\ *or formerly* **Pol·to·ratsk** \,päl-tə-'rätsk\ city ✱ of Turkmenistan *pop* 412,200

Ash·land \'ash-lənd\ **1** city NE Ky. on the Ohio *pop* 23,622 **2** city N *central* Ohio *pop* 20,079

Ash·ley \'ash-lē\ river 40 *mi* (64 *km*) S S.C. flowing SE into Charleston harbor

Ash·qe·lon \'ash-kə-,län\ ancient city & port SW Palestine, site in Israel WSW of Jerusalem

Ash Sha·ri·qah \,ash-'shä-rē-kə\ *or* **Shar·jah** \'shär-jə\ sheikhdom, member of United Arab Emirates

Ash·ta·bu·la \,ash-tə-'byü-lə\ city NE Ohio on Lake Erie *pop* 21,633

Asia \'ā-zhə, -shə\ continent of the eastern hemisphere N of equator forming a single landmass with Europe (the conventional dividing line between Asia & Europe being the Ural Mountains & main range of the Caucasus Mountains); has numerous large offshore islands including Cyprus, Sri Lanka, Malay Archipelago, Taiwan, the Japanese chain, & Sakhalin *area* 17,139,445 *sq mi* (44,391,162 *sq km*)

Asia Minor peninsula forming W extremity of Asia between Black Sea on N, Mediterranean Sea on S, & Aegean Sea on W — see ANATOLIA

Asir \a-'sir\ province S Saudi Arabia on Red Sea SE of Hejaz ✱ As Sabya *area* 40,130 *sq mi* (103,937 *sq km*)

As·ma·ra \az-'mär-ə, -'mar-ə\ city ✱ of Eritrea *pop* 342,706

As·nières \än-'yer\ commune N France NW of Paris

Aso \'ä-(,)sō\ *or* **Aso-san** \'ä-sō-,sän\ volcanic mountain Japan in *central* Kyushu; has five volcanic cones grouped around crater 15 *mi* (24 *km*) long with walls 2000 *ft* (610 *m*) high

Aso·lo \'ä-zò-,lō\ commune NE Italy NW of Treviso

Asphaltites, Lacus — see DEAD SEA

As·sam \ə-'sam, a-; 'a-,sam\ state NE India on edge of Himalayas ✱ Dispur *area* 30,318 *sq mi* (78,827 *sq km*), *pop* 22,414,322

As·sen \'ä-s°n\ commune NE Netherlands ✱ of Drenthe *pop* 50,880

As·sin·i·boine \ə-'si-nə-,bòin\ river 665 *mi* (1070 *km*) Canada rising in SE Saskatchewan & flowing S & E across S Manitoba into Red River

Assiniboine, Mount mountain 11,870 *ft* (3618 *m*) Canada in SW Alberta on British Columbia border

As·si·si \ə-'si-sē, -'sē-, -zē\ commune *central* Italy ESE of Perugia *pop* 24,669

As·syr·ia \ə-'sir-ē-ə\ *or biblical* **As·sur** \ä-'sur, 'ä-,\ *or* **Ashur** \'ä-,shùr\ ancient empire W Asia extending along middle Tigris & over foothills to the E; early ✱ Calah, later ✱ Nineveh

Astacus — see IZMIT

Asti \'äs-tē\ commune NW Italy W of Alessandria *pop* 74,649

As·tra·khan \'as-trə-,kan, -kən\ city Russia in Europe, on the Volga at head of its delta *pop* 512,000

As·tu·ri·as \ə-'stùr-ē-əs, a-, -'styùr-\ **1** region & old kingdom NW Spain on Bay of Biscay **2** province NW Spain *area* 4079 *sq mi* (10,565 *sq km*), *pop* 1,093,937 — **As·tu·ri·an** \-ē-ən\ *adjective or noun*

Asun·ción \ä-sün-'syōn\ city ✱ of Paraguay on Paraguay River at confluence with the Pilcomayo *pop* 502,426

As·wân \a-'swän, ä-\ *or ancient* **Sy·e·ne** \sī-'ē-nē\ city S Egypt on right bank of the Nile near site of dam built 1898–1902 & of **Aswân High Dam** (completed 1970 to form **Lake Nas·ser** \'nä-sər, 'na-\) *pop* 191,461

As·yût \äs-'yüt\ city *central* Egypt on left bank of the Nile *pop* 273,191

Ata·ca·ma \,ä-tä-'kä-mä\ — see PUNA DE ATACAMA

Atacama Desert desert N Chile between Copiapó & Peru border

Atas·ca·de·ro \ə-,tas-kə-'der-(,)ō\ city W Calif. *pop* 23,138

At·ba·ra \'at-bə-rə, 'ät-\ river *about* 500 *mi* (805 *km*) NE Africa rising in N Ethiopia & flowing through E Sudan into the Nile

Atchaf·a·laya \(ə-),cha-fə-'lī-ə\ river 225 *mi* (362 *km*) S La. flowing S into **Atchafalaya Bay** (inlet of Gulf of Mexico)

Ath·a·bas·ca *or* **Ath·a·bas·ka** \,a-thə-'bas-kə, ,ä-\ river 765 *mi* (1231 *km*) Canada in Alberta flowing NE & N into Lake Athabasca

Athabasca, Lake lake Canada on Alberta–Saskatchewan boundary *area* 3058 *sq mi* (7951 *sq km*)

Ath·ens \'a-thənz\ **1** city NE Ga. *pop* 45,734 **2** city SE Ohio *pop* 21,265 **3** *or Greek* **Athí·nai** \ä-'thē-(,)ne\ *or ancient* **Athe·nae** \ə-'thē-(,)nē\ city ✱ of Greece near Saronic Gulf *pop* 748,110 — **Athe·nian** \ə-'thē-nē-ən, -nyən\ *adjective or noun*

Athos \'a-,thòs, 'ä-\ mountain NE Greece at E end of Acte Peninsula; site of a number of monasteries comprising **Mount Athos** (autonomous area)

Ati·tlán \,ä-tē-'tlän\ lake 12 *mi* (19 *km*) long SW Guatemala at 4700 *ft* (1432 *m*) altitude occupying a crater 1000 *ft* (305 *m*) deep N of **Atitlán Volcano**

At·ka \'at-kə, 'ät-\ island SW Alaska in Andreanof group

At·lan·ta \ət-'lan-tə, at-\ city NW *central* Ga., its ✳ *pop* 394,017 — **At·lan·tan** \-'lan-tᵊn\ *adjective or noun*

At·lan·tic City \ət-'lan-tik, at-\ city SE N.J. on Atlantic coast *pop* 37,986

Atlantic Ocean ocean separating N. & S. America from Europe & Africa *area* 31,814,640 *sq mi* (82,399,918 *sq km*); often divided into **North Atlantic Ocean** & **South Atlantic Ocean**

Atlantic Provinces the Canadian provinces of Newfoundland, New Brunswick, Nova Scotia, & Prince Edward Island — see MARITIME PROVINCES

At·las Mountains \'at-ləs\ mountains NW Africa extending from SW Morocco to NE Tunisia; its highest peaks are in the **Grand**, or **High, Atlas** in SW *central* Morocco — see TOUBKAL (Jebel)

Atrek \ä-'trek\ *or* **Atrak** \-'trak\ river 300 *mi* (483 *km*) NE Iran flowing into the Caspian Sea on Turkmenistan border

Atropatene — see AZERBAIJAN

At·ta·wa·pis·kat \ˌa-tə-wə-'pis-kət\ river 465 *mi* (748 *km*) Canada in N Ontario flowing E into James Bay

At·ti·ca \'a-ti-kə\ region E Greece, chief city Athens; a state of ancient Greece

At·tle·boro \'a-tᵊl-ˌbər-ō\ city SE Mass. *pop* 38,383

At·tu \'a-(ˌ)tü\ island SW Alaska, most westerly of the Aleutians, in Near group — see WRANGELL (Cape)

At·wa·ter \'at-ˌwȯ-tər, -ˌwä-\ city *central* Calif. *pop* 22,282

Aube \'ōb\ river 154 *mi* (248 *km*) N *central* France flowing into the Seine

Au·ber·vil·liers \ˌō-bər-ˌvēl-'yä\ commune N France *pop* 72,859

Au·burn \'ȯ-bərn\ **1** city E Ala. *pop* 33,830 **2** city SW Maine *pop* 24,309 **3** city *central* N.Y. *pop* 31,258 **4** city W Wash. *pop* 33,102

Auck·land \'ȯ-klənd\ city & port N New Zealand on North Is. *pop* 315,668 — **Auck·land·er** \-klən-dər\ *noun*

Audenarde — see OUDENAARDE

Au·ghrim *or* **Aghrim** \'ȯ-grəm\ town W Ireland in E Galway

Au·gra·bies Falls \ȯ-'grä-bēz\ waterfall 480 *ft* (146 *m*) Republic of S. Africa in Orange River in Northern Cape province

Augs·burg \'ȯgz-ˌbərg, 'au̇gz-ˌbu̇rk\ city S Germany in Bavaria on the Lech *pop* 256,877

Au·gus·ta \ȯ-'gəs-tə, ə-\ **1** city E Ga. on Savannah River *pop* 44,639 **2** city ✳ of Maine on the Kennebec *pop* 21,325

Au·lis \'ȯ-ləs\ harbor E Greece in Boeotia on Evripos Strait

Au·nis \ō-'nēs\ former province W France on Gironde Estuary & Bay of Biscay ✳ La Rochelle

Au·rang·a·bad \au̇-'rəŋ-gə-ˌbäd, -'rəŋ-ə-, -ˌbad\ city W India in *central* Maharashtra ENE of Bombay *pop* 573,272

Au·rès \ō-'res\ massif *about* 7600 *ft* (2316 *m*) NE Algeria in Saharan Atlas

Au·ri·gnac \ˌȯ-rēn-'yak\ village SW France SW of Toulouse

Au·ril·lac \ˌȯ-rē-'yak\ city S *central* France *pop* 32,654

Au·ro·ra \ə-'rȯr-ə, ȯ-, -'rör-\ **1** city N *central* Colo. E of Denver *pop* 222,103 **2** city NE Ill. *pop* 99,581 **3** town Canada in SE Ontario *pop* 29,454

Au·sa·ble \ȯ-'sā-bəl\ river 20 *mi* (32 *km*) NE N.Y. flowing E into Lake Champlain through **Ausable Chasm** gorge

Auschwitz — see OŚWIECIM

Austerlitz — see SLAVKOV

Aus·tin \'ȯs-tən, 'äs-\ **1** city S Minn. *pop* 21,907 **2** city ✳ of Tex. on the Colorado *pop* 465,622

Austral Islands islands S Pacific S of Tahiti belonging to France *pop* 6509

Aus·tral·asia \ˌȯs-trə-'lā-zhə, ˌäs-, -'lā-shə\ Australia, New Zealand, & Melanesia — **Aus·tral·asian** \-zhən, -shən\ *adjective or noun*

Aus·tra·lia \ȯ-'strāl-yə, ä-, ə-\ **1** continent of the eastern hemisphere SE of Asia & S of the equator *area* 2,948,366 *sq mi* (7,665,751 *sq km*) **2** *or* **Commonwealth of Australia** dominion of the Commonwealth of Nations including the continent of Australia & island of Tasmania ✳

Canberra *area* 2,967,909 *sq mi* (7,716,563 *sq km*), *pop* 17,562,000

Australian Alps mountain range SE Australia in E Victoria & SE New S. Wales forming S end of Great Dividing Range

Australian Capital Territory *or formerly* **Federal Capital Territory** district SE Australia including two areas, one around Canberra & the other on Jervis Bay, surrounded by New S. Wales *area* 939 *sq mi* (2441 *sq km*), *pop* 229,000

Aus·tra·sia *or* **Os·tra·sia** \ȯ-'strā-zhə, ä-, -shə\ the E dominions of the Merovingian Franks extending from the Meuse to Böhmerwald — **Aus·tra·sian** \-zhən, -shən\ *adjective or noun*

Aus·tria \'ȯs-trē-ə, 'äs-\ *or German* **Ös·ter·reich** \'ᵉ̄-sta(r)-ˌrīk\ country *central* Europe in & N of E Alps with the Danube crossing it in N; a republic ✳ Vienna *area* 32,375 *sq mi* (84,175 *sq km*), *pop* 7,812,100 — **Aus·tri·an** \-ən\ *adjective or noun*

Austria–Hun·ga·ry \-'həŋ-gə-rē\ dual monarchy 1867–1918 *central* Europe including Bohemia, Moravia, Bukovina, Transylvania, Galicia, and what is now Austria, Hungary, Slovenia, Croatia, & NE Italy — **Aus·tro–Hun·gar·i·an** \ˌȯs-(ˌ)trō-ˌhəŋ-'gar-ē-ən, ˌäs-, -'ger-\ *adjective or noun*

Aus·tro·ne·sia \ˌȯs-trə-'nē-zhə, ˌäs-, -'nē-shə\ **1** the islands of the S Pacific **2** area extending from Madagascar through the Malay Peninsula & Archipelago to Hawaii & Easter Is.

Au·teuil \ō-'tᴐi, -'tə(r)\ district in W Paris, France

Au·vergne \ō-'vernʸ, -'vərn\ region & former province S *central* France ✳ Clermont (now Clermont-Ferrand)

Auvergne Mountains mountains S *central* France; highest in the Massif Central — see SANCY (Puy de)

Aux Cayes — see CAYES

Aux Sources, Mont \ˌmōⁿ-ˌtō-'su̇rs\ mountain 10,822 *ft* (3298 *m*) N Lesotho in Drakensberg Mountains on South Africa border

Au·yán·te·puí \au̇-ˌyän-tä-'pwē\ *or* **Devil Mountain** plateau *about* 20 *mi* (32 *km*) long SE Venezuela in valley of the Caroní — see ANGEL FALLS

Au·yuit·tuq National Park \au̇-'yü-ə-tək\ reservation NE Canada in E Baffin Is.

Av·a·lon \'a-və-ˌlän\ peninsula Canada in SE Newfoundland

Avalon, Isle of — see ISLE OF AVALON

Ave·bury \'āv-b(ə)-rē, *United States also* -ˌber-ē\ village S England in Wiltshire E of Bristol; has megalithic remains

Avel·la·ne·da \ˌä-vä-zhä-'nä-thä\ city E Argentina, E suburb of Buenos Aires, on Río de la Plata *pop* 346,620

Avenches \a-'väⁿsh\ *or ancient* **Aven·ti·cum** \ə-'ven-ti-kəm\ town W Switzerland in Vaud canton ✳ of ancient Helvetia

Av·en·tine \'a-vən-ˌtīn, -ˌtēn\ hill in Rome, Italy, one of seven (including also the Caelian, Capitoline, Esquiline, Palatine, Quirinal, & Viminal) on which the ancient city was built

Aver·nus, Lake \ə-'vər-nəs\ *or Italian* **Lago d'Aver·no** \ˌlä-gō-dä-'ver-(ˌ)nō\ lake S Italy in crater of extinct volcano W of Naples

Avi·gnon \ˌa-(ˌ)vēn-'yōⁿ\ city SE France *pop* 89,440

Ávi·la \'ä-vi-lə, -vē-ˌlä\ **1** province *central* Spain *area* 3107 *sq mi* (8047 *sq km*), *pop* 174,378 **2** city, its ✳, WNW of Madrid *pop* 45,977

Avlona — see VLORË

Avon \'ā-vən, 'a-, *United States also* 'ā-ˌvän\ **1** river 96 *mi* (154 *km*) *central* England rising in Northamptonshire & flowing WSW past Stratford-upon-Avon into Severn River at Tewkesbury **2** river 65 *mi* (105 *km*) S England rising near Devizes in Wiltshire & flowing S into English Channel **3** river 75 *mi* (121 *km*) SW England rising in Gloucestershire & flowing S & W through city of Bristol into Bristol Channel at Avonmouth **4** \'a-vən\ — see SWAN **5** \'ā-vən, 'a-, *United States also* 'ā-ˌvän\ county SW England ✳ Bristol *area* 535 *sq mi* (1386 *sq km*), *pop* 919,800

Avranches \av-'räⁿsh\ town NW France in SW Normandy

Awa·ji \ä-'wä-jē\ island Japan S of Honshu & NE of Shikoku

Awash \'ä-ˌwäsh\ river 500 *mi* (805 *km*) E Ethiopia flowing NE

Ax·el Hei·berg \'ak-səl-'hī-ˌbərg\ island N Canada in the Sverdrup Islands W of Ellesmere Is. *area* 15,779 *sq mi* (41,025 *sq km*)

Axum — see AKSUM — **Ax·um·ite** \'ak-sə-ˌmīt\ *adjective or noun*

Aya·cu·cho \ˌī-ä-'kü-(ˌ)chō\ town S Peru SE of Lima *pop* 101,600

Ay·dın \ˌī-'din\ city SW Turkey SE of Izmir *pop* 107,011

Ayers Rock \'arz, 'erz\ outcrop *central* Australia in SW Northern Territory; 1143 *ft* (348 *m*) high

Ayles·bury \'ālz-b(ə-)rē, *United States also* -ˌber-ē\ borough SE *central* England ✳ of Buckinghamshire *pop* 41,288

Ayl·mer \'āl-mər\ town Canada in SW Quebec *pop* 32,244

Ayr \'ar, 'er\ **1** *or* **Ayr·shire** \-ˌshir, -shər\ former county SW Scotland **2** burgh & port SW Scotland in Strathclyde *pop* 49,481

Ayut·tha·ya \ä-yü-'tī-ə\ *or in full* **Phra Na·khon Si Ayutthaya** \ˌprä-nä-'kȯn-sē-\ city S Thailand N of Bangkok *pop* 60,561

Azer·bai·jan \ˌa-zər-ˌbī-'jän, ˌä-\ independent country SE Europe bordering on Caspian Sea; a constituent republic of the U.S.S.R. 1936–91 ✳ Baku *area* 33,200 *sq mi* (86,320 *sq km*), *pop* 7,029,000

Azerbaijan *or ancient* **At·ro·pa·te·ne** \ˌa-trō-pə-'tē-nē\ *or* **Me·dia Atropatene** \ˌmē-dē-ə\ region NW Iran; chief city Tabriz

Azincourt — see AGINCOURT

Azores \'ā-ˌzȯrz, -ˌzȯrz, ə-'\ *or Portuguese* **Aço·res** \ə-'sȯr-ēsh\ islands N Atlantic belonging to Portugal & lying *about* 800 *mi* (1287 *km*) off coast of Portugal; chief town Ponta Delgada *area* 905 *sq mi* (2344 *sq km*), *pop* 236,500 — **Azor·e·an** *or* **Azor·i·an** \ā-'zȯr-ē-ən, -'zȯr-, ə-\ *adjective or noun*

Azov, Sea of \'a-ˌzȯf, 'ä-; ə-'zȯf\ gulf of the Black Sea E of Crimea connected with the Black Sea by the Kerch Strait *area* 14,517 *sq mi* (37,599 *sq km*)

Az·tec Ruins National Monument \'az-ˌtek\ reservation NW N.Mex. NE of Farmington; site of a prehistoric pueblo

Azu·sa \ə-'sü-sə\ city SW Calif. ENE of Los Angeles *pop* 41,333

Az Zaqāzīq — see ZAGAZIG

Baal·bek \'bä-əl-ˌbek, 'bäl-ˌbek\ town E Lebanon N of Damascus on site of ancient city of **He·li·op·o·lis** \ˌhē-lē-'ä-p(ə-)ləs\

Ba·bar Islands \'bä-ˌbär\ islands Indonesia ENE of Timor

Bab el Man·deb \'bäb-el-'män-dəb\ strait between SW Arabia & Africa connecting Red Sea & Gulf of Aden

Ba·bel·thu·ap \ˌbä-bəl-'tü-ˌäp\ island W Pacific, chief island in Palau *area* 143 *sq mi* (372 *sq km*)

Babruysk — see BOBRUYSK

Ba·bu·yan \ˌbä-bü-'yän\ chief island of the Babuyan group

Babuyan Islands *or* **Ba·bu·ya·nes** \ˌbä-bü-'yä-nās\ islands of N Philippines N of Luzon *area* 225 *sq mi* (585 *sq km*)

Bab·y·lon \'ba-bə-lən, -ˌlän\ ancient city ✳ of Babylonia; its site *about* 55 *mi* (89 *km*) S of Baghdad near the Euphrates

Bab·y·lo·nia \ˌba-bə-'lō-nyə, -nē-ə\ ancient country in valley of the lower Euphrates & the Tigris ✳ Babylon

Ba·cau \bə-'kau̇\ city E *central* Romania *pop* 193,269

Back \'bak\ river 605 *mi* (974 *km*) Canada in Northwest Territories flowing ENE into Arctic Ocean

Ba·co·lod \bä-'kō-ˌlȯd\ city Philippines on Negros Is. *pop* 364,000

Bactra — see BALKH

Bac·tria \'bak-trē-ə\ ancient country SW Asia between Hindu Kush & Oxus River ✳ Bactra — see BALKH — **Bac·tri·an** \'bak-trē-ən\ *adjective or noun*

Ba·da·joz \ˌbä-thä-'hōs, ˌbä-də-'hōz\ **1** province SW Spain in valley of the Guadiana *area*

\ə\ abut \ᵊ\ kitten \ər\ further \a\ ash \ā\ ace \ä\ mop, mar \au̇\ out \ch\ chin \e\ bet \ē\ easy \g\ go \i\ hit \ī\ ice \j\ job \ŋ\ sing \ō\ go \ȯ\ law \ȯi\ boy \th\ thin \t͟h\ the \ü\ loot \u̇\ foot \y\ yet \zh\ vision *see also* Guide to Pronunciation

8362 *sq mi* (21,658 *sq km*), *pop* 650,388 **2** city, its ✳ *pop* 122,225

Ba·da·lo·na \,bä-thä-'lō-nä, ,bä-d⁰l-'ō-nə\ city & port NE Spain on the Mediterranean NE of Barcelona *pop* 218,725

Bad Ems — see EMS

Ba·den \'bä-d⁰n\ **1** region SW Germany bordering on Switzerland & France; formerly a grand duchy (1805–1918), a state of the Weimar Republic (1918–33), an administrative division of the Third Reich (1933–49), & a state of the Bonn Republic (1949–51) ✳ Karlsruhe — see BADEN·WÜRTTEMBERG **2** BADEN-BADEN

Ba·den–Ba·den \,bä-d⁰n-'bä-d⁰n\ *or* **Baden** city & spa SW Germany in Baden-Württemberg SSW of Karlsruhe *pop* 52,524

Ba·den–Würt·tem·berg \,bä-d⁰n-'wər-təm-,bərg, -'wür-; -'vərt-təm-,berk\ state SW Germany W of Bavaria; formed 1951 from former Baden, Württemberg-Baden, & Württemberg-Hohenzollern states ✳ Stuttgart *area* 13,803 *sq mi* (35,750 *sq km*), *pop* 9,822,000

Bad Godesberg — see GODESBERG

Bad Hom·burg \'bät-'hōm-,bûrk, -'häm-,bərg\ city SW *central* Germany N of Frankfurt am Main *pop* 51,663

Badlands National Park reservation SW S.Dak. E of Black Hills comprising an area of badlands topography

Bad Mergentheim — see MERGENTHEIM

Baer·um \'bar-əm\ city SE Norway, a suburb of Oslo *pop* 89,221

Baf·fin Bay inlet of the Atlantic between W Greenland & E Baffin Is.

Baffin Island island NE Canada N of Hudson Strait; largest in Arctic Archipelago *area* 183,810 *sq mi* (477,906 *sq km*)

Ba·fing \bə-'faŋ, bá-'fēnʸ\ river 350 *mi* (560 *km*) W Africa in W Mali & Guinea; the upper course of the Senegal

Bagh·dad \'bag-,dad, ,bäg-'däd\ city ✳ of Iraq on the middle Tigris *pop* 3,841,268 — **Bagh·dadi** \bag-'da-dē\ *noun*

Ba·guio \,bä-gē-'ō\ city, summer ✳ of the Philippines in NW *central* Luzon *pop* 183,000

Ba·ha·mas \bə-'hä-məz, *by outsiders also* -'hā-\ islands in the Atlantic SE of Fla.; an independent member of the Commonwealth of Nations since 1973 ✳ Nassau *area* 4404 *sq mi* (11,450 *sq km*), *pop* 268,000 — see TURKS AND CAICOS — **Ba·ha·mi·an** \bə-'hā-mē-ən, -'hä-\ *adjective or noun*

Ba·ha·wal·pur \bə-'hä-wəl-,púr\ region Pakistan in SW Punjab; until 1947 a princely state of India

Ba·hia \bə-'hē-ə, bä-'ē-ə\ **1** *or formerly* **Ba·ía** \bä-'ē-ə\ state E Brazil ✳ Salvador *area* 216,612 *sq mi* (561,025 *sq km*), *pop* 11,801,810 **2** — see SALVADOR — **Ba·hi·an** \-ən\ *adjective or noun*

Ba·hía Blan·ca \bə-,hē-ə-'blaŋ-kə, bä-,ē-ə-'bläŋ-kä\ city & port E Argentina SW of Buenos Aires *pop* 271,467

Bahnasa, El — see OXYRHYNCHUS

Bah·rain *also* **Bah·rein** \bä-'rān\ **1** islands in Persian Gulf off coast of Arabia; an independent sultanate ✳ Manama (on Bahrain Is.) *area* 255 *sq mi* (661 *sq km*), *pop* 485,600 **2** island, largest of the group, 27 *mi* (43 *km*) long — **Bah·raini** *or* **Bah·reini** \-'rā-nē\ *adjective or noun*

Bahr al–Gha·zal \,bär-ál-gà-'zál\ river 445 *mi* (716 *km*) SW Sudan flowing E to unite with the Bahr el Jebel forming the White Nile

Ba·ia–Ma·re \,bä-yä-'mä-rā\ city NW Romania *pop* 150,456

Baie–Co·meau \,bā-kō-(,)mō, ,bā-kə-'mō\ town Canada in SE Quebec *pop* 26,012

Bai·kal, Lake *or* **Lake Bay·kal** \bī-'käl, -'kal\ lake Russia in Asia; 5715 *ft* (1742 *m*) deep, *about* 395 *mi* (636 *km*) long

Baile Atha Cliath — see DUBLIN

Ba·ja California \'bä-(,)hä\ peninsula 760 *mi* (1216 *km*) long NW Mexico between the Pacific & Gulf of California; divided into the states of **Baja California** (to the N ✳ Mexicali *area* 27,071 *sq mi or* 70,114 *sq km*, *pop* 1,660,855) & **Baja California Sur** \'súr\ (to the S ✳ La Paz *area* 28,447 *sq mi or* 73,678 *sq km*, *pop* 317,764)

Bakan — see SHIMONOSEKI

Ba·ker Island \'bā-kər\ atoll *central* Pacific near the equator at 176°31′W; belongs to U.S.

Baker, Mount mountain 10,778 *ft* (3266 *m*) NW Wash. in Cascade Range

Baker Lake — see DUBAWNT

Ba·kers·field \'bā-kərz-,fēld\ city S *central* Calif. on the Kern *pop* 174,820

Bākh·ta·rān \,bäk-tə-'rän\ *or formerly* **Ker·man·shah** \,ker-,män-'shä\ city W Iran *pop* 560,514

Ba·ku \bä-'kü\ city, ✳ of Azerbaijan *pop* 1,150,000

Bakwanga — see MBUJI-MAYI

Ba·la·kla·va \,ba-lə-'klä-və, -'kla-; bä-lə-'klä-və\ village in Crimea SE of Sevastopol

Bal·a·ton, Lake \'ba-lə-,tän, 'bó-ló-,tón\ *or German* **Plat·ten·see** \'plä-t⁰n-,zā\ lake W Hungary; largest in *central* Europe *area* 232 *sq mi* (601 *sq km*)

Bal·boa Heights \,bal-'bō-ə\ town Panama at Pacific entrance to Panama Canal adjacent to Panama (city); former administrative center of Canal Zone

Bald·win \'ból-dwən\ borough SW Pa. S of Pittsburgh *pop* 21,923

Baldwin Park city SW Calif. E of Los Angeles *pop* 69,330

Bâle — see BASEL

Bal·e·ar·es \,ba-lē-'är-ēz, ,bä-lē-'är-ās\ **1** BALEARIC ISLANDS **2** province E Spain comprising the Balearic Islands ✳ Palma *area* 1936 *sq mi* (5034 *sq km*), *pop* 709,138

Bal·e·ar·ic Islands \,ba-lē-'ar-ik\ islands E Spain in the W Mediterranean — see BALEARES, IBIZA, MAJORCA, MINORCA

Ba·li \'bä-lē, 'ba-\ island Indonesia off E Java *area* 2147 *sq mi* (5582 *sq km*), *pop* 2,777,811 — **Ba·li·nese** \,bä-li-'nēz, ,ba-, -'nēs\ *adjective or noun*

Ba·li·ke·sir \,bä-li-ke-'sir\ city NW Turkey in Asia *pop* 170,589

Ba·lik·pa·pan \,bä-lik-'pä-,pän\ city & port Indonesia on SE Borneo on inlet of Makassar Strait *pop* 309,492

Bal·kan Mountains \'ból-kən\ mountain range *central* Bulgaria extending from Yugoslavia border to Black Sea; highest point Botev Peak 7793 *ft* (2375 *m*)

Balkan Peninsula peninsula SE Europe between Adriatic & Ionian seas on W & Aegean & Black seas on E — **Balkan** *adjective* — **Balkan·ic** \ból-'ka-nik\ *adjective*

Bal·kans \'ból-kənz\ *also* **Balkan States** the countries occupying the Balkan Peninsula: Slovenia, Croatia, Bosnia and Herzegovina, Macedonia, Yugoslavia, Romania, Bulgaria, Albania, Greece, & Turkey in Europe

Bal·kar·ia \ból-'kar-ē-ə, bal-, -'ker-\ mountain region S Russia in Europe, in S Kabardino-Balkaria Republic

Balkh \'bälk\ **1** district N Afghanistan corresponding closely to ancient Bactria **2** *or ancient* **Bac·tra** \'bak-trə\ town N Afghanistan ✳ of ancient Bactria

Bal·khash, Lake \bal-'kash, bäl-'käsh\ lake 376 *mi* (605 *km*) long SE Kazakhstan *area about* 7100 *sq mi* (18,390 *sq km*)

Bal·la·rat \'ba-lə-,rat\ city SE Australia in *central* Victoria *pop* 34,501

Bal·ly·me·na \,ba-lē-'mē-nə\ district NE Northern Ireland, established 1974 *area* 246 *sq mi* (640 *sq km*), *pop* 56,032

Bal·ly·mon·ey \,ba-lē-'mə-nē\ district N Northern Ireland, established 1974 *area* 162 *sq mi* (421 *sq km*), *pop* 23,984

Bal·sas \'ból-səs, 'bäl-säs\ river 426 *mi* (682 *km*) *central* Mexico flowing from Tlaxcala to the Pacific on border between Michoacán & Guerrero

Bal·tic Sea \'ból-tik\ arm of the Atlantic N Europe enclosed by Denmark & Scandinavia *area about* 160,000 *sq mi* (256,000 *sq km*)

Bal·ti·more \'ból-tə-,mōr, -,mór, -mər; *by residents usually* 'ból-tə-,mōr *or* 'ból-mər\ city & port N *central* Md. on the Patapsco estuary near Chesapeake Bay *pop* 736,014 — **Bal·ti·mor·e·an** \,ból-tə-'mōr-ē-ən, -'mór-\ *noun*

Bal·ti·stan \,ból-tə-'stan, -bəl-, -'stän\ region Ladakh district N Kashmir; under Pakistani control

Ba·lu·chi·stan \bə-,lü-chə-'stan, -'stän; bə-'lü-chə-\ **1** arid region S Asia bordering on Arabian Sea in SW Pakistan & SE Iran S & SW of Afghanistan **2** province SW Pakistan ✳ Quetta *pop* 4,305,000

Ba·ma·ko \'bä-mä-,kō\ city ✳ of Mali on Niger River *pop* 745,787

Bam·ba·ri \,bäm-bä-rē\ town S *central* Central African Republic *pop* 52,100

Bam·berg \'bam-,bərg, 'bäm-,berk\ city S *central* Germany in N Bavaria NNW of Nuremberg *pop* 70,689

Ba·na·ba \bä-'nä-bä\ *or* **Ocean Island** island W Pacific SW of Nauru; belongs to Kiribati *area over* 2 *sq mi* (5 *sq km*), *pop* 284

Ba·na·hao, Mount \bä-'nä-,haú\ extinct volcano 7141 *ft* (2142 *m*) Philippines on S Luzon SE of Manila

Banana River \bə-'na-nə\ lagoon E Fla. between Canaveral Peninsula & Merritt Is.

Banaras — see VARANASI

Ba·nat \bə-'nät, 'bä-,nät\ region SE *central* Europe in Danube basin between the Tisza & the Mures & the Transylvanian Alps; once entirely in Hungary, divided 1919 between Yugoslavia & Romania

Ban·bridge \ban-'brij\ district SE Northern Ireland, established 1974 *area* 171 *sq mi* (445 *sq km*), *pop* 33,102

Ban·da Islands \'ban-də, 'bän-\ islands Indonesia in Moluccas S of Ceram *area* 16 *sq mi* (42 *sq km*)

Banda Sea sea E Malay Archipelago SE of Sulawesi, S of the Moluccas, W of Aru Islands, & NE of Timor

Ban·da Ori·en·tal \'bän-də-,ōr-ē-,en-'täl, -,ór-\ URUGUAY — a former name, used with reference to its position on E shore of Río de la Plata

Bandar — see MACHILIPATNAM

Bandar 'Abbas *or* **Bandar–e–Abbas** \,bən-dər(-ē)-ə-'bäs\ city S Iran on Strait of Hormuz *pop* 201,642

Bandar–e Khomeyni *or* **Bandar Khomeyni** \,bən-dər(-ē)-,kō-mā-'nē, -,kō-'mā-nē\ town & port SW Iran at head of Persian Gulf ENE of Abadan *pop* 49,355

Bandar Lampung — see TANJUNGKARANG

Ban·dar Se·ri Be·ga·wan \,bən-dər-,ser-ē-bə-'gä-wán\ *or formerly* **Brunei** town, ✳ of Brunei *pop* 21,484

Ban·de·lier National Monument \,ban-də-'lir\ reservation N *central* N.Mex. W of Santa Fe containing cliff-dweller ruins

Ban·dung *or Dutch* **Ban·doeng** \'bän-,dûŋ\ city Indonesia in W Java SE of Jakarta *pop* 2,057,442

Banff \'bam(p)f\ *or* **Banff·shire** \-,shir, -shər\ former county NE Scotland ✳ Banff

Banff National Park reservation W Canada in SW Alberta on E slope of Rocky Mountains

Ban·ga·lore \'baŋ-gə-,lōr, -,lór\ city S India W of Madras ✳ of Karnataka *pop* 3,302,296

Bang·ka *or* **Ban·ka** \'baŋ-kə\ island Indonesia off SE Sumatra; chief town Pangkalpinang *area* 4609 *sq mi* (11,983 *sq km*), *pop* 251,639

Bang·kok \'baŋ-,käk, baŋ-'\ *or Thai* **Krung Thep** \'krúŋ-'tep\ city & port ✳ of Thailand on the Chao Phraya *about* 25 *mi* (40 *km*) above its mouth *pop* 5,620,591

Ban·gla·desh \,bäŋ-glə-'desh, ,baŋ-, ,bən-, -'däsh\ country S Asia E of India on Bay of Bengal; a republic in the Commonwealth of Nations since 1971 ✳ Dhaka *area* 55,126 *sq mi* (143,328 *sq km*), *pop* 115,075,000 — see EAST PAKISTAN — **Ban·gla·deshi** \-'de-shē, -'dä-\ *adjective or noun*

Ban·gor \'baŋ-,gór & 'ban-,gór (*these usual for* 1), 'baŋ-gər\ **1** city E *central* Maine on the Penobscot *pop* 33,181 **2** town SE Northern Ireland in North Down district *pop* 46,585 **3** borough & city NW Wales in Gwynedd *pop* 12,174

Ban·gui \bäŋ-'gē\ city ✳ of Central African Republic, on the Ubangi *pop* 300,723

Bang·we·u·lu, Lake \,bäŋ-gwē-(,)lü\ lake *about* 50 *mi* (80 *km*) long N Zambia in swamp region; its area fluctuates seasonally; drains into the Luapula, a headstream of Congo River

Ban·jar·ma·sin \,bän-jär-'mä-sin\ city Indonesia in S Borneo *pop* 481,371

Ban·jul \'bän-jül\ *or formerly* **Bath·urst** \'ba-(,)thərst\ city & port ✳ of Gambia on island of St. Mary in Gambia River *pop* 44,188

Banks Island \'baŋks\ island N Canada at W end of Canadian Arctic Archipelago *area about* 27,000 *sq mi* (69,900 *sq km*)

Banks Islands islands SW Pacific N of Vanuatu *pop* 5521

Ban·nock·burn \\'ba-nək-,bərn, ,ba-nək-'-\\ town *central* Scotland in Central region SSE of Stirling

Ban·tam \\'ban-təm\\ village Indonesia in NW corner of Java; once ✳ of Sultanate of Bantam

Ban·try Bay \\'ban-trē\\ bay SW Ireland in SW County Cork

Bao·ding *or* **Pao·ting** \\'baù-'diŋ\\ *or formerly* **Tsing·yuan** \\'chiŋ-yü-'en\\ city NE China SW of Beijing *pop* 483,155

Bao·ji *or* **Pao·chi** \\'baù-'jē\\ city N *central* China in SW Shaanxi on the Wei W of Xi'an *pop* 337,765

Bao·tou *or* **Pao·t'ou** \\'baù-'tō\\ city N China in SW Inner Mongolia on the Huang *pop* 983,508

Ba·paume \\bä-'pōm, ba-\\ town N France S of Arras *pop* 3683

Ba·ra·cal·do \\,bä-rä-'käl-dō\\ commune N Spain W of Bilbao *pop* 104,883

Ba·ra·coa \\,bä-rä-'kō-ä\\ city & port E Cuba on N coast near E tip of island *pop* 76,873

Ba·ra·na·gar \\bə-'rä-nə-gər\\ city E India in W. Bengal N of Calcutta *pop* 223,770

Ba·ra·nof \\'bar-ə-,nöf, bə-'rä-nəf\\ island SE Alaska in Alexander Archipelago S of Chichagof Is. *area about* 1600 *sq mi* (4160 *sq km*)

Bar·a·tar·ia Bay \\,bar-ə-'ter-ē-ə, -'ter-\\ lagoon SE La. on coast NW of delta of Mississippi River

Bar·ba·dos \\bär-'bā-(,)dōs, -dəs, -(,)dōz\\ island Brit. West Indies in Lesser Antilles E of the Windward group; a dominion of the Commonwealth of Nations since 1966 ✳ Bridgetown *area* 166 *sq mi* (432 *sq km*), *pop* 260,000 — **Bar·ba·di·an** \\-'bā-dē-ən\\ *adjective or noun*

Bar·ba·ry \\'bär-b(ə-)rē\\ region N Africa on **Barbary Coast** extending from Egyptian border to the Atlantic & including the former **Barbary States** (Morocco, Algiers, Tunis, & Tripoli) — a chiefly former name

Bar·bers Point \\'bär-bərz\\ *or* **Ka·la·e·loa Point** \\,kä,lä-(,)ä-'lō-ä\\ cape Hawaii at SW corner of Oahu W of Pearl Harbor

Bar·ber·ton \\'bär-bər-tən\\ city NE Ohio SW of Akron *pop* 27,623

Bar·bi·zon \\,bär-bē-'zōⁿ, 'bär-bə-,zän\\ village N France SSE of Paris

Bar·bu·da \\bär-'bü-də\\ island Brit. West Indies in the Leewards *area* 62 *sq mi* (161 *sq km*) — see ANTIGUA 1

Bar·ce·lo·na \\,bär-sə-'lō-nə\\ **1** province NE Spain in Catalonia on the Mediterranean *area* 2986 *sq mi* (7734 *sq km*), *pop* 4,654,407 **2** city & port, its ✳ *pop* 1,623,542 **3** city NE Venezuela near coast *pop* 109,061 — **Bar·ce·lo·nan** \\-'lō-nən\\ *noun* — **Bar·ce·lo·nese** \\-lō-'nēz, -'nēs, -'nēz\\ *adjective or noun*

Bar·di·yah *or* **Bar·dia** \\'bär-dē-ə, bär-'dē-ə\\ town & port Libya in NE Cyrenaica

Ba·reil·ly *or* **Ba·re·li** \\bə-'rā-lē\\ **1** city N India in NW *central* Uttar Pradesh ESE of Delhi *pop* 590,661 **2** — see ROHILKHAND

Bar·ents Sea \\'bar-ən(t)s, 'bär-\\ sea comprising the part of the Arctic Ocean between Spitsbergen & Novaya Zemlya

Ba·ri \\'bär-ē\\ *or ancient* **Bar·i·um** \\'bar-ē-əm, 'ber-\\ commune & port SE Italy ✳ of Puglia on the Adriatic *pop* 341,273

Ba·ri·lo·che \\,bä-rē-'lō-chä\\ *or* **San Car·los de Bariloche** \\sän-'kär-lōs-thä-\\ town SW Argentina on Lake Nahuel Huapí *pop* 15,995

Ba·ri·nas \\bä-'rē-näs\\ town W *central* Venezuela *pop* 152,853

Bar·i·sal \\'bar-ə-,säl\\ city S Bangladesh in Ganges delta *pop* 180,014

Bar·ka \\'bär-kə\\ town Libya in NW Cyrenaica

Bar·king and Dag·en·ham \\'bär-kiŋ-ən(d)-'dag-ᵊn-ᵊm\\ borough of E Greater London, England *pop* 139,900

Bar·let·ta \\bär-'le-tə\\ commune & port SE Italy in Puglia on the Adriatic *pop* 88,074

Bar·na·ul \\,bär-nə-'ül\\ city Russia in Asia on the Ob ✳ of Altay territory *pop* 606,000

Bar·ne·gat Bay \\'bär-ni-,gat, -gət\\ inlet of the Atlantic E N.J.

Barnes \\'bärnz\\ former municipal borough SE England, now part of Richmond

Bar·net \\'bär-nət\\ borough of N Greater London, England *pop* 283,000

Barns·ley \\'bärnz-lē\\ town N England in S. Yorkshire *pop* 217,300

Barn·sta·ble \\'bärn-stə-bəl\\ town SE Mass. *pop* 40,949

Ba·ro·da \\bə-'rō-də\\ **1** former state W India near head of Gulf of Khambhat ✳ Baroda *area* 8176 *sq mi* (21,258 *sq km*) **2** — see VADODARA

Ba·rot·se·land \\bä-'rōt-sā-,land\\ region W Zambia; formerly a protectorate

Bar·qui·si·me·to \\,bär-kē-sə-'mā-(,)tō\\ city NW Venezuela *pop* 602,622

Bar·ran·quil·la \\,bär-än-'kē-yä\\ city & port N Colombia on the Magdalena *pop* 1,018,800

Barren Grounds treeless plains N Canada W of Hudson Bay

Bar·rie \\'bar-ē\\ city Canada in SE Ontario *pop* 62,728

Bar·row, Point \\'bar-(,)ō\\ most northerly point of Alaska & of the U.S., at *about* 71°25′N, 156°30′W

Bar·row–in–Fur·ness \\,bar-ō-in-'fər-nəs\\ port NW England in S Cumbria *pop* 71,900

Bar·stow \\'bär-,stō\\ city S Calif. NNE of San Bernardino *pop* 21,472

Bar·tles·ville \\'bär-tᵊlz-,vil\\ city NE Okla. *pop* 34,256

Bart·lett \\'bärt-lət\\ **1** village NE Ill. W of Chicago *pop* 19,373 **2** city SW Tenn. *pop* 26,989

Ba·rú \\bä-'rü\\ *or formerly* **Chi·ri·quí** \\,chē-rē-'kē\\ volcano 11,400 *ft* (3475 *m*) Panama near Costa Rican border

Ba·sel \\'bä-zəl\\ *or French* **Bâle** *or older* **Basle** \\'bäl\\ **1** former canton NW Switzerland, now divided into two half cantons: **Ba·sel–Land** \\'bä-zəl-,länt\\ (✳ Liestal *area* 165 *sq mi or* 429 *sq km, pop* 234,910) & **Ba·sel–Stadt** \\-,shtät\\ (✳ Basel *area* 14 *sq mi or* 36 *sq km, pop* 197,403) **2** city NW Switzerland ✳ of Basel-Stadt *pop* 171,465

Ba·shan \\'bä-shən\\ region in ancient Palestine E & NE of Sea of Galilee

Ba·shi Channel \\'bä-shē\\ strait between Philippines & Taiwan

Bash·kor·to·stan \\bäsh-'kör-tə-,stän, -,stan\\ *or* **Bash·kir Republic** \\,bash-'kir, ,bäsh-\\ autonomous republic E Russia in Europe, in S Ural Mountains ✳ Ufa *area* 55,443 *sq mi* (143,597 *sq km*), *pop* 4,008,000

Ba·si·lan \\'bä-sə-,län\\ **1** island Philippines SW of Mindanao *area* 495 *sq mi* (1287 *sq km*) **2** city comprising Basilan Is. and several small nearby islands

Bas·il·don \\'ba-zəl-dən\\ town SE England in Essex *pop* 157,500

Ba·si·li·ca·ta \\bä-,zē-lē-'kä-tä\\ *or formerly* **Lu·ca·nia** \\lü-'kā-nyə, 'kä-\\ region S Italy on Gulf of Taranto ✳ Potenza *pop* 591,897

Basin Ranges — see GREAT BASIN

Basque Country \\'bask, 'bäsk\\ autonomous region N Spain on Bay of Biscay including provinces of Álava, Guipúzcoa, & Vizcaya

Bas·ra \\'bäs-rə, 'bəs-, 'bas-, 'bäz-, 'bəz-, 'baz-\\ *or* **Al–Bas·rah** \\al-'\\ city & port S Iraq on Shatt-al-Arab *pop* 310,950

Bass Strait \\'bas\\ strait separating Tasmania & continent of Australia

Bas·sein \\bə-'sān\\ city S Myanmar W of Yangon *pop* 126,045

Basse·terre \\bas-'ter, bäs-\\ town & port Brit. West Indies ✳ of St. Kitts Is. & of St. Kitts-Nevis state *pop* 14,725

Basse–Terre \\bas-'ter, bäs-\\ **1** island French West Indies constituting the W part of Guadeloupe *area* 364 *sq mi* (946 *sq km*) **2** town & port ✳ of Guadeloupe *pop* 14,107

Bas·tia \\'bas-tē-ə, 'bäs-\\ city & port France on NE coast of Corsica *pop* 38,728

Bas·togne \\ba-'stōn, -'stò-nyə\\ town SE Belgium in the Ardennes *pop* 12,187

Basutoland — see LESOTHO

Ba·ta \\'bä-tä\\ city ✳ of Mbini, Equatorial Guinea *pop* 30,474

Ba·taan \\bə-'tan, -'tän\\ peninsula Philippines in W Luzon on W side of Manila Bay

Ba·ta·via \\bə-'tā-vē-ə\\ — see JAKARTA — **Ba·ta·vi·an** \\-vē-ən\\ *adjective or noun*

Batavian Republic the Netherlands under the French (1795–1806)

Bath \\'bath\\ city SW England in Avon *pop* 79,900

Bath·urst \\'ba-(,)thərst\\ — see BANJUL

Bathurst Island island N Canada in Parry group

Bat·on Rouge \\,ba-tᵊn-'rüzh\\ city ✳ of La. on Mississippi River *pop* 219,531

Bat·ter·sea \\'ba-tər-sē\\ former metropolitan borough SW London, England, on S bank of the Thames, now part of Wandsworth

Bat·tle Creek \\,ba-tᵊl-'krēk\\ city S Mich. *pop* 53,540

Ba·tu·mi \\bä-'tü-mē\\ city & port SW Republic of Georgia on Black Sea ✳ of Adjarian Republic *pop* 137,500

Baut·zen \\'baùt-sən\\ city E Germany on the Spree ENE of Dresden *pop* 47,131

Ba·var·ia \\bə-'ver-ē-ə, -'var-\\ *or German* **Bay·ern** \\'bī-ərn\\ state SE Germany bordering on Austria & the Czech Republic ✳ Munich *area* 27,239 *sq mi* (70,549 *sq km*), *pop* 11,448,800

Ba·ya·món \\,bī-ä-'mōn\\ city NE *central* Puerto Rico *pop* 220,262

Bay City city E Mich. near head of Saginaw Bay *pop* 38,936

Ba·yeux \\bī-'yü, bä-; bä-'yə(r); bá-'yœ\\ town NW France WNW of Caen *pop* 15,106

Baykal, Lake — see BAIKAL (Lake)

Bay·onne \\bā-'ōn\\ city & port NE N.J. *pop* 61,444

Ba·yonne \\bā-'ōn, bä-'yòn\\ city SW France on the Adour near Bay of Biscay *pop* 41,846

Bay·reuth \\bī-'ròit, 'bī-,\\ city Germany in Bavaria NE of Nuremberg *pop* 72,777

Bay·town \\'bā-,taùn\\ city SE Tex. on Galveston Bay *pop* 63,850

Beachy Head \\'bē-chē\\ headland SE England on coast of E. Sussex

Bear \\'bar, 'ber\\ river 350 *mi* (563 *km*) N Utah, SW Wyo., & SE Idaho flowing to Great Salt Lake

Beard·more \\'bird-,mōr, -,mór\\ glacier Antarctica descending to Ross Ice Shelf at *about* 170°E

Bear Mountain mountain 1305 *ft* (398 *m*) SE N.Y. on the Hudson

Bé·arn \\bā-'arn\\ region & former province SW France in Pyrenees SW of Gascony ✳ Pau

Be·as *or* **Bi·as** \\'bē-,äs\\ river *about* 300 *mi* (483 *km*) N India in the Punjab

Beau·fort Sea \\'bō-fərt\\ sea comprising the part of the Arctic Ocean NE of Alaska & NW of Canada

Beau·mar·is \\bō-'mar-əs\\ borough NW Wales in Gwynedd on E Anglesey Is. on **Beaumaris Bay** *pop* 2088

Beau·mont \\'bō-,mänt, bō-'\\ city & port SE Tex. on the Neches *pop* 114,323

Beaune \\'bōn\\ commune E France SSW of Dijon *pop* 22,171

Beau·port \\bō-'pòr, 'bō-(,)pórt\\ city Canada in S Quebec *pop* 69,158

Beau·so·leil \\,bō-sə-'lā\\ commune SE France N of Monaco

Beau·vais \\bō-'vā\\ commune N France NNW of Paris *pop* 56,278

Bea·ver \\'bē-vər\\ **1** river 280 *mi* (451 *km*) NW Okla. forming upper course of the N. Canadian **2** river 305 *mi* (491 *km*) Canada in Alberta & Saskatchewan flowing E into the Churchill

Bea·ver·creek \\'bē-vər-,krēk\\ city SW Ohio E of Dayton *pop* 33,626

Bea·ver·head Mountains \\'bē-vər-,hed\\ mountains on Idaho-Mont. boundary; SE part of Bitterroot Range of the Rockies — see GARFIELD MOUNTAIN

Bea·ver·ton \\'bē-vər-tən\\ city NW Oreg. W of Portland *pop* 53,310

Bé·char \\bā-'shär\\ *or formerly* **Co·lomb–Bé·char** \\kə-,lōⁿ-\\ commune NW Algeria SSE of Oran *pop* 107,311

Bech·u·a·na·land \\,bech-wä-nə-,land, ,be-chə-\\ **1** region S Africa N of Orange River & including Kalahari Desert & Okanvango Swamps **2** — see BOTSWANA **3** *or* **British Bechuanaland** former Brit. colony in the region S of the Molopo; became part of Union of South Africa 1895 — **Bech·u·a·na** \\,bech-wä-nə, ,be-chə-\\ *adjective or noun*

Beck·en·ham \'be-kə-nəm, 'bek-nəm\ former urban district SE England in Kent, now part of Bromley

Bed·ford \'bed-fərd\ **1** city N Tex. *pop* 43,762 **2** borough SE *central* England of Bedfordshire *pop* 74,245

Bed·ford·shire \'bed-fərd-,shir, -shər\ or **Bedford** \'bed-fərd\ county SE *central* England *area* 494 *sq mi* (1279 *sq km*), *pop* 514,200

Bedloe's Island — see LIBERTY ISLAND

Bę·dzin \'ben-,jēn\ commune S Poland in Silesia *pop* 75,800

Beer·she·ba \bir-'shē-bə, ber-, bər-\ town S Israel in N Negeb, in biblical times marking extreme S limit of Palestine *pop* 128,400

Behistun — see BISITUN

Bei·jing \'bā-'jiŋ\ or **Pe·king** \'pē-'kiŋ, 'pā-\ or formerly **Pei·ping** \'pā-'piŋ, 'bā-\ municipality NE China, its ✱ *pop* 10,819,407

Bei·ra \'bā-rə\ town & port SE Mozambique; chief port for central Mozambique & landlocked Zimbabwe & Malawi *pop* 298,847

Bei·rut \bā-'rüt\ or ancient **Be·ry·tus** \bə-'rī-təs\ city & port ✱ of Lebanon — **Bei·ruti** \bā-'rü-tē\ noun

Be·jaïa \bā-'zhī-ə\ or formerly **Bou·gie** \bü-'zhē\ city & port NE Algeria *pop* 89,500

Be·kaa \bi-'kä\ or **Al Biqa** \,äl-be-'kä\ or ancient **Coe·le–Syr·ia** \,sē-lē-'sir-ē-ə\ valley Lebanon between Lebanon & Anti-Lebanon mountain ranges

Be·la·rus \bē-lə-'rüs, ,bye-lə-\ or **Bye·la·rus** \bē-,e-lə-, ,bye-lə-\ independent country N *central* Europe; a constituent republic (**Belorussia** or **Byelorussia**) of the U.S.S.R. 1919–91 ✱ Minsk *area* 80,154 *sq mi* (207,599 *sq km*), *pop* 10,353,000

Belau — see PALAU

Be·la·wan \bā-'lä-,wän\ town & port Indonesia in NE Sumatra

Be·la·ya \'bye-lə-yə\ river Russia in Europe rising in the S Urals & flowing S, W, & NW to the Kama

Be·lém \be-'lem\ or **Pa·rá** \pä-'rä\ city N Brazil ✱ of Pará state on Pará River *pop* 1,200,000

Bel·fast \'bel-,fast, bel-'\ **1** district E Northern Ireland, established 1974 *area* 54 *sq mi* (140 *sq km*), *pop* 283,746 **2** city & port ✱ of Northern Ireland at head of **Belfast Lough** (inlet) *pop* 295,100

Bel·fort \bel-'fòr, bā-'fòr\ commune E France commanding **Belfort Gap** (wide pass between Vosges & Jura mountains) *pop* 51,913

Belgian Congo — see CONGO 2

Belgian East Africa — see RUANDA-URUNDI

Bel·gium \'bel-jəm\ or French **Bel·gique** \bel-'zhēk\ or Flemish **Bel·gië** \'bel-kē-ə\ country W Europe bordering on North Sea; a constitutional monarchy ✱ Brussels *area* 11,781 *sq mi* (30,513 *sq km*), *pop* 9,978,681

Bel·go·rod–Dnes·trov·ski or **Belgorod–Dnes·trov·skiy** \'bel-gə-,räd-(,)ne-'stròf-skē, -'stròv-, 'byel-gə-rət-dne-\ or formerly Turkish & Russian **Ak·ker·man** \'ä-kər-,män\ city SW Ukraine on the Dniester estuary *pop* 29,000

Bel·grade \'bel-,grād, -,gräd, -,grad, bel-'\ or **Beo·grad** \bā-'ò-,gräd\ city ✱ of Yugoslavia & of Serbia *pop* 1,553,854

Bel·gra·via \bel-'grā-vē-ə\ district of W *central* London, England, in Kensington and Chelsea borough S of Hyde Park

Be·li·tung \bä-'lē-təŋ\ or **Bil·li·ton** \-,tän\ island Indonesia between Sumatra & Borneo *area* 1866 *sq mi* (4852 *sq km*), *pop* 102,375

Be·lize \bə-'lēz\ or formerly **British Honduras** country Central America bordering on the Caribbean; an independent member of the Commonwealth of Nations ✱ Belmopan *area* 8867 *sq mi* (22,966 *sq km*), *pop* 184,340 — **Be·liz·ean** \-'lē-zē-ən\ adjective or noun

Belize City seaport Belize; former ✱ of British Honduras *pop* 45,158

Bell \'bel\ city SW Calif. SE of Los Angeles *pop* 34,365

Bel·la Coo·la \,be-lə-'kü-lə\ river about 60 *mi* (96 *km*) Canada in British Columbia flowing W to Burke Channel E of Queen Charlotte Sound

Bel·leau \be-'lō, 'be-,\ village N France NW of Château-Thierry & N of **Belleau Wood** (French **Bois de Bel·leau** \bwä-də-be-'lō\)

Belle Fourche \bel-'füsh\ river NE Wyo. & W S.Dak. flowing NE & E into Cheyenne River

Belle Isle, Strait of \bel-'īl\ channel between N tip of Newfoundland (island) & SE Labrador

Belle·ville \'bel-,vil\ **1** city SW Ill. *pop* 42,785 **2** town NE N.J. N of Newark *pop* 34,213 **3** city Canada in SE Ontario *pop* 37,243

Belle·vue \'bel-,vyü\ **1** city E Nebr. S of Omaha *pop* 30,982 **2** city W Wash. E of Seattle *pop* 86,874

Bell·flow·er \'bel-,flaù(-ə)r\ city SW Calif. E of Los Angeles *pop* 61,815

Bell Gardens city SW Calif. E of Los Angeles *pop* 42,355

Bel·ling·ham \'be-liŋ-,ham\ city & port NW Wash. on **Bellingham Bay** (inlet at N end of Puget Sound) *pop* 52,179

Bel·lings·hau·sen Sea \'be-liŋz-,haù-z°n\ sea comprising a large bay of the S Pacific W of base of Antarctic Peninsula

Bel·lin·zo·na \,be-lən-'zō-nə\ commune S Switzerland E of Locarno ✱ of Ticino *pop* 17,142

Bell·wood \'bel-,wùd\ village NE Ill. W of Chicago *pop* 20,241

Bel·mont \'bel-,mänt\ **1** city W Calif. SE of San Francisco *pop* 24,127 **2** town E Mass. W of Boston *pop* 24,720

Bel·mo·pan \,bel-mō-'pän\ city ✱ of Belize *pop* 3687

Be·lo Ho·ri·zon·te \'bā-lō-,òr-ē-'zòn-tē\ city E Brazil ✱ of Minas Gerais *pop* 2,300,000

Be·loit \bə-'lòit\ city S Wis. on Ill. border *pop* 35,573

Be·lo·rus·sia \,be-lō-'rə-shə, ,bye-lō-\ or **Bye·lo·rus·sia** \bē-,e-lō-, ,bye-lō-\ constituent republic of the U.S.S.R. bordering on Poland, Lithuania, & Latvia; became independent 1991 — see BELARUS

Beloye More — see WHITE SEA

Bel·sen \'bel-zən, -sən\ or **Ber·gen–Belsen** \,ber-gən-, ,bər-\ locality N Germany on Lüneburg Heath NW of Celle; site of Nazi concentration camp during World War II

Be·lu·kha \bə-'lü-kə\ mountain 15,157 *ft* (4620 *m*) Russia in Asia; highest in Altai mountain range

Benares — see VARANASI

Ben·brook \'ben-,brùk\ village N Tex. SW of Fort Worth *pop* 19,564

Bend \'bend\ city *central* Oreg. on the Deschutes *pop* 20,469

Ben·di·go \'ben-di-,gō\ city SE Australia in N Victoria NNW of Melbourne *pop* 30,133

Be·ne·lux \'be-nəl-,əks\ economic union comprising Belgium, the Netherlands, & Luxembourg; formed 1947

Be·ne·ven·to \bā-nā-'ven-(,)tō\ commune S Italy in Campania NE of Naples *pop* 62,683

Ben·gal \ben-'gòl, beŋ-, -'gäl\ region E India (subcontinent) including delta of the Ganges & the Brahmaputra; formerly a presidency & (1937–47) a province of Brit. India; divided 1947 between Pakistan & India (republic) — see EAST BENGAL, EAST PAKISTAN, WEST BENGAL — **Ben·gal·ese** \,beŋ-gə-'lēz, ,ben-, -'lēs\ adjective or noun

Bengal, Bay of arm of the Indian Ocean between India & Sri Lanka on the W & Myanmar & Malay Peninsula on the E

Beng·bu or **Pang–pu** or **Peng–pu** \all 'bəŋ-'bü\ city E China in N Anhui *pop* 449,245

Ben·gha·zi \ben-'gä-zē, beŋ-, -'ga-\ or ancient **Ber·e·ni·ce** \,ber-ə-'nī-sē\ city & port NE Libya, a former ✱ of Libya *pop* 446,250

Ben·gue·la \ben-'gwā-lä\ city & port W Angola *pop* 40,996

Be·ni \'bā-nē\ river about 1000 *mi* (1609 *km*) *central* & N Bolivia flowing N to unite with Mamoré River forming Madeira River

Be·ni·cia \bə-'nē-shə\ city *central* Calif. NNE of Oakland *pop* 24,437

Be·nin \be-'nēn, -'nin; 'be-nin\ **1** river about 100 *mi* (161 *km*) S Nigeria W of the Niger flowing into Bight of Benin **2** former kingdom W Africa on lower Niger River; incorporated in Nigeria after 1897 **3** or formerly **Da·ho·mey** \də-'hō-mē\ country W Africa on Gulf of Guinea; a republic, formerly a territory of French West Africa ✱ Porto-Novo *area* 43,483 *sq mi* (112,621 *sq km*), *pop* 5,074,000 **4** or **Benin City** city SW Nigeria in W delta of Niger River *pop*

202,800 — **Be·ni·nese** \bə-,ni-'nēz, -,nē-, -'nēs; ,be-ni-'nēz, -'nēs\ adjective or noun

Benin, Bight of the N section of Gulf of Guinea W Africa SW of Nigeria

Be·ni Su·ef \be-nē-sü-'af\ city N *central* Egypt on W bank of the Nile *pop* 174,000

Ben Lomond — see LOMOND (Ben)

Ben Nev·is \ben-'ne-vəs\ mountain 4406 *ft* (1343 *m*) W Scotland in Grampian Hills; highest in Great Britain

Be·no·ni \bə-'nō-nē\ city NE Republic of South Africa in Gauteng on the Witwatersrand E of Johannesburg *pop* 151,294

Be·nue \'bān-(,)wā\ river 870 *mi* (1400 *km*) W Africa flowing W into Niger River

Ben Ve·nue \,ben-və-'nü, -'nyü\ mountain 2393 *ft* (729 *m*) *central* Scotland S of Loch Katrine

Ben·xi \'bən-'shē\ or **Pen–hsi** \'ben-'shē\ or **Pen–ch'i** \-'chē\ city NE China in E *central* Liaoning *pop* 768,778

Be·rar \bā-'rär, bə-\ region W *central* India; in Central Provinces & Berar 1903–47, in Madhya Pradesh 1947–56, in Bombay 1956–60, in Maharashtra since 1960; chief city Amravati

Ber·be·ra \'bər-b(ə-)rə\ town & port N Somalia *pop* 12,219

Be·rea \bə-'rē-ə\ **1** city NE Ohio SW of Cleveland *pop* 19,051 **2** — see VEROIA

Be·re·zi·na \bə-'rā-z°n-ə, -'re-\ river 365 *mi* (587 *km*) Belarus flowing SE into the Dnieper

Bergama — see PERGAMUM

Ber·ga·mo \'ber-gä-,mō, 'bər-\ commune N Italy in Lombardy NE of Milan *pop* 115,655

Ber·gen 1 \'bər-gən, 'ber-\ city & port SW Norway *pop* 211,826 **2** — see MONS

Ber·gen·field \'bər-gən-,fēld\ borough NE N.J. *pop* 24,458

Be·ring Sea \'bir-iŋ, 'ber-\ arm of the N Pacific between Alaska & NE Siberia & between the Aleutians & Bering Strait *area* 885,000 *sq mi* (2,292,150 *sq km*)

Bering Strait strait at narrowest point 53 *mi* (85 *km*) wide separating Asia (Russia) from N. America (Alaska)

Berke·ley \'bər-klē\ city W Calif. on San Francisco Bay N of Oakland *pop* 102,724

Berk·shire \'bərk-,shir, -shər\ **1** hills W Mass. W of Connecticut River — see GREYLOCK (Mount) **2** \British usually 'bärk-\ county S England in Thames River basin ✱ Reading *area* 502 *sq mi* (1300 *sq km*), *pop* 716,500

Ber·lin \(,)bər-'lin, German ber-'lēn\ city, official ✱ of (reunified) Germany on Spree River, before 1945 ✱ of Germany & of Prussia, divided under postwar occupation between E. & W. Germany, E. Berlin being made ✱ of E. Germany (1949) & W. Berlin being a state (not formally incorporated) of W. Germany — **Ber·lin·er** \(,)bər-'li-nər\ noun

Ber·me·jo \ber-'mā-(,)hō\ river 650 *mi* (1046 *km*) N Argentina rising on Bolivian frontier & flowing SE into Paraguay River

Ber·mond·sey \'bər-mən(d)-zē\ former metropolitan borough E *central* London, England, now part of Southwark

Ber·mu·da \(,)bər-'myü-də\ islands W Atlantic ESE of Cape Hatteras; a self-governing Brit. colony ✱ Hamilton *area* 20 *sq mi* (52 *sq km*), *pop* 61,700 — **Ber·mu·di·an** \-dē-ən\ or **Ber·mu·dan** \-d°n\ adjective or noun

Bermuda Triangle triangular area N. Atlantic Ocean between Bermuda, Fla., & Puerto Rico; site of numerous reported disappearances of planes & ships

Bern \'bərn, 'bern\ **1** canton NW & W *central* Switzerland *area* 2327 *sq mi* (6027 *sq km*), *pop* 942,721 **2** city, its ✱ & ✱ of Switzerland on the Aare *pop* 135,825 — **Ber·nese** \(,)bər-'nēz, -'nēs\ adjective or noun

Bern·burg \'bərn-,bùrg, 'bern-,bùrk\ city *central* Germany W of Dessau *pop* 39,006

Ber·ner Al·pen \,ber-nər-'äl-pən\ or **Ber·nese Ober·land** \(,)bər-'nēz-'ō-bər-,länt, -'nēs-\ or **Bernese Alps** or **Oberland** section of the Alps S Switzerland in Bern & Valais cantons between Lake of Thun & Brienz on the N & the valley of the upper Rhône on the S

Ber·ni·cia \(,)bər-'ni-sh(ē-)ə\ Anglian kingdom of 6th century A.D. located between Tyne & Forth rivers ✱ Bamborough

Ber·ni·na \(ˌ)ber-'nē-nə\ the S extension of Rhaetian Alps on border between Italy & Switzerland; highest peak **Piz Bernina** \ˌpēts-\ (highest in the Rhaetian Alps) 13,200 ft (4023 m)

Beroea 1 — see ALEPPO **2** — see VEROIA

Ber·ry \be-'rē\ former province central France * Bourges

Ber·thoud Pass \'bər-thəd\ mountain pass 11,315 ft (3449 m) N Colo. in Front range WNW of Denver

Ber·wick \'ber-ik\ or **Ber·wick·shire** \-ˌshir, -shər\ former county SE Scotland * Duns

Ber·wyn \'bər-wən\ city NE Ill. W of Chicago pop 45,426

Berytus — see BEIRUT

Be·san·çon \bə-'zan(t)-sən, bə-zäⁿ-'sōⁿ\ city E France E of Dijon pop 119,194

Bes·kids \'bes-ˌkidz, be-'skēdz\ mountain ranges central Europe in W Carpathians; include **West Beskids** (in Poland, Slovakia, & the Czech Republic) & **East Beskids** (in Poland & NE Slovakia)

Bes·sa·ra·bia \ˌbe-sə-'rä-bē-ə\ region SE Europe between the Dniester & Prut rivers; now mostly in Moldova — **Bes·sa·ra·bi·an** \-bē-ən\ adjective or noun

Bes·se·mer \'be-sə-mər\ city N central Ala. pop 33,497

Beth·a·ny \'be-thə-nē\ **1** city central Okla. pop 20,075 **2** or now **Al-'Ay·zar·ī·yah** \ˌál-ˌī-zà-'rē-yə\ biblical village Palestine E of Jerusalem on Mount of Olives pop 3560

Beth·el \'be-thəl, be-'thel\ ruined town Palestine in W Jordan N of Jerusalem

Beth·el Park \'be-thəl\ borough SW Pa. pop 33,823

Be·thes·da \bə-'thez-də\ population center Md., a N suburb of Washington, D.C. pop 62,936

Beth·le·hem \'beth-li-ˌhem, -lē-həm, -lē-əm\ **1** city E Pa. on the Lehigh pop 71,428 **2** city Palestine in Judea SW of Jerusalem pop 34,180

Beth·nal Green \'beth-nəl\ former metropolitan borough E London, England, now part of Tower Hamlets

Beth·sa·i·da \beth-'sā-ə-də\ ruined town Palestine on NE side of Sea of Galilee E of the Jordan; its site in SE Syria

Be·tio \'bā-chē-ˌō, -shē-\ islet & village W Pacific in N Kiribati at S end of Tarawa

Bet·ten·dorf \'be-tⁿn-ˌdorf\ city E Iowa E of Davenport pop 28,132

Beuthen — see BYTOM

Bev·er·ley \'be-vər-lē\ town N England in Humberside pop 109,500

Bev·er·ly \'be-vər-lē\ city NE Mass. pop 38,195

Beverly Hills \'be-vər-lē\ city SW Calif. within city of Los Angeles pop 31,971

Bex·ley \'bek-slē\ borough of E Greater London, England pop 211,200

Bey·o·glu \ˌbā-ȯ-'glü\ or formerly **Pera** \'per-ə\ section of Istanbul, Turkey, comprising area N of the Golden Horn

Bé·ziers \bāz-'yā\ city S France SW of Montpellier pop 72,362

Bezwada — see VIJAYAWADA

Bha·gal·pur \'bä-gəl-ˌpur\ city E India on the Ganges in E Bihar pop 254,993

Bhak·ra Dam \'bə-krə, 'bä-\ hydroelectric & irrigation dam 740 ft (226 m) N India in Punjab NW of Bilaspur in gorge of the Sutlej

Bha·mo \bə-'mò, -'mō\ city N Myanmar on the upper Irrawaddy pop 13,767

Bhat·pa·ra \bät-'pär-ə\ city E India in W. Bengal pop 315,976

Bhav·na·gar or **Bhau·na·gar** \baù-'nə-gər\ city & port W India in S Gujarat on Gulf of Khambhat pop 402,338

Bho·pal \bō-'päl\ **1** former state N central India in & N of Vindhya Mountains * Bhopal; now part of Madhya Pradesh **2** city N central India NW of Nagpur * of Madhya Pradesh pop 1,062,771

Bhu·ba·nes·war or **Bhu·ba·nesh·war** \ˌbù-və-'näsh-wər\ city E India S of Cuttack * of Orissa pop 411,542

Bhu·tan \bü-'tän, -'tan\ country Asia in Himalayas on NE border of India; a protectorate of India * Thimphu area 18,000 sq mi (46,800 sq km), pop 1,546,000 — **Bhu·ta·nese** \ˌbü-tⁿn-'ēz, -'ēs\ adjective or noun

Bi·a·fra \bē-'ä-frə, bī-, -'a-\ name adopted by the SE part of Nigeria during its secession 1967–70 — **Bi·a·fran** \-frən\ adjective or noun

Biafra, Bight of or **Bight of Bon·ny** \'bä-nē\ the E section of Gulf of Guinea, W Africa

Bi·ak \bē-'yäk\ island off W New Guinea; largest of the Schoutens

Bia·ły·stok \bē-'ä-li-ˌstòk, byà-'wi-stòk\ city NE Poland pop 268,085

Biar·ritz \byä-'rēts\ commune SW France on Bay of Biscay pop 28,887

Bias — see BEAS

Bid·de·ford \'bi-də-fərd\ city SW Maine SW of Portland pop 20,710

Biel \'bēl\ or French **Bienne** \bē-'en\ commune NW Switzerland in Bern canton pop 52,670

Bie·le·feld \'bē-lə-ˌfelt\ city W central Germany E of Münster pop 322,132

Biel·sko–Bia·ła \bē-ˌel-skò-bē-'ä-lə, ˌbyel-skò-'byä-wä\ city S Poland pop 179,879

Big Bend 1 area W Tex. in large bend of the Rio Grande; partly included in **Big Bend National Park 2** section of Columbia River E central Wash.

Big Black river 330 mi (531 km) W central Miss. flowing to Mississippi River

Big Diomede — see DIOMEDE ISLANDS

Big·horn \'big-ˌhòrn\ river 336 mi (541 km) N Wyo. & SE Mont. flowing N into Yellowstone River — see WIND

Bighorn Mountains mountains N Wyo. extending S from Mont. border E of Bighorn River — see CLOUD PEAK

Big Sandy river 22 mi (35 km) between W.Va. & Ky. flowing N into Ohio River

Big Sioux \'sü\ river 420 mi (676 km) S.Dak. & Iowa flowing S to Missouri River & forming Iowa-S.Dak. boundary

Big Spring city W Tex. NE of Odessa pop 23,093

Big Stone lake about 30 mi (48 km) long between W Minn. & NE S.Dak. — see MINNESOTA 1

Big Sur \'sər\ region W Calif. centering on Big Sur River & extending about 80 mi (129 km) along coast SE of Point Sur

Big Thicket wilderness area E Tex. NE of Houston area about 450 sq mi (1170 sq km)

Bi·har \bi-'här\ **1** state NE India bordering on Nepal; winter * Patna, summer * Ranchi area 67,184 sq mi (174,006 sq km), pop 86,374,465 **2** city central Bihar state SE of Patna pop 200,976

Bi·ka·ner \ˌbi-kə-'nir, 'be-kə-ˌner\ city NW India in N Rajasthan in Thar Desert pop 416,289

Bi·ki·ni \bi-'kē-nē\ island (atoll) W Pacific in Marshall Islands — **Bi·ki·ni·an** \-nē-ən\ noun

Bi·las·pur \bə-'läs-ˌpùr\ city E central India in SE Madhya Pradesh SE of Jabalpur pop 233,570

Bil·bao \bil-'bä-ˌō, -'baù, -'bä-(ˌ)ō\ city N Spain * of Vizcaya pop 369,839

Bil·ler·i·ca \(ˌ)bil-'ri-kə\ town NE Mass. pop 37,609

Bil·lings \'bi-liŋz\ city S central Mont. pop 81,151

Billiton — see BELITUNG

Bi·loxi \bə-'lək-sē, -'läk-\ city & port SE Miss. pop 46,319

Bim·i·ni \'bi-mə-nē\ two islands of Bahamas NW of Andros

Bing·en \'biŋ-ən\ city W Germany pop 24,272

Bing·ham·ton \'biŋ-əm-tən\ city S central N.Y. pop 53,008

Binh Dinh — see AN NHON

Bío–Bío \ˌbē-ō-'bē-(ˌ)ō\ river 238 mi (383 km) S central Chile flowing into the Pacific at Concepción

Bi·o·ko \bē-'ō-(ˌ)kō\ or formerly **Fer·nan·do Póo** \fer-'nän-(ˌ)dō-'pō\ or 1973–79 **Ma·cí·as Ngue·ma Bi·yo·go** \mä-'sē-äs-əŋ-'gwä-mə-bē-'yō-(ˌ)gō\ island Equatorial Guinea in Bight of Biafra area 779 sq mi (2018 sq km)

Bir·ken·head \'bər-kən-ˌhed, ˌbər-kən-'\ borough NW England in Merseyside on the Mersey estuary opposite Liverpool pop 123,907

Bir·ming·ham \'bər-miŋ-ˌham, British usually -miŋ-əm\ **1** city N central Ala. pop 265,968 **2** city SE Mich. N of Detroit pop 19,997 **3** city & borough W central England in West Midlands pop 934,900

Bi·ro·bi·dzhan \ˌbir-ō-bi-'jän, -'jan\ city Russia in Asia * of Jewish Autonomous Oblast pop 86,300

Biscay or **Biscaya** — see VIZCAYA — **Bis·cay·an** \bis-'kī-ən, -'kā-\ adjective or noun

Bis·cay, Bay of \'bis-ˌkā, 'bis-\ inlet of the Atlantic between W coast of France & N coast of Spain

Bis·cayne Bay \bis-'kān, 'bis-\ inlet of the Atlantic SE Fla.; S part forms **Biscayne National Park**

Bish·kek \bish-'kek\ or 1926–91 **Frun·ze** \'frün-zi\ city on Chu River * of Kyrgyzstan pop 641,400

Bi·sho \'bē-(ˌ)shō\ town S Republic of South Africa; formerly * of Ciskei

Bi·si·tun \ˌbē-sə-'tün\ or **Be·his·tun** \ˌbā-his-\ or **Bi·su·tun** \ˌbē-sə-\ ruined town W Iran E of Kermanshah

Bis·kra \'bis-krə, -(ˌ)krä\ city NE Algeria at an oasis on S edge of Atlas Mountains pop 128,747

Bis·marck \'biz-ˌmärk\ city * of N.Dak. on Missouri River pop 49,256

Bismarck Archipelago archipelago W Pacific N of E end of New Guinea area 19,173 sq mi (49,658 sq km)

Bismarck Range mountain range North-East New Guinea NW of Owen Stanley Range; highest Mt. Wilhelm

Bismarck Sea sea comprising the part of the W Pacific enclosed by the islands of the Bismarck Archipelago

Bis·sau \bi-'saù\ city & port * of Guinea-Bissau pop 125,000

Bi·thyn·ia \bə-'thi-nē-ə\ ancient country NW Asia Minor bordering on the Sea of Marmara & Black Sea — **Bi·thyn·i·an** \-nē-ən\ adjective or noun

Bi·to·la \'bi-tō-lä\ or **Bi·tolj** \-ˌtȯl(-yə), -ˌtȯi\ or **Mon·a·stir** \ˌmä-nə-'stir\ city S Macedonia pop 122,173

Bitter Lakes two lakes (Great Bitter Lake & Little Bitter Lake) in NE Egypt N of Suez; connected & traversed by the Suez Canal

Bit·ter·root Range \'bi-tə(r)-ˌrüt, -ˌrùt\ range of the Rocky Mountains on Idaho-Mont. boundary — see BEAVERHEAD MOUNTAINS, GARFIELD MOUNTAIN

Bi·wa \'bē-(ˌ)wä\ lake 40 mi (64 km) long Japan on W central Honshu

Biysk \'bēsk\ city Russia in Asia, in E Altay territory pop 235,000

Bi·zerte \bə-'zər-tē, bi-'zert\ or **Bi·zer·ta** \bə-'zər-tə\ city & port N Tunisia on **Lake Bizerte** (a deep lagoon) pop 62,856

Black or in China **Amo** \'ä-ˌmō\ or in Vietnam **Da** \'dä\ river 500 mi (805 km) SE Asia rising in central Yunnan, China & flowing SE to Red River in N Vietnam

Black·burn \'blak-(ˌ)bərn\ borough NW England in Lancashire pop 132,800

Blackburn, Mount mountain 16,390 ft (4996 m) S Alaska; highest in the Wrangell Mountains

Black Canyon 1 canyon of Colorado River between Ariz. & Nev. S of Hoover Dam **2** canyon of the Gunnison SW central Colo. partly in **Black Canyon of the Gunnison National Monument**

Black Forest or German **Schwarz·wald** \'shvärts-ˌvält\ forested mountain region SW Germany along the upper Rhine between the Neckar River & Swiss border

Black Hills mountains W S.Dak. & NE Wyo. — see HARNEY PEAK

Black Mountains mountains W N.C., a range of the Blue Ridge Mountains — see MITCHELL (Mount)

Black·pool \'blak-ˌpül\ borough NW England in Lancashire on Irish Sea pop 144,500

Blacks·burg \'blaks-ˌbərg\ city W Va. W of Roanoke pop 34,590

Black Sea or ancient **Pon·tus Eux·i·nus** \ˌpän-təs-ˌyük-'sī-nəs\ or **Pontus** sea between Europe & Asia connected with Aegean Sea through the Bosporus, Sea of Marmara, & Dardanelles area more than 160,000 sq mi (414,400 sq km)

Black Volta — see VOLTA

\ə\ abut \ᵊ\ kitten \ər\ further \a\ ash \ā\ ace \ä\ mop, mar \aù\ out \ch\ chin \e\ bet \ē\ easy \g\ go \i\ hit \ī\ ice \j\ job \ŋ\ sing \ō\ go \ȯ\ law \ȯi\ boy \th\ thin \t̠h\ the \ü\ loot \ù\ foot \y\ yet \zh\ vision see also Guide to Pronunciation

Black Warrior river 178 *mi* (*286 km*) central Ala. flowing into the Tombigbee

Bla·go·vesh·chensk \,blä-gə-'vyäsh-chən(t)sk\ city Russia in Asia on the Amur *pop* 214,000

Blaine \'blān\ city E Minn. N of St. Paul *pop* 38,975

Blain·ville \'blān-,vil, blēⁿ-'vēl\ town Canada in S Quebec *pop* 22,679

Blanc, Cape \'blaŋk, 'blä\ **1** cape N Tunisia; northernmost point of Africa, at 37°14′N **2** promontory NW Africa on the Atlantic in Mauritania at SW tip of Río de Oro

Blanc, Mont — see MONT BLANC

Blan·ca Peak \'blaŋ-kə, 'bläŋ-\ mountain 14,345 *ft* (*4372 m*) S Colo.; highest in Sangre de Cristo Mountains

Blan·co, Cape \'blaŋ-(,)kō\ cape SW Oreg.

Blan·tyre \'blan-,tīr\ city S Malawi *pop* 333,120

Blar·ney \'blär-nē\ town SW Ireland in *central* County Cork *pop* 1952

Blen·heim \'ble-nəm\ or **Blind·heim** \'blint-,hīm\ village S Germany in Bavaria NNW of Augsburg *pop* 1619

Bli·da \'blē-də\ city N Algeria SW of Algiers *pop* 170,182

Block Island \'bläk\ island R.I. in the Atlantic at E entrance to Long Island Sound

Bloem·fon·tein \'blüm-fən-,tān, -,fän-\ city *central* Republic of South Africa, judicial ✳ of the Republic *pop* 149,836

Blois \'blwä\ city N *central* France SW of Orléans *pop* 51,549

Bloom·field \'blüm-,fēld\ **1** town N *central* Conn. NW of Hartford *pop* 18,608 **2** town NE N.J. *pop* 45,061

Bloo·ming·ton \'blü-miŋ-tən\ **1** city *central* Ill. *pop* 51,972 **2** city SW *central* Ind. *pop* 60,633 **3** village SE Minn. *pop* 86,335

Blooms·bury \'blümz-b(ə-)rē, *United States also* -,ber-ē\ district of N *central* London, England, in borough of Camden

Blue Grotto sea cave Italy on N shore of Capri

Blue Island city NE Ill. S of Chicago *pop* 21,203

Blue Mountains **1** mountains NE Oreg. & SE Wash.; highest Rock Creek Butte 9105 *ft* (*2775 m*) **2** mountains SE Australia in Great Dividing Range in E New S. Wales; highest 4460 *ft* (*1359 m*) **3** mountains E Jamaica; highest Blue Mountain Peak 7402 *ft* (*2256 m*)

Blue Nile river 850 *mi* (*1368 km*) Ethiopia & Sudan flowing from Lake Tana NNW into the Nile at Khartoum — see ABBAI

Blue Ridge the E range of the Appalachians E U.S. extending from South Mountain, S Pa. into N Ga. — see MITCHELL (Mount)

Blue Springs city W Mo. SE of Independence *pop* 40,153

Bluff \'bləf\ town S New Zealand; port for Invercargill *pop* 2720

Blythe·ville \'blī-vəl, 'blīth-,vil\ city NE Ark. *pop* 22,906

Bo·bo–Diou·las·so \'bō-(,)bō-dyü-'lä-(,)sō\ town W Burkina Faso *pop* 300,000

Bo·bruysk *or* **Ba·bruysk** \bə-'brü-isk\ city *central* Belarus on the Berezina *pop* 223,000

Bo·ca Ra·ton \,bō-kə-rə-'tōn\ city SE Fla. N of Fort Lauderdale *pop* 61,492

Bo·chum \'bō-kəm\ city W Germany in Ruhr valley *pop* 398,578

Bodensee — see CONSTANCE (Lake)

Bodh Ga·ya \'bōd-'gī-ä\ *or* **Bud·dha Gaya** \'bu̇-də\ *or* **Buddh Gaya** \'bu̇d\ village NE India in *central* Bihar *pop* 21,686

Bod·min \'bäd-min\ borough SW England, a ✳ of Cornwall and Isles of Scilly *pop* 12,148

Boe·o·tia \bē-'ō-sh(ē-)ə\ *or New Greek* **Voi·o·tía** \,vē-ō-'tē-ä\ district E *central* Greece NW of Attica — **Boe·o·tian** \bē-'ō-shən\ *adjective or noun*

Boetoeng — see BUTON

Bo·go·tá \,bō-gō-'tä, -'tȯ, 'bō-gə-\ city ✳ of Colombia on plateau in the Andes *pop* 4,921,300

Bo Hai *or* **Po Hai** \'bō-'hī\ *or* **Gulf of Chih·li** \'chē-'lē, 'jir\ arm of Yellow Sea NE China bounded on NE by Liaodong Peninsula & on SE by Shandong Peninsula

Bo·he·mia \bō-'hē-mē-ə\ *or* **Če·chy** \'che-kē, -kē\ region W Czech Republic; once a kingdom, later a province ✳ Prague

Bohemian Forest *or German* **Böh·mer Wald** \'bȫ-mər-,vält\ forested mountain region Czech Republic & Germany along boundary between E Bavaria & SW Bohemia

Bo·hol \bō-'hȯl\ island S *central* Philippines, one of the Visayan Islands, N of Mindanao *area* 1492 *sq mi* (*3879 sq km*)

Bois de Belleau — see BELLEAU

Bois de Bou·logne \,bwä-də-bü-'lȯn, -'lȯ-nyə, -'lȯin\ park France W of Paris

Boi·se \'bȯi-sē, -zē\ city ✳ of Idaho on Boise River (60 *mi or* 96 *km* long) *pop* 125,738

Bo·ja·dor, Cape \'bä-jə-,dȯr\ headland NW Africa in the Atlantic on W coast of Western Sahara

Bokhara — see BUKHARA

Boks·burg \'bäks-,bərg\ city NE Republic of South Africa in Gauteng E of Johannesburg *pop* 110,832

Bo·lan Pass \bō-'län\ mountain pass 5900 *ft* (*1798 m*) Pakistan in W Baluchistan

Bolbitine — see ROSETTA

Bo·ling·brook \'bō-liŋ-,bru̇k\ city NE Ill. SW of Chicago *pop* 40,843

Bo·lí·var, Cer·ro \'ser-(,)ō-bō-'lē-,vär\ *or formerly* **La Pa·ri·da** \,lä-pä-'rē-dä\ iron mountain 2018 *ft* (*615 m*) E Venezuela SE of Ciudad Bolívar

Bo·lí·var, Pi·co \'pē-(,)kō-bō-'lē-,vär\ mountain 16,427 *ft* (*5007 m*) W Venezuela in Cordillera de Mérida; highest in Venezuela

Bo·liv·ia \bə-'li-vē-ə\ country W *central* S. America; a republic; administrative ✳ La Paz, constitutional ✳ Sucre *area about* 424,200 *sq mi* (*1,102,920 sq km*), *pop* 7,715,000 — **Bo·liv·i·an** \-vē-ən\ *adjective or noun*

Bo·lo·gna \bə-'lō-nyä\ *or ancient* **Bo·no·nia** \bə-'nō-nē-ə\ commune N Italy ✳ of Emilia-Romagna at foot of the Apennines *pop* 404,322 — **Bo·lo·gnan** \bə-'lō-nyən\ *or* **Bo·lo·gnese** \,bō-lə-'nēz, -'nēs, -'nyēz, -'nyēs\ *adjective or noun*

Bol·se·na, Lake \bȯl-'sā-nə\ lake *central* Italy in NW Lazio

Bol·ton \'bōl-tⁿn\ borough NW England in NW Greater Manchester *pop* 253,300

Bol·za·no \bōlt-'sä-(,)nō, bōl-'zä-\ **1** former province N Italy in S Tirol, now part of Trentino-Alto Adige region **2** commune in Trentino-Alto Adige region *pop* 98,233

Bo·ma \'bō-mə\ city & port W Republic of the Congo on Congo River *pop* 246,207

Bom·bay \bäm-'bā\ **1** former state W India ✳ Bombay; divided 1960 into Gujarat & Maharashtra states; once a presidency & (1937–47) a province of Brit. India **2** *or* **Mum·bai** \'məm-,bī\ city & port W India ✳ of Maharashtra & city in Parts of former Bombay state *area about* 9,925,891

Bombay Island island W India on which city of Bombay is situated *area* 24 *sq mi* (*62 sq km*)

Bo·mu \'bō-(,)mü\ *or* **Mbo·mou** \əm-'bō-(,)mü\ river 500 *mi* (*805 km*) W *central* Africa forming boundary between Democratic Republic of the Congo & Central African Republic & uniting with the Uele to form the Ubangi

Bon, Cape \'bōⁿ\ *or Arabic* **Ra's at Tib** \,räs-ät-'tēb\ headland NE Tunisia on **Cape Bon Peninsula**

Bo·na, Mount \'bō-nə\ mountain *about* 16,500 *ft* (*5030 m*) S Alaska at W end of Wrangell Mountains

Bon·aire \bə-'nar, -'ner\ island Netherlands Antilles E of Curaçao *area* 111 *sq mi* (*287 sq km*), *pop* 11,058

Bon·di \'bän-,dī\ town SE Australia, SE suburb of Sydney, S of entrance to Port Jackson on **Bondi Beach**

Bône — see ANNABA

Bo·nin Islands \'bō-nən\ *or* **Oga·sa·wa·ra Islands** \(,)ō-,gä-sä-'wär-ä\ islands W Pacific *about* 600 *mi* (*966 km*) SSE of Tokyo; belong to Japan; administered by U.S. 1945–68 *area* 40 *sq mi* (*104 sq km*), *pop* 1507

Bonn \'bän, 'bȯn\ city W Germany on the Rhine SSE of Cologne; seat of German parliament and ✳ of Federal Republic of Germany (sometimes called **Bonn Republic**) before reunification *pop* 296,244

Bon·ne·ville Salt Flats \'bä-nə-,vil\ broad level area of Great Salt Lake Desert E of Wendover, Utah

Bonny, Bight of — see BIAFRA, BIGHT OF

Booker T. Washington National Monument historic site W *central* Va. SE of Roanoke

Boo·thia, Gulf of \'bü-thē-ə\ gulf N Canada between Baffin Is. & Melville Peninsula on E & Boothia Peninsula on W

Boothia Peninsula peninsula N Canada W of Baffin Is.; its N tip (at *about* 72°N, 94°W) is the northernmost point on N. American mainland

Boo·tle \'bü-tⁿl\ borough NW England in W Merseyside *pop* 62,463

Bo·phu·tha·tswa·na \,bō-(,)pü-tät-'swä-nä\ former group of noncontiguous black enclaves in the Republic of South Africa ✳ Mmabatho; granted independence 1977; abolished 1994

Bo·ra–Bo·ra \,bȯr-ə-'bȯr-ə, ,bȯr-ə-'bȯr-ə\ island S Pacific in Leeward group of the Society Islands NW of Tahiti *area about* 15 *sq mi* (*38 sq km*)

Bo·rah Peak \'bȯr-ə, 'bȯr-\ mountain 12,662 *ft* (*3859 m*) E *central* Idaho in Lost River Range; highest point in state

Bo·rås \bü-'rȯs\ city SW Sweden E of Göteborg *pop* 102,840

Bor·deaux \bȯr-'dō\ city & port SW France on the Garonne *pop* 213,274 — **Bor·de·lais** \,bȯr-dⁿl-'ā\ *noun*

Bor·ders \'bȯr-dərz\ region S Scotland, established 1975 ✳ Newtown St. Boswells *area* 1814 *sq mi* (*4698 sq km*), *pop* 105,300

Bor·di·ghe·ra \,bȯr-di-'ger-ə\ commune & port NW Italy in Liguria *pop* 11,559

Borgne, Lake \'bȯrn\ inlet of the Mississippi Sound E of New Orleans, La.

Bor·neo \'bȯr-nē-,ō\ island Malay Archipelago SW of Philippines *area* 290,320 *sq mi* (*751,929 sq km*) — see BRUNEI, KALIMANTAN, SABAH, SARAWAK — **Bor·ne·an** \-nē-ən\ *adjective or noun*

Born·holm \'bȯrn-,hōlm, -,hōm\ island Denmark in Baltic Sea ✳ Rönne *area* 227 *sq mi* (*588 sq km*), *pop* 45,991

Bos·nia \'bäz-nē-ə, 'bȯz-\ region S Europe in the Balkans; with Herzegovina forms independent state of **Bosnia and Her·ze·go·vi·na** \,hert-sə-gō-'vē-nə, ,hərt-, -'gō-və-nə\; a federated republic of Yugoslavia 1946–92 ✳ Sarajevo *area* 19,904 *sq mi* (*51,750 sq km*), *pop* 4,422,000 — **Bos·ni·an** \-nē-ən\ *adjective or noun*

Bos·po·rus \'bäs-p(ə-)rəs\ *or* **Bos·pho·rus** \-f(ə-)rəs\ strait *about* 18 *mi* (*29 km*) long between Turkey in Europe & Turkey in Asia connecting Sea of Marmara & Black Sea — **Bos·po·ran** \-pə-rən\ *adjective*

Bos·sier City \'bō-zhər\ city NW La. *pop* 52,721

Bos·ton \'bȯs-tən\ **1** city & port ✳ of Mass. on Massachusetts Bay *pop* 535,721 **2** borough & port E England in SE Lincolnshire in Parts of Holland *pop* 52,600 — **Bos·to·nian** \bȯ-'stō-nē-ən, -nyən\ *adjective or noun*

Boston Mountains mountains NW Ark. & E Okla. in Ozark Plateau

Bo·ta·fo·go Bay \,bō-tä-'fō-(,)gō\ inlet of Guanabara Bay in Rio de Janeiro, Brazil

Bot·a·ny Bay \'bä-tⁿn-ē\ inlet of the S Pacific SE Australia in New South Wales on S border of city of Sydney

Both·nia, Gulf of \'bäth-nē-ə\ arm of Baltic Sea between Sweden & Finland

Bo·tswa·na \bät-'swä-nə\ country S Africa N of the Molopo; an independent republic since 1966, formerly Brit. protectorate of **Bechuanaland** ✳ Gaborone *area about* 220,000 *sq mi* (*569,800 sq km*), *pop* 1,406,000

Bot·trop \'bä-,träp\ city W Germany NNW of Essen *pop* 118,758

Bou·cher·ville \'bü-shər-,vil, ,bü-shä-'vēl\ town Canada in S Quebec NE of Montreal *pop* 33,796

Bou·gain·ville \'bü-gən-,vil, ,bō-, 'bü-\ island S Pacific, largest of the Solomons; chief town Kieta *area* 3880 *sq mi* (*10,088 sq km*)

Bougie — see BEJAIA

Bouil·lon \bü-'yōⁿ\ town SE Belgium in the Ardennes *pop* 5468

Boul·der \'bōl-dər\ city N *central* Colo. *pop* 83,312

Boulder Dam — see HOOVER DAM

Bou·logne \bü-'lōn, -'lȯ-nyə, -'lȯin\ *or* **Bou·logne–sur–Mer** \-,sür-'mer\ city & port N France on English Channel *pop* 44,244

Boulogne–Bil·lan·court \-,bē-,yäⁿ-'kür\ commune N France SW of Paris on the Seine *pop* 103,527

Boundary Peak mountain 13,140 *ft* (*4005 m*) SW Nev. in White Mountains; highest in state

Boun·ti·ful city N Utah N of Salt Lake City *pop* 36,659

Bour·bon·nais \,bür-bò-'nā\ former province *central* France W of Burgundy

Bourges \'bürzh\ commune *central* France SSE of Orléans *pop* 78,773

Bourgogne — see BURGUNDY

Bourne·mouth \'bōrn-məth, 'bórn-, 'bùrn-\ town S England in Dorset on English Channel *pop* 154,400

Bou·vet \'bü-(,)vā\ island S Atlantic SSW of Cape of Good Hope at *about* 54˚S, 5˚E; belongs to Norway

Bow \'bō\ river 315 *mi* (507 *km*) Canada in SW Alberta rising in Banff National Park

Bow·ie \'bü-ē\ town Md. NE of Washington, D.C. *pop* 37,589

Bowling Green 1 city S Ky. *pop* 40,641 **2** city NW Ohio S of Toledo *pop* 28,176

Boyne \'bóin\ river 70 *mi* (113 *km*) E Ireland in Leinster flowing to Irish Sea S of Drogheda

Boyn·ton Beach \'bóin-t°n\ city SE Fla. *pop* 46,194

Bo·yo·ma Falls \bói-'ō-mä\ *or formerly* **Stanley Falls** series of seven cataracts NE Democratic Republic of the Congo in the Lualaba near head of Congo River with total fall of *about* 200 *ft* (61 *m*) in 60 *mi* (96 *km*)

Boz·caa·da \,bōz-jä-'dä\ *or ancient* **Ten·e·dos** \'te-nə-,däs\ island Turkey in NE Aegean Sea S of the Dardanelles

Boze·man \'bōz-mən\ city SW Mont. *pop* 22,660

Bra·bant \'brä-bənt; brə-'bant, -'bänt\ **1** old duchy of W Europe including region now forming N. Brabant province of Netherlands & of Brabant & Antwerp provinces of Belgium **2** province *central* Belgium ✱ Brussels *pop* 1,302,577

Bra·den·ton \'brä-d°n-tən\ city & port W Fla. N of Sarasota *pop* 43,779

Brad·ford \'brad-fərd\ city N England in W. Yorkshire *pop* 280,691

Bra·ga \'brä-gə\ commune NW Portugal NNE of Porto *pop* 63,033

Bra·gan·ça \brə-'gán-sə\ commune NE Portugal near Spanish border *pop* 14,181

Brah·ma·pu·tra \,brä-mə-'pü-trə\ river *about* 1800 *mi* (2900 *km*) S Asia flowing from the Himalays in Tibet to the Ganges delta in E India (subcontinent) — see JAMUNA, TSANGPO

Bra·i·la \brə-'ē-lə\ city E Romania on the Danube *pop* 242,595

Brain·tree \'brān-(,)trē\ town E Mass. S of Boston *pop* 33,836

Brak·pan \'brak-,pan\ city NE Republic of South Africa in Gauteng on the Witwatersrand S of Johannesburg *pop* 85,044

Bramp·ton \'bramp-tən\ city Canada in SE Ontario W of Toronto *pop* 234,445

Bran·co, Rio \,rē-ō-'brán-kü\ river 350 *mi* (563 *km*) N Brazil flowing S into Negro River

Bran·den·burg \'bran-dən-,bərg, 'brän-dən-,bùrk\ **1** region & former province NE *central* Germany **2** city E Germany *pop* 88,760

Bran·don \'bran-dən\ city Canada in SW Manitoba *pop* 38,567

Bran·dy·wine \'bran-dē-,wīn\ creek *about* 20 *mi* (32 *km*) SE Pa. & N Del. flowing SE to Wilmington, Del.

Bran·ford \'bran-fərd\ town S Conn. E of New Haven *pop* 27,603

Brant·ford \'brant-fərd\ city Canada in SE Ontario *pop* 81,997

Bras d'Or Lake \bra-'dór\ tidal lake *about* 50 *mi* (80 *km*) long Canada in Nova Scotia on Cape Breton Is.

Bra·sí·lia \brə-'zil-yə\ city ✱ of Brazil in Federal District *metropolitan area pop* 1,803,478

Bra·sov \brä-'shóv\ *or formerly* **Sta·lin** \'stä-lən, 'sta-, -,lēn\ *or* **Ora·sul Stalin** \,ò-,rä-shü, -shùl\ city *central* Romania in foothills of Transylvanian Alps *pop* 352,640

Bra·ti·sla·va \,bra-tə-'slä-və, ,brä-\ *or German* **Press·burg** \'pres-,bərg, -,bùrk\ *or Hungarian* **Po·zsony** \'pō-,zhō-nyə\ city W Slovakia, its ✱, on the Danube *pop* 441,453

Bratsk \'brätsk\ city Russia in Asia, NNE of Irkutsk near site of **Bratsk Dam** (in the Angara) *pop* 259,000

Braunschweig — see BRUNSWICK

Bravo, Río — see RIO GRANDE

Bray \'brā\ town & port E Ireland *pop* 25,101

Bra·zil *or Portuguese* **Bra·sil** \brə-'zil\ country E S. America; a federal republic ✱ Brasília *area about* 3,280,000 *sq mi* (8,495,200 *sq km*), *pop* 150,051,784 — **Bra·zil·ian** \brə-'zil-yən\ *adjective or noun*

Braz·os \'bra-zəs\ river *about* 840 *mi* (1350 *km*), *central* Tex. flowing SE into Gulf of Mexico

Braz·za·ville \'bra-zə-,vil, 'brä-zə-,vēl\ city & port ✱ of Republic of the Congo on W bank of Pool Malebo in Congo River *pop* 937,579

Brea \'brā-ə\ city SW Calif. SE of Los Angeles *pop* 32,873

Brec·on \'bre-kən\ *or* **Breck·nock** \'brek-,näk, -,nək\ **1** *or* **Brec·on·shire** *or* **Breck·nock·shire** \-,shir, -shər\ former county SE Wales ✱ Brecon **2** borough SE Wales in Powys *pop* 7422

Brecon Beacons two mountain peaks SE Wales in S Powys

Bre·da \'brā-dä\ commune S Netherlands in N. Brabant province *pop* 162,951

Bre·genz \'brā-,gents\ commune W Austria on Lake Constance ✱ of Vorarlberg *pop* 27,236

Bre·men \'bre-mən, 'brā-\ **1** former duchy N Germany between the lower Weser & the lower Elbe **2** state NW Germany *area* 156 *sq mi* (404 *sq km*), *pop* 681,700 **3** city & port, its ✱, on the Weser *pop* 552,746

Bre·mer·ha·ven \'bre-mər-,hä-v°n, ,brä-mər-'hä-f°n\ city & port NW Germany in Bremen state at mouth of the Weser; includes former city of Wesermünde *pop* 130,938

Brem·er·ton \'bre-mər-tən, -t°n\ city & port W Wash. on Puget Sound *pop* 38,142

Bren·ner Pass \'bre-nər\ mountain pass *about* 4495 *ft* (1370 *m*) in the Alps between Austria & Italy

Brent \'brent\ *or formerly* **Brent·ford and Chis·wick** \'brent-fərd-°n-'chi-zik\ borough of W Greater London, England *pop* 226,100

Bren·ta \'bren-tä\ river 100 *mi* (161 *km*) N Italy flowing SE into the Adriatic S of Chioggia

Bre·scia \'bre-shä, 'brā-\ *or ancient* **Brix·ia** \'brik-sē-ə\ commune N Italy in E Lombardy ENE of Milan *pop* 200,722

Breslau — see WROCŁAW

Brest \'brest\ **1** *or formerly* **Brest Li·tovsk** \li-'tófsk\ city SW Belarus on Bug River *pop* 277,000 **2** commune & port NW France in Brittany *pop* 153,099

Bre·ton, Cape \kāp-'bre-t°n, kə-'bre-, -'bri-\ headland Canada, easternmost point of Cape Breton Is. & of Nova Scotia, at 59˚48'W

Bridge·port \'brij-,pórt, -port\ city SW Conn. on Long Island Sound *pop* 141,686

Bridge·town \'brij-,taùn\ city & port Brit. West Indies ✱ of Barbados *pop* 6070

Bridge·wa·ter \'brij-,wò-tər, -,wä-\ city SE Mass. S of Brockton *pop* 21,249

Brie \'brē\ district & medieval county NE France E of Paris; chief town Meaux

Bri·enne \brē-'en\ **1** former county NE France in Champagne NNE of Troyes **2** town, its ✱

Bri·enz \brē-'ents\ town Switzerland in SE Bern canton at NE end of **Lake of Brienz** (9 *mi* or 14 *km* long, in course of the Aare)

Brigh·ton \'brī-t°n\ borough S England in E. Sussex on English Channel *pop* 133,400

Brin·di·si \'brin-də-(,)zē, 'brēn-\ *or ancient* **Brun·di·si·um** \,brən-'di-zē-əm, -zhē-\ city & port SE Italy in Puglia *pop* 91,778

Bris·bane \'briz-bən, -,bān\ city & port E Australia ✱ of Queensland on **Brisbane River** (215 *mi* or 344 *km*) near its mouth *pop* 751,115

Bris·tol \'bris-t°l\ **1** city W *central* Conn. WSW of Hartford *pop* 60,640 **2** town E R.I. SE of Providence *pop* 21,625 **3** city NE Tenn. *pop* 23,421 **4** city & port SW England in Avon on Avon River near Severn estuary *pop* 370,300 — **Bris·to·li·an** \bri-'stō-lē-ən, -'stól-yən\ *noun*

Bristol Bay arm of Bering Sea SW Alaska W of Alaska Peninsula

Bristol Channel channel between S Wales & SW England

Brit·ain \'bri-t°n\ **1** *or Latin* **Bri·tan·nia** \brə-'ta-nyə, -nē-ə\ the island of Great Britain **2** UNITED KINGDOM **3** COMMONWEALTH OF NATIONS

British America 1 *or* **British North America** CANADA **2** all Brit. possessions in & adjacent to N. & S. America

British Bechuanaland — see BECHUANALAND

British Cameroons former Brit. trust territory W equatorial Africa comprising two areas in the Cameroons between Nigeria & Cameroon ✱ Buea; divided 1961 between Nigeria (N section) & Cameroon (S section)

British Columbia province W Canada on Pacific coast ✱ Victoria *area* 344,663 *sq mi* (892,677 *sq km*), *pop* 3,282,061 — **British Co·lum·bi·an** \kə-'ləm-bē-ən\ *noun or adjective*

British Commonwealth COMMONWEALTH OF NATIONS — a former name

British East Africa 1 KENYA — a former name **2** the former Brit. dependencies in E Africa: Kenya, Uganda, Zanzibar, & Tanganyika

British Empire Great Britain & the Brit. dominions & dependencies — a former usage

British Guiana — see GUYANA

British Honduras — see BELIZE

British India the part of India formerly under direct Brit. administration — see INDIAN STATES

British Indian Ocean Territory Brit. colony in Indian Ocean comprising Chagos Archipelago & formerly Aldabra, Farquhar, & Desroches islands (returned to Seychelles 1976) *area* 23 *sq mi* (60 *sq km*)

British Isles island group W Europe comprising Great Britain, Ireland, & adjacent islands

British Malaya former dependencies of Great Britain in Malay Peninsula & in Malay Archipelago including Malaya (federation), Singapore, N. Borneo, Sarawak, & Brunei

British Solomon Islands former Brit. protectorate comprising the Solomons (except Bougainville, Buka, & adjacent small islands) & the Santa Cruz Islands ✱ Honiara (on Guadalcanal)

British Somaliland former Brit. protectorate E Africa bordering on Gulf of Aden ✱ Hargeisa; since 1960 part of Somalia

British Virgin Islands the E islands of the Virgin Islands group; a Brit. possession ✱ Road Town (on Tortola Is.) *area* 59 *sq mi* (153 *sq km*), *pop* 14,786

British West Indies islands of the West Indies including Jamaica, Bahamas, Caymans, Brit. Virgin Islands, Brit. Leeward & Windward Islands, Trinidad, & Tobago

Brit·ta·ny \'bri-t°n-ē\ *or French* **Bre·tagne** \brə-'tän'\ region & former province NW France SW of Normandy

Br·no \'bər-(,)nō\ *or German* **Brünn** \'brœn, 'brün\ city E Czech Republic, chief city of Moravia *pop* 387,986

Broad \'bród\ **1** river 220 *mi* (354 *km*) N.C. & S.C. — see SALUDA **2** river 70 *mi* (113 *km*) S S.C. flowing into the Atlantic

Broads \'bródz\ low-lying district E England in Norfolk (the **Norfolk Broads**) & Suffolk (the **Suffolk Broads**)

Brock·en \'brä-kən\ mountain 3747 *ft* (1142 *m*) *central* Germany near former E. Germany–W. Germany border; highest in Harz Mountains

Brock·ton \'bräk-tən\ city SE Mass. *pop* 92,788

Brock·ville \'bräk-,vil\ city Canada in SE Ontario *pop* 21,582

Bro·ken Ar·row \'brō-kən-'ar-ō\ city NE Okla. SE of Tulsa *pop* 58,043

Broken Hill 1 city SE Australia in W New South Wales *pop* 23,739 **2** — see KABWE

Bromberg — see BYDGOSZCZ

Brom·ley \'bräm-lē\ borough of SE Greater London, England *pop* 281,700

Bronx \'bränks\ *or* **The Bronx** borough of New York City on the mainland NE of Manhattan Is. *pop* 1,203,789

Brook·field \'brúk-,fēld\ city SE Wis. W of Milwaukee *pop* 35,184

Brook·line \'brúk-,līn\ town E Mass. W of Boston *pop* 54,718

\ə\ abut	\°\ kitten	\ər\ **further**	\a\ ash \ā\ **ace**
\ä\ mop, mar	\aù\ **out**	\ch\ **chin**	\e\ bet \ē\ **easy**
\g\ go	\i\ hit	\ī\ **ice**	\j\ **job** \ŋ\ sing \ō\ go
\ò\ law	\ói\ **boy**	\th\ **thin**	\th\ **the** \ü\ **loot** \ù\ **foot**
\y\ **yet**	\zh\ **vision**	*see also* Guide to Pronunciation	

Brook·lyn \'brú-klən\ borough of New York City at SW end of Long Is. *pop* 2,300,664 — **Brook·lyn·ite** \-klə-ˌnīt\ *noun*

Brooklyn Center village SE Minn. NW of Minneapolis *pop* 28,887

Brooklyn Park village E Minn. NW of Minneapolis *pop* 56,381

Brook Park \'brúk\ city NE Ohio *pop* 22,865

Brooks Range \'brúks\ mountain range N Alaska extending from Kotzebue Sound to Canadian border; highest peak over 9000 *ft* (2740 *m*)

Broom·field \'brüm-ˌfēld, 'brúm-\ city N *central* Colo. NNW of Denver *pop* 24,638

Bros·sard \brō-'sär(d)\ town Canada in S Quebec *pop* 64,793

Browns·ville \'braúnz-ˌvil, -vəl\ city & port S Tex. *pop* 98,962

Bruce \'brüs\ peninsula SE Ontario, Canada, projecting between Lake Huron & Georgian Bay

Brug·ge \'brü-gə, 'brœ-kə\ *or French* **Bruges** \'brüzh, brœzh\ commune NW Belgium ✳ of W. Flanders *pop* 116,700

Bru·nei \brü-'nī, 'brü-ˌnī\ **1** independent sultanate & former Brit. protectorate NW Borneo ✳ Bandar Seri Begawan *area* 2226 *sq mi* (5788 *sq km*), *pop* 260,863 **2** — see BANDAR SERI BEGAWAN — **Bru·nei·an** \brü-'nī-ən\ *adjective or noun*

Bruns·wick \'brənz-(ˌ)wik\ **1** town SW Maine *pop* 20,906 **2** city NE Ohio SSW of Cleveland *pop* 28,230 **3** *or German* **Braun·schweig** \'braún-ˌshvīk\ former state *central* Germany ✳ Brunswick **4** *or German* **Braun·schweig** city N *central* Germany W of Berlin *pop* 259,127

Brus·sels \'brə-səlz\ *or French* **Bru·xelles** \brœ(k)-'sel\ *or Flemish* **Brus·sel** \'brœ-səl\ city ✳ of Belgium & of Brabant *pop* 136,424 — **Bru·xel·lois** \brœ-sel-'wä *also* brœk-\ *adjective or noun*

Bruttium — see CALABRIA

Bry·an \'brī-ən\ city E *central* Tex. *pop* 55,002

Bry·ansk \brē-'änsk\ city Russia in Europe SW of Moscow *pop* 461,000

Bryce Canyon National Park \'brīs\ reservation S Utah NE of Zion National Park

Bu·bas·tis \byü-'bas-təs\ ancient city N Egypt near modern Zagazig

Bu·ca·ra·man·ga \ˌbü-kä-rä-'mäŋ-gä\ city N Colombia NNE of Bogotá *pop* 349,400

Bu·cha·rest \'bü-kə-ˌrest, 'byü-\ *or Romanian* **Bu·cu·reș·ti** \ˌbü-kə-'reshty, -'resh-tē\ city ✳ of Romania *pop* 2,036,894

Bu·chen·wald \'bü-kən-ˌwóld, -ˌvält\ village *central* Germany NW of Weimar; site of Nazi concentration camp

Buck·ing·ham·shire \'bə-kiŋ-əm-ˌshir, -shər, *United States also* -kiŋ-ˌham-\ *or* **Buckingham** *or* **Bucks** \'bəks\ county SE *central* England ✳ Aylesbury *area* 753 *sq mi* (1950 *sq km*), *pop* 651,700

Buck Island Reef National Monument \'bək\ reservation St. Croix, Virgin Islands; contains marine gardens

Bu·da·pest \'bü-də-ˌpest *also* 'bú-, 'byü-, -ˌpesht\ city ✳ of Hungary on the Danube *pop* 2,008,546

Buddha Gaya, Buddh Gaya — see BODH GAYA

Budweis — see CESKE BUDEJOVICE

Bue·na Park \'bwā-nə\ city Calif. W of Anaheim *pop* 68,784

Bue·na·ven·tu·ra \ˌbwā-nä-ven-'tü-rä\ city & port W Colombia on the Pacific *pop* 115,770

Bue·nos Ai·res \ˌbwā-nəs-'ar-ēz, *Spanish* ˌbwä-nōs-'ī-rās\ city & port ✳ of Argentina on Río de la Plata *pop* 2,960,976

Buenos Aires, Lake lake 80 *mi* (129 *km*) long S Argentina & S Chile

Buf·fa·lo \'bə-fə-ˌlō\ city & port W N.Y. on Lake Erie & the Niagara *pop* 328,123 — **Buf·fa·lo·ni·an** \ˌbə-fə-'lō-nē-ən\ *noun*

Buffalo Grove city NE Ill. *pop* 36,427

Bug \'büg\ **1** river over 450 *mi* (720 *km*) *central* Poland rising in W Ukraine, & flowing into the Vistula **2** river over 500 *mi* (805 *km*) SW Ukraine flowing SE to the Dnieper estuary

Bu·gan·da \bü-'gän-də, byü-\ region & former native kingdom E Africa in SE Uganda ✳ Kampala

Bu·jum·bu·ra \ˌbü-jəm-'búr-ə\ *or formerly* **Usum·bu·ra** \ˌü-səm-\ city ✳ of Burundi on Lake Tanganyika *pop* 236,334

Bu·ka \'bü-kä\ island W Pacific in the Solomons N of Bougainville *pop* 33,770

Bu·ka·vu \bü-'kä-(ˌ)vü\ *or formerly* **Cos·ter·mans·ville** \'käs-tər-mənz-ˌvil\ city E Democratic Republic of the Congo at S end of Lake Kivu *pop* 209,566

Bu·kha·ra \bü-'kär-ə, -'kar-, -'kär-\ *or* **Bo·kha·ra** \bō-\ **1** former emirate W Asia around city of Bukhara **2** city W Uzbekistan E of the Amu Darya *pop* 249,600 — **Bu·kha·ran** *or* **Bo·kha·ran** \-ən\ *adjective or noun*

Bu·ko·vi·na *or* **Bu·co·vi·na** \ˌbü-kō-'vē-nə\ region E *central* Europe in foothills of E Carpathians; now in NE Romania & W Ukraine

Bu·la·wa·yo \ˌbü-lä-'wä-yō\ city SW Zimbabwe, chief town of Matabeleland *pop* 495,317

Bul·gar·ia \ˌbəl-'gar-ē-ə, bül-, -'ger-\ country SE Europe on Black Sea; a republic ✳ Sofia *area* 42,823 *sq mi* (110,912 *sq km*), *pop* 8,466,000

Bull·head City \'búl-ˌhed\ city W Ariz., across Colorado River from Nev. *pop* 21,951

Bull Run \'búl-'rən\ stream 20 *mi* (32 *km*) N Va. W of Washington, D.C., flowing into Occoquan Creek (small tributary of the Potomac)

Bun·del·khand \'bún-dəl-ˌkənd\ region N *central* India containing headwaters of the Yamuna; now chiefly in N Madhya Pradesh

Bundesrepublik Deutschland — see GERMANY

Bun·ker Hill \'bəŋ-kər\ height in Charlestown section of Boston, Mass.

Bur·bank \'bər-ˌbaŋk\ **1** city SW Calif. *pop* 93,643 **2** city NE Ill. *pop* 27,600

Bur·gas \búr-'gäs\ city & port NE Bulgaria *pop* 204,915

Bur·gen·land \'bər-gən-ˌland, 'búr-gən-ˌlänt\ province E Austria SE of Vienna on Hungarian border ✳ Eisenstadt

Bur·gos \'búr-ˌgōs\ **1** province N Spain *area* 5509 *sq mi* (14,268 *sq km*), *pop* 352,722 **2** city, its ✳ & once W of Old Castile *pop* 160,278

Bur·gun·dy \'bər-gən-dē\ *or French* **Bour·gogne** \búr-'gón'\ **1** region & with varying limits former kingdom, duchy, & province E France S of Champagne **2** former county France E of Burgundy province; later called **Franche-Com·té** \ˌfrä'nsh-kō'n-'tā\ — **Bur·gun·di·an** \(ˌ)bər-'gən-dē-ən\ *adjective or noun*

Bur·ki·na Fa·so \búr-'kē-nə-'fä-sō, bər-\ *or formerly* **Upper Vol·ta** \'vōl-tə, 'vól-, -'väl-\ republic W Africa; until 1958 a French territory ✳ Ouagadougou *area* 105,869 *sq mi* (274,201 *sq km*), *pop* 9,780,000

Bur·lin·game \'bər-lin-ˌgām\ city W Calif. *pop* 26,801

Bur·ling·ton \'bər-liŋ-tən\ **1** city SE Iowa *pop* 27,208 **2** town NE Mass. *pop* 23,302 **3** city N *central* N.C. *pop* 39,498 **4** city NW Vt. *pop* 39,127 **5** city Canada in SE Ontario N of Hamilton *pop* 129,575

Burma — see MYANMAR

Bur·na·by \'bər-nə-bē\ municipality Canada in SW British Columbia *pop* 158,858

Burn·ley \'bərn-lē\ borough NW England in SE Lancashire *pop* 89,000

Burns·ville \'bərnz-ˌvil\ village SE Minn. S of Minneapolis *pop* 51,288

Bur·rard Inlet \bə-'rärd\ inlet of Strait of Georgia W Canada in British Columbia; city of Vancouver is situated on it

Bur·sa \búr-'sä, 'bər-sə\ *or formerly* **Bru·sa** \brü-'sä, 'brü-sə\ city NW Turkey in Asia near Sea of Marmara *pop* 834,576

Bur·ton \'bər-tᵊn\ city SE *central* Mich. SE of Flint *pop* 27,617

Bu·run·di \bü-'rün-dē, -'rún-\ *or formerly* **Urun·di** \ú-'rün-\ country E *central* Africa; a republic ✳ Bujumbura *area about* 10,700 *sq mi* (27,700 *sq km*), *pop* 5,665,000 — see RUANDA-URUNDI — **Bu·run·di·an** \-dē-ən\ *adjective or noun*

Bury \'ber-ē\ borough NW England in Greater Manchester NNW of Manchester *pop* 172,200

Bur·yat·ia \búr-'yä-tē-ə\ *or* **Bur·yat Republic** \búr-'yät, ˌbúr-ē-'ät\ autonomous republic S Russia in Asia adjacent to Mongolia & E of Lake Baikal ✳ Ulan-Ude *area* 135,637 *sq mi* (351,300 *sq km*), *pop* 1,059,000 — **Buryat** *noun*

Bury Saint Ed·munds \ˌber-ē-sänt-'ed-mən(d)z, -sənt-\ borough SE England in Suffolk *pop* 28,914

Bu·shehr \bü-'sher\ city & port SW Iran *pop* 120,787

Bu·ta·ri·ta·ri \bü-ˌtä-rē-'tä-rē\ atoll W Pacific at N end of Kiribati *area* 4 *sq mi* (10 *sq km*)

Bute \'byüt\ **1** island SW Scotland W of Firth of Clyde **2** *or* **Bute·shire** \-ˌshir, -shər\ former county SW Scotland comprising several islands in the Firth of Clyde ✳ Rothesay (on Bute)

Bu·ton \'bü-ˌtón\ *or* **Bu·tung** *or* **Du Boe·toeng** \'bü-ˌtúŋ\ island Indonesia off SE Sulawesi *area about* 2000 *sq mi* (5200 *sq km*) *pop* 253,262

Butte \'byüt\ city SW Mont. in plateau of Rockies *pop* 33,336

Bu·zau \bə-'zō, -'zaú\ city E Romania *pop* 145,423

Buz·zards Bay \'bə-zərdz\ inlet of the Atlantic SE Mass. W of Cape Cod

Byd·goszcz \'bid-ˌgósh(ch)\ *or German* **Brom·berg** \'bräm-ˌbárg, 'bróm-ˌberk\ city NW *central* Poland NE of Poznan *pop* 380,385

Byelarus — see BELARUS

Byelorussia — see BELORUSSIA — **Bye·lo·rus·sian** \bē-ˌe-lō-'rə-shən, ˌbye-lō-\ *adjective or noun*

By·tom \'bē-ˌtóm, 'bi-\ *or German* **Beu·then** \'bói-tᵊn\ city SW Poland in Silesia *pop* 229,851

Byzantium — see ISTANBUL

Ca·ba·na·tuan \ˌkä-bä-nä-'twän\ city Philippines in S *central* Luzon *pop* 173,000

Ca·bi·mas \kä-'bē-mäs\ city NW Venezuela on NE coast of Lake Maracaibo *pop* 165,755

Ca·bin·da \kä-'bin-dä\ territory W equatorial Africa on the Atlantic between Republic of the Congo & Democratic Republic of the Congo; belongs to Angola ✳ Cabinda *area* 3000 *sq mi* (7800 *sq km*), *pop* 58,547

Cab·ot Strait \'ka-bət\ strait *about* 70 *mi* (113 *km*) wide E Canada between SW Newfoundland & Cape Breton Is. connecting Gulf of Saint Lawrence with the Atlantic

Ca·bril·lo National Monument \kə-'brē-(ˌ)yō\ historic site SW Calif. on San Diego Bay

Ca·ca·hua·mil·pa \ˌkä-kē-wä-'mēl-pä\ caverns S Mexico in Guerrero NNE of Taxco

Cá·ce·res \'kä-sə-ˌräs\ **1** province W Spain in N Extremadura *area* 7701 *sq mi* (19,946 *sq km*), *pop* 411,464 **2** city, its ✳ *pop* 74,589

Cache la Pou·dre \ˌkash-lə-'pü-dər\ river 125 *mi* (201 *km*) N Colo. flowing into the S. Platte

Cad·do Lake \'ka-(ˌ)dō\ lake 20 *mi* (32 *km*) long NW La. & NE Tex. draining to Red River

Cá·diz \kə-'diz; 'kä-dəz, 'kä-, 'ka-; *Spanish* 'kä-(ˌ)dēs\ **1** province SW Spain in Andalusia *area* 2851 *sq mi* (7384 *sq km*), *pop* 1,078,404 **2** *or ancient* **Ga·dir** \'gä-dər\ *or* **Ga·des** \'gā-(ˌ)dēz\ city & port, its ✳, on Bay of Cádiz NW of Gibraltar *pop* 154,347

Cadiz, Gulf of arm of the Atlantic SW Spain

Cae·li·an \'sē-lē-ən\ hill in Rome, Italy, one of seven on which the ancient city was built — see AVENTINE

Caen \'kä'n\ city NW France in Normandy *pop* 115,624

Caerdydd — see CARDIFF

Caer·nar·von *or* **Caer·nar·fon** \kär-'när-vən, kə(r)-\ **1** *or* **Caer·nar·von·shire** \-ˌshir, -shər\ former county NW Wales **2** borough NW Wales ✳ of Gwynedd *pop* 9506

Cae·sa·rea \ˌsē-zə-'rē-ə, ˌse-sə-, ˌse-zə-\ **1** ancient seaport Palestine S of Haifa **2** *or* **Cae·sarea Mazaca** — see KAYSERI

Caesarea Phi·lip·pi \'fi-lə-ˌpī, fə-'li-ˌpī\ ancient city N Palestine SW of Mt. Hermon; site at modern village of Baniyas \ˌba-nē-'yas\ in SW Syria

Caesena — see CESENA

Ca·ga·yan \ˌkä-gä-'yän\ *or* **Rio Gran·de de Ca·gayan** \ˌrē-ō-'grän-dā-dä-\ river 220 *mi* (354 *km*) Philippines in NE Luzon flowing N

Ca·glia·ri \'käl-yä-ˌrē\ commune & port Italy ✳ of Sardinia *pop* 219,095

Ca·guas \'kä-ˌgwäs\ town E *central* Puerto Rico *pop* 92,429

Ca·ho·kia Mounds \kə-'hō-kē-ə\ group of prehistoric Indian mounds Ill. ENE of E. St. Louis

Ca·hors \kä-'ór\ city SW France N of Toulouse *pop* 20,787

Caicos — see TURKS AND CAICOS

Cairn·gorm \'karn-ˌgórm, 'kern-\ mountain 4084 *ft* (1245 *m*) in Cairngorm Mountains on boundary between Highlands and Grampian regions

Cairngorm Mountains mountain range of the Grampians NE *central* Scotland; highest point Ben Macdhui 4296 *ft* (1309 *m*)

Cairns \'karnz, 'kernz\ city & port NE Australia in NE Queensland *pop* 54,862

Cai·ro \'kī-(ˌ)rō\ city N Egypt, its ✳ *pop* 6,663,000 — **Cai·rene** \kī-'rēn\ *adjective or noun*

Caith·ness \'kāth-nis, ˌkāth-'nes\ *or* **Caith·ness–shire** \-nish-ˌshir, -shər; -'nesh-\ former county N Scotland ✳ Wick

Ca·ja·mar·ca \ˌkä-hə-'mär-kä\ city NW Peru *pop* 92,600

Ca·jon Pass \kə-'hōn\ pass 4301 *ft* (1303 *m*) S Calif. NW of San Bernardino between San Bernardino Mountains & San Gabriel Mountains

Cal·a·bar \'ka-lə-ˌbär\ city & port SE Nigeria *pop* 153,900

Ca·la·bria \kə-'lā-brē-ə, -'lä-\ **1** district of ancient Italy comprising area forming heel of the Italian Peninsula; now the S part of Puglia **2** *or Italian* **Le Ca·la·brie** \lä-kä-'lä-brē-ā\ *or ancient* **Brut·ti·um** \'brü-tē-əm, 'brü-shē-\ region S Italy occupying toe of the Italian Peninsula ✳ Catanzaro *area* 5822 *sq mi* (15,079 *sq km*), *pop* 2,152,539 — **Ca·la·bri·an** \kə-'lā-brē-ən, -'lä-\ *adjective or noun*

Ca·lah \'kā-lə\ ancient city ✳ of Assyria on the Tigris 20 *mi* (32 *km*) SE of modern Mosul, Iraq; site now called **Nim·rud** \nim-'rüd\

Ca·lais \ka-'lā, kä-'le\ city & port N France on Strait of Dover *pop* 75,836

Calais, Pas de — see DOVER (Strait of)

Ca·la·mian \ˌkä-lä-mē-'än\ islands W Philippines NE of Palawan Is.

Cal·ca·sieu \'kal-kə-ˌshü\ river 200 *mi* (322 *km*) SW La. flowing through **Calcasieu Lake** (*about* 15 *mi or* 24 *km* long) & **Calcasieu Pass** (channel 5 *mi or* 8 *km* long) into Gulf of Mexico

Cal·cut·ta \kal-'kə-tə\ city & port E India on the Hugli ✳ of W. Bengal *metropolitan area pop* 11,021,915 — **Cal·cut·tan** \-'kə-tᵊn\ *noun*

Cal·e·don \'ka-lə-dən\ town Canada in SE Ontario *pop* 34,965

Cal·e·do·nia \ˌka-lə-'dō-nyə, -nē-ə\ **1** town SE Wisconsin *pop* 20,999 **2** — see SCOTLAND — **Cal·e·do·nian** \-nyən, -nē-ən\ *adjective or noun*

Caledonian Canal ship canal N Scotland connecting Loch Linnhe & Moray Firth & uniting Lochs Ness, Oich, Lochy, & Eil

Cal·ga·ry \'kal-gə-rē\ city Canada in SW Alberta *pop* 710,677 — **Cal·gar·i·an** \kal-'gar-ē-ən, -'ger-\ *noun*

Ca·li \'kä-lē\ city W Colombia on the Cauca *pop* 1,624,400

Cal·i·cut \'ka-li-(ˌ)kət\ *or* **Ko·zhi·kode** \'kō-zhə-ˌkōd\ city & port SW India on Malabar Coast in Kerala *pop* 456,618

Cal·i·for·nia \ˌka-lə-'fór-nyə\ state SW U.S. ✳ Sacramento *area* 158,706 *sq mi* (411,048 *sq km*), *pop* 29,760,020 — **Cal·i·for·nio** \-nyō\ *noun* — **Cal·i·for·nian** \-nyən\ *adjective or noun*

California, Gulf of arm of the Pacific NW Mexico between Baja California & states of Sonora & Sinaloa

Cal·lao \kä-'yä-(ˌ)ō, -'yaù\ city & port W Peru on Callao Bay W of Lima *pop* 588,600

Ca·loo·sa·hatch·ee \kə-ˌlü-sə-'ha-chē\ river 75 *mi* (121 *km*) S Fla. flowing W into Gulf of Mexico

Calpe — see GIBRALTAR (Rock of)

Cal·ta·nis·set·ta \ˌkal-tä-nis-'se-tä\ commune Italy in *central* Sicily *pop* 60,162

Cal·u·met \'kal-yə-ˌmet, -mət\ industrial region NW Ind. & NE Ill. SE of & adjacent to Chicago; includes chiefly cities of E. Chicago, Gary, & Hammond, Ind., & Calumet City & Lansing, Ill.

Calumet City city NE Ill. S of Chicago *pop* 37,840

Cal·va·dos Reef \ˌkal-və-'dōs\ *or French* **Ro·chers du Calvados** \rō-ˌshä-dē-\ long reef of rocks NW France in English Channel at mouth of the Orne

Cal·va·ry \'kal-v(ə-)rē\ *or Hebrew* **Gol·go·tha** \'gäl-gə-thə, gäl-'gä-thə\ place outside ancient Jerusalem where Jesus was crucified

Cal·y·don \'ka-lə-ˌdän, -dᵊn\ ancient city *central* Greece in S Aetolia near Gulf of Patras — **Cal·y·do·ni·an** \ˌka-lə-'dō-nyən, -nē-ən\ *adjective*

Cam \'kam\ river 40 *mi* (64 *km*) E *central* England in Cambridgeshire flowing into the Ouse

Ca·ma·güey \ˌkä-mä-'gwā\ city E *central* Cuba *pop* 283,008

Ca·margue \kä-'märg\ *or* **La Camargue** \ˌlä-\ marshy island S France in delta of the Rhône

Cam·a·ril·lo \ˌka-mə-'rē-(ˌ)ō\ city SW Calif. W of Los Angeles *pop* 52,303

Cambay — see KHAMBHAT

Cambay, Gulf of — see KHAMBHAT (GULF OF)

Cam·ber·well \'kam-bər-ˌwel, -wəl\ **1** city SE Australia in S Victoria E of Melbourne *pop* 83,799 **2** former metropolitan borough S London, England, now part of Southwark

Cam·bo·dia \kam-'bō-dē-ə\ *or* **Kam·pu·chea** \ˌkam-pù-'chē-ə\ *or 1970–75* **Khmer Republic** \kə-'mer\ country SE Asia bordering on Gulf of Thailand ✳ Phnom Penh *area about* 70,000 *sq mi* (181,300 *sq km*), *pop* 9,287,000

Cam·brai *or formerly* **Cam·bray** \käm-'brā, kän-'bre\ city N France on the Schelde *pop* 34,210

Cam·bria \'kam-brē-ə\ — see WALES

Cam·bri·an \'kam-brē-ən\ mountains *central* Wales

Cam·bridge \'kām-brij\ **1** city E Mass. W of Boston *pop* 95,802 **2** city Canada in SE Ontario *pop* 92,772; includes former cities of Galt & Preston **3** *or Medieval Latin* **Can·ta·brig·ia** \ˌkan-tə-'bri-j(ē-)ə\ city & borough E England ✳ of Cambridgeshire *pop* 92,772

Cam·bridge·shire \'kām-brij-ˌshir, -shər\ *or* **Cambridge** *or formerly* **Cambridgeshire and Isle of Ely** \'ē-lē\ county E England ✳ Cambridge *area* 1364 *sq mi* (3533 *sq km*), *pop* 640,700

Cam·den \'kam-dən\ **1** city & port SW N.J. on Delaware River opposite Philadelphia, Pa. *pop* 87,492 **2** borough of N Greater London, England *pop* 170,500

Cam·er·oon \ˌka-mə-'rün\ **1** massif *about* 13,350 *ft* (4069 *m*) Cameroon (republic) NW of Buea **2** *or* **Cam·er·oun** \-'rün\ country W equatorial Africa in Cameroons region; a republic, formerly a trust territory under France ✳ Yaoundé *area about* 183,590 *sq mi* (475,500 *sq km*), *pop* 13,103,000 — **Cam·er·oo·nian** \-'rü-nē-ən, -nyən\ *adjective or noun*

Cam·er·oons \ˌka-mə-'rünz\ region W Africa bordering on NE Gulf of Guinea formerly comprising Brit. & French Cameroons but now divided between Nigeria & Cameroon — **Cam·er·oo·nian** \-'rü-nē-ən, -nyən\ *adjective or noun*

Ca·mi·guin \ˌkä-mē-'gēn\ **1** island N Philippines N of Luzon; site of Camiguin Volcano 2602 *ft* (793 *m*) **2** island S Philippines off N coast of Mindanao — see HIBOKHIBOK

Ca·mo·tes Sea \kä-'mō-ˌtās\ sea S *central* Philippines W of Leyte

Cam·pa·gna di Ro·ma \käm-ˌpä-nyä-dē-'rō-mä, -'pa-\ *or* **Roman Campagna** region *central* Italy around Rome

Cam·pa·nia \käm-'pä-nyä, käm-'pā-nyə\ region S Italy bordering on Tyrrhenian Sea ✳ Naples *area* 5250 *sq mi* (13,598 *sq km*), *pop* 5,808,705 — **Cam·pa·nian** \-nyən, -nē-ən\ *adjective or noun*

Camp·bell \'kam-bel, 'ka-məl\ city W Calif. SW of San José *pop* 36,048

Cam·pe·che \käm-'pe-chē, käm-'pā-chä\ **1** state SE Mexico in W Yucatán Peninsula *area* 21,666 *sq mi* (56,115 *sq km*), *pop* 535,185 **2** city & port, its ✳, on Bay of Campeche *pop* 172,208

Campeche, Bay of the SW section of Gulf of Mexico

Cam·pi·na Gran·de \ˌkàm-ˌpē-nə-'grán-dē\ city E Brazil in Paraíba *pop* 326,153

Cam·pi·nas \käm-'pē-nəs\ city SE Brazil in E São Paulo state *pop* 846,084

Cam·po·bel·lo \ˌkam-pə-'be-(ˌ)lō\ island Canada in SW New Brunswick

Cam·po·for·mi·do \ˌkam-(ˌ)pō-'fór-mə-ˌdō\ *or formerly* **Cam·po For·mio** \-mē-ˌō\ village NE Italy SW of Udine

Cam·po Gran·de \ˌkàm-(ˌ)pü-'grän-dē\ city SW Brazil ✳ of Mato Grosso do Sul *pop* 525,612

Cam·pos \'käm-pəs\ city SE Brazil in Rio de Janeiro state on the Paraíba *pop* 349,036

Cam Ranh Bay \'käm-'rän\ inlet of S. China Sea SE Vietnam *about* 180 *mi* (290 *km*) NE of Ho Chi Minh City

Ca·na \'kā-nə\ village in Galilee NE of Nazareth; now in Israel

Ca·naan \'kā-nən\ ancient region corresponding vaguely to later Palestine

Can·a·da \'ka-nə-də\ country N N. America including Newfoundland & Arctic islands N of mainland; a dominion of the Commonwealth of Nations ✳ Ottawa *area* 3,851,809 *sq mi* (10,014,703 *sq km*), *pop* 27,296,859

Ca·na·di·an \kə-'nā-dē-ən\ *or, above its junction with the N. Canadian,* **South Canadian** river 906 *mi* (1458 *km*) S *central* U.S. flowing E from NE N. Mex. to Arkansas River in E Okla.

Canadian Shield *or* **Lau·ren·tian Plateau** \lò-'ren(t)-shən\ plateau region E Canada & NE U.S. extending from Mackenzie River basin E to Davis Strait & S to S Quebec, NE Minn., N Wis., NW Mich., & NE N.Y. including the Adirondacks

Canal Zone *or* **Panama Canal Zone** strip of territory Panama; ceased to exist as a formal political entity Oct. 1, 1979, but remains under U.S. control through 1999 for administration of the Panama Canal

Can·an·dai·gua \ˌka-nən-'dā-gwə\ lake 15 *mi* (24 *km*) long W *central* N.Y.; one of the Finger Lakes

Ca·nary Islands \kə-'ner-ē\ islands in the Atlantic off NW Africa belonging to Spain *area* 2796 *sq mi* (7242 *sq km*), *pop* 1,493,784 — see LAS PALMAS, SANTA CRUZ DE TENERIFE — **Ca·nar·i·an** \kə-'ner-ē-ən\ *adjective or noun*

Ca·nav·er·al, Cape \kə-'nav-rəl, -'na-və-\ *or 1963–1973 officially* **Cape Ken·ne·dy** \'ke-nə-dē\ cape on E shore of Canaveral Peninsula; site of Air Force Missile Test Center & John F. Kennedy Space Center

Canaveral Peninsula peninsula E Fla. enclosing Indian River (lagoon)

Can·ber·ra \'kan-b(ə-)rə, -ˌber-ə\ city ✳ of Australia in Australian Capital Territory SW of Sydney

Can·cún \ˌkan-'kün, kän-\ resort SE Mexico on island off NE coast of Yucatán Peninsula

Can·dia \'kan-dē-ə, kän-\ **1** CRETE **2** — see IRAKLION

Candia, Sea of — see CRETE (Sea of)

Ca·nea \kə-'nē-ə\ *or ancient* **Cy·do·nia** \sī-'dō-nē-ə, -nyə\ city & port Greece ✳ of Crete *pop* 50,077

Can·i·a·pis·kau \ˌka-nē-ə-'pis-(ˌ)kō\ river 575 *mi* (925 *km*) Canada in N Quebec flowing N to unite with the Larch forming the Koksoak

Can·nae \'ka-(ˌ)nē\ ancient town SE Italy in Puglia WSW of modern Barletta

Can·na·nore \'ka-nə-ˌnōr, -ˌnòr\ **1** *or* **Ka·na·nur** \ˌkä-nə-'nùr\ city SW India in Kerala NNW of Calicut *pop* 65,233 **2** — see LACCADIVE ISLANDS

Cannes \'kan, 'kàn\ commune & port SE France SW of Nice *pop* 69,363

Ca·no·pus \kə-'nō-pəs\ ancient city N Egypt E of Alexandria at modern Abu Qir — **Ca·no·pic** \kə-'nō-pik, -'nä-\ *adjective*

Can·so, Cape \'kan(t)-(ˌ)sō\ cape Canada on NE Nova Scotia mainland

Canso, Strait of narrow channel Canada separating Cape Breton Is. from Nova Scotia mainland

Can·ta·bria \kän-'tä-brē-ä\ *or formerly* **San·tan·der** \ˌsän-'tän-der\ province N Spain in N Old Castile bordering on Bay of Biscay ✳ Santander *area* 2042 *sq mi* (5289 *sq km*), *pop* 527,326

Can·ta·bri·an Mountains \kan-'tä-brē-ən\ mountains N & NW Spain running E–W near coast of Bay of Biscay — see CERREDO

Cantabrigia — see CAMBRIDGE

Can·ter·bury \'kan-tə(r)-ˌber-ē, -b(ə-)rē\ **1** city SE Australia in E New South Wales, SW suburb of Sydney *pop* 129,232 **2** city & county borough SE England in Kent *pop* 34,404 — **Can·ter·bu·ri·an** \ˌkan-tə(r)-'byùr-ē-ən\ *adjective*

Can·ti·gny \ˌkäⁿˌtē-ˈnyē\ village N France S of Amiens

Can·ton \ˈkan-tᵊn\ **1** city NE Ohio SSE of Akron *pop* 84,161 **2** — see GUANGZHOU

Canyon de Chelly National Monument \də-ˈshä\ reservation NE Ariz. containing cliff-dweller ruins

Can·yon·lands National Park \ˈkan-yən-ˌlan(d)z\ reservation SE Utah surrounding junction of Colorado & Green rivers

Cap d'An·tibes \ˌkàp-däⁿ-ˈtēb\ cape SE France SW of Antibes

Cap de la Hague \ˌkàp-də-là-ˈàg\ cape NW France at tip of Cotentin Peninsula

Cap-de-la-Ma·de·leine \ˌkàp-də-là-ˌmàd-ˈlen\ city Canada in S Quebec on St. Lawrence River ENE of Trois-Rivières *pop* 33,716

Cape Breton — see BRETON (Cape)

Cape Bret·on Highlands National Park \ˈkàp-ˈbret-ᵊn, -ˈbre-, -ˈbri-\ reservation Canada in NE Nova Scotia near N end of Cape Breton Is.

Cape Breton Island island Canada in NE Nova Scotia *area* 3970 *sq mi* (10,322 *sq km*)

Cape Cod — see COD (Cape)

Cape Cod Bay the S end of Massachusetts Bay W of Cape Cod

Cape Cor·al \ˈkȯr-əl, ˈkär-\ city SW Fla. *pop* 74,991

Cape Fear \ˈfir\ **1** river 202 *mi* (325 *km*) central & SE N.C. flowing SE into the Atlantic **2** — see FEAR (Cape)

Cape Gi·rar·deau \jə-ˈrär-ˌdō, jə-ˈrä-də\ city SE Mo. on Mississippi River *pop* 34,438

Cape Kru·sen·stern National Monument \ˈkrü-zən-ˌstərn\ reservation NW Alaska on Chukchi Sea

Cape of Good Hope 1 — see GOOD HOPE (Cape of) **2** or **Cape Province** or **Kaapland** \ˈkäp-ˌlänt\ or earlier **Cape Colony** former province S Republic of South Africa ✳ Cape Town *area* 278,465 *sq mi* (724,009 *sq km*)

Ca·per·na·um \kə-ˈpər-nā-əm, -nē-\ city of ancient Palestine on NW shore of Sea of Galilee

Cape Sable — see SABLE (Cape)

Cape Sa·ble Island \ˈsā-bəl\ island 7 *mi* (11 *km*) long Canada off S coast of Nova Scotia

Cape Town \ˈkàp-ˌtaun\ city & port, legislative ✳ of Republic of South Africa & formerly ✳ of Cape of Good Hope, on Table Bay *pop* 776,617 — **Cape·to·ni·an** \ˈkàp-ˈtō-nē-ən\ *noun*

Cape Verde — see VERDE (Cape)

Cape Verde \ˈvərd\ country E Atlantic comprising the Cape Verde Islands; until 1975 belonged to Portugal ✳ Praia *area* 1557 *sq mi* (4048 *sq km*), *pop* 350,000 — **Cape Verd·ean** \ˈvər-dē-ən\ *adjective or noun*

Cape Verde Islands islands in the Atlantic off W Africa

Cape York Peninsula \ˈyȯrk\ peninsula NE Australia in N Queensland having at its N tip **Cape York** (on Torres Strait)

Cap Hai·tien \ˌkàp-ˈhā-shən\ or French **Cap-Ha·ï·tien** \ˌkà-pà-ē-ˈsyaⁿ, -ē-tyaⁿ\ city & port N Haiti *pop* 92,122

Cap·i·to·line \ˈka-pə-tᵊl-ˌīn, British often kə-ˈpi-tᵊl-\ hill in Rome, Italy, one of seven on which the ancient city was built — see AVENTINE

Capitol Reef National Park reservation S central Utah containing archaeological remains, petrified forests, & unusual erosion forms

Capodistria — see KOPER

Caporetto — see KOBARID

Cap·pa·do·cia \ˌka-pə-ˈdō-sh(ē-)ə\ ancient district E Asia Minor chiefly in valley of the upper Kizil Irmak in modern Turkey ✳ Caesarea Mazaca — **Cap·pa·do·cian** \-sh(ē-)ən\ *adjective or noun*

Ca·pri \kä-ˈprē, kə-; kä-ˌprē, ˈka-\ or ancient **Cap·re·ae** \ˈka-prē-ˌē\ island Italy S Bay of Naples *area* 4 *sq mi* (10 *sq km*) — **Ca·pri·ote** \ˈka-prē-ˌōt, ˈkä-, -prē-ət\ *noun*

Capsa — see GAFSA

Cap·ua \ˈka-pyü-wə, ˈkä-pü-ä\ commune S Italy on the Volturno N of Naples NW of site of ancient city of Capua *pop* 17,967

Cap·u·lin, Mount \ˈka-pyü-lən, -pü-\ cinder cone 8368 *ft* (2550 *m*) NE N. Mex.; main feature of **Capulin Volcano National Monument**

Cap Vert — see VERT (Cape)

Ca·ra·cas \kä-ˈrä-käs, -ˈra-\ city ✳ of Venezuela near Caribbean coast *metropolitan area pop* 1,824,892

Car·bon·dale \ˈkär-bən-ˌdāl\ city SW Ill. *pop* 27,033

Car·cas·sonne \ˌkär-kà-ˈsȯn, -ˈsōn\ city S France *pop* 44,991

Car·che·mish \ˈkär-kə-ˌmish, kär-ˈkē-mish\ ruined city S Turkey on the Euphrates at Syrian border N of modern Jarabulus, Syria

Cár·de·nas \ˈkär-thā-ˌnäs\ city & port N Cuba E of Matanzas *pop* 75,651

Car·diff \ˈkär-dif\ or Welsh **Caer-dydd** \kīr-ˈdēth\ borough & port ✳ of Wales & of S. Glamorgan *pop* 272,600

Car·di·gan \ˈkär-di-gən\ or **Car·di·gan·shire** \-ˌshir, -shər\ former county W Wales ✳ Aberystwyth

Cardigan Bay inlet of St. George's Channel on W coast of Wales

Ca·ren·tan \ˌkà-räⁿ-ˈtäⁿ\ town NW France at base of Cotentin Peninsula

Car·ia \ˈkar-ē-ə, ˈker-\ ancient region SW Asia Minor bordering on Aegean Sea ✳ Halicarnassus — **Car·i·an** \-ē-ən\ *adjective or noun*

Ca·rib·be·an Sea \ˌkar-ə-ˈbē-ən, kə-ˈri-bē-\ arm of the Atlantic bounded on N & E by West Indies, on S by S. America, & on W by Central America

Car·ib·bees \ˈkar-ə-ˌbēz\ LESSER ANTILLES

Car·i·boo \ˈkar-ə-ˌbü\ mountains W Canada in E central British Columbia W of the Rocky Mountains; highest point *about* 11,750 *ft* (3581 *m*)

Ca·rin·thia \kə-ˈrin(t)-thē-ə\ region central Europe in E Alps; once a duchy, Austrian crown land 1849–1918, divided between Austria & Yugoslavia 1918 — **Ca·rin·thi·an** \-thē-ən\ *adjective or noun*

Car·lisle \kär-ˈlīl, kər-, ˈkär-\ city & borough NW England ✳ of Cumbria *pop* 99,800

Car·low \ˈkär-ˌlō\ **1** county SE Ireland in Leinster *area* 346 *sq mi* (900 *sq km*), *pop* 40,942 **2** town, its ✳ *pop* 11,275

Carls·bad \ˈkär(-ə)lz-ˌbad\ **1** caverns SE N. Mex. in **Carlsbad Caverns National Park 2** city SW Calif. NNW of San Diego *pop* 63,126 **3** city SE N. Mex. on the Pecos *pop* 24,952

Carmana, Carmania — see KERMAN

Car·mar·then \kär-ˈmär-thən, kə(r)-\ **1** or **Car·mar·then·shire** \-ˌshir, -shər\ former county S Wales ✳ Carmarthen **2** borough & port S Wales ✳ of Dyfed *pop* 54,800

Car·mel \ˈkär-məl\ city W Calif. S of Monterey Bay *pop* 4239 **2** \ˈkär-məl\ city central Ind. N of Indianapolis *pop* 25,380

Car·mel, Mount \ˈkär-məl\ mountain ridge NW Israel; highest point 1791 *ft* (546 *m*)

Car·men de Pat·a·go·nes \ˈkär-men-thä-ˌpä-tä-ˈgō-näs\ town Argentina on the Negro River opposite Viedma *pop* 13,981

Car·nat·ic \kär-ˈna-tik\ region SE India between Eastern Ghats & Coromandel coast now in Andhra Pradesh & Karnataka

Car·nic Alps \ˈkär-nik\ mountain range E Alps between Austria & Italy

Car·nio·la \kär-nē-ˈō-lə, kär-ˈnyō-\ region S & W Slovenia NE of Istrian Peninsula — **Car·nio·lan** \-lən\ *adjective*

Car·o·li·na \ˌkar-ə-ˈlī-nə\ English colony 1663–1729 on E coast of N. America divided 1729 into N.C. & S.C. (the **Car·o·li·nas** \-nəz\) — **Car·o·lin·i·an** \ˌkar-ə-ˈli-nē-ən, -nyən\ *noun*

Ca·ro·li·na \ˌkä-rō-ˈlē-nä\ city NE central Puerto Rico *pop* 177,806

Car·o·line Islands \ˈkar-ə-ˌlīn, -lən\ islands W Pacific Ocean comprising Palau & the Federated States of Micronesia; formerly part of Trust Territory of the Pacific Islands

Car·ol Stream \ˈkar-əl\ village NE Ill. W of Chicago *pop* 31,716

Ca·ro·ní \ˌkä-rō-ˈnē\ river E Venezuela flowing N into the Orinoco

Car·pa·thi·an Mountains \kär-ˈpā-thē-ən\ mountain system E central Europe along boundary between Slovakia & Poland & extending through Ukraine & E Romania — see GERLACHOVKA, TATRY, TRANSYLVANIAN ALPS

Carpathian Ruthenia, Carpatho–Ukraine — see ZAKARPATS'KA

Car·pen·tar·ia, Gulf of \ˌkär-pən-ˈter-ē-ə, -ˈtar-\ inlet of Arafura Sea on N coast of Australia

Car·pen·ters·ville \ˈkär-pən-tərz-ˌvil\ village NE Ill. NW of Chicago *pop* 23,049

Car·qui·nez Strait \kär-ˈkē-nəs\ strait 8 *mi* (13 *km*) long Calif. joining San Pablo & Suisun bays

Car·ran·tuo·hill \ˌkar-ən-ˈtü-əl\ mountain 3414 *ft* (1041 *m*) SW Ireland in County Kerry; highest in Macgillicuddy's Reeks & in Ireland

Car·ra·ra \kä-ˈrär-ä\ commune N Italy ESE of La Spezia *pop* 68,528

Car·rhae \ˈkar-(ˌ)ē\ ancient city N Mesopotamia SSE of modern Urfa

Car·rick·fer·gus \ˌkar-ik-ˈfər-gəs\ district E Northern Ireland, established 1974 *area* 34 *sq mi* (88 *sq km*), *pop* 32,439

Car·rick on Shan·non \ˈkar-ik-ȯn-ˈsha-nən, -än-\ town N central Ireland ✳ of County Leitrim *pop* 1621

Car·roll·ton \ˈkar-əl-tən\ city N Tex. *pop* 82,169

Car·shal·ton \kär-ˈshȯl-tᵊn, kər-\ former urban district S England in Surrey, now part of Sutton

Carso — see KARST

Car·son \ˈkär-sᵊn\ **1** river W Nev. flowing NE into **Carson Lake 2** city SW Calif. SE of Los Angeles *pop* 83,995

Carson City city ✳ of Nev. E of Lake Tahoe *pop* 40,443

Carson Sink intermittent lake W Nev. S of Humboldt Lake

Carstensz, Mount — see PUNCAK JAYA

Car·ta·ge·na \ˌkär-tä-ˈgā-nä, -ˈhā-, -ˈjē-\ **1** city & port NW Colombia *pop* 688,300 **2** city & port SE Spain on the Mediterranean *pop* 166,736

Car·ta·go \kär-ˈtä-(ˌ)gō\ city central Costa Rica *pop* 21,753

Car·ter·et \ˌkär-tə-ˈret\ borough NE N.J. S of Elizabeth *pop* 19,025

Car·thage \ˈkär-thij\ or ancient **Car·tha·go** \kär-ˈtä-(ˌ)gō, -ˈthä-\ ancient city & state N Africa on coast NE of modern Tunis — **Car·tha·gin·ian** \ˌkär-thə-ˈji-nyən, -nē-ən\ *adjective or noun*

Cary \ˈkar-ē, ˈker-ē\ city E central N.C. *pop* 43,858

Ca·sa·blan·ca \ˌka-sə-ˈblaŋ-kə, ˌkä-sə-ˈbläŋ-, -zə-\ or Arabic **Dar el Bei·da** \ˌdär-ˌel-bā-ˈdä\ city & port W Morocco on the Atlantic *pop* 3,102,000

Casa Gran·de Ruins National Monument \ˌka-sə-ˈgran-dē\ reservation S Ariz. SE of Phoenix; prehistoric ruins

Cas·cade Range \(ˌ)kas-ˈkād\ mountain range W U.S., N continuation of the Sierra Nevada extending N from Lassen Peak across Oreg. & Wash. — see COAST MOUNTAINS, COAST RANGES, RAINIER (Mount)

Cas·co Bay \ˈkas-(ˌ)kō\ inlet of the Atlantic S Maine

Ca·ser·ta \kä-ˈzer-tä, -ˈzər-\ commune S Italy *pop* 68,811

Cash·el \ˈka-shəl\ town S Ireland in central Tipperary at base of **Rock of Cashel** (hill with ruins of cathedral & castle) *pop* 2473

Cashmere — see KASHMIR

Ca·si·quia·re or **Cas·si·quia·re** \ˌkä-sē-ˈkyä-rä\ river S Venezuela connecting the upper course of Negro River with Orinoco River

Cas·per \ˈkas-pər\ city central Wyo. on N. Platte River *pop* 46,742

Cas·pi·an Gates \ˈkas-pē-ən\ pass on W shore of Caspian Sea near Derbent

Caspian Sea sea (salt lake) between Europe & Asia; about 90 *ft* (27 *m*) below sea level *area* 143,550 *sq mi* (371,795 *sq km*)

Cas·si·no \kä-ˈsē-(ˌ)nō\ commune central Italy ESE of Frosinone; site of Monte Cassino monastery *pop* 32,803

Cas·tel Gan·dol·fo \(ˌ)kä-ˌstel-gän-ˈdȯl-(ˌ)fō\ commune central Italy on Lake Albano SE of Rome *pop* 6784

Cas·tel·lón \ˌkä-stēl-ˈyōn\ province E Spain *area* 2579 *sq mi* (6680 *sq km*), *pop* 446,744

Cas·tel·lón de la Pla·na \ˌkäs-tel-ˈyōn-thä-lä-ˈplä-nä\ city & port, ✳ of Castellón province, Spain, on the Mediterranean NE of Valencia *pop* 133,180

Castellorizo or **Castelrosso** — see KASTELLORIZON

Cas·tile \ka-ˈstēl\ or Spanish **Cas·til·la** \kä-ˈstēl-yä, -ˈstē-yä\ region & ancient kingdom central & N Spain divided by the Sierra de Guadarrama into regions & old provinces of **Old Castile** or Spanish **Castilla la Vie·ja** \lä-ˈvyä-hä\ (to the N,

✳ Burgos) & **New Castile** or Spanish **Castilla la Nue·va** \lä-'nwä-vä\ (to the S, ✳ Toledo)

Cas·til·lo de San Mar·cos National Monument \ka-'stē-yō-də-san-'mär-(,)kōs\ historic site NE Fla.; contains a Spanish fort

Cas·tle·bar \,ka-səl-'bär\ town NW Ireland ✳ of Mayo pop 6071

Castle Clin·ton National Monument \'klin-tⁿn\ historic site Manhattan Is. SE N.Y.; contains a fort

Cast·le·reagh \'ka-səl-(,)rā\ district E Northern Ireland, established 1974 area 33 sq mi (85 sq km), pop 60,649

Castres \'kästr\ city S France E of Toulouse pop 46,292

Cas·tries \'kas-,trēz, -,trēs\ city & port ✳ of St. Lucia pop 11,147

Ca·strop–Raux·el \käs-,tróp-'raùk-səl\ city W Germany SSW of Münster pop 79,065

Ça·tal·ca \chä-t³l-'jä\ city Turkey in Europe W of Istanbul

Cat·a·li·na \,ka-t³l-'ē-nə\ or **San·ta Catalina** \'san-tə\ island SW Calif. in Channel Islands area 70 sq mi (182 sq km)

Cat·a·lo·nia \,ka-t³l-'ō-nyə, -nē-ə\ or Spanish **Ca·ta·lu·ña** \,kä-tä-'lü-nyä\ autonomous region NE Spain bordering on France & the Mediterranean; chief city Barcelona area 12,328 sq mi (31,930 sq km), pop 6,059,494 — **Cat·a·lo·nian** \-'ō-nyən, -nē-ən\ adjective or noun

Ca·ta·mar·ca \,kä-tä-'mär-kä\ city NW Argentina pop 110,489

Ca·ta·nia \kə-'tä-nyə, -tä-\ or ancient **Cat·a·na** \'ka-tə-nə\ commune Italy in E Sicily on E coast on Gulf of Catania pop 330,037

Ca·tan·za·ro \,kä-,tänd-'zär-(,)ō, -,tänt-'sär-\ city S Italy ✳ of Calabria pop 93,464

Ca·taw·ba \kə-'tó-bə\ river 250 mi (402 km) flowing S from W N.C. into S.C. — see WATEREE

Ca·thay \ka-'thā\ CHINA — an old name

Cathedral City city SW Calif. pop 30,085

Catherine, Mount — see KATHERINA (Gebel)

Ca·toc·tin Mountain \kə-'täk-tən\ mountain ridge NW Md. & N Va. in Blue Ridge Mountains

Cats·kill Mountains \'kat-,skil\ mountains SE N.Y. in the Appalachian system W of Hudson River — see SLIDE MOUNTAIN

Cattaro — see KOTOR

Cau·ca \'kaù-kä\ river 838 mi (1348 km) W Colombia flowing N into the Magdalena

Cau·ca·sia \kó-'kä-zhə, -shə\ or **Cau·ca·sus** \'kó-kə-səs\ region SE Europe between the Black & Caspian seas; divided by Caucasus Mountains into **Cis·cau·ca·sia** \,sis-\ (to the N) & **Trans·cau·ca·sia** \,tran(t)s-\ (to the S)

Caucasus Indicus — see HINDU KUSH

Caucasus Mountains mountain system SE Europe in Russia, Georgia, Azerbaijan, and Armenia

Cau·dine Forks \'kó-,dīn, -,dēn\ two mountain passes S Italy in the Apennines between Benevento & Capua

Caul·field \'kól-,fēld\ city SE Australia in S Victoria SE of Melbourne; part of Greater Melbourne pop 67,776

Causses \'kōs\ limestone region S central France on S border of Massif Central

Cau·ve·ry \'kò-və-rē\ or **Kā·ve·ri** \'kä-və-rē\ river 475 mi (764 km) S India flowing E & entering Bay of Bengal in a wide delta

Cauvery Falls or **Kā·ve·ri Falls** \'kä-və-rē\ waterfall India in the Cauvery on Karnataka-Tamil Nadu boundary

Cav·an \'ka-vən\ **1** county NE Ireland (republic) in Ulster area 730 sq mi (1898 sq km), pop 52,756 **2** town, its ✳ pop 3332

Ca·vi·te \kä-'vē-tē\ city Philippines in Luzon on **Cavite Peninsula** in Manila Bay SW of Manila pop 92,000

Ca·xi·as \kä-'shē-əs\ **1** town NE Brazil in Maranhão WNW of Teresina pop 145,709 **2** — see DUQUE DE CAXIAS **3** or **Caxias do Sul** \də-'sül\ city S Brazil in Rio Grande do Sul pop 290,968

Cay·enne \kī-'en, kä-\ city & port ✳ of French Guiana on island in Cayenne River near the coast pop 37,097

Cayes \'kī\ or **Aux Cayes** \ō-'kī\ city & port SW Haiti pop 105,383

Ca·yey \kä-'yā\ city SE central Puerto Rico pop 46,553

Cay·man Islands \(,)kā-'man, attributively 'kā-mən\ islands W. Indies NW of Jamaica; a Brit. colony ✳ George Town (on **Grand Cayman**, chief island) area 100 sq mi (259 sq km), pop 23,881 — **Cay·man·i·an** \kā-'ma-nē-ən\ adjective or noun

Ca·yu·ga \kā-'yü-gə, kī-, kē-, kə-\ lake 40 mi (64 km) long W central N.Y.; one of the Finger Lakes

Ce·a·rá \,sā-ə-'rä\ state NE Brazil bordering on the Atlantic ✳ Fortaleza area 57,147 sq mi (148,011 sq km), pop 6,353,346

Ce·bu \sā-'bü\ **1** island E central Philippines, one of the Visayans area 1707 sq mi (4438 sq km) **2** city on E Cebu Is. pop 610,000

Čechy — see BOHEMIA

Ce·dar \'sē-dər\ river 329 mi (529 km) SE Minn. & E Iowa flowing SE into the Iowa

Cedar Breaks National Monument reservation SW Utah NE of Zion National Park containing unusual erosion forms

Cedar Falls city NE Iowa NW of Waterloo pop 34,298

Cedar Hill town NE Tex. SW of Dallas pop 19,976

Cedar Rapids city E Iowa on the Cedar pop 108,751

Ce·le·bes \'se-lə-,bēz, sə-'lē-bēz\ — see SULAWESI

Celebes Sea arm of W Pacific enclosed on N by Mindanao & the Sulu Archipelago, on S by Sulawesi, & on W by Borneo — **Cel·e·be·sian** \,se-lə-'bē-zhən\ adjective

Celestial Empire the former Chinese Empire

Cel·le \'(t)se-lə\ city N central Germany NE of Hannover pop 72,609

Celt·ic Sea \'kel-tik, 'sel-\ inlet of the Atlantic in British Isles SE of Ireland, SW of Wales, & W of Cornwall

Ce·nis, Mont \,mōⁿ-sə-'nē\ **1** mountain pass 6831 ft (2082 m) between France & Italy over Mont Cenis massif in Graian Alps **2** or **Fré·jus** \frā-'zhüs, -'zhēs\ railroad tunnel 8.5 mi (13.6 km) long piercing the Fréjus massif SW of Mont Cenis

Cen·ter·ville \'sen-tər-,vil, -vəl\ city SW Ohio pop 21,082

Central region central Scotland, established 1975 ✳ Stirling area 1017 sq mi (2635 sq km), pop 272,900

Central African Republic or 1976–79 **Central African Empire** or earlier **Ubangi–Shari** republic N central Africa ✳ Bangui area 240,376 sq mi (624,978 sq km), pop 2,998,000

Central America **1** the narrow S portion of N. America connecting with S. America & extending from the Isthmus of Tehuantepec to the Isthmus of Panama **2** the republics of Guatemala, El Salvador, Honduras, Nicaragua, & Costa Rica & often also Panama & Belize

Central Europe the countries of central Europe — usually considered as including the countries extending from Baltic Sea on the N to Alps on the S and from Russia, Lithuania, Belarus, & Ukraine on the E to North Sea & France on the W

Central India former group of 89 Indian states N central India ✳ Indore; area now chiefly in W & N Madhya Pradesh

Central Karroo — see KARROO

Central Provinces and Be·rar \bā-'rär, bə-\ former province of India reorganized 1950 & renamed Madhya Pradesh

Central Valley valley central Calif. comprising the valleys of the Sacramento & San Joaquin rivers

Ceos — see KEA

Ceph·a·lo·nia \,se-fə-'lō-nyə, -nē-ə\ or New Greek **Ke·fal·li·nía** \,ke-fä-lä-'nē-ä\ island W Greece in the Ionians area 288 sq mi (746 sq km)

Ce·ram or **Se·ram** \'sā-,räm\ island E Indonesia in central Moluccas area 6621 sq mi (17,215 sq km), pop 96,797

Ce·res \'sir-(,)ēz\ city central Calif. SE of Modesto pop 26,314

Cernauti — see CHERNIVTSI

Cer·re·do \se-'rā-(,)thó\ or **Tor·re de Cerredo** \'tòr-ā-thā-\ mountain 8787 ft (2678 m) N Spain SW of Santander; highest in the Cantabrians

Cer·ri·tos \sə-'rē-təs\ city SW Calif. NE of Long Beach pop 53,240

Cerro Bolívar — see BOLÍVAR (Cerro)

Cer·ro de Pas·co \'ser-ō-thā-'päs-(,)kō\ **1** mountain 15,100 ft (4602 m) central Peru NE of Lima **2** city near the mountain pop 170,500

Cerro de Pun·ta \thā-'pün-tä\ mountain about 4390 ft (1338 m), central Puerto Rico in Cordillera Central; highest on the island

Cerro Gor·do \'gòr-(,)dō\ mountain pass E Mexico between Veracruz & Jalapa

Cervin, Mont — see MATTERHORN

Ce·se·na \chā-'zā-nä\ or ancient **Cae·se·na** \sə-'zē-nə\ commune N Italy in Emilia-Romagna SE of Forlì pop 89,606

Ces·ke Bu·de·jo·vi·ce \'ches-ke-'bú-de-,yò-vět-se\ or German **Bud·weis** \'bút-,vīs\ city Czech Republic in S Bohemia pop 97,283

Ce·ti·nje \'(t)se-tē-,nyä\ town S Yugoslavia SE of Kotor near coast; formerly ✳ of Montenegro pop 20,258

Cette — see SÈTE

Ceu·ta \'thā-ü-,tä, 'syü-tä\ city & port N Morocco opposite Gibraltar; a Spanish presidio pop 73,483

Cé·vennes \sā-'ven\ mountain range S France W of the Rhône at E edge of Massif Central — see MÉZENC

Cey·lon \si-'län, sā-\ **1** or Arabic **Ser·en·dib** \'ser-ən-,dib, -,dip\ or Latin & Greek **Ta·prob·a·ne** \tə-'prä-bə-(,)nē\ island 270 mi (434 km) long & 140 mi (225 km) wide in Indian Ocean off S India **2** — see SRI LANKA — **Cey·lon·ese** \,sā-lə-'nēz, ,sē-, ,se-, -'nēs\ adjective or noun

Chaco — see GRAN CHACO

Chad or French **Tchad** \'chad\ country N central Africa ✳ N'Djamena; a republic; until 1959 a territory of French Equatorial Africa area 495,752 sq mi (1,288,955 sq km), pop 5,200,000 — **Chad·ian** \'cha-dē-ən\ adjective or noun

Chad, Lake shallow lake N central Africa at junction of boundaries of Chad, Niger, & Nigeria

Chae·ro·nea \,ker-ə-'nē-ə, ,kir-\ ancient city E central Greece in W Boeotia SE of Mt. Parnassus

Cha·gos Archipelago \'chä-gəs\ archipelago central Indian Ocean S of Maldives; comprises Brit. Indian Ocean Territory — see DIEGO GARCIA

Cha·gres \'chä-grəs, 'cha-\ river Panama flowing through Gatun Lake to the Caribbean

Cha·gua·ra·mas \,chä-gwä-'rä-mäs\ district NW Trinidad W of Port of Spain on **Chaguaramas Bay** (inlet of Gulf of Paria)

Cha·har \'chä-'här\ former province NE China in E Inner Mongolia ✳ Kalgan

Chalcedon — see KADIKOY

Chal·ci·di·ce \kal-'si-də-(,)sē\ or Greek **Khal·ki·di·kí** \,käl-kē-thē-'kē\ peninsula NE Greece in E Macedonia projecting SE into N Aegean Sea; terminates in three peninsulas: Kassandra (ancient Pallene), Sithonia, & Acte — see ACTE

Chalcis — see KHALKIS — **Chal·cid·i·an** \kal-'si-dē-ən\ adjective or noun

Chal·dea \kal-'dē-ə\ ancient region SW Asia on Euphrates River & Persian Gulf

Cha·leur Bay \shə-'lür, -'lər\ inlet of Gulf of St. Lawrence SE Canada between N New Brunswick & Gaspé Peninsula, Quebec

Cha·lon \shä-'lōⁿ\ or **Chalon–sur–Saône** \-,sür-'sòn\ city E central France N of Mâcon pop 56,259

Châ·lons \shä-'lōⁿ\ or **Châlons–sur–Marne** \-,sür-'märn\ commune NE France on the Marne pop 51,533

Cham·bal \'chəm-bəl\ river 650 mi (1046 km) central India flowing from Vindhya Mountains E into the Yamuna

Cham·bé·ry \,shän-bā-'rē\ city E France E of Lyon pop 55,603

Cham·bord \shän-'bòr\ village N central France NE of Blois pop 214

Cha·mi·zal \,sha-mə-'zäl, ,chä-mi-'säl\ tract of land 437 acres (177 hectares) on N bank of the Rio Grande formerly in El Paso, Tex.; ceded to Mexico 1963 — see CORDOVA ISLAND

Cha·mo·nix \,shä-mō-'nē\ **1** valley SE France NW of Mont Blanc **2** or **Chamonix–Mont–Blanc** \-(,)mōⁿ-'blä\ town SE France in Chamonix valley pop 5907

Cham·pagne \sham-'pān\ region & former province NE France W of Lorraine & N of Burgundy ✳ Troyes

Cham·paign \sham-'pān\ city E central Ill. pop 63,502

Cham·pi·gny–sur–Marne \shäⁿ-(ˌ)pē-'nyē-ˌsür-'märn\ commune N France, SSE suburb of Paris pop 80,189

Cham·plain, Lake \sham-'plān\ lake 125 mi (201 km) long between N.Y. & Vt. extending N into Quebec area 430 sq mi (1114 sq km)

Chan–chiang — see ZHENJIANG

Chan·der·na·gore \ˌchən-dər-nə-'gōr, -'gór\ or **Chan·dan·na·gar** \ˌchən-də-'nə-gər\ or **Chan·dar·na·gar** \-dər-'nə-gər\ or **Chan·der·na·gor** \-nə-'gōr\ city E India in W. Bengal N of Calcutta; before 1950 part of French India pop 421,256

Chan·di·garh \'chən-dē-gər\ city N India N of Delhi; a union territory administered by the national government; ✳ of Punjabi Suba & of Haryana; founded 1953, pop 510,565

Chan·dler \'chan(d)-lər\ city SW central Ariz. pop 90,533

Chan·dra·pur \ˌchən-drə-'pùr\ or formerly **Chan·da** \'chən-də\ town central India in E Maharashtra pop 225,841; ✳ of ancient Gond dynasty

Chang \'chäŋ\ or **Yang·tze** \'yaŋ-'sē, 'yaŋ(k)t-'sē; 'yän-'tsə\ river 3434 mi (5525 km) central China flowing from Kunlun Mountains in SW Qinghai E into E. China Sea

Changan — see XI'AN

Ch'ang–chia–k'ou — see ZHANGJIAKOU

Chang–chou — see ZHANGZHOU

Chang·chun \'chäŋ-'chùn\ city NE China ✳ of Jilin pop 1,679,270

Chang·de or **Ch'ang–te** \'chäŋ-'də\ city SE central China in N Hunan on the Yuan pop 301,276

Chang·sha \'chäŋ-'shä\ city SE central China ✳ of Hunan on the Xiang pop 1,113,212

Chang·zhou or **Ch'ang–chou** \'chäŋ-'jō\ or formerly **Wu·tsin** \'wüd-'zin\ city E China in S Jiangsu pop 531,470

Channel Islands **1** or **Santa Barbara Islands** Calif. in the Pacific off SW coast — see CATALINA, SAN CLEMENTE ISLAND, SANTA CRUZ, SANTA ROSA ISLAND **2** islands in English Channel; a possession of Brit. Crown area 75 sq mi (195 sq km), pop 135,694 — see ALDERNEY, GUERNSEY, JERSEY, SARK

Channel Islands National Park reserve SW Calif. in Channel Islands including areas on Anacapa Islands (E of Santa Cruz Is.) & Santa Barbara Is. (W of Santa Catalina Is.)

Chan·til·ly \ˌshäⁿ-tē-'yē, shan-'ti-lē\ town N France NNE of Paris pop 11,525

Chao·'an \'chaù-'än\ or **Chao·zhou** or **Ch'ao·chou** or **Chao·chow** \'chaù-'jō\ city E China in NE Guangdong on Han River pop 101,000

Chao Phra·ya \chaù-'prī-ə, prä-'yä\ or **Me Nam** \mä-'näm\ river 227 mi (365 km) W central Thailand formed by confluence of Nan & Ping rivers & flowing S into Gulf of Thailand

Cha·pa·la, Lake \chä-'pä-lä\ lake 50 mi (80 km) long W central Mexico in Jalisco & Michoacán SE of Guadalajara

Chapel Hill town N N.C. SW of Durham pop 38,719

Cha·rente \shä-'räⁿt\ river about 225 mi (362 km) W France flowing W into Bay of Biscay

Cha·ri or **Sha·ri** \'shär-ē\ river about 590 mi (949 km) N central Africa in Chad flowing NW into Lake Chad

Char·i·ton \'shar-ə-tⁿn\ river 280 mi (451 km) S Iowa & N Mo. flowing S into the Missouri

Charle·roi \ˌshär-lə-'rói, -lə-ˌwä\ city SW Belgium in Hainaut pop 206,800

Charles \'chär(-ə)lz\ river 47 mi (76 km) Mass. flowing into Boston harbor

Charles, Cape cape E Va. N of entrance to Chesapeake Bay

Charles·bourg \shärl-'bür, 'chär(-ə)lz-ˌbərg\ city Canada in SE Quebec NE of Quebec city pop 70,788

Charles·ton \'chär(-ə)l-stən\ **1** city E central Ill. pop 20,398 **2** city & port SE S.C. pop 80,414 **3** city ✳ W. Va. on the Kanawha pop 57,287 — **Charles·to·nian** \ˌchär(-ə)l-'stō-nē-ən, -nyən\ noun

Charleston Peak mountain 11,919 ft (3633 m) SE Nev. WNW of Las Vegas

Charles·town \'chär(-ə)lz-ˌtaùn\ section of Boston, Mass., on Boston harbor between mouths of Charles & Mystic rivers

Char·lotte \'shär-lət\ city S N.C. near S.C. border pop 395,934

Charlotte Ama·lie \ə-'mäl-yə, 'a-mə-lē\ or formerly **Saint Thomas** city & port ✳ of Virgin Islands of the U.S., on St. Thomas Is. pop 12,331

Charlotte Harbor inlet of Gulf of Mexico SW Fla.

Char·lottes·ville \'shär-ləts-ˌvil, -vəl\ city central Va. pop 40,341

Char·lotte·town \'shär-lət-ˌtaùn\ city & port Canada ✳ of Prince Edward Island on Northumberland Strait pop 15,396

Chartres \'shärt, 'shärtrᵉ\ city N central France SW of Paris pop 41,850

Châ·teau·guay \'sha-tə-ˌgä\ town Canada in S Quebec SW of Montreal pop 39,833

Châ·teau·roux \ˌshä-tō-'rü\ commune central France S of Orléans pop 35,691

Châ·teau–Thier·ry \ˌshä-ˌtō-tye-'rē\ town N France on the Marne SW of Reims pop 15,830

Chat·ham \'cha-təm\ **1** — see SAN CRISTÓBAL **2** city Canada in SE Ontario E of Lake Saint Clair pop 43,557 **3** borough SE England in Kent pop 43,557

Chatham Islands islands S Pacific belonging to New Zealand & comprising two islands (Chatham & Pitt) area 372 sq mi (967 sq km)

Chatham Strait strait SE Alaska between Admiralty Is. & Kuiu Is. on E & Baranof Is. & Chichagof Is. on W

Chat·ta·hoo·chee \ˌcha-tə-'hü-chē\ river 436 mi (702 km) SE U.S. rising in N Ga., flowing SW & S along Ala.-Ga. boundary into Lake Seminole

Chat·ta·noo·ga \ˌcha-tə-'nü-gə, ˌcha-tⁿn-'ü-\ city SE Tenn. on Tennessee River pop 152,466

Chau·tau·qua \shə-'tó-kwə\ lake 18 mi (29 km) long SW N.Y.

Che·bok·sa·ry \ˌche-bäk-'sär-ē\ city Russia in Europe ✳ of Chuvash Republic WNW of Kazan pop 442,000

Che·cheno–In·gush Republic \chə-ˌche-nō-in-'güsh\ former autonomous republic U.S.S.R. on N slopes of Caucasus Mountains; split into republics of Chechnya and Ingushetia within Russia 1992

Chech·nya or **Chech·e·nya** or **Chech·e·nia** \chech-'nyä, chech-nyə\ or **Che·chen Republic** \chi-'chen\ republic SE Russia in Europe on N slopes of Caucasus Mountains

Che·du·ba \chə-'dü-bə\ island W Myanmar area 202 sq mi (523 sq km), pop 2635

Chefoo — see YANTAI

Che·ju \'chä-ˌjü\ or formerly **Quel·part** \'kwel-ˌpärt\ island S. Korea in N E. China Sea area 706 sq mi (1829 sq km)

Chekiang — see ZHEJIANG

Che·lan, Lake \shə-'lan\ lake about 55 mi (88 km) long N central Wash.

Chelms·ford \'chemz-fərd also 'chelmz-\ **1** town NE Mass. S of Lowell pop 32,383 **2** \'chelmz-, 'chemz-\ borough SE England ✳ of Essex pop 150,000

Chel·sea \'chel-sē\ **1** city E Mass. NE of Boston pop 28,710 **2** former metropolitan borough SW London, England, on N bank of Thames River, now part of Kensington and Chelsea

Chel·ten·ham \'chelt-nəm, 'chel-tⁿn-əm, United States also -tⁿn-ˌham\ borough SW central England in Gloucestershire pop 85,900

Che·lya·binsk \chel-'yä-bən(t)sk\ city W Russia in Asia S of Sverdlovsk pop 1,143,000

Che·lyu·skin, Cape \chel-'yü-skən\ headland Russia in Asia on Taymyr Peninsula; northernmost point of Asian mainland, at 77°35′N, 105°E

Chem·nitz \'kem-ˌnits, -nəts\ or 1953–90 **Karl–Marx–Stadt** \(ˌ)kärl-'märk-ˌshtät, -ˌstät\ city E Germany SE of Leipzig pop 287,511

Chemulpo — see INCHON

Che·nab \chə-'näb\ river about 600 mi (965 km) NW India (subcontinent) in Kashmir & the Punjab flowing SW to unite with the Sutlej forming the Panjnad

Chen–chiang — see ZHENJIANG

Cheng–chou — see ZHENGZHOU

Cheng·de or **Ch'eng–te** \'chəŋ-'də\ or **Je·hol** \jə-'hòl, 'rō-'hòl\ city NE China in NE Hebei NE of Beijing pop 246,799

Cheng·du or **Ch'eng–tu** \'chəŋ-'dü\ city SW central China ✳ of Szechwan on Min River pop 1,713,255

Chenstokhov — see CZESTOCHOWA

Cher \'sher\ river 217 mi (349 km), central France flowing into the Loire

Cher·bourg \'sher-ˌbùr(g), sher-'bür\ city & port NW France on Cotentin Peninsula on English Channel pop 28,773

Che·rem·kho·vo \chə-'rem-kə-vō, ˌcher-əm-'kò-və\ city Russia in Asia NW of Irkutsk pop 73,600

Cher·kessk \chir-'kyesk\ city S Russia in Europe in N Caucasus region SE of Stavropol ✳ of Karachay-Cherkessia pop 119,000

Cher·ni·gov \chir-'nē-gəf\ city N Ukraine pop 306,000

Cher·niv·tsi \chir-'nift-sē\ or **Cher·nov·tsy** \chir-'nòft-sē\ or Romanian **Cer·na·u·ti** \ˌcher-nə-'üts, -'üt-sē\ city W Ukraine on the Prut near Romania border pop 259,000

Cher·no·byl \chər-'nō-bəl, (ˌ)cher-\ site N Ukraine of town abandoned after 1986 nuclear accident

Cher·o·kee Outlet \'cher-ə-(ˌ)kē\ strip of land N Okla. along S border of Kans. E of 100°W opened to settlement 1893; 50 mi (80 km) wide, about 220 mi (354 km) long

Cher·so·nese \'kər-sə-ˌnēz, -ˌnēs\ or ancient **Cher·so·ne·sus** \ˌkər-sə-'nē-səs\ any of several peninsulas: as (1) Jutland (the **Cim·bri·an Chersonese** \'sim-brē-ən\ or **Cim·bric Chersonese** \-brik\); (2) the Malay Peninsula (the **Golden Chersonese**); (3) the Crimea (the **Tau·ric Chersonese** \'tòr-ik\); (4) the Gallipoli Peninsula (the **Thra·cian Chersonese** \'thrā-shən\)

Cher·well \'chär-wəl\ river 30 mi (48 km) central England in Northamptonshire & Oxfordshire flowing S into the Thames at Oxford

Ches·a·peake \'che-sə-ˌpēk, 'ches-ˌpēk\ city SE Va. S of Norfolk pop 151,976

Chesapeake Bay inlet of the Atlantic 193 mi (311 km) long in Va. & Md.

Chesh·ire \'che-shər, -ˌshir\ **1** town S Conn. SW of Meriden pop 25,684 **2** or **Ches·ter** \'ches-tər\ county NW England ✳ Chester area 929 sq mi (2406 sq km), pop 937,300

Ches·ter \'ches-tər\ **1** city SE Pa. pop 41,856 **2** city NW England ✳ of Cheshire on Dee River pop 58,436

Ches·ter·field \'ches-tər-ˌfēld\ **1** city E Mo. W of St. Louis pop 37,991 **2** borough N central England in Derbyshire S of Sheffield pop 99,700

Chesterfield Inlet inlet N Canada on NW coast of Hudson Bay

Che·tu·mal \ˌchä-tü-'mäl\ city SE Mexico ✳ of Quintana Roo

Chev·i·ot \'che-vē-ət, 'che-\ peak 2676 ft (816 m) highest in the Cheviot Hills

Cheviot Hills hills extending NE to SW along English-Scottish border

Chey·enne \shī-'an, -'en\ **1** river 527 mi (850 km) S. Dak. flowing NE into Missouri River **2** city ✳ of Wyo. pop 50,008

Chia–i \'jyä-'ē\ city W central Taiwan pop 258,664

Chia–mu–ssu — see JIAMUSI

Chiang Mai \'jyäŋ-'mī\ city NW Thailand on the Ping pop 161,541

Chi·a·pas \chē-'ä-päs\ state SE Mexico bordering on the Pacific ✳ Tuxtla Gutiérrez area 28,528 sq mi (73,888 sq km), pop 3,210,496

Chi·ba \'chē-bä\ city E Japan in Honshu on Tokyo Bay E of Tokyo pop 829,467

Chi·ca·go \shə-'kä-(ˌ)gō, -'kò-, -gə\ **1** river Chicago, Ill., having two branches (N. Branch & S. Branch) & originally flowing E into Lake Michigan but now flowing S through S. Branch & Chicago Sanitary & Ship Canal into Des Plaines River **2** city & port NE Ill. on Lake Michigan pop 2,783,726 — **Chi·ca·go·an** \-'kä-gō-ən, -'kò-\ noun

Chicago Heights city NE Ill. S of Chicago pop 33,072

Chich·a·gof \'chi-chə-ˌgóf, -ˌgäf\ island SE Alaska in Alexander Archipelago N of Baranof Is. area 2100 sq mi (5460 sq km)

Chi·chén It·zá \chē-ˌchen-ēt-ˈsä, -ˈēt-sə\ village SE Mexico in Yucatán ESE of Mérida at site of ruins of important Mayan city

Chich·es·ter \ˈchi-chəs-tər\ city & borough S England ENE of Portsmouth ✳ of W. Sussex *pop* 24,189

Ch'i–ch'i–ha–erh — see QIQIHAR

Chick·a·hom·i·ny \ˌchi-kə-ˈhä-mə-nē\ river 90 *mi* (145 *km*) E Va. flowing SE into James River

Chi·cla·yo \chē-ˈklī-(ˌ)ō\ city NW Peru near coast *pop* 419,600

Chi·co \ˈchē-(ˌ)kō\ city W Calif. N of Sacramento *pop* 40,079

Chic·o·pee \ˈchi-kə-(ˌ)pē\ city SW Mass. *pop* 56,632

Chi·cou·ti·mi \shə-ˈkü-tə-mē\ **1** river 100 *mi* (161 *km*) Canada in S Quebec flowing N into the Saguenay **2** city Canada in S *central* Quebec on the Saguenay *pop* 62,670

Chihli — see HEBEI

Chihli, Gulf of — see BO HAI

Chi·hua·hua \chē-ˈwä-(ˌ)wä, chə-, -wə\ **1** state N Mexico bordering on the U.S. *area* 95,400 *sq mi* (247,086 *sq km*), *pop* 2,441,873 **2** city, its ✳ *metropolitan area pop* 530,487

Chi·le \ˈchi-lē, ˈchē-(ˌ)lā\ country S S. America between the Andes & the Pacific; a republic ✳ Santiago *area* 292,257 *sq mi* (756,946 *sq km*), *pop* 11,275,440 — **Chil·ean** \ˈchi-lē-ən, chə-ˈlā-ən\ *adjective or noun*

Chil·koot \ˈchil-ˌküt\ pass 3502 *ft* (1067 *m*) between SE Alaska & SW Yukon Territory, Canada, in N Coast Mountains

Chil·li·cothe \ˌchi-lə-ˈkä-thē, -ˈkȯ-\ city S Ohio *pop* 21,923

Chil·li·wack \ˈchi-lə-ˌwak\ municipality Canada in S British Columbia *pop* 49,531

Chi·loé \ˌchē-lō-ˈā\ island S *central* Chile *area* 4700 *sq mi* (12,220 *sq km*), *pop* 65,161

Chil·pan·cin·go \ˌchēl-pän-ˈsēn-(ˌ)gō\ city S Mexico ✳ of Guerrero *pop* 136,243

Chil·tern Hills \ˈchil-tərn\ hills S *central* England in Oxfordshire, Buckinghamshire, Hertfordshire, & Bedfordshire

Chi·lung \ˈjē-ˈlüŋ\ or **Keelung** \ˈkē-ˈlüŋ\ city & port N Taiwan *pop* 347,828

Chim·bo·ra·zo \ˌchēm-bō-ˈrä-(ˌ)zō\ mountain 20,561 *ft* (6267 *m*) W *central* Ecuador

Chimkent — see SHYMKENT

Chi·na, People's Republic of \ˈchī-nə\ country E Asia; a republic ✳ Beijing; *area* 3,691,502 *sq mi* (9,597,905 *sq km*), *pop* 1,179,467,000

China, Republic of — see TAIWAN

Chinan — see JINAN

China Sea the E. & S. China seas

Chin–chou, Chinchow — see JINZHOU

Chin·co·teague Bay \ˌshiŋ-kə-ˈtēg\ bay Md. & Va. on Atlantic coast

Chin·dwin \ˈchin-ˈdwin\ river NW Myanmar flowing S into the Irrawaddy

Chinese Turkestan region W China in W & *central* Xinjiang Uygur

Ch'ing Hai — see QINGHAI

Chin Hills \ˈchin\ hills W Myanmar; highest Mt. Victoria 10,016 *ft* (3053 *m*)

Ch'in–huang–tao, Chin·wang·tao — see QINHUANGDAO

Chinkiang — see ZHENJIANG

Chinnampo — see NAMPO

Chinnereth, Sea of — see GALILEE (Sea of)

Chi·no \ˈchē-(ˌ)nō\ city SW Calif. E of Los Angeles *pop* 59,682

Chiog·gia \kē-ˈȯ-jä\ commune & port NE Italy on island in Lagoon of Venice *pop* 52,582

Chi·os \ˈkī-ˌäs\ or *New Greek* **Khí·os** \ˈkē-ˌós\ **1** island E Greece in the Aegean off W coast of Turkey *area* 325 *sq mi* (842 *sq km*) *pop* 52,691 **2** city & port Greece on E coast of Chios Is. — **Chi·an** \ˈkī-ən\ *adjective or noun*

Chip·pe·wa \ˈchi-pə-ˌwȯ, -ˌwä, -ˌwā, -wə\ river 183 *mi* (294 *km*) NW Wis. flowing S into Mississippi River

Chir·i·ca·hua National Monument \ˌchir-ə-ˈkä-wə, *locally also* ˈchir-ə-ˌkaú\ reservation SE Ariz. containing curious natural rock formations

Chiriquí — see BARÚ

Chis·holm Trail \ˈchi-zəm\ pioneer cattle trail between San Antonio (Tex.) & Abilene (in E *central* Kans.), used especially 1866–85

Chi·și·nău \ˌkē-shē-ˈnaú\ or **Ki·shi·nev** \ˌki-shi-ˈnȯf; ˈki-shə-ˌnef, -ˌnev\ city *central* Moldova, its ✳ *pop* 665,000

Chis·le·hurst and Sid·cup \ˈchi-zəl-ˌhərst-ən(d)-ˈsid-kəp\ former urban district SE England in Kent, now partly in Bexley, partly in Bromley

Chi·ta \chi-ˈtä, ˈchē-\ city Russia in Asia E of Lake Baikal *pop* 377,000

Chi·tral \chi-ˈträl\ river 300 *mi* (483 *km*) N Pakistan & Afghanistan flowing SW into Kabul River

Chit·ta·gong \ˈchi-tə-ˌgäŋ, -ˌgȯŋ\ city & port SE Bangladesh on Bay of Bengal *pop* 1,566,070

Chi·tun·gwi·za \chē-tüŋ-ˈgwē-zä\ city NE *central* Zimbabwe, SSE of Harare *pop* 274,035

Chiu·si \ˈkyü-sē\ or *ancient* **Clu·si·um** \ˈklü-zhē-əm, -zē-\ town *central* Italy in Tuscany SE of Siena

Chkalov — see ORENBURG

Choaspes — see KARKHEH

Choi·seul \shwä-ˈzə(r)l, -ˈzēl\ island W Pacific in the Solomons SE of Bougainville Is.; nearly surrounded by barrier reef

Choi·sy \shwä-ˈzē\ or **Choi·sy–le–Roi** \shwä-ˌzē-lər-ˈwä\ commune E France on the Seine SSE of Paris *pop* 38,629

Cho·lon \shə-ˈlōn, chə-ˈlän\ former city S Vietnam, now part of Ho Chi Minh City

Cho·lu·la \chō-ˈlü-lä\ town SE *central* Mexico in Puebla state

Cho·mo Lha·ri \ˌchō-mō-ˈlär-ē\ mountain 23,997 *ft* (7314 *m*) in the Himalayas between Tibet & NW Bhutan; sacred to Buddhists

Chomolungma — see EVEREST (Mount)

Ch'ong·ju \ˈchȯŋ-jü\ city W *central* S. Korea N of Taejon *pop* 350,256

Chong·qing or **Ch'ung–ch'ing** \ˈchuŋ-ˈchiŋ\ or **Chung·king** \ˈchuŋ-ˈkiŋ\ city SE Sichuan on the Chang; ✳ of China 1937–43 *pop* 2,266,772

Chon·ju \ˈjən-jü\ city SW S. Korea SW of Taejon *pop* 426,473

Cho Oyu \ˈchō-ō-ˈyü\ mountain 26,750 *ft* (8153 *m*) Nepal & Tibet in the Himalayas; 6th highest in the world

Cho·ras·mia \kə-ˈraz-mē-ə\ province of ancient Persia on Oxus River extending W to Caspian Sea; equivalent to Khwarazm — see KHIVA

Cho·rzow \ˈkȯ-ˌzhüf, ˈkȯ-, -ˌzhüv\ city SW Poland in Silesia *pop* 132,674

Chosen — see KOREA

Cho·ta Nag·pur \ˌchō-tə-ˈnäg-ˌpur\ plateau region E India N of Mahanadi basin in N Orissa & S Bihar

Chou–shan — see ZHOUSHAN

Cho·wan \chə-ˈwän\ river 50 *mi* (80 *km*) NE N.C. flowing into Albemarle Sound

Christ·church \ˈkrīs(t)-ˌchərch\ city New Zealand on E coast of South Is. *pop* 292,858 — see LYTTELTON

Christiania — see OSLO

Chris·tian·sted \ˈkris-chən-ˌsted, ˈkrish-\ town Virgin Islands of the U.S. on N coast of St. Croix Is. *pop* 2555

Christ·mas Island \ˈkris-məs\ **1** island E Indian ocean 225 *mi* (360 *km*) S of W end of Java; administered by Australia *area* 52 *sq mi* (135 *sq km*), *pop* 1000 **2** — see KIRITIMATI

Chu \ˈchü\ **1** — see ZHU **2** river *over* 1000 *mi* (1609 *km*) SE Kazakhstan flowing E into Issyk Kul

Ch'üan–chou, Chuanchow — see QUANZHOU

Chubb Crater — see NEW QUEBEC CRATER

Chu·but \chü-ˈbüt, -ˈbut\ river 500 *mi* (805 *km*) S Argentina flowing E across Patagonia into the Atlantic

Chu–chou, Chuchow — see ZHUZHOU

Chudskoe — see PEIPUS

Chu·gach Mountains \ˈchü-ˌgach *also* -ˌgash\ mountains S Alaska extending along coast from Cook Inlet to St. Elias Range; highest 13,176 *ft* (4016 *m*)

Chuk·chi Peninsula \ˈchək-chē, ˈchuk-\ peninsula NE Russia in Asia, between Bering & Chukchi seas

Chukchi Sea sea of the Arctic Ocean N of Bering Strait

Chu·la Vis·ta \ˌchü-lə-ˈvis-tə\ city SW Calif. S of San Diego *pop* 135,163

Chu·lym or **Chu·lim** \chə-ˈlim\ river Russia in Asia flowing W into the Ob

Ch'ung–ch'ing, Chungking — see CHONGQING

Chur \ˈkur\ or *French* **Coire** \ˈkwär\ commune E Switzerland ✳ of Graubünden canton *pop* 31,078

Chur·chill \ˈchər-ˌchil\ **1** river *about* 1000 *mi* (1609 *km*) Canada flowing E across N Saskatchewan & N Manitoba into Hudson Bay **2** or *formerly* **Hamilton** river 208 *mi* (335 *km*) Canada in Newfoundland in S *central* Labrador flowing E to Lake Melville

Churchill Falls or *formerly* **Grand Falls** waterfall 245 *ft* (75 *m*) high Canada in W Labrador in Churchill River

Chuuk \ˈchuk\ or **Truk** \ˈtrək, ˈtruk\ islands *central* Carolines, part of Federated States of Micronesia

Chu·vash Republic \chü-ˈväsh\ autonomous republic E *central* Russia in Europe S of the Volga ✳ Cheboksary *area* 7066 *sq mi* (18,301 *sq km*), *pop* 1,393,000

Chu·zen·ji \chü-ˈzen-jē\ lake Japan in *central* Honshu W of Nikko

Cí·bo·la \ˈsē-bə-lə, ˈsi-\ historical region in present N N. Mex. including seven pueblos (the **Seven Cities of Cíbola**) believed by early Spanish explorers to contain vast treasures

Cic·ero \ˈsi-sə-ˌrō\ town NE Ill. W of Chicago *pop* 67,436

Cien·fue·gos \syen-ˈfwä-(ˌ)gōs\ city & port W *central* Cuba on S coast on **Cienfuegos Bay** *pop* 123,600

Cie·szyn \ˈche-shin\ or *German* **Te·schen** \ˈte-shən\ region *central* Europe in Silesia; once an Austrian duchy; divided 1920 between Poland & Czechoslovakia (now the Czech Republic)

Ci·la·cap or **Tji·la·tjap** \chē-ˈlä-ˌchäp\ city & port Indonesia in S Java ESE of Bandung

Ci·li·cia \sə-ˈli-sh(ē-)ə\ ancient country SE Asia Minor extending along Mediterranean coast S of Taurus Mountains — see LITTLE ARMENIA — **Ci·li·cian** \-ˈli-shən\ *adjective or noun*

Cilician Gates mountain pass S Turkey in Taurus Mountains

Cim·ar·ron \ˈsi-mə-ˌrän, -ˌrōn, -rən\ river flowing E from N N. Mex. through SW Kans. into Arkansas River in NE Okla.

Cimbrian Chersonese, Cimbric Chersonese — see CHERSONESE

Cim·me·ri·an Bosporus \sə-ˈmir-ē-ən\ KERCH STRAIT

Cin·cin·nati \ˌsin(t)-sə-ˈna-tē, -ˈna-tə\ city SW Ohio on Ohio River *pop* 364,040 — **Cin·cin·nat·i·an** \-ˈna-tē-ən\ *noun*

Cinque Ports \ˈsiŋk\ group of seaport towns SE England on coast of Kent & Sussex, originally five (Dover, Sandwich, Romney, Hastings, & Hythe) to which were later added Winchelsea, Rye, & other minor places, granted special privileges (abolished in 19th century) in return for services in coast defense

Cintra — see SINTRA

Circars — see NORTHERN CIRCARS

Cir·cas·sia \(ˌ)sər-ˈka-sh(ē-)ə\ region S Russia in Europe on Black Sea N of W end of Caucasus Mountains

Ci·re·bon \ˌchē-re-ˈbȯn\ city Indonesia in W Java on N coast E of Jakarta *pop* 245,307

Cirenaica — see CYRENAICA

Cis·al·pine Gaul \(ˌ)sis-ˈal-ˌpīn\ the part of Gaul lying S & E of the Alps

Ciscaucasia — see CAUCASIA

Cis·kei \ˈsis-ˌkī\ former black enclave in the Republic of South Africa ✳ Bisho; granted independence 1981; abolished 1994 — **Cis·kei·an** \(ˌ)sis-ˈkī-ən\ *adjective or noun*

Ci·thae·ron \sə-ˈthē-ˌrän\ or *New Greek* **Ki·thai·rón** \ˌkē-the-ˈrȯn\ or *formerly* **El·a·tea** \ˌe-lə-ˈtē-ə\ mountain 4623 *ft* (1409 *m*) Greece on NW border of ancient Attica

Ci·tlal·te·petl \ˌsēt-ˌläl-ˈtä-ˌpe-tᵊl\ or **Ori·za·ba** \ˌȯr-ə-ˈzä-bə, ˌō-rē-ˈsä-vä\ inactive volcano 18,700 *ft* (5700 *m*) SE Mexico on Puebla-Veracruz boundary; highest mountain in Mexico & 3d highest in N. America

Citrus Heights urban center N *central* Calif. NE of Sacramento *pop* 107,439

Città del Vaticano — see VATICAN CITY

Ci·u·dad Bo·lí·var \syü-'thäth-bō-'lē-,vär, ,sē-ù-'dad-\ city & port E *central* Venezuela on the Orinoco *pop* 225,846

Ciudad Gua·ya·na \gwä-'yä-nä\ city E Venezuela near junction of the Caroní & the Orinoco *pop* 536,506

Ciudad Juá·rez *or* **Juárez** \'hwär-es, 'wär-\ city Mexico in Chihuahua on Rio Grande opposite El Paso, Tex. *pop* 789,522

Ciudad Re·al \rā-'äl\ **1** province S *central* Spain *area* 7625 *sq mi* (17,749 *sq km*), *pop* 475,435 **2** commune, its ✳, S of Toledo *pop* 56,315

Ciudad Trujillo — see SANTO DOMINGO

Ciudad Vic·to·ria \vik-'tōr-ē-ə, -'tōr-\ city E *central* Mexico ✳ of Tamaulipas *pop* 94,304

Ci·vi·ta·vec·chia \,chē-vē-tä-'ve-(,)kyä\ commune & port *central* Italy in Lazio on Tyrrhenian Sea WNW of Rome *pop* 50,856

Clack·man·nan \klak-'ma-nən\ *or* **Clack·man·nan·shire** \-,shir, -shər\ **1** former county *central* Scotland bordering on the Forth **2** town, its ✳

Clac·ton \'klak-tən\ *or* **Clacton–on–Sea** town SE England in Essex on North Sea *pop* 43,571

Clare \'klar, 'kler\ county W Ireland in Munster ✳ Ennis *area* 1231 *sq mi* (3201 *sq km*), *pop* 90,918

Clare·mont \-,mänt\ city SW Calif. E of Los Angeles *pop* 32,503

Clark Fork \'klärk\ river 300 *mi* (483 *km*) W Mont. & N Idaho flowing NW into Pend Oreille Lake

Clarks·dale \'klärks-,dāl\ city NW Miss. *pop* 19,717

Clarks·ville \'klärks-,vil, -vəl\ **1** town S Ind. *pop* 19,833 **2** city N Tenn. NW of Nashville *pop* 75,494

Clear·field \'klir-,fēld\ city N Utah S of Ogden *pop* 21,435

Clear·wa·ter \'klir-,wȯ-tər, -,wä-\ city W Fla. NW of St. Petersburg on Gulf of Mexico *pop* 98,784

Clearwater Mountains mountains N *central* Idaho; highest about 8000 *ft* (2438 *m*)

Cle·burne \'klē-bərn\ city NE *central* Tex. *pop* 22,205

Clee Hills \'klē\ hills W England in S Shropshire

Cler·mont–Fer·rand \,kler-,mō°-fe-'rä°\ city *central* France in Allier valley on edge of Auvergne Mountains *pop* 140,167

Cleve·land \'klēv-lənd\ **1** city & port NE Ohio on Lake Erie *pop* 505,616 **2** city SE Tenn. ENE of Chattanooga *pop* 30,354 **3** county N England N of N. Yorkshire ✳ Middlesbrough *area* 233 *sq mi* (603 *sq km*), *pop* 541,100; includes the **Cleveland Hills** — **Cleve·land·er** \-lən-dər\ *noun*

Cleveland, Mount mountain 10,455 *ft* (3185 *m*) N Mont., highest in Glacier National Park

Cleveland Heights city NE Ohio E of Cleveland *pop* 54,052

Cli·chy \klē-'shē\ commune N France NW of Paris *pop* 48,204

Cliff·side Park \'klif-(,)sīd\ borough NE N.J. *pop* 20,393

Clif·ton \'klif-tən\ city NE N.J. N of Newark *pop* 71,742

Clinch \'klinch\ river *about* 300 *mi* (480 *km*) SW Va. & E Tenn. flowing SW into Tennessee River

Cling·mans Dome \'kliŋ-mənz\ mountain 6643 *ft* (2025 *m*) on N.C.-Tenn. boundary; highest in Great Smoky Mountains

Clin·ton \'klin-t°n\ **1** city E Iowa on Mississippi River *pop* 29,201 **2** town SW *central* Miss. *pop* 21,847

Clon·mel \klän-'mel\ town S Ireland ✳ of County Tipperary *pop* 11,759

Cloud Peak mountain 13,165 *ft* (4013 *m*) N Wyo.; highest in Bighorn Mountains

Clo·vis \'klō-vəs\ **1** city *central* Calif. NE of Fresno *pop* 50,323 **2** city E N. Mex. *pop* 30,954

Cluj–Na·po·ca \'klüzh-'nä-pō-kə\ city NW *central* Romania in Transylvania *pop* 317,914

Clu·ny \'klü-nē, klü-\ town E *central* France NNW of Lyon *pop* 4724

Clusium — see CHIUSI

Clu·tha \'klü-thə\ river 210 *mi* (338 *km*) New Zealand in SE South Is. flowing SE into the Pacific

Clwyd \'klü-id\ county NE Wales ✳ Mold *area* 937 *sq mi* (2436 *sq km*), *pop* 401,900

Clyde \'klīd\ river 106 *mi* (171 *km*) SW Scotland flowing NW into **Firth of Clyde** (estuary)

Clyde·bank \'klīd-,baŋk\ burgh W *central* Scotland in Strathclyde on Clyde River *pop* 46,920

Clydes·dale \'klīdz-,dāl\ valley of the upper Clyde River in Scotland

Cni·dus \'nī-dəs\ ancient town SW Asia Minor in Caria

Cnossus — see KNOSSOS

Coa·chel·la Valley \kō-'che-lə\ valley SE Calif. between Salton Sea & San Bernardino Mountains

Coa·hui·la \kō-ä-'wē-lä, kwä-'wē-\ state N Mexico bordering on the U.S. ✳ Saltillo *area* 58,522 *sq mi* (151,572 *sq km*), *pop* 1,972,340

Coast Mountains mountains Canada in W British Columbia; N continuation of Cascade Range

Coast Ranges mountain ranges W N. America extending along Pacific coast W of Sierra Nevada & Cascade Range & N through Vancouver Is., British Columbia, to Kenai Peninsula & Kodiak Is., Alaska — see LOGAN (Mount)

Coat·bridge \'kōt-(,)brij\ burgh S *central* Scotland in Strathclyde *pop* 50,866

Coats Land \'kōts\ section of Antarctica SE of Weddell Sea

Cobh \'kōv\ *or formerly* **Queens·town** \'kwēnz-,taùn\ town & port SW Ireland on island in Cork harbor *pop* 6369

Coblenz — see KOBLENZ

Co·burg **1** \'kō-,bərg\ city SE Australia in S Victoria, N suburb of Melbourne *pop* 50,625 **2** \-,bȯrg, -,bùrk\ city *central* Germany in N Bavaria NW of Bayreuth *pop* 44,693

Co·cha·bam·ba \,kō-chä-'bäm-bä\ city W *central* Bolivia *pop* 404,102

Co·chin \kō-'chin\ region SW India in Kerala on Malabar Coast — see TRAVANCORE

Co·chin China \'kō-,chin\ region S Vietnam bordering on S. China Sea & Gulf of Thailand *area* 29,974 *sq mi* (77,932 *sq km*)

Cochinos, Bahía de — see PIGS (Bay of)

Co·co \'kō,(,)kō\ *or formerly* **Se·go·via** \sā-'gō-vyä, sə-, -vē-ə\ river *over* 450 *mi* (724 *km*) N Nicaragua flowing NE into the Caribbean & forming part of Honduras-Nicaragua boundary

Co·co·ni·no Plateau \,kō-kə-'nē-(,)nō, -'nē-nə\ plateau NW Ariz. S of Grand Canyon

Coconut Creek city SE Fla. NNW of Fort Lauderdale *pop* 27,485

Co·cos Islands \'kō-kəs\ *or* **Kee·ling Islands** \'kē-liŋ\ islands E Indian Ocean belonging to Australia *area* 5.5 *sq mi* (14 *sq km*), *pop* 600

Cod, Cape \'käd\ peninsula 65 *mi* (105 *km*) long SE Mass. — **Cape Cod·der** \'kä-dər\ *noun*

Coele–Syria — see BEKAA

Coeur d'Alene \,kȯr-d°l-'ān\ city N Idaho *pop* 24,563

Coeur d'Alene Lake lake *about* 37 *mi* (59 *km*) long N Idaho E of Spokane, Wash.; drained by Spokane River

Co·glians, Mon·te \,mōn-tā-kōl-'yän(t)s\ mountain 9217 *ft* (2809 *m*) on Austria-Italy border; highest in the Carnic Alps

Coim·ba·tore \,kȯim-bə-'tōr, -'tȯr\ city S India in W Tamil Nadu on S slope of Nilgiri Hills *pop* 816,321

Co·im·bra \kō-'im-brə, kù-\ city W *central* Portugal *pop* 145,724

Coire — see CHUR

Col·ches·ter \'kōl-,ches-tər, -chəs-\ borough SE England in Essex *pop* 141,100

Col·chis \'käl-kəs\ ancient country bordering on Black Sea S of Caucasus Mountains; area now constitutes W part of Republic of Georgia — **Col·chi·an** \'käl-kē-ən\ *adjective or noun*

Cole·raine \kōl-'rān, 'kōl-\ district N Northern Ireland, established 1974 *area* 187 *sq mi* (484 *sq km*), *pop* 51,062

Co·li·ma \kō-'lē-mä\ **1** volcano SW Mexico in S Jalisco **2** state SW Mexico bordering on the Pacific *area* 2106 *sq mi* (5454 *sq km*), *pop* 428,510 **3** city, its ✳, SSW of Guadalajara *pop* 106,967

College Park 1 city NW Ga. S of Atlanta *pop* 20,457 **2** city SW Md. NE of Washington, D.C. *pop* 21,927

College Station city E *central* Tex. SE of Bryan *pop* 52,456

Col·lins·ville \'kä-lənz-,vil\ city SW Ill. NE of E. St. Louis *pop* 22,446

Col·mar *or* German **Kol·mar** \'kōl-,mär, kōl-'\ commune NE France at E edge of Vosges Mountains *pop* 64,889

Co·logne \kə-'lōn\ *or* German **Köln** \'kœln\ city W Germany in N. Rhine-Westphalia on the Rhine *pop* 956,690

Colomb–Béchar — see BÉCHAR

Co·lombes \kə-'lō°b, -'lōm\ commune N France, NW suburb of Paris *pop* 79,058

Co·lom·bia \kə-'ləm-bē-ə *also* -'lōm-\ country NW S. America bordering on Caribbean Sea & Pacific Ocean ✳ Bogotá *area* 439,735 *sq mi* (1,138,914 *sq km*), *pop* 26,525,670 — **Co·lom·bi·an** \-bē-ən\ *adjective or noun*

Co·lom·bo \kə-'ləm-(,)bō\ city & port ✳ of Sri Lanka *pop* 615,000

Co·lón \kō-'lōn\ city & port N Panama on the Caribbean at entrance to Panama Canal *pop* 54,469

Colón, Archipiélago de — see GALÁPAGOS ISLANDS

Col·o·phon \'kä-lə-fən, -,fän\ ancient city W Asia Minor in Lydia

Col·o·ra·do \,kä-lə-'ra-(,)dō, -'rä-\ **1** river 1450 *mi* (2334 *km*) SW U.S. & NW Mexico rising in N Colo. & flowing SW into Gulf of California **2** river 600 *mi* (950 *km*) S Tex. flowing SE into Gulf of Mexico **3** state W U.S. ✳ Denver *area* 104,247 *sq mi* (271,042 *sq km*), *pop* 3,294,394 **4** river 530 *mi* (853 *km*) *central* Argentina flowing SE to the Atlantic — **Col·o·ra·dan** \-'ra-d°n, -'rä-\ *adjective or noun* — **Col·o·ra·do·an** \-'ra-dō-ən, -'rä-\ *adjective or noun*

Colorado Desert desert SE Calif. W of Colorado River

Colorado National Monument reservation W Colo. W of Grand Junction containing many unusual erosion formations

Colorado Plateau plateau SW U.S. W of Rocky Mountains in Colorado River basin in N Ariz., S & E Utah, W Colo., & NW N. Mex

Colorado Springs city *central* Colo. E of Pikes Peak *pop* 281,140

Co·los·sae \kə-'lä-(,)sē\ ancient city SW *central* Asia Minor in SW Phrygia — **Co·los·sian** \kə-'lä-shən\ *adjective or noun*

Col·ton \'kōl-t°n\ city SW Calif. S of San Bernardino *pop* 40,213

Co·lum·bia \kə-'ləm-bē-ə\ **1** river 1214 *mi* (1953 *km*) SW Canada & NW U.S. rising in SE British Columbia & flowing S & W into the Pacific **2** city *central* Mo. *pop* 69,101 **3** city ✳ of S.C. *pop* 98,052 **4** city *central* Tenn. *pop* 28,583 — **Co·lum·bi·an** \-bē-ən\ *adjective or noun*

Columbia, Cape cape N Canada on Ellesmere Is.; northernmost point of Canada, at 83°07′N

Columbia, District of — see DISTRICT OF COLUMBIA

Columbia Plateau plateau E Wash., E Oreg., & SW Idaho in Columbia River basin

Co·lum·bus \kə-'ləm-bəs\ **1** city W Ga. on the Chattahoochee *pop* 178,681 **2** city S *central* Ind. *pop* 31,802 **3** city E Miss. *pop* 23,799 **4** city E Nebr. *pop* 19,480 **5** city *central* Ohio, its ✳ *pop* 632,910

Col·ville \'kōl-,vil, 'käl-\ river 375 *mi* (603 *km*) N Alaska flowing NE into Beaufort Sea

Col·wyn Bay \'käl-wən\ borough N Wales in Clwyd *pop* 26,278

Co·mil·la *or* **Ku·mil·la** \kù-'mi-lə\ city E Bangladesh SE of Dhaka *pop* 184,509

Commander — see KOMANDORSKIE ISLANDS

Common Market — see EUROPEAN ECONOMIC COMMUNITY

Commonwealth of Independent States association of the former constituent republics of the U.S.S.R. except for Lithuania, Latvia, & Estonia; formed 1991

Commonwealth of Nations *or* **Commonwealth** political organization consisting of nations loyal to the British monarch

Communism Peak *or* Russian **Pik Kom·mu·niz·ma** \'pēk-kə-mü-'nēs-mə\ mountain 24,590 *ft* (7495 *m*) NE Tajikistan in Pamirs; highest in Tajikistan & former U.S.S.R.

Co·mo \'kō-(,)mō\ commune N Italy in Lombardy at SW end of **Lake Como** (37 *mi* or 59 *km* long) *pop* 85,955

Co·mo·do·ro Ri·va·da·via \ˌkō-mō-'thōr-(ˌ)ō-ˌrē-vä-'thä-vē-ä\ city & port S Argentina *pop* 96,865

Com·o·rin, Cape \'kä-mə-rən; kə-'mōr-ən, -'mór-, -'mär-\ cape S India in Tamil Nadu; southernmost point of India, at 8°5'N

Com·o·ros \'kä-mə-ˌrōz\ group of islands forming a country off SE Africa between Mozambique & Madagascar; formerly a French possession; a republic (except for Mayotte Is., which remains French) since 1975 ✳ Moroni *area* 719 *sq mi* (1862 *sq km*), *pop* 519,527

Com·piègne \kōⁿ-'pyenʸ\ town N France on the Oise *pop* 44,703

Compostela — see SANTIAGO 3

Comp·ton \'käm(p)-tən\ city SW Calif. SSE of Los Angeles *pop* 90,454

Com·stock Lode \'käm-ˌstäk\ gold & silver lode at Virginia City, Nev.

Con·a·kry \'kä-nə-krē\ city & port ✳ of Guinea on the Atlantic *pop* 581,000

Co·nan·i·cut Island \kə-'na-ni-kət\ island R.I. in Narragansett Bay W of Aquidneck Is.

Con·cep·ción \kōn-sep-'syōn\ city S central Chile *pop* 267,891

Con·chos \'kōn-ˌchōs\ river 300 *mi* (483 *km*) N Mexico flowing NE into Rio Grande

Con·cord 1 \'kän-ˌkórd, 'kän-\ city W Calif. NE of Oakland *pop* 111,348 **2** \'kän-ˌkərd\ town E Mass. NW of Boston *pop* 17,076 **3** \'kän-kərd\ city ✳ of N.H. on the Merrimack *pop* 36,006 **4** \'kän-ˌkórd, 'kän-\ city S central N.C. *pop* 27,347

Co·ney Island \'kō-nē\ resort section of New York City in S Brooklyn; formerly an island

Con·ga·ree \'käŋ-gə-(ˌ)rē\ river 60 *mi* (96 *km*) central S.C. flowing SE to unite with the Wateree forming the Santee

Congaree Swamp National Monument reservation central S.C. S of Columbia

Con·go \'käŋ-(ˌ)gō\ **1** *or* **Zaire** river more than 2700 *mi* (4344 *km*) central Africa flowing N, W, & SW into the Atlantic — see LUALABA **2** *or* **Democratic Republic of the Congo** *or* *1971–97* **Za·ire** \zä-'ir\ *or* *1908–60* **Belgian Congo** *or* *1885–1908* **Congo Free State** country central Africa comprising most of Congo River basin E of lower Congo River ✳ Kinshasa *area* 905,356 *sq mi* (2,344,872 *sq km*), *pop* 43,775,000 **3** *or* **Republic of the Congo** *or* *formerly* **Middle Congo** country W central Africa W of the lower Congo ✳ Brazzaville *area* 132,047 *sq mi* (342,002 *sq km*), *pop* 2,775,000 — SEE FRENCH EQUATORIAL AFRICA — **Con·go·lese** \ˌkäŋ-gə-'lēz, -'lēs\ *adjective or noun*

Con·nacht \'kä-ˌnót\ *or formerly* **Con·naught** province W Ireland *area* 6611 *sq mi* (17,189 *sq km*), *pop* 422,909

Con·nect·i·cut \kə-'ne-ti-kət\ **1** river 407 *mi* (655 *km*) NE U.S. rising in N.H. & flowing S into Long Island Sound **2** state NE U.S. ✳ Hartford *area* 5018 *sq mi* (12,997 *sq km*), *pop* 3,287,116

Con·ne·ma·ra \ˌkä-nə-'mär-ə\ district Ireland in W Galway

Con·roe \'kän-(ˌ)rō\ city E Tex. *pop* 27,610

Con·stance \'kän(t)-stən(t)s\ *or German* **Kon·stanz** \'kón-ˌstänts\ commune S Germany on Lake Constance *pop* 76,162

Constance, Lake *or German* **Bo·den·see** \'bō-d'n-ˌzā\ lake 46 *mi* (74 *km*) long W Europe on border between Germany, Austria, & Switzerland

Con·stan·a \kən-'stän(t)-sə\ city & port SE Romania on Black Sea *pop* 315,917

Con·stan·tine \'kän(t)-stən-ˌtēn\ city NE Algeria *pop* 440,842

Constantinople — see ISTANBUL — **Con·stan·ti·no·pol·i·tan** \ˌkän-ˌstan-t'n-ō-'pä-lə-t'n\ *adjective*

Continental Divide *or* **Great Divide** the watershed of N. America comprising the line of highest points of land separating the waters flowing W from those flowing N or E, coinciding with various ranges of the Rockies, and extending SSE from NW Canada to NW S. America

Con·way \'kän-ˌwā\ city central Ark. N of Little Rock *pop* 26,481

Cooch Be·har \ˌküch-bə-'här\ former state NE India W of Assam; since 1947 attached to West Bengal

Cook, Mount \'kúk\ *or formerly* **Ao·rangi** \aú-'räŋ-ē\ mountain 12,349 *ft* (3764 *m*) New Zealand in W central South Is.; highest peak in Southern Alps & New Zealand

Cooke·ville \'kúk-ˌvil, -vəl\ city N central Tenn. *pop* 21,744

Cook Inlet inlet of the Pacific S Alaska W of Kenai Peninsula

Cook Islands islands S Pacific SW of Society Islands; self-governing territory of New Zealand ✳ Avarua (on Rarotonga Is.) *area* 92 *sq mi* (238 *sq km*), *pop* 17,614

Cooks·town \'kúks-ˌtaún\ district central Northern Ireland, established 1974 *area* 241 *sq mi* (627 *sq km*), *pop* 30,808

Cook Strait strait New Zealand between North Is. & South Is.

Coon Rapids \'kün\ city E Minn. N of St. Paul *pop* 52,978

Coo·per City \'kü-pər\ city SE Fla. WNW of Hollywood *pop* 20,791

Coorg *or* **Kurg** \'kúrg\ former state S India ✳ Mercara; merged with Mysore state (now Karnataka) 1956

Coo·sa \'kü-sə\ river 286 *mi* (460 *km*) NW Ga. & N Ala. flowing SW to join Tallapoosa River forming Alabama River

Coos Bay \'küs\ inlet of the Pacific SW Oreg.

Co·pán \kō-'pän\ ruins of Mayan city W Honduras

Co·pen·ha·gen \ˌkō-pən-'hā-gən, -'hä-; 'kō-pən-ˌ\ *or Danish* **Kø·ben·havn** \ˌkȳ-bən-'haún\ city & port ✳ of Denmark on E Sjælland Is. & N Amager Is. *pop* 467,850 — **Co·pen·ha·gen·er** \ˌkō-pən-'hā-gə-nər, -'hä-; 'kō-pən-ˌ\ *noun*

Co·pia·pó \ˌkō-pyä-'pō\ city N central Chile *pop* 79,268

Cop·per·as Cove \'kä-p(ə-)rəs\ city central Tex. *pop* 24,079

Cop·per·mine \'kä-pər-ˌmīn\ river 525 *mi* (845 *km*) N Canada in Northwest Territories flowing NW into Arctic Ocean

Coquilhatville — see MBANDAKA

Coral Gables city SE Fla. SW of Miami *pop* 40,091

Coral Sea arm of the SW Pacific bounded on W by Queensland, Australia, on N by the Solomons, & on E by Vanuatu & New Caledonia

Coral Springs city SE Fla. *pop* 79,443

Cor·co·va·do \ˌkór-kō-'vä-(ˌ)dü\ mountain 2310 *ft* (704 *m*) SE Brazil on S side of city of Rio de Janeiro

Cor·dil·le·ra Cen·tral \ˌkór-d'l-'yer-ə-ˌsen-'träl, ˌkór-də-'ler-, ˌkór-dē-'yer-\ **1** range of the Andes in Colombia **2** range of the Andes in Peru E of the Marañón **3** chief range of the Dominican Republic **4** range Philippines in N Luzon — see PULOG (Mount) **5** range S central Puerto Rico — see CERRO DE PUNTA

Cordillera de Mé·ri·da \thä-'mā-rē-ˌthä\ *or* **Sier·ra Ne·va·da de Mé·ri·da** \'syer-ä-ne-'vä-thä-ˌthä\ mountain range W Venezuela — see BOLÍVAR (Pico)

Cór·do·ba \'kór-də-bə, 'kór-thō-ˌvä\ **1** province S Spain *area* 5297 *sq mi* (13,179 *sq km*) *pop* 754,452 **2** *or* **Cor·do·va** \'kór-də-və, 'kór-thō-ˌvä\ city, its ✳, on the Guadalquivir *pop* 300,229 **3** city N central Argentina *pop* 1,179,067 — **Cor·do·ban** \-bən\ *adjective or noun*

Cor·do·va Island \'kór-də-və, 'kór-thō-ˌvä\ tract on the Rio Grande 385 *acres* (156 *hectares*) adjoining Chamizal, formerly belonging to Mexico; 193 *acres* (78 *hectares*) ceded to U.S. in 1963

Cor·fu \'kór-ˌfü; 'kór-(ˌ)fü, -(ˌ)fyü\ *or New Greek* **Kér·ky·ra** \'ker-kē-ˌrä\ *or ancient* **Cor·cy·ra** \kór-'sī-rə\ **1** island NW Greece, one of the Ionian Islands *area* 229 *sq mi* (593 *sq km*) *pop* 105,043 **2** city & port on E Corfu *pop* 36,875 — **Cor·fi·ote** \'kór-fē-ˌōt, -ət\ *noun*

Cor·inth \'kór-ən(t)th, 'kär-\ *or New Greek* **Kó·rin·thos** \'kór-ēn-ˌthós\ *or Lat* **Co·rin·thia** \kə-'rin(t)-thē-ə\ region of ancient Greece occupying most of Isthmus of Corinth & part of NE Peloponnese

Corinth, Gulf of inlet of Ionian Sea central Greece W of Isthmus of Corinth (neck of land 20 *mi* or 32 *km* long connecting Peloponnese with rest of Greece)

Cork \'kórk\ **1** county SW Ireland in Munster *area* 2880 *sq mi* (7459 *sq km*), *pop* 283,116 **2** city & port, its ✳, at head of Cork harbor *pop* 127,024

Corn \'kórn\ two small islands Nicaragua in the Caribbean

Cor·ner Brook \'kór-nər-ˌbrúk\ city Canada on W Newfoundland on Gulf of Saint Lawrence *pop* 22,410

Corneto — see TARQUINIA

Cor·no, Mon·te \'món-tā-'kór-(ˌ)nō\ mountain 9560 *ft* (2897 *m*) central Italy NE of Rome; highest in the Apennines

Corn·wall \'kórn-ˌwòl, -wəl\ **1** city Canada in SE Ontario *pop* 47,137 **2** *or since 1974* **Cornwall and Isles of Scil·ly** \'si-lē\ county SW England ✳ Bodmin & ✳ Truro *area* 1418 *sq mi* (3673 *sq km*), *pop* 469,300

Co·ro \'kór-(ˌ)ō, 'kór-\ city NW Venezuela near coast *pop* 124,616

Cor·o·man·del \ˌkór-ə-'man-d'l, ˌkär-\ coast region SE India on Bay of Bengal S of the Krishna

Co·ro·na \kə-'rō-nə\ city SW Calif. E of Los Angeles *pop* 76,095

Cor·o·na·do \ˌkór-ə-'nä-(ˌ)dō, ˌkär-\ city SW Calif. on San Diego Bay opposite San Diego *pop* 26,540

Cor·pus Chris·ti \ˌkór-pəs-'kris-tē\ city & port S Tex. on **Corpus Christi Bay** (inlet of Gulf of Mexico) at mouth of the Nueces *pop* 257,453

Cor·reg·i·dor \kə-'re-gə-ˌdór\ island N Philippines at entrance to Manila Bay *area* about 2 *sq mi* (5 *sq km*)

Cor·rien·tes \ˌkór-ē-'en-ˌtäs\ city NE Argentina *pop* 267,742

Cor·si·ca \'kór-si-kə\ *or French* **Corse** \'kórs\ island France in the Mediterranean N of Sardinia *area* 3360 *sq mi* (8702 *sq km*), *pop* 250,634 — **Cor·si·can** \'kór-si-kən\ *adjective or noun*

Cor·si·ca·na \ˌkór-sə-'ka-nə\ city NE central Tex. *pop* 22,911

Cor·ti·na *or* **Cortina d'Am·pez·zo** \kór-'tē-nä-ˌdäm-'pet-(ˌ)sō\ resort village N Italy in the Dolomites E of Belluno

Cort·land \'kórt-lənd\ city S central N.Y. *pop* 19,801

Cor·to·na \kór-'tō-nä\ commune central Italy NW of Perugia *pop* 22,352

Coruña, La; Corunna — see LA CORUÑA

Cor·val·lis \kór-'va-ləs\ city W Oreg. SW of Salem *pop* 44,757

Cos — see KOS

Co·sen·za \kō-'zen(t)-sä\ commune S Italy in Calabria *pop* 87,140

Cos·ta Bra·va \ˌkós-tä-'brä-vä, ˌkōs-\ coast region NE Spain in Catalonia on the Mediterranean extending NE from Barcelona

Costa del Sol \-del-'sōl, -thel-, -'sól\ coast region S Spain on the Mediterranean extending E from Gibraltar

Costa Me·sa \'mā-sə\ city SW Calif. SE of Long Beach on Pacific coast *pop* 96,357

Costa Ri·ca \'rē-kə\ country Central America between Nicaragua & Panama; a republic ✳ San José *area* 19,652 *sq mi* (50,899 *sq km*), *pop* 3,199,000 — **Cos·ta Ri·can** \-kən\ *adjective or noun*

Costermansville — see BUKAVU

Côte d'A·zur \ˌkōt-də-ˌzúr, -dä-'zűr\ coast region SE France on the Mediterranean; part of the Riviera

Côte d'Ivoire — see IVORY COAST

Côte d'Or \ˌkōt-'dór\ range of hills E France SW of Dijon

Co·ten·tin Peninsula \ˌkō-ˌtäⁿ-'taⁿ\ peninsula NW France projecting into English Channel W of mouth of the Seine

Côte–Saint–Luc \ˌkōt-saⁿ-'lük, -sänt-, -sənt-\ city Canada in S Quebec W of Montreal *pop* 28,700

Co·to·nou \ˌkō-tō-'nü\ city & port S Benin, former ✳ of Dahomey *pop* 449,000

Co·to·paxi \ˌkō-tō-'päk-sē\ volcano 19,347 *ft* (5897 *m*) N central Ecuador

\ə\ abut \ˈə\ kitten \ər\ further \a\ ash \ā\ ace
\ä\ mop, mar \aú\ out \ch\ chin \e\ bet \ē\ easy
\g\ go \i\ hit \ī\ ice \j\ job \ŋ\ sing
\ō\ law \ói\ boy \th\ thin \t̲h̲\ the \ü\ loot \ú\ foot
\y\ yet \zh\ vision *see also* Guide to Pronunciation

Cots·wold \'kät-ˌswōld, -swəld\ hills SW *central* England in Gloucestershire; highest point Cleeve Cloud 1031 *ft* (314 *m*)

Cottage Grove city E Minn. *pop* 22,935

Cott·bus *or* **Kott·bus** \'kät-bəs, -ˌbùs\ city E Germany on Spree River SE of Berlin *pop* 123,321

Cot·ti·an Alps \'kä-tē-ən\ range of W Alps France & Italy — see VISO

Coun·cil Bluffs \'kaùn(t)-səl-ˈbləfs\ city SW Iowa on Missouri River *pop* 54,315

Cou·ran·tyne \'kōr-ən-ˌtīn, \-ˌtīn\ *or Dutch* **Co·ran·tijn** \-ˌtīn\ river *about* 475 *mi* (764 *km*) N S. America flowing N into the Atlantic & forming boundary between Guyana & Suriname

Cour·be·voie \ˌkür-bə-ˈvwä\ commune N France on the Seine NW of Paris *pop* 65,649

Cour·land \'kùr-lənd, ˈkür-ˌlänt\ region W Latvia bordering on the Baltic & Gulf of Riga

Courland Lagoon *or German* **Kur·isch·es Haff** \'kùr-i-shəs-ˈhäf\ *or Russian* **Kur·skiy Za·liv** \'kùr-skē-ˈzä-lif\ inlet of the Baltic on border between Lithuania & Russia *area* 625 *sq mi* (1625 *sq km*)

Cour·ma·yeur \ˌkür-mə-ˈyər\ resort village NW Italy in Valle d'Aosta SE of Mont Blanc

Courtrai — see KORTRIJK

Cov·en·try **1** \'kə-vən-trē\ town W R.I. *pop* 31,083 **2** \'kä-, ˈkə-\ city *central* England in W. Midlands *pop* 292,500

Co·vi·na \kō-ˈvē-nə\ city SW Calif. E of Los Angeles *pop* 43,207

Cov·ing·ton \'kə-viŋ-tən\ city N Ky. *pop* 43,264

Cowes \'kaùz\ town S England on Isle of Wight *pop* 19,663

Cow·litz \'kaù-ləts\ river 130 *mi* (209 *km*) SW Wash. flowing into Columbia River

Co·zu·mel \ˌkō-sü-ˈmel, ˌkä-zə-\ island SE Mexico off Quintana Roo

Cracow — see KRAKÓW

Craig·av·on \krā-ˈga-vən\ district *central* Northern Ireland, established 1974 *area* 147 *sq mi* (381 *sq km*), *pop* 74,494

Cra·io·va \krä-ˈyō-vä\ city S Romania *pop* 300,030

Cran·ston \'kran(t)-stən\ city E R.I. S of Providence *pop* 76,060

Cra·ter Lake \'krā-tər\ lake 1932 *ft* (589 *m*) deep SW Oreg. in Cascade Range at altitude of 6164 *ft* (1879 *m*); main feature of **Crater Lake National Park**

Craters of the Moon National Monument reservation SE *central* Idaho including lava flows & other volcanic formations

Cré·cy \krā-ˈsē, ˈkre-sē\ *or* **Cré·cy–en–Pon·thieu** \krā-ˈsē-ˌäⁿ-pōⁿ-ˈtya(r), -ˈtyœ\ commune N France NW of Amiens

Cre·mo·na \krā-ˈmō-nä\ commune N Italy in Lombardy on the Po ESE of Milan *pop* 73,404 — **Crem·o·nese** \ˌkre-mə-ˈnēz, -ˈnēs\ *adjective*

Crete \'krēt\ *or Greek* **Krí·ti** \'krē-tē\ island Greece in the E Mediterranean ✻ Canea *area* 3189 *sq mi* (8260 *sq km*), *pop* 536,980 — **Cretan** \'krē-tᵊn\ *adjective or noun*

Crete, Sea of *or formerly* **Sea of Can·dia** \'kan-dē-ə\ the S section of Aegean Sea between Crete & the Cyclades

Crewe \'krü\ borough NW England in Cheshire *pop* 47,759

Cri·mea \krī-ˈmē-ə, krə-\ *or Russian* **Krim** \'krim\ peninsula SE Europe, extending into Black Sea SW of Sea of Azov — **Cri·me·an** \krī-ˈmē-ən, krə-\ *adjective*

Cris·to·bal \kri-ˈstō-bəl\ *or Spanish* **Cris·tó·bal** \krē-ˈstō-väl\ town N Panama adjoining Colón at Caribbean entrance to Panama Canal

Cro·a·tia \krō-ˈā-sh(ē-)ə\ independent country SE Europe; a constituent republic of Yugoslavia 1946–91 comprising Croatia, Slavonia, & most of Istria & the Dalmatian coast ✻ Zagreb *area* 21,829 *sq mi* (56,537 *sq km*), *pop* 4,821,000

Crocodile — see LIMPOPO

Cros·by \'krōz-bē\ *or* **Great Crosby** borough NW England in Merseyside on Irish Sea NNW of Liverpool *pop* 53,660

Cross \'krós\ river 300 *mi* (483 *km*) W Africa in W Cameroon & SE Nigeria flowing W & S into Gulf of Guinea

Cro·to·ne \krō-ˈtō-nā\ *or ancient* **Cro·to·na** \-nə\ *or* **Cro·ton** \'krō-ˌtän, ˈkrō-tᵊn\ commune S Italy in Calabria on Gulf of Taranto *pop* 55,633

Croy·don \'kròi-dᵊn\ borough of S Greater London, England *pop* 299,600

Cro·zet Islands \krō-ˈzā\ islands S Indian Ocean WNW of Kerguelen; a French dependency

Crys·tal \'kris-tᵊl\ city SE Minn. N of Minneapolis *pop* 23,788

Crystal Lake city N Ill. *pop* 24,512

Cte·si·phon \'te-sə-ˌfän, ˈtē-\ ancient city *central* Iraq on the Tigris opposite Seleucia ✻ of Parthia & of later Sassanid empire

Cuan·za *or* **Kwan·za** \'kwän-zä\ river 600 *mi* (965 *km*) SW Africa in *central* Angola flowing NW into the Atlantic

Cu·ba \'kyü-bə, ˈkü-vä\ **1** island in the W. Indies N of Caribbean Sea *area* 41,620 *sq mi* (107,800 *sq km*) **2** country largely coextensive with island; a republic ✻ Havana *area* 42,804 *sq mi* (110,862 *sq km*), *pop* 10,892,000 — **Cu·ban** \'kyü-bən\ *adjective or noun*

Cubango — see OKAVANGO

Cú·cu·ta \'kü-kü-tä\ city N Colombia near Venezuela border *pop* 450,300

Cud·a·hy \'kə-də-(ˌ)hē\ city SW Calif. NW of Downey *pop* 22,817

Cuen·ca \'kweŋ-kä\ **1** city S Ecuador *pop* 194,981 **2** province E *central* Spain *area* 6587 *sq mi* (17,060 *sq km*), *pop* 205,198 **3** commune, its ✻, ESE of Madrid *pop* 42,615

Cuer·na·va·ca \ˌkwer-nä-ˈvä-kä, -ˈvä-\ city S *central* Mexico S of Mexico City ✻ of Morelos *pop* 281,752

Cu·lia·cán \ˌkül-yä-ˈkän\ **1** river 175 *mi* (282 *km*) NW Mexico flowing SW into the Pacific at mouth of Gulf of California **2** city NW Mexico on the Culiacán ✻ of Sinaloa *pop* 602,114

Cul·lo·den Moor \kə-ˈlä-dᵊn, -ˈlō-\ moorland N Scotland in Highland region E of Inverness

Cul·ver City \'kəl-vər\ city SW Calif. *pop* 38,793

Cu·mae \'kyü-(ˌ)mē\ ancient town S Italy on Tyrrhenian coast W of modern Naples — **Cu·mae·an** \kyü-ˈmē-ən\ *adjective*

Cu·ma·ná \ˌkü-mä-ˈnä\ city & port NE Venezuela on the Caribbean NE of Barcelona *pop* 212,492

Cum·ber·land \'kəm-bər-lənd\ **1** river 687 *mi* (1106 *km*) S Ky. & N Tenn. flowing W into Ohio River **2** city NW Md. on the Potomac *pop* 23,706 **3** town NE R.I. *pop* 29,038 **4** former county NW England ✻ Carlisle — see CUMBRIA **5** settlement Canada in SE Ontario on Ottawa River NE of Ottawa *pop* 40,697

Cumberland Caverns caverns *central* Tenn. SE of McMinnville

Cumberland Falls falls SE Ky. in upper course of Cumberland River

Cumberland Gap mountain pass 1640 *ft* (500 *m*) NE Tenn. through a ridge of the Cumberlands SE of Middlesboro, Ky.

Cumberland Plateau mountain region E U.S., part of the S Appalachian Mountains W of Tennessee River extending from S W.Va. to NE Ala.

Cumbre, La — see USPALLATA

Cum·bria \'kəm-brē-ə\ **1** — see STRATHCLYDE **2** county NW England including former counties of Cumberland & Westmorland ✻ Carlisle *area* 2724 *sq mi* (7055 *sq km*), *pop* 486,900 — **Cum·bri·an** \'kəm-brē-ən\ *adjective or noun*

Cumbrian Mountains mountains NW England chiefly in Cumbria & Lancashire — see SCAFELL PIKE

Cu·naxa \kyü-ˈnak-sə\ town in ancient Babylonia NW of Babylon

Cu·ne·ne *or* **Ku·ne·ne** \kü-ˈnä-nə\ river 700 *mi* (1126 *km*) SW Africa in SW Angola flowing S & W into the Atlantic

Cu·par \'kü-pər\ burgh E Scotland ✻ of Fife *pop* 6642

Cu·per·ti·no \ˌkü-pər-ˈtē-(ˌ)nō\ city W Calif. W of San José *pop* 40,263

Cu·ra·çao \ˌkür-ə-ˈsaù, ˌkyür-, -ˈsō, -ˈsä-ˌō\ island Netherlands Antilles in the S Caribbean; chief town Willemstad *area* 182 *sq mi* (471 *sq km*), *pop* 143,816

Cu·ri·ti·ba \ˌkür-ə-ˈtē-bə\ city S Brazil ✻ of Paraná *pop* 1,966,426

Cush *or* **Kush** \'kəsh, ˈkùsh\ ancient country NE Africa in Nile valley S of Egypt — **Cush·ite** \'kə-ˌshīt, ˈkü-\ *adjective or noun* — **Cush·it·ic** \kə-ˈshi-tik, kù-\ *adjective*

Cus·ter Battlefield National Monument \'kəs-tər\ site SE Mont. on the Little Bighorn of battle 1876

Cut·tack \'kə-tək\ city E India in Orissa *pop* 440,295

Cux·ha·ven \'kùks-ˌhä-fᵊn\ city & port NW Germany on North Sea at mouth of the Elbe *pop* 56,328

Cuy·a·ho·ga \ˌkī-(ə-)ˈhò-gə, kə-ˈhò-, -ˈhä-, -ˈhò-\ river 100 *mi* (161 *km*) NE Ohio flowing into Lake Erie at Cleveland

Cuyahoga Falls city NE Ohio N of Akron *pop* 48,950

Cu·yu·ni \kü-ˈyü-nē\ river 350 *mi* (563 *km*) N S. America rising in E Venezuela & flowing E into the Essequibo in N Guyana

Cuz·co *or* **Cus·co** \'küs-(ˌ)kō\ city S Peru *pop* 316,804

Cwm·bran \kùm-ˈbrän\ urban town SE Wales ✻ of Gwent

Cyc·la·des \'si-klə-ˌdēz\ *or New Greek* **Ki·klá·dhes** \kē-ˈklä-(ˌ)thes\ islands Greece in the S Aegean *area* 993 *sq mi* (2572 *sq km*) *pop* 95,083 — **Cy·clad·ic** \sī-ˈkla-dik, sī-\ *adjective*

Cydonia — see CANEA — **Cy·do·nian** \sī-ˈdō-nē-ən, -nyən\ *adjective or noun*

Cymru — see WALES

Cy·press \'sī-prəs\ city SW Calif. SE of Los Angeles *pop* 42,655

Cy·prus \'sī-prəs\ **1** island E Mediterranean S of Turkey **2** country coextensive with the island; a republic of the Commonwealth of Nations ✻ Nicosia *area* 3572 *sq mi* (9287 *sq km*), *pop* 764,000 — **Cyp·ri·ot** \'si-prē-ət, -ˌät\ *or* **Cyp·ri·ote** \-ˌōt, -ət\ *adjective or noun*

Cy·re·na·ica \ˌsir-ə-ˈnä-ə-kə, ˌsī-rə-\ *or Italian* **Ci·re·na·ica** \same *or* ˌchē-rä-ˈnä-ē-(ˌ)kä\ **1** *or* **Cy·re·ne** \sī-ˈrē-(ˌ)nē\ ancient coastal region N Africa dominated by city of Cyrene **2** region E Libya, formerly a province — **Cy·re·na·ic** \ˌsir-ə-ˈnä-ik, ˌsī-rə-\ *adjective or noun* — **Cy·re·na·ican** \-ˈnä-ə-kən\ *adjective or noun*

Cy·re·ne \sī-ˈrē-(ˌ)nē\ ancient city N Africa on the Mediterranean in NE Libya — **Cy·re·ni·an** \-nē-ən\ *adjective or noun*

Cyz·i·cus \'si-zi-kəs\ **1** — see KAPIDAGI **2** ancient city in Mysia on isthmus leading to Kapidagi Peninsula

Czech·o·slo·va·kia \ˌche-kə-slō-ˈvä-kē-ə, -slə-, -ˈva-\ country 1918–92 *central* Europe; a republic ✻ Prague *area* 49,371 *sq mi* (127,871 *sq km*), *pop* 15,567,666; divided Jan. 1, 1993 into separate countries of Czech Republic & Slovakia — **Czech·o·slo·vak** \-ˈslō-ˌväk, -ˌvak\ *adjective or noun* — **Czech·o·slo·va·ki·an** \-slō-ˈvä-kē-ən, -slə-, -ˈva-\ *adjective or noun*

Czech Republic country *central* Europe; a constituent republic of Czechoslovakia 1918–92 ✻ Prague *area* 30,450 *sq mi* (78,866 *sq km*), *pop* 10,332,000

Cze·sto·cho·wa \ˌchen(t)-stə-ˈkō-və\ *or Russian* **Chen·sto·khov** \chen(t)-stə-ˈkóf, -ˈkóv\ city S Poland on the Warta *pop* 258,700

Da — see BLACK

Da·bro·wa Gor·ni·cza \dòⁿ-ˈbrò-vä-gùr-ˈnē-chä\ city S Poland *pop* 139,200

Dacca — see DHAKA

Da·chau \'dä-ˌkaù, -ˌkaù\ city S Germany in S Bavaria *pop* 35,892; site of Nazi concentration camp

Da·cia \'dā-sh(ē-)ə\ ancient country & Roman province SE Europe roughly equivalent to Romania & Bessarabia — **Da·cian** \-shən\ *adjective or noun*

Da·dra and Na·gar Ha·ve·li \də-ˈdrä . . . ˌnə-gər-ə-ˈvä-lē\ union territory India bordering on Gujarat and Maharashtra *area* 189 *sq mi* (491 *sq km*), *pop* 138,477

Dag·en·ham \'da-gə-nəm, ˈdag-nəm\ former municipal borough SE England in Essex, now part of Barking and Dagenham

Da·ge·stan *or* **Da·ghe·stan** \ˌda-gə-ˈstan, ˌdä-gə-ˈstän\ autonomous republic SE Russia in Europe, on W shore of the Caspian ✻ Makhachkala *area* 19,421 *sq mi* (50,300 *sq km*), *pop* 1,890,000

Dahomey — see BENIN — **Da·ho·man** \də-ˈhō-mən\ *adjective or noun* — **Da·ho·me·an** \-ˈmē-ən\ *or* **Da·ho·mey·an** \-ˈmē-ən\ *adjective or noun*

Da·kar \'da-,kär, dä-'kär\ city & port ✳ of Senegal *pop* 1,729,823

Dakh·la \'dä-klə\ *or formerly* **Vil·la Cis·ne·ros** \,vē-yə-sis-'ner-ōs\ town & port NW Africa in Western Sahara ✳ of Río de Oro

Da·ko·ta \də-'kō-tə\ **1** — see JAMES 1 **2** territory (1861–89) NW U.S. divided 1889 into states of N.D. & S.D. (the **Da·ko·tas** \-təz\) — **Da·ko·tan** \-'kō-t°n\ *adjective or noun*

Dal·e·car·lia \,da-lə-'kär-lē-ə\ region W *central* Sweden — **Dal·e·car·li·an** \-ən\ *adjective*

Da·lian *or* **Ta·lien** \'dä-'lyen\ *or* **Lu·da** *or* **Lu·ta** \'lü-'dä\ *or* **Dai·ren** \'dī-'ren\ city NE China in S Liaoning on Liaodong Peninsula *pop* 1,723,302

Dal·las \'da-ləs, -lis\ city NE Tex. on Trinity River *pop* 1,006,877 — **Dal·las·ite** \'da-lə-,sīt\ *noun*

Dal·ma·tia \dal-'mā-sh(ē-)ə\ region W Balkan Peninsula on the Adriatic — **Dal·ma·tian** \-shən\ *adjective or noun*

Dal·ton \'dȯl-t°n\ city NW Ga. *pop* 21,761

Da·ly City \'dā-lē\ city W Calif. S of San Francisco *pop* 92,311

Da·man \də-'män, -'man\ *or* **Da·mão** \də-'maůn\ district W India on Gulf of Khambhat; a constituent part of the union territory of **Daman and Diu** *(area* 36 *sq mi or* 93 *sq km, pop* 101,586) — see GOA, PORTUGUESE INDIA

Da·man·hûr \,dä-mən-'hûr\ city N Egypt E of Alexandria *pop* 216,000

Da·mas·cus \də-'mas-kəs\ city SW Syria, its ✳ *pop* 1,451,000

Dam·a·vand \'da-mə-,vand\ *or* **Dem·a·vend** \'de-mə-,vend\ mountain 18,934 *ft* (5771 *m*) N Iran; highest in Elburz Mountains

Dam·i·et·ta \,da-mē-'e-tə\ city & port N Egypt *pop* 93,488

Dammam — see AD DAMMAM

Da·mo·dar \'dä-mə-,där\ river 368 *mi* (592 *km*) NE India in *central* Bihar & W. Bengal flowing ESE into the Hugli

Dan \'dan\ **1** river 180 *mi* (290 *km*) S Va. & N N.C. flowing E into Roanoke River **2** ancient village at N extremity of Palestine

Da Nang \(,)dä-'näŋ, -'naŋ\ *or formerly* **Tou·rane** \tü-'rän\ city & port *central* Vietnam in Annam *pop* 369,734

Da·na Point \'dā-nə\ coastal city S Calif. *bet* Los Angeles and San Diego *pop* 31,896

Dan·bury \'dan-,ber-ē, -b(ə-)rē\ city SW Conn. *pop* 65,585

Dan·dong \'dän-'důŋ\ *or* **An·tung** \'än-'důŋ\ *or* **Tan·tung** \'dän-'důŋ\ city & port NE China in SE Liaoning at mouth of the Yalu *pop* 523,699

Danger Islands — see PUKAPUKA

Danish West Indies the W islands of the Virgin Islands group that were until 1917 a Danish possession & now constitute the Virgin Islands of the U.S.

Danmark — see DENMARK

Dan·ube \'dan-(,)yüb\ *or German* **Do·nau** \'dō-,naů\ *or ancient* **Da·nu·bi·us** \də-'nü-bē-əs, da-, -'nyü-\ *or* **Is·ter** \'is-tər\ river 1771 *mi* (2850 *km*) *central* & SE Europe flowing SE from SW Germany into Black Sea — **Da·nu·bi·an** \da-'nyü-bē-ən\ *adjective*

Dan·vers \'dan-vərz\ town NE Mass. N of Lynn *pop* 24,174

Dan·ville \'dan-,vil\ **1** city W Calif. E of Oakland *pop* 31,306 **2** city E Ill. *pop* 33,828 **3** city S Va. on Dan River *pop* 53,056

Dan·zig \'dan(t)-sig, 'dän(t)-\ **1** — see GDANSK **2** territory surrounding & including Gdansk that (1920–39) constituted a free city under the League of Nations

Danzig, Gulf of — see GDANSK, GULF OF

Dar·da·nelles \,där-d°n-'elz\ *or* **Hel·les·pont** \'he-lə-,spänt\ *or ancient* **Hel·les·pon·tus** \,he-lə-'spän-təs\ strait NW Turkey connecting Sea of Marmara with the Aegean

Dar el Beida — see CASABLANCA

Dar es Sa·laam \,där-,e(s)-sə-'läm\ city & port ✳ of Tanzania & of Tanganyika on Indian Ocean *pop* 1,360,850

Dar·fur \där-'fůr\ region W Sudan; chief city El Fasher

Dar·i·én \,där-ē-'en, ,der-, ,där-\ Spanish colonial settlement Central America W of Gulf of Darien

Darien, Gulf of inlet of the Caribbean between E Panama & NW Colombia

Darien, Isthmus of — see PANAMA (Isthmus of)

Dar·jee·ling *or* **Dar·ji·ling** \där-'jē-liŋ\ city NE India in W. Bengal on Sikkim border

Dar·ling \'där-liŋ\ river *about* 1700 *mi* (2735 *km*) SE Australia in Queensland & New South Wales flowing SW into Murray River

Darling Range mountain range SW Western Australia extending *about* 250 *mi* (400 *km*) N–S along coast; highest point Mt. Cooke 1910 *ft* (582 *m*)

Dar·ling·ton \'där-liŋ-tən\ town N England in Durham *pop* 96,700

Darm·stadt \'därm-,stat, -,shtät, -,stät\ city *central* Germany in Hesse SSW of Frankfurt am Main *pop* 140,040

Dar·nah \'där-nə, 'dar-\ *or* **Der·na** \'der-\ city & port NE Libya

Dart·moor \'därt-,mùr, -,mōr, -,mȯr\ tableland SW England in S Devon *area* 365 *sq mi* (945 *sq km*)

Dart·mouth \'därt-məth\ **1** town SE Mass. W of New Bedford *pop* 27,244 **2** city Canada in S Nova Scotia on Halifax harbor opposite Halifax *pop* 67,798 **3** town & port SW England in S Devon on Dart River *pop* 6599

Dar·win \'där-wən\ city & port N Australia ✳ of Northern Territory on Port Darwin (inlet of Timor Sea) *pop* 70,071

Da·tong \'dä-'tůŋ\ *or* **Ta·tung** \'dä-'tůŋ\ city NE China in N Shanxi *pop* 798,319

Dau·gav·pils \'daů-gəf-,pilz\ *or Russian* **Dvinsk** \də-'vin(t)sk\ city E Latvia on Dvina River *pop* 129,000

Dau·phi·né \,dō-fē-'nā\ region & former province SE France N of Provence ✳ Grenoble

Da·vao \'dä-,vaů, -,vaù\ city Philippines on Davao Gulf *pop* 850,000

Davao Gulf gulf of the Pacific, Philippines in SE Mindanao

Dav·en·port \'da-vən-,pȯrt, -,pȯrt\ city E Iowa on Mississippi River *pop* 95,333

Da·vid \dä-'vēth\ town W Panama *pop* 65,635

Da·vie \'dā-vē\ city SE Fla. *pop* 47,217

Da·vis \'dā-vəs\ city W Calif. W of Sacramento *pop* 46,209

Davis Mountains mountains W Tex. N of the Big Bend of the Rio Grande

Davis Strait strait connecting Baffin Bay with the Atlantic

Daw·son \'dȯ-s°n\ city N Canada in Yukon *pop* 972

Dax \'däks\ commune SW France in the Landes on the Adour NE of Biarritz *pop* 20,119

Day·ton \'dā-t°n\ city SW Ohio on Miami River *pop* 182,044

Day·to·na Beach \dā-'tō-nə, də-\ city NE Fla. *pop* 61,921

Da Yunhe — see GRAND CANAL

Dead Sea *or biblical* **Salt Sea** *or Latin* **La·cus As·phal·ti·tes** \'lā-kəs-,as-,fȯl-'tī-tēz\ salt lake *about* 50 *mi* (80 *km*) long on boundary between Israel & Jordan *area* 370 *sq mi* (962 *sq km*), surface 1312 *ft* (400 *m*) below sea level

Dean, Forest of \'dēn\ forested district SW England in W Gloucester between Severn & Wye rivers; an ancient royal forest

Dear·born \'dir-,bȯrn, -bərn\ city SE Mich. *pop* 89,286

Dearborn Heights city SE Mich. W of Detroit *pop* 60,838

Death Valley arid valley E Calif. & S Nev. containing lowest point in the U.S. at 282 *ft* (86 *m*) below sea level; most of area included in **Death Valley National Monument**

Deau·ville \'dō-,vil, dō-'vēl\ town NW France on Bay of the Seine SSW of Le Havre *pop* 4380

De·bre·cen \'de-bret-,sen\ city E Hungary *pop* 222,300

De·cap·o·lis \di-'ka-pə-ləs\ confederation of 10 ancient cities N Palestine in region chiefly SE of Sea of Galilee

De·ca·tur \di-'kā-tər\ **1** city N Ala. *pop* 48,761 **2** city *central* Ill. *pop* 83,885

Dec·can \'de-kən, -,kan\ plateau region S *central* India lying between Eastern Ghats & Western Ghats

Ded·ham \'de-dəm\ town E Mass. SW of Boston *pop* 23,782

Dee \'dē\ **1** river 87 *mi* (140 *km*) NE Scotland flowing E into North Sea **2** river 50 *mi* (80

km) S Scotland flowing S into Solway Firth **3** river 70 *mi* (113 *km*) N Wales & W England flowing E & N into Irish Sea

Deep South region SE U.S. — usually considered as including Ala., Ga., La., Miss., N.C., S.C., and all or part of the adjacent states of Fla., Va., Tenn., Ark., & Tex.

Deer·field Beach \'dir-,fēld\ city SE Fla. N of Fort Lauderdale *pop* 46,325

Deer Park city SE Tex. *pop* 27,652

De·hi·wa·la—Mount La·vin·ia \,dā-hē-'wä-lə . . . lə-'vi-nē-ə\ town W Sri Lanka on coast S of Colombo *pop* 193,000

Deh·ra Dun \,der-ə-'dün\ city N India in NW Uttar Pradesh *pop* 270,028

De Kalb \di-'kalb\ city N Ill. *pop* 34,925

De·la·goa Bay \,de-lə-'gō-ə\ inlet of Indian Ocean S Mozambique

De·la·no \də-'lā-(,)nō\ city S Calif. NNW of Bakersfield *pop* 22,762

Del·a·ware \'de-lə-,war, -,wer, -wər\ **1** river 296 *mi* (476 *km*) E U.S. flowing S from S N.Y. into Delaware Bay **2** state E U.S. ✳ Dover *area* 2057 *sq mi* (5348 *sq km*), *pop* 666,168 **3** city *central* Ohio NNW of Columbus *pop* 20,030 — **Del·a·war·e·an** \,de-lə-'war-ē-ən, -'wer-\ *noun*

Delaware Bay inlet of the Atlantic between SW N.J. & E Del.

Del City \'del\ city *central* Okla. E of Oklahoma City *pop* 23,928

De·lé·mont \də-lā-'mō"\ commune NW Switzerland ✳ of Jura canton *pop* 11,467

Delft \'delft\ commune SW Netherlands *pop* 90,066

Del·ga·do, Cape \del-'gä-(,)dō\ cape NE Mozambique

Del·hi \'de-lē\ **1** union territory N India W of Uttar Pradesh ✳ Delhi *area* 573 *sq mi* (1484 *sq km*), *pop* 9,420,644 **2** city, its ✳ *pop* 7,206,704 — see NEW DELHI

Dells of the Wisconsin *or* **Wisconsin Dells** \'delz\ gorge of Wisconsin River in S *central* Wis.

Del·mar·va Peninsula \del-'mär-və\ peninsula E U.S. between Chesapeake & Delaware bays comprising Del. & parts of Md. & Va. — see EASTERN SHORE

Del·men·horst \'del-mən-,hȯrst\ city NW Germany in Lower Saxony WSW of Bremen *pop* 75,967

De·los \'dē-,läs\ *or Greek* **Dhí·los** \'thē-,lȯs\ island Greece in *central* Cyclades *area* 2 *sq mi* (5.2 *sq km*) — **De·lian** \'dē-lē-ən, 'dēl-yən\ *adjective or noun*

Del·phi \'del-,fī\ ancient town *central* Greece in Phocis on S slope of Mt. Parnassus near present village of **Dhel·foi** \thel-'fē\

Del·ray Beach \'del-,rā\ city SE Fla. S of Palm Beach *pop* 47,181

Del Rio \del-'rē-(,)ō\ city S Tex. on Rio Grande *pop* 30,705

Del·ta \'del-tə\ municipality Canada in SW British Columbia *pop* 88,978

Delta, The region NW Miss. between Mississippi & Yazoo rivers

Demavend — see DAMAVAND

Dem·e·ra·ra \,de-mə-'rär-ə, -'rar-\ river 200 *mi* (322 *km*) Guyana flowing N into the Atlantic

Denali, Denali National Park — see MCKINLEY (Mount)

Den·bigh \'den-bē\ *or* **Den·bigh·shire** \-,shir, -shər\ former county N Wales ✳ Ruthin

Den·der·mon·de \,den-dər-'män-də\ *or French* **Ter·monde** \ter-'mō"d\ commune NW *central* Belgium *pop* 42,499

Den Hel·der \dən-'hel-dər\ commune W Netherlands in N. Holland on an outlet from Wadden Zee to North Sea *pop* 61,149

Den·i·son \'de-nə-sən\ city NE Tex. on Red River *pop* 21,505

De·niz·li \,de-nəz-'lē\ city SW Turkey SE of Izmir *pop* 204,118

Den·mark \'den-,märk\ *or Danish* **Dan·mark** \'dän-,märk\ country N Europe occupying most of

Jutland Peninsula & adjacent islands in Baltic & North seas; a kingdom ✳ Copenhagen *area* 16,629 *sq mi* (43,069 *sq km*), *pop* 5,129,778

Denmark Strait strait 130 *mi* (209 *km*) wide between SE Greenland & Iceland connecting Arctic Ocean with the Atlantic

Dent Blanche \dän-'blän¹sh\ mountain 14,295 *ft* (4357 *m*) S Switzerland in Pennine Alps

Dent du Mi-di \dän-dū-mē-'dē\ mountain 10,686 *ft* (3257 *m*) SW Switzerland in W Alps

Den-ton \'den-t⁹n\ city N Tex. NW of Dallas *pop* 66,270

D'En-tre-cas-teaux Islands \,dän-trə-'kas-(,)tō\ islands SW Pacific N of E tip of New Guinea belonging to Papua New Guinea *area* 1200 *sq mi* (3120 *sq km*), *pop* 38,894

Den-ver \'den-vər\ city N central Colo., its ✳ *pop* 467,610 — **Den-ver-ite** \-və-,rīt\ *noun*

Dept-ford \'det-fərd\ former metropolitan borough SE London, England, now part of Lewisham

Der-be \'dər-(,)bē\ ancient town S Asia Minor in S Lycaonia on border of Cilicia; exact site unknown

Der-bent *or* **Der-bend** \dər-'bent\ city S Russia in Europe in Dagestan on Caspian Sea *pop* 81,500

Der-by \'där-bē, *chiefly United States* 'dər-\ city N central England in Derbyshire *pop* 214,000

Der-by-shire \'där-bē-,shir, -shər; *United States also* -,shir\ *or* **Derby** county N central England ✳ Matlock *area* 1052 *sq mi* (2725 *sq km*), *pop* 914,600

Derna — *see* DARNAH

Der-ry \'der-ē\ **1** city SE N.H. SE of Manchester *pop* 29,603 **2** *or* **Lon-don-der-ry** \,lən-dən-'der-ē; 'lən-dən-,der-ē, -d(ə-)rē\ district NW Northern Ireland, established 1974 *area* 148 *sq mi* (383 *sq km*), *pop* 94,918 **3** *or* **Londonderry** county borough & port, NW Derry district *pop* 62,697

Der-went \'dər-wənt\ river more than 105 *mi* (170 *km*) Australia in Tasmania flowing SE into Tasman Sea

Derwent Water lake NW England in Lake District in Cumbria

Desaguadero — *see* SALADO

Des-chutes \dā-'shüt\ river 250 *mi* (402 *km*) central & N Oreg. E of Cascade Range flowing N into Columbia River

Des-er-et \,de-zə-'ret\ provisional state of the U.S. S of 42d parallel & W of the Rockies organized 1849 by Mormons

Des Moines \di-'móin\ **1** river 327 *mi* (526 *km*) Iowa flowing SE into Mississippi River **2** city ✳ of Iowa on Des Moines River *pop* 193,187

Des-na \dyi-'snä\ river 550 *mi* (885 *km*) SW Russia in Europe & N Ukraine flowing S into the Dnieper

De So-to \di-'sō-(,)tō\ city NE Tex. S of Dallas *pop* 30,544

Des Plaines \des-'plänz\ **1** river 150 *mi* (241 *km*) NE Ill. flowing S to unite with Kankakee River forming Illinois River **2** city NE Ill. NW of Chicago *pop* 53,223

Des-roches \dā-'rōsh\ island NW Indian Ocean NNE of Madagascar belonging to Seychelles

Des-sau \'de-,saú\ city central Germany NE of Halle *pop* 95,097

De-troit \di-'tróit, *locally also* 'dē-,\ **1** river 31 *mi* (50 *km*) Ontario & SE Mich. connecting Lake Erie & Lake Saint Clair **2** city SE Mich. on Detroit River *pop* 1,027,974 — **De-troit-er** \di-'trói-tər\ *noun*

Detskoe Selo — *see* PUSHKIN

Deur-ne \'dər-nə, 'dərn\ commune N Belgium, E suburb of Antwerp

Deutsche Demokratische Republik — *see* GERMANY

Deutschland — *see* GERMANY

De-ven-ter \'dā-vən-tər\ commune E Netherlands *pop* 68,004

Devil Mountain — *see* AUYÁN-TEPUÍ

Devil's Island *or French* **Île du Dia-ble** \,ēl-dū-'dyäbl¹\ island French Guiana in the Safety Islands group; former penal colony

Devils Post-pile \'pōst-,pīl\ lava formation E central Calif. SE of Yosemite National Park; feature of **Devils Postpile National Monument**

Devils Tower *or* **Ma-to Tepee** \'mä-(,)tō\ columnar rock formation NE Wyo. rising 865 *ft* (264 *m*) in **Devils Tower National Monument**

Dev-on \'de-vən\ *or* **Dev-on-shire** \'de-vən-,shir, -shər\ county SW England ✳ Exeter *area* 2686 *sq mi* (6957 *sq km*), *pop* 998,200

Devon Island island Northwest Territories, Canada in E Parry Islands N of Baffin Is. *area* 20,861 *sq mi* (54,239 *sq km*)

Dews-bury \'düz-,ber-ē, 'dyüz-, -b(ə-)rē\ town N England in W. Yorkshire S of Leeds *pop* 48,339

Dez \'dez\ river 250 *mi* (402 *km*) W Iran flowing S to the Karun

Dezh-nev, Cape \'dezh-nyif\ *or Russian* **Mys Dezh-ne-va** \'mis-,dezh-'nyò-və, ,desh-\ cape NE Russia in Asia at E end of Chukchi Peninsula

Dhah-ran \dä-'rän, thäh-'ran\ town SE Saudi Arabia on Persian Gulf near Bahrain Islands *pop* 12,500

Dha-ka \'dä-kə\ *or* **Dac-ca** \'da-kə, 'dä-\ city ✳ of Bangladesh *pop* 3,637,892

Dhau-la-gi-ri, Mount \,daù-lə-'gir-ē\ mountain 26,810 *ft* (8172 *m*) W central Nepal in the Himalayas

Di-a-blo, Mount \dē-'ä-(,)blō, dī-'a-\ mountain 3849 *ft* (1173 *m*) central Calif. at N end of **Diab-lo Range**

Di-a-man-ti-na **1** \,dī-ə-,man-'tē-nə\ intermittent river maximum length 560 *mi* (901 *km*) E central Australia in SW Queensland flowing SW into the Warburton **2** \dē-ə-\ city E Brazil in central Minas Gerais *pop* 26,075

Di-a-mond \'dī-(ə-)mənd\ *or* **Kum-gang** \'kùm-,gän\ mountains SE N. Korea; highest 5374 *ft* (1638 *m*)

Diamond Bar city S Calif. E of Los Angeles *pop* 53,672

Diamond Head promontory Hawaii on Oahu Is. in SE Honolulu

Die-go Gar-cia \dē-,ā-gō-,gär-'sē-ə\ island in Indian Ocean, chief island of Chagos Archipelago

Diégo–Suarez — *see* ANTSIRANANA

Dien Bien Phu \,dyen-,byen-'fü\ village NW Vietnam

Dieppe \'dyep\ city & port N France N of Rouen *pop* 25,607

Di-jon \dē-'zhòⁿ\ city E France *pop* 151,636

Diks-mui-de *or* **Dix-mui-de** \dik-'smī-də\ *or* **Dix-mude** \dēk-'smüd\ town W Belgium in W. Flanders N of Ieper *pop* 15,273

Di-li *or* **Dil-li** \'di-lē\ city & port N Timor, formerly ✳ of Portuguese Timor

Di-mi-trov-grad \də-'mē-trəf-,grad, -,grät\ city S Bulgaria on the Maritsa ESE of Plovdiv *pop* 56,882

Dimitrovo — *see* PERNIK

Di-nar-ic Alps \də-'nar-ik\ range of E Alps W Slovenia, W Croatia, Bosnia and Herzegovina, & Montenegro; highest point 8274 *ft* (2522 *m*)

Din-gle Bay \'diŋ-gəl\ inlet of the Atlantic SW Ireland

Ding-wall \'diŋ-,wòl\ burgh N Scotland NW of Inverness *pop* 4815

Dinosaur National Monument reservation NW Colo. & NE Utah at junction of Green & Yampa rivers; rich fossil deposits

Di-o-mede Islands \'dī-ə-,mēd\ islands in Bering Strait comprising **Big Diomede** (Russia) & **Little Diomede** (U.S.)

Diospolis — *see* THEBES

Di-re Da-wa \,dē-rä-'daú-ä\ city E Ethiopia *pop* 121,887

Disko — *see* QEQERTARSUAQ

Dismal Swamp *or* **Great Dismal Swamp** swamp SE Va. & NE N.C. between Chesapeake Bay & Albemarle Sound *about* 37 *mi* (60 *km*) long, 10 *mi* (16 *km*) wide

District of Co-lum-bia \kə-'ləm-bē-ə\ federal district E U.S. coextensive with city of Washington *area* 69 *sq mi* (179 *sq km*), *pop* 609,909

Dis-tri-to Fe-de-ral \di-'strē-tō-,fā-thā-'räl\ **1** district E Argentina largely comprising ✳ city of Buenos Aires *area* 77 *sq mi* (199 *sq km*), *pop* 2,960,976 **2** — *see* FEDERAL DISTRICT 1 **3** *or* **Federal District** district central Mexico including ✳ city of Mexico City *area* 579 *sq mi* (1500 *sq km*), *pop* 8,235,744 **4** *or* **Federal District** district N Venezuela including ✳ city of Caracas *area* 745 *sq mi* (1937 *sq km*), *pop* 2,103,661

Diu \'dē-(,)ü\ district W India at S end of Kathiawar Peninsula; a constituent part of the union territory of Daman and Diu — *see* GOA, PORTUGUESE INDIA

Di-yar-ba-kir \di-,yär-bä-'kir\ *or* **Di-ar-bekr** \-'be-kər\ city SE Turkey on the Tigris *pop* 381,144

Djakarta — *see* JAKARTA

Djawa — *see* JAVA

Djerba — *see* JERBA

Dji-bou-ti \jə-'bü-tē\ **1** *or formerly* **French Territory of the Afars and the Is-sas** \'ä-,fär(z) . . . ē-'sä(z)\ *or earlier* **French Somaliland** country E Africa on Gulf of Aden; a republic *area* 8880 *sq mi* (23,088 *sq km*), *pop* 510,000 **2** city, its ✳ *pop* 300,000

Dnie-per \'nē-pər\ river 1420 *mi* (2285 *km*) Ukraine, E Belarus, & W Russia in Europe rising in S Valdai Hills & flowing S into Black Sea

Dnies-ter \'nēs-tər\ river 877 *mi* (1411 *km*) W Ukraine & E Moldova rising on N slope of Carpathian Mountains near Polish border & flowing SE into Black Sea

Dni-pro-dzer-zhyns'k *or* **Dne-pro-dzer-zhinsk** \də-,nye-prə-dzir-'zhēnsk\ city E central Ukraine on the Dnieper W of Dnipropetrovs'k *pop* 284,000

Dni-pro-pe-trovs'k *or* **Dne-pro-pe-trovsk** \də-,nye-prə-pə-'tròfsk\ *or formerly* **Eka-te-ri-no-slav** \i-,kä-ti-'rē-nə-,släf, -,släv\ city E Ukraine *pop* 1,189,000

Do-be-rai \'dō-bə-,rī\ *or formerly* **Vo-gel-kop** \'vō-gəl-,käp\ peninsula Indonesia in NW W. Irian

Do-bru-ja *or* **Do-bru-dja** \'dō-brü-jä, -jə\ region S Europe in Romania & Bulgaria on Black Sea S of the Danube

Do-de-ca-nese \dō-'de-kə-,nēz, -,nēs; ,dō-di-kə-'\ islands Greece in the SE Aegean comprising the Southern Sporades S of Ikaria & Samos; belonged to Italy 1923–47 *area* 486 *sq mi* (1264 *sq km*) *pop* 162,439 — *see* RHODES — **Do-de-ca-ne-sian** \,dō-di-kə-'nē-zhən, ,dō-,de-kə-'nē-zhən, ,dō-di-kə-, -shən\ *adjective or noun*

Dodge City \'däj\ city S Kans. on Arkansas River *pop* 21,129

Do-do-ma \dō-'dō-(,)mä\ town NE central Tanzania, since 1974 designated as the future national ✳

Dog-ger Bank \'dò-gər, 'dä-\ submerged sandbank *about* 150 *mi* (241 *km*) long in North Sea E of N England

Do-ha \'dō-(,)hä\ city & port ✳ of Qatar on Persian Gulf *pop* 217,294

Dol-gel-lau \dòl-'ge-(,h)lī, -'geth-,lī\ town W Wales in Gwynedd, formerly ✳ of Merionethshire

Dol-lard–des–Or-meaux \dò-'lär-,dā-,zór-'mō\ town Canada in S Quebec NW of Montreal *pop* 46,922

Do-lo-mites \'dō-lə-,mīts, 'dä-\ range of E Alps NE Italy between Adige & Piave rivers — *see* MARMOLADA

Dol-ton \'dōl-t⁹n\ village NE Ill. S of Chicago *pop* 23,930

Dôme, Puy de \,pwē-də-'dōm\ mountain 4806 *ft* (1465 *m*) S central France in Auvergne Mountains

Dom-i-ni-ca \,dä-mə-'nē-kə, ÷də-'mi-nə-kə\ island Brit. West Indies in the Lesser Antilles; a republic of the Commonwealth of Nations since 1978 ✳ Roseau *area* 289 *sq mi* (749 *sq km*), *pop* 74,000

Do-min-i-can Republic \də-'mi-ni-kən\ *or formerly* **San-to Do-min-go** \,san-tə-də-'miŋ-(,)gō, ,sän-tō-thō-\ *or* **San Domingo** \san-də-, ,sän-dō-\ country W. Indies on E Hispaniola; a republic ✳ Santo Domingo *area* 18,657 *sq mi* (48,322 *sq km*), *pop* 7,634,000 — **Dominican** *adjective or noun*

Don \'dän\ river 1224 *mi* (1969 *km*) Russia in Europe flowing SE & then SW into Sea of Azov

Donau — *see* DANUBE

Don-cas-ter \'däŋ-kəs-tər\ borough N England in S. Yorkshire *pop* 81,610

Don-e-gal \,dä-ni-'gòl, ,də-\ county NW Ireland (republic) in Ulster ✳ Lifford *area* 1865 *sq mi* (4849 *sq km*), *pop* 128,117

Donegal Bay inlet of the Atlantic NW Ireland

Do-nets \'nets, -'nyets\ river *over* 630 *mi* (1014 *km*) SE Ukraine & SW Russia in Europe flowing SE into Don River

Donets Basin *or* **Don·bass** *or* **Don·bas** \ˌdän-'bas\ region E Ukraine SW of the Donets

Do·netsk \də-'nyetsk\ *or formerly* **Sta·li·no** \'stä-lyi-ˌnō, 'sta-\ *or* **Sta·lin** \'stä-lyin, 'sta-, -ˌlēn\ city E Ukraine in Donets Basin *pop* 1,121,000

Don·ner Pass \'dä-nər\ mountain pass *about* 7090 *ft* (2160 *m*) E Calif. in Sierra Nevada

Don·ny·brook \'dä-nē-ˌbrük\ city E Ireland in Leinster, SE suburb of Dublin

Doornik — see TOURNAI

Door Peninsula \'dōr, 'dȯr\ peninsula E Wis. between Green Bay & Lake Michigan

Dor·ches·ter \'dȯr-chəs-tər, -ˌches-\ borough S England ✳ of Dorset *pop* 14,049

Dor·dogne \dȯr-'dōn, -'dȯ-nyə\ river 293 *mi* (471 *km*) SW France flowing SW & W to unite with the Garonne forming the Gironde Estuary

Dor·drecht \'dȯr-ˌdrekt, -ˌdrekt\ commune SW Netherlands in S. Holland on the Meuse *pop* 112,687

Dore, Monts \mōⁿ-'dōr, -'dȯr\ mountain group S *central* France in Auvergne Mountains — see SANCY (Puy de)

Do·ris \'dōr-əs, 'dȯr-, 'där-\ **1** ancient country *central* Greece between Mounts Oeta & Parnassus **2** ancient district SW Asia Minor on coast of Caria

Dor·noch \'dȯr-nək, -nәk\ royal burgh N Scotland in Highland region N of Inverness

Dorpat — see TARTU

Dor·set \'dȯr-sət\ *or* **Dor·set·shire** \-ˌshir, -shər\ county S England ✳ Dorchester *area* 1062 *sq mi* (2750 *sq km*), *pop* 645,200

Dort·mund \'dȯrt-ˌmùnt, -mənd\ city W Germany in the Ruhr *pop* 601,007

Do·than \'dō-thən\ city SE Ala. *pop* 53,589

Dou·ai \dü-'ā\ city N France S of Lille *pop* 44,195

Dou·a·la \dü-'ä-lä\ city & port SW Cameroon on Bight of Biafra *pop* 810,000

Doug·las \'də-gləs\ borough ✳ of Isle of Man *pop* 22,214

Dou·ro \'dȯr-(ˌ)ü, 'dȯr-\ *or Spanish* **Due·ro** \'dwä-rō\ river 556 *mi* (895 *km*) N Spain & N Portugal flowing W into the Atlantic

Do·ver \'dō-vər\ **1** city *central* Del., its ✳ *pop* 27,630 **2** city SE N.H. *pop* 25,042 **3** borough SE England in Kent on Strait of Dover *pop* 32,843

Dover, Strait of *or French* **Pas de Ca·lais** \ˌpäd-kȧ-'lā\ channel between SE England & N France, easternmost section of English Channel; 20 *mi* (32 *km*) wide at narrowest point

Down \'daùn\ **1** district SE Northern Ireland, established 1974 *area* 250 *sq mi* (650 *sq km*), *pop* 57,511 **2** traditional county SE Northern Ireland

Dow·ners Grove \'daù-nərz\ village NE Ill. *pop* 46,858

Dow·ney \'daù-nē\ city SW Calif. SE of Los Angeles *pop* 91,444

Down·pat·rick \daùn-'pa-trik\ town SE Northern Ireland in Down district *pop* 8245

Downs \'daùnz\ **1** two ranges of hills SE England — see NORTH DOWNS, SOUTH DOWNS **2** roadstead in English Channel along E coast of Kent protected by the Goodwin Sands

Down Under Australia or New Zealand

Dra·chen·fels \'drä-kən-ˌfelz\ hill 1053 *ft* (321 *m*) W Germany in the Siebengebirge on the Rhine S of Bonn

Dra·cut \'drā-kət\ town NE Mass. N of Lowell *pop* 25,594

Dra·kens·berg \'drä-kənz-ˌbərg\ *or* **Kwath·lam·ba** \kwät-'läm-bə\ mountains S Republic of S. Africa & in Lesotho; highest Thabana Ntlenyana 11,425 *ft* (3482 *m*)

Drake Passage \'drāk\ strait S of S. America between Cape Horn & S. Shetlands

Dram·men \'drä-mən\ city & port SE Norway *pop* 51,978

Dran·cy \dräⁿ-'sē\ commune N France, NE of Paris *pop* 60,928

Dra·va *or* **Dra·ve** \'drä-və\ river 447 *mi* (719 *km*) S Austria, NE Slovenia, & N tip of Croatia flowing SE into the Danube

Dren·the \'dren-tə\ province NE Netherlands ✳ Assen *area* 1037 *sq mi* (2686 *sq km*), *pop* 448,256

Dres·den \'drez-dən\ city E Germany in Saxony *pop* 485,132

Dri·na \'drē-nə\ river 285 *mi* (459 *km*) flowing N along the border between Bosnia & Serbia into the Sava

Dro·ghe·da \'drȯi-ə-də, 'drȯ-i-də\ town & port E Ireland in County Louth on the Boyne *pop* 23,845

Drug — see DURG

Drum·mond·ville \'drə-mən(d)-ˌvil\ town Canada in S Quebec NE of Montreal *pop* 35,462

Dry Tor·tu·gas \tȯr-'tü-gəz\ island group S Fla. W of Key West; site of **Dry Tortugas National Monument**

Duar·te \'dwär-tē, dü-'är-\ city SW Calif. *pop* 20,688

Du·bawnt \dü-'bȯnt\ river 580 *mi* (933 *km*) N Canada flowing NE through Dubawnt Lake to **Ba·ker Lake** \'bā-kər\ (W expansion of Chesterfield Inlet)

Dubawnt Lake lake N Canada in SE Northwest Territories E of Great Slave Lake

Du·bayy *or* **Du·bai** \(ˌ)dü-'bī\ **1** sheikhdom, member of United Arab Emirates 1500 *sq mi* (3885 *sq km*) **2** city, its ✳ *pop* 265,702

Dub·lin \'də-blən\ *or for 2 and 3 Irish Gaelic* **Bai·le Atha Cli·ath** \blä-'klē-ə\ **1** city W Calif. ESE of Oakland *pop* 23,229 **2** county E Ireland in Leinster *area* 356 *sq mi* (926 *sq km*), *pop* 546,915 **3** city & county borough & port ✳ of Ireland (republic) & of County Dublin at mouth of the Liffey on **Dublin Bay** (inlet of Irish Sea) *pop* 477,675 — **Dub·lin·er** \'də-blə-nər\ *noun*

Du·brov·nik \'dü-ˌbrȯv-nik, dú-'brȯv-nik\ city & port S Croatia *pop* 55,638

Du·buque \də-'byük\ city E Iowa on Mississippi River *pop* 57,546

Dud·ley \'dəd-lē\ borough W *central* England in W. Midlands WNW of Birmingham *pop* 300,400

Duis·burg \'dü-əs-ˌbərg, 'düz-, 'dyüz-, *German* 'dēs-ˌbùrk\ *or formerly* **Duis·burg–Ham·born** \-ˌhäm-ˌbȯrn\ city W Germany at junction of Rhine & Ruhr rivers *pop* 537,441

Du·luth \də-'lüth\ city & port NE Minn. at W end of Lake Superior *pop* 85,493 — **Du·luth·ian** \-'lü-thē-ən\ *adjective or noun*

Dul·wich \'də-lij, -lich\ a SE district of London, England

Dum·bar·ton \ˌdəm-'bär-t^ən\ **1** burgh W *central* Scotland in Strathclyde *pop* 79,750 **2** *or* **Dum·bar·ton·shire** \-ˌshir, -shər\ DUNBARTON

Dum·fries \ˌdəm-'frēs, -'frēz\ **1** *or* **Dum·fries·shire** \-'frēsh-ˌshir, -shir, -shər\ former county S Scotland ✳ Dumfries **2** burgh S Scotland of Dumfries and Galloway *pop* 32,084

Dumfries and Gal·lo·way \'ga-lə-ˌwā\ region S Scotland, established 1975 ✳ Dumfries *area* 2481 *sq mi* (6425 *sq km*), *pop* 147,900

Dun·bar·ton \ˌdən-'bär-t^ən\ *or* **Dun·bar·ton·shire** \-ˌshir, -shər\ former county W *central* Scotland ✳ Dumbarton

Dun·can \'dəŋ-kən\ city S Okla. *pop* 21,732

Dun·can·ville \'dəŋ-kən-ˌvil, -vəl\ city NE Tex. *pop* 35,748

Dun·dalk \ˌdən-'dȯ(l)k\ town & port NE Ireland (republic) on **Dundalk Bay** (inlet of Irish sea) ✳ of County Louth *pop* 26,669

Dun·das \'dən-dəs\ town Canada in SE Ontario *pop* 21,868

Dun·dee \ˌdən-'dē\ city & port E Scotland ✳ of Tayside on Firth of Tay *pop* 172,860

Dun·e·din \ˌdə-'nē-d^ən\ **1** city W Fla. N of Clearwater *pop* 34,012 **2** — see EDINBURGH **3** city New Zealand on SE coast of South Is. at head of Otago Harbor *pop* 116,577

Dun·ferm·line \ˌdən-'fərm-lən\ royal burgh E Scotland in Fife *pop* 129,910

Dun·gan·non \ˌdən-'ga-nən\ district S Northern Ireland, established 1974 *area* 301 *sq mi* (783 *sq km*), *pop* 45,322

Dun·kerque *or* **Dun·kirk** \'dən-ˌkərk, ˌdən-'\ city & port N France on Strait of Dover *pop* 71,071

Dun Laoghai·re \ˌdən-'ler-ə\ *or formerly* **Kings·town** \'kiŋz-ˌtaùn\ borough & port E Ireland in Leinster on Dublin Bay *pop* 54,715

Dun·net Head \'də-nət\ headland N Scotland on N coast W of John o'Groat's; northernmost point of mainland, at 58°50'N

Duns \'dənz\ burgh SE Scotland in Borders region *pop* 2249

Du·que de Ca·xi·as \ˌdü-kē-dē-kə-'shē-əs\ city SE Brazil in Rio de Janeiro state N of city of Rio de Janeiro *pop* 664,643

Du·ran·go \dü-'raŋ-(ˌ)gō, dyü-; dü-'räŋ-gō\ **1** state NW *central* Mexico *area* 46,196 *sq mi* (119,648 *sq km*), *pop* 1,349,378 **2** city, its ✳ *pop* 414,015

Dur·ban \'dər-bən\ city & port E Republic of South Africa in E KwaZulu-Natal on Natal Bay *pop* 736,852

Durg \'dùrg\ *or formerly* **Drug** \'drüg\ city E *central* India in SE Madhya Pradesh E of Nagpur *pop* 150,513

Dur·ham \'dər-əm, 'də-rəm, 'dùr-əm\ **1** city NE *central* N.C. NW of Raleigh *pop* 136,611 **2** county N England bordering on North Sea *area* 974 *sq mi* (2523 *sq km*), *pop* 589,800 **3** city, its ✳, S of Newcastle *pop* 26,442

Dur·res \'dùr-əs\ *or Italian* **Du·raz·zo** \dü-'rät-(ˌ)sō\ *or ancient* **Ep·i·dam·nus** \ˌe-pə-'dam-nəs\ *or* **Dyr·ra·chi·um** \də-'rā-kē-əm\ city & port Albania on Adriatic Sea W of Tiranë *pop* 85,500

Du·shan·be \dü-'sham-bə, dyü-, -'shäm-; 'dyü-; ˌdyü-shäm-'bä\ *or formerly* **Sta·lin·a·bad** \stä-lyi-nə-ˌbäd, ˌsta-li-nə-'bad\ city ✳ of Tajikistan *pop* 595,000

Düs·sel·dorf \'dü-səl-ˌdȯrf, 'dyü-, 'dœ-\ city W Germany on the Rhine N of Cologne ✳ of N. Rhine-Westphalia *pop* 577,561

Dutch Borneo — see KALIMANTAN

Dutch Guiana — SEE SURINAME

Dutch New Guinea — see IRIAN JAYA

Dvi·na \dvē-'nä, 'dvē-nə\ river 466 *mi* (750 *km*) N Russia in Europe flowing NW into White Sea

Dvina, Western river 634 *mi* (1020 *km*) Latvia, W Belarus, & W Russia in Europe rising in Valdai Hills & flowing W into Gulf of Riga

Dvina Gulf *or* **Dvina Bay** *or formerly* **Gulf of Arch·an·gel** \'är-ˌkān-jəl\ arm of White Sea N Russia in Europe

Dvinsk — see DAUGAVPILS

Dy·fed \'də-ved, -vəd\ county SW Wales ✳ Carmarthen *area* 2227 *sq mi* (5768 *sq km*), *pop* 341,600

Dzaudzhikau — see VLADIKAVKAZ

Dzer·zhinsk \dzər-'zhēn(t)sk\ city *central* Russia in Europe on Oka River W of Nizhniy Novgorod *pop* 287,000

Dzungaria *or* **Dzungarian Basin** — see JUNGGAR

Ea·gan \'ē-gən\ city SE Minn. *pop* 47,409

Ea·gle Lake \'ē-gəl\ lake 13 *mi* (21 *km*) long N Calif. ENE of Lassen Peak

Eagle Pass city SW Tex. on Rio Grande *pop* 20,651

Ea·ling \'ē-liŋ\ borough of W Greater London, England *pop* 263,600

East An·glia \'aŋ-glē-ə\ region E England including Norfolk & Suffolk; one of kingdoms in Anglo-Saxon heptarchy *pop* 1,366,300 — **East An·gli·an** \-ən\ *adjective or noun*

East Antarctica — see ANTARCTICA

East Bengal the part of Bengal now in Bangladesh

East Beskids — see BESKIDS

East·bourne \'ēs(t)-ˌbȯrn, -ˌbȯrn\ town S England in E. Sussex on English Channel *pop* 83,200

East Chicago city NW Ind. SE of Chicago, Ill. *pop* 33,892

East China Sea sea W Pacific between China (on W), S. Korea (on N), Japan & Ryukyu Islands (on E), & Taiwan (on S)

East Cleveland city NE Ohio NE of Cleveland *pop* 33,096

East Detroit city SE Mich. NE of Detroit *pop* 35,283

East·er Island \'ē-stər\ *or* **Ra·pa Nui** \ˌrä-pə-'nü-ē\ *or Spanish* **Is·la de Pas·cua** \ˌēs-lä-thā-'päs-kwä\ island Chile in SE Pacific 2000 *mi* (3200 *km*) W of coast *area* 46 *sq mi* (119 *sq km*) — **Easter Islander** *noun*

\ə\ abut \ᵊ\ kitten \ər\ further \a\ ash \ā\ ace \ä\ mop, mar \aù\ out \ch\ chin \e\ bet \ē\ easy \g\ go \i\ hit \ī\ ice \j\ job \ŋ\ sing \ō\ go \ȯ\ law \ȯi\ boy \th\ thin \t̷h\ the \ü\ loot \ù\ foot \y\ yet \zh\ vision *see also* Guide to Pronunciation

Eastern Cape or **Oos Kaap** \ōs-'käp\ province SE Republic of South Africa area 65,483 sq mi (169,600 sq km), pop 6,504,000

Eastern Ghats \'gäts, 'góts, 'gəts\ chain of mountains SE India extending SW & S from near delta of the Mahanadi in Orissa to W Tamil Nadu; highest point Mt. Dodabetta (in Nilgiri Hills) 8640 ft (2633 m) — see WESTERN GHATS

Eastern Rumelia region S Bulgaria including Rhodope Mountains & the Maritsa valley

Eastern Samoa — see AMERICAN SAMOA

Eastern Shore region E Md. & E Va. E of Chesapeake Bay; sometimes considered as including Del. — see DELMARVA PENINSULA

Eastern Thrace — see THRACE

Eastern Transvaal — see MPUMALANGA

East Flanders province NW central Belgium ✳ Ghent area 1151 sq mi (2981 sq km), pop 1,335,793

East Frisian — see FRISIAN ISLANDS

East Germany the German Democratic Republic — see GERMANY

East Ham \'ēst-'ham\ former county borough SE England in Essex, now part of Newham

East Hartford town central Conn. pop 50,452

East Ha·ven \'ēst-,hā-vən\ town S Conn. SE of New Haven pop 26,144

East Indies 1 or **East India** southeastern Asia including India, Indochina, Malaya, & Malay Archipelago — a chiefly former name 2 the Malay Archipelago — **East Indian** adjective or noun

East·lake \'ēst-,lāk\ city NE Ohio NE of Cleveland pop 21,161

East Lansing city S Mich. pop 50,677

East London city & port S Republic of South Africa in SE Eastern Cape on Indian Ocean pop 119,727

East Los Angeles urban center SW Calif. pop 126,379

East Lo·thi·an \'lō-thē-ən\ or **Had·ding·ton** \'ha-diŋ-tən\ or **Had·ding·ton·shire** \-,shir, -shər\ former county SE Scotland ✳ Haddington — see LOTHIAN

East·main \'ēst-,mān\ river about 500 mi (804 km) in W Quebec

East Malaysia the parts of Malaysia on the island of Borneo, comprising Sabah and Sarawak

East Moline city NW Ill. on Mississippi River pop 20,147

Eas·ton \'ēs-tən\ 1 city SE Mass. SW of Brockton pop 19,807 2 city E Pa. NE of Allentown pop 26,276

East Orange city NE N.J. NW of Newark pop 73,552

East Pakistan the former E division of Pakistan comprising the E portion of Bengal — see BANGLADESH

East Palo Alto city W Calif. pop 23,451

East Peoria city central Ill. pop 21,378

East Point \'ēst-,póint\ city NW central Ga. SW of Atlanta pop 34,402

East Providence city E R.I. pop 50,380

East Prussia region N Europe bordering on the Baltic E of Pomerania; formerly a province of Prussia, for a time (1919–39) separated from rest of Prussia by Polish Corridor; divided 1945 between Poland & U.S.S.R. (Russia & Lithuania)

East Punjab — see PUNJAB

East Ridge \'ēst-,rij\ town SE Tenn. SE of Chattanooga pop 21,101

East Riding — see YORK

East River strait SE N.Y. connecting Upper New York Bay with Long Island Sound & separating Manhattan Is. from Long Is.

East Saint Louis city SW Ill. pop 40,944

East Siberian Sea sea, arm of Arctic Ocean N of E Russia in Asia extending from New Siberian Islands to Wrangel Is.

East Strouds·burg \'straúdz-,bərg\ borough E Pa. pop 8781

East Suffolk — see SUFFOLK

East Sus·sex \'sə-siks, United States also -,seks\ county SE England ✳ Lewes area 718 sq mi (1860 sq km), pop 670,600

East York borough Canada in SE Ontario near Toronto pop 102,696

Eau Claire \ō-'klar, -'kler\ city W Wis. pop 56,856

Eb·bw Vale \'e-bü-'väl\ town SE Wales in W Gwent pop 24,422

Eboracum — see YORK

Ebro \'ā-(,)brō\ river 565 mi (909 km) NE Spain flowing from Cantabrian Mountains ESE into the Mediterranean

Ecbatana — see HAMADAN

Ec·ua·dor \'e-kwə-,dór\ or \,e-kwä-'thòr\ country W S. America bordering on the Pacific; a republic ✳ Quito area 109,483 sq mi (283,561 sq km), pop 10,985,000 — **Ec·ua·dor·an** \,e-kwə-'dór-ən, -'dór-\ adjective or noun — **Ec·ua·dor·ean** or **Ec·ua·dor·ian** \-ē-ən\ adjective or noun

Edam \ē-dəm, -,dam, Dutch ā-'däm\ commune NW Netherlands on the IJsselmeer NNE of Amsterdam pop 23,853

Ede 1 \'ā-də\ commune E Netherlands NW of Arnhem pop 96,044 2 \'ā-,dā\ city SW Nigeria NE of Ibadan pop 271,000

Eden Prairie \'ē-d°n\ village SE central Minn., a suburb of Minneapolis pop 39,311

Edes·sa \i-'de-sə\ 1 city N Greece in W Macedonia; ancient ✳ of Macedonian kings pop 17,624 2 — see URFA

Edi·na \i-'dī-nə\ village SE Minn. SW of Minneapolis pop 46,070

Ed·in·boro \'e-d°n-,bər-ə, -,bə-rə\ borough NW corner of Pa. pop 7736

Ed·in·burg \'e-d°n-,bərg\ city S Tex. NW of Brownsville pop 29,885

Ed·in·burgh \'e-d°n-,bər-ə, -,bə-rə, -b(ə-)rə\ 1 or Scottish Gaelic **Dun·e·din** \,də-'nē-d°n\ city ✳ of Scotland & of Lothian region on Firth of Forth pop 434,520 2 or **Ed·in·burgh·shire** \-,shir, -shər\ — see MIDLOTHIAN

Edir·ne \ā-'dir-nə\ or formerly **Adri·a·no·ple** \,ā-drē-ə-'nō-pəl\ city Turkey in Europe on the Maritsa pop 102,345

Ed·is·to \'e-də-,stō\ river 150 mi (241 km) S S.C. flowing into the Atlantic

Edith Ca·vell, Mount \'ē-dəth-'ka-vəl, -kə-'vel\ mountain 11,033 ft (3363 m) Canada in SW Alberta in Jasper National Park

Ed·mond \'ed-mənd\ city central Okla. N of Oklahoma City pop 52,315

Ed·monds \'ed-mən(d)z\ city W Wash. N of Seattle pop 30,744

Ed·mon·ton \'ed-mən-tən\ 1 city Canada ✳ of Alberta on the N. Saskatchewan pop 616,741 2 former municipal borough SE England in Middlesex, now part of Enfield — **Ed·mon·to·ni·an** \,ed-mən-'tō-nē-ən, -nyən\ noun

Edo — see TOKYO

Edom \'ē-dəm\ or **Id·u·maea** or **Id·u·mea** \,i-dyü-'mē-ə\ ancient country SW Asia S of Judea & the Dead Sea

Ed·ward, Lake \'ed-wərd\ lake E Africa SW of Lake Albert on boundary between NE Democratic Republic of the Congo & SW Uganda area 830 sq mi (2158 sq km)

Ed·wards \'ed-wərdz\ plateau 2000–5000 ft (610–1524 m) SW Tex.

Efa·te \ā-'fä-,tā\ or French **Va·té** \vä-'tā\ island SW Pacific in central Vanuatu; chief town Port‣ Vila ✳ of Vanuatu) area 353 sq mi (914 sq km), pop 30,422

Effigy Mounds National Monument site NE Iowa on Mississippi River NW of Dubuque including prehistoric mounds

Ega·di Islands \'e-gə-dē\ or ancient **Ae·ga·tes Islands** \ē-'gä-tēz\ islands Italy off W coast of Sicily area 15 sq mi (6 sq km), pop 4335

Eger \'ā-gər\ or Czech **Ohře** \'ór-zhə\ river 193 mi (311 km) E Germany & NW Czech Republic flowing NE into the Elbe

Eg·mont, Mount \'eg-,mänt\ or **Ta·ra·na·ki** \,tä-rä-'nä-kē\ mountain 8260 ft (2518 m) New Zealand in W central North Is.

Egypt \'ē-jipt\ or Arabic **Miṣr** \'misrⁿ\ country NE Africa bordering on Mediterranean & Red seas ✳ Cairo area 386,900 sq mi (1,002,071 sq km), pop 57,673,000 — see UNITED ARAB REPUBLIC

Ei·fel \'ī-fəl\ plateau region W Germany NW of the Moselle & NE of Luxembourg

Ei·ger \'ī-gər\ mountain 13,025 ft (3970 m) W central Switzerland NE of the Jungfrau

Eind·ho·ven \'īnt-,hō-və(n), 'änt-\ commune S Netherlands in N. Brabant pop 193,966

Eire — see IRELAND

Ei·se·nach \'ī-z°n-,äk, -,äk\ city central Germany in Thuringia W of Erfurt pop 44,266

Ekaterinodar — see KRASNODAR

Ekaterinoslav — see DNIPROPETROVS'K

El Aiún — see AAIÚN, EL

El Al·a·mein \,el-,a-lə-'mān\ village NW Egypt on the Mediterranean N of NE corner of Qattara Depression

Elam \'ē-ləm\ or **Su·si·ana** \,sü-zē-'a-nə, -'ä-, -'ä-\ ancient kingdom SW Asia E of Persian Gulf E of Babylonia ✳ Susa — **Elam·ite** \'ē-lə-,mīt\ adjective or noun

Elat \ā-'lat, ā-'lät\ town & port S Israel at head of Gulf of Aqaba pop 29,900

Elatea — see CITHAERON

Elath \'ē-,lath\ — see AQABA

Ela·zig \,e-lə-'zə, -'zē(g)\ city E central Turkey in valley of the upper Murat pop 204,603

El·ba \'el-bə\ island Italy in the Mediterranean between Corsica & mainland; chief town Portoferraio area 86 sq mi (224 sq km)

El Bahnasa — see OXYRHYNCHUS

El·be \'el-bə, 'elb\ or Czech **La·be** \'lä-be\ river 720 mi (1159 km) N Czech Republic & NE Germany flowing NW into North Sea

El·bert, Mount \'el-bərt\ mountain 14,433 ft (4399 m) central Colo. in Sawatch Range; highest in Colo. & Rocky Mountains

El·blag \'el-,blóŋk\ or German **El·bing** \'el-biŋ\ city & port N Poland near the Frisches Haff pop 125,154

El'·brus or **El·brus** \el-'brüz, -'brüs\ mountain 18,510 ft (5642 m) S Russia in Europe; highest in the Caucasus & in Europe

El·burz Mountains \el-'bùrz\ mountains N Iran parallel with S shore of Caspian Sea — see DAMAVAND

El Ca·jon \,el-kə-'hōn\ city SW Calif. E of San Diego pop 88,693

El Cen·tro \el-'sen-(,)trō\ city S Calif. in Imperial Valley pop 31,384

El Cer·ri·to \,el-sə-'rē-(,)tō\ city W Calif. on San Francisco Bay N of Berkeley pop 22,869

El·che \'el-(,)chā\ city SE Spain SW of Alicante pop 188,062

El Do·ra·do \,el-də-'rā-(,)dō, -'rä-də\ city S Ark. pop 23,146

Electric Peak mountain 10,992 ft (3350 m) S Mont. in Yellowstone National Park; highest in Gallatin Range

El·e·phan·ta \,e-lə-'fan-tə\ or **Gha·ra·pu·ri** \,gär-ə-'pùr-ē\ island W India in Bombay harbor

El·e·phan·ti·ne \,e-lə-,fan-'tī-nē, -fən-, -'tī-\ island S Egypt in the Nile opposite Aswân pop 1814

Eleu·sis \i-'lü-səs\ ancient deme W Attica NW of Athens; ruins at modern town of **Elev·sís** \,elef-'sēs\ in E Greece — **El·eu·sin·i·an** \,el-yü-'si-nē-ən\ adjective or noun

Eleu·thera \i-'lü-thə-rə\ island Bahamas E of New Providence Is. area 164 sq mi (426 sq km)

El Fai·yûm \,el-fā-'yüm, -,()fī-\ or **Al Fay·yūm** \,al-\ city N Egypt SSW of Cairo pop 166,910

El Fa·sher \el-'fa-shər\ city W Sudan in Darfur

El Fer·rol \,el-fe-'ról\ or **El Ferrol del Cau·dil·lo** \,thel-kaú-'thē-(,)yō, -'thēl-(,)yōl\ city & port NW Spain on the Atlantic pop 83,045

El Gezira — see GEZIRA

El·gin 1 \'el-jən\ city NE Ill. pop 77,010 2 \'el-gən\ or **El·gin·shire** \-,shir, -shər\ — see MORAY 3 \'el-gən\ royal burgh NE Scotland in Moray district of Grampian region pop 18,905

El Giza — see GIZA

El·gon, Mount \'el-,gän\ extinct volcano 14,178 ft (4321 m) E Africa on boundary between Uganda & Kenya NE of Lake Victoria

Elikón — see HELICON

Elis \'ē-ləs\ or New Greek **Ilía** \ē-'lē-ä\ region S Greece in NW Peloponnese S of Achaea bordering on Ionian Sea

Elisabethville — see LUBUMBASHI

Elisavetgrad — see KIROVOGRAD

Elisavetpol — see GANCA

Elis·ta \e-'lyē-stə, ē-'lis-tə\ town S Russia in Europe ✳ of Kalmykia pop 95,200

Eliz·a·beth \i-'li-zə-bəth\ 1 short river SE Va. flowing between cities of Norfolk & Portsmouth into Hampton Roads 2 city & port NE N.J. SW of Newark on Newark Bay pop 110,002

Elizabeth Islands islands SE Mass. between Buzzards Bay & Vineyard Sound

Elk Grove Village village NE Ill. NW of Chicago pop 33,429

Elk·hart \'el-,kärt\ city N Ind. E of S. Bend pop 43,627

Elk Island National Park reservation Canada in E central Alberta

Ellás — see GREECE

Elles·mere Island \'elz-ˌmir\ island Canada in Northwest Territories W of NW Greenland — see COLUMBIA (Cape)

Ellice — see TUVALU

El·lis Island \'e-ləs\ island SE N.Y. in Upper New York Bay; served as immigrant station 1892–1954

El·lo·ra \e-'lōr-ə, -'lór-\ village W India in central Maharashtra NW of Aurangabad; caves

Ells·worth Land \'elz-(ˌ)wərth\ region W Antarctica on Bellingshausen Sea

El Maghreb al Aqsa — see MAGHREB

El Ma·hal·la El Ku·bra \el-mə-'ha-lə-,el-'kü-brə\ city N Egypt in Nile delta NE of Tanta pop 400,000

El Man·sû·ra \,el-man-'sùr-ə\ or **Al Man·su·rah** \,al-\ city N Egypt in Nile delta

Elm·hurst \'elm-,hərst\ city NE Ill. W of Chicago pop 42,029

El Min·ya \el-'min-yə\ or **Al Minya** \al-\ city central Egypt on the Nile

El·mi·ra \el-'mī-rə\ city S N.Y. pop 33,724

El Misti — see MISTI

El Mon·te \el-'män-tē\ city SW Calif. E of Los Angeles pop 106,209

El Mor·ro National Monument \el-'mär-(ˌ)ō, -'mór-\ reservation W N.Mex. SE of Gallup; rock carvings, pueblo

Elm·wood Park \'elm-,wùd\ village NE Ill. pop 23,206

El Obeid \,el-ō-'bād\ city central Sudan in Kordofan pop 66,270

El Paso \el-'pa-(ˌ)sō\ city Tex. at W tip on Rio Grande pop 515,342 — **El Paso·an** \-'pa-sō-ən\ noun

El Sal·va·dor \el-'sal-və-ˌdór, ˌsal-və-'; ˌel-ˌsäl-vä-'thór\ country Central America bordering on the Pacific; a republic ✻ San Salvador area 8260 sq mi (21,393 sq km) pop 5,517,000 — **El Sal·va·dor·an** \-,sal-və-'dór-ən\ noun or adjective

Elsass — see ALSACE

Elsene — see IXELLES

Elu·ru \e-'lùr-(ˌ)ü\ or formerly **El·lore** \e-'lór, -'lór\ city SE India in E Andhra Pradesh pop 212,918

Ely \'ē-lē\ town E England in N central Cambridgeshire

Ely, Isle of district & former administrative county (✻ Ely) E England in Cambridgeshire — see CAMBRIDGESHIRE

Elyr·ia \i-'lir-ē-ə\ city NE Ohio SW of Cleveland pop 56,746

Em·bar·ras or **Em·bar·rass** \'am-,brò—sic\ river 185 mi (298 km) E Ill. flowing SE into the Wabash

Em·den \'em-dən\ city & port NW Germany at mouth of Ems River pop 51,103

Emesa — see HOMS

Emi·lia \ā-'mēl-yä\ **1** district N Italy comprising the W part of Emilia-Romagna region **2** — see EMILIA-ROMAGNA

Emilia–Ro·ma·gna \-rō-'mä-nyä\ or formerly **Emilia** or ancient **Ae·mil·ia** \ē-'mil-yə\ region N Italy bounded by the Po, the Adriatic, & the Apennines ✻ Bologna area 8543 sq mi (22,126 sq km), pop 3,921,597

Em·me \'e-mə\ river about 50 mi (80 km) central Switzerland in E Bern canton

Em·men \'e-mən\ commune NE Netherlands pop 93,107

Em·po·ria \em-'pór-ē-ə, -'pór-\ city E central Kans. pop 25,512

Empty Quarter RUB' AL KHALI

Ems \'emz, 'em(p)s\ **1** river 231 mi (372 km) NW Germany flowing N into North Sea **2** or **Bad Ems** \,bät-\ town W Germany SE of Koblenz pop 10,358

Enchanted Mesa sandstone butte W N.Mex. NE of Acoma

En·ci·ni·tas \,en(t)-sə-'nē-təs\ city S Calif. on coast N of San Diego pop 55,386

En·der·bury \'en-dər-,ber-ē\ island (atoll) central Pacific in the Phoenix Islands chain of Kiribati

En·di·cott Mountains \'en-di-kət, -də-,kät\ mountains N Alaska, the central range of Brooks Range

En·field \'en-,fēld\ **1** town N Conn. pop 45,532 **2** borough of N Greater London, England pop 248,900

En·ga·dine \,eŋ-gə-'dēn, 'eŋ-gə-,\ valley of upper Inn River 60 mi (96 km) long E Switzerland in Graubünden

En·gland \'iŋ-glənd, 'iŋ-lənd\ **1** or Late Latin **An·glia** \'aŋ-glē-ə\ country S Great Britain; a division of the United Kingdom of Great Britain and Northern Ireland ✻ London area 50,333 sq mi (130,362 sq km), pop 46,161,000 **2** England & Wales **3** UNITED KINGDOM

En·gle·wood \'eŋ-gəl-,wùd\ **1** city N central Colo. S of Denver pop 29,387 **2** city NE N.J. on the Hudson pop 24,850

English Channel or French **La Manche** \lä-'mänsh\ strait between S England & N France connecting North Sea & Atlantic Ocean

Enid \'ē-nəd\ city N Okla. pop 45,309

Eni·we·tok \,e-ni-'wē-,täk\ island (atoll) W Pacific in the NW Marshalls

En·na \'e-nä\ commune Italy in central Sicily pop 28,296

En·nis \'e-nəs\ town W Ireland ✻ of County Clare pop 13,746

En·nis·kil·len \,e-nə-'ski-lən\ or **In·nis·kil·ling** \,i-nə-'ski-liŋ\ town SW Northern Ireland in central Fermanagh district

Enns \'enz, 'en(t)s\ river 160 mi (257 km) central Austria flowing E & N from Styria into the Danube

En·sche·de \'en(t)-skə-,dā, -skə-\ commune E Netherlands in Overijssel near German frontier pop 147,199

En·se·na·da \en(t)-sə-'nä-də, ,en-sä-'nä-thä\ city & port NW Mexico in Baja California on the Pacific SE of Tijuana pop 260,905

En·teb·be \en-'te-bə, -bē\ town S Uganda on N shore of Lake Victoria; former ✻ of Uganda pop 41,638

En·ter·prise \'en-tə(r)-,prīz\ city SE Ala. pop 20,123

Eph·e·sus \'e-fə-səs\ ancient city W Asia Minor in Ionia near Aegean coast; its site SSE of Izmir — **Ephe·sian** \i-'fē-zhən\ adjective or noun

Ephra·im \'ē-frē-əm\ **1** or **Mount Ephraim** hilly region central Palestine in N Jordan E of Jordan River **2** — see ISRAEL

Epidamnus — see DURRES

Ep·i·dau·rus \,e-pə-'dòr-əs\ ancient town S Greece in Argolis on Saronic Gulf

Épi·nal \,ā-pi-'näl\ commune NE France on the Moselle pop 39,480

Epi·rus \i-'pī-rəs\ or Greek **Epei·ros** \'ē-pē-,rós\ region NW Greece bordering on Ionian Sea — **Epi·rote** \i-'pī-,rōt, -rət\ noun

Ep·ping Forest \'e-piŋ\ forested region SE England in Essex NE of London & S of town of **Epping**

Equatorial Guinea country W Africa on Bight of Biafra comprising former Spanish Guinea; an independent republic since 1968 ✻ Malabo area 10,825 sq mi (28,037 sq km), pop 376,000 — see SPANISH GUINEA

Erbil — see ARBIL

Er·ci·yas \,er-jē-'yäs\ mountain 12,848 ft (3916 m) central Turkey; highest in Asia Minor

Er·e·bus, Mount \'er-ə-bəs\ volcano 12,450 ft (3795 m) E Antarctica on Ross Is. in SW Ross Sea

Ere·gli \,er-ā-'lē, -'glē\ **1** city S Turkey SSE of Ankara pop 74,332 **2** town & port NW Turkey in Asia on Black Sea pop 63,776

Er·furt \'er-fərt, -,fùrt\ city central Germany WSW of Leipzig pop 204,912

Erie \'ir-ē\ city & port NW Pa. on Lake Erie pop 108,718

Erie, Lake lake E central N. America on boundary between the U.S. & Canada; one of the Great Lakes area 9910 sq mi (25,667 sq km)

Erie Canal canal 363 mi (584 km) long N N.Y. from Hudson River at Albany to Lake Erie at Buffalo; built 1817–25; superseded by **New York State Barge Canal** (about 525 mi or 840 km long)

Eriha — see JERICHO

Er·in \'er-ən\ IRELAND — a poetic name

Er·i·trea \,er-ə-'trē-ə, -'trā-\ country NE Africa bordering on Red Sea ✻ Asmara; incorporated (1962) into Ethiopia; voted (1993) in favor of in-

dependence area 45,405 sq mi (117,599 sq km), pop 3,317,611 — **Er·i·tre·an** \-ən\ adjective or noun

Er·lang·en \'er-,läŋ-ən\ city S Germany in Bavaria NNW of Nuremberg pop 102,433

Er·moú·po·lis or **Her·moú·po·lis** \er-'mü-pə-lis, -,pō-,lēs\ or **Sí·ros** \'sī-,räs, 'sē-,rós\ town & port Greece on Síros; chief town of the Cyclades pop 12,987

Er Rif or **Er Riff** \er-'rif\ mountain range N Morocco on the Mediterranean

Erz·ge·bir·ge \'erts-gə-,bir-gə\ mountain range Germany & NW Czech Republic on boundary between Saxony & Bohemia; highest Klinovec (in Czech Republic) 4080 ft (1244 m)

Er·zin·can \,er-zin-'jän\ city E central Turkey on the Euphrates pop 90,799

Er·zu·rum \,er-zù-'rüm\ city NE Turkey in mountains of W Turkish Armenia pop 242,391

Es·bjerg \'es-,byer(g)\ city & port SW Denmark in SW Jutland Peninsula on North Sea pop 81,843

Escaut — see SCHELDT

Es·con·di·do \,es-kən-'dē-(ˌ)dō\ city SW Calif. N of San Diego pop 108,635

Es·dra·e·lon, Plain of \,ez-drə-'ē-lən\ plain N Israel NE of Mt. Carmel in valley of the upper Qishon

Es·fa·hān \,es-fə-'hän, -'han\ or **Is·fa·han** \,is-\ or formerly **Is·pa·han** \,is-pə-\ city W central Iran; former ✻ of Persia pop 986,753

Esher \'ē-shər\ town S England in N Surrey pop 61,446

Es·kils·tu·na \'es-kəl-,stü-nə\ city SE Sweden pop 89,584

Es·ki·se·hir \,es-ki-shə-'hir\ or **Es·ki·shehr** \-'sher\ city W central Turkey on tributary of the Sakarya pop 413,082

España — see SPAIN

Española — see HISPANIOLA

Es·pí·ri·to San·to \ə-'spir-ə-,tü-'sàn-(ˌ)tü\ state E Brazil bordering on the Atlantic ✻ Vitória area 17,658 sq mi (45,734 sq km), pop 2,598,231

Es·pí·ri·tu San·to \ə-'spir-ə-,tü-'sàn-(ˌ)tü\ island SW Pacific in NW Vanuatu largest in the group area 1420 sq mi (3678 sq km), pop 22,663

Es·poo \'es-(ˌ)pō\ town S Finland W of Helsinki pop 175,806

Es·qui·line \'es-kwə-,līn, -lən\ hill in Rome, Italy, one of seven on which the ancient city was built — see AVENTINE

Es·sa·oui·ra \,e-sə-'wir-ə\ or formerly **Mog·a·dor** \'mä-gə-,dor\ city & port W Morocco on the Atlantic W of Marrakech pop 30,061

Es·sen \'e-s³n\ city W Germany in the Ruhr pop 626,989

Es·se·qui·bo \,e-sə-'kē-(ˌ)bō\ river 630 mi (1014 km) Guyana flowing N into the Atlantic through a wide estuary

Es·sex \'e-siks\ county SE England bordering on North Sea & N shore of Thames River; one of kingdoms in Anglo-Saxon heptarchy ✻ Chelmsford area 1470 sq mi (3807 sq km), pop 1,495,600

Ess·ling·en \'es-liŋ-ən\ city SW Germany on the Neckar pop 91,829

Es·te·rel \,es-tə-'rel\ forested mountain region SE France on coast between Fréjus & Cannes; highest point 2020 ft (616 m)

Es·tes Park \'es-tēz\ valley N Colo. in Front Range of the Rocky Mountains at E border of Rocky Mountain National Park

Es·to·nia \e-'stō-nē-ə, -nyə\ or **Es·tho·nia** \es-'stō-, es-'thō-\ country N Europe bordering on Baltic Sea; one of the Baltic Provinces of Russia 1721–1917, an independent republic 1918–40, a constituent republic (**Estonian Republic**) of the U.S.S.R. 1940–91 ✻ Tallinn area 17,413 sq mi (45,100 sq km), pop 1,536,000

Es·to·ril \,ēsh-tə-'ril\ resort town Portugal on coast W of Lisbon pop 2524

Es·tre·ma·du·ra \,es-trə-mə-'dùr-ə\ region & old province W central Portugal ✻ Lisbon

Ethi·o·pia \,ē-thē-'ō-pē-ə\ **1** ancient country NE Africa bordering on Red Sea and extending

\ə\ abut \³\ kitten \ər\ further \a\ ash \ā\ ace
\ä\ mop, mar \aù\ out \ch\ chin \e\ bet \ē\ easy
\g\ go \i\ hit \ī\ ice \j\ job \ŋ\ sing \ō\ go
\ó\ law \ói\ boy \th\ thin \th\ the \ü\ loot \ù\ foot
\y\ yet \zh\ vision see also Guide to Pronunciation

from S Egypt to N (present-day) Ethiopia **2** or **Ab·ys·sin·ia** \ˌa-bə-'sin-yə, -'si-nē-ə\ country E Africa; formerly an empire, since 1975 a republic ✱ Addis Ababa *area* 471,776 *sq mi* (1,226,618 *sq km*), *pop* 55,699,000

Et·na, Mount \'et-nə\ volcano 10,902 *ft* (3323 *m*) Italy in NE Sicily

Eto·bi·coke \e-'tō-bi-ˌkō—*sic*\ city Canada in SE Ontario *pop* 309,993

Eton \'ē-tⁿn\ town SE *central* England in Berkshire

Etru·ria \i-'trúr-ē-ə\ ancient country *central* Italy coextensive with modern Tuscany & part of Umbria; home of the Etruscans

Et·trick Forest \'e-trik\ region, formerly a forest & hunting ground, in SE Scotland in Borders region

Eu·boea \yủ-'bē-ə\ or **Ev·voia** \'e-vē-ä\ island 90 *mi* (145 *km*) long E Greece in the Aegean NE of Attica & Boeotia *area* 1411 *sq mi* (3654 *sq km*) — **Eu·boe·an** \yủ-'bē-ən\ *adjective or noun*

Eu·clid \'yü-kləd\ city NE Ohio NE of Cleveland *pop* 54,875

Eu·ga·ne·an Hills \yủ-'gā-nē-ən, ˌyü-gə-'nē-\ hills NE Italy in SW Veneto between Padua & the Adige

Eu·gene \yủ-'jēn\ city W Oreg. on the Willamette *pop* 112,669

Eu·less \'yü-ləs\ city NE Tex. NE of Fort Worth *pop* 38,149

Eu·pen \'ói-pən; ˌə(r)-'pen, ˌē-'\ commune E Belgium E of Liège; formerly in Germany, transferred (with Malmédy) to Belgium 1919 *pop* 17,161

Eu·phra·tes \yủ-'frā-(ˌ)tēz\ river 1700 *mi* (2736 *km*) SW Asia flowing from E Turkey SW & SE to unite with the Tigris forming the Shatt-al-Arab — see KARA SU — **Eu·phra·te·an** \ˌyü-'frā-tē-ən\ *adjective*

Eur·asia \yủ-'rā-zhə, -shə\ name given to Asia & Europe as one continent

Eure \'ər, 'œr\ river 140 *mi* (225 *km*) NW France flowing N into the Seine

Eu·re·ka \yủ-'rē-kə\ city & port NW Calif. *pop* 27,025

Eu·rope \'yúr-əp\ **1** continent of the eastern hemisphere between Asia & the Atlantic *area* 3,997,929 *sq mi* (10,354,636 *sq km*), *pop* 498,000,000 **2** the European continent exclusive of the British Isles

European Economic Community or **Common Market** economic organization subsumed within the European Union

European Union or *formerly* **European Communities** or **European Community** economic, scientific, and political organization consisting of Belgium, France, Italy, Luxembourg, Netherlands, Germany, Denmark, Greece, Ireland, United Kingdom, Spain, Portugal, Austria, Finland, & Sweden

Ev·ans, Mount \'e-vənz\ mountain 14,264 *ft* (4348 *m*) N *central* Colo. in Front Range WSW of Denver

Ev·ans·ton \'e-vən(t)-stən\ city NE Ill. N of Chicago *pop* 73,233

Ev·ans·ville \'e-vənz-,vil\ city SW Ind. on Ohio River *pop* 126,272

Ev·er·est, Mount \'ev-rəst, 'e-və-\ or *Tibetan* **Cho·mo·lung·ma** \chō-mō-'lúŋ-mə\ mountain 29,028 *ft* (8848 *m*) S Asia on border between Nepal & Tibet in the Himalayas; highest in the world

Ev·er·ett \'ev-rət, 'e-və-\ **1** city E Mass. N of Boston *pop* 35,701 **2** city NW *central* Wash. on Puget Sound N of Seattle *pop* 69,961

Ev·er·glades \'e-vər-,glādz\ swamp region S Fla. S of Lake Okeechobee; now partly drained; SW part forms **Everglades National Park**

Evergreen Park village NE Ill. S of Chicago *pop* 20,874

Eve·sham \'ēv-shəm\ borough W *central* England in Hereford and Worcester S of Birmingham in **Vale of Evesham** *pop* 15,271

Évian or **Évian–les–Bains** \ˌā-vyäⁿ-le-'baⁿ\ commune E France on Lake Geneva; health resort *pop* 7027

Évo·ra \'e-vú-rə\ city S *central* Portugal *pop* 34,851

Évreux \āv-'rœ̄, -'rə(r)\ commune N France WNW of Paris *pop* 51,452

Ev·ri·pos \'ev-ri-ˌpós\ narrow strait E Greece between Euboea & mainland

Évros — see MARITSA

Ex·e·ter \'ek-sə-tər\ city SW England ✱ of Devon *pop* 101,100

Ex·moor \'eks-ˌmủr, -ˌmōr, -ˌmór\ moorland SW England in Somerset & Devon *area* 32 *sq mi* (83 *sq km*)

Ex·tre·ma·du·ra \ˌek-strə-mə-'dúr-ə, ˌes-trä-mä-'thü-rä\ region & old province W Spain bordering on Portugal; area included in present Cáceres & Badajoz provinces

Ex·u·ma \ik-'sü-mə, ig-'zü-\ islands in *central* Bahamas S of **Exuma Sound** (SE of New Providence Is.); chief island **Great Exuma**

Eyre, Lake intermittent lake *central* Australia in NE S. Australia

Eyre Peninsula \'ar, 'er\ peninsula Australia in S S. Australia W of Spencer Gulf

Eyzies, Les — see LES EYZIES

Fa·en·za \fä-'en-zä, -'en(t)-sä\ commune N Italy *pop* 54,118

Faer·oe Islands or **Far·oe Islands** \'far-(ˌ)ō, 'fer-\ islands Denmark in the NE Atlantic NW of the Shetlands ✱ Torshavn *area* 540 *sq mi* (1404 *sq km*), *pop* 47,653

Fa·ial \fə-'yäl, -'äl\ island *central* Azores *area* 66 *sq mi* (171 *sq km*)

Fair·banks \'far-ˌbaŋks, 'fer-\ city E *central* Alaska *pop* 30,843

Fair·born \'far-ˌbórn, 'fer-\ city SW *central* Ohio *pop* 31,300

Fair·fax \'far-ˌfaks, 'fer-\ city NE Va. *pop* 19,622

Fair·field \'far-ˌfēld, 'fer-\ **1** city W Calif. NE of Berkeley *pop* 77,211 **2** city SW Conn. SW of Bridgeport *pop* 53,418 **3** city SW Ohio *pop* 39,729

Fair Lawn borough NE N.J. NE of Paterson *pop* 30,548

Fair·mont \'far-ˌmänt, 'fer-\ city N W.Va. *pop* 20,210

Fair·weath·er, Mount or **Fairweather Mountain** \'far-ˌwe-thər, 'fer-\ mountain 15,300 *ft* (4663 *m*) on boundary between Alaska & British Columbia

Fai·sa·la·bad \ˌfī-sä-lə-'bäd, -ˌsa-lə-'bad\ or *formerly* **Lyall·pur** \lē-ˌäl-'púr\ city NE Pakistan W of Lahore *pop* 1,092,000

Faiyūm, El — see EL FAIYŪM

Faiz·a·bad \'fī-zə-ˌbad, -ˌbäd, **1** or **Fey·za·bad** \'fā-zə-ˌbäd\ city NE Afghanistan *pop* 70,871 **2** city N India in Uttar Pradesh *pop* 125,012

Fa·ka·ra·va \ˌfä-kä-'rä-vä\ island (atoll) S Pacific, principal island of the Tuamotu Archipelago *pop* 651

Fa·laise \fä-'lāz\ town NW France SSE of Caen *pop* 8387

Fal·kirk \'fól-(ˌ)kərk\ royal burgh *central* Scotland in Central region ENE of Glasgow *pop* 36,875

Falk·land Islands \'fó-klənd, 'fól-\ or *Spanish* **Is·las Mal·vi·nas** \ˌēs-läs-mäl-'vē-näs\ islands SW Atlantic E of S end of Argentina; a Brit. crown colony ✱ Stanley *area* 4700 *sq mi* (12,173 *sq km*), *pop* 2100

Falkland Islands Dependencies islands & territories in the S Atlantic & in Antarctica administered by the British from Falkland Islands, including S. Orkney, S. Sandwich, & S. Shetland Islands, S. Georgia Is., Antarctic Peninsula, & Palmer Archipelago

Fall River \'fól\ city & port SE Mass. *pop* 92,703

Fal·mouth \'fal-məth\ town SE Mass. on Cape Cod *pop* 27,960

False Bay \'fóls\ inlet Republic of South Africa in SW Western Cape province E of Cape of Good Hope

Fal·ster \'fäl-stər, 'fól-\ island Denmark in Baltic Sea S of Sjælland *pop* 42,841

Fa·ma·gus·ta \ˌfä-mä-'gús-tä, ˌfa-\ city & port E Cyprus on **Famagusta Bay** (inlet of the Mediterranean) *pop* 42,500

Fanning — see TABUAERAN

Far·al·lon Islands \'far-ə-ˌlän\ islands in the Pacific W *central* Calif. W of San Francisco

Far East the countries of E Asia & the Malay Archipelago — usually considered as comprising the Asian countries bordering on the Pacific but

sometimes as including also India, Sri Lanka, Bangladesh, Tibet, & Myanmar — **Far Eastern** *adjective*

Fare·well, Cape \'far-ˌwel, 'fer-\ cape Greenland at S tip

Far·go \'fär-(ˌ)gō\ city E N.Dak. on Red River *pop* 74,111

Farm·ers Branch \'fär-mərz\ city NE Tex. *pop* 24,250

Far·ming·ton \'fär-miŋ-tən\ **1** town N Conn. W of Hartford *pop* 20,608 **2** city NW N.Mex. *pop* 33,997

Farmington Hills city SE Mich. *pop* 74,652

Far·quhar Islands \'fär-kwər, -kər\ island group NW Indian Ocean NE of Madagascar belonging to Seychelles

Far·rukh·a·bad \fə-'rü-kə-ˌbad, -ˌbäd\ city N India in Uttar Pradesh on the Ganges WNW of Lucknow *pop* 160,927

Fársala — see PHARSALUS

Fashoda — see KODOK

Fá·ti·ma \'fa-tə-mə, 'fä-tē-\ village *central* Portugal NNE of Lisbon

Fatshan — see FOSHAN

Fay·ette·ville \'fā-ət-ˌvil, -vəl; 2 *is also* 'fed-vəl\ **1** city NW Ark. *pop* 42,099 **2** city SE *central* N.C. on Cape Fear River *pop* 75,695

Fear, Cape \'fir\ cape SE N.C. at mouth of Cape Fear River

Feath·er \'fe-thər\ river 100 *mi* (161 *km*) N *central* Calif. flowing S into Sacramento River

Federal Capital Territory — see AUSTRALIAN CAPITAL TERRITORY

Federal District 1 or *Portuguese* **Dis·tri·to Fe·de·ral** \dish-'trē-tü-ˌfe-di-'räl\ district E *central* Brazil including ✱ city of Brasília *area* 2245 *sq mi* (5814 *sq km*), *pop* 1,596,174 **2** — see DISTRITO FEDERAL 3 — see DISTRITO FEDERAL 4

Federated Malay States former Brit. protectorate (1895–1945) comprising the Malay states of Negeri Sembilan, Pahang, Perak, & Selangor ✱ Kuala Lumpur

Federated Shan States — see SHAN

Fen \'fən, 'fen\ river 300 *mi* (483 *km*) N China in *central* Shanxi flowing SSE into the Huang

Fengtien 1 — see LIAONING **2** — see SHENYANG

Fer·ga·na \fər-'gä-nə\ valley W *central* Asia in the Tian Shan in Kyrgyzstan, Tajikistan, & Uzbekistan SE of Tashkent

Fer·gu·son \'fər-gə-sən\ city E Mo. N of St. Louis *pop* 22,286

Fer·man·agh \fər-'ma-nə\ **1** district SW Northern Ireland, established 1974 *area* 724 *sq mi* (1875 *sq km*), *pop* 54,062 **2** traditional county W Northern Ireland

Fer·nan·do de No·ron·ha \fər-ˌnän-(ˌ)dü-dē-nò-'rō-nyə\ island Brazil in the Atlantic NE of city of Natal *area* 10 *sq mi* (26 *sq km*)

Fernando Póo — see BIOKO

Fern·dale \'fərn-ˌdāl\ city SE Mich. N of Detroit *pop* 25,084

Fer·ra·ra \fe-'rär-ä\ commune N Italy in Emilia-Romagna NE of Bologna near the Po *pop* 137,336

Ferro — see HIERRO

Ferrol, El — see EL FERROL

Ferryville — see MENZEL-BOURGUIBA

Fertile Crescent semicircle of fertile land stretching from SE coast of Mediterranean around Syrian Desert N of Arabia to Persian Gulf

Fez \'fez\ or **Fès** \'fes\ city N *central* Morocco *pop* 448,823

Fez·zan \fe-'zan\ region SW Libya, chiefly desert

Fich·tel·ge·bir·ge \'fik-tⁿl-gə-ˌbir-gə\ mountains Germany in NE Bavaria; highest Schneeberg 3453 *ft* (1052 *m*)

Fie·so·le \'fyā-zō-ˌlā\ or *ancient* **Fae·su·lae** \'fē-zə-ˌlē\ commune *central* Italy in Tuscany NE of Florence *pop* 15,056

Fife \'fīf\ or **Fife·shire** \-ˌshir, -shər\ region, formerly a county E Scotland between Firths of Tay & Forth ✱ Cupar *area* 509 *sq mi* (1319 *sq km*), *pop* 351,200

Fi·ji \'fē-(ˌ)jē\ islands SW Pacific E of Vanuatu constituting (with Rotuma Is.) an independent dominion of the Commonwealth of Nations ✱ Suva (on Viti Levu) *area* 7055 *sq mi* (18,272 *sq km*), *pop* 715,735 — **Fi·ji·an** \'fē-(ˌ)jē-ən, fi-'\ *adjective or noun*

Filch·ner Ice Shelf \'filk-nər\ area of shelf ice Antarctica in Weddell Sea

Filipinas, República de — see PHILIPPINES

Finch·ley \'finch-lē\ former municipal borough SE England in Middlesex, now part of Barnet

Find·lay \'fin(d)-lē\ city NW Ohio *pop* 35,703

Fin·gal's Cave \'fiŋ-gəlz\ sea cave W Scotland on Staffa Is.

Fin·ger Lakes \'fiŋ-gər\ group of long narrow lakes W *central* N.Y. comprising Cayuga, Seneca, Keuka, Canandaigua, Skaneateles, Owasco, & several smaller lakes

Fin·is·terre, Cape \,fi-nə-'ster, -'ster-ē\ cape NW Spain on coast of La Coruña province; westernmost point of Spanish mainland, at 9°18′W

Fin·land \'fin-lənd\ *or Finnish* **Suo·mi** \'swȯ-mē\ country N Europe bordering on Gulf of Bothnia & Gulf of Finland; a republic ✳ Helsinki *area* 130,128 *sq mi* (337,032 *sq km*), *pop* 5,058,000 — **Fin·land·er** *noun*

Finland, Gulf of arm of Baltic Sea between Finland & Estonia

Fin·lay \'fin-lē\ river 250 *mi* (402 *km*) Canada in N *central* British Columbia flowing SE to unite with **Pars·nip** \'pär-snip\ River (145 *mi or* 232 *km*) forming Peace River

Fins·bury \'finz-,ber-ē, -b(ə-)rē\ former metropolitan borough E *central* London, England, now part of Islington

Fin·ster·aar·horn \,fin(t)-stər-'är-,hȯrn\ mountain 14,019 *ft* (4273 *m*) S Switzerland; highest of the Berner Alpen

Fiord·land \fē-'ȯrd-,land, 'fē-,; 'fyȯrd-\ mountain region S New Zealand in SW South Is.

Fitch·burg \'fich-,bərg\ city N *central* Mass. *pop* 41,194

Fiume — see RIJEKA

Fiu·mi·ci·no \,fyü-mē-'chē-(,)nō\ town *central* Italy on Tyrrhenian Sea SW of Rome & WNW of Ostia

Flag·staff \'flag-,staf\ city N *central* Ariz. *pop* 45,857

Flam·bor·ough \'flam-,bər-ə, -,bə-rə, -b(ə-)rə\ town Canada in SE Ontario near Hamilton *pop* 29,616

Flamborough Head promontory NE England on Humberside coast

Flan·ders \'flan-dərz\ *or French* **Flan·dre** \'fläⁿdr^ə\ *or Flemish* **Vlaan·de·ren** \'vlän-də-rə(n)\ **1** medieval county along coast of what is now Belgium and adjacent parts of France & Netherlands ✳ Lille **2** semiautonomous region W Belgium — see EAST FLANDERS, WEST FLANDERS

Flat·head \'flat-,hed\ river 245 *mi* (394 *km*) SE British Columbia & NW Mont. flowing S through **Flathead Lake** (reservoir in Mont.) into Clark Fork

Flat·tery, Cape \'fla-tə-rē\ cape NW Wash. at entrance to Strait of Juan de Fuca

Flens·burg \'flenz-,bərg, 'flen(t)s-,bùrk\ city & port N Germany on inlet of the Baltic near Danish border *pop* 87,241

Fletsch·horn \'flech-,hȯrn\ mountain 13,107 *ft* (3995 *m*) S Switzerland in Pennine Alps S of Simplon Pass

Flevo·land \'fle-vō-,land\ province *central* Netherlands ✳ Lelystad *area* 549 *sq mi* (1422 *sq km*), *pop* 243,441

Flin·ders \'flin-dərz\ river 520 *mi* (837 *km*) Australia in *central* Queensland flowing NW into Gulf of Carpentaria

Flinders Ranges mountain ranges Australia in E S. Australia E of Lake Torrens

Flint \'flint\ **1** river 265 *mi* (426 *km*) W Ga. flowing S & SW into Lake Seminole **2** city SE *central* Mich. NNW of Detroit *pop* 140,761 **3** *or* **Flint·shire** \-,shir, -shər\ former county NE Wales ✳ Mold

Flod·den \'flä-d°n\ hill N England in N Northumberland near Scottish border

Flor·ence \'flȯr-ən(t)s, 'flär-\ **1** city NW Ala. on Tennessee River *pop* 36,426 **2** city E S.C. *pop* 29,813 **3** *or Italian* **Fi·ren·ze** \fē-'rent-sä\ commune *central* Italy on the Arno ✳ of Tuscany *pop* 402,316 — **Flor·en·tine** \'flȯr-ən-,tēn, 'flär-, -,tīn\ *noun*

Flo·res \'flȯr-əs, 'flȯr-\ **1** island NW Azores *area* 58 *sq mi* (150 *sq km*) **2** island Indonesia in Lesser Sunda Islands

Flo·ri·a·nó·po·lis \,flȯr-ē-ə-'nō-pù-lis\ city S Brazil ✳ of Santa Catarina state on island off coast *pop* 254,944

Flor·i·da \'flȯr-ə-də, 'flär-\ state SE U.S. ✳ Tallahassee *area* 58,664 *sq mi* (151,940 *sq km*), *pop* 12,937,926 — **Flo·rid·i·an** \flə-'ri-dē-ən\ *adjective or noun* — **Flor·i·dan** \'flȯr-ə-d°n, 'flär-\ *adjective or noun*

Florida, Straits of channel between Florida Keys (on NW) & Cuba & Bahamas (on S & E) connecting Gulf of Mexico with the Atlantic

Flor·i·da Island \'flȯr-ə-də, 'flär-; flə-'rē-də\ island W Pacific in SE Solomons N of Guadalcanal

Florida Keys chain of islands S Florida extending SW from S tip of the peninsula

Flo·ris·sant \'flȯr-ə-sənt, 'flȯr-\ city E Mo. NNW of St. Louis *pop* 51,206

Florissant Fossil Beds National Monument reservation *central* Colo.

Flush·ing \'flə-shiŋ\ **1** section of New York City on Long Is. in Queens **2** — see VLISSINGEN

Fly \'flī\ river 650 *mi* (1046 *km*) S New Guinea flowing SW into Gulf of Papua

Fog·gia \'fȯ-(,)jä\ commune SE Italy in Puglia *pop* 155,042

Foggy Bottom section of Washington, D.C., near the Potomac where the State Department building is located

Foix \'fwä\ region & former province S France in the Pyrenees SE of Gascony

Folke·stone \'fōk-stən, *United States also* -,stōn\ borough SE England in Kent on Strait of Dover *pop* 43,742

Fol·som \'fōl-səm\ city Calif. NE of Sacramento *pop* 29,802

Fond du Lac \'fän-d°l-,ak, 'fän-jə-,lak\ city E Wis. on Lake Winnebago *pop* 37,757

Fon·se·ca, Gulf of \fȯn-'sä-kä\ *or* **Fonseca Bay** inlet of the Pacific in Central America in El Salvador, Honduras, & Nicaragua

Fon·taine·bleau \'fän-t°n-,blō, ,fȯⁿ-ten-'blō\ commune N France *pop* 18,037

Fon·ta·na \fän-'ta-na\ city SW Calif. E of Los Angeles *pop* 87,535

Foochow — see FUZHOU

For·a·ker, Mount \'fȯr-i-kər, 'fär-\ mountain 17,400 *ft* (5304 *m*) S Alaska in Alaska Range SW of Mt. McKinley

For·far \'fȯr-fər\ **1** *or* **For·far·shire** \-,shir, -shər\ — see ANGUS **2** royal burgh E Scotland in Tayside *pop* 12,742

Fo·ril·lon National Park \,fȯr-ē(l)-'yōⁿ\ reservation E Canada in Gaspé Peninsula

For·lì \fȯr-'lē\ commune N Italy in Emilia-Romagna SE of Bologna *pop* 109,228

Formosa — see TAIWAN — **For·mo·san** \fȯr-'mō-s°n, fər-, -z°n\ *adjective or noun*

For·mo·sa Strait \fȯr-'mō-sə, fər-, -zə\ strait between Taiwan & China mainland connecting E. China & S. China seas

For·ta·le·za \,fȯr-t°l-'ā-zə\ city & port NE Brazil on the Atlantic ✳ of Ceará *pop* 1,700,000

Fort Col·lins \'kä-lənz\ city N Colo. *pop* 87,758

Fort–de–France \,fȯr-də-'fräⁿs\ city French West Indies ✳ of Martinique on W coast *pop* 93,598

Fort Dodge \'däj\ city NW *central* Iowa *pop* 25,894

Fort Erie \'ir-ē\ town Canada in SE Ontario on Niagara River *pop* 26,006

Fort Fred·e·ri·ca National Monument \,fre-də-'rē-kə, fre-'drē-\ reservation SE Ga. on W shore of St. Simons Is. containing site of fort built by Oglethorpe 1736

Fort George \'jȯrj\ river 480 *mi* (772 *km*) Canada in *central* Quebec flowing W into James Bay

Forth \'fȯrth, 'fȯrth\ river 116 *mi* (187 *km*) S *central* Scotland flowing E into **Firth of Forth** (estuary 48 *mi or* 77 *km* long, inlet of North Sea)

Fort Knox \'näks\ military reservation N *central* Ky. SSW of Louisville; location of U.S. Gold Bullion Depository

Fort–Lamy — see N'DJAMENA

Fort Lau·der·dale \'lȯ-dər-,dāl\ city SE Fla. on the Atlantic *pop* 149,377

Fort Lee \'lē\ borough NE N.J. on the Hudson *pop* 31,997

Fort Ma·tan·zas National Monument \mə-'tan-zəs\ reservation SSE of St. Augustine, Fla., containing fort built *about* 1736 by the Spanish

Fort Mc·Hen·ry National Monument \mə-'ken-rē\ site in Baltimore, Md., of a fort bombarded 1814 by the British

Fort Mc·Mur·ray \mək-'mər-ē\ city Canada in NE Alberta *pop* 34,706

Fort My·ers \'mī-(ə)rz\ city SW Fla. *pop* 45,206

Fort Nel·son \'nel-sən\ river 260 *mi* (418 *km*) Canada in NE British Columbia flowing NW into the Liard

Fort Peck Lake \'pek\ reservoir *about* 130 *mi* (209 *km*) long NE Mont. formed in Missouri River by **Fort Peck Dam**

Fort Pierce \'pirs\ city E Fla. on the Atlantic *pop* 36,830

Fort Pu·las·ki National Monument \pə-'laskē, pyü-\ reservation E Ga. comprising island in mouth of Savannah River, site of a fort built 1829–47 to replace Revolutionary Fort Greene

Fort Smith \'smith\ city NW Ark. on Arkansas River *pop* 72,798

Fort Stan·wix National Monument \'stan-(,)wiks\ historic site E *central* N.Y. in Rome

Fort Sum·ter National Monument \'səm(p)-tər\ reservation S.C. at entrance to Charleston harbor containing site of Fort Sumter

Fort Union National Monument reservation NE N.Mex. ENE of Santa Fe containing site of military post 1851–91

Fort Wal·ton Beach \'wȯl-t°n\ city NW Fla. E of Pensacola *pop* 21,471

Fort Wayne \'wān\ city NE Ind. *pop* 173,072

Fort William — see THUNDER BAY

Fort Worth \'wərth\ city N Tex. W of Dallas *pop* 447,619

Fo·shan \'fō-'shän\ *or formerly* **Fat·shan** \'fät-'shän\ city SE China in *central* Guangdong SW of Guangzhou *pop* 303,160

Fossil Butte National Monument reservation SW Wyo. containing aquatic fossils

Fos·ter City \'fȯs-tər, 'fäs-\ city W Calif. SSE of San Francisco *pop* 28,176

Fountain Valley city SW Calif. SE of Los Angeles *pop* 53,691

Four Forest Cantons the cantons of Uri, Schwyz, Unterwalden, & Lucerne in *central* Switzerland surrounding Lake of Lucerne

Fou·ta Djal·lon \,fü-tə-jə-'lōⁿ\ mountain region W Guinea; highest point *about* 4970 *ft* (1515 *m*)

Fox \'fäks\ **1** river 220 *mi* (354 *km*) SE Wis. & NE Ill. flowing S into Illinois River **2** river 175 *mi* (282 *km*) E Wis. flowing NE & N through Lake Winnebago into Green Bay

Foxe Basin \'fäks\ inlet of the Atlantic N Canada in E Northwest Territories W of Baffin Is.; connected with Hudson Bay by **Foxe Channel**

Fox Islands islands SW Alaska in E Aleutians — see UMNAK, UNALASKA, UNIMAK

Foyle \'fȯil\ river *about* 20 *mi* (32 *km*) N Ireland flowing NE past city of Derry into **Lough Foyle** (inlet of the Atlantic 18 *mi or* 29 *km* long)

Fra·ming·ham \'frā-miŋ-,ham\ town E Mass. WSW of Boston *pop* 64,989

France \'fran(t)s, 'fräⁿs\ country W Europe between English Channel & the Mediterranean; a republic ✳ Paris *area* 212,918 *sq mi* (551,458 *sq km*), *pop* 54,257,300

Franche–Com·té \,fräⁿsh-kōⁿ-'tä\ region & former county & province E France E of the Saône — see BURGUNDY

Fran·cis Case, Lake \'fran(t)-səs-'kās\ reservoir *about* 100 *mi* (161 *km*) long S S.Dak. formed in Missouri River by **Fort Ran·dall Dam** \'ran-d°l\

Fran·co·nia \fraŋ-'kō-nē-ə, -nyə\ former duchy in Austrasia, now included chiefly in Baden-Wurtemburg, Bavaria, & Hesse states, Germany — **Fran·co·ni·an** \-nē-ən, -nyən\ *adjective or noun*

Frank·fort \'fraŋk-fərt\ city ✳ of Ky., on Kentucky River E of Louisville *pop* 25,968

Frank·furt \'fraŋk-fərt, 'frän-,fùrt\ **1** *or in full* **Frankfurt am Main** \,äm-'mīn\ city W Germany on Main River *pop* 654,679 **2** *or in full* **Frankfurt an der Oder** \,än-dər-'ō-dər\ city E Germany on Oder River *pop* 85,357

\ə\ abut	\ᵊ\ kitten	\ər\ further \a\ ash \ā\ ace
\ä\ mop, mar	\aù\ out	\ch\ chin \e\ bet \ē\ easy
\g\ go	\i\ hit	\ī\ ice \j\ job
\ŋ\ sing	\ō\ go	\ȯ\ law \ȯi\ boy \th\ thin \th\ the \ü\ loot \ù\ foot
\y\ yet	\zh\ vision	*see also* Guide to Pronunciation

Frank·lin \'fraŋ-klən\ **1** town E *central* Mass. *pop* 22,095 **2** town *central* Tenn. S of Nashville *pop* 20,098 **3** city SE Wis., a SSW suburb of Milwaukee *pop* 21,855 **4** former district Canada in N Northwest Territories including Arctic islands & Boothia & Melville peninsulas

Franklin D. Roosevelt Lake reservoir 151 *mi* (243 *km*) long NE Wash. formed in Columbia River by Grand Coulee Dam

Franks Peak \'fraŋks\ mountain 13,140 *ft* (4005 *m*) NW Wyo.; highest in Absaroka Range

Franz Jo·sef Land \frants-'jō-zəf-,land, -səf; ,fränts-'yō-zəf-,länt\ archipelago Russia in Arctic Ocean N of Novaya Zemlya

Fras·ca·ti \frä-'skä-tē\ commune *central* Italy in Lazio SE of Rome *pop* 20,043

Fra·ser \'frā-zər, -zhər\ river 850 *mi* (1368 *km*) Canada in S *central* British Columbia flowing into Strait of Georgia

Frau·en·feld \'frau̇-(ə)n-,felt\ commune NE Switzerland ✳ of Thurgau canton *pop* 19,538

Fred·er·ick \'fre-drik, 'fre-də-rik\ city N Md. *pop* 40,148

Fred·er·icks·burg \'fre-driks-,bərg, 'fre-də-riks-\ city NE Va. SW of Alexandria *pop* 19,027

Fred·er·ic·ton \'fre-drik-tən, 'fre-də-rik-\ city Canada ✳ of New Brunswick on St. John River *pop* 46,466

Fred·er·iks·berg \'fre-driks-,bərg, 'fre-də-riks-\ city Denmark on Sjælland Is., W suburb of Copenhagen *pop* 85,327

Free·port \'frē-,pōrt, -,pȯrt\ **1** city N Ill. W of Rockford *pop* 25,840 **2** village SE N.Y. on Long Is. *pop* 39,894 **3** city NW Bahamas on *central* Grand Bahama Is. *pop* 26,574

Free State *or* **Vry·staat** \'frā-,stät, 'frī-\ *or formerly* **Or·ange Free State** \'ȯr-inj, 'är-, -ənj\ *or* **Oran·je Vrystaat** \ō-'rän-yə-\ province E *central* Republic of South Africa between Orange & Vaal rivers *area* 49,992 *sq mi* (129,480 *sq km*), *pop* 2,767,000

Free·town \'frē-,taun\ city & port ✳ of Sierra Leone on the Atlantic *pop* 178,600

Frei·burg \'frī-,bu̇rg, -,bȯrg, -,bu̇rk\ *or* **Freiburg im Breis·gau** \im-'brīs-,gau̇\ city SW Germany at W foot of Black Forest *pop* 193,775

Fréjus — *see* CENIS (Mont) 2

Fré·jus, Mas·sif du \mä-,sēf-dē-frā-'zhēs\ mountain on border between France & Italy at SW end of Graian Alps

Fre·man·tle \'frē-,man-tᵊl\ city Australia in SW Western Australia at mouth of Swan River; port for Perth *pop* 23,834

Fre·mont \'frē-mänt\ **1** city W Calif. SE of Oakland *pop* 173,339 **2** city E Nebr. *pop* 23,680

French Broad \'brȯd\ river 210 *mi* (338 *km*) flowing from W N.C. to E Tenn.

French Community former federation comprising France, its overseas departments & territories, & the former French territories in Africa that chose to maintain their ties with France

French Equatorial Africa *or earlier* **French Congo** former country W *central* Africa N of Congo River comprising a federation of Chad, Gabon, Middle Congo, & Ubangi-Shari territories ✳ Brazzaville

French Guiana country N S. America; an overseas department of France ✳ Cayenne *area* 35,126 *sq mi* (90,976 *sq km*), *pop* 128,000

French Guinea — *see* GUINEA

French India former French possessions in India including Chandernagore (ceded to India 1950) & Pondicherry, Karikal, Yanaon, & Mahé (ceded to India 1954) ✳ Pondicherry

French Indochina — *see* INDOCHINA

French Morocco — *see* MOROCCO

French Polynesia *or formerly* **French Oceania** islands in S Pacific belonging to France & including Society, Marquesas, Tuamotu, Gambier, & Tubuai groups ✳ Papeete (on Tahiti) *pop* 212,000

French Somaliland — *see* DJIBOUTI

French Sudan — *see* MALI

French Territory of the Afars and the Is·sas — *see* DJIBOUTI

French Togo — *see* TOGOLAND

French Union former federation (1946–58) comprising metropolitan France & its overseas departments, territories, & associated states — *see* FRENCH COMMUNITY

French West Africa former federation of French dependencies W Africa consisting of Dahomey, French Guinea, French Sudan, Ivory Coast, Mauritania, Niger, Senegal, & Upper Volta

French West Indies islands of the W. Indies belonging to France & including Guadeloupe, Martinique, Désirade, Les Saintes, Marie Galante, St. Barthélemy, & part of St. Martin

Fres·no \'frez-(,)nō\ city S *central* Calif. SE of San Francisco *pop* 354,202

Fria, Cape \'frē-ə\ cape NW Namibia on the Atlantic

Fri·bourg \frē-'bu̇r\ **1** canton W *central* Switzerland *area* 645 *sq mi* (1670 *sq km*), *pop* 203,878 **2** commune, its ✳, SW of Bern *pop* 33,913

Frid·ley \'frid-lē\ city SE Minn. N of St. Paul *pop* 28,335

Friends·wood \'fren(d)z-,wu̇d\ city SE Tex. SE of Houston *pop* 22,814

Fries·land \'frēs-,land, 'frēz-, -lənd; 'frēs-,länt\ **1** old region N Europe bordering on North Sea **2** province N Netherlands ✳ Leeuwarden *area* 1464 *sq mi* (3792 *sq km*), *pop* 603,998

Frio, Cape \'frē-(,)ō\ cape SE Brazil E of Rio de Janeiro

Fri·sches Haff \'fri-shəs-,häf\ lagoon N Poland & W Russia in Europe; inlet of Gulf of Gdansk

Fri·sian Islands \'fri-zhən, 'frē-\ islands NW Europe in North Sea including **West Frisian Islands** (off N Netherlands), **East Frisian Islands** (off NW Germany), & **North Frisian Islands** (off NW Germany & Denmark, including Helgoland & Sylt)

Fri·u·li \frē-'ü-lē\ district N Italy in Friuli-Venezia Giulia on Slovenia border — **Fri·u·li·an** \frē-'ü-lē-ən\ *adjective or noun*

Friuli–Ve·ne·zia Giu·lia \-ve-'net-sē-ə-'jül-yä\ region N Italy E of Veneto ✳ Trieste *area* 3028 *sq mi* (7842 *sq km*), *pop* 1,202,877

Fro·bi·sher Bay \'frō-bi-shər\ inlet of the Atlantic N Canada in E Northwest Territories on SE coast of Baffin Is.

Front Range \'frənt\ range of the Rockies extending from *central* Colo. N into SE Wyo. — *see* GRAYS PEAK

Frost·belt \'frȯst-,belt\ the N & NE states of the U.S.

Fro·ward, Cape \'frō-(w)ərd\ headland S Chile N of Strait of Magellan; southernmost point of mainland of S. America at *about* 53°54′S

Frunze — *see* BISHKEK

Fu–chou — *see* FUZHOU

Fujairah *or* **Fujayrah, Al** — *see* AL FUJAYRAH

Fu·ji \'fü-jē\ *or* **Fu·ji·ya·ma** \,fü-jē-'yä-mä\ *or* **Fu·ji–san** \-'sän\ mountain 12,388 *ft* (3776 *m*) Japan in S *central* Honshu; highest in Japan

Fu·jian \'fü-'jyen\ *or* **Fu·kien** \'fü-'kyen, -'jyen\ province SE China bordering on Formosa Strait ✳ Fuzhou *area* 47,529 *sq mi* (123,575 *sq km*), *pop* 30,048,224

Fu·ji·sa·wa \,fü-jē-'sä-wä\ city Japan on Honshu *pop* 358,757

Fu·ku·o·ka \,fü-kü-'ō-kä\ city & port Japan on N Kyushu on inlet of Tsushima Strait *pop* 1,261,658

Fu·ku·ya·ma \,fü-kə-'yä-mä\ city Japan on SW Honshu *pop* 365,615

Ful·da \'fu̇l-də\ city *central* Germany *pop* 57,180

Ful·ham \'fu̇-ləm\ former metropolitan borough SW London, England, now part of Hammersmith

Ful·ler·ton \'fu̇-lər-tən\ city SW Calif. NE of Long Beach *pop* 114,144

Fu·na·ba·shi \,fü-nä-'bä-shē\ city Japan on Honshu, a suburb of Tokyo *pop* 537,614

Fu·na·fu·ti \,fü-nä-'fü-tē\ island (atoll) S Pacific in *central* Tuvalu Islands; contains ✳ of the group *pop* 1328

Fun·chal \fün-'shäl, ,fən-\ city & port Portugal ✳ of Madeira Islands *pop* 126,021

Fun·dy, Bay of \'fən-dē\ inlet of the Atlantic SE Canada between New Brunswick & Nova Scotia

Fundy National Park reservation SE Canada in New Brunswick on upper Bay of Fundy

Fur·neaux \'fər-(,)nō\ islands Australia off NE Tasmania

Fur·ness \'fər-nəs\ district N England comprising peninsula in Irish Sea in SW Cumbria

Fürth \'fu̇rt, 'fu̇ert\ city S *central* Germany NW of Nuremberg *pop* 105,297

Fu·shun \'fü-'shùn\ city NE China in NE Liaoning E of Shenyang *pop* 1,202,388

Fu·tu·na \fü-'tü-nä\ **1** island SW Pacific in Futuna Islands **2** island SW Pacific in SE Vanuatu

Futuna Islands *or* **Hoorn Islands** \'hōrn, 'hȯrn\ islands SW Pacific NE of Fiji; formerly a French protectorate, since 1959 part of Wallis & Futuna Islands territory *pop* 4732

Fu·xin *or* **Fu·sin** \'fü-'shin\ city NE China in *central* Liaoning

Fu·zhou \'fü-jō\ *or* **Foo·chow** *or* **Fu–chou** \'fü-,jō, -'chau̇\ *or formerly* **Min·how** \'min-'hō\ city & port SE China ✳ of Fujian on Min River *pop* 874,809

Fyn \'fin\ island Denmark in the Baltic between Sjælland & Jutland; chief city Odense *area* 1149 *sq mi* (2987 *sq km*), *pop* 458,111

Ga·bès \'gä-,bes\ city & port SE Tunisia on **Gulf of Gabès** *or ancient* **Syr·tis Minor** \'sər-təs\ (arm of the Mediterranean) *pop* 83,610

Ga·bon \gá-'bōⁿ\ **1** *or* **Ga·boon** *or* **Ga·bun** \gə-'bün, ga-\ river NW Gabon flowing into the Atlantic through long wide estuary **2** country W Africa on the Atlantic; formerly a territory of French Equatorial Africa, since 1958 a republic ✳ Libreville *area* 102,317 *sq mi* (265,001 *sq km*), *pop* 1,280,000 — **Gab·o·nese** \,ga-bə-'nēz, -'nēs\ *adjective or noun*

Ga·bo·rone \,gä-bō-'rō-(,)nā, ,kä-\ *or formerly* **Ga·be·ro·nes** \-'rō-nəs\ town SE Botswana, its ✳ *pop* 133,468

Gad·a·ra \'ga-də-rə\ ancient town Palestine SE of Sea of Galilee — **Gad·a·rene** \'ga-də-,rēn, ,ga-də-'\ *adjective or noun*

Gades *or* **Gadir** — *see* CADIZ — **Gad·i·tan** \'ga-də-tan\ *adjective or noun*

Gads·den \'gadz-dən\ city NE Ala. on the Coosa *pop* 42,523

Gadsden Purchase tract of land S of Gila River in present Ariz. & N.Mex. purchased 1853 by the U.S. from Mexico *area* 29,640 *sq mi* (77,064 *sq km*)

Ga·e·ta \gä-'ä-tä\ city & port *central* Italy in Lazio on **Gulf of Gaeta** (inlet of Tyrrhenian Sea N of Bay of Naples) *pop* 22,393

Gaf·sa \'gaf-sə\ *or ancient* **Cap·sa** \'kap-sə\ oasis W *central* Tunisia

Ga·han·na \gə-'ha-nə\ city *central* Ohio NE of Columbus *pop* 27,791

Gaines·ville \'gānz-,vil, -vəl\ city N *central* Fla. *pop* 84,770

Gaird·ner, Lake \'gärd-nər, 'gerd-\ salt lake Australia in S. Australia W of Lake Torrens *area* 1840 *sq mi* (4784 *sq km*)

Gai·thers·burg \'gā-thərz-,bərg\ town W Md. NW of Washington, D.C. *pop* 39,542

Ga·lá·pa·gos Islands \gə-'lä-pə-gəs, -'la-, -,gōs\ *or* **Ar·chi·pié·la·go de Co·lón** \,är-chē-'pyä-lä-gō-thä-kō-'lōn\ island group Ecuador in the Pacific W of mainland ✳ on San Cristóbal Is. *area* 3093 *sq mi* (8010 *sq km*), *pop* 9785 — *see* ISABELA

Ga·la·ta \'ga-lə-tə\ port & commercial section of Istanbul, Turkey

Ga·la·ți \gä-'läts, -'lät-sē\ city E Romania on the Danube *pop* 307,376

Ga·la·tia \gə-'lā-sh(ē-)ə\ ancient country & Roman province *central* Asia Minor in region centered on modern Ankara, Turkey — **Ga·la·tian** \-shən\ *adjective or noun*

Gald·hø·pig·gen \'gäl-,hœ-,pē-gən\ mountain 8100 *ft* (2469 *m*) S *central* Norway in Jotunheim Mountains

Gales·burg \'gā(ə)lz-,bərg\ city NW Ill. WNW of Peoria *pop* 33,530

Ga·li·cia \gə-'li-sh(ē-)ə\ **1** region E *central* Europe including N slopes of the Carpathians & valleys of the upper Vistula, Dniester, Bug, & Seret rivers; former Austrian crown land; belonged to Poland between the two world wars; now divided between Poland & Ukraine **2** region & ancient kingdom NW Spain bordering on the Atlantic — **Ga·li·cian** \-'li-shən\ *adjective or noun*

Gal·i·lee \'ga-lə-,lē\ hill region N Israel N of Plain of Esdraelon — **Gal·i·le·an** \,ga-lə-'lē-ən\ *adjective or noun*

Galilee, Sea of *or modern* **Lake Ti·be·ri·as** \tī-'bir-ē-əs\ *or biblical* **Lake of Gen·nes·a·ret** \gə-'ne-sə-,ret, -rət\ *or* **Sea of Tiberias** *or* **Sea of Chin·ne·reth** \'ki-nə-,reth\ *or Hebrew* **Yam Kin·ne·ret** \'yäm-'ki-nə-,ret\ lake 13 *mi*

(21 *km*) long & 7 *mi* (11 *km*) wide N Israel on Syrian border traversed by Jordan River; *about* 700 *ft* (212 *m*) below sea level

Gal·la·tin \\'ga-lə-t^ə n\\ river 125 *mi* (201 *km*) SW Mont. — see THREE FORKS

Gallatin Range mountain range S Mont. — see ELECTRIC PEAK

Gal·li·nas, Point \\gä-'yē-näs\\ cape N Colombia; northernmost point of S. America, at 12°15′ N

Gal·lip·o·li \\gə-'li-pə-lē\\ *or Turkish* **Ge·li·bo·lu** \\ge-'lē-bó-,lü\\ peninsula Turkey in Europe between the Dardanelles & Saros Gulf — see CHERSONESE

Gal·lo·way \\'ga-lə-,wä\\ former district SW Scotland comprising area formerly in counties of Wigtown & Kirkcudbright — see DUMFRIES AND GALLOWAY — **Gal·we·gian** \\gal-'wē-j(ē-)ən\\ *adjective or noun*

Gal·lup \\'ga-ləp\\ city NW N.Mex. near Indian reservations *pop* 19,154

Galt \\'gólt\\ former city, Ontario, Canada — see CAMBRIDGE

Gal·ves·ton \\'gal-vəs-tən\\ city SE Tex. on **Galveston Island** (30 *mi or* 48 *km* long) at entrance to **Galveston Bay** (inlet of Gulf of Mexico) *pop* 59,070 — **Gal·ves·to·nian** \\,gal-və-'stō-nē-ən, -nyən\\ *noun*

Gal·way \\'gól-,wä\\ **1** county W Ireland in Connacht bordering on the Atlantic *area* 2293 *sq mi* (5962 *sq km*), *pop* 129,511 **2** municipal borough & port, its ✻, on **Galway Bay** (inlet) *pop* 50,842

Gam·bia \\'gam-bē-ə, 'gäm-\\ **1** river 700 *mi* (1126 *km*) W Africa flowing from Fouta Djallon in W Guinea W through Senegal into the Atlantic in Gambia **2** *or* **The Gambia** country W Africa; a republic in the Commonwealth of Nations ✻ Banjul *area* 4003 *sq mi* (10,368 *sq km*), *pop* 687,817 — **Gam·bi·an** \\-bē-ən\\ *adjective or noun*

Gam·bier Islands \\'gam-,bir\\ islands S Pacific SE of Tuamotu Archipelago belonging to France *pop* 620 — see MANGAREVA

Gan *or* **Kan** \\'gän\\ river over 500 *mi* (800 *km*) SE China in Jiangxi

Gana — see GHANA

Gan·ca \\'gän-jä\\ *or* **Gyan·dzha** \\gyän-'jä\\ *or 1935–90* **Ki·ro·va·bad** \\,kē-rə-və-'bät\\ *or earlier* **Eli·sa·vet·pol** *or* **Ye·li·za·vet·pol** \\yi-li-zə-'vyet-,pól\\ city W Azerbaijan *pop* 282,200

Gand — see GHENT

Gan·dhi·na·gar \\'gən-də-,nə-gər\\ town W India ✻ of Gujarat *pop* 121,746

Gan·ges \\'gan-,jēz\\ river 1550 *mi* (2494 *km*) N India flowing from the Himalayas SE & E to unite with the Brahmaputra & empty into Bay of Bengal through the vast **Ganges Delta** — see HUGLI — **Gan·get·ic** \\gan-'je-tik\\ *adjective*

Gangetic Plain low-lying plains region India & Bangladesh formed by Ganges River & its tributaries

Gang·tok \\gəŋ-'täk, 'gəŋ-\\ town NE India ✻ of Sikkim *pop* 24,971

Gan·nett Peak \\'ga-nət\\ mountain 13,804 *ft* (4208 *m*) central Wyo.; highest in Wind River Range & in the state

Gan·su *or* **Kan·su** \\'gän-'sü\\ province N central China ✻ Lanzhou *area* 137,104 *sq mi* (356,470 *sq km*), *pop* 22,371,141

Gar \\'gär\\ *or* **Ka·erh** \\'kä-ər\\ town China in W Tibet

Gar·da, Lake \\'gär-də\\ lake *about* 35 *mi* (56 *km*) long N Italy between Lombardy & Veneto draining through the Mincio into the Po

Gar·de·na \\gär-'dē-nə\\ city SW Calif. S of Los Angeles *pop* 49,847

Garden City **1** city W Kans. on Arkansas River *pop* 24,097 **2** city SE Mich. *pop* 31,846 **3** village SE N.Y. on Long Is. *pop* 21,686

Garden Grove city SW Calif. SW of Los Angeles *pop* 143,050

Gard·ner \\'gärd-nər\\ city N central Mass. *pop* 20,125

Gar·field \\'gär-,fēld\\ city NE N.J. N of Newark *pop* 26,727

Garfield Heights city NE Ohio SSE of Cleveland *pop* 31,739

Garfield Mountain mountain 10,961 *ft* (3341 *m*) SW Mont. near Idaho border; highest in Beaverhead & Bitterroot ranges

Ga·ri·glia·no \\,gär-ēl-'yä-(,)nō\\ river 100 *mi* (161 *km*) central Italy in Lazio flowing SE & SW into Gulf of Gaeta

Gar·land \\'gär-lənd\\ city NE Tex. NNE of Dallas *pop* 180,650

Gar·misch–Par·ten·kir·chen \\'gär-mish-'pärt^ə n-,kir-kən\\ city S Germany in Bavaria SW of Munich in foothills of the Alps *pop* 27,094

Ga·ronne \\gə-'rän, gä-'ron\\ river *about* 355 *mi* (571 *km*) SW France flowing NW to unite with the Dordogne forming Gironde Estuary

Gar·ri·son Dam \\'gar-ə-sən\\ dam 210 *ft* (64 *m*) high in Missouri River W central N. Dak. — see SAKAKAWEA (Lake)

Gary \\'gar-ē, 'ger-\\ city NW Ind. on Lake Michigan *pop* 116,646

Gas·co·nade \\,gas-kə-'näd\\ river 265 *mi* (426 *km*) S central Mo. flowing NE into Missouri River

Gas·co·ny \\'gas-kə-nē\\ *or French* **Gas·cogne** \\gä-'skòn'\\ region & former province SW France ✻ Auch

Ga·sher·brum \\gə-shər-,brüm, -,brüm\\ mountain 26,470 *ft* (8068 *m*) N Kashmir in Karakoram Range SE of K2

Gas·pé Peninsula \\ga-'spā, 'ga-,\\ peninsula Canada in SE Quebec between mouth of St. Lawrence River & Chaleur Bay — **Gas·pe·sian** \\ga-'spē-zhən\\ *adjective*

Gas·ti·neau Channel \\'gas-tə-,nō\\ channel SE Alaska between Douglas Is. & mainland; Juneau is situated on it

Gas·to·nia \\ga-'stō-nē-ə, -nyə\\ city SW N.C. W of Charlotte *pop* 54,732

Gates·head \\'gāts-,hed\\ borough N England in Tyne and Wear county on the Tyne opposite Newcastle *pop* 196,500

Gates of the Arctic National Park wilderness area N central Alaska in Brooks Range N of the Arctic Circle

Gath \\'gath\\ city of ancient Philistia ENE of Gaza

Gat·i·neau \\,ga-t^ə n-'ō\\ **1** river 240 *mi* (386 *km*) Canada in SW Quebec flowing S into Ottawa River at Hull **2** town Canada in SW Quebec *pop* 92,284

Ga·tun Lake \\gä-'tün\\ lake central Panama formed by the **Gatun Dam** in the Chagres; formerly in Canal Zone

Gaul \\'gól\\ *or Latin* **Gal·lia** \\'ga-lē-ə\\ ancient country W Europe comprising chiefly the region occupied by modern France & Belgium & at one time including also the Po valley in N Italy — see CISALPINE GAUL, TRANSALPINE GAUL

Gau·teng \\'gaú-,teŋ\\ *or formerly* **Pretoria–Witwatersrand–Vereeniging** province central NE Republic of South Africa *area* 7262 *sq mi* (18,810 *sq km*), *pop* 6,864,000

Ga·var·nie \\gä-vàr-'nē\\ waterfall 1385 *ft* (422 *m*) SW France S of Lourdes in the **Cirque de Gavarnie** \\,sērk-də-\\ (natural amphitheater at head of Gave de Pau) — see PAU

Gave de Pau — see PAU

Gav·ins Point Dam \\'ga-vənz\\ dam SE S.Dak. & NE Nebr. in Missouri River — see LEWIS AND CLARK LAKE

Gäv·le \\'yev-lə\\ city & port E Sweden on Gulf of Bothnia NNW of Stockholm *pop* 89,194

Ga·ya \\gə-'yä\\ city NE India in central Bihar *pop* 291,220

Ga·za *or Arabic* **Ghaz·ze** \\'gä-zə, 'ga-\\ city S Palestine near the Mediterranean; with surrounding coastal district (**Gaza Strip,** adjoining Sinai Peninsula), administered 1949–67 by Egypt, subsequently by Israel, self-rule accord signed 1994 *pop* 57,000 — **Ga·zan** \\-zən\\ *noun*

Ga·zi·an·tep \\,gä-zē-(,)än-'tep\\ *or formerly* **Ain·tab** \\in-'täb\\ city S Turkey N of Aleppo, Syria *pop* 603,434

Gdansk \\gə-'dän(t)sk, -'dan(t)sk\\ *or German* **Dan·zig** \\'dan(t)-sig, 'dän(t)-sik\\ city & port N Poland on Gulf of Gdansk *pop* 464,649

Gdansk, Gulf of *or* **Gulf of Danzig** inlet of S Baltic Sea in N Poland & W Russia

Gdyn·ia \\gə-'di-nē-ə\\ city & port N Poland on Gulf of Gdansk NNW of Gdansk *pop* 250,936

Gebel Katherina — see KATHERINA (Gebel)

Gebel Musa — see MUSA (Gebel)

Ge·diz \\gə-'dēz\\ *or* **Sa·ra·bat** \\,sär-ä-'bät\\ river 217 *mi* (349 *km*) W Turkey in Asia flowing W into Gulf of Izmir

Gee·long \\jə-'lóŋ\\ city & port SE Australia in S Victoria on Port Phillip Bay SW of Melbourne *pop* 13,036

Geelvink Bay — see SARERA BAY

Gel·der·land \\'gel-dər-,land, 'kel-dər-,länt\\ province E Netherlands bordering on IJsselmeer ✻ Arnhem *area* 1981 *sq mi* (5131 *sq km*), *pop* 1,839,883

Gelibolu — see GALLIPOLI

Gel·sen·kir·chen \\,gel-z^ə n-'kir-kən\\ city W Germany in the Ruhr W of Dortmund *pop* 293,839

General San Martín — see SAN MARTIN

Gen·e·see \\,je-nə-'sē\\ river 144 *mi* (232 *km*) W N.Y. flowing N into Lake Ontario

Ge·ne·va \\jə-'nē-və\\ *or French* **Ge·nève** \\zhə-'nev\\ *or German* **Genf** \\'genf\\ **1** canton SW Switzerland *area* 109 *sq mi* (282 *sq km*), *pop* 377,108 **2** city, its ✻, at SW tip of Lake Geneva on the Rhône *pop* 167,934 — **Gen·e·vese** \\,je-nə-'vēz, -'vēs\\ *adjective or noun*

Geneva, Lake *or* **Lake Le·man** \\'lē-mən, 'le-; lə-'man; lā-'män\\ lake 45 *mi* (72 *km*) long on border between SW Switzerland & E France; traversed by the Rhône

Gennesaret, Lake of — see GALILEE (Sea of)

Gen·oa \\'je-nō-ə\\ *or Italian* **Ge·no·va** \\'je-nō-(,)vä\\ *or ancient* **Gen·ua** \\'jen-yə-wə\\ commune & port NW Italy ✻ of Liguria at foot of the Apennines & at head of **Gulf of Genoa** (arm of Ligurian Sea) *pop* 675,639 — **Gen·o·ese** \\,je-nō-'ēz, -'ēs\\ *adjective or noun* — **Gen·o·vese** \\-'vēz, -'vēs\\ *adjective or noun*

Gen·tof·te \\'gen-,tóf-tə\\ city Denmark on Sjælland Is., N suburb of Copenhagen *pop* 65,032

George \\'jórj\\ river 345 *mi* (555 *km*) Canada in NE Quebec flowing N into Ungava Bay

George, Lake **1** lake 14 *mi* (22 *km*) long NE Fla. in course of St. Johns River WNW of Daytona Beach **2** lake 33 *mi* (53 *km*) long E N.Y. S of Lake Champlain

Georges Bank \\'jór-jəz\\ submerged sandbank E of Mass.

George·town \\'jórj-,taùn\\ **1** section of Washington, D.C., in W part of the city **2** city & port ✻ of Guyana on the Atlantic *pop* 162,000

George Town \\'jórj-,taùn\\ **1** town ✻ of Cayman Islands on Grand Cayman Is. **2** *or* **Penang** \\pə-'naŋ, -'nän\\ city & port Malaysia ✻ of Penang on Penang Is. *pop* 234,930

George Washington Birthplace National Monument historic site E Va.

George Washington Carver National Monument historic site SW Mo. SE of Joplin

Geor·gia \\'jór-jə\\ **1** state SE U.S. ✻ Atlanta *area* 58,910 *sq mi* (152,577 *sq km*), *pop* 6,478,216 **2** *or* **Republic of Georgia** independent country SE Europe bordering on Black Sea; an ancient & medieval kingdom & later (1936–91) a constituent republic of the U.S.S.R. ✻ Tbilisi *area* 26,911 *sq mi* (69,699 *sq km*), *pop* 5,493,000

Georgia, Strait of channel 150 *mi* (241 *km*) long NW Wash. & SW British Columbia between S Vancouver Is. & mainland NW of Puget Sound

Georgian Bay inlet of Lake Huron, Canada, in SE Ontario

Georgian Bay Islands National Park reservation SE Canada including Flowerpot Is. SE of Manitoulin Is. & a group of small islands N of Midland, Ontario

Geor·gi·na \\jór-'jē-nə\\ town Canada in SE Ontario *pop* 29,746

Ge·ra \\'ger-ə\\ city E Germany ESE of Erfurt *pop* 126,521

Ger·la·chov·ka \\'ger-lə-,kóf-kə, -,kóv-\\ *or* **Ger·la·chov·sky** \\-skē\\ mountain 8711 *ft* (2655 *m*) N Slovakia in Tatra Mountains; highest in Carpathians

German East Africa former country E Africa comprising Tanganyika & Ruanda-Urundi (now Rwanda & Burundi); a German protectorate 1885–1920

Ger·ma·nia \\(,)jər-'mā-nē-ə, -nyə\\ **1** region of ancient Europe E of the Rhine & N of the Danube **2** region of Roman Empire just W of the Rhine

in what is now NE France & part of Belgium & the Netherlands

German Southwest Africa — see NAMIBIA

Ger·man·town \'jər-mən-ˌtaún\ **1** city SW Tenn. *pop* 32,893 **2** a NW section of Philadelphia, Pa.

Ger·ma·ny \'jər-mə-nē\ *or German* **Deutsch·land** \'dóich-ˌlänt\ country central Europe bordering on North & Baltic seas, divided 1949–90 into two republics: **Federal Republic of Germany** *or* **Bun·des·re·pu·blik Deutschland** \ˌbún-dəs-ˌrä-pü-ˈblēk\ to the W (✳ Bonn, *area about* 96,000 *sq mi or* 249,600 *sq km*) & **German Democratic Republic** *or* **Deutsche De·mo·krat·ische Re·pu·blik** \ˌdói-chə-ˌdä-mō-ˈkrä-ti-shə-ˌrä-pü-ˈblēk\ to the E (✳ East Berlin *area about* 42,000 *sq mi or* 108,780 *sq km*); ✳ Berlin *area* 137,735 *sq mi* (356,734 *sq km*), *pop* 80,974,900

Ger·mis·ton \'jər-məs-tən\ city NE Republic of South Africa in Gauteng E of Johannesburg *pop* 221,972

Ge·ro·na \hä-ˈrō-nä, jə-\ **1** province NE Spain in NE Catalonia *area* 2273 *sq mi* (5887 *sq km*), *pop* 509,628 **2** *or* **Gi·ro·na** \hē-\ commune, its ✳ *pop* 68,656

Ge·zi·ra \jə-ˈzē-rə\ *or* **Gezira, El** \el-\ *or* **Al Ja·zi·rah** \ˌal-jə-ˈzē-rə\ region E central Sudan between the Blue Nile & the White Nile

Gha·da·mis *or* **Gha·da·mis** *or* **Ghu·da·mis** \gə-ˈdä-məs, -ˈdä-\ oasis & town NW Libya in Tripolitania near Algerian border

Gha·gha·ra \'gä-gə-rä\ river 570 *mi* (1207 *km*) S central Asia flowing S from SW Tibet through Nepal into the Ganges in N India

Gha·na \'gä-nə, 'ga-\ **1** *or* **Ga·na** ancient empire W Africa in what is now W Mali; flourished 4th–13th centuries **2** *or formerly* **Gold Coast** country W Africa bordering on Gulf of Guinea; a republic within the Commonwealth of Nations; formerly (as Gold Coast) a Brit. territory comprising Gold Coast colony, Ashanti, Northern Territories, & Togoland trust territory ✳ Accra *area* 92,100 *sq mi* (238,539 *sq km*), *pop* 15,636,000 — **Gha·na·ian** \gä-ˈnā-ən, ga-, -ˈnī-ən\ *adjective or noun* — **Gha·nian** \'gä-nē-ən, 'ga-, -nyən\ *adjective or noun* — **Gha·nese** \gä-ˈnēz, ga-, -ˈnēs\ *adjective*

Gharapuri — see ELEPHANTA

Ghar·da·ïa \gär-ˈdī-ə\ commune N central Algeria *pop* 89,415

Ghats — see EASTERN GHATS, WESTERN GHATS

Ghazal, Bahr el — see BAHR EL GHAZAL

Ghaz·ni \'gäz-nē\ city E central Afghanistan; once ✳ of a Muslim kingdom extending from the Tigris to the Ganges *pop* 35,900

Ghazze — see GAZA

Ghent \'gent\ *or Flemish* **Gent** \'kent\ *or French* **Gand** \gäⁿ\ city NW central Belgium ✳ of E. Flanders *pop* 230,246

Giant's Causeway formation of prismatic basaltic columns Northern Ireland on N coast of Moyle

Gib·e·on \'gi-bē-ən\ city of ancient Palestine NW of Jerusalem — **Gib·e·on·ite** \-ə-ˌnīt\ *noun*

Gi·bral·tar \jə-ˈbról-tər\ town & port on Rock of Gibraltar; a Brit. colony *area* 2.5 *sq mi* (6.5 *sq km*), *pop* 29,760 — **Gi·bral·tar·i·an** \jə-ˌbról-ˈter-ē-ən, ji-ˌbról-, -ˈtar-\ *noun*

Gibraltar, Rock of *or ancient* **Cal·pe** \'kal-(ˌ)pē\ headland on S coast of Spain at E end of Strait of Gibraltar; highest point 1396 *ft* (426 *m*) — see PILLARS OF HERCULES

Gibraltar, Strait of passage between Spain & Africa connecting the Atlantic & Mediterranean *about* 8 *mi* (12.8 *km*) wide at narrowest point

Gies·sen \'gē-sᵊn\ city W central Germany N of Frankfurt am Main *pop* 73,763

Gi·fu \'gē-(ˌ)fü\ city Japan in central Honshu *pop* 410,318

Gi·jón \hē-ˈhōn\ city & port NW Spain in Asturias province on Bay of Biscay *pop* 259,067

Gi·la \'hē-lə\ river 630 *mi* (1014 *km*) N.Mex. & Ariz. flowing W into Colorado River

Gila Cliff Dwellings National Monument reservation SW N.Mex. including cliff-dweller ruins

Gil·bert \'gil-bərt\ town SW central Ariz. SE of Mesa *pop* 29,188

Gilbert and El·lice \'e-lis\ island group W Pacific; until 1976 a Brit. colony; now divided into the independent countries of Kiribati and Tuvalu

Gilbert Islands islands Kiribati in central Pacific — **Gil·bert·ese** \ˌgil-bər-ˈtēz, -ˈtēs\ *noun or adjective*

Gil·boa, Mount \gil-ˈbō-ə\ mountain 1631 *ft* (497 *m*) N Palestine W of Jordan River & S of Plain of Esdraelon

Gil·e·ad \'gi-lē-əd\ mountainous region of Palestine E of Jordan River; now in Jordan — **Gil·e·ad·ite** \-lē-ə-ˌdīt\ *noun*

Gil·git \'gil-gət\ **1** region NW Kashmir; under Pakistani control **2** town NW Kashmir on Gilgit River (tributary of the Indus) *pop* 4671

Gil·ling·ham \'ji-liŋ-əm\ town SE England in Kent *pop* 93,300

Gil·roy \'gil-ˌrói\ city W Calif. SE of San Jose *pop* 31,487

Gin·za \'gin-zə, 'gēn-zä\ shopping street & entertainment district in downtown Tokyo, Japan

Gi·re·sun \gir-ə-ˈsün\ *or* **Ke·ra·sun** \ˌker-ə-\ city & port NE Turkey on Black Sea W of Trabzon *pop* 67,536

Girgenti — see AGRIGENTO

Gi·ronde \jə-ˈränd, zhə-; zhē-ˈrōⁿd\ estuary 45 *mi* (72 *km*) W France formed by junction of the Garonne & the Dordogne & flowing NW into Bay of Biscay

Gis·borne \'giz-bərn, -ˌbórn\ borough & port New Zealand on E North Is. *pop* 31,400

Gi·za \'gē-zə\ *or* **El Giza** \el-\ *or* **Al Ji·zah** \äl-ˈjē-zə\ city N Egypt on W bank of the Nile near Cairo *pop* 2,096,000

Gju·he·zes, Cape \jü-ˈhə-ˌzəs\ *or formerly* **Cape Lin·guet·ta** \liŋ-ˈgwe-tä\ *or* **Cape Glos·sa** \'glä-sä, 'glò-\ cape SW Albania projecting into Strait of Otranto

Gla·cier Bay \'glā-shər *also* -zhər\ inlet SE Alaska at S end of St. Elias Range in **Glacier Bay National Park**

Glacier National Park 1 — see WATERTON-GLACIER INTERNATIONAL PEACE PARK **2** reservation W Canada in SE British Columbia in Selkirk Mountains W of Yoho National Park

Glad·beck \'glät-ˌbek, 'glad-\ city W Germany in the Ruhr *pop* 80,127

Glades — see EVERGLADES

Glad·sak·se \'gläth-ˌsäk-sə\ city Denmark; a suburb of Copenhagen *pop* 61,198

Glad·stone \'glad-ˌstōn\ city W Mo. N of Kansas City *pop* 26,243

Gla·mor·gan \glə-ˈmór-gən\ *or* **Gla·mor·gan·shire** \-ˌshir, -shər\ former county SE Wales ✳ Cardiff — see MID GLAMORGAN, SOUTH GLAMORGAN, WEST GLAMORGAN

Gla·rus \'glär-əs\ *or French* **Gla·ris** \glä-ˈrēs\ **1** canton E central Switzerland *area* 264 *sq mi* (684 *sq km*), *pop* 37,686 **2** commune, its ✳ *pop* 5623

Glas·gow \'glas-(ˌ)kō, 'glas-(ˌ)gō, 'glaz-(ˌ)gō\ city & port S central Scotland on the Clyde ✳ of Strathclyde *pop* 681,470 — **Glas·we·gian** \gla-ˈswē-jən, glaz-\ *noun or adjective*

Glas·ton·bury 1 \'glas-tən-ˌber-ē\ town central Conn. SE of Hartford *pop* 27,901 **2** \'glas-tən-b(ə-)rē, 'gläs-\ town SW England in Somerset *pop* 6773

Glen Canyon Dam \'glen\ dam N Ariz. in Glen Canyon of Colorado River forming **Lake Powell** \'paú(-ə)l\ (chiefly in SE Utah)

Glen·coe \glen-ˈkō\ valley W Scotland SE of Loch Leven

Glen Cove \'glen-ˈkōv\ city SE N.Y. on NW Long Is. *pop* 24,149

Glen·dale \'glen-ˌdāl\ **1** city central Ariz. NW of Phoenix *pop* 148,134 **2** city SW Calif. just N of Los Angeles *pop* 180,038

Glendale Heights city NE Ill. *pop* 27,973

Glen·do·ra \glen-ˈdór-ə, -ˈdor-\ city SW Calif. *pop* 47,828

Glen El·lyn \gle-ˈne-lən\ village NE Ill. W of Chicago *pop* 24,944

Glen More \glen-ˈmōr, -ˈmór\ valley *about* 50 *mi* (80 *km*) long N Scotland running SW to NE & connecting Loche Linnhe & Moray Firth — see CALEDONIAN CANAL

Glen·view \'glen-ˌvyü\ village NE Ill. NNW of Chicago *pop* 37,093

Glit·ter·tind \'gli-tər-ˌtin\ mountain 8110 *ft* (2472 *m*) S central Norway in Jotunheim Mountains; highest in Scandinavia

Gli·wi·ce \gli-ˈvēt-se\ *or German* **Glei·witz** \'glī-(ˌ)vits\ city SW Poland in Silesia W of Katowice *pop* 222,084

Glouces·ter \'gläs-tər, 'glòs-\ **1** city NE Mass. on Cape Ann *pop* 28,716 **2** city Canada in SE Ontario near Ottawa *pop* 101,677 **3** town SW central England ✳ of Gloucestershire *pop* 91,800

Glouces·ter·shire \'gläs-tər-ˌshir, -shər, 'glòs-\ *or* **Glouces·ter** \'gläs-tər, 'glòs-\ county SW central England *area* 1055 *sq mi* (2732 *sq km*), *pop* 520,600

Gnossus — see KNOSSOS

Goa *or Portuguese* **Gôa** \'gō-ə\ state W India on Malabar Coast; before 1962 belonged to Portugal; with Daman & Diu constituted a union territory 1962–1987; ✳ Panaji *area* 1404 *sq mi* (3636 *sq km*), *pop* 1,169,793 — see PORTUGUESE INDIA — **Go·an** \'gō-ən\ *adjective or noun* — **Goa·nese** \ˌgō-ə-ˈnēz, -ˈnēs\ *adjective or noun*

Go·bi \'gō-(ˌ)bē\ desert E central Asia in Mongolia & China *area about* 500,000 *sq mi* (1,300,000 *sq km*)

Go·da·va·ri \gō-ˈdä-və-rē\ river 900 *mi* (1448 *km*) central India flowing SE across the Deccan into Bay of Bengal

Go·des·berg \'gō-dəs-ˌbərg, -ˌberk\ *or* **Bad Godesberg** \ˌbät-\ former commune W Germany on the Rhine; became part of Bonn 1969

Godthåb — see NUUK

Godwin Austen — see K2

Go·ge·bic \gō-ˈgē-bik\ iron range N Wis. & NW Mich.

Goi·â·nia *or formerly* **Goy·a·nia** \gói-ˈyä-nyə\ city W central Brazil ✳ of Goiás *pop* 920,838

Goi·ás *or formerly* **Goi·az** *or* **Goy·az** \gói-ˈäs\ state SE central Brazil ✳ Goiânia *area* 131,339 *sq mi* (340,168 *sq km*), *pop* 4,024,547

Gök·çe·ada \ˌgœk-jä-ə-ˈdä\ *or formerly* **Im·roz** \im-ˈrôz\ island Turkey in NE Aegean *area* 110 *sq mi* (286 *sq km*)

Go·lan Heights \'gō-ˌlän, -lən\ hilly region NE of Sea of Galilee; annexed by Israel 1981

Gol·con·da \gäl-ˈkän-də\ ruined city central India in W Andhra Pradesh W of Hyderabad ✳ (1512–1687) of Golconda kingdom

Gold Coast 1 region W Africa on N shore of Gulf of Guinea between the Ivory Coast (on W) & the Slave Coast (on E) **2** see GHANA **3** former Brit. colony in S Gold Coast region ✳ Accra; now part of Ghana

Golden Chersonese — see CHERSONESE

Golden Gate strait 2 *mi* (3.2 *km*) wide W Calif. connecting San Francisco Bay with Pacific Ocean

Golden Horn inlet of the Bosporus, Turkey; harbor of Istanbul

Golden Valley village E Minn. W of Minneapolis *pop* 20,971

Golds·boro \'gōl(d)z-ˌbər-ō\ city E central N.C. *pop* 40,709

Golgotha — see CALVARY

Go·ma·ti \'gō-mə-tē\ *or formerly* **Gum·ti** \'güm-tē\ river *about* 500 *mi* (805 *km*) N India flowing SE into the Ganges

Go·mel \gó-ˈmel, -ˈmyel\ *or* **Ho·mel** \hó-\ *or* **Ho·myel** \ˈkō-ˈmyel\ city SE Belarus *pop* 503,300

Go·mor·rah \gə-ˈmór-ə, -ˈmär-\ city of ancient Palestine in the plain of Jordan River

Go·nâve, Gulf of \gō-ˈnäv\ arm of Caribbean Sea on W coast of Haiti

Gon·der \'gón-dər\ *or* **Gon·dar** \-dər, -ˌdär\ city NW Ethiopia N of Lake Tana ✳ of Amhara & former ✳ of Ethiopia *pop* 98,352

Gond·wa·na·land \gän-ˈdwä-nə-ˌland\ *or* **Gond·wa·na** \-ˈdwä-nə\ hypothetical land area believed to have once connected the Indian subcontinent & the landmasses of the southern hemisphere

Gong·ga Shan \'gäŋ-gə-ˈshän\ *or* **Min·ya Kon·ka** \ˌmi-nyə-ˈkäŋ-kə\ mountain 24,790 *ft* (7556 *m*) W China in SW central Szechwan; highest in China

Good Hope, Cape of \ˌgúd-ˈhōp\ cape S Republic of South Africa in SW Western Cape province W of False Bay, at 34°21′ S — see CAPE OF GOOD HOPE 2

Good·win Sands \'gu̇d-win\ shoals SE England in Strait of Dover off E coast of Kent — see DOWNS

Goose Creek city SE S.C. *pop* 24,692

Go·rakh·pur \'gȯr-ək-ˌpu̇r, 'gȯr-\ city NE India in E Uttar Pradesh N of Varanasi *pop* 505,566

Go·ri·zia \gō-'rēt-syä\ commune NE Italy in Venetia *pop* 37,999

Gorki — see NIZHNIY NOVGOROD

Gör·litz \'ger-ˌlits, -ləts\ city E Germany on Neisse River *pop* 70,448

Gor·lov·ka \'gȯr-lȯf-kə\ *or* **Hor·liv·ka** \'hȯr-\ city E Ukraine in the Donets Basin N of Donetsk *pop* 337,000

Gor·no–Al·tay \'gȯr-nə-ˌäl-'tī\ *or formerly* **Oyrot** \'ȯi-rət\ autonomous region S Russia in Asia in SE Altay Territory in Altay Mountains ✻ **Gorno–Altaysk** \-'tīsk\ *area* 35,753 *sq mi* (92,600 *sq km*), *pop* 197,000

Gor·no–Ba·dakh·shan \'gȯr-(ˌ)nō-bä-däk-'shän\ autonomous region SE Tajikistan in the Pamirs ✻ Khorog *area* 24,595 *sq mi* (63,701 *sq km*), *pop* 167,100

Gor·zow Wiel·ko·pol·ski \gȯ-zhüf-ˌvyel-kȯ-'pȯl-skē\ city W Poland *pop* 123,350

Go·shen \'gō-shən\ **1** city N Ind. *pop* 23,797 **2** district of ancient Egypt E of the Nile delta

Gos·port \'gäs-ˌpȯrt, -ˌpȯrt\ town S England in Hampshire on Portsmouth harbor *pop* 72,800

Gö·te·borg \ˌyœ̅-tə-'bȯr-ē\ *or* **Goth·en·burg** \'gä-thən-ˌbərg\ city & port SW Sweden on the Kattegat *pop* 433,811

Go·tha \'gō-tə, 'gō-thə\ city central Germany W of Erfurt *pop* 53,372

Goth·am \'gä-thəm\ NEW YORK CITY — an informal name — **Goth·am·ite** \-thə-ˌmīt\ *noun*

Got·land \'gät-ˌland, -ˌländ\ island Sweden in the Baltic off SE coast; chief town Visby *area* 1225 *sq mi* (3173 *sq km*), *pop* 56,840

Göt·ting·en \'gœ-tiŋ-ən, 'ge-tiŋ-\ city central Germany SSW of Brunswick *pop* 124,331

Gou·da \'gau̇-də, 'gü-, ˈkau̇-\ commune SW Netherlands *pop* 67,146

Gow·er \'gau̇-(-ə)r\ peninsula S Wales W of Swansea

Gra·ham Land \'grā-əm, 'gra-(-ə)m\ the N section of the Antarctic Peninsula

Gra·hams·town \'grā-əmz-ˌtau̇n, 'gra-(-ə)mz-\ city S Republic of South Africa in Eastern Cape province ENE of Port Elizabeth *pop* 41,302

Gra·ian Alps \'grā-ən, 'grī-\ section of W Alps S of Mont Blanc on border between France & Italy — see GRAN PARADISO

Grain Coast \'grān\ region W Africa in Liberia on Gulf of Guinea

Gram·pi·an \'gram-pē-ən\ region NE central Scotland, established 1975 ✻ Aberdeen *area* 3358 *sq mi* (8698 *sq km*), *pop* 528,100

Grampian Hills hills central Scotland between the Lowlands & the Highlands — see BEN NEVIS

Gra·na·da \grə-'nä-də, grä-'nä-thä\ **1** city SW Nicaragua on NW shore of Lake Nicaragua *pop* 56,232 **2** medieval Moorish kingdom S Spain **3** province S Spain in Andalusia bordering on the Mediterranean *area* 4838 *sq mi* (12,530 *sq km*), *pop* 790,515 **4** city, ✻ of Granada province, Spain, in the Sierra Nevada *pop* 254,034

Gran·by \'gran-bē\ town Canada in S Quebec *pop* 42,804

Gran Cha·co \'grän-'chä-(ˌ)kō\ *or* **Chaco** region S central S. America drained by the Paraguay & its chief W tributaries the Pilcomayo & Bermejo; divided between Argentina, Bolivia, & Paraguay

Grand **1** river 260 *mi* (418 *km*) SW Mich. flowing N & W into Lake Michigan **2** river 300 *mi* (483 *km*) NW Mo. flowing SE into Missouri River **3** river 200 *mi* (322 *km*) N S.Dak. flowing E into Missouri River **5** the Colorado River from its source to junction with Green River in SE Utah — a former name **6** — see NEOSHO

Grand Atlas — see ATLAS

Grand Bahama island Bahamas, NW island of group *area* 530 *sq mi* (1373 *sq km*)

Grand Banks shoals in W Atlantic SE of Newfoundland

Grand Canal *or* **Da Yun·he** \'dä-'yün-'hə\ canal *about* 1000 *mi* (1609 *km*) long E China from Hengshui to Tianjin

Grand Canary *or Spanish* **Gran Ca·na·ria** \ˌgrän-kä-'när-yä\ island Spain in the Canaries; chief city Las Palmas *area* 592 *sq mi* (1533 *sq km*)

Grand Canyon gorge of the Colorado NW Ariz. extending from mouth of the Little Colorado W to the Grand Wash Cliffs; over 1 *mi* (1.6 *km*) deep; area largely comprised in **Grand Canyon National Park** — see MARBLE CANYON

Grand Cayman — see CAYMAN

Grand Cou·lee \'kü-lē\ valley E Wash. extending SSW from S wall of canyon of Columbia River where it turns W in forming the Big Bend

Grand Coulee Dam dam NE central Wash. in Columbia River — see FRANKLIN D. ROOSEVELT LAKE

Grande Prai·rie \'grand-'prer-ē, -'prä-rē\ city Canada in W Alberta *pop* 28,271

Grande, Rio **1** \ˌrē-ō-'grand, -'gran-dē\ river U.S. & Mexico — see RIO GRANDE **2** \ˌrē-ō-'gran-də, -dē\ river 680 *mi* (1094 *km*) E Brazil in Minas Gerais flowing W to unite with Paranaíba River forming Paraná River

Grande–Terre \grän-'ter\ island French West Indies constituting the E portion of Guadeloupe *area* 220 *sq mi* (572 *sq km*)

Grand Falls — see CHURCHILL FALLS

Grand Forks city E N.Dak. on Red River *pop* 49,425

Grand Island city SE central Nebr. near Platte River *pop* 39,386

Grand Junction city W Colo. on Colorado River *pop* 29,034

Grand Lac — see TONLE SAP

Grand Ma·nan Island \mə-'nan\ island 20 *mi* (32 *km*) long Canada in New Brunswick at entrance to Bay of Fundy

Grand Portage National Monument historic site NE Minn. on Lake Superior

Grand Prairie city NE central Tex. W of Dallas *pop* 99,616

Grand Rapids city SW Mich. on Grand River *pop* 189,126

Grand Te·ton \'tē-ˌtän, 'tē-t'n\ mountain 13,770 *ft* (4197 *m*) W Wyo. in Grand Teton National Park; highest in Teton Range

Grand Teton National Park reservation NW Wyo. including Jackson Lake & main part of Teton Range

Grand Trav·erse Bay \'tra-vərs\ inlet of Lake Michigan in Mich. on NW coast of Lower Peninsula

Grand Turk — see TURKS AND CAICOS

Grand·view \'grand-ˌvyü\ city W Mo. *pop* 24,967

Grange·mouth \'grānj-ˌmau̇th, -ˌmau̇th\ burgh & port central Scotland in Central region on Firth of Forth *pop* 21,666

Granicus — see KOCABAS

Granite City city SW Ill. on Mississippi River *pop* 32,862

Granite Peak mountain 12,799 *ft* (3901 *m*) S Mont. NE of Yellowstone National Park in Beartooth Range (spur of Absaroka Range); highest point in state

Gran Pa·ra·di·so \grän-ˌpär-ä-'dē-(ˌ)zō\ mountain 13,323 *ft* (4061 *m*) NW Italy in NW Piedmont; highest in Graian Alps

Grape·vine \'grāp-ˌvīn\ city N Tex. NE of Fort Worth *pop* 29,202

Gras·mere \'gras-ˌmir\ lake 1 *mi* (1.6 *km*) long NW England in Cumbria in Lake District

Grasse \'gras, 'gräs\ commune SE France W of Nice *pop* 42,077

Grass·lands National Park \'gras-ˌlandz, -ˌləndz\ reservation Canada in SW Saskatchewan

Grau·bün·den \grau̇-'bün-dən, -'bu̇en-\ *or French* **Gri·sons** \grē-'zōⁿ\ canton E Switzerland ✻ Chur *area* 2745 *sq mi* (7110 *sq km*), *pop* 177,096

Graudenz — see GRUDZIADZ

Gravenhage, 's — see HAGUE (The)

Graves·end \ˌgrāvz-'end\ town SE England in Kent on Thames estuary *pop* 52,963

Grays Harbor \'grāz\ inlet of the Pacific W Wash.

Grays Peak mountain 14,270 *ft* (4349 *m*) central Colo., highest in Front Range

Graz \'gräts\ city S Austria ✻ of Styria on the Mur *pop* 232,155

Great Abaco — see ABACO

Great Australian Bight wide bay on S coast of Australia; part of Indian Ocean

Great Barrier Reef coral reef 1250 *mi* (2012 *km*) long Australia in Coral Sea off NE coast of Queensland; in part comprises a marine park

Great Basin region W U.S. between Sierra Nevada & Wasatch Range including most of Nev. & parts of Calif., Idaho, Utah, Wyo., & Oreg. & having no drainage to ocean; contains many isolated mountain ranges (the **Basin Ranges**)

Great Basin National Park reservation E Nev. including Wheeler Peak & Lehman Caves

Great Bear Lake lake Canada in W Northwest Territories *area* over 12,000 *sq mi* (31,200 *sq km*)

Great Brit·ain \'bri-t'n\ *or* **Britain** **1** island W Europe comprising England, Scotland, & Wales *area* 88,150 *sq mi* (228,300 *sq km*), *pop* 53,917,000 **2** UNITED KINGDOM

Great Crosby — see CROSBY

Great Dismal — see DISMAL

Great Divide — see CONTINENTAL DIVIDE

Great Dividing Range mountain system E Australia extending from Cape York Peninsula to S Victoria &, interrupted by Bass Strait, into Tasmania — see KOSCIUSKO (Mount)

Greater Antilles group of islands in the West Indies including Cuba, Hispaniola, Jamaica, & Puerto Rico

Greater London — see LONDON 2

Greater Manchester metropolitan area NW England comprising Manchester and nearby boroughs *area* 514 *sq mi* (1331 *sq km*), *pop* 2,454,800

Greater Sunda Islands — see SUNDA ISLANDS

Greater Walachia — see MUNTENIA

Great Exuma — see EXUMA

Great Falls **1** waterfall 35 *ft* (11 *m*) in the Potomac N of Washington, D.C. **2** city W central Mont. on the Missouri River WSW of the **Great Falls of the Missouri** (waterfall, now in modified form) *pop* 55,097

Great Inagua — see INAGUA

Great Indian Desert — see THAR DESERT

Great Kabylia — see KABYLIA

Great Karroo — see KARROO

Great Lakes **1** chain of five lakes (Superior, Michigan, Huron, Erie, & Ontario) central N. America in the U.S. & Canada draining through St. Lawrence River into the Atlantic **2** group of lakes E central Africa including Lakes Turkana, Albert, Victoria, Tanganyika, & Malawi

Great Namaqualand — see NAMAQUALAND

Great Ouse — see OUSE

Great Plains elevated plains region W central U.S. & W Canada E of Rocky Mountains & chiefly W of 100th meridian extending from NE British Columbia & NW Alberta SE & S to include the Llano Estacado of N.Mex. & Tex.

Great Rift Valley depression SW Asia & E Africa extending with several breaks from valley of Jordan River S to central Mozambique

Great Saint Ber·nard \ˌsänt-bər-'närd\ mountain pass 8090 *ft* (2468 *m*) through Pennine Alps between Switzerland & Italy

Great Salt Lake lake *about* 80 *mi* (130 *km*) long N Utah having strongly saline waters & no outlet

Great Salt Lake Desert flat barren region NW Utah

Great Sand Dunes National Monument reservation S Colo. on W slope of Sangre de Cristo Mountains

Great Slave Lake \'slāv\ lake NW Canada in S Northwest Territories receiving Slave River on S & draining into Mackenzie River on W *area about* 11,000 *sq mi* (28,490 *sq km*)

Great Smoky Mountains mountains on N.C.–Tenn. boundary partly in **Great Smoky Mountains National Park** — see CLINGMANS DOME

Great Stour — see STOUR 3

Great Yarmouth — see YARMOUTH

Greece \'grēs\ *or New Greek* **El·lás** \e-'läs\ *or ancient Greek* **Hel·las** \'he-ləs\ country S Europe at S end of Balkan Peninsula; a republic ✻ Athens *area* 50,944 *sq mi* (131,945 *sq km*), *pop* 10,310,000

Gree·ley \'grē-lē\ city N Colo. *pop* 60,536

\ə\ abut \ᵊ\ kitten \ər\ further \a\ ash \ā\ ace
\ä\ mop, mar \au̇\ out \ch\ chin \e\ bet \ē\ easy
\g\ go \i\ hit \ī\ ice \j\ job \ŋ\ sing \ō\ go
\ȯ\ law \ȯi\ boy \th\ thin \th\ the \ü\ loot \u̇\ foot
\y\ yet \zh\ vision *see also* Guide to Pronunciation

Green \'grēn\ river 730 *mi* (1175 *km*) W U.S. flowing from Wind River Range in W Wyo. S into Colorado River in SE Utah

Green Bay 1 inlet of NW Lake Michigan 120 *mi* (193 *km*) long in NW Mich. & NE Wis. **2** city NE Wis. on Green Bay *pop* 96,466

Green·belt \'grēn-,belt\ city *central* Md. *pop* 21,096

Green·field \'grēn-,fēld\ city SE Wis. near Milwaukee *pop* 33,403

Green·land \'grēn-lənd, -,land\ *or native* **Ka·laal·lit Nu·naat** \kä-'lät-,lēt-nü-'nät, -'lä-\ island in N Atlantic off NE N. America belonging to Denmark ✳ Nuuk *area* 839,999 *sq mi* (2,175,597 *sq km*), *pop* 55,171 — **Green·land·er** \-lən-dər, -,lan-\ *noun*

Greenland Sea arm of Arctic Ocean between Greenland & Spitsbergen

Green Mountains mountains E N. America in Appalachian system extending from S Quebec S through Vt. into W Mass. — see MANSFIELD (Mount)

Gree·nock \'grē-nək\ burgh & port SW Scotland in Strathclyde on Firth of Clyde *pop* 57,324

Greens·boro \'grēnz-,bər-ō\ city N *central* N.C. *pop* 183,521

Green·ville \'grēn-,vil, -vəl\ **1** city W Miss. on Mississippi River *pop* 45,226 **2** city E N.C. *pop* 44,972 **3** city NW S.C. *pop* 58,282 **4** city NE Tex. NE of Dallas on the Sabine *pop* 23,071

Green·wich 1 \'gre-nich, 'grēn-,wich, 'grin-,wich\ town SW Conn. on Long Island Sound *pop* 58,441 **2** \'gri-nij, 'gre-, -nich\ borough of E Greater London, England *pop* 200,800

Green·wich Village \'gre-nich-\ section of New York City in Manhattan on lower W side

Green·wood \'grēn-,wùd\ **1** city *central* Ind. *pop* 26,265 **2** city S S.C. *pop* 20,807

Gre·na·da \grə-'nā-də\ island Brit. West Indies in S Windward Islands; with S Grenadines, independent member of the Commonwealth of Nations since 1974 ✳ St. George's *area* 133 *sq mi* (346 *sq km*), *pop* 98,000 — **Gre·na·dan** \-'nā-d'n\ *adjective or noun* — **Gre·na·di·an** \-'nā-dē-ən\ *adjective or noun*

Gren·a·dines \,gre-nə-'dēnz, 'gre-nə-,\ islands Brit. West Indies in *central* Windward Islands between Grenada & St. Vincent; divided administratively between Grenada & St. Vincent and the Grenadines

Gre·no·ble \grə-'nō-bəl, -'nòbl°\ city SE France on the Isère *pop* 153,973

Gresh·am \'gre-shəm\ city NW Oreg. E of Portland *pop* 68,235

Grey·lock, Mount \'grā-,läk\ mountain 3491 *ft* (1064 *m*) NW Mass.; highest in Berkshire Hills & in state

Grif·fin \'gri-fən\ city W *central* Ga. *pop* 21,347

Grims·by \'grimz-bē\ borough E England in Humberside near mouth of the Humber *pop* 92,147

Grin·del·wald \'grin-d°l-,wóld, -,vält\ valley & village *central* Switzerland in Bern canton in the Berner Alpen E of Interlaken

Gri·qua·land West \'gri-kwə-,land, 'grē-\ district NW Republic of South Africa in NE Northern Cape N of Orange River; chief town Kimberley

Gris–Nez, Cape \grē-'nā\ headland N France projecting into Strait of Dover

Grisons — see GRAUBÜNDEN

Grod·no \'gräd-(,)nō, 'gród-nə\ *or* **Hrod·na** *or* **Hrod·no** \'kród-nə\ city W Belarus on the Neman *pop* 284,800

Gro·ning·en \'grō-niŋ-ən, 'krō-niŋ-ə(n)\ **1** province NE Netherlands *area* 934 *sq mi* (2419 *sq km*), *pop* 555,397 **2** city, its ✳ *pop* 169,387

Gros Morne National Park \grō-'mórn\ reservation Canada in Newfoundland (island)

Gross·glock·ner \grōs-'glók-nər\ mountain 12,457 *ft* (3797 *m*) SW Austria, highest in the Hohe Tauern & in Austria

Gros Ventre \'grō-,vänt\ river 100 *mi* (161 *km*) W Wyo. flowing W into Snake River

Grot·on \'grä-t°n\ town SE Conn. E of New London *pop* 45,144

Grove City \'grōv-\ city *central* Ohio *pop* 19,661

Groz·ny *or* **Groz·nyy** \'gróz-nē, 'gräz-\ city S Russia in Europe, N of Caucasus Mountains *pop* 388,000

Gru·dziadz \'grü-jònts\ *or German* **Grau·denz** \'graú-,dents\ city N Poland on the Vistula NE of Bydgoszcz *pop* 100,861

Gua·da·la·ja·ra \,gwä-d°l-ə-'här-ə, ,gwä-thä-lä-'hä-rä\ **1** city W *central* Mexico ✳ of Jalisco *pop* 1,628,617 **2** province E *central* Spain in NE New Castile *area* 4707 *sq mi* (12,191 *sq km*), *pop* 145,593 **3** commune, ✳ of Guadalajara province, Spain *pop* 62,943

Gua·dal·ca·nal \,gwä-d°l-kə-'nal, ,gwä-də-kə-\ island W Pacific in the SE Solomons *pop* 23,922 — see HONIARA

Gua·dal·qui·vir \,gwä-d°l-ki-'vir, -'kwi-vər\ river 408 *mi* (656 *km*) S Spain flowing W & SW into Gulf of Cádiz

Gua·da·lupe \,gwä-d°l-,üp\ river SE Tex. flowing SE into San Antonio River

Gua·da·lupe Hi·dal·go \,gwä-d°l-,üp-hi-'dal-(,)gō, ,gwä-thä-'lü-pā-ē-'thäl-(,)gō\ **1** former city *central* Mexico N of Mexico City now part of city of Gustavo A. Madero **2** GUSTAVO A. MADERO (villa)

Guadalupe Mountains mountains S N.Mex. & W Tex., the S extension of Sacramento Mountains; highest point **Guadalupe Peak,** 8749 *ft* (2667 *m*) in **Guadalupe Mountains National Park** (in Tex.)

Gua·de·loupe \'gwä-d°l-,üp, ,gwä-d°l-'\ two islands, Basse-Terre (or Guadeloupe proper) & Grande-Terre, in French West Indies in *central* Leeward Islands; an overseas department of France ✳ Basse-Terre (on Basse-Terre Is.) *area* 582 *sq mi* (1507 *sq km*), *pop* 418,000 — **Gua·de·lou·pe·an** \,gwä-d°l-,ü-pē-ən\ *noun*

Gua·di·a·na \,gwä-'thyä-nä\ river 515 *mi* (829 *km*) Spain & Portugal flowing W & S into Gulf of Cádiz

Guairá — see SETE QUEDAS

Guam \'gwäm\ island W Pacific in S Marianas belonging to U.S. ✳ Agana *area* 209 *sq mi* (541 *sq km*), *pop* 143,000 — **Gua·ma·ni·an** \gwä-'mä-nē-ən\ *adjective or noun*

Gua·na·ba·coa \,gwä-nä-bä-'kō-ä\ city W Cuba E of Havana *pop* 100,452

Gua·na·ba·ra Bay \,gwä-nä-'bär-ə\ inlet of Atlantic Ocean SE Brazil

Gua·na·jua·to \,gwä-nä-'hwä-(,)tō\ **1** state *central* Mexico *area* 11,810 *sq mi* (30,588 *sq km*), *pop* 3,982,593 **2** city, its ✳ *pop* 113,580

Guang·dong \'gwäŋ-'dùŋ\ *or* **Kwang·tung** \'gwäŋ-'dùŋ, 'kwäŋ-, -'tùŋ\ province SE China bordering on S. China Sea & Gulf of Tonkin ✳ Guangzhou *area* 76,220 *sq mi* (197,410 *sq km*), *pop* (with Hainan) 62,829,236

Guang·xi Zhuang·zu \'gwäŋ-'shē-'jwäŋ-'dzü\ *or* **Kwang·si Chuang** \'gwäŋ-'shē-'jwäŋ\ region & former province S China W of Guangdong ✳ Nanning *area* 85,096 *sq mi* (221,250 *sq km*), *pop* 42,245,765

Guang·zhou *or* **Kuang–chou** \'gwäŋ-'jō\ *or* **Can·ton** \'kan-,tän, kan-'\ city & port SE China ✳ of Guangdong on Zhu River *pop* 2,914,281

Guan·tá·na·mo \gwän-'tä-nə-,mō\ city SE Cuba NW of **Guantánamo Bay** (inlet of the Caribbean; site of U.S. naval station) *pop* 200,381

Gua·po·ré \,gwä-pō-'rā\ **1** *or* **Ité·nez** \ē-'tä-nes\ river 1087 *mi* (1749 *km*) W Brazil & NE Bolivia flowing NW to the Mamoré **2** — see RONDÔNIA

Guar·da·fui, Cape \,g(w)är-dä-'fwē, -'fü-ē\ cape NE Somalia at entrance to Gulf of Aden

Guá·ri·co \'gwär-i-,kō\ river W Venezuela flowing SW & S into the Apure

Gua·te·ma·la \,gwä-tə-'mä-lə, -tä-'mä-lä\ **1** country Central America S of Mexico bordering on the Pacific & the Caribbean; a republic *area* 42,042 *sq mi* (109,309 *sq km*), *pop* 9,713,000 **2** *or* **Guatemala City** city, its ✳ *pop* 1,132,730 — **Gua·te·ma·lan** \-'mä-lən\ *adjective or noun*

Gua·via·re \,gwä-'vyä-rä\ river 650 *mi* (1046 *km*) Colombia flowing E into the Orinoco

Gua·ya·ma \,gwä-'yä-mä\ town SE Puerto Rico *pop* 21,692

Gua·ya·quil \,gwī-ə-'kē(ə)l, -'kil\ city & port W Ecuador on Guayas River 40 *mi* (64 *km*) from **Gulf of Guayaquil** (inlet of the Pacific) *pop* 1,508,444

Gua·yas \'gwī-äs\ river W Ecuador forming delta in Gulf of Guayaquil

Guay·mas \'gwī-mäs\ city & port NW Mexico in Sonora on Gulf of California *pop* 128,960

Guay·na·bo \gwī-'nä-(,)bō, -(,)vō\ city NE *central* Puerto Rico *pop* 73,385

Guelph \'gwelf\ city Canada in SE Ontario *pop* 87,976

Guern·sey \'gərn-zē\ island English Channel in the Channel Islands ✳ St. Peter Port *area* 24 *sq mi* (62 *sq km*), *pop* 55,421

Guer·re·ro \gə-'rä-rō\ state S Mexico bordering on the Pacific ✳ Chilpancingo *area* 24,631 *sq mi* (63,794 *sq km*), *pop* 2,620,637

Gui \'gwē\ *or* **Kuei** \'gwä\ river 200 *mi* (322 *km*) SE China in E Guangxi Zhuangzu flowing S into the Xi

Gui·a·na \gē-'a-nə, -'ä-nə; gī-'a-nə\ region N S. America bordering on the Atlantic & bounded on W & S by Orinoco, Negro, & Amazon rivers; includes Guyana, French Guiana, Suriname, & adjoining parts of Brazil & Venezuela — **Gui·a·nan** \-nən\ *adjective or noun* — **Gui·a·nese** \,gī-ə-'nēz, gē-ə-, -'nēs\ *adjective or noun*

Gui·enne *or* **Guy·enne** \gwē-'yen\ region & former province SW France bordering on Bay of Biscay ✳ Bordeaux — see AQUITAINE

Guil·ford \'gil-fərd\ city S Conn. on Long Island Sound *pop* 19,848

Gui·lin \'gwē-'lin\ *or* **Kuei–lin** *or* **Kwei·lin** \'gwä-'lin\ city S China in NE Guangxi Zhuangzu on the Gui *pop* 364,130

Guin·ea \'gi-nē\ *or French* **Gui·née** \gē-'nā\ **1** region W Africa bordering on the Atlantic from Gambia (on N) to Angola (on S) **2** *or formerly* **French Guinea** republic W Africa bordering on the Atlantic; formerly a territory of French West Africa ✳ Conakry *area* 94,925 *sq mi* (245,836 *sq km*), *pop* 7,300,000 — **Guin·ean** \'gi-nē-ən\ *adjective or noun*

Guinea, Gulf of arm of the Atlantic W *central* Africa; includes Bights of Benin & Biafra

Guin·ea–Bis·sau \,gi-nē-bi-'saú\ *or formerly* **Portuguese Guinea** republic W Africa S of Senegal; until 1974 a Portuguese colony ✳ Bissau *area* 13,948 *sq mi* (36,265 *sq km*), *pop* 1,036,000

Gui·púz·coa \gē-'püs-kō-ə, -'püth-kō-ä\ province N Spain; in Basque Country ✳ San Sebastian *area* 771 *sq mi* (1997 *sq km*), *pop* 676,488

Gui·yang \'gwē-'yäŋ\ *or* **Kuei–yang** *or* **Kwei·yang** \'gwä-'yäŋ\ city S China ✳ of Guizhou *pop* 1,018,619

Gui·zhou \'gwē-'jō\ *or* **Kwei·chow** \'gwä-'jō, 'kwä-\ province S China S of Szechwan ✳ Guiyang *area* 67,181 *sq mi* (174,671 *sq km*), *pop* 32,391,066

Gu·ja·rat *or* **Gu·je·rat** \,gü-jə-'rät, ,gú-\ **1** region W India where Gujarati is spoken **2** state W India N & E of Gulf of Khambhat ✳ Gandhinagar *area* 72,236 *sq mi* (187,091 *sq km*), *pop* 41,309,582

Guj·ran·wala \,güj-rən-'wä-lə, ,gúj-\ city NE Pakistan N of Lahore *pop* 785,000

Gulf·port \'gəlf-,pórt, -,pòrt\ city & port SE Miss. *pop* 40,775

Gulf Stream warm current in N Atlantic flowing from Gulf of Mexico NE along U.S. coast to Nantucket & thence eastward

Gulja — see YINING

Gumti — see GOMATI

Gun·ni·son \'gə-nə-sən\ river 150 *mi* (241 *km*) W *central* Colo. flowing W & NW into Colorado River — see BLACK CANYON

Gun·tur \,gùn-'túr\ city E India in *central* Andhra Pradesh W of Machilipatnam *pop* 471,051

Gus·ta·vo A. Ma·de·ro, Vil·la \'vē-yä-gü-'stä-vō-,ä-mä-'thä-rō\ city *central* Mexico in Distrito Federal N of Mexico City *pop* 1,182,895

Guy·ana \gī-'a-nə\ *or formerly* **British Guiana** country N S. America on Atlantic coast; a republic within the Commonwealth of Nations since 1970 ✳ Georgetown *area* 83,000 *sq mi* (215,800 *sq km*), *pop* 755,000 — **Guy·a·nese** \,gī-ə-'nēz, -'nēs\ *adjective or noun*

Gwa·dar *or* **Gwa·dur** \'gwä-dər\ town & port SW Pakistan on Arabian Sea; until 1958 belonged to Sultan of Oman *pop* 17,000

Gwa·li·or \'gwä-lē-,ór\ **1** former state N *central* India ✳ Lashkar; part of Madhya Pradesh since 1956 **2** city N *central* India in NW Madhya Pradesh SSE of Agra *pop* 690,765

Gwent \'gwent\ county SE Wales ✳ Cwmbran *area* 531 *sq mi* (1381 *sq km*), *pop* 432,300

Gwyn·edd \'gwi-neth\ county NW Wales ✳ Caernarvon *area* 1494 *sq mi* (3869 *sq km*), *pop* 238,600

Gyandzha — see GANCA

Gyor \'jœr\ city NW Hungary WNW of Budapest *pop* 134,200

Haar·lem \'här-ləm\ city W Netherlands ✳ of N. Holland *pop* 149,788

Habana, La — see HAVANA

Ha·chi·o·ji \,hä-chē-'ō-jē\ city Japan on Honshu *pop* 466,373

Hack·en·sack \'ha-kⁿn-,sak\ city NE N.J. *pop* 37,049

Hack·ney \'hak-nē\ borough of N Greater London, England *pop* 164,200

Had·ding·ton \'ha-diŋ-tən\ **1** *or* **Had·ding·ton·shire** \-shir, -shər\ — see EAST LOTHIAN **2** royal burgh Scotland in Lothian *pop* 8117

Ha·dra·mawt *or* **Ha·dhra·maut** \,hä-drə-'maut\ region S Arabia bordering on Arabian Sea E of Aden, Yemen; chief town Al Mukalla *area* 58,500 *sq mi* (152,100 *sq km*)

Hadrumetum — see SOUSSE

Hae·ju \'hī-(,)jü\ city SW N. Korea on inlet of Yellow Sea *pop* 195,000

Ha·erh·pin — see HARBIN

Ha·gen \'hä-gⁿn\ *or* **Hagen in West·fa·len** \in-,vest-'fä-lən\ city W Germany ENE of Düsseldorf *pop* 214,085

Ha·gers·town \'hā-gərz-,taun\ city N Md. *pop* 35,445

Hague, Cap de la — see CAP DE LA HAGUE

Hague, The \thə-'hāg\ *or Dutch* **'s Gra·ven·ha·ge** \'skrä-vⁿn-,hä-kə\ city SW Netherlands in S. Holland near coast of North Sea; de facto ✳ of the Netherlands *pop* 445,287

Haidarabad — see HYDERABAD

Hai·fa \'hī-fə\ city & port NW Israel at foot of Mt. Carmel *pop* 251,000

Hai·kou \'hī-'kō\ city & port SE China ✳ of Hainan *pop* 280,153

Hai·nan \'hī-'nän\ island SE China in S. China Sea; a province ✳ Haikou *area* 13,124 *sq mi* (33,991 *sq km*), *pop* 6,557,482

Hai·naut \ā-'nō, hā-\ **1** medieval county in Low Countries SE of Flanders in modern SW Belgium & N France **2** province SW Belgium ✳ Mons *area* 1463 *sq mi* (3789 *sq km*), *pop* 1,278,791

Hai·phong \'hī-'fòŋ, -'fäŋ\ city & port N Vietnam in Tonkin in delta of Red River *pop* 449,747

Hai·ti \'hā-tē *also* hä-'ē-tē\ **1** — see HISPANIOLA **2** country W. Indies on W Hispaniola; a republic ✳ Port-au-Prince *area* 10,714 *sq mi* (27,856 *sq km*), *pop* 6,902,000

Ha·ko·da·te \,hä-kō-'dä-tā\ city & port Japan in SW Hokkaido on Tsugaru Strait *pop* 307,251

Hal·ber·stadt \'häl-bər-,shtät, -,stät\ city *central* Germany SE of Brunswick *pop* 47,713

Ha·le·a·ka·la Crater \,hä-lā-,ä-kä-'lä\ crater of dormant volcano 10,023 *ft* (3055 *m*) Hawaii on E Maui; more than 2500 *ft* (762 *m*) deep, 20 *mi* (32 *km*) in circumference; in **Haleakala National Park**

Hal·i·car·nas·sus \,ha-lə-kär-'na-səs\ ancient city SW Asia Minor in SW Caria on Aegean Sea

Hal·i·fax \'ha-lə-,faks\ **1** city & port Canada ✳ of Nova Scotia *pop* 114,455 **2** borough N England in W. Yorkshire *pop* 87,488 — **Hal·i·go·ni·an** \,ha-lə-'gō-nē-ən\ *noun*

Hal·lan·dale \'ha-lən-,dāl\ city SE Fla. S of Fort Lauderdale *pop* 30,996

Hal·le \'hä-lə\ city E *central* Germany on the Saale NW of Leipzig *pop* 232,396

Hall·statt \'hòl-,stat, 'häl-,shtät, -,stät\ village W *central* Austria on shore of **Hall·stät·ter Lake** \'hòl-,ste-tər; 'häl-,shte-, -,ste-\

Hal·ma·hera \,hal-mə-'her-ə, ,häl-\ island E Indonesia in Moluccas; lies on the equator & is largest in group *area* 6928 *sq mi* (18,013 *sq km*), *pop* 54,000

Halm·stad \'hälm-,stä(d)\ city & port SW Sweden *pop* 81,084

Halq al-Wa·di \'hálk-ál-'wä-dē\ *or* **La Gou·lette** \,lä-gü-'let\ city N Tunisia on Bay of Tunis; port for Tunis *pop* 67,685

Hälsingborg — see HELSINGBORG

Hal·tom City \'hòl-təm\ village N Tex. NE of Fort Worth *pop* 32,856

Hal·ton Hills \'hòl-tⁿn\ town Canada in S Ontario *pop* 36,816

Halys — see KIZIL IRMAK

Ha·ma *or* **Ha·mah** \'hà-,mä\ *or biblical* **Ha·math** \'hā-,math\ city W Syria on the Orontes *pop* 229,000

Ha·mad, Al \,ál-hə-'mád\ the SW portion of Syrian Desert

Ha·ma·dan \,ha-mə-'dan, ,hä-mə-'dän\ *or ancient* **Ec·bat·a·na** \ek-'ba-tⁿn-ə\ city W Iran WSW of Tehran *pop* 272,499

Ha·ma·ma·tsu \,hä-mä-'mät-(,)sü\ city Japan in S Honshu SE of Nagoya near Pacific coast *pop* 534,624

Ham·burg \'ham-,bərg; 'häm-,burg, -,burk\ city & port N Germany on the Elbe 68 *mi* (109 *km*) from its mouth; a state of the Federal Republic of Germany 1948–90 & of reunified Germany since then *area* 288 *sq mi* (749 *sq km*), *pop* 1,668,800 — **Ham·burg·er** \-,bər-gər, -,bur-\ *noun*

Ham·den \'ham-dən\ town S Conn. N of New Haven *pop* 52,434

Ha·meln \'hä-məln\ *or formerly* **Ham·e·lin** \'ha-mə-lən\ city N *central* Germany in Lower Saxony SW of Hannover *pop* 58,906

Ham·hung \'häm-,huŋ\ city E *central* N. Korea near coast *pop* 701,000

Ham·il·ton \'ha-məl-tən\ **1** city SW Ohio N of Cincinnati *pop* 61,368 **2** town & port ✳ of Bermuda *pop* 1100 **3** — see CHURCHILL **4** city & port Canada in SE Ontario on Lake Ontario *pop* 318,499 **5** city New Zealand on *central* North Is. *pop* 103,600

Hamilton, Mount mountain 4261 *ft* (1299 *m*) W Calif. E of San Jose

Hamilton Inlet inlet of the Atlantic 150 *mi* (241 *km*) long (with Lake Melville) Canada in SE Labrador

Hamm \'häm, 'ham\ city W Germany on Lippe River *pop* 180,323

Ham·mer·fest \'ha-mər-,fest, 'hä-\ town & port N Norway on island in Arctic Ocean; northernmost town in Europe, at 70°38'N *pop* 6934

Ham·mer·smith and Ful·ham \'ha-mər-,smith-ənd-'fu-ləm\ borough of SW Greater London, England *pop* 136,500

Ham·mond \'ha-mənd\ city NW Ind. SE of Chicago *pop* 84,236

Hamp·shire \'hamp-,shir, -shər\ *or* **Hants** \'hants\ county S England on English Channel ✳ Winchester *area* 1509 *sq mi* (3908 *sq km*), *pop* 1,511,900

Hamp·stead \'hamp-stəd, -,sted\ former metropolitan borough NW London, England, now part of Camden

Hamp·ton \'hamp-tən\ city & port SE Va. E of Newport News on Hampton Roads *pop* 133,793

Hampton Roads channel SE Va. through which James & Elizabeth rivers flow into Chesapeake Bay

Han \'hän\ **1** river E *central* China in Shaanxi & Hubei flowing SE into the Chang **2** river *about* 300 *mi* (483 *km*) N *central* S. Korea flowing W & NW into Yellow Sea

HaNegev — see NEGEV

Han·ford \'han-fərd\ city S *central* Calif. SE of Fresno *pop* 30,897

Hang·zhou \'häŋ-'jō\ *or* **Hang·chou** \-'jō\ *or* **Hang·chow** \'haŋ-'chau, 'häŋ-'jō\ city E China ✳ of Zhejiang at head of **Hangzhou Bay** (inlet of E. China Sea) *pop* 1,099,660

Han·ko \'haŋ-,kō\ *or Swedish* **Hangö** \'häŋ-,œ\ town & port SW Finland on Hanko (Hangö) Peninsula in the Baltic SE of Turku

Han·kow \'haŋ-'kau, -'kō; 'hän-'kō\ former city E *central* China — see WUHAN

Han·ni·bal \'ha-nə-bəl\ city NE Mo. on Mississippi River *pop* 18,004

Han·o·ver \'ha-nō-vər, -nə-vər, *German* hä-'nō-fər\ city N *central* Germany WNW of Brunswick *pop* 517,476

Ha·noi \ha-'nòi, hə-, hä-\ city ✳ of Vietnam in Tonkin on Red River; formerly ✳ of French Indochina & of N. Vietnam *metropolitan area pop* 1,089,760

Han·o·ver Park \'ha-,nō-vər, -nə-vər\ city NE Ill. *pop* 32,895

Han·yang \'hän-'yäŋ\ former city E *central* China — see WUHAN

Haora — see HOWRAH

Ha·rap·pa \hə-'ra-pə\ locality W Pakistan in Indus valley NE of Multan; center of a prehistoric civilization

Ha·ra·re \hə-'rä-(,)rā\ *or formerly* **Salisbury** city ✳ of Zimbabwe *pop* 1,184,169

Har·bin \'här-bən, här-'bin\ *or* **Ha·erh·pin** \'hä-'ər-bin\ *or formerly* **Pin·kiang** \'bin-'jyäŋ\ city NE China ✳ of Heilongjiang on Songhua River *pop* 2,443,398

Ha·rer \'här-ər\ city E Ethiopia E of Addis Ababa *pop* 76,890

Ha·ri \'har-ē\ *or* **Ha·ri Rud** \'rüd\ *or ancient* **Ari·us** \'ar-ē-əs, 'er-; ə-'rī-əs\ river 700 *mi* (1126 *km*) NW Afghanistan, NE Iran, & S Turkmenistan flowing W & N into Kara Kum Desert

Har·in·gey \'har-iŋ-,gā\ borough of N Greater London, England *pop* 187,300

Har·lem \'här-ləm\ **1** river channel SE N.Y. NE of Manhattan Is.; with Spuyten Duyvil Creek, connects Hudson & East rivers **2** section of New York City in NE Manhattan bordering on Harlem & East rivers **3** HAARLEM — **Har·lem·ite** \-lə-,mīt\ *noun*

Har·lin·gen **1** \'här-lən-jən\ city S Tex. NNW of Brownsville *pop* 48,735 **2** \-liŋ-ən\ town & port N Netherlands in Friesland

Har·ney Lake \'här-nē\ intermittent salt lake SE Oreg. in **Harney Basin** (depression, *area* 2500 *sq mi* or 6500 *sq km*)

Harney Peak mountain 7242 *ft* (2207 *m*) SW S.Dak.; highest in Black Hills & in state

Harris — see LEWIS WITH HARRIS

Har·ris·burg \'har-əs-,bərg\ city ✳ of Pa. *pop* 52,376

Har·ri·son \'har-ə-sən\ village SE N.Y. on Long Island Sound *pop* 23,308

Har·ri·son·burg \'har-ə-sən-,bərg\ city N Va. *pop* 30,707

Har·ro·gate \'har-ə-gət, -,gāt\ borough N England in N. Yorkshire N of Leeds *pop* 66,475

Har·row \'har-(,)ō\ borough of NW Greater London, England *pop* 194,300

Hart·ford \'härt-fərd\ city N *central* Conn., its ✳ *pop* 139,739 — **Hart·ford·ite** \-fər-,dīt\ *noun*

Har·tle·pool \'härt-lē-,pül\ borough N England in Cleveland on North Sea *pop* 88,200

Har·vard, Mount \'här-vərd\ mountain 14,420 *ft* (4395 *m*) *central* Colo. in Sawatch Mountains SE of Mt. Elbert

Har·vey \'här-vē\ city NE Ill. S of Chicago *pop* 29,771

Har·wich \'har-ij, -ich\ borough SE England in Essex on North Sea *pop* 15,076

Ha·ry·a·na \,hə-rē-'ä-nə\ state NW India in E Punjab formed 1966 from southern part of former state of Punjab ✳ Chandigarh *area* 17,010 *sq mi* (44,226 *sq km*), *pop* 16,463,648

Harz \'härts\ mountains *central* Germany between the Elbe & the Leine — see BROCKEN

Hasa *or* **Hasa, Al—** — see AL-HASA

Has·selt \'hä-səlt\ commune NE Belgium ✳ of Limburg *pop* 66,611

Has·tings \'hās-tiŋz\ **1** city S Nebr. *pop* 22,837 **2** borough SE England in E. Sussex on Strait of Dover *pop* 78,100

Ha·tay \hä-'tī\ district S Turkey E of Gulf of Iskenderun

Hat·ter·as Island \'ha-tə-rəs\ island N.C. between Pamlico Sound & Atlantic Ocean; a long barrier island

Hatteras, Cape cape N.C. on SE Hatteras Is.

Hat·ties·burg \'ha-tēz-,bərg\ city SE Miss. *pop* 41,882

Hau·ra·ki Gulf \hau-'ra-kē, -'rä-\ inlet of the S Pacific N New Zealand on E coast of North Is.

Haute–Vol·ta \,ōt-vòl-'tä\ UPPER VOLTA — French name

Ha·va·na \hə-'va-nə\ *or Spanish* **La Ha·ba·na** \,lä-ä-'vä-nä\ city & port ✳ of Cuba on Gulf of Mexico *pop* 2,096,054 — **Ha·van·an** \hə-'va-nən\ *adjective or noun*

Hav·ant \'ha-vənt\ town S England in Hampshire NE of Portsmouth *pop* 117,400

Ha·vel \'hä-fⁿl\ river 212 *mi* (341 *km*) NE Germany flowing SW through Berlin into the Elbe

Have·lock \'hav-,läk, -lək\ city SE N.C. *pop* 20,268

Hav·er·ford·west \ˌha-vər-fərd-'west, ˌhär-fərd-\ borough & port SW Wales in Dyfed *pop* 9936

Ha·ver·hill \'hāv-rəl, 'hā-və-rəl\ city NE Mass. *pop* 51,418

Ha·ver·ing \'hāv-riŋ, 'hā-və-riŋ\ borough of NE Greater London, England *pop* 224,400

Ha·ví·rov \hä-vēr-,zhóf\ city E Czech Republic *pop* 86,267

Havre — see LE HAVRE

Ha·waii \hə-'wä-yē, -'wä-,ē *also* -'vä-ē or -'wó; *sometimes* -yə\ **1** *or* **Ha·wai·ian Islands** \-yən\ *or formerly* **Sand·wich Islands** \'sand-ˌwich\ group of islands central Pacific belonging to U.S. **2** island SE Hawaii, largest of the group; chief city Hilo *area* 4021 *sq mi* (10,455 *sq km*) **3** state of the U.S. comprising Hawaiian Islands except Midway Islands; annexed 1898, a territory 1900–59 ✳ Honolulu *area* 6471 *sq mi* (16,760 *sq km*), *pop* 1,108,229

Hawaii Volcanoes National Park reservation Hawaii including Mauna Loa & Kilauea volcanoes on Hawaii Island (island)

Hawke Bay \'hók\ inlet of the S Pacific N New Zealand on SE coast of North Is.

Haw·thorne \'hó-ˌthórn\ **1** city SW Calif. SW of Los Angeles *pop* 71,349 **2** borough NE N.J. N of Paterson *pop* 17,084

Hay \'hā\ river 530 *mi* (853 *km*) Canada in N Alberta & SW Mackenzie district flowing NE into Great Slave Lake

Hayes \'hāz\ **1** river 300 *mi* (483 *km*) Canada in E Manitoba flowing NE into Hudson Bay **2** *or* **Hayes and Har·ling·ton** \'här-liŋ-tən\ former urban district SE England in Middlesex, now part of Hillingdon

Hay·ward \'hā-wərd\ city W Calif. SE of Oakland *pop* 111,498

Ha·zel Park \'hā-zəl\ city SE Mich. N of Detroit *pop* 20,051

Ha·zle·ton \'hā-zəl-tən\ city E Pa. S of Wilkes-Barre *pop* 24,730

Heard \'hərd\ island S Indian Ocean SE of Kerguelen, at 53°10'S, 74°10'E; claimed by Australia

He·bei \hə-'bā\ *or* **Ho·peh** *or* **Ho·pei** \'hō-'bā *or formerly* **Chih·li** \'chē-'lē, 'jir-'lē\ province NE China ✳ Shijiazhuang *area* 77,079 *sq mi* (199,635 *sq km*), *pop* 61,082,439

Heb·ri·des \'he-brə-ˌdēz\ islands W Scotland in the Atlantic divided by Little Minch into **Inner Hebrides** (near the mainland) & **Outer Hebrides** (to NW) *area* 2900 *sq mi* (7540 *sq km*), *pop* 30,660 — see LEWIS WITH HARRIS, WESTERN ISLES — **Heb·ri·de·an** \ˌhe-brə-'dē-ən\ *adjective or noun*

He·bron \'hē-brən\ *or ancient* **Kir·jath–ar·ba** \ˌkər-yəth-'är-bə, ˌkir-\ city central Palestine SSW of Jerusalem in modern Jordan *pop* 79,087

Hec·ate Strait \'he-kət\ strait Canada in W British Columbia, inlet of the Pacific between Queen Charlotte Islands & the coast

Heer·len \'her-lən\ commune SE Netherlands in Limburg NE of Maastricht *pop* 95,001

He·fei *or* **Ho·fei** \'hə-'fā\ *or formerly* **Lu·chow** \'lü-'jō\ city E China ✳ of Anhui W of Nanjing *pop* 733,278

Hei·del·berg \'hī-dᵊl-ˌbərg, -ˌberk\ city SW Germany on the Neckar SE of Mannheim *pop* 139,392

Heil·bronn \'hīl-ˌbrän, hīl-'brón\ city SW Germany on the Neckar N of Stuttgart *pop* 117,427

Heilong, Hei·lung — see AMUR

Hei·long·jiang *or* **Hei·lung·kiang** \'hā-'lùŋ-'jyän\ province NE China in N Manchuria bordering on the Amur ✳ Harbin *area* 178,996 *sq mi* (465,390 *sq km*), *pop* 35,214,873

He·jaz \hē-'jaz, hi-\ *or* **Al Hi·jāz** \ˌál-hi-'jaz\ region W Saudi Arabia on Red Sea; a viceroyalty ✳ Mecca *area* 134,600 *sq mi* (348,614 *sq km*), *pop* 1,400,000

Hek·la *or* **Hec·la** \'he-klä\ volcano 4747 *ft* (1447 *m*) SW Iceland

Hel·e·na \'he-lə-nə\ city W central Mont., its ✳ *pop* 24,569

Hel·go·land \'hel-gō-ˌland, -ˌlänt\ *or* **Hel·i·go·land** \'he-lə-gō-\ island NW Germany in North Sea, in N. Frisian Group

Hel·i·con \'he-lə-ˌkän, -li-kən\ *or New Greek* **Eli·kón** \ˌe-lē-'kón\ mountain 5735 *ft* (1748 *m*) E central Greece in SW Boeotia near Gulf of Corinth

He·li·op·o·lis \ˌhē-lē-'ä-pə-lis\ **1** — see BAAL-BEK **2** ancient ruined city N Egypt S of modern Cairo **3** ancient ruined city NE of modern Cairo

Hellas — see GREECE

Hel·les, Cape \'he-(ˌ)lēz\ headland Turkey in Europe at S tip of Gallipoli Peninsula

Hellespont, Hellespontus — see DARDANELLES

Hell Gate a narrow part of East River in New York City between Long Is. & Manhattan Is.

Hells Canyon \'helz\ canyon of Snake River on Idaho-Oreg. border

Hel·mand *or* **Hel·mund** \'hel-mənd\ river SW Afghanistan flowing SW & W into a morass on Iran border

Hel·mond \'hel-ˌmónt\ commune S Netherlands *pop* 70,574

Helm·stedt \'helm-ˌshtet, -ˌstet\ city central Germany E of Brunswick near former E. Germany–W. Germany border *pop* 27,072

Hel·sing·borg *or* **Häl·sing·borg** \'hel-siŋ-ˌbórg, -ˌbor-ē\ city & port SW Sweden on Øresund opposite Helsingør, Denmark *pop* 108,359

Hel·sing·ør \ˌhel-siŋ-'œr\ city & port Denmark on N Sjælland Is. *pop* 56,754

Hel·sin·ki \'hel-ˌsiŋ-kē, hel-'\ *or Swedish* **Hel·sing·fors** \'hel-siŋ-ˌfórs\ city & port ✳ of Finland on Gulf of Finland *pop* 490,629

Hel·vel·lyn \hel-'ve-lən\ mountain 3118 *ft* (950 *m*) NW England in Cumbria SW of Ullswater

Helvetia — see SWITZERLAND — **Hel·ve·tian** \hel-'vē-shən\ *adjective or noun*

Hem·et \'he-mət\ city SE Calif. S of San Bernardino *pop* 36,094

Hemp·stead \'hem(p)-ˌsted, -stəd\ village SE N.Y. on Long Is. *pop* 49,453

He·nan \'hə-'nän\ *or* **Ho·nan** \'hō-'nan\ province E central China ✳ Zhengzhou *area* 64,479 *sq mi* (167,645 *sq km*), *pop* 85,509,535

Hen·der·son \'hen-dər-sən\ **1** city NW Ky. *pop* 25,945 **2** city S Nev. *pop* 64,942

Hen·der·son·ville \'hen-dər-sən-ˌvil, -vəl\ city N Tenn. NE of Nashville *pop* 32,188

Hen·don \'hen-dən\ former urban district SE England in Middlesex, now part of Barnet

Heng·e·lo \'heŋ-ə-ˌlō\ commune E Netherlands in Overijssel *pop* 76,726

Heng·yang \'həŋ-'yäŋ\ city SE central China in SE Hunan on the Xiang *pop* 487,148

Hen·ley \'hen-lē\ *or* **Henley on Thames** borough SE central England in Oxfordshire W of London *pop* 31,744

Hen·lo·pen, Cape \hen-'lō-pən\ headland SE Del. at entrance to Delaware Bay

Hen·ry, Cape \hen-rē\ headland SE Va. S of entrance to Chesapeake Bay

He·rat \he-'rät, hə-\ *or ancient* **Aria** \'ar-ē-ə, 'er; ə-'rī-ə\ city NW Afghanistan on the Hari *pop* 177,300

Her·cu·la·ne·um \ˌhər-kyə-'lā-nē-əm\ ancient city S Italy in Campania on Tyrrhenian Sea; destroyed A.D. 79 by eruption of Mt. Vesuvius

Her·e·ford \'her-ə-fərd, United States also 'hər-fərd\ **1** *or* **Her·e·ford·shire** \-ˌshir, -shər\ former county W England on Welsh border **2** town W England in Hereford and Worcester *pop* 49,800

Hereford and Worces·ter \'wús-tər\ county W England ✳ Worcester *area* 1571 *sq mi* (4069 *sq km*), *pop* 667,800

Her·ford \'her-fórt\ city W central Germany in N. Rhine-Westphalia NE of Bielefeld *pop* 64,732

He·ri·sau \'her-ə-ˌzaú\ commune NE Switzerland ✳ of Appenzell Outer Rhodes half canton *pop* 15,560

Her·mon, Mount \'hər-mən\ mountain 9232 *ft* (2814 *m*) on border between Syria & Lebanon; highest in Anti-Lebanon Mountains

Her·mo·sil·lo \ˌer-mō-'sē-(ˌ)yō\ city NW Mexico ✳ of Sonora on Sonora River *pop* 449,472

Hermoúpolis — see ERMOÚPOLIS

Her·ne \'her-nə\ city W Germany in the Ruhr *pop* 179,137

Her·ning \'her-niŋ, 'har-niŋ\ city Denmark in central Jutland *pop* 56,376

Her·ten \'her-tᵊn\ city W Germany in N. Rhine-Westphalia N of Essen *pop* 69,374

Hert·ford \'här-fərd, 'härt-, United States also 'härt-\ borough SE England ✳ of Hertfordshire *pop* 21,412

Hert·ford·shire \'här-fərd-ˌshir, 'härt-, -shər, United States also 'härt-, County SE England *area* 654 *sq mi* (1699 *sq km*), *pop* 951,500

Hertogenbosch, 's — see 'S HERTOGENBOSCH

Her·ze·go·vi·na \ˌhert-sə-gō-'vē-nə, ˌhart-, -'gō-və-nə\ *or Serbian* **Her·ce·go·vi·na** \'kert-sə-gō-vē-nə\ region S Europe S of Bosnia & NW of Montenegro; part of Bosnia and Herzegovina — **Her·ze·go·vi·nian** \ˌhert-sə-gō-'vē-nē-ən, ˌhart-, -nyən\ *noun*

Hes·pe·ria \he-'sper-ē-ə\ city SE Calif. N of San Bernardino *pop* 50,418

Hesse \'hes, 'he-sē\ *or German* **Hes·sen** \'he-sᵊn\ **1** region W central Germany N of Baden-Württemberg divided into **Hesse–Darmstadt** (in the S) & **Hesse–Cas·sel** \-'ka-sᵊl, -'kä-\ (in the N), the latter being united with Prussia in 1866 as part of the province of **Hesse–Nassau** along with the duchy of Nassau & the city of Frankfurt am Main **2** state of the Weimar Republic, equivalent to Hesse-Darmstadt **3** state of Germany & formerly of W. Germany including larger part of Hesse-Darmstadt & part of Hesse-Nassau ✳ Wiesbaden *area* 8151 *sq mi* (21,111 *sq km*), *pop* 5,763,300

Hes·ton and Isle·worth \'hes-tən-ənd-'ī-zəl-(ˌ)wərth, 'hes-ᵊn-\ former municipal borough SE England in Middlesex, now part of Hounslow

Hi·a·le·ah \ˌhī-ə-'lē-ə\ city SE Fla. N of Miami *pop* 188,004

Hibernia — see IRELAND

Hick·o·ry \'hi-kə-rē\ city W central N.C. *pop* 28,301

Hi·dal·go \hi-'dal-(ˌ)gō, ē-'thäl-(ˌ)gō\ state central Mexico ✳ Pachuca *area* 8103 *sq mi* (20,987 *sq km*), *pop* 1,888,366

Hierosolyma — see JERUSALEM

Hier·ro \'yer-(ˌ)ō\ *or* **Fer·ro** \'fer-(ˌ)ō\ island Spain, westernmost of the Canary Islands *area* 107 *sq mi* (278 *sq km*)

Hi·ga·shi·osa·ka \hē-ˌgä-shē-'ō-sä-kä\ city Japan in S Honshu; suburb of Osaka *pop* 518,251

High Atlas — see ATLAS

High·land \'hī-lənd\ **1** city SE Calif. E of San Bernardino *pop* 34,439 **2** town NW Ind. S of Hammond *pop* 23,696 **3** region N Scotland, established 1975 ✳ Inverness *area* 9806 *sq mi* (25,398 *sq km*), *pop* 206,900

Highland Park **1** city NE Ill. N of Chicago *pop* 30,575 **2** city SE Mich. within city of Detroit *pop* 20,121

High·lands \'hī-ləndz\ the chiefly mountainous N part of Scotland N of a line connecting Firth of Clyde & Firth of Tay

Highlands of Navesink — see NAVESINK (Highlands)

Highlands of the Hudson hilly region SE N.Y. on both sides of Hudson River; includes Storm King (W of the Hudson) 1355 *ft* (413 *m*)

High Plains the Great Plains especially from Nebr. southward

High Point \'hī-ˌpóint\ city N central N.C. SW of Greensboro *pop* 69,496

High Sierra the Sierra Nevada (in Calif.)

High Wyc·ombe \'wi-kəm\ borough SE central England in Buckinghamshire WNW of London *pop* 60,516

Hii·u·maa \'hē-ə-,mä\ island Estonia in Baltic Sea N of Sarema Is. *area* 373 *sq mi* (966 *sq km*)

Hijāz, Al — see HEJAZ

Hil·des·heim \'hil-dəs-,hīm\ city N central Germany SSE of Hannover *pop* 105,674

Hil·ling·don \'hi-liŋ-dən\ borough of W Greater London, England *pop* 225,800

Hills·boro \'hilz-,bər-ō\ city NW Oreg. W of Portland *pop* 37,520

Hi·lo \'hē-(ˌ)lō\ city & port Hawaii in E Hawaii (island) *pop* 37,808

Hil·ton Head Island \'hil-tᵊn-'hed\ island comprising a town of S.C. coast *pop* 23,694

Hil·ver·sum \'hil-vər-səm\ city central Netherlands in N. Holland SE of Amsterdam *pop* 84,674

Hi·ma·chal Pra·desh \hi-'mä-chəl-prə-'desh, -'däsh\ state NW India NW of Uttar Pradesh ✳ Simla *area* 21,490 *sq mi* (55,659 *sq km*), *pop* 5,170,877

Hi·ma·la·ya, the \ˌhi-mə-'lā-ə; hə-'mäl-yə, -'mä-lē-ə\ *or* **the Hi·ma·la·yas** \-əz\ mountains S Asia on border between India & Tibet & in

Kashmir, Nepal, & Bhutan — see EVEREST (Mount) — **Hi·ma·la·yan** \ˌhi-mə-ˈlā-ən; hə-ˈmäl-yən, -ˈmäl-ē-ən\ *adjective*

Hi·me·ji \hē-ˈmā-jē\ city Japan in W Honshu *pop* 454,360

Hindenburg — see ZABRZE

Hin·du Kush \ˈhin-(ˌ)dü-ˈkush, -ˈkəsh\ *or ancient* **Cau·ca·sus In·di·cus** \ˈkȯ-kə-səs-ˈin-di-kəs\ mountain range *central* Asia SW of the Pamirs on border of Kashmir & in Afghanistan — see TIRICH MIR

Hin·du·stan \ˌhin-(ˌ)dü-ˈstan, -də-, -ˈstän\ **1** region N India N of the Deccan including the plain drained by the Indus, the Ganges, & the Brahmaputra **2** the subcontinent of India **3** the Republic of India

Hines·ville \ˈhīnz-ˌvil, -vəl\ town SE Ga. *pop* 21,603

Hing·ham \ˈhiŋ-əm\ town E Mass. SE of Boston *pop* 19,821

Hip·po \ˈhi-(ˌ)pō\ *or* **Hippo Re·gi·us** \ˈrē-jəs, -jē-əs\ ancient city N Africa S of modern Bône, Algeria; chief town of Numidia

Hi·ra·ka·ta \ˌhe-rä-ˈkä-tä\ city Japan on Honshu *pop* 390,790

Hi·ro·shi·ma \ˌhir-ə-ˈshē-mə, hə-ˈrō-shə-mə\ city & port Japan in SW Honshu on Inland Sea *pop* 1,096,919

His·pa·nia \hi-ˈspā-nē-ə, -ˈspä-nyə, -ˈspä-\ IBERIAN PENINSULA

His·pan·io·la \ˌhis-pə-ˈnyō-lə\ *or Spanish* **Es·pa·ño·la** \ˌes-ˌpä-ˈnyō-lä\ *or formerly* **Hai·ti** \ˈhā-tē\ *or* **San·to Do·min·go** \ˌsan-tə-də-ˈmiŋ-(ˌ)gō\ *or* **San Domingo** \ˌsan-də-\ island West Indies in the Greater Antilles; divided between Haiti (on W) & Dominican Republic (on E) *area* 29,371 *sq mi* (76,071 *sq km*)

His·sar·lik \ˌhi-sər-ˈlik\ site of ancient Troy NW Turkey in Asia 4 *mi* (6.4 *km*) SE of mouth of the Dardanelles

Hi·was·see \hī-ˈwä-sē\ river 150 *mi* (241 *km*) E U.S. flowing from NE Ga. WNW through W N.C. into Tennessee River in Tenn.

Ho·bart 1 \ˈhō-bərt\ city NW Ind. *pop* 21,822 **2** \-ˌbärt\ city & port Australia ✳ of Tasmania *pop* 47,106

Hobbs \ˈhäbz\ city SE corner of N.Mex. *pop* 29,115

Ho·bo·ken \ˈhō-ˌbō-kən\ city NE N.J. N of Jersey City *pop* 33,397

Ho Chi Minh City \ˈhō-ˌchē-ˈmin\ *or formerly* **Sai·gon** \sī-ˈgän, ˈsī-ˌ\ city & port S Vietnam; formerly (as Saigon) ✳ of S. Vietnam *pop* 2,899,753

Hodeida — see AL HUDAYDAH

Hof \ˈhōf, ˈhȯf\ city Germany in Bavaria on the Saale near former E. Germany–W. Germany border *pop* 52,859

Hofei — see HEFEI

Hoff·man Estates \ˈhäf-mən, ˈhȯf-\ village NE Ill. *pop* 46,561

Hofuf — see AL HUFUF

Hoggar — see AHAGGAR

Ho·hen·zol·lern \ˈhō-ən-ˌzä-lərn, -ˌtsȯ-lərn\ region SW Germany, formerly a province of Prussia — see WÜRTTEMBERG

Ho·he Tau·ern \ˌhō-ə-ˈtaú-(ə)rn\ range of the E Alps W Austria between Carinthia & Tirol — see GROSSGLOCKNER

Hoh·hot \ˈhō-ˈhȯt\ *or* **Hu·he·hot** \ˈhü-(ˌ)hā-ˈhȯt\ *or* **Hu·ho·hao·t'e** \ˈhü-ˈhȯ-haú-tə-\ city N China ✳ of Inner Mongolia *pop* 652,534

Ho·ho·kam Pi·ma National Monument \ˌhō-ˈhō-kəm-ˈpē-mə\ reservation SE of Phoenix, Ariz.; not open to the public

Hok·kai·do \hȯ-ˈkī-(ˌ)dō\ *or formerly* **Ye·zo** \ˈye-(ˌ)zō\ island N Japan N of Honshu *area with adjacent small islands* 30,313 *sq mi* (78,511 *sq km*), *pop* 5,643,715

Hol·guín \(ˌ)hȯl-ˈgēn\ city E Cuba in plateau region *pop* 228,052

Hol·land \ˈhä-lənd\ **1** city W Mich. on Lake Michigan *pop* 30,745 **2** medieval county of Holy Roman Empire bordering on North Sea, now forming N. & S. Holland provinces of the Netherlands **3** — see NETHERLANDS — **Hol·land·er** \-lən-dər\ *noun*

Holland, Parts of district & former administrative county E England in SE Lincolnshire ✳ Boston *area* 418 *sq mi* (1083 *sq km*)

Hollandia — see JAYAPURA

Hol·lis·ter \ˈhä-lə-stər\ city W Calif. E of Monterey Bay *pop* 19,212

Hol·ly·wood \ˈhä-lē-ˌwúd\ **1** section of Los Angeles, Calif. NW of the downtown district **2** city SE Fla. N of Miami *pop* 121,697

Hol·stein \ˈhōl-ˌstīn, -ˌstēn; ˈhȯl-ˌstīn\ region N Germany S of Jutland Peninsula adjoining Schleswig; once a duchy of Denmark, became a part of Prussia 1866 — see SCHLESWIG-HOLSTEIN

Hol·ston \ˈhōl-stən\ river 140 *mi* (225 *km*) E Tenn. flowing SW to unite with French Broad River forming the Tennessee River

Holy Cross, Mount of the mountain 14,005 *ft* (4269 *m*) NW *central* Colo. in Sawatch Range

Holy·head \ˈhä-lē-ˌhed\ **1** island NW Wales in St. George's Channel off W coast of Anglesey **2** urban area & port NW Wales in Gwynedd on Holy Is.

Ho·ly Island \ˈhō-lē\ *or* **Lin·dis·farne** \ˈlin-dəs-ˌfärn\ island N England off NE coast of Northumberland; connected to mainland at low tide *pop* 190

Holy Land a name for Palestine first used in Zechariah 2:12

Holy Loch inlet of Firth of Clyde W Scotland on NW shore of the firth opposite mouth of the Clyde

Hol·yoke \ˈhōl-ˌyōk\ city SW Mass. N of Springfield *pop* 43,704

Holy Roman Empire realm of *central* Europe in medieval & modern periods; of varying extent, but with Germany as chief component

Homel *or* **Homyel'** — see GOMEL

Home·stead \ˈhōm-ˌsted\ city SE Fla. SW of Miami *pop* 26,866

Homestead National Monument site SE Nebr. (W of Beatrice) of first homestead entered under General Homestead Act of 1862

Home·wood \ˈhōm-ˌwúd\ **1** city *central* Ala. *pop* 22,922 **2** village NE Ill. S of Chicago *pop* 19,278

Homs \ˈhōmz, ˈhúms\ *or ancient* **Em·e·sa** \ˈe-mə-sə\ city W Syria on the Orontes *pop* 354,508

Honan — see HENAN

Hon·du·ras \hän-ˈdúr-əs, -ˈdyúr-; ȯn-ˈdü-räs\ country Central America bordering on the Caribbean & the Pacific; a republic ✳ Tegucigalpa *area* 43,277 *sq mi* (112,087 *sq km*), *pop* 4,604,800 — **Hon·du·ran** \-ən\ *adjective or noun* — **Hon·du·ra·ne·an** *or* **Hon·du·ra·ni·an** \ˌhän-dú-ˈrä-nē-ən, -dyú-\ *adjective or noun*

Honduras, Gulf of inlet of the Caribbean between S Belize, E Guatemala, & N Honduras

Hon·fleur \ōⁿ-ˈflœr\ town & port N France on Seine estuary *pop* 8346

Hong — see RED

Hong Kong \ˈhäŋ-ˌkäŋ, -ˈkäŋ; ˈhȯŋ-ˌkȯŋ, -ˈkȯŋ\ **1** territory China on SE coast E of mouth of Zhu River including Hong Kong Is., Kowloon Peninsula & adjacent area (New Territories) on mainland, & nearby islands; formerly a Brit. crown colony ✳ Victoria *area* 398 *sq mi* (1031 *sq km*), *pop* 4,986,560 **2** — see VICTORIA — **Hong·kong·er** *noun*

Hong·shui *or* **Hung·shui** \ˈhúŋ-ˈshwē\ river S China flowing from E Yunnan E to E Guangxi Zhuangzu

Hong·ze *or* **Hung·tse** \ˈhúŋ-ˈdzə\ lake 65 *mi* (105 *km*) long E China in W Jiangsu; traversed by the Huang

Ho·ni·a·ra \ˌhō-nē-ˈär-ə\ town W Pacific ✳ of Solomon Islands on Guadalcanal Is. *pop* 35,288

Ho·no·lu·lu \ˌhä-nə-ˈl-ü-(ˌ)lü, ˌhō-nə-ˈl-ü-l-\ city & port ✳ of Hawaii on Oahu *pop* 365,272 — **Ho·no·lu·lan** \-ˈl-ü-lən\ *noun*

Hon·shu \ˈhän-(ˌ)shü, ˈhȯn-\ *or* **Hon·do** \-(ˌ)dō\ island Japan, chief island of the group *area* 86,246 *sq mi* (223,377 *sq km*), *pop* 100,254,208

Hood, Mount \ˈhúd\ mountain 11,235 *ft* (3424 *m*) NW Oreg. in Cascade Range; highest point in state

Hood Canal inlet of Puget Sound 80 *mi* (129 *km*) long W Wash. along E shore of Olympic Peninsula

Hoofd·dorp \ˈhōft-ˌdȯrp\ commune W Netherlands *pop* 100,659

Hooghly — see HUGLI

Hook of Holland \ˈhúk\ headland SW Netherlands in S. Holland on coast SW of The Hague

Hoorn Islands — see FUTUNA ISLANDS

Hoo·sac Mountains \ˈhü-sək\ mountain range NW Mass. & SW Vt., a southern extension of Green Mountains

Hoo·ver \ˈhü-vər\ city *central* Ala. *pop* 39,788

Hoover Dam *or formerly* **Boul·der Dam** \ˈbōl-dər\ dam 726 *ft* (221 *m*) high in Colorado River between Nev. & Ariz. — see MEAD (Lake)

Ho·pat·cong, Lake \hə-ˈpat-ˌkän, -ˌkäŋ\ lake 8 *mi* (13 *km*) long N N.J.

Hopeh *or* **Hopei** — see HEBEI

Hope·well \ˈhōp-ˌwel, -wəl\ city SE Va. *pop* 23,101

Hop·kins·ville \ˈhäp-kənz-ˌvil\ city SW Ky. *pop* 29,809

Ho·reb, Mount \ˈhȯr-ˌeb, ˈhȯr-\ *or* **Mount Si·nai** \ˈsī-ˌnī *also* -nē-ˌī\ mountain where according to the Bible the Law was given to Moses; thought to be in the Gebel Musa on Sinai Peninsula

Horlivka — see GORLOVKA

Hor·moz \hȯr-ˈmȯz\ *or* **Hor·muz** \same *or* hȯr-ˈmúz\ island SE Iran in Strait of Hormuz

Hor·muz *or* **Or·muz** \ˈhȯr-ˌmȯz, hȯr-ˈmúz\ ancient town S Iran on **Strait of Hormuz** (strait connecting Persian Gulf & Gulf of Oman)

Horn \ˈhȯrn\ *or* **North Cape** cape NW Iceland

Horn, Cape headland S Chile on **Horn Island** in Tierra del Fuego; southernmost point of S. America, at 55°59′S

Horn·church \ˈhȯrn-ˌchərch\ former urban district SE England in Essex, now part of Havering

Horn of Africa the easternmost projection of Africa; variously used of Somalia, SE or all of Ethiopia & sometimes Djibouti; its E tip is Cape Guardafui

Hor·sens \ˈhȯr-sⁿz, -sⁿn(t)s\ city & port Denmark *pop* 54,940

Hos·pi·ta·let \ˌ(h)äs-ˌpi-tⁿl-ˈet, ˌōs-pē-tä-ˈlet\ city NE Spain in Barcelona province, SW suburb of Barcelona *pop* 269,241

Ho·tan \ˈhō-ˈtän\ *or* **Ho·t'ien** \ˈhō-ˈtyen\ *or* **Kho·tan** \ˈkō-ˈtän\ town & oasis W China in SW Xinjiang Uygur on S edge of the Taklimakan

Hot Springs city W *central* Ark. adjoining **Hot Springs National Park** (reservation containing hot mineral springs) *pop* 32,462

Hou·ma \ˈhō-mə, ˈhü-\ city SE La. *pop* 30,495

Houns·low \ˈhaúnz-(ˌ)lō\ borough of SW Greater London, England *pop* 193,400

Hou·sa·ton·ic \ˌhü-sə-ˈtä-nik, ˌhü-zə-\ river 148 *mi* (238 *km*) W Mass. & W Conn. flowing from Berkshire Hills S into Long Island Sound

Hous·ton \ˈhyü-stən, ˈyü-\ city & port SE Tex. connected with Galveston Bay by ship canal *pop* 1,630,553 — **Hous·to·nian** \hyü-ˈstō-nē-ən, yü-, -nyən\ *noun* — **Hous·ton·ite** \ˈhyü-stə-ˌnīt, ˈyü-\ *noun*

Hove \ˈhōv\ town S England in E. Sussex *pop* 82,500

Ho·ven·weep National Monument \ˈhō-vən-ˌwēp\ site SE Utah & SW Colo. of prehistoric pueblos & cliff dwellings

How·rah *or* **Hao·ra** \ˈhaú-rə\ city E India in W. Bengal on the Hugli opposite Calcutta *pop* 950,435

Hra·dec Kra·lo·ve \ˈ(h)rä-ˌdets-ˈkrä-lȯ-ˌvä\ *or German* **Kö·nig·grätz** \ˌkœ-nik-ˈgrets\ city N *central* Czech Republic *pop* 99,889

Hrodna *or* **Hrodno** — see GRODNO

Hsi — see XI

Hsia·men — see XIAMEN

Hsiang — see XIANG

Hsiang–t'an — see XIANGTAN

Hsin·chu \ˈshin-ˈchü\ city & port China in NW Taiwan on coast SW of Taipei *pop* 332,524

Hsin–hsiang — see XINXIANG

Hsi–ning — see XINING

Hsinkao — see YÜ SHAN

Hsüan–hua — see XUANHUA

Hsü–chou — see XUZHOU

Huai \hü-ˈī, ˈhwī\ river *over* 600 *mi* (966 *km*) E China flowing from S Henan E into Hongze Lake

Huai·nan \hü-ˈī-ˈnän, ˈhwī-\ city E China in N *central* Anhui SW of Bengbu *pop* 703,934

Hual·la·ga \wä-ˈyä-gä, kwä-\ river 700 *mi* (1126 *km*) N *central* Peru flowing N into the Marañón

Huam·bo \'wäm-(,)bō, 'hwäm-\ *or formerly* **No·va Lis·boa** \'nò-və-lēzh-'bò-ə\ city Angola in W central highlands *pop* 49,823

Huang *or* **Hwang** \'hwäŋ\ *or* **Yellow** river *about* 3000 *mi* (4828 *km*) N China flowing from Kunlun Mountains in Qinghai E into Bo Hai

Huang·pu *or* **Whang·poo** \'hwäŋ-'pü\ river 70 *mi* (113 *km*) E China flowing E & N past Shanghai into the Chang

Huas·ca·rán \,wäs-kä-'rän\ mountain 22,205 *ft* (6768 *m*) W Peru; highest in the country

Hu·bei *or* **Hu·peh** *or* **Hu·pei** \'hü-'bā, -'pā\ province E central China ✳ Wuhan area 72,394 sq mi (188,224 sq km), pop 53,969,210

Hu·ber Heights \'hyü-bər, 'yü-\ city W Ohio pop 38,696

Hu·bli–Dhar·war \,hùb-lē-,där-'wär\ city SW India in W Karnataka pop 648,298

Hudaydah, Al — see AL HUDAYDAH

Hud·ders·field \'hə-dərz-,fēld\ borough N England in W. Yorkshire NE of Manchester pop 123,888

Hud·son \'həd-sən\ river 306 *mi* (492 *km*) E N.Y. flowing from Adirondack Mountains S into New York Bay — **Hud·so·ni·an** \,həd-'sō-nē-ən\ adjective

Hudson Bay inlet of the Atlantic in N Canada; an inland sea 850 *mi* (1368 *km*) long

Hudson Strait strait 450 *mi* (724 *km*) long NE Canada between S Baffin Is. & N Quebec connecting Hudson Bay with the Atlantic

Hue *or French* **Hué** \'hwā, 'wā, hü-'ā, hyü-'ā\ city & port central Vietnam in Annam; formerly ✳ of Annam *pop* 211,718

Huel·va \'wel-vä, 'hwel-\ **1** province SW Spain in Andalusia on Gulf of Cádiz area 3894 sq mi (10,085 sq km), pop 443,476 **2** city, its ✳ pop 127,822

Hues·ca \'wes-kä, 'hwes-\ **1** province NE Spain in Aragon area 6051 sq mi (15,672 sq km), pop 207,810 **2** commune, its ✳ pop 44,165

Hufuf, Al — see AL HUFUF

Hu·gli *or* **Hoo·ghly** \'hü-glē\ river 120 *mi* (193 *km*) E India flowing S into Bay of Bengal; most westerly channel of the Ganges in its delta

Huhehot — see HOHHOT

Hui·la \'wē-(,)lä, 'hwē-\ volcano 18,865 *ft* (5750 *m*) SW central Colombia

Hull \'həl\ **1** town Canada in SW Quebec on Ottawa River opposite Ottawa, Ontario pop 60,707 **2** *in full* **Kings·ton upon Hull** \'kiŋ(k)-stən\ city & borough & port N England in Humberside pop 242,200

Hu·ma·cao \,ü-mə-'kaù\ town E Puerto Rico pop 21,306

Hum·ber \'həm-bər\ estuary 40 *mi* (64 *km*) E England formed by Ouse & Trent rivers & flowing E & SE into North Sea

Hum·ber·side \'həm-bər-,sīd\ county E England; area formerly in Yorkshire; ✳ Kingston upon Hull area 1405 sq mi (3639 sq km), pop 835,200

Hum·boldt \'həm-,bōlt\ river 290 *mi* (467 *km*) N Nev. flowing W & SW into Rye Patch reservoir & formerly into Humboldt Lake

Humboldt Bay bay NW Calif. on which Eureka is situated

Humboldt Glacier glacier NW Greenland

Humboldt Lake lake W Nev. formerly receiving Humboldt River; has no outlet, but has an intermittent S extension **Humboldt Sink**

Hum·phreys Peak \'həmp-frēz\ mountain peak 12,633 *ft* (3851 *m*) N central Ariz. — see SAN FRANCISCO PEAKS

Hu·nan \'hü-'nän\ province SE central China ✳ Changsha area 81,274 sq mi (211,312 sq km), pop 60,659,754

Hun·ga·ry \'həŋ-gə-rē\ *or Hungarian* **Ma·gyar·or·szag** \,mò-jòr-'òr-,säg\ country central Europe; formerly a kingdom, since 1946 a republic ✳ Budapest area 35,919 sq mi (93,030 sq km), pop 10,296,000

Hungshui — see HONGSHUI

Hungtse — see HONGZE

Hun·ter \'hən-tər\ river 287 *mi* (462 *km*) SE Australia in E New South Wales flowing E into the Pacific

Hun·ting·don \'hən-tiŋ-dən\ **1** *or* **Hun·ting·don·shire** \,shir, -shər\ *or* **Huntingdon and Pe·ter·bor·ough** \'pē-tər,bər-ō\ *or* **Hunts** \'hənts\ former county E central England ✳

Huntingdon; since 1974 part of Cambridgeshire **2** town E central England in Cambridgeshire pop 2859

Hun·ting·ton \'hən-tiŋ-tən\ city W W.Va. on Ohio River pop 54,844

Huntington Beach city SW Calif. SE of Los Angeles pop 181,519

Huntington Park city SW Calif. S of Los Angeles pop 56,065

Hunts·ville \'hənts-,vil, -vəl\ **1** city N Ala. pop 159,789 **2** city E Tex. N of Houston pop 27,925

Hu·on Gulf \'hyü-,än\ inlet of Solomon Sea on SE coast of North-East New Guinea S of Huon Peninsula

Hu·ron, Lake \'hyùr-,än, 'yùr-\ lake E central N. America between the U.S. & Canada; one of the Great Lakes area 23,010 sq mi (59,826 sq km)

Hurst \'hərst\ city NE Tex. NE of Fort Worth pop 33,574

Hutch·in·son \'hə-chən-sən\ city central Kans. pop 39,308

Huy \'wē, 'hwē\ commune E Belgium SW of Liège pop 18,197

Huy·ton with Ro·by \'hī-t°n-with-'rō-bē, -with-\ town NW England in Lancashire E of Liverpool pop 57,671

Hwaining — see ANQING

Hy·bla \'hī-blə\ ancient town in Sicily on S slope of Mt. Etna

Hydaspes — see JHELUM

Hy·der·a·bad \'hī-d(ə-)rə-,bad, -,bäd\ **1** former state S central India in the Deccan ✳ Hyderabad **2** *or* **Hai·dar·a·bad** city S central India ✳ of Andhra Pradesh pop 3,145,939 **3** city S Pakistan in Sind on the Indus pop 795,000

Hy·dra \'hī-drə\ *or New Greek* **Ídhra** \'ēth-rä\ island Greece in S Aegean Sea off E coast of Peloponnese area 20 sq mi (52 sq km), pop 2794 — **Hy·dri·ot** \'hī-drē-ət, -drē-,ät\ *or* **Hy·dri·ote** \-,ōt, -ət\ noun

Hydraotes — see RAVI

Hy·ères \ē-'er, 'yer\ commune SE France on Côte d'Azur E of Toulon pop 50,122

Hyères Islands *or French* **Îles d'Hyères** \,ēl-dē-'er, ,ēl-'dyer\ islands in the Mediterranean off SE coast of France

Hy·met·tus \hī-'me-təs\ mountain ridge *about* 3370 *ft* (1027 *m*) central Greece E & SE of Athens — **Hy·met·ti·an** \-'me-tē-ən\ adjective

Hyr·ca·nia \(,)hər-'kā-nē-ə\ province of ancient Persia on SE coast of Caspian NE of Media & NW of Parthia — **Hyr·ca·ni·an** \-nē-ən\ adjective

Ia·si \'yäsh, 'yä-shē\ *or* **Jas·sy** \'yä-sē\ city NE Romania pop 330,195

Iba·dan \i-'bä-d°n, -'ba-\ city SW Nigeria NNE of Lagos pop 1,263,000

Ibe·ria \ī-'bir-ē-ə\ **1** ancient Spain **2** IBERIAN PENINSULA **3** ancient region S of the Caucasus W of Colchis in modern Republic of Georgia

Ibe·ri·an Peninsula \-ē-ən\ peninsula SW Europe between the Mediterranean & the Atlantic occupied by Spain & Portugal

Ibi·cuí \,ē-bi-'kwē\ river S Brazil in Rio Grande do Sul flowing W into Uruguay River

Ibi·za \ē-'vē-thä, -'bē-, -sə, -zə\ island Spain in the Balearics SW of Majorca area about 220 sq mi (570 sq km)

Içá — see PUTUMAYO

Icaria — see IKARIA — **Icar·i·an** \ī-'ker-ē-ən, i-, -'kar-\ adjective or noun

Ice·land \'īs-lənd, 'īs-,land\ *or Danish* **Is·land** \'ēs-,län\ *or Icelandic* **Ís·land** \'ē-,slänt\ island between the Arctic & the Atlantic SE of Greenland; a republic formerly (1380–1918) belonging to Denmark, later (1918–44) an independent kingdom in personal union with Denmark ✳ Reykjavík area 39,702 sq mi (102,828 sq km), pop 255,855 — **Ice·land·er** \'īs-,lan-dər, 'īs-lən-\ noun

I–ch'ang — see YICHANG

Ichi·ka·wa \ē-'chē-,kä-wə\ city Japan in SE Honshu E of Tokyo pop 436,597

Iconium — see KONYA

Ida — see KAZ DAGI

Ida·ho \'ī-də-,hō\ state NW U.S. ✳ Boise area 83,557 sq mi (217,248 sq km), pop 1,006,749 — **Ida·ho·an** \,ī-də-'hō-ən\ adjective or noun

Idaho Falls city SE Idaho on Snake River pop 43,929

Id·fu \'id-(,)fü\ city S Egypt on the Nile pop 34,858

Ídhi \'ē-thē\ *or* **Ida** \'ī-də\ mountain 8058 *ft* (2456 *m*) Greece in central Crete; highest on island

Idumaea *or* **Idumea** — see EDOM — **Id·u·mae·an** *or* **Id·u·me·an** \,i-dyü-'mē-ən\ adjective or noun

Ie·per \'yä-pər\ *or French* **Ypres** \'ēpr'\ commune NW Belgium in W. Flanders pop 35,235

Ife \'ē-(,)fä\ city SW Nigeria NE of Ibadan pop 209,100

If·ni \'if-nē\ former territory SW Morocco; administered by Spain 1934–69 ✳ Sidi Ifni

Igua·çú *or* **Igua·zú** \,ē-gwə-'sü\ river S Brazil in Paraná state flowing W into Alto Paraná River; contains **Iguazú Falls** (waterfall over 2 *mi* or 3.2 *km* wide composed of numerous cataracts averaging 200 *ft* or 61 *m* in height)

IJs·sel \'ī-səl, 'ā-\ river 70 *mi* (113 *km*) E Netherlands flowing out of the Rhine N into IJsselmeer

IJs·sel·meer \,ī-səl-'mer, ,ā-\ *or* **Lake Ijs·sel** \'ī-səl, 'ā-\ freshwater lake N Netherlands separated from North Sea by a dike & bordered by reclaimed lands; part of former Zuider Zee (inlet of North Sea)

Ika·ria \ē-kä-'rē-ä\ *or* **Ni·ka·ria** \,nē-\ *or ancient* **Icar·ia** \ī-'kar-ē-ə, i-\ island Greece in Southern Sporades WSW of Samos area 99 sq mi (257 sq km)

Île–de–France \,ēl-də-'frä⁽ⁿ⁾s\ region & former province N central France bounded on N by Picardy, on E by Champagne, on S by Orléanais, & on W by Normandy ✳ Paris

Ile des Pins \,ēl-dā-'pa⁽ⁿ⁾\ *or* **Isle of Pines** \'pīnz\ island SW Pacific in New Caledonia territory SE of New Caledonia Is. area 58 sq mi (151 sq km)

Île du Diable — see DEVIL'S ISLAND

Îles de la Société — see SOCIETY ISLANDS

Îles du Vent — see WINDWARD ISLANDS

Îles sous le Vent — see LEEWARD ISLANDS

Il·ford \'il-fərd\ former municipal borough SE England in Essex, now part of Redbridge

Il·fra·combe \'il-frə-,küm\ town SW England in Devon on Bristol Channel pop 10,133

Ili \'ē-'lē\ river 800 *mi* (1287 *km*) central Asia flowing from W Xinjiang Uygur, China, W & NW into Lake Balkhash in Kazakhstan

Ilía — see ELIS

Il·i·am·na \,i-lē-'am-nə\ volcano 10,016 *ft* (3053 *m*) NE of Iliamna Lake

Iliamna Lake lake 80 *mi* (129 *km*) long SW Alaska NE of Bristol Bay

Ilion *or* **Ilium** — see TROY — **Il·i·an** \'i-lē-ən\ adjective or noun

Il·lam·pu \ē-'yäm-(,)pü\ **1** *or* **So·ra·ta** \sə-'rä-tə\ massif in the Andes W Bolivia E of Lake Titicaca — see ANCOHUMA **2** peak 20,867 *ft* (6360 *m*) in the Illampu massif

Il·li·ma·ni \ē-yē-'mä-nē\ mountain 21,201 *ft* (6462 *m*) Bolivia E of La Paz

Il·li·nois \,i-lə-'nòi also -'nòiz\ **1** river 273 *mi* (439 *km*) N. flowing SW into Mississippi River **2** state central U.S. ✳ Springfield area 56,400 sq mi (146,640 sq km), pop 11,430,602 — **Il·li·nois·an** \,i-lə-'nòi-ən also -'nòi-z°n\ adjective or noun

Il·lyr·ia \i-'lir-ē-ə\ ancient region S Europe in Balkan Peninsula bordering on the Adriatic — **Il·lyr·ic** \-'lir-ik\ adjective

Il·lyr·i·cum \i-'lir-i-kəm\ province of Roman Empire in Illyria

Il·men \'il-mən\ lake W Russia in Europe S of Lake Ladoga

Ilo·ilo \,ē-lō-'ē-(,)lō\ city Philippines on Panay Is. pop 311,000

Im·pe·ria \im-'pir-ē-ə, -'per-\ commune & port NW Italy in Liguria SW of Genoa pop 40,171

Im·pe·ri·al Beach \im-'pir-ē-əl\ city SW Calif. S of San Diego pop 26,512

Imperial Valley valley U.S. & Mexico in SE Calif. & NE Baja California in Colorado Desert; most of area below sea level

Imp·hal \'imp-,həl\ city NE India ✳ of Manipur pop 196,268

Imroz — see GÖKÇEADA

Ina·gua \i-'nä-gwə\ two islands in SE Bahamas: **Great Inagua** (50 *mi* or 80 *km* long) & **Little Inagua** (8 *mi* or 13 *km* long)

In·chon \\'in-,chän\ *or formerly* **Che·mul·po** \jə-'mùl-(,)pō\ city & port NW S. Korea W of Seoul *pop* 1,386,911

In·de·pen·dence \,in-də-'pen-dən(t)s\ city W Mo. E of Kansas City *pop* 112,301

In·dia \\'in-dē-ə\ **1** peninsula region (often called a subcontinent) S Asia S of the Himalayas between Bay of Bengal & Arabian Sea occupied by India, Pakistan, & Bangladesh & formerly often considered as also including Burma (but not Ceylon) **2** those parts of India until 1947 under Brit. rule or protection together with Baluchistan & the Andaman & Nicobar islands &, prior to 1937, Burma **3** country comprising major portion of peninsula; a republic within the Commonwealth of Nations; until 1947 a part of the Brit. Empire ✱ New Delhi *area* 1,195,063 *sq mi* (3,095,472 *sq km*), *pop* 896,567,000

In·di·ana \,in-dē-'a-nə\ state E *central* U.S. ✱ Indianapolis *area* 36,291 *sq mi* (94,357 *sq km*), *pop* 5,544,159 — **In·di·an·an** \-'a-nən\ *adjective or noun* — **In·di·an·i·an** \-'a-nē-ən\ *adjective or noun*

Indiana Harbor harbor district in E. Chicago, Ind., on Lake Michigan

In·di·a·nap·o·lis \,in-dē-ə-'na-pə-lis\ city *central* Ind., its ✱ *pop* 731,327

In·di·an Ocean \'in-dē-ən\ ocean E of Africa, S of Asia, W of Australia & Tasmania, & N of Antarctica *area about* 28,350,500 *sq mi* (73,427,795 *sq km*)

Indian River lagoon 165 *mi* (266 *km*) long E Fla. between mainland & coastal islands

Indian States *or* **Native States** former semi-independent states of the Indian Empire ruled by native princes subject to varying degrees of Brit. authority — see BRITISH INDIA

Indian Territory former territory S U.S. in present state of Okla.

In·dies \'in-(,)dēz\ **1** EAST INDIES **2** WEST INDIES

In·di·gir·ka \,in-də-'gir-kə\ river *over* 1000 *mi* (1609 *km*) E *central* Russia in Asia in NE Sakha Republic flowing N into E. Siberian Sea

In·dio \'in-dē-,ō\ city SE Calif. SE of San Bernardino *pop* 36,793

In·do·chi·na \,in-(,)dō-'chī-nə\ **1** peninsula SE Asia; includes Myanmar, Cambodia, Laos, Malay Peninsula, Thailand, & Vietnam **2** *or* **French Indochina** former country SE Asia comprising Annam, Cochin China, & Tonkin (all now a part of Vietnam), Cambodia, & Laos ✱ Hanoi

In·do·ne·sia \,in-də-'nē-zhə, -shə\ **1** country SE Asia in Malay Archipelago comprising Sumatra, Java, S & E Borneo, Sulawesi, Timor, W New Guinea, the Moluccas, & many adjacent smaller islands; formerly (as **Netherlands East Indies**) an overseas territory of the Netherlands ✱ Jakarta *area* 779,675 *sq mi* (2,019,358 *sq km*), *pop* 188,216,000 **2** MALAY ARCHIPELAGO

In·dore \in-'dōr, -'dor\ **1** former state *central* India in Narmada valley ✱ Indore; area now in Madhya Pradesh **2** city NW *central* India in W Madhya Pradesh *pop* 1,091,674

In·dus \'in-dəs\ river 1800 *mi* (2897 *km*) S Asia flowing from Tibet NW & SSW through Pakistan into Arabian Sea

In·gle·wood \'in-gəl-,wùd\ city SW Calif. SW of Los Angeles *pop* 109,602

In·gol·stadt \'in-gəl-,shtät, -,stät\ city S Germany in *central* Bavaria *pop* 107,375

In·gu·she·tia \,iŋ-gü-'shē-shə\ *or* **In·gu·she·ti·ya** \-'she-tē-yə\ *or* **Ingush Republic** \in-'güsh, iŋ-\ autonomous republic S Russia in Europe N of Caucasus Mts. ✱ Nazran *area* 1242 *mi* (3217 *sq km*), *pop* 1,234,000

Ink·ster \'iŋk-stər\ village SE Mich. W of Detroit *pop* 30,772

In·land Empire \'in-,land, -lənd\ region NW U.S. between Cascade Range & Rocky Mountains in E Wash., N Idaho, NW Mont., & NE Oreg.

Inland Sea inlet of the Pacific 240 *mi* (386 *km*) long SW Japan between Honshu on E & N, Kyushu on W, & Shikoku on S

Inn \'in\ river 320 *mi* (515 *km*) flowing from SE Switzerland NE through Austria into the Danube in SE Germany — see ENGADINE

Inner Hebrides — see HEBRIDES

Inner Mon·go·lia \män-'gōl-yə, mäŋ-, -'gō-lē-ə\ *or* **Nei Mong·gol** \'nā-'män-,gōl, -'mäŋ-\ region N China in SE Mongolia & W Manchuria ✱ Hohhot *area* 454,633 *sq mi* (1,182,046 *sq km*), *pop* 21,456,798

In·nis·fil \'i-nəs-,fil, -fəl\ town Canada in SE Ontario *pop* 21,667

Inniskilling — see ENNISKILLEN

Inns·bruck \'inz-,brúk, 'in(t)s-\ city W Austria *pop* 118,112

Inside Passage protected shipping route from Puget Sound, Wash., to Skagway, Alaska, following channels between mainland & coastal islands

In·ter·la·ken \'in-tər-,lä-kən\ commune W *central* Switzerland in Bern canton on the Aare between Lake of Thun & Lake of Brienz *pop* 5500

International Zone — see MOROCCO

In·ver·car·gill \,in-vər-'kär-gil\ borough New Zealand on S coast of South Is. *pop* 56,059 — see BLUFF

Inver Grove Heights \'in-vər\ city SE Minn. *pop* 22,477

In·ver·ness \,in-vər-'nes\ **1** *or* **In·ver·ness·shire** \-'nesh-,shir, -shər\ former county NW Scotland **2** burgh NW Scotland ✱ of Highland region *pop* 63,090

Io·an·ni·na \yō-'ä-nē-(,)nä\ city NW Greece in N Epirus *pop* 56,496

Io·na \ī-'ō-nə\ island Scotland in S Inner Hebrides off SW tip of Mull Is. *area* 6 *sq mi* (16 *sq km*), *pop* 120

Io·nia \ī-'ō-nē-ə\ ancient region W Asia Minor bordering on the Aegean W of Lydia & Caria — **Io·ni·an** \-nē-ən\ *adjective or noun*

Io·ni·an Islands \ī-'ō-nē-ən\ islands W Greece in Ionian Sea *pop* 191,003

Ionian Sea arm of the Mediterranean Sea between SE Italy & W Greece

Io·wa \'ī-ə-wə\ **1** river 291 *mi* (468 *km*) Iowa flowing SE into Mississippi River **2** state *central* U.S. ✱ Des Moines *area* 56,275 *sq mi* (145,752 *sq km*), *pop* 2,776,755 — **Io·wan** \-wən\ *adjective or noun*

Iowa City city E Iowa *pop* 59,738

I-pin — see YIBIN

Ipoh \'ē-(,)pō\ city Malaysia (federation) in Perak *pop* 125,766

Ips·wich \'ip-(,)swich\ **1** city E Australia in SE Queensland *pop* 73,299 **2** borough SE England ✱ of Suffolk *pop* 115,500

Iqa·lu·it \ē-'ka-lü-ət\ town Canada, on Baffin Is., Northwest Territories *pop* 3552

Iqui·que \ē-'kē-kā\ city & port N Chile on the Pacific *pop* 148,511

Iqui·tos \ē-'kē-(,)tōs\ city NE Peru on the Amazon *pop* 269,500

Irák·li·on \i-'ra-klē-ən, ē-'rä-klē-,ón\ *or* **Can·dia** \'kan-dē-ə\ city & port Greece on N coast of Crete *pop* 117,167

Iran \i-'rän, -'ran; ī-'ran\ *or especially formerly* **Per·sia** \'pər-zhə, *especially British* -shə\ country SW Asia bordering in N on Caspian Sea & in S on Persian Gulf & Gulf of Oman; an Islamic republic since 1979, formerly an empire ✱ Tehran *area* 635,932 *sq mi* (1,647,064 *sq km*), *pop* 59,570,000 — **Irani** \i-'rä-nē, -'ra-\ *adjective or noun*

Iraq \i-'räk, -'rak\ country SW Asia in Mesopotamia; a republic since 1958, formerly a kingdom ✱ Baghdad *area* 168,927 *sq mi* (437,521 *sq km*), *pop* 18,838,000 — **Iraqi** \-'rä-kē, -'ra-\ *adjective or noun*

Irbīl — see ARBIL

Ire·land \'īr-lənd\ **1** *or Latin* **Hi·ber·nia** \hī-'bər-nē-ə\ island W Europe in the Atlantic, one of the British Isles *area* 32,052 *sq mi* (83,015 *sq km*); divided between Ireland (republic) & Northern Ireland **2** *or* **Ei·re** \'er-ə\ country occupying major portion of the island; a republic since 1949; a division of the United Kingdom of Great Britain and Ireland 1801–1921 & (as **Irish Free State**) a dominion of the Commonwealth of Nations 1922–37 ✱ Dublin *area* 26,602 *sq mi* (69,165 *sq km*), *pop* 3,523,401 **3** — see NORTHERN IRELAND

Iri·an Ja·ya \ir-ē-,än-'jī-ä\ *or* **West Irian** *or formerly* **Dutch New Guin·ea** \'gi-nē\ *or* **Netherlands New Guinea** territory of Indonesia comprising the W half of New Guinea & adjacent islands; belonged to the Netherlands until 1963 ✱ Jayapura *area* 162,927 *sq mi* (421,981 *sq km*), *pop* 1,648,708

Irish Sea arm of the Atlantic between Great Britain & Ireland

Ir·kutsk \ir-'kütsk, ,ər-\ city S Russia in Asia on the Angara near Lake Baikal *pop* 639,000

Iron Gate \'ī-(ə)rn\ gorge 2 *mi* (3.2 *km*) long of the Danube where it cuts around Transylvanian Alps on border between Romania & Yugoslavia

Ir·ra·wad·dy \,ir-ə-'wä-dē\ river 1300 *mi* (2092 *km*) Myanmar flowing S into Bay of Bengal through several mouths

Ir·tysh \ir-'tish, ,ər-\ river *over* 2600 *mi* (4180 *km*) *central* Asia flowing from Altai mountains in China, NW & N through Kazakhstan & into the Ob in W Russia in Asia

Irún \ē-'rün\ commune N Spain in Guipúzcoa *pop* 52,828

Ir·vine \'ər-,vīn\ city SW Calif. SE of Santa Ana *pop* 110,330

Ir·ving \'ər-viŋ\ city NE Tex. W of Dallas *pop* 155,037

Is·a·bela Island \,i-zə-'be-lə, ,ē-sä-'vä-lä\ island Ecuador; largest of the Galápagos *area* 1650 *sq mi* (4290 *sq km*), *pop* 336

Isar \'ē-,zär\ river 163 *mi* (262 *km*) W Europe flowing from Tirol, Austria, through Bavaria, Germany, into the Danube

Isau·ria \ī-'sór-ē-ə\ ancient district in E Pisidia S Asia Minor on N slope of W Taurus Mountains — **Isau·ri·an** \-ē-ən\ *adjective or noun*

Is·chia \'is-kē-ə\ island Italy in Tyrrhenian Sea WSW of Naples *area* 18 *sq mi* (47 *sq km*)

Ise Bay \'ē-,sā\ inlet of the Pacific S Japan on S coast of Honshu

Iseo, Lake \ē-'zā-(,)ō\ lake 14 *mi* (22 *km*) long N Italy in Lombardy

Isère \ē-'zer\ river 150 *mi* (241 *km*) SE France flowing from Graian Alps WSW into the Rhône

Iser·lohn \,ē-zər-'lōn, 'ē-zər-,\ city W Germany *pop* 96,976

Isfahan — see ESFAHĀN

Ishim \i-'shim\ river 1330 *mi* (2140 *km*) flowing from N Kazakhstan N into the Irtysh in W Russia in Asia

Isis \'ī-səs\ the Thames River, England, at & upstream from Oxford

Is·ken·de·run \(,)is-,ken-də-'rün\ *or formerly* **Al·ex·an·dret·ta** \,a-lig-(,)zan-'dre-tə, ,e-\ city & port S Turkey on **Gulf of Iskenderun** (inlet of the Mediterranean) *pop* 154,807

Is·lam·a·bad \is-'lä-mə-,bäd, iz-, -'la-mə-,bad\ city of Pakistan in NE Pakistan NE of Rawalpindi *pop* 250,000

Island *or* **Ísland** — see ICELAND

Is·lay \'ī-(,)lā, -lə\ island Scotland in S Inner Hebrides *area* 234 *sq mi* (608 *sq km*), *pop* 3855

Isle au Haut \,ī-lə-'hō(t), ,ē-lə-'hō\ island Maine at entrance to Penobscot Bay — see ACADIA NATIONAL PARK

Isle of Av·a·lon \'a-və-,län\ district, originally an island, SW England in Somerset including Glastonbury

Isle of Ely — see ELY (Isle of)

Isle of Man — see MAN (Isle of)

Isle of Pines — see YOUTH (Isle of)

Isle of Wight — see WIGHT (Isle of)

Isle Roy·ale \'īl-'rói(-ə)l\ island Mich. in NW Lake Superior in **Isle Royale National Park**

Is·ling·ton \'iz-liŋ-tən\ borough of N Greater London, England *pop* 155,200

Is·ma·i·lia \,iz-mä-ə-'lē-ə, ,is-\ city NE Egypt on the Suez Canal *pop* 247,000

Isole Eolie — see LIPARI ISLANDS

Ison·zo \ē-'zón(t)-(,)sō\ *or* **So·ča** \'sò-chä\ river *about* 80 *mi* (129 *km*) W Slovenia & NE Italy flowing S into Gulf of Trieste

Ispahan — see ESFAHĀN

Is·par·ta \,is-(,)pär-'tä\ city SW Turkey N of Antalya *pop* 112,117

Is·ra·el \'iz-rē-əl, -(,)rā- *also* 'is- *or* 'iz-rəl\ **1** ancient kingdom Palestine comprising the lands occupied by the Hebrew people; established *about* 1025 B.C.; divided *about* 933 B.C. into a S

kingdom (Judah) & a N kingdom (Israel) **2** *or* **Northern Kingdom** *or* **Ephra·im** \'ē-frē-əm\ the N portion of the Hebrew kingdom after the division ✳ Samaria **3** country Palestine bordering on the Mediterranean; a republic established 1948 ✳ Jerusalem *area* 7993 *sq mi* (20,782 *sq km*), *pop* 4,037,620 — see PALESTINE

Is·sus \'i-səs\ ancient town S Asia Minor N of modern Iskenderun

Is·syk Kul *or* **Ys·yk-Köl** \,i-sik-'kəl, -'kœl\ lake 115 *mi* (185 *km*) long in NE Kyrgyzstan *area* 2355 *sq mi* (6099 *sq km*)

Is·tan·bul \,is-tən-'bül, -,tan-, -,tän-, -'bùl, 'is-tən-,, *or with* m *for* n\ *or formerly* **Con·stan·ti·no·ple** \,kän-,stan-t³n-'ō-pəl\ *or ancient* **By·zan·ti·um** \bə-'zan-tē-əm, -'zan-sh(ē-)əm\ city NW Turkey on the Bosporus & Sea of Marmara; former ✳ of Turkey & of Ottoman Empire *pop* 6,620,241

Ister — see DANUBE

Is·tria \'is-trē-ə\ *or* **Is·tra** \-trə\ *or* **Is·tri·an Peninsula** \-trē-ən\ peninsula in Croatia & Slovenia projecting into the N Adriatic — **Istrian** *adjective or noun*

Itai·pu \ē-'tī-pü\ dam in Paraná River between Brazil & Paraguay

Italian East Africa former territory E Africa comprising Eritrea, Ethiopia, & Italian Somaliland

Italian Somaliland former Italian colony E Africa bordering on Indian Ocean ✳ Mogadishu; since 1960 part of Somalia

It·a·ly \'i-t³l-ē\ *or Italian* **Ita·lia** \ē-'täl-yä\ *or Latin* **Ita·lia** \ə-'tal-yə, i-\ **1** peninsula 760 *mi* (1223 *km*) long S Europe projecting into the Mediterranean between Adriatic & Tyrrhenian seas **2** country comprising the peninsula of Italy, Sicily, Sardinia, & numerous other islands; a republic since 1946, formerly a kingdom ✳ Rome *area* 116,313 *sq mi* (302,251 *sq km*), *pop* 57,235,000

Ita·na·gar \ē-tə-'nə-gər\ town NE India ✳ of Arunachal Pradesh

Itas·ca, Lake \ī-'tas-kə\ lake NW *central* Minn.; generally considered as source of Mississippi River

Iténez — see GUAPORÉ

Ith·a·ca \'i-thi-kə\ **1** city S *central* N.Y. on Cayuga Lake *pop* 29,541 **2** *or New Greek* **Ithá·ki** \ē-'thä-kē\ island W Greece in the Ionian Islands NE of Cephalonia *area* 37 *sq mi* (96 *sq km*) — **Ith·a·can** \'i-thi-kən\ *adjective or noun*

Itsu·ku·shi·ma \ēt-,sü-kə-'shē-mä\ island *about* 5 *mi* (8 *km*) long Japan in Inland Sea SW of Hiroshima

It·u·raea *or* **It·u·rea** \i-tyü-'rē-ə\ ancient country NE Palestine S of Damascus — **It·u·rae·an** *or* **It·u·re·an** \-'rē-ən\ *adjective or noun*

Iva·no-Fran·kivs'k \i-'vä-nə-frän-'kifsk\ *or formerly* **Sta·ni·slav** \stä-nə-'släf, -'släv\ city SW Ukraine *pop* 226,000

Iva·no·vo \i-'vä-nə-və\ *or formerly* **Ivanovo Voz·ne·sensk** \,vəz-nə-'sen(t)sk\ city *central* Russia in Europe WNW of Nizhniy Novgorod *pop* 480,000

Ivory Coast *or* **Côte d'Ivoire** \,kōt-dē-'vwär\ **1** region W Africa bordering on the Atlantic W of the Gold Coast **2** country W Africa including the Ivory Coast & its hinterland; a republic; formerly a territory of French West Africa ✳ Abidjan *area* 124,503 *sq mi* (322,463 *sq km*), *pop* 13,459,000 — **Ivor·i·an** \(,)ī-'vōr-ē-ən, -'vör-\ *adjective or noun* — **Ivory Coast·er** \-'kō-stər\ *noun*

Iwo \'ē-(,)wō\ city SW Nigeria NE of Ibadan *pop* 319,500

Iwo Ji·ma \,ē-(,)wō-'jē-mə\ island Japan in W Pacific in the Volcano Islands *area* 8 *sq mi* (21 *sq km*)

Ix·elles \ēk-'sel\ *or Flemish* **El·se·ne** \'el-sə-nə\ commune *central* Belgium in Brabant; suburb of Brussels *pop* 72,610

Ix·ta·ci·huatl *or* **Iz·tac·ci·huatl** \,ēs-(,)tä-sē-,wä-t³l\ extinct volcano 17,343 *ft* (5286 *m*) S Mexico N of Popocatepetl

Iza·bal, Lake \,ē-zä-'bäl, -sä-'väl\ lake 25 *mi* (40 *km*) long E Guatemala

Izal·co \i-'zal-(,)kō, ē-'säl-\ volcano 7828 *ft* (2386 *m*) W El Salvador

Izhevsk \'ē-,zhefsk\ *or 1985–1987* **Usti·nov** \'üs-ti-,nóf, -,nóv\ city E Russia in Europe ✳ of Udmurtia *pop* 651,000

Iz·ma·il *or Romanian* **Is·ma·il** \,iz-ma-'ēl, ,is-\ city SW Ukraine on the Danube delta *pop* 95,000

Iz·mir \iz-'mir\ *or formerly* **Smyr·na** \'smər-nə\ city & port W Turkey in Asia on an inlet of the Aegean *pop* 1,757,414

Iz·mit *or* **Is·mid** \iz-'mit\ *or ancient* **As·ta·cus** \'as-tə-kəs\ *or* **Nic·o·me·dia** \,ni-kə-'mē-dē-ə\ city & port NW Turkey in Asia on **Gulf of Izmit** (E arm of Sea of Marmara) *pop* 256,882

Iz·nik \iz-'nik\ lake 14 *mi* (22 *km*) long NW Turkey in Asia

Jabal Katrinah — see KATHERINA (Gebel)

Ja·bal·pur \'jə-bəl-,pùr\ city *central* India in *central* Madhya Pradesh *pop* 739,961

Jack·son \'jak-sən\ **1** city S Mich. *pop* 37,446 **2** city ✳ of Miss. on Pearl River *pop* 196,637 **3** city W Tenn. *pop* 48,949

Jackson Hole valley NW Wyo. E of Teton Range & partly in Grand Teton National Park; contains **Jackson Lake** (reservoir)

Jack·son·ville \'jak-sən-,vil\ **1** city *central* Ark. NE of Little Rock *pop* 29,101 **2** city NE Fla. near mouth of St. Johns River *pop* 635,230 **3** city W *central* Ill. *pop* 19,324 **4** city E N.C. *pop* 30,013

Jadotville — see LIKASI

Ja·én \hä-'ān\ **1** province S Spain in N Andalusia *area* 5212 *sq mi* (13,499 *sq km*), *pop* 637,633 **2** commune, its ✳ *pop* 101,938

Jaf·fa \'ja-fə, 'ya-, 'yä-\ *or* **Ya·fo** \yä-'fō\ *or ancient* **Jop·pa** \'jä-pə\ former city W Israel, since 1950 a S section of Tel Aviv

Jaff·na \'jäf-nə\ city N Sri Lanka on Jaffna Peninsula *pop* 129,000

Jaffna Peninsula peninsula N extremity of Sri Lanka extending into Palk Strait

Jain·tia Hills \'jīn-tē-ə\ hills E India in N *central* Assam E of Khasi Hills

Jai·pur \'jī-,pùr\ **1** former state NW India; now part of Rajasthan **2** city, its ✳, now ✳ of Rajasthan *pop* 1,458,183

Ja·kar·ta *or* **Dja·kar·ta** \jə-'kär-tə\ *or formerly* **Ba·ta·via** \bə-'tä-vē-ə\ city & port ✳ of Indonesia in NW Java *pop* 6,503,449

Ja·lan·dhar \'jə-lən-dər\ city NW India in Punjab *pop* 509,510

Ja·la·pa \hə-'lä-pə\ city E Mexico ✳ of Veracruz *pop* 279,451

Ja·lis·co \hä-'lis-(,)kō\ state W *central* Mexico ✳ Guadalajara *area* 30,941 *sq mi* (80,137 *sq km*), *pop* 5,302,689

Jal·u·it \'ja-lù-wət, 'jal-yù-wət\ island (atoll) W Pacific, in Ralik chain of the Marshalls

Ja·mai·ca \jə-'mā-kə\ island West Indies in the Greater Antilles; a dominion of the Commonwealth of Nations since 1962; formerly a Brit. colony ✳ Kingston *area* 4471 *sq mi* (11,580 *sq km*), *pop* 2,464,000 — **Ja·mai·can** \-kən\ *adjective or noun*

Jamaica Bay inlet of Atlantic Ocean SE N.Y. in SW Long Is.

Jam·bi \'jäm-bē\ city & port Indonesia in SE *central* Sumatra *pop* 340,066

James \'jāmz\ **1** *or officially* **Da·ko·ta** \də-'kō-tə\ river 710 *mi* (1143 *km*) N.Dak. & S.Dak. flowing S to Missouri River **2** river 340 *mi* (547 *km*) Va. flowing E into Chesapeake Bay at Hampton Roads

James Bay the S extension of Hudson Bay 280 *mi* (448 *km*) long & 150 *mi* (240 *km*) wide Canada between NE Ontario & W Quebec

James·town \'jāmz-,taùn\ **1** city SW N.Y. *pop* 34,681 **2** ruined village E Va. SW of Williamsburg on James River; first permanent English settlement in America (1607)

Jam·mu \'jə-(,)mü\ city S of Srinagar, winter ✳ of Jammu & Kashmir *pop* 135,522

Jammu and Kash·mir \'kash-,mir, 'kazh-, kash-', kazh-\ *or* **Kashmir** state N India including Kashmir region & Jammu (to the S); claimed also by Pakistan; summer ✳ Srinagar, winter ✳ Jammu *area* 53,665 *sq mi* (138,992 *sq km*), *pop* 7,718,700

Jam·na·gar \jäm-'nə-gər\ city W India in W Gujarat on Gulf of Kachchh *pop* 350,544

Jam·shed·pur \'jäm-,shed-,pùr\ city E India in S Bihar SE of Ranchi *pop* 751,368

Ja·mu·na \'jə-mü-nə\ the lower Brahmaputra

Janes·ville \'jānz-,vil\ city S Wis. SE of Madison *pop* 52,133

Ja·nic·u·lum \jə-'ni-kyə-ləm\ hill in Rome, Italy, on right bank of the Tiber opposite the seven hills on which the ancient city was built — see AVENTINE

Jan Ma·yen Island \yän-'mī-ən\ island in Arctic Ocean E of Greenland & NNE of Iceland belonging to Norway *area* 147 *sq mi* (382 *sq km*)

Ja·pan \jə-'pan, ja-\ *or Japanese* **Nip·pon** \ni-'pän, nē-'pó³\ country E Asia comprising Honshu, Hokkaido, Kyushu, Shikoku, & other islands in the W Pacific; a constitutional monarchy ✳ Tokyo *area* 143,619 *sq mi* (371,973 *sq km*), *pop* 123,611,541

Japan, Sea of arm of the N Pacific W of Japan

Ja·pu·rá \,zhä-pü-'rä\ river 1750 *mi* (2816 *km*) S Colombia & NW Brazil flowing SE into the Amazon

Ja·ra·bu·lus \jə-'rä-bù-,lùs\ *or* **Je·ra·blus** \je-'rä-,blùs\ town N Syria on the Euphrates near Turkish border

Jar·vis \'jär-vis\ island *central* Pacific in the Line Islands; claimed by the U.S.

Jas·per National Park \'jas-pər\ reservation W Canada in W Alberta on E slopes of the Rockies NW of Banff National Park

Jassy — see IASI

Ja·strze·bie-Zdroj \yäs-'jä-bēz-'drói\ city S Poland *pop* 102,661

Ja·va \'jä-və, 'ja-\ *or Indonesian* **Dja·wa** \'jä-və\ island Indonesia SE of Sumatra; chief city Jakarta *area* 51,007 *sq mi* (132,618 *sq km*), *pop* 107,581,306

Java Head cape Indonesia at W end of Java on Sunda Strait

Ja·va·rí \,zhä-vä-'rē\ *or Spanish* **Ya·va·rí** \,yä-vä-'rē\ *or formerly* **Ya·ca·ra·na** \,yä-kä-'rä-nä\ river *about* 600 *mi* (965 *km*) Peru & Brazil flowing NE on the boundary & into the Amazon

Java Sea arm of the Pacific bounded on S by Java, on W by Sumatra, on N by Borneo, & on E by Sulawesi

Jaxartes — see SYR DARYA

Jaya, Puncak — see PUNCAK JAYA

Ja·ya·pu·ra \,jä-yä-'pü-rä\ *or formerly* **Hol·lan·dia** \hó-'län-dē-ə\ *or* **Ko·ta·ba·ru** \,kō-tä-bä-rü\ *or* **Su·kar·na·pu·ra** \sù-'kär-nä-,pü-rä\ city & port Indonesia ✳ of Irian Jaya

Ja·ya·pu·ra \,jä-yä-'pü-rä\ *or formerly* **Hol·lan·dia** \hó-'län-dē-ə\ *or* **Ko·ta·ba·ru** \,kō-tä-bä-rü\ *or* **Su·kar·na·pu·ra** \sù-'kär-nä-,pü-rä\ city & port Indonesia ✳ of Irian Jaya

Jazirah, Al — see GEZIRA

Jebel, Bahr el — see BAHR EL GHAZAL

Je·bel ed Druz \'je-bəl-ed-'drüz\ *or* **Jebel Druz** region S Syria E of Sea of Galilee on border of Jordan

Jebel Musa — see MUSA (Gebel)

Jebel Toubkal — see TOUBKAL (Jebel)

Je·bus \'jē-bəs\ a Biblical name for Jerusalem

Jed·burgh \'jed-b(ə-)rə\ royal burgh SE Scotland in Borders region

Jef·fer·son \'je-fər-sən\ river over 200 *mi* (321 *km*) SW Mont. — see THREE FORKS

Jefferson, Mount mountain 10,495 *ft* (3199 *m*) NW Oreg. in Cascades

Jefferson City city ✳ of Mo. on Missouri River *pop* 35,481

Jef·fer·son·town \'je-fər-sən-,taùn\ city N Ky. E of Louisville *pop* 23,221

Jef·fer·son·ville \'je-fər-sən-,vil\ city S Ind. *pop* 21,841

Jehol — see CHENGDE

Je·mappes \zhə-'máp\ commune SW Belgium W of Mons

Je·na \'yā-nə\ city E *central* Germany E of Erfurt *pop* 100,967

Je·qui·ti·nho·nha \zhe-,kē-tē-'nyō-nyə, -'nō-nyə\ river 500 *mi* (805 *km*) E Brazil flowing NE into the Atlantic

Jer·ba *or* **Djer·ba** \'jər-bə, 'jer-\ *or* **Jar·bah** \'jär-bə\ island SE Tunisia in the Mediterranean at entrance to Gulf of Gabes *area* 197 *sq mi* (510 *sq km*)

Je·rez \hə-'rās, hā-'reth, -'res\ *or* **Je·rez de la Fron·te·ra** \tthä-lä-frōn-'tā-rä\ *or formerly* **Xe·res** \'sher-ēz\ city SW Spain NE of Cádiz *pop* 182,939

Jer·i·cho \'jer-i-,kō\ **1** *or Arabic* **Eri·ha** \ā-'rē-hä\ town W Jordan 5 *mi* (8 *km*) NW of Dead

Sea **2** ancient Palestinian city near site of modern Jericho

Jer·sey \'jər-zē\ **1** island English Channel in the Channel Islands ✻ St. Helier *area* 45 *sq mi* (117 *sq km*) **2** NEW JERSEY — **Jer·sey·an** \-ən\ *noun* — **Jer·sey·ite** \-ˌīt\ *noun*

Jersey City city & port NE N.J. *pop* 228,537

Je·ru·sa·lem \jə-'rü-s(ə-)ləm, -'rü-z(ə-)ləm\ *or ancient* **Hi·ero·sol·y·ma** \ˌhī-(ə-)rō-'sä-lə-mə\ city *central* Palestine NW of Dead Sea; divided 1948–67 between Jordan (old city) & Israel (new city) ✻ of Israel since 1950 & formerly ✻ of ancient kingdoms of Israel & Judah; old city under Israeli control since 1967 *pop* 544,200 — **Je·ru·sa·lem·ite** \-lə-ˌmīt\ *noun*

Jer·vis Bay \'jär-vis\ inlet of the Pacific SE Australia on SE coast of New South Wales on which is situated district (*area* 28 *sq mi or* 73 *sq km*) that is part of Australian Capital Territory

Jesselton — see KOTA KINABALU

Jewel Cave National Monument limestone cave SW S.Dak.

Jewish Autonomous Oblast *or* **Ye·vrey·ska·ya** \yi-'vrä-skə-yə\ autonomous oblast E Russia in Asia, bordering on the Amur & Birobidzhan *area* 13,900 *sq mi* (36,001 *sq km*)

Jez·re·el \'jez-rē-ˌel, -ˌrēl\ ancient town *central* Palestine in Samaria NW of Mt. Gilboa in Valley of Jezreel; now in N Israel

Jezreel, Valley of the E end of the Plain of Esdraelon

Jhan·si \'jän(t)-sē\ city N India in S Uttar Pradesh *pop* 313,491

Jhe·lum \'jā-ləm\ *or ancient* **Hy·das·pes** \hī-'das-(ˌ)pēz\ river 450 *mi* (724 *km*) NW India (subcontinent) flowing from Kashmir S & SW into the Chenab

Jia·mu·si \'jyä-'mü-'sē\ *or* **Chia–mu–ssu** \'jyä-'mü-'sü\ *or* **Kia·mu·sze** \'jyä-'mü-'sə\ city NE China in E Heilongjiang *pop* 493,409

Jiang·su *or* **Kiang·su** \'jyän-'sü\ province E China bordering on Yellow Sea ✻ Nanjing *area* 40,927 *sq mi* (106,001 *sq km*), *pop* 67,056,519

Jiang·xi *or* **Kiang·si** \'jyän-shē\ province SE China ✻ Nanchang *area* 63,629 *sq mi* (165,435 *sq km*), *pop* 37,710,281

Jiao·zhou *or* **Kiao·chow** \'jyaü-'jō\ bay of Yellow Sea E China in E Shandong *area* 200 *sq mi* (520 *sq km*)

Jid·da *or* **Jid·dah** \'ji-də\ *or* **Jed·da** *or* **Jed·dah** \'je-də\ city W Saudi Arabia in Hejaz on Red Sea; port for Mecca *pop* 561,104

Jih–k'a–tse — see XIGAZÊ

Ji·lin \'jē-'lin\ *or* **Ki·rin** \'kē-'rin\ **1** province NE China in E Manchuria ✻ Changchun *area* 72,201 *sq mi* (187,723 *sq km*), *pop* 24,658,721 **2** *or formerly* **Yung·ki** \'yüŋ-jē\ city NE China in E *central* Jilin *pop* 1,036,858

Ji·nan *or* **Chi·nan** *or* **Tsi·nan** \'jē-'nän\ city E China ✻ of Shandong *pop* 1,500,000

Jin·ja \'jin-jä\ city & port SE Uganda on Lake Victoria *pop* 60,979

Jinmen — see QUEMOY

Jin·zhou *or* **Chin·chow** *or* **Chin–chou** \'jin-'jō\ city NE China in SW Liaoning *pop* 400,000

Jizah, Al — see GIZA

João Pes·soa \zhwaüⁿ-pe-'sō-ə\ *or formerly* **Pa·ra·í·ba** \ˌpär-ä-'ē-bə\ city NE Brazil ✻ of Paraíba *pop* 497,214

Jodh·pur \'jäd-pər, -ˌpùr\ **1** *or* **Mar·war** \'mär-ˌwär\ former state NW India bordering on Thar Desert & Rann of Kachchh; since 1949 part of Rajasthan state **2** city, its ✻ *pop* 666,279

Jod·rell Bank \'jä-drəl\ locality W England in NE Cheshire near Macclesfield

Jogjakarta — see YOGYAKARTA

Jo·han·nes·burg \jō-'hä-nəs-ˌbərg, -'ha-\ city NE Republic of South Africa in Gauteng *pop* 654,232

John Day \'jän-'dā\ river 281 *mi* (452 *km*) N Oreg. flowing W & N into Columbia River

John Day Fossil Beds National Monument reservation N *central* Oreg.

John o' Groat's \ˌjän-ō-'grōts\ *or* **John o' Groat's House** locality N Scotland; popularly considered the northernmost point of mainland of Scotland & Great Britain — see DUNNET HEAD

John·son City \'jän(t)-sən\ city NE Tenn. S of Va. border *pop* 49,381

John·ston \'jän(t)-stən\ **1** island (atoll) *central* Pacific SW of Honolulu, Hawaii; belongs to the U.S. **2** town N R.I. SW of Providence *pop* 26,542

Johns·town \'jänz-ˌtaün\ city SW *central* Pa. *pop* 28,134

Jo·hor \jə-'hōr, -'hòr\ state Malaysia in Peninsular Malaysia at S end of Malay Peninsula ✻ Johor Baharu *area* 7360 *sq mi* (19,062 *sq km*), *pop* 2,074,297

Johor Ba·ha·ru \'bä-hə-ˌrü\ city S Malaysia (federation) ✻ of Johor on an inlet opposite Singapore Is. *pop* 135,936

Join·vi·le *or formerly* **Join·vil·le** \zhäⁿ-'vē-lē\ city S Brazil NNW of Florianópolis *pop* 346,095

Jo·li·et \ˌjō-lē-'et, *chiefly by outsiders* ˌjä-\ city NE Ill. *pop* 76,836

Jo·lo \hō-'lō\ island S Philippines, chief island of Sulu Archipelago *area* 345 *sq mi* (897 *sq km*)

Jones·boro \'jōnz-ˌbər-ō\ city NE Ark. *pop* 46,535

Jön·kö·ping \'yœn-ˌshē-piŋ\ city S Sweden at S end of Vättern Lake *pop* 309,867

Jon·quière \zhōⁿ-'kyer\ town Canada in S *central* Quebec *pop* 57,933

Jop·lin \'jä-plin\ city SW Mo. *pop* 40,961

Joppa — see JAFFA

Jor·dan \'jòr-d°n\ **1** river *central* Utah flowing from Utah Lake N into Great Salt Lake **2** river 200 *mi* (322 *km*) NE Palestine flowing from Anti-Lebanon Mountains S through Sea of Galilee into Dead Sea **3** *or formerly* **Trans·jor·dan** \(ˌ)tran(t)s-, (ˌ)tranz-\ country SW Asia in NW Arabia ✻ Amman *area* 34,575 *sq mi* (89,549 *sq km*), *pop* 3,636,000 — **Jor·da·ni·an** \jòr-'dā-nē-ən\ *adjective or noun*

Josh·ua Tree National Monument \'jä-shə-wä\ reservation S Calif. N of Salton Sea containing unusual desert flora

Jo·tun·heim \'yō-t°n-ˌhäm\ *or Norwegian* **Jo·tun·hei·men** \-ˌhä-mən\ mountains S *central* Norway — see GLITTERTIND

Juana Dí·az \ˌwä-nə-'dē-ˌäs, ˌhwä-nä-'thē-äs\ municipality S Puerto Rico *pop* 45,198

Juan de Fu·ca, Strait of \ˌwän-də-'fyü-kə, ˌhwän-dä-'fü-kä\ strait 100 *mi* (161 *km*) long between Vancouver Is., British Columbia, & Olympic Peninsula, Wash.

Juan Fer·nán·dez \ˌwän-fər-'nän-dəs, ˌhwän-fer-'nän-dās\ group of three islands SE Pacific W of Chile; belongs to Chile *area* 70 *sq mi* (182 *sq km*)

Juan–les–Pins \ˌzhwäⁿ-lā-'paⁿ\ town SE France on Cap d'Antibes

Juárez — see CIUDAD JUÁREZ

Jub·ba *or* **Ju·ba** \'jü-bə\ river 1000 *mi* (1609 *km*) E Africa flowing from S Ethiopia S through Somalia into Indian Ocean

Ju·by, Cape \'jü-bē, 'yü-\ cape NW Africa on NW coast of Western Sahara

Jú·car \'hü-ˌkär\ river over 300 *mi* (483 *km*) E Spain flowing S & E into the Mediterranean S of Valencia

Ju·daea *or* **Ju·dea** \jü-'dē-ə, -'dā-\ ancient region Palestine constituting the S division (Judah) of the country under Persian, Greek, & Roman rule; bounded on N by Samaria, on E by Jordan River & Dead Sea, on SW by Sinai Peninsula, & on W by the Mediterranean — **Ju·dae·an** *or* **Ju·de·an** \-ən\ *adjective or noun*

Ju·dah \'jü-də\ ancient kingdom S Palestine ✻ Jerusalem — see ISRAEL

Jugoslavia — see YUGOSLAVIA — **Ju·go·slav** \ˌyü-gō-'släv, -'slav\ *or* **Ju·go·sla·vi·an** \-'slä-vē-ən\ *adjective or noun*

Juiz de Fo·ra \ˌzhwēzh-də-'fōr-ə, -'fòr-\ city E Brazil in S Minas Gerais *pop* 385,756

Ju·juy \hü-'hwē\ city NW Argentina N of Tucumán *pop* 44,188

Ju·lian Alps \'jül-yən\ section of E Alps W Slovenia & Italy N of Istrian Peninsula; highest peak Triglav 9395 *ft* (2864 *m*)

Julian Venetia — see VENEZIA GIULIA

Junction City city NE *central* Kans. *pop* 20,604

Ju·neau \'jü-(ˌ)nō, jü-'\ city & port ✻ of Alaska in SE coastal strip *pop* 26,751

Jung·frau \'yuŋ-ˌfraü\ mountain 13,642 *ft* (4158 *m*) SW *central* Switzerland in Berner Alpen between Bern & Valais cantons

Jung·gar \'juŋ-'gär\ *or* **Dzun·gar·ian Basin** \ˌzəŋ-'gar-ē-ən, ˌjuŋ-, -'ger-\ *or* **Dzun·gar·ia** \-ē-ə\ region W China in N Xinjiang Uygur N of the Tian Shan

Ju·ni·ata \ˌjü-nē-'a-tə\ river 150 *mi* (241 *km*) S *central* Pa. flowing E into the Susquehanna

Ju·nín \hü-'nēn\ **1** city E Argentina W of Buenos Aires *pop* 62,080 **2** town *central* Peru at S end of **Lake Junín** (25 *mi or* 40 *km* long)

Ju·pi·ter \'jü-pə-tər\ town SE Fla. *pop* 24,986

Jupiter Island island SE Fla. in the Atlantic

Ju·ra \'jur-ə\ **1** canton W Switzerland *area* 322 *sq mi* (834 *sq km*), *pop* 65,376 **2** mountains France & Switzerland extending *about* 145 *mi* (233 *km*) along the boundary; highest Mount Neige (in France) 5652 *ft* (1723 *m*) **3** island 24 *mi* (39 *km*) long W Scotland in the Inner Hebrides S of Mull

Juramento — see SALADO

Ju·ruá \ˌzhùr-(ə-)'wä\ river NW *central* S. America flowing from E *central* Peru NE into the Solimões in NW Brazil

Ju·rue·na \ˌzhùr-'wä-nə\ river 600 *mi* (966 *km*) W *central* Brazil flowing N to unite with the Teles Pires forming the Tapajoz

Jut·land \'jət-lənd\ *or Danish* **Jyl·land** \'yœ-ˌlän\ **1** peninsula N Europe projecting into North Sea & comprising mainland of Denmark & N portion of Schleswig-Holstein, Germany **2** the mainland of Denmark

Kaapland — see CAPE OF GOOD HOPE

Ka·ba·le·ga Falls \kə-bä-'lē-gä, 'kä-\ *or* **Ka·ba·re·ga Falls** \-'rä-\ *or* **Mur·chi·son Falls** \'mər-chə-sən\ waterfall 130 *ft* (40 *m*) W Uganda in the Victoria Nile

Kab·ar·di·no–Bal·kar·ia \ˌka-bər-'dē-nō-ˌbòl-'kar-ē-ə, -ˌbal-\ autonomous republic S Russia in Europe on N slopes of the Caucasus ✻ Nalchik *area* 4826 *sq mi* (12,499 *sq km*), *pop* 784,000 — **Kab·ar·din·ian** \ˌka-bər-'dē-nē-ən\ *adjective or noun*

Ka·bul \'kä-bəl, kə-'bül\ **1** river 435 *mi* (700 *km*) Afghanistan & N Pakistan flowing E into the Indus **2** city W of Afghanistan on Kabul River *pop* 1,424,400 — **Ka·buli** \'kä-bə-(ˌ)lē, kə-'bü-lē\ *adjective or noun*

Ka·bwe \'kä-(ˌ)bwä\ *or formerly* **Bro·ken Hill** \'brō-kən\ city *central* Zambia *pop* 166,519

Ka·by·lia \kə-'bē-lē-ə, -'bi-\ mountainous region N Algeria on coast E of Algiers; comprises two areas: **Great Kabylia** (to W) & **Little Kabylia** (to E)

Kachchh, Gulf of \'kəch\ *or* **Gulf of Kutch** \'kəch\ inlet of Arabian Sea W India N of Kathiawar

Kachchh, Rann of *or* **Rann of Kutch** salt marsh in S Pakistan & W India stretching in an arc from the mouths of the Indus to the head of Gulf of Kachchh

Ka·desh–bar·nea \ˌkā-(ˌ)desh-'bär-nē-ə, -bär-'nē-ə\ ancient town S Palestine SW of Dead Sea; exact location uncertain

Ka·di·koy \kä-'di-kòi\ *or ancient* **Chal·ce·don** \'kal-sə-ˌdän, kal-'sē-d°n\ former city Asia on the Bosporus; now a district of Istanbul

Kadiyevka — see STAKHANOV

Kaerh — see GAR

Kae·song \'kā-ˌsòŋ\ city SW N. Korea SE of Pyongyang *pop* 331,000

Kaf·fe·klub·ben \'ka-fə-ˌklü-bən, -ˌklə-\ island in Arctic Ocean off N coast of Greenland; northernmost point of land in the world, at 83°40′N

Kaf·frar·ia \kə-'frar-ē-ə, ka-, -'frer-\ region Republic of South Africa in Eastern Cape province S of Lesotho & bordering on Indian Ocean

Kafiristan — see NURISTAN

Ka·fue \kä-'fü-ä\ river 600 *mi* (965 *km*) Zambia flowing into the Zambezi

Ka·ge·ra \kä-'gä-rä\ river 430 *mi* (692 *km*) Burundi, Rwanda, & NW Tanzania flowing N & E into Lake Victoria on Uganda border

Ka·go·shi·ma \kä-gō-'shē-mä, kä-'gō-shē-\ city & port S Japan in S Kyushu on **Kagoshima Bay** (inlet of the Pacific) *pop* 536,685

Ka·hoo·la·we \,kä-hō-ō-'lä-(,)vä, -(,)wä\ island Hawaii SW of Maui *area* 45 *sq mi* (117 *sq km*)

Kai·bab Plateau \'kī-,bab\ plateau N Ariz. & SW Utah N of Grand Canyon

Kai·e·teur Falls \'kī-ə-,tür, ,kī-'chür\ waterfall 741 *ft* (226 *m*) high & 350 *ft* (107 *m*) wide *central* Guyana

Kai·feng \'kī-'fəŋ\ city E *central* China in NE Henan *pop* 318,000

Kai·lua \kī-'lü-ä\ city Hawaii in NE Oahu *pop* 36,818

Kair·ouan \ker-'wän\ city NE Tunisia *pop* 54,546

Kai·sers·lau·tern \,kī-zərz-'laü-tərn\ city SW Germany W of Ludwigshafen *pop* 100,541

Ka·ki·na·da \,kä-kə-'nä-də\ city & port E India in NE Andhra Pradesh on Bay of Bengal *pop* 279,875

Kalaallit Nunaat — see GREENLAND

Ka Lae \kä-'lä\ *or* **South Cape** headland Hawaii, southernmost point of Hawaii (island)

Kalaeloa Point — see BARBERS POINT

Kal·a·ha·ri Desert \,ka-lə-'här-ē, ,kä-\ desert region S Africa N of Orange River & S of Lake Ngami in Botswana & NW Republic of South Africa

Kal·a·ma·zoo \,ka-lə-mə-'zü\ city SW Mich. *pop* 80,277

Ka·lat *or* **Khe·lat** \kə-'lät\ region NW Pakistan including S & *central* Baluchistan; a former princely state ✱ Kalat

Ka·le·mie \kä-'lä-mē\ *or formerly* **Al·bert·ville** \,al-,ber-'vēl, 'al-bərt-,vil\ city & port E Democratic Republic of the Congo on Lake Tanganyika *pop* 96,212

Kalgan — see ZHANGJIAKOU

Kal·goor·lie–Boul·der \kal-'gür-lē-'bōl-dər\ town Australia in S *central* W. Australia *pop* 25,016

Ka·li·man·tan \,ka-lə-'man-,tan, ,kä-lē-'män-,tän\ **1** an Indonesian name for Borneo **2** the S & E part of Borneo belonging to Indonesia; formerly (as **Dutch Borneo**) part of Netherlands India

Kalinin — see TVER'

Ka·li·nin·grad \kə-'lē-nən-,grad, -nyən-, -,grät\ *or German* **Kö·nigs·berg** \'kä-nigz-,bərg, *German* 'kœ-niks-,berk\ city & port W Russia in Europe near the Frisches Haff; formerly ✱ of E. Prussia *pop* 411,000

Ka·lisz \'kä-lēsh\ commune *central* Poland W of Lodz *pop* 106,087

Kal·mar \'käl-,mär, 'kal-\ city & port SE Sweden *pop* 56,863

Kal·myk·ia \(,)kal-'mi-kē-ə\ autonomous republic S Russia in Europe on NW shore of Caspian Sea W of the Volga ✱ Elista *area* 29,305 *sq mi* (75,900 *sq km*), *pop* 322,000

Ka·lu·ga \kə-'lü-gə\ city W *central* Russia in Europe on Oka River WNW of Tula *pop* 347,000

Ka·ma \'kä-mə\ river E Russia in Europe flowing SW into the Volga S of Kazan

Ka·ma·ku·ra \,kä-'mä-kə-,rä, ,kä-mä-'kür-ä\ city Japan in SE Honshu on Sagami Sea S of Yokohama *pop* 174,299

Kam·chat·ka \kam-'chat-kə, -'chät-\ peninsula 750 *mi* (1207 *km*) long E Russia in Asia between Sea of Okhotsk & Bering Sea

Ka·met \'kə-mät, kə-'\ mountain 25,447 *ft* (7756 *m*) N India in Uttar Pradesh in the NW Himalayas

Kam·loops \'kam-,lüps\ city Canada in S British Columbia *pop* 67,057

Kam·pa·la \käm-'pä-lä, kam-\ city ✱ of Uganda N of Lake Victoria *pop* 773,463

Kampuchea — see CAMBODIA — **Kam·pu·che·an** \,kam-pù-'chē-ən\ *adjective*

Kan — see GAN

Ka·nan·ga \kä-'näŋ-gä\ *or formerly* **Lu·lua·bourg** \,lü-lwä-'bür\ city S *central* Democratic Republic of the Congo *pop* 371,862

Kananur — see CANNANORE

Ka·na·ta \kə-'nä-tə\ city Canada in SE Ontario *pop* 37,344

Ka·na·wha \kə-'nò-(w)ə\ river 97 *mi* (156 *km*) W W.Va. flowing NW into Ohio River

Ka·na·za·wa \,kä-'nä-zä-wä, ,kä-nä-'zä-wä\ city & port Japan in W *central* Honshu near Sea of Japan *pop* 442,872

Kan·chen·jun·ga \,kən-chən-'jəŋ-gə, -'jüŋ-\ *or* **Kang·chen·jun·ga** \,kəŋ-\ mountain 28,169 *ft*

(8586 *m*) Nepal & Sikkim in the Himalayas; 3d highest in world

Kan·chi·pu·ram \kän-'chē-pə-rəm\ city SE India in N Tamil Nadu SW of Madras *pop* 145,028

Kan·da·har *or* **Qan·da·har** \'kən-də-,här\ city SE Afghanistan *pop* 130,212

Kan·dy \'kan-dē\ city W *central* Sri Lanka ENE of Colombo *pop* 104,000 — **Kan·dy·an** \-dē-ən\ *adjective*

Kane Basin \'kān\ section of the passage between NW Greenland & Ellesmere Is. N of Baffin Bay

Ka·ne·o·he Bay \,kä-nē-'ō-ā, -'ō-(,)hā\ inlet Hawaii on E Oahu

Kan·ka·kee \,kaŋ-kə-'kē\ **1** river 135 *mi* (217 *km*) Ind. & Ill. flowing SW & W to unite with Des Plaines River forming Illinois River **2** city NE Ill. on Kankakee River *pop* 27,575

Kan·nap·o·lis \kə-'na-pə-lis\ town S *central* N.C. *pop* 29,696

Ka·no \'kä-(,)nō\ city N *central* Nigeria *pop* 594,800

Kan·pur \'kän-,pùr\ city N India in S Uttar Pradesh on the Ganges *pop* 1,879,420

Kan·sas \'kan-zəs\ **1** *or* **Kaw** \'kò\ river 169 *mi* (272 *km*) E Kans. flowing E into Missouri River — see SMOKY HILL **2** state *central* U.S. ✱ Topeka *area* 82,277 *sq mi* (213,097 *sq km*), *pop* 2,477,574 — **Kan·san** \'kan-zən\ *adjective or noun*

Kansas City 1 city NE Kans. adjacent to Kansas City, Mo. *pop* 149,767 **2** city W Mo. on Missouri River *pop* 435,146

Kansu — see GANSU

Kan·ton Island \'kan-tⁿn\ island (atoll) *central* Pacific in Phoenix Islands

Kan·to Plain \'kän-(,)tō\ region Japan in E *central* Honshu; Tokyo is situated on it

Kao·hsiung \'kaú-'shyùŋ, 'gaú-\ city & port SW Taiwan *pop* 1,405,860

Ka·pi·da·gi \,kä-pi-'daú\ *or ancient* **Cyz·i·cus** \'si-zi-kəs\ peninsula NW Turkey in Asia projecting into Sea of Marmara

Ka·ra·chay–Cher·kes·sia \,kär-ə-'chī-chir-'ke-syə\ *or formerly* **Ka·ra·cha·ye·vo–Cher·kess** \,kär-ə-'chī-ə-,vō-chir-'kes\ autonomous region SE Russia in Europe in N Caucasus *area* 5444 *sq mi* (14,100 *sq km*), *pop* 431,000 ✱ Cherkessk

Ka·ra·chi \kə-'rä-chē\ city & port S Pakistan ✱ of Sind *pop* 5,103,000

Karafuto — see SAKHALIN

Ka·ra·gan·da \,kä-rə-'gän-də\ *or* **Qa·ra·ghan·dy** \-dē\ city *central* Kazakhstan *pop* 608,600

Ka·raj \kä-'räj\ city N Iran NW of Tehran *pop* 275,100

Ka·ra·kal·pak \,kar-ə-,kál-'pák\ autonomous republic NW Uzbekistan SE of Aral Sea ✱ Nukus *area* 63,938 *sq mi* (165,599 *sq km*), *pop* 1,273,800

Kar·a·ko·ram Pass \,kär-ə-'kòr-əm, -'kòr-\ mountain pass 18,290 *ft* (5575 *m*) NE Kashmir through Karakoram Range

Karakoram Range mountain system S *central* Asia in N Kashmir & NW Tibet on Xinjiang Uygur border; westernmost system of the Himalaya complex, connecting the Himalayas with the Pamirs — see K2

Kar·a·ko·rum \,kär-ə-'kòr-əm\ ruined city Mongolia on the upper Orkhon ✱ of Mongol Empire

Ka·ra–Kum \,kär-ə-'küm, ,kär-\ desert Turkmenistan S of Aral Sea between the Caspian Sea & the Amu Darya *area* 115,830 *sq mi* (300,000 *sq km*)

Kara Sea arm of Arctic Ocean off coast of Russia E of Novaya Zemlya

Ka·ra Su \,kar-ə-'sü, ,kär-\ the Euphrates above its junction with the Murat in E *central* Turkey

Kar·ba·la' \'kär-bə-lə, ,kär-bə-lä\ city *central* Iraq SSW of Baghdad *pop* 83,301

Ka·re·lia \kə-'rē-lē-ə, -'rēl-yə\ autonomous republic NW Russia in Europe; formerly (1940–56), as the **Ka·re·lo–Finn·ish Republic** \kə-'rē-(,)lō-'fi-nish\ constituent republic of the U.S.S.R. ✱ Petrozadovsk *area* 66,564 *sq mi* (172,401 *sq km*), *pop* 800,000

Ka·re·lian Isthmus \kə-'rē-lē-ən, -'rēl-yən\ isthmus Russia in Europe between Gulf of Finland & Lake Ladoga

Ka·ri·ba \kə-'rē-bä\ lake 175 *mi* (282 *km*) long SE Zambia & N Zimbabwe formed in the Zambezi by **Kariba Dam**

Ka·ri·kal \,kär-ə-'käl\ **1** territory of former French India S of Pondicherry; incorporated 1954 in India *area* 52 *sq mi* (135 *sq km*) **2** *or* **Ka·rai·kal** \,kä-ri-'käl\ city & port, its ✱, on Bay of Bengal *pop* 22,252

Kar·kheh *or* **Ker·kheh** \kər-'kä\ *or ancient* **Cho·as·pes** \kō-'as-(,)pēz\ river flowing from W Iran S & W into marshlands E of the Tigris in SE Iraq

Karl–Marx–Stadt — see CHEMNITZ

Karls·kro·na \kär-(ə)lz-'krü-nə\ city & port SE Sweden on Baltic Sea *area pop* 59,753

Karls·ru·he \'kärl-(ə)lz-,rü-ə\ city SW Germany in Baden-Württemberg on the Rhine *pop* 278,579 — **Karls·ru·her** \-,rü-ər\ *noun*

Karl·stad \'kär(-ə)l-,stä(d)\ city SW Sweden *pop* 77,290

Kar·nak \'kär-,nak\ town S Egypt on the Nile N of Luxor on N part of site of ancient Thebes

Kar·na·ta·ka \kər-'nä-tə-kə\ *or formerly* **My·sore** \mī-'sòr, -'sòr\ state SW India ✱ Bangalore *area* 74,037 *sq mi* (191,756 *sq km*), *pop* 44,977,201

Ka·roo *or* **Kar·roo** \kə-'rü\ plateau region W Republic of South Africa W of Drakensberg Mountains divided into **Little Karoo** *or* **Southern Karoo** (in *central* Western Cape province); **Great Karoo** *or* **Central Karoo** (in Western Cape & Eastern Cape provinces); and **Northern Karoo** *or* **Upper Karoo** (in Northern Cape, Free State, & North West provinces)

Kár·pa·thos \'kär-pä-,thòs\ island Greece in the S Dodecanese *area* 118 *sq mi* (307 *sq km*), *pop* 8129

Kars \'kärz, 'kärs\ city NE Turkey *pop* 79,496

Karst \'kärst\ *or* **Kras** \'kräs\ *or Italian* **Car·so** \'kär-(,)sō\ limestone plateau NE of Istrian Peninsula in E Italy, W Slovenia, & W Croatia

Ka·run \kä-'rün\ river over 500 *mi* (804 *km*) W Iran flowing into Shatt-al-Arab

Ka·sai \kə-'sī\ **1** river 1338 *mi* (2153 *km*) N Angola & W Democratic Republic of the Congo flowing N & W into Congo River **2** region S *central* Democratic Republic of the Congo

Kashi \'ka-shē, 'kä-\ *or* **Kash·gar** \'kash-,gär, 'käsh-\ city W China in SW Xinjiang Uygur *pop* 174,570

Ka·shi·wa \kä-shē-(,)wä\ city Japan on Honshu *pop* 305,060

Kash·mir \'kash-,mir, 'kazh-, kash-', kazh-'\ **1** *or formerly* **Cash·mere** mountainous region N India (subcontinent) W of Tibet & SW of Xinjiang Uygur; includes valley (**Vale of Kashmir**) watered by the Jhelum **2** — see JAMMU AND KASHMIR

Kas·kas·kia \ka-'skas-kē-ə\ river 320 *mi* (515 *km*) SW Ill. flowing SW into Mississippi River

Kas·sa·la \kä-'sä-lə\ city NE Sudan *pop* 99,000

Kas·sel \'ka-səl, 'kä-\ city *central* Germany WNW of Erfurt *pop* 196,828

Kas·ser·ine Pass \'ka-sə-,rēn\ mountain pass *central* Tunisia

Ka·stel·lór·i·zon \,käs-te-'lòr-ē-,zòn\ *or* **Ca·stel·lo·ri·zo** \,käs-tə-'lòr-ə-,zō\ *or Italian* **Cas·tel·ros·so** \,käs-,tel-'rò-(,)sō\ island Greece in the E Dodecanese off SW coast of Turkey *area* 9 *sq mi* (23 *sq km*)

Ká·stron \'käs-,tròn\ town Greece on Lemnos

Ka·tah·din, Mount \kə-'tä-dⁿn\ mountain 5268 *ft* (1606 *m*) N *central* Maine; highest point in state

Katanga — see SHABA — **Ka·tan·gese** \kə-täŋ-'gēz, -taŋ-, -'gēs\ *adjective*

Ka·te·ri·ni \,kä-te-'rē-nē\ town N Greece *pop* 46,304

Kath·er·i·na, Ge·bel \'je-bəl,-ka-thə-'rē-nə\ *or* **Ja·bal Kat·ri·nah** \'jä-bəl-kä-'trē-nə\ *or* **Mount Cath·er·ine** \'ka-th(ə-)rən\ mountain 8652 *ft* (2637 *m*) NE Egypt on Sinai Peninsula; highest in the Gebel Musa

Ka·thi·a·war \,kä-tē-ə-'wär\ peninsula W India in Gujarat between Gulf of Kachchh & Gulf of Khambhat

Kath·man·du *or* **Kat·man·du** \,kat-,man-'dü, ,kät-,män-\ city ✱ of Nepal *pop* 235,211

Kat·mai, Mount \'kat-,mī\ volcano 6715 *ft* (2047 *m*) S Alaska in Aleutian Range at NE end of Alaska Peninsula

Katmai National Park reservation S Alaska including Mt. Katmai & Valley of Ten Thousand Smokes

Ka·to·wi·ce \kä-tȯ-'vēt-se\ city S Poland in Silesia *pop* 367,041

Kat·rine, Loch \'ka-trən\ lake 9 *mi* (*14 km*) long *central* Scotland in Central region E of Loch Lomond

Ka·tsi·na \'kät-sē-nä\ city N Nigeria ✳ of old kingdom of Katsina *pop* 182,400

Kat·te·gat \'ka-ti-ˌgat\ arm of North Sea between Sweden & Jutland Peninsula of Denmark

Kau·ai \kä-'wä-ē\ island Hawaii WNW of Oahu *area* 555 *sq mi* (*1437 sq km*)

Kau·nas \'kau̇-nəs, -ˌnäs\ *or Russian* **Kov·no** \'kȯv-(ˌ)nō, -nə\ city *central* Lithuania on the Neman; a former (1918–40) ✳ of Lithuania *pop* 433,600

Ka·vá·la *or* **Ka·vál·la** \kä-'vä-lä\ city & port NE Greece in Macedonia *pop* 58,576

Kāveri — see CAUVERY

Kāveri Falls — see CAUVERY FALLS

Kaw — see KANSAS

Ka·wa·goe \kä-'wä-gō-wä\ city Japan on SE *central* Honshu *pop* 304,860

Ka·wa·gu·chi \kä-wä-'gü-chē, kä-'wä-gü-(ˌ)chē\ city Japan in E Honshu N of Tokyo *pop* 438,667

Ka·war·tha Lakes \kə-'wȯr-thə\ group of lakes Canada in SE Ontario E of Lake Simcoe; traversed by Trent Canal system

Ka·wa·sa·ki \kä-wä-'sä-kē\ city Japan in E Honshu on Tokyo Bay, S suburb of Tokyo *pop* 1,173,606

Kay·se·ri \ˌkī-zə-'rē\ *or ancient* **Cae·sa·rea** \ˌsē-zə-'rē-ə, ˌse-zə-, ˌse-sə-\ *or* **Maz·a·ca** \'ma-zə-kə\ *or* **Caesarea Mazaca** city *central* Turkey in Asia at foot of Erciyas Dagi; chief city of ancient Cappadocia *pop* 421,362

Ka·zakh·stan \ˌka-(ˌ)zak-'stan; ˌkä-(ˌ)zäk-'stän *also* kə-\ independent country NW *central* Asia extending from Caspian Sea to Altay mountain range; a constituent republic of the U.S.S.R. 1936–91 ✳ Alma-Ata 1,048,300 *sq mi* (2,715,097 *sq km*), *pop* 17,186,000

Ka·zan **1** \kə-'zan\ river 455 *mi* (*732 km*) Canada flowing through a series of lakes into Baker Lake **2** \kə-'zan, -'zän, -'zä-nyə\ city E *central* Russia in Europe ✳ of Tatarstan *pop* 1,098,000

Kazan Retto — see VOLCANO

Kaz·bek \käz-'bek\ mountain 16,558 *ft* (*5047 m*) between Georgia & Russia in Europe in *central* Caucasus Mountains

Kaz Da·gi \ˌkäz-'dī\ *or* **Ida** \'ī-də\ mountain 5797 *ft* (*1767 m*) NW Turkey in Asia SE of ancient Troy

Kazvin — see QAZVIN

Kea \'kā-ä\ *or ancient* **Ce·os** \'sē-ˌäs\ island Greece in NW Cyclades; chief town Kea *area* 67 *sq mi* (*174 sq km*)

Ke·a·la·ke·kua Bay \kä-ə-lä-kä-'kü-ä\ inlet of the Pacific Hawaii in W Hawaii (island) on Kona coast W of Mauna Loa

Kear·ney \'kär-nē\ city S *central* Nebr. on Platte River *pop* 24,396

Kear·ny \'kär-nē\ town NE N.J. N of Newark *pop* 34,874

Kecs·ke·met \'kech-ke-ˌmāt\ city *central* Hungary *pop* 108,000

Ked·ah \'ke-də\ state Malaysia in N Peninsular Malaysia bordering on Strait of Malacca ✳ Alor Star *area* 3660 *sq mi* (*9516 sq km*), *pop* 1,304,800

Keeling — see COCOS

Keelung — see CHI-LUNG

Keene \'kēn\ city SW N.H. *pop* 22,430

Kee·wa·tin \kē-'wä-tᵊn, -'wä-\ former district Canada in E Northwest Territories N of Manitoba & Ontario & including the islands in Hudson Bay

Kefallinía — see CEPHALONIA

Kef·la·vik \'kye-blä-ˌvēk, 'ke-flə-\ town SW Iceland WSW of Reykjavík *pop* 7520

Keigh·ley \'kēth-lē— *sic*\ borough N England in W. Yorkshire, NW of Leeds *pop* 57,451

Kei·zer \'kī-zər\ city NW Oreg. N of Salem *pop* 21,884

Kej·im·ku·jik National Park \ˌke-jə-mə-'kü-jik, ˌkej-mə-\ reservation Canada in SW Nova Scotia

Ke·lan·tan \kə-'lan-ˌtan\ state Malaysia in N Peninsular Malaysia on S. China Sea ✳ Kota Baharu *area* 5780 *sq mi* (*14,970 sq km*), *pop* 1,181,680

Ke·low·na \kə-'lau̇-nə\ city Canada in S British Columbia *pop* 75,950

Keltsy — see KIELCE

Ke·me·ro·vo \'kye-mə-rə-və; 'ke-mə-ˌrō-və, -rə-ˌvō\ city Russia in Asia in Kuznetsk Basin on Tom River *pop* 521,000

Ke·nai Peninsula \'kē-ˌnī\ peninsula S Alaska E of Cook Inlet; site of **Kenai Fjords National Park** (ice field)

Ken·dal \'ken-dᵊl\ borough NW England in Cumbria *pop* 23,411

Ken·il·worth \'ke-nᵊl-ˌwərth\ town *central* England in Warwickshire *pop* 19,315

Ke·ni·tra \kə-'nē-trə\ *or formerly* **Port Lyau·tey** \ˌpȯr-lyō-'tā\ city N Morocco NE of Rabat *pop* 139,206

Ken·ne·bec \'ke-ni-ˌbek, ˌke-ni-'\ river 150 *mi* (*240 km*) S Maine flowing S from Moosehead Lake into the Atlantic

Kennedy, Cape — see CANAVERAL (Cape)

Ken·ne·dy, Mount \'ke-nə-dē\ mountain 13,905 *ft* (*4238 m*) NW Canada in Yukon Territory in St. Elias Range near Alaska border

Ken·ner \'ke-nər\ city SE La. W of New Orleans *pop* 72,033

Ken·ne·saw Mountain \'ke-nə-ˌsȯ\ mountain 1809 *ft* (*551 m*) NW Ga. NW of Atlanta

Ken·ne·wick \'ke-nə-ˌwik\ city SE Wash. *pop* 42,155

Ke·no·sha \kə-'nō-shə\ city SE Wis. S of Racine *pop* 80,352

Ken·sing·ton and Chel·sea \'ken-ziŋ-tən-ənd-'chel-sē, 'ken(t)-siŋ-\ borough of W Greater London, England *pop* 127,600; includes former boroughs of Kensington & Chelsea

Kent \'kent\ **1** city NE Ohio SE of Cleveland *pop* 28,835 **2** city W Wash. S of Seattle *pop* 37,960 **3** county SE England bordering on Strait of Dover; one of kingdoms in Anglo-Saxon heptarchy ✳ Maidstone *area* 1493 *sq mi* (*3867 sq km*), *pop* 1,485,100 — **Kent·ish** \'ken-tish\ *adjective*

Kent Island island Md. in Chesapeake Bay 15 *mi* (*25 km*) long; largest island in the bay

Ken·tucky \kən-'tə-kē\ **1** river 259 *mi* (*417 km*) N *central* Ky. flowing NW into Ohio river **2** state E *central* U.S. ✳ Frankfort *area* 40,395 *sq mi* (*105,027 sq km*), *pop* 3,685,296 — **Ken·tuck·i·an** \-kē-ən\ *adjective or noun*

Kent·wood \'kent-ˌwu̇d\ city SW Mich. *pop* 37,826

Ke·nya \'ke-nyə, 'kē-\ **1** extinct volcano 17,058 *ft* (*5199 m*) *central* Kenya near equator **2** republic E Africa S of Ethiopia bordering on Indian Ocean; member of the Commonwealth of Nations, formerly Brit. crown colony & protectorate ✳ Nairobi *area* 224,960 *sq mi* (*584,896 sq km*), *pop* 28,113,000 — **Ke·nyan** \-nyən\ *adjective or noun*

Ker·a·la \'ker-ə-lə\ state SW India bordering on Arabian Sea ✳ Trivandrum *area* 15,007 *sq mi* (*38,868 sq km*), *pop* 29,098,518

Kerasun — see GIRESUN

Kerch \'kerch\ **1** peninsula projecting E from the Crimea **2** city & port in the Crimea on Kerch Strait *pop* 178,000

Kerch Strait strait between Kerch & Taman peninsulas connecting Sea of Azov & Black Sea

Ker·gue·len \'kər-gə-lən, ˌker-gə-'len\ island in the Kerguelen Archipelago

Kerguelen Islands archipelago S Indian Ocean belonging to France *area* 2394 *sq mi* (*6200 sq km*)

Ke·rin·ci *or* **Ke·rin·tji** \kə-'rin-chē\ volcano 12,484 *ft* (*3805 m*) Indonesia in W *central* Sumatra; highest on the island

Kerkheh — see KARKHEH

Kerk·ra·de \'kerk-ˌrä-də\ commune SE Netherlands *pop* 53,364

Kérkyra — see CORFU

Ker·mad·ec Islands \(ˌ)kər-'ma-dək\ islands SW Pacific NE of New Zealand; belong to New Zealand *area* 13 *sq mi* (*34 sq km*), *pop* 9

Ker·man \kər-'män, ker-\ **1** *or ancient* **Car·ma·nia** \kär-'mā-nē-ə, -nyə\ region SE Iran bordering on Gulf of Oman & Persian Gulf S of ancient Parthia **2** *or ancient* **Car·ma·na** \kär-'mā-nə, -'ma-, -'mä-\ city SE *central* Iran in NW Kerman region *pop* 257,284

Kermanshah — see BAKHTARAN

Kern \'kərn\ river 150 *mi* (*241 km*) S *central* Calif. flowing SW into a reservoir

Ker·ry \'ker-ē\ county SW Ireland in Munster ✳ Tralee *area* 1815 *sq mi* (*4719 sq km*), *pop* 121,894

Ker·u·len \'ker-ə-ˌlen\ river E Mongolia flowing S & E into the Argun in Manchuria

Kes·te·ven, Parts of \'ke-ˌstē-vən, 'kes-ti-vən\ district & former administrative county E England in SW Lincolnshire ✳ Sleaford *area* 734 *sq mi* (*1901 sq km*)

Kes·wick \'ke-zik\ town NW England in Cumbria in Lake District

Ket·ter·ing \'ke-tə-riŋ\ city SW Ohio S of Dayton *pop* 60,569

Keu·ka Lake \'kyü-kə, kā-'yü-kä\ lake 18 *mi* (*29 km*) long W *central* N.Y.; one of the Finger Lakes

Kew \'kyü\ **1** city SE Australia in S Victoria, NE suburb of Melbourne *pop* 27,291 **2** parish S England in Surrey, now in the Greater London borough of Richmond upon Thames

Ke·wee·naw Peninsula \'kē-wə-ˌnȯ\ peninsula NW Mich. projecting from Upper Peninsula into Lake Superior W of **Keweenaw Bay**

Key Lar·go \'lär-(ˌ)gō\ island S Fla. in the Florida Keys

Key West \'west\ city SW Fla. on Key West (island) at W end of Florida Keys *pop* 24,832 — **Key West·er** \'wes-tər\ *noun*

Kha·ba·rovsk \kə-'bär-əfsk, kə-\ **1** territory E Russia in Asia bordering on Sea of Okhotsk *area* 318,378 *sq mi* (*824,599 sq km*), *pop* 1,855,000 **2** city, its ✳, on the Amur *pop* 615,000

Kha·kas·sia \kə-'käs-yə, kə-; kə-'kä-zhə\ autonomous region S Russia in Asia in SW Krasnoyarsk Territory N of the Sayan Mountains ✳ Abakan *area about* 24,000 *sq mi* (*62,400 sq km*), *pop* 581,000

Khalkidikí — see CHALCIDICE

Khal·kís \käl-'kēs, käl-\ *or* **Chal·cis** \'kal-səs, -kəs\ city *central* Greece ✳ of Euboea on Evripos Strait *pop* 51,482

Kham·bhat \'kəm-bət\ *or* **Cam·bay** \kam-'bā\ city W India in Gujarat W of Vadodara *pop* 76,724

Khambhat, Gulf of *or* **Gulf of Cambay** inlet of Arabian Sea in India N of Bombay

Khan·ka \'kaŋ-kə\ lake E Asia between Maritime Territory, Russia & Heilongjiang, China *area* 1700 *sq mi* (*4420 sq km*)

Khan–Ten·gri \ˌkän-'teŋ-grē\ mountain 22,949 *ft* (*6995 m*) on border between Kyrgyzstan & Xinjiang Uygur (China) in Tian Shan

Kha·rag·pur \'kär-əg-ˌpu̇r, 'kər-\ *or* **Kha·rak·pur** \'kär-əg-ˌpu̇r, 'kər-\ city E India in SW W. Bengal WSW of Calcutta *pop* 279,736

Khar·kiv \'kär-kəf, 'kär-\ *or* **Khar·kov** \'kär-ˌkȯf, 'kär-, -ˌkȯv, -kəf\ city NE Ukraine, its ✳ 1921–34, on edge of Donets Basin *pop* 1,623,000

Khar·toum \kär-'tüm\ city ✳ of Sudan at junction of White Nile & Blue Nile rivers *pop* 1,950,000

Khartoum North *or* **North Khartoum** city *central* Sudan *pop* 151,000

Kha·si Hills \'kä-sē\ hills E India in NW *central* Assam

Kha·tan·ga \kə-'täŋ-gə, -'taŋ-\ river 800 *mi* (*1287 km*) N Russia in Asia, in NE Krasnoyarsk Territory flowing N into Laptev Sea

Khelat — see KALAT

Kher·son \ker-'sȯn\ city & port S Ukraine on the Dnieper near its mouth *pop* 365,000

Khí·os \'kē-ˌȯs, 'kē-\ — see CHIOS

Khir·bat Qum·ran *or* **Khir·bet Qum·ran** \kir-'bat-küm-'rän\ locality Palestine in NW Jordan on Wadi Qumran near NW shore of Dead Sea; site of an Essene community (*about* 100 B.C.–A.D. 68) near a series of caves in which the Dead Sea Scrolls were found

Khi·va \'kē-və\ **1** *or* **Kho·rezm** \kə-'re-zəm\ oasis Uzbekistan on the lower Amu Darya **2** *or* **Khwa·razm** \kwə-'ra-zəm, kwä-\ *or* former khanate *central* Asia including Khiva oasis **3** town in the oasis, ✳ of the khanate *pop* 41,300

Khmer Republic — see CAMBODIA

Khor·a·san \ˌkȯr-ə-ˌsän, ˌkȯr-\ *or* **Khu·ra·san** \ˌku̇r-ə-ˌsän, ˌku̇r-\ region NE Iran; chief city Mashhad

Khor·ra·ma·bad \kó-'ra-mə-ˌbäd, -ˌbad\ *or* **Khur·ra·ma·bad** \kū-'rä-\ city W Iran *pop* 208,592

Khor·ram·shahr \ˌkȯr-əm-'shä(-hə)r, ˌkȯr-\ city & port W Iran in Khuzistan on Shatt-al-Arab NNW of Abadan

Khotan — see HOTAN

Khums, Al — see AL KHUMS

Khu·zi·stan \ˌkü-zi-'stän, -'stan\ region SW Iran bordering on Persian Gulf; chief city Khorramshahr

Khy·ber Pass \'kī-bər\ mountain pass 33 *mi* (53 *km*) long on border between Afghanistan & Pakistan in Safed Koh Range WNW of Peshawar

Kiamusze — see JIAMUSI

Kiangsi — see JIANGXI

Kiangsu — see JIANGSU

Kiaochow — see JIAOZHOU

Ki·bo \'kē-ˌ)bō\ mountain peak 19,340 *ft* (5895 *m*) Tanzania in NE Tanganyika; highest peak of Kilimanjaro & highest point in Africa

Kid·der·min·ster \'ki-dər-ˌmin(t)-stər\ borough W central England in Hereford and Worcester SW of Birmingham *pop* 51,261

Kid·ron \'ki-drən, 'kī-\ valley central Palestine between Jerusalem & Mount of Olives; source of stream (Kidron) flowing E to Dead Sea

Kiel \'kēl\ **1** city & port N Germany ✷ of Schleswig-Holstein on SE coast of Jutland Peninsula *pop* 247,107 **2** *or* **Nord–Ost·see** \ˌnȯrt-ˌȯst-'zā\ ship canal 61 *mi* (98 *km*) N Germany across base of Jutland Peninsula connecting Baltic Sea & North Sea

Kiel·ce \kē-'elt-ˌ)sä, 'kyelt-\ *or Russian* **Kelt·sy** \'kelt-sē\ city S Poland S of Warsaw *pop* 212,901

Ki·ev *or* **Ki·yev** \'kē-ˌef, -ˌev, -if\ city ✷ of Ukraine on the Dnieper *pop* 2,587,000 — **Ki·ev·an** \'kē-ˌe-fən, -vən\ *adjective or noun*

Ki·ga·li \kē-'gä-lē\ city central Rwanda, its ✷ *pop* 232,733

Kikládhes — see CYCLADES

Ki·lau·ea \ˌkē-ˌlä-'wā-ä\ volcanic crater 2 *mi* (3.2 *km*) wide Hawaii on Hawaii (island) in Hawaii Volcanoes National Park on E slope of Mauna Loa

Kil·dare \kil-'dar, -'der\ county E Ireland in Leinster ✷ Naas *area* 654 *sq mi* (1700 *sq km*), *pop* 122,656

Kil·i·man·ja·ro \ˌki-lə-mən-'jär-(ˌ)ō, -'jar-\ mountain Tanzania on NE mainland near Kenya border — see KIBO

Kil·ken·ny \kil-'ke-nē\ **1** county SE Ireland in Leinster *area* 796 *sq mi* (2070 *sq km*), *pop* 73,635 **2** town, its ✷ *pop* 8513

Kil·lar·ney, Lakes of \ki-'lär-nē\ three lakes SW Ireland in County Kerry

Kill Dev·il \'kil-ˌde-vəl\ hill E N.C. near village of **Kit·ty Hawk** \'ki-tē-ˌhȯk\ on sand barrier opposite Albemarle Sound

Kil·leen \ki-'lēn\ city central Tex. N of Austin *pop* 63,535

Kil·lie·cran·kie \ˌki-lē-'kran-kē\ mountain pass central Scotland in Tayside in the SE Grampians NW of Pitlochry

Kill Van Kull \ˌkil-(ˌ)van-'kəl, -vən-\ channel between N.J. & Staten Is., N.Y., connecting Newark Bay & Upper New York Bay

Kil·mar·nock \kil-'mär-nək\ burgh SW Scotland in Strathclyde *pop* 52,080

Kim·ber·ley \'kim-bər-lē\ city Republic of South Africa in E Northern Cape WNW of Bloemfontein *pop* 105,258

Kimberley Plateau *or* **The Kimberley** plateau region N Western Australia N of 19°30′S lat.

Kin·a·ba·lu *or* **Kin·a·bu·lu** \ˌkē-nä-'bä-lü\ mountain 13,455 *ft* (4101 *m*) N central N. Borneo; highest in Borneo

Kin·car·dine \kin-'kär-d°n\ *or* **Kin·car·dine·shire** \-ˌshir, -shər\ *or* **The Mearns** \'mərnz, 'mernz\ former county E Scotland ✷ Stonehaven

Ki·nesh·ma \'kē-nish-mə\ city central Russia in Europe NE of Moscow *pop* 104,000

King·man \'kiŋ-mən\ reef central Pacific at N end of Line Islands

King's — see OFFALY

Kings Canyon National Park \'kiŋz\ reservation SE central Calif. in the Sierra Nevada N of Sequoia National Park

King's Lynn \'kiŋz-'lin\ *or* **Lynn** *or* **Lynn Regis** \'rē-jəs\ borough E England in Norfolk near The Wash *pop* 33,340

Kings Mountain ridge N.C. & S.C. SW of Gastonia, N.C.

Kings Peak mountain 13,528 *ft* (4123 *m*) NE Utah in Uinta Mountains; highest point in state

Kings·port \'kiŋz-ˌpȯrt, -ˌpȯrt\ city NE Tenn. on the Holston *pop* 36,365

Kings·ton \'kiŋ-stən\ **1** city SE N.Y. on the Hudson *pop* 23,095 **2** city Canada in SE Ontario on Lake Ontario near head of St. Lawrence River; ✷ of Canada 1841–44 *pop* 56,597 **3** *or in full* **Kingston upon** (*or* **on**) **Thames** royal borough of SW Greater London, England ✷ of Surrey *pop* 130,600 **4** city & port ✷ of Jamaica on **Kingston Harbor** (inlet of the Caribbean) *pop* 103,771

Kingston upon Hull — see HULL

Kings·town \'kiŋz-ˌtaün\ **1** town & port ✷ of St. Vincent and the Grenadines on St. Vincent Is. at head of Kingstown Bay *pop* 15,670 **2** — see DUN LAOGHAIRE

Kings·ville \'kiŋz-ˌvil, -vəl\ city S Tex. *pop* 25,276

Kinneret, Yam — see GALILEE (Sea of)

Kin·ross \kin-'rȯs\ *or* **Kin·ross–shire** \-'rȯsh-ˌshir, -shər\ former county E central Scotland ✷ Kinross

Kin·sha·sa \kin-'shä-sə\ *or formerly* **Lé·o·pold·ville** \'lē-ə-ˌpōld-ˌvil, 'lā-\ city ✷ of Democratic Republic of the Congo on Congo River at outlet of Pool Malebo *pop* 3,804,000

Kin·ston \'kin-stən\ city E N.C. *pop* 25,295

Kin·tyre \kin-'tīr\ peninsula 40 *mi* (64 *km*) long SW Scotland between the Atlantic & Firth of Clyde; terminates in **Mull of Kintyre** \'məl\ (cape in N. channel)

Kioga — see KYOGA

Kirghiz Republic *or* **Kirgiz Republic** *or* **Kirghizia** — see KYRGYZSTAN

Ki·ri·bati \'kir-ə-ˌbas—*sic*\ island nation W Pacific SSE of the Marshalls comprising Ocean Island and the Gilbert, Line, & Phoenix groups ✷ Tarawa *area* 277 *sq mi* (717 *sq km*), *pop* 78,600

Ki·rik·ka·le \kə-'ri-kə-ˌlä\ city central Turkey E of Ankara *pop* 185,431

Kirin — see JILIN

Ki·riti·mati \kə-'ris-məs—*sic*\ *or* **Christ·mas** \'kris-məs\ island (atoll) in the Line Islands; largest atoll in the Pacific *area* 234 *sq mi* (608 *sq km*), *pop* 674

Kirjath–arba — see HEBRON

Kirk·caldy \(ˌ)kər-'kȯ-dē, -'kȯl-, -'kä-\ royal burgh & port E Scotland in Fife on Firth of Forth N of Edinburgh *pop* 46,314

Kirk·cud·bright \(ˌ)kər-'kü-brē\ *or* **Kirk·cud·bright·shire** \-ˌshir, -shər\ former county S Scotland ✷ Kirkcudbright

Kirk·land \'kərk-lənd\ city W Wash. NE of Seattle *pop* 40,052

Kirk·pat·rick, Mount \ˌkərk-'pa-trik\ mountain 14,856 *ft* (4528 *m*) E Antarctica in Queen Alexandra Range S of Ross Sea

Kir·kuk \kir-'kük\ city NE Iraq SE of Mosul *pop* 175,303

Kirk·wall \'kərk-ˌwȯl\ burgh & port N Scotland ✷ of Orkney, on Mainland Is. *pop* 5947

Kirk·wood \'kərk-ˌwüd\ city E Mo. W of St. Louis *pop* 27,291

Ki·rov \'kē-ˌrȯf, -ˌrȯv, -rəf\ *or* **Vyat·ka** \vē-'at-kə, -'ät-\ city E central Russia in Europe *pop* 493,000

Kirovabad — see GANCA

Ki·ro·vo·grad \ki-'rō-və-ˌgrad, -ˌgrät\ *or* **Ki·ro·vo·hrad** \-ˌkrät\ *or formerly* **Zi·nov·ievsk** \zə-'nȯv-ˌyefsk\ *or* **Eli·sa·vet·grad** \i-ˌli-zə-'vet-ˌgrad, -ˌgrät\ city S central Ukraine *pop* 278,000

Ki·ru·na \'kē-rü-ˌnä\ city N Sweden in Lapland *pop* 26,217

Ki·san·ga·ni \ˌkē-sän-'gä-nē\ *or formerly* **Stan·ley·ville** \'stan-lē-ˌvil\ city NE Democratic Republic of the Congo on Congo River *pop* 373,397

Kish \'kish\ ancient city of Sumer & Akkad E of site of Babylon

Kishinev — see CHIŞINĂU

Kis·ka \'kis-kə\ island SW Alaska; largest & westernmost of Rat Islands of the Aleutians

Kis·maa·yo \kēs-'mä-yō\ *or* **Kis·ma·yu** \kis-'mī-(ˌ)ü\ city & port S Somalia *pop* 30,115

Kis·sim·mee \ki-'si-mē\ **1** river 140 *mi* (225 *km*) S central Fla. flowing SSE from Tohopekaliga Lake through **Lake Kissimmee** (12 *mi or* 19 *km* long) into Lake Okeechobee **2** city Fla. on Tohopekaliga Lake *pop* 30,050

Kistna — see KRISHNA

Ki·su·mu \kē-'sü-(ˌ)mü\ city W Kenya on Lake Victoria *pop* 152,643

Ki·ta·kyu·shu \kē-ˌtä-'kyü-(ˌ)shü\ city & port Japan in N Kyushu formed 1963 by amalgamation of former cities of Kokura, Moji, Tobata, Wakamatsu, & Yawata *pop* 1,026,467

Kitch·e·ner \'kich-nər, 'ki-chə-\ city Canada in SE Ontario *pop* 168,282

Kithairon — see CITHAERON

Kí·thi·ra *or* **Ky·the·ra** *or* **Ký·thi·ra** \'kē-thē-(ˌ)rä\ island W Greece, southernmost of Ionian Islands ✷ Kíthira *area* 110 *sq mi* (286 *sq km*)

Kit·ta·tin·ny Mountain \ˌki-tə-'ti-nē\ ridge E U.S. in the Appalachians extending from SE N.Y. through NW N.J. into E Pa.

Kit·tery Point \'ki-tə-rē\ cape Maine at S tip

Kitty Hawk — see KILL DEVIL

Kitz·bü·hel \'kits-ˌbyü(-ə)l, -ˌbü̇(-ə)l\ resort town W Austria in the Tirol *pop* 8119

Ki·vu, Lake \'kē-(ˌ)vü\ lake 60 *mi* (96 *km*) long & 30 *mi* (48 *km*) wide E Democratic Republic of the Congo in Great Rift Valley N of Lake Tanganyika *area* 1042 *sq mi* (2699 *sq km*)

Ki·zil Ir·mak \kə-ˌzil-ir-'mäk\ *or ancient* **Ha·lys** \'hā-ləs\ river 715 *mi* (1150 *km*) N central Turkey flowing W & NE into Black Sea

Kjö·len Mountains \'chē-lən\ mountains on border between NE Norway & NW Sweden; highest Kebnekaise (in Sweden) 6965 *ft* (2123 *m*)

Kla·gen·furt \'klä-gən-ˌfürt\ city S Austria ✷ of Carinthia WSW of Graz *pop* 89,415

Klai·pe·da \'klī-pə-də\ *or* **Me·mel** \'mā-məl\ city & port W Lithuania on the Baltic *pop* 208,300

Klam·ath \'kla-məth\ river 250 *mi* (402 *km*) S Oreg. & NW Calif. flowing from Upper Klamath Lake SW into the Pacific

Klamath Mountains mountains S Oreg. & NW Calif. in the Coast Ranges; highest Mt. Eddy (in Calif.) 9038 *ft* (2755 *m*)

Kle·ve \'klā-və\ city W Germany WSW of Münster *pop* 46,450

Klon·dike \'klän-ˌdīk\ **1** river 90 *mi* (145 *km*) Canada in central Yukon Territory flowing W into the Yukon **2** the Klondike River valley

Klu·ane National Park \klü-'ō-nē, -'ä-\ reservation Canada in SW Yukon Territory

Kly·az·ma \klē-'az-mə\ river about 390 *mi* (630 *km*) central Russia in Europe flowing E to join the Oka W of Nizhniy Novgorod

Knos·sos *or* **Cnos·sus** *or* **Gnos·sus** \'nä-səs\ ruined city ✷ of ancient Crete near N coast SE of modern Iraklion

Knox·ville \'näks-ˌvil, -vəl\ city E Tenn. on Tennessee River *pop* 165,121

Knud Ras·mus·sen Land \'(k)nüd-'ras-mə-sən, -'räs-ˌmü-s°n\ region N & NW Greenland NE of Baffin Bay

Ko·ba·rid \'kō-bə-ˌrēd\ *or Italian* **Ca·po·ret·to** \ˌka-pə-'re-(ˌ)tō, ˌkä-pō-\ village W Slovenia on the Isonzo NE of Udine, Italy

Ko·be \'kō-bē, -ˌbā\ city & port Japan in S Honshu on Osaka Bay *pop* 1,477,423

København — see COPENHAGEN

Ko·blenz *or* **Co·blenz** \'kō-ˌblents\ city W Germany SSE of Cologne at confluence of the Rhine & the Moselle *pop* 109,046

Ko·buk Valley National Park \kō-'bük\ reservation W Alaska N of the arctic circle along **Ko·buk River**

Ko·ca \kō-'jä\ river about 75 *mi* (121 *km*) S Turkey flowing SW & S into the Mediterranean

Ko·ca·bas \ˌkō-jə-'bäsh\ *or ancient* **Gra·ni·cus** \grə-'nī-kəs\ river NW Turkey in Asia flowing NE to Sea of Marmara

Ko·chi \'kō-chē\ city & port Japan in S Shikoku *pop* 317,090

Ko·di·ak \'kō-dē-ˌak\ island S Alaska in Gulf of Alaska E of Alaska Peninsula

Ko·dok \'kō-ˌdäk\ *or formerly* **Fa·sho·da** \fə-'shō-də\ town SE Sudan on White Nile River

Ko·ha·la Mountains \kō-'hä-lä\ mountains Hawaii in N Hawaii (island); highest about 5500 *ft* (1676 *m*)

Ko·hi·ma \kō-'hē-mə, 'kō-hē-\ town NE India ✷ of Nagaland *pop* 53,122

Koil — see ALIGARH

Ko·kand \kō-'kand\ *or* **Qŭ·qon** \ku̇-'kȯn\ **1** region & former khanate E Uzbekistan **2** city in Kokand region SE of Tashkent *pop* 175,000

Ko·ko·mo \'kō-kə-ˌmō\ city N *central* Ind. *pop* 44,962

Koko Nor — see QINGHAI

Kok·so·ak \'käk-sō-ˌak\ river 85 *mi* (136 *km*) Canada N Quebec formed by confluence of the Caniapiskau and the Larch and flowing into Ungave Bay

Ko·la Peninsula \'kō-lə\ peninsula 250 *mi* (402 *km*) long & 150 *mi* (241 *km*) wide NW Russia in Europe between Barents & White seas

Ko·lar Gold Fields \kō-'lär\ city S India in SE Karnataka *pop* 156,398

Kold·ing \'kȯl-leŋ\ city & port Denmark *pop* 57,128

Kol·ha·pur \'kō-lə-ˌpu̇r\ city W India in SW Maharashtra SSE of Bombay *pop* 406,370

Kolmar — see COLMAR

Köln — see COLOGNE

Ko·ly·ma *or* **Ko·li·ma** \kə-'lē-mə, ˌkə-li-'mä\ river 1110 *mi* (1786 *km*) NE Russia in Asia flowing from Kolyma Mountains NE into E. Siberian Sea

Kolyma Mountains *or* **Kolima Mountains** mountain range Russia in Asia in NE Khabarovsk Territory parallel to coast of Penzhinskaya Bay

Ko·man·dor·ski Islands \kə-'man-ˌdȯr-skē\ *or* **Com·mand·er Islands** \kə-'man-dər\ islands E Russia in Asia in Bering Sea E of Kamchatka Peninsula *area* 850 *sq mi* (2210 *sq km*)

Ko·ma·ti \kō-'mä-tē\ river 500 *mi* (805 *km*) S Africa flowing from N Drakensberg Mountains in NE Republic of South Africa E & N into Delagoa Bay in S Mozambique

Ko·mi Republic \'kō-mē\ autonomous republic NE Russia in Europe W of N Ural Mountains ✱ Syktyvkar *area* 160,579 *sq mi* (415,900 *sq km*), *pop* 1,255,000

Kommunizma, Pik — see COMMUNISM PEAK

Ko·mo·do \kə-'mō-(ˌ)dō\ island Indonesia in the Lesser Sundas E of Sumbawa Is. & W of Flores Is. *area* 185 *sq mi* (481 *sq km*)

Kom·so·molsk \ˌkäm-sə-'mȯlsk\ city E Russia in Asia in S Khabarovsk Territory on the Amur

Ko·na \'kō-nä\ coast region Hawaii in W Hawaii (island)

Königgrätz — see HRADEC KRALOVE

Königsberg — see KALININGRAD

Kö·niz \'kā-nəts, 'kə(r)-, 'kē-\ commune W *central* Switzerland SW of Bern *pop* 36,101

Kon·kan \'käŋ-kən\ region W India in W Maharashtra bordering on Arabian Sea & extending from Bombay S to Goa

Konstanz — see CONSTANCE

Kon·ya \kȯ-'nyä\ *or ancient* **Ico·ni·um** \ī-'kō-nē-əm\ city SW *central* Turkey on edge of *central* plateau *pop* 513,346

Ko·o·lau \ˌkō-ō-'lä-(ˌ)u̇\ mountains Hawaii in E Oahu

Koo·te·nai *or (in Canada)* **Koo·te·nay** \'kü-tᵉn-ˌā, -tᵉn-ē\ river 407 *mi* (655 *km*) SW Canada & NW U.S. in British Columbia, Mont., & Idaho flowing through **Kootenay Lake** (65 *mi or* 104 *km* long, in British Columbia) into Columbia River

Kootenay National Park reservation Canada in SE British Columbia including section of the upper Kootenay River

Ko·per \'kō-per\ *or* **Ko·par** \-ˌpär\ *or Italian* **Ca·po·dis·tria** \ˌka-pə-'dis-trē-ə, ˌkä-pō-'dēs-\ town & port SW Slovenia at N end of Istrian Peninsula SSW of Trieste *pop* 25,272

Ko·peysk \kō-'pāsk\ city SW Russia in Asia SE of Chelyabinsk *pop* 78,300

Kor·do·fan \ˌkȯr-də-'fan\ region *central* Sudan W & N of White Nile River; chief city El Obeid

Ko·rea \kə-'rē-ə, *especially South* (ˌ)kō-\ **1** peninsula 600 *mi* (966 *km*) long & 135 *mi* (217 *km*) wide E Asia between Yellow Sea & Sea of Japan **2** *or Japanese* **Cho·sen** \'chō-'sen\ country coextensive with the peninsula; once a kingdom & (1910–45) a Japanese dependency ✱ Seoul; divided 1948 at 38th parallel into republics of **North Korea** (✱ Pyongyang *area* 46,609 *sq mi or* 120,717 *sq km, pop* 22,646,000), & **South Korea** (✱ Seoul *area* 38,022 *sq mi or* 98,477 *sq km, pop* 44,042,000)

Korea Bay arm of Yellow Sea between Liaodong Peninsula & N. Korea

Korea Strait strait 120 *mi* (193 *km*) wide between S S. Korea & SW Japan connecting Sea of Japan & Yellow Sea

Kórinthos — see CORINTH

Kort·rijk \'kȯrt-ˌrīk\ *or* **Cour·trai** \ku̇r-'trā\ commune NW Belgium in W. Flanders on the Leie NNE of Lille *pop* 76,141

Kos *or* **Cos** \'käs, 'kȯs\ **1** island Greece in the Dodecanese *area* 111 *sq mi* (289 *sq km*) **2** chief town on the island

Kos·ci·us·ko, Mount \ˌkä-zē-'əs-(ˌ)kō, ˌkä-sē-\ mountain 7310 *ft* (2228 *m*) SE Australia in SE New South Wales; highest in Great Dividing Range & in Australia

Ko·shi·ga·ya \kō-'shē-gä-yä; ˌkō-shi-'gī-ə\ city Japan on Honshu *pop* 285,280

Ko·si·ce \'kȯ-shēt-ˌsä\ city E Slovakia *pop* 234,840

Ko·so·vo \'kȯ-sȯ-ˌvō, 'kä-\ autonomous province S Yugoslavia *area* 4203 *sq mi* (10,886 *sq km*), *pop* 1,954,747

Kos·rae \'kȯs-ˌrī\ islands E Carolines, part of Federated States of Micronesia

Ko·stro·ma \ˌkäs-trə-'mä\ city *central* Russia in Europe on the Volga *pop* 282,000

Ko·sza·lin \kȯ-'shä-ˌlēn\ city NW Poland *pop* 107,580

Kotabaru — see JAYAPURA

Ko·ta Ba·ha·ru \ˌkō-tə-'bä-hä-ˌrü\ city Malaysia in N Peninsular Malaysia ✱ of Kelantan *pop* 281,161

Ko·ta Kin·a·ba·lu \'kō-tə-ˌki-nə-bə-'lü\ *or formerly* **Jes·sel·ton** \'je-səl-tən\ city & port Malaysia ✱ of Sabah *pop* 112,758

Ko·tor \'kō-ˌtȯr\ *or Italian* **Cat·ta·ro** \'kä-tä-ˌrō\ town & port SW Yugoslavia in Montenegro on an inlet of the Adriatic *pop* 22,496

Kottbus — see COTTBUS

Kot·te \'kō-(ˌ)tä\ town W Sri Lanka, a suburb ESE of Colombo *pop* 109,000

Kot·ze·bue Sound \'kät-si-ˌbyü\ arm of Chukchi Sea NW Alaska NE of Bering Strait

Kou·chi·bou·guac National Park \ˌkü-ˌshē-bü-'gwäk\ reservation SE Canada in E New Brunswick

Kou·dou·gou \ˌkü-'dü-(ˌ)gü\ town *central* Burkina Faso *pop* 106,000

Kovno — see KAUNAS

Kow·loon \'kau̇-'lün\ **1** peninsula SE China in Hong Kong opposite Hong Kong Is. **2** city on Kowloon Peninsula

Koy·u·kuk \kī-ə-ˌkək\ river *about* 500 *mi* (800 *km*) N *central* Alaska flowing from Brooks Range SW into Yukon River

Kozhikode — see CALICUT

Kra, Isthmus of \'krä\ isthmus S Thailand in N *central* Malay Peninsula; 40 *mi* (64 *km*) wide at narrowest part

Krak·a·tau \ˌkra-kə-'tau̇\ *or* **Krak·a·toa** \-'tō-ə\ island & volcano Indonesia between Sumatra & Java

Kra·ków *or* **Cra·cow** \'krä-ˌkau̇, 'kra-, 'krä-, -(ˌ)kō, *Polish* 'krä-ˌküf\ city S Poland on the Vistula *pop* 748,356

Kras — see KARST

Kras·no·dar \ˌkräs-nə-'där\ **1** territory S Russia in Europe in N Caucasus region *area* 32,278 *sq mi* (83,600 *sq km*), *pop* 5,004,000 **2** *or formerly* **Eka·te·ri·no·dar** \i-ˌkä-tə-'rē-nə-ˌdär\ city, its ✱, on the Kuban *pop* 635,000

Kras·no·yarsk Territory \ˌkräs-nə-'yärsk\ **1** territory W *central* Russia in Asia extending along valley of the Yenisey from Arctic Ocean to Sayan Mountains *area* 927,258 *sq mi* (2,401,598 *sq km*), *pop* 3,122,000 **2** city, its ✱, on the upper Yenisey *pop* 925,000

Kre·feld \'krā-ˌfelt\ *or formerly* **Krefeld–Uerding·en** \-'u̇r-diŋ-ən, -'ˌuer-\ city W Germany on the Rhine WSW of Essen *pop* 245,772

Krim — see CRIMEA

Krish·na \'krish-nə\ *or formerly* **Kist·na** \'kist-nə\ river 800 *mi* (1287 *km*) S India flowing from Western Ghats E into Bay of Bengal

Kristiania — see OSLO

Kris·tian·sand \ˌkris-chən-ˌsand, 'kris-tē-ən-ˌsän\ city & port SW Norway on the Skagerrak SW of Oslo *pop* 64,888

Kris·tian·sund \ˌkris-chən-ˌsend, 'kris-tē-ən-ˌsün\ city & port W Norway *pop* 17,121

Kríti — see CRETE

Kri·voy Rog \ˌkri-ˌvȯi-'rȯg, -'rȯk\ *or* **Kryv·yy Rih** \kri-'vē-'rik\ city SE *central* Ukraine NE of Odessa *pop* 724,000

Kron·shtadt \'krȯn-ˌshtät\ city W Russia in Europe on island in E Gulf of Finland W of St. Petersburg *pop* 45,300

Kru·ger National Park \'krü-gər\ game reserve NE Republic of South Africa in E parts of Northern & Mpumalanga provinces on Mozambique border

Kru·gers·dorp \'krü-gərz-ˌdȯrp\ city NE Republic of South Africa in Gauteng W of Johannesburg *pop* 92,725

Krung Thep — see BANGKOK

K2 \ˌkä-'tü\ *or* **God·win Aus·ten** \ˌgä-dwən-'ȯs-tən, ˌgȯ-, -'äs-\ mountain 28,250 *ft* (8611 *m*) N Kashmir in Karakoram Range; 2d highest in the world

Kua·la Lum·pur \ˌkwä-lə-'lu̇m-ˌpu̇r, -'ləm-, ˌlu̇m-\ city ✱ of Malaysia in Peninsular Malaysia *pop* 1,145,075

Kuang–chou — see GUANGZHOU

Ku·ban \ku̇-'ban', -'bän\ river over 550 *mi* (885 *km*) S Russia in Europe flowing from the Caucasus N & W into Sea of Azov

Ku·ching \'kü-chiŋ\ city & port Malaysia ✱ of Sarawak *pop* 231,490

Ku·dus \'kü-ˌdüs\ city Indonesia in *central* Java NE of Semarang

Kuei — see GUI

Kuei–lin — see GUILIN

Kuei–yang — see GUIYANG

Kufra — see AL KUFRAH

Ku·iu Island \'kü-(ˌ)yü\ island SE Alaska in *central* Alexander Archipelago

Ku·la Gulf \'kü-lə\ body of water 17 *mi* (27 *km*) long in the Solomons between New Georgia & adjacent islands

Kuldja — see YINING

Kum \'küm\ river 247 *mi* (398 *km*) *central* S. Korea flowing into Yellow Sea

Ku·ma·mo·to \ˌkü-mä-'mō-(ˌ)tō\ city Japan in W Kyushu *pop* 636,144

Ku·ma·si \kü-'mä-sē, -'ma-\ city S *central* Ghana in Ashanti *pop* 385,192

Kumgang — see DIAMOND

Kumilla — see COMILLA

Kunene — see CUNENE

Kun·lun \'kün-'lün\ mountains W China extending from the Pamirs & Karakoram Range E along N edge of Tibetan plateau to SE Qinghai — see MUZTAG

Kun·ming \'kün-'miŋ\ *or formerly* **Yun·nan** \'yü-'nän\ *or* **Yun·nan·fu** \-'fü\ city S China ✱ of Yunnan *pop* 1,127,411

Kun·san \'gün-ˌsän\ city & port W S. Korea on Yellow Sea at mouth of the Kum *pop* 218,216

Kuo·pio \'kwȯ-pē-ˌō\ city S *central* Finland *pop* 81,391

Ku·pre·a·nof \ˌkü-prē-'a-ˌnȯf\ island SE Alaska in E Alexander Archipelago

Ku·ra \kə-'rä, 'ku̇r-ə\ river 941 *mi* (1514 *km*) W Asia flowing from NE Turkey ESE through Georgia & Azerbaijan into Caspian Sea

Ku·ra·shi·ki \ku̇-'rä-shē-kē, ˌku̇r-ä-'shē-kē\ city Japan on Honshu *pop* 416,703

Kur·di·stan \ˌku̇r-də-'stan, ˌkər-, -'stän; 'kər-də-ˌ\ region SW Asia chiefly in E Turkey, NW Iran, & N Iraq

Kur·gan \ku̇r-'gan, -'gän\ city SW Russia in Asia E of Chelyabinsk *pop* 365,000

Ku·ria Mu·ria Islands \ˌku̇r-ē-ə-'mu̇r-ē-ə, ˌkyu̇r-, -'myu̇r-\ islands Oman in Arabian Sea off SW coast *area* 28 *sq mi* (73 *sq km*), *pop* 85

Ku·ril Islands *or* **Ku·rile Islands** \'kyu̇r-ˌēl, 'ku̇r-; kyu̇-'rēl, ku̇-\ islands Russia in the Pacific between S Kamchatka & NE Hokkaido, Japan; belonged 1875–1945 to Japan *area* 6023 *sq mi* (15,600 *sq km*)

Kurisches Haff — see COURLAND LAGOON

Kur·nool \kər-'nül\ city S India in W Andhra Pradesh SSW of Hyderabad *pop* 236,313

Kursk \'kùrsk\ city SW Russia in Europe on the Seym *pop* 435,000

Kush — see CUSH

Kus·ko·kwim \'kəs-kə-ˌkwim\ river *about* 600 *mi* (965 *km*) SW Alaska flowing SW into **Kuskokwim Bay** (inlet of Bering Sea)

Kut, Al — see AL KUT

Ku·tah·ya or **Ku·ta·iah** \kü-'tä-yə\ city W *central* Turkey *pop* 130,944

Kutch \'kəch\ former principality & state W India N of Gulf of Kachchh ✳ Bhuj; now part of Gujarat

Kutch, Gulf of — see KACHCHH (Gulf of)

Kutch, Rann of — see KACHCHH (Rann of)

Ku·wait \kù-'wät\ **1** country SW Asia in Arabia at head of Persian Gulf; a sheikhdom, before 1961 under Brit. protection *area* 6880 *sq mi* (17,819 *sq km*), *pop* 1,355,827 **2** city & port, its ✳ *pop* 181,774 — **Ku·waiti** \-'wä-tē\ *adjective or noun*

Kuybyshev — see SAMARA

Kuz·netsk \küz-'netsk\ city SE *central* Russia in Europe *pop* 101,000

Kuznetsk Basin basin of the Tom W *central* Russia in Asia extending from Novokuznetsk to Tomsk

Kwa·ja·lein \'kwä-jə-lən, -ˌlān\ island (atoll) 78 *mi* (126 *km*) long W Pacific in Ralik chain of the Marshalls

Kwan·do \'kwän-(ˌ)dō\ river *about* 500 *mi* (804 *km*) S Africa flowing from *central* Angola SE & E into the Zambezi just above Victoria Falls

Kwang·cho·wan \'gwän-'jō-'wän, 'kwän-\ former territory SE China in Kwangtung on Leizhou Peninsula; leased 1898–1946 to France ✳ Fort Bayard *area* 325 *sq mi* (845 *sq km*)

Kwang·ju \'gwän-(ˌ)jü, 'kwän-\ city SW S. Korea *pop* 905,896

Kwangsi Chuang — see GUANGXI ZHUANGZU

Kwangtung — see GUANGDONG

Kwan·tung \'gwän-'dùn, 'kwän-'tùn\ former territory NE China in S Manchuria at tip of Liaodong Peninsula; leased to Russia 1898–1905, to Japan 1905–45, to Russia again 1945–55; included cities of Port Arthur & Dairen

Kwanza — see CUANZA

Kwathlamba — see DRAKENSBERG

Kwa·Zu·lu \kwä-'zü-(ˌ)lü\ former group of noncontiguous black enclaves in E Republic of South Africa; incorporated into KwaZulu-Natal 1994

KwaZulu–Natal province E Republic of South Africa between Drakensberg Mountains & Indian Ocean *area* 35,591 *sq mi* (92,180 *sq km*), *pop* 8,553,000

Kweichow — see GUIZHOU

Kweilin — see GUILIN

Kyo·ga or **Kio·ga** \kē-'ō-gə\ lake *central* Uganda N of Lake Victoria traversed by the Victoria Nile

Kyo·to \'kyō-(ˌ)tō\ city Japan in W *central* Honshu NNE of Osaka; formerly (794–1869) ✳ of Japan *pop* 1,461,140

Kyr·gyz·stan \ˌkir-gi-'stan, -'stän; 'kir-gi-ˌ\ independent country W *central* Asia; a constituent republic (**Kir·giz Republic** or **Kir·ghiz Republic** \(ˌ)kir-'gēz\) of the U.S.S.R. 1936–91; ✳ Bishkek *area* 76,641 *sq mi* (198,500 *sq km*), *pop* 4,526,000

Kythera or **Kýthira** — see KÍTHIRA

Kyu·shu \'kyü-(ˌ)shü\ island S Japan S of W end of Honshu *area* over 16,200 *sq mi* (41,958 *sq km*), *pop* 13,296,054

Ky·zyl \ki-'zil\ town S Russia in Asia ✳ of Tuva Republic *pop* 88,000

Laayoune — see AAIÚN, EL

Labe — see ELBE

Lab·ra·dor \'la-brə-ˌdòr\ **1** peninsula E Canada between Hudson Bay & the Atlantic; divided between Quebec & Newfoundland *area* 625,000 *sq mi* (1,618,750 *sq km*) **2** the section of the peninsula belonging to Nfld. 102,485 *sq mi* (265,436 *sq km*) — **Lab·ra·do·re·an** or **Lab·ra·do·ri·an** \ˌla-brə-'dòr-ē-ən, -'dòr-\ *adjective or noun*

Labrador Sea arm of the Atlantic between Labrador & Greenland

La·bu·an \lä-'bü-än\ island Malaysia off W coast of Sabah *pop* 14,904

La Ca·na·da–Flint·ridge \ˌlä-kə-ˌnyä-də-'flint-(ˌ)rij\ city SW Calif. NW of Pasadena *pop* 19,378

Lac·ca·dive Islands \'la-kə-ˌdēv, -ˌdīv, -div\ or **Can·na·nore Islands** \'ka-nə-ˌnòr\ islands India in Arabian Sea N of Maldive Islands

Lacedaemon — see SPARTA — **Lac·e·dae·mo·nian** \ˌla-sə-di-'mō-nē-ən, -nyən\ *adjective or noun*

La·cey \'lā-sē\ city W Wash. E of Olympia *pop* 19,279

La Chaux–de–Fonds \lä-ˌshō-də-'fōⁿ\ commune W Switzerland in Neuchâtel canton in Jura Mountains WNW of Bern *pop* 36,107

La·chine \lə-'shēn\ town Canada in S Quebec above the **Lachine Rapids** on St. Lawrence River SW of Montreal *pop* 35,266

La·chish \'lā-kish\ ancient city S Palestine W of Hebron

Lach·lan \'lä-klən\ river 800 *mi* (1287 *km*) SE Australia in *central* New South Wales flowing W into the Murrumbidgee

Lack·a·wan·na \ˌla-kə-'wä-nə\ city W N.Y. *pop* 20,585

Lac Mai–Ndombe — see MAI-NDOMBE (Lac)

La·co·nia \lə-'kō-nē-ə, -nyə\ ancient country S Greece in SE Peloponnese bordering on the Aegean & the Mediterranean ✳ Sparta — **La·co·ni·an** \-nē-ən, -nyən\ *adjective or noun*

Laconia, Gulf of inlet of the Mediterranean on S coast of Greece in Peloponnese between Capes Matapan & Malea

La Co·ru·ña \lä-kō-'rü-nyä\ **1** province NW Spain in Galicia bordering on the Atlantic *area* 3041 *sq mi* (7876 *sq km*), *pop* 1,096,966 **2** or **Co·run·na** \kə-'rə-nə\ commune & port, its ✳ *pop* 246,953

La Crosse \lə-'krós\ city W Wis. *pop* 51,003

La·dakh \lə-'däk\ district N India in E Kashmir on border of Tibet ✳ Leh *area* 45,762 *sq mi* (118,981 *sq km*) — **La·dakhi** \-'dä-kē\ *adjective or noun*

Lad·o·ga, Lake \'la-də-gə, 'lä-\ lake W Russia in Europe near St. Petersburg *area* 6835 *sq mi* (17,703 *sq km*); largest in Europe

Ladrone — see MARIANA

La·dy·smith \'lā-dē-ˌsmith\ city E Republic of South Africa in W KwaZulu-Natal *pop* 28,920

Lae \'lä-ˌā\ city Papua New Guinea on Huon Gulf *pop* 80,655

La·fay·ette \ˌla-fē-'et, lä-\ **1** city W Calif. E of Berkeley *pop* 23,501 **2** city W *central* Ind. *pop* 43,764 **3** city S La. *pop* 94,440

La·gash \'lä-ˌgash\ ancient city of Sumer between the Euphrates & the Tigris at modern village of Telloh \te-'lō\ in S Iraq

Lagoa dos Patos — see PATOS (Lagoa dos)

La·gos \'lä-ˌgäs, -ˌgōs\ city & port, former ✳ of Nigeria on an offshore island in Bight of Benin & on mainland opposite the island *pop* 1,340,000

La Goulette — see HALQ AL-WADI

La Grange \lə-'grānj\ city W Ga. *pop* 25,597

La Granja — see SAN ILDEFONSO

La Guai·ra \lə-'gwī-rə\ city N Venezuela on the Caribbean; port for Caracas *pop* 20,344

La·gu·na Beach \lə-'gü-nə\ city SW Calif. SE of Long Beach *pop* 23,170

Laguna Madre — see MADRE (Laguna)

La·gu·na Ni·guel \lä-'gü-nə-nē-'gel\ city Calif. *pop* 44,400

La Habana — see HAVANA

La Ha·bra \lə-'hä-brə\ city SW Calif. SE of Los Angeles *pop* 51,266

Lake Hav·a·su City \'ha-və-ˌsü\ city Ariz. *pop* 24,363

La Hogue \lə-'hōg\ roadstead NW France in English Channel off E coast of Cotentin Peninsula

La·hore \lə-'hòr, -'hór\ city Pakistan in E Punjab province near the Ravi *pop* 2,922,000

Lah·ti \'lä-tē\ city S Finland NNE of Helsinki *pop* 93,132

La Jol·la \lə-'hói-ə\ a NW section of San Diego, Calif.

Lake Charles \'chär(-ə)lz\ city SW La. *pop* 70,580

Lake Clark National Park \'klärk\ reservation S *central* Alaska WSW of Anchorage

Lake District area NW England in S Cumbria & NW Lancashire containing many lakes & peaks

Lake Jack·son \'jak-sən\ city SE Tex. *pop* 22,776

Lake·land \'lāk-lənd\ city *central* Fla. E of Tampa *pop* 70,576

Lake Os·we·go \ä-'swē-(ˌ)gō\ city NW Oreg. S of Portland *pop* 30,576

Lake·ville \'lāk-ˌvil\ village SE Minn. SE of Minneapolis *pop* 24,854

Lake·wood \'lāk-ˌwùd\ **1** city SW Calif. NE of Long Beach *pop* 73,557 **2** city N *central* Colo. W of Denver *pop* 126,481 **3** city NE Ohio on Lake Erie W of Cleveland *pop* 59,718

Lake Worth \'wərth\ city SE Fla. on Lake Worth (lagoon) S of W. Palm Beach *pop* 28,564

Lak·shad·weep \lək-'shä-ˌdwēp\ or formerly **Lac·ca·dive, Min·i·coy, and Amin·di·vi Islands** \'la-kə-ˌdēv, -ˌdīv; 'mi-ni-ˌkói; ˌə-mən-'dē-vē\ union territory India comprising the Laccadive group ✳ Kavaratti *area* 11 *sq mi* (29 *sq km*), *pop* 51,707

La Lí·nea \lä-'lē-nä-ä\ commune SW Spain on Bay of Algeciras *pop* 57,918

La Man·cha \lä-'män-chä, lə-'man-chə\ region S *central* Spain in S New Castile — **Man·che·gan** \man-'chē-gən, män-chä-\ *adjective or noun*

La Mau·ri·cie National Park \lä-ˌmòr-ē-'sē\ reservation SE Canada in S Quebec

Lam·ba·ré·né \ˌläm-bä-rā-'nä\ city W Gabon *pop* 17,770

Lam·beth \'lam-bəth, -ˌbeth\ borough of S Greater London, England *pop* 220,100

La Me·sa \lə-'mā-sə\ city SW Calif. NE of San Diego *pop* 52,931

La·mia \lä-'mē-ä\ city E *central* Greece NW of Thermopylae *pop* 43,898

La Mi·ra·da \ˌlä-mə-'rä-də\ city SW Calif. SE of Los Angeles *pop* 40,452

Lam·mer·muir \'la-mər-ˌmyùr\ or **Lam·mer·moor** \-ˌmùr\ hills SE Scotland in Lothian & Borders regions

Lam·pe·du·sa \ˌlam-pə-'dü-sə, ˌläm-pe-'dü-zə\ island Italy in the Pelagians

La·nai \lə-'nī, lä-\ island Hawaii W of Maui *area* 141 *sq mi* (367 *sq km*)

Lan·ark \'la-nərk\ **1** or **Lan·ark·shire** \-ˌshir, -shər\ former county S *central* Scotland; chief city Glasgow **2** burgh *central* Scotland in Strathclyde SE of Glasgow *pop* 9778

Lan·ca·shire \'laŋ-kə-ˌshir, -shər\ or **Lan·cas·ter** \'laŋ-kəs-tər\ county NW England bordering on Irish Sea ✳ Preston *area* 1217 *sq mi* (3152 *sq km*), *pop* 1,365,100

Lan·cas·ter \'laŋ-kəs-tər; 'lan-ˌkas-tər, 'laŋ-\ **1** city SW Calif. NE of Los Angeles *pop* 97,291 **2** city S *central* Ohio SE of Columbus *pop* 34,507 **3** city SE Pa. *pop* 55,551 **4** city NE Tex. S of Dallas *pop* 22,117 **5** city NW England in Lancashire *pop* 125,600 — **Lan·cas·tri·an** \laŋ-'kas-trē-ən, lan-\ *adjective or noun*

Landes \'länd\ coastal region SW France on Bay of Biscay between Gironde Estuary & the Adour

Land's End \ˌlandz-'end\ cape SW England at SW tip of Cornwall; extreme W point of England, at 5°41′W

Lang·dale Pikes \'laŋ-ˌdāl\ two mountain peaks NW England in Cumbria in Lake District

Lang·ley \'laŋ-lē\ city Canada in British Columbia ESE of Vancouver *pop* 66,040

Lan·gue·doc \ˌläŋ-gə-'däk, ˌläⁿg-'dòk\ region & former province S France extending from Auvergne to the Mediterranean

Lan·sing \'lan-siŋ\ **1** village NE Ill. SSE of Chicago *pop* 28,086 **2** city S Mich., its ✳ *pop* 127,321

Lan Tau \'län-'daú\ island Hong Kong, China W of Hong Kong Is. *area* 58 *sq mi* (151 *sq km*)

La·nús \lä-'nüs\ city E Argentina S of Buenos Aires *pop* 466,755

Lan·zhou or **Lan–chou** \'län-'jō\ city N *central* China ✳ of Gansu *pop* 1,194,640

La·od·i·cea \(ˌ)lā-ˌä-də-'sē-ə, -ˌad-ə-\ **1** ancient city W *central* Asia Minor in Phrygia **2** — see LATAKIA — **La·od·i·ce·an** \-'sē-ən\ *adjective or noun*

Laoighis \'lāsh, 'lēsh\ or **Leix** \'lāsh, 'lēsh\ or formerly **Queen's** county *central* Ireland in Leinster ✳ Portlaoighise *area* 664 *sq mi* (1726 *sq km*), *pop* 52,314

Laon \'läⁿ\ commune N France NE of Paris *pop* 28,670

Laos \'laús, 'lä-(ˌ)ōs, 'lä-ˌäs\ country SE Asia; a republic, until 1975 a kingdom; formerly a state of French Indochina; ✳ Vientiane *area* 91,428 *sq mi* (236,799 *sq km*), *pop* 4,533,000

La Pal·ma \lä-'päl-mä\ island Spain in Canary Islands; chief town Santa Cruz de la Palma *area* 280 *sq mi* (728 *sq km*)

La Paz \lä-'päz, -'päs, -'paz\ **1** city, administrative ✳ of Bolivia E of Lake Titicaca at altitude of 12,001 *ft* (3658 *m*), *metropolitan area pop* 711,036 **2** town W Mexico ✳ of Baja California Sur on **La Paz Bay** (inlet of Gulf of California) *pop* 46,011

Lap·land \'lap-,land, -lənd\ region N Europe above the arctic circle in N Norway, N Sweden, N Finland, & Kola Peninsula of Russia — **Lap·land·er** \-,lan-dər, -lən-\ *noun*

La Pla·ta \lä-'plä-tä\ city E Argentina SE of Buenos Aires *pop* 542,567

La Plata Peak \lə-'pla-tə, -'plä-\ mountain 14,336 *ft* (4370 *m*) *central* Colo. in Sawatch Mountains

La Porte \lə-'pört, -'pòrt\ **1** city N Ind. *pop* 21,507 **2** city SE Tex. on Galveston Bay *pop* 27,910

Lap·tev Sea \'lap-,tef, -,tev\ *or formerly* **Norden·skjöld Sea** \'nör-d°n-,shəld, -,shúld, -,shĕld\ arm of Arctic Ocean Russia between Taymyr Peninsula & New Siberian Islands

La Pu·en·te \lä-'pwen-tā\ city SW Calif. ESE of Los Angeles *pop* 36,955

L'Aqui·la \'lä-kwē-lä\ commune *central* Italy NE of Rome ✳ of Abruzzi *pop* 66,863

Lar·a·mie \'lar-ə-mē\ **1** river 216 *mi* (348 *km*) N Colo. & SE Wyo. flowing N & NE into N. Platte River **2** city SE Wyo. *pop* 26,687

Larch \'lärch\ river 270 *mi* (434 *km*) Canada in W Quebec flowing NE to unite with the Caniapiskau forming Koksoak River

La·re·do \lə-'rā-(,)dō\ city S Tex. on Rio Grande *pop* 122,899

Lar·go \'lär-(,)gō\ town W Fla. S of Clearwater *pop* 65,674

La Rio·ja \lä-rē-'ō-hä\ province N Spain along the upper Ebro ✳ Logroño *area* 1944 *sq mi* (5035 *sq km*), *pop* 263,434

La·ris·sa \lə-'ri-sə\ city N *central* Greece in E Thessaly *pop* 113,426

Lar·i·stan \,lar-ə-'stan\ region S Iran bordering on Persian Gulf

Larne \'lärn\ district NE Northern Ireland, established 1974 *area* 131 *sq mi* (341 *sq km*), *pop* 29,181

La Ro·chelle \,lä-rō-'shel\ city & port W France *pop* 72,936

Lar·vik \'lär-vik\ town & port SE Norway *pop* 38,019

La·Salle \lə-'sal\ town Canada in S Quebec on the St. Lawrence *pop* 73,804

Las·caux \lä-'skō\ cave SW *central* France near town of Montignac

Las Cru·ces \läs-'krü-səs\ city S N.Mex. *pop* 62,126

La Se·re·na \lä-sā-'rā-nä\ city N *central* Chile *pop* 83,283

Las Pal·mas \läs-'päl-mäs\ **1** province Spain comprising the E Canary Islands *area* 1569 *sq mi* (4064 *sq km*), *pop* 767,969 **2** city & port, its ✳, in NE Grand Canary Is. *pop* 342,040

La Spe·zia \lä-'spet-sē-ä\ city & port NW Italy in Liguria *pop* 104,511

Las·sen Peak \'la-s°n\ volcano 10,457 *ft* (3187 *m*) N Calif. at S end of Cascade Range; central feature of **Lassen Volcanic National Park**

Las Ve·gas \läs-'vā-gəs\ city SE corner of Nev. *pop* 258,295

Lat·a·kia \,la-tə-'kē-ə\ **1** region NW Syria bordering on the Mediterranean **2** *or ancient* **La·od·i·cea** \(,)lā-,ä-də-'sē-ə, ,lā-ä-\ city & port, its chief town, on the Mediterranean *pop* 284,000

La·ti·na \lä-'tē-nä\ commune *central* Italy *pop* 105,543

Latin America 1 Spanish America & Brazil **2** all of the Americas S of the U.S. — **Latin-American** *adjective* — **Latin American** *noun*

Latin Quarter section of Paris, France, S of the Seine frequented by students & artists

Lat·via \'lat-vē-ə\ independent country N *central* Europe bordering on the Baltic; an independent republic 1918–40, a constituent republic (**Lat·vi·an Republic**) of the U.S.S.R. 1940–91; ✳ Riga *area* 24,595 *sq mi* (63,701 *sq km*), *pop* 2,596,000

Lau·der·dale Lakes \'lò-dər-,dāl\ city SE Fla. *pop* 27,341

Lau·der·hill \'lò-dər-,hil\ city SE Fla. *pop* 49,708

Laun·ces·ton \'lòn(t)-səs-tən, 'län(t)-\ city & port Australia in N Tasmania *pop* 62,504

Lau·ra·sia \lò-'rā-zhə, -shə\ hypothetical land area believed to have once connected the landmasses of the northern hemisphere except for the Indian subcontinent

Lau·rel \'lòr-əl, 'lär-\ town S *central* Md. NNE of Washington, D.C. *pop* 19,438

Lau·ren·tian Mountains \lò-'ren(t)-shən\ range Canada in S Quebec N of the St. Lawrence on S edge of Canadian Shield

Laurentian Plateau — see CANADIAN SHIELD

Lau·ri·um \'lòr-ē-əm, 'lär-\ mountain SE Greece at SE tip of Attica

Lau·sanne \lō-'zän, -'zan\ commune W Switzerland ✳ of Vaud canton on Lake Geneva *pop* 124,897

Lausitz — see LUSATIA

Lava Beds National Monument reservation N Calif. SE of Lower Klamath Lake

La·val \lə-'val\ town Canada in S Quebec NW of Montreal *pop* 314,398

La Vendée — see VENDÉE

La Verne \lə-'vərn\ city SW Calif. E of Los Angeles *pop* 30,897

Lawn·dale \'lòn-,dāl, 'län-\ city SW Calif. SSW of Los Angeles *pop* 27,331

Law·rence \'lòr-ən(t)s, 'lär-\ **1** town *central* Ind. NE of Indianapolis *pop* 26,763 **2** city NE Kans. WSW of Kansas City *pop* 65,608 **3** city NE corner of Mass. *pop* 70,207

Law·ton \'lò-t°n\ city SW Okla. *pop* 80,561

La'youn — see AAIÚN, EL

Lay·san \'lī-,sän\ island Hawaii in the Leewards NW of Niihau

Lay·ton \'lā-t°n\ city N Utah N of Salt Lake City *pop* 41,784

La·zio \'lät-sē-,ō\ *or* **La·tium** \'lā-sh(ē-)əm\ region *central* Italy bordering on Tyrrhenian Sea & traversed by the Tiber ✳ Rome *pop* 5,170,672

League City \'lēg\ city SE Tex. *pop* 30,159

Leam·ing·ton \'le-miŋ-tən\ *or* **Royal Leamington Spa** borough S *central* England in Warwickshire *pop* 44,989

Leav·en·worth \'le-vən-,wərth\ city NE Kans. on Missouri River NW of Kansas City *pop* 38,495

Lea·wood \'lē-,wúd\ city E Kans. S of Kansas City *pop* 19,693

Leb·a·non 1 \'le-bə-nən\ city SE *central* Pa. E of Harrisburg *pop* 24,800 **2** \-nən, -,nän\ country SW Asia bordering on the Mediterranean; a republic since 1944, formerly (1920–44) a French mandate ✳ Beirut *area* 3949 *sq mi* (10,225 *sq km*), *pop* 2,909,000 — **Leb·a·nese** \,le-bə-'nēz, -'nēs\ *adjective or noun*

Lebanon Mountains *or ancient* **Lib·a·nus** \'li-bə-nəs\ mountains Lebanon running parallel to coast W of Bekaa Valley

Le Bour·get \lə-,bùr-'zhā\ commune N France, NE suburb of Paris

Lec·ce \'lā-chā, 'le-\ commune SE Italy in Puglia *pop* 100,233

Lec·co \'lā-(,)kō, 'le-\ commune N Italy in Lombardy on SE arm (**Lake Lecco**) of Lake Como *pop* 45,859

Lech \'lek, 'lek\ river Austria & Germany flowing from Vorarlberg N into the Danube

Le·do \'lē-(,)dō, 'lā-\ town NE India in NE Assam

Leeds \'lēdz\ city N England in W. Yorkshire *pop* 674,400

Lee's Summit \'lēz\ city W Mo. SE of Kansas City *pop* 46,418

Leeu·war·den \'lā-ü-,vär-də(n)\ commune N Netherlands ✳ of Friesland *pop* 86,405

Lee·ward Islands \'lē-wərd, 'lü-ərd\ **1** island chain *central* Pacific extending 1250 *mi* (2012 *km*) WNW from main islands of the Hawaiian group; includes Nihoa, Necker, Laysan, Midway, & Kure islands **2** *or French* **Îles sous le Vent** \ēl-sü-lə-'vä\ islands S Pacific, W group of the Society Islands *pop* 22,232 **3** islands West Indies in the N Lesser Antilles extending from Virgin Islands (on N) to Dominica (on S) **4** former colony Brit. West Indies in the Leewards including Antigua, St. Kitts-Nevis, & Montserrat

Leg·horn \'leg-,hòrn\ *or Italian* **Li·vor·no** \lē-'vòr-(,)nō\ commune & port *central* Italy in Tuscany on Tyrrhenian Sea *pop* 171,346

Leg·ni·ca \leg-'nēt-sä\ city SW Poland *pop* 104,196

Leh \'lā\ town India in E Kashmir on the Indus ✳ of Ladakh

Le Ha·vre \lə-'hävr', -'häv\ *or* **Havre** *or formerly* **Le Havre–de–Grâce** \-də-'gräs\ city & port N France on English Channel on N side of Seine estuary *pop* 197,219

Le·high \'lē-,hī\ river 100 *mi* (161 *km*) E Pa. flowing SW & SE into Delaware River

Leh·man Caves \'lē-mən\ limestone caverns E Nev. on E slope of Wheeler Peak in Great Basin National Park

Leices·ter \'les-tər\ city *central* England ✳ of Leicestershire *pop* 270,600

Leices·ter·shire \'les-tər-,shir, -shər\ *or* **Leicester** county *central* England ✳ Leicester *area* 1021 *sq mi* (2644 *sq km*), *pop* 860,500

Lei·den *or* **Ley·den** \'lī-d°n, *Dutch usually* 'lā-də, -yə\ city W Netherlands in S. Holland on a branch of the lower Rhine *pop* 112,976

Leie — see LYS

Lei·ne \'lī-nə\ river 119 *mi* (192 *km*) *central* Germany

Lein·ster \'len(t)-stər\ province E Ireland *area* 7581 *sq mi* (19,635 *sq km*), *pop* 1,382,560

Leip·zig \'līp-sig, -sik\ city E Germany in Saxony *pop* 503,191

Lei·ria \lā-'rē-ə\ town W *central* Portugal SSW of Coimbra *pop* 101,325

Leith \'lēth\ port section of Edinburgh, Scotland, on Firth of Forth

Lei·tha \'lī-(,)tä\ river 112 *mi* (180 *km*) E Austria & NW Hungary flowing SE into the Raba

Lei·trim \'lē-trəm\ county NW Ireland in Connacht ✳ Carrick on Shannon *area* 589 *sq mi* (1531 *sq km*), *pop* 25,301

Leix — see LAOIGHIS

Lei·xões \lā-'shòi°sh\ town NW Portugal on the Atlantic; port for Porto

Lei·zhou *or* **Lei·chou** \lā-'jō\ *or* **Lui·chow** \'lwē-'jō, -'chaù\ peninsula SE China in Guangdong between S. China Sea & Gulf of Tonkin

Lek \'lek\ river 40 *mi* (64 *km*) Netherlands flowing W into the Atlantic; the N branch of the lower Rhine

Lely·stad \'lā-lē-,stät\ commune *central* Netherlands ✳ of Flevoland

Le Maine — see MAINE

Leman, Lake — see GENEVA (Lake)

Le Mans \lə-'mä\ city NW France on the Sarthe *pop* 148,465

Lemberg — see LVIV

Lem·nos \'lem-,näs, -nəs\ *or New Greek* **Lím·nos** \'lēm-,nòs\ island Greece in the Aegean ESE of Chalcidice peninsula; chief town Kástron *area* 177 *sq mi* (458 *sq km*)

Lemon Grove city S Calif. E of San Diego *pop* 23,984

Le·na \'lē-nə, 'lā-; 'lye-nə\ river *about* 2700 *mi* (4345 *km*) E Russia in Asia flowing from mountains W of Lake Baikal NE & N into Laptev Sea through wide delta

Le·nexa \lə-'nek-sə\ city E Kans. SW of Kansas City *pop* 34,034

Leningrad — see SAINT PETERSBURG 2 — **Len·in·grad·er** \'le-nən-,gra-dər, -,grä-\ *noun*

Le·nin Peak \'le-nən, 'lyä-nēn\ mountain 23,405 *ft* (7134 *m*) on border between Kyrgyzstan & Tajikistan; highest in Trans Alai Range

Lens \'lä\ city N France SW of Lille *pop* 35,278

Leom·in·ster \'le-mən-stər\ city *central* Mass. N of Worcester *pop* 38,145

Le·ón \lā-'ōn\ **1** *or* **León de los Al·da·mas** \dä-,lòs-äl-'dä-mäs, thä-\ city *central* Mexico in Guanajuato *pop* 872,453 **2** city W Nicaragua *pop* 90,897 **3** region & ancient kingdom NW Spain W of Old Castile **4** province NW Spain in N León region *area* 5972 *sq mi* (15,467 *sq km*), *pop* 525,896 **5** city, its ✳ *pop* 144,021

Le·o·ne, Mon·te \mòn-tā-lā-'ō-nā\ mountain 11,657 *ft* (3553 *m*) on border between Switzerland & Italy SW of Simplon Pass; highest in Lepontine Alps

Leopold II, Lake — see MAI-NDOMBE (Lac)

Léopoldville — see KINSHASA

Le·pon·tine Alps \li-'pän-ˌtīn, 'le-pən-\ range of *central* Alps on border between Switzerland & Italy — see LEONE (Monte)

Lep·tis Mag·na \ˌlep-təs-'mag-nə\ ancient seaport N Africa near present-day Al Khums

Lé·ri·da \'ler-i-də, 'lā-rē-thä\ **1** province NE Spain in NW Catalonia *area* 4644 *sq mi* (12,028 *sq km*), *pop* 353,455 **2** commune, its ✳ *pop* 111,880

Ler·wick \'lər-(ˌ)wik, 'ler-\ burgh & port N Scotland ✳ of Shetland on Mainland Is. *pop* 7223

Les·bos \'lez-ˌbäs, -bəs, -ˌvós\ *or* **Myt·i·le·ne** \ˌmit-ᵊl-'ē-nē, ˌmē-tē-'lē-\ island Greece in the Aegean off NW Turkey *area* 630 *sq mi* (1632 *sq km*), *pop* 103,700

Les Ey·zies \ˌlāz-ā-'zē\ commune SW *central* France SE of Périgueux

Le·so·tho \lə-'sō-(ˌ)tō, -'sü-(ˌ)tü\ *or formerly* **Ba·su·to·land** \bə-'sü-tō-ˌland\ country S Africa surrounded by Republic of South Africa; a constitutional monarchy, in the Commonwealth of Nations ✳ Maseru *area* 11,716 *sq mi* (30,462 *sq km*), *pop* 1,903,000

Lesser Antilles islands in the W. Indies including Virgin, Leeward, & Windward Islands, Trinidad, Barbados, Tobago, & islands in the S Caribbean N of Venezuela

Lesser Armenia — see LITTLE ARMENIA

Lesser Slave Lake \'slāv\ lake Canada in *central* Alberta draining through the **Lesser Slave River** to Athabasca River *area* 461 *sq mi* (1199 *sq km*)

Lesser Sunda Islands — see SUNDA ISLANDS

Leth·bridge \'leth-(ˌ)brij\ city Canada in S Alberta *pop* 60,974

Le·ti·cia \lä-'tē-sē-ä\ town SE Colombia on the Amazon

Leuc·tra \'lük-trə\ ancient village Greece in Boeotia SW of Thebes

Leuven — see LOUVAIN

Le·val·lois–Per·ret \lə-ˌvál-'wä-pə-'rā\ commune N France on the Seine, NW suburb of Paris *pop* 47,788

Le·vant \lə-'vant\ the countries bordering on the E Mediterranean — **Le·van·tine** \'le-vən-ˌtīn, -ˌtēn, lə-'van-\ *adjective or noun*

Levant States — see SYRIA

Le·ven, Loch \'lē-vən\ **1** inlet of Loch Linnhe W Scotland in Highland region **2** lake 4 *mi* (6.4 *km*) long E Scotland SSE of Perth

Le·ver·ku·sen \'lā-vər-ˌkü-zᵊn\ city W Germany on the Rhine SE of Düsseldorf *pop* 161,147

Lé·vis–Lau·zon \'lē-vəs-lō-'zōⁿ, lā-'vē-\ town Canada in S Quebec *pop* 39,452

Lev·kás \lef-'käs\ island Greece in the Ionians at entrance to Ambracian Gulf *area* 111 *sq mi* (289 *sq km*)

Lew·es \'lü-əs\ **1** the upper Yukon River S of its junction with the Pelly **2** borough S England ✳ of E. Sussex on Ouse River S of London

Lewis and Clark Caverns \'lü-əs-ənd-'klärk\ *or formerly* **Mor·ri·son Cave** \'mòr-ə-sən, 'mär-\ cavern *central* Mont. WNW of Bozeman

Lewis and Clark Lake lake 30 *mi* (48 *km*) long SE S.Dak. & NE Nebr. formed by Gavins Point Dam

Lew·i·sham \'lü-ə-shəm\ borough of SE Greater London, England *pop* 215,300

Lew·is·ton \'lü-əs-tən\ **1** city NW Idaho on Wash. border *pop* 28,082 **2** city SW Maine on the Androscoggin opposite Auburn *pop* 39,757

Le·wis·ville \'lü-əs-ˌvil, -vəl\ city N Tex. *pop* 46,521

Lewis with Har·ris \'lü-əs-with-'har-əs, -with-\ island NW Scotland in the Outer Hebrides divided administratively into **Lewis** (in the N; chief town & port Stornoway) & **Harris** (in the S); largest of the Hebrides, in Western Isles regional division *area* 770 *sq mi* (2002 *sq km*)

Lex·ing·ton \'lek-siŋ-tən\ **1** city N *central* Kentucky ESE of Frankfort *pop* 225,366 **2** town NE Mass. NW of Boston *pop* 28,974

Leyden — see LEIDEN

Ley·te \'lā-tē\ island Philippines in the Visayans W of **Leyte Gulf** (inlet of the Pacific); chief town Tacloban *area* 2785 *sq mi* (7241 *sq km*)

Ley·ton \'lā-tᵊn\ former municipal borough SE England in Essex, now part of Waltham Forest

Lha·sa \'lä-sə, 'la-\ city SW China ✳ of Tibet *pop* 106,885

Lho·tse \'lōt-'sā, 'hlōt-\ mountain 27,923 *ft* (8511 *m*) in Mt. Everest massif S of Mt. Everest; 4th highest in the world

Lian·yun·gang \'lyän-'yün-ˌgän\ *or* **Lien–yün·kang** \'lē-'ən-'yün-'gän\ *or formerly* **Tung·hai** \'dùn-'hī\ city E China in N Jiangsu *pop* 354,139

Liao \'lyaù\ river 700 *mi* (1126 *km*) NE China flowing into Gulf of Liaodong

Liao·dong *or* **Liao·tung** \'lyaù-'dùn\ peninsula NE China in S Liaoning between Korea Bay & **Gulf of Liaodong** (arm of Bo Hai)

Liao·ning \'lyaù-'niŋ\ *or formerly* **Feng·tien** \'fəŋ-'tyen\ province NE China in S Manchuria ✳ Shenyang *area* 58,301 *sq mi* (151,583 *sq km*), *pop* 39,459,697

Liao·si \'lyaù-'shē\ former province (1948–54) NE China in S Manchuria bordering on Gulf of Liaodong ✳ Chin-chou

Liao·yang \'lyaù-'yän\ city NE China in *central* Liaoning NE of Anshan *pop* 492,559

Liaoyuan — see SHUANGLIAO

Li·ard \'lē-ərd\ river 755 *mi* (1215 *km*) W Canada flowing from Stikine Mountains in Yukon Territory E & N into Mackenzie River

Libanus — see LEBANON MOUNTAINS

Lib·e·rec \'li-be-ˌrets\ city N Czech Republic in N Bohemia *pop* 104,158

Li·be·ria \lī-'bir-ē-ə\ country W Africa, a republic ✳ Monrovia *area* 43,000 *sq mi* (111,800 *sq km*), *pop* 2,101,628 — **Li·be·ri·an** \-ē-ən\ *adjective or noun*

Lib·er·ty \'li-bər-tē\ city NW Mo. NNE of Kansas City *pop* 20,459

Liberty Island *or formerly* **Bed·loe's Island** \'bed-ˌlōz\ island S N.Y. in Upper New York Bay; comprises **Statue of Liberty National Monument**

Lib·er·ty·ville \'li-bər-tē-ˌvil, -vəl\ city NE Ill. *pop* 19,174

Li·bre·ville \'lē-brə-ˌvil, -ˌvēl\ city & port ✳ of Gabon at mouth of Gabon River *pop* 352,000

Lib·ya \'li-bē-ə\ **1** the part of Africa N of the Sahara between Egypt & Syrtis Major (Gulf of Sidra) — an ancient name **2** N Africa W of Egypt — an ancient name **3** country N Africa bordering on the Mediterranean; a colony of Italy 1912–43, an independent kingdom 1951–69, a republic since 1969 ✳ Tripoli *area* 679,358 *sq mi* (1,766,331 *sq km*), *pop* 4,573,000

Lib·y·an Desert \'li-bē-ən\ desert N Africa W of the Nile in Libya, Egypt, & Sudan

Lich·field \'lich-ˌfēld\ city W *central* England in Staffordshire *pop* 90,700

Lick·ing \'li-kiŋ\ river 320 *mi* (515 *km*) NE Ky. flowing into Ohio river

Li·di·ce \'li-də-sē, 'lē-dyét-ˌsä\ village W *central* Czech Republic in W *central* Bohemia

Li·do \'lē-(ˌ)dō\ island Italy in the Adriatic separating Lagoon of Venice & Gulf of Venice

Liech·ten·stein \'lik-tən-ˌstīn, 'lik-tən-ˌshtin\ country W Europe between Switzerland & Austria bordering on the Rhine; a principality ✳ Vaduz *area* 62 *sq mi* (161 *sq km*), *pop* 28,877 — **Liech·ten·stein·er** \-ˌstī-nər, -ˌshtī-\ *noun*

Li·ège \lē-'ezh, -'āzh\ *or Flemish* **Luik** \'līk, 'lœik\ **1** province E Belgium *area* 1497 *sq mi* (3877 *sq km*), *pop* 999,646 **2** city, its ✳ *pop* 195,800

Lie·pa·ja \lē-'e-pə-yə, 'lye-pä-yä\ *or German* **Li·bau** \'lē-ˌbaù\ city & port W Latvia on the Baltic *pop* 114,900

Lif·fey \'li-fē\ river 50 *mi* (80 *km*) E Ireland flowing into Dublin Bay

Lif·ford \'li-fərd\ town NW Ireland (republic) in Ulster ✳ of county Donegal *pop* 1478

Li·gu·ria \lə-'gyùr-ē-ə\ region NW Italy bordering on Ligurian Sea ✳ Genoa *pop* 1,727,212 — **Li·gu·ri·an** \-ē-ən\ *adjective or noun*

Ligurian Sea arm of the Mediterranean N of Corsica

Li·ka·si \lē-'kä-sē\ *or formerly* **Ja·dot·ville** \ˌzha-dō-'vēl, zha-ˌdō-ˌvil\ city SE Democratic Republic of the Congo in SE Shaba *pop* 279,839

Lille \'lēl\ *or formerly* **Lisle** \'lēl, 'līl\ city N France; medieval ✳ of Flanders *pop* 178,301

Li·long·we \li-'lóŋ-(ˌ)gwä\ city ✳ of Malawi *pop* 223,318

Li·ma **1** \'lī-mə\ city NW Ohio *pop* 45,549 **2** \'lē-mə\ city ✳ of Peru, on the Rímac *pop* 5,825,900

Lim·a·vady \ˌli-mə-'va-dē\ district N Northern Ireland, established 1974 *area* 226 *sq mi* (588 *sq km*), *pop* 29,201

Li·may \lē-'mī\ river 250 *mi* (402 *km*) W Argentina flowing out of Lake Nahuel Huapí & joining the Neuquén forming Negro River

Lim·burg \'lim-ˌbərg\ **1** region W Europe E of the Meuse including parts of present Limburg province, Netherlands, & Limburg province, Belgium **2** province NE Belgium ✳ Hasselt *area* 935 *sq mi* (2422 *sq km*), *pop* 750,435 **3** province SE Netherlands ✳ Maastricht *area* 853 *sq mi* (2209 *sq km*), *pop* 1,119,942

Lime·house \'līm-ˌhaùs\ district E London, England, in Tower Hamlets on N bank of Thames River

Lim·er·ick \'li-mə-rik, 'lim-rik\ **1** county SW Ireland in Munster *area* 1037 *sq mi* (2696 *sq km*), *pop* 109,873 **2** city & county borough & port, its ✳, on the Shannon *pop* 52,040

Límnos — see LEMNOS

Li·moges \lē-'mōzh, li-\ city SW *central* France *pop* 136,407

Li·món \lē-'mōn\ *or* **Puer·to Limón** \'pwer-tō\ city & port E Costa Rica on the Caribbean *pop* 50,939

Li·mou·sin \ˌlē-mü-'zaⁿ\ region & former province S *central* France W of Auvergne ✳ Limoges

Lim·po·po \lim-'pō-(ˌ)pō\ *or* **Croc·o·dile** \'krä-kə-ˌdīl\ river 1000 *mi* (1609 *km*) S Africa flowing from Northern province, Republic of South Africa, into Indian Ocean in Mozambique

Li·na·res \lē-'när-ās\ commune S Spain N of Jaén *pop* 58,039

Lin·coln \'liŋ-kən\ **1** city SE Nebr., its ✳ *pop* 191,972 **2** city E England ✳ of Lincolnshire *pop* 81,900

Lincoln Park city SE Mich. SW of Detroit *pop* 41,832

Lin·coln·shire \'liŋ-kən-ˌshir, -shər\ *or* **Lincoln** county E England ✳ Lincoln *area* 2354 *sq mi* (6097 *sq km*), *pop* 573,900

Lin·den \'lin-dən\ city NE N.J. SSW of Elizabeth *pop* 36,701

Lin·den·hurst \'lin-dən-ˌhərst\ village SE N.Y. in *central* Long Is. *pop* 26,879

Lin·des·nes \'lin-dəs-ˌnäs\ cape Norway at S tip on North Sea

Lindisfarne — see HOLY

Lind·sey, Parts of \'lin-zē\ district & former administrative county E England in N Lincolnshire ✳ Lincoln *area* 1520 *sq mi* (3952 *sq km*)

Line Islands \'līn\ islands Kiribati in *central* Pacific S of Hawaii formerly divided between the U.S. (Kingman Reef & Palmyra) & Great Britain (Teraina, Tabuaeran, & Kiritimati) *pop* 4782

Lin·ga·yen Gulf \ˌliŋ-gä-'yen\ inlet of S. China Sea Philippines in NW Luzon

Linguetta, Cape — see GJUHEZES (Cape)

Lin·kö·ping \'lin-ˌshə(r)-piŋ, -ˌshē-\ city SE Sweden *pop* 126,377

Lin·lith·gow \lin-'lith-(ˌ)gō\ **1** *or* **Lin·lith·gow·shire** \-ˌshir, -shər\ — see WEST LOTHIAN **2** burgh SE Scotland in Lothian region W of Edinburgh *pop* 9524

Linn·he, Loch \'li-nē\ inlet of the Atlantic on W coast of Scotland extending NE from head of Firth of Lorne

Linz \'lints, 'linz\ city N Austria on the Danube *pop* 203,044

Li·on, Gulf of \'lī-ən\ *or French* **Golfe du Lion** \ˌgôlf-dē-'lyōⁿ\ arm of the Mediterranean on S coast of France

Lip·a·ri \'li-pə-rē\ *or ancient* **Lip·a·ra** \'li-pə-rä\ island, chief of the Lipari Islands

Lipari Islands *or Italian* **Iso·le Eo·lie** \'ē-zò-ˌlā -ā-'ò-lē-ˌā\ islands Italy in SE Tyrrhenian Sea off NE Sicily *area about* 45 *sq mi* (117 *sq km*) — see STROMBOLI

Li·petsk \'lē-ˌpetsk, -ˌpitsk\ city SW *central* Russia in Europe N of Voronezh *pop* 464,000

Lip·pe \'li-pə\ **1** river *about* 150 *mi* (241 *km*) W Germany flowing from Teutoburger Wald W into the Rhine **2** former principality & state W Germany between Teutoburger Wald & the Weser ✳ Detmold

Li·ri \'lir-ē\ river 100 *mi* (161 *km*) *central* Italy flowing into Gulf of Gaeta

Lis·bon \'liz-bən\ *or Portuguese* **Lis·boa** \lēzh-'vō-ə\ city & port ✳ of Portugal on Tagus estuary *pop* 677,790 — **Lis·bo·an** \liz-'bō-ən\ *noun*

Lis·burn \'liz-(ˌ)bərn\ district E Northern Ireland, established 1974 *area* 171 *sq mi* (445 *sq km*), *pop* 99,162

Lis·burne, Cape \'liz-(ˌ)bərn\ cape NW Alaska projecting into Arctic Ocean near W end of Brooks Range

Li·sieux \lēz-'yə(r), -'yœ\ city NW France E of Caen *pop* 24,506

Lisle \'līl\ village NE Ill. *pop* 19,512

Li·ta·ni \li-'tä-nē\ river 90 *mi* (144 *km*) S Lebanon flowing into Mediterranean

Lith·u·a·nia \ˌli-thə-'wā-nē-ə, -li-thyə-, -nyə\ *or Lithuanian* **Lie·tu·va** \lye-'tü-vä\ country N *central* Europe bordering on the Baltic; remnant of a medieval principality extending from Baltic Sea to Black Sea; a republic 1918–40, a constituent republic (**Lithuanian Republic**) of the U.S.S.R. 1940–91; ✳ Vilnius *area* 25,174 *sq mi* (65,201 *sq km*), *pop* 3,753,000

Little Abaco — see ABACO

Little Armenia *or* **Lesser Armenia** region S Turkey corresponding to ancient Cilicia

Little Bighorn river 80 *mi* (129 *km*) N Wyo. & S Mont. flowing N into Bighorn River

Little Colorado river *about* 300 *mi* (483 *km*) NE Ariz. flowing NW into Colorado River

Little Diomede — see DIOMEDE ISLANDS

Little Inagua — see INAGUA

Little Kabylia — see KABYLIA

Little Karroo — see KARROO

Little Minch — see MINCH

Little Missouri river 560 *mi* (901 *km*) W U.S. flowing from NE Wyo. N into Missouri River in W N.Dak.

Little Namaqualand — see NAMAQUALAND

Lit·tle Rock \'li-t°l-ˌräk\ city ✳ of Ark. on Arkansas River *pop* 175,795

Little Saint Ber·nard \ˌsänt-bər-'närd\ mountain pass 7178 *ft* (2188 *m*) over Savoy Alps between France & Italy S of Mont Blanc

Lit·tle·ton \'li-t°l-tən\ town N *central* Colo. S of Denver *pop* 33,685

Little Walachia — see OLTENIA

Liv·er·more \'li-vər-ˌmōr, -ˌmȯr\ city W Calif. SE of Oakland *pop* 56,741

Liv·er·pool \'li-vər-ˌpül\ city & port NW England in Merseyside on Mersey estuary *pop* 448,300 — **Liv·er·pud·li·an** \ˌli-vər-'pəd-lē-ən\ *adjective or noun*

Liv·ing·stone \'li-viŋ-stən\ city S Zambia on the Zambezi *pop* 82,218

Livingstone Falls rapids in lower Congo River W equatorial Africa below Pool Malebo; a series of cascades dropping *nearly* 900 *ft* (273 *m*) in 220 *mi* (352 *km*)

Li·vo·nia \lə-'vō-nē-ə, -nyə\ **1** region *central* Europe bordering on the Baltic in Latvia & Estonia **2** city SE Mich. W of Detroit *pop* 100,850 — **Li·vo·ni·an** \-nē-ən, -nyən\ *adjective or noun*

Livorno — see LEGHORN

Lizard Head *or* **Lizard Point** headland SW England in S Cornwall at S tip of **The Lizard** (peninsula projecting into English Channel); extreme S point of Great Britain at 49°57′30″N, 5°12′W

Lju·blja·na \lē-ü-blē-'ä-nə\ city *central* Slovenia, its ✳ *pop* 323,291

Llan·ber·is \lan-'ber-əs, hlan-\ village NW Wales in Gwynedd near Snowdon at entrance to **Pass of Llanberis** (1169 *ft* or 354 *m*)

Llan·drin·dod Wells \lan-'drin-ˌdȯd, hlan-\ town E Wales in Powys

Llan·dud·no \lan-'did-(ˌ)nō, hlan-, -'dəd-\ town NW Wales on coast of Gwynedd *pop* 18,991

Lla·nel·li *or* **Lla·nel·ly** \hla-'ne-hlē; hla-'ne-lē, hla-\ borough & port S Wales in Dyfed *pop* 73,500

Llan·gef·ni \lan-'gev-nē, hlan-\ town NW Wales in Gwynedd on Anglesey Is. *pop* 4265

Lla·no Es·ta·ca·do \'la-(ˌ)nō-ˌes-tə-'kä-(ˌ)dō, 'lä-, 'yä-\ *or* **Staked Plain** \'stāk(t)-\ plateau region SE N.Mex. & NW Tex.

Llu·llai·lla·co \ˌyü-yī-'yä-(ˌ)kō\ volcano 22,057 *ft* (6723 *m*) N Chile in Andes on Argentina border SE of Antofagasta

Lo·an·ge \lō-'aŋ-gə\ *or Portuguese* **Lu·an·gue** \lü-'aŋ-gə\ river 425 *mi* (684 *km*) NE Angola & SW Republic of the Congo flowing N into Kasai River

Lo·bi·to \lō-'bē-(ˌ)tō\ city & port W Angola *pop* 59,528

Lo·bos, Point \'lō-(ˌ)bōs\ **1** promontory Calif. in San Francisco on S side of entrance to the Golden Gate **2** promontory Calif. on the Pacific SW of Monterey

Lo·car·no \lō-'kär-(ˌ)nō\ commune SE *central* Switzerland *pop* 14,430

Loch·gilp·head \läk-'gilp-ˌhed, läk-\ burgh W Scotland on Loch Fyne

Lock·port \'läk-ˌpȯrt, -ˌpȯrt\ city W N.Y. NE of Buffalo *pop* 24,426

Lo·cris \'lō-krəs, 'lä-\ region of ancient Greece N of Gulf of Corinth — **Lo·cri·an** \-krē-ən\ *adjective or noun*

Lod \'lōd\ city *central* Israel *pop* 45,500

Lo·di 1 \'lō-ˌdī\ city *central* Calif. SSE of Sacramento *pop* 51,874 **2** \'lō-ˌdī\ borough NE N.J. SE of Paterson *pop* 22,355 **3** \'lō-(ˌ)dē\ commune N Italy in Lombardy SE of Milan *pop* 42,770

Lodz \'lüj, 'lädz\ city *central* Poland WSW of Warsaw *pop* 851,690

Lo·fo·ten \'lō-ˌfō-t°n\ island group Norway off NW coast SW of Vesterålen *area* 475 *sq mi* (1235 *sq km*)

Lo·gan \'lō-gən\ city N Utah *pop* 32,762

Logan, Mount mountain 19,524 *ft* (5951 *m*) Canada in SW Yukon Territory; highest in St. Elias & Coast ranges & in Canada & 2d highest in N. America

Lo·gro·ño \lō-'grō-(ˌ)nyō\ commune ✳ of La Rioja province, Spain, on the Ebro *pop* 121,066

Loire \lə-'wär, 'lwär\ river 634 *mi* (1020 *km*) *central* France flowing from the Massif Central NW & W into Bay of Biscay

Lol·land \'lä-lənd\ island Denmark in the Baltic S of Sjælland *area* 477 *sq mi* (1240 *sq km*), *pop* 73,564

Lo·ma·mi \lō-'mä-mē\ river *central* Democratic Republic of the Congo flowing N into Congo River

Lo·mas \'lō-ˌmäs\ *or* **Lo·mas de Za·mo·ra** \dä-zä-'mōr-ä, ˌtha-sä-'mō-rä\ city E Argentina SW of Buenos Aires *pop* 572,769

Lom·bard \'läm-ˌbärd\ village NE Ill. W of Chicago *pop* 39,408

Lom·bar·dy \-ˌbär-dē, -bər- *also* 'ləm-\ *or Italian* **Lom·bar·dia** \ˌläm-bər-'dē-ə, ˌlōm-\ region N Italy chiefly N of the Po ✳ Milan *pop* 8,911,995

Lom·blen \läm-'blen\ island Indonesia in the Lesser Sundas E of Flores *area* 468 *sq mi* (1217 *sq km*)

Lom·bok \läm-'bäk\ island Indonesia in the Lesser Sundas E of Bali; chief town Mataram *area* 1825 *sq mi* (4745 *sq km*), *pop* 1,300,234

Lo·mé \lō-'mā\ city & port ✳ of Togo *pop* 229,400

Lo·mi·ta \lō-'mē-tə\ city SW Calif. S of Los Angeles *pop* 19,382

Lo·mond, Ben \ben-'lō-mənd\ mountain 3192 *ft* (973 *m*) S *central* Scotland on E side of Loch Lomond

Lomond, Loch lake 24 *mi* (39 *km*) long S *central* Scotland in Strathclyde & Central regions; largest in Scotland

Lom·poc \'läm-ˌpōk\ city SW Calif. W of Santa Barbara *pop* 37,649

Lon·don \'lən-dən\ **1** city Canada in SE Ontario on Thames River *pop* 303,165 **2** city & port SE England formerly constituting an administrative county ✳ of United Kingdom; comprises **City of London** *or* **The City** (approximately coextensive with *ancient* **Lon·din·i·um** \län-'di-nē-əm,ˌlon-\; *pop* 4000) & 32 other boroughs which together are referred to as the metropolitan county of **Greater London** (*area* 632 *sq mi or* 1637 *sq km*, *pop* 6,377,900) — **Lon·don·er** \-də-nər\ *noun*

Lon·don·der·ry 1 \'lən-dən-ˌder-ē\ town SE N.H. NE of Nashua *pop* 19,781 **2** — see DERRY **3** \'lən-dən-der-ē, 'lən-dən-ˌder-ē\ traditional county N Northern Ireland

Long Beach 1 city & port SW Calif. SE of Los Angeles *pop* 429,433 **2** city SE N.Y. on island S of Long Is. *pop* 33,510

Long Branch city E *central* N.J. on the Atlantic *pop* 28,658

Long·ford \'lȯŋ-fərd\ **1** county E *central* Ireland in Leinster *area* 403 *sq mi* (1048 *sq km*), *pop* 30,296 **2** town, its ✳ *pop* 6393

Long Island island 118 *mi* (190 *km*) long SE N.Y. S of Conn. *area* 1723 *sq mi* (4462 *sq km*)

Long Island City section of New York City in NW Queens

Long Island Sound inlet of the Atlantic between Conn. & Long Is.

Long·mont \'lȯŋ-ˌmänt\ city N Colo. N of Denver *pop* 51,555

Longs Peak \'lȯŋz\ mountain 14,255 *ft* (4345 *m*) N *central* Colo. in Front Range in Rocky Mountain National Park

Lon·gueuil \lȯŋ-'gāl\ town Canada in S Quebec E of Montreal *pop* 129,874

Long·view 1 \'lȯŋ-ˌvyü\ city NE Tex. *pop* 70,311 **2** city SW Wash. on Columbia River *pop* 31,499

Long Xuy·en \'lȯŋ-'swē-ən\ city S Vietnam in SW Cochin China on S side of Mekong delta *pop* 128,817

Lookout, Cape cape E N.C. on the Atlantic SW of Cape Hatteras

Lookout Mountain ridge 2126 *ft* (648 *m*) SE Tenn., NW Ga., & NE Ala. near Chattanooga, Tenn.

Lo·rain \lə-'rān, lō-\ city N Ohio on Lake Erie W of Cleveland *pop* 71,245

Lor·ca \'lȯr-kə\ commune SE Spain SW of Murcia *pop* 65,832

Lord Howe Island \lȯrd-'haü\ island Australia in Tasman Sea ENE of Sydney belonging to New South Wales *area* 5 *sq mi* (13 *sq km*)

Lo·re·to \lȯ-'rā-(ˌ)tō, -'re-\ commune *central* Italy in Marche S of Ancona *pop* 10,797

Lo·ri·ent \lȯr-ē-'äⁿ\ commune & port NW France in Brittany on Bay of Biscay *pop* 61,630

Lorn, Firth of \'lȯrn\ *or* **Firth of Lorne** \'lȯrn\ strait W Scotland between E Mull Is. & mainland

Lor·raine \lə-'rān, lȯ-\ *or German* **Lo·thring·en** \'lō-triŋ-ən\ region & former duchy NE France around the upper Moselle & the Meuse; remnant (Upper Lorraine) of medieval kingdom of **Lo·tha·rin·gia** \ˌlō-thə-'rin-jē-ə\ including also territory to N (Lower Lorraine) between the Rhine & the Schelde — see ALSACE-LORRAINE

Los Al·tos \lȯs-'al-(ˌ)tōs\ city W Calif. SSE of Palo Alto *pop* 26,303

Los An·ge·les \lȯs-'an-jə-ləs *also* -ˌlēz, *sometimes* -'aŋ-gə-, ˌlēz\ city & port SW Calif. on the Pacific *pop* 3,485,398 — **Los An·ge·le·no** \-ˌan-jə-'lē-(ˌ)nō *also* -ˌaŋ-gə-'lē-\ *noun*

Los Án·ge·les \lōs-'äŋ-hā-ˌläs\ city S *central* Chile *pop* 142,136

Los Gat·os \lȯs-'ga-təs\ city W Calif. S of San José *pop* 27,357

Lot \'lät, 'lȯt\ river 300 *mi* (483 *km*) S France flowing W into the Garonne

Lo·thi·an \'lō-thē-ən\ region S Scotland bordering on Firth of Forth, established 1975 ✳ Edinburgh *area* 662 *sq mi* (1716 *sq km*), *pop* 753,900; formerly divided into three counties (the **Lothians**): East Lothian, Midlothian, & West Lothian

Louang·phra·bang \'lwän-prä-'bäŋ\ *or* **Luang Pra·bang** \'lwäŋ-prä-\ city NW Laos on the Mekong NNW of Vientiane

Lough·bor·ough \'ləf-ˌbər-ə, -ˌbə-rə, -b(ə-)rə\ borough *central* England in Leicestershire S of Nottingham *pop* 47,647

Lou·ise, Lake \lu̇-'ēz\ lake W Canada in SW Alberta in Banff National Park

Lou·i·si·ade Archipelago \ˌlü-ˌē-zē-'äd, -'ad\ island group in Solomon Sea SE of New Guinea; belongs to Papua New Guinea *pop* 14,599

Lou·i·si·ana \lu̇-ˌē-zē-'a-nə, ˌlü-ə-zē-, lü-zē-\ state S U.S. ✳ Baton Rouge *area* 48,523 *sq mi* (126,160 *sq km*), *pop* 4,219,973 — **Lou·i·si·an·an** \-'a-nən\ *adjective or noun* — **Lou·i·si·an·i·an** \-'a-nē-ən, -'a-nyən\ *adjective or noun*

Louisiana Purchase region W *central* U.S. between Mississippi River & the Rockies purchased 1803 from France *area* 885,000 *sq mi* (2,301,000 *sq km*)

Lou·is·ville \'lü-i-,vil, -vǝl\ city N Ky. on Ohio River *pop* 269,063

Loup \'lüp\ river 290 *mi* (467 *km*) with longest headstream (the Middle Loup) E *central* Nebr. flowing E into Platte River

Lourdes \'lürd, 'lürdz\ commune SW France on the Gave de Pau SSW of Tarbes *pop* 16,581

Lourenço Marques — see MAPUTO

Louth \'laúth\ county E Ireland in Leinster bordering on Irish Sea ✳ Dundalk *area* 317 *sq mi* (824 *sq km*), *pop* 90,707

Lou·vain \lü-'vaⁿ\ *or Flemish* **Leu·ven** \'lǝ(r)-vǝ(n), 'lȫ-\ city *central* Belgium in Brabant E of Brussels *pop* 85,200

Love·land \'lǝv-lǝnd\ city N Colo. N of Denver *pop* 37,352

Loveland Pass mountain pass N *central* Colo. in Front Range of Rocky Mountains

Low Countries region W Europe bordering on North Sea & comprising modern Belgium, Luxembourg, & the Netherlands

Low·ell \'lō-ǝl\ city NE Mass. NW of Boston *pop* 103,439

Lower Canada the province of Canada 1791–1841 corresponding to modern Quebec — see UPPER CANADA

Lower 48 the continental states of the U.S. excluding Alaska

Lower Klamath Lake lake N Calif. on Oreg. border SSE of Upper Klamath Lake (in Oreg.)

Lower Peninsula S part of Mich., S of Straits of Mackinac

Lower Saxony *or German* **Nie·der·sach·sen** \,nē-dǝr-'zäk-sǝn\ state of Germany & formerly of W. Germany bordering on North Sea ✳ Hannover *area* 18,305 *sq mi* (47,410 *sq km*), *pop* 7,387,200 — see SAXONY

Lowes·toft \'lō-stǝf(t), -,stóft\ borough & port E England in E. Suffolk on North Sea *pop* 55,231

Low·lands \'lō-lǝndz, -,landz\ the *central* & E part of Scotland lying between the Highlands & the Southern Uplands

Loyalty Islands islands SW Pacific E of New Caledonia; a dependency of New Caledonia *area* about 755 *sq mi* (1955 *sq km*), *pop* 17,912

Lu·a·la·ba \,lü-ä-'lä-bä\ river 400 *mi* (640 *km*) SE Democratic Republic of the Congo flowing N to join the **Lu·a·pu·la** \-'pü-lä\ (outlet of Lake Bangweulu) forming Congo River

Lu·an·da \lü-'än-dǝ\ city & port ✳ of Angola *pop* 1,544,400

Luange — see LOANGE

Lub·bock \'lǝ-bǝk\ city NW Tex. *pop* 186,206

Lü·beck \'lü-,bek, 'lȫ-\ city & port N Germany NE of Hamburg *pop* 215,999

Lu·blin \'lü-blǝn, -,blēn\ city E Poland SE of Warsaw *pop* 349,672

Lu·bum·ba·shi \,lü-büm-'bä-shē\ *or formerly* **Elis·a·beth·ville** \i-'li-zǝ-bǝth-,vil\ city SE Democratic Republic of the Congo in SE Shaba *pop* 739,082

Lucania — see BASILICATA

Lu·ca·nia, Mount \lü-'kä-nē-ǝ, -nyǝ\ mountain 17,147 *ft* (5226 *m*) Canada in SW Yukon Territory in St. Elias Range N of Mt. Logan

Luc·ca \'lü-kǝ\ commune *central* Italy in Tuscany NW of Florence *pop* 86,188

Lu·cerne \lü-'sǝrn\ *or German* **Lu·zern** \lüt-'sern\ **1** canton *central* Switzerland *area* 577 *sq mi* (1494 *sq km*), *pop* 316,210 **2** commune, its ✳, on Lake of Lucerne *pop* 59,932

Lucerne, Lake of *or German* **Vier·wald·stät·ter See** \fir-'vält-,shte-tǝr-,zā\ lake 24 *mi* (39 *km*) long *central* Switzerland *area* 44 *sq mi* (114 *sq km*)

Luchow — see HEFEI

Luck·now \'lǝk-,naú\ city N India ESE of Delhi ✳ of Uttar Pradesh *pop* 1,619,115

Lüda — see DALIAN

Lü·de·ritz \'lü-dǝ-rits, 'lȫ-\ town & port SW Namibia *pop* 6000

Lu·dhi·a·na \lü-dē-'ä-nǝ\ city NW India in Punjab SE of Amritsar *pop* 1,042,740

Lud·wigs·burg \'lüd-vigz-,búrg, 'lüt-viks-,búrk\ city SW Germany in Baden-Württemberg N of Stuttgart *pop* 83,913

Lud·wigs·ha·fen am Rhein \,lüd-vigz-'hä-f^ǝn-äm-'rīn, ,lüt-viks-\ city SW Germany on the Rhine opposite Mannheim *pop* 165,368

Luf·kin \'lǝf-kǝn\ city E Tex. NNE of Houston *pop* 30,206

Lu·ga·no \lü-'gä-(,)nō\ commune S Switzerland in Ticino canton on Lake Lugano *pop* 26,530

Lugano, Lake lake on border between Switzerland & Italy E of Lake Maggiore *area* 19 *sq mi* (49 *sq km*)

Lu·gansk \lü-'gän(t)sk\ *or* **Lu·hansk** \-'hän(t)sk\ *or alternately since 1935* **Vo·ro·shi·lov·grad** \,vór-ǝ-'shē-lǝf-,grad, ,vär-, -lǝv-, -,gräd\ city E Ukraine in Donets Basin *pop* 504,000

Lu·go \'lü-(,)gō\ **1** province NW Spain in NE Galicia on Bay of Biscay *area* 3785 *sq mi* (9803 *sq km*), *pop* 384,365 **2** commune, its ✳ *pop* 82,658

Luichow — see LEIZHOU

Luik — see LIÈGE

Lu·lea \'lü-lä-,ō\ city & port N Sweden near head of Gulf of Bothnia *pop* 68,924

Lu·le·bur·gaz \,lü-lǝ-búr-'gäz, ,lȫ-\ city *central* Turkey in Europe

Luluabourg — see KANANGA

Lund \'lünd, 'lǝnd\ city SW Sweden NE of Malmö *pop* 92,027

Lun·dy Island \'lǝn-dē\ island SW England at mouth of Bristol Channel off coast of Devon *area* 2 *sq mi* (5.2 *sq km*)

Lü·ne·burg \'lü-nǝ-,búrg, 'lȫ-nǝ-,búrk\ city N Germany SE of Hamburg & NE of **Lüneburg Heath** *or German* **Lü·ne·bur·ger Hei·de** \-,búr-gǝr-,hī-dǝ\ (tract of moorland *about* 55 *mi or* 88 *km* long) *pop* 62,944

Lü·nen \'lü-nǝn, 'lȫ-\ city W Germany S of Münster *pop* 88,443

Lu·nen·burg \'lü-nǝn-,bǝrg\ town Canada in S Nova Scotia *pop* 25,720

Lu·né·ville \'lü-nǝ-,vil, lȫ-ne-'vēl\ city NE France on the Meurthe SE of Nancy *pop* 22,393

Lungki — see ZHANGZHOU

Luo·yang \lu̇-'wō-'yäŋ\ *or* **Lo·yang** \'lō-'yäŋ\ city E China in N Henan in the Huang basin *pop* 759,752

Lu·ray Caverns \'lü-,rā, lü-'\ caverns N Va. in Blue Ridge Mountains

Lu·ri·stan \'lúr-ǝ-,stan, -,stän\ region W Iran; chief town Burujird

Lu·sa·ka \lü-'sä-kä\ city ✳ of Zambia *pop* 982,362

Lu·sa·tia \lü-'sā-sh(ē-)ǝ\ *or German* **Lau·sitz** \'laú-(,)zits\ region E Germany NW of Silesia E of the Elbe

Lü·shun \'lü-'shún, 'lȫ-\ *or* **Port Ar·thur** \'är-thǝr\ city & port NE China in S Liaoning at tip of Liaodong Peninsula *pop* 200,000

Lusitania — see PORTUGAL — **Lu·si·ta·ni·an** \,lü-sǝ-'tā-nē-ǝn, -nyǝn\ *adjective or noun*

Lu·ta — see DALIAN

Lutetia — see PARIS

Lu·ton \'lü-t^ǝn\ borough SE *central* England in SE Bedfordshire *pop* 167,300

Lüt·zen \'lüt-sǝn, 'lȫt-\ town E Germany in Saxony SW of Leipzig

Lux·em·bourg *or* **Lux·em·burg** \'lǝk-sǝm-,bǝrg, 'lúk-sǝm-,búrk\ **1** province SE Belgium ✳ Arlon *area* 1706 *sq mi* (4418 *sq km*), *pop* 232,813 **2** country W Europe between Belgium, France, & Germany; a grand duchy *area* 999 *sq mi* (2597 *sq km*), *pop* 392,000 **3** city, its ✳ *pop* 75,377 — **Lux·em·bourg·er** *or* **Lux·em·burg·er** \-,bǝr-gǝr, -,búr-\ *noun* — **Lux·em·bourg·i·an** *or* **Lux·em·burg·i·an** \,lǝk-sǝm-'bǝr-gē-ǝn, -,búr-\ *adjective*

Lux·or \'lǝk-,sór, 'lúk-\ city S Egypt on the Nile on S part of site of ancient Thebes *pop* 142,000

Lu·zon \lü-'zän\ island N Philippines, chief island of the group *area* 41,765 *sq mi* (108,171 *sq km*), *pop* 23,900,796

Lviv \lǝ-'vēf, -'vēv\ *or* **Lvov** \lǝ-'vóf, -'vòv\ *or Polish* **Lwów** \lǝ-'vüf, -'vüv\ *or German* **Lem·berg** \'lem-,bǝrg, -,berk\ city W Ukraine *pop* 802,000

Lyallpur — see FAISALABAD

Ly·ca·bet·tus *or Greek* **Ly·ka·bet·tos** \,li-kǝ-'be-tǝs, ,lī-\ mountain 909 *ft* (277 *m*) in NE part of Athens, Greece

Ly·ca·o·nia \,li-kā-'ō-nē-ǝ, ,lī-, -nyǝ\ ancient region & Roman province SE *central* Asia Minor N of Cilicia

Ly·cia \'li-sh(ē-)ǝ\ ancient region & Roman province SW Asia Minor on coast SE of Caria

Lyd·ia \'li-dē-ǝ\ ancient country W Asia Minor bordering on the Aegean ✳ Sardis

Lyn·brook \'lin-,brúk\ village SE N.Y. on Long Is. *pop* 19,208

Lynch·burg \'linch-,bǝrg\ city S *central* Va. on James River *pop* 66,049

Lynn \'lin\ **1** city NE Mass. NE of Boston *pop* 81,245 **2** *or* **Lynn Regis** — see KING'S LYNN

Lynn Canal narrow inlet of the Pacific 80 *mi* (129 *km*) long SE Alaska extending N from Juneau

Lynn·wood \'lin-,wúd\ city W Wash. N of Seattle *pop* 28,695

Lyn·wood \'lin-,wúd\ city SW Calif. S of Los Angeles *pop* 61,945

Ly·on·nais *or* **Ly·o·nais** \,lē-ǝ-'nā\ former province *central* France NE of Auvergne & W of the Saône & the Rhône ✳ Lyon

Lyon \'lyōⁿ\ *or* **Ly·ons** \lē-'ōⁿ, 'lī-ǝnz\ *or ancient* **Lug·du·num** \,lúg-'dü-nǝm, ,lǝg-\ city SE *central* France at confluence of the Saône & the Rhône *pop* 422,444

Lys \'lēs\ *or in Belgium* **Leie** \'lā-ǝ, 'lī-ǝ\ river 120 *mi* (193 *km*) France & Belgium flowing NE into the Schelde

Lyt·tel·ton \'li-t^ǝl-tǝn\ borough New Zealand on South Is.; port for Christchurch, on **Port Lyttelton** (inlet) *pop* 3190

Maarianhamina — see MARIEHAMN

Maas — see MEUSE

Maas·tricht *or* **Maes·tricht** \'mä-,strikt, -,strikt; mä-'\ commune SE Netherlands on the Meuse ✳ of Limburg *pop* 118,152

Ma·cao *or* **Ma·cau** \mǝ-'kaú\ **1** peninsula SE China in Guangdong in Xi delta W of Hong Kong **2** Portuguese overseas territory comprising peninsula on SE Macao Is. & adjacent islands *area* 6 *sq mi* (16 *sq km*), *pop* 488,000 **3** city & port, its ✳ *pop* 161,252 — **Mac·a·nese** \,mä-kǝ-'nēz, -'nēs\ *noun*

Ma·ca·pá \,mä-kǝ-'pä\ city & port N Brazil ✳ of Amapá *pop* 179,609

Macassar — see MAKASSAR — **Ma·cas·sar·ese** \mǝ-,ka-sǝ-'rēz, -'rēs\ *noun*

Mac·cles·field \'ma-kǝlz-,fēld\ borough W England in E Cheshire SSE of Manchester *pop* 147,000

Mac·don·nell Ranges \mǝk-'dä-n^ǝl\ series of mountain ridges *central* Australia in S Northern Territory; highest point Mt. Ziel 5023 *ft* (1531 *m*)

Mac·e·do·nia \,ma-sǝ-'dō-nē-ǝ, -nyǝ\ **1** region S Europe in Balkan Peninsula in NE Greece, the former Yugoslav section of Macedonia, & SW Bulgaria including territory of ancient kingdom of Macedonia (*or* **Mac·e·don** \'ma-sǝ-dǝn, -,dän\ ✳ Pella) **2** country S *central* Balkan Peninsula; a federated republic of Yugoslavia 1946–92 ✳ Skopje *area* 9928 *sq mi* (25,714 *sq km*), *pop* 2,063,000

Ma·ceió \,ma-sā-'ō\ city NE Brazil ✳ of Alagoas *pop* 628,209

Mac·gil·li·cud·dy's Reeks \mǝ-'gi-lǝ-,kǝ-dēz-'rēks\ mountain range SW Ireland in County Kerry — see CARRANTUOHILL

Ma·ches·ney Park \mǝ-'chez-nē\ village N Ill. N of Rockford *pop* 19,033

Ma·chi·da \'mä-'chē-dä, ,mä-chē-,dä\ city Japan on Honshu *pop* 355,843

Ma·chi·li·pat·nam \,mǝ-chǝ-lǝ-'pǝt-nǝm\ *or* **Ban·dar** \'bǝn-dǝr\ city & port SE India in E Andhra Pradesh SW of Kakinada *pop* 159,007

Ma·chu Pic·chu \,mä-(,)chü-'pē-(,)chü, -'pēk-\ site SE Peru of ancient Inca city on a mountain NW of Cuzco

Macías Nguema Biyogo — see BIOKO

Mac·ken·zie \mǝ-'ken-zē\ **1** river 1120 *mi* (1802 *km*) NW Canada flowing from Great Slave Lake NW into Beaufort Sea; sometimes considered to include the Finlay, Peace, & Slave rivers (total length 2635 *mi or* 4216 *km*) **2** former district Canada in W Northwest Territories in basin of Mackenzie River

Mackenzie Mountains mountain range NW Canada in the Rockies in Yukon Territory & W Northwest Territories

Mack·i·nac \'ma-kə-ˌnȯ, -ˌnak\ *or formerly* **Mich·i·li·mack·i·nac** \ˌmi-shə-lē-\ island N Mich. in Straits of Mackinac

Mackinac, Straits of channel N Mich. connecting Lake Huron & Lake Michigan; 4 *mi* (6.4 *km*) wide at narrowest point

Ma·comb \mə-'kōm\ city W Ill. SW of Peoria *pop* 19,952

Ma·con \'mā-kən\ city *central* Ga. on the Ocmulgee *pop* 106,612

Mâ·con \mä-'kōⁿ\ city E *central* France *pop* 38,508

Mac·quar·ie \mə-'kwär-ē\ river 590 *mi* (949 *km*) SE Australia in E *central* New South Wales flowing NNW to Darling River

Mac·tan \mäk-'tän\ island S *central* Philippines off E coast of Cebu

Mad·a·gas·car \ˌma-də-'gas-kər, -kär\ island W Indian Ocean off SE Africa; formerly a French territory; became (1958) a republic of the French Community as the **Mal·a·gasy Republic** \ˌma-lə-'ga-sē\ *or French* **Ré·pu·blique Mal·gache** \rä-pū̇-'blēk-mäl-'gäsh\ *or since 1975* **Democratic Republic of Madagascar** ✳ Antananarivo *area* 226,657 *sq mi* (589,308 *sq km*), *pop* 13,255,000 — **Mad·a·gas·can** \ˌma-də-'gas-kən\ *adjective or noun*

Ma·dei·ra \mə-'dir-ə, -'der-ə\ **1** river 2013 *mi* (3239 *km*) W Brazil formed at Bolivian border by confluence of the Mamoré & the Beni & flowing NE to the Amazon **2** islands in N Atlantic N of the Canaries belonging to Portugal ✳ Funchal *area* 308 *sq mi* (798 *sq km*), *pop* 253,000 **3** island, chief of group *area* 285 *sq mi* (741 *sq km*) — **Ma·dei·ran** \-'dir-ən, -'der-\ *adjective or noun*

Ma·de·ra \mə-'der-ə\ city S *central* Calif. NW of Fresno *pop* 29,281

Ma·dhya Bha·rat \ˌmä-dyə-'bär-ət\ former state *central* India; a union of 20 states including Gwalior, Indore, & Malwa formed 1948; became part of Madhya Pradesh 1956

Madhya Pra·desh \prə-'desh, -'dāsh\ state *central* India ✳ Bhopal *area* 171,220 *sq mi* (443,460 *sq km*), *pop* 66,181,170 — see CENTRAL PROVINCES AND BERAR, MADHYA BHARAT

Ma·di·nat ash Sha'b \ˌmä-ˌdē-ˌnə-tash-'shab\ city S Yemen; formerly a national ✳ of People's Democratic Republic of Yemen & (as **Al It·ti·had** \al-ˌi-tə-'had\) ✳ of Federation of South Arabia

Mad·i·son \'ma-də-sən\ **1** river 180 *mi* (290 *km*) SW Mont. — see THREE FORKS **2** city S Wis., its ✳ *pop* 191,262

Madison Heights city SE Mich. N of Detroit *pop* 32,196

Ma·dras \mə-'dras, -'dräs\ **1** — see TAMIL NADU **2** city & port S India ✳ of Tamil Nadu *pop* 3,841,396 — **Ma·drasi** \-'dra-sē, -'drä-\ *noun*

Ma·dre, La·gu·na \lə-ˌgü-nə-'mä-drä\ inlet of Gulf of Mexico S Tex. between Padre Is. & mainland

Ma·dre de Dios \ˌmä-drä-(ˌ)dā-dē-'ōs\ river *about* 700 *mi* (1126 *km*) rising in SE Peru & flowing E into the Beni in Brazil

Ma·drid \mə-'drid\ **1** province *central* Spain in NW New Castile *area* 3087 *sq mi* (7995 *sq km*), *pop* 4,947,555 **2** city, its ✳ & ✳ of Spain *pop* 2,909,792 — **Mad·ri·le·nian** \ˌma-drə-'lē-nē-ən, -dri-, -nyən\ *adjective or noun* — **Ma·dri·le·ño** \ˌmä-drə-'lā-(ˌ)nyō, -drē-\ *noun*

Ma·du·ra *or Dutch* **Ma·doe·ra** \mə-'du̇r-ə\ island Indonesia off coast of NE Java *area* (with adjacent islands) 2113 *sq mi* (5494 *sq km*), *pop* 1,858,183 — **Mad·u·rese** \ˌma-də-'rēz, ˌma-jə-, -'rēs\ *adjective or noun*

Ma·du·rai \ˌmä-də-'rī\ city S India in Tamil Nadu *pop* 940,989

Maeander — see MENDERES

Ma·fia \'ma-fē-ə, 'ma-\ island Tanzania in Indian Ocean S of Zanzibar *area* 170 *sq mi* (442 *sq km*), *pop* 16,748

Maf·i·keng \'ma-fə-kiŋ\ town N Republic of South Africa in North West province *pop* 6515

Ma·ga·dan \ˌmä-gə-'dan, -'dän\ city & port E Russia in Asia on N shore of Sea of Okhotsk *pop* 152,000

Ma·ga·dha \'mə-gə-də, 'mä-\ ancient kingdom, India including Bihar S of the Ganges

Magallanes — see PUNTA ARENAS

Mag·da·la \'mag-də-lə\ ancient city N Palestine on W shore of Sea of Galilee N of Tiberias

Mag·da·le·na \ˌmag-də-'lā-nə, -'lē-\ river 956 *mi* (1538 *km*) Colombia flowing N into the Caribbean

Mag·da·len Islands \'mag-də-lən\ *or French* **Îles de la Ma·de·leine** \ˌēl-də-lä-mád-'len, -ˌmä-də-'len\ islands Canada in Quebec in Gulf of St. Lawrence between Newfoundland & Prince Edward Island *area* 102 *sq mi* (265 *sq km*), *pop* 13,991

Mag·de·burg \'mäg-də-ˌbu̇rk, 'mag-də-ˌbərg\ city *central* Germany on the Elbe WSW of Berlin *pop* 275,238

Ma·gel·lan, Strait of \mə-'je-lən, *chiefly British* -'ge-\ strait 350 *mi* (563 *km*) long at S end of S. America between mainland & Tierra del Fuego (Archipelago)

Magerøy — see NORTH CAPE

Mag·gio·re, Lake \mä-'jȯr-ā, -'jȯr-\ lake 40 *mi* (64 *km*) long N Italy & S Switzerland traversed by Ticino River

Magh·er·a·felt \'mär-ə-ˌfelt, 'ma-kə-rə-ˌfelt\ district *central* Northern Ireland, established 1974 *area* 221 *sq mi* (575 *sq km*), *pop* 35,874

Ma·ghreb *or* **Ma·ghrib** \'mä-grəb\ **1** NW Africa, at time of the Moorish occupation, Spain; now considered as including Morocco, Algeria, Tunisia, & sometimes Libya **2** *or* **El Ma·ghreb al Aq·sa** \el-'mä-grəb-äl-'äk-sä\ MOROCCO — **Ma·ghre·bi** *or* **Ma·ghri·bi** \'mä-grə-bē\ *adjective or noun* — **Ma·ghreb·i·an** \mə-'grē-bē-ən\ *or* **Ma·ghrib·i·an** \-'gri\ *adjective or noun*

Mag·na Grae·cia \ˌmag-nə-'grē-shə\ the ancient Greek colonies in S Italian Peninsula including Tarentum, Sybaris, Crotona, Heraclea, & Neapolis

Mag·ne·sia \mag-'nē-shə, -zhə\ — see MANISA

Mag·ni·to·gorsk \mag-'nē-tə-ˌgȯrsk\ city W Russia in Asia on Ural River *pop* 441,000

Magyarország — see HUNGARY

Ma·ha·jan·ga \ˌmə-hə-'jəŋ-gə\ city & port NW Madagascar *pop* 121,967

Mahalla El Kubra, El \mə-'hä-nə-dē\ — see EL MAHALLA EL KUBRA

Ma·ha·na·di \mə-'hä-nə-dē\ river *about* 560 *mi* (900 *km*) E India flowing into Bay of Bengal in Orissa through several mouths

Ma·ha·rash·tra \ˌmä-hə-'räsh-trə\ **1** region W *central* India S of the Narbada; the original home of the Marathas **2** state W India bordering on Arabian Sea formed 1960 from SE part of former Bombay state ✳ Bombay *area* 118,637 *sq mi* (307,270 *sq km*), *pop* 78,937,187

Ma·hé \mä-'hā\ **1** island in Indian Ocean, chief of the Seychelles group *pop* 61,183 **2** *or formerly* **May·ya·li** \mī-'yä-lē\ town SW India in N Kerala; a settlement of French India until 1954 *pop* 10,437

Ma·hil·yow *or* **Mo·gi·lev** \mə-gil-'yȯf\ city E Belarus on the Dnieper *pop* 363,000

Ma·hón \mə-'hȯn, mä-'ōn\ *or* **Port Ma·hon** \mə-'hȯn\ city & port Spain on Minorca Is. *pop* 21,564

Ma·hone Bay \mə-'hōn\ inlet of the Atlantic E Canada in S Nova Scotia

Maid·en·head \'mā-dᵊn-ˌhed\ borough S England in Berkshire on Thames River W of London *pop* 49,038

Maid·stone \'mād-stən, -ˌstōn\ borough SE England ✳ of Kent on the Medway ESE of London *pop* 133,200

Main \mīn, 'mān\ river 325 *mi* (523 *km*) S *central* Germany rising in N Bavaria in the Fichtelgebirge & flowing W into the Rhine

Mai–Ndom·be, Lac \ˌlak-ˌmīn-'dȯm-bā\ *or formerly* **Lake Leo·pold II** \'lē-ə-ˌpōld\ lake W Democratic Republic of the Congo

Maine \'mān\ **1** state NE U.S. ✳ Augusta *area* 33,265 *sq mi* (86,156 *sq km*), *pop* 1,227,928 **2** *or* **Le Maine** \lə-'men\ region & former province NW France S of Normandy ✳ Le Mans **3** — see MAYENNE — **Main·er** \'mā-nər\ *noun*

Main·land \-ˌland, -lənd\ **1** HONSHU **2** island N Scotland, largest of the Orkneys **3** island N Scotland, largest of the Shetlands

Mainz \'mīnts\ *or French* **Ma·yence** \mä-'yäⁿs\ city SW *central* Germany on the Rhine ✳ of Rhineland-Palatinate *pop* 182,867

Mait·land \'māt-lənd\ city SE Australia in E New South Wales *pop* 46,909

Ma·jor·ca \mä-'jȯr-kə, mə-, -'yȯr-\ *or Spanish* **Ma·llor·ca** \mä-'yȯr-kä\ island Spain, largest of the Balearic Islands; chief city Palma *area* 1405 *sq mi* (3653 *sq km*) — **Ma·jor·can** \-'jȯr-kən, -'yȯr-\ *adjective or noun*

Ma·ju·ro \mä-'ju̇r-(ˌ)ō\ island (atoll) W Pacific in SE Marshall Islands; contains ✳ of the group

Ma·ka·lu \'mə-kə-ˌlü\ mountain 27,824 *ft* (8481 *m*) in the Himalayas in NE Nepal SE of Mt. Everest; 5th highest in world

Ma·kas·sar \mə-'ka-sər\ **1** *or* **Ma·cas·sar** strait Indonesia between E Borneo & W Sulawesi **2** — see UJUNG PANDANG — **Ma·kas·sa·rese** \ˌmə-ˌka-sə-'rēz, -'rēs\ *noun*

Ma·ke·yev·ka \mə-'kā-yəf-kə\ city E Ukraine in Donets Basin NE of Donetsk *pop* 424,000

Ma·kga·di·kga·di Pans \ˌmä-ˌkä-dē-'kä-dē\ large salt basin NE Botswana

Ma·khach·ka·la \ˌmä-ˌkäch-kə-'lä\ *or formerly* **Pe·trovsk** \pə-'trȯfsk\ city SE Russia in Europe on the Caspian ✳ of Dagestan *pop* 339,000

Mal·a·bar Coast \'ma-lə-ˌbär\ region SW India on Arabian Sea in Karnataka & Kerala states

Ma·la·bo \mä-'lä-(ˌ)bō\ *or formerly* **San·ta Is·a·bel** \ˌsan-tə-'i-zə-ˌbel\ city ✳ of Equatorial Guinea on Bioko Is. *pop* 37,237

Malacca — see MELAKA — **Ma·lac·can** \-kən\ *adjective*

Ma·lac·ca, Strait of \mə-'la-kə, -'lä-\ channel 500 *mi* (805 *km*) long between S Malay Peninsula & island of Sumatra

Má·la·ga \'ma-lə-gə, 'mä-lä-gä\ **1** province S Spain in Andalusia *area* 2809 *sq mi* (7275 *sq km*), *pop* 1,160,843 **2** city & port, its ✳, NE of Gibraltar *pop* 512,136

Malagasy Republic — see MADAGASCAR

Ma·lai·ta \mə-'lā-tə\ island SW Pacific in the SE Solomons NE of Guadalcanal

Ma·lang \mə-'läŋ\ city Indonesia in E Java S of Surabaja *pop* 695,618

Mä·lar·en \ˌmä-ˌlär-ən\ lake SE Sweden extending from Baltic Sea 70 *mi* (113 *km*) inland

Ma·la·tya \ˌmä-lä-ˌtyä\ *or ancient* **Mel·i·te·ne** \ˌme-lə-'tē-nē\ city E Turkey NE of Gaziantep *pop* 281,776

Ma·la·wi \mə-'lä-wē\ *or formerly* **Ny·asa·land** \nī-'a-sə-ˌland, nē-\ country SE Africa bordering on Lake Malawi; formerly a Brit. protectorate; independent member of the Commonwealth of Nations since 1964; a republic since 1966 ✳ Lilongwe *area* 45,747 *sq mi* (118,485 *sq km*), *pop* 10,581,000 — **Ma·la·wi·an** \-ən\ *adjective or noun*

Malawi, Lake *or* **Lake Ny·asa** \nī-'a-sə, nē-\ lake SE Africa in Great Rift Valley in Malawi, Mozambique, & Tanzania

Ma·laya \mə-'lā-ə, ma-\ **1** MALAY PENINSULA **2** BRITISH MALAYA **3** *or* **Federation of Malaya** former country SE Asia; a Brit. dominion 1957–63, since 1963 a territory (now called **Peninsular Malaysia**) of Malaysia ✳ Kuala Lumpur *area* 50,690 *sq mi* (131,794 *sq km*)

Ma·lay Archipelago \mə-'lā, 'mā-(ˌ)lā\ archipelago SE Asia including Sumatra, Java, Borneo, Sulawesi, Moluccas, & Timor; usually considered as including also the Philippines & sometimes New Guinea

Malay Peninsula peninsula 700 *mi* (1126 *km*) long SE Asia divided between Thailand & Malaysia

Ma·lay·sia \mə-'lā-zh(ē-)ə, -sh(ē-)ə\ **1** MALAY ARCHIPELAGO **2** *or* **Federation of Malaysia** country SE Asia, a union of Malaya, Sabah (N. Borneo), Sarawak, & (until 1965) Singapore; a limited constitutional monarchy in the Commonwealth of Nations ✳ Kuala Lumpur *area* 128,727 *sq mi* (333,403 *sq km*), *pop* 19,077,000 — **Ma·lay·sian** \mə-'lā-zhən, -shən\ *adjective or noun*

Malay Sea sea SE Asia surrounding the Malay Archipelago

Mal·den \'mȯl-dən\ **1** city E Mass. N of Boston *pop* 53,884 **2** island *central* Pacific, one of the Line Islands

\ə\ abut \ᵊ\ kitten \ər\ further \a\ ash \ā\ ace
\ä\ mop, mar \au̇\ out \ch\ chin \e\ bet \ē\ easy
\g\ go \i\ hit \ī\ ice \j\ job \ŋ\ sing \ō\ go
\ȯ\ law \ȯi\ boy \th\ thin \t͟h\ the \ü\ loot \u̇\ foot
\y\ yet \zh\ vision *see also* Guide to Pronunciation

Mal·dives \'mȯl-ˌdēvz, -ˌdīvz- *also* 'mal-, -divz\ islands in Indian Ocean S of the Laccadives; a sultanate under Brit. protection until 1965; now an independent member of the Commonwealth of Nations ✳ Male *area* 115 *sq mi* (299 *sq km*), *pop* 143,046 — **Mal·div·i·an** \mȯl-'di-vē-ən, mal-\ *adjective or noun*

Ma·le \'mä-lē\ island (atoll), chief of the Maldives; contains the nation's ✳

Ma·lea, Cape \mä-'lē-ä\ cape S Greece at extremity of E peninsula of the Peloponnese

Ma·le·bo, Pool *or* **Malebo Pool** \mä-'lā-ˌbō\ *or* **Stanley Pool** expansion of Congo River *about* 20 *mi* (32 *km*) long 300 *mi* (483 *km*) above its mouth between Republic of the Congo & Democratic Republic of the Congo

Mal·e·ku·la *or* **Mal·a·ku·la** \ˌma-lə-'kü-lə\ island SW Pacific in Vanuatu *area* 781 *sq mi* (2023 *sq km*), *pop* 19,289

Malgache, République — see MADAGASCAR

Mal·heur Lake \mal-'hu̇r\ lake SE Oreg. in Harney Basin

Ma·li \'mä-lē, 'ma-\ **1** federation 1959–60 of Senegal & Sudanese Republic **2** *or formerly* **Sudanese Republic** country W Africa in W Sahara & Sudan regions; a republic; before 1958 constituted **French Sudan** (a territory of France); ✳ Bamako *area* 478,652 *sq mi* (1,239,709 *sq mi*), *pop* 8,646,000 — **Ma·li·an** \-lē-ən\ *adjective or noun*

Malines — see MECHLIN

Mal·in Head \'ma-lən\ cape Ireland (republic) in county Donegal; northernmost tip of Ireland

Mal·mé·dy \ˌmal-mə-'dē\ commune E Belgium SE of Liège; formerly in Germany, transferred (with Eupen) to Belgium 1919 *pop* 10,291

Malmö \'mal-ˌmē, -(ˌ)mō\ city & port SW Sweden on Øresund opposite Copenhagen, Denmark *pop* 232,908

Mal·ta \'mȯl-tə\ *or ancient* **Mel·i·ta** \'me-lə-tə, mə-'lē-tə\ **1** *or* **Mal·tese Islands** \mȯl-'tēz, -'tēs\ group of islands in the Mediterranean S of Sicily; a dominion of the Commonwealth of Nations since 1964 ✳ Valletta *area* 122 *sq mi* (317 *sq mi*), *pop* 362,000 **2** island, chief of the group *area* 95 *sq mi* (247 *sq km*)

Maluku — see MOLUCCAS

Mal·vern Hills \'mȯ(l)-vərn\ hills W England in Hereford and Worcester

Malvinas, Islas — see FALKLAND ISLANDS

Mam·be·ra·mo \ˌmäm-bə-'rä-(ˌ)mō\ river 500 *mi* (805 *km*) W. New Guinea flowing NW into the Pacific

Mam·moth Cave \'ma-məth\ limestone caverns SW central Kentucky in **Mammoth Cave National Park**

Ma·mo·ré \ˌmä-mō-'rā\ river 1200 *mi* (1931 *km*) Bolivia flowing N to unite with the Beni on Brazilian border forming Madeira River

Man, Isle of \'man\ *or ancient* **Mo·na·pia** \mō-'nā-pē-ə\ *or* **Mo·na** \'mō-nə\ island British Isles in Irish Sea; a possession of the Brit. Crown; has own legislature & laws ✳ Douglas *area* 221 *sq mi* (575 *sq km*), *pop* 60,496 — **Manx·man** \'maŋks-mən\ *noun*

Ma·na·do *or* **Me·na·do** \mə-'nä-(ˌ)dō\ city & port Indonesia on NE Sulawesi Is. on Celebes Sea *pop* 318,796

Ma·na·gua \mä-'nä-gwä\ city ✳ of Nicaragua on Lake Managua *pop* 552,900

Managua, Lake lake 38 *mi* (61 *km*) long W Nicaragua draining S to Lake Nicaragua

Ma·na·ma \mə-'na-mə\ city ✳ of Bahrain *pop* 136,999

Ma·nas·sas \mə-'na-səs\ city NE Va. *pop* 27,957

Ma·naus \mə-'nau̇s\ city W Brazil ✳ of Amazonas on Negro River 12 *mi* (19 *km*) from its junction with the Amazon *pop* 1,010,558

Mancha, La — see LA MANCHA

Manche, La — see ENGLISH CHANNEL

Man·ches·ter \'man-ˌches-tər, -chəs-tər\ **1** town *central* Conn. E of Hartford *pop* 51,618 **2** city S N.H. on the Merrimack *pop* 99,567 **3** city NW England ENE of Liverpool *pop* 406,900 — SEE GREATER MANCHESTER — **Man·cu·ni·an** \man-'kyü-nē-ən, -nyən\ *adjective or noun*

Man·chu·kuo \ˌman-'chü-'kwō, ˌman-'chü-\ former country (1931–45) E Asia in Manchuria & E Inner Mongolia ✳ Changchun

Man·chu·ria \man-'chu̇r-ē-ə\ region NE China S of the Amur including Heilongjiang, Jilin, & Lia-

oning provinces & part of Inner Mongolia — **Man·chu·ri·an** \-ē-ən\ *adjective or noun*

Man·da·lay \ˌman-də-'lā\ city central Myanmar *pop* 453,000

Man·ga·ia \män-'gī-ə\ island S Pacific in SE Cook Islands; completely encircled by reef *area* 20 *sq mi* (52 *sq km*)

Man·ga·lore \'maŋ-gə-ˌlȯr, -ˌlȯr\ city S India in Karnataka on Malabar Coast W of Bangalore *pop* 272,819

Man·ga·re·va \ˌmäŋ-gä-'rā-vä, ˌmäŋ-ä-\ island S Pacific, chief of the Gambier Islands *area* 7 *sq mi* (18 *sq km*)

Man·hat·tan \man-'ha-tᵊn, mən-\ **1** city NE central Kans. on Kansas River *pop* 37,712 **2** island 13 *mi* (21 *km*) long SE N.Y. on New York Bay **3** borough of New York City comprising Manhattan Is., several small adjacent islands, & a small area (Marble Hill) on mainland *pop* 1,487,536 — **Man·hat·tan·ite** \-ˌīt\ *noun*

Manhattan Beach city SW Calif. SW of Los Angeles *pop* 32,063

Ma·ni·hi·ki \ˌma-nē-'hē-kē\ island, chief of the Northern Cook Islands; an atoll *pop* 408

Manihiki Islands — see NORTHERN COOK ISLANDS

Ma·ni·la \mə-'ni-lə\ city & port ✳ of the Philippines on W coast of Luzon on **Manila Bay** (inlet of S. China Sea) *pop* 1,587,000

Man·i·pur \ˌma-nə-'pu̇r, mə-\ **1** river 210 *mi* (338 *km*) NE India & W Myanmar flowing into the Chindwin **2** state NE India between Assam & Myanmar ✳ Imphal *area* 8628 *sq mi* (22,433 *sq km*)

Ma·ni·sa *or* **Ma·nis·sa** \ˌmä-nē-'sä\ *or ancient* **Mag·ne·sia** \mag-'nē-shə, -zhə\ city W Turkey NE of Izmir *pop* 158,928

Man·i·to·ba \ˌma-nə-'tō-bə\ province S central Canada ✳ Winnipeg *area* 211,468 *sq mi* (547,703 *sq km*), *pop* 1,091,942 — **Man·i·to·ban** \-bən\ *adjective or noun*

Manitoba, Lake lake over 120 *mi* (193 *km*) long Canada in S Manitoba *area* 1817 *sq mi* (4724 *sq km*)

Man·i·tou·lin Island \ˌma-nə-'tü-lən\ island 80 *mi* (129 *km*) long Canada in Ontario in Lake Huron *area* 1068 *sq mi* (2777 *sq km*)

Man·i·to·woc \'ma-nə-tə-ˌwäk\ city E Wis. *pop* 32,520

Ma·ni·za·les \ˌma-nə-'zä-ləs, ˌmä-nē-'sä-läs\ city W central Colombia in Cauca valley *pop* 327,100

Man·ka·to \man-'kā-(ˌ)tō\ city S Minn. *pop* 31,477

Man·nar, Gulf of \mə-'när\ inlet of Indian Ocean between Sri Lanka & S tip of India S of Palk Strait

Mann·heim \'man-ˌhīm, 'män-\ city SW Germany at confluence of the Rhine & the Neckar *pop* 314,685

Mans·field \'manz-ˌfēld, 'man(t)s-\ **1** town central Conn. *pop* 21,103 **2** city N central Ohio *pop* 50,627 **3** town N central England in Nottinghamshire N of Nottingham *pop* 98,800

Mansfield, Mount mountain 4393 *ft* (1339 *m*) N Vt.; highest in Green Mountains & in state

Mansûra, El *or* **Mansurah, Al** — see EL MANSURA

Man·te·ca \man-'tē-kə\ city central Calif. S of Stockton *pop* 40,773

Man·tua \'man-chə-wə, 'manch-wə, 'män-tü-ä\ *or* **Man·to·va** \'män-tō-vä\ commune N Italy in Lombardy WSW of Venice *pop* 52,948 — **Man·tu·an** \'man-chə-wən, 'manch-wən, 'man-tə-wən\ *adjective or noun*

Ma·nu·a Islands \'mä-ˌnü-ä\ islands SW Pacific in American Samoa E of Tutuila *area* 22 *sq mi* (57 *sq km*)

Ma·nus \'mä-nəs\ island SW Pacific in Admiralty Islands; largest of group *area* 600 *sq mi* (1560 *sq km*)

Man·za·la, Lake \man-'zä-lə\ *or ancient* **Ta·nis** \'tā-nəs\ lagoon N Egypt in Nile delta W of N entrance of Suez Canal

Man·za·nil·lo \ˌman-zə-'ni-lō, ˌmän-sä-'nē-yō\ **1** city & port E Cuba on the Caribbean *pop* 107,650 **2** city & port SW Mexico in Colima *pop* 92,168

Mao·ke Mountains \'mau̇-kä\ *or formerly* **Snow Mountains** \'snō\ mountains W. Irian, Indonesia — see PUNCAK JAYA

Maple Grove city SE central Minn. *pop* 38,736

Maple Heights city NE Ohio SE of Cleveland *pop* 27,089

Maple Ridge municipality Canada in SW British Columbia E of Vancouver *pop* 48,422

Ma·ple·wood \'mā-pəl-ˌwu̇d\ village SE Minn. *pop* 30,954

Ma·pu·to \mä-'pü-(ˌ)tō\ *or formerly* **Lou·ren·ço Mar·ques** \lō-'rän-sü-'mär-kish\ city & port ✳ of Mozambique on Delagoa Bay *pop* 755,300

Ma·quo·ke·ta \mə-'kō-kə-tə\ river 150 *mi* (241 *km*) E Iowa flowing SE into Mississippi River

Mar·a·cai·bo \ˌmar-ə-'kī-(ˌ)bō, ˌmär-ä-\ city NW Venezuela on channel between Lake Maracaibo & Gulf of Venezuela *pop* 1,207,513

Maracaibo, Lake the S extension of Gulf of Venezuela in NW Venezuela *area* over 5000 *sq mi* (12,950 *sq km*)

Maracanda — see SAMARQAND

Ma·ra·cay \ˌmär-ä-'kī\ city N Venezuela WSW of Caracas *pop* 354,428

Marais des Cygnes \ˌmer-də-'zēn, -'sēn\ river 150 *mi* (241 *km*) E Kans. & W Mo. flowing into the Osage

Ma·ra·nhão \ˌmär-ə-'nyau̇ⁿ\ state NE Brazil bordering on the Atlantic ✳ São Luis *area* 127,242 *sq mi* (329,557 *sq km*), *pop* 4,922,339

Ma·ra·ñón \ˌmär-ə-'nyōn\ river N Peru flowing from the Andes NNW & E to join the Ucayali forming the Amazon

Mar·a·thon \'mar-ə-ˌthän\ **1** plain E Greece in Attica NE of Athens on the Aegean **2** ancient town on the plain

Marble Canyon canyon of Colorado River N Ariz. just above the Grand Canyon, sometimes considered its upper portion

Mar·ble·head \'mär-bəl-ˌhed, ˌmär-bəl-'\ town E Mass. *pop* 19,971

Mar·burg \'mär-ˌbu̇rk, -ˌbərg\ city W central Germany in Hesse N of Frankfurt am Main *pop* 75,331

Marche \'märsh\ **1** region & former province central France NW of Auvergne **2** region central Italy on the Adriatic NW of Abruzzi ✳ Ancona *pop* 1,430,726

Mar·cus Island \'mär-kəs\ island W Pacific E of the Bonin Islands, belonging to Japan; occupied 1945–68 by U.S. *area* 1 *sq mi* (2.6 *sq km*)

Mar·cy, Mount \'mär-sē\ mountain 5344 *ft* (1629 *m*) NE N.Y.; highest in Adirondack Mountains & in state

Mar del Pla·ta \ˌmär-del-'plä-tä\ city & port E Argentina SSE of Buenos Aires *pop* 407,024

Mare Island \'mar, 'mer\ island W Calif. in San Pablo Bay

Ma·rem·ma \mä-'re-mä\ low-lying district W Italy on Tyrrhenian coast in SW Tuscany; formerly swampland

Ma·ren·go \mä-'reŋ-(ˌ)gō\ village NW Italy in SE Piedmont

Mar·e·o·tis \ˌmar-ē-'ō-təs\ *or Arabic* **Mar·yūt** \mər-'yüt\ lake N Egypt in Nile delta; Alexandria is situated between it & the Mediterranean

Ma·reth \'mär-əth, 'mar-\ town SE Tunisia SSE of Gabes

Mar·ga·ri·ta \ˌmär-gä-'rē-tä\ island N Venezuela in the Caribbean, chief of the **Nue·va Es·par·ta** \'nwä-vä-e-'spär-tä\ group; chief town & port Porlamar *area* 414 *sq mi* (1072 *sq km*)

Mar·gate \'mär-ˌgāt\ **1** city SE Fla. *pop* 42,985 **2** \-ˌgāt, -gət\ borough SE England in Kent on coast of Isle of Thanet *pop* 53,280

Mar·i·ana Islands \ˌmar-ē-'a-nə, -mar-ē-\ *or formerly* **La·drone Islands** \lə-'drōn\ islands W Pacific S of Bonin Islands; comprise commonwealth of Northern Mariana Islands & Guam

Ma·ri·a·nao \ˌmär-ē-ä-'nau̇\ city W Cuba, W suburb of Havana *pop* 133,671

Ma·ri·án·ské Láz·ně \'mär-ē-ˌän(t)-ske-'läz-ne\ *or German* **Ma·ri·en·bad** \mə-'rē-ən-ˌbad, -ˌbät; 'mar-ē-ən-, -ˌbät\ town W Czech Republic in NW Bohemia NE of Plzeň *pop* 15,378

Ma·ri·as \mə-'rī-əs, -əz\ river 210 *mi* (338 *km*) NW Mont. flowing SE to Missouri River

Marias Pass mountain pass 5215 *ft* (1590 *m*) NW Mont. in Lewis Range at SE corner of Glacier National Park

Ma·ri·bor \'mär-ē-ˌbȯr\ city NE Slovenia *pop* 153,053

Ma·rie Byrd Land \mə-ˌrē-'bərd\ region W Antarctica E of Ross Ice Shelf & Ross Sea

Ma·rie Ga·lante \mȧ-,rē-gȧ-'länt\ island E W. Indies in the Leewards; a dependency of Guadeloupe *area* 60 *sq mi* (156 *sq km*), *pop* 13,463

Ma·rie·hamn \mȯ-'rē-ȯ-,häm-ȯn\ *or* **Maa·rian·ha·mi·na** \'mär-yän-,hä-mȯ-,nä\ seaport SW Finland ✳ of Ahvenanmaa *pop* 10,067

Mar·i·et·ta \,mar-ē-'e-tȯ, ,mer-\ city NW Ga. NW of Atlanta *pop* 44,129

Ma·ri·na \mȯ-'rē-nȯ\ city W Calif. on Monterey Bay *pop* 26,436

Ma·rin·du·que \,mar-ȯn-'dü-(,)kā, ,mär-ēn-\ island Philippines in Sibuyan Sea S of Luzon; chief town Boac *area* 355 *sq mi* (923 *sq km*), *pop* 173,715

Mar·i·on \'mer-ē-ȯn, 'mar-\ **1** city N *central* Ind. *pop* 32,618 **2** city E Iowa NE of Cedar Rapids *pop* 20,403 **3** city *central* Ohio *pop* 34,075

Ma·ri El *or* **Ma·riy El** \'mä-rē-'el\ autonomous republic E *central* Russia in Europe ✳ Yoshkar-Ola *area* 8958 *sq mi* (23,201 *sq km*), *pop* 762,000

Maritime Alps section of the W Alps SE France & NW Italy extending to the Mediterranean; highest point Punta Argentera 10,817 *ft* (3297 *m*)

Maritime Provinces *or* **Maritimes** the Canadian provinces of New Brunswick, Nova Scotia, Prince Edward Island & sometimes thought to include Newfoundland — see ATLANTIC PROVINCES

Maritime Territory *or Russian* **Pri·mor·skiy Kray** *or* **Pri·mor·ski Krai** \prē-'mȯr-skē-'krī\ territory E Russia in Asia bordering on Sea of Japan ✳ Vladivostok *area* 64,054 *sq mi* (165,900 *sq km*), *pop* 2,309,000

Ma·ri·tsa \mȯ-'rēt-sȯ\ *or Greek* **Év·ros** \'ev-,rós\ *or Turkish* **Me·riç** \me-'rēch\ river *about* 300 *mi* (480 *km*) S Europe flowing from W Rhodope Mountains in S Bulgaria E & S through Thrace into the Aegean

Ma·ri·u·pol' \,mar-ē-'ü-,pȯl, -pȯl\ *or 1949–1989* **Zhda·nov** \zhȯ-'dä-nȯf\ city E Ukraine *pop* 417,000

Mark·ham \'mär-kȯm\ **1** town Canada in SE Ontario NE of Toronto *pop* 153,811 **2** river 200 *mi* (322 *km*) Papua New Guinea flowing S & SE into Solomon Sea

Markham, Mount mountain 14,275 *ft* (4351 *m*) Antarctica W of Ross Ice Shelf

Marl \'märl\ city W Germany in the Ruhr *pop* 91,864

Marl·bor·ough \'märl-,bȯr-ō, 'mȯl-\ city E Mass. E of Worcester *pop* 31,813

Mar·ma·ra, Sea of \'mär-mȯ-rȯ\ *or ancient* **Pro·pon·tis** \prȯ-'pän-tȯs\ sea NW Turkey connected with Black Sea by the Bosporus & with Aegean Sea by the Dardanelles *area* 4429 *sq mi* (11,471 *sq km*)

Mar·mo·la·da \,mär-mō-'lä-dä\ mountain 10,965 *ft* (3342 *m*) NE Italy; highest in the Dolomites

Marne \'märn\ river 325 *mi* (523 *km*) NE France flowing W into the Seine

Ma·ro·ni \mä-'rō-nē\ *or Dutch* **Ma·ro·wij·ne** \'mär-ō-,vī-nȯ\ river 450 *mi* (720 *km*) on border between Suriname & French Guiana flowing N into the Atlantic

Maros — see MURES

Mar·que·sas Islands \mär-'kā-zȯz, -zȯs, -sȯz, -sȯs\ *or French* **Îles Mar·quises** \,ēl-mär-'kēz\ islands S Pacific N of Tuamotu Archipelago in French Polynesia ✳ Taiohae (on Nuku Hiva) *area* 480 *sq mi* (1248 *sq km*), *pop* 7358

Mar·quette \mär-'ket\ city NW Mich. in Upper Peninsula on Lake Superior *pop* 21,977

Mar·ra·kech *or* **Mar·ra·kesh** \'mar-ȯ-,kesh, mȯ-'rä-kish\ *or formerly* **Mo·roc·co** \mȯ-'rä-(,)kō\ city *central* Morocco in foothills of the Grand Atlas *pop* 439,728

Mar·sa·la \mär-'sä-lä\ city & port Italy on W coast of Sicily S of Trapani *pop* 77,218

Marsa Matruh — see MATRUH

Mar·seille \mär-'sā\ *or* **Mar·seilles** \mär-'sā, -'sālz\ *or ancient* **Mas·sil·ia** \mȯ-'si-lē-ȯ\ city & port SE France on Gulf of Lion *pop* 807,726 — **Mar·seil·lais** \,mär-sȯ-'yā, -'yāz; -sȯ-'lā, -'lāz\ *noun*

Mar·shall \'mär-shȯl\ city NE Tex. *pop* 23,682

Marshall Islands islands W Pacific ✳ Majuro; part of former Trust Territory of the Pacific Islands; internally self-governing since 1980 — **Mar·shall·ese** \,mär-shȯ-'lēz, -'lēs\ *adjective or noun*

Mar·shall·town \'mär-shȯl-,taún\ city *central* Iowa *pop* 25,178

Marsh·field \'märsh-,fēld\ **1** town E Mass. N of Plymouth *pop* 21,531 **2** city N *central* Wis. *pop* 19,291

Mar·ston Moor \'mär-stȯn\ locality N England in N. Yorkshire W of York

Mar·ta·ban, Gulf of \,mär-tȯ-'ban, -'bän\ arm of Andaman Sea S Myanmar

Mar·tha's Vineyard \'mär-thȯz\ island 20 *mi* (32 *km*) long SE Mass. in the Atlantic off SW coast of Cape Cod WNW of Nantucket — **Vine·yard·er** \'vin-yȯr-dȯr\ *noun*

Mar·ti·nez \mär-'tē-nȯs\ city W Calif. NE of Oakland *pop* 31,808

Mar·ti·nique \,mär-tᵊn-'ēk\ island W. Indies in the Windwards; department of France ✳ Fort-de-France *area* 425 *sq mi* (1101 *sq km*), *pop* 377,000 — **Mar·ti·ni·can** \-'ē-kȯn\ *adjective* — **Mar·ti·ni·quais** \-,tē-ni-'kā\ *adjective*

Marwar — see JODHPUR

Maryborough — see PORTLAOIGHISE

Mary·land \'mer-ȯ-lȯnd, *locally also* 'mer-lȯn(d)\ state E U.S. ✳ Annapolis *area* 10,460 *sq mi* (27,091 *sq km*), *pop* 4,781,468 — **Mary·land·er** \-lȯn-dȯr, -,lan-\ *noun*

Maryland Heights city E Mo. W of St. Louis *pop* 25,407

Mary·ville \'mer-ē-,vil, 'mar-ē-, 'mä-rē-, -vȯl\ city E Tenn. *pop* 19,208

Ma·sa·da \mȯ-'sä-dȯ\ fortress town of ancient Palestine, site in SE Israel W of Dead Sea

Ma·san \'mä-,sän\ *or formerly* **Ma·sam·po** \'mä-,säm-,pō\ city & port SE S. Korea on an inlet of Korea Strait E of Pusan *pop* 448,746

Mas·ba·te \mäz-'bä-tē, mäs-\ island *central* Philippines in the Visayans NE of Panay *area* 1571 *sq mi* (4085 *sq km*)

Mas·ca·rene Islands \,mas-kȯ-'rēn\ islands W Indian Ocean E of Madagascar including Mauritius, Réunion, and Rodrigues

Mas·couche \ma-'sküsh\ town Canada in S Quebec N of Montreal *pop* 25,828

Mas·e·ru \'ma-sȯ-,rü, -zȯ-\ city ✳ of Lesotho *pop* 71,500

Mash·had \mȯ-'shad\ city NE Iran *pop* 1,463,508

Ma·son City \'mā-sᵊn\ city N Iowa *pop* 29,040

Mason-Dix·on Line \-'dik-sȯn\ the boundary line from the SW corner of Del. N to Pa. & W to approximately the SW corner of Pa. & often considered the boundary between the N & S states

Mas·qat \'mȯs-,kät\ *or* **Mus·cat** \-,kät, -,kat, -kȯt\ town & port ✳ of Oman on Gulf of Oman *pop* 100,000

Mas·sa·chu·setts \,ma-sȯ-'chü-sȯts, -zȯts\ state NE U.S. ✳ Boston *area* 8284 *sq mi* (21,456 *sq km*), *pop* 6,016,425

Massachusetts Bay inlet of the Atlantic E Mass.

Mas·sa·nut·ten Mountain \,ma-sȯ-'nȯ-tᵊn\ ridge N Va. in Blue Ridge Mountains

Mas·sa·wa \mȯ-'sä-wȯ, -'saú-ȯ\ *or* **Mits·'i·wa** \mit-'sē-wȯ\ city & port Eritrea on an inlet of Red Sea *pop* 16,579

Mas·sif Cen·tral \ma-'sēf-(,)sen-'träl, -(,)sän-\ plateau *central* France rising sharply just W of the Rhône-Saône valley & sloping N to the Paris basin & W to the basin of Aquitaine

Mas·sil·lon \'ma-sȯ-lȯn, -,län\ city NE Ohio *pop* 31,007

Mas·sive, Mount \'ma-siv\ mountain 14,421 *ft* (4396 *m*), *central* Colo. in Sawatch Range N of Mt. Elbert

Ma·su·ria \mȯ-'zúr-ē-ȯ, -'súr-\ *or German* **Ma·su·ren** \mȯ-'zúr-ȯn\ region NE Poland SE of Gulf of Gdansk; formerly in E. Prussia, Germany — **Ma·su·ri·an** \mȯ-'zúr-ē-ȯn, -'súr-\ *adjective*

Mat·a·be·le·land \,ma-tȯ-'bē-lē-,land, ,mä-tȯ-'bā-lä-\ region SW Zimbabwe between the Limpopo & the Zambezi; chief town Bulawayo

Ma·ta·di \mä-'tä-dē\ town & port W Democratic Republic of the Congo *pop* 172,926

Mat·a·gor·da Bay \,ma-tȯ-'gȯr-dȯ\ inlet of Gulf of Mexico 30 *mi* (48 *km*) long SE Tex.

Ma·ta·mo·ros \,mä-tä-'mȯr-ōs\ city NE Mexico in Tamaulipas on Rio Grande opposite Brownsville, Tex. *pop* 303,392

Mat·a·nus·ka \,ma-tȯ-'nüs-kȯ\ river 90 *mi* (145 *km*) S Alaska flowing SW to head of Cook Inlet

Ma·tan·zas \mȯ-'tan-zȯs, mä-'tän-säs\ city & port W Cuba on Straits of Florida E of Havana *pop* 113,724

Matapan — see TAÍNARON

Ma·thu·ra \'mȯ-tȯ-rȯ\ *or* **Mut·tra** \'mȯ-trȯ\ city N India in W Uttar Pradesh NW of Agra *pop* 226,850

Mat·lock \'mat-,läk\ town N England ✳ of Derbyshire *pop* 20,610

Ma·to Gros·so *or formerly* **Mat·to Gros·so** \,mä-tȯ-'grō-(,)sō, -(,)sü\ **1** state SW Brazil ✳ Cuiabá *area* 352,400 *sq mi* (912,716 *sq km*), *pop* 2,020,581 **2** plateau region in E *central* Mato Grosso state

Ma·to Gros·so do Sul \dō-'sül, -dù-\ state SW Brazil ✳ Campo Grande *area* 140,219 *sq mi* (350,548 *sq km*), *pop* 1,778,494

Mato Tepee — see DEVILS TOWER

Ma·truh \mȯ-'trü\ *or* **Mar·sa Matruh** \'mar-sȯ\ town NW Egypt

Mats·qui \'mat-skwē\ municipality Canada in SW British Columbia SE of Vancouver *pop* 68,064

Mat·su \'mät-'sü, 'mat-, -(,)sü\ island off SE China in Formosa Strait; administered by Taiwan *pop* 11,002

Mat·su·do \mät-'sü-(,)dō\ city Japan on Honshu, a suburb of Tokyo *pop* 456,211

Mat·su·shi·ma \,mät-sü-'shē-mȯ, mät-'sü-shē-mȯ\ group of over 200 islets Japan off N Honshu NE of Sendai

Mat·su·ya·ma \,mät-sü-'yä-mȯ\ city & port Japan in W Shikoku *pop* 443,317

Mat·tag·a·mi \mȯ-'ta-gȯ-mē\ river 275 *mi* (442 *km*) Canada in E Ontario

Mat·ta·po·ni \,ma-tȯ-pȯ-'nī\ river 125 *mi* (201 *km*) E Va.

Mat·ter·horn \'ma-tȯr-,hȯrn, 'mä-\ *or French* **Mont Cer·vin** \,mōⁿ-ser-'vaⁿ\ mountain 14,691 *ft* (4478 *m*) in Pennine Alps on border between Switzerland & Italy

Ma·tu·rín \,mä-tü-'rēn\ city NE Venezuela *pop* 207,382

Maui \'maú-ē\ island Hawaii NW of Hawaii (island) *area* 728 *sq mi* (1893 *sq km*)

Mau·mee \mȯ-'mē\ river 175 *mi* (282 *km*) NE Ind. & NW Ohio flowing NE into Lake Erie at Toledo

Mau·na Kea \,maú-nä-'kā-ä, ,mó-\ extinct volcano 13,796 *ft* (4205 *m*) Hawaii in N *central* Hawaii (island)

Mauna Loa \-'lō-ȯ\ volcano 13,680 *ft* (4170 *m*) Hawaii in S *central* Hawaii (island) in Hawaii Volcanoes National Park — see KILAUEA

Maures, Monts des \,mōⁿ-dā-'mȯr, -'mȯr\ mountains SE France along the Riviera SW of Fréjus

Mau·re·ta·nia *or* **Mau·ri·ta·nia** \,mȯr-ȯ-'tā-nē-ȯ, ,mär-, -nyȯ\ ancient country N Africa W of Numidia in modern Morocco & W Algeria — **Mau·re·ta·ni·an** *or* **Mau·ri·ta·ni·an** \-nē-ȯn, -nyȯn\ *adjective or noun*

Mauritania *or French* **Mau·ri·ta·nie** \mȯ-rē-tä-'nē\ country NW Africa bordering on the Atlantic N of Senegal River; a republic within the French Community, formerly a territory ✳ Nouakchott *area* 397,955 *sq mi* (1,030,807 *sq km*), *pop* 2,171,000 — **Mau·ri·ta·ni·an** \mȯr-ȯ-'tā-nē-ȯn, ,mär-, -nyȯn\ *adjective or noun*

Mau·ri·ti·us \mȯ-'ri-sh(ē-)ȯs\ island in Indian Ocean in *central* Mascarenes; constitutes with Rodrigues & other dependencies a dominion of the Commonwealth of Nations ✳ Port Louis *area* 720 *sq mi* (1872 *sq km*), *pop* 1,103,000 — **Mau·ri·tian** \-'ri-shȯn\ *adjective or noun*

May, Cape \'mā\ cape S N.J. at entrance to Delaware Bay

May·a·gua·na \,mä-ȯ-'gwä-nȯ\ island in SE Bahamas NNE of Great Inagua Is. *area* 110 *sq mi* (285 *sq km*)

Ma·ya·güez \,mī-ä-'gwez, -'gwes\ city & port W Puerto Rico *pop* 100,371

Ma·ya·pán \,mī-ä-'pän\ ruined city ✳ of the Mayas SE Mexico in Yucatán SSE of Mérida

Mayence — see MAINZ

GEO

Ma·yenne \mä-'yen\ river 125 *mi* (201 *km*) NW France uniting with the Sarthe to form the **Maine** \'mān, 'men\ (8 *mi* or 13 *km* long, flowing into the Loire)

May·fair \'mā-,fer, -,fer\ district of W London, England, in Westminster borough

May·field Heights \'mā-,fēld\ city NE Ohio E of Cleveland *pop* 19,847

May·kop \mī-'kòp\ city S Russia in Europe ✳ of Adygea *pop* 163,000

May·nooth \mā-'nüth\ town E Ireland in County Kildare *pop* 4768

Mayo 1 \'mī-(,)ō\ river 250 *mi* (402 *km*) NW Mexico in Sonora flowing SW into Gulf of California **2** \'mā-(,)ō\ county NW Ireland in Connacht ✳ Castlebar *area* 2084 *sq mi* (5418 *sq km*), *pop* 110,713

Ma·yon \mä-'yōn\ volcano 8077 *ft* (2462 *m*) Philippines in SE Luzon

Ma·yotte \mä-'yät, -'yot\ island of the Comoro group; a French dependency *area* 144 *sq mi* (374 *sq km*) *pop* 90,000 — see COMORO ISLANDS

May·wood \'mā-,wùd\ **1** city SW Calif. W of Whittier *pop* 27,850 **2** village NE Ill. W of Chicago *pop* 27,139

Mayyali — see MAHÉ

Mazaca — see KAYSERI

Ma·za·tlán \,mä-zət-'län, -sät-\ city & port W Mexico in Sinaloa on the Pacific *pop* 314,249

Mba·ba·ne \,əm-bä-'bä-nä\ town ✳ of Swaziland *pop* 23,109

Mban·da·ka \,əm-bän-'dä-kä\ *or formerly* **Co·quil·hat·ville** \,kō-kē-'at-,vil\ city W Democratic Republic of the Congo on Congo River *pop* 165,623

Mbi·ni \əm-'bē-nē\ *or formerly* **Río Mu·ni** \,rē-ō-'mü-nē\ mainland portion of Equatorial Guinea bordering on Gulf of Guinea ✳ Bata *area* 10,040 *sq mi* (26,104 *sq km*)

Mbomou — see BOMU

Mbu·ji-Ma·yi \əm-,bü-jē-'mī-,yē\ *or formerly* **Ba·kwan·ga** \bä-'kwän-gä\ city S Democratic Republic of the Congo *pop* 613,027

Mc·Al·len \mə-'ka-lən\ city S Tex. WNW of Brownsville *pop* 84,021

Mc·Kees·port \mə-'kēz-,pōrt, -,pórt\ city SW Pa. S of Pittsburgh *pop* 26,016

Mc·Kin·ley, Mount \mə-'kin-lē\ *or* **De·na·li** \də-'nä-lē\ mountain 20,320 *ft* (6194 *m*) central Alaska in Alaska Range; highest in U.S. & N. America; in **Denali National Park**

Mc·Kin·ney \mə-'ki-nē\ city NE Tex. N of Dallas *pop* 21,283

M'·Clure Strait \mə-'klür\ channel N Canada between Banks Is. & Melville Is. opening on the W into Arctic Ocean

Mc·Mur·do Sound \mək-'mər-dō\ inlet of W Ross Sea Antarctica between Ross Is. & coast of Victoria Land

Mead, Lake \'mēd\ reservoir NW Ariz. & SE Nev. formed by Hoover Dam in Colorado River

Mearns, The — see KINCARDINE

Meath \'mēth, *by outsiders also* 'mēth\ county E Ireland in NE Leinster ✳ Trim *area* 903 *sq mi* (2348 *sq km*), *pop* 105,370

Meaux \'mō\ commune N France ENE of Paris *pop* 49,409

Mec·ca \'me-kə\ city Saudi Arabia ✳ of Hejaz *pop* 366,801 — **Mec·can** \-kən\ *adjective or noun*

Mech·lin \'me-klən\ *or Flemish* **Me·che·len** \'mā-kə-lə(n)\ *or French* **Ma·lines** \må-'lēn\ commune N Belgium *pop* 75,700

Meck·len·burg \'me-klən-,bərg, -,búrk\ region NE Germany SE of Jutland Peninsula & E of the Elbe; in 18th & 19th centuries divided into duchies of **Mecklenburg–Schwe·rin** \-shvä-'rēn\ & **Mecklenburg–Stre·litz** \-'shtrā-ləts, 'strä-\ which became grand duchies 1815 & states of Weimar Republic 1919

Me·dan \mā-'dän\ city Indonesia in NE Sumatra *pop* 1,730,752

Me·del·lín \,me-d'l-'ēn, ,mā-thā-'yēn\ city NW Colombia NW of Bogotá *pop* 1,581,400

Med·ford \'med-fərd\ **1** city E Mass. N of Boston *pop* 57,407 **2** city SW Oreg. *pop* 46,951

Me·dia \'mē-dē-ə\ ancient country & province of Persian Empire SW Asia in NW modern Iran — **Me·di·an** \-dē-ən\ *adjective or noun*

Media Atropatene — see AZERBAIJAN

Med·i·cine Bow \'me-də-sən-,bō\ river 120 *mi* (193 *km*) S Wyo. flowing into N. Platte River

Medicine Bow Mountains mountains N Colo. & S Wyo. in the Rockies; highest **Medicine Bow Peak** (in Wyo.) 12,013 *ft* (3662 *m*)

Medicine Hat city Canada in SE Alberta *pop* 43,625

Me·di·na 1 \mə-'dī-nə\ city N Ohio WNW of Akron *pop* 19,231 **2** \mə-'dē-nə\ city W Saudi Arabia *pop* 198,186

Mediolanum — see MILAN

Med·i·ter·ra·nean Sea \,me-də-tə-'rā-nē-ən, -nyən\ sea 2300 *mi* (3700 *km*) long between Europe & Africa connecting with the Atlantic through Strait of Gibraltar & with Red Sea through Suez Canal

Mé·doc \mā-'däk, -'dòk\ district SW France N of Bordeaux

Med·way \'med-,wā\ river 70 *mi* (113 *km*) SE England in Kent flowing NE into Thames River

Mee·rut \'mā-rət, 'mir-ət\ city N India in NW Uttar Pradesh NE of Delhi *pop* 753,778

Meg·a·ra \'me-gə-rə\ city & port Greece on Saronic Gulf W of Athens *pop* 17,294; chief town of ancient **Meg·a·ris** \'me-gə-rəs\ (district between Saronic Gulf & Gulf of Corinth) — **Me·gar·i·an** \mə-'gar-ē-ən, me-, -'ger-\ *adjective or noun*

Me·gha·la·ya \,mā-gə-'lā-ə\ state NE India ✳ Shillong *area* 8665 *sq mi* (22,442 *sq km*), *pop* 1,774,778

Megh·na \'meg-nə\ the lower course of the Surma, India

Me·gid·do \mi-'gi-(,)dō\ ancient city N Palestine N of Samaria

Meis·sen \'mī-s°n\ city E Germany NW of Dresden *pop* 33,997

Méjico — see MEXICO

Mek·nes \mek-'nes\ city N Morocco WSW of Fez; former ✳ of Morocco *pop* 248,369

Me·kong \'mā-'kòn, -'kän; 'mā-,\ river 2600 *mi* (4184 *km*) SE Asia flowing from Qinghai (China) S & SE into S. China Sea in S Vietnam

Mel·aka *or* **Ma·lac·ca** \mə-'la-kə, -'lä-\ **1** state Malaysia on W coast of Peninsular Malaysia *area* 640 *sq mi* (1648 *sq km*), *pop* 504,502 **2** city, its port *pop* 250,635

Mel·a·ne·sia \,me-lə-'nē-zhə, -shə\ the islands in the Pacific NE of Australia & S of Micronesia including Bismarck Archipelago, the Solomons, Vanuatu, New Caledonia, & the Fijis

Mel·bourne \'mel-bərn\ **1** city E Fla. SSW of Cape Canaveral *pop* 59,646 **2** city & port SE Australia ✳ of Victoria on Port Phillip Bay *metropolitan area pop* 2,761,995 — **Mel·bour·ni·an** *or* **Mel·bur·ni·an** \mel-'bər-nē-ən\ *noun*

Me·lil·la \mə-'lē-yə\ city & port NE Morocco on coast NE of Fez; a Spanish presidio *pop* 56,497

Melita — see MALTA

Melitene — see MALATYA

Me·li·to·pol \,me-lə-'tò-pəl\ city S Ukraine near Sea of Azov *pop* 177,000

Melos — see MÍLOS

Mel·rose \'mel-,rōz\ city E Mass. N of Boston *pop* 28,150

Melrose Park village NE Ill. W of Chicago *pop* 20,859

Mel·ville, Lake \'mel-,vil\ lake Canada in Newfoundland in Labrador; the inner basin of Hamilton Inlet *area* 1133 *sq mi* (2946 *sq km*)

Melville Island island Canada in N Northwest Territories in Parry Islands *area over* 16,250 *sq mi* (42,088 *sq km*)

Melville Peninsula peninsula Canada in E Northwest Territories between Foxe Basin & an arm of Gulf of Boothia

Memel — see KLAIPEDA

Mem·phis \'mem(p)-fəs\ **1** city SW Tenn. on Mississippi River *pop* 610,337 **2** ancient city N Egypt on the Nile S of modern Cairo; once ✳ of Egypt — **Mem·phi·an** \-fē-ən\ *adjective or noun* — **Mem·phite** \'mem-,fīt\ *adjective or noun*

Mem·phre·ma·gog, Lake \,mem(p)-fri-'mā-,gäg\ lake 30 *mi* (48 *km*) long on border between Canada & the U.S. in Quebec & Vt.

Menado — see MANADO

Men·ai Strait \'me-,nī\ strait 14 *mi* (22 *km*) long N Wales between Anglesey Is. & mainland

Me Nam — see CHAO PHRAYA

Men·den·hall \'men-dən-,hól\ glacier SE Alaska N of Juneau

Men·de·res \,men-də-'res\ **1** *or ancient* **Mae·an·der** \mē-'an-dər\ river 240 *mi* (386 *km*) W Turkey in Asia flowing SW & W into the Aegean **2** *or ancient* **Sca·man·der** \skə-'man-dər\ river 60 *mi* (96 *km*) NW Turkey in Asia flowing from Mt. Ida W & NW across the plain of ancient Troy into the Dardanelles

Men·dip \'men-,dip, -dəp\ hills SW England in NE Somerset; highest Blackdown 1068 *ft* (326 *m*)

Men·do·ci·no, Cape \,men-də-'sē-(,)nō\ headland NW Calif. SSW of Eureka; extreme W point of Calif., at 124°8'W

Men·do·ta, Lake \men-'dō-tə\ lake 6 *mi* (9.6 *km*) long S Wis. NW of Madison

Men·do·za \men-'dō-zə\ city W Argentina SE of Aconcagua *pop* 121,696

Men·lo Park \'men-(,)lō\ city W Calif. SE of San Francisco *pop* 28,040

Me·nom·i·nee \mə-'nä-mə-nē\ river 125 *mi* (201 *km*) NE Wis. flowing SE on Mich.-Wis. border into Green Bay

Menominee Range iron-rich mountain range NE Wis. & NW Mich. in Upper Peninsula

Me·nom·o·nee Falls \mə-'nä-mə-nē\ village SE Wis. *pop* 26,840

Menorca — see MINORCA

Men·ton \mäⁿ-'tōⁿ\ *or Italian* **Men·to·ne** \men-'tō-nä\ city SE France on the Mediterranean ENE of Nice *pop* 29,474

Men·tor \'men-tər\ city NE Ohio NE of Cleveland *pop* 47,358

Men·zel Bour·gui·ba \men-'zel-búr-'gē-bə\ *or formerly* **Fer·ry·ville** \'fer-ē-,vil\ city N Tunisia on Lake Bizerte *pop* 42,111

Me·ra·no \mā-'rä-(,)nō\ commune N Italy in Trentino-Alto Adige NW of Bolzano *pop* 32,600

Mer·ced \mər-'sed\ **1** river 150 *mi* (241 *km*) central Calif. flowing W through Yosemite Valley into the San Joaquin **2** city central Calif. in San Joaquin valley *pop* 56,216

Mer·cer Island \'mər-sər\ city W Wash. E of Seattle *pop* 20,816

Mer·cia \'mər-sh(ē-)ə\ ancient Anglian kingdom central England; one of kingdoms in the Anglo-Saxon heptarchy

Mer·gent·heim \'mer-gənt-,hīm\ *or* **Bad Mergentheim** \,bät-\ town S Germany in Baden-Württemberg NNE of Stuttgart

Meriç — see MARITSA

Mé·ri·da \'mer-ə-də, 'mā-rē-thä\ **1** city SE Mexico ✳ of Yucatán *pop* 557,340 **2** city W Venezuela S of Lake Maracaibo *pop* 167,992

Mer·i·den \'mer-ə-d°n\ city S *central* Conn. S of Hartford *pop* 59,479

Me·rid·i·an \mə-'ri-dē-ən\ city E *central* Miss. *pop* 41,036

Merín — see MIRIM (Lake)

Mer·i·on·eth \,mer-ē-'ä-nəth\ *or* **Mer·i·on·eth·shire** \-,shir, -shər\ former county NW Wales ✳ Dolgellau

Mer·oë \'mer-ō-(,)ē\ ancient city, site in N *central* Sudan on the Nile — **Me·ro·ite** \'mer-ō-,īt\ *noun* — **Mero·it·ic** \,mer-ō-'i-tik\ *adjective*

Meroë, Isle of ancient region E Sudan between the Nile & Blue Nile rivers & the Atbara

Mer·rill·ville \'mer-əl-,vil, -vəl\ town NW Ind. *pop* 27,257

Mer·ri·mack \'mer-ə-,mak\ **1** river 110 *mi* (177 *km*) S N.H. & NE Mass. flowing S & NE into the Atlantic **2** town S N.H. *pop* 22,156

Mer·ritt Island \'mer-ət\ island 40 *mi* (64 *km*) long E Fla. W of Canaveral Peninsula between Indian & Banana rivers

Mer·sey \'mər-zē\ river 70 *mi* (113 *km*) NW England flowing NW & W into Irish Sea through a large estuary

Mer·sey·side \'mər-zē-,sīd\ metropolitan county NW England ✳ Liverpool *area* 261 *sq mi* (676 *sq km*), *pop* 1,376,800

Mer·sin \mer-'sēn\ city & port S Turkey on the Mediterranean WSW of Adana *pop* 422,357

Mer·thyr Tyd·fil \,mər-thər-'tid-,vil\ borough SE Wales in Mid Glamorgan *pop* 59,300

Mer·ton \'mər-t°n\ borough of SW Greater London, England *pop* 161,800

Me·ru, Mount \,mā-(,)rü\ mountain 14,979 *ft* (4566 *m*) NE Tanzania

Me·sa \'mā-sə\ city SW *central* Ariz. E of Phoenix *pop* 288,091

Me·sa·bi Range \mə-'sä-bē\ range of hills NE Minn. NW of Duluth containing large deposits of iron

Me·sa Verde National Park \'mā-sə-'vərd, -'vər-dē\ reservation SW Colo. containing prehistoric cliff dwellings

Me·se·ta \me-'sä-tə\ the central plateau of Spain

Me·so·amer·i·ca \,me-zō-ə-'mer-i-kə, ,mē-, -sō-\ region of S N. America that was occupied during pre-Columbian times — **Me·so·amer·i·can** \-kən\ adjective

Mes·o·po·ta·mia \,mes-(ə-)pə-'tā-mē-ə, -myə\ **1** region SW Asia between the Tigris & the Euphrates extending from the mountains of E Asia Minor to the Persian Gulf **2** the entire Tigris-Euphrates valley — **Mes·o·po·ta·mian** \-mē-ən, -myən\ adjective or noun

Mes·quite \mə-'skēt, me-\ city NE Tex. E of Dallas pop 101,484

Mes·se·ne or New Greek **Mes·sí·ni** \me-'sē-nē\ town S Greece in SW Peloponnese, ancient ✱ of Messenia

Mes·se·nia \mə-'sē-nē-ə, -nyə\ region S Greece in SW Peloponnese bordering on Ionian Sea

Messenia, Gulf of inlet of the Mediterranean S Greece on S coast of Peloponnese

Mes·si·na \me-'sē-nä\ or ancient **Mes·sa·na** \mə-'sä-nə\ or **Zan·cle** \'zan-(,)klē\ city & port Italy in NE Sicily pop 272,461

Messina, Strait of channel between S Italy & NE Sicily

Mes·ta \me-'stä\ or Greek **Nés·tos** \'nes-,tós\ river 150 mi (240 km) SW Bulgaria & NE Greece flowing from W end of Rhodope Mountains SE into the Aegean

Me·ta \'mā-tä\ river over 620 mi (998 km) NE Colombia flowing into the Orinoco on Venezuela-Colombia boundary

Met·air·ie \'me-tə-rē\ population center SE La. pop 149,428

Me·tau·ro \mə-'taúr-(,)ō\ or ancient **Me·tau·rus** \-'tór-əs\ river 70 mi (113 km) E central Italy flowing E into the Adriatic

Me·thu·en \mə-'thü-ən, -'thyü-\ town NE Mass. pop 39,990

Metz \'mets, French 'mes\ city NE France on the Moselle pop 123,920

Meurthe \'mərt, 'mœrt\ river about 100 mi (161 km) NE France flowing NW from Vosges Mountains to the Moselle

Meuse \'myüz, 'mœ(r)z, 'mœz\ or Dutch **Maas** \'mäs\ river about 580 mi (933 km) W Europe flowing from NE France through S Belgium into North Sea in the Netherlands

Mewar — see UDAIPUR

Mex·i·cali \,mek-si-'ka-lē, -sē-'kä-\ city NW Mexico ✱ of Baja California state on Mexico-Calif. border pop 602,390

Mex·i·co \'mek-si-,kō\ or Spanish **Mé·ji·co** \'me-hē-(,)kō\ or Mexican Spanish **Mé·xi·co** \'me-hē-(,)kō\ **1** country S N. America S of the U.S.; a republic ✱ Mexico area 759,530 sq mi (1,972,544 sq km), pop 89,995,000 **2** state S central Mexico ✱ Toluca area 8286 sq mi (21,461 sq km), pop 9,815,795 **3** or **Mexico City** city ✱ of Mexico (republic) in Federal District (area surrounded on three sides by state of Mexico) — see TENOCHTITLAN

Mexico, Gulf of inlet of the Atlantic on SE coast of N. America

Mé·zenc, Mount \mā-'zeŋk\ volcanic mountain 5755 ft (1754 m) S France; highest in the Cévennes

Mez·zo·gior·no \,met-sō-'jór-(,)nō, ,med-zō-\ the Italian Peninsula S of about the latitude of Rome

Mi·ami \mī-'a-mē\ city & port SE Fla. on Biscayne Bay pop 358,548 — **Mi·ami·an** \-mē-ən\ noun

Miami Beach city SE Fla. pop 92,639

Mich·i·gan \'mi-shi-gən\ state N U.S. in Great Lakes region including an upper (NW) & a lower (SE) peninsula ✱ Lansing area 58,527 sq mi (151,585 sq km), pop 9,295,297 — **Mich·i·gan·der** \,mi-shi-'gan-dər\ noun — **Mich·i·gan·ite** \'mi-shi-gə-,nīt\ noun

Michigan, Lake lake N central U.S.; one of the Great Lakes area 22,400 sq mi (58,240 sq km)

Michigan City city N Ind. on Lake Michigan pop 33,822

Michilimackinac — see MACKINAC

Mi·cho·a·cán \,mē-chō-ä-'kän\ state SW Mexico bordering on the Pacific ✱ Morelia area 23,114 sq mi (59,865 sq km), pop 3,548,199

Mi·cro·ne·sia \,mī-krə-'nē-zhə, -shə\ the islands of the W Pacific E of the Philippines & N of Melanesia including the Caroline, Kiribati, Mariana, & Marshall groups

Micronesia, Federated States of islands W Pacific in the Carolines comprising Kosrae, Pohnpei, Chuuk, & Yap; part of former Trust Territory of the Pacific Islands; internally self-governing since 1986

Mid·del·burg \'mi-d³l-,bərg\ city SW Netherlands on Walcheren Is. ✱ of Zeeland pop 39,828

Middle Congo former French territory W central Africa — see CONGO, FRENCH EQUATORIAL AFRICA

Middle East the countries of SW Asia & N Africa — usually considered as including the countries extending from Libya on the W to Afghanistan on the E — **Middle Eastern** or **Mid·east·ern** \,mid-'ē-stərn\ adjective — **Middle Easterner** noun

Mid·dles·brough \'mi-d³lz-brə\ town N England ✱ of Cleveland on Tees River pop 141,100

Mid·dle·sex \'mi-d³l-,seks\ former county SE England, now absorbed in Greater London

Mid·dle·town \'mi-d³l-,taún\ **1** city central Conn. S of Hartford pop 42,762 **2** city SE N.Y. pop 24,160 **3** city SW Ohio SW of Dayton pop 46,022 **4** town S R.I. N of Newport pop 19,460

Mid Gla·mor·gan \'mid-glə-'mór-gən\ county SE Wales area 393 sq mi (1022 sq km), pop 526,500

Mi·di \mē-'dē\ the south of France

Mid·i·an \'mi-dē-ən\ ancient region NW Arabia E of Gulf of Aqaba

Mid·land \'mid-lənd\ **1** city central Mich. NW of Saginaw pop 38,053 **2** city W Tex. NE of Odessa pop 89,443

Mid·lands \'mid-ləndz\ the central counties of England usually considered as comprising Bedfordshire, Buckinghamshire, Cambridgeshire, Derbyshire, Leicestershire, Lincolnshire, Northamptonshire, Nottinghamshire, Oxfordshire, Staffordshire, Warwickshire, W. Midlands, & part of Hereford and Worcester

Mid·lo·thi·an \mid-'lō-thē-ən\ or earlier **Ed·in·burgh** \'e-d³n-,bər-ə, -,bə-rə, -b(ə-)rə\ or **Ed·in·burgh·shire** \-,shir, -shər\ former county SE Scotland ✱ Edinburgh — see LOTHIAN

Mid·way \'mid-,wā\ islands (atoll) central Pacific 1300 mi (2092 km) WNW of Honolulu, Hawaii, belonging to the U.S., in Hawaiian group but not incorporated in state of Hawaii area 2 sq mi (5.2 sq km)

Mid·west \mid-'west\ or **Middle West** region N central U.S. including area around Great Lakes & in upper Mississippi valley from Ohio & sometimes Ky. on the E to N.Dak., S.Dak., Nebr., & Kans. on the W — **Mid·west·ern** \,mid-'wes-tərn\ or **Middle Western** adjective — **Mid·west·ern·er** \,mid-'wes-tə(r)-nər\ or **Middle Westerner** noun

Midwest City city central Okla. E of Oklahoma City pop 52,267

Mie·res \mē-'er-əs, 'myā-räs\ commune NW Spain in Asturias province pop 53,379

Míkonos — see MYKONOS

Mi·lan \mə-'lan, -mē-'län\ or Italian **Mi·la·no** \mē-'lä-(,)nō\ or ancient **Me·dio·la·num** \,mē-dē-ō-'lä-nəm\ commune N Italy ✱ of Lombardy pop 1,449,403 — **Mil·a·nese** \,mi-lə-'nēz, -'nēs\ adjective or noun

Mi·laz·zo \mē-'lät-(,)sō\ or ancient **My·lae** \'mī-(,)lē\ city & port Italy in NE Sicily W of Messina pop 31,559

Mi·le·tus \mī-'lē-təs, mə-\ ancient city on W coast of Asia Minor in Caria near mouth of Maeander River

Mil·ford \'mil-fərd\ **1** city S Conn. on Long Island Sound pop 49,938 **2** town E Mass. SE of Worcester pop 25,355

Milford Haven town & port SW Wales in Dyfed on Milford Haven (inlet of St. George's Channel) pop 13,934

Milk \'milk\ river 625 mi (1006 km) Canada & U.S. in Alberta & Mont. flowing SE into Missouri River

Mill·brae \'mil-,brā\ city W Calif. on San Francisco Bay S of San Francisco pop 20,412

Mille Lacs \mil(l)-'lak(s)\ lake 20 mi (32 km) long E central Minn.

Mill·ville \'mil-,vil\ city S N.J. pop 25,992

Mí·los or **Me·los** \'mē-,lòs\ island Greece in SW Cyclades area 57 sq mi (148 sq km)

Mil·pi·tas \mil-'pē-təs\ city W Calif. N of San José pop 50,686

Mil·ton \'mil-t³n\ **1** town E Mass. S of Boston pop 25,725 **2** town Canada in SE Ontario SW of Toronto pop 32,075

Mil·wau·kee \mil-'wò-kē\ city & port SE Wis. on Lake Michigan pop 628,088 — **Mil·wau·kee·an** \-kē-ən\ noun

Min \'min\ **1** river 350 mi (563 km) central China in Szechwan flowing SE into the Chang **2** river 250 mi (402 km) SE China in Fujian flowing SE into E. China Sea

Mi·nas Basin \'mī-nəs\ landlocked bay E Canada in central Nova Scotia; the NE extension of Bay of Fundy; connected with it by **Minas Channel**

Mi·nas de Río·tin·to \'mē-näs-thä-,rē-ō-'tēn-tō\ commune SW Spain in Huelva province NE of Huelva pop 5480

Mi·nas Ge·rais \,mē-nəs-zhə-'rīs\ state E Brazil ✱ Belo Horizonte area 226,707 sq mi (587,171 sq km), pop 15,746,200

Minch \'minch\ channel NW Scotland comprising **North Minch** & **Little Minch** between Outer Hebrides & NW coast of Scotland

Min·cio \'mēn-(,)chō, 'min-chē-,ō\ or ancient **Min·cius** \'min(t)-sh(ē-)əs, -sē-əs\ river 115 mi (185 km) N Italy issuing from Lake Garda & emptying into the Po

Min·da·nao \,min-də-'nä-,ō, -'naú\ island S Philippines area (including adjacent islands) 38,254 sq mi (99,078 sq km), pop 13,966,000

Mindanao Sea sea S Philippines N of Mindanao

Min·do·ro \min-'dōr-(,)ō, -'dór-\ island central Philippines SW of Luzon area 3759 sq mi (9773 sq km), pop 473,940

Minhow — see FUZHOU

Min·i·coy \'mi-ni-,kòi\ island India, southernmost of the Laccadives

Min·ne·ap·o·lis \,mi-nē-'a-pə-lis\ city SE Minn. on Mississippi River pop 368,383 — **Min·ne·a·pol·i·tan** \,mi-nē-ə-'pä-lə-t³n\ noun

Min·ne·so·ta \,mi-nə-'sō-tə\ **1** river 332 mi (534 km) S Minn. flowing from Big Stone Lake to Mississippi River **2** state N U.S. ✱ St. Paul area 84,068 sq mi (218,577 sq km), pop 4,375,099 — **Min·ne·so·tan** \-'sō-t³n\ adjective or noun

Min·ne·ton·ka \,mi-nə-'täŋ-kə\ city SE Minn. E of **Lake Minnetonka** (12 mi or 19 km long) pop 48,370

Minni — see ARMENIA

Mi·nor·ca \mə-'nòr-kə\ or Spanish **Me·nor·ca** \mā-'nór-kä\ island Spain in the Balearic Islands ENE of Majorca; chief city Mahón — **Mi·nor·can** \mə-'nòr-kən\ adjective or noun

Mi·not \'mī-,nät, -nət\ city NW central N.Dak. pop 34,544

Minsk \'min(t)sk\ city ✱ of Belarus pop 1,589,000

Minya, Al or **Minya, El** — see EL MINYA

Minya Konka — see GONGGA SHAN

Mi·que·lon \'mi-kə-,län, ,mē-kə-'lōⁿ\ island off S coast of Newfoundland, Canada, belonging to France — see SAINT PIERRE

Mir·a·mar \'mir-ə-,mär\ city SE Fla. pop 40,663

Mi·rim, Lake \mə-'rim\ or Spanish **Me·rín** \mā-'rēn\ lake 108 mi (174 km) long on boundary between Brazil & Uruguay near Atlantic coast

Mir·za·pur \'mir-zə-,púr\ city N India in SE Uttar Pradesh on the Ganges SW of Varanasi pop 169,368

Mi·se·num \mī-'sē-nəm\ ancient port & naval station S Italy at NW corner of Bay of Naples

Mish·a·wa·ka \,mi-shə-'wò-kə, -'wä-\ city N Ind. pop 42,608

Mis·kolc \'mish-,kōlts\ city NE Hungary NE of Budapest pop 207,300

Misr — see EGYPT

Mis·sion \'mi-shən\ **1** city S Tex. *pop* 28,653 **2** municipality Canada in SW British Columbia *pop* 26,202

Missionary Ridge mountain SE Tenn. & NW Ga. SE of Chattanooga

Mission Vie·jo \-vē-'ā-(,)hō\ city SW Calif. SE of Santa Ana *pop* 72,820

Mis·sis·sau·ga \,mi-sə-'sò-gə\ city Canada in S Ontario SW of Toronto *pop* 463,388

Mis·sis·sip·pi \,mi-sə-'si-pē\ **1** river 2340 *mi* (3765 *km*) *central* U.S. flowing from N *central* Minn. to Gulf of Mexico — see ITASCA (Lake) **2** river 105 *mi* (169 *km*) Canada in SE Ontario flowing NE & N into Ottawa River **3** state S U.S. ✱ Jackson *area* 47,689 *sq mi* (123,514 *sq km*), *pop* 2,573,216

Mississippi Sound inlet of Gulf of Mexico E of Lake Pontchartrain

Mis·sou·la \mə-'zü-lə\ city W Mont. *pop* 42,918

Mis·sou·ri \mə-'zùr-ē, *by some residents* mə-'zùr-ə\ **1** river 2466 *mi* (3968 *km*) W U.S. flowing from SW Mont. into Mississippi River in E Mo. — see THREE FORKS **2** state *central* U.S. ✱ Jefferson City *area* 69,697 *sq mi* (180,515 *sq km*), *pop* 5,117,073 — **Mis·sou·ri·an** \-'zùr-ē-ən\ *adjective or noun*

Missouri City city SE Tex. *pop* 36,176

Mis·tas·si·ni \,mis-tə-'sē-nē\ **1** lake Canada in S *central* Quebec draining W to James Bay *area* 840 *sq mi* (2184 *sq km*) **2** river 185 *mi* (298 *km*) Canada in S Quebec flowing S into Lake Saint-Jean

Mis·ti, El \el-'mēs-tē, -'mis-\ dormant volcano 19,101 *ft* (5822 *m*) S Peru

Mitch·am \'mi-chəm\ former municipal borough S England in Surrey, now part of Merton

Mitch·ell, Mount \'mi-chəl\ mountain 6684 *ft* (2037 *m*) W N.C. in Black Mountains of the Blue Ridge Mountains; highest point in U.S. E of Mississippi River

Mits'iwa — see MASSAWA

Mix·co \'mēs-(,)kō\ city S *central* Guatemala, a suburb of Guatemala City

Mi·ya·za·ki \mē-,yä-'zä-kē, mē-'yä-zä-(,)kē\ city & port Japan in Kyushu on SE coast *pop* 287,367

Mi·zo·ram \mi-'zòr-əm\ state NE India *area* 8142 *sq mi* (21,169 *sq km*), *pop* 689,756

Mma·ba·tho \mä-'bä-(,)tō\ town N Republic of South Africa near Botswana border; formerly ✱ of Bophuthatswana

Mo·ab \'mō-,ab\ region Jordan E of Dead Sea; in biblical times a kingdom between Edom & the country of the Amorites

Mo·bile \mō-'bēl, 'mō-,bēl\ **1** river 38 *mi* (61 *km*) long SW Ala. formed by Alabama & Tombigbee rivers & flowing S into **Mobile Bay** (inlet of Gulf of Mexico) **2** city & port SW Ala. *pop* 196,278

Moçambique — see MOZAMBIQUE

Moçâmedes — see NAMIBE

Mo·cha \'mō-kə\ *or Arabic* **Al Mu·khā** \,äl-mù-'kä\ town & port SW Yemen on the Red Sea

Mod·der \'mä-dər\ river 180 *mi* (290 *km*) Republic of South Africa in Free State; a tributary of the Vaal

Mo·de·na \'mō-dᵊn-ə, 'mó-dā-nä\ *or ancient* **Mu·ti·na** \'myü-tᵊn-ə\ commune N Italy in Emilia SW of Venice *pop* 176,857 — **Mod·e·nese** \,mō-dᵊn-'ēz, -mó-, -'ēs\ *noun*

Mo·des·to \mə-'des-(,)tō\ city *central* Calif. on the Tuolumne *pop* 164,730

Moe·sia \'mē-sh(ē-)ə\ ancient country & Roman province SE Europe in modern Serbia & Bulgaria S of the Danube from the Drina to Black Sea

Mog·a·di·shu \,mä-gə-'di-(,)shü, -mō-, -'dē-\ *or* **Mog·a·di·scio** \-(,)shō\ city & port ✱ of Somalia on Indian Ocean *pop* 349,245

Mogador — see ESSAOUIRA

Mogilev — see MAHILYOW

Mo·gol·lon Mountains \,mə-gə-'yōn, -mō-\ mountains SW N.Mex.; highest Whitewater Baldy 10,895 *ft* (3320 *m*)

Mo·hacs \'mō-,hach, -,häch\ town S Hungary *pop* 20,700

Mo·hawk \'mō-,hòk\ river 148 *mi* (238 *km*) E *central* N.Y. flowing E into Hudson River

Mo·hen·jo Da·ro \mō-'hen-(,)jō-'där-(,)ō\ prehistoric city Pakistan in Indus valley NE of modern Karachi

Mo·ja·ve Desert *or* **Mo·ha·ve Desert** \mə-'hä-vē, mō-\ desert S Calif. SE of S end of the Sierra Nevada

Mo·ji \'mō-(,)jē\ former city Japan in N Kyushu on Shimonoseki Strait — see KITAKYUSHU

Mok·po \'mäk-(,)pō\ city & port SW S. Korea on Yellow Sea SW of Kwangju *pop* 236,085

Mold \'mōld\ town NE Wales in Clwyd

Mol·da·via \mäl-'dā-vē-ə, -vyə\ **1** region Europe in NE Romania & Moldova between the Carpathians & Transylvanian Alps on the W & the Dniester on the E **2** — see MOLDOVA — **Mol·da·vian** \-vē-ən, -vyən\ *adjective or noun*

Mol·do·va \mäl-'dō-və, mòl-\ independent country in E Moldavia region; formerly (as **Moldavian Republic** or **Moldavia**) a constituent republic N of the U.S.S.R.; ✱ Chişinău *area* 13,012 *sq mi* (33,701 *sq km*), *pop* 4,362,000

Mo·len·beek \'mō-lən-,bāk\ *or* **Molenbeek–Saint–Jean** \-sa°-'zhä°\ commune *central* Belgium in Brabant W of Brussels *pop* 68,759

Mo·line \mō-'lēn\ city NW Ill. on Mississippi River *pop* 43,202

Mo·li·se \mō-'lē-zā\ region *central* Italy between the Apennines & the Adriatic S of Abruzzi ✱ Campobasso *pop* 335,348 — see ABRUZZI

Mo·lo·kai \,mä-lə-'kī, -mō-lō-'kä-ē\ island *central* Hawaii *area* 259 *sq mi* (673 *sq km*)

Mo·lo·po \mō-'lō-(,)pō\ river 600 *mi* (966 *km*) S Africa flowing W along border between Botswana & Republic of South Africa & thence S into Orange River, now usually dry

Molotov — see PERM

Mo·luc·cas \mə-'lə-kəz\ *or Indonesian* **Ma·lu·ku** \mä-'lü-(,)kü\ islands Indonesia in Malay Archipelago between Sulawesi & New Guinea *area* 32,307 *sq mi* (83,675 *sq km*), *pop* 1,857,790 — see HALMAHERA — **Mo·luc·ca** \mə-'lə-kə\ *or* **Mo·luc·can** \-kən\ *adjective*

Mom·ba·sa \mäm-'bä-sə\ **1** island Kenya on coast N of Pemba **2** city & port on Mombasa Is. & adjacent mainland *pop* 341,148

Mona 1 — see ANGLESEY **2** *or* **Monapia** — see MAN (Isle of)

Mo·na·co \'mä-nə-,kō *also* mə-'nä-(,)kō\ **1** country S Europe on the Mediterranean coast of France; a principality *area* 368 *acres* (147 *hectares*), *pop* 30,500 **2** commune, its ✱ — **Mo·na·can** \'mä-nə-kən, mə-'nä-kən\ *adjective or noun* — **Mon·e·gasque** \,mä-ni-'gask\ *adjective or noun*

Mo·nad·nock, Mount \mə-'nad-,näk\ mountain 3165 *ft* (965 *m*) SW N.H.

Mon·a·ghan \'mä-nə-hən, -,han\ **1** county NE Ireland (republic) in Ulster *area* 498 *sq mi* (1290 *sq km*), *pop* 51,293 **2** town, its ✱ *pop* 5754

Mo·na Passage \'mō-nə\ strait West Indies between Hispaniola & Puerto Rico connecting the Caribbean & the Atlantic

Monastir — see BITOLA

Mön·chen·glad·bach \,mən-kən-'glät-,bäk, -mən-kən-'glät-,bäk\ *or formerly* **Mün·chen–Glad·bach** \,m(y)ün-kən-, -,mən-kən-\ city W Germany W of Düsseldorf *pop* 262,581

Monc·ton \'məŋk-tən\ city Canada in E New Brunswick *pop* 57,010

Mon·go·lia \män-'gōl-yə, mäŋ-, -'gō-lē-ə\ **1** region E Asia E of Altay Mountains; includes Gobi Desert **2** *or* **Outer Mongolia** country E Asia comprising major portion of Mongolia region; a republic ✱ Ulaanbaatar *area* 604,247 *sq mi* (1,565,000 *sq km*), *pop* 2,182,000 **3** INNER MONGOLIA

Mon·he·gan \män-'hē-gən\ island Maine E of Portland

Mon·mouth \'män-məth, 'mən-\ *or* **Mon·mouth·shire** \-,shir, -shər\ former county SE Wales, often regarded as part of England ✱ Newport

Mo·noc·a·cy \mə-'nä-kə-sē\ river 60 *mi* (96 *km*) S Pa. & N Md. flowing S into the Potomac

Mo·no Lake \'mō-(,)nō\ saline lake 14 *mi* (22 *km*) long E Calif.

Mo·non·ga·he·la \mə-,nän-gə-'hē-lə, -,näŋ-gə-, -'hä-lə\ river 128 *mi* (206 *km*) N W.Va. & SW Pa. flowing N to unite with Allegheny River at Pittsburgh forming Ohio River

Mon·roe \(,)mən-'rō\ **1** city N La. *pop* 54,909 **2** city SE Mich. SSW of Detroit on Lake Erie *pop* 22,902

Mon·roe·ville \(,)mən-'rō-,vil\ borough SW Pa. E of Pittsburgh *pop* 29,169

Mon·ro·via \(,)mən-'rō-vē-ə\ **1** city SW Calif. E of Pasadena *pop* 35,761 **2** city & port ✱ of Liberia, on the Atlantic *pop* 243,243

Mons \'mō°s\ *or Flemish* **Ber·gen** \'ber-kə(n)\ commune SW Belgium ✱ of Hainaut *pop* 92,300

Mon·tana \män-'ta-nə\ state NW U.S. ✱ Helena *area* 147,046 *sq mi* (380,849 *sq km*), *pop* 799,065 — **Mon·tan·an** \-nən\ *adjective or noun*

Mont·au·ban \män-tō-'bän, mō°-tō-'bä°\ city SW France on the Tarn N of Toulouse *pop* 53,278

Mon·tauk Point \'män-,tòk\ headland SE N.Y. at E tip of Long Is.

Mont Blanc \mō°-'blä°\ mountain peak 15,771 *ft* (4807 *m*) on border of France, Italy, and Switzerland in Savoy Alps; highest of the Alps

Mont Blanc Tunnel tunnel 7½ *mi* (12 *km*) long France & Italy under Mont Blanc

Mont·clair \mänt-'klar, -'kler\ city SW Calif. E of Los Angeles *pop* 28,434

Mon·te Al·bán \,män-tē-äl-'bän, ,mōn-tä-äl-'vän\ ruined city of the Zapotecs S Mexico in Oaxaca state SW of Oaxaca

Mon·te·bel·lo \,män-tə-'be-(,)lō\ city SW Calif. *pop* 59,564

Mon·te Car·lo \,män-tē-'kär-(,)lō, ,mòn-tä-\ commune Monaco *pop* 14,702

Mon·te·go Bay \män-,tē-(,)gō\ city & port NW Jamaica on Montego Bay (inlet of the Caribbean) *pop* 83,446

Mon·te·ne·gro \,män-tə-'nē-(,)grō, -'nā-, -'ne-\ federated republic S Yugoslavia on the Adriatic; formerly a kingdom (✱ Cetinje) ✱ Podgorica *area* 5333 *sq mi* (13,812 *sq km*), *pop* 616,327 — **Mon·te·ne·grin** \-grən\ *adjective or noun*

Mon·te·rey \,män-tə-'rā\ city W Calif. on peninsula at S end of **Monterey Bay** (inlet of the Pacific) *pop* 31,954

Monterey Park city SW Calif. E of Los Angeles *pop* 60,738

Mon·ter·rey \,män-tə-'rā\ city NE Mexico ✱ of Nuevo León *pop* 1,064,197

Mon·te·vi·deo \,män-tə-və-'dā-(,)ō, -'vi-dē-,ō; ,món-tä-vē-'thā-ō\ city & port ✱ of Uruguay on N shore of Río de la Plata *pop* 1,260,753

Mon·te·zu·ma Castle National Monument \,män-tə-'zü-mə\ reservation *central* Ariz. containing prehistoric cliff dwellings

Mont·gom·ery \(,)mən(t)-'gə-mə-rē, män(t)-, -'gä-; -'gəm-rē, -'gäm-\ **1** city ✱ of Ala. on Alabama River *pop* 187,106 **2** *or* **Mont·gom·ery·shire** \-,shir, -shər\ former county E Wales ✱ Welshpool

Mont·mar·tre \mō°-'märtrᵊ\ section of Paris, France, on a hill in N *central* part of the city

Mont·mo·ren·cy \,mänt-mə-'ren(t)-sē, mō°-mò-rä°-'sē\ commune N France, N suburb of Paris *pop* 20,927

Mont·mo·ren·cy Falls \,mänt-mə-'ren(t)-sē\ waterfall *over* 270 *ft* (82 *m*) Canada in S Quebec NE of Quebec (city) in **Montmorency River** (60 *mi* or 96 *km* flowing S into St. Lawrence River)

Mont·par·nasse \,mō°-(,)pär-'näs, -'nas\ section of Paris, France, in S *central* part of the city — **Mont·par·nas·sian** \-'na-shən, -'na-sē-ən\ *adjective*

Mont·pe·lier \mänt-'pēl-yər, -'pil-\ city ✱ of Vt. *pop* 8247

Mont·pel·lier \mō°-pel-'yā\ city S France WNW of Marseille *pop* 210,866

Mon·tre·al \,män-trē-'òl, ,mən-\ *or* **Mont·ré·al** \,mō°-rā-'al\ city & port Canada in S Quebec on **Montreal Island** (32 *mi* or 51 *km* long, in St. Lawrence River) *pop* 1,017,666 — **Mon·tre·al·er** \,män-trē-'ò-lər, ,mən-\ *noun*

Montreal North *or* **Montréal–Nord** \-'nòr\ town Canada in S Quebec on Montreal Is. *pop* 85,516

Mon·treuil \mō°-'trœi\ *or* **Montreuil–sous–Bois** \-,sü-'bwä\ commune N France, E suburb of Paris *pop* 95,038

Mont–Royal \mō°-rwä-'yäl\ *or* **Mount Roy·al** \maùnt-'ròi(-ə)l\ height 769 *ft* (234 *m*) in Montreal, Quebec

Mont–Saint–Mi·chel \mō°-sa°-mē-'shel\ small island NW France in Gulf of St-Malo

Mont·ser·rat \,män(t)-sə-'rat\ island Brit. West Indies in the Leewards SW of Antigua ✱ Plymouth *area* 40 *sq mi* (104 *sq km*), *pop* 12,100

Monument Valley region NE Ariz. & SE Utah containing red sandstone buttes, mesas, & arches

Mon·za \'mȯnt-sä, 'män-zə\ commune N Italy in Lombardy SE of Milan *pop* 121,151

Moore \'mȯr, 'mȯr\ city *central* Okla. S of Oklahoma City *pop* 40,318

Mo·oréa \,mō-ō-'rä-ä\ island S Pacific in Society Islands NW of Tahiti *area* over 50 *sq mi* (130 *sq km*)

Moor·head \'mȯr-,hed, 'mȯr-, 'mu̇r-\ city W Minn. on Red River opposite Fargo, N.Dak. *pop* 32,295

Moor·park \'mȯr-,pärk, 'mȯr-\ city SW Calif. W of Los Angeles *pop* 25,494

Moose \'müs\ river 50 *mi* (80 *km*) Canada in NE Ontario flowing NE into James Bay; estuary of Abitibi, Mattagami, & other rivers

Moose·head Lake \'müs-,hed\ lake 35 *mi* (56 *km*) long NW *central* Maine

Moose Jaw city Canada in S Saskatchewan W of Regina *pop* 33,593

Mo·rad·a·bad \mə-'rä-də-,bäd, -'rä-də-,bad\ city N India in NW Uttar Pradesh ENE of Delhi *pop* 429,214

Mo·ra·tu·wa \mə-'rə-tə-wə, 'mȯr-ə-,tü-wə\ city W Sri Lanka on Indian Ocean S of Colombo *pop* 170,000

Mo·ra·va \'mȯr-ä-və\ **1** river *about* 220 *mi* (354 *km*), *central* Europe flowing S from E Czech Republic & forming part of the borders between the Czech Republic & Slovakia and Austria & Slovakia before entering the Danube **2** river 134 *mi* (216 *km*) Serbia flowing N into the Danube

Mo·ra·via \mə-'rä-vē-ə\ *or* **Mo·ra·va** \'mȯr-ä-və\ region E Czech Republic S of Silesia traversed by Morava River; once an independent kingdom, later under shifting jurisdictions; chief city Brno

Mo·ra·vi·an Gate \mə-'rä-vē-ən\ mountain pass *central* Europe between Sudety & Carpathian mountains

Moravska Ostrava — see OSTRAVA

Mor·ay \'mər-ē\ *or* **Mor·ay·shire** \-,shir, -shər\ *or* **El·gin** \'el-gən\ *or* **El·gin·shire** \-,shir, -shər\ former county NE Scotland bordering on North Sea ✱ Elgin

Moray Firth inlet of North Sea N Scotland

Mord·vin·ia \mȯrd-'vi-nē-ə\ *or* **Mor·do·via** \(,)mȯr-'dō-vē-ə\ *or* **Mor·do·vi·an Republic** \-vē-ən\ autonomous republic *central* Russia in Europe S & W of the middle Volga ✱ Saransk *area* 10,116 *sq mi* (26,200 *sq km*), *pop* 964,000 — **Mordvinian** *noun*

Mo·reau \'mȯr-(,)ō, 'mȯr-\ river 290 *mi* (467 *km*) NW S.Dak. flowing E into Missouri River

More·cambe and Hey·sham \'mȯr-kəm-ənd-'hē-shəm, 'mȯr-\ borough NW England in N Lancashire on **Morecambe Bay** (inlet of Irish Sea) *pop* 41,187

Mo·re·lia \mə-'rāl-yə, mō-'rāl-yä\ city SW Mexico ✱ of Michoacán *pop* 489,756

Mo·re·los \mə-'rä-ləs, mō-'rä-lōs\ state S *central* Mexico ✱ Cuernavaca *area* 1908 *sq mi* (4942 *sq km*), *pop* 1,195,059

Mo·re·no Valley \mə-'rē-(,)nō\ city S Calif. E of Riverside *pop* 118,779

More·ton Bay \'mȯr-t³n, 'mȯr-\ inlet of the Pacific Australia in SE Queensland at mouth of Brisbane River

Mor·gan Hill \'mȯr-gən\ city W Calif. SE of San Jose *pop* 23,928

Mor·gan·town \'mȯr-gən-,tau̇n\ city N W.Va. *pop* 25,879

Mo·ri·ah \mə-'rī-ə\ hill *central* Palestine in E part of Jerusalem

Mo·roc·co \mə-'rä-(,)kō\ **1** country NW Africa bordering on the Atlantic & the Mediterranean; a kingdom ✱ Rabat, summer ✱ Tangier *area* 172,413 *sq mi* (446,550 *sq km*), *pop* 20,419,555; formerly (1911–56) divided into **French Morocco** (protectorate ✱ Rabat), **Spanish Morocco** (protectorate ✱ Tetuán), **Southern Morocco** (Spanish protectorate, chief town Cabo Yubi), & the **International Zone** of Tangier **2** — see MARRAKECH — **Mo·roc·can** \-kən\ *adjective or noun*

Mo·ro Gulf \'mȯr-(,)ō\ arm of Celebes Sea S Philippines off SW coast of Mindanao

Mo·ro·ni \mȯ-'rō-nē\ city ✱ of Comoros *pop* 23,432

Mor·ris Jes·up, Cape \'mȯr-əs-'je-səp, 'mär-\ headland N Greenland in Peary Land on Arctic Ocean; is world's northernmost dry land

Morrison, Mount — see YU SHAN

Morrison Cave — see LEWIS AND CLARK CAVERN

Mor·ris·town \'mȯr-əs-,tau̇n, 'mär-\ city E Tenn. ENE of Knoxville *pop* 21,385

Mor·ton Grove \'mȯr-t³n\ village NE Ill. W of Evanston *pop* 22,408

Mos·cow \'mäs-(,)kō, -,kau̇\ *or Russian* **Mos·kva** \mäsk-'vä\ **1** river 315 *mi* (507 *km*) W *central* Russia in Europe flowing E into Oka River **2** city ✱ of Russia & *formerly* of U.S.S.R. & of Soviet Russia on Moscow River *pop* 8,769,000 — see MUSCOVY

Mo·selle \mō-'zel\ *or German* **Mo·sel** \'mō-zəl\ river *about* 340 *mi* (545 *km*) E France & W Germany flowing from Vosges Mountains into the Rhine at Koblenz

Mosquito Coast *or* **Mos·qui·tia** \mə-'skē-tē-ə\ region Central America bordering on the Caribbean in E Honduras & E Nicaragua

Mos·sel Bay \'mȯ-səl\ city & port S Republic of South Africa in S Western Cape on Mossel Bay (inlet of Indian Ocean) *pop* 17,574

Moss Point city SE Miss. E of Gulfport *pop* 17,837

Mos·tag·a·nem \mə-'sta-gə-,nem\ city & port NW Algeria *pop* 114,534

Mo·sul \mō-'sül, 'mō-səl\ city N Iraq on the Tigris *pop* 264,146

Moul·mein \mül-'mān, mȯl-, -'mīn\ city S Myanmar on Gulf of Martaban at mouth of the Salween *pop* 171,977

Mound City Group National Monument reservation S Ohio N of Chillicothe containing prehistoric mounds

Mountain Brook city N *central* Ala. E of Birmingham *pop* 19,810

Mountain View city W Calif. NW of San Jose *pop* 67,460

Mount De·sert Island \də-'zərt, 'de-zərt\ island S Maine in the Atlantic E of Penobscot Bay *area* 100 *sq mi* (260 *sq km*)

Mount·lake Terrace \'mau̇nt-,lāk\ city W Wash. N of Seattle *pop* 19,320

Mount Pearl town Canada in Newfoundland *pop* 23,689

Mount Pleasant 1 city *central* Mich. NW of Saginaw *pop* 23,285 **2** town SE S.C. on the coast *pop* 30,108

Mount Pros·pect \'prä-,spekt\ village NE Ill. *pop* 53,170

Mount Rainier National Park — see RAINIER (Mount)

Mount Rev·el·stoke National Park \'re-vəl-,stōk\ reservation Canada in SE British Columbia on a plateau including Mt. Revelstoke W of Selkirk Mountains

Mount Royal — see MONT-ROYAL

Mount Saint Helens National Volcanic Monument — see SAINT HELENS (Mount)

Mount Ver·non \'vər-nən\ city SE N.Y. *pop* 67,153

Mourne Mountains mountains SE Northern Ireland

Moyle \'mȯil\ district N Northern Ireland, established 1974 *area* 191 *sq mi* (497 *sq km*), *pop* 14,617

Mo·zam·bique \,mō-zəm-'bēk\ *or Portuguese* **Mo·çam·bi·que** \,mü-sám-'bē-kə\ **1** channel 950 *mi* (1529 *km*) long SE Africa between Madagascar & Mozambique **2** *or formerly* **Portuguese East Africa** country SE Africa bordering on Mozambique Channel; a republic, until 1975 a dependency of Portugal ✱ Maputo *area* 297,846 *sq mi* (771,421 *sq km*), *pop* 15,243,000 — **Mo·zam·bi·can** \,mō-zəm-'bē-kən\ *adjective or noun*

Mpu·ma·lan·ga \əm-,pü-mä-'län-gä\ *or formerly* **Eastern Transvaal** province NE Republic of South Africa *area* 30,259 *sq mi* (78,370 *sq km*), *pop* 2,911,000

Mtwa·ra \əm-'twär-ä\ city & port Tanzania in SE mainland

Mu·dan·jiang *or* **Mu-tan—chiang** *or* **Mu·tan·kiang** \'mü-'dän-'jyän\ city NE China in S Heilongjiang on the **Mudan River** (310 *mi* or 496 *km* flowing NE into Songhua River) *pop* 571,705

Mu·gu, Point \mə-'gü\ cape SW Calif. W of Los Angeles

Muir Woods National Monument \'myu̇r\ reservation N Calif. NW of San Francisco containing a redwood grove

Mui·zen·berg \'mī-z³n-,bərg\ town Republic of South Africa on False Bay, SSE suburb of Cape Town

Mukalla — see AL MUKALLA

Mukden — see SHENYANG

Mukhā, Al — see MOCHA

Mül·heim \'mül-,hīm, 'myül-, 'mēl-\ *or* **Mülheim an der Ruhr** \än-də(r)-'ru̇r\ city W Germany on Ruhr River *pop* 177,042

Mul·house \mə-'lüz\ commune NE France in Alsace *pop* 109,905

Mull \'məl\ island W Scotland in the Inner Hebrides *area* 351 *sq mi* (913 *sq km*), *pop* 1499

Mul·lin·gar \,mə-lən-'gär\ town N *central* Ireland ✱ of Westmeath *pop* 8077

Mul·tan \mu̇l-'tän\ city NE Pakistan SW of Lahore *pop* 742,000

Mult·no·mah Falls \,məlt-'nō-mə\ waterfall 620 *ft* (189 *m*) NW Oreg. E of Portland in a tributary of Columbia River

Mumbai — see BOMBAY 2

München–Gladbach — see MONCHENGLADBACH

Mun·cie \'mən(t)-sē\ city E *central* Ind. *pop* 71,035

Mun·de·lein \'mən-də-,līn\ village NE Ill. NW of Chicago *pop* 21,215

Mu·nich \'myü-nik\ *or German* **Mün·chen** \'mu̇en-ken\ city S Germany ✱ of Bavaria on the Isar *pop* 1,229,052

Mun·ster \'mən(t)-stər\ **1** town NW Ind. *pop* 19,949 **2** province S Ireland *area* 9316 *sq mi* (24,168 *sq km*), *pop* 789,869

Mün·ster \'mən(t)-stər, 'mu̇n(t)-, 'mu̇en-\ city W Germany; formerly ✱ of Westphalia *pop* 264,181

Mun·te·nia \mu̇n-'tē-nē-ə, mən-'tē-\ *or* **Greater Walachia** region SE Romania in E part of Walachia

Mur \'mu̇r\ *or* **Mu·ra** \'mu̇r-ə\ river 279 *mi* (449 *km*) Austria, NE Slovenia, & N tip of Croatia flowing into the Drava

Mu·rat \mu̇-'rät\ *or ancient* **Ar·sa·ni·as** \är-'sä-nē-əs\ river 380 *mi* (612 *km*) E Turkey flowing WSW into the Euphrates

Mur·chi·son \'mər-chə-sən\ river 440 *mi* (708 *km*) Australia in W Western Australia flowing W into Indian Ocean

Murchison Falls — see KABALEGA FALLS

Mur·cia \'mər-sh(ē-)ə\ **1** region & ancient kingdom SE Spain bordering on the Mediterranean **2** province SE Spain bordering on the Mediterranean *area* 4369 *sq mi* (11,316 *sq km*), *pop* 1,045,601 **3** commune, its ✱ & ✱ of ancient kingdom of Murcia *pop* 318,838

Mu·res \'mü-,resh\ *or Hungarian* **Ma·ros** \'mȯr-,ōsh\ river 450 *mi* (725 *km*), *central* Romania & E Hungary flowing W into the Tisza

Mur·frees·bo·ro \'mər-f(r)ēz-,bər-ō\ city *central* Tenn. *pop* 44,922

Mur·mansk \mu̇r-'man(t)sk, -'män(t)sk\ city & port NW Russia in Europe on an inlet of Barents Sea *pop* 468,000

Mur·ray \'mər-ē, 'mə-rē\ **1** city N Utah *pop* 31,282 **2** river 1609 *mi* (2589 *km*) SE Australia flowing from near Mt. Kosciusko in E Victoria W into Indian Ocean in SE S. Australia

Mur·rum·bidg·ee \,mər-əm-'bi-jē, ,mə-rəm-\ river *almost* 1000 *mi* (1609 *km*) SE Australia in New South Wales flowing W into Murray River

Murviedro — see SAGUNTO

Mu·sa, Ge·bel \'je-bəl-'mü-sə\ mountain group NE Egypt in S Sinai Peninsula — see HOREB (MOUNT), KATHERINA (Gebel)

Mu·sa, Je·bel \'je-bəl-'mü-sə\ *or ancient* **Ab·i·la** *or* **Ab·y·la** \'a-bə-lə\ mountain 2775 *ft* (846 *m*) N Morocco opposite Rock of Gibraltar — see PILLARS OF HERCULES

Muscat — see MASQAT

Muscat and Oman — see OMAN

Mus·ca·tine \ˌməs-kə-'tēn\ city E Iowa *pop* 22,881

Mus·co·vy \'məs-kə-vē\ **1** the principality of Moscow (founded 1295) which in 15th century came to dominate Russia **2** RUSSIA — a former name

Mus·ke·gon \mə-'skē-gən\ **1** river 200 *mi* (322 *km*) W central Mich. flowing SW into Lake Michigan **2** city & port SW Mich. *pop* 40,283

Mus·kin·gum \mə-'skiŋ-əm, -gəm\ river 120 *mi* (193 *km*) E Ohio flowing SSE into Ohio River

Mus·ko·gee \(ˌ)mə-'skō-gē\ city E Okla. *pop* 37,708

Mus·ko·ka, Lake \mə-'skō-kə\ lake Canada in SE Ontario E of Georgian Bay & N of Lake Simcoe *area* 54 *sq mi* (140 *sq km*)

Mus·sel·shell \'mə-səl-ˌshel\ river 300 *mi* (483 *km*) central Mont. flowing E & N into Missouri River

Mutina — see MODENA

Mu·tsu Bay \'müt-(ˌ)sü\ inlet N Japan on NE Honshu on Tsugaru Strait

Muttra — see MATHURA

Muz·tag \müs-'täg, məz-\ *or* **Ulugh Muz·tagh** \ˌü-lə-müs-'täg,-məz-\ mountain 25,340 *ft* (7724 *m*) W China in S Xinjiang Uygur; highest in Kunlun Mountains

Mwe·ru \'mwā-rü\ lake 76 *mi* (122 *km*) long on border between Democratic Republic of the Congo & Zambia SW of Lake Tanganyika

Myan·mar \'myän-ˌmär\ *or formerly* **Bur·ma** \'bər-mə\ country SE Asia on Bay of Bengal; a federal republic ✳ Yangon *area* 261,789 *sq mi* (680,651 *sq km*), *pop* 45,573,000

Myc·a·le \'mi-kə-(ˌ)lē\ promontory W Turkey opposite Samos Is.

My·ce·nae \mī-'sē-(ˌ)nē\ ancient city S Greece in NE Peloponnese

My·ko·la·yiv \ˌmē-kə-'lä-yif\ *or* **Ni·ko·la·yev** \ˌnē-\ city & port S Ukraine

Myk·o·nos \'mi-kə-ˌnōs\ *or New Greek* **Mí·ko·nos** \'mē-kō-ˌnós\ island Greece in the Aegean in NE Cyclades *area* 35 *sq mi* (91 *sq km*)

Mylae — see MILAZZO

My·men·singh \ˌmī-mən-'siŋ\ city N Bangladesh *pop* 198,662

My·ra \'mī-rə\ ancient city S Asia Minor on coast of Lycia

Myr·tle Beach \'mər-tᵊl\ city E S.C. on the Atlantic *pop* 24,848

My·sia \'mi-sh(ē-)ə\ ancient country NW Asia Minor bordering on the Propontis — **My·sian** \-sh(ē-)ən\ *adjective or noun*

My·sore \'mī-ˌsōr, -'sor\ **1** — see KARNATAKA **2** city S India in S Karnataka *pop* 606,755

Mys·tic \'mis-tik\ river E Mass. flowing SE into Boston harbor

Mytilene — see LESBOS

Naas \'näs\ town E Ireland in Leinster ✳ of Kildare *pop* 11,140

Nab·a·taea *or* **Nab·a·tea** \ˌna-bə-'tē-ə\ ancient Arab kingdom SE of Palestine — **Nab·a·tae·an** *or* **Nab·a·te·an** \-'tē-ən\ *adjective or noun*

Na·be·rezh·nye Chel·ny \nä-bə-ˌrezh-nə-'chel-nē, nä-bir-'yezh-ni-yə-chil-'nē\ city E Russia in Europe in Tatarstan *pop* 514,000

Nab·lus \'na-bləs, 'nä-\ *or* **Nā·bu·lus** \'nä-bù-lùs\ *or ancient* **She·chem** \'she-kəm, -ˌkem\ *or* **Ne·ap·o·lis** \nē-'a-pə-lis\ city central Palestine in Samaria; now in W Jordan *pop* 106,944

Nac·og·do·ches \ˌna-kə-'dō-chəz, -chəs\ city E Tex. *pop* 30,872

Nafud *or* **Nafūd, An** — see AN NAFUD

Na·ga Hills \'nä-gə\ hills E India & N Myanmar SE of the Brahmaputra; highest Saramati 12,553 *ft* (3826 *m*)

Na·ga·land \'nä-gə-ˌland\ state E India N of Manipur in Naga Hills ✳ Kohima *area* 6366 *sq mi* (16,488 *sq km*), *pop* 1,209,546

Na·ga·no \nä-'gä-(ˌ)nō\ city Japan on Honshu *pop* 350,673

Na·ga·sa·ki \ˌnä-gä-'sä-kē, ˌnä-gə-'sa-kē\ city & port Japan in W Kyushu on E. China Sea *pop* 442,373

Na·gor·no–Ka·ra·bakh \nə-ˌgor-(ˌ)nō-'kär-ə-ˌbäk\ autonomous oblast SW Azerbaijan ✳ Stepanakert *area* 1700 *sq mi* (4420 *sq km*), *pop* 193,300

Na·goya \nə-'gói-ə, 'nä-gò-(ˌ)yä\ city Japan in S central Honshu *pop* 2,154,664

Nag·pur \'näg-ˌpùr\ city E central India in NE Maharashtra *pop* 1,624,752

Na·ha \'nä-(ˌ)hä\ city & port Ryukyu Islands in SW Okinawa Is. ✳ of Okinawa *pop* 304,896

Na·han·ni National Park \nä-'hä-nē\ reservation W Canada in SW Northwest Territories

Na·huel Hua·pí \nä-'wel-wä-'pē\ lake SW Argentina in the Andes in **Nahuel Huapí National Park**

Nairn \'narn, 'nern\ **1** *or* **Nairn·shire** \-ˌshir, -shər\ former county NE Scotland **2** burgh, its ✳, on Moray Firth *pop* 10,420

Nai·ro·bi \nī-'rō-bē\ city S central Kenya, its ✳ *pop* 1,504,000

Najd — see NEJD — **Najdi** \'näj-dē, 'nazh-\ *adjective or noun*

Nal·chik \'näl-chik\ town S Russia in Europe ✳ of Kabardino-Balkaria *pop* 242,000

Na·ma·qua·land \nä-'mä-kwä-ˌland\ *or* **Na·ma·land** \'nä-mə-\ region SW Africa; divided by Orange River into **Great Namaqualand** (in Namibia) & **Little Namaqualand** (in Northern Cape province, Republic of South Africa, chief town Springbok)

Na·mi·be \nä-'mē-bä\ *or formerly* **Mo·çâ·me·des** \mə-'sä-mə-dish\ town & port SW Angola

Na·mib·ia \nə-'mi-bē-ə\ *or formerly* **South–West Africa** *or 1884–1919* **South-west Africa** country SW Africa on the Atlantic; until 1990 a territory administered by South Africa which captured it from Germany in World War I ✳ Windhoek *area* 318,321 *sq mi* (824,451 *sq km*), *pop* 1,511,600 — **Na·mib·ian** \-bē-ən, -byən\ *adjective or noun*

Nam·pa \'nam-pə\ city SW Idaho W of Boise *pop* 28,365

Nam·po \'nam-(ˌ)pō, 'näm-\ *or formerly* **Chin·nam·po** \'chē(n)-ˌnäm-(ˌ)pō\ city & port SW N. Korea SW of Pyongyang *pop* 130,000

Na·mur \nə-'mùr, -'myùr\ **1** province S Belgium *area* 1413 *sq mi* (3674 *sq km*), *pop* 423,317 **2** commune, its ✳ *pop* 104,200

Nan \'nän\ river 390 *mi* (628 *km*) N Thailand flowing S to join the Ping forming the Chao Phraya

Na·nai·mo \nä-'nī-(ˌ)mō\ city Canada in British Columbia on SE Vancouver Is. *pop* 60,129

Nan·chang \'nän-'chäŋ\ city SE China ✳ of Jiangxi on the Gan SW of Poyang Lake *pop* 1,086,124

Nan·cy \nän(t)-sē, näⁿ-'sē\ city NE France on the Meurthe *pop* 102,410

Nan·da De·vi \ˌnən-də-'dä-vē\ mountain 25,645 *ft* (7816 *m*) N India in the Himalayas in Uttar Pradesh

Nan·di *or* **Na·di** \'nän-(ˌ)dē\ village Fiji on W Viti Levu Is.

Nan·ga Par·bat \ˌnəŋ-gə-'pər-bət\ mountain 26,660 *ft* (8126 *m*) NW Kashmir in the W Himalayas

Nan·jing \'nän-'jiŋ\ *or* **Nan·king** \'nan-'kiŋ, 'nän-\ city E China on the Chang ✳ of Jiangsu & (1928–37 & 1946–49) ✳ of China *pop* 2,090,204

Nan Ling \'nän-'liŋ\ mountain system SE China roughly separating Guangdong & Guangxi Zhuangzu from Hunan & Guizhou

Nan·ning \'nän-'niŋ\ *or formerly* **Yung·ning** \'yùŋ-'niŋ\ city S China ✳ of Guangxi Zhuangzu *pop* 721,877

Nan·terre \näⁿ-'ter\ commune N France W of Paris *pop* 86,627

Nantes \'nan(t)s, 'näⁿt\ city NW France on the Loire *pop* 252,029

Nan·ti·coke \'nan-ti-ˌkōk\ city Canada in SE Ontario *pop* 22,727

Nan·tong \'nän-'tùŋ\ *or* **Nan·tung** \-'tùŋ\ city & port E China in SE Jiangsu on Chang estuary NW of Shanghai *pop* 343,341

Nan·tuck·et \nan-'tə-kət\ island Mass. S of Cape Cod on **Nantucket Sound** (inlet of the Atlantic) *pop* 6012 — **Nan·tuck·et·er** \-kə-tər\ *noun*

Napa \'na-pə\ city W Calif. N of Vallejo *pop* 61,842

Na·per·ville \'nä-pər-ˌvil\ city NE Ill. W of Chicago *pop* 85,351

Na·pi·er \'nä-pē-ər\ borough & port New Zealand in E North Is. on Hawke Bay *pop* 51,645

Na·ples \'nä-pəlz\ **1** city SW Fla. *pop* 19,505 **2** *or Italian* **Na·po·li** \'nä-pō-lē\ *or ancient* **Ne·ap·o·lis** \nē-'a-pə-ləs\ city & port S Italy on **Bay of Naples** (inlet of Tyrrhenian Sea) ✳ of Campania *pop* 1,054,601

Na·po \'nä-(ˌ)pō\ river 550 *mi* (885 *km*) NW S. America rising near Mt. Cotopaxi in central Ecuador & flowing E & SE into the Amazon

Na·ra \'när-ä\ city Japan in W central Honshu E of Osaka; an early ✳ of Japan *pop* 349,356

Nar·bonne \när-'bän, -'bən\ city S France *pop* 47,086

Na·rew \'när-ˌef, -ˌev\ *or Russian* **Na·rev** \'när-if\ river NE Poland flowing W & SW into Bug River

Nar·ma·da \nər-'mə-də\ river 800 *mi* (1287 *km*) central India flowing W between Vindhya Mountains & Satpura Range into Gulf of Khambhat

Nar·ra·gan·sett Bay \ˌnar-ə-'gan(t)-sət\ inlet of the Atlantic SE R.I.

Nar·vik \'när-vik\ town & port N Norway *pop* 18,736

Nash·ua \'na-shə-wə *also* -ˌwä\ city S N.H. *pop* 79,662

Nash·ville \'nash-ˌvil, -vəl\ city N central Tenn., its ✳ *pop* 488,374

Nas·sau **1** \'na-ˌsò\ city & port ✳ of Bahamas on New Providence Is. *pop* 172,196 **2** \-ˌsò, *German* 'nä-ˌsaù\ region Germany N & E of the Rhine; chief city Wiesbaden **3** — see SUDIRMAN

Nasser, Lake — see ASWAN

Na·tal \nə-'tal, -'täl\ **1** city & port NE Brazil ✳ of Rio Grande do Norte *pop* 606,541 **2** former province E Republic of South Africa between Drakensberg Mountains & Indian Ocean *area* 35,320 *sq mi* (91,479 *sq km*)

Natch·ez \'na-chəz\ city SW Miss. on Mississippi River *pop* 19,460

Natchez Trace pioneer road between Natchez, Miss., & Nashville, Tenn., used in the early 19th century

Na·tick \'nä-tik\ town E Mass. W of Boston *pop* 30,510

National City city SW Calif. S of San Diego *pop* 54,249

Native States — see INDIAN STATES

Natural Bridges National Monument reservation SE Utah

Nau·cra·tis \'nò-krə-təs\ ancient Greek city N Egypt in Nile delta

Nau·ga·tuck \'nò-gə-ˌtək\ borough SW central Conn. *pop* 30,625

Nau·plia \'nò-plē-ə\ *or* **Nau·pli·on** \-plē-ən\ *or New Greek* **Náv·pli·on** \'näf-plē-ˌón\ town & port S Greece in E Peloponnese near head of Gulf of Argolis *pop* 11,453

Na·u·ru \nä-'ü-(ˌ)rü\ *or formerly* **Pleas·ant Island** \'ple-zᵊnt\ island (atoll) W Pacific 26 *mi* (42 *km*) S of the equator; formerly a joint Brit., New Zealand, & Australian trust territory; since 1968 an independent republic *area* 8 *sq mi* (21 *sq km*), *pop* 10,000 — **Na·u·ru·an** \-'ü-rə-wən\ *adjective or noun*

Na·va·jo National Monument \'nä-və-ˌhō-, 'nä-\ reservation N Ariz. SW of Monument Valley near Utah boundary containing cliff dwellings

Na·varre \nə-'vär\ *or Spanish* **Na·var·ra** \nä-'vär-ä\ **1** region & former kingdom N Spain & SW France in W Pyrenees **2** province N Spain ✳ Pamplona *area* 4024 *sq mi* (10,422 *sq km*), *pop* 519,277

Navigators Islands — see SAMOA

Náv·pak·tos \'näf-ˌpäk-tòs\ town & port Greece on N shore of strait connecting Gulf of Corinth & Gulf of Patras

Nax·ci·van \ˌnək-chi-'vän\ *or* **Na·khi·che·van** \ˌnä-ki-chə-'vän\ **1** exclave of Azerbaijan separated from the rest of the country by Armenia *area* 2124 *sq mi* (5501 *sq km*), *pop* 305,700 **2** city, its ✳, on the Araks *pop* 61,700

Nax·os \'nak-səs, -ˌsäs\ **1** *or New Greek* **Ná·xos** \'näk-ˌsòs\ island Greece, largest of the Cyclades *area* 165 *sq mi* (427 *sq km*) **2** oldest Greek colony in Sicily; ruins SW of Taormina

Na·ya·rit \ˌnä-yä-'rēt\ state W Mexico bordering on the Pacific ✳ Tepic *area* 10,664 *sq mi* (27,620 *sq km*), *pop* 824,543

Naz·a·reth \'na-zə-rəth\ city N Israel in Galilee SE of Haifa *pop* 49,800

Naze, The \'näz\ headland SE England on E coast of Essex

Na·zil·li \ˌnä-zē-'lē\ city SW Turkey SE of Izmir

Naz·ran \'näz-rənʸ\ town S Russia in Europe ✳ of Ingushetia

N'Dja·me·na \ən-jä-'mä-nä, -'mē-\ *or formerly* **Fort–La·my** \ˌför-lə-'mē\ city on the Chari ✴ of Chad *pop* 687,800

Neagh, Lough \'nä\ lake *central* Northern Ireland *area* 153 *sq mi* (398 *sq km*); largest in British Isles

Neapolis 1 — see NABLUS **2** — see NAPLES

Near Islands \'nir\ islands SW Alaska at W end of the Aleutians — see ATTU

Near East 1 the Ottoman Empire at its greatest extent — a former usage **2** the countries of SW Asia & NE Africa — **Near Eastern** *adjective*

Nebo, Mount — see PISGAH (Mount)

Ne·bras·ka \nə-'bras-kə\ state *central* U.S. ✴ Lincoln *area* 77,355 *sq mi* (200,349 *sq km*), *pop* 1,578,385 — **Ne·bras·kan** \-kən\ *adjective or noun*

Ne·chako \ni-'cha-(ˌ)kō\ river 287 *mi* (462 *km*) Canada in *central* British Columbia flowing N & E into the Fraser

Ne·ches \'ne-chəz\ river E Tex. flowing S & SE into Sabine Lake

Neck·ar \'ne-kər, -ˌkär\ river 228 *mi* (367 *km*) SW Germany rising in the Black Forest & flowing N & W into the Rhine

Neck·er \'ne-kər\ island Hawaii in Leewards NW of Niihau Is.

Need·ham \'nē-dəm\ town E Mass. WSW of Boston *pop* 27,557

Nee·nah \'nē-nə\ city E Wis. on Lake Winnebago *pop* 23,219

Ne·ge·ri Sem·bi·lan \'ne-grē-səm-'bē-lən\ state Malaysia in Peninsular Malaysia on Strait of Malacca ✴ Seremban *area* 2590 *sq mi* (6708 *sq km*), *pop* 691,200

Neg·ev \'ne-ˌgev\ *or* **Ha·Neg·ev** \ˌhä-\ *or* **Neg·eb** \-ˌgeb\ region S Israel, a triangular wedge of desert touching Gulf of Aqaba in S

Ne·gro \'nā-(ˌ)grō, 'ne-\ **1** river 400 *mi* (640 *km*) S *central* Argentina flowing E into the Atlantic **2** river 1400 *mi* (2253 *km*) E Colombia & N Brazil flowing into the Amazon **3** river 434 *mi* (698 *km*) *central* Uruguay flowing SW into Uruguay River

Ne·gros \'nā-(ˌ)grōs, 'ne-\ island S *central* Philippines in the Visayas SE of Panay Is. *area* 4905 *sq mi* (12,753 *sq km*)

Neige, Mount — see JURA 2

Nei·jiang *or* **Nei–chiang** \'nā-'jyäŋ\ city *central* China in S *central* Szechwan SE of Chengdu *pop* 256,012

Nei Monggol — see INNER MONGOLIA

Neis·se \'nī-sə\ **1** *or* **Lau·sitz·er Neisse** \'laú-zit-sər-\ river 159 *mi* (256 *km*) N Europe flowing from N Czech Republic N into the Oder **2** — see NYSA

Nejd \'nejd, 'nezhd\ *or* **Najd** \'najd, 'nazhd\ region *central* & E Saudi Arabia; *area* 447,000 *sq mi* (1,162,200 *sq km*), *pop* 1,200,000 — **Nejdi** \'nej-dē, 'nezh-\ *adjective or noun*

Nel·son \'nel-sən\ **1** river 400 *mi* (644 *km*) Canada in Manitoba flowing from N end of Lake Winnipeg to Hudson Bay **2** city & port New Zealand on N coast of South Is. *pop* 37,943

Ne·man \'ne-mən\ *or* **Ne·mu·nas** \'ne-mü-ˌnäs\ river 582 *mi* (936 *km*) *central* Europe flowing from *central* Belarus N & W through Lithuania & along border with exclave of Russia into Courland Lagoon

Ne·mea \'nē-mē-ə\ valley & town Greece in NE Peloponnese W of Corinth — **Ne·me·an** \'nē-mē-ən, ni-'mē-\ *adjective*

Ne·o·sho \nē-'ō-(ˌ)shō, -shə\ *or in Oklahoma* **Grand** river 460 *mi* (740 *km*) SE Kans. & NE Okla. flowing SE & S into Arkansas River; now largely submerged in dam-created lakes and reservoirs in its lower course

Ne·pal \nə-'pól, nä-, -'päl *also* nə-'pal\ country Asia on NE border of India in the Himalayas; a kingdom ✴ Kathmandu *area* 54,362 *sq mi* (140,798 *sq km*), *pop* 20,220,000 — **Nep·a·lese** \ˌne-pə-'lēz, -'lēs\ *adjective or noun*

Ne·pe·an \'nē-pē-ən\ city Canada in SE Ontario SW of Ottawa *pop* 107,627

Ness, Loch \'nes\ lake 23 *mi* (37 *km*) long NW Scotland in Highland region

Néstos — see MESTA

Neth·er·lands \'ne-thər-ləndz\ **1** LOW COUNTRIES — an historical usage **2** *or* **Hol·land**

\'hä-lənd\ *or Dutch* **Ne·der·land** \'nā-dər-ˌlänt\ country NW Europe on North Sea; a kingdom, official ✴ Amsterdam, de facto ✴ The Hague *area* 16,033 *sq mi* (41,525 *sq km*), *pop* 15,009,000 — **Neth·er·land** \'ne-thər-lənd\ *adjective* — **Neth·er·land·er** \-ˌlan-dər, -lən-\ *noun* — **Neth·er·land·ic** \ˌlan-dik\ *adjective* — **Neth·er·land·ish** \-ˌlan-dish, -lən-\ *adjective*

Netherlands Antilles Dutch overseas territory, W. Indies comprising Bonaire, Curaçao, Saba, St. Eustatius, & S part of St. Martin ✴ Willemstad (on Curaçao) *area* over 370 *sq mi* (958 *sq km*), *pop* 190,566

Netherlands East Indies — see INDONESIA

Netherlands Guiana — see SURINAME

Netherlands New Guinea — see IRIAN JAYA

Netherlands Timor — see TIMOR

Néthou, Pic de — see ANETO (Pico de)

Net·tu·no \ne-'tü-(ˌ)nō\ commune Italy on Tyrrhenian Sea SSE of Rome adjoining Anzio *pop* 34,653

Neu·châ·tel \ˌnü-shä-'tel, ˌnyü-, -ˌnə(r)-, ˌnœ-\ *or German* **Neu·en·burg** \'nói-ən-ˌbərg, -ˌbúrk\ **1** canton W Switzerland in Jura Mountains *area* 308 *sq mi* (798 *sq km*), *pop* 159,543 **2** commune, its ✴, on **Lake of Neuchâtel** (*area* 84 *sq mi* or 218 *sq km*), *pop* 32,757

Neuil·ly–sur–Seine \ˌnə(r)-yē-sùr-'sān, ˌnœ-'yē-sūr\ commune N France NW of Paris near the Bois de Boulogne *pop* 65,941

Neu·mün·ster \nói-'mœn-stər\ city N Germany SSW of Kiel *pop* 81,175

Neu·quén \nyü-'kän, nä-ü-\ river 320 *mi* (515 *km*) W Argentina flowing from the Andes E to join the Limay forming Negro River

Neuse \'nüs, 'nyüs\ river E *central* N.C. flowing SE into Pamlico Sound

Neuss \'nóis\ city W Germany W of Düsseldorf *pop* 147,663

Neus·tria \'nü-strē-ə, 'nyü-\ **1** the western part of the dominions of the Franks after the conquest by Clovis in 511, comprising the NW part of modern France between the Meuse, the Loire, & the Atlantic **2** a name for Normandy used after 912 — **Neus·tri·an** \-ən\ *adjective or noun*

Ne·va \'nē-və, 'nä-, nye-'vä\ river 40 *mi* (64 *km*) W Russia in Europe flowing from Lake Ladoga to Gulf of Finland at St. Petersburg

Ne·va·da \nə-'va-də, -'vä-\ state W U.S. ✴ Carson City *area* 110,561 *sq mi* (286,353 *sq km*), *pop* 1,201,833 — **Ne·va·dan** \-'va-dⁿn, -'vä-\ *or* **Ne·va·di·an** \-'va-dē-ən, -'vä-\ *adjective or noun*

Ne·vers \nə-'ver\ city *central* France SE of Orléans *pop* 43,889

Ne·ves \'nā-vəs\ city SE Brazil on Guanabara Bay *pop* 151,067

Ne·vis \'nē-vəs\ island Brit. West Indies, part of St. Kitts-Nevis, in the Leewards; chief town Charlestown *area* 50 *sq mi* (130 *sq km*) — **Ne·vis·ian** \nə-'vi-zh(ē-)ən\ *adjective*

New Albany city S Ind. on Ohio River *pop* 36,322

New Amsterdam town founded 1625 on Manhattan Is. by the Dutch; renamed New York 1664 by the British

New·ark \'nü-ərk, 'nyü-; *especially 2 & 4* 'nü-ˌärk, 'nyü-\ **1** city W Calif. SE of San Francisco *pop* 37,861 **2** city NE Del. W of Wilmington *pop* 25,098 **3** city & port NE N.J. on **Newark Bay** (W extension of Upper New York Bay) *pop* 275,221 **4** city *central* Ohio *pop* 44,389

New Bedford city & port SE Mass. on W side of Buzzards Bay *pop* 99,922

New Ber·lin \'bər-lən\ city SE Wis. W of Milwaukee *pop* 33,592

New Braun·fels \'braún-fəlz\ city SE *central* Tex. *pop* 27,334

New Brighton village SE Minn. N of St. Paul *pop* 22,207

New Britain 1 city *central* Conn. *pop* 75,491 **2** island Bismarck Archipelago; largest of group *area* 14,160 *sq mi* (36,674 *sq km*), *pop* 263,500

New Brunswick 1 city N *central* N.J. *pop* 41,711 **2** province SE Canada bordering on Gulf of Saint Lawrence & Bay of Fundy ✴ Fredericton *area* 27,633 *sq mi* (71,569 *sq km*), *pop* 723,900

New·burgh \'nü-ˌbərg, 'nyü-\ city SE N.Y. on Hudson River S of Poughkeepsie *pop* 26,454

New Caledonia island SW Pacific SW of Vanuatu; with nearby islands, constitutes an overseas department of France ✴ Nouméa *area* 7367 *sq mi* (19,081 *sq km*), *pop* 183,100

New Castile — see CASTILE

New·cas·tle \'nü-ˌka-səl, 'nyü-, *3 is locally* nü-', nyü-'\ **1** city & port SE Australia in E New South Wales at mouth of Hunter River *metropolitan area pop* 262,331 **2** town Canada in SE Ontario ENE of Toronto *pop* 49,479 **3** *or in full* **Newcastle upon Tyne** \'tīn\ city & port N England ✴ of Tyne and Wear *pop* 263,000 **4** *or in full* **Newcastle under Lyme** \'līm\ borough W *central* England in Staffordshire *pop* 117,400

New Delhi city ✴ of India in Delhi Territory S of city of (old) Delhi *pop* 294,149

New England 1 the NE U.S. comprising the states of Maine, N.H., Vt., Mass., R.I., & Conn. **2** region SE Australia in NE New South Wales; in area of **New England Range** (part of Great Dividing Range) — **New En·gland·er** \'iŋ-glən-dər *also* 'iŋ-lən-\ *noun* — **New En·glandy** \-dē\ *adjective*

New Forest forested area S England in Hampshire between the Avon & Southampton Water; once a royal hunting ground

New·found·land \'nü-fən(d)-lənd, 'nyü-, -ˌland; ˌnü-fən(d)-'land, ˌnyü-\ **1** island Canada in the Atlantic E of Gulf of St. Lawrence *area* 43,359 *sq mi* (112,300 *sq km*) **2** province E Canada comprising Newfoundland (island) & part of Labrador ✴ St. John's *area* 143,488 *sq mi* (371,634 *sq km*), *pop* 568,474 — **New·found·land·er** \-lən-dər, -ˌlan-; -ˌlan-dər\ *noun*

New France the possessions of France in N. America before 1763

New Georgia 1 island group W Pacific in *central* Solomon Islands **2** island 50 *mi* (80 *km*) long, chief island of the group

New Gra·na·da \grə-'nä-də\ Spanish viceroyalty in NW S. America 1717–1819 comprising area included in modern Panama, Colombia, Venezuela, & Ecuador

New Guinea 1 island in Malay Archipelago N of E Australia divided between Irian Jaya on W & Papua New Guinea on E *area* over 315,000 *sq mi* (815,850 *sq km*) **2** the NE portion of the island of New Guinea with the Bismarck Archipelago, Bougainville, Buka, & adjacent small islands; part of Papua New Guinea — see NORTH-EAST NEW GUINEA — **New Guin·ean** \'gi-nē-ən\ *adjective or noun*

New·ham \'nü-əm, 'nyü-\ borough of E Greater London, England *pop* 200,200

New Hamp·shire \'hamp-shər, -ˌshir\ state NE U.S. ✴ Concord *area* 9279 *sq mi* (24,033 *sq km*), *pop* 1,109,252 — **New Hamp·shire·man** \-mən\ *noun* — **New Hamp·shir·ite** \-ˌīt\ *noun*

New Ha·ven \'hā-vən\ city & port S Conn. *pop* 130,474 — **New Ha·ven·er** \'hā-və-nər\ *noun*

New Hebrides — see VANUATU

New Hope \'nü-ˌhōp, 'nyü-\ village E Minn. N of Minneapolis *pop* 21,853

New Iberia city S La. SE of Lafayette *pop* 31,828

New·ing·ton \'nü-iŋ-tən, 'nyü-\ town *central* Conn. SW of Hartford *pop* 29,208

New Ireland island W Pacific in Bismarck Archipelago N of New Britain ✴ Kavieng *area* 3340 *sq mi* (8684 *sq km*), *pop* (with adjacent islands) 48,774

New Jersey state E U.S. ✴ Trenton *area* 7787 *sq mi* (20,168 *sq km*), *pop* 7,730,188 — **New Jer·sey·an** \-ən\ *noun* — **New Jer·sey·ite** \-ˌīt\ *noun*

New London city & port SE Conn. on Long Island Sound at mouth of Thames River *pop* 28,540

New·mar·ket \'nü-ˌmär-kət, 'nyü-\ **1** town Canada in SE Ontario N of Toronto *pop* 45,474 **2** town E England in Suffolk *pop* 16,235

New Mex·i·co \'mek-si-ˌkō\ state SW U.S. ✳ Santa Fe *area* 121,593 *sq mi* (314,926 *sq km*), *pop* 1,515,069 — **New Mex·i·can** \-si-kən\ *adjective or noun*

New Milford city W Conn. *pop* 23,629

New Neth·er·land \'ne-thər-lənd\ Dutch colony in N. America 1613–64 occupying lands bordering on Hudson River & later also on lower Delaware River ✳ New Amsterdam

New Or·leans \'ȯr-lē-ənz, 'ȯr-lənz, 'ȯrl-yənz, (ˌ)ȯr-'lēnz\ city & port SE La. between Lake Pontchartrain & Mississippi River *pop* 496,938 — **New Or·lea·nian** \(ˌ)ȯr-'lē-nyən, -nē-ən\ *noun*

New·port \'nü-ˌpȯrt, 'nyü-, -ˌpȯrt\ **1** city & port SE R.I. on Narragansett Bay *pop* 28,227 **2** borough S England ✳ of Isle of Wight *pop* 23,570 **3** borough SE Wales in Gwent WNW of Bristol *pop* 129,900 — **New·port·er** \-ˌpȯr-tər, -ˌpȯr-\ *noun*

Newport Beach city SW Calif. SE of Long Beach *pop* 66,643

New·port News \'nü-ˌpȯrt-'nüz, 'nyü-ˌpȯrt-'nyüz, -ˌpȯrt-, -pərt-\ city & port SE Va. on James River & Hampton Roads *pop* 170,045

New Providence island in NW *central* Bahamas E of Andros; site of Nassau 80 *sq mi* (207 *sq km*)

New Quebec region Canada in N Quebec N of the Eastmain between Hudson Bay & Labrador — see UNGAVA

New Quebec Crater *or formerly* **Chubb Crater** \'chəb\ large water-filled meteoric crater Canada in N Quebec, in N Ungava Peninsula

New Ro·chelle \rə-'shel\ city SE N.Y. on Long Island Sound E of Mount Vernon *pop* 67,265

New·ry and Mourne \'nü-rē, 'nyü- . . . 'mȯrn\ district S Northern Ireland *area* 345 *sq mi* (894 *sq km*), *pop* 82,288

New Siberian Islands islands NE Russia in Asia in Arctic Ocean between Laptev & E. Siberian seas *area* 11,000 *sq mi* (28,600 *sq km*)

New South Wales state SE Australia bordering on the Pacific ✳ Sydney *area* 309,433 *sq mi* (801,431 *sq km*), *pop* 5,732,032

New Spain Spanish viceroyalty 1535–1821 including territory now in SW U.S., Mexico, Central America N of Panama, much of the West Indies, & the Philippines ✳ Mexico City

New Sweden Swedish colony in N. America 1638–55 bordering on W bank of Delaware River from modern Trenton, N.J., to its mouth

New Territories Hong Kong exclusive of Hong Kong Is. & Kowloon Peninsula

New·ton \'nü-tᵊn, 'nyü-\ city E Mass. W of Boston *pop* 82,585

New·town \'nü-ˌtau̇n, 'nyü-\ town SW Conn. E of Danbury *pop* 20,779

New·town·ab·bey \ˌnü-tᵊn-'a-bē, ˌnyü-\ district E Northern Ireland, established 1974 *area* 58 *sq mi* (150 *sq km*), *pop* 73,832

New·town Saint Bos·wells \'nü-ˌtau̇n-sənt-'bäz-wəlz, ˌnyü-, -sänt-\ village S Scotland W of Kelso ✳ of Borders region

New West·min·ster \wes(t)-'min(t)-stər\ city Canada in SW British Columbia on the Fraser ESE of Vancouver *pop* 43,585

New Windsor — see WINDSOR

New York **1** state NE U.S. ✳ Albany *area* 49,576 *sq mi* (121,898 *sq km*), *pop* 17,990,456 **2** *or* **New York City** city & port SE N.Y. at mouth of Hudson River; includes boroughs of Bronx, Brooklyn, Manhattan, Queens, & Staten Is. *pop* 7,322,564 **3** the borough of Manhattan in New York City — **New York·er** \'yȯr-kər\ *noun*

New York Bay inlet of the Atlantic SE N.Y. & NE N.J. at mouth of Hudson River forming harbor of metropolitan New York & consisting of **Upper New York Bay** & **Lower New York Bay** connected by the **Narrows** (strait separating Staten Is. & Long Is.)

New York State Barge Canal — see ERIE

New Zea·land \'zē-lənd\ country SW Pacific ESE of Australia comprising chiefly North Is. & South Is.; a dominion of the Commonwealth of Nations ✳ Wellington *area* 103,736 *sq mi* (269,714 *sq km*), *pop* 3,175,737 — **New Zea·land·er** \-lən-dər\ *noun*

Ngaliema, Mount — see STANLEY (Mount)

Nga·mi, Lake \ən-'gä-mē\ marshy depression NW Botswana N of Kalahari Desert; formerly a large lake

Ngau·ru·hoe \əŋ-ˌgau̇-rə-'hō-ē\ volcano 7515 *ft* (2291 *m*) New Zealand in *central* North Is. in Tongariro National Park

Ni·ag·a·ra Falls \(ˌ)nī-'a-g(ə-)rə\ **1** waterfalls on border between N.Y. & Ontario in the **Niaga·ra River** (36 *mi or* 58 *km* flowing from Lake Erie N into Lake Ontario); divided by Goat Is. into Horseshoe, *or* Canadian, Falls (158 *ft or* 48 *m* high) & American Falls (167 *ft or* 51 *m* high) **2** city W N.Y. at the falls *pop* 61,840 **3** city Canada in SE Ontario *pop* 75,399

Nia·mey \nē-'ä-(ˌ)mā, nyä-'mā\ city ✳ of Niger *pop* 392,165

Ni·as \'nē-ˌäs\ island Indonesia in Indian Ocean off W coast of Sumatra *area* 1569 *sq mi* (4079 *sq km*), *pop* 314,829 — **Ni·as·san** \'nē-ə-sən\ *noun*

Ni·caea \nī-'sē-ə\ *or* **Nice** ancient city of Byzantine Empire, site at modern village of Iznik in NW Turkey in Asia at E end of Iznik Lake — **Ni·cae·an** \nī-'sē-ən\ *adjective*

Nic·a·ra·gua \ˌni-kə-'rä-gwə, ˌnē-kä-'rä-gwä\ **1** lake *about* 100 *mi* (161 *km*) long S Nicaragua **2** country Central America bordering on the Pacific & the Caribbean; a republic ✳ Managua *area* 49,579 *sq mi* (128,410 *sq km*), *pop* 4,265,000 — **Nic·a·ra·guan** \-'rä-gwən\ *adjective or noun*

Nice \'nēs\ *or ancient* **Ni·caea** \nī-'sē-ə\ city & port SE France on the Mediterranean *pop* 345,674

Nic·o·bar Islands \'ni-kə-ˌbär\ islands India in Indian Ocean S of Andaman Islands *area* 740 *sq mi* (1917 *sq km*), *pop* 14,563 — see ANDAMAN AND NICOBAR

Nicomedia — see IZMIT

Ni·cop·o·lis \nə-'kä-pə-lis, nī-\ ancient city NW Greece in Epirus

Nic·o·sia \ˌni-kə-'sē-ə\ city *central* Cyprus, its ✳ *pop* 168,800

Nidwald, Nidwalden — see UNTERWALDEN

Niedersachsen — see LOWER SAXONY

Nieuw·poort *or* **Nieu·port** \'nü-ˌpȯrt, 'nyü-, -ˌpȯrt, *French* nyœ̄-'pȯr\ commune NW Belgium in W. Flanders on the Yser *pop* 9572

Ni·ger \'nī-jər, nē-'zher\ **1** river 2600 *mi* (4184 *km*) W Africa flowing from Fouta Djallon NE, SE, & S into Gulf of Guinea **2** country W Africa; a republic, until 1958 a territory of French West Africa ✳ Niamey *area* 459,073 *sq mi* (1,188,999 *sq km*), *pop* 8,516,000 — **Ni·ger·ois** \ˌnē-zhər-'wä, -zher-\ *noun*

Ni·ge·ria \nī-'jir-ē-ə\ country W Africa bordering on Gulf of Guinea; a republic within the Commonwealth of Nations, formerly a colony & protectorate ✳ Abuja *area* 356,669 *sq mi* (927,339 *sq km*), *pop* 88,514,501 — **Ni·ge·ri·an** \-ē-ən\ *adjective or noun*

Nii·ga·ta \nē-'gä-tä, 'nē-gä-ˌtä\ city & port Japan in N Honshu on Sea of Japan *pop* 486,087

Nii·hau \'nē-ˌhau̇\ island Hawaii WSW of Kauai *area* 72 *sq mi* (187 *sq km*)

Nij·me·gen \'nī-ˌmā-gən, 'nā-, -kə(n)\ commune E Netherlands in Gelderland on the Waal S of Arnhem *pop* 146,344

Nikaria — see IKARIA

Nikolayev — see MYKOLAYIV

Ni·ko·pol \'nē-kə-ˌpȯl, 'nyē-, -pəl\ city E *central* Ukraine on the Dnieper *pop* 159,000

Nile \'nīl\ river 4160 *mi* (6693 *km*) E Africa flowing from Lake Victoria in Uganda N into the Mediterranean in Egypt; in various sections called specifically: **Vic·to·ria Nile** \vik-'tȯr-ē-ə, -'tȯr-\ *or* **Som·er·set Nile** \'sə-mər-sət, -ˌset\ between Lake Victoria & Lake Albert; **Al·bert Nile** \'al-bərt\ between Lake Albert & Lake No; & **White Nile** from Lake No to Khartoum — see BLUE NILE

Niles \'nīlz\ **1** village NE Ill. NW of Chicago *pop* 28,284 **2** city NE Ohio SE of Warren *pop* 21,128

Nil·gi·ri Hills \'nil-gə-rē\ hills S India in W Tamil Nadu; highest point Mt. Dodabetta 8640 *ft* (2633 *m*)

Nimes \'nēm\ city S France NE of Montpellier *pop* 133,607

Nimrud — see CALAH

Nin·e·veh \'ni-nə-və\ *or Latin* **Ni·nus** \'nī-nəs\ ancient city ✳ of Assyria; ruins in Iraq on the Tigris opposite Mosul

Ning·bo *or* **Ning·po** \'niŋ-'bō\ *or formerly* **Ning·hsien** \'niŋ-'shyen\ city E China in N Zhejiang ESE of Hangzhou *pop* 552,540

Ninghsia, Ningsia — see YINCHUAN

Ning·xia Hui·zu \'niŋ-'shyä-'hwē-'dzü\ *or* **Ning·sia Hui** \'niŋ-'shyä-'hwē\ region N China; formerly a province ✳ Yinchuan *area* 30,039 *sq mi* (78,101 *sq km*), *pop* 4,655,451

Ni·o·brara \ˌnī-ə-'brar-ə, -'brer-\ river 431 *mi* (694 *km*) E Wyo. & N Nebr. flowing E into Missouri River

Niort \nē-'ȯr\ city W France ENE of La Rochelle *pop* 58,660

Nip·i·gon, Lake \'ni-pə-ˌgän\ lake Canada in W Ontario N of Lake Superior *area* 1870 *sq mi* (4862 *sq km*)

Nip·is·sing, Lake \'ni-pə-siŋ\ lake Canada in SE Ontario NE of Georgian Bay *area* over 320 *sq mi* (829 *sq km*)

Nippon — see JAPAN

Nip·pur \ni-'pu̇r\ ancient city of Sumer SSE of Babylon

Nis *or* **Nish** \'nish, 'nēsh\ city E Yugoslavia in E Serbia *pop* 247,898

Ni·shi·no·mi·ya \ni-shē-'nō-mē-ˌyä\ city Japan in *central* Honshu on Osaka Bay E of Kobe *pop* 426,919

Ni·te·rói *or formerly* **Nic·the·roy** \ˌnē-te-'rȯi\ city SE Brazil on Guanabara Bay opposite Rio de Janeiro *pop* 416,123

Ni·tra \'nī-trə, 'nyē-trä\ city W Slovakia *pop* 89,888

Ni·u·a·fo·'ou \nē-ˌü-ä-ˌfō-ō\ island SW *central* Pacific in the N Tongas *pop* 763

Ni·ue \nē-'ü-(ˌ)ā\ island S *central* Pacific; a self-governing territory of New Zealand *area* 100 *sq mi* (260 *sq km*), *pop* 2244 — **Ni·ue·an** \nyü-'wā-ən, 'nyü-ˌwā-\ *noun*

Ni·velles \nē-'vel\ commune *central* Belgium *pop* 23,217

Ni·ver·nais \ˌnē-vər-'nā\ region & former province *central* France E of the upper Loire ✳ Nevers

Nizh·niy Nov·go·rod *or* **Nizh·ni Novgorod** \'nizh-nē-'näv-gə-ˌräd, -'nȯv-gə-rət\ *or* 1932–89 **Gor·ki** \'gȯr-kē\ city *central* Russia in Europe at confluence of Oka & Volga rivers *pop* 1,433,000

Nizhniy Ta·gil *or* **Nizhni Tagil** \tə-'gil\ city W Russia in Asia on E slope of the Urals *pop* 437,000

No, Lake \'nō\ lake S *central* Sudan where Bahr el Jebel & Bahr el Ghazal join to form the White Nile *area* 40 *sq mi* (104 *sq km*)

No·gal·es \nə-'ga-ləs, -'gä-läs\ **1** city S Ariz. on Mexican border *pop* 19,489 **2** city NW Mexico in Sonora *pop* 107,119

Nome, Cape \'nōm\ cape W Alaska on S side of Seward Peninsula

Noordwes — see NORTH WEST

Noot·ka Sound \'nu̇t-kə, 'nüt-\ inlet of the Pacific Canada in SW British Columbia on W coast of Vancouver Is.

Nor·co \'nȯr-(ˌ)kō, 'nȯr-\ city SE Calif. W of Palm Springs *pop* 23,302

Nordenskjöld Sea — see LAPTEV SEA

Nord·kyn, Cape \'nȯr-kən, 'nȯr-; 'nür-ˌkēn\ cape NE Norway on Barents Sea; northernmost point of European mainland, at 71°8′N

Nord–Ostsee — see KIEL 2

Nor·folk \'nȯr-fək, *United States also* -ˌfȯk, -ˌfȯrk\ **1** city NE Nebr. *pop* 21,476 **2** city SE Va. on Elizabeth River S of Hampton Roads *pop* 261,229 **3** county E England bordering on North Sea ✳ Norwich *area* 2152 *sq mi* (5574 *sq km*), *pop* 736,400

Norfolk Broads — see BROADS

Norfolk Island island S Pacific between New Caledonia & New Zealand; administered by Australia *area* 13 *sq mi* (34 *sq km*), *pop* 1912

Norge — see NORWAY

Nor·i·cum \'nȯr-i-kəm, 'när-\ ancient country & Roman province S *central* Europe S of the Danube in modern Austria & S Germany

No·rilsk \nə-'rēlsk\ city N Russia in Asia, N of arctic circle near mouth of the Yenisey *pop* 165,000

Nor·mal \'nȯr-məl\ town *central* Ill. N of Bloomington *pop* 40,023

Nor·man \'nȯr-mən\ city *central* Okla. on Canadian River *pop* 80,071

Nor·man·dy \'nȯr-mən-dē\ *or French* **Nor·man·die** \nȯr-män-dē\ region & former province NW France NE of Brittany ✻ Rouen

Nor·ris·town \'nȯr-əs-,taùn, 'när-\ borough SE Pa. *pop* 30,749

Norr·kö·ping \'nȯr-,shē-piṅ\ city & port SE Sweden SW of Stockholm at head of an inlet of the Baltic *pop* 120,798

North·al·ler·ton \nȯr-'tha-lər-t⁰n\ town N England ✻ of N. Yorkshire

North America continent of the western hemisphere NW of S. America bounded by Atlantic, Arctic, & Pacific oceans *area* 9,361,791 *sq mi* (24,247,039 *sq km*) — **North American** *adjective or noun*

North·amp·ton \nȯr-'tham(p)-tən, nȯrth-'ham(p)-\ **1** city W *central* Mass. on Connecticut River N of Holyoke *pop* 29,289 **2** borough *central* England ✻ of Northamptonshire *pop* 145,421

North·amp·ton·shire \-,shir, -shər\ *or* **Northampton** county *central* England ✻ Northampton *area* 947 *sq mi* (2453 *sq km*), *pop* 572,900

North Andover town NE Mass. E of Lawrence *pop* 22,792

North Atlantic — see ATLANTIC OCEAN

North At·tle·bor·ough *or* **North At·tle·boro** \'a-t⁰l-,bər-ō\ town SE Mass. *pop* 25,038

North Bay \'nȯrth-,bā\ city Canada in SE Ontario *pop* 55,405

North Borneo — see SABAH

North Brabant *or Dutch* **Noord–Bra·bant** \,nȯrt-'brä-,bänt\ province S Netherlands ✻ 's Hertogenbosch *area* 1971 *sq mi* (5105 *sq km*), *pop* 2,243,546

North·brook \'nȯrth-,brùk\ village NE Ill. NW of Chicago *pop* 32,308

North Canadian river *about* 800 *mi* (1287 *km*) S *central* U.S. flowing ESE from NE N.Mex. into Canadian River in E Okla. — see BEAVER

North Cape **1** cape New Zealand at N tip of North Is. **2** cape NE Norway on **Ma·ger·öy** \,mä-gə-'rȯi\ island (*area* 111 *sq mi or* 289 *sq km*) at 71°10′27″N **3** — see HORN

North Car·o·li·na \,kar-(ə)-'lī-nə\ state E U.S. ✻ Raleigh *area* 52,669 *sq mi* (136,413 *sq km*), *pop* 6,628,637 — **North Car·o·lin·ian** \-'li-nē-ən, -'li-nyən\ *adjective or noun*

North Cas·cades National Park \kas-'kādz, 'kas-,\ reservation N *central* Wash. on Canadian border

North Channel strait between NE Ireland & SW Scotland connecting Irish Sea & the Atlantic

North Charleston city SE S.C. *pop* 70,218

North Chicago city NE Ill. S of Waukegan *pop* 34,978

North Da·ko·ta \də-'kō-tə\ state NW *central* U.S. ✻ Bismarck *area* 70,665 *sq mi* (183,729 *sq km*), *pop* 638,800 — **North Da·ko·tan** \-'kō-t⁰n\ *adjective or noun*

North Down district E Northern Ireland, established 1974 *area* 28 *sq mi* (73 *sq km*), *pop* 70,308

North Downs hills S England chiefly in Kent & Surrey

North East Frontier Agency — see ARUNACHAL PRADESH

North–East New Guinea the NE part of mainland Papua New Guinea

Northern *or* **Noord** \'nȯrd, 'nȯrt\ *or formerly* **Northern Transvaal** province NE Republic of South Africa *area* 47,598 *sq mi* (123,280 *sq km*), *pop* 5,013,000

Northern Cape province W Republic of South Africa *area* 139,691 *sq mi* (361,800 *sq km*), *pop* 749,000

Northern Cir·cars \(,)sər-'kärz\ historic name for the coast region of E India now in E Andhra Pradesh

Northern Cook Islands \'kùk\ *or* **Ma·ni·hi·ki Islands** \,mä-nē-'hē-kē\ islands S *central* Pacific N of Cook Islands; belong to New Zealand

Northern Ireland country NE Ireland; a division of the United Kingdom of Great Britain and Northern Ireland ✻ Belfast *area* 5452 *sq mi* (14,121 *sq km*), *pop* 1,543,000 — see ULSTER

Northern Karroo — see KARROO

Northern Kingdom — see ISRAEL

Northern Mar·i·ana Islands \,mar-ē-'a-nə, ,mer-\ islands W Pacific; in Trust Territory of the Pacific Islands 1947–76 & a U.S. commonwealth since 1986; *area* 184 *sq mi* (478 *sq km*), *pop* 45,400

Northern Rhodesia — see ZAMBIA

Northern Sporades — see SPORADES

Northern Territory territory *central* & N Australia bordering on Arafura Sea ✻ Darwin *area* 520,280 *sq mi* (1,347,525 *sq km*), *pop* 169,300

Northern Yukon National Park reservation NW Canada

North Frisian — see FRISIAN ISLANDS

North·glenn \'nȯrth-,glen\ city N *central* Colo. NE of Denver *pop* 27,195

North Ha·ven \'nȯrth-,hā-vən\ town S Conn. *pop* 22,247

North Holland *or Dutch* **Noord–Hol·land** \,nȯrt-'hȯ-,länt\ province NW Netherlands ✻ Haarlem *area* 1124 *sq mi* (2911 *sq km*), *pop* 2,440,165

North Island island N New Zealand *area* 44,297 *sq mi* (114,729 *sq km*), *pop* 2,553,413

North Khartoum — see KHARTOUM, NORTH

North Kings·town \'kiṅ-stən\ town S R.I. *pop* 23,786

North Korea — see KOREA — **North Korean** *adjective or noun*

North Las Vegas city SE Nev. *pop* 47,707

North Lau·der·dale \'lȯ-dər-,dāl\ city SE Fla. *pop* 26,506

North Little Rock city *central* Ark. *pop* 61,741

North Miami city SE Fla. *pop* 49,998

North Miami Beach city SE Fla. *pop* 35,359

North Minch — see MINCH

North Olm·sted \'əm-,sted\ city NE Ohio *pop* 34,204

North Ossetia — see ALANIA

North Pacific — see PACIFIC OCEAN

North Platte **1** river 680 *mi* (1094 *km*) W U.S. flowing from N Colo. N & E through Wyo. into Nebr. to unite with the S. Platte forming Platte River **2** city SW *central* Nebr. *pop* 22,605

North Providence town NE R.I. *pop* 32,090

North Rhine–Westphalia *or German* **Nord·rhein–West·fa·len** \'nȯrt-,rīn-,vest-'fä-lən\ state of Germany & formerly of W. Germany formed 1946 by union of former Westphalia province, Lippe state, & N Rhine Province ✻ Düsseldorf *area* 13,142 *sq mi* (34,038 *sq km*), *pop* 17,349,700

North Rich·land Hills \'rich-lənd\ town N Tex. *pop* 45,895

North Ridge·ville \'rij-,vil\ village N Ohio *pop* 21,564

North Riding — see YORK

North River estuary of Hudson River between SE N.Y. & NE N.J.

North Roy·al·ton \'rȯi(-ə)l-tən\ city N Ohio *pop* 23,197

North Saskatchewan — see SASKATCHEWAN

North Sea arm of the Atlantic 600 *mi* (966 *km*) long & 350 *mi* (563 *km*) wide E of Great Britain

North Slope region N Alaska between Brooks Range & Arctic Ocean

North Tonawanda city W N.Y. N of Buffalo *pop* 34,989

North Truchas Peak — see TRUCHAS PEAK

North·um·ber·land \nȯr-'thəm-bər-lənd\ county N England ✻ Newcastle upon Tyne *area* 2013 *sq mi* (5214 *sq km*), *pop* 300,600

Northumberland Strait strait 180 *mi* (290 *km*) long Canada in Gulf of St. Lawrence between Prince Edward Island & the mainland

North·um·bria \nȯr-'thəm-brē-ə\ ancient country Great Britain between the Humber & Firth of Forth; one of kingdoms in Anglo-Saxon heptarchy

North Vancouver city Canada in SW British Columbia *pop* 38,436

North Vietnam — see VIETNAM

North West *or* **Noord–wes** \,nȯrd-'wes, ,nȯrt-\ province N Republic of South Africa *area* 44,861 *sq mi* (116,190 *sq km*), *pop* 3,349,000

North–West Frontier Province province of Pakistan & formerly of Brit. India on Afghanistan border ✻ Peshawar *pop* 11,658,000

Northwest Passage a passage by sea between the Atlantic & the Pacific along the N coast of N. America

Northwest Territories territory N Canada comprising the Arctic islands, the mainland N 60° between Yukon Territory & Hudson Bay, & the islands in Hudson Bay; ✻ Yellowknife *area* 1,253,432 *sq mi* (3,246,389 *sq km*), *pop* 57,649

North York city Canada in SE Ontario N of Toronto *pop* 562,564

North Yorkshire county N England ✻ Northallerton *area* 3327 *sq mi* (8617 *sq km*), *pop* 698,700

Nor·ton Shores \'nȯr-t⁰n\ city W Mich. S of Muskegon *pop* 21,755

Norton Sound arm of Bering Sea W Alaska between Seward Peninsula & the mouths of Yukon River

Nor·walk \'nȯr-,wȯk\ **1** city SW Calif. SE of Los Angeles *pop* 94,279 **2** city SW Conn. on Long Island Sound *pop* 78,331

Nor·way \'nȯr-,wā\ *or Norwegian* **Nor·ge** \'nȯr-gə\ country N Europe in Scandinavia bordering on Atlantic & Arctic oceans; a kingdom ✻ Oslo *area* 154,790 *sq mi* (400,906 *sq km*), *pop* 4,308,000

Nor·we·gian Sea \nȯr-'wē-jən\ arm of the N Atlantic W of Norway

Nor·wich **1** \'nȯr-(,)wich; 'nȯr-ich, 'när-\ city SE Conn. *pop* 37,391 **2** \'när-ij, -ich\ city E England ✻ of Norfolk *pop* 120,700

Nor·wood \'nȯr-,wùd\ **1** town E Mass. SW of Boston *pop* 28,700 **2** city SW Ohio within city of Cincinnati *pop* 23,674

Not·ta·way \'nä-tə-,wā\ river 400 *mi* (644 *km*) Canada in SW Quebec flowing NW into James Bay

Not·ting·ham \'nä-tiṅ-əm, *United States also* -,ham\ borough N *central* England ✻ of Nottinghamshire *pop* 261,500

Not·ting·ham·shire \'nä-tiṅ-əm-,shir, -shər, *United States also* -,ham-\ *or* **Nottingham** *or* **Notts** \'näts\ county N *central* England ✻ Nottingham *area* 866 *sq mi* (2243 *sq km*), *pop* 980,600

Nouak·chott \nù-'äk-,shät\ city ✻ of Mauritania near coast in SW *pop* 393,325

Nou·méa \nü-'mā-ə\ city & port ✻ of New Caledonia *pop* 65,110

No·va Igua·çu \,nȯ-və-,ē-gwə-'sü\ city SE Brazil in Rio de Janeiro state NW of Rio de Janeiro *pop* 1,286,337

Nova Lisboa — see HUAMBO

No·va·ra \nō-'vär-ä\ commune NW Italy in Piedmont *pop* 102,473

No·va Sco·tia \,nō-və-'skō-shə\ province SE Canada comprising a peninsula (375 *mi or* 600 *km* long) & Cape Breton Is. ✻ Halifax *area* 20,402 *sq mi* (52,840 *sq km*), *pop* 899,942 — see ACADIA — **No·va Sco·tian** \-shən\ *adjective or noun*

No·va·to \nō-'vä-(,)tō\ city W Calif. N of San Francisco *pop* 47,585

No·va·ya Zem·lya \'nō-və-yə-,zem-lē-'ä\ two islands NE Russia in Arctic & Arctic Ocean between Barents Sea & Kara Sea *area* 31,382 *sq mi* (81,279 *sq km*), *pop* 400

Nov·go·rod \'näv-gə-,räd, 'nȯv-gə-rət\ **1** medieval principality E Europe extending from Lake Peipus & Lithuania to the Urals **2** city W Russia in Europe *pop* 235,000

No·vi \'nō-,vī\ village SE Mich. NW of Detroit *pop* 32,998

No·vi Sad \,nō-vē-'säd\ city N Yugoslavia on the Danube; chief city of Vojvodina *pop* 264,533

No·vo·kuz·netsk \,nō-(,)vō-kúz-'netsk, ,nȯ-və-küz-'nyetsk\ *or formerly* **Sta·linsk** \'stä-lin(t)sk, 'sta-; 'stäl-yin(t)sk\ city S Russia in Asia at S end of Kuznetsk Basin *pop* 600,000

No·vo·si·birsk \,nō-(,)vō-sə-'birsk, ,nȯ-və-\ *or formerly* **No·vo·ni·ko·la·evsk** \-,ni-kə-'lī-əfsk\ city S Russia in Asia on the Ob *pop* 1,442,000

Nu·bia \'nü-bē-ə, 'nyü-\ region & ancient kingdom NE Africa along the Nile in S Egypt & N Sudan

Nu·bi·an Desert \'nü-bē-ən, 'nyü-\ desert NE Sudan E of the Nile

Nu·e·ces \nü-'ā-səs, nyü-\ river over 300 *mi* (483 *km*) S Tex. flowing S & SE into Nueces Bay at head of Corpus Christi Bay

Nueva Esparta — see MARGARITA

Nue·vo La·re·do \'nwä-(,)vō-lä-'rä-(,)dō, -thō\ city N Mexico in Tamaulipas on Rio Grande opposite Laredo, Tex. *pop* 217,912

Nuevo Le·ón \lā-'ōn\ state N Mexico in the Sierra Madre Oriental ✱ Monterrey *area* 24,925 *sq mi* (64,556 *sq km*), *pop* 3,098,736

Nu·ku·'a·lo·fa \,nü-kü-ä-'lō-fä\ town ✱ of Tonga on Tongatapu Is. *pop* 21,383

Nu·ku Hi·va \,nü-kü-'hē-vä\ island S Pacific in the Marquesas; largest in group *area about* 60 *sq mi* (155 *sq km*), *pop* 2100; chief town Taiohae

Null·ar·bor Plain \'nə-lə-,bòr\ treeless plain SW Australia in Western Australia & S. Australia bordering on Great Australian Bight

Num·foor \'nüm-,fòr, -,fór\ island Irian Jaya in W Schouten Islands *area* 28 *sq mi* (73 *sq km*)

Nu·mid·ia \nü-'mi-dē-ə, nyü-\ ancient country N Africa of Mauretania in modern Algeria; chief city Hippo — **Nu·mid·i·an** \-dē-ən\ *adjective or noun*

Nun·ea·ton \,nə-'nē-t°n\ borough *central* England in Warwickshire E of Birmingham *pop* 71,530

Nu·ni·vak \'nü-nə-,vak\ island 50 *mi* (80 *km*) long W Alaska in Bering Sea

Nu·rem·berg \'nùr-əm-,bərg, 'nyùr-\ *or German* **Nürn·berg** \'nùrn-,berk\ city S Germany in N central Bavaria *pop* 497,496

Nu·ri·stan \,nùr-i-'stän, -'stän\ *or formerly* **Kaf·iri·stan** \,ka-fə-ri-'stan, -'stän\ district E Afghanistan S of the Hindu Kush ✱ Puchal

Nuuk \'nük\ *or* **Godt·håb** \'gòt-,hòp\ town ✱ of Greenland on SW coast *pop* 12,181

Nyasa, Lake — see MALAWI (Lake)

Nyasaland — see MALAWI

Nyir·a·gon·go \nē-,ir-ə-'gòn-(,)gō, -'gän-, ,nyir-\ volcano *about* 11,400 *ft* (3475 *m*) E Democratic Republic of the Congo in Virunga Mountains NE of Lake Kivu

Nyí·regy·há·za \'nē-,rej-,hä-zò\ city NE Hungary *pop* 120,600

Nysa \'ni-sə\ *or German* **Neis·se** \'nī-sə\ river 120 *mi* (193 *km*) SW Poland flowing NE into the Oder

Oa·he Reservoir \ō-'ä-(,)hē\ reservoir *about* 225 *mi* (362 *km*) long N S.Dak. & S N.Dak. formed in Missouri River by **Oahe Dam**

Oa·hu \ō-'ä-(,)hü\ island Hawaii, site of Honolulu *area* 589 *sq mi* (1531 *sq km*)

Oak Creek city SE Wis. *pop* 19,513

Oak Forest village NE Ill. S of Chicago *pop* 26,203

Oak·ham \'ō-kəm\ town E *central* England in E Leicestershire; ✱ of former county of Rutland-shire *pop* 7996

Oak·land \'ō-klənd\ city & port W Calif. on San Francisco Bay opposite San Francisco *pop* 372,242

Oakland Park city SE Fla. N of Fort Lauderdale *pop* 26,326

Oak Lawn village NE Ill. SW of Chicago *pop* 56,182

Oak Park **1** village NE Ill. W of Chicago *pop* 53,648 **2** city SE Mich. N of Detroit *pop* 30,462

Oak Ridge city E Tenn. W of Knoxville *pop* 27,310

Oak·ville \'ōk-,vil\ town Canada in SE Ontario SW of Toronto *pop* 114,670

Oa·xa·ca \wä-'hä-kä\ **1** state SE Mexico bordering on the Pacific *area* 36,820 *sq mi* (95,364 *sq km*), *pop* 3,019,560 **2** city, its ✱ *pop* 212,943 — **Oa·xa·can** \-kən\ *adjective*

Ob \'äb, 'ób\ river over 2250 *mi* (3620 *km*) W Russia in Asia flowing NW & N into **Gulf of Ob** (inlet of Arctic Ocean 500 *mi or* 800 *km* long)

Ober·am·mer·gau \,ō-bər-'ä-mər-,gaú\ town S Germany in Bavaria SSW of Munich *pop* 4906

Ober·hau·sen \'ō-bər-,haú-z°n\ city W Germany in the Ruhr WNW of Essen *pop* 224,559

Oberland — see BERNER ALPEN

Oberpfalz — see PALATINATE

Obwald *or* **Obwalden** — see UNTERWALDEN

Ocala \ō-'ka-lə\ city N *central* Fla. S of Gainesville *pop* 42,045

Oce·a·nia \,ō-shē-'a-nē-ə, -'ā-\ the lands of the *central* & S Pacific including Micronesia, Melanesia, Polynesia (including New Zealand), often Australia, & sometimes the Malay Archipelago — **Oce·a·ni·an** \-nē-ən\ *adjective or noun*

Ocean Island 1 — see BANABA **2** — see KURE ATOLL

Ocean·side \'ō-shən-,sīd\ city SW Calif. NNW of San Diego *pop* 128,398

Oc·mul·gee \ōk-'məl-gē\ river 255 *mi* (410 *km*) *central* Ga. flowing SE to join the **Oco·nee** \ō-'kō-nē\ (250 *mi or* 402 *km*) forming the Altamaha

Ocmulgee National Monument reservation *central* Ga. at Macon containing American Indian mounds & other remains

Ocra·coke Island \'ō-krə-,kōk\ island off *central* N.C. coast between Pamlico Sound & the Atlantic — see CROATAN

Oden·se \'ō-d°n-sə, 'ü-ən-zə\ city Denmark in N Fyn Is. *pop* 174,948

Oder \'ō-dər\ *or* **Odra** \'ò-drə\ river *about* 565 *mi* (909 *km*) *central* Europe rising in the mountains of Silesia, Czech Republic & flowing N to join Neisse River & thence N into the Baltic Sea

Odes·sa \ō-'de-sə\ **1** city W Tex. *pop* 89,699 **2** city & port S Ukraine on Black Sea *pop* 1,101,000

Oea — see TRIPOLI

Oe·ta \'ē-tə\ mountains *central* Greece, E spur of Pindus Mountains; highest point 7060 *ft* (2152 *m*)

Of·fa·ly \'ò-fə-lē, 'ä-\ *or formerly* **King's** county *central* Ireland in Leinster ✱ Tullamore *area* 771 *sq mi* (2005 *sq km*), *pop* 58,494

Of·fen·bach \'ò-fən-,bäk, -,bäk\ city SW *central* Germany on Main River E of Frankfurt am Main *pop* 115,790

Oga·den \ō-'gä-,dän\ plateau region SE Ethiopia

Ogasawara Islands — see BONIN ISLANDS

Og·bo·mo·sho \,ōg-bō-'mō-(,)shō\ city W Nigeria *pop* 644,200

Og·den \'òg-dən, 'äg-\ city N Utah *pop* 63,909

Ogee·chee \ō-'gē-chē\ river 250 *mi* (402 *km*) E Ga. flowing SE into the Atlantic

Ohio \ō-'hī-(,)ō, ə-, -ə\ **1** river *about* 975 *mi* (1569 *km*) E U.S. flowing from junction of Allegheny & Monongahela rivers in W Pa. into Mississippi River **2** state E *central* U.S. ✱ Columbus *area* 41,222 *sq mi* (107,177 *sq km*), *pop* 10,847,115 — **Ohio·an** \-'hī-ō-ən\ *noun*

Ohře — see EGER

Oise \'wäz\ river 188 *mi* (302 *km*) N France flowing SW into the Seine

Oi·ta \'ōi-,tä, ō-'ē-tä\ city & port Japan in NE Kyushu *pop* 417,051

Ojos del Sa·la·do \'ō-(,)hōs,-del-sä-'lä-(,)dō, -,thel-, -thō\ mountain 22,664 *ft* (6908 *m*) NW Argentina in the Andes W of Tucumán

Oka \ō-'kä\ **1** river 530 *mi* (853 *km*) S *central* Russia in Asia flowing N from the Sayan Mountains into the Angara **2** river 919 *mi* (1479 *km*) *central* Russia in Europe flowing into the Volga

Oka·nog·an *or in Canada* **Oka·na·gan** \,ō-kə-'nä-gən\ river 300 *mi* (483 *km*) U.S. & Canada flowing from **Okanagan Lake** (in SE British Columbia) into Columbia River in NE Wash.

Oka·van·go \,ō-kä-'väŋ-(,)gō\ *or Portuguese* **Cu·ban·go** \kü-'bäŋ-(,)gü\ river 1000 *mi* (1609 *km*) SW *central* Africa rising in *central* Angola & flowing S & E to empty into **Okavango Swamps** *or* **Okavango Delta** (great marsh area N of Lake Ngami in NW Botswana)

Oka·ya·ma \,ō-kä-'yä-mä\ city & port Japan in W Honshu on Inland Sea *pop* 601,094

Oka·za·ki \,ō-kä-'zä-kē, ō-'kä-zä-kē\ city Japan in S *central* Honshu SE of Nagoya *pop* 306,821

Okee·cho·bee, Lake \,ō-kə-'chō-bē\ lake 37 *mi* (60 *km*) long S *central* Fla.

Oke·fe·no·kee \,ō-kə-fə-'nō-kē, ,ō-kē- *also* 'ōk-fə-,nōk\ swamp over 600 *sq mi* (1554 *sq km*) SE Ga. & NE Fla.

Okhotsk, Sea of \ō-'kätsk, ə-'kótsk\ inlet of the Pacific E Russia in Asia W of Kamchatka Peninsula & Kuril Islands

Oki Archipelago \ō-(,)kē\ archipelago Japan in Sea of Japan off SW Honshu

Oki·na·wa \,ō-kə-'nä-wə, -'naú-ə\ **1** island group Japan in *central* Ryukyu Islands ✱ Naha; occupied by the U.S. 1945–1972 **2** island in the group; largest in the Ryukyus *area* 454 *sq mi* (1176 *sq km*) — **Oki·na·wan** \-'nä-wən, -'naú-ən\ *adjective or noun*

Okla·ho·ma \,ō-klə-'hō-mə\ state S *central* U.S. ✱ Oklahoma City *area* 69,956 *sq mi* (181,186 *sq km*), *pop* 3,145,585 — **Okla·ho·man** \-mən\ *adjective or noun*

Oklahoma City city ✱ of Okla. on the N. Canadian *pop* 444,719

Öland \'ä(r)-,länd, 'ē-\ island Sweden in Baltic Sea off SE coast; chief town Borgholm *area* 519 *sq mi* (1349 *sq km*)

Ola·the \ō-'lā-thə\ city NE Kans. SW of Kansas City *pop* 63,352

Old Castile — see CASTILE

Ol·den·burg \'ōl-dən-,bərg, -,bùrk\ **1** former state NW Germany bordering on North Sea **2** city NW Germany W of Bremen *pop* 145,161

Old·ham \'ōl-dəm\ borough NW England in Greater Manchester *pop* 211,400

Old Point Comfort cape SE Va. on N shore of Hampton Roads

Old Sar·um \'sar-əm, 'ser-\ *or ancient* **Sor·bi·o·du·num** \,sòr-bē-ə-'dü-nəm, -'dyü-\ ancient city S England in Wiltshire N of Salisbury

Ol·du·vai Gorge \'ōl-də-,vī\ canyon Tanzania in N mainland SE of Serengeti Plain; fossil beds

Olek·ma \ō-'lek-mə\ river 794 *mi* (1278 *km*) E Russia in Asia rising in Yablonovy Mountains & flowing N into the Lena

Ole·nek \,ō-lə-'nyòk\ river N Russia in Asia flowing NE into Laptev Sea W of the Lena

Oli·fants \'ä-lə-fən(t)s\ river 350 *mi* (563 *km*) S Africa in Republic of South Africa & Mozambique flowing into the Limpopo

Olives, Mount of *or* **Ol·i·vet** \'ä-lə-,vet, ,ä-lə-'\ mountain ridge 2680 *ft* (817 *m*) W Jordan running N & S on E side of Jerusalem

Olo·mouc \'ò-lə-,mōts\ *or German* **Ol·mütz** \'òl-,müts, -,myüts, -,mœts\ city E Czech Republic in *central* Moravia *pop* 105,690

Olsz·tyn \'òl-shtən\ *or German* **Al·len·stein** \'ä-lən-,shtīn\ city N Poland NNW of Warsaw *pop* 161,238

Olt \'òlt\ river 308 *mi* (496 *km*) S Romania flowing S through the Transylvanian Alps into the Danube

Ol·te·nia \äl-'tē-nē-ə\ *or* **Little Walachia** region S Romania W of the Olt; the W division of Walachia

Olym·pia \ə-'lim-pē-ə, ō-\ **1** city ✱ of Wash. on Puget Sound *pop* 33,840 **2** plain S Greece in NW Peloponnese along the Alpheus — **Olym·pi·an** \-pē-ən\ *adjective or noun* — **Olym·pic** \-pik\ *adjective*

Olympic Mountains mountains NW Wash. in *central* Olympic Peninsula — see OLYMPUS (Mount)

Olympic National Park reservation NW Wash. including part of Olympic Mountains & strip of land along coast to W

Olympic Peninsula peninsula NW Wash. W of Puget Sound

Olym·pus \ə-'lim-pəs, ō-\ massif NE Greece in Thessaly near coast of Gulf of Salonika; highest point 9570 *ft* (2917 *m*)

Olympus, Mount 1 mountain 7965 *ft* (2428 *m*) NW Wash.; highest in Olympic Mountains **2** — see ULU DAG

Olyn·thus \ō-'lin(t)-thəs\ ancient city NE Greece in Macedonia on Chalcidice Peninsula

Om \'òm\ river 450 *mi* (724 *km*) SW Russia in Asia flowing into the Irtysh

Omagh \'ō-mə, -(,)mä\ **1** district W Northern Ireland, established 1974 *area* 436 *sq mi* (1134 *sq km*), *pop* 45,343 **2** town W Northern Ireland in *central* Omagh district *pop* 17,280

Oma·ha \'ō-mə-,hó, -,hä\ city E Nebr. on Missouri River *pop* 335,795

Oman \ō-'män, -'man\ *or formerly* **Muscat and Oman** country SW Asia in SE Arabia bordering on Arabian Sea; a sultanate ✱ Muscat *area* 82,000 *sq mi* (213,200 *sq km*), *pop* 2,000,000 — **Omani** \ō-'mä-nē, -'ma-\ *adjective or noun*

Oman, Gulf of arm of Arabian Sea between Oman & SE Iran

Om·dur·man \,äm-dər-'man, -'män\ city *central* Sudan on the Nile opposite Khartoum & Khartoum North *pop* 526,287

Omi·ya \ō-'mē-,yä, ō-'mē-ä\ city Japan on Honshu, a suburb of Tokyo *pop* 403,779

Omo·lon \,ä-mə-'lòn\ river 715 *mi* (1150 *km*) E Russia in Asia flowing from the Kolyma Range N into Kolyma River

Omsk \'óm(p)sk, 'äm(p)sk\ city SW Russia in Asia at confluence of the Irtysh & the Om *pop* 1,169,000

Omu·ra \'ō-mü-,rä, ō-'mü-rä\ city & port Japan in NW Kyushu on **Omura Bay** (inlet of E. China Sea) NNE of Nagasaki

One·ga, Lake \ō-'ne-gə\ lake NW Russia in Europe in S Karelia *area* over 3700 *sq mi* (9583 *sq km*)

Onei·da Lake \ō-'nī-də\ lake *about* 22 *mi* (35 *km*) long *central* N.Y. NE of Syracuse

On·tar·io \än-'ter-ē-,ō, -'tar-\ **1** city SW Calif. NW of Riverside *pop* 133,179 **2** province E Canada between Great Lakes & Hudson Bay ✳ Toronto *area* 353,951 *sq mi* (916,733 *sq km*), *pop* 10,084,885 — **On·tar·i·an** \-ē-ən\ *adjective or noun*

Ontario, Lake lake U.S. & Canada in N.Y. & Ontario; easternmost of the Great Lakes *area about* 7600 *sq mi* (19,684 *sq km*)

Oos Kaap — see EASTERN CAPE

Ope·li·ka \,ō-pə-'lī-kə\ city E Alabama *pop* 22,122

Opo·le \ō-'pò-le\ *or German* **Op·peln** \'ò-pəln\ city SW Poland on the Oder *pop* 127,653

Oporto — see PORTO

Oquirrh Mountains \'ō-kər\ mountain range N *central* Utah S of Great Salt Lake; highest point *about* 11,000 *ft* (3353 *m*)

Ora·dea \ò-'rä-dē-ə\ city NW Romania in Transylvania near Hungarian border *pop* 225,416

Oral \ò-'räl\ *or* **Uralsk** \ü-'rälsk, yù-'ralsk\ city W Kazakhstan on Ural River *pop* 98,640

Oran \ò-'rän\ city & port NW Algeria *pop* 628,558

Or·ange \'är-inj, 'är-(-ə)nj, 'òr-inj, 'òr(-ə)nj\ **1** city SW Calif. N of Santa Ana *pop* 110,658 **2** city E Tex. E of Beaumont on the Sabine *pop* 19,381 **3** river 1300 *mi* (2092 *km*) S Africa flowing from the Drakensberg in Lesotho W into the Atlantic

Orange \ò-'rä[n]zh\ city SE France N of Avignon *pop* 28,136

Orange Free State *or* **Oranje Vrystaat** — see FREE STATE

Orasul Stalin — see BRASOV

Ordzhonikidze — see VLADIKAVKAZ

Ōre·bro \,ær-ə-'brü\ city S *central* Sweden *pop* 123,188

Or·e·gon \'òr-i-gən, 'är-, *chiefly by outsiders* -,gän\ **1** the Columbia River — an old name used especially prior to discovery of mouth & renaming of river (1791) by Capt. Robert Gray **2** state NW U.S. ✳ Salem *area* 97,073 *sq mi* (251,419 *sq km*), *pop* 2,842,321 — **Or·e·go·nian** \,òr-i-'gō-nē-ən, ,är-, -nyən\ *adjective or noun*

Oregon Caves limestone caverns SW Oreg. SW of Medford in **Oregon Caves National Monument**

Oregon Country region W N. America between Pacific coast & the Rockies and between N Calif. & Alaska — so called *about* 1818–46

Oregon Trail pioneer route to the Pacific Northwest *about* 2000 *mi* (3219 *km*) long from vicinity of Independence, Mo., to Fort Vancouver, Wash.; used especially 1842–60

Orel \ò-'rel, òr-'yòl\ city Russia in Europe SSW of Moscow

Orem \'òr-əm, 'òr-\ city N *central* Utah N of Provo *pop* 67,561

Oren·burg \'òr-ən-,bərg, 'òr-, -,bùrg\ *or formerly* **Chka·lov** \chə-'kä-ləf\ city SE Russia in Europe on Ural River *pop* 557,000

Oren·se \ò-'ren-(,)sā\ **1** province NW Spain *area* 2810 *sq mi* (7278 *sq km*), *pop* 353,491 **2** city, its ✳ *pop* 101,623

Øre·sund \'ər-ə-,sən\ strait between Sjælland Is., Denmark, & S Sweden connecting Kattegat with Baltic Sea

Organ Pipe Cactus National Monument reservation S Ariz. on Mexican border

Or·hon \'òr-,hòn, -,kòn\ *or* **Or·khon** \'òr-,kòn, -,kòn\ river N Mongolia flowing NE from N edge of the Gobi into the Selenga

Oril·lia \ò-'ril-yə\ city Canada in SE Ontario on Lake Simcoe *pop* 25,925

Ori·no·co \,òr-ē-'nō-(,)kō, ,òr-\ river 1600 *mi* (2575 *km*) Venezuela flowing from Brazilian border to Colombia border & thence into the Atlantic through wide delta

Oris·sa \ò-'ri-sə\ state E India bordering on Bay of Bengal ✳ Bhubaneswar *area* 60,178 *sq mi* (155,861 *sq km*), *pop* 31,659,736

Ori·za·ba \,ò-ri-'zä-bə, ,òr-, ,ō-rē-'sä-vä\ **1** — see CITLALTEPETL **2** city E Mexico in Veracruz state *pop* 113,516

Ork·ney Islands \'òrk-nē\ islands N Scotland constituting a region ✳ Kirkwall (on Mainland Is.) *area* 376 *sq mi* (978 *sq km*), *pop* 19,570 — **Ork·ney·an** \'òrk-nē-ən, òrk-'\ *adjective or noun*

Or·lan·do \òr-'lan-(,)dō\ city E *central* Fla. NE of Tampa *pop* 164,693

Or·land Park \'òr-lənd\ village NE Ill. SW of Chicago *pop* 35,720

Or·lé·a·nais \,òr-lā-ə-'nä\ region & former province N *central* France ✳ Orléans

Or·lé·ans \,òr-lā-'ä[n]\ commune N *central* France on the Loire SSW of Paris *pop* 107,965

Or·ly \òr-'lē, 'òr-lē\ commune France, SSE suburb of Paris

Or·moc Bay \'òr-,mäk\ inlet of Camotes Sea Philippines in NW Leyte Is.

Or·mond Beach \'òr-mənd\ city E Fla. upcoast from Daytona Beach *pop* 29,721

Ormuz — see HORMUZ

Orne \'òrn\ river 95 *mi* (153 *km*) NW France flowing N into Bay of the Seine

Oron·tes \ò-'rän-(,)tēz\ river 246 *mi* (396 *km*) Syria & Turkey rising in Lebanon in the Bekaa & flowing into the Mediterranean

Or·ping·ton \'òr-pin-tən\ former urban district SE England in Kent, now part of Bromley

Or·re·fors \'òr-ə-,fòrz, -'fòrsh\ town SE Sweden NW of Kalmar

Orsk \'òrsk\ city SE Russia in Europe on Ural River S of Magnitogorsk *pop* 273,000

Or·te·gal, Cape \,òr-tē-'gäl\ cape NW Spain

Ort·les \'òrt-,läs\ *or German* **Ort·ler** \-,lər\ mountain range of E Alps N Italy between Venezia Tridentina & Lombardy; highest peak Ortles 12,792 *ft* (3899 *m*)

Orū·mī·yeh \,ùr-ü-'mē-yə\ *or formerly* **Re·zā·'ī·yeh** \,re-zä-'ē-yə\ **1** shallow saline lake NW Iran *area* 1815 *sq mi* (4701 *sq km*) **2** city NW Iran *pop* 300,746

Oru·ro \ò-'ri-rō\ city W Bolivia *pop* 183,194

Or·vie·to \òr-'vyä-(,)tō, -'vye-\ *or ancient* **Vel·su·na** \vel-'sü-nə\ *or* **Vol·sin·ii** \väl-'si-nē-,ī\ commune *central* Italy WNW of Terni *pop* 21,302

Osage \ō-'sāj, 'ō-,\ river E Kans. & Mo. flowing E into Missouri River; now partly submerged in Lake of the Ozarks

Osa·ka \ō-'sä-kä, 'ō-sä-,kä\ city & port Japan in S Honshu on **Osaka Bay** (inlet of the Pacific) *pop* 2,623,831

Osh·a·wa \'ä-shə-wə, -,wä, -,wò\ city Canada in SE Ontario on Lake Ontario ENE of Toronto *pop* 129,344

Osh·kosh \'äsh-,käsh\ city E Wis. on Lake Winnebago *pop* 55,006

Osi·jek \'ō-sē-,yek\ city E Croatia in Slavonia *pop* 129,792

Os·lo \'äz-(,)lō, 'äs-\ *or formerly* **Chris·ti·a·nia** *or* **Kris·ti·a·nia** \,kris-chē-'a-nē-ə, ,krish-chē-, ,kris-tē-, -'ä-\ city ✳ of Norway at N end of **Oslo Fjord** (inlet of the Skagerrak) *pop* 458,364

Os·na·brück \'äz-nə-,brük, ,òs-nə-'brœk\ city NW Germany in Lower Saxony *pop* 165,143

Osor·no \ō-'sòr-(,)nō\ volcano 8727 *ft* (2644 *m*) S *central* Chile in lake district

Os·sa, Mount \'ä-sə\ mountain 6490 *ft* (1967 *m*) NE Greece in E Thessaly

Os·se·tia \ä-'sē-sh(ē-)ə\ region SE Russia in Europe in *central* Caucasus — see ALANIA, SOUTH OSSETIA

Os·si·ning \'ä-s[ə]n-in\ village SE N.Y. *pop* 22,582

Ost·end \ä-'stend, 'ä-,\ *or Flemish* **Oost·en·de** \ō-'sten-də\ *or French* **Os·tende** \ò-'stä[n]d\ city & port NW Belgium *pop* 68,500

Ös·ter·reich — see AUSTRIA

Os·tia \'äs-tē-ə\ town *central* Italy at mouth of the Tiber E of site of ancient town of the same name which was the port for Rome

Ostrasia — see AUSTRASIA

Os·tra·va \'òs-trə-və\ *or formerly* **Mo·rav·ska Ostrava** \'mòr-əf-skə\ city *central* E Czech Republic in Moravia *pop* 327,553

Osu·mi Islands \'ō-sü-(,)mē, ō-'sü-mē\ island group Japan in N Ryukyus

Os·we·go \ä-'swē-(,)gō\ city N N.Y. on Lake Ontario *pop* 19,195

Oś·wię·cim \,òsh-'fyen-chēm\ *or* **Ausch·witz** \'aùsh-,vits\ commune S Poland W of Kraków; site of Nazi concentration camp during World War II *pop* 45,282

Ota·go Harbor \ō-'tä-gō\ inlet of the Pacific S New Zealand on E coast of South Is.; Dunedin is situated on it

Otran·to \ō-'tran-(,)tō, 'ō-trän-,tō\ commune & port S Italy on coast at SE tip of Puglia *pop* 5152

Otranto, Strait of strait between SE Italy & W Albania connecting Adriatic Sea & Ionian Sea

Ot·ta·wa \'ä-tə-wə, -,wä, -,wò\ **1** river 696 *mi* (1120 *km*) E Canada in SE Ontario & S Quebec flowing E into St. Lawrence River **2** city ✳ of Canada in SE Ontario *pop* 313,987

Ot·to·man Empire \'ä-tə-mən\ former Turkish sultanate (✳ Constantinople) in SE Europe, W Asia, & N Africa including at greatest extent Turkey, Syria, Mesopotamia, Palestine, Arabia, Egypt, Barbary States, Balkans, & parts of Russia & Hungary

Ot·tum·wa \ə-'təm-wə, ō-'təm-\ city SE Iowa *pop* 24,488

Oua·chi·ta \'wä-shə-,tò\ river 605 *mi* (974 *km*) SW Ark. & E La. flowing into Black River

Ouachita Mountains mountains W Ark. & SE Okla. S of Arkansas River

Oua·ga·dou·gou \,wä-gä-'dü-(,)gü\ city *central* Burkina Faso, its ✳ *pop* 366,000

Ouar·gla \'wòr-glə, 'wär-, -,glä\ town & oasis Algeria in the Sahara *pop* 81,721

Oubangui — see UBANGI

Oubangui–Chari — see UBANGI-SHARI

Ou·den·aar·de \,aù-d[ə]n-'är-də, ,ō-\ *or French* **Au·de·narde** \,ō-d[ə]n-'ärd\ commune Belgium in E Flanders on the Schelde *pop* 27,162

Oudh \'aùd\ region N India in E *central* Uttar Pradesh ✳ Lucknow

Oudts·hoorn \'ōts-,hòrn\ city S Republic of South Africa in Western Cape province E of Cape Town *pop* 26,907

Oues·sant, Île d' \ēl-dwe-'sä[n]\ *or* **Ush·ant** \'ə-shənt\ island NW France off tip of Brittany *pop* 1814

Ouj·da *or* **Oudj·da** \ùzh-'dä\ *or* **Ar Ujda** \'ùj-də\ city NE Morocco near Algerian border *pop* 260,082

Ou·lu \'aù-(,)lü, 'ō-\ *or Swedish* **Uleå·borg** \'ü-lä-ō-,bòr-ē\ city N *central* Finland on Gulf of Bothnia *pop* 100,281

Ou·ro Prê·to \,ō-(,)rü-'prä-(,)tü\ city E Brazil in Minas Gerais *pop* 62,483

Ouse \'üz\ **1** *or* **Great Ouse** river 160 *mi* (257 *km*) *central* & E England flowing into The Wash **2** river 60 *mi* (96 *km*) NE England flowing SE to unite with Trent River forming the Humber

Outer Banks chain of sand islands & peninsulas along N.C. coast

Outer Hebrides — see HEBRIDES

Outer Mongolia — see MONGOLIA — **Outer Mongolian** *adjective or noun*

Out Islands islands of the Bahamas group excepting New Providence

Ou·tre·mont \'ü-trə-,mänt, *French* ü-trə-'mō[n]\ town Canada in S Quebec on Montreal Is. *pop* 22,935

Oval·le \ō-'vī-,ä, -'vä-,yä\ city N *central* Chile

Over·ijs·sel \,ō-və-'rī-səl\ province E Netherlands ✳ Zwolle *area* 1518 *sq mi* (3932 *sq km*), *pop* 1,039,083

Over·land Park \'ō-vər-lənd\ city NE Kans. S of Kansas City *pop* 111,790

Ovie·do \,ō-vē-'ā-(,)dō, ,ō-'vyä-<u>th</u>ō\ **1** — see ASTURIAS 2 **2** city NW Spain ✳ of Asturias province *pop* 194,919

Owas·co Lake \ō-'wäs-(,)kō\ lake 11 *mi* (18 *km*) long *central* N.Y.; one of the Finger Lakes

Owa·ton·na \,ō-wə-'tä-nə\ city SE Minn. *pop* 19,386

Ow·en Falls \'ō-ən\ former waterfall E Africa in Uganda in the Nile N of Lake Victoria; now submerged in water behind **Owen Falls Dam**

Ow·ens \'ō-ənz\ river E Calif. formerly flowing into **Owens Lake** (now dry), now supplying water to city of Los Angeles by way of Los Angeles Aqueduct

Ow·ens·boro \'ō-ənz-,bər-ō\ city NW Ky. *pop* 53,549

Owen Sound city Canada in SE Ontario on Georgian Bay *pop* 21,674

Owen Stan·ley Range \'stan-lē\ mountain range E New Guinea; highest peak Mt. Victoria 13,363 *ft* (4073 *m*)

Owy·hee \ō-'wī-(,)(h)ē\ river 250 *mi* (402 *km*) SW Idaho & SE Oreg. flowing N into Snake River

Ox·ford \'äks-fərd\ *or Medieval Latin* **Ox·o·nia** \äk-'sō-nē-ə\ city S *central* England ✱ of Oxfordshire *pop* 109,000 — **Ox·ford·ian** \äks-'fŏr-dē-ən, -'fŏr-\ *adjective or noun*

Ox·ford·shire \'äks-fərd-,shir, -shər\ *or* **Oxford** county S *central* England ✱ Oxford *area* 1044 *sq mi* (2704 *sq km*), *pop* 553,800

Ox·nard \'äks-,närd\ city S Calif. SE of Santa Barbara *pop* 142,216

Oxus — see AMU DAR'YA

Oxy·rhyn·chus \,äk-si-'riŋ-kəs\ *or Arabic* **El Bah·na·sa** \el-'bä-nə-,sä\ archaeological site Egypt N of El Minyā & S of El Faiyûm

Oyrot — see GORNO-ALTAY

Ozark Plateau \'ō-,zärk\ *or* **Ozark Mountains** eroded tableland region 1500–2500 *ft* (457–762 *m*) high *central* U.S. N of Arkansas River in N Ark., S Mo., & NE Okla. with E extension in S Ill. — **Ozark·er** \'ō-,zär-kər\ *noun* — **Ozark·ian** \ō-'zär-kē-ən\ *adjective or noun*

Ozarks, Lake of the \'ō-,zärks\ reservoir 125 *mi* (200 *km*) long *central* Mo. formed in Osage River by Bagnell Dam

Pa·ca·rai·ma Mountains \,pä-kä-'rī-mä\ mountain range N S. America in SE Venezuela, N Brazil, & W Guyana — see RORAIMA

Pa·chu·ca \pä-'chü-kä\ city *central* Mexico ✱ of Hidalgo *pop* 179,440

Pa·cif·i·ca \pə-'si-fi-kə\ city W Calif. S of San Francisco on the Pacific *pop* 37,670

Pa·cif·ic Islands, Trust Territory of the \pə-'si-fik\ former trust territory in association with U.S. comprising the Carolines & the Marshalls; with the Marianas (except Guam) constituted a Japanese mandate 1919–45

Pacific Ocean ocean extending from the arctic circle to the antarctic regions & from W N. America & W S. America to E Asia & Australia *area* 69,375,000 *sq mi* (180,375,000 *sq km*); often divided into **North Pacific Ocean** & **South Pacific Ocean**

Pacific Rim the countries bordering on or located in the Pacific Ocean — used especially of the rapidly developing Asian countries on the Pacific

Pacific Rim National Park reservation SW Canada in Vancouver Island

Pac·to·lus \pak-'tō-ləs\ river Asia Minor in ancient Lydia flowing into the Hermus (modern Gediz) near Sardis

Pa·dang \'pä-,däŋ\ city & port Indonesia in W Sumatra *pop* 631,543

Pad·ding·ton \'pa-diŋ-tən\ former metropolitan borough NW London, England, now part of Westminster

Pa·dre Island \'pä-drē, -drā\ island 113 *mi* (182 *km*) long S Tex. between Laguna Madre & Gulf of Mexico

Pad·ua \'pa-jə-wə, 'pa-dyü-wə\ *or Italian* **Pa·do·va** \'pä-dō-,vä\ commune NE Italy W of Venice *pop* 215,025 — **Pad·u·an** \'pa-jə-wən, 'pa-dyü-\ *adjective or noun*

Pa·du·cah \pə-'dü-kə, -'dyü-\ city W Ky. on Ohio River *pop* 27,256

Padus — see PO

Paes·tum \'pes-təm, 'pēs-\ *or earlier* **Po·sei·do·nia** \,pä,sī-'dō-nē-ə, ,pō-\ ancient city S Italy in W Lucania on Gulf of Salerno (ancient **Bay of Paestum**)

Pa·go Pa·go \,pä-(,)gō-'pä-(,)gō, ,päŋ-(,)ō-'päŋ-(,)ō\ town & port ✱ of American Samoa on Tutuila Is.

Pa·hang \pə-'haŋ\ state E Malaysia (federation) bordering on S. China Sea ✱ Kuala Lipis *area* 13,920 *sq mi* (36,053 *sq km*), *pop* 1,036,724

Painted Desert region NE Ariz. E of the Little Colorado

Pais·ley \'pāz-lē\ burgh SW Scotland in Strathclyde *pop* 84,789

Pa·kan·ba·ru \,pä-kən-'bär-ü\ *or* **Pe·kan·ba·ru** \,pä-\ city Indonesia in *central* Sumatra *pop* 398,694

Pa·ki·stan \'pa-ki-,stan, ,pä-ki-'stän\ country S Asia originally comprising an E division & a W division; a dominion 1947–56, an Islamic republic since 1956, & a member of the Commonwealth of Nations 1956–72; formed from parts of former Brit. India; ✱ Islamabad *area* 310,403 *sq mi* (807,048 *sq km*), *pop* 131,434,000 — see EAST PAKISTAN, WEST PAKISTAN — **Pa·ki·stani** \,pa-ki-'sta-nē, ,pä-ki-'stä-\ *adjective or noun*

Pa·lat·i·nate \pə-'la-t°n-ət\ *or German* **Pfalz** \'(p)fälts\ either of two districts SW Germany once ruled by counts palatine of the Holy Roman Empire: **Rhenish Palatinate** *or* **Rhine Palatinate** *or German* **Rheinpfalz** \'rīn-,(p)fälts\ (on the Rhine E of Saarland) & **Upper Palatinate** *or German* **Ober·pfalz** \'ō-bər-,(p)fälts\ (on the Danube around Regensburg) — see RHINELAND-PALATINATE

Pal·a·tine \'pa-lə-,tīn\ **1** hill in Rome, Italy, one of seven on which the ancient city was built — see AVENTINE **2** village NE Ill. NW of Chicago *pop* 39,253

Pa·lau \pə-'laù\ *or* **Be·lau** \bə-\ island group W Pacific comprising a trust territory in association with U.S.; usually considered part of the Carolines — **Pa·lau·an** \pə-'laù-ən\ *noun*

Pa·la·wan \pə-'lä-wən, -,wän\ island 278 *mi* (445 *km*) long W Philippines W of the Visayans *area* 4550 *sq mi* (11,830 *sq km*), *pop* (with adjacent islands) 528,287

Pa·lem·bang \,pä-ləm-'bäŋ\ city & port Indonesia in SE Sumatra *pop* 1,141,036

Pa·len·cia \pä-'len-syä, -thyä\ **1** province N Spain *area* 3100 *sq mi* (8029 *sq km*), *pop* 185,479 **2** city, its ✱, NNE of Valladolid *pop* 77,772

Pa·len·que \pä-'leŋ-(,)kā\ ruined Mayan city S Mexico in N Chiapas SW of modern town of Palenque

Pa·ler·mo \pə-'lər-(,)mō, pä-'ler-\ *or ancient* **Pan·or·mus** \pa-'nòr-məs\ *or* **Pan·hor·mus** \pan-'hòr-\ city & port Italy ✱ of Sicily *pop* 697,162 — **Pa·ler·mi·tan** \pə-'lər-mə-t°n, -'ler-\ *adjective or noun*

Pal·es·tine \'pa-lə-,stīn\ *or Latin* **Pal·aes·ti·na** \,pa-lə-'stē-nə, -'stī-\ **1** ancient region SW Asia bordering on E coast of the Mediterranean & extending E of Jordan River **2** country bordering on the Mediterranean on W & Dead Sea on E; a part of the Ottoman Empire 1516–1917, a Brit. mandate 1923–48; now divided between Israel & Jordan — **Pal·es·tin·ian** \,pa-lə-'sti-nē-ən, -nyən\ *adjective or noun*

Pal·i·sades \,pa-lə-'sādz\ line of cliffs 15 *mi* (24 *km*) long SE N.Y. & NE N.J. on W bank of Hudson River

Palk Strait \'pò(l)k\ strait 40 *mi* (64 *km*) wide between N Sri Lanka & SE India connecting Gulf of Mannar & Bay of Bengal

Pal·ma \'päl-mä\ *or* **Palma de Mal·lor·ca** \dä-mä-'yòr-kä, thä-\ commune & port Spain ✱ of Baleares province on Majorca *pop* 296,754

Pal·mas, Cape \'päl-məs\ cape Liberia on extreme SE coast

Palm Bay city E Fla. *pop* 62,632

Palm Beach Gardens city SE Fla. *pop* 22,965

Palm·dale \'päm-,dāl, 'pälm-\ city SW Calif. NE of Los Angeles *pop* 68,842

Palm Desert city SW Calif ESE of Riverside *pop* 23,252

Palm·er Archipelago \'pä-mər, 'päl-\ *or formerly* **Antarctic Archipelago** islands W of N end of Antarctic Peninsula in Falkland Islands Dependencies

Palmer Peninsula — see ANTARCTIC PENINSULA

Palmer Land the S section of Antarctic Peninsula

Palm·er·ston \'pä-mər-stən, 'päl-mər-\ island (atoll) *central* Pacific NW of Rarotonga Is.; belongs to New Zealand *area* 1 *sq mi* (2.6 *sq km*)

Palmerston North city New Zealand on S North Is. NE of Wellington *pop* 70,318

Palm Springs city SW Calif. E of Los Angeles *pop* 40,181

Pal·my·ra \pal-'mī-rə\ *or biblical* **Tad·mor** \'tad-,mòr\ *or* **Ta·mar** \'tä-,mär, -mər\ ancient city Syria on N edge of Syrian Desert NE of Damascus — **Pal·my·rene** \,pal-mə-'rēn, -mī-\ *adjective or noun*

Palmyra Atoll island *central* Pacific in Line Islands *area* 1 *sq mi* (2.6 *sq km*)

Palo Al·to \,pa-lō-'al-(,)tō\ city W Calif. SE of San Francisco on San Francisco Bay *pop* 55,900

Pal·o·mar, Mount *or* **Palomar Mountain** \'pa-lə-,mär\ mountain 6138 *ft* (1871 *m*) S Calif. NNE of San Diego

Pa·los \'pä-,lōs\ *or* **Pa·los de la Fron·te·ra** \thä-lä-fròn-'tä-rä\ town & former port SW Spain SE of Huelva

Pa·louse \pə-'lüs\ **1** river *about* 140 *mi* (225 *km*) NW Idaho & SE Wash. flowing W & S into Snake River **2** fertile hilly region E Wash. & NW Idaho N of Snake & Clearwater rivers

Pa·mirs \pə-'mirz\ *or* **Pa·mir** \-'mir\ mountain region *central* Asia in Tajikistan & on borders of Xinjiang Uygur, Kashmir, & Afghanistan from which radiate Tian Shan to N, Kunlun & Karakoram to E, & Hindu Kush to W; has many peaks over 20,000 *ft* (6096 *m*)

Pam·li·co \'pam-li-,kō\ river E N.C., estuary of Tar River, flowing E into **Pamlico Sound** (inlet of the Atlantic between the mainland & offshore islands)

Pam·pa \'pam-pə\ city NW Tex. ENE of Amarillo *pop* 19,959

Pam·phyl·ia \pam-'fi-lē-ə\ ancient district & Roman province S Asia Minor on coast S of Pisidia — **Pam·phyl·i·an** \-lē-ən\ *adjective or noun*

Pam·plo·na \pam-'plō-nə, päm-'plō-nä\ *or formerly* **Pam·pe·lu·na** \,pam-pə-'lü-nə\ city N Spain ✱ of Navarra province & once ✱ of Navarre kingdom *pop* 179,251

Pan·a·ji \pə-'nä-jē\ town & port W India ✱ of Goa & formerly ✱ of Portuguese India *pop* 42,915

Pan·a·ma *or Spanish* **Pa·na·má** \'pa-nə-,mä, -,mò, ,pa-nə-'; ,pä-nä-'mä\ **1** country S Central America; a republic; before 1903 part of Colombia *area* (including Canal Zone) 33,659 *sq mi* (87,177 *sq km*), *pop* 2,563,000 **2** *or* **Panama City** city & port, its ✱, on Gulf of Panama *pop* 411,549 **3** ship canal 51 *mi* (82 *km*) *central* Panama connecting the Atlantic (Caribbean Sea) & the Pacific (Gulf of Panama) — **Pan·a·ma·ni·an** \,pa-nə-'mä-nē-ən\ *adjective or noun*

Panama, Gulf of inlet of the Pacific on S coast of Panama

Panama, Isthmus of *or formerly* **Isthmus of Dar·i·en** \,dar-ē-'en, ,der-, ,där-\ isthmus Central America connecting N. America & S. America & comprised in Panama (republic)

Panama Canal Zone — see CANAL ZONE

Panama City 1 city & port NW Fla. on Gulf of Mexico *pop* 34,378 **2** — see PANAMA

Pan·a·mint Mountains \'pa-nə-,mint, -mənt\ mountains E Calif. W of Death Valley — see TELESCOPE PEAK

Pa·nay \pə-'nī\ island Philippines in the Visayans; chief town Iloilo *area* 4446 *sq mi* (11,560 *sq km*)

Pan·gaea \pan-'jē-ə\ hypothetical land area believed to have once connected the landmasses of the southern hemisphere with those of the northern hemisphere — see GONDWANALAND, LAURASIA

Pang–pu — see BENGBU

Pa·ni·pat \'pä-ni-,pət\ city NW India in SE Haryana state *pop* 191,010

Panjab — see PUNJAB

Panj·nad \,pənj-'näd\ river 50 *mi* (80 *km*) Pakistan, the combined stream of the Chenab & the Sutlej, flowing SW into the Indus

Pan·kow \'päŋ-(,)kō\ NE suburb of Berlin, Germany; formerly seat of E. German government

Pan·mun·jom \,pän-,mùn-'jəm\ village on N. Korea–S. Korea border SE of Kaesong

Pan·no·nia \pə-'nō-nē-ə\ Roman province SE Europe including territory W of the Danube now in Hungary & adjacent parts of Croatia & Vojvodina

Pantar — see ALOR

Pan·tel·le·ria \,pan-,te-lə-'rē-ə\ island Italy in the Mediterranean between Sicily & Tunisia

Pá·nu·co \'pä-nü-,kō\ river *central* Mexico flowing from Hidalgo state NE into Gulf of Mexico

Pao-chi — see BAOJI

Pão de Açú·car \ˌpauⁿ-dē-ə-'sü-kər\ *or* **Sugar·loaf Mountain** peak 1296 *ft* (395 *m*) SE Brazil in city of Rio de Janeiro on W side of entrance to Guanabara Bay

Paoking — see SHAOYANG

Pao–ting — see BAODING

Pao–t'ou — see BAOTOU

Papal States temporal domain of the popes in *central* Italy 755–1870

Pa·pee·te \ˌpä-pē-'ā-tē, pə-'pā-tē, -'pē-\ commune & port Society Islands on Tahiti ✳ of French Polynesia *pop* 23,555

Paph·la·go·nia \ˌpa-flə-'gō-nē-ə, -nyə\ ancient country & Roman province N Asia Minor bordering on Black Sea — **Paph·la·go·nian** \-nē-ən, -nyən\ *adjective or noun*

Pa·phos \'pā-ˌfäs, 'pä-ˌfòs\ town SW Cyprus on coast 10 *mi* (16 *km*) WNW of site of ancient city of Paphos *pop* 27,800

Pa·pua \'pa-pyü-wə, 'pä-pù-wə\ the SE portion of the island of New Guinea; part of Papua New Guinea

Papua, Gulf of arm of Coral Sea SE New Guinea

Papua New Guinea country comprising territories of Papua & New Guinea; independent from 1975, formerly a United Nations trust territory administered by Australia ✳ Port Moresby *area* 178,260 *sq mi* (461,693 *sq km*), *pop* 3,918,000 — **Papua New Guinean** *adjective or noun*

Pa·rá \pə-'rä\ **1** river 200 *mi* (322 *km*) N Brazil, the E mouth of the Amazon **2** state N Brazil S of the Amazon ✳ Belém *area* 481,869 *sq mi* (1,248,041 *sq km*), *pop* 5,084,726 **3** — see BELÉM

Par·a·dise \'par-ə-ˌdīs, -ˌdīz\ **1** town N Calif. N of Sacramento *pop* 25,408 **2** population center Nev. *pop* 124,682

Par·a·guay \'par-ə-ˌgwī, -ˌgwä; ˌpä-rä-'gwī\ **1** river 1584 *mi* (2549 *km*) *central* S. America flowing from Mato Grosso plateau in Brazil S into Paraná River in Paraguay **2** country *central* S. America traversed by Paraguay river; a republic ✳ Asunción *area* 157,043 *sq mi* (406,741 *sq km*), *pop* 4,643,000 — **Par·a·guay·an** \ˌpar-ə-'gwī-ən, -'gwä\ *adjective or noun*

Pa·ra·í·ba \ˌpar-ə-'ē-bə\ **1** *or* **Paraíba do Nor·te** \dü-'nòr-tē\ river *about* 180 *mi* (290 *km*) NE Brazil flowing E into the Atlantic **2** *or* **Paraíba do Sul** \dü-'sül\ river *about* 600 *mi* (965 *km*) SE Brazil flowing NE into the Atlantic **3** state NE Brazil bordering on the Atlantic ✳ João Pessoa *area* 20,833 *sq mi* (53,957 *sq km*), *pop* 3,200,620

Par·a·mar·i·bo \ˌpar-ə-'mar-ə-ˌbō, ˌpär-ä-'mär-ē-ˌbō\ city & port ✳ of Suriname on Suriname River *pop* 200,000

Par·a·mount \'par-ə-ˌmaunt\ city SW Calif. N of Long Beach *pop* 47,669

Pa·ram·us \pə-'ra-məs\ borough NE N.J. *pop* 25,067

Pa·ra·ná \ˌpär-ä-'nä\ **1** *or in upper course* **Al·to Paraná** \'al-(ˌ)tō, 'äl-\ river *about* 2500 *mi* (4022 *km*) *central* S. America flowing from junction of Rio Grande & Paranaíba River in Brazil SSW into the Río de la Plata in Argentina **2** state S Brazil E of Paraná River ✳ Curitiba *area* 76,959 *sq mi* (199,324 *sq km*), *pop* 8,415,659 **3** city NE Argentina on Paraná River *pop* 277,338

Pa·ra·na·í·ba *or formerly* **Pa·ra·na·hi·ba** \ˌpar-ə-nə-'ē-bə, ˌpär-ä-nä-\ river S Brazil flowing SW to unite with the Rio Grande forming Paraná River

Par·du·bi·ce \'pär-dü-ˌbit-se\ city *central* Czech Republic in Bohemia on the Elbe E of Prague *pop* 94,857

Pa·ria Peninsula \'pär-ē-ä\ peninsula NE Venezuela

Paria, Gulf of inlet of the Atlantic between Trinidad & Venezuela

Pa·ri·cu·tín \pä-ˌrē-kü-'tēn\ volcano *about* 9100 *ft* (2775 *m*) SW Mexico in NW Michoacán; first eruption 1943

Parida, La — see BOLIVAR (Cerro)

Par·is \'par-əs, *French* pá-'rē\ **1** city NE Tex. *pop* 24,699 **2** *or ancient* **Lu·te·tia** \lü-'tē-sh(ē-)ə\ city ✳ of France on the Seine *pop* 2,175,200 — **Pa·ri·sian** \pə-'ri-zhən, -'rē-\ *adjective or noun*

Par·kers·burg \'pär-kərz-ˌbərg\ city NW W.Va. *pop* 33,862

Park Forest village NE Ill. S of Chicago *pop* 24,656

Park Ridge city NE Ill. NW of Chicago *pop* 36,175

Par·ma \'pär-mə\ **1** city NE Ohio S of Cleveland *pop* 87,876 **2** commune N Italy in Emilia-Romagna *pop* 168,905

Parma Heights city NE Ohio S of Cleveland *pop* 21,448

Par·na·í·ba *or formerly* **Par·na·hy·ba** \ˌpär-nə-'ē-bə\ river NE Brazil flowing NE into the Atlantic

Par·nas·sus \pär-'na-səs\ *or New Greek* **Par·nas·sós** \ˌpär-nä-'sòs\ mountain 8061 *ft* (2457 *m*), *central* Greece N of Gulf of Corinth

Pá·ros \'pär-ˌòs\ island Greece in *central* Cyclades W of Naxos *area* 75 *sq mi* (194 *sq km*)

Par·ra·mat·ta \ˌpar-ə-'ma-tə\ city SE Australia, W suburb of Sydney, on **Parramatta River** (estuary, W arm of Port Jackson) *pop* 132,798

Par·ris Island \'par-əs\ island S S.C. in Port Royal Sound

Par·ry Islands \'par-ē\ islands Canada in N Northwest Territories in Arctic Ocean N of Victoria Is.

Parsnip — see FINLAY

Par·thia \'pär-thē-ə\ ancient country SW Asia in NE modern Iran

Pas·a·de·na \ˌpa-sə-'dē-nə\ **1** city SW Calif. E of Glendale *pop* 131,591 **2** city SE Tex. E of Houston *pop* 119,363 — **Pas·a·de·nan** \-nən\ *noun*

Pa·sar·ga·dae \pə-'sär-gə-ˌdē\ city of ancient Persia built by Cyrus the Great; ruins NE of site of later Persepolis

Pa·say \'pä-ˌsī\ municipality Philippines in Luzon on Manila Bay S of Manila *pop* 354,000

Pas·ca·gou·la \ˌpas-kə-'gü-lə\ city & port SE Miss. *pop* 25,899

Pas·co \'pas-(ˌ)kō\ city SE Wash. *pop* 20,337

Pasco, Cerro de — see CERRO DE PASCO

Pascua, Isla de — see EASTER

Pas de Calais — see DOVER (Strait of)

Pa·sig \'pä-sig\ river 14 *mi* (23 *km*) Philippines in Luzon flowing from the Laguna de Bay through Manila into Manila Bay

Pas·sa·ic \pə-'sā-ik\ **1** river 80 *mi* (130 *km*) NE N.J. flowing into Newark Bay **2** city NE N.J. SSE of Paterson *pop* 58,041

Pas·sa·ma·quod·dy Bay \ˌpa-sə-mə-'kwä-dē\ inlet of Bay of Fundy between E Maine & SW New Brunswick at mouth of St. Croix River

Pas·se·ro, Cape \'pä-sə-ˌrō, 'pa-\ headland Italy at SE tip of Sicily

Pas·sy \pa-'sē\ section of Paris, France, on right bank of the Seine near the Bois de Boulogne

Pas·ta·za \pä-'stä-zə, -sä\ river 400 *mi* (644 *km*) Ecuador & Peru flowing S into the Marañón

Pat·a·go·nia \ˌpa-tə-'gō-nyə, -nē-ə\ region S. America in S Argentina & S Chile between the Andes & the Atlantic S of *about* 40° S lat.; sometimes considered as including Tierra del Fuego — **Pat·a·go·nian** \-nyən, -nē-ən\ *adjective or noun*

Pa·tan \'pä-ˌtən\ city E *central* Nepal adjoining Kathmandu *pop* 96,109

Pa·tap·sco \pə-'tap-(ˌ)skō, -si-ˌkō\ river 80 *mi* (129 *km*) N *central* Md. flowing SE into Chesapeake Bay

Pat·er·son \'pa-tər-sən\ city NE N.J. N of Newark *pop* 140,891

Pa·ti·a·la \ˌpə-tē-'ä-lə\ **1** former state NW India, now part of Punjab state **2** city, its ✳, SW of Simla *pop* 253,341

Pat·mos \'pat-məs, 'pät-ˌmòs\ island Greece in the NW Dodecanese

Pat·na \'pət-nə\ city NE India on the Ganges, ✳ of Bihar

Pa·tos, La·goa dos \lə-ˌgō-ə-dəs-'pa-təs, -düs-ˌpä-(ˌ)tüs\ lagoon 124 *mi* (200 *km*) long S Brazil in Rio Grande do Sul

Pa·tras \pə-'tras, pə-'tras\ *or Greek* **Pa·trai** \'pä-ˌtre\ *or ancient* **Pa·trae** \'pā-(ˌ)trē\ city & port W Greece in N Peloponnese on Gulf of Patras *pop* 155,180

Patras, Gulf of *or Greek* **Pa·tra·ï·kós Kól·pos** \ˌpä-trä-ē-ˌkòs-'kòl-(ˌ)pòs\ inlet of Ionian Sea W Greece W of Gulf of Corinth

Patrimony of St. Peter — see ROME (Duchy of)

Pa·tux·ent \pə-'tək-sənt\ river 100 *mi* (161 *km*) *central* Md. flowing S & SE into Chesapeake Bay

Pau \'pō\ **1** *or French* **Gave de Pau** \ˌgäv-də-'pō\ river 100 *mi* (161 *km*) SW France rising in the Pyrenees SW of Pau & flowing to the Adour — see GAVARNIE **2** commune SW France on Pau River *pop* 83,928

Pa·via \pə-'vē-ä\ commune N Italy S of Milan *pop* 76,418

Pav·lof \'pav-ˌlòf\ volcano 8261 *ft* (2518 *m*) SW Alaska on SW Alaska Peninsula in Aleutian Range

Paw·tuck·et \pə-'tə-kət, pò-\ city NE R.I. *pop* 72,644

Pay·san·dú \ˌpī-ˌsän-'dü\ city & port W Uruguay *pop* 62,412

Pea·body \'pē-bə-dē, -ˌbä-dē\ city NE Mass. N of Lynn *pop* 47,039

Peace \'pēs\ river 1195 *mi* (1923 *km*) W Canada flowing E & NE in N British Columbia & N Alberta into Slave River — see FINLAY

Peach·tree City \'pēch-ˌtrē\ city NW *central* Ga. SSW of Atlanta *pop* 19,027

Pearl \'pər(-ə)l\ **1** river *about* 410 *mi* (660 *km*) S Miss. flowing S into Gulf of Mexico **2** city S *central* Miss. *pop* 19,588 **3** — see ZHU

Pearl City city Hawaii in S Oahu *pop* 30,993

Pearl Harbor inlet Hawaii on S coast of Oahu W of Honolulu; site of U.S. Navy base

Pea·ry Land \'pir-ē\ region N Greenland on Arctic Ocean

Pe·chen·ga \'pe-chən-gə, pe-'chen-gä\ *or Finnish* **Pet·sa·mo** \'pet-sä-ˌmō\ town & port NW Russia in Europe on inlet of Barents Sea in district that belonged to Finland 1920–44 *pop* 3500

Pe·cho·ra \pi-'chòr-ə, -'chòr-\ river *over* 1100 *mi* (1770 *km*) NE Russia in Europe flowing N into Barents Sea

Pe·cos \'pā-kəs\ river E N.Mex. & W Tex. flowing SE into the Rio Grande

Pecos National Monument archaeological site N *central* N.Mex. SE of Santa Fe containing Indian villages & a Spanish mission

Pecs \'pāch\ city S Hungary W of the Danube *pop* 179,000

Ped·er·nal·es \ˌpər-d°n-'a-ləs\ river *central* Tex. flowing E into Colorado River

Pee·bles \'pē-bəlz\ **1** *or* **Pee·bles·shire** \'pē-bəl-ˌshir, -shər\ *or* **Tweed·dale** \'twēd-ˌdāl\ former county SE Scotland including upper course of the Tweed **2** burgh SE Scotland in Borders region

Pee Dee \'pē-ˌdē\ river 233 *mi* (375 *km*) N.C. & S.C. flowing SE into Winyah Bay — see YADKIN

Peeks·kill \'pēk-ˌskil\ city SE N.Y. N of Yonkers *pop* 19,536

Peel \'pēl\ river 425 *mi* (684 *km*) NW Canada rising in W Yukon Territory & flowing E & N into the Mackenzie

Pee·ne \'pā-nə\ river 70 *mi* (113 *km*) NE Germany flowing E through Pomerania and forming **Peene Estuary** which flows N–S

Pee·ne·mün·de \ˌpā-nə-'mün-də, -'myün-, -'muⁿ-\ village NE Germany on island at mouth of Peene Estuary

Pei·pus \'pī-pəs\ *or Estonian* **Peip·si** \'pāp-sē\ *or Russian* **Chud·skoe** \chüt-'skò-yə, -'skòi-(y)ə\ lake Europe, between Estonia & Russia *area* 1390 *sq mi* (3600 *sq km*)

Pekanbaru — see PAKANBARU

Pe·kin \'pē-kən, -ˌkin\ city N *central* Ill. SSW of Peoria *pop* 32,254

Peking — see BEIJING

Pe·la·gian Islands \pə-'lā-j(ē-)ən\ islands Italy in the Mediterranean S of Sicily between Malta & Tunisia

Pe·lée, Mount \pə-'lā\ volcano French West Indies in N Martinique; erupted 1902

Pelee, Point — see POINT PELEE NATIONAL PARK

Pe·lee Island \'pē-lē\ island SE Canada in W Lake Erie SW of Point Pelee, Ontario *area* 18 *sq mi* (47 *sq km*), *pop* 272

Pel·e·liu \ˌpe-lə-'lē-(ˌ)ü, 'pe-lel-ˌyü\ island W Pacific at S end of Palau Islands

\ə\ abut \ᵊ\ kitten \ər\ further \a\ ash \ā\ ace \ä\ mop, mar \aù\ out \ch\ chin \e\ bet \ē\ easy \g\ go \i\ hit \ī\ ice \j\ job \ŋ\ sing \ō\ go \ò\ law \òi\ boy \th\ thin \t͟h\ the \ü\ loot \ù\ foot \y\ yet \zh\ vision *see also* Guide to Pronunciation

Pe·li·on \'pē-lē-ən\ *or New Greek* **Pí·lion** \'pēl-,yón\ mountain 5089 *ft* (1551 *m*) NE Greece in E Thessaly SE of Mt. Ossa

Pel·la \'pe-lə\ ancient city NE Greece, ancient ✳ of Macedonia

Pel·ly \'pe-lē\ river 330 *mi* (531 *km*) NW Canada in Yukon Territory flowing W into Yukon River

Pel·o·pon·nese \'pe-lə-pə-,nēz, -,nēs, ,pe-lə-pə-'\ *or* **Pel·o·pon·ne·sus** \,pe-lə-pə-'nē-səs\ *or* **Pel·o·pon·ni·sos** \,pe-lə-'pò-nē-,sòs\ peninsula forming S part of mainland of Greece — **Pel·o·pon·ne·sian** \,pə-lə-pə-'nē-zhən, -shən\ *adjective or noun*

Pe·lo·tas \pā-'lō-təs\ city S Brazil in SE Rio Grande do Sul at S end of Lagoa dos Patos *pop* 289,484

Pem·ba \'pem-bə\ island Tanzania in Indian Ocean N of island of Zanzibar *pop* 265,039

Pem·broke \'pem-,brúk, *United States also* -,brōk\ *or* **Pem·broke·shire** \-,shir, -shər\ former county SW Wales ✳ Haverfordwest

Pem·broke Pines \'pem-,brōk\ city SE Fla. *pop* 65,452

Pe·nang \pə-'nan\ **1** island SE Asia at N end of Strait of Malacca *area* 108 *sq mi* (281 *sq km*) **2** state Malaysia (federation) comprising Penang Island & mainland opposite: until 1948 one of the Straits Settlements ✳ George Town *area* 400 *sq mi* (1036 *sq km*), *pop* 1,065,075 **3** — see GEORGE TOWN

Pen-ch'i — see BENXI

Pen·del·i·kón \,pen-de-lē-'kón\ mountain 3638 *ft* (1109 *m*) E Greece in Attica NE of Athens

Pend Oreille \,pän-də-'rā\ river 100 *mi* (161 *km*) N Idaho & NE Wash. flowing from **Pend Oreille Lake** (35 *mi* or 56 *km* long, in Idaho) W & N into Columbia River in British Columbia

Penedos de São Pedro e São Paulo — see SAINT PETER AND SAINT PAUL ROCKS

Pe·ne·us \pə-'nē-əs\ *or New Greek* **Pi·niós** \pē-'nyós\ *or formerly* **Sa·lam·bria** \sə-'lam-brē-ə\ river 125 *mi* (201 *km*) N Greece in Thessaly flowing E into Gulf of Salonika

P'eng-hu \'pəŋ-'hü\ *or* **Pes·ca·do·res** \,pes-kə-'dór-ēz, -'dór-, -əs\ islands E China in Formosa Strait, attached to Taiwan; chief town Makung (on P'eng-hu, chief island) *area* 49 *sq mi* (127 *sq km*)

Peng-pu — see BENGBU

Pen-hsi — see BENXI

Peninsular Malaysia — see MALAYA

Pen·nine Alps \'pe-,nīn\ section of Alps on border between Switzerland & Italy NE of Graian Alps — see ROSA (Monte)

Pennine Chain mountains N England extending from Scotland border to Derbyshire & Staffordshire; highest Cross Fell 2930 *ft* (893 *m*)

Penn·syl·va·nia \,pen(t)-səl-'vā-nyə, -nē-ə\ state NE U.S. ✳ Harrisburg *area* 45,333 *sq mi* (117,866 *sq km*), *pop* 11,881,643

Pe·nob·scot \pə-'näb-,skät, -skət\ river 101 *mi* (162 *km*) central Maine flowing S into **Penob·scot Bay** (inlet of the Atlantic)

Pen·rhyn \pen-'rin, 'pen-,\ *or* **Ton·ga·re·va** \,täŋ-(g)ä-'rā-vä\ island S Pacific in the Manihiki Islands

Pen·sa·co·la \,pen(t)-sə-'kō-lə\ city & port NW Fla. on **Pensacola Bay** (inlet of Gulf of Mexico) *pop* 58,165

Pen·tap·o·lis \pen-'ta-pə-ləs\ any one of several groups of five ancient cities in Italy, Asia Minor, & Cyrenaica

Pen·te·cost \'pen-ti-,kòst, -'käst\ island SW Pacific in Vanuatu *pop* 11,336

Pen·tic·ton \pen-'tik-tən\ city Canada in S British Columbia *pop* 27,258

Pent·land Firth \'pent-lənd\ channel between Orkneys & mainland of Scotland

Pentland Hills hills S Scotland in Borders, Lothian, & Strathclyde regions; highest peak Scald Law 1898 *ft* (578 *m*)

Pen·za \'pen-zə\ city S central Russia in Europe W of Kuibyshev *pop* 552,000

Pen·zance \pen-'zan(t)s, pən-\ borough & port SW England in Cornwall on English Channel *pop* 19,521

Pen·zhin·ska·ya \,pen-'zhin(t)-skə-yə, 'pen-,zhin(t)-\ *or* **Pen·zhi·na** \pen-zhə-nə\ bay, an arm of Sea of Okhotsk, E Russia in Asia between Kamchatka Peninsula & mainland

People's Democratic Republic of Yemen — see YEMEN

People's Republic of China China exclusive of Taiwan

Pe·o·ria \pē-'òr-ē-ə, -'òr-\ **1** town SW central Ariz. *pop* 50,618 **2** city N central Ill. on Illinois River *pop* 113,504

Pep·in, Lake \'pi-pən, 'pe-\ expansion of upper Mississippi River 34 *mi* (55 *km*) long between SE Minn. & W Wis.

Pera — see BEYOGLU

Pe·raea *or* **Pe·rea** \pə-'rē-ə\ ancient region of Palestine E of Jordan River

Pe·rak \'per-ə, 'pir-ə, 'per-,ak\ state Malaysia in W Peninsular Malaysia on Strait of Malacca ✳ Kuala Kangsar *area* 8030 *sq mi* (20,798 *sq km*), *pop* 1,880,016

Per·di·do \pər-'dē-(,)dō\ river 60 *mi* (96 *km*) rising in SE Ala. & flowing S into Gulf of Mexico forming part of Ala.-Fla. boundary

Per·ga \'pər-gə\ ancient city S Asia Minor in Pamphylia

Per·ga·mum \'pər-gə-məm\ *or* **Per·ga·mus** \-məs\ *or* **Per·ga·mos** \-məs, -,mäs\ **1** ancient Greek kingdom covering most of Asia Minor; at its height 263–133 B.C. **2** *or modern* **Ber·ga·ma** \bər-'gä-mə\ city W Turkey NNE of Izmir ✳ of ancient Pergamum

Pé·ri·gord \,per-ə-'gór\ old division of N Guienne in SW France ✳ Périgueux

Pé·ri·gueux \,per-ə-'gə(r), pā-rē-'gœ\ commune SW France NE of Bordeaux *pop* 34,848

Pe·rim \pə-'rim, -'rēm\ island in Bab el Mandeb Strait at entrance to Red Sea; belongs to Yemen

Per·lis \'per-lis\ state Malaysia bordering on Thailand & Andaman sea ✳ Kangar *area* 310 *sq mi* (803 *sq km*), *pop* 184,070

Perm \'pərm, 'perm\ *or formerly* **Mo·lo·tov** \'mä-lə-,tóf, 'mò-, 'mō-, -,tóv\ city E Russia in Europe *pop* 1,099,000

Per·nam·bu·co \,pər-nəm-'bü-(,)kō, -'byü-; ,pernəm-'bü-(,)kü\ **1** state N Brazil ✳ Recife *area* 39,005 *sq mi* (101,023 *sq km*), *pop* 7,109,626 **2** — see RECIFE

Per·nik \'per-nik\ *or formerly* **Di·mi·tro·vo** \də-'mē-trə-,vò\ city W Bulgaria S of Sofia *pop* 99,643

Per·pi·gnan \per-pē-'nyäⁿ\ city S France SE of Toulouse near Mediterranean coast *pop* 108,049

Per·ris \'per-əs\ city SE Calif. *pop* 21,460

Per·sep·o·lis \pər-'se-pə-lis\ city of ancient Persia, site in SW Iran NE of Shiraz

Persia — see IRAN

Persian Gulf arm of Arabian Sea between SW Iran & Arabia

Persian Gulf States Kuwait, Bahrain, Qatar, & United Arab Emirates

Per·sis \'pər-sis\ ancient region SW Iran

Perth \'pərth\ **1** city ✳ of Western Australia on Swan River *pop* 80,517 — see FREMANTLE **2** *or* **Perth·shire** \-,shir, -shər\ former county central Scotland **3** burgh central Scotland *pop* 41,998

Perth Am·boy \,pərth-'am-,bói\ city & port NE N.J. on Raritan Bay at mouth of Raritan River *pop* 41,967

Pe·ru \pə-'rü, pā-\ country W S. America; a republic ✳ Lima *area* 496,222 *sq mi* (1,285,215 *sq km*), *pop* 22,916,000 — **Pe·ru·vi·an** \-'rü-vē-ən\ *adjective or noun*

Pe·ru·gia \pə-'rü-j(ē-)ə, pā-\ commune central Italy between Lake Trasimeno & the Tiber ✳ of Umbria *pop* 143,698

Pe·sa·ro \'pā-zä-,rō\ commune & port central Italy on the Adriatic NW of Ancona *pop* 88,500

Pe·sca·ra \pe-'skär-ä\ commune & port central Italy on the Adriatic *pop* 121,367

Pe·sha·war \pə-'shä-wər, -'shaú(-ə)r\ city N Pakistan ESE of Khyber Pass *pop* 555,000

Pe·tach Tik·va *or* **Pe·tah Tiq·wa** \'pe-tə(k)-'tik-(,)vä, pā-\ city W Israel *pop* 148,900

Pet·a·lu·ma \,pe-tᵊl-'ü-mə\ city W Calif. N of San Francisco *pop* 43,184

Pe·ta·re \pe-'tär-(,)ā\ city N Venezuela, a SE suburb of Caracas *pop* 531,866

Pe·ter·bor·ough \'pē-tər-,bər-ō, -,bər-ō\ **1** city Canada in SE Ontario *pop* 68,371 **2** borough E central England *pop* 88,346

Peterborough, Soke of \'sōk\ former administrative county E central England in Northampton-shire; later part of Huntingdonshire & since 1974 in Cambridgeshire

Pe·ters·burg \'pē-tərz-,bərg\ **1** city SE Va. *pop* 38,386 **2** SAINT PETERSBURG

Pet·it·co·di·ac \,pe-tē-'kō-dē-,ak\ river 60 *mi* (96 *km*) SE Canada in SE New Brunswick flowing to head of Bay of Fundy

Pe·tra \'pē-trə, 'pe-\ ancient city of NW Arabia on slope of Mt. Hor, site now in SW Jordan; ✳ of the Edomites & Nabataeans

Petrified Forest National Park reservation E Ariz. in Painted Desert containing natural exhibit of petrified wood

Pe·tro·dvo·rets \,pi-trə-dvär-'yets\ *or formerly* **Pe·ter·hof** \'pē-tər-,hòf, -,häf\ town W Russia in Europe W of St. Petersburg

Petrograd — see SAINT PETERSBURG 2

Pet·ro·pav·lovsk \,pe-trə-'pav-,lòfsk, ,pi-trə-'pàv-ləfsk\ city N Kazakhstan *pop* 248,300

Petropavlovsk–Kam·chat·skiy \-kam-'chat-skē, -'chät-\ city & port E Russia in Asia on Kamchatka Peninsula *pop* 273,000

Pe·tró·po·lis \pə-'trò-pü-lēs\ city SE Brazil in Rio de Janeiro state *pop* 255,211

Petrovsk — see MAKHACHKALA

Pet·ro·za·vodsk \,pi-trə-zə-'vótsk\ city NW Russia in Europe ✳ of Karelia on Lake Onega *pop* 280,000

Petsamo — see PECHENGA

Pfalz — see PALATINATE

Pforz·heim \'(p)fòrts-,hīm\ city SW Germany SE of Karlsruhe *pop* 115,547

Phar·os \'far-,äs, 'fer-\ peninsula N Egypt in city of Alexandria; formerly an island

Pharr \'fär\ city S Tex. E of McAllen *pop* 32,921

Phar·sa·lus \fär-'sā-ləs\ *or modern* **Phar·sa·la** \'fär-sə-lə\ *or New Greek* **Fár·sa·la** \'fär-sä-lä\ town NE Greece in E Thessaly in ancient district of **Phar·sa·lia** \fär-'sāl-yə, -'sä-lē-ə\

Phe·nix City \'fē-niks\ city E Ala. *pop* 25,312

Phe·rae \'fir-ē\ ancient town SE Thessaly

Phil·a·del·phia \,fi-lə-'del-fyə, -fē-ə\ **1** city & port SE Pa. on Delaware River *pop* 1,585,577 **2** — see ALASEHIR **3** — see AMMAN — **Phil·a·del·phian** \-fyən, -fē-ən\ *adjective or noun*

Phi·lae \'fī-(,)lē\ former island S Egypt in the Nile above Aswân; now submerged

Philippeville — see SKIKDA

Phi·lip·pi \'fi-lə-,pī, fə-'li-,pī\ ancient town NE Greece in N central Macedonia — **Phi·lip·pi·an** \fə-'li-pē-ən\ *adjective or noun*

Phil·ip·pine Islands \,fi-lə-'pēn, 'fi-lə-,\ islands of the Malay Archipelago NE of Borneo — see PHILIPPINES

Phil·ip·pines \-'pēnz, -,pēnz\ *or Spanish* **Re·pú·bli·ca de Fi·li·pi·nas** \re-'pü-blē-kä-thä-fē-lē-'pē-(,)näs\ *or Pilipino* **Re·pu·bli·ka ng Pi·li·pi·nas** \-näŋ-,pē-lē-'pē-(,)näs\ country E Asia comprising the Philippine Islands; a republic; once a Spanish possession & (1898–1945) a U.S. possession ✳ Manila *land area* 115,651 *sq mi* (299,536 *sq km*), *pop* 64,954,000 — **Philippine** *adjective*

Philippine Sea sea comprising the waters of the W Pacific E of & adjacent to the Philippine Islands

Philippopolis — see PLOVDIV

Phi·lis·tia \fə-'lis-tē-ə\ ancient country SW Palestine on the coast; the land of the Philistines

Phnom Penh \(pə-)'näm-'pen, (pə-)'nòm-\ city ✳ of Cambodia, on the Mekong *pop* 800,000

Pho·caea \fō-'sē-ə\ ancient city of Asia Minor on Aegean Sea in N Ionia — **Pho·cae·an** \-ən\ *adjective or noun*

Pho·cis \'fō-səs\ region central Greece N of Gulf of Corinth — **Pho·cian** \'fō-sē-ən, -shən\ *adjective or noun*

Phoe·ni·cia \fi-'ni-sh(ē-)ə, -'nē-\ ancient country SW Asia at E end of the Mediterranean in modern Syria & Lebanon

Phoe·nix \'fē-niks\ city ✳ of Ariz. on Salt River *pop* 983,403

Phoenix Islands islands central Pacific belonging to Kiribati

Phra Nakhon Si Ayutthaya — see AYUTTHAYA

Phry·gia \'fri-j(ē-)ə\ ancient country W central Asia Minor divided *about* 400 B.C. into **Greater Phrygia** (the inland region) & **Lesser Phrygia** (region along the Hellespont)

Pia·cen·za \pyä-'chen-sä\ *or ancient* **Pla·cen·tia** \plə-'sen(t)-sh(ē-)ə\ commune N Italy on the Po SE of Milan *pop* 102,252

Pi·auí *or formerly* **Pi·au·hy** \pyaü-'ē, pē-,aü-\ state NE Brazil bordering on the Atlantic E of Parnaíba River ✻ Teresina *area* 97,017 *sq mi* (251,274 *sq km*), *pop* 2,581,054

Pia·ve \'pyä-(,)vā, pē-'ä-\ river 137 *mi* (220 *km*) NE Italy flowing S & SE into the Adriatic

Pic·ar·dy \'pi-kər-dē\ *or French* **Pi·car·die** \pē-kár-'dē\ region & former province N France bordering on English Channel N of Normandy ✻ Amiens — **Pi·card** \'pi-,kärd, -kərd; pi-'kärd\ *adjective or noun*

Pi·ce·num \pī-'sē-nəm\ district of ancient Italy on the Adriatic SE of Umbria

Pick·er·ing \'pi-k(ə-)riŋ\ town Canada in SE Ontario *pop* 68,631

Pi·co Ri·ve·ra \,pē-(,)kō-rə-'vir-ə\ city SW Calif. *pop* 59,177

Pied·mont \'pēd-,mänt\ **1** upland region E U.S. lying E of the Appalachian Mountains between SE N.Y. & *central* Ala. **2** *or Italian* **Pie·mon·te** \pyä-'mōn-(,)tā\ region NW Italy bordering on France & Switzerland W of Lombardy ✻ Turin *pop* 4,357,559 — **Pied·mon·tese** \,pēd-mən-'tēz, -(,)män-, -'tēs\ *adjective or noun*

Pie·dras Ne·gras \pē-'ä-drəs-'nā-grəs, 'pyä-thräs-'nä-gräs\ city N Mexico in Coahuila on the Rio Grande opposite Eagle Pass, Tex. *pop* 98,177

Pi·er·ia \pī-'ir-ē-ə, -'er-\ ancient region NE Greece in Macedonia W of Thessaly

Pierre \'pir\ city ✻ of S.Dak. on Missouri River *pop* 12,906

Pierre·fonds \pē-,er-'fōⁿ, pyer-\ town Canada in S Quebec W of Montreal *pop* 48,735

Pie·ter·mar·itz·burg \,pē-tər-'mar-əts-,bərg\ city E Republic of South Africa in S *central* KwaZulu-Natal *pop* 128,598

Pigs, Bay of \'pigz\ *or* **Ba·hía de Co·chi·nos** \bä-'ē-ä-thä-kō-'chē-nōs\ bay W Cuba on S coast

Pikes Peak \'pīks\ mountain 14,110 *ft* (4301 *m*) E *central* Colo. at S end of Front Range

Pik — see POBEDA PEAK

Pi·la·tus \pē-'lä-,tús\ mountain 6983 *ft* (2128 *m*) *central* Switzerland in Unterwalden SW of Lucerne

Pil·co·ma·yo \,pēl-kō-'mä-yō\ river 1000 *mi* (1609 *km*) S *central* S. America rising in Bolivia & flowing SE on Argentina-Paraguay boundary into Paraguay River

Pílion — see PELION

Pillars of Her·cu·les \'hər-kyə-,lēz\ the two promontories at E end of Strait of Gibraltar: Rock of Gibraltar (in Europe) & Jebel Musa (in Africa)

Pí·los \'pē-,lòs\ town & port SW Greece in SW Peloponnese

Pim·li·co \'pim-li-,kō\ district of W London, England, in SW Westminster

Pi·nar del Río \pē-'när-thel-'rē-(,)ō\ city & port W Cuba *pop* 121,774

Pi·na·tu·bo, Mount \,pē-nä-'tü-(,)bō, ,pi-nə-\ volcano N Philippines on Luzon

Pin·dus Mountains \'pin-dəs\ mountains N Greece between Epirus & Thessaly

Pine Bluff \'pīn-'bləf, -,bləf\ city SE *central* Ark. *pop* 57,140

Pi·nel·las Park \pī-'ne-ləs\ city W Fla. NW of St. Petersburg *pop* 43,426

Pinellas Peninsula peninsula W Fla. W of Tampa Bay

Pines, Isle of — see YOUTH (Isle of) **2** — see ILE DES PINS

Ping \'piŋ\ river 360 *mi* (579 *km*) W Thailand flowing SSE to join Nan River forming the Chao Phraya

Piniós — see PENEUS

Pinkiang — see HARBIN

Pinnacles National Monument reservation W *central* Calif. in Coast Range SSE of Hollister

Pinsk \'pin(t)sk\ city SW Belarus *pop* 123,800

Pio·tr·ków Try·bu·nal·ski \'pyò-tər-,küf-,tri-bü-'näl-skē, pē-'ò-, -,kúv-\ commune *central* Poland SSE of Lodz *pop* 80,529

Pipe Spring National Monument reservation NW Ariz. on Kaibab Plateau containing old Mormon fort

Pipe·stone National Monument \'pīp-,stōn\ reservation SW Minn. containing quarry once used by Indians

Piq·ua \'pi-(,)kwä, -kwə\ city W Ohio N of Dayton *pop* 20,612

Pi·rae·us \pī-'rē-əs, pi-'rä-\ *or* **Pi·rai·evs** \,pē-re-'efs\ city E Greece on Saronic Gulf; port of Athens *pop* 169,622

Pirineos — see PYRENEES

Pir·ma·sens \'pir-mə-,zen(t)s\ city SW Germany near French border E of Saarbrücken *pop* 47,801

Pir·na \'pir-nə\ city E Germany SE of Dresden *pop* 48,001

Pi·sa \'pē-zə, *Italian* -sä\ commune W *central* Italy in Tuscany on the Arno *pop* 98,006 — **Pi·san** \'pē-zᵊn\ *adjective or noun*

Pis·cat·a·qua \pi-'ska-tə-,kwò\ river 12 *mi* (19 *km*) Maine & N.H. formed by junction of Cocheco & Salmon Falls rivers & flowing SE on Maine-N.H. boundary into the Atlantic

Pis·gah, Mount \'piz-gə\ ridge Palestine in Jordan E of N end of Dead Sea; highest point over 2630 *ft* (802 *m*) was alternatively called **Mount Ne·bo** \'nē-bō\

Pi·sid·ia \pə-'si-dē-ə, pī-\ ancient country S Asia Minor N of Pamphylia — **Pi·sid·i·an** \-dē-ən\ *adjective*

Pi·sto·ia \pē-'stō-yä\ commune *central* Italy NW of Florence *pop* 87,275

Pit \'pit\ river N Calif. flowing SW into the Sacramento

Pit·cairn Island \'pit-,karn, -,kern\ island S Pacific SE of Tuamotu Archipelago; a Brit. colony, with several smaller islands *pop* 62

Pi·tes·ti \pē-'tesht, -'tesh-tē\ city S *central* Romania *pop* 162,395

Pitts·burg \'pits-,bərg\ city W Calif. NE of Oakland on San Joaquin River *pop* 47,564

Pitts·burgh \'pits-,bərg\ city SW Pa. at confluence of the Allegheny & the Monongahela where they form the Ohio *pop* 369,879 — **Pitts·burgh·er** \-,bər-gər\ *noun*

Pitts·field \'pits-,fēld\ city W Mass. *pop* 48,622

Piz Bernina — see BERNINA

Pla·cen·tia \plə-'sen(t)-shə\ city SW Calif. *pop* 41,259

Placentia Bay inlet of the Atlantic E Canada in SE Newfoundland

Plac·id, Lake \'pla-səd\ lake 5 *mi* (8 *km*) long NE N.Y. in the Adirondacks

Plain·field \'plān-,fēld\ city NE N.J. *pop* 46,567

Plains of Abra·ham \'ā-brə-,ham\ plateau Canada in W part of city of Quebec

Plain·view \'plān-,vyü\ city NW Tex. N of Lubbock *pop* 21,700

Pla·no \'plā-(,)nō\ city NE Tex. N of Dallas *pop* 128,713

Plantation city SE Fla. W of Fort Lauderdale *pop* 66,692

Plant City \'plant\ city W *central* Fla. E of Tampa *pop* 22,754

Plas·sey \'pla-sē\ village NE India in W. Bengal N of Calcutta

Pla·ta, Río de la \,rē-ō-thä-lä-'plä-tä\ *or* **River Plate** \'plāt\ estuary of Paraná & Uruguay rivers S. America between Uruguay & Argentina

Pla·taea \plə-'tē-ə\ *or* **Pla·tae·ae** \-,ē\ ancient city Greece in SE Boeotia S of Thebes — **Pla·tae·an** \-'tē-ən\ *adjective or noun*

Platte \'plat\ **1** river 310 *mi* (499 *km*) *central* Nebr. formed by junction of the N. Platte & S. Platte & flowing E into the Missouri **2** river 300 *mi* (483 *km*) SW Iowa & NW Mo. flowing into the Missouri

Plattensee — see BALATON (Lake)

Platts·burgh \'plats-,bərg\ city NE N.Y. on Lake Champlain *pop* 21,255

Plau·en \'plaü-ən\ *or* **Plauen im Vogt·land** \im-'fōkt-,länt\ city E Germany on the Weisse Elster *pop* 70,856

Pleasant — see NAURU

Pleasant Hill city W Calif. ENE of Oakland *pop* 31,585

Pleas·an·ton \'ple-zᵊn-tən\ city W Calif. SE of Oakland *pop* 50,553

Plenty, Bay of inlet of the S. Pacific N New Zealand on NE coast of North Is.

Ple·ven \'ple-vən\ city NW Bulgaria *pop* 138,323

Plock \'plòtsk\ commune NE *central* Poland *pop* 121,996

Plo·iesti *or* **Plo·esti** \plò-'yesht, -'yesh-tē\ city SE *central* Romania *pop* 247,502

Plov·div \'plòv-,dif, -,div\ *or Greek* **Phil·ip·pop·o·lis** \,fē-lē-'pò-pò-,lēs\ city S Bulgaria on the Maritsa N of the Rhodope Mountains *pop* 379,083

Plum \'pləm\ city SW Pa. *pop* 25,609

Plym·outh \'pli-məth\ **1** town SE Mass. *pop* 45,608 **2** village SE Minn. NW of Minneapolis *pop* 50,889 **3** city & port SW England in Devon *pop* 238,800

Plzeň \'pᵊl-,zen\ city W Czech Republic in Bohemia WSW of Prague *pop* 173,129

Po \'pō\ *or ancient* **Pa·dus** \'pā-dəs\ river 405 *mi* (652 *km*) N Italy flowing from slopes of Mt. Viso E into the Adriatic through several mouths

Po·be·da Peak \pō-'be-də, pə-, -'bye-\ *or Russian* **Pik Po·be·dy** \pik-pə-'bye-dē, -'be-dē\ mountain 24,406 *ft* (7439 *m*) E Kyrgyzstan; highest in Tian Shan

Po·ca·tel·lo \,pō-kə-'te-(,)lō, -lə\ city SE Idaho *pop* 46,080

Po·co·no Mountains \'pō-kə-,nō\ mountains E Pa. NW of Allentinny Mountain; highest *about* 1600 *ft* (488 *m*)

Pod·go·ri·ca \'pòd-,gör-ēt-sä\ *or 1946–92* **Ti·to·grad** \'tē-(,)tō-,grad, -,gräd\ city S Yugoslavia ✻ of Montenegro *pop* 152,242

Po·do·lia \pə-'dō-lē-ə, -'dōl-yə\ *or Russian* **Po·dolsk** \pə-'dòlsk\ region W Ukraine N of middle Dniester River

Po·dolsk \pə-'dòlsk\ city W *central* Russia in Europe S of Moscow *pop* 208,000

Po Hai — see BO HAI

Pohn·pei \'pōn-,pā\ *or* **Po·na·pe** \'pō-nə-,pā\ island E Carolines, part of Federated States of Micronesia

Pointe-à-Pi·tre \,pwan-tə-'pētrᵊ\ city & port French West Indies in Guadeloupe on Grande-Terre *pop* 26,083

Pointe–Claire \'pòint-'klar, pwant-\ town Canada in S Quebec on St. Lawrence River SW of Montreal *pop* 27,647

Pointe–Noire \,pwant-'nwär\ city & port SW Republic of the Congo on the Atlantic; formerly ✻ of Middle Congo *pop* 576,206

Point Pe·lee National Park \pòint-'pē-lē\ reservation Canada in SE Ontario on **Point Pelee** (cape projecting into Lake Erie)

Poi·tiers *or formerly* **Poic·tiers** \pwä-'tyā, 'pwä-tē-,ā\ city W *central* France SW of Tours *pop* 82,507

Poi·tou \pwä-'tü\ region & former province W France SE of Brittany ✻ Poitiers

Po·land \'pō-lənd\ *or Polish* **Pol·ska** \'pòl-skä\ country E *central* Europe bordering on Baltic Sea; in medieval period a kingdom, at one time extending to the lower Dnieper; partitioned 1772, 1793, 1795 among Russia, Prussia, & Austria; again a kingdom 1815–30; lost autonomy 1830–1918; since 1918 a republic ✻ Warsaw *area* 120,756 *sq mi* (312,758 *sq km*), *pop* 38,038,400

Polesye — see PRIPET

Polish Corridor strip of land N Europe in Poland that between World War I & World War II separated E. Prussia from main part of Germany; area was before 1919 part of Germany

Pol·ta·va \pəl-'tä-və\ city *central* Ukraine on Vorskla River WSW of Kharkiv *pop* 320,000

Poltoratsk — see ASHKHABAD

Poly·ne·sia \,pä-lə-'nē-zhə, -shə\ the islands of the *central* & S Pacific including Hawaii, the Line, Phoenix, Tonga, Cook, & Samoa islands, Tuvalu, Easter Is., French Polynesia, & often New Zealand

Pom·er·a·nia \,pä-mə-'rā-nē-ə, -nyə\ *or German* **Pom·mern** \'pò-mərn\ *or Polish* **Po·mo·rze** \pò-'mò-zhe\ **1** region N Europe on Baltic Sea; formerly in Germany, now mostly in Poland **2** former province of Prussia

Pom·er·e·lia \,pä-mə-'rē-lē-ə, -'rēl-yə\ *or German* **Pom·me·rel·len** \,pò-mə-'re-lən\ region E Europe on the Baltic W of the Vistula & E of Pomerania; originally part of Pomerania

Po·mo·na \pə-'mō-nə\ city SW Calif. E of Los Angeles *pop* 131,723

\ə\ **abut** \ᵊ\ **kitten** \ər\ **further** \a\ **ash** \ā\ **ace** \ä\ **mop, mar** \aú\ **out** \ch\ **chin** \e\ **bet** \ē\ **easy** \g\ **go** \i\ **hit** \ī\ **ice** \j\ **job** \ŋ\ **sing** \ō\ **go** \ò\ **law** \òi\ **boy** \th\ **thin** \t̲h\ **the** \ü\ **loot** \ú\ **foot** \y\ **yet** \zh\ **vision** *see also* Guide to Pronunciation

Pom·pa·no Beach \'päm-pə-,nō, 'pəm-\ city SE Fla. on the Atlantic N of Fort Lauderdale *pop* 72,411

Pom·pe·ii \päm-'pā, -'pā-,ē\ ancient city S Italy SE of Naples destroyed A.D. 79 by eruption of Mt. Vesuvius — **Pom·pe·ian** *or* **Pom·pei·ian** \-'pā-ən\ *adjective or noun*

Pon·ca City \'päŋ-kə\ city N Okla. on Arkansas River *pop* 26,359

Pon·ce \'pón(t)-(,)sā\ city & port S Puerto Rico *pop* 187,749

Pon·di·cher·ry \,pän-də-'cher-ē, -'sher-\ *or French* **Pon·di·ché·ry** \pōⁿ-dē-shä-'rē\ **1** union territory SE India SSW of Madras surrounded by Tamil Nadu; a settlement of French India before 1954, *area* 183 *sq mi* (474 *sq km*), *pop* 807,785 **2** city & port, its ✳ *pop* 202,648

Pon·ta Del·ga·da \,pōn-tə-del-'gä-də\ city & port Azores on São Miguel Is. *pop* 21,091

Pont·char·train, Lake \'pänt-shər-,trān, ,pänt-shər-\ lake SE La. E of the Mississippi & N of New Orleans *area about* 630 *sq mi* (1632 *sq km*)

Pon·te·fract \'pän-ti-,frakt, *formerly also* 'pəm(p)-frət, 'päm(p)-\ borough N England in W. Yorkshire, SE of Leeds *pop* 31,971

Pon·te·ve·dra \,pón-tā-'vā-drä\ **1** province NW Spain in SW Galicia on the Atlantic *area* 1729 *sq mi* (4478 *sq km*), *pop* 896,847 **2** commune & port, its ✳, NW of Vigo *pop* 68,645

Pon·ti·ac \'pän-tē-,ak\ city SE Mich. NW of Detroit *pop* 71,166

Pon·ti·a·nak \,pän-tē-'ä-,näk\ city Indonesia on SW coast of Borneo *pop* 398,357

Pon·tine Islands \'pän-,tīn, -,tēn\ islands Italy in Tyrrhenian Sea W of Naples; chief islands **Pon·za** \'pónt-sä\ & **Pon·ti·ne** \'pän-,tīn, -,tēn\ pōn-'tē-nä\

Pontine Marshes district *central* Italy in SW Lazio, separated from sea by low sand hills that prevent natural drainage; now reclaimed

Pon·tus \'pän-təs\ **1** ancient country NE Asia Minor; a kingdom 4th century B.C. to 66 B.C., later a Roman province **2** *or* **Pontus Euxinus** — see BLACK SEA

Pon·ty·pool \,pän-tə-'pül\ town SE Wales in Gwent *pop* 36,761

Pon·ty·pridd \,pän-tə-'prēth\ town SE Wales in Mid Glamorgan *pop* 32,992

Poole \'pül\ borough S England in Dorset on English Channel *pop* 130,900

Poona — see PUNE

Po·o·pó, Lake \,pō-ō-'pō, (,)pō-'pō\ lake 60 *mi* (96 *km*) long W *central* Bolivia S of Lake Titicaca at altitude of 12,000 *ft* (3658 *m*)

Pop·lar \'pä-plər\ former metropolitan borough E London, England, on N bank of the Thames, now part of Tower Hamlets

Po·po·ca·te·petl \,pō-pə-'ka-tə-,pe-tᵊl, -,katə-'; ,pō-pō-kä-'tä-,pet-ᵊl\ volcano 17,887 *ft* (5452 *m*) SE *central* Mexico in Puebla

Porcupine river 448 *mi* (721 *km*) in N Yukon Territory & NE Alaska flowing N & W into the Yukon

Po·ri \'pór-ē\ city & port SW Finland *pop* 76,456

Pork·ka·la Peninsula \'pór-kä-,lä\ peninsula S Finland W of Helsinki

Por·la·mar \,pór-lə-'mär\ city & port NE Venezuela on Margarita Is.

Port Ad·e·laide \'a-dᵊl-,ād\ city SE S. Australia on Gulf of St. Vincent at mouth of Torrens River; port for Adelaide *pop* 38,205

Por·tage \'pór-tij, 'pór-\ **1** city NW Ind. E of Gary *pop* 29,060 **2** city SW Mich. S of Kalamazoo *pop* 41,042

Port Ar·thur \'är-thər\ **1** city & port SE Tex. on Sabine Lake *pop* 58,724 **2** — see THUNDER BAY **3** — see LÜ-SHUN

Port-au-Prince \,pórt-ō-'prin(t)s, ,pórt-; ,pór-(t)ō-'praⁿs\ city & port ✳ of Haiti on SE shore of Gulf of Gonave *pop* 752,600

Port Blair \'blar, 'bler\ town & port India on S. Andaman Is. ✳ of Andaman and Nicobar union territory

Port Ches·ter \'pórt-,ches-tər, 'pórt-\ village SE N.Y. NE of New Rochelle on Long Island Sound *pop* 24,728

Port Co·quit·lam \kō-'kwit-ləm\ city Canada in SW British Columbia E of Vancouver *pop* 36,773

Port Eliz·a·beth \i-'li-zə-bəth\ city & port S Republic of South Africa in S Eastern Cape province on Algoa Bay *pop* 468,797

Por·ter·ville \'pór-tər-,vil, 'pór-\ city S *central* Calif. *pop* 29,563

Port Ev·er·glades \'e-vər-,glādz\ seaport SE Fla. on the Atlantic S of Fort Lauderdale

Port Hed·land \'hed-lənd\ port Western Australia

Port Hue·ne·me \wī-'nē-mē\ city S Calif. near Oxnard *pop* 20,319

Port Hu·ron \'hyūr-,än, 'yūr-, -ən\ city E Mich. on Lake Huron & St. Clair River *pop* 33,694

Port Jack·son \'jak-sən\ inlet of S Pacific SE Australia in New South Wales; the harbor of Sydney

Port·land \'pórt-lənd, 'pórt-\ **1** city & port SW Maine on Casco Bay *pop* 64,358 **2** city & port NW Oreg. at confluence of Columbia & Willamette rivers *pop* 437,319

Portland Canal inlet of the Pacific *about* 80 *mi* (129 *km*) long Canada & U.S. between British Columbia & SE tip of Alaska

Port·laoigh·i·se \pórt-'lē-shə, pórt-, -'lā-ə-\ *or* **Port Laoi·se** \'lē-shə\ *or* **Mary·bor·ough** \'mar-ē-,bər-ō\ town *central* Ireland ✳ of County Laoighis *pop* 3773

Port Lou·is \'lü-əs, 'lü-ē\ city & port ✳ of Mauritius *pop* 142,645

Port Lyautey — see KENITRA

Port Mahon — see MAHÓN

Port Mores·by \'mórz-bē, 'mórz-\ city & port SE New Guinea in Papua ✳ of Papua New Guinea *pop* 193,242

Por·to \'pór-(,)tü, 'pór-\ *or* **Opor·to** \ō-'pór-(,)tü, -'pór-\ city & port NW Portugal on the Douro *pop* 310,600 — see LEIXÕES

Pôr·to Ale·gre \,pór-(,)tü-ä-'lā-grē\ city & port S Brazil ✳ of Rio Grande do Sul state at N end of Lagoa dos Patos *pop* 1,300,000

Por·to·be·lo \,pór-tō-'be-(,)lō, ,pór-\ town & port Panama on Caribbean coast; the great emporium of S. American trade in 17th & 18th centuries

Port of Spain city & port ✳ of Trinidad and Tobago, on NW Trinidad Is. *pop* 50,878

Por·to-No·vo \,pór-tō-'nō-(,)vō, ,pór-\ city & port ✳ of Benin *pop* 192,000

Port Or·ange \'är-inj, 'är-(ə)nj, 'ór-inj, 'ór-(ə)nj\ city E Fla. *pop* 35,317

Porto Rico — see PUERTO RICO

Port Phil·lip Bay \'fi-ləp\ inlet of Bass Strait SE Australia in Victoria; the harbor of Melbourne

Port Roy·al \'rói-(ə)l\ town Jamaica at entrance to Kingston Harbor; early ✳ of Jamaica, destroyed by earthquakes 1692 & 1907 & partly engulfed by the sea

Port Royal Sound inlet of the Atlantic S S.C.

Port Said \sä-'ēd, 'sīd\ city & port NE Egypt on the Mediterranean at N end of Suez Canal *pop* 262,760

Port Saint Lu·cie \,sänt-'lü-sē\ city E Fla. *pop* 55,866

Ports·mouth \'pórts-məth, 'pórts-\ **1** city & port SE N.H. on the Atlantic *pop* 25,925 **2** city S Ohio at junction of Ohio & Scioto rivers *pop* 22,676 **3** city & port SE Va. on Elizabeth River opposite Norfolk *pop* 103,907 **4** city S England in Hampshire on **Port·sea** \'pórt-sē, 'pórt-\ (island in English Channel) *pop* 174,700

Port Stanley — see STANLEY

Port Sudan city & port NE Sudan on Red Sea *pop* 100,700

Por·tu·gal \'pór-chi-gəl, 'pór-; ,pür-tü-'gäl\ *or ancient* **Lu·si·ta·nia** \,lü-sə-'tā-nē-ə, -nyə\ country SW Europe in W Iberian Peninsula bordering on the Atlantic; a kingdom before 1910; now a republic ✳ Lisbon *area* (not including Azores & Madeira) 35,383 *sq mi* (91,642 *sq km*), *pop* 10,429,000

Portuguese East Africa — see MOZAMBIQUE

Portuguese Guinea — see GUINEA-BISSAU

Portuguese India former Portuguese possessions on W coast of India peninsula, annexed 1962 by India; comprised territory of Goa & districts of Daman & Diu

Portuguese Timor — see TIMOR

Portuguese West Africa — see ANGOLA

Port-Vi·la \,pórt-'vē-lə, pórt-\ *or* **Vila** town & port ✳ of Vanuatu in SW Efate Is. *pop* 18,905

Porz am Rhein \,pórts-äm-'rīn\ city W Germany ESE suburb of Cologne *pop* 76,762

Poseidonia — see PAESTUM

Potch·ef·stroom \'pó-chəf-,strōm\ city NE Republic of South Africa in E North West province SW of Johannesburg *pop* 51,800

Po·to·mac \pə-'tō-mək, -mik\ river 287 *mi* (462 *km*) E U.S. flowing from W.Va. into Chesapeake Bay & forming S boundary of Md.

Po·to·sí \,pō-tō-'sē\ city S Bolivia *pop* 112,291

Pots·dam \'päts-,dam\ city NE Germany SW of Berlin *pop* 139,025

Potts·town \'päts-,taún\ borough SE Pa. ESE of Reading *pop* 21,831

Pough·keep·sie \pə-'kip-sē, pō-\ city SE N.Y. *pop* 28,844

Po·way \'paú-(,)wā\ city S Calif., a suburb of San Diego *pop* 43,516

Pow·der \'paú-dər\ **1** river 150 *mi* (241 *km*) E Oreg. flowing into the Snake **2** river 375 *mi* (604 *km*) N Wyo. & SE Mont. flowing N into the Yellowstone

Powell, Lake — see GLEN CANYON DAM

Pow·ys \'pō-əs\ county E *central* Wales ✳ Llandrindod Wells *area* 1960 *sq mi* (5096 *sq km*), *pop* 116,500

Po·yang \'pō-'yäŋ\ lake 90 *mi* (145 *km*) long E China in N Jiangxi

Poz·nan \'pōz-,nan, 'póz-,nän\ *or German* **Po·sen** \'pō-zᵊn\ city W *central* Poland on the Warta *pop* 588,715

Poz·zuo·li \pót-'swó-lē\ *or ancient* **Pu·te·o·li** \pyü-'tē-ə-,lī, pü-\ commune & port S Italy in Campania W of Naples *pop* 76,121

Prague \'präg\ *or Czech* **Pra·ha** \'prä-(,)hä\ city ✳ of Czech Republic & formerly of Czechoslovakia in Bohemia on Vltava River *pop* 1,214,772

Praia \'prī-ə\ town ✳ of Cape Verde on São Tiago Is. *pop* 61,797

Prairie Provinces the Canadian provinces of Manitoba, Saskatchewan, & Alberta

Prairie Village city NE Kans. S of Kansas City *pop* 23,186

Pra·to \'prä-tō\ commune *central* Italy in Tuscany *pop* 165,888

Pratt·ville \'prat-,vil, -vəl\ city *central* Ala. NW of Montgomery *pop* 19,587

Pres·cott \'pres-kət, -,kät\ city *central* Ariz. *pop* 26,455

Presque Isle \presk-'īl\ peninsula NW Pa. in Lake Erie forming **Presque Isle Bay** (harbor of Erie, Pa.)

Pressburg — see BRATISLAVA

Pres·ton \'pres-tən\ **1** former town, Ontario, Canada — see CAMBRIDGE **2** borough NW England NNW of Liverpool ✳ of Lancashire *pop* 126,200

Prest·wich \'prest-(,)wich\ borough NW England in Greater Manchester NNW of Manchester *pop* 31,198

Prest·wick \'prest-(,)wik\ burgh SW Scotland in Strathclyde N of Ayr *pop* 13,532

Pre·to·ria \pri-'tōr-ē-ə, -'tór-\ city, administrative ✳ of Republic of South Africa & formerly ✳ of Transvaal *pop* 303,684

Pretoria–Witwatersrand–Vereeniging — see GAUTENG

Prib·i·lof Islands \'pri-bə-,lóf\ islands Alaska in Bering Sea

Prich·ard \'pri-chərd\ city SW Ala. N of Mobile *pop* 34,311

Primorski Krai *or* **Primorskiy Kray** — see MARITIME TERRITORY

Prince Al·bert \'al-bərt\ city Canada in *central* Saskatchewan *pop* 34,181

Prince Albert National Park reservation Canada in *central* Saskatchewan in watershed area

Prince Ed·ward Island \'ed-wərd\ island SE Canada in Gulf of Saint Lawrence off E New Brunswick & N Nova Scotia; a province ✳ Charlottetown *area* 2185 *sq mi* (5660 *sq km*), *pop* 129,765

Prince Edward Island National Park reservation Canada on N coast of Prince Edward Island

Prince George \'jórj\ city Canada in E *central* British Columbia *pop* 69,653

Prince of Wales, Cape \'wālz\ cape Alaska at W tip of Seward Peninsula; most westerly point of mainland of N. America, at 168°W

Prince of Wales Island 1 island SE Alaska, largest in Alexander Archipelago **2** island N Canada between Victoria Is. & Somerset Is. *area* 12,830 *sq mi* (33,358 *sq km*)

Prince Ru·pert's Land \'rü-pərts\ historical region N & W Canada comprising drainage basin of

Hudson Bay granted 1670 by King Charles II to Hudson's Bay Company; purchased 1869 by the Dominion

Prince Wil·liam Sound \'wil-yəm\ inlet of Gulf of Alaska S Alaska E of Kenai Peninsula

Prín·ci·pe Island \'prin(t)-si-pē\ island W Africa in Gulf of Guinea N of São Tomé — see SÃO TOMÉ

Prip·et \'pri-,pet, -pət\ or Russian **Pri·pyat** \'pri-pyat\ river 500 mi (805 km) E central Europe in NW Ukraine & S Belarus flowing E through the marshlands called **Po·les·ye** \pó-'les-ye\ or **Pripet Marshes** or **Pripyat Marshes** to the Dnieper

Pro·gre·so \prə-'gre-(,)sō\ city SE Mexico on Yucatán Peninsula; port for Mérida pop 37,806

Pro·ko·pyevsk \prə-'kó-pyəfsk\ city S Russia in Asia at S end of Kuznetsk Basin NW of Novokuznetsk pop 272,000

Propontis — see MARMARA (Sea of)

Pro·vence \prə-'vän(t)s, prō-'väs\ region & former province SE France bordering on the Mediterranean ✽ Aix-en-Provence

Prov·i·dence \'prä-və-dən(t)s, -,den(t)s\ city & port N R.I., its ✽ pop 160,728

Pro·vo \'prō-(,)vō\ city N central Utah on Utah Lake pop 86,835

Prud·hoe Bay \'prü-(,)dō, 'prə-; 'prüd-(,)hō, 'prəd-\ inlet of Beaufort Sea N Alaska

Prus·sia \'prə-shə\ or German **Preus·sen** \'prói-s°n\ **1** historical region N Germany bordering on Baltic Sea **2** former kingdom & state of Germany ✽ Berlin — see EAST PRUSSIA, WEST PRUSSIA — **Prus·sian** \'prə-shən\ adjective or noun

Prut \'prüt\ river 565 mi (909 km) E Europe flowing from the Carpathians SSE into the Danube; forming the Romanian boundary (World War II to 1991) with the U.S.S.R. & (since 1991) with Moldova & Ukraine

Pskov \pə-'skóf, -'skóv\ city W Russia in Europe near **Lake Pskov** (S arm of Peipus Lake) pop 209,000

Ptol·e·ma·ïs \,tä-lə-'mā-əs\ **1** ancient town in upper Egypt on left bank of the Nile NW of Thebes **2** ancient town in Cyrenaica NW of Barka; site at modern village of Tolmeta **3** — see ACRE

Pu·chon \'pü-,chón\ city NW S. Korea pop 456,292

Pueb·la \'pwe-blä\ **1** state SE central Mexico area 13,096 sq mi (33,919 sq km), pop 4,126,101 **2** or **Puebla de Za·ra·go·za** \dä-,zar-ə-'gó-zə, thä-,sär-ä-'gó-sä\ city, its ✽, SE of Mexico (City) pop 1,054,921

Pueb·lo \'pwe-,blo\ city SE central Colo. on the Arkansas pop 98,640

Puer·to Bar·rios \'pwer-tō-'bär-ē-,ōs\ city & port E Guatemala on Gulf of Honduras pop 39,088

Puerto La Cruz \lä-'krüz, -'krüs\ city NE Venezuela NE of Barcelona pop 60,546

Puerto Limón — see LIMÓN

Puerto Montt \'mónt\ city & port S central Chile pop 84,410

Puer·to Ri·co \,pórtə-'rē-(,)kō, ,pwer-tō-\ or formerly **Por·to Rico** \,pór-tə, ,pór-tō\ island W. Indies E of Hispaniola; a self-governing commonwealth in union with the U.S. ✽ San Juan area 3435 sq mi (8931 sq km), pop 3,612,000 — **Puerto Ri·can** \'rē-kən\ adjective or noun

Pu·get Sound \'pyü-jət\ arm of the Pacific extending 80 mi (129 km) S into W Wash. from E end of Strait of Juan de Fuca

Pu·glia \'pül-yä\ or **Apu·lia** \ä-'pül-yä\ or **Le Puglie** \lə-'pül-yä\ region SE Italy on the Adriatic & Gulf of Taranto ✽ Bari pop 4,069,359

Pu·ka·pu·ka \,pü-kä-'pü-kä\ or **Dan·ger Islands** \'dān-jər\ atoll central Pacific N of Cook Islands; chief island Pukapuka; administered with Cook Islands by New Zealand

Pu·la \'pü-lä\ city & port W Croatia at tip of Istrian Peninsula pop 62,690

Pul·ko·vo \'pül-kə-və, -,vō\ village W Russia in Europe S of St. Petersburg

Pull·man \'púl-mən\ city SE Wash. pop 23,478

Pu·log, Mount \'pü-,lóg\ mountain 9606 ft (2928 m) Philippines in N Luzon at S end of Cordillera Central; highest in Luzon

Pu·na de Ata·ca·ma \'pü-nä-,thä-,ä-tä-'kä-mä\ high plateau region NW Argentina NW of San Miguel de Tucumán

Pun·cak Jaya \,pún-,chäk-'jä-yə\ or formerly **Mount Car·stensz** \'kär-stənz\ mountain 16,535 ft (5040 m) in Sudirman Range, Irian Jaya, Indonesia; highest in New Guinea

Pu·ne \'pü-nə\ or **Poo·na** \'pü-nə\ city W India in Maharashtra ESE of Bombay pop 1,566,651

Pun·jab or **Pan·jab** \,pən-'jäb, -'jab, 'pən-,\ **1** region NW Indian subcontinent in Pakistan & NW India occupying valleys of the Indus & its five tributaries; formerly a province of Brit. India ✽ Lahore **2** or **East Punjab** former state NW India in E Punjab divided 1966 into two states of Punjabi Suba & Haryana **3** or formerly **West Punjab** province NE Pakistan ✽ Lahore **4** or **Pun·jabi Su·ba** \,pən-'jä-bē-'sü-bə, -,\'ja-\ state NW India formed from N part of former state of Punjab ✽ Chandigarh area 19,448 sq mi (50,370 sq km), pop 20,289,969

Punt \'pünt\ ancient Egyptian name for a part of Africa not certainly identified, probably Somaliland

Pun·ta Are·nas \,pün-tä-ä-'rä-näs\ or formerly **Ma·gal·la·nes** \,mä-gä-'yä-näs\ city & port S Chile on Strait of Magellan pop 95,332

Punta del Es·te \thel-'es-tā\ town S Uruguay E of Montevideo pop 5272

Pu·ra·cé \,pü-rä-'sā\ volcano 15,604 ft (4756 m) SW central Colombia

Pur·beck, Isle of \'pər-,bek\ peninsula region S England in Dorset extending E into English Channel

Pur·ga·toire \,pər-gə-,twär, 'pi-kə-,twīr\ river 190 mi (306 km) SE Colo. flowing into the Arkansas

Pu·ri \'púr-ē\ city & port E India in SE Orissa on Bay of Bengal pop 124,835

Pu·rus \pə-'rüs\ river 2000 mi (3219 km) NW central S. America rising in the Andes in SE Peru & flowing NE into the Amazon in Brazil

Pu·san \'pü-,sän\ city & port SE S. Korea on Korea Strait pop 3,825,000

Push·kin \'púsh-kən\ or formerly **Tsar·skoye Se·lo** \'(t)sär-skə-yə-sə-'ló\ or **Det·skoe Selo** \'dyet-skə-yə\ city W Russia in Europe S of St. Petersburg pop 95,300

Puteoli — see POZZUOLI

Put-in-Bay \,pút-,in-'bā\ inlet of Lake Erie in Ohio on S. Bass Is. N of Sandusky Bay; site of **Perry's Victory and International Peace Memorial Monument**

Pu·tu·ma·yo \,pü-tü-'mī-(,)ō\ or (in Brazil) **Içá** \ē-'sä\ river 980 mi (1577 km) NW S. America flowing from SW Colombia into the Amazon in NW Brazil

Puy·al·lup \pyü-'a-ləp\ city W central Wash. pop 23,875

Puy de Dôme — see DÔME (Puy de)

Puy de Sancy — see SANCY (Puy de)

Pya·ti·gorsk \pi-tē-'górsk\ city S Russia in Europe in N Caucasus SE of Stravropol pop 132,000

Pyd·na \'pid-nə\ ancient town Macedonia on W shore of Gulf of Salonika

Pyong·yang \'pyón-,yaŋ, 'pyəŋ-, -'yäŋ\ city ✽ of N. Korea on the Taedong pop 2,355,000

Pyramid Lake lake 30 mi (48 km) long NW Nev. NE of Reno

Pyr·e·nees \'pir-ə-,nēz\ or French **Py·ré·nées** \pē-rā-'nā\ or Spanish **Pi·ri·ne·os** \,pē-rē-'nä-(,)ōs\ mountains along French-Spanish border from Bay of Biscay to Gulf of Lion — see ANETO (Pico de) — **Pyr·e·ne·an** \,pir-ə-'nē-ən\ adjective or noun

Qandahar — see KANDAHAR

Qaraghandy — see KARAGANDA

Qa·tar \'kä-tər, 'gä-, 'gə-; kə-'tär\ country E Arabia on peninsula projecting into Persian Gulf; an independent emirate ✽ Doha area 4400 sq mi (11,395 sq km), pop 539,000 — **Qa·tari** \kə-'tär-ē, gə-\ adjective or noun

Qat·ta·ra Depression \kə-'tär-ə\ region NW Egypt, a low area 40 mi (64 km) from coast; lowest point 440 ft (134 m) below sea level

Qaz·vin or **Kaz·vin** \käz-'vēn\ city NW Iran S of Elburz Mountains & NW of Tehran pop 248,591

Qe·na \'ke-nə, 'kä-\ city S Egypt N of Luxor pop 137,000

Qe·qer·tar·su·aq \,ke-ker-,tär-'sü-äk\ or **Dis·ko** \'dis-kō\ island W Greenland in Davis Strait

Qeshm \'ke-shəm\ island S Iran in Strait of Hormuz pop 15,000

Qing·dao \'chiŋ-'daú\ or **Tsing·tao** \'chiŋ-'daú, '(t)siŋ-'daú\ city & port E China in E Shandong on Jiaozhou Bay pop 1,459,195

Qing·hai 1 \'chiŋ-'hī\ or **Ko·ko Nor** \,kō-(,)kō-'nór\ or **Ch'ing Hai** \'chiŋ-'hī\ low saline lake W central China in NE Qinghai province at altitude of 10,515 ft (3205 m) **2** or **Tsing·hai** \'chiŋ-'hī\ province W China ✽ Xining area 278,378 sq mi (723,783 sq km), pop 4,456,946

Qin·huang·dao or **Ch'in–huang–tao** or **Chin·wang·tao** \'chin-'hwäŋ-'daú, -'wäŋ-\ city & port NE China in NE Hebei pop 210,000

Qi·qi·har \'chē-'chē-'här\ or **Ch'i–ch'i–ha·erh** \'chē-'chē-'hä-'ər\ or **Tsi·tsi·har** \'(t)sēt-sē-,här, 'chē-chē-\ city NE China in W Heilongjiang pop 1,500,000

Qi·shon \'kē-,shón, kē-'\ river 45 mi (72 km) N Israel flowing NW through Plain of Esdraelon to the Mediterranean

Qom \'kúm\ city NW central Iran pop 543,139

Quad Cities \'kwäd\ the cities of Davenport, Iowa, Moline, Ill., Rock Island, Ill., & Bettendorf, Iowa

Quan·zhou or **Ch'üan–chou** or **Chuan·chow** \'chwän-'jō\ city SE China in SE Fujian on Formosa Strait pop 110,000

Qu'Ap·pelle \kwə-'pel\ river 270 mi (434 km) Canada in S Saskatchewan flowing E into the Assiniboine

Que·bec \kwi-'bek, ki-\ or **Qué·bec** \kā-'bek\ **1** province E Canada extending from Hudson Bay to Gaspé Peninsula area 524,251 sq mi (1,357,811 sq km), pop 6,895,963 **2** city & port, its ✽, on the St. Lawrence pop 167,517 — **Que·bec·er** or **Que·beck·er** \kwi-'be-kər, ki-\ noun

Queen Char·lotte Islands \'shär-lət\ islands Canada in W British Columbia in Pacific Ocean area about 4000 sq mi (10,360 sq km)

Queen Charlotte Sound sound S of Queen Charlotte Islands

Queen Eliz·a·beth Islands \i-'li-zə-bəth\ islands N Canada N of water passage extending from M'Clure Strait to Lancaster Sound; include Parry, Sverdrup, Devon, & Ellesmere islands

Queen Maud Land \'mód\ section of Antarctica on the Atlantic

Queens \'kwēnz\ borough of New York City on Long Is. E of Brooklyn pop 1,951,598

Queen's — see LAOIGHIS

Queens·land \'kwēnz-,land, -lənd\ state NE Australia ✽ Brisbane area 667,000 sq mi (1,727,530 sq km), pop 3,116,200 — **Queens·land·er** \-,lan-dər, -lən-\ noun

Queenstown — see COBH

Quelpart — see CHEJU

Que·moy \ki-'mói, kwi-; 'kwē-,\ or Chin **Jin·men** \'jin-'mən\ island SE China in Formosa Strait 15 mi (24 km) E of Amoy; garrisoned by Taiwan since 1950 pop 60,544

Que·ré·ta·ro \kā-'rā-tä-,rō\ **1** state central Mexico area 4544 sq mi (11,769 sq km), pop 1,051,235 **2** city, its ✽ pop 454,049

Quet·ta \'kwe-tə\ city Pakistan in N Baluchistan pop 285,000

Que·zal·te·nan·go \ke(t)-,säl-tā-'näŋ-(,)gō\ city SW Guatemala pop 72,745

Que·zon City \'kā-,són\ city Philippines in Luzon NE of Manila; former (1948–76) official ✽ of the Philippines pop 1,632,000

Quil·mes \'kēl-,mäs, -,mes\ city E Argentina SE of Buenos Aires pop 509,445

Quim·per \kaⁿ-'per\ commune NW France W of Rennes near Bay of Biscay pop 62,541

Qui·nault \kwi-'nólt\ river 65 mi (105 km) W Wash. flowing to the Pacific

Quin·cy 1 \'kwin(t)-sē\ city W Ill. on the Mississippi pop 39,681 **2** \'kwin-zē\ city E Mass. SE of Boston pop 84,985

Quin·ta·na Roo \kēn-,tä-nä-'rō\ state SE Mexico in E Yucatán ✽ Chetumal area 16,228 sq mi (42,030 sq km), pop 493,277

Quin·te, Bay of \'kwin-tē\ inlet of Lake Ontario in Canada in SE Ontario; connected with Georgian Bay by Trent Canal

Quir·i·nal \'kwir-ə-nᵊl\ hill in Rome, Italy, one of seven on which the ancient city was built — see AVENTINE

Qui·to \'kē-(,)tō\ city ✻ of Ecuador *pop* 1,100,847

Qumran, Khirbat — see KHIRBAT QUMRAN

Quoddy Bay PASSAMAQUODDY BAY

Qūqon — see KOKAND

Ra·ba \'rä-bə\ river 160 *mi* (257 *km*) SE Austria & W Hungary flowing E & NE into the Danube

Ra·bat \rə-'bät\ city ✻ of Morocco on Atlantic coast *pop* 518,616

Ra·baul \rä-'baúl\ city Bismarck Archipelago at E end of New Britain; formerly ✻ of Territory of New Guinea *pop* 17,022

Rabbah Ammon, Rabbath Ammon — see AMMAN

Race, Cape \'rās\ headland, SE point of Newfoundland, Canada

Ra·ci·bórz \rä-'chē-,bûsh\ *or German* **Ra·ti·bor** \'rä-tə-,bór\ city SW Poland in Silesia on the Oder *pop* 62,833

Ra·cine \rə-'sēn, rä-\ city SE Wis. S of Milwaukee *pop* 84,298

Rad·cliff \'rad-,klif\ city central Ky. *pop* 19,772

Rad·nor \'rad-nər, -,nór\ *or* **Rad·nor·shire** \-,shir, -shər\ former county E Wales ✻ Llandrindod Wells

Ra·dom \'rä-,dóm\ commune Poland NE of Kielce *pop* 226,317

Raetia — see RHAETIA — **Rae·tian** \'rē-shən\ *adjective or noun*

Ragae or Rages — see RHAGAE

Ra·gu·sa \rə-'gü-zə\ commune Italy in SE Sicily *pop* 68,850

Rah·way \'ró-,wä\ city NE N.J. SW of Elizabeth *pop* 25,325

Rainbow Bridge National Monument reservation S Utah near Ariz. boundary containing **Rainbow Bridge** (large natural bridge)

Rai·nier, Mount \rə-'nir, rā-\ *or formerly* **Mount Ta·co·ma** \tə-'kō-mə\ mountain 14,410 *ft* (4392 *m*) W central Wash., highest in the Cascade Range & in Wash.; in **Mount Rainier National Park**

Rainy \'rā-nē\ river 80 *mi* (129 *km*) on Canada-U.S. boundary between Ontario & Minn. flowing from Rainy Lake into Lake of the Woods

Rainy Lake lake Canada & U.S. between Ontario & Minn. *area* 360 *sq mi* (932 *sq km*)

Rai·pur \'rī-,púr\ city E India in SE Madhya Pradesh E of Nagpur *pop* 438,639

Rai·sin \'rā-zᵊn\ river about 115 *mi* (185 *km*) SE Mich. flowing into Lake Erie

Ra·jah·mun·dry \,rä-jə-'mùn-drē\ city E India in E Andhra Pradesh on Godavari River W of Kakinada *pop* 324,881

Ra·jas·than \'rä-jə-,stän\ state NW India bordering on Pakistan ✻ Jaipur *area* 132,149 *sq mi* (342,266 *sq km*), *pop* 44,005,990

Raj·kot \'räj-,kōt\ **1** former state W India in N central Kathiawar Peninsula **2** city, its ✻, now in Gujarat *pop* 612,458

Raj·pu·ta·na \,räj-pə-'tä-nə\ *or* **Rajasthan** region NW India bordering on Pakistan & including part of Thar Desert

Ra·leigh \'ró-lē, 'rä-lē\ city E central N.C., its ✻ *pop* 207,951

Ra·lik \'rä-lik\ the W chain of the Marshall Islands

Ram·a·po Mountains \,rä-mə-,pō\ mountains of the Appalachians N N.J. & S N.Y.; highest point 1164 *ft* (355 *m*)

Ra·mat Gan \rə-,mät-'gän, ,rä-mät-\ city W Israel E of Tel Aviv *pop* 122,700

Ram·bouil·let \rä''-bü-'yā\ town N France SW of Paris *pop* 25,293

Ram·gan·ga \räm-'gən-gə\ river about 350 *mi* (563 *km*) N India in Uttar Pradesh flowing S into the Ganges

Ram·pur \'räm-,púr\ **1** former state N India NW of Bareilly, now in Uttar Pradesh **2** city, its ✻, ENE of Delhi *pop* 242,752

Rams·gate \'ramz-,gāt, -gət\ borough SE England in Kent on North Sea N of Dover *pop* 39,642

Ran·ca·gua \rän-'kä-gwä, räŋ-\ city central Chile *pop* 139,925

Ran·chi \'rän-chē\ city E India in Bihar NW of Calcutta *pop* 599,306

Ran·cho Cu·ca·mon·ga \'ran-(,)chō-,kü-kə-'moŋ-gə, 'rän-, -'mäŋ-\ city SW Calif. NW of Riverside *pop* 101,409

Rancho Pal·os Ver·des \,pa-ləs-'vər-dēz\ city SW Calif. on coast S of Torrance *pop* 41,659

Rand \'rand, 'ränd\ WITWATERSRAND

Ran·ders \'rä-nərs\ city & port NE Denmark *pop* 61,137

Ran·dolph \'ran-,dälf\ town E Mass. S of Boston *pop* 30,093

Range·ley Lakes \'ranj-lē\ chain of lakes W Maine & N N.H.

Ran·goon \ran-'gün, raŋ-\ **1** *or* **Yan·gon** \,yäŋ-'gōn\ river 25 *mi* (40 *km*) S Myanmar, the E outlet of the Irrawaddy **2** — see YANGON

Ran·noch, Loch \'ra-nək, -nək̲\ lake 9 *mi* (14 *km*) long central Scotland

Rann of Kachchh — see KACHCHH (Rann of)

Ra·pa \'rä-pə\ island S Pacific in SE Tubuai group *area* 15 *sq mi* (39 *sq km*) *pop* 516

Ra·pal·lo \rə-'pä-(,)lō\ commune NW Italy in Liguria ESE of Genoa on Gulf of Rapallo (inlet of Ligurian Sea) *pop* 29,790

Rapa Nui — see EASTER

Rap·i·dan \,ra-pə-'dan\ river 70 *mi* (113 *km*) N Va. rising in Blue Ridge Mountains & flowing E into the Rappahannock

Rap·id City \'ra-pəd\ city W S.Dak. in Black Hills *pop* 54,523

Rap·pa·han·nock \,ra-pə-'ha-nək\ river 212 *mi* (341 *km*) NE Va. flowing into Chesapeake Bay

Rap·ti \'räp-tē\ river 400 *mi* (644 *km*) Nepal & N India flowing SE into the Gogra

Rar·i·tan \'rar-ə-tᵊn\ river 75 *mi* (121 *km*) N central N.J. flowing E into **Raritan Bay** (inlet of the Atlantic S of Staten Is., N.Y.)

Rar·o·ton·ga \,rar-ə-'täŋ-gə, -'täŋ-ə\ island S Pacific in SW part of Cook Islands; site of Avarua, ✻ of the group *pop* 9826

Ra's al Khay·mah *or* **Ras al–Khai·mah** \,räs-al-'kī-mə, -'kī-\ sheikhdom, member of United Arab Emirates

Ras Da·shen \,räs-də-'shen\ mountain 15,158 *ft* (4260 *m*) N Ethiopia NE of Lake Tana; highest in Ethiopia

Ra's at Tīb — see BON (Cape)

Rashid — see ROSETTA

Rasht \'rasht\ city NW Iran near the Caspian *pop* 2,900,897

Ra·tak \'rä-,täk\ the E chain of the Marshall Islands

Rat Islands \'rat\ islands SW Alaska in W Aleutians — see AMCHITKA, KISKA

Ra·ton \ra-'tōn, rə-, -'tün; *usually* -'tōn *in N Mex*, -'tün *in Colo*\ pass 7834 *ft* (2388 *m*) SE Colo. just N of Colo.-N.Mex. border in **Raton Range** (E spur of Sangre de Cristo Mountains)

Ra·ven·na \rä-'ve-nä\ commune N Italy NE of Florence *pop* 135,435

Ra·vi \'rä-vē\ *or ancient* **Hy·dra·o·tes** \,hī-drə-'ō-(,)tēz\ river 450 *mi* (724 *km*) N India flowing SW to the Chenab & forming part of boundary between E. Punjab (India) & W. Punjab (Pakistan)

Ra·wal·pin·di \,rä-wəl-'pin-dē, raúl-', ról-'\ city NE Pakistan NNW of Lahore *pop* 966,000

Ray·town \'rä-,taún\ city W Mo. SE of Kansas City *pop* 30,601

Read·ing \'re-diŋ\ **1** town E Mass. N of Boston *pop* 22,539 **2** city SE Pa. on the Schuylkill *pop* 78,380 **3** borough S England ✻ of Berkshire *pop* 122,600

Re·bild \'rä-,bil\ village N Denmark in N Jutland S of Ålborg in **Rebild Hills** (site of **Rebild National Park**)

Re·ci·fe \rə-'sē-fē\ *or formerly* **Per·nam·bu·co** \,pər-nəm-'bü-(,)kō, -'byü-; ,per-nəm-'bü-(,)kü\ city & port NE Brazil ✻ of Pernambuco state *municipal area pop* 1,300,000

Reck·ling·hau·sen \,re-kliŋ-'hau-zᵊn\ city W Germany SW of Münster *pop* 125,966

Red \'red\ **1** river 1018 *mi* (1638 *km*) flowing E on Okla.-Tex. boundary & into the Atchafalaya & Mississippi in La. **2** river N central U.S. & S central Canada flowing N on Minn.-N.Dak. boundary & into Lake Winnipeg in Manitoba **3** — see ARCTIC RED **4** *or* **Hong** \'hóŋ\ *or (in China)* **Yuan** \yü-'än, -an\ river 500 *mi* (805 *km*) SE Asia rising in central Yunnan, China, & flowing SE across N Vietnam into Gulf of Tonkin

Red·bridge \'red-(,)brij\ borough of NE Greater London, England *pop* 220,600

Red Deer **1** river 385 *mi* (620 *km*) Canada in S Alberta flowing E & SE into the S. Saskatchewan **2** city Canada in S central Alberta S of Edmonton *pop* 58,134

Red·ding \'re-diŋ\ city N Calif. *pop* 66,462

Red Lake lake 38 *mi* (61 *km*) long N Minn. divided into **Upper Red Lake** & **Lower Red Lake**; drained by **Red Lake River** (196 *mi or* 315 *km* flowing W into Red River)

Red·lands \'red-lən(d)z\ city S Calif. SE of San Bernardino *pop* 60,394

Red·mond \'red-mənd\ city W central Wash. NE of Seattle *pop* 35,800

Re·don·do Beach \ri-'dän-dō\ city SW Calif. *pop* 60,167

Red Sea sea 1450 *mi* (2334 *km*) long between Arabia & NE Africa

Red Volta river 200 *mi* (322 *km*) S Burkina Faso & N Ghana flowing into Lake Volta

Red·wood City \'red-,wúd\ city W Calif. SE of San Francisco *pop* 66,072

Redwood National Park reservation NW Calif.; groves of redwoods

Reel·foot \'rēl-,fút\ lake NW Tenn. near the Mississippi

Re·gens·burg \'rā-gənz-,bərg, -gəns-,búrk\ city SE Germany in Bavaria on the Danube NNE of Munich *pop* 123,002

Reg·gane \re-'gän, -'gan\ oasis central Algeria in Tanezrouft SSE of Béchar

Reg·gio \'re-(,)jō, -jē-(,)ō\ **1** *or* **Reggio di Ca·la·bria** \dē-kä-'lä-brē-ä\ *or* **Reggio Calabria** *or ancient* **Rhe·gi·um** \'rē-jē-əm\ commune & port S Italy on Strait of Messina *pop* 169,709 **2** *or* **Reggio nel·l'Emi·lia** \,ne-le-'mēl-yä\ *or* **Reggio Emilia** commune N Italy in Emilia-Romagna NW of Bologna *pop* 131,419

Re·gi·na \ri-'jī-nə\ city Canada ✻ of Saskatchewan *pop* 179,178

Reims *or* **Rheims** \'rēmz, *French* 'raⁿs\ city NE France ENE of Paris *pop* 185,164

Reindeer Lake lake Canada on Manitoba-Saskatchewan border *area about* 2500 *sq mi* (6475 *sq km*)

Re·ma·gen \'rä-,mä-gən\ town W Germany on W bank of the Rhine NW of Koblenz *pop* 15,460

Rem·scheid \'rem-,shīt\ city W Germany in N. Rhine-Westphalia ESE of Düsseldorf *pop* 123,618

Ren·do·va \ren-'dō-və\ island W Pacific in central Solomon Islands off SW central coast of New Georgia Is.

Ren·frew \'ren-,frü\ *or* **Ren·frew·shire** \-,shir, -shər\ former county SW Scotland ✻ Paisley

Rennes \'ren\ city NW France N of Nantes *pop* 203,533

Re·no \'rē-(,)nō\ city W Nev. NNE of Lake Tahoe *pop* 133,850

Ren·ton \'ren-tᵊn\ city W Wash. SE of Seattle *pop* 41,688

Re·pen·ti·gny \rə-,päⁿ-tē-'nyē\ town Canada in S Quebec NE of Montreal *pop* 49,630

Republican river 445 *mi* (716 *km*) Nebr. & Kans. rising in E Colo. & flowing E to unite with the Smoky Hill forming Kansas River

Re·thondes \rə-'tōⁿd\ village N France E of Compiègne

Ré·union \rē-'yü-nyən, ,rā-ᴇ-'nyōⁿ\ island W Indian Ocean in the W Mascarenes ✻ St.-Denis; an overseas department of France *area* 970 *sq mi* (2522 *sq km*), *pop* 634,000

Reut·ling·en \'róit-liŋ-ən\ city S Germany in Baden-Württemberg S of Stuttgart *pop* 105,835

Revel — see TALLINN

Re·vere \ri-'vir\ city E Mass. NE of Boston *pop* 42,786

Re·vil·la Gi·ge·do \rä-'vē-yä-hē-'hä-(,)thō\ islands Mexico in the Pacific SW of S end of Baja California

Re·vil·la·gi·ge·do Island \ri-,vi-lə-gə-'gē-(,)dō, -'ge-\ island SE Alaska in SE Alexander Archipelago E of Prince of Wales Is.

Reyes, Point \'rāz\ cape W Calif. at S extremity of peninsula extending into the Pacific NW of Golden Gate

Reyk·ja·vík \'rā-kyə-,vik, -,vēk\ city & port ✻ of Iceland *pop* 97,648

Reyn·olds·burg \'re-nᵊl(d)z-,bərg\ village central Ohio *pop* 25,748

Rey·no·sa \rā-'nō-sə\ city NE Mexico in Tamaulipas on the Rio Grande *pop* 281,618
Rezāīyeh — see ORŪMĪYEH
Rhae·tia *or* **Rae·tia** \'rē-sh(ē-)ə\ ancient Roman province *central* Europe S of the Danube including most of modern Tirol & Vorarlberg regions of Austria & Graubünden canton of E Switzerland — **Rhae·tian** \-shən\ *adjective or noun*
Rhaetian Alps section of Alps E Switzerland in E Graubünden — see BERNINA
Rha·gae *or* **Ra·gae** \-(,)jē, -jī\ *or biblical* **Ra·ges** \'rā-jəz\ city of ancient Media; ruins at modern village of **Rai** \'rī\ S of Tehran, Iran
Rheinpfalz — see PALATINATE
Rhenish Palatinate — see PALATINATE
Rheydt \'rīt\ city W Germany S of Mönchengladbach *pop* 100,300
Rhine \'rīn\ *or German* **Rhein** \'rīn\ *or French* **Rhin** \'raⁿ\ *or Dutch* **Rijn** \'rīn\ river 820 *mi* (1320 *km*) W Europe flowing from SE Switzerland to North Sea in Netherlands; forms W boundary of Liechtenstein & Austria & SW boundary of Germany — **Rhe·nish** \'re-nish, 'rē-\ *adjective*
Rhine·land \'rīn-,land, -lənd\ *or German* **Rhein·land** \'rīn-,länt\ **1** the part of Germany W of the Rhine **2** RHINE PROVINCE — **Rhine·land·er** \'rīn-,lan-dər, -lən-\ *noun*
Rhineland–Palatinate *or German* **Rhein·land–Pfalz** \'(p)fälts\ state of Germany & formerly of W. Germany chiefly W of the Rhine ✳ Mainz *area* 7654 *sq mi* (19,900 *sq km*), *pop* 3,642,482
Rhine Palatinate — see PALATINATE
Rhine Province former province of Prussia, Germany, bordering on Belgium ✳ Koblenz
Rhode Is·land \rōd-'ī-lənd\ **1** *or officially* **Rhode Island and Providence Plantations** state NE U.S. ✳ Providence *area* 1212 *sq mi* (3139 *sq km*), *pop* 1,003,464 **2** — see AQUIDNECK — **Rhode Islander** *noun*
Rhodes \'rōdz\ *or New Greek* **Ró·dhos** \'rō-,thôs\ **1** island Greece in the SE Aegean, chief island of the Dodecanese *area* 540 *sq mi* (1399 *sq km*) *pop* 103,295 **2** city, its ✳ *pop* 43,619 — **Rho·di·an** \'rō-dē-ən\ *adjective or noun*
Rho·de·sia \rō-'dē-zh(ē-)ə\ **1** region *central* S Africa S of Democratic Republic of the Congo comprising Zambia & Zimbabwe; contains rich archaeological findings **2** — see ZIMBABWE 2 — **Rho·de·sian** \-zh(ē-)ən\ *adjective or noun*
Rhodesia and Nyasaland, Federation of former country S Africa comprising S. Rhodesia, N. Rhodesia, & Nyasaland; a federal state within the Commonwealth; dissolved 1963
Rhod·o·pe \'rä-də-(,)pē, rō-'dō-pē\ mountains S Bulgaria & NE Greece; highest Musala 9596 *ft* (2925 *m*)
Rhon·dda \'rän-də, '(h)rän-thə\ borough SE Wales in Mid Glamorgan *pop* 76,300
Rhône \'rōn\ river 505 *mi* (813 *km*) Switzerland & France rising in the Alps and flowing through Lake Geneva into Gulf of Lion inlet of the Mediterranean
Rhyl \'ril\ town & port NE Wales in Clwyd at mouth of the Clwyd *pop* 22,714
Ri·al·to \rē-'al-(,)tō\ **1** city SW Calif. W of San Bernardino *pop* 72,388 **2** island & district of Venice, Italy
Ri·au *or* **Du Ri·ouw** \'rē-,au̇\ archipelago Indonesia S of Singapore; chief island Bintan *area* 2279 *sq mi* (5925 *sq km*) *pop* 278,966
Ri·bei·rão Prê·to \'rē-bə-'rau̇ⁿ-'prä-(,)tü\ city SE Brazil in N *central* São Paulo state *pop* 430,805
Rich·ard·son \'ri-chərd-sən\ city NE Tex. N of Dallas *pop* 74,840
Rich·e·lieu \'ri-shə-,lü, rē-shəl-'yœ̄\ river 210 *mi* (338 *km*) Canada in S Quebec flowing N from Lake Champlain to head of Lake St. Peter in the St. Lawrence
Rich·field \'rich-,fēld\ village SE Minn.; a S suburb of Minneapolis *pop* 35,710
Rich·land \'rich-lənd\ city SE Wash. at confluence of Yakima & Columbia rivers *pop* 32,315
Rich·mond \'rich-mənd\ **1** city W Calif. NNW of Oakland on San Francisco Bay *pop* 87,425 **2** city E Ind. *pop* 38,705 **3** city *central* Ky. *pop* 21,155 **4** borough of New York City — see STATEN ISLAND **5** city ✳ of Va. on the James *pop* 203,056 **6** city Canada in SW British Columbia S of Vancouver *pop* 126,624 **7** *or in*

full **Richmond upon Thames** borough of SW Greater London, England *pop* 154,600 — **Richmond·er** \-mən-dər\ *noun*
Richmond Hill town Canada in SE Ontario N of Toronto *pop* 80,142
Ri·deau Canal \ri-'dō\ canal system Canada 124 *mi* (200 *km*) long in SE Ontario connecting Lake Ontario & Ottawa River & including **Rideau Lake** (20 *mi* or 32 *km* long) & **Rideau River** (flowing into the Ottawa)
Ridge·crest \'rij-,krest\ city S Calif. NE of Bakersfield *pop* 27,725
Ridge·field \'rij-,fēld\ town SW Conn. NW of Norwalk *pop* 20,919
Ridge·wood \'rij-,wu̇d\ village NE N.J. NNE of Paterson *pop* 24,152
Rid·ing Mountain National Park \'rī-diŋ\ reservation Canada in SW Manitoba; has game preserve
Rift Valley GREAT RIFT VALLEY
Ri·ga \'rē-gə\ city & port ✳ of Latvia at S extremity of the Gulf of Riga *pop* 915,000
Riga, Gulf of inlet of Baltic Sea bordering on Estonia & Latvia
Ri·je·ka *or* **Ri·e·ka** \rē-'ye-kə\ *or Italian* **Fiu·me** \'fyü-(,)mā, fē-'ü-\ city & port W Croatia *pop* 167,964
Rijs·wijk \'rīs-,vīk\ commune SW Netherlands *pop* 47,456
Rí·mac \'rē-,mäk\ river 80 *mi* (129 *km*) W Peru flowing SW through Lima into the Pacific
Ri·mi·ni \'ri-mi-(,)nē, 'rē-\ *or ancient* **Arim·i·num** \ə-'ri-mə-nəm\ commune & port N Italy on the Adriatic ESE of Ravenna *pop* 128,119
Ri·mou·ski \ri-'müs-kē\ town Canada in E Quebec on Gaspé Peninsula *pop* 30,873
Ring of Fire belt of volcanoes & frequent seismic activity nearly encircling the Pacific
Rio \'rē-(,)ō\ RIO DE JANEIRO
Rio Bran·co \,rē-(,)ō-'braŋ-(,)kō, ,rē-(,)ō-'bräŋ-(,)kü\ **1** — see BRANCO **2** city W Brazil, ✳ of Acre *municipal area pop* 196,923
Rio de Ja·nei·ro \'rē-(,)ō-dā-zhə-'ner-(,)ō, -de-; 'rē-ü-dē-zhà-'nā-rü\ **1** state SE Brazil *area* 17,092 *sq mi* (44,268 *sq km*), *pop* 12,584,108 **2** city, its ✳ & port on Guanabara Bay; former ✳ of Brazil *pop* 6,100,000
Río de la Plata — see PLATA (Río de la)
Río de Oro \,rē-(,)ō-dē-'ōr-(,)ō, -'ȯr-\ territory NW Africa comprising the S zone of Western Sahara
Rio Grande **1** \,rē-(,)ō-'grand, -'gran-dē *also* ,rī-ō-'grand *or Mexican Spanish* **Río Bra·vo** \,rē-(,)ō-'brä-(,)vō\ river 1885 *mi* (3034 *km*) SW U.S. forming part of Mexico-U.S. boundary & flowing from San Juan Mountains in SW Colo. to Gulf of Mexico **2** *or* **Rio Gran·de do Sul** \,rē-ü-'gran-dē-dü-'sül\ city S Brazil in Rio Grande do Sul state W of entrance to Lagoa dos Patos *pop* 172,435 **3** \,rē-(,)ō-'grän-dā, -dē\ municipality NE Puerto Rico *pop* 45,648 **4** — see GRANDE (Rio)
Rio Grande de Cagayan — see CAGAYAN
Rio Gran·de do Nor·te \'rē-(,)ü-'grän-dē-dü-'nȯr-tē\ state NE Brazil ✳ Natal *area* 20,528 *sq mi* (53,168 *sq km*), *pop* 2,413,618
Rio Grande do Sul \-'sül\ state SE Brazil bordering on Uruguay ✳ Pôrto Alegre *area* 108,951 *sq mi* (282,183 *sq km*), *pop* 9,127,611
Rioja, the — see LA RIOJA
Río Muni — see MBINI
Río Pie·dras \'rē-(,)ō-'pyä-drəs, -thräs\ former city, since 1951 part of San Juan, Puerto Rico
Rio Ran·cho \,rē-(,)ō-'ran-(,)chō, -'rän-\ city *central* N.Mex., a N suburb of Albuquerque *pop* 32,505
Rip·on Falls \'ri-pən, -,pän\ former waterfall in the Victoria Nile N of Lake Victoria; submerged by Owen Falls Dam
Riv·er·side \'ri-vər-,sīd\ city S Calif. *pop* 226,505
Riv·i·era \,ri-vē-'er-ə\ coast region SE France & NW Italy bordering on the Mediterranean — see CÔTE D'AZUR
Riviera Beach city SE Fla. N of W. Palm Beach *pop* 27,639
Ri·yadh \rē-'yäd\ city ✳ of the Nejd & of Saudi Arabia *pop* 666,840
Rju·kan \rē-'ü-,kän\ town S Norway W of Oslo near **Rjukan Falls** (waterfall 780 *ft* or 238 *m*)

Ro·a·noke \'rō-(ə-),nōk\ **1** river 380 *mi* (612 *km*) S Va. & NE N.C. flowing E & SE into Albemarle Sound **2** city W *central* Va. *pop* 96,397
Roanoke Island island N.C. S of entrance to Albemarle Sound
Rob·erts, Point \'rä-bərts\ cape NW Wash., tip of a peninsula extending S into Strait of Georgia from British Columbia & separated from U.S. mainland by Boundary Bay
Rob·son, Mount \'räb-sən\ mountain 12,972 *ft* (3954 *m*) W Canada in E British Columbia; highest in Canadian Rockies
Ro·ca, Cape \'rō-kə\ *or Portuguese* **Ca·bo da Ro·ca** \'kȧ-bü-də-'rȯ-kə\ cape Portugal; westernmost point of continental Europe, at 9°30′W
Roch·dale \'räch-,dāl\ borough NW England in Greater Manchester NNE of Manchester *pop* 92,704
Roche·fort \rȯsh-'fȯr, 'rȯsh-fȯrt\ *or* **Rochefort–sur–Mer** \-,sür-'mer\ city W France SSE of La Rochelle *pop* 26,949
Roch·es·ter \'rä-chəs-tər, -,ches-tər\ **1** city SE Minn. *pop* 70,745 **2** city SE N.H. *pop* 26,630 **3** city W N.Y. on the Genesee *pop* 231,636 **4** city SE England in Kent *pop* 52,505
Rochester Hills city SE Mich. N of Detroit *pop* 61,766
Rock \'räk\ river 300 *mi* (483 *km*) S Wis. & N Ill. flowing S & SW into the Mississippi at Rock Island
Rock·all \'rä-,kȯl\ islet N Atlantic NW of Ireland, at 57°36′N, 13°41′W
Rock·ford \'räk-fərd\ city N Ill. NW of Chicago *pop* 139,426
Rock·hamp·ton \räk-'ham(p)-tən, rä-'kam(p)-\ city & port E Australia in E Queensland on Fitzroy River *pop* 61,631
Rock Hill city N S.C. SSW of Charlotte, N.C. *pop* 41,643
Rock Island city NW Ill. on the Mississippi *pop* 40,552
Rock·lin \'rä-klin, -klən\ city E Calif. NE of Sacramento *pop* 19,033
Rock Springs city SW Wyo. near Utah border *pop* 19,050
Rock·ville \'räk-,vil, -vəl\ city SW Md. *pop* 44,835
Rockville Centre village SE N.Y. in W *central* Long Is. *pop* 24,727
Rocky Mount \'rä-kē\ city NE *central* N.C. *pop* 48,997
Rocky Mountain National Park reservation N Colo.
Rocky Mountains *or* **Rock·ies** \'rä-kēz\ mountains W N. America extending from N Alaska SE to N.Mex. — see ELBERT (Mount), ROBSON (Mount)
Rocky River city NE Ohio on Lake Erie W of Cleveland *pop* 20,410
Ró·dhos — see RHODES
Ro·dri·gues \rō-'drē-gəs\ island Indian Ocean in the Mascarenes; a dependency of Mauritius; chief town Port Mathurin *area* 40 *sq mi* (104 *sq km*), *pop* 37,782
Rog·ers \'rä-jərz\ city NW Ark. *pop* 24,692
Rogers Pass mountain pass Canada in SE British Columbia in Selkirk Mountains
Rogue \'rōg\ river *about* 200 *mi* (320 *km*) SW Oreg. rising in Crater Lake National Park & flowing W & SW into the Pacific
Ro·hil·khand \'rō-,hil-,kənd\ *or* **Ba·reil·ly** \bə-'rā-lē\ region N India in Uttar Pradesh; chief city Bareilly
Rohn·ert Park \'rō-nərt\ city W Calif. S of Santa Rosa *pop* 36,326
Rolling Meadows city NE Ill. NW of Chicago *pop* 22,591
Ro·ma·gna \rō-'mä-nyä\ district N Italy on the Adriatic comprising the E part of Emilia–Romagna region
Roman Campagna — see CAMPAGNA DI ROMA
Ro·ma·nia \rü-'mā-nē-ə, rō-, -nyə\ *or* **Ru·ma·nia** \rü-\ country SE Europe bordering on Black Sea ✳ Bucharest *area* 91,699 *sq mi* (237,500 *sq km*), *pop* 22,789,000

\ə\ abut \ᵊ\ kitten \ər\ further \a\ ash \ā\ ace \ä\ mop, mar \au̇\ out \ch\ chin \e\ bet \ē\ easy \g\ go \i\ hit \ī\ ice \j\ job \ŋ\ sing \ō\ go \ȯ\ law \ȯi\ boy \th\ thin \th̠\ the \ü\ loot \u̇\ foot \y\ yet \zh\ vision *see also* Guide to Pronunciation

Rom·blon \räm-'blōn\ **1** islands Philippines in N Visayan Islands in Sibuyan Sea *area* 524 *sq mi* (1357 *sq km*) **2** island in the group

Rome \'rōm\ **1** city NW Ga. NW of Atlanta *pop* 30,326 **2** city E *central* N.Y. NW of Utica *pop* 44,350 **3** *or Italian* **Ro·ma** \'rō-mä\ *or ancient* **Ro·ma** \'rō-mə\ city ✳ of Italy on the Tiber *pop* 2,693,383 **4** the Roman Empire

Rome, Duchy of division of Byzantine Empire 6th to 8th century *central* Italy comprising most of modern Lazio; later a province of the Papal States called **Patrimony of Saint Pe·ter** \'pē-tər\

Rom·ford \'räm(p)-fərd, 'rəm(p)-\ former municipal borough SE England in Essex, now part of Havering

Rom·u·lus \'rä-myə-ləs\ city SE Mich. *pop* 22,897

Ron·ces·va·lles \,rón(t)-səs-'vī-əs\ *or French* **Ron·ce·vaux** \,rō"s-'vō, rō"-sə-\ commune N Spain 5 *mi* (8 *km*) from French boundary in the Pyrenees near **Pass of Roncesvalles**

Ron·dô·nia \rō"-'dō-nyə\ *or formerly* **Gua·po·ré** \,gwä-pó-'rä\ state W Brazil ✳ Porto Velho *area* 93,839 *sq mi* (243,043 *sq km*), *pop* 1,130,400

Rong·er·ik \'räŋ-ə-,rik, 'rōŋ-\ island W *central* Pacific in the Marshalls in Ratak chain E of Bikini

Ron·ne Ice Shelf \'rō-nə, 'rə-nə\ area of shelf ice Antarctica in Weddell Sea

Roo·de·poort \'rō-də-,pórt, 'rō-i-,pórt, -,pòrt\ city Republic of South Africa in Gauteng W of Johannesburg *metropolitan pop* 141,764

Roo·se·velt \'rō-zə-,velt, -vəlt *also* 'rü-\ river *about* 400 *mi* (644 *km*) W *central* Brazil flowing from W Mato Grosso state N into the Aripuanã

Ro·rai·ma \rə-'rī-mä\ mountain 9094 *ft* (2772 *m*) N S. America in Pacaraima Mountains on boundary between Venezuela, Guyana, & Brazil; has flat top

Ror·schach \'rór-,shäk, 'rōr-, -,shäk\ commune NE Switzerland on S shore of Lake Constance *pop* 9878

Ro·sa, Mon·te \'món-tä-'rō-zä\ mountain 15,203 *ft* (4634 *m*) on Swiss-Italian border; highest in Pennine Alps

Ro·sa·rio \rō-'zär-ē-,ō, -'sär-\ city E *central* Argentina on the Paraná *pop* 591,428

Ros·com·mon \räs-'kä-mən\ **1** county *central* Ireland in Connacht *area* 951 *sq mi* (2473 *sq km*), *pop* 51,897 **2** town, its ✳ *pop* 1363

Rose, Mount \'rōz\ mountain 10,778 *ft* (3285 *m*) W Nev. in Carson Range SW of Reno

Ro·seau \rō-'zō\ seaport ✳ of Dominica *pop* 15,853

Ro·selle \rō-'zel\ **1** city NE Ill. *pop* 20,819 **2** borough NE N.J. W of Elizabeth *pop* 20,314

Rose·mead \'rōz-,mēd\ city SW Calif. E of Los Angeles *pop* 51,638

Ro·sen·berg \'rō-zʰn-,bərg\ city SE Tex. *pop* 20,183

Ro·set·ta \rō-'ze-tə\ *or Arabic* **Ra·shīd** \rä-'shēd\ *or ancient* **Bol·bi·ti·ne** \,bäl-bə-'tī-nē\ **1** river 146 *mi* (235 *km*) N Egypt forming W branch of the Nile in its delta **2** city N Egypt on the Rosetta *pop* 36,711

Rose·ville \'rōz-,vil\ **1** city W Calif. NE of Sacramento *pop* 44,685 **2** city SE Mich. NE of Detroit *pop* 51,412 **3** village SE Minn. N of St. Paul *pop* 33,485

Ross and Crom·ar·ty \'rós-ənd-'krä-mər-tē\ former county N Scotland ✳ Dingwall

Ross Dependency section of Antarctica lying between 160°E and 150°W long.; claimed by New Zealand

Ross Ice Shelf area of shelf ice Antarctica in S Ross Sea

Ross Sea arm of S Pacific extending into Antarctica E of Victoria Land

Ros·tock \'räs-,täk, 'rós-,tók\ city & port NE Germany on Warnow River near the Baltic coast *pop* 234,475

Ros·tov \rə-'stóf, -'stóv\ *or* **Rostov–on–Don** \-,än-'dän, -,ón-\ city S Russia in Europe on the Don *pop* 1,027,000

Ros·well \'räz-,wel, -wəl\ **1** city NW *central* Ga. N of Atlanta *pop* 47,923 **2** city SE N.Mex. *pop* 44,654

Ro·ta \'rō-tə\ **1** island W Pacific at S end of the Marianas *area* 35 *sq mi* (91 *sq km*) **2** town & port SW Spain on the Atlantic NW of Cádiz

Roth·er·ham \'rä-thə-rəm\ borough N England in S. Yorkshire NE of Sheffield *area pop* 247,100

Rothe·say \'räth-sē\ royal burgh SW Scotland on island of Bute in Strathclyde *pop* 5408

Ro·to·rua \,rō-tō-'rü-ə\ city New Zealand in N central North Is. *pop* 53,700

Rot·ter·dam \'rä-tər-,dam, -,däm\ city & port SW Netherlands on the Nieuwe Maas *pop* 589,707 — **Rot·ter·dam·mer** \-,da-mər, -,dä-\ *noun*

Ro·tu·ma \rō-'tü-mə\ island SW Pacific N of Fiji Islands *area* 14 *sq mi* (36 *sq km*); belongs to Fiji

Rou·baix \rü-'bä\ city N France NE of Lille *pop* 98,179

Rou·en \rü-'ä"\ city & port N France on the Seine *pop* 105,470

Round Rock town *central* Tex. N of Austin *pop* 30,923

Rous·sil·lon \,rü-sē-'yō"\ region & former province S France bordering on the Pyrenees & the Mediterranean ✳ Perpignan

Rou·yn–No·ran·da \'rü-ən-nə-'ran-də, rü-'a"-\ town Canada in SW Quebec *pop* 26,448

Row·lett \'raù-lət\ city NE Tex., a suburb of Dallas *pop* 23,260

Rox·burgh \'räks-,bər-ə, -,bə-rə, -b(ə-)rə\ *or* **Rox·burgh·shire** \-,shir, -shər\ former county SE Scotland ✳ Jedburgh

Roy \'rói\ city NE Utah SW of Ogden *pop* 24,603

Royal Gorge section of the canyon of Arkansas River S *central* Colo.

Royal Leamington Spa — see LEAMINGTON

Royal Oak city SE Mich. N of Detroit *pop* 65,410

Royal Tun·bridge Wells *or* **Tunbridge Wells** \'tən-brij\ borough SE England in Kent *pop* 44,506

Ru·an·da–Urun·di \rü-'än-dä-ü-'rün-dē\ *or* **Belgian East Africa** former country E *central* Africa bordering on Lake Tanganyika & comprising two districts, **Ruanda** (✳ Kigali) & **Urundi** (✳ Usumbura), administered by Belgium under League of Nations mandate 1919–45 & under United Nations trusteeship 1946–62 ✳ Usumbura — see BURUNDI, RWANDA

Ru·a·pe·hu, Mount \,rü-ə-'pā-(,)hü\ volcano 9175 *ft* (2796 *m*) New Zealand, highest peak in North Is., in Tongariro National Park

Rub' al–Kha·li \,rüb-al-'kä-lē, *Arabic* -äl-'kä-\ desert region S Arabia extending from Nejd S to Hadhramaut *area about* 250,000 *sq mi* (647,500 *sq km*)

Ru·bi·con \'rü-bi-,kän\ river 15 *mi* (24 *km*) N *central* Italy flowing E into the Adriatic

Ru·da Śląs·ka \,rü-də-'shlō"-skə\ commune S Poland *pop* 169,789

Rudolf, Lake — see TURKANA (Lake)

Ru·fisque \rü-'fēsk\ city & port W Senegal *pop* 137,150

Rug·by \'rəg-bē\ town *central* England in Warwick on the Avon *pop* 83,400

Rü·gen \'rü-gən, 'rᴜᴇ-\ island NE Germany in Baltic Sea off coast of Pomerania *area* 358 *sq mi* (927 *sq km*); chief town Bergen

Ruhr \'rür\ **1** river 146 *mi* (235 *km*) W Germany flowing NW & W to the Rhine **2** industrial district in valley of the Ruhr

Ruis·lip North·wood \'rīs-ləp-'nórth-,wùd\ former urban district S England in Middlesex, now part of Hillingdon

Ru·me·lia \rü-'mēl-yə, -'mē-lē-ə\ a division of the old Ottoman Empire including Albania, Macedonia, & Thrace

Run·ny·mede \'rə-nē-,mēd\ meadow S England in Surrey at Egham on S bank of the Thames

Ru·pert \'rü-pərt\ river 380 *mi* (612 *km*) Canada in W Quebec flowing W into James Bay

Rupert's Land PRINCE RUPERT'S LAND

Ru·se \'rü-(,)sä\ *or Turkish* **Rus·chuk** \'rüs-'chük\ city NE Bulgaria on the Danube S of Bucharest *pop* 192,365

Rush·more, Mount \'rəsh-,mōr, -,mór\ mountain 5600 *ft* (1707 *m*) W S.Dak. in Black Hills on which are carved faces of presidents Washington, Jefferson, Lincoln, Theodore Roosevelt; a national memorial

Rus·sell Cave National Monument \'rə-səl\ reservation NE Ala. including cavern where remains of early pre-Columbian humans have been found

Rus·sell·ville \'rə-səl-,vil\ city NW *central* Ark. *pop* 21,260

Rus·sia \'rə-shə\ *or Russian* **Ros·si·ya** \rä-'sē-yə\ **1** former empire E Europe & N Asia coextensive (except for Finland & Kars region) with the U.S.S.R. ✳ St. Petersburg **2** the U.S.S.R. **3** *or officially* **Russian Federation** independent country in E Europe & N Asia bordering on Arctic & Pacific oceans & on Baltic & Black seas; a constituent republic (**Russian Republic** *or* **Soviet Russia**) of the U.S.S.R. 1922–91 ✳ Moscow *area* 6,592,812 *sq mi* (17,075,383 *sq km*), *pop* 148,000,000

Russian Turkestan region formerly comprising the republics of Soviet Central Asia

Rus·ton \'rəs-tən\ city N La. *pop* 20,027

Ruthenia — see ZAKARPATS'KA — **Ru·thene** \rü-'thēn\ *noun* — **Ru·the·nian** \-'thē-nyən, -nē-ən\ *adjective or noun*

Rut·land \'rət-lənd\ *or* **Rut·land·shire** \-lənd-,shir, -shər\ former county E *central* England ✳ Oakham

Ru·vu·ma *or Portuguese* **Ro·vu·ma** \rü-'vü-mə\ river *about* 450 *mi* (724 *km*) SE Africa rising in S Tanzania & flowing E into Indian Ocean

Ru·wen·zo·ri \,rü-ən-'zōr-ē, -'zór-\ mountain group E *central* Africa between Lake Albert & Lake Edward, on boundary between Uganda & Democratic Republic of the Congo — see STANLEY (Mount)

Rwan·da \rü-'än-dä\ *or formerly* **Ru·an·da** country E *central* Africa; a republic ✳ Kigali *area* 10,169 *sq mi* (26,338 *sq km*), *pop* 7,584,000 — see RUANDA-URUNDI — **Rwan·dan** \-dən\ *adjective or noun* — **Rwan·dese** \rü-,än-'dēz, -'dēs\ *adjective or noun*

Rya·zan \,rē-ə-'zan, -'zän\ city W *central* Russia in Europe on Oka River SE of Moscow *pop* 529,000

Ry·binsk \'ri-bən(t)sk\ *or 1946–57* **Shcher·ba·kov** \,sh(ch)er-bə-'kóf, -'kòv\ *or 1984–89* **An·dro·pov** \an-'dró-,pòf, -'pòv\ city W *central* Russia in Europe *pop* 252,000

Ryb·nik \'rib-nik\ commune S Poland *pop* 142,588

Rye \'rī\ borough SE England in E. Sussex *pop* 4293

Ryu·kyu Islands \rē-'yü-(,)kyü, -(,)kü\ islands W Pacific extending between Kyushu, Japan, & Taiwan; belonged to Japan 1895–1945; occupied by U.S. 1945; returned to Japan in 1953 (N islands) and 1972 (S islands) *area about* 850 *sq mi* (2202 *sq km*), *pop* 1,222,458 — see AMAMI, OKINAWA, OSUMI ISLANDS, SAKISHIMA ISLANDS, TOKARA ISLANDS — **Ryu·kyu·an** \-,kyü-ən, -,kü-\ *adjective or noun*

Rze·szow \'zhe-,shüf\ commune SE Poland *pop* 150,754

Saa·le \'zä-lə, 'sä-\ river 265 *mi* (426 *km*) E *central* Germany rising in NE Bavaria in the Fichtelgebirge & flowing N into the Elbe

Saan·ich \'sä-nich\ municipality Canada in British Columbia on SE Vancouver Is. N of Victoria *pop* 95,577

Saar \'sär, 'zär\ **1** *or French* **Sarre** \'sär\ river *about* 150 *mi* (241 *km*) Europe flowing from Vosges Mountains in France N to the Moselle in W Germany **2** *or* **Saar·land** \-,land, 'zär-\ region W Europe in basin of Saar River between France & Germany; once part of Lorraine, became part of Germany in 19th century; administered by League of Nations 1919–35; became a state of Germany 1935; came under control of France after World War II; to W. Germany by a plebiscite Jan. 1, 1957, as a state (**Saarland**) ✳ Saarbrücken *area* 991 *sq mi* (2567 *sq km*), *pop* 1,073,000

Saar·brück·en \zär-'brü-kən, sär-, -'brᴜᴇ-\ city SW Germany ✳ of Saarland *pop* 192,030

Saaremaa — see SAREMA

Sa·ba **1** \'sä-bə, 'sä-bə\ island SE W. Indies in Leeward Islands; part of Netherlands Antilles ✳ The Bottom *area* 5 *sq mi* (13 *sq km*), *pop* 1119 **2** — see SHEBA

Sa·ba·dell \,sä-bə-'del, ,sä-\ commune NE Spain NW of Barcelona *pop* 184,460

Sa·bah \'sä-bə\ *or formerly* **North Borneo** state Malaysia in NE Borneo, formerly a Brit. colony ✳ Kota Kinabalu *area* 29,507 *sq mi* (76,423 *sq km*), *pop* 1,736,902

Sa·bar·ma·ti \,sä-bər-'mə-tē\ river *ab* 250 *mi* (402 *km*) W India flowing S into head of Gulf of Khambhat

Sa·bi \'sä-bē\ *or in Mozambique* **Sa·ve** \'sä-və\ river 400 *mi* (644 *km*) SE Africa rising in *central* Zimbabwe & flowing E across S Mozambique to Indian Ocean

Sa·bine \sə-'bēn\ river E Tex. & W La. flowing SE through **Sabine Lake** (15 *mi or* 24 *km* long) & **Sabine Pass** (channel) into Gulf of Mexico

Sa·ble, Cape \'sā-bəl\ **1** cape at SW tip of Fla., southernmost point of U.S. mainland, at *about* 25°7′N **2** headland E Canada on an islet S of **Cape Sable Island** (7 *mi or* 11 *km* long, at S end of Nova Scotia)

Sable Island island Canada 20 *mi* (32 *km*) long in the Atlantic SE of Cape Canso; belongs to Nova Scotia

Sab·ra·tha \'sa-brə-thə\ *or ancient* **Sab·ra·ta** \-tə\ town Libya on the coast WNW of Tripoli *pop* 30,836

Sachsen — see SAXONY

Sa·co \'sò-(,)kō\ river 104 *mi* (167 *km*) E N.H. & SW Maine flowing SE into the Atlantic

Sac·ra·men·to \,sa-krə-'men-(,)tō\ **1** river 382 *mi* (615 *km*) N Calif. flowing S into Suisun Bay **2** city ✳ of Calif. on Sacramento River NE of San Francisco *pop* 369,365

Sacramento Mountains mountains S N.Mex. — see GUADALUPE MOUNTAINS, SIERRA BLANCA PEAK

Sa·fed Koh \sə-,fed-'kō\ mountain range E Afghanistan on Pakistan border; a S extension of the Hindu Kush

Sa·fi \'sa-fē\ city & port W Morocco SW of Casablanca *pop* 129,113

Sa·ga·mi Sea \sä-'gä-mē\ inlet of the Pacific Japan in *central* Honshu SW of Tokyo Bay

Sa·ga·mi·ha·ra \sä-,gä-mē-'här-ä\ city Japan on Honshu *pop* 531,562

Saghalien — see SAKHALIN

Sag·i·naw \'sa-gə-,nò\ city E *central* Mich. NNW of Flint *pop* 69,512

Saginaw Bay inlet of Lake Huron in E Mich.

Sa·gres \'sä-grish\ village SW Portugal E of Cape Saint Vincent

Sa·gua·ro National Monument \sə-'gwär-ō, -'wär-\ reservation SE Ariz. E of Tucson

Sag·ue·nay \'sa-gə-,nā, ,sa-gə-'\ river 105 *mi* (169 *km*) Canada in S Quebec flowing from Lake Saint Jean E into the St. Lawrence

Sa·guia el Ham·ra \'sa-gyə-el-'ham-rə\ territory NW Africa, the N zone of Western Sahara

Sa·gun·to \sä-'gün-(,)tō\ *or formerly* **Mur·vie·dro** \,mùr-vē-'ä-(,)drō, mùr-'vyä-thrō\ commune E Spain NNE of Valencia *pop* 55,457

Sa·ha·ra \sə-'har-ə, -'her-, -'här-\ desert region N Africa N of the Sudan region extending from the Atlantic coast to Red Sea or, as sometimes considered, to the Nile — **Sa·ha·ran** \-ən\ *adjective*

Sa·ha·ran·pur \sə-'här-ən-,pùr\ city N India in NW Uttar Pradesh NNE of Delhi *pop* 374,945

Sa·hel \sä-hil, sə-'hil\ the semidesert S fringe of the Sahara that stretches from Mauritania to Chad — **Sa·hel·ian** \sə-'hil-yən\ *adjective*

Saida — see SIDON

Saigon — see HO CHI MINH CITY — **Sai·gon·ese** \,sī-gə-'nēz, -'nēs\ *adjective or noun*

Sai·maa \'sī-,mä\ group of lakes SE Finland of which **Lake Saimaa** is the largest

Saint Al·bans \'òl-bənz\ borough SE England in Hertfordshire *pop* 122,400

Saint Al·bert \'al-bərt\ city Canada in *central* Alberta *pop* 42,146

Saint Bar·thé·le·my \,saⁿ-bár-tā-lə-'mē\ island French West Indies in department of Guadeloupe; chief town Gustavia *pop* 2351

Saint Bernard — see GREAT SAINT BERNARD, LITTLE SAINT BERNARD

Saint–Bru·no–de–Mon·tar·ville \sänt-'brü-,nō-də-'män-tər-,vil, sənt-; ,saⁿ-brü-'nō-də-,mōⁿ-tär-'vēl\ town Canada in S Quebec E of Montreal *pop* 23,849

Saint Cath·a·rines \'ka-th(ə-)rənz\ city Canada in SE Ontario NW of Niagara Falls on Welland Canal *pop* 129,300

Saint Charles \'chär(-ə)lz\ **1** city NE Ill. *pop* 22,501 **2** city E Mo. on the Missouri *pop* 54,555

Saint Clair, Lake \'klar, 'kler\ lake SE Mich. & SE Ontario *area* 460 *sq mi* (1196 *sq km*), connected by **Saint Clair River** (40 *mi or* 64 *km*) with Lake Huron & draining through Detroit River into Lake Erie

Saint Clair Shores city SE Mich. NE of Detroit *pop* 68,107

Saint–Cloud \sänt-'klaùd, sənt-; saⁿ-'klü-\ commune France, WSW suburb of Paris *pop* 28,673

Saint Cloud \'klaùd\ city *central* Minn. on the Mississippi *pop* 48,812

Saint Croix \sänt-'kròi, sənt-\ **1** river 129 *mi* (208 *km*) Canada & U.S. between New Brunswick & Maine **2** river 164 *mi* (264 *km*) NW Wis. & E Minn. flowing into the Mississippi **3** *or* **San·ta Cruz** \,san-tə-'krüz\ island W. Indies, largest of the Virgin Islands of the U.S. *area* 80 *sq mi* (208 *sq km*) *pop* 50,139; chief town Christiansted

Saint Croix Island International Historic Site reservation E Maine on Canada border on island in St. Croix River

Saint–Cyr–l'École \saⁿ-'sir-lā-'kòl\ commune N France W of Versailles *pop* 17,795

Saint–De·nis \,saⁿ(t)-də-'nē\ **1** commune N France NNE of Paris *pop* 90,806 **2** commune ✳ of Réunion Is. *pop* 100,926

Sainte–Foy \sänt-'fòi, sənt-; saⁿt-'fwä, saⁿ-tə-\ town Canada in SE Quebec SW of Quebec city *pop* 71,133

Saint Eli·as, Mount \i-'lī-əs\ mountain 18,008 *ft* (5489 *m*) on Alaska-Canada boundary in St. Elias Range

Saint Elias Range mountain range of the Coast Ranges SW Yukon Territory & E Alaska — see LOGAN (Mount)

Sainte–Thé·rèse \,sänt-tə-'rāz, ,saⁿt-tā-'rez\ town Canada in S Quebec *pop* 24,158

Saint–Étienne \saⁿ-tā-'tyen\ city SE *central* France *pop* 201,569

Saint–Eus·tache \,saⁿ-tyü-'stash\ town Canada in S Quebec *pop* 37,278

Saint Eu·sta·ti·us \,sänt-yü-'stā-sh(ē-)əs\ *or* **Sta·tia** \'stä-shə\ island W. Indies in Netherlands Antilles NW of St. Kitts *area* 7 *sq mi* (18 *sq km*) *pop* 1715

Saint Fran·cis \sänt-'fran(t)-səs, sənt-\ **1** river 425 *mi* (684 *km*) SE Mo. & E Ark. flowing S into the Mississippi **2** *or* **Saint Fran·çois** \saⁿ-frä-'swä\ river 165 *mi* (266 *km*) Canada in S Quebec flowing NW into the St. Lawrence

Saint Francis, Lake expansion of St. Lawrence River Canada above Valleyfield, Quebec

Saint Gall \sänt-'gòl, sənt-; saⁿ-'gäl\ *or German* **Sankt Gal·len** \zäŋkt-'gä-lən\ **1** canton NE Switzerland *area* 778 *sq mi* (2015 *sq km*), *pop* 416,578 **2** commune, its ✳ *pop* 73,889

Saint George \'jòrj\ city SW corner of Utah *pop* 28,502

Saint George's \'jòr-jəz\ town ✳ of Grenada *pop* 29,400

Saint George's Channel strait British Isles between SW Wales & Ireland

Saint–Ger·main \,saⁿ-zhər-'maⁿ\ *or* **Saint–Ger·main–en–Laye** \,saⁿ-,zhər-,maⁿ-,ä"-'lā\ commune N France WNW of Paris *pop* 41,710

Saint–Gilles \saⁿ-'zhēl\ *or Flemish* **Sint–Gil·lis** \sint-'gil-ləs, -'kil-\ commune *central* Belgium near Brussels *pop* 42,684

Saint Gott·hard \sänt-'gä-tərd, sənt-, 'gät-hərd, ,saⁿ-gə-'tär\ **1** mountains Switzerland in Lepontine Alps between Uri & Ticino cantons **2** mountain pass 6916 *ft* (2108 *m*) in St. Gotthard Range

Saint He·le·na \sänt-ᵉl-'ē-nə, ,sänt-hə-'lē-\ island S Atlantic; a Brit. colony ✳ Jamestown *area* 47 *sq mi* (122 *sq km*), *pop* 5644

Saint Hel·ens \sänt-'he-lənz, sənt-\ borough NW England in Merseyside ENE of Liverpool *pop* 98,769

Saint Helens, Mount volcanic peak 8366 *ft* (2550 *m*) SW Wash. in Cascades; in **Mount Saint Helens National Volcanic Monument**

Saint Hel·ier \'hel-yər\ town Channel Islands ✳ of Jersey *pop* 28,123

Saint–Hu·bert \sänt-'hyü-bərt, sənt-; ,saⁿ-yü-'ber\ town Canada in S Quebec E of Montreal *pop* 74,027

Saint–Hy·a·cinthe \sänt-'hī-ə-(,)sin(t)th, sənt-; ,sant-yə-'sant\ town Canada in S Quebec E of Montreal *pop* 39,292

Saint–Jean, Lake *or* **Lac Saint–Jean** \läk-saⁿ-zhäⁿ\ lake Canada in S Quebec draining through the Saguenay to the St. Lawrence *area* 414 *sq mi* (1072 *sq km*)

Saint–Jean–de–Luz \saⁿ-,zhäⁿ-də-'lüz, -'lᵫz\ town SW France on Bay of Biscay SW of Biarritz *pop* 13,181

Saint–Jean–sur–Ri·che·lieu \sä"-'zhäⁿ-sᵫr-'ri-shə-,lü, -,rē-shəl-'yᵫ\ town Canada in S Quebec SE of Montreal *pop* 37,607

Saint–Jé·rôme \,saⁿ-zhā-'rōm, ,sänt-jə-'rōm\ town Canada in S Quebec NW of Montreal *pop* 23,384

Saint John \sänt-'jän, sənt-\ **1** river 418 *mi* (673 *km*) NE U.S. & SE Canada flowing from N Maine into Bay of Fundy in New Brunswick **2** city & port Canada in S New Brunswick at mouth of the St. John *pop* 74,969

Saint John Island island W. Indies, one of the Virgin Islands of the U.S. *area* 20 *sq mi* (52 *sq km*), *pop* 3504

Saint Johns \sänt-'jänz, sənt-\ river 285 *mi* (459 *km*) NE Fla. flowing N & E into the Atlantic

Saint John's \sänt-'jänz, sənt-\ **1** city Brit. West Indies ✳ of Antigua and Barbuda on Antigua Is. **2** city & port Canada ✳ of Newfoundland *pop* 95,770

Saint Jo·seph \'jō-zəf *also* -səf\ city NW Mo. *pop* 71,852

Saint Kitts \'kits\ *or* **Saint Chris·to·pher** \'kris-tə-fər\ island Brit. West Indies in the Leewards; chief town Basseterre *area* 68 *sq mi* (177 *sq mi*); with Nevis, forms independent state of **Saint Kitts–Nevis** (✳ Basseterre *area* 104 *sq mi or* 269 *sq km*, *pop* 41,800) — **Kit·ti·tian** \kə-'ti-shən\ *noun*

Saint–Lau·rent \,saⁿ-lò-'räⁿ, sänt-lò-'rent\ town Canada in S Quebec bordering on Montreal Is. *pop* 72,402

Saint Law·rence \sänt-'lòr-ən(t)s, sənt-, -'lär-\ river 760 *mi* (1223 *km*) E Canada in Ontario & Quebec bordering on the U.S. in N.Y., flowing from Lake Ontario NE into the Atlantic, & forming at its mouth a wide bay (the **Gulf of Saint Lawrence**)

Saint Lawrence, Lake expansion of St. Lawrence River Canada & U.S. WSW of Cornwall, Ontario

Saint Lawrence Island island 95 *mi* (153 *km*) long W Alaska in N Bering Sea

Saint Lawrence Islands National Park reservation SE Canada in SE Ontario

Saint Lawrence Seaway waterway Canada & U.S. in & along the St. Lawrence River between Lake Ontario & Montreal

Saint–Lé·o·nard \,saⁿ-,lā-ə-'när; sänt-'le-nərd, sənt-\ town Canada in S Quebec N of Montreal *pop* 73,120

Saint–Lô \sänt-'lō, sənt-; saⁿ-'lō\ commune NW France *pop* 22,819

Saint–Lou·is \,saⁿ-lü-'ē\ **1** city & port Senegal on island at mouth of Senegal River; formerly ✳ of Senegal *pop* 125,717 **2** city & port Réunion

Saint Lou·is \sänt-'lü-əs, sənt-\ **1** river 160 *mi* (257 *km*) NE Minn. flowing to W tip of Lake Superior **2** city E Mo. on the Mississippi *pop* 396,685 — **Saint Lou·i·san** \-zən\ *noun* — **Saint Lou·i·sian** \'lü-ə-zhən, -shən\ *noun*

Saint Lou·is, Lake \sänt-'lü-ē, sənt-\ expansion of St. Lawrence River Canada above Lachine Rapids

Saint Lou·is Park \'lü-əs\ city SE Minn. *pop* 43,787

Saint Lu·cia \sänt-'lü-shə, sənt-\ island Brit. West Indies in the Windwards S of Martinique; an independent member of the Commonwealth of

\ə\ abut \ᵊ\ kitten \ər\ further \a\ ash \ā\ ace
\ä\ mop, mar \aù\ out \ch\ chin \e\ bet \ē\ easy
\g\ go \i\ hit \ī\ ice \j\ job \ŋ\ sing \ō\ go
\ò\ law \òi\ boy \th\ thin \th\ the \ü\ loot \ù\ foot
\y\ yet \zh\ vision *see also* Guide to Pronunciation

Nations since 1979 ✱ Castries *area* 238 *sq mi* (616 *sq km*), *pop* 148,183

Saint–Ma·lo \saⁿ-mə-'lō\ city & port NW France in Brittany on island in Gulf of Saint-Malo *pop* 49,274

Saint–Malo, Gulf of arm of English Channel NW France between Cotentin Peninsula & Brittany

Saint Mar·tin \sänt-'mär-tⁿn, sənt-\ *or Dutch* **Sint Maar·ten** \sint-\ island W. Indies in the N Leewards; divided between France & Netherlands *area* 33 *sq mi* (86 *sq km*)

Saint Mar·ys \'mer-ēz, 'mar-ēz, 'mā-rēz\ **1** river 175 *mi* (282 *km*) on Fla.-Ga. border flowing from Okefenokee Swamp to the Atlantic **2** river *about* 70 *mi* (115 *km*) between Canada & U.S. in Ontario & Upper Peninsula of Mich. flowing from Lake Superior into Lake Huron; descends 20 *ft* (6.1 *m*) in a mile at **Saint Marys Falls** — see SAULT SAINTE MARIE CANALS

Saint–Maur–des–Fos·sés \saⁿ-,mȯr-dā-fō-'sā\ commune N France SE of Paris on the Marne *pop* 77,492

Saint Mau·rice \sänt-'mȯr-əs, sənt-, -'mär-; saⁿ-mə-'rēs\ river 325 *mi* (523 *km*) Canada in S Quebec flowing S into the St. Lawrence

Saint–Mi·hiel \saⁿ-mē-'yel\ town NE France on the Meuse *pop* 5435

Saint Mo·ritz \sänt-mə-'rits, ,saⁿ-mə-\ *or German* **Sankt Mo·ritz** \zäŋkt-mə-'rits\ town E Switzerland in Graubünden canton SSE of Chur *pop* 5900

Saint–Na·zaire \,saⁿ-nə-'zar, -'zer\ commune & port NW France at mouth of the Loire *pop* 66,087

Sain·tonge \saⁿ-'tōⁿzh\ region & former province of France on Bay of Biscay N of the Gironde ✱ Saintes

Saint–Ouen \saⁿ-'twäⁿ\ commune France, N suburb of Paris *pop* 42,611

Saint Pan·cras \sänt-'paŋ-krəs, sənt-\ former metropolitan borough NW London, England, now part of Camden

Saint Paul \'pȯl\ city E Minn., its ✱ *pop* 272,235 — **Saint Paul·ite** \-'līt\ *noun*

Saint Pe·ter, Lake \sänt-'pē-tər, sənt-\ expansion of St. Lawrence River Canada between Sorel & Trois-Rivières, Quebec

Saint Peter and Saint Paul Rocks *or Portuguese* **Pe·ne·dos de São Pe·dro e São Pau·lo** \pə-'nā-dūs-dē-,saúⁿ-'pād-rü-ē-,saúⁿ-'paú-lò\ rocky islets in the Atlantic 600 *mi* (966 *km*) NE of Natal, Brazil; belong to Brazil

Saint Peter Port town Channel Islands ✱ of Guernsey *pop* 16,648

Saint Pe·ters \'pē-tərz\ city E Mo. WNW of St. Louis *pop* 45,779

Saint Pe·ters·burg \'pē-tərz-,bərg\ **1** city W Fla. on Pinellas Peninsula SW of Tampa *pop* 238,629 **2** *or 1914–24* **Pet·ro·grad** \'pe-trə-,grad, -,grät\ *or 1924–91* **Le·nin·grad** \'le-nən-,grad, -,grät\ city W Russia in Europe, at E end of Gulf of Finland; ✱ of Russian Empire 1712–1917, *pop* 4,952,000

Saint Pierre and Mi·que·lon \saⁿ-'pyer-ən(d)-,mē-kə-'lōⁿ\ French islands in the Atlantic off S Newfoundland ✱ St. Pierre, *area* 93 *sq mi* (242 *sq km*), *pop* 6400

Saint–Quen·tin \sänt-'kwen-tⁿn, sənt-, *French* saⁿ-käⁿ-'taⁿ\ commune N France on the Somme NW of Laon *pop* 62,085

Saint Si·mons Island \sänt-'sī-mənz, sənt-\ island SE Ga. in the Atlantic

Saint Thom·as \'tä-məs\ **1** island W. Indies, one of the Virgin Islands of the U.S. *area* 32 *sq mi* (83 *sq km*) **2** — see CHARLOTTE AMALIE **3** city Canada in SE Ontario SE of London *pop* 29,990

Saint–Tro·pez \,saⁿ-trȯ-'pā\ commune SE France on the Mediterranean SW of Cannes *pop* 4484

Saint Vin·cent \sänt-'vin(t)-sənt, sənt-\ island Brit. West Indies in *central* Windwards; with N Grenadines became independent 1979 as **Saint Vincent and the Grenadines** ✱ Kingstown *area* 150 *sq mi* (390 *sq km*), *pop* 109,000

Saint Vincent, Cape *or Portuguese* **Ca·bo de São Vi·cen·te** \'ká-bü-dē-,saúⁿ-vē-'säⁿ-tē\ cape SW Portugal

Saint Vincent, Gulf inlet of Indian Ocean Australia in S. Australia E of Yorke Peninsula

Sai·pan \sī-'pan, -'pän, 'sī-,\ island W Pacific in S central Marianas *area* 70 *sq mi* (182 *sq km*), *pop*

38,896 — **Sai·pa·nese** \,sī-pə-'nēz, -'nēs\ *adjective or noun*

Sa·ïs \'sā-is\ ancient city Egypt in Nile delta

Sa·ja·ma \sä-'hä-mä\ mountain 21,391 *ft* (6520 *m*) W Bolivia near Chilean boundary

Sa·kai \(,)sä-'kī\ city Japan in S Honshu on Osaka Bay *pop* 807,859

Sak·a·ka·wea, Lake \,sa-kə-kə-'wē-ə\ reservoir *about* 200 *mi* (322 *km*) long W N.Dak. formed in the Missouri by the Garrison Dam

Sa·kar·ya \sə-'kär-yə\ river *about* 500 *mi* (804 *km*) NW Turkey in Asia flowing into the Black Sea E of the Bosporus

Sa·kha \'sä-kə\ *or* **Ya·ku·tia** \yə-'kü-sh(ē-)ə\ autonomous republic E *central* Russia in Asia ✱ Yakutsk *area* 1,198,146 *sq mi* (3,103,198 *sq km*), *pop* 1,093,000

Sa·kha·lin \'sa-kə-,lēn, -lən; ,sä-kä-'lēn\ *or formerly* **Sa·gha·lien** \,sa-gə-,lēn, ,sa-gə-\ *or Japanese* **Ka·ra·fu·to** \kä-'rä-fə-,tō\ island SE Russia in Asia in Sea of Okhotsk N of Hokkaido; formerly (1905–45) divided between Russia & Japan *area more than* 28,500 *sq mi* (73,815 *sq km*)

Sa·ki·shi·ma Islands \,sä-kē-'shē-mä, sä-'kē-shē-mä\ island group Japan in S Ryukyus off E coast of N Taiwan; occupied 1945–72 by the U.S. *area* 343 *sq mi* (892 *sq km*)

Sakkara — see SAQQÁRA

Sa·kon·net River \sə-'kä-nət\ inlet of the Atlantic SE R.I., E of Aquidneck Is.

Sal·a·ber·ry–de–Val·ley·field \'sa-lə-,ber-ē-də-'va-lē-,fēld\ *or* **Valleyfield** town Canada in S Quebec SW of Montreal *pop* 27,598

Sa·la·do \sə-'lä-(,)dō, sä-'lä-thō\ **1** *or in upper course* **Ju·ra·men·to** \,hü-rä-'men-(,)tō\ river 1120 *mi* (1802 *km*) N Argentina flowing from the Andes SE into the Paraná **2** *or in upper course* **Des·agua·de·ro** \,thä-,sä-gwä-'ther-ō\ river 850 *mi* (1368 *km*) W *central* Argentina flowing S into the Colorado

Sal·a·man·ca \,sa-lə-'maŋ-kə, ,sä-lä-'mäŋ-kä\ **1** province W Spain *area* 4763 *sq mi* (12,336 *sq km*), *pop* 357,801 **2** commune, its ✱, WNW of Madrid *pop* 162,888

Sal·a·maua \,sä-lä-'maú-ä\ town Papua New Guinea on Huon Gulf

Salambria — see PENEUS

Sal·a·mis \'sa-lə-məs\ **1** ancient city Cyprus on E coast **2** island Greece in Saronic Gulf off Attica

Sal·da·nha Bay \sal-'da-nyə\ inlet of the Atlantic on W coast of Western Cape province, Republic of South Africa

Sa·lé \sa-'lä\ *or formerly* **Sal·lee** \'sa-lē\ city & port NW Morocco, N suburb of Rabat *pop* 289,391

Sa·lem \'sā-ləm\ **1** city & port NE Mass. NE of Lynn *pop* 38,091 **2** town SE N.H. E of Nashua *pop* 25,746 **3** city ✱ of Oreg. on Willamette River *pop* 107,786 **4** town W *central* Va. WNW of Roanoke *pop* 23,756 **5** city S India in N Tamil Nadu SW of Madras *pop* 366,712

Sa·ler·no \sə-'ler-(,)nō, sä-'ler-\ commune & port S Italy on **Gulf of Salerno** (inlet of Tyrrhenian Sea) ESE of Naples *pop* 152,159 — **Sa·ler·ni·tan** \-'lər-nə-tən, -'ler-\ *adjective or noun*

Sal·ford \'sȯl-fərd\ urban area NW England in Greater Manchester *pop* 98,024

Sa·li·na \sə-'lī-nə\ city *central* Kans. on Smoky Hill River *pop* 42,303

Sa·li·nas \sə-'lē-nəs\ **1** river 150 *mi* (241 *km*) W Calif. flowing NW into Monterey Bay **2** city W Calif. near Monterey Bay *pop* 108,777

Salinas National Monument reservation *central* N. Mex. containing archaeological ruins

Sal·is·bury \'sȯlz-,ber-ē, -b(ə-)rē, *United States also* 'salz-\ **1** city SE Md. *pop* 20,592 **2** city W *central* N.C. SSW of Winston-Salem *pop* 23,087 **3** — see HARARE **4** city & borough S England in Wiltshire on the Avon *pop* 35,355

Salisbury Plain plateau S England in Wiltshire NW of Salisbury

Salm·on \'sa-mən\ river 420 *mi* (676 *km*) *central* Idaho flowing into Snake River

Salmon River Mountains mountains *central* Idaho; many peaks over 9000 *ft* (2743 *m*)

Salonika — see THESSALONÍKI

Sa·lon·i·ka, Gulf of \sə-'lä-ni-kə\ *or Greek* **Therma·ï·kós Kól·pos** \ther-,mä-ē-'kós-'kȯl-pòs\ arm of Aegean Sea N Greece W of Chalcidice

Sal·op — see SHROPSHIRE — **Sa·lo·pi·an** \sə-'lō-pē-ən\ *adjective or noun*

Salt \'sȯlt\ **1** river 200 *mi* (322 *km*) Ariz. flowing W into the Gila **2** river 100 *mi* (161 *km*) N *central* Ky. flowing into Ohio River **3** river 200 *mi* (322 *km*) NE Mo. flowing SE into Mississippi River

Sal·ta \'säl-tä\ city NW Argentina *pop* 373,857

Sal·til·lo \säl-'tē-(,)yō, sal-\ city NE Mexico ✱ of Coahuila *pop* 440,845

Salt Lake City city N Utah, its ✱ *pop* 159,936

Sal·to \'säl-(,)tō\ city & port NW Uruguay on Uruguay River *pop* 74,881

Sal·ton Sea \'sȯl-tⁿn\ saline lake *about* 235 *ft* (72 *m*) below sea level SE Calif. at N end of Imperial Valley formed by diversion of water from Colorado River into depression called **Salton Sink**

Salt Sea — see DEAD SEA

Sa·lu·da \sə-'lü-də\ river 200 *mi* (322 *km*) W *central* S.C. flowing SE to unite with Broad River forming the Congaree

Sal·va·dor \'sal-və-,dȯr, ,sal-və-\ **1** EL SALVADOR **2** *or formerly* **São Salvador** \saúⁿ-\ *or* **Ba·hia** \bä-'ē-ə\ city & port NE Brazil ✱ of Bahia *pop* 2,000,000 — **Sal·va·dor·an** \,sal-və-'dȯr-ən, -'dór-\ *adjective or noun* — **Sal·va·dor·ean** *or* **Sal·va·dor·ian** \-ē-ən\ *adjective or noun*

Sal·ween \sal-'wēn\ river *about* 1500 *mi* (2415 *km*) SE Asia flowing from Tibet S into Gulf of Martaban in Myanmar

Salz·burg \'sȯlz-,bərg, 'sälz-, 'salz-, 'sȯlts-, *German* 'zälts-,bùrk\ city W Austria ESE of Munich, Germany *pop* 143,971

Salz·git·ter \'zälts-,gi-tər\ *or formerly* **Wa·tenstedt–Salzgitter** \'vä-tⁿn-,shtet-, -,stet-\ city N *central* Germany SW of Brunswick *pop* 115,381

Salz·kam·mer·gut \'zälts-,kä-mər-,gút\ district N Austria E of Salzburg; chief town Bad Ischl

Samanala — see ADAM'S PEAK

Sa·mar \'sä-,mär\ island *central* Philippines in the Visayans N of Leyte *area* 5050 *sq mi* (13,130 *sq km*)

Sa·ma·ra \sə-'mär-ə\ *or 1935–91* **Kuy·by·shev** \'kwē-bə-,shef, 'kü-ē-bə-, -,shev\ city E Russia in Europe in valley of the Volga *pop* 1,239,000

Sa·mar·ia \sə-'mer-ē-ə, -'mar-\ **1** district of ancient Palestine W of the Jordan between Galilee & Judaea **2** city, its ✱ & ✱ of the Northern Kingdom (Israel); rebuilt by Herod the Great & renamed **Se·bas·te** \sə-'bas-tē\; site in Jordan at modern village of Sebastye

Sa·ma·rin·da \,sa-mə-'rin-də\ city Indonesia in E Borneo *pop* 407,339

Sa·mar·qand *or* **Sam·ar·kand** \'sa-mər-,kand\ *or ancient* **Mar·a·can·da** \,mar-ə-'kan-də\ city E Uzbekistan *pop* 370,500

Sam·ni·um \'sam-nē-əm\ ancient country S *central* Italy

Sa·moa \sə-'mō-ə\ *or formerly* **Navigators Islands** islands SW *central* Pacific N of Tonga Islands; divided at long. 171°W into American, or Eastern, Samoa & Western Samoa *area* 1209 *sq mi* (3143 *sq km*)

Sa·mos \'sā-,mäs, 'sä-,mòs\ island Greece in the Aegean off coast of Turkey N of the Dodecanese *area* 184 *sq mi* (477 *sq km*) *pop* 41,850 — **Sa·mi·an** \'sā-mē-ən\ *adjective or noun*

Sam·o·thrace \'sa-mə-,thrās\ *or New Greek* **Sa·mo·thrá·ki** \,sä-mò-'thrä-kē\ island Greece in the NE Aegean — **Sam·o·thra·cian** \,sa-mə-'thrā-shən\ *adjective or noun*

Sam·sun \säm-'sün\ city & port N Turkey on Black Sea NW of Ankara *pop* 303,979

San·aa *or* **Sana** \sa-'nä, 'sa-,nä\ city S Arabia ✱ of Yemen & formerly ✱ of Yemen Arab Republic *pop* 125,093

Sa·nan·daj \,sä-nən-'däj\ city NW Iran *pop* 204,537

San An·dre·as Fault \,san-an-'drā-əs\ zone of faults Calif. extending from N coast toward head of Gulf of California

San An·ge·lo \san-'an-jə-,lō\ city W *central* Tex. *pop* 84,474

San An·to·nio \,san-ən-'tō-nē-,ō\ **1** river *about* 200 *mi* (322 *km*) S Tex. flowing SE into Gulf of Mexico **2** city S Tex. on San Antonio River *pop* 935,933 — **San An·to·ni·an** \-nē-ən\ *noun*

San Be·ni·to \,san-bə-'nē-(,)tō\ city S Tex. NW of Brownsville *pop* 20,125

San Ber·nar·di·no \\,san-,bər-nə(r)-'dē-(,)nō\ city SW Calif. E of Los Angeles *pop* 164,164

San Bernardino Mountains mountains S Calif. S of Mojave Desert; highest **San Gor·go·nio Mountain** \\,san-gȯr-'gō-nē-(,)ō\ 11,502 *ft* (3506 *m*)

San Bru·no \\san-'brü-(,)nō\ city W Calif. S of San Francisco *pop* 38,961

San Buenaventura — see VENTURA

San Car·los \\san-'kär-lōs\ city W Calif. SE of San Francisco *pop* 26,167

San Carlos de Bariloche — see BARILOCHE

San Cle·men·te \\,san-klə-'men-tē\ city SW Calif. NW of San Diego *pop* 41,100

San Clemente Island island S Calif., southernmost of Channel Islands

San Cris·to·bal \\,san-kri-'stō-bəl\ island W Pacific in SE Solomons

San Cris·tó·bal \\,san-kri-'stō-bəl\ **1** *or* **Chatham Island** island Ecuador in the Galápagos *pop* 1404 **2** city W Venezuela SSW of Lake Maracaibo *pop* 220,697

Sanc·ti Spí·ri·tus \\,säŋk-tē-'spē-rē-,tüs\ city W *central* Cuba SE of Santa Clara *pop* 85,499

San·cy, Puy de \\,pwē-də-,säⁿ-'sē\ mountain 6188 *ft* (1886 *m*) S *central* France; highest in the Monts Dore & Auvergne Mountains

San·da·kan \\san-'dä-kən\ city & port Malaysia in Sabah on Sulu Sea; former ✱ of N. Borneo *pop* 118,417

Sand·hurst \\'sand-,hərst\ village S England in E Berkshire SE of Reading *pop* 6445

San·dia Mountains \\san-'dē-ə\ mountains N *central* N.Mex. E of Albuquerque; highest **Sandia Crest** 10,678 *ft* (3255 *m*)

San Di·e·go \\,san-dē-'ā-(,)gō\ city & port W Calif. on **San Diego Bay** (inlet of the Pacific) *pop* 1,110,549 — **San Di·e·gan** \\-gən\ *adjective or noun*

San Di·mas \\san-'dē-məs\ city SW Calif. NW of Pomona *pop* 32,397

San Domingo 1 — see HISPANIOLA **2** — see DOMINICAN REPUBLIC **3** — see SANTO DOMINGO

San·dring·ham \\'san-driŋ-əm\ village E England in NW Norfolk

San·dus·ky \\sən-'dəs-kē, san-\ **1** river 150 *mi* (241 *km*) N Ohio flowing N into Lake Erie **2** city N Ohio at entrance to **Sandusky Bay** (inlet of Lake Erie) *pop* 29,764

Sand·wich \\'san(d)-(,)wich\ town SE England in Kent on Stour River *pop* 4227

Sandwich Islands — see HAWAII

Sandy \\'san-dē\ city N Utah S of Salt Lake City *pop* 75,058

Sandy Hook peninsula E N.J. extending N toward New York Bay

San Fer·nan·do \\,san-fər-'nan-(,)dō\ **1** valley S Calif. NW of Los Angeles; partly within Los Angeles city limits **2** city SW Calif. in San Fernando Valley *pop* 22,580

San·ford \\'san-fərd\ **1** city NE Fla. *pop* 32,387 **2** town SW Maine *pop* 20,463

Sanford, Mount mountain 16,237 *ft* (4949 *m*) S Alaska at W end of Wrangell Mountains

San Fran·cis·co \\,san-frən-'sis-(,)kō\ city & port W Calif. on **San Francisco Bay** & the Pacific *pop* 723,959 — **San Fran·cis·can** \\-kən\ *adjective or noun*

San Francisco Peaks mountain N *central* Ariz. N of Flagstaff; includes three peaks: Mt. Humphreys 12,633 *ft* (3851 *m*), highest point in the state; Mt. Agassiz 12,340 *ft* (3761 *m*); & Mt. Fremont 11,940 *ft* (3639 *m*)

San Ga·bri·el \\san-'gā-brē-əl\ city SW Calif. S of Pasadena *pop* 37,120

San Gabriel Mountains mountains S Calif. SW of Mojave Desert & NE of Los Angeles; highest San Antonio Peak 10,080 *ft* (3072 *m*)

San·ga·mon \\'san-gə-mən\ river *about* 250 *mi* (400 *km*) *central* Ill. flowing SW & W into Illinois River

San·gay \\sän-'gī\ volcano 17,159 *ft* (5230 *m*) SE *central* Ecuador

San·gi·he Islands \\säŋ-gē-'ā\ *or* **San·gi Islands** \\'säŋ-gē\ islands Indonesia NE of Sulawesi *pop* 194,253; largest of the group **Sangihe** *or* **Sangi**

San Gi·mi·gna·no \\,sän-jē-mē-'nyä-(,)nō\ commune *central* Italy NW of Siena

San·gre de Cris·to Mountains \\,saŋ-grē-də-'kris-(,)tō\ mountains S Colo. & N N.Mex. in Rocky Mountains — see BLANCA PEAK

San·i·bel Island \\'sa-nə-bəl, -,bel\ island SW Fla. SW of Fort Myers

San Il·de·fon·so \\,san-,il-də-'fän(t)-(,)sō, ,sän-,ēl-dā-'fȯn-sō\ *or* **La Gran·ja** \\lä-'grän-(,)hä\ commune *central* Spain SE of Segovia

San Isi·dro \\,san-ə-'sē-(,)drō\ city E Argentina *pop* 299,022

San Ja·cin·to \\,san-jə-'sin-tō\ river SE Tex. flowing S into Galveston Bay

San Joa·quin \\,san-wä-'kēn, -wȯ-\ river 350 *mi* (563 *km*) *central* Calif. flowing from the Sierra Nevada SW & then NW into Sacramento River

San Jo·se \\,san-(h)ō-'zā\ city W Calif. SSE of San Francisco *pop* 782,248

San Jo·sé \\,sän-hō-'sā, ,san-(h)ō-'zā\ city *central* Costa Rica, its ✱ *pop* 289,456

San Juan \\san-'wän, ,sän-'hwän\ **1** river 360 *mi* (579 *km*) SW Colo., NW N.Mex., & SE Utah flowing W into Colorado River **2** city & port NE Puerto Rico, its ✱ *pop* 437,745 **3** city W Argentina N of Mendoza *pop* 106,564 — **San Jua·ne·ro** \\,san-'wä-\ *noun*

San Juan Cap·is·tra·no \\,ka-pə-'strä-(,)nō\ city SW Calif. SE of Los Angeles *pop* 26,183

San Juan Hill hill E Cuba near Santiago de Cuba

San Juan Islands islands NW Wash. between Vancouver Is. & the mainland

San Juan Mountains mountains SW Colo. in the Rocky Mountains — see UNCOMPAHGRE PEAK

Sankt An·ton am Arl·berg \\zäŋkt-'än-,tōn-,äm-'är(-ə)l-,bȯrg, -,berk\ village W Austria in Tirol W of Innsbruck

Sankt Gallen — see SAINT GALL

Sankt Moritz — see SAINT MORITZ

San Le·an·dro \\san-lē-'an-(,)drō\ city W Calif. SE of Oakland *pop* 68,223

San Lo·ren·zo \\,sän-lō-'ren-(,)zō\ city S Paraguay E of Asunción

San Lu·cas, Cape \\san-'lü-kəs\ headland NW Mexico, the S extremity of Baja California

San Lu·is \\san-'lü-əs\ valley S Colo. & N N.Mex. along the upper Rio Grande between the San Juan & Sangre de Cristo mountains

San Lu·is Obis·po \\,san-,lü-əs-ə-'bis-(,)pō\ city W Calif. W of Santa Barbara *pop* 41,958

San Lu·is Po·to·sí \\,sän-,lü-,ēs-,pō-tə-'sē\ **1** state *central* Mexico *area* 24,266 *sq mi* (62,849 *sq km*), *pop* 2,003,187 **2** city, its ✱, NE of León *pop* 525,819

San Mar·cos \\san-'mär-kəs, -kōs\ **1** city SW Calif. NNW of San Diego *pop* 38,974 **2** city S Tex. NE of San Antonio *pop* 28,743

San Ma·ri·no \\,san-mə-'rē-(,)nō\ **1** country S Europe on Italian Peninsula SSW of Rimini; a republic *area* 24 *sq mi* (62 *sq km*), *pop* 24,000 **2** town, its ✱ — **Sam·mar·i·nese** \\sa(m)-,mar-ə-'nēz, -'nēs\ *noun* — **San Mar·i·nese** \\,san-,mar-\ *adjective or noun*

San Mar·tín \\san-mär-'tēn\ *or* **Ge·ne·ral San Martín** \\,hā-nā-'räl\ city E Argentina, NW suburb of Buenos Aires *pop* 407,506

San Ma·teo \\,san-mə-'tā-(,)ō\ city W Calif. SSE of San Francisco *pop* 85,486

San Mi·guel de Tu·cu·mán \\,sän-mē-'gel-dä-,tü-kü-män\ *or* **Tucumán** city NW Argentina at foot of E ranges of the Andes *pop* 473,014

San Pa·blo \\san-'pa-(,)blō\ city W Calif. N of Oakland on **San Pablo Bay** (N extension of San Francisco Bay) *pop* 25,158

San Pe·dro Channel \\san-'pē-(,)drō, -'pā-\ channel SW Calif. between Santa Catalina Is. & the mainland

San Pe·dro Su·la \\sän-'pā-(,)thrō-'sü-lä\ city NW Honduras *pop* 300,400

San Ra·fael \\san-rə-'fel\ city W Calif. N of San Francisco on San Pablo Bay *pop* 48,404

San Ra·mon \\san-rə-'mōn\ city W Calif. E of Oakland *pop* 35,303

San Re·mo \\san-'rā-(,)mō, san-'rē-\ city & port NW Italy in Liguria near French border *pop* 55,786

San Sal·va·dor \\san-'sal-və-,dȯr, ,sän-'säl-vä-,thȯr\ **1** island *central* Bahamas *area* 60 *sq mi* (156 *sq km*) **2** city W *central* El Salvador, its ✱ *pop* 349,333

San Stefano — see YESILKOY

San·ta Ana \\,san-tə-'a-nə, ,sän-tä-'ä-nä\ **1** city SW Calif. ESE of Long Beach *pop* 293,742 **2** city NW El Salvador NW of San Salvador *pop* 168,047

Santa Bar·ba·ra \\'bär-b(ə-)rə\ city S Calif. *pop* 85,571

Santa Barbara Channel channel SW Calif. between the N Channel Islands & mainland

Santa Barbara Islands — see CHANNEL ISLANDS

Santa Catalina — see CATALINA

San·ta Ca·ta·ri·na \\,san-tə-,ka-tə-'rē-nə\ state S Brazil bordering on the Atlantic ✱ Florianópolis *area* 37,060 *sq mi* (95,985 *sq km*), 4,536,433

Santa Clara \\'klar-ə, 'kler-\ **1** city W Calif. NW of San Jose *pop* 93,613 **2** city W *central* Cuba *pop* 194,354

San·ta Cla·ri·ta \\klə-'rē-tə\ city Calif. *pop* 110,642

Santa Cruz \\'krüz\ **1** island SW Calif. in NW Channel Islands **2** city W Calif. S of San Jose on Monterey Bay *pop* 49,040 **3** — see SAINT CROIX **4** river 250 *mi* (402 *km*) S Argentina flowing E into the Atlantic **5** city E Bolivia *pop* 694,616

San·ta Cruz de Te·ne·ri·fe \\,sän-tä-'krüs-dä-,te-nə-'rē-(,)fā, -'rēf, -'rif\ **1** province Spain comprising W Canary Islands *area* 1239 *sq mi* (3209 *sq km*), *pop* 725,815 **2** city & port, its ✱, on NE Tenerife Is. *pop* 189,317

Santa Cruz Islands islands SW Pacific in SE Solomons N of Vanuatu; until 1978 administratively attached to Brit. Solomon Islands *area* 362 *sq mi* (938 *sq km*)

San·ta Fe \\,san-tə-'fā\ **1** city ✱ of N.Mex. *pop* 55,859 **2** city *central* Argentina on Salado River *pop* 442,214 — **Santa Fe·an** \\'fā-ən\ *noun*

Santa Fe Trail pioneer route to the Southwest used especially 1821–80 from vicinity of Kansas City, Mo., to Santa Fe, N.Mex.

San·ta Is·a·bel \\,san-tə-'i-zə-,bel\ **1** island W Pacific in the E *central* Solomons NE of Guadalcanal *area about* 1500 *sq mi* (3900 *sq km*) **2** — see MALABO

Santa Ma·ria \\mə-'rē-ə\ city W Calif. NW of Santa Barbara *pop* 61,284

San·ta Ma·ría \\,sän-tä-mə-'rē-ə\ volcano *about* 12,400 *ft* (3780 *m*) W Guatemala

Santa Mar·ta \\'mär-tə\ city & port N Colombia on the Caribbean E of Barranquilla *pop* 286,500

San·ta Mon·i·ca \\,san-tə-'mä-ni-kə\ city SW Calif. adjacent to Los Angeles on **Santa Monica Bay** (inlet of the Pacific) *pop* 86,905

San·tan·der \\,sän-,tän-'der, ,san-,tan-\ **1** — see CANTABRIA **2** city & port N Spain on Bay of Biscay ✱ of Cantabria province *pop* 191,079

San·ta Pau·la \\,san-tə-'pȯ-lə\ city SW Calif. NW of Los Angeles *pop* 25,062

San·ta·rém \\,san-tə-'rem\ city N Brazil in W Pará at confluence of the Tapajoz & the Amazon *pop* 265,105

San·ta Ro·sa \\,san-tə-'rō-zə\ city W Calif. N of San Francisco *pop* 113,313

Santa Rosa Island island SW Calif. in NW Channel Islands

San·tee \\(,)san-'tē, 'san-\ **1** river 143 *mi* (230 *km*) S.C. flowing SE into the Atlantic — see CONGAREE **2** city S Calif., a suburb of San Diego *pop* 52,902

San·ti·a·go \\,san-tē-'ä-(,)gō, ,sän-\ **1** city *central* Chile, its ✱ *metropolitan area pop* 3,902,356 **2** *or* **Santiago de los Ca·bal·le·ros** \\thä-lōs-,kä-vä-'yer-(,)ōs\ city N *central* Dominican Republic *pop* 382,244 **3** *or* **Santiago de Com·pos·te·la** \\də-,käm-pə-'ste-lə, -,kȯm-\ commune NW Spain *pop* 87,807 — **San·ti·a·gan** \\,san-tē-'ä-gən, ,sän-\ *noun*

Santiago de Cu·ba \\də-'kyü-bə, thä-'kü-vä\ city & port SE Cuba *pop* 405,354

Santiago del Es·te·ro \\(,)del-ə-'ster-(,)ō, (,)thel-ā-'stä-rō\ city N Argentina SE of San Miguel de Tucumán *pop* 201,709

\\ə\ abut \\ˈ\ kitten \\ər\ further \\a\ ash \\ā\ ace \\ä\ mop, mar \\au̇\ out \\ch\ chin \\e\ bet \\ē\ easy \\g\ go \\i\ hit \\ī\ ice \\j\ job \\ŋ\ sing \\ō\ go \\ȯ\ law \\ȯi\ boy \\th\ thin \\th̲\ the \\ü\ loot \\u̇\ foot \\y\ yet \\zh\ vision *see also* Guide to Pronunciation

San·to Do·min·go \,san-tə-də-'miŋ-(,)gō\ **1** *or* **Santo Domingo de Guz·mán** \,sän-tō-thō-'mēŋ-gō-thä-güs-'män\ *or formerly* **Tru·jil·lo** \trü-'hē-(,)yō\ *or* **Ciu·dad Trujillo** \,syü-thä(th), ,sē-ù-'dad\ city & port ✻ of Dominican Republic on Caribbean Sea *pop* 654,757 **2** — see HISPANIOLA **3** — see DOMINICAN REPUBLIC — **San·to Do·min·gan** \,san-tə-də-'miŋ-gən\ *adjective or noun*

San·tos \'san-tüs\ city & port SE Brazil in SE São Paulo state SSE of São Paulo on an island in a tidal inlet *pop* 428,526

San·tur·ce \san-'tür-(,)sā\ a NE section of San Juan, Puerto Rico

São Fran·cis·co \,saủⁿ-frən-'sēs-(,)kü\ river 1800 *mi* (2897 *km*) E Brazil flowing from S *central* Minas Gerais NE & E into the Atlantic

São Luís \,saủⁿ-lù-'ēs\ city & port NE Brazil ✻ of Maranhão state on Maranhão Is. *pop* 695,780

São Manuel — see TELES PIRES

São Mi·guel \,saủⁿ-mē-'gel\ island Portugal in E Azores; chief town Ponta Delgada *area* 288 *sq mi* (746 *sq km*)

Saône \'sōn\ river 298 *mi* (479 *km*) E France flowing SSW into the Rhône

São Pau·lo \,saủⁿ-'paủ-(,)lü, -(,)lō\ **1** state SE Brazil *area* 95,852 *sq mi* (248,257 *sq km*), *pop* 31,192,818 **2** city, its ✻ *pop* 10,900,000

São Ro·que, Cape \,saủⁿ-'rò-kə\ headland NE Brazil N of Natal

São Salvador — see SALVADOR

São Tia·go \,saủⁿ-tē-'ä-(,)gü, -(,)gō\ island Cape Verde Islands, largest of the group; chief town Praia *area* 383 *sq mi* (992 *sq km*)

São To·mé \,saủⁿ-tə-'mā\ island W Africa in Gulf of Guinea; with Príncipe Is., forms the republic (until 1975 a Portuguese territory) of **São Tomé and Príncipe** (✻ São Tomé *area* 372 *sq mi or* 963 *sq km, pop* 128,000)

São Vicente, Cabo de — see SAINT VINCENT (Cape)

Sap·po·ro \'sä-pō-,rō; sä-'pōr-(,)ō\ city Japan on W Hokkaido *pop* 1,671,765

Saq·qâ·ra *or* **Saq·qā·rah** *or* **Sak·ka·ra** \sə-'kär-ə\ village N Egypt SW of ruins of Memphis

Sarabat — see GEDIZ

Sar·a·gos·sa \,sar-ə-'gä-sə\ *or Spanish* **Za·ra·go·za** \,thä-rä-'gō-thä, ,sä-rä-'gō-sə\ city, ✻ of Zaragoza province, Spain *pop* 594,394

Sa·ra·je·vo \,sar-ə-'yä-(,)vō, ,sär-ə-; 'sär-ə-ye-,vò\ city SE *central* Bosnia and Herzegovina, its ✻

Sar·a·nac \'sar-ə-,nak\ river 100 *mi* (161 *km*) NE N.Y. flowing NE from **Saranac Lakes** (three lakes in the Adirondacks: Upper Saranac, Middle Saranac, & Lower Saranac) into Lake Champlain

Sa·ransk \sə-'rän(t)sk, -'ran(t)sk\ city *central* Russia in Europe ✻ of Mordvinia *pop* 322,000

Sar·a·so·ta \,sar-ə-'sō-tə\ city W Fla. S of Tampa *pop* 50,961

Sar·a·to·ga \,sar-ə-'tō-gə\ city W Calif. SW of San Jose *pop* 28,061

Saratoga Lake lake 7 *mi* (11 *km*) long E N.Y. S of Lake George

Saratoga Springs city NE N.Y. *pop* 25,001

Sa·ra·tov \sə-'rä-təf\ city S *central* Russia in Europe on a reservoir of the Volga *pop* 909,000

Sa·ra·wak \sə-'rä-(,)wäk, -,wak\ state Malaysia in N Borneo, formerly a Brit. colony ✻ Kuching *area* 48,342 *sq mi* (125,206 *sq km*), *pop* 1,648,217

Sardica — see SOFIA

Sar·din·ia \sär-'din-ē-ə, -'di-nyə\ *or Italian* **Sar·de·gna** \sär-'dā-nyä\ island Italy S of Corsica; with surrounding smaller islands, constitutes a region of Italy ✻ Cagliari *area about* 9300 *sq mi* (24,087 *sq km*), *pop* 1,645,192

Sar·dis \'sär-dəs\ *or* **Sar·des** \'sär-(,)dēz\ ancient city W Asia Minor ✻ of ancient kingdom of Lydia; site E of Izmir — **Sar·di·an** \'sär-dē-ən\ *adjective or noun*

Sa·re·ma *or Estonian* **Saa·re·maa** \'sär-ə-,mä\ island Estonia at mouth of Gulf of Riga *area about* 1050 *sq mi* (2720 *sq km*)

Sa·re·ra Bay \sə-'rer-ə\ *or formerly* **Geel·vink Bay** \'gāl-(,)viŋk, 'kāl-\ inlet Indonesia in N W. Irian

Sar·gas·so Sea \sär-'ga-(,)sō\ tract of comparatively still water N Atlantic lying chiefly between 25° & 35°N & 40° & 70°W

Sark \'särk\ island in the English Channel, one of the Channel Islands; a dependency of Guernsey *area* 2 *sq mi* (5.2 *sq km*) — **Sark·ese** \,sär-'kēz, -'kēs\ *noun*

Sar·ma·tia \sär-'mā-sh(ē-)ə\ ancient region E Europe in modern Poland & Russia between the Vistula & the Volga — **Sar·ma·tian** \-shən\ *adjective or noun*

Sar·nia–Clear·wa·ter \'sär-nē-ə-'klir-,wò-tər, -,wä-\ city Canada in SE Ontario on St. Clair River opposite Port Huron, Mich. *pop* 74,376

Sa·ron·ic Gulf \sə-'rä-nik\ inlet of the Aegean SE Greece between Attica & the Peloponnese

Sa·ros Gulf \'sar-,äs, 'ser-\ inlet of the Aegean SW Turkey in Europe N of Gallipoli Peninsula

Sarre — see SAAR

Sarthe \'särt\ river 175 *mi* (282 *km*) NW France flowing S to unite with the Mayenne forming Maine River

Sarum OLD SARUM

Sa·se·bo \'sä-se-,bō\ city & port Japan in NW Kyushu on an inlet of E. China Sea *pop* 245,017

Sas·katch·e·wan \sə-'ska-chə-wən, sa-, -,wän\ **1** river 340 *mi* (547 *km*) S *central* Canada formed by confluence in *central* Saskatchewan of two branches rising in the Rockies in Alberta, the **North Saskatchewan** (760 *mi or* 1216 *km*) & the **South Saskatchewan** (865 *mi or* 1384 *km*), & flowing E into Lake Winnipeg **2** province SW Canada ✻ Regina *area* 220,121 *sq mi* (570,113 *sq km*), *pop* 988,928 — **Sas·katch·e·wan·ian** \-,ska-chə-'wä-nē-ən\ *adjective or noun*

Sas·ka·toon \,sas-kə-'tün\ city Canada in *central* Saskatchewan on S. Saskatchewan River *pop* 186,058

Sas·sa·ri \'sä-sä-(,)rē\ commune Italy in NW Sardinia *pop* 116,989

Sa·til·la \sə-'ti-lə\ river 220 *mi* (354 *km*) SE Ga. flowing E into the Atlantic

Sat·pu·ra Range \'sät-pə-rə\ range of hills W *central* India between the Narmada & the Tapi

Sa·tu–Ma·re \,sä-(,)tü-'mär-(,)ā\ city NW Romania in Transylvania on the Somes *pop* 136,881

Sau·di Arabia \'saủ-dē, 'sò-dē, sä-'ü-dē\ country SW Asia occupying most of Arabian Peninsula; a kingdom, comprising former kingdoms of Nejd & Hejaz & principality of Asir ✻ Riyadh *area* 865,000 *sq mi* (2,240,350 *sq km*), *pop* 17,419,000 — **Saudi** *adjective or noun* — **Saudi Arabian** *adjective or noun*

Sau·gus \'sò-gəs\ town NE Mass. W of Lynn *pop* 25,549

Sault Sainte Ma·rie \'sü-(,)sänt-mə-'rē\ city Canada in Ontario, across the St. Marys River from Michigan *pop* 81,476

Sault Sainte Marie Canals *or* **Soo Canals** \'sü\ three ship canals, two in the U.S. & one in Canada, at rapids in St. Marys River connecting Lake Superior & Lake Huron

Sau·mur \sō-'mür, -'myür, -'mēr\ commune NW France on the Loire SE of Angers *pop* 31,894

Sau·rash·tra \saủ-'räsh-trə\ former state (1948–56) W India on Kathiawar Peninsula; in Bombay state 1956–60 & since 1960 in Gujarat

Sa·va \'sä-və\ river 584 *mi* (940 *km*) flowing from Italian border E through Slovenia, into Croatia, along Croatia-Bosnia and Herzegovina border, & into Yugoslavia where it flows into the Danube at Belgrade

Sa·vaii \sə-'vī-,ē\ island SW *central* Pacific, largest in Samoa, in W. Samoa

Sa·van·nah \sə-'va-nə\ **1** river 314 *mi* (505 *km*) E Ga. flowing SE to the Atlantic & forming Ga.-S.C. boundary **2** city & port E Ga. at mouth of Savannah River *pop* 137,560

Save — see SABI

Sa·vo \'sä-(,)vō\ island W Pacific in SE Solomons N of W Guadalcanal

Sa·vo·na \sä-'vō-nä\ commune & port NW Italy SW of Genoa *pop* 67,137

Sa·voy \sə-'vòi\ *or French* **Sa·voie** \sà-'vwà\ *or Italian* **Sa·vo·ia** \sä-'vò-yä\ region SE France in Savoy Alps SW of Switzerland & bordering on Italy; duchy 1416–1720, part of kingdom of Sardinia 1720–1860; became part of France 1860 — **Sa·voy·ard** \sə-'vòi-,ärd, ,sa-,vòi-'ärd, ,sa-,vwä-'yär(d)\ *adjective or noun*

Savoy Alps section of W Alps SE France — see MONT BLANC

Sa·watch Range \sə-'wäch\ mountain range *central* Colo. in Rocky Mountains — see ELBERT (Mount)

Saxe \'saks\ SAXONY — its French form, used in English chiefly in names of former duchies in Thuringia: **Saxe–Al·ten·burg** \-'äl-t°n-,bùrg\, **Saxe–Co·burg** \-'kō-,bərg\, **Saxe–Go·tha** \-'gō-tə, -thə\, **Saxe–Mei·ning·en** \-'mī-niŋ-ən\, & **Saxe–Wei·mar–Ei·se·nach** \-'vī-,mär-'ī-z°n-,äk, -,äk\

Sax·o·ny \'sak-s(ə-)nē\ *or German* **Sach·sen** \'zäk-sən\ **1** region & former duchy NW Germany S of Jutland Peninsula between the Elbe & the Rhine — see LOWER SAXONY **2** region & former state E Germany N of the Erzgebirge — see SAXE

Sa·yan Mountains \sə-'yän\ mountains S Russia in Asia on border of Tuva N of Altay Mountains

Sayre·ville \'sar-,vil, 'ser-\ borough E *central* N.J. *pop* 34,986

Sa·zan \'sä-,zän\ *or Italian* **Sa·se·no** \sə-'zā-(,)nō, sä-\ island Albania in N Strait of Otranto

Sca Fell \skò-'fel\ mountain 3162 *ft* (964 *m*) NW England in Cumbrians SW of Keswick; second highest peak in England

Sca·fell Pike \,skò-'fel\ mountain 3210 *ft* (978 *m*) NW England in Cumbria NE of Sca Fell; highest in the Cumbrians & in England

Scamander — see MENDERES

Scan·di·na·via \,skan-də-'nā-vē-ə, -vyə\ **1** peninsula N Europe occupied by Norway & Sweden **2** Denmark, Norway, Sweden, & sometimes also Iceland, the Faeroe Islands, & Finland

Scapa Flow \,ska-pə-'flō\ sea basin N Scotland in the Orkneys

Scar·bor·ough \'skär-,bər-ō\ **1** city Canada in SE Ontario near Toronto *pop* 524,598 **2** town & port NE England in N. Yorkshire *pop* 107,800

Schaer·beek *or Flemish* **Schaar·beek** \'skär-,bāk, 'skar-\ commune *central* Belgium, NE suburb of Brussels *pop* 102,702

Schaff·hau·sen \shäf-'haủ-z°n\ **1** canton N Switzerland bordering on SW Germany *area* 115 *sq mi* (298 *sq km*), *pop* 71,210 **2** commune, its ✻ *pop* 34,101

Schaum·burg \'shäm-(,)bərg\ village NE Ill. NW of Chicago *pop* 68,586

Schaum·burg–Lip·pe \'shaủm-,bùrk-'li-pə\ state of Germany 1918–33 in NW between Westphalia & Hannover

Schel·de \'skel-də\ *or* **Scheldt** \'skelt\ *or French* **Es·caut** \e-'skō\ river 270 *mi* (434 *km*) W Europe flowing from N France through Belgium into North Sea in Netherlands

Sche·nec·ta·dy \skə-'nek-tə-dē\ city E N.Y. *pop* 65,566

Scher·er·ville \'shir-ər-,vil\ town NW Ind. *pop* 19,926

Sche·ve·ning·en \'skā-və-,niŋ-ə(n), 'skä-\ town SW Netherlands on North Sea W of The Hague

Schie·dam \skē-'däm, skē-\ commune SW Netherlands *pop* 71,117

Schles·wig \'shles-(,)wig, -(,)vik\ **1** *or Danish* **Sles·vig** \'slis-vē\ region N Germany & S Denmark in S Jutland Peninsula **2** city N Germany *pop about* 26,938

Schleswig–Hol·stein \-'hōl-,stīn, -,shtīn\ state of Germany & formerly of W. Germany consisting of Holstein & part of Schleswig ✻ Kiel *area* 6046 *sq mi* (15,659 *sq km*), *pop* 2,626,100

Scho·field Barracks \'skō-,fēld\ city Hawaii in *central* Oahu *pop* 19,597

Schou·ten Islands \'skaủ-t°n\ islands Indonesia in N W. Irian at mouth of Sarera Bay *area* 1230 *sq mi* (3198 *sq km*)

Schuyl·kill \'skü-k°l, 'skül-,kil\ river 131 *mi* (211 *km*) SE Pa. flowing SE into Delaware River at Philadelphia

Schwaben — see SWABIA

Schwarzwald — see BLACK FOREST

Schwein·furt \'shvīn-,fürt\ city S *central* Germany on Main River *pop* 54,520

Schweiz — see SWITZERLAND

Schwe·rin \shvā-'rēn\ city N Germany E of Hamburg *pop* 125,959

Schwyz \'shvēts\ **1** canton E *central* Switzerland *area* 351 *sq mi* (909 *sq km*), *pop* 108,576 **2** town, its ✻, E of Lucerne *pop* 12,596

Scil·ly, Isles of \'si-lē\ island group SW England off Land's End comprising 140 islands ✳ Hugh Town (on St. Mary's, largest island) *area* 6 *sq mi* (16 *sq km*), *pop* 2900 — see CORNWALL 2
Scil·lo·ni·an \si-'lō-nē-ən\ *adjective or noun*
Sci·o·to \sī-'ō-tə\ river 237 *mi* (381 *km*) Ohio flowing S into Ohio River
Scone \'skün\ locality E Scotland NE of Perth *pop* 3713
Sco·pus, Mount \'skō-pəs\ mountain Palestine in W Jordan in small area belonging to Israel
Scores·by Sound \'skōrz-bē, 'skôrz-\ inlet of Norwegian Sea E Greenland N of 70°N
Sco·tia Sea \'skō-shə\ part of the S Atlantic SE of Falkland Islands, W of S. Sandwich Islands, & N of S. Orkney Islands
Scot·land \'skät-lənd\ *or Latin* **Cal·e·do·nia** \,ka-lə-'dō-nyə, -nē-ə\ *Medieval Latin* **Sco·tia** \'skō-shə\ country N Great Britain; a division of United Kingdom of Great Britain and Northern Ireland ✳ Edinburgh *area* 29,797 *sq mi* (77,174 *sq km*), *pop* 5,102,400
Scotts Bluff National Monument \'skäts\ reservation W Nebr. on N. Platte River including **Scotts Bluff** (high butte that was a landmark on the Oregon Trail)
Scotts·dale \'skäts-,dāl\ city SW *central* Ariz. E of Phoenix *pop* 130,069
Scran·ton \'skran-t⁸n\ city NE Pa. *pop* 81,805
Scun·thorpe \'skən-,thôrp\ borough E England in Humberside WSW of Hull *pop* 60,500
Scu·ta·ri, Lake \'skü-tə-rē\ lake NW Albania & S Yugoslavia in Montenegro *area* 143 *sq mi* (370 *sq km*)
Scyth·ia \'si-thē-ə, -thē-\ the country of the ancient Scythians comprising parts of Europe & Asia in regions N & NE of Black Sea & E of Aral Sea
Sea Islands islands SE U.S. in the Atlantic off coast of S.C., Ga., & Fla. between mouths of Santee & St. Johns rivers
Seal Beach city SW Calif. SE of Los Angeles *pop* 25,098
Sea·side \'sē-,sīd\ city W Calif. on Monterey Bay *pop* 38,901
Se·at·tle \sē-'a-t⁸l\ city & port W Wash. between Puget Sound & Lake Washington *pop* 516,259 — **Se·at·tle·ite** \-t⁸l-,īt\ *noun*
Se·ba·go Lake \sə-'bā-(,)gō\ lake 13 *mi* (21 *km*) long SW Maine
Sebaste **1** *or* **Sebastia** — see SIVAS **2** — see SAMARIA
Se·cun·der·a·bad \si-'kən-də-rə-,bad, -,bäd\ city S *central* India in Andhra Pradesh, NE suburb of Hyderabad *pop* 167,461
Se·da·lia \sə-'dāl-yə\ city W *central* Mo. *pop* 19,800
Se·dan \si-'dan, *French* sə-'dä⁸\ city NE France on the Meuse NE of Reims *pop* 22,407
Sedge·moor \'sej-,mùr, -,mōr, -,môr\ tract of moorland SW England in *central* Somerset
Se·dom \sə-'dōm\ town Israel near S end of Dead Sea
Se·go·via \sā-'gō-vyə, sə-, -vē-ə\ **1** — see COCO **2** province N *central* Spain in Old Castile *area* 2683 *sq mi* (6949 *sq km*), *pop* 147,188 **3** commune, its ✳, NW of Madrid *pop* 54,142
Seim — see SEYM
Seine \'sān, 'sen\ river 480 *mi* (772 *km*) N France flowing NW into **Bay of the Seine** (inlet of English Channel)
Se·lang·or \sə-'läŋ-ər, -'laŋ-,gôr\ state *central* Malaysia (federation) on Strait of Malacca *area* 3074 *sq mi* (7962 *sq km*), *pop* 2,289,236
Sel·en·ga \,se-lən-'gä\ river N *central* Asia rising in W Mongolia & flowing into Lake Baikal
Se·leu·cia \sə-'lü-sh(ē-)ə\ **1** *or* **Seleucia Tra·che·o·tis** \,trā-kē-'ō-təs\ ancient city Asia Minor in Cilicia SW of Tarsus **2** ancient city, chief city of the Seleucid Empire; ruins now in Iraq on the Tigris SSE of Baghdad **3** *or* **Seleucia Pi·er·ia** \pī-'ir-ē-ə, -'er-\ ancient city Asia Minor N of mouth of the Orontes; port for Antioch
Sel·kirk \'sel-,kərk\ **1** *or* **Sel·kirk·shire** \-,shir, -shər\ former county SE Scotland **2** burgh *central* Borders region SE of Edinburgh *pop* 5417

Selkirk Mountains mountains SW Canada in SE British Columbia W of the Rockies; highest Mt. Sir Sandford 11,555 *ft* (3522 *m*)
Sel·ma \'sel-mə\ city *central* Ala. W of Montgomery *pop* 23,755
Se·ma·rang \sə-'mär-,äŋ\ city & port Indonesia in *central* Java W on N coast *pop* 1,250,971
Se·mey \'se-mā\ *or* **Sem·i·pa·la·tinsk** \,se-mi-pə-'lä-,tin(t)sk\ city NE Kazakhstan on the Irtysh *pop* 841,900
Sem·i·nole, Lake \'se-mə-,nōl\ reservoir SW Ga. & NW Fla. formed by confluence of Chattahoochee & Flint rivers & emptying by the Apalachicola
Sen·dai \(,)sen-'dī\ city Japan in NE Honshu *pop* 918,378
Sen·e·ca Lake \'se-ni-kə\ lake 35 *mi* (56 *km*) long W *central* N.Y.; one of the Finger Lakes
Sen·e·gal \,se-ni-'gôl, -'gäl, 'se-ni-,\ **1** river 1015 *mi* (1633 *km*) W Africa flowing from Fouta Djallon NW & W into the Atlantic **2** country W Africa on the Atlantic; a republic of the French Community, formerly a territory of French West Africa ✳ Dakar *area* 76,124 *sq mi* (197,161 *sq km*), *pop* 7,899,000 — **Sen·e·ga·lese** \,se-ni-gə-'lēz, -'lēs\ *adjective or noun*
Sen·e·gam·bia \,se-nə-'gam-bē-ə\ **1** region W Africa around Senegal & Gambia rivers **2** confederation of Senegal & Gambia 1982–89 — **Sen·e·gam·bi·an** \-ən\ *adjective or noun*
Sen·lac \'sen-,lak\ hill SE England in Sussex NW of Hastings
Sen·lis \sä⁸-lēs\ commune N France NNE of Paris *pop* 15,226
Sen·nar *or* **Sen·naar** \sə-'när\ region E Sudan chiefly between White Nile & Blue Nile rivers; an ancient kingdom
Sens \'sä⁸s\ city NE *central* France WSW of Troyes *pop* 27,755
Seoul \'sōl\ city NW S. Korea on Han River; formerly ✳ of Korea, since 1948 ✳ of S. Korea *pop* 9,639,110
Se·pik \'sā-pik\ river 600 *mi* (966 *km*) N Papua New Guinea
Sept-Îles \se-'tēl\ *or* **Seven Islands** town Canada in E Quebec at the mouth of St. Lawrence River *pop* 24,848
Se·quoia National Park \si-'kwói-ə\ reservation SE *central* Calif.; includes Mt. Whitney
Seram — see CERAM
Ser·bia \'sər-bē-ə\ *or formerly* **Ser·via** \-vē-ə\ federated republic *central* Yugoslavia traversed by Morava River; once a kingdom ✳ Belgrade *area* 34,115 *sq mi* (88,358 *sq km*), *pop* 9,823,000
Serbs, Croats, and Slovenes, Kingdom of the — see YUGOSLAVIA
Serdica — see SOFIA
Se·re·kun·da \,se-re-'kùn-də\ city W Gambia *pop* 68,824
Serendib — see CEYLON
Ser·en·ge·ti Plain \,ser-ən-'ge-tē\ area N Tanzania including **Serengeti National Park** (wild game reserve)
Ser·gi·pe \sər-'zhē-pə\ state NE Brazil ✳ Aracajú *area* 8441 *sq mi* (21,862 *sq km*), *pop* 1,492,400
Se·rin·ga·pa·tam \sə-,riŋ-gə-pə-'tam\ town S India N of city of Mysore
Se·ro·we \sə-'rō-ā\ city E Botswana *pop* 30,264
Ser·ra da Es·tre·la \'ser-ə-(,)dä-ish-'tre-lə\ mountain range Portugal; highest point Malhão da Estrela (highest in Portugal) 6532 *ft* (1991 *m*)
Serra do Mar \dü-'mär\ mountain range S Brazil along coast
Ser·rai \'ser-(,)e, -,ä\ city N Greece *pop* 50,875
Ser·ra Pa·ri·ma \'ser-ə-pə-'rē-mə\ mountain range N S. America on Venezuela-Brazil border SW of Pacaraima Mountains; source of the Orinoco
Ses·tos \'ses-təs\ ruined town Turkey in Europe on the Dardanelles (Hellespont) at narrowest point
Ses·to San Gio·van·ni \'ses-tō-,sän-jō-'vä-nē\ commune N Italy *pop* 89,517
Sète \'set\ *or formerly* **Cette** \'set\ commune & port S France SSW of Montpellier *pop* 41,916
Se·te Que·das \'se-tē-'kä-dəsh\ *or formerly* **Guaí·ra** \'gwī-(,)rä\ former cataract in Alto Paraná River on Brazil-Paraguay boundary; now submerged in reservoir formed by Itaipu Dam
Sé·tif \sā-'tēf\ commune NE Algeria *pop* 144,200

Se·tú·bal \sə-'tü-bəl, -,bäl\ city & port SW Portugal *pop* 77,285
Se·van \sə-'vän\ lake N Armenia *area* 525 *sq mi* (1360 *sq km*)
Se·vas·to·pol \sə-'vas-tə-,pōl, -,pól, -pəl\ ;se-və-'stō-pəl, -'stō-\ *or formerly* **Se·bas·to·pol** \'-bas-,; se-bə-\ city & port SW Crimea *pop* 366,000
Sev·ern \'se-vərn\ **1** inlet (**Severn River**) of Chesapeake Bay, in Md., on which Annapolis is situated **2** river 610 *mi* (982 *km*) Canada in NW Ontario flowing NE into Hudson Bay **3** river 210 *mi* (338 *km*) Great Britain flowing from E *central* Wales into Bristol Channel in England
Se·ver·na·ya Zem·lya \'se-vər-nə-yə-,zem-lē-'ä, 'sye-vər-nə-yə-zim-'lyä\ islands N Russia in Asia N of Taymyr Peninsula in Arctic Ocean between Kara & Laptev seas *area* 14,300 *sq mi* (37,180 *sq km*)
Se·vier \sə-'vir\ river 280 *mi* (451 *km*) SW *central* Utah flowing into **Sevier Lake** (25 *mi* or 40 *km* long; saline)
Se·ville \sə-'vil\ *or Spanish* **Se·vil·la** \sā-'vē-(,)yä\ **1** province SW Spain *area* 5406 *sq mi* (14,002 *sq km*), *pop* 1,619,703 **2** city, its ✳, on the Guadalquiver *pop* 659,126
Sè·vres \'sevr⁸\ commune N France SW of Paris *pop* 22,057
Sew·ard Peninsula \'sü-ərd\ peninsula 180 *mi* (290 *km*) long & 130 *mi* (209 *km*) wide W Alaska projecting into Bering Sea between Kotzebue & Norton sounds — see PRINCE OF WALES (Cape)
Sey·chelles \sā-'shel(z)\ island group W Indian Ocean NE of Madagascar; formerly a Brit. colony, a republic in the Commonwealth of Nations since 1976 ✳ Victoria (on Mahé Is.) *area* 107 *sq mi* (277 *sq km*), *pop* 68,598
Sey·han \sā-'hän\ **1** *or* **Sei·hun** \-'hün\ river Turkey flowing SSW into the Mediterranean **2** — see ADANA
Seym *or* **Seim** \'säm\ river 460 *mi* (740 *km*) N Ukraine & Russia in Europe flowing W into the Desna
Sfax \'sfaks\ city & port Tunisia on Gulf of Gabes *pop* 221,770
's Gravenhage — see HAGUE (The)
Shaan·xi \'shän-'shē\ *or* **Shen·si** \'shen-'sē, 'shən-'shē\ province N *central* China bordering on the Huang ✳ Xi'an *area* 75,598 *sq mi* (195,799 *sq km*), *pop* 32,882,403
Sha·ba \'shä-bə\ *or formerly* **Ka·tan·ga** \kə-'täŋ-gə, -'taŋ-\ region SE Democratic Republic of the Congo; chief city Lubumbashi
Shah·ja·han·pur \,shä-jə-'hän-,pùr\ city N India in *central* Uttar Pradesh NNW of Kanpur *pop* 237,663
Shah·pur \shä-'pùr\ ancient city SW Iran W of Shiraz
Shak·er Heights \'shā-kər\ city NE Ohio E of Cleveland *pop* 30,831
Shakh·ty \'shäk-tē, 'shak-\ *or formerly* **Ale·ksan·drovsk Gru·shev·ski** \,a-lik-'sän-drəfsk-grü-'shef-skē\ city S Russia in Europe NE of Rostov *pop* 228,000
Shan \'shän, 'shan\ *or formerly* **Federated Shan States** state E Myanmar comprising a mountainous region (the **Shan Hills**) ✳ Taunggyi
Shan·dong \'shän-'dòŋ\ **1** *or* **Shan–tung** \'shän-'təŋ, 'shän-'dùŋ\ peninsula E China projecting ENE between Yellow Sea & Bo Hai **2** province E China including Shandong Peninsula ✳ Jinan *area* 59,189 *sq mi* (153,300 *sq km*), *pop* 84,392,827
Shang·hai \shaŋ-'hī\ municipality & port E China on the Huangpu near the Chang estuary *pop* 7,469,509
Shang·qiu *or* **Shang–ch'iu** \'shäŋ-'chyü\ city E China in E Henan *pop* 164,880
Shan·non \'sha-nən\ river 230 *mi* (370 *km*) W Ireland flowing S & W into the Atlantic
Shan·tou \'shän-'tō\ *or* **Swa·tow** \'swä-'taù\ city & port SE China in E Guangdong on S. China Sea *pop* 578,630

\ə\ abut \⁸\ kitten \ər\ further \a\ ash \ā\ ace
\ä\ mop, mar \aù\ out \ch\ chin \e\ bet \ē\ easy
\g\ go \i\ hit \ī\ ice \j\ job \ŋ\ sing \ō\ go
\ò\ law \òi\ boy \th\ thin \th\ the \ü\ loot \ù\ foot
\y\ yet \zh\ vision *see also* Guide to Pronunciation

Shan·xi \\'shän-'shē\\ *or* **Shan·si** \\-'sē, -'shē\\ province N China bordering on the Huang ✳ Taiyuan *area* 60,656 *sq mi* (157,099 *sq km*), *pop* 28,759,014

Shao·xing *or* **Shao–hsing** \\'shaú-'shiŋ\\ city E China in N Zhejiang SE of Hangzhou *pop* 179,818

Shao·yang \\'shaú-'yäŋ\\ *or formerly* **Pao·king** \\'baú-'chiŋ\\ city SE China in *central* Hunan W of Hengyang *pop* 247,227

Shari — see CHARI

Sharjah — see ASH SHARIQAH

Shark Bay inlet of Indian Ocean 150 *mi* (241 *km*) long W Western Australia, at *about* 25°S

Shar·on, Plain of \\'shar-ən, 'sher-\\ region Israel on coast between Mt. Carmel & Jaffa

Sha·shi \\'shä-'shē\\ *or* **Sha–shih** \\-'shir, -'shē\\ city E *central* China in S Hubei on the Chang *pop* 281,352

Shas·ta, Mount \\'shas-tə\\ mountain 14,162 *ft* (4316 *m*) N Calif. in Cascade Range; an isolated volcanic cone

Shatt al Ar·ab \\,shat-al-'ar-əb\\ river 120 *mi* (193 *km*) SE Iraq formed by the Tigris & the Euphrates & flowing SE into Persian Gulf

Shaw·an·gunk Mountains \\'shäŋ-gəm, shə-'wän-(,)gəŋk\\ mountain ridge SE N.Y.; part of Kittatinny Mountain

Shaw·nee \\shó-'nē, 'shó-,; shä-'nē, 'shä-\\ **1** city NE Kans. S of Kansas City *pop* 37,993 **2** city *central* Okla. *pop* 26,017

Shcherbakov — see RYBINSK

She·ba \\'shē-bə\\ *or* **Sa·ba** \\'sä-bə\\ ancient country S Arabia, probably Yemen

She·boy·gan \\shi-'bói-gən\\ city & port E Wis. *pop* 49,676

Shechem — see NABLUS

Shef·field \\'she-,fēld\\ city N England in S. Yorkshire *pop* 499,700

Shel·i·kof \\'she-li-,kóf\\ strait S Alaska between Alaska Peninsula & islands of Kodiak & Afognak

Shel·ton \\'shel-t°n\\ city SW Conn. *pop* 35,418

Shen·an·do·ah \\,she-nən-'dō-ə, ,sha-nə-'dō-ə\\ river 55 *mi* (88 *km*) N Va. flowing NE between Allegheny & Blue Ridge Mountains across NE tip of W.Va. & into the Potomac; forms **Shenandoah Valley**

Shenandoah National Park reservation N Va. in Blue Ridge Mountains

Shensi — see SHAANXI

Shen·yang \\shən-'yäŋ\\ *or* **Muk·den** \\'múk-dən, 'mək-; múk-'den\\ *or formerly* **Feng·tien** \\'fəŋ-'tyen\\ city NE China in S of Liaoning; chief city of Manchuria *pop* 3,603,712

Sher·brooke \\'shər-,brúk\\ town E Canada in S Quebec *pop* 76,429

Sher·man \\'shər-mən\\ city NE Tex. N of Dallas *pop* 31,601

's Her·to·gen·bosch \\,ser-,tō-gən-'bós, -kən-\\ city S Netherlands ✳ of N. Brabant *pop* 81,471

Sher·wood Forest \\'shər-,wúd- *also* 'sher-\\ ancient royal forest *central* England chiefly in Nottinghamshire

Shet·land \\'shet-lənd\\ **1** islands N Scotland NE of the Orkneys **2** *or* **Zet·land** \\'zet-\\ region comprising the Shetlands ✳ Lerwick (on Mainland Is.) *area* 550 *sq mi* (1430 *sq km*), *pop* 22,270 — **Shet·land·er** \\'shet-lən-dər\\ *noun*

Siam — see THAILAND

Siam, Gulf of — see THAILAND (Gulf of)

Sian — see XI'AN

Siangtan — see XIANGTAN

Shey·enne \\shī-'an, -'en\\ river 325 *mi* (523 *km*) SE *central* N.Dak. flowing into Red River

Shi·bīn al–Kawm *or* **Shi·bīn el Kôm** \\shi-,bēn-el-'kōm\\ city N Egypt *pop* 153,000

Shigatse — see XIGAZE

Shi·jia·zhuang *or* **Shih–chia–chuang** \\'shir-'jyä-'jwäŋ, 'shē-\\ city NE China ✳ of Hebei *pop* 1,068,439

Shi·kar·pur \\shi-'kär-,púr\\ city S *central* Pakistan in Sind *pop* 88,000

Shi·ko·ku \\shē-'kō-(,)kü\\ island S Japan E of Kyushu *area* 7245 *sq mi* (18,765 *sq km*) *pop* 4,195,106

Shil·ka \\'shil-kə\\ river 345 *mi* (555 *km*) SE Russia in Asia flowing NE to unite with the Argun forming the Amur

Shil·long \\shi-'lóŋ\\ city NE India ✳ of Meghalaya *pop* 222,273

Shi·loh \\'shī-(,)lō\\ **1** locality SW Tenn., site of Civil War battle **2** ancient village Palestine W of Jordan River on slope of Mt. Ephraim

Shi·mi·zu \\shē-'mē-(,)zü, 'shē-mē-,zü\\ city & port Japan in *central* Honshu on Suruga Bay; port for Shizuoka *pop* 241,524

Shi·mo·da \\shē-'mō-də, -,dä\\ city & port Japan in S Honshu SW of Yokohama on Sagami Sea *pop* 30,081

Shi·mo·no·se·ki \\,shē-mō-nō-'se-kē\\ *or formerly* **Ba·kan** \\'bä-,kän\\ city & port Japan in SW Honshu on Shimonoseki Strait *pop* 262,643

Shimonoseki Strait strait Japan between Honshu & Kyushu connecting Inland Sea & Korea Strait

Shi·nar \\'shī-nər, -,när\\ a country known to the early Hebrews as a plain in Babylonia; probably Sumer

Ship Rock isolated mountain 7178 *ft* (2188 *m*) N.Mex. in NW corner

Shi·raz \\shi-'räz, -'raz\\ city SW *central* Iran *pop* 848,289

Shi·re \\'shē-(,)rā, 'shir-ē\\ river 250 *mi* (400 *km*) S Malawi & *central* Mozambique flowing from Lake Malawi S into the Zambezi

Shi·shal·din \\shi-'shal-dən\\ volcano 9372 *ft* (2856 *m*) SW Alaska on Unimak Is.; highest in Aleutian Range

Shi·zu·o·ka \\,shē-zü-'wō-kä\\ city Japan in *central* Honshu near Suruga Bay SW of Shimizu *pop* 472,199

Shko·dër \\'shkō-dər\\ city NW Albania *pop* 81,800

Sho·la·pur \\'shō-lə-,púr\\ *or* **So·la·pur** \\'sō-\\ city W India in SE Maharashtra SE of Bombay *pop* 514,461

Shore·ditch \\'shór-,dich, 'shór-\\ former metropolitan borough N *central* London, England, now part of Hackney

Shore·view \\'shór-,vyü, 'shór-\\ city E Minn. *pop* 24,587

Short·land Islands \\'shórt-lənd\\ islands W Pacific in the Solomons off S end of Bougainville

Sho·sho·ne \\shə-'shō-nē, shə-'shōn\\ river 120 *mi* (193 *km*) NW Wyo. flowing NE into Bighorn River

Shoshone Falls waterfall 210 *ft* (64 *m*) S Idaho in Snake River

Shreve·port \\'shrēv-,pōrt, -,pórt\\ city NW La. on Red River *pop* 198,525

Shrews·bury **1** \\'sh(r)üz-,ber-ē, -,b(ə-)rē\\ town E Mass. E of Worcester *pop* 24,146 **2** \\British often 'shrōz-\\ borough W England ✳ of Shropshire *pop* 59,826

Shrop·shire \\'shräp-shər, -,shir\\ *or* **Sal·op** \\'sa-ləp, -,läp\\ county W England bordering on Wales ✳ Shrewsbury *area* 1396 *sq mi* (3616 *sq km*), *pop* 401,600

Shuang·liao \\'shwäŋ-'lyaú\\ *or formerly* **Liao·yuan** \\'lyaú-'ywen\\ city NE China in W Jilin S of Changchun on the Liao

Shu·ma·gin \\'shü-mə-gən\\ islands SW Alaska S of Alaska Peninsula; largest Unga

Shushan — see SUSA

Shym·kent \\shim-'kent\\ *or* **Chim·kent** \\chim-\\ city S Kazakhstan N of Tashkent *pop* 438,800

Si — see XI

Si·al·kot \\sē-'äl-,kōt\\ city NE Pakistan NNE of Lahore *pop* 308,000

Si·be·ria \\sī-'bir-ē-ə\\ region N Asia in Russia extending from the Urals to the Pacific; roughly coextensive with Russia in Asia — **Si·be·ri·an** \\-ən\\ *adjective or noun*

Si·biu \\sē-'byü\\ city W *central* Romania in Transylvania *pop* 184,036

Si·bu·yan Sea \\,sē-bü-'yän\\ body of water *central* Philippines bounded by Mindoro, S Luzon, & the Visayan Islands

Sic·i·ly \\'si-s(ə-)lē\\ *or Italian* **Si·ci·lia** \\sē-'chēl-yä\\ *or ancient* **Si·cil·ia** \\sə-'sil-yə\\ *or* **Tri·nac·ria** \\trə-'na-krē-ə, trī-\\ island S Italy in the Mediterranean; a region ✳ Palermo *area* 9925 *sq mi* (25,706 *sq km*), *pop* 5,172,785 — **Si·cil·ian** \\sə-'sil-yən\\ *adjective or noun*

Si·cy·on \\'si-shē-,än, 'si-sē-\\ *or Greek* **Sik·y·on** \\'sē-kē-,ón\\ ancient city S Greece in NE Peloponnese NW of Corinth

Si·di Bar·râ·ni \\'sē-dē-bə-'rä-nē\\ village NW Egypt on coast

Sidi Bel Ab·bès \\'sē-dē-,bel-ə-'bes\\ commune NW Algeria *pop* 152,778

Si·don \\'sī-d°n\\ *or Arabic* **Sai·da** \\'sī-də\\ city & port SW Lebanon; a chief city of ancient Phoenicia — **Si·do·ni·an** \\sī-'dō-nē-ən\\ *adjective or noun*

Sid·ra, Gulf of \\'si-drə\\ *or* **Gulf of Sir·te** \\'sir-tə\\ *or ancient* **Syr·tis Major** \\'sər-təs\\ inlet of the Mediterranean on coast of Libya

Sie·ben·ge·bir·ge \\'zē-bən-gə-,bir-gə\\ hills W Germany on right bank of the Rhine SSE of Bonn — see DRACHENFELS

Si·ena *or* **Si·en·na** \\sē-'e-nä\\ commune *central* Italy in Tuscany *pop* 58,278 — **Si·en·ese** *or* **Si·en·nese** \\,sē-ə-'nēz, -'nēs\\ *adjective or noun*

Si·er·ra Blan·ca Peak \\sē-,er-ə-'blaŋ-kə, 'syer-ä-'bläŋ-kä\\ mountain 12,003 *ft* (3658 *m*) S *central* N.Mex. in Sierra Blanca Range of the Sacramento Mountains

Sierra de Gre·dos \\dā-'grā-(,)dōs, thā-\\ mountain range W *central* Spain, SW extension of Sierra de Guadarrama; highest peak Plaza de Almanzor *about* 8500 *ft* (2591 *m*)

Sierra de Gua·dar·ra·ma \\dā-,gwä-dä-'rä-mä\\ mountain range *central* Spain; highest peak Pico de Peñalara 7970 *ft* (2429 *m*)

Sier·ra Le·one \\sē-,er-ə-lē-'ōn, ,sir-ə-, -lē-'ō-nē\\ country W Africa on the Atlantic; a dominion of the Commonwealth of Nations ✳ Freetown *area* 27,699 *sq mi* (71,740 *sq km*), *pop* 4,491,000 — **Sierra Le·on·ean** \\-'ō-nē-ən\\ *adjective or noun*

Si·er·ra Ma·dre del Sur \\sē-,er-ə-'mä-drä-del-'sür, 'syer-ä-'mä-thrä-thel-'sür\\ mountain range S Mexico along Pacific coast in Guerrero & Oaxaca

Sierra Madre Oc·ci·den·tal \\,äk-sə-,den-'täl, ,ók-sē-,then-'täl\\ mountain range NW Mexico parallel to the Pacific coast

Sierra Madre Ori·en·tal \\,ōr-ē-,en-'täl, ,ór-\\ mountain range E Mexico parallel to coast of Gulf of Mexico

Sierra Mo·re·na \\mō-'rā-nä\\ mountain range SW Spain between the Guadiana & the Guadalquivir; highest peak Estrella 4339 *ft* (1322 *m*)

Sierra Ne·va·da \\nə-'va-də, -'vä-\\ **1** mountain range E Calif. — see WHITNEY (Mount) **2** mountain range S Spain; highest peak Mulhacén *about* 11,410 *ft* (3478 *m*)

Sierra Nevada de Mérida — see CORDILLERA DE MERIDA

Sierra Nevada de San·ta Mar·ta \\dā-,santə-'märt-ə, thä-,sän-tä-\\ mountain range N Colombia on Caribbean coast

Sierra Vis·ta \\'vis-tə\\ city SE Ariz. *pop* 32,983

Si·kang \\'shē-'käŋ\\ former province S China ✳ Yaan

Si·kho·te–Alin \\'sē-kə-,tä-ə-'lēn\\ mountain range SE Russia in Asia in Maritime Territory

Sik·kim \\'si-kəm, -,kim\\ former country SE Asia on S slope of the Himalayas between Nepal & Bhutan; since 1975 a state of India ✳ Gangtok *area* 2744 *sq mi* (7107 *sq km*), *pop* 406,457 — **Sik·kim·ese** \\,si-kə-'mēz, -'mēs\\ *adjective or noun*

Si·le·sia \\sī-'lē-zh(ē-)ə, sə-, -sh(ē-)ə\\ region E *central* Europe in valley of the upper Oder bordering on Sudety Mountains; formerly chiefly in Germany, now chiefly in E Czech Republic & SW Poland — **Si·le·sian** \\-zh(ē-)ən, -sh(ē-)ən\\ *adjective or noun*

Sim·birsk \\sim-'birsk\\ *or 1924–91* **Ul·ya·novsk** \\úl-'yä-nəfsk\\ city SE *central* Russia in Europe on the Volga *pop* 656,000

Sim·coe, Lake \\'sim-(,)kō\\ lake E Canada in SE Ontario SE of Georgian Bay *area* 280 *sq mi* (728 *sq km*)

Sim·fe·ro·pol \\,sim(p)-fə-'ró-pəl, -'rō-\\ city in the Crimea *pop* 353,000

Si·mi Valley \\sē-'mē\\ city SW Calif. W of Los Angeles *pop* 100,217

Sim·la \\'sim-lə\\ city N India N of Delhi ✳ of Himachal Pradesh & former summer ✳ of India *pop* 81,443

Si·mons·town \\'sī-mənz-,taún\\ town & port SW Republic of South Africa in Western Cape province on False Bay S of Cape Town

Sim·plon Pass \\'sim-,plän\\ mountain pass 6590 *ft* (2009 *m*) in Lepontine Alps between Switzerland & Italy in Valais & Piedmont

Simplon Tunnel tunnel *about* 12 *mi* (19 *km*) long through Monte Leone near Simplon Pass

Sims·bury \'simz-ˌber-ē, -b(ə-)rē\ town N Conn. pop 22,023

Si·nai \'sī-ˌnī also -nē-ˌī\ peninsula extension of continent of Asia NE Egypt between Red Sea & the Mediterranean — **Si·na·it·ic** \ˌsī-nē-'i-tik\ adjective

Sinai, Mount — see HOREB (Mount)

Si·na·loa \ˌsē-nä-'lō-ä\ state W Mexico bordering on Gulf of California ✳ Culiacán area 22,429 sq mi (58,091 sq km), pop 2,204,054

Sind or **Sindh** \'sind\ province S Pakistan in lower Indus valley ✳ Karachi

Sin·ga·pore \'siŋ-ə-ˌpōr, -ˌpȯr also 'siŋ-gə-\ **1** island Malay Archipelago in S. China Sea off S end of Malay Peninsula; formerly a Brit. crown colony, from 1963 to 1965 a state of Malaysia (federation), an independent republic in the Commonwealth of Nations since 1965, area 225 sq mi (585 sq km), pop 2,685,400 **2** city & port, its ✳, on Singapore Strait pop 206,500 — **Sin·ga·por·ean** \ˌsiŋ-ə-'pōr-ē-ən, -'pȯr- also 'siŋ-gə-\ adjective or noun

Singapore Strait channel SE Asia between Singapore Is. & Riau Archipelago connecting Strait of Malacca & S. China Sea

Sining — see XINING

Sinkiang Uighur — see XINJIANG UYGUR

Si·nop \sə-'nȯp\ or ancient **Si·no·pe** \-'nō-pē\ town & port N Turkey on peninsula in Black Sea NW of Ankara pop 25,631

Sinsiang — see XINXIANG

Sint–Gillis — see SAINT-GILLES

Sint Maarten — see SAINT MARTIN

Sin·tra or **Cin·tra** \'sēn-trə\ city W Portugal NW of Lisbon pop 262,447

Sin·ui·ju \'sin-'wē-'jü\ city W N. Korea on the Yalu opposite Antung, China pop 289,000

Sion 1 \sē-'ō̃\ or German **Sit·ten** \'zi-t°n, 'si-\ commune SW central Switzerland ✳ of Valais pop 25,350 **2** — see ZION 2

Sioux City \'sü\ city NW Iowa on Missouri River pop 80,505

Sioux Falls city SE S.Dak. on the Big Sioux pop 100,814

Si·ping \'sə-'piŋ\ or **Ssu–p'ing** \'sə-'piŋ\ or formerly **Sze·ping·kai** \'sə-'piŋ-'gī\ city NE China in Jilin SW of Changchun pop 317,223

Sip·par \si-'pär\ ancient city of Babylonia on the Euphrates SSW of modern Baghdad; Sargon's capital

Siracusa — see SYRACUSE

Si·ret \si-'ret\ river 280 mi (450 km) E Romania flowing from the Carpathians SE into the Danube

Sí·ros \'sē-ˌrȯs\ **1** or **Syros** island Greece in the Cyclades S of Andros **2** — see ERMOÚPOLIS

Sis·ki·you Mountains \'sis-ki-ˌyü\ mountains N Calif. & SW Oreg., a range of Klamath Mountains; highest Mt. Ashland (in Oreg.) 7533 ft (2296 m)

Sit·tang \'si-ˌtäŋ\ river 260 mi (418 km) E central Myanmar flowing S into Gulf of Martaban

Sit·twe \'si-ˌtwä\ or formerly **Ak·yab** \a-'kyab\ city & port N Myanmar; chief town of Arakan coast pop 42,329

Si·vas \si-'väs\ or ancient **Se·bas·te** \sə-'bas-tē\ or **Se·bas·tia** \sə-'bas-ch(ē-)ə, -tē-ə\ city E central Turkey on the upper Kizil Irmak pop 221,512

Si·wa \'sē-wə\ or ancient **Am·mo·ni·um** \ə-'mō-nē-əm\ oasis & town NW Egypt W of Qattara Depression pop 4999

Si·wa·lik Range \si-'wä-lik\ foothills of the Himalayas N India extending SE from N Punjab into Uttar Pradesh

Sjæl·land \'she-ˌlän\ island, largest of islands of Denmark; site of Copenhagen area 2709 sq mi (7043 sq km) pop 1,971,946

Skag·er·rak \'ska-gə-ˌrak\ arm of the North Sea between Norway & Denmark

Skag·it \'ska-jət\ river 163 mi (262 km) SW British Columbia & NW Wash. flowing S & W into Puget Sound

Skan·e·at·e·les Lake \ˌska-nē-'at-ləs, ˌski-nē-\ lake 16 mi (26 km) long central N.Y. SW of Syracuse; one of the Finger Lakes

Skaw, The \'skȯ\ or **Ska·gens Od·de** \'skä-gənz-ˌȯ-də\ cape Denmark at N extremity of Jutland

Skee·na \'skē-nə\ river 360 mi (579 km) Canada in W British Columbia flowing S & W into Hecate Strait

Skid·daw \'ski-ˌdȯ\ mountain 3053 ft (930 m) NW England in NW central Cumbria

Skik·da \'skik-(ˌ)dä\ or formerly **Phi·lippe·ville** \'fi-ləp-ˌvil, fi-ˌlēp-'vēl\ city & port NE Algeria N of Constantine pop 128,747

Ski·ros \'skē-ˌrȯs\ island Greece in the Northern Sporades E of Euboea

Sko·kie \'skō-kē\ village NE Ill. N of Chicago pop 59,432

Skop·je \'skȯ-pye, -pyə\ city ✳ of Macedonia on the Vardar pop 563,301

Skunk river 264 mi (425 km) SE Iowa flowing SE into Mississippi River

Skye \'skī\ island Scotland, one of the Inner Hebrides area 670 sq mi (1742 sq km)

Slave \'släv\ river 258 mi (415 km) Canada flowing from W end of Lake Athabasca N into Great Slave Lake

Slave Coast region W Africa bordering on Bight of Benin between Benin & Volta rivers

Slav·kov \'släf-ˌkȯf, 'släv-ˌkȯv\ or **Aus·ter·litz** \'ȯ-stər-ˌlits, 'aú-\ town SE Czech Republic ESE of Brno

Sla·vo·nia \slə-'vō-nē-ə, -nyə\ region E Croatia between the Sava, the Drava, & the Danube — **Sla·vo·ni·an** \-nē-ən, -nyən\ adjective or noun

Slea·ford \'slē-fərd\ town E England in SW Lincolnshire SSE of Lincoln

Slesvig — see SCHLESWIG

Sli·dell \slī-'del\ town SE La. NE of New Orleans pop 24,124

Slide Mountain \'slīd\ mountain 4204 ft (1281 m) SE N.Y. W of Kingston; highest in the Catskills

Sli·go \'slī-(ˌ)gō\ **1** county N Ireland (republic) in N Connacht area 693 sq mi (1795 sq km), pop 54,756 **2** municipal borough & port, its ✳, on **Sligo Bay** (inlet of Atlantic Ocean) pop 17,297

Slough \'slaú\ borough SE central England in Berkshire pop 98,600

Slo·va·kia \slō-'vä-kē-ə, -'va-\ or **Slo·ven·sko** \'slō-ven-ˌskȯ\ country central Europe; a constituent republic of Czechoslovakia 1918–92 ✳ Bratislava area 18,923 sq mi (49,011 sq km), pop 5,329,000

Slo·ve·nia \slō-'vē-nē-ə, -nyə\ country S Europe N & W of Croatia; a federated republic of Yugoslavia 1946–91 ✳ Ljubljana area 7819 sq mi (20,251 sq km), pop 1,997,000

Smith·field \'smith-ˌfēld\ city N R.I. NW of Providence pop 19,163

Smoky Hill river 540 mi (869 km) central Kans. flowing E to unite with Republican River forming the Kansas River

Smo·lensk \smō-'len(t)sk\ city W Russia in Europe on the upper Dnieper WSW of Moscow pop 352,000

Smyr·na \'smər-nə\ **1** town NW Ga. NW of Atlanta pop 30,981 **2** — see IZMIR

Snake \'snāk\ river 1038 mi (1670 km) NW U.S. flowing from NW Wyo. across S Idaho & into Columbia River in Wash.

Snake Range mountain range E Nevada

Sno·qual·mie Falls \snō-'kwäl-mē\ waterfall 270 ft (80 m) W central Wash. in **Snoqualmie River** 70 mi (118 km)

Snow — see MAOKE

Snow·don \'snō-d°n\ massif 3560 ft (1085 m) NW Wales in Gwynedd; highest point in Wales

Snow·do·nia \snō-'dō-nē-ə, -nyə\ mountain region NW Wales centering around Snowdon

Snowy river 278 mi (447 km) SE Australia flowing from Snowy Mountains to the Pacific in SE Victoria

Snowy Mountains mountains SE Australia in SE New South Wales

So·bat \'sō-ˌbat\ river 460 mi (740 km) W Ethiopia & SE Sudan flowing W into White Nile River

Soča — see ISONZO

So·chi \'sō-chē\ city & port S Russia in Europe on NE coast of Black Sea pop 344,000

So·ci·e·ty Islands \sə-'sī-ə-tē\ or French **Îles de la So·ci·é·té** \ēl-də-lä-sō-syā-'tā\ islands S Pacific belonging to France ✳ Papeete (on Tahiti) area 621 sq mi (1608 sq km), pop 162,573

So·cor·ro \sə-'kȯr-(ˌ)ō\ town Tex., a S suburb of El Paso pop 22,995

So·co·tra \sə-'kō-trə\ island Indian Ocean E of Gulf of Aden ✳ Tamrida (Hadibu) area 1400 sq mi (3640 sq km), pop 8000

Sö·der·täl·je \ˌsə(r)-dər-'tel-yə, ˌsœ-\ town SE Sweden, a suburb of Stockholm pop 81,460

Sod·om \'sä-dəm\ city of ancient Palestine in plain of Jordan River

So·fia \'sō-fē-ə, 'sȯ-, sō-'\ or Bulgarian **So·fi·ya** \'sȯ-fē-ə\ or ancient **Ser·di·ca** \'sər-di-kə\ or **Sar·di·ca** \'sär-\ city W Bulgaria, its ✳ pop 1,141,142

Sog·di·a·na \ˌsäg-dē-'a-nə, -'ä-nə, -'ā-nə\ province of ancient Persian Empire between the Jaxartes (Syr Darya) & Oxus (Amu Darya) ✳ Maracanda (Samarqand)

Sog·ne Fjord \'sȯŋ-nə\ inlet of Norwegian Sea SW Norway; longest fjord in Norway

So·hâg \sō-'haj\ city central Egypt on the Nile SE of Asyût pop 85,300

So·ho \'sō-ˌhō\ district of central London, England, in Westminster

Sois·sons \swä-'sō̃\ commune N France NW of Paris pop 32,144

Solapur — see SHOLAPUR

So·lent, The \'sō-lənt\ channel S England between Isle of Wight & the mainland

So·li·hull \ˌsō-li-'həl\ borough central England in W. Midlands SE of Birmingham pop 194,100

So·li·mões \ˌsü-lē-'mȯĩnsh\ the upper Amazon, Brazil, from Peruvian border to the mouth of Negro River

So·ling·en \'zō-liŋ-ən, 'sō-\ city W Germany in the Ruhr ESE of Düsseldorf pop 165,924

Sol·na \'sȯl-ˌnä\ city E Sweden, N suburb of Stockholm pop 51,427

Sol·o·mon Islands \'sä-lə-mən\ islands W Pacific E of New Guinea divided between Papua New Guinea & the independent country (formerly a Brit. protectorate) of the Solomon Islands (✳ Honiara) area 11,500 sq mi (29,785 sq km), pop 349,000

Solomon Sea arm of Coral Sea W of Solomon Islands

So·lo·thurn \'zō-lə-ˌtúrn, 'sō-\ or French **So·leure** \sō-'lər, -'lœr\ **1** canton NW Switzerland area 305 sq mi (790 sq km), pop 223,803 **2** commune, its ✳, on the Aare pop 15,531

Sol·way Firth \'säl-ˌwä\ inlet of Irish Sea in Great Britain on boundary between England & Scotland

So·ma·lia \sō-'mä-lē-ə, sə-, -'mäl-yə\ country E Africa bordering on Gulf of Aden & Indian Ocean; formed 1960 by union of Brit. Somaliland & Italian Somaliland ✳ Mogadishu area 246,154 sq mi (637,539 sq km), pop 8,050,000 — **So·ma·lian** \-'mä-lē-ən, -'mäl-yən\ adjective or noun

So·ma·li·land \sō-'mä-lē-ˌland, sə-\ region E Africa comprising Somalia, Djibouti, & the Ogaden region of E Ethiopia

Som·er·set \'sə-mər-ˌset, -sət\ or **Som·er·set·shire** \-ˌshir, -shər\ county SW England ✳ Taunton area 1383 sq mi (3582 sq km), pop 459,100

Somerset Island island N Canada in Northwest Territories N of Boothia Peninsula area 9370 sq mi (24,362 sq km)

Somerset Nile — see NILE

Som·er·ville \'sə-mər-ˌvil\ city E Mass. N of Cambridge pop 76,210

So·mes \sō-'mesh\ or Hungarian **Sza·mos** \'sȯ-ˌmȯsh\ river NE Hungary & NW Romania flowing NW into the Tisza

Somme \'säm, 'sȯm\ river about 150 mi (241 km) N France flowing NW into the English Channel

Song·hua \'sȯŋ-'hwä\ or **Sun·ga·ri** \'süŋ-gə-rē\ river over 1000 mi (1609 km) NE China in E Manchuria flowing from N. Korea border NW & NE into the Amur; dammed in upper part to form Songhua Reservoir

Song·nam \'sȯŋ-ˌnäm\ city NW S. Korea pop 447,692

So·no·ra \sə-'nȯr-ə, -'nȯr-\ **1** river 250 mi (400 km) NW Mexico flowing NW into upper Gulf of California **2** state NW Mexico bordering on U.S. & Gulf of California ✳ Hermosillo

area 71,403 *sq mi* (184,934 *sq km*), *pop* 1,823,606 — **So·no·ran** \-ən\ *adjective or noun*
Sonoran Desert desert SW U.S. & NW Mexico in S Ariz., SE Calif., & N Sonora
Soo Canals — see SAULT SAINTE MARIE CANALS
Soochow — see SUZHOU
Sop·ron \'shō-ˌprōn\ city W Hungary *pop* 57,500
Sorata — see ILLAMPU
Sorbiodunum — see OLD SARUM
So·ria \'sōr-ē-ə, 'sȯr-\ **1** province N central Spain *area* 3972 *sq mi* (10,287 *sq km*), *pop* 94,537 **2** commune, its ✳, W of Saragossa *pop* 32,360
So·ro·ca·ba \ˌsȯr-ə-'ka-bə, ˌsōr-, -'kä-\ city SE Brazil in SE São Paulo state *metropolitan area pop* 377,270
Sor·ren·to \sə-'ren-(ˌ)tō\ *or ancient* **Sur·ren·tum** \sə-'ren-təm\ commune & port S Italy on S side of Bay of Naples
Sos·no·wiec \sä-'snō-ˌvyets\ city SW Poland NE of Katowice *pop* 259,269
Sou·frière \ˌsü-frē-'er\ **1** volcano 4813 *ft* (1467 *m*) French West Indies in S Basse-Terre, Guadeloupe **2** volcano 4048 *ft* (1234 *m*) Brit. West Indies on St. Vincent Is.
Sou·ris \'sȯr-əs\ river 450 *mi* (724 *km*) Canada & U.S. flowing from SE Saskatchewan SE into N N.Dak. & N into the Assiniboine in SW Manitoba
Sousse \'süs\ *or ancient* **Had·ru·me·tum** \ˌha-drə-'mē-təm\ city & port NE Tunisia *pop* 69,530
South Africa, Republic of country S Africa S of the Limpopo, Molopo, & Orange rivers bordering on Atlantic & Indian oceans; a republic, until 1961 (as **Union of South Africa**) a Brit. dominion; administrative ✳ Pretoria, legislative ✳ Cape Town, judicial ✳ Bloemfontein *area* 471,445 *sq mi* (1,221,043 *sq km*), *pop* 30,193,000
Sou·thall \'saú-ˌthȯl\ former municipal borough S England in Middlesex, now part of Ealing
South America continent of the western hemisphere lying between the Atlantic & Pacific oceans SE of N. America & chiefly S of the equator *area* 6,880,706 *sq mi* (17,821,029 *sq km*) — **South American** *adjective or noun*
South·amp·ton \saú-'ham(p)-tən, saúth-'ham(p)-\ city & port S England in Hampshire on **Southampton Water** (estuary of Test River) *pop* 194,400
Southampton Island island N Canada in Northwest Territories, between Hudson Bay & Foxe Channel *area* 15,700 *sq mi* (40,820 *sq km*)
South Arabia, Federation of former Brit. protectorate comprising crown colony of Aden & numerous semi-independent Arab sultanates & emirates; made part of People's Democratic Republic of Yemen 1967
South Atlantic — see ATLANTIC OCEAN
South Australia state S Australia ✳ Adelaide *area* 380,070 *sq mi* (988,182 *sq km*), *pop* 1,462,900
South Bend \'bend\ city N Ind. NW of Fort Wayne *pop* 105,511
South Canadian — see CANADIAN
South Cape — see KA LAE
South Car·o·li·na \ˌkar-(ə)-'lī-nə\ state SE U.S. ✳ Columbia *area* 31,113 *sq mi* (80,583 *sq km*), *pop* 3,486,703 — **South Car·o·lin·ian** \-'li-nē-ən, -'li-nyən\ *adjective or noun*
South China Sea part of W Pacific enclosed by SE China, Taiwan, Philippines, Indochina, Malaya, & Borneo
South Da·ko·ta \də-'kō-tə\ state NW central U.S. ✳ Pierre *area* 77,116 *sq mi* (199,730 *sq km*), *pop* 696,004 — **South Da·ko·tan** \-'kō-tᵊn\ *adjective or noun*
South Downs hills S England chiefly in Sussex
South El Monte city SW Calif. SE of Los Angeles *pop* 20,850
South·end on Sea \ˌsaú-thend-ˌȯn-'sē, -ˌän-\ borough SE England in Essex at mouth of Thames estuary *pop* 153,700
Southern Alps mountain range New Zealand in W South Is. extending almost the length of the island — see COOK (Mount)
Southern Morocco — see MOROCCO
Southern Ocean the Antarctic Ocean
Southern Rhodesia — see ZIMBABWE
Southern Up·lands \'əp-lən(d)z, -ˌlan(d)z\ elevated moorland region S Scotland in Dumfries and Galloway, Borders, Lothian, & SE Strathclyde administrative regions

Southern Yemen — see YEMEN
South Euclid city NE Ohio E of Cleveland *pop* 23,866
South·field \'saúth-ˌfēld\ city SE Mich. NW of Detroit *pop* 75,728
South·gate \'saúth-ˌgāt\ city SE Mich. S of Detroit *pop* 30,771
South Gate \ˌgāt\ city SW Calif. SE of Los Angeles *pop* 86,284
South Georgia island S Atlantic E of Tierra del Fuego in Falkland Islands Dependencies *area* 1450 *sq mi* (3770 *sq km*)
South Glamorgan county SE Wales ✳ Cardiff *area* 161 *sq mi* (417 *sq km*), *pop* 383,300
South Holland **1** village NE Ill. S of Chicago *pop* 22,105 **2** *or Dutch* **Zuid–Hol·land** \zīt-'hȯ-ˌlänt\ province SW Netherlands ✳ Rotterdam *area* 1259 *sq mi* (3261 *sq km*), *pop* 3,295,522
South·ing·ton \'sə-thiŋ-tən\ town W central Conn. *pop* 38,518
South Island island S New Zealand *area* 59,439 *sq mi* (153,947 *sq km*), *pop* 881,537
South Kings·town \'kiŋ-stən, 'kiŋz-ˌtaún\ town S R.I. *pop* 24,631
South Korea — see KOREA
South Lake Tahoe city E Calif. on Lake Tahoe *pop* 21,586
South Milwaukee city SE Wis. on Lake Michigan *pop* 20,958
South Mountain ridge S Pa. & W Md. at N end of Blue Ridge
South Na·han·ni \nə-'ha-nē\ river 350 *mi* (563 *km*) Canada in SW Northwest Territories flowing SE into the Liard
South Orkney Islands islands S Atlantic SE of the Falkland Islands Dependencies *area* 240 *sq mi* (622 *sq km*)
South Os·se·tia \ä-'sē-shə\ autonomous region N Georgia ✳ Tskhinvali *area about* 1500 *sq mi* (3900 *sq km*), *pop* 99,000
South Pacific — see PACIFIC OCEAN
South Pasadena city SW Calif. *pop* 23,936
South Pass broad level valley SW central Wyo. crossing Continental Divide
South Plainfield borough NE N.J. SW of Elizabeth *pop* 20,489
South Platte river 424 *mi* (682 *km*) Colo. & Nebr. flowing E to join N. Platte River forming the Platte River
South·port \'saúth-ˌpȯrt, -ˌpȯrt\ borough NW England in Merseyside on coast N of Liverpool *pop* 89,745
South Portland city SW Maine *pop* 23,163
South Saint Paul city SE Minn. on Mississippi River *pop* 20,197
South Sandwich Islands islands S Atlantic SE of S. Georgia Is. in Falkland Islands Dependencies *area* 120 *sq mi* (312 *sq km*)
South San Francisco city W Calif. *pop* 54,312
South Saskatchewan — see SASKATCHEWAN
South Seas the areas of the Atlantic, Indian, & Pacific oceans in the southern hemisphere, especially the S Pacific
South Shetland Islands British islands S Atlantic SE of Cape Horn off tip of Antarctic Peninsula
South Shields \'shēldz\ borough N England in Tyne and Wear at mouth of the Tyne E of Newcastle *pop* 87,203
South Tirol — see ALTO ADIGE
South Vietnam — see VIETNAM
South·wark \'sə-thərk, 'saúth-wərk\ borough of S London, England *pop* 196,500
South–West Africa — see NAMIBIA
South Windsor town N Conn. NE of Hartford *pop* 22,090
South Yemen — see YEMEN — **South Ye·me·ni** \'ye-mə-nē\ *adjective*
South Yorkshire metropolitan county N England ✳ Barnsley *area* 624 *sq mi* (1616 *sq km*), *pop* 1,248,500
So·vetsk \sə-'vyetsk\ *or German* **Til·sit** \'til-sət, -zit\ city W Russia in Europe on the Neman *pop* 42,300
So·vet·ska·ya Ga·van \sə-'vyet-skə-yə-'gä-vən, -'gä-və-nyə\ city & port SE Russia in Asia on Tatar Strait *pop* 35,400
Soviet Central Asia the portion of *central* Asia formerly belonging to the U.S.S.R. & comprising

the Kyrgyzstan, Tajikistan, Turkmenistan, & Uzbekistan republics & sometimes Kazakhstan
Soviet Russia 1 — see RUSSIA **2** the U.S.S.R.
Soviet Union — see UNION OF SOVIET SOCIALIST REPUBLICS
So·we·to \sō-'wä-tō, -'we-, -tü\ township NE Republic of South Africa in Gauteng adjoining SW Johannesburg; a black residential complex
Spa \'spä\ town E Belgium SE of Liège *pop* 10,140
Spain \'spān\ *or Spanish* **Es·pa·ña** \ā-'spä-nyä\ country SW Europe in the Iberian Peninsula; a kingdom ✳ Madrid *area* 194,881 *sq mi* (504,742 *sq km*), *pop* 39,141,000
Span·dau \'shpän-ˌdaú, 'spän-\ a W section of Berlin, Germany
Spanish America 1 the Spanish-speaking countries of the Americas **2** the parts of America settled & formerly governed by the Spanish
Spanish Guinea former Spanish colony W Africa bordering on Gulf of Guinea including Río Muni (Mbini), Fernando Póo (Bioko) & other islands — see EQUATORIAL GUINEA
Spanish Main \'mān\ **1** the mainland of Spanish America especially along N coast of S. America **2** the Caribbean Sea & adjacent waters especially at the time when region was infested with pirates
Spanish Morocco — see MOROCCO
Spanish Peaks two mountains (**East Spanish Peak** 12,683 *ft or* 3866 *m* & **West Spanish Peak** 13,623 *ft or* 4152 *m*) S Colo.
Spanish Sahara former Spanish possessions Río de Oro & Saguia el Hamra — see WESTERN SAHARA
Spanish Town town SE *central* Jamaica W of Kingston; former ✳ of Jamaica
Sparks \'spärks\ city W Nev. E of Reno *pop* 53,367
Spar·ta \'spär-tə\ *or* **Lac·e·dae·mon** \ˌla-sə-'dē-mən\ ancient city S Greece in Peloponnese ✳ of Laconia
Spar·tan·burg \'spär-tᵊn-ˌbərg\ city NW S.C. *pop* 43,467
Spen·cer Gulf \'spen(t)-sər\ inlet of Indian Ocean SE S. Australia
Spey \'spā\ river 110 *mi* (177 *km*) NE Scotland flowing into Moray Firth
Spey·er \'shpī(-ə)r, 'spī(-ə)r\ *or* **Spires** \'spīrz\ city SW Germany on W bank of the Rhine SW of Heidelberg *pop* 47,456
Spezia, La — see LA SPEZIA
Spits·ber·gen \'spits-ˌbər-gən\ group of islands in Arctic Ocean N of Norway; belongs to Norway *area* 23,641 *sq mi* (61,230 *sq km*) — see SVALBARD
Split \'split\ city & port S Croatia on Dalmatian coast *pop* 200,459
Spo·kane \spō-'kan\ **1** river 120 *mi* (193 *km*) N Idaho & E Wash. flowing from Coeur d'Alene Lake W into Columbia River **2** city E Wash. at Spokane Falls in Spokane River *pop* 177,196
Spo·le·to \spō-'lā-(ˌ)tō, -'lē-\ commune central Italy SE of Perugia *pop* 37,057
Spor·a·des \'spȯr-ə-ˌdēz, 'spär-\ two island groups Greece in the Aegean: the **Northern Sporades** (chief island Skíros, N of Euboea & E of Thessaly) & the **Southern Sporades** (chiefly Samos, Ikaria, & the Dodecanese, off SW Turkey)
Sprat·ly Islands \'sprat-lē\ islands *central* S. China Sea SE of Cam Ranh Bay, Vietnam; claimed by several countries
Spree \'shprā, 'sprā\ river 247 *mi* (397 *km*) E Germany flowing N into the Havel
Spree·wald \-ˌvält\ marshy district E Germany in Spree valley
Spring·dale \'spriŋ-ˌdāl\ city NW Ark. *pop* 29,941
Spring·field \'spriŋ-ˌfēld\ **1** city ✳ of Ill. on the Sangamon *pop* 105,227 **2** city SW Mass. on Connecticut River *pop* 156,983 **3** city SW Mo. *pop* 140,494 **4** city W central Ohio NE of Dayton *pop* 70,487 **5** city W Oreg. on the Willamette E of Eugene *pop* 44,683
Springs \'spriŋz\ city NE Republic of South Africa in Gauteng *pop* 142,812
Spring Valley village SE N.Y. N of New York City *pop* 21,802

Spuy·ten Duy·vil Creek \,spī-t°n-'dī-vəl\ channel New York City N of Manhattan Is. connecting Hudson & Harlem rivers

Sri Lan·ka \(,)srē-'län-kə, (,)shrē-, -'laŋ-\ *or formerly* **Cey·lon** \si-'län, sā-\ country coextensive with island of Ceylon; an independent republic in the Commonwealth of Nations ✳ Colombo *area* 25,332 *sq mi* (65,863 *sq km*), *pop* 17,829,500 — **Sri Lan·kan** \-'län-kən, -'laŋ\ *adjective or noun*

Sri·na·gar \srē-'nə-gər\ city India, summer ✳ of Jammu and Kashmir, in W Kashmir on the Jhelum NNE of Lahore *pop* 423,253

Ssu-p'ing — see SIPING

Staf·fa \'sta-fə\ islet W Scotland in the Inner Hebrides W of Mull — see FINGAL'S CAVE

Staf·ford \'sta-fərd\ borough W *central* England ✳ of Staffordshire *pop* 117,000

Staf·ford·shire \'sta-fərd-,shir, -shər\ *or* **Stafford** county W *central* England ✳ Stafford *area* 1086 *sq mi* (2813 *sq km*), *pop* 1,020,300

Staked Plain — see LLANO ESTACADO

Sta·kha·nov \stə-'kä-nəf, -'kä-\ *or formerly* **Ka·di·yev·ka** \kə-'dē-yəf-kə\ city E Ukraine *pop* 113,000

Stalin **1** — see BRASOV **2** — see DONETSK **3** — see VARNA

Stalinabad — see DUSHANBE

Stalingrad — see VOLGOGRAD

Stalino — see DONETSK

Stalinsk — see NOVOKUZNETSK

Stam·ford \'stam-fərd\ city SW Conn. *pop* 108,056

Stanislav — see IVANO-FRANKIVS'K

Stan·ley \'stan-lē\ *or* **Port Stanley** town ✳ of the Falklands

Stanley, Mount *or in Democratic Republic of the Congo* **Mount Nga·lie·ma** \əŋ-gäl-'yā-mä\ mountain with two peaks (higher Margherita Peak 16,763 *ft or* 5109 *m*) E *central* Africa; highest of Ruwenzori

Stanley Falls — see BOYOMA FALLS

Stanley Pool — see MALEBO, POOL

Stanleyville — see KISANGANI

Stan·o·voy \,sta-nə-'vói\ mountain range SE Russia in Asia N of the Amur

Stan·ton \'stan-t°n\ city SW Calif. SE of Los Angeles *pop* 30,491

Sta·ra Za·go·ra \,stär-ə-zə-'gór-ə, -'gór-\ city *central* Bulgaria *pop* 164,553

State College borough *central* Pa. NE of Altoona *pop* 38,923

Stat·en Island \'sta-t°n\ **1** island SE N.Y. SW of mouth of Hudson River **2** *or formerly* **Rich·mond** \'rich-mənd\ borough of New York City including Staten Is. *pop* 378,977

Statia — see SAINT EUSTATIUS

Statue of Liberty National Monument — see LIBERTY ISLAND

Staun·ton \'stan-t°n\ city NW *central* Va. *pop* 24,461

Sta·vang·er \stə-'väŋ-ər, -'vaŋ-\ city & port SW Norway *pop* 97,570

Stav·ro·pol \sta-'vró-pəl, -'vró-, 'stä-vrə-pəl\ **1** territory S Russia in Europe N of the Caucasus *area* 31,120 *sq mi* (80,600 *sq km*), *pop* 2,536,000 **2** city, its ✳ *pop* 332,000 **3** — see TOL'YATTI

Stę·bark \'stem-,bärk\ *or German* **Tan·nen·berg** \'ta-nən-,bərg, 'tä-nən-,berk\ village NE Poland SW of Olsztyn

Steens Mountain \'stēnz\ mountain mass SE Oreg.; highest point *about* 9700 *ft* (2955 *m*)

Stel·len·bosch \'ste-lən-,bäs, -,bäsh, *Afrikaans* ,ste-ləm-'bós\ city SW Republic of South Africa in SW Western Cape province *pop* 29,955

Step·ney \'step-nē\ former metropolitan borough E London, England, on N bank of Thames River, now part of Tower Hamlets

Ster·ling Heights \'stər-liŋ\ city SE Mich. N of Detroit *pop* 117,810

Steu·ben·ville \'stü-bən-,vil, 'styü-\ city E Ohio *pop* 22,125

Ste·vens Point \'stē-vənz\ city *central* Wis. *pop* 23,006

Stew·art \'stü-ərt, 'styü-\ river 331 *mi* (532 *km*) Canada in *central* Yukon Territory flowing W into Yukon River

Stewart Island island New Zealand S of South Is. *area* 675 *sq mi* (1748 *sq km*)

Sti·kine \sti-'kēn\ river 335 *mi* (539 *km*) Canada & Alaska flowing from **Stikine Mountains** (in British Columbia & Yukon Territory) into the Pacific

Still·wa·ter \'stil-,wó-tər, -,wä-\ city N *central* Okla. *pop* 36,676

Stir·ling \'stər-liŋ\ **1** *or* **Stir·ling·shire** \-,shir, -shər\ former county *central* Scotland **2** burgh *central* Scotland ✳ of Central region *pop* 38,638

Stock·holm \'stäk-,hō(l)m\ city & port ✳ of Sweden on Mälaren Lake *pop* 684,576 — **Stock·holm·er** \-,hō(l)-mər\ *noun*

Stock·port \'stäk-,pórt, -,pórt\ borough NW England in Greater Manchester S of Manchester *pop* 276,800

Stock·ton \'stäk-tən\ city *central* Calif. on the San Joaquin *pop* 210,943

Stoke New·ing·ton \stók-'nü-iŋ-tən, -'nyü-\ former metropolitan borough N London, England, now part of Hackney

Stoke on Trent \'stók-,än-'trent, -,ón-\ city W *central* England in Staffordshire *pop* 244,800

Stone·ham \'stō-nəm, 'stōn-,ham\ town E Mass. *pop* 22,203

Stone·ha·ven \stōn-'hā-vən, stän-'hī\ burgh & port E Scotland in Grampian region *pop* 7885

Stone·henge \'stōn-,henj, (,)stōn-'\ assemblage of megaliths S England in Wiltshire on Salisbury Plain erected by prehistoric peoples

Stone Mountain mountain 1686 *ft* (514 *m*) NW *central* Ga. E of Atlanta

Stones \'stōnz\ river 60 *mi* (96 *km*) *central* Tenn. flowing NW into Cumberland River

Ston·ey Creek \'stō-nē\ city Canada in SE Ontario *pop* 49,968

Stor·mont \'stór-mənt\ E suburb of Belfast, Northern Ireland; site of Parliament House

Stor·no·way \'stór-nə-,wā\ burgh NW Scotland in Lewis ✳ of Western Isles region *pop* 8660

Stough·ton \'stō-t°n\ town E Mass. NW of Brockton *pop* 26,777

Stour **1** \'stúr\ river 47 *mi* (76 *km*) SE England flowing E between Essex & Suffolk into the North Sea **2** \'stúr\ river 55 *mi* (88 *km*) S England in Dorset & Hampshire flowing SE into Avon River **3** *or* **Great Stour** \'stúr *also* 'staúr\ river 40 *mi* (64 *km*) SE England in Kent flowing NE into the North Sea **4** \'staúr, 'stór\ river 20 *mi* (32 *km*) *central* England in Oxfordshire & Warwickshire flowing NW into Avon River **5** *same as* 4\ river 20 *mi* (32 *km*) W *central* England in Staffordshire & Hereford and Worcester flowing S into Severn River

Stour·bridge \'staúr-(,)brij, 'stór-\ borough W *central* England in W. Midlands W of Birmingham *pop* 54,661

Stow \'stō\ city NE Ohio NE of Akron *pop* 27,702

Stra·bane \strə-'ban\ district N Northern Ireland, established 1974 *area* 336 *sq mi* (874 *sq km*), *pop* 35,668

Straits Settlements former country SE Asia bordering on Strait of Malacca & comprising Singapore Is., Penang, & Melaka; now divided between Singapore (republic) & Malaysia (federation) *area* 1242 *sq mi* (3229 *sq km*)

Stral·sund \'shträl-,zúnt, 'sträl-, -,súnt\ city & port NE Germany on the Baltic opposite Rügen Is. *pop* 71,618

Stras·bourg \'sträs-,búrg, 'sträz-, -,bərg\ *or German* **Strass·burg** \'shträs-,búrk\ city NE France on Ill River *pop* 255,937

Strat·ford \'strat-fərd\ **1** town SW Conn. *pop* 49,389 **2** city Canada in SE Ontario W of Kitchener *pop* 27,666

Stratford–upon–Avon \-'ā-vən, -'a-\ borough *central* England in Warwickshire SSE of Birmingham *pop* 20,858

Strath·clyde \strath-'klīd\ **1** Celtic kingdom of 6th to 11th centuries S Scotland & NW England ✳ Dumbarton; its S part called **Cum·bria** \'kəm-brē-ə\ **2** former SW Scotland, established 1975; ✳ Glasgow *area* 5214 *sq mi* (13,503 *sq km*), *pop* 2,286,800

Strath·more \strath-'mór, -'mór\ great valley of E *central* Scotland S of the Grampians

Stream·wood \'strēm-,wúd\ village NE Ill. E of Elgin *pop* 30,987

Stre·sa \'strā-zə\ town NW Italy in Piedmont on Lake Maggiore

Stret·ford \'stret-fərd\ borough NW England in Greater Manchester SW of Manchester *pop* 47,600

Stri·món, Gulf of \strē-'món\ *or* **Stri·mon·i·kós Kól·pos** \strē-,mó-nē-'kós-'kól-pós\ *or* **Stry·mon·ic Gulf** \strī-'mä-nik\ inlet of the Aegean NE Greece NE of Chalcidice Peninsula

Strom·bo·li \'sträm-bō-(,)lē\ *or ancient* **Stron·gy·le** \'strän-jə-,lē\ **1** island Italy in Lipari Islands **2** volcano 3038 *ft* (926 *m*) on the island

Strom·lo, Mount \'sträm-(,)lō\ hill 2500 *ft* (758 *m*) SE Australia in Australian Capital Territory W of Canberra

Strongs·ville \'stróŋz-,vil\ city NE Ohio SW of Cleveland *pop* 35,308

Stry·mon \'strī-,män\ *or Bulgarian* **Stru·ma** \'strü-mə\ river W Bulgaria & NE Greece flowing SE into Gulf of Strimón

Stutt·gart \'shtút-,gärt, 'stút-, 'stət-\ city SW Germany ✳ of Baden-Württemberg on the Neckar *pop* 591,946

Styr \'stir\ river 271 *mi* (436 *km*) NW Ukraine flowing N into the Pripet in the Pripet Marshes

Styr·ia \'stir-ē-ə\ *or German* **Stei·er·mark** \'shtī-(ə)r-,märk, 'stī-(ə)r-\ region *central* & SE Austria; chief city Graz — **Styr·i·an** \'stir-ē-ən\ *adjective or noun*

Sua·kin \'swä-kən\ town & port NE Sudan on Red Sea

Su·bic \'sü-bik\ town Philippines in W Luzon at head of **Subic Bay** (inlet of S. China Sea NW of Bataan Peninsula) *pop* 30,340

Su·bo·ti·ca \'sü-bó-,tēt-sä\ city N Yugoslavia in N Vojvodina near Hungarian border *pop* 150,666

Süchow **1** — see XUZHOU **2** — see YIBIN

Su·cre \'sü-(,)krā\ city, constitutional ✳ of Bolivia, SE of La Paz *pop* 130,952

Su·dan \sü-'dan, -'dän\ **1** region N Africa between the Atlantic & the upper Nile S of the Sahara including basins of Lake Chad & Niger River & the upper Nile **2** country NE Africa S of Egypt; a republic, until 1956 a territory (**Anglo–Egyptian Sudan**) under joint Brit. & Egyptian rule ✳ Khartoum *area* 967,500 *sq mi* (2,515,500 *sq km*), *pop* 25,000,000 — **Su·da·nese** \,süd°n-'ēz, -'ēs\ *adjective or noun*

Sudanese Republic — see MALI

Sud·bury \'səd-,ber-ē, -b(ə-)rē\ city Canada in SE Ontario N of Georgian Bay *pop* 92,884

Sudd \'səd\ swamp region S Sudan drained by White Nile River

Su·de·ten·land \sü-'dā-t°n-,land, -,länt\ region N Czech Republic in Sudety Mountains

Su·de·ty \Czech 'sú-de-tē, Polish sù-'de-tē\ *or* **Su·de·ten** \sü-'dā-t°n\ mountains *central* Europe W of the Carpathians between Czech Republic & Poland — **Sudeten** *adjective or noun*

Su·dir·man Range \sü-'dir-mən\ *or formerly* **Nas·sau Range** \'na-,só\ mountain range *central* W. Irian — see DJAJA (Mount)

Su·ez \sü-'ez, 'sü-,ez, *chiefly British* 'sü-iz\ city & port NE Egypt at S end of Suez Canal on **Gulf of Suez** (arm of Red Sea) *pop* 376,000

Suez, Isthmus of isthmus NE Egypt between Mediterranean & Red seas connecting Africa & Asia

Suez Canal canal over 100 *mi* (161 *km*) long NE Egypt traversing Isthmus of Suez

Suf·folk \'sə-fək, *United States also* -,fók\ **1** city SE Va. W of Chesapeake *pop* 52,141 **2** county E England bordering on North Sea ✳ Ipswich *area* 1520 *mi* (3937 *km*), *pop* 629,900; formerly divided into administrative counties of **East Suffolk** (✳ Ipswich) & **West Suffolk** (✳ Bury St. Edmunds)

Suffolk Broads — see BROADS

Sugar Land city SE Tex. SW of Houston *pop* 24,529

Sugarloaf Mountain — see PAO DE AÇÚCAR

Suisse — see SWITZERLAND

Sui·sun Bay \sə-'sün\ the E extension of San Pablo Bay *central* Calif.

Sui·sun City \sə-'sün\ city *central* Calif. SW of Sacramento *pop* 22,686

\ə\ abut \°\ kitten \ər\ further \a\ ash \ā\ ace \ä\ mop, mar \aú\ out \ch\ chin \e\ bet \ē\ easy \g\ go \i\ hit \ī\ ice \j\ job \ŋ\ sing \ō\ go \ò\ law \ói\ boy \th\ thin \t̷h\ the \ü\ loot \ú\ foot \y\ yet \zh\ vision *see also* Guide to Pronunciation

Su·i·ta \'sü-'ē-tä\ city Japan on Honshu *pop* 345,187

Sukarnapura — see JAYAPURA

Su·khu·mi \'sü-kə-mē, sü-'kü-mē\ city & port NW Georgia ✻ of Abkhaz Republic on Black Sea *pop* 120,000

Suk·kur \'sü-kər\ city Pakistan in N Sind on the Indus *pop* 193,000

Su·la·we·si \,sü-lä-'wä-sē\ *or* **Ce·le·bes** \'se-lə-,bēz, sə-'lē-bēz\ island Indonesia E of Borneo ✻ Ujung Pandang *area* 72,775 *sq mi* (188,487 *sq km*), *pop* 12,520,711

Sul·grave \'səl-,grāv\ village England in S Northamptonshire

Sul·phur \'səl-fər\ city SW La. *pop* 20,125

Su·lu Archipelago \'sü-(,)lü\ archipelago SW Philippines SW of Mindanao

Sulu Sea sea W Philippines N of Celebes Sea

Su·ma·tra \sü-'mä-trə\ island W Indonesia S of Malay Peninsula *area* 182,542 *sq mi* (472,784 *sq km*) — **Su·ma·tran** \-trən\ *adjective or noun*

Sum·ba \'süm-bə\ island Indonesia in the Lesser Sundas *area* 4306 *sq mi* (11,196 *sq km*), *pop* 251,126

Sum·ba·wa \süm-'bä-wə\ island Indonesia in the Lesser Sundas *area* 5693 *sq mi* (14,802 *sq km*), *pop* 195,554

Su·mer \'sü-mər\ the S division of ancient Babylonia — see AKKAD, SHINAR

Sum·ga·it \süm-'gī-it\ *or* **Sum·qay·it** \-'kī-\ city & port Azerbaijan on the Caspian NW of Baku *pop* 236,200

Sum·mer·ville \'sə-mər-,vil\ town SE S.C. NW of Charleston *pop* 22,519

Sum·mit \'sə-mət\ city NE N.J. W of Newark *pop* 19,757

Sum·ter \'səm-tər\ city E *central* S.C. E of Columbia *pop* 41,943

Sun·belt \'sən-,belt\ region S & SW U.S.

Sun·da Islands \'sün-də, 'sən-\ islands Malay Archipelago comprising the **Greater Sunda Islands** (Sumatra, Java, Borneo, Sulawesi, & adjacent islands) & the **Lesser Sunda Islands** (extending E from Bali to Timor); with exception of N Borneo, belongs to Indonesia

Sunda Strait strait between Java & Sumatra

Sun·der·land \'sən-dər-lənd\ borough N England in Tyne and Wear on North Sea *pop* 286,800

Sunds·vall \'sən(t)s-,väl, 'sündz-\ city & port E Sweden on Gulf of Bothnia *pop* 94,329

Sungari — see SONGHUA

Sun·ny·vale \'sə-nē-,vāl\ city W Calif. WNW of San Jose *pop* 117,229

Sun·rise \'sən-,rīz\ city SE Fla. *pop* 64,407

Sunset Crater volcanic crater N *central* Ariz. in **Sunset Crater National Monument**

Suomi — see FINLAND

Su·pe·ri·or \sü-'pir-ē-ər\ city & port NW Wis. on Lake Superior *pop* 27,134

Superior, Lake lake U.S. & Canada; largest, northernmost, & westernmost of the Great Lakes *area* 31,800 *sq mi* (82,362 *sq km*)

Superstition Mountains range S *central* Ariz. E of Phoenix

Sur \'sür\ *or* **Tyre** \'tīr\ town S Lebanon on the coast; ancient ✻ of Phoenicia

Sur, Point \'sər\ promontory Calif. on the Pacific SSW of Monterey — see BIG SUR

Su·ra·ba·ya \,sür-ə-'bī-ə\ city & port Indonesia in NE Java on **Surabaya Strait** (between Java & W end of Madura) *pop* 2,483,871

Su·ra·kar·ta \,sür-ə-'kär-tə\ city Indonesia in *central* Java *pop* 504,176

Su·rat \'sür-ət, sə-'rat\ city W India in SE Gujarat *pop* 1,505,872

Sur·bi·ton \'sər-bə-t°n\ former municipal borough S England in Surrey WSW of London, now part of Kingston upon Thames

Su·ri·ba·chi, Mount \,sür-ē-'bä-chē\ volcano 548 *ft* (167 *m*) in the Volcano Islands at S end of Iwo Jima

Su·ri·na·me \,sür-ə-'nä-mə\ **1** *or formerly* **Dutch Guiana** *or* **Netherlands Guiana** country N S. America between Guyana & French Guiana; a republic, until 1975 territory of the Netherlands ✻ Paramaribo *area* 63,251 *sq mi* (163,820 *sq km*), *pop* 403,000 **2** river N Suriname flowing N into the Atlantic — **Su·ri·nam·er** \'sür-ə-,nä-mər, ,sür-ə-'nä-\ *noun* — **Su·ri·nam·ese** \,sür-ə-nə-'mēz, -'mēs\ *adjective or noun*

Sur·ma \'sür-mə\ river 560 *mi* (901 *km*) NE India (subcontinent) in Manipur & Bangladesh — see MEGHNA

Surrentum — see SORRENTO

Sur·rey \'sər-ē, 'sə-rē\ **1** county SE England S of London ✻ Kingston upon Thames *area* 662 *sq mi* (1714 *sq km*), *pop* 998,000 **2** municipality Canada in SW British Columbia SE of Vancouver *pop* 245,173

Surts·ey \'sərt-,sā, 'sürt-\ island Iceland off S coast *area* 1 *sq mi* (2.6 *sq km*); formed 1963 by volcanic eruption

Su·ru·ga Bay \'sür-ə-gə, sü-'rü-gä\ inlet of the Pacific Japan on coast of SE Honshu W of Sagami Sea

Su·sa \'sü-zə\ *or biblical* **Shu·shan** \'shü-shən, -,shan\ ancient city ✻ of Elam; ruins in SW Iran

Susiana — see ELAM

Sus·que·han·na \,səs-kwə-'ha-nə\ river 444 *mi* (714 *km*) E U.S. flowing from *central* N.Y. S through Pa. & into Chesapeake Bay in N Md.

Sus·sex \'sə-siks, *United States also* -,seks\ former county SE England bordering on English Channel; one of kingdoms in Anglo-Saxon heptarchy — see EAST SUSSEX, WEST SUSSEX

Suth·er·land \'sə-thər-lənd\ *or* **Suth·er·land·shire** \-lən(d)-,shir, -shər\ former county N Scotland ✻ Dornoch

Sutherland Falls waterfall 1904 *ft* (580 *m*) New Zealand in SW South Is.

Sut·lej \'sət-,lej\ river *about* 900 *mi* (1448 *km*) N India (subcontinent) flowing from Tibet W & SW through the Punjab to join the Chenab

Sut·ton \'sə-t°n\ borough of S Greater London, England *pop* 164,300

Sutton Cold·field \'kōl(d)-,fēld\ borough *central* England in W. Midlands NE of Birmingham *pop* 86,494

Sutton–in–Ash·field \-'ash-,fēld\ town N *central* England in Nottinghamshire N of Nottingham *pop* 41,270

Su·va \'sü-və\ city & port ✻ of Fiji, on Viti Levu Is. *pop* 63,628

Su·wał·ki \sü-'vau-kē\ **1** district NE Poland **2** city in the district

Su·wan·nee \sə-'wä-nē, 'swä-\ river 250 *mi* (400 *km*) SE Ga. & N Fla. flowing SW into Gulf of Mexico

Su·won \'sü-,wän\ city NW S. Korea S of Seoul *pop* 430,752

Su·zhou \'sü-'jō\ *or* **Soo·chow** \-'jō, -'chaü\ *or formerly* **Wu·hsien** \'wü-'shyen\ city E China in SE Jiangsu W of Shanghai *pop* 706,459

Sval·bard \'sväl-,bär\ islands in the Arctic Ocean including Spitsbergen, Bear Is., & other small islands *area* 23,958 *sq mi* (62,052 *sq km*); under Norwegian administration

Sverdlovsk — see YEKATERINBURG

Sver·drup Islands \'sver-drəp\ islands N Canada W of Ellesmere Is. including Axel Heiberg, Ellef Ringnes, & Amund Ringnes islands

Swa·bia \'swä-bē-ə\ *or German* **Schwa·ben** \'shvä-bən\ region and medieval county SW Germany chiefly in area comprising modern Baden-Wurttemberg & W Bavaria — **Swa·bi·an** \'swä-bē-ən\ *adjective or noun*

Swan \'swän\ *or in its upper course* **Av·on** \'a-vən\ river *about* 240 *mi* (386 *km*) SW Western Australia flowing W into Indian Ocean

Swan Islands two islands in the Caribbean NE of Honduras

Swan·sea \'swän-zē *also* -,sē\ city & port SE Wales ✻ of W. Glamorgan *pop* 182,100

Swat \'swät\ river 400 *mi* (644 *km*) Pakistan flowing into Kabul River

Swatow — see SHANTOU

Swa·zi·land \'swä-zē-,land\ country SE Africa between Republic of South Africa & Mozambique; a former Brit. protectorate, an independent kingdom since 1968 ✻ Mbabane *area* 6705 *sq mi* (17,433 *sq km*), *pop* 494,534

Swe·den \'swē-d°n\ *or Swedish* **Sve·ri·ge** \'sve-rē-yə\ country N Europe on Scandinavian Peninsula W of Baltic Sea; a kingdom ✻ Stockholm *area* 173,665 *sq mi* (449,792 *sq km*), *pop* 8,727,000

Swin·don \'swin-dən\ borough S England in NE Wiltshire *pop* 91,136

Świ·no·ujś·cie \,shfē-nō-'ü-ēsh,che\ city & port NW Poland on N coast of Uznam (Usedom) Is. NNW of Szczecin *pop* 42,886

Swin·ton and Pen·dle·bury \'swin-t°n-ənd-'pen-d°l-,ber-ē, -b(ə-)rē\ borough NW England in Greater Manchester NW of Manchester *pop* 39,621

Swit·zer·land \'swit-sər-lənd\ *or French* **Suisse** \'swᵉēs\ *or German* **der Schweiz** \der-'shvīts\ *or Italian* **Sviz·ze·ra** \'zvēt-tsä-rä\ *or Latin* **Hel·ve·tia** \hel-'vē-sh(ē-)ə\ country W Europe in the Alps; a federal republic ✻ Bern *area* 15,940 *sq mi* (41,444 *sq km*), *pop* 6,996,000

Syb·a·ris \'si-bə-rəs\ ancient Greek city S Italy on Gulf of Tarentum; destroyed 510 B.C.

Syd·ney \'sid-nē\ **1** city & port SE Australia on Port Jackson ✻ of New South Wales *metropolitan area pop* 3,097,956 **2** city Canada in NE Nova Scotia on Cape Breton Is. *pop* 26,063 — **Syd·ney·ite** \-,īt\ *noun* — **Syd·ney·sid·er** \-,sī-dər\ *noun*

Syene — see ASWÂN

Syk·tyv·kar \,sik-tif-'kär\ town NE Russia in Europe ✻ of Komi Republic *pop* 226,000

Sylt \'zilt, 'silt\ island NW Germany, chief of the N. Frisian Islands *area* 36 *sq mi* (94 *sq km*)

Syr·a·cuse \'sir-ə-,kyüs, -,kyüz\ **1** city *central* N.Y. near Oneida Lake *pop* 163,860 **2** *or Italian* **Si·ra·cu·sa** \,sē-rä-'kü-zä\ *or ancient* **Syr·a·cu·sae** \,sir-ə-'kyü-(,)sē, -(,)zē\ city & port Italy in SE Sicily *pop* 124,606 — **Syr·a·cu·san** \,sir-ə-'kyü-s°n, -'kyü-\ *adjective or noun*

Syr Dar·ya \sir-'där-yə\ *or ancient* **Jax·ar·tes** \jak-'sär-(,)tēz\ river *about* 1370 *mi* (2204 *km*) Kyrgyzstan & S Kazakhstan flowing from Tian Shan W & NW into Lake Aral

Syr·ia \'sir-ē-ə\ **1** ancient region SW Asia bordering on the Mediterranean & covering modern Syria, Lebanon, Israel, & Jordan **2** *or* French mandate (1920–44) comprising the **Levant States** \lə-'vant\ (Syria, Lebanon, Latakia, & Jebel ed Druz), administrative ✻ Beirut, legislative ✻ Damascus **3** country SW Asia bordering on the Mediterranean; a republic 1944–58 & since 1961; a province of United Arab Republic 1958–61 ✻ Damascus *area* 71,498 *sq mi* (185,180 *sq km*), *pop* 13,398,000 — **Syr·i·an** \'sir-ē-ən\ *adjective or noun*

Syrian Desert desert W Asia between Mediterranean coast & the Euphrates covering N Saudi Arabia, NE Jordan, SE Syria, & W Iraq

Syros — see SÍROS 1

Syrtis Major — see SIDRA (Gulf of)

Syrtis Minor — see GABÈS (Gulf of)

Szamos — see SOMEŞ

Szcze·cin \'shche-,chēn\ city & port NW Poland *pop* 412,058

Sze·chwan \'sech-'wän, 'sesh-\ *or* **Si·chuan** \'sēch-'wän\ province SW China ✻ Chengdu *area* 219,691 *sq mi* (571,197 *sq km*), *pop* 107,218,173

Sze·ged \'se-,ged\ city S Hungary *pop* 184,000

Sze·kes·fe·her·var \'sā-,kesh-,fe-hār-,vär\ city W *central* Hungary *pop* 111,200

Szepingkai — see SIPING

Szol·nok \'sōl-,nōk\ city E *central* Hungary *pop* 82,900

Szom·bat·hely \'sōm-,bót-,hā\ city W Hungary *pop* 87,700

Ta·bas·co \tə-'bas-(,)kō\ state SE Mexico on the Caribbean SW of Yucatán Peninsula ✻ Villahermosa *area* 9522 *sq mi* (24,662 *sq km*), *pop* 1,501,744

Ta·blas \'tä-bläs\ island *central* Philippines in Romblon group

Table Bay harbor of Cape Town, Republic of South Africa

Table Mountain mountain 3563 *ft* (1086 *m*) Republic of South Africa S of Cape Town

Ta·bor, Mount \'tā-bər, -,bór\ mountain 1929 *ft* (588 *m*) N Palestine E of Nazareth

Ta·bo·ra \tä-'bór-ä, -'bór-\ city W *central* Tanzania *pop* 67,392

Ta·briz \tə-'brēz\ city NW Iran in Azerbaijan *pop* 971,482

Ta·bu·a·er·an \tə-,bü-ə-'er-ən\ *or formerly* **Fanning Island** \'fa-niŋ\ island *central* Pacific in the Line Islands *area* 15 *sq mi* (39 *sq km*), *pop* 376

Tac·na \'täk-nä\ city S Peru near Chilean border *pop* 150,200; in region (**Tacna–Ari·ca** \-ä-'rē-kä\) occupied 1884–1930 by Chile & now divided between Chile & Peru

Ta·co·ma \tə-'kō-mə\ city & port W Wash. on Puget Sound S of Seattle *pop* 176,664

Tacoma, Mount — see RAINIER (Mount)

Ta·con·ic Range \tə-'kä-nik\ mountains along N part of Conn.-N.Y. boundary, entire Mass.-N.Y. boundary & in SW Vt.; highest Mt. Equinox (in Vt.) 3816 *ft* (1163 *m*)

Ta·djou·ra, Gulf of \tə-'jūr-ə\ inlet of Gulf of Aden in E Djibouti

Tadmor — see PALMYRA

Tae·dong \ta-'dùŋ, tī-\ river *central* N. Korea flowing SW into Korea Bay

Tae·gu \ta-'gü, tī-\ city SE S. Korea NNW of Pusan *pop* 2,248,000

Tae·jon \ta-'jòn, tī-\ city *central* S. Korea NW of Taegu *pop* 1,064,000

Ta·gan·rog \'ta-gən-,räg\ city S Russia in Europe on **Gulf of Taganrog** (NE arm of Sea of Azov) *pop* 293,000

Ta·gus \'tā-gəs\ *or Spanish* **Ta·jo** \'tä-(,)hō\ *or Portuguese* **Te·jo** \'tā-(,)zhü\ river 626 *mi* (1007 *km*) Spain & Portugal flowing W into the Atlantic

Ta·hi·ti \tə-'hē-tē\ island S Pacific in Windward group of the Society Islands; chief town Papeete *area* 402 *sq mi* (1045 *sq km*), *pop* 131,309

Ta·hoe, Lake \'tä-,hō\ lake 22 *mi* (35 *km*) long on Calif.-Nev. boundary

Tai·chung \'tī-'chùŋ\ city W Taiwan *pop* 779,370

Tai Hu \'tī-'hü\ lake *about* 45 *mi* (72 *km*) long E China in Jiangsu

T'ai–nan \'tī-'nän\ city SW Taiwan *pop* 702,237

Taí·na·ron \'tā-nä-,ròn\ *or* **Mat·a·pan** \,ma-tə-'pan\ cape S Greece at S tip of Peloponnese between Gulfs of Laconia & Messenia

Tai·o·hae \,tī-ō-'hē\ town Nuku Hiva Is. ✷ of the Marquesas

Tai·pei \'tī-'pā, -'bā\ city ✷ of (Nationalist) Republic of China, on Taiwan *pop* 2,651,419

Tai Shan \'tī-'shän\ mountain 5000 *ft* (1524 *m*) E China in W Shandong

Tai·wan \'tī-'wän\ *or* **For·mo·sa** \fòr-'mō-sə, fər-, -zə\ island China off SE coast E of Fujian; belonged to Japan 1895–1945; since 1949 seat of (Nationalist) Republic of China ✷ Taipei) *area* 13,807 *sq mi* (35,760 *sq km*) *pop* 20,926,000 — **Tai·wan·ese** \,tī-wə-'nēz, -'nēs\ *adjective or noun*

Tai·yu·an \'tī-'ywen, -'ywän\ *or formerly* **Yangku** \'yäŋ-'kü\ city N China ✷ of Shanxi *pop* 1,533,884

Tai·zhou *or* **T'ai–chou** \'tī-'jō\ city E China in *central* Jiangsu

Ta·jik·i·stan \tä-,ji-ki-'stan, tə-, -,jē, -'stän; -'ji-ki-,, -jē\ country W *central* Asia bordering on China & Afghanistan; a constituent republic (**Tadzhik Republic** \tä-'jik, tə-, -'jēk\ *or* **Ta·dzhik·i·stan** *same as* TAJIKISTAN\) of the U.S.S.R. 1929–91 ✷ Dushanbe *area* 55,251 *sq mi* (143,100 *sq km*), *pop* 5,705,000

Ta·ju·mul·co \,tä-hü-'mül-(,)kō\ mountain 13,845 *ft* (4220 *m*) W Guatemala; highest in Central America

Ta·ka·mat·su \,tä-kä-'mät-(,)sü, tä-'kä-mät-,sü\ city & port Japan in NE Shikoku on Inland Sea *pop* 329,695

Ta·kat·su·ki \tä-'kät-sù-(,)kē\ city Japan in S Honshu *pop* 359,867

Tak·ka·kaw \'ta-kə-,kò\ waterfall 1650 *ft* (503 *m*) Canada in SE British Columbia in Yoho National Park; highest in Canada

Ta·kli·ma·kan *or* **Ta·kla Ma·kan** \,tä-klə-mə-'kän\ desert W China in *central* Xinjiang Uygur between Tian Shan & Kunlun mountains

Ta·la·ud Islands \'tä-,lä-,üd\ *or* **Ta·laur Islands** \-,lä-,ür\ islands Indonesia NE of Sulawesi *area* 494 *sq mi* (1284 *sq km*), *pop* 194,253

Tal·ca \'täl-kä\ city *central* Chile S of Santiago *pop* 128,544

Tal·ca·hua·no \,täl-kä-'wä-(,)nō, -'hwä-\ city & port S *central* Chile NW of Concepción *pop* 202,368

Ta·lien — see DALIAN

Tal·la·has·see \,ta-lə-'ha-sē\ city ✷ of Fla. *pop* 124,773

Tal·la·hatch·ie \,ta-lə-'ha-chē\ river 230 *mi* (370 *km*) N Miss. flowing SW

Tal·la·poo·sa \,ta-lə-'pü-sə\ river 268 *mi* (431 *km*) NW Ga. & E Ala. flowing SW to join the Coosa forming Alabama River

Tal·linn \'ta-lən, 'tä-\ *or formerly* **Re·vel** \'rā-vəl\ city & port ✷ of Estonia *pop* 482,000

Ta·ma·le \tä-'mä-lā\ town N Ghana *pop* 135,952

Tam·al·pais, Mount \,ta-məl-'pī-əs\ mountain 2572 *ft* (784 *m*) W Calif. NW of San Francisco

Ta·man \tə-'män\ peninsula S Russia in Europe in Ciscaucasia between Sea of Azov & Black Sea

Tam·an·ras·set \,ta-mən-'ra-sət\ wadi & oasis SE Algeria

Ta·mar \'tā-mər\ **1** river 40 *mi* (64 *km*) Australia in N Tasmania flowing N to Bass Strait **2** river 60 *mi* (96 *km*) SW England flowing SE from NW Devon into English Channel **3** — see PALMYRA

Tam·a·rac \'ta-mə-,rak\ city SE Fla. *pop* 44,822

Tamatave — see TOAMASINA

Ta·mau·li·pas \,tä-,maù-'lē-päs, tə-\ state NE Mexico bordering on Gulf of Mexico ✷ Ciudad Victoria *area* 30,822 *sq mi* (79,829 *sq km*), *pop* 2,249,581

Tam·bo·ra \täm-'bòr-ə, -'bòr-\ volcano 9350 *ft* (2850 *m*) Indonesia on Sumbawa Is.

Tam·bov \täm-'bòf, -'bòv\ city S *central* Russia in Europe SE of Moscow *pop* 311,000

Tam·il Na·du \,ta-məl-'nä-(,)dü, ,tä-\ *or formerly* **Madras** state SE India bordering on Bay of Bengal ✷ Madras *area* 50,180 *sq mi* (129,966 *sq km*), *pop* 55,858,946

Tam·pa \'tam-pə\ city W Fla. on **Tampa Bay** (inlet of Gulf of Mexico) *pop* 280,015 — **Tam·pan** \-pən\ *adjective or noun*

Tam·pe·re \'tam-pe-,rā, 'täm-\ city SW Finland *pop* 171,561

Tam·pi·co \tam-'pē-(,)kō\ city & port E Mexico in S Tamaulipas on the Pánuco 7 *mi* (11 *km*) from its mouth *pop* 271,636

Ta·na \'tä-nä\ river 440 *mi* (708 *km*) E Africa in Kenya flowing into Indian Ocean

Ta·na, Lake \'tä-nä\ lake NW Ethiopia; source of Blue Nile River *area* 1418 *sq mi* (3687 *sq km*)

Ta·na·gra \'ta-nə-grə, tə-'na-grə\ village E *central* Greece E of Thebes; an important town of ancient Boeotia

Tan·a·na \'ta-nə-,nò\ river 550 *mi* (885 *km*) E & *central* Alaska flowing NW into Yukon River

Tananarive, Tananarivo — see ANTANANARIVO

Tan·ez·rouft \,ta-nəz-'rüft\ extremely arid region of W Sahara in SW Algeria & N Mali

Tan·ga \'taŋ-gə\ city & port Tanzania on NE mainland *pop* 187,634

Tan·gan·yi·ka \,tan-gə-'nyē-kə, ,taŋ-gə-, -'nē-\ former country E Africa between Lake Tanganyika & Indian Ocean; administered by Britain 1920–61; became an independent member of the Commonwealth of Nations 1961 ✷ Dar es Salaam; since 1964 united with Zanzibar as Tanzania — see GERMAN EAST AFRICA — **Tan·gan·yi·kan** \-kən\ *adjective or noun*

Tanganyika, Lake lake E Africa in Great Rift Valley between Democratic Republic of the Congo & Tanzania *area* 12,700 *sq mi* (33,020 *sq km*)

Tan·gier \tan-'jir\ **1** city & port N Morocco on Strait of Gibraltar; summer ✷ of Morocco *pop* 187,894 **2** the International Zone of Tangier — see MOROCCO — **Tan·ger·ine** \,tan-jə-'rēn\ *adjective or noun*

Tang·shan \'däŋ-'shän, 'täŋ-\ city NE China in E Hebei *pop* 1,044,194

Ta·nim·bar Islands \tə-'nim-,bär, tä-\ islands Indonesia in SE Moluccas ENE of Timor *pop* 50,000

Ta·nis \'tä-nəs\ *or biblical* **Zo·an** \'zō-,an\ ancient city N Egypt in E Nile delta near Lake Tanis

Tanis, Lake — see MANZALA (Lake)

Tan·jung·ka·rang \tän-jùŋ-'kä-räŋ\ *or* **Ban·dar Lam·pung** \'bən-dər-'läm-pùŋ\ city & port Indonesia in S Sumatra *pop* 636,706

Tan·jung·pri·ok \tän-jùŋ-prē-'ók\ port of Jakarta, Indonesia

Tan·na \'tä-nə\ island SW Pacific in Vanuatu *pop* 19,825

Tannenberg — see STĘBARK

Tan·ta \'tän-tə\ city N Egypt in *central* Nile delta *pop* 372,000

Tan·tung — see DANDONG

Tan·za·nia \,tan-zə-'nē-ə, ,tän-\ republic E Africa formed 1964 by union of Tanganyika & Zanzibar ✷ Dar es Salaam *area* 364,900 *sq mi* (945,091 *sq km*), *pop* 26,542,000 — **Tan·za·ni·an** \-'nē-ən\ *adjective or noun*

Taor·mi·na \taùr-'mē-nä\ *or ancient* **Tau·ro·me·ni·um** \,tòr-ə-'mē-nē-əm\ commune Italy in NE Sicily

Ta·pa·jos *or* **Ta·pa·joz** \,ta-pə-'zhòs, ,tä-\ river N Brazil flowing NE into the Amazon — see JURUENA

Ta·pi \'tä-pē\ river 436 *mi* (702 *km*) W India S of Satpura Range flowing W into Gulf of Khambhat

Tap·pan Zee \,ta-pən-'zē\ expansion of Hudson River SE N.Y.

Taprobane — see CEYLON

Ta·qua·ri \,ta-kwə-'rē, ,tä-\ river 350 *mi* (565 *km*) S *central* Brazil rising in S *central* Mato Grosso & flowing WSW into Paraguay River

Tar \'tär\ river 215 *mi* (346 *km*) NE N.C. — see PAMLICO

Tara \'tar-ə\ village Ireland in County Meath NW of Dublin near **Hill of Tara** (seat of ancient Irish kings)

Tarabulus — see TRIPOLI

Taranaki — see EGMONT (Mount)

Ta·ran·to \'tär-än-,tō, tə-'ran-,(,)tō\ *or ancient* **Ta·ren·tum** \tə-'ren-təm\ city & port SE Italy on **Gulf of Taranto** (inlet of Ionian Sea) *pop* 244,512

Ta·ra·wa \tə-'rä-wə, 'tar-ə-,wä\ island *central* Pacific ✷ of Kiribati *area* 8 *sq mi* (21 *sq km*), *pop* 28,802

Tarbes \'tärb\ city SW France ESE of Pau *pop* 50,228

Ta·ri·fa, Cape \tä-'rē-fə, tə-\ cape S Spain; southernmost point of continental Europe, at 36°01′N

Ta·rim \'dä-'rēm, 'tä-\ river 1250 *mi* (2012 *km*) W China in Xinjiang Uygur in the Taklimakan flowing E & SE into a marshy depression

Tar·lac \'tär-,läk\ city Philippines in *central* Luzon *pop* 688,457

Tarn \'tärn\ river 233 *mi* (375 *km*) S France flowing W into the Garonne

Tar·nów \'tär-,nüf\ city S Poland E of Kraków *pop* 120,385

Tar·qui·nia \tär-'kwē-nyə, -'kwi-, -nē-ə\ *or formerly* **Cor·ne·to** \kòr-'nä-(,)tō\ *or ancient* **Tar·quin·ii** \tär-'kwi-nē-,ī\ town *central* Italy in N Lazio NW of Viterbo

Tar·ra·go·na \,tar-ə-'gō-nə, ,tär-ä-'gō-nä\ **1** province NE Spain on the Mediterranean *area* 2426 *sq mi* (6283 *sq km*), *pop* 542,004 **2** commune & port, its ✷, SW of Barcelona *pop* 110,003

Tar·ra·sa \tä-'rä-sä\ commune NE Spain NNW of Barcelona *pop* 154,360

Tar·shish \'tär-(,)shish\ ancient maritime country referred to in the Bible, some located in S Spain & identified with Tartessus

Tar·sus \'tär-səs\ city S Turkey near the Cilician Gates ✷ of ancient Cilicia *pop* 187,508

Tar·tes·sus *or* **Tar·tes·sos** \tär-'te-səs\ ancient kingdom on SW coast of Spanish peninsula — see TARSHISH

Tar·tu \'tär-(,)tü\ *or German* **Dor·pat** \'dòr-,pät\ city E Estonia W of Lake Peipus *pop* 113,410

Tash·kent \tash-'kent, täsh-\ city E of the Syr Darya ✷ of Uzbekistan *pop* 2,073,000

Tas·man, Mount \'taz-mən\ mountain 11,475 *ft* (3498 *m*) New Zealand in South Is. in Southern Alps NE of Mt. Cook

Tas·ma·nia \taz-'mā-nē-ə, -nyə\ *or formerly* **Van Die·men's Land** \van-'dē-mənz\ island SE Australia S of Victoria; a state ✷ Hobart *area* 26,383 *sq mi* (68,332 *sq km*), *pop* 471,400 — **Tas·ma·ni·an** \taz-'mā-nē-ən, -nyən\ *adjective or noun*

Tasman Sea the part of the S Pacific between SE Australia & W New Zealand

Ta·ta·ban·ya \'tò-tò-,bä-(,)nyò\ city NW Hungary *pop* 75,300

Ta·tar·stan \,ta-tər-'stan, ,tä-tər-'stän\ autonomous republic E *central* Russia in Europe ✷ Kazan *area* 26,255 *sq mi* (68,000 *sq km*), *pop* 3,696,000

Ta·tar Strait \'tä-,tär, tə-'tär\ strait between Sakhalin Is. & mainland of Asia

Ta·try \'tä-trē\ *or* **Ta·tra** \'tä-trə\ mountain group N Slovakia & S Poland in *central* Carpathian Mountains — see GERLACHOVKA

Tatung — see DATONG

\ə\ abut \ᵊ\ kitten \ər\ **further** \a\ **ash** \ā\ **ace**
\ä\ mop, mar \aù\ **out** \ch\ **chin** \e\ **bet** \ē\ **easy**
\g\ **go** \i\ **hit** \ī\ **ice** \j\ **job** \ŋ\ **sing** \ō\ **go**
\ò\ **law** \òi\ **boy** \th\ **thin** \t̲h̲\ **the** \ü\ **loot** \ù\ **foot**
\y\ **yet** \zh\ **vision** *see also* Guide to Pronunciation

Tau·ghan·nock Falls \tə-'ga-nək\ waterfall 215 *ft* (66 *m*) S central N.Y. NW of Ithaca

Taung·gyi \'taun-jē\ town E Myanmar ✻ of Shan state *pop* 8652

Taun·ton \'tón-tᵊn, 'tän-\ city SE Mass. *pop* 49,832

Tau·nus \'tau̇-nəs\ mountain range SW *central* Germany E of the Rhine & N of lower Main River; highest peak Grosser Feldberg 2886 *ft* (880 *m*)

Tauric Chersonese — see CHERSONESE

Tau·rus \'tȯr-əs\ *or* Turkish **To·ros** \tȯ-'rȯs\ mountains S Turkey parallel to Mediterranean coast

Tax·co \'täs-(ˌ)kō\ *or* **Taxco de Alar·cón** \thä-ˌä-ˌlär-'kȯn\ city S Mexico in Guerrero SSW of Mexico City *pop* 86,811

Tay \'tā\ river 120 *mi* (193 *km*) E *central* Scotland flowing into North Sea through **Loch Tay** and **Firth of Tay**

Tay·lor \'tā-lər\ city SE Mich. SW of Detroit *pop* 70,811

Tay·myr Peninsula \tī-'mir\ peninsula N Russia in Asia between the Yenisey & the Khatanga — see CHELYUSKIN (Cape)

Tay·side \'tā-ˌsīd\ region E *central* Scotland, established 1975 ✻ Dundee *area* 2893 *sq mi* (7492 *sq km*), *pop* 395,200

Tbi·li·si \tə-'bē-lə-sē, tə-bə-'lē-sē\ *or* **Tif·lis** \'ti-fləs, tə-'flēs\ city ✻ of Republic of Georgia on the Kura *pop* 1,260,000

Tchad — see CHAD

Teche, Bayou \'tesh\ stream 175 *mi* (282 *km*) S La. flowing SE into the Atchafalaya

Tees \'tēz\ river 70 *mi* (113 *km*) N England flowing E into North Sea

Tees·side \'tēz-ˌsīd\ former county borough (1968–74) N England; since 1974 part of Cleveland

Te·gu·ci·gal·pa \tə-ˌgü-sə-'gal-pə, tä-ˌgü-sē-'gäl-pä\ city ✻ of Honduras *district pop* 608,100

Te·hach·a·pi Mountains \ti-'ha-chə-pē\ mountains SE Calif. N of Mojave Desert running E–W between S end of Sierra Nevada & the Coast Ranges; highest Double Mountain 7988 *ft* (2435 *m*); at E end is **Tehachapi Pass** 3793 *ft* (1156 *m*)

Teh·ran \tā-(ə-)'ran, te-'ran, -'rän\ city ✻ of Iran at foot of S slope of Elburz Mountains *pop* 6,042,584

Teh·ri \'tā-rē\ *or* **Tehri Garh·wal** \(ˌ)gər-'wäl\ former state N India in NW Uttar Pradesh on Tibet border; chief town Tehri

Te·huan·te·pec, Isthmus of \tā-'wän-tə-ˌpek\ the narrowest section of Mexico, between **Gulf of Tehuantepec** (on Pacific side) & Bay of Campeche; 137 *mi* (220 *km*) wide at narrowest point

Tejo — see TAGUS

Tel Aviv \ˌtel-ə-'vēv\ city W Israel on the Mediterranean *pop* 353,200 — see JAFFA — **Tel Avi·van** \-'vē-vən\ *noun*

Tel el Amar·na \'tel-ˌel-ə-'mär-nə\ locality *central* Egypt on E bank of the Nile NW of Asyût; site of ruins

Tel·e·mark \'te-lə-ˌmärk\ mountain region SW Norway

Telescope Peak mountain 11,049 *ft* (3368 *m*) E Calif., highest in Panamint Mountains

Te·les Pi·res \'tä-lēs-'pē-rēs\ *or formerly* **São Ma·nuel** \ˌsau̇ⁿ-mä-'nwel\ river 600 *mi* (966 *km*) E Brazil flowing NW to join the Juruena forming the Tapajos

Te·ma \'tā-mä\ city & port Ghana E of Accra *pop* 100,052

Te·mec·u·la \tə-'me-kyü-lə\ city S Calif. between Riverside & San Diego *pop* 27,099

Temeš — see TIMIŞ

Tem·pe \'tem-pē, *chiefly by outsiders* 'tem-pē\ city S *central* Ariz. SE of Phoenix *pop* 141,865

Tempe, Vale of \'tem-pē\ *or New Greek* **Tém·bi** \'tem-bē\ valley in NE Thessaly between Mounts Olympus & Ossa

Tem·ple \'tem-pəl\ city NE *central* Tex. SSW of Waco *pop* 46,109

Temple City city SW Calif. SE of Pasadena *pop* 31,100

Te·mu·co \tā-'mü-(ˌ)kō\ city S *central* Chile *pop* 157,634

Tenedos — see BOZCAADA

Te·ne·ri·fe \ˌte-nə-'ré-(ˌ)fä, -'rēf, -'rif\ *or formerly* **Ten·er·iffe** \ˌte-nə-'rif, -'rēf\ island Spain, largest of the Canary Islands; chief town Santa Cruz de Tenerife *area* 795 *sq mi* (2059 *sq km*)

Ten·nes·see \ˌte-nə-'sē, 'te-nə-,\ **1** river 652 *mi* (1049 *km*) E U.S., in Tenn., Ala., & Ky. flowing into Ohio River **2** state SE *central* U.S. ✻ Nashville *area* 42,144 *sq mi* (109,153 *sq km*), *pop* 4,877,185 — **Ten·nes·se·an** *or* **Ten·nes·see·an** \ˌte-nə-'sē-ən\ *adjective or noun*

Tennessee–Tom·big·bee Waterway \-'täm-'big-bē\ waterway 234 *mi* (374 *km*) long from Tennessee River on Tenn.-Miss. border to Tombigbee River in W *central* Ala.

Te·noch·ti·tlán \tā-ˌnȯch-tēt-'län\ name for Mexico City when it was capital of the Aztec Empire

Ten·sas \'ten-ˌsȯ\ river 250 *mi* (402 *km*) NE La. uniting with Ouachita River to form Black River

Ten·saw \'ten-ˌsȯ\ river 40 *mi* (64 *km*) SW Ala. formed by Tombigbee & Alabama rivers & flowing S into Mobile Bay

Te·o·ti·hua·cán \ˌtā-ō-ˌtē-wä-'kän\ city S *central* Mexico in Mexico state NE of Mexico City; once ✻ of the Toltecs *pop* 2238

Te·pic \tā-'pēk\ city W Mexico ✻ of Nayarit *pop* 238,101

Te·quen·da·ma Falls \ˌtā-kän-'dä-mä\ waterfall *central* Colombia S of Bogotá

Te·rai·na \te-'rī-nə\ *or formerly* **Washington Island** island *central* Pacific in the Line Islands *pop* 437

Ter·cei·ra \tər-'ser-ə, -'sir-\ island *central* Azores *area* 153 *sq mi* (396 *sq km*)

Te·re·si·na \ˌtär-ä-'zē-nə\ city NE Brazil ✻ of Piauí *pop* 598,449

Termonde — see DENDERMONDE

Ter·na·te \ter-'nä-(ˌ)tä\ **1** island Indonesia in N Moluccas off W Halmahera *pop* 33,964 **2** city & port, chief city on Ternate *pop* 24,287

Ter·ni \'ter-nē\ commune *central* Italy NNE of Rome *pop* 110,020

Ter·ra·ci·na \ˌter-ä-'chē-nä\ city & port *central* Italy in Lazio SE of Pontine Marshes *pop* 39,393

Ter·ra No·va National Park \ˌter-ə-'nō-və\ reservation E Canada in E Newfoundland (island)

Terre·bonne \ˌter-ə-'bän, ter-'bȯn\ town Canada in Quebec N of Montreal *pop* 39,678

Ter·re Haute \ˌter-ə-'hȯt *also* -'hät\ city W Ind. on the Wabash *pop* 57,483

Te·ruel \ˌter-ü-'wel\ **1** province E Spain in S Aragon *area* 5715 *sq mi* (14,802 *sq km*), *pop* 143,680 **2** commune, its ✻, S of Saragossa *pop* 28,487

Teschen — see CIESZYN

Tessin — see TICINO

Te·thys \'tē-thəs\ hypothetical sea believed to have extended into E Pangaea & later to have separated Laurasia to the N & Gondwanaland to the S with the Mediterranean being a remnant of it — **Te·thy·an** \-thē-ən\ *adjective*

Te·ton Range \'tē-ˌtän, -tᵊn\ mountain range NW Wyo. — see GRAND TETON

Té·touan \tā-'twän\ *or Spanish* **Te·tuán** \te-'twän\ city & port N Morocco on the Mediterranean *pop* 139,105

Teu·to·burg Forest \'tü-tə-ˌbərg, 'tyü-\ *or German* **Teu·to·bur·ger Wald** \'tȯi-tə-ˌbu̇r-gər-ˌvält\ range of forested hills W Germany in region between Ems & Weser rivers; highest point 1530 *ft* (466 *m*)

Tewkes·bury \'tüks-ˌber-ē, 'tyüks-, 'tu̇ks-, -b(ə-)rē\ borough SW *central* England in Gloucestershire on Avon & Severn rivers *pop* 9554

Tewks·bury \'tüks-ˌber-ē, 'tyüks-, 'tu̇ks-, -b(ə-)rē\ town NE Mass. *pop* 27,266

Tex·ar·kana \ˌtek-sər-'ka-nə, -sär-\ **1** city SW Ark. *pop* 22,631 **2** city NE Tex. adjacent to Texarkana, Ark. *pop* 31,656

Tex·as \'tek-səs, -siz\ state S U.S. ✻ Austin *area* 266,807 *sq mi* (691,030 *sq km*), *pop* 16,986,510 — **Tex·an** \-sən\ *adjective or noun*

Texas City city & port SE Tex. on Galveston Bay *pop* 40,822

Tex·co·co \tes-'kō-(ˌ)kō\ city *central* Mexico in Mexico state E of Mexico City *pop* 18,044

Thai·land \'tī-ˌland, -lənd\ *or formerly* **Si·am** \sī-'am\ country SE Asia on Gulf of Thailand; a kingdom ✻ Bangkok *area* 198,455 *sq mi* (513,998 *sq km*), *pop* 57,829,000 — **Thai·land·er** \-ˌlan-dər, -lən-\ *noun*

Thailand, Gulf of *or formerly* **Gulf of Siam** arm of S China Sea between Indochina & Malay Peninsula

Thames **1** \'temz, 'thämz, 'tämz\ river 15 *mi* (24 *km*) SE Conn., an estuary flowing S into Long Island Sound **2** \'temz\ river 135 *mi* (217 *km*) Canada in SE Ontario flowing S & SW into Lake St. Clair **3** \'temz\ river *over* 200 *mi* (322 *km*) S England flowing from the Cotswolds in Gloucestershire E into the North Sea — see ISIS

Than·et, Isle of \'tha-nət\ tract of land SE England in NE Kent cut off from mainland by arms of Stour River *area* 42 *sq mi* (109 *sq km*)

Thar Desert \'tär\ *or* **Great Indian Desert** desert S Asia in Pakistan & India between Aravalli Range & the Indus

Thá·sos \'thä-ˌsȯs\ island Greece in the N Aegean E of Chalcidice Peninsula *area* 146 *sq mi* (378 *sq km*)

The·ba·id \thi-'bā-əd, 'thē-bā-ˌid\ ancient district surrounding Thebes in Egypt or in Greece

Thebes \'thēbz\ **1** *or ancient* **The·bae** \'thē-(ˌ)bē\ *or* **Di·os·po·lis** \dī-'äs-pə-lis\ ancient city S Egypt on the Nile S of modern Qena — see KARNAK, LUXOR **2** ancient city E Greece in Boeotia NNW of Athens — **The·ban** \'thē-bən\ *adjective or noun*

The Colony city N Tex. *pop* 22,113

The Hague — see HAGUE (The)

The·o·dore Roosevelt National Park \'thē-ə-ˌdȯr, -ˌdȯr, -dər\ reservation W N.Dak. comprising three areas in badland region on the Little Missouri

Thermaïkós Kólpos — see SALONIKA (Gulf of)

Ther·mop·y·lae \(ˌ)thər-'mä-pə-(ˌ)lē\ locality E Greece between Mt. Oeta & Gulf of Lamia; once a narrow pass along the coast, now a rocky plain 6 *mi* (9.6 *km*) from the sea

Thes·sa·lo·ní·ki \the-sä-lō-'nē-kē\ *or formerly* **Sa·lo·ni·ka** \sə-'lä-ni-kə, -lä-'nē-kə\ *or ancient* **Thes·sa·lo·ni·ca** \ˌthe-sə-lä-ni-kə, -lə-'nē-kə\ city & port N Greece in Macedonia *pop* 402,443

Thes·sa·ly \'the-sə-lē\ *or Greek* **Thes·sa·lía** \ˌthe-sä-'lē-ä\ region E Greece between Pindus Mountains & the Aegean — **Thes·sa·lian** \the-'sā-lē-ən, -'säl-yən\ *adjective or noun*

Thim·phu \thim-'pü\ city W *central* Bhutan, its ✻

Thí·ra \'thir-ə\ *or ancient* **The·ra** \'thir-ə\ island Greece in S Cyclades 29 *sq mi* (75 *sq km*)

Tho·hoy·an·dou \tō-ˌhȯi-an-'dü\ town NE Republic of South Africa; formerly ✻ of Venda

Thomp·son \'täm(p)-sən\ river 304 *mi* (489 *km*) Canada in S British Columbia flowing S (as the **North Thompson**) & thence W & SW into the Fraser; joined by a branch, the **South Thompson**

Thorn·ton \'thȯrn-tᵊn\ city NE *central* Colo. N of Denver *pop* 55,031

Thousand Islands island group Canada & U.S. in St. Lawrence River in Ontario & N.Y.

Thousand Oaks city SW Calif. W of Los Angeles *pop* 104,352

Thrace \'thrās\ region SE Europe in Balkan Peninsula N of the Aegean; as ancient country (**Thra·cia** \'thrā-(ˌ)sē\ *or* **Thra·cia** \'thrā-sh(ē-)ə\), extended to the Danube; modern remnant divided between Greece (**Western Thrace**) & Turkey (**Eastern Thrace**, constituting Turkey in Europe) — **Thra·cian** \'thrā-shən\ *adjective or noun*

Thracian Chersonese — see CHERSONESE

Three Forks locality SW Mont. where Missouri River is formed by confluence of Gallatin, Jefferson, & Madison rivers *pop* 1203

Three Rivers TROIS-RIVIÈRES

Thu·le \'tü-lē\ settlement & district NW Greenland N of Cape York

Thun \'tün\ commune E *central* Switzerland *pop* 37,950

Thun, Lake of \'tün\ *or* **Thun·er·see** \'tü-nər-ˌzā\ lake 10 *mi* (16 *km*) long *central* Switzerland; an expansion of Aare River

Thunder Bay city & port Canada in SW Ontario on Lake Superior, formed 1970 by consolidation of Fort William & Port Arthur *pop* 113,946

Thur·gau \'tu̇r-ˌgau̇\ *or French* **Thur·go·vie** \tu̇r-gȯ-'vē\ canton NE Switzerland ✻ Frauenfeld *area* 389 *sq mi* (1008 *sq km*), *pop* 201,773

Thu·rin·gia \thú-'rin-j(ē-)ə, thyú-\ *or German* **Thü·ring·en** \'tǖ-riŋ-ən\ region *central* Germany including the **Thu·rin·gian Forest** \thú-'rin-j(ē-)ən, thyú-\ *or German* **Thü·ring·er Wald** \'tǖ-riŋ-ər-ˌvält\ (wooded mountain range between the upper Werra & the Czech border)

Thur·rock \'thər-ək, 'thə-rək\ former urban district SE England in Essex

Thursday Island island NE Australia off N Queensland in Torres Strait

Thyatira — see AKHISAR

Ti·a·hua·na·co \ˌtē-ä-wä-'nä-(ˌ)kō\ locality W Bolivia near SE end of Lake Titicaca; site of prehistoric ruins

Tian·jin \'tyän-'jin\ *or* **Tien·tsin** \'tyen-'tsin, 'tin-\ municipality & port NE China SE of Beijing *pop* 7,764,141

Tian Shan \'tyän-'shän, -'shan\ *or* **Tien Shan** \'tyen-\ mountain system *central* Asia extending from the Pamirs NE into Xinjiang Uygur — see POBEDA PEAK

Ti·ber \'tī-bər\ *or Italian* **Te·ve·re** \'tā-vä-rā\ river 252 *mi* (405 *km*) *central* Italy flowing through Rome into Tyrrhenian Sea

Ti·be·ri·as \tī-'bir-ē-əs\ city N Palestine in Galilee on W shore of Sea of Galilee; now in NE Israel *pop* 23,900

Tiberias, Lake *or* **Tiberias, Sea of** — see GALILEE (Sea of)

Ti·bes·ti Mountains \tə-'bes-tē\ mountains N *central* Africa in the Sahara in NW Chad; highest Emi Koussi 11,204 *ft* (3415 *m*)

Ti·bet \tə-'bet\ *or* **Xi·zang** \'shēd-'zäŋ\ region SW China on high plateau (average altitude 16,000 *ft or* 4877 *m*) N of the Himalayas ✳ Lhasa *area* 471,660 *sq mi* (1,226,316 *sq km*), *pop* 2,196,010

Ti·bu·rón \ˌtē-bü-'rōn\ island 34 *mi* (55 *km*) long NW Mexico in Gulf of California off coast of Sonora

Ti·ci·no \tə-'chē-(ˌ)nō\ **1** river 154 *mi* (248 *km*) Switzerland & Italy flowing from slopes of St. Gotthard Range SE & SW through Lake Maggiore into the Po **2** *or French* **Tes·sin** \teˈsaⁿ\ canton S Switzerland bordering on Italy ✳ Bellinzona *area* 1085 *sq mi* (2821 *sq km*), *pop* 286,537 — **Ti·ci·nese** \ˌti-chə-'nēz, -'nēs\ *adjective or noun*

Tientsin — see TIANJIN

Tier·ra del Fue·go \tē-'er-ə-(ˌ)del-fü-'ā-(ˌ)gō, 'tyer-ä-(ˌ)thel-'fwä-gō\ **1** archipelago off S. America S of Strait of Magellan; in Argentina & Chile *area* over 28,400 *sq mi* (73,556 *sq km*) **2** chief island of the archipelago; divided between Chile and Argentina *area* 18,530 *sq mi* (48,178 *sq km*)

Tiflis — see TBILISI

Ti·gard \'tī-gərd\ city NW Oreg. SSW of Portland *pop* 29,344

Ti·gre **1** \'tē-(ˌ)grā\ city E Argentina, NW suburb of Buenos Aires, on islands in Paraná delta *pop* 256,005 **2** \ti-'grā, 'ti-(ˌ)grā\ region N Ethiopia bordering on Eritrea — **Ti·gre·an** \ti-'grā-ən\ *adjective or noun*

Ti·gris \'tī-grəs\ river 1180 *mi* (1899 *km*) Iraq & SE Turkey flowing SSE & uniting with the Euphrates to form the Shatt al Arab

Ti·jua·na \bē-ə-'wä-nə, tē-ə-'wä-nä\ city NW Mexico on U.S. border in Baja California *pop* 742,686

Ti·kal \tē-'käl\ ancient Mayan city N Guatemala

Til·burg \'til-bərg\ commune S Netherlands SE of Rotterdam *pop* 160,618

Til·bury \'til-b(ə-)rē, *United States also* -ˌber-ē\ town & port SE England in Essex on Thames River E of London

Til·la·mook Bay \'ti-lə-ˌmək, -ˌmúk\ inlet of the Pacific NW Oreg.

Tilsit — see SOVETSK

Ti·ma·ga·mi, Lake \tə-'mä-gə-mē\ lake Canada in Ontario N of Lake Nipissing

Timbuktu — see TOMBOUCTOU

Tim·gad \'tim-ˌgad\ ancient Roman city NE Algeria

Ti·miş \'tē-mēsh\ *or* **Te·meš** \'te-mesh\ river about 200 *mi* (322 *km*) Romania & Yugoslavia flowing W & S into the Danube downstream from Belgrade

Ti·mi·soa·ra \ˌtē-mē-'shwär-ä\ city W Romania *pop* 333,365

Tim·mins \'ti-mənz\ city Canada in E Ontario N of Sudbury *pop* 47,461

Ti·mor \'tē-ˌmór, tē-'\ **1** island E Indonesia in Lesser Sunda Islands *area* 13,094 *sq mi* (34,044 *sq km*), *pop* 3,000,000; W part (formerly **Neth·erlands Timor**) belonged to the Dutch until 1946, E part (formerly **Portuguese Timor**) to Portugal until 1975 **2** sea between Timor Is. & Australia — **Ti·mor·ese** \(ˌ)tē-ˌmò-'rēz, -'rēs\ *adjective or noun*

Tim·pa·no·gos, Mount \ˌtim-pə-'nō-gəs\ mountain 12,008 *ft* (3660 *m*) N *central* Utah N of Provo; highest in Wasatch Range

Timpanogos Cave National Monument series of limestone caverns N *central* Utah on N slope of Mt. Timpanogos

Ti·ni·an \ˌti-nē-'an\ island W Pacific in the S Marianas

Tin·ley Park \'tin-lē\ city NE Ill. *pop* 37,121

Ti·nos \'tē-ˌnòs\ island Greece in N Cyclades SE of Andros

Tin·tag·el Head \tin-'ta-jəl\ headland SW England in NW Cornwall

Tip·pe·ca·noe \ˌti-pē-kə-'nü\ river 200 *mi* (322 *km*) N Ind. flowing SW into the Wabash

Tip·per·ary \ˌti-pə-'rer-ē\ **1** county S Ireland in Munster ✳ Clonmel *area* 1643 *sq mi* (4272 *sq km*), *pop* 132,772 **2** town in SW County Tipperary *pop* 4783

Ti·ra·në *or* **Ti·ra·na** \ti-'rä-nə, tē-\ city *central* Albania, its ✳ *pop* 243,000

Tir·gu–Mu·res \ˌtir-(ˌ)gü-'mü-ˌresh\ city NE *central* Romania ESE of Cluj-Napoca *pop* 164,781

Ti·rich Mir \ˌtir-ich-'mir\ mountain *about* 25,260 *ft* (7699 *m*) Pakistan on Afghan border; highest in the Hindu Kush

Ti·rol *or* **Ty·rol** \tə-'rōl; 'tī-ˌrōl, tī-'; 'tir-əl\ *or Italian* **Ti·ro·lo** \tē-'rò-(ˌ)lō\ region Europe in E Alps chiefly in Austria; the section S of Brenner Pass has belonged since 1919 to Italy — **Ti·ro·le·an** \tə-'rō-lē-ən, tī-; ˌtir-ə-', ˌtī-rə-\ *adjective or noun* — **Ti·ro·lese** \ˌtir-ə-'lēz, ˌtī-rə-, -'lēs\ *adjective or noun*

Ti·ruch·chi·rap·pal·li \ˌtir-ə-chə-'rä-pə-lē\ city S India in *central* Tamil Nadu *pop* 711,862

Ti·ryns \'tir-ənz, 'tī-rənz\ city of pre-Homeric Greece; ruins in E Peloponnese SE of Argos

Ti·sza \'ti-ˌsó\ river *about* 600 *mi* (965 *km*) E Europe flowing from the Carpathians in W Ukraine W & SW into the Danube

Ti·ti·ca·ca, Lake \ˌti-ti-'kä-kä, ˌtē-tē-\ lake on Peru-Bolivia boundary at altitude of 12,500 *ft* (3810 *m*), *area* 3200 *sq mi* (8320 *sq km*)

Titograd — see PODGORICA

Ti·tus·ville \'tī-təs-ˌvil, -vəl\ city E Fla. E of Orlando *pop* 39,394

Tiv·o·li \'tē-və-lē, 'tē-vō-\ *or ancient* **Ti·bur** \'tī-bər\ commune *central* Italy in Lazio ENE of Rome *pop* 50,559

Tjilatjap — see CILACAP

Tlax·ca·la \tlä-'skä-lä\ **1** state *central* Mexico *area* 1511 *sq mi* (3913 *sq km*), *pop* 761,277 **2** city, its ✳, E of Mexico City *pop* 50,631

Tlem·cen \tlem-'sen\ *or* **Ti·lim·sen** \tə-lim-'sen\ city NW Algeria *pop* 126,882

Toa Al·ta \ˌtō-ä-'äl-tä\ municipality NE *central* Puerto Rico *pop* 44,101

Toa Ba·ja \ˌbä-(ˌ)hä\ municipality NE Puerto Rico W of San Juan *pop* 89,454

To·a·ma·si·na \ˌtō-ə-mə-'sē-nə\ *or formerly* **Ta·ma·tave** \ˌtə-mə-'täv, ˌtä-\ city & port E coast of Madagascar *pop* 145,431

To·ba·go \tə-'bā-(ˌ)gō\ island SE W. Indies, a territory of Trinidad and Tobago; chief town Scarborough *area* 116 *sq mi* (302 *sq km*), *pop* 50,282 — **To·ba·go·ni·an** \ˌtō-bə-'gō-nē-ən, -nyən\ *noun*

To·bol \tə-'ból\ river N Kazakhstan & SW Russia in Asia flowing from SE foothills of the Urals NNE into the Irtysh

To·bruk \tō-'brúk, 'tō-,\ city & port NE Libya *pop* 34,200

To·can·tins \ˌtō-kən-'tēnz, ˌtü-kən-'tēⁿs\ river *about* 1700 *mi* (2736 *km*) E *central* & NE Brazil rising in S *central* Goiás & flowing N into Pará River

To·go \'tō-(ˌ)gō\ republic W Africa on Bight of Benin ✳ Lomé *area* 21,853 *sq mi* (56,599 *sq km*), *pop* 3,810,000 — **To·go·lese** \ˌtō-gə-'lēz, -'lēs\ *adjective or noun*

To·go·land \'tō-(ˌ)gō-ˌland\ region W Africa on Gulf of Guinea between Benin & Ghana; until 1919 a German protectorate, then divided into two trust territories: **British Togoland** (in W; since 1957 part of Ghana) & **French Togo** (in E; since 1958 Togo) — **To·go·land·er** \'tō-(ˌ)gō-ˌlan-dər\ *noun*

To·ho·pe·kal·i·ga Lake \tə-ˌhō-pi-'ka-li-gə\ lake *central* Fla. S of Orlando

To·ka·ra Islands \tō-'kär-ä\ island group Japan in N Ryukyus

To·ke·lau Islands \'tō-kə-ˌláu\ islands *central* Pacific N of Samoa belonging to New Zealand *pop* 1690 — **To·ke·lau·an** \ˌtō-kə-'láu-ən\ *noun*

To·ko·ro·za·wa \ˌtō-kō-'rō-zä-(ˌ)wä\ city Japan on Honshu, a suburb of Tokyo *pop* 303,047

To·ku·shi·ma \ˌtō-kü-'shē-mä\ city & port Japan on E coast of Shikoku Is. *pop* 264,503

To·kyo \'tō-kē-ō, -ˌō, -ˌkyō\ *or formerly* **Edo** \'e-(ˌ)dō\ *or* **Ye·do** \'ye-(ˌ)dō\ city ✳ of Japan in SE Honshu on **Tokyo Bay** (inlet of the Pacific) *pop* 11,854,987 — **To·kyo·ite** \'tō-kē-(ˌ)ō-ˌīt\ *noun*

To·le·do \tə-'lē-(ˌ)dō, -'lē-də, *for 2 & 3 also* tō-'lā-thō\ **1** city & port NW Ohio on the Maumee River *pop* 332,943 **2** province *central* Spain in W New Castile *area* 5934 *sq mi* (15,369 *sq km*), *pop* 489,543 **3** commune, its ✳ *pop* 59,563 — **To·le·dan** \-'lē-d'n\ *adjective or noun* — **To·le·do·an** \-'lē-də-ən\ *adjective or noun*

To·li·ma \tō-'lē-mä\ dormant volcano W *central* Colombia 17,110 *ft* (5215 *m*)

To·lu·ca \tō-'lü-kä\ *or* **Toluca de Ler·do** \thä-'ler-(ˌ)dō\ city *central* Mexico ✳ of Mexico state *pop* 487,630

Toluca, Ne·va·do de \nä-'vä-thō-thä-\ extinct volcano 15,016 *ft* (4577 *m*) S *central* Mexico in Mexico state

Tol'·yat·ti *or* **To·gliat·ti** \tól'-'yä-tē\ *or formerly* **Stav·ro·pol** \stav-'ró-pəl, -'rō-; 'stä-vrə-ˌpəl\ city SE *central* Russia in Europe NW of Samara *pop* 666,000

Tom \'täm, 'tóm\ river 450 *mi* (724 *km*) S Russia in Asia rising in NW Altay Mountains & flowing into the Ob

Tom·big·bee \täm-'big-bē\ river NE Miss. & W Ala. flowing S to Mobile & Tensaw rivers

Tom·bouc·tou \tōⁿ-bük-'tü\ *or* **Tim·buk·tu** \ˌtim-ˌbək-'tü, tim-'bək-(ˌ)tü\ town W Africa in Mali near Niger River *pop* 31,925

Tomsk \'täm(p)sk, 'tóm(p)sk\ city S *central* Russia in Asia on Tom River near its junction with the Ob *pop* 505,000

Ton·ga \'täŋ-gə, 'täŋ-ə\ islands SW Pacific E of Fiji; a kingdom in the Commonwealth of Nations ✳ Nukualofa *area* 270 *sq mi* (702 *sq km*), *pop* 94,649

Tongareva — see PENRHYN

Ton·ga·ri·ro \ˌtäŋ-gə-'rir-(ˌ)ō, ˌtäŋ-ə-\ volcano 6516 *ft* (1986 *m*) New Zealand in *central* North Is. in **Tongariro National Park**

Tong·hua \'tùŋ-'hwä, 'tóŋ-'wä\ *or* **T'ung–hua** *or* **Tung·hwa** \'túŋ-\ city NE China in S Jilin *pop* 158,000

Tongue \'təŋ\ river 246 *mi* (396 *km*) N Wyo. & S Mont. flowing N into Yellowstone River

Ton·kin \'tän-kən; 'tän-'kin, 'täŋ-\ *or* **Tong·king** \'täŋ-kiŋ\ region N Indochina bordering on China, since 1946 forming N part of Vietnam; chief city Hanoi — **Ton·kin·ese** \ˌtäŋ-kə-'nēz, ˌtän-, -'nēs\ *or* **Tong·king·ese** \ˌtäŋ-kiŋ-'ēz, -'ēs\ *adjective or noun*

Tonkin, Gulf of arm of S. China Sea E of N Vietnam

Ton·le Sap \ˌtän-ˌlā-'sap\ *or French* **Grand Lac** \gräⁿ-'läk\ lake 87 *mi* (140 *km*) long SW Indochina in W Cambodia

Ton·to National Monument \ˌtän-(ˌ)tō\ reservation S *central* Ariz. E of Phoenix containing cliff-dweller ruins

Too·woom·ba \tə-'wüm-bə\ city E Australia in SE Queensland *pop* 81,043

To·pe·ka \tə-'pē-kə\ city ✳ of Kans. on Kansas River *pop* 119,883

To·po·lo·bam·po \tō-ˌpō-lō-'bäm-(ˌ)pō\ town & port NW Mexico in Sinaloa on Gulf of California

Tor·bay \(,)tȯr-'bā\ former county borough SW England in Devon on **Tor Bay** (inlet of English Channel); included Brixham, Paignton, & Torquay

Tor·cel·lo \tȯr-'che-(,)lō\ island Italy in Lagoon of Venice

Tor·de·sil·las \,tȯr-dā-'sē-yäs, -'sēl-yäs\ village NW Spain SW of Valladolid

Torino — see TURIN

Tor·ne \'tȯr-nə\ or Finnish **Tor·nio** \'tȯr-nē-,ō\ river 354 mi (570 km) NE Sweden flowing S, forming part of Finnish-Swedish border, to head of Gulf of Bothnia

To·ron·to \tə-'rän-(,)tō, -rän-tə\ city & port Canada ✳ of Ontario on Lake Ontario pop 635,395 — **To·ron·to·ni·an** \tə-,rän-'tō-nē-ən; ,tȯr-ən-, ,tär-ən-\ adjective or noun

Toros — see TAURUS

Tor·rance \'tȯr-ən(t)s, 'tär-\ city SW Calif. SSW of Los Angeles pop 133,107

Tor·re An·nun·zi·a·ta \'tȯr-ā-ä-,nün(t)-sē-'ä-tä\ commune S Italy on Bay of Naples SE of Naples pop 56,471

Torre de Cerredo — see CERREDO

Tor·re del Gre·co \'tȯr-ā-del-'gre-(,)kō, -'grä-\ commune S Italy on Bay of Naples pop 103,577

Tor·rens, Lake \'tȯr-ənz, 'tär-\ salt lake Australia in E S. Australia N of Spencer Gulf 92 ft (28 m) above sea level

Tor·re·ón \tȯr-ā-'ōn\ city N Mexico in Coahuila pop 459,809

Tor·res Strait \'tȯr-əs\ strait 80 mi (129 km) wide between island of New Guinea & N tip of Cape York Peninsula, Australia

Tor·res Ve·dras \,tȯr-iz-'ve-drəsh\ town W Portugal N of Lisbon

Tor·ring·ton \'tȯr-iŋ-tən, 'tär-\ city NW Conn. pop 33,687

Tórs·havn \'tȯrs-,haùn\ town & port ✳ of the Faeroe Islands pop 16,091

Tor·to·la \tȯr-'tō-lə\ island Brit. West Indies, chief of the Brit. Virgin Islands; site of Road Town area 21 sq mi (54 sq km), pop 9730

Tor·tu·ga \tȯr-'tü-gə\ island NW Haiti off N coast; a resort of pirates in 17th century pop 13,723

To·ruń \'tȯr-,ün, ,ü-nyə\ city N Poland on the Vistula pop 200,822

Toscana — see TUSCANY

Tot·ten·ham \'tä-tⁿ-əm\ former municipal borough SE England in Middlesex, now part of Haringey

Toub·kal, Je·bel \'je-bəl-tüb-'käl\ mountain 13,665 ft (4165 m) W central Morocco; highest in Atlas Mountains

Toug·gourt \tə-'gùrt\ town & oasis NE Algeria S of Biskra pop 70,645

Tou·lon \tü-'lōⁿ\ commune & port SE France on the Mediterranean pop 170,167

Tou·louse \tü-'lüz\ city SW France on the Garonne pop 365,933

Tou·raine \tù-'ren, -'ren\ region & former province NW central France ✳ Tours

Tourane — see DA NANG

Tour·coing \tùr-'kwaⁿ\ city N France NE of Lille pop 94,425

Tour·nai or **Tour·nay** \tùr-'nā\ or Flemish **Door·nik** \'dȯr-nik, 'dȯr-\ commune SW Belgium on the Schelde pop 67,732

Tours \'tùr\ city NW central France pop 133,403

Tower Hamlets borough of E Greater London, England pop 153,500

Towns·ville \'taùnz-,vil, -vəl\ city & port NE Australia in NE Queensland pop 101,398

To·ya·ma \tō-'yä-mä\ city Japan in central Honshu near **Toyama Bay** (inlet of Sea of Japan) pop 321,259

To·yo·ha·shi \,tȯi-ō-'hä-shē\ city Japan in S Honshu SE of Nagoya pop 337,988

To·yo·na·ka \,tȯi-ō-'nä-kə\ city Japan on Honshu pop 409,843

To·yo·ta \tȯi-'ō-tä\ city Japan on Honshu pop 332,336

Trab·zon \trab-'zän\ or **Treb·i·zond** \'tre-bə-,zänd\ or ancient **Trap·e·zus** \'tra-pi-zəs\ city & port NE Turkey on Black Sea pop 143,941

Tra·cy \'trā-sē\ city central Calif. SSW of Stockton pop 33,558

Tra·fal·gar, Cape \trə-'fal-gər, Spanish ,trä-fäl-'gär\ cape SW Spain SE of Cádiz at W end of Strait of Gibraltar

Tra·lee \trə-'lē\ seaport SW Ireland ✳ of Kerry pop 17,109

Trans Alai \,tran(t)s-ə-'lī, ,tranz-\ mountain range Kyrgyzstan & Tajikistan in NW Pamirs — see LENIN PEAK

Transalpine Gaul the part of Gaul included chiefly in modern France & Belgium

Transcaucasia — see CAUCASIA — **Trans·cau·ca·sian** \,tran(t)s-kȯ-'kā-zhən, -'ka-\ adjective or noun

Transjordan — see JORDAN — **Trans·jor·da·ni·an** \,tran(t)s-jȯr-'dā-nē-ən, ,tranz-\ adjective or noun

Trans·kei \(,)tran(t)s-'kī\ former black enclave in the Republic of South Africa ✳ Umtata; granted independence 1976; abolished 1994 — **Trans·kei·an** \-ən\ adjective or noun

Trans·vaal \tran(t)s-'väl, tranz-\ former province NE Republic of South Africa between the Vaal & the Limpopo; in 19th century a Boer republic (**South African Republic**) ✳ Pretoria area 109,621 sq mi (283,918 sq km)

Tran·syl·va·nia \,tran(t)-səl-'vā-nyə, -nē-ə\ or Romanian **Tran·sil·va·nia** \,tran(t)-səl-'vā-nyə, -nē-ə\ region W Romania bounded on the N, E, & S by the Carpathians & the Transylvanian Alps; part of Hungary 1867–1918 — **Tran·syl·va·nian** \-nyən, -nē-ən\ adjective or noun

Transylvanian Alps a S extension of the Carpathian Mountains in central Romania

Tra·pa·ni \'trä-pä-nē\ commune & port Italy at NW tip of Sicily pop 69,273

Tra·si·me·no, Lake \,trä-zē-'mā-nō\ lake 10 mi (16 km) wide central Italy W of Perugia

Trav·an·core \'tra-vən-,kȯr, -,kȯr\ region & former state SW India on Malabar Coast extending N from Cape Comorin; included (1949–56) in former **Travancore and Co·chin** \'kō-chən\ state (✳ Trivandrum) — see KERALA

Trav·erse, Lake \'tra-vərs\ lake NE S.Dak. & W Minn.; drained by the Bois de Sioux (headstream of Red River)

Treb·bia \'tre-bē-ä\ or ancient **Tre·bia** \'trē-bē-ə\ river 71 mi (114 km) NW Italy flowing N into the Po

Treb·i·zond \'tre-bə-,zänd\ 1 — see TRABZON 2 Greek empire 1204–1461, an offshoot of Byzantine Empire; at greatest extent included Georgia, Crimea, & S coast of Black Sea E of the Sakarya

Treng·ga·nu \treŋ-'gä-(,)nü\ state Malaysia in NE Peninsular Malaysia on S. China Sea ✳ Kuala Trengganu area 5000 sq mi (12,950 sq km)

Trent \'trent\ 1 river 150 mi (241 km) Canada in SE Ontario flowing from Kawartha Lakes through Rice Lake into Lake Ontario (Bay of Quinte) 2 river 170 mi (274 km) central England flowing NNE & uniting with Ouse River to form the Humber

Trent Canal canal system Canada 224 mi (360 km) long in SE Ontario connecting Lake Huron (Georgian Bay) with Lake Ontario (Bay of Quinte)

Tren·ti·no–Al·to Adi·ge \tren-'tē-nō-,äl-tō-'ä-dē-,jä\ region N Italy ✳ Trento area 5526 sq mi (13,613 sq km), pop 886,679

Tren·to \'tren-(,)tō\ commune N Italy pop 101,430

Tren·ton \'tren-tⁿn\ 1 city SE Mich. on Detroit River pop 20,586 2 city ✳ of N.J. on Delaware River pop 88,675

Tre·vi·so \trā-'vē-(,)zō\ commune NE Italy NW of Venice pop 83,222

Trier \'trir\ city W Germany on the Moselle near Luxembourg border pop 98,752

Tri·este \trē-'est, -'es-tē, -'es-tā\ or Serbo-Croatian **Trst** \'tərst\ city & port NE Italy ✳ of Friuli-Venezia Giulia, on **Gulf of Trieste** (inlet at head of the Adriatic NW of the Istrian Peninsula) pop 229,216; once belonged to Austria; part of Italy 1919–47; in 1947 made with surrounding territory the **Free Territory of Trieste** under administration of the United Nations; city with N part of Free Territory returned to Italy 1953, S part of territory having previously been absorbed into Yugoslavia — **Tri·es·tine** \trē-'es-tən, -,tēn\ adjective

Trik·ka·la or **Trik·ka·la** \tri-kə-lə, 'trē-kä-lä\ city central Greece pop 48,810

Trim \'trim\ town E Ireland ✳ of County Meath pop 1781

Trinacria — see SICILY — **Tri·nac·ri·an** \trə-'na-krē-ən, trī-\ adjective

Trin·co·ma·lee \,triŋ-kō-mə-'lē, triŋ-'kə-mə-lē\ city & port NE Sri Lanka on Bay of Bengal pop 50,000

Trin·i·dad \'tri-nə-,dad\ island SE W. Indies off coast of NE Venezuela pop 1,184,106; with Tobago, a dominion (**Trinidad and Tobago**) of the Commonwealth of Nations since 1962; formerly a Brit. colony ✳ Port of Spain area 1980 sq mi (5128 sq km), pop 1,234,388 — **Trin·i·da·di·an** \,tri-nə-'dā-dē-ən, -'da-\ adjective or noun

Trin·i·ty \'tri-nə-tē\ river E Tex. flowing SE into Galveston Bay

Trip·o·li \'tri-pə-lē\ 1 or Arabic **Ta·rā·bu·lus** \tə-'rä-bə-ləs\ or ancient **Trip·o·lis** \'tri-pə-ləs\ city & port NW Lebanon NNE of Beirut pop 127,611 2 or Arabic **Tarābulus** or ancient **Oea** \'ē-ə\ city & port NW Libya, its ✳ pop 591,062 3 Tripolitania when it was one of the Barbary States — **Trip·ol·i·tan** \tri-'pä-lə-tⁿn\ adjective or noun

Tri·po·li·ta·nia \tri-,pä-lə-'tā-nyə, ,tri-pə-lə-\ or ancient **Trip·o·lis** \'tri-pə-ləs\ region & former province NW Libya bordering on the Mediterranean — **Tri·po·li·ta·nian** \tri-,pä-lə-'tā-nyən, ,tri-pə-lə-\ adjective or noun

Tri·pu·ra \'tri-pə-rə\ state E India between Bangladesh & Assam ✳ Agartala area 4035 sq mi (10,451 sq km), pop 2,757,205

Tris·tan da Cu·nha \,tris-tən-də-'kü-nə, -nyə\ island S Atlantic, chief of the Tristan da Cunha Islands attached to Brit. colony of St. Helena area 38 sq mi (98 sq km), pop 296; volcanic eruptions 1961

Tri·van·drum \tri-'van-drəm\ city & port S India NW of Cape Comorin ✳ of Kerala pop 699,872

Tro·as \'trō-,as\ 1 or **Tro·ad** \-,ad\ territory surrounding the ancient city of Troy in NW Mysia, Asia Minor 2 ancient city of Mysia S of site of Troy — **Tro·ad·ic** \trō-'a-dik\ adjective

Tro·bri·and \'trō-brē-,änd, -,and\ islands SW Pacific in Solomon Sea; attached to Papua New Guinea area 170 sq mi (442 sq km) — **Tro·bri·and·er** \,trō-brē-'än-dər, -'an-\ noun

Trois–Ri·vières \,t(r)wä-ri-'vyer\ town Canada in S Quebec NE of Montreal on N bank of St. Lawrence River pop 49,426

Trom·sö \'träm-,sō, -,sœ\ city & port N Norway pop 50,548

Trond·heim \'trän-,hām\ city & port central Norway on **Trondheim Fjord** (80 mi or 128 km long), pop 137,346

Tros·sachs \'trä-səks, -,saks\ valley central Scotland between Loch Katrine & Loch Achray

Trou·ville \trü-'vēl\ or **Trouville–sur–Mer** \-(,)sūr-'mer\ town & port N France on English Channel S of Le Havre pop 5645

Trow·bridge \'trō-(,)brij\ town S England ✳ of Wiltshire pop 22,984

Troy \'trȯi\ 1 city SE Mich. N of Detroit pop 72,884 2 city E N.Y. on Hudson River NNE of Albany pop 54,269 3 city W Ohio pop 19,478 4 or **Il·i·um** \'i-lē-əm\ or **Il·i·on** \'i-lē-,än, -lē-ən\ or **Tro·ja** \'trō-jə, -yə\ ancient city NW Asia Minor in Troas SW of the Dardanelles

Troyes \'t(r)wä\ city NE France SE of Paris pop 60,755

Tru·chas Peak \'trü-chəs\ or **North Truchas Peak** mountain 13,110 ft (3996 m) N N.Mex. in Sangre de Cristo Mountains NE of Santa Fe; highest of three peaks forming **Truchas Peaks**

Trucial Oman, Trucial States — see UNITED ARAB EMIRATES

Truck·ee \'trə-kē\ river 120 mi (193 km) E Calif. & W Nev. flowing from Lake Tahoe into Pyramid Lake

Tru·ji·llo \trü-'hē-(,)yō\ 1 city NW Peru NW of Lima pop 193,528 2 — see SANTO DOMINGO

Trujillo Al·to \-'äl-(,)tō\ municipality NE central Puerto Rico pop 61,120

Truk Islands \'trək, 'trük\ islands central Carolines, part of Federated States of Micronesia

Trum·bull \'trəm-bəl\ town SW Conn. N of Bridgeport pop 32,016

Tru·ro \'trü-(,)rō\ city & borough SW England ✳ of Cornwall and Isles of Scilly pop 16,277

Tsang·po \'(t)säŋ-'pō\ the upper Brahmaputra in Tibet

Tsaritsyn — see VOLGOGRAD

Tsarskoye Selo — see PUSHKIN

Tsinan — see JINAN

Tsinghai — see QINGHAI

Tsingtao — see QINGDAO

Tsitsihar — see QIQIHAR

Tskhin·va·li \'(t)skin-və-lē\ town N Republic of Georgia NW of Tbilisi ✷ of S. Ossetia Autonomous Oblast *pop* 42,600

Tsu·ga·ru Strait \'(t)sü-gä-,rü\ strait Japan between Honshu & Hokkaido

Tsu·shi·ma \(t)sü-'shē-mä\ island Japan in Korea Strait separated from Kyushu and Honshu by **Tsushima Strait** (the SE part of Korea Strait) *area* 271 *sq mi* (705 *sq km*)

Tu·a·mo·tu Archipelago \,tü-ä-'mō-(,)tü\ archipelago S Pacific E of Society Islands; belongs to France *area* 330 *sq mi* (858 *sq km*), *pop* 11,754

Tü·bing·en \'tü-biŋ-ən, 'tyü-, 'tē-\ city SW Germany on the Neckar S of Stuttgart *pop* 82,483

Tuc·son \'tü-,sän, *especially locally* tü-'sän\ city SE Ariz. *pop* 405,390 — **Tuc·son·an** \'tü-,sä-nən\ *noun*

Tucumán — see SAN MIGUEL DE TUCUMÁN

Tu·ge·la \tü-'gā-lä\ river 312 *mi* (502 *km*) E Republic of South Africa in *central* KwaZulu-Natal flowing E to Indian Ocean; near its source on Mont Aux Sources are the **Tugela Falls** (3110 *ft or* 948 *m*)

Tu·la \'tü-lä\ **1** *or* **Tula de Al·len·de** \(,)thä-ä-'yen-dā\ city *central* Mexico in SW Hidalgo N of Mexico City; ancient ✷ of the Toltecs *pop* 71,622 **2** city SW *central* Russia in Europe S of Moscow on a tributary of Oka River *pop* 541,000

Tu·la·gi \tü-'lä-gē\ island S Pacific in S *central* Solomons

Tu·lare \tü-'lar(-ē), -'ler(-ē)\ city S *central* Calif. SE of Fresno *pop* 33,249

Tulare Lake former lake S *central* Calif. S of Hanford; drained for farmland

Tul·la·more \,tə-lə-'mōr, -'mór\ town *central* Ireland ✷ of county Offaly *pop* 8623

Tul·sa \'təl-sə\ city NE Okla. on Arkansas River *pop* 367,302 — **Tul·san** \-sən\ *noun*

Tu·ma·ca·co·ri National Monument \,tü-mə-'kä-kə-rē\ historic site S Ariz. S of Tucson; contains remains of Franciscan mission

Tu·men \'tü-'mən\ river 324 *mi* (521 *km*) E Asia on border between N. Korea, China, & Russia flowing NE & SE into Sea of Japan

Tu·muc–Hu·mac Mountains \,tü-,mü-kü-'mäk\ *or Portuguese* **Ser·ra Tu·mu·cu·ma·que** \'se-rə-tü-,mü-kü-'mä-kä, -kē\ range of low mountains NE Brazil on Suriname-French Guiana boundary

Tunbridge Wells — see ROYAL TUNBRIDGE WELLS

T'ung–hua — see TONGHUA

Tun·gu·ska \tún-'gü-skə, tən-\ any of three rivers in *central* Russia in Asia, tributaries of the Yenisey: **Lower Tunguska**, **Stony Tunguska**, & **Upper Tunguska** (lower course of the Angara)

Tu·nis \'tü-nəs, 'tyü-\ **1** city ✷ of Tunisia near site of ancient Carthage *pop* 620,149 **2** TUNISIA — used especially of the former Barbary State

Tu·ni·sia \tü-'nē-zh(ē-)ə, tyü-, -'ni-\ country N Africa bordering on the Mediterranean; formerly one of the Barbary States; a French protectorate 1881–1956, a monarchy 1956–57, & a republic since 1957 ✷ Tunis *area* 63,378 *sq mi* (164,149 *sq km*), *pop* 8,530,000 — **Tu·ni·sian** \-zh(ē-)ən\ *adjective or noun*

Tu·ol·um·ne \tü-'ä-lə-mē\ river 155 *mi* (249 *km*) *central* Calif. flowing W from Yosemite National Park into the San Joaquin

Tu·pe·lo \'tü-pə-,lō, 'tyü-\ city NE Miss. *pop* 30,685

Tu·pun·ga·to \,tü-püŋ-'gä-(,)tō\ mountain 22,310 *ft* (6800 *m*) in the Andes on Argentina-Chile boundary ENE of Santiago, Chile

Tu·rin \'túr-ən, 'tyúr-; tü-'rin, tyü-\ *or Italian* **To·ri·no** \tō-'rē-(,)nō\ commune NW Italy on the Po ✷ of Piedmont *pop* 961,916 — **Tu·rin·ese** \,túr-ə-'nēz, ,tyúr-, -'nēs\ *adjective or noun*

Tur·ka·na, Lake \tər-'ka-nə\ *or* **Lake Ru·dolf** \'rü-,dólf, -,dälf\ lake N Kenya in Great Rift Valley *area* 2473 *sq mi* (6405 *sq km*)

Tur·key \'tər-kē\ country W Asia & SE Europe between Mediterranean & Black seas; formerly center of an empire (✷ Constantinople), since

1923 a republic ✷ Ankara *area* 301,380 *sq mi* (780,574 *sq km*), *pop* 50,664,458 — see OTTOMAN EMPIRE

Tur·ki·stan *or* **Tur·ke·stan** \,tər-kə-'stan, -'stän; 'tər-kə-,\ region *central* Asia between Iran & Siberia; now divided between Turkmenistan, Uzbekistan, Tajikistan, Kyrgyzstan, Kazakhstan, China, & Afghanistan — see CHINESE TURKESTAN, RUSSIAN TURKESTAN

Turk·men·i·stan \,tərk-,me-nə-'stan, -'stän; (,)tərk-'me-nə-,\ country *central* Asia bordering on Afghanistan, Iran, & the Caspian Sea; a constituent republic (**Turk·men Republic** \'tərk-mən\) of the U.S.S.R. 1925–91 ✷ Ashkhabad *area* 188,455 *sq mi* (488,098 *sq km*), *pop* 3,958,000 — **Turk·man** \'tərk-mən\ *noun, pl* **Turk·men** \-mən\ — **Turkmen** *noun, pl* **Turk·mens** \-mənz\ — **Turkmen** *adjective* — **Turk·me·ni·an** \,tərk-'mē-nē-ən\ *adjective*

Turks and Cai·cos \'tərks-ənd-'kā-kəs, -,kōs\ two groups of islands (Turks Islands & Caicos Islands) Brit. West Indies at SE end of Bahamas; a Brit. colony; seat of government on **Grand Turk** (7 *mi* or 11 *km* long) *area* 166 *sq mi* (432 *sq km*), *pop* 12,350

Tur·ku \'túr-(,)kü\ city & port SW Finland *pop* 159,469

Tur·lock \'tər-,läk\ city *central* Calif. SE of Modesto *pop* 42,198

Turn·hout \'túrn-,haút, túr-'nüt\ commune N Belgium *pop* 38,100

Tur·tle Bay \'tər-tᵊl\ section of New York City in E *central* Manhattan on East River; site of United Nations headquarters

Tus·ca·loo·sa \,təs-kə-'lü-sə\ city W *central* Ala. on Black Warrior River SW of Birmingham *pop* 77,759

Tus·ca·ny \'təs-kə-nē\ *or Italian* **To·sca·na** \tō-'skä-nä\ region NW *central* Italy bordering on Ligurian & Tyrrhenian seas ✷ Florence *area* 8876 *sq mi* (22,989 *sq km*), *pop* 3,560,582

Tus·cu·lum \'təs-kyə-ləm, -kə-\ ancient town Italy in Lazio SE of Rome

Tus·tin \'təs-tən\ city SW Calif. E of Santa Ana *pop* 50,689

Tu·tu·i·la \,tü-tü-'wē-lä\ island, chief of American Samoa group *area* 52 *sq mi* (135 *sq km*) — **Tu·tu·i·lan** \-lən\ *adjective or noun*

Tu·va Republic \'tü-və\ autonomous republic S Russia in Asia N of Mongolia ✷ Kyzyl *area* 65,380 *sq mi* (169,334 *sq km*), *pop* 306,000

Tu·va·lu \tü-'vä-(,)lü, -'vär-(,)ü\ *or formerly* **El·lice Islands** \'e-lis\ islands W Pacific N of Fiji; a Brit. territory 1976–78; became an independent member of the Commonwealth of Nations 1978 ✷ Funafuti *area* 9 *sq mi* (23 *sq km*), *pop* 9700 — see GILBERT AND ELLICE

Tux·tla \'tüst-lə\ *or* **Tuxtla Gu·tiér·rez** \gü-'tyer-es\ city SE Mexico ✷ of Chiapas *pop* 295,615

Tu·zi·goot National Monument \'tü-zi-,güt\ reservation *central* Ariz. SW of Flagstaff containing ruins of prehistoric pueblo

Tver' \'tver\ *or* 1932–90 **Ka·li·nin** \kä-'lē-nin\ city W *central* Russia in Europe on the Volga *pop* 456,000

Tweed \'twēd\ river 97 *mi* (156 *km*) SE Scotland & NE England flowing E into North Sea

Tweeddale — see PEEBLES

Twick·en·ham \'twi-kᵊn-əm, 'twit-nəm\ former municipal borough SE England in Middlesex, now part of Richmond upon Thames

Twin Cities the cities of Minneapolis & St. Paul, Minn.

Twin Falls city S Idaho SW of Twin Falls (waterfall in *central* Snake River) *pop* 27,591

Two Sic·i·lies \'si-s(ə-)lēz\ former kingdom consisting of Sicily & S Italy

Ty·chy \'ti-kē, -ki\ town S Poland *pop* 189,874

Ty·ler \'tī-lər\ city E Tex. ESE of Dallas *pop* 75,450

Tyn·dall, Mount \'tin-dᵊl\ **1** mountain 14,018 *ft* (4273 *m*) S *central* Calif. in Sierra Nevada NW of Mt. Whitney **2** mountain 8280 *ft* (2524 *m*) New Zealand in *central* South Is. in Southern Alps

Tyne \'tīn\ river 30 *mi* (48 *km*) N England flowing E into North Sea

Tyne and Wear \'wir\ metropolitan county N England ✷ Newcastle upon Tyne *area* 216 *sq mi* (559 *sq km*), *pop* 1,087,000

Tyne·mouth \'tīn-,maúth, -,məth\ borough N England in Tyne and Wear on North Sea at mouth of the Tyne *pop* 60,022

Tyre — see SUR — **Tyr·i·an** \'tir-ē-ən\ *adjective*

Ty·ree, Mount \tī-'rē\ mountain 16,290 *ft* (4965 *m*) W Antarctica in Ellsworth Mountains NW of Vinson Massif

Tyrol — see TIROL — **Ty·ro·le·an** \tə-'rō-lē-ən, tī-; ,tir-ə-, ,tī-rə-\ *adjective or noun* — **Ty·ro·lese** \,tir-ə-'lēz, ,tī-rə-, -'lēs\ *adjective or noun*

Ty·rone \ti-'rōn\ former county W *central* Northern Ireland ✷ Omagh *area* 1218 *sq mi* (3167 *sq km*)

Tyr·rhe·ni·an Sea \tə-'rē-nē-ən\ the part of the Mediterranean W of Italy, N of Sicily, & E of Sardinia & Corsica

Tyu·men \tyü-'men\ city W Russia in Asia on the **Tu·ra** \tù-'rä\ (a tributary of the Tobol) *pop* 496,000

Tzu–kung — see ZIGONG

Tzu–po — see ZIBO

Uap — see YAP

Uau·pés \waú-'pes\ *or Spanish* **Vau·pés** \vaú-\ river Colombia & Brazil flowing ESE into Negro River

Uban·gi \ü-'bäŋ-gē, yü-'baŋ-\ *or French* **Ou·ban·gui** \ü-bä⁽n⁾-'gē\ river 700 *mi* (1126 *km*) W *central* Africa on NW border of Democratic Republic of the Congo flowing W & S into Congo River — see UELE

Ubangi–Sha·ri \-'shär-ē\ *or French* **Oubangui–Cha·ri** \-shä-'rē\ former French territory N *central* Africa — see CENTRAL AFRICAN REPUBLIC

Uca·ya·li \,ü-kä-'yä-lē\ river *about* 1000 *mi* (1609 *km*) *central* & N Peru flowing N to unite with the Marañón forming the Amazon

Uc·cle \'ükl\, **'ēkl\ *or Flemish* **Uk·kel** \'ə-kəl, 'œ-\ commune *central* Belgium *pop* 73,721

Udai·pur \ú-'dī-,púr\ **1** *or* **Me·war** \mā-'wär\ former state N India, now part of Rajasthan state **2** city, its ✷, *pop* 307,682

Udi·ne \'ü-dē-,nā\ commune NE Italy NE of Venice in Friuli-Venezia Giulia region *pop* 99,157

Ud·mur·tia \úd-'múr-shə, -shē-ə\ *or* **Ud·mur·ti·ya** \-tē-yə\ autonomous republic E Russia in Europe in W foothills of the Urals ✷ Izhevsk *area* 16,255 *sq mi* (42,101 *sq km*), *pop* 1,637,000

Ue·le \'we-lē\ river 700 *mi* (1126 *km*) *central* Africa flowing W in N Democratic Republic of the Congo to unite with the Bomu forming Ubangi River

Ufa \ü-'fä\ **1** river E Russia in Europe in S Urals flowing NW & SW into the Belaya **2** city E Russia in Europe ✷ of Bashkortostan *pop* 1,097,000

Ugan·da \ü-'gän-də, yü-'gän-\ republic E Africa N of Lake Victoria; member of the Commonwealth of Nations ✷ Kampala *area* 91,134 *sq mi* (236,037 *sq km*), *pop* 17,741,000 — **Ugan·dan** \-dən\ *adjective or noun*

Uga·rit \ü-'gär-it, yü-\ ancient city, Syria on Mediterranean coast

Uin·ta Mountains \yü-'in-tə\ mountain range NE Utah — see KINGS PEAK

Ujda — see OUJDA

Uj·jain \'ü-,jin\ city NW *central* India in W Madhya Pradesh NNW of Indore *pop* 362,633

Ujung Pan·dang \ü-,jùŋ-(,)pän-'däŋ\ *or formerly* **Ma·kas·sar** \mə-'ka-sər\ city & port Indonesia in SW Sulawesi *pop* 944,685

Ukraine \yü-'krān, 'yü-,, *also* yü-'krīn\ *or* **the Ukraine** country E Europe on N coast of Black Sea; a constituent republic of the U.S.S.R. 1923–91 ✷ Kiev *area* 233,089 *sq mi* (603,701 *sq km*), *pop* 52,344,000

Ulaan·baa·tar *or* **Ulan Ba·tor** \,ü-,län-'bä-,tór\ *or formerly* **Ur·ga** \'úr-gə\ city N *central* Mongolia (republic), its ✷ *pop* 548,400

Ulan–Ude \ü-,län-ü-'dā\ *or formerly* **Verkh·ne·u·dinsk** \,verk-nə-'ü-din(t)sk\ city E Russia in Asia ✷ of Buryatia on the Selenga *pop* 366,000

Uleåborg — see OULU

Ulls·wa·ter \'əlz-,wȯ-tər, -,wä-\ lake 7 *mi* (11 *km*) long NW England in Cumbria

Ulm \'ùlm\ city S Germany in E Baden-Württemberg *pop* 112,173

Ul·san \'ùl-'sän\ city SE S. Korea *pop* 551,014

Ul·ster \'əl-stər\ **1** region N Ireland (island) comprising Northern Ireland & N Ireland (republic); ancient kingdom, later a province comprising nine counties, three of which in 1921 joined Irish Free State (now Ireland) while the rest remained with United Kingdom **2** province N Ireland (republic) comprising counties Cavan, Donegal, & Monaghan *area* 3093 *sq mi* (8042 *sq km*), *pop* 232,206 **3** Northern Ireland comprising districts Antrim, Armagh, Down, Fermanagh, Londonderry, & Tyrone ✳ Belfast — **Ul·ster·ite** \-stə-,rīt\ *noun* — **Ul·ster·man** \-stər-mən\ *noun*

Ulu Dag \,ü-lə-'dä(g)\ *or ancient* **Mount Olympus** \ə-'lim-pəs, ō-\ mountain 8343 *ft* (2543 *m*) NW Turkey in Asia SE of Bursa

Ulugh Muztagh — see MUZTAG

Ulyanovsk — see SIMBIRSK

Uma·til·la \,yü-mə-'ti-lə\ river 80 *mi* (129 *km*) NE Oreg. flowing W & N into Columbia River

Um·bria \'əm-brē-ə\ region *central* Italy in the Apennines ✳ Perugia *pop* 820,316

Umeå \'ü-mä-(,)ō\ city & port N Sweden on Gulf of Bothnia *pop* 94,912

Umm al Qay·wayn *or* **Umm al–Qai·wain** \'ùm-äl-kī-'wīn\ sheikhdom, member of United Arab Emirates

Um·nak \'üm-,nak\ island SW Alaska in Fox Islands

Ump·qua \'əm(p)-,kwȯ\ river 200 *mi* (322 *km*) SW Oreg. flowing into the Pacific

Um·ta·ta \ùm-'tä-tə\ city Republic of South Africa, formerly ✳ of Transkei

Un·alas·ka \ə-nə-'las-kə\ island SW Alaska in Fox Islands

Unalaska Bay bay SW Alaska on N coast of Unalaska Is.

Un·com·pah·gre Peak \,ən-kəm-'pä-grē\ mountain 14,309 *ft* (4361 *m*) SW Colo.; highest in San Juan Mountains

Uncompahgre Plateau tableland W Colo. SW of the Gunnison

Un·ga·va \,ən-'ga-və\ region Canada N of the Eastmain & W of Labrador including Ungava Peninsula, divided 1927 between Quebec & Newfoundland — see NEW QUEBEC

Ungava Bay inlet of Hudson Strait Canada in N Quebec

Ungava Peninsula peninsula Canada in N Quebec between Hudson Bay & Ungava Bay

Uni·mak \'yü-nə-,mak\ island SW Alaska in Fox Islands

Union City **1** city W Calif. S of Oakland *pop* 53,762 **2** city NE N.J. N of Jersey City *pop* 58,012

Union of South Africa — see SOUTH AFRICA (Republic of)

Union of Soviet Socialist Republics *or* **Soviet Union** country 1922–91 E Europe & N Asia bordering on the Arctic & Pacific oceans & Baltic & Black seas; a union of 15 constituent republics ✳ Moscow *area* 8,649,512 *sq mi* (22,402,236 *sq km*)

United Arab Emirates *or formerly* **Tru·cial States** \'trü-shəl\ *or* **Trucial Oman** \ō-'män, -'man\ country NE Arabia on Persian Gulf between Qatar & Oman; a republic composed of seven sheikdoms (Abu Dhabi, 'Ajman, Al Fujayrah, Ash Shariqah, Dubayy, Ra's al Khaymah, & Umm al Qaywayn formerly under Brit. protection ✳ Abu Dhabi *area* 30,000 *sq mi* (77,700 *sq km*), *pop* 1,986,000

United Arab Republic former name (1961–71) of republic of Egypt & previously (1958–61) of union of Egypt & Syria

United Kingdom **1** *or* **United Kingdom of Great Britain and Northern Ireland** country W Europe in British Isles comprising Great Britain & Northern Ireland ✳ London *area* 94,251 *sq mi* (244,110 *sq km*), *pop* 58,421,700 **2** *or* **United Kingdom of Great Britain and Ireland** country 1801–1921 comprising Great Britain & Ireland

United Nations political organization established 1945; headquarters in New York City in E *central* Manhattan overlooking East River — see TURTLE BAY

United Provinces *or* **United Provinces of Agra and Oudh** former province N India formed 1902 ✳ Allahabad; as Uttar Pradesh, became a state of India (republic) 1950

United States of America *or* **United States** \yü-'nī-təd-'stāts, *especially Southern* 'yü-,\ country N. America bordering on Atlantic, Pacific, & Arctic oceans; a federal republic ✳ Washington *area* 3,619,969 *sq mi* (9,375,720 *sq km*), *pop* 249,632,692

University City city E Mo. WNW of St. Louis *pop* 40,087

University Park city NE Tex. within city of Dallas *pop* 22,259

Un·ter·wal·den \'ùn-tər-,väl-dən\ former canton *central* Switzerland, now divided into two cantons (formerly half cantons): **Nid·wal·den** \'nēt-,väl-dən\ *or French* **Nid·wald** \nēd-'vȧld\ (✳ Stans *area* 106 *sq mi* (276 *sq km*, *pop* 35,393) & **Ob·wal·den** \'ȯp-,väl-dən\ *or French* **Ob·wald** \ȯb-'vȧld\ (✳ Sarnen *area* 189 *sq mi* (490 *sq km*), *pop* 30,837)

Up·land \'əp-lənd\ city SW Calif. W of San Bernardino *pop* 63,374

Upo·lu \ü-'pō-(,)lü\ island S Pacific in Western Samoa

Upper Adige — see ALTO ADIGE

Upper Arlington city *central* Ohio W of Columbus *pop* 34,128

Upper Canada the Canadian province 1791–1841 corresponding to modern Ontario — see LOWER CANADA

Upper Karroo — see KARROO

Upper Klamath Lake lake 30 *mi* (48 *km*) long S Oreg. SSE of Crater Lake National Park drained by Klamath River — see LOWER KLAMATH LAKE

Upper Palatinate — see PALATINATE

Upper Peninsula the N part of Mich. between Lakes Superior & Michigan

Upper Volta — see BURKINA FASO — **Upper Vol·tan** \'väl-tᵊn, 'vōl-, 'vȯl-\ *adjective or noun*

Upp·sa·la \'ùp-,sä-lə, 'üp-, -lä\ city E Sweden NNW of Stockholm *pop* 174,554

Ur \'ər, 'ùr\ city of ancient Sumer; site in S Iraq NW of Basra

Ural \'yùr-əl\ river over 1500 *mi* (2414 *km*) Russia & Kazakhstan rising at S end of Ural Mountains & flowing S into the Caspian

Ural Mountains mountain system Russia & Kazakhstan extending from Kara Sea to steppes N of Aral Sea; usually considered the dividing line between Asia & Europe; highest Narodnaya 6214 *ft* (1894 *m*)

Uralsk — see ORAL

Ura·ri·coe·ra \ù-,rär-i-'kwer-ə\ river *about* 300 *mi* (483 *km*) N Brazil, a headstream of the Branco

Ura·wa \ù-'rä-wä\ city Japan in Honshu N of Tokyo *pop* 434,976

Ur·ba·na \,ər-'ba-nə\ city E *central* Ill. *pop* 36,344

Ur·ban·dale \'ər-bən-,dāl\ city S *central* Iowa *pop* 23,500

Ur·bi·no \ùr-'bē-(,)nō\ commune *central* Italy *pop* 15,125

Ur·fa \'ùr-fä\ *or ancient* **Edes·sa** \i-'de-sə\ city SE Turkey *pop* 276,528

Urga — see ULAANBAATAR

Uri \'ùr-ē\ canton *central* Switzerland S of Lake of Lucerne ✳ Altdorf *area* 415 *sq mi* (1079 *sq km*), *pop* 34,042

Urmia, Lake — see REZĀIYEH

Uru·bam·ba \,ùr-ü-'bäm-bä\ river 450 *mi* (724 *km*) *central* Peru flowing NNW to unite with the Apurímac forming the Ucayali

Uru·guay \'ùr-ə-,gwī, 'yùr-; 'yùr-ə-,gwä; ,ü-rü-'gwī\ **1** river *about* 1000 *mi* (1609 *km*) SE S. America rising in Brazil & flowing into the Río de la Plata **2** *or* **Re·pú·bli·ca Ori·en·tal del Uru·guay** \rä-'pü-blē-(,)kä-,ōr-ē-,en-'täl-thel-\ country SE S. America between the lower Uruguay & the Atlantic; a republic ✳ Montevideo *area* 68,039 *sq mi* (176,221 *sq km*), *pop* 3,149,000 — see BANDA ORIENTAL — **Uru·guay·an** \,ùr-ə-'gwī-ən, ,yùr-; ,yùr-ə-'gwä-\ *adjective or noun*

Ürüm·qi \'ē-'rüm-'chē\ *or* **Urum·chi** \ù-'rùm-chē, ,ùr-əm-'\ *or* **Wu–lu–mu–ch'i** \wü-'lü-mü-'chē\ city NW China ✳ of Xinjiang Uygur on N side of Tian Shan *pop* 1,046,898

Urundi — see BURUNDI

Ushant — see OUESSANT, ÎLE D'

Us·hua·ia \ü-'swī-ä\ town S Argentina on S coast of Tierra del Fuego Is., at 54°48′S; southernmost city in the world *pop* 10,998

Usk \'əsk\ river 60 *mi* (96 *km*) S Wales & W England flowing E & S into Severn estuary

Üs·kü·dar \,üs-kē-'där\ suburb of Istanbul, Turkey, on Asian side of the Bosporus

Us·pal·la·ta Pass \,üs-pä-'yä-tä, -'zhä-\ *or* **La Cum·bre** \lä-'küm-(,)brä\ mountain pass (12,572 *ft or* 3832 *m*) & tunnel S S. America in the Andes between Mendoza, Argentina & Santiago, Chile

Us·su·ri \ù-'sùr-ē\ river 365 *mi* (587 *km*) E Asia on border between Russia & China flowing N into the Amur

Usti nad La·bem \'üs-tē-'näd-lä-,bem\ city NW Czech Republic in N Bohemia on the Elbe *pop* 99,739

Ustinov — see IZHEVSK

Usumbura — see BUJUMBURA

Utah \'yü-,tȯ, -,tä\ state W U.S. ✳ Salt Lake City *area* 84,899 *sq mi* (219,888 *sq km*), *pop* 1,722,850 — **Utah·an** \-,tȯ(-ə)n, -,tä(-ə)n\ *adjective or noun* — **Utahn** \-,tȯ(-ə)n, -,tä(-ə)n\ *noun*

Utah Lake lake 23 *mi* (37 *km*) long N *central* Utah drained by Jordan River

Uti·ca \'yü-ti-kə\ **1** city E *central* N.Y. on Mohawk River *pop* 68,637 **2** ancient city N Africa on Mediterranean coast NW of Carthage

Utrecht \'yü-,trekt, 'ē-,trekt\ **1** province *central* Netherlands S of the IJsselmeer *area* 538 *sq mi* (1393 *sq km*), *pop* 1,047,035 **2** city, its ✳ *pop* 232,705

Utsu·no·mi·ya \,üt-sə-'nō-mē-,yä\ city Japan in *central* Honshu N of Tokyo *pop* 426,809

Ut·tar Pra·desh \,ù-tər-prə-'desh, -'däsh\ state N India bordering on Tibet & Nepal ✳ Lucknow *area* 113,655 *sq mi* (294,366 *sq km*), *pop* 139,112,287 — see UNITED PROVINCES

Ux·bridge \'əks-(,)brij\ former municipal borough SE England in Middlesex, now part of Hillingdon

Ux·mal \üsh-'mäl, üs-\ site of ancient Maya city SE Mexico in N Yucatán

Uz·bek·i·stan \(,)ùz-,be-ki-'stan, ,əz-, -'stän; -'be-ki-,\ country W *central* Asia E of the Amu Darya; a constituent republic (**Uz·bek Republic** \'ùz-,bek, 'əz-, üz-'\) of the U.S.S.R. 1924–91 ✳ Tashkent *area* 173,591 *sq mi* (449,601 *sq km*), *pop* 21,179,000

Uzh·go·rod \'üzh-gə-rət\ city SW Ukraine ✳ of Zakarpats'ka *pop* 123,000

Vaal \'väl\ river 720 *mi* (1158 *km*) Republic of South Africa rising in Mpumalanga & flowing W into Orange River in Northern Cape province

Vaa·sa *or Swedish* **Va·sa** \'vä-sə\ city & port W Finland *pop* 53,364

Vaca·ville \'va-kə-,vil\ city W Calif. SW of Sacramento *pop* 71,479

Va·do·da·ra \və-'dō-də-,rä\ *or* **Ba·ro·da** \bə-'rō-də\ city W India in SE Gujarat SE of Ahmadabad *pop* 1,061,598

Va·duz \vä-'düts\ commune ✳ of Liechtenstein on the upper Rhine

Váh \'vä(k)\ *or Hungarian* **Vág** \'väg\ river over 240 *mi* (386 *km*) W Slovakia rising in Tatry Mountains & flowing W & S into the Danube

Va·lais \va-'lā\ *or German* **Wal·lis** \'vä-lis\ canton SW *central* Switzerland bordering on France & Italy ✳ Sion *area* 2020 *sq mi* (5232 *sq km*), *pop* 249,473

Val·dai Hills \väl-'dī\ hills W Russia in Europe SE of Lake Ilmen; highest point 1053 *ft* (321 *m*)

Val·di·via \väl-'dē-vē-ä\ city & port S *central* Chile *pop* 100,046

Val d'Or \'val-,dȯr\ town Canada in SW Quebec *pop* 23,842

Val·dos·ta \val-'däs-tə\ city S Ga. *pop* 39,806

Va·lence \va-'lä⁼s\ commune SE France S of Lyon *pop* 65,026

Va·len·cia \və-'len(t)-sh(ē-)ə, -sē-ə\ **1** region & ancient kingdom E Spain between Andalusia & Catalonia **2** province E Spain *area* 4156 *sq mi* (10,764 *sq km*), *pop* 2,117,927 **3** commune & port on the Mediterranean, its ✳ *pop* 752,909 **4** city N Venezuela WSW of Caracas *pop* 903,706

Va·len·ci·ennes \və-ˌlen(t)-sē-'en(z)\ city N France pop 39,276

Va·len·tia \və-'len(t)-sh(ē-)ə\ island SW Ireland in County Kerry in the Atlantic S of entrance to Dingle Bay

Val·la·do·lid \ˌva-lə-də-'lid, ˌvä-yä-thō-'lēth\ **1** province NW central Spain area 3166 sq mi (8200 sq km), pop 494,207 **2** commune, its ✱, NNW of Madrid pop 320,293

Val·lau·ris \ˌvä-lô-'rēs\ village SE France NE of Cannes

Val·le·cas \vä-'yä-käs\ commune central Spain, SE suburb of Madrid

Val·le d'Ao·sta \ˌvä-lā-dä-'ôs-tä\ or **Val d'Aosta** \ˌväl-dä-\ autonomous region NW Italy bordering on France & Switzerland NW of Piedmont ✱ Aosta 1260 sq mi (3263 sq km), pop 115,270

Val·le·jo \və-'lā-(ˌ)ō\ city W Calif. on San Pablo Bay pop 109,199

Val·let·ta \və-'le-tə\ city & port ✱ of Malta pop 9210

Valley East town Canada in S Ontario N of Sudbury pop 21,939

Valleyfield — see SALABERRY-DE-VALLEYFIELD

Valley of Ten Thousand Smokes volcanic region SW Alaska in Katmai National Monument

Valley Stream village SE N.Y. on Long Is. pop 33,946

Va·lois \'val-ˌwä, ˌvàl-'wä\ medieval county & duchy N France in NE Île-de-France ✱ Crépy-en-Valois

Valona — see VLORË

Val·pa·rai·so \ˌval-pə-'rā-(ˌ)zō\ city NW Ind. SE of Gary pop 24,414 **2** \-'rī-(ˌ)zō, -'rā-\ or Spanish **Val·pa·ra·í·so** \ˌväl-pä-rä-'ē-sō\ city & port central Chile WNW of Santiago pop 265,718

Van \'van\ salt lake E Turkey in Armenia area 1419 sq mi (3675 sq km)

Van·cou·ver \van-'kü-vər\ **1** city SW Wash. on Columbia River opposite Portland, Oreg. pop 46,380 **2** city & port Canada in SW British Columbia on Burrard Inlet pop 471,844 — **Van·cou·ver·ite** \-və-ˌrīt\ noun

Vancouver, Mount mountain 15,700 ft (4785 m) on Alaska-Yukon boundary in St. Elias Range

Vancouver Island island W Canada in British Columbia off SW coast; chief city Victoria area 12,408 sq mi (32,261 sq km)

Van Die·men Gulf \van-'dē-mən\ inlet of Arafura Sea N Australia in N Northern Territory

Van Diemen's Land — see TASMANIA

Vä·nern \'ve-nərn\ lake SW Sweden area 2156 sq mi (5584 sq km)

Van·taa \'vän-(ˌ)tä\ town S Finland N of Helsinki pop 159,462

Va·nua Le·vu \və-ˌnü-ə-'le-(ˌ)vü, ˌvän-wä-'lä-\ island S Pacific in the Fijis NE of Viti Levu area 2137 sq mi (5535 sq km)

Van·u·a·tu \ˌvan-wä-'tü, ˌvän- also -'wä-(ˌ)tü\ or formerly **New Heb·ri·des** \'he-brə-ˌdēz\ islands SW Pacific NE of New Caledonia & W of Fiji; formerly under joint Brit. & French administration, a republic since 1980 ✱ Vila (on Efate) area 5700 sq mi (14,820 sq km) pop 142,419

Va·ra·na·si \və-'rä-nə-sē\ or **Ba·na·ras** or **Be·na·res** \bə-'när-əs\ city N India in SE Uttar Pradesh pop 932,399

Var·dar \'vär-ˌdär\ river 241 mi (388 km) Macedonia (country) & N Greece flowing S into Gulf of Salonika

Va·re·se \vä-'rä-sä\ commune N Italy NW of Milan pop 85,461

Var·na \'vär-nə\ or formerly **Sta·lin** \'stä-lən, 'sta-, -ˌlēn\ city & port E Bulgaria on Black Sea pop 314,913

Väs·ter·ås \ˌves-tə-'rôs\ city E Sweden on Mälaren Lake NW of Stockholm pop 120,889

Vaté — see EFATE

Vat·i·can City \'va-ti-kən\ or Italian **Cit·tà del Va·ti·ca·no** \chēt-'tä-del-ˌvä-tē-'kä-nō\ independent papal state within commune of Rome, Italy; created Feb. 11, 1929 area 109 acres (43 hectares), pop 771

Vät·tern \'ve-tərn\ lake S Sweden area 738 sq mi (1911 sq km)

Vaud \'vō\ or German **Waadt** \'vät\ canton W Switzerland N of Lake Geneva ✱ Lausanne area 1240 sq mi (3212 sq km), pop 576,319

Vaughan \'vòn, 'vän\ city Canada in SE Ontario N of Toronto pop 111,359

Vaupés — see UAUPÉS

Ve·ga Ba·ja \ˌvā-gə-'bä-(ˌ)hä\ municipality N Puerto Rico pop 55,997

Vegas LAS VEGAS

Ve·ii \'vē-ˌī, 'vā-\ ancient city of Etruria in central Italy NNW of Rome

Vej·le \'vī-lə\ city & port Denmark pop 50,879

Vel·bert \'fel-bərt\ city W Germany in N. Rhine-Westphalia in Ruhr valley NE of Düsseldorf pop 89,347

Vel·la La·vel·la \ˌve-lə-lə-'ve-lə\ island SW Pacific in central Solomons

Vel·lore \və-'lòr, ve-, -'lòr\ city SE India in N Tamil Nadu WSW of Madras pop 172,467

Vel·sen \'vel-sən, -zən\ commune N Netherlands; outer port for Amsterdam pop 61,506

Velsuna — see ORVIETO

Vence \'väⁿs\ commune SE France W of Nice pop 7332

Ven·da \'ven-də\ former black enclave in the Republic of South Africa ✱ Thohoyandou; granted independence 1979; abolished 1994

Ven·dée \väⁿ-'dā\ or **La Vendée** \lä-\ region W France bordering on Bay of Biscay S of Brittany

Ven·dôme \väⁿ-'dōm\ town N central France WSW of Orléans

Ve·ne·tia \və-'nē-sh(ē-)ə\ or Italian **Ve·ne·zia** \ve-'net-sē-ä\ **1** area NE Italy, W Slovenia, & W Croatia including territory between the lower Po & the Alps **2** VENEZIA EUGANEA — **Ve·ne·tian** \-'nē-shən\ adjective

Ve·ne·to \və-nā-ˌtō, 'vä-\ region NE Italy comprising most of Venezia Euganea ✱ Venice area 7096 sq mi (18,379 sq km), pop 4,385,023

Ve·ne·zia Eu·ga·nea \vä-'net-sē-ä-ˌä-ü-'gä-nē-ä\ the S portion of Venetia

Venezia Giu·lia \'jül-yä\ the E portion of Venetia including Julian Alps & Istria; now mainly in Slovenia & Croatia

Venezia Tri·den·ti·na \ˌtrē-ˌden-'tē-nä\ the NW portion of Venetia N of Lake Garda; included in Trentino-Alto Adige region

Ven·e·zu·e·la \ˌve-nə-'zwā-lə, -zə-'wä; ˌbä-nā-'swä-lä\ country N S. America; a republic ✱ Caracas area 352,143 sq mi (912,050 sq km), pop 20,609,000 — **Ven·e·zu·e·lan** \-lən\ adjective or noun

Venezuela, Gulf of inlet of the Caribbean NW Venezuela N of Lake Maracaibo

Ven·iam·i·nof Crater \ve-'nya-mə-ˌnòf\ volcano 8225 ft (2507 m) SW Alaska on central Alaska Peninsula in Aleutian Range

Ven·ice \'ve-nəs\ or Italian **Ve·ne·zia** \ve-'net-sē-ä\ or Latin **Ve·ne·tia** \və-'nē-sh(ē-)ə\ city & port NE Italy W of Veneto, on islands in **Lagoon of Venice** (inlet of Gulf of Venice) pop 308,717 — **Ve·ne·tian** \və-'nē-shən\ adjective or noun

Venice, Gulf of arm of the Adriatic between Po delta & Istria

Ven·lo or **Ven·loo** \'ven-(ˌ)lō\ commune SE Netherlands on Maas River near German border pop 64,890

Ven·ta \'ven-tə\ river 217 mi (349 km) in Lithuania & Latvia flowing into the Baltic

Ven·ti·mi·glia \ˌven-tē-'mēl-yä\ commune NW Italy on Ligurian Sea W of San Remo near Menton, France pop 25,221

Vents·pils \'vent-ˌspils, -ˌspilz\ or German **Win·dau** \'vin-ˌdaù\ city & port Latvia at mouth of the Venta pop 50,400

Ven·tu·ra \ven-'tùr-ə, -'tyùr-\ or officially **San Buen·a·ven·tu·ra** \(ˌ)san-ˌbwe-nə-ˌven-\ city & port SW Calif. on Santa Barbara Channel ESE of Santa Barbara pop 92,575

Venue, Ben — see BEN VENUE

Ve·ra·cruz \ˌver-ə-'krüz, -'krüs\ **1** state E Mexico ✱ Jalapa area 28,114 sq mi (72,815 sq km), pop 6,228,239 **2** or **Vera Cruz Lla·ve** \'yä-(ˌ)vä\ city & port E Mexico in Veracruz state on Gulf of Mexico pop 327,522

Ver·cel·li \ver-'che-lē, (ˌ)vər-\ commune NW Italy pop 48,597

Ver·di·gris \'vər-də-grəs\ river 351 mi (565 km) SE Kans. & NE Okla. flowing into Arkansas River

Ver·dun \(ˌ)vər-'dən, ver-\ **1** town Canada in S Quebec on Montreal Is. pop 61,307 **2** or **Verdun–sur–Meuse** \-ˌsùr-\ city NE France on the Meuse ESE of Reims pop 23,427

Ver·ee·ni·ging \fə-'rā-nə-ˌgiŋ, -nə-ˌkəŋ\ city NE Republic of South Africa in Gauteng on the Vaal S of Johannesburg pop 94,500

Verkhneudinsk — see ULAN-UDE

Ver·mont \vər-'mänt\ state NE U.S. ✱ Montpelier area 9609 sq mi (24,983 sq km), pop 562,758 — **Ver·mont·er** \-'män-tər\ noun

Ver·non \'vər-nən\ **1** town N central Conn. NE of Hartford pop 29,841 **2** city Canada in S British Columbia pop 23,514

Vernyi — see ALMA-ATA

Vé·roia \'ver-yä\ or ancient **Be·rea** or **Be·roea** \bə-'rē-ə\ town NE Greece in Macedonia W of Thessaloníki

Ve·ro·na \ve-'rō-nä\ commune NE Italy on the Adige pop 252,689 — **Ver·o·nese** \ˌver-ə-'nēz, -'nēs\ adjective or noun

Ver·sailles \(ˌ)vər-'sī, ver-\ city N France, WSW suburb of Paris pop 91,029

Vert, Cap \'vərt\ or **Cape Vert** \'vərt\ promontory W Africa in Senegal; westernmost point in Africa at 17°30′ W

Ver·viers \ver-'vyä\ commune E Belgium E of Liège pop 53,700

Ves·ta·via Hills \ve-'stā-vē-ə\ city central Ala. S of Birmingham pop 19,749

Ves·ter·ål·en \'ves-tə-ˌrò-lən\ island group Norway off NW coast NE of Lofoten island group

Ve·su·vi·us \və-'sü-vē-əs\ or Italian **Ve·su·vio** \vä-'sü-vyō, -'zü-\ volcano 4190 ft (1277 m) Italy in campania on Bay of Naples

Ve·tlu·ga \vet-'lü-gə\ river 528 mi (850 km) central Russia in Europe flowing S into the Volga

Ve·vey \və-'vā\ commune W Switzerland in Vaud on NE shore of Lake Geneva pop 16,139

Vi·cen·te Ló·pez \vē-'sen-tē-'lō-ˌpez, -ˌpes\ city E Argentina, N suburb of Buenos Aires, on Río de la Plata pop 289,142

Vi·cen·za \vē-'chen-sä\ commune NE Italy W of Venice pop 107,076

Vi·chu·ga \vi-'chü-gə\ city central Russia in Europe NE of Moscow pop 49,700

Vi·chy \'vi-shē, 'vē-\ commune central France on the Allier pop 28,048

Vicks·burg \'viks-ˌbərg\ city W Miss. pop 20,908

Vic·to·ria \vik-'tòr-ē-ə, -'tòr-\ **1** city SE Tex. on Guadalupe River pop 55,076 **2** city Canada ✱ of British Columbia on SE Vancouver Is. pop 71,228 **3** river 350 mi (563 km) Australia in NW Northern Territory flowing N & NW to Timor Sea **4** state SE Australia ✱ Melbourne area 87,884 sq mi (228,498 sq km), pop 4,244,221 **5** or **Hong Kong** \'häŋ-ˌkäŋ, -'käŋ; 'hòŋ-ˌkòŋ, -'kòŋ\ city & port ✱ of Hong Kong territory, China on NW Hong Kong Is. pop 1,026,870 — **Vic·to·ri·an** \vik-'tòr-ē-ən, -'tòr-\ adjective or noun

Victoria, Lake lake E Africa in Tanzania, Kenya, & Uganda area 26,828 sq mi (69,484 sq km)

Victoria Falls waterfall 355 ft (108 m) S Africa in the Zambezi on border between Zambia & Zimbabwe

Victoria Island island N Canada SE of Banks Is. area 81,930 sq mi (213,018 sq km)

Victoria Land region E Antarctica S of New Zealand on W shore of Ross Sea & Ross Ice Shelf

Victoria Nile — see NILE

Vic·tor·ville \'vik-tər-ˌvil\ city SE Calif. N of San Bernardino pop 40,674

Vied·ma \'vyäd-mä\ town S central Argentina pop 24,338

Vi·en·na \vē-'e-nə, -'a-\ or German **Wien** \'vēn\ city ✱ of Austria on the Danube pop 1,539,848 — **Vi·en·nese** \ˌvē-ə-'nēz, -'nēs\ adjective or noun

Vi·enne \vē-'en\ **1** river 217 mi (349 km) SW central France flowing NW into the Loire **2** city SE France on the Rhône pop 30,386

Vien·tiane \(ˌ)vyen-'tyän\ city ✱ of Laos, near Thailand border pop 132,253

Vie·ques \vē-'ā-käs\ island W. Indies off E Puerto Rico, belonging to Puerto Rico; chief town Isabel Segunda

\ə\ abut \ᵊ\ kitten \ər\ further \a\ ash \ā\ ace \ä\ mop, mar \aù\ out \ch\ chin \e\ bet \ē\ easy \g\ go \i\ hit \ī\ ice \j\ job \ŋ\ sing \ō\ go \ò\ law \òi\ boy \th\ thin \t̲h̲\ the \ü\ loot \ù\ foot \y\ yet \zh\ vision see also Guide to Pronunciation

Vierwaldstätter See — see LUCERNE (Lake of)

Viet·nam \vē-'et-'näm, vyet-, ,vē-ət-, vēt-, -'nam\ country SE Asia in Indochina; state, including Tonkin & N Annam, set up 1945–46; with S Annam & Cochin China, an associated state of French Union 1950–54; after civil war, divided 1954–75 at 17th parallel into republics of **North Vietnam** (✻ Hanoi) & **South Vietnam** (✻ Saigon) reunited 1975 (✻ Hanoi) *area* 127,207 *sq mi* (330,738 *sq km*), *pop* 70,454,000

Vi·go \'vē-(,)gō\ city & port NW Spain on **Vigo Bay** (inlet of the Atlantic) *pop* 276,109

Viipuri — see VYBORG

Vi·ja·ya·na·gar \,vi-jə-yə-'nə-gər\ Hindu kingdom (1336–1565) S India S of the Krishna

Vi·ja·ya·wa·da \,vi-jə-yə-'wä-də\ *or formerly* **Bez·wa·da** \be-'zwä-də\ city SE India in E Andhra Pradesh on the Krishna, at head of its delta *pop* 701,827

Vila — see PORT-VILA

Villa Cisneros — see DAKHLA

Villa Gustavo A. Madero — see GUSTAVO A. MADERO, VILLA

Vil·la·her·mo·sa \,vē-yä-,er-'mō-sä\ city SE Mexico ✻ of Tabasco state *pop* 158,216

Vil·la Park \'vi-lə\ village NE Ill. W of Chicago *pop* 22,253

Ville·franche \,vēl-'fräⁿsh, ,vē-lə-\ **1** *or* **Villefranche–sur–Mer** \-'su͝er-'mer\ commune & port SE France E of Nice *pop* 8123 **2** *or* **Villefranche–sur–Saône** \-'sōn\ commune E central France NNW of Lyon *pop* 29,889

Vil·leur·banne \(,)vē-,yœr-'ban, -'bän\ commune E France, E suburb of Lyon *pop* 119,848

Vil·ni·us \'vil-nē-əs\ city ✻ of Lithuania *pop* 582,000

Vi·lyui *or* **Vi·lyuy** \vil-'yü-ē\ river over 1500 *mi* (2414 *km*) central Russia in Asia flowing E into the Lena

Vim·i·nal \'vi-mə-n°l\ hill in Rome, Italy, one of seven upon which the ancient city was built — see AVENTINE

Vi·my Ridge \'vē-mē, vi-'mē\ ridge near Vimy commune N France N of Arras

Vi·ña del Mar \'vē-nyä-(,)thel-'mär\ city & port central Chile E of Valparaiso *pop* 249,977

Vin·cennes \vin-'senz; *for 2, French* vaⁿ-'sen\ **1** city SW Ind. *pop* 19,859 **2** commune N France, E suburb of Paris *pop* 42,651

Vin·dhya Mountains \'vin-dyə, -dē-ə\ mountain range N central India N of & parallel to the Narmada River

Vindhya Pra·desh \prə-'desh, -'dāsh\ former state NE central India ✻ Rewa; became (1956) part of Madhya Pradesh

Vine·land \'vīn-lənd\ city S N.J. *pop* 54,780

Vin·land \'vin-lənd\ a portion of the coast of N. America visited & so called by Norse voyagers *about* A.D. 1000; perhaps N tip of Newfoundland

Vin·ny·tsya *or* **Vin·ni·tsa** \'vi-nət-syə\ city W central Ukraine *pop* 381,000

Vin·son Massif \'vin(t)-sən\ mountain 16,066 *ft* (4897 *m*) W Antarctica S of Ellsworth Land in Ellsworth Mountains; highest in Antarctica

Vir·gin \'vər-jən\ river 200 *mi* (322 *km*) SW Utah & SE Nev. flowing to Lake Mead

Vir·gin·ia \vər-'ji-nyə, -'ji-nē-ə\ state E U.S. ✻ Richmond *area* 40,767 *sq mi* (105,586 *sq km*), *pop* 6,187,358 — **Vir·gin·ian** \-nyən, -nē-ən\ *adjective or noun*

Virginia Beach city SE Va. on the Atlantic *pop* 393,069

Virginia Capes Cape Charles & Cape Henry in Va. forming entrance to Chesapeake Bay

Virgin Islands group of islands W. Indies E of Puerto Rico — see BRITISH VIRGIN ISLANDS, VIRGIN ISLANDS OF THE UNITED STATES

Virgin Islands National Park reservation W. Indies in Virgin Islands of the U.S. on St. John Is.

Virgin Islands of the United States the W islands of the Virgin Islands group including St. Croix, St. John, & St. Thomas; a territory ✻ Charlotte Amalie (on St. Thomas Is.) *area* 132 *sq mi* (343 *sq km*), *pop* 101,809 — see DANISH WEST INDIES

Vi·run·ga \vē-'ru͝ŋ-gä\ volcanic mountain range E central Africa in E Democratic Republic of the Congo, SW Uganda & NW Rwanda N of Lake Kivu; highest peak Karisimbi 14,780 *ft* (4505 *m*)

Vi·sa·lia \vī-'sāl-yə\ city S central Calif. SE of Fresno *pop* 75,636

Vi·sa·yan Islands \və-'sī-ən\ islands central Philippines between Luzon & Mindanao — see BOHOL, CEBU, LEYTE, MASBATE, NEGROS, PANAY, ROMBLON, SAMAR

Vis·by \'viz-bē\ city & port Sweden on Gotland Is. in the Baltic *pop* 19,319

Vish·a·kha·pat·nam \vi-,shä-kə-'pət-nəm\ *or* **Vi·sa·kha·pat·nam** \vi-,sä-\ city & port E India in NE Andhra Pradesh *pop* 752,037

Vi·so \'vē-(,)zō\ mountain 12,602 *ft* (3841 *m*) NW Italy in Piedmont SW of Turin near French border; highest in Cottian Alps

Vis·ta \'vis-tə\ city SW Calif. N of San Diego *pop* 71,872

Vis·tu·la \'vis-chə-lə, 'vish-chə-, 'vis-tə-\ *or Polish* **Wis·ła** \'vē-(,)swä\ river over 660 *mi* (1062 *km*) Poland flowing N from the Carpathians into Gulf of Gdansk

Vistula Lagoon FRISCHES HAFF

Vi·tebsk \'vē-,tepsk, -,tebsk, və-\ *or* **Vit·syebsk** \'vēt-syipsk\ city NE Belarus on Dvina River *pop* 1,434,200

Vi·ter·bo \vi-'ter-(,)bō\ commune central Italy in Lazio *pop* 58,353

Vi·ti Le·vu \,vē-tē-'le-(,)vü\ island SW Pacific, largest of the Fiji group *area* 4010 *sq mi* (10,386 *sq km*)

Vi·tim \və-'tēm\ river 1133 *mi* (1823 *km*) S Russia in Asia flowing NE into the Lena

Vi·to·ria \vi-'tōr-ē-ə, -'tȯr-\ city N Spain ✻ of Álava province SSE of Bilbao *pop* 204,961

Vi·tó·ria \vi-'tōr-ē-ə, -'tȯr-\ city & port E Brazil ✻ of Espírito Santo state on Espírito Santo Is. *pop* 258,243

Vi·try·sur–Seine \vē-,trē-,su͝er-'san, -'sen\ commune N France, SSE suburb of Paris *pop* 82,820

Viz·ca·ya \vēs-'kī-ä\ *or* **Bis·ca·ya** \bēs-\ *or* **Bis·cay** \'bis-,kā, -kē\ province N Spain on Bay of Biscay; in Basque Country ✻ Bilbao *area* 853 *sq mi* (2209 *sq km*), *pop* 1,155,106

Vlaanderen — see FLANDERS

Vlaar·ding·en \'vlär-diŋ-ə(n)\ commune & port SW Netherlands W of Rotterdam *pop* 73,893

Vlad·i·kav·kaz \,vla-də-,käf-'käz, -,kaf-'kaz\ *or 1932–43 & 1955–91* **Or·dzha·ni·kid·ze** \,ȯr-jä-nə-'kid-zə\ *or 1944–54* **Dzau·dzhi·kau** \(d)zau̇-'jē-,kau̇\ city S Russia in Europe *pop* 325,000

Vla·di·mir \'vla-də-,mir, vlə-'dē-,mir\ city central Russia in Europe on the Klyazma E of Moscow *pop* 356,000

Vlad·i·vos·tok \,vla-də-və-'stäk, -'väs-,täk\ city & port SE Russia in Asia ✻ of Maritime Territory *pop* 648,000

Vlis·sing·en \'vli-siŋ-ə(n)\ *or* **Flush·ing** \'flə-shiŋ\ city & port SW Netherlands on Walcheren Is. *pop* 43,913

Vlo·rë \'vlȯr-ə, 'vlȯr-\ *or* **Va·lo·na** \və-'lō-nə\ *or formerly* **Av·lo·na** \av-'lō-nə\ city & port S Albania *pop* 73,800

Vlta·va \'vəl-tə-və\ river 270 *mi* (434 *km*) W Czech Republic in Bohemia flowing N into the Elbe

Vogelkop — see DOBERAI

Voiotía — see BOEOTIA

Voj·vo·di·na \'vȯi-və-,dē-nä\ autonomous region N Yugoslavia N of the Danube; chief city Novi Sad *area* 8683 *sq mi* (22,576 *sq km*), *pop* 2,012,605

Volcano Islands *or Japanese* **Ka·zan Ret·to** \,kä-,zän-'re-(,)tō\ islands W Pacific S of Bonin Islands; belong to Japan; under U.S. control 1945–68 *area* 11 *sq mi* (29 *sq km*) — see IWO JIMA

Vol·ga \'väl-gə, 'vȯl-, 'vōl-\ river *about* 2300 *mi* (3700 *km*) Russia in Europe rising in Valdai Hills & flowing into the Caspian

Vol·go·grad \'väl-gə-,grad, 'vȯl-, 'vōl-, -,grät\ *or formerly* **Sta·lin·grad** \'stä-lən-,grad, 'sta-, -,grät\ *or* **Tsa·ri·tsyn** \(t)sə-'rēt-sən\ city S Russia in Europe on the Volga *pop* 1,006,000

Vo·log·da \'vȯ-ləg-də\ city central Russia in Europe NNE of Moscow *pop* 290,000

Vó·los \'vȯ-,lȯs\ city & port E Greece on **Gulf of Volos** (inlet of the Aegean)

Volsinii — see ORVIETO

Vol·ta \'väl-tə, 'vȯl-, 'vōl-\ river W Africa flowing from **Lake Volta** (reservoir *area* 3275 *sq mi or* 8515 *sq km*) receiving the **Black Volta** &

White Volta) in N central Ghana & flowing S into Bight of Benin — see RED VOLTA

Vol·ta Re·don·da \'väl-tə-ri-'dän-də, ,vōl-, 'vȯl-\ city E Brazil on Paraíba River NW of city of Rio de Janeiro *pop* 220,086

Vol·tur·no \väl-'tu͝r-(,)nō, vōl-, vȯl-\ river 110 *mi* (177 *km*) S central Italy flowing from the Apennines SE & SW into Gulf of Gaeta

Vor·arl·berg \'fȯr-,ärl-,bərg, 'fȯr-, -,berk\ province W Austria W of Tirol bordering on Switzerland ✻ Bregenz *pop* 333,128

Vo·ro·nezh \və-'rȯ-nish\ city S central Russia in Europe near Don River *pop* 902,000

Voroshilovgrad — see LUGANSK

Vosges \'vōzh\ mountains NE France on W side of Rhine valley; highest 4672 *ft* (1424 *m*)

Voy·a·geurs National Park \vȯi-ə-'zhərz\ reservation N Minn. on Canadian border S of Rainy Lake

Vrangelya — see WRANGEL

Vrystaat — see FREE STATE

Vyat·ka \vē-'ät-kə\ **1** river *about* 800 *mi* (1287 *km*) E central Russia in Europe flowing into the Kama **2** — see KIROV

Vy·borg \'vē-,bȯrg\ *or Finnish* **Vii·pu·ri** \'vē-pü-rē\ city & port W Russia in Europe on arm of Gulf of Finland; belonged to Finland 1917–40 *pop* 81,100

Vy·cheg·da \'vi-chig-də\ river 700 *mi* (1120 *km*) NE central Russia in Europe flowing W to the Northern Dvina

Waadt — see VAUD

Waal \'väl\ river Netherlands, the S branch of the lower Rhine

Wa·bash \'wȯ-,bash\ river 475 *mi* (764 *km*) Ind. & Ill. flowing into Ohio River

Wa·co \'wā-(,)kō\ city NE central Tex. on the Brazos *pop* 103,590

Wad·den Zee \,vä-d°n-'zā\ inlet of North Sea N Netherlands between W. Frisian Islands & IJsselmeer

Wad·ding·ton, Mount \'wä-diŋ-tən\ mountain 13,104 *ft* (3994 *m*) W Canada in SW British Columbia in Coast Mountains; highest in the province

Wadi al–'Arabah, Wadi 'Arabah, Wadi el–'Arabah — see 'ARABAH, WADI

Wad Me·da·ni \,wäd-'me-d°n-ē\ city E central Sudan on the Blue Nile *pop* 106,715

Wa·gram \'vä-,gräm\ village Austria NE of Vienna

Wai·a·le·a·le, Mount \,wī-,ä-lā-'ä-lā\ mountain 5200 *ft* (1585 *m*) Hawaii in central Kauai

Wai·ka·to \wī-'kä-(,)tō\ river 264 *mi* (425 *km*) New Zealand in NW North Is. flowing NW into Tasman Sea

Wai·ki·ki \,wī-ki-'kē\ resort section of Honolulu, Hawaii NW of Diamond Head on **Waikiki Beach**

Wai·mea Canyon \wī-'mā-ä\ gorge Hawaii on SW coast of Kauai

Wai·pa·hu \wī-'pä-(,)hü\ city Hawaii in SW Oahu *pop* 31,435

Wai·ta·ki \wī-'tä-kē\ river 130 *mi* (209 *km*) New Zealand in SE central South Is. flowing ESE into the Pacific

Wa·ka·ya·ma \,wä-kä-'yä-mä\ city & port Japan in SW Honshu on Inland Sea *pop* 396,554

Wake Island \'wāk\ island N Pacific N of Marshall Islands belonging to the U.S.

Wake·field \'wāk-,fēld\ **1** town E Mass. N of Boston *pop* 24,825 **2** city & borough N England ✻ of W. Yorkshire *pop* 60,540

Wa·la·chia *or* **Wal·la·chia** \wä-'lā-kē-ə\ region S Romania between the Transylvanian Alps & the Danube; includes Muntenia & Oltenia; chief city Bucharest — **Wa·la·chi·an** *or* **Wal·la·chi·an** \-ən\ *adjective or noun*

Wał·brzych \'vau̇b-,zhik, -,zhik\ city SW Poland *pop* 141,139

Wal·deck \'väl-,dek\ former county, principality, & state of Germany between Westphalia & Hesse-Nassau ✻ Arolsen

Wal·den Pond \'wȯl-dən\ pond NE Mass. S of Concord

Wales \'wālz\ *or Welsh* **Cym·ru** \'kəm-,rē\ *or Medieval Latin* **Cam·bria** \'kam-brē-ə\ principality SW Great Britain; a division of the United Kingdom of Great Britain and Northern Ireland ✻ Cardiff *area* 8016 *sq mi* (20,761 *sq km*), *pop* 2,799,000

Wal·la·sey \'wä-lə-sē\ borough NW England in Merseyside on coast W of Liverpool *pop* 90,057

Wal·la Wal·la \,wä-lə-'wä-lə, 'wä-lə-,\ city SE Wash. *pop* 26,478

Wal·ling·ford \'wä-liŋ-fərd\ town S Conn. NNE of New Haven *pop* 40,822

Wallis — see VALAIS

Wal·lis Islands \'wä-ləs\ islands SW Pacific NE of Fiji Islands; with Futuna Islands, constitute a French overseas territory (**Wallis and Futuna Islands** *pop* 14,000)

Wal·lops Island \'wä-ləps\ island E Va. in the Atlantic SW of Chincoteague Bay

Wal·lowa Mountains \wä-'laù-ə\ mountains NE Oreg. E of Blue Mountains; highest Sacajawea Peak 9838 *ft* (2999 *m*)

Walnut city SW Calif. E of Los Angeles *pop* 29,105

Walnut Canyon National Monument reservation N *central* Ariz. ESE of Flagstaff containing cliff dwellings

Walnut Creek city W Calif. E of Berkeley *pop* 60,569

Wal·pole \'wòl-,pōl, 'wäl-\ town E Mass. SW of Boston *pop* 20,212

Wal·sall \'wòl-,sòl, -səl\ borough W *central* England in W. Midlands NNW of Birmingham *pop* 255,600

Wal·tham \'wòl-,tham, *chiefly by outsiders* -thəm\ city E Mass. W of Boston *pop* 57,878

Wal·tham Forest \'wòl-thəm\ borough of NE Greater London, England *pop* 203,400

Wal·tham·stow \'wòl-thəm-,stō\ former municipal borough SE England in Essex, now part of Waltham Forest

Wal·vis Bay \'wòl-vəs\ town & port W Namibia on Walvis Bay (inlet) W of Windhoek; formerly an exclave of Republic of South Africa forming a district (*area* of district) 434 *sq mi* (1124 *sq km*)

Wands·worth \'wän(d)z-(,)wərth\ borough of SW Greater London, England *pop* 237,500

Wang·a·nui \,wäŋ-gə-'nü-ē, ,wäŋ-ə-\ **1** river 180 *mi* (290 *km*) New Zealand in SW *central* North Is., flowing into Tasman Sea **2** city & port New Zealand in North Is. on Tasman Sea *pop* 41,400

Wan·ne–Eick·el \'vä-nə-'ī-kəl\ city W Germany in the Ruhr N of Bochum *pop* 100,300

Wan·stead and Wood·ford \'wän-stəd-ᵊn-'wùd-fərd\ former municipal borough S England in Essex, now part of Redbridge

Wap·si·pin·i·con \,wäp-si-'pi-ni-kən\ river 225 *mi* (362 *km*) SE Minn. & E Iowa flowing SE into Mississippi River

Wa·ran·gal \wə-'rəŋ-gəl\ city S *central* India in N Andhra Pradesh NE of Hyderabad *pop* 447,653

War·bur·ton Creek \'wòr-(,)bər-tᵊn\ river 275 *mi* (442 *km*) Australia in NE S. Australia flowing SW into Lake Eyre

Ware·ham \'war-əm, 'wer-, -,ham\ city SE Mass. ENE of New Bedford *pop* 19,232

War·ley \'wòr-lē\ town W *central* England, a NW suburb of Birmingham *pop* 152,455

War·ner Rob·ins \'wòr-nər-'rä-bənz\ city *central* Ga. *pop* 43,726

War·ren \'wòr-ən, 'wär-\ **1** city SE Mich. N of Detroit *pop* 144,864 **2** city NE Ohio NW of Youngstown *pop* 50,793

War·ring·ton \'wòr-iŋ-tən, 'wär-\ borough NW England in Cheshire on the Mersey E of Liverpool *pop* 57,389

War·saw \'wòr-,sò\ or Polish **War·sza·wa** \vär-'shä-vä\ city ✳ of Poland on the Vistula *pop* 1,655,063

War·ta \'vär-tə\ or German **War·the** \'vär-tə\ river 502 *mi* (808 *km*) Poland flowing NW & W into the Oder

War·wick \'wär-ik, *United States also* 'wòr-ik, 'wòr-(,)wik\ **1** city *central* R.I. S of Providence on Narragansett Bay *pop* 85,427 **2** town *central* England N of Warwickshire *pop* 21,936

War·wick·shire \'wär-ik-,shir, -shər, *United States also* 'wòr-ik-, 'wòr-(,)wik-\ or **Warwick** county *central* England ✳ Warwick *area* 792 *sq mi* (2051 *sq km*), *pop* 477,000

Wa·satch Range \'wò-,sach\ mountain range SE Idaho & N & *central* Utah — see TIMPANOGOS (Mount)

Wash, The \'wòsh, 'wäsh\ inlet of North Sea E England between Norfolk & Lincoln

Wash·ing·ton \'wò-shiŋ-tən, 'wä-, *chiefly Midland also* 'wòr-shiŋ- *or* 'wär-\ **1** state NW U.S. ✳ Olympia *area* 68,192 *sq mi* (177,299 *sq km*), *pop* 4,866,692 **2** city ✳ of the U.S., coextensive with District of Columbia *pop* 609,909 **3** — see TERAINA — **Wash·ing·to·nian** \,wò-shiŋ-'tō-nē-ən, ,wä-, -nyən\ *adjective or noun*

Washington, Lake lake 20 *mi* (32 *km*) long W Wash. E of Seattle

Washington, Mount mountain 6288 *ft* (1916 *m*) N N.H.; highest in White Mountains

Wash·i·ta \'wä-shə-,tò, 'wò-\ river 500 *mi* (805 *km*) NW Tex. & SW Okla. flowing SE into Red River

Wa·tau·ga \wä-'tò-gə\ **1** river 60 *mi* (96 *km*) NW N.C. & NE Tenn. flowing into S fork of the Holston **2** town N Tex. *pop* 20,009

Watenstedt–Salzgitter — see SALZGITTER

Wa·ter·bury \'wò-tə(r)-,ber-ē, 'wä-\ city W *central* Conn. *pop* 108,961

Wa·ter·ee \'wò-tə-,rē, 'wä-\ river S.C., lower course of the Catawba — see CONGAREE

Wa·ter·ford \'wò-tər-fərd, 'wä-\ **1** county S Ireland in Munster *area* 710 *sq mi* (1846 *sq km*), *pop* 51,296 **2** city & port, its ✳ *pop* 40,345

Wa·ter·loo \,wò-tər-'lü, 'wä-; 'wò-tər-,lü, 'wä-\ **1** city NE *central* Iowa *pop* 66,467 **2** town *central* Belgium S of Brussels *pop* 27,860 **3** city Canada in SE Ontario W of Kitchener *pop* 71,181

Wa·ter·ton–Glacier International Peace Park \'wò-tər-tᵊn, 'wä-\ reservation comprising **Glacier National Park** (reservation NW Mont.) & **Waterton Lakes National Park** (reservation Canada in Rocky Mountains in S Alberta)

Wa·ter·town \'wò-tər-,taùn, 'wä-\ **1** town SW Conn. NW of Waterbury *pop* 20,456 **2** town E Mass. W of Boston *pop* 33,284 **3** city N *central* N.Y. SE of Kingston, Ontario *pop* 29,429 **4** city SE Wis. *pop* 19,142

Wat·ford \'wät-fərd\ town SE England in Hertfordshire NW of London *pop* 72,100

Wat·son·ville \'wät-sən-,vil\ city W Calif. *pop* 31,099

Wat·ten·scheid \'vä-tᵊn-,shīt\ city W Germany E of Essen *pop* 80,527

Watts \'wäts\ section of Los Angeles, Calif. S of the downtown district

Wau·ke·gan \wò-'kē-gən\ city NE Ill. N of Chicago *pop* 69,392

Wau·ke·sha \'wò-kə-,shò\ city SE Wis. *pop* 56,958

Wau·sau \'wò-,sò, -sə\ city N *central* Wis. *pop* 37,060

Wau·wa·to·sa \,wò-wə-'tō-sə\ city SE Wis. *pop* 49,366

Wayne \'wān\ village SE Mich. SW of Detroit *pop* 19,899

Wa·zir·i·stan \wə-,zir-i-'stan, -'stän\ region W Pakistan on border of Afghanistan NE of Baluchistan

Weald \'wēld\ region SE England in Kent, Surrey, & Sussex, between N. Downs & S. Downs; once heavily forested

Wear \'wir\ river 67 *mi* (108 *km*) N England flowing into North Sea at Sunderland

Web·ster Groves \'web-stər\ city E Mo. *pop* 22,987

Wed·dell Sea \wə-'del, 'we-dᵊl\ arm of the S Atlantic E of Antarctic Peninsula

Wei \'wā\ river *about* 535 *mi* (860 *km*) N *central* China flowing E to join the Huang

Wei·fang \'wā-'fäŋ\ city E China in E *central* Shandong *pop* 428,522

Wei·hai \'wā-'hī\ city & port E China in NE Shandong on Yellow Sea *pop* 128,888

Wei·mar \'vī-,mär, 'wī-\ city E *central* Germany E of Erfurt *pop* 64,000

Weimar Republic the German republic 1919–33

Weir·ton \'wir-tᵊn\ city N W.Va. on Ohio River *pop* 22,124

Wel·land \'we-lənd\ city Canada in SE Ontario SW of Niagara Falls *pop* 47,914

Welland Canal or **Welland Ship Canal** canal 27 *mi* (44 *km*) Canada in SE Ontario connecting Lake Erie & Lake Ontario

Welles·ley \'welz-lē\ town E Mass. WSW of Boston *pop* 26,615

Wel·ling·ton \'we-liŋ-tən\ city & port ✳ of New Zealand in SW North Is. on Port Nicholson (Wellington Harbor) on Cook Strait *pop* 149,400

Wells \'welz\ city & borough SW England in Somerset *pop* 8374

Welsh·pool \'welsh-,pül\ town E Wales in Powys *pop* 7317

Wel·wyn Garden City \'we-lən\ town SE England in Hertfordshire N of London *pop* 40,369

Wem·bley \'wem-blē\ former municipal borough SE England in Middlesex, now part of Brent

We·natch·ee \wə-'na-chē\ city *central* Wash. *pop* 21,756

Wen·zhou or **Wen·chow** or **Wen–chou** \'wən-'jō\ city & port E China in S Zhejiang on E. China Sea *pop* 401,871

Wer·ra \'ver-ə\ river 180 *mi* (290 *km*), *central* Germany flowing N

We·ser \'vā-zər\ river 273 *mi* (439 *km*) *central* & NW Germany flowing into North Sea

Wes·la·co \'wes-li-,kō\ city S Tex. W of Harlingen *pop* 21,877

Wes·sex \'we-siks\ ancient Anglian kingdom S England ✳ Winchester; one of kingdoms in Anglo-Saxon heptarchy

West Al·lis \'a-ləs\ city SE Wis. *pop* 63,221

West Antarctica — see ANTARCTICA

West Bank area Palestine W of Jordan River; occupied by Israel since 1967 — **West Bank·er** \'baŋ-kər\ *noun*

West Bend \'bend\ city SE Wis. NNW of Milwaukee *pop* 23,916

West Bengal state E India comprising the W third of former Bengal province ✳ Calcutta *area* 33,852 *sq mi* (87,677 *sq km*), *pop* 68,077,965

West Beskids — see BESKIDS

West Brom·wich \'brä-mich\ borough W *central* England in W. Midlands NW of Birmingham *pop* 154,930

West Co·vi·na \kō-'vē-nə\ city SW Calif. *pop* 96,086

West Des Moines city S *central* Iowa *pop* 31,702

Wes·ter·ly \'wes-tər-lē\ town SW R.I. *pop* 21,605

Western — see HEBRIDES

Western Australia state W Australia on Indian Ocean ✳ Perth *area* 975,920 *sq mi* (2,537,392 *sq km*), *pop* 1,676,400

Western Cape or **Wes–Kaap** \'wes-,käp, 'ves-\ province SW Republic of South Africa *area* 49,950 *sq mi* (129,370 *sq km*), *pop* 3,635,000

Western Ghats \'gäts, 'gòts, 'gəts\ chain of mountains SW India extending SSE parallel to coast from mouth of the Tapi to Cape Comorin; highest 8842 *ft* (2695 *m*) — see EASTERN GHATS

Western Isles 1 the Outer Hebrides, constituting since 1975 a region of W Scotland ✳ Stornoway *area* 1120 *sq mi* (2912 *sq km*), *pop* 29,410 **2** — used unofficially for the entire Hebrides group

Western Reserve tract of land NE Ohio on S shore of Lake Erie; part of W lands of Conn., ceded 1800 *area about* 5470 *sq mi* (14,222 *sq km*)

Western Sahara or *formerly* **Spanish Sahara** territory NW Africa *area* 102,703 *sq mi* (266,001 *sq km*) *pop* 213,000; formerly a Spanish possession, divided 1975 between Mauritania, which gave up its claim in Aug. 1979, & Morocco, which subsequently occupied the entire territory

Western Samoa group of islands of Samoa W of 171°W; until 1962 a territory administered by New Zealand; became an independent member of the Commonwealth of Nations 1962 ✳ Apia (on Upolu Is.) *area* 1100 *sq mi* (2850 *sq km*), *pop* 156,349

Western Thrace — see THRACE

Wes·ter·ville \'wes-tər-,vil, -vəl\ city *central* Ohio *pop* 30,269

West·field \'west-,fēld\ **1** city SW Mass. WNW of Springfield *pop* 38,372 **2** town NE N.J. WSW of Elizabeth *pop* 28,870

\ə\ abut \ᵊ\ kitten \ər\ further \a\ ash \ā\ ace
\ä\ mop, mar \aù\ out \ch\ chin \e\ bet \ē\ easy
\g\ go \i\ hit \ī\ ice \j\ job \ŋ\ sing \ō\ go
\ò\ law \òi\ boy \th\ thin \th\ the \ü\ loot \ù\ foot
\y\ yet \zh\ vision *see also* Guide to Pronunciation

West Flanders province NW Belgium bordering on North Sea ✳ Brugge *area* 1210 *sq mi* (3134 *sq km*), *pop* 1,106,829

West Frisian — see FRISIAN ISLANDS

West Germany — see GERMANY

West Glamorgan county SE Wales ✳ Swansea *area* 317 *sq mi* (820 *sq km*), *pop* 357,800

West Ham \'ham\ former county borough SE England in Essex, now part of Newham

West Hartford town *central* Conn. *pop* 60,110

West Ha·ven \'west-,hā-vən\ city S Conn. *pop* 54,021

West Hollywood city SW Calif. *pop* 36,118

West Indies 1 the islands lying between SE N. America & N S. America bordering the Caribbean & comprising the Greater Antilles, Lesser Antilles, & Bahamas 2 *or* **West Indies Federation** former country including all of the Brit. West Indies except the Bahamas & the Brit. Virgin Islands; established 1958, dissolved 1961 — **West Indian** *adjective or noun*

West Irian — see IRIAN JAYA

West Jordan city N *central* Utah *pop* 42,892

West Lafayette city W *central* Ind. *pop* 25,907

West·lake \'west-,lāk\ city N Ohio W of Cleveland *pop* 27,018

West·land \'west-lənd\ city SE Mich. W of Detroit *pop* 84,724

West Lo·thi·an \'lō-thē-ən\ *or earlier* **Lin·lith·gow** \lin-'lith-(,)gō\ *or* **Lin·lith·gow·shire** \-,shir, -shər\ former county SE Scotland bordering on Firth of Forth ✳ Linlithgow — see LOTHIAN

West Malaysia the peninsular part of Malaysia — see MALAYA 3

West·meath \(,)west-'mēth, -'mēth\ county E *central* Ireland in Leinster ✳ Mullingar *area* 681 *sq mi* (1771 *sq km*), *pop* 61,880

West Memphis city E Ark. on Mississippi River *pop* 28,259

West Midlands metropolitan county W *central* England ✳ Birmingham *area* 360 *sq mi* (932 *sq km*), *pop* 2,499,300

West Miff·lin \'mi-flən\ borough SW Pa. SE of Pittsburgh *pop* 23,644

West·min·ster \'wes(t)-,min(t)-stər\ 1 city SW Calif. E of Long Beach *pop* 78,118 2 city N *central* Colo. NW of Denver *pop* 74,625 3 *or* **City of Westminster** borough of W *central* Greater London, England *pop* 181,500

West·mont \'west-,mänt\ city NE Ill. *pop* 21,228

West·mor·land \'west-mər-lənd, *United States also* west-'mōr- *or* -'mȯr-\ former county NW England ✳ Kendal

West New York town NE N.J. on Hudson River *pop* 38,125

Wes·ton–su·per–Mare \'wes-tən-,sü-pər-'mar, -'mer\ borough SW England in Avon on Bristol Channel *pop* 57,980

West Pakistan the former W division of Pakistan, now coextensive with Pakistan

West Palm Beach city SE Fla. on Lake Worth inlet *pop* 67,643

West·pha·lia \west-'fāl-yə, -'fā-lē-ə\ *or German* **West·fa·len** \vest-'fä-lən\ region W Germany bordering on Netherlands E of the Rhine; includes Ruhr valley; a province of Prussia 1816–1945 ✳ Münster — see NORTH RHINE–WESTPHALIA — **West·pha·lian** \west(t)-'fāl-yən, -'fā-lē-ən\ *adjective or noun*

West·port \'west-,pȯrt, -,pȯrt\ town SW Conn. *pop* 24,410

West Prussia region N Europe bordering on the Baltic between Pomerania & E. Prussia; since 1945 in Poland

West Punjab — see PUNJAB

West Quod·dy Head \'kwä-dē\ cape NE Maine at entrance to Passamaquoddy Bay

Wes·tra·lia \we-'strāl-yə, -'strā-lē-ə\ WESTERN AUSTRALIA

West Riding — see YORK

West Sacramento city Calif. *pop* 28,898

West Saint Paul city SE Minn. S of St. Paul *pop* 19,248

West Springfield town SW Mass. on Connecticut River *pop* 27,537

West Suffolk — see SUFFOLK

West Sus·sex \'sə-siks, *United States also* -,seks\ county S England ✳ Chichester *area* 806 *sq mi* (2088 *sq km*), *pop* 692,800

West Valley City city N Utah bordering Salt Lake City on the S *pop* 86,976

West Vancouver municipality Canada in SW British Columbia N of Vancouver *pop* 38,783

West Virginia state E U.S. ✳ Charleston *area* 24,181 *sq mi* (62,871 *sq km*), *pop* 1,793,477 — **West Virginian** *adjective or noun*

West Warwick town *central* R.I. *pop* 29,268

West Yorkshire metropolitan county NW England ✳ Wakefield *area* 816 *sq mi* (2113 *sq km*), *pop* 1,984,700

Weth·ers·field \'we-thərz-,fēld\ town *central* Conn. *pop* 25,651

Wex·ford \'weks-fərd\ 1 county SE Ireland in Leinster *area* 908 *sq mi* (2352 *sq km*), *pop* 102,069 2 town & port, its ✳ *pop* 9537

Wey·mouth \'wā-məth\ town E Mass. SE of Boston *pop* 54,063

Whales, Bay of inlet of Ross Sea Antarctica in Ross Ice Shelf

Whangpoo — see HUANGPU

Whea·ton \'hwē-t²n, 'wē-\ city NE Ill. W of Chicago *pop* 51,464

Wheat Ridge city N *central* Colo. W of Denver *pop* 29,419

Whee·ler Peak \'hwē-lər, 'wē-\ 1 mountain 13,065 *ft* (3980 *m*) E Nev. in Snake Range 2 mountain 13,160 *ft* (4010 *m*) N N.Mex. in Sangre de Cristo Mountains; highest in the state

Whee·ling \'hwē-liŋ, 'wē-\ 1 village NE Ill. NNE of Chicago *pop* 29,911 2 city N W.Va. on Ohio River *pop* 34,882

Whid·bey Island \'hwid-bē, 'wid-\ island 40 *mi* (64 *km*) long NW Wash. at N end of Puget Sound E of Admiralty Inlet

Whit·by \'hwit-bē, 'wit-\ town Canada in S Ontario *pop* 61,281

White 1 river 690 *mi* (1110 *km*) N Ark. & SW Mo. flowing SE into Mississippi River 2 river NW Colo. & E Utah flowing W into Green River 3 river 50 *mi* (80 *km*) SW Ind. flowing W into the Wabash 4 river 325 *mi* (523 *km*) S S.Dak. flowing E into Missouri River 5 river NW Tex.

White Bear Lake city E Minn. NE of St. Paul *pop* 24,704

White·chap·el \'hwit-,cha-pəl, 'wit-\ district of E London, England, N of Thames River in Tower Hamlets

White·friars \'hwit-,frī(-ə)rz, 'wit-\ district of *central* London, England, on Thames River

White·hall \-,hȯl\ city *central* Ohio, E suburb of Columbus *pop* 20,572

White·horse \'hwit-,hȯrs, 'wit-\ city NW Canada ✳ of Yukon Territory on upper Yukon River *pop* 17,925

White Mountains 1 mountains E Calif. & SE Nev. 2 mountains N N.H. in the Appalachians — see WASHINGTON (Mount)

White Nile — see NILE

White Pass mountain pass 2890 *ft* (881 *m*) SE Alaska N of Skagway

White Plains city SE N.Y. NE of Yonkers *pop* 48,718

White Sands National Monument reservation S N.Mex. SW of Alamogordo comprising an area of gypsum sand dunes

White Sea *or Russian* **Be·lo·ye Mo·re** \'bye-lə-yə-'mȯr-yə, 'be-lə-\ inlet of Barents Sea NW Russia in Europe enclosed on the N by Kola Peninsula

White Volta — see VOLTA

Whit·ney, Mount \'hwit-nē, 'wit-\ mountain 14,495 *ft* (4418 *m*) SE *central* Calif. in Sierra Nevada in Sequoia National Park; highest in the U.S. outside of Alaska

Whit·ti·er \'hwi-tē-ər, 'wi-\ city SW Calif. SE of Los Angeles *pop* 77,671

Wich·i·ta \'wi-chə-,tȯ\ 1 city S *central* Kans. on Arkansas River *pop* 304,011 2 river 250 *mi* (402 *km*) N Tex. flowing ENE into Red River

Wichita Falls city N Tex. on Wichita River *pop* 96,259

Wichita Mountains mountains SW Okla.; highest Mt. Scott 2464 *ft* (751 *m*)

Wick·low \'wi-(,)klō\ 1 county E Ireland in Leinster *area* 782 *sq mi* (2033 *sq km*), *pop* 97,265 2 town & port, its ✳, SSE of Dublin *pop* 5847

Wicklow Mountains mountains Ireland along E coast; highest Lugnaquilla 3039 *ft* (926 *m*)

Wien — see VIENNA

Wies·ba·den \'vēs-,bä-d²n\ city SW *central* Germany on the Rhine W of Frankfurt am Main ✳ of Hesse *pop* 264,022

Wig·an \'wi-gən\ borough NW England in Greater Manchester W of Manchester *metropolitan area pop* 301,900

Wight, Isle of \'wīt\ island S England in English Channel constituting **Isle of Wight** county (✳ Newport *area* 152 *sq mi or* 394 *sq km*, *pop* 126,600)

Wig·town \'wig-tən, -,taün\ *or* **Wig·town·shire** \-,shir, -shər\ former county SW Scotland ✳ Wigtown

Wilderness Road trail from SW Va. to *central* Ky. through Cumberland Gap blazed to site of Boonesborough by Daniel Boone 1775 & later extended to falls of the Ohio at Louisville

Wil·helms·ha·ven \,vil-,helmz-'hä-fən, 'vi-ləmz-,\ city & port NW Germany NW of Bremen *pop* 91,149

Wilkes–Barre \'wilks-,bar-ə, -,bar-ē, -,bar\ city NE Pa. on the Susquehanna SW of Scranton *pop* 47,523

Wilkes Land \'wilks\ coast region E Antarctica extending along Indian Ocean S of Australia

Wil·kins·burg \'wil-kənz-,bərg\ borough SW Pa. *pop* 21,080

Wil·lam·ette \wə-'la-mət\ river 300 *mi* (485 *km*) NW Oreg. flowing N into Columbia River

Wil·la·pa Bay \'wi-lə-,pȯ, -,pä\ inlet of the Pacific SW Wash.

Wil·lem·stad \'vi-ləm-,stät\ city ✳ of Netherlands Antilles on Curaçao Is. *pop* 43,547

Willes·den \'wilz-dən\ former municipal borough SE England in Middlesex, now part of Brent

Wil·liams·burg \'wil-yəmz-,bərg\ city SE Va. NNW of Newport News; ✳ of Virginia 1699–1780; site of large-scale restoration (Colonial Williamsburg) *pop* 11,530

Wil·liam·son, Mount \'wil-yəm-sən\ mountain 14,375 *ft* (4382 *m*) SE *central* Calif. in Sierra Nevada NNW of Mt. Whitney

Wil·liams·port \'wil-yəmz-,pȯrt, -,pȯrt\ city N *central* Pa. on W branch of the Susquehanna *pop* 31,933

Wil·lough·by \'wi-lə-bē\ city NE Ohio NE of Cleveland *pop* 20,510

Wil·mette \wil-'met\ village NE Ill. N of Chicago *pop* 26,690

Wil·ming·ton \'wil-miŋ-tən\ 1 city & port N Del. *pop* 71,529 2 city & port SE N.C. *pop* 55,530

Wil·son \'wil-sən\ city E *central* N.C. E of Raleigh *pop* 36,930

Wilson, Mount mountain 5710 *ft* (1740 *m*) SW Calif. NE of Pasadena

Wilt·shire \'wilt-,shir, -shər\ county S England ✳ Trowbridge *area* 1392 *sq mi* (3605 *sq km*), *pop* 553,300

Wim·ble·don \'wim-bəl-dən\ former municipal borough SE England in Surrey, now part of Merton

Win·ches·ter \'win-,ches-tər, -chəs-tər\ 1 town E Mass. NW of Boston *pop* 20,267 2 city N Va. *pop* 21,947 3 city & borough S England ✳ of Hampshire *pop* 30,642

Wind \'wind\ river W *central* Wyo., the upper course of Bighorn River

Windau — see VENTSPILS

Wind Cave limestone cavern SW S. Dak. in Black Hills in **Wind Cave National Park**

Win·der·mere \'win-də(r)-,mir\ lake 10 *mi* (16 *km*) long NW England in Cumbria; largest in England

Wind·ham \'win-dəm\ town E *central* Conn. *pop* 22,039

Wind·hoek \'vint-,húk\ city ✳ of Namibia *pop* 144,558

Wind River Canyon gorge of Bighorn River W *central* Wyo.

Wind River Range mountain range W *central* Wyo. — see GANNETT PEAK

Wind·sor \'win-zər\ 1 town N *central* Conn. N of Hartford *pop* 27,817 2 city Canada in SE Ontario on Detroit River opposite Detroit, Mich. *pop* 191,435 3 *or* **New Windsor** royal borough S England in Berkshire on Thames River W of London *pop* 30,065

Wind·ward Islands \'wind-wərd\ 1 islands W. Indies in the S Lesser Antilles extending S from Martinique but not including Barbados,

Tobago, or Trinidad **2** former colony Brit. West Indies comprising territories of St. Lucia, St. Vincent, & Grenada in the Windward group & Dominica in the Leewards **3** *or French* **Îles du Vent** \ēl-dü̅e̅-vä"\ islands S Pacific, E group of the Society Islands, including Tahiti *pop* 140,341

Win·ne·ba·go, Lake \,wi-nə-'bā-(,)gō\ lake 30 *mi* (48 *km*) long E Wis.

Win·ni·peg \'wi-nə-,peg\ **1** river *about* 500 *mi* (804 *km*) Canada in W Ontario & SE Manitoba flowing from Lake of the Woods to Lake Winnipeg **2** city Canada ✳ of Manitoba *pop* 616,790 — **Win·ni·peg·ger** \-,pe-gər\ *noun*

Winnipeg, Lake lake *about* 260 *mi* (418 *km*) long Canada in S central Manitoba drained by Nelson River

Win·ni·pe·go·sis, Lake \,wi-nə-pə-'gō-səs\ lake Canada in W Manitoba W of Lake Winnipeg *area* 2075 *sq mi* (5374 *sq km*)

Win·ni·pe·sau·kee, Lake \,wi-nə-pə-'sò-kē\ lake central N.H. *area* 71 *sq mi* (185 *sq km*)

Wi·no·na \wə-'nō-nə\ city SE Minn. *pop* 25,399

Wi·noo·ski \wə-'nüs-kē\ river 100 *mi* (161 *km*) N central Vt. flowing into Lake Champlain

Win·ston–Sa·lem \,win(t)-stən-'sā-ləm\ city N N.C. *pop* 143,485

Winter Haven city central Fla. E of Lakeland *pop* 24,725

Winter Park city E Fla. N of Orlando *pop* 22,242

Winter Springs city E central Fla. N of Orlando *pop* 22,151

Win·ter·thur \'vin-tər-,tùr\ commune N Switzerland in Zurich canton NE of Zurich *pop* 86,600

Win·yah Bay \'win-,yò\ inlet of the Atlantic E S.C.

Wis·con·sin \wi-'skän(t)-sən\ **1** river 430 *mi* (692 *km*) central Wis. flowing S & W into Mississippi River **2** state N central U.S. ✳ Madison *area* 56,154 *sq mi* (145,439 *sq km*), *pop* 4,891,769 — **Wis·con·sin·ite** \-sə-,nīt\ *noun*

Wisconsin Dells — see DELLS OF THE WISCONSIN

Wisła — see VISTULA

Wis·mar \'vis-,mär, 'wiz-,mär\ city & port N Germany *pop* 54,471

Wis·sa·hick·on Creek \,wi-sə-'hi-kən\ stream SE Pa. flowing into the Schuylkill at Philadelphia

With·la·coo·chee \,with-lə-'kü-chē\ **1** river 110 *mi* (177 *km*) S Ga. & NW Fla. flowing SE into the Suwannee **2** river 120 *mi* (193 *km*) NW central Fla. flowing NW into Gulf of Mexico

Wit·ten \'vi-t³n\ city W Germany SW of Dortmund *pop* 105,242

Wit·ten·berg \'wi-t³n-,bərg, 'vi-t³n-,berk\ city E central Germany E of Dessau *pop* 48,718

Wit·wa·ters·rand \'wit-,wò-tərz-,rand, -,wä-, -,ränd, -,ränt\ ridge of auriferous rock 62 *mi* (100 *km*) long & 23 *mi* (37 *km*) wide NE Republic of South Africa in Gauteng and North West provinces

Wło·cła·wek \vwòt-'swä-,vek\ commune N central Poland on the Vistula *pop* 120,823

Wo·burn \'wü-bərn, 'wō-\ city E Mass. NW of Boston *pop* 35,943

Wo·dzi·sław Ślą·ski \vò-'jē-swäf-'shlòn-skē\ town S Poland *pop* 111,329

Wolds, The \'wōldz\ chalk hills NE England in N. Yorkshire, Humberside, & N Lincolnshire

Wolfs·burg \'wùlfs-,bərg, 'vòlfs-,bùrk\ city N central Germany *pop* 128,995

Wol·lon·gong \'wù-lən-,gäŋ, -,gòŋ\ city SE Australia in E New South Wales S of Sydney *pop* 211,417

Wol·ver·hamp·ton \,wùl-vər-'ham(p)-tən\ borough W central England in W. Midlands NW of Birmingham *pop* 239,800

Won·san \'wən-,sän\ city & port N. Korea on E coast *pop* 274,000

Wood Buffalo National Park reservation W Canada in N Alberta & S Northwest Territories

Wood·bury \'wùd-,ber-ē, -,bə-rē\ city E Minn., a suburb of St. Paul *pop* 20,075

Wood Green former municipal borough SE England in Middlesex, now part of Haringey

Wood·land \'wùd-lənd\ city N Calif. NW of Sacramento *pop* 39,802

Wood·lark \'wùd-,lärk\ island W Pacific in Solomon Sea off SE end of New Guinea; attached to Papua New Guinea *area* 400 *sq mi* (1040 *sq mi*)

Wood·ridge \'wùd-(,)rij\ city NE Ill. *pop* 26,256

Woods, Lake of the lake S Canada & N U.S. in Ontario, Manitoba, & Minn. SE of Lake Winnipeg *area* 1679 *sq mi* (4349 *sq km*)

Wood·stock \'wùd-,stäk\ city Canada in SE Ontario *pop* 30,075

Wool·wich \'wù-lij, -lich\ former metropolitan borough E London, England, now part of Greenwich

Woom·era \'wù-mə-rə\ town S. Australia W of Lake Torrens

Woon·sock·et \wün-'sä-kət, 'wün-\ city N R.I. *pop* 43,877

Woos·ter \'wùs-tər\ city N central Ohio SW of Akron *pop* 22,191

Worces·ter \'wùs-tər\ **1** city E central Mass. W of Boston *pop* 169,759 **2** *or* **Worces·ter·shire** \-tə(r)-,shir, -,shər\ former county W central England — see HEREFORD AND WORCESTER **3** city, ✳ of Hereford and Worcester *pop* 81,000

Worms \'wərmz, 'vòrm(p)s\ city SW Germany on the Rhine NNW of Mannheim *pop* 77,429

Worth, Lake \'wərth\ inlet (lagoon) of the Atlantic SE Fla.

Wor·thing \'wər-thiŋ\ borough S England in W. Sussex on English Channel *pop* 94,100

Wound·ed Knee \,wün-dəd-'nē\ locality SW S. Dakota; site of 1890 massacre of American Indians by U.S. troops

Wran·gel \'raŋ-gəl\ *or Russian* **Vran·ge·lya** \'vrán-gəl-yə\ island in Arctic Ocean off NE coast of Russia in Asia

Wran·gell \'raŋ-gəl\ island SE Alaska NE of Prince of Wales Is.

Wrangell, Cape cape on Attu Is. in Aleutians

Wrangell, Mount active volcano 14,163 *ft* (4317 *m*) S Alaska in Wrangell Mountains NW of Mt. Blackburn

Wrangell Mountains mountain range S Alaska NW of St. Elias Range — see BLACKBURN (Mount)

Wrangell–Saint Eli·as National Park \-sänt-i-'lī-əs\ reservation S central Alaska; largest park in the world covering 8,331,604 *acres* (3,374,300 *hectares*)

Wrath, Cape \'rath, *Scots* 'ròth *or* 'räth\ extreme NW point of Scotland, at 58°35′N

Wrex·ham \'rek-səm\ borough NE Wales in Clwyd *pop* 40,272

Wro·cław \'vrót-,swäf, -,släv\ *or German* **Bres·lau** \'bres-,laù, 'brez-\ city SW Poland, chief city of Silesia *pop* 642,334

Wu \'wü\ river 700 *mi* (1126 *km*) central China rising in W Guizhou & flowing through Szechwan into the Chang

Wu·chang \'wü-'chäŋ\ former city E central China — see WUHAN

Wu·han \'wü-'hän\ city E central China ✳ of Hubei at junction of Han & Chang rivers; formed from the former separate cities of Hankow, Hanyang, & Wuchang *pop* 3,284,229

Wuhsien — see SUZHOU

Wu·hu \'wü-'hü\ city E China in E Anhui *pop* 425,740

Wu–lu–mu–ch'i — see ÜRÜMQI

Wu·pat·ki National Monument \wü-'pat-kē\ reservation N Ariz. NNE of Flagstaff containing prehistoric Indian dwellings

Wup·per·tal \'vü-pər-,täl\ city W Germany in Ruhr valley ENE of Düsseldorf *pop* 385,463

Würt·tem·berg \'wər-təm-,bərg, 'wùr-; 'vùrt-təm-,berk\ region SW Germany between Baden & Bavaria; chief city Stuttgart; once a duchy, kingdom 1813–1918, state 1918–45; divided 1945–51, S part being joined to Hohenzollern forming **Württemberg–Hohenzollern** state & N part to N Baden forming **Württemberg–Baden** state; since 1951 part of Baden-Württemberg state

Würz·burg \'wərts-,bərg, 'wùrts-; 'vùrts-,bùrk\ city S central Germany on Main River in N Bavaria NW of Nuremberg *pop* 128,512

Wu·xi *or* **Wu–hsi** *or* **Wu·sih** \'wü-'shē\ city E China in S Jiangsu NW of Suzhou

Wu·zhou *or* **Wu–chou** *or* **Wu·chow** \'wü-'jō\ city S China in E Guangxi Zhuangzu at junction of the Gui & the Xi *pop* 210,452

Wy·an·dotte \'wī-ən-,dät *also* 'wīn-\ city SE Mich. *pop* 30,938

Wye \'wī\ river 130 *mi* (209 *km*) E Wales & W England flowing into Severn River

Wy·o·ming \wī-'ō-miŋ\ **1** state NW U.S. ✳ Cheyenne *area* 97,914 *sq mi* (254,576 *sq km*), *pop* 453,588 **2** valley NE Pa. along the Susquehanna **3** city SW Mich. *pop* 63,891 — **Wy·o·ming·ite** \-miŋ-,īt\ *noun*

Xan·thus \'zan(t)-thəs\ city of ancient Lycia; its site near mouth of Koca River in SW Turkey

Xe·nia \'zē-nyə, -nē-ə\ city SW central Ohio *pop* 24,664

Xeres — see JEREZ

Xi *or* **Hsi** *or* **Si** \'shē\ river 300 *mi* (483 *km*) SE China in Guangxi Zhuangzu & Guangdong flowing E into S. China Sea

Xia·men *or* **Hsia–men** \'shyä-'mən\ *or* **Amoy** \ä-'mòi, a-, ə-\ city & port SE China in S Fujian on two islands *pop* 308,000

Xi'·an *or* **Si·an** \'shē-'än\ *or formerly* **Chang·an** \'chäŋ-'än\ city E central China ✳ of Shaanxi on the Wei *pop* 1,959,044

Xiang *or* **Hsiang** \'shyaŋ\ river 350 *mi* (560 *km*) SE central China flowing from N Guangxi Zhuangzu N into Hunan

Xiang·tan *or* **Hsiang–t'an** *or* **Siang·tan** \'shyän-,tän, -,tan\ city SE China in E Hunan on the Xiang S of Changsha *pop* 441,968

Xi·ga·zê *or* **Shi–ga·dzu** \shē-'gä-'dzə\ *or* **Shi·ga·tse** \shi-'gä-dzə\ *or* **Jih–k'a–tse** \'zhir-'kä-'dzə\ town W China in SE Tibet on the Tsangpo W of Lhasa

Xin·gu \shēŋ-'gü\ river 1230 *mi* (1979 *km*) central & N Brazil rising on Mato Grosso plateau & flowing N into the Amazon near its mouth

Xi·ning *or* **Si·ning** *or* **Hsi–Ning** \'shē-'niŋ\ city NW China ✳ of Qinghai *pop* 551,776

Xin·jiang Uy·gur *or* **Sin·kiang Ui·ghur** \'shin-'jyäŋ-'wē-gər\ region W China between the Kunlun & Altay mountains; formerly a province ✳ Ürümqi *area* 635,829 *sq mi* (1,653,154 *sq km*), *pop* 15,155,778

Xin·xiang *or* **Hsin–hsiang** *or* **Sin–siang** \'shin-'shyäŋ\ city E China in N Henan N of Zhengzhou *pop* 473,762

Xizang — see TIBET

Xo·chi·mil·co \,sō-chē-'mēl(,)-kō, ,sō-shi-, -'mil-\ city S central Mexico, SE suburb of Mexico City *pop* 271,020

Xuan·hua *or* **Hsüan–hua** \'shwän-'hwä, 'shwan-, -'wä\ city NE China in NW Hebei NW of Beijing *pop* 114,000

Xu·zhou *or* **Hsü–chou** *or* **Sü–chow** \'shü-'jō, 'sü-; 'sü-'chaù\ city E China in NW Jiangsu *pop* 805,695

Ya·blo·no·vy Mountains *or* **Ya·blo·no·vyy Mountains** \,yä-blə-nə-'vē\ mountain range S Russia in Asia

Yacarana — see JAVARI

Yad·kin \'yad-kən\ river 202 *mi* (325 *km*) central N.C., the upper course of the Pee Dee

Yafo — see JAFFA

Yak·i·ma \'ya-kə-,mò\ **1** river 200 *mi* (322 *km*) S Wash. flowing SE into Columbia River **2** city S central Wash. *pop* 54,827

Yak·u·tat Bay \'ya-kə-,tat\ inlet of the Pacific SE Alaska

Yakutia — see SAKHA

Ya·kutsk \yə-'kütsk\ city E central Russia in Asia *pop* 198,000

Ya·long *or* **Ya·lung** \'yä-'lùŋ\ river SW China in W Szechwan flowing S into the Chang

Yal·ta \'yòl-tə\ city & port on S coast of Crimea *pop* 89,000

Ya·lu \'yä-(,)lü\ river *about* 500 *mi* (804 *km*) SE Manchuria & NW N. Korea flowing N, W, & SW into Korea Bay

Ya·mal \yə-'mäl\ peninsula NW Russia in Asia at N end of Ural Mountains between Gulf of Ob & Kara Sea

Ya·mous·sou·kro \,yä-mə-'sü-krō\ town central Ivory Coast

Yam·pa \'yam-pə\ river 250 *mi* (400 *km*) NW Colo. flowing W into Green River in Dinosaur National Monument

Ya·mu·na \'yə-mə-nə\ river 860 *mi* (1384 *km*) N India in Uttar Pradesh flowing from the Himalayas S & SE into the Ganges

Ya·na \'yä-nä\ river N Russia in Asia flowing N into Laptev Sea

Yan'an \'yä-'nän\ *or* **Yen·an** \'ye-'nän\ city NE central China in *central* Shaanxi *pop* 113,277

Yangku — see TAIYUAN

Yan·gon \,yän-'gōn\ **1** — see RANGOON 1 **2** *or formerly* **Rangoon** city & port ✳ of Myanmar on Rangoon River 21 *mi* (34 *km*) from its mouth *pop* 1,717,649

Yang·quan *or* **Yang·chüan** \'yän-'chwän, -'chwen\ city N China in E Shanxi E of Taiyuan *pop* 362,268

Yangtze — see CHANG

Yang·zhou *or* **Yang–chou** \'yäŋ-'jō\ city E China in SW Jiangsu NE of Nanjing *pop* 312,892

Yan·tai \'yän-'tī\ *or* **Yen–t'ai** \'yən-\ *or* **Che·foo** \'jə-'fü\ city & port E China in NE Shandong on Shandong Peninsula on Bo Hai *pop* 452,127

Yao \'yaü\ city Japan on Honshu, a suburb of Osaka *pop* 277,724

Yaoun·dé *or* **Yaun·de** \yaün-'dā\ city ✳ *central* Cameroon, its ✳ *pop* 649,000

Yap \'yap, 'yäp\ *or* **Uap** \'wäp\ islands W Carolines, part of Federated States of Micronesia — **Yap·ese** \ya-'pēz, yä-, -'pēs\ *adjective*

Ya·quí \yä-'kē\ river 420 *mi* (676 *km*) NW Mexico in Sonora flowing SW into Gulf of California

Yar·kand \yär-'kand\ *or* **Yar·kant** \-'känt\ river Kashmir & China flowing from Karakoram Range N & W to join the Hotan in Xinjiang Uygur forming the Tarim

Yar·mouth \'yär-məth\ **1** city SE Mass. E of Barnstable *pop* 21,174 **2** *or* **Great Yarmouth** borough & port E England in Norfolk on North Sea *pop* 50,152

Ya·ro·slavl \,yär-ə-'slä-vᵊl\ city *central* Russia in Europe on the Volga NE of Moscow *pop* 637,000

Yau·co \'yaü-,kō\ municipality SW Puerto Rico *pop* 42,058

Yavari — see JAVARI

Ya·wa·ta \yä-'wä-tä\ former city Japan in N Kyushu — see KITAKYUSHU

Yazd \'yazd\ *or* **Yezd** \'yezd\ city *central* Iran *pop* 230,483

Yaz·oo \ya-'zü, 'ya-(,)zü\ river 189 *mi* (304 *km*) Miss. flowing SW into Mississippi River

Yedo — see TOKYO

Ye·gor'·yevsk \yə-'gòr-yəfsk, -əfsk\ city W *central* Russia in Europe SE of Moscow *pop* 74,200

Ye·ka·te·rin·burg \yi-'ka-tə-rən-,bərg, yi-,kä-ti-rēm-'bùrk\ *or* 1924–91 **Sverd·lovsk** \sverd-'lòfsk\ city W Russia in Asia in *central* Ural Mountains *pop* 1,371,000

Yelizavetpol — see GANCA

Yellow — see HUANG

Yel·low·knife \'ye-lō-,nīf\ city Canada ✳ of Northwest Territories on Great Slave Lake *pop* 15,179

Yellow Sea inlet of E. China Sea between N China, N. Korea, & S. Korea

Yel·low·stone \'ye-lō-,stōn\ river 671 *mi* (1080 *km*) NW Wyo. & S & E Mont. flowing N through **Yellowstone Lake** (area 140 *sq mi or* 364 *sq km*) & **Grand Canyon of the Yellowstone** in Yellowstone National Park & NE into Missouri River in NW N.Dak. near Mont. border

Yellowstone Falls two waterfalls NW Wyo. in Yellowstone River at head of Grand Canyon of the Yellowstone; upper fall 109 *ft* (33 *m*), lower fall 308 *ft* (94 *m*)

Yellowstone National Park reservation NW Wyo., E Idaho, & S Mont. including plateau region notable for numerous geysers & hot springs

Ye·men \'ye-mən\ country S Arabia bordering on Red Sea & Gulf of Aden; a republic formed 1990 by merger of **Yemen Arab Republic** (✳ Sanaa) with **People's Democratic Republic of Yemen** *or* **Southern Yemen** (✳ Aden) ✳ Sanaa *area* 203,849 *sq mi* (527,969 *sq km*), *pop* 12,961,000 — **Ye·me·ni** \'ye-mə-nē\ *adjective or noun* — **Ye·men·ite** \-mə-,nīt\ *noun or adjective*

Yen·i·sey \,yi-ni-'sā\ river over 2500 *mi* (4022 *km*) Russia in Asia flowing N into Arctic Ocean

Yen–t'ai — see YANTAI

Ye·re·van \,yer-ə-'vän\ city ✳ of Armenia *pop* 1,199,000

Ye·şil Ir·mak \yə-'shēl-ir-'mäk\ river N Turkey in Asia flowing N into Black Sea

Ye·şil·koy \ye-(,)shēl-'kòi\ *or formerly* **San Ste·fa·no** \san-'ste-fə-,nō\ town Turkey in Europe on Sea of Marmara W of Istanbul

Yevreyskaya — see JEWISH AUTONOMOUS OBLAST

Yezo — see HOKKAIDO

Yi·bin \'yē-'bēn\ *or* **I–pin** \'ē-'bēn, -'pin\ *or formerly* **Su–chow** \shü-'jō, 'sü-; 'sü-'chaü\ city *central* China in S Szechwan *pop* 805,695

Yi·chang \'yē-'chäŋ\ *or* **I–ch'ang** \'ē-'chäŋ\ city *central* China in W Hubei *pop* 371,601

Yin·chuan \'yin-chwän, -'chwen\ *or formerly* **Ning·sia** *or* **Ning·hsia** \'niŋ-'shyä\ city N China ✳ of Ningxia Huizu on the Huang *pop* 356,652

Ying·kou \'yiŋ-'kō\ *or* **Ying·kow** \'yiŋ-'kaü, -'kō\ city & port NE China in *central* Liaoning on Gulf of Liaodong *pop* 421,589

Yi·ning \'yē-'niŋ\ *or* **Gul·ja** \'gül-(,)jä\ *or* **Kul·dja** \'kül-(,)jä\ city W China in NW Xinjiang Uygur *pop* 177,193

Yog·ya·kar·ta \,yō-gyə-'kär-tə\ *or* **Jog·ja·kar·ta** \,jōg-yə-\ city Indonesia in S Java *pop* 412,392

Yo·ho National Park \'yō-(,)hō\ reservation W Canada in SE British Columbia on Alberta border

Yo·ko·ha·ma \,yō-kō-'hä-mä\ city & port Japan in SE Honshu on Tokyo Bay S of Tokyo *pop* 3,220,350

Yo·ko·su·ka \yō-'kò-s(ə-)kä\ city & port Japan in Honshu W of entrance to Tokyo Bay *pop* 433,361

Yon·kers \'yäŋ-kərz\ city SE N.Y. N of New York City *pop* 188,082

Yonne \'yän, 'yòn\ river 182 *mi* (293 *km*) NE *central* France flowing NNW into the Seine

Yor·ba Lin·da \,yòr-bə-'lin-də, ,yòr-\ city SW Calif. SE of Los Angeles *pop* 52,422

York \'yòrk\ **1** city SE Pa. SE of Harrisburg *pop* 42,192 **2** city Canada in SE Ontario near Toronto *pop* 140,525 **3** *or* **York·shire** \-,shir, -shər\ former county N England bordering on North Sea comprising city of York & (former) administrative counties of **East Rid·ing** \'rī-diŋ\ (✳ Beverley), **North Riding** (✳ Northallerton), & **West Riding** (✳ Wakefield) — see HUMBERSIDE, NORTH YORKSHIRE, SOUTH YORKSHIRE, WEST YORKSHIRE **4** *or ancient* **Ebo·ra·cum** \i-'bòr-ə-kəm, -'bär-\ city N England in N. Yorkshire on Ouse River *pop* 100,600

York, Cape — see CAPE YORK PENINSULA

Yorke Peninsula \'yòrk\ peninsula Australia in SE S. Australia between Spencer Gulf and Gulf St. Vincent

York River estuary 40 *mi* (64 *km*) E Va. flowing SE into Chesapeake Bay

Yo·sem·i·te Falls \yō-'se-mə-tē\ waterfall E *central* Calif. descending from rim of Yosemite Valley in two falls (upper fall 1430 *ft or* 436 *m*, lower fall 320 *ft or* 98 *m* connected by a cascade)

Yosemite Valley glaciated valley of Merced River E *central* Calif. on W slope of Sierra Nevada in **Yosemite National Park**

Yosh·kar–Ola \yəsh-'kär-ə-'lä\ town E Russia in Europe ✳ of Mari El *pop* 249,000

Yo·su \'yō-(,)sü\ city & port S S. Korea on Korea Strait *pop* 171,933

Yough·io·ghe·ny \,yä-kə-'gā-nē, ,yò-hə-, -'ge-nē\ river 135 *mi* (217 *km*) NE W.Va., NW Md., & SW Pa. flowing N & NW into the Monongahela

Youngs·town \'yəŋz-,taün\ city NE Ohio E of Akron *pop* 95,732

Youth, Isle of *or formerly* **Isle of Pines** island W Cuba in the Caribbean *area* 1180 *sq mi* (3068 *sq km*)

Ypres — see IEPER

Yp·si·lan·ti \,ip-sə-'lan-tē\ city SE Mich. *pop* 24,846

Yser \ē-'zer\ river 48 *mi* (77 *km*) France & Belgium flowing into North Sea

Ysyk–Köl — see ISSYK KUL

Yu·an \'ywen, 'ywän\ **1** river 500 *mi* (805 *km*) SE *central* China flowing from Guizhou NE to NE Hunan **2** — see RED

Yu·ba City \'yü-bə\ city N Calif. N of Sacramento *pop* 27,437

Yu·cai·pa \yü-'kī-pə\ city S Calif. E of Riverside *pop* 32,824

Yu·ca·tán \,yü-kə-'tan, -kä-'tän\ **1** peninsula SE Mexico & N Central America including Belize & part of Guatemala **2** state SE Mexico at N end of Yucatán Peninsula ✳ Mérida *area* 16,749 *sq mi* (43,380 *sq km*), *pop* 1,362,940 — **Yu·ca·te·can** \-'te-kən\ *adjective*

Yucatán Channel channel between Yucatán & W end of Cuba

Yuc·ca House National Monument \'yə-kə\ reservation SW Colo.; contains prehistoric ruins

Yu·go·sla·via *also* **Ju·go·sla·via** \,yü-gō-'slä-vē-ə, ,yü-gə-\ country S Europe on Balkan Peninsula comprising Serbia, Montenegro, Vojvodina, & Kosovo; together with Slovenia, Croatia, Bosnia and Herzegovina, & Macedonia established 1918 as a kingdom (**Kingdom of the Serbs, Croats, and Slovenes**), became a federal republic 1945; ✳ Belgrade *area* 39,449 *sq mi* (102,173 *sq km*), *pop* 10,561,000 — **Yu·go·slav** \,yü-gō-'släv, -'slav; 'yü-gō-,\ *or* **Yu·go·sla·vi·an** \,yü-gō-'slä-vē-ən, -gə-\ *adjective or noun*

Yu·kon \'yü-,kän\ **1** city *central* Okla. *pop* 20,935 **2** river 1979 *mi* (3185 *km*) NW Canada & Alaska flowing NW & SW into Bering Sea — see LEWES **3** *or* **Yukon Territory** territory NW Canada between Alaska & British Columbia bordering on Arctic Ocean ✳ Whitehorse *area* 205,345 *sq mi* (531,843 *sq km*), *pop* 27,797

Yu·ma \'yü-mə\ city SW Ariz. on Colorado River *pop* 54,923

Yungki — see JILIN

Yungning — see NANNING

Yun·nan \'yü-'nän\ **1** province SW China bordering on Indochina & Myanmar ✳ Kunming *area* 168,417 *sq mi* (437,884 *sq km*), *pop* 36,972,610 **2** *or* **Yunnanfu** — see KUNMING — **Yun·nan·ese** \,yü-nə-'nēz, -'nēs\ *adjective or noun*

Yun·que, El \el-'yün-(,)kā\ mountain 3496 *ft* (1066 *m*) E Puerto Rico

Yü Shan \'yē-'shän, 'yü-\ *or* **Hsin·kao** \'shin-'kaü\ *or* **Mount Mor·ri·son** \'mòr-ə-sən, 'mär-\ mountain 13,113 *ft* (3997 *m*) *central* Taiwan; highest on island

Yver·don \ē-ver-'dōⁿ\ commune W Switzerland N of Lausanne *pop* 20,802

Zaan·dam \zän-,däm\ commune W Netherlands *pop* 129,341

Zab·rze \'zäb-(,)zhä\ *or German* **Hin·den·burg** \'hin-dən-bərg, -,bùrk\ city SW Poland in Silesia *pop* 203,367

Za·ca·te·cas \,za-kə-'tā-kəs, ,sä-kä-'tā-käs\ **1** state N *central* Mexico *area* 28,973 *sq mi* (75,040 *sq km*), *pop* 1,276,323 **2** city, its ✳ *pop* 100,051

Za·dar \'zä-,där\ *or Italian* **Za·ra** \'zär-ä\ city & port Croatia; held by Italy 1920–47 *pop* 80,355

Zag·a·zig \'za-gə-,zig\ *or* **Az–Za·qā·zīq** \,az-zə-,kä-'zēk\ city N Egypt NNE of Cairo *pop* 279,000

Za·greb \'zä-,greb\ city ✳ of Croatia *pop* 867,865

Zag·ros Mountains \'za-grəs, -,grōs\ mountains W & S Iran bordering on Turkey, Iraq, & Persian Gulf; highest over 14,000 *ft* (4267 *m*)

Za·he·dan \zä-hi-'dän\ city E Iran *pop* 281,923

Zaire \zä-'yir\ **1 2** — see CONGO 2 — **Zair·ean** *or* **Zair·ian** \zä-'ir-ē-ən\ *adjective or noun*

Za·kar·pat·s'ka \,zä-kər-'pät-skə\ *or formerly* **Car·pa·thi·an Ru·the·nia** \kär-'pā-thē-ən-rü-'thē-nyə, -nē-ə\ *or* **Ruthenia** region W Ukraine S of the Carpathian Mountains; part of Hungary before 1918 & 1939–45; a province of Czechoslovakia 1918–38 ✳ Uzhgorod *area* 4942 *sq mi* (12,800 *sq km*) *pop* 1,265,900

Zá·kin·thos \'zä-kēn-,thòs\ **1** island W Greece, one of the Ionian Islands, SSE of Cephalonia *area* 157 *sq mi* (407 *sq km*) *pop* 32,746 **2** its chief town *pop* 10,205

Za·ma \'zä-mə, 'zä-\ ancient town N Africa SW of Carthage

Zam·be·zi *or* **Zam·be·si** \zam-'bē-zē, zäm-'bä-zē\ river *about* 1700 *mi* (2735 *km*) SE Africa flowing from NW Zambia into Mozambique Channel

Zam·bia \'zam-bē-ə\ *or formerly* **Northern Rhodesia** country S Africa; formerly a Brit. protectorate; independent republic within the Commonwealth of Nations since 1964 ✳ Lusaka *area* 290,585 *sq mi* (752,615 *sq km*), *pop* 9,132,000 — **Zam·bi·an** \'zam-bē-ən\ *adjective or noun*

Zam·bo·an·ga \ˌzam-bō-ˈäŋ-gə\ city & port Philippines on SW coast of Mindanao *pop* 442,000

Za·mo·ra \zə-ˈmōr-ə, -ˈmór-\ **1** province NW Spain in *central* León *area* 4077 *sq mi* (10,559 *sq km*), *pop* 213,668 **2** city, its ✳ *pop* 64,631

Zancle — see MESSINA

Zanes·ville \ˈzānz-ˌvil\ city E *central* Ohio *pop* 26,778

Zan·jan \zan-ˈjän\ city NW Iran *pop* 215,261

Zan·zi·bar \ˈzan-zə-ˌbär\ **1** island E Africa off NE Tanzania mainland *area* 600 *sq mi* (1554 *sq km*), *pop* 375,539; formerly a sultanate, with Pemba & adjacent islands forming a Brit. protectorate; became independent 1963; united 1964 with Tanganyika to form Tanzania **2** city & port ✳ of the island & formerly of protectorate *pop* 157,634 — **Zan·zi·bari** \ˌzan-zə-ˈbär-ē\ *noun or adjective*

Za·po·rizh·zhya *or Russian* **Za·po·rozh'·ye** \ˌzä-pə-ˈró-zhə\ *or formerly* **Ale·ksan·drovsk** \a-lik-ˈsan-drəfsk\ city SE Ukraine *pop* 897,000

Za·ra·go·za \ˌzar-ə-ˈgō-zə\ *or* **Sar·a·gos·sa** \ˌsar-ə-ˈgä-sə\ **1** province NE Spain in W Aragon *area* 6639 *sq mi* (17,195 *sq km*), *pop* 837,327 **2** — see SARAGOSSA

Zee·brug·ge \ˈzā-ˌbrə-gə, -ˌbrü-\ town NW Belgium; port for Brugge

Zee·land \ˈzē-lənd, ˈzā-; ˈzā-ˌlänt\ province SW Netherlands ✳ Middelburg *area* 1043 *sq mi* (2701 *sq km*), *pop* 361,195

Zeist \ˈzīst\ commune *central* Netherlands E of Utrecht *pop* 59,096

Zem·po·al·te·pec \ˌzem-pō-ˈäl-tā-ˌpek\ *or* **Zem·po·al·te·petl** \-ˌäl-ˈtā-ˌpe-tʰl, -ˌäl-tə-ˈ\ mountain 11,138 *ft* (3395 *m*) SE Mexico in Oaxaca

Zer·matt \(t)ser-ˈmät\ village SW *central* Switzerland in Valais in Pennine Alps NE of the Matterhorn

Zetland — see SHETLAND

Zhang·jia·kou \ˈjäŋ-ˈjyä-ˈkō\ *or* **Ch'ang–chia·k'ou** \ˈchäŋ-ˈjyä-ˈkō\ *or* **Kal·gan** \ˈkal-ˈgan\ city NE China in NW Hebei NW of Beijing *pop* 529,136

Zhang·zhou *or* **Chang–chou** \ˈjäŋ-ˈjō\ *or formerly* **Lung·ki** \ˈlùŋ-kē\ city SE China in S Fujian

Zhda·nov — see MARIUPOL

Zhe·jiang *or* **Che·kiang** \ˈjə-ˈjyäŋ\ province E China bordering on E. China Sea ✳ Hangzhou *area* 39,305 *sq mi* (102,193 *sq km*), *pop* 41,445,930

Zheng·zhou *or* **Cheng–chou** *or* **Cheng·chow** \ˈjəŋ-ˈjō\ city NE *central* China ✳ of Henan on the Huang *pop* 1,159,679

Zhen·jiang *or* **Chen–chiang** \ˈjən-ˈjyäŋ\ city & port E China in NW *central* Jiangsu *pop* 368,316

Zhi·to·mir *or* **Zhy·to·myr** \zhi-ˈtò-ˌmir\ city W Ukraine *pop* 298,000

Zhou·shan *or* **Chou–shan** \ˈjō-ˈshän\ archipelago E China in E. China Sea at entrance to Hangzhou Bay

Zhu \ˈjü\ *or* **Chu** \ˈjü, ˈchü\ *or* **Pearl** river SE China SE of Guangzhou

Zhu·zhou *or* **Chu–chou** *or* **Chu·chow** \ˈjü-ˈjō\ city SE China in E Hunan *pop* 409,924

Zi·bo *or* **Tzu–po** \ˈ(d)zə-ˈbō\ city E China in *central* Shandong *pop* 1,138,074

Zie·lo·na Go·ra \zhe-ˈlò-nä-ˈgùr-ä\ city W *central* Poland *pop* 113,322

Zi·gong *or* **Tzu–kung** \ˈ(d)zə-ˈgùŋ\ city S *central* China in S *central* Szechwan *pop* 393,184

Zi·li·na \ˈzhē-lē-ˌnä\ city N Slovakia *pop* 83,853

Zim·ba·bwe \zim-ˈbä-bwē, -(ˌ)bwā\ **1** archaeological site NE Zimbabwe (country) **2** *or formerly* **Southern Rhodesia** *or 1970–79* **Rhodesia** country S Africa S of the Zambezi; a self-governing Brit. colony which declared itself a republic 1970; adopted majority rule 1979 ✳ Harare *area* 150,820 *sq mi* (390,624 *sq km*), *pop* 7,550,000 — **Zim·ba·bwe·an** \-ən\ *adjective or noun*

Zinovievsk — SEE KIROVOGRAD

Zi·on \ˈzī-ən\ **1** city NE Ill. N of Waukegan *pop* 19,775 **2** *or* **Mount Zion** *or* **Sion** \ˈsī-ən, ˈzī-\ **Mount Sion** hill E Jerusalem, Israel; originally the stronghold of Jerusalem conquered by David; occupied in ancient times by the Jewish Temple

Zi·on National Park \ˈzī-ən\ reservation SW Utah centering around **Zion Canyon** of Virgin River

Zi·pan·gu \zə-ˈpaŋ-(ˌ)gü\ the name for Japan used by Marco Polo

Zi·pa·qui·rá \ˌsē-pä-kē-ˈrä\ town *central* Colombia N of Bogotá

Zla·to·ust \ˌzlä-tə-ˈüst\ city W Russia in Asia in the S Urals *pop* 208,000

Zoan — see TANIS

Zom·ba \ˈzäm-bə, ˈzōm-\ city SE Malawi S of Lake Malawi *pop* 51,838

Zon·gul·dak \ˌzòŋ-gəl-ˈdäk\ city & port NW Turkey *pop* 116,725

Zug \ˈ(t)sük, ˈzüg\ *or French* **Zoug** \ˈzüg\ **1** canton N *central* Switzerland *area* 92 *sq mi* (238 *sq km*), *pop* 84,742 **2** commune, its ✳, on Lake of Zug *pop* 21,752

Zug, Lake of lake N *central* Switzerland in Zug & Schwyz cantons N of Lake of Lucerne *area* 15 *sq mi* (39 *sq km*)

Zug·spit·ze \ˈ(t)sük-ˌshpit-sə, ˈzüg-, -ˌspit-\ mountain 9721 *ft* (2963 *m*) S Germany; highest in Bavarian Alps & in Germany

Zui·der Zee \ˌzī-dər-ˈzā, -ˈzē\ former inlet of North Sea N Netherlands — see IJSSELMEER

Zuidholland — see SOUTH HOLLAND

Zu·lu·land \ˈzü-(ˌ)lü-ˌland\ territory E Republic of South Africa in NE KwaZulu-Natal bordering on Indian Ocean N of the Tugela *area* 10,362 *sq mi* (26,838 *sq km*)

Zu·rich \ˈzùr-ik\ *or German* **Zü·rich** \ˈtsē-rik\ **1** canton N Switzerland *area* 668 *sq mi* (1730 *sq km*), *pop* 1,152,769 **2** city, its ✳, at NW end of Lake of Zurich *pop* 347,021 — **Zü·rich·er** \-i-kər, -ri-kər\ *noun*

Zurich, Lake of lake 25 *mi* (40 *km*) long N *central* Switzerland

Zut·phen \ˈzət-fən\ commune E Netherlands on the IJssel *pop* 31,117

Zwick·au \ˈtsfi-ˌkaù, ˈzwi-\ city E Germany S of Leipzig *pop* 112,565

Zwol·le \ˈzvò-lə, ˈzwò-\ city E Netherlands ✳ of Overijssel *pop* 98,318

\ə\ abut \ˈə\ kitten \ər\ further \a\ ash \ā\ ace
\ä\ mop, mar \aù\ out \ch\ chin \e\ bet \ē\ easy
\g\ go \i\ hit \ī\ ice \j\ job \ŋ\ sing \ō\ go
\ò\ law \òi\ boy \th\ thin \t͟h\ the \ü\ loot \ù\ foot
\y\ yet \zh\ vision *see also* Guide to Pronunciation

Signs and Symbols

Astronomy

SUN, GREATER PLANETS, ETC.

⊙	the sun; Sunday
◐, ☾, or ☽	the moon; Monday
●	new moon
☽, ◐, ☽,)	first quarter
○ or 🌝	full moon
☾, ◐, ☾, (	last quarter
☿	Mercury; Wednesday
♀	Venus; Friday
⊕, ⊖, or ♁	the earth
♂	Mars; Tuesday
♃	Jupiter; Thursday
♄ or ♄	Saturn; Saturday
♅, ♅, or ♅	Uranus
♆, ♆, or ♆	Neptune

♇ Pluto

☄ comet

* or ✶ fixed star

ASPECTS AND NODES

☌ conjunction—indicating that the bodies have the same longitude, or right ascension

□ quadrature—indicating a difference of 90° in longitude, or right ascension

△ trine—indicating a difference of 120° in longitude, or right ascension

☍ opposition—indicating a difference of 180° in longitude, or right ascension; as ☍ ♆ ⊙ opposition of Neptune to the Sun

☊ ascending node

☋ descending node

Biology

○ an individual, specifically, a female—used chiefly in inheritance charts

□ an individual, specifically, a male—used chiefly in inheritance charts

♀ female

♂ or ♁ male

× crossed with; hybrid

+ wild type

F_1 offspring of the first generation

F_2 offspring of the second generation

F_3, F_4, F_5 offspring of the third, fourth, fifth, etc., generation

Business and Finance

a/c	account ⟨in a/c with⟩
@	at; each ⟨4 apples @ 5¢ = 20¢⟩
P	principal; present value
i, r	rate of interest
n	number of periods (as of interest) and especially years
/ or ℗	per
c/o	care of
#	number if it precedes a numeral ⟨track #3⟩; pounds if it follows ⟨a 5 # sack of sugar⟩
℔	pound; pounds

% percent

‰ per thousand

$ dollars

¢ cents

£ pounds

/ shillings (for other currency symbols see MONEY table)

© copyrighted

® registered trademark

Chemistry

+ signifies "plus", "and", "together with", and is used between the symbols of substances brought together for, or produced by, a reaction; placed to the right of a symbol above the line, it signifies a unit charge of positive electricity: Ca^{++} denotes the ion of calcium, which carries two positive charges; the plus sign is used also to indicate a dextrorotatory compound [as (+) tartaric acid]

− signifies a unit charge of negative electricity when placed to the right of a symbol above the line: Cl^- denotes a chlorine ion carrying a negative charge; the minus sign is used to indicate a levorotatory compound [as (−) quinine]; it is also used to indicate the removal of a part from a compound (as − CO_2)

— signifies a single bond and is used between the symbols of elements or groups which unite to form a compound: H—Cl for HCl, H—O—H for H_2O

· is used to separate parts of a compound regarded as loosely joined (as $CuSO_4 \cdot 5H_2O$); the centered dot is also used to denote the presence of a single unpaired electron (as H·)

◯ or ⬡ denotes the benzene ring

= indicates a double bond; placed to the right of a symbol above the line, it signifies two unit charges of negative electricity (as $SO_4^=$, the negative ion of sulfuric acid, carrying two negative charges)

≡ signifies a triple bond or a triple negative charge

: is used to indicate an unshared pair of electrons (as in : NH_3); is sometimes used to indicate a double bond (as in $CH_2:CH_2$)

() marks groups within a compound [as in $C_6H_4(CH_3)_2$, the formula for xylene which contains two methyl groups (CH_3)]

⌐ or ⌐ joins attached atoms or groups in structural formulas for cyclic compounds, as that for glucose

$$CH_2OHCH(CHOH)_3CHOH$$

= give or form

→ gives, leads to, or is converted to

⇋ forms and is formed from, is in equilibrium with

↓ indicates precipitation of the substance

↑ indicates that the substance passes off as a gas

≡ is equivalent—used in statements to show how much of one substance will react with a given quantity of another so as to leave no excess of either

1-, 2-, etc. used initially in names, referring to the positions of substituting groups, attached to the first, etc., of the numbered atoms of the parent compound

H enthalpy

^{2}H also H^2 deuterium

^{3}H also H^3 tritium

M metal

R organic group, alkyl or aryl group

S entropy

X halogen atom

Z atomic number (for element symbols see ELEMENT table)

′ is used to distinguish between different substituents of the same kind (as R′, R″, R‴ to indicate different organic groups)

Mathematics

+ plus; positive ⟨$a+b=c$⟩—used also to indicate omitted figures or an approximation

− minus; negative

± plus or minus ⟨the square root of $4a^2$ is $\pm 2a$⟩

× multiplied by; times ⟨$6 \times 4 = 24$⟩—also indicated by placing a dot between the factors ⟨$6 \cdot 4 = 24$⟩ or by writing the factors one after the other, often enclosed in parentheses, without explicitly indicating multiplication ⟨$(4)(5)(3) = 60$⟩ ⟨$-4abc$⟩

÷ or : divided by ⟨$24 \div 6 = 4$⟩—also indicated by writing the divisor under the dividend with a line between ⟨$\frac{24}{6} = 4$⟩ or by writing the divisor after the dividend with an oblique line between ⟨3/8⟩

E times 10 raised to an indicated exponent ⟨$4.52E5 = 4.52 \times 10^5$⟩—used especially in calculator and computer displays

= equals ⟨$6 + 2 = 8$⟩

≠ or ≠ is not equal to

> is greater than ⟨$6 > 5$⟩

< is less than ⟨$3 < 4$⟩

≧ or ≥ is greater than or equal to

≦ or ≤ is less than or equal to

≯ is not greater than

≮ is not less than

≈ is approximately equal to

≡ is identical with

~ is similar to; the negation of; the negative of

≅ is congruent to

∝ varies directly as; is proportional to

: is to; the ratio of

∴ therefore

∞ infinity

∠ angle; the angle ⟨∠ ABC⟩

∟ right angle ⟨∟ ABC⟩

⊥ the perpendicular; is perpendicular to ⟨AB ⊥ CD⟩

∥ parallel; is parallel to ⟨AB ∥ CD⟩

⊙ or ○ circle

⌒ arc of a circle

△ triangle

□ square

▭ rectangle

√ or √ root—used without a figure to indicate a square root (as in $\sqrt{4} = 2$) or with an index above the sign to indicate a higher degree (as in $\sqrt[3]{3}$, $\sqrt[5]{7}$); also denoted by a fractional index at the right of a number whose denominator expresses the degree of the root ⟨$3^{1/3} = \sqrt[3]{3}$⟩

() parentheses
[] brackets } indicate that the quantities enclosed by them are to be taken together
{ } braces

— (above the quantities) vinculum

Δ the operation of finding the difference between two nearby values of a variable (as y) or of a function (as f) for two values of its independent variable (as x) differing by a small nonzero amount (as h) ⟨$\Delta y = y_2 - y_1$⟩ ⟨$\Delta f(x) = f(x + h) - f(x)$⟩

∫ integral; integral of ⟨$\int 2x\,dx = x^2 + C$⟩

$\int_b^a$ the integral taken from the value b to the value a of the variable

$\frac{df(x)}{dx}$ the derivative of the function $f(x)$ with respect to x

$\frac{\partial f(x,y)}{\partial x}$ the partial derivative of the function $f(x,y)$ with respect to x

δ_j^i Kronecker delta

s standard deviation of a sample taken from a population

σ standard deviation of a population

Σ sum; summation ⟨$\sum_{i=1}^n x_i = x_1 + x_2 + ... + x_n$⟩

$\bar{x}$ arithmetic mean of a sample of a variable x

μ (1) micrometer (2) arithmetic mean of a population

μ_2 or σ^2 variance

X^2 chi-square

P the probability of obtaining a result as great as or greater than the observed result in a statistical test if the null hypothesis is true

r correlation coefficient

$E(x)$ expected value of the random variable x

π pi; the number 3.14159265+; the ratio of the circumference of a circle to its diameter

$\prod$ product $\langle \prod_{i=1}^{n} x_i = (x_1)(x_2)...(x_n) \rangle$

! factorial $\langle n! = n(n-1)(n-2)...1 \rangle$

e or ϵ (1) the number 2.7182818+; the base of the natural system of logarithms (2) the eccentricity of a conic section

i the positive square root of minus one $\sqrt{-1}$

n an unspecified number (as an exponent) especially when integral

° degree $\langle 60° \rangle$

′ minute; foot $\langle 30' \rangle$—used also to distinguish between different values of the same variable or between different variables (as a', a'', a''', usually read a prime, a double prime, a triple prime) or between the first and higher derivatives of a function (as f', f'' or $f'(x)$, $f''(x)$ for the first and second derivatives of f or $f(x)$)

″ second; inch $\langle 30'' \rangle$

$^0, ^1, ^2, ^3$, etc. —used as exponents placed above and at the right of an expression to indicate that it is raised to a power whose degree is indicated by the figure $\langle a^0$ equals 1 $\rangle$ $\langle a^1$ equals $a \rangle$ $\langle a^2$ is the square of $a \rangle$

$^{-1}, ^{-2}, ^{-3}$, etc. —used as exponents placed above and at the right of an expression to indicate that the reciprocal of the expression is raised to the power whose degree is indicated by the figure $\langle a^{-1}$ equals $1/a \rangle$ $\langle a^{-2}$ equals $1/a^2 \rangle$

$\sin^{-1}x$ arc sine of x

$\cos^{-1}x$ arc cosine of x

$\tan^{-1}x$ arc tangent of x

f function

f^{-1} the inverse of the function f

$|z|$ the absolute value of z

$[a_{ij}]$ matrix with element a_{ij} in the ith row and jth column

$|a_{ij}|$ determinant of a square matrix with elements a_{ij}

$\|A\|$ or $\|x\|$ norm of matrix A or the vector x

A^{-1} inverse of the matrix A

A^T transpose of the matrix A

$\oplus$ an operation in a mathematical system (as a group or ring) with $A \oplus B$ indicating the sum of the two elements A and B

$\otimes$ an operation in a mathematical system (as a group or ring) with $A \otimes B$ indicating the product of the two elements A and B

$[x]$ the greatest integer not greater than x

(a,b) the open interval $a < x < b$

$[a,b]$ the closed interval $a \leq x \leq b$

$\aleph_0$ aleph-null

ω the ordinal number of the positive integers

$\ni$ or : such that $\langle$ choose a and $b \ni a + b = 6 \rangle$

$\exists$ there exists $\langle \exists\ a \ni a + 2 = 4 \rangle$

$\forall$ for every, for all $\langle \forall\ a \ni a$ is a real number, $a^2 \geq 0 \rangle$

$\cup$ union of two sets

$\cap$ intersection of two sets

$\subset$ is included in, is a subset of

$\supset$ contains as a subset

$\in$ or ϵ is an element of

$\notin$ is not an element of

Λ or 0 or ϕ or { } empty set, null set

Medicine

$\overline{AA}$, $\overline{A}$, or $\overline{aa}$ ana; of each

℞ take—used on prescriptions; prescription; treatment

☠ poison

APOTHECARIES' MEASURES

℥ ounce

f℥ fluid ounce

f℈ fluid dram

min or ℳ minim

APOTHECARIES' WEIGHTS

℔ pound

℥ ounce (as ℥ i or ℥ j, one ounce; ℥ ss, half an ounce; ℥ iss or ℥ jss, one ounce and a half; ℥ ij, two ounces)

℈ dram

℈ scruple

Miscellaneous

& and

&c et cetera; and so forth

" or " ditto marks

/ diagonal or slant or solidus or virgule; used to mean "or" (as in and/or), "and/or" (as in dead/wounded), "per" (as in feet/second); indicates end of a line of verse; separates the figures of a date (4/4/73)

☞ index or fist

< derived from
> whence derived } used in linguistics
+ and

* hypothetical, ungrammatical

† died—used especially in genealogies

✡ Magen David

+ cross (for variations see CROSS illustration)

☧ monogram from Greek XP signifying Christ

☥ ankh

℣ versicle

℟ response

✲ —used in Roman Catholic and Anglican service books to divide each verse of a psalm, indicating where the response begins

✠ or + —used in some service books to indicate where the sign of the cross is to be made; also used by certain Roman Catholic and Anglican prelates as a sign of the cross preceding their signatures

LXX Septuagint

Ⓤ or Ⓚ kosher certification

$f/$ or f: relative aperture of a photographic lens

🛆 civil defense

☮ peace

x by $\langle 3 \times 5$ cards $\rangle$

卐 swastika

Physics

α	alpha particle	E	electric field, energy, illumination, modulus of elasticity, potential difference
β	beta particle, beta ray	h	Planck's constant
γ	gamma, photon, surface tension	H	magnetic field strength
ϵ	permittivity	J	angular momentum
η	efficiency, viscosity	L	inductance, self-inductance
λ	wavelength	n	index of refraction, neutron
μ	micro-, permeability	p	momentum of a particle, proton
ν	frequency, neutrino	S	entropy
ρ	density, resistivity	T	absolute temperature, period
σ	conductivity, cross section, surface tension	V	electrical potential
ϕ	luminous flux, magnetic flux	W	work
Ω	ohm	X	power of magnification, reactance
B	magnetic induction, magnetic field	Y	admittance
c	speed of light	Z	impedance
e	electron, electronic charge		

Reference marks

*	asterisk or star	§	section or numbered clause
†	dagger	‖	parallels
‡	double dagger	¶ or ⁋	paragraph

Stamps and stamp collecting

⊙ or ○ or 0	used	⊞	block of four
★ or *	unused	⊠	entire cover or card
★★ or **	unused with original gum intact and never mounted with a stamp hinge		

Weather

Barometer, changes of:

╱	Rising, then falling	▬	warm front
⟋	Rising, then steady; or rising, then rising more slowly	▲▲	occluded front
∕	Rising steadily, or unsteadily	⌁	stationary front
✓	Falling or steady, then rising; or rising, then rising more quickly	)(	funnel clouds
—	Steady, same as 3 hours ago	∞	haze
╲	Falling, then rising, same or lower than 3 hours ago	●	hurricane
╲	Falling, then steady; or falling, then falling more slowly	Ọ	tropical storm
╲	Falling steadily, or unsteadily	↔	ice needles
╲	Steady or rising, then falling; or falling, then falling more quickly	●	rain
◎	calm	⁂	rain and snow
○	clear	⩌	rime
◑	cloudy (partly)	⥮	sandstorm or dust storm
●	cloudy (completely overcast)	∇	shower(s)
⊹	drifting or blowing snow	∇̇	shower of rain
⁹	drizzle	⊖	shower of hail
≡	fog	△	sleet
∽	freezing rain	✳	snow
▲▲	cold front	⏃	thunderstorm
		⎡	visibility reduced by smoke

Punctuation

The English writing system uses punctuation marks to separate groups of words for meaning and emphasis; to convey an idea of the variations of pitch, volume, pauses, and intonations of speech; and to help avoid contextual ambiguity. The use of the standard English punctuation marks is discussed in the following pages; examples are provided to illustrate the general rules.

' Apostrophe

1. Indicates the possessive case of nouns and indefinite pronouns. The possessive case of almost all singular nouns may be formed by adding 's. Traditionally, however, only the apostrophe is added when the s would not be pronounced in normal speech. The possessive case of plural nouns ending in s or in an \s\ or \z\ sound is generally formed by adding an apostrophe only; the possessive of irregular plurals is formed by adding 's.

 her mother-in-law's car

 anyone's guess

 the boy's mother

 the boys' mothers

 Degas's drawings

 Knox's products

 Aristophanes' play

 for righteousness' sake

 the Stephenses' house

 children's laughter

2. Marks omission of letters in contracted words.

 didn't

 o'clock

 hang 'em up

3. Marks omission of digits in numbers.

 class of '83

4. Is often used to form plurals of letters, figures, punctuated abbreviations, symbols, and words referred to as words.

 Dot your *i*'s and cross your *t*'s.

 His *1*'s and his *7*'s looked alike.

 Two of the junior faculty have Ph.D's.

 She has trouble pronouncing her *the*'s.

[] Brackets

1. Set off interpolated editorial matter within quoted material.

 He wrote, "I ain't [sic] going."

 Vaulting ambition, which o'erleaps itself
 And falls on the other [side].
 —Shakespeare

2. Function as parentheses within parentheses.

 Bowman Act (22 Stat., ch. 4, § [or sec.] 4, p. 50)

3. Set off phonetic symbols and transcriptions.

 [t] in British *duty*

 the word is pronounced ['ek-sə-jənt]

: Colon

1. Introduces a clause or phrase that explains, illustrates, amplifies, or restates what has gone before.

 The sentence was poorly constructed: it lacked both unity and coherence.

2. Directs attention to an appositive.

 He had only one pleasure: eating.

3. Introduces a series.

 Three abstained: England, France, and Belgium.

4. Introduces lengthy quoted material set off from the rest of a text by indentation but not by quotation marks.

 I quote from the text of Chapter One:

5. Separates elements in page references, in bibliographical and biblical citations, and in set formulas used to express ratios and time.

Journal of the American Medical Association 48:356

Stendhal, *Love* (New York: Penguin, 1975)

John 4:10 a ratio of 3:5 8:30 a.m.

6. Separates titles and subtitles (as of books).

Battle Cry of Freedom: The Era of the Civil War

7. Follows the salutation in formal correspondence.

Dear Sir or Madam:

Ladies and Gentlemen:

8. Punctuates headings in memorandums and formal correspondence.

TO: VIA:
SUBJECT: REFERENCE:

Comma ,

1. Separates main clauses joined by a coordinating conjunction (such as *and, but, or, nor,* or *for*), and sometimes short parallel clauses not joined by conjunctions.

She knew very little about him, and he volunteered nothing.

I came, I saw, I conquered.

2. Sets off an adverbial clause or a long adverbial phrase that precedes or interrupts the main clause.

When she discovered the answer, she reported it to us.

The report, after being read aloud, was put up for consideration.

3. Sets off transitional words and expressions (such as *on the contrary, on the other hand*), conjunctive adverbs (such as *consequently, furthermore, however*), and expressions that introduce an illustration or example (such as *namely, for example*).

My partner, on the other hand, remains unconvinced.

The regent's whim, however, threw the negotiations into chaos.

She responded as completely as she could; that is, she answered each of the individual questions specifically.

4. Sets off contrasting and opposing expressions within sentences.

The cost is not $65.00, but $56.65.

He changed his style, not his ethics.

5. Separates words, phrases, or clauses in series. (Many omit the comma before the conjunction introducing the last item in a series when no ambiguity results.)

He was young, eager, and restless.

It requires one to travel constantly, to have no private life, and to live on almost nothing.

Be sure to pack a flashlight, a sweater and an extra pair of socks.

6. Separates coordinate adjectives modifying a noun. However, a comma is not used between two adjectives when the first modifies the combination of the second adjective and the word or phrase it modifies.

The harsh, damp, piercing wind cut through his jacket.

a low common denominator

7. Sets off parenthetical elements such as nonrestrictive clauses and phrases.

Our guide, who wore a blue beret, was an experienced traveler.

We visited Gettysburg, site of the famous battle.

The book's author, Marie Jones, was an accomplished athlete.

8. Introduces a direct quotation, terminates a direct quotation that is neither a question nor an exclamation, and sets off split quotations. The comma is not used with quotations that are tightly integrated into the sentences in which they appear (e.g., as subject or predicate nominatives) or those that do not represent actual dialogue.

Mary said, "I am leaving."

"I am leaving," Mary said.

"I am leaving," Mary said with determination, "even if you want me to stay."

"The computer is down" was the reply she feared.

The fact that he said he was about to "faint from hunger" doesn't mean he actually fainted.

9. Sets off words in direct address, absolute phrases, and mild interjections.

You may go, John, if you wish.

I fear their encounter, his temper being what it is.

Ah, that's my idea of an excellent dinner.

10. Separates a tag question from the rest of the sentence.

It's a fine day, isn't it?

11. Indicates the omission of a word or words used in a parallel construction earlier in the sentence. When the meaning of the sentence is quite clear without the comma, the comma is omitted.

Common stocks are preferred by some investors; bonds, by others.

He was in love with her and she with him.

12. Is used to avoid ambiguity that might arise from adjacent words.

To Mary, Jane was someone special.

13. Is used to divide digits in numbers into groups of three; however, it is generally not used in pagination, in dates, or in street numbers, and sometimes not used in numbers with four digits.

Smithville, pop. 100,000

4,550 cars

but

page 1411 4507 Main St.

3600 rpm the year 1983

14. Punctuates an inverted name.

Morton, William A.

15. Separates a surname from a following title or degree and often from the words "Junior" and "Senior" and their abbreviations.

Sandra H. Cobb, Vice President

Jesse Ginsburg, D.D.M.

16. Sets off geographical names (such as state or country from city), elements of dates, and addresses. When just the month and the year are given in a date, the comma is usually omitted.

Shreveport, Louisiana, is the site of a large air base.

On Sunday, June 23, 1940, he was wounded.

Number 10 Downing Street, London, is a famous
address.

She began her career in April 1993 at a modest salary.

17. Follows the salutation in informal correspondence, and follows the complimentary close of a letter.

Dear Mark,

Affectionately,

Very truly yours,

— Dash

1. Usually marks an abrupt change or break in the continuity of a sentence.

When in 1960 the stockpile was sold off—indeed,
dumped as surplus—natural rubber sales were hard
hit.—Barry Commoner

2. Is sometimes used in place of commas or parentheses when special emphasis is required.

The presentations—and especially the one by Ms.
Dow—impressed the audience.

3. Introduces a statement that explains, summarizes, or expands on what precedes it.

Oil, steel, and wheat—these are the sinews of
industrialization.

The motion was then tabled—that is, removed indefinitely from consideration.

4. Often precedes the attribution of a quotation.

My foot is on my native heath. . . .—Sir Walter Scott

5. Sets off an interrupting clause or phrase. The dash takes the place of a comma that would ordinarily set off the clause, but an exclamation point or question mark is retained.

If we don't succeed—and the critics say we won't—
then the whole project is in jeopardy.

They are demanding that everything—even the marshland!—be transferred to the new trust.

Your question—it was *your* question, wasn't it, Mr.
Jones?—just can't be answered.

. Ellipsis (or
Suspension Points)

1. Indicates the omission of one or more words within a quoted passage. When four dots are used, the ellipsis indicates the omission of one or more sentences within the passage or the omission of words at the end of a sentence. The first or the last of the four dots is a period.

In the little world in which children have their
existence, . . . there is nothing so finely perceived and
so finely felt as injustice.—Charles Dickens

Security is mostly a superstition. . . . Avoiding danger
is no safer in the long run than outright
exposure. . . . Life is either a daring adventure or
nothing.—Helen Keller

2. Usually indicates omission of one or more lines of poetry when ellipsis is extended the length of the line.

I think that I shall never see
A poem lovely as a tree
.
Poems are made by fools like me,
But only God can make a tree.
—Joyce Kilmer

3. Indicates halting speech or an unfinished sentence in dialogue.

"I'd like to . . . that is . . . if you don't mind. . . ."

! Exclamation Point

1. Ends an emphatic phrase or sentence.

Get out of here!

Her notorious ostentation—she flew her friends to Bangkok
for her birthday parties!—was feasted on by the popular press.

2. Ends an emphatic interjection.

Encore!

All of this proves—at long last!—that we were right from the start.

- Hyphen

The hyphen is often used between parts of a compound. The styling of such words varies; when in doubt, see the entry in the dictionary at its own place or in a list of undefined words at an individual prefix. For unentered compounds, advice will be found in *Merriam-Webster's Manual for Writers and Editors* or a comparable guide.

1. Is often used between a prefix and root, especially whenever the root is capitalized, when two identical vowels come together, or when the resulting word could be confused with another identically spelled word.

pre-Renaissance

co-opted

anti-inflationary

re-cover a sofa

 but

recover from an illness

2. Is used in some compounds, especially those containing prepositions.

president-elect sister-in-law

good-for-nothing over-the-counter

falling-out write-off

3. Is often used in compound modifiers in attributive position.

traveling in a fast-moving van

She has gray-green eyes.

a come-as-you-are party

4. Suspends the first element of a hyphenated compound or a prefix (hyphenated or not) when the second element or base word is part of a following hyphenated compound or derived form.

a six- or eight-cylinder engine

pre- and postadolescent trauma

5. Marks division of a word at the end of a line.

 The ruling pas-
sion of his life

6. Is used in writing out compound numbers between 21 and 99.

 thirty-four

 one hundred thirty-eight

7. Is often used between the numerator and the denominator in writing out fractions, especially when they are used as modifiers. However, fractions used as nouns are often written as open compounds, especially when either the numerator or the denominator already contains a hyphen.

 a two-thirds majority of the vote

 three fifths of her paycheck

 one seventy-second of an inch

8. Serves as an equivalent of *through* or (*up*) *to and including* when used between indicators of range such as numbers and dates. (In typeset material the longer en dash is used.)

 pages 40–98

 the years 1980–89

9. Serves as the equivalent of *to, and,* or *versus* in indicating linkage or opposition. (In typeset material the longer en dash is used.)

 the New York–Paris flight

 the Hardy–Weinberg law

 the Lincoln–Douglas Debates

 The final score was 7–2.

Hyphen, Double ⸗

Is used at the end-of-line division of a hyphenated compound to indicate that the compound is hyphenated and not closed.

self ⸗ [end of line] seeker

 but

self- [end of line] same

Parentheses ()

1. Enclose words, numbers, phrases, or clauses that provide examples, explanations, or supplementary material that does not essentially alter the meaning of the sentence.

 Three old destroyers (all now out of commission) will be scrapped.

 He has followed the fortunes of the modern renaissance (*al-Nahdad*) in the Arabic-speaking world.

2. Enclose numerals that confirm a written number in a text.

 Delivery will be made in thirty (30) days.

3. Enclose numbers or letters in a series.

 We must set forth (1) our long-term goals, (2) our immediate objectives, and (3) the means at our disposal.

4. Enclose abbreviations that follow their spelled-out forms or spelled-out forms that follow their abbreviations.

 a ruling by the Federal Communications Commission (FCC)

 the manufacture and disposal of PVC (polyvinyl chloride)

5. Indicate alternative terms.

 Please indicate the lecture(s) you would like to attend.

6. Enclose publication data in footnotes and endnotes.

 Marguerite Yourcenar, *The Dark Brain of Piranesi and Other Essays* (New York: Farrar, Straus and Giroux, 1985), p. 9.

7. Are used with other punctuation marks in the following ways:

If the parenthetic expression is an independent sentence standing alone, its first word is capitalized and a period is included *inside* the last parenthesis. However, if the parenthetic expression, even if it could stand alone as a sentence, occurs within a sentence, it is uncapitalized and has no sentence period but may have an exclamation point, a question mark, a period for an abbreviation, or quotation marks within the closing parenthesis.

 The discussion was held in the boardroom. (The results are still confidential.)

 Although we liked the restaurant (their Italian food was the best), we seldom went there.

 After waiting in line for an hour (why do we do these things?), we finally left.

 Years ago, someone (I wish I could remember who!) told me about it.

 What was once informally known as A.B.D. status is now often recognized by the degree of Master of Philosophy (M. Phil.).

 He was depressed ("I must resign") and refused to do anything.

No punctuation mark should be placed directly before parenthetical material in a sentence; if a break is required, punctuation should be placed *after* the final parenthesis.

 I'll get back to you tomorrow (Friday), when I have more details.

Period .

1. Ends sentences or sentence fragments that are neither interrogatory nor exclamatory.

 Not bad.

 Give it your best.

 I gave it my best.

 He asked if she had given it her best.

2. Follows some abbreviations and contractions.

 Dr. A.D. ibid. i.e.

 Jr. etc. cont.

3. Is normally used with an individual's initials.

 F. Scott Fitzgerald

 T. S. Eliot

4. Is used after numerals and letters in vertical enumerations and outlines.

 Required skills are:
 1. Shorthand
 2. Typing
 3. Transcription

 I. Objectives
 A. Economy
 1. low initial cost
 2. low maintenance cost
 B. Ease of operation

? Question Mark

1. Ends a direct question.

 How did she do it?

 "How did she do it?" he asked.

2. Ends a question that is part of a larger sentence, but not an indirect question.

 How did she do it? was the question on each person's mind.

 He wondered, Will it work?

 He wondered whether it would work.

3. Indicates the writer's ignorance or uncertainty.

 Geoffrey Chaucer, English poet (1342?–1400)

" " Quotation Marks, Double

1. Enclose direct quotations but not indirect quotations.

 She said, "I am leaving."

 She said that she was leaving.

2. Enclose words or phrases borrowed from others, words used in a special way, and words of marked informality when introduced into formal writing.

 Much of the population in the hellish future he envisions is addicted to "derms," patches that deliver potent drug doses instantaneously through the skin.

 He called himself "emperor," but he was really just a dictator.

 He was arrested for smuggling "smack."

3. Enclose titles of poems, short stories, articles, lectures, chapters of books, short musical compositions, and radio and TV programs.

 Robert Frost's "After Apple-Picking"

 Cynthia Ozick's "Rosa"

 The third chapter of *Treasure Island* is entitled "The Black Spot."

 "All the Things You Are"

 Debussy's "Clair de lune"

 NBC's "Today Show"

4. Are used with other punctuation marks in the following ways:

 The period and the comma fall *within* the quotation marks.

 "I am leaving," she said.

 It was unclear how she maintained such an estate on "a small annuity."

 The colon and semicolon fall *outside* the quotation marks.

 There was only one thing to do when he said "I may not run": promise him a large campaign contribution.

 He spoke of his "little cottage in the country"; he might better have called it a mansion.

 The dash, the question mark, and the exclamation point fall *within* the quotation marks when they refer to the quoted matter only; they fall *outside* when they refer to the whole sentence.

 "I can't see how—" he started to say.

 He asked, "When did she leave?"

 What is the meaning of "the open door"?

The sergeant shouted "Halt!"

Save us from his "mercy"!

5. Are not used with *yes* or *no* except in direct discourse.

 She said yes to all our requests.

6. Are not used with lengthy quotations set off from the text.

 He took the title for his biography of Thoreau from a passage in *Walden*:

 > I long ago lost a hound, a bay horse, and a turtle-dove, and am still on their trail. . . . I have met one or two who had heard the hound, and the tramp of the horse, and even seen the dove disappear behind a cloud, and they seemed as anxious to recover them as if they had lost them themselves.

 However, the title *A Hound, a Bay Horse, and a Turtle-Dove* probably puzzled some readers.

' ' Quotation Marks, Single

1. Enclose a quotation within a quotation in American usage. When both single and double quotation marks occur at the end of a sentence, the period typically falls within *both* sets of marks.

 The witness said, "I distinctly heard him say, 'Don't be late,' and then heard the door close."

 The witness said, "I distinctly heard him say, 'Don't be late.' "

2. Are sometimes used in place of double quotation marks, especially in British usage. In this case a quotation within a quotation is set off by double quotation marks.

 The witness said, 'I distinctly heard him say, "Don't be late," and then heard the door close.'

; Semicolon

1. Links independent clauses not joined by a coordinating conjunction.

 Some people have the ability to write well; others do not.

2. Links clauses joined by a conjunctive adverb (such as *consequently, furthermore, however*).

 Speeding is illegal; furthermore, it is very dangerous.

3. Often occurs before expressions that introduce expansions or series (such as *for example, for instance, that is, e.g.,* or *i.e.*).

 As a manager she tried to do the best job she could; that is, to keep her project on schedule and under budget.

4. Separates phrases that contain commas.

 The country's resources consist of large ore deposits; lumber, waterpower, and fertile soils; and a strong, rugged people.

 Send copies to our offices in Portland, Maine; Springfield, Illinois; and Savannah, Georgia.

5. Is placed outside quotation marks and parentheses.

 They again demanded "complete autonomy"; the demand was again rejected.

Virgule (or Slash) /

1. Separates alternatives.

 high-heat and/or high-speed applications

 . . . sit hour after hour . . . and finally year after year
 in a catatonic/frenzied trance rewriting the Bible
 —William Saroyan

2. Replaces the word *to* or *and* between related terms that are compounded.

 the fiscal year 1983/1984

 in the May/June issue

3. Divides run-in lines of poetry.

 Say, sages, what's the charm on earth/Can turn death's
 dart aside?—Robert Burns

4. Divides elements in dates and divides numerators and denominators in fractions.

 offer expires 5/19/94

 Fifteen and 44/100 dollars

5. Often represents *per* or *to* when used with units of measure or to indicate the terms of a ratio.

 9 ft/sec

 29 mi/gal

 risk/reward trade-off

6. Sets off phonemes and phonemic transcription.

 /b/ as in *but*

Capitalization

Capitals are used for two broad purposes in English: they mark a beginning (as of a sentence) and they signal a proper noun, pronoun, or adjective. The following principles, each with examples, describe the most common uses of capital letters.

Beginnings

1. The first word of a sentence or sentence fragment is capitalized.

 The play lasted nearly three hours.

 How are you feeling?

 Bravo!

2. The first word of a sentence contained within parentheses is capitalized if it does not occur within another sentence. The first word of a parenthetical sentence within another sentence is not capitalized.

 The discussion was held in the boardroom. (The results are still confidential.)

 Although we liked the restaurant (their Italian food was the best), we seldom ate there.

 After waiting in line for an hour (why do we do these things?), we finally left.

3. The first word of a direct quotation is capitalized. However, if the quotation is interrupted in the middle of a sentence, the second part does not begin with a capital. When a quotation, whether a sentence fragment or a complete sentence, is syntactically dependent on the sentence in which it occurs, the quotation does not begin with a capital.

 The President said, "We have rejected this report entirely."

 "We have rejected this report entirely," the President said, "and we will not comment on it further."

 The President made it clear that "there is no room for compromise."

4. The first word of a sentence within a sentence is usually capitalized when it represents a direct question, a motto or aphorism, or spoken or unspoken dialogue. The first word following a colon may be either lowercased or capitalized if it introduces a complete sentence. While the former is more usual, the latter is common when the sentence is fairly lengthy and distinctly separate from the preceding clause.

 The question, as Disraeli said, is this: Is man an ape or an angel?

 My first thought was, How can I avoid this assignment?

 The advantage of this particular system is clear: it's inexpensive.

 The situation is critical: This company cannot hope to recoup the fourth-quarter losses that were sustained in five operating divisions.

5. The first word of a line of poetry is traditionally capitalized; however, in much twentieth-century poetry the line beginnings are lowercased.

 The best lack all conviction, while the worst
 Are full of passionate intensity.

 —W. B. Yeats

6. The first words of run-in enumerations that form complete sentences are capitalized, as are usually the first words of vertical lists and enumerations.

However, enumerations of words or phrases run in with the introductory text are generally lowercased.

 Do the following tasks at the end of the day:
 1. Clear your desktop of papers. 2. Cover office machines. 3. Straighten the contents of your desk drawers, cabinets, and bookcases.

 This is the agenda:
 Call to order
 Roll call
 Minutes of the previous meeting
 Treasurer's report

 On the agenda will be (1) call to order, (2) roll call, (3) minutes of the previous meeting, (4) treasurer's report. . . .

7. The first word in an outline heading is capitalized.

 I. Editorial tasks

 II. Production responsibilities
 A. Cost estimates
 B. Bids

8. The first word of the salutation of a letter and the first word of a complimentary close are capitalized.

 Dear Mary,

 Ladies and Gentlemen:

 Sincerely yours,

Proper Nouns, Pronouns, and Adjectives

Capitals are used with almost all proper nouns—that is, nouns that name particular persons, places, or things (including abstract entities), distinguishing them from others of the same class—and proper adjectives—that is, adjectives that take their meaning from what is named by the proper noun. The essential distinction in the use of capitals and lowercase letters at the beginnings of words lies in this individualizing significance of capitals as against the generalizing significance of lowercase. The following subject headings are in alphabetical order.

ARMED FORCES

1. Branches and units of the armed forces are capitalized, as are easily recognized short forms of full branch and unit designations. However, the words *army, navy*, etc., are lowercased when used in their plural forms or when they are not part of an official title.

 United States Army

 a contract with the Army

 Corps of Engineers

 a bridge built by the Engineers

 allied armies

AWARDS

2. Names of awards and prizes are capitalized.

 the Nobel Prize in Chemistry

 Distinguished Service Cross

 Academy Award

DERIVATIVES OF PROPER NAMES

3. Derivatives of proper names are capitalized when used in their primary sense. However, if the derived term has taken on a specialized meaning, it is usually not capitalized.

 Roman customs

 Shakespearean comedies

 Edwardian era

 but

 quixotic

 herculean

 bohemian tastes

GEOGRAPHICAL REFERENCES

4. Divisions of the earth's surface and names of distinct areas, regions, places, or districts are capitalized, as are most derivative adjectives and some derivative nouns and verbs.

 The Eastern Hemisphere

 Midwest

 Tropic of Cancer

 Springfield, Massachusetts

 the Middle Eastern situation

 an Americanism

 but

 french fries

 a japan finish

 manila envelope

5. Popular names of localities are capitalized.

the Corn Belt	the Loop
The Big Apple	the Gold Coast
the Pacific Rim	

6. Words designating global, national, regional, or local political divisions are capitalized when they are essential elements of specific names. However, they are usually lowercased when they precede a proper name or stand alone. (In legal documents, these words are often capitalized regardless of position.)

the British Empire	Washington State
New York City	Ward 1
but	
the fall of the empire	the state of Washington
the city of New York	fires in three wards

7. Generic geographical terms (such as *lake, mountain, river, valley*) are capitalized if they are part of a specific proper name.

Hudson Bay	Long Island
Niagara Falls	Crater Lake
the Shenandoah Valley	

8. Generic terms preceding names are usually capitalized.

 Lakes Michigan and Superior

 Mounts Whitney and Rainier

9. Generic terms following names are usually lowercased, as are singular or plural generic terms that are used descriptively or alone.

 the Himalaya and Andes mountains

 the Atlantic coast of Labrador

 the Hudson valley

 the river valley

 the valley

10. Compass points are capitalized when they refer to a geographical region or when they are part of a street name, but they are lowercased when they refer to simple direction.

 up North

 back East

 the Northwest

 West Columbus Avenue

 Park Avenue South

 but

 west of the Rockies

 the east coast of Florida

11. Adjectives derived from compass points and nouns designating the inhabitants of some geographical regions are capitalized. When in doubt, see the entry in the dictionary.

 a Southern accent

 Northerners

12. Terms designating public places are capitalized if they are part of a proper name.

 Brooklyn Bridge

 Lincoln Park

 the St. Regis Hotel

 Independence Hall

 but

 Wisconsin and Connecticut avenues

 the Plaza and St. Regis hotels

GOVERNMENTAL AND JUDICIAL BODIES

13. Full names of legislative, deliberative, executive, and administrative bodies are capitalized, as are short forms of these names. However, nonspecific noun and adjective references to them are usually lowercased.

 the U.S. House of Representatives

 the House

 the Federal Bureau of Investigation

 but

 both houses of Congress

 a federal agency

14. Names of international courts, the U.S. Supreme Court, and other higher courts are capitalized. However, names of city and county courts are usually lowercased.

 The International Court of Arbitration

 the Supreme Court of the United States

 the Supreme Court

 the United States Court of Appeals for the Second Circuit

 the Michigan Court of Appeals

 Lawton municipal court

 Newark night court

HISTORICAL PERIODS AND EVENTS

15. Names of congresses, councils, and expositions are capitalized.

the Yalta Conference

the Republican National Convention

16. Names of historical events, some historical periods, and some cultural periods and movements are capitalized. When in doubt, consult the entry in the dictionary, especially for periods.

the Boston Tea Party

the Renaissance

Prohibition

the Augustan Age

the Enlightenment

but

the space age

neoclassicism

17. Numerical designations of historical time periods are capitalized when they are part of a proper name; otherwise they are lowercased.

the Third Reich

the Roaring Twenties

but

the eighteenth century

the eighties

18. Names of treaties, laws, and acts are capitalized.

Treaty of Versailles

The Clean Air Act of 1990

ORGANIZATIONS

19. Names of firms, corporations, schools, and organizations and their members are capitalized. However, common nouns occurring after the names of two or more organizations are lowercased. The word *the* at the beginning of such names is only capitalized when the full legal name is used.

Thunder's Mouth Press

University of Wisconsin

European Community

Rotary International

Kiwanians

American and United airlines

20. Words such as *group, division, department, office,* or *agency* that designate a corporate and organizational unit are capitalized only when used with its specific name.

in the Editorial Department of Merriam-Webster

but

a notice to all department heads

PEOPLE

21. Names of persons are capitalized. However, the capitalization of particles such as *de, della, der, du, l', la, ten,* and *van* varies widely, especially in names of people in English-speaking countries.

Noah Webster

W.E.B. Du Bois

Daphne du Maurier

Wernher von Braun

Anthony Van Dyck

22. Titles preceding the name of a person and epithets used instead of a name are capitalized. However, titles following a name or used alone are usually lowercased.

President Roosevelt

Professor Kaiser

Queen Elizabeth

Old Hickory

the Iron Chancellor

but

Henry VIII, king of England

23. Corporate titles are capitalized when used with an individual's name; otherwise, they are lowercased.

Lisa Dominguez, Vice President

The sales manager called me.

24. Words of family relationship preceding or used in place of a person's name are capitalized; however, these words are lowercased if they are part of a noun phrase used in place of a name.

Cousin Julia

I know when Mother's birthday is.

but

I know when my mother's birthday is.

25. Words designating peoples, nationalities, religious groups, tribes, races, and languages are capitalized. Other terms used to refer to groups of people are often lowercased. Designations based on color are usually lowercased.

Canadians	Iroquois
Ibo	African-American
Latin	Indo-European
highlander (an inhabitant of a highland)	
Highlander (an inhabitant of the Highlands of Scotland)	
black	white

PERSONIFICATIONS

26. Personifications are capitalized.

She dwells with Beauty—Beauty that must die;
And Joy, whose hand is ever at his lips
Bidding adieu.

—John Keats

obey the commands of Nature

PRONOUNS

27. The pronoun I is capitalized. For pronouns referring to the Deity, see rule 29 below.

. . . no one but I myself had yet printed any of my work.—Paul Bowles

RELIGIOUS TERMS

28. Words designating the Deity are capitalized.

An anthropomorphic, vengeful Jehovah became a spiritual, benevolent Supreme Being.—A.R. Katz

29. Personal pronouns referring to the Deity are usually capitalized, even when they closely follow their antecedent. However, many writers never capitalize such pronouns.

All Thy works, O Lord, shall bless Thee.

—Oxford American Hymnal

God's in his heaven—
All's right with the world!
—Robert Browning

30. Traditional designations of revered persons, such as prophets, apostles, and saints, are often capitalized.

our Lady

the Prophet

the Lawgiver

31. Names of religions, creeds and confessions, denominations, and religious orders are capitalized, as is the word *Church* when used as part of a proper name.

Judaism

Apostles' Creed

the Thirty-nine Articles of the Church of England

Society of Jesus

Hunt Memorial Church

but

the local Baptist church

32. Names for the Bible or parts, versions, or editions of it and names of other sacred books are capitalized but not italicized. Adjectives derived from the names of sacred books are irregularly capitalized or lowercased; when in doubt, see the entry in the dictionary.

Authorized Version	New English Bible
Old Testament	Pentateuch
Apocrypha	Gospel of Saint Mark
Talmud	Koran
biblical	Koranic

SCIENTIFIC TERMS

33. Names of planets and their satellites, asteroids, stars, constellations and groups of stars, and other unique celestial objects are capitalized. However, the words *sun, earth,* and *moon* are usually lowercased unless they occur with other astronomical names.

Venus	Ganymede
Sirius	the Pleiades

the Milky Way

enjoying the beauty of the moon

probes heading for the Moon and Mars

34. New Latin genus names in zoology and botany are capitalized; the second term in binomial scientific names, identifying the species, is not.

a cabbage butterfly (*Pieris rapae*)

a common buttercup (*Ranunculus acris*)

35. New Latin names of all groups above genus in zoology and botany (such as class or family) are capitalized; however, their derivative adjectives and nouns are not.

Gastropoda	*but*	gastropod
Mantidae	*but*	mantid

36. Names of geological eras, periods, epochs, and strata and names of prehistoric divisions are capitalized.

Silurian period	Pleistocene epoch
Age of Reptiles	Neolithic age

SEASONS, MONTHS, DAYS

37. Names of months, days of the week, and holidays and holy days are capitalized.

January	Ramadan
Tuesday	Thanksgiving
Yom Kippur	Easter

38. Names of seasons are not capitalized except when personified.

last spring

the sweet breath of Spring

TITLES OF PRINTED MATTER AND WORKS OF ART

39. Words in titles are capitalized, with the exception of internal conjunctions, prepositions, and articles. In some publications, prepositions of five or more letters are capitalized also.

Of Mice and Men

"The Man Who Would Be King"

"To His Coy Mistress"

Slouching Towards Bethlehem

40. Capitalization of the titles of movies, plays, paintings, sculpture, and musical compositions follow similar conventions. For more details, see the Italicization section below.

41. Major sections of books, long articles, or reports are capitalized when they are referred to within the same material.

See the Appendix for further information.

The Introduction explains the scope of this book.

discussed later in Chapter 4

42. Nouns used with numbers or letters to designate major reference headings are capitalized. Nouns designating minor elements are typically lowercased.

Volume V	Table 3
page 101	note 10

TRADEMARKS

43. Registered trademarks and service marks are capitalized.

Express Mail	Orlon
Kleenex	Walkman

VEHICLES

44. Names of ships, aircraft, and spacecraft are capitalized.

Titanic

Lindbergh's *Spirit of St. Louis*

Apollo 13

Italicization

The following are usually italicized in print and underlined in manuscript and typescript.

1. Words and passages that are to be emphasized.

 This was their fatal error: there *was* no cache of supplies in the now-abandoned depot.

2. Titles of books, magazines, newspapers, plays, long poems, movies, paintings, sculpture, and long musical compositions (but not musical compositions identified by the name of their genre).

 Dickens's *Bleak House*

 National Geographic

 Christian Science Monitor

 Shakespeare's *Othello*

 Eliot's *The Waste Land*

 the movie *Back to the Future*

 Gainsborough's *Blue Boy*

 Mozart's *Don Giovanni*

 but

 Schubert's Sonata in B-flat Major, D. 960

 NOTE: In the plurals of such italicized titles, the *s* or *es* endings are usually in roman type.

 hidden under a stack of *New Yorker*s

3. Names of ships, aircraft, and spacecraft.

 Titanic

 Lindbergh's *Spirit of St. Louis*

 Apollo 13

4. Words, letters, and figures when referred to as such.

 The *g* in *align* is silent.

 The first *2* and the last *0* are barely legible.

5. Unfamiliar words when first introduced and defined in a text.

 Heart failure is often accompanied by *edema,* an accumulation of fluid which tends to produce swelling of the lower extremities.

6. Foreign words and phrases that have not been naturalized in English. In general, any word entered in the main A–Z vocabulary of this dictionary need not be italicized.

 c'est la vie

 aere perennius

 che sarà, sarà

 sans peur et sans reproche

 but

 pasta ad hoc ex officio

7. New Latin scientific names of genera, species, subspecies, races, and varieties (but not groups of higher rank, such as phyla, classes, or orders) in botanical or zoological names.

 a thick-shelled American clam (*Mercenaria mercenaria*)

 a mallard (*Anas platyrhynchos*)

 but

 the family Hominidae

8. Case titles in legal citations, both in full and shortened form; "v." for "versus" is set in either roman or italic.

 Jones v. *Ohio*

 Smith et al v. Jones

 the *Jones* case

 Jones

Documentation of Sources

Writers and editors use various methods to indicate the source of a quotation or piece of information borrowed from another work. In works published for the general public and traditionally in scholarly works in the humanities, footnotes or endnotes have been preferred. In this system, sequential numbers within the text refer the reader to notes at the bottom of the page or at the end of the article, chapter, or book; these notes contain full bibliographical information on the works cited. In scholarly works in the social and natural sciences, and increasingly in the humanities as well, parenthetical references within the text refer the reader to an alphabetically arranged list of sources at the end of the work. The system of footnotes or endnotes is the more flexible, in that it allows for commentary on the work or subject and can also be used for brief peripheral discussions not tied to any specific work. However, style manuals tend to encourage the use of parenthetical references in addition to or instead of footnotes or endnotes, since for most kinds of material they are efficient and convenient for both writer and reader. In a carefully documented work, a bibliography or list of sources normally follows the entire text (including any endnotes) regardless of which system is used.

Though different publishers and journals have adopted slightly varying styles, the following examples illustrate standard styles for references, notes, and bibliographic entries. For more extensive treatment than can be provided here, *Merriam-Webster's Manual for Writers and Editors, The Chicago Manual of Style, The MLA Style Manual,* or the *Publication Manual of the American Psychological Association* may be consulted.

Footnotes and Endnotes

Footnotes and endnotes are indicated by superscript Arabic numerals placed immediately after the material to be documented. The numbering is consecutive throughout an article or monograph; in a book, it usually starts over with each new chapter or section. Footnotes appear at the bottom of the page; endnotes, which take the same form as footnotes, are gathered at the end of the article, chapter, or book. Endnotes are generally preferred over footnotes by writers and publishers because they are easier to handle when preparing both manuscript and printed pages, though they can be less convenient for the reader. All of the examples shown reflect humanities citation style. All of the cited works appear again in the Lists of Sources section below.

Books

One author	[1]Elizabeth Bishop, *The Complete Poems: 1927–1979* (New York: Farrar, Straus & Giroux, 1983), 46.
Two or more authors	[2]Bert Holldobler and Edward O. Wilson, *The Ants* (Cambridge, Mass.: Belknap–Harvard Univ. Press, 1990), 119.
	[3]Randolph Quirk et al., *A Comprehensive Grammar of the English Language* (London: Longman, 1985), 135.
Edition and/or translation	[4]Arthur S. Banks, ed., *Political Handbook of the World: 1992* (Binghamton, N.Y.: CSA Publications, 1992), 293–95.
	[5]Simone de Beauvoir, *The Second Sex,* trans. and ed. H. M. Parshley (New York: Knopf, 1953; Random House, 1974), 446.
Second or later edition	[6]Albert C. Baugh and Thomas Cable, *A History of the English Language,* 3d ed. (Englewood Cliffs, N.J.: Prentice Hall, 1978), 14.
Article in a collection or festschrift	[7]Ernst Mayr, "Processes of Speciation in Animals," in *Mechanisms of Speciation,* ed. C. Barigozzi (New York: Alan R. Liss, 1982), 1–3.
Work in two or more volumes	[8]Ronald M. Nowak, *Walker's Mammals of the World,* 5th ed. (Baltimore: Johns Hopkins Univ. Press, 1991), 2:661.
Corporate author	[9]Commission on the Humanities, *The Humanities in American Life* (Berkeley: Univ. of California Press, 1980), 46.
Book lacking publication data	[10]*Photographic View Album of Cambridge* [England], n.p., n.d., n.pag.
Subsequent reference	[11]Baugh and Cable, 18–19.

Articles

Journal paginated consecutively throughout annual volume

[12]Stephen Jay Gould and Niles Eldredge, "Punctuated Equilibria: The Tempo and Mode of Evolution Reconsidered," *Paleobiology* 3 (1977): 121.

Journal paginated consecutively only within each issue

[13]Roseann Duenas Gonzalez, "Teaching Mexican American Students to Write: Capitalizing on the Culture," *English Journal* 71.7 (Nov. 1982): 22–24.

Monthly magazine

[14]John Lukacs, "The End of the Twentieth Century," *Harper's,* Jan. 1993: 40.

Weekly magazine

[15]Richard Preston, "A Reporter at Large: Crisis in the Hot Zone," *New Yorker,* 26 Oct. 1992: 58.

Newspaper

[16]William J. Broad, "Big Science Squeezes Small-Scale Researchers," *New York Times,* 29 Dec. 1992: C1.

Signed review

[17]George Steiner, review of *Oeuvres en Prose Complètes, Tome 3,* by Charles Péguy, *Times Literary Supplement,* 25 Dec. 1992: 3.

Parenthetical References

Parenthetical references are highly abbreviated bibliographical citations that appear within the text itself, enclosed in parentheses. Such references direct the reader to a detailed bibliography or list of sources at the end of the work, often removing the need for footnotes or endnotes. The parenthetical references usually include only the author's last name and a page reference. (In the social and natural sciences, the year of publication is included after the author's name, and the page number is often omitted.) Any element of the reference that is clear from the context may be omitted. To distinguish among cited works published by the same author, the author's name may be followed by the specific work's title, which is usually shortened. (If the author-date system is being used, a lowercase letter can be added after the year—e.g., 1992a, 1992b—to distinguish between works published in the same year.) Each of the following references is keyed to an entry in the Lists of Sources section below.

Humanities style

(Quirk et al., 135)
(Baugh and Cable, *History,* 14)
(Commission on the Humanities, 46)

Sciences style

(Mayr 1982, 1–3)
(Nowak 1991, 2:661)
(Gould and Eldredge 1977)

Lists of Sources

A bibliography or list of sources in alphabetical order usually appears at the end of the work. The following lists of cited works illustrate standard styles employed in, respectively, the humanities and the social and natural sciences. The principal differences between the two styles are these. In the sciences, (1) an initial is generally used instead of the author's first name, (2) the date is placed directly after the author's name, (3) all words in titles are lowercased except the first word and the first word of any subtitle as well as proper nouns and adjectives, and (4) article titles are not set off by quotation marks. (In some scientific publications, book and journal titles are not italicized.)

Humanities style

Baugh, Albert C., and Thomas Cable. *A History of the English Language.* 3d ed. Englewood Cliffs, N.J.: Prentice Hall, 1978.

Beauvoir, Simone de. *The Second Sex.* Trans. and ed. H. M. Parshley. New York: Alfred A. Knopf, 1953. Reprint. New York: Random House, 1974.

Bishop, Elizabeth. *The Complete Poems: 1927–1979.* New York: Farrar, Straus & Giroux, 1983.

Commission on the Humanities. *The Humanities in American Life.* Berkeley: University of California Press, 1980.

Gonzalez, Roseann Duenas. "Teaching Mexican American Students to Write: Capitalizing on the Culture." *English Journal* 71.7 (November 1982): 22–24.

Lukacs, John. "The End of the Twentieth Century." *Harper's,* January 1993: 39–58.

Photographic View Album of Cambridge [England]. N.d., n.p., n. pag.

Quirk, Randolph, Sidney Greenbaum, Geoffrey Leech, and Jan Svartvik. *A Comprehensive Grammar of the English Language.* London: Longman, 1985.

Steiner, George. Review of *Oeuvres en Prose Complètes, Tome 3,* by Charles Péguy. *Times Literary Supplement,* 25 December 1992: 3–4.

Sciences style

Banks, A. S., ed. 1992. *Political handbook of the world: 1992.* Binghamton, N.Y.: CSA Publications.

Broad, W. J. 1992. Big science squeezes small-scale researchers. *New York Times,* 29 Dec.: C1+.

Gould, S. J., and N. Eldredge. 1977. Punctuated equilibria: The tempo and mode of evolution reconsidered. *Paleobiology* 3: 115–151.

Holldobler, B., and E. O. Wilson. 1990. *The ants.* Cambridge, Mass.: Belknap–Harvard Univ. Press.

Mayr, E. 1982. Processes of speciation in animals. In C. Barigozzi, ed., *Mechanisms of speciation.* New York: Alan R. Liss: 1–19.

Nowak, R.M. 1991. *Walker's mammals of the world.* 5th ed. 2 vols. Baltimore: Johns Hopkins Univ. Press.

Preston, R. 1992. A reporter at large: Crisis in the hot zone. *New Yorker,* 26 Oct.: 58–81.

Index

Abbreviations and Symbols for Chemical Elements 2157
Alphabet Table ... 51
Animals, Names of ... 19a
Apostrophe, use of .. 2325
Astronomy signs and symbols 2321
Attributive Nouns ... 12a
Beaufort Scale (table) 156
Bells, Ship's (table) 162
Bible (table) ... 171
Biographical Names .. 2176
Biology signs and symbols 2321
Brackets, use of .. 2325
Business and Finance signs and symbols 2321
Calendar, Gregorian (table) 1187
Calendar, Islamic (table) 1187
Calendars, Jewish (tables) 991, 1187
Calendars, Principal, Months of (table) 1187
Capitalization 12a, 2331
Centered Dots, use of 8a
Chemical Elements (table) 587
Chemistry signs and symbols 2321
Colon, use of ... 2325
Combining Forms ... 21a
Comma, use of ... 2326
Compounds, styling of 7a, 2327
Contents .. 5a
Cross-Reference ... 20a
Dash, use of .. 2327
Dates ... 14a
Definitions ... 17a
Diacritics (table) .. 500
Division of Senses .. 17a
Division of Words ... 8a
Documentation of Sources 2336
Double Hyphen, use of 2328
Easter Dates (table) 572
Elements, Chemical (table) 587
Ellipsis, use of .. 2327
End-of-Line Division 8a
Entries, discussion of 7a
Etymology ... 12a
Exclamation Point, use of 2327
Explanatory Notes ... 7a
Finance signs and symbols 2321
Footnotes, use of ... 2336
Foreign Words and Phrases 2169
Functional Labels ... 10a
Geographical Names .. 2225
Geologic Time (table) 768
Guide to Pronunciation 23a
Guide Words ... 7a
Handbook of Style ... 2325
Histories, Word ... 14a
Homographs .. 7a
Hyphen, use of .. 2327
Hyphen, Double, use of 2328
Illustrative Quotations 16a
Indo-European Languages (table) 937
Inflected Forms ... 10a
Islamic Calendar (table) 1187
Italicization ... 2335
Jewish Years (table) 991
Labels, Functional .. 10a
Labels, Status .. 15a
Labels, Subject ... 16a
Labels, Usage ... 15a
Language Research Service 2340
Languages, Indo-European (table) 937

Languages with over Forty Million Speakers, Home
 (table) ... 1031
Lists of Undefined Words 22a
Mathematical signs and symbols 2322
Measures and Weights (table) 2097
Medicine signs and symbols 2323
Metric System (table) 1153
Money (table) ... 1181
Months of the Principal Calendars (table) 1187
Morse Code (table) .. 1191
Names of Plants and Animals 19a
Numbers (table) ... 1254
Omission of a Sense 18a
Order of Senses ... 18a
Origins of Words (Etymology) 12a
Parentheses, use of 2328
Period, use of .. 2328
Periodic Table (table) 1358
Physics signs and symbols 2324
Planets (table) ... 1396
Plants, Names of .. 19a
Plurals ... 10a
Preface ... 6a
Prefixes .. 21a
Pronunciation 9a, 23a
Pronunciation Symbols 28a
Proofreaders' Marks (table) 1466
Punctuation Marks (table) 1485
Punctuation, use of 2325
Question Mark, use of 2329
Quotation Marks, Double, use of 2329
Quotation Marks, Single, use of 2329
Quotations, Illustrative 16a
Radio Frequencies (table) 1512
Reference Marks ... 2324
Run-on Entries .. 8a
Semicolon, use of ... 2329
Sense Division .. 17a
Sense Omission .. 18a
Sense Order ... 18a
Ship's Bells (table) 162
Signs and Symbols ... 2321
Slash, use of ... 2330
Stamps and Stamp Collecting signs and symbols 2324
Status Labels ... 15a
Style, Handbook of .. 2325
Subject Labels .. 16a
Suffixes .. 21a
Suspension Points, use of 2327
Symbols ... 2321
Synonyms .. 21a
Taxonomic Entries ... 19a
Truth Table (table) 1985
Undefined Words, Lists of 22a
Usage ... 15a
Usage Labels .. 15a
Usage Notes ... 16a
Usage Paragraphs .. 17a
Variants .. 8a
Verbal Illustrations 16a
Virgule, use of ... 2330
Volume Formulas (table) 2071
Weather signs and symbols 2324
Weights and Measures (table) 2097
Word History Paragraphs 14a
Word Origins (Etymology) 12a
Zodiac (table) .. 2153

Merriam-Webster's
Language Research Service

The Language Research Service offers owners of this dictionary the opportunity to take advantage of the editorial resources of America's foremost dictionary publisher—*at no cost*.

The Language Research Service answers *specific* questions about words and their origin, spelling, pronunciation, meaning, or usage. If you have a question about a particular word, such as who first used it or why it has not been entered in the dictionary, a letter to the Language Research Service will bring a prompt, accurate, and concise reply from a member of the Merriam-Webster editorial staff, the largest dictionary staff in America. Questions about the specific features of your dictionary are also welcome, though you will find most such questions can be answered easily by referring to the Explanatory Notes section, beginning on page 7a.

The editorial resources at Merriam-Webster include a collection of more than 15 million citations (examples of words used in context) and a data-gathering program that produces many thousands of new citations every year. As the owner of this dictionary you are offered privileged access to these resources and assured of current, carefully researched replies.

You don't have to be a scholar to benefit from the Language Research Service. It makes Merriam-Webster's experience and resources available to professionals, students, and laymen alike in a way no other dictionary publisher has ever attempted.

Letters from correspondents in the U.S. should include a self-addressed stamped envelope. To assure a prompt response, we request that no more than three specific questions be asked in any one letter.

Take advantage of this unique offer. Send your questions to Language Research Service, P.O. Box 281, Springfield, Massachusetts 01102.